GUIDE TO MICROFORMS IN PRINT

AUTHOR
TITLE

Incorporating International Microforms in Print

VOL. 1

1999

A – K

K · G · SAUR

Edited by:
Irene Izod

CIP-Kurztitelaufnahme der Deutschen Bibliothek
[Guide to microforms in print / Author, title]
Guide to microforms in print :
incorporating international microforms in print.
Author, title. – Munich : Saur
ISSN 0164-0747
Erscheint jährlich. – Früher im Verl. Meckler,
Westport, CT. – Aufnahme nach 1990

1990 –
Verl.-Wechsel

Library of Congress Catalog Card Number: 61-7082

Part of Reed Elsevier

Computer-controlled data preparation
and automatic data processing
by Microcomposition, München

Cover art by William Pownall

Printed and bound by Legoprint S.r.l., Trento, Italy

ISSN 0164-0747
ISBN 3-598-11392-7

Table of Contents

Vol. 1

Vol. 2

Foreword

Guide to Microforms in Print is a title main entry listing, with cross-references from all authors and editors to titles. In addition, cross-references from variant authors and titles are provided where needed.

The **Author-Title Guide** provides access to international microform publications. Publications listed include books, journals, newspapers, government publications, archival material, collections and other projects currently available from microform publishers throughout the world provided they are for sale on a regular and current basis.

Alphabetical Arrangement of Entries

Main entries and cross-references are interfiled to form a single list arranged alphabetically by word according to Anglo-American practice. Personal name entries (name references) precede other kinds of entries beginning with the same word or group of words.

Entries beginning with initial letters file before words beginning with the same letter. Acronyms file as multi-letter words. The ampersand (&) does not file. The following initial articles do not file:

a, al, an, das, dat, dem, den, der, des, det, die, dit, een, eene, ein, eine, einem, einen, einer, eines, eit, el, en, ett, gli, het, il, la, las, le, les, lo, los, o, os, the, um, uma, un, una, unas, une, uno, unos.

U.S., Mc and St. are filed as though spelled out when they occur at the beginning of an entry.

Numbers file before letters of the alphabet; the user looking for a title that begins with the date 1981, for example, should search under "Nineteen Eighty-one" in the N alphabet as well as under "1981" in the numerical arrangement preceding the A alphabet.

Roman numerals are being changed successively to arabic numerals. Search under both the arabic numeral as well as roman numerals as though they were letters.

Authors

As many as two personal authors or editors may be listed for a given title. If more than two authors or editors are responsible for a given work, only the name of the first is provided followed by et al.

Form and Content of Entries

The main form of entry is as follows:

Title (in capital letters). Author(s) or editor(s). Place of publication. Date of Publication. Collation information. Type of microform code. Price. ISBN. Extra distributor or co-publisher information. Further title information. Publisher code. Subject classes.

The numbers given in square brackets following the publisher's name designate the classes based on a modified Dewey Decimal Classification System, in which materials of related interest may be found in the **GMIP Subject Guide**.

Prices

In previous editions of Guide to Microforms in Print, the word apply was used to indicate that price information was to be obtained directly from the publisher. While the word apply is still to be found in this edition, it has been removed when possible. Where no price is given, the user should contact the publisher directly.

When no currency symbol appears before a price, the US$ is meant.

The prices listed are inclusive, unless they are followed by a coded symbol as follows:

Price Code:		
	c	per card; e. g., $5.00c
	dc	per double-sided card; e. g., $.75dc
	f	per fiche; e. g., $1.25f
	r	per reel, e. g., $1.05r
	t	per title (of a collection); e. g., $2.00t
	v	per volume; e. g., $3.00v
	y	per year; e. g., $4.00y

Type of Microform

The numerical code designation for the type of microform in which a title is available now precedes the price. The coding for the type of microform is as follows:

1	reel microfilm; 35mm. [See also no. 13 & 14]
2	micro-opaque cards; 75 x 125mm (3 x 5″)
3	micro-opaque cards; 6 x 9″
4	micro-opaque cards; 5 x 8″
5	reel microfilm; 16mm. [See also no. 6]
6	reel microfilm; 16mm. (cartridge or cassette)
7	microfiche; 75 x 125mm. (3 x 5″)
8	microfiche; 9 x 12cm.
9	microfiche; 105 x 148mm. (4 x 6″)

10	micro-opaque cards; 105 x 148mm. (4 x 6″)
11	text-fiche; case bound volume with full size front and end matter, including index; text on 4 x 6″ pocket-held microfiche
12	ultramicrofiche; 4 x 6″, 2500 or 3200 pages per fiche
13	reel microfilm; 35mm. (cartridge or cassette)
14	reel microfilm; 35mm. in color
15	color microfiche; 105 x 148 mm. (4 x 6″)
16	other; description necessary
17	COM fiche

Ordering information

Publishers are identified in the main entry by an abbreviation preceded by a two character country-of-publication code in lower-case letters. This code and the abbreviation are arranged alphabetically in the section **Publishers and Distributors** where full ordering information can be found. In addition, an alphabetical **Index to Publishers and Distributors** is provided.

Please note that books listed in **GMIP** cannot be ordered through K. G. Saur.

Country-of-Publication Codes*

aa Albania
ae Algeria
ag Argentina
ao Angola
aq Antigua and Barbuda
at Australia
au Austria

ba Bahrain
bb Barbados
be Belgium
bg Bangladesh
bh Belize
bl Brazil
bm Bermuda
bn Bosnia-Hercegovina
bo Bolivia
bs Botswana
bt Bhutan
bu Bulgaria
bw Belarus

cc China, People's Republic
ce Sri Lanka
cf Congo
ch China, Republic
ci Croatia
ck Columbia
cl Chile
cm Cameroon
cn Canada
cr Costa Rica
cw Cook Islands
cy Cyprus

dk Denmark

ec Ecuador
er Estonia
et Ethiopia

fi Finland
fj Fiji
fr France

gd Grenada
gh Ghana
gm Gambia
gr Greece
gt Guatemala
gw Germany, Federal Republic
gy Guyana

hk Hong Kong
hu Hungary

ic Iceland
ie Ireland
ii India
io Indonesia
ir Iran
is Israel
it Italy

ja Japan
jm Jamaica
jo Jordan

ke Kenya
kn Korea, Democratic People's Republic
ko Korea, Republic
kr Ukraine
ku Kuwait

lb Liberia
le Lebanon
lh Liechtenstein
li Lithuania
lo Lesotho
lu Luxembourg
lv Latvia

mc Monaco
md Moldova
mf Mauritius
mg Madagaskar
mh Macao
mj Monserrat
mm Malta
mr Morocco
mw Malawi
mx Mexico
my Malaysia

na Netherlands Antilles
ne Netherlands
ng Niger
no Norway
np Nepal
nr Nigeria
nz New Zealand

pe Peru
ph Philippines
pk Pakistan

pl	Poland	tr	Trinidad and Tobago
po	Portugal	ts	United Arab Emirates
pp	Papua New Guinea	tu	Turkey
pr	Puerto Rico	tz	Tanzania
rm	Romania	ua	Egypt
ru	Russia	ug	Uganda
		ui	Channel Islands
sa	South Africa	uk	United Kingdom
se	Seychelles	us	United States
sg	Senegal		
si	Singapore	vc	Vatican City
sj	Sudan	ve	Venezuela
sl	Sierra Leone	vn	Vietnam
so	Somalia		
sp	Spain	xm	St. Vincent and the Grenadines
sq	Swaziland	xn	Macedonia
sr	Surinam	xo	Slovak Republic
su	Saudi Arabia	xr	Czech Republic
sw	Sweden	xv	Slovenia
sx	Namibia		
sy	Syria	yu	Yugoslavia
sz	Switzerland		
		za	Zambia
th	Thailand	zi	Zimbabwe
ti	Tunisia	zr	Zaire
to	Tonga		

* Please note that not every country for which a country-of-publication code or currency symbol is listed is represented in GMIP

Abbreviations

abr	abridged
ac	audiocassette(s)
Amer	American
annot	annotation(s), annotated
apply	apply to publisher for price
approx	approximately
bd	bound
bk(s)	books
Bro	brother
ca	circa
cl	hardback
coll	collection
comp(s)	compiler(s)
corp	corporation
dept	department
dist	distributor
doc(s)	document(s)
ea	each
ed(s)	editor(s); edition(s)
enl	enlarged
f	microfiche(s)
facs	facsimile
fasc	fascicule
FAX	telefax
fiche(s)	microfiche(s)
hb	hardback
ill, illus	illustrated, illustration(s), illustrator(s)
impr	imprint
in prep	in preparation
incl	includes, including
inst	institute
ISBN	International Standard Book Number
lea	leather
ltd ed	limited edition
mf	microfiche(s)
mins	minutes
ms, mss	manuscript, manuscripts
natl	national
no, nos	number, numbers
o/p	out-of-print
o/s	out-of-stock
orig	original
p, pp	pages
pb	softback
pseud	pseudonym
pt(s)	parts
pub, publ	published, publisher, publishing
r	reel(s)
rb	looseleaf; ringbound
repr	reprint
rev	revised
sb	softback
St.	Saint
subsc	subscription; subscribers
suppl	supplement
T	telephone
TA	cable address
tba	to be arranged
tr, trans	translator, translated, translation
TX	telex
v	volume(s)
vol(s)	volume(s)

Currency Symbols

A$	Australian dollar
Arg$	Argentine peso
Br	birr (Ethiopia)
B/	balboa (Panama)
B$	Bahamian dollar
BD$	Bermuda dollar
Bf	Belgian franc
Bo	bólivar (Venezuela)
C	new cedi (Ghana)
C$	córdoba (Nicaragua)
C£	Cyprus pound
Can$	Canadian dollar
CEsc	Cape Verde escudo
CFAf	CFA franc
Col	colón (Costa Rica, El Salvador)
Col$	Columbian peso
Cruz	cruzeiro (Brazil)
Cub$	Cuban peso
DA	Algerian Dinar
Dfl or DG	Dutch florin
DH	United Arab Emirates dirham
Din	Yugoslavian dinar
Dir	dirham (Morocco)
DKr	Danish krone
DM	Deutsche Mark
Dr	drachma (Greece)
DT	Tunesian dinar
E°	Chilean escudo, peso
EC$	East Caribbean dollar
ECU	European Community Unit
ESC	escudo (Portugal)
F or FF	French franc
FCFP	franc CFP (French Polynesia)
FD	franc Djibouti
FMG	franc malgache (Madagascar)
Fmk	markka (Finland)
Ft	forint (Hungary)
G	gourde (Haiti)
G̸	guarani (Paraguay)
G$	Guyana dollar
G£	dalasi (Gambia)
Gld	guilder (Netherlands)
HK$	Hong Kong dollar
HL	lempira (Honduras)
I£	Israeli pound
Ikr	Iceland krona
Ir£	Irish pound
J$	Jamaican dollar
K	kina (Papua New Guinea)
Kčs	koruna (Czechoslovakia)
KD	Kuwait dinar
Kr	Swedish krona
KSh	Kenya shilling
L	Italian lira
L£	Lebanese pound
Le	leone (Sierra Leone)
Lei	lei (Romania)
Lek	lek (Albania)
Lfr	Luxembourg franc
Lv	lev (Bulgaria)
M$	Malaysian ringitt
Mex$	Mexican peso
MK	Malawi kwacha
MR	Mauritius rupee
N	naira (Nigeria)
NAf	Netherlands Antilles florin
NIS	new schekel (Israel)
Nkr	Norwegian krone
NR	Nepalese rupee
NT$	new Taiwan dollar (Republic of China)
NZ$	New Zealand dollar
ÖS	Austrian Schilling (also S)
P	pula (Botswana)
PakRs	Pakistani rupee
Pat	pataca (Macao)
PP	Philippine (Macao)
PS	English pound
Pta	peseta (Spain)
Q̸	q̸etzal (Guatemala)
Q	Qatar riyal
R	South African rand
Rb	ruble
RD$	Dominican peso
Re	Indian rupee
RI	rial (Iran)
RMBY	Renminbi yuan (People's Republic of China)

Rp	rupiah (Indonesia)
Rs	Indian rupee
S	Schilling (Austria)
S/	sol (Peru)
S$	Singapore dollar
S£	Sudanese pound
Sfr	Swiss franc
SI	sucre (Ecuador)
SL£	Solomon dollar
SLR	Sri Lanka rupee
SmS	Somali shilling
SR	Seychelles rupee
SRI	Saudi riyal
T$	Pa'anga (Tonga)
THB	baht (Thailand)
Tk	taka (Bangladesh)
TL	Turkish pound, lira
TSh	Tanzanian shilling
TT$	Trinidad/Tobago dollar
UR$	Uruguay peso
USh	Uganda shilling
W	won (Korea)
WS$	tala (Samoa)
Y	yen (Japan)
Z	zaiire
Z$	Zimbabwean dollar
zl	zloty (Poland)
ZK	kwacha (Zambia)
$	United States dollar
$b	Bolivian peso
$F	Fiji dollar
£	English pound
£E	Egyptian pound
£M	Malta pound
£S	Syrian pound

Survey of Classes

Divisions marked with (*) have been modified. See Guidelines.

*GENERALITIES[1]

000 Generalities
010 General Bibliography
011 Bibliography of Philosophy and Psychology
012 Bibliography of Religion
013 Bibliography of Social Sciences
014 Bibliography of Language and Literature Studies
015 Bibliography of Science
016 Bibliography of Technology
017 Bibliography of the Arts
018 Bibliography of Belles-Lettres
019 Bibliography of Geography and History
020 Library and Information Science
025 Archives
030 Encyclopedic Works
040 Language Dictionaries
050 Generalities Dictionaries
051 Philosophy and Related Disciplines Dictionaries
052 Religion Dictionaries
053 Social Science Dictionaries
054 Linguistics and Literature Dictionaries
055 Science Dictionaries
056 Techology (Applied Science) Dictionaries
057 Dictionaries of the Arts
059 Geography and History Dictionaries
060 General Organizations/Museology
070 Journalism/Publishing/Newspapers
071 Newspapers – United States
072 Newspapers – Non U.S.
073 Periodicals
080 General Collections
090 Manuscripts and Book Rarities

PHILOSOPHY AND RELATED DISCIPLINES

100 Philosophy and Related Disciplines
110 Metaphysics (Speculative Philosophy)
120 Epistemology/Causation/Humankind
130 Paranormal Phenomena and Arts
140 Specific Philosophical Viewpoints
150 Psychology
160 Logic
170 Ethics (Moral Philosophy)
180 Ancient, Medieval, Eastern Philosophy
190 Modern Western Philosophy

*RELIGION

200 Religion
210 Religious Beliefs and Attitudes
220 Bible
230 Comparative Religion
240 Christianity
250 Classical (Greek and Roman) Religions
260 Judaism
280 Indic Religions/Buddhism
290 Miscellaneous Religions

SOCIAL SCIENCES[2]

300 Social Sciences
301 Sociology
302 Social Interaction
303 Social Processes
304 Relation of Natural Factors to Social Processes
305 Social Stratification
306 Culture and Institutions
307 Communities
310 Statistics
320 Political Science
321 Theory of the State
323 Constitutional History and Government
324 Official Government Documents
327 International Relations
330 Economies
331 Labor Economics
332 Financial Economics
333 Land Economics
334 Cooperatives
335 Socialism and Related Systems
336 Public Finance
337 International Economics
338 Production Economics
339 Macroeconomics and Related Topics

SOCIAL SCIENCES cont'd.

340	Law
350	Public Administration/Executive Branch of Government
355	Military Science / Military History
360	Social Problems and Services/ Association
370	Education
380	Commerce/Communications/ Transportation
390	Customs/Etiquette/Folklore

*LANGUAGE/LINGUISTICS/ LITERATURE

400	General Language Studies
410	General Literature Studies
420	English Language and Literature
430	Germanic Languages and Literatures
440	Romance Languages and Literatures
450	Latin and Greek Languages and Literatures
460	Balto-Slavic Languages and Literatures
470	Afro-Asiatic Languages and Literatures
480	Sino-Tibetan and Japanese Languages and Literatures
490	Other Languages and Literatures

PURE SCIENCES[3]

500	Pure Sciences
510	Mathematics
520	Astronomy and Allied Sciences
530	Physics
540	Chemistry and Allied Sciences
550	Sciences of the Earth and Other Worlds
560	Paleontology/Paleozoology
570	Life Sciences
572	Human Races
573	Physical Anthropology
574	Biology
575	Organic Evolution/Genetics
576	Microbes
577	General Nature of Life
578	Microscopy in Biology
579	Collection and Preservation of Biological Specimens
580	Botanical Sciences
590	Zoological Sciences

TECHNOLOGY (APPLIED SCIENCES)[4]

600	Technology (Applied Sciences)
610	Medicine/Nursing
611	Human Anatomy/Cytology/Tissue Biology
612	Human Physiology
613	General and Personal Hygiene
614	Public Health and Related Topics
615	Pharmaecology/Therapeutics
616	Diseases
617	Surgery
618	Gynecology/Obstetrics/Pediatrics/ Geriatrics
619	Experimental Medicine
620	Engineering and Allied Operations
621	Applied Physics
622	Mining and Related Operations
623	Military and Nautical Engineering
624	Civil Engineering
625	Railroads/Roads/Highways
627	Hydraulic Engineering
628	Sanitary and Municipal Engineering
629	Other Branches of Engineering
630	Agriculture/Veterinary Science
631	Plant Culture
634	Forestry
636	Animal Husbandry
639	Hunting, Gamekeeping, Fishing
640	Home Economics and Family Living
650	Management and Auxilliary Services
660	Chemical and Related Technologies
670	Manufacturers
680	Manufacture of Products for Specific Uses
690	Buildings

THE ARTS

700	The Arts
710	Civic and Landscape Art
720	Architecture
730	Plastic Arts/Sculpture
740	Drawing/Decorative and Minor Arts
750	Painting and Paintings
760	Graphic Arts/Printmaking and Prints
770	Photography and Photographs
780	Music
790	Recreational and Performing Art

*Belles Lettres

800 General Collections of Belles Lettres
810 Poetry
820 Drama
830 Fiction
840 Literary Essays
850 Speeches
860 Letters
870 Satire and Humor
880 Miscellaneous Writings
890 Unassigned Belles-Lettres

*GEOGRAPHY/HISTORY AND AREA STUDIES

900 Geography and History
910 General Geography Travel
920 General Biography and Genealogy
930 Ancient History/Archeology
940 European History
941 British/Scottish/Irish History
943 Central European/German History
944 French/Monacan History
945 Italian History
946 Spanish/Portuguese History
947 Eastern European/Russian History
948 Northern European/Scandinavian History
949 History of Other Parts of Europe
950 Asian History
956 Middle Eastern History
960 African History
970 History of the Americas
971 General History of Canada
972 General History of Mexico, Middle and South America
975 General History of the United States
976 United States: Slavery/Civil War Period
977 United States: War with Spain to Present
978 United States: Local History and Geography
980 History of Oceania
990 History of Other Areas and Worlds

1) Includes expansion of class 010, Bibliography
2) Includes expansion of class 300, Social Sciences, and class 330, Economics. Subclasses 308 and 309 not assigned.
3) Includes expansion of class 570, Life Sciences. Subclass 571 not assigned.
4) Includes expansion of class 610, Medical Sciences, class 620, Engineering and Allied Operations. (Subclass 626 not assigned), and, slightly modified, class 630, Agriculture. Subclasses 632, 633, 635, 637 and 638 not assigned.

Survey of Subjects

Publishers and Distributors

at Aboriginal
Aboriginal Studies Press, Division of Australian Institute of Aboriginal and Torres Strait Islander Studies (AIATSIS), Acton House, Marcus Clarke St, Acton, GPOB 553, Canberra City ACT 2601, Australia / T: (02) 62461191, Fax: 62497310, E-mail: atf@aiatsis.gov.au – ISBN 0-85575
Orders
Peribo, 58 Beaumont Rd, Mount Kuring-Gai, NSW 2080, Australia / T: (02) 94570011, Fax: 94570022 – ISBN 1-86322

at A.G.S.M.
Australian Graduate School of Management, University of New South Wales, c/o Univ of NSW, AGSM Company Information, Sydney, NSW 2052, Australia / T: (02) 99319393, Fax: 96622451
Orders
Styfox Pty Ltd, 1/21 Dale St, POB 914, Brookvale NSW 2100, Australia / T: (02) 99056722, Fax: 99056127, E-mail: styfox@infoflex.com.au, Internet: www.styfox.com.au

at Archives
Australian Archives, POB 34, Dickson ACT 2602, Australia / T: (02) 62093443, Fax: 62093447

at AusInfo
AusInfo, Government Info Shop, GPOB 84, Canberra ACT 2601, Australia / T: (02) 62954411, (1800) 132447, Fax: 62954888, Internet: www.ausinfo.gov.au – ISBN 0-642; 0-634; 0-644

at A.U.S.L.I.G.
Australian Surveying and Land Information Group (AUSLIG), c/o Dept of Administrative Services, POB 2, Belconnen ACT 2616, Australia / T: (02) 62014300, Fax: 62014381

at Baillieu Libr
Baillieu Library, University of Melbourne, Parkville, Vic. 3052, Australia / T: (03) 93444000, Fax: 93481142 – ISBN 0-949302

at BISA
BISA School of Information, Library and Archive Studies, SILAS, Univ of New South Wales, Sydney, NSW 2052, Australia / T: (02) 93853438, Fax: 93853430, Tx: AA26054 – ISBN 0-86758

at Butterworths
Butterworths, 271-273 Lane Cove Rd, POB 345, North Ryde NSW 2113, Australia / T: (02) 93353333, 93354555, (1800) 620618, Fax: 93354611, 93354644, (008) 800122, Internet: www.butterworths.com.au – ISBN 0-409
Branch of
Butterworth & Co (Publishers) Ltd, Halsbury House, 35 Chancery Lane, POB 3000, London WC2A 1EL, United Kingdom / T: (0171) 4002500, Fax: 4002842, 4002969, Tx: 95678, Internet: www.butterworths.co.uk – ISBN 0-406; 0-407; 0-408; 0-409; 0-592
Orders
Canada: Butterworths Canada Ltd, 75 Clegg Rd, Markham, ON L6G 1A1, Canada / T: (905) 479-2665, (800) 668-6481, Fax: 479-2826, (800) 461-3275, Tx: 6525350, E-mail: orders@butterworths.ca, Internet: www.butterworths.ca – ISBN 0-409
Hong Kong: Butterworths Asia, c/o 19/F Eight Commercial Tower, 8 Sun Yip St, Chai Wan, Hong Kong / T: 29651400, (800) 7145, Fax: 29760840 – ISBN 962-8105; 0-409
India: Butterworth & Co (Asia) Pte Ltd, c/o G-2 Vardaan House, 7/28 Mahavir St, Ansari Rd, Daryanj, New Delhi, India / T: (011) 3282580, Fax: 3282650
Ireland: Butterworth (Ireland) Ltd, 16 Upper Ormand Quay, Dublin, Ireland / T: (01) 8731555, Fax: 8731876 – ISBN 1-85475
NZ: Butterworths of New Zealand Ltd, 203-207 Victoria St, POB 472, Wellington 1, New Zealand / T: (04) 3851479, (800) 800986, Fax: 3851598, Tx: 31306, E-mail: bonzl!wgpo!nieuj@bwthsnz.attmail.com – ISBN 0-40970
Pakistan: Butterworth & Co (Publishers) Ltd, 7 Jahangir St, Islamia Pk Poonch Rd, Lahore, Pakistan / T: (042) 415226
S Africa: Butterworth Publishers (Pty) Ltd, 8 Walter Pl, Mayville, POB 4, Mayville 4058, South Africa / T: (031) 2683111, Fax: 2683118, E-mail: vanessa.griffiths@butterworths.co.za, Internet: www.butterworths.co.za – ISBN 0-409
Singapore: Butterworths Asia, 1 Temasek Av, #17-01 Millenia Twr, Singapore, Singapore / T: 3369661, Fax: 3369662 – ISBN 9971-70; 0-409
UK: Butterworth & Co (Publishers) Ltd, Halsbury House, 35 Chancery Lane, POB 3000, London WC2A 1EL, United Kingdom / T: (0171) 4002500, Fax: 4002842, 4002969, Tx: 95678, Internet: www.butterworths.co.uk – ISBN 0-406; 0-407; 0-408; 0-409; 0-592
USA: Michie, 701 E Water St, Charlottesville VA 22906-7587, U.S.A. / T: (804) 972-7600, Fax: 972-7656
Branches
Australia: Butterworth-Heinemann, 22 Salmon St, POB 251, Port Melbourne Vic. 3207, Australia / T: (03) 92457111, Fax: 92457577, E-mail: bhau.marketing@reededucation.com.au, Internet: www.bh.com – ISBN 0-7506; 0-409
United Kingdom: Butterworth Law Publishers, Halsbury House, 35 Chancery Lane, POB 3000, London WC2A 1ER, United Kingdom / T: (0171) 4002500, Fax: 4002969, Tx: 95678
U.S.A.: Michie, 701 E Water St, Charlottesville VA 22906-7587, U.S.A. / T: (804) 972-7600, Fax: 972-7656
Canada: Butterworths Vancouver, 409 Granville St, Suite 1455, Vancouver BC V6C 1T2, Canada / T: (604) 684-4116, Fax: 682-5779
South Africa: Digma Publications, POB 65042, Benmore 2010, South Africa / T: (011) 8834854, Fax: 8836540 – ISBN 0-86984; 1-86829
Information
Only Australian titles listed

at Corangamite
Corangamite Regional Library Corporation, Warrnambool Microfilm Unit, POB 784, Warrnambool Vic. 3280, Australia / T: (03) 55621425, Fax: 55621425 – ISBN 0-909928

at Grainger Mus
Grainger Museum Board, University of Melbourne, Parkville, Vic. 3052, Australia / T: (03) 93445270, Fax: 93491707 – ISBN 0-909454, 86839

at G.S.N.T.
Genealogical Society of the Northern Territory Inc, POB 37212, Winnellie NT 0801, Australia / T: (08) 89321716 – ISBN 0-949124

at Hutchinson
Fabian Hutchinson, POB 218, Carlton South Vic. 3053, Australia / T: (03) 4896670, (08) 89532380, Fax: (06) 2573678

at Libertarian Micro
Libertarian Microfiche Publishing, c/o John Zube, 7 Oxley St, Berrima, NSW 2577, Australia / T: (02) 48771436

at Nat'l Libr
National Library of Australia, Parkes Place, Canberra, ACT 2600, Australia / T: (02) 62621367, (800) 800100, Fax: 62731084, 62734493, E-mail: nlasales@nla.gov.au – ISBN 0-642

at N.S.W. Archives
Archives Authority of New South Wales, Lvl 3, 66 Harrington St, The Rocks, Sydney, NSW 2000, Australia / T: (02) 92370137, 92370200, Fax: 92370142, E-mail: aonsw@records.nsw.gov.au – ISBN 0-7305
Orders
Styfox Pty Ltd, 1/21 Dale St, POB 914, Brookvale NSW 2100, Australia / T: (02) 99056722, Fax: 99056127, E-mail: styfox@infoflex.com.au, Internet: www.styfox.com.au

at Pacific Mss
Pacific Manuscripts Bureau (Pambu), Australian National University, RSPAS, Australian National Univ, Canberra, ACT 0200, Australia / T: (02) 62492521, Fax: 62490198, Tx: AA62694 SOPAC, E-mail: pambu@coombs.anu.edu.au
Information
A$60.00r silver A$50.00r vesicular (Australia); A$70.00r silver A$60.00r vesicular (overseas)

at Parliament
New South Wales Parliament, Parliament Hs, Macquarie St, Sydney, NSW 2000, Australia / T: (02) 92302380, Fax: 92311932
Orders
Styfox Pty Ltd, 1/21 Dale St, POB 914, Brookvale NSW 2100, Australia / T: (02) 99056722, Fax: 99056127, E-mail: styfox@infoflex.com.au, Internet: www.styfox.com.au
Information
Styfox Pty Ltd is the sole distributor of microfiche for the New South Wales Parliament. Catalogue available upon request

at Pascoe
W. & F. Pascoe Pty Ltd, 7 Hayes St, Balgowlah, NSW 2093, Australia / T: (02) 99491133, Fax: 99494389, E-mail: pascoe@zip.com.au – ISBN 0-9593336

at R.A.O.U.
Royal Australasian Ornithologists Union (RAOU), 21 Gladstone St, Moonee Pondsn, Vic. 3039, Australia / T: (03) 3701422, Fax: 3709194 – ISBN 0-9599823; 1-875122

at Seanachas
Seanachas Press, POB 169, Maroubra NSW 2035, Australia

at State Libr Vic
State Library of Victoria, 328 Swanston St, Melbourne, Vic. 3000, Australia / T: (03) 96699935, Fax: 96699958

at Statistics
Australian Bureau of Statistics (ABS), (Central Office), Australian Capital Territory, Cameron Offices, Chandler St, Belconnen, ACT 2616, POB 10, Belconnen ACT 2616, Australia / T: (02) 62526684, Fax: 62525988, Tx: 62020, E-mail: susan.pitt@abs.gov.au – ISBN 0-642
Branches
Australia: Australian Bureau of Statistics, New South Wales Office, St. Andrew's Hs, Sydney Sq, GPOB 796, Sydney NSW 2001, Australia / T: (02) 92684611, 92684620, Fax: 92647527, Tx: 20819, E-mail: stat.info@abs.telememo.au
Australia: Australian Bureau of Statistics, Northern Territory Office, 6th Floor MLC Bldg, 81 Smith St, Darwin, NT 0800, POB 3796, Darwin NT 0801, Australia / T: (08) 89813456, Fax: 89811218, E-mail: stat.info@abs.telememo.au
Australia: Australian Bureau of Statistics, Queensland Office, 313 Adelaide St, Brisbane, Qld. 4000, POB 9817, Brisbane Qld. 4001, Australia / T: (07) 32226351, Fax: 32296042, Tx: 40271, E-mail: stat.info@abs.telememo.au
Australia: Australian Bureau of Statistics, South Australian Office, 41 Currie St, Adelaide, SA 5000, POB 2272, Adelaide SA 5001, Australia / T: (08) 82377100, 82377582, Fax: (08) 82377566, Tx: 82106, E-mail: stat.info@abs.telememo.au
Australia: Australian Bureau of Statistics, Tasmanian Office, 1st Floor, 175 Collins St, GPOB 66A, Hobart Tas. 7001, Australia / T: (03) 62205800, Fax: 62205824, Tx: 58098, E-mail: stat.info@abs.telememo.au
Australia: Australian Bureau of Statistics, Victorian Office, Rialto N Twr, 525 Collins St, GPOB 2796Y, Melbourne Vic. 3001, Australia / T: (03) 96157000, Fax: 96157798, Tx: 30086, E-mail: stat.info@abs.telememo.au
Australia: Australian Bureau of Statistics, Western Australian Office, Hyatt Ctr, 30 Terrace Rd, GPOB K881, Perth WA 6001, Australia / T: (08) 93235140, Fax: 92212374, E-mail: stat.info@abs.telememo.au

at Thorpe Mf
D.W. Thorpe, POB 146, 18 Salmon St, Port Melbourne Vic. 3207, Australia / T: (03) 92457370, Fax: 92457395, (1800) 639798, E-mail: hugh.forster@thorpe.com.au, Internet: www.reedbooks.com.au/index.html – ISBN 0-909532; 1-875589; 0-7506
Orders
Continental Europe: K.G. Saur Verlag GmbH & Co KG, Ortlerstr. 8, 81373 München, Postf 70 16 20, 81316 München Germany / T: (089) 769020, Fax: 76902150, 76902250, E-mail: 100730.1341@compuserve.com, Internet: www.saur.de – ISBN 3-7940; 3-598
UK & Ireland: Bowker-Saur Ltd, Windsor Crt, East Grinstead House, East Grinstead, West Sussex, United Kingdom / T: (01342) 326972, Fax: 335612, E-mail: nicci@bowker-saur.co.uk.com – ISBN 0-86291
USA & Canada: R.R. Bowker, 121 Chanlon Rd, New Providence, NJ 07974, U.S.A. / T: (908) 464-6800 Sales USA (800) 521-8110, Fax: 771-7725 Ulrich's, 665-3502 BIP & ABPR, Tx: 12-7703, E-mail: ulrichs@reedref.com (Ulrich); dgravesande@reedref.com (BIP); blamar@reedref.com (ABPR) – ISBN 0-8352

at U.N.S.W. Library
University of New South Wales Library, UNSW, Sydney, NSW 2052, Australia / T: (02) 93852618, Fax: 93851260 – ISBN 0-909283

at Vine
Nick Vine Hall, 386 Ferrars St, Albert Park, Vic. 3206, Australia / T: (03) 96999548, Fax: 96962382 – ISBN 0-9597208; 1-86404; 1-875652

be Academie Royale
Académie Royale de Belgique, Rue Dacale 1, 1000 Bruxelles Belgium / T: (02) 5502206, 5502221, Fax: 5502205 – ISBN 90-6569; 2-8031
Orders
Brepols Publishers, Steenweg op Tielen 68, 2300 Turnhout, Belgium / T: (014) 402500, Fax: 428919, E-mail: publishers@brepols.com, Internet: www.brepols.com/publishers/ – ISBN 2-503; 90-72100

be Brepols
Brepols Publishers, Steenweg op Tielen 68, 2300 Turnhout, Belgium / T: (014) 402500, Fax: 428919, E-mail: publishers@brepols.com, Internet: www.brepols.com/publishers/ – ISBN 2-503; 90-72100
Orders
France: Editions Brepols, 23 rue des Grands Augustins, 75006 Paris, France / T: (1) 44412000, Fax: 43262377, Tx: 200307 f

be E.A.S.
European Aquaculture Society, Coupure Rechts 168, 9000 Gent, Belgium / T: (09) 2237722, Fax: 2237604

bl Biblioteca
Fundação Biblioteca Nacional, Avenida Rio Branco 219, 20040-008 Rio de Janeiro, Brazil / T: (021) 262.8255 x 220, 218, 219, 311, Fax: 2204173, Tx: 22941 bnrj br – ISBN 85-7017

bs U.B. Nat'l Inst
University of Botswana, National Institute of Development Research & Documentation (NIR), Private Bag 0022, Gaborone Botswana / T: 356364/5, Fax: 356591, Tx: 2429 BD – ISBN 99912-2
Orders
Botswana Book Centre, The Mall, POB 91, Gaborone Botswana / T: 352931, Fax: 374315, Tx: 2327

cc Globe
Globe Microfilms, c/o Editor, 57 Xuanwumen Xidajie, Beijing, China, People's Republic
Orders
N America: Norman Ross Publishing Inc, 330 W 58th St, New York, NY 10019, U.S.A. / T: (212) 765-8200, (800) 648-8850, Fax: 765-2393, E-mail: info@nross.com, Internet: www.nross.com – ISBN 0-8287; 0-88354

cc Haifu Micro
Haifu Microfilm Producing Center, Nanjing China, People's Republic

Orders
China National Publications Import & Export Corporation, Shanghai Branch, 537 Yan An Road (M), Shanghai, China, People's Republic

cc Microforms
China National Microforms Import & Export Corporation, A Subsidiary of China International Book Trading Corporation, 35 Chegongzhuang Xilu, POB 399-A, Beijing China, People's Republic / T: 8412255, 8413842, Fax: 8412023, Tx: 22496 cibtc cn

ch Transmission
Transmission Books & Microforms Company, Ltd, POB 96-337, Taipei, R.O.C. China, Republic / T: (02) 7367071, 7361058, Fax: 7363001, Tx: 26026

cn Bibl Nat
Bibliothèque Nationale du Québec, Service de Microphotographie, 125 rue Sherbrooke Ouest, Montréal, QC H2X 1X4, Canada / T: (514) 873-1100, Fax: 873-4310

cn Can Microfilming
Canadian Microfilming Co Ltd, Société Canadienne du Microfilm Inc, 464 rue Saint-Jean, Montreal, QC H2Y 2S1, Canada / T: (514) 288-5404, Fax: 843-4690

cn Carswell
Carswell, A Division of Thomson Canada Ltd, 2075 Kennedy Rd, 1 Corporate Plaza, Scarborough, ON M1T 3V4, Canada / T: (416) 759-4411, (800) 387-5164, Fax: 398-5082, 759-5415 – ISBN 0-459; 0-88820

Orders
H.B. Fenn & Co, Ltd, 1090 Lorimar Dr, Mississauga, ON L5S 1R7, Canada / T: (905) 670-3366, (800) 267-3366, Fax: 670-3422 – ISBN 0-919768; 1-55168

Branches
Canada: Richard De Boo Publishers, A Division of Thomson Canada Limited, 81 Curlew Dr, Don Mills, ON M3A 3P7, Canada / T: (416) 445-4940, (800) 268-6452, Fax: 445-5352 – ISBN 0-88820

cn C.I.H.M.
Canadian Institute for Historical Microreproductions, Institut canadien de microreproductions historiques, POB 2428, Stn D, Ottawa ON K1P 5W5, Canada / T: (613) 235-2628, Fax: 235-9752, E-mail: cihmicmh@nlo.nlc-bnc.ca, Internet: www.nlc-bnc.ca/cihm/

cn Commonwealth Micro
Commonwealth Microfilm Products, A Division of West Canadian Industries Group, 202 Amber St, Markham, ON L3R 3J8, Canada / T: (905) 415-9498, Fax: 415-9616

Information
Shipping and handling charges are NOT included in prices given

cn Communication
Canada Communication Group – Publishing, Groupe Communication Canada – Edition, Ottawa, ON K1A 0S9, Canada / T: (819) 956-4800, (800) 661-2868, Fax: 994-1498, (800) 661-1743, Tx: 534296, E-mail: publishing@ccg-gcc.ca – ISBN 0-660; 0-662; 0-315

Orders
Books Express, POB 10 Saffron Walden, Essex CB11 4EW, United Kingdom / T: (01799) 513726, Fax: 513248

USA: ISBS International Specialized Book Services Inc, 5804 NE Hassalo St, Portland, OR 97213-3644, U.S.A. / T: (503) 287-3093, (800) 944-6190, Fax: 280-8832, E-mail: orders@isbs.com – ISBN 0-89955

Information
Order co-published titles directly from co-publisher indicated

cn Geography
Geography Publications University of Waterloo, c/o Kate Evans, Department of Geography, Waterloo, ON N2L 3G1, Canada / E-mail: bkevans@cousteau.uwaterloo.ca – ISBN 0-921083

cn Globe Info
Globe Information Services, A Division of the Globe and Mail, 1120 Brichmont Rd, Scarborough, ON M1K 5G4, Canada / T: (416) 585-5090, (800) 701-9130, Fax: 585-5249, 752-9646 – ISBN 0-921925

cn I.D.R.C.
International Development Research Centre, Centre de Recherches pour le Développement International, 250 Albert St, POB 8500, Ottawa ON K1G 3H9, Canada / T: (613) 236-6163, Fax: 238-7230, Tx: 053-3753, E-mail: order@idrc.ca, Internet: www.idrc.ca – ISBN 0-88936; 1-55250

Orders
Germany: Siegfried Toeche-Mittler GmbH, Tropical Scientific Books, Hindenburgstr 33, 64295 Darmstadt, Germany / T: (06151) 33665, Fax: 314048 – ISBN 3-87820

India: Oxford Book and Stationery Company, Scindia House, New Delhi 110 001, India / T: (011) 45896, Fax: 3322639

Malaysia: University of Malaya Co-operative Bookshop Ltd, Kedai Buku Koperasi, Universiti Malaya, Jalan Pantai Baru, POB 1127, 59700 Kuala Lumpur Malaysia / T: (603) 7565000, Fax: (603) 7554424 – ISBN 967-9939

Singapore: Select Books Pte Ltd, c/o Lim U Wen Lena, 19 Tanglin Rd, #03-15 Tanglin Shopping Ctr, Singapore, Singapore / T: 7321515, Fax: 7360855, E-mail: selectbk@cyberway.com.sg

Tanzania: Tanzania Publishing House, 47 Independence Ave, POB 2138, Dar es Salaam Tanzania / T: (051) 32164/5/6, Tx: 41000 tptc tz – ISBN 9976-1

UK: Intermediate Technology Publications Ltd, 103-105, Southampton Row, London WC1B 4HH, United Kingdom / T: (0171) 4369761, Fax: 4362013, Tx: 268312 wescom g – ISBN 0-903031; 0-946688

USA: Unipub Bernan Associates, Kraus Organization Ltd, 4611-F Assembly Dr, Lanham MD 20706-4391, U.S.A. / T: (301) 459-7666, (800) 274-4888 USA, (800) 233-0504 Canada, Fax: 459-0056, E-mail: query@kraus.com

cn Library Assoc
Canadian Library Association, c/o Publications, 200 Elgin St, Suite 602, Ottawa, ON K2P 1L5, Canada / T: (613) 232-9625, Fax: 563-9895 – ISBN 0-88802

Orders
Microfilm Titles: Commonwealth Microfilm Products, A Division of West Canadian Industries Group, 202 Amber St, Markham, ON L3R 3J8, Canada / T: (905) 415-9498, Fax: 415-9616

USA: American Library Association, 50 E Huron St, Chicago, IL 60611, U.S.A. / T: (312) 280-4271, (800) 545-2433, Fax: 440-9374 – ISBN 0-8389

cn McLaren
McLaren Micropublishing Ltd, POB 972, Station F, Toronto ON M4Y 2N9, Canada / T: (416) 960-4801, Fax: 964-3745, E-mail: mmicro@interlog.com

cn Micromedia
Micromedia Limited, 20 Victoria St, Toronto, ON M5C 2N8, Canada / T: (416) 362-5211, (800) 387-2689, Fax: 362-6161, (800) 387-2689, E-mail: info@micromedia.on.ca – ISBN 0-88892

cn Municipal
Municipal World Inc, Elgin County Rd 27, Union, ON N0L 2L0, Box 399, Station Main, St. Thomas ON N5P 3V3, Canada / T: (519) 633-0031, Fax: 633-1001, E-mail: mwadmin@municipalworld.com – ISBN 0-919779

cn Nash Info
Nash Information Services, Inc, 1975 Bel Air Dr, Ottawa, ON K2C 0X1, Canada / T: (613) 225-3781, Fax: 225-6553

cn Nat'l Library
National Library of Canada/Bibliothèque nationale du Canada, Canadian Theses Service, 395 Wellington St, Ottawa, ON K1A 0N4, Canada / T: (819) 953-6221, Fax: 997-7517, Tx: 0534311, 0534312 – ISBN 0-612; 0-315

cn Pontif
Pontifical Institute of Medieval Studies, 59 Queen's Park Cres E, Toronto, ON M5S 2C4, Canada / T: (416) 926-7144, Fax: 926-7258, E-mail: pontifex@chass.utoronto.ca, Internet: www.chass.utoronto.ca:8080/ pontifex/pubs/ index.html – ISBN 0-88844

Orders
Europe: Brepols Publishers, Steenweg op Tielen 68, 2300 Turnhout, Belgium / T: (014) 402500, Fax: 428919, E-mail: publishers@brepols.com, Internet: www.brepols.com/publishers/ – ISBN 2-503; 90-72100

cn Precision
Precision Micrographic Services Ltd, 204 W 6th Av, Vancouver, BC V5Y 1K8, Canada / T: (604) 873-2681, Fax: 873-2683

cn Preston
Preston Microfilming Services, 2215 Queen St E, Toronto, ON M4E 1E8, Canada / T: (416) 699-7154, Fax: 699-7155

cn Telebook
Canadian Telebook Agency, 2 Gloucester St, Suite 301, Toronto, ON M4Y 1L5, Canada / T: (416) 929-7332, Fax: 929-3015

cn Thunder Bay
Thunder Bay Historical Museum Society, 425 Donald St E, Thunder Bay, ON P7E 5V1, Canada / T: (807) 623-0801, Fax: 622-6880, E-mail: tbhms@tbaytel.net, Internet: www.tbaytel.net/tbhms – ISBN 0-920119

Orders
Singing Shield Productions, 104 Ray Blvd, Thunder Bay, ON P7B 4C4, Canada / T: (807) 344-8355, Fax: 344-8355, E-mail: pebarr@tbaytel.net – ISBN 0-9691717

cn U.B.C. Preserve
University of British Columbia, Facilities and Preservation Office, Main Library, 1956 Main Mall, Vancouver, BC V6T 1Z1, Canada / T: (604) 822-3858, Fax: 822-3335, 822-9272, E-mail: namor@unixg.ubc.ca

cn U.T. Pr
University of Toronto Press, 10 St. Mary St, Ste 700, Toronto, ON M4Y 2W8, Canada / T: (416) 978-2239, (800) 565-9532, Fax: 978-4738 – ISBN 0-8020

Orders
Australia, NZ & Canada: University of Toronto Press, Publications Order Department, 10 St. Mary St, Ste 700, Toronto, ON M4Y 2W8, Canada / T: (416) 667-7791, (800) 565-9523, Fax: 667-7832, (800) 221-9985, E-mail: utpbooks@utpress.utoronto.ca

Europe: Marston Book Service Ltd, POB 269, Abingdon, Oxfordshire OX14 4YN, United Kingdom / T: (01235) 465500, Fax: 465555, E-mail: direct.order@marston.co.uk

Japan: UPS United Publishers Services Ltd, c/o Kenkyu-Sha Bldg, 9 Kanada Surugadai 2-chome, Chiyoda-ku, Tokyo, Japan / T: (03) 32927160, 32928610, Fax: 32928610, 32914541, Tx: 33331, E-mail: ups@beehive.twics.com

Branches
U.S.A.: University of Toronto Press, 250 Sonwil Dr, Buffalo, NY 14225, U.S.A. / T: (800) 565-9523, Fax: (800) 221-9985, E-mail: utpbooks@gpu.utcc.utoronto.ca, Internet: www.utpress.utoronto.ca

cn W.L.U. Press
Wilfrid Laurier University Press, WLU Press, 75 University Av W, Waterloo, ON N2L 3C5, Canada / T: (519) 884-0710 ext 6124, Fax: 725-1399, E-mail: press@mach1.wlu.ca – ISBN 0-88920

Orders
Australia: Wilfrid Laurier University Press, 4408 Milestrip Rd, Blasdell, NY 14219-2599, Box 277, Blasdell NY 14219-2599, U.S.A. / T: (519) 884-0710, Fax: 725-1399, E-mail: press@mach1.wlu.ca, Internet: info.wlu.ca/wwwpress

Europe: Wilfrid Laurier University Press, c/o University Book Marketing, 114-115 Tottenham Court Rd, London, United Kingdom / T: (0171) 3888500, Fax: 3885950

USA: Humanities Press International, Inc, 165 First Av, Atlantic Highlands NJ 07716-1289, U.S.A. / T: (201) 872-1441, (800) 221-3845, Fax: 872-0717, Tx: 752233 Hilarious – ISBN 0-391

et ILRI
International Livestock Research Institute (ILRI), POB 5689, Addis Ababa Ethiopia / T: (01) 613215, Fax: 611892, Tx: 21207 ilca et, E-mail: ilri-ethiopia@cgnet.com – ISBN 92-9053; 92-9146

Orders
Europe: TRIOPS, Hindenburgstr 33, 64295 Darmstadt, Germany / T: (06151) 33665

N America: Agribookstore, Winrock International, 1611 N Kent St, Suite 600, Arlington VA 22209, U.S.A. / T: (703) 525-9455, Fax: (703) 525-1744, Tx: 6491106, E-mail: (Dialcom) 41:tcn408

Information
ILCA pubs. are free to readers in Africa if ordered from ILCA headquarters in Ethiopia and sent to an African address. Prices include airmail postage. The ILCA and ILRAD have merged to form ILRI.

fi H.U. Libr
Helsingin yliopiston kirjasto, Helsinki University Library, Unioninkatu 36, POB 15, 00014 University of Helsinki Finland / T: (09) 19122732, Fax: 19122742, Tx: 121538 hyk, E-mail: anna-maija.pietilä@cc.helsinki.fi

fr A.C.R.P.P.
Association pour la Conservation et la Reproduction Photographique de la Presse, B.P. 21, 77313 Marne-La-Vallée Cedex 2, France

Information
ALL correspondence and orders to Mikrofilmarchiv in Dortmund

fr A.C.R.P.P.
A.C.R.P.P., Association pour la Conservation et la Reproduction photographique de la Presse, Le Parc aux Vignes, 11 allée des Sarments, 77183 Croissy-Beaubourg, BP 21, 77313 Marne-La-Vallée Cedex 2, France / T: (01) 60176810, 60177213, Fax: 60176805

Orders
Mikrofilmarchiv der deutschsprachigen Presse e.V., Münsterstr 9-11, 44122 Dortmund, Germany / T: (0231) 5023249, 5023216, Fax: 5026018, E-mail: pbohrman@stadtdor.de

N America: Norman Ross Publishing Inc, 330 W 58th St, New York, NY 10019, U.S.A. / T: (212) 765-8200, (800) 648-8850, Fax: 765-2393, E-mail: info@nross.com, Internet: www.nross.com – ISBN 0-8287; 0-88354

fr Armell
ARMELL, Agence Régionale des Métiers du Livre et de la Lecture des Pays de la Loire, Bibliothèque Jean Vilar, Place Jean Vilar, 49000 Angers, France / T: (01) 41440691, Fax: 41684589

fr Atelier National
Atelier National de Reproduction des Thèes de Lille, Université de Lille III, 9, rue Auguste Angellier, 59046 Lille, France / T: (03) 20308673, Fax: 20542195 – ISBN 02-284

Orders
Outside France: Société Nouvelle Didier érudition, 6, Rue de la Sorbonne, 75005 Paris France / T: (1) 43544757, Fax: 40517385

Information
F45.00 per title up to the 11th fiche. After this add F3.00 per fiche

fr Augustiniennes
Institut d'Etudes Augustiniennes, 3 Rue de l'Abbaye, 75006 Paris France / T: (01) 43548025 – ISBN 2-85121

fr Bibl Nationale
Bibliothèque Nationale de France, Service commercial, 58 rue de Richelieu, 75002 Paris, France / T: (01) 47038898, Fax: 47038172 – ISBN 2-7177

Orders
N & S America: Norman Ross Publishing Inc, 330 W 58th St, New York, NY 10019, U.S.A. / T: (212) 765-8200, (800) 648-8850, Fax: 765-2393, E-mail: info@nross.com, Internet: www.nross.com – ISBN 0-8287; 0-88354

fr CHANGE
CHANGE, Editions Numismatiques et Changes, 12, Rue Poincaré, 55800 Revigny, France

fr C.R.D.P.
Centre Régional de Documentation Pédagogique de Franche-Comté, CRDP Besançon, 6 rue des Fusillés de la Résistance, 25003 Besançon Cédex, France / T: (05) 81250250, Fax: 81250255

fr Electre
Electre, 35 rue Grégoire de Tours, 75279 Paris Cedex 06, France / T: (01) 44412800, Fax: 44412855 – ISBN 2-7654

fr Ethnologie
Institut d'Ethnologie du Muséum National d'Histoire Naturelle, Collection Archives et Documents, micro-edition, c/o Musée de l'Homme, Palais de Chaillot, 17, Pl du Trocadéro, 75116 Paris, France / T: (01) 44057345 – ISBN 2-85265

fr F.F.G.
Fédération Française de Généologie, F.F.G., Centre des Provinces Françaieses, 2 rue Achille Luchaire, 75014 Paris, BP 63, 75261 Paris Cedex 06, France

fr Hachette
Microéditions Hachette, 79 blvd St-Germain, 75006 Paris France / T: (01) 46348634 – ISBN 2-01
Orders
Norman Ross Publishing Inc, 330 W 58th St, New York, NY 10019, U.S.A. / T: (212) 765-8200, (800) 648-8850, Fax: 765-2393, E-mail: info@nross.com, Internet: www.nross.com – ISBN 0-8287; 0-88354

fr I.C.S.
International Communications Services, 23, avenue Villemain, 75014 Paris, France / T: (01) 45438260, Fax: 45438140
Orders
N America: Norman Ross Publishing Inc, 330 W 58th St, New York, NY 10019, U.S.A. / T: (212) 765-8200, (800) 648-8850, Fax: 765-2393, E-mail: info@nross.com, Internet: www.nross.com – ISBN 0-8287; 0-88354

fr Illustration
Archives de L'Illustration / Keystone, 21 rue du Renard, 75004 Paris, France
Orders
Norman Ross Publishing Inc, 330 W 58th St, New York, NY 10019, U.S.A. / T: (212) 765-8200, (800) 648-8850, Fax: 765-2393, E-mail: info@nross.com, Internet: www.nross.com – ISBN 0-8287; 0-88354

fr I.S.S.N.
ISSN International Centre, 20 rue Bachaumont, 75002 Paris, France / T: (01) 44882220, Fax: 40263243, Tx: 219847 f

fr Journal Officiel
Journal Officiel, Editeur des Journaux Officiels, 26 rue Desaix, 75727 Paris, France / T: (01) 40587500, 40587600

fr Orientalistes
Publications Orientalistes de France, 1 blvd de l'Oise, 95030 Cergy, France / T: (01) 34223002, Fax: 30734400 – ISBN 2-7169
Orders
Distique, 5 rue de Maréchal-Leclerc, 28600 Luisant, France / T: (02) 37305700, Fax: 37305712
N America: Norman Ross Publishing Inc, 330 W 58th St, New York, NY 10019, U.S.A. / T: (212) 765-8200, (800) 648-8850, Fax: 765-2393, E-mail: info@nross.com, Internet: www.nross.com – ISBN 0-8287; 0-88354

fr Réunion
Editions de la Réunion des Musées Nationaux (R.M.N.), 49 rue Etienne Marcel, 75001 Paris, France / T: (01) 40134800, Fax: 42225073 – ISBN 2-7118

fr S.E.M.P.
S.E.M.P., S.A., 26 rue Le Brun, 75013 0aris, France / T: (01) 44084646, Fax: 44084640, Tx: 203046 f

fr UNESCO
UNESCO, United Nations Educational, Scientific and Cultural Organization, 1 rue Miollis, 75732 Paris, France / T: (01) 45681000, Fax: 42733007, Tx: 204461 Paris, Internet: www.unesco.org/publishing – ISBN 92-3
Orders
All microfiche titles: Archives and Micrography Section (DIT/AM), UNESCO, 7, place de Fontenoy, 75352 Paris 07 SP, France / T: (01) 45681945, 45684300, Fax: 45671690, 45685741, Tx: 204461 Paris, Internet: www.unesco.org/publishing
Australia: Educational Supplies Pty Ltd, 8 Cross St, POB 33, PO, Brookvale NSW 2100, Australia / T: (02) 99050201, Fax: 99055209
Canada: Renouf Publishing Co Ltd, Editions Renouf Ltée, 5369 Canotek Rd, Ottawa, ON K1J 9J3, Canada / T: (613) 745-2665, Fax: 745-7660, Internet: fox.nstn.ca/ renouf
Germany: S. Karger GmbH, Lörracher Str 16A, 79115 Freiburg, Postfach, 79095 Freiburg Germany / T: (0761) 452070, Fax: 4520714 – ISBN 3-8055
UK: Her Majesty's Stationery Office (HMSO), c/o Agency Section, 51 Nine Elms Lane, POB 276, London SW8 5DT, United Kingdom / T: (0171) 8738365, Fax: 8738203, Tx: 2971138 – ISBN 0-10; 0-11; 0-337
USA: Unipub Bernan Associates, Kraus Organization Ltd, 4611-F Assembly Dr, Lanham MD 20706-4391, U.S.A. / T: (301) 459-7666, (800) 274-4888 USA, (800) 233-0504 Canada, Fax: 459-0056, E-mail: query@kraus.com
Information
Orders sent to above address should be accompanied by by a cheque or money order in French francs or the equivalent sum in US dollars. All out-of-print titles available on microfiche. Includes International Bureau of Education publications

gw Alpha Com
Alpha Com GmbH, Sportalle 6, 22335 Hamburg, Postf 630654, 22316 Hamburg Germany / T: (040) 513020, Fax: 51302111
Orders
N America: Norman Ross Publishing Inc, 330 W 58th St, New York, NY 10019, U.S.A. / T: (212) 765-8200, (800) 648-8850, Fax: 765-2393, E-mail: info@nross.com, Internet: www.nross.com – ISBN 0-8287; 0-88354

gw Beck
C.H. Beck'sche Verlagsbuchhandlung, Wilhelmstr 9, 80801 München, Postf 400340, 80703 München Germany / T: (089) 38189238, Fax: 38189661 – ISBN 3-406

gw Belser Wiss
Belser Wissenschaftlicher Dienst, Gartenstr 1, 72218 Wildberg, Postf 126, 72215 Wildberg Germany / T: (07054) 2475, Fax: 2639, E-mail: 101553.3467@compuserve.com – ISBN 3-628

gw Böhner
Dr. Claus-Peter Böhner, Wilhelm-Wundt-Str. 18, 68199 Mannheim, Germany / T: (0621) 861627, Fax: 856410 – ISBN 3-930263

gw Boorberg
Richard Boorberg Verlag GmbH & Co, Scharrstr 2, 70563 Stuttgart, Postf 800260, 70502 Stuttgart Germany / T: (0711) 73850, Fax: 732694

gw D.M.A.
Deutsches Musikgeschichtliches Archiv, Gießbergstr 41-47, 34127 Kassel, Germany / T: (0561) 899940

gw Fischer
Harald Fischer Verlag GmbH, Theaterplatz 31, 91054 Erlangen, Postf 1565, 91005 Erlangen Germany / T: (09131) 205620, Fax: 206028, E-mail: haraldfischerverlag@fen.baynet.de – ISBN 3-89131

gw Hänsel
Verlag Dr. Hänsel-Hohenhausen, Verlag der Deutschen Hochschulschriften (DHS), Boschring 21-23, Postf 1212, 63324 Egelsbach Germany / T: (06103) 44940, Fax: 44944 – ISBN 3-89349; 3-8267

gw Heinz
Hans-Dieter Heinz, Akademischer Verlag Stuttgart, Steiermärker Str 132, 70469 Stuttgart, Germany / T: (0711) 812413, Fax: 1353186 – ISBN 3-88099

gw IOS
IOS-ECHO, Publikationen auf Mikrofiche, Eichenallee 12, Postf 141, 21517 Wohltorf Germany / T: (04104) 80120, Fax: 80329

gw Keip
Antiquariat und Verlag Keip GmbH, Bayernstr 9, 63773 Goldbach, Germany / T: (06021) 59050, Fax: 590542, E-mail: antiquariat.keip@t-online.de, Internet: keip.net – ISBN 3-8051

gw Lengenfelder
Edition Helga Lengenfelder, Schönstr 51, 81543 München, Germany / T: (089) 663845 – ISBN 3-89219

gw Mikro Press
Mikro Press GmbH, Siemensstr 17-19, 53121 Bonn, Germany / T: (0228) 231688, Fax: 628868
Orders
N America: Norman Ross Publishing Inc, 330 W 58th St, New York, NY 10019, U.S.A. / T: (212) 765-8200, (800) 648-8850, Fax: 765-2393, E-mail: info@nross.com, Internet: www.nross.com – ISBN 0-8287; 0-88354

gw Mikrofilm
Mikrofilmarchiv der deutschsprachigen Presse e.V., Münsterstr 9-11, 44122 Dortmund, Germany / T: (0231) 5023249, 5023216, Fax: 5026018, E-mail: pbohrman@stadtdor.de
Information
Inquire for prices

gw Misc Inst
Miscellaneous Institutions, see gw Mikrofilm, Germany
Information
All institutes, libraries whose masters are available for filming through Mikrofilmarchiv

gw Olms
Georg Olms Verlag AG, Hagentorwall 7, 31134 Hildesheim, Germany / T: (05121) 15010, Fax: 150150, E-mail: olms@georg-olms.hi.eunet.de – ISBN 3-487
Orders
VVA – Vereinigte Verlagsauslieferung, An der Autobahn, 33334 Gütersloh, Postf 7600, 33310 Gütersloh Germany / T: (05241) 808077, 803844, Fax: 806007, 8060250
Austria: Mohr Morawa, Buchvertrieb GmbH, Sulzengasse 2, 1232 Wien, Postf 260, 1101 Wien Austria / T: (01) 6846140, 6876420, Fax: 687130, Tx: 131912 momo
N America: Norman Ross Publishing Inc, 330 W 58th St, New York, NY 10019, U.S.A. / T: (212) 765-8200, (800) 648-8850, Fax: 765-2393, E-mail: info@nross.com, Internet: www.nross.com – ISBN 0-8287; 0-88354
Branches
Switzerland: Edition Olms AG, Färberstr 28, 8008 Zürich Switzerland / T: (01) 2610270, Fax: 2617103 – ISBN 3-283
U.S.A.: Georg Olms AG, 111 West 57 St, New York, NY 10019, U.S.A. / T: (212) 757-5237

gw Saur
K.G. Saur Verlag GmbH & Co KG, Ortlerstr. 8, 81373 München, Postf 70 16 20, 81316 München Germany / T: (089) 769020, Fax: 76902150, 76902250, E-mail: 100730.1341@compuserve.com, Internet: www.saur.de – ISBN 3-7940; 3-598
Orders
Australia: D.W. Thorpe, POB 146, 18 Salmon St, Port Melbourne Vic. 3207, Australia / T: (03) 92457370, Fax: 92457395, (1800) 639798, E-mail: hugh.forster@thorpe.com.au, Internet: www.reedbooks.com.au/index.html – ISBN 0-909532; 1-875589; 0-7506
N America: R.R. Bowker, 121 Chanlon Rd, New Providence, NJ 07974, U.S.A. / T: (908) 771-8626, Fax: 771-8784, E-mail: nan.hudes@bowker.com – ISBN 0-89664
UK & Ireland: Bowker-Saur Ltd, Windsor Crt, East Grinstead House, East Grinstead, West Sussex, United Kingdom / T: (01342) 326972, Fax: 335612, E-mail: nicci@bowker-saur.co.uk.com – ISBN 0-86291

gw V.C.H.
VCH Verlagsgesellschaft mbH, Pappelallee 3, 69469 Weinheim, Postfach 101161, 69451 Weinheim Germany / T: (06201) 606152, 606427, Fax: 606184, 606117, Tx: 465516 vchwhd – ISBN 3-527
Orders
DECHEMA e.V., Theodor-Heuss-Allee 25, 60486 Frankfurt am Main, Postf 150104, 60061 Frankfurt am Main Germany / T: (069) 7564275, Fax: 7564201, Tx: 412490 dcha d – ISBN 3-926959
Australia, NZ: Jacaranda Wiley Ltd, 33 Park Rd, POB 1226, Milton Qld. 4064, Australia / T: (07) 38599755, (800) 777474, Fax: 38599715, (800) 802258, E-mail: custservice@jacwiley.com.au – ISBN 0-7016
Malaysia, Singapore, Brunei, Burma: Parry's Press, Parry's Book Center, 60 Jalan Negara, Taman Melawati, 53100 Kuala Lumpur, POB 10960, 50730 Kuala Lumpur Malaysia / T: (03) 4087235, 4079176, Fax: 4079180, Tx: parry's ma 33243, E-mail: haja@msn.com
Philippines: National Bookstore, Inc, 701 Rizal Av, Sta Cruz, POB 1934, Manila Philippines / T: (02) 494306, Tx: 27890, 41144 – ISBN 971-08
S Korea: Kumi Trading Co Ltd, CPOB 3553, Seoul 100-635, Korea, Republic / T: (02) 5886667, Fax: (02) 5888291
Taiwan: Maw Chang Book Company, 84.4 Sing Sung South Rd, Section 3, POB 58911, Taipei 107, China, Republic / T: 3210698
UK & Ireland: International Thomson Publishing Services Ltd, Cheriton House, North Way, Andover Hants SP10 5BE, United Kingdom / T: (01264) 342910, Fax: 342787
Branches
Japan: VCH Shuppan K.K., Eikow Bldg, 10-9 Hongo 1-chome, Bunkyo-ku, Tokyo, Japan / T: (03) 38163146, Fax: 38163758
Switzerland: VCH, Hardstr 10, 4020 Basel Switzerland / T: (061) 2710606, Fax: 2710618, Tx: 911527 dmsch
United Kingdom: VCH Publishers (UK) Ltd, 8 Wellington Court, Cambridge CB1 1HZ, United Kingdom / T: (01223) 321111, Fax: 313321, Tx: 825372 turping g
Singapore: Parry's Book Centre Pte Ltd, 528-A Macpherson Rd, Singapore, Singapore / T: 7448673, Fax: 7448676

ie European Micro
European Micropublishing Services Ltd, Unit 56, Sandyford Industrial Estate, Dublin, Ireland / T: (01) 2897912, Fax: 2897913

ie Irish Times
The Irish Times Ltd, 10-16 D'Olier St, POB 74, Dublin 2, Ireland / T: (01) 6792022, Fax: 6797991, Tx: 93639 – ISBN 0-907011

ie Microforms
Irish Microforms Ltd, Sentry Hall, Industrial Estate, Sentry, Dublin, Ireland / T: (01) 8424144, Fax: 8424052
Orders
N America: Norman Ross Publishing Inc, 330 W 58th St, New York, NY 10019, U.S.A. / T: (212) 765-8200, (800) 648-8850, Fax: 765-2393, E-mail: info@nross.com, Internet: www.nross.com – ISBN 0-8287; 0-88354

ii ICRISAT
ICRISAT, International Crops Research Institute for the Semi-Arid Tropics, Information Services, Patancheru PO, Andhra Pradesh 502 324, India / T: (0842) 224016, Fax: 241239, Tx: 422203 icri in, 4256366 icri in. Dialcom: 157:CG1505 – ISBN 92-9066
Orders
N America: Agribookstore, Winrock International, 1611 N Kent St, Suite 600, Arlington VA 22209, U.S.A. / T: (703) 525-9455, Fax: (703) 525-1744, Tx: 6491106, E-mail: (Dialcom) 41:tcn408
Information
All out-of-print titles are available as microfiche at flat-rate page charges inclusive of postage

is I.T.T.I.
I.T.T.I. Ltd, 39 Hayarkon St, Bnei-Brak, Israel / T: (03) 5707881, Fax: 5700291

it F.A.O.
FAO, Food and Agriculture Organization of the United Nations, Viale delle Terme di Caracalla, 00100 Roma, Italy / T: (06) 52251, Fax: 52253152, 52255155, Tx: 610181 fao i, E-mail: publications-sales@fao.org, Internet: www.fao.org – ISBN 92-5
Information
Inquire about titles on microfiche. Inquire about inclusive subscriptions at $200.00 per year for FAO Yearbooks and Annuals

ja CEACS
The Centre for East Asian Cultural Studies for Unesco, The Toyo Bunko, Honkomagome 2-28-21, Bunkyo-ku, Tokyo, Japan / T: (03) 39420124, Fax: 39420120, E-mail: ceacs@toyo-bunko.or.jp – ISBN 4-89656
Orders
Kinokuniya Co Ltd, Publishing Department, 38-1 Sakuragaoka 5-chome Setagaya-ku, Tokyo, Japan / T: (03) 34390172, Fax: 34390173, Tx: 2424344 – ISBN 4-314

ja Japan Micro
Japan Microfilm Service Center Co, Ltd, 1-10-11 Hongo, Bunkyo-ku, Tokyo, Japan / T: (03) 38151231, Fax: 38158177

ja Journal of Physics
Japanese Journal of Applied Physics, c/o Daini Toyokaiji Bldg, 4-24-8 Shinbashi, Minato-ku, Tokyo, Japan / Fax: (03) 3432-0728, E-mail: customer@jjap.or.jp, Internet: www.soc.nacsis.ac.jp/jjap

ja Nat'l Diet
National Diet Library, 1-10-1 Nagata-cho, Chiyoda-ku, Tokyo 100, Japan / T: (03) 35812331, Fax: (03) 35979104 – ISBN 4-87582

ja Nihon Keizai
Nihon Keizai Shimbun, Inc, 1-9-5 Otemachi, Chiyoda-ku, Tokyo, Japan / T: (03) 32700251, Fax: 52552864, Tx: 22308 nikkei – ISBN 4-532
Orders
Europe: Nihon Keizai Shimbun Europe Ltd, Bush House, North West Wing, Aldwych, London WC2BN 4PJ, United Kingdom / T: (0171) 3794994, Fax: 3790378, Tx: 918553 nikeg

ja Nippon Tech
Nippon Technical Service Co, Ltd, Kohjimachi 4 Chome Bldg, Kohjimachi 4-3, Chiyoda-Ku, Tokyo, Japan / T: (03) 32651955, 32651956, Fax: 32341956, Tx: 02324870 tecser j

ja Physical Soc
The Physical Society of Japan, Rm No. 211, Kikai-Shinko Bldg, 3-5-8 Shiba-Koen, Minato-Ku, Tokyo, Japan / T: (03) 34342671, Fax: 34320997, E-mail: pubpub@jps.or.jp, Internet: www.soc.nacsis.ac.jp/jps/jpsj/ – ISBN 4-89027

ja U.N. Univ
United Nations University Press (UNU), 53-70 Jingumae 5-chome, Shibuya-ku, Tokyo, Japan / T: (03) 34992811, Fax: 34067345, E-mail: sales@hq.unu.edu, Internet: www.unu.edu – ISBN 92-808; 952-9520
Orders
Australia: Hunter Publications, 58A Gipps St, Collingwood, Vic. 3066, Australia / T: (03) 94175361, Fax: 94197154
Germany: UNO – Verlag, Poppelsdorfer Allee 55, 53115 Bonn, Germany / T: (0228) 212940, Fax: 217492
India: Segment Book Distributors, B-23/25 Kailash Colony, New Delhi, India / T: (011) 6443013, Fax: 16470472
Italy: Licosa, Libreria Commissionaria Sansoni s.p.a., Via Benedetto Fortini, 120/10, POB 552, 50125 Firenze Italy / T: (055) 645415, Fax: 641257, Tx: 343509
N America: Unipub Bernan Associates, Kraus Organization Ltd, 4611-F Assembly Dr, Lanham MD 20706-4391, U.S.A. / T: (301) 459-7666, (800) 274-4888 USA, (800) 233-0504 Canada, Fax: 459-0056, E-mail: query@kraus.com
S Korea: Median Media Ltd, 99-13 Chungjungro 2-ga, Seodaemun-ku, Seoul, Korea, Republic / T: (02) 3937583, Fax: 3925431
Singapore: Chopmen Publishers, 865 Mountbatten Rd #05-28, Singapore, 1543, Singapore / T: 3441495, Fax: 3440180, E-mail: mighty@singnet.com.sg – ISBN 9971-68
Spain: Mundi Prensa Libros SA, Castelló 37, 28001 Madrid, Spain / T: (91) 4313399, Fax: 5753998, Tx: 49370 mpli e
Sweden: Fritzes Kungl. Hovbokhandel, Regeringsgaten 12, Box 16356, 10327 Stockholm Sweden / T: (08) 238900, Fax: 205021
Switzerland: United Nations Publications, Vereinte Nationen Veröffentlichungen, C115 Palais des Nations, 1211 Genève, Switzerland / T: (022) 9172606, 9172613, Fax: 9170027, E-mail: unpubli@unog.ch, Internet: www.un.org/pubs/sales.htm – ISBN 92-1; 92-806; 92-9045; 92-9771
UK: Her Majesty's Stationery Office (HMSO), c/o Agency Section, 51 Nine Elms Lane, POB 276, London SW8 5DT, United Kingdom / T: (0171) 8738365, Fax: 8738203, Tx: 2971138 – ISBN 0-10; 0-11; 0-337

ja Yushodo
Yushodo Co., Ltd, 29 San-ei-cho, Shinjuku-ku, Tokyo, Japan / T: (03) 33571411, Fax: 33515855, Tx: 2324136

lu EEC
Office for Official Publications of the European Communities, 2 Rue Mercier, 2985 Luxembourg, Luxembourg / T: 292942505, Fax: 292942709 – ISBN 92-77; 92-825; 92-826; 92-827; 92-828
Orders
Canada: Renouf Publishing Co Ltd, Editions Renouf Ltée, 5369 Canotek Rd, Ottawa, ON K1J 9J3, Canada / T: (613) 745-2665, Fax: 745-7660, Internet: fox.nstn.ca/ renouf
Japan: Kinokuniya Co Ltd, Publishing Department, 38-1 Sakuragaoka 5-chome Setagaya-ku, Tokyo, Japan / T: (03) 34390172, Fax: 34390173, Tx: 2424344 – ISBN 4-314
UK: Her Majesty's Stationery Office (HMSO), c/o Agency Section, 51 Nine Elms Lane, POB 276, London SW8 5DT, United Kingdom / T: (0171) 8738365, Fax: 8738203, Tx: 2971138 – ISBN 0-10; 0-11; 0-337
USA: Unipub Bernan Associates, Kraus Organization Ltd, 4611-F Assembly Dr, Lanham MD 20706-4391, U.S.A. / T: (301) 459-7666, (800) 274-4888 USA, (800) 233-0504 Canada, Fax: 459-0056, E-mail: query@kraus.com

mx El Nacional
El Nacional, Ignacio Mariscal 25, 06030 Mexico, Mexico
Orders
Norman Ross Publishing Inc, 330 W 58th St, New York, NY 10019, U.S.A. / T: (212) 765-8200, (800) 648-8850, Fax: 765-2393, E-mail: info@nross.com, Internet: www.nross.com – ISBN 0-8287; 0-88354

ne Brill
Brill, Academic Publishers, Plantijnstraat 2, 2321 JC Leiden, Postbus 9000, 2300 PA Leiden Netherlands / T: (071) 5353566, Fax: 5317532, E-mail: cs@brill.nl – ISBN 90-04
Branches
Denmark: Scandinavian Science Press Ltd, Langaåsen 4, Ganløse, 2760 Målv, Denmark / T: (02) 183021 – ISBN 87-87491
Germany: Brill, Academic Publishers, Antwerpener Str 6-12, 50672 Köln, Germany / T: (0221) 516488, Fax: 518533, E-mail: 00221516488-0001@t-online.de – ISBN 3-7652
Japan: Brill, Academic Publishers, c/o Bureau A. Hosoya, Stork Yotsuzya no. 104, 24-5 Sakamachi, Shinjuku-ku, Tokyo, Japan / T: (03) 3580692, Fax: 3580693
U.S.A.: Brill, Academic Publishers, 112 Water St, Ste 400, Boston, MA 02109, U.S.A. / T: (617) 263-2323, (800) 962-4406, Fax: 263-2324, E-mail: 103740.2612@compuserve.com – ISBN 0-9004

ne IDC
IDC Publishers bv, Hogewoerd 151, POB 11205, 2301 EE Leiden Netherlands / T: (071) 5142700, Fax: 5131721, E-mail: info@idc.nl, Internet: www.idc.nl – ISBN 3-85750
Information
For a distributor in your area / country, please contact IDC Publishers. You can also find a list of distributors at our website (How to contact us).

ne MMF Publ
MMF Publications, Heereweg 331a, POB 287, 2160 AG Lisse Netherlands / T: (0252) 417250, Fax: 418658, E-mail: 100315.315@compuserve.com
Branch of
Microformat Systems B.V. / Microformat Publications, Heereweg 331A, POB 287, 2160 AG Lisse Netherlands / T: (2521) 17250, Fax: 18658
Orders
Norman Ross Publishing Inc, 330 W 58th St, New York, NY 10019, U.S.A. / T: (212) 765-8200, (800) 648-8850, Fax: 765-2393, E-mail: info@nross.com, Internet: www.nross.com – ISBN 0-8287; 0-88354

ne Schierenberg
Dieter Schierenberg BV, Rare Books and Periodicals on Natural Sciences, Prinsengracht 485-487, 1016 HP Amsterdam, Netherlands / T: (020) 6225730, Fax: 6265650, Tx: 13408 schie

ne Sdu MICRO
NV Sdu Publishers (MICRO), Christoffel Plantijnstraat 2, Postb 20014, 2500 EA Den Haag Netherlands / T: (070) 3789534, Fax: 3835709, Tx: 32486 stdru

ne Slangenburg
Microlibrary Slangenburg Abbey, Abdijlaan 1, Slangenburg, 7004 JL Doetinchem, Netherlands / T: (0315) 298268, Fax: 298798, E-mail: info@willibrords-abbey.nl

ne Swets
Swets & Zeitlinger B.V., Heereweg 347b, Postbus 810, 2160 SZ Lisse Netherlands / T: (0252) 435111, Fax: 415888, Tx: 41325 szlis nl, E-mail: wverbeek@swets.nl, Internet: www.swets.nl – ISBN 90-265
Branches
Germany: Swets & Zeitlinger GmbH, Schaubstr 16, 60596 Frankfurt am Main, Germany / T: (069) 633988-0, Fax: 6314216/17, Tx: 4189720
United Kingdom: Swets United Kingdom Ltd, 32 Blacklands Way, Abingdon Business Park, Abingdon Oxon OX14 1SX, United Kingdom / T: (01235) 530809, Fax: 535055, Tx: 83649
U.S.A.: Swets & Zeitlinger Inc, 440 Creamery Way, Suite A, Exton, PA 19341, U.S.A. / T: (610) 524-5355, Fax: (610) 524-5366

nz BAB
BAB Microfilming, 4 Kathryn Av, Mt. Roskill, Auckland, New Zealand / T: (09) 6259778, Fax: 6259778 – ISBN 0-908797; 0-908989

nz Butterworths
Butterworths of New Zealand Ltd, 203-207 Victoria St, POB 472, Wellington 1, New Zealand / T: (04) 3851479, (800) 800986, Fax: 3851598, Tx: 31306, E-mail: bonzl!wgpo!nieuj@bwthsnz.attmail.com – ISBN 0-40970
Branch of
Butterworth & Co (Publishers) Ltd, Halsbury House, 35 Chancery Lane, POB 3000, London WC2A 1EL, United Kingdom / T: (0171) 4002500, Fax: 4002842, 4002969, Tx: 95678, Internet: www.butterworths.co.uk – ISBN 0-406; 0-407; 0-408; 0-409; 0-592
Orders
Australia: Butterworths, 271-273 Lane Cove Rd, POB 345, North Ryde NSW 2113, Australia / T: (02) 93353333, 93354555, (1800) 620618, Fax: 93354611, 93354644, (008) 800122, Internet: www.butterworths.com.au – ISBN 0-409
Canada: Butterworths Canada Ltd, 75 Clegg Rd, Markham, ON L6G 1A1, Canada / T: (905) 479-2665, (800) 668-6481, Fax: 479-2826, (800) 461-3275, Tx: 6525350, E-mail: orders@butterworths.ca, Internet: www.butterworths.ca – ISBN 0-409
Hong Kong: Butterworths Asia, c/o 19/F Eight Commercial Tower, 8 Sun Yip St, Chai Wan, Hong Kong / T: 29651400, (800) 7145, Fax: 29760840 – ISBN 962-8105; 0-409
India: Butterworth & Co (Asia) Pte Ltd, c/o G-2 Vardaan House, 7/28 Mahavir St, Ansari Rd, Daryanj, New Delhi, India / T: (011) 3282580, Fax: 3282650
Ireland: Butterworth (Ireland) Ltd, 16 Upper Ormand Quay, Dublin, Ireland / T: (01) 8731555, Fax: 8731876 – ISBN 1-85475
Pakistan: Butterworth & Co (Publishers) Ltd, 7 Jahangir St, Islamia Pk Poonch Rd, Lahore, Pakistan / T: (042) 415226
S Africa: Butterworth Publishers (Pty) Ltd, 8 Walter Pl, Mayville, POB 4, Mayville 4058, South Africa / T: (031) 2683111, Fax: 2683118, E-mail: vanessa.griffiths@butterworths.co.za, Internet: www.butterworths.co.za – ISBN 0-409
Singapore: Butterworths Asia, 1 Temasek Av, #17-01 Millenia Twr, Singapore, Singapore / T: 3369661, Fax: 3369662 – ISBN 9971-70; 0-409
UK: Butterworth & Co (Publishers) Ltd, Halsbury House, 35 Chancery Lane, POB 3000, London WC2A 1EL, United Kingdom / T: (0171) 4002500, Fax: 4002842, 4002969, Tx: 95678, Internet: www.butterworths.co.uk – ISBN 0-406; 0-407; 0-408; 0-409; 0-592
USA: Michie, 701 E Water St, Charlottesville VA 22906-7587, U.S.A. / T: (804) 972-7600, Fax: 972-7656

nz Forest
New Zealand Institute of Forestry, Inc, POB 19-840, Christchurch New Zealand / T: (03) 3842432, Fax: 3842432, E-mail: sheppars@lincoln.ac.nz

nz Libr & Info
NZ Library and Information Association, 86-90 Lambton Quay, Level 8, POB 12-212, Wellington 1, New Zealand / T: (04) 4735834, Fax: 4991480 – ISBN 0-908560

nz Nat'l Libr
National Library Shop, A Division of the National Library of New Zealand, Cnr Molesworth & Aitken St, POB 1467, Wellington 6001, New Zealand / T: (04) 4743000, Fax: 4743035, E-mail: shop@natlib.govt.nz

nz SROW
Society for Research on Women in New Zealand Inc, POB 13-078, Johnsonville Wellington, New Zealand – ISBN 0-908621

sa Books in Print
Books in Print Information Services, POB 15129, Vlaeberg, Cape Town 8018, South Africa / Fax: (021) 4615467

sa Juta
Juta & Company Ltd, Mercury Cres, Hillstar Ind Township, Wetton, POB 14373, Kenwyn 7790, South Africa / T: (021) 7975101, Fax: 7627424, E-mail: books@juta.co.za – ISBN 0-7021
Branches
South Africa: Juta & Co Ltd, Fleming Rd, Route 24, Meadowdale Ext 1, Germiston, POB 163, Isando 1600, South Africa / T: (011) 3924040, Fax: 3924170

sa Microfile
Microfile, Halco House, 20 Harrison Street South, Johannesburg, POB 61328, Marshalltown 2107, South Africa / T: (011) 8344161 (Head Office), 8369660 (Factory), Fax: 8344179

sa SA Libr
South African Library, Queen Victoria St, Cape Town, POB 496, Cape Town 8000, South Africa / T: (021) 246320, Fax: 244848, E-mail: macmahon@salib.ac.za – ISBN 0-86968

sa State Archives
State Archives and Heraldic Services, Private Bag X236, Pretoria 0001, South Africa / T: (012) 3235300, Fax: 3235287, E-mail: arg02@acts2.pwv.gov.za – ISBN 0-7970

sa State Libr
State Library, Staatsbiblioteek, Vermeulen St, POB 397, Pretoria 0001, South Africa / T: (012) 3861661, Fax: 3255984, Tx: 322171 sa, E-mail: statelib@statelib.pwv.gov.za – ISBN 0-7989

sp Bibl Santa Ana
Biblioteca Santa Ana, Calle Ortega Munoz s/n, Apartado de Correos 90, 06200 Almendralejo (Badajoz) Spain / T: (924) 661689, 661178

sp Boletín
Boletín Oficial del Estado, Av de Manoteras 54, 28050 Madrid, Spain / T: (91) 3841715, 3841700, Fax: 3841710, 3841714
Orders
N America: Norman Ross Publishing Inc, 330 W 58th St, New York, NY 10019, U.S.A. / T: (212) 765-8200, (800) 648-8850, Fax: 765-2393, E-mail: info@nross.com, Internet: www.nross.com – ISBN 0-8287; 0-88354

sp Cultura
Ministerio de Cultura, Servicio de Reproducción de Documentos de Archivos Estatales, Calle Serrano, 115, 28006 Madrid, Spain / T: (91) 5628011, 5628458, Fax: 4116669

sp Iglesias
Editorial Pablo Iglesias, Monte Esquinza, 30, 2° Dcha, 28010 Madrid, Spain / T: (91) 3104313, 3102839, Fax: 3194585 – ISBN 84-85691

sp Pentalfa
Pentalfa Microediciones, Apartado 360, 33080 Oviedo, Spain / T: (985) 5985386, Fax: 5985512

su Okaz
Okaz for Press and Publishing, POB 1508, Jeddah 21441, Saudi Arabia / T: (02) 6722630, Fax: 6728150, Tx: 6013060 SJ OKAZ – ISBN 9960-706

sw G.U.
Gothenburg University Library, Göteborgs Universitetsbibliotek, Renströmsgt 4, Box 5096, 402 22 Göteborg Sweden / T: (031) 7731733, Fax: 163797, E-mail: jan.ahman@ub.gu.se, Internet: www.ub.gu.se/ub-doc/acta.htm – ISBN 91-7346; 91-85206

sw Kungliga
Kungliga Biblioteket, The Royal Library, National Library of Sweden, Humlegården, Stockholm, POB 5039, 102 41 Stockholm Sweden / T: (08) 4634071, Fax: 4634300, E-mail: per.kjellberg@kb.se

sz Elsevier
Elsevier Science S.A., 50 Avenue de la Gare, 1003 Lausanne, BP 564, 1001 Lausanne 1, Switzerland / T: (021) 207381, Fax: 235444, Tx: 450620 ELSA CH
Branch of
Elsevier Science B.V., POB 211, 1000 AE Amsterdam Netherlands / T: (020) 4853757, Fax: 4853432, E-mail: nlinfo-f@elsevier.nl, Internet: www.elsevier.com – ISBN 0-7204; 0-444; 90-219; 2-906077
Orders
UMI University Microfilms International, A Bell & Howell Company, 300 N Zeeb Rd, POB 1346, Ann Arbor MI 48106-1346, U.S.A. / T: (313) 761-4700, (800) 521-0600, Fax: 973-7007, Tx: 211607 umi ur – ISBN 0-8357
Branches
Netherlands: Elsevier Science, Lifesciences Department, Molenwerf 1, 1014 AG Amsterdam, Postbus 1527, 1000 BM Amsterdam Netherlands / T: (20) 5803911, Tx: 18582 – ISBN 0-7204; 0-444
Netherlands: Excerpta Medica base, An Imprint of Elsevier Science, Postbus 1126, 1000 BC Amsterdam Netherlands / T: (020) 5803911, Tx: 14664 Elnet – ISBN 90-219; 0-444
Netherlands: North-Holland Publishing Company, An Imprint of Elsevier Science, Postbus 211, 1000 AE Amsterdam Netherlands – ISBN 0-444
United Kingdom: Elsevier Science Ltd, The Boulevard, Langford Lane, Kidlington, United Kingdom / T: (01865) 843000, Fax: 843010 – ISBN 0-08
U.S.A.: Elsevier Science Inc, 655 Ave of the Americas, New York NY 10010, U.S.A. / T: (212) 989-5800, Fax: (212) 633-3990, Tx: 137328 – ISBN 0-08
Information
Formerly Elsevier Sequoia

sz I.C.J.
International Commission of Jurists, Centre for the Independence of Judges and Lawers, 26, chemin de Joinville, BP 160, 1216 Cointrin Genève, Switzerland / T: (022) 7884747, Fax: 7884880, Tx: 418531 icj ch – ISBN 92-9037

sz I.L.O.
International Labour Office, Bureau International du Travail, Publications Bureau, 4 Rte des Morillons, 1211 Genève, Switzerland / T: (022) 7997301, Fax: 7996938, Tx: 415647 ilo ch, E-mail: pubvente@ilo.org – ISBN 92-2
Orders
Canada: Canadian Scholars' Press Inc, 180 Bloor St W, Ste 402, Toronto, ON M5S 2V6, Canada / T: (416) 929-2774, Fax: 929-1926, E-mail: orders@cspi.org – ISBN 0-921627; 1-55130
Ethiopia: ILO Regional Office for Africa, Jobs and Skills Programme for Africa, POB 2788, Addis Ababa Ethiopia / T: (01) 517320, Fax: 513633
Germany: Internationales Arbeitsamt – Veröffentlichungen / Bibliothek, Hohenzollernstr 21, 53173 Bonn, Germany / T: (0228) 362322, 363988, Fax: 352186, Tx: 23726
India: International Labour Office, East Court, 3rd Flr, India Habitat Centre, Lodi Rd, New Delhi, India / T: 4602101/4, Fax: 4602111
Japan: International Labour Office, 8th Flr, The UNU Headquarters Bldg, 53-70, Jingumae 5-chome, Shibuya-ku, Tokyo, Japan / T: (03) 54672701/3, Fax: (03) 54672700
UK: International Labour Office, Vincent House, Vincent Square, London, United Kingdom / T: (0171) 8286401, Fax: 2335925
USA: ILO Branch Office, International Labour Organization, 1828 L St NW, Washington, DC 20036, U.S.A. / T: (202) 653-7652, Fax: 653-7687, E-mail: burrylee@ilo.org, Internet: us.ilo.org
Branches
United Kingdom: CSP Publications, 224A London Rd, Hadleigh, Essex SS7 2DE, United Kingdom / T: (01702) 552912, Fax: 556095
U.S.A.: CSPI, 519 Mill St, POB 336, Lockport NY 14095, U.S.A. / T: (416) 929-2994, Fax: 929-1926

sz Infoprint
Infoprint S.A., CP 113, 6513 Monte Carasso Switzerland / T: (021) 8815067, (077) 862974, Fax: 8821584

sz I.T.U.
International Telecommunication Union, ITU, Pl des Nations, 1211 Genève, Switzerland / T: (022) 7305318, Fax: 7305194, Tx: 421000 uit ch – ISBN 92-61; 92-71; 92-72; 92-73; 92-74

sz Petro
Petroconsultants S.A., International Energy Services, 24 Chemin de la Mairie, POB 152, 1258 Perly-Geneva Switzerland / T: (022) 7211717, 7211900, Fax: 7211919, 7211894, Tx: 413541 petr ch, E-mail: sales@petroconsultants.com, Internet: www.petroconsultants.com

uk Academic
Academic Microforms Ltd, 7 Deronda Rd, London, SE24 9BQ, United Kingdom / T: (0181) 6743335, Fax: 6743335

uk Altair
Altair Publishing, Nanholme Mill, Shaw Wood Rd, Todmorden, United Kingdom / T: (01706) 818948, (01422) 843214, Fax: 818948 – ISBN 1-871132

uk Ariel
Ariel House Publications, c/o Ariel Cottage, 8 Hadland Terrace, West Cross, Swansea, United Kingdom / T: (01792) 405267, Fax: 405267 – ISBN 0-906948

uk Athenaeum
Athenaeum Liverpool, Church Alley, Liverpool, United Kingdom / T: (0151) 7097770

uk Barbour
Barbour Microfiles, New Lodge Drift Rd, Windsor, Berks SL4 4RQ, United Kingdom / T: (01344) 884121, Fax: 884845

uk Bell
Peter Bell, 4 Brandon St, Edinburgh, United Kingdom / T: (0131) 5662198, Fax: 6522805, Tx: 72165 (ref: INTERFICHE)

uk British Libr
British Library National Bibliographic Service, Boston Spa, Wetherby, West Yorkshire LS23 7BQ, United Kingdom / T: (01937) 546610, Fax: 546586, Tx: 557831 – ISBN 0-7123; 0-900220

uk British Libr Docs
British Library Document Supply Centre, Boston Spa, Wetherby, United Kingdom / T: (01937) 546080, Fax: 546286, E-mail: dsc-publishing-section@bl.uk – ISBN 0-7123

uk British Libr Humanities
British Library Publications. Humanities and Social Sciences, 41 Russell Square, London, United Kingdom / T: (0171) 3237704, Fax: 3237768
Orders
Turpin Distribution Services Ltd, Blackhorse Road, Letchworth, Herts SG6 1HN, United Kingdom / T: (01462) 672555, Fax: 480947

uk British Libr Newspaper
British Library Newspaper Library, c/o Microfilm Administration, Colindale Av, London, United Kingdom / T: (0171) 4127351, Fax: 4127396, Tx: 21462
Information
Price per reel £45.00 plus VAT and postage

uk British Univ Film
British Universities Film & Video Council (BUFVC), 55 Greek St, London, United Kingdom / T: (0171) 7343687, Fax: 2873914, E-mail: bufvc@open.ac.uk – ISBN 0-901299

uk Business
Business Archives Council, Archives, University of Glasgow, Glasgow, United Kingdom / T: (0141) 3305516, Fax: 3304158

uk Carfax
Carfax Publishing Company, POB 25, Abingdon, Oxfordshire OX14 3UE, United Kingdom / T: (01235) 401000, Fax: 401550, Tx: 9312131582 jog
Branches
Australia: Carfax Publishing Company, POB 352, Cammeray NSW 2062, Australia
U.S.A.: Carfax Publishing Company, 875-81 Massachusetts Ave, Cambridge MA 02139, U.S.A.

uk Chadwyck
Chadwyck-Healey Ltd, The Quorum, Barnwell Rd, Cambridge, United Kingdom / T: (01223) 215512, Fax: 215514, Tx: 9312102281 ch g, E-mail: mail@chadwyck.co.uk, Internet: www.chadwyck.co.uk – ISBN 0-85964
Branches
France: Chadwyck-Healey France S.A., 50 rue de Paradis, 75010 Paris France / T: (1) 44838181, Fax: 44838183 – ISBN 2-86976
Spain: Chadwyck-Healey Espanña S.L., Juan Bravo 18, 2°C, Madrid, 28006, Spain / T: (91) 5755597, Fax: 5759885
U.S.A.: Chadwyck-Healey Inc, 1101 King St, Suite 380, Alexandria, VA 22314, U.S.A. / T: (703) 683-4890, (800) 752-0515, Fax: 683-7589, E-mail: mktg@chadwyck.com – ISBN 0-85964

uk Chivers
Cedric Chivers Ltd, 9a/9b Aldermoor Way Longwell Green, Bristol, United Kingdom / T: (0117) 9352617, Fax: 9618446
Orders
N America: Norman Ross Publishing Inc, 330 W 58th St, New York, NY 10019, U.S.A. / T: (212) 765-8200, (800) 648-8850, Fax: 765-2393, E-mail: info@nross.com, Internet: www.nross.com – ISBN 0-8287; 0-88354

uk Dawson
William Dawson & Sons Ltd, Cannon House, Park Farm Rd, Folkestone, Kent, United Kingdom / T: (01303) 850101, Fax: 850440, Tx: 96392 – ISBN 0-85210; 0-7129

uk Derwent
Derwent Information Ltd, 14 Great Queen St, London, United Kingdom / T: (0171) 3442800, Fax: 4902138 – ISBN 0-901157
Branches
U.S.A.: Derwent Publications Inc, 1313 Dolley Madison Blvd, Suite 401, McLean VA 22101, U.S.A. / T: (703) 790-0400, Fax: 790-1426

uk Emmett
Emmett Publishing Ltd, Glenthorne, Hill Rd, Hindhead, Surrey GU26 6QN, United Kingdom / T: (01428) 609099, Fax: 609099, E-mail: info@emmetpub.demon.co.uk, Internet: www.emmettpub.co.uk – ISBN 0-907696; 1-869934
Branches
U.S.A.: Emmett Publishing Ltd, 1683 Novato Blvd, Suite 5, Novato, CA 94947, U.S.A. / T: (800) 898-EMET, Fax: (415) 898-3180

uk FIAF
Fédération Internationale des Archives du Film (FIAF), 6 Nottingham St, London W1M 3RB, United Kingdom / T: (0171) 2240991, Fax: 2241203
Orders
International Index to Film / Television Periodicals, 113 Canalot Studios, 222 Kensal Rd, London W10 5BN, United Kingdom / T: (0181) 9601001

uk G.B.P.R.O.
Great Britain Public Record Office, Ruskin Av, Kew, Richmond, United Kingdom / T: (0181) 8763444, Fax: 3925266, 8788905, E-mail: alawes.pro.kew@gtnet.gov.uk

uk Hall
G.K. Hall & Co, c/o Prentice Hall, Campus 400, Maylands Av, Hemel Hempstead, Herts HP2 7EZ, United Kingdom / T: (01442) 881900, Fax: 257115 – ISBN 0-8161; 0-7838

uk Herald
Caledonian Newspapers Ltd, Herald & Evening Times, 195 Albion St, Glasgow, United Kingdom / T: (0141) 5526255, Fax: 2642

uk INSPEC
INSPEC, Michael Faraday House, Six Hills Way, Stevenage, Herts SG1 2AY, United Kingdom / T: (01438) 313311, Fax: 742840, Tx: 825578 ieestv g

uk I.O.P.
IOP Publishing Ltd, Techno House, Redcliffe Way, Bristol, United Kingdom / T: (0117) 9297481, Fax: 9294318, Tx: 449149 instp g, E-mail: custserv@ioppublishing.co.uk, Internet: www.iop.org – ISBN 0-85498; 0-85274; 0-7503
Orders
N America & Mexico: American Institute of Physics, c/o T. Kusma, 500 Sunnyside Blvd, Woodbury, NY 11797-2999, U.S.A. / T: (516) 576-2270, (800) 344-6902, Fax: 349-9704, Tx: 960983 – ISBN 0-88318

uk I.P.C.
IPC Magazines Limited, King's Reach Tower, Stamford St, London, United Kingdom / T: (0171) 2615000, Fax: 2615041

uk Libr Preservation
Library Preservation Systems International Ltd, POB 8, Southend, Reading RG7 6AQ, United Kingdom / T: (01734) 810755, Fax: 810422

uk L.I.S.E.
Librarians of Institutes and Schools of Education (LISE), c/o Education Library (UCS), Hendrefoilan, Gower Rd, Swansea, United Kingdom / T: (01792) 205678 ext 2059 – ISBN 0-901922

uk Liverpool Bib
Liverpool Bibliographical Society, 2 Staplands Rd, Liverpool, L14 3LL, United Kingdom / T: (0151) 2289480

uk Manchester Libr
Manchester Public Libraries, Central Library, Saint Peter's Sq, Manchester, Lancs M2 5PD, United Kingdom / T: (0161) 2341900, Fax: 2341963, Tx: 669475 – ISBN 0-901315

uk Mansell Publ
Mansell Publishing Ltd, An Imprint of Cassell, Wellington House, 125 Strand, London, United Kingdom / T: (0171) 4205555, Fax: 24085314

uk Matthew
Adam Matthew Publications, 8, Oxford St, Marlborough, Wilts SN8 1AP, United Kingdom / T: (01672) 511921, Fax: 511663

uk Micro Graphix
Micro Graphix, 15 Bridge St Mill, Bridge St, Witney, Oxon OX8 6YH, United Kingdom / T: (01993) 776396, Fax: 779050

uk Microform Academic
Microform Academic Publishers, A Division of Microform (Wakefield) Ltd, Main St, East Ardsley, Wakefield, W Yorkshire WF3 2AT, United Kingdom / T: (01924) 825700, Fax: 871005, E-mail: micro_image@cix.compulink.co.uk – ISBN 1-85117

uk Mindata
Mindata Ltd, Bathwick Hill, Bath, United Kingdom / T: (01225) 466447, Fax: 482841

uk Pordes
H. Pordes Ltd, Publishers & Booksellers, 383 Cockfosters Rd, Cockfosters, HERTS EN4 OJS, United Kingdom / T: (0181) 4492524, Fax: 4419595 – ISBN 0-85376

uk Scot News
Scottish Newspapers Microfilming Unit, 4 Bankhead Medway, Sighthill Industrial Estate, Edinburgh, United Kingdom / T: (0131) 4536872, Fax: 4536872

uk Skinner
M. Skinner & Company Ltd, 5 The Parade, St. John's Hill, London, United Kingdom / T: (0171) 2237724

uk Tech
Technical Indexes Ltd, Willoughby Rd, Bracknell, United Kingdom / T: (01344) 426311, Fax: 424971 – ISBN 0-86041

uk UNIMICRO
UNIMICRO, The Old School House, 34 Pevensey Rd, St. Leonards, United Kingdom / T: (01424) 432909, Fax: 434338

uk Voltaire
Voltaire Foundation, 99 Banbury Rd, Oxford, United Kingdom / T: (01865) 284600, Fax: 284610 – ISBN 0-7294; 0-903588; 0-9502162

uk Whitaker
Whitaker Bibliographic Services, 12 Dyott St, London, United Kingdom / T: (0171) 4206000, Fax: 8362909 – ISBN 0-85021

uk World
World Microfilms Publications Ltd, Microworld House, 4 Foscote Mews, London, United Kingdom / T: (0171) 2662202, Fax: 2662314, E-mail: microworld@ndirect.co.uk – ISBN 1-85035; 1-86013
Orders
N America: Norman Ross Publishing Inc, 330 W 58th St, New York, NY 10019, U.S.A. / T: (212) 765-8200, (800) 648-8850, Fax: 765-2393, E-mail: info@nross.com, Internet: www.nross.com – ISBN 0-8287; 0-88354

us A.B.H.S.
American Baptist Historical Society, 1106 S Goodman St, Rochester, NY 14620, U.S.A. / T: (716) 473-1740 – ISBN 0-910056

us A.C.S.
American Chemical Society (ACS), 1155 16th St NW, Washington, DC 20036, U.S.A. / T: (202) 872-4376, (800) 227-5558, Fax: 872-6303, E-mail: m_neville@acs.org – ISBN 0-8412
Branches
U.S.A.: Chemical Abstracts Service (CAS), 2540 Olentangy River Rd, POB 3012, Columbus OH 43210-0012, U.S.A. / T: (614) 447-3600, Fax: 447-3709, Tx: 6842086

us Advanced Libr
Advanced Library Systems Inc, 100 Brickstone Sq, POB 246, Andover MA 01810-0005, U.S.A. / T: (508) 470-0610, Fax: 475-1072, E-mail: advlibsy@shore.net

us Aero
Micro Aero Charts, Subsidiary of Color Microimaging, 5078 List Dr, Colorado Springs, CO 80919-3316, U.S.A. / T: (719) 594-9202, (800) 421-8717, Fax: 594-9202

us African Imprint
African & Caribbean Imprint Library Services, POB 350, North Falmouth MA 02574, U.S.A. / T: (508) 540-5378, Fax: 548-6801

us A.G.L.L.
American Genealogical Lending Library (AGLL), 593 West 100 North, POB 329, Bountiful UT 84011-0329, U.S.A. / T: (801) 298-5446, Fax: 298-5468, E-mail: roy@agll.com

us A.G.U.
American Geophysical Union, 2000 Florida Ave NW, Washington, DC 20009, U.S.A. / T: (202) 462-6900, (800) 966-2481, Fax: 328-0566 – ISBN 0-87590

us A.I.A.
American Institute of Architects, 1735 New York Av NW, Washington, DC 20006, U.S.A. / T: (202) 626-7474, Fax: 626-7420 – ISBN 1-57165; 1-879304
Orders
Norman Ross Publishing Inc, 330 W 58th St, New York, NY 10019, U.S.A. / T: (212) 765-8200, (800) 648-8850, Fax: 765-2393, E-mail: info@nross.com, Internet: www.nross.com – ISBN 0-8287; 0-88354

us AIChE
American Institute of Chemical Engineers, 345 E 47th St, New York, NY 10017-2395, U.S.A. / T: (212) 705-8100, (800) 242-4363, Fax: 705-8400, E-mail: xpress@aiche.org – ISBN 0-8169
Orders
Quarterlies and other periodicals: UMI University Microfilms International, A Bell & Howell Company, 300 N Zeeb Rd, POB 1346, Ann Arbor MI 48106-1346, U.S.A. / T: (313) 761-4700, (800) 521-0600, Fax: 973-7007, Tx: 211607 umi ur – ISBN 0-8357

us A.I.I.M.
Association for Information and Image Management, 1100 Wayne Av, Suite 1100, Silver Spring, MD 20910, U.S.A. / T: (301) 587-8202, Fax: 587-2711 – ISBN 0-89258

us A.I.P.
American Institute of Physics, c/o T. Kusma, 500 Sunnyside Blvd, Woodbury, NY 11797-2999, U.S.A. / T: (516) 576-2270, (800) 344-6902, Fax: 349-9704, Tx: 960983 – ISBN 0-88318

us Aircraft Tech
Aircraft Technical Publishers, 101 South Hill Dr, Brisbane, CA 94005-1203, U.S.A. / T: (415) 330-9500, (800) 227-4610, Fax: 468-1596, Tx: 171048, E-mail: mhuggins@atp.com

us A.J.P.C.
American Jewish Periodical Center, c/o Hebrew Union College, Jewish Institute of Religion, 3101 Clifton Av, Cincinnati, OH 45220-2488, U.S.A. / T: (513) 221-1875, Ext 294

us A.L.A.
American Library Association, 50 E Huron St, Chicago, IL 60611, U.S.A. / T: (312) 280-4271, (800) 545-2433, Fax: 440-9374 – ISBN 0-8389

us Alper
Jerry Alper Inc, 271 Main St, POB 218, Eastchester NY 10707, U.S.A. / T: (914) 793-2100, Fax: 793-7811

us Americana
Americana Unlimited, POB 50447, Tucson AZ 85703, U.S.A. / T: (602) 792-3453

us Amistad
Amistad Research Center, Tilton Hall, Tulane University, New Orleans, LA 70118-5665, U.S.A. / T: (504) 865-5535

us Antiquarian
Antiquarian and Landmarks Society, Inc, 394 Main St, Hartford, CT 06103-9857, U.S.A. / T: (203) 247-8998
Orders
UMI University Microfilms International, A Bell & Howell Company, 300 N Zeeb Rd, POB 1346, Ann Arbor MI 48106-1346, U.S.A. / T: (313) 761-4700, (800) 521-0600, Fax: 973-7007, Tx: 211607 umi ur – ISBN 0-8357

us Appropriate Tech
Appropriate Technology Project, Volunteers in Asia, Inc, POB 4543, Stanford CA 94309, U.S.A. / T: (415) 725-7977, Fax: 725-1805

us Archival
Center for Archival Collections, c/o B.G. Univ, Jerome Libr, 5th Fl, 1001 E Wooster St, Bowling Green, OH 43403-0175, U.S.A. / T: (419) 372-2411, Fax: 372-0155

us Asia Libr
Asia Library Services, POB 2296, Springfield VA 22152, U.S.A. / E-mail: asialib@idsonline.com

us A.T.B.I.
Alvina Treut Burrows Institute, Inc, POB 49, Manhasset NY 11030, U.S.A. / T: (516) 869-8457

us A.T.L.A.
American Theological Library Association, ATLA Preservation Programs, 820 Church St, Suite 300, Evanston, IL 60201-5613, U.S.A. / T: (847) 869-7788, Fax: 869-8513, E-mail: atla@atla.com – ISBN 0-8370; 0-7905; 0-524
Information
Inquire for prices

us Auto-Graphics
Auto-Graphics, Inc, 3201 Temple Av, Pomona, CA 91768, U.S.A. / T: (909) 595-7204, (800) 325-7961

us Baptist
The Southern Baptist Convention Historical Library and Archives, 901 Commerce St, Suite 400, Nashville, TN 37203-3630, U.S.A. / T: (615) 244-0344, Fax: 782-4821, E-mail: bsumners@edge.net – ISBN 0-939804

us BIOSIS
BIOSIS, BioSciences Information Service, 2100 Arch St, Philadelphia, PA 19103-1399, U.S.A. / T: (215) 587-4800, (800) 523-4806, Fax: 587-2016, Tx: 831739, E-mail: info@mail.biosis.org

us Bloch
Bloch and Company, POB 18058, Cleveland OH 44118, U.S.A. / T: (216) 371-0979

us Bowker
R.R. Bowker, 121 Chanlon Rd, New Providence, NJ 07974, U.S.A. / T: (908) 464-6800 Sales USA (800) 521-8110, Fax: 771-7725 Ulrich's, 665-3502 BIP & ABPR, Tx: 12-7703, E-mail: ulrichs@reedref.com (Ulrich); dgravesande@reedref.com (BIP); blamar@reedref.com (ABPR) – ISBN 0-8352
Orders
Australia: D.W. Thorpe, POB 146, 18 Salmon St, Port Melbourne Vic. 3207, Australia / T: (03) 92457370, Fax: 92457395, (1800) 639798, E-mail: hugh.forster@thorpe.com.au, Internet: www.reedbooks.com.au/index.html – ISBN 0-909532; 1-875589; 0-7506
German-Speaking Europe: K.G. Saur Verlag GmbH & Co KG, Ortlerstr. 8, 81373 München, Postf 70 16 20, 81316 München Germany / T: (089) 769020, Fax: 76902150, 76902250, E-mail: 100730.1341@compuserve.com, Internet: www.saur.de – ISBN 3-7940; 3-598
UK, Ireland & Europe: Bowker-Saur Ltd, Windsor Crt, East Grinstead House, East Grinstead, West Sussex, United Kingdom / T: (01342) 326972, Fax: 335612, E-mail: nicci@bowker-saur.co.uk.com – ISBN 0-86291

us Buckmaster
Buckmaster Publishing, Whitehall, 6196 Jefferson Hwy, Mineral, VA 23117, U.S.A. / T: (540) 894-5777, (800) 282-5628, Fax: 894-9141, E-mail: info@buck.com

us Buffalo
Buffalo and Erie County Historical Society, 25 Nottingham Court, Buffalo, NY 14216-3199, U.S.A. / T: (716) 873-9644, Fax: 873-8754

us Career
Career Guidance Foundation, College Catalog Library, 8090 Engineer Rd, San Diego, CA 92111-1988, U.S.A. / T: (619) 560-8051, (800) 854-2670

us Chicago
University of Chicago Press, 5801 Ellis Ave, Chicago, IL 60637, U.S.A. / T: (312) 702-7706, (800) 621-2736, Fax: 702-9756, E-mail: marketing@press.uchicago.edu, Internet: www.press.uchicago.edu – ISBN 0-226
Orders
Europe: John Wiley & Sons Ltd, Distribution Centre, 1 Oldlands Way, Bognor Regis W. Sussex PO22 9SA, United Kingdom / T: (01243) 779777, Fax: 820250, E-mail: customer@wiley.co.uk – ISBN 0-470; 0-471

us Chinese Res
Center for Chinese Research Materials, POB 3090, Oakton VA 22124, U.S.A. / T: (703) 281-7731, Fax: 281-1835

us CIS
CIS, Congressional Information Service, Inc, 4520 East-West Hwy, Ste 800, Bethesda, MD 20814-3389, U.S.A. / T: (301) 654-1550, (800) 638-8380, Fax: 657-3203, 654-4033, E-mail: info@cispubs.com, Internet: www.cispubs.com – ISBN 0-912380; 0-88692
Orders
Japan: Maruzen Company Ltd, 2-3-10 Nihonbashi, Chuo-ku, Tokyo, POB 5050, Tokyo International 100-31, Japan / T: (03) 32727211, Fax: 56842458, Tx: 26516, 26517 – ISBN 4-621; 4-89580; 4-8395
Branches
U.S.A.: Maruzen International Co Ltd, 1251 Av of the Americas, Suite 1780, New York NY 10020, U.S.A. / T: (212) 541-9090, Tx: 235485

us CLASS
Cooperative Library Agency for Systems and Services, CLASS, 1415 Koll Circle, Suite 101, San Jose, CA 95112-4698, U.S.A. / T: (408) 453-0444, Fax: 453-5379, Tx: ONTYME: CLASSHQ

us Comics
MicroComics Inc, POB 243, Ridgewood NJ 07450, U.S.A. / T: (201) 445-3450, Fax: 445-2924, E-mail: arah@aol.com

us Congressional Digest
Congressional Digest Corporation, 3231 P St, NW, Washington, DC 20007, U.S.A. / T: (202) 333-7332, Fax: 625-6670
Orders
UMI University Microfilms International, A Bell & Howell Company, 300 N Zeeb Rd, POB 1346, Ann Arbor MI 48106-1346, U.S.A. / T: (313) 761-4700, (800) 521-0600, Fax: 973-7007, Tx: 211607 umi ur – ISBN 0-8357

us Contemporary Arts
Contemporary Arts Press / ART COM, Division of La Mamelle, Inc, POB 193123, Rincon Center, San Francisco CA 94119-3123, U.S.A. / T: (415) 431-7524, Fax: 431-7841, Tx: 4946074 art com – ISBN 0-931818

us Continnuus
Continnuus, POB 416, Denver CO 80201-0416, U.S.A. / T: (303) 575-5676

us Corning Mus
The Corning Museum of Glass, Microform Publications, One Museum Way, Corning, NY 14830-2253, U.S.A. / T: (607) 937-5371, Fax: 937-3352 – ISBN 0-87290

us Creative
Creative MicroLibraries, Inc, A Division of Svobodny Development Corporation, POB 49, Manhasset NY 11030, U.S.A. / T: (516) 869-8457

us C.S.A.
Cambridge Scientific Abstracts, A Division of Cambridge Information Group, Inc, 7200 Wisconsin Ave, Bethesda, MD 20814-4823, U.S.A. / T: (301) 961-6750, (800) 843-7751, Fax: 961-6720

us Current
The Current Digest, 3857 N High St, Columbus, OH 43214, U.S.A. / T: (614) 292-4234, Fax: 267-6310, E-mail: fowler.40@osu.edu – ISBN 0-913601

us Dartmouth
Dartmouth College Library, Baker Library, Hanover, NH 03755-3525, U.S.A. / T: (603) 646-2235, Fax: 646-3702

us Dataflow
Dataflow Systems Inc, 7758 Wisconsin Av, Bethesda, MD 20814-3530, U.S.A. / T: (301) 654-9133, Fax: 654-9133

us Disclosure
Disclosure, Inc, 5161 River Rd, Bethesda, MD 20816, U.S.A. / T: (301) 951-1300

us East View
East View Publications, 3020 Harbor Lane North, Minneapolis, MN 55447-5137, U.S.A. / T: (612) 550-0961, (800) 477-1005, Fax: 559-2931 – ISBN 1-879944

us EDRS
ERIC Document Reproduction Service, EDRS, 7420 Fullerton Rd, Suite 110, Springfield, VA 22153-2852, U.S.A. / T: (703) 440-1400, Fax: 440-1403

us Ei
Engineering Information Inc, Ei, 1 Castle Point Terrace, Hoboken, NJ 07030-5996, U.S.A. / T: (201) 216-8500, (800) 221-1044 (Canada & USA), Fax: 216-8532, Tx: 4990438, E-mail: ei@ei.org – ISBN 0-911820; 0-87394

us E.T.S.
Educational Testing Service, Rosedale Rd, Princeton, NJ 08541-0001, U.S.A. / T: (609) 734-5689, Fax: 683-7186, Tx: 843420, E-mail: pstanley@ets.org – ISBN 0-88685

us Facts
Facts on File, Inc, A Subsidiary of Infobase Holdings, Inc, 460 Park Ave S, New York, NY 10016-7382, U.S.A. / T: (212) 683-2244, (800) 322-8755, Fax: 683-3633, Tx: 2596469 mci uw – ISBN 0-8160

us Fairchild Micro
Fairchild Microfilm (Publications), Inc, 7 W 34 St, New York, NY 10001, U.S.A. / T: (212) 630-3880, (800) 247-6622, Fax: 630-3868, Tx: 125308 – ISBN 0-87005

us Gabriel Micro
Gabriel Micrographics, POB 611, DeKalb IL 60115, U.S.A. / T: (815) 895-6842

us Gale
Gale Research Inc, A Subsidiary of The Thomson Corporation, 835 Penobscot Bldg, Detroit, MI 48226-4094, U.S.A. / T: (313) 961-2242, (800) 877-4253, Fax: 961-6083, Tx: 810-221-7086 – ISBN 0-8103; 0-7876

us Gaunt
Gaunt, Inc, Gaunt Bldg, 3011 Gulf Dr, Holmes Beach, FL 34217-2199, U.S.A. / T: (941) 778-5211, 778-4832, (800) 942-8683, Fax: 778-5252, E-mail: gauntinc.@worldnet.att.net – ISBN 0-912004; 1-56169

us Genetic Eng
Genetic Engineering News, A Division of Mary Ann Liebert, Inc, 1651 Third Av, New York, NY 10128, U.S.A. / T: (212) 722-3708, Fax: 289-4697

us Geological Soc
Geological Society of America, Inc, 3300 Penrose Pl, POB 9140, Boulder CO 80301, U.S.A. / T: (303) 447-2020, (800) 472-1988, Fax: 447-1133, Internet: www.geosociety.org – ISBN 0-8137

us Godfrey
Godfrey Memorial Library, 134 Newfield St, Middletown, CT 06457, U.S.A. / T: (860) 346-4375

us Gordon
Gordon & Breach, Science Publishers, c/o International Publishers Distributor, 820 Town Center Drive, Langhorne, PA 19047, U.S.A. / T: (215) 750-2642 ext 133, (800) 545-8398, Fax: 750-6343, Tx: 236735 gopubur – ISBN 0-677

Branches

U.S.A.: Harwood Academic Publishers, c/o International Publishers Distributor, 820 Town Center Drive, Langhorne, PA 19047, U.S.A. / T: (215) 750-2642, (800) 545-8398, Fax: 750-6343, Tx: 236735 Gopub Ur – ISBN 3-7186

United Kingdom: Harwood Academic, 42 William IV St, London WC2N 4DE, United Kingdom

us Gov't Printing
United States Government Printing Office (USG), 732 N Capitol St NW, Washington, DC 20401, U.S.A. / T: (202) 512-1800, Fax: 512-2250 – ISBN 0-16

Orders

Mail orders: US Government Printing Office (GPO), c/o Superintendent of Documents, POB 371954, Pittsburgh PA 15250-7954, U.S.A.

us Haworth
The Haworth Press, Inc, 10 Alice St, Binghamton, NY 13904-1580, U.S.A. / T: (607) 722-5857, (800) 342-9678, Fax: 722-6362, (800) 895-0582, E-mail: getinfo@haworth.com

Information

$30.00 per reel for US customers; outside US $42.00 per reel.

us Hayes
Rutherford B. Hayes Presidential Center, 1337 Hayes Ave, Spiegel Grove, Fremont, OH 43420-2796, U.S.A. / T: (419) 332-2081, Fax: 332-4952

us Heather
Heather Press, 2605 W Berkshire, Muncie, IN 47304-1226, U.S.A. / T: (317) 284-8295

us Hein
William S. Hein & Co, Inc, Hein Bldg, 1285 Main St, Buffalo, NY 14209-1987, U.S.A. / T: (716) 882-2600, (800) 828-7571, Fax: 883-8100, Tx: 91209 wms hein buf, E-mail: wsheinco@class.org – ISBN 0-89941; 0-930342; 1-57598

Information

Includes Rothman microform titles

us Historical Soc
State Historical Society of Wisconsin, 816 State St, Madison, WI 53706-1482, U.S.A. / T: (608) 264-6530 – ISBN 0-87020

Information

Address orders to the Library Acquisitions Section. Please do not make prepayment. You will be invoiced when the microfilm is mailed at a rate of $30.00r for in-state orders and $45.00r for out-of-state orders

us H.M.M.L.
Hill Monastic Manuscript Library (HMML), Bush Center, St. John's University, POB 7300, Collegeville MN 56321-7300, U.S.A. / T: (612) 363-3514, Fax: 363-3222 – ISBN 0-940250

us Holbrook
Holbrook Research Institute, 4 Mayfair Circle, Oxford, MA 01540-2722, U.S.A. / T: (508) 987-0881

Information

$6.00 per fiche

us Holland
Holland Land Company Project, Reed Library, State Univ of NY, Fredonia, NY 14063, U.S.A. / T: (716) 673-3194

us Hoover Inst Photo
Hoover Institution Photographic Services, Stanford University, Stanford, CA 94305-6010, U.S.A. / T: (415) 723-3166, Fax: 723-4655, Tx: 348402 Stanford stnu – ISBN 0-8179

Orders

Europe: Clio Distribution Services, 55 St. Thomas' St, Oxford OX1 1JG, United Kingdom / T: (01865) 250333, Fax: 790358, Tx: 83130

us H.R.A.F.
Human Relations Area Files Press, Affiliate of Yale University, 755 Prospect St, New Haven, CT 06511, U.S.A. / T: (203) 764-9401, Fax: 764-9404, E-mail: hrafmem@minerva.cis.yale.edu – ISBN 0-87536

us H.S.P.
Historical Society of Pennsylvania, 1300 Locust St, Philadelphia, PA 19107-5699, U.S.A. / T: (215) 732-6200 – ISBN 0-910732

us H.U. College Libr
Harvard College Library, Photographic Services Division, Widener Rm 90, Cambridge, MA 02138, U.S.A. / T: (617) 495-3995

us H.U. Law
Harvard Law School Library, Microform Proj, Rm 539, Langdell Hall, Cambridge, MA 02138, U.S.A. / T: (617) 495-4722

us H.U. Library
Harvard University Library, Photographic Services Division, Widener Library, Rm 90, Cambridge, MA 02138, U.S.A. / T: (617) 495-3995, Fax: 495-0403

us I.A.C.
Information Access Company (IAC), 362 Lakeside Dr, Foster City, CA 94404, U.S.A. / T: (415) 378-5000, (800) 227-8431, Fax: 378-5369, (800) 676-2345

us I.A.S.W.R.
The Institute for Advanced Studies of World Religions (IASWR), Rd 2, Rt 301, Carmel, NY 10512, U.S.A. / T: (914) 225-1445, Fax: 225-1485 – ISBN 0-915078

us IDC
IDC Publishers Inc, 3265 Johnson Av, Riverdale, NY 10463, U.S.A. / T: (718) 432-1400, (800) 757-7441, Fax: 432-0020, E-mail: info@idcpublishers.com, Internet: www.idc.nl

us I.E.A.H.C.
Institute of Early American History and Culture, POB 8781, Williamsburg VA 23187-8781, U.S.A. / T: (804) 221-1116 – ISBN 0-910776

us I.E.E.E.
Institute of Electrical and Electronics Engineers, Inc (IEEE), PPL/IEEE Service Center, 445 Hoes Lane, POB 1331, Piscataway NJ 08855-1331, U.S.A. / T: (908) 981-0060 (for sales information), Fax: 981-0027, Tx: 833233 – ISBN 0-85296; 0-8631

us I.H.R.C.
Immigration History Research Center, c/o University of Minnesota, 826 Berry St, Saint Paul, MN 55114, U.S.A. / T: (612) 627-4208, Fax: 627-4190

us I.H.S.
Indiana Historical Society, 315 W Ohio St, Indianapolis, IN 46202-3299, U.S.A. / T: (317) 232-1882, (800) 447-1830, TDD (317) 233-6615, Fax: 233-3109

us IL Archives
Illinois State Archives, Margaret Cross Norton Bldg, Springfield, IL 62756, U.S.A. / T: (217) 782-3674, Fax: 524-3930

Orders

The Society of American Archivists, 600 South Federal St, Suite 504, Chicago, IL 60605, U.S.A. / T: (312) 922-0140, Fax: 347-1452, E-mail: info@saa.mhs.compuserve.com – ISBN 0-931828

us IL Hist
Illinois State Historical Library, A Division of the Illinois Historic Preservation Agency, 1 Old State Capitol Plaza, Springfield, IL 62701, U.S.A. / T: (217) 785-7942 – ISBN 0-912226

us I.M.R.
IMR Limited, 1591 S. 19th St, Harrisburg, PA 17104, POB 1777, Harrisburg PA 17105, U.S.A. / T: (717) 985-1000, (800) 446-2826, E-mail: rootski@juno.com

us Indices
Indices Publishing, 228 Sandy Neck Way, Vallejo, CA 94591-7850, U.S.A. / T: (707) 554-4814, Fax: 554-4814 – ISBN 0-9641213

us Info Handling
Information Handling Services, c/o Inverness Business Park, 15 Inverness Way E, Englewood, CO 80112, U.S.A. / T: (303) 790-0600, (800) 716-3447 (ext 009), Fax: 397-2410, (800) 716-6447 – ISBN 0-89847

us Info Resources
Information Resources Press (IRP), A Division of Herner & Co, 1110 N Glebe Rd, Ste 550, Arlington, VA 22201, U.S.A. / T: (703) 558-8270, Fax: 558-4979 – ISBN 0-87815

us Ingram
Ingram Distribution Group Inc, One Ingram Blvd, POB 3006, La Vergne TN 37086-1986, U.S.A. / T: (615) 793-5000, Fax: 793-3976

us I.R.C.
Effective Information Resource Corporation, 15578 Graham St, Huntington Beach, CA 92649, U.S.A. / T: (714) 373-4544, Fax: 373-0177

us I.R.E.
International Research & Evaluation, Information & Technology Transfer Database, 21098 IRE Control Center, Eagan, MN 55121-0098, U.S.A. / T: (612) 888-9635, Fax: 888-9124, Tx: 291008 – ISBN 0-930318

us I.U. Libraries
Indiana University Libraries, Preservation Microfilming, Preservation Department, Bloomington, IN 47405, U.S.A. / T: (812) 855-8820

us Knoedler
Knoedler Gallery, 19 E 70th St, New York, NY 10021, U.S.A. / T: (212) 794-0567, Fax: 570-6616

us KS Hist
Kansas State Historical Society, c/o Historical Soc Research Ctr, 6425 SW 6th Av, Topeka, KS 66615-1099, U.S.A. / T: (913) 272-8681, Fax: 272-8682, Internet: history.cc.ukans.edu/heritage/kshs – ISBN 0-87726

us L of C Cataloging
Library of Congress, Cataloging Distribution Service (CDS), Customer Services/Dept FG, Washington, DC 20541-5017, U.S.A. / T: (202) 707-6100, (800) 255-3666, Fax: 707-1334, E-mail: cdsinfo@mail.loc.gov – ISBN 0-8444

Orders

Selected titles: Scholarly Resources Inc, 104 Greenhill Av, Wilmington, DE 19805-1897, U.S.A. / T: (302) 654-7713, (800) 772-8937, Fax: 654-3871, E-mail: sales@scholarly.com – ISBN 0-8420

us L of C Photodup
Library of Congress, Photoduplication Service, 101 Independence Av SE, Washington, DC 20540-4574, U.S.A. / T: (202) 707-5640, Fax: 707-1771, Tx: 7108220185, E-mail: dmcn@loc.gov

Orders

All titles relating to E Asia: Scholarly Resources Inc, 104 Greenhill Av, Wilmington, DE 19805-1897, U.S.A. / T: (302) 654-7713, (800) 772-8937, Fax: 654-3871, E-mail: sales@scholarly.com – ISBN 0-8420

us Lawrence Pub
Lawrence Publications, c/o College of Arts and Architecture, 206 Engineering Unit C, University Park, PA 16802-1425, U.S.A. / T: (814) 863-0972

us Library Micro
Library Microfilms, A Division of Bay Microfilm, Inc, 1115 E Arques Av, Sunnyvale, CA 94086, U.S.A. / T: (408) 736-7444, Fax: 736-4397

us L.L.M.C.
Law Library Microform Consortium, University of Hawaii – Windward Campus, POB 1599, Kaneohe HI 96744, U.S.A. / T: (808) 235-2200, (800) 235-4446, Fax: 235-1755

us Lomond
Lomond Publications, Inc., POB 88, Mount Airy MD 21771, U.S.A. / T: (301) 829-1496 – ISBN 0-912338

us MARC Applied
MARC Applied Research Company, A Division of the Library Corporation, Research Park, Inwood, WV 25428, U.S.A. / T: (304) 229-0100, (800) 624-0559, Fax: 229-0295

us McGilvery
Laurence McGilvery, POB 852, La Jolla CA 92038-0852, U.S.A. / T: (619) 454-4443 – ISBN 0-910938

us MD Archives
Maryland State Archives, Hall of Records, 350 Rowe Blvd, Annapolis, MD 21401, U.S.A. / T: (410) 974-3915, Fax: 974-3895, Internet: www.mdarchives.state.md.us

us Mecklermedia
Mecklermedia Corporation, 20 Ketchum St, Westport, CT 06880-5808, U.S.A. / T: (203) 226-6967, Fax: 454-5840, Tx: 955239 tlx srvc – ISBN 0-88736; 0-930466
Branches
United Kingdom: Mecklermedia Ltd, Artillery House, Artillery Row, London SW1P 1RT, United Kingdom / T: (0171) 9760405, Fax: 9760506

us MEDOC
The University of Chicago, Middle East Documentation Center (MEDOC), 5828 South University Ave, 201 Pick Hall, Chicago, IL 60637-1501, U.S.A. / T: (312) 702-8425, Fax: 753-0569, E-mail: mideast-library@uchicago.edu
Information
Checks are payable in US$ to the University of Chicago. The date of publication refers to the Hijri calendar unless: in square brackets (Gregorian), followed by an M (Mali), by a K (Kameriye) or by an S (Semsi calandar)

us MELSA
Metropolitan Library Service Agency (MELSA), c/o 201 Hamline Park Plaza Bldg, 570 Asbury St, St. Paul, MN 55104-1849, U.S.A. / T: (612) 645-5731, Fax: 649-3169

us MESDA
Museum of Early Southern Decorative Arts (MESDA), 924 South Main St, POB 10310, Winston-Salem NC 27108-0310, U.S.A. / T: (910) 721-7366, Fax: 721-7367

us M.H.S.
Minnesota Historical Society, Division of Library and Archives, 345 Kellogg Blvd W, St. Paul, MN 55102, U.S.A. / T: (612) 296-6980, Fax: 296-9961

us Microfilm
Microfilm Company of California, Inc, 1977 S Los Angeles St, Los Angeles, CA 90011, U.S.A. / T: (213) 749-2463, Fax: 749-8943

us Microform Publ
Microform Publications, International Institute for Sport and Human Performance, 1243 University of Oregon, Eugene, OR 97403-1243, U.S.A. / T: (541) 346-4117, Fax: 346-0935, E-mail: hheiny@oregon.uoregon.edu, Internet: darkwing.uoregon.edu/ micropub/
Information
Please apply to publisher for information on titles prior to 1991

us Micromedex
Micromedex, Inc, 6200 S Syracuse Way, Suite 300, Englewood, CO 80111-4740, U.S.A. / T: (303) 486-6400, (800) 525-9083, Fax: 486-6464

us Mitchell Int'l
Mitchell International, 9889 Willow Creek Rd, POB 26260, San Diego CA 92196-0260, U.S.A. / T: (619) 578-6550, (800) 854-7030, Fax: 578-4752

us Moody's
Moody's Investors Service, Inc, 99 Church St, New York, NY 10007, U.S.A. / T: (212) 553-0300

us MRTS
MRTS, State Univ of NY at Binghamton, Binghamton, NY 13902-6000, U.S.A. / T: (607) 777-6758, Fax: 777-2408 – ISBN 0-86698

us Nat'l Archives
National Archives Trust Fund, National Archives and Records Administration, Publication Sales, Washington, DC 20408, U.S.A. / T: (202) 501-6056, Fax: 501-6175 – ISBN 0-911333
Orders
Scholarly Resources Inc, 104 Greenhill Av, Wilmington, DE 19805-1897, U.S.A. / T: (302) 654-7713, (800) 772-8937, Fax: 654-3871, E-mail: sales@scholarly.com – ISBN 0-8420
Information
$23.00 per roll for U.S. customers; outside U.S. $30.00 per reel (includes shipping)

us NC Archives
North Carolina Division of Archives and History, 109 E Jones St, Raleigh, NC 27601-2807, U.S.A. / T: (919) 733-3952, Fax: 733-1354, E-mail: archives@ncsl.dcr.state.nc.us

us N.C.J.R.S.
National Institute of Justice / NCJRS, POB 6000, Rockville MD 20850, U.S.A. / T: (301) 251-5255, (800) 851-3420, Fax: 251-5212

us NE Hist
Nebraska State Historical Society, 1500 R Street, POB 82554, Lincoln NB 68501-2554, U.S.A. / T: (402) 471-4751, Fax: 471-3100

us New England
New England Historic Genealogical Society, 101 Newbury St, Boston, MA 02116-3087, U.S.A. / T: (617) 536-5740, Fax: 536-7307

us New York Law
New York Law Publishing Company, 345 Park Ave S, New York, NY 10010, U.S.A. / T: (212) 545-6170, Fax: 696-1848

us NewsBank
NewsBank, Inc, 58 Pine St, New Canaan, CT 06840-5426, U.S.A. / T: (203) 966-1100, Fax: 966-6254 – ISBN 0-737

us NM Archives
New Mexico State Records Center and Archives, State Rules Division, 404 Montezuma, Santa Fe, NM 87503, U.S.A. / T: (505) 827-7332, Fax: 827-7331

us N.T.I.S.
National Technical Information Service (NTIS), c/o U.S. Department of Commerce, 5285 Port Royal Rd, Springfield, VA 22161, U.S.A. / T: (703) 487-4650

us NY Public
New York Public Library, Copy Services, 5th Av & 42nd St, Rm 315 R, New York, NY 10018-2788, U.S.A. / T: (212) 930-0814, Fax: 221-3423 – ISBN 0-87104
Orders
New York Public Library, Branch Libraries, 455 5th Av, New York NY 10016, U.S.A. / T: (212) 340-0897

us Ohio Hist
Ohio Historical Society, c/o Ohio Historical Ctr, Microfilm Dept, 1982 Velma Av, Columbus, OH 43211-2497, U.S.A. / T: (614) 297-2300 – ISBN 0-87758

us OmniSys
OmniSys Corporation, 32 Wexford St, Needham Heights, MA 02194, U.S.A. / T: (617) 444-4123, Fax: 444-5590, E-mail: omnisys@gis.net – ISBN 1-884719

us Optical Soc
Optical Society of America, 2010 Massachusetts Av NW, Washington, DC 20036-1023, U.S.A. / T: (202) 223-8130, Fax: 223-1096, Tx: 510 600 3965, Internet: www.osa.org – ISBN 0-9600380; 1-55752

us Opus
OPUS Publications, Inc, 250 Dodge Av, East Haven, CT 06512-3358, U.S.A. / T: (203) 466-5055, Fax: 466-5054 – ISBN 0-940983

us Oregon Hist
Oregon Historical Society Library, 1200 SW Park Av, Portland, OR 97205, U.S.A. / T: (503) 222-1741, Ext. 54, Fax: 221-2035, E-mail: orhist@ohs.org

us ORS Publ
ORS Publishing, 4948 St. Elmo Ave, Suite 207, Bethesda, MD 20814, U.S.A. / T: (301) 656-8611

us Oryx
Oryx Press, 4041 North Central Ave, No. 700, Phoenix, AZ 85012-3397, U.S.A. / T: (602) 265-2651, (800) 279-6799, Fax: 265-6250, (800) 279-4663

us Paper
Institute of Paper Science and Technology, Inc, 500 Tenth St NW, Atlanta, GA 30318-5794, U.S.A. / T: (404) 894-5726, Fax: 894-4778 – ISBN 0-87010

us Partington
Paul G. Partington, 7320 S Gretna Av, Whittier, CA 90606, U.S.A. / T: (310) 695-7960 – ISBN 0-9602538

us Penn Academy
Pennsylvania Academy of the Fine Arts, 1820 Chestnut St, Philadelphia, PA 19103, U.S.A. / T: (215) 972-7642, Fax: 972-5564 – ISBN 0-943836

us Penn Hist
Pennsylvania Historical and Museum Commission, Division of Publications and Sales, POB 1026, Harrisburg PA 17108-1026, U.S.A. / T: (717) 783-2618 – ISBN 0-911124; 0-89271
Orders
Scholarly Resources Inc, 104 Greenhill Av, Wilmington, DE 19805-1897, U.S.A. / T: (302) 654-7713, (800) 772-8937, Fax: 654-3871, E-mail: sales@scholarly.com – ISBN 0-8420

us Penn State
Pennsylvania State University Press, 820 N University Dr, University Park, PA 16802-1003, U.S.A. / T: (814) 865-1327, Fax: 863-1408 – ISBN 0-271

us Perceptual
Perceptual and Motor Skills, POB 9229, Missoula MT 59807, U.S.A. / T: (406) 728-1710

us Philosophy
Philosophy Documentation Center, c/o Bowling Green State University, 209E Harshman, Bowling Green, OH 43403-0189, U.S.A. / T: (419) 372-2419, Fax: 372-6987, E-mail: phildoc@opie.bgsu.edu, Internet: www.bgsu.edu/pdc/ – ISBN 0-912632

us P.K. Yonge
P.K. Yonge Library of Florida History, 1 Library East, University of Florida, Gainesville, FL 32611, U.S.A. / T: (904) 392-0319, Fax: 392-4788

us Presbyterian
Presbyterian Historical Society, 425 Lombard St, Philadelphia, PA 19147-1516, U.S.A. / T: (215) 627-1852, Fax: 627-0509 – ISBN 0-912686

us Preston Publ
Preston Publications, Inc, A Division of Preston Industries, Inc, 7800 Merrimac Av, POB 48312, Niles IL 60714-0312, U.S.A. / T: (708) 965-0566, Fax: 965-7639 – ISBN 0-912474

us Primary
Primary Source Media, 12 Lunar Dr, Woodbridge, CT 06525, U.S.A. / T: (203) 397-2600, (800) 444-0799, Fax: 397-3893, Tx: 465-6345, E-mail: sales@psmedia.com; cmullen@psmedia.com – ISBN 0-89235
Branches
United Kingdom: Research Publications Limited, 50 Milford Rd, POB 45, Reading RG1 8HF, United Kingdom / T: (01734) 583247, Fax: 394334, Tx: 848336 rpl

us Princeton Micro
Princeton Microfilm Corporation, 43 Highstown Rd, POB 235, Princeton Junction NJ 08550, U.S.A. / T: (609) 452-2066, (800) 257-9502, Fax: 275-6201

us Psychological
Psychological Reports, POB 9229, Missoula MT 59807, U.S.A. / T: (406) 728-1710

us Readex
Readex Microprint Corp., 58 Pine St, New Canaan, CT 06840-5426, U.S.A. / T: (813) 263-6004, Fax: 263-3004

us Res Libr
Center for Research Libraries, 6050 South Kenwood Av, Chicago, IL 60637-2804, U.S.A. / T: (312) 955-4545, Fax: 955-4339, E-mail: rudeen@crlmail.uchicago.edu – ISBN 0-932486

us Roosevelt
Franklin D. Roosevelt Library, 511 Albany Post Rd, Hyde Park, NY 12538, U.S.A. / T: (914) 229-8114, Fax: 229-0872, E-mail: library@roosevelt.nara.gov

us Ross
Norman Ross Publishing Inc, 330 W 58th St, New York, NY 10019, U.S.A. / T: (212) 765-8200, (800) 648-8850, Fax: 765-2393, E-mail: info@nross.com, Internet: www.nross.com – ISBN 0-8287; 0-88354
Information
$80.00 per reel

us Roth
Roth Publishing, Inc, 175 Great Neck Rd, Great Neck, NY 11021, POB 406, Great Neck NY 11021, U.S.A. / T: (516) 466-3676, (800) 899-7684, Fax: 829-7746 – ISBN 0-8486
Orders
Australia: Mason's Book Centre, 13 Catalina Dr, Tullamarine, Vic. 3043, Australia / T: (03) 83383044, Fax: 83382225
Europe: MMF Publications, Heereweg 331a, POB 287, 2160 AG Lisse Netherlands / T: (0252) 417250, Fax: 418658, E-mail: 100315.315@compuserve.com
Branches
Japan: Publishers International Corporation, 2nd Newfield Bldg, 42-3 Ohtsuka 3-Chome Brunk-ku, Tokyo 112, Japan
Netherlands: Moran Information and Publishing Co, Singel 357, Amsterdam 1012 WK, Netherlands

us S.A.A.
The Society of American Archivists, 600 South Federal St, Suite 504, Chicago, IL 60605, U.S.A. / T: (312) 922-0140, Fax: 347-1452, E-mail: info@saa.mhs.compuserve.com – ISBN 0-931828

us S.A.E.
Society of Automotive Engineers, Inc, SAE, 400 Commonwealth Dr, Warrendale, PA 15096-0001, U.S.A. / T: (412) 776-4841, Fax: 776-0790, Tx: 866355 – ISBN 1-56091

us SC Archives
South Carolina Department of Archives and History, 1430 Senate St, POB 11,669, Capitol Stn, Columbia SC 29211-1669, U.S.A. / T: (803) 734-8590, Fax: 734-8820

us Schnappsburg
Schnappsburg University Press, 101 Thornwood Rd, Jamestown, NC 27282, U.S.A. / T: (910) 454-0828, Fax: 299-2326

us Schnase
Schnase Microfilm Systems, 120 Brown Rd, POB 119, Scarsdale NY 10583, U.S.A. / T: (914) 725-1284, (603) 253-6583, Fax: 723-3485

us Scholarly Res
Scholarly Resources Inc, 104 Greenhill Av, Wilmington, DE 19805-1897, U.S.A. / T: (302) 654-7713, (800) 772-8937, Fax: 654-3871, E-mail: sales@scholarly.com – ISBN 0-8420
Orders
Canada: Scholarly Book Services Inc, 77 Mowat Ave, Suite 403, Toronto ON M6K 3E3, Canada / T: (416) 533-5490, Fax: (416) 533-5652
Europe: Eurospan Ltd, 3 Henrietta St, Covent Garden, London WC2E 8LU, United Kingdom / T: (0171) 2400856
Japan: Far Eastern Book-Sellers, Kanda, POB 72, Tokyo Japan / T: (03) 32657532
Taiwan: Transmission Books & Microforms Company, Ltd, POB 96-337, Taipei, R.O.C. China, Republic / T: (02) 7367071, 7361058, Fax: 7363001, Tx: 26026
Information
Scholarly Resources acquired the Michael Glazier microfilm collection in 1991.

us Scholars' Facs
Scholars' Facsimiles & Reprints, Subs of Academic Resources Corp, POB 344, Delmar NY 12054, U.S.A. / T: (313) 741-0344 – ISBN 0-8201

us Shkurkin
Vlad Shkurkin, Publisher, 6025 Rose Arbor, San Pablo, CA 94806-4147, U.S.A. / T: (510) 232-7742, Fax: 236-7050, E-mail: shkurkin@ix.netcom.com – ISBN 0-932732

us S.I.A.M.
Society for Industrial and Applied Mathematics (SIAM), 3600 University City Science Center, Philadelphia, PA 19104-2688, U.S.A. / T: (215) 382-9800, Fax: 386-7999, Tx: 446715, E-mail: siam@siam.org, Internet: www.siam.org – ISBN 0-89871

us Sibley
Sibley Music Library Microform Service, c/o Eastman School of Music, 27 Gibbs St, Rochester, NY 14604-2596, U.S.A. / T: (716) 274-1305

us S.M.E.
Society of Manufacturing Engineers (SME), One SME Drive, POB 930, Dearborn MI 48121-0930, U.S.A. / T: (313) 271-1500, Fax: 271-2861, Tx: 297742 – ISBN 0-87263

us South Carolina Historical
South Carolina Historical Society, Fireproof Bldg, 100 Meeting St, Charleston, SC 29401-2299, U.S.A. / T: (803) 723-3225

us Spaulding
Spaulding Co, Inc, Document Conversion Services, 80 Hawes Way, Stoughton, MA 02072, U.S.A. / T: (617) 828-8090, Fax: 341-4113

us Standard & Poor's
Standard & Poor's Corporation, 25 Broadway, New York, NY 10004, U.S.A. / T: (212) 208-8000, Fax: 412-0543

us Stemmons
Stemmons Publishing Co, POB 612, West Jordan UT 84088, U.S.A. / T: (801) 254-2152

us Striker
Paul S. Striker, Aesthetic Plastic Surgery, 660 Park Av, New York, NY 10021, U.S.A. / T: (212) 744-4265, Fax: 861-5800

us S.U. Libraries
Stanford University Libraries, Publ Sales, Cecil H. Green Libr, Stanford, CA 94305-6004, U.S.A. / T: (415) 723-0461

us Tax
Tax Analysts, 6830 N Fairfax Dr, Arlington, VA 22213, U.S.A. / T: (703) 533-4400, Fax: 533-4444 – ISBN 0-918255

us Trans-Media
Trans-Media / Philip F. Cohen Legal Associates, Inc, John Marshall Bookstore, 40 Cedar St, Dobbs Ferry, NY 10522, U.S.A. / T: (914) 693-1100, Fax: 693-0402 – ISBN 0-913338; 0-379

us TX Culture
The University of Texas, Institute of Texan Cultures at San Antonio, 801 South Bowie St, San Antonio, TX 78205-3296, U.S.A. / T: (210) 458-2300, (800) 776-7651, Fax: 458-2205

us U.C. Orient
The Oriental Institute of the University of Chicago, 1155 E 58th St, Chicago, IL 60637, U.S.A. / T: (773) 702-5967, Fax: 702-9853 – ISBN 0-918986; 1-885923
Orders
University of Chicago Press, 5801 Ellis Ave, Chicago, IL 60637, U.S.A. / T: (312) 702-7706, (800) 621-2736, Fax: 702-9756, E-mail: marketing@press.uchicago.edu, Internet: www.press.uchicago.edu – ISBN 0-226

us UMI
UMI University Microfilms International, A Bell & Howell Company, 300 N Zeeb Rd, POB 1346, Ann Arbor MI 48106-1346, U.S.A. / T: (313) 761-4700, (800) 521-0600, Fax: 973-7007, Tx: 211607 umi ur – ISBN 0-8357
Orders
Europe, Africa, the Mid East & Australasia: Information Publications International Ltd, White Swan House, Godstone, Surrey RH9 8LW, United Kingdom / T: (01883) 744123, Fax: 744024, Tx: 85195212 ipi g – ISBN 0-902741
Latin America, Caribbean & Bermuda: EMC International Inc, 3622 West Liberty, Ann Arbor, MI 48103, U.S.A. / T: (313) 769-6065, Fax: (313) 769-4880, Tx: 3717930
SE Asia & Far East: Information Publications/Pte Ltd, 41 Kallang Pudding, Unit 04-03, Golden Wheel Bldg, Singapore, Singapore / T: 7415166, Fax: 7429356, Tx: 50785 ipl
Information
Inquire for prices

us U.N. Pubs
United Nations Publications, c/o Sales Section, United Nations Plaza, Rm DC2-853, Dept C005, New York, NY 10017, U.S.A. / T: (212) 963-8302, (800) 253-9646, Fax: 963-3489, E-mail: publications@un.org, Internet: www.un.org/pubs/sales.htm – ISBN 0-680; 92-1
Orders
Europe: United Nations, Palais des Nations, Microform Sales, Office C 115, 1211 Genève 10, Switzerland / T: (022) 9172613, Fax: 9170027, Tx: 412962 uno ch, E-mail: unpubli@unog.ch – ISBN 92-1
Information
The fiche quantity is shown after each language symbol E/F (Eng/Fr); E (Eng); F(French); S(Spanish); R(Russian). Except for the "Commodity Trade Statistics", which are diazo mf, all mf are silver halide. Price: Silver $2.50 per mf; Diazo $2.00

us U.N.C. Southern Hist
University of North Carolina at Chapel Hill, Southern Historical Collection, Wilson Library, CB 3926, Chapel Hill, NC 27514-8890, U.S.A. / T: (919) 962-1345, Fax: 962-0484

us U.N.D.
University of North Dakota, Chester Fritz Library, Elwyn B. Robinson Dept of Special Collections, POB 9000, Grand Forks ND 58202-9000, U.S.A. / T: (701) 777-4625, Fax: 777-3319, E-mail: slater@plains.nodak.edu

us U.N.D. Archives
Archives of the University of Notre Dame, 607 Hesburgh Library, Notre Dame, IN 46556, U.S.A. / T: (219) 631-6448, Fax: 631-7980, E-mail: archives.1@nd.edu

us UNIFO
UNIFO Publishers, Inc, POB 3858, Sarasota FL 34230-3858, U.S.A. / T: (813) 953-7900, Fax: 953-7900 – ISBN 0-89111

us Univ Ill Libr
University of Illinois at Urbana-Champaign, Graduate School of Library and Information Science, 501 East Daniel St, Champaign, IL 61820-6211, U.S.A. / T: (217) 333-1359, Fax: 244-7329
Information
All orders must be prepaid in US dollars through US banks. Make checks payable to the University of Illinois

us Univelt
Univelt Inc., POB 28130, San Diego CA 92198-0198, U.S.A. / T: (760) 746-4005, Fax: 746-3139 – ISBN 0-912183; 0-87703

us Universal
Universal Serials and Book Exchange (USBE), United States Book Exchange, 2969 W 25th St, Cleveland, OH 44113-5399, U.S.A. / T: (216) 241-6960, Fax: 241-6966
Orders
Norman Ross Publishing Inc, 330 W 58th St, New York, NY 10019, U.S.A. / T: (212) 765-8200, (800) 648-8850, Fax: 765-2393, E-mail: info@nross.com, Internet: www.nross.com – ISBN 0-8287; 0-88354

us U.O. Library
University of Oregon Knight Library, 1501 Kincaid, Eugene, OR 97403-1299, U.S.A. / T: (503) 686-3080

us UPA
University Publications of America UPA, An Imprint of CIS, 4520 East-West Hwy, Bethesda, MD 20814-3389, U.S.A. / T: (301) 657-3200, (800) 692-6300, Fax: 657-3203, E-mail: info@upapubs.com, Internet: www.upapubs.com
Information
Greenwood Press's existing microform collections were transferred to University Publications of America, which now owns and distributes them

us Updata
Updata Publications, Inc, 1736 Westwood Blvd, Los Angeles, CA 90024, U.S.A. / T: (310) 474-5900, Fax: 474-4095, E-mail: cdrom@updata.com – ISBN 0-9607840

us U.W. Libraries
University of Washington Libraries, c/o Microforms Special Collections, Allen Library, Box 352900, Seattle WA 98195-2900, U.S.A. / T: (206) 543-1929, Fax: 685-8049

us U.W. Library
University of Wisconsin, Memorial Library, 728 State St, Room B108, Madison, WI 53706, U.S.A. / T: (608) 262-1193, Fax: 262-4649, E-mail: arolich@macc.wisc.edu

us Value
Value Line Publishing, Inc, 220 E 42nd St, New York, NY 10017, U.S.A. / T: (212) 907-1680, Fax: 818-9733

us V.C.H.
VCH Publishers Inc, 220 East 23rd St, New York, NY 10010-4606, U.S.A. / T: (212) 683-8333, (800) 422-8824, Fax: 481-0897, Tx: 5101011104 – ISBN 0-89573; 1-56081
Branch of
VCH Verlagsgesellschaft mbH, Pappelallee 3, 69469 Weinheim, Postfach 101161, 69451 Weinheim Germany / T: (06201) 606152, 606427, Fax: 606184, 606117, Tx: 465516 vchwhd – ISBN 3-527
Orders
VCH Publishers Inc, 303 NW 12th Av, Deerfield Beach, FL 33442-1788, U.S.A. / T: (305) 428-5566, (800) 367-8249, Fax: (800) 367-8247, Tx: 5101011104 vchpub
UK & Ireland: International Thomson Publishing Services Ltd, Cheriton House, North Way, Andover Hants SP10 5BE, United Kingdom / T: (01264) 342910, Fax: 342787
Information
Formerly Verlag Chemie International Inc

us Washington
Washington Service Bureau, Inc, 655 15th St NW, Washington, DC 20005, U.S.A. / T: (202) 508-0600, (800) 955-5219, Fax: 508-0694

us Western Res
The Western Reserve Historical Society, Library, 10825 East Blvd, Cleveland, OH 44106-1777, U.S.A. / T: (216) 721-5722, Fax: 721-5702 – ISBN 0-911704

us Williams
Williams & Wilkins, A Waverly Company, 428 E Preston St, Baltimore, MD 21202-3993, U.S.A. / T: (301) 528-4000, (800) 638-6423, Fax: (410) 528-8596, Tx: 87669 – ISBN 0-683

us Wilson
H.W. Wilson Co, 950 University Av, Bronx, NY 10452, U.S.A. / T: (718) 588-8400, (800) 367-6770, Fax: 590-4276 – ISBN 0-8242

us Women's Hist
Women's History Research Center, 2325 Oak St, Berkeley, CA 94708-1697, U.S.A. / T: (510) 524-1582 – ISBN 0-912374

Index to Publishers and Distributors

Aboriginal Studies Press, Canberra City *see* at Aboriginal
Academic Microforms Ltd, London *see* uk Academic
Académie Royale de Belgique, Bruxelles *see* be Academie Royale
A.C.R.P.P, Marne-La-Vallée *see* fr A.C.R.P.P.
Adam Matthew Publications, Marlborough *see* uk Matthew
Advanced Library Systems Inc, Andover *see* us Advanced Libr
African & Caribbean Imprint Library Services, North Falmouth *see* us African Imprint
Aircraft Technical Publishers, Brisbane *see* us Aircraft Tech
Alper, Eastchester *see* us Alper
Alpha Com GmbH, Hamburg *see* gw Alpha Com
Altair Publishing, Todmorden *see* uk Altair
Alvina Treut Burrows Institute, Inc, Manhasset *see* us A.T.B.I.
American Baptist Historical Society, Rochester *see* us A.B.H.S.
American Chemical Society (ACS), Washington *see* us A.C.S.
American Genealogical Lending Library (AGLL), Bountiful *see* us A.G.L.L.
American Geophysical Union, Washington *see* us A.G.U.
American Institute of Architects, Washington *see* us A.I.A.
American Institute of Chemical Engineers, New York *see* us AIChE
American Institute of Physics, Woodbury *see* us A.I.P.
American Jewish Periodical Center, Cincinnati *see* us A.J.P.C.
American Library Association, Chicago *see* us A.L.A.
American Theological Library Association, Evanston *see* us A.T.L.A.
Americana Unlimited, Tucson *see* us Americana
Amistad Research Center, New Orleans *see* us Amistad
Antiquarian and Landmarks Society, Inc, Hartford *see* us Antiquarian
Appropriate Technology Project, Stanford *see* us Appropriate Tech
Archives Authority of New South Wales, Sydney *see* at N.S.W. Archives
Archives de L'Illustration / Keystone, Paris *see* fr Illustration
Archives of the University of Notre Dame, Notre Dame *see* us U.N.D. Archives
Ariel House Publications, Swansea *see* uk Ariel
ARMELL, Angers *see* fr Armell
Asia Library Services, Springfield *see* us Asia Libr
Association for Information and Image Management, Silver Spring *see* us A.I.I.M.
Association pour la Conservation et la Reproduction, Marne-La-Vallée *see* fr A.C.R.P.P.
Atelier National de Reproduction des Thèes de Lille, Lille *see* fr Atelier National
Athenaeum Liverpool, Liverpool *see* uk Athenaeum
AusInfo, Canberra *see* at AusInfo
Australian Archives, Dickson *see* at Archives
Australian Bureau of Statistics (ABS), Belconnen *see* at Statistics
Australian Graduate School of Management, Sydney *see* at A.G.S.M.
Australian Surveying and Land Information Group (AUSLIG), Belconnen *see* at A.U.S.L.I.G.
Auto-Graphics, Inc, Pomona *see* us Auto-Graphics
BAB Microfilming, Mt. Roskill, Auckland *see* nz BAB
Baillieu Library, Parkville *see* at Baillieu Libr
Barbour Microfiles, Windsor *see* uk Barbour
Beck'sche, München *see* gw Beck
Bell, Edinburgh *see* uk Bell
Belser Wissenschaftlicher Dienst, Wildberg *see* gw Belser Wiss
Biblioteca Nacional, Rio de Janeiro *see* bl Biblioteca
Biblioteca Santa Ana, Almendralejo (Badajoz) *see* sp Bibl Santa Ana
Bibliothèque Nationale de France, Paris *see* fr Bibl Nationale
Bibliothèque Nationale du Québec, Montréal *see* cn Bibl Nat
BIOSIS, Philadelphia *see* us BIOSIS
BISA, Sydney *see* at BISA
Bloch and Company, Cleveland *see* us Bloch
Böhner, Mannheim *see* gw Böhner
Boletín Oficial del Estado, Madrid *see* sp Boletín
Books in Print Information Services, Vlaeberg, Cape Town *see* sa Books in Print
Boorberg, Stuttgart *see* gw Boorberg
Bowker, New Providence *see* us Bowker
Brepols Publishers, Turnhout *see* be Brepols
Brill, Leiden *see* ne Brill
British Library Document Supply Centre, Wetherby *see* uk British Libr Docs
British Library National Bibliographic Service, Wetherby *see* uk British Libr
British Library Newspaper Library, London *see* uk British Libr Newspaper
British Library Publications. Humanities and Social Sciences, London *see* uk British Libr Humanities
British Universities Film & Video Council (BUFVC), London *see* uk British Univ Film
Buckmaster Publishing, Mineral *see* us Buckmaster
Buffalo and Erie County Historical Society, Buffalo *see* us Buffalo
Business Archives Council, Glasgow *see* uk Business
Butterworths, North Ryde *see* at Butterworths
Butterworths of New Zealand Ltd, Wellington *see* nz Butterworths
Caledonian Newspapers Ltd, Glasgow *see* uk Herald
Cambridge Scientific Abstracts, Bethesda *see* us C.S.A.
Canada Communication Group – Publishing, Ottawa *see* cn Communication
Canadian Institute for Historical Microreproductions, Ottawa *see* cn C.I.H.M.
Canadian Library Association, Ottawa *see* cn Library Assoc
Canadian Microfilming Co Ltd, Montreal *see* cn Can Microfilming
Canadian Telebook Agency, Toronto *see* cn Telebook
Career Guidance Foundation, San Diego *see* us Career
Carfax Publishing Company, Abingdon, Oxfordshire *see* uk Carfax
Carswell, Scarborough *see* cn Carswell
Center for Archival Collections, Bowling Green *see* us Archival
Center for Chinese Research Materials, Oakton *see* us Chinese Res
Center for Research Libraries, Chicago *see* us Res Libr
The Centre for East Asian Cultural Studies for Unesco, Tokyo *see* ja CEACS
Centre Régional de Documentation Pédagogique de Franche-Comté, Besançon Cédex *see* fr C.R.D.P.
Chadwyck-Healey Ltd, Cambridge *see* uk Chadwyck
CHANGE, Revigny *see* fr CHANGE
China National Microforms Import & Export Corporation, Beijing *see* cc Microforms
Chivers, Bristol *see* uk Chivers
CIS, Bethesda *see* us CIS
Commonwealth Microfilm Products, Markham *see* cn Commonwealth Micro
Congressional Digest Corporation, Washington *see* us Congressional Digest
Contemporary Arts Press / ART COM, San Francisco *see* us Contemporary Arts
Continnuus, Denver *see* us Continnuus
Cooperative Library Agency for Systems and Services, San Jose *see* us CLASS
Corangamite Regional Library Corporation, Warrnambool Microfilm Unit, Warrnambool *see* at Corangamite
Creative MicroLibraries, Inc, Manhasset *see* us Creative
The Current Digest, Columbus *see* us Current
Dartmouth College Library, Hanover *see* us Dartmouth
Dataflow Systems Inc, Bethesda *see* us Dataflow
Dawson, Folkestone, Kent *see* uk Dawson
Derwent Information Ltd, London *see* uk Derwent
Deutsches Musikgeschichtliches Archiv, Kassel *see* gw D.M.A.
Disclosure, Inc, Bethesda *see* us Disclosure
East View Publications, Minneapolis *see* us East View
Educational Testing Service, Princeton *see* us E.T.S.
Effective Information Resource Corporation, Huntington Beach *see* us I.R.C.
El Nacional, Mexico *see* mx El Nacional
Electre, Paris *see* fr Electre
Elsevier Science S.A., Lausanne *see* sz Elsevier
Emmett Publishing Ltd, Hindhead *see* uk Emmett
Engineering Information Inc, Hoboken *see* us Ei
ERIC Document Reproduction Service, Springfield *see* us EDRS
European Aquaculture Society, Gent *see* be E.A.S.
European Micropublishing Services Ltd, Dublin *see* ie European Micro
Facts on File, Inc, New York *see* us Facts
Fairchild Microfilm (Publications), Inc, New York *see* us Fairchild Micro
FAO, Roma *see* it F.A.O.
Fédération Française de Généologie, Paris *see* fr F.F.G.
Fédération Internationale des Archives du Film (FIAF), London *see* uk FIAF
Fischer, Erlangen *see* gw Fischer
Gabriel Micrographics, DeKalb *see* us Gabriel Micro
Gale Research Inc, Detroit *see* us Gale
Gaunt, Inc, Holmes Beach *see* us Gaunt
Genealogical Society of the Northern Territory Inc, Winnellie *see* at G.S.N.T.
Genetic Engineering News, New York *see* us Genetic Eng
Geography Publications, Waterloo *see* cn Geography
Geological Society of America, Inc, Boulder *see* us Geological Soc
Globe Information Services, Scarborough *see* cn Globe Info
Globe Microfilms, Beijing *see* cc Globe
Godfrey Memorial Library, Middletown *see* us Godfrey
Gordon & Breach, Science Publishers, Langhorne *see* us Gordon
Gothenburg University Library, Göteborg *see* sw G.U.
Grainger Museum Board, Parkville *see* at Grainger Mus
Great Britain Public Record Office, Richmond *see* uk G.B.P.R.O.
Haifu Microfilm Producing Center, Nanjing *see* cc Haifu Micro
Hall, Hemel Hempstead *see* uk Hall
Hänsel-Hohenhausen, Egelsbach *see* gw Hänsel
Harvard College Library, Cambridge *see* us H.U. College Libr
Harvard Law School Library, Cambridge *see* us H.U. Law
Harvard University Library, Cambridge *see* us H.U. Library
Hayes, Fremont *see* us Hayes
Heather Press, Muncie *see* us Heather
Hein, Buffalo *see* us Hein
Heinz, Stuttgart *see* gw Heinz
Helsingin yliopiston kirjasto, University of Helsinki *see* fi H.U. Libr
Hill Monastic Manuscript Library (HMML), Collegeville *see* us H.M.M.L.
Historical Society of Pennsylvania, Philadelphia *see* us H.S.P.
Holbrook Research Institute, Oxford *see* us Holbrook
Holland Land Company Project, Fredonia *see* us Holland
Hoover Institution Photographic Services, Stanford *see* us Hoover Inst Photo
Human Relations Area Files Press, New Haven *see* us H.R.A.F.
Hutchinson, Carlton South *see* at Hutchinson
ICRISAT, Patancheru PO *see* ii ICRISAT
IDC Publishers bv, Leiden *see* ne IDC
Iglesias, Madrid *see* sp Iglesias
Illinois State Archives, Springfield *see* us IL Archives
Illinois State Historical Library, Springfield *see* us IL Hist
Immigration History Research Center, Saint Paul *see* us I.H.R.C.
IMR Limited, Harrisburg *see* us I.M.R.
Indiana Historical Society, Indianapolis *see* us I.H.S.
Indiana University Libraries, Bloomington *see* us I.U. Libraries
Indices Publishing, Vallejo *see* us Indices
Infoprint S.A., Monte Carasso *see* sz Infoprint
Information Access Company (IAC), Foster City *see* us I.A.C.
Information Handling Services, Englewood *see* us Info Handling
Information Resources Press (IRP), Arlington *see* us Info Resources
Ingram Distribution Group Inc, La Vergne *see* us Ingram
INSPEC, Stevenage *see* uk INSPEC
Institut d'Ethnologie du Muséum National d'Histoire Naturelle, Paris *see* fr Ethnologie
Institut d'Etudes Augustiniennes, Paris *see* fr Augustiniennes
Institute of Early American History and Culture, Williamsburg *see* us I.E.A.H.C.
Institute of Electrical and Electronics Engineers, Inc (IEEE), Piscataway *see* us I.E.E.E.
Institute of Paper Science and Technology, Inc, Atlanta *see* us Paper
International Commission of Jurists, Cointrin *see* sz I.C.J.
International Communications Services, Paris *see* fr I.C.S.
International Development Research Centre, Ottawa *see* cn I.D.R.C.
International Labour Office, Genève *see* sz I.L.O.
International Livestock Research Institute (ILRI), Addis Ababa *see* et ILRI
International Research & Evaluation, Eagan *see* us I.R.E.
International Telecommunication Union, ITU, Genève *see* sz I.T.U.
IOP Publishing Ltd, Bristol *see* uk I.O.P.
IOS-ECHO, Wohltorf *see* gw IOS
IPC Magazines Limited, London *see* uk I.P.C.
Irish Microforms Ltd, Sentry, Dublin *see* ie Microforms
ISSN International Centre, Paris *see* fr I.S.S.N.
I.T.T.I. Ltd, Bnei-Brak *see* is I.T.T.I.
Japan Microfilm Service Center Co, Ltd, Tokyo *see* ja Japan Micro
Japanese Journal of Applied Physics, Tokyo *see* ja Journal of Physics
Journal Officiel, Editeur des Journaux Officiels, Paris *see* fr Journal Officiel
Juta & Company Ltd, Kenwyn *see* sa Juta
Kansas State Historical Society, Topeka *see* us KS Hist
Keip GmbH, Goldbach *see* gw Keip
Knoedler Gallery, New York *see* us Knoedler
Kungliga Biblioteket, Stockholm *see* sw Kungliga
Law Library Microform Consortium, Kaneohe *see* us L.L.M.C.
Lawrence, University Park *see* us Lawrence Pub
Lengenfelder, München *see* gw Lengenfelder
Libertarian Microfiche Publishing, Berrima *see* at Libertarian Micro
Librarians of Institutes and Schools of Education (LISE), Swansea *see* uk L.I.S.E.
Library Microfilms, Sunnyvale *see* us Library Micro
Library of Congress, Washington *see* us L of C Cataloging
Library of Congress, Washington *see* us L of C Photodup
Library Preservation Systems International Ltd, Reading *see* uk Libr Preservation
Liverpool Bibliographical Society, Liverpool *see* uk Liverpool Bib
Lomond Publications, Inc., Mount Airy *see* us Lomond
McGilvery, La Jolla *see* us McGilvery
McLaren Micropublishing Ltd, Toronto *see* cn McLaren
Manchester Public Libraries, Manchester *see* uk Manchester Libr
Mansell Publishing Ltd, London *see* uk Mansell Publ

MARC Applied Research Company, Inwood *see* us MARC Applied
Maryland State Archives, Annapolis *see* us MD Archives
Mecklermedia Corporation, Westport *see* us Mecklermedia
Metropolitan Library Service Agency (MELSA), St. Paul *see* us MELSA
Micro Aero Charts, Colorado Springs *see* us Aero
Micro Graphix, Witney *see* uk Micro Graphix
MicroComics Inc, Ridgewood *see* us Comics
Microéditions Hachette, Paris *see* fr Hachette
Microfile, Marshalltown *see* sa Microfile
Microfilm Company of California, Inc, Los Angeles *see* us Microfilm
Microform Academic Publishers, Wakefield *see* uk Microform Academic
Microform Publications, Eugene *see* us Microform Publ
Microlibrary Slangenburg Abbey, Doetinchem *see* ne Slangenburg
Micromedex, Inc, Englewood *see* us Micromedex
Micromedia Limited, Toronto *see* cn Micromedia
Mikro Press GmbH, Bonn *see* gw Mikro Press
Mikrofilmarchiv der deutschsprachigen Presse e.V., Dortmund *see* gw Mikrofilm
Mindata Ltd, Bath *see* uk Mindata
Ministerio de Cultura, Madrid *see* sp Cultura
Minnesota Historical Society, St. Paul *see* us M.H.S.
Miscellaneous Institutions, see gw Mikrofilm *see* gw Misc Inst
Mitchell International, San Diego *see* us Mitchell Int'l
MMF Publications, Lisse *see* ne MMF Publ
Moody's Investors Service, Inc, New York *see* us Moody's
MRTS, Binghamton *see* us MRTS
Municipal World Inc, St. Thomas *see* cn Municipal
Museum of Early Southern Decorative Arts (MESDA), Winston-Salem *see* us MESDA
Nash Information Services, Inc, Ottawa *see* cn Nash Info
National Archives Trust Fund, Washington *see* us Nat'l Archives
National Diet Library, Tokyo *see* ja Nat'l Diet
National Institute of Justice / NCJRS, Rockville *see* us N.C.J.R.S.
National Library of Australia, Canberra *see* at Nat'l Libr
National Library of Canada/Bibliothèque nationale du Canada, Ottawa *see* cn Nat'l Library
National Library Shop, Wellington *see* nz Nat'l Libr
National Technical Information Service (NTIS), Springfield *see* us N.T.I.S.
Nebraska State Historical Society, Lincoln *see* us NE Hist
New England Historic Genealogical Society, Boston *see* us New England
New Mexico State Records Center and Archives, State Rules Division, Santa Fe *see* us NM Archives
New South Wales Parliament, Sydney *see* at Parliament
New York Law Publishing Company, New York *see* us New York Law
New York Public Library, New York *see* us NY Public
New Zealand Institute of Forestry, Inc, Christchurch *see* nz Forest
NewsBank, Inc, New Canaan *see* us NewsBank
Nihon Keizai Shimbun, Inc, Tokyo *see* ja Nihon Keizai
Nippon Technical Service Co, Ltd, Tokyo *see* ja Nippon Tech
North Carolina Division of Archives and History, Raleigh *see* us NC Archives
NV Sdu Publishers (MICRO), Den Haag *see* ne Sdu MICRO
NZ Library and Information Association, Wellington *see* nz Libr & Info
Office for Official Publications of the European Communities, Luxembourg *see* lu EEC
Ohio Historical Society, Columbus *see* us Ohio Hist
Okaz for Press and Publishing, Jeddah *see* su Okaz
Olms, Hildesheim *see* gw Olms
OmniSys Corporation, Needham Heights *see* us OmniSys
Optical Society of America, Washington *see* us Optical Soc
OPUS Publications, Inc, East Haven *see* us Opus
Oregon Historical Society Library, Portland *see* us Oregon Hist
ORS Publishing, Bethesda *see* us ORS Publ
Oryx Press, Phoenix *see* us Oryx
Pacific Manuscripts Bureau (Pambu), Canberra *see* at Pacific Mss
Partington, Whittier *see* us Partington
Pascoe, Balgowlah *see* at Pascoe
Pennsylvania Academy of the Fine Arts, Philadelphia *see* us Penn Academy
Pennsylvania Historical and Museum Commission, Harrisburg *see* us Penn Hist
Pennsylvania State University Press, University Park *see* us Penn State
Pentalfa Microediciones, Oviedo *see* sp Pentalfa
Perceptual and Motor Skills, Missoula *see* us Perceptual
Petroconsultants S.A., Perly-Geneva *see* sz Petro
Philosophy Documentation Center, Bowling Green *see* us Philosophy
The Physical Society of Japan, Tokyo *see* ja Physical Soc
Pontifical Institute of Medieval Studies, Toronto *see* cn Pontif
Pordes, Cockfosters *see* uk Pordes
Precision Micrographic Services Ltd, Vancouver *see* cn Precision
Presbyterian Historical Society, Philadelphia *see* us Presbyterian
Preston Microfilming Services, Toronto *see* cn Preston
Preston Publications, Inc, Niles *see* us Preston Publ
Primary Source Media, Woodbridge *see* us Primary
Princeton Microfilm Corporation, Princeton Junction *see* us Princeton Micro
Psychological Reports, Missoula *see* us Psychological
Publications Orientalistes de France, Cergy *see* fr Orientalistes
Readex Microprint Corp., New Canaan *see* us Readex
Editions de la Réunion des Musées Nationaux (R.M.N.), Paris *see* fr Réunion
Roosevelt, Hyde Park *see* us Roosevelt
Ross, New York *see* us Ross
Roth Publishing, Inc, Great Neck *see* us Roth
Royal Australasian Ornithologists Union (RAOU), Moonee Pondsn *see* at R.A.O.U.
Saur, München *see* gw Saur
Schierenberg, Amsterdam *see* ne Schierenberg
Schnappsburg University Press, Jamestown *see* us Schnappsburg
Schnase Microfilm Systems, Scarsdale *see* us Schnase
Scholarly Resources Inc, Wilmington *see* us Scholarly Res
Scholars' Facsimiles & Reprints, Delmar *see* us Scholars' Facs
Scottish Newspapers Microfilming Unit, Edinburgh *see* uk Scot News
Seanachas Press, Maroubra *see* at Seanachas
S.E.M.P., S.A., 0aris *see* fr S.E.M.P.
Shkurkin, San Pablo *see* us Shkurkin
Sibley Music Library Microform Service, Rochester *see* us Sibley
Skinner, London *see* uk Skinner
Society for Industrial and Applied Mathematics (SIAM), Philadelphia *see* us S.I.A.M.
Society for Research on Women in New Zealand Inc, Johnsonville *see* nz SROW
Society of Automotive Engineers, Inc, Warrendale *see* us S.A.E.
Society of Manufacturing Engineers (SME), Dearborn *see* us S.M.E.
South African Library, Cape Town *see* sa SA Libr
South Carolina Department of Archives and History, Columbia *see* us SC Archives
South Carolina Historical Society, Charleston *see* us South Carolina Historical
Spaulding Co, Inc, Stoughton *see* us Spaulding
Standard & Poor's Corporation, New York *see* us Standard & Poor's
Stanford University Libraries, Stanford *see* us S.U. Libraries
State Archives and Heraldic Services, Pretoria *see* sa State Archives
State Historical Society of Wisconsin, Madison *see* us Historical Soc
State Library, Pretoria *see* sa State Libr
State Library of Victoria, Melbourne *see* at State Libr Vic
Stemmons Publishing Co, West Jordan *see* us Stemmons
Striker, New York *see* us Striker
Swets & Zeitlinger B.V., Lisse *see* ne Swets
Tax Analysts, Arlington *see* us Tax
Technical Indexes Ltd, Bracknell *see* uk Tech
The Corning Museum of Glass, Corning *see* us Corning Mus
The Haworth Press, Inc, Binghamton *see* us Haworth
The Institute for Advanced Studies of World Religions (IASWR), Carmel *see* us I.A.S.W.R.
The Irish Times Ltd, Dublin *see* ie Irish Times
The Oriental Institute of the University of Chicago, Chicago *see* us U.C. Orient
The Society of American Archivists, Chicago *see* us S.A.A.
The Southern Baptist Convention Historical Library and Archives, Nashville *see* us Baptist
The University of Chicago, Chicago *see* us MEDOC
The University of Texas, Institute of Texan Cultures at San Antonio, San Antonio *see* us TX Culture
The Western Reserve Historical Society, Cleveland *see* us Western Res
Thorpe, Port Melbourne *see* at Thorpe Mf
Thunder Bay Historical Museum Society, Thunder Bay *see* cn Thunder Bay
Trans-Media / Philip F. Cohen Legal Associates, Inc, Dobbs Ferry *see* us Trans-Media
Transmission Books & Microforms Company, Ltd, Taipei, R.O.C. *see* ch Transmission
UMI University Microfilms International, Ann Arbor *see* us UMI
UNESCO, Paris *see* fr UNESCO
UNIFO Publishers, Inc, Sarasota *see* us UNIFO
UNIMICRO, St. Leonards *see* uk UNIMICRO
United Nations Publications, New York *see* us U.N. Pubs
United Nations University Press (UNU), Tokyo *see* ja U.N. Univ
United States Government Printing Office (USG), Washington *see* us Gov't Printing
Univelt Inc., San Diego *see* us Univelt
Universal Serials and Book Exchange (USBE), Cleveland *see* us Universal
University of Botswana, National Institute of Development Research & Documentation (NIR), Gaborone *see* bs U.B. Nat'l Inst
University of British Columbia, Vancouver *see* cn U.B.C. Preserve
University of Chicago Press, Chicago *see* us Chicago
University of Illinois at Urbana-Champaign, Champaign *see* us Univ Ill Libr
University of New South Wales Library, Sydney *see* at U.N.S.W. Library
University of North Carolina at Chapel Hill, Southern Historical Collection, Chapel Hill *see* us U.N.C. Southern Hist
University of North Dakota, Grand Forks *see* us U.N.D.
University of Oregon Knight Library, Eugene *see* us U.O. Library
University of Toronto Press, Toronto *see* cn U.T. Pr
University of Washington Libraries, Seattle *see* us U.W. Libraries
University of Wisconsin, Memorial Library, Madison *see* us U.W. Library
University Publications of America UPA, Bethesda *see* us UPA
Updata Publications, Inc, Los Angeles *see* us Updata
Value Line Publishing, Inc, New York *see* us Value
VCH Publishers Inc, New York *see* us V.C.H.
VCH Verlagsgesellschaft mbH, Weinheim *see* gw V.C.H.
Vine Hall, Albert Park *see* at Vine
Voltaire Foundation, Oxford *see* uk Voltaire
Washington Service Bureau, Inc, Washington *see* us Washington
Whitaker Bibliographic Services, London *see* uk Whitaker
Wilfrid Laurier University Press, Waterloo *see* cn W.L.U. Press
Williams & Wilkins, Baltimore *see* us Williams
Wilson, Bronx *see* us Wilson
Women's History Research Center, Berkeley *see* us Women's Hist
World Microfilms Publications Ltd, London *see* uk World
Yonge Library of Florida History, Gainesville *see* us P.K. Yonge
Yushodo Co., Ltd, Tokyo *see* ja Yushodo

Author-Title List
A–K

Title main entries with references
from authors, editors

0 14 DE JULHO – Pilar, Alagoas. 14 Jul 1889 – 1,5,6 – bl Biblioteca [072]
EL 1 CONGRESO NACIONAL DE BRUJOLOGIA EN SAN SEBASTIAN / Gutierrez Macias, Valeriano – Badajoz: Dip. Provincial, 1973. Sep. REE – 1 – sp Bibl Santa Ana [946]
1 CONSEJO SINDICAL COMARCAL. DELEGACION COMARCAL DE AZUAGA / Delegacion Provincial de Sindicatos – Azuaga: Tip. Domenech, 1959 – sp Bibl Santa Ana [946]
1 KNIGI SVIASHCHENNOGO PISANIIA / Akademiia Nauk. Okhrannaia opis' Rukopisnogo otdeleniia Biblioteki imp – Comp. by V. I. Sreznevskii. Spb. 1905. BR-7307 2 – 8 – ne IDC [010]
1 LA CHANSON FRANCAISE A TRAVERS LES SIECLES : REVUE HISTORIQUE DE SES AUTEURS ET DE LEURS INTERPRETES / Morin, Victor – (2: Operetta-Dinner: A gastronomico-musical fantasy in two acts) – Toronto, 1939. SEM105P812 – 1mf – 9 – Can$2.25 – cn Bibl Nat [780]
1 REUNION HISPANO PORTUGUESA DE HEMATOLOGIA / Asociacion Espanola de Hematologia y Hemoterapia, 12 Reunion – Badajoz: Elvas, Doncel, I.G., 1969 – sp Bibl Santa Ana [060]
1 SAMUEL 1-7, 1 : TEXT- UND QUELLENKRITISCH UNTERSUCHT / Holtz, Kurt – Leipzig: W Drugulin, 1904 – 1mf – 9 – 0-8370-3630-5 – 1985-1630 – us A.T.L.A. [220]
1 STAR EVENING NEWS EDITION – Fort Worth. Texas. 1966- – 1 – us UMI [071]
1 STAR EVENING SUB-EDITION – Fort Worth. Texas. 1933-65 – 1 – us UMI [071]
1 STAR STATE FINAL EDITION – Fort Worth. Texas. 1967- – 1 – us UMI [071]
1ER MAZURKA POUR LE PIANO, OP. 21 / Saint-Saens, Camille – Paris: Durand & fils, [188-] – 1 – us Sibley [780]
1ER QUINTETTO POUR 2 VIOLONS, 2 ALTOS ET BASSE / Widekehr, J – (5 pts) – Paris: Imbault, 179- – 1 – us Sibley [780]
1ST BAYONA Y LA POLITICA DE NAPOLEON EN AMERICA... Y 2ND HISTORIA DE LA PRIMERA REPUBLICA DE VENEZUELA... / Parra Perez, C – Madrid: Razon y Fe, 1940 – 1 – sp Bibl Santa Ana [320]
1ST CAMPEONATO DE PESCA EN LA MODALIDAD DE C. GRUPO IBERDUERO. EMBALSE DE ALCANTARA EN AGUAS DEL RIO TAJO. FINCA LA CARRASCOSA. DIA 21 DE JUNIO DE 1975. REGLAMENTO Y PROGRAMA DE ACTOS / Campeonato de Pesca 1, 1975 – Caceres: Imp. Rodriguez, 1975 – 1 – sp Bibl Santa Ana [946]
1ST CONCURSO HIPICO NACIONAL 26 AL 28 AGOSTO... – Caceres: Tip. Extremadura, 1972 – 1 – sp Bibl Santa Ana [946]
1ST CONGRESO REGIONAL AGRARIO DE EXTREMADURA. DISCURSOS, DESARROLLO, PONENCIAS, Y CONCLUSIONES. CACERES-BADAJOZ NOVIEMBRE DE 1949 – Caceres: Tip. El Noticiero, s.a. – sp Bibl Santa Ana [360]
1ST CONGRESO SINDICAL AGRARIO DE EXTREMADURA 2. PONENCIA REGINEN DE PRECIOS Y MERCADOS EN LA AGRICULTURA / Corral Acedo, Francisco et al – Caceres: Tip. El Noticiero s.a., 1949 – sp Bibl Santa Ana [630]
1ST CONGRESO SINDICAL AGRARIO DE EXTREMADURA 3 PONENCIA. PLAN NACIONAL DE TRANSFORMACION EN EL CAMPO / Sierra, Francisco et al – Caceres: Tip. El Noticiero s.a., 1949 – sp Bibl Santa Ana [630]
1ST CONGRESO SINDICAL AGRARIO DE EXTREMADURA. PONENCIA 4 SERVICIOS ECONOMICOS DE LAS HERMANDADES / Sanz Catalan, Jose & Masa Campos, Antonio – Caceres: Tip. El Noticieros. s.a., 1949 – sp Bibl Santa Ana [630]
1ST CONGRESO SINDICAL AGRARIO DE EXTREMADURA. PONENCIA 5 MUTUALIDADES AGRICOLAS / Diaz Montilla, Rafael et al – Tip. El Noticiero s.a., 1949 – sp Bibl Santa Ana [630]
1ST CONGRESO SINDICAL AGRARIO DE EXTREMADURA. PONENCIA 6. MECANIZACION E INDUSTRIALIZACION DEL CAMPO / Muriel Jimenez, Vicente et al – Caceres: Tip. El Noticiero s.a., 1949 – sp Bibl Santa Ana [630]
1ST CONGRESO SINDICAL AGRARIO DE EXTREMADURA. PONENCIA 7. SITUACION DE LA, PRODUCCION GANADERA / Moreno de Arteaga, Antonio & Blazquez Izquierdo, Jose – Caceres: Tip. El Noticiero, s.a., 1949 – sp Bibl Santa Ana [630]
1ST CONGRESO SINDICAL AGRARIO DE EXTREMADURA. PONENCIA 7, SOLUCIONES URGENTES A LOS PROBLEMAS FUNDAMENTALES DEL CAMPO EXTREMENOS / Sana Catalan, Jose et al – Caceres: Tip. El Noticiero, s.a. (1949) – sp Bibl Santa Ana [630]
1ST CONGRESO SINDICAL AGRARIO DE EXTREMADURA, PONENCIA I ESTRUCTURA Y FINES DEL SINDICALISMO AGRARIO / Donoso Cortes y Donoso Cortes, E et al – Caceres: Tip. El Noticiero, s.a. 1949 – sp Bibl Santa Ana [946]
1ST EXPOSICION COLECTIVA DEL GRUPO ARTISTICO EL CANCHAL. 1976 – Caceres: Tip. Extremadura, 1976 – 1 – sp Bibl Santa Ana [700]
1ST REGIMENT, OVLA, RECORDS, MS 2894 – 1861-1862 – 1 reel – 1 – us Western Res [976]
1ST REGIMENT, OVLA, RECORDS, MS 3965 – 1861 – 1reel – 1 – us Western Res [976]
1ST REPORT / Great Britain. Advisory Council on Art Education – 1960 – 9 – uk Microform Academic [324]
1ST VUELTA CICLISTA A CACERES 1970. ORGANIZA CLUB POLIDEPORTIVO UNION. COLABROA FEDERACION EXTREMENA DE CICLISMO. CACERES, FERIA DE 1970 / Vuelta Ciclista – Plasencia: Graf. Sandoval, 1970 – 1 – sp Bibl Santa Ana [946]
1ST-8TH ANNUAL REPORT AND PROCEEDINGS...SESSION 1836/7-43/44 / Botanical Society of Edinburgh – Edinburgh, 1841 v1, 1838-44 v 2-5 – 3 – us Readex [580]
1X2 LAS QUINIELAS AL ALCANCE DE TODOS / Correyero, M – Don Benito: Tip. Trejo, 1969 – sp Bibl Santa Ana [946]
2 CONCURSO PROVINCIAL DE FORMACION PROFESIONAL, MAYO 1948 / Delegacion Provincial del Frente de Juventudas, Seccion de Centros de Trabajo – Caceres: Tip. El. Noticiero, S.A. – sp Bibl Santa Ana [946]
2 CONGRESO SINDICAL AGRARIO DE EXTREMADURA : DISCURSOS, PONENCIAS, CONCLUSIONES / Delegacion Provincial de Sindicatos – Badajoz: Imp. Bartolome Garcia, 1951 – sp Bibl Santa Ana [946]
2 JUEGOS DEPORTIVOS / Caceres. Delegacion Provincial de Organizaciones del Movimiento – Caceres, Caceres: Imp. San Guiro, 1965 – 1 – sp Bibl Santa Ana [790]
2 MANUSCRIPTS IN CURSIVE HEBREW, BOUND, CONTAINING ESSAYS AND LETTERS SUPPOSEDLY BY / Menahem Mendell of Lublin – n.p., n.d – 1 – us U.W. Library [470]
2 PLAN DE FOMENTO (1959-1964) / Portugal. Assembleia Nacional – 3v. Lisboa. 1959 – 9 – ne IDC [338]
2 PLAN QUINQUENAL / Argentine Republic. Subsecretaria de Informaciones – Buenos Aires. 1953 – 9 – ne IDC [338]
2 PLANO DE FOMENTO (1959-1964) – D-1129 1. 1959 – 9 – ne IDC [338]
2 PLANO DE FOMENTO 1959-1964 – D-1118 1. 1959 – 9 – ne IDC [330]
[2] SELECT AIRS WITH VARIATIONS / Gelinek, J – (2 vol in 1) – London: Preston, 181- – 1 – us Sibley [780]
2. SONATE, OP. 21, PIANO SOLO / Szymanowski, K – Wien: Universal ed, c1912 – 1 – us Sibley [780]
2 STAR EVENING HOME EDITION – Fort Worth. Texas. 1902-1966 – 1 – us UMI [071]
2 STAR MORNING EDITION – Fort Worth. Texas. 1966- – 1 – us UMI [071]
2. TIMOTHY 2:15 : A COURSE OF STUDY IN PERSONAL WORK / Pope, Howard Walter – Boston:United Society of Christian Endeavor, c1910 – 1mf – 9 – 0-8370-2611-3 – 1985-0611 – us A.T.L.A. [240]
2 X 2 EQUALS 5. LISTY IMAZHINISTA / Shershenevich, V – M. 1920. BR-1083 2 – 8 – ne IDC [490]
2-D AND 3-D METAPHORICALLY EQUIVOCAL SPACE – Pattee, University Park, PA. 1989 – 62p 6mf – 9 – $0.50f – us Lawrence Pub [720]
2E CONFERENCE AU SOMMET : ORGANISATION DES ETATS RIVERAINS DU SENEGAL – [Conakry]: Impr nationale "Partice Lumumba", 1970 – us Res Libr [960]
2E PLAN DE MODERNISATION ET D'EQUIPEMENT RAPPORT GENERAL DE LA COMMISSION D'ETUDE. DES TERRITORIES D'OUTRE-MER / France. Commissariat General du Plan – Paris. 1954. BD-559 1 – 9 – ne IDC [338]
2E PLAN FRANCE, RAPPORT GENERAL DE LA COMMISSION D'ETUDE. ALGERIE / France. Commissariat General du Plan – Paris, Commissariat General du Plan. 1954 – 9 – ne IDC [338]
2E PLAN FRANCE, RAPPORT GENERAL DE LA COMMISSION D'ETUDE. MAROC – Paris, Commisariat General du Plan. 1954. BD-560 1 – 9 – ne IDC [330]
2E PLAN FRANCE, RAPPORT GENERAL DE LA COMMISSION D'ETUDE. TUNISIE / France. Commission d'Etude Tunisie – Paris, Commissariat General du Plan. 1954 – 9 – ne IDC [338]
2E PLAN QUADRIENNAL 1974-1977 / Algeria – Rapport general.1974. BD-1805-1 – 9 – ne IDC [960]
2E PLAN RAPPORT GENERAL DE LA COMMISSION D'ETUDE ET DE COORDINATION DES PLANS. DES DEPARTEMENTS D'OUTRE-MER / France. Commissariat General du Plan – Paris. 1954 – 9 – ne IDC [338]
LE 2EME PLAN QUINQUENNAL 1917-1975 / Togo – Summary in French. Bulletin de l'Afrique Noire. numero special, 3rd ed. Paris. 1975. BD-1859 1 – 9 – ne IDC [338]
2ND CONGRESO (1. ORDINARIO) DEL COMITE CONTRA EL RACISMO Y ANTISEMITISMO DE LA ARGENTINA : REALIZADO EL 9 DE SEPTIEMBRE DE 1939 EN LA CIUDAD DE BUENOS AIRES / Comite Contra el Racismo y el Antisemitismo de la Argentina – Buenos Aires: El Comite, 1939 – 1 – CSUXAHZ2349-B – us Hoover Inst Photo [305]
2ND CONGRESO DE GEOGRAFIA E HISTORIA HISPANO-AMERICANAS / Bayle, Constantino – Madrid: Razon y Fe, 1921 – 1 – sp Bibl Santa Ana [972]
2ND FESTIVALES DE ESPANA. PLASENCIA, 13 AL 16 DE JUNIO 1970 – Plasencia: Imp. La Victoria, 1970 – 1 – sp Bibl Santa Ana [390]
2ND GALA DEL DEPORTE COMARCAL / Delegacion de Deportes – Coriz: Gr. Planta, 1980 – 1 – sp Bibl Santa Ana [946]
2ND [I.E. SEGUNDO] PLAN QUINQUENAL : MANUAL DOCTRINARIO Y PRACTICO / Argentina. Ministerio de Asistencia Social y Salud Publica – [Buenos Aires], 1954 – 1 – CSUXADJ8067-B – us Hoover Inst Photo [972]
2ND JORNADAS DE PROMOCION DEL DEPORTE LABORAL 1976 / Obra Sindical de Educacion y Descanso – Caceres: Tip. Extremadura, 1976 – 1 – sp Bibl Santa Ana [790]
2ND JUEGOS DIDACTICO-DEPORTIVOS NACIONALES DE LAS ESCUELAS NORMALES. FASE DE SECTOR. CACERES 1 AL 4 DE ABRIL 1971 – Caceres: Tip. Extremadura, 1971 – 1 – sp Bibl Santa Ana [370]
THE 2ND SET OF BATESON'S MADRIGALS : SCORED BY PROF. E. TAYLOR / Bateson, T – Ms score, London, 1846. Never published – 1 – us Sibley [780]
2TES TRIO FUER PIANO, VIOLINE UND VIOLONCELLE, OP. 20 / Bargiel, Woldemar – Leipzig: F E C Leuckart; New York: Scharfenberg & Luis [186-?] – 1 – us Sibley [780]
3 DAGAR – Vaexjoe, 1993-94 – 9 – sw Kungliga [072]
3 DISCURSOS. / Primo de Rivera, Jose Antonio – n.p., 1936? Fiche W1502. (Blodgett Collection of Spanish Civil War Pamphlets) – 9 – us H.U. College Libr [946]
3 FERIA REGIONAL DEL CAMPO EXTREMENO / Zafra. Ayuntamiento – Zafra: Comision de Ferias y Fiestas del Ayuntamiento, 1968 – sp Bibl Santa Ana [946]
3 PIECES FOR PIANO, OP. 54 / Moszkowski, M – New York: John Church Co, 1895 – 1 – us Sibley [780]
3 PLANO DE FOMENTO PARA 1968-1973 / Mozambique. (Portugal). Presidencia do Conselho – D-1130 1. 1968 – 9 – ne IDC [338]
3 PLANO DE FOMENTO, PROGRAM DE EXECUCAO 1973 / Portugal. Presidencia do Conselho. Secreteriado Tecnico – Lisbon. 1973. BD-2019 1 – 9 – ne IDC [338]
3 PLANO DE FOMENTO. PROGRAMA DE EXECUCAO, 1970 / Portugal. Presidencia do Conselho – (III Development Plan. Implementation Program, 1970). Lisboa. 1970. BD-1737 1 – 9 – ne IDC [338]
3 PLANO DE FOMENTO. PROGRAMA DE EXECUCAO, 1971 / Portugal. Presidencia do Conselho – (III Development Plan. Implementation Program, 1971). Lisboa. 1971. BD-1739 1 – 9 – ne IDC [338]
3 PLANO DE FOMENTO. PROGRAMA DE EXECUCAO, 1972 / Portugal. Presidencia do Conselho – (III Development Plan. Implementation Program, 1972). Lisboa. 1972. BD-1740 1 – 9 – ne IDC [338]
3 RAID HIPICO INTERNACIONAL. BADAJOZ-CACERES-BADAJOZ (14 Y 15 DE MARZO 1970) / Sociedad Hipica Lebrera de Badajoz – Badajoz: Imp. Comercial M. Cordon, 1970 – sp Bibl Santa Ana [946]
3 STAR COMPLETE MARKET EDITION – Fort Worth. Texas. 1926- – 1 – us UMI [071]
3 STAR EVENING EDITION – Fort Worth. Texas. 1967- – 1 – us UMI [071]
3E PLAN, 1958-1961 RAPPORT GENERAL DE LA COMMISSION DE MODERNISATION ET D'EQUIPEMENT DES DEP. D'OUTRE-MER / France. Commissariat General du Plan – Paris. 1959 – 9 – ne IDC [338]
3E PLAN DE MODERNISATION ET D'EQUIPEMENT 1958-1961 (DECRET NO. 59-443 DU 19 MAR 1959) / France – Paris. 1959. BD-524 1 – 9 – ne IDC [324]
3EME MAZURKA, OP. 17 / Liapunov, S – [19–] – 1 – us Sibley [780]
3RD EXPOSICION FILATELICA CACERNA / C.N.S. Vicesecretaria Provincial de O. Sindicales de E.D. – Caceres: Tip. El Noticiero, 1955 – 1 – sp Bibl Santa Ana [946]
A 3RD SET OF SIX CONCERTOS FOR THE HARPSICHORD... OP. 13 / Bach, Johann Christian – London: Printed and sold by I Walker, [1777] – 5 – us Sibley [780]
EL 4 CENTENARIO DEL DESCUBRIMIENTO DE CALIFORNIA / Bayle, Constantino – Madrid: Razon y Fe, 1932 – 1 – sp Bibl Santa Ana [978]
4. COMISION NO 1 A: AGRICULTURA / Consejo Economico Sindical Provincial – Badajoz: Imprenta Inca, 1965 – sp Bibl Santa Ana [630]
4. COMISION NO 1 B: REPOBLACION FORESTAL / Consejo Economico Sindical Provincial – Badajoz: Imprenta Inca, 1965 – sp Bibl Santa Ana [630]
4. COMISION NO 1: GANADERIA / Consejo Economico Sindical Provincial – Badajoz: Imp. Inca, 1965 – sp Bibl Santa Ana [630]
4. COMISION NO 7: ENSENANZA Y FORMACION PROFESIONAL / Consejo Economico Sindical Provincial – Badajoz: Graficas Jimenez, 1965 – sp Bibl Santa Ana [330]
4 CONSEJO ECONOMICO SINDICAL / Laguna Sanz, Eduardo – 1st Prov.Comision (Ganaderia). Badajoz: Imp. Inca, 1966 – 1 – sp Bibl Santa Ana [330]
4 CONSEJO ECONOMICO SINDICAL 11TH PROV. COMISION. SANIDAD Y ASISTENCIA SOCIAL / Lopez Santamaria, Luis – Diciembre, 1965. Badajoz. Imp.Inca, 1965 – 1 – sp Bibl Santa Ana [330]
4 CONSEJO ECONOMICO SINDICAL 14TH PROV. COMISION. TRABAJO / Masa Godoy, Jose – Badajoz: Impenta Inca, 1966 – 1 – sp Bibl Santa Ana [330]
4 DE OUTUBRO – Maceio, Alagoas. 4 Out 1886; 4 Out 1888 – 1,5,6 – bl Biblioteca [072]
4 DISCURSOS. / Primo de Rivera, Pilar – Barcelona, 1939. Fiche W1121. (Blodgett Collection of Spanish Civil War Pamphlets) – 9 – us H.U. College Libr [946]
4 FESTIVALES DE ESPANA. PLASENCIA 23-29 JUNIO 1972 / Festivales de Espana N. Plasencia, 1972 – Plasencia: Imp. La Victoria, 1972 – 1 – sp Bibl Santa Ana [390]
4 (I.E EMPAT) / Said, M. – Besar Imam Madzhab: Abu Hanifah, Malik Bin Anas, Moh. Bin Idris Assjafi'i (Dan) Amhad Bin Hanbal. 1963? – 9 – SE-5898 1 – ne IDC [270]
LES 4 [I.E. QUATRE] CANDIDATS A LA PRESIDENCE – Paris, [1848?] – us Res Libr [320]

4 MARCHA PENITENCIAL NOCTURNA AL SANTUARIO DEL PALANCAR (CACERES) – Madrid: Graf. Calleja, 1967 – 1 – sp Bibl Santa Ana [240]

4 OEUVRES MICROFILMEES ENSEMBLE / Weyher, Charles-L – (Experiences reproduisant les proprietes des aimants... Paris: Gauthier-Villars, 1899; Sur l'ether. Paris: Gauthier-Villars, 1903; Sur les tourbillons: conference... Paris: Gauthier-Villars,[ca 1905]; Toujours les tourbillons. Paris: Gauthier-Villars, 1910) – 1 – F75.90 – fr Armell [944]

4 PLAN DE DEVELOPPEMENT ECONOMIQUE ET SOCIAL. 1973-1976 *see* QUATRIEME PLAN DE DEVELOPPEMENT ECONOMIQUE ET SOCIAL. 1973-1976

4 PLENO : REGLAMENTO / Consejo Economico Sindical – Badajoz: Imprenta Inca, 1963 – sp Bibl Santa Ana [330]

4 PLENO DEL CONSEJO ECONOMICO SINDICAL. CONCLUSIONES DEFINITIVAS / Organizacion Sindical de Badajoz – Badajoz: Imprenta Inca, 1966 – sp Bibl Santa Ana [330]

4 RAID HIPICO INTERNACIONAL-BADAJOZ-CACERES-BADAJOZ (18-19 DE MARZO 1971) / Sociedad Hipica Lebrera de Badajoz – Badajoz: Imprenta Comercial C. Oudrid, 1971 – sp Bibl Santa Ana [946]

4 SONATAS AND TWO DUETTS FOR THE HARPSICHORD OR PIANOFORTE WITH AN ACCOMPANYMENT FOR A GERMAN FLUTE OR VIOLIN, OPERA 18 / Bach, Johann Christian – London: Welcker, 1775? – 1 – us Sibley [780]

4 STAR EVENING EDITION – Fort Worth, Texas. 1966 – 1 – us UMI [071]

4 STAR MORNING CITY HOME EDITION – Fort Worth, Texas. 1944-1965 – 1 – us UMI [071]

4E PLAN, 1962-1965 LA RECHERCHE SCIENTIFIQUE ET TECHNIQUE / France. Commissariat General du Plan – Paris. 1962. BD-284 1 – 9 – ne IDC [500]

4E PLAN, 1962-1965 RAPPORT DE LA COMMISSION DE L'ARTISANAT / France. Commissariat General du Plan – 2v. Paris. 1961. BD-286 1 – 9 – ne IDC [330]

4E PLAN, 1962-1965 RAPPORT DE LA COMMISSION DES PECHES MARITIMES / France. Commissariat General du Plan – Paris. 1961. BD-296 1 – 9 – ne IDC [639]

4E PLAN, 1962-1965 RAPPORT GENERAL DE LA COMMISSION DE LA CHIMIE / France. Commissariat General du Plan – Paris. 1961. BD-288 1 – 9 – ne IDC [660]

4E PLAN, 1962-1965 RAPPORT GENERAL DE LA COMMISSION DE LA RADIODIFFUSION ET DE LA TELEVISION / France. Commissariat General du Plan – Paris. 1961. BD-298 1 – 9 – ne IDC [380]

4E PLAN, 1962-1965 RAPPORT GENERAL DE LA COMMISSION DE L'AGRICULTURE / France. Commissariat General du Plan – Paris. 1961 – 9 – ne IDC [630]

4E PLAN, 1962-1965 RAPPORT GENERAL DE LA COMMISSION DE L'ECONOMIE GENERALE ET DU FINANCEMENT / France. Commissariat General du Plan – Paris. 1961 – 9 – ne IDC [332]

4E PLAN, 1962-1965 RAPPORT GENERAL DE LA COMMISSION DE L'ENERGIE / France. Commissariat General du Plan – Paris. 1961. BD-290 1 – 9 – ne IDC [333]

4E PLAN, 1962-1965 RAPPORT GENERAL DE LA COMMISSION DE L'EQUIPEMENT SCOLAIRE, UNIVERSITAIRE ET SPORTIF / France. Commissariat General du Plan – Paris. 1961 – 9 – ne IDC [370]

4E PLAN 1962-1965 RAPPORT GENERAL DE LA COMMISSION DE L'EQUIPEMENT URBAIN / France. Commissariat General du Plan – Paris. 1961. BD-294 1 – 9 – ne IDC [338]

4E PLAN, 1962-1965 RAPPORT GENERAL DE LA COMMISSION DES CARBURANTS / France. Commissariat General du Plan – Paris. 1961 – 9 – ne IDC [330]

4E PLAN, 1962-1965 RAPPORT GENERAL DE LA COMMISSION DES INDUSTRIES AGRICOLES ET ALIMENTAIRES / France. Commissariat General du Plan – Paris. 1961 – 9 – ne IDC [630]

4E PLAN, 1962-1965 RAPPORT GENERAL DE LA COMMISSION DES POSTES ET TELECOMMUNICATIONS / France. Commissariat General du Plan – Paris. 1961 – 9 – ne IDC [380]

4E PLAN, 1962-1965 RAPPORT GENERAL DE LA COMMISSION DU TOURISME / France. Commissariat General du Plan – Paris. 1961 – 9 – ne IDC [910]

4E PLAN DE DEVELOPPEMENT ECONOMIQUE ET SOCIAL (1962-1965) RAPPORT GENERAL DE LA COMMISSION DE LA MAIN-D'OEUVRE / France. Commissariat General du Plan – Paris. 1961. BD-615 1 – 9 – ne IDC [338]

4EME MAZURKA, OP. 19 / Liapunov, S – [19–] – 1 – us Sibley [780]

LE 4EME PLAN QUADRIENNAL 1973-1977 / Senegal – Summary in French. Bulletin de l'Afrique Noire. numero special 3rd ed. Paris. 1975. BD-1861 1 – 9 – ne IDC [338]

LE 4EME PLAN QUADRIENNAL DE DEVELOPPEMENT ECONOMIQUE ET SOCIAL 1974-1977 – Plans regionaux. 7v. BD-2000 1 – 9 – ne IDC [338]

4-H CIRCULAR/JUNIOR CIRCULAR / New Hampshire. Cooperative Extension Service – v. 1-70. 1926-68 – 1,5,6 – us Spaulding [630]

4-H Club, Willing Workers, Reno County, KS *see* RECORDS

4-H REVIEW / Mississippi State University. Cooperative Extension Service – No.1-6. 1974-79. 1 reel – 1,5 – us Spaulding [630]

4-H SERVICE BULLETIN, SERIES 100 / New Mexico State University. Cooperative Extension Service – 1970-82.Series 100 A-S. 1 reel – 1,5 – us Spaulding [630]

4-H SHORT COURSE / Louisiana State University. Cooperative Extension Service – No.63-70. 1977-84. 1 reel – 1,5 – us Spaulding [630]

4TH ASAMBLEA PLENARIA DEL CONSEJO ECONOMICO SINDICAL. PONENCIAS Y CONCLUSIONES / Consejo Economico Sincial – Caceres: Tip. El Noticiero, 1956 – 1 – sp Bibl Santa Ana [330]

EL 4TH CENTENARIO DE LA FUNDACION DE LIMA / Bayle, Constantino – Madrid: Razon y Fe, 1935 – 1 – sp Bibl Santa Ana [972]

4TH CENTENARIO DE SAN PEDRO DE ALCANTARA – Madrid: Arch. Ibero Americano, 1961 – 1 – sp Bibl Santa Ana [240]

4th International Missionary Council *see* PROCEEDINGS (CCC337)

4TH JUEGOS NACIONALES DE LA EDUCACION GENERAL BASICA / Delegacion Provincial de la Juventud – Caceres: Sergio Dorado, 1973 – 1 – sp Bibl Santa Ana [370]

4TH KONGRESS KOMINTERNA : DOKLADY T.T. LENINA, TROT SKOGO, KLARY T SETKIN I DR.: STENOGRAFICHESKI I OTCHET. CHETVERTY I KONGRESS KOMINTERNA / Communist International. Congress (4th: 1922: Petrograd and Moscow, R.S.F.S.R.) – Kharkov: Kharkovskoe kooperativnoe izd-vo "Proletari i", 1922 – 1 – CSUX89-B4288 – us Hoover Inst Photo [320]

4TH PLAN QUINQUENNAL DE DEVELOPPEMENT ECONOMIQUE, SOCIAL ET CULTUREL (1976-1981) – (In French) – 1r – $49.50 – us African Imprint [330]

4-YEAR PLAN FOR SOCIAL AND ECONOMIC DEVELOPMENT, 1971-1975 – D-1124 1. 2 v. 1971 – 9 – ne IDC [338]

5 BROCHURES MICROFILMEES ENSEMBLE / Mathorez, Jules – (Les Italiens a Nantes et dans le pays nantais (extr. du "Bulletin italien", XIII, 2, avril-juin 1913; Notes sur la colonie hollandaise de Nantes (extr. de "La Revue du Nord", fevr. 1913; Notes sur la colonie hollandaise de Nantes du 14e au 18e siecle. Paris: la Bretagne nouvelle,[1913?]; Note sur la colonie irlandaise de Nantes du 16e au 18e siecle (extr. du "Bulletin de la Societe archeologique de Nantes et de la Loire-Inferieure", T.53, 1913); Note sur les Espagnols et les Portugais a Nantes (extr. du "Bulletin hispanique", T.XIV et XV: 1912-1913)) – 1 – F138.52 – fr Armell [944]

5 CITIES TIMES PRESS RECORDER – Arroyo Grande, CA. 1970-1979 – 36r – 1 – $1,800.00 – B02023 – us Library Micro [071]

5 CITIES TIMES PRESS RECORDER – Avila Beach, CA. 1972-79 – 32r – 1 – $1,600.00 – B02037 – us Library Micro [071]

5 CITIES TIMES PRESS RECORDER *see* ARROYO GRANDE VALLEY HERALD RECORDER

5 CONCURSO DE EMBELLECIMIENTO DE PUEBLOS – Badajoz: Imp. Provincial, 1973 – sp Bibl Santa Ana [946]

5 DE SEPTIEMBRE – Cienfuegos, Cuba. Aug-Nov 1982; Feb-July 1983; Feb 17 1984-1990 – 9r – 1 – us L of C Photodup [072]

05 DE SETEMBRO – [s.l.] 5 Set 1905 – 1,5,6 – bl Biblioteca [072]

5 STAR MORNING CITY EDITION – Fort Worth. Texas. 1926-1966 – 1 – us UMI [071]

5 THEMES – Pattee, University Park, PA, 1990 – 68p 3 cards – 9 – us Lawrence Pub [720]

5 YEAR PHASED PROGRAM OF ECONOMIC DEVELOPMENT AS REVISED / Jordan. Development Board – Oct 1954. BNE-9784 1 – 9 – ne IDC [338]

5 YEAR PLAN OF AGRICULTURAL DEVELOPMENT IN INDONESIA; RESULTS OF INSPECTORS' CONFERENCE OF MINISTRY OF AGRICULTURE HELD IN DJAKARTA FROM APRIL 28, 1954 TILL MAY 5, 1954 / Indonesia. Kementerian Pertanian – SE-5539 1. 1954 – 9 – ne IDC [630]

5 YEAR PLAN; RESULTS OF CONFERENCE BETWEEN HEADS AND INSPECTORS OF MINISTRY OF AGRICULTURE, DJAKARTA, APR. 28-MAY 5, 1954 / Indonesia. Kementerian Pertanian – SE-5540 1 – 9 – ne IDC [630]

5 YEAR PROGRAM FOR ECONOMIC DEVELOPMENT 1962-1967 / Jordan. Development Board – 1961. BNE-9783 1 – 9 – ne IDC [338]

5E PLAN, 1966-1970 COMMISSION DE L'HABITATION / France. Commissariat General du Plan – Paris. 1966 – 9 – ne IDC [338]

5E PLAN, 1966-1970 ECONOMIC AND SOCIAL DEVELOPMENT PLAN / France. Commissariat General du Plan – Paris. 1966. BD-609 1 – 9 – ne IDC [338]

5E PLAN, 1966-1970 ENFANCE INADAPTEE, RAPPORT DE L'INTERGROUPE / France. Commissariat General du Plan – Paris 1967 – 9 – ne IDC [338]

5E PLAN, 1966-1970 ORIENTATION ET FINANCEMENT DE LA POLITIQUE FONCIERE / France. Commissariat General du Plan – Paris 1966. BD-264 1 – 9 – ne IDC [332]

5E PLAN, 1966-1970 ORIENTATIONS DE LA POLITIQUE D'URBANISME / France. Commissariat General du Plan – Paris 1966 – 9 – ne IDC [338]

5E PLAN, 1966-1970 RAPPORT GENERAL DE LA COMMISSION CENTRALE DES DEPARTEMENTS D'ONTRE-MER / France. Commissariat General du Plan – Paris. 1967 – 9 – ne IDC [338]

5E PLAN, 1966-1970 RAPPORT GENERAL DE LA COMMISSION DE LA CHIMIE / France. Commissariat General du Plan – Paris. 1966. BD-268 1 – 9 – ne IDC [660]

5E PLAN, 1966-1970 RAPPORT GENERAL DE LA COMMISSION DE LA MAIN-D'OEUVRE / France. Commissariat General du Plan – Paris. 1966. BD-271 1 – 9 – ne IDC [331]

5E PLAN, 1966-1970. RAPPORT GENERAL DE LA COMMISSION DE LA PRODUCTIVITE / France. Commissariat General du Plan – Paris. 1966 – 9 – ne IDC [338]

5E PLAN, 1966-1970 RAPPORT GENERAL DE LA COMMISSION DE L'EAU / France. Commissariat General du Plan – Paris. 1966 – 9 – ne IDC [338]

5E PLAN, 1966-1970 RAPPORT GENERAL DE LA COMMISSION DE L'ENERGIE / France. Commissariat General du Plan – Paris. 1966. BD-257 1 – 9 – ne IDC [333]

5E PLAN, 1966-1970 RAPPORT GENERAL DE LA COMMISSION DE L'EQUIPEMENT SCOLAIRE, UNIVERSITAIRE ET SPORTIF / France. Commissariat General du Plan – Paris. 1966. BD-266 1 – 9 – ne IDC [338]

5E PLAN, 1966-1970 RAPPORT GENERAL DE LA COMMISSION DE L'EQUIPEMENT URBAIN / France. Commissariat General du Plan – Paris. 1966. Bd-262 1 – 9 – ne IDC [338]

5E PLAN, 1966-1970 RAPPORT GENERAL DE LA COMMISSION DES CARBURANTS / France. Commissariat General du Plan – Paris. 1966 – 9 – ne IDC [330]

5E PLAN, 1966-1970 RAPPORT GENERAL DE LA COMMISSION DES INDUSTRIES AGRICOLES ET ALIMENTAIRES / France. Commissariat General du Plan – Paris. 1966. BD-315 1 – 9 – ne IDC [630]

5E PLAN, 1966-1970 RAPPORT GENERAL DE LA COMMISSION DES INDUSTRIES DE TRANSFORMATION / France. Commissariat General du Plan – Paris. 1966 – 9 – ne IDC [338]

5E PLAN, 1966-1970 RAPPORT GENERAL DE LA COMMISSION DES PECHES MARITIMES / France. Commissariat General du Plan – Paris. 1966. BD-259 1 – 9 – ne IDC [639]

5E PLAN, 1966-1970 RAPPORT GENERAL DE LA COMMISSION DES POSTES ET TELECOMMUNICATIONS / France. Commissariat General du Plan – Paris. 1966 – 9 – ne IDC [380]

5E PLAN, 1966-1970 RAPPORT GENERAL DE LA COMMISSION DU COMMERCE / France. Commissariat General du Plan – Paris. 1966 – 9 – ne IDC [380]

5E PLAN, 1966-1970 RAPPORT GENERAL DE LA COMMISSION DU SECTEUR DES METIERS ET DE L'ARTISANAT / France. Commissariat General du Plan – Paris. 1966 – 9 – ne IDC [331]

5E PLAN, 1966-1970 RAPPORT GENERAL DE L'EQUIPEMENT SANITAIRE ET SOCIAL / France. Commissariat General du Plan – Paris. 1966. BD-270 1 – 9 – ne IDC [338]

5E PLAN DE DEVELOPPEMENT ECONOMIQUE ET SOCIAL (1966-1970) / France – 2v. Paris. 1965 – 9 – ne IDC [338]

5E PLAN DE DEVELOPPEMENT ECONOMIQUE ET SOCIAL LA RECHERCHE SCIENTIFIQUE ET TECHNIQUE / France. Commissariat General du Plan – 2v. Paris. 1966. BD-254 1 – 9 – ne IDC [338]

5TH EXPOSICION REGIONAL FILATELICA CACERENA / Vicesecretaria provincial de obras sindicales – Caceres: Tip. Extremadura, 1959 – 1 – sp Bibl Santa Ana [338]

THE 5TH PLAN / Iran. Iran Trade and Industry Publication. (suppl. nr. 200) – Teheran. March. 1973. BD-1803 1 – 9 – ne IDC [956]

A 5TH SET OF SONATAS FOR PIANOFORTE OR HARPSICHORD. H. 16, NOS. 33, 34, 43 / Haydn, Joseph – London: Birchall, 1783? – 1 – us Sibley [780]

5TH UNITED NATIONS CRIME CONGRESS : GENEVA – 1975, PAPERS AND PROCEEDINGS – (Includes 1,800+ pages, plus printed index) – 43mf – 9 – $100.00 – 0-89111-006-2 – us UNIFO [360]

6 ARTICULOS PERIODISTICOS DE PERON / Peron, Juan Domingo – Buenos Aires?: Subsecretaria de Informaciones de la Presidencia de la Nacion, 1948? – 1 – CSUXADJ3393-B – us Hoover Inst Photo [320]

6 BROCHURES, LA PLUPART EXTRAITES DE "REVUE DE BRETAGNE" / Angot, Joseph – (Coups de crayon (1906); Etude sommaire sur Saint-Martin-de-Vertou, 527-601 (1905); Le Missel de Barbechat, 12e Siecle...(1906); Notes de bibliographie liturgique bretonne... (1907); Le Sauvetage d'un vieux sanctuaire vendeen:... Sallertaine... -[S.l.: s.n.], 1910; Vers le regionalime integral... – Paris: Nouv. Librairie nationale, 1911) – 1 – F212.53 – fr Armell [944]

6 CORNET PIECES, WITH AN INTRODUCTION FOR THE DIAPASONS AND A FUGUE *see* SIX CORNET PIECES, WITH AN INTRODUCTION FOR THE DIAPSONS AND A FUGUE

6 FESTIVAL IBERICO DE MUSICA – Badajoz: Dip. Provincial y Ayuntamiento de Badajoz e Institucion Cultural Pedro de Valencia, 1978 – sp Bibl Santa Ana [780]

6 SONATE A TRE, DUE VIOLINI E FLAUTI E BASSO / Locatelli, Pietro – 1737? – 9 – us Sibley [780]

6 SONATES A UNE FLUTE TRAVERSIERE, UN HAUTBOIS OU VIOLON ET BASSE CONTINUE...20ME OUVRAGE, LIVRE SECOND / Schickhard, Johann Christian – Amsterdam: M C le Cene, [1720?] – 1 – us Sibley [780]

6 SUITEES POUR LE CLAVECIN, S. 812-817 / Bach, Johann Sebastian – Leipsic: Hoffmeister et Kuhnel, 1803 – 1 – us Sibley [780]

6 THEMES OF DESIGN – Pattee, University Park, PA. 1989 – 43p 2mf – 9 – $0.50f – us Lawrence Pub [720]

LA 6E CONFERENCE ECONOMIQUE NATIONALE 1977 – Conakry: Impr nationale "Partice Lumumba", [1978] – us Res Libr [330]

6EME BALLADE...OP. 85 / Gottschalk, L M – (Oeuvre posthume, publies sur manuscrits originaux) – Mayence: Schotts Sohne, 188- – 1 – us Sibley [780]

6TH BIENAL EXTREMENA DE PINTURA – Merida: Bimilenario de Merida, Tip. Vadillo, 1976 – 1 – sp Bibl Santa Ana [946]

6TH UNITED NATIONS CRIME CONGRESS : CARACAS – 1980, PAPERS AND PROCEEDINGS – (Includes 1,800+ pages, plus printed index) – 45mf – 9 – $110.00 – 0-89111-017-8 – us UNIFO [360]

7 BROCHURES MICROFILMEES ENSEMBLE, DONT 6 EXTRAITES DU "BULLETIN DE LA SOCIETE ARCHEOLOGIQUE DE NANTES ET DE LA LOIRE-INFERIEURE" / Veillecheze, Alfred de – (La Chapelle de Bethleem, 1905; La Chapelle du Crucifix: Le Croisic, 1905; Le Croisic: vieux logis, vieilles gens, 1902; Famille Rene de Veillecheze: documents et actes de l'Etat-civil. Vannes: Lafolye, 1899; Madame de Bulkeley et le chateau du Givre... 1903; Prieure du Pellerin... 1907; Saint-Goustan... 1908) – 1 – F136.63 – fr Armell [930]

7 DE OCTUBRE: UNA NUEVA ERA EN EL CAMPO / Spain. Ministerio de Agricultura – Madrid, 1936. Fiche W1161. (Blodgett Collection of Spanish Civil War Pamphlets) – 9 – us H.U. College Libr [946]

7 GIORNI (SUPPL. CORRIERE DELLA SERA) – 1987-1995 – 3r per y – 5,6 – Sfr668.00 – sz Infoprint [072]

7 PEINTRES BELGES / Reunion des musees nationaux. Paris – 1946. 1 fiche – 9 – fr Réunion [700]

7 SONATAS A OBOE SOLO CON IL BASSO; 18 SONATAS A FLUTA TRAVERSIER CON IL BASSO; 1 SONATA A? SOLO CON IL BASSO / Sammartini, Giuseppe – ca. 1760 – 9 – us Sibley [780]

DI 7 TEG ILLUSTRIRT = LES 7 JOURS ILLUSTRES – (In Yiddish) – Paris (and London). no5 13 Jul 1928-no13 7 Sep 1928 – 1r – 1 – $25.00 – cn Can Microfilming [072]

7 TRII PER VIOLINO DUE E CETRA / Canaletti, G – (Parts) – London: Longman, Lukey & Co, 177- – 1 – us Sibley [780]

7EME BALLADE...OP. 87 / Gottschalk, L M – (Oeuvre posthume, publies sur manuscrits originaux) – Mayence: Schotts Sohne, 188- – 1 – us Sibley [780]

LE 7IEME JOUR : PUBLIEE DURANT LA GREVE DES EMPLOYES DU "SOLEIL" – Quebec, 19 mar 1978-1 avr 1978 – 1r – 1 – Can$30.00 – cn Can Microfilming [072]

7TH UNITED NATIONS CRIME CONGRESS : MILAN – 1985 – (Includes 3,200+ pages, including printed index) – ca 60mf – 9 – $165.00 – 0-89111-024-0 – us UNIFO [360]

8 DOCUMENTS MAN. INTERESSANT LA FRANC-MACONNERIE, DONNES PAR A. LE BEAU A LA BIBL. MUNIC. DE NANTES = 8 HANDWRITTEN DOCUMENTS ABOUT FREEMASONRY / Franc-Maconnerie – 1 – F85.40 – fr Armell [360]

8 MARTA / Maiakovskii, Vladimir – M. 1936. BR-1010 2 – 8 – ne IDC [460]

8 MM MOVIE MAKER AND CINE CAMERA *see* AMATEUR CINE WORLD

8 SIDOR – Stockholm, 1995- – 9 – sw Kungliga [072]

8EME BALLADE...OP. 90 / Gottschalk, L M – (Oeuvre posthume, publies sur manuscrite originaux) – Mayence: Schotts Sohne, 188- – 1 – us Sibley [780]

8EMES CONGRES NATIONAUX J R D A-C N T G – Conakry: Impr nationale "Partice Lumumba", 1975 – us Res Libr [320]

DAS 9. BUCH INNERHALB DER PHARSALIA DES LUCAN UND DIE FRAGE DER VOLLENDUNG DES EPOS / Voegler, Gudrun – Frankfurt a.M., 1967 – 1mf – 9 – DM48.00 – 3-89349-771-4 – gw Hänsel [430]

9EME CONGRES NATIONAL DU PDG (9TH: 1972 CONKARY) / Parti democratique de Guinee Congres nationale – Conakry: Impr Nationale "Patrice Lumumba," 1973 – us Res Libr [960]

9-OE IANVARIA : OCHERK / Gorky, Maksim – Peterburg: Gos. izd-vo, 1920 – 1 – CSUX88-B5294 – us Hoover Inst Photo [947]

10 ANOS DE ENSENANZA LABORAL EN TRUJIULLO / Trujillo. Centro de Ensenanza Media y Profesional Garcia de Paredes – Trujillo (Caceres): Imp. Moderna, 1960 – 1 – sp Bibl Santa Ana [370]

10 LET RABOTY ARTELI "METALLIST" / Vlasov, P A – Serpukhov, 1928 – 1mf – 9 – COR-417/1 – ne IDC [334]

10 SONATAS FOR 2 GERMAN FLUTES OR 2 VIOLINS WITH A THOROUGH BASS... / Fesch, W de – London: B Cooke, 1732? – 1 – us Sibley [780]

10 VARIATIONEN FUER KLAVIER UEBER EIN ALLEGRETTO AUS SARTIS OPER "I FINTO EREDI" / Mozart, Wolfgang Amadeus – (Authenticity doubtful. Koechel attributed it to Emanuel Aloys Forster. K.V. Anh. 289) – London: Preston, 179- – 1 – us Sibley [780]

10TH CERTAMEN DE EXPERIENCIAS TEATRALES PARA LA JUVENTUD / Delegacion Provincial de la Juventud – Caceres: Imp. M. Sergio Dorado, 1973 – 1 – sp Bibl Santa Ana [946]

10TH FERIA REGIONAL DEL CAMPO EXTREMENO. OCTUBRE 1975 / Zafra. Ayuntamiento – Zafra: Ind Tip. Extremenas, 1975 – 1 – sp Bibl Santa Ana [240]

11 OEUVRES CONCERNANT ELISA MERCOEUR, MICROFILMEES ENSEMBLE ET SIGNEES = 11 WORKS ABOUT ELISA MERCOEUR MICROFILMED TOGETHER – fr Armell [920]

11TH CAMPEONATO DE ESPANA DE LA CLASE DE...Y COPA NACIONAL JUVENIL 1974: INSTRUCCIONES DE REGATA / Club Nautico Lago Gabriel y Galan. Plasencia – Plasencia: Graf. Sandoval, 1974 – 1 – sp Bibl Santa Ana [790]

11TH COMISION. SANIDAD Y ASISTENCIA SOCIAL / Consejo Economico Sindical Provincial – Badajoz: Tmorenta Inca, 1965 – sp Bibl Santa Ana [330]

THE 11TH DYNASTY TEMPLE AT DEIR EL-BAHARI (MEES VOL 28) : PART 1 / Naville, E – London, 1907 – 7mf – 8 – Dfl28.00 – ne Slangenburg [720]

THE 11TH DYNASTY TEMPLE AT DEIR EL-BAHARI (MEES VOL 30) : PART 2 / Naville, E – London, 1910 – 4mf – 8 – Dfl19.00 – ne Slangenburg [720]

THE 11TH DYNASTY TEMPLE AT DEIR EL-BAHARI (MEES VOL 32) : PART 3 / Naville, E & Hall, H R – London, 1913 – 5mf – 8 – Dfl22.00 – ne Slangenburg [720]

LES 12 CHANSONS DU SAGUENAY – Montreal: le Repertoire regional canadien, [1939]. SEM105P1475 – 1mf – 9 – Can$2.25 – cn Bibl Nat [780]

12 ETUDES, OP. 11. VOL 1 / Liapunov, S – [19–] – 1 – us Sibley [780]

12 FACSIMILES OF OLD ENGLISH MANUSCRIPTS / Skeat, W W – 1892 – 1 – uk Microform Academic [420]

12 SINFONIE A QUATTRO... DUE VIOLINE, ALTO, ORGANO ET VIOLONCELLO / Alberti, G M – London: J Walsh, 1730? – 1 – us Sibley [780]

12 SONATES POUR LE VIOLONCELLE ET BASSE CONTINUE / Azais, P H – Sorese, Revel/Paris: Bognon, 1780 – 1 – us Sibley [780]

12 STUDES, OP. 11. VOL 2 / Liapunov, S – [19–] – 1 – us Sibley [780]

12 UHR BLATT *see* NEUE BERLINER ZEITUNG

DAS 12-UHR-BLATT *see* NEUE BERLINER ZEITUNG

13 IA ARMIZ / U.S.S.R. Army. Tsentral'nyi Arkhiv RKKA – (Obzor fonda no. 198). Comp. by Iu. Levetskii. M. 1939. BR-11,077 1 – 9 – ne IDC [355]

13 LET BOR'BY ZA REVOLIUTSIONNO-MARKSISTSKUIU TEORIIU PRAVA / Stuchka, Petr Ivanovich – M. 1931 – 5mf – 9 – ne IDC [340]

13 ORAISONS FUNEBRES OU DESCRIPTIONS DU CATAFALQUE DE LOUIS 15, RELIEES ET MICROFILMEES ENSEMBLE = 13 FUNERAL ORATIONS OR DESCRIPTIONS OF THE CATAFALQUE OF THE FRENCH KING LOUIS THE 15TH, BOUND AND MICROFILMED TOGETHER – fr Armell [944]

DIE 13 PUNKTE, FUER WELCHE SPANIEN KAEMPFT – Barcelona, 1938. Fiche W845. (Blodgett Collection of Spanish Civil War Pamphlets) – 9 – us H.U. College Libr [946]

13TH GALA DEL DEPORTE PROVINCIAL. 1977. HOMENAJE A LA EXCMA. DIPUTACION PROVINCIAL / Delegacion Provincial de Educacion Fisica y Deportes – Caceres: Tip. Extremadura, 1977 – 1 – sp Bibl Santa Ana [370]

14 DEKABRIA / Merezhkovskii, Dimitrii – Paris. 1921. BR-757 2 – 8 – ne IDC [460]

14 DEKABRIA / Merezhkovskii, Dimitrii – (Tsarstvo zveria). Petrograd. 1918. BR-756 2 – 8 – ne IDC [460]

LOS 14 EL AUXILIAR DEL QUINIELISTA POR CACERES / Martin y Bueso, Tomas – Imprenta Sanguino. 1953 – sp Bibl Santa Ana [946]

14 MIESIATSEV VO VLASTI BOLSHEVIKOV : PERMSKIE UZHASY. CHETYRNADTSAT MIESIATSEV VO VLASTI BOLSHEVIKOV / Deborogii-Mokrievich, Vladimir Karpovich – Ekaterinburg: Tip. Russk. o-vo pech. di ela, 1919 – 1 – CSUX88-B6932 – us Hoover Inst Photo [947]

LE 14 NOVEMBRE OU JAMAIS... : PARTI LIBERAL DU QUEBEC – Montreal, 14 nov 1962 – 1r – 1 – Can$25.00 – cn Can Microfilming [072]

14. T *see* DIE BRIEFE PETRI UND DER BRIEF JUDAE

14TH WARD NEWS – Toledo, Ohio. 1933-1970 – 1r – 1 – $32.50r – us Archival [071]

15 DE OUTUBRO – Maceio, Alagoas. 15 Out 1886 – 1,5,6 – bl Biblioteca [072]

15 LET RUSSKOGO FUTURIZMA. 1912-1927 / Kruchenykh, A – M. 1928. BR-1352 2 – 8 – ne IDC [700]

15 S"EZD VKP(B) I KOOPERATSIIA / Vladilenkina, E – M., L., 1928 – 1mf – 9 – COR-148/1 – ne IDC [334]

15 TO 18: REPORT / Great Britain. Central Advisory Council for Education – 1859-1960. (Crowther report). v1. Report; v2. Surveys – 9 – uk Microform Academic [370]

15-I DOKLAD V KOMISSIIU IMPERATORSKOGO MOSKOVSKOGO OBSHCHESTVA SEL'SKOGO KHOZIAISTVA PO VOPROSU O KHUTORAKH I SOVRENMENNYKH USLOVIIAKH KREST'IANSKOGO KHOZIAISTVA / Stolypin, D A – M., 1884 – 1mf – 9 – COR-112/1 – ne IDC [334]

15TH CAMPEONATO NACIONAL FEDERAL DE CANARICULTURA Y PAJAROS EXOTICOS E INDIGENAS Y 7TH CONCURSO EXPOSICION DE LA U.C.E... / Federacion Ornitologica Espanola – Caceres: Tip. La Minerva, 1962 – 1 – sp Bibl Santa Ana [590]

15TH CERTAMEN NACIONAL DEL AHORRO / Caja Postal de Ahorros – Badajoz, S.L., 1947 – 1 – sp Bibl Santa Ana [946]

16 DOCUMENTS DIVERS CONCERNANT L'ERDRE, RIVIERE DE LOIRE-ATLANTIQUE = 16 DOCUMENTS ABOUT THE RIVER L'ERDRE (DEPARTMENT OF LOIRE-ATLANTIQUE) – Nantes, Paris, 1712-1928 – fr Armell [910]

16TH GALA DEL DEPORTE PROVINCIAL / Delegacion Provincial Consejo Superior de Deportes – Caceres – 1 – sp Bibl Santa Ana [946]

16th Guam Legislature *see* A REASSESSMENT OF GUAM'S POLITICAL RELATIONSHIP WITH THE UNITED STATES

17 DE OCTUBRE : JORNADA HEROICA DEL PUEBLO Y PARA EL PUEBLO / Peron, Juan Domingo – [Buenos Aires, 1950?] – 1 – CSUXADQ7371-B – us Hoover Inst Photo [972]

17 DE OCTUBRE : OSVALDO Y LIBERTAD / Chaminaud, Ricardo – Rosario, Agentina: Editorial Santos Vega, 1950 – 1 – CSUXADQ3302-B – us Hoover Inst Photo [830]

17 DE OCTUBRE DE 1945 Y SUS EVOCACIONES EN LOS ANOS 1946, 1947, 1948, 1949 Y 1950 / Argentina. Presidencia. Subsecretaria de Informaciones – [Buenos Aires, 1951?] – 1 – CSUXAHZ7751-B – us Hoover Inst Photo [320]

17 [I.E DIECISIETE] DE OCTUBRE : LA REVOLUCION DE LOS DESCAMISADOS / Colom, Eduardo – Buenos Aires: Editorial La Epoca, [1946] – 1 – CSUXADP9912-B – us Hoover Inst Photo [320]

EL 17 [I.E. DIECISIETE] DE OCTUBRE / Gambini, Hugo – [Buenos Aires]: Centro Editor de America Latina, [1971] – 1 – CSUXADJ2573-B – us Hoover Inst Photo [972]

17 OPUSCULES / Valdes, Juan de – London: Truebner, 1882 – 1mf – us A.T.L.A. [240]

17TH AND 18TH CENTURY BOOK PROSPECTUSES – (Guide available separately $20. Gough Coll 11mf $92. Johnson Coll 27mf $172.50) – 38mf coll + guide – 9 – $264.50 – us UMI [080]

18 DE JULIO; DOS ANOS DE GUERRA – Bilbao, 1939. Fiche W837. (Blodgett Collection of Spanish Civil War Pamphlets) – 9 – us H.U. College Libr [946]

THE 18 NOTEBOOKS WRITTEN DURING THE VOYAGE OF THE BEAGLE / Darwin, Charles – 1831-36 – 1 – uk Microform Academic [910]

19 BAHMAN DANISHJU'I – London. Shumarah-'i 1-7 (Bahman 1354-Farvardin 1356 [Jan/Feb 1976-Mar/Apr 1977]) – 1 reel – 1 – $50.00 – us MEDOC [950]

19 OEUVRES MICROFILMEES ENSEMBLE = 19 WORKS MICROFILMED TOGETHER / Pellerin, Joseph-Michel – fr Armell [944]

LE 19. SIECLE: TABLEAUX DES PREMIERES ANNEES : BONAPARTE ET PIE 7 ; LE CONCORDAT DE 1801 / Gosselin, Auguste – Quebec: L J Demers & frere..., 1901. SEM105P467 – 1mf – 9 – Can$2.25 – cn Bibl Nat [944]

LE 19E SIECLE : JOURNAL POLITIQUE QUOT. – Paris: Edmond About, 10 nov 1871-juin 1921 – 1 – fr A.C.R.P.P. [320]

19TH CENTURY EUROPEAN PAINTINGS AND DRAWINGS – (Over 50,000 reproductions, 8,500 artists) – $2,900.00 – 1-900853-80-9 – uk Mindata [750]

19TH CENTURY PAINTINGS – (Almost 8,000 reproductions) – 131mf – 9 – $825.00 – 0-907006-77-9 – uk Mindata [750]

19TH CENTURY RUSSIA: CONTEMPORARY FRENCH OPINION / ed by Cadot, Michel – 41 titles in French – 9 – fr Hachette [947]

20 [I.E. SEGUNDO] PLAN QUINQUENAL / Argentine Republic. Presidente. Subsecretaria de Informaciones – [Buenos Aires, 1953] – 1 – CSUXADJ8073-B – us Hoover Inst Photo [320]

20. [I.E. SEGUNDO] PLAN QUINQUENAL DE LA NACION : PLAN GENERAL DE GOBIERNO, 1953-1957 (LEY 14.184. DECRETO NO. 13.751/54) RESPONSABILIDAD DE EJECUCI ON DE LOS MINISTERIOS DEL PODER EJECUTIVO / Argentine Republic. Secretaria de Prensa y Difusion – Buenos Aires, 1954 – 1 – CSUXADQ3355-B – us Hoover Inst Photo [320]

20 JAHRE CAFE DES WESTENS / Pauly, Ernst; ed by Pauly, Ernst – 1913. 1 fiche (29x) – 9 – 1.00f – at Libertarian Micro [320]

20 LET RABOTY NAZAR'EVSKOI ARTELI / Vlasov, P A – M., 1929 – 1mf – 9 – COR-416/1 – ne IDC [334]

20 MELODIES, DEUXIEME RECUEIL / Faure, J B – Paris: Heugel, 188- – 1 – us Sibley [780]

20 MELODIES, QUATRIEME RECUEIL / Faure, J B – Paris: Heugel, 188- – 1 – us Sibley [780]

20 OKTOBAR – Belgrade, Yugoslavia. Feb 1945-Mar 1952 – 3r – 1 – us L of C Photodup [949]

20. PLAN QUINQUENAL / Buenos Aires (Argentina: Province) – Buenos Aires: Direccion de Impresiones Oficiales de la Provincia de Bs. As. (Eva Peron), [1952?]. 5v – 1 – CSUXADL7546-B – us Hoover Inst Photo [320]

20 WOOD PROJECTS FOR UNDER $75 – (1986- 1,5,6) – 1983- – 9 – us UMI [640]

20 YEARS OF INDONESIAN FICTION 1940-1960 : A BIBLIOGRAPHY SELECTED FROM THE IDC COLLECTION / ed by Elly, Julia – 1981 – A$10.00 – 0-86758-060-7 – at BISA [830]

20TH CENTURY HISTORICAL AND BIOGRAPHICAL RECORD OF ELKHART / Deahl, Anthony – Chicago: Lewis Publ. Co., 1905. Indiana Reel 11. (The Cox Library Collection) – 5 – us Americana [978]

A 20TH CENTURY HISTORY AND BIOGRAPHICAL RECORD OF BRANCH COUNTY / Collin, Henry P – Chicago: Lewis Publishing Company, 1906.Michigan Reel 6. (The Cox Library Collection) – 5 – us Americana [978]

20TH CENTURY HISTORY AND BIOGRAPHY OF YOUNGSTOWN AND MAHONING COUNTY / Sanderson, Thomas W – Chicago: Biographical Publ. Co., 1907. Ohio Reel 47. (The Cox Library Collection) – 5 – us Americana [978]

A 20TH CENTURY HISTORY OF ALLEGAN COUNTY / Thomas, Henry F – Chicago: Lewis Publishing Co., 1907. Michigan Reel 4. (The Cox Library Collection) – 5 – us Americana [978]

20TH CENTURY HISTORY OF ALTOONA AND BLAIR COUNTIES / Sell, Jesse C – Chicago, Richmond-Arnold Publ. Co., 1911. Pennsylvania Reel 12. (The Cox Library Collection) – 5 – us Americana [978]

A 20TH CENTURY HISTORY OF BERRIEN COUNTY / Coolidge, Orville W – Chicago: Lewis Publishing Company, 1906.Michigan Reel 6. (The Cox Library Collection) – 5 – us Americana [978]

A 20TH CENTURY HISTORY OF CASS COUNTY / Glover, L H – Chicago: Lewis Publishing Company, 1906.Michigan Reel 8. (The Cox Library Collection) – 5 – us Americana [978]

20TH CENTURY HISTORY OF FINDLAY AND HANCOCK COUNTY AND REPRESENTATIVE CITIZENS / Kimmell, J A – Chicago: Richmond-Arnold Publ. Co., 1910. Ohio Reel 37. (The Cox Library Collection) – 5 – us Americana [978]

A 20TH CENTURY HISTORY OF HARDIN COUNTY / Kohler, Minnie I – Chicago: Lewis Publ. Co., 1910. Vols. 1-2. Ohio Reel 38. (The Cox Library Collection) – 5 – us Americana [978]

20TH CENTURY HISTORY OF JEFFERSON COUNTY AND REPRESENTATIVE CITIZENS / Doyle, Joseph B – Chicago: Richmond-Arnold Publ. Co., 1910. Ohio Reel 40. (The Cox Library Collection) – 5 – us Americana [978]

20TH CENTURY HISTORY OF SANDUSKY COUNTY AND REPRESENTATIVE CITIZENS / Meek, Basil – Chicago: Richmond-Arnold Publ. Co., 1909. Ohio Reel 57. (The Cox Library Collection) – 5 – us Americana [978]

20TH CENTURY HISTORY OF SPRINGFIELD AND CLARK COUNTY / Rockel, William Mahlon – Chicago: Biographical Publ. Co., 1908. Ohio Reel 20. (The Cox Library Collection) – 5 – us Americana [978]

20TH CENTURY HISTORY OF TRUMBUL COUNTY / Upton, Harriet Taylor – Chicago: Lewis Publ. Co., 1909. Vols. 1-2. Ohio Reel 63. (The Cox Library Collection) – 5 – us Americana [978]

20TH CENTURY HISTORY OF WASHINGTON COUNTY AND CITY / McFarland, Joseph F – Chicago, Richmond-Arnold, 1910. Pennsylvania Reel 42. (The Cox Library Collection) – 5 – us Americana [978]

21 DIAS EN EL ASILO SAN MIGUEL *see* VEINTI UN DIAS EN EL ASILO SAN MIGUEL

THE 21ST CENTURY IN SPACE – (Suppl to v70, Advances) – 1990 – 1mf – 9 – $10.00 – 0-87703-316-1 – us Univelt [629]

22 DE JANEI RO DE 1903 – Manoas, Amazonas. 22 Jan 1903 – 1,5,6 – bl Biblioteca [072]

22 PIECES CONCERNANT LA SOCIETE POPULAIRE DE NANTES SOUS LA REVOLUTION = 22 BOOKLETS ABOUT THE POPULAR SOCIETY OF NANTES DURING THE FRENCH REVOLUTION: PROCLAMATIONS, MINUTES OF SESSIONS, ADDRESSES, ETC, MICROFILMED TOGETHER : PROCLAMATIONS, PROCES-VERBAUX DE SEANCES, ADRESSES, ETC, MICROFILMEES ENSEMBLE / Societe Populaire, Nantes, Revolution francaise – fr Armell [910]

O 23 DE JULHO : HOMENAGEM AO EXMO. SR. CORONEL ANTONIO CLEMENTE RIBEIRO BITTENCOURT – Manaos, Amazonas. 23 Jul 1908 – 1,5,6 – bl Biblioteca [072]

23 PIECES CONCERNANT LA FAMILLE DE PARTHENAY L'ARCHEVEQUE, SEIGNEURS DE TAILLEBOURG, LE PARC, SOUBISE, MOUCHAMPS, ETC / Parthenay l'Archeveque, famille de – 1329-1610 – 1 – F142.32 – fr Armell [920]

24 HEURES – 1930-1949 – 3r per y – 5,6 – Sfr1,016.00 – sz Infoprint [072]

24 HEURES – 1950-1995 – 6r per y – 5,6 – Sfr1,176.00 – sz Infoprint [949]

24 HEURES – (Also available on CD-ROM) – 1879-1929 – 2r per y – 5,6 – Sfr829.00 – sz Infoprint [072]

24 HEURES, SWITZERLAND – (Yrly reel count varies) – 1879- – 5 – us Ross [072]

24 MENUETTOS FOR TWO VIOLINS AND A BASS / Schwindl, F – (Separate parts) – London: Samuel & Ann Thompson, [1778] – 1 – us Sibley [780]

24 ORE – Milan, Italy. -d. 15 Feb 1950-22 April 1962. Imperfect. 55 reels – 1 – uk British Libr Newspaper [072]

24 VIOLIN EXERCISES, OP. 37 / Dont, J – New York: C Fisher, ca 1898 – 1 – us Sibley [780]

25 ANIVERSARIO DE LA SOCIEDAD ESPANOLA DE PSICOLOGIA / Caudeli Peiro, Jesus – 1952-78. Libros en Microficha no 18. 1985 – 2mf – 9 – Pta1,500.00 – 84-85422-55-4 – sp Pentalfa [150]

25 ANOS A TRAVES DEL ESTADO DE ANTIOQUIA / Gomez Barrientos, Estanislao – Medellin (Colombia), 1927 – 1 – sp Bibl Santa Ana [946]

25 CHORALE, MIT ACHTERLY GENERAL BAESSEN / Kittel, J C – (MS) – 1791 – 1 – us Sibley [780]

25 DE MARCO : ORGAO DO PARTIDO CONSERVADOR – Curitiba, 25 Mar-17 Nov 1876 – 1,5,6 – bl Biblioteca [972]

25 JAHRE GEWERKVEREIN CHRISTLICHER BERGARBEITER / Imbusch, H – Essen, 1919 – 1 – DM30.00 – gw Mikro Press [331]

25 SERMON...SAN JUAN DE LA MATA / Solano de Figueroa y Altamirano, Juan – 1670 – 9 – $1.50f – sp Bibl Santa Ana [240]

25TH SERMON EN LA FESTIVIDAD DEL GLORIOSO PATRIARCA SAN JUAN DE LA MATA, FUNDADOR DE LA ORDEN DE LA SANTISIMA TRINIDAD... / Solano de Figueroa y Altamirano, Juan – Madrid: Joseph Fernandez de Buendia, 1670 – 1 – sp Bibl Santa Ana [240]

25-YEAR AWARDS – (Also available on mf) – 1992, 1996, 1997 – 3r – 1 – $240.00 – us Ross [720]

26 au 28 mai 1901, Lyon *see* COMPTE RENDU STENOGRAPHIQUE

26 JUEGOS ESCOLARES NACIONALES. FASE FACIONAL DE BALONCESTO. CATEGORIAS: JUVENIL E INFANTIL – Caceres: Imp. M. Sergio Dorado, 1974 – 1 – sp Bibl Santa Ana [946]

26 SCHLUSZREDEN DIE BALTHAZAR FRIDBERGER DEM J. ECKIO / Fridberger, B – 9 – BME-35 1 – ne IDC [943]

26TH CONCURSO HIPICO NACIONAL 1969 – Caceres: Imp. Moderna, 1963 – 1 – sp Bibl Santa Ana [946]

EL 26TH CONGRESO INTERNACIONAL DE AMERICANISTAS / Bayle, Constantino – Madrid: Razon y Fe, 1935 – 1 – sp Bibl Santa Ana [970]

EL 27 / Pena El 27 – Caceres: Imp. Fernandez, 1971 – 1 – sp Bibl Santa Ana [946]

EL 27 JUNIO 1975 / Pena El 27 – Plasencia: Imp. IERSA, 1975 – 1 – sp Bibl Santa Ana [946]

27EME ANNIVERSAIRE DU PARTIE DEMOCRATIQUE DE GUINEE – Conakry: Impr nationale "Partice Lumumba", 1974 – us Res Libr [320]

DER 29TH PSALM AUSGELEGT... / Bugenhagen, J – [Wittemberge], 1542 – 1mf – 9 – ne IDC [240]

30 CARICATURAS DE LA GUERRA / Spain. Ministerio de Propaganda – Valencia, 1937. Fiche W1189. (Blodgett Collection of Spanish Civil War Pamphlets) – 9 – us H.U. College Libr [946]

30 YUNIYU – Khartoum, Sudan, may 20-jun 19; jul 14-dec 15 1990; jan 1-may 11; may 25-aug 10 1991 – 1r – 1 – us Res Libr [960]

[31 CANTATA, FOR ONE VOICE WITH A THOROUGH BASS] / Scarlatti, Alessandro – Mansucript, [1725?] – 1 – us Sibley [780]

31 CANTATAS / Scarlatti, Alessandro – For voice with thorough bass. 1725? Mss – 1 – us Sibley [780]

31P METABOLIC RESPONSES TO ACTIVITY OF NONSPECIFICALLY TRAINED MUSCLE TISSUE IN ELITE ENDURANCE ATHLETES AND IN HEALTHY, SEDENTARY SUBJECTS AS OBSERVED BY 31P MAGNETIC SPECTROSCOPY / Brown, Richard L & Klug, Gary A – 1992 – 3mf – $12.00 – us Microform Publ [612]

31-PHOSPHOROUS, NUCLEAR MAGNETIC RESONANCE SPECTROSCOPY STUDIES OF EXERCISING HUMAN MUSCLE / Marsh, Gregory D & Taylor, A W – 1992 – 2mf – $8.00 – us Microform Publ [612]

32 DOC. MANUSCRITS INTERESSANT L'HISTOIRE BRETONNE, MICROFILMES ENSEMBLE = SET OF 32 HANDWR. DOCUMENTS ABOUT LOCAL HISTORY OF BRITTANY, MICROFILMED TOGETHER / Praud de la Nicolliere-Teijeiro, Stephane – 19th c. – 10r – fr Armell [910]

LES 35 VOTES PRINCIPAUX DE L'ASSEMBLEE NATIONALE CONSTITUANTE – Paris, 1849 – us Res Libr [323]

THE 39 ARTICLES OF OUR ESTABLISHED CHURCH – 1571 : THE ORIGINAL LATIN, COLLATED WITH EARLY EDITIONS / ed by Budd, Henry – (In English and Latin) – London: Edward Lumley, [18–?] – 1mf – 9 – 0-8370-8802-X – 1986-2802 – us A.T.L.A. [240]

DIE 50 GEISTLICHEN HOMILIEN DES MARKARIOS / Doerries et al – Berlin, 1964 – 7mf – 8 – ne Slangenburg [240]

50 LET POTREBITEL'SKOI KOOPERATSII V ROSSII : ISTORICHESKII OCHERK I SOVREMENNOE SOSTOIANIE / Kheisin, M L – Pg., 1915 – 1mf – 9 – COR-135/1 – ne IDC [334]

50 LET PUSHKINSKOGO DOMA / Pushkinskii dom – Moscow, Leningrad, 1956.247p. BR-10,960/1 – 9 – ne IDC [025]

50 THESEN ZU DEN KIRCHLICHEN FRAGEN DER GEGENWART ALS POSITIVE GEGENANTWORT AUF DIE PAEPSTLICHE EINLADUNG ZUM CONCIL – Neuwied: J H Heuser, 1869 – 1mf – 9 – 0-8370-8938-7 – 1986-2938 – us A.T.L.A. [240]

50 YEARS' DOCUMENTS OF THE FOUNDATION OF THE REPUBLIC OF CHINA – Taipei, 1961. 21v – 7r – 5 – 330.00 – ch Transmission [950]

57 TH. MORALE SINNE-BEELDEN, AEN SIJNE HOOGHEYDT, DEN DOORLUCHTIGEN ENDE HOOGH-GHE BOREN VORST FREDRICK HENDRICK PRINCE VAN ORANGIEN... / Barbonius, J – Amsterdam, 1641 – 2mf – 9 – ne IDC [700]

61 BEZONDERE ZINNE-BEELDEN, VOOR-GESTELD DOOR ZOO VEELE KONSTIG IN KOOPER GESNEEDENE PLAATJES : OF NUT EN VERMAAKLYK TYD-VERDRYF; VERRYKT MET STIGTENDE EN TE GELYK LEERZAAME VEERTHIEN-REGULIGE VEERSJES – Amsterdam, [c1780] – 1mf – 9 – O-3022/1 – ne IDC [700]

67 SPECIAL REPORTS AND BIBLIOGRAPHIES / Iron and Steel Institute – 7 – uk Microform Academic [670]

70 HORAS TRAGICAS. LOS FUSILAMIENTO DE JUNIO EN LA ARGENTINA – Montevideo. (1957) – 1 – us Res Libr [972]

'70 ONWARD PREPARATION MATERIALS / Southern Baptist Convention – 1966-70 – 1 – 61.67 – us Baptist [240]

72 DNIA PERVOGO RUSKOGO PARLAMENTA / Tsitron, A – Spb., 1906. 165p – 2mf – 9 – ne IDC [320]

72 INVENTORIES TO THE ARCHIVES OF THE IISH / International Institute of Social History. Amsterdam – 129mf – 9 – HI-2400/1-HI-2471/1 – ne IDC [025]

73 AMATEUR RADIO TODAY – 1960- – over 600mf – 9 – $285.00 – us Buckmaster [621]

73 AMATEUR RADIO'S TECHNICAL JOURNAL – v263-. 1982- – 1,5,6,9 – us UMI [073]

75 MILLION CAMPAIGN / Southern Baptist Convention – Scrapbook of Frank Burkhalter, 1924. Books and pamphlets. 460p – 1 – 16.10 – us Baptist [240]

94 POINTS AGAINST COMPULSORY VOTING / Zube, John – 1mf – 9 – at Libertarian Micro [320]

100 JAHRE WALLRAF-RICHARTZ MUSEUM 1861-1961 / Wallraf-Richartz-Museum. Cologne – 1961 – 1mf – 9 – uk Chadwyck [700]

100 SILBERNE BLECHBESTECKE : ERLEBTE HEITERE GESCHICHTEN / Wiese, Ernst August – Leipzig: Amthorsche Verlagsbuchhandlung, 1942 – 1 – us U.W. Library [870]

100 YEARS OF THE COMMERCIAL APPEAL 1840-1940 / Kelley, Robert; ed by Kelley, Robert – Memphis: Mephis Publ. Co., 1940. Tennessee Reel 2. (The Cox Library Collection) – 5 – us Americana [978]

101 ONE HUNDRED ONE / Said, M – (Seratus Satu) hadits tentang budi luhur. Inc. quotations from Hadith in Arabic. SE 5746 1. 1964? – 9 – ne IDC [290]

103 DNIA VTOROI DUMY / Tsitron, A – Spb., 1907. 188p – 3mf – 9 – ne IDC [320]

115 VERSETTEN UND CADENZEN FUER DIE ORGEL. / Eberlin, Johann E – Ch. 1. 180? – 9 – us Sibley [780]

125TH ANNIVERSARY REPORT / American Sunday School Union – 1942 – 1 – $5.00 – us Baptist [240]

DER 128TH PSALM VOM GLUECK, SEGEN, GEDEIEN DER EHELEUT... / Corvinus, A – [Hildensheim], 1543 – 3mf – 9 – ne IDC [240]

132 PUBLICATIONS IN THE LOMA LANGUAGE / Loma Literacy Center – 3r – 1 – $148.50 – us African Imprint [490]

136TH FERIA DE SANTIAGO PARA TODA CLASE DE GANADOS 1971 / Casatejada. Ayuntamiento – Caceres: Imp. La Minerva, 1971 – 1 – sp Bibl Santa Ana [390]

139 FOTOGRAFIAS DEL MOVIMIENTO NACIONAL EN SEVILLA – Sevilla, 193? Fiche W 800. (Blodgett Collection of Spanish Civil War Pamphlets) – 9 – us H.U. College Libr [946]

141ST FERIA DE SANTIAGO 1976 – Caceres: Imp. La Minerva, 1976 – 1 – sp Bibl Santa Ana [390]

142ND FERIA DE SANTIAGO PARA TODA CLASE DE GANADOS / Casatejada. Ayuntamiento – Caceres: Imp. La Minerva, 1977 – sp Bibl Santa Ana [390]

144TH FERIA DE SANTIAAGO. JULIO DE 1979 / Casatejada. Ayuntamiento – Caceres: Tip. La Minerva, 1979 – 1 – sp Bibl Santa Ana [390]

196 ART EXHIBITION CATALOGS ON MICROFICHE / North America. Museums and Galleries – 1935-76 – 252mf – 9 – $78.80 – uk Chadwyck [700]

300 YEARS : CORTEZ TO FREMONT – 1845 (Regional History) – 1 – us Ross [970]

321 MANUSCRIPTS AND LETTERS FROM 21 CHURCHES, 1775-1819 / Northamptonshire Baptist Association, England – 1 – 28.56 – us Baptist [240]

371 VERSTIMMEGE CHORALGESANG. DRITTE AUFLAGE / Bach, Johann Sebastian – Leipzig: Breitkopf & Hartel, 1831 – 1 – us Sibley [780]

700 YEARS OF HOLLIDAYS / Holliday, Omar – 1939 – 1 – 5.00 – us Baptist [390]

900 = NEUF CENTS – no. 1-5. Rome, Florence. 1926-27 – 1 – fr A.C.R.P.P. [073]

1000 TAGE WESTFRONT : DIE ERLEBNISSE EINES EINFACHEN SOLDATEN / Wallenborn, Franz – Leipzig: Hesse & Becker, 1929 – 1 – us U.W. Library [890]

1001 DECORATING IDEAS – 1940-80 – 1 – us UMI [073]

1001 HOME IDEAS – (1984-. 5,6,9) – Aug 1981- – 1 – us UMI [073]

1001 HOME-DECORATING IDEAS – Jan-Jul 1981 – 1 – us UMI [073]

1001 (I.E. SERIBU SATU) / Triandhy, A S – Tafsir Mimpi; Fungsi Dan Kenjataan Pengertian Dari Beberapa Bidang Peri Hidup Manusia. SE 5466 1963 – 9 – ne IDC [950]

1001 SOAL-SOAL HIDUP / Amrullah, Abdul Malik Karim – 1962 – 9 – SE-4978 1 – ne IDC [950]

1297 [1880] SENE-I HICRIYESINE MAHSUS SALNAME-I KAMERI / Tevfik, Ebuezziya – Istanbul: Mihran Matbaasi – $50.00 – us MEDOC [956]

1335 SENESI TUERK SANAYI SERGISI KATALOGU – Istanbul: Tuerk Duenyasi Matbaasi, 1335 [1919] – 9 – $20.00 – us MEDOC [380]

THE 1745 REBELLION PAPERS, 1745-1753 / Great Britain. Treasury Solicitor – TS 20 – 8r – 1 – us Ross [941]

1798 U.S. DIRECT TAX CENSUS FOR MAINE AND MASSACHUSETTS – (Maine: Reel 1: Hancock, Washington, Lincoln, Cumberland; Reel 2: York; Massachusetts: Reel 3: Essex; Reel 4: Essex; Reel 5: Essex, Suffolk, Norfolk; Reel 6: Suffolk, Norfolk; Reel 7: Middlesex; Reel 8: Middlesex; Reel 9: Middlesex, Bristol, Plymouth, Barnstable, Dukes, Nantucket; Reel 10: Bristol, Plymouth, Barnstable, Dukes, Nantucket; Reel 11: Bristol, Plymouth, Barnstable, Dukes, Nantucket; Reel 12: Worcester; Reel 13: Worcester; Reel 14: Worcester; Reel 15: Hampshire; Reel 16: Hampshire; Reel 17: Hampshire; Reel 18: Berkshire; Guide included free with each complete set ordered) – 1979 – 18r – 1 – $540.00 set $30.00r – us New England [978]

1800 CENSUS / Delaware – Comp. by Doris Ollar and Gerald M. Maddux, 1964.Indexed. 4 fiches. F-0925 – 9 – us A.G.L.L. [920]

1812: DOKUMENTY GOSUDARSTVENNOGO I S. PETERSBURGSKOGO GLAVNOGO ARKHIVOV / Goriainov, S M – St. Petersburg, 1912. 2pts. 19, 552p; 184p. BR-10,998/1 – 9 – ne IDC [947]

1820 FEDERAL CENSUS FOR INDIANA / Indiana.Census – Comp. by Willard Heiss. 5 fiches. F-0933 – 9 – us A.G.L.L. [310]

1820 FEDERAL CENSUS OF ILLINOIS / Illinois. Census – Item D. Listed alphabetically. 77p. SW16-0075 – 5 – us A.G.L.L. [920]

1820 FEDERAL CENSUS OF ILLINOIS / Illinois. Census; ed by Volkel, Lowell M & Gill, James V – 1966. F-1305 – 2mf – 9 – us A.G.L.L. [920]

1830 FEDERAL POPULATION CENSUS FOR INDIANA : INDEX / Alig, Tobey – 1981 – 9 – $12.00 – us I.H.S. [920]

1830 INDIANA CENSUS INDEX – Indianapolis, IN: Indiana Historical Society – 3mf – 9 – $14.00 – us A.G.L.L. [975]

1832 SPEECH IN DEFENCE OF THE AMERICAN SYSTEM / Clay, Henry – 22p – 9 – 1.00f – at Libertarian Micro [320]

1833 OU L'ANNEE DE LA MERE / Barrault, Emile – Lyon, Mme S. Durval, 2 livraisons datees de janvier et fevrier 1833, 47 et 45 p. Les Saint-Simoniens, 1825-1834. 6928 – 9 – fr Hachette [335]

1837: MY CONNECTION WITH IT / Brown, Thomas Storrow – Quebec: R. Renault, 1898. 00318. (Pre-1900 Canadiana) – 9 – cn C.I.H.M. [971]

1840 FEDERAL POPULATION CENSUS, INDIANA : INDEX / Genealogy Division, Indiana State Library – 1975 – 9 – $12.00 – us I.H.S. [920]

1840 INDIANA CENSUS INDEX – Indianapolis, IN: Indiana Historical Society – 4mf – 9 – $14.00 – us A.G.L.L. [975]

THE 1840 IOWA CENSUS / Iowa. Census – (Mortality Schedules, 1850, 1860, 1870, 1880. T1156-0054 to 0062. 1) – By Rowene T. Obert, et al, 1968.Census of the 18 orig. counties & several precincts. 6 fiches. F-1267 – 9 – us A.G.L.L. [310]

1851 / Calendario de Extremadura – (1849, 1852, 1833, 1828, 1845, 1857) – Madrid: Est.Tip.de los Sres. Martinez y Minuesa, 1850 – 1 – sp Bibl Santa Ana [946]

1851 CENSUS ENUMERATORS' RETURNS – (With printed guide) – 145mf – 9 – £545.00 – uk Chadwyck [920]

1860 INDIA CENSUS INDEX – Indianapolis: Indiana Historical Society, 1981 – 159mf – 9 – $5.00mf – us I.H.S. [920]

1860 INDIANA CENSUS INDEX : ALPHABETICAL – Indianapolis, IN: Indiana Historical Society – 50mf – 9 – $300.00 – us A.G.L.L. [975]

1860 INDIANA CENSUS INDEX : BY COUNTY – Indianapolis, IN: Indiana Historical Society – 96mf – 9 – $500.00 – us A.G.L.L. [975]

1880, ALABAMA CENSUS / McNutt, Minnie Morrow – 1982. 201p. Typed ms. Includes name index. Z101-0001 – 5 – us A.G.L.L. [310]

1889. DIE ERSTE ERHEBUNG DER BERGARBEITER. ZUR ERINNERUNG AN DEN GROSSEN BERGARBEITERSTREIK VOR 20 JAHREN / Bredenbeck, Anton – Dortmund, 1905 – 1 – DM30.00 – gw Mikro Press [331]

1900 CENSUS SCHEDULES / U.S. Bureau of the Census – 1854 rolls. T623. Arrangd by state or territory and thereunder by county. Names of large cities may appear. Not in strict alphabetical order. Printed catalog available to use as a finding aid "The 1900 Federal Population Census." – 1 – us Nat'l Archives [324]

1900 [MILLENOVECENTO]-1901 [MILLENOVECENTUNO] – New York, NY, 1901 – 1mf or 1r – 1,9 – us I.H.R.C. [978]

1901 NORTHERN TERRITORY CENSUS – 2mf – A$10.00 – 0-949124-15-X – item 2 – at G.S.N.T. [920]

1903 VICTORIAN ELECTORAL ROLL – 5v – 125mf – 9 – A$150.00 – at State Libr Vic [320]

1905 GOD V DEREVNE / Goncharskaia, S – Moskva: Gos. izd-vo, 1926 – 1 – CSUX88-B754 – us Hoover Inst Photo [947]

1905, K GODOVSHCHINE PERVO I RUSSKO I REVOLIUTSII : 1905-1925, KATALOG KNIG / Gosudarstvennoe izdatelstvo (R.S.F.S.R.) – Moskva, Leningrad: Gos. izd-vo, 1925 – 1 – CSUX91-B3172 – us Hoover Inst Photo [947]

1905 NA I AKHROME / Chudnovtsev, M I – Moskva: Moskovski i rabochi i, 1925 – 1 – CSUX88-B1187 – us Hoover Inst Photo [947]

1908 VICTORIAN ELECTORAL ROLL – 22v – 149mf and hard copy contents list – 9 – A$150.00 – at State Libr Vic [320]

1910 CENSUS SCHEDULES / U.S. Bureau of the Census – 1784 rolls. T624. Arranged by state or territory and thereunder by county. Names of large cities may appear. Not in strict alphabetical order. Printed catalog available to use as finding aid "the 1910 Federal Population Census."' – 1 – us Nat'l Archives [324]

1912 VICTORIAN ELECTORAL ROLL – 22v – 157mf and hard copy contents list – 9 – A$150.00 – at State Libr Vic [320]

DIE 1920 ALS "DICHTERISCHE BEKENNTNISSE" VON ARTHUR TREBITSCH HERAUSGEGEBENE TEXTSAMMLUNG "DEUTSCHER GEIST AUS OESTERREICH" / Boehner, Claus-Peter – repr 1992 – 109p – 9 – DM98.00 – 3-89349-456-1 – gw Hänsel [430]

1920 CENSUS – Population Census Schedules. 2,076 rolls; Sound Index. 8,590 rolls – 1 – $23.00r – us A.G.L.L. [975]

1924: A MAGAZINE OF THE ARTS – Woodstock, New York. no. 1-4. July-Dec 1924 – 1 – us NY Public [700]

1924 SUPPLEMENT TO ROSBROOK ON NEW YORK CORPORATIONS (2D ED.) AND BENDER'S CORPORATION MANUAL. / Rosbrook, Alden Ivan – Albany: Bender, 1924. 114 numb. leaves. LL-1471 – 1 – us L of C Photodup [340]

1926 SENESI ZIRAAT ISTATISTIKLERI – Istanbul, 1926 – 9 – $20.00 – us MEDOC [350]

"THE 1927 EXCAVATIONS AT BEISAN" / Rowe, Alan – University of Pennsylvania Museum Journal: Jun 1928 – 9 – $10.00 – us I.R.C. [930]

1933: A YEAR MAGAZINE – Philadelphia. June c 1933-Dec 1933 Apr 1934 – 1 – us NY Public [073]

THE 1941 SOVIET WAR GAME : AN ARCHIVAL RECORD / Russian State Military Archive – Minneapolis: East View Publications, 1993 – 40mf – 9 – $1,000.00 – us East View [355]

"1948" / Eckdall, Ella – [1927-1973], Scrapbook of clippings, correspondence, notes, excerpts, pictures and cartoons relating to Major General Funston, 1927-1973 – 1 – us KS Hist [920]

THE 1953 PILOT POPULATION CENSUS FOR THE FIRST POPULATION CENSUS IN SUDAN / Sudan. Dept. of Statistics – 1955. BNE-7630 1 – 9 – ne IDC [310]

1956 POPULATION CENSUS, 8TH APRIL 1956 : REPORT / Taylor, D H – Maseru: Basutoland Govt, 1958 – us Res Libr [310]

1958 ANNUAL REPORT KABUPATEN OF MALANG, EASTERN JAVA / Mintarum – SE-1149 1. 1959 – 9 – ne IDC [025]

1960 AGRICULTURAL CENSUS, BASUTOLAND / Morojele, C M H – Maseru: Statistics Dep. pt1-6. 1962-65 – us Res Libr [630]

1962 FEDERAL SOCIAL PLAN. THE 1962 FEDERAL BUDGET / Yugoslavia – BD 1785 1 – 9 – ne IDC [350]

1962 REVIEW OF THE AGENCY FOR INTERNATIONAL DEVELOPMENT AND UNIVERSITY OF KENTUCKY COOPERATIVE PROGRAM AT BANDUNG INSTITUTE OF TECHNOLOGY, BANDUNG / Baker, Merl – SE-3319 1 – 9 – ne IDC [370]

1966 POPULATION CENSUS REPORT : KINGDOM OF LESOTHO / Lesotho. Bureau of Statistics – Maseru: the Bureau, 1966? – us Res Libr [310]

1967 GENERAL ELECTIONS MANIFESTOES – New Delhi: Educational Resources Ctr, 1967 – us Res Libr [320]

1970 ANNUAL PROGRAMME / Abu Dhabi. Planning Board – Abu Dhabi. 1970. BD-1604 1 – 9 – ne IDC [330]

1970 COLORADO COMPREHENSIVE OUTDOOR RECREATION PLAN / Colorado. Dept of Natural Resources. Div of Game, Fish and Parks – [Denver]: Div of Game, Fish & Parks, [1970?] – us Res Libr [790]

1970 DECENNIAL CENSUS GUIDE AND MICROFICHE / U.S. Bureau of the Census – (Coll includes printed aid. Subsets include: 1970 Census of Housing (incl Block Reports and Maps): $3,950 silver, $3,355 diazo. Census of Population: $1,670 silver, $1,420 diazo. Census of Population and Housing: $1,470 silve $1,250 diazo) – 3857mf – 9 – $6,380.00 silver $5,425.00 diazo – us CIS [310]

1970 WORLD CENSUS OF AGRICULTURE : ANALYSIS AND INTERNATIONAL COMPARISON OF THE RESULTS – 1981 – 300p – it F.A.O. [630]

1971 ANNUAL PROGRAMME / Abu Dhabi. Planning Board – Abu Dhabi. 1971. BD-1605 1 – 9 – ne IDC [330]

1972 YILI PROGRAMI, IKINCI BES YIL 1968-1972 / Turkey. Basbakanlik Devlet Planlama Teskilati – (1972 Annual Program, Second Five Year Development Plan). Ankara. 1972. BD-1769 – 9 – ne IDC [330]

1973 ANNUAL PROGRAMME / Abu Dhabi. Planning Board – Abu Dhabi. 1972. BD-1606 1 – 9 – ne IDC [330]

1974 PROCEEDINGS OF THE SOCIETY ON THE HISTORY OF PHYSICAL EDUCATION AND SPORT IN ASIA AND PACIFIC AREA / Israel. Ministry of Education and Culture. Sports Authority – By Uriel Simri. Tel Aviv. Apr 1975. 117 p – 9 – 3.00 – is I.T.T.I. [790]

1975 EDUCATION PLAN / Papua New Guinea. Department of Education – Port Moresby, 1975 – 3mf – 9 – DE-225/1 – ne IDC [370]

1976 COLORADO COMPREHENSIVE OUTDOOR RECREATION PLAN – [Denver: Colorado Div of Parks & Outdoor Recreation, Comprehensive Planning], 1975 – us Res Libr [790]

THE 1979 FEDERAL DISTRICT COURT TIME STUDY / Flanders, Steven – Washington: FJC, Oct 1980 – 2mf – 9 – $3.00 – LLMC 95-825 – us L.L.M.C. [340]

1980 DECENNIAL CENSUS GUIDE AND MICROFICHE / U.S. Bureau of the Census – (Basic coll excl block reports and maps 3767mf $6,295 silver $5,350 diazo. Subsets include: 1980 Census of Housing: $1,755 silver, $1,490 diazo. Census of Population: $2,330 silver, $1,980 diazo. Census of Population and Housing (excludes Block Reports and Maps): $2,915 silver $2,480 diazo. Block Reports and Maps: $6,615 silver $5,625 diazo. Guide avaliable free with mf, $195 if purchased separately) – 6828mf – 9 – $12,910.00 silver $10,975.00 diazo – us CIS [310]

THE 1981 BANKRUPTCY COURT TIME STUDY – Washington: FJC, Nov 1982 – 2mf – 9 – $3.00 – LLMC 95-832 – us L.L.M.C. [340]

1983 WORLD LIST OF SEED PROCESSING EQUIPMENT – 1983 – 252p – it F.A.O. [660]

1984 VICTORIAN ELECTORAL ROLL – 40v – 164mf – 9 – A$200.00 – at State Libr Vic [320]

1988 PRESIDENTIAL ELECTION POLLS : THE GALLUP/CONUS REPORTS / Gallop Organization – (With printed guide) – 1990 – 5r – 1 – $425.00 – S3210 – us Scholarly Res [977]

THE 1989 USSR CENSUS : A BILINGUAL (RUSSIAN/ENGLISH) COMPANION GUIDE TO THE MICROFICHE EDITION / East View PublicationsStatisticheskii komitet Sodruzhestva Nezavisimykh Gosudarstv; ed by Bronshteyn, Karen – Minneapolis: East View Publications, 1994 – 3mf – 9 – $29.95 – 1-879944-34-0 – us East View [304]

1990 DECENNIAL CENSUS GUIDE AND MICROFICHE / U.S. Bureau of the Census – (Subsets include: 1990 Census of Housing: $2,295 silver $1,950 diazo. Census of Population: $2,865 silver $2,435 diazo. Census of Population and Housing: $8,995 silver $7,645 diazo. Census Tract and Block Numbering Area Maps only: $2 ,970 silver $2,525 diazo. Related Commerce Dept, GAO, & congressional background reports (guides not included) $580 silver $495 diazo. Guide free with mf, $345 if purchased separately) – 4216mf – 9 – $9,995.00 silver $8,495.00 diazo – us CIS [310]

1991 CENSUS : COLLECTION DISTRICT CONVERSION LIST – 9 – at Statistics [304]

1991 CENSUS : COLLECTION DISTRICT MAPS – 9 – at Statistics [304]

1991 CENSUS : STATE MATRIXES, AUSTRALIAN CAPITAL TERRITORY – 9 – at Statistics [304]

1991 CENSUS : STATE MATRIXES, NEW SOUTH WALES – 9 – at Statistics [304]

1991 CENSUS : STATE MATRIXES, NORTHERN TERRITORY – 9 – at Statistics [304]

1991 CENSUS : STATE MATRIXES, QUEENSLAND – 9 – at Statistics [304]

1991 CENSUS : STATE MATRIXES, SOUTH AUSTRALIA – 9 – at Statistics [304]

1991 CENSUS : STATE MATRIXES, TASMANIA – 9 – at Statistics [304]

1991 CENSUS : STATE MATRIXES, VICTORIA – 9 – at Statistics [304]

1991 CENSUS : STATE MATRIXES, WESTERN AUSTRALIA – 9 – at Statistics [304]

4,000 DOLLARS REWARD = 4,000 PIASTRES DE RECOMPENSE – Quebec, 1837. SEM105P922 – 1mf – 9 – Can$2.25 – cn Bibl Nat [971]

1814-4 IIULIA 1914. PUSHKIN V PECHATI. 1814-1837. KHRONOLOGICHESKII UKAZATEL' PROIZVEDENII PUSHKINA, NAPCCHATANNYKH PRI EGO ZHIZNI / Siniavskii, N & Tsiavlovskii, M – M. 1914 – 8 – BR-7257 2 – ne IDC [460]

150,000.000 / Maiakovskii, Vladimir – Spb. 1921 – 8 – BR-1004 2 – ne IDC [460]

1734-1884: SESQUI-CENTENNIAL...SILVER SPRINGS PRESBYTERIAN CHURCH / Ferguson, Thomas James – 1885 – 1 – $50.00 – us Presbyterian [240]

1856-57 VICTORIAN ELECTORAL ROLL – 39mf and hard copy contents list – 9 – A$100.00 – at State Libr Vic [320]

THE 1905-1907 BREASTED EXPEDITIONS TO EGYPT AND THE SUDAN : A PHOTOGRAPHIC SURVEY, VOL 1 / Oriental Institute. University of Chicago – (14p accompanying text) – 1976 – 6mf – 9 – $15.00f – 0-226-69471-2 – us Chicago [910]

THE 1905-1907 BREASTED EXPEDITIONS TO EGYPT AND THE SUDAN : A PHOTOGRAPHIC SURVEY, VOL 2 / Oriental Institute. University of Chicago – (16p accompanying text) – 1976 – 7mf – 9 – $15.00f – 0-226-69472-0 – us Chicago [910]

THE 1919-20 BREASTED EXPEDITION TO THE NEAR EAST / Marcanti, Ruth – (30p accompanying text) – 1977 – 2mf – 9 – $20.50f – 0-226-69473-9 – us Chicago [910]

1925-1926 TUERKIYE CUMHURIYETI DEVLET SALNAMESI – 1926 – $90.00 – us MEDOC [956]

A+ – v1- 1983- – 1,5,6,9 – us UMI [073]

A. A. BLOK / Kniazhnii, V – Petrograd. 1922. BR-1337 2 – 8 – ne IDC [920]

A AND C ADULT AND CHILD – (Cont by: A and C Medical Challenge. Former titles: Adult and Child (may 1969-dec 1970)) – Chicago. v1-3. 1969-1971* – 1 – D6952 – us UMI [610]

A AND C MEDICAL CHALLENGE – (Cont by: Medical Challenge. Cont: A & C Adult and Child) – Chicago. r4 jan-dec 1972 (incomplete); r5 jan-sep 1973 – 1 – r4 inquire r5 $40.80y – D6952.01 – us UMI [610]

A AND E – Mendocino, CA. v5 no9 1980-v11 no11/12 1986-1987 – 3r – 1 – $150.00 – B06035 – us Library Micro [071]

A. BI ULLETEN T SENTRALNOGO STATISTICHESKOGO UPRAVLENII A. *see* BI ULET EN T SENTRALNAE STATYSTYCHNAE UPRAVY

A CAZA DE TESTAMENTOS. UNA PIEZA MAYOR / Bayle, Constantino – Madrid: Razon y Fe, 1925 – 1 – sp Bibl Santa Ana [972]

A CELEBRAR EN CACERES DEL 5 AL 11 DE OCTUBRE DE 1969 / Caceres, 34th Asamblea de la Federacion Espanola de Centros de Iniciativas y Turismo – Plasencia: Imp. Sanguino, 1969 – 1 – sp Bibl Santa Ana [338]

A CIDADE *see* A CIDADE DE VICOSA

A DONDE NOS LLEVA ESTA DICTADURA? Y QUE DEBEMOS HACER? / Gonzalez Alberdi, Paulino – [Buenos Aires?]: Editorial Anteo, [1962?] – 1 – CSUXAHZ7349-B – us Hoover Inst Photo [320]

A DONDE VA PERON? : DE BERLINA WALL STREET / Damonte Taborda, Raul – Montevideo: Ediciones de la Resistencia Revolucionaria Argentina, [1955] – 1 – CSUXADJ4129-B – us Hoover Inst Photo [330]

A EXTREMADURA / Pelaez, Florentino – S.l. Imp. de los Menores de Ramos, s.a. – 1 – sp Bibl Santa Ana [946]

A. F. KERENSKII PAMPHLET COLLECTION – 1917-1918 – 1 – CSUXANS1160-B – us Hoover Inst Photo [331]

A F L OFFICIAL DOCUMENTS / American Federation of Labor – (Cont in pt by: AFL-CIO Publications) – Washington. 1910-55* – 1 – D9493 – us UMI [331]

A. GERIN-LAJOIE: D'APRES SES MEMOIRES / Casgrain, Henri-Raymond – Montreal: Beauchemin & Valois, 1886. c1885. 00890. (Pre-1900 Canadiana) – 9 – cn C.I.H.M. [920]

A. I. BOGDANOV, 1692-1766 / Koblents, I N – (Iz proshlogo russkoi istoricheskoi nauki i knigovedeniia). M. 1958. BR-6212 2 – 8 – ne IDC [920]

A LA BRUNANTE: CONTES ET RECITS / Faucher de Saint-Maurice, Narcisse – Montreal: Duvernay, et Dansereau, 1874. 03056. (Pre-1900 Canadiana) – 9 – cn C.I.H.M. [971]

A LA CONQUETE DE LA LIBERTE : LES CONSTITUTIONS DU CANADA / DeCelles, Alfred Duclos – 1914. SEM105P518 – 1mf – 9 – Can$2.25 – cn Bibl Nat [323]

A LA CORSE / Cayol, C – Toulon, impr. Baunie, 1833, 8 p. Les Saint-Simoniens, 1825-1834. 6923 – 9 – fr Hachette [335]

A LA COTE OCCIDENTALE D'AFRIQUE / Laumann, E M – Paris, Firmin Didot et Cie. 1894 – 9 – 7.50 – fr Orientalistes [960]

A LA DECOUVERTE DE SHAKESPEARE / Lefranc, Abel – Paris: Michel, (1945-50). plates, ports., facsims – 1 – us U.W. Library [420]

A LA FUTURA MADRE. BARCELONA, 1930 / Roca Puig, P – Madrid: Razon y Fe, 1930 – 1 – sp Bibl Santa Ana [946]

A LA LEGION CANTOS DE AMOR Y DE DOLOR DE ESPANA POR... / Gordo Moreno, Angel – Alcala de Henares: Imp. Talleres Penitenciarios Alcala, 1941 – sp Bibl Santa Ana [780]

A LA MEMOIRE DE ALPHONSE LUSIGNAN: HOMMAGE DE SES AMIS ET CONFRERES: AVEC UN PORTRAIT PAR JULIEN – Montreal: Desaulniers et Leblanc, 1892. 02380. (Pre-1900 Canadiana) – 9 – cn C.I.H.M. [971]

A LA MEMOIRE DE L'HONORABLE CHARLES SERAPHIN RODIER: AVOCAT, EX-MAIREE BATAILLON, FONDATEUR DE L'ASILE DE BETHLEEM, ETC., ETC., ETC – 1874?. 05671. (Pre-1900 Canadiana) – 9 – cn C.I.H.M. [971]

A LA MEMOIRE DE SOEUR DE LA NATIVITE DE LA CONGREGATION DE NOTRE DAME DECEDEE A LA VILLA MARIA, JEUDI, 23 DECEMBRE 1875 – Montreal: Lovell, 1876. 02381. (Pre-1900 Canadiana) – 9 – cn C.I.H.M. [240]

A LA MEMOIRE DU REV. MESSIRE JOSEPH F.L. DUHAMEL, SECRETAIRE DU DIOCESE D'OTTAWA – s.l., s.n. 1881. 00003. (Pre-1900 Canadiana) – 9 – cn C.I.H.M. [920]

A LA NATION ARTESIENNE, SUR LA NECESSITE DE REFORMER LES ETATS D'ARTOIS / Robespierre, Maximilien de – Reprod. de l'ed. s.l., s.n., s.d. 83p. Manuscrits. 1 fiche. (Political Science Collection) – 9 – 6.00 – fr Bibl Nationale [320]

A LA RECHERCHE DU GRAND-AXE : CONTRIBUTION AUX ETUDES TRANSSAHARIENNES, AVEC QUARANTE-DEUX PHOTOGRAPHIES ET CINQ CARTES / Gradis, Gaston – Paris: Plon.Nourrit, [1924] – 1 – us Res Libr [960]

A LA VEILLEE: CONTES ET RECITS / Faucher de Saint-Maurice, Narcisse – Quebec: C. Darveau, 1877. 03057. (Pre-1900 Canadiana) – 9 – cn C.I.H.M. [971]

A LA VIRGEN DE LOS CHINATOS, LA SANTISIMA VIRGEN DE LA LUZ. ABRIL 1970 – Plasencia: Imp. La Victoria, 1970 – 1 – sp Bibl Santa Ana [946]

A L'ARMEE : DISCOURS DU GENERAL LE FLO, PRONONCE A L'ASSEMBLEE NATIONALE LE 11 MAI 1849 – [Paris], 1849 – us Res Libr [355]

A LOS INTELECTUALES DE ESPANA – (Hernandez, Jesus). Barcelona, 1937. Fiche W 940. (Blodgett Collection of Spanish Civil War Pamphlets) – 9 – us H.U. College Libr [946]

A LOS LECTORES ANTIGUOS Y NUEVOS DE "RAZON Y FE" / Bayle, Constantino – Madrid: Razon y Fe, 1926 – 1 – sp Bibl Santa Ana [946]

A LYON MENILMONTANT, LE 23 NOVEMBRE 1832 / Chevalier, Michel – Paris, impr. Duvergier, 8 p. Les Saint-Simoniens, 1825-1834. 6964 – 9 – fr Hachette [335]

A M *see* USLOVII A I KHOD PROIZROSTANII A KHLEBOV UROZHAI A 1918-1919 S.-KH. G. V KIEVSKO I GUB

A MARIA SANTISIMA QUE BAJO LA ADVOCACION DE NUESTRA SENORA DE LA PIEDAD SE VENERA EN ALMENDRALEJO – Madrid: Imp. Asilo Huerfanos, 1902 – 1 – sp Bibl Santa Ana [946]

A MES AMIS RUSSES ET POLONAIS / Bakounine, M A – (Russia – 19th C. series). 1862 – 9 – fr Hachette [947]

A MES SOEURS ET FRERES DE PARIS, DE LYON, DE GRENOBLE / Biard, Gustave – Paris, impr. de Setier, 1833, 8 p. Les Saint-Simoniens, 1825-1834. 6967 – 9 – fr Hachette [335]

A MI TIERRA! SUITE MUSICANA PARA GRAN ORQUESTRA / Perez Casas, B – Manuscript, 191- – 1 – us Sibley [780]

A. N. OSTROVSKII, N. S. LESKOV RUKOPISI, PEREPISKA, DOKUMENTY / Ostrovskii, AN & Kashin, N P; ed by Kashin, N P – (Biulleteni Gosudarstvennogo literaturnogo muzeia, nr. 3). M. 1938. BR-10,807 1 – 9 – ne IDC [920]

A N S: ADVANCES IN NURSING SCIENCE – v1- 1978- – 1,5,6,9 – us UMI [073]

A NOS SEIGNEURS DE PARLEMENT SUPPLIE HUMBLEMENT MARIE BENOIST DITE DE LA BUCAILLE – Rouen. 1699 – 9 – fr Hachette [360]

A ORILLAS DEL ORINOCO Y A ORILLAS DEL TAMESIS / Bayle, Constantino – Madrid: Razon y Fe, 1930 – 1 – sp Bibl Santa Ana [946]

A. POR EL EXCMO. SR. CONDE DE MONTIJO...SRA. DONA MARIANA ENRIQUEZ / Garcia Jalon, Miguel – 1741 – 9 – $1.50f – sp Bibl Santa Ana [946]

A PROPOS – (1986- 5,6,9) – 1964- – 1 – us UMI [073]

A PROPOS – Quebec, Canada. 16 sep 1973-17 aut 1974 – 6r – 1 – Can$55.00r – cn Can Microfilming [072]

A PROPOS DE LA DEFINITION DE L'INDIEN AU GUATEMALA / Demyk, M – 9 – F50.00 – fr Ethnologie [306]

A PROPOS DE LA GUERRE HISPANO-AMERICAINE / Chapman, William – Quebec: L. Brousseau, 1898. 00571. (Pre-1900 Canadiana) – 9 – cn C.I.H.M. [977]

A PROPOS D'EDUCATION : LETTRES A M. L'ABBE BAILLARGE DU COLLEGE DE JOLIETTE / Frechette, Louis-Honore – rev ed. Montreal: Desaulniers, 1893 SEM16P43 – 1r – 5 – Can$9.00 – cn Bibl Nat [370]

A PROPOSITO DE LOS CONDES DE LA GOMERA "FUE ANTANO REGULAR LA SUCESION DE ESTE TITULO" / Darias y Padron, Dacio V – Madrid, s.i., 1956 – 1 – sp Bibl Santa Ana [946]

A PROPOSITO DE UN DOCUMENTO. NOTICIAS SOBRE LOS SANCHEZ DE BADAJOZ / Rodriguez Amaya, Esteban – Badajoz: Imp. Provincial, 1945 – 1 – sp Bibl Santa Ana [946]

A QUOI BON LA SOCIETE ABERDEEN / Aberdeen and Temair, Ishbel Gordon, Marchioness of – 1885?. 04000. (Pre-1900 Canadiana) – 9 – cn C.I.H.M. [360]

A REBOURS / Huysmans, Joris Karl – Paris: A. Charpentier, 1884. 294p. 4 fiches. (Literature Collection) – 9 – 10.00 – fr Bibl Nationale [830]

A SA GRANDEUR MONSIGNEUR CHARLES LAROCQUE, EVEQUE DE ST HYACINTHE / Dessaulles, L A – s.l.: s.n., 1868?. 02160. (Pre-1900 Canadiana) – 9 – cn C.I.H.M. [971]

A SALAMANCA DIAK / Espronceda, Jose de – Maqyar Helikon, 1961 – 1 – sp Bibl Santa Ana [946]

A. SHATTUCKS BOOK / Shattuck, Abel – Manuscript, ca. 1801. Solos for treble instrument, some with second parts. Includes: "Hail Columbia," "Irish Washerwoman," and "Yankee Doodle." MUSIC 1975 – 1 – us L of C Photodup [780]

A SOLAS CON MI ALMA / Ramos Aparicio, Juan – Caceres: Imprenta Moderna, 1955 – sp Bibl Santa Ana [780]

A SON EXCELLENCE DOM HENRI SMEULDERS, COMMISSAIRE APOSTOLIQUE AU CANADA – 1883?. 00865. (Pre-1900 Canadiana) – 9 – cn C.I.H.M. [971]

A SON EXCELLENCE MGR. DOM HENRI SMEULDERS A JOLIETTE: COMPTE-RENDU / Baillairge, Frederic Alexandre – Joliette: Impr. du College Joliette, 1885. 00085. (Pre-1900 Canadiana) – 9 – cn C.I.H.M. [971]

A SON EXCELLENCE MONSEIGNEUR DONAT SBARRETTI: ARCHEVEQUE D'EPHESE, DELEGUE APOSTOLIQUE AU CANADA ET AUX REVERENDISSIMES PERES DU PREMIER CONCILE PLENIER DU CANADA – Quebec: s.n., 1909. SEM105P690 – 1mf – 9 – Can$2.25 – cn Bibl Nat [240]

A TOUS ET A TOUTES / Biard, Gustave – Grenoble, impr. J.-H. Barnel, s. d., 2 p. Chants Saint-Simoniens, ibid, 8 p. Sambuc, Jules. Parallele du Saint-Simonien et du Republicain. Lettre adressee au President de la reunion des Amis de l'Egalite. Ibid., 1831, 15 p. Les Saint-Simoniens, 1825-1834. 6926 – 9 – fr Hachette [335]

A TRAVERS LA VIE / Michel, Louise – Paris: Fayard, 1894. 155p. (Les Femmes Collection) – 2mf – 9 – $6.00 – fr Bibl Nationale [640]

A TRAVERS L'AFRIQUE CENTRALE DE CONGO AU NIGER: 1892-1893 / Maistre, C – Paris. 1895. BA-179 – 8 – ne IDC [910]

A TRAVERS L'AFRIQUE CENTRALE DU CAP AU LAC NYASSA / Foa, Edouard – Paris, E. Plon, Nourrit et Cie. 1897 – 9 – 12.50 – fr Orientalistes [910]

A TRAVERS L'AFRIQUE. VOYAGE DE ZANZIBAR A BANGUELA / Cameron, Verney L – (African Library). Paris. Hachette. 1878 – 9 – fr Hachette [960]

A TRAVERS L'AFRIQUE, VOYAGE DE ZANZIBAR A BENGUELA / Cameron, Verney L – Paris, Hachette & Cie. 1878 – 9 – 15.00 – fr Orientalistes [910]

A TRAVERS L'AMERIQUE: NOUVELLES ET RECITS / Biart, Lucien – Vingt-huit dessins hors texte par F. Lix. Gravures de Gerard. Paris: A. Hennuyer, 1876? 03582. (Pre-1900 Canadiana) – 9 – cn C.I.H.M. [910]

A TRAVERS LE FOUTA-DIALLON ET LE BAMBOUC (SOUDAN OCCIDENTAL) / Noirot, Ernest – Paris, 1885? – 1 – us Res Libr [960]

A TRAVERS LE FOUTA-DIALLON ET LE BAMBOUC (SOUDAN OCCIDENTAL) / Noirot, Ernst – Paris: E Flammarion, [1885?] – us Res Libr [960]

A TRAVERS LE NORD-OUEST CANADIEN / Bouthillier Chavigny, Charles de – Montreal: Eusebe Senecal et fils, 1893. SEM105P10 – 3mf – 9 – Can$6.75 – cn Bibl Nat [910]

A TRAVERS LE NORD-OUEST CANADIEN: DE MONTREAL AUX MONTAGNES ROCHEUSES: NOTES DE VOYAGE / Bouthillier Chavigny, Charles de – Montreal: E. Senecal, 1893. 00223. (Pre-1900 Canadiana) – 9 – cn C.I.H.M. [910]

A TRAVERS LE ZANZIBAR, VOYAGE DANS L'OUDOE, L'OUZIGOUA, L'OUKWERE, L'OUKAMI ET L'OUSAGARA / Baur et le Roy, (Pere); ed by Mame, Alfred et fils – 1886 – 9 – 10.00 – fr Orientalistes [910]

A TRAVERS LES DOCUMENTS OFFICIELS: CE QUE NOUS AVONS PAYE ET CE QU'IL NOUS RESTE – s.l., s.n., 188?. 00764 (Pre-1900 Canadiana) – 9 – cn C.I.H.M. [971]

A TRAVERS LES MISSIONS DU TOGO ET DU DAHOMEY / Boucher, Andre – 1926 – 1 – us A.T.L.A. [960]

A TRAVERS LES REGISTRES / Tanguay, Cyprien – Montreal: Librairie Saint Josephe; Cadieux et Derome, 1886. SEM105P5 – 3mf – 9 – Can$6.75 – cn Bibl Nat [920]

A. V. BADAJOZ LA TIENDA ASILO. POEMA. – 1889 – 9 – 1.50f – sp Bibl Santa Ana [810]

A. V. CHAIANOV PAMPHLET COLLECTION – 1964 – 1 – CSUXANS0747-B – us Hoover Inst Photo [331]

A VARIAS TINTAS / Gutierrez Cunado, Antolin – Caceres: Ed. Extremadura, 1929 – 1 – sp Bibl Santa Ana [946]

A VISO A SVLTAN SELIM DE LA ROTTA DE LA SUA ARMADA, ET LA MORTE DE I SUOI CAPITANI, ... – [1571] – 1mf – 9 – H-8180/1 – ne IDC [956]

A. Warner and Co *see*
- HISTORY OF ALLEGHENY COUNTY
- HISTORY OF BEAVER COUNTY
- HISTORY OF THE COUNTIES OF WOODBURY AND PLYMOUTH

Aa, Abraham Jacob von der *see* BESCHRIJVING DER NEDERLANDSCHE BEZITTINGEN IN OOST-INDIE

AA (THE ALUMINUM ASSOCIATION, INC.) – Printed index. Updated every 60 days – 6,9 – us Info Handling [670]

A.A. TITOV COLLECTION. OKHRANNYI KATALOG SLAVIANO-RUSSKIKH RUKOPISEI A.A. TITOVA. V G. ROSTOVE IAROSLAVSKOI GUBERNII / Saltykov-Shchedrin Library – v1-2. Rostov, 1881-83; v3-6. M. 1888-95. PKG-F-15.4 BR-11,206 1 – 9 – ne IDC [010]

AAAS BULLETIN *see* BULLETIN – AMERICAN ASSOCIATION FOR THE ADVANCEMENT OF SCIENCE

AAAS SCIENCE BOOKS – (Cont by: Science Books and Films. Former title: Science Books – a Quarterly Review) – Washington. v1-5 apr 1965-mar 1970. cum index v1-2 1; v6-10 may 1970-mar 1975 1,5,9 – 1,5,9 – D5926 – us UMI [500]

AACE BULLETIN / American Association of Cost Engineers (AACE) – (Cont by: Cost Accounting) – Morgantown. cum index 1-5; v1-20 nov 1958-jun 1978 1; v15-20 feb 1973-jun 1978 5; v17-20 feb 1975-jun 1978 9 – 1,5,9 – D8768 – us UMI [650]

AACHENER ALLGEMEINE ZEITUNG – Aachen, 1916-jun 1918 (incomplete) – 4r – 1 – Dist. gw Mikrofilm – uk British Libr Newspaper [072]

AACHENER ANZEIGER *see*
- AACHENER ANZEIGER – POLITISCHES TAGEBLATT
- ECHO DER GEGENWART

AACHENER ANZEIGER – POLITISCHES TAGEBLATT – (Cont: Aachener Anzeiger, -jul 1878) – Aachen, 1885, 1887-93, 1901-43 – 1 – Dist. gw Mikrofilm – gw Misc Inst [943]

AACHENER FREMDENBLATT – Aachen, 1848-jan 1 1849 – 1r – 1 – Dist. gw Mikrofilm – gw Misc Inst [943]

AACHENER NACHRICHTEN – Aachen, 1963-68 – 27r – 1 – gw Mikrofilm [072]

AACHENER NACHRICHTEN – Aachen, 1968- – ca 7r per yr – 1 – Dist. gw Mikrofilm – gw Misc Inst [072]

AACHENER NACHRICHTEN – Aachen, jan 24, feb 21 1945-nov 29 1952 (incomplete) – 17r – 1 – uk British Libr Newspaper [943]

AACHENER VOLKSZEITUNG – (Cont by: Aachener Zeitung, mar 6 1996) – Aachen, apr 20 1946-nov 26 1952 – 17r – 1 – uk British Libr Newspaper [943]

AACHENER VOLKSZEITUNG *see* HEINSBERGER VOLKSZEITUNG

AACHENER ZEITUNG – (Cont: Journal de la Roer, -jan 1814; Stadt-Aachener Zeitung, -1848) – Aachen, 1811-jan 31 1847, 1848-68, 1876-sep 30 1888 – 1 – Dist. gw Mikrofilm – gw Misc Inst [943]

AACHENER ZEITUNG *see* AACHENER VOLKSZEITUNG

AACN CLINICAL ISSUES – (Cont: AACN Clinical Issues in Critical Care Nursing) – Philadelphia. v6-8. feb 1995-nov 1997+ – 1,5,9 – D19707.01 – us UMI [610]

AACN CLINICAL ISSUES *see* AACN CLINICAL ISSUES IN CRITICAL CARE NURSING

AACN CLINICAL ISSUES IN CRITICAL CARE NURSING – (Cont by: AACN Clinical Issues) – Philadelphia. v1-2 may 1990-91* 1; v3-5 feb 1992-94 1,5*,9 – 1,5,9 – D19707 – us UMI [610]

AACN CLINICAL ISSUES IN CRITICAL CARE NURSING *see* AACN CLINICAL ISSUES

AACN NURSING SCAN IN CRITICAL CARE – Philadelphia, 1991-94* 1; 1995-97+ 1,5,9 – 1,5,9 – D21644 – us UMI [610]

AAESPH REVIEW – American Assoc. for the Education of the Severely-Profoundly Handicapped. v1-4. 1975-79. See also: JASH: Journal of the Assoc. for the Severely Handicapped – 1 – us UMI [370]

AAESPH REVIEW / American Association for the Education of the Severely/Profoundly Handicapped – (Cont by: JASH, Journal of the Association for the Severely Handicapped. Former title: Review (sep 1975-may 1976)) – Baltimore. v1-4. sep 1975-Win 1979 – 1,5*,9 – D12077 – us UMI [360]

AAG NEWSLETTER / Association of American Geographers – (1975- . 5,6,9) – 1967- – 1 – us UMI [550]

AAHE BULLETIN / American Association for Higher Education – (Cont: College and University Bulletin) – Washington. v31-. sep 1978- – 1,5,9 – D6980.01 – us UMI [370]

AALBORG STIFTSBOG – 1958-92 (complete) – Inquire – 1 – ATLA S0768 – us A.T.L.A. [073]

Aalders, G *see* THE PROBLEM OF THE BOOK OF JONAH

AALS *see* SCIENCE OF LEGAL METHOD

AALTEN EN BREDEVOORT IN VERVLOGEN TIJDEN / Rots, B D – Aalten, 1950 – Dfl13.00 – ne Slangenburg [240]
AAN DE RAND DE DIBESE / Denolf, Prosper – Brussels, 1954 – 1 – us Res Libr [960]
AANA JOURNAL / American Association of Nurse Anesthetists (AANA) – (Microed includes vols of: AANA (American Association of Nurse Anesthetists Newsbulletin. Cont: Journal of the American Association of Nurse Anesthetists) – Park Ridge. v42-63. feb 1974-dec 1995 1; v43-63 feb 1975-dec 1995 5; v44-47 feb 1976-dec 1995 9; v64-65 feb 1996-dec 1997+ 1,5,9 – 1,5,9 – D2083.01 – us UMI [073]
AANA NEWSBULLETIN *see* AANA JOURNAL
AANMERKINGEN, OP OTTO VAN VEENS ZINNEBEELDEN DER GODDELIJKE LIEFDE / Bruin, C – O 564. 1726 – 9 – ne IDC [760]
AANNT JOURNAL / American Association of Nephrology Nurses and Technicians (AANNT) – (Cont: Journal of the American Association of Nephrology Nurses & Technicians. Cont by: ANNA Journal) – Pitman. v8-11. feb 1981-may 1984* – 1,5,9 – D21622.01 – us UMI [073]
AANNT JOURNAL *see* ANNA JOURNAL
AANTEKENINGEN VAN EEN COLLEGE IN ETHNOLOGIE – SE-5212 1. 1948-1949 – 9 – ne IDC [306]
AANTEKENINGEN VAN F.V.H.A. DE STUERS GEHOUDEN BIJ HET OVERBRENGEN VAN DIPONEGORO VAN MAGELANG NAAR BATAVIA – 1830. KITLV,H 342. BSD-102/1 mf.46 – 9 – ne IDC [950]
AAOHN JOURNAL : OFFICIAL JOURNAL OF THE AAOHN / American Association of Occupational Health Nurses (AAOHN) – (Cont: Occupational Health Nursing) – Atlanta. v34-45. jan 1986-dec 1997+ – 1,5,9 – D11478.02 – us UMI [610]
AAPG BULLETIN / American Association of Petroleum Geologists – (Former titles: Bulletin of the Southwestern Association of Petroleum Geologists (1917); Bulletin of the American Association of Petroleum Geologists (1918-dec 1966); American Association of Petroleum Geologists Bulletin (jan 1967-dec 1973)) – Tulsa. v181 jan 1917-dec 1997+ 1; v44-81 jan 1960-dec 1997+ 5; v54-81 jan 1970-dec 1997+ 9 – 1,5,9 – D903 – us UMI [550]
AAR MIT GEBROCHENER SCHWINGE : CLEMENS BRENTANO, ANNETTE VON DROSTE-HUELSHOFF / Schneider, Reinhold – (Includes bibliographical references) – 2. Aufl. Heidelberg: F H Kerle, 1948 – 1 – us U.W. Library [830]
AARCTIMES – (Cont: AARTimes – and Official Publication of the American Association for Respiratory Therapy) – Dallas. v11-21. jan 1987-dec 1997+ – 1,5,9 – D14134.01 – us UMI [610]
AARCTIMES *see* AARTIMES
AARD EN DOEL VAN... / Hamaker, H J – Leiden, 1878 – 1mf – 1 – ILM-394/1 – ne IDC [327]
Aaron, Elizabeth A *see* THE OXYGEN COST OF EXERCISE HYPERNEA
Aaron, P *see* TRATTATO DELLA NATURA ET COGNITIONE DI TUTTI GLI TUONI DI CANTO FIGURATO NO DA ALTRUI PIU SCRITTI
AARTIMES : AN OFFICIAL PUBLICATION OF THE AART / American Association for Respiratory Therapy (A A RT) – (Cont by: AARCTimes) – Dallas. v1-6 jul 1977-82* 1; v7-10 jan 1983-dec 1986 1,5,9 – 1,5,9 – D14134 – us UMI [610]
AARTIMES *see* AARCTIMES
AAS MICROFICHE SERIES (1968-), VOL 1 *see* SEARCH FOR EXTRATERRESTRIAL LIFE
AAS MICROFICHE SERIES (1968-), VOL 2 *see* SPACE FLIGHT MECHANICS SPECIALIST SYMPOSIUM
AAS MICROFICHE SERIES (1968-), VOL 3 *see* COMMERCIAL UTILIZATION OF SPACE
AAS MICROFICHE SERIES (1968-), VOL 4 *see* SATURN 5/APOLLO AND BEYOND
AAS MICROFICHE SERIES (1968-), VOL 5 *see* USE OF SPACE SYSTEMS FOR PLANETARY GEOLOGY AND GEOPHYSICS
AAS MICROFICHE SERIES (1968-), VOL 6 *see* ASTRONAUTICS INTERNATIONAL
AAS MICROFICHE SERIES (1968-), VOL 7 *see*
– ASTRODYNAMICS SPECIALIST CONFERENCE
AAS MICROFICHE SERIES (1968-), VOL 8 *see* SPACE PROJECTIONS
AAS MICROFICHE SERIES (1968-), VOL 9 *see* SOUTHEASTERN SYMPOSIUM ON MISSILES AND AEROSPACE VEHICLE SCIENCES
AAS MICROFICHE SERIES (1968-), VOL 10 *see* ROCKY MOUNTAIN RESOURCES FOR AEROSPACE SCIENCE AND TECHNOLOGY
AAS MICROFICHE SERIES (1968-), VOL 11 *see* SPACE AS A NATIONAL RESOURCE
AAS MICROFICHE SERIES (1968-), VOL 12 *see* SPACE TECHNOLOGY AND EARTH PROBLEMS
AAS MICROFICHE SERIES (1968-), VOL 13 *see* PLANNING CHALLENGES OF THE 70'S IN THE PUBLIC DOMAIN
AAS MICROFICHE SERIES (1968-), VOL 14 *see* PLANNING CHALLENGES OF THE 70'S IN SPACE
AAS MICROFICHE SERIES (1968-), VOL 15 *see* OPERATIONS RESEARCH
AAS MICROFICHE SERIES (1968-), VOL 16 *see* OPERATIONS RESEARCH
AAS MICROFICHE SERIES (1968-), VOL 17 *see* OPERATIONS RESEARCH
AAS MICROFICHE SERIES (1968-), VOL 18 *see* SPACECRAFT AND SPACE TECHNOLOGY
AAS MICROFICHE SERIES (1968-), VOL 19 *see* SPACE EXPLORATION, SPACE SCIENCE, AND APPLICATIONS
AAS MICROFICHE SERIES (1968-), VOL 21 *see* AAS/AIAA ASTRODYNAMICS SPECIALIST CONFERENCE, 1973
AAS MICROFICHE SERIES (1968-), VOL 22 *see* SKYLAB RESULTS
AAS MICROFICHE SERIES (1968-), VOL 23 *see* INTERNATIONAL SPACE SAFETY AND RESCUE SYMPOSIA
AAS MICROFICHE SERIES (1968-), VOL 24 *see* INTERNATIONAL SPACE SAFETY AND RESCUE SYMPOSIA
AAS MICROFICHE SERIES (1968-), VOL 25 *see* SPACE SHUTTLE MISSIONS OF THE 80'S
AAS MICROFICHE SERIES (1968-), VOL 26 *see* AAS/AIAA ASTRODYNAMICS CONFERENCE, 1975
AAS MICROFICHE SERIES (1968-), VOL 27 *see* AAS/AIAA ASTRODYNAMICS CONFERENCE, 1977
AAS MICROFICHE SERIES (1968-), VOL 28 *see* INDUSTRIALIZATION OF SPACE
AAS MICROFICHE SERIES (1968-), VOL 29 *see* GUIDANCE AND CONTROL CONFERENCE
AAS MICROFICHE SERIES (1968-), VOL 30 *see* THE FUTURE U.S. SPACE PROGRAM
AAS MICROFICHE SERIES (1968-), VOL 31 *see* GUIDANCE AND CONTROL
AAS MICROFICHE SERIES (1968-), VOL 32 *see* AAS/AIAA ASTRODYNAMICS CONFERENCE, 1979
AAS MICROFICHE SERIES (1968-), VOL 33 *see* SPACE SHUTTLE
AAS MICROFICHE SERIES (1968-), VOL 34 *see* COMMERCIAL OPERATIONS IN SPACE
AAS MICROFICHE SERIES (1968-), VOL 35 *see* SPACE
AAS MICROFICHE SERIES (1968-), VOL 36 *see* GUIDANCE AND CONTROL
AAS MICROFICHE SERIES (1968-), VOL 37 *see* AAS/AIAA ASTRODYNAMICS CONFERENCE
AAS MICROFICHE SERIES (1968-), VOL 38 *see* GUIDANCE AND CONTROL
AAS MICROFICHE SERIES (1968-), VOL 39 *see* INTERNATIONAL SPACE SAFETY AND RESCUE SYMPOSIUM
AAS MICROFICHE SERIES (1968-), VOL 40 *see* INTERNATIONAL SPACE SAFETY AND RESCUE SYMPOSIA
AAS MICROFICHE SERIES (1968-), VOL 41 *see* INTERNATIONAL SPACE SAFETY AND RESCUE SYMPOSIA
AAS MICROFICHE SERIES (1968-), VOL 42 *see* SPACELAB, SPACE PLATFORMS AND THE FUTURE
AAS MICROFICHE SERIES (1968-), VOL 43 *see* ENGINEERING SCIENCES AND MECHANICS
AAS MICROFICHE SERIES (1968-), VOL 44 *see* GUIDANCE AND CONTROL
AAS MICROFICHE SERIES (1968-), VOL 45 *see* ASTRODYNAMICS 1983
AAS MICROFICHE SERIES (1968-), VOL 46 *see* SPACE
AAS MICROFICHE SERIES (1968-), VOL 47 *see* SPACE OPERATIONS FOR THE 80S AND 90S
AAS MICROFICHE SERIES (1968-), VOL 48 *see* GUIDANCE AND CONTROL
AAS MICROFICHE SERIES (1968-), VOL 49 *see* CAREERS IN SPACE
AAS MICROFICHE SERIES (1968-), VOL 50 *see* GUIDANCE AND CONTROL
AAS MICROFICHE SERIES (1968-), VOL 51 *see* ASTRODYNAMICS 1985
AAS MICROFICHE SERIES (1968-), VOL 53 *see* GUIDANCE AND CONTROL
AAS MICROFICHE SERIES (1968-), VOL 54 *see* AEROSPACE CENTURY 21
AAS MICROFICHE SERIES (1968-), VOL 55 *see* ASTRODYNAMICS 1987
AAS MICROFICHE SERIES (1968-), VOL 56 *see* GUIDANCE AND CONTROL
AAS MICROFICHE SERIES (1968-), VOL 57 *see* ORBITAL MECHANICS AND MISSION DESIGN
AAS MICROFICHE SERIES (1968-), VOL 58 *see* THE 21ST CENTURY IN SPACE
AAS MICROFICHE SERIES (1968-), VOL 59 *see* ASTRODYNAMICS 1989
AAS MICROFICHE SERIES (1968-), VOL 60 *see* GLOBAL ENVIRONMENTAL CHANGE
AAS MICROFICHE SERIES (1968-), VOL 61 *see* SPACE BUSINESS OPPORTUNITIES FOR THE NEXT DECADE
AAS MICROFICHE SERIES (1968-), VOL 62 *see* SPACEFLIGHT MECHANICS 1991
AAS MICROFICHE SERIES (1968-), VOL 63 *see* ASTRODYNAMICS 1991
AAS MICROFICHE SERIES (1968-), VOL 64 *see* GUIDANCE AND CONTROL
AAS MICROFICHE SERIES (1968-), VOL 65 *see* SPACEFLIGHT MECHANICS 1992
AAS MICROFICHE SERIES (1968-), VOL 66 *see* SPACE BUSINESS OPPORTUNITIES-2
AAS MICROFICHE SERIES (1968-), VOL 67 *see* GUIDANCE AND CONTROL 1993
AAS MICROFICHE SERIES (1968-), VOL 68 *see* SPACEFLIGHT MECHANICS 1993
AAS MICROFICHE SERIES (1968-), VOL 69 *see* SPACEFLIGHT DYNAMICS 1993
AAS MICROFICHE SERIES (1968-), VOL 70 *see* ASTRODYNAMICS 1993
AAS MICROFICHE SERIES (1968-), VOL 71 *see* SPACEFLIGHT MECHANICS 1995
AAS MICROFICHE SERIES (1968-), VOL 72 *see* ASTRODYNAMICS 1995
AAS MICROFICHE SERIES (1968-), VOL 73 *see* SPACEFLIGHT MECHANICS 1996
AAS MICROFICHE SERIES, VOL 52 *see* SPACE EXPLOITATION AND UTILIZATION
AASA OFFICIAL REPORT / American Association of School Administrators – (All that is currently offered. Superseded by cassette available fr American Association of School Administrators) – Arlington, 1971-72 – 1,5,9 – D6482 – us UMI [370]
AAS/AIAA ASTRODYNAMICS CONFERENCE – (Suppl to v46, Advances) – 1981 – 21mf – 9 – $40.00 – 0-87703-163-0 – us Univelt [629]
AAS/AIAA ASTRODYNAMICS CONFERENCE, 1975 – (Suppl to v33, Advances) – 1976 – 36mf – 9 – $40.00 – 0-87703-142-8 – us Univelt [629]
AAS/AIAA ASTRODYNAMICS CONFERENCE, 1977 – 31mf – 9 – $50.00 – 0-87703-241-6 – us Univelt [629]
AAS/AIAA ASTRODYNAMICS CONFERENCE, 1979 – (Suppl to v40, Advances) – 1979 – 13mf – 9 – $20.00 – 0-87703-139-8 – us Univelt [629]
AAS/AIAA ASTRODYNAMICS SPECIALIST CONFERENCE, 1973 – 28mf – 9 – $35.00 – 0-87703-238-6 – us Univelt [629]
AASHTO (AMERICAN ASSOCIATION OF STATE HIGHWAY AND TRANSPORTATION OFFICIALS) – Printed index. Updated every 60 days – 6,9 – us Info Handling [625]
AASTARAAMAT / Tartu. Esti Rahva Muuseum – 1925-45 – 2r – 1 – us Ross [947]
AATCC (AMERICAN ASSOCIATION OF TEXTILE CHEMISTS AND COLORISTS) – Gives complete test methods. Printed index. Updated every 60 days – 6,9 – us Info Handling [660]
AATSEEL'S NEWSLETTER / American Association of Teachers of Slavic and East European Languages – (All that is currently available) – San Antonio. v15. oct 1973-apr 1974 – 1 – D8715 – us UMI [460]
AAU NEWS : (AMATEUR ATHLETIC UNION OF THE UNITED STATES) – (Cont by: Info AAU (Amateur Athletic Union of the United States)) – Indianapolis. v1-43 1930-72*. v44-51 jan 1973-dec 1980 1; v46-47 1975-76. v48-49 1977-78*. v50-51 1979-80 5; v46 1975*. v47-51 1976-80 9 – 1,5,9 – D8556 – us UMI [790]
AAU NEWS *see* INFO AAU
AAUP BULLETIN / American Association of University Professors (AAUP) – (Cont by: Academe. Former title: Bulletin of the American Association of University Professors (dec 1915-Win 1955)) – Washington. cum index 1-20 1915-34; v1-64 1915-dec 1978 1; v54-64 Spr 1968-dec 1978 5; v58-64 mar 1972-dec 1978 9 – 1,5,9 – D974 – us UMI [370]
AAUP BULLETIN *see* ACADEME
AAUW (American Association of University Women) *see* JOURNAL
AAUW JOURNAL / American Association of University Women (AAUW) – (Cont by: Graduate Woman. Former titles: Publications of the Association of Collegiate Alumnae (1882-jun 1910); Journal of the American Association of University Women (oct 1921-oct 1961)) – Washington. 1s-3s: v1-12 1882-1905. 3s: v1-71 1906-may 1978 1; v62-63 oct 1968-may 1970 5 – 1,5 – D904 – us UMI [370]
Aav, Yrjo *see*
– ESTONIAN PERIODICALS AND BOOKS IN FINNISH LIBRARIES
– RUSSIAN BIBLIOGRAPHIES: BIBLIOGRAPHIES AND BOOKS ON LIBRARIANSHIP PRINTED IN RUSSIAN CHARACTERS IN THE HELSINKI LIBRARY
– RUSSIAN DICTIONARIES
AB DAFUER, NACH AFRIKA : EINE BUBENGESCHICHTE AUS VERGANGENEN TAGEN / Weller, Anton Friedrich Tuedel – Muenchen: F Eher, [194-?] – 1 – us U.W. Library [830]
Ab Ithel, J Williams *see*
– ANNALES CAMBRIAE (A.D. 444-1288) (RS20)
– BRUT Y TYWYSOGION (RS17)
AB URBE CONDITA LIBRI 1,2,21,22: ADIUNCTAE SUNT PARTES E SELECTAE EX LIBRIS 3,4,5,6,7,26,29 / Livy – Wien: Tempsky, 1906. 52p. fold. map – 1 – us U.W. Library [930]
ABA BANK COMPLIANCE – (Cont: Bank Compliance) – Washington. v6-13. 1985-92* 1; v14-15 1993-94*. v16-18 1995-97+ 1,5,9 – 1,5,9 – D15700.01 – us UMI [332]
ABA BANK SECURITY AND FRAUD PREVENTION – (Cont in pt: Bank Insurance & Protection Bulletin) – Washington. v1 sep 1994*. v2-4 1995-97+ – 1,5,9 – D21295 – us UMI [073]
ABA BANKING JOURNAL – American Bankers' Association. v.71- 1979- – 1,5,6,9 – us UMI [073]
ABA BANKING JOURNAL – v71- 1979- – 1,5,6,9 – us UMI [336]
ABA BANKING JOURNAL / American Bankers Association – (Shipped qrtly or yrly. Cont: Banking) – New York. v71-. apr 1979- – 1,5,9 – D6992.01 – us UMI [332]
ABA Commission of Inquiry *see* NOTES OF EVIDENCE
ABA JOURNAL / American Bar Association (ABA) – (Cont: American Bar Association Journal) – Chicago. v70-83. jan 1984-dec 1997+ – 1,5,9 – D1897.01 – us UMI [340]
ABA JOURNAL – (Title varies: v1-69 1915-83 as American Bar Association Journal) – v1-81. 1915-1995 – 9 – $1,451.00 set – us Hein [340]
ABA JOURNAL *see* AMERICAN BAR ASSOCIATION JOURNAL
ABA MANAGEMENT UPDATE OF PERSONAL TRUST AND PRIVATE BANKING – Washington. 1988-92* 1; Win 1993-94*. jan-feb 1995 1,5,9 – 1,5,9 – D20256 – us UMI [332]
ABA SECTION OF CORPORATION BANKING AND BUSINESS LAW : PROCEEDINGS – 1939-50 – 1,5,6 – $45.00 – us Hein [340]
ABA SECTION OF INTERNATIONAL AND COMPARATIVE LAW : BULLETIN – v1-10. 1957-66 – 1,5,6 – $45.00 – us Hein [340]
ABA SECTION OF INTERNATIONAL AND COMPARATIVE LAW : PROCEEDINGS – 1942-65 – 1,5,6 – $135.00 – us Hein [340]
LES ABABUA (CONGO BELGE) / Halkin, Joseph – Bruxelles: A DeWit [etc], 1911 – us Res Libr [960]
ABACUS – New York. v1-5. 1983-88* – 1 – inquire – D16972 – us UMI [380]
ABACUS – Sydney. v1-33 sep 1965-sep 1997+ 1; v10-33 jun 1974-sep 1997+ 5; v12-33 jun 1976-sep 1997+ 9 – 1,5,9 – D9848 – us UMI [073]
ABAD PEMIKIRAN / Snyder, Louis Leo – Translation of The age of reason. SE 3465 1. 1962 – 9 – ne IDC [950]

Abadia, Ignacio *see* RESUMEN SACADO DEL INVENTARIO GENERAL...DE LOS ARNESES DE LA REAL ACADEMIA

Abadie, M *see* LES RACES DU HAUT-TONKIN DE PHONG-THO A LANG-SON

O ABADIENSE – Martinho Campos, Brazil. May-Jul 1934 – 1 – bl Biblioteca [072]

Abadilla, A G *see* ANG MAIKLING KATHANG TAGALOG

Abadjief, C *see* DIE HANDELSPOLITIK BULGARIENS

Abaelardus, Petrus *see*
- EPITOME THEOLOGIAE CHRISTIANAE
- OPERA
- THEOLOGIA

O ABAETE – Abaete, Aug-Dec 1948; Jan-Mar, May-Jul 1949 – 1,5,6 – bl Biblioteca [072]

O ABAETE – Abaete, Sep-Dec 1904; Jan-Jun, Aug-Nov 1905 – 1,5,6 – bl Biblioteca [072]

ABAETE-JORNAL – Abaete, Dec 1934; 1935; Jan-Sep 1937; Feb, May, Dec 1940; May, Nov-Dec 1941; Jan-Feb, May-Jul 1942; Feb-Dec 1943; Jan-May 1944; Jun-Dec 1945; Jan 1946 – 1,5,6 – bl Biblioteca [072]

ABAGABE B'ANKOLE – (Filmed with: Rowe, John A "Selected articles on the Bataka" (Bukalasa, 1922-23). Kagwa, Apolo "The Clans of the Baganda (Mengo, 1949). Gray, J M "Mutesa of Buganda" (1934)) – Kampala: Eagle Press, 1955 – 9 – us Res Libr [960]

Abajian, James de T *see* BLACKS IN SELECTED NEWSPAPERS, CENSUSES AND OTHER SOURCES: AN INDEX TO NAMES AND SUBJECTS

ABAKAMA BA BUNYORO KITARA : TRANSLATION (P. 33-162) / Rowe, J A – (Filmed with: Daudi Chawa 2: Kabaka of Buganda – Why Sir Apolo Kaggwa..resigned [Kampala, 1964]) – Kampala, Uganda, 1964 – us Res Libr [960]

ABANTU BATHO – Johannesburg, South Africa. 24 Apr 1930-23 Jul 1931. 1 reel – 1, 16 diazo available at reduced price – sa SA Libr [072]

Abarca, Mariano *see* LA INDUSTRIALIZACION DE LA AGENTINA

ABA'S CONSUMER BANKING DIGEST – (Cont by: Retail Banking Digest) – Washington. v1-12 may 1982-92* 1; v13 1993* 1,5,9 – 1,5,9 – D20201 – us UMI [332]

ABA'S FINANCIAL SERVICES INDUSTRY TRENDS – Washington, 1987-92* 1; 1993-94*. 1995-97+ 1,5,9 – 1,5,9 – D20286 – us UMI [332]

Abasolo-Enriquez, Lorenza *see* FILIPINO LANGUAGE LEXICON

Abastecimiento de aguas *see* AFOROS EN LA SIERRA DE MONTANCHEZ. ANO 1818

Abate, Giuseppe *see* LA CASA NATALE DI S. FRANCESCO...SECOLO 13. ROMA (1966)

O ABATIRA – Santo Amaro, BA. 11-24 Dez 1850; Jan, Maio-15 Jul 1851 – 1,5,6 – bl Biblioteca [072]

Abauzit (Firmin) *see* DISCOURS HISTORIQUE SUR L'APOCALYPSE

Abba Tecle Mariam Semhary Selam *see* DE SS. SACRAMENTIS SECUNDUM RITUM AETHIOPICUM

Abbadie, Arnauld d' *see*
- CATALOGUE RAISONNE DE MANUSCRITS ETHIOPIENS
- DOUZE ANS DANS LA HAUTE-ETHIOPIE (ABYSSINIE)

Abbas, Ahmed *see* LA LOI MUNICIPALE DU 5 AVRIL 1884 ET L'ALGERIE

Abbas, Hassan *see*
- BEGINILAH TJARA BERISTERI
- DITJELAH-TJELAH KEHIDUPAN NABI MUHAMMAD S.A.W

ABBAUES ET PRIEURES DE L'ANCIENNE FRANCE / Beaunier, Dom. – (Ed. Besse). Province Ecclesiastique de Tours. Tome 7. 1920 – Dfl30.00 – ne Slangenburg [240]

A L'ABBAYE DE MONTMAJOUR : LES ORIGINES DE LA REFORME DE SAINT-MAUR. (MEMOIRES DE L'INSTITUT HISTORIQUE DE PROVENCE, T. 4, 1927) / Benoit, F – Marseille, 1927 – Dfl6.00 – ne Slangenburg [240]

L'ABBAYE EXEMPTE DE CLUNY ET LE SAINT-SIEGE / Letonnelier, G – 1923 – Dfl19.00 – ne Slangenburg [240]

ABBAYES ET PRIEURES DE L'ANCIENNE FRANCE / Beaunier, Dom. – (Ed. Besse). Province Ecclesiastique de Bourges. Tome 5. 1912 – Dfl28.00 – ne Slangenburg [240]

ABBAYES ET PRIEURES DE L'ANCIENNE FRANCE / Beaunier, Dom. – (Ed. Besse). Province Ecclesiastique de Rouen. Tome 7. 1914 – Dfl25.00 – ne Slangenburg [240]

ABBAYES ET PRIEURES DE L'ANCIENNE FRANCE / Beaunier, Dom. – (Ed. Besse). Province Ecclesiastique de Sens. Tome 6. 1913 – Dfl19.00 – ne Slangenburg [240]

ABBAYES ET PRIEURES DE L'ANCIENNE FRANCE / Beaunier, Dom. – (Ed. Besse). Tome 4: Provinces Ecclesiastiques d'Alby, de Narbonne et de Toulouse, 1911 – Dfl30.00 – ne Slangenburg [240]

ABBAYES ET PRIEURES DE L'ANCIENNE FRANCE / Besse, J et al – Tome 9. Province Ecclesiastique de Vienne, 1932 – Dfl25.00 – ne Slangenburg [240]

ABBAYES ET PRIEURES DE L'ANCIENNE FRANCE / Beyssac, J – Tome 9. Province Ecclesiastique de Lyon, Pt 1 1933 – Dfl19.00 – ne Slangenburg [240]

ABBAYES ET PRIEURES DE L'ANCIENNE FRANCE / Laurent, J & Claudon, F – Tome 12: Province Ecclesiastique de Lyon, Pt 3 1941 – Dfl46.00 – ne Slangenburg [240]

ABBAYES ET PRIEURES DE L'ANCIENNE FRANCE. PROVINCES ECCLESIASTIQUES D'AUCH ET DE BORDEAUX : ARCHIVES DE LA FRANCE MONASTIQUE, VOL 10 / Beaunier, Dom.; ed by Besse, Dom J M – Tome 3. 1910 – 6mf – 8 – Dfl32.00 – ne Slangenburg [240]

Abbayes, H des *see* REVISION MONOGRAPHIQUE DES CLADONIA DU SOUS-GENRE CLADINA (LICHENS) RENNES, 1939

ABBAYES, PRIEUR ES ET COUVENTS D'HOMMES EN FRANCE / Lecestre, Leon – Paris, 1902 – 1mf – 9 – F30.00 – fr F.F.G. [240]

L'ABBE A. L. DE BARBARIN – s.n. 1875. 02138. (Pre-1900 Canadiana) – 9 – cn C.I.H.M. [920]

L'ABBE C. H. LAVERDIERE / Faucher de Saint-Maurice, Narcisse – s.l.: s.n., 18??. 03058. (Pre-1900 Canadiana) – 9 – us UMI [971]

L'ABBE DE L'EPEE / Bouilly, Jean Nicolas – (French Theatre Series). Paris. Andre, an VIII. 1799 – 9 – fr Hachette [820]

L'ABBE DESFONTAINES ET SON ROLE DANS LA LITTERATURE DE SON TEMPS / Morris, Thelma – (Studies on Voltaire and the eighteenth century, vol. 19) – Oxford. 1961 – 9 – $54.00 – 0-7294-0072-7 – uk Voltaire [920]

L'ABBE DOHERTY: SES PRINCIPAUX ECRITS EN FRANCAIS: PRECEDES D'UN PORTRAIT ET D'UNE NOTICE BIOGRAPHIQUE / Doherty, Patrick John – par un ami. Quebec: A. Cote, 1872. 02730. (Pre-1900 Canadiana) – 9 – cn C.I.H.M. [971]

L'ABBE ET LE RABBIN / Holbach, Paul-Thiry d' – (D'Holbach Series) – 9 – fr Hachette [240]

L'ABBE EUSEBE RENAUDOT : ESSAI SUR SA VIE ET SON OEUVRE LITURGIQUE / Villien, A – Paris, 1904 – 4mf – 8 – Dfl19.00 – ne Slangenburg [240]

L'ABBE GABRIEL RICHARD, CURE DE DETROIT / Dionne, Narcisse Eutrope – Quebec: S.A. Demers..., 1902. SEM105P503 – 1mf – 9 – Can$2.25 – cn Bibl Nat [240]

L'ABBE H.-R. CASGRAIN / Laflamme, Joseph Clovis Kemner – [Quebec]: [s.n.], [1905?]. SEM105P736 – 1mf – 9 – Can$2.25 – cn Bibl Nat [240]

L'ABBE JEAN HOLMES ET SES CONFERENCES DE NOTRE-DAME: ETUDE LITTERAIRE ET BIOGRAPHIQUE / Chauveau, Pierre J O – Quebec: A. Cote, 1876. 00587. (Pre-1900 Canadiana) – 9 – cn C.I.H.M. [920]

L'ABBE JOSEPH AUBRY / Chandonnet, Thomas Aime – (Montreal: C. Beauchemin & Valois, 1875). 00554. (Pre-1900 Canadiana) – 9 – cn C.I.H.M. [240]

Abbey, Charles J *see*
- THE ENGLISH CHURCH AND ITS BISHOPS, 1700-1800
- THE ENGLISH CHURCH IN THE EIGHTEENTH CENTURY
- RELIGIOUS THOUGHT IN OLD ENGLISH VERSE

Abbey, Richard *see* DIUTURNITY

ABBILDUNG UND BESCHREIBUNG BLUEHENDER CAKTEEN / Pfeiffer, L K G & Otto, C F – 2v. Cassel. 1838-1843-50. B-5635 2 – 8 – ne IDC [580]

Abbondio-Kuenzle, Christine *see* CHRUT UND UCHRUT IM SEELEGAERTLI

ABBONIS DE BELLO PARISIACO LIBRI 3 (MGH 7: 1.BD) – 1871 – Dfl9.00 – ne Slangenburg [240]

ABBOT ENGINEER – Camp Abbot, OR. -w. 21 May 1943-17 Jun 1944. 1 roll – 1 – us U.O. Library [071]

Abbot, Ezra *see*
- THE AUTHORSHIP OF THE FOURTH GOSPEL
- LITERATURE OF THE DOCTRINE OF A FUTURE LIFE
- THE LITERATURE OF THE DOCTRINE OF A FUTURE LIFE
- NOTES ON SCRIVENER'S PLAIN INTRODUCTION TO THE CRITICISM OF THE NEW TESTAMENT

Abbot, Ezra et al *see* THE FOURTH GOSPEL

Abbot, Francis Ellingwood *see*
- IS ROMANISM REAL CHRISTIANITY?
- SCIENTIFIC THEISM
- THE WAY OUT OF AGNOSTICISM

ABBOTSFORD SUMAS AND MATSQUI NEWS – British Columbia, CN. 1923- – 4r per yr – 1 – Can$55.00r – cn Commonwealth Micro [072]

Abbott *see*
- HISTORY OF BRANCH COUNTY
- HISTORY OF LIVINGSTON COUNTY. BIOGRAPHICAL SKETCHES

Abbott, Albert Holden *see* THOUGHTS ON PHILOSOPHY AND PHILOSOPHY AND THEOLOGY

Abbott, Austin *see*
- ABBOTT'S NEW YORK DIGEST
- A BRIEF FOR THE TRIAL OF CRIMINAL CASES
- A BRIEF ON THE MODES OF PROVING THE FACTS MOST FREQUENTLY IN ISSUE.

Abbott, Benjamin Vaughan *see*
- ABBOTT'S NEW YORK DIGEST
- ABBOTT'S REPORTS OF CASES IN ADMIRALTY FOR THE SOUTHERN DISTRICT OF NEW YORK
- ABBOTT'S REPORTS OF U.S. CIRCUIT AND DISTRICT COURT DECISIONS
- JUDGE AND JURY
- THE PATENT LAWS OF ALL NATIONS
- A TREATISE UPON THE UNITED STATES COURTS.

Abbott, Charles *see*
- A TREATISE OF THE LAW RELATIVE TO MERCHANT SHIPS AND SEAMEN.

Abbott, Edwin Abbott *see*
- ANGLICAN CAREER OF CARDINAL NEWMAN
- APOLOGIA
- CLUE
- COMMON TRADITION OF THE SYNOPTIC GOSPELS
- ILLUSION IN RELIGION
- JOHANNINE VOCABULARY
- JOHANNINE VOCABULARY:...THE WORDS OF THE FOURTH GOSPEL WITH THOSE OF THE THREE
- KERNEL AND THE HUSK
- THE MESSAGE OF THE SON OF MAN
- ONESIMUS
- PHILOCHRISTUS: MEMOIRS OF A DISCIPLE OF THE LORD
- ST. THOMAS OF CANTERBURY

Abbott, Ernest Hamlin *see* RELIGIOUS LIFE IN AMERICA

Abbott, Frank F *see* A HISTORY AND DESCRIPTION OF ROMAN POLITICAL INSTITUTIONS

Abbott, George F *see* THE HOLY WAR IN TRIPOLI

Abbott, J C *see*
- FERTILIZER MARKETING
- MARKETING EGGS AND POULTRY
- MARKETING FRUITS AND VEGETABLES
- MARKETING IMPROVEMENT IN THE DEVELOPING WORLD

Abbott, Jacob *see* THE CORNER-STONE, OR, A FAMILIAR ILLUSTRATION OF THE PRINCIPLES OF CHRISTIAN TRUTH

Abbott, Je'Anna Lanza *see* JOURNAL OF CONVENTION AND EXHIBITION MANAGEMENT

Abbott, John Stevens Cabot *see*
- THE HISTORY OF CHRISTIANITY
- HISTORY OF MARIE ANTOINETTE

Abbott, Lyman *see*
- AMERICA IN THE MAKING
- CHRISTIANITY AND SOCIAL PROBLEMS
- THE EPISTLE OF PAUL THE APOSTLE TO THE ROMANS
- EPISTLE OF PAUL THE APOSTLE TO THE ROMANS
- THE EVOLUTION OF CHRISTIANITY
- HENRY WARD BEECHER
- AN ILLUSTRATED COMMENTARY ON THE ACTS OF THE APOSTLES
- ILLUSTRATED COMMENTARY ON THE GOSPEL ACCORDING TO MATTHEW
- AN ILLUSTRATED COMMENTARY ON THE GOSPEL ACCORDING TO ST. JOHN
- ILLUSTRATED COMMENTARY ON THE GOSPEL ACCORDING TO ST JOHN
- ILLUSTRATED COMMENTARY ON THE GOSPEL OF LUKE
- ILLUSTRATED COMMENTARY ON THE GOSPELS ACCORDING TO MARK AND LUKE
- IMPRESSIONS OF A CARELESS TRAVELER
- IN AID OF FAITH
- LAICUS, OR, THE EXPERIENCES OF A LAYMAN IN A COUNTRY PARISH
- LIFE AND LETTERS OF PAUL THE APOSTLE
- THE LIFE AND LITERATURE OF THE ANCIENT HEBREWS
- LIFE AND LITERATURE OF THE ANCIENT HEBREWS
- OLD TESTAMENT SHADOWS OF NEW TESTAMENT TRUTHS
- THE PERSONALITY OF GOD
- PROBLEMS OF LIFE
- REMINISCENCES
- THE RIGHTS OF MAN
- THE SPIRIT OF DEMOCRACY
- A STUDY IN HUMAN NATURE
- THE SUPERNATURAL
- SUPERNATURAL: AN ADDRESS
- THE THEOLOGY OF AN EVOLUTIONIST

Abbott, Thomas Kingsmill *see*
- CRITICAL AND EXEGETICAL COMMENTARY ON THE EPISTLES TO THE EPHESIANS AND...COLOSSIANS
- THE ENGLISH BIBLE AND OUR DUTY WITH REGARD TO IT
- ESSAYS CHIEFLY ON THE ORIGINAL TEXTS OF THE OLD AND NEW TESTAMENTS

ABBOTTEMPO – (Ceased publ) – Montreal. v1-3. mar 1963-nov 1965 – 1 – D1908 – us UMI [073]

ABBOTT'S APPEALS DECISIONS : UNREPORTED / New York. (State) – (A Pre-NRS title) – v1-4. 1852-69 (all publ) – 28mf – 9 – $42.00 – LLMC 80-053 – us L.L.M.C. [340]

ABBOTT'S MONTHLY – v1-7. 1930-33 – 3r – 1 – us Ross [975]

ABBOTT'S NEW CASES / New York. (State) – v1-32. 1876-94 (all publ) – 213mf – 9 – $319.00 – LLMC 78-094 – us L.L.M.C. [340]

ABBOTT'S NEW YORK DIGEST / Abbott, Benjamin Vaughan & Abbott, Austin – New York: Voohris. v1-8. 1813-69 (all publ) – 67mf – 9 – $100.00 – LLMC 79-518 – us L.L.M.C. [340]

ABBOTT'S PRACTICE REPORTS / New York. (State) – os: v1-19. 1854-65; ns: v1-16. 1865-75 (all publ) – 227mf – 9 – $340.00 – LLMC 78-090 – us L.L.M.C. [340]

ABBOTT'S REPORTS OF CASES IN ADMIRALTY FOR THE SOUTHERN DISTRICT OF NEW YORK / Abbott, Benjamin Vaughan – Boston: Little-Brown. 1v. 1857 (all publ) – 7mf – 9 – $10.50 – LLMC 81-427 – us L.L.M.C. [324]

ABBOTT'S REPORTS OF U.S. CIRCUIT AND DISTRICT COURT DECISIONS / Abbott, Benjamin Vaughan – New York: Diossy, 1863-1871 – 14mf – 9 – $21.00 – LLMC 81-428 – us L.L.M.C. [340]

ABBOTT'S WEEKLY AND ILLUSTRATED NEWS – Chicago. Ill. v. 1, no. 2-15; 6, no. 8-14. 1933-1934 – 1 – incomplete – us NY Public [071]

ABBREGE DES METHODES DE TRAICTER DES CONTROVERSES / Veron, F – Ed 20. [Paris], 1636 – 9mf – 9 – CA-152/1 – ne IDC [240]

L'ABBREGEE HISTOIRE DU GRAND MIRACLE PAR NOSTRE SAUVEUR / Boulaese, Jehan – Paris. 1573 – 9 – fr Hachette [360]

ABBREVIATIONS USED BY FAO FOR INTERNATIONAL ORGANIZATIONS, CONGRESSES, COMMISSIONS, COMMITTEES, ETC – 4th rev ed 1988 – 210p – it F.A.O. [400]

L'ABC – Port-au Prince: Impr Vve J Chenet, 1re annee, n2-28. 27 mars-31 juli 1897 – us Res Libr [072]

ABC – Baja, MX. 1974- – 26+ r – $1,300.00 ($70.00y) – R04159 – us Library Micro [072]

ABC – Lisbon, Portugal. 15 Jul 1920-24 Sep 1931 – 12r – 1 – uk British Libr Newspaper [072]

ABC – Madrid: Prensa Espanola, 1956-feb 1993 – 1 – us Res Libr [072]

ABC – Madrid SP. Apr 16 1922-Apr 4 1974 – 1 – us U.O. Library [071]

ABC – Madrid, Spain. 1942-55 – 84r – 1 – us L of C Photodup [072]

ABC : ORGAM LITTERARIO, CRITICO E DE PROPAGANDA COMMERCIAL – Manaos, Amazonas. 13-27 Jan 1918 – 1,5,6 – bl Biblioteca [072]
AN ABC AGAINST NUCLEAR WAR A HANDBOOK OF IDEAS ON THE PREVENTION OF NUCLEAR WAR MAINLY THROUGH THE EXTENSION OF RIGHTS AND LIBERTIES / Zube, John – 3fiches. (24x) – 9 – 1.00f – at Libertarian Micro [320]
ABC ARMENISCH UND DEUTSCH, ODER NAMENBUECHLEIN ZUM GEBRAUCHE DER ARMENISCHEN JUGEND IN SIEBENBUERGEN – Triest, 1788 – 1mf – ne IDC [460]
THE ABC CATECHISM (CCC265) / Price, P F – (In Chinese) – Hankow: Religious Tract Society, 1938 – 1r – 1 – 1984-6604 – us A.T.L.A. [240]
ABC DEL ALCOHOLISMO / Curado Garcia, Blas – Barcelona: Offset industrial, S.A. 1972 – 1 – sp Bibl Santa Ana [360]
ABC DIARIO MUSICO – Biographical notices of the musicians, composers, and singers of the period. 1780 – 9 – us Sibley [780]
ABC DIRECTORY – West Coast. 1936-1937 – 1r – 1 – $50.00 – D134 – us Library Micro [978]
ABC NEWS – Sept 1984. 4p. Bullion Dealers – 9 – 1.00f – at Libertarian Micro [320]
ABC NEWS TRANSCRIPTS AND INDEX – (Full text of television news transcripts with printed indexes. Cumulative 1970-85; annual 1986-) – 1970 – 9 – us Primary [000]
THE ABC OF THE GOVERNMENT OF THE UNITED STATES / Morse, Perley – NY: Perley Morse & Co, 1916 – 1mf – 9 – $1.50 – LLMC 96-057 – us L.L.M.C. [323]
THE ABC OF THE KNIGHTS OF THE KU KLUX KLAN / Simmons, W J – Atlanta: The Klan, c1917 – us Res Libr [360]
THE ABC OF WALL STREET / ed by S.A.N. – NY: DOUBLEDAY, PAGE & CO, 1916 – 2mf – 9 – $3.00 – LLMC 96-061 – us L.L.M.C. [332]
ABC POLITIK. KAWTOKAKE MITURUT PESENAN C.D.B.-P.K.I. DJAWA TENGAH / Communist Party. Indonesia – SE-4719 1. Sala, 1964 – 9 – ne IDC [335]
THE ABC RAILWAY AND STEAMBOAT TRAVELLERS' GUIDE – Montreal: J.T. Robinson, [1880-188-? or 189-?] – 9 – cn C.I.H.M. [380]
THE ABC REPORTER *see* INTERNATIONAL ASSOCIATION OF INDUSTRIAL ACCIDENT BOARDS AND COMMISSION REPORTER
ABCA BULLETIN – (v36-47, no.4. 1973-84. 5,6. v38-47, no.4. 1975-84. 9) – American Business Communication Association. v1-47, no.4. Dec 1936-84 – 1 – us UMI [380]
ABCA BULLETIN / American Business Communication Association – (Cont by: Bulletin of the Association for Business Communication. Former titles: ACTBW Bulletin (dec 1936-apr 1937); ABWA Bulletin (may 1937-1967)) – Urbana. v1-47 dec 1936-dec 1984 1*; v36-47 1973-dec 1984 5; v38-47 mar 1975-dec 1984 9 – 1,5,9 – D8090 – us UMI [650]
ABCEDARIO PITTORICO / Orlandi, Pellegrino Antonio – O-382. 1704 – 9 – ne IDC [760]
ABCEDARIUM ANGLICO LATINUM / Huloet, Richard – 1552. 457p. (English Linguistics Series 1500-1800) – 9 – us UMI [420]
ABC'S OF COPYRIGHT – 3rd ed 1986 – 73p – 9 – 92-3-101889-2 – fr UNESCO [340]
ABCS OF FREEDOM / Read, Leonard E – 1976. Also: Meditations on Freedom; Instead of Violence, 1973, 31p.; Pattern For Revolt,Rev. ed., 1973, 31p. Together with: Laissez-faire Definitions, by John Zube, comp. (cont'd). 1 fiche (24x) – 9 – 1.00f – at Libertarian Micro [320]
Abd Al Aziz Ibn Othman, Al Kabisi *see* ALCABITII AD MAGISTERIUM JUDICIORUM ISAGOGE...
Abd Al-Baqi Niha Vandi *see* MA'ASIR I RAHIMI
Abd Al-Hamid Lahawri *see* BADSHAH NAMAH
Abd Al-Qadir Bin-i-Maluk *see* MUNTAKHAB AL-TAWARIKH
Abd al-Rahman ibn' Abd Allah *see* DOCUMENTS ARABES RELATIFS A L'HISTOIRE DU SOUDAN
Abdallah, A *see* L'ORDINAMENTO LITURGICO DI GABRIELE 5, 88E PATRIARCA COPTO
ABDIAS / Stifter, Adalbert – Berlin: Schreiter, [1914?] – 1 – us U.W. Library [830]
ABDOMINAL IMAGING – (Formed by the union of: Gastrointestinal Radiology and, Urologic Radiology) – Heidelberg. v18-22. jan 1993-dec 1997+ – 1,5,9 – D19607 – us UMI [616]
THE ABDUCTION OF MARY ANN SMITH BY THE ROMAN CATHOLICS / Mattison, Hiram – 1868 – 9 – us A.T.L.A. [240]
ABDUELHAMID'IN KAYGULARI / Sami, Ebuesuereyya – Istanbul: Kader Matbaasi, 1330 [1914] – $37.00 – us MEDOC [956]
Abduelkadir, Gulami *see* DIVAN
Abduelkadir, Mehmed *see* MUEKEMMEL VE MUFASSAL TUERKIYE CUMHURIYETI ATLASI
ABDUL BAHA IN EGYPT / Sohrab, Mirza Ahmad – London: Rider, (1929). 390p – 1 – us U.W. Library [290]
ABDUL BAHA ON DIVINE PHILOSOPHY / Chamberlain, Isabel Fraser – Boston: Tudor Press, c1918.189p – 1 – us U.W. Library [290]
Abdul Rahman daeng Matamman *see* BERZANDJI TERDJEMAH BAHASA BUGIS
ABDULHAMID 2, SULTAN OF TURKEY PAMPHET COLLECTION – 1909-1931 – 1 – CSUXANQ7699-B – us Hoover Inst Photo [947]
ABDULLAH ABDURAHMAN FAMILY PAPERS, 1906-1962 – Chicago: Uni of Chicago, Photodup Dept, [1977] – us Res Libr [920]
Abdullah, Z *see* BUDI LUHUR; BUKU BATJAAN AGAMA UNTUK SEKOLAH RAKJAT OLAN MADRASAH-MADRASAH. DIHIASI OLEH M. LUBIS
Abdulmuin, M Taib T *see* ICHTISAR ILMU TAUHID
Abdulrachman, Moch *see* PETUNDJUK STATISTIK PERTANIAN RAKJAT
Abdulsalam *see* A PICTORIAL REVIEW OF INDONESIA'S HISTORY OF INDEPENDENCE
Abdur Rahman, A F M *see* INSTITUTES OF MUSSALMAN LAW, A TREATISE ON PERSONAL LAW ACCORDING TO THE HANAFITE SCHOOL, WITH REFERENCES TO ORIGINAL ARABIC SOURCES...1795 TO 1906
Abdurahman, Fuad *see* PENGETAHUAN TENTANG TELEVISI
L'ABEILLE – Quebec: Petit Seminaire de Quebec, 1848-1881 – 9 – cn C.I.H.M. [370]
L'ABEILLE : REVUE MENSUELLE CATHOLIQUE / Giraud, Philippe – Montreal. v7 n1. 1905 – 1r – 1 – Can$25.00 – cn Can Microfilming [073]
ABEILLE : MEMOIRES. JOURNAL D'ENTOMOLOGIE / ed by Marseul, S A de – (1869/1870-1874/1875, v7-12[S.2, v1-6]; 1875-1881, v13-18[S.3, v1-6]; 1880-1886/1887, v19-24[S.4, v1-6]; 1888-1889, v25-26[S.5, v1-2]; 1890/1892-1935/1938, v27-36) – Paris, 1864-1869. v1-6 – 290mf – 9 – Z-915c/2 – ne IDC [590]
L'ABEILLE CANADIENNE / ed by Garneau, F-X – Quebec, Canada. 7 dec 1833-8 fev 1834 – 1r – 1 – Can$25.00 – cn Can Microfilming [072]
L'ABEILLE CANADIENNE / ed by Mezieres, Henri – Montreal. 1 aut 1818-15 jan 1819 – 1r – 1 – Can$30.00 – cn Can Microfilming [072]
L'ABEILLE CANADIENNE – Montreal, Canada. 4 aut-11 aut 1843 – 1r – 1 – Can$25.00 – cn Can Microfilming [072]
L'ABEILLE DE LA NOUVELLE-ORLEANS – New Orleans, LA. 16 sep 1845-26 fev 1899 – 1r – 1 – Can$30.00 – cn Can Microfilming [071]
L'ABEILLE MEDICALE : REVUE – Montreal, Canada. jan 1879-jan 1882 – 1r – 1 – Can$40.00 – cn Can Microfilming [610]
L'ABEILLE PAROISSIALE – Montreal: Granger Greres, 1895-1896 – 9 – cn C.I.H.M. [971]
LA ABEJA ESPANOLA – Anos 1812-1813 (12-IX/31-VIII) – 49mf – 9 – sp Cultura [946]
Abejon, Carlos *see* LA MUJER ARGENTINA ANTES Y DESPUES DE EVA PERON
ABEL : EN PLATTDEUTSCH STUECKSCHEN MERRN UT DE MARSCH UN MERRN UT'T LEBEN / Trede, Paul – 2. Opl. Garding: H Luehr & Dircks, [1896] – 1r – 1 – us U.W. Library [430]
Abel, C *see* NARRATIVE OF A JOURNEY TO THE INTERIOR OF CHINA
Abel, F *see* GESTES DE LA VIE QUOTIDIENNE DANS LE CONSTANTINOIS
Abel, F M *see*
- GEOGRAPHIE DE LA PALESTINE
- LES LIVRES DES MACCABEES (ETB)

Abel, K F *see* SIX SYMPHONIES A DEUX VIOLINS, DEUX HAUTBOIS, DEUX CORS DE CHASSE, ALTO VIOLA E BASSE.
ABEL LARKIN FAMILY PAPERS *see* LARKIN, ABEL, FAMILY PAPERS, MS 924
Abel, Ludwig *see* KEILSCHRIFTTEXTE
ABELARD : SA VIE, SA PHILOSOPHIE & SA THEOLOGIE / Remusat, Charles de – Paris: Didier, 1855 – 3mf – us A.T.L.A. [240]
ABELARD AND THE ORIGIN AND EARLY HISTORY OF UNIVERSITIES / Compayre, Gabriel – New York: Charles Scribner, 1893. (The Great educators) – 1mf – us A.T.L.A. [370]
A ABELHA : JORNAL POLITICO, LITTERARIO E NOTICIOSO – [s.l.]. 17 Fev 1860 – 1,5,6 – bl Biblioteca [072]
A ABELHO DA CHINA – [Macao]: Na Typographia do Governo, sep 12 1822-mar 20 1823 – 1r – 1 – us Res Libr [950]
O ABELHUDO : FOLHA DOS CURIOSOS – Sao Luiz, 27 Nov 1898-26 Mar 1899 – 1,5,6 – bl Biblioteca [072]
Abella Blasco, Mario *see* HISTORIA DEL SINDICALISMO
Abelly, L *see*
- TRAITTE DES HERESIES, CONTENANT LES CAUSES DES HERESIES, LES MOEURS ET ARTIFICES...
- LA VIE DU VENERABLE SERVITEUR DE DIEU VINCENT DE PAUL

Abel-Remusat *see*
- MEMOIRES SUR LES RELATIONS POLITIQUES DES PRINCES CHRETIENS ET PARTICULIEREMENT DES ROIS DE FRANCE, AVEC LES EMPEREURS MONGOLS
- NOTICE SUR LE DICTIONNAIRE INTITULE

Abelson, J *see* THE IMMANENCE OF GOD IN RABBINICAL LITERATURE
ABENAKI INDIAN LEGENDS, GRAMMAR AND PLACE NAMES / Masta, Henry Lorne – Victoriaville: l'Imprimerie de Victoriaville, 1932. SEM105P1640 – 2mf – 9 – Can$4.50 – cn Bibl Nat [390]
DER ABEND – Berlin, 1976-jan 23 1981 – 21r – 1 – Dist. gw Mikrofilm – gw Misc Inst [072]
DER ABEND – Berlin, DE. 1928-32; 1946-49; 1955-70 – 64r – 1 – us L of C Photodup [072]
DER ABEND – Berlin, mar 24-dec 1892 – 2r – 1 – Dist. gw Mikrofilm – gw Misc Inst [943]
DER ABEND – Berlin, oct 14 1946-mar 22 1952 – 17r – 1 – uk British Libr Newspaper [943]
DER ABEND – West Berlin, oct 10, 1946-sep 30, 1950 – 5r – 1 – gw Mikrofilm [072]
DAS ABEND BLATT – New York etc. v1. no. 1-v9. no. 2337. Oct 15 1894-Apr 12 1902 – 1 – us NY Public [071]
DAS ABEND BLATT – New York. N.Y. The evening paper. 1894-1902 – 1 – us A.J.P.C. [071]
ABEND BLATT FUER DIE ARBEITER ZEITUNG – New York. v1-9. 1894-1902 – 18r – 1 – us Ross [071]
ABEND POST = THE EVENING POST – London, UK. 26 Feb 1915-12 May 1916 – 1 – uk British Libr Newspaper [072]
ABEND POST – San Francisco, CA. 1863-1864 – 1r – 1 – $50.00 – C03663 – us Library Micro [071]
ABENDECHO *see* HAMBURG-ALTONAER VOLKSBLATT
DIE ABENDLAENDISCHE MESSE : VOM FUENFTEN BIS ZUM ACHTEN JAHRHUNDERT / Probst, Ferdinand – Muenster i.W.: Aschendorff, 1896 – 2mf – us A.T.L.A. [240]
ABENDLAENDISCHE PALAESTINAPILGER DES ERSTEN JAHRTAUSENDS UND IHRE BERICHTE : EINE KULTURGESCHICHTLICHE SKIZZE / Baumstark, Anton – Koeln: J.P. Bachem, 1906 – 1mf – us A.T.L.A. [306]
DER ABENDLAENDISCHE TEXT DER APOSTELGESCHICHTE UND DIE WIR-QUELLE: EINE STUDIE / Pott, August – Leipzig: J.C. Hinrichs, 1900. 1 fiche. 8370-4786-2 – 9 – us A.T.L.A. [240]
ABENDLAND : UNABHAENGIGE DEUTSCHE EUROPAEISCHE STIMMEN FUER CHRISTLICHE GESELLSCHAFTSERNEUERUNG – Prag (Praha), Czechoslovakia. Feb 1938 – 1 – gw Mikrofilm [073]
DAS ABENDLAND – Central Organe fuer alle zeitgemaessen Interessen des Judenthums. Prague: Bruenn, v1-6, 1864-69. Incomplete. 1 reel. B1. (Leo Baeck Institute. German-Jewish Periodicals) – 1 – $75.00 – us UPA [260]
ABENDLIED, SCHLUMMERLIED AND DIE BLUMENSPRACHE / Schubert, Franz – 2 songs, autograph manuscript D. 527, 519. 1817 – 9 – us Sibley [780]
ABENDPOST : AUSGABE SUED-HANNOVER – Goettingen. feb 6, 1947-mar 3, 1949 – 1r – 1 – gw Mikrofilm [072]
ABENDPOST – Hannover, West Germany. 1947-48 – 1 – gw Mikrofilm [072]
ABENDPOST – (Issues for 1904, 1906-07, 1939 filmed consecutively with: Sonntagpost 1904, 1906-07, 1922-38, 1939) – Chicago, IL: Glogauer & Co. Chicago ed – 1 – us Res Libr [071]
ABENDPOST – Rochester. N.Y. 1912; 1937-1966 – 1 – us UMI [071]
ABENDPOST – Weimar, 1947 – 1r – 1 – DM75.00 – gw Mikro Press [072]
ABENDPOST – Weimar, East-Germany. 1947. Incomplete – 1 – gw Mikrofilm [072]
ABENDPOST UND MILWAUKEE DEUTSCHE ZEITUNG – Chicago, 1972-84 – 20r – 1 – gw Mikrofilm [071]
ABENDPOST UND SONNTAG POST – (Includes the evening and sunday eds) – Chicago, sep 1889-dec 1921; 1922-73*; 1974-76*; jan 1977-dec 1979; 1980-sep 1991* – 1 – inquire – D10213 – us UMI [072]
ABENDPOST-NACHTAUSGABE – Frankfurt Main, West Germany. 1976-1988 – 1 – gw Mikrofilm [072]
ABEND-ZEITUNG – Dresden, DE. Jul-Dec 1825 – 1r – 1 – gw Mikrofilm [072]
ABENDZEITUNG – Munchen, DE. 1951- – ca 8r per yr – 1 – gw Mikrofilm [072]
ABENDZEITUNG – Munich. DE. 1979- – ca 365mf per yr – mf – gw Alpha Com [072]
ABENDZEITUNG *see* DIE°ABENDZEITUNG
DIE ABENDZEITUNG – (Cont: Die Tageszeitung since 1948 n41. Cont by: Abendzeitung, jul 1 1950) – Muenchen, may 5 1948-50 – 5r – 1 – gw Mikrofilm [072]
ABENTEUER EINES BLAUSTRUEMPFCHENS / Heyse, Paul – Stuttgart: C Krabbe, [1897] – 1r – 1 – us U.W. Library [830]
EINE ABENTEUERLICHE REISE = LA FOLLE AVENTURE : ROMAN / Lichtenberger, Andre – Leipzig: Philipp Reclam jun., [19–?] – 1r – 1 – us U.W. Library [830]
DER ABENTEUERLICHE SIMPLICISSIMUS / Grimmelshausen, Hans Jakob Christoph von; ed by Klee, Gotthold – Bielefeld: Velhagen & Klasing, 1912 – 1r – 1 – us U.W. Library [830]
ABENTEURER- UND LUIQUIDATORENTUM / Rudas, L – Die Politiek Bela Kuns und die Krise der K.P.U. Wien. 1922. B-498 2 – 8 – ne IDC [943]
Abercrombie, Nigel *see* CULTURAL POLICY IN THE UNITED KINGDOM
ABERDARE LEADER – Aberdare, Wales. 1902-to date – 1 – uk Microform Academic [072]
ABERDEEN – Aberdeen. Mississippi. -w. 1902-32 – 1 – us UMI [071]
Aberdeen. Allenvale Cemetery *see* REGISTERS OF BURIALS
Aberdeen and Temair, Ishbel Gordon *see*
- CANADA'S LATE PREMIER
- GOOD-BYE
- INAUGURAL MEETING OF THE LOCAL COUNCIL OF WOMEN OF HALIFAX
- THE NATIONAL COUNCIL OF WOMEN OF CANADA
- WHERE DWELLS "OUR LADY OF THE SUNSHINE"

Aberdeen and Temair, Ishbel Gordon, Marchioness of *see*
- A QUOI BON LA SOCIETE ABERDEEN
- ADDRESS: AT A PUBLIC MEETING, OTTAWA, 1898
- LADY ABERDEEN'S ADDRESS: AT A PUBLIC MEETING HELD IN THE TOWN HALL, PORT ARTHUR, ON TUESDAY, SEPT. 25
- PRESIDENT'S CLOSING ADDRESS AT THE FIFTH ANNUAL MEETING OF THE NATIONAL COUNCIL OF WOMEN OF CANADA
- WHAT IS THE USE OF THE VICTORIAN ORDER OF NURSES FOR CANADA?

Aberdeen Association *see*
- THE MISSION OF THE OLD MAGAZINE
- REPORT

THE ABERDEEN DOCTORS : A NOTABLE GROUP OF SCOTTISH THEOLOGIANS OF THE FIRST EPISCOPAL PERIOD, 1610-1638... / Macmillan, D – London: Hodder & Stoughton, 1909 – 1mf – us A.T.L.A. [240]
ABERDEEN HERALD – Scotland, 6 Jan 1844-11 Nov 1876 – 28r – 1 – uk British Libr Newspaper [072]

THE ABERDEEN HERALD – Aberdeen, South Africa. 20 Jul 1889-28 Nov 1891. 2 reels – 1, 16 diazo available at reduced price – sa SA Libr [072]
ABERDEEN JOURNAL – Scotland, 21 Nov 1752; 1 Apr, 12 May 1760; 27 Jul, 8 May 1780-15 Dec 1783; 28 Nov 1785; 2,9 Jan, 24 Jul-7 Aug, 4,11,25 Sep, 2-23 Oct 1786; 28 Jan, 11 Feb 1799. (10 Aug 1767; 1 Nov 1773; 2 June 1777; 30 Nov 1778; 11 Jan 1779) – 1r – 1 – uk British Libr Newspaper [072]
ABERDEEN SATURDAY POST – Scotland, 27 Jul-26 Oct 1861 – 19ft – 1 – uk British Libr Newspaper [072]
ABERDEEN-ANGUS JOURNAL – (Cont by: Angus Journal n11969) – Webster City. v1-60. aug 1919-jun 1979 1; v52-59 aug 1970-jul 1978. v60 aug 1978-jun 1979* 5; v56-59 aug 1974-jul 1978*. v60 aug 1978-jun 1979 9 – 1,5,9 – inquire – D177 – us UMI [630]
ABERDEEN'S CONCRETE CONSTRUCTION – (Cont: Concrete Construction) – Addison. v35-40. feb 1990-dec 1997+ – 1,5,9 – D6545.01 – us UMI [690]
ABERDEEN'S MAGAZINE OF MASONRY CONSTRUCTION – (Cont: Magazine of Masonry Construction) – Addison. v3-10. mar 1990-dec 1997+* – 1 – D16704.01 – us UMI [690]
ABERDEENSHIRE, 1837 : BRITISH ISLES CENSUS DIRECTORIES PROJECT, SCOTLAND. VOL 27 – 1mf – 9 – A$9.00 – at Vine [941]
ABERDEENSHIRE (ABERDEEN), 1820 : BRITISH ISLES CENSUS DIRECTORIES PROJECT, SCOTLAND. VOL 59 – 1mf – 9 – A$9.00 – at Vine [941]
ABERGELE AND PENSARN VISITOR – Wales, 17 Jul 1869-Dec 1903 – 14r – 1 – uk British Libr Newspaper [072]
ABERGLAUBE ODER VOLKSWEISHEIT? / Fischer, Hanns – 1939 – 1 – us I.U. Libraries [390]
ABERGLAUBE, SAGE UND MAERCHEN BEI GRIMMELSHAUSEN / Amersbach, Karl – (Includes bibliographical references) – Baden-Baden: E Koelblin, 1891-1893 – 1r – 1 – us U.W. Library [430]
Abernethy, Alonzo *see* A HISTORY OF IOWA BAPTIST SCHOOLS
Abernethy, J *see* SURGICAL OBSERVATIONS ON THE CONSTITUTIONAL ORIGIN AND TREATMENT OF LOCAL DISEASES AND ON ANEURISMS
Abert, Hermann *see* GOETHE UND DIE MUSIK
ABESSINIEN : EINE LANDESKUNDE NACH REISEN UND STUDIEN IN DEN JAHREN 1907-1913 / Rein, G Kurt – Berlin: D Reimer (E Vohsen), 1918-20 – 1 – us Res Libr [960]
Abeyesooriya, Samson *see*
- DE FONSEKA FAMILY OF KALUTARA (CEYLON)
- LIFE OF LADY CATHERINE DE SOYSA
- WHO'S WHO OF CEYLON

ABF RESEARCH REPORTER – American Bar Foundation. v.1-6. Spr 1971-Sum 1975. See Also: American Bar Foundation Research Reporter – 1 – us UMI [340]
DIE ABFASSUNGSZEIT DER SCHRIFTEN TERTULLIANS (T.U.U. 1-5/2A) / Noeldechen, Ernst – Leipzig, 1888 – 3mf – 9 – ne Slangenburg [240]
DIE ABFASSUNGSZEIT DES GALATERBRIEFES : EIN BEITRAG ZUR NEUTESTAMENTLICHEN EINLEITUNG UND ZEITGESCHICHTE / Steinmann, Alphons – (Includes indexes) – Muenster i.W.: Aschendorff, 1906 – 1mf – 9 – 0-8370-6779-0 – 1986-0779 – us A.T.L.A. [220]
ABFASSUNGSZEIT UND ABSCHLUSS DES PSALTERS ZUR PRUEFUNG DER FRAGE NACH MAKKABAEERPSALMEN / Ehrt, Carl – Leipzig: J.A. Barth, 1869. 1 fiche – 9 – us A.T.L.A. [220]
ABGASUNTERSUCHUNGEN AN EINEM PFLANZENOELBETRIEBENEN VORKAMMER-DIESELMOTOR / Fischer, Tim – 1995 – 2mf – 9 – DM80.00 – 3-8267-2127-6 – gw Hänsel [628]
DIE ABHAENGIGKEIT DER PFLANZENGESTALT VON KLIMA UND BODEN / Kerner von Marilaun, A – Innsbruck. 1869. B-6492 2 – 8 – ne IDC [580]
ABHANDLUNG UEBER DEN URSPRUNG DER SPRACHE / Herber, J G – (Linguistic series). v. 5. 1789 – 9 – fr Hachette [400]
ABHANDLUNG UEBER DES ATHIOPISCHEN BUCHES HENOKH / Ewald, Heinrich – 1854 – 9 – us A.T.L.A. [240]
ABHANDLUNG UEBER DIE ARZNEIKRAEFTE DER PFLANZEN,... / Dierbach, J H – Lemgo, 1831 – 5mf – 9 – ne IDC [615]
ABHANDLUNG UEBER DIE FRAGE OB DIE MUSIK BEY DEM GOTTESDIENSTE DER CHRISTEN ZU DULDEN, ODER NICHT / Albrecht, J L – 1764 – 9 – us Sibley [780]
ABHANDLUNG UEBER DIE RECHENKUNST ODER PRACTISCHE ARITHMETIK ZUM GEBRAUCH FUER SCHULEN / ed by Benner, Enos – Sumnytaun (U.S.A) 3rd ed 1853 – 2mf – DM62.00 – 3-8267-3029-1 – gw Hänsel [510]
ABHANDLUNG VON DEM GELDUMLAUF / Buesch, Johann Georg – 1800, Auszug, 90 – 9 – 1.00f – at Libertarian Micro [335]
ABHANDLUNG VON DEM VERDERBEN DES GESCHMACKS IN DER FRANZOESISCHEN MUSIK / Bollioud de Mermet, L – 1750. BP-642 1 – 9 – ne IDC [780]
EINE ABHANDLUNG VON DEN MUSICALISCHEN INTERVALLEN UND GESCHLECHTEN.. / Scheibe, Johann Adolph – 1739 – 2 – us Sibley [780]
ABHANDLUNG VON DER FUGE / Marpurg, Friedrich Wilhelm – 1753-54. 2v – 9 – us Sibley [780]
ABHANDLUNG VON DER FUGE NACH DEM GRUNDSAETZEN UND EXEMPELN DER BESTEN DEUTSCHEN UND AUSLAENDISCHEN MEISTER ENTWORFEN VON FRIEDRICH WILHELM MARPURG / Marpurg, Friedrich Wilhelm – Berlin. 1753. BP-709 1 – 9 – ne IDC [780]
ABHANDLUNG VON INSECTEN / Schaeffer, J C – Regensburg, 1752-79. 3v. Z-1597/2 – 8 – ne IDC [590]
ABHANDLUNGEN / Akademie der Wissenschaften. Berlin – 1804-1907 – 1 – us Schnase [500]
ABHANDLUNGEN / Akademie der Wissenschaften. Goettingen – v1-38 1838-92 BH-642 2 – 8 – ne IDC [500]
ABHANDLUNGEN / Deutscher Seefischereiverein – v1-13 1897-1922 – 1 – us Res Libr [639]
ABHANDLUNGEN / Naturforschende Gesellschaft zu Halle – bd.1-bd.25; n.F. no.1-n.F. no.7. 1854-1919 – 3 – us Readex [500]
ABHANDLUNGEN / Naturforschende Gesselschaft. Dessau – Dessau und Leipzig. 1783. v.1 – 3 – us Readex [530]
ABHANDLUNGEN / Naturforschenden Gesellschaft in Zurich – 1761-66 – 3 – us Readex [500]
ABHANDLUNGEN / Naturwissenschaftlicher Verein zu Bremen – Bd. 1-32; 1886 68-1951. Film Mas C 575 – 1 – us H.U. Library [580]
ABHANDLUNGEN DER CHURFUERSTLICH-BAIERISCHEN AKADEMIE DER WISSENSCHAFTEN / Akademie der Wissenschaften. Munich – Munich, 1763-76 – 3 – us Readex [500]
ABHANDLUNGEN DER KOENIGLICH PREUSSISCHEN AKADEMIE DER WISSENSCHAFTEN : PHILOSOPHISCH-HISTORISCHE KLASSE – Berlin, 1908-1941 – 653mf – 9 – H-636c/2 – ne IDC [100]
ABHANDLUNGEN DER KOENIGLICH PREUSSISCHEN AKADEMIE DER WISSENSCHAFTEN : PHYSIKALISCH-MATHEMATISCHE KLASSE – Berlin, 1908-1938 – 197mf – 9 – H-418/2 – ne IDC [510]
ABHANDLUNGEN DER KOENIGLICHEN AKADEMIE DER WISSENSCHAFTEN IN BERLIN, 1804-1907 : PHYSIKALISCHE, MATHEMATISCHE, PHILOSOPHISCHE, HISTORISCH-PHILOLOGISCHE KLASSE – Berlin, 1815-1907 – 2,459mf – 9 – H-641/2 – ne IDC [510]
ABHANDLUNGEN DER KOENIGLICHEN GESELLSCHAFT DER WISSENSCHAFTEN ZU GOETTINGEN – Goettingen, 1838-1892. v1-38 – 455mf – 9 – H-642/2 – ne IDC [510]
ABHANDLUNGEN DER MATHEMATISCHEN KLASSE DER KOENIGLICH-PREUSSISCHEN AKADEMIE DER WISSENSCHAFTEN, 1804-1907 – Berlin, 1815-1907 – 336mf – 9 – H-1099/2 – ne IDC [510]
ABHANDLUNGEN DER MATHEMATISCH-PHYSISCHEN CLASSE DER KOENIGLICH SAECHSISCHEN GESELLSCHAFT DER WISSENSCHAFTEN – Leipzig: Weidmannsche Buchhandlung, [1849- v15 1890] – 1r – 1 – us Res Libr [500]
ABHANDLUNGEN DER NATURFORSCHENDEN GESELLSCHAFT IN ZURICH – 1761-66 – 3 – us Readex [500]
ABHANDLUNGEN DES ZOOLOGISCH-MINERALOGISCHEN VEREINES IN REGENSBURG / Naturwissenschaftlicher Verein. Regensburg – 1849-78 – 3 – us Readex [590]
ABHANDLUNGEN UEBER DIE GESCHICHTE DES FRIEDENSSCHLUSSES ZU UTRECHT / Faesi, J K – Leipzig, 1790 – 6mf – 1 – ILM-2789/1 – ne IDC [327]
ABHANDLUNGEN UEBER FLECHTEN / Reinke, J – (Jahrbuecher fuer wissenschaftliche Botanik (Pringsheim) v. 26, 1894; v. 28, 1895; v. 29, 1896). B-5386 2 – 8 – ne IDC [580]
ABHANDLUNGEN ZU GOETHES LEBEN UND WERKEN / Duentzer, Heinrich – Leipzig: E Wartig, 1885 – 1r – 1 – us U.W. Library [430]
Abhedananda, Swami *see* SCIENCE OF PSYCHIC PHENOMENA
ABHIJAN – Bishnupur. v1-32 n40. jun 29 1941-mar 1973 – 7r – 1 – us Res Libr [950]
ABI NEWSLETTER – (Cont by: American Bankruptcy Institute Journal) – Washington, 1983-92* – 1 – D22553 – us UMI [073]
ABIB – New York. 1915 – 1 – us A.J.P.C. [073]
Abicht, J H *see* KURZE DARSTELLUNG
THE ABIDING COMFORTER...THE PERSON, THE PRESENCE, AND THE POWER OF THE HOLY SPIRIT / Stone, E A – Chicago: Fleming H. Revell, 1889. 1 fiche – 9 – us A.T.L.A. [240]
ABIDING FAITH FOR A NATION IN CRISIS (CCC340) = TA SHIH TAI TI TSUNG CHIAO HSIN YANG / Wu, Yao-tsung – (In Chinese) – Shanghai: Association Press of China, 1938 – 1r – 1 – 1984-6679 – us A.T.L.A. [210]
ABIDING KNOWLEDGE OF CHRISTIAN TRUTH (CCC202) / Huang, Samuel K – (In Chinese) – Shanghai: Christian Literature Society, 1934 – 1r – 1 – 1984-B500 – us A.T.L.A. [240]
Abilene. Kansas *see* ORDINANCE BOOK
THE ABILITY OF SARCOPLASMIC RETICULUM TO REGULATE INTRACELLULAR CALCIUM FOLLOWING A FATIGUING BOUT OF EXERCISE / Favero, Terence G & Klug, Gary A – 1990 – 1mf – 9 – $4.00 – us Microform Publ [612]
THE ABILITY OF UNDERGRADUATE PHYSICAL EDUCATION MAJORS TO VERBALLY IDENTIFY AND VISUALLY DISCRIMINATE CRITICAL ELEMENTS OF SELECT SPORT SKILLS / Edkins, C E – 1991 – 2mf – 9 – $8.00 – us Microform Publ [150]
Abineno, Johannes Ludwig Chrysostomus *see* PENGGEMBALAAN
ABINGDON AND READING HERALD – Abingdon, England. 10 Jun 1871-1873 – 2 1/2r – 1 – uk British Libr Newspaper [072]
ABINGDON EXPRESS – England, 5 Feb 1887-30 Jun 1888 – 1r – 1 – uk British Libr Newspaper [072]
ABINGDON FREE PRESS AND DIDCOT NEWS – (Missing: 1911) – England, Jun 1902-Mar 1916 – 9r – 1 – uk British Libr Newspaper [072]
ABINGDON MONTHLY MESSENGER – England, Jan-Jul 1875 – 8ft – 1 – uk British Libr Newspaper [072]
ABINGDON NEWS – England, 4 Jan 1878-21 Jun 1879 – 1r – 1 – uk British Libr Newspaper [072]
ABINGTON 1691-1849 – (Mf 1T: Deaths 1721-71. Mf 1T-37: Births 1691-1759. Mf 3T: Marrs & Intents 1712-61. Mf 4T-5T: Births 1759-88. Mf 5T: Deaths 1772-96. Mf 6T: Births 1727-96. Mf 6T-7T: Intentions 1761-1800. Mf 7T-8T: Births 1777-99. Mf 8T: Deaths. Mf 8T-9T: Marriages 1760-99. Mf 9T-11T: Births 1800-21. Mf 11T: Out-of-Town Marrs 1715-99. Mf 11T-12T: Intentions 1801-21. Mf 12T-13T: Marriages 1794-1820; Deaths 1800-21. Mf 14T-20T: Births 1821-49; Deaths 1821-44; Intentions 1821-49; Marriages 1821-44. Mf 25T: Vitals 1837-49. Mf 25T-26T: Marriages 1844-49. Mf 26T-27T: Deaths 1844-49) – (mf ed 1994) – 27mf – 9 – 0-87623-196-2 – us Holbrook [920]
ABINGTON 1691-1892 – (Mf 1-5: Town & Vital 1691-1777. Mf 6-9: Town Records 1712-66. Mf 9-10: Vital Records 1691-1777. Mf 11-15: Town & Vital 1727-1820. Mf 16-22: Town & Vital 1715-1856. Mf 23-25: Birth & Death 1821-51. Mf 26-32: Town Records 1766-1821. Mf 33-38: Town Records 1821-52. Mf 39-43: Town Records 1822-1918. Mf 44-49: Marriages 1821-60. Mf 50-51: Birth Index 1850-61. Mf 52-54: Births 1851-61. Mf 55-56: Birth Index 1862-91. Mf 57-60: Births 1862-91. Mf 61-62: Marr Index 1850-61. Mf 63-64: Marriages 1852-62. Mf 65-66: Marr Index 1862-91. Mf 67-71: Marriages 1863-91. Mf 72: Death Index 1850-61. Mf 73-74: Deaths 1851-61. Mf 75-76: Death Index 1862-91. Mf 77-79: Deaths 1862-91) – (mf ed 1992) – 79mf – 9 – 0-87623-159-8 – us Holbrook [920]
Abington Abbey *see* CHRONICON MONASTERII DE ABINGTON (RS2)
Abi-Saab, Georges *see* CONCEPT OF INTERNATIONAL ORGANIZATION
ABISMO...Y DISCURSO...VIRGEN MARIA / Guerrero, Alonso – 1686 – 9 – 1.50f – sp Bibl Santa Ana [240]
L'ABITIBI / ed by Authier, Henri – (Cont by and filmed with: LA GAZETTE DU NORD: 29 jun 1922-29 nov 1929; 16 fev 1940-31 mai 1951) – Amos, Canada. 29 jan 1920-22 jun 1922 – 12r – 1 – Can$65.00r – cn Can Microfilming [072]
ABITIBI-DIMANCHE. L'HEBDO-MAGAZINE DU NORD-QUEST QUEBECOIS – Montreal: Bibliotheque nationale du Quebec. v1-2. 1973. SEM35P11 – 2r – 1 – Can$95.00 – cn Bibl Nat [073]
ABITO Y ARMADURA ESPIRITUAL...CON PRIVILEGIO IMPERIAL. 1544 / Cabranes, Diego de – 9 – 1.50f – sp Bibl Santa Ana [240]
DER ABITURIENTENTAG : DIE GESCHICHTE EINER JUGENDSCHULD / Werfel, Franz – Berlin: P Zsolnay, 1928 – 1r – 1 – us U.W. Library [430]
DER ABLASS : SEINE GESCHICHTE UND BEDEUTUNG IN DER HEILSOEKONOMIE / Groene, V – Regensburg: G.J. Manz, 1863 – 1mf – us A.T.L.A. [240]
DER ABLASSSTREIT / Dieckhoff, A W – Gotha: F.A. Perthes, 1886 – 1mf – us A.T.L.A. [240]
THE ABLE MINISTER / Evans, Hugh – A sermon preached in Broadmead before the Britol Education Society. 1773 – 1 – 5.00 – us Baptist [240]
Ablesimov, A O *see* SOCHINENIIA
ABLONCZY, PAL/NAPI KOENYV (DIARY) – us I.H.R.C. [090]
ABNER CREEK BAPTIST CHURCH. SPARTANBURG COUNTY, SOUTH CAROLINA : CHURCH RECORDS – Sept. 1834-June 1990 – 2r – 1 – $99.81 – us Baptist [240]
ABODA ZARA: DER MISCHNATRAKTAT GOETZENDIENST / Strack, Hermann Leberecht – Berlin: H. Reuther, 1888. 1 fiche – 9 – us A.T.L.A. [270]
ABODAH ZARA. MISCHNA UND TOSEFTA / Blaufuss, H – Nuremberg. 1916. BJ-32-10 1 – 9 – ne IDC [270]
ABOGADO Y NOTORIO / Escalante, D – Guatemala, 1915 – 1mf – 1 – ILM-2510/1 – ne IDC [327]
LA ABOLICION DE LA ESOLAVITUD EN EL ORDERN ECONOMICO / Labra y Cadrana, Rafael Maria de – Madrid: J. Noguera, 1873 – 1 – us U.W. Library [305]
ABOLICION OFICIAL DEL LAICISMO EN LAS ESCUELAS / Bayle, Constantino – Madrid: Razon y Fe, 1937 – 1 – sp Bibl Santa Ana [370]
O ABOLICIONISTA : ORGAO DA SOCIEDADE BRASILEIRA CONTRA A ESCRAVIDAO – Rio de Janeiro, 1 Nov 1880-1 Dec 1881 – 1,5,6 – bl Biblioteca [072]
O ABOLICIONISTA – [s.l.]. 30 Abr, Jul 1871; 1 Mar-15 Abr 1872 – 1,5,6 – bl Biblioteca [072]
ABOLICIONSTA DO AMAZONAS – Manaos, Amazonas. 4 Maio-10 Jul 1884 – 1,5,6 – bl Biblioteca [072]
Abolina, A *see* AGITAT SII A I PROPAGANDA V DEREVNE
ABOLITION AND EMANCIPATION : PAPERS OF THOMAS CLARKSON, WILLIAM LLOYD GARRISON, ZACHARY MACAULAY, HARRIET MARTINEAU, HARRIET BEECHER STOWE AND WILLIAM WILBERFORCE – (Guide included) – 1996 – 7r – 1 – $840.00 – uk Matthew [976]
L'ABOLITION DE LA MISERE PAR L'ELEVATION DES SALAIRES / Girardin, Emile de – (Condition of 19th C. French working class series). 1850 – 9 – fr Hachette [331]
L'ABOLITION DE L'ESCLAVAGE (27 AVRIL 1848) / Martin, Gaston – Paris. 1948. (La Condition Ouvriere. Part Two.) – 9 – 2.50 – fr Bibl Nationale [360]

ABOLITION DE L'ESCLAVAGE. PROCES VERBAUX RAPPORTS ET PROJETS DE DECRETS DE LA COMMISSION INSTITUEE POUR PREPARER L'ACTE D'ABOLITION IMMEDIATE DE L'ESCLAVAGE – (Slave Trade and Abolitionism in France Series). 1848 – 9 – fr Hachette [360]
ABOLITION INTELLIGENCER AND MISSIONARY MAGAZINE – (Ceased publ. Issues 8,9,12 not available for filming) – Shelbyville. v1. may 1822-mar 1823 – 1 – D4406 – us UMI [240]
ABOLITION OF SLAVERY IN THE ANGLO-SAXON WORLD – George Carter and Peter Ripley, eds – 1 – uk World [900]
ABOLITIONIST : OR RECORD OF THE NEW ENGLAND ANTI-SLAVERY SOCIETY – (Ceased publ) – Boston. v1. jan-dec 1833 – 1 – D3912 – us UMI [976]
DER ABOLITIONIST, 1. 1902 – 32. 1933 (HQ 28) : ORGAN FUER DIE BESTREBUNGEN DER INT. FOEDERATION DER STAATLICH REGLEMENTIERTEN PROSTITUTION / ed by Scheven, Katharina – 1902-33 (mf ed 1997) – 40mf – 9 – DM410.00 – 3-89131-140-0 – gw Fischer [305]
L'ABOLITIONNISTE FRANCAIS – Paris. 1844-50 – 1 – fr A.C.R.P.P. [073]
L'ABORDAGE INTERNATIONAL... / Cholet, C – Paris, 1898 – 3mf – 1 – ILM-375/1 – ne IDC [327]
LES ABORIGENES AUSTRALIENS / Elkin, Aldophus Peter – Paris: Gallimard, 1967 – fr Armell [305]
LOS ABORIGENES DEL PAIS DE CUYO / Cabrera, Pablo – Cordoba (Argentina), 1929; Madrid: Razon y Fe, 1931 – 1 – sp Bibl Santa Ana [305]
ABORIGINAL AMERICAN AUTHORS AND THEIR PRODUCTIONS: ESPECIALLY THOSE IN THE NATIVE LANGUAGES: A CHAPTER IN THE HISTORY OF LITERATURE / Brinton, Daniel Garrison – Philadelphia: D. Brinton, 1883. 00278. (Pre-1900 Canadiana) – 9 – cn C.I.H.M. [490]
ABORIGINAL AMERICAN HARPOONS / Mason, Otis Tufton – BN 313 2. 1902 – 8 – ne IDC [639]
ABORIGINAL CRICKETERS IN ENGLAND – 1868. Score Book – 1r – 1 – at Corangamite [790]
THE ABORIGINAL TRIBES OF HYDERABAD.. / Fuerer-Haimendorf, Christoph von – London: Macmillan & Co., 1943 – 1 – us U.W. Library [305]
THE ABORIGINES' PROTECTION SOCIETY – 1997 – ca 3r – 1 – ca £220.00 – 1-897955-59-6 – uk Academic [360]
ABORIINAL LAW CENTRE – Kensington. 16 docs. 1985-1991 – 6mf – 9 – ne IDC [340]
Abos, Alvaro *see* LA COLUMNA VERTEBRAL
Abott *see* NATURALIZATION AND ALLEGIANCE
ABOU NADDARA – Paris. 1878-90, 1898-99 – 1 – fr A.C.R.P.P. [073]
Aboussouan, B *see* LE PROBLEME POLITIQUE SYRIEN
About, Edmond *see* GREECE AND THE GREEKS OF THE PRESENT DAY
ABOUT THE HOUSE – (Ceased publ) – London. v1-3 nov 1962-Sum 1972 1; v4-8 Chr 1972-Sum 1992 1,5,9 – 1,5,9 – D8594 – us UMI [073]
Abraham a Sancta Clara *see*
- AUF, AUF IHR CHRISTEN
- ETWAS FUER ALLE
- MERCURIALIS OF WINTERGROEN
- NUTTELIJK MENGELMOES
- DE WELVOORZIENE WYNKELDER...
- ZEEDELYKE GESCHIEDENISSE OF AANGENAAM WINTER-GROEN

ABRAHAM A SANCTA CLARA (1644-1709) : ZUR ZWEIHUNDERTSTEN WIEDERKEHR SEINES TODESTAGES: EINE AUSWAHL AUS SEINEN WERKEN MIT EINER EINLEITUNG VERSEHEN / Keller, Gottfried – Bern: G Grunau, 1909 – 1r – 1 – us U.W. Library [240]
Abraham Lincoln Association *see* PAPERS OF THE ABRAHAM LINCOLN ASSOCIATION
ABRAHAM LINCOLN PAPERS – (With guide) – 97r – 1 – $3,395.00 – Dist. us Scholarly Res – us L of C Photodup [975]
ABRAHAM LINCOLN QUARTERLY – (Ceased publ) – Springfield. v5-7. mar 1948-dec 1952 – 1 – D189 – us UMI [073]
ABRAHAM: RECENT DISCOVERIES AND HEBREW ORIGINS / Woolley, Leonard – Farber & Farber, 1936 – 9 – $12.00 – us I.R.C. [220]
Abraham, Roy Clive *see*
- A DICTIONARY OF THE TIV LANGUAGE
- THE GRAMMAR OF TIV
- THE PRINCIPLES OF IDOMA
- THE PRINCIPLES OF TIV

ABRAHAM SCHELLENBERG PAPERS / Schellenberg, Theodore R – 1875-1921 – 1 – us KS Hist [920]
ABRAHAM VAN WICQUEFORT... / Everwijn, D – Leiden, 1857 – 4mf – 1 – ILM-380/1 – ne IDC [327]
Abrahams, Israel *see*
- THE BOOK OF DELIGHT AND OTHER PAPERS
- CHAPTERS ON JEWISH LITERATURE
- JEWISH LIFE IN THE MIDDLE AGES
- JUDAISM

Abram, A *see*
- ENGLISH LIFE AND MANNERS IN THE LATER MIDDLE AGES
- SOCIAL ENGLAND IN THE FIFTEENTH CENTURY

ABRAM FISHER AND 13 OTHERS – ((Case history)) – 10r – 1 – sa Microfile [960]
ABRAMOS LOS OJOS / Anchorena de Acevedo, Ines – Buenos Aires, 1946 – 1 – CSUXADL6469-B – us Hoover Inst Photo [972]
Abramov, A *see*
- CHTO SDELALO ZEMSTVO I CHTO ONO DALAET?
- OKTIABR'SKAIA POEMA MAIAKOVSKOGO

Abramov, A V et al *see* NASTOL'NYI ENTSIKLOPEDICHESKII SLOVAR'
Abramov, N *see*
- POLNYI SLOVAR' RUSSKIKH RIFM
- SLOVAR'RUSSKIKH SINONIMOV I SKHODNYKH PO SMYSLU SLOV

Abramova *see* VRAGILI TRUDOVOMU NARODU EVREI
Abramovich, D I *see*
- KATALOG SOBRANIIA RUKOPISEI PROF. I. V. POMIALOVSKOGO NYNE PRINADLEZHASHCHIKH IMP. PUBLICHNOI BIBLIOTEKE
- OPISANIE RUKOPISEI S. PETERSBURGSKOI DEKHOVNOI AKADEMII. SOFFIISKAIA BIBLIOTEKA

Abramovich, N Ia *see*
- KHUDOZHNIKI I MYSLITELI. II KNIGA LITERATURNO-KRITICHESKIKH OCHERKOV
- LITERATURNO-KRITICHESKIE OCHERKI
- V OSENNIKH SADAKH, LITERATURA SEGODNIASHNIAGO DNIA

Abramovich, S D *see* FINANSOVYE PERSPEKTIVY RAZVITII A PROMYSHLENNOSTI
Abramowitsch, S J *see* TOLEDOT HA-TEVA
Abrams, Charles *see* CHARLES ABRAMS
ABRASIVE ENGINEERING – (Former titles: Grinding and Finishing (mar 1955, feb 1961-jan 1965, aug 1965-jun 1968); GF, Grinding and Finishing (may 1955-jan 1961); Grinding/Finishing (feb 1965-jul 1965)) – Wheaton. v1-20 mar 1955-dec 1974 1*; v17-20 jan 1971-dec 1974 5 – 1,5 – D1651 – us UMI [620]
ABRASIVES – v. 1-19. 1920-1938 – 1,5,6 – us Princeton Micro [621]
Abravanel, I *see* LE PRINCIPE DE LA FOI
ABRECHNUNG FOLGT / Grosz, Georg – 57 politische Zeichnungen. Berlin c1923 – 1 – us U.W. Library [760]
ABRECHNUNG-RANDBEMERKUNGEN ZU LEBEN UND ARBEIT / MacKay, John Henry – (Geldanarchie, by Urjo Rey. 1931. 64p. A Vindication of Natural Society..., by Edmund Burke. 1756. 54p. On Law, by Wm. Godwin. 16p) – 1mf (24x) – 9 – 1.00f – at Libertarian Micro [320]
ABREGE DE LA VIE DE BERNADETTE, SOEUR MARIE BERNARD / R, H – Montreal: J. Rolland, 1879. 04001. (Pre-1900 Canadiana) – 9 – cn C.I.H.M. [240]
ABREGE DE LA VIE DES PLUS FAMEUX PEINTRES / Dezallier d'Argenville, Antoine Joseph – O-225. 3 v. 1745-1752 – 9 – ne IDC [920]
ABREGE DE LA VIE DES PLUS FAMEUX PEINTRES... / Dezallier d'Argenville, A J – Paris. 3v. 1745-1752 – 30mf – ne IDC [750]
ABREGE DE LA VIE DES SAINTS. CHACUNE SUIVIE DE TROIS REFLEXIONS – Saint-Philippe: Impr. Ecclesiastique, 1825. SEM16P63 – 1r – 5 – Can$9.00 – cn Bibl Nat [240]
ABREGE DE L'EXPOSITION DE LA DOCTRINE CHRETIENNE / Reticius, FE C – Montreal: les Freres des ecoles chretiennes, 1942. SEM105P712 – 6mf – 9 – Can$13.50 – cn Bibl Nat [240]
ABREGE DE L'HISTOIRE ECCLESIASTIQUE DE FLEURY – (D'Holbach series). 1767 – 9 – fr Hachette [240]
ABREGE DE L'HISTOIRE SAINTE, DE L'HISTOIRE DE FRANCE ET DE L'HISTOIRE DU CANADA A L'USAGE. – Montreal, J. Rolland, 1875. 00770. (Pre-1900 Canadiana) – 9 – cn C.I.H.M. [971]
ABREGE DU CATECHISME A L'USAGE DE LA TRIBU DES CRIS – Montreal. 1872. 04002. (Pre-1900 Canadiana) – 9 – cn C.I.H.M. [240]
ABREGE HISTORIQUE DE L'ESTABLISSEMENT DE L'HOPITAL DES ENFANS-TROUVES / Arrault, Charles – Paris, Thibioust, 1746. 14 p. 1 fiche. (Statistics: Medical Studies Series) – 9 – 6.00 – fr Bibl Nationale [310]
Abregu Virreira, Carlos *see* LA PROTECCION DEL ABORIGEN EN EL 20. PLAN QUINQUENAL
Abreu Bertodano, Jose Antonio *see*
- COLECCION DE TRATADOS DE PAZ. TOMO 1
- COLECCION DE TRATADOS DE PAZ. TOMO 2
- COLECCION DE TRATADOS DE PAZ. TOMO 3
- COLECCION DE TRATADOS DE PAZ. TOMO 4
- COLECCION DE TRATADOS DE PAZ. TOMO 5
- COLECCION DE TRATADOS DE PAZ. TOMO 6
- COLECCION DE TRATADOS DE PAZ. TOMO 7
- COLECCION DE TRATADOS DE PAZ. TOMO 8
- COLECCION DE TRATADOS DE PAZ. TOMO 9
- COLECCION DE TRATADOS DE PAZ. TOMO 10
- COLECCION DE TRATADOS DE PAZ. TOMO 11
- COLECCION DE TRATADOS DE PAZ. TOMO 12

Abreu, F J de *see*
- TRADADO JURIDICO-POLITICO SOBRE PRESSAS DE MAR, ...
- TRAITE JURIDICO-POLITIQUE SUR LES PRISES MARITIMES, ...

L'ABRI CHAPADA DOS CRUZES, SITE DE LA VARIETE SERRA DA CAPIVARA ET DE STYLE SERRA DO TAPUIO, SUD-EST DU PIAUI, BRESIL / Guidon, N & Ogel-Ros, L – 9 – F60.00 – fr Ethnologie [306]
L'ABRI DE SUCUPIRA: UN SITE D'ART RUPESTRE DE LA REGION DE LA SERRA DO CIPO, MINAS GERAIS, BRESIL / Anthonioz-Russel, S & Monzon, S – Couverture photographique – 9 – F150.00 – fr Ethnologie [306]
UN ABRI DECORE DE LA SERRA NOVA, REGION DE SAO RAIMUNDO NONATO, ETAT DU PIAUI, BRESIL / Guidon, N. et al – 9 – F110.00 – fr Ethnologie [306]
UN ABRI LIMITROPHE DE L'AIRE DE SAO RAIMUNDO NONATO: LA TOCA DA PEDRA SOLTA DO BOM JESUS, BRESIL / Ogel-Ros, L – 9 – F100.00 – fr Ethnologie [306]
UN ABRI PEINT LIMITROPHE DE L'AIRE DE SAO RAIMUNDO NONATO, LA TOCA DAS LETRAS, SUD DU PIAUI, BRESIL / Ogel-Ros, L – 9 – F70.00 – fr Ethnologie [306]
L'ABRI TOCA DA BOA VISTA I, UN SITE DE L'AIRE DE SAO RAIMUNDO NONATO, SUD-EST DU PIAUI, BRESIL / Rocha Silva, G – 9 – F80.00 – fr Ethnologie [306]
L'ABRI TOCA DO BAIXAO DO CAPIM, SITE DES SOUS-TRADITIONS VARZEA GRANDE ET SERRA DO TAPIUO / Rocha Silva, G – 9 – F60.00 – fr Ethnologie [306]
L'ABRI TOCA DO CALDEIRAO DOS RODRIGUEZ 2, SITE DU STYLE VARZEA GRANDE, SUD-OUEST DU PIAUI, BRESIL / Manenti, F – 9 – Fr60.00 – fr Ethnologie [306]
L'ABRI TOCA DO CALDEIRAO DOS RODRIGUEZ I, SITE DU STYLE VARZEA GRANDE, SUD-EST DU PIAUI, BRESIL / Manenti, F – 9 – F70.00 – fr Ethnologie [306]
ABRI TOCA DO PINGA DO BOI, SITE TYPIQUE DE LA VARIETE SERRA BRANCA, STYLE VARZEA GRANDE, BRESIL / Guidon, N & Maranca, S & Ogel-Ros, L – 9 – F100.00 – fr Ethnologie [306]
L'ABRI TOCA DO SALITRE, SITE TYPIQUE DE LA SOUS-TRADITION SALITRE / Ogel-Ros, L & Ros, D – 11 fiches – 9 – F120.00 – fr Ethnologie [306]
Abribat, J M *see* LE DETROIT DE MAGELLAN...
Abricht, J *see* DIVINE EMBLEMS
ABRIDGED GRAMMARS OF THE LANGUAGES OF THE CUNEIFORM INSCRIPTIONS : CONTAINING 1. – A SUMERO-AKKADIAN GRAMMAR, 2. – AN ASSYRO-BABYLONIAN GRAMMAR, 3. – A VANNIC GRAMMAR, 4. – A MEDIC GRAMMAR, 5. – AN OLD PERSIAN GRAMMAR / Bertin, George – London: Truebner, 1888 – 1mf – 9 – 0-8370-8563-2 – 1986-2563 – us A.T.L.A. [470]
ABRIDGED INDEX MEDICUS – Bethesda. v1-28 jan 1970-dec 1997+ 1*; v5-28 jan 1974-dec 1997+ 5*,9 – 1,5,9 – D6285 – us UMI [610]
AN ABRIDGEMENT OF MILITARY LAW / Winthrop, W – (This is the 1st of eight eds of the Abridgement) – Washington, DC: W H Morrison, 1887 – 5mf – 9 – $7.50 – LLMC 96-094 – us L.L.M.C. [340]
AN ABRIDGMENT OF CHRISTIAN DOCTRINE – Montreal: J Brown, 1812. SEM16P28 – 1r – 5 – Can$9.00 – cn Bibl Nat [240]
AN ABRIDGMENT OF THE COMPILED LAWS OF THE STATE OF MICHIGAN, 1897. / Michigan. Laws, Statutes, etc – Lansing, MI: Smith, 1899. 977p. L.C. copy imperfect: p. 975-977 wanting. LL-951 – 1 – us L of C Photodup [340]
Abril, Manuel *see* FELIPE TRIGO. EXPOSICION Y GLOSA DE SU VIDA, SU FILOSOFIA, SU MORAL, SU ARTE, SU ESTILO
Abril, P *see* APUNTAMIENTOS...DE COMO SE DEBEN REFORMAR...LAS DOCTRINAS Y LA MANERA DE...
ABRIS PEINTS DE LA SERRA BRANCA ET DE LA SERRA NOVA, REGION DE VARZEA GRANDE, ETAT DU PIAUI, BRESIL / Guidon, N – 9 – F320.00 – fr Ethnologie [306]
ABRIS PEINTS DE LA SERRA DO CAPIVARA, REGION DE VARZEA GRANDE, ETAT DU PIAUI, BRESIL / Guidon, N – 9 – F320.00 – fr Ethnologie [306]
LES ABRIS TOCAS DO BAIXAO DO PERNA 1 ET 2, SITES DU STYLE VARZEA GRANDE, SUD-EST DU PIAUI, BRESIL / Guidon, N & Ogel-Ros, L – 9 – Fr120.00 – fr Ethnologie [306]
ABRISS DER DEUTSCHEN LITERATURGESCHICHTE IN TABELLEN / Schmitt, Fritz & Goeres, Joern – (Includes bibliographical references and index) – Frankfurt am Main: Athenaeum, 1963 – 1r – 1 – us U.W. Library [430]
ABRISS DER DEUTSCHEN LITERATURGESCHICHTE IN TABELLEN / Schmitt, Fritz & Goeres, Joern – (Includes bibliographical references and index) – Frankfurt am Main: Athenaeum-Verlag, 1965 – 1 – us U.W. Library [430]
ABRISS DER EINLEITUNG ZUM ALTEN TESTAMENT IN TABELLENFORM : AN STELLE DER DRITTEN AUSGABE VON HERTWIG'S EINLEITUNGSTABELLEN / Kleinert, Paul – (Includes bibliographies & index) – Berlin: G W F Mueller, 1878 – 1mf – 9 – 0-8370-3917-7 – 1985-1917 – us A.T.L.A. [220]
ABRISS DER GESAMTEN KIRCHENGESCHICHTE / Herzog, Johann J – Erlangen: E. Besold, 1890-1892 – 4mf – us A.T.L.A. [240]
ABRISS EINER GESCHICHTE DER PROTESTANTISCHEN MISSIONEN : VON DER REFORMATION BIS AUF DIE GEGENWART: EIN BEITRAG ZUR NEUEREN KIRCHENGESCHICHTE / Warneck, Gustav – (Includes bibliographical references and indexes) – 7. Aufl. Berlin: Martin Warneck, 1901 – 1mf – 9 – 0-8370-6627-1 – 1986-0627 – us A.T.L.A. [240]
ABR'OLHOS : ORGAM SEMANARIO, HUMORISTICO E CRITICO – Manaos, Amazonas. 15 Ago 1926-25 Fev 1927 – 1,5,6 – bl Biblioteca [072]
ABRUF VERBALER ODER VISUELLER INOFRMATIONEN BEIM ENTSTEHEN EINER KINDERZEICHNUNG / Seidel, Kerstin – 1994 – 1mf – DM60.00 – 3-8267-2052-0 – gw Hänsel [370]
ABRUZZO-MOLISE – (Previous title: Marsica Nuova (11/26/1918-1923), Pueblo, CO) – Rochester, NY, 1918-1923, 1926 – 1r – 1 – us I.H.R.C. [978]
ABS, AMERICAN BEHAVIORAL SCIENTIST – (1966-. 5,6. 1975-. 9) – v1-. 1957- – 1 – us UMI [150]
ABS (AMERICAN BUREAU OF SHIPPING) – Printed index. Updated every 60 days – 6,9 – us Info Handling [380]

Absal *see* AN ALLEGORY. TRANSLATED FROM THE PERSIAN OF JAMI

ABSALOM, ABSALOM! – Concordance to the novel – 12mf – 9 – us UMI [420]

ABSATZWIRTSCHAFT – 1958- 1; 1974- 5,6; 1975- 9 – us UMI [380]

ABSCHID DER STETTE ZUERICH, BERN UND SANT GALLEN, VON WEGEN DER WIDERTEUEFFER AUSZGANGEN – 1527. BME-7 1 – 9 – ne IDC [340]

ABSCHIEBUNG IST MORD – Oct 1986 – 9 – 1.00f – at Libertarian Micro [320]

ABSCHIED VOM PARADIES : EIN ROMAN UNTER KINDERN / Thiess, Frank – Stuttgart: I Engelhorn, 1927 – 1r – 1 – us U.W. Library [830]

THE ABSENCE OF PRECISION IN THE FORMULARIES OF THE CHURCH OF ENGLAND SCRIPTURAL, AND SUITABLE TO A STATE OF PROBATION: IN EIGHT SERMONS / Bode, John Ernest – Oxford: J. Wright, 1855 – 1mf – us A.T.L.A. [240]

ABSIDE – (All that is currently offered) – San Luis Potosi. v39-42 jan 1975-dec 1978 1; v 40-42 jan 1976-dec 1978 5*,9* – 1,5,9 – D451 – us UMI [073]

ABSOLIUTIZM V ROSSII (XVII-XVIII VV.) – Sbornik statei semidesiatiletiiu. B.B. Kafengausa, Moscow, 1964. 517,(4)p. BR-6065 2 – 8 – ne IDC [947]

ABSOLUTE ODER RELATIVE WAHRHEIT DER HEILIGEN SCHRIFT / Egger, Franz – Brixen: A. Weger, 1909. 1 fiche – 9 – us A.T.L.A. [240]

ABSOLUTE RELIGION : A VIEW OF THE ABSOLUTE RELIGION, BASED ON PHILOSOPHICAL PRINCIPLES AND THE DOCTRINES OF THE BIBLE / Upham, Thomas Cogswell – New York: G P Putnam, 1873 – 1mf – 9 – 0-8370-5650-0 – 1985-3650 – us A.T.L.A. [230]

THE ABSOLUTIVE AND THE RELATIVE IN ESKIMO / Thalbitzer, W – Grammatical miscellany to Otto Jespersen's 70th birthday. BN 420 2. 1930 – 8 – ne IDC [170]

LO ABSOLUTO / Campoamor y Campoosorio, Ramon de – 1865. Libros en Microficha no 16 – 1mf – 9 – Pta1,000.00 – 84-85422-43-0 – sp Pentalfa [170]

ABSONDERLICHE CHARAKTERE BEI WILHELM RAABE / Jansen, Werner – Greifswald, 1914 – 1mf – DM48.00 – 3-8267-3085-2 – gw Hänsel [430]

ABSORPTION ET DIGESTION CHEZ ACTINIA EQUINA L., NUTRITION DES ACTINIAIRES / Van-Praet, M – 9 – F90.00 – fr Ethnologie [590]

THE ABSTAINER – Halifax, Canada. v4 n12. 15 mar 1860 – 1r – 1 – Can$25.00 – cn Can Microfilming [072]

THE ABSTAINER – Halifax, N.S.: J. Barnes, v1 no 1 (Oct 15 1856) – 9 – cn C.I.H.M. [072]

ABSTRACT AND CONSTRUCTIVIST ART : SUBJECT COLLECTIONS – (Individual titles not listed separately) – 87 catalogues on 106mf – 9 – £670.00 – uk Chadwyck [700]

ABSTRACT BULLETIN / The Institute of Paper Science & Technology, Inc – v1-. September 1930- – 5,6,9 – us Paper [670]

ABSTRACT BY...OF COKE ESTATE DEEDS / Bedingfield, Christopher – 1708 – 1 – uk Microform Academic [941]

ABSTRACT OF PROCEEDINGS FOR THE ACADEMIC YEAR... – 1941; 1942; 1949; 1950 (complete) – Inquire – 1 – ATLA 1944-S524 – us A.T.L.A. [370]

ABSTRACT OF PROCEEDINGS FOR THE YEAR... – 1891/92-1940/41 (complete) – Inquire – 1 – ATLA 1994-S523 – us A.T.L.A. [073]

ABSTRACT OF RESEARCHES ON MAGNETISM AND ON CERTAIN ALLIED SUBJECTS INCLUDING A SUPPOSED NEW IMPONDERABLE / Reichenbach, Karl Ludwig Friedrich – Trans. and abr. from the German by William Gregory. London: Taylor and Walton, 1846. x,112p – 1 – us U.W. Library [530]

AN ABSTRACT OF THE CHARACTERS OF OCHSENHEIMER'S GENERA OF THE LEPIDOPTERA OF EUROPE / Children, J G – London, 1828-30.150p. (Phil. Mag., v4-8). Z1136/2 – 8 – ne IDC [590]

ABSTRACT OF THE COLLECTION AND BUSINESS LAWS OF COLORADO TERRITORY / Morrison, Robert Stewart – Denver: Rocky Mountain News, 1872. 53,2p. LL-932 – 1 – us L of C Photodup [340]

ABSTRACT OF THE FORMER ARTICLES OF FAITH CONFESSED BY THE ORIGINAL BAPTIST CHURCH – (Free Will Baptist 1812) – 1 – 5.00 – us Baptist [240]

AN ABSTRACT OF THE GEOLOGY OF INDIA / Duncan, P M – G-158 2. 1876 – 8 – ne IDC [550]

AN ABSTRACT OF THE LOIX DE POLICE, OR, PUBLIC REGULATIONS FOR THE ESTABLISHMENT OF PEACE AND GOOD ORDER, THAT WERE OF FORCE IN THE PROVINCE OF QUEBEC. – London: Printed Charles Eyre and William Strahan, 1772. SEM105P370 – 1mf – 9 – Can$2.25 – cn Bibl Nat [360]

AN ABSTRACT OF THE MOST MATERIAL PARTS OF AN ACT...INTITULED AN ACT FOR MAKING, REPAIRING AND ALTERING THE HIGHWAYS AND BRIDGES WITHIN THIS PROVINCE. / Canada. Bas-Canada. Laws, Statutes, etc – Montreal: Printed at the Office of the Morning Courier, 1839. SEM105P145 – 1mf – 9 – Can$2.25 – cn Bibl Nat [324]

ABSTRACT OF THE PROCEEDINGS OF THE COUNCIL OF THE GOVERNOR-GENERAL OF INDIA ASSEMBLED FOR THE PURPOSE OF MAKING LAWS AND REGULATIONS 1862-1920 – (Missing: 1868, v7(p. 189-215, 364, 368, 370, 374, 376, 382-384)) – Calcutta, 1863-1921. v1-59 – 942mf – 9 – I-11/2 – ne IDC [340]

AN ABSTRACT OF THE SEVERAL ROYAL EDICTS AND DECLARATIONS, AND PROVINCIAL REGULATIONS AND ORDINANCES, THAT WERE IN FORCE IN THE PROVINCE OF QUEBEC IN THE TIME OF THE FRENCH GOVERNMENT.. / Cugnet, Francois Joseph – London: Printed by Charles Eyre and William Strahan, 1772. SEM105P371 – 9 – Can$2.25 – cn Bibl Nat [971]

AN ABSTRACT OF THE STATUTORY LAW OF CORPORATIONS AS RESPECTS THEIR FORMATION, OFFICERS, MEETINGS, LIABILITY OF MEMBERS, ETC / Collins, Fred K – Cleveland, Schenck, 1881. 79 p. LL-494 – 1 – us L of C Photodup [340]

AN ABSTRACT OF THOSE PARTS OF THE CUSTOM OF THE VISCOUNTY AND PROVOSTSHIPS OF PARIS, WHICH WERE RECEIVED AND PRACTIFIED IN THE PROVINCE OF QUEBEC. – London: Printed by Charles Eyre and William Strahan, 1772. SEM105P368 – 1mf – 9 – Can$2.25 – cn Bibl Nat [360]

ABSTRACT OF VOTES (HARDIN CO) / Defiance County, Ohio. Board of Elections – 1839 – 1r – 1 – $32.50r – us Archival [324]

ABSTRACT OF VOTES (PAULDING CO) / Defiance County, Ohio. Board of Elections – 1839 – 1r – 1 – $32.50r – us Archival [324]

ABSTRACTS / American Ceramic Society – v1-34. 1922-55 – 1,5,6 – us Princeton Micro [540]

ABSTRACTS / Zinc Development Association – 1943-64 – 1 £845.25 7 £210.00 – uk Microform Academic [660]

ABSTRACTS AND REVIEWS / Royal Institution of Chartered Surveyors – 1965-92. Continued annually – 1 – £525.00 – uk World [720]

ABSTRACTS FOR SOCIAL WORKERS – (Cont by: Social Work Research and Abstracts) – New York. v1-13 Spr 1965-Spr 1977 1; v7-13 Spr 1971-Spr 1977 5; v11-13 Spr 1975-Spr 1977 9 – 1,5,9 – D5852 – us UMI [360]

ABSTRACTS IN SOCIAL GERONTOLOGY – (Cont: Current Literature on Aging) – Thousand Oaks. v33-40. mar 1990-dec 1997+* – 1,5,9 – D17949.03 – us UMI [618]

ABSTRACTS OF BOOK REVIEWS IN CURRENT LEGAL PERIODICALS – repr 1987 – 9 – $150.00 set – 0-89941-584-9 – us Hein [340]

ABSTRACTS OF CLINICAL CARE GUIDELINES – Chicago. v1-4 1989-1992 1*; v5-9 1993-1997+* 1,5,9 – 1,5,9 – D20756 – us UMI [610]

ABSTRACTS OF DECLASSIFIED DOCUMENTS – (Ceased publ. Cont by: Nuclear Science Abstracts) – Washington. cum index 1-2; v1-2. jul 1947-jun 1948 – 1 – D8570 – us UMI [530]

ABSTRACTS OF ENGLISH STUDIES – Calgary. v1-34 jan 1958-dec 1991. v35 mar-dec 1994*. v36-38 mar-dec 1997+ 1; v14-34 sep 1970-dec 1991 5. v35 mar-dec 1994*. v36-38 mar-dec 1995-97+ 5,9; v19-34 sep 1975-dec 1991 9 – 1,5,9 – inquire – D1603 – us UMI [420]

ABSTRACTS OF FOLKLORE STUDIES – (Ceased publ) – Arlington. cum index 1-2; v1-7 jan 1963-Win 1969 1; v8-13 Spr 1970-Win 1975 1,5 – 1,5 – D5897 – us UMI [390]

ABSTRACTS OF HEALTH CARE MANAGEMENT STUDIES – (Cont: Abstracts of Hospital Management Studies n10526) – Ann Arbor. v15-23. jun 1979-may 1987 – 1,5,9 – $83.70y – D10526.01 – us UMI [350]

ABSTRACTS OF HEALTH CARE MANAGEMENT STUDIES *see* ABSTRACTS OF HOSPITAL MANAGEMENT STUDIES

ABSTRACTS OF HOSPITAL MANAGEMENT STUDIES – (Cont by: Abstracts of Health Care Management Studies) – Ann Arbor. v1-14 jun 1965-78 1; v11-14 jun 1975-78 5,9 – 1,5,9 – inquire – D10526 – us UMI [610]

ABSTRACTS OF HOSPITAL MANAGEMENT STUDIES *see* ABSTRACTS OF HEALTH CARE MANAGEMENT STUDIES

ABSTRACTS OF NORTH AMERICAN GEOLOGY – (Ceased publ) – Washington, jan 1966-dec 1971 1; jan 1970-dec 1971 5 – 1,5 – D3292 – us UMI [550]

ABSTRACTS OF NORTH AMERICAN GEOLOGY (WASHINGTON) / U.S. Department of the Interior – (All published. U.S. Dept. of Interior Geology Survey.) 1966-1971 – 1,5,6 – us Princeton Micro [550]

ABSTRACTS OF OREGON DONATION LAND CLAIMS, 1852-1903 / U.S. Bureau of Land Management – 6rolls. M145. Printed guide – 1 – us Nat'l Archives [324]

ABSTRACTS OF PAPERS PRESENTED AT THE 1974-76 SEMINAR OF THE GEOLOGICAL SURVEY OF ISRAEL / Israel. Ministry of Commerce, Industry and Tourism. Geological Survey – By Yosef Bartov and Aline Ehrlich. Jerusalem. Mar 1977. 48 p – 9 – 2.00 – is I.T.T.I. [550]

ABSTRACTS OF PAPERS PRESENTED TO THE AMERICAN MATHEMATICAL SOCIETY – Providence. v1-18. jan 1980-nov 1997+ – 1,5*9 – inquire – D12051 – us UMI [510]

ABSTRACTS OF PHOTOGRAPHIC SCIENCE AND ENGINEERING LITERATURE – (Ceased publ) – Wasghinton. v1-11. mar 1962-dec 1972 – 1 – D6700 – us UMI [770]

ABSTRACTS OF ROAD TAXES / Lucas County, Ohio. Sylvania Township Township Clerk – 1837-1882 – 3r – 1 – $32.50r – us Archival [324]

ABSTRACTS OF SERVICE RECORDS OF NAVAL OFFICERS ("RECORDS OF OFFICERS"), 1798-1893 / U.S. Navy. Bureau of Naval Personnel – 19r – 1 – M330 – us Nat'l Archives [355]

ABSTRACTS OF SERVICE RECORDS OF NAVAL OFFICERS ("RECORDS OF OFFICERS"), 1829-1924 – 18r – 1 – M1328 – us Nat'l Archives [355]

ABSTRACTS OF TAX / Allen County. Ohio. Auditor – 1878-82 – 1 – $32.50r – us Archival [978]

ABSTRACTS OF TAX / Putnam County. Ohio. Auditor – 1870-1875 – 1r – 1 – $32.50r – us Archival [324]

ABSTRACTS OF TAXES / Wood County. Ohio. Auditor – 1825-30 – 1r – 1 – $32.50r – us Archival [978]

ABSTRACTS OF THE FINANCIAL REPORTS / Massachusetts. Comptroller's Division – 1922-77. 56 fiches. (Harvard Law School Library Collection.) – 9 – 1.50f – us H.U. Law [324]

ABSTRACTS OF THE PAPERS PRINTED IN THE PHILOSOPHICAL TRANSACTIONS OF THE ROYAL SOCIETY – (Cont as: Proceedings of the Royal Society of London v7-75 1854/55-1904/05) – London. v1-6. 1800-1854 – 815mf – 9 – H-624/2 – ne IDC [100]

ABSTRACTS OF THE PROCEEDINGS OF THE LEGISLATIVE COUNCIL FOR THE NORTH-WESTERN PROVINCES AND OUDH, ... – Allahabad, 1887-1920. v1-13 – 323mf – 9 – I-79/2 – ne IDC [340]

ABSTRACTS OF THE RECORDS OF THE SOCIETY OF FRIENDS IN INDIANA / ed by Heiss, Willard – 6v 32mf – 9 – $55.00 – us A.G.L.L. [060]

ABSTRACTS OF WASHINGTON DONATION LAND CLAIMS, 1855-1902 / U.S. Bureau of Land Management – 1roll. M203. Printed guide – 1 – us Nat'l Archives [324]

ABSTRACTS OF WILLS OF CHATHAM COUNTY, 1773-1817 / LaLar & Wilson – Washington, DC, National Gen. Soc., 1963. Georgia Reel 3. (The Cox Library Collection) – 5 – us Americana [920]

ABSTRACTS OF WILLS PROVED IN 1625-1792 / Jamaica – British Museum ADD. Ms 34184. BRRAM – 1 – uk Microform Academic [972]

ABSTRACTS OF WORKING PAPERS IN ECONOMICS – New York. v1-6 1986-1990 1*; v7-18 1991-1998+* 1,5,9 – 1,5,9 – D17114 – us UMI [330]

ABSTRACTS OF WORLD MEDICINE – (Ceased publ) – London. v1-36 jan 1947-dec 1971 1; v45 jan-dec 1971 5 – 1,5 – D1365 – us UMI [610]

ABSTRACTS ON CRIME AND JUVENILE DELINQUENCY – Base collection with index 1968-75; annual updates with indexes 1976- – 769mf complete collection; 261mf base collection – 9 – $3230.00 complete collection to 1988; base collection $860.00 – us UMI [360]

ABSTRACTS ON CRIME AND JUVENILE DELINQUENCY – (Price includes hardbound User Indexes) – 1968-1985 + cumulative indexes – 9 – $2,700.00 set – 0-89941-411-7 – us Hein [360]

ABSTRACTS ON HYGIENE – (Cont by: Abstracts on Hygiene and Communicable Diseases. Former title: Bulletin of Hygiene) – London. v1-50 jan 1926-dec 1975* 1; v51-55 jan 1976-dec 1980 1,5,9 – 1,5,9 – inquire – D11151 – us UMI [610]

ABSTRACTS ON HYGIENE *see* ABSTRACTS ON HYGIENE AND COMMUNICABLE DISEASES

ABSTRACTS ON HYGIENE AND COMMUNICABLE DISEASES – (Cont: Abstracts on Hygiene) – London. v56-72. jan 1981-dec 1997+* – 1,5,9 – D11151.01 – us UMI [614]

ABSTRACTS ON HYGIENE AND COMMUNICABLE DISEASES *see* ABSTRACTS ON HYGIENE

ABSTRAKTE ARBEIT UND ABSTRAKTWERDEN DER KUNST / Fiebig, Wilfried – Berlin, 1974 – 4mf – DM90.00 – 3-89349-998-9 – gw Hänsel [700]

Abteilung neuere deutsche Literaturgeschichte *see* NEUE DEUTSCHE FORSCHUNGEN

ABTICS (ABSTRACT AND BOOK TITLE INDEX CARD SERVICE) – London. v1-66. 1960-71 – 5 – $9,933.00 set $150.50r – D40000 – us UMI [020]

Abu Dhabi. Abu Dhabi Fund for Arab Economic Development *see* FIRST ANNUAL REPORT 1974-1975

Abu Dhabi. Directorate General of Planning and Coordination *see* FIVE YEAR DEVELOPMENT PLAN, 1968-1972

Abu Dhabi. Planning Board *see*
- 1970 ANNUAL PROGRAMME
- 1971 ANNUAL PROGRAMME
- 1973 ANNUAL PROGRAMME

ABU TELFAN, ODER, DIE HEIMKEHR VOM MONDGEBIRGE : ROMAN / Raabe, Wilhelm Karl – Berlin: Aufbau-Verlag, 1961 – 1r – 1 – us U.W. Library [830]

Abubakar, H *see* TECHNIK CHOETBAH, TOENTOENAN NGARANG CHOETBAH DJOEM'AH, DENING M. 'AFWAN SHD(JAVANESE OR ARABIC) SE-5290/1. 1947

Abudacnus, Jos. *see* HISTORIA JACOBITARUM

Abu-el-Fazl *see* AKBARNAMA

ABUFAR OU LA FAMILLE ARABE / Ducis – (French Theatre Series). Paris. Barba, an III. 1795 – 9 – fr Hachette [820]

Abulafia, T *see* GAN HA-MESHALIM VE-HA-HIDOT

ABULFEDAE ANNALES MUSLEMICI ARABICE ET LATINE / Reiskii, J J – Hafniae v1-5 1789-1794 – 112mf – 8 – Dfl392.00 – ne Slangenburg [030]

ABUNDANT LIFE MAGAZINE – Tulsa. v29-33 jan 1975-dec 1979 1; v29 1975. v30-33 jan 1976-dec 1979* 5,9 – $83.70y – D10336 – us UMI [240]

ABU-NUAS : ORGAO CRITICO ARABE – Manaus, Amazonas. 1 Nov-Dez 1915; Jan-Ago, Out 1916 – 1,5,6 – bl Biblioteca [072]

ABUS DE L'ANCIENNE EDUCATION, DEVOILES ET REFORMES PAR LES PROGRES DE LA RAISON / Degranthe – Paris. Desseine. 1790. 6748 – 9 – fr Hachette [944]
Abushady, M *see* CENTRAL BANKING IN EGYPT
ABUZAR OU LA FAMILLE EXTRAVAGANTE / Barre, Radet et Desfontaines – (French Theatre Series). Paris. "Au Theatre de Vaudeville," an V. 1795 – 9 – fr Hachette [820]
ABWA BULLETIN *see* ABCA BULLETIN
DIE ABWEGE, ODER IRRUNGEN UND VERSUCHUNGEN, GUTWILLIGER UND FROMMER MENSCHEN, AUS BEYSTIMMUNG DES GOTTSELIGEN ALTERTHUMS ANGEMERCKET / Arnold, Gottfried – 1708 – 1 – us A.T.L.A. [240]
DIE ABWEHR – Warnsdorf, may 1 1926-apr 21 1929 – 7r – 1 – gw Mikrofilm [072]
ABWEHR-BLAETTER / Verein zur Abwehr des Antisemitismus – (Lacks: n1,13) – 1892-1906. v2-16. – 3r – 1 – us Ross [270]
ABYDOS (MEES VOL 22) : PART 1 / Flinders Petrie, W M – London, 1902 – 9mf – 8 – Dfl32.00 – ne Slangenburg [930]
ABYDOS (MEES VOL 24) : PART 2 / Flinders Petrie, W M – London, 1903 – 8mf – 8 – Dfl30.00 – ne Slangenburg [930]
ABYDOS (MEES VOL 25) : PART 3 / Ayrton, Edward R et al – London, 1904 – 9mf – 8 – Dfl32.00 – ne Slangenburg [930]
Abykeeva, A T *see* ZEMELNOE PRAVO V PERVYI GOD SOVETSKOI VLASTI (1917-18)
THE ABYSSINIAN CHURCH / Dowling, Theodore Edward – London: Cope & Fenwick, [1909?] – 1mf – us A.T.L.A. [240]
ABYSSINIAN SCRAPBOOKS : COMPRISED OF CLIPPINGS AND PHOTOGRAPHS RELATING TO HIS DIPLOMATIC MISSION TO ETHIOPIA IN 1903-1904 / Skinner, Robert Peet – Annapolis, MD: US Naval Academy Library, 1963 – 9 – us Res Libr [960]
ABYSSINIE / Desvergers, Noel – Paris, Firmin Didot Freres. 1847 – 9 – 5.00 – fr Orientalistes [960]
L'ABYSSINIE ET LES ITALIENS / Castonnet des Fosses, Henri – Paris: P Tequi, 1897 – 1 – us Res Libr [960]
ABZ : ARBEIT IN BILD UND ZEIT – Berlin, 1933 n1-19 – 1 – Dist. gw Mikrofilm – gw Misc Inst [072]
A/C FLYER – New York, 1972-94*; 1995-97+ – 1 – D18208 – us UMI [073]
AC POLITIK / Communist Party. Indonesia – Djakarta. SE-1255 1. 1958 – 9 – ne IDC [335]
AC SPARKLER – Flint. Mich. 1943- – 1 – us UMI [071]
A.C. WILLIAMS PAPERS *see* WILLIAMS, A.C., PAPERS, MS 593
ACA BULLETIN / Association for Communication Administration – (Cont: Bulletin of the Departments & Administrators in Speech Communication. Cont by: JACA – Journal of the Association of Communication Administration) – Annandale. r13-20. 1975-76*; r21-82. aug 1977-oct 1992 1; r21-24. aug 1977-apr 1978*; r25-82. aug 1978-oct 1992 5; r21-82. aug 1977-oct 1992 9 – inquire – us UMI [410]
ACA JOURNAL – Scottsdale. v1-3 Aut 1992-Win 1995*. v4-6 Spr 1995-Win 1998+ – 1,5,9 – D19586 – us UMI [073]
ACA JOURNAL OF CHIROPRACTIC / American Chiropractic Association – v1- 1963- 1; v12-1975- 5,6,9 – us UMI [610]
ACA JOURNAL OF CHIROPRACTIC / American Journal of Chiropractic – (Cont by: Journal of chiropractic) – Des Moines. v1-18 1964-dec 1981 1*; v12-18 jan 1975-dec 1981 5,9 – 1,5,9 – D10579 – us UMI [615]
ACA NEWS – (Absorbed: Legislative Scene, and: Resources, Sep 1992) – Scottsdale. v1-35 1969-92* 1; v36-37 jan 1993-dec 1994*. v38-40 jan 1995-dec 1997+ 1,5,9 – 1,5,9 – D18675 – us UMI [073]
ACADEME – (Absorbed by: Academe) – Washington. v1-12 jan 1967-dec 1978 1; v12 1978* 5,9 – 1,5,9 – $40.80y – D6517 – us UMI [370]
ACADEME / Association of University Professors – (Cont: AAUP Bulletin n974. Absorbed: Academe 1979 n6517) – Washinton. v65-83. feb 1979-1997+ – 1,5,9 – D974.01 – us UMI [370]
ACADEMIA – Djakarta. (incomplete) SE-447 1. 1948-1952 – 9 – ne IDC [073]
Academia das Sciencias de Lisboa *see* MEMORIAS
Academia de Bellas Artes de San Fernando *see* HOMENAJE A EUGENIO HERMOSO
Academia de la Historia. Madrid *see*
- BOLETIN
- MEMORIAL HISTORICO ESPANA9OL
- MEMORIAL HISTORICO ESPANOL

Academia de la Lengua *see*
- DICCIONARIO DE LA LENGUA CASTELLANA. TOMO 1
- DICCIONARIO DE LA LENGUA CASTELLANA. TOMO 2
- DICCIONARIO DE LA LENGUA CASTELLANA. TOMO 3
- DICCIONARIO DE LA LENGUA CASTELLANA. TOMO 4
- DICCIONARIO DE LA LENGUA CASTELLANA. TOMO 5
- DICCIONARIO DE LA LENGUA CASTELLANA. TOMO 6

La Academia de Musica y Banda Municipal de Caceres *see* REGLAMENTO
Academia Espanola *see*
- COLECCION OBRAS PREMIADAS. OBRAS DE ELOCUENCIA
- COLECCION OBRAS PREMIADAS. OBRAS DE POESIA
- GRAMATICA DE LA LENGUA CASTELLANA
- ORTOGRAFIA

ACADEMIA MUSICO-POETICO BIPARTITA. ODER: HOHE SCHUEL DER MUSICALISCHEN COMPOSITION IN ZWEY THEIL EINGETHEILT / Murschhauser, F X. – P 732. 1721 – 9 – ne IDC [780]
Academia Portuhuesa da Historia *see* GUIA DE BIBLIOGRAFIA HISTORICA PORTUGUESA
ACADEMIA QUE SE CELEBRO EN BADAJOZ EN CASA DE DON MANUEL MENESES – 1684 – 9 – $1.50f – sp Bibl Santa Ana [946]
L'ACADEMIA TODESCA... / Sandrart, J von – Nuernberg, Frankfurt, 1675-1679 – 2v – 9 – ne IDC [700]
ACADEMIAE CAESAREO-LEOPOLDINAE NATURAE CURIOSORUM EPHEMERIDES... – Francofurti, 1712-1772. v1-10 – 84mf – 9 – H-569/2 – ne IDC [520]
Academiae Scientiarum Fennicae *see* ANNALES MATHEMATICA
Academia...Valencia. Academia Socialista Preparatoria para el Ingreso en las Escuelas Populares de Guerra *see* CIRCULAR DE LA AGRUPACION SOCIALISTA DE VALENCIA
ACADEMIC CURRICULUM, OFFICER'S GENERAL EDUCATION OF THE A.M.N / Magelang Indonesia. Akademi Militer Nasional – (National Military Academy). SE-2211 1. Academic year 1958-1959 – 9 – ne IDC [370]
ACADEMIC EMERGENCY MEDICINE – Philadelphia. v1-4. jan 1994-1997+* – 1,5,9 – D21605 – us UMI [610]
ACADEMIC FREEDOM UNDER ISRAELI MILITARY OCCUPATION – 1984 – sz I.C.J. [320]
THE ACADEMIC INN – Leaflet, 1986. 1p – 9 – 1.00f – at Libertarian Micro [320]
ACADEMIC MEDICINE – (Cont: Journal of Medical Education) – Philadelphia. v64-72. jan 1989-dec 1997+ – 1,5,9 – D171.01 – us UMI [610]
ACADEMIC MONTHLY = HSUEH SHU YUEH PAO – v3 no 1-10. Feb-Nov 1899 (incomplete) – 1r – 1 – ATLA S0296K – us A.T.L.A. [073]
ACADEMIC PERFORMANCE, ATTENDANCE, AND SCHEDULE RIGOR OF EXTRACURRICULAR PARTICIPANTS AND NONPARTICIPANTS / Patranella, Kenneth W – 1987 – 2mf – 9 – $8.00 – us Microform Publ [370]
ACADEMIC PSYCHIATRY – (Cont: Journal of Psychiatric Education) – Washington. v13-21. Spr 1989-Win 1997+ – 1,5*,9 – D11182.01 – us UMI [616]
ACADEMIC QUESTIONS : AQ – New Brunswick. v1-9. Win 1987-Fal 1998+ – 1,5*,9 – D16937 – us UMI [073]
ACADEMIC THERAPY – (Cont by: Intervention in School and Clinic n6344:01. Former title: Academic Therapy Quarterly (Fall 1965-Sum 1968)) – San Rafael. v1-25 fall 1965-may 1990 1; v7-25 fall 1971-may 1990 5; v11-25 fall 1975-may 1990 9 – 1,5,9 – inquire – D6344 – us UMI [150]
ACADEMIC THERAPY QUARTERLY *see* ACADEMIC THERAPY
ACADEMICIAN – (Ceased publ) – New York. v1. feb 1818-jan 1820 – 1 – D3533 – us UMI [073]
O ACADEMICO – Manoas, Amazonas. 28 Set-Dez 1926; Jan-Jun, Set-Out 1927; Fev, Set 1928 – 1,5,6 – bl Biblioteca [072]
O ACADEMICO : PERIODICO DEDICADO A MEDICINA E A LITERATURA – [s.l.]. 15 Ago 1872 – 1,5,6 – bl Biblioteca [072]
O ACADEMICO : PERIODICO SCIENTIFICO E LITTERARIO – [s.l.]. Maio, Ago 1853 – 1,5,6 – bl Biblioteca [072]
Academie de Dijon *see* MEMOIRES DE L'ACADEMIE DE DIJON
L'ACADEMIE DE L'ART POETIQUE / Deimier, P de – 1610 – 9 – fr I.C.S. [440]
Academie de Musique de Quebec *see* REGLEMENTS ET CONSTITUTION
Academie de St. Augustin *see* COMPTE RENDU DE LA DISTRIBUTION DES PRIX ET DE LA PRESENTATION D'UNE MEDAILLE D'HONNEUR OFFERTE PAR S.E. LE GOUVERNEUR GENERAL ET LA PRINCESSE LOUISE AUX ELEVES.
Academie des inscriptions et belles lettres, Paris *see* RECUEIL DES HISTORIENS DES GAULES ET DE LA FRANCE
Academie des Inscriptions et Belles-Lettres de Paris *see* REPERTOIRE D'EPIGRAPHIE SEMITIQUE
Academie des Inscriptions et Belles-Lettres. Paris. Commission de la Fondation Piot *see* MONUMENTS ET MEMOIRES
Academie des Sciences, Belles-lettres et arts. Besancon *see* PROCES-VERBAUX ET MEMOIRES
Academie des Sciences d'Outre-Mer *see* COMPTES RENDUS
Academie des Sciences, Inscriptions et Belles-Lettres de Toulouse *see* MEMOIRES
Academie des Sciences Morales et Politiques *see* LE SUFFRAGE DES FEMMES
Academie des Sciences. Paris *see*
- COMPTES RENDUS HEBDOMADAIRES DES SEANCES
- COMPTES RENDUS-SERIE A: SCIENCES MATHEMATIQUES
- COMPTES RENDUS-SERIE B: SCIENCES PHYSIQUES
- COMPTES RENDUS-SERIE C: SCIENCES CHIMIQUES
- COMPTES RENDUS-SERIE D: SCIENCES NATURELLES
- HISTOIRE DE L'ACADEMIE ROYALE DES SCIENCES...AVEC LES MEMOIRES DE MATHEMATIQUE & DE PHYSIQUE...TIRES DES REGISTRES DE CETTE ACADEMIE
- MEMOIRES DE L'ACADEMIE ROYALE DES SCIENCES
- MEMOIRES DE MATHEMATIQUE ET DE PHYSIQUE, PRESENTES A L'ACADEMIE ROYALE DES SCIENCES, PAR DIVERS SCAVANS, ET LUS DANS SES ASSEMBLEES
- THE PHILOSOPHICAL HISTORY AND MEMOIRES OF THE ROYAL ACADEMY OF SCIENCES AT PARIS

Academie des Sciences. Russie *see* COMPTES RENDUS
Academie Francaise *see* DICTIONNAIRE DE L'ACADEMIE
Academie Imperiale des Sciences. St. Petersburg *see* MELANGES ASIATIQUES TIRES DE BULLETIN HISTORICO-PHILOSOPHIQUE DE L'ACADEMIE IMPERIALE DES SCIENCES DE ST PETERSBOURG
Academie Nationale des Sciences, Arts et Belles-Lettres. Caen *see* MEMOIRES
THE ACADEMIE OF ELOQUENCE / Blount, Thomas – 1654. 247p. (English Linguistics Series 1500-1800) – 9 – us UMI [420]
Academie Polonaise Des Sciences *see*
- BULLETIN

Academie Royale des Sciences *see* DESCRIPTION DES ARTS ET METIERS
ACADEMIES OF SCIENCE PUBLICATIONS – 71 titles – 9 – ne IDC [500]
ACADEMY : LUTHERANS IN PROFESSION – (Cont: Lutheran Scholar) – v1-40. 1943-86 (complete) – 4r – 1 – ATLA S0732 – us A.T.L.A. [073]
ACADEMY *see* ACADEMY AND LITERATURE
THE ACADEMY – Pictou, N.S.: [s.n., 1884?-18– or 19–] – 9 – cn C.I.H.M. [370]
ACADEMY AND LITERATURE – (Former titles: Academy; Academy and Literature) – London. v1-90. oct 1869-sep 1916 – 1 – $3,828.50 – 69 – us UMI [900]
ACADEMY ARCHITECTURE AND ARCHITECTURAL REVIEW – (Ceased publ) – London. cum index 1-21; v1-62. 1889-1931 – 1 – D5896 – us UMI [720]
THE ACADEMY GOSSIP / Mount Allison Wesleyan Academy – Sackville, N.B.: Chignecto Post, [1871-18– or 19–] – 9 – cn C.I.H.M. [370]
THE ACADEMY OF ARMORY / Holme, Randle – 1688. 1146p. (English Linguistics Series, 1500-1800) – 9 – us UMI [920]
ACADEMY OF MANAGEMENT EXECUTIVE – (Cont by: Executive) – Mississippi. v1-3. feb 1987-nov 1989 – 1,5,9 – D16369 – us UMI [650]
ACADEMY OF MANAGEMENT EXECUTIVE – (Cont: Executive) – Briarcliff Manor. v7-11. may 1993-nov 1997+ – 1,5,9 – D16369.02 – us UMI [650]
ACADEMY OF MANAGEMENT JOURNAL – (Shipped yrly or qrtly. Former title: Journal of the Academy of Management. With Jan 1976 superseded in part by: Academy of Mangement Review) – Mississippi. v1-40 apr 1958-dec 1997+ 1; v13-40 mar 1970-dec 1997+ 5; v18-40 mar 1975-dec 1997+ 9 – 1,5,9 – D5393 – us UMI [650]
ACADEMY OF MANAGEMENT JOURNAL *see* ACADEMY OF MANAGEMENT REVIEW
ACADEMY OF MANAGEMENT REVIEW – (Supersedes in part: Academy of Management Journal) – Mississippi. v1-22 jan 1976-oct 1997+ 1,5; v2-22 jan 1977-oct 1997+ 9 – 1,5,9 – D10726 – us UMI [650]
ACADEMY OF MANGEMENT : BEST PAPERS PROCEEDINGS – (Cont: Proceedings, Academy of Managment) – Columbia. 1986-1997+ – 1,5,9 – D6576.01 – us UMI [650]
ACADEMY OF MANGEMENT REVIEW *see* ACADEMY OF MANAGEMENT JOURNAL
ACADEMY OF MARKETING SCIENCE : JOURNAL – (1984-1987 includes: Developments in Marketing Science) – Greenvale. v1-25 1973-1997+ 1,5; v3-25 1975-1997+ 9 – 1,5,9 – D10335 – us UMI [650]
Academy of Marketing Science *see* JOURNAL
ACADEMY OF NURSING OF THE PHILIPPINES – v1- 1966- – 1,5,6,9 – us UMI [073]
ACADEMY OF PARISH CHURCH : JOURNAL / Academy of Parish Clergy – (Superseded by: Sharing the Practice) – v1-5. Apr 1971-Aug 1975 (incomplete) – 1r – 1 – ATLA T0002 – us A.T.L.A. [240]
ACADEMY OF PARISH CLERGY *see* SHARING THE PRACTICE
Academy of Parish Clergy *see* ACADEMY OF PARISH CHURCH
Academy of Political Science *see* PROCEEDINGS
ACADEMY OF RELIGION AND PSYCHICAL RESEARCH : JOURNAL – v2-12. 1979-89 (complete) – 2r – 1 – ATLA S0841 – us A.T.L.A. [073]
Academy of Sciences of the USSR Section: Geochemistry *see* PROCEEDINGS
Academy of Sciences of the U.S.S.R. Section: Geological Sciences *see* PROCEEDINGS
ACADIA ATHENAEUM – (Cont by: Athenaeum (Wolfville, N.S.)) – Wolfville [N.S.]: Students of Acadia College, [1874-1961] v1 no 1 (Nov 1874-) – 9 – cn C.I.H.M. [370]
Acadia College. Halifax *see* JUBILEE...AND MEMORIAL EXERCISES
Acadia Provident Association *see* PROSPECTUS
ACADIAN RECORDER – Halifax, Canada. 1817-69 – 9r – 1 – $585.00 – cn Library Assoc [971]
ACADIAN RECORDER – Halifax, Canada. Jan 1913-Jun 1922 – 26r – 1 – uk British Libr Newspaper [072]
THE ACADIAN SCIENTIST – (Cont by: Canadian Science Monthly) – Wolfville, N.S.: Acadian Science Club, [1883?-1884] – 9 – cn C.I.H.M. [500]
THE ACADIAN SCIENTIST *see* THE CANADIAN SCIENCE MONTHLY
L'ACADIE LIBERALE – Meteghan, Nova Scotia. 18 oct 1890 – 1r – 1 – Can$25.00 – cn Can Microfilming [072]
L'ACADIE NOUVELLE – Caraquet, New Brunswick, CN. 1984- – 12r per yr – 1 – Can$55.00r – cn Commonwealth Micro [072]
L'ACADIEN – Moncton, Canada. 1913-26 – 6r – 1 – $390.00 – cn Library Assoc [971]
L'ACADIEN – Moncton, New Brunswick. v7 n86. 3 sep 1920 – 1r – 1 – Can$25.00 – cn Can Microfilming [072]
ACADIENSIS – Fredericton. v1- 1971- – 9 – Price varies – cn Micromedia [073]
ACADIENSIS – v1-8. 1901-Oct. 1908 – 1 – cn Precision [073]
ACANTHA – Choteau. Mont. 1904-1950; 1956-1959; 1966-74 – 1 – us UMI [071]

ACANTHA – Dupuyer. Mont. 1895-1904 – 1 – us UMI [071]

ACAO DIREITA – Rio de Janeiro, BL. 1946-1958 – 1r – $50.00 – R04165 – us Library Micro [320]

ACARI, MYRIPODA ET SCORPIONES HUCUSQUE IN ITALIA REPERTA / Berlese – Patavii, 1882-1903. 9v – 89mf – 9 – 784/2 – ne IDC [590]

THE ACARN-HOG ECONOMY OF THE OAK WOOD LANDS... / Parsons James, J – New York: American geographical Society, 1962 – 1 – sp Bibl Santa Ana [338]

ACC CURRENT JOURNAL REVIEW – New York. v1-3 nov 1992-94*. v4-6 1995-97+ – 1 – D42672 – us UMI [073]

ACC OUTLOOK / American Crafts Council – (Ceased publ. Former titles: ACC outlook (mar 1960-jul 1964); American Craft Council Outlook (1964-1969)) – New York. v19 Spr 1975-Spr 1976 – 1 – D9966 – us UMI [740]

ACC OUTLOOK *see* ACC OUTLOOK

Accademia del Cimento. Florence *see* ATTI E MEMORIE INEDITE E NOTIZIE ANEDDOTE DEI PROGRESSI DELLE SCIENZE IN TOSCANA...COMINCIANDO DA GALILEO GALILEI, FINO A FRANCESCO REDI ED A VINCENZO VIVIANI INCLUSIVE

Accademia delle scienze dell'Instituto di Bologna *see* DE BONONIENSI SCIENTIARUM ET ARTIUM INSTITUTO ATQUE ACADEMIA COMMENTARII

Accademia nazionale Luigi Cherubini di Musica. Lettere e Arti figurative *see* ATTI

Accademia Patavina di Scienze, Lettere ed Arti *see* SAGGI SCIENTIFICI E LETTERARI DELL' ACCADEMIA DI PADOVA

Accademia Romana di Archeologia. Rome *see* ATTI DELLA PONTIFICIA ACCADEMIA ROMANA DI ARCHEOLOGIA

ACCADEMIE E BIBLIOTECHE D'ILALIA – (Publication suspended 1943-1949) – Rome. v1-65 jul 1927-dec 1997+ 1; v38-65 jan 1970-dec 1997+* 5; v44-65 jan 1976-dec 1997+* 9 – 1,5,9 – D2147 – us UMI [370]

ACCAO COLONIAL – Porto: Accao colonial, jun 30 1930-jan 1934 – us Res Libr [072]

ACCAO NACIONAL – Lourenco Marques: [Accao Nacional de Mocambique, apr 5-aug 6, sep 11-24 1926 (reel 15); oct 1-8, nov 5-dec 3 1926 (reel 18) – us Res Libr [072]

ACCAO SOCIAL – Sao Joao del-Rei, Brazil. May-Jun 1918; May 1919 – 1 – bl Biblioteca [072]

ACCEDENCE / Stanbridge, John – ca. 1496. 36p. (English Linguistics Series 1500-1800) – 9 – us UMI [400]

ACCEDENCE COMMENC'T GRAMMAR / Milton, John – 1669. 72p. (English Linguistics Series 1500-1800) – 9 – us UMI [450]

ACCENT – Devon. n1-84 jan 1976-dec 1982 1,5. n8-22 jan 1993-dec 1997+ 1; n8-11 jan 1983-dec 1986. n12-19 jan 1987-dec 1994*. n20-22 jan 1995-dec 1997+ 5; n1-48 jan 1976-dec 1979*. n49-60 1980. n61-84 jan 1981-dec 1982*. n8-22 jan 1983-dec 1997+ 9 – 1,5,9 – inquire – D11778 – us UMI [073]

ACCENT ON LIVING – Bloomington. v1-42 1956-spr 1998+ 1; v17-42 sum 1972-spr 1998+ 5; v19-42 sum 1974-spr 1998+ 9 – 1,5,9 – inquire – D7406 – us UMI [610]

ACCENT ON THE RIGHT / Read, Leonard E – 1968. 125p. Together with: Talking to Myself. 1970. 177p. 1 fiche (24x) – 9 – 1.00f – at Libertarian Micro [320]

ACCEPTANCE OF CESSIONS OF CERTAIN SAMOAN ISLANDS : REPORT OF THE SENATE COMMITTEE ON TERRITORIAL AND INSULAR POSSESSIONS / American Samoa. US Congress – 70th Congress 1st sess. Senate report no 984. n.p. 3 May 1928 – 1mf – 9 – $1.50 – LLMC 82-100C Title 33 – us L.L.M.C. [327]

ACCEPTANCES AND ORDER FOR COMMISSIONS IN THE RECORDS OF THE DEPARTMENT OF STATE / U.S. Department of State – 1789-1828. 2 rolls. T645 – 1 – us Nat'l Archives [975]

L'ACCES DES FRANCAIS DEVANT LES TRIBUNAUX ALLEMANDS ET LA CAUTION "JUDICATUM SOLVI" / Casteljau, X de – N.p., [1922] – 1mf – 1 – ILM-3924/1 – ne IDC [327]

ACCESS – (Cont: Online Data Access. Cont by: Access to Wang) – Austin. 1985-1988* – 1 – D19756.01 – us UMI [000]

ACCESS : SOME WESTERN MODELS OF COMMUNITY MEDIA – 1977 – 229p – 9 – 92-3-101432-3 – fr UNESCO [380]

ACCESS : TECHNOLOGY AND ACCESS TO COMMUNICATION MEDIA – 1975 – 44p – 9 – 92-3-101271-1 – fr UNESCO [000]

ACCESS – Washington. n1-182 jan 1975-jul 1985 1; n1-58 jan 1975-dec 1977*. n59-111 oct 1978-dec 1980. n112-182 jan 1981-jul 1985* 5; n1-46 jan 1975-dec 1976*. n47-182 jan 1977-jul 1985 9 – 1,5,9 – inquire – D11715 – us UMI [380]

ACCESS *see* ACCESS TO WANG

ACCESS CONTROL – (Cont: Access Control, Fence Industry. Cont by: Access Control & Security Systems Integration) – Atlanta. v31-38. sep 1988-jun 1995* – 1 – D7706.03 – us UMI [073]

ACCESS CONTROL *see*
- ACCESS CONTROL AND SECURITY SYSTEMS INTEGRATION
- ACCESS CONTROL, FENCE INDUSTRY

ACCESS CONTROL AND SECURITY SYSTEMS INTEGRATION – (Cont: Access Control) – Atlanta. v38-40. jul 1995-dec 1997+ – 1 – D7706.04 – us UMI [073]

ACCESS CONTROL AND SECURITY SYSTEMS INTEGRATION *see* ACCESS CONTROL

ACCESS CONTROL, FENCE INDUSTRY – (Cont: Fence Industry Access Control. Cont by: Access Control) – Atlanta. v30-31. aug 1987-aug 1988* – 1 – D7706.02 – us UMI [073]

ACCESS CONTROL, FENCE INDUSTRY *see* ACCESS CONTROL

ACCESS MAGAZINE – 1p flyer – 9 – 1.00f – at Libertarian Micro [320]

ACCESS TO WANG – (Cont: Access) – Austin. 1988-1994* 1; 1995-1997+ 1,5,9 – 1,5,9 – D19756.02 – us UMI [073]

ACCESS TO WANG *see* ACCESS

ACCESSIBLE FIELD SPORTS: THE EXPERIENCES OF A SPORTSMAN IN NORTH AMERICA / Gillmore, Parker – London: Chapman and Hall, 1869. 02321. (Pre-1900 Canadiana) – 9 – cn C.I.H.M. [790]

ACCESSOIREX 93 – (See also Sempex-Parapharmex-Accessoirex) – 1992. Microfiches C: Accessoires et Divers Vendus en Officine – 9 – FF491.00 – fr S.E.M.P. [610]

AN ACCIDENCE TO THE ENGLISH TONGUE / Jones, Hugh – 1724. 85p. (English Linguistics Series 1500-1800) – 9 – us UMI [420]

ACCIDENT – Pattee, University Park, PA. 1989 – 18p 1mf – 9 – $0.50f – us Lawrence Pub [720]

ACCIDENT ANALYSIS AND PREVENTION – Oxford. v1-29 1969-dec 1997+ 1,5; v1-29 1969-dec 1997+ 9 – 1,5,9 – inquire – D49000 – us UMI [073]

EL ACCIDENTE DE ABORDAJE / Gay de Montella, R – Barcelona, 1908 – 1mf – 1 – ILM-3327/1 – ne IDC [327]

EL ACCIDENTE DE TRABAJO EN LA HISTORIA Y EN LA REALIDAD ESPANOLA / Rodriguez Bautista, Ambrosio – Caceres: Tip. El Noticiero, 1950 – sp Bibl Santa Ana [331]

ACCION CHILENA – Santiago. v. 1-7. no. 1. Jan. 1934-Jan. 1938 – 1 – us NY Public [073]

LA ACCION DEL PODER EJECUTIVO DESDE EL 1. DE ABRIL DE 1947 HASTA EL 31 DE MARZO DE 1948 : ORDENADA CRONOLOGICAMENTE / Peron, Juan – Buenos Aires, 1948 – 1 – CSUXADH9367-B – us Hoover Inst Photo [320]

ACCION ECONOMICA : PLANES DE GOBIERNO DEL GENERAL JUAN D. PERON – Buenos Aires: Ediciones de la Liberacion: [distribuye, El Coloquio], 1st ed 1973 – 1 – CSUXAHZ5158-B – us Hoover Inst Photo [330]

ACCION EDUCATIVA DEL GOBIERNO FEDERAL DEL... / Mexico. Secretaria de Educacion Publica – Mexico: La Secretaria, [1952/54-1954/55] – us Res Libr [370]

Accion Regional Extremena *see* AREX. DECLARACION PROGRAMATICA

Accion Social Universitaria *see* REFORMA DE LA CONSTITUCION ARGENTINA

ACCIS GUIDE TO UNITED NATIONS INFORMATION SOURCES ON FOOD AND AGRICULTURE : ACCIS GUIDE TO UNITED NATIONS INFORMATION SOURCES NO 1 – 1987 – 133p – it F.A.O. [630]

Accoldi, B *see* LA GVERRA FATTA DA CHRISTIANI CONTRA BARBARI PER LA RICVPERATIO...

Accolti, B *see* ...DE BELLO A CHRISTIANIS CONTRA BARBAROS GESTO PRO CHRISTI SEPVLCHRO ET 4 DAEA RECVPERANDIS

ACCOMPLISHMENTS IN ONCOLOGY/ GENERAL MOTORS CANCER RESEARCH FOUNDATION – v1- . 1986- – 1,5,6,9 – us UMI [073]

ACCOMPLISSEMENT DES PROPHETIES... / Du Moulin, P – Sedan, 1624 – 5mf – 9 – CA-128/1 – ne IDC [240]

ACCORDS COMMERCIAUX CONCLUS PAR L'ALGERIE / Algeria – 1965. BNE-8601 1 – 9 – ne IDC [380]

ACCORDS PASSES ENTRE LA FRANCE ET L'ALGERIE DE JUILLET 1962 AU 31 DEC 1963 / France. Direction de la Documentation – 1964. BNE-8641 1 – 9 – ne IDC [944]

ACCOUNT, 1801-1838, V3-6, 8 / Marsden, G – (Coll title: The People Called Methodists, Phase 3: Primary Sources, 1801-1850) – 5mf – 9 – MP-676/1 – ne IDC [240]

ACCOUNT BOOK – 1890-95.Farm Manager. Mostly detailing expenses incurred in running a farm in Charleston County (SC). 1 fiche – 9 – us South Carolina Historical [978]

ACCOUNT BOOK / Aimar, C P – 1861-94.2 fiches – 9 – us South Carolina Historical [978]

ACCOUNT BOOK / Bluffton General Store. Bluffton, South Carolina – 1852-57.7 fiches – 9 – us South Carolina Historical [978]

ACCOUNT BOOK / Elfe, Thomas – 1768-75. 12 fiches – 9 – us South Carolina Historical [025]

ACCOUNT BOOK / Elliott, Juliet Georgiana – 1844-74. 3 fiches – 9 – us South Carolina Historical [025]

ACCOUNT BOOK / Ewing, Clymer and Co. Westport, Mo – 1839-40 – 1 – us KS Hist [025]

ACCOUNT BOOK / Grant, George – 1873-77 – 1 – us KS Hist [920]

ACCOUNT BOOK / Grinstead, William – 1850-1951 – 1 – us KS Hist [920]

ACCOUNT BOOK / Grinter, Moses – 1855-82 – 1 – us KS Hist [920]

ACCOUNT BOOK / Ottawa County. Ohio. Carroll Township. Township Treasurer – 1905-1923 – 1r – 1 – $32.50r – us Archival [324]

ACCOUNT BOOK / Putnam County. Ohio. Auditor – (Incomplete) – 1839-1874 – 1r – 1 – $32.50r – us Archival [324]

ACCOUNT BOOK / Roberts, Isaac N – 1857-78 – 1 – us KS Hist [978]

ACCOUNT BOOK / South Carolina. Militia. Fourth Brigade – 1861. 1 fiche – 9 – us South Carolina Historical [976]

ACCOUNT BOOK / Verdier, John Mark – 1785-91.54 fiches – 9 – us South Carolina Historical [978]

ACCOUNT BOOK, MS 1627 / Mishimens, Isaac – 1833-47 – 1r – 1 – us Western Res [978]

ACCOUNT BOOK OF ORDERS ISSUED / Ottawa County. Ohio. Carroll Township. Township Clerk – 1878-1893 – 1r – 1 – $32.50r – us Archival [324]

ACCOUNT BOOKS / Krall, William – 1900-1925, Farm account books of William Krall, Atchison County, KS – 1 – us KS Hist [380]

ACCOUNT BOOKS / Ottawa County. Ohio. Carroll Township. Board of Trustees – 1859-1893 – 1r – 1 – $32.50r – us Archival [324]

ACCOUNT BOOKS / Ottawa County. Ohio. Carroll Township. Township Clerk – 1905-1927 – 2r – 1 – $32.50r – us Archival [324]

ACCOUNT BOOKS AND MISCELLANEOUS PAPERS / Harrouff, George – (Diary. 1872-1944. 1) – 1874-1944 – 1 – us KS Hist [920]

ACCOUNT BOOKS, MS 1880 / Jackson, Andrew 2 – 1845-77 – 1r – 1 – us Western Res [920]

ACCOUNT BOOKS OF HIS EXPENSES ABROAD / Coke, T – 1712-18; 1714-18. Holkham mss. 733, 734. Holkham Hall, Norfolk, England – 1 – uk Microform Academic [025]

ACCOUNT, GUIDE AND FORM BOOK FOR ADMINISTRATORS AND EXECUTORS IN THE STATE OF OHIO / Gale, John T – Columbus, O.: Ruggles-Gale Co., 1895. 72,51p. LL-18 – 1 – us L of C Photodup [340]

AN ACCOUNT OF A LATE RIOT AT EXETER / Cennick, J – London, 1745 – 1mf – 9 – MP-320/1 – ne IDC [240]

ACCOUNT OF A VOYAGE FOR THE DISCOVERY OF A NORTHWEST PASSAGE / Drage – by the Clerk of California. BN 194 2. v. 1-2. 1748-1749 – 8 – ne IDC [910]

ACCOUNT OF A VOYAGE OF DISCOVERY OF THE NORTHEAST OF SIBERIA / Sarytchew, G – BN 381 2. 1806-07 – 8 – ne IDC [910]

AN ACCOUNT OF AN EMBASSY TO THE COURT OF THE TESHOO LAMA, IN TIBET; ... / Turner, S – London, 1800 – 10mf – 9 – ne IDC [610]

ACCOUNT OF COUNTY OF CUMBERLAND / Denton, John – 17th cent. Holkham ms. 760. Holkham Hall, Norfolk, England – 1 – uk Microform Academic [941]

AN ACCOUNT OF DISTEMPERS INCIDENT TO SEAFARING PEOPLE / Cockburn, W – M 327. 1696. m – 9 – ne IDC [610]

AN ACCOUNT OF INDIAN SERPENTS / Russell, P – Z 288 2. 2 v. 1796-1801 – 8 – ne IDC [590]

ACCOUNT OF MARRIAGES SOLEMNIZED BY TOLAVER ROBERTSON SINCE OCT 1842 – 1 – 5.00 – us Baptist [240]

ACCOUNT OF MARRIAGES SOLEMNIZED BY TOLAVER ROBERTSON SINCE OCTOBER 1842, AN / Robertson, Tolaver – South Carolina. 34p – 1 – $5.00 – us Baptist [306]

AN ACCOUNT OF SOUTH-WEST BARBARY: CONTAINING WHAT IS MOST REMARKABLE IN THE TERRITORIES OF THE KING OF FEZ AND MOROCCO / Ockley, Simon – London, 1713. SEM105P554 – 3mf – 9 – Can$6.75 – cn Bibl Nat [960]

AN ACCOUNT OF THE AMERICAN BAPTIST MISSION TO THE BURMAN EMPIRE / Judson, A H – London, 1823 – 4mf – 9 – ne IDC [950]

ACCOUNT OF THE ANCIENT FLEMISH SCHOOL OF PAINTING / Guicciardini, L – O-989 1. 1795 – 9 – ne IDC [750]

AN ACCOUNT OF THE BILIOUS REMITTING YELLOW FEVER / Rush, B – M 139 2. 1794 – 8 – ne IDC [610]

AN ACCOUNT OF THE CANADIAN PROTEST AGAINST THE INTRODUCTION INTO CANADA OF MUSICAL EXAMINATIONS BY OUTSIDE MUSICAL EXAMINING BODIES / Canadian Protesting Committee – Ed., comp. and publ. by order of the Canadian Protesting Committee. Toronto, 1899. 00443. (Pre-1900 Canadiana) – 9 – cn C.I.H.M. [780]

AN ACCOUNT OF THE CONQUEST OF GUATEMALA IN 1524 / Alvarado, Pedro de; ed by Mackie, Sedley J – New York: The Cortes Society, 1924 – 1 – sp Bibl Santa Ana [972]

AN ACCOUNT OF THE CRUSTACAE OF NORWAY / Sars, G O – 1249 2. v. 1-8. 1895-1921 – 8 – ne IDC [590]

AN ACCOUNT OF THE DANES AND NORWEGIANS IN ENGLAND.. / Worsaae, Jens Jakob Asmussen – London: J. Murray, 1852.xxiii,359p. Illus. 1 reel. 1272 – 1 – us U.W. Library [941]

AN ACCOUNT OF THE DISCOVERIES OF THE PORTUGUESE IN THE INTERIOR OF ANGOLA AND MOZAMBIQUE : FROM ORIGINAL MANUSCRIPTS: TO WHICH IS ADDED A NOTE BY THE AUTHOR, ON A GEOGRAPHICAL ERROR OF MUNGO PARK IN HIS LAST JOURNAL INTO THE INTERIOR OF AFRICA / Bowditch, Thomas Edward – London: J Booth, 1824 – 1 – us Res Libr [910]

AN ACCOUNT OF THE DISTRICTS OF BIHAR AND PATNA IN 1811-1812 / Buchanan, Francis Hamilton – Printed from Buchanan mss. in the India Office Library. 2v. 1 illus. fold. map, fold. plan, tables – 1 – us U.W. Library [950]

AN ACCOUNT OF THE EMPIRE OF CHINA / Fernandez Navarette, D – London. v1. 1704 – 10mf – 9 – ne IDC [910]

AN ACCOUNT OF THE EMPIRE OF CHINA... / Escalante, B de – London. v2. 1745 – 2mf – 9 – ne IDC [910]

AN ACCOUNT OF THE EXCAVATIONS AT TELL ATCHANA / Woolley, Leonard – Oxford, 1955 – 9 – $18.00 – us I.R.C. [930]

AN ACCOUNT OF THE EXPENDITURE OF THE OFFICE AND ESTABLISHMENT OF LORD GOSFORD, AS GOVERNOR GENERAL AND COMMISSIONER IN CANADA, FOR ONE YEAR – [London, England: s.n., 1838]. SEM105P1391 – 1mf – 9 – Can$2.25 – cn Bibl Nat [336]

ACCOUNT OF THE FLOWERING PLANTS, FERNS AND ALLIES OF HARLESTON / Galpin, F W – London and Harleston. 1888. B-7188 2 – 8 – ne IDC [580]
AN ACCOUNT OF THE FOXGLOVE, AND SOME OF ITS MEDICAL USES / Withering, W – M 245. 1785 – 9 – ne IDC [615]
AN ACCOUNT OF THE GOLD COAST OF AFRICA / Meredith, H – 1812 – 7 – uk Microform Academic [330]
AN ACCOUNT OF THE ISLAND OF CEYLON / Percival, R – Z-287 2. 1803 – 8 – ne IDC [910]
AN ACCOUNT OF THE KURNOOL DISTRICT / Benson, C – Madras. 1889. BI-150-19 2 – 8 – ne IDC [950]
ACCOUNT OF THE LIFE AND WRITINGS OF JAMES BRUCE : AUTHOR OF TRAVELS TO DISCOVER THE SOURCE OF THE NILE, IN THE YEARS 1768-1773 / Murray, Alexander – Edinburgh: A Constable & Co [etc], 1808 – us Res Libr [910]
AN ACCOUNT OF THE LIFE AND WRITINGS OF S. IRENAEUS, BISHOP OF LYONS AND MARTYR : INTENDED TO ILLUSTRATE THE DOCTRINE, DISCIPLINE, PRACTICES, AND HISTORY OF THE CHURCH, AND THE TENETS AND PRACTICES OF THE GNOSTIC HERETICS, DURING THE SECOND CENTURY / Beaven, James – London: Rivington, 1841 – 1mf – us A.T.L.A. [240]
AN ACCOUNT OF THE LIFE OF DR. WILLIAM AUGUSTUS CARLETON / Hayatt, Alice Nelson – 1905-80. Apostle to the West – 1 – $5.00 – us Baptist [240]
AN ACCOUNT OF THE LIVES AND WORKS OF THE MOST EMINENT SPANISH PAINTERS, SCULPTORS AND ARCHITECTS / Palomino, A A – O-1060 1. 1739 – 2mf – 9 – ne IDC [920]
AN ACCOUNT OF THE MUSICAL PERFORMANCES IN WESTMINSTER ABBEY, AND THE PANTHEON / Burney, Charles – 1785 – 9 – us Sibley [780]
AN ACCOUNT OF THE MUSICAL PERFORMANCES IN WESTMINSTER-ABBEY AND THE PANTHEON / Burney, Charles – P 649. 1785 – 9 – ne IDC [780]
AN ACCOUNT OF THE NATIVE AFRICANS IN THE NEIGHBOURHOOD OF SIERRA LEONE / Winterbottom, T – 2v. London. 1803. BA-357 2 – 8 – ne IDC [960]
ACCOUNT OF THE PROCEEDINGS OF H.M.S. ENTERPRISE FROM BEHRING STRAIT TO CAMBRIDGE BAY / Collinson, Richard – BN 167 2. 1855 – 8 – ne IDC [910]
AN ACCOUNT OF THE REMARKABLE MUSICAL TALENTS OF SEVERAL MEMBERS OF THE WESLEY FAMILY / ed by Winters, W – London: F. Davis, 1874 – 1mf – us A.T.L.A. [780]
AN ACCOUNT OF THE ROMANSH LANGUAGE / Planta, Joseph – 1776. 36p. (English Linguistics Series 1500-1800) – 9 – us UMI [440]
ACCOUNT OF THE RUSSIAN DISCOVERIES BETWEEN ASIA AND AMERICA, TO WHICH ARE ADDED THE CONQUEST OF SIBERIA AND / Coxe, D – 3rd ed. BN-177 2. 1787 – 8 – ne IDC [910]
ACCOUNT OF THE RUSSIAN DISCOVERIES BETWEEN ASIA AND AMERICA. TO WHICH ARE ADDED THE CONQUEST OF SIBERIA, AND THE HISTORY OF THE TRANSACTIONS AND COMMERCE BETWEEN RUSSIA AND CHINA / Coxe, William – 4th ed., enl. London: Cadell and Davies, 1803. xxiv,492p. maps – 1 – us U.W. Library [910]
AN ACCOUNT OF THE SORE THROAT ATTENDED WITH ULCERS / Fothergill, J – M-100.m 1748 – 9 – ne IDC [610]
AN ACCOUNT OF THE TONIC SOL-FA METHOD OF TEACHING TO SING / Curwen, John Spencer – London: Ward & Co, 1860 – 1 – us Sibley [780]
AN ACCOUNT OF THE TRIAL OF EDWARD SMYTH, LATE CURATE OF BALLYCULTER IN THE DIOCESE OF DOWN / Smyth, Edward Coffin – Dublin, 1777 – 2mf – 9 – MP-520/1 – ne IDC [240]
ACCOUNT OF THE T'U-JUHUN IN THE HISTORY OF THE CHIN DYNASTIE / Carroll, T D – (trans. and annotated). University of California Press. CDHT, nr. 4. 1953. BU-585 2 – 8 – ne IDC [950]
AN ACCOUNT OF TIMBUCTOO / Shabeeny, H A S – 1820 – 7 – uk Microform Academic [910]
AN ACCOUNT OF TIMBUCTOO AND HOUSA, TERRIT. IN THE INTERIOR OF AFRICA / Jackson, J G – London. 1820. Index. BA-143 2 – 8 – ne IDC [960]
ACCOUNT OF TOWNSHIP FUNDS / Paulding County. Ohio. Crane Township. Township Clerk – 1905-1930 – 2r – 1 – $32.50r – us Archival [324]
ACCOUNT RECORDS / Hancock County. Ohio. Biglick Township. Township Clerk – 1895-1928 – 1r – 1 – $32.50r – us Archival [324]
ACCOUNT RECORDS / Monroe County. Mich, Bedford Township. Township Treasurer – 1863-1958 – 2r – 1 – $32.50r – us Archival [324]
ACCOUNT RECORDS / Monroe County. Mich, Bedford Township. Township Treasurer – 1933-1959 – 1r – 1 – $32.50r – us Archival [324]
ACCOUNT RECORDS / Wood County. Ohio. Bradner, Village. Village Council – 1890-1898 – 1r – 1 – $32.50r – us Archival [324]
ACCOUNTABILITY IN RESEARCH : POLICIES AND QUALITY ASSURANCE / ed by Annau, Zoltan & Baldwin, Judith – 9,5,1 – us Gordon [574]
ACCOUNTANCY – 1958-to date – 1 – uk Microform Academic [650]
ACCOUNTANCY – (v1-34 1889-sep 1928 not available for filming. Former title: Incorporated Accountants' Journal (1889-1938)) – London. v35-120 oct 1928-dec 1997 1; v83-120 jan 1972-dec 1997+ 5; v88-120 jan 1977-dec 1997+ 9 – 1,5,9 – inquire – D2162 – us UMI [650]
ACCOUNTANCY AGE – London. v1-11 1969-dec 1997+ 1*; v6-11 jan 1975-dec 1997+ 5*,9* – 1,5,9 – D8880 – us UMI [650]
ACCOUNTANCY IRELAND – Dublin. 1969-1974 1*; v7-29 feb 1975-dec 1997+ 1,5*,9 – 1,5,9 – D8595 – us UMI [650]
ACCOUNTANT – London. n1-171 oct 1874-dec 1974*. n172-194 jan 1975-dec 1986. n5793-5928 jan 1987-dec 1997+ 1,5,9; n172-173 1975* 5. n174-194 jan 1976-dec 1986 5,9 – 1,5,9 – inquire – D10491 – us UMI [380]
ACCOUNTANT IN AUSTRALIA – (Cont by: Chartered Accountant in Australia) – Sydney. v1-3. dec 1930-jun 1933* – 1 – D18680 – us UMI [650]
ACCOUNTANTS DIGEST – Syracuse. v1-38 sep 1935-sep 1937*. v39.54 sep 1973-sep 1988 1; v40-54 sep 1974-sep 1988 5,9 – 1,5,9 – D10202 – us UMI [380]
ACCOUNTANTS' INDEX – (Annual cumulations offered. Cont by: Accounting and Tax Index n20133) – New York. 1950-87* 1; 1988-dec 1991* 1,5,9 – 1,5,9 – D12389 – us UMI [650]
ACCOUNTANTS' INDEX *see* ACCOUNTING AND TAX INDEX
ACCOUNTANT'S MAGAZINE – (Cont by: CA) – Edinburgh. v1-79 1897-dec 1975* 1; v80-97 jan 1976-may 1993 1,5,9 – 1,5,9 – D11283 – us UMI [650]
ACCOUNTANT'S MAGAZINE : EDINBURGH – London. v1-87. 1897-1984 – 1 – $3,000.00 – us Alper [330]
ACCOUNTANTS RECORD – 1974- – 9 – uk Microform Academic [380]
ACCOUNTANTS REVIEW-RECORD-COMPANY ACCOUNTANT – 1974-to date – 9 – uk Microform Academic [380]
ACCOUNTANTS WEEKLY – London. oct 1972-nov 1981* – 1 – D12799 – us UMI [650]
ACCOUNTING AND BUSINESS RESEARCH – 1970- – 9 – uk Microform Academic [650]
ACCOUNTING AND BUSINESS RESEARCH – London. v1-28 1970-aut 1998+ 1; v6-28 win 1975-aut 1998+ 5,9 – 1,5,9 – D9976 – us UMI [650]
ACCOUNTING AND FINANCE – (Cont: Accounting Education) – Clayton. v19-37 1979-Nov 1997+ 1*; v26-37 may 1986-nov 1997+ 5*,9 – 1,5,9 – D15002.02 – us UMI [650]
ACCOUNTING AND FINANCE *see* ACCOUNTING EDUCATION
ACCOUNTING AND TAX INDEX – (Cont: Accountants' Index) – Ann Arbor. v1-6. 1qr 1992-4qr 1997+* – 1,5,9 – D20133 – us UMI [650]
ACCOUNTING AND TAX INDEX *see* ACCOUNTANTS' INDEX
ACCOUNTING, AUDITING, AND ACCOUNTABILITY – (Cont by: Accounting, Auditing and Accountability Journal) – Bradford. v1. 1988* – 1 – D18876 – us UMI [650]
ACCOUNTING, AUDITING, AND ACCOUNTABILITY *see* ACCOUNTING, AUDITING, AND ACCOUNTABILITY JOURNAL
ACCOUNTING, AUDITING AND ACCOUNTABILITY JOURNAL *see* ACCOUNTING, AUDITING, AND ACCOUNTABILITY
ACCOUNTING, AUDITING, AND ACCOUNTABILITY JOURNAL – (All that is currently available. Cont: Accounting, Auditing, and Accountability) – Bradford. v2-3 1989-1990 1*; v4-8 1991-1995* 1,5,9 – 1,5,9 – D18876.01 – us UMI [650]
ACCOUNTING EDUCATION – (Cont: New Bulletin. Cont by: Accounting and Finance) – Clayton. 1970-1978* – 1 – D15002.01 – us UMI [650]
ACCOUNTING EDUCATION *see* ACCOUNTING AND FINANCE
ACCOUNTING EDUCATION NEWS – Sarasota. v1-18 1973-aug 1991 1*; oct 1991-1998+* 1,5,9 – 1,5,9 – D19047 – us UMI [650]
ACCOUNTING ENQUIRIES – Scarborough. 1991-1994* 1; aug 1995-1997+ 1,5,9 – 1,5,9 – D24857 – us UMI [650]
ACCOUNTING FORUM – New York. v1-43 1930-73*. v44-55 may 1974-jan 1986 1; v44 may 1974-dec 1974 5. v46-55 may 1976-jan 1986 5,9 – 1,5,9 – D10279 – us UMI [380]
ACCOUNTING HISTORIAN – (Cont by: Accounting Historians Journal) – v1-3. 1974-Fal 1976* – 1 – D18978 – us UMI [650]
ACCOUNTING HISTORIAN *see* ACCOUNTING HISTORIANS JOURNAL
ACCOUNTING HISTORIANS JOURNAL – (Cont: Accounting Historian) – v4-24. Spr 1977-dec 1997+ 1*; v18-24 jun 1991-dec 1997+* 5,9 – 1,5,9 – D18978.01 – us UMI [650]
ACCOUNTING HISTORIANS JOURNAL *see* ACCOUNTING HISTORIAN
ACCOUNTING HORIZONS – Sarasota. v1-11. mar 1987-dec1997+ 1,5*,9 – 1,5,9 – D16393 – us UMI [650]
ACCOUNTING, MANAGEMENT AND INFORMATION TECHNOLOGIES – New York. v1 1991. v2 1992*. v3-7 1993-97+ 1,5; v1-7 1991-97+ 9 – 1,5,9 – $382.50y – D49616 – us UMI [650]
ACCOUNTING, ORGANIZATIONS AND SOCIETY – Oxford. v1-22. 1976-97+ 1,5,9 – 1,5,9 – D49090 – us UMI [650]
ACCOUNTING RESEARCH – London.1948-57; 1970. Continued annually – 1 – £795.00 – uk World [380]
ACCOUNTING REVIEW – Sarasota. v1-47 mar 1926-oct 1972 1. v48-72 jan 1973-oct 1997+ 1,5; v53-72 jan 1978-oct 1997+ 9 – 1,5,9 – D8788 – us UMI [650]
ACCOUNTING SERIES / U.S. Securities and Exchange Commission – v. 1-140. 1937-1973 – 9 – us UMI [650]
ACCOUNTING SERIES RELEASES / U.S. Securities and Exchange Commission – nos 1-195. 6 Jan 1937-18 Jan 1973 (all publ) – 6mf – 9 – $9.00 – LLMC 84-359 – us L.L.M.C. [340]
ACCOUNTING TECHNOLOGY – (Cont: Computers in Accounting) – Boston. v9-13. feb 1993-dec 1997+ – 1,5*,9 – D16340.01 – us UMI [650]
ACCOUNTING TODAY – New York. v1-11 1987-dec 1997+ 1*; v5-11 jan 1991-dec 1997+* 5,9 – 1,5,9 – D18748 – us UMI [650]
ACCOUNTS / Fullwood, R H & Boyle, C – 1846-55, 1859-62. 10 fiches – 9 – us South Carolina Historical [025]
ACCOUNTS / Holkham Hall. Norfolk. England – 1789-1814 – 1 – uk Microform Academic [640]
ACCOUNTS / Myers, T A – 1882-98.2 fiches – 9 – us South Carolina Historical [978]
ACCOUNTS / Pickens, Francis W – 1860-61. 1 fiche – 9 – us South Carolina Historical [025]
ACCOUNTS / Pinckney, Thomas, Jr. – 1827-64.9 fiches – 9 – us South Carolina Historical [025]
ACCOUNTS AUDITED OF CLAIMS GROWING OUT OF THE REVOLUTION IN SOUTH CAROLINA / South Carolina. Department of Archives and History – 165r – 1 – $75.00r – Out-of-state orders: us Scholarly Res – us SC Archives [975]
ACCOUNTS OF BRITISH TRADE IN AMERICA / Blathwayt, William – 1682-1714 – 1 – 12.00 – us L of C Photodup [975]
ACCOUNTS OF CHEMICAL RESEARCH / American Chemical Society – Easton. v1-30. 1968-1997+ 1,5; v7-30 1974-1997+ 9 – 1,5,9 – D50000 – us UMI [650]
ACCOUNTS OF CHEMICAL RESEARCH – v1-1968- – 1,5,6,9 – us A.C.S. [073]
ACCOUNTS OF THE NET REVENUE AND EXPENDITURE OF THE PROVINCE OF LOWER CANADA, FOR THE YEARS 1825, 1826, AND 1827 – London: Printed by William Clowes, 1828. SEM105P397 – 1mf – 9 – Can$2.25 – cn Bibl Nat [336]
ACCOUNTS OF THE WORKS OF ART BOUGHT IN ROME / Brettingham, Matthew – 1746. Holkham ms. 744. Holkham Hall, Norfolk, England – 1 – uk Microform Academic [920]
ACCOUNTS RELATING TO THE FOREIGN TRADE AND NAVIGATION OF INDIA / India. Dept. of Commercial Intelligence and Statistics – Delhi. 1869 70-1908. (Scattered issues wanting) – 1 – 336.00 – us L of C Photodup [950]
ACCOUNTS RELATING TO TRADE AND NAVIGATION 1847/48-1964 – (Coll title: British Government Publications...1801-1977, Foreign Trade) – 125r – 1 (£15,875.00 foreign trade set of 220r + 824mf) – uk Chadwyck [380]
ACCP NEWS – Silver Spring, 1972-94* 1; 1995-97+ 1,5,9 – 1,5,9 – D22783 – us UMI [073]
THE ACCRA EVENING NEWS – (26 no. issued between Sept. 3, 1948 and Oct. 6, 1951 and v.8, no. 80) – Accra, Ghana: Kwame Nkrumah, 1948- – 1 – CSUX86-S93 – us Hoover Inst Photo [960]
Accra. Gold Coast Public Relations Dept *see* ACHIEVEMENT IN THE GOLD COAST
ACCREDITATION AND QUALITY ASSURANCE – Berlin. v1-2. 1996-1997+ – 1,5,9 – D22944 – us UMI [650]
ACCRINGTON ADVERTISER *see* ACCRINGTON WEEKLY ADVERTISER
ACCRINGTON WEEKLY ADVERTISER – England, 24 May 1889-26 Dec 1896; 4 Jan 1898-8 Dec 1905; 29 Apr-9 Dec 1911; 11 Apr, 23 May 1914; 30 Jan, 13 Feb, 27 Mar, 24 Apr, 1 May, 5 Jun 1915 – 11r – 1 – uk British Libr Newspaper [072]
ACCURACY OF A TREADMILL SCORING SYSTEM FOR PREDICTION OF CORONARY ARTERY DISEASE IN FEMALE SUBJECTS / Sheehan, Laurieanne & Sanborn, Charlotte F – 1991 – 1mf – 9 – $4.00 – us Microform Publ [612]
THE ACCURACY OF HEART RATE AS AN INDICATOR OF METABOLIC RATE WHILE PERFORMING STEP AEROBICS / Hartman, Greta B – University of North Carolina at Chapel Hill, 1995 – 1mf – 9 – $4.00 – PH1463 – us Microform Publ [612]
ACCURACY OF PERCEIVED HEAVINESS AND PERCEIVED JOINT PLACEMENT IN NORMAL AND INJURED SHOULDER JOINTS / Spoerl, J J – 1991 – 1mf – 9 – $4.00 – us Microform Publ [612]
THE ACCURACY OF VARIOUS INDIRECT DETERMINATIONS OF BODY COMPOSITION : COMPARISON WITH A MULTICOMPONENT CRITERION MODEL / Wegner, Michael S – Oregon State University, 1995 – 2mf – 9 – $8.00 – PE 3677 – us Microform Publ [617]
ACE *see* HANDBALL
ACE G-MAN – (Ceased publ) – New York. may 1936-apr 1943* – 1 – D8279 – us UMI [073]
ACE HIGH DETECTIVE – (Ceased publ) – New York. aug 1936-feb 1937* – 1 – D2894 – us UMI [073]
ACE HIGH WESTERN – (Ceased publ) – New York. aug 1936-feb 1937* – 1 – D8302 – us UMI [073]
Acedo, Federico *see*
- CORRESPONDIENTE EN CACERES DE LA R.A. DE LA HISTORIA
- DE LOS NOMBRES ATRIBUIDOS A TRUJILLO
- FALLECIMIENTO EN CACERES
- GUIA DE TRUJILLO

ACEHI JOURNAL – v18- 1992- – 9 – Can$20.00y – cn Micromedia [073]
Acemel, Isidoro *see* PARTIDA DE BAUTISMO DEL P. ANDRES DE GUADALUPE
ACEPHALE – no. 1. Paris. 24 juin 1936; no. double. 21 janv 1937; no. 3-4. juil 1937; no. 5. juin 1939; n.s., no. 1. 1938 – 1 – fr A.C.R.P.P. [073]
Acero, Liliana *see* TEXTILE WORKERS IN BRAZIL AND ARGENTINA
L'ACETYLENE – Paris, France. June 1901-June 1903 – 1r – 1 – uk British Libr Newspaper [072]

Aceuchal *see*
- FIESTAS PATRONALES DE NUESTRA SENORA LA SANTISIMA VIRGEN DE LA SOLEDAD
- MUSEO TAURINO DE MAHIZFLOR. CATALOGO GUIA 1950

Acevedo, Alfonso de *see*
- COMMENTARII JURIS CIVILIS.
- COMMENTARIORUM CONTINUATIO AD LEGES REGIAS.
- COMMENTARIORUM IURIS CIVILIS
- COMMENTARIORUM IURIS CIVILIS, TOMUS QUINTUS
- COMMENTARIORUM IURIS CIVILIS, TOMUS SECUNDUS
- COMMENTARIORUM IURIS CIVILIS, TOMUS SEXTUS
- COMMENTARIUM JURIS CIVILIS...SALMANTICAL, DIDACUSCUSIO, 1591
- CONSILIA...PERFECTA...PER JOHANNEM DE ACEVEDO
- OPERA DOCTORIS...IN HIS PANIAE REGIAS CONSTITUTIONES
- TRACTATUS DE CURIA PISANA..

Acevedo, Alonso de *see* CREACION DEL MUNDO

Acevedo, E O *see* CHANGES IN COGNITIVE APPRAISALS AND METABOLIC INDICES OF PHYSICAL EXERTION DURING AT TWO-HOUR RUN

THE ACH INDEX OF NUTRITIONAL STATUS / Franzen, Raymond H & Palmer, G T – 1934 – 1mf – 9 – $3.00 – us Microform Publ [612]

ACHA ACTION / American College Health Association – Rockville. v8 jul 1977-jun 1978; v10-11 jul 1979-may 1981 1; v8 jul 1977-jun 1978*; v10 jul 1979-jun 1980*; v11 jul 1980-may 1981 5; v8 jul 1977-jun 1978*; v10-11 jul 1979-may 1981* – 1,5,9 – $83.70y – D11548 – us UMI [610]

Acharius, E *see*
- LICHENOGRAPHIA UNIVERSALIS
- LICHENOGRAPHIAE SUECICAE PRODROMUS
- METHODUS QUA OMNES DETECTOS LICHENES SECUNDUM ORGANA
- SYNOPSIS METHODICA LICHENUM

Acharya Girjashankar Vallabhaji *see* HISTORICAL INSCRIPTIONS OF GUJARAT (FROM ANCIENT TIMES TO THE END OF THE VAGHELA DYNASTY)

Acharya, M P T *see* HOW LONG CAN CAPITALISM SURVIVE?

ACHAWAH : MAANDBLAD VAN DEN BOND VAN ISRAELIETISCHE GODSDIENSTONDERWIJZERS IN NEDERLAND – Amsterdam, 1894-1940. v1-45 – 71mf – 9 – J-261-4/1 – ne IDC [240]

ACH-CHIHEB – Constantine. 1925-27; 1929-aout 1939 – 1 – fr A.C.R.P.P. [073]

Achdut Haawoda Poale Zion/Histradut *see*
- DAVAR

ACHEEN, AND THE PORTS ON THE NORTH AND EAST COASTS OF SUMATRA / Anderson, J – London, 1840 – 3mf – 9 – ne IDC [950]

Achelis, Ernst Christian *see*
- DER DEKALOG ALS KATECHETISCHES LEHRSTUCK
- DIE ENTSTEHUNGSZEIT VON LUTHER'S GEISTLICHEN LIEDERN
- ZUR SYMBOLFRAGE

Achelis, Hans *see*
- ACTA SS. NEREI ET ACHILLEI (T.U.U. 1-11/2)
- DIE AELTESTEN QUELLEN DES ORIENTALISCHEN KIRCHENRECHTES (T.U.U. 1-6/4
- DAS CHRISTENTUM IN DEN ERSTEN DREI JAHRHUNDERTEN
- HIPPOLYTSSTUDIEN (T.U.U. 2-16/4)
- DIE MARTYROLOGIEN
- DAS SYMBOL DES FISCHES UND DIE FISCHDENKMAELER DER ROEMISCHEN KATAKOMBEN
- DIE SYRISCHE DIDASKALIA
- DIE SYRISCHE DIDASKALIA (T.U.U. 2-25/2)
- VIRGINES SUBINTRODUCTAE

Achelis, Johannes *see* DER RELIGIONSGESCHLICHTLICHE GEHALT DER PSALMEN

Achelis, T *see* DIE ENTWICKLUNG DER EHE

Achenbach, E *see* DER BRIEFLICHE UND TELEGRAPHISCHE VERTRAG...

ACHER- UND BUEHLER BOTE – (Cont: Acher Bote, -jun 1896; Buehler Bote (alternating with Acher Bote), -mar 1899. Cont by: Mittelbadischer Bote, jan 1 1936; Acher- und Buehler Bote, oct 29 1949. Today Bereichsausgabe der Badischen Neuesten Nachrichten, Karlsruhe) – Buehl, 1894, 1896-nov 1899, 1900-mar 31 1943, oct 29 1949-may 5 1955, 1988- – 1 – Inquire at Mikrofilmarchiv for details – gw Misc Inst [943]

ACHER- UND BUEHLER BOTE – Karlsruhe, DE. 1988- – 9r – 1 – gw Mikrofilm [072]

ACHER-BOTE *see* ACHER- UND BUEHLER BOTE

ACHERLAND : E PSALM / Wueest, Josef – Luzern: E Haag, 1928 – 1r – 1 – us U.W. Library [810]

Achermann, Franz Heinrich *see* DAEMONENTAENZER DER URZEIT

ACHER-RENCH-ZEITUNG – Oberkirch, Germany. 1 Jun 1983- – 1 – gw Mikrofilm [072]

Achery, D'Dom Luc *see* VETERUM ALIQUOT SCRIPTORUM. SPICILEGIUM

Acheson, Archibald Earl of Gosford *see* LOWER CANADA

Acheson, Dean *see* OFFICIAL CONVERSATIONS AND MEETINGS OF DEAN ACHESON, 1949-53

Acheson, Gambrell, Toomey, Acheson, Jr *see* TEXANS WHO'S WHO

Acheson, George *see* BIOLOGICAL STUDY OF THE TAP WATER IN THE SCHOOL OF PRACTICAL SCIENCE, TORONTO

ACHIEVEMENT – Sevenoaks. v41-64 1939-dec 1997+ 1*; v42-49 feb 1983-dec 1982 5*,9 – 1,5,9 – D1399 – us UMI [073]

ACHIEVEMENT IN THE GOLD COAST : ASPECTS OF DEVELOPMENT IN A BRITISH WEST AFRICAN TERRITORY / Accra. Gold Coast Public Relations Dept – Accra, 1951 – us Res Libr [960]

ACHIEVEMENT MOTIVATION AMONG ANGLO-AMERICAN AND HAWAIIAN PHYSICAL-ACTIVITY PARTICIPANTS : INDIVIDUAL DIFFERENCES AND SOCIAL CONTEXTUAL FACTORS / Hayashi, Carl T – 1994 – 3mf – $12.00 – us Microform Publ [150]

ACHIEVEMENTS OF THE FIRST OF SEPTEMBER REVOLUTION / Libya. Ministry of Information and Culture. Public Relations Department – 1972. Cover circle: First of September revolution: third anniversary. BNE-531 1 – 9 – ne IDC [956]

ACHILLE : DRAMME PER MUSICA IN TRE ATTI / Paer, F – Partition. 2v. Ms 180- – 1 – us Sibley [780]

ACHILLE ET POLIXENE / Colasse, Pascal – 1687 – 1 – us Sibley [780]

ACHIM VON ARNIM / Seidel, Ina – Stuttgart: J G Cotta, c1944 – 1r – 1 – us U.W. Library [430]

ACHIMER KREISBLATT – (Cont: Neues Wochenblatt fuer die Amtsbezirke Achim und Thedinghausen -apr 1885. Kreisblatt fuer den Kreis Achim, may 6 1885-1911) – Achim, 1878, 1880-81, 1883, 1885, mar 27 1888-90, 1892-nov 16 1929, 1930-dec 24 1944 (incomplete) – 54r – 1 – Dist. gw Mikrofilm – gw Misc Inst [943]

ACHIMER KURIER *see* WESER-KURIER

Achintre, A *see* LE FIGARO

Achintre, Auguste *see*
- APROPOS SIC: AU PUBLIC DU MONTREAL POUR LES ADIEUX DE LA COMPAGNIE
- CANTATE, LA CONFEDERATION
- PORTRAITS ET DOSSIERS PARLEMENTAIRES DU PREMIER PARLEMENT DE QUEBEC

Achleitner, Arthur *see*
- ANGELA
- BERGGESCHICHTEN
- DER FINANZER
- GRUENE BRUECHE
- HALALI!
- IM GRUENEN TANN
- IN DEN BERGEN, DA LAUERT DER WILDSCHUETZ
- IN TREUE FEST

Achleitner, Richard *see* DIE UNENTWEGTEN

ACHMAD. TIGA ORANG ANAK PETUALWNG / Saerozi, A M – SE 5130 1. 1963 – 9 – ne IDC [950]

ACHPER HEALTHY LIFESTYLES JOURNAL – (Cont: ACHPER National Journal) – Kingswood. v41-44 Aut 1994-Sum 1997+ 1,5,9; v41 Aut-Sum 1994* 5 – 1,5,9 – D10250.03 – us UMI [640]

ACHPER HEALTHY LIFESTYLES JOURNAL *see* ACHPER NATIONAL JOURNAL

ACHPER NATIONAL JOURNAL – (Cont: Australian Journal for Health, Physical Education and Recreation (AJHPER). Cont by: ACHPER Healthy Lifestyles Journal) – Kingswood. v99-138 Aut 1983-Sum 1992. v140 Aut-Sum 1993 – 1,5,9 – D10250.02 – us UMI [613]

ACHPER NATIONAL JOURNAL *see* ACHPER HEALTHY LIFESTYLES JOURNAL

Ach-San *see* TJARIOS NENG OMAH

ACHT MEMORIES BETREFFENDE JAVAANSE HOVEN, 1773-1803 – 17-22mf – 9 – ne IDC [950]

ACHT U. DREYSSIG SCHLUSZREDE / Prugner, N & Fridberger, B – 1524. BME-33 1 – 9 – ne IDC [240]

ACHT-EN-DERTIG KONSTIGE ZINNEBEELDEN : MET DICHTKUNDIGE UITLEGGINGEN VERRYKT, DOOR EEN LIEFHEBBER DER NEDERDUITSCHE POEZY – Amsterdam, 1737 – 1mf – 9 – ne IDC [430]

ACHT-UHR-ABENDBLATT *see* NATIONAL-ZEITUNG

DER ACHTUNDSECHZIGSTE PSALM:...UND NEUEREN AUSLEGER / Grill, Julius – Tuebingen: H. Laupp, 1883. 1 fiche – 9 – us A.T.L.A. [220]

EIN ACHTUNDVIERZIGER : ERLEBTES UND GEDACHTES / Wagner, Philipp – Brooklyn, NY: J Wagner, 1882 – 1r – 1 – us U.W. Library [920]

ACHTZEHEN SCHLUSZREDE / Fridberger, B – 1524. BME-34 1 – 9 – ne IDC [240]

ACHTZEHNHUNDERTNEUNUNDACHTZIG *see* 1889. DIE ERSTE ERHEBUNG DER BERGARBEITER. ZUR ERINNERUNG AN DEN GROSSEN BERGARBEITERSTREIK VOR 20 JAHREN

ACI (AMERICAN CONCRETE INSTITUTE) – All ACI standards and Technical Committee reports. Printed index. Updated every 60 days – 6,9 – us Info Handling [690]

ACI MATERIALS JOURNAL – (Cont in pt: Journal of the American Concrete Institute) – Detroit. v84-94. jan 1987-dec 1997+ – 1,5,9 – D16080 – us UMI [690]

ACI STRUCTURAL JOURNAL – (Cont in pt: Journal of the American Concrete Institute) – Detroit. v84-94. jan 1987-dec 1997+ – 1,5,9 – D16079 – us UMI [690]

ACIATE YEARBOOK – 1977- – 1 – us UMI [080]

ACID DEPOSITION AND THE ENVIRONMENT : THE INTERNATIONAL ANNUAL "GREY LITERATURE" ENVIRONMENTAL REFERENCE COLLECTION – (Part 1: The Basic set to 1988; Part 2: 1989 Update) – 410mf – 9 – us Primary [360]

ACID RAIN FICHE – Subscription service of current titles in acid rain information. 400 titles yearly from scholarly, scientific, industrial, technical and general periodicals from U.S. government documents and worldwide literature, conferences and organizations. Cross-indexed. Bi-monthly. Includes abstract journal. Merged with Environment Abstracts (Environment Fiche) from Jan 1991. Publ. ceased Nov./Dec. 1990 – 9 – $3,100.00 – us Bowker [574]

ACIK SOEZ – Kastamonu: Kastamonu Matbaasi, 1919-1928 – 9 – $20.00 – us MEDOC [956]

ACIS AND GALATEA AND ALEXANDER'E FEA VOLS 1 AND 4 FROM THE VOCAL WORKS OF HANDEL, WITH A SEPARATE ACCOMPANYMENT ARRANGED FOR THE ORGAN OR PIANOFORTE BY DR. JOHN CLARK / Handel, George Frederic – Philadelphia: G E Blake, 1823 – 1 – us Sibley [780]

ACIS ET GALATEE, PAROLES DE CAMPISTRON, MUSIQUE DE LULLI / Campistron, Jean-G de & Lulli, Jean-B – 17th c. – fr Armell [780]

ACIS ET GALATEE: PASTORALE HEROIQUE... / Lully, Jean-Baptiste – Paris: Christophe Ballard, 1686 – 1 – us Sibley [780]

ACIVILICAO CATOLICA E OS ERROS MODERNOS / Donoso Cortes, Juan Francisco – Petropolis: Editora Vozes limitada, 1960 – 1 – sp Bibl Santa Ana [240]

Acka, Sohuily Felix *see* DROIT ET SCIENCE DANS LA PENSEE DE HANS KELSEN (CONTRIBUTION A LA THEORIE PURE DU DROIT)

Ackelsberg, Martha A *see* THE PRACTICE OF ANARCHIST REVOLUTION: THE POSITION OF WOMEN IN SPANISH ANARCHIST COLLECTIVES

Acker, L van *see* OPERA OMNIA

Ackerman, George Everett *see*
- MAN
- MAN, A REVELATION OF GOD

Ackermann, Johannes *see* TOLSTOI UND DAS NEUE TESTAMENT

Ackermann, Richard *see* THE REPOSITORY OF ARTS, LITERATURE, FASHIONS AND MANUFACTURING

Ackermann, Werner *see* DIE COSMOPOLITISCHE UNION; THE COSMOPOLITAN UNION

Ackermann's Advertising & News Service Ltd *see* PAZIFISCHE RUNDSCHAU

ACKERMAN'S JUVENILE FORGET-ME-NOT – 1830-32 – 10mf – 9 – £85.00 – uk Chadwyck [800]

THE ACKNOWLEDGED DOCTRINES OF THE CHURCH OF ROME : BEING AN EXPOSITION OF ROMAN CATHOLIC DOCTRINES AS SET FORTH BY ESTEEMED DOCTORS OF THE SAID CHURCH, AND CONFIRMED BY REPEATED PUBLICATION, WITH THE SANCTION OF BISHOPS AND MINISTERS OF HER COMMUNION – London: Charles Gilpin, 1850 – 2mf – 9 – 0-8370-8325-7 – 1986-2325 – us A.T.L.A. [240]

THE ACKNOWLEDGMENT OF DEEDS, CONTAINING ALL THE STATUTES, TERRITORIAL AND STATE, OF ILLINOIS. / Hunt, John Eddy – 1st ed. Chicago, 1896. 206p. LL-611 – 1 – us L of C Photodup [340]

Ackworth, New Hampshire.First Baptist Church *see* RECORDS

Ackworth. Yorkshire *see* PARISH REGISTERS

Acland, Hugh Dyke *see* GLORIOUS RECOVERY BY THE VAUDOIS OF THEIR VALLEYS, FROM THE ORIGINAL WITH A COMPENDIOUS HISTORY OF THAT PEOPLE, PREVIOUS AND SUBSEQUENT TO THAT EVENT, BY HUGH DYKE ACLAND

ACLS NEWSLETTER / American Council of Learned Societies – Richmond. v1- 1949-1; v25- 1974- 5; v25- 1974- 9 – 1,5,9 – inquire – D9638 – us UMI [000]

ACLU *see*
- AMERICAN CIVIL LIBERTIES UNION RECORDS AND PUBLICATIONS, 1917-1990
- JOURNAL

ACM COMPUTING SURVEYS / Association for Computing Machinery – v3-. 1971-. Continues: Computing Surveys – 1,5,6,9 – us UMI [073]

ACM COMPUTING SURVEYS – (Cum index v3-9 1971-77. Cont: Computing Surveys) – Baltimore. v3-29. mar 1971-dec 1997+ – 1,5,9 – D12685.01 – us UMI [520]

ACM TRANSACTIONS ON COMPUTER SYSTEMS – Baltimore. v1-3 feb 1983-85* 1; v4-15 feb 1986-nov 1997+ 1,5,9 – 1,5,9 – D16265 – us UMI [000]

ACM TRANSACTIONS ON DATABASE SYSTEMS / Association for Computing Machinery – (D12686) – New York. v1-2 mar 1976-77* 1; v3-20 mar 1978-dec 1995; v21 mar-dec 1996; v22 mar-dec 1997 1,5,9 – 1,5,9 – inquire – D – us UMI [073]

ACM TRANSACTIONS ON GRAPHICS – New York. v1-4 jan 1982-85* 1; v5-16 jan 1986-oct 1997+ 1,5,9 – 1,5,9 – D16266 – us UMI [000]

ACM TRANSACTIONS ON INFORMATION SYSTEMS – (Cont: ACM Transactions on Office Information Systems) – New York. v7-15. jan 1989-oct 1997+ – 1,5,9 – D16267.01 – us UMI [000]

ACM TRANSACTIONS ON INFORMATION SYSTEMS *see* ACM TRANSACTIONS ON OFFICE INFORMATION SYSTEMS

ACM TRANSACTIONS ON MATHEMATICAL SOFTWARE / Association for Computing Machinery – (Only subsc to the paper copy can purchase the latest 2 complete publ yrs) – New York. v1-3 mar 1975-77* 1; v4-21 mar 1978-dec 1995; v22 mar-dec 1996; v23 mar-dec 1997 1,5,9 – 1,5,9 – inquire – D12687 – us UMI [073]

ACM TRANSACTIONS ON OFFICE INFORMATION SYSTEMS – (Cont by: ACM Transactions on Information Systems) – New York. v1-3 jan 1983-85* 1; v4-6 jan 1986-oct 1988 1,5,9 – 1,5,9 – D16267 – us UMI [000]

ACM TRANSACTIONS ON OFFICE INFORMATION SYSTEMS *see* ACM TRANSACTIONS ON INFORMATION SYSTEMS

ACM TRANSACTIONS ON PROGRAMMING LANGUAGES AND SYSTEMS – New York. v1-7 jul 1979-86* 1; v8-19 jan 1986-nov 1997 1,5,9 – 1,5,9 – D16268 – us UMI [000]

ACOG CURRENT JOURNAL REVIEW – New York. v1-6 1987-92* 1; v7-11 1993-97+ 1,5,9 – 1,5,9 – D42749 – us UMI [073]

Acomb. Yorkshire *see* PARISH REGISTERS

Acominati, Nicetae *see* HISTORIA (CBH 13)

ACONTECEU : ESPECIAL / Centro Ecumenico de Documentacao e Informacao. Rio de Janeiro – (Suppl to: Aconteceu. Filmed together n202-289) – Rio de Janeiro: CEDI, n10 12-16 apr 1982, apr 1983-1986 – us Res Libr [073]

ACORDS DEL PLE EXTRAORDINARI DEL COMITE NACIONAL DE LA UNION GENERAL DE TRABAJADORES – Valencia, 27-30 d'octubre del 1937. (Union General de Trabajadores de Espana.) Barcelona, 1937. Fiche W 701. (Blodgett Collection of Spanish Civil War Pamphlets) – 9 – us H.U. College Libr [946]

ACORN – Oakland. Iowa. -w. 1950-71 – 1 – us UMI [071]

Acornley, John Holmes *see* THE COLORED LADY EVANGELIST: BEING THE LIFE, LABORS AND EXPERIENCES OF MRS. HARRIET A. BAKER

Acosta, C *see*
- TRACTADO DELAS DROGAS, Y MEDICINAS DE LAS INDIAS ORIENTALES,...
- TRATADO DE LAS DROGAS Y MEDICINAS DE LAS INDIAS ORIENTALES CON SUS PLANTAS...

Acosta, E *see* RERUM A SOCIETATE JESU IN ORIENTO GESTARUM AD ANNUM USQUE

Acosta, J *see* DE NATURA NOVI ORBIS LIBRI DUO ET DE PROMULGATIONE EVANGELI APUD...

ACOUSTICAL IMAGING AND HOLOGRAPHY – v. 1-. 1978- – 1,5,6,9 – us UMI [770]

ACOUSTICAL PHYSICS – v1- 1955- – 1,5,6 – us A.I.P. [530]

O ACOUTE DOS DESPOTAS – Salvador, Brazil. Set-out 1832 (incomplete) – 1,5,6 – bl Biblioteca [072]

ACQUIRE : THE MAGAZINE FOR COLLECTORS – (Cont by: Collector Editions Quarterly) – New York. v1-5 jun 1973-jul 1977 1; v2-5 mar 1974-jul 1977 5,9* – 1,5,9 – D8740 – us UMI [073]

ACQUISITIONS LIBRARIAN / Haworth Press – New York. v1-9. 1989-1997+ – 1,9 – D51075 – us UMI [020]

THE ACQUISITIONS LIBRARIAN / ed by Katz, Bill – v1- 1989- – 1, 9 ($135.00 in US $189.00 outside hardcopy subsc) – us Haworth [020]

Acquoy, J G R *see*
- HANDLEIDING TOT DE KERKGESCHIEDVORSCHING EN KERKGESCHIEDSCHRIJVING
- HET KLOOSTER TE WINDESHEIM EN ZIJN INVLOED

O ACRE : ORGAM DOS INTERESSES GERAES – Senna Madureira, Acre. 5-30 Jul 1916 – 1,5,6 – bl Biblioteca [072]

O ACRE : ORGAM OFFICIAL – Rio Branco, Acre. 18 Ago 1929-Out 1936; Mar-Abr 1937; Ago, Out 1940; Jan 1941; Jan 1943-Out 1944; Maio 1946-Mar, Maio, Jul-Dez 1962; Jan-Fev 1963; Fev 1965; Jun-9 Dez 1972 – 1,5,6 – bl Biblioteca [072]

O ACRE : ORGAO DOS INTERESSES ACREANOS – Xapury, Acre. 24 Jun-1 Out 1907; 16 Mar-1 Jun 1913 – 1,5,6 – bl Biblioteca [072]

ACREANO : ORGAO DO CLUB POLITICO 24 DE JANEIRO – Xapury, Acre. 15 Nov 1907-26 Jun 1912 – 1,5,6 – bl Biblioteca [072]

L'ACROBATE – Montreal, Canada. 5 sep 1874 – 1r – 1 – Can$25.00 – cn Can Microfilming [072]

Acronivs, R *see* SEER GRONDIGHE ENDE WT GODES WOORDT WEL GHEFONDEERDE ONDERRICHTINGE, TEGHENS DE LASTERINGHE ENDE HET GESCHREY, DAT DE WEDERDOOPEREN

Acropolitae, Georgii *see* HISTORIA

ACROSS AFRICA / Cameron, Verney L – v. 1-2, Index. London. 1877. BA-168 2 – 8 – ne IDC [960]

ACROSS CENTRAL AMERICA / Boddam-Whetham, John W – London: Hurst and Blackett, 1877. xii,353p – 1 – us U.W. Library [972]

ACROSS THE BOARD – (Cont: Conference Board Record) – New York. v13-20 oct 1976-1983* 1; v21-34 jan 1984-dec 1997+ 1,5,9 – 1,5,9 – D14582.01 – us UMI [073]

ACROSS THE CANADIAN PRAIRIES: A TWO MONTHS' HOLIDAY IN THE DOMINION / Colmer, Joseph Grose – London: European Mail, 1895. 03389. (Pre-1900 Canadiana) – 9 – cn C.I.H.M. [910]

ACROSS THE CONTINENT VIA THE CANADIAN PACIFIC RAILWAY: A LECTURE DELIVERED...23RD MARCH, 1887 / Beaugrand, Honore – Montreal?, 1887?. 02978. (Pre-1900 Canadiana) – 9 – cn C.I.H.M. [910]

ACROSS THE VATNA JOKULL; OR, SCENES IN ICELAND; BEING A DESCRIPTION OF HITHERTO UNKNOWN REGIONS / Watts, William Lord – London: Longmans and Co., 1876. 202p. 2 maps (1 fold.) – 1 – us U.W. Library [910]

ACS MAGAZINE – (Cont: Automotive Chain Store. Cont by: Automotive Chain Store) – Akron. v31. jan-jul 1983* – 1 – inquire – D13832.01 – us UMI [073]

ACSM BULLETIN – (Cont: American Congress on Surveying and Mapping Bulletin) – Falls Church. n75- Nov 1981- – 1 – inquire – D12485.01 – us UMI [520]

ACSM-ASP FALL CONVENTION : TECHNICAL PAPERS – (Formed by the merger of: ASP-ACSM Fall Techincal Meeting – Technical Papers of the American Congress on Surveying & Mapping, and: American Society of Photogrammetry – Technical Papers. Cont by: ACSM-ASPRS Fall Convention – Technical Papers) – Falls Church. sep 1982-84* – 1 – D16421.02 – us UMI [520]

ACSM-ASP FALL CONVENTION TECHNICAL PAPERS *see* ASP-ACSM (AMERICAN CONGRESS ON SURVEYING AND MAPPING) TECHNICAL PAPERS

ACSM-ASPRS FALL CONVENTION : TECHNICAL PAPERS – (Split into: ASPRS-ACSM Fall Convention Technical Papers, and: ASPRS Technical Papers. Cont: ACSM-ASP Fall convention Technical Papers) – sep 1985* – 1 – D16421-03 – us UMI [520]

ACSUS NEWSLETTER / Association for Canadian Studies in the United States – (Cont by: American Review of Canadian Studies) – Washington. v1-2. Spr 1971-Aut 1972* – 1 – inquire – D12073 – us UMI [073]

THE ACT AND TESTIMONY OF THE MINORITY *see* THEOLOGICAL MISCELLANY 1

AN ACT AUTHORIZING THE FORMATION OF CORPORATIONS FOR MANUFACTURING, MINING. – New York, Banks, 1875. 94 p. LL-478 – 1 – us L of C Photodup [340]

THE ACT AUTHORIZING THE FORMATION OF CORPORATIONS FOR MANUFACTURING, MINING, MECHANICAL, CHEMICAL. / New York. (State). Laws, Statutes, etc – New York: Baker, Voorhis, 1884. 84p. LL-1685 – 1 – us L of C Photodup [340]

ACT BOOKS OF THE ARCHBISHOPS OF CANTERBURY: 1663-1914 / Lambeth Palace. Library – 1 – PS395.00 – uk World [240]

AN ACT CONCERNING BANKRUPTS, AND THE ADMINISTRATION OF THEIR EFFECTS / Canada. Laws, Statutes, etc – Kingston: Printed by S Derbishire and G Desbarats, 1843. SEM105P200 – 1mf – 9 – Can$2.25 – cn Bibl Nat [324]

THE ACT CONCERNING CORPORATIONS IN THE STATE OF NEW JERSEY, APPROVED APRIL 7, 1875 / Corbin, William Horace – Jersey City: Linn, 1889. 108p. LL-227 – 1 – us L of C Photodup [340]

AN ACT CONCERNING CORPORATIONS (REVISION OF 1896), TAKING EFFECT JULY 4, 1896, IN THE STATE OF NEW JERSEY. / Corbin, William Horace – 10th ed. Newark: Soney & Sage, 1897. 109p. LL-839 – 1 – us L of C Photodup [340]

AN ACT FOR LIMITING THE TIME OF SERVICE IN THE ARMY / Canada. Laws, Statutes, etc – Quebec: Printed by J N Duquet, 1865. SEM105P318 – 4mf – 9 – Can$9.00 – cn Bibl Nat [355]

AN ACT FOR THE ABOLITION OF FEUDAL RIGHTS AND DUTIES IN LOWER CANADA / Canada. Laws, Statutes, etc – Quebec: Printed by Stewart Derbishire and George Desbarats, 1854. SEM105P265 – 1mf – 9 – Can$2.25 – cn Bibl Nat [340]

ACT OF 1800 BANKRUPTCY CASE FILES OF THE U.S. DISTRICT COURT OF MARYLAND / U.S. Circuit and District Courts – 1800-03 – 2r. – 1 – M1031 – us Nat'l Archives [324]

ACT OF 1800 BANKRUPTCY RECORDS OF THE U.S. DISTRICT COURT FOR THE EASTERN DISTRICT OF PENNSYLVANIA / U.S. Circuit and District Courts. Pennsylvania – 1800-06 – 24r – 1 – M993 – us Nat'l Archives [324]

ACT OF 1800 BANKRUPTCY RECORDS OF THE U.S. DISTRICT COURT FOR THE SOUTHERN DISTRICT OF NEW YORK / U.S. Circuit and District Courts. New York – 1800-09 – 11r – 1 – M933 – us Nat'l Archives [324]

THE ACT OF BAPTISM IN THE HISTORY OF THE CHRISTIAN CHURCH / Burrage, Henry S – Philadelphia: American Baptist Publication Society, c1879 – 1mf – us A.T.L.A. [240]

ACT OF THE INDONESIAN COUNCIL FOR THE SCIENCES / Indonesia. Laws, Statutes, etc – In Indonesian and English. SE-6871 1. 1956? – 9 – ne IDC [324]

AN ACT RESPECTING THE MILITIA, EXTRACTED FROM CONSOLIDATED STATUTES OF CANADA / Canada. Laws, Statutes, etc – Quebec: Printed by Stewart Derbishire and George Desbarats, 1861. SEM105P181 – 1mf – 9 – Can$2.25 – cn Bibl Nat [324]

AN ACT RESPECTING THE PRESERVATION OF THE PUBLIC HEALTH / Canada. Laws, Statutes, etc – s.l: Printed for the Bureau of Agriculture and Statistics, 1866. SEM105P198 – 1mf – 9 – Can$2.25 – cn Bibl Nat [614]

AN ACT TO AMEND AND CONSOLIDATE THE LAW RELATING TO EDUCATION / Malaya (Federation) – Federal Government Gazette, April 1961 (p389-460) – 1mf – 9 – DE-201/1 – ne IDC [370]

AN ACT TO AMEND THE ACTS RELATING TO THE GRAND TRUNK RAILWAY COMPANY OF CANADA / Canada. Laws, Statutes, etc – Quebec: Stewart Derbishire and George Desbarats, 1855. SEM105P1761 – 1mf – 9 – Can$2.25 – cn Bibl Nat [380]

AN ACT TO AMEND THE ACTS RELATING TO THE GRAND TRUNK RAILWAY COMPANY OF CANADA / Canada. Laws, Statutes, etc – [S.l.: s.n., 1858 ?]. SEM105P1767 – 1mf – 9 – Can$2.25 – cn Bibl Nat [380]

ACT TO APPROVE THE COMPACT OF FREE ASSOCIATION WITH PALAU : 99TH CONG, 2ND SESS / U.S. Congress – P.L. 99-658, nov 14, 1986 – 1mf – 9 – $1.50 – LLMC 82-100G, Title 32 – us L.L.M.C. [327]

AN ACT TO AUTHORIZE THE GRAND TRUNK RAILWAY COMPANY OF CANADA TO CONSTRUCT A BRIDGE OVER THE RIVER ST CLAIR AT SARNIA / Canada. Laws, Statutes, etc – Toronto: S Derbishire and G Desbarats, [1858 ?]. SEM105P1766 – 1mf – 9 – Can$2.25 – cn Bibl Nat [380]

AN ACT TO ESTABLISH A UNIFORM SYSTEM OF BANKRUPTCY THROUGHOUT THE UNITED STATES / Blumenstiel, Alexander – New York, Blumenstiel 1880 75 p. LL-1457 – 1 – us L of C Photodup [340]

AN ACT TO GRANT ADDITIONAL AID TO THE GRAND TRUNK RAILWAY COMPANY OF CANADA / Canada. Laws, Statutes, etc – Toronto: S Derbishire and G Desbarats, [1856?]. SEM105P1765 – 1mf – 9 – Can$2.25 – cn Bibl Nat [380]

AN ACT TO MAKE A NEW AND MORE CONVENIENT SUBDIVISION OF THE PROVINCE INTO COUNTIES,... – [s.l.]: [s.n.], [1829?]. SEM105P529 – 1mf – 9 – Can$2.25 – cn Bibl Nat [323]

AN ACT TO MAKE TEMPORARY PROVISION FOR THE GOVERNMENT OF LOWER CANADA / Bas-Canada. Laws, Statutes etc – Montreal: A H Armour and H Ramsay, 1838. SEM105P1908 – 1mf – 9 – Can$2.25 – cn Bibl Nat [323]

AN ACT TO PROVIDE FOR THE ORGANIZATION AND REGULATION OF CERTAIN BUSINESS CORPORATIONS / McMaster, Robert Bach – (New York, Baker, Voorhis, 1884. 50 p. LL-668. New York, Baker, Voorhis, 1887. 94 p. LL-684. New York, Baker, Voorhis, 1890. LL-919) – New York, Baker, Voorhis, 1875. 33, xvii p. LL-706 – 1 – us L of C Photodup [340]

ACTA ACADEMIAE ELECTORALIS MOGUNTINAE SCIENTIARUM QUAE ERFURTI EST, AD ANNUM 1776-95 / Akademie Gemeinnuetziger Wissenschaften zu Erfurt – 3 – us Readex [500]

ACTA ACADEMIAE ELECTORALIS MOGUNTINAE SCIENTIARUM UTILIUM QUAE ERFORDIAE EST / Akademie Gemeinnuetziger Wissenschaften zu Erfurt – Erfordiae et Gothae, 1757-61. v.1-2 – 3 – us Readex [500]

ACTA ACADEMIAE SCIENTIARUM IMPERIALIS PETROPOLITANAE – Petropoli, 1777-1782. v1-6 – 132mf – 9 – R-5816/2 – ne IDC [500]

ACTA AGRICULTURAE SCANDINAVICA – (Ceased publ. Split into: Acta Agriculturae Scandinavica, Section A; Acta Agriculturae Scandinavica, Section B) – Uppsala. 1950-1991* – 1 – D22134 – us UMI [630]

ACTA AGRICULTURAE SCANDINAVICA *see*
- ACTA AGRICULTURAE SCANDINAVICA, SECTION A
- ACTA AGRICULTURAE SCANDINAVICA, SECTION B

ACTA AGRICULTURAE SCANDINAVICA, SECTION A : ANIMAL SCIENCE – (Cont in part: Acta Agriculturae Scandinavica) – Copenhagen. v42-44 1992-1994 1*; v45-47 1995-1997+ 1,5,9 – 1,5,9 – D22135 – us UMI [636]

ACTA AGRICULTURAE SCANDINAVICA, SECTION A *see* ACTA AGRICULTURAE SCANDINAVICA

ACTA AGRICULTURAE SCANDINAVICA, SECTION B : SOIL AND PLANT SCIENCE – (Cont in part: Acta Agriculturae Scandinavica) – Copenhagen. v42-44 1992-1994 1*; v45-47 1995-1997+ 1,5,9 – 1,5,9 – D22136 – us UMI [630]

ACTA AGRICULTURAE SCANDINAVICA, SECTION B *see* ACTA AGRICULTURAE SCANDINAVICA

ACTA ALLERGOLOGICA *see* ALLERGY

ACTA AMAZONICA – Manaus. v1-27. apr 1971-1997+* – 1 – D8161 – us UMI [972]

ACTA ANATOMICA – Basel. v63-160 jan 1966-1997+* 1,5; v75-160 jan 1970-1997+ 9* – 1,5,9 – D2043 – us UMI [611]

ACTA ANATOMICA – (International Archives of Anatomy, Histology, Embryology, and Cytology). v. 1-16. 1945-52 – 1,5,6 – us Princeton Micro [611]

ACTA ANATOMICA – v91- 1975- – 1,5,9 – us UMI [073]

ACTA APOSTOLICAE SEDIS – 19(1909)-60(1968) – 920mf – 9 – Dfl3,220.00 – ne Slangenburg [073]

ACTA APOSTOLICAE SEDIS – Romae, 1909-1942. v1-34 – 590mf – 9 – H-194/2 – ne IDC [240]

ACTA APOSTOLICAE SEDIS – (Supersedes: Acta Sanctae Sedis) – Vatican City. v1-89 jan 1909-dec 1997+ 1; v63-89 jan 1971-dec 1997+ 5; v68-89 jan 1971-dec 1997+ 9 – 1,5,9 – D3202 – us UMI [240]

ACTA APOSTOLICAE SEDIS *see* ACTA SANCTAE SEDIS

ACTA APOSTOLORUM : GRAECE ET LATINE EDIDIT ACTUS APOSTOLORUM EXTRA CANONEM RECEPTUM ADDIDIT / ed by Hilgenfeld, A – Berolini, 1899 – 6mf – 8 – Dfl3.50ea – ne Slangenburg [250]

ACTA APOSTOLORUM, SIVE, LUCAE AD THEOPHILUM LIBER ALTER : SECUNDAM FORMAM QUAE VIDETUR ROMANUM / ed by Blass, Fridericus – Lipsiae [Leipzig]: B G Teubner, 1896 – 1mf – 9 – 0-8370-2366-1 – 1985-0366 – us A.T.L.A. [220]

ACTA APOSTOLORVM. ANNOTATIONUM LUCAE LOSSIJ, IN NOVUM TESTAMENTUM IESU CHRISTI NAZARAENI,...DUODECIM CAPITUM ACTORUM APOSTOLICORUM / Lossius, L – Francoforti, 1558. V.3 – 7mf – ne IDC [240]

ACTA APPLICANDAE MATHEMATICAE – v1-. 1983- – 1,5,6,9 – us UMI [073]

ACTA ASTRONAUTICA – (1974 (1) and v17-18 1988 (9) incomplete. Cont: Astronautica Acta) – Elmsford. n1-41. 1974-97+ 1,5,9 – 1,5,9 – D49001 – us UMI [073]

ACTA AUDIOLOGICA Y FONIATRICA HISPANOAMERICANA – (All that is currently available) – Mexico City. v9. jan-dec 1972 – 1,5 – D7771 – us UMI [073]

ACTA BIOLOGICA ACADEMIAE SCIENTIARUM HUNGARICAE – Budapest, 1953-1954. v4-5 – 31mf – 9 – 598/2 – ne IDC [574]

ACTA BIOLOGICA VENEZUELICA – Caracas. v9. sep 1975-oct 1978 – 1,5,9 – $83.70y – D7261 – us UMI [574]

ACTA BORUSSICA NEUE FOLGE : PREUSSISCHE STAATS-MINISTERRATSPROTOKOLLE VON 1817-1934/38 – ca 900mf – 9 – subsc: DM4,900.00 diazo DM5,900.00 silver – gw Olms [943]

ACTA BOTANICA BOHEMICA – Prag, 1922-1944. v1-16 – 24mf – 9 – 8552/1 – ne IDC [580]

ACTA BOTANICA FENNICA – Helsinki, 1925-1931. v1-10 – 18mf – 9 – 8554/1 – ne IDC [580]

ACTA BOTANICA NEERLANDICA – Amsterdam. v1-46 1952-dec 1997+ 1*; v36-46 feb 1987-dec 1997+ 5*,9* – 1,5,9 – D16732 – us UMI [580]

ACTA CAPITULARIA CONGREGATIONIS DE SEPTEM FONTIBUS – 1847-1891 – 4mf – 8 – Dfl19.00 – ne Slangenburg [240]

ACTA CAPITULI WINDESHEMENSIS : KERKHISTORISCHE STUDIEN 4 / ed by Woude, Utig S v. d. – 's-Gravenhage, 1953 – 5mf – 8 – Dfl22.00 – ne Slangenburg [240]

ACTA CHEMICA SCANDINAVICA – Kopenhagen. v1-14. 1947-60. 732/2 – 8 – ne IDC [073]

ACTA CHIRURGICA SCANDINAVICA – (Ceased publ. Cont: Nordiskt Medicinskt Arkiv. Cont by: European Journal of Surgery) – Stockholm. v85-156. 1920-1990* – 1 – D22159.02 – us UMI [617]

ACTA COLLOQUIJ MONTIS BELLIGARTENSIS... / Andreae d.A E, J – Tvbingae, 1587 – 7mf – 9 – ne IDC [240]

ACTA CONCILIORUM ET EPISTOLAE DECRETALES AC CONSTITUTIONES : SUMMORUM PONTIFICUM / Harduinus, Johannes – Parisiis. Tom 1-11. 1714-1715 – Dfl1,589.00 – ne Slangenburg [240]

ACTA CONCILIORUM ET EPISTOLAE DECRETALES AC CONSTITUTIONES SUMMORUM PONTIFICUM / Harduinus, Johannes – Parisiis, 1714-1715. 11v – 9 – Bf36,750.00 set – 1-799-00202-0 – be Brepols [240]

ACTA CONCILIORUM OECUMENICORUM / ed by Schwartz, Eduard – Berolini, Lipsiae, 1927-28 – 8 – BC-2/2 – ne IDC [240]

ACTA CONCILIORUM OECUMENICORUM / ed by Schwartz, Eduard – Berolini. Tom 1-4. 1927 Ss – Dfl613.00 – ne Slangenburg [240]

ACTA CRYSTALLOGRAPHICA – v. 1-21. 1948-66 – 1,5,6 – us Princeton Micro [540]

ACTA CYTOLOGICA – Chicago. v1-41 1957-dec 1997+ 1*; v27-41 jan 1983-dec 1997+ 5*,9 – 1,5,9 – D1570 – us UMI [616]

ACTA CYTOLOGICA – v1-30. 1957-86 – 1,5,6 – us Princeton Micro [574]

ACTA DA SESSAO / Angola. Conselho Legislativo – Luanda, 1963-70 – 1r – 1 – us Ross [324]

ACTA DE 22 DE OCTUBRE DE 1918 / Comision de Monumentos – Madrid: Fortanet, 1919. B.R.A.H. lxxiv/pp. 268-272 – 1 – sp Bibl Santa Ana [946]

ACTA DE CONSTITUCION Y REGLAMENTO DE "EL ALBA" SOCIEDAD OBRERA DE SOCORROS MUTUOS DE ALDEA DEL CA NO – (Caceres): Tip. La Minerva Cacerena de Serafin Ronda s.a., 1915? – 1 – sp Bibl Santa Ana [350]

ACTA DE LA SESION DE 1 DE OCTUBRE DE 1920 / Comision de Monumentos – Madrid: Ed. Reus, 1921. B.R.A.H. 78. pp. 88-90. Tambien: 12 de noviembre de 1920 – 1 – sp Bibl Santa Ana [946]

ACTA DE LA SESION DE 9 DE DICIEMBRE DE 1918 / Subcomision de monumentos – Madrid: Fortanet, 1919. B.R.A.H. 74. pp. 287-289 – 1 – sp Bibl Santa Ana [946]

ACTA DE LA SESION DE 22 DE MARZO DE 1920 / Comision de Monumentos – Madrid: Fortanet, 1920. B.R.A.H. 77. pp. 86-92 y 383 – 1 – sp Bibl Santa Ana [946]

ACTA DE LA SESION DEL 14 DE MARZO DE 1920 / Comision de Monumentos – Madrid: Fortanet, 1920. B.R.A.H. 77. pp. 365-379 – 1 – sp Bibl Santa Ana [946]

ACTA DER DISPUTATION ZU FLENSBURG, DIE SACHE DES HOCHWIRDIGEN SACRAMENTS BETREFFEND, IM 1529. JAR. GESCHEHEN – Wittemberg, J. Kluck. 1529. BME-324 1 – 9 – ne IDC [240]

ACTA DER PROVINCIALE EN PARTICULIERE SYNODEN : GEHOUDEN IN DE NOORDELIJKE NEDERLANDEN, 1572-1620 / ed by Reitsma, A S & Veen, S D Van – Groningen. v1-8. 1892-1899 – 65mf – 8 – Dfl228.00 – ne Slangenburg [240]

ACTA DERMATO-VENEREOLOGICA – (Cont: Acta Diabetologica Latina) – Stockholm. v1-78 1920-1997+ 1*; v76-78 1995-1997+ 5,9 – 1,5,9 – D22137 – us UMI [616]

ACTA DES COLLOQUIJ, ZWISCHEN DEN WUERTENBERGISCHEN THEOLOGEN VND D. IOANNE PISTORIO, ZU BADEN GEHALTEN... / Heerbrand, J – Tuebingen, 1590 – 5mf – ne IDC [240]

ACTA DIABETOLOGICA *see* ACTA DIABETOLOGICA LATINA

ACTA DIABETOLOGICA LATINA – (Cont by: Acta Diabetologica) – Milano. v1-20 jan 1964-dec 1983*; v21-28 jan 1984-mar 1991 – 1 – D11544 – us UMI [610]

ACTA DIABETOLOGICA LATINA *see* ACTA DERMATO-VENEREOLOGICA

ACTA ELECTRONICA – Paris. 1956-61 – 1 – fr A.C.R.P.P. [073]

ACTA ENDOCRINOLOGICA – (Cont by: European Journal of Endocrinology) – Oslo. 1948-1993* – 1 – D22153 – us UMI [616]

ACTA ERUDITORUM; NOVA ACTA ERUDITORUM / ed by Mencke, Otto et al – Leipzig, 1682-1782. Hildesheim 1981 – 850mf – 9 – DM5,300.00 diazo DM6,100.00 silver – gw Olms [100]

ACTA ET DECRETA CONCILIORUM : COLL. LACENSUS 7: CONCILIUM VATICANUM 1 – Freiburg Brg., 1890 – Dfl1,12.00 – ne Slangenburg [240]

ACTA ET SCRIPTA THEOLOGORVM VVIRTEMBERGENSIVM, ET PATRIARCHAE CONSTANTINOPOLITANI D. HIEREMIAE... / Andreae d.A E, J – Vvitebergae, 1584 – 5mf – 9 – ne IDC [240]

ACTA EX IIS DECERPTA QUAE APUD SANCTAM SEDEM GERUNTUR *see* ACTA SANCTAE SEDIS

ACTA FORESTALIA FENNICA – Helsingforsae, 1913-1920. v1-14 – 115mf – 9 – H-419/2 – ne IDC [634]

ACTA GEOLOGICA SINICA – (English ed. Ceased publ) – Beijing. v1-5. 1988-1992* – 1,5,9 – D49590 – us UMI [550]

ACTA HAEMATOLOGICA – Basel. v35-98 jan 1966-dec 1997+ 1*,5*; v91-98 jan 1994-dec 1997+ 9* – 1,5,9 – D2045 – us UMI [616]

ACTA HAEMATOLOGICA – v52-. 1975- – 1,5,9 – us UMI [073]

ACTA: HANDLUNGEN: LEGATION VND SCHRIFFTE. GESPRECHE VND DISPUTATION ANTONIJ CORUINI VND JOANNIS KYMEI, MIT DEM MUENSTERISCHEN KOENIG / Corvinus, A – Wittemberg, G. Rhaw. 1536. BME-161 1 – 9 – ne IDC [240]

ACTA: HANDLUNGEN: LEGATION VND SCHRIFFTE: SO DURCH DEN...HERRN PHILIPSEN LANDGRAVEN ZU HESSEN ETC... / Corvinus, A – Wittemberg, 1536 – 2mf – 9 – ne IDC [240]

ACTA HELVETICA, PHYSICO-MATHEMATICO-ANATOMICO-BOTANICO-M EDICA, FIGURIS AENEIS. – Basileae, 1751-77. v.1-8. Also: Nova Acta helvetica,..., Basileae, 1787. v.1 – 3 – us Readex [500]

ACTA HEPATO-GASTROENTEROLOGICA – (Cont by: Hepato-gastroenterology. Former Titles: Acta Hepatologica (1953-1958); Acta Hepato-Splenologica (1959-dec 1971)) – Stuttgart. v1-25 1953-dec 1978 1*; v23-25 jan 1976-dec 1978 5*,9 – 1,5,9 – D10151 – us UMI [616]

ACTA HEPATOLOGICA *see* ACTA HEPATO-GASTROENTEROLOGICA

ACTA HEPATO-SPLENOLOGICA *see* ACTA HEPATO-GASTROENTEROLOGICA

ACTA HISTOCHEMICA – v11-51. Jena. 1960-1974 – 5,9 – Dfl4,510.00; Dfl110.00v – ne Swets [610]

ACTA HISTOCHEMICA – v1-65. 1954-79 – 1,5,6 – us Princeton Micro [540]

ACTA HISTOCHEMICA ET CYTOCHEMICA – Kyoto. v1-30 1968-1997+ 1*; v7-30 1974-1997+ 5*,9* – 1,5,9 – D7937 – us UMI [073]

ACTA HORTI BERGIANI – Stockholm, 1890-1939. v1-12 – 66mf – 9 – 8555/1 – ne IDC [580]

ACTA HORTI PETROPOLITANI – (v32(2); v33(2); v36(2) have not been published) – Trudy Imperatorskago. S. Peterburgskago Botanicheskago Sada. Spb., 1871-1920. v1-36. Index 1871-1913 – 241mf – 9 – 7475/1 – ne IDC [580]

ACTA INFORMATICA – Heidelberg. v1-14 1971-80*. v15-34 1981-nov 1997+ 1; v1-34 1971-nov 1997+ 5,9 – 1,5,9 – D13128 – us UMI [073]

ACTA LITERARIA ET SCIENTIARUM SVECIAE – Upsala, 1720-1739 – 3 – us Readex [400]

ACTA MARTYRUM : OPERA AC STUDIO – (Includes index) – Ratisbonae [Regensburg]: G Josephi Manz, 1859 – 2mf – 9 – 0-8370-6938-6 – 1986-0938 – us A.T.L.A. [920]

ACTA MARTYRUM SELECTA = AUSGEWAEHLTE MAERTYRERACTEN : UND ANDERE URKUNDEN AUS DER VERFOLGUNGSZEIT DER CHRISTLICHEN KIRCHE / Gebhardt, Oscar von – Berlin: A. Duncker, 1902 – 1mf – us A.T.L.A. [240]

ACTA MATERIALIA – (Cont: Acta Metallurgica et Materialia) – v44-45. jan 1996-dec 1997+ – 1,5,9 – D49002.02 – us UMI [660]

ACTA MATERIALIA *see* ACTA METALLURGICA ET MATERIALIA

ACTA MATHEMATICA – (Stockholm). v. 1-116. 1882-1966 – 1,5,6 – us Princeton Micro [510]

ACTA MECHANICA – Wien. v1-85 1965-dec 1990*. v86-101 1991-93. v102-107 1994*. v108-121 1995-97+ – 1 – D13256 – us UMI [620]

ACTA MECHANICA SOLIDA SINICA – 1,5,6,9 – us UMI [620]

ACTA MEDICA DEL VALLE – (All that is currently available) – Cali. v3-4. 1972-1973 – 1 – D7675 – us UMI [610]

ACTA MEDICA SCANDINAVICA – (Stockholm). v. 87-139. 1935-1950 – 1,5,6 – us Princeton Micro [610]

ACTA MEDICA SCANDINAVICA SUPPLEMENT – nos. 1-249. 1921-50 – 1,5,6 – us Princeton Micro [610]

ACTA METALLURGICA – (Cont by: Acta Metallurgica et Materialia) – Elmsford. v1-37 1953-dec 1989 1,5,9 – 1,5,9 – D49002 – us UMI [660]

ACTA METALLURGICA *see* ACTA METALLURGICA ET MATERIALIA

ACTA METALLURGICA ET MATERIALIA – (Cont: Acta Metallurgica. Cont by: Acta Materialia) – Elmsford. v38-43. jan 1990-dec 1995 – 1,5,9 – $1,365.00y – D49002.01 – us UMI [660]

ACTA METALLURGICA ET MATERIALIA *see*
– ACTA MATERIALIA
– ACTA METALLURGICA

ACTA METEOROLOGICA SINICA = CHI HSIANG HSUEH PAO – Beijing, 1987-94* 1; 1995-97+ 1,5,9 – 1,5,9 – D22003 – us UMI [550]

ACTA NEUROCHIRURGICA – Wien. v1-74 feb 1950-84* 1; v74-149 1985-97+ 1,5,9 – 1,5,9 – D13257 – us UMI [617]

ACTA NEUROLOGICA BELGICA – (All that is currently available. Former Titles: Journal de Neurologie (1895-1923); Journal de Neurologie et de Psychiatrie (1924-1932); Journal Belge de Neurologie et de Psychiatrie (1933-1947); Acta Neurologica et Psychiatrica Belgica (1948-1969)) – Brussels. v75-80. jan 1975-dec 1980 – 1,5,9 – D10527 – us UMI [616]

ACTA NEUROLOGICA BELGICA – (Former titles: Journal de Neurologie; Neurologie, Psychiatrie, Psychologie; Journal de Neurologie et de Psychiatrie; Journal Belge de Neurologie et de Psychiatrie; Acta Neurologica et Psychiatrica Belgica) – Brussels. v75-80 jan 1975-dec 1980 1; v76 jan 1975*. v76 jan 1976. v77-80 jan 1977-dec 1980* 5; v75-80 jan 1975-dec 1980 9 – 1,5,9 – $83.70y – D10527 – us UMI [616]

ACTA NEUROLOGICA ET PSYCHIATRICA BELGICA *see*
– ACTA NEUROLOGICA BELGICA

ACTA NEUROLOGICA SUPPLEMENTUM *see* ACTA NEUROPATHOLOGICA

ACTA NEUROPATHOLOGICA – (Includes: Acta Neurologica Supplementum 1962-83) – Heidelberg. v1-52 may 1961-may 1980*. v53-94 jan 1981-dec 1997 1; v53-58 jan 1981-dec 1982. v59-84 jan 1983-nov 1992*. v85-94 dec 1992-dec 1997+ 5; v53-94 jan 1981-dec 1997+ 9 – 1,5,9 – D13100 – us UMI [073]

ACTA NEUROVEGETATIVA – (Cont by: Journal of Neuro-Visceral Relations) – Wien. v1-30. 1950-1967* – 1 – D13266 – us UMI [612]

ACTA NUMERICA – Cambridge. v4-6. 1995-1997+ – 1,5,9 – D21006 – us UMI [510]

ACTA OCEANOLOGICA SINICA = HAI YANG HSUEH PAO – Beijing. v1-3 jun 1982-84*. v4-16 1qr 1996-4qr 1997+ 1; v1-5 jun 1982-86*. v6-12 1qr 1987-4qr 1993; v13 1994*. v14-16 1qr 1995-4qr 1997+ 5,9 – 1,5,9 – D49587 – us UMI [550]

ACTA ODER GESCHICHT WIE ES VFF DEM GESPRECH IN ZUERICH ERGANGEN IST / Haetzer, L – Zuerich, Chr. Froschouer. 1523. BME-47 1 – 9 – ne IDC [240]

ACTA ODONTOLOGICA SCANDINAVICA – (Has suppl: Acta Odontologica Scandinavica) – Oslo. v1-55 1939-1997+ 1; v53-55 1995-1997+ 5,9 – 1,5,9 – D13593 – us UMI [617]

ACTA ODONTOLOGICA SCANDINAVICA : SUPPLEMENT – (Suppl to: Acta Odontologica Scandinavica) – Aarhus. 1940-1997+ 1*; 1995-1997+ 5,9 – 1,5,9 – D13594 – us UMI [617]

ACTA ODONTOLOGICA SCANDINAVICA *see*
– ACTA ODONTOLOGICA SCANDINAVICA

ACTA ONCOLOGICA – (Cont: Acta Radiologica) – Oslo. v26-36. 1987-1997+ – 1,5*,9 – D6042.04 – us UMI [616]

ACTA ORIENTALIA / Magyar Tudomanyos Akademia – (In Russian, English, French and German) – Budapest, 1950-67.-v1-20 – 138mf – 8 – CH-100/20 – ne IDC [950]

ACTA ORIENTALIA / ed by Societas Orientalis Batava – Lugduni Batavorum. v1-3 1923-40.-v1-18 – 114mf – 8 – CH-101c/2 – ne IDC [950]

ACTA ORTHOPAEDICA SCANDINAVICA – Copenhagen. 1930-1997+ 1*; 1995-1997+ 5,9 – 1,5,9 – D16132 – us UMI [617]

ACTA OTO-LARYNGOLOGICA – Oslo. v1-80 1918-1997+ 1*; v78-80 1995-1997+ 5,9 – 1,5,9 – D22138 – us UMI [617]

ACTA PACIFICATIONIS ... INTER ... HISPANIARUM & ... AUSTRIAE, ... BELGII ... – Lugduni, 1580 – 4mf – 9 – ILM-970/1 – ne IDC [340]

ACTA PAEDIATRICA – (Micro-ed includes suppl. Cont: Acta Paediatrica Scandinavica) – Oslo. v81-84. jan 1992-dec 1997+ – 1,5,9 – D2174.01 – us UMI [618]

ACTA PAEDIATRICA *see* ACTA PAEDIATRICA SCANDINAVICA

ACTA PAEDIATRICA JAPONICA – Tokyo. v5-39 1963-dec 1997+ 1*; v34-39 feb 1992-dec 1997+ 5*,9* – 1,5,9 – D19970 – us UMI [618]

ACTA PAEDIATRICA SCANDINAVICA – (Includes suppls. Cont by: Acta Paediatrica. Former titles: Acta Paediatrica) – Stockholm. v1-80 1921-dec 1991, cum index 2-31 1922-43 1; v55-80 jan 1966-dec 1991 5; v59-61 jan 1970-nov 1972. v63-80 jan 1974-dec 1991 – 1,5,9 – D2174 – us UMI [618]

ACTA PAEDIATRICA SCANDINAVICA *see* ACTA PAEDIATRICA

ACTA PALAEONTOLOGICA SINICA – v1-13, 14 (nos 1-2). 1953-66 – 8 – Dfl1,000.00 – ne Schierenberg [560]

ACTA PATHOLOGICA JAPONICA – (Cont by: Pathology International) – Tokyo. v1-43 1950-93* 1; v22-37 feb-nov 1972. v24-25 jan 1974-nov 1975*. v26-27 jan 1976-nov 1977. v28-30 jan 1978-nov 1980*. v31 1981. v32-37 jan 1982-dec 1987* 5; v24-37 jan 1982-dec 1987 9 – 1,5,9 – D7164 – us UMI [616]

ACTA PHARMACEUTICA NORDICA – (Ceased publ. Absorbed: Acta Pharmaceutica Suecica. Absorbed in part by: European Journal of Pharmaceutical Sciences) – Stockholm. v1-4. 1989-1992 – 1,5*,9 – D17721 – us UMI [615]

ACTA PHARMACEUTICA NORDICA *see* ACTA PHARMACEUTICAL SUECICA

ACTA PHARMACEUTICA SUECICA *see* ACTA PHARMACEUTICA NORDICA

ACTA PHARMACEUTICAL SUECICA – (Absorbed by: Acta Pharmaceutica Nordica) – Stockholm. v1-13 apr 1964-apr 1976* 1; v14-25 1977-88 1,5,6,9 – D11578 – us UMI [615]

ACTA PHARMACOLOGICA ET TOXICOLOGICA – v. 1-39. 1945-1976 – 1,5,6 – us Princeton Micro [610]

ACTA PHILOLOGICA SCANDINAVICA – Copenhagen. v1-33. 1926-82 – 5,9 – Dfl1,980.00; Dfl60.00v – ne Swets [400]

ACTA PHYSICA AUSTRIACA – (Ceased publ. Has suppl: Acta Physica Austriaca) – Wien. v1-57. mar 1947-1985* – 1 – D13259 – us UMI [610]

ACTA PHYSICA AUSTRIACA – (Has suppl: Acta Physica Austriaca – Supplement) – Wien. v1-57. mar 1947-85* – 1 – D13259 – us UMI [073]

ACTA PHYSICA AUSTRIACA : SUPPLEMENTUM – (Ceased publ. Suppl to: Acta Physica Austriaca) – Wien. 1964-1985* – 1 – D13260 – us UMI [610]

ACTA PHYSICA AUSTRIACA *see*
– ACTA PHYSICA AUSTRIACA

ACTA PHYSICOCHIMICA U.S.S.R – v. 1-22. 1934-1947 – 1,5,6 – us Princeton Micro [540]

ACTA PHYSICO-MEDICA ACADEMIAE : CAESAREAE LEOPOLDINO-CAROLINAE / Deutsche Akademie der Naturforscher – Norimbergae, 1727-54.-v1-10 – 175mf – 8 – H-540/2 – ne IDC [610]

ACTA PHYSIOLOGICA ACADEMIAE SCIENTARUM HUNGARICUM – v. 8, 10-45. 1955-1974 – 1,5,6 – us Princeton Micro [610]

ACTA PHYSIOLOGICA ET PHARMACOLOGICA LATINOAMERICANA : ORGANO DE LA ASOCIACION LATINOAMERICANA DE CIENCIAS FISIOLOGICAS Y DE LA ASOCIACION LATINOAMERICANA DE FARMACOLOGIA – (Cont: Acta Physiologica Latinoamericana. Cont by: Acta

Physiologica, Pharmacologica et Therapeutica Latinoamericana) – Buenos Aires. v34-40. 1984-1990* – 1 – D8789.01 – us UMI [615]

ACTA PHYSIOLOGICA ET PHARMACOLOGICA LATINOAMERICANA *see* – ACTA PHYSIOLOGICA LATINOAMERICANA – ACTA PHYSIOLOGICA, PHARMACOLOGICA ET THERAPEUTICA LATINOAMERICANA

ACTA PHYSIOLOGICA ET PHARMACOLOGICA NEDERLANDICA – v.2-5; 7-11. 1951-57; 1958-69 – 1,5,6 – 2264.00 – us Princeton Micro [612]

ACTA PHYSIOLOGICA LATINOAMERICANA – (Cont by: Acta Physiologica et Pharmacologica Latinoamericana) – Buenos Aires. v1-33 1950-1983 1; v24-33 1974-1983 5,9 – 1,5,9 – D8789 – us UMI [612]

ACTA PHYSIOLOGICA LATINOAMERICANA *see* ACTA PHYSIOLOGICA ET PHARMACOLOGICA LATINOAMERICANA

ACTA PHYSIOLOGICA, PHARMACOLOGICA ET THERAPEUTICA LATINOAMERICANA : ORGANO DE LA ASOCIACION LATINOAMERICANA DE CIENCIAS FISIOLOGICAS Y DE LA ASOCIACION LATINOAMERICANA DE FARMACOLOGIA – (Cont: Acta Physiologica et Pharmacologica Latinoamericana) – Buenos Aires. v41-47. 1991-1997*+ – 1 – D8789.02 – us UMI [615]

ACTA PHYSIOLOGICA, PHARMACOLOGICA ET THERAPEUTICA LATINOAMERICANA *see* ACTA PHYSIOLOGICA ET PHARMACOLOGICA LATINOAMERICANA

ACTA PHYSIOLOGICA SCANDINAVICA – Oxford. v31-83 jun 1954-dec 1971; suppls 1969-71; v84-161 jan 1972-dec 1997+ 1; v84-161 jan 1972-dec 1997+ 5; v90-161 jan 1974-dec 1997+ 9 – 1,5,9 – D6924 – us UMI [612]

ACTA PHYSIOLOGICA SCANDINAVICA – Stockholm, Sweden. 1940-61 – 8r – 1 – sw Kungliga [073]

ACTA PHYSIOLOGICA SCANDINAVICA – v1-107. 1940-79 – 1,5,6 – us Princeton Micro [612]

ACTA PHYSIOLOGICA SCANDINAVICA: SUPPLEMENTS – Nos. 1-447. 1940-1979 – 1,5,6 – us Princeton Micro [612]

ACTA PHYTOTAXONOMICA SINICA – (Missing: 1951, v1(2); 1952, v2(2); 1953-1954, v2(4)-3) – Peking, 1951-1966. v1-11 – 114mf – 9 – 7647/2 – ne IDC [560]

ACTA POLYTECHNICA SCANDINAVICA : APPLIED PHYSICS SERIES – (Cont: Acta Polytechnica Scandinavica Physics Including Nucleonics Series) – Helsinki, 1976-97+ – 1 – D7064.01 – us UMI [621]

ACTA POLYTECHNICA SCANDINAVICA : CHEMISTRY INCLUDING METALLURGY SERIES – (Cont by: Acta Polytechnica Scandinavica Chemical Technology and Metallurgy Series) – Helsinki. cum index 1958-1970; v1-152 1958-1983 – 1 – D7059 – us UMI [660]

ACTA POLYTECHNICA SCANDINAVICA : CHEMISTRY TECHNOLOGY AND METALLURGY SERIES – (Cont: Acta Polytechnica Scandinavica Chemistry including Metallurgy Series) – Helsinki, 1983-97+ – 1 – D7059.01 – us UMI [540]

ACTA POLYTECHNICA SCANDINAVICA : CIVIL ENGINEERING AND BUILDING CONSTRUCTION SERIES – Helsinki, 1958-70 cum index. 1958-88. 1989-94*. 1995-97+ – 1 – D7060 – us UMI [624]

ACTA POLYTECHNICA SCANDINAVICA : ELECTRICAL ENGINEERING SERIES – Helsinki, 1958-70 cum index. 1958-71. v30-76 1972-93. v74-75 1994*. v76-81 1995-97+ 1; v38-51 1976-83*. v52-54 1984. v55-76 1985-93*. v74-75 1994*. v76-81 1995-97+ 5; v38-42 1976-78*. v43-47 1980-81. v48-51 1982-83*. v52-54 1984. v56-76 1986-93. v74-75 1994*. v76-81 1995-97+ – 1,5,9 – D7061 – us UMI [621]

ACTA POLYTECHNICA SCANDINAVICA : MATHEMATICS AND COMPUTER SCIENCE SERIES – (Cont: Acta Polytechnica Scandinavica – Mathematics and Computing Machinery Series. Cont by: Acta Polytechnica Scandinavica – Mathematics and Computing in Engineering Series) – Helsinki, 1975-93 1; 1976, 1978-93* 5; 1976-78*, 1979, 1980*, 1981-82, 1983*, 1984-93 9 – 1,5,9 – D7062.01 – us UMI [073]

ACTA POLYTECHNICA SCANDINAVICA : MATHEMATICS AND COMPUTING IN ENGINEERING SERIES – (Cont: Acta Polytechnica Scandinavica – Mathematics and Computer Science Series) – Helsinki. 1994-1997*+ – 1,5,9 – D7062.02 – us UMI [620]

ACTA POLYTECHNICA SCANDINAVICA : MATHEMATICS AND COMPUTING MACHINERY SERIES – (Cont by: Acta Polytechnica Scandinavica – Mathematics and Computer Science Series) – Helsinki, 1972-74*; cum index 1958-70 – 1 – D7062 – us UMI [510]

ACTA POLYTECHNICA SCANDINAVICA : MECHANICAL ENGINEERING SERIES – (Suspended publ with n91 (1985). Resumed publ with n92 (1988)) – Helsinki, 1958-70 cum index; 1958-93; 1994*; 1995-97+ – 1 – D7063 – us UMI [621]

ACTA POLYTECHNICA SCANDINAVICA : PHYSICS INCLUDING NUCLEONICS SERIES – (Cont by: Acta Polytechnica Scandinavica – Applied Physics Series) – Helsinki, 1958-70 cum index; 1958-75 – 1 – D7064 – us UMI [530]

ACTA POLYTECHNICA SCANDINAVICA – APPLIED PHYSICS SERIES *see* ACTA POLYTECHNICA SCANDINAVICA

ACTA POLYTECHNICA SCANDINAVICA CHEMICAL TECHNOLOGY AND METALLURGY SERIES *see* ACTA POLYTECHNICA SCANDINAVICA

ACTA POLYTECHNICA SCANDINAVICA – CHEMISTRY *see* ACTA POLYTECHNICA SCANDINAVICA

ACTA POLYTECHNICA SCANDINAVICA – MATHEMATICS AND COMPUTER SCIENCE SERIES *see* – ACTA POLYTECHNICA SCANDINAVICA

ACTA POLYTECHNICA SCANDINAVICA – MATHEMATICS AND COMPUTING MACHINERY SERIES. CONT BY: ACTA POLYTECHNICA SCANDINAVICA – MATHEMATICS AND COMPUTING IN ENGINEERING SERIES *see* ACTA POLYTECHNICA SCANDINAVICA

ACTA POLYTECHNICA SCANDINAVICA PHYSICS INCLUDING NUCLEONICS SERIES *see* ACTA POLYTECHNICA SCANDINAVICA

ACTA PSYCHOLOGICA – Amsterdam. v1-96 1935-Dec 1997+ 1,5; v67-96 mar 1988-dec 1997+ 9 – 1,5,9 – D42005 – us UMI [150]

ACTA PSYCHOLOGICA – v1-57. 1936-84 – 1,5,6,13 – sz Elsevier [073]

ACTA RADIOLOGICA – (Cont: Acta Radiologica – Diagnosis) – Stockholm. v28-38. jan 1987-nov 1997+ – 1,5,9 – D2542.01 – us UMI [616]

ACTA RADIOLOGICA : DIAGNOSIS – (Cont in pt by: Acta Radiologica – Therapy, Physics, Biology with 1963. Microed includes v1-8 1963-69 of Acta Radiologica...) – Stockholm. v1-58 jan 1921-dec 1962; ns 1-5 jan 1963-jan 1966 1; ns 6-12 jan 1967-nov 1972, ns 14-27 jan 1973-dec 1986 1,5; ns 10-12 jan 1970-nov 1972, ns 14-27 jan 1973-dec 1986 9 – 1,5,9 – D2542 – us UMI [616]

ACTA RADIOLOGICA : ONCOLOGY – (Cont: Acta Radiologica – Oncology, Radiation, Therapy, Physics and Biology. Cont by: Acta Oncologica) – Stockholm. v23-25 1984-dec 1986 – 1,5,9 – D6042.03 – us UMI [073]

ACTA RADIOLOGICA : ONCOLOGY, RADIATION THERAPY, PHYSICS AND BIOLOGY – (Cont: Acta Radiologica – Oncology, Radiation, Physics, Biology. Cont by: Acta Radiologica – Oncology) – Stockholm. v19-22. 1980-83 – 1,5,9 – $172.50y – D6042.02 – us UMI [616]

ACTA RADIOLOGICA : ONCOLOGY, RADIATION THERAPY, PHYSICS AND BIOLOGY - (Cont: Acta Radiologica – Therapy, Physics, Biology. Cont by: Acta Radiologica – Oncology, Radiation Therapy, Physics and Biology) – Stockholm. v17-18. 1978-79 – 1,5,9 ($172.50y) – D6042.01 – us UMI [073]

ACTA RADIOLOGICA : THERAPY, PHYSICS AND BIOLOGY – (V1-8 1963-69 included in microed of Acta Radiologica – Diagnosis. Cont by: Acta Radiologica – Oncology, Radiation, Physics, Biology) – Stockholm. n9-16. 1970-77 – 1,5,9 – D6042 – us UMI [616]

ACTA RADIOLOGICA : THERAPY, PHYSICS, BIOLOGY – (Cont by: Acta Radiologica – Oncology, Radiation, Physics, Biology. Vols 1-8 1963-1969 incl in micro-ed of: Acta Radiologica – Diagnosis) – Stockholm. v9-16. feb 1970-dec 1977 – 1,5,9 – D6042 – us UMI [616]

ACTA RADIOLOGICA *see* ACTA ONCOLOGICA

ACTA RADIOLOGICA – DIAGNOSIS *see* – ACTA RADIOLOGICA

ACTA RADIOLOGICA – ONCOLOGY, RADIATION, PHYSICS, BIOLOGY *see* ACTA RADIOLOGICA

ACTA RIDDLEIANA / Ridley College – St. Catharines [Ont.]: The College, [1891?]- – 9 – cn C.I.H.M. [370]

ACTA SANCTAE SEDIS : EPHEMERIDES ROMANAE A SSMO D. N. PIO PP. X AUTHENTICAE ET OFFICALES APOSTOLICAE SEDIS ACTIS PUBLICE EVULGANDIS DECLARATAE – (Ceased publ. Superseded by: Acta Apostolicae Sedis. Former title: Acta ex Iis Decerpta Quae Apud Sanctam Sedem Geruntur) – Rome. cum index 1-41 1865-1908; v1-41 1865-1908 – 1 – D3156 – us UMI [240]

ACTA SANCTAE SEDIS – Rome. v1-41. 1865-1908/1909 – 386mf – 9 – ne IDC [240]

ACTA SANCTAE SEDIS *see* ACTA APOSTOLICAE SEDIS

ACTA SANCTORUM : ACTA SANCTORUM. JANUARY-NOVEMBER. BRUSSELS, PARIS, 1863-1931. PROPYLAEUM...NOVEMBRIS ET DECEMBRIS, 1902, 1940 – 2,096mf – 9 – ne IDC [240]

ACTA SANCTORUM : APRILIS – (v1 1-10 1866 Dfl95.00. v2 11-21 1866 Dfl98.00. v3 22-30 1866 Dfl102.00) – ne Slangenburg [240]

ACTA SANCTORUM : AUGUSTUS – (v1 1-4 1867 Dfl91.00. v2 5-12 1867 Dfl74.00. v3 13-19 1867 Dfl77.00. v4 20-24 1867 Dfl94.00. v5 25-26 1868 Dfl98.00. v6 27-31 1868 Dfl84.00) – ne Slangenburg [240]

ACTA SANCTORUM / ed by Bollandus, J & Henschenius, G – (Individual titles also listed) – Editio Novissima. Paris. v1-69. 1863-1940 – Dfl5,887.00 – ne Slangenburg [240]

ACTA SANCTORUM : FEBRUARIUS – (v1 1-6 1863 Dfl95.00. v2 7-16 1864 Dfl88.00. v3 17-28 1864 Dfl77.00) – ne Slangenburg [240]

ACTA SANCTORUM : JANUARIUS – (v1 1-11 1863 Dfl81.00. v2 12-21 1863 Dfl77.00. v3 22-31 1863 Dfl77.00) – ne Slangenburg [240]

ACTA SANCTORUM : JULIUS – (v1 1-3 1867 Dfl67.00. v2 4-9 1867 Dfl81.00. v3 10-14 1867 Dfl81.00 v4 15-19 1868 Dfl77.00. v5 20-25 1868 Dfl78.00. v6 25-28 1868 Dfl74.00. v7 29-31 1868 Dfl84.00) – ne Slangenburg [240]

ACTA SANCTORUM : JUNIUS – (v1 1-6 1867 Dfl109.00. v2 7-11 1867 Dfl60.00. v3 12-15 1867 Dfl60.00. v4 16-19. 1867 Dfl91.00 v5 20-21 1867 Dfl98.00. v6 22-24 1867. Martyrologium Usuardi Monachi Dfl84.00. v7 25-30 1867 Dfl98.00) – ne Slangenburg [240]

ACTA SANCTORUM : MAIUS – (v1 1-5 1866 Dfl88.00. v2 5-11 1866 Dfl81.00. v3 12-16 1866 Dfl77.00. v4 17-19 1866 Dfl 60.00. v5 20-24 1866 Dfl67.00. v6 24-28 1866 Dfl95.00. v7 29-31 1866 Dfl95.00. Propyleum Ad Septem Tomos Maii 1866 Dfl70.00) – ne Slangenburg [240]

ACTA SANCTORUM : MARTIUS – (v1 1-8 1865 Dfl91.00. v2 9-18 1865 Dfl95.00. v3 19-31 1866 Dfl95.00) – ne Slangenburg [240]

ACTA SANCTORUM : NOVEMBER – (v1 1-3 1887 Dfl95.00. v2/1 4 1894 Dfl84.00. v2/2 4 1931 Dfl67.00. v3 5-8 1910 Dfl91.00. v4 9-10 1920 Dfl70.00. Propyleum Ad Acta Sanctorum Novembris 1902 Dfl56.00. Propyleum Ad Acta Sanctorum Decembris 1940 Dfl63.00) – ne Slangenburg [240]

ACTA SANCTORUM : OCTOBER – (v1 1-2 1866 Dfl77.00. v2 3-4 1866 Dfl102.00. v3 5-7 1868 Dfl98.00. v4 8-9 1866 Dfl105.00. v5 10-11 1866 Dfl84.00. v6 12-14 1906 Dfl67.00. v7/1 15 1869 Dfl81.00. v7/2 16 1869 Dfl39.00. v8 17-20 1866 Dfl105.00. v9 21-22 1869 Dfl91.00. v10 23-24 1869 Dfl91.00. Kalendarii, Oct v11, 25 1870 Dfl105.00. v12 26-29 1884 Dfl95.00. v13 29-31 1883 Dfl95.00. Vol Complectens Auctoria Octobris, 1877 Dfl25.00. Index Hagiologicus Actorum Sanctorum Decem Priorum Mensium 1875 Dfl53.00) – ne Slangenburg [240]

ACTA SANCTORUM : SEPTEMBER – (v1 1-3 1868 Dfl77.00. v2 4-6 1869 Dfl84.00. v3 7-11 1868 Dfl91.00. v4 12-14 1868 Dfl81.00. v5 15-18 1866 Dfl102.00. v6 19-24 1867 Dfl95.00. v7 25-28 1867 Dfl91.00. v8 29-30 1867 Dfl84.00) – ne Slangenburg [240]

ACTA SANCTORUM BELGII SELECTA / Ghesquiere, J – Bruxellis. v1-6. 1783-1794 – 123mf – 8 – Dfl431.00 – ne Slangenburg [240]

ACTA SANCTORUM ORDINIS ST BENEDICTI / ed by Mabillon, Jean & Ruinart, Thierry – Seculum 1-6. (500-1100). Paris, 1668-1701. – 96mf – 9 – subsc: DM700.00 diazo DM800.00 silver – gw Olms [240]

ACTA SANCTORUM O.S.B. / ed by d'Achery, L, Mabillon, J – Lut. Parisiorum, 1668-1701 – 347mf – 8 – ne Slangenburg [240]

ACTA SANCTORUM O.S.B. / ed by d'Achery, L & Mabillon, J – Lut. Parisiorum. v1-9. 1668-1701 – Dfl1,215.00 – ne Slangenburg [240]

ACTA SANCTORUM O.S.B. / Mabillon, Jean – Venetiis. v1-9. 1733 – 314mf – 8 – Dfl1,099.00 – ne Slangenburg [240]

ACTA SCIENTARUM MATHEMATICARUM – v.1-37. 1922-75 – 1,5,6 – us Princeton Micro [510]

ACTA SCIENTIARUM MATHEMATICARUM – (Fomer titles: Acta Litterarum ac Scientarium Regiae Universitatis Hungaricae Francisco-Josephinae. Sectio Scientiarum Mathematicarum) – Szeged. 1922-75*; v38-58 1976-93; 1994* 1; v61-66 1995-97+ 1,5,9; v38-52 1976-88; v53-60 1989-94* 5; v38-58 1976-93; v59-60 1994* 9 – 1,5,9 – D9178 – us UMI [510]

ACTA SEMINARII PHILOLOGICI ERLANGENSIS – Erlangae, 1878-1891. v1-5 – 43mf – 9 – H-358/2 – ne IDC [400]

ACTA SOCIETATIS PRO FAUNA ET FLORA FENNICA – Helsingforsiae, 1875-1934. v1-57 – 331mf – 9 – 8553/1 – ne IDC [580]

ACTA SOCIETATIS REGIAE SCIENTIARUM UPSALIENSIS – Stockholm, 1774-51.-5v – 16mf – 8 – 307/2 – ne IDC [500]

ACTA SOCIETATIS REGIAE SCIENTIARUM UPSALIENSIS / Vetenskaps-Societeten i Upsala – Stockholmiae, 1744-51 – 3 – us Readex [500]

ACTA SOCIOLOGICA – Copenhagen. v1-15. 1956-72 – 5,9 – Dfl1,350.00; Dfl90.00v – ne Swets [300]

ACTA SOCIOLOGICA – Koepenhamn. v1-3. 1956-58. 1121/2 – 8 – ne IDC [073]

ACTA SOCIOLOGICA – Oslo. v1-25 1973-82*; v26-40 mar 1983-97+ 1; v26-36 mar 1983-dec 1993; v37 jun-dec 1994*; v38-40 apr 1995-dec 1997+ 5; v26-40 mar 1983-dec 1997+ 9 – 1 – D13020 – us UMI [073]

ACTA SS. D.N. PII PP. 9 : EX QUIBUS EXCERPTUS EST SYLLABUS EDITUS DIE 8 DECEMBRIS 1864 / Pius 9th, Pope – Romae: Typis Rev Camerae Apostolicae, 1865 – 1mf – 9 – 0-8370-8463-6 – 1986-2463 – us A.T.L.A. [240]

ACTA SS. NEREI ET ACHILLEI (T.U.U. 1-11/2) / Achelis, Hans – Leipzig, 1893 – 2mf – 9 – ne Slangenburg [240]

ACTA SYNODI NATIONALIS DORDRACENSE 1618-1619 – Leiden, 1620 – 40mf – 8 – Dfl140.00 – ne Slangenburg [943]

ACTA SYNODI NATIONALIS DORDRACENSE 1618-1619 1500 LEIDEN, 1620 – 40mf – 9 – ne IDC [240]

ACTA TROPICA – Basel. v47-67. jan 1990-dec 1997*+ – 1,5,9 – D42470 – us UMI [073]

ACTA VAN DE NEDERL. SYNODE DER ZESTIENDE EEUW / ed by Rutgers, F – Marnix Vereeniging 2/3. Utrecht, 1889 – 12mf – 8 – Dfl49.00 – ne Slangenburg [073]

ACTA VAN DE NEDERLANDSCHE SYNODEN DER ZESTIENDE EEUW (DE WERKEN..2,3) / ed by Rutgers, F L – Utrecht, 1889 – Dfl42.00 – ne Slangenburg [240]

ACTA VITAMINOLOGICA *see* ACTA VITAMINOLOGICA ET ENZYMOLOGICA

ACTA VITAMINOLOGICA ET ENZYMOLOGICA – (Vol 27 not available for filming. Former title: Acta Vitaminologica (feb 1947-66)) – Milano. v1-32 feb 1947-78. ns 1-7 1979-85 1; v28-32. ns 1-7 1979-85 5; v28-31 1974-77. v32 1978*. ns 1-7 9 – 1,5,9 – D8742 – us UMI [615]

ACTA ZOOLOGICA – Stockholm. v1-67. 1920-86 1; v68-78 1987-dec 1997+ 1,5,9 – 1,5,9 – D49553 – us UMI [590]

ACTA ZOOLOGICA ET PATHOLOGICA ANTVERPIENSIA – (Former title: Bulletins de la Societe Royale de Zoologie d'Anvers (juil 1953-mars 1966)) – Antwerp. v55-57 1953-73*; v58-75 feb 1974-oct 1980; v76-82 1981-feb 1992* – 1,5,9 – D7519 – us UMI [590]

ACTAS / Mexico. Convencion Nacional Bautista – v. 1 and 2. 1903-20, 1921-27 – 1 – 27.93 – us Baptist [240]

ACTAS CAPITULARES (1479-1510) – Cordoba – 1r – 5,6 – sp Cultura [946]

ACTAS CAPITULARES (ANNO 1518) – Avila – 1r – 5,6 – sp Cultura [946]

ACTAS CAPITULARES (ANNO 1520) – Avila – 1r – 5,6 – sp Cultura [946]

ACTAS CAPITULARES (ANNO 1522-1542) – Avila – 1r – 5,6 – sp Cultura [946]

ACTAS CAPITULARES (ANNO 1541-1599) – Avila – 1r – 5,6 – sp Cultura [946]

ACTAS CAPITULARES (ANNO 1543-1556) – Caceres – 1r – 5,6 – sp Cultura [946]

ACTAS CAPITULARES SOBRE EL GRAN CAPITAN (ANNO 1498-1512) – Cordoba – 1r – 5,6 – sp Cultura [946]

ACTAS DAS SESSOES DA SOCIEDADE DE GEOGRAPHIA DE LISBOA – Lisboa: Imprensa Nacional. v1-13. 1876/81-1893 – 6r – 1 – us Res Libr [946]

ACTAS DE LA COMISION DE ARMAMENTO Y DEFENSA DE LA PROVINCIA DE EXTREMADURA – 1835 – 9 – 1.50f – sp Bibl Santa Ana [355]

ACTAS DE SESSAO / Angola. Conselho Legislativo – 1935-36, 1956-Nov. 11, 1963 – 1 – us NY Public [324]

ACTAS DEL CABILDO DE CARACAS. TOMO 1. CARACAS, 1943 / Bayle, Constantino – Madrid: Razon y Fe, 1946 – 1 – sp Bibl Santa Ana [946]

ACTAS, INFORMES, RESOLUCIONES Y DOCUMENTACION GENERAL DE LA ALTA COMISION... – Buenos Aires, 1916 – 12mf – 9 – ILM-4019/1 – ne IDC [340]

ACTBW BULLETIN *see* ABCA BULLETIN

L'ACTE D'AGRICULTURE ET L'ACTE D'AMENDEMENT DES MUNICIPALITES ET CHEMINS DU BAS-CANADA DE 1857 / Canada. Laws, Statutes, etc – Toronto: Impr. par Stewart Derbishire and George Desbarats, 1857. SEM105P187 – 1mf – 9 – Can$2.25 – cn Bibl Nat [324]

ACTE D'AMENDEMENT DES MUNICIPALITES ET DES CHEMINS DU BAS-CANADA, DE 1856, AVEC SOMMAIRE ET INDEX / Canada. Laws, Statutes, etc – Toronto: Imprime par S Derbishire et G Desbarats. 1856. SEM105P185 – 1mf – 9 – Can$2.25 – cn Bibl Nat [324]

L'ACTE D'AMENDEMENT SEIGNEURIAL DE 1859 / Canada. Laws, Statutes, etc – Toronto: Impr. par Stewart Derbishire and George Desbarats, 1859. SEM105P274 – 1mf – 9 – Can$2.25 – cn Bibl Nat [340]

ACTE DES MUNICIPALITES ET DES CHEMINS DE 1855. / Canada. Laws, Statutes, etc – Quebec: Imprime par Stewart Derbishire and George Desbarats, 1855. SEM105P192 – 3mf – 9 – Can$6.75 – cn Bibl Nat [324]

ACTE DES MUNICIPALITES ET DES CHEMINS DE 1855...LES ACTES DE LA REPRESENTATION PARLEMENTAIRE...ET LES ACTES SEIGNEURIAUX... / Canada. Laws, Statutes, etc – Quebec: Stewart Derbishire and George Desbarats..., 1855. SEM105P192 – 3mf – 9 – Can$6.75 – cn Bibl Nat [333]

ACTE DU CONGRES DE VIENNE DU 9 JUIN 1815, AVEC SES ANNEXES – Vienne, [1815] – 4mf – 9 – ILM-2946/1 – ne IDC [340]

L'ACTE MUNICIPAL DU BAS CANADA DE 1860 / Canada. Laws, Statutes, etc – Quebec: Impr. par Stewart Derbishire et George Desbarats, 1860. SEM105P195 – 2mf – 9 – Can$4.50 – cn Bibl Nat [324]

ACTE POUR ABROGER CERTAINES LOIS Y MENTIONNEES POUR MIEUX POURVOIR A LA DEFENSE DE CETTE PROVINCE ET POUR EN REGLER LA MILICE / Canada. Laws, Statutes, etc – Montreal: Stewart Derbishire and George Desbarats, 1846. SEM105P1784 – 1mf – 9 – Can$2.25 – cn Bibl Nat [971]

ACTE POUR ABROGER CERTAINS ACTES Y MENTIONNES ET ETABLIR DE MEILLEURES DISPOSITIONS RELATIVEMENT A L'ADMISSION DES ARPENTEURS ET A L'ARPENTAGE DES TERRES EN CETTE PROVINCE / Canada. Laws, Statutes, etc – Quebec: Augustin Cote, 1855. SEM105P1789 – 1mf – 9 – Can$2.25 – cn Bibl Nat [971]

ACTE POUR ABROGER CERTAINS ACTES Y MENTIONNES, ET POUR AMENDER, REFONDRE ET RESUMER EN UN SEUL ACTE..... / Canada. Laws, Statutes, etc – Quebec: Stewart Derbishire and George Desbarats, 1851. SEM105P1459 – 2mf – 9 – Can$4.50 – cn Bibl Nat [971]

ACTE POUR AMENDER ET REFONDRE LES DIFFERENTS ACTES CONCERNANT LE NOTARIAT / Canada (Province) Acte Pour Amender et Refondre... – Quebec: Imprime par Charles-Francois Langlois, [1875] – 1mf – 9 – Can$2.25 – cn Bibl Nat [340]

ACTE POUR AMENDER L'ACTE MUNICIPAL REFONDU DU BAS-CANADA / Canada. Province. Acte Pour Amender l'Acte Municipal du Bas-Canada – Quebec: Imprime par Stewart Derbishire et George Desbarats, 1861 – 1mf – 9 – Can$2.25 – cn Bibl Nat [340]

ACTE POUR AMENDER LES LOIS EN FORCE CONCERNANT LA VENTE DES LIQUEURS ENIVRANTES ET L'OCTROI DE LICENCES A CET EFFET. / Canada. Laws, Statutes, etc – Quebec: Imprime par George Desbarats et Malcom Cameron, 1864. SEM105P182 – 1mf – 9 – Can$2.25 – cn Bibl Nat [324]

ACTE POUR AMENDER LES LOIS RELATIVES A LA MILICE DE CETTE PROVINCE ET LES RENDRE PERMANENTES / Canada. Laws, Statutes, etc – Toronto: Imprime par Stewart Derbishire et George Desbarats, 1859. SEM105P178 – 1mf – 9 – Can$2.25 – cn Bibl Nat [324]

ACTE POUR FAIRE DE PLUS AMPLES DISPOSITIONS POUR L'INCORPORATION DE LA VILLE DES TROIS-RIVIERES / Canada. Laws, Statutes, etc – Toronto: Imprime par Stewart Derbishire et George Desbarats, 1857. SEM105P184 – 1mf – 9 – Can$2.25 – cn Bibl Nat [324]

ACTE POUR FAIRE UNE DIVISION NOUVELLE ET PLUS COMMODE DE LA PROVINCE EN COMTES AFIN D'AVOIR UNE REPRESENTATION (SIC) DANS L'ASSEMBLEE PLUS EGALE.. / (Canada). Bass-Canada. Chambre d'Assemblee – 1829. SEM105P529 – 1mf – 9 – Can$2.25 – cn Bibl Nat [324]

ACTE POUR L'ABOLITION DES DROITS ET DEVOIRS FEODAUX DANS LE BAS-CANADA / Canada. Laws, Statutes, etc – Quebec: Imprime par Stewart Derbishire et George Desbarats, 1854. SEM105P264 – 1mf – 9 – Can$2.25 – cn Bibl Nat [340]

ACTE POUR POURVOIR A LA DECISION SOMMAIRE DES PETITES CAUSES, DANS LE BAS-CANADA / Canada. Laws, Statutes, etc – Kingston: Imprime par S Derbishire et G Desbarats, 1844. SEM105P189 – 1mf – 9 – Can$2.25 – cn Bibl Nat [324]

ACTE POUR POURVOIR PLUS AMPLEMENT A L'INCORPORATIN DE LA VILLE DE ST HYACINTHE, ET POUR ETENDRE SES LIMITES / Canada – Quebec: Stewart Derbishire et George Desbarats, 1853. SEM105P1559 – 1mf – 9 – Can$2.25 – cn Bibl Nat [971]

ACTE POUR REGLER LA MILICE DE CETTE PROVINCE ET POUR ABROGER LES ACTES MAINTENANT EN FORCE A CETTE FIN / Canada. Laws, Statutes, etc – Quebec: Imprime par Stewart Derbishire et George Desbarats, 1855. SEM105P180 – 1mf – 9 – Can$2.25 – cn Bibl Nat [324]

DIE ACTEN DES KARPUS, DES PAPYLUS UND DER AGATHONIKE (T.U.U. 1-3/4B) / Harnack, Adolf von – Leipzig, 1888 – 1mf – 9 – ne Slangenburg [240]

ACTEN VAN DE CLASS. EN SYNOD. VERG. DER VERSCH. GEMEENTEN IN HET LAND VAN CLEEF : KEULEN EN AKEN 1571-1589 / ed by Janssen, H Q. & Toornenebergen, J van – Marnix-Ver. II/2. Utrecht 1882 – 3mf – 8 – ne Slangenburg [073]

ACTEN VAN DE CLASSICALE EN SYNODALE VERGADERINGEN DER VERSCHILLENDEN GEMEENTEN IN HET LAND VAN CLEEFF, STICHT VAN KEULEN EN AKEN 1571-1589 (DE WERKEN..2,2) / ed by Janssen, H Q & Toorenbergen, J J van – Utrecht, 1882 – Dfl13.00 – ne Slangenburg [240]

ACTEN VAN DE COLLOQUIA DER NEDERLANSCHE GEMEENTEN IN ENGELAND 1575-1624 (DE WERKEN..2,1) / ed by Toorenbergen, J J van – Utrecht, 1872 – Dfl28.00 – ne Slangenburg [240]

ACTENSTUECKE UND BELEGE UEBER DEN BRUCH DER NEUTRALITAET PREUSSENS GEGEN POLEN – Fuerth, 1832 – 2mf – 9 – ILM-2945/1 – ne IDC [340]

ACTENSTUECKE UND BRIEFE ZUR GESCHICHTE KAISER KARL 5. / Lanz, K – Wien, 1853 – 10mf – 9 – ne IDC [943]

ACTENSTUEKKE, DIE VERBESSERUNG DES BUERGERLICHE ZUSTANDES DER ISRAELITEN BETREFFEND / ed by Buchholz, C A – Stuttgard. Tuebingen. 1815. BJ-23-107 1 – 9 – ne IDC [943]

ACTES / Congres International d'Ethnologie Europeenne. (Premier) – (Commission 1: Bibliographie. F20.00. Commission 2: Outillage et techniques agricoles. F30.00. Commission 3: Poetique populaire Ballades. F90.00. Commission 4: Coutumes calendaires et fetes contemporaines. F60.00. Commission 5: Architecture populaire et musees ethnographiques de plein air. F30.00. Commission 6: Organisation familiale. F30.00. Commission 7: Films. F20.00. Commission 8: Relations intertechniques dans l'Europe contemporaine. F50.00. Commission 9: La Culture populaire et son expression museographique. F50.00) – 9 – F300.00 – fr Ethnologie [306]

ACTES / Societe d'histoire naturelle de Paris – Paris. 1792 – 3 – us Readex [580]

ACTES CONCERNANT L'EDUCATION ET LES ECOLES DANS LE BAS-CANADA / Canada. Laws, Statutes, etc – Quebec: Imprime par Stewart Derbishire et George Desbarats, 1861. SEM105P183 – 1mf – 9 – Can$2.25 – cn Bibl Nat [324]

ACTES DE LA SOCIETE D'HISTOIRE NATURELLE DE PARIS – Paris-Strasbourg, 1792. v1(1) – 9mf – 9 – 7390/2 – ne IDC [500]

ACTES DE LA SOCIETE DU CHEMIN DE FER OTTOMAN – (Comes in French and Ottoman) – 1889-1913 – 38mf – $75.00 – us MEDOC [650]

ACTES DE PHILIPPE IER, DIT LE NOBLE, COMTE ET MARQUIS DE NAMUR (1196-1212) / Walraet, M – Brussel, 1949 – 8mf – 8 – Dfl3.50ea – ne Slangenburg [200]

ACTES DE PHILIPPE IER, DIT LE NOBLE, COMTE ET MARQUIS DE NAMUR (1196-1212) / Walraet, M – Bruxelles, 1949 – Dfl30.00 – ne Slangenburg [240]

LES ACTES DE SA SAINTETE LE PAPE JEAN 23 (OCTOBRE 1958-JANVIER 1962) : BIBLIOGRAPHIE ANALYTIQUE / Saint-Philippe-Andre, Soeur – 1963. SEM105P4 – 3mf – 9 – cn Bibl Nat [240]

ACTES D'EDUCATION ELEMENTAIRE ET LES CIRCULAIRES Y RELATIVES NOS. 9 ET 12 DU SURINTENDANT DE L'EDUCATION POUR LE BAS-CANADA / Canada. Bas-Canada. Departement de l'Instruction publique – Montreal: Imp. par Stewart Derbishire et Georges Desbarats, 1849. SEM105P323 – 2mf – 9 – Can$4.50 – cn Bibl Nat [324]

ACTES D'EDUCATION ELEMENTAIRE ET POUR L'ETABLISSEMENT D'ECOLES NORMALES... / Canada. Lois, etc – Quebec: Stewart Derbishire and George Desbarats, 1852. SEM105P1521 – 1mf – 9 – Can$2.25 – cn Bibl Nat [370]

LES ACTES DES APOTRES – Pelletiers, etc. Paris (VII-XI). 1790-91 – 1 – fr A.C.R.P.P. [240]

LES ACTES DES APOTRES : TRADUCTION NOUVELLE AVEC INTRODUCTION ET NOTES / Loisy, A – Paris, 1925 – 6mf – 8 – Dfl3.50ea – ne Slangenburg [220]

ACTES DES COMTES DE NAMUR DE LA PREMIERE RACE (946-1196) / Rousseau, F – Bruxelles, 1936 – Dfl35.00 – ne Slangenburg [240]

ACTES DES ETATS GENERAUX DES ANCIENS PAYS-BAS / Cuvelier, J – Bruxelles. Tom. 1 (1424-1477). 1948 – Dfl42.00 – ne Slangenburg [240]

LES ACTES DES MARTYRS DE L'EGLISE COPTE : ETUDE CRITIQUE / Amelineau, E – Paris: E. Leroux, 1890 – 1mf – us A.T.L.A. [240]

LES ACTES DES MARTYRS DE L'EGYPTE : TIRES DES MANUSCRITS COPTES DE LA BIBLIOTHEQUE VATICANE ET DU MUSEE BORGIA / Hyvernat, Henri – Paris: E. Leroux, 1886 – 1mf – us A.T.L.A. [240]

ACTES DES MUNICIPALITES DU BAS-CANADA / Canada. Laws, Statutes, etc – Toronto: Imprime par Stewart Derbishire et George Desbarats, 1851. SEM105P170 – 2mf – 9 – Can$4.50 – cn Bibl Nat [324]

ACTES DES PRINCES-EVEQUES DE LIEGE : HUGUES DE PIERREPONT 1200-1229 / Poncelet, E – Bruxelles, 1941 – Dfl49.00 – ne Slangenburg [240]

LES ACTES. DU 2 IEME SEMINAIRE D'ETUDES SUR LE DEVELOPPEMENT RURAL DANS LES PAYS DU BASSIN MEDITERRANEEN / Lebanon. Office du Developpement Social – Beirut. 1967. BNE-19.713 1 – 9 – ne IDC [338]

ACTES DU CONGRES PANAFRICAIN DE PREHISTOIRE... : 7E SESSION / Congres Panafricain de Prehistoire, 1976 – Addis-Abeba: Abebe [et al], 1976 – 1 – F266,61 – fr Armell [500]

ACTES ET DELIBERATIONS...LES 25, 26 ET 27 JUIN 1880: ANNUAIRE NO. 3 DU CERCLE CATHOLIQUE DE QUEBEC, 1879-80 / Congres Catholique Canadien francais. Ier: 1880. Quebec, Quebec – Montreal: E. Senecal, 1880. 00126. (Pre-1900 Canadiana) – 9 – cn C.I.H.M. [240]

ACTES POUR PROMOUVOIR L'EDUCATION DANS LE BAS CANADA / Canada. Laws, Statutes, etc – Toronto: Imprime par Stewart Derbishire et George Desbarats, 1857. SEM105P202 – 1mf – 9 – Can$2.25 – cn Bibl Nat [324]

ACTES RELATIFS A LA RECONSTRUCTION DE L'ABBAYE DE DAOULAS (15 AVRIL 1722-18 AOUT 1723 / Daoulas abbaye – (Microfilme avec/microfilmed with: – Explication des blasons qui sont dans la grande verriere de l'eglise abbatiale de Daoulas) – 18th cent. 2v – 1 – F50.00 – fr Armell [240]

ACTES RELATIFS AUX CHEMINS A BARRIERES ET PONTS DANS ET PRES QUEBEC / Canada (Province) Lois, etc. – Quebec: Imprime par Stewart Derbishire et George Desbarats, 1853 – 1mf – 9 – Can$2.25 – cn Bibl Nat [340]

ACTES RELATIFS AUX POUVOIRS, AUX DEVOIRS ET A LA PROTECTION DES JUGES DE PAIX DANS LE BAS-CANADA AVEC UN INDEX ANALYTIQUE / Canada. Laws, Statutes, etc – Quebec: Imprime par Stewart Derbishire et George Desbarats, 1853. SEM105P175 – 2mf – 9 – Can$4.50 – cn Bibl Nat [324]

ACTES RELATIFS AUX POUVOIRS, AUX DEVOIRS ET A LA PROTECTION DES JUGES DE PAIX DANS LE BAS-CANADA, AVEC UN INDEX ANALYTIQUE COMPLET / Canada. Laws, Statutes, etc – Toronto: Imprime par S Derbishire et G Desbarats, 1858. SEM105P177 – 2mf – 9 – Can$4.50 – cn Bibl Nat [324]

LES ACTES SEIGNEURIAUX: SAVOIR: L'ACTE SEIGNEURIAL DE 1854...L'ACTE D'AMENDEMENT SEIGNEURIAL DE 1855. – Toronto: Imprime par S. Derbishire et G. Desbarats, 1856. SEM105P267 – 1mf – 9 – Can$2.25 – cn Bibl Nat [323]

ACTI DEL CONGRESSO INTERNAZIONALE DI SCIENZE STORICHE – (Roma,1-9 Aprile 1903) v3. Roma, 1906 – 13mf – 9 – Dfl4.00 – ne Slangenburg [073]

ACTING THE DANCE : AN APPLICATION OF THE STANISLAVSKI ACTING METHOD / Plumlee, Linda K – 1989 – 106p 2mf – 9 – $8.00 – us Microform Publ [790]

L'ACTION – (Filmed as part of: Commune de Paris newspapers. Newspapers on these reels are filmed chronologically, not alphabetically) – [Paris]: Impr Balitout, apr 6,8-9 1871 – us Res Libr [072]

L'ACTION / ed by Fournier, Jules & Asselin, Olivar – Montreal, Canada. 15 avr 1911-29 avr 1916 – 1r – 1 – Can$45.00 – cn Can Microfilming [072]

L'ACTION – Paris. 29 mars 1903-1924 – 1 – fr A.C.R.P.P. [073]

L'ACTION – Port-au-Prince, Haiti: Impr du Petit Impartial, 1 annee n2-106. 1juin 1929-5 juin 1930 – us Res Libr [072]

L'ACTION – Port-au-Prince, Haiti: L'Action, 2eme annee n101-5eme annee n363. 9 sep 1948-25 aout 1952 – us Res Libr [072]

L'ACTION – Quebec, Canada. 3 jul 1962-8 sep 1973 – 67r – 1 – Can$55.00r – cn Can Microfilming [072]

L'ACTION : SUPPLEMENTS ET INDEX ANNUEL – Quebec, 1935-64 – 19r – 1 – Can$55.00r – cn Can Microfilming [072]

L'ACTION *see* L'ACTION DE MONTCALM

ACTION – Hollywood. v1-9 sep 1966-dec 1974 1; v 10 jan-dec 1975 1,5,9 – 1,5,9 – D10525 – us UMI [073]

ACTION – Issue Nos. 11-15 Apr 1939-Aug 1939 – 5mf – 15 – $31,95 – us Comics [760]

ACTION – Issue Nos. 1-5 Jun-Oct 1938 – 5mf – 15 – $31,95 – us Comics [760]

ACTION – Issue Nos. 16-20 Sept 1939-Jan 1940 – 5mf – 15 – $31,95 – us Comics [760]

ACTION – Issue Nos. 21-25 Feb 1940-Jun 1940 – 5mf – 15 – $31,95 – us Comics [760]

ACTION – Issue Nos. 26-30 Jul 1940-Nov 1940 – 5mf – 15 – $31.95 – us Comics [760]

ACTION – Issue Nos. 31-35 Dec 1940-Apr 1941 – 5mf – 15 – $31.95 – us Comics [760]

ACTION – Issue Nos. 36-40 May 1941-Sept 1941 – 5mf – 15 – $31.95 – us Comics [760]

ACTION – Issue Nos. 41-45 Oct 1941-Feb 1942 – 5mf – 15 – $31.95 – us Comics [760]

ACTION – Issue Nos. 46-50 Mar 1942-July 1942 – 5mf – 15 – $31.95 – us Comics [760]

ACTION – Issue Nos. 51-55 Aug 1942-Dec 1942 – 5mf – 15 – $31.95 – us Comics [760]

ACTION – Issue Nos. 6-10 Nov 1938-Mar 1939 – 5mf – 15 – $31,95 – us Comics [760]

ACTION – [New York: Action], feb 26 1973-feb 25 1974 – 1r – 1 – us Res Libr [071]

ACTION – New York, NY. 1969-83 – 1 – us A.J.P.C. [071]

ACTION – Paris. 9 sept 1944-9 mai 1952 – 1 – fr A.C.R.P.P. [073]

ACTION AND REACTION – [New York: Arabic-English Newspaper Inc]. apr 4 1977-apr 1 1983 – 1r – 1 – us Res Libr [071]

THE ACTION AND USES IN MEDICINE OF DIGITALIS / Cushny, A R – London, 1925 – 6mf – 9 – ne IDC [615]

L'ACTION ANTIMILITARISTE – Marseille. Mens. sept 1904-janv 1905 – 1 – fr A.C.R.P.P. [073]

L'ACTION CANADIENNE : LIGUE D'ACTION CANADIENNE – Trois-Rivieres, Canada. v3 n1. nov 1925 – 1r – 1 – Can$25.00 – cn Can Microfilming [072]

L'ACTION CANADIENNE – Riviere-du-Loup (Fraserville), Canada. 2 mai 1911-v4 n11. 21 oct 1914 – 1r – 1 – Can$30.00 – cn Can Microfilming [072]

ACTION CANADIENNE-FRANCAISE – v1-20. 1917-1928 – 1 – cn Precision [073]

L'ACTION CATHOLIQUE ET L'ACTION – Quebec, Canada. 1 fev. 1915-30 jun 1962 – 192r – 1 – Can$55.00r – cn Can Microfilming [072]

L'ACTION CONSERVATRICE : CARICATURES ET PHOTOS – Montreal, Canada. 19 oct 1934-v1 n49. 11 oct 1935 – 1r – 1 – Can$30.00 – cn Can Microfilming [072]

L'ACTION D'ART – Paris. No.1-18.Fevr-dec 1913.Mq. no.: 7,12 – 1 – fr A.C.R.P.P. [073]

L'ACTION DE MONTCALM – (Becomes: L'Action 18 sep 1974-5 oct 1977. Becomes: Journal L'Action 12 oct 1977-23 dec 1991) – Joliette, Canada. 28 aut 1974-11 sep 1974 – 32r – 1 – Can$70.00r – cn Can Microfilming [072]

ACTION DES CHRETIENS POUR L'ABOLITION DE LA TORTURE = CHRISTIAN ACTION FOR THE ABOLITION OF TORTURE – Paris. 133 docs. 1980-1991 – 83mf – 9 – ne IDC [320]

L'ACTION DES DEUX-MONTAGNES – St Eustache, Canada. jan 1962-v4 n19. 25 aut 1965 – 1r – 1 – Can$50.00 – cn Can Microfilming [072]

L'ACTION DES JEUNES / ed by Richer-Louveteau, H – Montreal, Canada. 23 mai 1935 – 1r – 1 – Can$25.00 – cn Can Microfilming [072]

L'ACTION DIRECTE – no. 4-31. Paris. fevr-sept 1908 – 1 – fr A.C.R.P.P. [073]

L'ACTION DIRECTE EXERCEE PAR LA VICTIME D'UN ACCIDENT ... / Bernays, J – Paris, 1933 – 2mf – 9 – ILM-3157/1 – ne IDC [327]

ACTION FOR HUMAN WELFARE – (Consists of v.3, no.6-7; v.6, no.3-4; v.9, no.4; v.10, no.3,7-10 (June-July 1945, Aug. 1946, Sept. 1947, Feb. 15, April-June 1948) – Norwalk, Ohio: Action Publishers – 1 – CSUX89-S89 – us Hoover Inst Photo [360]

L'ACTION FRANCAISE / ed by Groulx, Lionel – (Becomes: L'Action Nationale. jan 1933) – Montreal. v1 n1. jan 1917-dec 1921 – 1r – 1 – cn Can Microfilming [072]

L'ACTION FRANCAISE – Paris, Lyon. Quot. 21 mars 1908-24 aout 1944 – 1 – fr A.C.R.P.P. [072]

L'ACTION FRANCAISE – Paris, may 13 1938-jun 6 1940; mar 26-dec 17 1941 – 9r – 1 – us Res Libr [072]

ACTION IN TEACHER EDUCATION – Reston. v1-17 Sum 1978-Win 1996. v18 Spr 1996-Win 1997. v19 Spr 1997-Win 1998 – 1,5,9 – D11661 – us UMI [370]

L'ACTION INDOCHINOISE – no. 1. Saigon. 23 aout 1928 – 1 – fr A.C.R.P.P. [072]

ACTION INFORMATIQUE / ed by Tocco, Gil – Montreal, 23 mai 1988-11 fev 1991 – 1r – 1 – Can$75.00 – cn Can Microfilming [072]

ACTION LIBERALE / ed by Masson, Lorenzo – Quebec, Canada. 12 avr 1930-26 sep 1931 – 1r – 1 – Can$40.00 – cn Can Microfilming [072]

L'ACTION MUSICALE / ed by Lapierre, Eugene – Montreal, Canada. 9 avr 1932-23 jul 1932 – 1r – 1 – Can$25.00 – cn Can Microfilming [780]

L'ACTION NATIONALE – Port-au-Prince. Oct 30 1931-June 19 1934. Incomplete – 1 – us NY Public [072]

L'ACTION NATIONALE *see* L'ACTION FRANCAISE

AN ACTION PLAN OF ASSISTANCE FOR THE SMALL FARMERS OF NEW MEXICO / New Mexico State University – 1979. 1 reel – 1,5 – us Spaulding [630]

L'ACTION REGIONALISTE – Paris. fevr 1902; 1903-juin juil 1914; fevr-sept oct 1920; 1933-mars 1940; 1953-61; janv mars-juil sept 1968 – 1 – fr A.C.R.P.P. [073]

L'ACTION SOCIALE – Quebec, Canada. 21 dec 1907-30 jan 1915 – 16r – 1 – Can$55.00r – cn Can Microfilming [072]

ACTION SOCIALE DE LA FEMME ET LE LIVRE FRANCAIS – v1-39 10 Apr 1902-Nov 1939. Jan 1903 wanting – 1 – $109.00 – us L of C Photodup [305]

L'ACTION SOCIALE ET CATHOLIQUE : HEBDO – Quebec, Canada. 1908-1917 – 5r – 1 – Can$55.00r – cn Can Microfilming [072]

L'ACTION SYNDICALE – Lens. 17 janv 1904-2 oct 1910. Suite de: REVEIL SYNDICAL – 1 – fr A.C.R.P.P. [073]

L'ACTION UNIVERSITAIRE : REVUE DES ANCIENS DE L'UNIVERSITE DE MONTREAL – (Cont by: L'Inter avr 1961-sep 1972. Cont by: L'Interdit jan 1973-jun 1980 1r Can$60.00. Becomes: Les Diplomes sep 1980-1993 1r Can$60.00) – Montreal: Univ de Montreal. Dec 1934-Aut 1960 – 4r – 1 – Can$60.00r – cn Can Microfilming [370]

THE ACTIS AND DEIDIS OF SCHIR WILLIAM WALLACE / Henry the Minstrel – 1570 – 9 – $25.00 – us Scholars' Facs [810]

ACTITUD – C.1: v.1:no.1 1954:Feb.-v.1:no.11 (1954:Dec.) – 1 – CSUXAJA8261-S – us Hoover Inst Photo [946]

LA ACTITUD INTERNACIONAL: CEGUERA PARA EL VERDADERO PELIGRO – Madrid, 1936? Fiche W 702. (Blodgett Collection of Spanish Civil War Pamphlets) – 9 – us H.U. College Libr [946]

ACTIVE AND PASSIVE ELECTRONIC COMPONENTS / ed by Campbell, D S – 1,5,9 – us Gordon [621]

ACTIVIDADES DE EDUCACION FUNDAMENTAL EN LA PROVINCIA DE BADAJOZ / Ministerio de Educacion Nacional. Junta Nacional contra el analfabetismo – Madrid: Sucesores de Rivadeneyra S.A. – sp Bibl Santa Ana [370]

ACTIVIDADES DOS MISSIONARIOS... / Castelo-Branco, Fernando A – Madrid: Archivo Ibero Americano, 1960 – 1 – sp Bibl Santa Ana [240]

ACTIVIST – (Ceased publ) – Buffalo. v1-2. sep 1969-may 1971 – 1 – D7786 – us UMI [073]

ACTIVIST – (Ceased publ) – Oberlin. v1-15 oct 1960-Spr 1975 1; v11-15 1971-1975 5 – 1,5 – D2328 – us UMI [073]

ACTIVITE DU SECTEUR MINIER / Morocco. Direction des Mines et de la Geologie – 1971-72. BNE-3037 1 – 9 – ne IDC [622]

L'ACTIVITEA1 DE L'ASSEMBLEA1E PARLEMENTAIRE EUROPEA1ENE / European Parliamentary Assembly – Paris. Dec 1959 Jan 1960-Aug Sept 1961 – 1 – us NY Public [324]

LES ACTIVITES ET LES PUBLICATIONS DU CENTRE CANADIEN DES CERCLES LACORDAIRE ET SAINTE-JEANNE D'ARC DEPUIS SA FONDATION EN DECEMBRE 1939 / Lacroix, Denise – 1953. SEM105P4 – 1mf – 9 – cn Bibl Nat [240]

ACTIVITIES, ADAPTATION AND AGING / ed by Foster, Phyllis M – v1- 1980- – 1, 9 ($135.00 in US $189.00 outside hardcopy subsc) – us Haworth [618]

ACTON 1734-1849 – (Mf 1T-3T: Births & Deaths 1735-1816. Mf 3T-4T: Intentions 1734-1813. Mf 4T: Marriages 1739-1812. Mf 4T-5T: Births 1791-1851. Mf 5T: Deaths 1801-44; Out-of-Town Marriages 1738-99. Mf 5T-6T: Intentions 1813-50. Mf 6T-7T: Marriages 1812-49. Mf 7T: Births & Deaths 1844-49) – (mf ed 1994) – 7mf – 9 – 0-87623-197-0 – us Holbrook [920]

ACTON FREE PRESS – Acton, 1893-1984 – 63r – 1 – cn Preston [971]

ACTON FREE PRESS – Acton, Canada. 1875-95 – 7r – 1 – $455.00 – cn Library Assoc [971]

ACTON GAZETTE – London, 1967-81 – 30r – 1 – uk British Libr Newspaper [072]

Acton, John Emerich Edward Dalberg *see* LECTURES ON THE FRENCH REVOLUTION

Acton, John Emerich Edward Dalberg Acton, Baron *see* LECTURES ON MODERN HISTORY

Acton, Richard *see* OUR COLONIAL EMPIRE

ACTON ROOSTER – Acton, CA. Nov 1900-Dec 1913 – 1r – 1 – $50.00 – C02000 – us Library Micro [071]

ACTORS AND MANAGERS OF THE ENGLISH AND AMERICAN STAGE, SERIES 1 – (Pt 1: From Box 1-30. Pt 2: From Box 36-39) – Papers of Henry Irving and Ellen Terry from the Bram Stoker Collection, The Shakespeare Centre Library, Stratford-upon-Avon – 1 – us Primary [790]

ACTORS AND MANAGERS OF THE ENGLISH AND AMERICAN STAGE, SERIES 2 : THE PAPERS OF DAVID GARRICK – (Pt 1: Correspondence from the John Forster Collection at the National Art Library, Victoria and Albert Museum) – 1 – us Primary [790]

ACTORS' EQUITY ASSOCIATION COUNCIL MINUTES, 1913-1970 AND EXECUTIVE COMMITEE MINUTES, 1918-1924 – (Series 1: Council Minutes Council Proceedings. Includes index to the minutes 1918-25 & a file of motions to council 1919-25. Series 2: Executive Committee Minutes – Meetings 1918-24. No minutes for 1921) – 73r – 1 – £4,520.00 – uk Chadwyck [790]

ACTORS' EQUITY ASSOCIATION MAGAZINE : EQUITY – EQUITY NEWS – dec 1915-spr 1973 (Equity) aug 1973-dec 1981 (Equity News) – 255mf – 9 – £910.00 – uk Chadwyck [790]

ACTORUM ET GESTORUM SUECO-POLONICO-RUM SEMESTRALE SECUNDUM – N.p., 1657 – 1mf – 9 – ILM-1010/1 – ne IDC [340]

ACTS AND DOCUMENTS : CHARTER OF THE UNITED NATIONS, THE STATUTE AND RULES OF COURT AND OTHER DOCUMENTS / UN International Court of Justice – nos 1-4 – E/F21 – 9 – us U.N. Pubs [340]

THE ACTS AND NEGOTIATIONS : GENERAL PEACE, CONCLUDED AT RYSWICK, ... – London, 1698 – 4mf – 9 – ILM-830/1 – ne IDC [340]

ACTS AND ORDINANCES OF THE GOVERNOR AND COUNCIL OF NEW SOUTH WALES : AND ACTS OF PARLIAMENT ENACTED FOR, AND APPLIED TO, THE COLONY, WITH NOTES AND INDEX / Callaghan, Thomas – Sydney: W J Row. 2v + app. 1844 – 17mf – 9 – $25.00 – LLMC 96-002 – us L.L.M.C. [323]

ACTS: INTRODUCTION, AV, RV, WITH NOTES, INDEX / Bartlet, James Vernon – Edinburgh: Jack, (19–?). 1 fiche – 9 – us A.T.L.A. [240]

ACTS OF ENGLISH MARTYRS : HITHERTO UNPUBLISHED / Pollen, John Hungerford – London: Burns and Oates, 1891 – 1mf – us A.T.L.A. [240]

ACTS OF PARLIAMENT / Scotland. Parliament – 1124-1707 – 4r – 1 – $200.00 – us Trans-Media [324]

ACTS OF PARLIAMENT AND BENCH TABLE ORDERS OF THE INNER TEMPLE / England. Inns of Court – London, 1926 – 2mf – 9 – $3.00 – LLMC 84-269 – us L.L.M.C. [324]

ACTS OF THE APOSTLES : WITH NOTES, CRITICAL, EXPLANATORY, AND PRACTICAL... / Cowles, Henry – New York: D Appleton, 1883 – 1mf – 9 – 0-8370-2751-9 – 1985-0751 – us A.T.L.A. [220]

THE ACTS OF THE APOSTLES / Harnack, Adolf von – London: Williams & Norgate, 1909. 1 fiche – 9 – us A.T.L.A. [240]

THE ACTS OF THE APOSTLES / Stokes, George Thomas – New York: A.C. Armstrong, 1891. 2 fiches – 9 – us A.T.L.A. [240]

THE ACTS OF THE APOSTLES : WITH INTRODUCTION AND NOTES / Page, Thomas Ethelbert – (Includes bibliographical references, glossary, index) – London: Macmillan, 1895 – 1mf – 9 – 0-8370-4656-4 – 1985-2656 – us A.T.L.A. [220]

THE ACTS OF THE APOSTLES : WITH MAPS, INTRODUCTION AND NOTES / Lumby, Joseph Rawson – (Includes bibliographical references and indexes) – stereotyped ed. Cambridge: University Press; New York: Macmillan [distributor], 1897 – 1mf – 9 – 0-8370-6753-7 – 1986-0753 – us A.T.L.A. [220]

THE ACTS OF THE APOSTLES: IN GREEK AND ENGLISH: WITH NOTES / Rendall, Frederic – London: Macmillan, 1897.1 fiche – 9 – us A.T.L.A. [240]

ACTS OF THE CHURCH, 1531-1885 : THE CHURCH OF ENGLAND HER OWN REFORMER, AS TESTIFIED BY THE RECORDS OF HER CONVOCATIONS, WITH APPENDIX CONTAINING LEGAL INSTRUMENTS ANCIENT AND MODERN CONNECTED WITH THOSE ASSEMBLIES AND COMMENTS THEREON / Joyce, James Wayland – London: J. Whitaker, 1886 – 1mf – us A.T.L.A. [240]

ACTS OF THE DEACONS: BEING A COURSE OF LECTURES...ON ACTS / Goulburn, Edward Meyrick – London: Rivingtons, 1867. 1 fiche – 9 – us A.T.L.A. [240]

ACTS OF THE GENERAL ASSEMBLY OF THE COMMONWEALTH OF KENTUCKY / Kentucky. Laws, Statutes, etc – Frankfort. On film: 1900-72. LL-060 – 1 – us L of C Photodup [340]

ACTS OF THE ITALIAN PARLIAMENT, 1848-1870 – $3,000.00 – us UPA [320]

THE ACTS OF THE PARLIAMENTS OF SCOTLAND, 1124-1707 / Scotland – v1-12. 1814-44 – 1 – $480.00 – 0-89093-030-9 – us UPA [941]

ACTS OF THE PRIVY COUNCIL OF ENGLAND : COLONIAL SERIES, 1613-1783 / Grant, W L & Munro, James – v1-6. 1908-12 – 1 – $200.00 – 0-89093-031-7 – us UPA [941]

ACTS RELATING TO CAR TRUSTS, AS IN FORCE DOWN TO AUGUST 1, 1893 / Rawle, Francis – Philadelphia, 1893. 111 p. LL-1067 – 1 – us L of C Photodup [340]

THE ACTS RELATING TO COMMON SCHOOLS AND ALSO SEPARATE SCHOOLS IN ONTARIO:.. / ed by Hodgins, J George – Toronto: Hunter, Rose, 1870. 06798. (Pre-1900 Canadiana) – 9 – cn C.I.H.M. [971]

ACTS RELATING TO THE POWERS, DUTIES AND PROTECTION OF THE JUSTICES OF THE PEACE IN LOWER CANADA WITH A FULL SYNOPTICAL INDEX / Canada. Laws, Statutes, etc – Quebec: Derbishire et G Desbarats, 1853. SEM105P176 – 2mf – 9 – Can$4.50 – cn Bibl Nat [324]

THE ACTS TO REGULATE COMMERCE : INDEXED AND DIGESTED / Hamlin, Charles S – Boston: Little Brown, 1907 – 5mf – 9 – $7.50 – LLMC 80-525 – us L.L.M.C. [340]

ACTUACION DE LA JUNTA DE SENORAS DE LA CRUZ ROJA DE BADAJOZ DURANTE LA CAMPANA DE AFRICA DE 1921 Y 1922 / Badajoz, Cruz Roja – Badajoz: La Libertad, 1923 – 1 – sp Bibl Santa Ana [946]

LA ACTUACION INTERNACIONAL DE LAS SOCIEDADES / Basombrio y Echenique, C – Lima, 1919 – 1mf – 9 – ILM-3291/1 – ne IDC [340]

ACTUACION POLICIAL DE UNNEXTREMENO EN EL SIGLO 17 / Munoz de San Pedro, Miguel – D. Luis de Tapia y Paredes. Badajoz: Imp. Diput. Provincial. Sep. Rev. Est. Extremenos – 1 – sp Bibl Santa Ana [320]

ACTUAL SPECIFYING ENGINEER – (Cont by: Specifying Engineer) – Chicago. v1-34. 1958-75* – 1 – D14966 – us UMI [073]

ACTUALIDAD COLONIAL – Lisbon: Editorial Cosmos, n1-3. jan-mar/apr 1935 – us Res Libr [072]

ACTUALIDAD LINGUISTICA DE FRANCISCO SANCHEZ DE LAS BROZAS / Salinero, Fernando G – Badajoz: Imprenta Diputacion Provincial, 1973 – sp Bibl Santa Ana [410]

ACTUALIDAD LITURGICA – Mexico: Obra Nacional de la Buena Prensa, n20-109. 1978-92 – 6r – 1 – us Res Libr [072]

ACTUALIDAD PASTORAL – Buenos Aires: Actualidad Pastoral. v7 n68-v25 n195. feb 1974-1992 – 5r – 1 – us Res Libr [072]

A ACTUALIDADE : ORGAO DO PARTIDO LIBERAL – Ouro Preto, Mar 1878-Dec 1881 – 1,5,6 – bl Biblioteca [072]

ACTUALIDADE : JORNAL POLITICO, COMMERCIAL E AGRICOLA – Santo Amaro, BA. 18 Out 1884 – 1,5,6 – bl Biblioteca [072]

ACTUALIDADE : SEMANARIO, IMPARCIAL E POPULAR – Cidade de Santo Antonio de Jesus, BA. 30 Ago 1891 – 1,5,6 – bl Biblioteca [072]

O ACTUALIDADES – Manaos, Amazonas. 13-20 Jun 1904 – 1,5,6 – bl Biblioteca [072]

ACTUALISATION DES STATISTIQUES AGRICOLES MAROCAINES 1959/1960 A 1966/1967 / Morocco. Ministere de l'Agriculture – 1969. BNE-3067 1 – 9 – ne IDC [630]

L'ACTUALITE / ed by Levesque, D – Montreal, Canada. v2 n24. 27 mai 1928 – 1r – 1 – Can$25.00 – cn Can Microfilming [072]

L'ACTUALITE – Toronto, 1961- – 1,9 – Can$75.00y 1 Can$82.00y 9 – cn Micromedia [073]

ACTUALITE – Gaspe, Canada. avr 1961-jun 1966 – 2r – 1 – Can$55.00r – cn Can Microfilming [073]

ACTUALITE – Montreal. v1-22 sep 1976-dec 1997+ 1*; v14-22 1989-dec 1997+ 5*,9* – 1,5,9 – D17814 – us UMI [073]

L'ACTUALITE JURIDIQUE – (Droit administratif. 1950-92. 5. Propriete immobiliere. 1950-92. 5) – Paris. nov 1945-49. A partir de 1950, divise en deux parties – 5 – fr A.C.R.P.P. [073]

L'ACTUALITE LITTERAIRE, ARTISTIQUE, SCIENTIFIQUE – no. 1-26. Paris. 2 juin-24 nov 1861 – 1 – fr A.C.R.P.P. [073]

ACTUALITE PHARMACEUTIQUE – v1. 1993/94 – 1 – Can$85.00y – cn Micromedia [615]

L'ACTUALITEE – Port-au-Prince: Ambiard, 1re annee n1-2eme annee n90. 26 mai 1906-22 fevr 1908 – us Res Libr [072]

ACTUALITES AFRICAINES – Leopoldville: Impr de l'Avenir, jun 4,18-jul 9 1960 – us Res Libr [072]

ACTUALITES DE KIVU – Bukavu, mar 17-may 26, jun 9-aug 11 1962 – us Res Libr [072]

ACTUARIAL REVIEW – Arlington. v1-17 1974-90*. v18-24 feb 1991-97+ – 1 – D12639 – us UMI [310]

ACTUELLE GERONTOLOGIE *see* AKTUELLE GERONTOLOGIE

ACTUELLE TRAUMATOLOGIE *see* AKTUELLE TRAUMATOLGIE

ACTUELLE UROLOGIE *see* AKTUELLE UROLOGIE

ACUERDOS DEL EXTINGUIDO CABILDO DE BUENOS AIRES / Mallie, Augusto S – Madrid: Razon y Fe, 1926 – 1 – sp Bibl Santa Ana [972]

ACUERDOS DEL EXTINGUIDO CABILDO DE BUENOS AIRES... : SEVIE 3, TOMO 7 (1782-85) / Mallie, Augusto S – Buenos Aires, 1930; Madrid: Razon y Fe, 1931 – 1 – sp Bibl Santa Ana [350]

ACUERDOS DEL EXTINGUIDO CABILDO DE BUENOS AIRES. SERIE 2, TOMO 4 (1719 A 1722). BUENOS AIRES, 1927 / Mallie, Augusto S; ed by Bayle, Constantino – Madrid: Razon y Fe, 1928 – 9 – sp Bibl Santa Ana [972]

ACUERDOS DEL EXTINGUIDO CABILDO DE BUENOS AIRES. SERIE 2, TOMO 6 1729-1733; SERIE 3, TOMO 5 1774-76; SERIE 4, TOMO 5 1812-1813. BUENOS AIRES, 1918-1928 / Mallie, Augusto S – Madrid: Razon y Fe, 1929 – 1 – sp Bibl Santa Ana [946]

ACUERDOS DEL EXTINGUIDO CABILDO DE BUENOS AIRES. SERIE 2, TOMO 9 Y SERIE 3, TOMO 9 / Bayle, Constantino – Buenos Aires, 1931; Madrid: Razon y Fe, 1933 – 1 – sp Bibl Santa Ana [972]

Acuna, Cristobal de *see* NUEVO DESCUBRIMIENTO DEL GRAN RIO DE LAS AMAZONAS

Acuna de Figueroa, Francisco Esteban *see* OBRAS COMPLETAS

Acuna, Marcelo Luis *see* DE FRONDIZIA ALFONS IN

ACUPUNCTURE AND ELECTRO-THERAPEUTICS RESEARCH – Oxford. v1-10 1975-85. v11 1986*. v12-18 1987-93 1; v1-12 1975-87. v13 1988*. v14-18 1989-93 5; v1-18 1975-93 9. v19 1994*. v20-22 1995-97+ 1,5,9 – 1,5,9 – D49003 – us UMI [615]

ACUS – ANNUAL REPORTS / Administrative Conference of the U.S. (ACUS) – (Lacking: 1981) – 1969 thru 1993 – 36mf – 9 – $54.00 – LLMC 94-335 – us L.L.M.C. [340]

ACUS – RECOMENDATIONS AND REPORTS *see* ACUS – ANNUAL REPORTS

ACUS RECOMMENDATIONS AND REPORTS / U.S. Administrative Conference of the United States – (With composite index in v4 to all publ works prior to Dec 1977, including the reports of 2 temporary conferences of 1953 + 1961. Followed by annual reports and recommendations in 1 or 2 vols, from 1978-1992. Lacking: 1990. Updates planned) – Washington: GPO. v1-4. 8 Jan 1968-31 Dec 1977 – 9 – $258.00 – LLMC 82-207 – us L.L.M.C. [324]

ACUSADO A LA INQUISICION / Esquivel, Antonio – Madrid: Graf. Calleja, 1969 – 1 – sp Bibl Santa Ana [240]

ACUSHNET 1860-1900 – (Mf 1: Births 1860-85. Mf 2: Births 1886-1900. Mf 2: Marriages 1860-67. Mf 3: Marriages 1867-99. Mf 4: Marriages 1899-1900. Mf 4: Deaths 1860-85. Mf 5: Deaths 1886-1900) – (mf ed 1992) – 5mf – 9 – 0-87623-137-7 – us Holbrook [920]

ACUTE CARDIOVASCULAR RESPONSES OF CARDIAC PATIENTS TO DYNAMIC VARIABLE RESISTANCE EXERCISE OF VARYING INTENSITY / Stralow, C R – 1991 – 1mf – 9 – $4.00 – us Microform Publ [612]

THE ACUTE EFFECTS OF MODERATE ITENSITY CIRCUIT WEIGHT TRAINING ON LIPID-LIPOPROTEIN PROFILES / Lee, Y – 1991 – 2mf – 9 – $8.00 – us Microform Publ [612]

ACUTE EFFECTS OF STRENGTH TRAINING ON CARDIORESPIRATORY PARAMETERS DURING SUBSEQUENT AEROBIC EXERCISE / Wallis, Jason D – Oregon State University, 1995 – 1mf – 9 – PH 1514 – us Microform Publ [612]

THE ACUTE PHYSIOLOGICAL RESPONSES TO WALKING WITH AND WITHOUT POWER POLES IN PATIENTS WITH CARDIAC DISEASE / Walter, Patrick – University of Wisconsin-La Crosse, 1995 – 1mf – 9 – PH 1515 – us Microform Publ [612]

Acworth, W M *see* THE STATE IN RELATION TO RAILWAYS

Aczi *see* DIVAN

AD : UNITED CHURCH OF CHRIST EDITION – (Former titles: A.D. United Church Herald Edition; A.D. United Church of Christ Edition; A.D: the Magazine for the United Church of Christ Family) – New York. v1-12 sep 1972-aug 1983 1; v3 jan-dec 1974*; v5-6 jan 1976-dec 1977*; v7 jan-dec 1978; v8-12 jan 1979-aug 1983 5; v3 jan-dec 1974*; v5-7 jan 1976-dec 1978*; v8-12 jan 1979-aug 1983 – 1,5,9 – $83.70y – D9291 – us UMI [240]

AD : UNITED PRESBYTERIAN EDITION – (Supersedes: Presbyterian Life. Former titles: A.D. Presbyterian Life Edition; A.D. United Presbyterian Edition; A.D: the Magazine for the United Presbyterian Family) – New York. v1-12 sep 1972-aug 1983 1; v1 sep-dec 1972; v3 jan-dec 1974; v5-6 jan 1976-dec 1977; v7-8 jan 1978-dec 1979* ; v9 jan-dec 1980; v10-12 jan 1981-aug 1983* 5; v5-12 jan 1976-aug 1983 9 – 1,5,9 – $83.70y – us UMI [240]

AD AND D, AUTOMOTIVE DESIGN AND DEVELOPMENT – (Cont. Autoproducts) – Oak Park. v14-18 may 1976-may 1980 1; v15-18 jan 1977-may 1980 5,9; v15 1977* 9 – 1,5,9 – D7934.01 – us UMI [629]

AD ASTRA = TO THE STARS – (Microfiche shipped yrly or qrtly. Cont: Space World) – Washington. v1-9. jan 1989-dec 1997+ – 1,5,9 – D17079 – us UMI [520]

AD CAESAREM ORATIO PRO CHRISTIANA REPV... / Coptius, F – Romae, 1523 – 1mf – 9 – H-8230/1 – ne IDC [956]

AD CHRISTIANOS PRINCIPES DE SVSCEPTO PRO CHRISTIANA REP. CONTRA TURCAS BELLO COMMUNITER CONFICIENDO... / Ginius, L – Senis, 1572 – 1mf – 9 – H-8328/1 – ne IDC [956]

AD CLERUM / Parker, Joseph – 1873 – 9 – us A.T.L.A. [240]

AD FORUM – (Cont by: Adweek, National Marketing ed) – New York. v3-6 jan 1982-may 1985 1,9; v3-5 jan 1982-dec 1984*. v6 jan-may 1985 5 – 1 – D13435 – us UMI [073]

AD FORUM *see* ADWEEK

AD HISTORIAM CASSINENSIS ACCESSIONES / Gattula, Erasmus, OSB – Venetiis. v1-3. 1734 – Dfl140.00 – ne Slangenburg [240]

AD MAVORTIUM LOLLIANUM ASTRONOMICON, LIB. VIII / Firmicus Maternus, Julius – Per Nicolaum Prucknerum. Basileae: Ex officina I. Hervagii, 1533 – 1 – us U.W. Library [520]

AD MONACHOS DEHORTATIONES / Trithemius, J – Romae, 1898 – 10mf – 8 – Dfl35.00 – ne Slangenburg [240]

AD NURSE – (Cont by: Advancing Clinical Care) – Franksville. v1-4 jan 1986-apr 1989 – 1,5,9 – D16482 – us UMI [610]

AD NURSE *see* ADVANCING CLINICAL CARE

AD PHYSIOLOGUM / Epiphanius, Saint, Bishop of Constantia in Cyprus – O-841 1. 1587-1588 – 9 – ne IDC [612]

AD REVERENDISSIMUM IN CHRISTO PATREM ET D.D. ANTONIUM GALEAZ. DE BENTIVOLIS SEDIS APOSTOLICAE PROTHONOTARIUM B.M. JOHANNIS SPADARII IN MUSICA HUMILIMI... / Spataro, Giovanni – 1491 – 9 – us Sibley [780]

AD SANCTA SANCTORUM: OH BONE JESU MISERERE NOSTRI, SATB, LATIN TEXT / Palestrina, Giovanni Pierluigi – Ms score, 178- – 1 – us Sibley [780]

AD SUAM HISTORIAM AETHIOPICAM ANTEHAC EDITAM COMMENTARIUS. : IN QUO MULTA BREVITER DICTA FULSIUS NARRANTUR... / Ludolfi, Iobi (alias Leutholf dicti) – (Filmed with: his Relatio nova de hodierno Habessiniae statu...) – Francofurti ad Moenum: Sumptibus Johannis David Zunneri: Typis: Martini Jacqueti, 1691 – 9 – us Res Libr [960]

AD VIRUM NOBILEM DE CULTU CONFUCII PHILOSOPHI ET PROGENITORUM APUD SINAS / Dez. J – N.p., 1700 – 1mf – 9 – HTM-226/1 – ne IDC [180]

ADA COMMERCIAL – Ada, Ohio. 1877-1878 – 1r – 1 – $32.50r – us Archival [071]

ADA FIELD NOTES / Field, M J – Chicago: [Cooperative Africana Microfilming Project, CRL], 1973 (mf ed) – us Res Libr [960]

ADA FORECAST – (Cont by: Diabetes Forecast) – Chicago, 1948-74* – 1 – D19373 – us UMI [616]

ADA HERALD – Ada, Ohio. 1916- – 9r – 1 – $32.50r – us Archival [071]

ADA NEWS – Chicago. v1-20 jul 1970-89. v21-22 jan 1990-dec 1991*. v23 1992. v24-25 jan 1993-dec 1994*. v26-28 jan 1992-dec 1997+ 1; v10-25 jan 1979-dec 1994*. v26-28 jan 1995-dec 1997+ 5; v10 1979*. v11-20 jan 1980-dec 1989. v21-22 jan 1990-dec 1991*. v23 1992. v24-25 jan 1993-dec 1994*. v26-28 1995-dec 1997+ 9 – 1,5,9 – D7636 – us UMI [073]

Ada. Ohio. Ohio Northern University *see* REGISTRARS LEDGERS AND INDEX

ADA RECORD – Ada,Ohio. 1873-1907 – 9r – 1 – $32.50r – us Archival [071]

ADA USER – London. 1980-1993* v15-18 1994-1997+ 1; v15-18 1994-1997*+ 5,9 – 1,5,9 – D21473 – us UMI [073]

ADA WORLD – (Cont: Union for Democratic Action; UDA Congressional Newsletter) – 1947-71. v1-26 – 2r – 1 – us Ross [320]

ADA WORLD – Washington, DC. 1968-69 – 4r – 1 – $250.00 – R05500 – us Library Micro [071]

ADAIR COUNTY FREE PRESS – Greenfield. Iowa. -w. 1951-62 – 1 – us UMI [071]

Adair, E R *see* THE EXTERRITORIALITY OF AMBASSADORS...

Adair, Samuel Lyle and Florella (Brown) Family *see* COLLECTION

ADALBERT STIFTER : SEIN LEBEN IN SELBSTZEUGNISSEN, BRIEFEN UND BERICHTEN – Berlin: Verlag des Druckhauses Tempelhof, 1947, c1946 – 1r – 1 – us U.W. Library [920]

ADALBERT STIFTER UND WIEN / Eltz-Hoffmann, Lieselotte von – [Vienna]: Wiener Verlag, 1946 – 1r – 1 – us U.W. Library [920]

ADALBERT STIFTERS "WITIKO" / Conrath, Annemarie – (Includes bibliographical references) – Wuerzburg: K Triltsch, 1942 – 1r – 1 – us U.W. Library [430]

ADALBERTUS SAMARITANUS (MGH QUELLEN..: 3.BD) : PRAECEPTA DICTAMINUM – 1961 – Dfl9.00 – ne Slangenburg [240]

Adam, Adele Marion *see*
- THE RELIGIOUS TEACHERS OF GREECE
- THE VITALITY OF PLATONISM, AND OTHER ESSAYS

Adam, Adolf *see* DER POSTILLON VON LONJUMEAU

ADAM AND EVE : HISTORY OR MYTH? / Townsend, Luther Tracy – Boston: Chapple Publ, 1904 – 1mf – 9 – 0-8370-5558-X – 1985-3558 – us A.T.L.A. [220]

ADAM AND THE ADAMITE, OR, THE HARMONY OF SCRIPTURE AND ETHNOLOGY – London: Richard Bentley, 1872. 1 fiche – 9 – us A.T.L.A. [240]

ADAM CAST FORTH / Doughty, Charles Montagu – London: Duckworth, 1908 – 1r – 1 – 1-55879-390-9 – uk Libr Preservation [999]

Adam, D S *see* CARDINAL ELEMENTS OF THE CHRISTIAN FAITH

Adam, de Saint Victor *see* THE LITURGICAL POETRY OF ADAM OF ST VICTOR

ADAM DRAWINGS IN THE VICTORIA AND ALBERT MUSEUM – 1r – 1 – $95.00 – 1-900853-45-0 – uk Mindata [720]

ADAM ET EVE – Montreal, Canada. 26 oct 1929 – 1r – 1 – Can$25.00 – cn Can Microfilming [072]

Adam, George Jefferys *see* BEHIND THE SCENES AT THE FRONT

Adam, Graeme Mercer *see*
- AN ALGONQUIN MAIDEN: A ROMANCE OF THE EARLY DAYS OF UPPER CANADA
- CANADA, HISTORICAL AND DESCRIPTIVE, FROM SEA TO SEA
- ILLUSTRATED QUEBEC: THE GIBRALTER AND TOURISTS' MECCA OF AMERICA UNDER FRENCH AND ENGLISH OCCUPANCY
- ILLUSTRATED TORONTO: THE QUEEN CITY OF THE WEST
- MUSKOKA ILLUSTRATED: WITH DESCRIPTIVE NARRATIVE OF THIS PICTURESQUE REGION
- PROMINENT MEN OF CANADA: A COLLECTION OF PERSONS DISTINGUISHED IN PROFESSIONAL AND POLITICAL LIFE, AND IN THE COMMERCE AND INDUSTRY OF CANADA
- PUBLIC SCHOOL HISTORY OF ENGLAND AND CANADA: WITH INTRODUCTION, HINTS TO TEACHERS, AND BRIEF EXAMINATION QUESTIONS
- REFORM IN THE EDUCATION OFFICE: A LETTER TO THE HON. OLIVER MOWAT..
- TORONTO OF TODAY: WITH A GLANCE AT THE PAST
- TORONTO, OLD AND NEW: A MEMORIAL VOLUME...TO MARK THE HUNDREDTH ANNIVERSARY OF THE PASSING OF THE CONSTITUTIONAL ACT OF 1791.

ADAM GRAINGER / Wood, Ellen – British Fiction Archive: Unit 1 – 9 – uk Bell [830]

Adam, James *see*
- THE RELIGIOUS TEACHERS OF GREECE
- THE VITALITY OF PLATONISM, AND OTHER ESSAYS

Adam, John *see* EXPOSITION OF THE EPISTLE OF JAMES

Adam, Lucien *see*
- ESQUISSE D'UNE GRAMMAIRE COMPAREE DES DIALECTES CREE ET CHIPPEWAY
- SONATE POUR LE FORTEPIANO, OP. 8

ADAM MALIK; A SKETCH / Sluimers, B – 5635 1. 1966 – 9 – ne IDC [920]

Adam Murimuth *see* CONTINUATIO CHRONICARUM (RS93)

Adam Of Evesham *see* MAGNA VITA S. HUGONIS, EPISCOPI LINCOLNIENSIS (RS37)

Adam, Pastor *see*
- EEN CONCORDANTIE OFT REGISTER DER GANSCHER BIBEL...
- UNDERSCHEIT. TUSSCHEN RECHTE LEER VNDE VALSCHE LEER DER TWISTIGEN ARTICULEN

ADAM SMITH: RICHESSE DES NATIONS / Courcelle-Seneuil, Jean Gustave – Paris: Guillaumin, 1888.4 fiches. (Economics Collection) – 9 – 10.00 – fr Bibl Nationale [330]

ADAM THOM, L.L.D., 1802-1890 – 1898? 01000. (Pre-1900 Canadiana) – 9 – cn C.I.H.M. [920]

ADAM UND CHRISTUS : ROEM. 5, 12-21: EINE EXEGETISCHE MONOGRAPHIE / Dietzsch, August – (Includes bibliographical references) – Bonn: Adolph Marcus, 1871 – 1mf – 9 – 0-8370-3563-5 – 1985-1563 – us A.T.L.A. [220]

ADAM UND QUAIN IM LICHTE DER VERGLEICHENDEN MYTHENFORSCHUNG / Boeklen, Ernst – Leipzig: J.C. Hinrichs, 1907. 1 fiche – 9 – us A.T.L.A. [240]

ADAMAUA : BERICHT UEBER DIE EXPEDITION DES DEUTSCHEN KAMERUN-KOMITEES IN DEN JAHREN 1893/94 / Passarge, Siegfried – Berlin: D Reimer, 1895 – 1 – us Res Libr [960]

Adami, A *see*
- ARCANA PACIS WESTPHALICAE...
- DISCURSO MEDICO SOBRE EL VERDADERO METODO DE CURAR LAS VIRUELAS...

Adamov, E A *see*
- RAZDEL AZIATSKOI TURTSII PO...
- SBORNIK DOGOVOROV ROSSII S DRUGIMI GOSUDARSTVAMI

Adamovich, G *see*
- CHISTILISHCHE. STIKHI, KNIGA VTORAIA
- NA ZAPADE
- NESKOL'KO SLOV O MANDEL'SHTAME
- ODINOCHESTVO I SVOBODA. IZD. IMENI CHEKHOVA
- PO POVODU SOBRANIIA SOCHINENII OSIPA MANDEL'SHTAMA

Adams *see* GAZETTEER OF WASHINGTON COUNTY

ADAMS 1878-1894 – (Mf 1-3: Index to Deaths 1878-1907. Mf 4-8: Index to Deaths 1908-88. Mf 9-13: Deaths 1878-1907. Mf 14-15: Index to Marriages 1877-1900. Mf 16-19: Index to Marriages. Mf 20-24: Marriages 1878-1900. Mf 25-27: Index to Births 1878-97. Mf 28-32: Index to Births 1898-1930. Mf 33-36: Births 1878-94) – (mf ed 1989) – 36mf – 9 – 0-87623-092-3 – us Holbrook [920]

Adams, Andrew Leith *see*
- FIELD AND FOREST RAMBLES: WITH NOTES AND OBSERVATIONS ON THE NATURAL HISTORY OF EASTERN CANADA
- THE GENERA OF RECENT MOLLUSCA
- MONOGRAPH ON THE BRITISH FOSSIL ELEPHANTS
- THE ZOOLOGY OF THE VOYAGE OF H.M.S. SAMARANG DURING 1843-1846

Adams, Archibald G *see* A DIALOGUE ON CHRISTIANITY FOR MY CHINESE FRIENDS (CCC1)

Adams, Arvil V *see* EXPEDITING SETTLEMENT OF EMPLOYEE GRIEVANCES IN THE FEDERAL SECTOR

Adams, Brooks *see*
- THE EMANCIPATION OF MASSACHUSETTS
- THE LAW OF CIVILIZATION AND DECAY

ADAMS CENTINEL – Gettysburg. Pa. -w. 1800-67 – 1 – us UMI [071]

Adams, Charles Coffin *see*
- THE BIBLE
- BIBLE: A SCIENTIFIC REVELATION

Adams, Charles Francis *see*
- ANTINOMIANISM IN THE COLONY OF MASSACHUSETTS BAY, 1636-1638
- MASSACHUSETTS
- PAPERS OF CHARLES FRANCIS ADAMS 2, 1861-1933

Adams, Cleophas *see* LE MEGANTIC

ADAMS CO. INDEPENDENT – Littlestown, PA., 1860-1942 – 13 – $25.00r – us I.M.R. [071]

ADAMS COUNTY NEWS – Gettysburg. Pa. 1908-17 – 1 – us UMI [071]

ADAMS COUNTY VOICE – Kenesaw, NE. -w. Jul 1914; Feb 1915-Oct 1917; Jan 1918-May 1920; Oct 1921-Aug 1942 – 1 – us NE Hist [071]

Adams, Deborah *see* THE RELATIVE EFFECTIVENESS OF THREE INSTRUCTIONAL STRATEGIES ON THE LEARNING OF AN OVERARM THROW FOR FORCE

Adams, E D *see* BRITISH INTERESTS AND ACTIVITIES IN TEXAS, 1838-1846

Adams, Elenor B *see* DON DIEGO QUIJADA...

Adams, Elmer E et al *see* PAPERS

Adams, Ephraim *see* THE IOWA BAND

Adams, Faried *see*
- CROWN VS. ADAMS AND 29 OTHERS
- CROWN VS. ADAMS AND 29 OTHERS; PREPARATORY EXAMINATION ON A CHARGE OF HIGH TREASON, IN THE MAGISTRATE'S COURT OF JOHANNESBURG, 1956-1958

Adams, Franc L *see* PIONEER HISTORY OF INGHAM COUNTY

Adams, Frank Dawson *see*
- NODULAR GRANITE FROM PINE LAKE, ONTARIO
- ON THE GEOLOGY OF THE ST CLAIR TUNNEL
- ON THE ORIGIN AND RELATIONS OF THE GRENVILLE AND HASTINGS SERIES IN THE CANADIAN LAURENTIAN
- PRELIMINARY REPORT ON THE GEOLOGY OF A PORTION OF CENTRAL ONTARIO SITUATED IN THE COUNTIES OF VICTORIA
- REPORT ON THE GEOLOGY OF A PORTION OF THE LAURENTIAN AREA LYING TO THE NORTH OF THE ISLAND OF MONTREAL

Adams, H *see* THE GENERA OF RECENT MOLLUSCA

Adams, Henry *see*
- THE BIBLE VERSUS INFIDELITY
- THE CAUSE OF THE DEGRADATION OF MAN
- ESTHER
- HENRY ADAMS PAPERS, 1843-1938
- INFANT BAPTISM: WHEN-WHERE-WHY INSTITUTED
- TAHITI
- A TRUE PICTURE OF THE EFFECTS OF INTEMPERANCE

Adams, Herbert B *see* JOHNS HOPKINS UNIVERSITY STUDIES IN HISTORICAL AND POLITICAL SCIENCE

Adams, J *see*
- THE COUNTRY FROM CAPE PALMAS TO RIVER CONGO
- REMARKS ON THE COUNTRY EXTENDING FROM CAPE PALMAS TO THE RIVER CONGO

Adams, J N *see*
- BIBLIOGRAPHY OF EIGHTEENTH-CENTURY LEGAL LITERATURE
- A BIBLIOGRAPHY OF NINETEENTH-CENTURY LEGAL LITERATURE

Adams, James *see*
- EUPHONOLOGIA LINGUAE ANGLICANAE, ET MIRUM SONORUM ARTIFICIUM
- THE PRONUNCIATION OF THE ENGLISH LANGUAGE VINDICATED FROM IMPUTED ANOMALY AND CAPRICE

Adams, James Edward *see*
- THE MISSIONARY PASTOR
- THE MISSIONARY PASTOR: HELPS FOR DEVELOPING THE MISSIONARY LIFE IN HIS CHURCH

Adams, Jenny L *see* MAXIMAL POWER OUTPUT ON THE BICYCLE ERGOMETER

Adams, John *see* ISRAEL'S IDEAL: STUDIES IN OLD TESTAMENT THEOLOGY

Adams, John Coleman *see*
- CHRISTIAN TYPES OF HEROISM
- THE DOCTRINE OF EQUITY
- THE FATHERHOOD OF GOD

Adams, John Quincy *see*
- BAPTISTS, THE ONLY THOROUGH RELIGIOUS REFORMERS
- BAPTISTS, THOROUGH RELIGIOUS REFORMERS
- THE DUPLICATE LETTERS, THE FISHERIES AND THE MISSISSIPI...
- LETTERS AND OPINIONS OF THE MASONIC INSTITUTION

Adams, M *see* BRITISH ATTITUDE TO GERMAN COLONIAL DEVELOPMENT, 1880-1885

Adams, Myron Winslow *see*
- CONTINUOUS CREATION: AN APPLICATION OF THE EVOLUTIONARY PHILOSOPHY
- ST. PAUL'S VOCABULARY: ST PAUL AS A FORMER OF WORDS

Adams, Nehemiah *see* CHURCH PASTORALS

ADAMS PAPERS, 1639-1889 – (300,000p of ms. material, comprising the papers of John Adams, John Quincy Adams, Charles Francis Adams and of their wives and children) – Massachusetts Historical Society – 620r – 1 – $20,125.00 – us UMI [920]

Adams, R J *see* THE LORD'S SUPPER IN BAPTIST CHURCHES

Adams, Robert Chamblet *see*
- EVOLUTION: A LECTURE DELIVERED IN MONTREAL, MARCH 1883.
- THE HISTORY OF ENGLAND IN RHYME
- ON BOARD THE "ROCKET"
- PIONEER PITH, THE GIST OF LECTURES ON RATIONALISM
- TRAVELS IN FAITH FROM TRADITION TO REASON

Adams, Samuel Houston *see* COMPARING TORT LIABILITY KNOWLEDGE OF FUTURE TEACHER COACHES AND CURRENT PRACTICING TEACHER COACHES

ADAMS SOEHNE : ROMAN / Wilbrandt, Adolf von – 2. Aufl. Berlin: W Hertz, 1890 – 1r – 1 – us U.W. Library [830]

Adams, W A *see* ROMEO UND JULIA AUF DEM DORFE

ADAM'S WEEKLY COURANT – Chester, England. 4 Mar 1766-27 Dec 1785 – 4r – 1 – uk British Libr Newspaper [072]

ADAMS WEEKLY GLOBE – Adams, NE. Feb. 1890-Oct. 1902. Incomplete; Oct. 1907- – 1 – us NE Hist [071]

Adams, William *see*
- CONVERSATIONS OF JESUS CHRIST WITH REPRESENTATIVE MEN
- A DISCOURSE ON THE LIFE AND SERVICES OF PROFESSOR MOSES STUART
- HISTORICAL GAZETTEER AND BIOGRAPHICAL MEMORIAL OF CATTARAUGUS COUNTY

Adams, William H Davenport *see* ST. PAUL: HIS LIFE, HIS WORK AND HIS WRITINGS

Adams, William O *see* MUSICK BOOK

Adamson, Robert *see*
- THE DEVELOPMENT OF MODERN PHILOSOPHY
- ON THE PHILOSOPHY OF KANT

Adamson, Thomas *see*
- THE SPIRIT OF POWER
- SPIRIT OF POWER: AS SET FORTH IN THE BOOK OF THE ACTS OF THE APOSTLES
- STUDIES OF THE MIND OF CHRIST

Adamus, John *see* ZASTAW W PRAWIE LITEWSKIEM 15 I 16 WIEKU

ADANA TICARET REHBERI = GUIDE COMMERCIAL D'ADANA / Oguz, Remzi – Istanbul: Cihan Biraderler Matbaasi, 1340 [1924] – 9 – $75.00 – us MEDOC [380]

Adanson, Michel *see*
- FAMILLES DES PLANTES
- HISTOIRE NATURELLE DU SENEGAL AVEC LA RELATION ABREGEE D'UN VOYAGE FAIT EN CE PAYS PENDANT LES ANNEES 1749,-50,-51,-52 ET-53
- HISTOIRE NATURELLE DU SENEGAL (COQUILLAGE)

Adanya, S *see* LE REGIME INTERNATIONAL DE L'ESCAUT

ADAPTATION OF THE ELECTORAL LAW OF 1890 TO CUBA AND PORTO RICO : ROYAL DECREE OF 1897 – Washington: GPO, 1899 – 1mf – 9 – $1.50 – LLMC 92-307 – us L.L.M.C. [972]

ADAPTIVE AGRICULTURAL RESEARCH PROJECT, 1981-1985 / Dominican Republic – (This catalogue includes a printed guide) – 37mf – 9 – ne IDC [630]

ADAPTIVE BEAMFORMING APPLIED TO HYDROACOUSTIC COMMUNICATIONS / Stiller, Christoph – 1994 – 1mf – DM60.00 – 3-8267-2001-6 – gw Hänsel [380]

ADAPTIVE NATURE OF AGONISTIC BEHAVIOUR IN WINTER FLOCKS OF THE GREY-BREASTED SILVEREYE / Wilson, Janice – (PhD Thesis) – 1980 – microfiche – A$15.00 – at R.A.O.U. [590]

Adariukov, V Ia *see* BIBLIOGRAFICHESKII UKAZATEL' KNIG BROSHIUR, ZHURNAL'NYKH STATEI ZAMETOK PO ISTORII RUSSKOGO TEATRA

ADATDELICTENRECHT IN DE RAPAT-MARGA-RECHTSPRAAK VAN PALEMBANG / Lublink-Weddik, W F – 1939 – 4mf – 9 – ne IDC [340]

ADATRECHTBUNDELS – 's-Gravenhage, 1910-1916. v1-12 – 56mf – 9 – ne IDC [999]

ADBASTON PARISH REGISTERS, 1600-1760, ASHLEY PARISH REGISTERS, 1581-1733, BIDDULPH PARISH REGISTERS, 1558-1755, BILSTON, ST LEONARD PARISH REGISTERS, 1684-1837 / Staffordshire – 1 – uk Microform Academic [941]

Adcock, Arthur John *see* GODS OF MODERN GRUB STREET

Addams, Jane *see* JANE ADDAMS PAPERS, 1860-1960

ADDENDA ET EMENDANDA AD F. EHRLE HISTORIA BIBLIOTHECAE ROMANORUM PONTIFICUM TOMUS I / P ELZER, A – Romae, 1947 – Dfl32.00 – ne Slangenburg [240]

ADDICION AL PARECER DEL R.P. FR...ACERCA DE UNA ELECCION QUE DIO EN DOCE DE DICIEMBRE DE 1639 POR EL MISMO PADRE A PETICION DEL PADRE FR. SEBASTIAN DE MORATILLA VICARIO DE LA SANTA CASA DE GUADALUPE Y PROFESSO DELLA / Virgen, Juan de la – S.l., s.i., s.a. 1640 – 1 – sp Bibl Santa Ana [240]

ADDICTION = BRITISH JOURNAL OF ADDICTION – 1901- 88v – 9 – £439.00 – 0965-2140 – uk Carfax [616]

ADDICTION – (Cont: British Journal of Addiction) – Abingdon. v88-92. jan 1993-dec 1997*+ – 1,5,9 – D13420.03 – us UMI [616]

ADDICTION ABSTRACTS – 1995, Vol 2 – £181.00 – uk Carfax [616]

ADDICTION ABSTRACTS – Abingdon. v1-4. 1994-1997*+ – 1,5,9 – D20942 – us UMI [616]

ADDICTION AND RECOVERY – (Cont: Alcoholism and Addiction and Recovery Life. Cont by: Behavioral Health Management) – Cleveland. v10-13. jun 1990-dec 1993 – 1,5*,9 – D16861.04 – us UMI [616]

ADDICTION AND RECOVERY *see* ALCOHOLISM AND ADDICTION AND RECOVERY LIFE

ADDICTION RESEARCH / ed by Davies, John B & Drucker Ernest – 9,5,1 – us Harwood [616]

ADDICTIVE BEHAVIORS – Oxford. v1-22 1975-97+ – 1,5,9 – D49004 – us UMI [073]

Addis, William Edward *see* HEBREW RELIGION TO THE ESTABLISHMENT OF JUDAISM UNDER EZRA

ADDIS ZAMAN – Addis Ababa, Ethiopia. jun 7 1941-10 sep 1971 – 1 – us Res Libr [960]

Addison, Albert Christopher *see* THE STORY OF THE BIRKENHEAD: A RECORD OF BRITISH HEROISM

Addison, Charles Greenstreet *see*
- ADDISON ON TORTS
- A TREATISE ON THE LAW OF CONTRACTS.

Addison, Daniel Dulany *see* THE CLERGY IN AMERICAN LIFE AND LETTERS

Addison, Maine. Indian River Baptist Sewing Circle *see* RECORDS

Addison, Maine. Second Baptist Church *see* RECORDS

ADDISON ON TORTS / Addison, Charles Greenstreet – 6th ed., Toronto, Carswell, 1890. 935 p. LL-897 – 1 – us L of C Photodup [340]

Addison, T *see* ON THE CONSTITUTIONAL AND LOCAL EFFECTS OF DISEASE OF THE SUPRA-RENAL CAPSULES

Addison, William L T *see* ON CRYSTAL FORMATION OF THE ELEMENTS AND THEIR ALLOTROPIC MODIFICATIONS: WITH DEDUCTION OF THE ATOMIC FORMS THEREFROM

ADDISON'S REPORTS / Pennsylvania. Superior Court – (A Pre-NRS title) – 1v. 1791-99 – 2mf – 9 – $9.00 – LLMC 84-192 – us L.L.M.C. [340]

ADDITAMENTA AD G. A. PRITZELII THESAURUM LITERATURAE BOTANICAE / Zuchold, E A – Halis. 1853. B-6499 1 – 1mf – 9 – ne IDC [580]

ADDITAMENTA AD HISTORIAM MOLLUSCORUM, PISCIUM ET AMPHIBIORUM / Meckel, J F – Z-648 2. 1832 – 8 – ne IDC [590]

ADDITAMENTA AD SYNOPSIM THEOLOGIAE PRO ANNO 1908 / Tanquerey, Adolphe – (Includes bibliographical references) – Romae: Desclee & Socii, 1908 – 1mf – 9 – 0-8370-8391-5 – 1986-2391 – us A.T.L.A. [240]

ADDITAMENTA AD THESAURUM LITERATURAE BOTANICAE / Berg, E de – Index. Librorum botanicorum I. Halis. 1859. Index. Librorum botanicorum II. Petropoli. 1862. Lacking: Index Librorum botanicorum III. B-6498 1 – 2mf – 9 – ne IDC [580]

ADDITIONAL LETTERS BY HISTORICUS ON SOME QUESTIONS OF INTERNATIONAL LAW / [Harcourt, W G G Y V] – London, Cambridge, 1863 – 1mf – 1 – ILM-3840/1 – ne IDC [327]

ADDITIONAL OBSERVATIONS ON THE NATURE AND VALUE OF CIVIL LIBERTY, AND THE WAR WITH AMERICA / Price, R – London, 1777 – 3mf – 9 – ne IDC [320]

ADDITIONES AD VARIAS RESOLUTIONES. / Ayllon Laynez, Juan – 1653 – 9 – 1.50f – sp Bibl Santa Ana [946]

ADDITIONS AND CORRECTIONS TO THE BOOK OF GENESIS / Driver, Samuel Rolles – 1909 – 9 – $10.00 – us I.R.C. [220]

ADDITIONS ET CORRECTIONS A LA FAUNE COLEOPTEROLOGIQUE DE LA PROVINCE DE QUEBEC, 1879 / Provancher, Leon A – Quebec: C Darveau, 1879. SEM16P196 – 1r – 5 – Can$9.00 – cn Bibl Nat [590]

AD-DOURRA AL-FAAKHIRA. PREMI ERE PARTIE = DURRAH AL-FAKHIRAH FI KASHF O'ULUM AL-AKHIRAH : LA PERLE PRECIEUSE DE GHAZAALAI / Ghazzali – (In French and Arabic. No more publ. Includes bibliographical references) – Leipzig: G Kreysing, 1877 – 1mf – 9 – 0-8370-7698-6 – 1986-1698 – us A.T.L.A. [260]

ADDRESS – (Companys, Lluis). n.p. 1936? Fiche W 814. (Blodgett Collection of Spanish Civil War Pamphlets) – 9 – us H.U. College Libr [946]

ADDRESS: AT A PUBLIC MEETING, OTTAWA, 1898 / Aberdeen and Temair, Ishbel Gordon, Marchioness of – 1898. 00765. (Pre-1900 Canadiana) – 9 – cn C.I.H.M. [971]

ADDRESS AT NINTH PLENARY MEETING OF UNESCO 13TH GENERAL CONFERENCE / Pusponegoro, Sudjono Djuned – Paris, Oct 24 1964. SE-10,517 1 – 9 – ne IDC [370]

ADDRESS AT THE CONVOCATION OF THE UNIVERSITY OF TORONTO, JUNE 10TH, 1890 / Blake, Edward – Toronto: Rowsell & Hutchison, 1890. 02174. (Pre-1900 Canadiana) – 9 – cn C.I.H.M. [971]

ADDRESS AT THE FUNERAL OF HENRY GEORGE / Crosby, J Sherwin – 9 – 1.00f – at Libertarian Micro [335]

ADDRESS AT THE LIPI-NAS WORKSHOP ON FOOD IN DJAKARTA ON MAY 27 TO JUNE 1, 1968 / Hamengku, Buwono 9 – SE-6324 1 – 9 – ne IDC [630]

AN ADDRESS BEFORE THE COMMERCIAL EXCHANGE OF DES MOINES, IOWA, THURSDAY, DECEMBER 20, 1894 / Brown, William Carlos, 1853-1924 – 1894? 00970. (Pre-1900 Canadiana) – 9 – cn C.I.H.M. [380]

ADDRESS BEFORE THE GRAFTON AND COOS BAR ASSOCIATION / Chandler, William Eaton – Concord: Republican, 1888. 38p. LL-10 – 1 – us L of C Photodup [340]

ADDRESS BEFORE THE IMPERIAL INSTITUTE OF GREAT BRITAIN ON THE 10TH OF MARCH, 1898 / Bouthillier Chavigny, Charles de – Montreal: Gazette Print. Co., 1898. 02529. (Pre-1900 Canadiana) – 9 – cn C.I.H.M. [971]

ADDRESS BY AUTHOR, PRESIDENT OF ASIAN-AFRICAN-CONFERENCE / Sastroamidjojo, Ali – SE 5910 1. 1955 – 9 – ne IDC [950]

ADDRESS BY H. E. THE MINISTER OF SECURITY AND DEFENCE, ON JAN. 5, 1960,AT THE PRESS CLUB / Nasution, Abdul Haris – Djakarta. SE-2587 1 – 9 – ne IDC [025]

ADDRESS BY LEIMENA, ACTING FOREIGN MINISTER ON THE OCCASION OF UNITED NATIONS DAY / Indonesia. Departemen Luar Negeri – SE-4607 1. 1960 – 9 – ne IDC [327]

ADDRESS BY THE PROVINCIAL COUNCIL TO THE PEOPLE OF ONTARIO, DEALING MAINLY WITH SEPARATE SCHOOLS / Equal Rights Association for the Province of Ontario – Toronto: The Association, 1889?. 02918. (Pre-1900 Canadiana) – 9 – cn C.I.H.M. [971]

ADDRESS DELIVERED APRIL 18, 1937 – (Cannon, Walter Bradford). N.Y. 1937. Fiche W 772. (Blodgett Collection of Spanish Civil War Pamphlets) – 9 – us H.U. College Libr [946]

AN ADDRESS DELIVERED BEFORE THE UNIVERSITY OF NASHVILLE, 1839 / Howell, Robert Boyte C – 28p – 1 – 5.00 – us Baptist [240]

ADDRESS DELIVERED IN BOSTON MUSIC HALL, WEDNESDAY EVENING, JANUARY 31, 1894 / Blake, Edward – Boston: Municipal Council of the Irish National Federation of Boston and Vicinity. 1894? 02296. (Pre-1900 Canadiana) – 9 – cn C.I.H.M. [360]

AN ADDRESS DELIVERED IN CHANCELLORS HALL, STATE EDUCATION BUILDING, ALBANY, NY / Cardozo, Benjamin Nathan – Albany: Evory, 1925. 11p. LL-2265 – 1 – us L of C Photodup [340]

ADDRESS DELIVERED IN CONVOCATION HALL, QUEEN'S COLLEGE, KINGSTON, APRIL 28TH, 1885 / Fleming, Sandford – Ottawa: Citizen, 1885. 03122. (Pre-1900 Canadiana) – 9 – cn C.I.H.M. [971]

ADDRESS DELIVERED IN ST MARY'S CHURCH, ST JOHN'S, N.F., 22ND MAY, 1898, TO LODGE DUDLEY S.O.E / Botwood, Edward – 1898. 00908. (Pre-1900 Canadiana) – 9 – cn C.I.H.M. [971]

AN ADDRESS DELIVERED IN THE FIRST CHURCH, SALEM, AT THE FUNERAL SERVICES OF CHARLES W. UPHAM, JUNE 18, 1875 / Ellis, George E – And the sermon preached on the succeeding Sabbath by James T. Hewes. Salem, Mass.: Published by the family, 1875. 05235. (Pre-1900 Canadiana) – 9 – cn C.I.H.M. [971]

AN ADDRESS DELIVERED IN THE FIRST PARISH, BEVERLY, OCTOBER 2, 1867, ON THE TWO-HUNDREDTH ANNIVERSARY OF ITS FORMATION / Thayer, Christopher Toppan – 1868 – 1 – us A.T.L.A. [240]

ADDRESS, DELIVERED MAY 8, 1878, AT THE ANNUAL COMMENCEMENT OF THE CINCINNATI LAW SCHOOL / Drake, Charles Daniel – Washington City, McGill, 1878. 18 p. LL-410 – 1 – us L of C Photodup [340]

ADDRESS DELIVERED ON THE 30TH DAY OF OCTOBER, A.D. 1883, ON THE OCCASION OF THE OPENING OF A LAW SCHOOL IN CONNECTION WITH DALHOUSIE COLLEGE, HALIFAX, NOVA SCOTIA / Archibald, Adams George – Halifax?, 1883? 02473. (Pre-1900 Canadiana) – 9 – cn C.I.H.M. [370]

AN ADDRESS FROM THE CHARLESTON ASSOCIATION...CALLING FOR THE ORGANIZATION OF THE THE STATE BAPTIST CONVENTION OF SOUTH CAROLINA / Baptist Association. Charleston, South Carolina – Signed by Richard Furman. Ms. 46p – 1 – 5.00 – us Baptist [240]

AN ADDRESS HISTORIC AND REMINISCENT... MT. NEBO PRESBYTERIAN CHURCH / McCollough, Andrew W – 1905 – 9 – $50.00 – us Presbyterian [240]

ADDRESS OF HON. DANIEL H. CHAMBERLAIN TO THE GRADUATING CLASS AT THE COMMENCEMENT EXERCISES OF COLUMBIA COLLEGE LAW SCHOOL. / Chamberlain, Daniel Henry – New York: Evening Post Job Printing Office, 1886. 19p. LL-425 – 1 – us L of C Photodup [340]

ADDRESS OF PRESIDENT LLUIS COMPANYS TO THE PARLIAMENT OF CATALUNYA, MARCH 1, 1938 – (Companys, Lluis). Barcelona? 1938? Fiche W 815. (Blodgett Collection of Spanish Civil War Pamphlets) – 9 – us H.U. College Libr [946]

ADDRESS OF THE PRESIDENT, HON. WILLIAM WIRT HENRY, DELIVERED AT THE NINTH ANNUAL MEETING, HELD AT THE HOT SPRINGS OF VIRGINIA, AUGUST 3, 4 AND 5, 1897 / Henry, William Wirt – Richmond: Goode Printing Co, 1897 – 1 – LL-1197 – us L of C Photodup [340]

ADDRESS ON SUPPOSED MIRACLES / Buckley, James Monroe – New York: Hurd and Houghton, 1875. 1 fiche – 9 – us A.T.L.A. [240]

AN ADDRESS ON SUPPOSED MIRACLES : DELIVERED MONDAY, SEPTEMBER 20, 1875, BEFORE THE NEW YORK MINISTERS' MEETING OF THE M.E. CHURCH / Buckley, James Monroe – NY: Hurd and Houghton, 1875 – 1mf – 9 – 0-8370-2506-0 – 1985-0506 – us A.T.L.A. [240]

ADDRESS ON THE LIFE AND CHARACTER OF WILLIAM CRANCH, DELIVERED JANUARY 10TH, 1907, BY ALEXANDER B. HAGNER AT THE REQUEST OF THE BAR ASSOCIATION OF THE DISTRICT OF COLUMBIA / Hagner, Alexander Burton – Washington, D.C., 1913. 36 p. LL-469 – 1 – us L of C Photodup [340]

AN ADDRESS ON THE MISSIONARY CHARACTER / Smith, Eli – 1840 – 1 – us A.T.L.A. [240]

AN ADDRESS ON WOMAN'S WORK IN THE CHURCH / Heckman, George C – 1875 – 9 – us A.T.L.A. [240]

AN ADDRESS, THE PLACE OF BAPTISTS IN PROTESTANT CHRISTENDOM / Bliff, Geo. Ripley – 1 – 5.31 – us Baptist [240]

AN ADDRESS TO ALL THE COLORED CITIZENS OF THE UNITED STATES / Meachum, John B – 1846 – 9 – $50.00 – us Presbyterian [240]

AN ADDRESS TO SEAMEN, DELIVERED AT PORTLAND, 28 OCT 1821; AT THE REQUEST OF THE PORTLAND MARINE BIBLE SOCIETY / Payson, Edward – 1 – 5.00 – us Baptist [240]

AN ADDRESS TO STUDENTS OF LAW IN THE UNITED STATES. (CIRCULAR) / Hoffman, David – Baltimore: Toy, 1824. 15p. LL-383 – 1 – us L of C Photodup [340]

ADDRESS TO THE BRITISH ASSOCIATION FOR THE ADVANCEMENT OF SCIENCE / Dawson, John William – s.l.: s.n., 1886?. 02239. (Pre-1900 Canadiana) – 9 – cn C.I.H.M. [971]

AN ADDRESS TO THE BRITISH PUBLIC / Mission Saint-Simonienne – London, Rolandi, 1832, 36 p. Les Saint-Simoniens, 1825-1834. 6900 – 9 – fr Hachette [335]

AN ADDRESS TO THE MERCHANTS OF GREAT-BRITAIN... – London, n.d. – 1mf – 9 – ILM-2768/1 – ne IDC [340]

ADDRESS TO THE PUBLIC CONCERNING POLITICAL OPINIONS, AND PLANS LATELY ADOPTED TO PROMOTE RELIGION IN SCOTLAND / Haldane, Robert – 1800 – 1 – 5.00 – us Baptist [240]

ADDRESS TO THE SOCIETY FOR THE IMPROVEMENT OF BRITISH WOOL / Sinclair, J – 1791 – 7 – uk Microform Academic [636]

AN ADDRESS UPON THE USE AND ABUSE OF ALCOHOLIC DRINKS / Bayard, William – St. John, N.B.?, 1882?. 02996. (Pre-1900 Canadiana) – 9 – cn C.I.H.M. [360]

ADDRESS...DICKINSON COLLEGE / Nisbet, Charles – June, 1798 – 1 – $50.00 – us Presbyterian [240]

ADDRESSE A MM. LES ELECTEURS DU COMTE DE LOTBINIERE: SUIVIE DE DIVERS DOCUMENTS / Amyot, Guillaume – 187?. 00886. (Pre-1900 Canadiana) – 9 – cn C.I.H.M. [971]

ADDRESSE AUX PROLETAIRES ET OUVRIERS FRANCAIS SUR LA SITUATION PRESENTE. / Jouy (ouvrier menusier) – Paris. 1839. (La Condition Ouvriere. Part Two.) – 9 – 2.50 – fr Bibl Nationale [360]

ADDRESSE DE M. C. BEAUSOLEIL, CANDIDAT NATIONAL, AUX ELECTEURS DU COMTE BERTHIER / Beausoleil, Cleophas – 1886? 03528. (Pre-1900 Canadiana) – 9 – cn C.I.H.M. [971]

ADDRESSES / Brooks, Phillips – Introd. by Julius H. Ward. Boston: C.E. Brown, c1893. 204p. On cover: Perfect Freedom – 1 – us U.W. Library [240]

ADDRESSES / Evans, John – s.l.: s.n., 1897? (London: Spottiswoode). 02924. (Pre-1900 Canadiana) – 9 – cn C.I.H.M. [971]

ADDRESSES / Nugroho, Notosusanto – Remarks on certain problems of economic development in Indonesia; Remarks on developments in Indonesia which have some bearing on American-Indonesian relations; The third man in the 'silent war.' SE-2523 1. 1957-59 – 9 – ne IDC [950]

ADDRESSES AND CORRESPONDENCE, 1857-1908 / Blyden, Edward Wilmot – 1 – us Res Libr [920]

ADDRESSES AND LECTURES.. / New Orleans Baptist Theological Seminary – Faculty addresses, Layne Lectures, Carver-Barnes Lectures, evangelism lectures, missionary days, Tharp Lectures, Founders Day Addresses. 1953-70 – 1 – 43.82 – us Baptist [240]

ADDRESSES AND SERMONS FOR PREACHERS (CCC92) / Ch'en, Chin-yung – (In Chinese) – Shanghai: Christian Literature Society, 1927 – 1r – 1 – 1984-B500 – us A.T.L.A. [240]

ADDRESSES AT THE CELEBRATION OF THE TWO HUNDRED AND FIFTIETH ANNIVERSARY OF THE WESTMINSTER ASSEMBLY BY THE GENERAL ASSEMBLY OF THE PRESBYTERIAN CHURCH IN THE U.S.A. / ed by Roberts, W Henry – Philadelphia: Presbyterian Board of Publication and Sabbath-School Work, 1898 – 1mf – us A.T.L.A. [240]

ADDRESSES BEFORE THE MEMBERS OF THE BAR, OF WORCESTER COUNTY, MASSACHUSETTS: BY JOSEPH WILLARD, OCTOBER 2, 1829; EMORY WASHBURN, FEBRUARY 7, 1856; DWIGHT FOSTER, OCTOBER 3, 1878 / Worcester County. Massachusetts Bar – Worchester, Hamilton, 1879. 250 p. LL-1565 – 1 – us L of C Photodup [340]

ADDRESSES BEFORE THE NEW YORK STATE CONFERENCE OF RELIGION – 1903-15 (complete) – 1r – 1 – ATLA S0903 – us A.T.L.A. [073]

ADDRESSES DELIVERED AT AGINCOURT, APRIL 2ND AND MAY 7TH, 1878: AN ABLE EXPOSITION OF THE CAUSE OF THE HARD TIMES: THE BANKS, LOAN COMPANIES AND IMPORTING MERCHANTS CHIEFLY TO BLAME / Bradford, Robert – Toronto: Morton & McLean, 1878? 00232. (Pre-1900 Canadiana) – 9 – cn C.I.H.M. [332]

ADDRESSES DELIVERED AT THE 40TH ANNIVERSARY OF THE BOARDS OF HOME MISSIONS, FOREIGN MISSIONS AND CHURCH EXTENSION OF THE GENERAL SYNOD OF THE EVANGELICAL LUTHERAN CHURCH AT HARRISBURG... – Philadelphia: Lutheran Publ Society, c1909 – 1mf – 9 – 0-8370-6152-0 – 1986-0152 – us A.T.L.A. [240]

ADDRESSES, ESSAYS, LECTURES / Broadus, John A – 1851-95.v1-2. 844p – 1 – 37.98 – us Baptist [240]

ADDRESSES FOR LIBERTARIANS – A Compilation of Lists and directories. 4 fiches (29x) – 9 – 1.00f – at Libertarian Micro [320]

ADDRESSES ON FOREIGN MISSIONS / Storrs, Richard Salter – Boston: American Board of Commissioners for Foreign Missions, 1900 – 1mf – 9 – 0-8370-6399-X – 1986-0399 – us A.T.L.A. [240]

ADDRESSES ON HISTORICAL AND LITERARY SUBJECTS : IN CONTINUATION OF "STUDIES IN EUROPEAN HISTORY" / Doellinger, Ignaz von – London: J. Murray 1894 – 1mf – us A.T.L.A. [940]

ADDRESSES ON HOMELY AND RELIGIOUS SUBJECTS / Baar, Herman – New York: H.O.A. Ind. Sch., 1880-85. 2 fiches – 9 – us A.T.L.A. [240]

ADDRESSES ON THE ART OF PLEADING, DELIVERED TO THE GLASGOW LEGAL AND SPECULATIVE SOCIETY ON SEPTEMBER 29, 1860 / Moncreiff, James Moncreiff – London: Griffin, 1860. 23p. LL-2239 – 1 – us L of C Photodup [340]

ADDRESSES ON THE OCCASION OF THE GATHERING IN THE GORDON MEMORIAL COLLEGE, KHARTOUM ON THE 20TH FEBRUARY 1945 : TO CELEBRATE THE INAUGRATION OF THE COLLEGE IN ITS NEW FORM – [Khartoum, 1945] – us Res Libr [080]

ADDRESSES ON THE REVISED VERSION OF HOLY SCRIPTURE / Ellicott, Charles J – New York: E.S. Gorham, 1903. 1 fiche – 9 – us A.T.L.A. [240]

ADDRICH IM MOOS : HISTORISCHER ROMAN / Zschokke, Heinrich – 1. Aufl. Berlin: Buchverlag Der Morgen, 1966 – 1 – us U.W. Library [830]

Addy, Sidney Oldall *see* CHURCH AND MANOR

ADE BULLETIN / Association of Departments of English – (1975- . 5,6,9) – 1964- – 1 – us UMI [400]

ADEB-I SEDAT / Pasa, Ahmet Cevdet – Istanbul: Karabet ve Kasbar Matbaasi, 1303 [1886] – $16.00 – us MEDOC [470]

ADEL UND UNTERGANG / Weinheber, Josef – 5. Aufl. Wien: A Luser, c1934 – 1r – 1 – us U.W. Library [810]

THE ADELAIDE FREE PRESS – Adelaide, South Africa. 7 Jan 1905-21 Dec 1911.6 reels – 1, 16 diazo available at reduced price – sa SA Libr [072]

ADELAIDE LAW REVIEW – Adelaide. v1 1960-73* 1; v5-19 1973-97+ 1,5,9 – 1,5,9 – D9476 – us UMI [340]

ADELAIDE OBSERVER – Australia, Jan 1844-Sep 1857; Feb 1862-Dec 1870; Jan 1880-Jun 1922; Jan-Aug 1930 – 126 1/2r – 1 – uk British Libr Newspaper [072]

ADELAIDE OPINION – Adelaide, South Africa. 3 May-29 Nov 1882. 1 reel – 1, 16 diazo available at reduced price – sa SA Libr [072]

ADELAIDE PHOENIX – Adelaide, South Africa. 13 Jan-7 Jul 1883. 1 reel – 1, 16 diazo available at reduced price – sa SA Libr [072]

THE ADELAIDE RECORDER – Adelaide, South Africa. 1 Jul 1885-8 Nov 1887. 1 reel – 1, 16 diazo available at reduced price – sa SA Libr [072]

ADELAIDE STANDARD – Adelaide, South Africa. 2 Jan 1878-22 Feb 1882.2 reels – 1, 16 diazo available at reduced price – sa SA Libr [072]

ADELAIDE TIMES – Adelaide, South Africa. 14 Jul-29 Dec 1883. 1 reel – 1, 16 diazo available at reduced price – sa SA Libr [072]

ADELAIDE TIMES – Australia, Oct 1848-Dec 1856; June-Dec 1857 – 16r – 1 – uk British Libr Newspaper [072]

EL ADELANTADO HERNANDO DE SOTO : BREVE NOTICIAS, NUEVOS DOCUMENTOS PARA SU BIOGRAFIA Y RELACION DE LOS QUE LE ACOMPANARON A LA FLORIDA / Solar y Taboada, Antonio & Rigula y Ochotorena, Jose de – Badajoz: Ediciones Arqueros, 1929 – 1 – sp Bibl Santa Ana [946]

ADELANTE – Havana. v1-4. 1935-39 – 1r – 1 – us Ross [972]

ADELANTE – Villafranca de los Barros, 1920. 1 numero – 5 – sp Bibl Santa Ana [073]

ADELARDO LOPEZ DE AYALA / Blanco Garcia, Francisco – Madrid: Saenz de Jubera, 1909 – sp Bibl Santa Ana [440]

Adelon, Alard, Alibert et al *see* DICTIONNAIRE DES SCIENCES MEDICALES, PAR UNE SOCIETE DE MEDECINS ET DE CHIRURGIENS (AEL, ABT.3;5)

ADELPHI – uk Chadwyck [073]

ADELPHI PAPERS – Oxford. v1-302 nov 1963-jul 1996 1; v74-302 jan 1971-jul 1996 5*; v113-302 Spr 1975-jul 1996 9*; jan 1996-dec 1997+ 1,5,9 – 1,5,9 – D3175 – us UMI [073]

Adelung, F von *see* KRITISCH-LITERAERISCHE UEBERSICHT DER REISENDEN IN RUSSLAND BIS ZUM 1700, DEREN BERICHTE BEKANNT SIND

Adelung, J C *see*
- MITHRIDATES, ODER ALLGEMEINE SPRACHENKUNDE
- MITHRIDATES ODER ALLGEMEINE SPRACHENKUNDE...

- VERSUCH EINES VOLLSTAENDIGEN GRAMMATISCH-KRITISCHEN WORTERBUCHES DER HOCHDEUTSCHEN MUNDART...

Ademollo, Alessandro *see* I PRIMO FASTI DELLA MUSICA ITALIANA A PARIGI: 1645-1662

THE ADEN ANALYSIS – A Concise Analyis of Key Financial Markets – 9 – 1.00f – at Libertarian Micro [320]

Aden. Audit Department *see* REPORT ON THE AUDIT OF THE ACCOUNTS

ADEN CHRONICLE – Southern Yemen, 7 Jan-11 Feb, 7 Apr-19 May, 3 Nov 1960-20 Dec 1962; 9 Jan 1964-14 April 1966 (imperfect). – 10r – 1 – uk British Libr Newspaper [072]

Aden. Customs and Excise Department *see* STATEMENT OF EXTERNAL TRADE

Aden. Great Britain Colonial Office *see* REPORT ON THE ABYAN SCHEME

Aden. Treasury Department *see* ANNUAL REPORT BY THE CHIEF ACCOUNTANT

Adeney, Walter Frederic *see*
- EZRA, NEHEMIAH, AND ESTHER
- THE GREEK AND EASTERN CHURCHES
- THE HEBREW UTOPIA
- HEBREW UTOPIA: A STUDY OF MESSIANIC PROPHECY
- HOW TO READ THE BIBLE: HINTS FOR S-S TEACHERS AND OTHER BIBLE STUDENTS
- THE SONG OF SOLOMON AND THE LAMENTATIONS OF JEREMIAH
- SONG OF SOLOMON AND THE LAMENTATIONS OF JEREMIAH
- THEOLOGY OF THE NEW TESTAMENT
- THESSALONIANS AND GALATIANS
- WOMEN OF THE NEW TESTAMENT

ADENOGRAPHIA: SIVE, GLANDULARUM TOTIUS CORPORIS DESCRIPTIO / Wharton, T – M 271. 1656 – 9 – ne IDC [612]

Aderson, Susan McMurray *see* JOURNAL OF ELDER ABUSE AND NEGLECT

ADEVARUL – (Cont: Scinteia) – (Romania), 1976- – 1 – us Ross [072]

ADEVARUL *see* SCINTEIA

ADFL (Association of Departments of Foreign Languages) *see* BULLETIN

AD'GE PSALIE – Nal'chik, USSR. Apr 1991-1992 – 2r – 1 – us L of C Photodup [072]

ADHELMI OPERA (MGH 1: 15.BD) / ed by Ehwald, R – 1919 – Dfl70.00 – ne Slangenburg [240]

ADHERENT – Seattle. v1-4 oct 1974-77* 1; v5-10 apr 1978-Win 1983 1,5,9 – 1,5,9 – D11912 – us UMI [380]

ADHESIVE ABSTRACTS – Oxford. v1-10. jan 1988-dec 1997*+ – 1,5,9 – D49556 – us UMI [680]

ADHESIVE AND SEALANTS INDUSTRY – Troy. v1-4. Feb 1994-1997*+ – 1,5,9 – D21296 – us UMI [680]

ADHESIVES AGE – Atlanta. v1-40 oct 1958-dec 1997+ 1; v10-40 jan 1967-dec 1997+ 5; v19-40 jan 1976-dec 1997+ 9 – 1,5,9 – D2494 – us UMI [660]

Adi Koro, Raden Pandji *see* TJARETAH PANDJAHTANDARAN

Adi, S *see* PARIBASAN BEBASAN SALOKA

ADICION A LA RELACION DESCRIPTIVA DE LOS MAPAS PLANOS...ARCHIVO GENERAL DE INDIAS / Torre Revello, Jose; ed by Bayle, Constantino – Madrid: Razon y Fe, 1928 – 9 – sp Bibl Santa Ana [910]

ADICION A LAS AVENTURAS DE GIL BLAS. TOMO 6 / Lesage, Alano Renato – 1791 – 1mf – 9 – Pta1,000.00 – 84-7848-255-5 – sp Pentalfa [920]

ADICION A LAS AVENTURAS DE GIL BLAS. TOMO 7 / Lesage, Alano Renato – 1791 – 1mf – 9 – Pta1,000.00 – 84-7848-256-3 – sp Pentalfa [920]

ADICION A UN FOLLETO / Torre Isunza de Hita, Pedro – Cabra: Imp. Manuel Cordon, 1928 – sp Bibl Santa Ana [946]

ADICION AL DISCURSO...PROVANDO QUE NO SE DEVE SANGRAR EN EL SARAMPION... / Saavedra, J – Granada, 1626 – 1mf – 9 – sp Cultura [616]

ADICION DEL INVENTARIO DEL MUSEO DE LA COMISION PROVINCIAL DE MONUMENTOS HISTORICOS Y ARTISTICOS DE BADAJOZ / Solar y Taboada, Antonio – Badajoz: Minerva Extremena, 1919 – 1 – sp Bibl Santa Ana [060]

ADICIONES / Feijoo Montenegro, Benito J – 1mf – 9 – Pta1,000.00 – 84-7848-025-0 – sp Pentalfa [440]

ADIEU PARIS : JOURNAL D'UNE EVACUEE CANADIENNE / Routier, Simone – Ottawa: Ed du droit. 10 Mai-17 Juin 1940. SEM16P250 – 1r – 5 – Can$9.00 – cn Bibl Nat [920]

ADINAH – Shumarah-'i 1-30, 32. – Azar 1364-Isfand 1367 [Nov 1985-Feb 1989] – 1r – 1 – $35.00 – us MEDOC [956]

Adinegoro, Djamaludin *see*
- ILMU DJIWA SOSIAL DAN SESEORANG, OLEH ADI NEGORO
- KAMOES BAHASA INDONESIA-NIPPON DAN NIPPON INDONESIA

Adinolfi, S *see* DIRITTO INTERNAZIONALE PENALE

ADIOS A PERON : DOCE DISCURSOS – Chivilcoy [Argentina]: Ediciones Figaro, 1974 – 1 – CSUXADP3837-B – us Hoover Inst Photo [972]

ADISENDJAJA – Pengatar teoritis ke keradjinan di Indonesia. Revisi tjet-2. Djakarta Biro NALITBANG. Departemen Perindustrian Tekstil Keradjinan Rakjat. 1968. x, 253p. 1966. Title: pengantar keradjinan. BSEM-13870 1 – 9 – ne IDC [330]

Adisumarta, R J *see* KAPTIN. DEFICIT PEMERINTAH PADJAK-PADJAK DAN PEMBANGUNAN

ADJAN – Penuntun reparasi pulpen. Djakarta: Murnibaru, 1961. 48p. illus. SEM-11560 – 9 – ne IDC [950]

ADJARANADJARAN KARL MARX: 1964 / Lenin, Vladimir Ilyich – SE-5098 1 – 9 – ne IDC [335]

Adjarian, H *see* CLASSIFICATION DES DIALECTES ARMENIENS

LES ADJECTIFS DE QUALITE PHYSIQUE RELATIFS A L'ESPACE EN FRANCAIS MODERNE: ETUDE MORPHO-SYNTAXIQUE / Delomier, D – 9 – F120.00 – fr Ethnologie [440]

DAS ADJEKTIV BEI ULRICH VON LICHTENSTEIN / Lucas, Wilhelm – 1995 – 2mf – 9 – DM62.00 – 3-8267-3111-5 – gw Hänsel [430]

Adjitorop, Jusuf *see*
- DEMOKRASI SOSIALIS DALAM PEKERDJAAN PERADILAN DAN PEMBUATAN UNDANGUNDANG
- MADJULAH INTELIGENSIA INDONESIA, BERKERUMUN DISEKITAR MANIPOL

THE ADJUDGED CASES ON INSANITY AS A DEFENSE TO CRIME. / Lawson, John Davison – St. Louis, Thomas, 1884. 953 p. LL-332 – 1 – us L of C Photodup [340]

ADJUR-ADJER / Supardi – SE 3952 1. 1961 – 9 – ne IDC [950]

THE ADJUSTMENT OF ITALIAN-AMERICANS TO THE WAR CRISIS / Campisi, Paul – 1942 (Dec.) – 1r – 1 – us I.H.R.C. [305]

ADJUSTMENT OF LABOR-MANAGEMENT DISPUTES IN CALIFORNIA / California. State Conciliation Service – 1948-69. 11 fiches. (Harvard Law School Library Collection – 9 – 1.50f – us H.U. Law [331]

ADJUSTMENTS TO CHANGES IN FISHERIES LAW AND ECONOMICS – 1985 – 120p – it F.A.O. [340]

Adjutant General of the State *see* ROSTER OF NEBRASKA VOLUNTERES

Adkins, Nelson *see* AMERICAN PERIODICAL INDEX, 1730-1860

ADL ON THE FRONTLINE – (Cont: B'nai B'rith – Anti Defamation League – ADL Bulletin) – New York. v1 1991*. v2-7 jan 1992-dec 1997+ – 1,5,9 – D19564 – us UMI [073]

DER ADLER – Berlin, 1939-44 (incomplete) – 1 – Dist. gw Mikrofilm – gw Misc Inst [072]

Adler, Carl *see* MUNDARTLICH HEITERES

Adler, Elkan Nathan *see* AUTO DE FE AND JEW

Adler, Emma *see* GOETHE UND FRAU V. STEIN

Adler, Georg *see* GESCHICHTE DES SOZIALISMUS UND KOMMUNISMUS

Adler, Hans *see* KAMPF DEM TODE

Adler, K *see* APOLOGIA M. CASPARIS AQVILAE

Adler, Mortimer Jerome *see* HOW TO THINK ABOUT WAR AND PEACE

Adler, Ottilie *see* FRIEDRICH UND CAROLINE PERTHES

DER ADLERFLUG IM ROMISCHEN KONSERKRATIONSZEREMONIELL / Geyer, Ursula – Bonn, 1967 – 1 – DM30.00 – gw Mikro Press [930]

ADLERSHOFER TAGEBLATT – Berlin, jan-mar 1925 – 1r – 1 – Dist. gw Mikrofilm – gw Misc Inst [943]

Adlin, Rina *see* PENUNTUN WANITA AND PRIJA MODERN

Adloff, Virginia McLean *see* BIOGRAPHICAL FILE OF AFRICAN LEADERS

Adlung, Jacob *see*
- ANLEITUNG ZU DER MUSIKALISCHEN GELAHRTHEIT....1758
- ANLEITUNG ZUR MUSIKALISCHEN GELAHRTHEIT....1783
- MUSICA MECHANICA ORGANOEDI..

Admawiria, Sam Suhaedi *see* AN INVITATION TO BANDUNG REGION; OPAL OF THE ORIENT

ADMINISTATIVE AND FINANCIAL TERMS – 2nd rev ed 1986 – 216p – it F.A.O. [650]

ADMINISTERING AGRICULTURAL DEVELOPMENT FOR SMALL FARMERS : ISSUES IN DECENTRALIZATION AND PEOPLE'S PARTICIPATION – 1981 – 72p – it F.A.O. [338]

ADMINISTERING THE FEDERAL JUDICIAL CIRCUITS : A SURVEY OF CHIEF JUDGES' APPROACHES AND PROCEDURES / Wheeler, Russell R & Nihan, Charles W – Washington: FJC, Aug 1982 – 1mf – 9 – $1.50 – LLMC 95-348 – us L.L.M.C. [340]

ADMINISTRACION DE ESPANA EN EL REINADO DE LOS REYES CATOLICOS / Montero de Espinosa, Luis – Madrid, 1858 – 1 – sp Bibl Santa Ana [350]

L'ADMINISTRACION DE SACRAMENTOS EN TOLEDO DESPUES DEL CAMBIO DE RITO / Garcia, Alf. I – 1958 – 2mf – 8 – Dfl9.00 – ne Slangenburg [240]

ADMINISTRACION...REYES CATOLICOS / Montero de Espinosa, Luis – 1858 – 9 – 1.50f – sp Bibl Santa Ana [946]

ADMINISTRASI NEGARA, SEBUAH PEDOMAN KERDJA / Slamet Wijadi Atmosudarmo – SE 4058 1. 1961 – 9 – ne IDC [950]

L'ADMINISTRATION – Pointe-aux-Trembles, Canada. v4 n5. 2 feb 1918-v6 n12. 28 mar 1920 – 1r – 1 – Can$45.00 – cn Can Microfilming [072]

ADMINISTRATION AND CONFLICT MANAGEMENT IN JAPANESE COASTAL FISHERIES – 1987 – 99p – it F.A.O. [650]

ADMINISTRATION AND POLICY IN MENTAL HEALTH – (Cont: Administration in Mental Health) – New York. v16-25. Fal 1988-Jul 1998+ – 1,5,9 – D11427.01 – us UMI [360]

ADMINISTRATION AND SOCIETY – (Cont: Journal of Comparative Administration) – Beverly Hills. v6-29. may 1974-feb 1998+ – 1 – D12641.01 – us UMI [073]

L'ADMINISTRATION CHAPLEAU – Montreal: s.n., 1881. 00014. (Pre-1900 Canadiana) – 9 – cn C.I.H.M. [971]

ADMINISTRATION DOCKETS / Van Wert County. Ohio. Probate Court – 1862-1905 – 3r – 1 – $32.50r – us Archival [324]

ADMINISTRATION DOCKETS / Wyandot County. Ohio. Probate Court – 1845-1855 – 1r – 1 – $32.50r – us Archival [324]

ADMINISTRATION IN MENTAL HEALTH – (Vol 4 never publ. Cont by: Administration and Policy in Mental Health) – New York. v1-15. Win 1972-Sum 1988 – 1,5,9 – D11427 – us UMI [360]

ADMINISTRATION IN MENTAL HEALTH *see* ADMINISTRATION AND POLICY IN MENTAL HEALTH

ADMINISTRATION IN SOCIAL WORK / ed by Patti, Rino J – v1- 1977- – 1, 9 ($275.00 in US $385.00 outside hardcopy subsc) – us Haworth [650]

L'ADMINISTRATION MAROCAINE / Morocco. Institut International d'Administration Publique. Encyclopedie administrative – Paris. 1970. BNE-3208 1 – 9 – ne IDC [350]

THE ADMINISTRATION OF CECIL JOHN RHODES AS PRIME MINISTER OF THE CAPE COLONY, 1890-1896 / Jenkins, Stanley John – [Cape Town], 1951 – us Res Libr [960]

ADMINISTRATION OF CROWN LANDS DEPARTMENT UNDER THE MOWAT GOVERNMENT, ELEVEN YEARS OF EFFICIENT AND ECONOMICAL GOVERNMENT – 1883. 06460. (Pre-1900 Canadiana) – 9 – cn C.I.H.M. [971]

THE ADMINISTRATION OF ESTATES / Sheard, Terence – Rev. Toronto: Life Underwriters Association of Canada. 1942. 133p. LL-2322 – 1 – us L of C Photodup [340]

ADMINISTRATION OF FOREIGN ESTATES / Burgin, E L – London, 1913 – 4mf – 1 – ILM-2974/1 – ne IDC [327]

ADMINISTRATION OF JUSTICE IN A LARGE APPELLATE COURT : THE NINTH CIRCUIT INNOVATIONS PROJECT / Cecil, Joe S – Washington: FJC, 1985 – 2mf – 9 – $3.00 – LLMC 95-320 – us L.L.M.C. [340]

THE ADMINISTRATION OF LIEUT. GOVERNOR SIMCOE VIEWED IN HIS OFFICIAL CORRESPONDENCE / Cruikshank, Ernest Alexander – s.l.: s.n., 1891? 03631. (Pre-1900 Canadiana) – 9 – cn C.I.H.M. [971]

ADMINISTRATION OF NAURU GOVERNMENT GAZETTE – 1957-68 – 5r – 1 – us Ross [324]

THE ADMINISTRATION OF THE CONSOLIDATED HOUSING ACT, 1925 AND THE CONSOLIDATED TOWN PLANNING ACT, 1925 / Aldridge, Henry R – London, 1925. Second suppl. to Aldridge: The National Housing Manual, 1923 – 1 – £35.00r – uk Altair [710]

THE ADMINISTRATION OF THE TOWN PLANNING DUTIES OF LOCAL AUTHORITIES / Aldridge, Henry R – London. 1922 Supplement to Aldridge: The Case for Town Planning, 1915 – 1 – £35.00r – uk Altair [710]

ADMINISTRATION PAPERS / Uganda Institute of Public Administration – 1 – us Res Libr [960]

ADMINISTRATION POLICY IN MENTAL HEALTH *see* ADMINISTRATION IN MENTAL HEALTH

ADMINISTRATION REPORT : CENSUS OF INDIA – Peshwar: North-West Frontier Prov Govt Press, 1911-31 – 1 – us Res Libr [950]

ADMINISTRATION REPORT / India. Archaeological Department. Travancore – v1-13. Ernakulam. 1936/37-1951/52. BI-692 2 – 8 – ne IDC [930]

ADMINISTRATIVE ARCHIVES, 1833-1969 / Catholic Archdiocese of Papeete – 32r – 1 – PMB1080 – at Pacific Mss [980]

ADMINISTRATIVE CODE / California. Laws, Statutes, etc – 9 – us UMI [324]

Administrative Conference of the U.S. (ACUS) *see*
- ACUS – ANNUAL REPORTS
- ADMINISTRATIVE PROCEDURE SOURCEBOOK
- COLLOQUIUM ON REGULATORY DESIGN IN THEORY AND PRACTICE
- DIRECTORY OF ADMINISTRATIVE HEARING FACILITIES
- DRAFTING FEDERAL GRANT STATUTES
- EXECUTIVE CONTROL OF RULEMAKING
- EXPEDITING SETTLEMENT OF EMPLOYEE GRIEVANCES IN THE FEDERAL SECTOR
- FEDERAL ADMINISTRATIVE LAW JUDGE HEARINGS, STATISTICAL REPORTS
- FEDERAL USER FEES
- GOVERNMENT IN THE SUNSHINE ACT
- A GUIDE TO FEDERAL AGENCY RULEMAKING
- JUDICIAL REVIEW UNDER THE CLEAN AIR ACT AND FEDERAL WATER POLLUTION CONTROL ACT
- LEGISLATIVE VETO OF AGENCY RULES AFTER U.S. V. CHADHA
- LA MEDIACION
- MEDIATION
- NEGOTIATED RULEMAKING SOURCEBOOK
- THE OMBUNDSMAN
- REGULATORY AGENCY CHAIRMEN AND THE REGULATORY PROCESS

Administrative Conference of the U.S. (ACUS). Subcomm on Administrative Practice and Procedure od the Senate Judiciary Committee *see* TEMPORARY ADMINISTRATIVE CONFERENCE OF THE U.S.

ADMINISTRATIVE HISTORIES OF U.S. CIVILIAN AGENCIES : KOREAN WAR / U. S. – (178 histories produced by 21 civilian agencies) – 1 – us Primary [977]

ADMINISTRATIVE HISTORIES OF U.S. CIVILIAN AGENCIES : WORLD WAR 2 / U. S. – (423 histories produced by 57 civilian agencies) – 1 – us Primary [977]

ADMINISTRATIVE HISTORY, GENERAL HEADQUARTERS, UNITED STATES ARMY FORCES, PACIFIC / U.S. Army. Far East Command – 6 Apr 1945-31 Dec 1946. 25v – 1 – 69.00 – us L of C Photodup [977]

ADMINISTRATIVE LAW BULLETIN *see* ADMINISTRATIVE LAW REVIEW (ABA)

ADMINISTRATIVE LAW JUDGES DECISIONS / U.S. Dept of Labor – (Lacking: v1 no5. v6 nos5-6. v7 no3. Add vols planned) – v1-7 no5. 1987-Sep/Oct 1993 – 104mf – 9 – $156.00 – LLMC 95-002 – us L.L.M.C. [340]

ADMINISTRATIVE LAW REVIEW (ABA) – (Title varies: v1-12 1949-1960 as Administrative Law Bulletin) – v1-47. 1949-1995 – 9 – Inquire – us Hein [340]

ADMINISTRATIVE MANAGEMENT – (Formed by the union of: Office Administration and Automation & Information Management) – New York. v46-49. oct 1985-apr 1988 – 1,5,9 – D700.02 – us UMI [650]

ADMINISTRATIVE MANAGEMENT – (Merged with: Word Processing & Information Services to form: Office Administration and Automation. Former titles: Geyer's Office Equipment Digest; Office Equipment Digest (1941-sep 19459; Office Management & Equipment (oct 1945-apr 1953); Office Management: the Magazine for Management Executives (Jun 1953-apr 1960); Office Management and American Business (may 1960-apr 1961)) – New York. v1-43. jul 1940-dec 1982 1; v31-43 jan 1970-dec 1982 5; v36-43 jan 1975-dec 1982 9 – 1,5,9 – D700 – us UMI [650]

ADMINISTRATIVE PROCEDURE SOURCEBOOK : STATUTES AND RELATED MATERIALS / Administrative Conference of the U.S. (ACUS) – 1st ed 1985. Washington: GPO, 1985 (all publ) – 11mf – 9 – $16.50 – LLMC 94-335A – us L.L.M.C. [340]

ADMINISTRATIVE PROCEDURE SOURCEBOOK : STATUTES AND RELATED MATERIALS / Administrative Conference of the U.S. (ACUS) – 2nd ed 1992. Washington: GPO, 1992 (all publ) – 11mf – 9 – $16.50 – LLMC 94-335B – us L.L.M.C. [340]

ADMINISTRATIVE REPORT OF THE CENSUS OF COCHIN- Ernakulam: Printed at the Cochin Govt Press, pt3. 1901 – us Res Libr [310]

ADMINISTRATIVE REPORT OF THE CENSUS OPERATIONS IN THE BOMBAY PRESIDENCY – Bombay: Govt Central Press, 1901 – 1 – us Res Libr [324]

ADMINISTRATIVE RULES AND REGULATIONS OF THE GOVERNMENT OF GUAM, 1975 / Bohn, John A – (With revisions for 1981-82) – Agana: Guam Law Revision Commission. 2v. 1975-82 – 39mf – 9 – $58.00 – LLMC 82-100B Title 5 – us L.L.M.C. [324]

ADMINISTRATIVE SCIENCE QUARTERLY – Ithaca. v1-42 jun 1956-dec 1997+ 1; v16-42 mar 1971-dec 1997+ 5; v20-42 mar 1975-dec 1997+ 9 – 1,5,9 – D5139 – us UMI [323]

ADMINISTRATIVE SET UP OF THE EDUCATION DIVISION / Pakistan. Education Division – 1971 – 1mf – 9 – DE-581/1 – ne IDC [370]

Administrative Staff College of India *see* ASCI JOURNAL OF MANAGEMENT

ADMINISTRATIVE STRUCTURE IN LARGE DISTRICT COURTS : A REPORT TO THE CONFERENCE OF METROPOLITAN DISTRICT CHIEF JUDGES / Dubois, Philip – Washington: FJC, Dec 1981 – 1mf – 9 – $1.50 – LLMC 95-802 – us L.L.M.C. [340]

ADMINISTRATIVE STRUCTURE OF ATHLETIC DEPARTMENTS AND THE IMPACT OF TITLE IX / Derouin, Barbara – 1981 – 9 – 4.00 – us Microform Publ [790]

ADMINISTRATIVNOE ZAKONODATEL'STVO / ed by Askarkhanov, S S & Brodovich, S M – Moscow, 1936. 292p. BR-8420 1 – 9 – ne IDC [340]

ADMINISTRATOR'S DIGEST – (Cont: Library Administrator's Digest) – Orinda. v1-17 dec 1965-dec 1982 1; v6-17 jan 1971-dec 1982 5; v12-17 jan 1977-dec 1982 9 – 1,5,9 – D2738 – us UMI [020]

ADMINISTRATOR'S NOTEBOOK – (Ceased publ) – Chicago. cum index 1-17 v1-36 may 1952-1995 1; v20-36 sep 1971-1995 5; v25-36 1976-1995 9 – 1,5,9 – D1842 – us UMI [073]

ADMINISTRATORS SWAP SHOP – Washington. v18-21 oct 1971-apr 1974 1; v21-24 oct 1974-apr 1978* 1,5,9 – 1,5,9 – D9907 – us UMI [073]

ADMIRABLE CHANGEMENT DE VIE D'UN JEUNE ADVOCAT EN LA COUR NOUVELLEMENT OPEREE PAR LE MOYEN D'UN DEMON – La Fleche. 1634 – 9 – fr Hachette [360]

DER ADMIRAL : DREI NOVELLEN / Moeller, Eberhard Wolfgang – Muenchen: A Langen, G Mueller, 1937 – 1r – 1 – us U.W. Library [830]

ADMIRAL DUNCAN / Duncan, Robert Adam Haldane Philips – London: 1898 – 2mf – 1 – 1-55879-050-0 – uk Libr Preservation [355]

ADMIRAL NIMITZ COMMAND SUMMARY : RUNNING ESTIMATE AND SURVEY, 1941-1945 / U.S. Navy. Historical Center. Operational Archives Branch – 1985 – 3r – 1 – $255.00 – S1162 – us Scholarly Res [355]

ADMIRAL OF THE FLEET, SIR GEOFFREY PHIPPS HORNBY G.C.B.: A BIOGRAPHY / Egerton, Mrs. Fred – Edinburgh: W. Blackwood, 1896. 02891. (Pre-1900 Canadiana) – 9 – cn C.I.H.M. [971]

ADMIRAL OF THE FLEET: SIR PROVO W. P. WALLIS, C. C. B. ETC.: A MEMOIR / Brighton, John George – London: Hutchinson, 1892. 00272. (Pre-1900 Canadiana) – 9 – cn C.I.H.M. [920]

ADMIRAL OF THE FLEET SIR PROVO W.P. WALLIS : A MEMOIR / Brighton, John George – 1892 – 9 – $20.00 – uk Libr Preservation [920]

ADMIRAL SIR PHILIPP B.V. BROKE : A MEMOIR / Broke, Philipp BV – 1866 – 9 – $20.00 – uk Libr Preservation [355]

ADMIRALTY CASE FILES OF THE U.S. DISTRICT COURT FOR THE EASTERN DISTRICT OF PENNSYLVANIA / U.S. Circuit and District Courts. Pennsylvania – 1789-1840 – 18r – 1 – M988 – us Nat'l Archives [324]

ADMIRALTY CASE FILES OF THE U.S. DISTRICT COURT FOR THE EASTERN DISTRICT OF VIRGINIA, 1801-1861 – 18r – 1 – M1300 – us Nat'l Archives [340]

ADMIRALTY CASE FILES OF THE U.S. DISTRICT COURT FOR THE NORTHERN DISTRICT OF CALIFORNIA, 1850-1900 – 401r – 1 – M1249 – us Nat'l Archives [340]

ADMIRALTY CASE FILES OF THE U.S. DISTRICT COURT FOR THE SOUTHERN DISTRICT OF NEW YORK / U.S. Circuit and District Courts. New York – 1790-1842 – 62r – 1 – M919 – us Nat'l Archives [324]

ADMIRALTY FINAL RECORD BOOKS AND MINUTES..., 1790-1857 / U.S. District Courts. South Carolina – RG 21. 4 rolls – 1 – M1182 – us Nat'l Archives [340]

ADMIRALTY FINAL RECORD BOOKS OF THE U.S. DISTRICT COURT FOR THE SOUTHERN DISTRICT OF FLORIDA (KEY WEST), 1828-1911 – 19r – 1 – M1360 – us Nat'l Archives [340]

ADMIRALTY FINAL RECORD BOOKS, U.S. DISTRICT COURT, EASTERN DISTRICT OF NORTH CAROLINA, 1858-1907 – 1r – 1 – M1429 – us Nat'l Archives [340]

ADMIRALTY JURISDICTION: REPORT / New Zealand. Special Law Reform Committee on Admiralty Jurisdiction – Wellington 1972. 65p. LL-4199 – 1 – us L of C Photodup [340]

ADMIRANDA ORBIS CHRISTIANI : TOM. 1-2. POST EDITIONEM VENETAM SECUNDA IN GERMANIA / Bagatta, J B – Aug. Vindelicorum & Dilingae, 1700 – Dfl172.00 – ne Slangenburg [240]

ADMIRANDA ROMANARUM ANTIQUITATUM AC VETERIS SCULPTURAE VESTIGIA / Bartolt, P – O 1088. 1693 – 9 – ne IDC [930]

THE ADMISSIBILITY OF EVIDENCE OF "SYSTEM" IN CRIMINAL CASES; A READING DELIVERED IN THE HALL OF THE HONOURABLE SOCIETY OF THE MIDDLE TEMPLE BY THE AUTUMN READER, SIR FRED E. PRITCHARD, ON THURSDAY, 21 NOVEMBER, 1957 / Pritchard, Fred Eills – London: Flint, 1958?. 34p. LL-2261 – 1 – us L of C Photodup [340]

ADMISSIONS TO COUNTY HOSPITAL / Van Wert County. Ohio. Board of County Commissioners – 1919-1932 – 1r – 1 – $32.50r – us Archival [324]

ADMITTED ALIEN CREW LISTS OF VESSELS ARRIVING AT SAN FRANCISCO, 1896-1921 – 8r – 1 – M1436 – us Nat'l Archives [340]

ADMONITIO DE PRAECIPVIS CAPITIBVS CONTROVERSIARVM DE COENA DOMINI,... / Eitzen, P von – [Hamburg], 1561 – 1mf – 9 – ne IDC [240]

ADMONTER HAJNT = TO-DAY IN ADMONT – (Yiddish in Latin characters) – Admont, AU. no9. 4 Oct 1946 – 1 – 1 – $25.00 – cn Can Microfilming [072]

ADMONTER HAJNT – v1 no12 15 Jan-v2 no13 1 Apr 1947 – 1 – 1 – $25.00 – cn Can Microfilming [072]

Adney, Edwin Tappan *see* THE BARK CANOES AND SKIN BOATS OF NORTH AMERICA

ADOBES IN SAN MATEO COUNTY / Bowman, J N – San Mateo Co, CA. – 1r – 1 B40259 – $50.00 – us Library Micro [978]

ADOLESCENCE – (Microfiche shipped yrly or qrtly) – Roslyn Heights. v1-32 Spr 1966-Win 1997+ 1; v6-32 Spr 1971-Win 1997+ 5; v10-32 Spr 1975-Win 1997+ 9 – 1,5,9 – D2544 – us UMI [305]

ADOLESCENS ACADEMICUS SUB INSTITUTIONE SALOMONIS / Musart, C – Douai, 1633 – 8mf – 9 – ne IDC [370]

ADOLESCENT AND PEDIATRIC GYNECOLOGY – New York. v1-10. 1988-Fal 1997+ – 1,5,9 – D16973 – us UMI [618]

ADOLESCENT MEDICINE – Philadelphia. v1-8 1990-1997+ 1*; v5-8 1994-1997+ 5*,9* – 1,5,9 – D21686 – us UMI [305]

ADOLESCENT PSYCHIATRY – Hillsdale. v1-6 1971-78*. v7-22 1979-97+ 1; v7 1979*. v8-22 1980-97+ 5; v7-22 1979-97+ 9 – 1,5,9 – D12195 – us UMI [073]

"ADOL'F" BENZHAMENA KONSTANA V TVORCHESTVE PUSHKINA / Akhmatova, A – Pushkin. Vremennik Pushkinskoi Komissii. I, M.,-L., 1936. p.91-114. BR-3723 2 – 8 – ne IDC [460]

ADOLF BRUELL'S POPULAERWIS-SENSCHAFTLICHE MONATSBLAETTER ZUR BELEHRUNG UEBER DAS JUDENTHUM FUER GEBILDETE ALLER CONFESSIONEN – Frankfurt. v1-28. 1881-1908. Lacking: v21 (1901, except no. 10) and v27 (1907). 3 reels. B333. (Leo Baeck Institute. German-Jewish Periodicals, Pt 1) – 1 – $205.00 – us UPA [270]

ADOLF FRIEDRICH GRAF VON SCHACK : EIN POETISCHES CHARAKTERBILD / Manssen, W J – (Translated from the Dutch) – Stuttgart: J B Metzler, 1888 – 1r – 1 – us U.W. Library [430]

ADOLF FRIEDRICH GRAF VON SCHACK ALS UEBERSETZER / Walter, Erich – Leipzig: M Hesse, 1907 – 1r – 1 – us U.W. Library [430]

ADOLF HITLER PAMPHLET COLLECTION – 1925-1986 – 2r – 1 – CSUXANR9544-B – us Hoover Inst Photo [943]

ADOLF REICHWEIN (1898-1944) : LEBEN UND WERK DES POLITISCHEN PAEDAGOGEN IM WIDERSTAND GEGEN DAS NS-REGIME UNTER BESONDERER BERUECKSICHTIGUNG SEINER AUSEINANDERSETZUNG MIT KULTUR, POLITIK, WIRTSCHAFTS- UND SOZIALPROBLEMEN OSTASIENS / Wittig, Horst E – 1993 – 2mf – 9 – DM80.00 – 3-89349-762-5 – gw Hänsel [370]

ADOLF WILBRANDT ALS DRAMATIKER / Scharrer, Eduard – (Includes bibliographical references) – Muenchen: Hans Sachs-Verlag, 1912 – 1r – 1 – us U.W. Library [430]

ADOLPH EICHMANN PAMPHLET COLLECTION – 1958-1961 – 1 – CSUXANR9521-B – us Hoover Inst Photo [943]

THE ADOLPH GERMER PAPERS – 9 – $2,890.00 – 1-55655-026-X – us UPA [331]

Adolph, Karl *see*
- AM ERSTEN MAI
- DAUGHTERS OF VIENNA

Adolph, L *see* MANUEL PRACTIQUE DES SOCIETES ANONYMES ETRANGERES

[ADOLPHE ET CLARE] D'UN EPOUX CHERI / Dalayrac, N – Paris: ca 1800 – 1 – us Sibley [780]

ADOLPHUS AND ELLIS' REPORTS : REPORTS OF CASES ARGUED AND DETERMINED IN THE COURT OF KING'S BENCH... / Adolphus, John L & Ellis, Thomas F – (This series became "Queen's Bench Reports" with the accession of Victoria in 1838) – v1-12. 1834-41. London: Saunders and Benning, 1835-42 (all publ) – 133mf – 9 – $199.00 – LLMC 84-741 – us L.L.M.C. [324]

ADOLPHUS AND ELLIS' REPORTS, NEW SERIES / Adolphus, John L & Ellis, Thomas F – v1-18. 1841-52. London: Saunders & Benning, 1843-56 (all publ) – 215mf – 9 – $322.00 – LLMC 84-742 – us L.L.M.C. [324]

Adolphus, John L *see*
- ADOLPHUS AND ELLIS' REPORTS
- ADOLPHUS AND ELLIS' REPORTS, NEW SERIES
- BARNEWELL AND ADOLPHUS' REPORTS

ADONDE VA EL PERONISMO / Fernandez, E – [Buenos Aires]: Ediciones Politica Obrera, [1957] – 1 – CSUXAGP8723-B – us Hoover Inst Photo [320]

ADONDE VAMOS? : PROLOGO [DE] JUAN D. PERON / Barrios, Americo – [Ciudad Trujillo, 1959?] – 1 – CSUXADL6461-B – us Hoover Inst Photo [320]

ADONIRAM JUDSON : A BIOGRAPHY / Judson, Edward – (Includes list of Adoniram Judsons' publications and index) – Philadelphia: American Baptist Publ Society, c1894 – 1mf – 9 – 0-8370-6671-9 – 1986-0671 – us A.T.L.A. [920]

ADONIRAM JUDSON GORDON : A BIOGRAPHY WITH LETTERS AND ILLUSTRATIVE EXTRACTS DRAWN FROM UNPUBLISHED OR UNCOLLECTED SERMONS AND ADDRESSES / Gordon, Ernest B – New York: F.H. Revell, c1896 – 1mf – us A.T.L.A. [240]

ADONIS, ATTIS, OSIRIS : STUDIES IN THE HISTORY OF ORIENTAL RELIGION / Frazer, James George – London, New York: Macmillan, 1906 – 1 roll – 1 – 1-55879-767-X – uk Libr Preservation [280]

ADONIS OU LE BON NEGRE / Beraud & Rosny – French Theatre Series. Paris. Glisau, Pigoreau et Le Pan, an VI. 1798 – 9 – fr Hachette [820]

THE ADOPTED CHILD : A MUSCIAL DRAMA IN TWO ACTS, WITH PIANO ACCOMP / Attwood, T – London: Clementi & Co, 1805? – 1 – us Sibley [780]

ADOPTION AND LEGITIMATION OF CHILDREN / Joyce, Joseph Asbury – Oakland Oakland Tribune Publishing Co., 1890. 73 p. LL-1202 – 1 – us L of C Photodup [340]

DIE ADOPTION IM ALTBABYLONISCHEN RECHT / David, M – (Leipziger rechtwissenschaftliche Studien, Heft 23). Leipzig. 1927 – 9 – ne IDC [930]

DIE ADOPTION, LEGITIMATION UND DIE KINDESANERKENNUNG... / Fuehrer, J – Langensalza, 1926 – 1mf – 1 – ILM-3079/1 – ne IDC [327]

Adorers of the Blood of Christ. Wichita, KS *see* ANNALS

Adrario, A *see* PER LA VITTORIA DELL'ARMATA CHRISTIANA, ...

ADREM – 1990-92 (complete) – 1r – 1 – ATLA S0929 – us A.T.L.A. [073]

ADRESNAIA KNIGA KNIGOPRODAVTSEV, IZDATELEI, TORGOVTSEV NOTAMI, REDAKTSII GAZET I ZHURNALOV, BIBLIOTEK DLIA CHTENIIA I ZAVEDENII PECHATI V ROSSII / Ginlein, R E – 1903-04. Spb. 1903. BR-4601 2 – 8 – ne IDC [460]

ADRESSE AU PEUPLE BELGIQUE / Robespierre, Maximilien de – Reprod. d'une ed. s.l., s.n., s.d. 34p. 1 fiche. (Political Science Collection) – 9 – 6.00 – fr Bibl Nationale [320]

ADRESSE AUX ELECTEURS MUNICIPAUX DE LA VILLE DE LONGUEUIL / Electeur de Longueuil – s.l.: s.n., 18–. 00777. (Pre-1900 Canadiana) – 9 – cn C.I.H.M. [971]

ADRESSE DE BIENVENUE PAR M. BAILLAIRGE A LA SECTION DE MONTREAL DES ARCHITECTES DU CANADA:...LE 2 OCTOBRE, 1895 / Baillairge, Charles – 1895?. 00883. (Pre-1900 Canadiana) – 9 – cn C.I.H.M. [720]

ADRESSE DE L'ASSEMBLEE AUX FRANCAIS, DUE 10 AOUT 1792 / Condorcet, Marie Jean Antoine Nicolas de – Paris: Imp. nationale, s.d. 2p.1 fiche. (Political Science Collection) – 9 – 6.00 – fr Bibl Nationale [323]

ADRESSE DES REPRESENTANS DE LA COMMUNE DE PARIS A LEURS CONCITOYENS / Robespierre, Maximilien de – Paris: Imp. P.J. Duplain, 1792. 15p. 1 fiche. (Political Science Collection) – 9 – 6.00 – fr Bibl Nationale [323]

ADRESSEAVISEN – (Norway), 1992- – 12r per yr – 1 – us Ross [072]

ADRESY ZEMSTV 1894-1895 GG. I IKH POLITICHESKAI A PROGRAMMA – [S.l.: s.n., 1895?] – 1 – CSUX88-B9827 – us Hoover Inst Photo [320]

Adrian, Michigan. First Baptist Church *see* RECORDS

ADRIANO, SONGS IN THE OPERA / Veracini, F – (Full score) – Ms of the 18th century – 1 – us Sibley [780]

Adrianus 6 *see* BRIEFWECHSEL DECEMBER 1522 BIS FRUELING 1523

ADRIATIC QUESTION PAMPHLET COLLECTION – 1918?-1923? – 1 – CSUXANR0857-B – us Hoover Inst Photo [940]

ADULT AND CHILD *see* A AND C ADULT AND CHILD

ADULT BASIC EDUCATION – (Cont: Adult Literacy and Basic Education) – Athens. v1-7. Spr 1991-Fal 1997+ – 1,5*,9 – D18782 – us UMI [370]

ADULT BASIC EDUCATION *see* ADULT LITERACY AND BASIC EDUCATION

ADULT BIBLE CLASS QUARTERLY – Jan 1915-61 – 1 – 305.69 – us Baptist [240]

ADULT EDUCATION – (Cont by: Adults Learning. Former title: Journal of Adult Education) – London. v1-47 sep 1926-mar 1975 1; v48-61 may 1975-mar 1989 1,5; v49-61 may 1976-mar 1989 9 – 1,5,9 – D10228 – us UMI [370]

ADULT EDUCATION – (Microed includes v14 (Fall 1949-aug 1950) of: Adult Education Bulletin. Cont by: Adult Education Quarterly) – Chapel Hill. v1-33 oct 1950-Win 1983 1; v19-33 Fal 1970-Win 1983 5; v21-33 Fal 1970-Win 1983 9 – 1,5,9 – D268 – us UMI [370]

ADULT EDUCATION *see*
– ADULT EDUCATION QUARTERLY
– ADULTS LEARNING

ADULT EDUCATION: A PLAN FOR DEVELOPMENT / Great Britain. Committee of Inquiry – Report. 1973 – 9 – uk Microform Academic [324]

THE ADULT EDUCATION ANNUAL REPORT 1982 / Nigeria. Cross River State. Adult Education Division – Calabar – 3mf – 9 – DE-455/1 – ne IDC [370]

ADULT EDUCATION BULLETIN *see* ADULT EDUCATION

ADULT EDUCATION IN THAILAND / Thailand. Ministry of Education. Adult Education Division – Bangkok, 1976 – 1mf – 9 – DE-289/1 – ne IDC [370]

ADULT EDUCATION IN THE PEOPLE'S REPUBLIC OF BULGARIA / Micheva, P et al – Prague, 1982 – 2mf – 9 – DE-132/1 – ne IDC [370]

ADULT EDUCATION MEMORANDA / Masanawa, I – Kaduna, [1980] – 1mf – 9 – DE-129/1 – ne IDC [370]

ADULT EDUCATION MEMORANDA / Masanawa, I – 1973 – 1mf – 9 – DE-114/1 – ne IDC [370]

ADULT EDUCATION QUARTERLY – (Cont: Adult Education) – Washington. v33-48. Spr 1983-Sum 1998+ – 1,5,9 – D268.01 – us UMI [370]

ADULT EDUCATION QUARTERLY *see* ADULT EDUCATION

ADULT EDUCATION SECTION / Hong Kong. Education Department – Hong Kong, 1980 – 1mf – 9 – DE-175/1 – ne IDC [370]

ADULT FOSTER CARE JOURNAL – (Cont by: Adult Residential Care Journal) – New York. v1-2. Spr 1987-Win 1988 – 1,5*,9 – D16145 – us UMI [360]

ADULT FOSTER CARE JOURNAL *see* ADULT RESIDENTIAL CARE JOURNAL

ADULT LEADER – (All that is currently available. Supersedes: Adult Teacher) – Nashville. v1-12 sep 1968-aug 1980 1*; v4-12 sep 1971-aug 1980 5*; v9-12 spe 1976-aug 1980 9* – 1,5,9 – D3277 – us UMI [073]

ADULT LEADER *see* ADULT TEACHER

ADULT LEADERSHIP – (Cont by: Lifelong Learning: The Adult Years) – Washington. v1-25. 1952-77 1; v18-25 may 1969-jun 1977 5; v24-25 sep 1975-jun 1977 9 – 1,5,9 – D920 – us UMI [150]

ADULT LEARNING – (Cont: Lifelong Learning) – Washington. v1-9. sep 1989-aug 1998+ – 1,5,9 – D17359 – us UMI [370]

ADULT LEARNING – (Superceded by: Food for Thought. Ceased publ) – Toronto. v1-4. nov 1936-nov 1939 – 1 – D1177 – us UMI [370]

ADULT LITERACY : A PLAN FOR SEYCHELLES 1985 / Seychelles. Ministry of Education and Information – Mahe, 1984 – 3mf – 9 – DE-463/1 – ne IDC [370]

ADULT LITERACY AND BASIC EDUCATION – (Cont by: Adult Basic Education) – Auburn. v1-14 Spr 1977-90 1,9; v1 Spr 1977-Win 1978*. v2 Spr 1978-Win 1979. v3-4 Spr 1979-Win 1981*. v5 Spr-Win 1981. v6 Spr-Win 1982*. v7 1983. v8-12 1984-88*. v13-14 1989-90 5 – 1,5,9 – D11338 – us UMI [370]

ADULT LITERACY AND BASIC EDUCATION *see* ADULT BASIC EDUCATION

ADULT RESIDENTIAL CARE JOURNAL – (Cont: Adult Foster Care Journal) – New York. v3-11. Spr 1989-Fal 1997+ – 1,5*,9 – D16145.01 – us UMI [360]

ADULT RESIDENTIAL CARE JOURNAL *see* ADULT FOSTER CARE JOURNAL

ADULT TEACHER – (Ceased publ. Superseded by: Adult Leader) – Nashville. v1-21. oct 1947-aug 1968 – 1 – D2108 – us UMI [370]

ADULT TEACHER *see* ADULT LEADER

THE ADULT. (THE JOURNAL OF SEX) – London. 1897-99 – 1 – uk Microform Academic [613]

ADULTS LEARNING – (Cont: Adult Education) – Leicester. v1-9. sep 1989-jun 1998+ – 1,5,9 – D17416 – us UMI [370]

ADULTS LEARNING *see* ADULT EDUCATION

Aduriz, Joaquin *see* HOMBRE, MARXISMO Y CRISTIANISMO

ADVANCE – Caldwell. Kan. 1894-1901 – 1 – us UMI [071]

ADVANCE – Cape Town, SA: Competent Publ & Printing, [1952-nov 6-oct 21 1954] – 1 – us Res Libr [072]

ADVANCE – (Ceased publ) – St Louis. v1-22 1954-sep 1975 1*; v22 jan-sep 1975 5 – 1,5 – D8532 – us UMI [073]

ADVANCE – Ceredo. West Virginia. 1885-1891; 1893-1921; 1936-39 – 1 – us UMI [071]

ADVANCE – Chetopa. Kan. 1869-1973 – 1 – us UMI [071]

ADVANCE – Chicago, IL. 1934-49 (complete) – 5r – 1 – ATLA S0868 – us A.T.L.A. [073]

ADVANCE – Corning, CA. 1922-28 – 2r – 1 – $100.00 – B02138 – us Library Micro [071]

ADVANCE – Dunbar. West Virginia. 1917-21; 1927-40 – 1 – us UMI [071]

ADVANCE – Latrobe. Pa. 1873-1899 – 1 – us UMI [071]

ADVANCE : OFFICIAL ORGAN / Amalgamated Clothing Workers of America – New York, 30 Dec 1921-16 Nov 1928 (imperfect) – 3r – 1 – uk British Libr Newspaper [073]

ADVANCE – Sidney. Kan. 1882-1883 – 1 – us UMI [071]

ADVANCE *see* GUARDIAN

THE ADVANCE – Niagara-on-the-Lake Ontario, CN. 1919-88 – 33r – 1 – cn Commonwealth Micro [072]

THE ADVANCE – Providence. R.I. 1906-1936 – 1 – us UMI [071]

THE ADVANCE – St Louis, MO. v2-21. 1934-54 (complete) – 1r – 1 – ATLA S0532 – us A.T.L.A. [240]

THE ADVANCE – Zurich, Ontario, CN. 1986 – 1r – 1 – cn Commonwealth Micro [072]

ADVANCE ARGUS – Greenville, PA. -w 1898-1923. 9 rolls – 13 – $25.00r – us I.M.R. [071]

ADVANCE AUSTRALIA – Melbourne, 21 April 1914-15 Dec 1919 (imperfect) – 2r – 1 – uk British Libr Newspaper [072]

ADVANCE: CANADA'S FORWARD-LOOKING YOUTH PAPER – 1 – 75.00 – cn McLaren [971]

ADVANCE IN THE ANTILLES: THE NEW ERA IN CUBA AND PORTO RICO / Grose, Howard Benjamin – New York: Presb. Home Missions, 1910. xii,259p.1 fiche – 9 – us A.T.L.A. [240]

ADVANCE REPORTER – Stryker, Ohio. 1976-37r – 1 – $32.50r – us Archival [071]

ADVANCED CEMENT BASED MATERIALS (ACBM) – New York. v1-8. oct 1993-1997*+ – 1,5,9 – D42750 – us UMI [620]

ADVANCED DRUG DELIVERY REVIEWS – Amsterdam. v1-27 may 1987-1997+ 1*,5*; v2-27 oct 1988-1997+ 9* – 1,5,9 – D42548 – us UMI [615]

ADVANCED IMAGING – (Absorbed: AVC Presentation) – Woodbury. may 1986-1989 v5-12 1990-1997+ 1*; v5-12 1990-1997*+ 5,9 – 1,5,9 – D18083 – us UMI [073]

ADVANCED IMAGING *see* AVC PRESENTATION

ADVANCED LABANOTATION / ed by Guest, Ann Hutchinson – 9,5,1 – us Harwood [790]

ADVANCED MANAGEMENT *see* ADVANCED MANAGEMENT JOURNAL

ADVANCED MANAGEMENT JOURNAL – (Sep-dec 1963 issues not available for filming. Cont by: S A M Advanced Management Journal. Former titles: Society for the Advancement of Management Journal (jan 1936-jul 1939); Advanced Management: Quarterly Journal (Fall 1939-61); Advanced Management-Office Executive (jan 1962-aug 1963); Advanced Management Journal (sep 1963-sep 1968)) – Cincinnati. v1-49 jan 1936-Win 1984 1; v36-49 jan 1971-Win 1984 5,9 – 1,5,9 – D1959 – us UMI [650]

ADVANCED MANAGEMENT JOURNAL *see* ADVANCED MANAGEMENT JOURNAL

ADVANCED MANAGEMENT-OFFICE EXECUTIVE *see* ADVANCED MANAGEMENT JOURNAL

ADVANCED MANUFACTURING ENGINEERING (AME) – (Ceased publ. Absorbed by: Computer-Integrated Manufacturing Systems) – Guildford. v1-3. oct 1988-jan 1991 – 1,5*,9 – D17210 – us UMI [670]

ADVANCED MANUFACTURING PROCESSES – (Cont by: Advanced Materials and Manufacturing Processes) – New York. v1-2. 1986-1987* – 1 – D16470 – us UMI [670]

ADVANCED MANUFACTURING PROCESSES *see* ADVANCED MATERIALS AND MANUFACTURING

ADVANCED MATERIALS ABSTRACTS – (Ceased publ) – Oxford. v1-3. jan 1989-apr 1991 – 1,5*,9 – D49579 – us UMI [620]

ADVANCED MATERIALS AND MANUFACTURING – (Cont: Advanced Manufacturing Processes. Cont by: Materials and Manufacturing Processes) – New York. v3. 1988* – 1 – D16470.01 – us UMI [670]

ADVANCED MATERIALS AND MANUFACTURING PROCESSES *see* ADVANCED MANUFACTURING PROCESSES

ADVANCED MATERIALS AND PROCESSES – (Formed by the union of: Metal Progress & Advanced Materials and Processes) – Metals Park. v130-152. oct 1986-dec 1997+ – 1,5,9 – D15671 – us UMI [620]

ADVANCED MATERIALS AND PROCESSES – (Merged with: Metal Progress to form: Advanced Materials & Processes) – Metals Park. v1-2. sep 1985-86 – 1,5,9 – $43.00y – D14991 – us UMI [600]

ADVANCED MATERIALS AND PROCESSES *see*
– ADVANCED MATERIALS AND PROCESSES

ADVANCED MATERIALS FOR OPTICS AND ELECTRONICS – (Formed by the Union of: Journal of Molecular Electronics & Chemtronics) – Chichester. v1-7. feb 1992-dec 1997*+ – 1,5,9 – D19064 – us UMI [621]

ADVANCED NUCLEAR RESEARCH: HEARING. / U.S. Congress. House. Committee on Science and Astronautics. Subcommittee on Aeronautics and Space Technology – Washington, Govt. Print. Off., 1974. 75 p. LL-2362 – 1 – us L of C Photodup [340]

ADVANCED PRACTICE NURSING QUARTERLY – Gaithersburg. 1995-1997+ – 1,5,9 – D21633 – us UMI [610]

ADVANCED TECHNOLOGY LIBRARIES – Boston. v1-26. jan 1972-dec 1997+ – 1,5,9 – D7806 – us UMI [020]

ADVANCEMENT OF SCIENCE – (Ceased publ) – London. v1-27 oct 1939-jun 1971 1; v22-27 may 1965-jun 1971 5; v27 sep 1970-jun 1971 9* – 1,5,9 – D1278 – us UMI [500]

ADVANCES IN ANATOMIC PATHOLOGY – New York. 1994-1997*+ – 1,5,9 – D21155 – us UMI [611]

ADVANCES IN ASSESSMENT OF WORLD CEPHALOPED RESOURCES – 1983 – 467p – it F.A.O. [333]

ADVANCES IN BEHAVIOUR RESEARCH AND THERAPY – Oxford. v1-19. 1977-97+ – 1,5,9 – D49539 – us UMI [616]

ADVANCES IN CHEMICAL PHYSICS – (1984-. 5,6,9) – 1958- – 1 – us UMI [530]

ADVANCES IN COLLOID AND INTERFACE SCIENCE – v1-21. 1967-84 – 1,5,6,13 – sz Elsevier [073]

ADVANCES IN COMPETITIVENESS RESEARCH – Indiana. 1993-1997+ 1*; 1995-1997+ 5,9 – 1,5,9 – D23806 – us UMI [338]

ADVANCES IN CONTRACEPTION – Lancaster. v1-13 mar 1985-dec 1997+ 1; v5-13 1989-1997+ 5,9 – 1,5,9 – D16761 – us UMI [613]

ADVANCES IN EARTH-ORIENTED APPLICATIONS OF SPACE TECHNOLOGY – v. 1-. 1980- – 5,6,9 – us UMI [629]

ADVANCES IN ENGEERING SOFTWARE – BARKING *see* ADVANCES IN ENGINEERING SOFTWARE AND WORKSTATIONS

ADVANCES IN ENGINEERING SOFTWARE – (Cont: Advances in Engineering Software and Workstations) – Barking. v14-30. 1992-1997*+ – 1,5,9 – D42718.02 – us UMI [621]

ADVANCES IN ENGINEERING SOFTWARE – (Cont in part by: Advances in Engineering Software and Workstations) – Southampton. v1-12. dec 1978-oct 1990* – 1 – D42718 – us UMI [621]

ADVANCES IN ENGINEERING SOFTWARE AND WORKSTATIONS – (Cont in part: Advances in Engineering Software (Southampton ed). Cont by: Advances in Engeering Software (Barking ed)) – Southampton. v13. 1991* – 1 – D42718.01 – us UMI [621]

ADVANCES IN ENGINEERING SOFTWARE AND WORKSTATIONS *see*
– ADVANCES IN ENGINEERING SOFTWARE

ADVANCES IN ENGINEERING SOFTWARE – SOUTHAMPTON *see* ADVANCES IN ENGINEERING SOFTWARE AND WORKSTATIONS

ADVANCES IN ENZYME REGULATION – Oxford. v1-37 1963-97+ 1,5; v16 1978. v17 1979*. v18-37 1980-97+ 9 – 1,5,9 – D49006 – us UMI [073]

ADVANCES IN ENZYMOLOGY AND RELATED AREAS OF MOLECULAR BIOLOGY – (1985-. 5,6,9) – v29-. 1967- – 1 – us UMI [612]

ADVANCES IN ENZYMOLOGY AND RELATED SUBJECTS – v1-2. 1941-42 – 1 – us UMI [612]

ADVANCES IN ENZYMOLOGY AND RELATED SUBJECTS OF BIOCHEMISTRY – v3-28. 1943-66 – 1 – us UMI [612]

ADVANCES IN FREE RADICAL BIOLOGY AND MEDICINE – (Ceased publ. Merged with: Journal of Free Radicals in Biology and Medicine; to form: Free Radical Biology and Medicine) – Elmsford. v1-2. 1985-1986 – 1,5,9 – D49479 – us UMI [610]

ADVANCES IN GASTROENTEROLOGY, HEPATOLOGY AND CLINICAL NUTRITION – Philadelphia. 1996-1997+ – 1,5,9 – D23341 – us UMI [616]

ADVANCES IN INTERNAL MEDICINE – Chicago. 1942-94*; 1995-97+ – 1 – D13048 – us UMI [073]

ADVANCES IN ISRAEL RESEARCH ON WATER DESALINATION / Israel. Prime Minister's Office – Lectures given by the Israel scientists at the Int'l. Desalting and Environmental Assoc. Conf. held in Mexico City, 24-29 Oct 1976. 73 p., illus., diagr – 9 – 2.00 – is I.T.T.I. [660]

ADVANCES IN NEPHROLOGY FROM THE NECKER HOSPITAL – v1-5. 1971-75 – 1 – us UMI [073]

ADVANCES IN NEUROIMMUNOLOGY – Manchester. v1-3 jan 1991-oct 1993. v4 jan-oct 1994*. v5-7 jan 1995-oct 1997+ 1,5,9 – 1,5,9 – D49620 – us UMI [616]

ADVANCES IN ORTHOPAEDIC SURGERY – New York. v7-20 1983-1997+ 1*; v18-20 1995-1997+ 5,9 – 1,5,9 – D21154.01 – us UMI [617]

ADVANCES IN PEDIATRICS – v1-24. 1942-76 – 1 – us UMI [073]

ADVANCES IN PHYSICS – London. v1-46 1952-dec 1997+ 1*; v41-46 jan 1992-dec 1997+ 5*,9 – 1,5,9 – D17347 – us UMI [530]

ADVANCES IN PHYSICS – v.1-24. 1951-75. London – 9 – uk Dawson [530]

ADVANCES IN PHYSIOLOGY EDUCATION – Bethesda. v1-18. jun 1989-dec 1997*+ – 1,5,9 – D17272 – us UMI [612]

ADVANCES IN PLASTICS TECHNOLOGY – (Cont by: Advances in Polymer Technology) – New York. v1. jan-oct 1981 – 1,5,9 – $195.00y – D13076 – us UMI [660]

ADVANCES IN PLASTICS TECHNOLOGY *see* ADVANCES IN POLYMER TECHNOLOGY

ADVANCES IN POLYMER TECHNOLOGY – (Cont: Advances in Plastics Technology) – New York. v2-14 Win 1982-Win 1997+ 1,9; v2-9 Win 1982-Win 1989. v10-13 Spr 1990-Win 1994*. v14-16 Spr 1995-Win 1997+ 5 – 1,5,9 – D13076.01 – us UMI [660]

ADVANCES IN POLYMER TECHNOLOGY *see* ADVANCES IN PLASTICS TECHNOLOGY

ADVANCES IN SPACE RESEARCH – Oxford. v1-20. 1981-97+ 1,5,9; v8 1988* 5,9; v12 1992* 5 – 1,5,9 – D49540 – us UMI [520]

ADVANCES IN SURGERY – v1-12. 1965-78 – 1 – us UMI [617]

ADVANCES IN THE BIOSCIENCES – Oxford. v1-118. 1967-97+ . v89-100 1993-94* 1,5,9 – 1,5,9 – D49007 – us UMI [574]

ADVANCES IN THE CONTINUING EDUCATION OF ENGINEERS / Ovesen, N Krebs – 1980 – 200p – 9 – 92-3-101832-9 – fr UNESCO [370]

ADVANCES IN TUNNELLING TECHNOLOGY AND SURFACE USE = DEVELOPPEMENT DES TRAVAUX EN SOUTERRAIN – (Ceased publ. Merged in 1986 with: Underground Space; to form: Tunnelling and Underground Space Technology) – Oxford. v1-4. 1981-1984 – 1,5,9* – D49385 – us UMI [624]

ADVANCES IN WATER RESOURCES – Barking. v1-20 sep 1977-1997+ 1*; v15-20 1992-1997*+ 5,9 – 1,5,9 – D42703 – us UMI [333]
ADVANCING CLINICAL CARE – (Ceased publ. Cont: AD Nurse) – Franksville. v4-6. may 1989-dec 1991 – 1,5,9 – D16482.01 – us UMI [610]
ADVANCING CLINICAL CARE *see* AD NURSE
THE ADVANTAGE – Riverside, CA. Apr 1977-82 – 8r – 1 – $400.00 – R02713 – us Library Micro [071]
ADVANTAGES OF IMPERIAL FEDERATION: A LECTURE DELIVERED...JANUARY 30TH, 1891.. / Grant, George Monro – Toronto: C. Blackett, 1891. 05115. (Pre-1900 Canadiana) – 9 – cn C.I.H.M. [971]
ADVENT AND ASCENSION / Faunce, Daniel Webster – 1903 – 9 – us A.T.L.A. [240]
ADVENT CHRISTIAN QUARTERLY – Buchanan. v1-2. jul 1869-apr 1871* – 1 – D11584 – us UMI [240]
ADVENT HERALD – Boston. v1-14. mar 1840-jan 1848* – 1 – D11610 – us UMI [240]
THE ADVENT HERALD – Boston, MA (& New York City). v10 n18. 10 dec 1845; v12 n5. 9 sep 1846; v12 n7. 23 sep 1846 – 1r – 1 – Can$30.00 – cn Can Microfilming [071]
ADVENT MESSAGE TO THE DAUGHTERS OF ZION – Boston. v1. may-sep 1844* – 1 – D11585 – us UMI [240]
ADVENT MIRROR – Boston. v1. 1845* – 1 – D11586 – us UMI [240]
ADVENT REVIEW AND SABBATH HERALD – v151-155. 1974-78. Continued as: Adventist Review – 1 – us A.T.L.A. [240]
ADVENT SHIELD AND REVIEW – Boston. v1. may 1844-apr 1845* – 1 – D11587 – us UMI [240]
ADVENT TESTIMONY – (All that is currently offered) – Boston. v1 mar-apr 1846* – 1 – D11588 – us UMI [240]
ADVENTIST HERITAGE – Loma Linda. v1-18 jan 1974-Win 1998+ 1,5*,9 – 1,5,9 – D9335 – us UMI [240]
ADVENTIST REVIEW – v156-162. 1979-85, 1987. Continues: Advent Review and Sabbath Herald – 1 – us A.T.L.A. [240]
ADVENTURE – (Ceased publ) – New York. 1910-dec 1955* – 1 – D8309 – us UMI [073]
ADVENTURE – Issue Nos. 103-107 Apr 1946-Aug 1946 – 5mf – 15 – $31,95 – us Comics [760]
ADVENTURE – Issue Nos. 108-112 Sept 1946-Jan 1947 – 5mf – 15 – $31,95 – us Comics [760]
ADVENTURE – Issue Nos. 113-117 Feb 1947-Jun 1947 – 5mf – 15 – $31,95 – us Comics [760]
ADVENTURE – Issue Nos. 118-122 Jul 1947-Nov 1947 – 5mf – 15 – $31,95 – us Comics [760]
ADVENTURE – Issue Nos. 123-127 Dec 1947-Apr 1948 – 5mf – 15 – $31,95 – us Comics [760]
ADVENTURE. (BRIG) *see* JOURNAL OF VOYAGE FROM SALEM TOWARDS ST KITTS OF BRIG ADVENTURE
ADVENTURE FOR GOD / Brent, Charles H – New York: Longmans, Green, 1905 – 1mf – us A.T.L.A. [240]
ADVENTURES AMONG BOOKS / Lang, Andrew – London, New York, Bombay: Longmans, Green, 1905 – 1 roll – 1 – 1-55879-513-8 – uk Libr Preservation [420]
ADVENTURES IN CRITICISM / Quiller-Couch, Arthur Thomas – London: Cassell, 1896 – 1 roll – 1 – 1-55879-819-6 – uk Libr Preservation [420]
ADVENTURES IN NEW GUINEA / Chalmers, James – [London]: Religious Tract Society, 1889 – 1mf – 9 – 0-8370-8327-3 – 1986-2327 – us A.T.L.A. [980]
ADVENTURES IN NYASALAND. / Fotheringham, L Monteith – London. 1891 – 1 – us Res Libr [960]
ADVENTURES IN SIAM IN THE 17TH CENTURY / Hutchinson, E W – 1 – uk Microform Academic [910]
ADVENTURES IN THULE: THREE STORIES FOR BOYS / Black, William – British Fiction Archive: Unit 4 – 9 – uk Bell [830]
THE ADVENTURES OF A PROTESTANT IN SEARCH OF A RELIGION / Iota – New York, Montreal: D & J Sadlier & Co, 1879 – 4mf – 9 – Can$9.00 – cn Bibl Nat [240]
ADVENTURES OF AN ATTORNEY IN SEARCH OF PRACTICE / Warren, Samuel – Chicago: James Cockcroft & Co, 1872 – 5mf – 9 – $7.50 – LLMC 95-191 – us L.L.M.C. [340]
THE ADVENTURES OF MISS KANG (CCC327) / ed by Woman's Messenger Staff – (In Chinese) – Hong Kong: Bible Book and Tract Depot for Council on Christian Literature for Overseas Chinese, 1953 – 1r – 1 – 1984-6666 – us A.T.L.A. [830]
ADVERSARIA CRITICA SACRA : WITH A SHORT EXPLANATORY INTRODUCTION / Scrivener, Frederick Henry Ambrose – Cambridge: University Press; New York: Macmillan [distributor], 1893 – 1mf – 9 – 0-8370-5198-3 – 1985-3198 – us A.T.L.A. [220]
ADVERSE DRUG REACTION BULLETIN – Surrey. 1966-1972* v38-187 feb 1973-dec 1997+ 1; v56-187 feb 1976-dec 1997+ 5*,9 – 1,5,9 – D8330 – us UMI [615]
ADVERSE DRUG REACTIONS AND ACUTE POISONING REVIEWS – (Cont by: Adverse Drug Reactions and Toxicological Reviews) – Oxford. v1-9 Spr 1982-Win 1990 1,5*,9 – 1,5,9 – D14048.01 – us UMI [615]
ADVERSE DRUG REACTIONS AND ACUTE POISONING REVIEWS *see* ADVERSE DRUG REACTIONS AND TOLXICOLOGICAL REVIEWS
ADVERSE DRUG REACTIONS AND TOLXICOLOGICAL REVIEWS – (Cont: Adverse Drug Reactions and Acute Poisoning Reviews) – Oxford. v10-16. Spr 1991-Win 1997+ – 1,5*,9 – D14048.01 – us UMI [615]
ADVERSE DRUG REACTIONS AND TOXICOLOGICAL REVIEWS *see* ADVERSE DRUG REACTIONS AND ACUTE POISONING REVIEWS
ADVERSUS ELIPANDUM / Liebanensis, Beatus & Oxomensis, Eterius – 1984 – 6mf – 9 – Bf1,050.00 – 2-503-60592-3 – be Brepols [240]
ADVERSUS LUDAEOS (CCCM 63-63A) / Petrus Venerabilis – 1985 – 6mf – 9 – Bf1,450.00 – 2-503-30582-2 – be Brepols [240]
ADVERSUS OMNES HAERESES LIBRI 14 / Castro, Alf. A – Antverpiae, 1556 – 41mf – 8 – ne Slangenburg [240]
ADVERSUS OMNIA CATABAPTISTARVM PRAVA DOGMATA LIB. IIII. PER LEONEM JUDAE AUCTI / Bullinger, H – Tigvri, Christoph Froschover, 1535 – 5mf – 9 – PBU-547/1 – ne IDC [240]
ADVERSVS ANABAPTISTAS. IUDICIUM / Melanchthon, Philip – Item An Magistratus iure occidere anabaptistas Joh. Brentii Sententia. Item Articuli, inspectionis Ecclesiarum Saxoniae, emendati. n.d. BME-98 1 – 9 – ne IDC [240]
ADVERSVS IMPIOS ANABAPTISTARVM ERRORES. IUDITIUM / Dickius, L – Haganoae, J. Sec. 1530. BME-115 1 – 9 – ne IDC [240]
ADVERTENCIAS A LA ISTORIA (SIC) DE MERIDA / Gomez Bravo, Juan – 1638 – 9 – 1.50f – sp Bibl Santa Ana [946]
ADVERTENCIAS Y OBLIGACIONES...REJON / Trejo, Luis de – 1639 – 9 – 1.50f – sp Bibl Santa Ana [946]
ADVERTENTIEBLAD *see* DE ZUID-AFRIKAAN
ADVERTISEMENT COPIES – San Gabriel Valley, CA. 1992 – 34+ r – 1 – $1,700.00 ($850.00y) – R04104 – us Library Micro [071]
ADVERTISER – Alderson. West Virginia. 1900-1938 – 1 – us UMI [071]
ADVERTISER – Amory. Miss. 1936-1940 – 1 – us UMI [071]
ADVERTISER – Angelica. N.Y. 1877-1879 – 1 – us UMI [071]
ADVERTISER – Ardmore. Pa. 1962- – 1 – us UMI [071]
ADVERTISER – Bonyrigg, Scotland. 1984-85 – 4r – 1 – uk British Libr Newspaper [072]
ADVERTISER – Clinton. Iowa. 1913-1927 – 1 – us UMI [071]
ADVERTISER – Edgefield. S.C. -w. 1836-1902 – 1 – us UMI [071]
ADVERTISER – Elmira. N.Y. 1855-1920; 1923-50 – 1 – us UMI [071]
ADVERTISER – Etobicoke, 1925-1977 – 46r – 1 – cn Preston [971]
ADVERTISER – Grand Gulf. Miss. 1835-1838 – 1 – us UMI [071]
ADVERTISER – Hammond. N.Y. 1907-1910; 1913-1947 – 1 – us UMI [071]
ADVERTISER – Honolulu. Hawaii. 1882- – 1 – us UMI [071]
ADVERTISER – Hope Valley. R.I. 1881-1882; 1895-1941 – 1 – us UMI [071]
ADVERTISER – Huntington. West Virginia. 1895-1979 – 1 – us UMI [071]
ADVERTISER – Lexington. Miss. 1905-1915. 1938-1966 – 1 – us UMI [071]
ADVERTISER – Manhattan. Ohio. -w. 1838-41 – 1 – us UMI [071]
ADVERTISER – Milan. Ohio. 1880-84 – 1 – us UMI [071]
ADVERTISER – Moss Point. Miss. 1961-1962 – 1 – us UMI [071]
ADVERTISER – Newark. N.J. 1832-1907 – 1 – us UMI [071]
ADVERTISER – Newport. R.I. -w. 1850-64 – 1 – us UMI [071]
ADVERTISER – Oklahoma City. Okl. 1948-56 – 1 – us UMI [071]
ADVERTISER – Owen Sound, 1870-1921 – 23r – 1 – cn Preston [971]
ADVERTISER – Richmond, CA. 1933-34 – 1r – 1 – $50.00 – B02689 – us Library Micro [071]
ADVERTISER – Ripley. Miss. 1843-46; 1855-1856 – 1 – us UMI [071]
ADVERTISER – Salisbury. Md. 1871-1877; 1880; 1883-1912; 1914-18; 1924-1929 – 1 – us UMI [071]
ADVERTISER – Santa Maria. Calif. -w. 1956-64 – 1 – us UMI [071]
ADVERTISER – St. Albans. West Virginia. -w. 1948- – 1 – us UMI [071]
ADVERTISER – Utica. Miss. 1944-1952 – 1 – us UMI [071]
ADVERTISER – Wilmington. N.C. 1837-1841 – 1 – us UMI [071]
THE ADVERTISER – Auburn. N.Y. 1913-1931 – 1 – us UMI [071]
THE ADVERTISER – City of Cebu: Advertiser Press, jan 9 1942-mar 7 1942 – us Res Libr [072]
THE ADVERTISER – Ione, NV. Sep-Oct 1964 – 1r – 1 – $50.00 – U04589 – us Library Micro [071]
THE ADVERTISER – Kentville, Nova Scotia. v18 n25. 26 avr 1901 – 1r – 1 – Can$25.00 – cn Can Microfilming [072]
THE ADVERTISER – New York. N.Y. 1921, 1922 – 1 – us A.J.P.C. [071]
THE ADVERTISER – Waterford. Ireland. -w. 11 Mar-16 Sep 1848. (10 ft) – 1 – uk British Libr Newspaper [072]
THE ADVERTISER AND COUNTIES OF PRESCOTT AND RUSSELL ADVOCATE – L'Orignal, Ontario. v21 n44a. 8 nov 1888; 14 fev 1889 – 1r – 1 – Can$25.00 – cn Can Microfilming [072]
THE ADVERTISER AND EASTERN TOWNSHIPS SENTINEL – (Filmed together with: Waterloo Advertiser and Eastern Townships Advocates 8 dec 1864-13 jan 1870. Waterloo Advertiser and District of Bedford Times 21 jan 1870-21 dec 1888. Waterloo Advertiser 4 jan 1889-v68 n40 5 oct 1923) – Knowlton, Waterloo, Canada. 11 jan 1856-10 nov 1864 – 12r – 1 – Can$65.00r – cn Can Microfilming [072]
ADVERTISER AND SUNDAY – Montgomery. Ala. 1952- – 1 – us UMI [071]
THE ADVERTISER AND WATERFORD MARKET NOTE – Waterford. Ireland. -w. 4 Mar-15 Apr 1843. (7 ft) – 1 – uk British Libr Newspaper [072]
ADVERTISER ETC – (Portadown Recorder, 1895) – Portadown, Ireland. 1890-94 – 2r – 1 – uk British Libr Newspaper [072]
ADVERTISER (MARYBOROUGH) – 1949-1953. A1-5 – 5r – 1 – at Corangamite [072]
ADVERTISER NEWS – (1980-1992) – Pembroke, 1993 – 1 – cn Preston [971]
ADVERTISER NEWS – Portland OR. Mar 2 9 1949 – 1 – us U.O. Library [071]
ADVERTISER WEEKLY NEWS – London, UK. 2 Sep-30 Dec 1981; 6 Jan 1982-4 Jan 1983 – 1 1/2r – 1 – uk British Libr Newspaper [072]
ADVERTISER-MONITOR – Mount Clemens. Mich. 1937-40 – 1 – us UMI [071]
ADVERTISER'S WEEKLY – (All that is currently available) – London. 1957-1964* v147-174. jan 1950-dec 1956 – 1 – D476 – us UMI [650]
ADVERTISER-TRIBUNE – Tiffin, Ohio. 1933-1944 – 37r – 1 – $32.50r – us Archival [071]
ADVERTISER-TRIBUNE – Tiffin. Ohio. 1945- – 1 – us UMI [071]
ADVERTISING – (Cont: Advertising Quarterly. Cont by: Advertising Magazine) – London. v56-62. Sum 1978-1980* – 1 – D12475.01 – us UMI [650]
ADVERTISING *see*
– ADVERTISING MAGAZAINE
– ADVERTISING QUARTERLY
ADVERTISING AGE : ELECTRONIC MEDIA EDITION – (Cont by: Electronic Media) – Chicago. v1 may-jul 1982 1,5*,9 – 1,5,9 – D13840 – us UMI [650]
ADVERTISING AGE : [MIDWEST REGION EDITION] – (Absorbed: Promotion, 1974) – Chicago. shipped semiannually. v1-68 jan1930-dec 1997+ 1; v51-68 jan 1980-dec 1997+ 5; v46-68 jan 1975-dec 1997+ 9 – 1,5,9 – us UMI [650]
ADVERTISING AGE'S BUSINESS MARKETING – (Cont: Business Marketing. Microfiche shipped yrly or qrtly) – Chicago. v79-82. jan 1994-dec 1997 – 1,5,9 – D348.02 – us UMI [650]
ADVERTISING AND SALES PROMOTION – (Cont by: Promotion. Former title: Advertising Requirements (feb 1953-apr 1961)) – Chicago. v1-21. feb 1953-dec 1973 – 1,5,9 – D1174 – us UMI [650]
ADVERTISING AND SALES PROMOTION *see* PROMOTION
ADVERTISING MAGAZAINE – (Cont: Advertising. Cont by: Journal of Advertising) – London. v63-69. Spr 1980-Aut 1981* – 1 – D12475.02 – us UMI [650]
ADVERTISING MAGAZINE *see* ADVERTISING
ADVERTISING NEWS OF NEW YORK – (Cont by: Adweek, Eastern ed) – New York. v1-20. 1960-nov 1979* – 1 – D15417 – us UMI [650]
ADVERTISING NEWS OF NEW YORK *see* ADWEEK
ADVERTISING QUARTERLY – (Cont as: Advertising) – London. v1-55. Aut 1964-Spr 1978* – 1 – D12475 – us UMI [650]
ADVERTISING QUARTERLY *see* ADVERTISING
ADVERTISING REQUIREMENTS *see* ADVERTISING AND SALES PROMOTION
Advertising Research Foundation *see* ANNUAL CONFERENCE PROCEEDINGS
ADVERTISING: THE SOCIAL AND ECONOMIC PROBLEM / French, George, 1853-1935 – New York: The Ronald Press Company, 1915. 258p. illus – 1 – us U.W. Library [650]
ADVERTISING WORLD – London, UK. Oct-Dec 1901 – 9ft – 1 – uk British Libr Newspaper [072]
ADVERTISSEMENT A TOUS BONS ET LOYAUX SUBIECTZ DU ROY, ECCLESIASTIQUES, NOBLES, & DU TIERS ESTAT, POUR N'ESTRE SURPRINS & CIRCONUENUZ PAR LES PROPOSITIONS COLORES... – Paris: Pour I. Dallier, 1567 – 1 – us U.W. Library [944]
ADVERTISSEMENT SURLE FAICT DU CONCILE DE TRENTE: FAICT PAN MIL CING SENS SOIXANTE QUATRE / Mesnil, Jean Baptiste du – Imprime nourellement. s.l.: s.n., 1567 – 1 – us U.W. Library [900]
ADVICE TO STUDENTS HAVING IN VIEW THE CHRISTIAN MINISTRY ADDRESSED TO THEM AT THE ACADEMY AT BRITSOL / Evans, C – 1770 – 1 – 5.00 – us Baptist [240]
ADVICE TO YOUNG MAN : AND (INCIDENTALLY) TO YOUNG WOMEN, IN THE MIDDLE AND HIGHER RANKS OF LIFE... / Cobbett, William – London: The author, 1829 – 1 roll – 1 – 1-55879-367-4 – uk Libr Preservation [150]
ADVIENTO Y SERMONES VARIOS / Duran de Montijo, Juan – 1722. 5v – 9 – 1.50f – sp Bibl Santa Ana [240]
ADVIS AUX CRIMINALISTES SUR LES ABUS QUI SE GLISSENT DANS LES PROCES DE SORCELLERIE / Spee, P Friedrich von – Lyon. 1660 – 9 – fr Hachette [360]
ADVIS DE LA MAGNIFIQVE ET TRIOMPHANTE ENTREE DU SEIGNEUR MARC ANTOINE COLONNE, ... – Paris, 1572 – 1mf – 9 – H-8189/1 – ne IDC [944]
ADVIS ED DEVIS DES LENGUES; SUIVIS DE LAMARTIGENEE, CEST A DIRE DE LA SOURCE DE PECHE / Bonivard, Francois – Geneve: Jules-Guillaume Fick, 1865 – 1mf – 9 – 0-8370-8564-0 – 1986-2564 – us A.T.L.A. [490]
ADVIS NOVVELLEMENT VENVS DE MESSINE... – Paris, 1565 – 1mf – 9 – H-8164/1 – ne IDC [944]
ADVISER : OR, VERMONT EVANGELICAL MAGAZINE – (Ceased publ) – Middlebury. v1-7. jan 1809-dec 1815 – 1 – D3534 – us UMI [240]
THE ADVISER – Toronto: [s.n., 1861?-186- or 19–] – 9 – cn C.I.H.M. [971]
THE ADVISOR – Bartlett. Ill. 1965-71 – 1 – us UMI [071]
Advisory Council for the Northern Sudan. Khartoum *see* PROCEEDINGS, 1ST-2ND SESSIONS 1944, 4TH-8TH SESSIONS NOV 1944-1948
Advisory Council on Historic Preservation *see* TRUSTEESHIP TERMINATION

ADVOCATE – (Also: Colonial Advocate) – Queenston and Toronto, Canada. 1824-34 – 2r – 1 – $136.00 – cn Library Assoc [072]
ADVOCATE – Auburn. N.Y. 1913-31 – 1 – us UMI [071]
ADVOCATE – Bassett, NE. -w. Jul. 1892-Nov. 1892. Incomplete; May 1895-Dec. 1895 – 1 – us NE Hist [071]
ADVOCATE – Belleville. Ill. 1898-1958 – 1 – us UMI [071]
ADVOCATE – Bowling Green. 1866 – 1r – 1 – $32.50r – us Archival [071]
ADVOCATE – Columbus. Kan. -w. 1882-1936, 1942-45 – 1 – us UMI [071]
ADVOCATE – Ellinwood. Kan. 1888-1898 – 1 – us UMI [071]
ADVOCATE – Gainesville. Miss. 1845-1846 – 1 – us UMI [071]
ADVOCATE – Greenville. Ohio. 1930-39 – 1 – us UMI [071]
ADVOCATE – Jackson. Miss. 1941- – 1 – us UMI [071]
ADVOCATE – LaGrande OR. Aug 25 1899 – 1 – us U.O. Library [071]
ADVOCATE – Le Grande, CA. 1911-1942 – 10r – 1 – $500.00 – B06033 – us Library Micro [071]
ADVOCATE – Liberty. Miss. 1837-1846 – 1 – us UMI [071]
ADVOCATE – Los Angeles, CA. bw. nos. 211-. Mar. 1977-. y Continues: Los Angeles advocate. ISSN 0001-8996. OCLC 7927377 – 1 – us U.W. Library [073]
ADVOCATE – Manistee. Mich. -w. 1896-98, 1903-14 – 1 – us UMI [071]
ADVOCATE – Mullens. West Virginia. 1926- – 1 – us UMI [071]
ADVOCATE – Newark. Ohio. 1940- – 1 – us UMI [071]
ADVOCATE – Parsons. West Virginia. -w. 1896-1919; 1922- – 1 – us UMI [071]
ADVOCATE – Racine. Wis. 1853-54 – 1 – us UMI [071]
ADVOCATE – Racine. Wis. -w. 1842-84 – 1 – us UMI [071]
ADVOCATE – San Francisco, CA. 1979-1984 – 4r – 1 – $200.00 – R03470 – us Library Micro [071]
ADVOCATE – (Set incl. Beaver State Herald (Gresham); Beaver State Herald (Lents); Mt.Scott Herald (Lents); Mt. Scott Herald (Portland)) – Portland, OR. -w. 5 May 1923-2 Dec 1933. – 7r – 1 – us U.O. Library [071]
ADVOCATE – Stamford. Conn. 1840-1966; 1972- – 1 – us UMI [071]
ADVOCATE – Topeka. Kan. 1889-1899 – 1 – us UMI [071]
ADVOCATE – Utica. N.Y. 1908-1917 – 9 – us UMI [071]
ADVOCATE – Vicksburg. Miss. and Register. 1831-38 – 1 – us UMI [071]
ADVOCATE – (Weekly African-American Republican newspaper) – Cleveland, OH. May 15 1915-Jun 1 1918 – 2r – 1 – us Western Res [071]
ADVOCATE : A WEEKLY LAW JOURNAL – St Paul, Minneapolis, Chicago. v1-2. 1888-90 – 1 – $40.00 – us Hein [073]
ADVOCATE *see* HARVARD ADVOCATE
THE ADVOCATE – Bradner, Ohio. 1894-1954 – 16r – 1 – $32.50r – us Archival [071]
THE ADVOCATE – Huntingdon, Canada. v4 n2. 14 Jan 1886-v5 n1. 6 Jan 1887 – 1r – 1 – Can$40.00 – cn Can Microfilming [072]
THE ADVOCATE : A JOURNAL FOR MILITARY DEFENSE COUNSEL – (Cont by: The Army Lawyer) – v1-16 no 2. 1969-84 (all publ) – 9 – LLMC 84-237 – us L.L.M.C. [073]
THE ADVOCATE – Minneapolis. v1-2. 1888-90 (all publ) – 8mf – 9 – $12.00 – LLMC 84-395 – us L.L.M.C. [073]
THE ADVOCATE – Sydney, Nova Scotia. v13 n9. 1 jan 1885-v13 n10. 8 jan 1885 – 1r – 1 – Can$25.00 – cn Can Microfilming [072]
THE ADVOCATE – Toronto: L.P. Kribs, v1 no 1 (Feb 8 1894)- – 9 – cn C.I.H.M. [073]
THE ADVOCATE – (Updated regularly. Missing: v16 no 11, v24 nos 11-12, v26 nos 1-6) – Idaho State Bar. v1-29. 1957-86 – 66mf – 9 – $99.00 – LLMC 84-396 – us L.L.M.C. [073]
THE ADVOCATE (AND PRED. TITLES) – San Pablo, CA. Contra Costa Community College: 1950-1990 – 14r – 1 – $700.00 – B07455 – us Library Micro [370]
ADVOCATE AND PRESS – New Bloomfield, PA., 1889-1932 – 13 – $25.00r – us I.M.R. [071]
ADVOCATE AND THE WOODVILLE ADVOCATE – Beaverton, 1878-1888 – 3r – 1 – cn Preston [971]
ADVOCATE AND VALLEY VISTA *see* POST-ADVOCATE
ADVOCATE FOR THE TESTIMONY OF GOD : AS IT IS WRITTEN IN THE BOOKS OF NATURE AND REVELATION – (Ceased publ. Former title: Apostolic Advocate (may 1 1835-apr 1837)) – Librety. v1-5. may 1835-apr 1839 – 1 – D3711 – us UMI [240]
ADVOCATE (IDAHO STATE BAR JOURNAL) – v23-37. 1980-94 – 9 – $198.00 set – us Hein [340]
ADVOCATE MESSENGER – Danville. Ky. 1951- – 1 – us UMI [071]
ADVOCATE NEWS – Fort Bragg, CA. 1971-83 – 18r – 1 – $900.00 – B02238 – us Library Micro [071]
ADVOCATE OF PEACE – v1-95. Jun 1837-Sept 1932. 260 fiches – 9 – $1,050.00 – us UPA [320]
ADVOCATE OF PEACE AND CHRISTIAN PATRIOT – (Ceased publ) – Philadelphia. v1. sep 1828-jun 1829 – 1 – D4407 – us UMI [240]
ADVOCATE OF SCIENCE : A POPULAR SCIENTIFIC JOURNAL – (Ceased publ) – Philadelphia. v1. feb 1833-34 – 1 – D3913 – us UMI [500]
ADVOCATE OF SCIENCE AND ANNALS OF NATURAL HISTORY – (Ceased publ) – Philadelphia. v1. aug 1834-apr 1835 – 1 – D3914 – us UMI [500]
ADVOCATE (SUFFOLK) – (v1-16 1968-85 in reels $72.00. v17-24 1986-94 in mf $78.00) – v1-24. 1968-1994 – 5,6,9 – $150.00 set – us Hein [340]
ADVOCATE (VANCOUVER) – v1-53. 1943-1995 – 9 – $597.00 set – us Hein [340]
ADVOCATE-NEWS – Bridgetown, Barbados, 1930-49 – 93r – 1 – $4,603.50 – us African Imprint [072]
ADVOCATE-TRIBUNE – Bloomington, NE. -w. Feb. 1882-Nov. 1891. Incomplete; Jan. 1892-Oct. 1959 – 1 – us NE Hist [071]
ADWEEK – (Cont: Adweek – Midwest Advertising News) – Chicago. v1938 jan 1981-dec 1997+1*; v32-38 jan 1991-dec 1997+ 5*,9 – 1,5,9 – D18872.01 – us UMI [650]
ADWEEK – (Cont: Adweek Southeast Advertising News) – Atlanta. v5-18 1984- 1*; v12-18 jan 1991- 5*,9 – 1,5,9 – D18871.01 – us UMI [650]
ADWEEK : EASTERN EDITION – (Cont: Advertising News of New York) – New York. v20-38 nov 1979-dec 1997+ 1*; v26-38 jan 1985-dec 1997+ 5*,9 – 1,5,9 – D15417.01 – us UMI [650]
ADWEEK : MIDWEST ADVERTISING NEWS – (Cont by: Adweek – Midwest ed) – Chicago. v1-19. 1963-jan 1981* – 1 – D18872 – us UMI [650]
ADWEEK : NATIONAL MARKETING EDITION – (Cont: Ad Forum. Cont by: Adweek's Marketing Week – National Marketing Ed) – New York. v1-27. jul 1985-sep 1986 – 1,5,9 – D16149 – us UMI [650]
ADWEEK : NEW ENGLAND EDITION – (Cont: New England Advertising Week) – Boston. v23-27 feb 1986-dec 1997+* 1,5,9 – 1,5,9 – D18870.01 – us UMI [650]
ADWEEK : SOUTHEAST ADVERTISING NEWS – (Cont by: Adweek – Southeast ed) – Atlanta. v1-4. feb 1980-83* – 1 – D18871 – us UMI [650]
ADWEEK : WESTERN EDITION – New York. may 1980-1990* v41-47 1991- 1*; v41-47 1991-* 5,9 – 1,5,9 – D18806 – us UMI [650]
ADWEEK *see*
– AD FORUM
– ADVERTISING NEWS OF NEW YORK
ADWEEK : SOUTHWEST ADVERTISING NEWS – (Cont by: Adweek Southwest Ed) – Dallas. v1-4. sep 1979-1982* – 1 – D18873 – us UMI [650]
ADWEEK : SOUTHWEST ED – (Cont: Adweek Southwest Advertising News) – Dallas. v5-38 jan 1983- 1*; v13-38 jan 1991-* 5,9 – 1,5,9 – D18873.01 – us UMI [650]
ADWEEK – MIDWEST ADVERTISING NEWS *see* ADWEEK
ADWEEK – MIDWEST EDITION *see* ADWEEK
ADWEEK NATIONAL MARKETING ED *see* ADWEEK'S MARKETING WEEK
ADWEEK SOUTHEAST ADVERTISING NEWS *see* ADWEEK
ADWEEK – SOUTHEAST EDITION *see* ADWEEK
ADWEEK SOUTHWEST ADVERTISING NEWS *see* ADWEEK
ADWEEK SOUTHWEST ED *see* ADWEEK
ADWEEK'S COMPUTER AND ELECTRONICS MARKETING – (Cont: Computer and Electronics Marketing. Cont by: Marketing Computers) – New York. v6-7. jun 1985-aug 1987* – 1 – D18869.01 – us UMI [621]
ADWEEK'S MARKETING WEEK : NATIONAL MARKETING ED – (Cont: Adweek National Marketing Ed. Cont by: Brandweek) – New York. v27-33. sep 1986-jun 1992 – 1,5,9 – D16149.01 – us UMI [650]
ADWEEK'S MARKETING WEEK – NATIONAL MARKETING EDITION *see* ADWEEK
Adwick-le-Street. Yorkshire *see* PARISH REGISTERS
Adyar Library *see* BULLETIN
Adye, Ralph Willett *see* THE BOMBARDIER AND POCKET GUNNER
Adye, Stephen P *see* A TREATISE ON COURTS-MARTIAL
AE AGRICULTURAL ECONOMICS AND RURAL SOCIOLOGY REPORT / Clemson University. Agricultural Experiment Station – No.331-424. 1970-82 – 1,5 – us Spaulding [630]
AE INFORMATION SERIES / North Carolina. State University. Raleigh. Dept. of Economics – v.1-129. Sep 1937-Sep 1966 – 1,5 – us Spaulding [630]
AE SERIES / South Carolina. Agricultural Experiment Station. Clemson – n.101-330. Feb. 1951-Jan 1969 – 1,5 – us Spaulding [630]
AEA ADVOCATE – (Cont: Arizona Educator Advocate) – Phoenix. v5-15 apr 1979-aug 1989*. v16-24 sep 1989-jun 1998+ – 1 – D11260.01 – us UMI [340]
AEA INFORMATION SERIES / Louisiana State University. Agricultural Extension Service. Department of Agricultural Economics and Agribusiness – No.17-52. 1969-81. 1 reel – 1,5 – us Spaulding [630]
AEC / University of Kentucky. Department of Agricultural Economics – No.1-22.1973-83. 1 fiche – 9 – us Spaulding [630]
AEC MIMEOGRAPHED REPORT / Mississippi. Agricultural Experiment Station. State College – v. 25-56. 1959-69 – 1,5,6 – us Spaulding [630]
AEC. M.R / Mississippi State University. Agricultural Experiment Station. Agricultural and Forestry Experiment Station – No.57-102. 1969-80 – 1,5 – us Spaulding [630]
AEC STATISTICAL SERIES / Mississippi. Agricultural Experiment Station. State College – v. 1-94. 1962-63 – 1,5,6 – us Spaulding [630]
AEC TECHNICAL PUBLICATION / Mississippi. Agricultural Experiment Station. State College – v. 1-13. 1959-71 – 1,5,6 – us Spaulding [630]
AEC TECHNICAL PUBLICATION / Mississippi State University. Agricultural Experiment Station. Agricultural and Forestry Experiment Station – No.14-39. 1976-82 – 1,5 – us Spaulding [630]
AEDC JOURNAL – (Cont: AIDC Journal) – Kansas City. v16. jan-Fal 1981 – 1,5,9 – D2313.01 – us UMI [073]
AEDC JOURNAL *see* AIDC JOURNAL
AEDES WALPOLIANAE / Walpole, H – OR, A DESCRIPTION OF THE COLLECTION OF PICTURES AT Houghton-Hall in Norfolk. O 1173 1. 1752 – 9 – ne IDC [760]
AEDITIO / Colet, John – 1527. 85p. (English Linguistics Series 1500-1800) – 9 – us UMI [400]
AEDS BULLETIN *see* AEDS MONITOR
AEDS JOURNAL / Association for Educational Data Systems – (Cont by: Journal of Research on Computing in Education) – Washington. v1-7 sep 1967-sum 1974; v8-20 fall 1974-fall 1986 1; v8 fall 1974-sum 1975*; v10-11 fall 1976-sum 1978*; v12-20 fall 1978-fall 1986 5; v10-20 fall 1976-fall 1986 9 – 1,5,9 – D10379 – us UMI [370]
AEDS MONITOR / Association for Educational Data Systems – (Cont by: Monitor. Former titles: Association for Educational Data Systems (AEDS) Bulletin) – Washington. v1-13 dec 1962-jun 1975; v14-23 jul 1975-jun 1985; v24 jul-aug 1985 1; v16-23 jul 1977-jun 1985; v24 jul-aug 1985 5; v16-23 jul 1977-jun 1985; v24 jul-aug 1985 9 – 1,5,9 – D10380 – us UMI [370]
AEES / University of Kentucky. Department of Agricultural Engineering – No.1-34.1978-83. 5 fiches – 9 – us Spaulding [630]
AEF – Brazzaville, French Equatorial Africa. Jun 1943-Aug 1945 (imperfect) – 4r – 1 – uk British Libr Newspaper [072]
AEF NOUVELLE – Brazzaville. aout 1948-nov 1949 – 1 – fr A.C.R.P.P. [072]
Aegidius, of Assisi *see* DICTA BEATI AEGIDII ASSISIENSIS
THE AEGIS – Bel Air. Md. -w. 1857- – 1 – us UMI [071]
THE AEGIS AND WESTERN COURIER – Castlebar. Ireland. -w. 23 Jun 1841-26 Nov 1842. (43 ft) – 1 – uk British Libr Newspaper [072]
AEGYPTEN UND DIE BIBEL : DIE URGESCHICHTE ISRAELS IM LICHT DER AEGYPTISCHEN MYTHOLOGIE / Voelter, Daniel – (Includes bibliographical references) – 2. neubearb Aufl. Leiden: E J Brill, 1904 – 1mf – 9 – 0-8370-9276-0 – 1986-3276 – us A.T.L.A. [220]
AEGYPTEN-INDEX = EGYPTIAN INDEX. PICTORIAL DOCUMENTATION ON ART IN EGYPT : BILDDOKUMENTATION ZUR KUNST IN AEGYPTEN / ed by Bildarchiv Foto Marburg – Deutsches Dokumentationszentrum fuer Kunstgeschichte Philipps-Universitaet Marburg – (mf ed 1997) – 111mf (1:24) – 9 – silver DM4,800.00 – 3-598-33634-9 – gw Saur [700]
AEGYPTISCH-ARAMAEISCHE INSCHRIFTEN / Lauth, Franz Joseph – [S.l.: s.n.], 1878 – 1mf – 9 – 0-8370-7164-X – 1986-1164 – us A.T.L.A. [470]
AEGYPTISCHE GRABSTEINE UND DENKSTEINE AUS ATHEN UND KONSTANTINOPEL / Poertner, B – Strassbourg. 1908. BNE-391 1 – 9 – ne IDC [930]
AEGYPTISCHE GRABSTEINE UND DENKSTEINE AUS SUEDDEUTSCHEN SAMMLUNGEN / Poertner, B & Spiegelberg, W – I. Karlsruhe, Muelhausen, Strassburg, Stuttgart. II Muenchen. III Bonn, Darmstadt, Frankfurt a. M., Genf, Neuchatel. Strassbourg. 1902. BNE-390 2 – 9 – ne IDC [930]
AEGYPTISCHE LESESTUECKE / Sethe, K – ed. 2. Leipzig. 1928. BNE-486 1 – 9 – ne IDC [930]
DIE AEGYPTISCHE SAMMLUNG DER MUSEUM-MEERMANNO-WESTREENIANUM / Spiegelberg, W – Strassburg. 1896. BNE-392 – 9 – ne IDC [930]
DIE AEGYPTISCHE SAMMLUNG DES MUSEUM-MEERMANNO-WESTREENIANUM IM HAAG / Spiegelberg, W – Strassburg, 1896 – 1mf – 9 – ne IDC [930]
DAS AEGYPTISCHE VERBUM IM ALTAEGYPTISCHEN, NEUAEGYPTISCHEN UND KOPTISCHEN / Sethe, K – 3v. Leipzig. 1899-1902. BNE-495 1 – 9 – ne IDC [470]
AEGYPTOLOGISCHE RANDGLOSSEN ZUM ALTEN TESTAMENT / Spiegelberg, W – Strassburg. 1904. BNE-482 1 – 9 – ne IDC [220]
AEGYPTUS : RIVISTA ITALIANA DI EGITTOLOGIA E DI PAPIROLOGIA – 1(1920)-20(1940) – 152mf – 9 – Dfl532.00 – ne Slangenburg [073]
Aehrling, E *see* CARL VON LINNES BREFVEXLING
AEI ECONOMIST – (Merged with: Public Opinion to form: American Enterprise) – Washington. v1-13. sep 1977-89* – 1 – D17433 – us UMI [330]
AEI ECONOMIST *see* AMERICAN ENTERPRISE
AEI FOREIGN POLICY AND DEFENSE REVIEW – Washington. v1-6. 1979-86* – 1 – D14896 – us UMI [327]
Aelders, Etta P *see* APPEL AUX FRANCAISES SUR LA REGENERATION DES MOEURS ET NECESITE DE L'INFLUENCE DES FEMMES DANS UN GOUVERNEMENT LIBRE
AELFRIDA : DRAMA IN FUENF AUFZUEGEN / Loewenberg, Jakob – Hamburg: M Glogau, 1919 – 1r – 1 – us U.W. Library [820]
Aelred of Rievaulx, Saint *see* LIVES OF S. NINIAN AND S. KENTIGERN
DIE AELTERE WORMSER BRIEFSAMMLUNG (MGH EPISTOLAE 2: 3.BD) – 1949 – Dfl13.00 – ne Slangenburg [240]
DER AELTESTE ENGLISCHE MARIENHYMNUS "ON GOD UREISUN OF URE LEFDI" / Marufke, Willy – (Written in the first part of the 13th century in the Berkshire or Wiltshire dialect. Generally ascribed to Edmund Rich, Archbishop of Canterbury) – Leipzig: Quelle & Meyer, 1907 – 1 – us U.W. Library [420]
DAS AELTESTE GERMANISCHE CHRISTENTUM, ODER, DER SOGEN. "ARIANISMUS" DER GERMANEN : VORTRAG / Schubert, Hans von – Tuebingen: Mohr, 1909 – 1mf – us A.T.L.A. [240]

DER AELTESTE SOHN / Bethusy-Huc, Valeska von Reiswitz-Kaderzin, Graefin von – Stuttgart: Deutsche Verlags-Anstalt, 1889 – 1 – us U.W. Library [830]

DIE AELTESTE TERMINOLOGIE DER JUEDISCHEN SCHRIFTAUSLEGUNG : EIN WOERTERBUCH DER BIBELEXEGETISCHEN KUNSTSPRACHE DER TANNAITEN / Bacher, Wilhelm – (In Hebrew Includes bibliographical references) – Leipzig: J C Hinrichs, 1899 – 1mf – 9 – 0-8370-2134-0 – 1985-0134 – us A.T.L.A. [220]

DIE AELTESTEN APOLOGETEN : TEXTE MIT KURZEN EINLEITUNGEN / Goodspeed, Edgar J – Goettingen: Vandenhoeck & Ruprecht, 1914 – 1mf – us A.T.L.A. [240]

DIE AELTESTEN BIOGRAPHIEN DES HEILIGEN NORBERT / Rosenmund, R – Berlin, 1874 – 2mf – 8 – Dfl9.00 – ne Slangenburg [240]

DIE AELTESTEN QUELLEN DES ORIENTALISCHEN KIRCHENRECHTES (T.U.U. 1-6/4 / Achelis, Hans – Leipzig, 1891 – 5mf – 9 – ne Slangenburg [240]

DIE AELTESTEN ROEMISCHEN SACRAMENTARIEN UND ORDINES / Probst, Ferdinand – Muenster i.W.: Aschendorff, 1892 – 1mf – 9 – 0-8370-7185-2 – 1986-1185 – us A.T.L.A. [240]

AEN / University of Kentucky. Department of Agricultural Engineering – No.1-55.1972-82. 6 fiches – 9 – us Spaulding [630]

Aenchbacher, L E *see* THE RELATIONSHIP BETWEEN PHYSICAL ACTIVITY AND SELF-RATED DEPRESSION IN FREE-LIVING WOMEN AGED 60 YEARS AND OLDER

AENLEIDING TOT DE KENNISE VAN HET VERHEVENE DEEL DER NEDERDUITSCHE SPRAKE / Kate, Lambert ten – 2v. 1723. In French. (Linguistic Series) – 9 – fr Hachette [400]

AENMERKINGE OP DE MISSIVE VAN PARNAS,... / Groot, H de – The Hague, 1685 – 1mf – 1 – ILM-756/1 – ne IDC [327]

THE AEOLIAN QUARTERLY – New York, 1897-99 – 1 – £60.00 – uk Chadwyck [780]

Aepinus, J *see*
- BEKENTNISS VNND ERKLERUNG AUFFS INTERIM DURCH DER ERBARN STEDTE...
- D. IOANNES AEPINI IN PSALMUM 26 COMMENTARIU,...

AEQUATIONES MATHEMATICAE – Basel. 1968-1988* v37-54 1989- – 1 – D13939 – us UMI [510]

AERATION OF GRAIN IN SUBTROPICAL CLIMATES – 1982 – 125p – it F.A.O. [631]

AEREOPLASTES THEOSOPHICUS, SIVE EICONES MYSTICAE / Oraeus, Henricus – O 704. 1620-1621 – 9 – ne IDC [240]

AERIAL OPERATIONS DURING WORLD WAR 2 PAMPHLET COLLECTION – 1940-1944 – 1 – CSUXAMJ4290-B – us Hoover Inst Photo [350]

AERIAL PHOTO INTERPRETATION IN SOIL SURVEY – 1976 – 116p – it F.A.O. [631]

AEROBIC AND ANAEROBIC PERFORMANCE MEASURES IN ACTIVE AND INACTIVE YOUNG AND MIDDLE-AGED MALES / Ecker, KR – 1990 – 2mf – 9 – $8.00 – us Microform Publ [612]

AEROBIC AND FITNESS *see* AMERICAN FITNESS

AEROBIC CERTIFICATION / Jefferis, Shelly J – California State University, Northridge, 1995 – 1mf – 9 – PE 3655 – us Microform Publ [370]

AEROBIC EXERCISE RELATED TO FUNCTIONAL AEROBIC CAPACITY, REPETITIVE/INTERFERING BEHAVIOR, AND PLATELET SEROTONIN CONCENTRATION OF INDIVIDUALS WITH AUTISM / Schmidt, Gordon J – 1989 – 221p 3mf – 9 – $12.00 – us Microform Publ [617]

AEROBIC RESPONSES TO 12 WEEKS OF EXERSTRIDING OR WALKING TRAINING IN SEDENTARY ADULT WOMEN / Larkin, James M & Butts, Nancy Kay – 1992 – 1mf – $4.00 – us Microform Publ [612]

AEROBIC RESPONSES TO 12 WEEKS OF TRAINING ON VARIOUS MODES OF HOME EXERCISE EQUIPMENT IN SEDENTARY ADULTS / Angelini, Marc A – University of Wisconsin-La Crosse, 1995 – 1mf – 9 – $4.00 – PH1451 – us Microform Publ [613]

AEROBICS AND FITNESS *see* AFAA JOURNAL

AEROBICS AND FITNESS – (Cont: AFAA Journal. Cont by: American Fitness) – Sherman Oaks. mar 1984-1987* – 1 – D19374.01 – us UMI [613]

AERODOMES / Borie, Henri Jules – Paris, Morris, 1865. 4 fol., 45p., pl. (Architecture Series) – 9 – fr Hachette [720]

AERODYNAMICS THEORY / Durand, W F – v1-6. 26 fiches – 9 – 60.00 – us Updata [629]

AEROMEDICAL REVIEWS – (Ceased publ) – Washington, 1958-84* – 1 – D12398 – us UMI [073]

AERONAUT, A PERIODICAL PAPER, BY AN ASSOCIATION OF GENTLEMEN – (Ceased publ) – New York. v1-12. 1816-1822 – 1 – D3535 – us UMI [073]

AERONAUTICAL AND MISCELLANEOUS NOTEBOOKS / Cayley, George – 1799-1826 – 7 – uk Microform Academic [629]

AERONAUTICAL ENGINEERING REVIEW *see* AEROSPACE ENGINEERING

AERONAUTICAL JOURNAL – (Beginning with 1984, incorporates: Aeronautical Quarterly. Former titles: Aeronautical Journal (1897-1922); Journal of the Royal Aeronautical Society (jan 1923-dec 1967)) – London. v1-101 jan 1897-dec 1997+ 1; v70-101 jan 1966-dec 1997+ 5; v80-101 jan 1976-dec 1997+ 9 – 1,5,9 – D1281 – us UMI [629]

AERONAUTICAL JOURNAL *see* AERONAUTICAL JOURNAL

AERONAUTICAL QUARTERLY – (Incorporated with: Aeronautical Journal) – London. v1-34 may 1949-nov 1983 1; v17-34 feb 1966-nov 1983 5; v27-34 feb 1976-nov 1983 9 – 1,5,9 – D1280 – us UMI [629]

AERONAUTICAL QUARTERLY *see* AERONAUTICAL JOURNAL

Aeronautical Society of America *see* BULLETIN

AERONAUTICS – 1939-60 – 1 – uk Microform Academic [073]

AERONAUTICS – London. v. 1-45. Aug 1932-Mar 1962 – 1 – 90.00 – us L of C Photodup [629]

AERONAUTICS – v. 1-17. 1907-1915 – 1,5,6 – us Princeton Micro [629]

AERONAUTICS ACT AND REGULATIONS / Canada. Laws, Statutes, etc – (Amendment Service. YX76-A2-EM) – Basic set. YX76-A2-IEM – 9 – Can$40.00 – cn Communication [380]

AERONAUTICS AND SPACE REPORTS TO THE CONGRESS, 1958-84 – 8 reels with printed guide – 1 – $770.00 – 0-89093-985-3 – us UPA [629]

l'Aeropagite, Marie-de-Saint-Denis *see* BIBLIOGRAPHIE ANALYTIQUE, PRECEDEE D'UNE BIOGRAPHIE DE MONSEIGNEUR ALPHONSE-MARIE PARENT...

AEROPLANE *see* AEROPLANE

AEROPLANE – (Absorbed by: Flight International. Former Titles: Aeroplane (jun 8, 1911-apr 17, 1959); Aeroplane and Astronautics (apr 24, 1959-mar 8, 1962); Aeroplane and Commerical Aviation News (mar 15, 1962-apr 28-1966)) – London. v94-116. jan 1958-oct 1968 – 1 – D1276 – us UMI [629]

AEROPLANE AND ASTRONAUTICS *see* AEROPLANE

AEROPLANE AND COMMERICAL AVIATION NEWS *see* AEROPLANE

AEROPLANE MONTHLY – (All that is currently available) – Cheam. v2-19. jan 1974-dec 1991 – 1,5,9* – D8448 – us UMI [629]

AEROSOL AGE – (Cont by: Spray Technology and Marketing) – Cedar Grove. v1-36 may 1956-mar 1991 1; v14-36 jan 1969-mar 1991 5; v22-36 jan 1977-mar 1991 9 – 1,5,9 – D2100 – us UMI [660]

AEROSOL SCIENCE AND TECHNOLOGY – New York. v1-27 1982-* 1,5; v8-27 1988- 9* – 1,5,9 – D42397 – us UMI [660]

AEROSPACE – (1974-. 5,6. 1976-. 9) – Washington. v1-25 mar 1963-Sum 1987 1; v12-25 feb 1974-Sum 1987 5; v13-25 feb 1975-Win 1987 9 – 1,5,9 – D10065 – us UMI [629]

AEROSPACE – (Absorbed with July/Aug 1987 issue: Tech Air) – London. NS: v1-24 sep 1969-dec 1997+ 1*,5*,9* – 1 – D11492 – us UMI [629]

AEROSPACE AMERICA – (Cont: Astronautics and Aeronautics) – New York. v22-35. jan 1984- – 1,5,9 – D1605.01 – us UMI [629]

AEROSPACE AND AVIATION DOCUMENTS – 1982. Updated every 3 mos – 5,9 – uk Tech [629]

AEROSPACE CENTURY 21 – (Suppl to v64, Advances) – 1987 – 6mf – 9 – $25.00 – 0-87703-278-5 – us Univelt [629]

AEROSPACE ENGINEERING *see* AEROSPACE ENGINEERING

AEROSPACE ENGINEERING – (Ceased publ. Supersedes the Aeronautical review section of the Journal of Aeronautical Sciences. Merged with: Astronautics; to form: Astronautics and Aerospace Engineering, Astronautics and Aeronautics. Former titles: Aeronautical Engineering Review (apr 1942-apr 1958); Aero/space Engineering (may 1958-mar 1961)) – Easton. v1-22. apr 1942-jan 1963 – 1 – D5069 – us UMI [629]

AEROSPACE ENGINEERING – (Cont: SAE in Aerospace Engineering) – Warrendale. v3-17 mar 1983- 1*; v6-17 jan 1986- 5,9 – 1,5,9 – D16289.01 – us UMI [629]

AEROSPACE FACTS – (All that is currently available) – Brigham City. v1-15 mar 1965-Fal 1979 1; v8-15 jan 1972-Fal 1979 5*; v12-14 jan 1976-Fal 1979 9* – 1,5,9 – D7938 – us UMI [629]

AEROSPACE HISTORIAN – (Cont by: Air Power History. Former Titles: Air Power Historian (sep 1954-apr 1959); Airpower Historian (jul 1959-jul 1965)) – Washington. v1-35 sep 1954-dec 1988 1; v20-35 mar 1973-dec 1988 5,9 – 1,5,9 – D1519 – us UMI [629]

AEROSPACE HISTORIAN *see* AIR POWER HISTORY

AEROSPACE INTERNATIONAL – (Cont: Air Force/Space Digest International) – Washington. v2-7 nov 1966-apr 1972* 1; v8-17 may 1972-81 1,5,9 – 1,5,9 – D6701.01 – us UMI [629]

AEROSPACE INTERNATIONAL *see* AIR FORCE/SPACE DIGEST INTERNATIONAL

AEROSPACE MANAGEMENT – (Ceased publ. Former titles: Aircraft and Missiles Manufacturing (jan 1958-sep 1959); Aircraft and Missiles (oct 1959-jul 1961)) – Philadelphia. v1-7. jan 1958-apr 1964 – 1 – D1109 – us UMI [629]

AEROSPACE MANAGEMENT – (Ceased publ) – Philadelphia. v1-6. 1966-1971 – 5 – D6337 – us UMI [629]

AEROSPACE MATERIAL SPECIFICATIONS (AMS) / Society of Automotive Engineers – (Monthly Update Service is available for $1,725.00; (AMS) + Update Service are available as a set for $3,075.00) – 9 – $2,125.00 – us S.A.E. [629]

AEROSPACE MEDICINE – (Cont by: Aviation space and environmental medicine. Former title: Journal of aviation medicine (mar 1930-may 1959)) – Washington. v1-45. mar 1930-dec 1974* – 1 – D11403 – us UMI [610]

AEROSPACE MEDICINE AND BIOLOGY : AN ANNOTATED BIBLIOGRAPHY – (Ceased publ. Cont by: Aerospace Medicine and Biology. Former title: Aviation Medicine) – Washington. cum index 1-10 (1952-1961) v1-11 1952-1963 – 1 – D6286 – us UMI [629]

AEROSPACE MEDICINE AND BIOLOGY *see* AEROSPACE MEDICINE AND BIOLOGY

AEROSPACE MEDICINE AND BIOLOGY – (All that is available. Cont: Aerospace Medicine and Biology, an Annotated Bibliography) – Washington. v125-189. feb 1974-jan 1979 – 1,5,9* – D3139 – us UMI [629]

AEROSPACE MEDICINE AND BIOLOGY, AN ANNOTATED BIBLIOGRAPHY *see* AEROSPACE MEDICINE AND BIOLOGY

AEROSPACE RESEARCH AND DEVELOPMENT – (v24 1970, Science and Technology) – 9 – $40.00 – us Univelt [629]

AEROSPACE SAFETY – (Vols 1-5 not available for filming. Cont by: Flying Safety. Former titles: Flying Safety Journal (dec 1944-19??); Flying Safety (19??-jun 1960)) – Washington. v6-36 jan 1950-dec 1980 1; v30-36 jan 1974-dec 1980 5,9 – 1,5,9 – D6287 – us UMI [629]

AEROSPACE STANDARDS / Society of Automotive Engineers – (Monthly Update Service is available for $800.00; When purchased together the price for both is $1,895.00) – 9 – $1,575.00 – us S.A.E. [629]

AEROSVET – Belgrade, 12 Jan 1958-15 Dec 1962 – 2r – 1 – uk British Libr Newspaper [072]

AERZTE IN OST- UND WESTPREUSSEN : LEBEN UND LEISTUNG SEIT DEM 18. JAHRHUNDERT / ed by Scholz, Harry & Schroeder, Paul – (Includes bibliographical references and indexes) – Wuerzburg: Holzner Verlag, 1970 – 1 – us U.W. Library [610]

AERZTLICHE MISSIONEN / Christlieb, Theodor – Guetersloh: C. Bertelsmann, 1889 – 1mf – us A.T.L.A. [240]

AERZTLICHE PRAXIS – 1949- 1; 1974- 5,6 – us UMI [610]

AES : JOURNAL OF THE AUDIO ENGINEERING SOCIETY, AUDIO/ACOUSTICS/APPLICATIONS – (Cont: Journal of the Audio Engineering Society) – New York. v34-45. jan 1986-dec 1997+ – 1,5,9 – D6175.01 – us UMI [621]

AES INFO SERIES / South Dakota. State University. Agricultural Experiment Station – nos.1-9. 1968-74 – 1,5,6 – us Spaulding [630]

Aeschylus *see* THE AGAMEMNON OF AESCHYLUS

AESTHETIC AS SCIENCE OF EXPRESSION AND GENERAL LINGUISTIC / Croce, Benedetto – London, New York: Macmillan, 1909 – 1mf – us A.T.L.A. [140]

THE AESTHETIC MOVEMENT IN ENGLAND / Hamilton, Walter – London: Reeves & Turner, 1882 – 1 roll – 1 – 1-55879-824-2 – uk Libr Preservation [900]

AESTHETIC PAPERS – 9 – 15.00 – us Scholars' Facs [700]

AESTHETIC PLASTIC SURGERY – Heidelberg. v1-21 1976-Fall 1997+ 1*; v5-21 1981-Fall 1997+ 5*,9* – 1,5,9 – D13129 – us UMI [617]

AESTHETIC STANDARDS IN OLD TIME DANCING IN SOUTHWEST VIRGINIA : AFRICAN-AMERICAN AND EUROPEAN-AMERICAN THREADS / Spalding, Susan E & Dixon-Gottschild, Brenda – 1993 – 4mf – 9 – $16.00 – us Microform Publ [790]

AESTHETIC SURGERY *see* AESTHETIC SURGERY QUARTERLY

AESTHETIC SURGERY – (Cont by: Aesthetic Surgery Quarterly) – Long Beach. v1-14. 1981-1994* – 1 – D22105 – us UMI [617]

AESTHETIC SURGERY QUARTERLY – (Cont: Aesthetic Surgery) – Long Beach. v15-. 1995- – 1,5,9 – D22105.01 – us UMI [617]

AESTHETIC SURGERY QUARTERLY *see* AESTHETIC SURGERY

AESTHETICA. NOCIONES DE LA BELLEZA Y DE LAS ARTES / Gomez Bravo, Vicente – Madrid: Editorial Razon y Fe, 1934 – 1 – sp Bibl Santa Ana [700]

AESTHETIK DES JAHRMARKTS : UTOPIE IN DER GEGENWART? / Kletzka, Renate – 1995 – 1mf – 9 – DM60.00 – 3-8267-2268-X – gw Hänsel [700]

AESTHETISCHE FELDZUEGE : DEM JUNGEN DEUTSCHLAND GEWIDMET / Wienbarg, Ludolf – Hamburg: Hoffmann und Campe, 1834 – 1 – us U.W. Library [430]

DIE AESTHETISCHEN KONZEPTIONEN VON JOHN KEATS UND G.W.F. HEGELS VORLESUNGEN UEBER DIE AESTHETIK : ZUR DIALEKTIK DES AESTHETISCHEN / Scholze, Werner – Frankfurt a.M., 1975 – 2mf – 9 – DM62.00 – 3-89349-671-8 – gw Hänsel [110]

DIE AETHIOPISCHE BIBELUEBERSETZUNG...ALT- UND NEUTESTAMENTLICHE WISSENSCHAFT / Pfeiffer, Eduard – Leipzig: Eduard Pfeiffer, 1902. 1 fiche – 9 – us A.T.L.A. [240]

DIE AETHIOPISCHE UEBERSETZUNG DES ZACHARIAS, ERSTES HEFT : TEXT ZUM ERSTEN MALE HERAUSGEGEBEN, PROLEGOMENA, COMMENTAR / Kramer, Friedrich Oswald – (Includes bibliographical references) – Leipzig: Doerffling & Franke, 1898 – 1mf – 9 – 0-8370-3991-6 – 1985-1991 – us A.T.L.A. [220]

AETHJOPUM SERVUS : A STUDY IN CHRISTIAN ALTRUISM / Petre, Maude Dominica – London: Osgood, McIlvaine, 1896 – 1mf – us A.T.L.A. [240]

DIE AETIOLOGIE, DER BEGRIFF UND DIE PROPHYLAXIS DES KINDBETTFIEBERS / Semmelweis, I P – Pest, etc. 1861 – 10mf – 9 – ne IDC [618]

AETIOLOGY OF PSYCHOACTIVE SUBSTANCE USE : A REPORT AND CRITICALLY ANNOTATED BIBLIOGRAPHY ON RESEARCH INTO THE AETIOLOGY OF ALCOHOL, NICOTINE, OPIATE AND OTHER PSYCHOACTIVE SUBSTANCE USE / Fazey, C – 1977 – 226p – 9 – 92-3-101508-7 – fr UNESCO [613]

AETIOPATHOGENETISCHE VORSTELLUNG DES LUMBAGO-ISCHIALGIE-SYNDROMS IN DER DEUTSCHEN MEDIZINISCHEN WOCHENSCHRIFT VON 1900 BIS 1991 : ENTSTEHUNG EINES PARADIGMAS / Lutz, Gabriele K – 1995 – 3mf – 9 – DM98.00 – 3-8267-2223-X – gw Hänsel [616]

Aetius, Br *see* KAMUS DJERMAN-INDONESIA

THE AETNA – Hartford, CT. v17 n3. avr 1885 – 1r – 1 – Can$25.00 – cn Can Microfilming [071]

THE AETNA – Montreal: W.H. Orr, [1868-1911] – 9 – cn C.I.H.M. [971]

AF DI VEGN ZU DER NAYER SHUL – 1924-1928 – 1 – us NY Public [073]

AF EN ENDNU LEVENDES PAPIRER / Kierkegaard, Soren – Kjobenhavn: C.A. Reitzel, 1838 – 1mf – us A.T.L.A. [190]

AF OFL AUTO WORKER : 1939-1955 – (Coll title: Labor Union Periodicals, Pt 1) – 2r – 1 – $270.00 – 1-55655-225-4 – us UPA [331]

AF. Smirdin Biblioteka *see* ROSPIS' ROSSIISKIM KNIGAM DLIA CHTENIIA, IZ BIBLIOTEKI ALEKSANDRA SMIRDINA, SISTEMATICHESKIM PORIADKOM RASPOLOZHENNAIA

AFA BUNDESZEITUNG – Berlin, 1924-33 – 1 – gw Mikrofilm [072]

AFA : BUNDESZEITUNG ALLGEMEINER FREIER ANGESTELLTENBUND. V2-5. 1920-23 – Title varies. (Serial Publications of German Trade Unions in the Memorial Library, University of Wisconsin-Madison) – 1 – us U.W. Library [331]

AFA SCHRIFTEN SAMMLUNG / Allgemeiner Freier Angestelltenbund – Berlin. v2-5. 1921-24. (Serial publications of German trade unions in the Memorial Library, University of Wisconsin-Madison) – 1 – us U.W. Library [331]

AFAA JOURNAL – (Cont by: Aerobics & Fitness) – Sherman Oaks, 1983-84* – 1 – D19374 – us UMI [613]

AFAA JOURNAL *see* AEROBICS AND FITNESS

AFA-BUNDESZEITUNG – (Cont: Mitteilungsblatt der Arbeitsgemeinschaft freier Angestelltenverbaende, -nov 1920; Mitteilungsblatt des Allgemeinen Freien Angestelltenbundes, -mar 1922) – Berlin, 1919-33 n4 – 1 – Inquire at Mikrofilmarchiv for details – gw Misc Inst [331]

AFAK / ed by Kamil, A – Istanbul: Mahmut Bey Matbaasi, Matbaa-i Osmaniye, 1882-1883 – 9 – $50.00 – us MEDOC [956]

AFAR / American Friends of the Angolan Revolution – [New York]: AFAR, n2-3. apr-jun 1970 – us Res Libr [071]

AFBEELDING DER MENSCHELYKE BEZIGHEDEN, BESTAANDE IN HONDERT ONDERSCHEIDEN PRINTVERBEELDINGEN, VERTONENDE ALLERHANDE STANTSPERSONEN, ... / Luyken, J & Luyken, C – 1st ed. Amsterdam, n.d. – 2mf – 9 – O-3115/1 – ne IDC [760]

AFBEELDINGEN VAN MINNE : EMBLEMATA AMATORIA, EMBLEMES D'AMOUR / Heinsius, D – (First edition of "Het ambacht van Cupido". Titlepage (A1) missing) – Leiden, 1613 – 2mf – 9 – O-3079/1 – ne IDC [760]

AFBEELDINGEN VAN ZELDZAME GEWASSEN / Meerburgh, N – Leyden, 1775 1780. 18 pp., 40 pls. B-441 2 – 8 – ne IDC [580]

AFBMA (ANTI-FRICTION BEARING MANUFACTURERS ASSOCIATION) – All standards. Printed index. Updated every 60 days – 6,9 – us Info Handling [680]

AFE LANGBEIN'S SAEMMTLICHE GEDICHTE / Langbein, August Friedrich Ernst – Neue Ausg. Stuttgart: Rieger, 1855 – 1r – 1 – us U.W. Library [810]

Afevork, G J *see* GUIDE DU VOYAGEUR EN ABYSSINIE

AFFAERSEKONOMI – 1928-74 – 1 – us UMI [073]

L'AFFAIRE CLERFEYT. / Clerfeyt, Joseph Maximilian Louis – Bruxelles: Vanderauwera, 1873. 354p. LL-4030 – 1 – us L of C Photodup [340]

UNE AFFAIRE DE FAMILLE AU XIXE SIECLE: MEQUILLET-NOBLOT / Fohlen, C – 9 – F50.00 – fr Ethnologie [306]

L'AFFAIRE DE LA BAIE DES CHALEURS DEVANT LA COMMISSION ROYALE: APPRECIATION DE LA PREUVE – Quebec: Belleau, 1891. 02578. (Pre-1900 Canadiana) – 9 – cn C.I.H.M. [971]

EL "AFFAIRE" DE LA CORTE SUPREMA ARGENTINA / Gonzalez Roura, Octavio – [Buenos Aires]: L.J. Rosso, [1950] – 1 – CSUXADJ1811-B – us Hoover Inst Photo [360]

AFFAIRE DES TANNERIES – Seance du 25 novembre 1875 discours des honorables messieurs Angers, Ouiment, Chapleau, et de M. Taillon. s.l., s.n., 1875?. 02582. (Pre-1900 Canadiana) – 9 – cn C.I.H.M. [971]

L'AFFAIRE DREYFUS / Dreyfus, Alfred – (1908. 3 v. LL-4034) – Paris, Ligue francaise pour la defense des droits de l'homme et du citoyen, 1906. 2 v. LL-4035 – 1 – us L of C Photodup [340]

AFFAIRE GUIBORD: QUESTION DE REFUS DE SEPULTURE : RAPPORT DE LA CAUSE AVEC LE TEXTE DU JUGEMENT DE SON HONNEUR LE JUGE MONDELET / Brown, Henriette – Montreal: des presses a vapeur de La Minerve, 1870. SEM105P1449 – 2mf – 9 – Can$4.50 – cn Bibl Nat [971]

AFFAIRE GUIBORD: QUESTION DE REFUS DE SEPULTURE: RAPPORT DE LA CAUSE AVEC LE TEXTE DU JUGEMENT DE LA COUR SUPERIEURE.. – Montreal: Presses a vapeur de la Minerve, 1870. 00043. (Pre-1900 Canadiana) – 9 – cn C.I.H.M. [971]

L'AFFAIRE TYRRELL : UN EPISODE DE LA CRISE CATHOLIQUE / Gout, Raoul – (Includes bibliographical references) – Paris: Emile Nourry, 1909 – 1mf – 9 – 0-8370-8428-8 – 1986-2428 – us A.T.L.A. [240]

LES AFFAIRES : REVUE / ed by Beauchamp, Claude – Montreal, feb 1928-31 dec 1992 – 49r – 1 – Can$75.00r – cn Can Microfilming [073]

AFFAIRES DES FOURRURES – s.l., s.n. 18??. 02579. (Pre-1900 Canadiana) – 9 – cn C.I.H.M. [971]

AFFAIRES ENTRE LA VILLE ET LA FABRIQUE DE LONGUEUIL CONCERNANT LES TAXES SUR L'EGLISE – Montreal: s.n.. 1888. 04006. (Pre-1900 Canadiana) – 9 – cn C.I.H.M. [971]

L'AFFAME – no. 1-6. Marseille. mai-aout 1884 – 1 – fr A.C.R.P.P. [073]

AFFANI CRUDELI = GLI GIOCHI D'AGRIGENTO / Federici, V – London: T Skillern, 1793? – 1 – us Sibley [780]

AFFARSVARLDEN – (All that is currently offered) – Stockholm, jan 1977-dec 1979 1,5*,9* – 1,5,9 – D10230 – us UMI [336]

AN AFFECTIONATE ADDRESS TO THE MEMBERS OF THE METHODIST SOCIETY, IN LEEDS AND ELSEWHERE, RESPECTING THE LATE TRANSACTIONS AT BRISTOL;... / Terry, Garnet – Leeds, 1794 – 1mf – 9 – MP-585/1 – ne IDC [240]

AFFECTIONUM QUAE DICUNTUR HYSTERICAE ET HYPOCHONDRIACAE PATHOLOGIA... / Willis, Thomas – Londini, 1670 – 3mf – 9 – ne IDC [616]

Afferica, J *see* CONSIDERATIONS ON THE FORMATION OF THE HERMITAGE COLLECTION OF RUSSIAN MANUSCRIPTS

L'AFFICHE – Montreal, fev 1848-26 mai 1848. 3 affiches – 1r – 1 – Can$25.00 – cn Can Microfilming [072]

AFFICHES, ANNONCES, AVIS DIVERS DE TOULOUSE ET DU HAUT-LANGUEDOC – devenu: Journal universel et affiches de Toulouse et du Languedoc. devenu: Journal et affiches du department de Haute-Garonne. Toulouse. 1785-93 – 1 – F627.00 – fr A.C.R.P.P. [073]

AFFICHES, ANNONCES ET AVIS DIVERS DE JEVER *see* JEVERISCHE WOECHENTLICHE ANZEIGEN UND NACHRICHTEN

AFFICHES, ANNONCES ET AVIS DIVERS. FEUILLE COMMERCIALE DE NANTES / FEUILLE COMMERCIALE D'AFFICHES (...) / FEUILLE COMMERCIALE ET MARITIME D'AFFICHES (...) / FEUILLE COMMERCIALE.LLOYD NANTAIS – (Numerous missing numbers) – Quotid. de Nantes, dec. 1811-dec. 1836 (nombr. no. manq.) – 52r – 1 – F18253,96 – fr Armell [380]

AFFICHES D'ANGERS, CAPITALE DE L'APANAGE DE MONSEIGNEUR LE COMTE DE PROVENCE... [PUIS] JOURNAL POLITIQUE ET LITTERAIRE [DU DEPARTEMENT] DE MAINE-ET-LOIRE – July 1773 – Dec. 1830 – 35r – 1 – fr Armell [944]

AFFICHES DE NANTES ET DU DEPARTEMENT DE LOIRE-INFERIEURE – Bi- ou tri-hebdom., Nantes, janv. 1791-sept. 1794 – 2r – 1 – F1077,84 – fr Armell [073]

AFFICHES DE STRASBOURG – Strasbourg, France. 1862-98 – 1 – fr A.C.R.P.P. [072]

AFFICHES DU [PUIS DE] POITOU – Jan. 1777 – Dec. 1781 – 1r – fr Armell [910]

AFFILIA – Thousand Oaks. v1- Spr 1986- 1*; v3- Spr 1988 5*,9 – 1,5,9 – D17050 – us UMI [073]

AFFINITAS LINGUAE HUNGARICAE CUM LINGUIS FENNICAE ORIGINIS GRAMMATICE DEMONSTRATA / Gyarmathy, S – In Latin. (Linguistic series). 1799 – 9 – fr Hachette [490]

LES AFFINITES ELECTIVES DE GOETHE : ESSAI DE COMMENTAIRE CRITIQUE / Francois-Poncet, Andre – (Includes bibliographical references) – Paris: F Alcan, 1910 – 1r – 1 – us U.W. Library [430]

AFFIRMATIONS – (Cont: Sisterhood with which it is filmed) – v1-9. 1974-82 (complete) – 1r – 1 – ATLA S0343B – us A.T.L.A. [073]

AFFIRMATIONS / Ellis, Havelock – London: Walter Scott, 1898 – 1 roll – 1 – 1-55879-412-3 – uk Libr Preservation [150]

AFFIRMATIONS *see* SISTERHOOD

THE AFFLICTIONS OF THE RIGHTEOUS : AS DISCUSSED IN THE BOOK OF JOB AND IN THE LIGHT OF THE GOSPEL / Macleod, William B – London, New York: Hodder & Stoughton, [1913] – 1mf – 9 – 0-8370-6272-1 – 1986-0272 – us A.T.L.A. [220]

Affo, I *see*
- RAGIONAMENTO. SOPRA UNA STANZA DIPINTA DAL. A. ALLEGRI DA CORREGGIO NEL MONISTERO DI S. PAOLO IN PARMA
- VITA DEL GRAZIOSISSIMO PITTORE FRANCESCO MAZZOLA, DETTO IL PARMIGIANINO

Affolter, Ludwig *see* UEBER DIE VERNEHMUNG DER PARTEIEN ALS ZEUGEN IM CIVILPROZESS.

Affonso Celso, Affonso Celso de Assis Figueiredo, Conde de *see* PORQUE ME UFANO DO MEU PAIZ; RIGHT OR WRONG, MY COUNTRY

L'AFFRANCHI – (Filmed as pt of: Commune de Paris newspapers. Newspapers on these reels are filmed chronologically, not alphabetically) – [Paris]: Impr Schiller, apr 2-4, 6-7, 9-10, 12-13, 15, 17, 19-20, 23-25 1871 – 2r – 1 – us Res Libr [072]

AFFRAY AT BROWNSVILLE, AUGUST 13 AND 14 1906, COURT-MARTIAL, MACKLIN : PROCEEDINGS OF A GENERAL COURT-MARTIAL CONVENED AT HEADQUARTERS, DEPARTMENT OF TEXAS, APRIL 15 1907, IN THE CASE OF CAPTAIN EDGAR A. MACKLIN – Washington: GPO, 1907 – 3mf – 9 – $4.50 – LLMC 97-006 – us L.L.M.C. [340]

AFGHANISTAN : AN AMERICAN PERSPECTIVE – Treaties and agreements, federal agency reports, private contractor reports, technical and statistical reports, UN agency reports and documents. With printed guide. 755 fiches – 9 – $3,025.00 – us UPA [950]

AFGHANISTAN : THE MAKING OF U.S. POLICY, 1973-1990 – (With 2-vol printed guide & index £630.00) – 424mf – 9 – £2,940.00 – uk Chadwyck [327]

AFGHANISTAN / Reunion des musees nationaux. Paris – Arts ancien. 1935-37. 1938. 1 fiche – 9 – fr Réunion [700]

Afghanistan *see*
- THE FIVE-YEAR ECONOMIC DEVELOPMENT PLAN OF AFGHANISTAN
- RASMI JARIDA

Afghanistan. Ministry of Education Department of Planning *see* EDUCATIONAL STATISTICS IN AFGHANISTAN 1969-1972

Afghanistan. Ministry of National Economy *see* FIVE YEAR ECONOMIC DEVELOPMENT PLAN

Afghanistan. Ministry of Planning *see*
- SECOND FIVE YEAR PLAN, 1341-45. MAR 1962-MAR 1967
- SURVEY OF PROGRESS, 1960
- SURVEY OF PROGRESS, 1961-62
- THE THIRD FIVE YEAR ECONOMIC AND SOCIAL PLAN OF AFGHANISTAN, 1967-1971

AFISHA TIM = POSTER "TIM" – Moscow. n1-4. 1926-27 – 3mf – 9 – $50.00 – us Ross [790]

AFIYET – (Added title: Dilber Kontes) – Istanbul: Luesyen Matbaasi, 1913-1914 – 9 – $150.00 – us MEDOC [956]

AFKAR – Karachi, Maktab-i-Afkar. v6-17, 19, 32-33. -m – 1 – us U.W. Library [490]

AFL CANNERY REPORTER, 1949-1954 : UNITED DAIRY FARMER, 1941, 1944-1945 / California State Council of Cannery Unions, Teamsters & United Mine Workers – (Coll title: Labor Union Periodicals, Pt 3) – 1996 – 1r – 1 – $135.00 – 1-55655-613-6 – us UPA [331]

AFL, CIO, and AFL-CIO. Conventions *see* STATE LABOR PROCEEDINGS

AFL OFFICIAL DOCUMENTS *see* AFL-CIO PUBLICATIONS

AFL RANK-AND-FILE FEDERATIONIST – New York. v1-2. 1934-35 – 1 reel – 1 – $65.00 – us UPA [332]

AFLAK – (Purchase with Sitarah-'i Subh. Cont by: Khala) – Tehran, Shumarah-'i 14-8 Shahrivar 1304 [30 Aug 1925] – 1 – us MEDOC [956]

AFLAK *see* KHALQ

Aflalo, S *see* QUESTAO DE SUCCESSAO

AFL-CIO (American Federation of Labor-Congress of Industrial Organizations) *see*
- PROCEEDINGS
- PUBLICATIONS

AFL-CIO AMERICAN FEDERATIONIST / American Federation of Labor & Congress of Industrial Organizations – (With v89 n5 filmed as periodic suppl to AFL-CIO News. Cont: American Federationist) – Washington. v83-89. jul 1976-jun 1982 – 1;5;9 – $40.80y – D2232.01 – us UMI [331]

AFL-CIO AMERICAN FEDERATIONIST *see*
- AFL-CIO NEWS
- AMERICAN FEDERATIONIST

AFL-CIO. Library *see* AMERICAN FEDERATION OF LABOR AND CONGRESS OF INDUSTRIAL ORGANIZATIONS

AFL-CIO NEWS – (Includes as periodic suppl: AFL-CIO American Federationist, beginning July 1982) – Washington. v1-2 dec 1955-dec 1957; v3-4 jan 1958-jan 1959; v5-6 jan 1960-dec 1961; v7-8 jan 1962-dec 1963; v9-10 jan 1964-dec 1965; v11-12 jan 1966-dec 1967; v13-40 jan 1968-dec 1995; v41 jan-dec 1996; v42 jan-dec 1997+ – 1 – inquire – D3199 – us UMI [331]

AFL-CIO NEWS *see* AFL-CIO AMERICAN FEDERATIONIST

AFL-CIO PROCEEDINGS – (Formed by the union of: AFL Proceedings, and: Proceedings of the Constitutional Convention of the Congress of Industrial Organizations) – Washington. 1955-97+ 1; 1971-97+ 5; 1973-97+ 9; 1994* 1,5,9; 1975-79* 5 – 1,5,9 – D3284 – us UMI [331]

AFL-CIO PROCEEDINGS *see* AMERICAN FEDERATION OF LABOR PROCEEDINGS

-CIO PUBLICATIONS *see* A F L OFFICIAL DOCUMENTS

AFL-CIO PUBLICATIONS / American Federation of Labor & Congress of Industrial Organizations – (Cont in pt: AFL Official Documents) – Washington, 1956-81. 1982*. 1983-97+ 1; 1974-88* 5; 1974. 1976*. 1977-81. 1982*. 1984-88 9 – 1,5,9 – D9494 – us UMI [331]

AFNOR (ASSOCIATION FRANCAISE DE NORMALISATION) – Printed index. English updated every 60 days. French updated every 30 days – 6,9 – us Info Handling [380]

AFONSKIE LISTKI – nos1-350. 1899-1906 (complete) – 1r – 1 – ATLA S0193A – us A.T.L.A. [073]

AFOROS EN LA SIERRA DE MONTANCHEZ. ANO 1818 / Abastecimiento de aguas – Caceres: Tip. El Noticiero, 1818 – 1 – sp Bibl Santa Ana [946]

AFOROS PRACTICADOS EN LAS CUENCAS DE LOS RIOS GUADIANA – 1881 – 9 – 1.50f – sp Bibl Santa Ana [910]

AFRICA – 1928-to date – 1,9 – uk Microform Academic [073]

AFRICA : ANTROPOLOGIA DELLA STIRPE CAMITICA (SPECIE EURAFRICANA) / Sergi, Giuseppe – Torino: F Bocca, 1897 – 9 – us Res Libr [306]

AFRICA : DRAME EN CINQ ACTES, EN VERS / Deschamps, Edouard – Paris: E Dentu, 1893 – 9 – us Res Libr [820]

AFRICA – (Individual titles available, also listed separately) – 33,524mf + 118r – 9,1 – ne IDC [960]

AFRICA – London. v1-83 may 1971-nov 1986 1,5; v41-83 jan 1975-nov 1986 9 – 1,5,9 – D6109 – us UMI [073]

AFRICA / Reclus, Elisee; ed by Ravenstein, E G & Keane, A H – (v1-4 of The Earth and its Inhabitants) – New York, 1895-98 – 1r – 1 – us Ross [960]

AFRICA – White Sisters. v2-18. 1937-66 – 2r – 1 – us Ross [960]
Africa *see* GOVERNMENT PUBLICATIONS AND ANNUAL DEPARTMENTAL REPORTS RELATING TO AFRICAN COUNTRIES PRIOR TO INDEPENDENCE
AFRICA – (Ceased publ. Former Title: Messenger of Our Lady of Africa) – Metuchen. v1-21. 1931-1969 – 1 – D6661 – us UMI [073]
AFRICA – (Cont by: Africa Confindential) – London. 1960-1966* – 1 – D21836 – us UMI [960]
AFRICA : ECONOMIC, FINANCIAL AND TECHNICAL – (Cont by: Africa Research Bulletin, Economic Series) – London. jan 1964-dec 1964* – 1 – D18098 – us UMI [330]
AFRICA – Edinburgh. v1- jan 1928- 1*; v55-1985- 5*,9 – 1,5,9 – D15393 – us UMI [960]
AFRICA (#21836) *see* AFRICA CONFIDENTIAL
AFRICA: 1941-61 / U.S. Office of Strategic Services – 1980. Series: OSS State Department Intelligence and Research Reports, Pt 13 – 1 – $1,060.00 – us UPA [960]
AFRICA, 1946-76 / U.S. Central Intelligence Agency – Series: CIA Research Reports – 1 – $305.00 – us UPA [960]
AFRICA, 1962-1980 : SPECIAL STUDIES SERIES – (Supplements: 1980-85. 11r $1,210.00 ISBN 0-89093-679-X; 1985-88. 10r $1,105.00 ISBN 1-55655-114-2; 1989-91. 10r $1,105.00 ISBN 1-55655-428-1; 1992-94. 10r $1,190.00 ISBN 1-55655-534-2. With printed guides) – 7r – 1 – $770.00 – 0-89093-382-0 – us UPA [320]
AFRICA AND THE AMERICAN NEGRO : ADDRESSES AND PROCEEDINGS OF THE CONGRESS ON AFRICA HELD UNDER AUSPICES OF THE STEWART MISSIONARY FOUNDATION FOR AFRICA OF GAMMON THEOLOGICAL SEMINARY..COTTON STATES AND INTERNATIONAL EXPOSITION – dec 13-15 1895 – 9 – us Res Libr [960]
AFRICA AND THE BRUSSELS GEOGRAPHICAL CONFERENCE / Banning, Emile Theodore – London: Low, Marston, Searle & Rivington, 1877 – 9 – us Res Libr [910]
AFRICA AND THE SECOND WORLD WAR – 1985 – 9 – 92-3-102324-1 – fr UNESCO [960]
AFRICA CONFIDENTIAL – (Cont: Africa (#21836)) – London. 1967- 1*; 1995- 5,9 – 1,5,9 – D21836.01 – us UMI [960]
AFRICA CONFINDENTIAL *see* AFRICA
AFRICA CURRENTS – (Supersedes: Africa Digest) – London. v1-24. Spr 1975-jul 1981 – 1,5*,9 – D11520 – us UMI [960]
AFRICA CURRENTS *see* AFRICA DIGEST
AFRICA DIGEST *see* AFRICA CURRENTS
AFRICA DIGEST – (Ceased publ. Superseded by: Africa Currents) – London. cum index 15-18 1968-1971 v1-21 jul 1952-dec 1974 1; v19-21 jul 1972-dec 1974 5 – 1,5 – D6962 – us UMI [960]
Africa. Economic Commission for Africa *see* BIBLIOGRAPHY OF AFRICAN STATISTICAL PUBLICATIONS 1966-1973
AFRICA, ECONOMIC, FINANCIAL AND TECHNICAL *see* AFRICA RESEARCH BULLETIN
AFRICA EN EL PENSAMIENTO DE DONOSO CORTES / Donoso Cortes, Juan Francisco – Madrid, 1955 – 1 – sp Bibl Santa Ana [920]
AFRICA ET BUCOLICA / Petrarca – 16th cent. Holkham ms. 429. Holkham Hall, Norfolk, England – 1 – uk Microform Academic [760]
Africa Institute *see* BULLETIN
AFRICA INSTITUTE : BULLETIN – (Ceased publ. Former Title: Africa Institute, International Bulletin) – Pretoria. v1-16 feb 1963-1978 1; v10-16 jan 1972-1978 5; v14-16 1976-1978 9 – 1,5,9 – D7042 – us UMI [073]
AFRICA INSTITUTE, INTERNATIONAL BULLETIN *see* AFRICA INSTITUTE
AFRICA LETTER – (Ceased publ) – Calcutta. v1-52. 1971-jun 1972 – 1,5 – D7869 – us UMI [960]
AFRICA NEWS *see* AFRICA NEWS ONLINE
AFRICA NEWS – (Cont by: Africa News Online) – Durham. v1-38 jun 1973-may 1993 1*; v31-38 jan 1989-may 1993 5*,9 – 1,5,9 – D17766 – us UMI [960]
AFRICA NEWS ONLINE *see* AFRICA NEWS
AFRICA NEWS ONLINE – (Cont: Africa News) – Durham. v38-. may 1993- – 1,5,9 – D17766.01 – us UMI [960]
AFRICA NEWS SERVICE – Durham. 358 docs. 1980-1991 – 63mf – 9 – ne IDC [360]
AFRICA QUARTERLY – New Delhi. v1-37 apr 1961-1998+ 1*; v17-26 jul 1977-1987 5,9* – 1,5,9 – D6961 – us UMI [073]
AFRICA REPORT – (Publ ceased with v19 1974. Former title: Africa Special Report (jul 5 1956-60)) – New York. v17-19. 1972-74 – 1,5,9 – D11361 – us UMI [300]
AFRICA REPORT – (All that is currently available. Suspended with v40 n3 (may-jun 1995)) – New York. v1-40 jul 1956-jun 1995 1; v21-40 jan 1976-jun 1995 5,9 – 1,5,9 – D11066 – us UMI [960]
AFRICA RESEARCH BULLETIN : ECONOMIC SERIES – (Cont: Africa, Economic, Financial and Technical. Cont by: Africa Research Bulletin, Economic, Financial and Technical Series) – Exeter. v2-28 jan 1965-1992 1*; v27-28 1990-1992* 5,9 – 1,5,9 – D18098.01 – us UMI [330]
AFRICA RESEARCH BULLETIN : ECONOMIC, FINANCIAL, AND TECHNICAL SERIES – (Cont: Africa Research Bulletin, Economic Series) – Exeter. v29-. jan 1992-* – 1,5,9 – D18098.02 – us UMI [330]
AFRICA RESEARCH BULLETIN, ECONOMIC, FINANCIAL AND TECHNICAL SERIES *see* AFRICA RESEARCH BULLETIN
AFRICA RESEARCH BULLETIN, ECONOMIC SERIES *see*
– AFRICA
– AFRICA RESEARCH BULLETIN
AFRICA SOUTH OF THE SAHARA / Glazier, Kenneth M – A select and annotated bibliography: 1958-63. 1964. 165p – 1 – 35.00r – us Hoover Inst Photo [960]
AFRICA SOUTH OF THE SAHARA: INDEX TO PERIODICAL LITERATURE, 1900-1970 / U.S. Library of Congress – (First Suppl., 1973.-14,100 entries 1 reel. $120.00 ISBN: 0-8161-1351-3; Second Suppl., 1981.-41,000 entries 3 reels. $240.00 ISBN: 0-8161-1512-5) – 1971.-87,200 entries 8 reels.-ISBN: 0-8161-1256-8 – 1 – $400.00 – uk Hall [073]
AFRICA SPEAKS : A COLLECTION OF ORIGINAL VERSE WITH AN INTRODUCTION ON "POETRY IN AFRICA" – 2nd ed. Accra: Guinea Press, [1960?] – us Res Libr [810]
AFRICA SPECIAL REPORT *see* AFRICA REPORT
Africa. Swedish International Development Authority / International Labour Office *see* SKILL DEVELOPMENT FOR SELF RELIANCE
AFRICA THEOLOGICAL JOURNAL – (Publ suspended 1973-77) – Makumira. v1-26 1968-1997+ 1; v14-26 1985-1997+ 5*,9* – 1,5,9 – D15121 – us UMI [240]
AFRICA TODAY – Denver. v1- jan 1954- 1*; v23- 1976- 5; v24- jan 1977- 9 – 1,5,9 – D5714 – us UMI [960]
AFRICA, TODAY AND TOMORROW / New York. African Academy of Arts and Research – 1945 – 1r – 1 – us Ross [960]
AFRICA: TO-DAY AND TO-MORROW / African Academy of Arts and Research. New York – New York. April 1945 – 1 – us NY Public [073]
AFRICA VIEW / Huxley, J S – New York. London. 1931. BA-317 2 – 8 – ne IDC [960]
AFRICA WAITING : OR, THE PROBLEM OF AFRICA'S EVANGELIZATION / Thornton, Douglas Montagu – (Includes appendixes) – New York: Student Volunteer Movement for Foreign Missions, 1899 – 1mf – 9 – 0-8370-6530-5 – 1986-0530 – us A.T.L.A. [240]
AFRICA WATCH – (Missing: Doc. 6) – New York. 82 docs. 1988-1991 – 30mf – 9 – ne IDC [960]
Africa-Asia Islamic Organization. Central Council *see* DOCUMENTS OF THE FIRST CENTRAL COUNCIL MEETING, DJAKARTA, 3-4 FEB., 1966. SE-6613/1. 1966
AFRICAN : A JOURNAL OF AFRICAN AFFAIRS / Universal Ethiopian Students' Association – v1-6, no. 5 (all publ). 1937-48 – 1 reel – 1 – $65.00 – us UPA [960]
AFRICAN ABSTRACTS – 1950-1972 – 1 – uk Microform Academic [073]
AFRICAN ABSTRACTS – v. 1-23. 1950-72. London. All pub – 9 – 24100.00; 4.50v – uk Dawson [960]
African Academy of Arts and Research. New York *see* AFRICA: TO-DAY AND TO-MORROW
AFRICAN AFFAIRS – 1901-to date – 1,9 – uk Microform Academic [073]
AFRICAN AFFAIRS – (Cont: Journal of the Royal African Society) – London. v43-82 jul 1944-83* 1; v83-96 jan 1984-oct 1997+ 1,5,9 – 1,5,9 – D14338.02 – us UMI [960]
AFRICAN AMERICAN REVIEW – (Cont: Black American Literature Forum) – Terre Haute. v26-. Spr 1992- – 1,5,9 – D5044.02 – us UMI [420]
AFRICAN AMERICANS IN WORLD WAR 2 PAMPHLET COLLECTION – 1941-1942 – 1 – CSUXANN2582-B – us Hoover Inst Photo [350]
AFRICAN ANIMAL GENETIC RESOURCES : THEIR CHARACTERISATION, CONSERVATION AND UTILISATION. PROCEEDINGS OF THE RESEARCH PLANNING WORKSHOP HELD AT ILCA, ADDIS ABABA, ETHIOPIA, 19-21 FEBRUARY 1992 / ed by Rege, J E O & Lipner, M E – 1992 – 9 – $13.00 – 92-9053-238-6 – et ILRI [636]
AFRICAN ANIMAL TRYPANOSOMIASIS : SELECTED ARTICLES FROM THE WORLD ANIMAL REVIEW – 1983 – 86p – it F.A.O. [636]
AFRICAN ARCHAEOLOGICAL REVIEW – v1-12. 1983-94 – $50.00v – us UMI [930]
AFRICAN ARCHIVES INDEX / United Society for the Propagation of the Gospel – 1 – uk Microform Academic [240]
AFRICAN ARTS = ARTS D'AFRIQUE – Los Angeles. v5-30 Aut 1971-oct 1997+ 1; v1-30 Aut 1967-oct 1997+ 5; v10-30 oct 1976-oct 1997+ 9 – 1,5,9 – D6069 – us UMI [700]
THE AFRICAN AS SUCKLING AND AS ADULT / Ritchie, J F – 1 – uk Microform Academic [960]
THE AFRICAN AWAKENING / Davidson, Basil – London: Cape, 1955. 262p. illus – 1 – us U.W. Library [960]
AFRICAN BIOGRAPHICAL ARCHIVE (AFBA) = ARCHIVES BIOGRAPHIQUES AFRICAINES (AFBA) / Herrero Mediavilla, Victor – 1994-1997 – ca 450mf (1:24) in 12 installments – diazo DM19,800.00 (silver DM21,840.00 ISBN: 3-598-33100-2) – 3-598-33101-0 – Dist. ja Maruzen – gw Saur [920]
AFRICAN BOOKS NEWSLETTER – (All that is currently available) – Calcutta. v1-8. apr 1966-mar 1974 – 1 – D2308 – us UMI [070]
AFRICAN BUSINESS – London. v1-232 sep 1978-dec 1997+ 1,5*,9 – 1,5,9 – D12162 – us UMI [960]
AFRICAN BUSINESS SERIES – (Filmed with other titles) – [Legon]: Economic Res Div, Uni College of Ghana, n1-2. 1959-60 – us Res Libr [338]
AFRICAN CHRONICLE – Durban, South Africa. 1908-30 – 1 – sa State Libr [072]
African Civilization Society *see* ANNUAL REPORTS, 1859-1867
AFRICAN CLASSICS / Royal Commonwealth Society – 7 – uk Microform Academic [800]
AFRICAN COLONIZER – London, 22 Feb 1840-27 Mar 1841 – 25ft – 1 – uk British Libr Newspaper [072]
AFRICAN COMMENTARY – Northampton. v3-. 1991-* – 1 – D18033 – us UMI [960]
AFRICAN COMMUNIST – Johannesburg. v1-1960- 1*; v60- 1975- 5*; v68- 1977- 9 – 1,5,9 – D8332 – us UMI [320]
AFRICAN CONVERSATION-PIECE / Leith-Ross, Sylvia – London: Hutchison, [1944] – 9 – us Res Libr [960]
AFRICAN CULTURE AND ITS RELATION TO THE TRAINING OF AFRICAN NURSES – [Pretoria: South African Nursing Assoc, 1952?] – 9 – us Res Libr [960]
AFRICAN DEVELOPMENT – (Cont by: New African Development) – London. v1-10 1966-dec 1976 1; v9-10 jan 1975-dec 1976 5; v10 1976 9 – 1,5,9 – D9142 – us UMI [960]
AFRICAN DEVELOPMENT *see* NEW AFRICAN DEVELOPMENT
AFRICAN DEVELOPMENT SOURCEBOOK – (Available in English/French) – 1991 – 9 – 92-3-002736-7 – fr UNESCO [338]
AFRICAN DOCUMENTS – 1957- – 720r – 1 – $40,990.00 – us OmniSys [960]
AFRICAN DRUM – Johannesburg. v1-7. 1951-65 – 14r – 1 – us Ross [073]
THE AFRICAN DRUM – (Sale subject to copyright restrictions) – South Africa. 1951-52. Continued as: Drum, 1952-85. 33 reels – 1 – sa SA Libr [072]
AFRICAN EAGLE – Salisbury, Zimbabwe. 6 Jan 1959-25 Jan 1962 – 6r – 1 – uk British Libr Newspaper [072]
AFRICAN ETHNONYMS AND TOPONYMS – 1984 – 198p – 9 – 92-3-101944-9 – fr UNESCO [470]
AFRICAN EXPOSITOR – Raleigh, NC. Oct 1880, Jan 1883, Jan 1884, Jan 1888 – 1 – 15.50 – us A.B.H.S. [073]
African Institution *see*
– REPORTS
– REPORTS OF THE COMMITTEE
AFRICAN INTELLIGENCER – (Ceased publ) – Washington. v1. 1820 – 1 – D3536 – us UMI [073]
AFRICAN INTERPRETER / African Students' Association of the United States – v1. 1943-44 – 1r – 1 – us Ross [360]
AFRICAN INTERPRETER AND ADVOCATE – Freetown, Sierra Leone. 2 Feb, 20 Jul 1867; 4, 18 Jan-7 Mar 1868, 24 Apr 1869 – 11ft – 1 – uk British Libr Newspaper [072]
AFRICAN JOURNAL *see* SAM SLY'S AFRICAN JOURNAL
AFRICAN JOURNAL OF ECOLOGY – (Cont: East African Wildlife Journal) – Oxford. v17-. mar 1979- – 1,5*,9* – D15501.01 – us UMI [574]
AFRICAN JOURNAL OF MEDICAL SCIENCES *see* AFRICAN JOURNAL OF MEDICINE AND MEDICAL SCIENCES
AFRICAN JOURNAL OF MEDICAL SCIENCES – (Cont by: African Journal of Medicine and Medical Sciences) – Oxford. v1-4. jan 1970-1973* – 1 – D15502 – us UMI [610]
AFRICAN JOURNAL OF MEDICINE AND MEDICAL SCIENCES – (Cont: African Journal of Medical Sciences) – Ibadan. v5-. mar 1976- – 1 – D15502.01 – us UMI [610]
AFRICAN JOURNAL OF MEDICINE AND MEDICAL SCIENCES *see* AFRICAN JOURNAL OF MEDICAL SCIENCES
AFRICAN JOURNAL OF TROPICAL HYDROBIOLOGY AND FISHERIES – (All that is currently available) – Jinja. v1-2. 1971-1972 – 1 – D8328 – us UMI [574]
AFRICAN LANGUAGES AND CULTURES – London. v1- 1988- 1*; v8- 1995- 5,9 – 1,5,9 – D22910 – us UMI [470]
THE AFRICAN MAGICIAN / Powles, Francis – London, 1930 – 1r – 1 – us Ross [800]
AFRICAN MAIL – Lusaka, Zambia. 8 Mar 1960-25 May 1963 (imperfect) – 4r – 1 – uk British Libr Newspaper [072]
THE AFRICAN MAIL – v. 1-16. 4 Oct 1903-5 Jan 1917. v. 1, no. 1-77; v. 4, no. 183 wanting – 1 – 195.00 – us L of C Photodup [960]
AFRICAN MEMORANDA / Beaver, P – 1805 – 7 – uk Microform Academic [960]
African Methodist Episcopal Church of Nova Scotia *see* MISSIONARY ENTERPRISE AMONG THE COLORED PEOPLE OF THE MARITIME PROVINCES OF CANADA
AN AFRICAN MILLIONAIRE: EPISODES IN THE LIFE OF THE ILLUSTRIOUS COLONEL CLAY / Allen, Grant – London: G. Richards, 1898. 05000. (Pre-1900 Canadiana) – 9 – cn C.I.H.M. [920]
AFRICAN MIMS – Monthly Index of Medical Specialties. 1960-1975 – 1 – us UMI [615]
AFRICAN MIMS *see* MIMS AFRICA
AFRICAN MISSIONS : IMPRESSIONS OF THE SOUTH, EAST, AND CENTRE OF THE DARK CONTINENT / O'Rorke, Benjamin Garniss – London: S.P.C.K.; New York: E.S. Gorham, 1912 – 1mf – us A.T.L.A. [240]
THE AFRICAN MISSIONS OF THE WHITE FATHERS – Quebec: [White Fathers, 1909?-194-?] – 9 – cn C.I.H.M. [240]
AFRICAN MORNING POST – Accra, Ghana. Jun 1935-Sep 1938; Jan-Feb 1939; Oct-Dec 1950; Aug 1952-Mar 1953 – 5r – 1 – uk British Libr Newspaper [072]
THE AFRICAN MORNING POST – (60 no. issued between July 12, 1944 and March 9, 1951) – Accra, Ghana: African Morning Post – 1 – CSUX86-S84 – us Hoover Inst Photo [960]
THE AFRICAN NATIONAL TIMES – Accra. Ghana. 14, 25, 18 Aug; 11, 22, 25 Sep; 2, 16 Oct 1948 – 1 – us NY Public [072]
THE AFRICAN NATIONAL TIMES – (V.1, no.2, 5-6, 10, 16-18, 21; v.2, no. 41; v.3, no. 12, 19, 65; v.4, no. 338 (July 1948-Feb. 1951)) – Accra, Ghana: Ako Adjei – 1 – CSUX86-S91 – us Hoover Inst Photo [960]
AFRICAN NEWS...INFORMATION FROM AND ABOUT AFRICA – v1-2. 1889-90 – 1r – 1 – us Ross [240]

AFRICAN OBSERVER – A monthly journal... illustrative of the general character, and moral and political effects, of Negro slavery. Nos.1-12 (all publ.). 1827-1828 – 4mf – 9 – $55.00 – us UPA [976]
AFRICAN OFFICIAL STATISTICAL SERIALS, 1867-1982 – (Individual titles also listed and may be purchased separately) – 2,085mf – 9 – £9,040.00 coll – uk Chadwyck [960]
AFRICAN OFFICIAL STATISTICAL SERIALS, 1867-1982 *see*
- ALGERIA
- ANGOLA
- BENIN
- BOTSWANA
- BURUNDI
- CAMEROON
- CAPE VERDE ISLANDS
- CENTRAL AFRICAN REPUBLIC
- CHAD
- CONGO (FORMERLY FRENCH CONGO)
- EGYPT
- ETHIOPIA
- FRENCH EQUATORIAL AFRICA
- FRENCH WEST AFRICA
- GABON
- GAMBIA
- GHANA (FORMERLY GOLD COAST)
- GUINEA-BISSAU (FORMERLY PORTUGUESE GUINEA)
- IVORY COA LA COTE D'IVIORE EN CHIFFRES
- KENYA
- LESOTHO (FORMERLY BASUTOLAND)
- LIBYA
- MALAGASY REPUBLIC (MADAGASCAR)
- MALAWI (FORMERLY NYASALAND)
- MALI (FORMERLY FRENCH SUDAN)
- MAURITANIA
- MAURITIUS
- MOROCCO
- MOZAMBIQUE
- NIGER
- NIGERIA
- SENEGAL
- SIERRA LEONE
- SOMALIA
- SOUTH AFRICA
- SPANISH SAHARA
- SWAZILAND
- TANZANIA (FORMERLY TANGANYIKA AND ZANZIBAR)
- TOGO
- TUNISIA
- UGANDA
- UNITED ARAB REPUBLIC
- ZAIRE (FORMERLY BELGIAN CONGO)
- ZAMBIA
- ZIMBABWE (FORMERLY RHODESIA)
- ZIMBABWE. STATISTICAL YEARBOOK OF SOUTHERN RHODESIA

AFRICAN PASTURELAND ECOLOGY, WITH PARTICULAR REFERENCE TO THE PASTORAL ENVIRONMENT OF EASTERN AFRICA – 1980 – 203p – it F.A.O. [630]
AFRICAN REPOSITORY – (Former title: African Repository and Colonial Journal (mar 1825-aug 1850)) – Washington. v1-68. mar 1825-jan 1892 – 1 – D4570 – us UMI [960]
AFRICAN REPOSITORY AND COLONIAL JOURNAL *see* AFRICAN REPOSITORY
THE AFRICAN REPUBLIC OF LIBERIA AND THE BELGIAN CONGO : BASED ON THE OBSERVATIONS MADE AND MATERIAL COLLECTED DURING THE HARVARD AFRICAN EXPEDITION, 1926-1927 / Harvard African Expedition; ed by Strong, Richard P – 2v. 1930 – 1r – 1 – us Ross [960]
AFRICAN RESEARCHES / Park & Hornemann, Friedrich K – v. 2. 1792-1802 – 7 – uk Microform Academic [910]
AFRICAN SCHOLAR – (All that is currently available. Publ suspended 1971) – Washington. v1. aug 1968-aug 1970 – 1 – D8402 – us UMI [370]
AFRICAN SECTIONAL COMMITTEE RECORDS / Manchester Chamber of Commerce and Industry. Archives – 1829-1926 – 6r – 1 – £240.00 – uk Altair [960]
THE AFRICAN SKETCH-BOOK / Reade, Winwood – London: Smith, Elder & Co, 1873 – 1 – us Res Libr [960]
THE AFRICAN SLAVE TRADE / Buston, Thomas Fowell – London, 1839 – 1 – us Res Libr [305]
THE AFRICAN SLAVE TRADE / Buxton, Thomas Fowell – London. 1839. BA-288 2 – 8 – ne IDC [960]
AFRICAN SLAVE TRADE FROM THE FIFTEENTH TO THE NINETEENTH CENTURY – repr 1985 – 330p – 9 – 92-3-101672-5 – fr UNESCO [960]
African Society *see* JOURNAL OF THE AFRICAN SOCIETY
African Students' Association of the United States *see* AFRICAN INTERPRETER
AFRICAN STUDIES BULLETIN *see* AFRICAN STUDIES REVIEW
AFRICAN STUDIES BULLETIN – (Cont by: African Studies Review) – New York. v1-12. apr 1958-dec 1969 – 1 – D18291 – us UMI [960]
AFRICAN STUDIES IN THE USSR / Akademiia Nauk. USSR. Institute of Africa – M. 1962. BR-2474 2 – 8 – ne IDC [960]
AFRICAN STUDIES REVIEW – (Cont: African Studies Bulletin) – Atlanta. v13- apr 1970- 1*; v32- apr 1989- 5*,9 – 1,5,9 – D18291.01 – us UMI [960]
AFRICAN STUDIES REVIEW *see* AFRICAN STUDIES BULLETIN
AFRICAN TELEGRAPH AND GOLD COAST MIRROR – London, 14 Nov 1914-25 Feb 1915; Dec 1918-Dec 1919 – 29ft – 1 – uk British Libr Newspaper [072]
AFRICAN TIMES – London, Feb 1862-Dec 1902 – 8r – 1 – uk British Libr Newspaper [072]
AFRICAN TIMES – New York. v. 1-3. no. 16. Dec. 1948-May 1951 – 1 – us NY Public [073]
AFRICAN TIMES AND ORIENT REVIEW – London, Jul 1912-Aug 1914; Jan 1917-Oct 1918 – 2r – 1 – uk British Libr Newspaper [072]
AFRICAN TRADE REVIEW – Madrid. Dec 1967-Oct 1975; Oct 1977-Oct 1978 – 1 – 92.00 – us L of C Photodup [380]
AFRICAN TRYPANOSOMIASES – 1979 – 105p – it F.A.O. [634]
AFRICAN WEEKLY – Salisbury. Rhodesia. Jun 1952-Jan 1962. gaps – 1 – 35.00r – us Hoover Inst Photo [072]
AFRICAN WILDLIFE = AFRIKA-NATUURLEWE – Linden. v1-51 oct 1946-dec 1997+ 1; v36-42 jan 1982-dec 1988 5*,9 – 1,5,9 – D11426 – us UMI [590]
AFRICAN WORLD – (Some missing issues) – v10-112. 1905-30 – 1 – us L of C Photodup [073]
AFRICANA CONFERENCE PAPER INDEX / Northwestern University.Melville J. Herskovits Library of African Studies – 1972.-12,500 listings 2 reels.-ISBN: 0-8161-1532-X – 1 – $210.00 – uk Hall [960]
AFRICANA NOTES AND NEWS = AFRICANA AANTEKENININGE – (All that is currently offered) – Johannesburg. v22-23. mar 1976-dec 1979 1,5*,9* – 1,5,9 – D10378 – us UMI [960]
O AFRICANO – (Sample issue: dec 25 1908) – Lourenco Marques: Gremio Africano, [mar 1909-jan 3 1920] – 5r – 1 – us Res Libr [960]
Africanus, L *see* THE HISTORY AND DESCRIPTION OF AFRICA
AFRICA'S LUMINARY – v1-3. 1839-41 (complete) – 1r – 1 – ATLA B0124 – us A.T.L.A. [240]
THE AFRICO-AMERICAN PRESBYTERIAN, 1880-1938 – 4r – 1 – $340.00 – D3327 – Co-publ the Presbyterian Historical Society, Dept of History, Presbyterian Church (U.S.A.) 1995 – us Scholarly Res [240]
THE AFRICO-AMERICAN PRESBYTERIAN VOLS 46-59 (1925-1938) PARTIAL – Atlanta, GA – 4r – 1 – $200.00 – us Presbyterian [240]
AFRIKA 1956-1961 / ed by Potekhin, I I – M. 1961. BR-2473 2 – 8 – ne IDC [960]
AFRIKA DELILI – Mehmet Musin. Kahire: Al-Felah Ceridesi Matbaasi, 1312 [1895] – $200.00 – us MEDOC [956]
AFRIKA, DER DUNKLE ERDTHEIL IM LICHTE UNSERER ZEIT / Schweiger-Lerchenfeld, Amand – Wien: A. Hartleben, 1886. 952p.illus – 1 – us U.W. Library [960]
AFRIKA KWETU – Zanzibar, Tanzania. 8 Jan 1959-1 Feb 1962 – 1r – 1 – uk British Libr Newspaper [072]
AFRIKA NACHTRICHTEN – Leipzig, 1938-39 – 1r – 1 – gw Mikrofilm [072]
AFRIKAANSCHE BOERENVRIEND, DE – Colesberg, South Africa. 1 Jul 1882-30 Jun 1883. 1 reel. Absorbed by: Colesberg Advertiser – 1, 16 diazo available at reduced price – sa SA Libr [072]
AFRIKAANSCHE VOORSTANDER, DE – Port Elizabeth, South Africa. 3 May 1849-21 Mar 1850. 1 reel – 1, 16 diazo available at reduced price – sa SA Libr [072]
AFRIKAANSE PATRIOT *see* PAARL POST
DIE AFRIKA-LITERATUR / Paulitschke, Phillip Viktor – 1882 – 1 – uk Microform Academic [960]
AFRIKANER *see* MIDDELLANDSCHE AFRIKAANDER, DE
DIE AFRIKANER – (Issues for 1950-61 filmed with Midland News and Karoo Framer 1926-27, 1929-61, and with Middellandsche Afrikaander 1928,) – Cradock: [s.n.], 1933- (Cradock: Gedruk deur die here White & Boughton) – 1 – us Res Libr [072]
AFRIKANER IDISHE TSAYTUNG = THE AFRICAN JEWISH NEWSPAPER – Johannesburg, SA. v5 no 23 1935; v8 no 13 1938 – 1r – 1 – Can$25.00 – cn Can Microfilming [072]
DIE AFRIKANISCHE ARTEN DER GATTUNG FICUS LINN / Mildbread, J & Burret, M – (Engler Bot. Jahrb. 1911, v. 46, p. 163-269). B-2208 2 – 8 – ne IDC [580]
AFRIKANISCHE TRAUERSPIELE : CLEOPATRA, SOPHONISBE / Lohenstein, Daniel Casper von; ed by Just, Klaus Guenther – (Includes bibliographical references) – Stuttgart: Hiersemann, 1957 – 1 – us U.W. Library [820]
AFRIKANSKII ETNOGRAFICHESKII SBORNIK / Akademiia Nauk. SSSR – v. 1-4. 1956-62. BR-2471 2 – 8 – ne IDC [305]
AFRIQUE – no. 1-274; MQ no. 94, 107, 182, 249. Alger. avr. 1924-61 – 1 – fr A.C.R.P.P. [073]
AFRIQUE: 19TH AND 20TH CENTURIES – (Following authors from this series are also listed separately in this directory:. Aholi, Paul. Ancey, G. Arnaud, Jean-Claude. Baillon, D. Boisson, Claude. Castella, P. Chevassu, J. Clerc, Michel. Donnenfeld, J. Ferrari, Antoine. Lafargue, Fernand. Leblanc, C. Le Cour Grand Maison. Michotte, J. Pairault, Claude. Soulez. Tchoume, Mezan. Trouchaud, J.P) – Geographical articles, research reports and planning studies, dealing with Africa from the colonial period to the present. In French. Titles also available individually; inquire – 9 – fr Hachette [960]
AFRIQUE AUSTRALE, EMPIRE DU MAROC / Hoefer, Ferdinand – Paris: Firmin Didot Freres, 1848 – 9 – 15.00 – fr Orientalistes [960]
L'AFRIQUE BYZANTINE / Diehl, Charles – Histoire de la domination byzantine en Afrique. Paris. 1896. BA-621 2 – 8 – ne IDC [960]
L'AFRIQUE CENTRALE, EXPEDITIONS AU LAC VICTORIA-NYANZA ET AU MAKRAKA NIAM NIAM, A L'OUEST DU NIL BLANC / Chaille-Long – Paris, E. Plon and Cie. 1877 – 9 – 12.50 – fr Orientalistes [910]
L'AFRIQUE CENTRALE FRANCAISE, RECIT DU VOYAGE DE LA MISSION, APPENDICE PAR PELLEGRIN, ET AL / Chevalier, Auguste – Paris: A. Challamel, 1907. 776p. illus – 1 – us U.W. Library [910]
L'AFRIQUE CHRETIENNE / Leclercq, Henri – (Includes bibliographical references) – 2e ed. Paris: Victor Lecoffre. 2v. 1904 – 3mf – 9 – 0-8370-7643-9 – 1986-1643 – us A.T.L.A. [240]
AFRIQUE CHRETIENNE – Kinshasa, 7 Jan 1962-31 Dec 1967. BAF-110 3 – 1 – ne IDC [240]
L'AFRIQUE CONTEMPORAINE – Paris. avr mai 1962-nov dec 1979 – 1 – fr A.C.R.P.P. [073]
L'AFRIQUE DE MARMOL / Marmol (y Carvajal) – Trad. de l'Espagnol par N. Perrot d'Ablancourt; enrichie des cartes geographiques de M. Sanfon. 3 v. Paris. 1667. BA-123 2 – 8 – ne IDC [960]
L'AFRIQUE DU SUD / Aubert, Georges – Paris: Flammarion, [1898] – 1 – us Res Libr [960]
L'AFRIQUE EQUATORIALE / Compiegne – Okanda. Bangouens. Asyeba. Paris, Plon. 1876 – 9 – 12.50 – fr Orientalistes [960]
AFRIQUE EQUATORIALE FRANCAISE / Ziegle, H – Paris. 1951. BA-396 2 – 8 – ne IDC [960]
L'AFRIQUE ET LE PEUPLE AFFRIQUAIN / Lamiral, D H – Paris, Dessenne. 1789 – 9 – 12.50 – fr Orientalistes [305]
L'AFRIQUE ET LE PEUPLE AFRICAIN CONSIDERES DANS LEURS RAPPORTS AVEC NOTRE COMMERCE ET NOS COLONIES / Lamiral, D H – (Slave Trade and Abolitionism in France series). 1789 – 9 – fr Hachette [960]
L'AFRIQUE ET LE PEUPLE AFRICAIN CONSIDERES SOUS TOUS LEURS RAPPORTS AVEC NOTRE COMMERCE ET NOS COLONIES. DEDIE AU COMMERCE ET AUX COLONS FRANCAIS / Lamiral, D H – (African Library series) – 9 – fr Hachette [960]
AFRIQUE EXPLOREE ET CIVILISEE – Geneva. v1-15. 1879-94. 2 reels – 1 – $60.00r – us Ross [960]
AFRIQUE EXPLOREE ET CIVILISEE – Geneve-Paris-Bruxelles. juil 1879-juil 1894 – 1 – fr A.C.R.P.P. [073]
AFRIQUE EXPLOREE ET CIVILISEE – (Vol 1 not available for photography. Ceased publ) – Geneva. v2-15. 1880-1894 – 1 – D3326 – us UMI [960]
L'AFRIQUE FANTOME / Leiris, Michel – [Paris]: Gallimard, [1934] – 1 – us Res Libr [960]
L'AFRIQUE FRANCAISE – 1900-Apr. May 1940; July 1952-Jan. Apr. 1960. Suspended May 1940-Apr. 1952. Missing: no. 1, 1952 – 1 – 35.00r – us Hoover Inst Photo [960]
L'AFRIQUE FRANCAISE; BULLETIN MENSUEL DU COMITE DE L'AFRIQUE FRANCAISE ET DU COMITE DU MAROC – v. 1-50, 61-65. 1891-1940, 1952-56. V. 50, no. 1, 4-12 WANTING – 1 – 747.00 – us L of C Photodup [944]
AFRIQUE MAGAZINE *see* JEUNE AFRIQUE AND AFRIQUE MAGAZINE
L'AFRIQUE NOIRE OCCIDENTALE : ESQUISSE DES CADRES GEOGRAPHIQUES / Gautier, Emile Felix – Paris: E Larose, 1935 – 1 – us Res Libr [960]
AFRIQUE NOUVELLE – no. 1288. Dakar. 1960-15 juin 1972 – 1 – fr A.C.R.P.P. [073]
L'AFRIQUE OCCIDENTALE : ALGERIE, MZAB, TILDIKELT / Soleillet, Paul – Avignon: F Sequin aine, 1887 – 1 – us Res Libr [960]
L'AFRIQUE OCCIDENTALE FRANCAISE / Francois, Georges Alphonse Florent Octave – Paris: E Larose, 1907 – 1 – us Res Libr [960]
L'AFRIQUE OCCIDENTALE FRANCAISE : PAR L'ATLANTIQUE OU PAR LE SAHARA? / Tuaillon, Georges – Paris: Charles-Lavauzelle, 1936 – 1 – us Res Libr [960]
L'AFRIQUE OCCIDENTALE FRANCAISE DANS LA LITTERATURE FRANCAISE (DEPUIS 1870) / Lebel, Roland – Paris: E Larose, 1925 – 1 – us Res Libr [300]
L'AFRIQUE, OU HISTOIRE, MOEURS, USAGES ET COUTUMES DES AFRICAINS / Geoffroy de Villeneuve, Rene C – (African Library). Paris. Nepveu. 1814 – 9 – fr Hachette [960]
L'AFRIQUE, OU HISTOIRE, MOEURS, USAGES ET COUTUMES DES AFRICAINS: DAHOMEY (GUINEE) / Macleod, John – V, 11, traduction de l'anglais. Paris, Nepveu. 1821 – 9 – 5.00 – fr Orientalistes [390]
L'AFRIQUE, OU HISTOIRE, MOEURS, USAGES ET COUTUMES DES AFRICAINS: FEZZAN / Lyon, G F – V, 12, traduction de l'anglais. Paris: Nepvue. 1821 – 9 – 15.00 – fr Orientalistes [390]
L'AFRIQUE PITTORESQUE : LE CONTINENT AFRICAIN ET LES ILES. LECTURES CHOISIES – 2e ed. Paris: C Delagrave, 1890 – 1 – us Res Libr [960]
L'AFRIQUE SAUVAGE, NOUVELLES EXCURSIONS AU PAYS DES ASHANGOS / Du Chaillu, Paul Belloni – Paris, Michel Levy Freres. 1868 – 9 – 15.00 – fr Orientalistes [910]
AFRIQUE, TERRE QUI MEURT : LA DEGRADATION DES SOLS AFRICAINS SOUS L'INFLUENCE DE LA COLONISATION / Harroy, Jean-Paul – Bruxelles: M Hayez, 1944 – 1 – us Res Libr [960]
AFRISCOPE – (All that is currently available) – Yaba. v4-12 jan 1974-dec 1982 1,5; v6-12 jan 1976-dec 1982 9 – 1,5,9 – D1361 – us UMI [960]
AFRO AMERICAN – Baltimore. Md. (5 Star Ed.) 1935- – 1 – us UMI [071]
AFRO AMERICAN – Baltimore. Md. (Late City Ed.) 1933- – 1 – us UMI [071]
AFRO AMERICAN – Baltimore. Md. (Nat'l. Ed.) 1893- – 1 – us UMI [071]
AFRO AMERICAN – Newark. N.J. (N.J. Ed.) 1941- – 1 – us UMI [071]
AFRO AMERICAN – Philadelphia, PA. 1934-68 – 1 – us UMI [071]
AFRO AMERICAN – Washington. D.C. (Capital Ed.). 1932- – 1 – us UMI [071]
AFRO AMERICAN – Washington. D.C. (Red Star Ed.). 1949- – 1 – us UMI [071]
LES AFRO-AMERICAINS – Dakar: IFAN, 1952 [1953] – 1 – us Res Libr [960]
AFRO-AMERICAN – Richmond. Va. 1938- – 1 – us UMI [071]
Afro-American Clubwoman's Project *see* COLLECTED RECORDS

AFRO-AMERICAN FOLKSONGS : A STUDY IN RACIAL AND NATIONAL MUSIC / Krehbiel, Henry Edward – New York: G. Schirmer, c1914 – 1mf – us A.T.L.A. [780]
THE AFRO-AMERICAN HISTORY SERIES / ed by Whiteman, Maxwell – 1978 – 58mf – 9 – $261.00 – S1842 – 1167-6 – us L of C Photodup [305]
AFRO-AMERICAN STUDIES *see* ETHNIC GROUPS (INC. AFRO-AMERICAN STUDIES)
AFRO-AMERICAN STUDIES MATERIALS – (Collection of literature and primary source material from colonial times through the 19th century. 7200) – 7200v – 9 – us Primary [305]
AFRO-AMERICANA – New York. v1. Win 1969-Fal 1970 – 1 – D10111 – us UMI [073]
AFRO-ASIA AND NON-ALIGNMENT / Jansen, G H – SE-11,606 1. 1966 – 9 – ne IDC [950]
AFRO-ASIAN ECONOMIC REVIEW / Afro-Asian Organization for Economic Co-operation – Cairo. v3-6. 1961-64 – 2r – 1 – us Ross [330]
Afro-Asian Organization for Economic Co-operation *see* AFRO-ASIAN ECONOMIC REVIEW
AFRO-ASIAN TRADE DIRECTORY – SE-3350 1. 1957 – 9 – ne IDC [380]
AFRO-HISPANIC REVIEW – Columbia. v1- jan 1982- 1*; v10- jan 1991- 5*,9 – 1,5,9 – D19148 – us UMI [073]
AFS INTERNATIONAL CAST METALS JOURNAL / American Foundrymen's Society – v1-. 1976- – 1,5,6,9 – us UMI [670]
AFSCHRIFTEN UIT HET OUDARCHIEF VAN MODJOKERTO 1819-1850 MET INVENTARIS – 23-43mf – 9 – ne IDC [950]
AFSCHRIFTEN VAN PORTUGESE ARCHIEFSTUKKEN VOORNAMELIJK BETREFFENDE VESTIGINGEN IN DE MOLUKKEN EN OP MALAKKA – 1515-32.KITLV,H. 697b. BSD-102/1 mf. 3-7 – 9 – ne IDC [950]
AFSCHRIFTEN VAN PORTUGESE BRIEVEN OVER DE OUDSTE MISSIEPOSTEN IN OOST-INDIE – 1650. KITLV,H 697a. BSD-102/1 mf. 8 (1-2)-8(2-2) – 9 – ne IDC [950]
Aftalion, Albert *see*
- LA CRISE DE L'INDUSTRIE LINIERE ET LA CONCURRENCE VICTORIEUSE DE L'INDUSTRIE COTONNIERE
- LES CRISES PERIODIQUES DE SURPRODUCTION
- LE DEVELOPPEMENT DE LA FABRIQUE ET LE TRAVAIL A DOMICILE DANS LES INDUSTRIES DE L'HABILLEMENT

AFTENPOSTEN – Oslo: [s.n., jul 1938-] – 1 – us Res Libr [072]
AFTER CORONADO. SPANISH EXPLORATION NORTHEAST OF NEW MEXICO, 1696-1727... / Bernab y Thomas, Alfred – Madrid: Missionalia Hispanica, 1945 – 1 – sp Bibl Santa Ana [910]
AFTER CORONADO, SPANISH EXPLORATION NORTHEAST OF NEW MEXICO, 1696-1727. DOCUMENTS FROM THE ARCHIVES OF SPAIN, MEXICO AND NEW MEXICO...NORMAN, 1935 / Thomas, Alfred B – Madrid: Razon y Fe, 1936 – 1 – sp Bibl Santa Ana [910]
AFTER DARK – North Hollywood. v1-15 feb 1960-jan 1983 1; v12-15 may 1970-jan 1983 5; v7-15 may 1974-jan 1983 9 – 1,5,9 – D3228 – us UMI [073]
AFTER FIFTY YEARS, OR, LETTERS OF A GRANDFATHER : ON OCCASION OF THE JUBILEE OF THE FREE CHURCH OF SCOTLAND IN 1893 / Blaikie, William Garden – London; New York: T. Nelson, 1893 – 1mf – us A.T.L.A. [240]
AFTER MOTHER INDIA / Field, Harry Hubert – New York: Harcourt, Brace and Co., (c1929). xiv,325p. illus – 1 – us U.W. Library [950]
AFTER TEN YEARS, STILL: ONWARD, NEVER RETREAT / Sukarno, Pres. Indonesia – Address at 10th anniversary of First Afro-Asian Conference. SE 4965 1. Apr. 18, 1965 – 9 – ne IDC [324]
AFTER THE HELL IN SPAIN, THE REFUGEES SINK INTO ANOTHER HELL–THE FRENCH CAMPS – NY. 1939. Fiche W 703. (Blodgett Collection of Spanish Civil War Pamphlets) – 9 – us H.U. College Libr [946]
AFTER WHITSITT WHAT? / Mitchell, S C – 1 – 5.00 – us Baptist [240]
AFTER WORK : HOME READING FOR THE FAMILY CIRCLE – (Ceased publ) – London. ns1-10. jan 1874-1887 – 1 – D4744 – us UMI [640]
AFTER-ACTION REPORT, THIRD U.S. ARMY. 1 AUGUST 1944-9 MAY 1945 / U.S. Army – 3r – 1 – $255.00 – S1651 – Co-publ in cooperation with the Center for Military History – us Scholarly Res [355]
AFTER-DEATH COMMUNICATIONS / Bazett, L Margery – New York: H. Holt and Co., 1920.Introd. by J. Arthur Hill. 119p – 1 – us U.W. Library [150]
THE AFTERGLOW OF THE JAPANESE SUNSET / Slamet, Mas – SE 12,089 1. 1946 – 9 – ne IDC [950]
AFTERIMAGE – Rochester, NY. 1979-1989 – 7r – 1 – $350.00 – R04151 – us Library Micro [071]
AFTERIMAGE – Rochester. v1-. mar 1972-* – 1 – D10712 – us UMI [073]
AFTERMARKET BUSINESS – (Cont: Home and Auto) – Cleveland. v96- jul 1986- 1*; v103-1993-* 5,9 – 1,5,9 – D12961.03 – us UMI [073]
AFTONBLADET – Stockholm: Stockholms-Tidningen tr., jul 1938-aug 1939; dec 1943-jun 1945; 1948-jun 1950 – 1 – us Res Libr [072]
AFTONBLADET – Stockholm, Sweden. 1830- – 1 – sw Kungliga [072]
AFTONBLADET NEWSBILLS – Stockholm, 1935-78 – 9 – sw Kungliga [072]
AFTONPOSTEN – Goteborg, Sweden. 1951-56 – 40r – 1 – sw Kungliga [072]
AFTONTIDNINGEN – Stockholm, 1889-90 – 9 – sw Kungliga [072]
AFTONTIDNINGEN – Stockholm, Sweden. 1909-20 – 48r – 1 – sw Kungliga [072]
AFTONTIDNINGEN – Stockholm, Sweden. 1942-56 – 135r – 1 – sw Kungliga [072]
AFTONTIDNINGEN SEMIWEEKLY EDITION – Stockholm, 1914-20 – 9 – sw Kungliga [072]
AFVA EVALUATIONS – (Cont: EFLA Evaluations) – La Grange, 1988-92. 1993-94* 1; 1988. Win 1989-94* 5; 1988-92. 1993-94* 9; 1995-97+ 1,5,9 – 1,5,9 – D9916.01 – us UMI [020]
AFYON-KARAHISARDA NUR – Afyon, 1924-1928; Sahibi: Ahmed Sami [Onur], Mueduerue: Tahir Hayreddin. – Nos. 3, 5, 7, 10-13, 20-21, 23-24, 26-28, 31-32, 44-45, 47-48, 50, 52. – 1 Hazaran 1340 [1924]-15 Haziran 1928 – 6mf – 9 – $125.00 – us MEDOC [949]
AG / North Carolina State University.Agricultural Extension Service – No.1-299. 1976-82. 98 fiches – 9 – us Spaulding [630]
A.G. BLIUMKIN PAMPHLET COLLECTION – 193? – 1 reel – 1 – CSUXANS0733-B – us Hoover Inst Photo [947]
AG CHEM AND COMMERCIAL FERTILIZER *see*
- FARM CHEMICALS
- FARM CHEMICALS AND CROP LIFE

AG CHEM AND COMMERCIAL FERTILIZER – (Ceased publ. Merged with: Farm Chemicals and Crop Life; To form: Farm Chemicals. Absorbed: Commercial Fertilizer and Plant Food Industry, 1970. Former Title: Agricultural Chemicals) – Cedar Grove. v1-28 may 1946-apr 1973 1; v21-27 jan 1966-dec 1972 5 – 1,5 – D60 – us UMI [630]
AG CONSULTANT *see* AG CONSULTANT AND FIELDMAN
AG CONSULTANT – (Cont: Ag Consultant and Fieldman) – Willoughby. v42-. Fal 1986- – 1,5*,9 – D1415.04 – us UMI [073]
AG CONSULTANT AND FIELDMAN *see* AGRI-FIELDMAN AND CONSULTANT
AG CONSULTANT AND FIELDMAN – (Cont: Agri-Fieldman and Consultant. Cont by: Ag Consultant) – Willoughby. v36-42. jan 1980-aug 1986 – 1,5,9 – D1415.03 – us UMI [073]
AG CONSULTANT AND FIELDMAN *see* AG CONSULTANT
AG INSTITUTE NEWS / University of Tennessee.Institute of Agriculture – No.1-6. 1976-81. 1 reel – 1,5 – us Spaulding [630]
AG INSTITUTE REPORT / University of Tennessee.Institute of Agriculture – No.1-4. 1978-81. 1 reel – 1,5 – us Spaulding [630]
Ag Rhaly, A *see* RAPPORT SUR LA MISSION MEDICO-SCIENTIFIQUE FRANCO-MALIENNE
AGA (AMERICAN GAS ASSOCIATION) – Standards. Includes the National Fuel Gas Code. Printed index. Updated every 60 days – 6,9 – us Info Handling [660]
AGA: AMERICAN GAS ASSOCIATION MONTHLY – v1- 1919- 1; 1975- 5,6; 1976- 4 x 6 in9 – us UMI [622]
AGA MONTHLY – (Cont: American Gas Association Monthly. Cont by: American Gas) – Arlington. v66-70. oct 1984-dec 1988 – 1,5,9 – D10410.01 – us UMI [073]
AGA MONTHLY *see*
- AMERICAN GAS
- AMERICAN GAS ASSOCIATION MONTHLY

Aga, Silahdar Findiklili Mehmet *see* SILAHDAR TARIHI
DIE AGADA DER BABYLONISCHEN AMORAEER / Bacher, Wilhelm – Franfurt a.M.: J. Kauffmann, 1913. 1 fiche – 9 – us A.T.L.A. [270]
DIE AGADA DER BABYLONISCHEN AMORAEER / Bacher, Wilhelm – Frankfurt, 1913 – Dfl19.00 – ne Slangenburg [220]
DIE AGADA DER PALAESTINENSISCHEN AMORAEER / Bacher, Wilhelm – 3v. 1892-99. BJ-32-29 1 – 9 – ne IDC [900]
DIE AGADA DER PALAESTINENSISCHEN AMORAEER / Bacher, Wilhelm – Strassburg. bd 1-3. 1892-1899 – Dfl123.00 – ne Slangenburg [220]
DIE AGADA DER TANAITEN / Bacher, Wilhelm – 2v. Strassburg. 1890. BJ-32-27 – 9 – ne IDC [900]
DIE AGADA DER TANNAITEN / Bacher, Wilhelm – (Erster Band: Von Hillel bis Akiba. Strassburg 1884 8mf; Zweiter Band: Von Akiba's Tod bis zum Abschluss der Mischna. Strassburg 1890 10mf) – 8 – Dfl3.50ea – ne Slangenburg [270]
DIE AGADA DER TANNAITEN UND AMORAEER / Bacher, Wilhelm – Strassburg. 1902. BJ-32-30 1 – 9 – ne IDC [900]
AGAFII / Levchenko, M V – O tsarstvovanii Iustiniana. M. L. 1953. BU-529 2 – 8 – ne IDC [947]
AGAI-DICUTTA YACLU-A – (Paiate Indian newspaper) – Schurz, NV. 1975-1977; 1979 – 2r – 1 – $100.00 – U04897 – us Library Micro [071]
AGAINST CENSORSHIP / Botsford, David – 1986, LA Political Notes, No.20, 2p – 9 – 1.00f – at Libertarian Micro [335]
AGAINST THE PROFESSIONS / Davies, Stephen – LA Political Notes, No.19, 2p – 9 – 1.00f – at Libertarian Micro [320]
AGAMA ADALAH UNSUR MUTLAK DIDALAM NATION BUILDING / Sukarno, Pres. Indonesia – SE 10,293 1. 1962 – 9 – ne IDC [324]
AGAMEMNON / Lemercier – (French Theatre Series). Paris. Fayolle, an V. 1797 – 9 – fr Hachette [820]
THE AGAMEMNON OF AESCHYLUS / Aeschylus – London: Smith, Elder, 1877 – 1 roll – 1 – 1-55879-181-7 – uk Libr Preservation [820]
AGAPE, DANS LE N.T / Spicq, C – Paris, 1958. 3v – 20mf – 8 – Dfl3.50ea – ne Slangenburg [220]
Agapov, D V *see* ALFAVITNYI KATALOG RUSSKIKH KNIG PO MATEMATIKE, VYSHEDSHIKH V ROSSII S NACHALA KNIGOPECHATANIIA DO POSLEDNIAGO VREMENI
Agardh, C A *see*
- CONSPECTUS CRITICUS DIATOMACEARUM
- SPECIES ALGARUM...GRYPHISWALDIAE
- SYNOPSIS ALGARUM SCANDINAVIAE
- SYSTEMA ALGARUM

Agardh, J G *see*
- ANALECTA ALGOLOGICA
- NYA ALGER FRAN MEXICO
- SPECIES, GENERA ET ORDINES ALGARUM
- SYNOPSIS GENERIS LUPINI
- THEORIA SYSTEMATIS PLANTARUM
- TILL ALGERNESS SYSTEMATIK

THE AGARICACEAE OF MICHIGAN / Kauffman, C H – (Mich. Geol. and Bot. Survey. Publ. nr. 26, Biol. S. 5). 2 v. Michigan. 1918. B-433 2 – 8 – ne IDC [580]
Agassiz, J L R *see*
- BIBLIOGRAPHIA ZOOLOGIAE ET GEOLOGIAE
- NOMENCLATORIS ZOOLOGICI INDEX UNIVERSALIS

Agassiz, Louis *see*
- BIBLIOGRAPHIA ZOOLOGIAE ET GEOLOGIAE
- CONTRIBUTIONS TO THE NATURAL HISTORY OF THE UNITED STATES OF AMERICA
- RECHERCHES SUR LES POISSONS FOSSILES

Agassiz, Louis et al *see* SCIENTIFIC RESULTS OF A JOURNEY IN BRAZIL/BY LOUIS AGASSIZ AND HIS TRAVELLING COMPANIONS. GEOLOGY AND PHYSICAL GEOGRAPHY OF BRAZIL
AGATE – Edmonton. v1- 1987- – 9 – Can$20.00y – 0833-0603 – cn Micromedia [073]
AGAWAM 1855-1892 – (Mf 1-8: Births, Marriages, Deaths 1855-92. Mf 9-11: Index to Births 1855-92. Mf 12-14: Index to Marriages 1855-92. Mf 15-17: Index to Deaths 1855-92) – (mf ed 1987) – 17mf – 9 – 0-87623-011-7 – us Holbrook [920]
AGB REPORTS / Association of Governing Boards of Universities and Colleges – (v20-, 1977- . 5,6,9) – v. 1-. 1958- – 1 – us UMI [370]
AGDER BISPEDOMME : ARBOK – v1-33. 1951-83 (complete) – 3r – 1 – ATLA S0510 – us A.T.L.A. [073]
AGE – (Also known as: Review Journal) – Las Vegas, NV. 1905-47 (scats) – 13r – 1 – $650.00 – U04595 – us Library Micro [071]
AGE – Birmingham. Ala. 1886-1887 – 1 – us UMI [071]
AGE – Clinton. Iowa. 1871-1901 – 1 – us UMI [071]
AGE – Coshocton. Ohio. 1862-1914 – 1 – us UMI [071]
AGE – Melbourne, 1854-1977 – 730r – 1 – at Pascoe [072]
THE AGE – Boulder. Mont. 1888-1904 – 1 – us UMI [071]
THE AGE – London, England. -w. 15 May 1825-30 Dec 1843. 8 reels – 1 – uk British Libr Newspaper [072]
THE AGE – Melbourne, 1859- – 24r per y – 1 – us Ross [072]
THE AGE – Melbourne. Australia. 1978- – 1 – us Primary [072]
THE AGE – Melbourne, Australia. -d. Jan 1941-Oct 1974. 581 reels – 1 – uk British Libr Newspaper [072]
THE AGE – York, PA., 1890-1900 – 13 – $25.00r – us I.M.R. [071]
AGE AND AGE MONTHLY – 1 – F13,839.00 – sz Infoprint [073]
AGE AND AGE MONTHLY – 1978-1985 – 1 – F10,696.00 – sz Infoprint [073]
AGE AND AGE MONTHLY – 1986-1993 – 1 – F13,271.00 – sz Infoprint [073]
AGE AND AGING – Oxford. v1-13 feb 1972-84* 1; v14-26 jan 1985-nov 1997+ 1,5,9 – 1,5,9 – D15304 – us UMI [618]
AGE AND ARGUS *see* THE ARGUS
THE AGE AND THE CHURCH : BEING A STUDY OF THE AGE, AND OF THE ADAPTATION OF THE CHURCH TO ITS NEEDS / Stuckenberg, John Henry Wilburn – Hartford, Conn., U.S.A.: Student Publishing, c1893 – 1mf – us A.T.L.A. [240]
AGE DIFFERENCES IN PERFORMANCE OF A COINCIDENT ANTICIPATION TASK: APPLICATION OF A MODIFIED INFORMATION PROCESSING MODEL / Williams, Kathleen – 1982 – 9 – $12.00 – us Microform Publ [150]
L'AGE D'OR DE LA PEINTURE TOULOUSAINE / Reunion des musees nationaux. Paris – 1947. 8 illus. 1 fiche – 9 – fr Réunion [700]
THE AGE OF CHARLEMAGNE (CHARLES THE GREAT) / Wells, Charles Luke – New York: Christian Literature Co., 1898 – 2mf – us A.T.L.A. [940]
THE AGE OF CHARLEMAGNE (CHARLES THE GREAT) / Wells, Charles Luke – New York: The Christian Literature Co., 1898. xix,472p.(Ten Epochs of Church History IV). Bibliography – 1 – us U.W. Library [900]
THE AGE OF ERASMUS : LECTURES / Allen, Philip Schuyler – Oxford: Clarendon Press; New York: Oxford University Press, 1914 – 1mf – us A.T.L.A. [190]
THE AGE OF FAITH / Bradford, Amory Howe – Boston: Houghton, Mifflin, 1900.1 fiche – 9 – us A.T.L.A. [240]
AGE OF FREEDOM / Berlin Heights, OH. Lorain County 1858 – (Also: Good Time Coming, 1859. The New Campaign, 1871. Free love newspapers. Sold as a set) – 1858 – 1 – us Western Res [071]
THE AGE OF HILDEBRAND / Vincent, Marvin Richardson – New York: Christian Literature, 1896 – 2mf – us A.T.L.A. [240]
AGE OF INTRODUCTION AND CURRENT FREQUENCY OF PARTICIPATION IN LEAGUE AND CASUAL BOWLERS / Duray, Nicholas A – 1982 – 9 – $4.00 – us Microform Publ [790]

THE AGE OF REVOLUTION : BEING AN OUTLINE OF THE HISTORY OF THE CHURCH FROM 1648 TO 1815 / Hutton, William Holden – London: Rivingtons, 1908 (The Church universal; v. [7]) – 1mf – us A.T.L.A. [240]

THE AGE OF THE FATHERS : BEING CHAPTERS IN THE HISTORY OF THE CHURCH DURING THE FOURTH AND FIFTH CENTURIES / Bright, William – London; New York: Longmans, Green, 1903 – 3mf – us A.T.L.A. [240]

THE AGE OF THE GREAT WESTERN SCHISM / Locke, Clinton – New York: Christian Literature Co., 1896. (Ten epochs of church history; v8) – 1mf – us A.T.L.A. [240]

THE AGE OF THE RENASCENCE : AN OUTLINE SKETCH OF THE HISTORY OF THE PAPACY FROM THE RETURN FROM AVIGNON TO THE SACK OF ROME (1377-1527) / Dyke, Paul van – New York: Christian Literature, 1897 – 1mf – us A.T.L.A. [240]

Agee, James K *see* FIRE AND FUEL MANAGEMENT IN MEDITERRANEAN-CLIMATE ECOSYSTEMS

AGE-HERALD – Birmingham. Ala. 1888-1946 – 1 – us UMI [071]

AGEING AND SOCIETY – Cambridge. v1-1981- 1*; v7- mar 1987- 5,9 – 1,5,9 – D16514 – us UMI [073]

Agelov, E *see* KOLCHAK ILI LENIN?

Agence de Presse Libre du Quebec *see*
- BULLETIN POPULAIRE
- MOBILISATION

AGENCE ECONOMIQUE DES TERRITOIRES FRANCAIS SOUS MANDAT – n.s., no. 1-26. 1926-28. devenu: Togo-Cameroun. 1929-janv 1937. devenu: Cameroun. Paris. avr-dec 1937 – 1 – fr A.C.R.P.P. [073]

AGENCIA LATINOAMERICANA DE INFORMACION = LATIN AMERICAN INFORMATION AGENCY – Quito. 165 docs. 1981-1991 – 61mf – 9 – ne IDC [320]

THE AGENCY AND MERCANTILE, SHIPPING, AGRICULTURAL, ADVERTISING AND GENERAL REGISTER – Freetown. Sierra Leone. -w. 24 Oct-21 Nov 1884, 31 Dec 1886-15 Apr 1887. (8 ft) – 1 – uk British Libr Newspaper [072]

THE AGENCY CONTRACT AND THE POWER OF ATTORNEY APPLIED TO BUSINESS IN INDONESIA / Pratomo, R – Djakarta, 1972. LL-10032 – 1 – us L of C Photodup [340]

THE AGENCY OF A.B. STEINBERGER IN THE SAMOAN ISLANDS : MESSAGE FROM THE PRESIDENT OF THE UNITED STATES TO THE CONGRESS / Grant, President – 44th Congress 2nd sess. House Exec Doc no 44 24 Feb 1877. n.p,n.d. – 2mf – 9 – $3.00 – LLMC 82-100C Title 42 – us L.L.M.C. [327]

AGENCY SALES – (Former titles: Agency Sales Magazine (1970-oct 1972); Agency Sales Magazine with Agent and Representative (nov 1972-73); Agency Sales with Agent and Representative (1974-76); Agency Sales Magazine (nov 1976-aug 1979)) – Irvine. v1-27 1970-dec 1997+ 1*; v3-27 jan 1973-dec 1997+ 5*; v6-27 jan 1976-dec 1997+ 9 – 1,5,9 – D9623 – us UMI [650]

AGENCY SALES MAGAZINE *see* AGENCY SALES

AGENCY SALES MAGAZINE WITH AGENT AND REPRESENTATIVE *see* AGENCY SALES

AGENCY SALES WITH AGENT AND REPRESENTATIVE *see* AGENCY SALES

AGENDA – London. v1-35 jan 1959-Win 1998+ 1; v9-35 Win 1971-Win 1998+ 5; v13-35 Spr 1975-Win 1998+ 9 – 1,5,9 – D6612 – us UMI [073]

AGENDA : NATIONAL COUNCIL OF LA RAZA – (Ceased publ) – Washington. v1-11. jun 1971-dec 1981* – 1 – D14248 – us UMI [073]

AGENDA – (Cont by: Animals' Agenda) – Westport. v1-4. 1980-1984* – 1 – D18626 – us UMI [073]

AGENDA / National Council of La Raza – (Ceased publ) – Washington. v1-11. jun 1971-dec 1981* – 1 – D14248 – us UMI [073]

AGENDA BOOK OF THE SOUTH AFRICAN INDIAN CONGRESS CONFERENCE – [Johannesburg: The Congress]. v20 1952; v22 1956 – 1 – us Res Libr [960]

AGENDA BOOK OF THE...PROVINCIAL CONFERENCE / Natal Indian Congress – 1940-41, 1944, 1947-48, 1951-55, 1957 – 1 – us Res Libr [960]

AGENDA COLONIENSIS ECCLESIAE – 1614 – 9mf – 8 – Dfl32.00 – ne Slangenburg [240]

AGENDA COMMUNIS : DIE AELTESTE AGENDE IN DER DIOEZESE ERMLAND UND IM DEUTSCHORDENSTAATE PREUSSEN / Kolberg, A – Braunsberg, 1903 – 3mf – 8 – Dfl13.00 – ne Slangenburg [240]

DIE AGENDA DER DIOZESE NAUMBURG VON 1502 / ed by Schoenfelder, A – Paderborn, 1904 – 1mf – 8 – Dfl6.00 – ne Slangenburg [240]

Agenda Sindical *see* BADAJOZ-71

DIE AGENDE DER DIOZESE SCHWERIN VON 1521 / ed by Schoenfelder, A – Paderborn, 1906 – 3mf – 8 – Dfl13.00 – ne Slangenburg [240]

AGENOR : THE EUROPEAN REVIEW – (Britain and Europe since 1945) – 1967- – 9 – us Primary [073]

AGENSKALNA BAPTIST CHURCH, RIGA. RIGAS AGENSKALNA BAPTISTU DRAUDSES 50 GADI = FIFTY YEARS OF THE AGENSKALNA BAPTIST CHURCH OF RIGA – Riga, 1934. Publ. No. 6346,no. 3. One of six items on reel. Total Pages 152 – 1 – us Baptist [240]

DER AGENT : ROMAN / Lindau, Paul – New York: G E Stechert, 1899 – 1r – 1 – us U.W. Library [830]

EL AGENTE DE MATRIMONIOS / Lopez de Ayala, Adelardo – Madrid: Imprenta de Jose Rodriguez, 1862 – sp Bibl Santa Ana [780]

Agentina. Ministerio del Interior *see* LAS FUERZAS ARMADAS RESTITUYEN EL IMPERIO DE LA SOBERANIA POPULAR

AGENTS AND ACTIONS – (Cont by: Inflammation Research) – Basel. v1-43 jul 1969-dec 1994 1; v2-43 apr 1971-dec 1994 5; v4-43 mar 1974-dec 1994 9 – 1,5,9 – D5141 – us UMI [073]

THE AGENTS' COMPANION – London, Ont.: Companion Pub Co, [1874-18–?] – 9 – cn C.I.H.M. [070]

AGE-RELATED CHANGES IN THE RELEASE POINT, VELOCITY AND ACCELERATION IN GIRLS' OVERARM THROWING PERFORMANCE / Yan, Jin H & Payne, V Gregory – 1992 – 1mf – 9 – $4.00 – us Microform Publ [612]

THE AGES BEFORE MOSES : A SERIES OF LECTURES ON THE BOOK OF GENESIS / Gibson, John Monro – New York: Anson D F Randolph, c1879 – 1mf – 9 – 0-8370-3264-4 – 1985-1264 – us A.T.L.A. [220]

AGES BEFORE MOSES: A SERIES OF LECTURES ON THE BOOK OF GENESIS / Gibson, John Monro – New York: A.D.F. Randolph, 1879.1 fiche – 9 – us A.T.L.A. [220]

AGES OF CHRISTENDOM BEFORE THE REFORMATION / Stoughton, John – London: Jackson and Walford, 1857 – 2mf – us A.T.L.A. [240]

AGEXPORTER – (Cont: Foreign Agriculture) – Washington. v1-. jan 1989- – 1,5*,9 – D16928 – us UMI [380]

THE AGE/YORK PRESS – York, PA. -d 1897-1898 – 13 – $25.00r – us I.M.R. [071]

AGGADAT ARBA KOSOT / Pappenheim, S – Berlin. 1790. BJ-422-66 1 – 9 – ne IDC [100]

AGGIE TATLER / Nebraska. College of Agriculture – n.1-12. 1916-28 – 1,5 – us Spaulding [630]

AGGIUNTE ALLA ORNITOLOGIA DELLA PAPUASIA E DELLE MOLUCCHE / Salvador, T.A – (R. Accad. Sci. Torino. Mem, s. 2, v. 40). 3 pts. Torino. 1889-91. BZ-1900/2 – 8mf – 8 – ne IDC [590]

L'AGGLOMERATION DAKAROISE; QUELQUES ASPECTS SOCIOLOGIQUES ET DEMOGRAPHIQUES / Institut Francais d'Afrique Noire – Saint Louis, Senegal, 1954 – 1 – us Res Libr [310]

AGGREGATES OF POLLS, PROPERTY AND TAXES / Massachusetts. Dept. of Corporations and Taxation – 1861-1940. 94 fiches. (Harvard Law School Library Collection.) – 9 – 1.50f – us H.U. Law [324]

AGGRESSION AND VIOLENT BEHAVIOR – Tarrytown. 1996- – 1,5,9 – D49635 – us UMI [150]

AGHS LEGAL AID CELL – Lahore. 15 docs. 1989-1991 – 14mf – 9 – ne IDC [340]

Agia, Miguel *see* SERVIDUMBRES PERSONALES DE INDIOS

Agila *see* AGILA P'ALANTE

AGILA P'ALANTE / Agila – Trujullo: Imp. Gexme, 1981 – 1 – sp Bibl Santa Ana [946]

AGING – (Ceased publ) – Washington. v1-367 jan 1951-1996 1; v135-367 jan 1966-1996 5,9 – 1,5,9 – D2119 – us UMI [301]

AGING AND WORK – (Supersedes: Industrial Gerontology) – Washington. v1-7 Win 1978-1984 – 1,5,9 – D11717 – us UMI [331]

L'AGIOTEUR / Charlemagne, Armand – (French Theatre Series). Paris. Barga, an IV. 1796 – 9 – fr Hachette [820]

Agippa von Nettesheim, Heinrich Cornelius *see* THREE BOOKS OF ACCULT PHILOSOPHY

AGITAT SII A I PROPAGANDA V DEREVNE : POSOBIE DLI A DEREVENSKIKH I ACHEEK RKP I RLKSM, IZB-CHITALEN I SHEFSKIKH KOLLEKTIVOV / ed by Abolina, A – Leningrad: Pribo i, 1925 – 1 – CSUX89-B6244 – us Hoover Inst Photo [320]

L'AGITATEUR – I, no. 1-12. Marseille. mars-mai 1892; II, no. 1-6. janv-fevr 1893; n.s., no. 1-2. fevr-mars 1897 – 1 – fr A.C.R.P.P. [073]

AGITATOR – (All that is currently offered) – Moscow, 1961-67 – 1 – D16200 – us UMI [073]

AGITATOR – Marshfield OR. Mar 11 1911 – 1 – us U.O. Library [071]

AGITATOR : MONTHLY, LATER WEEKLY FREE LOVE/SPIRITUALIST NEWSPAPER – Cleveland, OH. Feb 1858-1 Apr 1860 – 1r – 1 – us Western Res [071]

AGITATOR : ZHURNAL T SENTRALNOGO KOMITETA KOMMUNISTICHESKO I PARTII SOVETSKOGO SOI UZA – (Includes 1958, no. 9-24; 1960-1989) – Moskva: Izd-vo "Pravda", 1956-1989 – 1 – CSUX89-S948 – us Hoover Inst Photo [320]

AGITATOR – Zhurnal tsentral'nogo komiteta kommunisticheskoi partii Sovetskogo Soiuza. Moscow, 1956-72. Lacking: 1956; 1957; 1958; 1961 (20). BR-10,381/1 – 9 – ne IDC [073]

DER AGITATOR – Berlin, 1870-71 – 1r – 1 – DM100.00 – gw Mikro Press [072]

DER AGITATOR – Berlin, Germany. 1870-1871 – 1 – gw Mikrofilm [072]

AGITATOR KAZAKHSTANA : ZHURNAL T SENTRALNOGO KOMITETA KP KAZAKHSTANA – (Dates include[1976-1989:29]) – [Alma-Ata]: Izd-vo T SK KP Kazakhstana, -1989 – 1 – CSUX90-S95 – us Hoover Inst Photo [947]

Agitprop T SK i MK VKP (b) *see* FAKTY I TSIFRY PROTIV DEMAGOGII I IZMYSHLENII OPPOZITSII

AGLA – Montijo, 1935. 2 numeros – 5 – sp Bibl Santa Ana [073]

AGLAJA / Puchner, Rudolph – Milwaukee, WI.: C N Caspar, 1887 – 1r – 1 – us U.W. Library [810]

Aglionby, W *see* PAINTING ILLUSTRATED IN THREE DIALLOGUES

Aglipay y Labayan, Gregorio *see* BIBLIA FILIPINA

AGLL CATALOG – 3v – 4mf – 9 – $5.00mf – us A.G.L.L. [978]

AGMA (AMERICAN GEAR MANUFACTURERS ASSOCIATION) – Standards. Printed index. Updated every 60 days – 6,9 – us Info Handling [680]

Agmer-Ben-Ab-Dala *see* TRATADO DE LAS AGUAS MEDICINALES DE SALAM-BIR (8S.A.). TRAD. M. PIZZI

Agnelli, Giovanni *see* TOPO-CRONOGRAFIA DEL VIAGGIO DANTESCO

Agnelli, J *see* GALLERIA DI PITTURE DELL'... TOMMASO RUFFO, VESCOVO DI PALESTRINA E DI FERRARA...

AGNES DE CHAILLOT : COMEDIE / Biancolelli, Pierre-Francois – 2nd ed. Paris: chez Francois Flahaut, 1723. SEM105P1362 – 1mf – 9 – Can$2.25 – cn Bibl Nat [870]

AGNES HARCOURT, OR, "FOR HIS SAKE" : A CANADIAN STORY ILLUSTRATIVE OF THE POWER OF A CHILD'S LIFE – Montreal: Montreal Women's Printing Office, 1879. 04007. (Pre-1900 Canadiana) – 9 – cn C.I.H.M. [830]

AGNETHELER WOCHENBLATT – (Cont by: Agnetheler Zeitung) – Agnetheln, mar 18 1922-nov 29 1924 – 1r – 1 – Dist. gw Mikrofilm – gw Misc Inst [949]

AGNETHELER ZEITUNG *see* AGNETHELER WOCHENBLATT

Agnew, David C A *see* PROTESTANT EXILES FROM FRANCE..

LES AGNI / Delafosse, Maurice – Paris: Masson, 1893 – 9 – 5.00 – fr Orientalistes [960]

AGNI BAWANA / Pakem Kedjaksaan Tinggi – (Monthly) – Djakarta, 1966 – 1mf – 9 – SE-1302/1 – ne IDC [950]

L'AGNI. VARIETE IALECTALE SANVI / Retor, Georges – (Africa series). 1970 – 9 – fr Hachette [999]

Agno, Lydia Navarro *see* KUNG PAANO NAMUMUHAY AT GUMAGAWA ANG MGA TAO.

THE AGNOSTIC GOSPEL : A REVIEW OF HUXLEY ON THE BIBLE: WITH RELATED ESSAYS / Parker, Henry Webster – New York: John B Alden, 1896, c1895 – 1mf – 9 – 0-8370-4667-X – 1985-2667 – us A.T.L.A. [220]

AGNOSTIC JOURNAL – 1889-1907 – 1 – uk Microform Academic [210]

AN AGNOSTIC LOOKS AT LIFE; CHALLENGES OF A MILITANT PEN / Haldeman-Julius, Emanuel – Girard, Kan.: Haldeman-Julius Co., c1926. 128p – 1 – us U.W. Library [240]

AGNOSTICISM : A DOCTRINE OF DESPAIR: A BACCALAUREATE SERMON, JUNE 27, 1880 / Porter, Noah – New York: American Tract Society, [1880?] – 1mf – 9 – 0-8370-5117-7 – 1985-3117 – us A.T.L.A. [210]

AGNOSTICISM AND THEISM IN THE NINETEENTH CENTURY; AN HISTORICAL STUDY OF RELIGIOUS THOUGHT / Armstrong, Richard Acland – Six lectures, with introd. by Philip H. Wicksteed. London: P. Green, 1905. 207p – 1 – us U.W. Library [000]

AGNOSTICISM: SERMONS / Momerie, Alfred Williams – Edinburgh: William Blackwood, 1891. 1 fiche. 8370-4462-6 – 9 – us A.T.L.A. [240]

AN AGNOSTIC'S APOLOGY : AND OTHER ESSAYS / Stephen, Leslie – New York: G P Putnam; London: Smith, Elder, 1893 – 1mf – 9 – 0-8370-5398-6 – 1985-3398 – us A.T.L.A. [210]

AN AGNOSTIC'S APOLOGY : AND OTHER ESSAYS / Stephen, Leslie – New York: G.P. Putnam's Sons; London: Smith, Elder, 1893 – 1 roll – 1 – 1-55879-924-9 – uk Libr Preservation [190]

AGNOSTOT THEOS : UNTERSUCHUNGEN ZUR FORMENGESCHICHTE RELIGIOESER REDE / Norden, E – Leipzig-Berlin, 1913 – 8mf – 8 – Dfl3.50ea – ne Slangenburg [240]

Agobardus Lugdunensis *see* OPERA OMNIA

AGOEDATH JISRAEEL – Rotterdam. v. 1-6. 1926-32. BJ-261-7 1 – 9 – ne IDC [072]

LA AGONIA DEL PRINCIPE DE LA PAZ. DISCURSO...1923-1924 / Ossorio, Angel – Madrid: Est. Tip. Anonima Mefar, 1923 – 1 – sp Bibl Santa Ana [972]

AGONISTES – Prague, CS. Dec 1953-Jan 1954 – 1r – 1 – us L of C Photodup [072]

Agorastes, Phil *see* AMPHIOXUS AND ASCIDIAN: OUR GELATINOUS ANCESTORS: HOW THE MISSING LINKS WERE DISCOVERED AND MADE KNOWN

Agosti, Hector Pablo *see* PERON Y LA SEGUNDA GUERRA MUNDIAL

Agostini, Edouard *see* LA FRANCE ET LE CANADA: RAPPORT AU SYNDICAT MARITIME ET FLUVIAL DE FRANCE

Agozino, Adalberto C *see* LOS ESTILOS POLITICOS EN LA ARGENTINA 1853-1955

AGPS CATALOGUE ON MICROFICHE – monthly – 9 – at AusInfo [013]

AGR / University of Kentucky. Department of Agronomy – No.1-103. 1972-83. 14 fiches – 9 – us Spaulding [630]

AGRA AKHBAR – Agra, India. 1947-53 – 1r – 1 – us L of C Photodup [072]

AGRA AND GWALIOR / India. Preservation of National Monuments; ed by Cole, H H – Calcutta, 1885. BI-681 2 – 8 – ne IDC [720]

AGRAMER TAGBLATT – Zagreb, 15 Feb 1909-30 Apr 1912; 1-31 Dec 1913; 2 Jan-28 Feb 1914; 27 Jun-27 Jul 1914; 21 Feb-2 Apr 1919 (imperfect) – 6r – 1 – uk British Libr Newspaper [072]

AGRAMER TAGBLATT – Zagreb, Yugoslavia. 1-7 Jun 1918 – 1r – 1 – us L of C Photodup [949]

Agranovski i, Abram Davidovich et al *see* LI UDI-VREDITELI, SHAKHTINSKOE DELO

AGRAPHA AUSSERCANONISCHE EVANGELIENFRAGMENTE (T.U.U. 1-5/4A) / Resch, A – Leipzig, 1899 – 8mf – 9 – ne Slangenburg [240]

AGRAPHA AUSSERCANONISCHE PARALLELTEXTE ZU DEN EVANGELIEN : HEFT 1 T/M 5 (T.U.U. 1-10/1.2.3.4.5.) / Resch, A – Leipzig, 1893-1897 – 32p – 9 – ne Slangenburg [240]

AGRAPHA AUSSERCANONISCHE SCHRIFTFRAGMENTE (T.U.U. 2-30/3.4.) / Resch, A – Leipzig, 1906 – 7mf – 9 – ne Slangenburg [240]

THE AGRARIAN / South Carolina. Agricultural Experiment Station. Clemson – Dec 1938-Summer 1965 – 1,5 – us Spaulding [630]

AGRARIAN LAW AND JUDICIAL SYSTEMS – 1975 – 100p – it F.A.O. [340]

AGRARIAN PERIODICALS IN THE UNITED STATES – 1920-60. 41 periodical titles; 8 pamphlets in 18 groups – 25r – 1 – $2,405.00 – us UPA [630]

AGRARIAN RECONSTRUCTION – 1968 – 82p – it F.A.O. [630]

THE AGRARIAN REFORM – (Spain. Embajada. United States). Washington, DC. n.d. Fiche W 1176. (Blodgett Collection of Spanish Civil War Pamphlets) – 9 – us H.U. College Libr [946]

AGRARIAN REFORM AND LAND RECLAMATION IN TEN YEARS / Egypt. Ministry of Agrarian Reform – 1962? BNE-4646 1 – 9 – ne IDC [630]

AGRARIAN REFORM AND RURAL DEVELOPMENT – 1979 – 124p – it F.A.O. [307]

AGRARNAI A REVOLIUTSIIA : V CHETYREKH TOMAKH. KRESTI ANSKOE DVIZHENIE V 1917 GODU – Moskva: Izd-vo Kommunistichesko i akademii, [192-?]- – 1 – CSUX88-B2848 – us Hoover Inst Photo [320]

AGRARNYI VOPROS I KOOPERATSIIA : DOKLAD, CHITANNYI V.V. KRAINSKIM, [...] 20 DEK. 1905 G / Krainskii, V V – Spb., 1906 – 1mf – 9 – COR-52/1 – ne IDC [334]

AGRARNYI VOPROS I KOOPERATSIIA / Oganovskii, N P – M., 1917 – 1mf – 9 – COR-80/1 – ne IDC [334]

AGRARNYI VOPROS O ZEMLE I ZEMEL'NYKH PORIADKAKH / Kondrat'ev, N D – M., 1917 – 1mf – 9 – COR-199/1 – ne IDC [334]

AGRARNYI VOPROS V ROSSII I EGO RESHENIE V PROGRAMMAKH RAZLICHNYKH PARTII / Rozhkov, N – M., 1906. 41p – 1mf – 9 – ne IDC [320]

AGREEMENT BETWEEN H.M.'S GOVERNMENT AND THE FRENCH GOVERNMENT RESPECTING THE BOUNDARY LINE BETWEEN SYRIA AND PALESTINE FROM THE MEDITERRANEAN TO EL HAMME / Great Britain – London. 1923. BJ-28-89 1 – 9 – ne IDC [956]

AGREEMENT BETWEEN PALESTINE AND SYRIA AND THE LEBANON AMENDING THE AGREEMENT OF 2 FEB 1926, REGARDING FRONTIER QUESTIONS / Palestine. Treaties – 3 Nov 1938. London. 1939. BJ-28-103 1 – 9 – ne IDC [956]

THE AGREEMENT BETWEEN UNION SEMINARY AND THE GENERAL ASSEMBLY / Prentiss, George L – New York: A.D.F. Randolph, c1892 – 1mf – us A.T.L.A. [240]

AGREEMENT ESTABLISHING AN ASSOCIATION BETWEEN THE EUROPEAN ECONOMIC COMMUNITY AND THE KINGDOM OF MAROCCO / Morocco. European Economic Community – Geneva. 1969. BNE-3051 1 – 9 – ne IDC [337]

AGREEMENT FOR TRANSPORT OF QUEENSLAND CONTINGENT TO SOUTH AFRICA, 1899-1899 / Chief Secretary's Office, Queensland – 5r – 1 – CRS B5176 – at Archives [920]

AGREEMENT OF EVOLUTION AND CHRISTIANITY / Phillips, Samuel Louis – Washington: Phillips, 1904. 1 fiche. 8370-4734-X – 9 – us A.T.L.A. [240]

THE AGREEMENT OF SCIENCE AND REVELATION / Wythe, Joseph Henry – Philadelphia: J.B. Lippincott, 1872. 1 fiche – 9 – us A.T.L.A. [240]

AGREGACION TEMPORAL PROCESOS ESTOCASTICOS DISCRETOS DE MEDIAS MOVILES / Carrion Garcia, Andres – 1mf – 9 – Pta1,000.00 – 84-85422-65-1 – sp Pentalfa [610]

LES AGREMENS DU LANGAGE / Gamaches, P E S de le – 1718 – 9 – fr I.C.S. [400]

L'AGREMENT DES CONCERTS DE LA RUE FEYDEAU. PAR LE CITOYEN N... S... – Paris: Laurens, 1795 – 1mf – 9 – us Sibley [780]

AG-RESEARCH BRIEFS / Georgia. Agricultural Experiment Station. Athens – v. 1-5. 1955-59 – 1,5,6 – us Spaulding [630]

THE AGREVIEW / Virginia. Polytechnic Institute. College of Agriculture – v. 1-26. 1926-64 – 1,5,6 – us Spaulding [630]

AGRI FINANCE – (Former titles: Agricultural Banker (nov 1959-oct 1962); Agricultural Banking and Finance (nov 1962-aug 1968)) – Niles. v1-39. 1959-1997+' – 1 – D15341 – us UMI [334]

AGRI MARKETING – Skokie. v1-35 Spr 1963-dec 1997+ 1'; v27-25 jan 1989-dec 1997+ 5',9 – 1,5,9 – D15342 – us UMI [380]

AGRI-BOOK MAGAZINE – Exeter. v15- 1989- – 9 – Can$20.00y – 0705-3878 – cn Micromedia [630]

Agribozli Nu'man Mahir, Beg *see* DIVAN

AGRIBUSINESS – New York. v1-13. Spr 1985-dec 1997+ 1,5',9 – 1,5,9 – D14802 – us UMI [338]

AGRICOL VIALA OU LE JEUNE HEROS DE LA DURANCE / Madelaine, Philipon de la & Jadin, L – French Theatre Series. Paris. Barba, an II. 1794 – 9 – fr Hachette [820]

AGRICOLA ARIDUS / Colorado. College of Agriculture – v.1-2. 1901-02 – 1,5,6 – us Spaulding [630]

Agricola, F *see* TRATTENIMENTI SULLE VERNICI, ED ALTRE MATERIE UTILI.

Agricola, F et al *see* ORATIO DE BELLO ADVERSVS TVRCAM, AD FERDINANDUM VNGARIAE ET BOHEMIAE REGEM, ET PRINCIPES

Agricola, Martin *see*
- MUSICA CHORALIS DEUDSCH
- MUSICA FIGURALIS DEUDSCH
- MUSICA INSTRUMENTALIS DEUDSCH
- MUSICA INSTRUMENTALIS DEUDSCH..
- QUAESTIONES VULGATIORES IN MUSICAN, PRO MAGDEBURGENSIS SCHOLAE PUERIS DIGESTAE
- RUDIMENTA MUSICES..

AGRICOLA'S SPRICHWORTER / Latendorf, Friedrich – 1862 – 1 – us I.U. Libraries [390]

L'AGRICULTEUR : J'L OFFICIEL DE LA CHAMBRE D'AGRICULTURE DU BAS-CANADA – Tome 9 n1. sep 1858-2 aut 1861 – 1 – cn Can Microfilming [072]

L'AGRICULTEUR : JOURNAL OFFICIEL DE LA CHAMBRE D'AGRICULTURE DU BAS-CANADA / La Chambre d'Agriculture du Bas-Canada. Montreal – Montreal. v11-13. Aug 1858-80 – 1r – 1 – Can$50.00 – cn Can Microfilming [630]

L'AGRICULTEUR – Montreal: De Montigny, [1857-1862?] – 9 – cn C.I.H.M. [630]

L'AGRICULTEUR – Saint-Boniface, Man.: A. Gauvin, [1889-1891] – 9 – cn C.I.H.M. [630]

AGRICULTEUR *see* REVUE AGRICOLE, MANUFACTURIERE, COMMERCIALE ET DE COLONISATION

L'AGRICULTEUR CANADIEN – Montreal: H.A. Chaput, v1 no 1 (juin 1886)- – 9 – cn C.I.H.M. [630]

L'AGRICULTEUR DE LA MAYENNE – Sept. 1930 – April 1941 – 2r – fr Armell [630]

AGRICULTEURS (INTEGRAUX) SUR BRULIS EN ASIE DU SUD-EST / Lenclud, G – 9 – F60.00 – fr Ethnologie [305]

EL AGRICULTOR – Aldeanueva del Camino, 1908. Numeros sueltos – 5 – sp Bibl Santa Ana [073]

O AGRICULTOR BAHIANO – [s.l.]-BA, Brazil. 27 Jan-21 Abr 1866 – 1 – bl Biblioteca [630]

AGRICULTOR SERGIPANO : ORGAO EXCLUSIVO DA AGRICULTURA DO COMMERICO – Aracaju, 9 Jun, Aug, 3 Nov 1881 – 1,5,6 – bl Biblioteca [072]

AGRICULTURA METODICA...NATURALEZA / Zepeda y Vivero, Juan A – 1791 – 9 – 1.50f – sp Bibl Santa Ana [630]

AGRICULTURA TECHNICA – (1980- 5,6,9) – 1944-. Continues Boletin de Sanidad Vegetal – 1 – us UMI [630]

AGRICULTURAL ADJUSTMENT IN DEVELOPED COUNTRIES – 1972 – 204p – it F.A.O. [631]

AGRICULTURAL ADMINISTRATION – v1-17. 1974-84 – 1,5,6,13 – sz Elsevier [630]

AGRICULTURAL ADMINISTRATION *see* AGRICULTURAL ADMINISTRATION AND EXTENSION

AGRICULTURAL ADMINISTRATION – (Cont by: Agricultural Administration and Extension) – Barking. v1-23. 1974-1986 – 1,5 – D42007 – us UMI [630]

AGRICULTURAL ADMINISTRATION AND EXTENSION – (Absorbed by: Agricultural Systems. Cont: Agricultural Administration) – Barking. v24-30 1987-1988 1,5; v28-30 1988 9 – 1,5,9 – D42007.01 – us UMI [630]

AGRICULTURAL ADMINISTRATION AND EXTENSION *see*
- AGRICULTURAL ADMINISTRATION
- AGRICULTURAL SYSTEMS

AGRICULTURAL AND BIOLOGICAL CHEMISTRY – v25-43. 1961-79 – 1,5,6 – us Princeton Micro [630]

AGRICULTURAL AND ECONOMIC STATISTICS / Egypt. Ministry of Agriculture – 1949 – 9 – ne IDC [630]

AGRICULTURAL AND FOREST METEOROLOGY – (Micro-ed includes Vol 1 of the supplement: Atlas. Former title: Agricultural Meteorology (mar 1964-jan 1984)) – Amsterdam. v1- 1964- 1,5; v41-oct 1987- 9 – 1,5,9 – D42239 – us UMI [634]

AGRICULTURAL AND HORTICULTURAL SEEDS – 2nd printing 1978 – 531p – it F.A.O. [634]

Agricultural and Industrial Exhibition (1878: Truro, Nova Scotia) *see* GENERAL REGULATIONS AND PRIZE LIST

Agricultural and Industrial Exhibition (1880: Kentville, Nova Scotia) *see* GENERAL REGULATIONS AND PRIZE LIST

AGRICULTURAL AND INDUSTRIAL MAGAZINE : CANADIAN QUARTERLY – Montreal. v1 n1. may 1938. v1 n2. aug 1838 – 1r – 1 – Can$25.00 – cn Can Microfilming [072]

Agricultural and Industrial Provincial Exhibition (1885: Kentville, Nova Scotia) *see* PRIZE LIST

Agricultural and Rural Workers *see* RURAL WORKER

Agricultural and Trades Association of Okanagan Mission Valley *see* A SHORT HISTORY OF KELOWNA AND ITS SURROUNDINGS IN THE PROVINCE OF BRITISH COLUMBIA, DOMINION OF CANADA

AGRICULTURAL BANKER *see* AGRI FINANCE

AGRICULTURAL BANKING AND FINANCE *see* AGRI FINANCE

AGRICULTURAL CAPITAL FORMATION IN SELECTED DEVELOPING COUNTRIES – 1973 – 43p – it F.A.O. [332]

AGRICULTURAL CENSUS LEGISLATION – 1984 – 122p – it F.A.O. [340]

AGRICULTURAL CENSUS OF EGYPT / Egypt. Ministry of Agriculture – 1939. 1946. BNE-4650 1 – 9 – ne IDC [630]

AGRICULTURAL CHEMICAL SERVICES SERIES / Clemson University. Agricultural Experiment Station – No.5-11.1970-82. 1 reel – 1,5 – us Spaulding [630]

AGRICULTURAL CHEMICAL SERVICES SERIES / South Carolina. Agricultural Experiment Station. Clemson – n.1-4. 1966-69 – 1,5 – us Spaulding [630]

AGRICULTURAL CHEMICALS *see* AG CHEM AND COMMERCIAL FERTILIZER

AGRICULTURAL CHEMICALS CONFERENCE FOR PESTICIDE DEALERS AND APPLICATORS 1967-82 / Oklahoma State University. Cooperative Extension Service – 1,5 – us Spaulding [630]

AGRICULTURAL CHEMICALS HANDBOOK / Clemson University. Agricultural Extension Division – 1982. 6 fiches – 9 – us Spaulding [630]

AGRICULTURAL COLLEGE SPECIAL BULLETIN: FOOD DEPT / North Dakota. Agricultural Experiment Station. Fargo – no.1-v.6, no.2. 1903-20 – 1,5,6 – us Spaulding [630]

AGRICULTURAL COMMITTEE / UN Economic Commission for Europe (ECE) – 1947-88 – E/F.85 E.2488 F.2436 R.2023 – 9 – us U.N. Pubs [340]

AGRICULTURAL COMMUNICATIONS RESEARCH REPORT / Illinois. College of Agriculture – Nos 1-20 1960-64 – 1,5 – us Spaulding [630]

AN AGRICULTURAL CONCILIATION COMMISSIONER'S GUIDE. / Rood, John Romain – Detroit: Detroit Law Book Co. 1934. 66p. LL-1104 – 1 – us L of C Photodup [340]

AGRICULTURAL COOPERATIVE MARKETING / Digby, M & Gretton, R – 1978 – 80p – it F.A.O. [334]

AGRICULTURAL CREDIT – 1978 rev ed 1983 – 381p – it F.A.O. [332]

AGRICULTURAL CREDIT BIBLIOGRAPHY. NO 4 (1985) – 1985 – 47p – it F.A.O. [332]

AGRICULTURAL CREDIT LEGISLATION IN SELECTED DEVELOPING COUNTRIES – 1974 – 144p – it F.A.O. [340]

AGRICULTURAL DEVELOPMENT AND EMPLOYMENT PERFORMANCE AND PLANNING : A COMPARATIVE ANALYSIS – 1974 – 144p – it F.A.O. [338]

AGRICULTURAL DEVELOPMENT AND RESEARCH IN SYRIA / American University of Beirut. Syria. (Faculty of agricultural sciences) – 1956. BNE-9725 1 – 9 – ne IDC [630]

AGRICULTURAL DEVELOPMENT IN MODERN JAPAN : THE SIGNIFICANCE OF THE JAPANESE EXPERIENCE – 1976 – 32p – it F.A.O. [630]

AGRICULTURAL DEVELOPMENT PROPOSALS, 1966-1970 / Ceylon. Ministry of Planning and Economic Affairs – Colombo. 1966 – 9 – ne IDC [630]

AGRICULTURAL ECONOMIC REPORT / North Dakota. Agricultural Experiment Station. Fargo – nos.1-111.1951-75 – 1,5,6 – us Spaulding [330]

AGRICULTURAL ECONOMIC RESEARCH / U.S. Department of Agriculture – v1-38. 1949-86.150 fiches – 9 – 180.00 – us Updata [338]

AGRICULTURAL ECONOMIC RESEARCH MONOGRAPH / Vermont. Agricultural Experiment Station – v. 1-45. 1947-68 – 1,5,6 – us Spaulding [330]

AGRICULTURAL ECONOMICS / Wisconsin. College of Agricultural and Life Sciences. Dept. of Agricultural Economics – no.1-55. Aug 1951-Sep 1969 – 1,5 – us Spaulding [338]

AGRICULTURAL ECONOMICS – Amsterdam. v1- dec 1986- 1,5; v2- 1988- 9 – 1,5,9 – D42498 – us UMI [630]

AGRICULTURAL ECONOMICS CIRCULAR / Tennessee. University. Agricultural Experiment Station – n.1-6, Mar 1958-Sep 1961 – 1,5 – us Spaulding [330]

AGRICULTURAL ECONOMICS EXTENSION SERIES AND INFORMATION SERIES / University of Kentucky. Cooperative Extension Service – No.1-52.1967-83. 22 fiches – 9 – us Spaulding [338]

AGRICULTURAL ECONOMICS MIMEOGRAPH / Alabama. Agricultural Experiment Station – 1963. 2 fiches – 9 – us Spaulding [630]

AGRICULTURAL ECONOMICS MISCELLANY REPORT / North Dakota. Agricultural Experiment Station. Fargo. Dept. of Agricultural Economics – nos.1-21. 1968-75 – 1,5,6 – us Spaulding [630]

AGRICULTURAL ECONOMICS PAMPHLETS / South Dakota. State University. Agricultural Experiment Station – nos.1-145. 1941-74 – 1,5,6 – us Spaulding [630]

AGRICULTURAL ECONOMICS REPORT / Kansas. State University. Agricultural Experiment Station – nos.1-106. 1940-65 – 1,5,6 – us Spaulding [338]

AGRICULTURAL ECONOMICS RESEARCH – (Cont by: Journal of Agricultural Economics Research) – Washingont. v1-39 jan 1949-Win 1987 1; v23-39 jan 1971-Fal 1987 5; v27-39 jan 1975-Win 1987 9 – 1,5,9 – D1846 – us UMI [630]

AGRICULTURAL ECONOMICS SERIES / Alabama. Agricultural Experiment Station – v. 1-20. 1963-70 – 1,5,6 – us Spaulding [630]

AGRICULTURAL ECONOMICS SERIES / Auburn University. Agricultural Experiment Station – no.21-33. 1970-79. 1 reel – 1, 5 – us Spaulding [338]

AGRICULTURAL ECONOMICS SPECIAL REPORT N.2 / Virginia. Agricultural Experiment Station. Blacksburg – 1fiche – 9 – us Spaulding [338]

AGRICULTURAL ECONOMICS STATISTICAL SERIES / North Dakota. Agricultural Experiment Station. Fargo. Dept. of Agricultural Economics – nos.1-21. 1967-75 – 1,5,6 – us Spaulding [630]

AGRICULTURAL ECONOMY / Egypt. Ministry of Agriculture – 1958. Suppl. BNE-4647 1 – 9 – ne IDC [630]

THE AGRICULTURAL ECONOMY OF THE SUDAN / U.S. Department of Agriculture – Warren, C. 1958. BNE-7697 1 – 9 – ne IDC [338]

THE AGRICULTURAL ECONOMY OF THE UNITED ARAB REPUBLIC / U.S. Department of Agriculture – Warren, C. J. 1964. BNE-4681 1 – 9 – ne IDC [630]

AGRICULTURAL EDUCATION *see* AGRICULTURAL EDUCATION MAGAZINE

AGRICULTURAL EDUCATION: A LECTURE DELIVERED BEFORE THE YOUNG MEN'S CHRISTIAN ASSOCIATION, CHARLOTTETOWN, P. E. ISLAND, ON THURSDAY EVENING, JANUARY 17, 1884 / Ferguson, Donald – s.l.: s.n., 1884? (Charlottetown, P.E. I.: J. Mitchell). 03087. (Pre-1900 Canadiana) – 9 – cn C.I.H.M. [370]

AGRICULTURAL EDUCATION MAGAZINE – (Former titles: Agricultural Education (jan 1929-may 1937); Agricultural Education Magazine (jul 1937-jun 1962); Agricultural Education (jul 1962-dec 1979)) – Henry. v1-70 jan 1929-jun 1998+ 1; v47-70 jul 1974-jun 1998+ 5; v48-70 jul 1975-jun 1998+ 9 – 1,5,9 – D10338 – us UMI [630]

Agricultural Education Survey Team *see* REPORT

AGRICULTURAL EMPLOYMENT IN DEVELOPING COUNTRIES – 1977 – 48p – it F.A.O. [331]

AGRICULTURAL ENGINEER – (Cont: Landwards. Former titles: Proceedings, Institution of British Agricultural Engineers, (1942-1948); Journal of the Institution of British Agricultural Engineers (1949-1957); Journal and Proceedings of the Institution of British Agricultural Engineers (1958-oct 1959); Journal and Proceedings of the Institution of Agricultural Engineers (1960-Win 1971)) – Rickmansworth. 1942-1972 v34-50 Spr 1979-Win 1995 1 – 1 – D8678 – us UMI [630]

THE AGRICULTURAL ENGINEER: FARM BUILDING / Nebraska. College of Agriculture. Extension Service – n.1-3. 1948-51 – 1, 5 – us Spaulding [620]

THE AGRICULTURAL ENGINEER: IRRIGATION / Nebraska. College of Agriculture. Extension Service – no 1 1949 – 1, 5 – us Spaulding [630]

THE AGRICULTURAL ENGINEER: RURAL ELECTRIFICATION / Nebraska. College of Agriculture. Extension Service – n.1 and 2. 1948-49 – 1, 5 – us Spaulding [630]

AGRICULTURAL ENGINEERING – (Cont in pt by: Resource) – St Joseph. v1-75 sep 1920-mar 1994 1; v47-75 jan 1966-mar 1994 5; v58-75 jan 1977-mar 1994 9 – 1,5,9 – D767 – us UMI [630]

AGRICULTURAL ENGINEERING DEPARTMENTAL SERIES / Auburn University. Agricultural Experiment Station – No.1. 1976. 1 reel – 1, 5 – us Spaulding [630]

AGRICULTURAL ENGINEERING HANDBOOK / Clemson University. Agricultural Extension Division – No.4-15.1970-82. 8 fiches – 9 – us Spaulding [630]

AGRICULTURAL ENGINEERING IN DEVELOPMENT : GUIDELINES FOR ESTABLISHMENT OF VILLAGE WORKSHOPS – 1988 – 71p – it F.A.O. [620]

AGRICULTURAL ENGINEERING NEWSLETTER / Minnesota. College of Agriculture. Department of Agricultural Engineering – 15 Apr 1932-15 Jun 1941. Nos 1-111 – 1,5,6 – us Spaulding [630]

AGRICULTURAL ENGINEERING PAMPHLET / South Dakota. State University. Agricultural Experiment Station – Nos 1-4 1941-49 – 1,5,6 – us Spaulding [630]

AGRICULTURAL ENGINEERING RESEARCH SERIES / Clemson University. Agricultural Experiment Station – No.12-25. 1970-82. 1 reel – 1,5 – us Spaulding [630]

AGRICULTURAL ENGINEERING RESEARCH SERIES / South Carolina. Agricultural Experiment Station. Clemson – Nos 1-11 1960-68 – 1,5 – us Spaulding [630]

AGRICULTURAL EXTENSION : A REFERENCE MANUAL – 1972 2nd ed 1984 – 273p – it F.A.O. [630]

AGRICULTURAL EXTENSION AND AGRICULTURAL RESEARCH, INDONESIA; REPORT FOR YEARS 1951-1956 / U.S. Operations Mission to Indonesia – SE 5686 1. 1957 – 9 – ne IDC [630]

AGRICULTURAL EXTENSION SYSTEMS IN SOME AFRICAN AND ASIAN COUNTRIES – 1984 – 80p – it F.A.O. [630]

AGRICULTURAL FINANCE REVIEW – (Publ suspended Vol 35 (oct 1974) and resumed Vol 36 (apr 1976)) – Washington. v1- may 1938- 1; v36- apr 1976- 5*,9 – 1,5,9 – D5755 – us UMI [630]

AGRICULTURAL GROWTH AND FACTOR PRODUCTIVITY IN DEVELOPING COUNTRIES – 1984 – 80p – it F.A.O. [338]

AGRICULTURAL HANDBOOKS / U.S. Department of Agriculture – Nos. 1-663. 1377 fiches – 9 – 2000.00 – us Updata [630]

AGRICULTURAL HISTORY – Berkeley. v1-71 jan 1927-Win/Fall 1997+ 1; v39-71 jan 1965-Win/Fall 1997+ 5; v49-71 jan 1975-Win/Fall 1997+ 9 – 1,5,9 – D901 – us UMI [630]

AGRICULTURAL HISTORY – Berkeley. v1- jan 1927- 1; v39- jan 1965- 5; v49- jan 1975- 9 – 1,5,9 – D901 – us UMI [630]

AGRICULTURAL HISTORY REVIEW – Reading. Cum index v1-18 1953-70; v1-45 1953-1997+ – 1,5,9 – D10687 – us UMI [630]

AGRICULTURAL HISTORY SERIES – (Ceased publ) – Washingont. cum index 1-7; v1-7. 1941-1943 – 1 – D5756 – us UMI [630]

AGRICULTURAL HOLDINGS IN THE 1970 WORLD CENSUS OF AGRICULTURE : A STATISTICAL ANALYSIS – 1984 – 49p – it F.A.O. [310]

AGRICULTURAL INSURANCE LEGISLATION – 1981 – 156p – it F.A.O. [340]

AGRICULTURAL ISSUES IN STRUCTURAL ADJUSTMENT PROGRAMS – 1987 – 92p – it F.A.O. [338]

AGRICULTURAL JOURNAL AND TRANSACTIONS OF THE LOWER CANADA AGRICULTURAL SOCIETY – (Cont: The Canadian Agricultural Journal) – Montreal: Lovell & Gibson, [1847?-1853] – 9 – cn C.I.H.M. [630]

AGRICULTURAL JOURNAL AND TRANSACTIONS OF THE LOWER CANADA AGRICULTURAL SOCIETY *see* THE CANADIAN AGRICULTURAL JOURNAL

AGRICULTURAL LABOUR MARKETS AND STRUCTURAL ADJUSTMENT IN SUB-SAHARAN AFRICA – 1991 – 90p – it F.A.O. [331]

AGRICULTURAL LAW JOURNAL – (Cont by: Journal of Agricultural Taxation and Law) – Wilmette. v1-4. Spr 1979-Win 1983* – 1 – D13454 – us UMI [073]

Agricultural Library, Wageningen, Netherlands *see* BIBLIOGRAPHY OF AGRICULTURAL BIBLIOGRAPHIES, 1960-1977

AGRICULTURAL MARKET INTERVENTION AND PRICING POLICIES IN AFRICA – 1990 – 256p – it F.A.O. [650]

AGRICULTURAL MARKETING – (Ceased publ) – Washington. v1-16. jul 1956-jul 1971 – 1 – D3191 – us UMI [630]

AGRICULTURAL MARKETING BOARDS : THEIR ESTABLISHMENT AND OPERATION – 1974 – 236p – it F.A.O. [650]

AGRICULTURAL MARKETING, SEED PRODUCTION FARM, AGRICULTURAL CREDIT, PUBLIC LAW, 480 CEREALS / Siple, V A – Jordan. 1959? BNE-9812 1 – 9 – ne IDC [380]

AGRICULTURAL MECHANIZATION IN DEVELOPMENT : GUIDELINES FOR STRATEGY FORMULATION – 1981 repr 1986 – 79p – it F.A.O. [631]

AGRICULTURAL METEOROLOGY – v1-32 1964-84 – 1,5,6,13 – sz Elsevier [550]

AGRICULTURAL METEOROLOGY *see* AGRICULTURAL AND FOREST METEOROLOGY

AGRICULTURAL MUSEUM – (Ceased publ) – Georgetown. v1-2. jul 1810-may 1812 – 1 – D3537 – us UMI [630]

AGRICULTURAL NEWS REPORT / Mississippi. State College. Agricultural Extension Service – v. 1, no. 1-4. 1937 – 1,5,6 – us Spaulding [630]

AGRICULTURAL NOTEBOOK: ENGINEERING NEWS / Nebraska. College of Agriculture – nos 1-124 1962-69 – 1,5 – us Spaulding [630]

AGRICULTURAL NOTEBOOK: INSECT LETTER / Nebraska. College of Agriculture – 1954-69 – 1,5 – us Spaulding [630]

AGRICULTURAL NOTEBOOK: PLANT PATHOLOGY / Nebraska. College of Agriculture – n.1-74 and index. 1967-69 – 1,5 – us Spaulding [630]

AGRICULTURAL OUTLOOK – (Cont: Agricultural Outlook Digest) – Washington. v1 1975-77* 1; v29-247 jan 1978-dec 1997+ 1,5,9 – 1,5,9 – D11789 – us UMI [630]

AGRICULTURAL OUTLOOK *see* AGRICULTURAL OUTLOOK DIGEST

AGRICULTURAL OUTLOOK DIGEST *see* AGRICULTURAL OUTLOOK

AGRICULTURAL OUTLOOK DIGEST – (Ceased publ. Cont by: Agricultural Outlook) – Washington. jan 1974-may 1975 – 1,5,9* – D7426 – us UMI [630]

AGRICULTURAL PLANNING COURSE 1963 – 1976 – 222p – it F.A.O. [338]

AGRICULTURAL PLANNING COURSE 1965 – 1976 – 208p – it F.A.O. [338]

AGRICULTURAL PLANNING COURSE, PORT-OF-SPAIN, 1969 – 1975 – 84p – it F.A.O. [338]

AGRICULTURAL PLANNING SERIES / Montana. Agricultural Extension Service – 1936-42 – 1,5,6 – us Spaulding [630]

AGRICULTURAL POLICIES, PROTECTIONISM AND TRADE : SELECTED WORKING PAPERS, 1985-1987 – 1988 – 65p – it F.A.O. [380]

AGRICULTURAL POLICY REVIEW / North Carolina. State University. Raleigh. Agricultural Policy Institute – v.1-10. 1961-70 – 1,5 – us Spaulding [630]

AGRICULTURAL PRICE POLICIES : ISSUES AND PROPOSALS – 1987 – 211p – it F.A.O. [338]

AGRICULTURAL PRICE POLICIES IN THE NEAR EAST : LESSONS OF EXPERIENCE – 1989 – 101p – it F.A.O. [338]

AGRICULTURAL PRICES AND EXPORT EARNINGS : THE EXPERIENCE OF DEVELOPING COUNTRIES IN THE 1970S – 1984 – 58p – it F.A.O. [380]

AGRICULTURAL PRODUCTION IN MISSISSIPPI / Mississippi. Agricultural Experiment Station. State College – 1943-49 – 1,5,6 – us Spaulding [338]

THE AGRICULTURAL PROGRAM UNDER TAIWANS THIRD 4-YEAR PLAN / China. Republic. Ministry of Economic Affairs.Agricultural Planning and Coordination Committee – Taipei. 1961. BD-432 1 – 9 – ne IDC [630]

AGRICULTURAL RAW MATERIALS : COMPETITION WITH SYNTHETIC SUBSTITUTES – 1984 – 65p – it F.A.O. [630]

AGRICULTURAL RESEARCH / U.S. Department of Agriculture – v1-34. 1953-86.360 fiches – 9 – 410.00 – us Updata [630]

AGRICULTURAL RESEARCH – Washington. v1- jan 1953- 1; v19- jul 1970- 5; v24- jul 1975- 9 – 1,5,9 – D1711 – us UMI [630]

AGRICULTURAL RESEARCH IN INDIA : AN OVERVIEW OF ITS ORGANIZATION, MANAGEMENT AND OPERATIONS – 1987 – 266p – it F.A.O. [630]

AGRICULTURAL RESEARCH POLICY AND DEVELOPMENT – 1987 – 257p – it F.A.O. [350]

AGRICULTURAL RESIDUES : BIBLIOGRAPHY 1975-81 AND QUANTITATIVE SURVEY – 1981 – 171p – it F.A.O. [631]

AGRICULTURAL RESIDUES : COMPENDIUM OF TECHNOLOGIES – 1982 – 632p – it F.A.O. [631]

AGRICULTURAL RESIDUES : WORLD DIRECTORY OF INSTITUTIONS – 1982 – 222p – it F.A.O. [060]

AGRICULTURAL SCIENCE REVIEW – (Ceased publ) – Washington. cum index 1-4 Fal 1963-1966; v1-11 Fal 1963-1973 1; v9-11 1971-1973 5 – 1,5 – D2412 – us UMI [630]

AGRICULTURAL SECTOR ANALYSIS AND MODELS IN DEVELOPING COUNTRIES – 1982 – 415p – it F.A.O. [338]

AGRICULTURAL SITUATION / U.S. Department of Agriculture – v1-63. 1921-79.155 fiches – 9 – 230.00 – us Updata [630]

AGRICULTURAL SITUATION *see* FARMLINE

AGRICULTURAL SITUATION – (Merged with: Farm Index; To form: Farmline. Former title: Monthly Notes, Farm Management and Farm Economics (jan 1922-jun 1922)) – Washington. v1-63 jan 1922-dec 1979 1; v55-63 jan 1971-dec 1979 5; v58-63 jan 1974-dec 1979 9* – 1,5,9 – D372 – us UMI [630]

AGRICULTURAL STABILIZATION AND STRUCTURAL ADJUSTMENT POLICIES IN DEVELOPING COUNTRIES – 1987 – 100p – it F.A.O. [338]

AGRICULTURAL STATISTICS / North Dakota. Agricultural Experiment Station. Fargo. Dept. of Agricultural Economics – nos.1-36. 1959-75 – 1,5,6 – us Spaulding [630]

AGRICULTURAL STATISTICS / Putnam County. Ohio. Auditor – 1912 – 1r – 1 – $32.50r – us Archival [324]

AGRICULTURAL STATISTICS : UNITED KINGDOM 1867-1975 – (Coll title: British Government Publications...1801-1977, Agriculture) – 9r – 1 – £490.00 – uk Chadwyck [630]

AGRICULTURAL STATISTICS / U.S. Department of Agriculture – 1936-85.364 fiches – 9 – 460.00 – us Updata [630]

AGRICULTURAL STATISTICS – Washington. 1936- 1,5; 1972- 9* – 1,5,9 – D5791 – us UMI [630]

AGRICULTURAL STATISTICS: BULLETIN / Sudan. Dept. of Agriculture – 7v. in 6. 1960-67. BNE-7609 1 – 9 – ne IDC [630]

AGRICULTURAL STATISTICS BY PLOT TO PLOT ENUMERATION IN BENGAL, 1944-45 / Bengal Govt. Department of Agriculture, Forest and Fisheries – Alipore: Bengal Govt Press, 1946-[194-?]. pts1-3 – 1 – us Res Libr [950]

AGRICULTURAL STATISTICS FOR CYRENAICA, 1959 / Libya. Provincial Government of Cyrenaica. Statistics Division – Mar 1960. Nazirate of Agriculture and Forests. BNE-1025 1 – 9 – ne IDC [310]

AGRICULTURAL STATISTICS IN LIBYA / Libya. Ministry of Agriculture – Tripoli. 1963. BNE-1005 1 – 9 – ne IDC [338]

AGRICULTURAL SUSTAINABILITY : DEFINITION AND IMPLICATIONS FOR AGRICULTURAL AND TRADE POLICY – 1992 – 115p – it F.A.O. [338]

AGRICULTURAL SYSTEMS – v1-15. 1976-84 – 1,5,6,13 – sz Elsevier [630]

AGRICULTURAL SYSTEMS *see* AGRICULTURAL ADMINISTRATION AND EXTENSION

AGRICULTURAL SYSTEMS – (Absorbed: Agricultural Administration and Extension (1989) & Research and Development in Agriculture (1989)) – Barking. v1- jan 1976- 1,5; v26- 1988- 9 – 1,5,9 – D42008 – us UMI [630]

AGRICULTURAL TAXATION IN ETHIOPIA – 1992 – 96p – it F.A.O. [336]

AGRICULTURAL TAXATION IN MALAYSIA – 1992 – 81p – it F.A.O. [336]

AGRICULTURAL TAXATION IN THE PHILIPPINES – 1992 – 119p – it F.A.O. [336]

AGRICULTURAL TRENDS / Vermont. Agricultural Extension Service – 1939-41 – 1,5,6 – us Spaulding [630]

AGRICULTURAL UNIONIST *see* SHARECROPPER'S VOICE, 1935-1937 : SOUTHERN FARM LEADER, 1936 : STFU NEWS, 1938-1939 : TENANT FARMER, 1941-1942 : FARM WORKER, 1943-1944 : FARM LABOR NEWS, 1946-1951 : THE UNION FARMER, 1952-1953 : AGRICULTURAL UNIONIST, 1952-1954

AGRICULTURAL WASTES – v1-11. 1979-84 – 1,5,6,13 – sz Elsevier [630]

AGRICULTURAL WASTES – (Cont by: Biological Wastes) – London. v1-18. feb 1979-1986 – 1,5 – D42009 – us UMI [630]

AGRICULTURAL WATER MANAGEMENT – v1-9. 1976-84 – 1,5,6,13 – sz Elsevier [631]

AGRICULTURAL WATER MANAGEMENT – Amsterdam. v1- dec 1976- 1,5*; v14- aug 1988- 9 – 1,5,9 – D42010 – us UMI [630]

AGRICULTURAL WEATHER RESEARCH SERIES / Clemson University. Agricultural Experiment Station – Nos 22-58 1970-82 – 1r – 1,5 – us Spaulding [630]

AGRICULTURAL WEATHER RESEARCH SERIES / South Carolina. Agricultural Experiment Station. Clemson – Nos 1-21 1964-69 – 1,5 – us Spaulding [630]

AGRICULTURAL WEATHER SERIES / Alabama. Agricultural Experiment Station – v1-12 1964-75 – 1,5,6 – us Spaulding [630]

AGRICULTURAL WEATHER SERIES / Auburn University. Agricultural Experiment Station – Nos 13-22 1976-82 – 1r – 1,5 – us Spaulding [630]

AGRICULTURAL WRITERS / McDonald, D – London, 1908. B-7648 1 – 4mf – 9 – ne IDC [630]

THE AGRICULTURALIST AND CANADIAN JOURNAL *see* THE CANADA FARMER

AGRICULTURE – (1: Dominican Republic; Adaptive Agricultural Research Project 1981-1985 (Agricultural University Wageningen) 37mf Dfl370.00; 2: Philippines; The Role of Social Anthropology/Sociology in Agricultural Research 1982-1986 (Wageningen – IRRI Program) 16mf Dfl160.00; 3: Sri Lanka; Popular participation in planned development at village level 1981-1985 (Agricultural University Wageningen) 134mf Dfl1,340.00; 4: Bibliography of Agricultural Bibliographies 1960-1977 (Agricultural University Wageningen) 222mf Dfl1,341.00) – 69 serials and 4 special collections – 9 – ne IDC [630]

AGRICULTURE / Nebraska. College of Agriculture – n.1-20. 1902-21 – 1,5 – us Spaulding [630]

AGRICULTURE – (Former titles: Journal of the Board of Agriculture (sep 1894-dec 1919); Journal of the Ministry of Agriculture (jan 1920-mar 1939)) – London. v56-79 apr 1949-dec 1972 1; v78-79 jan 1971-dec 1972 5 – 1,5 – D622 – us UMI [630]

AGRICULTURE ABROAD – (Ceased: v39 1984) – Ottawa. v1-39. 1945-84 – 95 – Can$20.00y – cn Micromedia [073]

L'AGRICULTURE ALGERIENNE A TRAVERS LES CHIFRES, 1970 / Algeria. Ministere de l'Agriculture – BNE-8657 1 – 9 – ne IDC [630]

AGRICULTURE AND ENVIRONMENT – v1-7. 1974-82 – 1,5,6,13 – sz Elsevier [630]

AGRICULTURE AND ENVIRONMENT *see*
– AGRICULTURE, ECOSYSTEMS AND ENVIRONMENT
– AGRO-ECOSYSTEMS

AGRICULTURE AND ENVIRONMENT – (Ceased publ. Merged with: Agro-Ecosystems; To form: Agriculture, Ecosystems and Environment) – Amsterdam. v1-7. jun 1974-nov 1982 – 1,5 – D42105 – us UMI [630]

AGRICULTURE AND EQUIPMENT INTERNATIONAL *see* AGRICULTURE INTERNATIONAL

AGRICULTURE AND EQUIPMENT INTERNATIONAL – (Cont: Agriculture International) – Horne. v44-. 1992- – 1,5*,9 – D16061.01 – us UMI [630]

AGRICULTURE AND FARMING, 1610-1900 : PART 1: MANUALS AND TEXT BOOKS A-D – (Part 2: Farming manuals and text books, F-Y. 134mf.$1120.00) – Marlborough: Adam Matthew Publications, 1993 – 127mf – 9 – $1,050.00 – uk Matthew [630]

AGRICULTURE AND FORESTRY BULLETIN *see* AGRICULTURE BULLETIN

AGRICULTURE AND POLITICS IN MERU-ARUSHA / University College of Dar es Salaam. History Dept. – [Dar es Salaam] Uni of Dar es Salaam, Photographic Unit, [19–?] – 1 – us Res Libr [960]

L'AGRICULTURE AU POINT DE VUE DE L'EMIGRATION: LECTURE DEVANT "L'UNION CATHOLIQUE", LE 27 OCTOBRE 1872 / Barnard, Edouard Andre – Montreal: La Minerve, 1872? 00909. (Pre-1900 Canadiana) – 9 – cn C.I.H.M. [971]

AGRICULTURE BULLETIN – (Cont by: Agriculture and Forestry Bulletin) – Edmonton. v1-18. apr 1962-Win 1977* – 1 – D7501 – us UMI [630]

AGRICULTURE DECISIONS / U.S. Department of Agriculture – (Updates planned) – v1-52. 1942-93 – 1028mf – 9 – $1,542.00 – LLMC 78-200 – us L.L.M.C. [340]

AGRICULTURE ECONOMIC REPORTS / U.S. Department of Agriculture – v1-564. 1961-86. 631 fiches – 9 – 700.00 – us Updata [324]

AGRICULTURE, ECOSYSTEMS AND ENVIRONMENT – v9-12. 1983-84 – 1,5,6,13 – sz Elsevier [630]

AGRICULTURE, ECOSYSTEMS AND ENVIRONMENT *see*
– AGRICULTURE AND ENVIRONMENT
– AGRO-ECOSYSTEMS

AGRICULTURE, ECOSYSTEMS AND ENVIRONMENT – (Formed by the union of: Agriculture and Environment & Agro-Ecosystems. Absorbed: Protection Ecology) – Amsterdam. v9- feb 1983- 1,5; v22- aug 1988- 9 – 1,5,9 – D42107 – us UMI [333]

L'AGRICULTURE ET LES CLASSES PAYSANNES / Raveau, Paul – Paris, 1926. (La Condition ouvriere. Part Two) – 9 – 10.00 – fr Bibl Nationale [360]

AGRICULTURE FROM THE PERSPECTIVE OF POPULATION GROWTH : SOME RESULTS FROM "AGRICULTURE: TOWARD 2000" – 1983 – 100p – it F.A.O. [630]

AGRICULTURE IN PUBLIC SCHOOLS: AN ADDRESS DELIVERED BEFORE THE MEMBERS OF THE ONTARIO TEACHER'S ASSOCIATION AT THEIR THIRTIETH ANNUAL CONVENTION HELD AT NIAGARA-ON-THE-LAKE, AUGUST, 1890 / Bryant, John Ebenezer – Toronto: Warwick, 1891. 00303. (Pre-1900 Canadiana) – 9 – cn C.I.H.M. [630]

AGRICULTURE IN THE NEAR EAST / United Nations. Food and Agriculture Organization – Development Outlook. Rome, Italy. Nov 1963. BNE-1001 1 – 9 – ne IDC [630]

AGRICULTURE IN WESTERN TRIPOLITANIA / Libya. Ministry of Agriculture and Livestock – Ed. 2. 1963. BNE-1029 1 – 9 – ne IDC [630]

AGRICULTURE INFORMATION BULLETINS / U.S. Department of Agriculture – Nos. 1-536. 1941-85. 517 fiches – 9 – $780.00 – us Updata [630]

AGRICULTURE INTERNATIONAL *see* AGRICULTURE AND EQUIPMENT INTERNATIONAL

AGRICULTURE INTERNATIONAL – (Formed by the union of: World Crops & Livestock International. Cont by: Agriculture and Equipment International) – Horne. v37-44. jul 1985-1992 – 1,5*,9 – D16061 – us UMI [630]

THE AGRICULTURE OF MOROCCO: PROGRAMS, PROGRESS, PROSPECTS / U.S. Department of Agriculture. Economic Research Service – Holm, H. M. 1961. BNE-3057 1 – 9 – ne IDC [630]

AGRICULTURE OF THE AMERICAS / U.S. Department of Agriculture – v1-7. 1941-47. 80 fiches – 9 – 120.00 – us Updata [630]

AGRICULTURE SCHEDULES, PENNSYLVANIA FEDERAL DECENNIAL CENSUSES / U.S. Bureau of the Census – 1850-80. 62 rolls. T1138 – 1 – us Nat'l Archives [324]

L'AGRICULTURE SYRIENNE ENTRE LES DEUX GUERRES / Traboulsi, I – Beyrouth. 1948. BNE-9743 1 – 9 – ne IDC [630]

AGRICULTURIST AND CANADIAN JOURNAL *see* CANADIAN AGRICULTURIST

THE AGRICULTURIST AND CANADIAN JOURNAL – Toronto: Brewer, McPhail, 1848 – 9 – cn C.I.H.M. [630]

AGRI-FIELDMAN – (Cont: Farm Technology and Agri-Fieldman. Cont by: Agri-Fieldman and Consultant) – Willoughby. v29-32 Sum 1973-may 1976 1,5; v32 jan-may 1976* 9 – 1,5,9 – D1415.01 – us UMI [630]

AGRI-FIELDMAN *see*
– AGRI-FIELDMAN AND CONSULTANT
– FARM TECHNOLOGY AND AGRI-FIELDMAN

AGRI-FIELDMAN AND CONSULTANT – (Cont: Agri-Fieldman. Cont by: Ag Consultant and Fieldman) – Willoughby. v32-35. Sum 1976-Fall 1979 – 1,5,9* – D1415.02 – us UMI [630]

AGRI-FIELDMAN AND CONSULTANT *see*
– AGRI-FIELDMAN
– AG CONSULTANT AND FIELDMAN

Agrippa *see* CHRONICON EPHRATENSE

Agrippa, Henricus Cornelius *see* DE L'INCERTITUDE, VANITE, ET ABUS DES SCIENCES

AGRI-PRACTICE – (Cont: Bovine Practice) – Santa Barbara. v4-18. jan 1983-dec 1997+ – 1 – D12427.01 – us UMI [636]

AGRIS FORESTRY : WORLD CATALOGUE OF INFORMATION AND DOCUMENTATION SERVICES – 1979 – 152p – it F.A.O. [634]

AGRISCIENCE – (Incorporates: Agrologist 1989) – Ottawa, 1989- – 9 – Can$20.00y – cn Micromedia [630]

AGRISCIENCE *see* AGROLOGIST

AGROCLIMATOLOGICAL DATA FOR AFRICA – 1988, 1984 – 2v 816p – it F.A.O. [550]

AGROCLIMATOLOGICAL DATA FOR ASIA – 1987 – 486p – it F.A.O. [550]

AGROCLIMATOLOGICAL DATA FOR LATIN AMERICA AND THE CARIBBEAN – 1985 – 600p – it F.A.O. [550]

AGRO-ECOLOGICAL LAND RESOURCES ASSESSMENT FOR AGRICULTURAL DEVELOPMENT PLANNING : A CASE STUDY OF KENYA: RESOURCES DATA BASE AND LAND PRODUCTIVITY; TECHNICAL ANNEX 1: LAND RESOURCES – 1991 – 158p – it F.A.O. [333]

AGRO-ECOSYSTEMS – v1-8. 1975-82 – 1,5,6,13 – sz Elsevier [630]

AGRO-ECOSYSTEMS *see*
– AGRICULTURE AND ENVIRONMENT
– AGRICULTURE, ECOSYSTEMS AND ENVIRONMENT

AGRO-ECOSYSTEMS – (Merged with: Agriculture and Environment; To form: Agriculture, Ecosystems and Environment) – Amsterdam. v1-8. jun 1974-feb 1983 – 1,5 – D42106 – us UMI [574]

AGROFORESTRY SYSTEMS – The Hague. v1-1982- 1*; v8- 1989-* 5,9 – 1,5,9 – D16762 – us UMI [634]

AGRO-KOOPERATIVNYI KRUZHOK / ed by Orleanskii, V L & Krivosheina, P I – Ed 2. M., 1929 – 2mf – 9 – COR-242/1 – ne IDC [334]

AGROLOGIST – (Cont: AIC Review. Incorporated in: AgriScience 1989) – Ottawa. v1- 1972- – 9 – Can$20.00y – cn Micromedia [073]

AGROLOGIST *see* AGRISCIENCE

AGRO-METEOROLOGICAL FIELD STATIONS – 1976 – 103p – it F.A.O. [630]

THE AGRONOMIST / New Mexico State University. Department of Agronomy – No.3-9. 1970/71-76/77. 1 reel – 1,5 – us Spaulding [630]

AGRONOMY AND SOILS RESEARCH SERIES / Clemson University. Agricultural Experiment Station – No.85-104. 1970-82. 1 reel – 1,5 – us Spaulding [630]

AGRONOMY AND SOILS RESEARCH SERIES / South Carolina. Agricultural Experiment Station. Clemson – n.1-84. Jun 1957-69 – 1,5 – us Spaulding [631]

AGRONOMY DEPARTMENT RESEARCH REPORT / University of Florida. Agricultural Experiment Station – 70/4-82/7. 1970-82 – 1, 5 – us Spaulding [630]

AGRONOMY FACTS / Illinois. Department of Agronomy – n.1-9. 1953 54-62 64 – 1,5 – us Spaulding [630]

AGRONOMY INFORMATION CIRCULAR / North Carolina. Agricultural Experiment Station. Raleigh – n.1-152. 1927-51 – 1,5 – us Spaulding [630]

AGRONOMY MIMEO REPORT / Florida. Agricultural Experiment Station – 55-1 – 70-3. 1954-69 – 1,5,6 – us Spaulding [630]

AGRONOMY MIMEOGRAPH CIRCULAR / North Dakota. Agricultural Experiment Station. Fargo – nos.51-110. 1929-75 – 1,5,6 – us Spaulding [630]

AGRONOMY MIMEOGRAPHED CIRCULAR / Virginia. Agricultural Experiment Station. Blacksburg – May 25 & Oct 20 1942. 1 fiche – 9 – us Spaulding [630]

AGRONOMY PAMPHLET / South Dakota. State University. Agricultural Experiment Station – nos.1-92. 1944-68 – 1,5,6 – us Spaulding [630]

AGRONOMY RESEARCH REPORT / Louisiana State University. Agricultural Experiment Station. Department of Agronomy – No.13-79 – 1,5 – us Spaulding [630]

AGRONOMY VIEWS / Nebraska. College of Agriculture. Dept. of Agronomy – n.1-234. 1955-69 – 1, 5 – us Spaulding [630]

AGROSTIDEA 3. : CALLUS OBCONICUS (STIPACEA) / Trinius, Carl Bernhard – Mem. Acad. Sc. St. Petersb. S6 v5(p1-189) 1843 – 6mf – 9 – ne IDC [580]

AGROSTOGRAPHIA CAPENSIS / Nees von Esenbeck, C G D – Halae, 1853. 490 pp. B-447 2 – 8 – ne IDC [580]

AGROSTOGRAPHIE DES DEPARTEMENTS DU NORD DE LA FRANCE / Desmazieres, J B H J – Lille. 1812. B-5895 2 – 8 – ne IDC [630]

AGROSTOLOGIA HELVETICA / Gaudin, J F A G P – 2v. Paris. 1811. B-680 2 – 8 – ne IDC [580]

AGSTATS ON MICROFICHE – 9 – at Statistics [630]

AGUAS AZOADAS.. / Bejarano y Sanchez, Eloy – 1888 – 9 – 1.50f – sp Bibl Santa Ana [946]

AGUAS BICARBONATADAS CALCICAS DE ALANGE / Berben, Abdon – Madrid: Imp. Leonardo Minon e hijos, 1895 – sp Bibl Santa Ana [331]

Aguas Monreal, Mariano *see*
– PROGRAMA DE CUADROS DE HISTORIA NATURAL
– TRATADO ELEMENTAL DE HISTORIA NATURAL

Aguascalientes. Mexico (State) *see* PERIODICO OFICIAL

Aguayo-Nayle, Lolita R *see* ARCHIVO BIOGRAFICO DE ESPANA, PORTUGAL E IBEROAMERICA (ABEPI 1)

AGUDAH NEWS REPORTER – New York, NY. 1974-78 – 1 – us A.J.P.C. [071]

Agudze-Vioka, B *see* L'HOMME ET LE MONDE A TRAVERS LES PROVERBES TOGOLAIS DE LANGUE EVE

Ague de Lassus, Lucien *see* CHEZ LE BEY DE TUNIS

Aguessy, C *see* CONTRIBUTION A L'ETUDE DE L'HISTOIRE DE L'ANCIEN ROYAUME DE PORTO-NOVA

Aguessy, H et al *see* TIME AND THE PHILOSOPHIES

Aguiar, T *see* APOLOGIA PRO CONSILIO MEDICINALI IN DIMINUTE VISIONES ADVERSUS DUAS EPITOLAS...

EL AGUILA EXTREMENA – v. 1. 1899 – 9 – 1.50f – sp Bibl Santa Ana [800]

Aguilar, Faustino *see* ANF LIHIM NG ISANG PULO: NOBELANG TAGALOG.

Aguilar, Francisco de *see* RELACION DE LA CONQUISTA DE LA NUEVA ESPANA

Aguilar, Fray Francisco de *see* HISTORIA DE LA NUEVA ESPANA

Aguilar Gallegos, Manuel *see*
– ORACION FUNEBRE...POR LOS FALLECIDOS... DE LA GUERRA CIVIL
– LA ROMERIA ESPANOLA AL VATICANO EN EL ANO DE 1876

Aguilera, M *see* ESTUDIO JURIDICO Y LEGAL...

Aguinaga, R *see* NOTAS PARA UNA BIBLIOGRAFIA GUADALUPANA

Aguirre Camara, Jose *see*
– ALGUNAS VERDADES SOBRE TARIFAS DE TELEFONOS, DICHAS EN EL PARLAMENTO
– CUATRO ARTICULOS
– DEMAGOGIA, INFLACION Y ARMAMENTISMO
– EL PAIS AL SERVICIO DEL CORONEL

Aguirre, Manuel de *see* INDAGACIONES SOBRE LA GEOGRAFIA

Agular, M Maria Esperanza *see* ESTUDIO BIBLIOGRAFICO DE DON MANUEL EDUARDO DE GOROSTIZA. MEXICO, 1932

Agulhon, Maurice *see* LES SAINT-SIMONIENS: 1825-1834

Agundez, Antonio *see* FORMULARIOS PARA LOS FISCALES MUNICIPALES Y COMARCALES

Agundez Fernandez, Antonio *see*
– BIOGRAFIA DE CACERES
– NOTAS PARA LA HISTORIA DE LA CIUDAD DE BADAJOZ A FINES DEL SIGLO 18
– SEGUALAZION ORIZZONTALI IN SPAGUE

Agundez Ferrandez, Antonio *see* SINTESIS BIOGRAFICA DE CACERES

Agus, G *see*
– ALLEMANDS DANCED AT THE KING'S THEATRE, SET FOR GERMAN FLUTE, VIOLIN OR HARPSICHORD
– SIX NOTTURNOS FOR TWO VIOLINS AND A VIOLONCELLO OBLIGATTO

AGUSTIN DE ITURBIDE : EMPERADOR DE MEJICO... / Mestas, Alberto de – Madrid: Razon y Fe, 1939 – 1 – sp Bibl Santa Ana [972]

Agustin, M *see* LIBRO DE LOS SECRETOS DE AGRICULTURA, CASA DE CAMPO PASTORIL

Agyei, Samuel Kwasi *see* A GUIDE TO RECORDS RELATING TO GHANA IN REPOSITORIES IN THE U.K. EXCLUDING THE PUBLIC RECORD OFFICE

Agyemang, K *see* EVALUATION OF THE PRODUCTIVITY OF CROSSBRED DAIRY CATTLE ON SMALLHOLDER AND GOVERNMENT FARMS IN THE REPUBLIC OF MALAWI

AHA NEWSLETTER – (Cont by: AHA Perspectives: Newsletter of the American Historical Association including EIB Notices) – Washington. v1-20 dec 1962-jun 1982 1; v10-20 jan 1972-jun 1982 5; v13 1975*. v14-15 jan 1976-dec 1977. v16 1978*. v17-20 jan 1979-jun 1982 – 1,5,9 – D8092 – us UMI [073]

AHA NEWSLETTER *see* AHA PERSPECTIVES

AHA PERSPECTIVES : NEWSLETTER OF THE AMERICAN HISTORICAL ASSOCIATION INCLUDING EIB NOTICES – (Cont: AHA Newsletter. Cont by: Perspectives Newsletter of the American Historical Association) – Washington. v20-22. sep 1982-feb 1984 – 1,5,9 – D8092.01 – us UMI [073]

AHA PERSPECTIVES *see* AHA NEWSLETTER

Ahagon, Marques de Laurencin *see* SERIES DE LOS MAS IMPORTANTES DOCUMENTOS DEL ARCHIVO Y BIBLIOTECA DEL EXCMO. SR. DUQUE DE MEDINACELI, ELEGIDOS POR SU ENCARGO Y PUBLICADOS A SUS EXPENSAS...

AHALI – Edirne, Sofya: Olyadsamaryaviza Matbaasi, 1919-1921 – 9 – $20.00 – us MEDOC [956]

AHALI – Samsun: Ahali Matbaasi. Sahib-i Imtiyaz: Ismail Cenani. Nos. 133 (14 Eyluel 1338 [1922] – 9 – $20.00 – us MEDOC [956]

AHANGAR – Tehran, Sal-'i 1, shumarah-'i 1-16. – 27 Farvardin 1358-16 Murdad 1358 [16 Apr 1979-7 Aug 1979] – 1r – 1 – $25.00 – us MEDOC [956]

AHASVERUS : DER EWIGE JUDE / Zirus, Werner – (Includes bibliographical references and index) – Berlin: W de Gruyter & Co, 1930 – 2r – 1 – us U.W. Library [430]

AHASVERUS, DER EWIGE JUDE / Zirus, Werner – 1930 – 1 – us I.U. Libraries [390]

AHAVAT HA-KADMONIM / Judaism.Liturgy. Fes – Yerushalayim: s.n., 649 1888 or 1889. Fasts and feasts – 1 – us U.W. Library [270]

AHAVAT ZIYYON / Simhah, ben Joshua of Zalozhstsy – Grodno. 1790. BJ-27-17 1 – 9 – ne IDC [900]

AHAVAT ZIYYON VI-YRUSHALAYIM / Ratner, DB – 3v. Vilna. Petrokov. 1901-17. BJ-32-20 1 – 9 – ne IDC [270]
AHAVAT ZIYYON VI-YRUSHALAYIM / Ratner, DB – Vilna, Petrokov. 3v. 1901-1917 – 10mf – 9 – ne IDC [947]
AHEA ACTION / American Home Economics Association – 1974- – 1 – us UMI [640]
AHEA ACTION / American Home Economics Association – Washington. v1-24 aug 1974-1*; v1-14 aug 1974-aug 1988* 5,9 – 1,5,9 – D10748 – us UMI [640]
AHEIM = AT HOME – (In Yiddish) – Leipheim, DE. no5. 21 Mar 1946 – 1r – 1 – $25.00 – cn Can Microfilming [072]
AHENK – Izmir: Ahenk Yurdu Matbaasi, 1895-1928 – 9 – $20.00 – us MEDOC [956]
Ahern, John *see* LECONS D'ANGLAIS D'APRES LA METHODE NATURELLE: PREMIER LIVRE DU MAITRE
Ahern, M J *see* NOTES POUR SERVIR A L'HISTOIRE DE LA MEDECINE DANS LE BAS-CANADA...
DIE AHHIJTAVIA-URKUNDEN / Sommer, F – (Abh. Bayerischen Ak. Wis. Philosophisch-historische Abt., Neue Folge 6). Muenchen. 1932 – 9 – ne IDC [090]
AHIASAF – 13 v. Warsaw. 1893-1904, 1923. BJ-100-105 – 9 – ne IDC [947]
AHIASAF – Warsaw. 1-13. 1893-1923 – 1 – us NY Public [073]
THE AHIMAN REZON : OR BOOK OF THE CONSTITUTION OF THE RIGHT, WORSHIPFUL GRAND LODGE OF FREE AND ACCEPTED MASONS OF PENNSYLVANIA – Philadelphia, 1902 – 3mf – 9 – $4.50 – LLMC 92-186 – us L.L.M.C. [360]
AHKAM-I SAL – Sene 1276 [1859] – 9 – $20.00 – us MEDOC [956]
THE AHKIMAL AWAWTOM – 1927-31. (American Indian Periodicals in the Princeton University Library) – 3mf – 9 – $45.00 – us UPA [305]
Ahlers, Rudolf *see*
- THOMAS TORSTEN
- DAS WEITE LAND

Ahmad, H A Malik *see* TAFSIR SINAR
AHMAD IBN HANBAL AND THE MIHNA / Patton, Walter Melville – A biography of the imam including an account of the Mohammadan inquisition called the Mihna, 218-234 A. H. 1897 – 1 – us A.T.L.A. [920]
Ahmad ibn Muhammad ibn Kathir, Al Farghani *see* MVHAMEDIS ALFRAGANI ARABIS CHRONOLIGCA ET ASTRONOMICA ELEMENTA, ...
Ahmad, Ibrahim A *see* JOURNAL OF NONPARAMETRIC STATISTICS
Ahmed, Muesellem *see* DIVAN
Ahmet, Servili Hafiz *see* AHTER-I KEBIR
AHNAS EL MEDINEH (MEES VOL 11) : (HERACLEOPOLIS MAGNA) / Naville, E – (Also: J.J. Tylor and L. Griffith: The Tomb of Paheri at El Kab) – London, 1894 – 7mf – 8 – Dfl28.00 – ne Slangenburg [720]
DER AHNENKULTUS UND DIE URRELIGION ISRAELS / Grueneisen, Carl – (Includes indexes) – Halle a. S:Max Niemeyer, 1900 – 1mf – 9 – 0-8370-3415-9 – 1985-1415 – us A.T.L.A. [270]
DIE AHNFRAU : TRAUERSPIEL IN FUENF AUFZUEGEN / Grillparzer, Franz – 3. Aufl. Stuttgart, Berlin: J G Cotta, 1902 – 1r – 1 – us U.W. Library [200]
Aholi, Paul *see* PATHOLOGIE DU PANCREAS ET MALNUTRITION PROTEIQUE EN ZONE INTERTROPICALE
AHORA – (In Spanish) – Reno, NV. 1987 – 7+ r – 1 – $350.00 ($50.00y) – N03709 – us Library Micro [071]
EL AHORRO Y LA POLITICA SOCIAL / Allue Salvador, Miguel – Caceres: Tip. Editorial Extremadura, 1956 – 1 – sp Bibl Santa Ana [320]
Ahrendts, C *see* ERSITZUNG BEWEGLICHER SACHEN IM INTERNATIONALEN PRIVATRECHT
Ahrens, A *see* FAUNA INSECTORUM EUROPAE
AHTER-I KEBIR / Ahmet, Servili Hafiz – Istanbul: Matbaa-i Ahmed Ihsan, 1321 [1903] – $200.00 – us MEDOC [470]
Ahuma, S R B Attoh *see* MEMOIRS OF WEST AFRICAN CELEBRITIES
Ahumada, P *see* QUESTION EN LA QUAL SE INTENTA AVERIGUAR COMO Y DE QUE VENAS Y DE QUE PARTE...SE DEBA SANGRAR
AHZAB – Tehran, 1980-. – Sal-i 1, shumarah-'i 1-18, 20-31. 9 Day 1359-13 Murdad 1360 [30 Dec 1980-2 Aug 1981] – 1r – 1 – $25.00 – us MEDOC [956]
AI AND SOCIETY – Berlin. v1-11 jul 1987-dec 1997+; v6-8 jan 1992-dec 1994* – 1,5,9 – D16971 – us UMI [073]
AI (ASPHALT INSTITUTE) – Printed index. Updated every 60 days – 6,9 – us Info Handling [690]
AI COMMUNICATIONS – Amsterdam. v1- 1988-1*; v7- 1994-* 5,9 – 1,5,9 – D21474 – us UMI [380]
AI EXPERT – San Francisco. v1-10. 1986-jun 1995 – 1,5,9 – D15989 – us UMI [073]
A.I. GUCHKOV V TRETEI GOSUDARSTVENNOI DUMIE, 1907-1912 GG : SBORNIK RIECHEI / Guchkov, Aleksandr Ivanovich – S.-Peterburg: "Novoe vremia", 1912 – 1 – CSUX89-B2399 – us Hoover Inst Photo [947]
AI MAGAZINE – La Canada. v1-5. spr 1980-84* 1; v6-16 spr 1985-win 1995; v17 spr-win 1996; v18 spr-win 1997+ 5 – 1,5,9 – D15622 – us UMI [073]
AI PARA TON IORDANEN LAURAI KALAMOONOS KAI AGIOU GERASIMOU : KAI OI BIOI TOU AGIOU GERASIMOU KAI KYRIAKOU YOU ANACHOORETOU / ed by Koikylides, K M – Jerusalem, 1902 – 3mf – 8 – Dfl9.00 – ne Slangenburg [240]
AI PARA TON IORDANENS LAURAI KALAMOONOS KAI AGIOU GERASIMOU... / ed by Kotkylides, K M – Jerusalem, 1902 – 3mf – 8 – Dfl3.50ea – ne Slangenburg [956]
AIA (AMERICAN INSTITUTE OF ARCHITECTS) – Printed index. Updated every 60 days – 6,9 – us Info Handling [620]
AIA AWARDS PROGRAMS – (Print index available for all awards programs for 1995-97) – 151r (includes 14 index reels) – 1 – $12,080.00 set – us Ross [720]
AIA JOURNAL / American Institute of Architects – (Cont: Octagon. Cont by: Architecture: the AIA journal. Former titles: Journal of the American Institue of Architects (jan 1944-apr 1957)) – Washington. v7-72 jan 1944-jun 1983 1; v55-72 jan 1971-jun 1983 5; v63-72 jan 1975-jun 1983 9 – 1,5,9 – D114 – us UMI [720]
AIA OUTGOING CORRESPONDENCE : NOVEMBER 13 1896-OCTOBER 25 1909 – (Gives insights into the projects and concerns of local architects during the late 19th and early 20th centuries) – 37v – 20r – 1 – $1,600.00 – us Ross [720]
AIA PROCEEDINGS 1867-1931, 1943-1967 – 12r – 1 – $969.00 – us Ross [720]
AIAA (American Institute of Aeronautics and Astronautics) *see* BULLETIN
AIAA BULLETIN / American Institute of Aeronautics and Astronautics (AIAA) – (Absorbed by: Astronautics and Aeronautics) – New York. v1-12 1964-dec 1975 1; v8-12 5; v11 1974*. v12 1975 9 – 1,5,9 – D5073 – us UMI [629]
AIAA JOURNAL / American Institute of Aeronautics and Astronautics – (Formed by the union of: ARS (American Rocket Society) Journal, and: Journal of the Aerospace Sciences) – New York. v1-35 jan 1963-dec 1997+ 1; v9-35 jan 1971-dec 1997+ 5; v14-35 jan 1976-dec 1997+ 9 – 1,5,9 – D1600 – us UMI [629]
AIAA STUDENT JOURNAL / American Institute of Aeronautics and Astronautics – New York. cum index v1-6 apr 1963-dec 1968; v1-35 apr 1963- 1; v9-35 Feb 1971- 5; v14-35 Spr 1976- 9* – 1,5,9 – D5027 – us UMI [629]
AIA/ALA LIBRARY BUILDING AWARDS – (Awards for submissions for 1987 also available in mf. 1987 index on microfilm) – 1985, 1989, 1993, 1997 – 8r – 1 – $640.00 – us Ross [720]
AIA/BIA BRICK IN ARCHITECTURE AWARDS OF EXCELLENCE – (1991 and 1993 available on mf) – 1995, 1997 – 6r – 1 – $480.00 – us Ross [720]
AIA/NAS (AEROSPACE INDUSTRIES ASSOCIATION OF AMERICA/NATIONAL AEROSPACE STANDARDS) – Printed index. Updated every 60 days – 6,9 – us Info Handling [629]
AIC REVIEW *see* AGROLOGIST
Aicard, Jean *see* POEMES DE PROVENCE
AICHACHER NACHRICHTEN – Aichach, dec 1959-73 – 1 – Dist. gw Mikrofilm – gw Misc Inst [072]
AICHE (AMERICAN INSTITUTE OF CHEMICAL ENGINEERS) – Standards. Printed index. Updated every 60 days – 6,9 – us Info Handling [540]
AICHE JOURNAL / American Institute of Chemical Engineers – New York. v1-43. mar 1955- – 1,5,9 – D12576 – us UMI [660]
Aichel, Margaret Hurkamp *see* LETTERS
Aicher, Georg *see* KAMEL UND NADELOEHR: EINE KRITISCH-EXEGETISCHE STUDIE UEBER MT. 19, 24 UND PARAL
Aickin, Joseph *see* THE ENGLISH GRAMMAR
AICPA TAX DIVISION NEWSLETTER / American Institute of Certified Public Accountants Tax Division – Washington. v8-13. Sum 1992-* – 1,5,9 – D19192 – us UMI [336]
AID FOR CHILDREN – n.p. 193? Fiche W 704. (Blodgett Collection of Spanish Civil War Pamphlets) – 9 – us H.U. College Libr [946]
AID FOR OLD PEOPLE – n.p. 193? Fiche W 705. (Blodgett Collection of Spanish Civil War Pamphlets) – 9 – us H.U. College Libr [946]
AIDA POLLUTION INSURANCE BULLETIN – (Association Internationale de Droit des Assurances) – 1,5,6,9 – us UMI [360]
AIDC JOURNAL – (Cont by: AEDC Journal) – Boston. v1-15 jan 1966-oct 1980 1; v6-10 jan 1971-oct 1975. v11 jan-oct 1976*. v12-15 jan 1977-oct 1980 5; v10-15 jan 1975-oct 1980 9 – 1,5,9 – D2313 – us UMI [073]
AIDC JOURNAL *see* AEDC JOURNAL
L'AIDE A LA FRANCE : COMITE D'ASSISTANCE – Montreal, Canada. 7,8 jun 1918 – 1r – 1 – Can$25.00 – cn Can Microfilming [360]
AIDE-MEMOIRE FROM OBSERVERS OF REPUBLIC OF INDONESIA TO THE U.N. MALAYSIA MISSION IN SARAWAK AND SABAH / Indonesia – SE-4704 1. 1963 – 9 – ne IDC [950]
Aidid, Abdullah *see* RENUNGAN DILEMBAH WAHJU
Aidit, Dipa Nusantara *see*
- ANTI-IMPERIALISME DAN FRONT NASIONAL
- INDONESIAN REVOLUTION AND THE IMMEDIATE TASKS OF THE COMMUNIST PARTY OF INDONESIA
- INDONESIAN SOCIETY AND THE INDONESIAN REVOLUTION
- PERKUAT PERSATUAN NASIONAL DAN PERSATUAN KOMUNIS
- PROBLEMS OF THE INDONESIAN REVOLUTION
- THE ROAD TO PEOPLE'S DEMOCRACY FOR INDONESIA: GENERAL REPORT ON THE POLITICAL AND ORGANISATIONAL SITUATION, DELIVERED AT 5TH NATIONAL CONGRESS OF COMMUNIST PARTY OF INDONESIA,MAR. 1954. SE-2604/1. 1955
- THE ROAD TO PEOPLE'S DEMOCRACY FOR INDONESIA: GENERAL REPORT ON THE POLITICAL AND ORGANISATIONAL SITUATION, DELIVERED AT THE 5TH NATIONAL CONGRESS OF THE COMMUNIST PARTY OF INDONESIA,MAR. 1954. SE-6271/1. 1968
- SOSIALISME INDONESIA DAN SJARAT-SJARAT PELAKSANAANNJA
- TENTANG MARXISME
- UNTUK DEMOKRASI, PERSATUAN DAN MOBILISASI
- VISIT TO FIVE SOCIALIST STATES

AIDS ABSTRACTS – (Cont: AIDS Information) – Abingdon. v9-10 jan 1993-94*. v11-13 1995-97* – 1,5,9 – D20900-01 – us UMI [616]
AIDS ABSTRACTS : INTERNATIONAL LITERATURE ON ACQUIRED IMMUNODEFICIENCY SYNDROM AND RELATED RETROVIRUSES – 1990- 9v. Formerly: AIDS Information – 9 – £162.00 – 0953-1580 – uk Carfax [616]
AIDS ABSTRACTS *see* AIDS INFORMATION
AIDS CARE – Abingdon. v1-4 1989-92* 1; v5-6 1993-94*. v7-9 1995-97+ 1,5,9 – 1,5,9 – D20901 – us UMI [616]
AIDS CARE: PSYCHOLOGICAL AND SOCIO-MEDICAL ASPECTS OF AIDS/HIV – 1989-5v – 9 – £169.50 – uk Carfax [610]
AIDS EDUCATION AND PREVENTION – New York. v1-9 Spr 1989-dec 1997+ 1,5,9; v1-6 Spr 1989-dec 1994* 5 – 1,5,9 – D17419 – us UMI [614]
AIDS INFORMATION – (Cont by: AIDS Abstracts) – Leeds. v1-8. 1989-92* – 1 – D20900 – us UMI [616]
AIDS INFORMATION *see* AIDS ABSTRACTS
AIDS RESEARCH ARCHIVES : OBSERVATIONS ON SOCIAL AND POLITICAL CHANGE 1980-90 – (Documents the history of AIDS growth and treatment as seen through the eyes of alternative media) – New York, 1994 – 9 – $675.00 – us Alper [301]
AIDS TO FAITH : A SERIES OF THEOLOGICAL ESSAYS / ed by Thomson, William – (Includes bibliographical references) – New York: D Appleton, 1862 – 2mf – 9 – 0-8370-5494-X – 1985-3494 – us A.T.L.A. [240]
AIDS TO SCRIPTURE STUDY / Gardiner, Frederic – (Includes index) – Boston: Houghton, Mifflin, 1890 – 1mf – 9 – 0-8370-3231-8 – 1985-1231 – us A.T.L.A. [220]
AIDS TO THE DEVOUT STUDY OF CRITICISM : PT 1: THE DAVID-NARRATIVES PT 2: THE BOOK OF PSALMS / Cheyne, Thomas Kelly – New York: Thomas Whittaker, 1892 – 1mf – 9 – 0-8370-2640-7 – 1985-0640 – us A.T.L.A. [220]
AIDS TO THE STUDY AND USE OF LAW BOOKS: A SELECTED LIST, CLASSIFIED AND ANNOTATED, OF PUBLICATIONS RELATING TO LAW LITERATURE, LAW STUDY AND LEGAL ETHICS / Hicks, Frederick Charles – New York: Baker, Voorhis, 1913. 129p. L.C. copy imperfect: supplement wanting. LL-220 – 1 – us L of C Photodup [340]
AIDS TO THE STUDY OF ACTS (CCC236) / Luce, H W – (In Chinese) – Shanghai: Mission Book Company, 1918 – 1r – 1 – 1984-6575 – us A.T.L.A. [220]
AIDS TO THE STUDY OF DANTE / Dinsmore, Charles Allen – Boston: Houghton Mifflin, 1903 – 1mf – us A.T.L.A. [450]
AIDS TO THE STUDY OF GERMAN THEOLOGY / Matheson, George – (Includes index) – 2nd ed. Edinburgh: T & T Clark, 1876 – 1mf – 9 – 0-8370-8768-6 – 1986-2768 – us A.T.L.A. [240]
AIDS WEEKLY PLUS – Atlanta, 1995-97+ – 1,5,9 – D22107 – us UMI [073]
AIEE TRANSACTIONS – 1884-1964 – 1,5,6 – 2550.00 – us I.E.E.E. [621]
Aiello, Kimberly A *see* DIFFERENCES IN PHYSIOLOGICAL AND MECHANICAL PROPERTIES OF STAIR CLIMBING ON THREE DIFFERENT APPARATUS
AIGENTLICHE BESCHREIBUNG DER RAISZ, SO ER VOR DISER ZEIT GEGEN AUFFGANG INN DIE MORGENLANDER, FUERNEMLICH SYRIAM, IUDAEAM, ARABIAM, MESOPOTAMIAM, BABYLONIAM, ASSYRIAM, ARMENIAM... / Rauwolff, L – Laugingen. 3pts. 1582 – 6mf – 9 – 9234/1 – ne IDC [956]
Aighan *see* BRUNEHAUT OU LES SUCCESSEURS DE CLOVIS
L'AIGLON – Beauceville, Canada. v12 n13. 28 mar 1952-21 jun 1956 – 1r – 1 – Can$50.00 – cn Can Microfilming [072]
L'AIGLON – Beauceville-Est, ca 1938?-73. SEM35P272 – 1 – cn Bibl Nat [072]
L'AIGLON – Lac Etchemin, Canada. v22 n44. 15 nov 1962-v23 n3. 24 jan 1963 – 1r – 1 – Can$35.00 – cn Can Microfilming [072]
L'AIGUILLON – Mont-Joli: C.B. Beaudet. v1-3. 1943-1945. SEM35P342 – 1r – 1 – Can$18.00 – cn Bibl Nat [072]
Aiguino da Brescia, Illuminato *see*
- LA ILLUMINATA DE TUTTI I TUONI DI CANTO FERMO..
- IL TESORO ILLUMINATO DI TUTTI I TUONI DI CANTO FIGURATO..

Aiguino, T *see* IL TESORO ILLVMINATO DI TVTTI I TVONI DI CANTO FIGVRATO, CON ALCVNI BELLISSIMI SECRETI
AIIE TRANSACTIONS / American Institute of Industrial Engineers – (Cont by: IIE transactions. Supersedes in part: Journal of industrial engineering) – New York. v1-13 mar 1969-dec 1981 1; v3-13 mar 1971-dec 1981 5; v9-13 mar 1977-dec 1981 9 – 1,5,9 – D3180 – us UMI [620]
AIIM (ASSOCIATION FOR INFORMATION AND IMAGE MANAGEMENT) – Printed index. Updated every 60 days – 6,9 – us Info Handling [650]
AIIM INDEX / Association for Information and Image Management – Information on microform and image processing applications, market studies, standards, technical processes, research, equipment evaluations, directories, guides, state-of-the-art reports. Updated quarterly – 9 – $250.00 (AIIM members); $300.00 (others) – us A.I.I.M. [770]

AIIM STANDARDS SET / Association for Information and Image Management – (All AIIM standards and list of micrographic and related standards) – 1992 – 9 – $475.00 (AIIM members); $525.00 (others) – us A.I.I.M. [650]
Aiken, Catharine *see* METHODS OF MIND-TRAINING; CONCENTRATED ATTENTION AND MEMORY
AIKEN FIRST BAPTIST CHURCH. AIKEN, SOUTH CAROLINA : CHURCH RECORDS – 1814-10 Jun 1889 – 1 – 29.61 – us Baptist [240]
Aiken, John *see* MISCELLANEOUS PAPERS
Aiken, Joseph Daniel *see* TYPESCRIPT OF TRAVEL DIARY
Aikens *see* MEN OF PROGRESS IN WISCONSIN
Aikens, Asa *see* PRACTICAL FORMS, WITH NOTES AND REFERENCES EXPLANATORY OF THE LAW GOVERNING THE CASES TO WHICH THEY ARE APPLICABLE.
AIKEN'S REPORTS / Vermont. Supreme Court – (A Pre-NRS title) – v1-2. 1825-1828 (all publ) – 10mf – 9 – $15.00 – LLMC 90-311 – us L.L.M.C. [340]
Aikhenvald, Iu *see*
- NASHA REVOLIUTSIIA
- POETY I POETESSY
- SILUETY RUSSKIKH PISATELEI
- VALERII BRIUSOV

Aikin, J *see* THE LIVES OF JOHN SELDEN, AND ARCHBISHOP USHER...
Aikin, Lucy *see* EPISTLES ON WOMEN
LES AILES – no. 1-984, inc. Paris. 1921-6 juin 1940 – 1 – fr A.C.R.P.P. [073]
AIM – (Cont by: Canadian Appraiser v29 1985) – Winnipeg. v1-28. 1957-84 – 9 – Can$20.00y – cn Micromedia [073]
AIM *see* CANADIAN APPRAISER
AIM INTERNATIONAL – (1985- . 5,6,9) – v67- . 1983- – 1 – us UMI [270]
AIM REPORT – (Accuracy in Media). v. 1-. 1972- – v1- 1972- 1; v7- 1978- 5,6,9 – us UMI [410]
Aimar, C P *see*
- ACCOUNT BOOK
- CASHBOOK
- LEDGER
- PLANTATION ACCOUNT BOOKS

Aimes, Hubert Hillary Suffern *see* A HISTORY OF SLAVERY IN CUBA, 1511 TO 1868
AIMS AND AIDS FOR GIRLS AND YOUNG WOMEN, ON THE VARIOUS DUTIES OF LIFE, INCLUDING PHYSICAL, INTELLECTUAL, AND MORAL DEVELOPMENT / Weaver, George Sumner – New York: Fowler and Wells, 1856. 224p – 1 – us U.W. Library [640]
THE AIMS AND OBJECTIVES OF EDUCATION IN BOTSWANA / Botswana. Ministry of Education – 1971 – 1mf – 9 – DE-420/1 – ne IDC [370]
AIMS IN THE PACIFIC / Indonesia. Kementerian Penerangan – SE-11,905 1. 1948? – 9 – ne IDC [324]
AIMS NEWSLETTER / American Institute for Marxist Studies – (Ceased publ) – New York. v1-22 1964-dec 1985 1*; v10-22 jan 1973-dec 1985 5*; v11-22 jan/dec 1974-jan/dec 1985 9* – 1,5,9 – D6580 – us UMI [335]
AINSLEE'S – (Former title: Ainslee's Magazine (feb 1898-sep 1902)) – New York. v1-58. feb 1898-dec 1926 – 1 – D6127 – us UMI [073]
Ainslie, J R *see* LIST OF PLANTS USED IN NATIVE MEDICINE IN NIGERIA
Ainslie, Peter *see* THE MESSAGE OF THE DISCIPLES FOR THE UNION OF THE CHURCH
Ainslie, W *see* MATERIA INDICA
Ainsworth, Barbara E *see*
- FACTORS ASSOCIATED WITH THE RECALL OF PHYSICAL ACTIVITY
- THE RELATIONSHIP BETWEEN SOCIAL PHYSIQUE ANXIETY AND PHYSICAL ACTIVITY

Ainsworth, Barbare E *see* USE OF THE EXERCISE BENEFITS/BARRIERS SCALE IN NORTH CAROLINA DEPARTMENT OF CORRECTION EMPLOYEES
AINSWORTH HERALD – Ainsworth, NE. -w. Jul. 1892-Mar. 1901. Incomplete – 1 – us NE Hist [071]
Ainsworth, John Dawson *see* JOHN AINSWORTH, PIONEER KENYA ADMINISTRATOR, 1864-1946
AINSWORTH JOURNAL – Ainsworth, NE. -w. Jul. 1884-May 1887. Incomplete – 1 – us NE Hist [071]
AINSWORTH STAR-JOURNAL – Ainsworth, NE. -w. Aug. 1886-Sep. 1890. Incomplete; Sep. 1890-Dec. 1908; Dec. 1908-Nov. 1921 – 1 – us NE Hist [071]
Ainsworth, William Francis *see* TRAVELS IN THE TRACK OF THE TEN THOUSAND GREEKS..
Ainsworth, William Harrison *see*
- THE GOOD OLD TIMES; THE STORY OF THE MANCHESTER REBELS OF '45
- JACK SHEPPARD
- THE TOWER OF LONDON
- WINDSOR CASTLE

AINSWORTH'S MAGAZINE – (Ceased publ) – London. v1-26. 1842-1854 – 1 – D4197 – us UMI [073]
AIN'T I A WOMAN – (All that is currently available) – Iowa city. v1-3. jun 1970-jul 1973 – 1 – D7939 – us UMI [305]
Ainzaft, Samuil Semenovich *see*
- ISTORIIA RABOCHEGO I PROFESSIONALNOGO DVIZHENIIA DEREVOOBDELOCHNIKOV DO REVOLIUTSII 1917 GODA
- PROFESSIONALNOE DVIZHENIE V ROSSII V 1905-1907 GG
- ZUBATOVSHCHINA I GAPONOVSHCHINA

L'AIOLI – Avignon, France. 7 Jan 1891-27 Dec 1899 – 2r – 1 – uk British Libr Newspaper [072]
AION – Athens, 2 Jul 1880-15 Jun 1885 (imperfect) – 6r – 1 – uk British Libr Newspaper [072]
AIPLA QUARTERLY JOURNAL – (Also as Apla Quarterly Journal) – v1-22. 1973-1994 – 9 – $260.00 set – us Hein [340]
AIR AGE NEWS – Sparks, NV. 1966-1968 – 1r – 1 – $50.00 – N04742 – us Library Micro [071]
AIR ALLEMAND VARIE POUR LE VIOLON AVEC ACCOMP. DE PIANO / Fontaine, A – (Parts) – Ms copy – 1 – us Sibley [780]
AIR AND SPACE – (Ceased publ) – Washington. v1-6. mar 1978-Sum 1983 – 1,5,9 – D11718 – us UMI [629]
AIR AND SPACE SMITHSONIAN – Washington. v1-12. apr 1986-mar 1998+ – 1,5,9 – D16012 – us UMI [629]
AIR AND SPACE SMITHSONIAN – Washington. v1-. apr 1986- – 1,5,9 – D16012 – us UMI [629]
AIR AND WASTE – (Cont & cont by: Journal of the Air and Waste Management Association) – Pittsburgh. v43-44. jan 1993-dec 1994 – 1,5,9 – D6210.03 – us UMI [628]
AIR AND WATER POLLUTION – (Split into: Atmospheric Environment, and: Water Research. Former titles: International Journal of Air Pollution (oct 1958-oct 1960 + jun 1961-sep/oct 1961)) – Oxford. v1-10 1958-66 – 1,5,9 – D49008 – us UMI [360]
AIR AVEC 24 VARIATIONS POUR L'ETUDE DE LA FLUTE, OP. 1 / Iusdorff, J – (2nd edition) – Offenbach sur la Mein: Jean Andre, 1809? – 1 – us Sibley [780]
AIR CARGO – (Guide section cont in: OAG Air Cargo Guide. Absorbed in pt by: Cargo Airlift. Vols 1&2 not available for filming) – Oak Brook. v3-15. jan 1959-jan/feb 1971 – 1 – D1755 – us UMI [380]
AIR CARGO *see* OAG AIR CARGO GUIDE
AIR CARGO MAGAZINE *see* AIR CARGO WORLD
AIR CARGO WORLD – (Cont: Air Cargo Magazine) – Atlanta. v73-87. jan 1983-dec 1997+ – 1,5,9 – D242.02 – us UMI [380]
AIR CLASSICS – Canoga Park. 1963- 1*; 1995- 5,9 – 1,5,9 – D24902 – us UMI [073]
AIR COMBAT – Canoga Park. 1973- 1*; 1995- 5,9 – 1,5,9 – D23401 – us UMI [073]
AIR CONDITIONING AND REFRIGERATION NEWS *see* AIR CONDITIONING, HEATING AND REFRIGERATION NEWS
AIR CONDITIONING, HEATING AND REFRIGERATION NEWS – (Absorbed: Air Engineering (mar 24 1969). Former titles: Electric Refrigeration News (sep 11 1926-sep 9 1936); Air Conditioning and Refrigeration News (sep 16 1936-nov 24 1958)) – Troy. v1-202 sep 1926-dec 1997+ 1; v113-202 jan 1968-dec 1997+ 5; v146-202 jan 1979-dec 1997+ 9 – 1,5,9 – D758 – us UMI [621]
AIR CONDITIONING, HEATING AND REFRIGERATION NEWS *see* AIR ENGINEERING
AIR CONDITIONING, HEATING AND VENTILATING – (Formerly: Heating and Ventilation. Now: Building Systems Design.) v. 28-46. 1931-1949 – 1,5,6 – us Princeton Micro [621]
AIR COOLED NEWS – Cazenovia. v27-44. 1980-mar 1998+* – 1 – D11384 – us UMI [621]
AIR CORPS NEWS LETTER *see* AIR FORCE MAGAZINE
AIR DES DEUX JUMEAUX DE BERGAME... : VARIE POUR LE VIOLON ET...AVEC UN ACCOMPAGNEMENT DE PIANOFORTE... OEUVRE 31, NO 3 / Desaugiers, M – (Score and parts) – Paris: Erard, [179-?] – 1 – us Sibley [780]
AIR ENGINEERING *see* AIR CONDITIONING, HEATING AND REFRIGERATION NEWS
AIR ENGINEERING – (Ceased publ. Absorbed by: Air Conditioning, Heating and Refrigeration News, 24 mar 1969) – Detroit. v1-11 apr 1959-feb 1969 – 1 – D1956 – us UMI [621]
AIR ET COSMOS – 1990-1995 – 2r per y – 6 – Sfr802.00 – sz Infoprint [073]
AIR FAVORI POUR LE PIANO-FORTE... / Latour, T – 2nd ed. Chez Jean Andre, [1805] – 1 – us Sibley [780]
AIR FORCE – v.1-46. Sept 21, 1918-Dec 1963 – 1 – 989.00 – us L of C Photodup [355]
AIR FORCE *see* AIR FORCE MAGAZINE
AIR FORCE AND SPACE DIGEST *see* AIR FORCE MAGAZINE
AIR FORCE CIVIL ENGINEER *see* AIR FORCE ENGINEERING AND SERVICES QUARTERLY
AIR FORCE CIVIL ENGINEER – (Cont by: Air Force Engineering and Services Quarterly) – Wright-Patterson AFB. v1-15 1960-nov 1974 1*; v13-15 feb 1972-nov 1974 5,9 – 1,5,9 – D6345 – us UMI [624]
AIR FORCE COMPTROLLER – Washington. v1-oct 1967- 1; v7- jan 1973- 5,9 – 1,5,9 – D6650 – us UMI [355]
AIR FORCE ENGINEERING AND SERVICES QUARTERLY *see*
- AIR FORCE CIVIL ENGINEER
- AIR FORCE ENGINEERING AND SERVICES QUARTERLY

AIR FORCE ENGINEERING AND SERVICES QUARTERLY – (Ceased publ. Cont: Air Force Civil Engineer. Former titles: Air Force Engineering and Services Quarterly (aug 1975-feb 1980); Engineering and Services, Air Force Engineering and Services Quarterly (may 1980-feb 1981); Air Force Engineering and Services Quarterly (Sum 1981-Fal 1982); Quarterly, Air Force Engineering and Services (Win 1982-Win 1983)) – Tyndall AFB. v16-27. aug 1975-Sum 1986 – 1,5,9 – D6345.01 – us UMI [629]
AIR FORCE LAW REVIEW / U.S. Army. Air Force – (v1-6 no 5 titled: U.S. Air Force JAG Bulletin. v6 no 6-v15 no 2 titled: JAG Law Review. Updates planned) – v1-38. Mar 1959-1994 – 156mf – 9 – $234.00 – LLMC 80-527 – us L.L.M.C. [340]
AIR FORCE LAW REVIEW – (Cont: United States Air Force JAG Law Review) – Maxwel AFB. v16- Spr 1974- 1; v17- Spr 1975- 5*; v18- Spr 1976- 9 – 1,5,9 – D5750.01 – us UMI [340]
AIR FORCE MAGAZINE – (Vols 1-9 (1918-25) & v19 n1-8 were not available for filming. Former titles: DMA Weekly News Letter (sep 21 1918-mar 29 1919); Air Service News Letter (apr 5 1919-jan 1927); Air Corps News Letter (feb 1927-aug 1941); Air Forces News Letter (sep 1941-42); Air Force (dec 1942-may 1959); Air Force and Space Digest (jun 1959-jan 1971)) – Washington. v10-80 1926-dec 1997+ 1; v49-80 jan 1966-dec 1997+ 5; v58-80 jan 1975-dec 1997+ 9 – 1,5,9 – D1541 – us UMI [350]
AIR FORCE RESEARCH REVIEW – (Ceased publ. Former title: OAR Research Review (feb 1962-jun 1970)) – Washington. v1-3. feb 1962-dec 1971 – 1 – D6288 – us UMI [355]
AIR FORCE TIMES – 1942-67. Some wanting – 1 – 1,127.00 – us L of C Photodup [629]
AIR FORCE TIMES – Springfield. v1-58 1947-aug 1998+ 1; v40-58 jul 1979-aug 1998+ 5,9 – 1,5,9 – D1760 – us UMI [350]
AIR FORCES NEWS LETTER *see* AIR FORCE MAGAZINE
AIR FORCE/SPACE DIGEST INTERNATIONAL *see* AEROSPACE INTERNATIONAL
AIR FORCE/SPACE DIGEST INTERNATIONAL – (Cont by: Aerospace International) – Washington. v1-2. jan 1965-oct 1966* – 1 – D6701 – us UMI [629]
AIR LAW REVIEW – New York University. v1-12. 1930-1941 (complete) – 61r – 1 – $91.00 – LLMC 95-111 – us L.L.M.C. [340]
AIR LAWS AND TREATIES OF THE WORLD / U.S. Library of Congress – Washington: GPO. 3v. 1965 (all publ) – 48mf – 9 – $72.00 – LLMC 81-408 – us L.L.M.C. [340]
AIR LINE PILOT – Herndon. v1- apr 1932- 1; v40- jan 1971- 5*; v45- jan 1976- 9 – 1,5,9 – D2766 – us UMI [380]
AN AIR OF MOZART, WITH VARIATIONS FOR A VIOLIN AND VIOLONCELLO / ed by Cohen, E G W – (Parts) – London, 1800 – 1 – us Sibley [780]
AIR POLLUTION : ALL KNOWN ARTICLES RELATING TO AIR POLLUTANTS AND AIR POLLUTION CONTROLS – (18,454 articles. Accession cards, author cards, subject cards available) – 139r – 1 – $6,950.00 – B70065 – us Library Micro [360]
Air Pollution Control Association *see*
- JOURNAL
- JOURNAL OF THE AIR POLLUTION CONTROL ASSOCIATION

AIR POLLUTION METEOROLOGY IN ISRAEL / Israel. Ministry of Transport Meteorological Service – National Survey. Part 1. 1976. 260 p – 9 – $5.00 – is I.T.T.I. [360]
AIR POLLUTION TITLES – (All that is currently available. The micro-ed is the nov/dec cumulative issue) – University Park. 1967-1971 v8-27 nov 1972-dec 1991 1; v8-15 nov 1972-dec 1979 5 – 1,5 – D7667 – us UMI [360]
AIR POWER – The Air Force quarterly. v. 1-7. 1953-60 – 1 – 60.00 – us L of C Photodup [629]
AIR POWER HISTORIAN – v. 1-10. 1954-63 – 1 – 37.00 – us L of C Photodup [629]
AIR POWER HISTORIAN *see* AEROSPACE HISTORIAN
AIR POWER HISTORY *see* AEROSPACE HISTORIAN
AIR POWER HISTORY – (Cont: Aerospace Historian) – Washington. v36-. Spr 1989- – 1,5,9 – D1519.01 – us UMI [629]
AIR PROGRESS – (Vols 1-16 not available for filming. Cont by: Air Progress Affordable Flying) – Canoga Park. v44-57 1982-sep 1995 1; v30-57 jan 1972-sep 1995 5; v34-57 jan 1974-sep 1995 – 1,5,9 – D6583 – us UMI [380]
AIR PROGRESS *see* AIR PROGRESS AFFORDABLE FLYING
AIR PROGRESS AFFORDABLE FLYING *see* AIR PROGRESS
AIR PROGRESS AFFORDABLE FLYING – (Cont: Air Progress) – Canoga Park. v57-. oct 1995- – 1,5,9 – D6583.01 – us UMI [629]
AIR REPAIR *see* JOURNAL OF THE AIR POLLUTION CONTROL ASSOCIATION
AIR RESCUE INFORMATION LETTER – 1951-56 – 1 – 41.00 – us L of C Photodup [629]
AIR RESERVE FORCES REVIEW *see* AIR RESERVIST
AIR RESERVIST – (Cont by: Citizen Airman. Former title: Air Reserve Forces Review (jun 1949-jun 1952)) – Washington. v26-37 may 1974-Fal 1985 1; v28-37 apr 1976-Fal 1985 5,9 – 1,5,9 – D7421 – us UMI [355]
AIR [SAXON] WITH VARIATIONS FOR THE PIANO / Gelinek, J – London: Bland & Weller, 181- – 1 – us Sibley [780]
AIR SERVICE AND AIR CORPS NEWS LETTER, 1918-1935 / U.S. Army – 5r – 1 – $425.00 – S1652 – us Scholarly Res [355]
AIR SERVICE NEWS LETTER *see* AIR FORCE MAGAZINE
AIR TRAILS *see* AMERICAN AIRCRAFT MODELER
AIR TRAILS AND SCIENCE FRONTIERS *see* AMERICAN AIRCRAFT MODELER
AIR TRAILS HOBBIES FOR YOUNG MEN *see* AMERICAN AIRCRAFT MODELER
AIR TRAILS PICTORIAL *see* AMERICAN AIRCRAFT MODELER
AIR TRANSPORT WORLD – New York. v1-11 1964-74* 1; v12-34 jan 1975-dec 1997+ 1,5,9 – 1,5,9 – D10339 – us UMI [380]
AIR UNIVERSITY DISPATCH – v. 1-17. 1947-63 – 1 – 186.00 – us L of C Photodup [629]
AIR UNIVERSITY QUARTERLY – v. 1-13. 1947-62 – 1 – 127.00 – us L of C Photodup [629]
AIR UNIVERSITY QUARTERLY REVIEW *see* AIR UNIVERSITY REVIEW

AIR UNIVERSITY REVIEW – (Cont by: Airpower Journal. Former title: Air University Quarterly Review (Spr 1947-Sum 1963)) – Maxwell AFB. v1-38 Spr 1947-mar 1987 1; v22-38 nov 1970-mar 1987 5; v27-38 nov 1975-mar 1987 9 – 1,5,9 – D1772 – us UMI [370]

AIR UNIVERSITY REVIEW / U.S. Army. Air Force – v1-38 no 2. 1947-Mar 1987 (all publ) – 372mf – 9 – $558.00 – LLMC 80-528 – us L.L.M.C. [073]

AIR UNIVERSITY REVIEW, UNITED STATES ED *see* AIRPOWER JOURNAL

AIR VARIE POUR VIOLON ET VIOLONCELLE / Barni, C – (Parts) – Paris: Hanry, ca 1806 – 1 – us Sibley [780]

AIR WEATHER SERVICE OBSERVER – v1-10 Nov 1954-63. Missing 1962 – 1 – $20.00 – us L of C Photodup [550]

Airay, Henry *see* LECTURES UPON THE WHOLE EPISTLE OF ST PAUL TO THE PHILIPPIANS

AIRCONDITIONING AND REFRIGERATION BUSINESS – (Cont by: Contracting Business. Former titles: Refrigeration Industry (jun 1944-mar 1949); Commercial Refrigeration and Air Conditioning (apr 1949-apr 1958); Refrigeration and Airconditioning Business (may 1958-feb 1964)) – Cleveland. v1-38 jun 1944-aug 1981 – 1,5*,9* – D797 – us UMI [621]

AIRCRAFT – A journal published in the interest of aviation. London. v. 1, no. 1-v. 3, no. 33. Aug. 1916-Dec. 25, 1918. Incomplete – 1 – us NY Public [073]

AIRCRAFT AND MISSILES *see* AEROSPACE MANAGEMENT

AIRCRAFT AND MISSILES MANUFACTURING *see* AEROSPACE MANAGEMENT

AIRCRAFT ECONOMICS – London, 1992- 1*; 1995- 5,9 – 1,5,9 – D22021 – us UMI [629]

AIRCRAFT ENGINEERING – v. 1-35. 1929-63 – 1 – 589.00 – us L of C Photodup [629]

The Aircraft Shop Stewards National Council *see* THE NEW PROPELLOR

AIRCRAFT TIMES – Los Angeles, CA. Sept 1941-Feb 1946 – 4r – 1 – $200.00 – C02367 – us Library Micro [071]

AIRDIE AND COATBRIDGE TELEGRAPH *see* WEEKLY TELEGRAPH

AIRDRIE ADVERTISER AND LINLITHGOWSHIRE STANDARD – Scotland, 1899-1957 – 52r – 1 – uk British Libr Newspaper [072]

AIRDRIE AND COATBRIDGE ADVERTISER – 1 – £42.00r – uk Scot News [072]

AIRDRIE AND COATBRIDGE ADVERTISER – Scotland, 1957-81 – 14r – 1 – uk British Libr Newspaper [072]

AIRDRIE AND COATBRIDGE ADVERTISER *see* AIRDRIE ADVERTISER AND LINLITHGOWSHIRE STANDARD

AIRDRIE AND COATBRIDGE LUMINARY – Scotland, 22 May-11 Sep 1847; 18,25 Dec 1851; 1 Jan-10 Mar 1852 – 1/4r – 1 – uk British Libr Newspaper [072]

Airdrie. New Monkland Cemetery *see* REGISTER OF BURIALS

AIRFINANCE JOURNAL – Coggeshall, 1980- 1*; jan 1991-* 5,9 – 1,5,9 – D19527 – us UMI [073]

AIRFIX MAGAZINE FOR MODELLERS – v19-1977- – 1,5,6,9 – us UMI [790]

AIRFIX MAGAZINE FOR PLASTIC MODELLERS – (v.15-18. 1975-77 5,6,9) – v.1-18. 1960-77 – 1 – us UMI [073]

Airi, Raghunath *see* CONCEPT OF SARASVATI (IN VEDIC LITERATURE)

THE AIRLIFTER – Dover. Del. -w. 1972-75 – 1 – us UMI [071]

AIRLINE EXECUTIVE – (Cont by: Airline Executive International) – Atlanta. v1-13 oct 1977-dec 1989 1*; v7-13 jan 1983-dec 1989 5*,9 – 1,5,9 – D14110 – us UMI [380]

AIRLINE EXECUTIVE *see* AIRLINE EXECUTIVE INTERNATIONAL

AIRLINE EXECUTIVE INTERNATIONAL *see* AIRLINE EXECUTIVE

AIRLINE EXECUTIVE INTERNATIONAL – (Ceased publ. Cont: Airline Executive) – Atlanta. v14-15. jan 1990-dec 1991 – 1,5,9 – D14110.01 – us UMI [380]

AIRMAN – v. 1-7. Aug 1957-63 – 1 – 85.00 – us L of C Photodup [355]

AIRMAN – Washington. v1- aug 1957- 1; v18-jan 1974- 5,9 – 1,5,9 – D7243 – us UMI [073]

AIRONE – 1991-1995 – 1r per y – 5,6 – Sfr401.00 – sz Infoprint [073]

AIRPORT AREA : CULVER CITY, EL SEGUNDO, GARDENA, REDONDO BEACH, SANTA MONICA, ETC. – 1975- – 33+ r – 1 – $1,650.00 – P00001 – us Library Micro [910]

AIRPOWER HISTORIAN *see* AEROSPACE HISTORIAN

AIRPOWER JOURNAL *see* AIR UNIVERSITY REVIEW

AIRPOWER JOURNAL – (Cont: Air University Review, United States Edition) – Maxwell AFB. v1-. Sum 1987- – 1,5,9 – D16177 – us UMI [073]

AIR-RAID OVER BARCELONA – (Richardson, Stanley). n.p. 193? Fiche W 1138. (Blodgett Collection of Spanish Civil War Pamphlets) – 9 – us H.U. College Libr [946]

AIRS CONNUS VARIES, RECUEIL D'. OP. 71 / Dussek, J L – Paris: Nadermann, 181- – 1 – us Sibley [780]

AIRS DETACHES DE MELIDE, OU LE NAVIGATEUR / Philidor, F A – Paris: de Boubers, 17– – 1 – us Sibley [780]

AIRS ET DUO DU MARIAGE SECRET [COMEDIE LYRIQUE] / Kohaut J – (In Process) – Paris, 1768? – 1 – us Sibley [780]

AIRS, MARCHES, MINUETTS... / McEwan – (Hautboy primo part only) – Leicester[?], 178- – 1 – us Sibley [780]

AIRTIGHT GRAIN STORAGE – 1973 repr 1980 – 71p – it F.A.O. [660]

AIR/WATER POLLUTION REPORT – Silver Spring. v1-35 oct 1963-dec 1997+ 1*; v12-35 jan 1974-dec 1997+ 5*,9* – 1,5,9 – D10200 – us UMI [360]

AIRWORTHINESS MANUAL – 1986. T51-13-1986 – 1mf – 9 – Can$41.00 – cn Communication [629]

AISC (AMERICAN INSTITUTE OF STEEL CONSTRUCTION) – Standards. Printed index. Updated every 60 days – 6,9 – us Info Handling [690]

AISI (AMERICAN IRON AND STEEL INSTITUTE) – Printed index. Updated every 60 days – 6,9 – us Info Handling [670]

Aisy, J *see* LE GENIE DE LA LANGUE FRANCOISE

Aitchison, C U. *see*
- A COLLECTION OF TREATIES, ENGAGEMENTS AND SANADS
- A COLLECTION OF TREATIES, ENGAGEMENTS AND SUNNUDS, RELATING TO INDIA AND NEIGHBOURING COUNTRIES

Aitchison, J E T *see* A CATALOGUE OF THE PLANTS OF THE PUNJAB AND SINDH

Aitchison, Jean *see* BIBLIOGRAPHY OF MONO- AND MULTILINGUAL VOCABULARIES, THESAURI, SUBJECT HEADINGS AND CLASSIFICATION SCHEMES IN THE SOCIAL SCIENCES

Aitken, Douglas J *see* NEW MEANING FOR EDUCATION

Aitken, George Atherton *see* THE LIFE AND WORKS OF JOHN ARBUTHNOT, M.D., FELLOW OF THE ROYAL COLLEGE OF PHYSICIANS

Aitken, Michael J *see* REGULATING TAXI OPERATORS: SOME HISTORICAL INSIGHTS

Aitken, William Benford *see* THE DOMINION OF CANADA: A STUDY OF ANNEXATION

Aitkin, George *see* SOLOMONS TOK TOK

Aiton, W *see*
- HORTUS KEWENSIS

Aiyar, P S *see* CONFLICT OF RACES IN SOUTH AFRICA

AIZ – ARBEITER-ILLUSTRIERTE ZEITUNG *see* SOWJETRUSSLAND IM BILD

AIZ ARBEITER-ILLUSTRIERTE ZEITUNG – Berlin and Prag.Nov 1924-12 Aug 1936 – 1 – gw Mikrofilm [072]

Aizcorbe, Roberto *see* ARGENTINA, THE PERONIST MYTH

L'AIZI. ESQUISSE PHONOLOGIQUE ET ENQUETE LEXICALE / Herault, G – (Africa series). 1971 – 9 – fr Hachette [470]

AJA – Banaras, India. Mar 1947-1959; 1961-94 – 185r – 1 – us L of C Photodup [072]

AJAX : A MONTHLY MAGAZINE FOR LOVERS OF LITERATURE – (Ceased publ) – Alton. v1-6. nov 1916-dec 1921 – 1 – D4640 – us UMI [073]

AJAX COMMANDER – Ajax, 1942-1965 – 1r – 1 – cn Preston [971]

AJAX GUARDIAN – Ajax, 1960-1973 – 8r – 1 – cn Preston [971]

Ajisafe, Ajayi Kolawole *see*
- HISTORY OF ABEOKUTA
- THE LAWS AND CUSTOMS OF THE YORUBA PEOPLE

AJOQ (ATELIER DE LA JEUNESSE OUVRIERE) – Montreal, nov 1971 – 1r – 1 – Can$20.00 – cn Can Microfilming [073]

AJOT : THE AMERICAN JOURNAL OF OCCUPATIONAL THERAPY – (Cont & cont by: American Journal of Occupational Therapy) – Bethesda. v32-33. jan 1978-dec 1979 – 1,5,9 – $82.90y – D10224.01 – us UMI [615]

AJOT *see*
- AMERICAN JOURNAL OF OCCUPATIONAL THERAPY

AJR : AMERICAN JOURNAL OF ROENTGENOLOGY – (Cont: American Journal of Roentgenology, Radium Therapy, and Nuclear Science) – Springfield. v126-169. jan 1976-dec 1997+ – 1,5,9 – D1574.01 – us UMI [615]

AJURICABA – Manaos, Amazonas. 10 Set 1934 – 1,5,6 – bl Biblioteca [072]

AJURICABA : PERIODICO NACIONALISTA – Manaos, Amazonas. 7 Abr 1920 – 1,5,6 – bl Biblioteca [072]

Akademi Angkatan Bersendjata Republik Indonesia *see* MADJALAH

AKADEMI AURI / Muljono, Sri – SE-4551 1. 1962 – 9 – ne IDC [950]

THE AKADEMI ILMU PELAJARAN; PAST, PRESENT AND FUTURE : REPORT OF PROGRESS MADE IN IMPROVING MARITIME TRAINING IN INDONESIA AND A BLUEPRINT FOR THE FUTURE / U.S. Agency for International Development – SE 4656 1. 1964 – 9 – ne IDC [370]

THE AKADEMI ILMU PELAJARAN; PAST, PRESENT AND FUTURE. INDONESIAN MARITIME TRANSPORTATION / U.S. Agency for International Development – SE 4657 1 – 9 – ne IDC [324]

AKADEMIA KIJOWSKO-MOHILANSKA / Jablonowski, A – Krakow. 1899-1900. BR-5556 2 – 8 – ne IDC [943]

Akademia Nauk SSSR Institut slaviano Vediniia *see* K STOLETIIU GEROICHESKOI BOR'BY ZA NASHU I VASHU SVOBODU

AKADEMICHESKIE ARKHIVY SSSR ZA 50 LET SOVETSKOI VLASTI (TRUDY 1-GO SOVESHCHANIIA ARKHIVISTOV AKADEMII NAUK SSSR I AKADEMII NAUK SOIUZNYKH RESPUBLIK, 17-23 MAIA 1967 G.) / ed by Levshin, B V – Moscow, 1968.313p. Articles surveying development of selected archives under Academy of Sciences. BR-10,948/1 – 9 – ne IDC [025]

Akademie der Wissenschaften. Berlin *see*
- ABHANDLUNGEN
- BERICHT
- BERLINER ASTRONOMISCHES JAHRBUCH
- GENERAL INDEX OF ALL PUBLICATIONS 1710-1899, OF "ABHANDLUNGEN" 1710-1870, OF "BERICHT" AND "MONATSBERICHT" 1836-58, 1859-73, 1874-81
- HISTOIRE
- HISTOIRE DE L'ACADEMIE
- HISTOIRE DE L'ACADEMIE ROYALE DES SCIENCES ET DES BELLES-LETTRES DE BERLIN
- JAHRBUCH
- MATHEMATISCH-NATURWISSENSCHAFTLICHE KLASSE ABHANDLUNGEN
- MATHEMATISCH-NATURWISSENSCHAFTLICHE KLASSE SITZUNGSBERICHTE
- MEMOIRES
- MEMOIRES DE L'ACADEMIE ROYALE DES SCIENCES ET BELLES-LETTRES DEPUIS L'AVENEMENT DE FREDERIC GUILLAUME 2 FREDERIC GUILLAUME 3 AU THRONE
- MISCELLANEA BEROLINENSIA
- MISCELLANEA BEROLINENSIA AD INCREMENTUM SCIENTIARUM, EX SCRIPTIS SOCIETATI REGIAE SCIENTIARUM EXHIBITIS EDITA, CUM FIGVRIS AENEIS ET INDICE MATERIARUM
- MONATSBERICHTE
- NOUVEAUX MEMOIRES
- NOUVEAUX MEMOIRES DE L'ACADEMIE ROYALE DES SCIENCES ET BELLES-LETTRES
- PHILOSOPHISCH-HISTORISCHE KLASSE: ABHANDLUNGEN
- PHILOSOPHISCH-HISTORISCHE KLASSE: SITZUNGSBERICHTE
- SAMMLUNG DER DEUTSCHEN ABHANDLUNGEN
- SITZUNGSBERICHTE
- SITZUNGSBERICHTE PHYSIKALISCH-MATHEMATISCHE KLASSE

Akademie der Wissenschaften. Goettingen *see*
- ABHANDLUNGEN
- COMMENTARII
- NOVI COMMENTARII SOCIETATIS REGIAE SCIENTIARUM GOETTINGENSIS

Akademie der Wissenschaften. Munich *see*
- ABHANDLUNGEN DER CHURFUERSTLICH-BAIERISCHEN AKADEMIE DER WISSENSCHAFTEN
- METEOROLOGISCHE EPHEMERIDEN.
- NEUE PHILOSOPHISCHE ABHANDLUNGEN
- PHYSIKALISCHE ABHANDLUNGEN.

Akademie der Wissenschaften. Vienna *see*
- MATHEMATISCH-NATURWISSENSCHAFTLICHE KLASSE: SITZUNGSBERICHTE

Akademie Gemeinnuetziger Wissenschaften zu Erfurt *see*
- ACTA ACADEMIAE ELECTORALIS MOGUNTINAE SCIENTIARUM QUAE ERFURTI EST, AD ANNUM 1776-95
- ACTA ACADEMIAE ELECTORALIS MOGUNTINAE SCIENTIARUM UTILIUM QUAE ERFORDIAE EST
- UEBERSETZUNGEN UND DEUTSCHE ABHANDLUNGEN WELCHE BEY DER CHURFURSTLICHE MAINZISCHEN.

Akademiia Dukhovnaia. Leningrad *see* OPISANIE KNIG GRAZHDANSKOI PECHATI

Akademiia Nauk *see*
- OPYT OBLASTNAGO VELIKORUSSKAGO SLOVARIA
- OTCHET O DEIATELNOSTI OTDELENIIA RUSSKAGO IAZYKA I SLOVESNOSTI
- SISTEMATICHESKII I ALFAVITNYIA UKAZATEL' STATEI, POMESHCHENYKH V PERIODICHESKIKH IZDANIIAKH I SBORNIKAKH IMP. AKADEMII NAUK, A TAKZHE SOCHINENII, IZDANNYKH AKADEMIEIU OTDEL'NO

Akademiia Nauk Azerbaidzhanskoi SSRAzaerbajgan. S S R Elmaer Akademiiasynyn Chaebaerlaeri *see* SERIIA GEOLOGO-GEOGRAFICHESKIKH NAUK

Akademiia Nauk Azerbaidzhanskoi SSRAzaerbajgan S S R Elmlaer Akademiiasynyn Chaebaerlaeri *see* SERIIA BIOLOGICHESKIKH I SEL'SKOKHOZIAISTVENNYKH NAUK

Akademiia Nauk. BSSR *see* COMPTES-RENDUS DE L'ACADEMIE DES SCIENCES DE RUSSIE

Akademiia Nauk Kazakhskoi SSSR *see* REVOLIUTSIIA 1905-1907 GODOV V KAZAKHSTANE

Akademiia Nauk. Kiev *see* ZAPYSKY ISTORYCHNO-FILOLOHICHNOHO VIDDILU UKRAJINS'KOI AKADEMIJI NAUK

Akademiia Nauk. Okhrannaia opis' Rukopisnogo otdeleniia Biblioteki imp *see* 1 KNIGI SVIASHCHENNOGO PISANIIA

Akademiia Nauk. Otdelyeniye Russakavo Yazyka i Slovesnosti. St Petersburg *see* SBORNIK

Akademiia Nauk. Saint Petersburg *see* SPISOK RUSSKIKH POVREMENNYKH IZDANII S 1703 PO 1899 GOD. PRINADLEZHASHCHIKH BIBLIOTEKE IMP

Akademiia Nauk. SSR Institut russkoi literatury. Pushkinskii dom *see* RUSSKII FOL'KLOR

Akademiia Nauk. SSSR *see*
- AFRIKANSKII ETNOGRAFICHESKII SBORNIK
- THE ANNALS OF THE RUSSIAN ACADEMY OF SCIENCE
- BOTANICHESKII ZHURNAL
- DAGESTANSIK FILIAL, MAKHACH-KALA
- DOKLADY
- DOKLADY I SOOBSHCHENIIA INSTITUTA ISTORII
- ISTORIIA BIBLIOTEKI AKADEMII NAUK SSSR, 1714-1964
- SBORNIK PO RUSSKOMU YAZYKU I SLOVESNOSTI
- SPRAVOCHNIK-PUTEVODITEL PO BIBLIOTEKE AKADEMII NAUK SSSR

Akademiia Nauk. SSSR Biblioteki *see* SPRAVOCHNIK

Akademiia Nauk. SSSR Institut Istorii *see* RUSSKAIA ARMIIA I FLOT V 18. VEKE (OCHERKI)

Akademiia Nauk. SSSR Institut mirovoi literatury im. A M *see* PROBLEMY REALIZMA V RUSSKOI LITERATURE XVIII VEKA

Akademiia Nauk. SSSR Institut Prava *see* OSNOVNYE ZADACHI NAUKI SOVETSKOGO SOTSIALISTICHESKOGO PRAVA

Akademiia Nauk. SSSR. Institut Russkoi Literatury *see* LITERATURA

Akademiia Nauk. SSSR Institut Russkovo Yazyka *see* DIALEKTOLOGICHESKI SEKTOR

Akademiia nauk SSSR, Institut vysokomolekuliarnykh soedinenii i Biblioteka Akademii nauk SSSR *see* BIBLIOGRAFICHESKII UKAZATEL RABOT NAUCHNYKH SOTRUDNIKOV INSTITUTA VYSOKOMOLEKULIARNYKH SOEDINENII AN SSSR

Akademiia Nauk. SSSR Opisanie Rukopisnogo otdeleniia Biblioteki Akademii nauk SSSR *see* RUKOPISI

Akademiia nauk SSSR, Otdelenie ordena Lenina Instituta khimicheskoi fiziki *see* GORENIE I VZRYV

Akademiia nauk SSSR, Sibirskoe otdelenie *see* CHISLENNYE METODY MEKHANIKI SPLOSHNOI SREDY

Akademiia nauk SSSR. Sibirskoe otdelenie, Gosudarstvennaia publichnaia nauchno-tekhnicheskaia biblioteka *see* IZ ISTORII KNIGI, BIBLIOTECHNOGO DELA I BIBLIOGRAFII V SIBIRI

Akademiia Nauk. URSR. Kiev. *see* ZVIDOMLENNYA

Akademiia Nauk. URSR. Kiev. Etnografichna Komisiia *see* ETNOGRAFICHNII VISNIK

Akademiia Nauk. URSR. Kiev. Instytut Budivel'noi Mekhaniky *see* NAUKOVI PRATSI

Akademiia Nauk. URSR. Kiev. Instytut Elektrozvaryuvannya *see* TRUDY PO AVTOMATICHESKOI SVARKE POD FLYUSOM

Akademiia Nauk. URSR. Kiev. Instytut Movy i Literatury *see* NAUKOVY ZAPYSKY

Akademiia Nauk. URSR. Kiev. Istorichna Sektsiia *see* ZAPISKI

Akademiia Nauk. URSR. Kiev. Istorichno-Filologichnii Viddil *see* ZAPISKI

Akademiia Nauk. URSR. Kiev. Istorychna Sektziya *see* KOMISSIYA ISTORYCHNOI PISENNOSTY UKRAYINS'KI NARODNI DUMY

Akademiia Nauk. USSR. Institute of Africa *see* AFRICAN STUDIES IN THE USSR

AKADEMIK VASILII ZUEV, EGO ZHIZN' I TRUDY / Raikov, BE – M., L. 1955. BR-7808 2 – 8 – ne IDC [920]

AKADEMISCHE FESTREDE ZU GRILLPARZERS HUNDERTSTEM GEBURTSTAGE : GEHALTEN IN DER AULA DES CAROLINUMS VON AUGUST SAUER / Sauer, August – Prag: J G Calve, 1891 – 1r – 1 – us U.W. Library [430]

AKALI – Jullundur, India. 1951-56; Apr-Jun 1971 – 5r – 1 – us L of C Photodup [072]

AKAN RELIGION AND THE CHRISTIAN FAITH / Williamson, S G – Accra, 1965 – 4mf – 8 – Dfl3.50ea – ne Slangenburg [290]

AKAN (TWI-FANTE) LANGUAGE COLLECTION / Warren, Denise M – Chicago: Uni of Chicago, Photodup Dept, [19–?] – 1 – us Res Libr [490]

AKASHVANI – New Delhi. v.7-26. May 1942-Oct 1961 – 1 – 230.00 – us L of C Photodup [410]

AKBARNAMA / Abu-el-Fazl – H. Beveridge (transl.). Bibliotheca Indica Series: Persian. Calcutta, 1899. 3 vols. (Asiatic Soc. Bengal. N.S. no. 940, 1077) Lacking: v. 3. BI-761 2 – 8 – ne IDC [890]

AKC GAZETTE – (Cont: Pure-Bred Dogs, American Kennel Gazette) – New York. v112-114. jan 1995-dec 1997+ – 1,5,9 – D8211.01 – us UMI [636]

Aken, Adolf Friedrich *see* DIE GRUNDZUEGE DER LEHRE VON TEMPUS UND MODUS IM GRIECHISCHEN

Akerman, J Y *see* REMAINS OF PAGAN SAXONDOM

Akerman, William *see* "THE BIBLE AND THE SQUARE": BEING A MASONIC MIRROR AND GUIDE, CONTAINING SCRIPTURAL AND MASONIC TEACHINGS, TO WHICH IS ADDED A SYMBOLIC CHART, WITH FULL EXPLANATIONS: A VALUABLE HANDBOOK TO THE CRAFT

Akeroyd, Ivy A *see* WHAT ARE HUMAN RIGHTS

Akesson, N B *see* USE OF AIRCRAFT IN AGRICULTURE

AKHBAR – Alger. janv-sept 1897, 1902-05, 1909-fevr 1934 – 1 – fr A.C.R.P.P. [073]

AKHBAR AL-'ALAM AL-ISLAMI – Mecca, Saudi Arabia. 1977-1992 – 15r – 1 – us L of C Photodup [072]

AKHBAR AL-YOUM – (Egypt), 1944- – 52mf per yr – 9 – $300.00y – us Ross [072]

AKHBAR-I IRAN – Tehran, 197?-. – Dawrah-'i jadid, sal-i 6, shumarah-'i 10-38. 26 Day 1358-22 Mihr 1360 [26 Jan 1980-14 Oct 1981] – 1r – 1 – $25.00 – us MEDOC [956]

AKHBAR-I JABHAH-'I MILLI-I IRAN – [Tehran]: Kumisyun-i Intisharat va tablighat-i Jabhah-'i Milli-i Iran, Shumarah-'i 1-48. – 14 Bahman 1340-17 Urdibihisht 1342 [3 Feb 1942-7 May 1963] – 1r – 1 – $25.00 – us MEDOC [956]

AKHEIR SA'AH – (Egypt), 1944- – 52mf per yr – 9 – $300.00y – us Ross [072]

Akhmatova, A *see*
- "ADOL'F" BENZHAMENA KONSTANA V TVORCHESTVE PUSHKINA
- ANNO DOMINI 1921 STIKHI
- ANNO DOMINI 1921. STIKHOTVORENIIA
- BELAIA STAIA
- BELAIA STAIA. STIKHOTVORENIIA
- CHETKI. STIKHI
- DVA STIKHOTVORENIIA
- IZ TRAGEDII "PROLOG, ILI SON VO SNE"
- IZBRANNYE STIKHOTVORENIIA. IZD. IMENI CHEKHOVA
- K POEME, STIKHOTVORENIE. DEN' POEZII 1962
- OSIP MANDEL'SHTAM (LISTKI IZ DNEVNIKA). VOZDUSHNYE PUTI
- PODOROZHNIK
- POEMA BEZ GEROIA. TRIPTIKH. VOZDUSHNYE PUTI
- POSLEDNIAIA SKAZKA PUSHKINA
- REKVIEM
- STIKHOTVORENIIA
- STIKHOTVORENIIA 1909-1960

AKHMATOVA I MAIAKOVSKII / Chukovskii, K – In the collection Dom iskusstv. no. 1. Peterburg. 1921. Reprinted in I. Oksenov (Ed.). Sovremennaia russkaia kritika. L. 1925. BR-3649 2 – 8 – ne IDC [460]

AKHTAR – Istanbul, Sal-i 2, adad 61-sal-i 3, adad 17. – 11 Jan 1877-4 Apr 1977); sal-i 5, shumarah-i 1-50. – 25 Dec 1878-10 Dec 1879; sal-i 6, shumarah-i 1-49. – 17 Dec 1879-29 Oct 1880; sal-i 7, shumarah-i 1-48. – 9 Dec 1880-17 Nov 1881; sal-i 8, shumarah-i 1-51. – 24 Nov 1881-8 Nov 1882 – 2mf – 1 – $155.00 – us MEDOC [949]

Akhun, Mikhail Ilich *see* BOLSHEVIKI I ARMII A V 1905-1917 GG

AKIF BEY / Kemal, Namik – Istanbul, 1290 [1873] – $35.00 – us MEDOC [470]

Akif, Mehmed *see* SEBIL UER-RESAD

THE AKIKUYU, THEIR CUSTOMS, TRADITIONS AND FOLKLORE / Cagnolo, C – Nyeri, Kenya: Printed by Akikuyu in the Mission Printing School, 1933 – 1 – us Res Libr [306]

Akimoto, S *see* KELOEARGA DAN ROEMAH TANGGA NIPPON. DISALIN DENGAN MERDEKA...OLEH TUN SRI LANANG

Akimov, A *see* NE MOGU MOLCHAT

Akimushkin, O F *see* MATERIALY DLIA BIBLIOGRAFII RABOT O PERSIDSKIKH RUKOPISIAKH

AKIN – Guemuelcine [Komotini] Greece. Nos. 17, 29, 31, 49, 53, 79 (31 Mayis 1957-17 Ekim 1958) – 9 – $20.00 – us MEDOC [956]

Akindele, Adolphe *see* CONTRIBUTION A L'ETUDE DE L'HISTOIRE DE L'ANCIEN ROYAUME DE PORTO-NOVA

Akins, Ann S *see* DANCING IN DIXIE'S LAND

Akinyotu, Adetunji *see* A BIBLIOGRAPHY ON DEVELOPMENT PLANNING IN NIGERIA, 1955-1968

Akita Prefectural Library *see* SATAKE MONJO

AKKADISCHE GOETTEREPITHETA / Tallgvist, K – (Studia Orientalia. v. 7. Helsingforsiae. 1938). BNE-403 1 – 9 – ne IDC [290]

DER AKKADISCHE WETTERGOTT IN MESOPOTAMIEN / Schlobies, H – (Mitteilungen der altorientalischen gesellschaft. v. 1, pt. 1). Leipzig. 1925. BNE-20,101 1 – 9 – ne IDC [290]

AKKORD : NOVOSTI IZ MUZYKAL'NOGO MIRA (PRILOZHENIE K ZHURN. "RADUGA") – Moscow, 1884-86 – 14mf – 9 – us Ross [780]

AKLAT NG PAGLULUTO / Ignacio, Rosendo – Maynila: J. Martinez, 1919. 161p. plates. ill – 1 – us U.W. Library [640]

AKMEIZM / Dolinin, A S – Zavety, 5. 1913. BR-3652 2 – 8 – ne IDC [460]

AKMEIZM / Mikhailovskii, BV – Literatura XX veka (s devianostykh godov XIX veka do 1917 g.). M. 1939. BR-1432 2 – 8 – ne IDC [460]

AKMEIZM ILI ADAMIZM / Sovsun, V – Literaturnaia entsiklopediia. v. 70-73. I. M. 1930. BR-3701 2 – 8 – ne IDC [460]

AKMOLINSKIE OBLASTNYE VEDOMOSTI – Omsk, 1871-1919 – 42r – 1 – $3,750.00 coll – us Ross [072]

Akovenko, Vasillii Grigorevich *see* ZAPISKI PARTIZANA

Akovlev, Akov Arkadevich *see*
- PARTII A V BORBE S BIUROKRATIZMOM
- RUSSKI I ANARKHIZM V VELIKO I RUSSKO I REVOLIUTSII

Akridge, Sharon A Hollenbeck *see* CINDERELLA FROM THE PAMPAS

AKRON AND ENVIRONS: HISTORICAL BIOGRAPHICAL AND GENEALOGICAL / Olin, Oscar E – Chicago: Lewis Publ. Co., 1917. Ohio Reel 61.(The Cox Library Collection) – 5 – us Americana [978]

AKRON AND SUMMIT COUNTY / Kenfield, Scott D – Biographical sketches. Chicago: S. J. Clarke Publ. Co, 1928. Vols. 1-3. Ohio Reel 62. (The Cox Library Collection) – 5 – us Americana [978]

AKRON BUSINESS AND ECONOMIC REVIEW – (Former title: University of Akron Business Review) – Akron. v1-22 Spr 1970-Win 1991 1; v7-22 Spr 1976-Win 1991 5,9 – 1,5,9 – D8214 – us UMI [338]

AKRON LAW REVIEW – v. 1-. 1967- – 1. – apply; v.11- 1977- 5,6,9 – us UMI [340]

AKRON LAW REVIEW – (v1-18 1969-95 reel $230.00. v19-28 mf $203.00) – v1-28. 1967-95 – 5,6,9 – $433.00 set – us Hein [340]

Akron, Ohio *see* MISCELLANEOUS EARLY NEWSPAPERS

AKRON TAX JOURNAL – University of Akron. v1-11. 1983-95 – 9 – $98.00 set – us Hein [336]

AKROPOLIS – Athens, 5 Oct 1888-28 Sep 1912 – 50r – 1 – uk British Libr Newspaper [072]

AKROPOLIS : GRIECHISCHE TAGESZEITUNG IN DEUTSCHLAND – Bonn, Germany. 1 Sep 1978-1 Aug 1989 – 1 – gw Mikrofilm [072]

AKROPOLIS : GRIECHISCHE TAGESZEITUNG IN DEUTSCHLAND – Bonn, sep 1 1978-aug 1 1989 – 31r – 1 – Inquire at Mikrofilmarchiv for details – gw Misc Inst [072]

DIE AKROTERFIGUREN DES TEMPELS DER ATHENER AUF DELOS / Wester, Ursula – Heidelberg, 1969 – 2mf – 9 – DM62.00 – 3-89349-675-0 – gw Hänsel [730]

Aksakov, I S *see*
- I.S. AKSAKOV V EGO PIS'MAKH
- POLNOE SOBRANIE SOCHINENII

Aksakov, K S *see* POLNOE SOBRANIE SOCHINENII

Aksakov, ST *see* BIBLIOGRAFICHESKII UKAZATEL' KNIG I STATEI I ZHIZNI I SOCHINENIIAKH EGO. 1816-1852

Aksakova, K S et al *see* MOSKOVSKII SBORNIK

AKSARIYAT – (Missing issues: 71-76, 109, 115, 118-119, 147) – West Germany: Sazman-i Fida'yan-i Khalq-i Iran Dar Kharij Az Kishvar. Shumarah-i 70-148 (28 Murdad 1364-11 Isfand 1365 [9 Aug 1985-2 Mar 1987]) – 9 – $25.00 – us MEDOC [956]

Akselrod, Pavel Borisovich *see*
- NARODNAIA DUMA I RABOCHI I SI EZD
- NARODNAIA DUMA I RABOCHI I SOI EZD
- RABOCHI I KLASS I REVOLIUTSIONNOE DVIZHENIE V ROSSII

AKSI AMBILALIH TONGGAK BERSEDJARAH MENGGANJANG "MALAYSIA." SE 4723/1. 1964 / Sentral Organisasi Buruh Seluruh Indonesia – 9 – ne IDC [025]

AKS-I SADA. ANADOLU SESLERI – Samsun. No. 1023 (25 Kanunisani 1336 [1920]) – 9 – $20.00 – us MEDOC [956]

AKTA GRODZKIE I ZIEMSKIE Z CZASOW RZECZYPOSPOLITEJ POLSKIEJ Z ARCHIWUM TAK ZWANEGO BERNARDYNSKIEGO WE LWOWIE – v. 1-25. 1868-1935 – 1 – 203.00 – us L of C Photodup [943]

DIE AKTEN DER EDESSENISCHEN BEKENNER CURJAS, SAMONAS UND ABIBOS (T.U.U. 3-37/2) / Gebhardt, Oscar von – Leipzig, 1911 – 5mf – 9 – ne Slangenburg [240]

AKTEN DER PARTEIKANZLEI DER NSDAP = FILES OF THE NATIONAL SOCIALIST PARTY CHANCELLERY : A RECONSTRUCTION OF LOST RECORDS / Institut fuer Zeitgeschichte Muenchen – 1983-1992 – 491mf (1:48) – 9 – silver DM9,800.00 – 3-598-30260-6 – gw Saur [943]

AKTEN DER PRINZIPALKOMMISSION DES IMMERWAEHRENDEN REICHSTAGES ZU REGENSBURG 1663-1806 – 1990-1992 – 5,118mf (1:24) – 9 – silver DM24,000.00 – 3-598-33080-4 – gw Saur [943]

DIE AKTEN DES VOGELSANGS : ERZAEHLUNG / Raabe, Wilhelm Karl – Leipzig: P Reclam, 1944 – 1r – 1 – us U.W. Library [830]

DIE AKTEN DES VOGELSANGS / Raabe, Wilhelm Karl – Berlin: Otto Janke, 1896 – 1r – 1 – us U.W. Library [830]

AKTEN UEBER DIE KRANKHEIT VON HEINRICH HEINES VATER – (Includes bibliographical references) – Kiel: Wissenschaftliche Gesellschaft fuer Literatur und Theater, 1928 – 1r – 1 – us U.W. Library [616]

AKTEN-STUECKE DIE REFORM DER JUEDISCHEN KOLONIEN IN DEN PREUSSISCHEN STAATEN BETREFFEND / Friedlaender, D – Berlin. 1793. BJ-23-110 1 – 9 – ne IDC [943]

AKTENSTUECKE ZUM CONCIL = SELECTIONS : DAS INFALLIBILITAETSSCHEMA UND DIE MINORITAETSGUTACHTEN / Vatican Council. 1st – (Texts in German and Latin) – Stuttgart: J G Cotta, 1870 – 1mf – 9 – 0-8370-8479-2 – 1986-2479 – us A.T.L.A. [240]

DIE AKTENSTUECKE ZUM FRIEDEN VON S. GERMANO 1230 (MGH EPISTOLAE 4: 4.BD) – 1926 – Dfl9.00 – ne Slangenburg [240]

Aktepe, M Muenir *see* TARIH-I LUTFI

DIE AKTION – Berlin, 1914-23, 1925-28 – 1 – Dist. gw Mikrofilm – gw Misc Inst [700]

DIE AKTION – Berlin, 1939-43 (incomplete) – 1 – Dist. gw Mikrofilm – gw Misc Inst [072]

DIE AKTION : ZEITSCHRIFT FUER DEN KOMMUNISMUS – v5-22. 1915-32 – 1r – 1 – us Ross [073]

AKTIONSARTEN MIT GRADUIERENDER SEMANTIK IN DER RUSSISCHEN SPRACHE DER GEGENWART / Suchy, Anke – 1995 – 2mf – 9 – DM80.00 – 3-8267-2130-6 – gw Hänsel [460]

AKTIVES ZUHOEREN UND BEHALTEN : EINE EMPIRISCHE UNTERSUCHUNG / Haensel, Anette – 1992 – 9 – DM98.00 – 3-89349-482-0 – gw Hänsel [400]

AKTSIONER – Gazeta promyshlennosti i torgovli. Pribavlenie k gazete "Den'". v. 1-52. M. 1863. Lacking: v. 6, 13, 22, 23, 24. BR-1502 2 – 8 – ne IDC [073]

AKTSIONER – Pribavlenie k Vestniku promyshlenosti. M. 1860-61. BR-1503 2 – 8 – ne IDC [073]

DER AKTUAR SALZMANN : GOETHE'S FREUND UND TISCHGENOSSE IN STRASSBURG: EINE LEBENS-SKIZZE, NEBST BRIEFEN VON GOETHE, LENZ, L. WAGNER, MICHAELIS, HUFELAND U.A. / Stoeber, August – (Includes bibliographical references) – Frankfurt a.M.: Th Voelcker, 1855 – 1 – us U.W. Library [920]

AKTUELLE DERMATOLOGIE – Stuttgart. v1-. feb 1977- – 1 – D10149 – us UMI [616]

AKTUELLE FRAUENARBEITSSCHUTZPOLITIK : URSACHEN UND KONSEQUENZEN (DER AUFHEBUNG) DES NACHTARBEITSVERBOTES / Anemueller, Susann – 1993 – 1mf – 9 – DM98.00 – 3-89349-680-7 – gw Hänsel [331]

AKTUELLE GERONTOLOGIE – (Cont: Actuelle Gerontologie) – Stuttgart. v4-13. jan 1974-nov 1983 – 1 – D10153.01 – us UMI [618]

AKTUELLE GESPRAECHE – (Lacking scattered issues) – v1-39. 1953-91 – 4r – 1 – ATLA S0851 – us A.T.L.A. [073]

DER AKTUELLE PRESSEDIENST *see* REICHSSENDER BRESLAU: NACHRICHTENDIENST

AKTUELLE TRAUMATOLGIE – (Former title: Actuelle Traumatologie) – Stuttgart. v1-. feb 1971-* – 1 – D10155 – us UMI [616]

AKTUELLE TRAUMATOLOGIE – Stuttgart. v1-. 1974-* – 1 – D10154 – us UMI [616]

AKTUELLE UROLOGIE – (Former title: Actuelle Urologie) – Stuttgart. v1-. 1970-* – 1 – D10156 – us UMI [616]

DIE AKTUELLE WEITERENTWICKLUNG IN DER ANLAGE-UMWELTDEBATTE DER INTELLIGENZ / Kostrzewa, Frank – 1993 – 2mf – 9 – DM98.00 – 3-89349-702-1 – gw Hänsel [150]

AKTUELLER FERNSEHDIENST – (Publ in Frankfurt/Main since mar 1958, in Bad Homburg vor der Hoehe since aug 3, 1966, in Muenchen since jun 1, 1971, in Berlin since jul 11, 1977) – Hamburg. sep 15, 1955-78 – 13r – 1 – gw Mikrofilm [072]

AKTUELT *see* SOCIAL-DEMOKRATEN; AKTUELT; DET FRI AKTUELT

AKTY / Russia. Kavkazskaya Arkheograficheskaya Kommissiya. Tiflis – v. 1-12. 181904 – 1 – us NY Public [324]

AKTY ISTORICHESKIE, SOBRANNYE I IZDANNYE ARKHEOGRAFICHESKOIU KOMMISSIEIU – St. Petersburg, 1841-72.17v. suppls. Historical records for 1334-1699 publ. in 1841-42 and suppl. with materials from the tenth to end of 17th cent. Much material of legal interest. B-1172/2 – 8 – ne IDC [947]
AKTY IURIDICHESKIE ILI SOBRANIE FORM STARINAGO DIELOPROIZVODSTA / Russia. Arkheograficheskaia Kommissiia – Leningrad, 1838 + index 1840 – 1r – 1 – us Ross [947]
AKTY IZDAVAEMYE VILENSKOIU ARKHEOGRAFICHESKOIU KOMMISSIEIU – Vilna, 1865-1915. v.1-39. B-1147 2 – 8 – ne IDC [930]
AKTY, OTNOSI ASHCHIESI A K ISTORII ZEMSKIKH SOBOROV – Moskva: Gos. izd-vo, 1920 – 1 – CSUX89-B1616 – us Hoover Inst Photo [999]
AKTY OTNOSIASHCHIESIA DO GRAZHDANSKOI RASPRAVY DREVNEI ROSSII – Kiev, 1860-63. 2v. B-68 2 – 8 – ne IDC [340]
AKTY, OTNOSIASHCHIESIA DO IURIDICHESKAGO BYTA DREVNEI ROSSII / Kalachov, N V – Moscow, 1857-64.BR-10,146/2 – 8 – ne IDC [947]
AKTY, OTNOSIASHCHIESIA K ISTORII IUZHNOI I ZAPADNOI ROSSII, SOBRANNYE I IZDANNYE ARKHEOGRAFICHESKOI KOMMISSIEIU – St. Petersburg, 1846-92. 15v. B-1068 2 – 8 – ne IDC [947]
AKTY, OTNOSYASHCHIESYA DO YURIDICHESKAGO BYTA DREVNEI ROSSII / Russia. Arkheograficheskaia Kommissiia – Leningrad, 1857-84 – 1r – 1 – us Ross [947]
AKTY, OTNOSYASHCHIESYA DO YURIDICHESKAGO BYTA DREVNEI ROSSII / Russia. Arkheograficheskaia Kommissiia – St Petersburg. 1857-1884 – 1 – us NY Public [930]
AKTY, SOBRANNYE V BIBLIOTEKAKH I ARKHIVAKH RUSSKOI IMPERATORSKOI ARKHEOGRAFICHESKOIU EKSPEDITSIEIU IMPERATORSKOI AKADEMII NAUK – Saint Petersburg, 1836-38. 4v. Documents collected in libraries and archives by the archeographical expedition of the Imperial Academy of Sciences concerning Russia social and economic history, 1294-1700. BR-112/2 – 8 – ne IDC [947]
AKTY SOTSIAL'NO-EKONOMICHESKOI ISTORII SEVEROVOSTOCHNOI RUSI KONTSA XIV-NACHALA XVI VV – Moscow, 1964. v3. BR-10,239/1 – 9 – ne IDC [947]
AKTY YURIDICHESKIYE / Russia. Arkheograficheskaia Kommissiia – St Petersburg. 1838 and Index, 1840 – 1 – us NY Public [930]
AKU PERTJAJA; SEBUAH URAIAN TENTANG INDJIL DAM SERUAN UNTUK PERTJAJA / Verkuyl, Johannes – SE 5162 1. 1961 – 9 – ne IDC [950]
Akubovskii, Georgii *see* LITERATURNYE PORTRETY, PISATELI KUZNITSY
Akushkin, Evgenii Evgenevich *see* FRANTSUZSKAIA INTERVENTSIIA NA IUGE 1918-1919
AKUSTISCHE ZEITSCHRIFT – (Ceased publ) – Leipzig. v1-9. sep 1936-jan 1944 – 1 – D185 – us UMI [621]
AKWESASNE NOTES – (Publ suspended in 1993 & 1994) – Mohawk Nation at Akwesasne. v1-23 feb 1969-Fal 1992 ns:1-Spr 1995- 1; v11-23 feb 1979-Fal 1992 ns:1- Spr 1995- 5,9 – 1,5,9 – D7156 – us UMI [978]
AKWESASNE NOTES – v1-9. 1969-81 – 168mf – 9 – $5.00f – us Ross [073]
AKZEPTANZPROBLEME BEIM EINSATZ INNOVATIVER INFORMATIONSTECHNOLOGIE IM BUERO- UND VERWALTUNGSBEREICH ANALYSIERT AM BEISPIEL EINES INDUSTRIEBETRIEBES / Wagner, Albert – Erlangen-Nuernberg, 1983 – 3mf – DM76.00 – 3-89349-902-4 – gw Hänsel [650]
Akzin, B *see* LES PROBLEMES FONDAMENTAUX DU DROIT INTERNATIONAL PUBLIC
AL COR – Asuncion, PY. 1964-1969 – 1r – $50.00 – R63578 – us Library Micro [072]
AL DIA SIGUIENTE / Amadeo, Mario – Buenos Aires, 1955 – 1 – CSUXADH2115-B – us Hoover Inst Photo [972]
AL FILO DEL MEDIO SIGLO / Carulla, Juan Emiliano – Buenos Aires: Editorial Huemul, [2nd ed 1964] – 1 – CSUXAJB7837-B – us Hoover Inst Photo [380]
AL LADO DEL GUADIANA / Vaca Morales, Francisco – Badajoz: Arqueros, 1943 – 1 – sp Bibl Santa Ana [946]
AL' MANAKH PECHATI – Sbornik svedenii o vsekh periodicheskikh izdaniiakh. Na 1909 god. Spb., 1909. BR-1647 2 – 8 – ne IDC [030]
Al Marrekoshi, Abdo-'L-Wahid *see* THE HISTORY OF THE ALMOHADES
AL PASAR ANTE LAS HORAS / Sanchez Arjona, Vicente – (Pensamientos vulgares) – Sevilla: Graficas T., Tomo 1. 1955. Tomo 2-5 – 1 – sp Bibl Santa Ana [946]
AL SINDICATO DE LA COMUNIDAD DE LABRADORES (PROYECTO DE COOPERATIVA VITICO-ALCOHOLERA EN ALMENDRALEJO) / Luengo, Juan – Badajoz: Uceda Hermanos, 1905 – 1 – sp Bibl Santa Ana [946]
AL ZURRIAGAZO ZURRIBANDA / Gallardo, Bartolome Jose – 1822 – 9 – 1.50f – sp Bibl Santa Ana [946]
ALA BULLETIN / American Library Association – (Ceased publ. Cont by: American Libraries. Former titles: Bulletin of the American Library Association (jan 1907-dec 1938)) – Chicago. v1-63 1907-dec 1969 1; v54-63 jan 1960-dec 1969 5* – 1,5 – D951 – us UMI [020]
ALA SANTISIMA VIRGEN DE LA LUZ 1978 / Asociacion Benefica Ntra. Sra. de la Luz. Malpartida de Plasencia – Imp. Sanchez Rodrigo, 1978 – sp Bibl Santa Ana [240]
ALA SANTISIMA VIRGEN DEL ROSARIO. ACTOS Y FESTEJOS EN SU HONOR, 1946 / Madronera. Ayuntamiento – Caceres: Tip. El Noticiero – sp Bibl Santa Ana [240]
ALABAMA – 13r – 1 – $1,040.00 – us Scholarly Res [370]
ALABAMA : CODE OF ALABAMA – Charlottesville: Michie Company, 1975-Aug 1996 – 9 – $1,137.00 set – us Hein [340]
ALABAMA : PERIODICO CRITICO, CHISTOSO, NOTICIOSO E LITTERARIO – [s.l.]. 17 Maio 1887 – 1,5,6 – bl Biblioteca [072]
ALABAMA : SESSION LAWS OF AMERICAN STATES AND TERRITORIES – 1818-1995 – 9 – $1,880.00 set – us Hein [340]
Alabama *see*
- BIENNIAL REPORTS (A-G), 1882-1936
- REPORTS PRE-NRS
- STATE REPORTS, POST-NRS

O ALABAMA : PERIODICO CRITICO E CHISTOSO – [s.l.]. 14 Jul 1866; Jul 1867; Jan 1869; Dez 1873; Nov 1876; Mar 1878; Maio, Nov 1879; Nov 1881; 11 Abr 1882 – 1,5,6 – bl Biblioteca [072]
Alabama Academy of Science *see* JOURNAL
ALABAMA AGRIBUSINESS / Auburn University. Cooperative Extension Service – v. 1-8. 1962-70 – 1,5,6 – us Spaulding [630]
ALABAMA AGRIBUSINESS / Auburn University. Extension Service – No.9-21.1970-82. 1 reel – 1, 5 – us Spaulding [630]
Alabama. Agricultural Experiment Station *see*
- AGRICULTURAL ECONOMICS MIMEOGRAPH
- AGRICULTURAL ECONOMICS SERIES
- AGRICULTURAL WEATHER SERIES
- BULLETIN
- CIRCULAR
- CORN VARIETIES FOR ALABAMA
- COTTON VARIETIES FOR ALABAMA
- FORESTRY DEPARTMENT SERIES
- GENERAL PUBLICATIONS
- GRAIN SORGHUM VARIETIES
- HIGHLIGHTS OF AGRICULTURAL RESEARCH
- HOME ECONOMICS RESEARCH DEPARTMENTAL SERIES
- LEAFLET
- PEANUT VARIETIES FOR ALABAMA
- POULTRY SCIENCE DEPARTMENTAL SERIES 1
- PROCEEDINGS OF THE ANNUAL STAFF CONFERENCE
- PROGRESS REPORT SERIES
- REPORT
- SMALL GRAIN VARIETY REPORT
- SPECIAL LEAFLET
- ZOOLOGY-ENTOMOLOGY DEPARTMENT SERIES

ALABAMA APPELLATE COURTS / Alabama. Supreme Court. Library – (2nd ed., Montgomery, 1970. 34p. LL-2276) – Montgomery, Ellis, 1968. 24 p. LL-2280 – 1 – us L of C Photodup [340]
ALABAMA ATTORNEY GENERAL REPORTS AND OPINIONS – (6 1882-1980 v178 $560.00. 9 1980-19954 v179-2364 $400.00) – v178. 1882-1995 – 6,9 – $960.00 set – us Hein [340]
ALABAMA BAPTIST – 4Feb 1843-Dec 1846, 1854-1963 – 1 – 2,455.63 – us Baptist [240]
ALABAMA BAPTIST – Birmingham. 1946-48; 1952-55; 1962-76 – 1 – 276.00 – us L of C Photodup [240]
ALABAMA BAR BULLETIN – 1939 – 9 – $5.00 set – us Hein [340]
Alabama. Canebrake Agricultural Experiment Station *see*
- BULLETIN
- REPORT

ALABAMA CENSUS RETURNS 1820 – 5 – us A.G.L.L. [310]
ALABAMA CHRISTIAN ADVOCATE *see* METHODIST CHRISTIAN ADVOCATE
Alabama Committee for Equal Justice *see* RELEASE
ALABAMA COURRIER – Athens, AL. 1931; 1941-49 – 1 – us UMI [071]
ALABAMA COURRIER AND LIMESTONE DEMOCRAT – Athens, AL. -w. 1950-68 – 1 – us UMI [071]
ALABAMA, HER HISTORY, RESOURCES, WAR RECORD AND PUBLIC MEN / Brewer, W – Montgomery: Barret and Brown Steam Printers and Bookbinders, 1872. Alabama Reel 2. (The Cox Library Collection) – 5 – us Americana [978]
ALABAMA INDEPENDENCE – Birmingham, AL. 1969 – 1 – us UMI [071]
ALABAMA JOURNAL – Montgomery. Ala. 1952- – 1 – us UMI [071]
ALABAMA LAW JOURNAL – Montgomery. v1-4. 1882-85 – 1 – $40.00 – us Hein [073]
THE ALABAMA LAW JOURNAL – (Cont by a modern series in 1925 but for copyright reasons is not offered at present by LLMC) – Montgomery, AL. v1-4. 1882-85 (complete) – 16mf – 9 – LLMC 82-900 – us L.L.M.C. [073]
ALABAMA LAW REVIEW – v1-46. 1948-1995 – 9 – $614.00 set – us Hein [340]
ALABAMA LAWYER – v1-56. 1940-1995 – 9 – $675.00 set – us Hein [340]
ALABAMA LIBRARIAN – Montgomery. cum index 1-10; v1- Dec 1949- 1; v21- jan 1970- 5*; v27- jan 1989- 9* – 1,5,9 – D2277 – us UMI [020]
Alabama. Polytechnic Institute. Extension Service *see*
- HOME AND FARM CONVENIENCES
- NINTH ALABAMA NATIONAL EGG LAYING DEMONSTRATION

Alabama. Polytechnic Institute. Extension Service. Negro Division *see* MONTHLY RADIO BROADCASTS
ALABAMA REVIEW – University. v1- jan 1948- 1*; v42- jan 1989- 5*,9 – 1,5,9 – D17983 – us UMI [370]
Alabama State Bar Association *see* REPORTS
Alabama. State Bar Association *see* PROCEEDINGS
ALABAMA STATE BAR ASSOCIATION REPORTS – (Regular updates) – nos 1-35. 1880-1912 – 84mf – 9 – $126.00 – LLMC 84-397 – us L.L.M.C. [073]
Alabama. Supreme Court *see*
- ALABAMA SUPREME COURT REPORTS
- MINOR'S REPORTS
- PORTER'S REPORTS
- STEWART AND PORTER'S REPORTS
- STEWART'S REPORTS

Alabama. Supreme Court. Library *see* ALABAMA APPELLATE COURTS
ALABAMA SUPREME COURT REPORTS / Alabama. Supreme Court – (Pre-NRS: v1-80 1840-87.696mf. $1,044.00. Updates planned) – v1-203. 1840-1918/19 – 1755mf – $2,632.00 – LLMC 82-980 – us L.L.M.C. [340]
ALABAMA SUPREME COURT REPORTS *see*
- MINOR'S REPORTS
- PORTER'S REPORTS
- STEWART AND PORTER'S REPORTS
- STEWART'S REPORTS

Alabaster, Henry *see* THE WHEEL OF THE LAW. BUDDHISM, ILLUSTRATED FROM SIAMESE SOURCES BY THE MODERN BUDDHIST, A LIFE OF BUDDHA, AND AN ACCOUNT OF THE PHRABAT
AL-ADWA – al-Khartum: [s.n.] sep 9 1986-jun 6 1987 – 2r – 1 – us Res Libr [072]
O ALAGOANO – Cidade de Alagoas, Alagoas. 5, 26 Nov 1890 – 1,5,6 – bl Biblioteca [072]
ALAGOAS : MENSARIO ILUSTRADO – Maceio, Alagoas. Ago-Out 1938 – 1,5,6 – bl Biblioteca [072]
O ALAGOAS : ORGAO CONSERVADOR – Maceio, Alagoas. 1-3 Jun 1887 – 1,5,6 – bl Biblioteca [072]
O ALAGOINHENSE : PERIODICO NOTICIOSO COMMERCIAL E RECREATIVO – Alagoinhas, BA. 14 Jun 1885 – 1,5,6 – bl Biblioteca [072]
AL-AHALI – Baghdad, Iraq. 1960-mar 28 1961 – 1 – us Res Libr [072]
AL-AHALI – (Egypt), 1978- – 52mf per yr – 9 – $300.00y – us Ross [072]
ALAHAMBRA – 1909-34; 1981; 1992-94; 1993- – 31+ r – 1 – $1,550.00 – P00002 – us Library Micro [910]
AL-AHRAM – 1876-1995 – 12 times per yr – 1 – F2,968.00 – sz Infoprint [072]
AL-AHRAM – 1986-1990 – 9 – F1,978.00 – sz Infoprint [072]
AL-AHRAM – (Egypt), 1876- – 12r per yr – 1 – $1,100.00y – us Ross [072]
AL-AHRAM AL EKTISADI – 1950-1995 – 8 times per yr – 1 – F1,978.00 – sz Infoprint [072]
AL-AHRAM AL-IQTISADI – (Egypt), 1950- – 1 – $400.00y – us Ross [072]
AL-AHRAR – (Egypt), 1977- – 52mf per yr – 9 – $300.00y – us Ross [072]
AL-AHRAR – (Scattered issues lacking) – Cairo, Egypt. Nov 14 1977-July 30 1979; Aug 4 1980-1991 – 7r – 1 – us L of C Photodup [072]
Alaiz, Felipe *see* DECADENCE OF POLITICAL SOCIALISM
AL-AKHBAR – (Egypt), 1953- – 365mf per yr – 9 – $800.00y – us Ross [072]
AL-ALAM-AL-AHMAR – Paris. nos1-4. mai-aout 1926 – 1 – fr A.C.R.P.P. [073]
ALAM-AL-AHMAR *see* AL-ALAM-AL-AHMAR
Alamanni, C *see* SUMMA...D. THOMAE AQUINATIS...IN ORDINEM CURSUS PHILOSOPHICI ACCOMMODATA
ALAMEDA ARGUS – Alameda, CA. Dec 1877-Dec 1885; Jan 1887-88; 1890-Jun 1910; Jan 1911-Sept 1912 – 33r – 1 – $1,650.00 – B02003 – us Library Micro [071]
ALAMEDA CITY DIRECTORIES INCLUDING BERKELEY AND OAKLAND – Alameda Co, CA. 1869-1901 – 26r – 1 – $1,300.00 – D001 – us Library Micro [910]
ALAMEDA, CONTRA COSTA, MONTEREY, SAN BENITO, SAN MATEO, SANTA CLARA AND SANTA CRUZ COUNTIES – Alameda Co, CA. 1879 – 1r – 1 – $50.00 – D002 – us Library Micro [978]
ALAMEDA, CONTRA COSTA, MONTEREY, SAN BENITO, SAN MATEO, SANTA CLARA AND SANTA CRUZ COUNTIES – Contra Costa Co, CA. 1879 – 1r – 1 – $50.00 – D002 – us Library Micro [978]
ALAMEDA, CONTRA COSTA, MONTEREY, SAN BENITO, SAN MATEO, SANTA CLARA AND SANTA CRUZ COUNTIES – Monterey Co, CA. 1879 – 1r – 1 – $50.00 – D002 – us Library Micro [978]
ALAMEDA, CONTRA COSTA, MONTEREY, SAN BENITO, SAN MATEO, SANTA CLARA AND SANTA CRUZ COUNTIES – San Benito Co, CA. 1879 – 1r – 1 – $50.00 – D002 – us Library Micro [978]
ALAMEDA, CONTRA COSTA, MONTEREY, SAN BENITO, SAN MATEO, SANTA CLARA AND SANTA CRUZ COUNTIES – San Mateo Co, CA. 1879 – 1r – 1 – $50.00 – D002 – us Library Micro [978]
ALAMEDA, CONTRA COSTA, MONTEREY, SAN BENITO, SAN MATEO, SANTA CLARA AND SANTA CRUZ COUNTIES – Santa Clara Co, CA. 1879 – 1r – 1 – $50.00 – D002 – us Library Micro [978]
ALAMEDA, CONTRA COSTA, MONTEREY, SAN BENITO, SAN MATEO, SANTA CLARA AND SANTA CRUZ COUNTIES – Santa Cruz Co, CA. 1879 – 1r – 1 – $50.00 – D002 – us Library Micro [978]
ALAMEDA COUNTY – 1901; 1903-05; 1929-34 – 13r – 1 – $650.00 – P00003 – us Library Micro [910]
ALAMEDA COUNTY GAZETTE – Alameda, CA. 1856-75 – 2r – 1 – $100.00 – B02004 – us Library Micro [071]
ALAMEDA COUNTY GAZETTE – San Leandro, CA. 1856-75 – 2r – 1 – $100.00 – C02897 – us Library Micro [071]
ALAMEDA COUNTY UNION LABOR RECORD – Oakland, CA. 1918-1928 – 4r – 1 – $200.00 – C03623 – us Library Micro [331]
ALAMEDA ENCINAL – Alameda, CA. 21 Sept, 1 Nov 1869; 16 Sept 1869-31 Dec 1874; Jan 1875-90; 23 Sept 1892-14 Sept 1895; Jan 1897-Dec 1906 – 27r – 1 – $1,350.00 – B02005 – us Library Micro [071]

ALAMEDA JOURNAL – Alameda, CA. 1935-1937; 1987 – 10+ r – 1 – $500.00 ($90.00y) – B05025 – us Library Micro [073]

ALAMEDA TIMES STAR – (Also known as: Evening Times Star and Daily Argus) – Alameda, CA. 1909-1956. 1959- – 566+ r – 1 BC02007 – $28,300.00 ($480.00y) – us Library Micro [071]

ALAMGIR-NAMAH / Muhammad Kazim – (Bibliotheca Indica: Oriental Works). Calcutta. 1868-73. (lacking: 1869-73). BI-764 2 – 8 – ne IDC [490]

Alamillo Salgado, Ildefonso *see* EL BROCENSE

Alamo, Gutierrez del *see* TEXTO DE DERECHO MARITIMO INTERNATIONAL...

THE ALAMO SAN JACINTO AND THE REPUBLIC OF TEXAS – 1 – us Ross [977]

Alamsjah, Z St *see* ILMU BUMI KABUPATEN 50 KOTA

THE ALAN G. BARBOUR SCREEN FACTS AND SCREEN NOSTALGIA ILLUSTRATED COLLECTION – (Guide available separately $15.00) – 154mf – 9 – $575.00 coll + guide – us UMI [790]

AL-ANBA – (Ceased in 1985) – Jerusalem, 1968(Oct.)-1985(Jan.) – 50r – 1 – J-93-1/3 – ne IDC [072]

Aland, Kurt *see*
- KLEINE SCHRIFTEN 1
- KLEINE SCHRIFTEN 2
- STUDIA PATRISTICA

Aland-Cross-Danielou *see* STUDIA EVANGELICA

ALANDSKII KONGRESS / Feigina, S A – Vnesniaia politika Rossii v Kontse severnoi voiny. Akademiia nauk SSSR, institut istorii. M. 1959. BR-10,524 1 – 9 – ne IDC [947]

ALANGE / Puerto Reyna, Juan Antonio – Sevilla: Eulogio de las Heras, 1913 – 1 – sp Bibl Santa Ana [946]

ALANGE / Puerto Reyna, Juan Antonio – Sevilla: Eulogio de las Heras, 1914 – 1 – sp Bibl Santa Ana [946]

ALANGE. NOTICIAS HISTORICAS ACERCA DE ESTA VILLA Y DE SUS FAMOSOS BANOS / Puerto Reyna, Juan Antonio – Sevilla: Prida, 3rd ed. 1925 – 1 – sp Bibl Santa Ana [946]

Al-Ani, Salman H *see* READINGS IN ARABIC LINGUISTICS

Alapont, Giuseppe *see* THE LIVES OF THE BLESSED LEONARD OF PORT MAURICE AND OF THE BLESSED NICHOLAS FATTORE

Alarcon, Pedro Antonio de *see* UNA VISITA AL MONASTERIO DE YUSTE

Alard, L *see* DE VETERUM MUSICA

ALARM : AN ANARCHIST WEEKLY FOR THE WORKERS – London, UK. 26 Jul-22 Nov 1896 – 4ft – 1 – uk British Libr Newspaper [072]

ALARM : KAMPFBLATT GEGEN VOLKSBETRUG – Berlin, jan 8-dec 24 1931, jan 7-dec 29 1932, jan 5-feb 16 1933 – 1 – Dist. gw Mikrofilm – gw Misc Inst [072]

ALARM : MITTEILUNGSBLATT DER LIGA FUER MENSCHENRECHTE – Porto Alegre, Brasil. 15 Feb-1 May 1937 – 1r – 1 – gw Mikrofilm [073]

ALARM : WORKING PEOPLE'S INTERNATIONAL ASSOCIATION – Series 1. v1-3. no.3 (all publ). 1884-1886. Series 2. v1-2. nos.1-47 (all publ). 1887-1889 – 1 reel – 1 – $65.00 – us UPA [335]

THE ALARM CLOCK – Montreal, Canada. v1 n3 mar 1933 – 1r – 1 – Can$25.00 – cn Can Microfilming [072]

ALARM SIGNAL – (Ceased publ. Cont: Signal) – Washington. jan 1980-apr 1983 – 1,5*,9 – D11019.01 – us UMI [073]

UNE ALARME – Comedie en un acte. Quebec?: s.n.. 1876. 04056. (Pre-1900 Canadiana) – 9 – cn C.I.H.M. [820]

ALAS: A NOVEL / Broughton, Rhoda – British Fiction Archive: Unit 4 – 9 – uk Bell [830]

Alas, Clarin *see* ENSAYOS Y REVISTAS: 1888-1892

Alas, Leonila E de las *see* PHILIPPINE ETHNOGRAPHIC SERIES

LAS ALAS ROTAS / Costa Duran, Maria – Barcelona, 1933; Madrid: Razon y Fe, 1933 – 1 – sp Bibl Santa Ana [999]

ALASKA / Erdmann, H – BN 204 2. 1909 – 8 – ne IDC [978]

ALASKA : SESSION LAWS OF AMERICAN STATES AND TERRITORIES – 1913-95 – 9 – $720.00 set – us Hein [340]

ALASKA *see* ALASKA SPORTSMAN

Alaska *see*
- REPORTS AND OPINIONS (A-G)
- STATE REPORTS, PRE-NRS

ALASKA – (Cont: Alaska Sportsman) – Anchorage. v35- oct 1969- 1*; v58- jan 1992- 5,9 – 1,5,9 – D18624.01 – us UMI [790]

ALASKA AND THE KLONDIKE: A JOURNEY TO THE NEW ELDORADO...OBSERVATIONS ON THE PHYSICAL HISTORY AND GEOLOGY OF THE GOLD REGIONS / Heilprin, Angelo – London: C.A. Pearson, 1899. 05536. (Pre-1900 Canadiana) – 9 – cn C.I.H.M. [971]

ALASKA ATTORNEY GENERAL REPORTS AND OPINIONS – (6 1917-1968 $245.00. 9 1979-1994 $965.00) – 1917-1994 – 6,9 – $1,210.00 set – us Hein [340]

ALASKA BAPTIST MESSENGER – 1946-48; 1952-91 – 1 – $190.08 – us Baptist [240]

ALASKA BAR RAG – v1-19. 1978-95 – 9 – $245.00 set – us Hein [340]

THE ALASKA BOUNDARY / Davidson, G – San Francisco, 1903 – 3mf – 1 – ILM-1524/1 – ne IDC [327]

THE ALASKA BOUNDARY / Davidson, George – 1903. 235p. Includes map of the N.W. Coast of America.V105-0001 – 1 – us A.G.L.L. [978]

ALASKA BUSINESS AND INDUSTRY *see* ALASKA INDUSTRY

ALASKA BUSINESS AND INDUSTRY – (Cont: Alaska Industry) – Anchorage. v14-16. mar 1982-may 1984 – 1,5,9 – D7464.01 – us UMI [338]

ALASKA BUSINESS MONTHLY – Anchorage. v1-13. jan 1985-dec 1997+ 1,5*,9 – 1,5,9 – D14900 – us UMI [338]

ALASKA CONSERVATION REVIEW – (Publ is believed to have ceased with v20, no. 4 (1979)) – Fairbanks. v13-20 Spr 1972-Win 1979 1; v1-20 mar 1960-Win 1979 5*; v15-20 spr 1974-Win 1979 9* – 1,5,9 – D6483 – us UMI [630]

"ALASKA FILE" OF THE OFFICE OF THE SECRETARY OF THE TREASURY, 1868-1903 / U.S. Fish and Wildlife Service – 25 rolls. M720. Printed guide – 1 – us Nat'l Archives [324]

ALASKA FILE OF THE REVENUE CUTTER SERVICE, 1867-1914 / U.S. Coast Guard – M641. Printed guide – 20r – 1 – us Nat'l Archives [978]

ALASKA FILE OF THE SPECIAL AGENTS DIVISION OF THE DEPARTMENT OF THE TREASURY / U.S. Department of the Treasury – 1867-1903. 16 rolls. M802 – 1 – us Nat'l Archives [336]

Alaska. Governor's Office *see* CHRONOLOGICAL FILES, 1884-1913

ALASKA HERALD – (In English and Russian) – San Francisco, CA. 1868-72 – 3r – 1 – $150.00 – B02786 – us Library Micro [071]

ALASKA HERALD – (Including the US constitution in Russian) – Anchorage, AL. 1868-72 – 3r – 1 – $150.00 – B01000 – us Library Micro [071]

ALASKA HERALD – San Francisco. Calif. v. 1, no. 1-v. 8, no. 196. Mar 1868-Mar 1876 – 1 – us NY Public [071]

ALASKA HIGHWAY NEWS – Fort St John, British Columbia, CN. Mar 1944-Mar 1977 – 28r – 1 – cn Commonwealth Micro [072]

THE ALASKA INDIAN LANGUAGE COLLECTION OF THE OREGON PROVINCE ARCHIVES OF THE SOCIETY OF JESUS / ed by Carriker, Robert C – (With printed guide) – 1976 – 28r – 1 – $2,380.00 – D3154 – us Scholarly Res [490]

ALASKA INDUSTRY *see* ALASKA BUSINESS AND INDUSTRY

ALASKA INDUSTRY – (Cont by: Alaska Business and Industry) – Anchorage. v1-14 jan 1969-feb 1982 1; v4-14 jan 1972-feb 1982 5; v5-14 jan 1973-feb 1982 9 – 1,5,9 – D7464 – us UMI [338]

ALASKA, ITS SOUTHERN COAST AND THE SITKAN ARCHIPELAGO / Scidmore, Eliza Ruhamah – Boston: D. Lothrop and Co., 1885. vii,333p. illus., map – 1 – us U.W. Library [910]

ALASKA JOURNAL OF COMMERCE – Anchorage. v1- 1976- 1*; v17- 1993-* 5,9 – 1,5,9 – D17827.01 – us UMI [380]

ALASKA LAW JOURNAL – v1-9. 1963-71 – 9 – $65.00 set – us Hein [340]

ALASKA MAPS : CITIES AND TOWNS – 1904-57. 121 maps. 23 towns. Sanborn Company fire insurance maps – 1 – $32.00r – us Shkurkin [910]

ALASKA MEDICINE – Anchorage. v1- mar 1959- 1; v9- mar 1967- 5; v18- jan 1976- 9 – 1,5,9 – D2460 – us UMI [610]

THE ALASKA MISSION COLLECTION OF THE OREGON PROVINCE ARCHIVES OF THE SOCIETY OF JESUS / ed by Carriker, Robert C – (With printed guide) – 1980 – 42r – 1 – $3,570.00 – D3153 – us Scholarly Res [240]

ALASKA NATIVE CLAIMS APPEALS BOARD DECISIONS AND ORDERS / U.S. Department of the Interior – Sept 1975-Jun 1982 (all publ) – 35mf – 9 – $52.00 – LLMC 82-201 – us L.L.M.C. [324]

ALASKA NATIVES AND THE LAND / U.S. Federal Field Committee for Development Planning in Alaska – 1968 – 9 – $5.00f – us Ross [970]

Alaska. Office of the Secretary *see* CORRESPONDENCE OF THE SECRETARY OF ALASKA

ALASKA REPORTS – v1-4. 1884-1914 – 12mf – 9 – $54.00 – LLMC 86-101 – us L.L.M.C. [340]

ALASKA REVIEW – v1-10. 1984-93 – 1,5 – $135.00 – us Hein [073]

ALASKA REVIEW – (Ceased publ) – Anchorage. v1-4. Win 1963-1972 – 1 – D10377 – us UMI [978]

ALASKA SPORTSMAN *see* ALASKA

ALASKA SPORTSMAN – (Cont by: Alaska) – Juneau. v1-35. 1935-sep 1969 – 1 – D18624 – us UMI [790]

ALASKA STATUTES ANNOTATED – Superseded vols. 1980- – 9 – Inquire – us Hein [340]

Alaska. Supreme Court *see* ALASKA SUPREME COURT REPORTS

ALASKA SUPREME COURT REPORTS / Alaska. Supreme Court – (No Pre-NRS vols. Add vols planned) – v1-5. 1884-1918 – 15mf – 9 – $67.50 – LLMC 86-101 – us L.L.M.C. [340]

Alaska. (Territory). Attorney General's Office *see* REPORT

THE ALASKA TREATY / Miller, David Hunter – 1 roll. T1024 – 1 – us Nat'l Archives [975]

ALASKA YUKON GAZETTEER 1923-24 / R.L. Polk and Co – Seattle, 1923. Alaska Reel 1. The Cox Library Collection – 5 – us Americana [978]

ALASKAN RUSSIAN CHURCH ARCHIVES – 1730-1930 – 1 – 8095.00 – us L of C Photodup [240]

THE ALASKAN WHALE CULT AND ITS AFFINITIES / Lantis, Margaret – BN-291 2. 1938 – 8 – ne IDC [306]

ALASKA-YUKON MAGAZINE – Juneau. v1-13. 1905-12 – 2r – 1 – us Ross [978]

ALASTOR : OR, THE SPIRIT OF SOLITUDE, AND OTHER POEMS / Shelley, Percy Bysshe – London: Printed for Baldwin, Cradock, and Joy, Carpenter and Son, 1816 – 1 roll – 1 – 1-55879-663-0 – uk Libr Preservation [810]

AL-ASWAR / ed by Ibrahim, Hanna et al – 'Akka al-Qadimah, Israel: Maktab al-Aswar. 1988- – $85.00 – us MEDOC [470]

AL-ASWAR / ed by Ibrahim, Hanna et al – Akka al-Qadimah, Israel: Maktab al-Aswar, 1988- – 9 – $345.00 – us MEDOC [956]

AL-ATMA AL-SIHYUNIYAH FI MIYAH AL-URDUN WA-AL-LITANI / al-Din al-Khayru, Izz – [al-Qahirah]: Jamiat al-Duwal al-Arabiyah, al-Munazzamah al-Arabiyah lil-Tarbiyah wa-al-Thaqafah wa-al-Ulum, Mahad al-Buhuth wa-al-Dirasat al-Arabiyah, 1977. – us Res Libr [072]

Alaydrus, Ali *see*
- IMADUDDIN
- KITAB PERUKUNAN

AL-AYYAM : AL-KHARTUM: SHARIKAT AL-AYY AM LIL-SIHAFAH AL-MAHDURAH, [MAR 27 1987-JUN 29 1989] – 9r – us Res Libr [072]

L'ALBA – Newport. R.I. 1913-1931; 1932-1935 – 1 – us UMI [071]

Alba, Jose *see* PERDIGON Y PERRUNILLA

L'ALBA SOCIALE – Tampa, FL, 1901 – 5mf or 1r – 1,9 – us I.H.R.C. [978]

AL-BADIL – al-Khartum: al-Badil, [sep 9 1985-feb 11 1989] – 1r – us Res Libr [072]

al-Badisi, "Abd al-Haqq ibn Ismail." *see* EL'MAQSAD (VIES DES SAINTES DU RIF).

Albaiges, J *see* INTERNATIONAL JOURNAL OF ENVIRONMENTAL ANALYTICAL CHEMISTRY

Albala-Bertrand, Luis *see* DEMOCRATIC CULTURE AND GOVERNANCE

AL-BALAD – al-Khartum: Dar al-Balad lil-Tibaah wa-al-Nashr, feb 11-may 1 1989 – 1r – us Res Libr [072]

AL-BALAGH AL-USBU'I – Cairo, 1926-1930. – vol 1, no 1- vol 4, no 174. 21 Jumada al-Ula 1345-20 Safar 1349 [26 November 1926-16 July 1930] – 3r – 1 – $395.00 – us MEDOC [949]

ALBAN STOLZ IN SEINER ENTWICKLUNG ALS SCHRIFTSTELLER / Hulshof, Franz – (Includes bibliographical references and index) – Graz: Waechter-Verlag, 1931 – 1r – 1 – us U.W. Library [430]

DIE ALBANESISCHEN UND SLAVISCHEN SCHRIFTEN / Geitler, L – Wien. 1883. BR-10,129 1 – 9 – ne IDC [460]

ALBANIA – Bruxelles. mars 1897-1907, 1909 – 1 – fr A.C.R.P.P. [949]

Albania *see*
- LA LOI SUR LE PLAN BIENNAL, 1949-1950
- RAPPORT SUR LES RESULTATS DE LA REALISATION DU 1ER PLAN
- REVUE ALBANAISE

ALBANIANS IN YUGOSLAVIA PAMPHLET COLLECTION – 1965-1987 – 1 – CSUXANQ5357-B – us Hoover Inst Photo [305]

ALBANIA'S BOUNDARIES AND ETHNOGRAPHY PAMPHLET COLLECTION – 1919-1921 – 1 – CSUXANQ8129-B – us Hoover Inst Photo [305]

ALBANIA'S FOREIGN RELATIONS PAMPHLET COLLECTION – 1913-1977 – 1 – CSUXANQ7849-B – us Hoover Inst Photo [320]

L'ALBANIE LIBRE – Milan, Italy. Mar 1947-30 May 1959 – 1r – 1 – uk British Libr Newspaper [072]

L'ALBANIE LIBRE – Milan, Italy. March 1947-30 May 1959 – 1r – 1 – uk British Libr Newspaper [072]

ALBANY ARGUS – Albany, NY. 1813-1820 – 3 – us Readex [071]

ALBANY BOUQUET AND LITERARY SPECTATOR – (Ceased publ) – Albany. v1. apr 1835-sep 1835 – 1 – D3716 – us UMI [070]

ALBANY CITIZEN – Albany, OR. -w. Mar 25, 1910- Sept 2, 1910 – 1 – us U.O. Library [071]

Albany Club *see* ...INCORPORATED 1882:... TO PROVIDE A CONVENIENT PLACE FOR SOCIAL AND BUSINESS PURPOSES

ALBANY COMMUNITY NEWS – Albany, CA. 1976-1983 – 1r – 1 – $50.00 – B06005 – us Library Micro [071]

ALBANY DEMOCRAT – Albany, OR. -d. 7 May 1888-1 Mar 1925 – 1 – us U.O. Library [071]

ALBANY DEMOCRAT – Albany, OR. -w, -sw. 27 Apr 1900-1 Jul 1926 – 1 – us U.O. Library [071]

ALBANY DEMOCRAT-HERALD – Albany, OR. -d. 2 Mar 1925-1 Jul 1978- – 1 – us U.O. Library [071]

ALBANY EVENING DEMOCRAT – Albany, OR. -d. 6 Dec 1875-3 June 1876 – 1 – us U.O. Library [071]

ALBANY FIRST BAPTIST CHURCH. ALBANY, GEORGIA : CHURCH RECORDS – Jul 1848-Sept 1987. Lacking minutes: 1861-99, 1901-16, 1937-42. History: 1836-1906. Includes: Ladies Aid Soc. records, 1895-1901 – 1 – 299.16 – us Baptist [240]

ALBANY FIRST BAPTIST CHURCH. ALBANY, KENTUCKY : CHURCH RECORDS – Sep 1841-May 1980. 1706p. Lacks Jul 1860-Jun 1866, Nov 1866-May 1870, Jan 1927-Feb 1933 – 1 – 76.77 – us Baptist [240]

THE ALBANY GAZETTE – Albany, NY. v30 n2849. 14 mar 1814 – 1r – 1 – Can$25.00 – cn Can Microfilming [071]

Albany. Georgia. First Baptist Church *see* THE WAY

ALBANY JOURNAL – Albany, OR. -w. 12 Mar 1864-23 Feb 1866. 1 roll – 1 – us U.O. Library [071]

ALBANY LAW ENVIRONMENTAL OUTLOOK JOURNAL – v1. 1995 – 9 – $10.00 – us Hein [340]

ALBANY LAW JOURNAL – v1-70. 1870-1908 – 1,5,6 – $640.00 – us Hein [073]

THE ALBANY LAW JOURNAL : A WEEKLY RECORD – (v1-62 weekly. v63-70 monthly. Titles added regularly) – v1-70. 1870-1909 – 140mf – 9 – $630.00 – LLMC 82-901 – us L.L.M.C. [073]

ALBANY LAW JOURNAL – (Ceased publ) – Albany. cum index 1-24 1870-1881; v1-70. jan 1870-dec 1908 – 1 – D4624 – us UMI [340]

ALBANY LAW REVIEW – (Cont: Albany Law Review of Recent Decisions) – Albany. v12-61 jun 1948-1998+ 1*; v45-61 Fall 1980-1998+ 5*,9 – 1,5,9 – D12612.02 – us UMI [340]
ALBANY LAW REVIEW – (No additions poss for copyright reasons) – Albany Law School: v1-19. 1931/32-1955 – 52mf – 9 – $78.00 – LLMC 95-110 – us L.L.M.C. [073]
ALBANY LAW REVIEW – (v1-49 1931-85 $563.00 reel or mf. v50-59 1985-96 $228.00 mf) – v1-59. 1931-96 – 5,6,9 – $791.00 set – us Hein [340]
ALBANY LAW REVIEW *see* ALBANY LAW REVIEW OF RECENT DECISIONS
ALBANY LAW REVIEW OF RECENT DECISIONS – (Cont by: Albany Law Review) – Albany. v6-11. 1936-42* – 1 – D12612.01 – us UMI [340]
ALBANY LAW REVIEW OF RECENT DECISIONS *see* ALBANY LAW REVIEW
ALBANY MEDICAL COLLEGE INAUGURAL THESES, 1839-91 – (Cataloging available) – 1866mf – 9 – $7,180.00 – us UMI [610]
Albany. Presbytery (Pres. Ch. in the U.S.A.) *see* RECORDS, 1790-1797
ALBANY REGISTER – Albany, OR. -w. 3 Oct 1868-31 Dec 1880. – 4r – 1 – us U.O. Library [071]
Albany. Synod (Pres. Church in the U.S.A.) *see* MINUTES
ALBANY TIMES – Albany, CA. 1935-1938; 1944-1948; 1979 – 18r – 1 – $900.00 – B06006 – us Library Micro [071]
ALBANY-DECATUR DAILY – Decatur. Ala. 1917-26 – 1 – us UMI [071]
Albarda, J H *see*
- AVES NEERLANDICAE

Albarellos, Juan *see* EFEMERIDES BURGALESCAS
AL-BARID AL-GAZA'IRI – no. 1-4. Alger. aout-sept 1913 – 1 – fr A.C.R.P.P. [073]
AL-BARQ – El Bark. 22 no. Constantine. 1927 – 1 – fr A.C.R.P.P. [073]
Albarran, Ramon *see* LOS TORPEDOS EN LA GUERRA MARITIMA
Albaspinaeus, Gabr. *see* OBSERVATIONUM LIBRI DUO
AL-BASSIR – Paris. 1881-82 – 1 – fr A.C.R.P.P. [073]
ALBAYRAK – Erzurum, 1913-1921. Mes'ul Mueduerue: Suelayman Necati – 9 – $20.00 – us MEDOC [956]
DER ALBBOTE *see* DER VOLKSFREUND
DER ALBBOTE TALGANG-ZEITUNG *see* DER VOLKSFREUND
Albeca, Alexandre L d' *see* LA FRANCE AU DAHOMEY
Albeca, Alexandre-L d' *see* LES ETABLISSEMENTS FRANCAIS DU GOLFE DU BENIN...
Albeck, H *see*
- UNTERSUCHUNGEN UEBER DIE HALACHISCHEN MIDRASCHIM
- UNTERSUCHUNGEN UEBER DIE REDAKTION DER MISCHNA

Albee, Ernest *see*
- THE BEGINNINGS OF ENGLISH UTILITARIANISM
- A HISTORY OF ENGLISH UTILITARIANISM

AL-BEIRAK-AL-AHMAR / Parti communiste S F IC – no. 1. Paris. sept 1926 – 1 – fr A.C.R.P.P. [335]
ALBEMARLE : A MONTHLY REVIEW – (Ceased publ) – London. v1-2. jan 1892-sep 1892 – 1 – D4198 – us UMI [073]
Albemarle, George Thomas Keppel, Earl *see* MEMOIRS OF THE MARQUIS OF ROCKINGHAM AND HIS CONTEMPORARIES
Albenino, Nicolao de *see* VERDADERA RELACION DELO SUSSEDIDO ENLOS REYNOS E PROVINCIAS DEL PERU DESDE LA YDA DEELLOS DEL VIREY BLASCO NUNES VELA...Y MUERTE DE GONCALO PICARRO. SEVILLA. 1549
Albenino, Nicolas de *see* VERDADERA RELACION DE LO SUSSEDIDO EN LOS REYNOS...DEL PERU...INTRODUCCION DE JOSE TORIBIO MEDINA. PARIS 1930
Albeniz, I *see*
- PARA PIANO. (NO 4 FROM RECUERDOS DE VLAJE)
- ...PAVANA-CAPRICHO, OP. 12. PIANO SOLO

Alber, E *see*
- EIN DIALOGUS ODER GESPRAECH ETLICHER PERSONEN VOM INTERIM...
- DAS EHBUECHLIN...
- DIE GROSSE WOLTHAT
- IVDICIVM ERASMI ALBERI, DE SPONGIA ERASMI ROTEROD...

Albergati, C *see* CANTATE MORALI A VOCE SOLA, OP. 3
ALBERNI VALLEY TIMES – Port Alberni, British Columbia, CN. Nov 1967- – 4r per yr – 1 – Can$55.00r – cn Commonwealth Micro [072]
L'ALBERO DI DIANA : DRAMMA GIOCOSO IN 2 ATTI / Martin y Solar, V – Manuscript, [1787?] – 1 – us Sibley [780]
L'ALBERO DI DIANA (VON V. MARTIN). CHE BEL SPASSETTO : THE FAVORITE AIR, INTRODUCED... IN THE COMIC OPERA L'ALBERO DI DIANNA / Mazzinghi, J – (Vocal score) – London: G Goulding – 1 – us Sibley [780]
Alberry, A J *see*
- AVICENNA ON THEOLOGY

Albers, B *see* CONSUETUDINES MONASTICAE
Albers, Emanuel *see* DIE QUELLENBERICHTE IN JOSUA 1-12
Albers, J C *see* MALACOGRAPHIA MADERENSIS
Albers, Robert H *see* JOURNAL OF MINISTRY IN ADDICTION AND RECOVERY
Albert, Albrecht *see* KID
ALBERT ANDERSSONS AFFARSBLAD – Uddevalla, Sweden. 1899-1902 – 1 reel – 1 – sw Kungliga [948]
ALBERT BITZIUS : LEBENSBILD EINES REPUBLIKANERS, NACH SEINEM HANDSCHRIFTLICHEN NACHLASSE / Gotthelf, Jeremias; ed by Balmer, Hans – Bern: Nydegger & Baumgart, 1888 – 1 – us U.W. Library [920]
Albert, Carlos L *see* THE WAR NEXT DOOR
ALBERT COLLEGE TIMES – [Belleville, Ont.?]: The College, v1 no 1 (Mar 1 1889)- – 9 – cn C.I.H.M. [370]
ALBERT EHRHARD UND DIE ERFORSCHUNG DER GRIECHISCH-BYZANTINISCHEN HAGIOGRAPHIE (T.U.U. 5-111) / Winkelmann, F – Berlin, 1971 – 2mf – 9 – ne Slangenburg [240]
Albert, F R *see*
- DIE BLUETEZEIT DER DEUTSCHEN PREDIGT IM MITTELALTER, 1100-1400
- DIE GESCHICHTE DER PREDIGT IN DEUTSCHLAND BIS AUF KARL DEN GROSSEN, 600-814
- SEIT WANN GIEBT ES EINE PREDIGT IN DEUTSCHER SPRACHE?

ALBERT GAZETTE – Burgersdorp, South Africa. 6 Jan 1894-24 Dec 1898. 3 reels – 1, 16 diazo available at reduced price – sa SA Libr [072]
ALBERT GIACOMETTI / Reunion des musees nationaux. Paris – 1969. 156 illus. 3 fiches – 9 – fr Réunion [750]
ALBERT JAMES MYER, FOUNDER OF THE ARMY SIGNAL CORPS: A BIOGRAPHICAL STUDY / Scheips, Paul Joseph – 1965 – 1 – us KS Hist [920]
THE ALBERT LEVITT PAPERS / Levitt, Albert – (Guide only $105.00) – 42r – 1 – $4,560.00 – 0-89093-807-5 – us UPA [920]
Albert, Maria *see* BIBLIOGRAPHIE DE MERE ISABELLE SORMANY, DITE LADAUVERSIERE, RELIGIEUSE HOSPITALIERE DE SAINT-JOSEPH, PREMIERE SUPERIEURE GENERALE 1897-1957...
Albert, Maurice *see* LES THEATRES DES BOULEVARDS: 1789-1848
ALBERT NORDEN : PAMPHLET COLLECTION – 1963-1975 – 1 – CSUXANS5590-B – us Hoover Inst Photo [920]
THE ALBERT PORTE PAPERS – 10r – $495.00 – us African Imprint [320]
THE ALBERT RECORD – Burgersdorp, South Africa. 7 Mar-22 Aug 1885. 1 reel – 1, 16 diazo available at reduced price – sa SA Libr [072]
ALBERT SCHWEITZER PAMPHLET COLLECTION – 19??-1984 – 1 – CSUXANR3440-B – us Hoover Inst Photo [610]
ALBERT TESSIER ET SON OEUVRE / Tessier, Albert – Montreal: Bibliotheque Nationale du Quebec, 1974. SEM35P95 – 1r – 1 – Can$23.00 – cn Bibl Nat [410]
ALBERT TIMES – Burgersdorp, South Africa. 4 Jan 1855-31 Dec 1859. 4 reels – 1, 16 diazo available at reduced price – sa SA Libr [072]
Alberta *see* LEGISLATIVE ASSEMBLY JOURNALS
ALBERTA BUSINESS – Calgary, mar 1984-1*; 1994-* 5,9 – 1,5,9 – D21674 – us UMI [338]
ALBERTA BUSINESS – (Publ suspended v10 1993. Reactivated 1994) – Calgary.0v1-1984- – 9 – Can$20.00y – cn Micromedia [380]
Alberta. Canada *see*
- ALBERTA LAW REPORTS
- ALBERTA STATUTES, SESSION LAWS AND REVISIONS

ALBERTA FARMER – Calgary, 1919-1931 – 10r – 1 – cn Preston [971]
ALBERTA GAZETTE – (1958-69 Can$1,200.00 1. 1970-82 Can$155.00y 5. 1996 Can$200.00y 9) – Edmonton. v53- 1958- – 1,6,9 – Price varies with yr – cn Micromedia [073]
ALBERTA GAZETTE – Edmonton, 1958-69 – 18r – 1 – us Ross [324]
ALBERTA GAZETTE PART 2 – (v91 1995 Can$180.00y 9) – Edmonton. v66- 1970- – 5,9 – Price varies with yr – cn Micromedia [073]
ALBERTA HISTORICAL REVIEW – (Cont by: Alberta History) – Calgary, cum index 1-15 1953-1967; v1-22. apr 1953-Aut 1974 – 1 – D7401 – us UMI [971]
ALBERTA HISTORICAL REVIEW *see* ALBERTA HISTORY
ALBERTA HISTORY *see* ALBERTA HISTORICAL REVIEW
ALBERTA HISTORY – (Cont: Alberta Historical Review) – Clagary. v23- Win 1975- 1*; v24-Win 1976-* 5,9 – 1,5,9 – D7401.01 – us UMI [971]
ALBERTA JOURNAL OF EDUCATIONAL RESEARCH – v39- 1993- – 9 – Can$20.00y – cn Micromedia [370]
ALBERTA LAW REPORTS / Alberta. Canada – (Cont by 2nd series which is not offered by LLMC) – 1st series: v1-26. 1908-33 (all publ) – 181mf – 9 – $271.00 – LLMC 81-018 – us L.L.M.C. [340]
ALBERTA LAW REVIEW – Edmonton. v1-35 1955-aug 1997+ 1; v9-35 1971-aug 1997+ 5*; v14-35 1976-aug 1997+ 9 – 1,5,9 – D2422 – us UMI [340]
ALBERTA LEARNING RESOURCES JOURNAL – (No issue publ in 1991. Cont by: Teacher-Librarian Today v1 1995) – Edmonton. v9-12. 1988-93 – 9 – Can$20.00y – cn Micromedia [020]
ALBERTA MODERN LANGUAGE JOURNAL – Edmonton. v1- 1962- – 9 – Can$20.00y – cn Micromedia [400]
ALBERTA NONPARTISAN – Alberta, CN. Oct 1917-Jul 1919 – 1r – 1 – cn Commonwealth Micro [072]
ALBERTA REPORT – (Cont: Saint John's Edmonton Report. Paper copy issue index 1973-86) – Edmonton. v7- 1979/80- – 9 – Can$73.00y – cn Micromedia [073]
ALBERTA SCRAPBOOK HANSARD – (Newspaper articles concerning the activities of the Alberta Legislative Assembly; in the Legislature Library in Edmonton) – Alberta, CN. 1906-64 – complete collection – 1 – $65.00r – cn Commonwealth Micro [971]
ALBERTA SOCIAL CREDIT CHRONICLE – Alberta, CN. Jul 1934-Jan 1936 – 1r – 1 – cn Commonwealth Micro [072]
ALBERTA STATUTES, SESSION LAWS AND REVISIONS / Alberta. Canada – (Updates planned) – 1906 Consolidated Statutes-1945 Parliament 2nd sess. 1906-45 – 331mf – 9 – $496.00 – LLMC 90-110 – us L.L.M.C. [340]
Alberta Teachers' Alliance *see* ATA MAGAZINE
Alberta Teachers Association *see* ATA NEWS
Alberta Teachers' Association *see* ATA NEWS
Alberta-Marie, Soeur *see* BIBLIOGRAPHIE DE MONSIEUR LE CURE L. BOISSEAU, CURE DE NEW CARLISLE
ALBERTAN – Calgary, Alberta, CN. 1897-1906; 1920-60; 1970-Aug 1980 – 358r – 1 – cn Commonwealth Micro [072]
ALBERTA-PAST AND PRESENT / Blue, John – Historical and Biographical. Chicago: Pioneer Historical Publ. Co., 1924. v1-3. Canada reel 4. (Cox Library Collection) – 5 – us Americana [971]
Alberti, Blas *see*
- PERONISMO, BUROCRACIA Y BURGUESIA NACIONAL
- EL PERONISMO POLEMICO

Alberti, Conrad *see*
- DIE ALTEN UND DIE JUNGEN
- BETTINA VON ARNIM
- LUDWIG BOERNE

ALBERTI DE BEZANIS ABBATIS S. LAURENTII CREMONENSIS CHRONICA (MGH 7: 3.BD) – 1908 – Dfl13.00 – ne Slangenburg [240]
Alberti, Eduard *see* LEXIKON DER SCHLESWIG-HOLSTEIN-LAUENBURGISCHEN UND EUTINISCHEN SCHRIFTSTELLER VON 1829-1882
Alberti, Fra Leandro *see* DESCRITTIONE DI TUTTA ITALIA
Alberti, G M *see* 12 SINFONIE A QUATTRO... DUE VIOLINE, ALTO, ORGANO ET VIOLONCELLO
Alberti, L B *see*
- LA ARCHITECTURA
- L'ARCHITECTURE ET ART DE BIEN BASTIR.
- L'ARCHITETTURA. TRADOTTA IN LINGUA FIORENTINA DA C. BARTOLI
- DE RE AEDIFICATORIA
- LOS DIEZ LIBROS DE ARCHITECTURA
- I DIECI LIBRI DE L'ARCHITETTURA

Alberti, Louis *see* DESCRIPTION PHYSIQUE ET HISTORIQUE DES CAFRES
Albertini, G *see* [VIRGINIA] LA MIA SPOSA. OVERTURE
Albertini, J B von *see* CONSPECTUS FUNGORUM IN LUSATIAE SUPERIORIS AGRO NISKIENSI CRESCENTIUM
Albertini, L E *see* DERECHO DIPLOMATICO...
Albertinus, Edm. *see* DE EUCHARISTIAE SIVE COENAE DOMINICAE SACRAMENTO LIBRI TRES
Albertinus Mussatus *see* CARMINA
Alberts, Juergen *see* ARBEITEROEF-FENTLICHKEIT UND LITERATUR
ALBERTUS MAGNUS : BEITRAEGE ZU SEINER WUERDIGUNG / Hertling, Georg von – Muenster i.W.: Aschendorff, 1914 – 1mf – us A.T.L.A. [920]
Albertus Magnus *see* DAS BUCH DER VERSAMLUNG; ORDER, DAS BUCH DER HEIMLIGKEITEN MAGNI ALBERTI, VON ARTZNEY VND TUGENDEN DER KRUTER VNND EDEL GSETEIN, VND VON ETLICHE WOLBEKANTEN THIERE
Alberus, E *see*
- CHRISTLICHER, NUETZLICHER, U. NOHTWENDIGER TRACTAT UND BERICHT VON DER KINDER TAUFF, WIDER DEN IRRTHUMB U. FALSCHE LEHRE DER SCHWERMER. EINER VORREDEN NIC. SELNECCERI VOM EXORCISMO
- DIT IS EEN SEER SCHOON CHRISTELIJCKE ONDERWIJSINGHE VANDEN DOOPSEL, TEGHEN DIE WEDERDOOPERS, PAPISTEN EN ALLE VALSCHE SECKTEN
- WIDER DIE VERFLUCHTE LERE DER CARLSTADER, VND ALLE FUERNEMSTE HEUBTER DER SACRAMENTIRER, ROTTENGEISTER, WIDERTEUFFER

Albery, Nicholas *see* BEST IDEAS, A DIRECTORY OF SOCIAL INVENTIONS
Albicini, C *see* LA NAZIONALITA
Albin, P *see*
- LES GRANDS TRAITES POLITIQUES ... DEPUIS 1815 JUSQU'A NOS JOURS
- LES GRANDS TRAITES POLITIQUES RECUEIL DES PRINCIPAUX TEXTES DIPLOMATIQUES DE 1815 A 1914 AVEC DES NOTICES HISTORIQUES ET DES NOTES
- LES GRANDS TRAITES POLITIQUES RECUEIL DES PRINCIPAUX TEXTES DIPLOMATIQUES DEPUIS 1815 JUSQU'A NOS JOURS AVEC DES NOTICES HISTORIQUES ET DES NOTES

ALBINA SUBCHASER – Portland OR. June 4 1942-Dec 23 1944, Mar 10 Apr June 1945 – 1 – us U.O. Library [071]
ALBINA WEEKLY COURIER – Portland, OR. 15 Feb 1890-23 Jun 1894. – 1r – 1 – us U.O. Library [071]
Albinana, Jose Maria *see* CONFINADO EN LAS HURDES (UNA VICTIMA DE LA INQUISICION REPUBLICANA)
Albinana Sanz, J *see* LOS CRIMINES DEL CACIQUISMO. LA TRAGEDIA DE EL POBO. DEFENSA DEL MEDICO...
ALBINUS AND THE HISTORY OF MIDDLE PLATONISM. CAMBRIDGE CLASSICAL STUDIES / Witt, R E – v3. Cambridge. 1937. B-347 2 – 8 – ne IDC [180]
ALBION – Boone. v1-29 1969-Win 1997+ 1*; v15-29 Spr 1983-Win 1997+ 5*,9 – 1,5,9 – D13915 – us UMI [073]
ALBION – New York, NY. v40 n1. 4 Jan 1862-v40 n52. 27 Dec 1862 – 1r – 1 – Can$50.00 – cn Can Microfilming [071]
THE ALBION – New York, 1822-25; 1855-62; 1868-71 – 5r – 1 – us Ross [073]
THE ALBION – New York. June 22 1822-Dec 28 1833; Jan 14 1834-Sept 29 1855; Jan 5 1856-Dec 26 1863; Mar 28 1868-Dec 18 1869; Jan 7 1871-Dec 30 1871; and Oct 25 1873-Jan 30 1875. Not collated – 1 – us NY Public [071]

ALBION : A JOURNAL OF NEWS, POLITICS, AND LITERATURE – (Ceased publ) – New York. v1-54. jun 1822-dec 1876 – 1 – D4409 – us UMI [073]

ALBION ARGUS – Albion, NE. -w. Dec. 1887-Aug. 1897. Incomplete; Sep. 1897-Apr. 1948 – 1 – us NE Hist [071]

THE ALBION HOTEL VISITOR'S GUIDE TO MONTREAL AND RIVER ST LAWRENCE – Montreal: Decker, Stearns & Murray, 1876. 00779. (Pre-1900 Canadiana) – 9 – cn C.I.H.M. [910]

Albion Mines. Nova Scotia *see* SPECIAL RULES FOR THE CONDUCT AND GUIDANCE OF THE PERSONS ACTING IN THE MANAGEMENT AND OF ALL PERSONS EMPLOYED IN...THE ALBION MINES

ALBION NEWS – Albion, NE. -w. Apr 1880-Aug 1895. Incomplete; Aug. 1895- – 1 – us NE Hist [071]

ALBION W. TOURGEE PAPERS / Tourgee, Albion W – 60r – 1 – $4440.00 – us UMI [920]

Albionic Consulting and Research *see* CONSPIRACY AND REVISIONIST LITERATURE

Albisetti, E *see* DIE EHESCHLIESSUNG, DIE TRENNUNG,...

Albitskii, N A *see* PODROBNAIA OPIS 962 RUKOPISIAM NACHALA 17 DO NACHALA 19 STOLETIJ DOLMATOVSKAGO ARKHIVA

Albo-Carbon Light Agency *see* THE PATENT ALBO-CARBON LIGHT

ALBOM PERVO I RUSSKO I REVOLIUTSII 1905-1907 G.G. / ed by Mitskevicha, S I – Moskva: Gos. izd-vo, 1926 – 1 – CSUX88-B1280 – us Hoover Inst Photo [320]

ALBOM REVOLIUTSIONNO I ROSSII = ALBUM OF REVOLUTIONARY RUSSIA – New York: Russian Socialist Federation, [1920?] – 1 – CSUX89-B7797 – us Hoover Inst Photo [320]

Albon, Robert *see*
- OCCUPATIONAL REGULATION AND THE PUBLIC INTEREST, COMPETITION OR MONOPOLY
- PRIVATE CORRESPONDENCE, COMPETITION OR MONOPOLY IN AUSTRALIA'S POSTAL SERVICES?
- RENT CONTROL, COSTS AND CONSEQUENCES

ALBOR : ORGAO INDEPENDENTE – Araguari, 28 Feb 1953; 8 Jun 1963 – 1,5,6 – bl Biblioteca [072]

Alboreda, A M *see* HISTORIA DE MONTSERRAT

ALBORES.ENSAYOS / Gutierrez, Miguel – 1881 – 9 – 1.50f – sp Bibl Santa Ana [840]

Albornoz, Alvaro de *see*
- EN LOS CAMINOS DE LA LIBERTAD
- EL FASCISMO Y LAS ARMAS Y LAS LETRAS ESPANOLAS

Albornoz de Videla, Graciela *see* EVITA

ALBOROTO Y MOTIN DE MEXICO DEL 8 DE JUNIO DE 1692. MEXICO, 1932 / Siguenza y Gongora, Carlos – Madrid: Razon y Fe, 1935 – 1 – sp Bibl Santa Ana [972]

Albrecht, Carl *see* DIE WISSENSCHAFTLICH GEORDNETE WELTANSICHT

Albrecht, Chr. *see* SCHLEIERMACHER'S LITURGIK

Albrecht, Erwin *see* WEGERECHT

Albrecht, Guenter et al *see* LEXIKON DEUTSCHSPRACHIGER SCHRIFTSTELLER VON DEN ANFAENGEN BIS ZUR GEGENWART

ALBRECHT HALLERS TAGEBUECHER SEINER REISEN NACH DEUTSCHLAND, HOLLAND UND ENGLAND : 1723-1727 / ed by Hirzel, Ludwig – ("Anhang: Ein bisher unbekanntes Gedicht Hallers aus dem Jahre 1721") – Leipzig: S Hirzel, 1883 – 1r – 1 – us U.W. Library [920]

Albrecht, Helmut *see* ENTWURF UND ERPROBUNG EINES KONZEPTS FUER DIE ITG IN DER LEHRERBILDUNG AN PAEDAGOGISCHEN HOCHSCHULEN

Albrecht, Hermann *see* DER PRAEZEPTORATSVIKARI

Albrecht, J L *see*
- ABHANDLUNG UEBER DIE FRAGE OB DIE MUSIK BEY DEM GOTTESDIENSTE DER CHRISTEN ZU DULDEN, ODER NICHT
- GRUENDLICHE EINLEITUNG IN DIE ANFANGSLEHREN DER TONKUNST

Albrecht, J W *see* TRACTATUS PHYSICUS DE EFFECTIBUS MUSICES IN CORPUS ANIMATUM

Albrecht, Julius *see* AUSGEWAEHLTE KAPITEL ZU EINER HANS-SACHS-GRAMMATIK

Albrecht, K *see*
- DIE IM TAHKEMONI VORKOMMENDEN ANGABEN UEBER HARIZIS LEBEN
- SHA'AR HA-SHIR
- STUDIEN ZU DEN DICHTUNGEN ABRAHAMS BEN EZRA

Albrecht, Karl *see* SHAOAR HA-SHIR

Albrecht, Luitgard *see* DER MAGISCHE IDEALISMUS IN NOVALIS' MAERCHENTHEORIE UND MAERCHENDICHTUNG

Albrecht, Otto *see* LUTHERS KATECHISMEN

ALBRECHT V. HALLERS SPRACHE IN IHRER ENTWICKLUNG DARGESTELLT / Kaeslin, Hans – (Includes bibliographical references) – [S.l.: s.n.], 1892 (Brugg: Buchdruckerei "Effingerhof") – 1r – 1 – us U.W. Library [430]

ALBRECHT VON HALLER : EINE STUDIE ZUR GEISTESGESCHICHTE DER AUFKLAERUNG / Irsay, Stephen d' – (Includes indexes) – Leipzig: G Thieme, 1930 – 1r – 1 – us U.W. Library [430]

ALBRECHT VON HALLER UND SEINE BEDEUTUNG FUER DIE DEUTSCHE CULTUR : VORTRAG, GEHALTEN IN DER LITERARISCHEN GESELLSCHAFT ZU DANZIG / Lissauer, Abraham – Berlin: Luederitz, 1873 – 1r – 1 – us U.W. Library [943]

ALBRECHT VON WALLENSTEIN,... : UNGEDRUCKTE, EIGENHAENDIGE VERTRAULICHE BRIEFE UND AMTLICHE SCHREIBEN AUS DEN JAHREN 1627 BIS 1634... / ed by Foerster, F – (Available: 1828. v1) – Berlin. 3v. 1828-1829 – 5mf – 9 – ne IDC [943]

Albrechtsberger, Johann G *see*
- GRUENDLICHE ANWEISUNG ZUR COMPOSITION
- JOHANN GEORG ALBRECHTSBERGERS... GRUENDLICHE ANWEISUNG ZUR COMPOSITION
- KURZGEFASSTE METHODE DEN GENERALBASS ZU ERLERNEN..
- QUATUOR POUR LE CLAVECIN, OU FORTEPIANO, DEUX VIOLONS
- QUINTUOR POUR TROIS VIOLONS, ALTO ET BASSE, CONTENANT UNE FUGUE A QUATRE SUJETS...
- SAEMMTLICHE SCHRIFTEN UEBER GENERALBASZ, HARMONIE-LEHRE UND TONSETZKUNST; ZUM SELBSUNTERRICHTE
- SECHS FUGEN FUER PIANOFORTE ODER ORGEL...11TES
- SEI QUARTETTI CON FUGHE PER DIVERSI STROMENTI...
- SIX FUGUES POUR LE PIANOFORTE...OP. 17
- SIX QUATUORS EN FUGUES, A DEUX VIOLONS, TAILLE ET BASSE...OEUVRE SECOND
- SIX QUATUORS POUR DEUX VIOLONS, ALTO ET VIOLONCELLE, OEUVRE 21
- SIX TRIOS CONCERTANS POUR VIOLON, VIOLA ET VIOLONCELLE, OEUVRE 9EME
- TROIS SEXTUORS POUR DEUX VIOLONS, DEUX ALTOS VIONLONCELLE ET BASSE, OP. 13, N.1

Albright, Cindy W *see* COMPARISON OF TWO METHODS OF TRAINING SPECIAL OLYMPICS VOLUNTEERS TO TEACH AND COACH BOWLING

Albright, W F *see*
- ARCHAEOLOGY AND THE RELIGION OF ISRAEL
- THE ARCHAEOLOGY OF PALESTINE
- THE ARCHAEOLOGY OF PALESTINE AND THE BIBLE

L'ALBUM – Paris. 1821-mars 1823; nov 1828-aout 1829 – 1 – fr A.C.R.P.P. [073]

O ALBUM – Rio de Janeiro, Jan 1893-Jan 1895 – 1,5,6 – bl Biblioteca [072]

ALBUM DE LA GRANDE GUERRE / Comite de Recrutement Canadien-Francais. Montreal – 1915 et 1917. SEM105P731 – 1mf – 9 – Can$2.25 – cn Bibl Nat [355]

L'ALBUM DE LA MINERVE – Montreal, Canada. 4v. 1872-74 – 2r – 1 – Can$50.00r – cn Can Microfilming [640]

ALBUM DE LA MINERVE : JOURNAL DE LA FAMILLE – v1-3. 1872-74. SEM35P136 – 1r – 1 – Can$72.00 – cn Bibl Nat [640]

ALBUM DE LA PAZ Y EL TRABAJO / Paz, Ireneo – Mexico: Impr., Litografia y Encuadernacion de I. Paz, 1911? – 1 – us U.W. Library [972]

ALBUM DE LA REVUE CANADIENNE – Montreal: La Revue, 1899. 06574. (Pre-1900 Canadiana) – 9 – cn C.I.H.M. [971]

ALBUM DE TERRE-SAINTE / Ghyvelde, Frederic de – 1905? SEM105P539 – 2mf – 9 – Can$4.50 – cn Bibl Nat [240]

ALBUM DEL BARDO. COLECCION DE ARTICULOS...DE VARIOS AUTORES – 9 – 1.50f – sp Bibl Santa Ana [800]

ALBUM DER BASLER MISSIONSGE-SELLSCHAFT.. / Ramseyer, Friedrich August – 1895 – 1 – us A.T.L.A. [240]

L'ALBUM DES FAMILLES *see* LE FOYER DOMESTIQUE / L'ALBUM DES FAMILLES

ALBUM DES FAMILLES – Ottawa: [Bureaux de "l'Album des familles"] 5e annee, no 2 (1er fevr. 1880)- – 9 – cn C.I.H.M. [930]

ALBUM DES LEGENDES – devenu: Le Livre des legendes. Paris. Mens. 1894-95 – 1 – fr A.C.R.P.P. [073]

ALBUM DES PERES DU CONCILE OECUMENIQUE DU VATICAN: COMMENCE LE 8 DECEMBRE 1869 – L. E. Desmarais. 1875? 02394. (Pre-1900 Canadiana) – 9 – cn C.I.H.M. [240]

ALBUM HENRI JULIEN : DESSINS ET CARICATURES / Librairie Beauchemin – Montreal, 1916 – 1r – 1 – Can$35.00 – cn Can Microfilming [760]

ALBUM HISTORICO DE LA PRIMERA ASAMBLEA FILIPINA / Tuohy, Anthony R – Fotografias reproducidas de La Revista filipina, supl. espanol del The Far Eastern Review. Manila: s.n., 1908. 104p. ill. 10 fold. col. maps in pocket – 1 – us U.W. Library [323]

ALBUM ILLUSTRATING THE MANUFACTURE OF BATIK / Batik – Balai Penelitian Batik, Java. SE-4538 1 – 9 – ne IDC [740]

L'ALBUM INDUSTRIEL – Montreal: T. Berthiaume, [1894-1895?] – 9 – cn C.I.H.M. [670]

ALBUM LITERARIO ESPANOL – 1846 – 9 – 1.50f – sp Bibl Santa Ana [800]

L'ALBUM LITTERAIRE – Saint-Hyacinthe, Canada. 12 jan-13 avr 1883 – 1r – 1 – Can$25.00 – cn Can Microfilming [800]

ALBUM LITTERAIRE ET MUSICAL DE LA REVUE CANADIENNE – v1-12. 1846-1847. SEM16P306 – 1r – 5 – Can$30.00 – cn Bibl Nat [073]

L'ALBUM MUSICAL – Montreal: A. Filiatreault, [1882-1884] – 9 – cn C.I.H.M. [780]

AN ALBUM OF 35 DRAWINGS, MAINLY OF BUILDINGS, ANTIQUE STATUES, ETC / Sanzio, Raffaelle – Holkham Red Book. Holkham mss. 701, 708, 772. Holkham Hall, Norfolk, England – 1 – uk Microform Academic [740]

ALBUM OF CHINESE CONTEMPORARY PAINTINGS – (Bilingual: English/Chinese) – 1995 – 214p – 9 – 92-3-002841-X – fr UNESCO [750]

ALBUM OF GENEALOGY AND BIOGRAPHY COOK COUNTY / Calumet Book and Engraving Co – Chicago, 1895. Illinois Reel 16. (The Cox Library Collection) – 5 – us Americana [920]

ALBUM OF HISTORY AND BIOGRAPHY OF MEEKER COUNTY / Alden, Ogle & Co – Chicago, 1888. Minnesota Reel 9. (The Cox Library Collection) – 5 – us Americana [978]

ALBUM OF NIAGARA FALLS – Portland, ME: Chisholm, 18??. 00022. (Pre-1900 Canadiana) – 9 – cn C.I.H.M. [971]

AN ALBUM OF THE ATTORNEYS OF RHODE ISLAND, WITH A PORTRAIT AND BRIEF RECORD OF THE LIFE OF EACH / Bowler, Ernest Constant – Bethel, Me., News Publishing Co., 1904. 208 p. LL-722 – 1 – us L of C Photodup [340]

ALBUM PALEOGRAPHICUM 17 PROVINCIARUM / Dekker, C et al – 1992 – 1mf – 9 – Bf2,731.00 – 90-72100-45-X – be Brepols [090]

ALBUM (POESIAS) / Rosado H de Sotomayor, Jose – Plasencia: Tip. Jose Hotiveros, 1934 – 1 – sp Bibl Santa Ana [810]

L'ALBUM SOUVENIR DES NOCES D'ARGENT DE LA SOCIETE SAINT JEAN BAPTISTE DU COLLEGE SAINT JOSEPH, MEMRAMCOOK, N.B.:.. – Montreal: C. Beauchemin, 1894?. 02395. (Pre-1900 Canadiana) – 9 – cn C.I.H.M. [971]

ALBUM SOUVENIR DU IIIE CENTENAIRE DU QUEBEC, 1608-1908 – Quebec: s.n., 1908. SEM105P479 – 1mf – 9 – Can$2.25 – cn Bibl Nat [971]

L'ALBUM UNIVERSEL / ed by Berthiaume, Treffle – Montreal, Canada. 1 nov 1901-12 oct 1907 – 5r – 1 – Can$60.00r – cn Can Microfilming [072]

ALBUM VERSES AND OTHER POEMS / Davin, Nicholas Flood – Ottawa?: s.n., 1882 (Ottawa: MacLean, Roger). 02590. (Pre-1900 Canadiana) – 9 – cn C.I.H.M. [810]

L'ALBUM-SOUVENIR DE L'OEUVRE DE LA CATHEDRALE – Numero unique. Montreal, sep 1891 – 1r – 1 – Can$25.00 – cn Can Microfilming [072]

THE ALBUQUERQUE INDIAN – 1905-06. (American Indian Periodicals in the Princeton University Library) – 9 – $45.00 – us UPA [305]

Al-Burhanpuri, Muhammad ibn Fadl Allah al-Hindi *see* THE GIFT ADDRESSED TO THE SPIRIT OF THE PROPHET,BY A. H. JOHNS. (ORIENTAL MONOGRAPH SERIES, NO. 1). ARABIC, JAVANESE AND ENGLISH. SE-11,438/1. 1965

Alburquerque. Ayuntamiento *see*
- FERIAS Y FIESTAS EN HONOR DE LA SANTISIMA VIRGEN DE CARRION, PATRONA DE ALBURQUERQUE
- FERIAS Y FIESTAS...SEPTIEMBRE, 1960 EN HONOR DE LA SANTISIMA VIRGEN DE CARRION
- FESTEJOS EN HONOR DE LA SANTISIMA VIRGEN DE CARRION, 1977

Alburquerque. Hermandad de Ntra. Sra. de Carrion *see* REGLAMENTO DE LA...PATRONA DE ALBURQUERQUE

ALBURY BANNER – Jan 3 1896-May 25 1950 – 9 – at Pascoe [072]

ALBURY BORDER POST – Australia, Jun 1889-Oct 1902 – 26r – 1 – uk British Libr Newspaper [072]

Albyn *see*
- DUPES ET DEMAGOGUES: A SOUVENIR
- MY MOTHER: IN MEMORIAM
- THE PREFACE: A POEM OF THE PERIOD
- RETRIBUTION: A LITERARY CONTRIBUTION TO THE NOVA SCOTIA DEPARTMENT OF THE PHILADELPHIA EXHIBITION
- RUSTICATING IN REALITY: A PIERIAN PARAPHRASE
- THE SABBATH IN DARTMOUTH

ALCABITII AD MAGISTERIUM JUDICIORUM ISAGOGE... / Abd Al Aziz Ibn Othman, Al Kabisi – (Relie et microfilme avec. THIBAULT (Jehan). – Declaration de la dignite des planetes... – Paris: Nyverd, 1543) – Paris: Simon de Colines, 1521 – 1 – F118.60 – fr Armell [944]

LAS ALCABOLAS DE ALBURQUERQUE O LOS CELEBRES BALDIOS / Duarte Insua, Lino – Badajoz: Dip. Provincial, 1946. Sep. de la Rev. de Estudios Extremenos – 1 – sp Bibl Santa Ana [340]

O ALCACAR : REVISTA SEMANAL LITTERARIA, CHISTOSA E ILLUSTRADA – S Salvador-BA, Brazil. 1 Jan 1871 – 1 – bl Biblioteca [072]

Alcala, Manuel *see* CESAR CORTES

EL ALCALDE DE ZALAMEA / Calderon de la Barca, Pedro – 1849 – 9 – 1.50f – sp Bibl Santa Ana [820]

ALCALDE DE ZALAMEA, EL / Calderon de la Barca, Pedro – Madrid: Rivadeneyra, 1849 – 1 – sp Bibl Santa Ana [946]

ALCANCE MISIONAL DE LA LITURGIA DEL CANACULO O EL PROBLEMA DE LA ADAPTACION / Morillo Trivino, Santiago – Granada: Imp. F. Roman, 1945 – 1 – sp Bibl Santa Ana [240]

Alcandre, J *see* LE MANDAT COLONIAL

Alcaniz, Florentino *see*
- LAS CRUZADAS DEL CORAZON DE JESUS
- LOS CRUZADOS DEL CORAZON DE JESUS. AVISOS PRACTICOS PARA SU FUNDACION Y ORGANIZACION

ALCANTARA – Caceres, 1945-1979 – 5 – sp Bibl Santa Ana [073]

Alcantara. Ayuntamiento *see*
- ESTATUTOS DEL PATRONATO DE VIVIENDAS SOCIALES DE ALCANTARA. 1971
- TRADICIONALES FERIAS Y FIESTAS DE PRIMAVERA, 1978
- TRADICIONALES FERIAS Y FIESTAS DE PRIMAVERA...1979

ALCANTARA (CACERES) / Junta Provincial de Turismo – (Fotos Gudiol) – Vitoria: Tip. Fournier, s.a. – 1 – sp Bibl Santa Ana [338]

Alcantara, San Pedro de *see* TRATADO DE LA ORACION Y MEDITACION

Alcantara. Spain *see* ORDENANZAS MUNICIPALES

Alcanzar Anguita, Eufrasio *see* TECNICA Y PERITACION CALIGRAFICA

Alcaraz Segura, Lorenzo *see* LOS NINOS (UN LIBRO PARA LOS GRANDES) CONSIDERACIONES SOBRE LA PRIMERA EDUCACION Y LA PRIMERA INSTRUCCION

Alcarotti, G F *see* DEL VIAGGIO DI TERRA SANTA

LA ALCAZABA ALMOHADE DE BADAJOZ / Torres Balbas, Leopoldo – Madrid. C.S.I.C. Granada. Al-Anadalus, 8, vol 6, fasc. 1. 1941 – 1 – sp Bibl Santa Ana [946]
ALCAZABA OF MERIDA. EARLY MUSLIM ARCHITECTURE / Hernandez, Felix – Oxford: Clasendon, 1940 – 1 – sp Bibl Santa Ana [720]
Alcazar Alenda, Jose Maria *see*
– CARTA PASTORAL
– CARTA PASTORAL DEL...CON OCASION DEL 4TH CENTENARIO DE LA MUERTE DE HERNANDO CORTES Y DEL HOMENAJE DE ESPANA A NUESTRA SENORA DE GUADALUPE
EN EL ALCAZAR DE LA REINA. ANTOLOGIA POETICA GUADALUPENSE. CACERES, 1967 / Corredor, Antonio – Madrid: Graf. Calleja, 1968 – 1 – sp Bibl Santa Ana [810]
EL ALCAZAR DE TOLEDO / Sanchez Arjona, Vicente – Sevilla: Imprenta Zambrano, s.a. – 1 – sp Bibl Santa Ana [946]
Alcazar Molina, Cayetano *see* LOS VIRREINATOS EN EL SIGLO 18. MADRID, 1945
ALCESTER CHRONICLE – England, Apr 1864-Dec 1887; 1889; 1897; 1910; Jun-Oct 1912; 1986- – 47+ r – 1 – uk British Libr Newspaper [072]
ALCESTER GAZETTE – Alcester, England. 29 Apr-30 Dec 1864 – 44ft – 1 – uk British Libr Newspaper [072]
ALCESTER LOCAL TIMES – Alcester, England. 14 Nov 1863-23 Sep 1865 – 46ft – 1 – uk British Libr Newspaper [072]
ALCESTE-TRAGEDIE : OPERA EN TROIS ACTES... / Gluck, CW – Paris: Au bureau d'Abonement musical, 1777 – 1 – us Sibley [780]
ALCESTIS: A POETRY QUARTERLY – New York. v. 1 no. 1-4 Oct 1934-July 1935 – 1 – us NY Public [420]
ALCHERINGA – ETHNOPOETICS – Boston. v1-5 Fall 1970-Sum 1973 ns: v1-4 1975-80 1*; v2-4 1976-80 5*,9* – 1,5,9 – D10362 – us UMI [410]
Alchevskaia, Kh. D *see* PEREDUMANNOE I PEREZHITOE DNEVNIKI, PISMA, VOSPOMINANIIA
Alciati, Andrea *see*
– EMBLEMATA
– EMBLEMATA: CUM CLAUDII MINOIS DIVIONENSIS AD EADEM COMMENTARIIS
– EMBLEMATA V. C. ANDREAE ALCIATI MEDIOLANENSIS IURISCONSULTI
– EMBLEMATUM LIBELLUS
ALCIDE AL BRIVO / Hasse, Johann Adolf – Lipsia: B C Breitkopf e figlio, 1763 – 1 – us Sibley [780]
ALCIMI ECDICII AVITI VIENNENSIS EPISCOPI OPERA QUAE SUPERSUNT (MGH 1: 6.BD. 2.TEIL) / ed by Reiper, R – 1883 – Dfl42.00 – ne Slangenburg [240]
Alcobendes, Severiano *see* LAS MISIONES FRANCISCANAS EN CHINA. CARTAS, INFORMES Y RELACIONES DEL PADRE BUENAVENTURA IBANEZ (1650-1690)
Alcock, A W *see* CATALOGUE OF THE INDIAN DECAPOD CRUSTACEA IN THE COLLECTION OF THE INDIAN MUSEUM
Alcock, Deborah *see* THE ROMANCE OF PROTESTANTISM
Alcock, John Congreve *see* OBSERVATIONS CONCERNING THE NATURE AND ORIGIN OF THE MEETINGS OF THE TWELVE JUDGES FOR THE CONSIDERATION OF CASES RESERVED FROM THE CIRCUITS
ALCOHOL – (Absorbed: Alcohol and Drug Research, 1987) – New York. v1-2 1984-85* 1; v3-14 jan 1986-dec 1997+ 1,5,9 – 1,5,9 – D49536 – us UMI [616]
ALCOHOL *see* ALCOHOL AND DRUG RESEARCH
ALCOHOL AND ALCOHOLISM : INTERNATIONAL JOURNAL OF THE MEDICAL COUNCIL ON ALCOHOLISM – (All that is currently offered. Cont: British Journal on Alcohol and Alcoholism. Cont by: Alcohol and Alcoholism) – Oxford. v18-29. Spr/Win 1983-nov 1994 – 1,5,9 – D49439 – us UMI [616]
ALCOHOL AND ALCOHOLISM : INTERNATIONAL JOURNAL OF THE MEDICAL COUNCIL ON ALCOHOLISM – (Cont: Alcohol and Alcoholism) – Oxford. v30-32. 1995-97+ – 1,5,9 – D25177 – us UMI [616]
ALCOHOL AND ALCOHOLISM *see*
– ALCOHOL AND ALCOHOLISM
ALCOHOL AND DRUG RESEARCH *see* ALCOHOL
ALCOHOL AND DRUG RESEARCH – (Ceased publ. Absorbed by: Alcohol. Former title: Substance and Alcohol Actions/Misuse (1980-1985)) – New York. v1-7. 1980-1987 – 1,5,9 – D49334 – us UMI [615]
ALCOHOL HEALTH AND RESEARCH WORLD – Washington. v1-21. Spr 1973-1997+ – 1,5,9 – D12110 – us UMI [610]
ALCOHOL IN HEALTH AND DISEASE / Bucke, Richard Maurice – London, Ont.: J. Bryce, 1880. 00322. (Pre-1900 Canadiana) – 9 – cn C.I.H.M. [360]
THE ALCOHOLIC BEVERAGE LAWS OF THE DISTRICT OF COLUMBIA, REV. TO JANUARY 1, 1948 / District of Columbia. Laws, Statutes, etc – Washington, Division of Printing and Publications, Govt. of the District of Columbia, 1948 58 p. LL-381 – 1 – us L of C Photodup [340]
ALCOHOLISM : CLINICAL AND EXPERIMENTAL RESEARCH – v5-20. 1981-96 – 16r – 1,5,6,9 – $95.00r – us Williams [360]
ALCOHOLISM *see* ALCOHOLISM AND ADDICTION MAGAZINE
ALCOHOLISM – (Cont by: Alcoholism and Addiction Magazine) – Seattle. v1-5. sep 1980-1985* – 1 – D16861 – us UMI [616]
ALCOHOLISM – Zagreb. v1- 1965- 1*; v9-1973- 5*,9 – 1,5,9 – D7237 – us UMI [616]
ALCOHOLISM AND ADDICTION – (Cont: Alcoholism and Addiction Magazine. Cont by: Alcoholism and Addiction and Recovery Life) – Cleveland. v8-9. feb 1988-dec 1988 – 1,5*,9 – D16861.02 – us UMI [616]
ALCOHOLISM AND ADDICTION *see*
– ALCOHOLISM AND ADDICTION AND RECOVERY LIFE
– ALCOHOLISM AND ADDICTION MAGAZINE
ALCOHOLISM AND ADDICTION AND RECOVERY LIFE *see* ADDICTION AND RECOVERY
ALCOHOLISM AND ADDICTION AND RECOVERY LIFE – (Cont: Alcoholism and Addiction. Cont by: Addiction and Recovery) – Cleveland. v9. oct-nov 1989 – 1,5*,9 – D16861.03 – us UMI [616]
ALCOHOLISM AND ADDICTION AND RECOVERY LIFE *see* ALCOHOLISM AND ADDICTION
ALCOHOLISM AND ADDICTION MAGAZINE – (Cont: Alcoholism. Cont by: Alcoholism and Addiction) – Cleveland. v5-8 aug 1985-dec 1987 1*; v8 sep-dec 1987 5*,9 – 1,5,9 – D16861.01 – us UMI [616]
ALCOHOLISM AND ADDICTION MAGAZINE *see*
– ALCOHOLISM
– ALCOHOLISM AND ADDICTION
ALCOHOLISM TREATMENT QUARTERLY / ed by McGovern, Thomas F – v1- 1984- – 1, 9 ($275.00 in US $385.00 outside hardcopy subsc) – us Haworth [360]
Alcollarin. Ayuntamiento *see* FIESTAS EN HONOR DE LOS EMIGRANTES. ALCOLLARIN, 7 Y 8 AGOSTO 1971
ALCONETAR / Sanchez Loro, Domingo – Caceres: Garcia Floriano, 1947 – 1 – sp Bibl Santa Ana [946]
ALCOOL ET ALCOOLISME (CAUSERIES SUR L'INTEMPERANCE) / Rousseau, Edmond – 2nd ed. Quebec: la Cie de publication "Le Soleil", 1906. SEM105P1670 – 3mf – 9 – Can$6.75 – cn Bibl Nat [360]
ALCORANI SEU LEGIS MAHOMETI ET EVANGELISTARUM COCORDIAE LIBER, IN QUO DE CALAMITATIBUS ORBI CHRISTIANO IMMINENTIBUS TRACTATUR / Postel, G – Parisiis, 1543 – 2mf – 9 – H-8269/1 – ne IDC [956]
Alcorta, C A *see* PRINCIPIOS DE DERECHO PENAL INTERNACIONAL
Alcott, Amos Bronson *see* ESSAYS ON EDUCATION TOGETHER WITH THE TOWN REPORTS FOR 1859-1861 AND THE SCHOOL REPORTS FOR 1861-1862 OF CONCORD, MASSACHUSETTS
Alcott, Blake *see* THE CONCEPT OF THE OBJECTIVE AND LIBERTARIANISM
Alcott, William A *see* LETTERS TO A SISTER, OR, WOMAN'S MISSION
ALCTS NEWSLETTER – (Cont: American Library Association – Resources and Technical Division – RTSD Newsletter) – Chicago. v1-8 1990-97+ 1,5,9; v1 1990*. v3-5 1992-94* 5 – 1,5,9 – D17556 – us UMI [020]
ALCTS NEWSLETTER *see* NEWSLETTER
Alcuesca R. Ayuntamiento *see* GRANDES FIESTAS EN HONOR DE LA VIRGEN DEL ROSARIO, 1977
Alcuescar *see* COMISION DE MONUMENTOS, ANTIGUEDADES ROMANAS
Alcuescar. Ayuntamiento *see*
– FIESTAS EN HONOR DE LA SANTISIMA VIRGEN DEL ROSARIO, 1971
– GRANDES FIESTAS EN HONOR DE LA SANTISIMA VIRGEN DEL ROSARIO. 1974
ALCUIN AND THE RISE OF THE CHRISTIAN SCHOOLS / West, Fleming – New York: Scribner, 1892 – 1mf – us A.T.L.A. [240]
ALCUIN CLUB COLLECTION – 1899-1958 – 1 – uk Microform Academic [240]
ALCUIN OF YORK : LECTURES / DELIVERED IN THE CATHEDRAL CHURCH OF BRISTOL IN 1907 AND 1908 / Browne, G F – London: S.P.C.K.; New York: E.S. Gorham, 1908 – 1mf – us A.T.L.A. [240]
ALCUIN UND SEIN JAHRHUNDERT : EIN BEITRAG ZUR CHRISTLICH-THEOLOGISCHEN LITERARGESCHICHTE / Werner, Karl – (Includes bibliographical references and index of names) – Paderborn: Ferdinand Schoeningh, 1876 – 1mf – 9 – 0-8370-7037-6 – 1986-1037 – us A.T.L.A. [920]
ALCUNI GENERI DI LICHENI NUOVAMENTE LIMITATI E DESCRITTI / Massalongo, A B – Verona. 1855. B-2338 2 – 8 – ne IDC [580]
ALDABADAS / Juez Nieto, Antonio – Badajoz: Tip. Clasica, 1944 – sp Bibl Santa Ana [946]
Aldama, J A *see* MORILLO, SANTIAGO. LAS IGLESIAS CRISTIANAS DE ORIENTE. TEXTO DE TEOLOGIA ORIENTAL. GRANADA, 1946
Aldana, Cosme de *see* OTTAVAS Y CANCIONES ESPIRITUALES
Aldana, Francisco de *see* EPISTOLARIO POETICO COMPLETO
Aldao, Andres *see*
– ARGENTINA
– PERONISMO
AL-DAWA – (Missing: No. 36 (May 1979)) – Sawt al-Haqq wa 'l-Quwwa wa 'l-Hurriya. Cairo, 1976-1981 – 77mf – 9 – NE-20322/1 – ne IDC [260]
Alday, P *see* TROIS QUATUORS
Aldea de Trujillo. Ayuntamiento *see* FERIAS Y FIESTAS EN HONOR DE SAN ISIDRO LABRADOR. MAYO DE 1951
Aldeacentenera *see* SOCIEDAD DE CAZADORES DE ALDEACENTENERA. REGLAMENTO
Aldeanueva del Camino. Ayuntamiento *see* ORDENANZAS MUNICIPALES
Aldeburgh. Suffolk *see* CORPORATION LETTER BOOKS
Alden, Henry M *see* HARPER'S PICTORIAL HISTORY OF THE GREAT REBELLION
Alden, Henry Mills *see* GOD IN HIS WORLD: AN INTERPRETATION
Alden, Ogle & Co *see*
– ALBUM OF HISTORY AND BIOGRAPHY OF MEEKER COUNTY
– ILLUSTRATED ALBUM OF BIOGRAPHY OF RED RIVER VALLEY AND PARK REGIONS
Alden Publishing Co *see*
– COMPENDIUM OF HISTORY, REMINISCENCE AND BIOGRAPHY OF NEBRASKA
– COMPENDIUM OF HISTORY, REMINISCENCE AND BIOGRAPHY OF WESTERN NEBRASKA
Alder, J *see*
– BRITISH NUCLIBRANCHIATE MOLLUSCA
– A MONOGRAPH OF BRITISH NUCLIBRANCHIATE MOLLUSCA
D'ALDERCHRISTELICSTE RELIGION ODER CERIMONIEN DIE MEN SACRAMENTLIJCKEN TER BETERINGE DES LICHAEMS CHRISTI INDER GHEMEENTEN BRUYCKEN SAL. ANDER MAEL VERBETERT ENDE GHEMEERDERT VAN DEN AUTHEUR SELUE / Joris, David – BME-379 1 – 9 – ne IDC [240]
DEN ALDERHEIJLICHSTEN NAEM VOOR EEN NIEUJAER-GIFT / Poirters, Adrianus – O 405. 1647 – 9 – ne IDC [760]
ALDERLEY AND WILMSLOW ADVERTISER – (Lacking: Jan-March 1896; Jan-Dec 1897; Jan-Feb 1911) – Alderley, Wilmslow, England. 7 Aug 1874-Dec 1924 – 40r – 1 – uk British Libr Newspaper [072]
ALDERSHOT AND DISTRICT TOWN CRIER – England, 1932 – 18ft – 1 – uk British Libr Newspaper [072]
ALDERSHOT NEWS – England, 1976-81 – 41r – 1 – uk British Libr Newspaper [072]
Alderson, Edward H *see* BARNEWELL AND ALDERSON'S REPORTS
Alderwerelt van Rosenburgh, C R W K van *see*
– MALAYAN FERNS
– MALAYAN FERNS ALLIES
– MALAYAN FERNS AND FERN ALLIES
AL-DIFA – (Missing: 1934(Jan.-March); 1935(Dec.); 1939(Jan.-Aug.); 1948(May)-1949(Feb.); 1952(Sept.)-195(Jan.)) – Jaffa, Jerusalem, 1934(April)-1966 – 57r – 1 – J-93-2/3 – ne IDC [072]
AL-DIFFAH AL-GHARBIYAH – (Filmed by the University of Chicago Library Photodup Laboratory for the Middle Eastern Microfilm Project at the Center for Research Libraries) – Chicago: The West Bank Publ, 1993 – 1 – us Res Libr [071]
AL-DIMUQRATI – [Khartoum?]: Dar al-Arabi lil-Tabaah wa-al-Nashr, nov 28 1985; apr 28-dec 17 1987 – 1r – us Res Libr [956]
al-Din al-Khayru, Izz *see* AL-ATMA AL-SIHYUNIYAH FI MIYAH AL-URDUN WA-AL-LITANI
ALDINE : THE ART JOURNAL OF AMERICA – (Ceased publ. Vols 1-2 were not available for photography. Former title: Aldine Press, a Typographic Art Journal (1868-1870)) – New York. v3-9. jan 1870-1879 – 1 – D5201 – us UMI [700]
ALDINE HISTORY OF NEW SOUTH WALES – Sydney: Aldine Publishing Co., 1888 – 15mf – 9 – A$40.00 – at State Libr Vic [980]
ALDINE PRESS, A TYPOGRAPHIC ART JOURNAL *see* ALDINE
ALDRE BISKOTSEL I SVERIGE OCH DANMAR / Sandklef, Albert – 1937 – 1 – us I.U. Libraries [390]
Aldred, Guy *see* WORKS
Aldredge, Robert Croom *see* THESIS
Aldrete, B *see* DEL ORIGEN, Y PRINCIPIO DE LA LENGVA CASTELLANA O ROMACE QUE OI SE USA EN ESPANA
Aldrete y Soto, L *see*
– CRISOL DE LA VERDAD ILUSTRADO CON DIVINAS Y HUMANAS LETRAS, PADRES Y DOCTORES...
– DEFENSA DE LA ASTROLOGIA Y CONJETURAS
– DISCURSO DEL COMETA DEL ANO 1680
– LUZ DE MEDICINA Y RESPUESTA A LAS OBJECIONES PUESTAS A LA UNIVERSAL
– LA VERDAD ACRISOLADA EN LAS LETRAS DIVINAS Y HUMANAS...RESPONDIENDO AL AUTO...
Aldrich *see*
– HISTORY OF ONTARIO COUNTY
– HISTORY OF WINDSOR COUNTY
– LAND MARKS OF STUEBEN COUNTY
Aldrich, Henry *see* ARTIS LOGICAE COMPENDIUM
Aldrich, Jeremiah K *see* CRITICAL EXAMINATION OF...THE TIME OF OUR SAVIOUR'S CRUCIFIXION
Aldrich, Lewis C *see*
– HISTORY OF ERIE COUNTY
– HISTORY OF HENRY AND FULTON COUNTIES
– HISTORY OF YATES COUNTY
Aldrich, Nelson W *see* PAPERS
Aldridge, Henry R *see*
– THE ADMINISTRATION OF THE CONSOLIDATED HOUSING ACT, 1925 AND THE CONSOLIDATED TOWN PLANNING ACT, 1925
– THE ADMINISTRATION OF THE TOWN PLANNING DUTIES OF LOCAL AUTHORITIES
– THE CASE FOR TOWN PLANNING
– GUIDE TO THE ADMINISTRATION OF THE HOUSING ACTS, 1923 AND 1924
– THE NATIONAL HOUSING MANUAL
Aleander, H *see* LEXICON GRAECOLATINUM...
ALEANDER UND LUTHER AUF DEM REICHSTAGE ZU WORMS : EIN BEITRAG ZUR REFORMATIONSGESCHICHTE / Hausrath, Adolf – Berlin: G. Grote, 1897 – 1mf – us A.T.L.A. [240]
Aleandro, Girolamo *see* DIE DEPESCHEN DES NUNTIUS ALEANDER VOM WORMSER REICHSTAGE 1521
Aleantara. Ayuntamiento *see* FERIAS Y FIESTAS DE PRIMAVERA 1972
ALEGACION AL DERECHO...DUQUE DE MEDINACELI / Santos Cuenda, Juan y Consortes – 1877 – 9 – 1.50f – sp Bibl Santa Ana [946]
ALEGACION EN DERECHO DE DON JUAN DE ARGUELLO SOBRE SU PRISION – 1736? Incompleto – 9 – $1.50f – sp Bibl Santa Ana [946]
ALEGACION EN DERECHO...VIRGEN DEL PUERTO...PLASENCIA / Garcia Mora, Jose – 1892 – 9 – 1.50f – sp Bibl Santa Ana [240]
ALEGACION...DEHESA DE LA SERENA...PLEITO...MARQUES DE PERALES / Torres, Manuel de – 1796 – 9 – 1.50f – sp Bibl Santa Ana [946]

ALEGATO CONTRA UNA GRAVE FALTA DE INSENSIBILIDAD HISTORICA – Madrid, 1936. Fiche W 708. (Blodgett Collection of Spanish Civil War Pamphlets) – 9 – us H.U. College Libr [946]
ALEGATO DE BUENA PRUEBA PRESENTADO / Cabrera de la Rocha, Juan – 1841 – 9 – 1.50f – sp Bibl Santa Ana [946]
LE ALEGREZZE FATTE IN VENETIA PER LA MIRACOLOSA VITTORIA OTTENUTA DALLA SANTISSIMA LIGA...1571 – [1571] – 1mf – 9 – H-8179/1 – ne IDC [910]
Alejandro-De Leon, Daniel see COMPARISON OF SKINFOLD MEASUREMENTS UNDER NORMALLY HYDRATED AND DEHYDRATED CONDITIONS IN FEMALES AGES TO 54
ALEKSANDER BLOK I EGO MAT' / Beketova, M – L. 1925. BR-1989 2 – 8 – ne IDC [920]
ALEKSANDER BLOK. SINKHRONICHESKIE TABOLTSY ZHIZNI I TVORCHESTVA 1880-1921 / Ashukin, N – Bibliografiia 1902-1923. "Novaia Moskva." 1923. BR-1977 2 – 8 – ne IDC [920]
ALEKSANDER BLOK / Mochul'skii, K – Paris. 1948. BR-1442 – 8 – ne IDC [920]
ALEKSANDR HERZEN PAMPHLET COLLECTION – 1858 – 1 – CSUXANS0673-B – us Hoover Inst Photo [335]
ALEKSANDR ILICH DUTOV : VO ISKOVO I ATAMAN ORENBURGSKAGO KAZACHI AGO VO ISKA GENERALLE ITENANT: KRATKAI A BIOGRAFIIA, VYBORKI IZ PECHATI, STATI I PROCH., OTNOSI ASHCHEESI A K DI EI ATELNOSTI VO ISKOVOGO ATAMANA – [Orenburg?: s.n., 1919?] – 1 – CSUX88-B8400 – us Hoover Inst Photo [335]
ALEKSANDR PERVYI / Merezhkovskii, Dimitrii – Ed. 3. 2 v. M. 1913. BR-746 2 – 8 – ne IDC [460]
Aleksandrenko, V N see
– RUSSKIE DIPLOMATICHESKIE AGENTY V LONDONE V 18 V.
– SOBRANIE VAZHNEISHIKH TRAKTATOV I KONVENTSII ZAKLIUCHENNYKH ROSSIEI S INOSTRANNYMI DERZHAVAMI (1774-1906)
ALEKSANDRIISKIIA PESNI / Kuzmin, M – Spb. 1906. BR-1189 2 – 8 – ne IDC [460]
Aleksandrov, B A see KOLONIAL'NYE MANDATY
Aleksandrov, M see SBORNIK ZAKONODATEL'NYKH MATERIALOV, INSTRUKTSII I RAZ"IASNENII PO KOOPERATSII INVALIDOV
Aleksandrov, P A see SEVERNAIA SISTEMA
Aleksandrovich, V see
– KPOZNANII U KHARAKTERA GRAZHDANSKOI VOINY
– UCHENIE O LITSAKH IURIDICHESKIKH, PO NACHALAM NAUKI
Aleksandrovskii, S V see GRAZHDANSKII KODEKS RSFSR S POSTATEINO-SISTEMATIZIROVANNYMI MATERIALAMI
Alekseev, Aleksandr Aleksandrovich see EDINAIA ILI FEDERATIVNAIA ROSSIIA
Alekseev, M P see
– DEKABRISTY I IKH VREMIA. MATERIALY I SOOBSHCHENIIA
– OCHERKI ISTORII ISPANO-RUSSKIH LITERATURNYKH OTNOSHENII. XVI-XIX VV
Alekseev, S A see
– FEVRAL'SKAIA REVOLIUTSIIA
– GRAZHDANSKAIA VOINA V SIBIRII SEVERNOI OBLASTI
– MANIFEST 17 OKTIABRIA 1905 G. I POLITICHESKOE DVIZHENIE, EGO VYZVAVSHEE
– SAMODERZHAVIE I LIBERALY V REVOLIUTSIIU 1905-1907 GODOV
Alekseev, T D see ZHILISHCHNYE ZAKONY
ALEKSEI PETROVICH ERMOLOV / Pogodin, M P – Materialy dlia ego biografii. M. 1864. BR-8298 2 – 8 – ne IDC [920]
ALEKSEI STEPANOVICH KHOMIAKOV / Berdiaev, N A – M. 1912. B-2210 2 – 8 – ne IDC [920]
Aleksh, (Vinogradov) Ieromonakh see KITAISKAIA BIBLIOTEKA I UCHENYE TRUDY CHLENOV IMP. ROSSIISKOI DUKHOVNOI I DIPLOMATICHESKOI MISSII V G. PEKINE
Aleksieev, V P see PERVYI RUSSKII PARLAMENT
Aleksii see O VOZROZHDENII KRESHCHENIEM": V" ZASHCHITU KRESHCHENIYA MLADENTSEV" PROTIV" BAPTISTOV"
Aleksinskii, Grigorii Alekseevich see
– VO IMIA SOTSIALIZMA
– VOINA I REVOLIUTSIIA
Alektorov, A E see UKAZATEL' KNIG, ZHURNAL'NYKH I GAZETNYKH STATEI I ZAMETOK O KIRGIZAKH
Alele, Joseph see DIARIES
ALEM – Istanbul: Bekir Efendi Matbaasi, 1908-1909 – 9 – $75.00 – us MEDOC [956]
Alemand, L A see NOUVELLES OBSERVATIONS OU GUERRE CIVILE DES FRANCOIS SUR LA LANGUE
ALEMANNIA ZEITSCHRIFT FUER SPRACHE, LITTERATUR UND VOLKSKUNDE DES ELSASSES UND OBERRHEINS / ed by Birlinger, Anton – Bonn, 1875-92 – 64mf – 9 – subsc: DM380.00 diazo DM460.00 silver – gw Olms [430]
Alemany Bolufer, Jose see ESTUDIO ELEMENTAL DE GRAMATICA HISTORICA DE LA LENGUA CASTELLANA
Alembert, Jean Le Rond d' see
– ELEMENTS DE MUSIQUE THEORIQUE ET PRATIQUE, SUIVANT LES PRINCIPES DE M RAMEAU
– ELEMENTS DE MUSIQUE THEORIQUE ET PRATIQUE, SUIVANT LES PRINCIPES DE M. RAMEAU
– OPUSCULES MATHEMATIQUES
– PREMIERS MEMOIRES MATHEMATIQUES
– REFLEXIONS SUR LA CAUSE GENERALE DES VENTS
– SYSTEMATISCHE EINLEITUNG IN DIE MUSICALISCHE SETZKUNST
ALENCAR : PERIODICO CRITICO E LITTERARIO – Itapagipe-BA, Brazil. 17 Jul 1883 – 1 – bl Biblioteca [072]
Alende, Oscar see LOS QUE MUEVEN LAS PALANCAS
Alepin, Sam see LE MORALISTE
Aler, F Vernon see ALER'S HISTORY OF MARTINSBURG AND BERKELEY COUNTY
ALER'S HISTORY OF MARTINSBURG AND BERKELEY COUNTY / Aler, F Vernon – Hagerstown, Mail Publishing Co., 1888. West Virginia Reel 2. (The Cox Library Collection) – 5 – us Americana [978]
ALERT – Amherst, NE. -w. May 1897-Dec. 1897 – 1 – us NE Hist [071]
ALERT – Rocky Hill. 1975-1991 v30- jan 1992- 1*,9*; v30- jan 1992- 5* – 1,5,9 – D19855 – us UMI [073]
ALERTA – 1963-. Guatemala. -w – 1 – us U.W. Library [072]
L'ALERTE – no. 29-47. Lyon. avr 1936-37 – 1 – fr A.C.R.P.P. [073]
Aleshintsev, I see ISTORIIA GIMNAZICHESKAGO OBRAZOVANIIA V ROSSII (XVIII I XIX VEK)
Alessandri see
– LE DROIT INTERNATIONAL PUBLIC...
– INTRODUCTION
Alessandri, F see SIX SONATAS FOR 2 VIOLINS AND CONTINUO
[ALESSANDRO NELLE INDIE. OVERTURE; ARR.] OPERA OVERTURES ADAPTED FOR THE HARPSICHORD OR PIANO FORTE WITH AN ACCOOMPANIMENT FOR A VIOLIN. NUMBER 6 / Tarchi, A – (Binder's collection, also contains other by works by Tarchi, Martin y Soler, Paisiello, Federici, and Andreozzi) – London: Longman & Broderip, [1789] – 1 – us Sibley [780]
ALETHIAN CRITIC : OR ERROR EXPOSED – (Ceased publ) – Lexington. v1. apr 1804-apr 1806 – 1 – D5205 – us UMI [073]
ALEUT HUNTING HEADGEAR AND ITS ORNAMENTATION / Ivanov, S V – BN 267 2. 1928 – 8 – ne IDC [390]
THE ALEUT LANGUAGE AND ITS RELATION TO THE ESKIMO DIALECTS / Jochelson, W – BN 277 2. 1913 – 8 – ne IDC [490]
AN ALEUTIAN BURIAL / Weyer, E M – BN 456 2. 1929 – 8 – ne IDC [306]
Alewyn, A see VERMEERDERDE ZEDE EN HARPGEZANGEN
ALEXANDER : EIN HOEFISCHER VERSROMAN DES 13. JAHRHUNDERTS / Ems, Rudolf von; ed by Junk, Victor – Leipzig: K W Hiersemann. 2v. 1928-29 – 1 – us U.W. Library [830]
ALEXANDER 3RD, EMPEROR OF RUSSIA PAMPHLET COLLECTION – 1894 – 1 – CSUXANS0716-B – us Hoover Inst Photo [947]
Alexander, Archibald see
– BIOGRAPHICAL SKETCHES OF THE FOUNDER AND PRINCIPAL ALUMNI OF THE LOG COLLEGE
– A BRIEF COMPEND OF BIBLE TRUTH
– CHRISTIANITY AND ETHICS
– EVIDENCES OF THE AUTHENTICITY, INSPIRATION, AND CANONICAL AUTHORITY OF THE HOLY SCRIPTURES
– A HISTORY OF COLONIZATION ON THE WESTERN COAST OF AFRICA
– SOME PROBLEMS OF PHILOSOPHY
– THEORIES OF THE WILL IN THE HISTORY OF PHILOSOPHY
– A THEORY OF CONDUCT
ALEXANDER BLOK / Orlov, V N – Ocherk tvorchestva. M. 1956. BR-1469 2 – 8 – ne IDC [920]
ALEXANDER BLOK ET SON TEMPS / Berberova, N N – Spb. 1922. BR-1994 2 – 8 – ne IDC [920]
ALEXANDER BLOK, PROPHET OF REVOLUTION / Kisch, C – London. 1960. BR-1333 1 – 9 – ne IDC [460]
Alexander Brown 1890 see THE GENESIS OF THE UNITED STATES
ALEXANDER CAMPBELL : LEADER OF THE GREAT REFORMATION OF THE NINETEENTH CENTURY / Grafton, Thomas W – St. Louis: Christian Publishing, 1897 – 1mf – us A.T.L.A. [240]
ALEXANDER CAMPBELL'S THEOLOGY : ITS SOURCES AND HISTORICAL SETTING / Garrison, Winfred Ernest – St. Louis: Christian Publishing Co., 1900 – 1mf – us A.T.L.A. [240]
Alexander, Charles Beatty see NOTES ON THE NEW YORK LAW OF LIFE INSURANCE
ALEXANDER CRUMMELL COLLECTION : FROM THE HOLDINGS OF THE SCHOMBURG CENTER FOR RESEARCH IN BLACK CULTURE, MANUSCRIPTS, ARCHIVES AND RARE BOOKS DIVISION: THE NEW YORK PUBLIC LIBRARY, ASTOR, LENOX AND TILDEN FOUNDATIONS – (Guide which covers all coll under "Civil Rights Advocates" sold separately for $20.00 D3305.G3) – 1995 – 10r – 1 – $850.00 – D3305P11 – Dist. us Scholarly Res – us L of C Photodup [240]
Alexander de Hales see GLOSSA IN QUATTUOR LIBROS
Alexander, Gilchrist G see THE TEMPLE OF THE NINETIES
Alexander, Gross see
– A HISTORY OF THE METHODIST CHURCH, SOUTH, THE UNITED PRESBYTERIAN CHURCH, THE CUMBERLAND PERSBYTERIAN CHURCH, AND THE PRESBYTERIAN CHURCH, SOUTH, IN THE UNITED STATES
– THE SON OF MAN
ALEXANDER HARPER FAMILY PAPERS see HARPER, ALEXANDER, FAMILY PAPERS MS 3231
ALEXANDER HELPHAND PAMPHLET COLLECTION – 1908 – 1 – CSUXANS1157-B – us Hoover Inst Photo [943]
Alexander, Henry Carrington see THE LIFE OF JOSEPH ADDISON ALEXANDER
ALEXANDER HERIOT MACKONOCHIE : A MEMOIR / Towle, Eleanor A; ed by Russell, Edward Francis – New York: E. & J.B. Young, 1890 – 1mf – us A.T.L.A. [240]
ALEXANDER HERZEN / Partridge, Monica – 1984 – 9 – 92-3-102255-5 – fr UNESCO [947]
Alexander, Isaac see CIVIL WAR CORRESPONDENCE
Alexander, J A see THE PSALMS TRANSLATED AND EXPLAINED
Alexander, James McKinney see THE ISLANDS OF THE PACIFIC
Alexander, James W see
– FORTY YEARS' FAMILIAR LETTERS OF JAMES W. ALEXANDER, D.D.
– THE LIFE OF ARCHIBALD ALEXANDER, D.D.
– THE NEW YORK PULPIT IN THE REVIVAL OF 1858
Alexander, John see REASONS FOR BECOMING A BAPTIST
Alexander, Joseph Addison see
– NOTES ON NEW TESTAMENT LITERATURE & ECCLESIASTICAL HISTORY
– THE PSALMS
Alexander Mack Historical Society see SCHWARZENAU
ALEXANDER MARX JUBILEE VOLUME / Marx, Alexander – 2v. New York. 1950. BJ-100-55 1 – 9 – ne IDC [900]
ALEXANDER MINORITA (MGH QUELLEN..: 1.BD) : EXPOSITIO IN APOCALYPSIM – 1955 – Dfl39.00 – ne Slangenburg [240]
ALEXANDER MURRAY, F.G.S., F.R.S.C., C.M.G / Bell, Robert – 1892?. 00100. (Pre-1900 Canadiana) – 9 – cn C.I.H.M. [920]
Alexander Neckam see ALEXANDRI NECKAM DE NATURIS RERUM, LIBRI DUO (RS34)
ALEXANDER PUSHKIN / Blagoj, Dmitrij – 1981 – 80p – 9 – 92-3-101814-0 – fr UNESCO [460]
Alexander, Rebecca see CIVIL WAR CORRESPONDENCE
Alexander, Robert Jackson see
– JUAN DOMINGO PERON
– LABOR RELATIONS IN ARGENTINA, BRAZIL, AND CHILE
– THE PERON ERA
– TROTSKYISM IN LATIN AMERICA
ALEXANDER SERGEVICH PUSHKIN V CHESHSKOI LITERATURE / Frantsev, V A – Bibliograficheskie materialy. Spb. 1898. BR-5897 2 – 8 – ne IDC [460]
Alexander, Sidney Arthur see THE CHRISTIANITY OF ST PAUL
Alexander, Thomas P see DIARY
ALEXANDER TURNBULL LIBRARY CATALOGUE – (General Catalogue 266mf NZ$360.00. New Zealand and Pacific Catalogue (Author/Title) 488mf NZ$165.60. New Zealand and Pacific Catalogue (Subject) 308mf NZ$90.00) – 9 – nz Nat'l Libr [980]
ALEXANDER UND GILGAMOS / Meissner, Bruno – (Includes bibliographical references) – Leipzig: Eduard Pfeiffer, [19–?] – 1mf – 9 – 0-8370-7088-0 – 1986-1088 – us A.T.L.A. [230]
ALEXANDER VARIAN JR. LETTERS see VARIAN, ALEXANDER, JR., LETTERS, MS 3141
Alexander, W see JOURNAL OF LORD MACARTNEY'S EMBASSY TO CHINA
Alexander, W E see
– HISTORY OF CHICKASAW AND HOWARD COUNTIES
– HISTORY OF WINNESHIEK AND ALLAMAKEE COUNTIES
Alexander, William see
– DEMONIC POSSESSION IN THE NEW TESTAMENT...HISTORICAL, MEDICAL, AND THEOLOGICAL
– THE EPISTLES OF ST. JOHN
– EPISTLES OF ST JOHN: 21 DISCOURSES: WITH GREEK TEXT, COMPARATIVE VERSIONS
– LEADING IDEAS OF THE GOSPELS: FIVE SERMONS
– THE LIFE INSURANCE COMPANY
– PRIMARY CONVICTIONS
– ST. PAUL AT ATHENS
– THE WITNESS OF THE PSALMS TO CHRIST AND CHRISTIANITY
– ZECHARIAH
Alexander Wright see CATECHISM OF PRIVATE AND PUBLIC HYGIENE
Alexander, Yonah see TERRORISM
ALEXANDER'S FINANCIAL HERALD – London, UK. 11 Sep-30 Oct 1895 – 1 – uk British Libr Newspaper [072]
ALEXANDER'S MAGAZINE – 1-7 (all publ). 1905-1909 – 29mf – 9 – $120.00 – us UPA [305]
ALEXANDER'S MAGAZINE – (Ceased publ) – Boston. v1-7. may 1905-apr 1909 – 1 – D3341 – us UMI [073]
Alexandre, P see EUROPE ET JUPITER, CONCERT FRANCOIS A DEUX VOIX
ALEXANDRI NECKAM DE NATURIS RERUM, LIBRI DUO (RS34) : WITH NECKAM'S POEM DE LAUDIBUS DIVINAE SAPIENTIAE / Alexander Neckam; ed by Wright, T – 1863 – Dfl39.00 – ne Slangenburg [240]
ALEXANDRIA ADVERTISER – Alexandria, Va. 1800-08 – 3 – us Readex [071]
ALEXANDRIA ARGUS – Alexandria, NE. -w. Nov. 1895-Dec. 1902. Incomplete; May 1904-Jan. 1948; Feb. 1950-Dec. 1972 – 1 – us NE Hist [071]
THE ALEXANDRIA FUTURES MARKET (ALEXANDRIA COTTON EXPORTERS' ASSOCIATION) / Barber, C R – 1951. BNE-4607 1 – 9 – ne IDC [332]
ALEXANDRIA GAZETTE – Alexandria, VA. 1808-1820 – 1,3 – us Readex [071]
Alexandria, Louisiana see MISCELLANEOUS EARLY NEWSPAPERS
ALEXANDRIA NEWS – Alexandria, NE. -w. Apr 1879-Jul 1880 – 1 – us NE Hist [071]
ALEXANDRIA TIMES – Alexandria. Va. 1797-1802 – 1,3 – us Readex [071]
ALEXANDRIAN AND CARTHAGINIAN THEOLOGY CONTRASTED : THE HULSEAN LECTURES, 1892-93 / Heard, J B – Edinburgh: T.& T. Clark; New York: Scribner [distributor], 1893 – 1mf – us A.T.L.A. [230]
DE ALEXANDRIJNSCHE VERTALING VAN HET DODEKAPROPHETON / Schuurmans Stekhoven, J Z – (Includes bibliographical references and index) – Leiden: E J Brill, 1887 – 1mf – 9 – 0-8370-9270-1 – 1986-3270 – us A.T.L.A. [220]

DIE ALEXANDRINISCHE UEBERSETZUNG DES BUCHES HOSEA, HEFT 1 : EIN BEITRAG ZU DEN SEPTUAGINTA-STUDIEN UND DER AUSLEGUNG DES PROPHETEN HOSEA / Treitel, Leopold – Karlsruhe:A Bielefeld, 1887 – 1mf – 9 – 0-8370-5568-7 – 1985-3568 – us A.T.L.A. [220]

DIE ALEXANDRINISCHE UEBERSETZUNG DES BUCHES JESAIAS: EINE RECTORSREDE / Scholz, Anton – Wuerzburg: Leo Woerl, 1880. 1 fiche – 9 – us A.T.L.A. [240]

ALEXIADIS LIBRI 15 (CSHB 49) / Comnena, Anna – Bonnae. v2. 1878 – Dfl53.00 – ne Slangenburg [240]

Alexis, Leon d' *see* TRAITE DES ENERGUMENES, SUIVY D'UN DISCOURS SUR LA POSSESSION DE MARTHE BROSSIER

Alexis M G *see* LE CONGO BELGE ILLUSTRE

Alexis, OFM *see* HISTOIRE DE LA PROVINCE ECCLESIASTIQUE D'OTTAWA ET DE LA COLONISATION DANS LA VALLEE DE L'OTTAWA

Alexis, R P *see*
- UNE AME SACERDOTALE, LE CHANOINE MICHEL
- L'ETAT RELIGIEUX ET POLITIQUE DE LA FRANCE CONTEMPORAINE
- UN VOYAGE A LA GUADELOUPE

Alexis, Willibald *see* ERINNERUNGEN

Aley, Peter *see* EDUARD MOERIKES KUENSTLERISCHES SELBSTVERSTAENDNIS. IM SPIEGEL SEINER GEDICHTE "DIE ELEMENTE", "GOETTLICHE REMINISZENZ" UND "NEUE LIEBE"

Alf Gold Mining Company *see* THE ALF GOLD MINING COMPANY

THE ALF GOLD MINING COMPANY / Alf Gold Mining Company – s.l., s.n. 1896. 00032. (Pre-1900 Canadiana) – 9 – cn C.I.H.M. [622]

ALFABET NOUVEAU DE LA VREE ET PURE ORTOGRAFE FRANSOIZE / Poisson, R – 1609 – 9 – fr I.C.S. [440]

ALFABETISCHE CATALOGUS : GEDENKBOEKEN EN ANDERE JUBILEUM UITGAVEN... / Economisch-Historische Bibliotheek – Amsterdam – 101mf – 9 – H-1784/1 – ne IDC [020]

ALFABETISCHE CATALOGUS VON DE BOEKEN EN BROCHURES VAN HET INTERNATIONAL INSTITUUT. / International Instituut vor Sociale Geschiedenis. Amsterdam – (First Supplement, 1974.-43,600 cards 2 reels. $275.00 ISBN: 0-8161-1552-4; Second Supplement, 1979.-50,200 cards 3 reels. $450.00 ISBN: 0-8161-1464-1) – 1970.-310,000 cards 12 reels.-ISBN: 0-8161-1551-6 – 1 – $1340.00 – uk Hall [360]

AL-FAJR – Jerusalem, 1972(April)-1992 – 64r – 1 – J-93-3/3 – ne IDC [072]

ALFAR MORUNO DE BADAJOZ / Melida, Jose Ramon & Fita, Fidel – Madrid: Fortanet, 1912. B.R.A.H. 60. pp. 161-162 – 1 – sp Bibl Santa Ana [946]

Alfaric, Prosper *see* FROM JEWISH MESSIANISM TO THE CHRISTIAN CHURCH

AL-FATAT – New York, dec 12 1917-nov 15 1918; may 24-31 jun 21-jul 5 1919 – 1r – 1 – us Res Libr [071]

AL-FATAWA AL-'ALAMGIRIYAH. FUTAWA ALEMGIRI : A COLLECTION OF OPINIONS AND PRECEPTS OF MOHAMMEDAN LAW – Calcutta, Education Press. 6v. 1828-35 – 1 – LL-12025 – us L of C Photodup [340]

ALFAVITNO-PREDMETNYI I UKAZATEL DEKRETOV I RASPORI AZHENI I – (C.1: 1920-1921) – Kazan: Narodny i komissariat i ustit sii A.T.T.S.S.R., 1921- – 1 – CSUXAKY5556-S – us Hoover Inst Photo [947]

ALFAVITNO-PREDMETNYI UKAZATEL DE ISTVUI USHCHIKH NESEKRETNYKH PRIKAZOV I TSIRKULIAROV PO RKKF ZA VREMIA S 1923 PO 1927 GOD – Leningrad: Izd. Upravlenii a v.-morskikh sil RKKA, 1928 – 1 – CSUX91-B3168 – us Hoover Inst Photo [947]

ALFAVITNO-PREDMETNYI UKAZATEL K DEKRETAM, POSTANOVLENIIAM I RASPORI AZHENIIAM / Barsegiants, OB – Moskva: Izd Otdela i ustit sii Moskovskogo soveta R., K. i K.D., 1922 – 1 – CSUX91-B1344 – us Hoover Inst Photo [947]

ALFAVITNO-PREDMETNYI UKAZATEL K POSTANOVLENIIAM I RASPORI AZHENIIAM MOSKOVSKOGO SOVETA R., K. I K.D. I EGO OTDELOV, OPUBLIKOVANNYKH V GAZETE "KOMMUNISTICHESKI I TRUD" : ZA VREMIA S L-GO I ANVARIA PO L-OENOI ABRIA 1921 G / Barsegiants, OB – Moskva: Gorodsko i ra ionny i sovet R., K. i K.D., 1921 – 1 – CSUX91-B3005 – us Hoover Inst Photo [947]

ALFAVITNO-PREDMETNYI UKAZATEL' K POSTANOVLENIIAM TSK KP LATVII I SOVETA MINISTROV LATVIISKOI SSR I RASPORIAZHENIIAM SOVETA MINISTROV LATVIISKOI SSR ZA 1940-1959 GG – Riga, 1960 – 5mf – 9 – ne IDC [320]

ALFAVITNO-PREDMETNYI UKAZATEL ZA IANVAR 1922 G. K DEKRETAM, POSTANOVLENIIAM, RASPORIAZHENIIAM I PRIKAZAM / Barsegiants, OB – Moskva: Izd. Narodnogo komissariata i ustit sii, 1922 – 1 – CSUX90-B9574 – us Hoover Inst Photo [947]

ALFAVITNYI KATALOG RUSSKIKH KNIG PO MATEMATIKE, VYSHEDSHIKH V ROSSII S NACHALA KNIGOPECHATANIIA DO POSLEDNIAGO VREMENI / Agapov, D V – Orenburg. 1908. BR-7049 2 – 8 – ne IDC [510]

ALFAVITNYI SPISOK / Russia. Tsentral'nyi Komitet Tsenzury Inostrannoi – 1866-69, 1882-92, 1894, 1896-99 – 1 – $69.00 – us L of C Photodup [324]

ALFAVITNYI SPISOK KNIG BIBLIOTEKI IURIDICHESKAGO FAKUL'TETA IMP. KAZANSKAGO UNIVERSITETA – Kazan, 1901. 133p. Catalog of the Library of the law faculty of Kazan University, arranged alphabetically. BR-4478- – 8 – ne IDC [340]

ALFAVITNYI SPISOK (OBSHII) KNIGAM NA ANGLISSKOM IAZYKE, POZVOLENNYM INOSTRANNOIU TSENSUROIU S ISKLIUCHENIEM MEST DLIA PUBLIKI I BEZYSSLOVNYM. S 1815 NO 1855 GOD VKLIUCHITEL'NO – St. Petersburg, 1856. 14p. Br-10,094 1 – 9 – ne IDC [947]

ALFAVITNYI SPISOK PERIODICHESKIKH IZDANII ROSSIISKOI IMPERII – St. Petersburg, 1899. 51p. BR-5858 2 – 8 – ne IDC [030]

ALFAVITNYI UKAZATEL' DRAMATICHESKIKH SOCHINENII NA RUSSKOM IAZYKE, DOZVOLENNYKH K PREDSTAVLENIIU BEZUSLOVNO S 1 IANVARIA 1897 GODA PO 1 IANVARIA 1902 GODA – St. Petersburg, 1902. 146p. BR-7050 2 – 8 – ne IDC [790]

ALFAVITNYI UKAZATEL K SOBRANIIU POSTANOVLENII I RASPORI AZHENII M.S.R. I K.D. ZA VREMI A OT L MAI A 1918 G. PO 31 IULIA 1919 G – Moskva: [s.n., 1919?] – 1 – CSUX91-B4178 – us Hoover Inst Photo [947]

ALFAVITNYI UKAZATEL K SOBRANIIU POSTANOVLENII I RASPORI AZHENII M.S.R. I K.D. ZA VREMIA OT L MAIA 1918 G. PO 31 IULIA 1919 G – Moskva: [s.n., 1919?] – 1 – CSUXADP9445-B – us Hoover Inst Photo [947]

ALFAVITNYI UKAZATEL' KNIGAM I BROSHIURAM, AREST NA KOTORYIA UTVERZHDEN SUDEBNYMI USTANOVLENIIAMI – St. Petersburg, 1907-14. 4v. Dop. BR-5859 2 – 8 – ne IDC [030]

Alfeevskii, S A *see* ARENDA TORGOVYKH PREDPRIIATII

ALFELDER ZEITUNG – Alfeld, 1987- – 5r per yr – 1 – Dist. gw Mikrofilm – gw Misc Inst [072]

Alfimov, M V *see* SCIENTIFIC AND APPLIED PHOTOGRAPHY

ALFIYYA (QUINTESSENCE DE LA GRAMMAIRE ARABE) / Ibn Malik – 1833 – 1 – uk Microform Academic [470]

ALFONS GORBACH PAMPHLET COLLECTION – 1961 – 1 – CSUXANQ2307-B – us Hoover Inst Photo [920]

ALFONSO 2 Y LUGARTENENCIA INFANTE PEDRO (ANNO 1289-1295) – Barcelona – 1r – 5,6 – sp Cultura [946]

Alfonso 4 *see* MAJORICARUM (ANNO 1416-1458)

Alfonso 10 el Sabio, Rey de Castilla *see*
- CANTIGAS DE SANTA MARIA
- CODIGO DE LAS SIETE PARTIDAS DEL REY D. ALFONSO EL SABIO GLOSADAS POR EL LIC. GREGORIO LOPEZ DE TOVAR
- QUINTA PARTIDA, COM. DE GREGORIO LOPEZ
- EL SABIO. LAS SIETE PARTIDAS (ANNO 1587)

Alfonso 10 el Sabio, Rey de Castilla Rey de Castilla *see*
- SETENA PARTIDA, COM. DE GREGORIO LOPEZ
- SEXTA PARTIDA, COM. DE GREGORIO LOPEZ

Alfonso 10th, King of Castille and Leon, 1221-1284 *see* CHRONICA DEL MUY ESCLARECIDO PRINCIPE, Y REY DON ALFONSO..

Alfonso de Orozco, Beato *see*
- COMMENTARIA QUAEDAM IN CANTICA CANTICORUM
- DECLAMATIONES QUADRAGESIMALES.

Alfonso, Francisco *see* DISPUTATIONES IN...ARISTOTELIS DE ANIMA

ALFORD 1759-1849 – (Mf 1T: Intentions 1808, 1810, 1820-49; Marriages 1803, 1820, 1841-44; Births & Deaths 1759-1825; Deaths 1842-43; Births 1839-42. Mf 2T: Births 1843-50; Marriages 1843-50; Deaths 1843-50) – (mf ed 1994) – 2mf – 9 – 0-87623-198-9 – us Holbrook [920]

ALFORD 1759-1906 – (Mf 1-4: Town Records 1773-1835. Mf 5-6: Town & Vital Records 1759-1844. Mf 7: Births 1843-74. Mf 8: Marriages 1843-75. Mf 8: Deaths 1843-74. Mf 9: Deaths 1875-1981. Mf 10: Deaths 1981-86. Mf 11: Marriages 1875-1987. Mf 12: Births 1875-1906) – (mf ed 1988) – 12mf – 9 – 0-87623-077-X – us Holbrook [920]

Alford, F S *see* THE GREATER ILLUSION, A CRITICAL REVIEW OF AUSTRALIA'S FISCAL POLICY

Alford, Henry *see*
- THE BOOK OF GENESIS, AND PART OF THE BOOK OF EXODUS
- ESSAYS AND ADDRESSES CHIEFLY ON CHURCH SUBJECTS
- HOW TO STUDY THE NEW TESTAMENT: THE EPISTLES (FIRST SECTION)
- HOW TO STUDY THE NEW TESTAMENT: THE GOSPELS: THE ACTS OF THE APOSTLES

ALFORD STANDARD / LINCOLNSHIRE STANDARD (ALFORD, MABLE THORPE AND SUTTON-ON-SEA) – England, 1987- – 34+ r – 1 – uk British Libr Newspaper [072]

ALFRED – Sydney, 1835 – 1r – 1 – A$31.00 silver A$27.00 vesicular – at Pascoe [072]

THE ALFRED ADVOCATE – Portland, ME: Libby & Smith, nov 4 1915-sep 28 1916 – 1r – 1 – us Res Libr [071]

THE ALFRED AND WESTMINSTER EVENING GAZETTE – London. -d. 12 May 1810-31 Dec 1811. (3 reels) – 1 – uk British Libr Newspaper [072]

Alfred Barron *see* HOME-TALKS

ALFRED BAUDRILLART PAMPHLET COLLECTION – 1919 – 1 – CSUXANQ3166-B – us Hoover Inst Photo [331]

ALFRED CHENEY JOHNSTON STUDIO PORTRAITS / U.S. Library of Congress. Prints and Photographs Division – Movie stars, theatrical performers of the 1920's and 1930's; studies for advertisements. 245 images. 1 reel. P&P8782 – 1 – 23.00r – us L of C Photodup [770]

ALFRED DREYFUS PAMPHLET COLLECTION – 1898-1931? – 1 – CSUXANQ4910-B – us Hoover Inst Photo [944]

ALFRED HITCHCOCK'S MYSTERY MAGAZINE – New York. v1-. dec 1956-* – 1 – D11961 – us UMI [790]

ALFRED LALLIE : 1 LIVRE ET 10 BROCHURES MICROFILMEES ENSEMBLE / Lallie, Alfred – 1 – F369,08 – fr Armell [944]

ALFRED LALLIE : 10 OEUVRES MICROFILMEES ENSEMBLE / Lallie, Alfred – 1 – F349.16 – fr Armell [944]

ALFRED MEISSNER - FRANZ HEDRICH : GESCHICHTE IHRES LITERARISCHEN VERHAELTNISSES AUF GRUNDLAGE DER BRIEFE, DIE ALFRED MEISSNER SEIT DEM JAHRE 1854 BIS ZU SEINEM TODE 1885 AN FRANZ HEDRICH GESCHRIEBEN / Hedrich, Franz – Berlin: Otto Janke, 1890 – 1r – 1 – us U.W. Library [430]

ALFRED PELLAN ET SON OEUVRE / Pellan, Alfred – SEM35P1 – 4r – 1 – Can$195.00 – cn Bibl Nat [700]

ALFRED THE GREAT: A SKETCH AND SEVEN STUDIES / Draper, Warwick Herbert – Preface by Right Rev. J. Percival. London: E. Stock, 1901. xv,143p. illus.plates, map, facsim – 1 – us U.W. Library [920]

ALFRED THOMPSON PAMPHLET COLLECTION – 1964 – 1 – CSUXANP3029-B – us Hoover Inst Photo [920]

ALFWAR OCH SKAMT *see* SUNDSVALLS TIDNING

ALGAE ANTARCTICA / Hooker, J D & Harvey, W H – London Journal of Botany, v.4, 1845 – 9 – uk Microform Academic [580]

ALGAE BRITANNICAE / Greville, R K – Edinburgh. 1830. B-985 2 – 8 – ne IDC [580]

Algamar, B *see* SAY IT IN: BAHASA INDONESIA, ENGLISH, NIPPONGO

Algar, D *see* STUDIES ON GROWTH, BODY COMPOSITION AND NUTRITION OF EMUS

AL-GARIDAH – Cairo. Sept 1 1909-Aug 30 1913 – 1 – us NY Public [072]

Algarotti, F *see* AN ESSAY ON PAINTING

ALGARUM UNICELLULARUM GENERA NOVA ET MINUS COGNITA / Braun, A C H – Lipsiae. 1855. B-5108 2 – 8 – ne IDC [580]

L'ALGARUM ZANARDINI. WITH BIOGRAPHY OF G. A. M. ZANARDINI BY G. MENEGHINI / Toni, G B de & Levi(-Morenos), D – Venezia. 1888. B-6357 2 – 8 – ne IDC [580]

AL-GAZA'IR : REVUE ALGERIENNE D'EDUCATION SOCIALE – Al Djazaier, Alger. n1-2. oct-nov 1908 – 1 – fr A.C.R.P.P. [073]

ALGAZEL'S METAPHYSICS : A MEDIAEVAL TRANSLATION / Al-Ghazali; ed by Muckle, J T – 1933 – xx/247p – 9 – Can$4.00 – 0-88844-555-5 – cn Pontif [110]

ALGEBRA AND LOGIC – New York. v7-36 jan 1968-dec 1997+ 1*,5*; v17-36 jan 1978-dec 1997+ 9* – 1,5,9 – D10875 – us UMI [510]

THE ALGEBRA OF MOHAMMED BEN MUSA / Khuwarazmu – 1831 – 1 – uk Microform Academic [510]

ALGEBRA UNIVERSALIS – Winnipeg. v1-. 1971-* – 1 – D17776 – us UMI [510]

ALGEBRAISCHE STRUKTUREN IN EINFACHEN WARTESCHLANGEN-NETZEN / Knaup, Werner – 1994 – 3mf – DM98.00 – 3-89349-878-8 – gw Hänsel [510]

L'ALGEBRE DE LA LOGIQUE / Couturat, Louis – Paris: E. Capiomont, 1905. 2 fiches. (Philosophy Collection) – 9 – 6.00 – fr Bibl Nationale [160]

ALGEMEEN DAGBLAD VAN NEDERLANDSCH INDIE, 1873-1886 / Netherlands. Royal Library. The Hague. Newspaper Department – Inclusive: Advertentie-Blad, 1874. KB004 – 323mf – 9 – Dfl1760.00 silver – ne MMF Publ [072]

ALGEMEEN DOOPSGEZIND WEEKBLAD – (Lacking some issues) – v19-47. 1964-92 – Inquire – 1 – ATLA S0336 – us A.T.L.A. [240]

ALGEMEEN HANDELSBLAD – 1828-1970 – 9,807mf – 9 – Dfl50,996.00 silver Dfl46,583.00 diazo – ne MMF Publ [072]

ALGEMEEN MAGAZYN, VAN WETENSCHAP, KONST EN SMAAK – Amsterdam, 1785-91. Behelzende: 1, Wysbegeerte en Zedekunde; 2, Natuurkunde en Natuurlyke historie; 3, Historiekunde; 4, Beschaafde letteren, fraaije kunsten, en mengelwerk – 3 – us Readex [700]

ALGEMEEN OVERZICHT VAN DE STAATKUNDIGE GESTELDHEID VAN NEDERL. INDIE – 1839-40.Arch. Kol. Geh. Exh. 31 jan 1851, 27 bis. BSD-100/1 mf.1-7 – 9 – ne IDC [950]

ALGEMEEN WEEKBLAD, VOOR CHRISTENDOM EN CULTUUR – v1-17. 1924-41 (complete) – 9r – 1 – ATLA S0110 – us A.T.L.A. [240]

Algemeene Vereeniging van Rubberplanters ter Oostkust van Sumatra *see* TUNTUNAN UNTUK DACTYLOSCOPISCH BUREAU DARI A.V.R.O.S

ALGEMENE KONST- EN LETTER-BODE, VOOR MEER- EN MIN-GEOEFENDEN : BEHELZENDE BERIGTEN UIT DE GELEERDE WAERELD, VAN ALLE LANDEN... – Haarlem. v1-72. 1788-1860 – 633mf – 9 – 8604/1 – ne IDC [073]

DIE ALGEN DER DALMATISCHEN KUESTE / Frauenfeld, G von – Wien. 1855. B-6365 2 – 8 – ne IDC [580]

DIE ALGEN DES TROPISCHEN AUSTRALIENS / Sonder, O W – (Abh. Naturw. Ver. Hamburg, 1871, v. 5, pt. 2, nr. 2, p. 35-74, 6 pls.). B-6406 1 – 9 – ne IDC [580]

DIE ALGENFLORA DER INSEL MORTIZHOLM... / Skuja, H L – Riga, 1931 – 1mf – 9 – ne IDC [580]

DIE ALGENFLORA DES MITTLEREN THEILES VON FRANKEN / Reinsch, P F – Nuernberg. 1867. B-6402 2 – 8 – ne IDC [580]

D'ALGER A TOMBOUCTOU, DES RIVES DE LA LOIRE AUX RIVES DU NIGER / Le More, Rene – Paris, 1913 – 1 – us Res Libr [960]

Alger, Horatio *see* HELPING HIMSELF: OR, GRANT THORNTON'S AMBITION

ALGER REPUBLICAIN – Algiers, Oct 1943-Jul 1945 (imperfect) – 2r – 1 – uk British Libr Newspaper [072]
Alger, William Rounseville *see* THE SCHOOL OF LIFE
ALGERIA : ANNUAIRE STATISTIQUE DE L'ALGERIE 1926-1964 / Algeria. Service Central de Statistique – (1961, 1962 not publ. Coll title: African Official Statistical Serials, 1867-1982) – 112mf – 9 – £5.00f (set £965.00 153mf) – uk Chadwyck [960]
ALGERIA : STATISTIQUE GENERALE DE L'ALGERIE 1867-1925 / Algeria. Service de la Statistique Generale – (1882-86 not publ. 1924 not available. Coll title: African Official Statistical Serials, 1867-1982) – 41mf – 9 – £7.00f (set £965.00 153mf) – uk Chadwyck [960]
Algeria *see*
- 2E PLAN QUADRIENNAL 1974-1977
- ACCORDS COMMERCIAUX CONCLUS PAR L'ALGERIE
- AL-JARIDAH AL-RASMIYAH
- EVOLUTION DE L'INDUSTRIE MANUFACTURIERE EN ALGERIE, 1962/1968
- JOURNAL OFFICIAL DE LA REPUBLIQUE ALGERIENNE
- JOURNAL OFFICIEL
- MONITEUR ALGERIEN
- PERSPECTIVES DECENNALES DE DEVELOPPEMENT ECONOMIQUE DE L'ALGERIE
- PLAN QUADRIENNAL 1970-1973 RAPPORT GENERAL
- RAPPORT GENERAL SUR LE DEUXIEME PLAN QUADRIENNAL DE MODERNISATION ET D'EQUIPEMENT DE L'ALGERIE
- SOCIETE NATIONALE POUR LA RECHERCHE, LA PRODUCTION, LE TRANSPORT ET LA COMMERCIALISATION DES HYDROCARBURES

Algeria. Banque Industrielle d l'Algerie et de la Mediterranee *see* RAPPORT ANNUEL
Algeria. Banque Nationale pour le Commerce et l'Industrie, Algiers *see* LES ENTREPRISES INDUSTRIELLES EN ALGERIE ET AU SAHARA
Algeria. Caisse Algerienne de Credit Agricole Mutuel *see* RAPPORT SUR LA PRODUCTION AGRICOLE ALGERIENNE ET SUR L'ACTIVITE DES INSTITUTIONS DE CREDIT MUTUEL ET DE COOPERATION AGRICOLES D'ALGERIE
Algeria. Caisse Algerienne de Developpement *see*
- EXERCISE: BILAN, COMPTES D'EXPLOITATION GENERALE, COMPTES DE PERTES ET PROFITS
- PROGRAMME D'EQUIPEMENT: NOMENCLATURE DU PROGRAMME D EQUIPEMENT PUBLIC; CONCOURS A TITRE DEFINITIF. 4 V. IN 5. 1963-66. BNE-8610/1
- RAPPORT D'ACTIVITE
- SITUATION DES PRETS EXTERIEURS
- SITUATION "EMPLOIS-RESSOURCES ETAT"

Algeria. Caisse Centrale Algerienne du Credit Populaire *see* ASSEMBLEE GENERALE ORDINAIRE
Algeria. Caisse Centrale des Societes Agricoles de Prevoyance de'Algerie *see* RAPPORT SUR LES OPERATIONS ET LES RESULTATS FINANCIERS
Algeria. Caisse d'Equipement pour le Developpement de l'Algerie *see*
- GUIDE DE L'INDUSTRIEL; RESUMES DES ETUDES DE BRANCHES
- PLAN DE CONSTANTINE: 2 ANS DE REALISATIONS
- PROGRAMME DE EQUIPEMENT
- LES REALISATIONS DE 1959 A 1962

Algeria. Centre de Coordination des Instituts de Technologie *see* LES INSTITUTS DE TECHNOLOGIE: BILAN D'UNE ANNEE DE FONCTIONEMENT
Algeria. Centre European pour le Developpement Industriel *see* JOURNEES D'INFORMATION ET DE DISCUSSION SUR LE DEVELOPPEMENT INDUSTRIEL DE L'ALGERIE
Algeria. Chambre de Commerce et d'Industrie d'Alger *see*
- L'ANNUAIRE ECONOMIQUE DE L'ALGERIE
- L'ARTISANAT ALGERIEN
- BILAN ECONOMIQUE D'UNE ANNEE D'INDEPENDANCE
- LES COOPERATIVES ET L'ALGERIE
- L'EAU EN ALGERIE
- SITUATION ECONOMIQUE DE L'ALGERIE
- LE SUCRE EN ALGERIE

Algeria. Commissariat National au Recensement de la Population *see*
- ETUDE STATISTIQUE NATIONALE DE LA POPULATION: PRESENTATION GENERALE DE L'ENQUETE
- ETUDE STATISTIQUE NATIONALE DE LA POPULATION: PRESENTATION GENERALE DE L'ENQUETE FECONDITE
- RECENSEMENT GENERAL DE LA POPULATION 1966: SITUATION DE RESIDENCE PAR COMMUNE
- RECENSEMENT GENERAL DE LA POPULATION ET DE L'HABITAT
- RECENSEMENT GENERAL DE LA POPULATION ET DE L'HABITAT, 1966
- RECENSEMENT GENERAL DE LA POPULATION ET DE L'HABITAT, 1966: CARACTERISTIQUES SOCIO-ECONOMIQUES DE LA POPULATION; EXPLOITATION PAR SONDAGE

Algeria. Commissariat National aux Recensements et Enquetes Statistiques *see* POPULATION ET HABITAT DES VILLES ET CHEFS-LIEUX AU RECENSEMENT DE 1966. POPULATION NON ALGERIENNE L'HABITAT DANS LES CHEFS-LIEUX URBANS
Algeria. Compagnie de Recherches et d'Exploitation de Petrole au Sahara *see* EXERCISE
Algeria. Compagnie Francaise des Petroles. (Algerie) *see* RAPPORT ANNUEL
Algeria. Credit Foncier d'Algerie et de Tunisie *see* ASSEMBLEE GENERAL ORDINAIRE. RAPPORT DU CONSEIL D'ADMINISTRATION, RAPPORT DU COMMITTEE DE CENSURE, RAPPORTS DE MM. LES COMMISSAIRES, RESOLUTIONS DE L'ASSEMBLEE
Algeria. Delegation generale du Gouvernement en Algerie *see* PLAN DE CONSTANTINE, 1959-1963: RAPPORT GENERAL
Algeria. Direction des Mines et de la Geologie *see* RAPPORT SUR L'INDUSTRIE MINIERE
Algeria. Direction du Travail et de l'Emploi *see*
- LEGISLATION EN VIGUEUR EN MATIERE DE CONTRACT DE TRAVAIL ET DE L'EMPLOI
- LEGISLATION EN VIGUEUR EN MATIERE DE FORMATION PROFESSIONNELLE ET D'APPRENTISSAGE

Algeria. Direction Generale du Plan et des Etudes Economiques *see*
- ANNUAIRE STATISTIQUE DE L'ALGERIE
- COMMERCE EXTERIEUR DE L'ALGERIE
- INDUSTRIE: DONNEES SUR L'INDUSTRIE ALGERIENNE, 1968, (1-3); 1968 (1-2)
- PLAN QUADRENNIAL, 1970-1973
- PLAN TRIENNAL 1967-1969, PROGRAMME D'EQUIPEMENT, NOMENCLATURE
- REGULATION DES NAISSANCES: OPINIONS ET ATTITUDES DES COUPLES ALGERIENS
- LA SITUATION ECONOMIQUE DE L'ALGERIE, AU LER JANVIER
- SITUATION ECONOMIQUE EN 1963

Algeria. Direction Nationale des Douanes *see*
- LE COMMERCE EXTERIEUR DE L'ALGERIE
- DOCUMENTS STATISTIQUES SUR LE COMMERCE EXTERIEUR DE L'ALGERIE

Algeria. Gouvernement General *see*
- EXPOSE DE LA SITUATION GENERALE DE L'ALGERIE
- PERSPECTIVES DECENNALES DE DEVELOPPEMENT ECONOMIQUE DE L'ALGERIE
- RAPPORT GENERAL SUR LE DEUXIEME PLAN QUADRIENNAL DE MODERNISATION ET D'EQUIPEMENT DE L'ALGERIE
- RAPPORT GENERAL SUR LES INVESTISSEMENTS PREVUS EN 1955 AU TITRE DU PLAN DE MODERNISATION ET D'EQUIPEMENT

Algeria. ILO *see* INSTITUT NATIONAL DE LA FORMATION PROFESSIONNELLE DES ADULTES RAPPORT
Algeria. Institut pour l'Etude et le Developpement de l'Industrie en Algerie *see*
- ETUDE DE LA MISE EN VALEUR DE LA REGION DU CHELIF
- ETUDE DU DEVELOPPEMENT ECONOMIQUE DE L'EST ALGERIEN
- ETUDE DU DEVELOPPEMENT ECONOMIQUE DE L'OUEST ALGERIEN
- ETUDE SUR LE DEVELOPPEMENT ECONOMIQUE DU CENTRE D'ARZEW
- ETUDES DES ENTREPRISES ET DES INDUSTRIES DU BATIMENT EN ALGERIE
- RAPPORT AU GOUVERNEMENT DE LA REPUBLIQUE ALGERIENNE SUR LE DEVELOPPEMENT DU MOUVEMENT COOPERATIF
- LE SECTEUR ALGERIEN DES INDUSTRIES AGRICOLES ET ALIMENTAIRES

Algeria. Maghreb Permanent Consultative Committee *see* TEXTES FONDAMENTAUX DES INSTITUTIONS MAGHREBINES
Algeria. Ministere de l'Agriculture *see*
- L'AGRICULTURE ALGERIENNE A TRAVERS LES CHIFRES, 1970
- L'EMPLOI DANS LE SECTEUR AUTOGERE AGRICOLE, CAMPAGNE 1967-1968
- PLAN QUADRIENNAL, 1970-1973
- SUPERFICIES ET PRODUCTIONS, STATISTIQUES AGRICOLES

Algeria. Ministere de l'Information et de la Culture *see*
- LA FORMATION PROFESSIONNELLE EN ALGERIE
- THE FOUR-YEAR PLAN (1970-73)
- SYSTEME ET STRUCTURE BANCAIRES EN ALGERIE

Algeria. Ministere de l'Orientation Nationale *see*
- ALGERIE AN 2, 1962-1964
- UNE ANNEE DE REVOLUTION SOCIALISTE, 1962

Algeria. Ministere du Travail *see* FORMATION PROFESSIONNELLE: PROJET DE PROGRAMME POUR LA PERIODE QUADRIENNALE 1970-1978
Algeria. Ministry of Industry and Power *see* ASPECTS OF THE ALGERIAN OIL POLICY 1965-1970
Algeria. Office Algerien d'Action Commerciale *see* STATISTIQUES DES EXPORTATIONS DES PRODUITS CONTROLES, CAMPAGNE
Algeria. Presidence du Conseil de la Revolution *see* PROJET DE CHARTE DE LA REVOLUTION AGRAIRE
Algeria. Secretariat Social d'Oran *see* REGARDS SUR L'ARRONDISSEMENT DE MASCARA
Algeria. Service Central de Statistique *see* ALGERIA
Algeria. Service de la Colonisation et de l'Hydraulique *see* PERIMETRES IRRIGABLES ET DEFENDUS; COMPTE RENDU
Algeria. Service de la Statistique Generale *see*
- ALGERIA
- ANNUAIRE STATISTIQUE DE L'ALGERIE
- LES COMPTES ECONOMIQUES DE L'ALGERIE ET DU SAHARA POUR LES ANNEES 1957 ET 1958
- RESULTATS STATISTIQUES DU DENOMBREMENT DE LA POPULATION EFFECTUE LE 13 OCT 1954
- STATISTIQUE GENERALE DE L'ALGERIE

Algeria. Service de Statistique Generale *see* ANNUAIRE STATISTIQUE DE L'ALGERIE
Algeria. Service des Statistiques Sociales *see* LES STATISTIQUES DU TRAVAIL ET DES RESSOURCES HUMAINES DANS QUATRE PAYS CHOISIS
Algeria. Societe Nationale de Recherche et d'Exploitation des Petroles en Algerie *see* RAPPORT ANNUEL D'ACTIVITE
Algeria. Union General des Travaillleurs Algeriens *see* CONGRES NATIONAL, 2ND, ALGIERS, 1965, ENSEMBLE DES TEXTES ADOPTES
ALGERIANS IN FRANCE PAMPHLET COLLECTION – 1961? – 1 – CSUXANQ3158-B – us Hoover Inst Photo [305]
ALGERIE AN 2, 1962-1964 / Algeria. Ministere de l'Orientation Nationale – BNE-8660 1 – 9 – ne IDC [338]
L'ALGERIE D'ABORD – no. 1-2. Alger. juil 1955 – 1 – fr A.C.R.P.P. [073]
ALGERIE OUVRIERE – Alger. 1930-aout 1939 – 1 – fr A.C.R.P.P. [073]
L'ALGERIEN EN FRANCE – no. 1-64. Paris. juil 1950-55 – 1 – fr A.C.R.P.P. [073]
ALGERIE-NOUVELLE – Alger. juil 1946-sept 1955. B.N. Jo. 86525. suite de: La Lutte sociale voir a ce titre – 1 – fr A.C.R.P.P. [073]
ALGER-REPUBLICAIN – Alger-republicain. oct 1938-oct 1939; fevr-avr 1940; oct 1943-sept 1955; oct 1962-64 – 1 – fr A.C.R.P.P. [072]
AL-GHADD – [Khartoum?]: al-Ghadd, apr 19, may 17, jun 7, 1989 – 1r – 1 – us Res Libr [956]
Al-Ghazali *see* ALGAZEL'S METAPHYSICS
Al-Ghaziri, Bernard Ghobaeira *see* ROME ET L'EGLISE SYRIENNE-MARONITE D'ANTIOCHE (517-1531)
Al-Ghazzali *see* MISHKAT AL-ANWAR
Al-Ghazzali, Iman *see*
- MENJINGKAP RAHASIA KEBAHAGIAAN
- PERDJUANGAN MELAWAN KESESATAN

ALGHE ITALIANE E DALMATICHE / Meneghini, G – Padova, 1842-1846. Fasc. 1-5. 384 pp., 5 pls. B-6383 1 – 9 – ne IDC [580]
LE ALGHE MARINE DELLA SICILIA ORIENTALE / Spinelli, V – Catania, 1905. 55 pp. (Atti Accad. Gioenia Sci. Nat. Catania, s. 4, v. 18, Mem. 13). B-6407 1 – 9 – ne IDC [580]
ALGHI DI AUSTRALIA, TASMANIA E NUOVA ZELANDA RACCOLTE DAL G. CAPRA NEL 1908-1909 / Toni, G B de & Forti, A – (Mem. R. Inst. Veneto, Venezia, v. 29, index, 1923). B-6510 2 – 8 – ne IDC [580]
ALGO MAS SOBRE LAS BULAS ALEJANDRINAS / Bayle, Constantino – Madrid: Razon y Fe, 1946 – 1 – sp Bibl Santa Ana [946]
ALGO SOBRE LOS DISCIPULOS Y SEGUIDORES DE ZURBARAN (1) / Torres Martin, Ramon – Badajoz: Imprenta Diput. Provincial, 1964 – sp Bibl Santa Ana [946]
ALGO SOBRE LOS DISCIPULOS Y SEGUIDORES DE ZURBARAN (2) / Torres Martin, Ramon – Badajoz: Imprenta Diputacion Provincial, 1965 – sp Bibl Santa Ana [946]
ALGOL – (Cont by: Starship) – New York. v12-23 may 1973-Win 1978 1*; v13-16 Win 1976-Win 1978 5*,9 – 1,5,9 – D9671 – us UMI [073]
ALGOLOGIA ADRIATICA / Naccari, F L – Bologna, 1828. 97 pp. B-6384 1 – 9 – ne IDC [580]
ALGOLOGISCHE NOTIZEN. 1-6 / Wille, N – (Nyt Mag. Naturv. v. 38, pt. 2). Christiania. 1900. B-6425 2 – 8 – ne IDC [580]
ALGOMA MISSIONARY NEWS – (Cont by: Algoma Anglican) – Sault Ste Marie, Ont.: [Algoma Missionary Press] v7 no 1 (Jan 1 1884)- – 9 – cn C.I.H.M. [240]
ALGOMA MISSIONARY NEWS AND SHINGWAUK JOURNAL – 1887-90 – 1 – 45.00 – cn McLaren [240]
ALGOMA MISSIONARY NEWS AND SHINGWAUK JOURNAL *see* ALGOMA QUARTERLY
ALGOMA QUARTERLY – (Cont by: Algoma Missionary News and Shingwauk Journal) – [Sault Ste. Marie, Ont.: s.n., 1874-1877] – 9 – cn C.I.H.M. [240]
ALGOMA REVIEW. – Sault Ste. Marie, Ont.: J.E. Dudley, [1882?-18– or 19–] – 9 – cn C.I.H.M. [073]
L'ALGONQUIN – Ville de Laval, Quebec. 31 mar 1955-v1 n4. 21 avr 1955 – 1r – 1 – Can$25.00 – cn Can Microfilming [072]
AN ALGONQUIN MAIDEN: A ROMANCE OF THE EARLY DAYS OF UPPER CANADA / Adam, Graeme Mercer – Montreal: J. Lovell, Toronto: Williamson, 1887, c1886. 00008. (Pre-1900 Canadiana) – 9 – cn C.I.H.M. [830]
Algora y Pontes, Loreto M *see* NACIONES ELEMENTALES DE ARITMETICA
AL-GOUMHURIYAH – (Egypt), 1953- – 365mf per yr – 9 – $600.00y – us Ross [072]
LES ALGUES DE LA FLORE DE BUITENZORG... / Wildeman, E de – Leide, 1900.-XI/457pp., 16 pls. Flore de Buitenzorg. v3 – 9mf – 9 – 6424/2 – ne IDC [580]
LES ALGUES DE P.K.A. SCHOUSBOE / Bornet, J BE – (Mem. Soc. Nat. Sci. Nat. et Math. de Cherbourg). v. 28. 1892. B-6344 2 – 8 – ne IDC [580]
ALGUNAS ACTAS CAPITULARES DE LA PROVINCIA DE SAN GABRIEL AL PRINCIPIO DEL SIGLO 17 (ANOS 1601-1608) / Barrado Manzano, Arcangel – Madrid: Archivo Ibero-Americano, 1960 – 1 – sp Bibl Santa Ana [946]
ALGUNAS IDEAS SOBRE EL ENGRANDECIMIENTO DE CACERES / Castel, Joaquin – 1898 – 9 – 1.50f – sp Bibl Santa Ana [000]
ALGUNAS PAGINAS DEL EXPEDIENTE...CONSTRUCCION DE UN CEMENTERIO / Fregenal de la Sierra. Spain – 1882 – 9 – 1.50f – sp Bibl Santa Ana [324]
ALGUNAS VERDADES SOBRE TARIFAS DE TELEFONOS, DICHAS EN EL PARLAMENTO / Aguirre Camara, Jose – Buenos Aires: Editorial Cerro, 1942 – 1 – CSUXADQ4944-B – us Hoover Inst Photo [380]
ALGUNOS DATOS SOBRE LA TRAGEDIA DE EUZKADI – Madrid, 1937. Fiche W 709. (Blodgett Collection of Spanish Civil War Pamphlets) – 9 – us H.U. College Libr [946]

ALGUNOS PUNTOS DE HISTORIA ACERCA DE LA HISTORIA DEL COLONIAJE EN EL ECUADOR / ed by Bayle, Constantino – Madrid: Razon y Fe, 1927 – 1 – sp Bibl Santa Ana [972]

ALGUNOS RASGOS DEL HOMBRE EXTREMENO / Caba, Pedro – Badajoz: Dip. Provincial, 1966 – sp Bibl Santa Ana [946]

ALGUNOS RASGOS SOBRE COMO DEBIERA ORGANIZARSE LA LUCHA ANTITUBERCULOSAS EN EL NUEVO ESTADO ESPANOL NACIONAL SINDICALISTA / Merino Hompanera, Jose – Caceres: Tip. La Minerva Cacerena, 1938 – sp Bibl Santa Ana [946]

ALGUNOS VERSOS : CON UN RETRATO DE SU AUTOR POR J. MORENO VILLA / Diez Canedo, Enrique – Madrid: s.i., 1924 – 9 – sp Bibl Santa Ana [999]

AL-HADAH AL-SIYASI – [al-Khartum, al-Sudan]: Hizb al-Bath al-Arabi al-Ishtirak, aug 15 1985-jun 29 1989] – 14r – 1 – us Res Libr [072]

Al-Haddad, Abdul-Rahman *see* CULTURAL POLICY IN THE YEMEN ARAB REPUBLIC

Alhaiza, Adolphe *see* HISTORIQUE DE L'ECOLE SOCIETAIRE FONDEE PAR CHARLES FOURIER SUIVI D'UN RESUME DE LA DOCTRINE FOURIERISTE ET DU SOMMAIRE DU GERANTISME ELUCIDE

ALHAMBRA – Belawan, Sumatra. illus. Lacking: 193? BSE-3500 1 – 1 – ne IDC [950]

ALHAMBRA COMMUNITY BOOK / Northrup, W M – San Gabriel, Monterey Park. Alhambra: Arthur H. Cawston, 1944. California Reel 17. (The Cox Library Collection) – 5 – us Americana [978]

ALHAMBRA PROGRESS *see* POST-ADVOCATE

AL-HAQ = LAW IN THE SERVICE OF MAN – Ramallah. 82 docs. 1981-1991 – 55mf – 9 – ne IDC [340]

AL-HAQIQAH : SAWT MUNAMZAMAT AL-MASIHIYIN AL-DIMUQRATIYIN – Bayrut: Munazamat al-Masihiyin al-Dimuqratiyin, feb 1980-nov 1981 – 1r – 1 – us Res Libr [956]

AL-HIKMA – Judeo-arabe. n1-32. Constantine, juil 1922-mai 1923. mq n1-5, 7-13, 19 – 1 – fr A.C.R.P.P. [073]

AL-HILAL – Cairo. Sept. 1892-Dec. 1960, Jan. 1962-Dec. 1967 – 1 – 35.00r – us Hoover Inst Photo [956]

AL-HILAL – (Yrly reel count varies (approx 2r/y)) – (Egypt), 1892- – 1 – $330.00y – us Ross [072]

AL-HILF AL-ATLASI WA-AL-SHARQ AL-AWSAT / Buhayri, Marwan – Bayrut: Muassasat al-Dirasat al-Filastiniyah, 1982 – 1r – 1 – us Res Libr [072]

AL-HMISHMAR – Israel, 1979- – 9 – $430.00y – us Ross [072]

O ALHO – Cruzeiro Do Sul, Acre. Jun-15 Ago 1908 – 1,5,6 – bl Biblioteca [072]

O ALHO : SEMANARIO HUMORISTICO E APIMENTADO – Maceio, Alagoas. 29 Mar 1902 – 1,5,6 – bl Biblioteca [072]

ALI AKBAR DIHHUDA (1879-1956) : LEBEN, WERK UND WIRKUNG ZWISCHEN POLITIK UND WISSENSCHAFT / Moghaddam, Abdollah Golijani – 1993 – 3mf – 9 – DM98.00 – 3-89349-806-0 – gw Hänsel [320]

Ali, Ameer *see* THE PERSONAL LAW OF THE MAHOMMEDANS, ACCORDING TO ALL THE SCHOOLS

ALI BABA : AGAINST THE FORTY THIEVES – Istanbul: Sabahattin Ali. – Nos 1-4, 1947 – 1mf – 9 – $10.50 – us MEDOC [949]

Ali Ibn Hamid *see* KUFI

ALI IKTISAD MECLISI RAPORLARI: BIRINCI ICTIMA DEVRESI : 1 MART 1928-19 MART 1928 – Istanbul: Tuerk Ocaklari Merkez Heyeti Matbaasi, 1928 – 9 – $20.00 – us MEDOC [350]

Ali, Is. *see*
- TARBUS PUSAKA
- WAN SALEH KEHILANGAN DJANGGUT

Ali, Khalid Ismail *see* STUDIEN UEBER HOMONYME WURZELN IM ARABISCHEN MIT BESONDERER BERUECKSICHTIGUNG DES MUCVGAM MAQAYIS AL-LUGA VON AHMAD IBN FARIS (GE 395/1005)

Ali Muhammad Khan *see* THE POLITICAL HISTORY OF GUJARAT

Ali, Mustafa *see* HEFT MECLIS

Ali, R Moh. *see*
- PENGANTUR ILMU SEDJARAH INDONESIA
- PERANAN BANGSA INDONESIA DALAM SEDJARAH ASIA TENGGARA

ALI THE LION: ALI OF TEBELENI, PASHA OF JANNINA, 1741-1822 / Plomer, William – London: J. Cape, 1936.288p. illus. plates.Bibliographic note – 1 – us U.W. Library [920]

ALI-ABA CLE REVIEW / American Law Institute-American Bar Association Committee on Continuing Professional Education – (Former titles: Joint Committee on Continuing Legal Education (US) ALI-ABA CLE Review (oct 1966-sep 1974)) – Philadelphia. v1-28 oct 1966- 1*; v7-28 jan 1976- 5*,9 – 1,5,9 – D8592 – us UMI [340]

ALI-ABA COURSE MATERIALS JOURNAL / American Law Institute-American Bar Association – Philadelphia. v1-14 1976-80*; v5-20 aug 1980-jun 1996; v21 aug 1996-jun 1997; v22 aug 1997-jun 1998+ 1; v5-6 aug 1980-jun 1982*; v 7 aug 1982-jun 1983; v8-19 aug 1983-jun 1995*; v20 aug 1995-jun 1996; v21 aug 1996-jun 1997 5; v5-20 aug 1980-jun 1996; v21 aug 1996-jun 1997; v22 aug 1997-jun 1998+ 9 – 1,5,9 – D12548 – us UMI [073]

ALI-ABA COURSE MATERIALS JOURNAL – v1-20. 1976-96 – 9 – $445.00 set – us Hein [340]

ALI-ABA ESTATE PLANNING COURSE MATERIALS JOURNAL : CMJ EP – Philadelphia. v1-3. apr 1995-97+ – 1,5,9 – D21704 – us UMI [073]

ALI-ABA ESTATE PLANNING COURSE MATERIALS JOURNAL – v1. 1995 – 9 – $12.00 – us Hein [340]

LOS ALIADOS – Malaga, Spain. 15 May-30 Oct 1915.-w. 9 ft – 1 – uk British Libr Newspaper [072]

Aliakrinskii, A *see* BRAK, SEMIA, OPEKA; RUKOVODSTVO DLIA ZAGS

Alias Pozas, Isabel Margarita *see* EL VALLE DEL JERTE, SUS REALIDADES Y ESPERANZAS

ALI-BABA *see* CLE JOURNAL AND REGISTER (ALI-ABA)

ALI-BABA OU LES QUARANTE VOLEURS ECTERMINES PAR UNE ESCLAVE / Galland, Antoine – 5 ed. Montreal: la Librairie Beauchemin limitee, [1955?]. SEM105P1825 – 1mf – 9 – Can$2.25 – cn Bibl Nat [420]

ALICAT. THE ONLINE CATALOG / Ok Park, Hye – Adelphi University, Garden City, NY. ED 244-639 – 9 – $0.91 – us EDRS [000]

ALICE DRIVE BAPTIST CHURCH. SUMTER COUNTY. SOUTH CAROLINA : CHURCH RECORDS – 1956-60 – 1 – 20.16 – us Baptist [240]

ALICE LORRAINE / Blackmore, Richard Doddridge – British Fiction Archive: Unit 3 – 9 – uk Bell [830]

THE ALICE TIMES – Alice, South Africa. 7 Mar 1874-24 Dec 1930. 42 reels – 1, 16 diazo available at reduced price – sa SA Libr [072]

AL-IDARAT AL-MAHA-LIYYAH AL-BALADIYYAH FI LUBNAN / Lebanon. Ministere du Plan – 1967. BNE-19.712 1 – 9 – ne IDC [338]

ALIEN CRITIC – (Cont by: Science Fiction Review) – Santa Monica. v2-3. feb 1973-nov 1974 – 1 – D7469 – us UMI [420]

ALIEN LABOR PROGRAM IN GUAM : HEARING BEFORE THE SPECIAL STUDY SUBCOMMITTEE OF THE HOUSE JUDICIARY COMMITTEE / Guam. US Congress – 93rd Congress 1st sess. 9 Aug 1973. Washington: GPO, 1973 – 3mf – 9 – $4.50 – LLMC 82-100B Title 20 – us L.L.M.C. [324]

ALIEN LAW : RECHTE UND PFLICHTEN DER AUSLAENDER / Germany. Laws, Statutes etc – Berlin, n.d. – 1mf – 1 – ILM-3786/1 – ne IDC [327]

L'ALIENATION MENTALE DEVANT LA JUSTICE CRIMINELLE / Gaultier, D Z – [Sorel]: Imprime au Sorelois, 1883. SEM105P1619 – 1mf – 9 – Can$2.25 – cn Bibl Nat [360]

L'ALIENE DEVANT LA PHILOSOPHIE, LA MORALE ET LA SOCIETE / Lemoine, Albert J F – French Precursors of Psychiatry Series. Paris. Didier. 1862 – 9 – fr Hachette [190]

L'ALIENE DEVANT LUI-MEME, L'APPRECIATION LEGALE, LA LEGISLATION, LES SYSTEMES, LA SOCIETE ET LA FAMILLE / Bonnet, Henry F A – Preface de Brierre de Boismont. (French Precursors of Psychiatry Series). Paris: V. Masson, 1866 – 9 – fr Hachette [150]

ALIENS IN THE UNITED STATES DURING WORLD WAR 2 PAMPHLET COLLECTION – 1940-1942 – 1 – CSUXANM9167-B – us Hoover Inst Photo [975]

ALIENS INDEX (BIRTHS) 1888-1922 (DEATHS) 1875-1922 OVERLANDERS (OR DROVERS) ARRIVING IN N.T. 1879-1883 MINING PERMITS 1896-1911 – 9 – A$15.00 – 0-949124-17-6 – item 4 – at G.S.N.T. [920]

ALIENS NATURALIZED IN NEW ZEALAND 1843-1916 : NAMES, ETC OF ALIEN FRIENDS WHO HAVE BEEN NATURALIZED IN NEW ZEALAND – (An alphabetical listing of full names, occupation, residential location and date of naturalization. Plus Copy of the Acts and Ordinances publ in the Statutes of New Zealnd, 1844-70 in chronological order) – Wellington, 1918 – 3mf – NZ$9.00 – 0-908797-08-7 – NZNB N1583 – nz BAB [980]

ALIENS OR AMERICANS? / Grose, Howard B – New York: Young People's Missionary Movement, c1906 (Forward mission study courses) – 1mf – us A.T.L.A. [240]

Aliesch, Peter *see*
- STUDIEN ZU THOMAS HARDY'S PROSASTIL

ALIFBA – Paris: Kitab-i Alifba, 1982-1983. – Dawrah-'i jadid: jild-i 1-4. – zimistan 1361-payiz 1362 [winter 1982-fall 1983] – 1r – 1 – $35.00 – us MEDOC [956]

Alig, Tobey *see* 1830 FEDERAL POPULATION CENSUS FOR INDIANA

Aligarh Institute *see* GAZETTE

ALIGARH MONTHLY – v. 1-6 (6). (v. 6 (7-12) not publ.). Aligarh, Cawnpore. 1903-08. Lacking: v. 5 (4). BI-366 2 – 8 – ne IDC [073]

AL-ILM WA-AL-TIKNULUJIYA FI AL-SIRA AL-ARABI-AL-ISRAILI / Zahlan, Antwan – Bayrut: Muassasat al-Dirasat al-Filastiniyah, 1981 – 1r – 1 – us Res Libr [956]

ALILOT GILGAMESH / Tchernichowsky, S – Warsaw. 1924. BJ-422-92 1 – 9 – ne IDC [470]

LA ALIMENTACION RACIONAL DEL GANADO / Diaz Montilla, Rafael – Badajoz: Graficas Iberia, 1944 – sp Bibl Santa Ana [946]

ALIMENTARY PHARMACOLOGY AND THERAPEUTICS – Oxford. v1-11 feb 1987-dec 1997+ 1,5*,9* – 1,5,9 – D15612 – us UMI [615]

L'ALIMENTATION HIVERNALE DU MERLAN (MERLANGIUS MERLANGUS L., 1758) EN MER DU NORD / Panafieu, J B de – 9 – F60.00 – fr Ethnologie [574]

ALIMENTOS PROCESADOS – Chicago. v1-. mar 1982-* – 1 – D16089 – us UMI [073]

Alimov, P *see* PRAKTICHESKOE RUKOVODSTVO PO PROPAGANDA PRAVA

ALINARI PHOTO ARCHIVE / ed by Couprie, L D – (The Alinari Collection: 66,444 photographs; The Anderson Collection: 27,244 photographs; The Brogi Collection: 25,382 photographs; Includes a printed guide and 7 plastic binders) – 1,339mf – 9 – ne IDC [770]

ALINGSAS TIDNING – Alingsas, Sweden. 1888-1978 – 156r – 1 – sw Kungliga [072]

ALINGSAS TIDNING – (Elfsborgs Lans Tidning, 1980-82; Gota Alvdalsnyheterna, 1979-82; Nya Lerums Tidning, 1980-82; Lerums Tidning, 1982) – Alingsas, Sweden. 1979- – 1 – sw Kungliga [072]

ALINGSAS WECKOBLAD – Alingsas, Sweden. 1865-88 – 11r – 1 – sw Kungliga [072]

Alinin, K *see* CHEKA

AL-INMA WA-AL-TASNIFI LUBNAN THIRD NATIONAL DEVELOPMENT CONFERENCE 18-20 APR 1968 / Lebanon. Development Studies Association – Beirut. 1968. BNE-19.701 1 – 9 – ne IDC [338]

Aliotta, Antonio *see* THE IDEALISTIC REACTION AGAINST SCIENCE

Alipili *see* CENTRUM NATURAE CONCENTRATUM: OR THE SALT OF NATURE REGENERATED

Aliquo, David *see* COMPARISON OF THE ASSOCIATION OF CERVICAL SPINAL CANAL STENOSIS AND INTERVERTEBRAL FORAMING CANAL STENOSIS AND TRANSIENT UPPER EXTREMITY PARASTHESIAS

ALIRAN ISLAM – Bandung. (incomplete) SE-326 1. 1948-1951 – 9 – ne IDC [260]

ALIRAN KESEDARAN NEGARA – Pulau Pinang. 153 docs. 1980-1991 – 104mf – 9 – ne IDC [950]

AL-IRFAN / Majallah Ilmiyah Adabiyah Akhlaqiyah Ijtima iyah. Saydun, Lebanon; ed by Al-Zayn, Ahmad 'Arif – (Missing issues: v64, nos. 1, 4-10; v66, nos. 6-7; v73, nos. 8-10) – v1-77 (1909-1993) – 9 – $50.00ea – us MEDOC [956]

AL-ISHTIRA KIYAH – [Khartoum?]: al-Hizb al-Ishtiraki al-Islami, jan 28 1988-jun 3 1989 – 1r – 1 – us Res Libr [956]

Alisjahbana, Sutan Takdir *see*
- THE FAILURE OF MODERN LINGUISTICS IN THE FACE OF LINGUISTIC PROBLEMS OF THE 20TH CENTURY
- INDONESIA: SOCIAL AND CULTURAL REVOLUTION
- KEGAGALAN ILMU BAHASA MODERN DALAM MENGHADAPI SOAL2 BAHASA ABAD KEDUA PULUH
- LAYAR TERKEMBANG
- PEMBIMBING KEFILSAFAT, I: METAFISIKA

AL'ISLAAH = THE REFORM – New York, NY, 1949-1958, 1962-1977 – 5r – 1 – us I.H.R.C. [978]

AL-ISLAH – Journal El-Islah. Dir. Taieb El Okbi. 16 no. Biskra. 1929-30 – 1 – fr A.C.R.P.P. [073]

ALISO VIEJO NEWS – South Co, CA. 1993 – 4r – 1 – $200.00 – R04116 – us Library Micro [071]

Alison, Archibald *see* REMARKS ON THE ADMINISTRATION OF CRIMINAL JUSTICE IN SCOTLAND.

Alison, Francis *see*
- MISCELLANEOUS MANUSCRIPTS, BIOGRAPHICAL DATA, AND DOCUMENTS
- SERMONS

ALIS'S BIRMINGHAM GAZETTE – England, 1835-42 – 3r – 1 – uk British Libr Newspaper [072]

AL-ITISAM – Cairo, 1977-1981 – 18mf – 9 – NE-20323/1 – ne IDC [260]

AL-ITTIHAD – Haifa, 1944(May)-1993(April) – 63r – 1 – J-93-4/3 – ne IDC [072]

AL-ITTIHAD = L'UNION : TITRE ET TEXTE EN CARACTERES ARABES – (Titre francais: L' Union sept-oct 1880) – Paris. n2-3 – 1 – fr A.C.R.P.P. [073]

AL-ITTIHAD – al-Khartum: al-Sharikah al-Arabiyah li-Khadamat al-Ilam wa-al Malumat, oct 11 1987-jul 18 1988 – 3r – 1 – us Res Libr [956]

AL-ITTIHADI – Khartoum. dec 21 1985-jun 15 1989 – us Res Libr [072]

ALIVE – (All that is currently available) – St Louis. v1-11 sep 1969-aug 1980 1; v4-11 sep 1972-aug 1980 5*; v8-11 sep 1976-aug 1980 9* – 1,5,9 – D7526 – us UMI [073]

ALIVIO DE LOS SEDIENTOS... / Micon, F – Barcelona, 1576 – 9 – sp Cultura [610]

THE ALIWAL NORTH STANDARD – Aliwal North, South Africa. 6 Mar 1872-19 Dec 1874. 2 reels – 1, 16 diazo available at reduced price – sa SA Libr [072]

THE ALIWAL OBSERVER – Aliwal North, South Africa. 5 Mar-31 Dec 1870. 1 reel – 1, 16 diazo available at reduced price – sa SA Libr [072]

ALIYE DIVAN-I HARB-I OERFIYESINDE TEDKIK OLUNAN MESELE-I SIYASIYE HAKKINDA IZAHAT – Istanbul: Tanin Matbaasi, 1332 [1916] – $60.00 – us MEDOC [956]

al-Jabarti *see* MERVEILLES BIOGRAPHIQUES ET HISTORIQUES

AL-JADID : SHAHRIYAH LIL-ADAB WA-AL-'ULUM WA-AL-FUNUN – (Missing Issues: mujallad. 12, 'adad. 11-12: mujallad) – Haifa, Israel: Hanna Naqqarah, 1953-1991 – $950.00 – us MEDOC [470]

AL-JAMAHIRIYAH – Tripoli, Libya. Sept 1980-Jan 1986; 1987 – 8r – 1 – us L of C Photodup [072]

AL-JAMI'AH AL-ARABIYYAH – Jerusalem, 1927-1935 – 15r – 1 – J-93-9/3 – ne IDC [072]

AL-JARIDA AL-RASMIYA – [Egypt], 1958- – 1 – $300.00y – us Ross [072]

AL-JARIDAH AL-RASMIYAH – (1980-) – 1970-79 – 12r – 1 – us L of C Photodup [324]

AL-JARIDAH AL-RASMIYAH / Algeria – (1978-. approx.25.00y; 1) – 1970-77. 6 reels – 1 – 125.00 – us L of C Photodup [324]

AL-JARIDAH AL-RASMIYAH – (Apr-Dec 1972. 1 reel. 20.00; 1. 1971, 1973-. approx.23.00y; LOC; 1) – 1970 – 1 – 23.00 – us L of C Photodup [324]

AL-JARIDAH AL-RASMIYAH / Libya – (1979-. approx.50.00y; 1) – 1970-78 – 1 – 276.00 – us L of C Photodup [324]

AL-JARIDAH AL-RASMIYAH / Morocco – (1980-. ca $65.00y) – 1970-79 – 29r – 1 – $580.00; outside North America add $1.25r – us L of C Photodup [324]

AL-JARIDAH AL-RASMIYAH / Oman – (1980-. ca $20.00y) – Apr 1973-Dec 1979 – 4r – 1 – $75.00; outside North America add $1.25r – us L of C Photodup [324]

AL-JARIDAH AL-RASMIYAH / Qatar – (1980-. approx.20.00y; 1) – 1970-79 – 1 – 69.00 – us L of C Photodup [324]
AL-JARIDAH AL-RASMIYAH / Syria – (1980-. ca $250.00y) – 1970-79 – 139r – 1 – $2780.00; outside North America add $1.25r – us L of C Photodup [324]
AL-JARIDAH AL-RASMIYAH / United Arab Emirates – (1978-. ca $20.00y) – Dec. 1971-1977 – 2r – 1 – $45.00; outside North America add $1.25r – us L of C Photodup [324]
AL-JARIDAH AL-RASMIYAH / Yemen – (1978-. ca $20.00y) – 1971-77 – 2r – 1 – $45.00; outside North America add $1.25r – us L of C Photodup [324]
AL-JARIDAH AL-RASMIYAH. / Jordan – (1979-. approx.50.00y; 1) – 1970-78 – 1 – 345.00 – us L of C Photodup [324]
AL-JARIDAH AL-RASMIYAH. / Lebanon – (1971-74. 12 reels. 276.00; 1. 1975-. approx.70.00y; LOC; 1) – 1940-45 – 1 – 161.00 – us L of C Photodup [324]
AL-JARIDAH AL-RASMIYAH LI-HUKUMAT DUBAYY WA-TAWABI'IHA – (1978-) – 1974-77 – 1r – 1 – us L of C Photodup [324]
AL-JARIDAH AL-RASMIYAH. (OFFICIAL GAZETTE) / Egypt – (1980-. ca $30.00y) – Mar 1958-79 – 32r – 1 – $736.00; outside North America add $1.25r – us L of C Photodup [324]
AL-JINAN – Beirut. 1870-1877; 1878, nos. 6, 21, 24; 1879, no. 11 – 1 – 35.00r – us Hoover Inst Photo [072]
AL-KASHKUL – Cairo. Mar. 1922-Apr. 1933, Feb. 16, Mar. 2, Mar. 9, 1934. Missing nos. 105, 523 – 1 – 35.00r – us Hoover Inst Photo [073]
AL-KATIB – Mujallad 13, 'adad 139-mujallad 14, 'adad 150 (Jan 1992-Feb 1993) – $50.00 – us MEDOC [470]
AL-KAZIRNA – (Bilingual) – Paris. n1-6 7. dec 1923-mai juin 1924 – 1 – fr A.C.R.P.P. [073]
Alker, Emmerich see DIE CHRONOLOGIE DER BUECHER DER KOENIGE UND PARALIPOMENON
Alker, Ernst see FRANZ GRILLPRARZER
AL-KHIDMAH AL-IJTIMAIYYAH AL-AHLIYYAH FI LUBNAN / Lebanon. Ministere du Plan – 1965. BNE-19.711 1 – 9 – ne IDC [338]
Alkhimov, V S see PERDAGANGAN LUAR-NEGERI URSS
ALKIBIADES / Bauernfeld, Eduard von – Dresden: L Ehlermann, 1889 – 1 – us U.W. Library [820]
AL-KINDAI : GENANNT "DER PHILOSOPH DER ARABER": EIN VORBILD SEINER ZEIT UND SEINES VOLKES / Fluegel, Gustav – (Text in German; bibliography in German and Arabic) – Leipzig: In Commission bei F A Brockhaus, 1857 – 1mf – 9 – 0-8370-7696-X – 1986-1696 – us A.T.L.A. [100]
AL-KUDS – Jerusalem, 1968(Nov.)-1992 – 83r – 1 – J-93-5/3 – ne IDC [072]
AL-KUWAYT AL-YAWM / Kuwait – (1980-. approx.160.00y; 1) – 1970-79 – 1 – 782.00 – us L of C Photodup [324]
ALL ABOUT JESUS / Dickson, Alexander – New York: Robert Carter, 1878, c1875 – 1mf – 9 – 0-8370-2906-6 – 1985-0906 – us A.T.L.A. [240]
ALL AFRICA CONFERENCE OF CHURCHES (AACC) – Nairobi. 83 docs. 1980-1990 – 41mf – 9 – ne IDC [240]
ALL ALONG THE RIVER / Braddon, Mary Elizabeth – British Fiction Archive: Unit 5 – 9 – uk Bell [830]
ALL CATEGORIES / The NewsBank Library – (Business and Economic Development Category. Consumer Affairs Category. Education Category. Employment Category. Environment Category. Government Structure Category. Health Category. Housing and land development Category. International Affairs and Defense Category. Law and legal systems Category. Political Development Category. Social Relations Category. Transportation Category. Welfare and Social Problems Category) – 1970-. Monthly index with cumulations – 9 – us NewsBank [071]
ALL CATEGORIES / The NewsBank Review of the Arts – 1975-. Monthly index with cumulations – 9 – us NewsBank [700]
ALL EXAMINATION QUESTIONS USED FOR TWELVE YEARS, IN THE REGULAR COURSES IN COLUMBIAN UNIVERSITY. / Howe, Frank Clifford – Washington, D.C. 1889. 93p. L.C. copy imperfect: p. 1-2 wanting. LL-1074 – 1 – us L of C Photodup [340]
ALL HALLOWS' IN THE WEST – [Yale, B.C.?]: All Hallows', [1899?-1901] – 9 – cn C.I.H.M. [971]
ALL HANDS : THE BUREAU OF NAVAL PERSONNEL INFORMATOIN BULLETIN – Jun 1945-63 – 1 – $320.00 – us L of C Photodup [355]
ALL HANDS – Washington. 1914-dec 1971; v659- dec 1971- 1*; v659- dec 1971- 5; v684- jan 1974- 9 – 1,5,9 – D6829 – us UMI [073]
ALL IN ONE: ALL USEFUL SCIENCE AND PROFITABLE ARTS IN ONE BOOK OF JEHOVAH AELOHIM / Bampfield, Francis – 1677 – 1 – 11.20 – us Baptist [240]
ALL IRELAND REVIEW – Dublin. v. 1-7. no. 3. Jan 6 1900-Jan 1907 – 1 – us NY Public [073]
ALL IRELAND REVIEW – Dublin. v1-7. 1900-072 reels – 2r – 1 – us Ross [073]
ALL OUTDOORS – v1-9, no.5 (all publ). Fall 1913-Feb 1922 – 4r – 1 – $465.00 – us UPA [790]
ALL SELECT – Issue Nos. 1-5 Fall 1943-Winter 1944-45 – 5mf – 15 – $31,95 – us Comics [760]
ALL SELECT – Issue Nos. 6-10 March 1945-Summer 1946 – 5mf – 15 – $31,95 – us Comics [760]
ALL STAR – Issue Nos. 11-15 Jun 1942-Feb 1943 – 5mf – 15 – $31.95 – us Comics [760]
ALL STAR – Issue Nos. 1-5 Summer 40-Jul 1941 – 5mf – 15 – $31,95 – us Comics [760]
ALL STAR – Issue Nos. 16-20 Apr 1943-Spring 44 – 5mf – 15 – $31.95 – us Comics [760]
ALL STAR – Issue Nos. 21-25 Summer 44-Summer 45 – 5mf – 15 – $31.95 – us Comics [760]
ALL STAR – Issue Nos. 26-30 Fall 45-Aug 1946 – 5mf – 15 – $31.95 – us Comics [760]
ALL STAR – Issue Nos. 31-35 Oct 1946-Jun 1947 – 5mf – 15 – $31.95 – us Comics [760]
ALL STAR – Issue Nos. 36-40 Aug 1947-Apr 1948 – 5mf – 15 – $31.95 – us Comics [760]
ALL STAR – Issue Nos. 41-45 Jun 1948-Feb 1949 – 5mf – 15 – $31.95 – us Comics [760]
ALL STAR – Issue Nos. 46-50 Apr 1949-Dec 1949 – 5mf – 15 – $31.95 – us Comics [760]
ALL STAR – Issue Nos. 51-57 Feb 1950-Feb 1951 – 6mf – 15 – $31.95 – us Comics [760]
ALL STAR – Issue Nos. 6-10 Aug 1941-May 1941 – 5mf – 15 – $31.95 – us Comics [760]
ALL THE YEAR ROUND – (Ceased publ) – London. cum index 1-20 1859-1868; v1-19 apr 1859-jun 1868; ns1-43 aug 1886-dec 1888;3s1-13 jan 1889-mar 1895 – 1 – D5202 – us UMI [073]
ALL WINNERS – Issue Nos. 11-15 Winter 1943-44-Spring 1945 – 5mf – 15 – $31,95 – us Comics [760]
ALL WINNERS – Issue Nos. 1-5 Summer 1941-Summer 1942 – 5mf – 15 – $31,95 – us Comics [760]
ALL WINNERS – Issue Nos. 16-21 Summer 1945-Winter 45-47. No. 20 not published – 5mf – 15 – $31,95 – us Comics [760]
ALL WINNERS – Issue Nos. 6-10 Fall 1942-Fall 1943 – 5mf – 15 – $31,95 – us Comics [760]
ALLA TEDESCA, ARR. AS A RONDO FOR PIANO / Dussek, J L – London: Lavenu & Mitchel, 1806 – 1 – us Sibley [780]
Allacci, L see DRAMMATURGIA. ACCRESCIUTA E CONTINUATA FINO ALL'ANNO 1755
Allah, Hajji Sayyid Farraj see UQYANUS
Allahabad, Oudh see DEMOCRACY NOT SUITED TO INDIA
Allain, Ernest see L'EGLISE ET L'ENSEIGNEMENT POPULAIRE
Allaire, J-B-A see NOS SAINTS PATRONS
Allam, Paul F W see SYSTEM 5
Allan, Alexander M see BEFORE THE MAST AND BEHIND THE PULPIT
Allan, Diane E see GENDER DIFFERENCES IN SPORT CENTRALITY
ALLAN FINE'S TRENDS IN INTEGRATED HEALTH CARE – (Cont: Hospital Managed Care and Direct Contracting) – Gaithersburg. 1995- – 1,5,9 – D19504.02 – us UMI [360]
Allan, George William see NOTES ON THE ORNITHOLOGY OF THE SEASONS: AS ILLUSTRATED BY THE ARRIVAL AND DEPARTURE OF SOME OF OUR MIGRATORY BIRDS
Allan Hancock Foundation see DE LAUBENFIL'S SPONGE FILE
ALLAN MORRISON PAPERS, 1940-1968 : FROM THE HOLDINGS OF THE SCHOMBURG CENTER FOR RESEARCH IN BLACK CULTURE, MANUSCRIPTS, ARCHIVES AND RARE BOOKS DIVISION: THE NEW YORK PUBLIC LIBRARY, ASTOR, LENOX AND TILDEN FOUNDATIONS – (Guide which covers all coll under "Literature and the Arts" sold separately for $20.00 D3305.G6) – 1995 – 3r – 1 – $255.00 – D3305P23 – Dist. us Scholarly Res – us L of C Photodup [070]
ALLAN QUATERMAIN : BEING AN ACCOUNT OF HIS FURTHER ADVENTURES UND DISCOVERIES IN COMPANY WITH SIR HENRY CURTIS, COMMANDER JOHN GOOD, AND ONE UMSLOPOGAAS / Haggard, Henry Rider – London: Longmans, Green, 1887 – 1 roll – 1 – 1-55879-707-6 – uk Libr Preservation [830]
Allan, T R see
- CATALOGUE OF A COLLECTION OF BIBLES AND PORTIONS OF THE BIBLE IN VARIOUS LANGUAGES...
- CATALOGUE OF A COLLECTION OF BIBLES AND PORTIONS OF THE BIBLE IN VARIOUS LANGUAGES AS ALSO OF BIBLIOGRAPHICAL WORKS ON BIBLES AND ESPECIALLY ON THOSE IN THE ABOVE COLLECTION...
- A CATALOGUE OF BOOKS CHIEFLY THEOLOGICAL...

Allan, W H et al see NEWCASTLE DISEASE VACCINES
Allan, William et al see LAND HOLDING AND LAND USAGE AMONG THE PLATEAU TONGA OF MAZABUKA DISTRICT
ALLANSFORD CELEBRATION COMMITTEE MINUTES – 1980-1981 – 2mf – 9 – at Corangamite [910]
ALLANSFORD C.W.A. MINUTES – 1947-1989 – 16mf – 9 – at Corangamite [910]
ALLANSFORD MECHANICS INSTITUTE MINUTES – 1905-1985 – 15r – 9 – at Corangamite [910]
ALLANSFORD PROGRESS ASSOCIATION MINUTES – 1966-1988 – 7mf – 9 – at Corangamite [360]
Allard, Alberic see HISTOIRE DE LA JUSTICE CRIMINELLE.
Allard, Paul see
- L'ART PAIEN SOUS LES EMPEREURS CHRETIENS
- LES DERNIERES PERSECUTIONS DU TROISIEME SIECLE (GALLUS, VAKERIEN, AURELIEN)
- LES ESCLAVES CHRETIENS : DEPUIS LES PREMIERS TEMPS DE L'EGLISE JUSQU'A LA FIN DE LA DOMINATION ROMAINE EN OCCIDENT
- ESCLAVES, SERFS ET MAINMORTABLES
- TEN LECTURES ON THE MARTYRS

L'ALLARME – Sommerville, MA, 1916 – 2mf or 1r – 1,9 – us I.H.R.C. [978]
Allart de Meritens, Hortense see
- LA FEMME ET LA DEMOCRATIE DE NOTRE TEMPS

AL-LATAIF – Cairo. May 1887-Apr. 1893 complete – 1 – 35.00r – us Hoover Inst Photo [072]
Allatius, L see
- BREVIARIUM HISTORICUM (CBH 12,1)
- DE ECCLESIAE OCCIDENTALIS ET ORIENTALIS PERPETUA CONSENSIONE
- HISTORIA
- SYMMICTA SIVE OPUSCULA GRAECA ET LATINA (CBH 30,5)

AL-LAYALI – Alger. 5nos. 1936-37 – 1 – fr A.C.R.P.P. [073]
ALLDEUTSCHE BLAETTER – Berlin, 1917-19 – 9r – 1 – gw Mikrofilm [072]
ALLDEUTSCHE BLAETTER – Berlin. v4-33. 1894-1923 – 8r – 1 – us Ross [320]
ALLDEUTSCHE BLAETTER – (Cont: Mitteilungen des Allgemeinen Deutschen Verbandes, -1893) – Berlin, 1891-1919 (incomplete) – 1 – Inquire at Mikrofilmarchiv for details – gw Misc Inst [943]
ALLDEUTSCHER VERBAND FLUGSCHRIFTEN – Munich. v. 1-25. 1897-1906 – 1 – us NY Public [073]
Alldridge, Thomas Joshua see THE SHERBRO AND ITS HINTERLAND
ALLE DE GEDICHTEN VAN HIERONYMUS SWEERTS / Sweerts, H – Amsterdam, 1697 – 10mf – 9 – ne IDC [810]
ALLE DEN VOLCKE – v28-34. 1934-40 (complete) – 1r – 1 – ATLA S0545 – us A.T.L.A. [073]
ALLE PROPHETEN NACH HEBRAISCHER SPRACH VERTEUETSCHT / Haetzer, L & Dengk, H – Worms, Peter Schoeffer. 1527. BME-55 1 – 9 – ne IDC [270]
ALLE PROPHETENN NACH HEBRIESCHER SPRACH VERDEUETSCHT / Haetzer, L & Dengk, H – Augspurg, H. Stayner. 1528. BME-56 1 – 9 – ne IDC [270]
ALLE WASSER BOEHMENS FLIESSEN NACH DEUTSCHLAND / Bodenreuth, Friedrich – Berlin: H von Hugo, 1937 – 1r – 1 – us U.W. Library [830]
ALLE WIPFEL RAUSCHEN HEIMAT : ROMAN / Zenker, Wolfgang – Leipzig: O Janke, 1943 – 1 – us U.W. Library [830]
ALLEGANY COUNTY AND ITS PEOPLE / Minard & Merrill – Centennial memorial history. Alfred: W. A. Fergusson and Co., 1896. New York Reel 8. (The Cox Library Collection) – 5 – us Americana [978]
ALLEGANY COUNTY REPUBLICAN – Angelica Court House. N.Y. 1879-1898 – 1 – us UMI [071]
ALLEGED DISCREPANCIES OF THE BIBLE / Bates, William Henry – Boston: Watchword & Truth, 1902.1 fiche – 9 – us A.T.L.A. [240]
ALLEGHENIAN – Allegheny. Pa. 1886-1893 – 1 – us UMI [071]
THE ALLEGHENIAN – Pittsburgh, PA. -w 1893-1896 – 13 – $25.00r – us I.M.R. [071]
ALLEGHENY BULLETIN – (Published during strike period of: Pittsburgh Press. Cont by: Pittsburgh Post-Gazette) – Pittsburgh, PA. aug 1992-jan 1993 – 1 – D60688 – us UMI [073]
ALLEGHENY COUNTY DEMOCRAT – Wellsville, NY. 1882-85; 1888-90; 1936-39; 1952-56; 1964-65 – 1 – us UMI [071]
THE ALLEGORICAL DRAMA OF CALDERON, AN INTRODUCTION TO THE AUTOS SACRAMENTALES / Parker, Alexander Augustine – Oxford: Dolphin Book, 1943 – 1 – us U.W. Library [440]
DIE ALLEGORIE IN IHRER EXEGETISCHEN ANWENDUNG BEI MAIMONIDES / Goldberger, Philipp – Wien: A. Fanto, 1894. 1 fiche – 9 – us A.T.L.A. [270]
DIE ALLEGORIE IN KUNST, WISSENSCHAFT UND KIRCHE / Bornemann, Wilhelm – Freiburg i.B.: J.C.B. Mohr, 1899 – 1mf – us A.T.L.A. [700]
ALLEGORISCHE PERSONEN ZUM GEBRAUCHE DER BILDENDEN KUENSTLER / Ramler, Karl Wilhelm – O 1262 1. 1788 – 9 – ne IDC [700]
AN ALLEGORY. TRANSLATED FROM THE PERSIAN OF JAMI / Salaman & Absal – London: J.W. Parker, 1856 – 1 roll – 1 – 1-55879-581-2 – uk Libr Preservation [390]
ALLEGRIDI BRAVURA POUR LE PIANOFORTE / Weyse, C E – Zuric: Naigueli et Co, 1810? – 1 – us Sibley [780]
ALLEGRO – New York. 1943-1976 – 1 – 207.00 – us L of C Photodup [780]
THE ALLEGRO QUMRAN COLLECTION ON MICROFICHE : SUPPLEMENT TO THE DEAD SEA SCROLLS ON MICROFICHE / ed by Brooke, George J – (Includes Companion Guide) – Leiden: E J Brill/IDC, May 1996 – 30mf – 9 – Dfl950.00 – ne Brill [200]
THE ALLEGRO QUMRAN PHOTOGRAPH COLLECTION / ed by Brooke, George J – 1996 – 35mf – 9 – Dfl950.00 – 90-04-10558-1 – ne Brill [270]
ALLEHANDA see MALMO ALLEHANDA
ALLEHANDA KARLSKOGA-DEGERFORS see NERIKES ALLEHANDA
DIE ALL-EINHEIT : GRUNDLINIEN DER WELT- UND LEBENSANSCHAUUNG IM GEISTE GOETHES UND SPINOZAS / Kronenberg, Moritz – Stuttgart: Strecker, 1924 – 1r – 1 – us U.W. Library [100]
ALLEMAGNE – Paris. 1949-avr 1967 – 1 – fr A.C.R.P.P. [073]
L'ALLEMAGNE CONTEMPORAINE 1919-1924. SA STRUCTURE ET SON EVOLUTION POLITIQUES / Vermeil, E – H 549 2 – 8 – ne IDC [943]
ALLEMANDS DANCED AT THE KING'S THEATRE, SET FOR GERMAN FLUTE, VIOLIN OR HARPSICHORD / Agus, G – London: Welcker, 1767? – 1 – us Sibley [780]
ALLEMANNISCHE GEDICHTE / Hebel, Johann Peter; ed by Heilig, Otto – Heidelberg: C Winter, 1902 – 1r – 1 – us U.W. Library [810]

ALLEMANNISCHE LIEDER : NEBST WORTERKLAERUNG UND EINER ALLEMANNISCHEN GRAMMATIK / Hoffmann von Fallersleben, August Heinrich – 5. verb. verm. Ausg. Mannheim: F Bassermann, 1843 – 1r – 1 – us U.W. Library [810]
Allemeier, Meredith Frances *see* CIAU ATHLETES' USE AND INTENTIONS TO USE PERFORMANCE ENHANCING DRUGS
Allen *see* CENTENNIAL HISTORY OF AKRON 1825-1925
Allen, A J C *see* THE CHURCH CATECHISM
Allen, Alexander V G *see*
- CHRISTIAN INSTITUTIONS
- JONATHAN EDWARDS
- RELIGIOUS PROGRESS

Allen, Arthur F *see* NORTHWESTERN IOWA: ITS HISTORY AND TRADITIONS 1804-1926
Allen, Arthur H *see* WHO'S WHO IN WASHINGTON STATE 1927
Allen, B F *see* HISTORY OF SAN MATEO COUNTY
Allen, B M *see* THE RT. HON. SIR ERNEST SATOW
Allen, Charles Edwin *see* REV. JACOB BAILEY, HIS CHARACTER AND WORKS
ALLEN COUNTY DEMOCRAT – Lima, Ohio. 1861-1891 – 7r – 1 – $32.50r – us Archival [071]
ALLEN COUNTY HERALD – Iola. Kan. 1891-1893 – 1 – us UMI [071]
Allen County. Kansas. School District 23 *see* RECORDS
Allen County. Ohio. Auditor *see*
- ABSTRACTS OF TAX
- COMMON SCHOOL LIBRARY FUNDS
- DOCKET OF COUNTY HOME BILLS
- ENUMERATIONS OF YOUTH
- SCHOOL LAND RECORDS
- TAX LEVIES
- TAX MAPS

Allen County. Ohio. Board of County Commissioners *see*
- COURTHOUSE SPECIFICATIONS
- INDEX TO JOURNAL, BILLS

Allen County. Ohio. Board of Elections *see* MINUTES
Allen County. Ohio. Board of Railroard Appraisers *see* RAILROAD APPRAISEMENT RECORDS
Allen County. Ohio. Board of Revision *see* MINUTES
Allen County. Ohio. Budget Commission *see* MINUTES
Allen County. Ohio. Circuit Court *see*
- COMPLETE RECORDS
- JOURNALS

Allen County. Ohio. Common Pleas. Civil Division *see*
- COMPLETE RECORDS
- NATURALIZATION RECORDS
- NATURALIZATIONS

Allen County. Ohio. Common Pleas. Criminal Div *see*
- COMPLETE RECORDS
- JOURNALS

Allen County. Ohio. Common Pleas. Juvenile Div *see*
- CASE FILES
- DETENTION HOME REGISTER
- JOURNALS
- MOTHER'S PENSION CASE FILES
- MOTHER'S PENSION DOCKETS/RECS
- MOTHER'S PENSION JOURNALS

Allen County. Ohio. Coroner *see*
- INQUESTS
- PROPERTY RECORDS

Allen County. Ohio. District Court *see* JOURNALS
Allen County. Ohio. Engineer *see*
- DITCH RECORDS
- FREE TURNPIKE RECORDS

Allen County. Ohio. Probate Court *see*
- CRIMINAL JOURNALS
- INDEX TO CRIMINAL RECORDS
- INHERITANCE TAX RECORDS
- RECORDS OF FEEBLE MINDED YOUTH
- REGISTER OF PATENTS
- TREASURER'S EXAMINATION RECORD

Allen County. Ohio. Recorder *see*
- DEED RECORDS
- SOLDIER'S DISCHARGE RECORDS

Allen County. Ohio. Soldiers Relief Commission *see* DISABILITY ALLOWANCE RECORDS
Allen County. Ohio. Trustees of the Sinking Fund *see* MINUTES
Allen, D M *see* THE COMPARISON OF RESTING METABOLIC RATE IN TRAINED VS. UNTRAINED FEMALES
Allen, Donna *see* COVERAGE OF THE SPIRITUAL DIMENSION OF HEALTH IN PERSONAL HEALTH TEXTBOOKS IN HIGHER EDUCATION
Allen, Edith H *see* HOME MISSIONS IN ACTION
Allen, Ethan *see* REASON, THE ONLY ORACLE OF MAN
Allen, Fred C *see* HANDBOOK OF THE NEW YORK STATE REFORMATORY AT ELMIRA
Allen, G G *see* BIBLIOGRAPHY OF MONO- AND MULTILINGUAL VOCABULARIES, THESAURI, SUBJECT HEADINGS AND CLASSIFICATION SCHEMES IN THE SOCIAL SCIENCES
Allen, Grant *see*
- AN AFRICAN MILLIONAIRE: EPISODES IN THE LIFE OF THE ILLUSTRIOUS COLONEL CLAY
- THE ATTIS OF CAIUS VALERIUS CATALLUS: TRANSLATED INTO ENGLISH VERSE..
- A BRIDE FROM THE DESERT
- CHARLES DARWIN
- CITIES OF BELGIUM
- THE COLOURS OF FLOWERS: AS ILLUSTRATED IN BRITISH FLORA
- THE COLOUR-SENSE: ITS ORIGIN AND DEVELOPMENT: AN ESSAY IN COMPARATIVE PSYCHOLOGY
- THE CRUISE OF THE ALBATROSS, OR WHEN WAS WEDNESDAY THE TENTH?
- THE DESIRE OF THE EYES AND OTHER STORIES
- THE DEVIL'S DIE: A NOVEL
- THE EUROPEAN TOUR
- FALLING IN LOVE: WITH OTHER ESSAYS ON MORE EXACT BRANCHES OF SCIENCE
- FLASHLIGHTS ON NATURE
- FLOWERS AND THEIR PEDIGREES
- THE INCIDENTAL BISHOP
- IVAN GREET'S MASTERPIECE, ETC
- THE JAWS OF DEATH: A NOVEL
- LINNET: A ROMANCE
- MICHAEL'S CRAG
- MISS CAYLEY'S ADVENTURES
- MOORLAND IDYLLS
- PARIS
- POST-PRANDIAL PHILOSOPHY
- RECALLED TO LIFE
- SCIENCE IN ARCADY
- A SPLENDID SIN
- TOM, UNLIMITED: A STORY FOR CHILDREN
- TWELVE TALES: WITH A HEADPIECE, TAILPIECE, AND AN INTERMEZZO: BEING SELECT STORIES
- VIGNETTES FROM NATURE
- WEDNESDAY THE TENTH: A TALE OF THE SOUTH PACIFIC
- THE WHITE MAN'S FOOT
- THE WOMAN WHO DID

Allen, H T *see* ATNATANAS: NATIVES OF COPPER RIVER, ALASKA
Allen, Hamilton Ford *see* THE INFINITIVE IN POLYBIUS COMPARED WITH THE INFINITIVE IN BIBLICAL GREEK
Allen, I M *see* THE U.S. BAPTIST ANNUAL REGISTER
Allen, J A *see* BULLETIN OF THE NUTTALL ORNITHOLOGICAL CLUB
Allen, Jacob D *see* POEMS
Allen, Jelisaveta Stanojevich *see*
- AUTHOR INDEX OF BYZANTINE STUDIES
- BYZANTINE STUDIES

Allen, Jeslisaveta Stanojevich *see* AUTHOR INDEX OF BYZANTINE STUDIES 2
Allen, Joe W *see* NEODESHA SCRAPBOOK
Allen, Joel Asaph *see* HISTORY OF NORTH AMERICAN PINNIPEDS: A MONOGRAPH OF THE WALRUSES, SEA-LIONS, SEA-BEARS AND SEALS OF NORTH AMERICA
Allen, John Slater *see* FROM APOLLYONVILLE TO THE HOLY CITY: A POEM
Allen, Joseph Antisell *see*
- DR. RYERSON: A REVIEW AND A STUDY
- MEMOIR OF THE LIFE AND SERVICES OF ADMIRAL SIR WILLIAM HARGOOD, ETC
- THE RELIGION OF THE POPE AND PRIMITIVE CHRISTIANITY: A CONTRAST

Allen, Joseph H *see* GREEK READER
Allen, Joseph Henry *see*
- CHRISTIAN HISTORY IN ITS THREE GREAT PERIODS
- A HISTORY OF THE UNITARIANS AND THE UNIVERSALISTS IN THE UNITED STATES
- OUR LIBERAL MOVEMENT IN THEOLOGY, CHIEFLY AS SHOWN IN RECOLLECTIONS OF THE HISTORY OF UNITARIANISM IN NEW ENGLAND
- OUTLINE OF CHRISTIAN HISTORY, A.D.50-1880

Allen, Marie-B *see* ELIE GOULET DE LA SOCIETE DES ECRIVAINS CANADIENS
Allen, Mary Montcrieff *see* TRAVEL DIARY
ALLEN MEMORIAL ART MUSEUM : BULLETIN / Allen Memorial Art Museum, Oberlin College – Oberlin. cum index 1-30; v1-oct 1944- 1; v34- 1976- 5*,9* – 1,5,9 – D6722 – us UMI [060]
Allen Memorial Art Museum, Oberlin College *see* ALLEN MEMORIAL ART MUSEUM
ALLEN MEMORIAL BAPTIST CHURCH. KINGS MOUNTAIN ASSOCIATION. GROVER, NORTH CAROLINA : CHURCH RECORDS – 1947-Oct 1963 – 1 – 13.86 – us Baptist [240]
ALLEN NEWS – Allen, NE. -w. Jun. 1892-Jan. 1896. Incomplete; Jan. 1896-Aug. 1896; Mar. 1897-Jan 1902. Incomplete; Jan. 1913-Sep. 1924; Jul. 1928-Sep. 1934. Incomplete; Sep. 1934-Oct. 1942; Apr. 1948-May 1948 – 1 – us NE Hist [071]
Allen, Otis *see* MEMOIR OF OTIS ALLEN.
Allen, Philip Schuyler *see*
- THE AGE OF ERASMUS
- IN LONGFELLOWS PANTOFFELN
- WILHELM MUELLER AND THE GERMAN VOLKSLIED

Allen, Richard *see* BRIEF VINDICATIONS OF AN ESSAY TO PROVE SINGING OF PSALMS, ETC
Allen, Samuel E S *see* EXPLORATIONS AMONG THE WATERSHED ROCKIES OF CANADA
Allen, Stephen Merrill *see* RELIGION AND SCIENCE: THE LETTERS OF ALPHA
Allen, Sue *see* VICTORIAN BOOKBINDINGS
Allen, T F *see* THE CHARACEAE OF AMERICA.
Allen, Thomas *see*
- HISTORY AND ANTIQUITIES OF LONDON, WESTMINSTER, SOUTHWARK AND PARTS ADJACENT
- PROBLEM OF CITY GOVERNMENT

Allen, W *see* STUDIES IN AFRICAN LAND USAGE IN NORTHERN RHODESIA
Allen, W C *see*
- THE ANNALS OF HAYWOOD COUNTY
- A BRIEF UNPUBLISHED HISTORY OF THE BAPTISTS OF SOUTH CAROLINA, 1683-1937
- HISTORY OF HALIFAX COUNTY

Allen, W G *see* WHEATLEY, BANNEKER AND HORTON
Allen, W W *see* CALIFORNIA GOLD BOOK
Allen, Wilkes *see* APOLLO
Allen, William *see*
- A NARRATIVE OF THE EXPEDITION TO THE RIVER NIGER IN 1841
- A NARRATIVE OF THE EXPEDITION TO THE RIVER NIGER IN 1841 UNDER THE COMMAND OF CAPTAIN H.D. TROTTER

Allen, William Francis *see* ESSAYS AND MONOGRAPHS
Allen, William G *see* HISTORY OF STORY COUNTY
Allen, William Henry *see* INVENTORY OF UNPUBLISHED MATERIAL FOR AMERICAN RELIGIOUS HISTORY IN PROTESTANT CHURCH ARCHIVES AND OTHER REPOSITORIES
Allen, William K *see* LACTATE THRESHOLD IN MASTERS ATHLETES AS COMPARED TO YOUNG ATHLETES
Allen, Y J *see* PAPERS, 1854-1924
ALLENDALE RECORDER – 1897-1901 – 1r – 1 – at Corangamite [980]
Allende, Alfredo E *see* HISTORIA DE UNA GRAN LEY
ALLENSTEINER KREISBLATT – (Cont by: Allensteiner Zeitung, 1881) – Allenstein, jan 4 1851-55, 1857-59 (incomplete), 1863-69, jul 2-sep 29 1912, jan 1-mar 31 1914, jul 1 1920-jun 30 1921 (incomplete) – 12r – 1 – Dist. gw Mikrofilm – gw Misc Inst [943]
ALLENSTEINER VOLKSBLATT – Allenstein, jan 6 1918-aug 6 1919 (incomplete) – 3r – 1 – uk British Libr Newspaper [943]
ALLENSTEINER ZEITUNG *see* ALLENSTEINER KREISBLATT
THE ALLENTOWN DEMOCRAT – Allentown, PA. -d 1879-1918 – 13 – $25.00r – us I.M.R. [071]
Allenwood, Pennsylvania.White Deer Baptist Church *see* MINUTES AND MEMBERS
ALLERGY – (v1-21. Dfl60.00v; v22-28. Dfl100.00v) – v1-28. Copenhagen. 1948-73. Continues: Acta Allergologica – 5,9 – Dfl1,960.00 – ne Swets [616]
ALLERGY INFORMATION *see* NEWSLETTER, ALLERGY INFORMATION ASSOCIATION
Allergy Information Association *see* NEWSLETTER, ALLERGY INFORMATION ASSOCIATION
ALLERHAND HUMORE : KLEINBAEUERLICHES, GROSSSTAEDTISCHES UND GEFABELTES / Anzengruber, Ludwig – Leipzig: Breitkopf und Haertel, 1883 – 1r – 1 – us U.W. Library [943]
ALLERHOECHST PRIVILEGIRTE SCHLESWIG-HOLSTEINISCHES ANZEIGEN – Glueckstadt. N.F. v. 29-43. 1865-79. Film Mas C 392 – 1 – us H.U. Library [073]
ALLERS : ILLUSTRERAD FAMILJEJOURNAL – Kobenhavn, Denmark; Helsingborg, Sweden. 1879-1955 – 1 – sw Kungliga [073]
ALLES UM LIEBE : GOETHES BRIEFE AUS DER ERSTEN HAELFTE SEINES LEBENS / ed by Hartung, Ernst – Duesseldorf: W Langewiesche-Brandt, 1907 – 1r – 1 – us U.W. Library [920]
Alletz, Pons Augustin *see*
- L'ART D'INTRUIRE ET DE TOUCHER LES AMES DANS LE TRIBUNAL DE PENITENCE
- DICTIONNAIRE DES RICHESSES DE LA LANGUE FRANCOISE

Alley, Bowen & Co *see* HISTORY OF SONOMA COUNTY
ALLEY-CROPPING AND MULCHING WITH ERYTHRINA POEPPIGIANA (WALP.) O.F. COOK AND GLIRICIDIA SEPIUM (JACQ.) WALP : EFFECTS ON MAIZE/ WEED COMPETITION AN NUTRIENT UPTAKE / Rippin, Markus – 1992 – 106p – DM98.00 – 3-89349-548-7 – gw Hänsel [630]
Allezt, Agustin *see*
- PRINCIPIOS FUNDAMENTALES DE LA RELIGION, 1
- PRINCIPIOS FUNDAMENTALES DE LA RELIGION, 2

ALLGAEUER ANZEIGEBLATT, ALLGAEUER ZEITUNG – Immenstadt, Germany. 1 Jun 1983- – 1 – gw Mikrofilm [072]
ALLGAEUER ZEITUNG, KEMPTER TAGBLATT – Kempten, West-Germany. 1977- – 1 – gw Mikrofilm [072]
ALLGAEUERER ZEITUNG, DER ALLGAEUER, NEUE KAUFBEURER ZEITUNG – Kaufbeuren, Germany. 1 Jun 1983- – 1 – gw Mikrofilm [072]
ALLGAU ALPS : PAMPHLET COLLECTION – 19?? – 1 – CSUXANS6067-B – us Hoover Inst Photo [910]
ALLGEMEINE ANNALEN DER GEWERBSKUNDE – Leipzig, 1803-04 – 1 – gw Mikrofilm [943]
ALLGEMEINE ARBEITER-ZEITUNG – Frankfurt Main, Germany. May 18-Jun 10 1848 – 1 – gw Mikrofilm [072]
ALLGEMEINE ARBEITERZEITUNG – Budapest, 1870 – 1r – 1 – Inquire at Mikrofilmarchiv for details – gw Misc Inst [943]
ALLGEMEINE ARBEITERZEITUNG – Budapest, Hungary. 1870 – 1 – gw Mikrofilm [072]
ALLGEMEINE AUSWANDERUNGS-ZEITUNG – Rudolstadt, Germany. 1846-56 – 1 – gw Mikrofilm [072]
ALLGEMEINE BADZEITUNG – (Cont by: Mittelrheinische Zeitung, apr 2 1849) – Baden-Baden, feb 16-jun 23 1849 – 1r – 1 – Dist. gw Mikrofilm – gw Misc Inst [790]
ALLGEMEINE BERG- UND HUETTENMAENNISCHE ZEITUNG – Quedlinburg, DE. 1859-63 – 2 1/2r – 1 – uk British Libr Newspaper [072]
ALLGEMEINE BERLINER ARCHITEKTENZEITUNG – Berlin, 1902-04 – 1 – gw Mikrofilm [072]
ALLGEMEINE BIBLIOTHEK DER BIBLISCHEN LITERATUR – v1-10. 1787-1800 (complete) – 5r – 1 – ATLA S0239 – us A.T.L.A. [073]
ALLGEMEINE BLUMENTHALER ZEITUNG *see* BLUMENTHALER ZEITUNG
DAS ALLGEMEINE CONCIL VON VATICAN : ZWEI HIRTENSCHREIBEN / Rauscher, Joseph Othmar – Wien: Wilhelm Braumueller, 1870 – 1mf – 9 – 0-8370-8372-9 – 1986-2372 – us A.T.L.A. [240]
ALLGEMEINE CORRESPONDENZ – London, UK. 1 Jun 1898-31 Oct 1901 – 1 – uk British Libr Newspaper [072]
ALLGEMEINE CORRESPONDENZ *see* DEUTSCHE KORRESPONDENZ
ALLGEMEINE DEUTSCHE ARBEITER-ZEITUNG *see*
- ARBEITER-ZEITUNG

ALLGEMEINE DEUTSCHE BIBLIOTHEK – Berlin-Stettin, 1766-94 – 913mf – 9 – DM4,170.00 – gw Mikro Press [072]

ALLGEMEINE DEUTSCHE BIBLIOTHEK 1765-1796/NEUE ALLGEMEINE DEUTSCHE BIBLIOTHEK 1793-1806 / ed by Nicolai, Friedrich – Berlin und Stettin, spaeter Kiel, 1765-1806 (mf ed 1993) – 770mf – 9 – DM7,800.00 – 3-89131-108-7 – gw Fischer [100]

ALLGEMEINE DEUTSCHE BIBLIOTHEK; NEUE DEUTSCHE BIBLIOTHEK / ed by Nicolai, Friedrich – Berlin, Stettin, Kiel, 1765-96. 118v. Berlin, Stettin, 1793-1806. 107v – 820mf – 9 – subsc: DM4,500.00 diazo DM5,500.00 silver – gw Olms [430]

ALLGEMEINE DEUTSCHE BIOGRAFIE – Leipzig. v56. 1875-1912 – 499mf – 9 – H-3026/1 – ne IDC [920]

ALLGEMEINE DEUTSCHE LEHRERZEITUNG – Berlin, 1919-33 – 1 – Dist. gw Mikrofilm – gw Misc Inst [370]

ALLGEMEINE DEUTSCHE MUSIK-ZEITUNG / ed by Reinsdorf, Otto et al – (Wochenschrift fuer das Gesammte Musikalische Leben der Gegenwart, 1882-, No 15-; Wochenschrift fuer die Reform des Gesammten Musiklebens der Gegenwart, 1882-, No 16-; Wochenschrift fuer die Reform des Musiklebens der Gegenwart, 1885-.- No 12-; Allgemeine Deutsche Musik-Zeitung, 1925-.-No 52-) – 1988 – 670mf (1:24) – 9 – diazo DM4,800.00 (silver DM5,980.00 ISBN: 3-598-32530-4) – 3-598-32531-2 – gw Saur [780]

ALLGEMEINE DEUTSCHE NATURHISTORISCHE ZEITUNG – Im Auftrage der Gesellschaft Isis in Dresden. Dresden & Leipzig, 1846-47. v.1-2. New Series, 1855-57. v.1-3 – 3 – us Readex [574]

ALLGEMEINE DEUTSCHE POLYTECHNISCHE ZEITUNG – Berlin, 1873-75, 1879-82, 1884 – 7r – 1 – uk British Libr Newspaper [620]

ALLGEMEINE DEUTSCHE REAL-ENCYCLOPAEDIE FUER DIE GEBILDETEN STAENDE (AEL, ABT 1; 35.17) : CONVERSATIONS-LEXIKON – 9. Aufl. Leipzig. 15 Bde. 1843-48 (mf ed 1997) – 75mf – 9 – DM1,190.00 – 3-89131-266-0 – gw Fischer [943]

ALLGEMEINE DEUTSCHE REAL-ENCYCLOPAEDIE FUER DIE GEBILDETEN STAENDE (AEL, ABT 1; 35.19) : CONVERSATIONS-LEXIKON – 11. Aufl. Leipzig. 1864-68 (mf ed 1997) – 90mf – 9 – DM1,590.00 – 3-89131-268-7 – gw Fischer [943]

ALLGEMEINE DEUTSCHE REAL-ENCYCLOPAEDIE FUER DIE GEBILDETEN STAENDE (CONVERSATIONS-LEXIKON) (AEL, ABT 1; 35.8) – 5. Aufl. Leipzig. 10 Bde. 1820 (mf ed 1997) – 61mf – 9 – DM1,150.00 – 3-89131-258-X – gw Fischer [943]

ALLGEMEINE DEUTSCHE REAL-ENCYCLOPAEDIE FUER DIE GEBILDETEN STAENDE (CONVERSATIONS-LEXIKON) (AEL, ABT 1; 35.11) – 6. Aufl. Leipzig. 10 Bde. 1824 (mf ed 1997) – 60mf – 9 – DM1,150.00 – 3-89131-261-X – gw Fischer [943]

ALLGEMEINE DEUTSCHE REAL-ENCYCLOPAEDIE FUER DIE GEBILDETEN STAENDE (CONVERSATIONS-LEXIKON) (AEL, ABT 1; 35.12) : SUPPLEMENTBAND FUER DIE BESITZER DER FUENFTEN UND FRUEHEREN AUFLAGEN – Leipzig, 1824 (mf ed 1997) – 7mf – 9 – DM180.00 – 3-89131-262-8 – gw Fischer [943]

ALLGEMEINE DEUTSCHE REAL-ENCYCLOPAEDIE FUER DIE GEBILDETEN STAENDE (CONVERSATIONS-LEXIKON) (AEL, ABT 1; 35.13) – 7. Aufl. Leipzig. 12 Bde. 1827 (mf ed 1997) – 75mf – 9 – DM1,100.00 – 3-89131-263-6 – gw Fischer [943]

ALLGEMEINE DEUTSCHE REAL-ENCYCLOPAEDIE FUER DIE GEBILDETEN STAENDE (CONVERSATIONS-LEXIKON) (AEL, ABT 1; 35.14) : SUPPLEMENTBAND FUER DIE BESITZER DER SECHSTEN UND FRUEHEREN AUFLAGEN UND DER NEUEN FOLGE – Leipzig, 1829 (mf ed 1997) – 7mf – 9 – DM190.00 – 3-89131-264-4 – gw Fischer [943]

ALLGEMEINE DEUTSCHE REAL-ENCYCLOPAEDIE FUER DIE GEBILDETEN STAENDE (CONVERSATIONS-LEXIKON) (AEL, ABT 1; 35.15) – 7. Aufl. Leipzig. 12 Bde. 1830 (mf ed 1997) – 99mf – 9 – DM1,100.00 – 3-89131-277-6 – gw Fischer [943]

ALLGEMEINE DEUTSCHE REAL-ENCYCLOPAEDIE FUER DIE GEBILDETEN STAENDE (CONVERSATIONS-LEXIKON) (AEL, ABT. 1; 35.16) – 8. Aufl. Leipzig. 12 Bde. 1833-37 (mf ed 1997) – 74mf – 9 – DM1,190.00 – 3-89131-265-2 – gw Fischer [943]

ALLGEMEINE DEUTSCHE REAL-ENCYCLOPAEDIE FUER DIE GEBILDETEN STAENDE (CONVERSATIONS-LEXIKON) (AEL, ABT 1; 35.18) – 10. Aufl. Leipzig. 15 Bde. 1851-55 (mf ed 1997) – 85mf – 9 – DM1,250.00 – 3-89131-267-9 – gw Fischer [943]

ALLGEMEINE DEUTSCHE SCHULZEITUNG – Berlin, 1889-90 – 1r – 1 – Dist. gw Mikrofilm – gw Misc Inst [370]

ALLGEMEINE DEUTSCHE THEATER-ZEITUNG – (Title change: 1809 Archiv fuer Theater und Literatur. 1810 Archiv fuer Literatur und Kunst) – Hamburg, DE. 1807-10 (incomplete) – 1 – gw Mikrofilm [072]

ALLGEMEINE DEUTSCHE ZEITUNG FUER RUMAENIEN *see*
– NEUER WEG

ALLGEMEINE ENCYCLOPAEDIE DER WISSENSCHAFTEN UND KUENSTE : 1ST SECTION: VOLS 1-99 LEIPZIG 1818-1882; 2ND SECTION: VOLS 1-43 LEIPZIG 1827-1889; 3RD SECTION: VOLS 1-25 LEIPZIG 1830-1850 / Ersch, J S & Gruber, J G – 1996 – 310mf (1:24) – 9 – silver DM8,800.00 – 3-598-33511-3 – gw Saur [030]

ALLGEMEINE ENCYCLOPAEDIE DER WISSENSCHAFTEN UND KUENSTE (AEL, ABT 1; 33) / Ersch, J S & Gruber, J G – Leipzig. 167 Bde. 1818-89 (mf ed 1995) – 462mf – 9 – DM7,500.00 – 3-89131-214-8 – gw Fischer [030]

ALLGEMEINE FLEISCHER ZEITUNG – Berlin, Nov 1916-Dec 1918 – 5r – 1 – uk British Libr Newspaper [072]

ALLGEMEINE FLEISCHER-ZEITUNG – Berlin, nov 1916-18 (incomplete) – 5r – 1 – uk British Libr Newspaper [640]

ALLGEMEINE FORSTZEITSCHRIFT – vol. 1-12. 1946-57. (Scattered issues lacking) – 1 – 30.00 – us L of C Photodup [634]

ALLGEMEINE GESCHICHTE DER LITERATUR DES MITTELALTERS IM ABENDLANDE / Ebert, Adolf – Leipzig, F. C. W. Vogel, 1874-87. 3 v. Film Mas 9227 – 1 – us H.U. Library [410]

ALLGEMEINE GESCHICHTE DER MUSIK / Forkel, J N – 2v. 1788-1801 – 9 – us Sibley [780]

ALLGEMEINE GESCHICHTE DER MUSIK / Forkel, J N – P 271. Bd. 1-2. 1788 – 9 – ne IDC [780]

ALLGEMEINE GESCHICHTE DER PHILOSOPHIE / Deussen, Paul – Leipzig, 1920, Bd. 1,1. – 7mf, Bd. 1,2. – 7mf, Bd. 1,3. – 13mf – 8 – Dfl3.50ea – ne Slangenburg [100]

ALLGEMEINE GESCHICHTE DES ZEITUNGSWESENS / Salomon, Ludwig – 1907 – 1 – DM30.00 – gw Mikro Press [943]

ALLGEMEINE GESCHICHTE IN EINZELDARSTELLUNGEN / ed by Oncken, Wilhelm – (I. Geschichte des Altertums. 10v. II. Geschichte des Mittelalters. 16v. III. Geschichte der neuern Zeit. 13v. IV. Geschichte der neuesten Zeit. 6v) – Berlin, G. Grote. 1879-93. 45v. Film Mas C 604 – 1 – us H.U. Library [080]

ALLGEMEINE GESUNDHEITSREGELN – Lobenstein, DE. 1790 – 9 – gw Mikrofilm [072]

ALLGEMEINE GEWERBE-ZEITUNG – Berlin. oct 2, 1874-75; 1877-79 – 1r – 1 – gw Mikrofilm [072]

ALLGEMEINE ILLUSTRIERTE JUDENZEITUNG *see* CARMEL

ALLGEMEINE ILLUSTRIERTE ZEITUNG – Leipzig, Germany. 1865-69 – 1 – gw Mikrofilm [072]

ALLGEMEINE ILLUSTRIRTE JUDENZEITUNG, CARMEL – (Buda-) Pest, 1860-jun 21 1861 – 1r – 1 – Inquire at Mikrofilmarchiv for details – gw Misc Inst [943]

ALLGEMEINE JUEDISCHE WOCHENZEITUNG : BEILAGE: ALLGEMEINE JUEDISCHE ILLUSTRIERTE – (Also known as: Allgemeine Wochenzeitung der Juden in Deutschland) – Duesseldorf. sep 1950-59. feb 1960-may 1968 – 2r – 1 – gw Mikrofilm [270]

ALLGEMEINE JUEDISCHE WOCHENZEITUNG – Duesseldorf, 1946-1994 – 39r – 1 – DM1,425.00 DM80.00y – gw Mikro Press [072]

ALLGEMEINE KINO-BOERSE – Leipzig, 1919 n5-sep 18 1922 (incomplete) – 1r – 1 – gw Mikrofilm [790]

ALLGEMEINE KIRCHEN- ZEITUNG – (Missing: 1822-1823, v1-2) – Darmstadt. v1-11. 1822-1832 – 287mf – 9 – ne IDC [240]

ALLGEMEINE KIRCHEN-ZEITUNG – 3(1824)-11(1832) – 287mf – 9 – Dfl1,005.00 – ne Slangenburg [073]

ALLGEMEINE KIRCHLICHE ZEITSCHRIFT – 1(1860)-9(1868) – 107mf – 9 – Dfl71.00 – ne Slangenburg [073]

ALLGEMEINE KIRCHLICHE ZEITSCHRIFT – Elberfeld. v1-13. 1860-1872 – 147mf – 9 – ne IDC [240]

ALLGEMEINE LITERATUR DER MUSIK / Forkel, J N – 1792 – 9 – us Sibley [780]

ALLGEMEINE LITERATUR DER MUSIK... : SYSTEMATISCH GEORDNET / Forkel, J N – Leipzig. 2pts. 1792 – 9mf – ne IDC [780]

ALLGEMEINE LITERATUR DER MUSIK. SYSTEMATISCH GEORDNET. ERSTER UND ZWEYTER THEIL / Forkel, J N – P 272. 1792 – 9 – ne IDC [780]

ALLGEMEINE LITERATURGESCHICHTE / Mundt, Theodor; ed by Garber, Klaus – Berlin. v1-3. 1846 – 15mf – 9 – subsc: DM120.00 – gw Olms [410]

ALLGEMEINE LITERATUR-ZEITUNG / ed by Schuetz, C G & Ersch, J S – Halle, 1804-1849 (mf ed 1996) – 9 – DM8,500.00 – 3-89131-109-5 – gw Fischer [430]

ALLGEMEINE LITERATUR-ZEITUNG / ed by Schuetz, Christian Gottfried – Leipzig, 1785-1803; Hildesheim, 1981 – 526mf – 9 – DM3,850.00 diazo DM4,600.00 silver – gw Olms [430]

ALLGEMEINE MEDIZINISCH-PHARMAZEUTISCHE FLORA,... / Kosteletzky, V F – (Missing: 1836. V.5) – Prag, 1831-1836. 6v – 21mf – 9 – ne IDC [615]

ALLGEMEINE MUSIKALISCHE ZEITUNG – Leipzig. v. 1-8. Oct. 1798-Sept. 1806 – 1 – us NY Public [073]

ALLGEMEINE MUSIKALISCHE ZEITUNG – (Siehe: (WIENER) ALLGEMEINE MUSIKALISCHE ZEITUNG) – 9 – gw Olms [780]

ALLGEMEINE MUSIKALISCHE ZEITUNG – v. 1-50. 1798-1848. n.s. 1-3. 1863-65. s.3. 1-17. 1866-82. Index, 1798-1848 – 1 – 544.00 – us L of C Photodup [780]

ALLGEMEINE MUSIKALISCHE ZEITUNG – With the first series was issued "Intelligenzblatt zur Allgemeinen Musikalischen Zeitung.". v. 1-50. 1798-1848 – 9 – us Sibley [780]

ALLGEMEINE MUSIKALISCHE ZEITUNG MIT BESONDERER RUCKSICHT – Auf den Osterreichischen Kaiserstaat. Vienna. 1817-1824 – 1 – us NY Public [073]

ALLGEMEINE MUSIKALISCHE ZEITUNG, MIT BESONDERER RUCKSICHT AUF DEN OESTERREICHISCHEN KAISERSTAAT – Wien. 1817-21. 1 reel – 1 – 25.00 – us L of C Photodup [780]

ALLGEMEINE MUSIKLEHRE / Marx, A B – (First edition) – Leipzig: Breitkopf & Hartel, 1839 – 1 – us Sibley [780]

ALLGEMEINE MUSIK-ZEITUNG – Berlin, Leipzig etc. v. 8-20, 26-70, no. 6. 1881-Mar 19 1943 – 1 – us NY Public [073]

ALLGEMEINE MUSIK-ZEITUNG – Zeitschrift fuer das Musikleben der Gegenwart. v1-70. Leipzig, Berlin. 1874-1943 – 1 – us Schnase [780]

ALLGEMEINE MUSIKZEITUNG : WOCHENSCHRIFT FUER DAS MUSIKLEBEN DER GEGENWART – v8-20, 26-66. 1899-1939 – 25r – 1 – us Ross [780]

ALLGEMEINE MUSIK-ZEITUNG: WOCHENSCHRIFT FUER DIE REFORM DES MUSIKLEBENS DER GEGENWART – Berlin. 1874-1943 – 1 – 1035.00 – us L of C Photodup [780]

ALLGEMEINE NACHRICHTEN FUER POMMERELLEN – (Cont: Briesener Zeitung) – Briesen, oct 16 1928-jun 28 1930, jan 3-nov 14 1931 – 1 – Inquire at Mikrofilmarchiv for details – gw Misc Inst [943]

ALLGEMEINE NACHRICHTEN FUER POMMERELLEN – (Former title: Briesener Zeitung) – Briesen (Wabrzezno), Germany. Oct 16, 1928-Jun 28, 1930; Jan 3-Nov 14, 1931 – 1 – gw Mikrofilm [072]

ALLGEMEINE ODER-ZEITUNG – (Cont by: Neue Oder-Zeitung, mar 27 1849) – Breslau, 1846-jun 1847, 1848-55 – 21r – 1 – Inquire at Mikrofilmarchiv for details – gw Misc Inst [943]

ALLGEMEINE ODER-ZEITUNG – (Title change: Neue Oder-Zeitung, Mar 27, 1849) – Breslau (Wroclaw), Germany. Apr 2, 1846-Dec 31, 1855 – 21r – 1 – gw Mikrofilm [072]

ALLGEMEINE PREUSSISCHE STAATS-ZEITUNG – (Suppl available from other sources, inquire: Mikrofilmarchiv Dortmund. Cont by: Allgemeine preussische Zeitung, jul 1 1843. Preussischer Staats-Anzeiger, may 1848. Koeniglich-preussischer Staatsanzeiger, jul 1 1851. Deutscher Reichsanzeiger und Preussischer Staatsanzeiger, jul 1871) – Berlin, 1819-apr 14 1945 – 553r – 1 – gw Mikro Press [943]

ALLGEMEINE PREUSSISCHE STAATS-ZEITUNG – (Title varies: 1843 Allgemeine preussische Zeitung. 1848 Preussischer Staats-Anzeiger. 1851 Koeniglich-preussischer Staatsanzeiger. 1871 Deutscher Reichsanzeiger und Preussischer Staatsanzeiger) – Berlin, 1848 – 2r – 1 – gw Mikrofilm [072]

ALLGEMEINE PREUSSISCHE ZEITUNG – (Also known as: Preussischer Staats-Anzeiger) – Berlin, Germany. Jan-Dec 1848 – 1 – gw Mikrofilm [072]

ALLGEMEINE PREUSSISCHE ZEITUNG *see*
– ALLGEMEINE PREUSSISCHE STAATS-ZEITUNG

ALLGEMEINE REALENCYCLOPAEDIE ODER CONVERSATIONS-LEXIKON FUER DAS KATHOLISCHE DEUTSCHLAND (AEL, ABT 1;6) / ed by Binder, Wilhelm – Regensburg (Manz), 1846-1850 (mf ed 1993) – 124mf – 9 – DM1,380.00 – 3-89131-104-4 – gw Fischer [030]

ALLGEMEINE SCHLOSSER- UND MASCHINENBAUER ZEITUNG – Luebeck, 1919-29 – 7r – 1 – DM525.00 – gw Mikro Press [072]

ALLGEMEINE SONNTAGSZEITUNG – Duesseldorf and Wuerzburg, West Germany.1956-76 – 1 – gw Mikrofilm [072]

ALLGEMEINE THEATER-CHRONIK – Leipzig, Oct 1852-Mar 1873 – 5r – 1 – gw Mikrofilm [072]

ALLGEMEINE THEATER-CHRONIK : ORGAN FUER DAS GESAMTINERESSE DER DEUTSCHEN BUEHNEN UND IHRER MITGLIEDER – Leipzig, 1852-1873 – 5r – 1 – DM500.00 – gw Mikro Press [790]

ALLGEMEINE THEORIE DER SCHOENEN KUENSTE / Sulzer, Johann Georg – O 438. 4 v. 1792-1794 – 9 – ne IDC [700]

ALLGEMEINE UND CHEMISCHE GEOLOGIE / Roth, J L A – 2511 2. 3 v. 1879-1893 – 8 – ne IDC [550]

ALLGEMEINE WELTGESCHICHTE MIT BESONDERER BERUECKSICHITIGUNG DES GEISTES$ UND CULTURLEBENS DER VOELKER UND MIT BENUTZUNG DER NEUEREN GESCHICHTLICHEN FORSCHUNGEN / Weber, Georg – Leipzig, 1857-1880. 15 v. & Register, 4 v., 1865-81. Film Mas C 468 – 1 – us H.U. Library [900]

ALLGEMEINE WOCHEN-CHRONIK – Bremen, aug 6 1854-jan 7 1855 – 1r – 1 – Inquire at Mikrofilmarchiv for details – gw Misc Inst [943]

ALLGEMEINE WOCHEN-CHRONIK – Bremen, Germany.6 Aug 1854-7 Jan 1855 – 1r – 1 – gw Mikrofilm [073]

ALLGEMEINE WOCHENZEITUNG DER JUDEN IN DEUTSCHLAND *see* ALLGEMEINE JUEDISCHE WOCHENZEITUNG

ALLGEMEINE ZEITUNG – Augsburg and Munich, Germany. Aug 3 1847-Dec 1855 and Jan 1877-Dec 1922. Not collated – 1 – us NY Public [943]

ALLGEMEINE ZEITUNG – Augsburg, (zunaechst: Tuebingen, Stuttgart, Ulm) 1798-1847 – 9 – gw Olms [320]

ALLGEMEINE ZEITUNG – (Cont: Cotta'sche Zeitung, Tuebingen, Stuttgart, Ulm, 1798-1807. Publ in Augsburg jan 16 1807-sep 1882, in Munich since oct 1882. Cont by: AZ am Abend; and: AZ am Morgen, mar 1925. Suppl 1891-1907 (incomplete) available from other sources, inquire: Mikrofilmarchiv Dortmund) – Augsburg, 1798-jun 30 1929 (incl Handelsbeilagen until 1865) – 366r; 27r Handelsbeilagen – 1 – Dist. gw Mikrofilm – gw Misc Inst [943]

ALLGEMEINE ZEITUNG : KREISBLATT FUER DEN KREIS COESFELD – Coesfeld, West Germany. 1981- – 1 – gw Mikrofilm [072]

ALLGEMEINE ZEITUNG – Mainz, Germany. Nov 1966-1967; May 1973-1980 – 98r – 1 – us L of C Photodup [072]

ALLGEMEINE ZEITUNG – Mainz, nov 29-dec 20 1946, jan 1-dec 17 1947, nov 2 1949-jun 29 1962 – 49r – 1 – gw Mikrofilm [072]
ALLGEMEINE ZEITUNG – Munich, 1908-16 – 5r – 1 – us Ross [072]
ALLGEMEINE ZEITUNG – (Suppl: Jan 1833-Dec 1847 42r) – Munich, DE. Jan 1799-Dec 1847 – 116r – 1 – uk British Libr Newspaper [072]
ALLGEMEINE ZEITUNG – Windhuk (Windhoek), Nambia. 1972-76; 1978-79 – 1 – gw Mikrofilm [430]
ALLGEMEINE ZEITUNG DER LUENEBURGER HEIDE – Uelzen, West-Germany. 1977- – 7r – 1 – gw Mikrofilm [072]
ALLGEMEINE ZEITUNG DES JUDENTHUMS – Leipzig. 1837-Apr 28 1922. Incomplete – 1 – us NY Public [072]
ALLGEMEINE ZEITUNG DES JUDENTHUMS – Leipzig, Berlin. v1-86. 1837-1922 – 24r – 1 – us Ross [270]
ALLGEMEINE ZEITUNG DES JUDENTUMS – Ein unparteiisches Organ fuer alles juedische Interesse. Leipzig. 1837-1922. BNE-349 1 – 9 – ne IDC [073]
ALLGEMEINE ZEITUNG DES JUEDENT(H)UMS – Leipzig, Germany. 1837-95; 1897-Mar 1917 (incomplete); 1918-28 Apr 1922 – 24r – 1 – gw Mikrofilm [072]
Allgemeinen Konferenz der Deutschen Sittlichkeitsvereine *see* MODERNE REALISTISCHE LITTERATUR IM LICHTE DER ETHIK UND AESTHETHIK
ALLGEMEINER ANZEIGER – Bielefeld, 1865-sep 30 1870 – 1 – Inquire at Mikrofilmarchiv for details – gw Misc Inst [072]
ALLGEMEINER ANZEIGER : FUER DIE KREISE WOLMIRSTEDT UND NEU-HALDENSLEBEN – Wolmirstedt, Germany. 1870-79 – 1 – gw Mikrofilm [072]
ALLGEMEINER ANZEIGER – Koeln, Germany. Apr-Dec 1849 – 1 – gw Mikrofilm [072]
ALLGEMEINER ARBEITER-KALENDER – Budapest, 1877, 1887, 1889, 1891-93 – 1r – 1 – Inquire at Mikrofilmarchiv for details – gw Misc Inst [072]
ALLGEMEINER ARBEITER-KALENDER – Budapest, Hungary. 1877, 1887, 1889, 1891-93 – 1r – 1 – gw Mikrofilm [073]
ALLGEMEINER BONNER ANZEIGER FUER INDUSTRIE; HANDEL UND GEWERBE – Bonn, dec 24 1859, jan 1-jun 28 1860 – 1 – Inquire at Mikrofilmarchiv for details – gw Misc Inst [380]
Allgemeiner deutscher Arbeiter-Verein *see* PROTOKOLL DER GENERALVERSAMMLUNG
ALLGEMEINER DEUTSCHER ARBEITERVEREIN PROTOKOLLE – (Generalversammlung: Frankfurt-Main 30 Nov 1865-1 Dec 1866; 1868 DM75.00. Generalversammlung: Berlin 19-25 May 1871 DM75.00. Vorstandssitzung: Hannover 3 Mar 1872 DM75.00. Generalversammlung: Hannover 26 May-5 Jun 1874 DM75.00. Generalversammlung: Berlin 18-24 May 1873 DM75.00) – gw Mikro Press [330]
Allgemeiner deutscher Gewerkschaftsbund *see*
- JAHRBUCH
- KORRESPONDENZBLATT..

Allgemeiner deutscher Gewerkschaftsbund. Ortsausschuss Berlin *see*
- BERICHT..
- GESCHAEFTSBERICHT

Allgemeiner deutscher Gewerkschaftsbund. Ortsausschuss Halle *see* BERICHT
Allgemeiner deutscher Gewerkschaftsbund. Ortsausschuss Muenchen *see* JAHRBUCH..
ALLGEMEINER DEUTSCHER LITERATUR-KALENDER – Bremen, 1881 – 1 – Inquire at Mikrofilmarchiv for details – gw Misc Inst [890]
ALLGEMEINER DEUTSCHER LITERATUR-KALENDER – Bremen, Germany.1881 – 1 – gw Mikrofilm [073]
ALLGEMEINER DEUTSCHER LITERATURKALENDER, 1879-1882 – (v1-13 (1879-91) DM46.00y; v14-39 (1892-1917) DM64.00y) – Deutscher Literaturkalender 1883-1902. Kuerschners Deutscher Literaturkalender 1903-1917 (mf ed 1993) – 355mf – 9 – DM1,950.00 – 3-89131-041-2 – gw Fischer [430]
Allgemeiner Eisenbahnerverband *see* PROTOKOLL DES DELEGIERTENTAGES
ALLGEMEINER FRAUENKALENDER, 1.1885-2.1886 DIE FRAUENBESTREBUNGEN UNSERER ZEIT, 3.1887 (HQ, 17) / Morgenstern, Lina – 1885-1887 (mf ed 1995) – 16mf – 9 – DM220.00 – 3-89131-129-X – gw Fischer [305]
Allgemeiner Freier Angestelltenbund *see*
- AFA SCHRIFTEN SAMMLUNG
- DIE ANGESTELLTEN-BEWEGUNG
- NIEDERSCHRIFT VOM GEWERKSCHAFTSKONGRESS
- PROTOKOLL VOM AFA-GEWERKSCHAFTKONGRESS

Allgemeiner freier Angestelltenbund. Bezirkskartell Brandenburg. Ortskartell Berlin *see* BERICHT UEBER DAS GESCHAFTSJAHR
Allgemeiner Heimarbeiterschutz-Kongress. 1st, Berlin. 1904 *see* PROTOKOLL DER VERHANDLUNGEN..
ALLGEMEINER LITTERARISCHER ANZEIGER 1796-1801. LITTERARISCHE BLAETTER 1802-1806. NEUER LITTERARISCHER ANZEIGER 1806-1808. ALLGEMEINES REGISTER 1811 – Leipzig, spaeter Nuernberg u.a., 1796-1811 (mf ed 1992) – 97mf – 9 – DM690.00 – 3-89131-055-2 – gw Fischer [430]
Allgemeiner Schutzkongress fuer alle in der Schiffahrt und im Schiffbau Beschaeftigten *see* PROTOKOLL DER VERHANDLUNGEN
ALLGEMEINES BERLINER INTELLIGENZBLATT – Berlin, 1860, apr-jul 1861 – 4r – 1 – Dist. gw Mikrofilm – gw Misc Inst [943]
ALLGEMEINES BUCHER-LEXICON / Heinsius, Wilhelm – 19v. 1812-94 – 1 – 281.00 – us L of C Photodup [430]
ALLGEMEINES BUECHERLEXIKON ODER VOLLSTAENDIGES VERZEICHNIS ALLER VON 1700 BIS ENDE 1892 ERSCHIENENEN BUECHER / Heinsius, Wilhelm – Leipzig. 19v. 1812-94 – 9 – subsc: DM1,400.00 – gw Olms [057]
ALLGEMEINES CONVERSTIONS-TASCHENLEXIKON (AEL, ABT 1;31) : ODER REAL-ENCYKLOPAEDIE DER FUER DIE GEBILDETEN STAENDE NOTWENDIGEN KENNTNISSE UND WISSENSCHAFTEN – Quedlinburg, Leipzig. 65 bde. 1828-1833 (mf ed 1995) – 67mf – 9 – DM1,980.00 – 3-89131-212-1 – gw Fischer [030]
ALLGEMEINES DEUTSCHES SACH-WOERTERBUCH ALLER MENSCHLICHEN KENNTNISSE UND FERTIGKEITEN (AEL, ABT 1;22) : 10 BAENDE UND 1 SUPPLEMENTBAND / ed by Liechtenstern, Joseph Freiherr von – Meissen, 1824-1834 (mf ed 1994) – 43mf – 9 – DM1,260.00 – 3-89131-172-9 – gw Fischer [030]
ALLGEMEINES DEUTSCHES VOLKS-CONVERSATIONS-LEXIKON UND FREMDWOERTERBUCH (AEL, ABT 1;23) : EIN UNENTBEHRLICHES HANDBUCH FUER JEDERMANN – Hamburg. 8 bde. 1844-1849 (mf ed 1994) – 73mf – 9 – DM750.00 – 3-89131-173-7 – gw Fischer [030]
ALLGEMEINES FRIEDBERGER WOCHENBLATT FUER STADT- UND LANDLEUTE – (Cont by: Gemeinnuetziges Wochenblatt fuer Friedberg und die Gegend, 1819. Wochenblatt fuer Friedberg und die Gegend, 1828. Friedberger Wochenblatt zu den Wetterauer Anzeigen, sep 13, 1834) – Friedberg. oct 2, 1809. 1811-aug 1, 1835 – 1 – gw Mikrofilm [072]
ALLGEMEINES GELEHRTEN-LEXICON / Joecher, Christian Gottlieb – Leipzig, Delmenhorst und Bremen 1750-1897. Hildesheim, 1984 – 143mf – 9 – DM960.00 diazo DM1150.000 silver – gw Olms [430]
ALLGEMEINES, HELVETISCHES, EYDGENOESSISCHES ODER SCHWEIZERISCHES LEXICON UND SUPPLEMENT ZUM ALLGEMEINEN HELVETISCH-EIDGENOESSISCHEN LEXICON HERRN BUERGERMEISTERS LEU HERAUSGEGEBEN VON HANS JACOB HOLZHALB (AEL, ABT.1;8) / Leu, Hans Jakob – Zuerich, 1747-1795 (mf ed 1992) – 171mf – 9 – DM1,380.00 – 3-89131-077-3 – gw Fischer [943]
ALLGEMEINES HISTORISCHES LEXIKON IN WELCHEM DAS LEBEN UND DIE THATEN DERER PATRIARICHEN, PROPHETEN, APOSTEL ... VORGESTELLET WERDEN (AEL, ABT 1; 37) – 3. verb. Aufl. Leipzig. 4 Bde. 1730-32 (mf ed 1997) – 51mf – 9 – DM580.00 – 3-89131-276-8 – gw Fischer [943]
ALLGEMEINES INTELLIGENZBLATT *see* FREIBURGER ZEITUNG
ALLGEMEINES JOURNAL DER CHEMIE – Leipzig, 1798-1803. (General journal of chemistry) – 3 – us Readex [540]
ALLGEMEINES OEKONOMISCHES MAGAZIN – Hamburg, DE. 1782-83 – 9 – gw Mikrofilm [073]
ALLGEMEINES REGISTER UEBER DIE GOETTINGISCHEN GELEHRTEN ANZEIGEN VON 1753 BIS 1782 / ed by Ekkard, Friedrich – Goettingen, 1784-1785; Hildesheim, 1980 – 25mf – 9 – DM190.00 – gw Olms [943]
ALLGEMEINES REPERTORIUM FUER DIE THEOLOGISCHE LITERATUR UND KIRCHLICHE STATISTIK – 1(1833)-80(1853) – 405mf – 9 – Dfl1,418.00 – ne Slangenburg [073]
ALLGEMEINES REPERTORIUM FUER DIE THEOLOGISCHE LITERATUR UND KIRCHLICHE STATISTIK – Berlin. v1-80. 1833-1853 – 405mf – 9 – ne IDC [240]
ALLGEMEINES VOLKSBLATT – Koeln, Germany. 1845. Incomplete – 1 – gw Mikrofilm [072]
ALLGEMEINES, VOLLSTAENDIGES NEUHEBRAEISCH-DEUTSCHES WOERTERBUCH : MIT INBEGRIFF ALLER IN DEN TALMUDISCHEN SCHRIFTEN UND IN DER NEUEN LITERATUR UEBERHAUPT VORKOMMENDEN FREMDWOERTER / Schulbaum, Moses – (Text in Hebrew. Occasional phrases in Greek or Latin) – Lemberg: Michael Wolf, 1880 – 1mf – 9 – 0-8370-7506-8 – 1986-1506 – us A.T.L.A. [470]
ALLGEMEINMEDIZIN – (Ceased publ) – Berlin. v14-19. may 1985-oct 1990* – 1,5,9 – D16974 – us UMI [610]
ALLGEMEINWISSENSCHAFTLICHE UND LITERARISCHE ZEITSCHRIFTEN DES 17. UND 18. JAHRHUNDERTS – (See individual titles: Allgemeine Literatur-Zeitung. Athenaeum-Eine Zeitschrift. Belustigungen des Verstandes und des Witzes. Beytraege zur critischen Historie der deutschen Sprache, Poesie und Beredsamkeit. Briefe, die neueste Literatur betreffend. Briefe ueber Merkwuerdigkeiten der Litteratur. Deutsche Monatsschrift-Neue deutsche Monatsschrift. Deutsches Museum-Neues deutsches Museum. Die Discourse der Mahlern. Frankfurter gelehrte Anzeigen. Die Horen-Eine Monatsschrift. Der Mahler der Sitten. Monatsgespraeche. Neue Beytraege zum Vergnuegen des Verstandes und des Witzes. Neue Thalia. Neuer Buechersaal der schoenen Wissenschaften und freyen Kuenste. Thalia) – Hildesheim, 1977-81 – 1632mf – 9 – DM10,700.00 diazo; DM12,600.00 silver – gw Olms [430]
ALLGEMEINWISSENSCHAFTLICHE UND LITERARISCHE ZEITSCHRIFTEN DES 17. UND 18. JAHRHUNDERTS *see*
- ALLGEMEINE LITERATUR-ZEITUNG
- ATHENAEUM
- BELUSTIGUNGEN DES VERSTANDES UND DES WITZES
- BEYTRAEGE ZUR CRITISCHEN HISTORIE DER DEUTSCHEN SPRACHE, POESIE UND BEREDSAMKEIT
- BRIEFE UEBER MERKWUERDIGKEITEN DER LITTERATUR
- DEUTSCHE MONATSSCHRIFT/NEUE DEUTSCHE MONATSSCHRIFT
- DEUTSCHES MUSEUM
- DIE DISCOURSE DER MAHLERN
- FRANKFURTER GELEHRTE ANZEIGEN
- DIE HOREN
- DER MAHLER DER SITTEN
- MONATSGESPRAECHE
- NEUE THALIA
- NEUER BUECHERSAAL DER SCHOENEN WISSENSCHAFTEN UND FREYEN KUENSTE
- THALIA

ALLIANCA : ORGAO DA CLASSE ESTUDANTESCA – Maceio, Alagoas. 1 Jun, 1 Set 1890 – 1,5,6 – bl Biblioteca [072]
L'ALLIANCE : CONSERVATEUR – St-Jean, Canada. 30 mars 1893-23 fev 1894 – 1r – 1 – Can$35.00 – cn Can Microfilming [072]
L'ALLIANCE / ed by Page, N – Hull, Canada. 2 oct 1886-16 jul 1887 – 1r – 1 – Can$25.00 – cn Can Microfilming [072]
L'ALLIANCE – Paris. 1 2 fevr-5 juil 1846 – 1 – fr A.C.R.P.P. [944]
L'ALLIANCE – Toronto. v1 n2. dec 1954-nov 1955 – 1r – 1 – Can$25.00 – cn Can Microfilming [072]
L'ALLIANCE AUTRICHIENNE / Broglie, J V A de – H-551 2. 1895 – 8 – ne IDC [943]
ALLIANCE DAILY TIMES-HERALD – Alliance, NE. Jan 1891- – 1 – us NE Hist [071]
L'ALLIANCE DEMOCRATIQUE – puis Bulletin interieur du Parti. Paris. 1934-39; 1947-avr 1955 – 1 – fr A.C.R.P.P. [335]
L'ALLIANCE ET LA PARENTE A VILLAREMBERT / Collomb, G – 9 – F30.00 – fr Ethnologie [305]
ALLIANCE HERALD – Alliance, NE. -w., sw. Jul. 1895-Jan. 1897; Jun. 1897; Mar. 1898-Aug. 1898; Jul. 1903-Dec. 1903. Incomplete; Jan 1904-Nov. 1905; Mar. 1908-Jun. 1922 – 1 – us NE Hist [071]
L'ALLIANCE ISRAELITE UNIVERSELLE. PAIX ET DROIT – Paris. 1921-janv mars 1940 – 1 – fr A.C.R.P.P. [340]
ALLIANCE LIFE *see* ALLIANCE WITNESS
ALLIANCE LIFE – (Cont: Alliance Witness) – Nyack. v122-. may 1987- – 1,5*,9 – D8790.01 – us UMI [073]
L'ALLIANCE NATIONALE – Montreal, Canada. v15 n1+2. jan/fev 1909-v25 n11+12. nov/dec 1919 – 1r – 1 – Can$40.00 – cn Can Microfilming [073]
L'ALLIANCE NATIONALE – Montreal: La Societe de secours mutuels l'"Alliance nationale" 1895-[1919] – 9 – cn C.I.H.M. [360]
ALLIANCE NEWS – Alliance, NE. -w. Oct. 1914; Jan. 1918-Apr. 1943 – 1 – us NE Hist [071]
ALLIANCE NEWS – Manchester, UK. 1895-1900 – 5r – 1 – uk British Libr Newspaper [072]
Alliance of Poles of America *see* RECORDS, MS P.P.
ALLIANCE OF TRANS. SAXONS – (Series 1,3) – Cleveland, Ohio, 1902-1981 – 37r – 1 – us I.H.R.C. [978]
ALLIANCE REPUBLICAINE DEMOCRATIQUE / Parti republicain democratique et social – Paris. 21 fevr 1902-janv 1921 – 1 – fr A.C.R.P.P. [320]
THE ALLIANCE SUN / Farmers Alliance of Burt County.Nebraska – Lyons, NE. 1888-. -w.Incomplete. Issues mutilated and poor print – 1 – us NE Hist [071]
ALLIANCE WEEKLY *see* ALLIANCE WITNESS
ALLIANCE WITNESS – (Cont by: Alliance Life. Former titles: Christian Alliance and Foreign Missionary Weekly (1887-1896); Christian and Missionary Alliance (1897-sep 1911); Alliance Weekly (oct 1911-dec 25, 1957)) – Nyack. v1-122 1887-apr 1987 1*; v110-122 jan 1975-apr 1987 5*,9* – 1,5,9 – D8790 – us UMI [073]
ALLIANCE WITNESS *see* ALLIANCE LIFE
Allibaco, W A *see*
- THE PHILOSOPHIC AND SCIENTIFIC ULTIMATUM
- PHILOSOPHIC AND SCIENTIFIC ULTIMATUM... FOR THE GUIDE OF NATIONS

Allibone, Samuel A *see* UNION BIBLE COMPANION: CONTAINING THE EVIDENCES...OF THE HOLY SCRIPTURES
Allied Forces. Southeast Asia Command. Netherlands Indies Civil Administration *see* RECHTSREGLEMENT VOOR BURGERLIJKE- EN STRAFZAKEN IN BORNEO EN DE GROOTE OOST
ALLIED HIGH COMMAND PAPERS – 1943-45 – 1 – uk Microform Academic [941]
ALLIED INTERVENTION IN RUSSIA FROM 1918 TO 1920 PAMPHLET COLLECTION – 1917-1969 – 1 – CSUXANS8421-B – us Hoover Inst Photo [350]
ALLIED NEWS – Grove City. Pa. 1969- – 1 – us UMI [071]
Allied Operational and Occupational Headquarters. World War II *see* REVIEWS OF THE YOKOHAMA CLASS B AND CLASS C WAR CRIMES TRIALS BY THE 8TH ARMY JUDGE ADVOCATE, 1946-1949
Allied Powers. Reparation Commission *see* REPARATION PAPERS OF THE ALLIED POWERS REPARATION COMMISSION
Allier, R *see*
- LES EGLISES DE LA REFORME ET LE PROBLEME DE LA PAIX AU COURS DU 19EME SIECLE
- LA PSYCHOLOGIE DE LA CONVERSION CHEZ LES PEUPLES NONCIVILISES

Allihn, F H Th *see* ZEITSCHRIFT FUER EXACTE PHILOSOPHIE IM SINNE DES NEUERN PHILOSOPHISCHEN REALISMUS, 1. 1861 – 20. 1896
ALLILUIA / Narbut, V – Stikhi. Spb. 1912. BR-1204 2 – 8 – ne IDC [460]
Allin, Thomas *see* THE AUGUSTINIAN REVOLUTION IN THEOLOGY
Allin, Thomas et al *see*
- THE JUBILEE OF THE METHODIST NEW CONNEXION
- THE JUBILEE OF THE METHODIST NEW CONNEXION; BEING A GRATEFUL MEMORIAL OF THE ORIGIN, GOVERNMENT AND HISTORY OF THE DENOMINATION

Allioni, C *see*
- AUCTUARIUM AD FLORAM PEDEMONTANAM CUM NOTIS ET EMENDATIONIBUS
- FLORA PEDEMONTANA, SIVE ENUMERATIO METHODICA STIRPIUM INDIGENARUM PEDEMONTII

ALLIORUM ADHUC COGNITORUM MONOGRAPHIA / Regel, E A von – Petropoli. 1875. B-5151 2 – 8 – ne IDC [580]

Allis, O T *see* THE FIVE BOOKS OF MOSES

ALLIS-CHALMERS ELECTRICAL REVIEW *see* ALLIS-CHALMERS ENGINEERING REVIEW

ALLIS-CHALMERS ENGINEERING REVIEW – (Ceased publ. Former title: Allis-Chalmers Electrical Review) – Milwaukee, cum index 1-15 1936-1950; v1-41 sep 1936-1976 – 1,5*,9* – D678 – us UMI [620]

Allison, L C *see* DISCOVERY OF TRIPOLI OR POLISHING POWDER NEAR ST JOHN:..

Allison, Leonard A *see* THE REV. OLIVER ARNOLD, FIRST RECTOR OF SUSSEX, N.B. WITH SOME ACCOUNT OF HIS LIFE, HIS PARISH AND HIS SUCCESSORS AND THE OLD INDIAN COLLEGE

Allison, Nathaniel T *see* HISTORY OF CHEROKEE COUNTY AND REPRESENTATIVE CITIZENS

Allison Peers, E *see* THE CHURCH IN SPAIN

Allison, William Henry *see*
- BAPTIST COUNCILS IN AMERICA
- INVENTORY OF UNPUBLISHED MATERIAL FOR AMERICAN RELIGIOUS HISTORY IN PROTESTANT CHURCH ARCHIVES AND OTHER REPOSITORIES

DEN ALLMAENNA RELIGIONSHISTORIEN OCH DEN KYRKLIGA TEOLOGIEN / Soederblom, Nathan – Uppsala: W. Schultz, [1901?] – 1mf – us A.T.L.A. [240]

Allman, E *see* DER DEUTSCHE SEEHANDEL...

Allman, G J *see*
- A MONOGRAPH OF THE FRESH-WATER POLYZOA, INCLUDING ALL THE KNOWN SPECIES, BOTH BRITISH AND FOREIGN
- A MONOGRAPH OF THE GYMNOBLASTIC OR TUBULARIAN HYDROIDS

ALLMANNA JOURNALEN – Stockholm, Sweden. 1813 – 1 reel – 1 – sw Kungliga [073]

Allmers, Hermann *see* MARSCHENBUCH

Allmers, Robert *see* KAMPF UM THURANT

Allo, E B *see*
- ST. PAUL

ALLO MONTREAL – Montreal, 13 avr 1974-26 mai 1974 – 1r – 1 – Can$40.00 – cn Can Microfilming [072]

ALLO POLICE – Montreal, Canada. 28 fev 1953-24 jun 1956 – 3r – 1 – Can$60.00r – cn Can Microfilming [360]

ALLO POLICE – Montreal. v1- 1953-. SEM35P306 – 67r – 1 – cn Bibl Nat [072]

ALLOA ADVERTISER – Scotland, 1850-1972 – 58r – 1 – uk British Libr Newspaper [072]

ALLOA ADVERTISER JOURNAL – Scotland, 1972-81 – 28mqn r – 1 – uk British Libr Newspaper [072]

ALLOA AND HILLFOOTS ADVERTISER – 1 – £42.00r – uk Scot News [072]

ALLOA AND HILLFOOTS ADVERTISER JOURNAL *see* ALLOA ADVERTISER JOURNAL

ALLOA JOURNAL – Scotland, 1859-1972 – 54r – 1 – uk British Libr Newspaper [072]

Alloa, Scotland. Greenside Cemetery *see* REGISTER OF BURIALS

ALLOCUTIONS TO THE CLERGY AND PASTORALS OF THE LATE RIGHT REV. DR. MORIARTY, BISHOP OF KERRY / Moriarty, David – Dublin: Browne and Nolan; London: Burns and Oates, 1884 – 1mf – 9 – 0-8370-7006-6 – 1986-1006 – us A.T.L.A. [240]

Allodi, L *see* PETRUS BOHERIUS

ALLOMETRIC SCALING OF GRIP STRENGTH BY BODY MASS AND LEAN BODY MASS IN COLLEGE-AGE MEN AND WOMEN / Lee, Siu Y – Springfield College, 1995 – 2mf – 9 – $8.00 – PE3606 – us Microform Publ [612]

Allotte de la Fuye *see* NOUVEAU CLASSEMENT DES MONNAIES ARSACIDES D'APRES LE CATALOGUE DU BRITISH MUSEUM

Alloway, Mary Wilson *see* FAMOUS FIRESIDES OF FRENCH CANADA

THE ALL-ROUND ROUTE GUIDE: THE HUDSON RIVER, TRENTON FALLS, NIAGARA, TORONTO, THOUSAND ISLANDS, RIVER ST LAWRENCE, OTTAWA, MONTREAL, QUEBEC.. – Montreal: Montreal Print. and Pub. Co., 1868. 05677. (Pre-1900 Canadiana) – 9 – cn C.I.H.M. [910]

All-Russian Trade Union of Civil Servants, Shop Assistants and Clerks *see* THE ALL-RUSSIAN TRADE UNION OF CIVIL SERVANTS, SHOP ASSISTANTS AND CLERKS

THE ALL-RUSSIAN TRADE UNION OF CIVIL SERVANTS, SHOP ASSISTANTS AND CLERKS / All-Russian Trade Union of Civil Servants, Shop Assistants and Clerks – Moscow: All-Russian Central Council of Trade Unions, 1920 – 1 – CSUX91-B1099 – us Hoover Inst Photo [331]

ALL'S WELL – Fayetteville Arkansas. v. 1, no. 9-v. 13, no. 5. Aug 1921-Dec 1935 – 1 – us NY Public [073]

ALL'S WELL : OR THE MIRROR REPOLISHED – (Ceased publ. Supersedes: Reedy's Mirror) – Fayetteville. v1-13. 1920-dec 1935* – 1 – D4644 – us UMI [073]

Allsopp, Henry *see* AN INTRODUCTION TO ENGLISH INDUSTRIAL HISTORY

Allston, Joseph Blyth *see* BIOGRAPHY

Allston, Robert FW *see* PAPERS

Allston, Washington *see* PAPERS OF WASHINGTON ALLSTON

ALL-STORY COMBINED WITH MUNSEY'S – (Ceased publ. Formed by the union of: Munsey's Magazine & a part of Argosy All-Story Weekly) – New York. v1-88. oct 1929-mar 1940* – 1 – D4773 – us UMI [420]

Allue Salvador, Miguel *see* EL AHORRO Y LA POLITICA SOCIAL

All-Union (Russian) Communist Party. Smolensk Archives *see* RECORDS

ALL-UNION UNION OF EVANGELICAL CHRISTIANS-BAPTISTS : CONGRESSES – Moscow, 1966, 1979 – 1r – 1 – $7.12 – us Baptist [420]

ALLYN K. FORD COLLECTION OF HISTORICAL MANUSCRIPTS – Over 1500 letters, cards and documents spanning five centuries (1472-1970) and several continents. 5 reels, including filmed inventory – 1 – $150.00; $30.00r – us M.H.S. [900]

AL'MA / Minskii, N – Tragediia iz sovremennoi zhizni v 3-kh deistviiakh. Spb. 1900. BR-803 2 – 8 – ne IDC [490]

EL ALMA CRISTIANA DE CORTES. EN EL CENTENARIO DE SU MUERTE / Bayle, Constantino – Madrid: Razon y Fe, 1948 – 1 – sp Bibl Santa Ana [920]

ALMA EMERITA – Merida, 1908 – 5 – sp Bibl Santa Ana [073]

ALMA EN LOS LABIOS / Trigo, Felipe – Madrid: Renacumiento, 7th ed 1920 – sp Bibl Santa Ana [946]

ALMA EXTREMENA – Caceres, 1905 y 1906. 2 numeros – 5 – sp Bibl Santa Ana [073]

ALMA RECORD – Alma, NE. -w. Oct. 1895-Jan. 1897. Incomplete; Jun. 1901-Mar. 1904; Jan. 1908-Jun. 1925 – 1 – us NE Hist [071]

ALMADEN-CAMBRIAN SUN – San Jose, CA. 1973-Aug 1976 – 11r – 1 – $550.00 – B02873 – us Library Micro [071]

ALMAE OPTIMORUM STUDIORUM MATRI VIADRINAE ACADEMIAE ILLUSTRISSIMAE / Fickert, Karl Rudolph – Wroclaw: W. Friedrich, 1861. 1 fiche – 9 – us A.T.L.A. [240]

THE ALMAFILIAN – St. Thomas, Ont.: Alma College, [188-?-189- or 19–] – 9 – cn C.I.H.M. [370]

ALMAGESTUM BOTANICUM MANTISSA / Plukenet, L – Londini. 1697-1700. B-5326 2 – 8 – ne IDC [580]

Al-Magrebi, Samuel *see* DES SAMUEL AL-MAGREBI ABHANDLUNG UEBER...PFLICHTEN DER PRIESTER UND RICHTER

AL-MAGRIB – Al Maghrib. Fond. Pierre Fontana. no. 1-32. Alger. avr-juil 1903. mq no. 20-24 – 1 – fr A.C.R.P.P. [073]

AL-MAGRIB AL-ARABI – (Ed. francaise. sept 1947-mai 1949. Ed. arabe. juin 1947-mai 1949, mars-mai 1956) – Dir.-gerant M.S. Zahiri. Alger – 1 – fr A.C.R.P.P. [073]

AL-MAGRIB EL-MAGHRIB – Dir. Taamout Aissa Ben Yahia. n1-38. Alger, 1930-31 – 1 – fr A.C.R.P.P. [073]

Almagro Basch, Martin *see*
- EXCAVACIONES DE RUINAS DE EPOCA VISIGODA EN LA ALDEA DE SAN PEDRO DE MERIDA
- GUIA DE MERIDA
- MERIDA. GUIDE DE LA VILLE ET DE SES MONUMENTS

ALMANAC OF SEAPOWER – (Suppl to: Sea Power into which it was absorbed in 1987) – Arlington, 1983-86* – 1 – D15173 – us UMI [355]

ALMANAC PANORAMA – Los Angeles, CA. 1980-86 – 1 – us A.J.P.C. [071]

ALMANACH ADMINISTRATIVO, HISTORICO E MERCANTIL DA PROVINCIA DO AMAZONAS – Manaos, Amazonas. 1884 – 1,5,6 – bl Biblioteca [072]

ALMANACH DAS FAMILIAS – [s.l.]. 1877 – 1,5,6 – bl Biblioteca [072]

ALMANACH DE LA GUADELOUPE ET DEPENDANCES – Basse-Terre. 1832-36; 1838-41; 1843-50 – 1 – fr A.C.R.P.P. [073]

ALMANACH DE LA LITTERATURE, DU THEATRE ET DES BEAUX-ARTS – Paris. 1853-69 – 1 – fr A.C.R.P.P. [410]

ALMANACH DE LA QUESTION SOCIALE ET DE LA LIBRE PENSEE – Paris. 1891-1900; 1902-03 – 1 – fr A.C.R.P.P. [073]

ALMANACH DES DAMES, POUR L'ANNEE 1807 / Plamondon, Louis – Quebec: Nouvelle-Imprimerie. SEM16P193 – 1r – 5 – Can$9.00 – cn Bibl Nat [030]

ALMANACH DES FEMMES – 2eme annee. Women's almanac for 1853 in English and French. Publ. by Jeanne Deroin. London: J. Watson, 1853. 230p. (Miscellaneous selections) – 3mf – 9 – $8.00 – fr Bibl Nationale [305]

ALMANACH DES FEMMES POUR 1854 – Publie par Jeanne Deroin. 3eme annee. Londres: J. Watson, 1854. 122p. (Miscellaneous selections) – 2mf – 9 – $6.00 – fr Bibl Nationale [640]

ALMANACH DES FRANCS-MACONS – La Haye, Amsterdam, 1751, 1757, 1761-1764-1766, 1768, 1769, 1772-1792 – 30mf – ne IDC [944]

ALMANACH DES TRADITIONS POPULAIRES / ed by Rolland, Eugene – Paris. 3v. 1882-1884 – 7mf – 9 – ne IDC [390]

ALMANACH DO PARANA – '(s.l.')-Curitiba, Brazil. 1896-1913; 1929 – 1,5,6 – bl Biblioteca [073]

ALMANACH DU BARREAU: LIVRE DE REFERENCES CONTENANT LE NOM ET L'ADRESSE DES JUGES, SHERIFS, PROTONOTAIRES, AVOCATS, NOTAIRES...DE LA PROVINCE DE QUEBEC – (Only 1887 filmed) – Montreal: E Senecal et Fils, 1887-. SEM105P912 – 2mf – 9 – Can$4.50 – cn Bibl Nat [030]

ALMANACH DU PEUPLE DE BEAUCHEMIN & PAYETTE POUR L'AN 1957 – Montreal: Beauchemin et Payette, 1857. SEM105P895 – 1mf – 9 – Can$2.25 – cn Bibl Nat [030]

ALMANACH FUER DAS JAHR / Bibliotheque de la Societe Psychanalytique de Paris – puis Der Psychoanalyse. Wien. 1926-38 – 1 – fr A.C.R.P.P. [616]

ALMANACH FUER FREUNDE DER SCHAUSPEILKUNST – Berlin. v. 1-17. 1836-53. Title varies: 1847, Wolff's Almanach fuer Freunde der Schauspielkunst. Cont'd by Deutscher Buehnen-Almanach. Film Mas C 487 – 1 – us H.U. Library [790]

ALMANACH FUER FREUNDE DER SCHAUSPIELKUN JAHRGANG (1)-(6), JAHRGANG 7-10 = GERMAN THEATRE ALMANACH AND YEARBOOKS / ed by Wolff, Ludwig – (Cont as: Wolff's Almanach fuer Freunde der Schauspielkunst: Jg. 11, 12-17. Deutscher Buehnen-Almanach: Jg. 18-57. Berlin 1837-1893) – 1988 – 463mf (1:24) – 9 – diazo DM3,700.00 (silver DM4,500.00 ISBN: 3-598-32323-9) – 3-598-32324-7 – gw Saur [790]

ALMANACH GENERAL DU COMMERCE DE LA GUADELOUPE – Basse-Terre. 1843 – 1 – fr A.C.R.P.P. [073]

ALMANACH HISTORIQUE ET CHRONOLOGIQUE DES SPECTACLES – devenu: Nouveau calendrier historique des theatres de l'Opera et des comedies francaise et italienne et des foires. devenu: Les Spectacles de Paris, ou suite du calendrier historique et chronologique des theatres. devenu: Almanach des spectacles de Paris. Paris. 1752-1815 (interruptions entre 1794 et l'an VIII puis entre l'an IX et 1815) – 1 – fr A.C.R.P.P. [790]

ALMANACH JUDICIAIRE DE LA PROVINCE DE QUEBEC / Audette, Louis Arthur – Levis, Quebec: Mercier, 1888. 00062. (Pre-1900 Canadiana) – 9 – cn C.I.H.M. [340]

ALMANACH LITTERARIO ALAGOANO DAS SENHORAS – Jaragua, Alagoas. Mar 1888; Jan 1889 – 1,5,6 – bl Biblioteca [072]

ALMANACH LITTERARIO E DE INDICACOES – [s.l.]. 1888-1889 – 1,5,6 – bl Biblioteca [072]

ALMANACH MENSUEL DE l'APOSTOLAT DE LA PRIERE – Montreal: Publie par le Directeur Superieur de l'Oeuvre, College Ste. Marie, [189-?-1966] – 9 – cn C.I.H.M. [240]

ALMANACH NATIONAL DU DEPARTEMENT DE LA LOIRE-INFERIEURE, CONTENANT LES DEPART ET ARRIVEE DES COURIERS ET MESSAGERIES,... – Nantes: Forest, [s.d.] – fr Armell [944]

ALMANACHS DE L'ACTION ET INDEX ANNUEL – Quebec, Canada. 1917-42 – 2r – 1 – Can$55.00r – cn Can Microfilming [072]

ALMANACHS ET ANNUAIRES DE LA VILLE DE QUEBEC DE 1780 A 1900 / Carrier, Nicole – 1964. SEM105P4 – 2mf – 9 – cn Bibl Nat [910]

ALMANAK – (In Icelandic) – Canada, 1895-1907 – 6r – 1 – cn Commonwealth Micro [072]

ALMANAK ADMINISTRATIVO, CIVIL E INDUSTRIAL DA PROVINCIA DE MINAS GERAIS – Ouro Preto, 1864-65; 1870; 1873; 1875 – 1,5,6 – bl Biblioteca [324]

ALMANAK ADMINISTRATIVO, COMMERCIAL E INDUSTRIAL DA PROVINCIA DA BAHIA PARA O ANNO DE 1873 – [s.l.]. 1872 – 1,5,6 – bl Biblioteca [072]

ALMANAK ADMINISTRATIVO DA PROVINCIA DAS ALAGOAS – [s.l.] Ver Alamanak da Provincia das Alagoas – 1,5,6 – bl Biblioteca [072]

ALMANAK ADMINISTRATIVO, MERCANTIL E INDUSTRIAL DA BAHIA – '(s.l.')-BA, Brazil. 1854-60; 1862-63 (incomplete) – 1,5,6 – bl Biblioteca [072]

ALMANAK ADMINISTRATIVO, MERCANTIL E INDUSTRIAL DO RIO DE JANEIRO – Rio de Janeiro: E H Laemmert. v1-4. 1844-47 – 1 – us Res Libr [030]

ALMANAK ADMINISTRATIVO, MERCANTIL, E INDUSTRIAL DO RIO DE JANEIRO – Rio de Janeiro, 1844-1915;1928 – 1,5,6 – bl Biblioteca [072]

ALMANAK "ASIA-RAYA" 2603 : TAHOEN KE-I. – Djakarta, Asia-Raya, Bagian Penerbitan (2603). 258p – 192-194mf – 9 – ne IDC [080]

ALMANAK "ASIA-RAYA" 2604 : TAHOEN KE-II. – Djakarta, Djawa Sjinboen Sja (2604). 280p – 195-197mf – 9 – ne IDC [080]

ALMANAK DA PROVINCIA DAS ALAGOAS – Maceio, Alagoas. 1873-1987; 1877-1878; 1880 – 1,5,6 – bl Biblioteca [072]

ALMANAK DAI TOA. (ASIA TIMOER RAJA) : DISOESOEN OLEH HASSAN NOEL 'ARIFIN – Medan, Toko Boekoe "Antara" (2602). 36p – 198mf – 9 – ne IDC [080]

ALMANAK DO ESTADO DE ALAGOAS – Maceio, Alagoas. 1891-1894 – 1,5,6 – bl Biblioteca [072]

ALMANAK EKONOMI – Jogjakarta. 1951-1953. SE-258 1. 1957 – 9 – ne IDC [330]

ALMANAK INDONESIA – Bandung. (incomplete) SE-603 1. 1949-1951 – 9 – ne IDC [950]

ALMANAK INDONESIA – Djakarta. v1-2. 1968 – 32mf – 9 – SE-1306/1 – ne IDC [950]

ALMANAK MAHADEWA – Ngajogjakarta. (incomplete) SE-612 1. 1952-1959 – 9 – ne IDC [030]

ALMANAK NAUTIKA / Pardi – SE-4370 1. 1963 – 9 – ne IDC [030]

ALMANAK SOEARA ASIA 2604 – Soerabaja, Soeara Asia, 2604. 216p – 205-207mf – 9 – ne IDC [080]

ALMANAK TANI – Djakarta. (incomplete) SE-607 1. 1955-1958 – 9 – ne IDC [030]

ALMANAK VAN HET LEIDSCHE STUDENTENCORPS : 119E JAARG. 1933 – Leiden, 1932 – 6mf – 9 – ne IDC [080]

ALMANAK VAN NEDERLANDSCH INDIE – Batavia, 1820-1864 – 275mf – 9 – ne IDC [080]

ALMANAK VETERAN R.I. MARKAS DAERAH LEGIUN VETERAN R.I. – (Annual. Only issue published) – Medan, 1966 – 4mf – 9 – SE-1309/1 – ne IDC [950]

ALMANAK WASPADA – Ngajogjakarta. (incomplete). SE-613 1. 1954-1965 – 9 – ne IDC [030]

AL'MANAKH – L'vivs'kii derzhavnii universitet im. I. Franka. Students'ka literaturna studiia L'viv, 1954-1956. v. 1-2. 124, (2), 189 pp. BR-1646 2 – 8 – ne IDC [030]

AL'MANAKH – Spb., 1906. v. 1-2. BR-5740 2 – 8 – ne IDC [030]

AL'MANAKH ARTELI PISATELEI "KRUG" – Moscow. 1923-1925, nos. 1-5 – 1 – 35.00r – us Hoover Inst Photo [460]

AL'MANAKH GRIF – M., 1903, 1904, 1905, 1914. BR-3313 2 – 8 – ne IDC [030]

AL'MANAKH MUZ – Petrograd. Izd. "Felana". 1916. 192, (10) pp. BR-1823 2 – 8 – ne IDC [030]

ALMANAKH NA PROSHCHANIE = ALMANACH NOS ADIEUX, FAREWELL ALMANAC / ed by Burnakina, A A – Konstantinopol: [s.n., 1924] – 1 – CSUX89-B6385 – us Hoover Inst Photo [460]

AL'MANAKH STIKHOV / Drakon – Spb. 1921. BR-1843 2 – 8 – ne IDC [460]

AL'MANAKHI "TVORCHESTVO" – M., Petrograd, 1917. v. 1-2. BR-1827 2 – 8 – ne IDC [030]

ALMANAKUMUM – Kutaradja, Atjeh, Atjeh Press Service. SE-5706 1 – 9 – ne IDC [030]

ALMANAQUE DEL MAESTRO / Pimentel y Donaire, Miguel – 1892 – 9 – 1.50f – sp Bibl Santa Ana [030]

ALMANAQUE DO ENSINO – Maceio, Alagoas. Jan 1937 – 1,5,6 – bl Biblioteca [072]

ALMANAQUE FILIPINO I GUIA DE FORASTEROS PARA EL ANO DE... – Manila: Impr de D Jose Maria Dayot por Tomas Oliva, [1835?-] – 1r – 1 – us Res Libr [950]

AL-MANAR – Cairo. 1897-1935 – 1 – 35.00r – us Hoover Inst Photo [260]

Almani, Muhammad Abdullah *see* CULTURAL POLICY IN THE KINGDOM OF SAUDI ARABIA

Almanzi, J *see* HIGGAYON BE-KHINNOR

Almaraz. Ayuntamiento *see* FIESTAS DE SAN ROQUE EN ALMARAZ 1980

AL-MAWAKIB – (Missing Mujallad 9 nos 9-12) – Mujallad 9, nos 5-6-Mujallad 11, nos 3-4 – $65.00 – us MEDOC [470]

AL-MAWAKIB – (Missing v9, Nos. 1-4, 9-12) – Nazareth: 1984-. Mujallad 1-11 (Jan 1984-Dec 1994) – 9 – $265.00 – us MEDOC [956]

AL-MAYDAN : JOURNAL SOCIAL, ECONOMIQUE ET POLITIQUE ALGERIAN – Constantine. n1-28. juil 1937-mars 1938. mq n1,10,13,15,17 – 1 – fr A.C.R.P.P. [073]

Almeida, Ferrand Pimentel d' *see* O SENTIMENTO DA NATUREZA NO FAUSTO DE GOETHE

Almeida, Jose Americo de *see*
- A PARAHYBA E SEUS PROBLEMAS

Almeida Santos, J *see* CONTRIBUICAO PARA E BIBLIOGRAFIA DAS LINGUAS "BANTU" DE ANGOLA

Almeida, W B d' *see* LIFE IN JAVA

Almendralejo *see*
- FERIA DE AGOSTO, 1927
- FERIAS Y FIESTAS. AGOSTO DE 1945
- PADRON GENERAL DEL ANO 1897
- REVISTA DE FERIAS, 1943. FESTIVIDAD DE NUESTRA SENORA DE LA PIEDAD

ALMENDRALEJO ASOCIACION DE ADORADORES DE JESUS SACRAMENTADO Y PRACTICAS RELIGIOSAS / Canciones – Almendralejo: Luciano Carballar, 1901 – 1 – sp Bibl Santa Ana [240]

Almendralejo. Ayuntamiento *see*
- FERIA DE LAS MERCEDES EN ALMENDRALEJO
- FERIA DE LAS MERCEDES EN ALMENDRALEJO DE 1913. CONCURSO DE GANADERIA

Almendralejo. El Obrero Extremeno *see* REGLAMENTO DE LA SOCIEDAD COOPERATIVA Y DE SOCORROS MUTUOS. EL OBRERO EXTREMENO. ALMENDRALEJO

ALMENDRALEJO. FERIAS Y FIESTAS 1942. NUESTRA SENORA DE LA PIEDAD – 1 – sp Bibl Santa Ana [946]

Almendralejo, Pedro de *see* ESCUDO DE LAS INDULGENCIAS DE LA RELIGION...DE S. FRANCISCO

Almendralejo. Spain *see*
- ESTATUTOS DE LA COFRADIA DEL SANTISIMO SACRAMENTO
- REGLAMENTO DE GUARDAS DE LA COMUNIDAD DE LABRADORES DE ALMENDRALEJO

Almendrallucas, Bernardo *see* DOCTRINAS SOCIALES, SUPERADAS POR...

Almeras, Henri d' *see* LA FEMME AMOUREUSE DANS LA VIE ET DANS LA LITTERATURE

ALMIRANTE – Dores da Boa Esperanca, 13 Feb-6, 13 Mar 1898 – 1,5,6 – bl Biblioteca [072]

EL ALMIRANTE DE CASTILLA HASTA LAS CAPITULACIONES DE SANTA FE. SEVILLA, 1944 / Perez Embrid, Florentino – Madrid: Razon y Fe, 1946 – 1 – sp Bibl Santa Ana [946]

AL-MISBAH – Oran. n1-34. juin 1904-fevr 1905 – 1 – fr A.C.R.P.P. [073]

AL-MITHAQ – (March 1980-July 1982: weekly; August 1982-July 1984: twice a week; August 1984-August 1986: daily. Ceased) – Jerusalem, 1980-1986 – 12r – 1 – J-93-10/3 – ne IDC [072]

AL-MI'YAR : GARIDA ADABIYA INTIQADIYA FUKAHIYA – Alger. n1-9. dec 1932-avr 1933 – 1 – fr A.C.R.P.P. [073]

AL-MOAYAD – Cairo. Nov 19 1907-Apr 1914 – 1 – us NY Public [073]

ALMOFADINHA – Manaos, Amazonas. 2 Jan 1922 – 1,5,6 – bl Biblioteca [072]

AL-MOGHREB AL-AKSA : TANGIER GAZETTE – Tangier, Morocco. 2 Jan 1897-28 May 1940; 27 May 1949-26 Aug 1960 – 21r – 1 – uk British Libr Newspaper [072]

Almoharin. Sociedad Mutua de Criadores de Ganado Vacuno *see* REGLAMENTO DE LA SOCIEDAD MUTUA DE CRIADORES DE GANADO VACUNO

Almon, John *see* A REVIEW OF THE REIGN OF GEORGE 2

Almond, Nina *see* THE TREATY OF ST GERMAIN

Almondbury. Yorkshire. All Hallows *see* PARISH REGISTERS

ALMONER : A PERIODICAL RELIGIOUS PUBLICATION – (Ceased publ) – Lexington. v1. apr 1814-may 1815 – 1 – D3538 – us UMI [240]

AL-MONTADA : CHRISTIAN NEWS BULLETIN – (Some pgs lacking) – nos 1-118. Apr 1967-85 – 3r – 1 – ATLA S0175 – us A.T.L.A. [240]

ALMONTE GAZETTE – (1979-1992.-15r) – Almonte, 1993 – 1r – 1 – cn Preston [971]

THE ALMOST CHRISTIAN DISCOVERED : OR, THE FALSE PROFESSOR TRIED AND CAST / Mead, Matthew – New York: Lewis Colby, 1850 – 1mf – 9 – 0-8370-7169-0 – 1986-1169 – us A.T.L.A. [240]

O ALMOTACE : PERIODICO LOCAL, CRITICO-DESPERTANTE – Cachoeira-BA, Brazil. 14 Dez 1850-12 Ago 1851 – 1 – bl Biblioteca [072]

Almqvist, S *see* OM DE SKANDINAVISKA ARTENA AF LAFSLAGTENA SCHISMATOMMA, OPEGRAPHA OCH BACTROSPORA

AL-MUBASSIR – (Arabic text. Bilingual: 1859-1861) – Alger, sept 1847-70, 1912-26 – 1 – fr A.C.R.P.P. [073]

Al-Muhailani, Abdul-Rahman S *see* THE INFLUENCE OF PHYSICAL CONDITIONING AND DECONDITIONING UPON CARDIAC STRUCTURE OF MALES AND FEMALES

AL-MUNTAHAB : EL-MOUNTAKHEB. JOURNAL DONNANT DES NOUVELLES DE L'ALGERIE ET DE L'ETRANGER SUR LA SITUATION ARABE – Alger. n1-40. avr 1882-janv 1883 – 1 – fr A.C.R.P.P. [073]

AL-MUQTABAS – Damascus, 1906-1911. V.1-6 – 52mf – 9 – NE-20327/1 – ne IDC [073]

AL'MUQTATAF – Cairo. 1876-Dec. 1952; Vol. 1, no. 1- Vol. 121, no. 5. Missing: scattered issues – 1 – 35.00r – us Hoover Inst Photo [072]

AL-MUSAWWAR – (Egypt), 1925- – 52mf per yr – 9 – $300.00y – us Ross [072]

AL-MUSHIR – (Lacking some pgs) – 1970-93 – 8r – 1 – ATLA S0735 – us A.T.L.A. [260]

AL-MUSTAQBAL – Paris. n1-151. mars 1916-19 – 1 – fr A.C.R.P.P. [073]

ALMUTH: THE MESSIANIC ENIGMA OF THE XLIX PSALM / Blackwood, James Stevenson – London: James Nisbet, 1880. 1 fiche – 9 – us A.T.L.A. [240]

AL-MUWATIN – Baghdad, [jun 6-aug 1962] – us Res Libr [072]

AL-NAGAH – Constantine, mai 1923-sept 1956 – 1 – fr A.C.R.P.P. [073]

AL-NAHAR – (Missing 1986(26); 1987(289); 1988(April 6, 12, 29-30; June 24, 29); 1989-1990; 1991(1403, 1443, 1459, 1576, 1619, 1679, 1683)) – Jerusalem, 1986(March)-1991 – 12r – 1 – J-93-11/3 – ne IDC [072]

AL-NAHLA – Beyrouth. n1. mai 1870 – 1 – fr A.C.R.P.P. [073]

AL-NIBRAS – Beirut, 1909-1910. V.1-2 – 10mf – 9 – NE-20334/1 – ne IDC [073]

AL-NOUR – [Egypt], 1981- – 52mf per yr – 9 – $300.00y – us Ross [072]

ALNWICK AND COUNTY GAZETTE – (Also known as: Northumberland Gazette) – 1889; 1909; 1912; 1950; 1965-68; 1993-Jun 1997 – 30 1/2r – 1 – uk British Libr Newspaper [072]

A.L.O.C. *see* THE STORY OF A DARK PLOT

ALOCUCION A LOS ACTORES ARGENTINOS. MANUSCRITO / Garcia Lorca, Federico – 1mf – 9 – sp Cultura [850]

Aloe, Carlos *see*
- BUENOS AIRES CON PERON
- DIA DE LA RECONQUISTA
- LA REVOLUCION SOCIAL ARGENTINA

ALOG : ARMY LOGISTICIAN – (Cont & cont by: Army Logistician) – Fort Lee. v16. sep 1984-apr 1987 – 1,5,9 – D5713.01 – us UMI [355]

ALOHA NEWS – Aloha, OR. -w. 19 Mar 1927-26 Jan 1951. – 6r – 1 – us U.O. Library [071]

ALOHA TIMES – Beaverton, OR. -sw. 6 Jun 1974-23 Nov 1977+. – 5r – 1 – us U.O. Library [071]

ALONE IN THE WIDE, WIDE WORLD: A MUSICALLY ILLUSTRATED SERVICE / Andrews, J R – Toronto: W. Briggs, 1891. 02409. (Pre-1900 Canadiana) – 9 – cn C.I.H.M. [240]

ALONG THE TRAILS OF YESTERDAY / Wishek, Nina F – A story of McIntosh County. Asheley-Tribune, 1921. North Dakota Reel 2. (The Cox Library Collection) – 5 – us Americana [978]

Alonso Chacon, Joseph *see* TRADICIONES Y MEMORIAS HISTORIALES DE DON GONZALO DE STUNIGA

Alonso Cortes, Narciso *see* ESPRONCEDA. ILUSTRACIONES BIOGRAFICAS Y CRITICAS

Alonso de la Avecilla, Pablo *see* CANCIONES GUERRERAS

Alonso de Llerena *see* ORACION FUNEBRE...5 DE JULIO DE 1736

ALONSO FERNANDEZ DE BARRANTES. SU TESTAMENTO (1390) APUNTES GENEALOGICOS DE SU CASA / Ciadoncha, Marques de – Madrid: Tip. Arch., 1931. B.R.A.H. 99, pp. 225-267 – sp Bibl Santa Ana [920]

Alonso Getino, G *see* INCENDIO DE CONVENTOS EN ESPANA Y SUPRESION DE COLEGIOS Y MISIONES ESPANOLAS EN ULTRAMAR

ALONSO GOLFIN. LEYENDA / Hurtado de Mendoza, Publio – 1894 – 9 – 1.50f – sp Bibl Santa Ana [830]

Alonso, Julio *see*
- VIAS FERREAS. ASIENTO Y CONSERVACION...
- VIAS FERREAS. ASIENTO Y CONSERVACION. ATLAS

ALONSO PEREZ DE GUZMAN / Justiniano Arribas, Juan – 1896 – 9 – 1.50f – sp Bibl Santa Ana [920]

Alonso Pineiro, Armendo *see* LA DICTADURA PERONISTA

Alonso y de los Ruizes de Fontecha, J *see*
- DIEZ PRIVILEGIOS PARA MUJERES PRENADAS...CON UN DICCIONARIO MEDICO
- DISPUTATIONES MEDICAE DE ANGINORUM ...

Alonzo, S *see* IL FENOMENO STORICO DI GINEVRA

ALOR – Badajoz, 1950-1958 – 5 – sp Bibl Santa Ana [073]

Alos, J *see* PHARMACO-MEDICA DISSERTATIO DE VIPERIIS TROCHISCIS

DIE ALPEN / Haller, Albrecht von; ed by Betteridge, Harold T – Berlin: Akademie-Verlag, 1959 – 1r – 1 – us U.W. Library [430]

ALPENKLAENGE UND LAWINENDONNER / Waelti, C – 2. Ausg. Thun und Aarau: J J Christen, 1844 – 1r – 1 – us U.W. Library [810]

Alpenvereins Buecherei. Munich *see* KATALOGE DER ALPENVEREINS BUECHEREI

ALPENZEITUNG – Bozen, 1938, may 2-dec 31 1939, apr 25 1940-41 (incomplete) – 7r – 1 – Inquire at Mikrofilmarchiv for details – gw Misc Inst [945]

Alpers, Wilhelm *see* DIE HELDENBRAUT

Alpert, Benjamin M *see*
- OUTLINE OF NEW YORK CRIMINAL LAW
- OUTLINE OF THE LAW OF PRIVATE CORPORATIONS.

DES ALPES AU NIGER : SOUVENIR D'UN MARSOUIN (1868-1891) / Descastes, Francois – Paris: F Juven, 1898 – 1 – us Res Libr [910]

THE ALPHA – Arthabaska, Canada. v7 n46. 13 oct 1887; v33 n2. 31 dec 1914 – 1r – 1 – Can$25.00 – cn Can Microfilming [072]

ALPHA 94 : LITERACY AND CULTURAL DEVELOPMENT STRATEGIES IN RURAL AREAS / ed by Hautecœur, Jean-Paul – 1995 – 348p – 9 – 92-820-1067-8 – Co-publ with Culture Concepts/UNESCO-UIE – fr UNESCO [370]

Alpha Gold Mining Company *see* PROSPECTUS, REPORTS AND STATISTICS.

ALPHA KAPPA DELTAN – (Cont by: Sociological Inquiry) – Austin. v1-30. 1930-60* – 1 – D12945 – us UMI [073]

Alpha Micro Users Society *see* AMUS NEWSLETTER

ALPHA MICRO USERS SOCIETY (AMUS) NEWSLETTER *see* AMUS.LOG

Alpha Pyram's Publishing *see* GIFT BASKET IDEA ENCYCLOPAEDIA

ALPHABET MALGACHE POUR SERVIR D'INTRODUCTION A UNE GRAMMAIRE / Webber, R P – Ile bourbon, Notre Dame de la Ressource. 1852 – 9 – $5.00 – fr Orientalistes [490]

ALPHABET MANTCHOU, REDIGE D'APRES LE SYLLABAIRE ET LE DICTIONNAIRE UNIVERSEL DE CETTE LANGUE / Langles, L – Ed. 3. Paris. 1807. BU-500 2 – 5mf – 8 – ne IDC [490]

AN ALPHABETICAL AND CHRONOLOGICAL ARRANGEMENT OF THE WESLEYAN METHODIST MINISTERS AND PREACHERS ON TRIAL IN CONNEXION WITH THE BRITISH AND IRISH CONFERENCES; ...FROM THE COMMENCEMENT OF THEIR ITINERANCY TO...1900; ... / Hill, W; ed by Waller, D J – 19th ed. London, 1900. x/262p – 3mf – 9 – ne IDC [240]

AN ALPHABETICAL AND CHRONOLOGICAL ARRANGEMENT OF THE WESLEYAN METHODIST MINISTERS AND PREACHERS ON TRIAL IN CONNEXION WITH THE BRITISH AND IRISH CONFERENCES; ...FROM THE COMMENCEMENT OF THEIR ITINERANCY TO...1912; ... / Hill, W; ed by Triggs, A – 22nd ed. London, 1912. xiii/317p – 3mf – 9 – ne IDC [240]

AN ALPHABETICAL AND CHRONOLOGICAL ARRANGEMENT OF THE WESLEYAN METHODIST MINISTERS AND PREACHERS ON TRIAL IN CONNEXION WITH THE BRITISH AND IRISH CONFERENCES; ...FROM THE COMMENCEMENT OF THEIR ITINERANCY TO...1916; ... / Hill, W; ed by Triggs, A – 23rd ed. London, 1916. xvi/328p – 4mf – 9 – ne IDC [240]

ALPHABETICAL AND CHRONOLOGICAL ARRANGEMENTS OF THE WESLEYAN METHODIST MINISTERS AND PROBATIONERS IN CONNEXION WITH THE BRITISH AND IRISH CONFERENCES; ...FROM THE COMMENCEMENT OF THEIR ITINERANCY TO...1922 / Hill, W; ed by Triggs, A – 24th ed. London, 1922. xvi/325p – 4mf – 9 – ne IDC [240]

AN ALPHABETICAL ARRANGEMENT : A SUPPLEMENT TO HILL'S ALPHABETICAL ARRANGEMENT OF THE WESLEYAN-METHODIST PREACHERS AND MISSIONARIES BELONGING TO THE BRITISH CONFERENCE;...FROM THE YEAR 1826 TO 1832;... / Hill, W – London, 1833. [2], 96p – 2mf – 9 – ne IDC [240]

AN ALPHABETICAL ARRANGEMENT OF ALL THE WESLEYAN METHODIST MINISTERS AND PREACHERS ON TRIAL IN CONNEXION WITH THE BRITISH AND IRISH CONFERENCES; ...FROM THE COMMENCEMENT OF THEIR ITINERANCY TO...1892; ... / Hill, W; ed by Waller, D J – 17th ed. London, 1892. xi/213p – 3mf – 9 – ne IDC [240]

AN ALPHABETICAL ARRANGEMENT OF ALL THE WESLEYAN METHODIST MINISTERS AND PREACHERS ON TRIAL IN CONNEXION WITH THE BRITISH AND IRISH CONFERENCES; ...FROM THE COMMENCEMENT OF THEIR ITINERANCY TO...1896; ... / Hill, W; ed by Waller, D J – 18th ed. London, 1896. xxxvi/228p – 3mf – 9 – ne IDC [240]

AN ALPHABETICAL ARRANGEMENT OF ALL THE WESLEYAN METHODIST PREACHERS AND MISSIONARIES, WHO ARE NOW TRAVELLING IN GREAT-BRITAIN AND IN DISTANT PARTS OF THE GLOBE,... / Hill, W – Bradford, 1819 – 2mf – 9 – ne IDC [240]

AN ALPHABETICAL ARRANGEMENT OF ALL THE WESLEYAN-METHODIST MINISTERS AND PREACHERS ON TRIAL, IN CONNECTION WITH THE BRITISH AND IRISH CONFERENCES : WITH SEVERAL OF THE MINISTERS OF THE AFFILIATED CONFERENCES...FROM THE COMMENCEMENT OF THEIR ITINERANCY TO...1869 / Hill, W; ed by Osborn, M C – 11th ed. London, 1869. [4], 224p – 3mf – 9 – ne IDC [240]

AN ALPHABETICAL ARRANGEMENT OF ALL THE WESLEYAN-METHODIST MINISTERS, AND PREACHERS ON TRIAL, IN CONNECTION WITH THE BRITISH AND IRISH CONFERENCES : WITH SEVERAL OF THE MINISTERS OF THE AFFILIATED CONFERENCES OF FRANCE AND AUSTRALASIA...FROM THE COMMENCEMENT OF THEIR ITINERANCY TO...1877 / Hill, W; ed by Osborn, M C – 13th ed. London, 1878. [5], 247p – 3mf – 9 – ne IDC [240]

AN ALPHABETICAL ARRANGEMENT OF ALL THE WESLEYAN-METHODIST MINISTERS, AND PREACHERS ON TRIAL, IN CONNECTION WITH THE BRITISH AND IRISH CONFERENCES; : WITH SEVERAL OF THE MINISTERS OF THE AFFILIATED CONFERENCES OF FRANCE AND AUSTRALASIA...FROM THE COMMENCEMENT OF THEIR ITINERANCY TO...1873 / Hill, W; ed by Osborn, M C – 12th ed. London, 1874. [4], 221p – 3mf – 9 – ne IDC [240]

AN ALPHABETICAL ARRANGEMENT OF ALL THE WESLEYAN-METHODIST MINISTERS, MISSIONARIES AND PREACHERS ON TRIAL, IN CONNEXION WITH THE BRITISH AND IRISH CONFERENCES : WITH SEVERAL OF THE MINISTERS OF THE AFFILIATED CONFERENCES OF FRANCE, AUSTRALASIA, CANADA AND EASTERN BRITISH AMERICA; ...FROM THE COMMENCEMENT OF THEIR ITINERANCY TO...1865 / Hill, W; ed by Haswell, J P – 10th ed. London, 1866. iv/207p – 3mf – 9 – ne IDC [240]

AN ALPHABETICAL ARRANGEMENT OF ALL THE WESLEYAN-METHODIST MINISTERS, MISSIONARIES AND PREACHERS ON TRIAL IN CONNEXION WITH THE BRITISH AND IRISH CONFERENCES OR WITH THE AFFILIATED CONFERENCES : FRANCE, AUSTRALASIA AND EASTERN BRITISH AMERICA...FROM THE COMMENCEMENT OF THEIR ITINERANCY TO...1857 / Hill, W; ed by Haswell, J P – 8th ed. London, 1858. iv/180p – 2mf – 9 – ne IDC [240]

AN ALPHABETICAL ARRANGEMENT OF ALL THE WESLEYAN-METHODIST MINISTERS, MISSIONARIES AND PREACHERS ON TRIAL IN CONNEXION WITH THE BRITISH AND IRISH CONFERENCES;...FROM THE COMMENCEMENT OF THEIR ITINERANCY TO...1846 / Hill, W; ed by Haswell, J P – 6th ed. London, 1847. [3], 230p – 3mf – 9 – ne IDC [240]

AN ALPHABETICAL ARRANGEMENT OF ALL THE WESLEYAN-METHODIST MINISTERS, MISSIONARIES AND PREACHERS ON TRIAL IN CONNEXION WITH THE BRITISH AND IRISH CONFERENCES;...FROM THE COMMENCEMENT OF THEIR ITINERANCY TO...1852 / Hill, W; ed by Haswell, J P – 7th ed. London, 1853. [3], 249p – 9 – ne IDC [240]

AN ALPHABETICAL ARRANGEMENT OF ALL THE WESLEYAN-METHODIST PREACHERS AND MISSIONARIES IN CONNEXION WITH THE BRITISH AND IRISH CONFERENCES;... FROM THE COMMENCEMENT OF THEIR ITINERANCY TO...1837 / Hill, W – 4th ed. London, 1838. [3], 152p – 2mf – 9 – ne IDC [240]

AN ALPHABETICAL ARRANGEMENT OF ALL THE WESLEYAN-METHODIST PREACHERS AND MISSIONARIES IN CONNEXION WITH THE BRITISH AND IRISH CONFERENCES;... FROM THE COMMENCEMENT OF THEIR ITINERANCY TO...1840 / Hill, W – 5th ed. London, 1841. [3], 219p – 3mf – 9 – ne IDC [240]

AN ALPHABETICAL ARRANGEMENT OF ALL THE WESLEYAN-METHODIST PREACHERS AND MISSIONARIES, WHO ARE NOW TRAVELLING IN GREAT-BRITAIN AND IN DISTANT PARTS OF THE GLOBE,... / Hill, W – Bradford, 1819. [4], 112p – 2mf – 9 – ne IDC [240]

AN ALPHABETICAL ARRANGEMENT OF ALL THE WESLEYAN-METHODIST PREACHERS AND MISSIONARIES WHO ARE NOW TRAVELLING, OR ARE LOCATED, IN GREAT BRITAIN, AND IN DISTANT PARTS OF THE GLOBE,... / Hill, W – 3rd ed. London, 1827. 166p – 2mf – 9 – ne IDC [240]

ALPHABETICAL CARD NAME INDEXES TO THE COMPILED SERVICE RECORDS OF VOLUNTEER SOLDIERS WHO SERVED IN UNION ORGANIZATIONS NOT RAISED BY STATES OR TERRITORIES, EXCEPTING THE VETERANS RESERVE CORPS AND THE U.S. COLORED TROOPS – 36r – 1 – M1290 – us Nat'l Archives [976]

ALPHABETICAL CATALOG / Johann Gottfried Herder Institute. Marburg-Lahn. Library – (First Suppl., 1971.-38,500 cards 4 reels. $235.00 ISBN: 0-8161-1399-8) – 1 – uk Hall [010]

ALPHABETICAL CATALOGUE OF THE LIBRARY OF THE HON. THE LEGISLATIVE COUNCIL OF CANADA: AUTHORS AND SUBJECTS / Canada. Parliament. Legislative Council. Library – Montreal: Printed by James Starkes and Co, 1845. SEM105P156 – 3mf – 9 – Can$6.75 – cn Bibl Nat [340]

ALPHABETICAL CATALOGUES / Jewish National and University Library. Jerusalem – 3597mf – 9 – J-10-16/1-J-10-20/1 – ne IDC [020]

AN ALPHABETICAL INDEX OF THE CODE OF CIVIL PROCEDURE OF LOWER CANADA / Coutlee, Louis William (1851-1917) – Montreal: Dawson Bros.., 1870. SEM105P47 – 1mf – 9 – Can$2.25 – cn Bibl Nat [340]

ALPHABETICAL INDEX TO CANADIAN BORDER ENTRIES THROUGH SMALL PORTS IN VERMONT, 1895-1924 – 6r – 1 – M1462 – us Nat'l Archives [340]

ALPHABETICAL INDEX TO REGISTER OF BRITISH SHIPS, 1948- / Collector of Customs, Sydney – A-Z Aimee – Zonda – 1 – CRS C5 – at Archives [920]

AN ALPHABETICAL INDEX TO THE NEW TESTAMENT – Philadelphia: American Sunday School Union, 1868. 1 fiche – 9 – us A.T.L.A. [240]

ALPHABETICAL LIST OF MERCHANTS, TRADERS AND HOUSEKEEPERS RESIDING IN MONTREAL / Doige, Thomas – Montreal, Canada. 1819 – 1r – 1 – Can$25.00 – cn Can Microfilming [910]

ALPHABETICAL LIST OF THE BOMBAY CIVIL SERVANTS, 1798-1839 / Dodwell & Miles – London. 1839. BI-337 2 – 8 – ne IDC [950]

AN ALPHABETICAL LIST OF THE FEASTS AND HOLIDAYS OF THE HINDUS AND MUHAMMADANS / Imperial Record Dept. India – Calcutta: Superintendent of Govt Printing, 1914 – us Res Libr [230]

ALPHABETICAL LIST OF THE MADRAS CIVIL SERVANTS, 1780-1838 / Dodwell & Miles – London. 1839. BI-338 2 – 8 – ne IDC [950]

ALPHABETICAL LIST OF THE OFFICERS OF THE INDIAN ARMY, 1760-1837 / Dodwell & Miles – London. 1838. BI-339 2 – 8 – ne IDC [920]

ALPHABETICAL RECORD: ENGINEERS AND SUPERINTENDENTS, ETC., AND THE PRINCIPAL PUBLIC WORKS ON WHICH THEY HAVE REPORTED OR BEEN EMPLOYED: CANADA, 1779 TO 1891 / Baillairge, George F – 1891?. 02219. (Pre-1900 Canadiana) – 9 – cn C.I.H.M. [920]

ALPHABETICAL ROLL OF WESTERN AUSTRALIAN CONTINGENTS IN SOUTH AFRICA, 1900-1903 – 3r – 1 – CRS B5165 – at Archives [920]

ALPHABETISCHER KATALOG / Institut fuer Zeitgeschichte. Muenchen.Bibliothek – (First suppl., 1973.-2reels. $155.00 ISBN: 0-8161-1404-8) – 1 – uk Hall [900]

ALPHABETISCHER KATALOG... – (See KATALOG, ALPHABETISCHER...) – gw Olms [020]

ALPHABETISCHER KATALOG DER BIBLIOTHEK DES JOHANN-GOTTFRIED-HERDER-INSTITUTS = ALPHABETICAL CATALOG OF THE LIBRARY OF THE JOHANN GOTTFRIED HERDER INSTITUTE / Johann-Gottfried-Herder-Institut. Marburg/Lahn, Germany – (First Supplement, 1971. 38,500 cards. 4 reels. $215.00 export $260.00. – ISBN 0-8161-1339-8) – uk Hall [014]

ALPHABETISCHER MUSIKALIENKATALOG DER PFAELZISCHEN LANDESBIBLIOTHEK SPEYER – 1991 – 55mf (1:42) – 9 – diazo DM2,400 – 3-598-33195-9 – gw Saur [780]

ALPHABETISCHES VERZEICHNIS ALLER BEKANNTEN FREIMAURER LOGEN... – Leipzig, 1778 – 2mf – ne IDC [360]

ALPHABETISCHES VERZEICHNIS ALLER IN BOISDUVAL'S SYSTEM DER EUROPAEISCHEN SCHMETTERLINGE / Fehr, J G – Erlangen, [1842] – 38p – ne IDC [590]

ALPHABETUM ARMENUM CUM ORIATIONE DOMINICALI... / Amaduzzi, J-C – Romae, 1784 – 1mf – ne IDC [460]

ALPHABETVM ARABICVM – Romae, 1592 – 1mf – 9 – H-8221/1 – ne IDC [470]

ALPHONSE DESJARDINS / Vaillancourt, Cyrille – Levis: Le Quotidien, 1950. SEM16P215 – 1r – 5 – Can$9.00 – cn Bibl Nat [336]

Alphonse, Francois J-B d' *see* MEMOIRE STATISTIQUE DU DEPARTEMENT DE L'INDRE

Alphonsus, Joao *see* ROLA-MOCA

ALPINE CHRONICLE – Silver Mountain, CA. 1870-1872 – 1r – 1 – $50.00 – C03653 – us Library Micro [071]

ALPINE ENTERPRISE – Markleeville, CA, NV. 1979 – 4+ r – 1 – $200.00 ($90.00y) – B03613 – us Library Micro [071]

ALPINE OBSERVER – 1921-1928 – 2mf – 9 – at Corangamite [980]

ALPINE POST – St Moritz, Switzerland. 29 Oct 1892-30 Mar 1901 – 9r – 1 – uk British Libr Newspaper [072]

THE ALPS, SWITZERLAND, AND THE NORTH OF ITALY / Williams, Charles – London: J. Cassell, 1854. viii,633p. map. illus – 1 – us U.W. Library [949]

AL-QANUN FI AL-TIBB. A SYSTEM OF MEDICINE, AND OTHER WORKS / Husain ibn 'abd (Abu 'Ali) – (In Arabic) – Typographic Medicea. Rome. 3pts. 1593 – 19mf – 9 – H-8435/1 – ne IDC [610]

AL-RA'ID AL-RASMI. / Tunisia – (1978-. ca $40.00y) – 1970-77 – 12r – 1 – $240.00; outside North America add $1.25r – us L of C Photodup [324]

AL-RAJA – Paris, mars-nov 1895, nov 1898-mai 1899 – 1 – fr A.C.R.P.P. [073]

ALRAUNE : DIE GESCHICHTE EINES LEBENDEN WESENS / Ewers, Hanns Heinz – Berlin: Sieben Staebe-Verlags- und Druckereigesellschaft m.b.h., 1928. 439,(3)p – 1 – us U.W. Library [830]

ALRAUNENMAEREN / List, Guido – 1903 – 1 – us I.U. Libraries [390]

ALRESFORD : ESSAYS FOR THE TIMES / Newnham, William Orde – London: Longmans, Green, 1891 – 1mf – 9 – 0-8370-3928-2 – 1985-1928 – us A.T.L.A. [240]

AL-RIYADH – al-Riyadh, Saudi Arabia: Muassasat al-Yamamah al-Sahafiyah, [1972-74]; [1977-78]; [1979-] – us Res Libr [072]

ALS ESKIMO UNTER DEN ESKIMOS / Klutschak, H W – BN 283 2. 1881 – 8 – ne IDC [306]

ALS ICH JUNG NOCH WAR : NEUE GESCHICHTEN AUS DER WALDHEIMAT / Rosegger, Peter – Leipzig: L Staackmann, 1895 – 1r – 1 – us U.W. Library [920]

ALS LANDRAT IN OSTPREUSSEN : RAGNIT-ALLENSTEIN / Pauly, Walter – Wuerzburg: Holzner-Verlag, 1957 – 10r – 1 – us U.W. Library [350]

ALS OESTERREICH ZERFIEL / Bartsch, Rudolf Hans – Wien: C W Stern, 1905 – 1r – 1 – us U.W. Library [830]

ALS SCHRIFTSTELLER LEBEN : GESPRAECHE MIT PETER HANDKE, FRANZ XAVER KROETZ, GERHARD ZWERENZ, WALTER JENS, PETER RUEHMKORF, GUENTER GRASS / Arnold, Heinz Ludwig – Reinbek bei Hamburg: Rowohlt, 1979 – 1r – 1 – us U.W. Library [430]

ALSA FORUM *see* LEGAL STUDIES FORUM

L'ALSACE EN 1789: TABLEAU DES DIVISIONS TERRITORIALES ET DES DIFFERENTES SEIGNEURIES D'ALSACE / Heitz, Frederic Charles – Strasbourg, 3rd ed 1860 – 1mf – 9 – F30.00 – fr F.F.G. [944]

L'ALSACE LIBERE – Strasbourg, France. 29 Nov 1944-31 Dec 1945 (imperfect) – 1r – 1 – uk British Libr Newspaper [072]

L'ALSACE NOBLE / Lehr – Paris, 1870. 3v – 5mf – 9 – F150.00 – fr F.F.G. [920]

L'ALSACIEN – Strasbourg. 1848-avr 1849 – 1 – fr A.C.R.P.P. [073]

AL-SA'IH – (Available: 1930, V.18(216-224); V.19(1-5)) – New York – 9mf – 9 – NE-20332/1 – ne IDC [073]

ALSBACHER, MOSES, DOCUMENT, MSS V.F. A – 1839 – 1r – 1 – us Western Res [978]

ALSC NEWSLETTER – (Association for Library Service to Children). v1- 1978- – 1,5,6,9 – us UMI [073]

Alsdorf, Ludwig *see* DEUTSCH-INDISCHE GEISTESBEZIEHUNGEN

AL-SEYASA AL DAWLIA – 1965-1995 – 6 times per yr – 1 – F618.00 – sz Infoprint [072]

AL-SHA'B – Cairo, Egypt. May 1 1979-1991 – 8r – 1 – us L of C Photodup [072]

AL-SHAB – Jerusalem, 1972(July)-1992 – 57r – 1 – J-93-6/3 – ne IDC [072]

AL-SHARQ / Majallah shahriyah ta ni bi-Shu"un al-Adab wa-al-Fann wa-al-Fikr – Jerusalem: Tasdur 'an Sahifat al-Anba'. al-Sanah 2, Adad al-Awwal-al-Sanah 23, al-Adad al-Rabi, June 1971-Nov/Dec 1993) – 9 – $700.00 – us MEDOC [956]

AL-SHARQ – Sanah 22, 'Adad l-Sanah 23, 'Adad 4 (Jan/Mar 1992-Nov/Dec 1993) – $200.00 – us MEDOC [470]

Al'shits, D N *see* ISTORICHESKAIA KOLLEKTSIA ERMITAZHNOGO SOBRANIIA RUKOPISEI

Alsinet, J *see*
- NUEVAS UTILIDADES DE LA QUINA
- NUEVO METODO PARA CURAR FLATOS, HIPOCONDRIAS, VAPORES Y ATAQUES HYSTERICOS...

ALSINO, NOVELA / Prado, Pedro – 2nd ed. Santiago, Chile: Nascimento, 1928. 4,leaf,(11)-302p – 1 – us U.W. Library [830]

AL-SIYASI – Cairo, Egypt. May 15 1977-1979; July 27 1980-Nov 1987; Jan 1988-1991 – 15r – 1 – us L of C Photodup [072]

AL-SIYASSA AL-DAWLIYA – [Egypt], 1965- – 1 – $300.00y – us Ross [072]

Alskii, M *see* NASHI FINANSY ZA VREMIA GRAZHDANSKOI VOINY I NEPA

ALSOGRAPHIA AMERICANA / Rafinesque-Schmaltz, Constantine S – 7608 2. 1838 – 8 – ne IDC [580]

ALSOGRAPHIA AMERICANA / Rafinesque-Schmaltz, Constantine S – Philadelphia. 1838; continuation of Sylva Telluriana, see I. D. C. nr. 8117. B-8092 1 – 9 – ne IDC [580]

Alston, Leonard *see*
- MODERN CONSTITUTIONS IN OUTLINE
- STOIC AND CHRISTIAN IN THE SECOND CENTURY
- THE WHITE MAN'S WORK IN ASIA AND AFRICA

Alston, R C *see*
- ENGLISH LINGUISTICS, 1500-1800
- LINGUISTICS SPECIALIST COLLECTION
- THE NINETEENTH CENTURY LITERATURE SPECIALIST COLLECTION
- PUBLISHING, THE BOOKTRADE AND THE DIFFUSION OF KNOWLEDGE SPECIALIST COLLECTION

AL-SUDAN AL-HADITH – Khartoum, Sudan. Aug 1989-1990 – 4r – 1 – us L of C Photodup [072]

Alt, Axel *see* DER TOD FUHR IM ZUG

EIN ALT CHRISTLICH CONCILIUM FUR 1200 JAREN ZU GANGRA JNN PAPHLAGONIA GEHALTEN / Kymeus, J – Item ein alt wunderbarliche Geschicht vnd auffrhur. von denen die Christum an Jueden vnd Heiden rechen wolten. Mit einer vorrhede M. Lutheri. Wittemberg, J. Klug. 1537. BME-96 – 9 – ne IDC [240]

Alt, Karl Hermann *see* GOETHE UND SEINE ZEIT

ALTA ADVOCATE – (Comic Section only: 1932-1938 1r $50.00) – Alta, CA. 1897-1906; 1907; 1932-1937; 1963-1964 – 15r – 1 – $750.00 – C03727 – us Library Micro [071]

ALTA CALIFORNIA – Alta, Calif. 1849-91 – 1 – us UMI [071]

ALTA CALIFORNIA – (Cont: California Star) – San Francisco, CA. 1849-91 – 138r – 1 – $6,900.00 – C02787 – us Library Micro [071]

ALTA CALIFORNIA *see* CALIFORNIA STAR

Alta Comision Interamericana *see* REGIMEN JURIDICO DE LAS SOCIEDAS ANONIMAS EXTRANJERAS...

Alta Comision Internacional *see*
- ESTUDIO SOBRE UNE LEGISLACION UNIFORME EN MATERIA DE LETRAS DE CAMBIO...
- INFORME PRELIMINAR SOBRE LA UNIFICACION DEL DERECHO RELATIVO AL CHEQUE

ALTA EXTREMADURA : CARNESTOLENDAS / Gutierrez Macias, Valeriano – Badajoz: Imp. Dip. Provincial, 1968 – sp Bibl Santa Ana [946]

ALTA FREQUENZA – (All that is currently available) – Milano. v45-51. jan 1976-dec 1982 – 1*,5,9* – D2021 – us UMI [073]

ALTADENA : THE WEEKLY – (Also known as: The Altadena Press, Altadena Chronicle, Pasadena: The Weekly) – Altadena, CA. 1929-1930; 1930-1935; 1936-1937; 1938-1952; 1955-1974; 1976-1980; 1982-1986 – 43r – 1 – $2,150.00 – H03134 – us Library Micro [071]

ALTADENA CHRONICLE *see* ALTADENA

ALTADENA PRESS *see* ALTADENA

ALTAEGYPTISCHE TEMPELINSCHRIFTEN IN DEN JAHREN 1863-1865 AN ORT UND STELLEN GESAMMELT / Duemichen, J – Leipzig, 1867. BNE-369 1 – 9 – ne IDC [410]

ALTAISKII KRESTIANIN – (Missing: 1916: v32; 1917: v7-12, 17, 24-25, 27, 44, 46-48) – Barnaul, 1912-18 – 96mf – 9 – COR-545/1 – ne IDC [334]

Altamira, Rafael *see* TECNICA DE INVESTIGACION...

Altaner, Bruno *see*
- DIETRICH VON BERN IN DER NEUEREN LITERATUR
- DIE DOMINIKANERMISSIONEN DES 13 JAHRHUNDERTS
- KLEINE SCHRIFTEN (T.U.U. 5-83)
- SPRACHKENNTNISSE UND DOLMETSCHERWESEN IM MISSIONARISCHEN UND DIPLOMATISCHEN VERKEHR ZWISCHEN ABENDLAND (PAEPSTLICHE KURIE) UND ORIENT IM 13 UND 14 JH

THE ALTAR AND THE THRONE – Montreal, Canada. v1 n3. 1 mar 1871-v1 n7. 26 avr 1871 – 1r – 1 – Can$25.00 – cn Can Microfilming [072]

ALTARBUCH...ALTKATHOLIKEN – Bonn, 1959 – 6mf – 8 – Dfl3.50ea – ne Slangenburg [240]

DAS ALTARWERK ZU LAUENSTEIN UND DIE ANFAENGE DES BAROCK IN SACHSEN / Carus, Victor A – Stuttgart, 1912 – 9 – DM48.00 – 3-89349-268-2 – gw Hänsel [730]

AL-TASAWWUF AL-ISLAMI / High Council of Sufism – Sharia wa Haqiqa wa Tariqa. Cairo, 1979-1982 – 34mf – 9 – NE-20326/1 – ne IDC [260]

AL-TAWHID – (Missing: Rabi al-Thani and Jumada 'l-Ula 1394. Shawwal, Dhu 'l-Qada, and Dhu 'l-Hijja 1395, Muharram and Safar 1396, and Safar 1401) – Cairo, 1973-1981 – 54mf – 9 – NE-20324/1 – ne IDC [260]

ALTBABYLONISCHE KEILSCHRIFTTEXTE : ZUM GEBRAUCHE BEI VORLESUNGEN / ed by Winckler, Hugo – Leipzig: Eduard Pfeiffer, 1892 – 1mf – 9 – 0-8370-8635-3 – 1986-2635 – us A.T.L.A. [470]

EIN ALTBABYLONISCHER FELDERPLAN : NACH MITTHEILUNGEN VON F.V. SCHEIL / ed by Eisenlohr, August – (In German and Sumerian. Includes bibliographical references) – Leipzig: J C Hinrichs, 1896 – 1mf – 9 – 0-8370-8570-5 – 1986-2570 – us A.T.L.A. [470]

Altbrechtsberger, J G *see* TROIS SEXTUORS POUR DEUX VIOLONS, DEUX ALTOS, VIOLONCELLE ET BASSE, OP. 13, N.2

ALTBUDDHISTISCHE KULSTAETTEN IN CHINESISCH-TURKISTAN / Gruenwedel, A – Bericht ueber archaeologische Arbeiten von 1906 bis 1907 bei Kuca, Qarasahr und in der Oase Turfan. Berlin. 1912. Illus. BU-626 2 – 8 – ne IDC [930]

DIE ALTCHRISTLICHE GRABESKUNST : EIN VERSUCH DER EINHEITLICHEN AUSLEGUNG / Styger, Paul – Muenchen, 1927 – 2mf – 9 – DM62.00 – 3-89349-314-X – gw Hänsel [730]

DIE ALTCHRISTLICHE LITERATUR UND IHRE ERFORSCHUNG SEIT 1880 : ALLGEMEINE UEBERSICHT UND ERSTER LITERATURBERICHT (1880-1884) / Ehrhardt, Albert – Freiburg im Breisgau, St. Louis, Mo.: Herder, 1894 -; 240mf – us A.T.L.A. [240]

DIE ALTCHRISTLICHE LITERATUR UND IHRE ERFORSCHUNG VON 1884-1900 / Ehrhardt, Albert – Freiburg im Breisgau, St. Louis, Mo.: Herder 1900 – 2mf – us A.T.L.A. [240]

ALTCHRISTLICHE LITURGISCHE STUECKE AUS DER KIRCHE AEGYPTENS (T.U.U. 2-17/3B1) / Wobbermin, G – Leipzig, 1899 – 1mf – 9 – ne Slangenburg [240]

ALTCHRISTLICHE MALEREI UND ALTKIRCHLICHE LITERATUR : EINE UNTERSUCHUNG UEBER DEN BIBLISCHEN CYKLUS DER GEMAELDE IN DEN ROEMISCHEN KATAKOMBEN / Hennecke, Edgar – Leipzig: Veit, 1896 – 1mf – us A.T.L.A. [240]

ALTCHRISTLICHE SAGEN UEBER DAS LEBEN JESU UND DER APOSTEL / Couard, Ludwig – Guetersloh: Bertelsmann, 1909. 1 fiche – 9 – us A.T.L.A. [240]

ALTCHRISTLICHE STAEDTE UND LANDSCHAFTEN 1, KONSTANTINOPEL (324-450) / Schultze, V – Leipzig, 1913 – Dfl25.00 – ne Slangenburg [240]

ALTCHRISTLICHE TEXTE / Schubart, W & C Smith – 979 2. 1910 – 8 – ne IDC [240]

ALTCHRISTLICHE UND MODERNE GEDANKEN UEBER FRAUENBERUF : DREI AUFSAETZE / Mausbach, Joseph – M. Gladbach: Volksvereins Verlag, 1910 – 1mf – us A.T.L.A. [305]

DER ALTE ANFANG UND DIE URSPRUENGLICHE FORM VON CYPRIANS SCHRIFT AD DONATUM (T.U.U. 2-19/1C) / Goetz, KG – Leipzig, 1899 – 1mf – 9 – ne Slangenburg [240]

ALTE BEKANNTE AUS DEM NEW YORKER DEUTSCHEN VIERTEL / Stuerenburg, E – New York: E Steiger, [1886] – 1r – 1 – us U.W. Library [430]

DER ALTE FRITZ : EIN NIEDERDEUTSCHER VOLKSMYTHUS / Winckler, Josef – Stuttgart: Deutsche Verlags-Anstalt, c1934 – 1r – 1 – us U.W. Library [390]

DI ALTE HEYM = L'ANCIEN FOYER – (In Yiddish) – Paris, FR. no1. Oct 1946 – 1 – 1 – $25.00 – cn Can Microfilming [072]

ALTE HOCH- UND NIEDERDEUTSCHE VOLKSLIEDER : MIT ABHANDLUNG UND ANMERKUNGEN / ed by Uhland, Ludwig – (v1 issued in 2pts. No more publ) – Stuttgart: J G Cotta, 1844-45 – 1r – 1 – us U.W. Library [780]

DAS ALTE KOENIGREICH KONGO / Ihle, A – Leipzig. 1929. BA-318 2 – 8 – ne IDC [960]

ALTE NESTER : ZWEI BUECHER LEBENSGESCHICHTEN / Raabe, Wilhelm Karl – 2. Aufl. Berlin: O Janke, 1897 – 1r – 1 – us U.W. Library [830]

DAS ALTE TESTAMENT IM NEUEN TESTAMENT: UEBER DIE CITATE DES ALTEN TESTAMENTS IM NEUEN TESTAMENT UND UEBER DEN OPFER- UND PRIESTERBEGRIFF IM ALTEN UND NEUEN TESTAMENTE / Tholuck, August – 3. verm. Aufl. Gotha, F. A. Perthes, 1868. Film Mas 9379 – 1 – us H.U. Library [220]

DAS ALTE TESTAMENT IN PREDIGTEN UND BIBELSTUNDEN : DAS ERSTE BUCH MOSE SEINEM HEIMGANG / Schlosser, Gustav; ed by Scriba, Otto – Bielefeld:Velhagen & Klasing, 1892 – 1mf – 9 – 0-8370-5099-5 – 1985-3099 – us A.T.L.A. [220]

DER ALTE UND DER NEUE GLAUBE : EIN BEKENNTNISS ALS ANTWORT AUF DAVID FRIEDRICH STRAUSS / Weis, Ludwig – Berlin: F Henschel, 1873 – 1mf – 9 – 0-8370-7436-3 – 1986-1436 – us A.T.L.A. [230]

DER ALTE UND DER NEUE GLAUBE: EIN BEKENNTNISS / Strauss, David Friedrich – Bonn: Emil Strauss, 1874. 1 fiche – 9 – us A.T.L.A. [240]

ALTE UND MODERNE KUNST – Vienna, 1956- (mf ed 1956-75) – 6r – 1 – £345.00 – uk Chadwyck [720]

ALTE UND NEUE GEDICHTE / Huch, Ricarda – Leipzig: Insel-Verlag, [1920?] – 1r – 1 – us U.W. Library [810]

ALTE UND NEUE QUELLEN ZUR GESCHICHTE DES TAUFSYMBOLS UND DER GLAUBENSREGEL / Caspari, C P – Christiana, 1879 – 6mf – 8 – Dfl25.00 – ne Slangenburg [210]

ALTE UND NEUE QUELLEN ZUR GESCHICHTE DES TAUFSYMBOLS UND DER GLAUBENSREGEL / Caspari, C P – Christiania: Mallingsche Buch., 1879. 1 fiche – 9 – us A.T.L.A. [240]

DER ALTE WEG ZUM ALTEN GOTT : GEDANKEN UND BETRACHTUNGEN UEBER WICHTIGE FRAGEN DES CHRISTLICHEN GLAUBENS / Bruckner, Albert – Schkenditz: W Schaefer, 1903 – 1mf – 9 – 0-8370-2490-0 – 1985-0490 – us A.T.L.A. [240]

DIE ALTEN LATEINISCHEN THOMASAKTEN (T.U.U. 5-122) / Zelzer, K – 1977 – 3mf – 9 – ne Slangenburg [220]

DIE ALTEN PETRUSAKTEN IM ZUSAMMENHANG MIT DER APOKRYPHEN APOSTELLITTERATUR (T.U.U. 2-24/1) / Schmidt, Carl – Leipzig, 1903 – 3mf – 9 – ne Slangenburg [240]

DIE ALTEN UND DIE JUNGEN : DRAMATISCHES GENREBILD IN EINEM AKT / Lorm, Hieronymus – Berlin: L Kolbe, 1862 – 1 – us U.W. Library [820]

DIE ALTEN UND DIE JUNGEN : SOZIALER ROMAN / Alberti, Conrad – Leipzig: W Friedrich, [190-] – 1r – 1 – us U.W. Library [830]

DIE ALTEN UND DIE JUNGEN : SOZIALER ROMAN / Alberti, Conrad – Leipzig: W Friedrich. 2v. [190-] – 1 – us U.W. Library [830]

ALTENAER KREISBLATT – (Cont: Wochenblatt fuer den Kreis Altena und die Stadt Altena -oct 1835. Wochenblatt fuer den Kreis Altena, -1869) – Altena, oct 4 1834-apr 13 1945, oct 28-dec 31 1949, 1958-60, 1988- – 1 – Dist. gw Mikrofilm – gw Misc Inst [943]

ALTENAER KREISBLATT. AMTLICHES NACHRICHTENBLATT *see* AMTLICHES NACHRICHTENBLATT FUER DEN KREIS ALTENA

Altenberg, Peter *see*
- MEIN LEBENSABEND
- WAS DER TAG MIR ZUTRAEGT
- WIE ICH ES SEHE

DER ALTENGLISCHE REGIUS-PSALTER : EINE INTERLINEAVERSION IN HS. ROYAL 2.B.5 DES BRIT. MUS. / ed by Roeder, F – Halle, 1904 – 6mf – 8 – Dfl25.00 – ne Slangenburg [240]

Alter, J Cecil *see* STORIED DOMAIN

ALTERATIONS IN 72 KILODALTON STRESS PROTEIN LEVELS FOLLOWING ECCENTRICALLY BIASED EXERCISE / Sim, James D & Noble, Earl G – 1992 – 2mf – $8.00 – us Microform Publ [612]

DIE ALTERCATIO SIMONIS JUDAEI ET THEOPHILI CHRISTIANI UND DIE ACTA ARCHELAI UND DAS DIATERSSARON TATIANS (T.U.U. 1-1/3) / Harnack, Adolf von – Leipzig, 1883 – 3mf – 9 – ne Slangenburg [240]

ALTERN IN DER ARBEITSGESELLSCHAFT : UEBER DIE SOZIALE KONSTRUKTION DES HOEHEREN LEBENSALTERS / Huf, Stefan – 1995 – 1mf – 9 – DM60.00 – 3-8267-2129-2 – gw Hänsel [360]

L'ALTERNATIVE *see* LE COMBAT

ALTERNATIVE / Committee for Non-violent Revolution – 1-3 2+5 (all publ). 1948-51 – 1mf – 9 – $35.00 – us UPA [335]

ALTERNATIVE : AN AMERICAN SPECTATOR – (Cont: Alternative. Cont by: American Spectator) – Bloomington. v8-10. oct 1974-sep 1977 – 1 – D7782.01 – us UMI [073]

ALTERNATIVE *see* ALTERNATIVE

ALTERNATIVE – (Cont by: Alternative, an American Spectator) – Bloomington. v6-7. oct 1972-sep 1974 – 1 – D7782 – us UMI [073]

ALTERNATIVE, AN AMERICAN SPECTATOR *see* ALTERNATIVE

ALTERNATIVE DISPUTE RESOLUTION IN A BANKRUPTCY COURT : THE MEDIATION PROGRAM IN THE SOUTHERN DISTRICT OF CALIFORNIA / Hartwell, Steven & Bermant, Gordon – Washington: GPO, 1988 – 2mf – 9 – $3.00 – LLMC 95-339 – us L.L.M.C. [340]

ALTERNATIVE ENERGY SOURCES FOR THE ISRAEL ECONOMY 1973-2000 : RESEARCH STUDY REPORT: PHASE ONE / Israel. Prime Minister's Office – Jerusalem. Dec 1973. 141p. Diagr – 9 – $3.00 – is I.T.T.I. [338]

ALTERNATIVE FUTURES – v.1-. Winter 1978- – 1,5,6,9 – us UMI [300]

ALTERNATIVE FUTURES – (Ceased publ) – Tory. v1-4. Spr 1978-Sum 1981 – 1,5*,9 – D12052 – us UMI [073]

ALTERNATIVE HIGHER EDUCATION – v. 1-. 1976- – 1,5,6,9 – us UMI [370]

ALTERNATIVE HIGHER EDUCATION – (Cont by: Innovative Higher Education) – New York. v1-7. Fal 1976-Sum 1983 – 1,5*,9 – D11172 – us UMI [370]

ALTERNATIVE LAW JOURNAL – (Title varies: v1-16 1974-91 as Legal Services Bulletin) – v1-20. 1974-95 – 9 – $208.00 set – us Hein [340]

ALTERNATIVE LIFESTYLES – v5-. 1982- – 1,5,6,9 – us UMI [073]

ALTERNATIVE LIFESTYLES – (Cont by: Lifestyles) – New York. v5-6. Fal 1982-Sum 1984 – 1,5*,9 – D14128 – us UMI [640]

ALTERNATIVE MEDIA : LINKING GLOBAL AND LOCAL – 1995 – 142p – 9 – 92-3-102852-9 – fr UNESCO [380]

ALTERNATIVE PRESS, 1986+ – (Ca 100 titles from around the world) – 3 Units – 122r – 1 – $8,400.00 – us UMI [073]

ALTERNATIVE REVIEW – Nos.1-9, Feb-Nov 1986. Libertarian Alliance, London – 9 – 1.00f – at Libertarian Micro [320]

ALTERNATIVE SOURCES OF ENERGY – (Cont by: Independent Power) – Milaca. v1-17. 1971-oct 1988 – 1,5,9 – D9535 – us UMI [333]

THE ALTERNATIVE TO SOCIALISM AND SPURIOUS CAPITALISM: NATURAL CAPITALISM / Woodbury, A M – 1fiche (29x) – 9 – 1.00f – at Libertarian Micro [320]

AN ALTERNATIVE WAY OF EXPLAINING THE GEORGIST THEORY / Costerus, W – 1982. 7p – 9 – 1.00f – at Libertarian Micro [335]

ALTERNATIVES – (All that is currently offered) – Oberlin. v1-3 Spr 1976-Win 1977 – 1,5,9 – D12353 – us UMI [073]

ALTERNATIVES – Boulder. v1-22 mar 1975-Fall 1997+ 1*; v5-22 jun 1979-Fall 1997+ 5*,9 – 1,5,9 – D12219 – us UMI [073]

ALTERNATIVES : A JOURNAL OF WORLD POLICY – (v1-10 1974-85 in reel $145.00. v11-20 1985-95 in mf $250.00) – v1-20. 1974-1995 – 5,6,9 – $395.00 set – us Hein [320]

ALTERNATIVES – Waterloo. v1-23 Sum 1971-sep 1998+ 1; v5-23 dec 1975-sep 1998+ 5,9 – 1,5,9 – D7598 – us UMI [073]

THE ALTERNATIVES OF FAITH AND UNBELIEF / Stanford, Charles – London: Relgious Tract Society, 1888. 1 fiche – 9 – us A.T.L.A. [240]

ALTERNATIVET – Stockholm, 1988-92 – 9 – sw Kungliga [072]

ALTEROSA – Belo Horizonte, Sept 1948-Dec 1961; Feb, Apr-Dec 1962; Jan 1963-25 Nov 1964 – 1,5,6 – bl Biblioteca [072]

Althamer, A *see*
- CONCILIATIONES LOCORUM SCRIPTURAE, QUI SPECIE TENVS INTER SE PUGNARE UIDENTUR, CENTURIAE DUAE..
- EIN KURTZE VNTTERRICHT DEN PFARHERRN VND PREDIGERN. VERORDENT, WES SIE DAS VOLCK WIDER ETLICHE VERFUERISCHE LERE, DER WIDERTAUFFER. AUSZ GOETTLICHER SCHRIFFT VERMANEN, VND VNTERRICHTEN SOLLEN

AL-THAQAFAH – Cairo. Jan 1939-Dec 1952 – 1 – 35.00r – us Hoover Inst Photo [072]

Althaus, Friedrich *see* THE ROMAN JOURNALS OF FERDINAND GREGOROVIUS 1852-1874

ALT-HEIDELBERG : SCHAUSPIEL IN 5 AUFZUEGEN / Meyer-Foerster, Wilhelm – Berlin: A Scherl, c1902 – 1r – 1 – us U.W. Library [820]

Altheim, Franz *see* DIE KRISE DER ALTEN WELT IM 3. JAHRHUNDERT N. ZW. UND IHRE URSACHEN

ALTHOCHDEUTSCHE LESESTUECKE / Wackernagel, Wilhelm – (Includes notes on vocabulary) – Basel: H Richter, 1875 – 1 – us U.W. Library [890]

DIE ALTHOCHDEUTSCHEN GLOSSEN / Steinmeyer, E & Sievers, E – Berlin. 5v. 1879-1922 – 66mf – ne IDC [430]

LA ALTISIMA / Trigo, Felipe – Madrid: Renacimiento, 8th ed 1907 – sp Bibl Santa Ana [946]

ALTISRAELITISCHE KULTSTAETTEN / Gall, August, Freiherr von – Giessen: J Ricker, 1898 – 1mf – 9 – 0-8370-3224-5 – 1985-1224 – us A.T.L.A. [220]

Altissiodorensis, Guillermus *see* SUMMA AUREA IN 4 LIBROS SENTENT

ALTITUDE 1350 – St Donat, Canada. Dec 1972-31 dec 1991 – 5r – 1 – Can$60.00r – cn Can Microfilming [072]

DIE ALTKANAANAEISCHEN FREMDWORTE UND EIGENNAMEN IM AEGYPTISCHEN / Burchardt, M – Leipzig. 1909. BNE-20,034 1 – 9 – ne IDC [930]

DER ALT-KATHOLIK – v58. 1965 (incomplete) – 1r – 1 – ATLA S0476 – us A.T.L.A. [073]

DER ALT-KATHOLIK *see* ALT-KATHOLISCHE KIRCHENZEITUNG

DIE ALTKATHOLISCHE KIRCHE DES ERZBISTHUMS UTRECHT : GESCHICHTLICHE PARALLELE ZUR ALTKATHOLISCHEN GEMEINDEBILDUNG IN DEUTSCHLAND / Nippold, Friedrich – Heidelberg: Fr. Bassermann, 1872 – 1mf – us A.T.L.A. [240]

DIE ALT-KATHOLISCHE KIRCHE IN DEUTSCHLAND : KIRCHLICHES JAHRBUCH / Die Alt-Katholische Kirche in Deutschland – 1974-85 (complete) – 1r – 1 – ATLA S0649 – us A.T.L.A. [073]

Die Alt-Katholische Kirche in Deutschland *see* DIE ALT-KATHOLISCHE KIRCHE IN DEUTSCHLAND

ALT-KATHOLISCHE KIRCHENZEITUNG – (Cont: Der Alt-Katholik) – Berlin, Germany. v19-25. 1966-74; 1982-89 (complete) – 4r – 1 – ATLA S0517 – us A.T.L.A. [073]

ALTKATHOLISCHE KIRCHENZEITUNG – Wien. v1-19, 28-34. 1966-90 (complete) – 3r – 1 – ATLA S0426 – us A.T.L.A. [240]

ALTKATHOLISCHER KIRCHENBOTE FUER STEIERMARK – (Title varies) – v1-6. 1902-07 (complete) – 1r – 1 – ATLA S0469 – us A.T.L.A. [240]

ALTKIRCHENSLAVISCH-GRIECHISCHES WOERTERBUCH DES CODEX SUPRASLIENSIS / Meyer, KH – Hamburg, 1935 – 6mf – ne IDC [460]

ALTKIRCHER KREISBLATT – Altkirch, 1880-aug 5 1914 – 1 – Dist. gw Mikrofilm – fr A.C.R.P.P. [944]

ALTKIRCHLICHE CHRISTOLOGIE UND DER EVANGELISCHE HEILSGLAUBE *see* COLLECTED WORKS

ALTMAERKER VOLKSFREUND – Stendal, apr 7 1919-nov 10 1923 – 8r – 1 – gw Mikrofilm [072]

Altman, S *see* JOURNAL OF URBAN ANALYSIS AND PUBLIC MANAGEMENT

Altmann, Otto *see* TEGEN DEN STROOM

DIE ALTMARK IM DREISSIGJAEHRIGEN KRIEGE / Zahn, W – Halle a.S.: Verein fuer Reformationsgeschichte, 1904 (Schriften des Vereins fuer Reformationsgeschichte: 21. Jahrg., Schrift 80) – 1mf – us A.T.L.A. [943]

ALTMARK-ZEITUNG – (Suppl ed to: Altmark-Zeitung, Salzwedel. Gardelegen, Kloetze) – Gardelegen, DE. 1992- – 8r per yr – 1 – gw Mikrofilm [072]

ALTMUEHL-BOTE, KELHEIMER ZEITUNG – (Since Jun 1972: Mittelbayerische Zeitung) – Kelheim, Germany. Jul 1952 – Jul 31, 1973 – 1 – gw Mikrofilm [072]

ALTNAYLAND – (In Yiddish) – Warsaw, PL. v3 no10 Apr 1925 – 1r – 1 – $25.00 – cn Can Microfilming [072]

ALTO ACRE : ORGAM DO PARTIDO CONSTRUCTOR ACREANO – Xapury, Acre. 15 Jun 1913-28 Abr 1914 – 1,5,6 – bl Biblioteca [072]

O ALTO JURUA : ORGAM DO MUNICIPIO – Cruzeiro do Sul, Acre. 12 Ago-30 Dez 1913 – 1,5,6 – bl Biblioteca [072]

ALTO MADEIRA : JORNAL INDEPENDENTE – Porto Velho, Amazonas. 6 Maio-Ago, Dez 1917; Jan-Abr, Jul-Set, Nov-Dez 1918; Out, 3 Dez 1925 – 1,5,6 – bl Biblioteca [072]

O ALTO PURUS : ORGAM OFFICIAL – Senna Madureira, Acre. 24 Fev, Mar, Jul 1908; Fev-Maio, Jul-Dez 1909; Jan, Jun 1910-Maio 1916; Out 1916; Mar-Jul, Set-Dez 1917; Jan-3 Mar 1918 – 1,5,6 – bl Biblioteca [072]

ALTO RIO DOCE : ORGAO DOS PODERES MUNICIPAIS – Alto Rio Doce, 26 Mar 1933 – 1,5,6 – bl Biblioteca [072]

ALTO S. FRANCISCO : ORGAM DO POVO – Piumhy, 21 Dec 1924; Jun-Aug, Oct-Dec 1933; Jan-Dec 1934; Jan-Apr, Jun, Aug-Dec 1935; Jan-May, Jul-Dec 1936; Jan, Mar-Jun, Oct 1938; Apr 1939; Feb 1940; 30 Oct 1943 – 1,5,6 – bl Biblioteca [072]

Altolaguirre, Angel de *see*
- COLECCION DE LAS MEMORIAS O RELACIONES QUE ESCRIBIERON LOS VIRREYES DEL PERU ACERCA DEL ESTADO EN QUE DEJABAN LAS COSAS GENERALES DEL REINO. TOMO 2
- DON PEDRO DE ALVARADO, CONQUISTADOR DEL REINO DE GUATEMALA. MADRID, 1927
- HERNANDO CORTES (ESTUDIO DE UN CARACTER) POR EL TENIENTE GENERAL MARQUES DE POLARIEGA
- PRUEBA HISTORICA DE LA INOCENCIA DE D. HERNANDO CORTES EN LA MUERTE DE SU ESPOSA, DE JUAN PALACIOS. INFORME
- RELACIONES GEOGRAFICAS DE LA GOBERNACION DE VENEZUELA (1767-68)
- LOS RESTOS DE HERNANDO CORTES (DE LUIS...OBREGON)

ALTON INDUSTRIAL-WILLIAMSON COUNTY / Baptist Associations. Illinois – 1971-78.37 associations, alphabetically arranged. 3 reels – 1 – 107.80 – us Baptist [240]

ALTON LOCKE, TAILOR AND POET : AN AUTOBIOGRAPHY / Kingsley, Charles – Cambridge: Macmillan, 1862 – 1 roll – 1 – 1-55879-954-0 – uk Libr Preservation [420]

ALTONAER MERKUR – Altona (Hamburg), Germany. 1848-49. Zeitung und Intelligenzblatt fuer die Herzogtuemer Schleswig, Holstein und Lauenburg – 1 – gw Mikrofilm [072]

ALTONAISCHE RELATION – Hamburg, DE. 1685; 1688; 1696 – 1 – gw Mikrofilm [072]

ALTONAISCHER MERCURIUS – Hamburg, Germany. 1752-1815 – 122r – 1 – gw Mikrofilm [072]

ALTOONA TIMES – Altoona, PA. -d. 1884-1919 – 13 – $25.00r – us I.M.R. [071]

ALTOONA TRIBUNE – Altoona, PA. -d. 1889-1957 – 13 – $25.00r – us I.M.R. [071]

Altorfina *see*
- EMBLEMATA ANNIVERSARIA ACADEMIAE ALTORFINAE STUDIORUM IUVENTUTIS
- EMBLEMATA ANNIVERSARIA ACADEMIAE NORIBERGENSIS, QUAE EST ALTORFFII

ALTORIENTALISCHEN STUDIEN / Meissner, B – (Mitteilungen der altorientalischen gesellschaft. v. 4, pt. 1). Leipzig. 1928-29. BNE-20,105 1 – 9 – ne IDC [930]

ALTORIENTALISCHER UND ISRAELITISCHER MONOTHEISMUS : EIN WORT ZUR REVISION DER ENTWICKLUNGSGESCHICHTLICHEN AUFFASSUNG DER ISRAELITISCHEN RELIGIONSGESCHICHTE / Baentsch, Bruno – Tuebingen: J C B Mohr, 1906 – 1mf – 9 – 0-8370-2149-9 – 1985-0149 – us A.T.L.A. [220]

ALTOSMANISCHEN ANONYMEN CHRONIKEN / ed by Giese, Friedrich – Breslau, [1922] – 14mf – 9 – $200.00 – us MEDOC [949]

ALTPREUSSISCHE GRAMMATIK / Endzelin, J – Riga. 1944. B-1477 2 – 4mf – 8 – ne IDC [430]

ALTPREUSSISCHE MONATSCHRIFT – Koeningsberg. v1-59. 1864-1922 – 713mf – 9 – ne IDC [947]

ALTPREUSSISCHE MONATSSCHRIFT – 1991. Koenigsberg, 1864-1923 (mf ed 1991) – 439mf – DM4,500.00 – 3-89131-039-0 – gw Fischer [942]

DIE ALTPREUSSISCHEN SPRACHDENKMAELER : EINLEITUNG, TEXTE, GRAMMATIK, WOERTERBUCH / Trautmann, R – Goettingen, 1910 – 9mf – 9 – ne IDC [460]

Altrichter, Gertrud *see* MIRKO, DER KNECHT

AN ALTRUIST / Ouida – British Fiction Archive: Unit 3 – 9 – uk Bell [830]

Altschul, Jakob *see* DER GEIST DES HOHEN LIEDES

DIE ALTSEMITISCHEN INSCHRIFTEN VON SENDSCHIRLI IN DEN KOENIGLICHEN MUSEEN ZU BERLIN : TEXT IN HEBRAEISCHER UMSCHRIFT, UEBERSETZUNG, COMMENTAR, GRAMMATISCHER ABRISS UND VOCABULAR / Mueller, David Heinrich – Wien: Alfred Hoelder, 1893 – 1mf – 9 – 0-8370-7315-4 – 1986-1315 – us A.T.L.A. [470]

Altsheler, Joseph Alexander *see* THE SUN OF SARATOGA: A ROMANCE OF BURGOYNE'S SURRENDER

AL'TSIONA – Al'manakh. 1. M., 1914. 242 pp. BR-1817 2 – 8 – ne IDC [030]

DIE ALTSYRISCHE EVANGELIENUEBERSETZUNG UND TATIANS DIATESSARON, BESONDERS IN IHREM GEGENSEITIGEN VERHAELTNIS / Hjelt, Arthur – 1903 – 1 – us A.T.L.A. [240]

DIE ALTTESTAMENTLICHE AUFERSTEHUNGSHOFFNUNG / Bertheau, Ernst – Hannover: Heinrich Feesche, 1905. 1 fiche – 9 – us A.T.L.A. [240]

ALTTESTAMENTLICHE KRITIK UND CHRISTENGLAUBE : EIN WORT ZUM FRIEDEN / Koenig, Eduard – (Includes bibliographical references) – Bonn: Eduard Weber (Julius Flittner), 1893 – 1mf – 9 – 0-8370-3962-2 – 1985-1962 – us A.T.L.A. [220]

DIE ALTTESTAMENTLICHE SCHAETZUNG DES GOTTESNAMENS / Giesebrecht, Friedrich – Koenigsberg: Thomas & Oppermann, 1901 – 9 – us A.T.L.A. [240]

ALTTESTAMENTLICHE THEOLOGIE / Riehm, Eduard – Halle: Eugen Strien, 1889. 2 fiches – 9 – us A.T.L.A. [240]

DER ALTTESTAMENTLICHE UNTERBAU DES REICHES GOTTES / Boehmer, Julius – Leipzig: J.C. Hinrichs, 1902. 1 fiche – 9 – us A.T.L.A. [240]

ALTTESTAMENTLICHE UNTERSUCHUNGEN, ERSTES HEFT / Riedel, Wilhelm – Leipzig: A. Deichert, 1902. 1 fiche – 9 – us A.T.L.A. [240]

DIE ALTTESTAMENTLICHEN CITATE BEI PAULUS : TEXTKRITISCH UND BIBLISCH-THEOLOGISCH GEWUERDIGT / Vollmer, Hans – (Includes bibliographical references and index) – Freiburg i.B.: J C B Mohr (Paul Siebeck), 1895 – 1mf – 9 – 0-8370-6440-6 – 1986-0440 – us A.T.L.A. [220]

DIE ALTTESTAMENTLICHEN CITATE IM NEUEN TESTAMENT / Boehl, Eduard – Wien: Wilhelm Braumuller, 1878. 1 fiche – 9 – us A.T.L.A. [240]

ALTTESTAMENTLICHEN UNTERSUCHUNGEN, 1. BUCH / Bachmann, Johannes – (Includes appendix) – Berlin: S Calvary, 1894 – 1mf – 9 – 0-8370-2137-5 – 1985-0137 – us A.T.L.A. [220]

ALTTURKESTANISCHE VOLKSPOESIE / Brockelmann, C – 2pts Pt 1: in: Asia Major. Probeband, 1923, p 1-22; pt 2 in: Asia Major, v1, fasc 1, 1924, p 24-44 – 8 – ne IDC [490]

Altube, Gregorio de *see* EL EXCMO. SR. D. XAVIER MARIA DE MUNIBE, CONDE DE PENAFLORIDA

ALTUN YURT – Adana: Yeni Adana Matbaasi, 1923-?; Mueduer-i Mes'ul: Agah Tugrul. – Nos 1-6. – 15 Mayis-11 Tesrinievvel 1339 – 3mf – 9 – $75.00 – us MEDOC [949]

Aluin, Juan *see* VIDA DE LA VENERABLE SIERRA DE DIOS MARIA DE S. FRANCISCO, LLAMADA COMUNMENTE LA ROZAS...

LOS ALUMBRADOS ESPANOLES DE LOS SIGLOS 16 Y 17 / Lorca, B – Madrid: Razon y Fe, 1934 – 1 – sp Bibl Santa Ana [946]

L'ALUMINIUM, ETC : JOURNAL DE L'ELECTROLYSE, L'ALUMINIUM, L'ACETYLENE – Paris, France. Jan 1896-15 Dec 1901 – 3r – 1 – uk British Libr Newspaper [073]

ALUMINIUM WORKERS NEWS DIGEST *see* CIO NEWS

Aluminium Workers of America, CIO *see* CIO NEWS

ALUMMAH, ME'ASSEF HA-AGUDDAH LE-MADDA'EI HA-YAHADUT BI-YERUSHALAYIM – Jerusalem. 1936. BJ-100-148 1 – 9 – ne IDC [956]

Alumnae Association of the Baptist WMU Training School. Louisville, Ky *see* ANNUAL BULLETIN

ALUMNI BULLETIN OF THE HARVARD INTERNATIONAL LAW CLUB *see* HARVARD INTERNATIONAL LAW JOURNAL

ALUMNI NEWSLETTER / Louisiana State University. Agricultural Experiment Station. School of Forestry and Wildlife Management – v26,no.2-v27,no.2. 1975-76. 1 reel – 1,5 – us Spaulding [634]

ALUMNI SOUVENIR ILLUSTRATING BUILDINGS AND FACULTIES OF THE UNIVERSITY OF TORONTO AND AFFILIATED COLLEGES – Toronto?: M.B. Aylsworth, 1892. 02446. (Pre-1900 Canadiana) – 9 – cn C.I.H.M. [370]

AL-'URWA AL-WUTQA = LE LIEN INDISSOLUBLE – (Reedition de 1958) – Paris. n1-18. mars-oct 1884 – 1 – fr A.C.R.P.P. [073]

Alva y Viamont, D *see* EL PERFECTO CAPITAN, INSTRUIDO EN LA DISCIPLINA MILITAR Y NUEVA CIENCIA DE ARTILLERIA

ALVAR GARCIA DE SANTA MARIA. / Cantera y Burgos, Francisco – Madrid. 1951 – 1 – us Res Libr [946]

Alvarado Garaicoa, Toedoro *see*
- VASCO NUNEZ DE BALBOA. ADELANTADO DE LA COSTA DEL MAR DEL SUR
- VIDA, PASION Y MUERTE DE VASCO NUNEZ DE BALBOA (DESCUBRIDOR DEL OCEANO PACIFICO) Y FRANCISCO DE ORELLANA (DESCUBRIDOR DEL RIO AMAZONAS)

Alvarado, Manuel *see*
- DISCURSO QUE...PRONUNCIO EL 23 DE ABRIL.
- VIDEO WORLD-WIDE

Alvarado, Pedro de *see* AN ACCOUNT OF THE CONQUEST OF GUATEMALA IN 1524

LOS ALVARADOS EN EL – NUEVO MUNDO / Solar y Taboada, Antonio & Rigula y Ochotorena, Jose de – Madrid: Tip. Rev. Arch, Bib. y Museos, 1934 – 1 – sp Bibl Santa Ana [946]

Alvares, Didac *see* DE AUXILIIS DIVINAE GRATIAE

Alvarez, Arturo *see*
- ATAIDE, ANTONIO DE
- LA CODIFICATION DU DROIT INTERNATIONAL
- CONSIDERATIONS GENERALES SUR LA CODIFICATION DU DROIT INTERNATIONAL AMERICAIN
- UN CURIOSO MANUSCRITO SOBRE EL CONVENTO DE SAN ONOFRE DE LA LAPA (BADAJOZ) (SU BIBLIOTECA Y SACRISTIA EN EL SIGLO 16)
- DESPUES DE LA GUERRA...
- LE DROIT INTERNATIONAL AMERICAIN...
- LE DROIT INTERNATIONAL DE L'AVENIR
- GUADALUPE, ARTE, DEVOCION Y...
- GUADALUPE EN LA AMERICA ANDINA. MADRID, 1969
- LAS MUNICIPALIDADES HISPANO-PORTUGUESAS. SU ORIGEN Y DESARROLLO HASTA EL SIGLO 15
- LE NOUVEAU DROIT INTERNATIONAL ET SA NOUVELLE METHODE D'ETUDE
- LE NOUVEAU DROIT INTERNATIONAL PUBLIC...
- LE PANAMERICANISME ET LA SIXIEME CONFERENCE PANAMERICAINE
- LOS PILARES DE LA HISPANIDAD SE FORJARON EN GUADALUPE
- TRADICION CONCEPTISTA EN LA PROVINCIA BETICA

Alvarez, C *see*
- GUERRA Y MARINA, EPOCA DE CARLOS 1 DE ESPANA...
- VALLADOLID. ARCHIVO GENERAL DE SIMANCAS. SECRETARIA DE GUERRA (S. 18)...HOJAS DE SERVICIOS DE AMERICA

Alvarez de la Rivera, Senen *see* BIBLIOTECA HISTORICO-GENEALOGICA ASTURIANA...

Alvarez de Sotomayor, Agustin *see* MEMORIA SOBRE LA CRIA CABALLAR

Alvarez del Manzano y Alvarez Rivera, F *see* LA LEY MERCANTIL...

Alvarez del Vayo, Juan *see* POESIAS

Alvarez del Vayo, Julio *see*
- ALVAREZ DEL VAYO'S ANSWER TO THE BRITISH CHARGE D'AFFAIRES
- DEUX DISCOURS
- L'ESPAGNE ACCUSE
- SPEECH DELIVERED BEFORE THE ASSEMBLY OF THE LEAGUE OF NATIONS, 25 SEPTEMBER 1936

ALVAREZ DEL VAYO'S ANSWER TO THE BRITISH CHARGE D'AFFAIRES / Alvarez del Vayo, Julio – n.p. 1937. Fiche W 713. (Blodgett Collection of Spanish Civil War Pamphlets) – 9 – us H.U. College Libr [946]

Alvarez, Emmanuel *see* DE CONSTRUCTIONE OCTO PARTIUM ORATIONIS LIBER

Alvarez, Fernando *see* EL PERONISMO, ANTECEDENTES Y GOBIERNO

Alvarez, Francois *see*
- HISTORIALE DESCRIPTION DE L'ETHIOPIE CONTENANT LA VRAIE RELATION DES TERRES ET PAYS DU GRAND ROI ET EMPEREUR PRETE-IAN, L'ASSIETTE DE SES ROYAUMES ET PROVINCES, LEURS COUTUMES, LOIS ET RELIGION
- REGIMIENTO CONTRA LA PESTE

Alvarez Guerra, Andres *see*
- CREDITO NACIONAL O SEA HACIENDA PUBLICA
- DESCRIPCION Y DISENO DEL TRILLO
- INVENTO CERES O SEA METODO DE PROCEDER...PROPIO POR DIEZ ANOS
- TERCER CUADERNO DE LOS INVENTOS CERES

Alvarez Guerra, Juan *see* CORRECCIONES AL TRILLO INVENTADO POR DON JUAN ALVAREZ GUERRA, EXECUTADAS POR DON JUAN FRANCISCO GUTIERREZ

Alvarez, Jose Ma. Leyendas *see* BARCELONA, 1933

Alvarez Joven, Arturo *see* LA GITANA EXTREMENA Y OTROS POEMAS

Alvarez Lencero, H *see* CANCIONES EN CARNE VIVA

Alvarez Lencero, Luis *see*
- HOMBRE. GRABADOS DE FRANCISCO MATEOS
- EL SURCO DE LA SANGRE

Alvarez Madariaga, Luz *see* CONTRATOS Y CUASICONTRATOS MINEROS EN LAS LEGISLACIONES SUDAMERICANAS

Alvarez Medina, Felipe *see* POESIAS

Alvarez Rubiano, Pablo *see* PEDRERIAS DAVILA. CONTRIBUCION AL ESTUDIO DE LA FIGURA DEL "GRAN JUSTADOR", GOBERNADOR DE CASTILLA DEL ORO Y NICARAGUA. MADRID, 1944

Alvarez Saenz de Buruaga, Jose *see*
- ANFITEATRO
- DATOS PARA EL ESTUDIO DE LAS ANTIGUEDADES DE MERIDA
- EL ESCUDO DE MERIDA Y SU ORIGEN ROMANO
- LA FUNDACION DE MERIDA
- LOCALIZACION DE LA RELIQUIA DE LA CABEZA DE SANTA EULALIA
- MERIDA EN EL SIGLO 27 (CONTINUACION DE LA "HISTORIA DE LA CIUDAD DE MERIDA" DE MORENO DE VARGAS)
- MERIDA Y LOS VIAJEROS
- MISCELANEA EMERITENSE DEL S. 16
- NUEVAS APORTACIONES AL ESTUDIO DE LA NECROPOLIS ORIENTAL DE MERIDA

- EL PALACIO DEL DUQUE DE LA ROCA, DE MERIDA
- LAS RUINAS DE EMERITA Y DE ITALICA A TRAVES DE NEBRIJA Y RODRIGO CARO

Alvarez, Santiago *see* EL PUEBLO DE GALICIA, CONTRA EL FASCISMO

Alvarez, Segis *see*
- LA JUVENTUD Y LOS CAMPESINOS
- NUESTRA ORGANIZACION Y NUESTROS CUADROS: J. S. U. DE ESPANA

Alvarez y Saenz de Buruaga, Jose *see* UN NUCLEO DE NETERRAMIENTOS ROMANOS EN LA CAMPINA DE MERIDA

ALVARO CORDOBES, OPERA (SIECLE 10) – Cordoba – 1r – 5,6 – sp Cultura [946]

ALVEISRUSISHER TSUZAMENFOR FUN YIDISHE POYERIM (2ND: 1928: MINSK, BYELORUSSIAN S.S.R.) *see* TSVEITER ALVEISRUSISHER TSUZAMENFOR FUN YIDISHE POYERIM

Alverdes, Paul *see*
- DANK UND DIENST
- DIE FLUCHT
- REINHOLD: ODER, DIE VERWANDELTEN
- VERGEBLICHER FISCHZUG
- DIE VERWANDELTEN
- DAS WINTERLAGER

Alverez, Felix *see* "PERFILES SACERDOTALES". BARCELONA, EDIT. HERNANDO. 1959...

Alverstone, Viscount *see* RECOLLECTIONS OF BENCH AND BAR

Alverthorpe. Yorkshire. St. Paul's *see* PARISH REGISTERS

ALVES SACRAMENTO : DICCIONARIO BIBLIOGRAPHICO BRAZILEIRO / Blake, A V – Rio de Janeiro: Typ. Nacional. v1,4-6. 1883-1900 – 22mf – 9 – ne IDC [972]

Alves, William *see* LECTURES ON THE EPISTLE OF PAUL THE APOSTLE TO THE EPHESIANS: CHAPTER 1: EXPOSITORY AND PRACTICAL

THE ALVINA TREUT BURROWS RESEARCH COLLECTION ON COMPOSITION / Svobodny, Dolly – 1900-86. 1500 titles on 300mf. Printed card indexes included – 9 – us A.T.B.I. [370]

O ALVINOPOLIS : ORGAO OFFICIAL DA CAMARA – Cidade de Alvinopolis, 15 Oct 1917; Jan, Mar 1919; 4 Dec 1927 – 1,5,6 – bl Biblioteca [072]

ALVIRA ALIAS OREA / Henderson, J Duff – Toronto: Hunter, Rose, 1899. 05539. (Pre-1900 Canadiana) – 9 – cn C.I.H.M. [830]

ALVO ADVANCE – Alvo, NE. -w. Nov. 1895-Jun. 1899. Incomplete; Dec. 1901-May 1903; Mar. 1908-Dec. 1920 – 1 – us NE Hist [071]

A ALVORADA : PERIODICO LITERARIO E NOTICIOSO – Villa Seabra, Acre. 14 Jul, Out 1913; Jan 1914; Mar-Maio, Ago-Out, Dez 1915; Abr, Jul-Ago, Out 1916; Fev-Mar 1917; 28 Fev 1919 – 1 – bl Biblioteca [072]

A ALVORADA – Piracicaba, Brazil. Jun-Nov 1880. Incomplete – 1 – bl Biblioteca [072]

A ALVORADA – Ponte Nova, 10 Mar 1906 – 1,5,6 – bl Biblioteca [072]

A ALVORADA : SEMANARIO LITTERARIO E NOTICIOSO – Manaos, Amazonas. 20 Maio 1895 – 1,5,6 – bl Biblioteca [072]

ALVORADA : ORGAM DEDICADO A DEFESA E EDUCACAO DA MULHER – Penedo, Alagoas. 15 Mar-15 Maio 1910 – 1,5,6 – bl Biblioteca [072]

ALVORADA : PERIODICO NOTICIOSO, LITTERARIO E CHISTOSO – Maceio, Alagoas. 23 Set 1887; 30 Abr 1888 – 1,5,6 – bl Biblioteca [072]

ALVORADA : REVISTA LITTERARIA, CRITICA E NOTICIOSA – Maceio, Alagoas. 25 Ago 1896 – 1,5,6 – bl Biblioteca [072]

ALVORADA : SEMANARIO CATOLICO – Sete Lagoas, 19 Oct 1941; May 1944; 20 Jan 1963 – 1,5,6 – bl Biblioteca [072]

ALVORADA – Villa do Aratuhipe, 25 Jan, 6 Sep 1891 – 1,5,6 – bl Biblioteca [072]

A ALVORADO : ORGAO LITTERARIO, CRITICO E NOTICIOSO – '(s.l.')-Sao Luis, Brazil. 8 Sep-10 Nov 1895 – 1,5,6 – bl Biblioteca [072]

ALVSBORGS NYHETER – Vanersborg, Sweden. 1982- – 1 – sw Kungliga [072]

ALVSBORGSPOSTEN – Uddevalle, Sweden. 1978- – 1 – sw Kungliga [072]

AL-WAFD – [Egypt], 1984- – 365mf per yr – 9 – $600.00y – us Ross [072]

Alwan, A S *see* A BIBLIOGRAPHY ON LAND TENURE AND RELATED QUESTIONS IN LIBYA

ALWAQAI ALIRAQIYA: OFFICIAL GAZETTE OF THE REPUBLIC OF IRAQ / Iraq – (1979-. ca 20.00y) – 1970-78. Formerly: Iraq weekly gazette – 1 – $92.00 – us L of C Photodup [324]

AL-WAQA'I AL-IRAQIYAH / Iraq – (1980-. ca $30.00y) – 1970-79 – 1 – $230.00 – us L of C Photodup [324]

AL-WAQAI AL-MISRIYA – [Egypt], 1950- – 1 – $300.00y – us Ross [072]

AL-WAQA'I' AL-MISRIYAH : EGYTIAN BULLETIN / Egypt – (1919-26, 1928-49, 1961-66, 1970-79 63r. 1980-.) – 1887-91, 1901, 1907-17 – 81r – 1 – us L of C Photodup [324]

Alward, Silas *see* THE JUBILEE YEAR: AN ORATION

AL-WATWANY – (Cont: L'Echo des Comores) – Moroni, Comoros. Sept 6 1985-Oct 11 1991 – 4r – 1 – us L of C Photodup [072]

Alymov, A A *see* VOPROSY SOVETSKOGO STROITEL'STVA: SBORNIK STATEI

AL-ZAHF AL-AKHDAR – Tripoli, Libya. 1980-1984; 1987 – 6r – 1 – us L of C Photodup [072]

AL-ZAHRA – Cairo, 1924-1928. V.1-5 – 39mf – 9 – NE-20329/1 – ne IDC [073]

Al-Zayn, Ahmad 'Arif *see* AL-IRFAN

Alzog, John *see* MANUA OF UNIVERSAL CHURCH HISTORY

AM *see* HA-'AM

AM ANDEREN MORGEN : ROMAN / Bauer, Josef Martin – Muenchen: R Piper, c1949 – 1r – 1 – us U.W. Library [830]

AM DA MALSHK GA NA DAMSH ST JOHN. LIGI – The Gospel according to St. John trans. into Zimshian. Halifax: J. Bowes, 1867. 00125. (Pre-1900 Canadiana) – 9 – cn C.I.H.M. [240]

A.M. ENFANTIN / Toussaint – Paris, impr. de Lachevardiere, 1832, 8 p. Transon, Abel. SIMPLE ECRIT. AUX SAINT-SIMONIENS, Paris, Everat, 1832, 32 p. Les Saint-Simoniens, 1825-1834. 6951 – 9 – fr Hachette [335]

AM ENGINEERING DATA BASE IN ORDER BY COUNTY AND STATE / U.S. National Technical Information Service – Monthly – 9 – us N.T.I.S. [000]

AM ENGINEERING DATA BASE IN ORDER BY STATE / U.S. National Technical Information Service – Monthly.Secondarily, in order by city – 9 – us N.T.I.S. [000]

AM ERSTEN MAI : EINE TRAGIKOMOEDIE DER ARBEIT AUS FRIEDENSTAGEN / Adolph, Karl – Leipzig: Neuer Akademischer Verlag, 1919 – 1r – 1 – us U.W. Library [820]

AM GOLDENEN STEIG UND ANDERE ERZAEHLUNGEN AUS DEM BAYER- UND BOEHMERWALD / Schmidt, Maximilian – 2. Aufl. Reutlingen: Ensslin & Laiblin, [1899?] – 1r – 1 – us U.W. Library [830]

A.M. GORKII I SOZDANIE ISTORII FABRIK I ZAVODOV / Gorkii, A M – Moscow, 1959. 364p. BR-10,671/1 – 9 – ne IDC [380]

THE AM HA-ARETZ : THE ANCIENT HEBREW PARLIAMENT / Sulzberger, Mayer – (Includes indexes) – Philadelphia: J H Greenstone, 1909 – 1mf – 9 – 0-8370-5465-6 – 1985-3465 – us A.T.L.A. [270]

AM I A JEW OR GENTILE? READ AND SEE / Davies, Thomas Alfred – New York: E.H. Coffin, c1889. 1 fiche – 9 – us A.T.L.A. [240]

AM KACHELOFEN / Bloesch, Hans – Bern: Gute Schriften, 1945 – 1 – us U.W. Library [890]

A.M. MACKAY : PIONEER MISSIONARY OF THE CHURCH MISSIONARY SOCIETY IN UGANDA / Mackay, Alexander Murdoch; ed by Harrison, Mrs J W – New York: A C Armstrong, 1890 – 2mf – 9 – 0-8370-6270-5 – 1986-0270 – us A.T.L.A. [920]

AMA ARCHIVES OF GERNERAL PSYCHIATRY *see* AMA ARCHIVES OF NEUROLOGY AND PSYCHIATRY

AMA ARCHIVES OF INDUSTRIAL HEALTH – (Cont by: Archives of Environmental Health. Former titles: Archives of Industrial Hygiene and Occupational Medicine (jan-sep 1950); AMA Archives of Industrial Hygiene and Occupational Medicine (oct 1950-dec 1954)) – Chicago. v1-21. 1950-jun 1960 – 1 – D407 – us UMI [360]

AMA ARCHIVES OF INDUSTRIAL HYGIENE AND OCCUAPTIONAL MEDICINE *see* AMA ARCHIVES OF INDUSTRIAL HEALTH

AMA ARCHIVES OF NEUROLOGY *see* AMA ARCHIVES OF NEUROLOGY AND PSYCHIATRY

AMA ARCHIVES OF NEUROLOGY AND PSYCHIATRY – v39-81. 1938-59 – 1,5,6 – us Princeton Micro [616]

AMA ARCHIVES OF NEUROLOGY AND PSYCHIATRY / American Medical Association – (Ceased publ. Superseded by: AMA Archives of Neurology, and: AMA Archives of Gerneral Psychiatry. Former titles: Archives of Neurology and Psychiatry (jan 1919-sep 1950)) – Chicago. v1-81. jan 1919-jan-jun 1959 – 1 – D69 – us UMI [616]

A'ma Yusuf Garibi, Efendi *see* DIVAN

Amabile, Luigi *see* IL SANTO OFFICIO DELLA INQUISIZIONE IN NAPOLI

Amadei, M *see* DELLA FORZA DEI GIUDICATI...

Amadeo, Eduardo *see* UNA PROPUESTA JUSTICIALISTA

Amadeo, Mario *see*
- AL DIA SIGUIENTE
- POR UNA SOLUCION NACIONAL

Amadeo, Tomas *see* LA FUNCION SOCIAL [CONFERENCIAS]

[AMADIS. SELECTIONS] : TOUS LES AIRS DE VIOLON DE L'OPERA D'AMADIS, COMPOSEZ PAR MONSIEUR LULLY... / Lully, Jean-Baptiste – Amsterdam: Antoine Pointel, [1688?] – 1 – us Sibley [780]

Amado, Jorge *see* DE COMO O MULATO PORCIUNCULA DESCARREGOU SEU DEFUNTO

Amado, Manuel *see*
- COMPENDIO HISTORICOS DE LAS VIDAS DE LOS SANTOS...DEL ORDEN DE PREDICADORES
- DIOS Y ESPANA: O SEA ENSAYO DE LO QUE DEBE A LA R. CATOLICA
- LA MONARQUIA Y LA RELIGION TRIUNFANTES DE LOS SOFISMAS
- LOS SIETE DIAS DE LA PASION O LECCIONES PRACTICAS DE VIRTUD

AMADOR DISPATCH – (Cont by: Ledger and Progress-News) – Jackson, CA. 1863-75; 1878-89; 1890-1980 – 57r – 1 BC02317 – $2,850.00 – us Library Micro [071]

AMADOR DISPATCH, JACKSON *see* AMADOR PROGESS-NEWS

AMADOR, EL DORADO, PLACER AND SACRAMENTO COUNTIES – Amador Co, CA. 1884-1885 – 1 – 1 – $50.00 – D005 – us Library Micro [978]

AMADOR, EL DORADO, PLACER AND SACRAMENTO COUNTIES – Placer Co, CA. 1884-1885 – 1r – 1 – $50.00 – D005 – us Library Micro [978]

AMADOR, EL DORADO, PLACER AND SACRAMENTO COUNTIES – Sacramento Co, CA. 1884-1885 – 1r – 1 – $50.00 – D005 – us Library Micro [978]

AMADOR, EL DORADO, SACRAMENTO AND PLACER COUNTIES – El Dorado Co, CA. 1884-1885 – 1r – 1 – $50.00 – D005 – us Library Micro [978]

AMADOR LEDGER AND AMADOR RECORD – Jackson, CA. 1900-18; 1921-1980 – 43r – 1 BC02318 – $2,150.00 – us Library Micro [071]

AMADOR PROGESS-NEWS – (Cont with: Amador Dispatch, Jackson) – Ione, CA. 1979 – 2r – 1 – $100.00 – B02307 – us Library Micro [071]

AMADOR/EL DORADO – 1928-38; 1992- – 13+ r – 1 – $650.00 – P00004 – us Library Micro [910]

Amaduzzi, J-C *see* ALPHABETUM ARMENUM CUM ORIATIONE DOMINICALI...

Amak Sjariffudin *see* KISAH KARTOSUWIRJO DAN MENJERAHNJA

AMAL VE-TIRSAH / Ha-Cohen, S – Roedelheim. 1812. BJ-422-79 – 9 – ne IDC [470]

AMALARII EPISCOPI OPERA / Hanssens, J M – (Liturgica Omnia 1948 Studi e Testi 138, Tomus, 1. 10mf; Studi e Testi 139 Tomus, 2. 15mf; Studi e Testi 140 Tomus, 3. 13mf) – Roma, 1948 – 8 – Dfl133.00 – ne Slangenburg [240]

Amalgamated Association of Iron, Steel, and Tin Workers of America *see*
- NATIONAL LABOR TRIBUNE

Amalgamated Clothing Workers of America *see* ADVANCE

Amalgamated Food Workers of America *see* FREE VOICE OF THE AMALGAMATED FOOD WORKERS

AMALGAMATED JOURNAL : 1988-1942 – (Coll title: Labor Union Periodicals, Pt 1) – 29r – 1 – $3,915.00 – 1-55655-226-2 – us UPA [331]

Amalgamated Lithographers of America *see* LITHOGRAPHER'S BULLETIN, 1901-1904 : OFFICIAL PUBLICATION OF THE LITHOGRAPHER'S INTERNATIONAL PROTECTIVE AND BENEFICIAL ASSOCIATION, 1910-1913 : THE LITHOGRAPHER'S JOURNAL, 1918-1955

Amalgamated Meat Cutters and Butcher Workmen of North America *see*
- BUTCHER WORKMAN
- OFFICIAL JOURNAL
- OFFICIAL JOURNAL OF THE AMALGAMATED MEATCUTTERS AND BUTCHER WORKMEN
- PACKINGHOUSE WORKER

AMALGAMATION OF THE GENERAL AND PARTICULAR BAPTIST IN ENGLAND / Baptist Missionary Society. Archives. London – 1889-91. 225p – 1 – $7.87 – us Baptist [240]

THE AMALGAMATION OF THE TWO BRANCHES OF THE LEGAL PROFESSION. / Saunders, Cornelius Thomas – London: Butterworths, 1870. 32p. LL-2245 – 1 – us L of C Photodup [340]

Amalgemated Marine Workers' Union. London, England *see* MARINE WORKER

AMALIE FUERSTIN VON GALLITZIN / Brentano, Maria Rafaela – Freiburg i.B., 1920. xii/154p – DM48.00 – 3-89349-207-0 – gw Hänsel [920]

AMAL-I-SALIH / Salih Kambo, M; ed by Yazdani, G – v. 3. Calcutta. 1939. BI-750 2 – 8 – ne IDC [490]

AMALKAN ILMU DARIPADA KEHIDUPAN SEHARI-HARI (THE SCHOOL OF LIFE) AMANAT PADA PERINGATAN HARI SARDJANA KE-4, 30 SEPT. 1963 / Sukarno, Pres. Indonesia – SE 4731 1. 1963 – 9 – ne IDC [324]

AMALS TIDNING – Amal, Sweden. 1874-85 – 4r – 1 – sw Kungliga [072]

AMALS WECKOBLAD – Amal, Sweden. 1846-47, 1856-74 – 4r – 1 – sw Kungliga [072]

AMALSPOSTEN – Amal, Sweden. 1883-97 – 10r – 1 – sw Kungliga [072]

AMANA, THE COMMUNITY OF TRUE INSPIRATION / Shambaugh, Bertha, MH – Iowa City, Iowa: State Historical Society of Iowa, c1908 – 1mf – us A.T.L.A. [240]

AMANAH PRESIDEN / Sukarno, Pres. Indonesia – SE 2046 1. 1946 – 9 – ne IDC [324]

AMANAT POLITIK PRESIDEN/PEMIMPIN BESAR REVOLUSI / Sukarno, Pres. Indonesia – SE 5018 1. 1965 – 9 – ne IDC [324]

Amand, D *see* FATALISME ET LIBERTE DANS L'ANTIQUITE GRECQUE

Amans, Georges *see* POUR SEDUIRE LES FEMMES

Amar, Djen *see* BANDUNG LAUTAN API

Amar, Jules *see* THE HUMAN MOTOR

Amar y Arguedas, J *see*
- INSTRUCCION CURATIVA DE LAS CALENTURAS CONOCIDAS...COMO TABARDILLO
- INSTRUCCION CURATIVA DE LAS VIRUELAS
- INSTRUCCION CURATIVA Y PRESERVATIVA DE LOS DOLORES DE COSTADO Y PULMONES

Amaral, Tancredo do *see*
- O ESTADO DE SAO PAULO..
- A HISTORIA DE SAO PAULO ENSINADA PELA BIOGRAPHIA DOS SAUS VULTOS MAIS NOTAVEIS

AMARANTH – Saint John, N.B.: R. Shives, [1841?-1843] – 9 – cn C.I.H.M. [971]

AMARANTH : A MONTHLY MAGAZINE OF NEW AND POPULAR TALES, POETRY, HISTORY, BIOGRAPHY – (Ceased publ) – New Brunswick. v1-3. jan 1841-dec 1843* – 1 – D5203 – us UMI [073]

AMARANTH : OR MASONIC GARLAND – (Ceased publ) – Boston. v1-2. spr 1828-oct 1829 – 1 – D3915 – us UMI [073]

AMARANTH : OR TOKEN OF REMEMBRANCE – (Ceased publ) – Boston, New York. v1. 1847-1855 – 1 – D3824 – us UMI [073]

AMARANTH : A SEMI-MONTHLY PUBLICATION DEVOTED TO POLITE LITERATURE, SCIENCE, POETRY AND AMUSEMENT – (Ceased publ) – Ashland. v1. feb-dec 1847 – 1 – D3757 – us UMI [073]

Amard, Louis Victor Frederic *see* TRAITE ANALYTIQUE DE LA FOLIE ET DES MOYENS DE LA GUERIR

AMARGOSA TIMES – Beatty-Beatty, NV. 1982-1983 – 1r – 1 – $50.00 – N03701 – us Library Micro [071]

AMAROC NEWS – Coblenz, Germany. v. 1, no. 1-v. 2, no. 255. Apr. 21, 1919-Dec. 31, 1920 – 1 – us NY Public [073]

Amaron, Calvin E *see* LE RETOUR DE L'EMIGRE

AMASYA TARIHI / Huseyin, Husameddin – Istanbul: Hikmet Matba'asi and Istikbal Matba'asi, 1912-1935 – 20mf – 9 – $42.00 – us MEDOC [949]

AMASYA'DA EMEL – Amasya, 1921-1923 – 9 – $20.00 – us MEDOC [956]

Amat, Juan Carlos *see*
- GUITARRA ESPANOLA, Y VANDOLA, EN DOS MANERAS DE GUITARRA, CASTELLANA
- QUATRE CENTS AFORISMES CATHALANS...

THE AMATEUR ATHLETE – v1-4, no.2 (all publ). Mar 1896-Sept 1897 – 1 reel – 1 – $185.00 – us UPA [790]

Amateur Athletic Union of the United States *see* INFO AAU

Amateur Basketball Association *see* HANDBOOK

AMATEUR CINE WORLD – (Material for 1964 was not available for photography. Merged with: 8 mm Movie Maker and Cine Camera; To form: Movie Maker) – London. v1-20 apr1934-dec 1961*; ns3-12 jan 1962-dec 1966 – 1 – D525 – us UMI [790]

AMATEUR MASTER FILE / U.S. National Technical Information Service – Twice a year. Data pertaining to amateur licensees and listed in call sign sequence – 9 – us N.T.I.S. [000]

AMATEUR MASTER FILE SUPPLEMENT / U.S. National Technical Information Service – Monthly – 9 – us N.T.I.S. [000]

L'AMATEUR, OU NOUVELLE PIECES ET DISSERTATIONS FRANCOISES ET ETRANGERES / Martinelli, V – P 716. 1762 – 9 – ne IDC [840]

AMATEUR PHOTOGRAPHER – (Former titles: Photography (nov 1888-1908); Photography and Focus (1908-18); Amateur Photographer and Photography (jun 19 1918-jul 27 1927); Amateur Photographer and Cinematographer (aug 3 1927-jun 13 1945)) – Sutton. nov 1888-dec 1997+ 1*; v171 jan 1985-dec 1997+ 5*,9* – D11258 – us UMI [770]

AMATEUR PHOTOGRAPHER *see* AMATEUR PHOTOGRAPHER AND PHOTOGRAPHIC NEWS

AMATEUR PHOTOGRAPHER AND CINEMATOGRAPHER *see* AMATEUR PHOTOGRAPHER

AMATEUR PHOTOGRAPHER AND PHOTOGRAPHIC NEWS – (Merged into: Amateur Photographer) – Sutton. v1-67. oct 1884-jun 1918* – 1 – D11257 – us UMI [770]

THE AMATEUR PHOTOGRAPHER AND PHOTOGRAPHIC NEWS – London: Hazell, Watson & Viney. v47-67 n1232-1758. may 12 1908-jun 10 1918 – 1 – us Res Libr [760]

AMATEUR PHOTOGRAPHER AND PHOTOGRAPHY *see* AMATEUR PHOTOGRAPHER

AMATEUR WORK : A MONTHLY MAGAZINE OF THE USEFUL ARTS AND SCIENCES – (Ceased publ) – Boston. v1-6. nov 1901-apr 1907 – 1 – D3212 – us UMI [073]

THE AMATEURA – [Upper Dorchester, N.B.]: U D L & M Society, [1888?-1889?] – 9 – cn C.I.H.M. [971]

AMAUTA – Lima. nos. 1-32. Sept. 1926-Aug. Sept. 1930 – 1 – us NY Public [073]

Amaya Delgado, Manuel *see* TRATADO DE LAS ASFIXIAS O MUERTES ASFIXIANTES

THE AMAZING MARRIAGE / Meredith, George – Westminster: Archibald Constable, 1895 – 1 roll – 1 – 1-55879-975-3 – uk Libr Preservation [820]

AMAZING SCIENCE FICTION – v20-49. Feb 1946-Nov 1975. (Science Fiction Periodicals, Series 2) – 1 – $2,405.00 – us UPA [830]

AMAZING STORIES – New York. v1-12. 1918-385 reels – 5r – 1 – us Ross [830]

AMAZING STORIES – v1-19. 1926-45 – 22r – 1 – $1,695.00 – us UPA [830]

AMAZING STORIES ANNUAL – (all publ). 1927 – 1 reel – 1 – $45.00 – us UPA [830]

AMAZING STORIES QUARTERLY – v1-7. (all publ). 1928-34 – 2r – 1 – $210.00 – us UPA [830]

THE AMAZON – vol.1, no.1-. Milwaukee: Amazon Collective, May 1972 – 1 – us U.W. Library [073]

AMAZON QUARTERLY – (Ceased publ) – Oakland. v1-3. Fal 1972-mar 1975 – 1,5 – D7940 – us UMI [073]

AMAZON VALLEY INDIAN – v29-39. Jul 1934-Feb 1944 (complete) – 1r – 1 – ATLA S0535 – us A.T.L.A. [240]

AMAZONAS – Manaos, Amazonas. 26 Set 1866-Dez 1872; Ago 1876; Jan 1878-Jul 1884; Jul 1890-Out 1891; Jul 1892-Nov 1893; Jun 1900; Abr, Jun-Set 1920 – 1,5,6 – bl Biblioteca [072]

AMAZONAS CATHOLICO – Manaos, Amazonas. 13 Jun 1894 – 1,5,6 – bl Biblioteca [072]

AMAZONAS COMMERCIAL – Manaos, Amazonas. 10 Mar 1895; Jul 1897; Fev, 26 Maio 1900 – 1,5,6 – bl Biblioteca [072]

AMAZONIA : JORNAL, BI-MENSARIO NOTI CIOSO, LITERARIO DE INTERESSES RE-GIO-NAIS – Manaus, Amazonas. 9 Fev 1948 – 1,5,6 – bl Biblioteca [072]

AMAZONIA. A TERRA E O HOMEM / Lima, Araujo – 2a. ed. Sao Paulo. 1937 – 1 – us Res Libr [972]

AMAZONIAN RAIN FOREST : THE STRUCTURE AND FUNCTION OF A NUTRIENT STRESSED ECOSYSTEM AND THE IMPACT OF SLASH-AND-BURN AGRICULTURE / ed by Jordan, C F – 1989 – 9 – 92-3-102629-1 – fr UNESCO [574]

O AMAZONICO : ORGAO DE INTERESSES GERAES DA REGIAO AMAZONICA – Manaos, Amazonas. 1 Jun 1929 – 1,5,6 – bl Biblioteca [072]

AMAZONIDA : ATUALIDADES – Manaos, Amazonas. Maio 1942 – 1,5,6 – bl Biblioteca [072]

L'AMBASCIATORE / Bragaccia, G – Padova, 1935 – 8mf – 1 – ILM-346/1 – ne IDC [327]

L'AMBASSADE DE D. GARCIAS DE SILVA FIGVEROA EN PERSE, CONTENANT... – Paris, 1667 – 6mf – 9 – ILM-1216/1 – ne IDC [340]

AMBASSADE EN CHINE ET AU JAPON / Moges – Souvenirs d'une ambassade en Chine et au Japon en 1857 et 1858. Paris, Hachette. 1860 – 9 – 10.00 – fr Orientalistes [950]

AMBASSADE EXTRAORDINAIRE DE MESSIEURS LES DUC DANGOULESME, COMTE DE BETHUNE,... – Paris, 1667 – 16mf – 9 – ILM-1161/1 – ne IDC [340]

AMBASSADES MEMORABLES VERS LES EMPEREURS DU JAPON – Amsterdam, 1680 – 10mf – 9 – ILM-1162/1 – ne IDC [340]

AMBASSADOR FOR INTERMEDIATES – Mar 1932-41 – 1 – 138.46 – us Baptist [240]

AMBASSADOR LEADER – Brotherhood Commission publication, SBC, Apr 1959-67 – 1 – 52.85 – us Baptist [240]

AMBASSADOR LIFE – 1946-67 – 1 – 277.48 – us Baptist [240]

AMBASSADORIAL AND SECRET SERVICE REPORTS ON REVOLUTIONARY AND NAPOLEONIC FRANCE, 1781-1815 / Great Britain. Public Record Office – (Part 1: FO27, v1-20, 1781-86.) – PRO Class FO27, France, General Correspondence. v1-20 – 1 – us Primary [941]

Ambelouis, R *see* DE L'EFFET DU CHANGEMENT DU STATUT PERSONNEL...

Amberley, John Russell *see* AN ANALYSIUS OF RELIGIOUS BELIEF

AMBIDEXTERITY AND MENTAL CULTURE / Macnaughton-Jones, Henry – Illus. New York: Rebman Co., n.d. 102p – 1 – us U.W. Library [150]

AMBIENTE AXIOLOGICO DE LA TEORIA PURA DEL DERECHO / Carrillo, Rafael – Bogota. Univ. Nacional de Colombia. 1947. 92p. LL-4068 – 1 – us L of C Photodup [340]

AMBIO – Stockholm. v1-. 1972-* – 1,5,9 – D49282 – us UMI [073]

AMBIT – London. 1959-1971*; v50-. 1972-* – 1 – D7641 – us UMI [073]

Ambler, Pennsylvania. Mount Pleasant Baptist Church *see* RECORDS

AMBON BEROEPT ZICH OP RECHT EN TROUW – Den Haag, 1950 – 1mf – 9 – ne IDC [950]

AMBON EN DE A.R. PARTIJ. DE VRIJHEIDSSTRIJD VAN DE REPUBLIEK DER ZUID-MOLUKKEN / Gerbrandy, P S – Kampen, 1956 – 1mf – 9 – ne IDC [320]

AMBON NU! : [VIER REPORTAGES] / Kloosterhuis, H – Wageningen, 1968 – 1mf – 9 – ne IDC [950]

Ambri, M *see* DONGENG-DONGENG SASAKALA, KENGING NGEMPELKEUN MOH. AMBRI

Ambrose, Stephen J *see* ASPECTS OF THE PHYSIOLOGICAL AND BEHAVIOURAL ECOLOGY OF THE WHITE-BROWED SCRUBWREN, SERICORNIS FRONTALIS (ACANTHIZIDAE) IN WESTERN AUSTRALIA

Ambrosini, G *see*
- PAESI SOTTO MANDATA...
- IL REGIME DEGLI STRETTI

Ambrosio de Montanchez *see* MISCELANEA SAGRADA DE VARIOS DISCURSOS PANEGIRICOS

AMBROSIO-FILMS – Berlin. 1910, p93 – 1911 – 1 – gw Mikrofilm [790]

AMBROSIUS VON MAILAND UND DER TOD KAISER VALENTINIANS 2 : EIN HISTORISCH-THEOLOGISCHER KOMMENTAR ZU DES BISCHOFS LEICHENREDE "DE OBITU VALENTINIANI" (1-14), NEBST EINER DEUTSCHEN UEBERSETZUNG DES GESAMTEN TEXTES / Schmitt, Bernhard – 1994 – 4mf – DM112.00 – 3-8267-2019-9 – gw Hänsel [240]

AMBTS-BRIEVEN: 1802-1842 / Falck, Anton Reinhard – Hague: W.P. van Stockum, 1878. xiv,360p – 1 – us U.W. Library [320]

DE AMBTSDATA VAN DE OUDSTE OPPERRABBIJNEN BIJ DE HOOGDUITSCHE JOODSCHE GEMEENTE TE AMSTERDAM / Sluys, D M – (van ongeveer 1640 tot 1706). Amsterdam. 1917. BJ-262-60 1 – 9 – ne IDC [949]

AMBULANTE SOZIALE DIENSTE IN DER ALTENHILFE : EIN BEITRAG ZUR ERHALTUNG EINER WEITGEHEND SELBSTAENDIGEN LEBENSFUEHRUNG ALTER MENSCHEN / Kieninger, Carmen – 1995 – 2mf – 9 – DM198.00 – 3-931223-06-X – gw Böhner [360]

AMBULATORY SURGERY – Oxford. v1-. mar 1993-* – 1,5,9 – D20363 – us UMI [617]

AMBUSHES AND SURPRISES: BEING A DESCRIPTION OF SOME OF THE MOST FAMOUS INSTANCES OF THE LEADING INTO AMBUSH AND THE SURPRISE OF ARMIES, FROM THE TIME OF HANNIBAL TO THE PERIOD OF THE INDIAN MUTINY / Malleson, George Bruce – London: W.H. Allen, 1885. x,434p. illus – 1 – us U.W. Library [355]

AMC JOURNAL – (Cont in pt by: Mining Voice. Former titles: Mining Congress Journal (jan 1915-dec 1977)) – Washington. v1-60 jan 1915-dec 1974 1; v6-80 jan 1975-dec 1994 1,5,9 – 1,5,9 – D10300 – us UMI [622]

AMCABEY – Istanbul, cilt 1, sayi 1-cilt 3, sayi 69. – 5 Birincikanun 1942-25 Mart 1944 [5 December 1942-25 March 1944] – 10mf – 9 – $50.00 – us MEDOC [949]

AMDDIFFYNYDD Y GWEITHIWR – Merthyr Tydfil, Wales. 8 Aug 1874-13 Nov 1875 – 43ft – 1 – uk British Libr Newspaper [072]

Amdrup, G *see* THE FORMER ESKIMO SETTLEMENTS ON THE EAST COAST OF GREENLAND BETWEEN SCORESBYSUND AND THE ANGMAGSSALIK DISTRICT

L'AME AMANTE DE SON DIEU, REPRESENTEE DANS LES EMBLEMES DE HERMANNUS HUGO SUR SES PIEUX DESIRS : ET DANS CEUX D'OTHON VAENIUS SUR L'AMOUR DIVIN / Hugo, H & Vaenius, O – Utrecht, 1750 – 4mf – 9 – O-3092/1 – ne IDC [760]

AME CHURCH REVIEW – African Methodist Episcopal Church. v1-26. 1884-1910 – 4r – 1 – us Ross [073]

AME CHURCH REVIEW – Nashville. v1-233 1884-1906*. v234-368 jan 1968-dec 1997+ 1; v238-240 jan-4qr 1969*. v241-244 1970. v245-276 jan 1971-dec 1973*. v277-279 1974. v280-282 1975*. v283-332 jan 1976-dec 1988. v333-356 jan 1989-dec 1994*. v357-368 jan 1995-dec 1997+ 5; v238-244 jan 1969-dec 1970*. v245-276 jan 1971-dec 1973. v277-279 1974*. v280-368 jan 1975-dec 1997+ 9 – 1,5,9 – D3102 – us UMI [240]

L'AME DU PYGMEE D'AFRIQUE / Trilles, H – Paris: Editions du Cerf, 1945 – 1 – us Res Libr [290]

L'AME D'UN PEUPLE AFRICAIN, LES BAMABARA, LEUR VIE PSYCHIQUE, ETHIQUE, SOCIALE, RELIGIEUSE / Henry, Jos – Munster: Verlag der Aschendorffschen Buchhandlung, 1910 – 1 – us Res Libr [306]

Ame, Emile *see* DICTIONNAIRE TOPOGRAPHIQUE DU DEPARTEMENT DE CANTAL

L'AME ROMANTIQUE ET LE REVE / Beguin, Albert – Paris: J. Corti, s.d. 5 fiches.(Literature Collection) – 9 – 12.00 – fr Bibl Nationale [440]

UNE AME SACERDOTALE, LE CHANOINE MICHEL / Alexis, R P – Ottawa: l'Echo de S Francois, [1912]. SEM105P687 – 1mf – 9 – Can$2.25 – cn Bibl Nat [240]

AMEDRA : ROMAN DE MOEURS NEGRES DU CONGO BELGE / Delhaise, Arnould M L – Bruxelles: Renaissance d'Occident, 1926 – 1 – us Res Libr [390]

Ameghino, F *see* OBRAS COMPLETAS Y CORRESPONDENCIA CIENTIFICA

Ameisenowa, Z *see* COMMENTARY ON THE SOBIESKY BOOK OF HOURS IN WINDSOR CASTLE LIBRARY

Amelander, M M *see* SHE-ERIT YISRA'EL

AMELIA, TAMERTON CHURCH-TOWER, ETC : WITH PREFATORY STUDY ON ENGLISH METRICAL LAW / Patmore, Coventry Kersey Dighton – London: G. Bell and Sons, 1878 – 1 roll – 1 – 1-55879-186-8 – uk Libr Preservation [810]

Amelineau, E *see*
- LES ACTES DES MARTYRS DE L'EGLISE COPTE
- CONTES ET ROMANS DE L'EGYPTE CHRETIENNE
- LES MOINES EYGPTIENS. VIE DE SCHNOUDI
- MONUMENTS POUR SERVIR A L'HISTOIRE DE L'EGYPTE CHRETIENNE

Ameller, C *see* ELEMENTOS DE GEOMETRIA Y FISICA EXPERIMENTAL...

Amelli, A M *see* MINIATURE SACRE E PROFANE DELL' ANNO 1023, ILLUSTRANTI L'ENCICLOPEDIA MEDIOEVALE DI RABANO MAURO

Amelotte, D *see* LA VIE DU PERE CHARLES DE CONDREN

LES AMEN DE MONSABRE: LECTURE FAITE AU CERCLE VILLE-MARIE DE MONTREAL / Beaubien, Charles Philippe – Montreal: E. Senecal, 1892. 03514. (Pre-1900 Canadiana) – 9 – cn C.I.H.M. [240]

AMEN SUGERENCIAS LITURGICAS / Aradillas Agudo, Antonio – Madrid: Studium, 1966 – sp Bibl Santa Ana [240]

L'AMENAGEMENT DE L'ESPACE : PLANIFICATION REGIONALE ET GEOGRAPHIQUE (EN ITALIE, BELGIQUE, GRANDE-BRETAGNE, VENEZUELA) / Gottmann, Jet al – F30.00 – fr Ethnologie [710]

AMENDED LIST OF ANCIENT MONUMENTS IN BURMA / Burma. Lists of Monuments – Rangoon, 1921. BI-1005 2 – 8 – ne IDC [324]

THE AMENDING OF THE FEDERAL CONSTITUTION / Orfield, Lester Bernhardt – Ann Arbor: University of Michigan, 1942. 242p. LL-1136 – 1 – us L of C Photodup [340]

AMENDMENT TO THE ORGANIC ACT OF GUAM : HEARING BEFORE THE SUBCOMMITTEE ON TERRITORIAL AND INSULAR AFFAIRS... / Guam. US Congress – 92nd Congress 2nd sess. 14 Sep 1972. Washington: GPO, 1972 – 1mf – 9 – $1.50 – LLMC 82-100B Title 16 – us L.L.M.C. [340]

AMENDMENTS TO ARTICLES 2 AND 36, UNIFORM CODE OF MILITARY JUSTICE : HEARINGS BEFORE THE MILITARY PERSONNEL SUBCOMMITTEE OF THE COMMITTEE ON ARMED SERVICES – House of Rep. 96th Congress, 1st session, June 11-12 1979. Washington: GPO, 1979 – 2mf – 9 – $3.00 – LLMC 96-079 – us L.L.M.C. [340]

AMENDMENTS TO THE CONSTITUTION OF NORTH CAROLINA, 1776-1974 / Sanders, John L – Chapel Hill: Institute of Government, University of North Carolina at Chapel Hill, 1975. LL-2395 – 1 – us L of C Photodup [340]

AMENIDADES NATURALES DE LAS ESPANAS / Lagasca y Segura, M – v. 1, NR. 1-2. Orihuela. 1811-21. B-5999 2 – 8 – ne IDC [580]

AMENIDADES...DE LA VERA ALTA Y BAXA / Azedo de la Berrueza, Gabriel – 1891 – 9 – 1.50f – sp Bibl Santa Ana [946]

Amenumey, Divine Edem Kobla *see* THE EWE PEOPLE AND THE COMING OF EUROPEAN RULE, 1850-1914

AMERASIA – v1-11. no.2, 7 (all publ). 1937-47 – 60mf – 9 – $345.00 – us UPA [335]

AMERASIA JOURNAL – Los Angeles. v1- mar 1971- 1*; v2- 1973- 5,9 – 1,5,9 – D7751 – us UMI [616]

AMERCAN JOURNAL OF SURGICAL PATHOLOGY – New York. v1-21 mar 1977-1*; v17-21 jan-dec 1993-* 5,9 – 1,5,9 – D18692 – us UMI [617]

AMERICA – Chicago, 7 Apr 1888-24 Sep 1891 – 7r – 1 – uk British Libr Newspaper [071]

AMERICA – Denver, CO. 1920-1930(?) – us I.H.R.C. [073]

AMERICA – Detroit, MI. 1906-66 – 1 – us Res Libr [071]

AMERICA – New York. v1-177 apr 1909-dec 1997+ 1; v118-177 jan 1968-dec 1997+ 5; v103-177 apr 1960-dec 1997+ 9. Shipped annually or qrtly – 1,5,9 – D320 – us UMI [073]

America *see*
- COLECCION DE DOCUMENTOS INEDITOS, RELATIVOS AL DESCUBRIMIENTO, CONQUISTA Y ORGANIZACION DE LAS ANTIGUAS POSESIONES ESPANOLAS DE AMERICA Y OCEANIA
- COLECCION DE LIBROS Y DOCUMENTOS REFERENTES A LA HISTORIA DE AMERICA

LA AMERICA – 1-15. 1910-25 – 1 – us NY Public [073]

LA AMERICA – Madrid. Spain. -w. 8 Mar 1857-13 Mar 1875. (12 reels) – 1 – uk British Libr Newspaper [072]

LA AMERICA – New York, NY. 1910-25 – 1 – us A.J.P.C. [071]

AMERICA, 1935-1946 / U.S. Library of Congress – (Northeastern states 434mf £1,930. Midwestern states 254mf £1,210. Northwestern states 153mf £795. Southern states 301mf £1,545. Southwestern states 205mf £1,090. Farwestern states 159mf £795. Guide and index £42) – 1981 – 1574mf – 9 – £6,230.00 coll – uk Chadwyck [975]

AMERICA, A PROPHECY / Blake, William – (Copy O). Linnell-Riches – 14 – uk Microform Academic [810]

AMERICA AND BRITTANIA. PEACE. A NEW MARCH / Taylor, Raynor – Composed by R. Taylor (and so arranged as to harmonize perfectly with Washingtons march played both together). Philadelphia: G. Willig n.d.. MUSIC 3082, Item 11 – 1 – us L of C Photodup [780]

AMERICA AND HER PROBLEMS / Estournelles de Constant, Paul Henri Benjamin Baron d' – New York: Macmillan, 1915 – 2mf – us A.T.L.A. [240]

AMERICA AND THE AMERICANS: A NARRATIVE OF A TOUR IN THE UNITED STATES AND CANADA: WITH CHAPTERS ON AMERICAN HOME LIFE / Craib, Alexander – Paisley Scotland: A. Gardner, 1892. 00273. (Pre-1900 Canadiana) – 9 – cn C.I.H.M. [971]

AMERICA AND WEST INDIES : ORIGINAL CORRESPONDENCE ETC 1606-1807 / Great Britain. Colonial Office – (CO5 46-63, 83-111: Military Dispatches, 1755-83 27r; CO5 65-82, 225: Indian Affairs, 1760-84 10r; CO5 358-380, 382-397, 400-405: South Carolina, 1699-1784 17r; CO5 751-769, 855-895, 898-921: Massachusetts and New England, 1620-1778 40r; CO5 1037-1078, 1081-1132: New York, 1664-1781 48r; CO5 1308-1334, 1337-1369: Virginia, 1606-1781 25r) – 1 – $80.00r – us Ross [941]

AMERICA, BRITAIN AND THE WAR OF INDEPENDENCE – (The papers and correspondence of Sir Jeffrey, 1st Baron Amherst (1717-97) from the Amherst MSS in the Kent Archives Office) – 1 – us Primary [941]

AMERICA EN PARIS – no. 1-33. Paris. 1891-mai 1892 – 1 – fr A.C.R.P.P. [073]

AMERICA EN TIEMPO DE FELIPE 2 SEGUN EL COSMOGRAFO CRONISTA JUAN LOPEZ DE VELASCO. EL TERRITORIO ESPANOL DE IFNI / Beltran y Rozpide, Ricardo; ed by Bayle, Constantino – Madrid: Razon y Fe, 1928 – 9 – sp Bibl Santa Ana [970]

AMERICA HEROLD-LINCOLN FREIE PRESSE – Omaha. 1972-82 – 1 – gw Mikrofilm [071]

AMERICA, HISTORICAL, STATISTIC, AND DESCRIPTIVE / Buckingham, James Silk – 3v. 1841 – 1r – 1 – us Ross [970]

AMERICA IN THE MAKING / Abbott, Lyman – New Haven: Yale University Press; London: Oxford University Press, 1911. (Yale lectures on the responsibilities of citizenship) – 1mf – us A.T.L.A. [975]

LA AMERICA INDIGENA. TOMO 1. EL HOMBRE AMERICANO. LOS PUEBLOS DE AMERICA. BARCELONA, 1935 / Pericot y Garcia, Luis – Madrid: Razon y Fe, 1936 – 1 – sp Bibl Santa Ana [970]

AMERICA LATINA : REVISTA DE ARTE E PENSAMENTO – Rio de Janeiro, Aug 1919-Feb 1920 – 1,5,6 – bl Biblioteca [072]

AMERICA LETTERS / Etelae-Pohjanmaa – 1890-1960 – 16r – 1 – us I.H.R.C. [860]

AMERICA: LIFE AND LABOR / American National Women's Trade Union League – 1911-21 – 1 – £180.00 – uk World [073]

AMERICA OF TO-MORROW / Klein, Felix – Chicago: A.C. McClurg, 1911 – 1mf – us A.T.L.A. [240]

AMERICA PICTURESQUE AND DESCRIPTIVE VOL. 1 / Cook, Joel – Philadelphia: H. T. Coates, 1900. 05241. (Pre-1900 Canadiana) – 9 – cn C.I.H.M. [971]

AMERICA PICTURESQUE AND DESCRIPTIVE. VOL. 2 / Cook, Joel – Philadelphia: H. T. Coates, 1900. 05242. (Pre-1900 Canadiana) – 9 – cn C.I.H.M. [910]

AMERICA PICTURESQUE AND DESCRIPTIVE. VOL. 3 / Cook, Joel – Philadelphia: H. T. Coates, 1900. 05243. (Pre-1900 Canadiana) – 9 – cn C.I.H.M. [910]

AMERICA SAMOA : REPORT OF A SPECIAL SUB-COMMITTEE ON TERRITORIAL AND INSULAR AFFAIRS OF THE HOUSE COMMITTEE ON INTERIOR AND INSULAR AFFAIRS / American Samoa. US Congress – 84th Congress 1st sess. Comm print no 4 Nov 1954. Washington: GPO, 1954 – 1mf – 9 – $1.50 – LLMC 82-100C Title 34 – us L.L.M.C. [327]

AMERICA, SU GEOGRAFIA, SU HISTORIA / Fernandez Pesquero, J – Madrid: Razon y Fe, 1930 – 1 – sp Bibl Santa Ana [972]

AMERICA (UNITED STATES) – 1936-63 – 1,5,6 – us Princeton Micro [975]

AMERICA–A NEW MARCH / Gram, Hans – Printed from movable type as a supplement to Vol. III, 1791, of "The Massachusetts Magazine." Scored on three staves, two treble and one bass, instrumentation unspecified. MUSIC 123, Item 3 – 1 – us L of C Photodup [780]

AMERICA-HEROLD – (Includes v.66, no.41-42,44-49,51-52; v.67, no.2-30,32-33,36,38-41,43-45, 47-50,52-v.69, no.45; Jan.1939-Jan.1942) – Winona, Minn.: National Weeklies, 19??- – 1 – CSUX86-S170 – us Hoover Inst Photo [978]

AMERICA-HEROLD – Omaha, NE. -w. 12 Mar 1975-18 Oct 1978. In German – 1 – us NE Hist [071]

AMERICA-LATINA – London, UK. 15 Feb 1915-Apr 1920 – 1 – uk British Libr Newspaper [072]

AMERICAN – Boston. Mass. 1951-1961 – 1 – us UMI [071]

AMERICAN – Brookville. Ind. 1872-1900; 1924-1939 – 1 – us UMI [071]

AMERICAN – Brookville. Pa. -w. 1958-71 – 1 – us UMI [071]

AMERICAN – Chicago. Ill. 1950-1969 – 1 – us UMI [071]

AMERICAN – Cleveland, OH: F J & J F Svoboda, [1918-sep 17 1936]; 1937-jun 3 1939 – 1 – us Res Libr [071]

AMERICAN – Crescent City. Calif. 1927-1969 – 1 – us UMI [071]

AMERICAN – Gary. Ind. -w. 1927-51, 1956-67 – 1 – us UMI [071]

AMERICAN – Hattiesburg. Miss. 1918- – 1 – us UMI [071]

AMERICAN – New York. N.Y. 1819-20 – 1,3 – us Readex [071]

AMERICAN – Providence. R.I. 1808-1809. Rhode Island American. 1809-1820 – 3 – us Readex [071]

AMERICAN – Santa Clara, CA. 1973-79 – 4r – 1 – $200.00 – B02944 – us Library Micro [071]

AMERICAN – Somerset. Pa. 1937- – 1 – us UMI [071]

AMERICAN – Vicksburg. Miss. 1902-1904 – 1 – us UMI [071]

AMERICAN – Waterbury. Conn. 1899-1921 – 1 – us UMI [071]

AMERICAN – Waterbury. Conn. -w. 1887-95, 1907-08 – 1 – us UMI [071]

THE AMERICAN – Jan. 10, 1893-Oct. 6, 1894 – 1 – us NY Public [073]

THE AMERICAN – Name changed from New York American for the Country. 1832-1836. Incomplete – 1 – us NY Public [073]

AMERICAN : A NATIONAL JOURNAL – (Ceased publ) – Philadelphia. v1-33. oct 1880-dec 1900 – 1 – D5204 – us UMI [975]

American Academic of Deans *see* PROCEEDINGS

American Academy in Rome *see* PAPERS AND MONOGRAPHS

American Academy of Arts and Sciences *see*
- BULLETIN
- MEMOIRS

American Academy of Arts and Sciences, Boston *see* MEMOIRS OF THE AMERICAN ACADEMY OF ARTS AND SCIENCES

American Academy of Dermatology *see* JOURNAL OF THE AMERICAN ACADEMY OF DERMATOLOGY

American Academy of Language and Belles Lettres *see* CIRCULAR

American Academy of Medicine. Conference on Prevention of Infant Mortality. 1909, New Haven, CT *see* PAPERS AND DISCUSSIONS

AMERICAN ACADEMY OF ORTHOPAEDIC SURGEONS BULLETIN – Chicago. v1- 1933- 1*; v38- jan 1990- 5*,9* – 1,5,9 – D2091 – us UMI [617]

American Academy of Physician Assistants *see* JAAPA

American Academy of Political and Social Science *see*
- ANNALS
- ANNALS OF THE AMERICAN ACADEMY OF POLITICAL AND SOCIAL SCIENCE
- ANNALS OF THE AMERICAN ACADEMY OF POLITICAL SCIENCE
- THE INITIATIVE, REFERENDUM AND RECALL.

American Academy of Political and Social Science. Philadelphia *see* ANNALS

American Academy of Psychiatry and the Law *see* BULLETIN OF THE AMERICAN ACADEMY OF PSYCHIATRY AND THE LAW

American Academy of Psychoanalysis *see* JOURNAL OF THE AMERICAN ACADEMY OF PSYCHOANALYSIS

AMERICAN ACADEMY OF PSYCHOANALYSIS: JOURNAL – v1-14. 1973-86 – 1,5,6 – us Princeton Micro [616]

American Academy of Religion *see* JOURNAL OF THE AMERICAN ACADEMY OF RELIGION

AMERICAN ACADEMY OF RELIGION BULLETIN *see* JOURNAL OF THE AMERICAN ACADEMY OF RELIGION

AMERICAN ACADEMY OF RELIGION JOURNAL *see* JOURNAL OF BIBLE AND RELIGION

AMERICAN ADVERTISING – Washington. v1- 1984- 1*; v6- Spr 1990- 5*,9* – 1,5,9 – D18543 – us UMI [650]

AMERICAN ADVOCATE OF PEACE – v1-2. 1834-36 – 7mf – 9 – $50.00 – us UPA [320]

AMERICAN AGENCY BULLETIN – (Cont by: Independent Agent) – New York. v1-66. jun 1903-dec 1968* – 1 – D12495 – us UMI [073]

AMERICAN AGENT AND BROKER – (Cont: Local Agent) – St Louis. v41-69 oct 1969-dec 1997+ 1*; v52-69 jan 1980-dec 1997+ 5*,9 – 1,5,9 – us UMI [332]

AMERICAN AGRICULTURIST AND THE RURAL NEW YORKER – (Absorbed: Farmers' Cabinet and American Herd-Book, 1848; American Farmer's Magazine, 1859; Genesee Farmer, jan 1866; American Farmer, 1897. Publ suspended 1852-aug 1853. Cont by: American Agriculturist, Rural New Yorker. Former Titles: American Agriculturist (apr 1842-may 18,1912); Orange Judd American Agriculturist (may 25,1912-may 14,1921); American Agriculturist (may 21,1921-nov 1964)) – Ithaca. v1-172. apr 1842-aug 1975 – 1 – D1985 – us UMI [630]

American Agricultural Economics Association *see* PAPERS

AMERICAN AGRICULTURIST *see*
- AMERICAN FARMER
- AMERICAN FARMERS' MAGAZINE
- FARMERS' CABINET AND AMERICAN HERD-BOOK

AMERICAN AGRICULTURIST : RURAL NEW YORKER – (Cont: American Agriculturist and the Rural New Yorker. Cont by: American Agriculturist) – Ithaca. v172-173. sep 1975-mar 1976 – 1 – D1985.01 – us UMI [630]

AMERICAN AGRICULTURIST *see*
- AMERICAN AGRICLUTURIST AND THE RURAL NEW YORKER
- AMERICAN AGRICULTURIST

AMERICAN AGRICULTURIST AND THE RURAL NEW YORKER *see* AMERICAN AGRICULTURIST

THE AMERICAN AGRICULTURIST LAW BOOK, A COMPENDIUM OF EVERY DAY LAW, FOR FARMERS, MECHANICS, BUSINESS MEN, MANUFACTURERS, ETC.. / Corey, Henry Bascom – New York: American Agriculturist, 1885. 404,xxp. LL-1550 – 1 – us L of C Photodup [340]

AMERICAN AGRICULTURIST, RURAL NEW YORKER *see* AMERICAN AGRICLUTURIST AND THE RURAL NEW YORKER

AMERICAN AIRCRAFT MODELER – (Ceased publ. Former titles: Bill Barnes Air Trails (feb 1934-jan 1937); Air Trails (feb 1937-jul 1942, sep 1950-mar 1954); Air Trails Pictorial (aug 1942-dec 1946, oct 1947-aug 1950); Air Trails and Science Frontiers (jan 1947-sep 1947); Air Trails Hobbies for Young Men (apr 1954-oct 1955); Young Men, Hobbies, Aviation, Careers (nov 1955-nov 1956); American Modeler (dec 1956-dec 1967)) – Washington. v76-79. jan 1973-mar 1975 – 1,5 – D7557 – us UMI [380]

American Alliance for Health, Physical Education and Recreation *see* RESEARCH QUARTERLY

AMERICAN ALMANAC AND REPOSITORY OF USEFUL KNOWLEDGE – (Ceased publ) – Boston. 1830-1861 – 1 – D3823 – us UMI [000]

AMERICAN ALMANAC AND TREASURY OF FACTS, STATISTICAL, FINANCIAL, AND POLITICAL – (Ceased publ) – New York. v1-12. jan 1878-dec 1889 – 1 – D2561 – us UMI [030]

AMERICAN ALPINE JOURNAL – New York. v1-1929- 1; v17- 1970- 5*; v21- 1977- 9* – 1,5,9 – D2379 – us UMI [073]

THE AMERICAN AMATEUR PHOTOGRAPHER – (Issues for 1905-06 filmed with: American Amateur Photographer and Camera & Dark-Room, Jan-Jun 1907) – Brunswick, ME: [s.n. v1-18. 1889-1906] – 6r – 1 – us Res Libr [770]

THE AMERICAN AMATEUR PHOTOGRAPHER AND CAMERA AND DARK-ROOM *see* THE AMERICAN AMATEUR PHOTOGRAPHER

AMERICAN ANCESTRY – By Thomas P. Hughes, 1887-1900. 12v. Indexes. SW16-0074, 0085, 0086 – 5 – us A.G.L.L. [978]

AMERICAN ANCESTRY / Hughes, Thomas P – (Vol. 1. Name and descent in the line of male Americans who settled in U.S. prior to the Declaration of Independence 1776 (New York Reel 6). Vol. 2. Name and descent in male line of Americans whose Ancestors settled in the U.S. previous to the Declaration of Independence 1776-Columbia County (New York Reel 13)) – Albany, Joel Munsell's Sons, 1887. 2 vols. (The Cox Library Collection) – 5 – us Americana [978]

AMERICAN ANCESTRY: GIVING THE NAME AND DESCENT IN THE MALE LINE – 12v. 1887-99 – 1 – 23.00 – us L of C Photodup [920]

AMERICAN AND COMMERCIAL ADVERTISER – Baltimore. Md. 1799-1920 – 1 – us UMI [071]

AMERICAN AND ENGLISH ANNOTATED CASES – 1901-18 – 31r – 1 – $1,150.00 – us Trans-Media [340]

AMERICAN AND ENGLISH ANNOTATED CASES – (Title merged in 1912 with the American State Reports, to become the American Annotated Cases) – Northport, NY: Thompson Co. v1-21. 1906-11 (all publ) – 287mf – 9 – $430.00 – LLMC 84-695 – us L.L.M.C. [340]

AMERICAN AND ENGLISH CORPORATION CASES – Northport, NY/Charlotteville: Thompson, Michie Co. 1st series: v1-48 + digest for vl-40. 1833-94. New series: v1-19. 1896-1904 (all publ) – 567mf – 9 – $850.00 – LLMC 80-432 – us L.L.M.C. [340]

AMERICAN AND ENGLISH DECISIONS IN EQUITY – Philadelphia: M Murphy Co. v1-10 + index for v1-5. 1895-1904 (all publ) – 92mf – 9 – $138.00 – LLMC 84-696 – us L.L.M.C. [340]

THE AMERICAN AND ENGLISH ENCYCLOPAEDIA OF LAW – v. 1-31. 1887-96 – 1 – 290.00 – us L of C Photodup [340]

AMERICAN AND ENGLISH ENCYCLOPEDIA OF LAW AND PRACTICE – 1st ed. Northport, NY: Ed Thompson. v1-31. 1877-96 (all publ) – 373mf – 9 – $559.00 – LLMC 82-507 – us L.L.M.C. [340]

AMERICAN AND ENGLISH ENCYCLOPEDIA OF LAW AND PRACTICE – 2nd ed. Northport, NY: Ed Thompson. v1-32 + suppl v1-5. 1896-1905 (all publ) – 508mf – 9 – $762.00 – LLMC 82-508 – us L.L.M.C. [340]

AMERICAN AND ENGLISH PATENT CASES – (v1-3 cover English court reports and v4-20 cover reports of the U.S. Supreme Court) – Washington: C R Brodix. v1-20. 1662-1890 (all publ) – 143mf – 9 – $214.00 – LLMC 81-420 – us L.L.M.C. [340]

AMERICAN AND ENGLISH RAILROAD CASES – (New series: v24-68 1902-13 entitled: Railroad Reports) – Northport, NY/ Charlottesville: Thompson/Michie 1st series: v1-61 + 4 index/digest vols; 1881-95 + new series: v1-68 + 6 index vols; 1894-1913 (all publ) – 1205mf – 9 – $1,807.00 – LLMC 80-433 – us L.L.M.C. [340]

AMERICAN AND EUROPEAN PRESSED GLASS IN THE CORNING MUSEUM OF GLASS / Spillman, Jane Shadel – 1981. 404p. 1500 illus., 16 color plates. 8 fiches. No.6660 – 9 – $12.50 – us Corning Mus [730]

AMERICAN AND EXPORT BULLETIN *see* AMERICAN IMPORT EXPORT BULLETIN

AMERICAN AND SCANDINAVIAN REVIEW – v1-62 1913-74 1; 1968-1974 5,6 – us UMI [073]

American Animal Hospital Association *see* JOURNAL OF THE AMERICAN ANIMAL HOSPITAL ASSOCIATION

AMERICAN ANNALS OF EDUCATION – (Former title: American Journal of Education (jan 1826-may 1830); American Journal of Education and Monthly Lyceum (jun 1830-jul 1830); American Annals of Education and Instruction (aug 1830-dec 1837)) – Boston. ns1 jan 1826-dec 1830; 3s1-9 aug 1830-dec 1839 – 1 – D3918 – us UMI [370]

AMERICAN ANNALS OF EDUCATION AND INSTRUCTION *see* AMERICAN ANNALS OF EDUCATION

AMERICAN ANNALS OF THE DEAF – (Publ suspended oct 1849-jul 1850 and sep 1861.jun 1868. Former title: American Annals of the Deaf and Dumb (oct 1847-jul 1886)) – Washington. cum index v1-100 1847-1955; v1-142 oct 1847-dec 1997+ 1; v112-142 jan 1967-dec 1997+ 5,9 – 1,5,9 – D2236 – us UMI [616]

AMERICAN ANNALS OF THE DEAF AND DUMB *see* AMERICAN ANNALS OF THE DEAF

AMERICAN ANNOTATED CASES – (Title changes to: Annotated Cases – American and English in mid-1916) – New York, San Francisco: Thompson Co, Bancroft-Whitney. v1912A-1916B (19 bks). 1912-16 (all publ) – 285mf – 9 – $427.00 – LLMC 84-695B – us L.L.M.C. [340]

AMERICAN ANNOTATED CASES *see* AMERICAN AND ENGLISH ANNOTATED CASES

AMERICAN ANNUAL REGISTER – (Ceased publ) – New York. cum index 5-8 1829-1833; v1-8 1825-1833 – 1 – D2772 – us UMI [975]

AMERICAN ANTHROPOLOGIST – New series v1-67. 1899-1965 – 1 – us Princeton Micro [301]

AMERICAN ANTHROPOLOGIST – Washington. cum index v1-50 1888-1948 1; v31-50 1929-48 5; v1-99 jan 1888-dec 1997+ 1,9; v9-99 jan 1907-dec 1997+ 5*. Shipped yrly or qrtly – 1,5,9 – D1829 – us UMI [301]

AMERICAN ANTIQUARIAN *see* AMERICAN ANTIQUARIAN AND ORIENTAL JOURNAL

AMERICAN ANTIQUARIAN AND ORIENTAL JOURNAL – (Absorbed: Biblia (jan 1906). Former title: American Antiquarian (apr1878-oct 1880)) – Toledo. v1-36. apr 1878-jan 1914 – 1 – D3886 – us UMI [073]

American Antiquarian Society *see*
- NEWS-LETTER
- NEWS-LETTER OF THE AMERICAN ANTIQUARIAN SOCIETY
- PROCEEDINGS
- PROCEEDINGS OF THE AMERICAN ANTIQUARIAN SOCIETY

AMERICAN ANTIQUITY – (Mf ed includes v9 1991 of: SAA Bulletin) – Washington. v1-62. jul 1935-oct 1997+ 1,5*,9 – 1,5,9 – D11734 – us UMI [930]

AMERICAN ANTI-SLAVERY REPORTER / American Anti-Slavery Society – Nos.1-8 (all publ). 1834 – 2mf – 9 – $55.00 – us UPA [976]

AMERICAN ANTI-SLAVERY REPORTER – (Ceased publ) – New York. v1. jan-aug 1834 – 1 – D4147 – us UMI [976]

American Anti-Slavery Society *see*
- AMERICAN ANTI-SLAVERY REPORTER
- ANNUAL REPORT
- ANTI-SLAVERY EXAMINER
- ANTI-SLAVERY RECORD
- ANTI-SLAVERY TRACTS

American Anti-Slavery Society. Free Soil Party *see* EMANCIPATOR AND REPUBLICAN

THE AMERICAN APOLLO – Boston, MA. 1792-94. The Federal Orrery, 1794-96 – 1,3 – us Readex [071]

AMERICAN APOLLO – (Ceased publ) – Boston. v1. jan 1792 – 1 – D3500 – us UMI [073]

AMERICAN APPEAL – v1-8 2+48 (all publ). 1920-1927 – 1 reel – 1 – $115.00 – us UPA [975]

THE AMERICAN APPEAL – 1926, 1927 (both incompl) – 1 – us Hoover Inst Photo [071]

American Arbitration Association *see*
- ARBITRATION IN THE SCHOOLS
- LABOR ARBITRATION AWARDS
- LABOR ARBITRATION IN GOVERNMENT

AMERICAN ARCHAEOLOGIST – (Former title: Antiquarian (jan 1897-jan 1899)) – Columbus. v1-3. jan 1897-jan 1899 – 1 – D2560 – us UMI [930]

AMERICAN ARCHITECT *see* AMERICAN ARCHITECT AND ARCHITECTURE

AMERICAN ARCHITECT AND ARCHITECTURE – (Absorbed: Inland Architect and News Record jan 1909. Absorbed by: Architect Record. Former titles: American Architect and Building News (jan 1 1876-dec 30 1908); American Architect (jan 6 1909-aug 17 1921); American Architect and the Architectural Review (aug 1921-dec 1924); American Architect (jan 14 1925-may 1938)) – New York. v1-152. jan 1876-feb 1938 – 1 – D4636 – us UMI [720]

AMERICAN ARCHITECT AND BUILDING NEWS – v. 1-118 and indexes. Boston, New York. 1876-1920. BO-1206 1 – 9 – ne IDC [073]

AMERICAN ARCHITECT AND BUILDING NEWS *see* AMERICAN ARCHITECT AND ARCHITECTURE

AMERICAN ARCHITECT AND THE ARCHITECTURAL REVIEW *see* AMERICAN ARCHITECT AND ARCHITECTURE

AMERICAN ARCHITECTURAL BOOKS – (Titles from Henry-Russell Hitchcock bibliography) – 1 – us Primary [720]

AMERICAN ARCHIVES OF REHABILITATION THERAPY – (Ceased publ) – North Little Rock. v14-35 mar 1966-Win 1987 1; cum index 1-3 1953-1955; v1-35 mar 1953-Win 1987 5; v22-35 mar 1974-Win 1987 9 – 1,5,9 – D2155 – us UMI [617]

AMERICAN ARCHIVIST – v. 1-21. 1938-58 – 1,5,6 – us Princeton Micro [900]

THE AMERICAN ARCHIVIST / Society of American Archivists – v1-49. 1938-86 – 1 – $280.00 – us S.A.A. [025]

AMERICAN ARCHIVIST – Chicago. v1- jan 1938- 1*; v50- Win 1987- 5*,9 – 1,5,9 – D16424 – us UMI [020]

AMERICAN ART – (Cont: Smithsonian Studies in American Art) – Oxford. v5-. Win 1991- – 1,5*,9 – D17039.01 – us UMI [700]

AMERICAN ART AND ANTIQUES – (Cont by: Art and Antiques) – New York. v1-2. jul 1978-dec 1979* – 1 – D12626 – us UMI [700]

AMERICAN ART IN THE BARBIZON MOOD / National Collection of Fine Arts. Smithsonian Institution; ed by Birmingham, Peter – 1976 – 2 color mf – 15 – $27.00f – 0-226-69413-5 – us Chicago [760]

AMERICAN ART JOURNAL – New York. v1-Spr 1969 1*; v4- Spr 1972- 5*; v8- may 1976- 9* – 1,5,9 – D6721 – us UMI [700]

AMERICAN ART REVIEW – (Ceased publ) – Boston. v1-2. nov 1879-oct 1881 – 1 – D3354 – us UMI [700]

AMERICAN ART UNION BULLETIN – 1847-53 – 15mf – 9 – £85.00 – uk Chadwyck [073]

AMERICAN ARTISAN *see* AMERICAN ARTISAN

AMERICAN ARTISAN : THE WARM HEATING AND SHEET METAL JOURNAL – (Vols 1-38, 40, 89, 90 were not available for photography. Former titles: American Artisan (1880-mar 26, 1892); American Artisan, Tinner and House Furnisher (apr 2, 1892-1897); American Artisan and Hardware Record (1898-feb 25, 1928)) – Chicago. v39-118. jan 1900-dec 1949 – 1 – D280 – us UMI [073]

AMERICAN ARTISAN AND HARDWARE RECORD *see* AMERICAN ARTISAN

AMERICAN ARTISAN, TINNER AND HOUSE FURNISHER *see* AMERICAN ARTISAN

AMERICAN ARTIST – (Mf ed includes the biannual of: Watercolor, Fall 1991-94. Former title: Art Instruction (apr 1937-dec 1939)) – Stamford. v1-61 apr 1937-dec 1997+ 1; v33-61 jan 1969-dec 1997+ 5; v24-61 jan 1960-dec 1997+ 9. Shipped yrly or qrtly – 1,5,9 – D1425 – us UMI [700]

AMERICAN ARTISTS / Courtauld Institute of Art – (Printed index of 4,000 artists included) – 1994 – 803mf – 9 – $5,800.00 – 1-869934-99-7 – uk Emmett [700]

AMERICAN ASIAN REVIEW – Queens. v1-Spr 1983- 1*; v12- 1994- 5*,9* – 1,5,9 – D21271 – us UMI [073]

AMERICAN ASSISTANCE TO INDONESIA : PROGRAM AND FINANCIAL DETAILS – SE-3209 1. 1960? – 9 – ne IDC [950]

AMERICAN ASSISTANCE TO INDONESIA : PROGRAM HIGHLIGHTS – SE-3025 1. 1960 – 9 – ne IDC [950]

American Association for Cancer Research *see* PROCEEDINGS

American Association for Health, Physical Education and Recreation *see* RESEARCH QUARTERLY

American Association for Higher Education *see* AAHE BULLETIN

AMERICAN ASSOCIATION FOR LABOR LEGISLATION, 1905-1943 – 71r – 1 – $4655.00 – us UMI [331]

AMERICAN ASSOCIATION FOR LABORATORY ACCREDIATION (A2LA) – (Updated Every 60 Days) – Information Handling Services – 5,9 – us Info Handling [500]

American Association for Respiratory Therapy (A A RT) *see* AARTIMES

American Association for the Advancement of Science *see*
- BULLETIN – AMERICAN ASSOCIATION FOR THE ADVANCEMENT OF SCIENCE
- PROCEEDINGS

AMERICAN ASSOCIATION FOR THE ADVANCEMENT OF SCIENCE, SCIENCE AND HUMAN RIGHTS PROGRAM, OFFICE OF SCIENTIFIC FREEDOM AND RESPONSIBILITY – (Missing: Doc 92) – Washington D.C. 94 docs. 1980-1991 – 36mf – 9 – ne IDC [320]

American Association for the Education of the Severely/Profoundly Handicapped *see* AAESPH REVIEW

American Association of Cereal Chemists *see* JOURNAL OF THE AMERICAN ASSOCIATION OF CEREAL CHEMISTS

American Association of Colleges of Pharmacy Teachers' Seminar *see* PROCEEDINGS – AMERICAN ASSOCIATION OF COLLEGES OF PHARMACY TEACHERS' SEMINAR

American Association of Cost Engineers (AACE) *see*
- AACE BULLETIN
- TRANSACTIONS

American Association of Equine Practitioners *see* PROCEEDINGS

AMERICAN ASSOCIATION OF INDUSTRIAL NURSES JOURNAL – (Cont by: Occupational Health Nursing) – New York. v1-16. oct 1953-dec 1968* – 1 – D11478 – us UMI [636]

American Association of Instructors and Investigators in Poultry Husbandry *see* JOURNAL

American Association of Law Libraries *see* LAW LIBRARY PACKAGE PLAN

American Association of Nephrology Nurses and Technicians (AANNT) *see* AANNT JOURNAL

AMERICAN ASSOCIATION OF NURSE ANESTHETICS – v35-46. 1967-78 – 1,5,6 – us Princeton Micro [610]

American Association of Nurse Anesthetists (AANA) *see* AANA JOURNAL

American Association of Occupational Health Nurses (AAOHN) *see* AAOHN JOURNAL

American Association of Petroleum Geologists *see*
- AAPG BULLETIN
- BULLETIN

AMERICAN ASSOCIATION OF PETROLEUM GEOLOGISTS BULLETIN *see* AAPG BULLETIN

American Association of School Administrators *see* AASA OFFICIAL REPORT

American Association of Teacher Educators in Agriculture *see* JOURNAL OF THE AMERICAN ASSOCIATION OF TEACHER EDUCATORS IN AGRICULTURE

American Association of Teachers of French *see* FRENCH REVIEW

American Association of Teachers of Slavic and East European Languages *see* AATSEEL'S NEWSLETTER

American Association of University Professors *see* BULLETIN

American Association of University Professors (AAUP) *see* AAUP BULLETIN

AMERICAN ASSOCIATION OF UNIVERSITY WOMEN : ARCHIVES, 1881-1976 – (Includes personal papers of Ida H. Hyde (1867-1947)) – 158r – 1 – $9,950.00 – us UMI [370]

American Association of University Women (AAUW) *see* AAUW JOURNAL

American Astronautical Society *see*
- COMPLETE AAS MICROFICHE SERIES COLLECTION
- OUT-OF-PRINT AAS BOOKS ON MICROFICHE

The American Astronomical Society *see* BULLETIN

AMERICAN ATHENAEUM, A REPOSITORY OF BELLES LETTRES, SCIENCE AND THE ARTS – (Absorbed into: New-York Literary Gazette, and American Athenaeum) – New York. v1. apr 1825-mar 1826 – 1 – D4410 – us UMI [073]

AMERICAN ATHLETE AND CYCLE TRADE REVIEW – v1-15, no. 13 (all publ). Mar 1887?-Mar 1895 – 6r – 1 – $655.00 – us UPA [790]

AMERICAN AVIATION – v1-33 1937-69 1; 1968-69 5,6 – us UMI [629]

AMERICAN BABY – (1985- 5,6,9) – v1- 1940- – 1 – us UMI [618]

AMERICAN BABY'S CHILDBIRTH EDUCATOR – (Ceased publ) – New York. v1-9. Fall 1981-Win 1990* – 1 – D15631 – us UMI [618]

AMERICAN BAKER – (Ceased publ. Cont: the monthly "Northwestern Miller and American Baker"; Issue of: Northwestern Miller) – Minneapolis. v9-28. jan 1941-jun 1960* – 1 – D375 – us UMI [640]

AMERICAN BANKER – (Index available. Not available for filming: 1885; jul 1887-feb 9 1888; 1889; jan-jun 1981; 2892; apr 8-jun 30 1896; dec 12-26 1914; may 14-jun 25 1923; 1938. Former title: Thompson's Bank Note and Commercial Recorder (1836-jan 22 1887)) – New York, 1884-1997 1; 1979-97 9 – 1,9 – D60533 – us UMI [332]

AMERICAN BANKER – New York, NY. 1974-1975 – 12r – 1 – $600.00 – R04900 – us Library Micro [071]

American Bankers Association *see*
- ABA BANKING JOURNAL
- PROTECTIVE BULLETIN

AMERICAN BANKERS ASSOCIATION JOURNAL *see* PROTECTIVE BULLETIN

AMERICAN BANKRUPTCY INSTITUTE JOURNAL *see* ABI NEWSLETTER

AMERICAN BANKRUPTCY INSTITUTE JOURNAL – (Cont: ABI Newsletter) – Washington. jul 1992- 1*; 1995- 5,9 – 1,5,9 – D22553.01 – us UMI [332]

AMERICAN BANKRUPTCY LAW JOURNAL – v1-69. 1926-1995 – 9 – $666.00 set – us Hein [340]

AMERICAN BANKRUPTCY LAW JOURNAL – (Former titles: Journal of the National Association of Referees in Bankruptcy (dec 1926-oct 1965); Journal of the National Conference of Referees in Bankruptcy (1966-oct 1970)) – Ft. Wayne. v1- 1927- 1*; v50-Win 1976- 5,9 – 1,5,9 – D6484 – us UMI [340]

AMERICAN BANKRUPTCY REPORTS *see* NATIONAL BANKRUPTCY NEWS AND REPORTS

AMERICAN BANKRUPTCY REPORTS, ANNOTATED – (Cont by: National Bankruptcy News and Reports. Title followed by a new series v1-57 1924-45. Not available from LLMC for copyright reasons) – Albany: M Bender. v1-49 + digest nos 1 + 2. 1899-1923 (all publ) – 560mf – 9 – $840.00 – LLMC 82-404 – us L.L.M.C. [340]

AMERICAN BAPTIST – (Cont: Crusader and Mission) – New York. v7-28. 1850-72 (complete) – 9r – 1 – ATLA R0103 – us A.T.L.A. [240]

AMERICAN BAPTIST *see* AMERICAN BAPTISTS IN MISSION

AMERICAN BAPTIST – (Formed by the union of: Baptist Missionary Magazine & Baptist Home Mission Monthly & Good Work. Cont: American Baptists in Mission. Former titles: Missions, American Baptist International Magazine (jan 1910-apr 1967); Mission (may 1967-mar 1970)) – Valley Forge. v1-190 jan 1910-aug 1992 1*; v175-190 jan 1977-aug 1992 5*,9* – 1,5,9 – D1979 – us UMI [240]

AMERICAN BAPTIST FLAG – Missouri. 1875-1937 – 1 – 1436.19 – us Baptist [240]

American Baptist Foreign Mission Societies *see* MISSIONARY CORRESPONDENCE

The American Baptist Historical Society, Chester, Pa *see* CHRONICLE
American Baptist Home Mission Societies *see* ANNUAL REPORTS AND DIRECTORIES
The American Baptist Missionary Union *see* MISSIONARY JUBILEE
American Baptist Publication Society *see* THE BAPTIST HARP
AMERICAN BAPTIST QUARTERLY – (Cont: Foundations) – Rochester. v1-16 oct 1982-dec 1997+ 1*; v4-16 mar 1985-dec 1997+ 5*,9 – 1,5,9 – D15659 – us UMI [240]
AMERICAN BAPTIST REGISTER FOR 1852 / Burrows, J. Lansing – 1 – 19.11 – us Baptist [240]
American Baptist Theological Seminary *see* BULLETINS
American Baptist Theological Seminary. Nashville, Tennessee *see* CATALOGS
AMERICAN BAPTIST YEARBOOK – 1841-1940 – 1 – 646.46 – us Baptist [240]
AMERICAN BAPTISTS IN MISSION *see* AMERICAN BAPTIST
AMERICAN BAPTISTS IN MISSION – (Cont: American Baptist) – Valley Forge. v191-. sep 1992- – 1,5*,9 – D1979.01 – us UMI [240]
AMERICAN BAR ASSOCIATION = SECTION OF INDIVIDUAL RIGHTS AND RESPONSIBILITIES – Chicago. 28 docs. 1980-1990 – 24mf – 9 – ne IDC [320]
American Bar Association *see*
- AMERICAN BAR ASSOCIATION JOURNAL
- CANONS OF PROFESSIONAL ETHICS
- REPORT OF THE SPECIAL COMMITTEE, APPOINTED TO CONSIDER AND REPORT WHETHER THE PRESENT DELAY AND UNCERTAINTY IN JUDICIAL ADMINISTRATION CAN BE LESSENED.

American Bar Association (ABA) *see* ABA JOURNAL
AMERICAN BAR ASSOCIATION ANNUAL REPORTS – (No additions poss for copyright reasons) – v1-85. 1878-1960 – 759mf – 9 – $1,138.00 – LLMC 81-400 – us L.L.M.C. [073]
AMERICAN BAR ASSOCIATION ARCHIVE COLLECTION – (Inception-1985 $27,995.00 set. 1986-92 $1,750.00y) – Inception-1992 – 9 – $35,000.00 set – us Hein [340]
American Bar Association. Committee on Canons of Professional Ethics *see* REPORT
American Bar Association. Committee on Unauthorized Practice of the Law *see* COMPENDIUM.
AMERICAN BAR ASSOCIATION JOURNAL – (Updates planned) – v1. 1915 – 7mf – 9 – $10.50 – LLMC 90-316 – us L.L.M.C. [073]
AMERICAN BAR ASSOCIATION JOURNAL *see*
- ABA JOURNAL

AMERICAN BAR ASSOCIATION JOURNAL / American Bar Association – (Cont by: ABA Journal) – Chicago. v1-69 jan 1915-dec 1983 1; v57-69 jan 1971-dec 1983 5; v63-69 jan 1977-dec 1983 9 – 1,5,9 – D1897 – us UMI [340]
AMERICAN BAR ASSOCIATION MODEL PROCUREMENT CODE SLIM / U.S. National Institute of Justice – 1985. 98 documents – 9 – $188.00 – us N.C.J.R.S. [360]
AMERICAN BAR ASSOCIATION. SECTION OF ANTITRUST LAW PROCEEDINGS *see* ANTITRUST LAW JOURNAL
AMERICAN BAR ASSOCIATION. SECTION OF FAMILY LAW *see* FAMILY LAW QUARTERLY (ABA)
American Bar Association. Section of Insurance, Negligence and Compensation *see* FORUM
American Bar Association, Section of Insurance Negligence and Compensation Law *see* PROCEEDINGS
AMERICAN BAR ASSOCIATION, SECTION OF INTERNATIONAL AND COMPARATIVE LAW. BULLETIN *see* INTERNATIONAL LAWYER
AMERICAN BAR ASSOCIATION: SECTION OF REAL PROPERTY, PROBATE AND TRUST LAW *see* REAL PROPERTY PROBATE AND TRUST JOURNAL (ABA)
AMERICAN BAR ASSOCIATION SECTION OF TAXATION. BULLETIN *see* TAX LAWYER (ABA)
AMERICAN BAR ASSOCIATION VISIT TO ENGLAND, SCOTLAND AND IRELAND, 1924 : MEMORIAL VOLUME – New York: ABA Committee on Publications, 1926 – 6mf – 9 – $9.00 – LLMC 92-127 – us L.L.M.C. [340]
American Bar Foundation *see* AMERICAN BAR FOUNDATION RESEARCH JOURNAL
AMERICAN BAR FOUNDATION RESEARCH JOURNAL / American Bar Foundation – (Cont by: Law and Social Inquiry) – Chicago. 1976-1987 1*; 1982-1987 5,9 – 1,5,9 – D13519 – us UMI [340]
AMERICAN BAR FOUNDATION RESEARCH REPORTER – (All that is currently offered) – Chicago. v13-23. Win 1979-Fall 1983 – 1,5,9 – D12104.01 – us UMI [340]
AMERICAN BAR NEWS – (Ceased publ) – Chicago. jul 1956-jul 1974*; v20-21 jan 1975-jun 1976 1; v21 feb-jun 1976 5*,9 – 1,5,9 – D10723 – us UMI [340]
THE AMERICAN BARON: A NOVEL / De Mille, James – New York: Harper, 1872. 05403. (Pre-1900 Canadiana) – 9 – cn C.I.H.M. [830]
AMERICAN BEACON – Norfolk. Va. 1815-20 – 1,3 – us Readex [071]
AMERICAN BEACON – Norfolk. Va. Title varies. 1815-1855 – 1 – us UMI [071]
AMERICAN BEE JOURNAL – v. 112-113. 1972-73 – 1,5,6 – us Princeton Micro [630]
AMERICAN BEE JOURNAL – (Publ suspended fom 1862-jun 1866) – Hamilton. v1- jan 1861- 1; v111- jan 1971- 5; v116- jan 1976- 9* – 1,5,9 – D317 – us UMI [073]
AMERICAN BEEF PRODUCER – (Former titles: Producer (jun 1919-may 1934); American Cattle Producer (jun 1934-mar 1969)) – Denver. v1-53 jun 1919-feb 1972 1; v52-53 jun 1970-feb 1972 5 – 1,5 – D1110 – us UMI [636]
AMERICAN BEHAVIORAL SCIENTIST – (Shipped qtrly or yrly. Fomer title: Political Research, Organization and Design (sep 1957-jun 1960)) – Beverly Hills. v1- sep 1957- 1; v10- sep 1966- 5; v19- sep 1975- 9 – 1,5,9 – D1598 – us UMI [150]
AMERICAN BENEDICTINE REVIEW – Richardton. v1- Spr 1950- 1; v22- mar 1971- 5*; v27- mar 1976- 9 – 1,5,9 – D2224 – us UMI [240]
AMERICAN BIBLE SOCIETY : ANNUAL REPORT / American Bible Society – (Lacking: some pgs) – 1817-1988 – 1 – ATLA S0670 – us A.T.L.A. [073]
AMERICAN BIBLE SOCIETY – (Lacking: 1860 p33-48) – v1-29, v1-130. 1843-48, 1856-1989 – 20r – 1 – ATLA S0515 – us A.T.L.A. [240]
American Bible Society *see* AMERICAN BIBLE SOCIETY
AMERICAN BIBLIOGRAPHY / Evans, Charles – 12 v. 1903-1934, plus v. 13, American Antiquarian Society, 1955 – 3 – us Readex [010]
AMERICAN BIBLIOPOLIST – (Ceased publ) – New York. v1-9. jan 1869-apr 1877 – 1 – D3355 – us UMI [020]
AMERICAN BIOGRAPHICAL ARCHIVE (ABA 1) = AMERIKANISCHES BIOGRAPHISCHES ARCHIV (ABA 1) / ed by Gibbs, Nanette & Worters, Garance – (Printed Index.- Distribution rights for German-speaking Europe and Eastern Europe only) – 1986-1991 – 1842mf (1:24) – 9 – diazo DM20,800.00 (silver DM22,800.00 ISBN: 3-598-30951-1) – 3-598-30950-3 – gw Saur [920]
AMERICAN BIOGRAPHICAL ARCHIVE (ABA 2) = AMERIKANISCHES BIOGRAPHISCHES ARCHIV : SERIES 2 (ABA 2) / Baillie, Laureen – 1993-1996 – 734mf (1:24) in 12 installments – 9 – diazo DM22,800.00 (silver DM24,600.00 ISBN: 3-598-33534-2) – 3-598-33520-2 – Dist. ja Maruzen – gw Saur [920]
AMERICAN BIOGRAPHICAL DIRECTORIES / Potomac Press – Concise biographies of District of Columbia's prominent and representative contemporary citizens and valuable statistical data 1908-1909. Washington, DC, 1908. District of Columbia Reel 1. (The Cox Library Collection) – 5 – us Americana [978]
AMERICAN BIOGRAPHICAL HISTORY OF EMINENT AND SELF-MADE MEN OF THE STATE OF MICHIGAN / Western Biographical Publishing Co – Cincinnati, 1878. Michigan Reel 2. (The Cox Library Collection) – 5 – us Americana [920]
AMERICAN BIOLOGY TEACHER – Washington. v1-59 oct 1938-dec 1997+ 1; v32-59 jan 1970-dec 1997+ 5; v37-59 jan 1975-dec 1997+ 9. Shipped yrly or qrtly – 1,5,9 – D1535 – us UMI [370]
AMERICAN BIRDS – (Supersedes sect 2 of: Audobon Magazine. Cont by: National Audobon Society Field Notes. Former title: Audobon Field Notes (jan 1974-dec 1970)) – New York. cum index 1-13 1949-59; v1-48 jan 1947-Spr 1994 1; v24-48 feb 1970-Spr 1994 5; v29-48 feb 1975-Spr 1994 9 – 1,5,9 – D1800 – us UMI [590]
THE AMERICAN BOARD IN CHINA 1830-1950 / Goodsell, Fred Field – Review and appraisal. 1969 – 1 – us A.T.L.A. [240]
American Board of Commissioners for Foreign Missions. Foochow *see* FOOCHOW MESSENGER
American Board of Commissioners for Foreign Missions. North China Mission. Fenchow Station *see* FENCHOW
AMERICAN BOAT MODELER – (Cont by: Radio Control Boat Modeler) – Wilton. v1. 1987* – 1 – D22547 – us UMI [629]
AMERICAN BOOK PUBLISHING RECORD – Newton. v1-10 feb 1960- 1; v18-19 jan 1977- 5*; v18 jan 1977- 9 – 1,5,9 – D3437 – us UMI [070]
AMERICAN BOOK REVIEW – Newark, NJ. 1977-1983 – 3r – 1 – $150.00 – R04977 – us Library Micro [073]
AMERICAN BOY – (All that is currently available) – Detroit. v1-11. nov 1899-nov 1910* – 1 – D3356 – us UMI [073]
AMERICAN BUILDER – (Ceased publ. Former titles: American Carpenter and Builder (apr 1905-jan 1917); American Builder (feb 1917-sep 1930); American Builder and Building Age (oct 1930-may 1948)) – New York. v1-102. apr 1905-feb 1969 (ns) – 1 – D288 – us UMI [690]
AMERICAN BUILDER *see* AMERICAN BUILDER
AMERICAN BUILDER AND BUILDING AGE *see* AMERICAN BUILDER
AMERICAN BULLETIN; THE WHITE MAN'S VIEWPOINT – New York. v. 1-2, no. 30. 28 Mar 1935-3 Nov 1936 – 1 – us NY Public [073]
American Bureau of Industrial Research *see* MANUSCRIPT COLLECTIONS ON THE EARLY AMERICAN LABOR MOVEMENT, 1862-1908
AMERICAN BUSINESS – (Ceased publ. Merged with: Office management, to form: Office Management and American business. Former titles: Office Equipment Salesman (oct 1930-oct 1932); American Salesman (dec 1932-jun 1934)) – Chicago. v3-30 jan 1933-apr 1960 – 1 – D447 – us UMI [650]
American Business Communication Association *see* ABCA BULLETIN
AMERICAN BUSINESS LAW : WITH LEGAL FORMS / Sullivan, John J – New York/ London: D Appleton, 1909 – 5mf – 9 – $7.50 – LLMC 92-170 – us L.L.M.C. [340]
AMERICAN BUSINESS LAW JOURNAL – Austin. v1-35 Spr 1963- 1; v9-35 Spr 1971- 5; v15-35 Spr 1977- 9 – 1,5,9 – D2428 – us UMI [340]
AMERICAN BUSINESS REVIEW – West Haven. v1-16 jun 1983- 1*; v11-16 1992-* 5,9 – 1,5,9 – D20145 – us UMI [650]
THE AMERICAN CARAVAN: A YEARBOOK OF AMERICAN LITERATURE – New York. 1927-1936 – 1 – us NY Public [800]
American Carpatho-Russian Youth *see* KALENDAR
AMERICAN CARPENTER AND BUILDER *see* AMERICAN BUILDER
AMERICAN CARTOGRAPHER – (Cont by: Cartography and Geographic Information Systems) – Falls Church. cum index 1-6; v1-16 apr 1974-oct 1989 1,5,9 – 1,5,9 – D12484 – us UMI [520]
AMERICAN CASES ON CONTRACT. / Huffcut, Ernest Wilson – 2d ed. Albany, N.Y.: Banks, 1900. 898p. LL-644 – 1 – us L of C Photodup [340]
AMERICAN CATHOLIC HISTORICAL RESEARCHES – (Ceased publ. Former titles: Historical researches in western Pennsylvania, principally Catholic (jul 1884-apr 1885); Catholic historical researches (jul 1885-oct 1886)) – Philadelphia. cum index v1-NS 1884-1912; v1-21 jul 1884-oct 1904; ns 1-8 jan 1905-jul 1912 – 1 – D5210 – us UMI [240]
AMERICAN CATHOLIC PHILOSOPHICAL QUARTERLY – (For suppl 1990. Proceedings of the American Catholic Philosophical Association. Cont: New scholasticism) – Washington. v64-71 Win 1990- – 1,5,9 – D430.01 – us UMI [240]
AMERICAN CATHOLIC QUARTERLY REVIEW – (Ceased publ) – Philedelphia. cum index v1-25 jan 1876-oct 1900; v1-49 jan 1876-jan 1924 – 1 – D5211 – us UMI [240]
AMERICAN CATHOLIC TRIBUNE – Cincinnati. v3-9. 1887-94 (complete) – 2r – 1 – ATLA S0333 – us A.T.L.A. [240]
AMERICAN CATTLE PRODUCER *see* AMERICAN BEEF PRODUCER
AMERICAN CENTENNIAL NEWSPAPERS – 1876 – 40r – 1 – us Ross [071]
American Ceramic Society *see*
- ABSTRACTS
- AMERICAN CERAMIC SOCIETY BULLETIN
- BULLETIN
- CERAMIC ABSTRACTS
- JOURNAL
- JOURNAL OF THE AMERICAN CERAMIC SOCIETY

AMERICAN CERAMIC SOCIETY BULLETIN / American Ceramic Society – (Vols 1-12 n6 1922-jun 1933 and v21 n1-4 jan-apr 1942 included in mf ed of: Journal of the American Ceramic Society. Vol 21 n5-v24 include: Ceramic Abstracts. Former title: Bulletin of the American Ceramic Society (1922-dec 15 1945)) – Columbus. cum index 1-38 1918-55; v12-76 jul 1933-dec 1997+ 1; v46-76 jan 1967-dec 1997+ 5; v54-76 jan 1975-dec 1997+ 9 – 1,5,9 – D1543 – us UMI [730]
AMERICAN CERAMIC SOCIETY BULLETIN *see* JOURNAL OF THE AMERICAN CERAMIC SOCIETY
THE AMERICAN CHAMBER OF COMMERCE JOURNAL/THE CHAMBER – 35v. illus. -m. Ceased publ. with v35, no.10 in Oct 1959? Suspended publ. 194?-Dec 1945 – 1 – us U.W. Library [380]
American Chamber of Commerce. Liverpool. BRRAM *see* THE MINUTE BOOKS
THE AMERICAN CHARACIDAE / Eigenmann, C H – Z-5 2. 1917-1929 – 8 – ne IDC [590]
AMERICAN CHEMICAL JOURNAL – v. 1-50. 1879-1913 – 1,5,6 – us Princeton Micro [540]
American Chemical Society *see*
- ACCOUNTS OF CHEMICAL RESEARCH
- CHEMICAL ABSTRACTS
- JOURNAL OF THE AMERICAN CHEMICAL SOCIETY
- PREPRINTS OF PAPERS

AMERICAN CHILD / National Child Labor Committee – v1-37 (1919-55) and Child Labor Bulletin 1-7 (1912-19) – 86mf – 9 – $305.00 – us UPA [331]
AMERICAN CHILDHOOD – (Ceased publ. Former titles: Kindergarten and First Grade: a magazine of practical help and suggestion for teachers of kindergarten and first primary grade (jan 1916-jun 1924); Kindergarten and First Grade Magazine (sep 1924-mar 1926)) – Springfield. v1-43. jan 1916-jun 1958 – 1 – D1116 – us UMI [370]
American Chiropractic Association *see* ACA JOURNAL OF CHIROPRACTIC
AMERICAN CHIROPRACTOR – Fort Wayne. v1-19 1979- – 1 – D16155 – us UMI [615]
AMERICAN CHRISTIAN EXPOSITOR – v1. 1831-32 – 1 – $50.00 – us Presbyterian [978]
AMERICAN CHURCH MONTHLY – (Ceased publ) – New York. v1-3 jan 1857-jun 1858 – 1 – D2773 – us UMI [240]
THE AMERICAN CHURCH MONTHLY – v1-42. 1917-37 (complete) – Inquire – 1 – ATLA 1994-S535 – us A.T.L.A. [073]
AMERICAN CHURCH NEWS – (Cont by: New Oxford review. Former titles: American Church Union. ACU news (1933-Jan 1959)) – Oakland. v22-32 apr 1955-jan 1977 1; v44 jan 1977 5; v44 jan 1977 9 – 1,5,9 – D2223 – us UMI [240]
AMERICAN CINEMATOGRAPHER – (Vol 1 was never publ) – Hollywood. v2-78 oct 1921-dec 1997+ 1; v49-78 jan 1968-dec 1997+ 5,9 – 1,5,9 – D2115 – us UMI [790]
AMERICAN CITIZEN – New York. N.Y. 1800-1810 – 3 – us Readex [071]
AMERICAN CITIZEN – Omaha, NE. -w. Jul 1938; Oct 1939-Dec 1964; Jan 1966 to date – 1 – us NE Hist [071]
AMERICAN CITIZEN – Portland OR. Dec 28 1933, Jan 23 1934 – 1 – us U.O. Library [071]
THE AMERICAN CITIZEN – Des Moines, IA. -w. 17 Jul 1925-29 Dec 1972. 12 reels, 600 feet – 1 – us I.H.R.C. [071]
THE AMERICAN CITIZEN – (In English) – Des Moines, IA. 1940-43 – 1r – 1 – $85.00 – D3366 – us Scholarly Res [071]
THE AMERICAN CITIZEN – New York. N.Y. 1912-14 – 1 – us A.J.P.C. [071]

AMERICAN CITY – (Cont by: American City and County) – Pittsfield. v1-90 sep 1909-aug 1975 1; v83-90 jan 1968-aug 1975 5; v85-90 jan 1970-aug 1975 9 – 1,5,9 – D12 – us UMI [073]

AMERICAN CITY *see* AMERICAN CITY AND COUNTY

AMERICAN CITY AND COUNTY – (Cont: American City) – Pittsfield. v90-112 sep 1975-dec 1997+ 1,5,9. Shipped yrly or qrtly – 1,5,9 – D12.01 – us UMI [073]

AMERICAN CITY AND COUNTY *see* AMERICAN CITY

AMERICAN CITY, VIRGINIA CITY, GOLD HILL AND SILVER CITY DIRECTORY – State of Nevada. 1864-1865 – 1r – 1 – $50.00 – D116 – us Library Micro [910]

AMERICAN CIVIL LAW JOURNAL – New York. v1. 1873 – 1 – $40.00 – us Hein [073]

American Civil Liberties Union *see* RECORDS AND PUBLICATIONS

AMERICAN CIVIL LIBERTIES UNION ARCHIVES – (Includes guide) – 1995 – 293r – 1 – $24,905.00 – D3306 – Co-publ with Princeton University, New York Public Library and ACLU – us Scholarly Res [320]

AMERICAN CIVIL LIBERTIES UNION RECORDS AND PUBLICATIONS, 1917-1990 – (Base collection (1917-75) $6630; updates 1974-78 $450; 1978-80 $295; 1981-1984 $755; 1985-89 n.p.) – 106r (base collection); 22r (updates) – 1 – $8130.00 complete – us UMI [323]

AMERICAN CLASSICAL LEAGUE NEWSLETTER – (1980- 5,6,9) – 1978- – 1 – us UMI [073]

AMERICAN COIN-OP – (Cont by: Coin-op) – Chicago. v21-38 jan 1980-* – 1 – D1675.01 – us UMI [730]

AMERICAN COLLECTION, 1940- *see*
- LITTLE MAGAZINES (COLLECTION)

AMERICAN COLLECTION, 1910-1919 *see*
- LITTLE MAGAZINES (COLLECTION)

AMERICAN COLLECTION, 1920-1929 *see*
- LITTLE MAGAZINES (COLLECTION)

AMERICAN COLLECTION, 1930-1939 *see*
- LITTLE MAGAZINES (COLLECTION)

THE AMERICAN COLLEGE / Sharpless, Isaac – Garden City, N.Y.: Doubleday, Page, 1915 – 1mf – us A.T.L.A. [370]

AMERICAN COLLEGE ATHLETICS / Savage, Howard J – 1929 – 8mf – 9 – $24.00 – us Microform Publ [370]

American College Health Association *see* ACHA ACTION

American College of Nursing Home Administrators *see* JOURNAL

American College of Surgeons *see*
- BULLETIN
- SURGICAL FORUM

AMERICAN COLONISTS IN ENGLISH RECORDS – Comp. by George Sherwood 1962.Item E. A guide to direct references in authentic records not in Hotten. Orig. publ. 1932 in London. Dates are from 1609-1773. Indexed, 215p. SW16-0078 – 5 – us A.G.L.L. [978]

American Colonization Society *see*
- ANNUAL REPORT OF THE AMERICAN COLONIZATION SOCIETY
- RECORDS

THE AMERICAN COLONIZATION SOCIETY – (With guide) – 323r – 1 – $11,305.00 – Dist. us Scholarly Res – us L of C Photodup [976]

American Committee for South Asian Art *see* ARCHIVES

AMERICAN COMMITTEE ON AFRICA AND THE AFRICA FUND – New York. 245 docs. 1980-1991 – 39mf – 9 – ne IDC [320]

THE AMERICAN COMMONWEALTH / Bryce, James – 2nd rev ed. London: MacMillan & Co. 2v. 1891 – 16mf – 9 – $24.00 – LLMC 95-063 – us L.L.M.C. [323]

THE AMERICAN COMMONWEALTH / Bryce, James – 3rd ed. New York: The Macmillan Co, 1908 – 18mf – 9 – $27.00 – LLMC 92-168 – us L.L.M.C. [323]

AMERICAN COMMUNITIES AND CO-OPERATIVE COLONIES / Hinds, William Alfred – Chicago: C.H. Kerr, 1908 – 2mf – us A.T.L.A. [334]

AMERICAN CONFERENCE ON INTERNATIONAL ARBITRATION HELD IN WASHINGTON, D.C. APRIL 22 AND 23 1896 – New York, 1896 – 3mf – 9 – ILM-4061/1 – ne IDC [340]

THE AMERICAN CONFLICT : A HISTORY OF THE GREAT REBELLION IN THE UNITED STATES OF AMERICA, 1860-1864 / Greeley, Horace – 2v. 1865-67 – 1r – 1 – us Ross [976]

American Congregational Association Library *see* BULLETIN OF THE CONGREGATIONAL LIBRARY

American Congregational Association. Library *see* BULLETIN

American Congress n Surveying and Mapping *see* JOINT PROCEEDINGS

American Congress on Surveying and Mapping *see*
- BULLETIN
- PAPERS
- PAPERS FROM THE ANNUAL MEETING
- PROCEEDINGS

AMERICAN CONGRESS ON SURVEYING AND MAPPING *see* TECHNICAL PAPERS

American Congress on Surveying and Mapping *see*
- TECHNICAL PAPERS

AMERICAN CONGRESS ON SURVEYING AND MAPPING BULLETIN *see* ACSM BULLETIN

American Congress on Surveying and Mapping Fall Technical Meeting *see* TECHNICAL PAPERS

AMERICAN CONGRESS ON SURVEYING AND MAPPING (FALL TECHNICAL MEETING9 TECHNICAL PAPERS *see* ASP-ACSM (AMERICAN CONGRESS ON SURVEYING AND MAPPING) TECHNICAL PAPERS

AMERICAN CONGRESS ON SURVEYING AND MAPPING JOINT PROCEEDING OF THE AMERICAN SOCIETY OF PHOTOGRAMMETRY *see* TECHNICAL PAPERS

American Congress on Surveying and Mapping. Meeting Technical Papers *see*
- ANNUAL MEETING ACSM
- ANNUAL MEETING OF THE AMERICAN CONGRESS ON SURVEYING AND MAPPING

AMERICAN CONSTELLATION – Petersburg. Va. 1825-1828; 1838 – 1 – us UMI [071]

THE AMERICAN CONSTITUTIONAL SYSTEM : AN INTRODUCTION TO THE STUDY OF THE AMERICAN STATE / Willoughby, Westel Woodbury – New York: The Century Co, 1919 – 4mf – 9 – $6.00 – LLMC 95-080 – us L.L.M.C. [323]

AMERICAN CONSTITUTIONS : CONSTITUTING THE CONSTITUTIONS OF EACH STATE IN THE UNION OF THE UNITED STATES / Hough, Franklin B – Albany: Weed-Parsons. 2v. 1871 – 6mf – 9 – $9.00 – LLMC 84-257 – us L.L.M.C. [323]

American Convention for Promoting the Abolition of Slavery, and Improving the Condition of the African Race *see* MINUTES

THE AMERICAN CONVEYANCER; CONTAINING A LARGE VARIETY OF LEGAL FORMS AND INSTRUMENTS, ADAPTED TO POPULAR WANTS AND PROFESSIONAL USE THROUGHOUT THE UNITED STATES. / Curtis, George Ticknor – New ed. Boston, Little, Brown, 1847. 283 p. LL-1089 – 1 – us L of C Photodup [340]

AMERICAN COPTIC ASSOCIATION – Jersey Cita. 49 docs. 1981-1991 – 19mf – 9 – ne IDC [360]

AMERICAN CORPORATION CASES – Chicago, IL: E B Myers Co. v1-10 + digest. 1868-87 (all publ) – 88mf – 9 – $132.00 – LLMC 80-431 – us L.L.M.C. [340]

AMERICAN CORRECTIONAL ASSOCIATION : PROCEEDINGS OF ANNUAL CONGRESSES – (Indexes for 1870, 1874, 1876 and 1884-1934. No meetings held in 1871-73, 1875 or 1877-82. Name of organization varies: 1871-1907 – The National Prison Association. 1908-54 – The American Prison Association. Lacking: Congress of 1870. Report 1918. Also missing p63-64, 137-138 1897. p323-338 1920) – 1874-1964 – 379mf – 9 – $568.00 – LLMC 84-267 – us L.L.M.C. [340]

American Correctional Association *see* ANNUAL CONGRESS ON CORRECTION PROCEEDINGS

AMERICAN CORRECTIVE THERAPY JOURNAL – (Cont by: Clinical kinesiology. Former tiles: Journal of the Association for Physical and Mental Rehabilitation (mar 1947-may 1948); Physical and mental rehabilitation journal: official publication of the Physical and Mental Rehabilitation Association (aug 1948-apr 1949); Journal of the Association of Physical and Mental Rehabilitation (jun 1949-jul-aug 1967)) – Houston. cum index v1-5 1947-1951 v1-41 mar 1947-dec 1987 1; v25-41 jan 1971-dec 1987 5; v30-41 jan 1976-dec 1987 9 – 1,5,9 – D3189 – us UMI [615]

THE AMERICAN CORRESPONDENCE / Royal Society of Arts – 1755-1840. BRRAM – 1 – uk Microform Academic [975]

THE AMERICAN CORRESPONDENCE OF J. BRYCE, 1871-1922. BRRAM / Bryce, James – 1 – uk Microform Academic [920]

American Council Against Nazi Propaganda *see* HOUR

American Council of Learned Societies *see* ACLS NEWSLETTER

American Council on Consumer Interests *see* NEWSLETTER

American Council on Consumer Interests. (ACCI) *see* NEWSLETTER

American Council on Industrial Arts Teacher Education *see* YEARBOOK

AMERICAN COUNCIL ON INDUSTRIAL ARTS TEACHER EDUCATION YEARBOOK – (Cont by: Yearbook. Council on Technology Teacher Education) – Bloomington. 1952-1986 1; 1976-1986 5*; 1976-1986 9 – 1,5,9 – D10486 – us UMI [370]

AMERICAN CRAFT – (Cont: Craft Horizons with Craft World) – New York. v39-57. jun 1979-jan 1998+. Shipped yrly or qrtly – 1,5,9 – D773.01 – us UMI [740]

AMERICAN CRAFT COUNCIL OUTLOOK *see* ACC OUTLOOK

American Crafts Council *see* ACC OUTLOOK

American Crafts Council.(ACC) *see* OUTLOOK

AMERICAN CRAFTSMAN – New York. v1-33. 1884-98 – 2r – 1 – us Ross [740]

AMERICAN CRIMINAL LAW QUARTERLY *see* AMERICAN CRIMINAL LAW REVIEW

AMERICAN CRIMINAL LAW REVIEW – (Former titles: Criminal Law Quarterly (nov 1962-feb 1963); American Criminal Law Quarterly (may 1963-Fall 1970)) – Chicago. cum index 1-4; v1-35 nov 1962-Spr 1998+ 1; v10-35 jul 1971-Spr 1998+ 5*; v13-35 Sum 1975-Spr 1998+ 9 – 1,5,9 – D6716 – us UMI [340]

AMERICAN CRIMINAL LAW REVIEW – v1-31. 1962-94 – 1,5,6 – $540.00 – us Hein [340]

AMERICAN CRIMINAL REPORTS – (With index) – Callaghan & Co. v1-15. 1878-1909 – 126mf – 9 – $189.00 – LLMC 84-263 – us L.L.M.C. [340]

THE AMERICAN CRITERION OF THE ENGLISH LANGUAGE / Carrol, James – 1795. 125p. (English Linguistics Series 1500-1800) – 9 – us UMI [420]

AMERICAN CRITIC AND GENERAL REVIEW – (Ceased publ) – Washington. v1 apr 1820 – 1 – D4411 – us UMI [073]

AMERICAN CULTURAL HISTORY, 1607-1829 / Knapp, Samuel Lorenzo – 9 – 20.00 – us Scholars' Facs [420]

AMERICAN CULTURE AND THE NORTHWEST COAST / Kroeber, A L – BN 288 2. 1923 – 8 – ne IDC [306]

AMERICAN CULTURE SERIES 2 (ACS 2) – (Includes American Culture Series 1; 12 individual units available separately) – 643r – 1 – $38,315.00 – us UMI [975]

AMERICAN CULTURE SERIES I (ACS I), 1493-1806 – 26r – 1 – $1900.00 – us UMI [975]

AMERICAN CYCLOPAEDIA – Classical Encyclopedias collection – 154mf – 9 – us UMI [030]

AMERICAN CYCLOPEDIA – A popular dictionary of general knowledge. v1-16. 1873. N.s. v1. 1876 – 1,5,6 – us Princeton Micro [073]

AMERICAN DAIRY REVIEW – (Ceased publ. Absorbed by: Dairy record) – Chicago. v1-43 aug 1939-may 1981 1; v33-43 jan 1971-may 1981 5; v38-43 jan 1976-may 1981 9 – 1,5,9 – D2471 – us UMI [630]

AMERICAN DECISIONS – San Francisco: Bancroft-Whitney. v1-100. 1760-1869 (all publ) – 938mf – 9 – $1,407.00 – LLMC 78-032 – us L.L.M.C. [340]

AMERICAN DECORATIVE ART – (Over 2,600 illustrations) – 45mf – 9 – $290.00 – 0-907006-62-0 – uk Mindata [749]

AMERICAN DEMOCRACY VS. THE SPANISH HIERARCHY / Spanish Information Bureau. New York – New York, 1937. Fiche W 716. (Blodgett Collection of Spanish Civil War Pamphlets) – 9 – us H.U. College Libr [946]

AMERICAN DEMOCRAT – Carlisle, PA. -w 1851-62 – 3 rolls – 13 – $25.00r – us I.M.R. [071]

AMERICAN DEMOGRAPHICS – Ithaca. v1-19. jan 1979-dec 1997+ – 1,5,9 – D13396 – us UMI [310]

American Dental Association *see* JOURNAL OF THE AMERICAN DENTAL ASSOCIATION

American Dietetic Association *see*
- JOURNAL
- JOURNAL OF THE AMERICAN DIETETIC ASSOCIATION

AMERICAN DIGEST SYSTEM : CENTURY EDITION – St Paul: West Publ Co. v1-50. 1658-1896 (all publ) – 753mf – 9 – $1,129.00 – LLMC 79-406 – us L.L.M.C. [340]

AMERICAN DIGEST SYSTEM – (Decennial eds also available) – 1658-1936 – 9 – $3,640.00 set – us Hein [340]

AMERICAN DIGEST SYSTEM : FIRST DECENNIAL EDITION – St Paul: West Publ Co. v1-25. 1897-1906 (all publ) – 548mf – 9 – $822.00 – LLMC 84-388 – us L.L.M.C. [340]

AMERICAN DOCTORAL DISSERTATIONS *see* DOCTORAL DISSERTATIONS ACCEPTED BY AMERICAN UNIVERSITIES

AMERICAN DOCTORAL DISSERTATIONS – (Cont: Doctoral dissertations accepted by American universities) – Ann Arbor. v16-jul 1955- 1*; 1966- 5*; 1975- 9* – 1,5,9 – D3047 – us UMI [370]

AMERICAN DOCUMENTATION *see* JOURNAL OF THE AMERICAN SOCIETY FOR INFORMATION SCIENCE

THE AMERICAN DRAUGHT PLAYER : OR, THE THEORY AND PRACTICE OF THE SCIENTIFIC GAME OF CHECKERS: SIMPLIFIED AND ILLUSTRATED WITH PRACTICAL DIAGRAMS CONTAINING UPWARDS OF SEVENTEEN HUNDRED GAMES AND POSITIONS / Spayth, Henry – 5th rev corr ed. New York: Dick & Fitzgerald, 1869, c1860 – us Res Libr [790]

AMERICAN DRUGGIST – (Former titles: New remedies (jul 1871-dec 1883); American druggist (1884-mar 1893); American druggist and pharmaceutical record (apr 21, 1893-dec 1922); American druggist (jan 1923-dec 11, 1972); American druggist merchandising (jan 1973-dec 1973)) – New York. v1-172 jul 1871-dec 1975 1*; v173-216 jan 1976- 5 – 1,5 – D3123 – us UMI [615]

AMERICAN DRUGGIST *see*
- AMERICAN DRUGGIST

AMERICAN DRUGGIST AND PHARMACEUTICAL RECORD *see* AMERICAN DRUGGIST

AMERICAN DRUGGIST MERCHANDISING *see* AMERICAN DRUGGIST

AMERICAN DRYCLEANER – Chicago. v1-64 1934-* – 1 – D9893 – us UMI [660]

AMERICAN DYESTUFF REPORTER – New York. v1-86 oct 1917-dec 1973 1; v55-86 jan 1966-dec 1997+ 5; v65-86 jan 1976-dec 1997+ 9 – 1,5,9 – D781 – us UMI [660]

AMERICAN DYESTUFF REPORTER – v26-44. 1937-55 – 1,5,6 – us Princeton Micro [660]

AMERICAN EAGLE – Estero. Fla. Jun 1965- – 1 – us P.K. Yonge [071]

AMERICAN EAGLE – (Single issue of this anti-Masonic newspaper) – Westfield, NY. v2 n23. May 7 1833 – 1r – 1 – us Western Res [071]

AMERICAN EAGLE – (Ceased publ) – New York. v1 jun-jul 1847 – 1 – D4412 – us UMI [073]

AMERICAN ECCLESIASTICAL REVIEW – (Ceased publ. Former titles: American ecclesiastical review (jan 1889-jun 1905); Ecclesiastical review (jul 1905-dec 1943)) – Washington. v1-169 jan 1889-dec 1975 1; v164-169 jan 1971-dec 1975 5 – 1,5 – D1929 – us UMI [240]

AMERICAN ECCLESIASTICAL REVIEW *see* AMERICAN ECCLESIASTICAL REVIEW

AMERICAN ECLECTIC – (Ceased publ. United with: The Museum of foreign literature, science and art, to form: Eclectic museum of foreign literature, music and art) – New York. v1-4 jan 1841-nov 1842 – 1 – D3919 – us UMI [073]

AMERICAN ECONOMIC ASSOCIATION QUARTERLY *see* AMERICAN ECONOMIC REVIEW

AMERICAN ECONOMIC ASSOCIATION QUARTERLY – (Ceased publ. Cont by: American economic review. Former titles: Publication of the American Economic Association) – Princeton. cum index 1886-1910; v1-11 mar 1886-aug 1896; ns-11 dec 1897-dec 1910 – 1 – D5212 – us UMI [330]

AMERICAN ECONOMIC REVIEW – v. 1-35. 1911-1945 – 1 – us Princeton Micro [330]

AMERICAN ECONOMIC REVIEW – (Vols for 1911 include the Papers and Proceedings of the American Economic Association. Cont: American Economic Association Quarterly) – Nashville. v1-87 mar 1911-dec 1997+ 1; v58-87 mar 1968-dec 1997+ 5; v60-87 mar 1970-dec 1997+ 9. Shipped yrly or qrtly – 1,5,9 – D533 – us UMI [330]

AMERICAN ECONOMIC REVIEW *see* AMERICAN ECONOMIC ASSOCIATION QUARTERLY

AMERICAN ECONOMIST – (Vol 1 not available for filming) – Los Angeles. v2-41 may 1957-Fall 1997+ 1; v15-41 Spr 1971-Fall 1997+ 5; v19-41 Spr 1975-Fall 1997+ 9 – 1,5,9 – us UMI [330]

AMERICAN EDITORIAL REVIEW – (Missing: n22; n67) – (West Newton, Mass.). n1 (May 1989)-n90 (29 Apr 1994) – 45ft – us A.J.P.C. [270]

AMERICAN EDUCATION – (Cont: Higher Education, and: School Life. Former title: American Education (dec 1964/jan 1965-apr 1980)) – Washington. v1-21 dec 1964-85 1,9; v15-21 jan 1979-1985 5 – 1,5,9 – D1696 – us UMI [370]

AMERICAN EDUCATION *see* AMERICAN EDUCATION

AMERICAN EDUCATIONAL RESEARCH JOURNAL – Washington. v1-34 jan 1964-Win 1997+ 1; v8-34 jan 1971-Win 1997+ 5; v9-34 Win 1972-Win 1997+ 9 – 1,5,9 – D1801 – us UMI [370]

AMERICAN EDUCATIONIST AND WESTERN SCHOOL JOURNAL – Cleveland. v1. feb-may 1852 – 1 – D3480 – us UMI [370]

AMERICAN EDUCATOR – Washington. v1-21. Win 1977-Win 1998+ – 1,5,9 – D11615 – us UMI [370]

AMERICAN ELECTRIC RAILWAY ASSOCIATION – v. 1-23. 1912-1932 – 1,5,6 – us Princeton Micro [629]

AMERICAN ELECTRICAL CASES, ANNOTATED – (v7 contains an index/digest for v1-7) – Albany: M Bender: v1-9. 1873-1908 (all publ) – 94mf – 9 – $141.00 – LLMC 82-400 – us L.L.M.C. [340]

American Electro-Chemical Society *see* MEETINGS

AMERICAN ELECTRO-CHEMICAL SOCIETY MEETINGS – (Cont by: Electrochemical Society meetings) – Pennington. v1-99. Spr 1902-Spr 1951 – 1 – D13067 – us UMI [660]

AMERICAN ENCROACHMENTS ON BRITISH RIGHTS / Atcheson, N – London, 1808 – 5mf – 9 – ILM-2545/1 – ne IDC [340]

AMERICAN ENGINEER AND RAILROAD JOURNAL *see* VAN NOSTRAND'S ENGINEERING MAGAZINE

AMERICAN ENTERPRISE *see* AEI ECONOMIST

AMERICAN ENTERPRISE : 150=WASHINGTON. V1-8. JAN 1990- – (Formed by the union of: AEI economist, and: Public opinion) – 1,5,9 – D17755 – us UMI [338]

AMERICAN ENTOMOLOGIST – (Cont: Bulletin of the Entomological Society of America) – Lanham. v36-43 Spr 1990- 1; v36-43 Spr 1990- 5*; v36-43 Spr 1990- 9 – 1,5,9 – D9056.01 – us UMI [580]

American Episcopal Diocese. Anking *see* ANKING NEWSLETTER

AMERICAN ETHNOLOGIST – Arlington. cum index 1-3 1974-76; v1-24 feb 1974-nov 1997+ 1,5,9 – 1,5,9 – D11754 – us UMI [305]

AMERICAN EXAMINER – New York. N.Y. 1958-68 – 1 – us A.J.P.C. [071]

AMERICAN EXPORTER – (Cont by: Export) – New York, 1877-1970* – 1 – D24430 – us UMI [380]

AMERICAN EXPOSITOR – (Ceased publ) – Mount Vernon. v1. may 1850 – 1 – D3920 – us UMI [073]

AMERICAN EXPRESSIONISTIC DRAMA; CONTAINING ANALYSES OF THREE OUTSTANDING AMERICAN PLAYS.. / Rama Murthy, V – O'Neill, The Hairy Ape; Williams, The Glass Menagerie; Miller, Death of a Salesman. 1st ed. Delhi: Doaba House, 1970. 102p. Bibliography – 1 – us U.W. Library [420]

AMERICAN FABIAN – v1-5 2+11 (all publ). 1895-1900 – 10mf – 9 – $55.00 – us UPA [335]

AMERICAN FAMILY PHYSICIAN – (Ceased publ. Merged with: GP, to become: American family physician/GP. Former titles: Family physician (jul 1961-may 1962)) – St Louis. v1-17. jul 1961-dec 1969 – 5 – D5873 – us UMI [610]

AMERICAN FAMILY PHYSICIAN – (Cont by: American family physician/GP) – Kansas City. v2-56 dec 1970- 1; v3-56 jan 1971- 5; v13-56 jan 1976- – 1,5,9 – D5888.01 – us UMI [610]

AMERICAN FAMILY PHYSICIAN *see* AMERICAN FAMILY PHYSICIAN/GP

AMERICAN FAMILY PHYSICIAN/GP – (Formed by the merger of: American family physician and: GP. Cont by: American family physician) – Kansas City. v1-2. jan-nov 1970 – 1 – D5888 – us UMI [610]

AMERICAN FAMILY PHYSICIAN/GP *see*
- AMERICAN FAMILY PHYSICIAN

AMERICAN FAMILY PHYSICIAN/GP (KANSAS CITY) – v. 1-5. 1970-1972 – 1,5,6 – us Princeton Micro [616]

AMERICAN FARMER – (Ceased publ. Absorbed by: American agriculturist. Former titles: American farmer (apr 2, 1819-mar 7, 1834); Farmer and gardener (may 9, 1834-may 22, 1839); American farmer, and spirit of the agricultural journals of the day (may 29, 1839-jun 1850); American farmer (jul 1850-july 1870); American farmer and Rural register (jan 1872-dec 1873)) – Balitmore. v1-13 apr 1819-mar 1832; 2s: v14-6 mar 1832-may 1839; 3s: v1-5 may 1839-may 1844; 3s-4s: v6 may 1844-jun 1851; 4s: v7-13 jul 1851-jun 1858; 4s-6s: v14-4 jul 1858-dec 1869; 7s-8s: v1-4 jan 1870-dec 1875; 8s: v5-9 jan 1876-dec 1880; 8s-11s: v10-1 jan 1888-dec 1892; ns: 25-90 jan 1893-feb 1897 – 1 – D4413 – us UMI [630]

AMERICAN FARMER *see*
- AMERICAN FARMER
- AMERICAN AGRICLUTURIST AND THE RURAL NEW YORKER

AMERICAN FARMER AND RURAL REGISTER *see* AMERICAN FARMER

AMERICAN FARMER, AND SPIRIT OF THE AGRICULTURAL JOURNALS OF THE DAY *see* AMERICAN FARMER

AMERICAN FARMERS' MAGAZINE – (Ceased publ. Absorbed by: American agriculturist. Cont in pt: Monthly journal of agriculture. Former titles: Plough, the loom, and the anvil (jul 1848-dec 1857) – New York. v1-12. jul 1848-jun 1859 – 1 – D3921 – us UMI [630]

AMERICAN FARMER'S MAGAZINE *see* AMERICAN AGRICLUTURIST AND THE RURAL NEW YORKER

THE AMERICAN FEDERAL SYSTEM / Smellie, Kingsley B – London: Williams & Norgate, 1928 – 2mf – 9 – $3.00 – LLMC 95-068 – us L.L.M.C. [323]

AMERICAN FEDERATION OF ARTS CATALOGUE – (Individual titles not listed separately) – New York, 1929-1975 – 57 catalogues on 76mf – 9 – £560.00 – uk Chadwyck [700]

American Federation of Labor *see*
- A F L OFFICIAL DOCUMENTS
- AFL-CIO AMERICAN FEDERATIONIST
- AFL-CIO PUBLICATIONS
- PRESIDENT'S OFFICE FILES, SERIES A
- STRIKES AND AGREEMENTS FILE, 1898-1953

AMERICAN FEDERATION OF LABOR (AFL) PROCEEDINGS *see* AFL-CIO PROCEEDINGS

AMERICAN FEDERATION OF LABOR AND CONGRESS OF INDUSTRIAL ORGANIZATIONS : PAMPHLETS / AFL-CIO. Library – (AFL Pamphlets, 1889-1955: 12r $1,370.00; CIO Pamphlets, 1935-55: 7r $820.00) – 1889-1955 – 19r – 1 – $1,970.00 set – us UPA [330]

AMERICAN FEDERATION OF LABOR ANNUAL MEETINGS AND REPORTS – 1st-74th conventions. 1881-1955 (all publ) – 9 – LLMC 84-345 – us L.L.M.C. [073]

American Federation of Labor. Missouri State Federation of Labor *see* LABOR HERALD

AMERICAN FEDERATION OF LABOR PROCEEDINGS – (Ceased publ. Cont in part by: AFL-CIO proceedings) – Washington, 1881-1955 – 1 – D5952 – us UMI [331]

AMERICAN FEDERATION OF LABOR RECORDS – (See also indiv. parts: Strikes and Agreements File; President's Office Files: William Green Papers) – 9 – $13,590.00 set – 0-89093-895-4 – us UPA [331]

American Federation of Musicians *see* INTERNATIONAL MUSICIAN

American Federation of Musicians. Local 103, Columbus, Ohio *see* RECORDS

American Federation of Photographic Societies *see* PHOTO-ERA MAGAZINE

AMERICAN FEDERATIONIST – (Cont by: AFL-CIO American Federationist) – Washington. v1-83 mar 1894-jun 1976 1; v78-83 jan 1971-jun 1976 5; v83 jan-jun 1976 9 – 1,5,9 – D2232 – us UMI [331]

AMERICAN FENCING – Colorado Springs. cum index v1-10 1949-1959; v1-47 nov 1949- 1; v26-47 sep 1974- 5; v26-47 sep 1947- 9 – 1,5,9 – D7179 – us UMI [630]

AMERICAN FERN JOURNAL – v. 1-50. 1910-60 – 1,5,6 – us Princeton Micro [580]

AMERICAN FERTILIZER *see* FARM CHEMICALS AND CROP LIFE

AMERICAN FERTILIZER AND ALLIED CHEMICALS *see* FARM CHEMICALS AND CROP LIFE

AMERICAN FICTION : 1774-1910 – (Titles from Lyle H. Wright bibliography and Library of Congress Shelf List of American Adult Fiction) – 1 – us Primary [830]

THE AMERICAN FIELD – New York, Chicago: American Field Publ Co. v16-20 jul 1980-83. v25-28 1886-87. v33-34 1890. v39-42 1893-94. v53-56 1900-01 – us Res Libr [073]

AMERICAN FIGHTS AND FIGHTERS: STORIES OF THE FIRST FIVE WARS OF THE UNITED STATES FROM THE WAR OF THE REVOLUTION TO THE WAR OF 1812 / Brady, Cyrus Townsend – New York: McClure, Phillips, 1900. 03715. (Pre-1900 Canadiana) – 9 – cn C.I.H.M. [975]

AMERICAN FILM – (Ceased publ) – New York. v1-17. oct 1975-feb 1992 – 1,5,9 – D11838 – us UMI [790]

American Fisheries Society *see*
- TRANSACTIONS

AMERICAN FITNESS – (Cont by: Aerobic and Fitness) – Sherman Oaks. v5-15 may 1987- 1*; v11-15 jan 1993- 5*,9* – 1,5,9 – D19374.02 – us UMI [613]

AMERICAN FITNESS *see* AEROBICS AND FITNESS

AMERICAN FLAG – (Biweekly newspaper publ in Mexico by Americans during the Mexican War) – Matamoros, Mexico. nov 28, 1846-nov 20, 1847 – 1 – us Western Res [071]

AMERICAN FOLKSONG TEXTS / Gordon, Robert Winslow – 1 – 318.00 – us L of C Photodup [780]

AMERICAN FORCES IN ACTION / U.S. Army. Office of Military History – 3rolls. T1107 – 1 – us Nat'l Archives [355]

AMERICAN FOREIGN POLICY AND TREATY INDEX MICROFICHE LIBRARY – (Access to US Government documents on world affairs) – 1993- – 9 – Apply for prices – us CIS [327]

AMERICAN FOREIGN POLICY SERIES : BASIC DOCUMENTS / U.S. Department of State – (Current Documents: 1956-67; 1981-84 (none publ 1968-80). Updates available) – 5bks. 1941-49; 1950-55; 1977-80 (all publ) – 697mf – 9 – $1,046.00 – LLMC 80-909 – us L.L.M.C. [977]

American Forensic Association *see* JOURNAL OF THE AMERICAN FORENSIC ASSOCIATION

AMERICAN FORESTRY *see* AMERICAN FORESTS

AMERICAN FORESTRY ASSOCIATION PROCEEDINGS – (Ceased publ) – Washington. v1-12; 1882-dec 1897 – 1 – D7189 – us UMI [634]

AMERICAN FORESTS – (Former titles: New Jersey Forester (jan-may 1 1895); Forester (jul 1 1895-dec 1901); Forestry and Irrigation (jan 1902-aug 1908); Conservation; Forests, Waters, Soils and Minerals (sep 1908-dec 1909); American Forestry (jan 1910-dec 1923); American Forests and Forest Life (jan 1924-dec 1930)) – Washington. v1-103 jan 1895-dec 1997+ 1; v78-103 jan 1972-dec 1997+ 5,9. Shipped yrly or qrtly – 1,5,9 – D6554 – us UMI [634]

AMERICAN FORESTS AND FOREST LIFE *see* AMERICAN FORESTS

American Foundation for the Blind. M.C. Migel Memorial Library, New York City *see* DICTIONARY CATALOG OF THE M.C. MIGEL MEMORIAL LIBRARY, AMERICAN FOUNDATION FOR THE BLIND

AMERICAN FOUNDRYMAN – v17-27. 1950-55 – 1,5,6 – us Princeton Micro [670]

American Foundrymen's Society *see*
- AFS INTERNATIONAL CAST METALS JOURNAL
- TRANSACTIONS

American Foundrymen's Society. New York *see* TRANSACTIONS

AMERICAN FREE PRESS (PHILADELPHIA, PA.) – (Includes v1, no 6 9-19 (May 1 1940-Jan 1 1941)) – Philadelphia, Pa.: American Free Press Pub. Co. – 1 – CSUX89-S81 – us Hoover Inst Photo [978]

AMERICAN FREEDMAN – (Ceased publ) – New York. v1-3. apr 1866-jul 1869 – 1 – D3081 – us UMI [073]

AMERICAN FREEDMEN'S BULLETIN – (Former titles: Freedmen's bulletin (jul 1864-nov 1865); Western freemen's bulletin (dec 1865-mar 1886)) – Chicago. v1-2. jun 1864-aug 1866 – 1 – D3346 – us UMI [073]

American Friends of Spanish Democracy *see* THE PERSECUTION OF PROTESTANTS IN FASCIST SPAIN

American Friends of the Angolan Revolution *see* AFAR

American Friends of the Chinese People *see* CHINA TODAY

AMERICAN FRIENDS PEACE CONFERENCE HELD AT PHILADELPHIA : TWELFTH MONTH 12TH, 13TH AND 14TH. 1901 – Philadelphia, 1902 – 3mf – 9 – ILM-4062/1 – ne IDC [340]

AMERICAN FRIENDS SERVICE COMMITTEE – Philadelphia. 194 docs. 1980-1990 – 72mf – 9 – ne IDC [320]

AMERICAN FRUIT GROWER – (Vols 1-16 not available for filming. Former titles: Green's Fruit Grower and Home Companion (1889-oct 1909); Green's Fruit Grower (nov 1909-sep 1917); Green's American Fruit Grower (oct 1917-aug 1918); American Fruit Grower (sep 1918-dec 1921); American Fruit Grower Magazine (jan 1922-dec 1930)) – Willoughby. v17-117 jan 1897-dec 1997+ 1; v91-117 jan 1971-dec 1997+ 5; v97-117 jan 1977-dec 1997+ 9 – 1,5,9 – D319 – us UMI [630]

AMERICAN FRUIT GROWER *see* AMERICAN FRUIT GROWER

AMERICAN FRUIT GROWER MAGAZINE *see* AMERICAN FRUIT GROWER

AMERICAN FUND FOR PUBLIC SERVICE RECORDS, 1922-1941 : FROM THE HOLDINGS OF THE RARE BOOKS AND MANUSCRIPTS DIVISION – (Guide may be purchased separately) – Center for the Humanities the New York Public Library; Astor, Lenox, and Tilden Foundations, 1966 – 36r – 1 – $3,060,00 – D3351 – us Scholarly Res [350]

AMERICAN GAS *see* AGA MONTHLY

AMERICAN GAS – (Cont: AGA monthly) – Arlington. v71-79 jan 1989- 1; v71-79 jan 1989- 5; v71-79 jan 1989 9 – 1,5,9 – D10410.02 – us UMI [333]

AMERICAN GAS ASSOCIATION MONTHLY *see* AGA MONTHLY

AMERICAN GAS ASSOCIATION MONTHLY – (Cont: AGA monthly) – Arlington. v1-66 jan 1919-sep 1984 1; v57-66 jan 1975-sep 1984 5; v58-66 jan 1976-sep 1984 9 – 1,5,9 – D10410 – us UMI [333]

American Genealogical Lending Library *see* GENEALOGICAL SERVICES

AMERICAN GENEALOGIST – (Former titles: New Haven genealogical magazine (1922/23-apr 1932); American genealogist and New Haven genealogical magazine (jul 1932-apr 1937)) – Des Moines. v1-72 jul 1922- 1; v47-72 jan 1971- 5*; v53-72 jan-oct 1977- 9 – 1,5,9 – D104 – us UMI [920]

AMERICAN GENEALOGIST AND NEW HAVEN GENEALOGICAL MAGAZINE *see* AMERICAN GENEALOGIST

American Geographical Society. Library. New York *see* RESEARCH CATALOGUE OF THE AMERICAN GEOGRAPHICAL SOCIETY

American Geographical Society. Library. New York. *see* INDEX TO MAPS IN BOOKS AND PERIODICALS

American Geographical Society of New York *see* BULLETIN

American Geophysical Union *see* EOS: TRANSACTIONS

AMERICAN GERMAN REVIEW – v. 1-15. 1934-49 – 1,5,6 – us Princeton Micro [073]

AMERICAN GIRL – (Ceased publ. Former titles: Rally; a scouting magazine for the American girl (oct 1917-may 1920)) – New York. v1-62 oct 1917-jul 1979 1; v56-62 jan 1973-jun 1979 5; v58-62 jan 1975-jul 1979 9 – 1,5,9 – D9807 – us UMI [790]

AN AMERICAN GIRL IN LONDON / Duncan, Sara Jeannette – With 80 illustrations by F. H. Townsend. Toronto: Williamson, 1891. 05290. (Pre-1900 Canadiana) – 9 – cn C.I.H.M. [910]

AMERICAN GLASS REVIEW – Clifton. v1-118 1882- 1*; v96-118 jul 1975-* 5,9 – 1,5,9 – D8380 – us UMI [670]

AMERICAN GLASS WORKER – Oittsburgh, PA: Barrows & Osborne, may 15 1885 (sample iss). v1 n1-26 jun 5 1885-jun 21 1886 – us Res Libr [670]

AMERICAN GLASS WORKER – Clifton. v1-3. 1882-sep 1887* – 1 – D8659 – us UMI [670]

AMERICAN GLEANOR AND VIRGINIA MAGAZINE – (Ceased publ) – Richmond. v1. jan-dec 1807 – 1 – D3539 – us UMI [073]

AMERICAN GOVERNMENT AND POLITICS / Beard, Charles A – New York: The Macmillan Co, 1911 – 8mf – 9 – $12.00 – LLMC 92-167 – us L.L.M.C. [323]

AMERICAN GUIDE SERIES – $950.00 – us UPA [910]

AMERICAN GYMNASIA AND ATHLETIC RECORD : A MONTHLY JOURNAL OF RATIONAL, PHYSICAL TRAINING (SUBTITLE VARIES) – v1-4, no. 8 (all publ). Sep 1904-Apr 1908 – 1 reel – 1 – $125.00 – us UPA [970]

AMERICAN HARMONY: CONTAINING A VARIETY OF AIRS SUITABLE FOR DIVINE WORSHIP, ON THANKSGIVINGS, ORDINATIONS, CHRISTMAS, FASTS, FUNERALS AND OTHER OCCASIONS / Holden, Oliver – Together with a number of psalm tunes, in three and four parts. Boston: Thomas and Andrews, 1792. MUSIC 123, Item 1 – 1 – us L of C Photodup [780]

American Health Care Association *see* JOURNAL

American Heart Association, Inc *see* ARTERIOSCLEROSIS

AMERICAN HEART JOURNAL – St Louis. v1-134 oct 1925-dec 1997+ 1; v69-134 jan 1965-dec 1997+ 5; v79-134 jan 1970-dec 1997+ 9 – 1,5,9 – D1884 – us UMI [610]

AMERICAN HEART JOURNAL – v1-49. 1925-44 – 1,5,6 – us Princeton Micro [610]

AMERICAN HEBREW ALMANAC – Philadelphia. 1881 – 1 – us A.J.P.C. [030]

AMERICAN HEBREW AND JEWISH MESSENGER – New York, 19 May 1905-13 Feb 1920 (imperfect) – 28r – 1 – uk British Libr Newspaper [071]

AMERICAN HEBREW NEWS – Portland OR. Mar 8 15 1895 – 1 – us U.O. Library [071]

AMERICAN HERITAGE – (Also available fr publ: cum index for dec 1954-oct 1982) – New York. cum index 6-15; v1-48 1949-dec 1997 1,9; v20-48 dec 1968-dec 1997+ 5. Shipped yrly or qrtly – 1,5,9 – D887 – us UMI [970]

AMERICAN HERITAGE INVENTION AND TECHNOLOGY – New York. v1-13. Sum 1985-Spr 1998+ – 1,5,9 – D15347 – us UMI [600]

AMERICAN HEROES ON MISSION FIELDS : BRIEF MISSIONARY BIOGRAPHIES / ed by Haydn, Hiram Collins – New York: American Tract Society, c1890 – 1mf – 9 – 0-8370-6239-X – 1986-0239 – us A.T.L.A. [240]

AMERICAN HERO-MYTHS: A STUDY IN THE NATIVE RELIGIONS OF THE WESTERN CONTINENT / Brinton, Daniel Garrison – Philadelphia: H.Watts, 1882. 02440. (Pre-1900 Canadiana) – 9 – cn C.I.H.M. [290]

American Historical Association *see*
- ANNUAL REPORT
- CAPTURED GERMAN DOCUMENTS FILMED AT BERLIN
- NEWSLETTER
- PROCEEDINGS
- PROGRAM OF THE ANNUAL MEETING
- REPORTS

AMERICAN HISTORICAL ASSOCIATION ANNUAL REPORT – (Micro-edition includes supplement: Writings on American history for 1909-1911 and 1918-1958) – Washington. v1-5 1884-1891 1889- 1*; 1964- 5*; 1964-9* – 1,5,9 – D1654 – us UMI [975]

AMERICAN HISTORICAL MAGAZINE – (Ceased publ) – New Haven. v1. jan-jun 1836 – 1 – D3715 – us UMI [975]

AMERICAN HISTORICAL MONTHLY *see* POTTER'S AMERICAN MONTHLY

AMERICAN HISTORICAL REGISTER AND MONTHLY GAZETTE OF THE HISTORIC, MILITARY AND PATRIOTIC-HEREDITARY SOCIETY OF THE UNITED STATES OF AMERICA – (Ceased publ) – Philadelphia. ns: v1. sep 1894-may 1897 – 1 – D3880 – us UMI [920]

AMERICAN HISTORICAL REVIEW – v. 1-35. 1895-1929 – 1 – us Princeton Micro [970]

AMERICAN HISTORICAL REVIEW – Washington. v1-12. 1895-1907 – 5r – 1 – us Ross [970]

AMERICAN HISTORICAL REVIEW – Wshington. cum index 1-40 1895-1936; v1-102 oct 1895-dec 1997+ 1; v73-102 oct 1967-dec 1997+ 5; v75-102 oct 1969-dec 1997+ 9. Shipped yrly or qrtly – 1,5,9 – D413 – us UMI [970]

American Historical Society *see*
- THE COUNTY OF LOS ANGELES
- ENCYCLOPEDIA OF CONNECTICUT BIOGRAPHY: GENEALOGICAL, MEMORIAL AND REPRESENTATIVE CITIZENS
- HISTORY OF NORTHAMPTON COUNTY AND THE GRAND VALLEY OF THE LEHIGH
- MONTANA

AMERICAN HISTORY – (Cont: American History Illustrated) – Harrisburg. v29-32. may 1994- – 1,5,9 – D12015.01 – us UMI [975]

AMERICAN HISTORY *see* AMERICAN HISTORY ILLUSTRATED

AMERICAN HISTORY AND CULTURE : THE NATIONAL PARK SYSTEM: CULTURAL RESOURCE REPORTS, 1935-1984 – (Also available by region. Guide: Cultutal Resources Management Bibliography 7116mf £58.00) – over 8000mf – 9 – £18,850.00 – uk Chadwyck [975]

AMERICAN HISTORY ILLUSTRATED *see* AMERICAN HISTORY

AMERICAN HISTORY ILLUSTRATED – (Cont by: American history) – Harrisburg. cum index v1-5 1966-feb 1971; v1-29 apr 1966-apr 1994 – 1,5,9 – D12015 – us UMI [975]

AMERICAN HISTORY VIGNETTE *see* MORSE AND THE TELEGRAPH

AMERICAN HISTORY VIGNETTES – 21r – 1 – us Ross [970]

AMERICAN HISTORY VIGNETTES *see*
- THE ALAMO SAN JACINTO AND THE REPUBLIC OF TEXAS
- CALIFORNIA, DISCOVERY OF GOLD IN
- COMMODORE PERRY IN JAPAN
- FLIGHT OF CHARLES A. LINDBERGH
- FULTON'S FOLLY
- JOHN BROWN'S RAID
- LEWIS AND CLARK EXPEDITION
- LINCOLN-DOUGLAS DEBATES
- LOUISIANA PURCHASE
- MONROE DOCTRINE
- PANAMA CANAL
- PURCHASE OF ALASKA
- SURRENDER AT APPOMATTOX
- WORLD WAR ONE ARMISTICE

AMERICAN HOME – (Absorbed by: Redbook) – New York. v1-81 oct 1928-feb 1978 1; v73-81 jan 1970-feb 1978 5,9 – 1,5,9 – D886 – us UMI [640]

American Home Economics Association *see*
- AHEA ACTION

American Home Missionary Society *see* PAPERS

AMERICAN HOMESTYLE – (Cont: Decorating and remodeling. Cont by: American homestyle and gardening) – New York. v8-10. 1993-mar 1995* – 1,5,9 – D22192.01 – us UMI [640]

AMERICAN HOMESTYLE *see* AMERICAN HOMESTYLE AND GARDENING

AMERICAN HOMESTYLE AND GARDENING – (Cont: American homestyle) – New York. v10. apr-dec 1995 1996- – 1,5,9 – D22192.02 – us UMI [640]

AMERICAN HOMESTYLE AND GARDENING *see* AMERICAN HOMESTYLE

AMERICAN HOROLOGIST *see* AMERICAN HOROLOGIST AND JEWELER

AMERICAN HOROLOGIST AND JEWELER – (Cont by: Watch and clock review. Former titles: American horologist (jan 1936-may 1946)) – Denver. v1-47 jan 1936-dec 1980 1; v43-47 jan 1976-dec 1980* 5,9 – 1,5,9 – D6705 – us UMI [730]

AMERICAN HORTICULTURAL MAGAZINE – (Former titles: National horticultural magazine (aug 1922-oct 1959); American horticultural magazine (1960-Fal 1971)) – Alexandria. cum index 39-50 1960-1971; v3-76 jan 1924- 1; v51-76 mar 1972- 5; v55-76 feb 1976- – 1,5,9 – D7008 – us UMI [630]

AMERICAN HORTICULTURAL MAGAZINE *see* AMERICAN HORTICULTURAL MAGAZINE

THE AMERICAN HOUSE TRAVELLER'S GUIDE FOR RIVER ST LAWRENCE AND THE CITIES OF MONTREAL, QUEBEC & OTTAWA – Montreal?, 1872. 05674. (Pre-1900 Canadiana) – 9 – cn C.I.H.M. [910]

AMERICAN HUMANE MAGAZINE – (Formed by the union of: National Humane Review, and: Animal Shelter Shoptalk) – Englewood. v64-66. nov 1976-dec 1978 1,5*,9* – 1,5,9 – D1510.01 – us UMI [636]

AMERICAN HUNGARIAN REVIEW – (Ceased publ) – St Louis. v11. 1973 – 1,5 – D7489 – us UMI [073]

AMERICAN HUNTER – Washington. v1-25 oct 1973- 1*; v16-25 jan 1988- 5*,9 – 1,5,9 – D16725 – us UMI [790]

AMERICAN ILLUSTRATED MAGAZINE *see* AMERICAN MAGAZINE

AMERICAN IMAGO – (Publ suspended aug 1942-feb 1946) – Detroit. cum index 1-20 1939-63; v1-54 1939-Win 1997+ 1; v28-54 Spr 1971-Win 1997+ 5,9. Shipped yrly or qrtly – 1,5,9 – D1837 – us UMI [150]

AMERICAN IMMIGRANT AUTOBIOGRAPHIES, PART 1 : MANUSCRIPT AUTOBIOGRAPHIES FROM THE IMMIGRATION HISTORY RESEARCH CENTER, UNIVERSITY OF MINNESOTA – 7r – 1 – $770.00 – 1-55655-052-9 – us UPA [304]

American Immigration and Citizenship Conference. Committee on Integration *see* DOUBLE UPROOTED: DUTCH INDONESIAN REFUGEES IN THE UNITED STATES

AMERICAN IMPORT EXPORT BULLETIN – (Cont by: American Import Export Management. Former title: American and Export Bulletin (jul 1934-mar 1974)) – Philadelphia. v1-95 jul 1934-sep 1981 1; v74-95 jan 1971-sep 1981 5; v86-95 jan 1977-sep 1981 9 – 1,5,9 – D311 – us UMI [380]

AMERICAN IMPORT EXPORT BULLETIN *see* AMERICAN IMPORT EXPORT MANAGEMENT

AMERICAN IMPORT EXPORT MANAGEMENT – (Cont: American import export bulletin. Cont by: American import-export management's global trade executive) – Philadelphia. v95-102. oct-dec 1981-apr 1985 – 1,5,9 – D311.01 – us UMI [650]

AMERICAN IMPORT EXPORT MANAGEMENT *see*
- AMERICAN IMPORT EXPORT BULLETIN
- AMERICAN IMPORT-EXPORT MANAGEMENT'S GLOBAL TRADE EXECUTIVE

AMERICAN IMPORT/EXPORT GLOBAL TRADE – (Cont: American import/export management's global trade. Cont by: Global trade) – Philadelphia. v107-108. nov 1987-jun 1988 – 1,5,9 – D311.06 – us UMI [337]

AMERICAN IMPORT/EXPORT GLOBAL TRADE *see* AMERICAN IMPORT/EXPORT MANAGEMENT'S GLOBAL TRADE

AMERICAN IMPORT/EXPORT MANAGEMENT'S GLOBAL TRADE – (Cont: American import-export management's global trade executive. Cont by: American import/export global trade) – Philadelphia. v106-107. mar-oct 1987 – 1,5,9 – D311.05 – us UMI [337]

AMERICAN IMPORT/EXPORT MANAGEMENT'S GLOBAL TRADE *see*
- AMERICAN IMPORT/EXPORT GLOBAL TRADE
- AMERICAN IMPORT-EXPORT MANAGEMENT'S GLOBAL TRADE EXECUTIVE

AMERICAN IMPORT-EXPORT MANAGEMENT'S GLOBAL TRADE EXECUTIVE – (Cont: American import export management. Cont by: Global trade executive) – Philadelphia. v102-103. may-nov 1985 – 1,5,9 – D311.02 – us UMI [650]

AMERICAN IMPORT-EXPORT MANAGEMENT'S GLOBAL TRADE EXECUTIVE – (Cont: Global trade executive. Cont by: American import/export management's global trade) – Philadelphia. v105-106. nov 1986-feb 1987 – 1,5,9 – D311.04 – us UMI [650]

AMERICAN IMPORT-EXPORT MANAGEMENT'S GLOBAL TRADE EXECUTIVE *see*
- AMERICAN IMPORT EXPORT MANAGEMENT
- AMERICAN IMPORT/EXPORT MANAGEMENT'S GLOBAL TRADE

AMERICAN IMPRINTS INVENTORY: NO.5 CHECK LIST OF KENTUCKY IMPRINTS, 1787-1810 – By Douglas C. McMurtrie.1939. Indexed. Includes index of printers. 3 fiches. F-0492 – 9 – us A.G.L.L. [070]

AMERICAN IMPRINTS INVENTORY: NO.25 SUPPLEMENTAL CHECK LIST OF KENTUCKY IMPRINTS, 1788-1820 – Comp. by John Wilson Townsend. 1942. Indexed. 3 fiches. F-0497 – 9 – us A.G.L.L. [070]

AMERICAN IN THE EAST : A GLANCE AT OUR HISTORY, PROSPECTS, PROBLEMS, AND DUTIES IN THE PACIFIC OCEAN / Griffis, William Elliot – New York: A.S. Barnes, 1899 – 1mf – us A.T.L.A. [978]

THE AMERICAN INDIAN / Association on American Indian Affairs – 1943-59. (American Indian Periodicals in the Princeton University Library) – 14mf – 9 – $70.00 – us UPA [305]

THE AMERICAN INDIAN – New York. no. 1-8. Nov. 1927-May 1932 – 1 – us NY Public [970]

THE AMERICAN INDIAN / Society of Oklahoma Indians – 1926-31. (American Indian Periodicals in the Princeton University Library) – 12mf – 9 – $65.00 – us UPA [305]

AMERICAN INDIAN CALENDAR / U.S. Bureau of Indian Affairs – 1968 – 9 – $5.00f – us Ross [970]

AMERICAN INDIAN CORRESPONDENCE / Presbyterian Historical Society – The Presbyterian Historical Society Collection of Missionaries' Letters, 1833-1893. Collection of 13,422 letters accompanied by hardcopy user's guide – 35r – 1 – $3,435.00 – us UPA [240]

American Indian Cultural Group *see* NEWSLETTER

AMERICAN INDIAN CULTURE AND RESEARCH JOURNAL – Los Angeles. v1-21. 1974-1997+ – 1,5*,9 – D11579 – us UMI [305]

American Indian Defense Association *see* AMERICAN INDIAN LIFE

AMERICAN INDIAN INDEX – 1953-68.(American Indian Periodicals in the Princeton University Library). 17 fiches – 9 – $75.00 – us UPA [305]

AMERICAN INDIAN JOURNAL – (Ceased publ) – Washington. v1-8 oct 1975-1982 1; v3-8 jan 1977-1982 5*,9 – 1,5,9 – D11412 – us UMI [073]

AMERICAN INDIAN JOURNAL – (Missing: 1983-85) – Institute for the Development of Indian Law. v1-9. 1975-87 – 9 – $92.00 set – us Hein [340]

AMERICAN INDIAN LAW NEWSLETTER – 1968-78. (American Indian Periodicals in the Princeton University Library). 29 fiches – 9 – $120.00 – us UPA [340]

AMERICAN INDIAN LAW REVIEW – (v1-11 1973-83 $88.00 reel. v12-19 1985-1994 $118.00 mf) – University of Oklahoma. v1-19. 1973-95 – 5,6,9 – $206.00 – us Hein [073]

AMERICAN INDIAN LIBRARIES NEWSLETTER – Chicago. v1-20 Fall1976-Sum 1998+ 1*; v8-20 Spr 1985-Sum 1998+ 5*,9 – 1,5,9 – D12516 – us UMI [020]

AMERICAN INDIAN LIFE / American Indian Defense Association – 1925-36. (American Indian Periodicals in the Princeton University Library) – 6mf – 9 – $45.00 – us UPA [305]

AMERICAN INDIAN MAGAZINE – Quarterly journal of the Society of American Indians. 1913-20. (American Indian Periodicals in the Princeton University Library). 25 fiches – 9 – $110.00 – us UPA [305]

AMERICAN INDIAN MAGAZINE – (Ceased publ. Former titles: Quarterly journal of the Society of American Indians (jan/apr 1913-oct/dec 1915)) – Washington. v1-7. jan 1913-aug 1920 – 1 – D7043 – us UMI [975]

AMERICAN INDIAN NEWS – 1968-73. Indian League of America. (American Indian Periodicals in the Princeton University Library). 3 fiches – 9 – $45.00 – us UPA [305]

THE AMERICAN INDIAN ON THE NEW TRAIL : THE RED MAN OF THE U.S. AND THE CHRISTIAN GOSPEL / Moffett, Thomas C – New York: Missionary Eduction Movement of the United States and Canada, 1914 – 1mf – us A.T.L.A. [306]

AMERICAN INDIAN PERIODICALS FROM THE STATE HISTORICAL SOCIETY OF WISCONSIN : 1884-1981 – 41 titles. 13 reels – 1 – $895.00 – us UPA [305]

AMERICAN INDIAN PERIODICALS IN THE PRINCETON UNIVERSITY LIBRARY – (Part 2: 34 titles. 401 fiches; 2 reels. $1,515.00) – Part 1: 95 titles. 2,286 fiches; 2 reels. Individual titles available – 1,9 – $7,525.00 – us UPA [305]

AMERICAN INDIAN POLICY / Taylor, Theodore W – 1983. 230p Index. ISBN: 0-912338-42-3 – 9 – 12.95 – us Lomond [321]

American Indian Press Association *see*
- INFORMATION LETTER
- NEWS SERVICE
- SPECIAL REPORT

AMERICAN INDIAN QUARTERLY – Berkeley. v1-21 Spr 1974-Fall 1997+ 1; v6-21 Spr 1982-Fall 1997+ 5*,9 – 1,5,9 – D14185 – us UMI [073]

American Indian Studies Dept. CSU San Francisco *see* NEWSPAPER AND NEWSLETTER COLLECTION "AKWESASNE NEWS THRU TREATY COUNSEL NEWS"

THE AMERICAN INDIANA – Blairsville, PA., 1826 – 13 – $25.00r – us I.M.R. [071]

AMERICAN INDONESIAN CHAMBER OF COMMERCE INC. INFORMATION BULLETIN – (Many vols missing) – New York. nos1-986. [195?]1955-1971 – 92mf – 9 – SE-703/1 – ne IDC [380]

American Industrial Hygiene Association *see* AMERICAN INDUSTRIAL HYGIENE ASSOCIATION JOURNAL

AMERICAN INDUSTRIAL HYGIENE ASSOCIATION JOURNAL / American Industrial Hygiene Association – (Former titles: Industrial Medicine – Industrial Hygiene Section (jan 1940-oct 1944); Industrial Hygiene (jan 1945-feb 1946); American Industrial Hygiene Association Quarterly (jun 1946-dec 1957)) – Akron. v1-58 jan 1940-dec 1997+ 1; v35-58 jan 1974-dec 1997+ 5; v36-58 jan 1975-dec 1997+ 9 – 1,5,9 – D10121 – us UMI [360]

AMERICAN INDUSTRIAL HYGIENE ASSOCIATION QUARTERLY *see* AMERICAN INDUSTRIAL HYGIENE ASSOCIATION JOURNAL

AMERICAN INK MAKER – (Cont: American inkmaker) – Melville. v56-75. jun 1981-* – 1 – D13973.02 – us UMI [680]

AMERICAN INK MAKER – (Cont by: American inkmaker) – Melville. v1-47. 1923-jul 1969* – 1 – D13973 – us UMI [680]

AMERICAN INK MAKER *see* AMERICAN INKMAKER

AMERICAN INKMAKER – (Cont: American ink maker. Cont by: American ink maker) – Melville. v47-59. aug 1969-may 1981* – 1 – D13973.01 – us UMI [680]

AMERICAN INKMAKER *see*
- AMERICAN INK MAKER

American Institute for Marxist Studies *see* AIMS NEWSLETTER

American Institute of Aeronautics and Astronautics *see*
- AIAA JOURNAL
- AIAA STUDENT JOURNAL

American Institute of Aeronautics and Astronautics (AIAA) *see* AIAA BULLETIN

American Institute of Architects *see*
- AIA JOURNAL
- PAPERS FROM THE AMERICAN INSTITUTE OF ARCHITECTS LIBRARY AND ARCHIVES

THE AMERICAN INSTITUTE OF ARCHITECTS (AIA) LIBRARY AND ARCHIVES MICROFORM COLLECTIONS – (Indvidual colls also listed separately) – 4 colls – 1,5 – $14,200.00 coll – us Ross [720]

THE AMERICAN INSTITUTE OF ARCHITECTS (AIA) LIBRARY AND ARCHIVES MICROFORM COLLECTIONS *see*
- AIA AWARDS PROGRAMS
- AIA OUTGOING CORRESPONDENCE
- AIA PROCEEDINGS 1867-1931, 1943-1967
- PAPERS OF THE WESTERN ASSOCIATION OF ARCHITECTS, 1884-1889

THE AMERICAN INSTITUTE OF ARCHITECTS (AIA) LIBRARY AND ARCHIVES MICROFORM COLLECTIONS, AWARDS PROGRAMS *see*
- 25-YEAR AWARDS
- AIA/ALA LIBRARY BUILDING AWARDS
- AIA/BIA BRICK IN ARCHITECTURE AWARDS OF EXCELLENCE
- HONOR AWARDS FOR ARCHITECTURE
- HONOR AWARDS FOR INTERIORS
- HONOR AWARDS FOR URBAN DESIGN
- RELIGIOUS ART AND ARCHITECTURE DESIGN AWARDS

American Institute of Biological Sciences. Biological Sciences Curriculum Study *see* BSCS NEWSLETTER

American Institute of Certified Public Accountants Tax Division *see* AICPA TAX DIVISION NEWSLETTER

American Institute of Chemical Engineers *see*
- AICHE JOURNAL
- MEETING PAPERS

American Institute of Electrical Engineers *see* TRANSACTIONS

American Institute of Industrial Engineers *see*
- AIIE TRANSACTIONS
- TECHNICAL PAPERS, INSTITUTE CONFERENCE AND CONVENTION

AMERICAN INSTITUTE OF INDUSTRIAL ENGINEERS CONFERENCE PROCEEDINGS *see* TECHNICAL PAPERS, INSTITUTE CONFERENCE AND CONVENTION

American Institute of Instruction *see* ANNUAL MEETING

American Institute of Mining *see* METALLURGICAL, AND PETROLEUM ENGINEERS TRANSACTIONS

American Institute of Mining and Metallurgical Engineers *see* TRANSACTIONS

AMERICAN INSTITUTE OF MINING AND METALLURGICAL ENGINEERS TRANSACTIONS *see* METALLURGICAL, AND PETROLEUM ENGINEERS TRANSACTIONS

American Institute of Mining Engineers *see* HALIFAX MEETING: SEPT 16-17, 1885

American Institute of Mining, Metallurgical and Petroleum Engineers *see* TRANSACTIONS

AMERICAN INSTITUTE OF MINING, METALLURGICAL AND PETROLEUM ENGINEERS TRANSACTIONS *see* TRANSACTIONS

American Institute of Physics *see*
- COMPUTERS IN PHYSICS
- JOURNAL OF CHEMICAL PHYSICS

American Institute of Planners *see* JOURNAL OF THE AMERICAN INSTITUTE OF PLANNERS

American Institution of Hemoeopathy *see* PHARMACOPEIA

AMERICAN INTRA-OCULAR IMPLANT SOCIETY, JOURNAL – (v.5-. 1979- 5,6,9) – v.2-. 1976- – 1 – us UMI [073]

AMERICAN INVESTOR – (Ceased publ. Former titles: American Stock Exchange investor (1956-1966)) – New York. v1-19. 1956-aug 1974* – 1 – D6656 – us UMI [332]

American Iris Society *see* BULLETIN

American Irish Historical Society *see* JOURNAL

American Iron and Steel Association *see* BULLETIN

AMERICAN IRON & STEEL INSTITUTE YEARBOOK – 1913-54 – 1,5,6 – us Princeton Micro [670]

AMERICAN ISRAELITE *see*
- ISRAELITE

AMERICAN ISSUE – National ed. Jan 1900-Dec 1933. Related Guide Book may be purchased separately from publisher – 11 35mm rolls in set – 1 – us Ohio Hist [360]

American Issue Publishing Company *see* PAPERS

THE AMERICAN JEFFERSON – Brookville, PA., 1826 – 13 – $25.00r – us I.M.R. [071]

AMERICAN JESUITS. NEW YORK 1934 / Walsh, James – Madrid: Razon y Fe, 1935 – 1 – sp Bibl Santa Ana [240]

THE AMERICAN JEW AS PATRIOT, SOLDIER AND CITIZEN / Wolf, Simon; ed by Levy, Louis Edward – Philadelphia: Levytype; New York: Brentano's, 1895 – 2mf – us A.T.L.A. [305]

THE AMERICAN JEWESS – New York. N.Y. 1895-99 – 1 – us A.J.P.C. [071]

AMERICAN JEWISH ARCHIVES – Cincinnati. v1-49 jun 1948-Win 1997+ 1*; v32-48 apr 1980-Win 1997+ 5*,9 – 1,5,9 – D12676 – us UMI [270]

American Jewish Archives. Cincinnati *see* MANUSCRIPT CATALOG OF THE AMERICAN JEWISH ARCHIVES

AN AMERICAN JEWISH BIBLIOGRAPHY, BEING A LIST OF BOOKS AND PAMPHLETS BY JEWS OR RELATING TO THEM; PRINTED... UNTIL 1850 / Rosenbach, A SW – Baltimore, 1926 – 6mf – ne IDC [270]

THE AMERICAN JEWISH CHRONICLE – New York. N.Y. 1916-18 – 1 – us A.J.P.C. [071]

American Jewish Committee. Library of Jewish Information *see* JEWS BEHIND THE IRON CURTAIN

AMERICAN JEWISH CONGRESS-NEWS – New York, NY. 1964-86 – 1 – us A.J.P.C. [071]

AMERICAN JEWISH HISTORICAL QUARTERLY / American Jewish Historical Society Inc – v1-68. 1893-1979 + index v1-20 – 14r – 1 – us Ross [270]

American Jewish Historical Society Inc *see* AMERICAN JEWISH HISTORICAL QUARTERLY

AMERICAN JEWISH JOINT DISTRIBUTION COMMITTEE – New York, NY. 1953-84 – 1 – us A.J.P.C. [071]

AMERICAN JEWISH LEDGER – (Vol. 8, no. 7 (Sept. 1952)) – Newark, N.J. – 1 – us A.J.P.C. [270]

AMERICAN JEWISH NEWS – New York. N.Y. 1918-19 – 1 – us A.J.P.C. [071]

AMERICAN JEWISH OUTLOOK – Pittsburgh. Pa. 1958-62 – 1 – us A.J.P.C. [071]

AMERICAN JEWISH REVIEW – Atlanta. Ga. 1913-15 – 1 – us A.J.P.C. [071]

AMERICAN JEWISH REVIEW – Buffalo. N.Y. 1917-25 – 1 – us A.J.P.C. [071]

AMERICAN JEWISH TIMES – Howell, N.J. v3, no. 1 (Sept. 1990); v3, no. 7 (Mar. 1991); v4, no. 8 (Apr. 1992) – us A.J.P.C. [071]

AMERICAN JEWISH WORLD – Minneapolis St. Paul. Minn. 1958-67 – 1 – us A.J.P.C. [071]

THE AMERICAN JEWS' ANNUAL – Cincinnati. 1884 85-97 – 1 – us A.J.P.C. [270]

AMERICAN JOURNAL – Providence. R.I. and General Advertiser. 1779-81 – 1 – us UMI [071]

THE AMERICAN JOURNAL – v1-31. Dec 1884-Mar 1915 – 1 – 650.00 – us Opus [073]

AMERICAN JOURNAL OF AGRICULTURAL ECONOMICS – (Former title: Journal of Farm Economics (1919-dec 1967)) – St Paul. cum index 1-20 jun 1919-dec 1938; v1-79 jun 1919-dec 1997+ 1; v52-79 feb 1970-dec 1997+ 5; v57-79 feb 1975-dec 1997+ 9 – 1,5,9 – D1936 – us UMI [630]

AMERICAN JOURNAL OF ANATOMY – Baltimore, 1901-1906; 1936-1939. V.1-5; V.58-65 – 132mf – 9 – ne IDC [611]

AMERICAN JOURNAL OF ANATOMY – Philadelphia. v123-147. 1968-76 – 5,9 – Dfl1,500.00; Dfl60.00v – ne Swets [611]

AMERICAN JOURNAL OF ANATOMY – v. 1-117. 1901-1965 – 1,5,6 – us Princeton Micro [611]

AMERICAN JOURNAL OF ARCHAEOLOGY – (Former title: American Journal of Archaeology and of the History of the Fine Arts (1885-96)) – Boston. cum index 1-10 1885-95; v1-9 jan 1885-dec 1894; cum index 2s 1-10 1897-1906; 2s v10-2-101 jan 1895-oct 1997+ 1; v69-101 jan 1965-oct 1997+ 5; v74-101 jan 1970-oct 1997+ 9 – 1,5,9 – D422 – us UMI [930]

AMERICAN JOURNAL OF ARCHAEOLOGY – o.s.v. 1-11. 1885-1896. n.s. v. 1-52. 1897-1948 – 1 – us Princeton Micro [930]

AMERICAN JOURNAL OF ARCHAEOLOGY AND OF THE HISTORY OF THE FINE ARTS *see* AMERICAN JOURNAL OF ARCHAEOLOGY

AMERICAN JOURNAL OF ART THERAPY – (Former title: Bulletin of Art Therapy (fall 1961-jul 1969)) – Washington. v1-36 Fall 1962-may 1998+ 1; v10-36 oct 1970-may 1998+ 5; v16-36 oct 1976-may 1998+ 9 – 1,5,9 – D1820 – us UMI [615]

AMERICAN JOURNAL OF AUDIOLOGY – Washington. v1-6 nov 1991- 1*; v3-6 mar/nov 1994- 5*,9 – 1,5,9 – D20817 – us UMI [612]

AMERICAN JOURNAL OF BOTANY – v. 1-50. 1914-1963 – 1,5,6 – us Princeton Micro [580]

AMERICAN JOURNAL OF CANCER – v. 1-40. 1916-1940 – 1,5,6 – us Princeton Micro [610]

AMERICAN JOURNAL OF CARDIAC IMAGING – Orlando. v4-11 1990- 1*; v6-11 1992-* 5,9 – 1,5,9 – D21077 – us UMI [616]

AMERICAN JOURNAL OF CARDIOLOGY – New York. cum index v1-7 1958-1961; v1-80 jan 1958- 1; v15-80 jan 1965- 5; v25-80 jan 1970- 9 – 1,5,9 – D1973 – us UMI [616]

AMERICAN JOURNAL OF CHINESE MEDICINE – (Cont by: Comparative Medicine East and West) – Garden City. v1-5. jan 1973-Spr 1977 – 1,5,9* – D10055 – us UMI [615]

AMERICAN JOURNAL OF CHINESE MEDICINE – (Cont: Comparative medicine East and West) – Garden City. v7-25. Spr 1979- – 1,5*,9 – D10055.02 – us UMI [615]

American Journal of Chiropractic *see* ACA JOURNAL OF CHIROPRACTIC

AMERICAN JOURNAL OF CLINICAL BIOFEEDBACK – (Cont by: Clinical Biofeedback and Health) – Des Plaines. v1-7. Sum 1978-Win 1984 – 1,5,9 – D11712 – us UMI [616]

AMERICAN JOURNAL OF CLINICAL HYPNOSIS – Des Plaines. cum index 1-6 jul 1958-jul 1964; v1-40 jul 1958- 1; v13-40 jul 1970- 5,9 – 1,5,9 – D2293 – us UMI [616]

AMERICAN JOURNAL OF CLINICAL NUTRITION – (Former title: Journal of Clinical Nutrition (sep 1952-may/jun 1954)) – Bethesda. v1-66 sep 1952-dec 1997+ 1; v18-66 jan 1966-dec 1997+ 5; v23-66 jan 1970-dec 1997+ 9. Shipped yrly or qrtly – 1,5,9 – D1963 – us UMI [612]

AMERICAN JOURNAL OF CLINICAL NUTRITION – New York. v8-19. 1960-66. M-13/2 – 8 – ne IDC [614]

AMERICAN JOURNAL OF CLINICAL ONCOLOGY : CANCER CLINICAL TRIALS – (Cont: Cancer clinical trials) – New York. v5-20 1982- 1*; v16-20 feb 1993- 5,9 – 1,5,9 – D18696.01 – us UMI [616]

AMERICAN JOURNAL OF CLINICAL PATHOLOGY / American Society of Clinical Pathologists – Baltimore. v33-34, 37-46. 1960, 1962-66. M-12/2 – 8 – ne IDC [073]

AMERICAN JOURNAL OF CLINICAL PATHOLOGY – Philadelphia. v1-108 jan 1931-dec 1997+ 1; v39-108 jan 1963-dec 1997+ 5*,9* – 1,5,9 – D94 – us UMI [616]

AMERICAN JOURNAL OF COMMUNITY PSYCHOLOGY – New York. 1973-v25 dec 1997+ 1; v17-25 feb 1989-dec 1997+ 5*,9 – 1,5,9 – D12399 – us UMI [150]

AMERICAN JOURNAL OF COMPARATIVE LAW – Berkeley. v1-45 Win 1952- 1; v20-45 Win 1972- 5; v22-45 Win/Fal 1974- – 1,5,9 – D6486 – us UMI [340]

AMERICAN JOURNAL OF CONTACT DERMATITIS – Philadelphia. v1-8 mar 1990- 1*; v3-4 mar 1992- 5,9 – 1,5,9 – D21078 – us UMI [616]

AMERICAN JOURNAL OF CORRECTION – (Cont: Prison world. Cont by: Corrections today) – Laurel. v16-40. sep 1954-dec 1978* – 1 – D12976.02 – us UMI [360]

AMERICAN JOURNAL OF CRIMINAL JUSTICE – (Cont: Southern journal of criminal justice) – Richmond. v9-21. Fall 1984- – 1,5*,9 – D13350.01 – us UMI [360]

AMERICAN JOURNAL OF CRIMINAL LAW – Austin. cum index 1-2; v1-2 feb 1972-Win 1974 1; v3-25 Sum 1974-Spr 1998+ – 1,5,9 – D10070 – us UMI [340]

AMERICAN JOURNAL OF CRIMINAL LAW – (v1-12 1972-84 $160.00 reel. v13-22 1985-95 $163.00 mf) – University of Texas. v1-22. 1972-95 – 5,6,9 – $346.00 – us Hein [340]

AMERICAN JOURNAL OF DANCE THERAPY – Columbia. v1-19 Spr 1977- 1*; v11-19 Spr 1989-* 5,9 – 1,5,9 – D17540 – us UMI [615]

AMERICAN JOURNAL OF DERMATOPHATHOLOGY – New York. v1-19 1979- 1*; v15-19 1993-* 5,9 – 1,5,9 – D18695 – us UMI [616]

AMERICAN JOURNAL OF DIAGNOSTIC GYNECOLOGY AND OBSTETRICS – (Cont by: Diagnostic gynecology and obstetrics) – New York. v1. 1979* – 1 – D16577 – us UMI [618]

AMERICAN JOURNAL OF DIGESTIVE DISEASES – (Cont by: Digestive diseases and sciences. Former titles: American journal of digestive diseases and nutrition (mar 1934-feb 1938)) – New York. v1-22 1934-1955; ns: v1-23 jan/dec 1956-jan/dec 1978 1*; ns: v2-23 jan 1957-jan/dec 1978 5* – 1,5 – D53 – us UMI [616]

AMERICAN JOURNAL OF DIGESTIVE DISEASES AND NUTRITION *see* AMERICAN JOURNAL OF DIGESTIVE DISEASES

AMERICAN JOURNAL OF DISEASES OF CHILDREN – (Cont by: Archives of Pediatrics and Adolescent Medicine. Former titles: American Journal of Diseases of Children (jan 1911-dec 1955); Journal of Diseases of Children (jan 1956-jun 1960)) – Chicago. v1-147 jan 1911-dec 1993 1; v109-147 jan 1965-dec 1993 5; v119-147 jan 1970-dec 1993 9 – 1,5,9 – D408 – us UMI [618]

AMERICAN JOURNAL OF DISEASES OF CHILDREN *see* AMERICAN JOURNAL OF DISEASES OF CHILDREN

AMERICAN JOURNAL OF DRUG AND ALCOHOL ABUSE – New York. v1-18 1974-92 1*; v19-23 mar 1993-dec 1997+ 1*,5*,9* – 1,5,9 – D12923 – us UMI [360]

AMERICAN JOURNAL OF ECONOMICS AND SOCIOLOGY – New York. v1-56 oct 1941-oct 1997+ 1; v28-56 jan 1969-oct 1997+ 5; v34-56 jan 1975-oct 1997+ 9 – 1,5,9 – D1084 – us UMI [300]

AMERICAN JOURNAL OF EDUCATION – (Cont: School Review) – Chicago. v88-106. nov 1979-aug 1998+. Shipped yrly or qrtly – 1,5,9 – D137.01 – us UMI [370]

AMERICAN JOURNAL OF EDUCATION – (Ceased publ) – New York. v1. feb-may 1847 – 1 – D4611 – us UMI [370]

AMERICAN JOURNAL OF EDUCATION – (Ceased publ. Former titles: American Journal of Education and College Review (aug 1855-jan 1856)) – Harford. cum index v1-16 aug 1855-dec 1866; v1-32 aug 1855-dec 1882 – 1 – D3873 – us UMI [370]

AMERICAN JOURNAL OF EDUCATION – St Bonaventure. v1-37. feb 1869-jun 1904 – 1 – D4813 – us UMI [370]

AMERICAN JOURNAL OF EDUCATION *see* AMERICAN ANNALS OF EDUCATION

AMERICAN JOURNAL OF EDUCATION AND COLLEGE REVIEW *see* AMERICAN JOURNAL OF EDUCATION

AMERICAN JOURNAL OF EDUCATION AND MONTHLY LYCEUM *see* AMERICAN ANNALS OF EDUCATION

AMERICAN JOURNAL OF EDUCATION (BARNARD'S) – v. 1-32. 1855-1882 – 1 – us Princeton Micro [370]

AMERICAN JOURNAL OF EDUCATION (CHICAGO) – v1-95. 1893-1987 – 1,5,6 – us Princeton Micro [073]

AMERICAN JOURNAL OF EMERGENCY MEDICINE – Philadelphia. v1-15. jul 1983- – 1,5,9 – D14729 – us UMI [610]

THE AMERICAN JOURNAL OF EMERGENCY MEDICINE – v1- 1983- – 1,5,6,9 – us UMI [617]

AMERICAN JOURNAL OF ENOLOGY – (Cont: American Society of Enologists. Proceedings, Annual Open Meeting. Cont by: American Journal of Enology and Viticulture) – Davis. v5-9. 1954-1958* – 1 – D13557.01 – us UMI [630]

AMERICAN JOURNAL OF ENOLOGY *see* AMERICAN JOURNAL OF ENOLOGY AND VITICULTURE

AMERICAN JOURNAL OF ENOLOGY AND VITICULTURE – (Cont: American Journal of Enology) – Davis. v10-48. 1959-* – 1 – D13557.02 – us UMI [630]

AMERICAN JOURNAL OF ENOLOGY AND VITICULTURE *see* AMERICAN JOURNAL OF ENOLOGY

AMERICAN JOURNAL OF FAMILY LAW – v1-8. 1987-1994 – 9 – $195.00 set – us Hein [340]

AMERICAN JOURNAL OF FAMILY THERAPY – (Cont: International Journal of Family Counseling) – New York. v7-25. Spr 1979- – 1,5,9 – D8240.02 – us UMI [360]

AMERICAN JOURNAL OF FORENSIC PSYCHIATRY – (v1-5 1978-84 in reel $68.00. v6-16 1985-95 in mf $223.00) – v1-16. 1978-95 – 5,6,9 – $291.00 set – us Hein [614]

AMERICAN JOURNAL OF FORENSIC PSYCHOLOGY – (v1-2 1983-84 in reel $45.00. v3-13 1985-95 in mf $224.00) – v1-13. 1983-95 – 5,6,9 – $269.00 set – us Hein [614]

AMERICAN JOURNAL OF GASTROENTEROLOGY – v77-91. 1982-96 – 15r – 1,5,6,9 – $110.00r – us Williams [616]

AMERICAN JOURNAL OF GASTROENTEROLOGY – (Former titles: Review of Gastroenterolgy (mar 1934-dec 1953)) – Baltimore. v16-76 jan 1949-dec 1981 1; v45-76 jan 1966-dec 1981 5; 53-76 jan 1970-dec 1981 9 – 1,5,9 – D5 – us UMI [616]

AMERICAN JOURNAL OF GERIATRIC PSYCHIATRY – Washington. v1-5. Win 1993-* – 1,5,9 – D20183 – us UMI [616]

AMERICAN JOURNAL OF HEALTH BEHAVIOR – (Cont: Health Values) – Star City. v20-21. jan-dec 1996 – 1,5,9 – D12296.01 – us UMI [073]

AMERICAN JOURNAL OF HEALTH PROMOTION – Birmingham. 1986- 1*; 1994-* 5,9 – 1,5,9 – D21657 – us UMI [613]

AMERICAN JOURNAL OF HEALTH-SYSTEM PHARMACY – (Cont: American Journal of Hospital Pharmacy) – Bethesda. v52-54. jan-dec 1995- – 1,5,9 – D1923.01 – us UMI [615]

AMERICAN JOURNAL OF HEALTH-SYSTEM PHARMACY *see* AMERICAN JOURNAL OF HOSPITAL PHARMACY

AMERICAN JOURNAL OF HOMEOPATHIA – (Ceased publ) – New York. v1. feb-aug 1835 – 1 – D3922 – us UMI [615]

AMERICAN JOURNAL OF HOMEOPATHY – (Ceased publ) – New York. v1. aug 1838-jul 1839 – 1 – D3924 – us UMI [615]

AMERICAN JOURNAL OF HOMOEPATHY – (Ceased publ) – New York. v1-9. apr 1846-aug 1854 – 1 – D3923 – us UMI [615]

AMERICAN JOURNAL OF HOSPITAL PHARMACY – (Absorbed: Clinical Pharmacy (1994). Cont by: American Journal of Health-System Pharmacy. Former titles: Official Bulletin (jun 1943-nov-dec 1944); Bulletin of the American Society of Hospital Pharmacists (jan-feb 1945-nov-dec 1949); Bulletin (jan-feb 1950-nov-dec 1957)) – Hamilton. v1-51 jun 1943-dec 1994 1; v28-51 jan 1971-dec 1994 5; v33-51 jan-dec 1976-dec 1994 9 – 1,5,9 – D1923 – us UMI [615]

AMERICAN JOURNAL OF HOSPITAL PHARMACY *see* AMERICAN JOURNAL OF HEALTH-SYSTEM PHARMACY

AMERICAN JOURNAL OF HUMAN GENETICS – Chicago. v1-61 sep 1949-dec 1997+ 1; v15-61 jan-dec 1997+ 5; v29-61 jan 1977-deec 1997+ 9 – 1,5,9 – D2740 – us UMI [573]

AMERICAN JOURNAL OF HYPERTENSION – New York. v1-10 jan 1988- 1*; v6-10 jan 1993- 5,9 – D42751 – us UMI [616]

AMERICAN JOURNAL OF INDIVIDUAL PSYCHOLOGY *see* JOURNAL OF INDIVIDUAL PSYCHOLOGY

AMERICAN JOURNAL OF INFECTION CONTROL – (Cont: Association for Practitioners in Infection Control. Apic Journal) – St Louis. v8-25. feb 1980- – 1,5,9 – D12232.03 – us UMI [614]

AMERICAN JOURNAL OF INSANITY *see* AMERICAN JOURNAL OF PSYCHIATRY

AMERICAN JOURNAL OF INTERNATIONAL LAW – (Absorbed: Proceedings of the American Society of International Law at the Meeting of the Executive Council. Superseded in pt by: Proceedings of the Annual Meeting, 1974) – Washington. v1-91 jan 1907-oct 1997+ 1; v59-91 jan 1965-oct 1997+ 5; v68-91 jan 1974-oct 1997+ 9 – 1,5,9 – D1763 – us UMI [340]

AMERICAN JOURNAL OF INTERNATIONAL LAW – v. 1-41. 1907-1947 – 1,5,6 – us Princeton Micro [340]

AMERICAN JOURNAL OF INTERNATIONAL LAW – v1-89. 1907-95 – 9 – $2,541.00 set – us Hein [340]

AMERICAN JOURNAL OF INTRAVENOUS THERAPY – (Cont: American Journal of I.V. Therapy. Cont by: American Journal of Intravenous Therapy & Clinical Nutrition) – Redding. v4-6. apr 1977-79* – 1 – D14121.01 – us UMI [615]

AMERICAN JOURNAL OF INTRAVENOUS THERAPY *see* AMERICAN JOURNAL OF INTRAVENOUS THERAPY AND CLINICAL NUTRITION

AMERICAN JOURNAL OF INTRAVENOUS THERAPY AND CLINICAL NUTRITION *see* AMERICAN JOURNAL OF INTRAVENOUS THERAPY

AMERICAN JOURNAL OF INTRAVENOUS THERAPY AND CLINICAL NUTRITION – (Cont: American Journal of Intravenous Therapy. Cont by: Intravenous Therapy News) – Georgetown. v6-11 apr 1979-may 1984 1*; v10-11 jan 1983-may 1984 5*,9 – 1,5,9 – D14121.02 – us UMI [615]

THE AMERICAN JOURNAL OF INTRAVENOUS THERAPY AND CLINICAL NUTRITION – (1983-. 1,5,6,9) – v6-11. 1979-84 – 1 – us UMI [073]

AMERICAN JOURNAL OF I.V. THERAPY – (Cont by: American of Intravenous Therapy) – Rowayton. v1-4. oct 1974-mar 1977* – 1 – D14121 – us UMI [615]

AMERICAN JOURNAL OF I.V. THERAPY *see* AMERICAN JOURNAL OF INTRAVENOUS THERAPY

AMERICAN JOURNAL OF JURISPRUDENCE – (v1-29 1956-84 in reel $235.00. v30-40 1985-95 in mf $185.00. Incl 20-yr index. Cont as: Natural Law Forum) – v1-40. 1956-95 – 5,6,9 – $420.00 set – us Hein [340]

AMERICAN JOURNAL OF JURISPRUDENCE – (Former titles: Natural Law Forum) – Notre Dame. v1-27 1956-1982 1; v16-27 1971-1982 5; v22-27 1977-1982 9 – 1,5,9 – D2722 – us UMI [340]

AMERICAN JOURNAL OF KIDNEY DISEASES – Philadelphia. v17-30 1990- 1*; v19-30 jan 1922-* 5,9 – 1,5,9 – D21079 – us UMI [616]

AMERICAN JOURNAL OF KNEE SURGERY – Thorofare. v1-10. 1988-* – 1 – D17271 – us UMI [617]

AMERICAN JOURNAL OF LAW AND MEDICINE – Boston. v1-4 mar 1975-79* 1; v5-23 Spr 1979-1997+ – 1,5,9 – D12087 – us UMI [073]

AMERICAN JOURNAL OF LAW AND MEDICINE – (v1-10 1975-85 in reel $160.00. v11-21 1985-95 in mf $290.00 set) – v1-21. 1975-95 – 5,6,9 – $450.00 set – us Hein [340]

AMERICAN JOURNAL OF LEGAL HISTORY – v1-36. 1957-92 – 1,5,6 – $315.00 – us Hein [340]

AMERICAN JOURNAL OF MATHEMATICS – Baltimore. cum index 1-75 1878-1953; v1-119 1878-dec 1997+ 1; v99-119 feb 1917-dec 1997+ 5,9 – 1,5,9 – D1913 – us UMI [510]

AMERICAN JOURNAL OF MATHEMATICS – v1-77. 1878-1955 – 1,5,6 – us Princeton Micro [510]

AMERICAN JOURNAL OF MEDICAL QUALITY – v1-11. 1986-96 – 11r – 1,5,6,9 – $65.00r – us Williams [610]

AMERICAN JOURNAL OF MEDICAL TECHNOLOGY – (Merged with: Journal of the American Medical Technologists to form: Journal of Medical Technology. Absorbed: Cadence of the Clinical Laboratory, 1977. Former titles: Official Publication of the American Society of Clinical Laboratory Technicians; Bulletin of...(jan-nov 1935); American Journal of Medical Technology (jan 1936-dec 1976); Medical Technology (jan-feb 1977)) – Houston. v1-49 nov 1934-dec 1983 1; v37-49 jan 1971-dec 1983 5; v41-49 jan 1975-dec 1983 9 – 1,5,9 – D2759 – us UMI [610]

AMERICAN JOURNAL OF MEDICAL TECHNOLOGY *see* AMERICAN JOURNAL OF MEDICAL TECHNOLOGY

AMERICAN JOURNAL OF MEDICINE – New York. v1-103 jul 1946-dec 1997+ 1; v38-103 jan 1965-dec 1997+ 5; v48-103 jan 1970-dec 1997+ 9. Shipped yrly or qrtly – 1,5,9 – D1964 – us UMI [610]

AMERICAN JOURNAL OF MENTAL DEFICIENCY – (Cont by: American Journal on Mental Retardation (AJMR). Former titles: Proceedings of the Association of Medical Officers of American Institutions for Idiotic and Feeble-Minded Persons (1876-95); Proceedings and Addresses of the American Association for the Study of the Feeble-Minded (1918-32); Proceedings and Addresses of the Annual Session of the American Association on Mental Deficiency (1933-39)) – Albany. v1-92 1876-sep 1987 1*; v71-92 jul 1966-sep 1987 5; v80-92 jul 1975-sep 1987 9 – 1,5,9 – D1558 – us UMI [616]

AMERICAN JOURNAL OF MENTAL DEFICIENCY *see* AMERICAN JOURNAL OF MENTAL RETARDATION

AMERICAN JOURNAL OF MENTAL RETARDATION – (Cont: American Journal of Mental Deficiency) – Washington. v92-102. nov 1987- – 1,5,9 – D1558.01 – us UMI [616]

AMERICAN JOURNAL OF MUSIC AND MUSICAL VISITOR – (Ceased publ) – Boston. v1-5. jul 1840-oct 1846 – 1 – D4148 – us UMI [780]

AMERICAN JOURNAL OF NEPHROLOGY – v1-. 1981- – 1,5,9 – us UMI [073]

AMERICAN JOURNAL OF NEUROLOGY AND PSYCHIATRY – (Ceased publ) – New York. v1-3. feb 1882-apr 1885 – 1 – D3210 – us UMI [615]

AMERICAN JOURNAL OF NONINVASIVE CARDIOLOGY – Basel. v1-11 jan 1987-1*; v7-11 1993-* 5,9 – 1,5,9 – D20573 – us UMI [616]

AMERICAN JOURNAL OF NUMISMATICS – (Former titles: American Journal of Numismatics, and Bulletin of the American Numismatic and Archaeological Society (may 1866-apr 1869); American Journal of Numismatics, and Bulletin of the American Numismatic and Archaeological Societies (may 1869-apr 1897)) – New York. cum index v1-50; v1-41 may 1866-apr 1907 – 1 – D4859 – us UMI [616]

AMERICAN JOURNAL OF NUMISMATICS, AND BULLETIN OF THE AMERICAN NUMISMATIC AND ARCHAEOLOGICAL SOCIETY *see* AMERICAN JOURNAL OF NUMISMATICS

AMERICAN JOURNAL OF NURSING – v1-55. 1923-55 – 1,5,6 – us Princeton Micro [610]

AMERICAN JOURNAL OF NURSING – New York. cum index v1-50 1900-1950; cum index v61-65 jan 1961-dec 1965; v1-97 1900- 1; v65-97 jan 1965- 5; v70-97 jan 1970- 9 – 1,5,9 – D835 – us UMI [610]

American Journal of Nursing. Sophia F. Palmer Memorial Library. New York *see* CATALOG OF THE SOPHIA F. PALMER MEMORIAL LIBRARY

AMERICAN JOURNAL OF OBSTETRICS AND GYNECOLOGY – v1-70. 1920-55.Continues: American Journal of Obstetrics and Diseases of Women and Children – 1,5,6 – us Princeton Micro [618]

AMERICAN JOURNAL OF OBSTETRICS AND GYNECOLOGY – St Louis. v1-177 oct 1920-1; v91-177 jan 1965- 5; v106-177 jan 1970-9 – 1,5,9 – D1881 – us UMI [618]

AMERICAN JOURNAL OF OCCUPATIONAL THERAPY – (Cont: AJOT) – Bethesda. v34-51. jan 1990-dec 1997+ – 1,5,9 – D10224.02 – us UMI [615]

AMERICAN JOURNAL OF OCCUPATIONAL THERAPY – (Cont by: AJOT - The American Journal of Occupational Therapy) – New York. v1-31 1947-77 1; v29-31 jan 1975-dec 1977 5; v30-31 jan 1976-dec 1977 9 – 1,5,9 – D10224 – us UMI [615]

AMERICAN JOURNAL OF OCCUPATIONAL THERAPY *see* AJOT

AMERICAN JOURNAL OF OPHTHALMOLOGY – Chicago. v1-34 apr 1884-dec 1917; ns: v1-60 jan 1918-jan-dec 1965; 3s: v61-124 jan 1966- 1; 3s: v59-124 jan 1966- 5; 3s v69-124 jan 1970- 9 – 1,5,9 – D99 – us UMI [617]

AMERICAN JOURNAL OF OPTOMETRY *see* AMERICAN JOURNAL OF OPTOMETRY AND ARCHIVES OF AMERICAN ACADEMY OF OPTOMETRY

AMERICAN JOURNAL OF OPTOMETRY AND ARCHIVES OF AMERICAN ACADEMY OF OPTOMETRY – (Cont by: American Journal of Optometry and Physiological Optics. Former titles: Northwest Journal of Optometry (jan 1924-july 1925); American Journal of Optometry (aug 1925-dec 1940)) – Minneapolis. v1-50 jan 1924-dec 1973 1; 45-50 jan 1968-dec 1973 5; v47-50 jan 1970-dec 1973 9 – 1,5,9 – D100 – us UMI [617]

AMERICAN JOURNAL OF OPTOMETRY AND ARCHIVES OF AMERICAN ACADEMY OF OPTOMETRY *see* AMERICAN JOURNAL OF OPTOMETRY AND PHYSIOLOGICAL OPTICS

AMERICAN JOURNAL OF OPTOMETRY AND PHYSIOLOGICAL OPTICS – (Cont: American Journal of Optometry and Archives of American Academy of Optometry) – Baltimore. v51-52. jan 1974-dec 1975 – 1 – D100.01 – us UMI [617]

AMERICAN JOURNAL OF OPTOMETRY AND PHYSIOLOGICAL OPTICS *see* AMERICAN JOURNAL OF OPTOMETRY AND ARCHIVES OF AMERICAN ACADEMY OF OPTOMETRY

AMERICAN JOURNAL OF ORTHODONTICS – (Superseded in jan 1948 by: Oral Surgery, Oral Medicine, Oral Pathology. Cont by: American Journal of Orthodontics and Dentofacial Orthopedics. Former titles: International Journal of Orthodontia (jan 1915-feb 1919); International Journal of Orthodontia and Oral Surgery (mar 1919-jan 1922); International Journal of Orthodontia, Oral Surgery and Radiography (feb 1922-dec 1932); International Journal of Orthodontia and Dentistry for Children (jan 1933-dec 1935); International Journal of Orthodontia and Oral Surgery (1936-1937); American Journal of Orthodontics and oral Surgery (1938-1947)) – St Louis. v1-89 jan 1915-jun 1986 1; v59-89 jan 1971-jun 1986 5; v65-89 jan 1974-jun 1986 – 1,5,9 – D1880 – us UMI [617]

AMERICAN JOURNAL OF ORTHODONTICS *see* AMERICAN JOURNAL OF ORTHODONTICS AND DENTOFACIAL ORTHOPEDICS

AMERICAN JOURNAL OF ORTHODONTICS AND DENTOFACIAL ORTHOPEDICS – (Cont: American Journal of Orthodontics) – St Louis. v90-112. jul 1986 – 1,5,9 – D1880.01 – us UMI [617]

AMERICAN JOURNAL OF ORTHODONTICS AND DENTOFACIAL ORTHOPEDICS *see* AMERICAN JOURNAL OF ORTHODONTICS

AMERICAN JOURNAL OF ORTHODONTICS AND ORAL SURGERY *see* AMERICAN JOURNAL OF ORTHODONTICS

AMERICAN JOURNAL OF ORTHOPSYCHIATRY – Albany. cum index 1-10 1930-1940 v1-67 oct 1930- – 1,5,9 – D5839 – us UMI [616]

AMERICAN JOURNAL OF OTOLARYNGOLOGY – v.1-. Fal 1979- – 1,5,6,9 – us UMI [073]

AMERICAN JOURNAL OF OTOLOGY – New York. v1-18. jul 1979- – 1,5*,9 – D12998 – us UMI [617]

AMERICAN JOURNAL OF PASTORAL COUNSELING / ed by Dayringer, Richard – (Cont: Journal of Pastoral Psychotherapy. Cont: Journal of Religion in Psychotherapy) – v1- 1990- – 1,9 ($60.00 in US $84.00 outside hardcopy subsc) – us Haworth [616]

AMERICAN JOURNAL OF PATHOLOGY – Hagerstown. cum index v1-20 v1-151 jan 1925- 1; v70-151 1973- 5; v78-151 jan-dec 1975- – 1,5,9 – D8777 – us UMI [574]

AMERICAN JOURNAL OF PERINATOLOGY – New York. v1-14. oct 1983- – 1,5*,9 – D12997 – us UMI [618]

AMERICAN JOURNAL OF PHARMACEUTICAL EDUCATION – v. 11-14. 1947-1950 – 1,5,6 – us Princeton Micro [615]

AMERICAN JOURNAL OF PHARMACEUTICAL EDUCATION – Alexandria. cum index v1-20 1937-1956 v1-61 jan 1937- 1; v32-61 feb 1968- 5; v35-61 jan 1971 9 – 1,5,9 – D1524 – us UMI [615]

AMERICAN JOURNAL OF PHARMACY – v1-142. 1829-1970 – 1,5,6 – us Princeton Micro [615]

AMERICAN JOURNAL OF PHARMACY *see* AMERICAN JOURNAL OF PHARMACY AND THE SCIENCES SUPPORTING PUBLIC HEALTH

AMERICAN JOURNAL OF PHARMACY AND THE SCIENCES SUPPORTING PUBLIC HEALTH – (Cont: Pharmacy Management) – Philadelphia. v153-169. oct 1981- – 1,5*,9 – D1.02 – us UMI [615]

AMERICAN JOURNAL OF PHARMACY AND THE SCIENCES SUPPORTING PUBLIC HEALTH – (Merged with: Pharmacy Management, to form: Journal of Philadelphia College of Pharmacy (apr 1829-jan 1835); American Journal of Pharmacy (1836-1936)) – Philadelphia. v1-150 dec 1825-dec 19781; v132-150 jan 1960-dec 1978 5; v142-150 jan 1970-dec 1978 9 – 1,5,9 – D1 – us UMI [615]

AMERICAN JOURNAL OF PHILOLOGY – 1-1880- 1; 1977 5,6,9 – us UMI [400]

AMERICAN JOURNAL OF PHILOLOGY – v. 1-83. 1880-1962 – 1 – us Princeton Micro [400]

AMERICAN JOURNAL OF PHOTOGRAPHY – (Ceased publ) – Philadelphia. v3-20. sep 1882-sep 1900 – 1 – D4634 – us UMI [770]

AMERICAN JOURNAL OF PHYSICAL ANTHROPOLOGY – (American Association of Physical Anthropologists.) v. 1-29, Old Series. 1918-1942. v. 1-26, New Series. 1943-1967 – 1 – us Princeton Micro [573]

AMERICAN JOURNAL OF PHYSICAL MEDICINE AND REHABILITATION – v1-75. 1922-96 – 1,5,6,9 – $90.00r – us Williams [617]

AMERICAN JOURNAL OF PHYSICS – v1-. 1933- – 1,5,6 – us A.I.P. [530]

AMERICAN JOURNAL OF PHYSICS – (Former titles: American Physics Teacher (feb 1933-dec 1939)) – Woodbury, 1993- – 1,5,9 – D38091 – us UMI [530]

AMERICAN JOURNAL OF PHYSIOLOGY – v. 1-195. 1898-1958 – 1,5,6 – us Princeton Micro [612]

AMERICAN JOURNAL OF PHYSIOLOGY – Bethesda. cum index v1-229 1898-1975 v1-273 jan 1898- 1; v208-273 jan 1965- 5; v218-273 jan 1970- 9 – 1,5,9 – D776 – us UMI [612]

AMERICAN JOURNAL OF PHYSIOLOGY : CELL PHYSIOLOGY – (Publ as a division of, and contains material also publ in: American Journal of Physiology) – Bethesda. v1-42. jan 1977- – 1*,5*,9 – D11160 – us UMI [612]

AMERICAN JOURNAL OF PHYSIOLOGY : ENDOCRINOLOGY AND METABOLISM – (Contains materials also publ in: American Journal of Physiology. Cont in pt: American Journal of Physiology: Endocrinology, Metabolism and Gastrointestinal Phsiology) – Bethesda. v1-36 jan 1980- 1*; v5-36 jan 1982- 5*; v5-36 jan 1982- 9 – 1,5,9 – D11945 – us UMI [612]

AMERICAN JOURNAL OF PHYSIOLOGY : ENDOCRINOLOGY, METABOLISM AND GASTROINTESTINAL PHYSIOLOGY – (Publ as a division of, and contains material also publ in: American Journal of Physiology. Cont by: American Journal of physiology: Endocrinology and Metabolism, and: American Journal of Physiology: Gastrointestinal and Liver Physiology) – Bethesda. v1-6 jan 1977-jan/dec 1979 1*; v1-4 jan-dec 1977-jan/dec 1978* 5,9 – 1,5,9 – D11156 – us UMI [612]

AMERICAN JOURNAL OF PHYSIOLOGY : GASTROINTESTINAL AND LIVER PHYSIOLOGY – (Contains material also publ in: American Journal of Physiology. Cont in pt: American Journal of Physiology: Endocrinology, Metabolism and Gastrointestinal Physiology) – Bethesda. v1-36. 1980-* – 1 – D11946 – us UMI [612]

AMERICAN JOURNAL OF PHYSIOLOGY : HEART AND CIRCULATORY PHYSIOLOGY – (Publ as a division, and contains materials publ in: American Journal of Physiology) – Bethesda. v1-42. jan 1977- – 1,5*,9 – D11157 – us UMI [612]

AMERICAN JOURNAL OF PHYSIOLOGY : LUNG CELLULAR AND MOLECULAR PHYSIOLOGY – Bethesda. v1-17. aug 1989-* – 1 – D17273 – us UMI [612]

AMERICAN JOURNAL OF PHYSIOLOGY : REGULATORY, INTEGRATIVE AND COMPARATIVE PHYSIOLOGY – (Publ as a division of, and contains material also publ in: American Journal of Physiology) – Bethesda. v1-42. jan 1977- – 1*,5*,9 – D11158 – us UMI [612]

AMERICAN JOURNAL OF PHYSIOLOGY : RENAL, FLUID AND ELECTROLYTE PHYSIOLOGY – (Publ as a division of, and contains material also publ in: American Journal of Physiology) – Bethesda. v7-42. jan 1980-* – 1 – D11159 – us UMI [612]

AMERICAN JOURNAL OF POLICE : AN INTERDISCIPLINARY JOURNAL OF THEORY AND RESEARCH – Cincinnati. v1-16 1981-1*; v4-16 Spr 1985- 5*,9 – 1,5,9 – D15308 – us UMI [360]

AMERICAN JOURNAL OF POLITICAL SCIENCE – (Cont: Midwest Journal of Political Science) – Austin. v17-41 feb 1973- 1,5; v20-41 feb 1976- 9 – 1,5,9 – D2539.01 – us UMI [320]

AMERICAN JOURNAL OF PREVENTIVE MEDICINE – New York. v1-13 jan 1985-1*; v4-13 jan 1988- 5*,9 – 1,5,9 – D17033 – us UMI [614]

AMERICAN JOURNAL OF PROCTOLOGY – (Cont by: American Journal of Proctology, Gastroenterology and Colon and Rectal Surgery) – East Stroudsburg. v1-28 mar 1950-dec 1977 1; v22-28 feb 1971-dec 1977 5; v28 feb-dec 1977 9 – 1,5,9 – D1996 – us UMI [617]

AMERICAN JOURNAL OF PROCTOLOGY *see* AMERICAN JOURNAL OF PROCTOLOGY, GASTROENTEROLOGY AND COLON AND RECTAL SURGERY

AMERICAN JOURNAL OF PROCTOLOGY, GASTROENTEROLOGY AND COLON AND RECTAL SURGERY – (Cont: American Journal of Proctology. Cont by: Gastroenterology and Endoscopy News) – Georgetown. v29-36. jan 1978-jan-feb 1985 – 1,5,9 – D1996.01 – us UMI [617]

AMERICAN JOURNAL OF PROCTOLOGY, GASTROENTEROLOGY AND COLON AND RECTAL SURGERY *see* AMERICAN JOURNAL OF PROCTOLOGY

AMERICAN JOURNAL OF PROGRESSIVE THERAPEUTICS – (Ceased publ. Former titles: America X-ray Journal (may 1897-nov 1904)) – Chicago. v1-19. may 1897-aug 1906 – 1 – D5729 – us UMI [615]

AMERICAN JOURNAL OF PSYCHIATRY – v1-111. 1844-1954 – 1,5,6 – us Princeton Micro [616]

AMERICAN JOURNAL OF PSYCHIATRY – (Former titles: American Journal of Insanity (jul 1844-apr 1921)) – Washington. v1-154 jul 1844- 1; v122-154 jul 1965- 5; v127-154 jul 1970 9 – 1,5,9 – D746 – us UMI [616]

AMERICAN JOURNAL OF PSYCHOANALYSIS – New York. cum index v1-25 1941-1965; v1-57 1941- 1; v27-55 may 1967- 5; v30-57 1970- 9 – 1,5,9 – D2394 – us UMI [150]

AMERICAN JOURNAL OF PSYCHOLOGY – v. 1-53. 1887-1940 – 1,5,6 – us Princeton Micro [150]

AMERICAN JOURNAL OF PSYCHOLOGY – Urbana. v1-110 nov 1887- 1; v78-110 mar 1965- 5; v83-110 mar 1970- 9 – 1,5,9 – D121 – us UMI [150]

AMERICAN JOURNAL OF PSYCHOTHERAPY – Bronx. v1-51 jan 1947- 1*; v43-51 jan 1989- 5*,9 – 1,5,9 – D18267 – us UMI [150]

AMERICAN JOURNAL OF PUBLIC HEALTH – (Cont: American Journal of Public Hygiene. Former titles: Journal of the American Public Health Association (jan 1911-dec 1911); American Journal of Public Health (jan 1912-dec 1927); American Journal of Public Health and the Nation's Health (jan 1928-dec 1970)) – Washington. cum index v1-35 1911-1945; v1-87 jan 1911- 1; v55-87 jan 1965- 5,9 – 1,5,9 – D8 – us UMI [614]

AMERICAN JOURNAL OF PUBLIC HEALTH *see* AMERICAN JOURNAL OF PUBLIC HEALTH

AMERICAN JOURNAL OF PUBLIC HEALTH AND THE NATION'S HEALTH *see* AMERICAN JOURNAL OF PUBLIC HEALTH

AMERICAN JOURNAL OF PUBLIC HYGIENE – (Ceased publ. Cont by: Journal of the American Public Health Association. Former titles: Massachusetts Association of Boards of Health Journal (jan 1891-aug 1904); American Journal of Public Hygiene; Journal of the Massachusetts Association of Boards of Health (nov 1904-nov 1906)) – cum index v1-6; v1-20 jan 1891-nov 1910 – 1 – D4782 – us UMI [614]

AMERICAN JOURNAL OF PUBLIC HYGIENE *see*
- AMERICAN JOURNAL OF PUBLIC HEALTH
- AMERICAN JOURNAL OF PUBLIC HYGIENE

THE AMERICAN JOURNAL OF RELIGIOUS PSYCHOLOGY AND EDUCATION – v1-4. 1904-11 (complete) – 1r – 1 – ATLA 1994-S518 – us A.T.L.A. [073]

AMERICAN JOURNAL OF RESPIRATORY AND CRITICAL CARE MEDICINE – (Cont: American Review of Respiratory Disease) – New York. v149-156. jan-dec 1994- – 1,5,9 – D102.01 – us UMI [610]

AMERICAN JOURNAL OF RESPIRATORY CELL AND MOLECULAR BIOLOGY – New York. v1-17. jul 1989-* – 1 – D18350 – us UMI [611]

AMERICAN JOURNAL OF ROENTGENOLOGY – 126- 1976- – 1,5,6,9 – us UMI [616]

AMERICAN JOURNAL OF ROENTGENOLOGY *see*
- AMERICAN JOURNAL OF ROENTGENOLOGY, RADIUM THERAPY, AND NUCLEAR MEDICINE

AMERICAN JOURNAL OF ROENTGENOLOGY AND RADIUM THERAPY *see* AMERICAN JOURNAL OF ROENTGENOLOGY, RADIUM THERAPY, AND NUCLEAR MEDICINE

AMERICAN JOURNAL OF ROENTGENOLOGY, RADIUM THERAPY, AND NUCLEAR MEDICINE – (Cont by: American Journal of Roentgenology. Former titles: American Quarterly of Roentgenology (oct 1906-sep 1913); American Journal of Roentgenology (nov 1913-dec 1922); American Journal of Roentgenology and Radium Therapy (jan 1923-dec 1951)) – Springfield. cum index v1-78 1906-1957; v1-5 oct 1906-sep 1913; ns: v1-125 nov 1913-dec 1975 1; v96-125 jan 1966-dec 1975 5; v108-125 jan 1970-dec 1975 9 – 1,5,9 – D1574 – us UMI [615]

AMERICAN JOURNAL OF ROENTGENOLOGY, RADIUM THERAPY, AND NUCLEAR SCIENCE *see* AJR

AMERICAN JOURNAL OF SCIENCE – v1-283. 1818-1983 – 1,5,6 – us Princeton Micro [500]

AMERICAN JOURNAL OF SCIENCE – (Former titles: American Journal of Science (1818-1819); American Journal of Science and Arts (apr 1820-1879)) – New Haven. cum index v1-49 1818-1846; v1-45 jun 1825-oct 1843; 2s: cum index v1-50 may 1846-nov 1870; v6-49 nov 1848-jan 1870; 3s: cum index v1-47; v6-47 dec 1873-jan 1894; 4s: cum index v1-20 jan 1894-dec 1906; v2-22 dec 1896-dec 1906; v247-260 jan 1949-dec 1962 – 1 – D517 – us UMI [500]

AMERICAN JOURNAL OF SCIENCE *see* AMERICAN JOURNAL OF SCIENCE

AMERICAN JOURNAL OF SCIENCE AND ARTS *see* AMERICAN JOURNAL OF SCIENCE

AMERICAN JOURNAL OF SEMITIC LANGUAGES AND LITERATURE – v. 1-58. 1884-1941 – 1 – us Princeton Micro [470]

AMERICAN JOURNAL OF SEMITIC LANGUAGES AND LITERATURES – (Superseded by: Journal of Near Eastern Studies, 1942. Former titles: Hebraica (mar 1884-apr/jul 1895)) – Chicago. v1-26. mar 1884-jul 1910 – 1 – D5655 – us UMI [470]

THE AMERICAN JOURNAL OF SEMITIC LANGUAGES AND LITERATURES – (Supersedes: Hebraica v1-11) – v1-58. Mar 1884-Oct 1941 (complete) – 9r – 1 – ATLA S0003 – us A.T.L.A. [470]

AMERICAN JOURNAL OF SMALL BUSINESS – (Cont by: Entrepreneurship Theory and Practice) – Baltimore. v1-12. jul 1976-Spr 1988 – 1,5,9 – D13012 – us UMI [650]

AMERICAN JOURNAL OF SOCIAL PSYCHIATRY – (Ceased publ) – Santa Barbara. v1-7 apr 1981-Fal 1987 1*; v4-7 Win 1984-Fal 1987 5,9 – 1,5,9 – D14094 – us UMI [616]

AMERICAN JOURNAL OF SOCIOLOGY – Chicago.v62. 1956. 1103/2 – 8 – ne IDC [073]

AMERICAN JOURNAL OF SOCIOLOGY – v. 1-59. 1895-1953 – 1 – us Princeton Micro [300]

AMERICAN JOURNAL OF SOCIOLOGY – Chicago. cum index v1-52 1895-1947; v1-103 jul 1895- 1; v71-103 jul 1965- 5; v83-103 jul 1977 9 – 1,5,9 – D492 – us UMI [301]

AMERICAN JOURNAL OF SPEECH-LANGUAGE PATHOLOGY – Washington. v1-6 sep 1991-1*; v3-6 jan-sep 1994- 5*; v3-6 jan 1994-9 – 1,5,9 – D20818 – us UMI [400]

AMERICAN JOURNAL OF SPORTS MEDICINE – (Cont: Journal of Sports Medicine) – Balitmore. v4-25 jan 1976- 1*; v14-25jan-dec 1986- 5*; v14-25 jan 1986- – 1,5,9 – D16280.01 – us UMI [617]

AMERICAN JOURNAL OF SURGERY – (Former titles: American Journal of Surgery and Gynecology) – New York. v11-40 jul 1898-jun 1926; ns: v1-174 jul 1926- 1; v109-174 jan 1965- 5; v119-174 jan 1970- 9 – 1,5,9 – D1965 – us UMI [617]

AMERICAN JOURNAL OF SURGERY AND GYNECOLOGY *see* AMERICAN JOURNAL OF SURGERY

AMERICAN JOURNAL OF TAX POLICY – University of Alabama. v1-12. 1982-95 – 9 – $168.00 set – us Hein [340]

AMERICAN JOURNAL OF TECHNOLOGY *see* JOURNAL OF THE AMERICAN MEDICAL TECHNOLOGISTS

AMERICAN JOURNAL OF THE MEDICAL SCIENCES – (Supersedes: Philadelphia Journal of the Medical and Physical Sciences. Absorbed: American Medical Recorder (jul 1829)) – Thorofare. v1-26 nov 1828-may 1840; ns: v1-314 1; v249-314 jan 1965- 5; v259-314 jan 1970- 9 – 1,5,9 – D1754 – us UMI [610]

THE AMERICAN JOURNAL OF THE MEDICAL SCIENCES – Old series, v1-26. 1827-40. New Series, v1-229. 1841-1955 – 1,5,6 – us Princeton Micro [610]

AMERICAN JOURNAL OF THEOLOGY – v1-24. 1897-Oct 1920 (complete) – 17r – 1 – ATLA S0173 – us A.T.L.A. [073]

AMERICAN JOURNAL OF THEOLOGY – (Ceased publ. Merged with: Biblical World, to form: Journal of Religion) – Chicago. cum index v1-24 1897-1920; v1-24 jan 1897- oct 1920 – 1 – D3308 – us UMI [240]

THE AMERICAN JOURNAL OF THEOLOGY – Chicago, 1(1897)-24(1920) – 326mf – 9 – Dfl1,141.00 – ne Slangenburg [073]

THE AMERICAN JOURNAL OF THEOLOGY – Chicago. v1-24. 1897-1920 – 326mf – 9 – ne IDC [240]

AMERICAN JOURNAL OF THEOLOGY AND PHILOSOPHY – v1-11. 1980-90 (complete) – 1r – 1 – ATLA S0803 – us A.T.L.A. [073]

AMERICAN JOURNAL OF THEOLOGY AND PHILOSOPHY – West Lafayette. v1-18 jan 1980- 1*; v6-18 jan 1985- 5*, 9 – 1,5,9 – D15392 – us UMI [240]

AMERICAN JOURNAL OF TRIAL ADVOCACY – Birmingham. v1-21 1977- 1*; v3-21 Sum 1979- 5,9 – 1,5,9 – D12035 – us UMI [340]

AMERICAN JOURNAL OF VETERINARY RESEARCH – Schaumberg. v1-58 oct 1940-1; v30-58 jan 1969- 5; v38-58 jan 1977-9 – 1,5,9 – D160 – us UMI [636]

AMERICAN JOURNAL ON ADDICTIONS – Washington. v1-6 Win-Fal 1992- 1*; v1-6 Win 1992- 5*; v1-6Win-Fal 1992- 9* – 1,5,9 – D20184 – us UMI [616]

AMERICAN JOURNAL ON MENTAL RETARDATION *see* AMERICAN JOURNAL OF MENTAL DEFICIENCY

AMERICAN JOURNALISM REVIEW – (Cont: Washington Journalism Review) – Adelphia. v15-19. mar 1993- – 1,5,9 – D12946.03 – us UMI [070]

AMERICAN JOURNALS / Fox, George T – 1831-68. BRRAM – 1 – uk Microform Academic [920]

AMERICAN JUBILEE – Nos. 1-12 (all publ). 1854-1855 – 2mf – 9 – $55.00 – us UPA [305]

AMERICAN JUBILEE – (Ceased publ. Superseded by: Radical Abolitionist.) – New York. v1. mar 1854-apr 1855 – 1 – D3082 – us UMI [073]

AMERICAN JUDAISM – New York. N.Y. 1951-65 – 1 – us A.J.P.C. [270]

AMERICAN JUDAISM – (Ceased publ) – New York. v1-16. nov 1951-Spr 1967 – 1 – D1537 – us UMI [270]

AMERICAN JUNIPERS-SECTION SABINA / Engelmann, G – 7537 2. 1877 – 8 – ne IDC [580]

AMERICAN JURISPRUDENCE – 1st series compl. collection; 2nd series superseded vol only – 9 – Inquire – us Hein [340]

AMERICAN JURISPRUDENCE. / Andrews, Charles – New Haven, Conn., Hoggson & Robinson, 1898. 30 p. LL-426 – 1 – us L of C Photodup [340]

AMERICAN JURIST AND LAW MAGAZINE – Boston. v1-28. 1829-1843 – 1,5,6 – $200.00 – us Hein [073]

AMERICAN JURIST AND LAW MAGAZINE – (Ceased publ) – Boston. cum index v1-21 1829-1839; v1-28 jan 1829-jan 1843 – 1 – D4155 – us UMI [340]

THE AMERICAN JURIST AND LAW MAGAZINE – v1-28. 1829-43 (all publ) – 9 – LLMC 82-902 – us L.L.M.C. [073]

THE AMERICAN JURY / Coughlin, Michael E – 1980 – 9 – 1.00f – at Libertarian Micro [320]

American Kennel Club *see* STUD BOOK REGISTER

THE AMERICAN KITCHEN MAGAZINE – Boston, MA: Home Science Publ Co. v3 n6-v18 n6. sep 1895-mar 1903 – 1 – us Res Libr [640]

American Labor Conference on International Affairs *see* MODERN REVIEW

AMERICAN LABOR LEGISLATION REVIEW – (Missing: v1-3, v5-16) – v1-32 no 4. 1911-41 (all publ) – 193mf – 9 – $289.00 – LLMC 84-346 – us L.L.M.C. [073]

AMERICAN LABOR LEGISLATION REVIEW – v. 1-32. 1911-1942 – 1,5,6 – us Princeton Micro [331]

AMERICAN LABOR UNIONS – (Constitutions and Proceedings; Officers' Reports; Supplementary Documents) – 1836-1988 – 2 Pts 481r; 5882mf – 1,9 – $36,230.00 – us UMI [331]

AMERICAN LABORER : DEVOTED TO THE CAUSE OF PROTECTION TO HOME INDUSTRY, EMBRACING THE ARGUMENTS, REPORTS AND SPEECHES OF THE ABLEST CIVILIANS OF THE UNTIED STATES IN FAVOR OF THE POLICY OF PROTECTION TO AMERICAN LABOR, WITH THE STATISTICS OF PRODUCTION IN THE UNITED STATES – (Ceased publ) – New York. v1. apr 1842-mar 1843 – 1 – D4354 – us UMI [331]

AMERICAN LADIES' MAGAZINE – (Absorbed by: Lady's Book. Former titles: Ladies' Magazine (Jan 1828-dec 1829); Ladies' Magazine and Literary Gazette (jan 1803-dec 1833); Ladies' Magazine (jan 1834)) – Boston. v1-9. jan 1828-dec 1836 – 1 – D3925 – us UMI [640]

AMERICAN LANGUAGE FOREIGN TEACHER – Detroit. v1. oct 1970-apr 1971 – 1 – D6963 – us UMI [400]

AMERICAN LANGUAGE JOURNAL – v1-. 1982- – 1,5,6,9 – us UMI [400]

AMERICAN LAUNDRY DIGEST – Detroit. v1-62 1936- 1*; v39-62 jan-dec 1974-* 5,9 – 1,5,9 – D9894 – us UMI [640]

AMERICAN LAW / Hilliard, Francis – New York: Peloubet, 1881. 2v. LL-747 – 1 – us L of C Photodup [340]

AMERICAN LAW / Hilliard, Francis – New York: Ward & Peloubet, 1877-78. 2v. LL-1684 – 1 – us L of C Photodup [340]

AMERICAN LAW. / Andrews, James deWitt – 2d ed. Chicago, Callaghan,1908. 2 v. LL-1409 – 1 – us L of C Photodup [340]

AMERICAN LAW AND PROCEDURE – (v1-12 ed by James P. Hall. v13-14 by James B. Andrews) – Chicago: LaSalle Ext University. v1-14. 1910 (all publ) – 70mf – 9 – $106.00 – LLMC 84-381 – us L.L.M.C. [340]

American Law Association *see* CATALOGUE.

American Law Institute *see* CODE OF CRIMINAL PROCEDURE: PRELIMINARY DRAFT

AMERICAN LAW INSTITUTE MICROFICHE ARCHIVES *see* AMERICAN LAW INSTITUTE MICROFICHE PUBLICATIONS

AMERICAN LAW INSTITUTE MICROFICHE PUBLICATIONS – (Backfile thru update 1996 no 2. Title varies: Backfile thru 1993 no 2 as American Law Institute Microfiche Archives) – 9 – $20,250.00 set – 0-89941-412-5 – us Hein [340]

American Law Institute. Philadelphia *see*
- THE INSTITUTE
- A STUDY OF THE BUSINESS OF THE FEDERAL COURTS.

AMERICAN LAW INSTITUTE PROCEEDINGS – 1st-68th. 1923-91 – 9 – $1,493.00 set – us Hein [340]

American Law Institute-American Bar Association *see* ALI-ABA COURSE MATERIALS JOURNAL

American Law Institute-American Bar Association Committee on Continuing Professional Education *see* ALI-ABA CLE REVIEW

AMERICAN LAW JOURNAL – NS: v1-4. 1848-1852 – 1,5,6 – $40.00 – us Hein [073]

AMERICAN LAW JOURNAL *see* THE AMERICAN LAW REGISTER AND REVIEW

AMERICAN LAW JOURNAL – (Ceased publ. Former titles: Pennsylvania Law Journal (1842-jun 1848)) – Philadelphia. v1-11. 1842-jun 1852 – 1 – D4141 – us UMI [340]

THE AMERICAN LAW JOURNAL – Columbus, OH. v1-2. 1884-85 (all publ) – 10mf – 9 – $15.00 – LLMC 84-398 – us L.L.M.C. [073]

THE AMERICAN LAW JOURNAL – (Title varies: v1-7 titled " Pennsylvania Law Journal". v8-11 titled "American Law Journal, New Series") – v1-11. 1842-52 (all publ) – 9 – LLMC 82-9031 – us L.L.M.C. [073]

THE AMERICAN LAW JOURNAL AND MISCELLANEOUS REPORTER – v1-3. 1808-10 (all publ) – 9 – LLMC 84-3991 – us L.L.M.C. [073]

AMERICAN LAW JOURNAL, NEW SERIES *see* THE AMERICAN LAW JOURNAL

THE AMERICAN LAW LIST – (Missing: v1. v11 no 3. v13 no 2. v15) – v1-15. 1898-1910 (all publ) – 119mf – 9 – $178.00 – LLMC 84-400 – us L.L.M.C. [073]

AMERICAN LAW MAGAZINE – Philadelphia. v1-6. 1843-1846 – 1,5,6 – $80.00 – us Hein [073]

AMERICAN LAW MAGAZINE – (Ceased publ) – Philadelphia. v1-6. apr 1843-jan 1846 – 1 – D4149 – us UMI [340]

THE AMERICAN LAW MAGAZINE – (Merged into: The Central Law Journal LLMC 82-912) – Chicago, IL. v1-2 no 2. 1882-83 (all publ) – 6mf – 9 – $9.00 – LLMC 84-401 – us L.L.M.C. [073]

THE AMERICAN LAW MAGAZINE – Philadelphia. v1-6. 1843-46 – 9 – LLMC 82-905 – us L.L.M.C. [073]

THE AMERICAN LAW OF REAL PROPERTY / Hilliard, Francis – 3d ed. New York: Banks, Gould, 1855. 2v. LL-1699 – 1 – us L of C Photodup [340]

THE AMERICAN LAW OF REAL PROPERTY. 3D ED / Tiedeman, Christopher Gustavus – St. Louis, Thomas, 1906. 1017 p. LL-1026 – 1 – us L of C Photodup [340]

THE AMERICAN LAW PRIMER, FOR PUBLIC AND PRIVATE SCHOOLS, FAMILIES, AND THE UNPROFESSIONAL GENERALLY / Leahy, Daniel F – San Francisco, Domestic Publishing Co., 1889. 181 p. LL-208 – 1 – us L of C Photodup [340]

THE AMERICAN LAW RECORD – Cincinnati, OH. v1-15. 1872-8 (all publ) – 45mf – 9 – $202.00 – LLMC 82-906 – us L.L.M.C. [073]

THE AMERICAN LAW REGISTER AND REVIEW – (Missing: ns v50. Cont: The American Law Journal LLMC 82-903. Cont by: The University of Pennsylvania Law Review) – v1-9. ns: v1-51 + digest. 1852-1912 – 177mf – 9 – $796.00 – LLMC 82-970 – us L.L.M.C. [073]

AMERICAN LAW REVIEW – (Ceased publ. Cont: Financial Trend) – Dallas. v16. jan-may 1985 – 1 – D9313.01 – us UMI [340]

AMERICAN LAW REVIEW – New York. cum index v1-13 1866-1878; v1-40 oct 1866-dec 1906 – 1 – D5466 – us UMI [340]

THE AMERICAN LAW REVIEW – (Title merged into: The United States Law Review publ by US Review Corporation NY. Not offered by LLMC for copyright reasons) – v1-63 no 3. 1866-1929 (all publ) – 203mf – 9 – $913.00 – LLMC 82-907 – us L.L.M.C. [073]

THE AMERICAN LAW SCHOOL REVIEW : AN INTERCOLLEGIATE LAW JOURNAL – (Lacking: v7) – St Paul: West Publ Co. 1902-47 (all publ) – 84mf – 9 – $126.00 – LLMC 84-402 – us L.L.M.C. [073]

AMERICAN LAW TIMES REPORTS *see* THE REPORTER

THE AMERICAN LAW TIMES REPORTS – (v1-2 of OS entitled: The Law Times (U.S.) Courts Reports. Cont by: The Law and Enquity Reporter after v6) – Washington/New York: American Law Times Assoc/Cox/Hurd & Houghton. 1st series: v1-6. 1868-74. ns: v1-4. 1874-77 (all publ) – 69mf – 9 – $103.00 – LLMC 81-412 – us L.L.M.C. [340]

AMERICAN LAWYER – (Ceased publ) – New York. v1-16. jan 1893-jul 1908 – 1 – D5219 – us UMI [340]

THE AMERICAN LAWYER – New York. v1-16. 1896-1908 – 106mf – 9 – $159.00 – LLMC 82-908 – us L.L.M.C. [073]

THE AMERICAN LAWYER AND BUSINESSMAN'S FORMBOOK... / Beadle, Delos White – New York: Ensign, Bridgman & Fanning, 1856 – 4mf – 9 – $6.00 – LLMC 91-501 – us L.L.M.C. [073]

AMERICAN LEADING CASES : BEING SELECT DECISIONS OF THE AMERICAN COURTS IN SEVERAL DEPARTMENTS OF LAW WITH SPECIAL REFERENCE TO MERCANTILE LAW / Clarke, J I & Wandle, H B – 5th enl ed. Philadelphia: T & T W Johnson. v1-2. 1871 – LLMC 95-115 – us L.L.M.C. [340]

AMERICAN LEADING CASES: BEING SELECT DECISIONS OF AMERICAN COURTS, IN SEVERAL DEPARTMENTS OF LAW; WITH ESPECIAL REFERENCE TO MERCANTILE LAW / Hare, John Innes Clark – 4th ed. Philadelphia: Johnson, 1857. 2v. LL-882 – 1 – us L of C Photodup [340]

American Leather Chemists' Association *see*
- JOURNAL

AMERICAN LEGAL RECORDS *see* MAYOR'S COURT, NEW YORK CITY

AMERICAN LEGION – (Supersedes: American Legion Weekly. Former titles: American Legion Monthly (jul 1926-jun 1937)) – Washington. v1-143 jan 1926- 1; v92-143 jan 1972- 5; v100-143 jan 1976- 9 – 1,5,9 – D6556 – us UMI [355]

AMERICAN LEGION MAGAZINE – (1972- 5,6 1975- 9) – v1- 1926- – 1 – us UMI [355]

AMERICAN LEGION MONTHLY *see*
- AMERICAN LEGION
- AMERICAN LEGION WEEKLY

AMERICAN LEGION WEEKLY – (Ceased publ. Superseded by: American Legion Monthly) – Indianapolis. v1-8. jul 1919-jun 1926 – 1 – D8558 – us UMI [355]

AMERICAN LEGION WEEKLY *see* AMERICAN LEGION

AMERICAN LIBERAL – San Francisco, CA. 1966 – 1r – 1 – $50.00 – R02788 – us Library Micro [071]

THE AMERICAN LIBERAL (NEW YORK, N.Y.: 1939) – (Includes March-April 1939) – New York, N.Y.: American Liberal Press, 1939- – 1 – CSUX89-S97 – us Hoover Inst Photo [978]

AMERICAN LIBRARIES – (v. 2-. 1971- 9) – v. 1- Jan 1970- – 1,5,6 – us UMI [020]

AMERICAN LIBRARIES – (Cont: American Library Association) – Chicago. v1-28. jan 1970- – 1,5,9 – D5731 – us UMI [020]

AMERICAN LIBRARIES *see* ALA BULLETIN

American Library Association *see* ALA BULLETIN

AMERICAN LIBRARY ASSOCIATION *see* AMERICAN LIBRARIES

American Library Association *see*
- BULLETIN
- COMPUTER OUTPUT MICROFILM (COM) HARDWARE AND SOFTWARE: THE STATE OF THE ART
- MICROGRAPHICS EDUCATION FOR LIBRARIANS
- SOME CURRENT REPROGRAPHIC CONCERNS RELATED TO INTERLIBRARY LOAN
- A SURVEY OF TELEFACSIMILE USE IN LIBRARIES IN THE UNITED STATES

American Library Association. Health and Rehabilitative Library Services Division *see* HRLSD JOURNAL

AMERICAN LIBRARY ASSOCIATION – HEALTH AND REHABILITATIVE LIBRARY SERVICES DIVISION: JOURNAL *see* HEALTH AND REHABILITATIVE LIBRARY SERVICES

American Library Association. Library Administration Division *see* LAD NEWSLETTER

A(MERICAN) L(IBRARY) A(SSOCIATION) PORTRAIT INDEX : INDEX TO PORTRAITS CONTAINED IN PRINTED BOOKS AND PERIODICALS / ed by Lane, W C & Browne, N E – Washington, DC, 1906 – 29mf – 9 – O-120/1 – ne IDC [020]

American Library Association. Resources and Technical Services Division *see* NEWSLETTER

AMERICAN LIBRARY ASSOCIATION – RTSD NEWSLETTER *see* ALCTS NEWSLETTER

THE AMERICAN LIBRARY IN PARIS – Paris, 1924-1926 – 4mf – 9 – ILM-3839/1 – ne IDC [340]

AMERICAN LITERARY ANNUALS AND GIFT BOOKS, 1825-65 – (Titles from Ralph Thompson bibliography) – 1 – us Primary [880]

AMERICAN LITERARY GAZETTE AND NEW YORK WEEKLY MIRROR – New York. v1-6. 1844-47 – 1r – 1 – us Ross [071]

AMERICAN LITERARY GAZETTE AND PUBLISHERS' CIRCULAR – (Ceased publ. Absorbed by: Publishers Weekly. Former titles: American Publishers' Circular and Literary Gazette (sep 1855-oct 1863)) – Philadelphia. v1-18. sep 1855-jan 1872 – 1 – D3758 – us UMI [070]

AMERICAN LITERARY HISTORY – New York. v1-9. Spr 1989- – 1,5,9 – D17034 – us UMI [420]

AMERICAN LITERARY MAGAZINE – (Ceased publ) – Albany. v1-5. jul 1847-aug 1849 – 1 – D3759 – us UMI [420]

AMERICAN LITERARY MANUSCRIPTS FROM THE HUNTINGTON LIBRARY SAN MARINO, CALIFORNIA – (Pt 1: The Birth of American Literature, 1650-1850) – 1 – us Primary [800]

AMERICAN LITERATURE : A JOURNAL OF LITERARY HISTORY, CRITICISM AND BIBLIOGRAPHY – Durham. v1-69 mar 1929- 1; v40-69 mar 1968- 5; v42-69 mar 1970- 9 – 1,5,9 – D1022 – us UMI [420]

AMERICAN LITERATURE ABSTRACTS – (Ceased publ) – San Jose. v1-5 dec 1967-jun 1972 1; v4-5 dec 1970-jun 1972 5 – 1,5 – D3443 – us UMI [420]

AMERICAN LLOYD'S REGISTER OF AMERICAN AND FOREIGN SHIPPING – New York, 1868, 1874, 1880-83 – 6r – 1 – us Ross [380]

AMERICAN LOYALIST CLAIMS 1776-1831 / Great Britain. Exchequer and Audit Department – (Series 2: 1780-1835 (AO 13) $7,250) – Series 1 (AO 12) – 30r – 1 – us Ross [941]

American Lung Association *see* BULLETIN

AMERICAN LUNG ASSOCIATION BULLETIN – (Ceased publ. Cont: National Tuberculosis and Respiratory Disease Association Bulletin) – New York. v59-69 jun 1973-jun 1983 1,5; v62-69 jan 1976-jun 1983 9 – 1,5,9 – D1974.01 – us UMI [616]

AMERICAN LUTHERAN – (Superseded by Lutheran Forum) – v6-49. 1923-66 (complete) – 9r – 1 – ATLA S0520 – us A.T.L.A. [240]

AMERICAN LUTHERAN CHURCH : ALMANAC YEARBOOK / American Lutheran Church – 1931-87 (complete) – 11r – 1 – ATLA S0668 – us A.T.L.A. [073]

American Lutheran Church *see* AMERICAN LUTHERAN CHURCH

AMERICAN LUTHERAN CHURCH. EASTERN DISTRICT : REPORTS AND ACTIONS – (Lacking some pages) – v1-26. 1961-86 – 4r – 1 – ATLA S0395 – us A.T.L.A. [240]

AMERICAN LUTHERAN SURVEY : A REVIEW OF WORLD PROGRESS & PROBLEMS – (Lacking some pages) – v1-20 no 9. Oct 1914-Jun 1928 – 15r – 1 – ATLA S0092 – us A.T.L.A. [073]

AMERICAN MACHINIST – v49-94 1918-1950 – 1,5,6 – us Princeton Micro [620]

AMERICAN MACHINIST – (Cont: American Machinist and Automated Manufacturing) – New York. v132-141. aug-dec 1988- – 1,5,9 – D30.02 – us UMI [620]

AMERICAN MACHINIST – (Cont by: American Machinist and Automated Manufacturing. Former titles: American Machinist (nov 1877-jan 1960); American Machinist, Metalworking Manufacturing (feb 1960-feb 1968)) – New York. v1-129 1877-dec 1985 1; v109-129 jan 1965-dec 1985 5; 114-129 jan 1971-dec 1985 9 – 1,5,9 – D30 – us UMI [620]

AMERICAN MACHINIST *see*
- AMERICAN MACHINIST
- AMERICAN MACHINIST AND AUTOMATED MANUFACTURING

AMERICAN MACHINIST AND AUTOMATED MANUFACTURING – (Cont: American Machinist. Cont by: American Machinist) – New York. v130-132. jan 1986-jan-jul 1988 – 1,5,9 – D30.01 – us UMI [620]

AMERICAN MACHINIST AND AUTOMATED MANUFACTURING *see*
- AMERICAN MACHINIST

AMERICAN MACHINIST, METALWORKING MANUFACTURING *see* AMERICAN MACHINIST

AMERICAN MAGAZINE : CONTAINING A MISCELLANEOUS COLLECTION OF ORIGINAL AND OTHER VALUABLE ESSAYS IN PROSE AND VERSE, AND CALCULATED BOTH FOR INSTRUCTION AND AMUSEMENT – (Ceased publ) – New York. v1-12. dec 1787-nov 1788 – 1 – D3502 – us UMI [073]

AMERICAN MAGAZINE – (Former titles: Frank Leslie's Popular Monthly (jan 1876-feb 1904); Leslie's Monthly Magazine (mar 1904-aug 1905); American Illustrated Magazine (sep 1905-may 1906)) – Springfield. v1-62. jan 1876-oct 1906 – 1 – D5221 – us UMI [073]

AMERICAN MAGAZINE : A MONTHLY MISCELLANY DEVOTED TO LITERATURE, SCIENCE, HISTORY, BIOGRAPHY AND THE ARTS, INCLUDING ALSO STATE PAPER AND PUBLIC DOCUMENTS – (Ceased publ) – Albany. v1. jun 1815-may 1816 – 1 – D3540 – us UMI [073]

AMERICAN MAGAZINE : OR A MONTHLY VIEW OF THE POLITICAL STATE OF THE BRITISH COLONIES – (Ceased publ) – Philadelphia. v1-3. jan-mar 1741 – 1 – D3503 – us UMI [975]

AMERICAN MAGAZINE : OR GENERAL REPOSITORY – (Ceased publ) – Philadelphia. v1-9. jan-sep 1769 – 1 – D3504 – us UMI [073]

AMERICAN MAGAZINE AND HISTORICAL CHRONICLE – (Ceased publ) – Boston. v1-3. sep 1743-dec 1746 – 1 – D3501 – us UMI [975]

AMERICAN MAGAZINE AND MONTHLY CHRONICLE FOR THE BRITISH COLONIES – (Ceased publ) – Philadelphia. v1. oct 1757-oct 1758 – 1 – D3505 – us UMI [975]

AMERICAN MAGAZINE, AND REPOSITORY OF USEFUL LITERATURE : DEVOTED TO SCIENCE, LITERATURE, AND ARTS, AND EMBELLISHED WITH NUMEROUS ENGRAVINGS – (Ceased publ) – Albany. v1-2. jul 1841-apr 1842 – 1 – D3926 – us UMI [073]

AMERICAN MAGAZINE OF USEFUL AND ENTERTAINING KNOWLEDGE – (Ceased publ) – Boston. v1-3. sep 1834-sep 1837 – 1 – D3741 – us UMI [073]

AMERICAN MAGAZINE OF WONDERS, AND MARVELOUS CHRONICLE – (Ceased publ) – New York. v1-2. 1809 – 1 – D3541 – us UMI [073]

AMERICAN MANUAL OF THE MULBERRY TREES / Rafinesque-Schmaltz, Constantine S – Philadelphia. 1839. B-8097 1 – 9 – ne IDC [580]

AMERICAN MANUSCRIPT MAPS IN BRITISH REPOSITORIES – (Phase 1: Revolutionary Period, 1763-83, From Public Record Office, London, £140.00; 1. Phase 2: The Colonial Era. From the Public Record Office, London. £105.00; MAP; 1) – BRRAM – uk Microform Academic [970]

American Marketing Association *see* CONFERENCE PROCEEDINGS

AMERICAN MARRIAGES BEFORE 1699 – By William H. Clemens, 1926. Item D. Social customs & history of colonies before 1699 in addition to marriage names & dates. 244p. Listed alphabetically. SW16-0003 – 5 – us A.G.L.L. [920]

AMERICAN MASONIC REGISTER AND LADIES' AND GENTLEMEN'S MAGAZINE – (Ceased publ) – New York. v1-2. sep 1820-jun 1823 – 1 – D3542 – us UMI [073]

AMERICAN MASONIC REGISTER AND LITERARY COMPANION : BEING A PERIODICAL DEVOTED TO MASONRY, ARTS AND SCIENCE, BIOGRAPHY, SKETCHES OF CHARACTER, ETC – (Ceased publ) – Albany. v1-8. aug 1839-oct 1847 – 1 – D4620 – us UMI [073]

AMERICAN MATERIAL IN THE LIVERPOOL PAPERS / Liverpool Papers – 1727-1828. BRRAM – 1 – uk Microform Academic [025]

AMERICAN MATERIAL IN THE NATIONAL LIBRARY OF WALES / Wales. National Library – 17th-19th Centuries. BRRAM – 1 – uk Microform Academic [975]

AMERICAN MATERIAL. PLUS INDEX / United Society for the Propagation of the Gospel – 1 – uk Microform Academic [240]

AMERICAN MATHEMATICAL MONTHLY – Washington. v1-104 1894- 1; v82-104 jan 1975- 5,9 – 1,5,9 – D10928 – us UMI [510]

American Mathematical Society *see*
- BULLETIN
- BULLETIN, NEW SERIES
- NOTICES
- PROCEEDINGS
- TRANSACTIONS

AMERICAN MCALL RECORD – v1-51 no 3. Oct 1883-May 1933 (complete) – 3r – 1 – ATLA S0218 – us A.T.L.A. [073]

AMERICAN MECHANICS' MAGAZINE : CONTAINING USEFUL ORIGINAL MATTER, ON SUBJECTS CONNECTED WITH MANUFACTURES, THE ARTS AND SCIENCES, AS WELL AS SELECTIONS FROM THE MOST APPROVED DOMESTIC AND FOREIGN JOURNALS – (Ceased publ) – New York. v1-2. feb 1825-feb 1826 – 1 – D3708 – us UMI [621]

AMERICAN MEDICAL AND PHILOSOPHICAL REGISTER : OR, ANNALS OF MEDICINE, NATURAL HISTORY, AGRICULTURE, AND THE ARTS – (Ceased publ) – New York. v1-4. jul 1810-apr 1814 – 1 – D4414 – us UMI [610]

American Medical Association *see*
- AMA ARCHIVES OF NEUROLOGY AND PSYCHIATRY
- JOURNAL (JAMA)

American medical association *see* JAMA, THE JOURNAL OF THE AMERICAN MEDICAL ASSOCIATION

American Medical Association. Division of Library and Archival Services *see* INDEX TO MEDICAL SOCIOECONOMIC LITERATURE, 1962-1970

AMERICAN MEDICAL BOTANY / Bigelow, J – 3V. M-246. 1817-1820 – 9 – ne IDC [610]

AMERICAN MEDICAL PERIODICALS, 1797-1900 – (19th-century medical periodicals from the holdings of the National Library of Medicine and other major institutions) – 1 – us Primary [073]

AMERICAN MEDICAL RECORDER *see* AMERICAN JOURNAL OF THE MEDICAL SCIENCES

American Medical Technologists *see* JOURNAL OF THE AMERICAN MEDICAL TECHNOLOGISTS

American Mental Health Counselors Association (AMHCA) *see* AMHCA JOURNAL

AMERICAN MERCURY – (1965-80. 5,6. 1970-80. 9) – 1-116. 1924-80 – 1 – us UMI [320]

AMERICAN MERCURY – Hartford. Conn. 1784-1820 – 1,3 – us Readex [071]

AMERICAN METAL MARKET – New York, 1946- – 1 – $300.00y – us Fairchild Micro [660]

American Meteorological Society *see* BULLETIN

AMERICAN METHODIST LADIES' ASSOCIATION-ITS CONNECTIONAL CHARACTER / Smart, James S – From: The Ladies Repository, XV, 26 Sept 1866. pp570-571 – 9 – us A.T.L.A. [240]

American Microscopical society *see* TRANSACTIONS

AMERICAN MIDLAND NATURALIST – (1970- . 5,6,9) – v. 1- 1909- – 1 – us UMI [500]

AMERICAN MIDLAND NATURALIST – v. 1-34. 1909-1945 – 1 – us Princeton Micro [574]

AMERICAN MILITARY NEWSPAPERS ON MICROFILM, PT 1 – 162 newspapers on 742r – 1 – $55,000.00 $90.00r – State Historical Society of Wisconsin – us Ross [071]

AMERICAN MILITARY OPERATIONS DURING WORLD WAR 2 PAMPHLET COLLECTION – 194?-1945 – 1 – CSUXANM9163-B – us Hoover Inst Photo [350]

AMERICAN MINERALOGIST – v1-50. 1916-1965 – 1,5,6 – us Princeton Micro [540]

AMERICAN MINERVA – New York. N.Y. 1793-96. And THE MINERVA. 1796-97. Sold as one unit – 1,3 – us Readex [071]

AMERICAN MINING CODE / Copp, Henry Norris – (9th ed. Washington, DC, 1896. 214p. LL-65) – Washington, DC, 1882. 226p. LL-66 – 1 – us L of C Photodup [340]

THE AMERICAN MISSION IN EGYPT, 1854 TO 1896 / Watson, Andrew – (Includes index) – Pittsburgh: United Presbyterian Board of Publ, 1898, c1897 – 2mf – 9 – 0-8370-7351-0 – 1986-1351 – us A.T.L.A. [240]

AMERICAN MISSIONARY – 1860-1927. (American Indian Periodicals in the Princeton University Library). 327 fiches – 9 – $1,225.00 – us UPA [240]

THE AMERICAN MISSIONARY / American Missionary Association – 1846-1934 – 1 – $350.00 – us Amistad [240]

THE AMERICAN MISSIONARY – (Lacking some issues) – v1-63 no 1-25. 1857-Mar 1933 – 19r – 1 – ATLA S0227 – us A.T.L.A. [073]

American Missionary Association *see*
- THE AMERICAN MISSIONARY
- ANNUAL REPORT
- ARCHIVES

AMERICAN MIZRACHI WOMEN – New York, NY. 1974-86/87. Continued by: The Amit Woman – 1 – us A.J.P.C. [071]

AMERICAN MODEL PRINTER : CRAFTSMAN *see* PRINTER'S CIRCULAR AND STATIONERS' AND PUBLISHERS' GAZETTE, 1866-1888 : AMERICAN MODEL PRINTER, 1879-1882 : CRAFTSMAN, 1884-1888

AMERICAN MODELER *see* AMERICAN AIRCRAFT MODELER

THE AMERICAN MUNICIPAL LAW REVIEW *see* LEGAL NOTES ON LOCAL GOVERNMENT

American Museum in Britain *see* MANUSCRIPTS

American Museum of Natural History *see* BULLETIN

AMERICAN MUSIC – v1-. 1983- – 1,5,6,9 – us UMI [073]

AMERICAN MUSIC: A VOLUME OF TUNES... FROM THE LIBRARY OF ROBERT CARTER OF VIRGINIA / Carter, J – Nomony Hall. c1750-70 – 9 – us Sibley [780]

AMERICAN MUSIC TEACHER – (1971- . 5,6. 1977- . 9) – v. 1- 1951- – 1 – us UMI [780]

THE AMERICAN MUSICAL JOURNAL – v. 1, no. 1-12. Oct 1834-Nov 1835 – 9 – us Sibley [780]

THE AMERICAN MUSICAL TIMES – v1-5. 1891-Aug 1895 – 1 – 375.00 – us Opus [073]

THE AMERICAN MUSICIAN – v13-16. 1889-90 – 2r – 1 – us Ross [780]

American National Standards Institute *see* ANSI. REPORTER

American National Women's Trade Union League *see* AMERICA: LIFE AND LABOR

AMERICAN NATURAL HISTORY – From Bibliography of American Natural History 1769-1865 by Max Meisel – 1 – us Primary [574]

AMERICAN NATURALIST – v. 1-97. 1868-1963 – 5,6 – us Princeton Micro [574]

AMERICAN NATURALIST – (v104- . 5,6. v111- , 1977- . 9) – v. 1- 1867- – 1 – us UMI [574]

AMERICAN NEGLIGENCE CASES / ed by Hamilton, T F – (A complete coll of all reported negligence cases decided in the Federal Courts of the US, the Courts of Last Resort of All the States and Territories from the Earliest Times...Topically arranged with notes of English cases and annotations. Publ as a retrospective companion set to: American Negligence Reports, Current Series) – New York: Remick & Schilling. v1-17. 1789-1897 (all publ) – 179mf – 9 – $268.00 – LLMC 84-697 – us L.L.M.C. [340]

AMERICAN NEGLIGENCE CASES *see*
- AMERICAN NEGLIGENCE REPORTS, CURRENT SERIES
- A COMMONSENSE DIGEST OF AMERICAN NEGLIGENCE CASES
- A KEY WORD INDEX TO THE NOTES IN AMERICAN NEGLIGENCE CASES

AMERICAN NEGLIGENCE CASES AND REPORTS *see*
- DIGEST TO AMERICAN NEGLIGENCE CASES AND REPORTS

AMERICAN NEGLIGENCE DIGEST : FROM 1897-1907 / Eagle, Walter – (A digest of all the Negligence Cases contained in the Series of American Negligence Reports, v1-20 inclusive) – New York: Remick & Schilling. 1v (all publ) – 18mf – 9 – $27.00 – LLMC 84-699B – us L.L.M.C. [340]

AMERICAN NEGLIGENCE DIGEST : FROM THE EARLIEST TIMES TO 1902 / Hook, Alfred J – Remick & Schilling. 1v. 1902 – 7mf – 9 – $10.50 – LLMC 84-699A – us L.L.M.C. [340]

AMERICAN NEGLIGENCE REPORTS *see*
- DIGEST TO AMERICAN NEGLIGENCE REPORTS
- NEGLIGENCE AND COMPENSATION CASES, ANNOTATED

AMERICAN NEGLIGENCE REPORTS, CURRENT SERIES / ed by Gardner, John M – (The "Current Series" references the fact that "American Negligence Cases" was being publ simultaneously to provide retrospective coverage in this subject area. Title cont by: Negligence Compensation Cases, Annotated. Individual titles under this series also listed separately) – New York: Remick & Schilling. v1-21. 1897-1910 (all publ) – 190mf – 9 – $285.00 – LLMC 84-698 – us L.L.M.C. [340]

AMERICAN NEGLIGENCE REPORTS, CURRENT SERIES *see* AMERICAN NEGLIGENCE CASES

THE AMERICAN NEGRO : WHAT HE WAS, WHAT HE IS, AND WHAT HE MAY BECOME; A CRITICAL AND PRACTICAL DISCUSSION / Thomas, William Hannibal – 1901 – 1r – 1 – us Ross [975]

American Negro Academy. Washington, D.C *see* OCCASIONAL PAPERS

AMERICAN NEGRO HISTORICAL SOCIETY COLLECTION, 1790-1905 – (With Guide) – ca 15r – 1 – ca $1,275.00 – S3362 – Co-publ with the Historical Society of Pennsylvania. Available Spring, 1997 – us Scholarly Res [976]

American Negro Labor Congress *see* THE LIBERATOR

AMERICAN NEPTUNE – (1971- . 5,6. 1977- . 9) – v. 1- 1941- – 1 – us UMI [970]

AMERICAN NEWS REPORT – (Scattered issues. Ceased publication) – Djakarta, 1961-1965 – 218mf – 9 – SE-1311/1 – ne IDC [950]

AMERICAN NEWSPAPERS AND PERIODICALS PUBLISHED IN THE U.K. AND EUROPE: 18TH-20TH CENTURIES – 26 titles. Printed index – 1 – £1,500.00 – uk World [071]

AMERICAN NINETEENTH CENTURY ART : SUBJECT COLLECTIONS – (Individual titles not listed separately) – 42 catalogues on 60mf – 9 – £440.00 – uk Chadwyck [700]

AMERICAN NONCONFORMIST – Winfield. Kan. 1886-1900 – 1 – us UMI [071]

AMERICAN NOTES AND QUERIES – Philadelphia: The Westminster Publishing Co, v1 nos 1-4 1857; ns v1-9 1888-92; ns v1-8 1941-50; ns v1-24 1962-86 – 7r – 1 – $550.00 – us OmniSys [420]

American Numismatic Society. New York *see*
- AUCTION CATALOGUE
- DICTIONARY CATALOGUE

American Numismatic Society. New York. Library *see* DICTIONARY AND AUCTION CATALOGS OF THE LIBRARY

THE AMERICAN NURSE – (1983-. 1,5,6,9) – v4-. 1972- – 1 – us UMI [073]

AMERICAN NURSERYMAN – (1970- . 5,6. 1975- . 9) – 1904- – 1 – us UMI [631]

THE AMERICAN OBSERVER (WASHINGTON, D.C.) – (100 scattered issues between Sept. 9, 1931 and Apr. 28, 1947) – Washington, D.C.: Civic Education Service, 1931- – 1 – CSUX86-S17 – us Hoover Inst Photo [978]

THE AMERICAN OCCUPATION IN GERMANY, 1918-1923 – (With printed guide) – 2r – 1 – $170.00 – S1679 – us Scholarly Res [943]

AMERICAN OF INTRAVENOUS THERAPY *see* AMERICAN JOURNAL OF I.V. THERAPY
American Oil Chemists' Society *see* JOURNAL OF THE AMERICAN OIL CHEMISTS' SOCIETY
American Oil Chemists' society *see* JOURNAL
THE AMERICAN ORATOR / Munn, Lewis C – Boston: Tappan & Whitmore, 1853 – 5mf – 9 – $7.50 – LLMC 91-505 – us L.L.M.C. [340]
THE AMERICAN ORGANIST – (1983-. 5,6,9) – v. 1-. 1967- – 1 – us UMI [780]
American Oriental Society *see*
- JOURNAL
- JOURNAL OF THE AMERICAN ORIENTAL SOCIETY

American Ornithologists' Union. Committee on Classification and Nomenclature *see* THE CODE OF NOMENCLATURE AND CHECK-LIST OF NORTH AMERICAN BIRDS.
AMERICAN ORNITHOLOGY / Wilson, A – 9v. 1801-24 – 8 – Z 1963 2 – ne IDC [590]
AMERICAN PAINTINGS – (Almost 7,500 pictures, drawings and sculpture including Latin American works) – 124mf – 9 – $780.00 – 0-907006-67-1 – uk Mindata [750]
AMERICAN PAPER CONVERTER – 1945-53.Continued by: Paper, Film and Foil Converter – 1 – us UMI [600]
AMERICAN PAPER CONVERTER *see* PAPER, FILM AND FOIL CONVERTER
AMERICAN PAPER INDUSTRY *see* PAPER INDUSTRY
AMERICAN PAPERS / Carr, Ralph – 1741-78. BRRAM – 1 – uk Microform Academic [941]
AMERICAN PAPERS OF W.S. LINDSAY – 1861-66 – 1 – uk Microform Academic [920]
AMERICAN PATRIOT – Apr 1912-Aug 1916. Related Guide Book may be purchased separately from publisher – 2 roll 35mm set – 1 – us Ohio Hist [360]
AMERICAN PATRIOT – Concord. N.H. 1808-1809. New Hampshire Patriot. 1809-1820. Sold as one unit – 1,3 – us Readex [071]
THE AMERICAN PATRIOT (SAPULPA, OKLA.) – (Includes v.37, no.16-17, 19-21; v.1, no. 1-3, 5, 8, 11, 17-20, 32 (April 17, 1952-Jan. 2, 1953)) – Sapulpa, Okla.: Oklahoma Citizens Committee – 1 – CSUX89-S96 – us Hoover Inst Photo [978]
AMERICAN PERFUMER AND ESSENTIAL OIL REVIEW – v16-81. 1921-66 – 1,5,6 – us Princeton Micro [660]
AMERICAN PERIODICAL INDEX, 1730-1860 / ed by Adkins, Nelson – 1960 – 3 – us Readex [073]
AMERICAN PERIODICALS SERIES (APS 1, 2, AND 3) – 1741-1900 – Series 1, Beginnings (1741-1800) 33r $1980.00; Series 2, Growth and Change (1800-1850) 1966r $102,750.00; Series 3, Crisis and Reconstruction (1850-1900) 771r $45,885.00 – 1 – us UMI [073]
American Pharmaceutical Association *see*
- BULLETIN
- JOURNAL OF THE AMERICAN PHARMACEUTICAL ASSOCIATION

AMERICAN PHARMACY – v. 18. 1978 – 1,5,6,9 – us UMI [615]
AMERICAN PHARMACY *see* JOURNAL OF THE AMERICAN PHARMACEUTICAL ASSOCIATION
American Philological Association *see* TRANSACTIONS AND PROCEEDINGS
American Philosophical Association *see* PROCEEDINGS AND ADDRESSES
American Philosophical Society *see*
- PROCEEDINGS
- TRANSACTIONS

THE AMERICAN PHILOSOPHY OF LAW. / Le Buffe, Francis Peter – 4th ed. New York, Crusader Press, 1947. 418 p. LL-304 – 1 – us L of C Photodup [340]
AMERICAN PHOTO-ENGRAVER *see* PLATE MAKERS' CRITERION, 1907-1909 : AMERICAN PHOTO-ENGRAVER, 1908-1955
AMERICAN PHOTOGRAPHER – (1980- 5,6,9) – 1978- – 1 – us UMI [760]
American Physical Education Association *see* PROCEEDINGS
AMERICAN PHYSICAL EDUCATION REVIEW – 1-34. 1896-1929 – 368mf – 9 – $1,104.00 – us Microform Publ [790]
The American Physical Society *see* BULLETIN
American Physical Society *see*
- BULLETIN
- REVIEWS OF MODERN PHYSICS

AMERICAN PHYSICS TEACHER *see* AMERICAN JOURNAL OF PHYSICS
AMERICAN PIONEER – (Publ by American forces in Mexico during the Mexican War) – Monterey, Mexico. mar 22, 1847 – 1 – us Western Res [071]
THE AMERICAN PLAN OF GOVERNMENT : THE CONSTITUTION AS INTERPRETED BY ACCEPTED AUTHORITIES / Bacon, Charles W – 4th rev ed. New York, London: G P Putnam's Sons, 1921 – 6mf – 9 – $9.00 – LLMC 95-088 – us L.L.M.C. [323]
AMERICAN POEMS – 1793 – 9 – 20.00 – us Scholars' Facs [810]
AMERICAN POETRY : 1609-1870 – Based on the Harris Collection, Brown University – 1 – us Primary [810]
AMERICAN POETRY REVIEW – Cambridge, MA. 1972-1979 – 2r – 1 – $100.00 – R04378 – us Library Micro [420]
AMERICAN POETRY REVIEW – (v. 8-. 1979-. 5,6,9) – v.1- 1972- – 1 – us UMI [420]
AMERICAN POLITICAL SCIENCE – Washington. 1968-70. 3v. BH-1808-1 – 9 – ne IDC [970]
American Political Science Association *see* PROCEEDINGS
AMERICAN POLITICAL SCIENCE REVIEW – v. 1-34. 1906-1940 – 1 – us Princeton Micro [320]
AMERICAN POLITICAL SCIENCE REVIEW – (v. 60-. 1966- 5,6. v. 64-. 1970- 9) – v. 1-1906- – 1 – us UMI [320]
AMERICAN POLITICAL SCIENCE REVIEW – v. 62-64. Menasha, Wisconsin. 1968-70. BH-1826 1 – 9 – ne IDC [320]
AMERICAN POLITICS QUARTERLY – (1983-. 1,5,6,9) – v1-. 1973- – 1 – us UMI [073]
AMERICAN POPULAR CULTURE, 1897-1949 – 48r – 1 – $2495.00 – us UMI [975]
AMERICAN POPULAR SONGS / New York Public Library. Lincoln Center Music Collection – 1890-1896 – 5r – 1 – us Ross [780]
THE AMERICAN PORTION OF THE HISTORICAL LIBRARY OF VICTOR MORIN / Morin, Victor – New York: American Art Association, Anderson Galleries, 1931. SEM105P758 – 1mf – 9 – Can$2.25 – cn Bibl Nat [020]
THE AMERICAN POST – Paterson. N.J. 1965-67 – 1 – us A.J.P.C. [071]
AMERICAN PRACTICE REPORTS : OFFICIAL LEADING CASES IN ALL STATE AND FEDERAL COURTS / ed by Ray, Charles A – Washington: Washington Law Book Co. v1-2. 1897-98 (all publ) – 18mf – 9 – $27.00 – LLMC 84-700 – us L.L.M.C. [340]
AMERICAN PRACTITIONER AND DIGEST OF TREATMENT – v1-13. 1950-62.Continues: American Practitioner (v1-4. 1946-49) – 1,5,6 – us Princeton Micro [610]
American Presbyterian Mission *see* HAINAN NEWSLETTER
AMERICAN PRESBYTERIANA 1 – 1 – $50.00 – us Presbyterian [240]
AMERICAN PRESBYTERIANA 2 – China Mission Resources. 1900-48 – 1 – $150.00 – us Presbyterian [240]
AMERICAN PRESBYTERIANA 3 – Evangelism Resources – 1 – $50.00 – us Presbyterian [240]
AMERICAN PRESBYTERIANISM : ITS ORIGIN AND EARLY HISTORY : TOGETHER WITH AN APPENDIX OF LETTERS AND DOCUMENTS, MANY OF WHICH HAVE RECENTLY BEEN DISCOVERED / Briggs, Charles Augustus – New York: Charles Scribner, 1885 – 2mf – us A.T.L.A. [240]
AMERICAN PRESS *see* AMERICAN SETTLER
AMERICAN PRESSMAN, 1890-1955 : SERVICE BUREAU NEWS BULLETIN OF THE INTERNATIONAL PRINTING PRESSMEN AND ASSISTANTS' UNION OF NORTH AMERICA, 1937- 1952 / International Printing Pressman and Assistants' Union of North America – (Coll title: Labour Union Periodicals, Pt 2) – 26r – 1 – $3,510.00 – us UPA [070]
AMERICAN PRIMERS – $6,020.00 – us UPA [370]
AMERICAN PRINTER AND LITHOGRAPHER – v182- . 1979- .Continues: Inland Printer American Lithographer – 1,5,6,9 – us UMI [073]
AMERICAN PRINTS, 1870-1950 / Baltimore Museum of Art; ed by Johnson, Robert Flynn – (34p accompanying text) – 1976 – 1 color mf – 15 – $18.00f – 0-226-68824-0 – us Chicago [760]
AMERICAN PRISONERS OF WAR, RECORDS RELATING TO – 1812-1815. BRRAM – 1 – uk Microform Academic [975]

AMERICAN PROBATE REPORTS – (Cont by: Probate Reports Annotated) – New York: Baker & Voorhis. v1-8. 1875-95 (all publ) – 58mf – 9 – $87.00 – LLMC 82-403 – us L.L.M.C. [340]
AMERICAN PROBATE REPORTS *see* PROBATE REPORTS ANNOTATED
AMERICAN PROFESSIONAL PHARMACIST – v.1-35. Apr 1935-Aug 1969. Continued as: Pharmacy Times – 1 – us UMI [073]
AMERICAN PROPAGANDA DURING WORLD WAR 1 PAMPHLET COLLECTION – 1916-1929 – 2r – 1 – CSUXANL5383-B – us Hoover Inst Photo [303]
AMERICAN PROPAGANDA DURING WORLD WAR 2 PAMPHLET COLLECTION – 1934-1945 – 1 – CSUXANN2833-B – us Hoover Inst Photo [303]
THE AMERICAN PROTESTANT MAGAZINE – v1-5. Jun 1845-49 (complete) – 1r – 1 – ATLA T0010 – us A.T.L.A. [073]
American Psychological Association *see* APA MONITOR
AMERICAN PSYCHOLOGIST – (v. 20-. 1965-5,6. v. 25-. 1970- 9) – v. 1- 1946- – 1 – us UMI [150]
AMERICAN PSYCHOLOGIST – v1-38. 1946-83 – 1,5,6 – us Princeton Micro [150]
AMERICAN PUBLIC OPINION – n.p. 193? Fiche W 719. (Blodgett Collection of Spanish Civil War Pamphlets) – 9 – us H.U. College Libr [946]
AMERICAN PUBLIC OPINION DATA – 1981-92. Responses to questions from more than 400 polling sources. Includes press releases, reports, newspaper stories, computer printouts etc – 9 – $100.00y (1981-86); $149.00 (1987-89); $174.50 (1991-92) – us ORS Publ [300]
AMERICAN PUBLIC OPINION INDEX – 1981-92. A listing of questions asked from more than 400 polling sources. Cross-listings – 9 – $125.00y (1981-86); $149.50 (1987-1989); $174.50 (1991-92) – us ORS Publ [300]
THE AMERICAN PUBLIC SCHOOL: A GENETIC STUDY OF PRINCIPLES, PRACTICES AND AND PRESENT PROBLEMS / Finney, Ross Lee – New York: Macmillan, 1921. xvi,355p. illus. diagrs. (The Modern Teacher's Series) – 1 – us U.W. Library [370]
AMERICAN PUBLISHERS' CIRCULAR AND LITERARY GAZETTE *see* AMERICAN LITERARY GAZETTE AND PUBLISHERS' CIRCULAR
THE AMERICAN PULPIT : SKETCHES, BIOGRAPHICAL AND DESCRIPTIVE, OF LIVING AMERICAN PREACHERS, AND OF THE RELIGIOUS MOVEMENTS AND DISTINCTIVE IDEAS WHICH THEY REPRESENT / Fowler, Henry T – New York: J.M. Fairchild, 1856 – 2mf – us A.T.L.A. [240]
THE AMERICAN PULPIT: SKETCHES, BIOGRAPHICAL / Fowler, Henry T – 1856 – 1 – $50.00 – us Presbyterian [920]
AMERICAN QUARTERLY – (v. 20-. 1968- 5,6. v. 27-. 1975- 9) – v. 1- 1949- – 1 – us UMI [420]
AMERICAN QUARTERLY JOURNAL OF PROPHECY – v. 1-3. 1858-1860 – 1 – us UMI [240]
AMERICAN QUARTERLY OF ROENTGENOLOGY *see* AMERICAN JOURNAL OF ROENTGENOLOGY, RADIUM THERAPY, AND NUCLEAR MEDICINE
THE AMERICAN RACE: A LINGUISTIC CLASSIFICATION AND ETHNOGRAPHIC DESCRIPTION OF THE NATIVE TRIBES OF NORTH AND SOUTH AMERICA / Brinton, Daniel Garrison – New York: N. Hodges, 1891. 00280. (Pre-1900 Canadiana) – 9 – cn C.I.H.M. [305]
AMERICAN RAILROAD AND CORPORATION REPORTS (OR REPORTER) / ed by Lewis, John – Chicago: Myers & Co. v-12. 1888-96 (all publ) – 108mf – 9 – $162.00 – LLMC 84-701 – us L.L.M.C. [380]
AMERICAN RAILROAD JOURNAL – v. 1-74. 1832-1900 – 1 – 980.00 – us L of C Photodup [380]
AMERICAN RAILWAY REPORTS : A COLLECTION OF ALL REPORTED DECISIONS RELATED TO RAILWAYS / Truman, J Henry – (Although issued between 1872-81, title retrospectively covers all R.R. cases prior to 1881) – New York: Cockcroft. v1-21. 1872-81 (all publ) – 136mf – 9 – $204.00 – LLMC 84-702 – us L.L.M.C. [380]
AMERICAN RECREATION JOURNAL *see* PARKS AND RECREATION

AMERICAN RECREATIONAL JOURNAL *see* PARKS AND RECREATION
AMERICAN REHABILITATION – (1979- 5,6,9) – 1975- – 1 – us UMI [610]
AMERICAN REPORTS – New York/San Francisco: Bancroft-Whitney. v1-60. 1870-87 (all publ) – 679mf – 9 – $1,018.00 – LLMC 78-036 – us L.L.M.C. [340]
AMERICAN REPUBLIC – Frankfort. Ky. 1810-1812 – 1 – us UMI [071]
THE AMERICAN REPUBLIC AND ITS GOVERNMENT : AN ANALYSIS OF THE GOVERNMENT OF THE UNITED STATES WITH A CONSIDERATION OF ITS FUNDAMENTAL PRINCIPLES AND OF ITS RELATIONS TO THE STATES AND TERRITORIES / Woodburn, James A – 2nd rev. ed. New York/London: G P Putnam's Sons, 1916 – 5mf – 9 – $7.50 – LLMC 95-087 – us L.L.M.C. [323]
THE AMERICAN REPUBLIC, ITS CONSTITUTION, TENDENCIES AND DESTINY / Brownson, Orestes A – New York: P O'Shea, 1865 – 5mf – 9 – $7.50 – LLMC 95-094 – us L.L.M.C. [323]
AMERICAN REPUBLICAN, AND BALTIMORE DAILY CLIPPER – Baltimore, Maryland. Nov 11-Dec 31 1944; 1945-1946 – 3r – 1 – us L of C Photodup [071]
AMERICAN RESTAURANT – 1919-Dec 1928 – 1 – us UMI [640]
AMERICAN RESTAURANT HOSPITALITY – (See also: American Restaurant Magazine; Hospitality: Restaurant; Restaurant Hospitality) – 1962-67 – 1 – us UMI [640]
AMERICAN RESTAURANT MAGAZINE – (See also: American Restaurant Hospitality; Hospitality: Restaurant; Restaurant Hospitality) – 1929-62 – 1 – us UMI [640]
AMERICAN REVIEW – New York. v1-9.1933-37. See also: Bookman – 1,5,6 – us Princeton Micro [073]
AMERICAN REVIEW OF CANADIAN STUDIES – (Index 1971-88) – Washington. v1- 1971- – 9 – Can$28.00y – cn Micromedia [073]
AMERICAN REVIEW OF CANADIAN STUDIES – (v9- 1979- 5,6,9) – v3- 1973- . Continues ACSUS Newsletter (Association for Canadian Studies in the United States) – 1 – us UMI [971]
AMERICAN REVIEW OF CANADIAN STUDIES *see* ACSUS NEWSLETTER
AMERICAN REVIEW OF INTERNATIONAL ARBITRATION – v1-5. 1990-1994 – 9 – $1,130.00 set – us Hein [340]
AMERICAN REVIEW OF RESPIRATORY DISEASE – (1965- 5,6. 1970- 9) – 1-1917- – 1 – us UMI [616]
AMERICAN REVIEW OF RESPIRATORY DISEASE *see* AMERICAN JOURNAL OF RESPIRATORY AND CRITICAL CARE MEDICINE
AMERICAN REVIEW OF RESPIRATORY DISEASES – v1-72. 1917-55 – 1,5,6 – us Princeton Micro [616]
American Revision Committee *see* HISTORICAL ACCOUNT OF THE WORK OF THE AMERICAN COMMITTEE OF REVISION OF THE AUTHORIZED ENGLISH VERSION OF THE BIBLE
THE AMERICAN REVOLUTION – 9 – $4,620.00 – us UPA [975]
THE AMERICAN REVOLUTION IN CONTEXT / ed by Brown, Wallace & Palmer, Greg – Collection of original documents from British and American Archives – 1 – £275.00 – uk World [025]
AMERICAN RIFLEMAN – (v124- , 1976- . 5,6. v123- , 1975- . 9) – v. 71-. 1923- – 1 – us UMI [790]
AMERICAN RIGHTS IN SAMOA : MESSAGE FROM THE PRESIDENT OF THE U.S. TO THE CONGRESS / Cleveland, President – 3rd Congress 1st sess. House Exec Doc No 238 2 Apr 1888. Washington: GPO, n.d. – 4mf – 9 – $6.00 – LLMC 82-100C Title 7 – us L.L.M.C. [327]
THE AMERICAN RONDO / Holst, G – London: J & L Ballo, [184?] – 1 – us Sibley [780]
AMERICAN RULING CASES, ANNOTATED – Chicago: National Law Book Co. v1-5. 1920 (all publ) – 79mf – 9 – $119.00 – LLMC 95-043 – us L.L.M.C. [340]
AMERICAN RUSSIAN FALCON *see* AMERIKANSKIJ RUSSKIJ SOKOL SOJEDINENIJA
AMERICAN SALESMAN *see* AMERICAN BUSINESS

AMERICAN SAMOA : A DESCRIPTIVE AND HISTORICAL PROFILE / Tansill, William R – Washington: Lib of Congress, 1974 – 1mf – 9 – $1.50 – LLMC 82-100C Title 45 – us L.L.M.C. [980]

AMERICAN SAMOA : HEARING BEFORE THE SUBCOMMITTEE ON TERRITORIAL AND INSULAR AFFAIRS OF THE HOUSE COMMITTEE ON INTERIOR AND INSULAR AFFAIRS / American Samoa. US Congress – 93rd Congress 1st sess 18 Apr 1973. Washington: GPO, 1973 – 1mf – 9 – $1.50 – LLMC 82-100C Title 37 – us L.L.M.C. [327]

AMERICAN SAMOA : WORKING PAPER PREPARED BY THE SECRETARIAT FOR THE GENERAL ASSEMBLY'S SPECIAL COMMITTEE ON THE SITUATION WITH REGARD TO THE IMPLEMENTATION OF THE DECLARATION ON THE GRANTING OF INDEPENDENCE TO COLONIAL COUNTRIES AND PEOPLES, JUNE 7 1974 – 1mf – 9 – $1.50 – LLMC 82-100C Title 39 – us L.L.M.C. [324]

American Samoa *see*
- THE AGENCY OF A.B. STEINBERGER IN THE SAMOAN ISLANDS
- AMERICAN RIGHTS IN SAMOA
- AMERICAN SAMOA CONGRESSIONAL HEARINGS, 1928
- AMERICAN SAMOA LEGISLATURE, SESSION LAWS
- AMERICAN SAMOAN COMMISSION
- THE AMERICAN SAMOAN COMMISSION'S VISIT TO SAMOA, SEPTEMBER-OCTOBER 1931
- AMERICAN SAMOAN REPORTS, 1ST SERIES
- ANNUAL REPORTS OF THE GOVERNOR OF AMERICAN SAMOA TO THE SECRETARY OF THE INTERIOR
- CODE OF AMERICAN SAMOA, 1946 EDITION
- CODE OF AMERICAN SAMOAN, 1973 EDITION
- RECORDS OF THE GOVERNMENT
- REVISED CONSTITUTION OF AMERICAN SAMOA, 1967
- SAMOAN AFFAIRS
- U.S. INSULAR AREAS, APPLICATION OF RELEVANT PROVISIONS OF THE U.S. CONSTITUTION

AMERICAN SAMOA ADMINISTRATIVE CODE, 1982 : A CODIFICATION OF THE ADMINISTRATIVE RULES OF AMERICAN SAMOA / American Samoa. Government – (With suppl thru Mar 1988 and a vol of superseded materials Samoa) – Seattle: Book Publ Co, 1982- – 30mf – 9 – $45.00 – LLMC 82-100C Title 15 – us L.L.M.C. [324]

American Samoa. Bar Association *see* THE SAMOAN PACIFIC LAW JOURNAL

AMERICAN SAMOA CONGRESSIONAL HEARINGS, 1928 : JOINT HEARINGS BEFORE THE SENATE COMMITTEE ON TERRITORIAL AND INSULAR POSSESSIONS AND THE HOUSE COMMITTEE ON INSULAR AFFAIRS / American Samoa – 70th Congress 1st sess 17-21 Jan 1928. Washington: GPO, 1928 – 2mf – 9 – $3.00 – LLMC 82-100C Title 32 – us L.L.M.C. [327]

American Samoa. Constitutional Convention *see* PROPOSED REVISED CONSTITUTION OF AMERICAN SAMOA, 1986

American Samoa. Department of Interior *see* THE APPLICATION OF FEDERAL LAWS IN AMERICAN SAMOA, GUAM, THE NORTHERN MARIANA ISLANDS, AND THE VIRGIN ISLANDS

American Samoa. Executive Branch *see* CODIFICATION OF THE REGULATIONS AND ORDERS FOR THE GOVERNMENT OF AMERICAN SAMOA

American Samoa. Government *see*
- AMERICAN SAMOA ADMINISTRATIVE CODE, 1982
- AMERICAN SAMOAN CODE ANNOTATED
- THE ASG REPORT

American Samoa. High Court *see* AMERICAN SAMOA REPORTS, 2ND SERIES

AMERICAN SAMOA, HOPE AND DESPAIR, 1947-1952 / McGrew, W L – n.p., n.d – 1mf – 9 – $1.50 – LLMC 82-100C Title 46 – us L.L.M.C. [980]

American Samoa. Interim Research Section *see* REVISED CODE OF AMERICAN SAMOA, 1961 EDITION

AMERICAN SAMOA LEGISLATURE, SESSION LAWS : 8TH LEGISLATURE 1963; 10-11TH LEGISLATURE 1968-1969; 13-20TH LEGISLATURE 1973-1988 / American Samoa – Legislative Reference Bureau, 1963-88 – 81mf – 9 – $121.50 – LLMC 82-100C Title 6 – us L.L.M.C. [324]

American Samoa. Office of Samoan Information *see* AMERIKA SAMOA

AMERICAN SAMOA REPORTS, 2ND SERIES / American Samoa. High Court – High Court of American Samoa. v1-18. 1983-90 – 43mf – 9 – $64.00 – LLMC 82-100C Title 4 – us L.L.M.C. [340]

AMERICAN SAMOA TREATIES : WITH THE UNITED KINGDOM, AUGUST 28 AND SEPTEMBER 2 1879; WITH THE UNITED KINGDOM, THE UNITED STATES AND GERMANY, SEPTEMBER 29 1883; AND THE FINAL ACT OF THE CONFERENCE ON THE AFFAIRS OF SAMOA (TREATY OF BERLIN) JUNE 14 1889 – 4mf – 9 – $6.00 – LLMC 82-100C Title 49 – us L.L.M.C. [324]

American Samoa. US Congress *see*
- ACCEPTANCE OF CESSIONS OF CERTAIN SAMOAN ISLANDS
- AMERICA SAMOA
- AMERICAN SAMOA
- CURRENT PROBLEMS IN AMERICAN SAMOA
- JURISDICTION OF SUBMERGED LANDS IN AMERICAN SAMOA, GUAM, AND THE VIRGIN ISLANDS
- STAFF STUDY ON AMERICAN SAMOA

American Samoa. US Congress. Subcomm National Parks and Insular Affairs *see* LEGISLATIVE HISTORY OF THE OMNIBUS INSULAR AREAS ACT OF 1979-1980

American Samoa. US Senate *see* U.S. SENATE STUDY MISSION TO EASTERN (AMERICAN) SAMOA

AMERICAN SAMOAN CODE ANNOTATED : 1981 EDITION / American Samoa. Government – Seattle: Book Publ Co, 1982-87? – 32mf – 9 – $48.00 – LLMC 82-100C Title 13 – us L.L.M.C. [324]

AMERICAN SAMOAN COMMISSION : HEARINGS BEFORE THE COMMISSION APPOINTED BY THE PRESIDENT IN ACCORDANCE WITH PUBLIC RESOLUTION NO 89, 70TH CONGRESS....ACCEPTING THE CESSION OF CERTAIN ISLANDS OF THE SAMOAN GROUP, SEPTEMBER-OCTOBER, 1931, HONOLULU AND PAGO PAGO / American Samoa – Washington: GPO, 1931 – 6mf – 9 – $9.00 – LLMC 82-100C Title 8 – us L.L.M.C. [327]

THE AMERICAN SAMOAN COMMISSION'S VISIT TO SAMOA, SEPTEMBER-OCTOBER 1931 / Moore, Reuel S & Farrington, Joseph R – Washington: GPO, 1931 – 1mf – 9 – $1.50 – LLMC 82-100C Title 29 – us L.L.M.C. [327]

AMERICAN SAMOAN REPORTS, 1ST SERIES : 1900-1975 / American Samoa – (Includes index for v1-4 and 1982) – Equity Publ Co. v1-4. 1977-78 – 36mf – 9 – $54.00 – LLMC 82-100C Title 4 – us L.L.M.C. [324]

AMERICAN SATURDAY COURIER – July 16, 1831-1835 – 1 – us Res Libr [073]

AMERICAN SCHOLAR – (1967- 5,6. 1970- 9) – 1- 1932- – 1 – us UMI [073]

AMERICAN SCHOLAR – Washington. A quarterly for the independent thinker. v1-26. 1932-57. Continues: Phi Beta Kappa Key – 1,5,6 – us Princeton Micro [370]

AMERICAN SCHOOL AND UNIVERSITY – New York, NY. 1965-67 – 3r – 1 – $150.00 – R04901 – us Library Micro [071]

AMERICAN SCHOOL AND UNIVERSITY – v. 1-14. 1928-1942 – 1,5,6 – us Princeton Micro [370]

AMERICAN SCHOOL AND UNIVERSITY – (v39- . 5,6. v48- . 9) – 1- 1928- – 1 – us UMI [370]

AMERICAN SCHOOL BOARD JOURNAL – (v. 154-. 1967- 5,6. v. 162-. 1975- 9) – 1-1891- – 1 – us UMI [370]

American School. Chicago *see* LAW OF REAL PROPERTY, PART 4, INSTRUCTION PAPER

American School of Classical Studies at Athens *see*
- CATALOGUE OF THE GENNADIUS LIBRARY, AMERICAN SCHOOL OF CLASSICAL STUDIES AT ATHENS

AMERICAN SCIENTIST – v1- 1913- 1; v53-5,6; v58- 9 – us UMI [500]

AMERICAN SCIENTIST – v31-43. 1943-55 – 1,5,6 – us Princeton Micro [500]

AMERICAN SECONDARY EDUCATION – v1-1970- 1; v9- 1978- 5,6,9 – us UMI [370]

AMERICAN SENTINEL – Westminster, Maryland. 1856-1928 – 1 – us MD Archives [071]

AMERICAN SENTINEL (ARKHANGELSK, RUSSIA) – (Includes c.1: 1919: Jan.17) – Arkhangellsk: Gub. tip. – 1 reel – 1 – CSUXANR1736-S – us Hoover Inst Photo [947]

AMERICAN SETTLER – London, 10 Jul 1880-26 Nov 1892 – 12r – 1 – uk British Libr Newspaper [072]

AMERICAN SETTLER – London, Jan 1872-19 Jun 1875 – 2r – 1 – uk British Libr Newspaper [072]

THE AMERICAN SHEPHERD / Morrell, L A – 1851 – 7 – uk Microform Academic [970]

American Ship Building Company. Cleveland, Ohio *see* NAVAL ARCHITECTURAL DRAWINGS

THE AMERICAN SLAVE CODE IN THEORY AND PRACTICE : ITS DISTINCTIVE FEATURES SHOWN BY ITS STATUTES, JUDICIAL DECISIONS, AND ILLUSTRATIVE FACTS / Goodell, William – 2nd ed. New York: American & Foreign Anti-Slavery Society, 1853 – 5mf – 9 – $7.50 – LLMC 92-101 – us L.L.M.C. [340]

AMERICAN SLAVERY DISTINGUISHED FROM SLAVERY OF ENGLISH THEORISTS, AND JUSTIFIED BY THE LAW OF NATURE / Seabury, Samuel – 1861 – 1 – us A.T.L.A. [240]

AMERICAN SLAVERY DISTINGUISHED FROM THE SLAVERY OF ENGLISH THEORISTS : AND JUSTIFIED BY THE LAW OF NATURE / Seabury, Samuel – New York, 1861 – 1r – 1 – us Ross [320]

AMERICAN SOCIAL AND RELIGIOUS CONDITIONS / Stelzele, Charles – New York: F.H. Revell, c1912 – 1mf – us A.T.L.A. [240]

AMERICAN SOCIALIST / Socialist Party. U.S.A – 1-4 (all publ). 1914-1917 – 1 reel – 1 – $110.00 – us UPA [335]

American Society for Artificial Internal Organs *see*
- ASAIO TRANSACTIONS
- ASIO JOURNAL
- TRANSACTIONS..

American Society For Engineering Education *see* PROCEEDINGS

American Society for Experimental Biology *see* FEDERATION PROCEEDINGS

American Society for Information Science *see*
- BULLETIN
- JOURNAL OF THE AMERICAN SOCIETY FOR INFORMATION SCIENCE

AMERICAN SOCIETY FOR INFORMATION SCIENCE: JOURNAL – v1-33. 1950-82 – 1,5,6 – us Princeton Micro [000]

American Society for Metals *see* TRANSACTIONS

American Society for Psychical Research *see* JOURNAL OF THE AMERICAN SOCIETY FOR PSYCHICAL RESEARCH

American Society for Technical Aid to Spanish Democracy *see* SPAIN IS FIGHTING FOR YOU

American Society for Testing and Materials *see*
- PROCEEDINGS
- STANDARDIZATION NEWS

AMERICAN SOCIETY FOR TESTING MATERIALS BULLETIN *see* ASTM BULLETIN

American Society of Agronomy *see* PROCEEDINGS OF THE AMERICAN SOCIETY OF AGRONOMY

AMERICAN SOCIETY OF CHURCH HISTORY : PAPERS – v1 no 1-8. 1888-96; v2 no 1-9. 1906-33 (complete) – 2r – 1 – ATLA S0001 – us A.T.L.A. [240]

American Society of Civil Engineers *see*
- COLLECTED JOURNALS
- DOCUMENTS ON TIME REFORM
- STANDARD TIME FOR THE UNITED STATES OF AMERICA, CANADA AND MEXICO
- STANDARD TIME: REPLIES TO QUESTIONS SUBMITTED BY SPECIAL COMMITTEE..
- TRANSACTIONS

American Society of Clinical Pathologists *see* AMERICAN JOURNAL OF CLINICAL PATHOLOGY

AMERICAN SOCIETY OF ENOLOGISTS. PROCEEDINGS, ANNUAL OPEN MEETING *see* AMERICAN JOURNAL OF ENOLOGY

AMERICAN SOCIETY OF HEATING AND AIR-CONDITIONING ENGINEERS – TRANSACTIONS *see* ASHRAE TRANSACTIONS

AMERICAN SOCIETY OF HEATING AND VENTILATING ENGINEERS – TRANSACTIONS *see* ASHRAE TRANSACTIONS

American Society of International Law *see* PROCEEDINGS OF THE ANNUAL MEETING

AMERICAN SOCIETY OF INTERNATIONAL LAW PROCEEDINGS – v1-89. 1907-95 – 9 – $1,059.00 set – us Hein [340]

American Society of Lubrication Engineers *see* ASLE TRANSACTIONS

American Society of Mechanical Engineers *see*
- TRANSACTIONS
- TRANSACTIONS (A.S.M.E.)

American Society of Pension Actuaries *see* PROCEEDINGS

AMERICAN SOCIETY OF PHOTOGRAMMETRY *see* ANNUAL MEETING OF THE AMERICAN CONGRESS ON SURVEYING AND MAPPING

AMERICAN SOCIETY OF PHOTOGRAMMETRY TECHNICAL PAPERS *see* ASP-ACSM (AMERICAN CONGRESS ON SURVEYING AND MAPPING) TECHNICAL PAPERS

American Society of Safety Engineers *see*
- ASSE JOURNAL
- PROCEEDINGS

AMERICAN SOCIOLOGICAL REVIEW – (v. 33-. 1968- 5,6. v. 35-. 1970- 9) – v. 1- 1936- – 1 – us UMI [300]

AMERICAN SOCIOLOGICAL REVIEW – Wisconsin. v1-15. 1936-50. B-278/2 – 8 – ne IDC [073]

AMERICAN SOCIOLOGIST – (1971- . 5,6. 1977- . 9) – v. 1- 1965- – 1 – us UMI [300]

AMERICAN SOCIOLOGIST – New York. 1965-70. BH-1812 1 – 9 – ne IDC [300]

AMERICAN SPECTATOR – 1-4 (all publ). 1932-1937 – 1 reel – 1 – $115.00 – us UPA [335]

AMERICAN SPECTATOR – (1979. 5,6,9) – v.11- .1977- – 1 – us UMI [073]

AMERICAN SPECTATOR *see* ALTERNATIVE

THE AMERICAN SPECTATOR: A LITERARY NEWSPAPER – New York. v. 1-4, no. 48. Nov. 1932-May 1937 – 1 – us NY Public [420]

AMERICAN SPEECH – (1967- . 5,6. 1975- . 9) – 30- 1955- – 1 – us UMI [420]

AMERICAN SPIDERS AND THEIR SPINNINGWORK / Maccook, H C – Z-2183 3 v. 1889-1893 – 8 – ne IDC [590]

AMERICAN SRBOBRAN – Pittsburgh, PA, 1906-1912, 1918-1940 – 28r – 1 – us I.H.R.C. [978]

AMERICAN STANDARD – San Francisco. v. 1, no. 9, 11, 13-16, 18-24, 26; v. 2, no. 31, 35, 49, 53; v. 3, no. 3. Oct. 19, 1888-Jan. 4, 1890 – 1 – us NY Public [073]

AMERICAN STAR – (Bi-weekly, later daily, newspaper publ in Mexico during the Mexican War) – Puebla, Mexico. july 25, 1847-may 27, 1848 – 1 – us Western Res [071]

AMERICAN STATE PAPERS / U. S. – Serial nos 1-38. 38v Jun 11 1789 – Mar 3 1838 – 3 – us Readex [976]

AMERICAN STATE PAPERS: DOCUMENTS, LEGISLATIVE AND EXECUTIVE, 1789-1838 – 20r – 1 – $1265.00 – us UMI [324]

AMERICAN STATE PAPERS: PUBLIC LANDS / U.S. Congress – v1-7, 1789-1835.v300-0069/0075 – 1 – us A.G.L.L. [324]

AMERICAN STATE REPORTS – (Individual titles under this coll also listed separately) – San Francisco: Bancroft-Whitney. v1-140. 1886-1911 (all publ) – 1585mf – 9 – $2,377.00 – LLMC 78-038 – us L.L.M.C. [340]

AMERICAN STATE REPORTS *see*
- AMERICAN AND ENGLISH ANNOTATED CASES
- NOTES ON THE AMERICAN DECISIONS AND REPORTS

AMERICAN STATE REPORTS PRIOR TO NATIONAL REPORTER SYSTEM – 1106 reels – 1 – $33,500.00 – us Trans-Media [340]

AMERICAN STATE REPORTS, TRINITY SERIES, PT 3 *see*
- CHURCH'S DIGEST OF CASES IN VOLS 25-48 OF THE AMERICAN STATE REPORTS
- GREEN'S DIGEST OF THE CASES IN THE AMERICAN STATE REPORTS
- INDEX/DIGEST TO THE MONOGRAPHIC NOTES IN THE AMERICAN STATE REPORTS
- MACK'S DIGEST OF CASES IN VOLS 1-24 OF THE AMERICAN STATE REPORTS
- MAGEE'S DIGEST OF CASES IN VOLS 49-72 OF THE AMERICAN STATE REPORTS
- MARTIN'S NUMERICAL TABLE OF CASES IN THE TRINITY SERIES
- RAPALJE'S DIGEST OF THE AMERICAN DECISIONS AND REPORTS
- TABLE OF CASES AND INDEX TO THE NOTES IN AMERICAN DECISIONS AND REPORTS

- TORBERT'S TABLE OF CASES IN THE TRINITY SERIES

AMERICAN STATE TRIALS : CRIMINAL CASES – (Add vols to be filmed) – St Louis: Thomas Law Book Co. v1-4. 1914-15 – 40mf – 9 – $60.00 – LLMC 90-352 – us L.L.M.C. [340]

AMERICAN STATESMAN – Lexington. Ky. 1811-13 – 1 – us UMI [071]

THE AMERICAN STATESMEN SERIES *see*
- CHARLES SUMMER
- DANIEL WEBSTER
- HENRY CLAY
- JAMES MADISON
- JOHN C. CALHOUN
- JOHN JAY
- PATRICK HENRY
- SALMON PORTLAND CHASE
- THADDEUS STEVENS
- THOMAS JEFFERSON
- WILLIAM HENRY SEWARD

American Statistical Association *see*
- JOURNAL
- PROCEEDINGS
- PROCEEDINGS OF THE SECTION ON STATISTICAL EDUCATION

AMERICAN STATISTICIAN – (1971- . 5,6. 1975- . 9) – v. 1- 1947- – 1 – us UMI [310]

AMERICAN STATISTICIAN – v. 1-23. 1947-69 – 1,5,6 – us Princeton Micro [510]

AMERICAN STATISTICS INDEX MICROFICHE LIBRARY – (Includes significant statistical publications of the U.S. Federal Government. Both depository and non-depository publications. From early 1960's onwards) – 1974- – 9 – Apply for prices – us CIS [310]

AMERICAN STOCK EXCHANGE INVESTOR *see* AMERICAN INVESTOR

AMERICAN STREET RAILWAY DECISIONS – (Covers US and Canada. Title originally intended to be retrospective reprint of all street railway cases from 1841 to date but only managed coverage for the years 1841-64) – Brooklyn, NY: American Street Railroad Assoc. v1-2. 1841-64 (all publ) – 12mf – 9 – $18.00 – LLMC 84-703 – us L.L.M.C. [380]

AMERICAN STUDIES IN SCANDINAVIA – (1981- . 1,5,6,9) – 1973- – 1 – us UMI [073]

AMERICAN STUDIES INTERNATIONAL – (v21- . 1982-. 1,5,6,9) – v1-11; v18-. 1962-72; 1979- – 1 – us UMI [073]

American Sunbathing Association *see* SUNSHINE AND HEALTH

American Sunday School Union *see*
- 125TH ANNIVERSARY REPORT
- ANNUAL REPORTS, 1825-1835

AMERICAN SUNDAY SCHOOL UNION PAPERS, 1817-1915 – 234r – 1 – $12,530.00 – us UMI [240]

THE AMERICAN SUPREME COURT AS AN INTERNATIONAL TRIBUNAL / Smith, Hebert Arthur – New York: Oxford 1920. 123p. LL-1496 – 1 – us L of C Photodup [340]

The American Swedish Foundation *see* THE JOHN ERICSSON COLLECTION OF THE AMERICAN SWEDISH HISTORICAL FOUNDATION

THE AMERICAN TAR: INDEPENDENT AND FREE / Taylor, Raynor – ca. 1796 – 9 – us Sibley [780]

AMERICAN TEACHER – (1978-. 5,6,9) – v. 1- 1912- – 1 – us UMI [370]

AMERICAN TELEGRAPH – Brownsville, PA.1814-18 – 1 – us Readex [071]

American Telephone and Telegraph Co *see* CLASSIFIED INDEX OF RATE CASES, YEARS 1925, 1926, 1927

AMERICAN TELEPHONE JOURNAL – v. 2-18. 1900-08 – 1,5,6 – us Princeton Micro [380]

American Temperance Union *see* JOURNAL

AN AMERICAN TEXT-BOOK OF PATHOLOGY : FOR THE USE OF STUDENTS AND PRACTITIONERS OF MEDICINE AND SURGERY / ed by Hektoen, Ludvig & Riesman, David – Philadelphia: W B Saunders & Co, 1901 – us Res Libr [617]

AMERICAN THEATRE PERIODICALS OF THE NINETEENTH AND EARLY TWENTIETH CENTURIES – 1 – us Primary [790]

AMERICAN THEOLOGICAL LIBRARY ASSOCIATION : SUMMARY OF PROCEEDINGS / American Theological Library Association – v1-19. 1947-65 (complete) – 2r – 1 – ATLA S0121 – us A.T.L.A. [020]

American Theological Library Association *see* AMERICAN THEOLOGICAL LIBRARY ASSOCIATION

THE AMERICAN THEOSOPHIST – 1979-90 (complete) – 4r – 1 – ATLA S0434 – us A.T.L.A. [073]

American Tract Society *see*
- FREEDMAN
- FREEDMAN'S JOURNAL

THE AMERICAN TRACT SOCIETY, ET AL., VS. LYDIA G. ATWATER, ET AL / Smith, Palmer Cone – Circleville, Ohio: Van Cleaf & Dresbach 1877?. 26p. LL-27 – 1 – us L of C Photodup [340]

AMERICAN TRADEMARK CASES. / Cox, Rowland – Cincinnati, Clark, 1871. 782 p. LL-548 – 1 – us L of C Photodup [340]

AMERICAN TRAVELLER – Typescript of letters. 1810. Letters apparently by and for Englishmen as an informal survey of American nature, people, institutions and developments. 4 fiches – 9 – us South Carolina Historical [910]

AMERICAN TRIAL LAWYERS ASSOCIATION NEWSLETTER – v.7-15. Sep 1964-Nov 1972. Continued as Association of Trial Lawyers of America Newsletter – 1 – us UMI [073]

AMERICAN TWENTIETH CENTURY ART : SUBJECT COLLECTIONS – (Individual titles not listed separately) – 225 catalogues on 282mf – 9 – £1,480.00 – uk Chadwyck [700]

AMERICAN UNIFORM MARRIAGE AND MARRIAGE LICENSE ACT / National Conference of Commissioners on Uniform State Laws – Williamsport, Pa.: Railway Printing Co. 1911. 29p. LL-950 – 1 – us L of C Photodup [340]

AMERICAN UNION – Ellicottville. N.Y. 1856-1859 – 1 – us UMI [071]

AMERICAN UNIONIST – Salem, OR. -w. 31 Dec 1866-31 Jul 1869. – 1r – 1 – us U.O. Library [071]

AMERICAN UNIVERSITY INTRAMURAL LAW REVIEW – v. 1-5. 1952-1956 – 1 – us UMI [340]

AMERICAN UNIVERSITY JOURNAL OF INTERNATIONAL LAW AND POLICY – v1-10. 1986-95 – 9 – $209.00 set – us Hein [340]

AMERICAN UNIVERSITY LAW REVIEW – (v1-34 1952-85 $460.00 reel. v35-44 1985-95 $253.00 mf) – v1-44. 1952-95 – 5,6,9 – $713.00 set – us Hein [340]

AMERICAN UNIVERSITY LAW REVIEW – (v28- 1978- 5,6,9) – v6- 1957- – 1 – us UMI [340]

American University of Beirut. Syria. (Faculty of agricultural sciences) *see* AGRICULTURAL DEVELOPMENT AND RESEARCH IN SYRIA

AMERICAN URBAN LIFE AND HEALTH – (Pt 1: Reports of the Charity Organisation of New York, 1883-1914) – 1 – us Primary [025]

AMERICAN VANGUARD – v9-15; ns: n4-46. 1912-18; 1921-24 – 1r – 1 – us Ross [360]

American Venereal Disease Association *see* JOURNAL OF THE AMERICAN VENEREAL DISEASE ASSOCIATION

AMERICAN VERSUS ENGLISH METHODS OF BRIDGE DESIGNING – Tokyo, 1886. 02536. (Pre-1900 Canadiana) – 9 – cn C.I.H.M. [624]

American Veterinary Medical Association *see* JOURNAL OF THE AMERICAN VETERINARY MEDICAL ASSOCIATION

AMERICAN VETERINARY MEDICAL ASSOCIATION: JOURNAL – v. 29-127. 1905-55 – 1, 5, 6 – 960.00 – us Princeton Micro [636]

AMERICAN VETERINARY REVIEW *see* JOURNAL OF THE AMERICAN VETERINARY MEDICAL ASSOCIATION

AMERICAN VOCATIONAL JOURNAL – (1966-78. 5,6. 1971-78. 9) – 1-53. 1926-78 – 1 – us UMI [650]

AMERICAN VOCATIONAL JOURNAL *see* VOCED

AMERICAN VOLUNTEER – Carlisle, PA. -w 1842-1905; 1814-1909. 24 rolls – 13 – $25.00r – us I.M.R. [071]

AMERICAN WALDENSIAN AID SOCIETY : NEWSLETTER – 1953-89 (complete) – 2r – 1 – ATLA S0404 – us A.T.L.A. [240]

AMERICAN WATCHMAN – Wilmington. Del. 1809-1820 – 1,3 – us Readex [071]

American Water Works Association *see* JOURNAL

THE AMERICAN WEEKLY MERCURY – Philadelphia. Pa. 1719-49 – 1,3 – us Readex [071]

AMERICAN WEST – (v. 6-. 1969- 5,6. v. 8-. 1971- 9) – 1- 1964- – 1 – us UMI [975]

AMERICAN WIVES AND ENGLISH HUSBANDS: A NOVEL / Atherton, Gertrude – Toronto: Copp, Clark, 1898. 03988. (Pre-1900 Canadiana) – 9 – cn C.I.H.M. [830]

THE AMERICAN WOMAN – v3-10,19. 1890-94,1909-10 – 3r – 1 – us Ross [305]

AMERICAN WOMEN'S DIARIES – Segment 1-3. New England Women, Southern Women, Western Women; Diaries of women representing how they viewed themselves – 1 – us Readex [920]

American Workers Party *see* LABOR AGE

AMERICAN WRITERS OF TO-DAY / Vedder, Henry Clay – New York: Silver, Burdett, 1910 – 1mf – us A.T.L.A. [420]

AMERICAN X-RAY JOURNAL *see* AMERICAN JOURNAL OF PROGRESSIVE THERAPEUTICS

AMERICAN ZIONIST – 1- 1921- 1; 1970- 5,6; 1977- 4 x 6 in9 – us UMI [270]

AMERICAN ZIONIST – New York, NY. 1921-79 – 1 – us A.J.P.C. [071]

AMERICAN ZIONIST – New York, NY. Nov/Dec 1979-Oct/Nov 1985. Ceased publication – 1 – us A.J.P.C. [071]

AMERICAN ZIONIST CASE / American Zionist Emergency Council – Statement submitted to the Anglo-American Committee of Inquiry by the American Zionist Emergency Council. Jan 1946. BJ-28-27 1 – 9 – ne IDC [956]

American Zionist Emergency Council *see*
- AMERICAN ZIONIST CASE
- A REPORT OF ACTIVITIES, 1940-1946

AMERICAN ZOOLOGIST – (1971- . 5,6. 1976- . 9) – 1- 1961- – 1 – us UMI [590]

AMERICANA : MAGAZINE OF PICTORIAL SATIRE – New York: American Group Inc, feb 1932-nov 1933 – 1 – us Res Libr [870]

AMERICANA – Portland OR. Apr 20 27 May 4 Sep 7 1940 – 1 – us U.O. Library [071]

AMERICANA NOT IN SABIN – 69 reels plus Group V on 62 fiches. Group V: See: France and America During the French Revolution: The Rise of Independent Haiti – 1 – $5,150.00 – us OmniSys [970]

AMERICAN-ARAB AFAIRS – (Cont by: Middle East Policy) – Washington. v1-38 Sum 1982-Sum 1991 1*; v10-38 Fal 1984-Sum 1991 5,9 – 1,5,9 – D14796 – us UMI [327]

AMERICAN-ARAB AFFAIRS – v1-. 1982- – 1,5,6,9 – us UMI [073]

L'AMERICANISME / Houtin, Albert – (Includes index) – Paris: Emile Nourry, 1904 – 2mf – 9 – 0-8370-8827-5 – 1986-2827 – us A.T.L.A. [240]

AMERICANISMS, OLD AND NEW: A DICTIONARY OF WORDS, PHRASES AND COLLOQUIALISMS PECULAIR TO THE UNITED STATES, BRITISH AMERICA, THE WEST INDIES, ETC., ETC., THEIR DERIVATION, MEANING AND APPLICATION : TOGETHER WITH NUMEROUS ANECDOTAL, HISTORICAL, EXPLANATORY AND FOLK-LORE NOTES / Farmer, John Stephen – London: Privately printed by T. Poulter, 1889. 02949. (Pre-1900 Canadiana) – 9 – cn C.I.H.M. [420]

AMERICANO – Portland OR. July 1915 – 1 – us U.O. Library [071]

O AMERICANO – Cachoeira, BA. 12 Maio 1872; Mar 1878; Jan 1882; Out 1883; Ago 1884; Jan-Fev 1885; Mar 1886 – 1,5,6 – bl Biblioteca [072]

O AMERICANO : ORGAO REPUBLICANO – Manaos, Amazonas. 21 Nov-5 Dez 1889 – 1,5,6 – bl Biblioteca [072]

AMERICANS FOR DEMOCRATIC ACTION PAPERS, 1932-1973 – (With printed guide £48.00) – 142r – 1 – £6,595.00 – uk Chadwyck [977]

AMERICANS FOR HAGANAH – (V1, No1, (15 Aug. 1947)-v1, No7, (15 Dec. 1947); Continued by: Haganah Speaks) – New York, N.Y. – us A.J.P.C. [270]

AMERICANS FOR HAGANAH *see* HAGANAH SPEAKS

AMERICANS FOR JUSTICE IN THE MIDDLE EAST – Beirut. 87 docs. 1980-1991 – 23mf – 9 – ne IDC [320]

AMERICANS FOR MIDDLE EAST UNDERSTANDING – New York. 48 docs. 1980-1991 – 14mf – 9 – ne IDC [320]

AMERICANS FROM CROATIA / Tomasic, Dinko A – June 1983 – 1r – 1 – us I.H.R.C. [920]

AMERICANS IN BLACK AFRICA UP TO 1865 / Clendenen, Clarence C & Duignan, Peter – 1964. 109p – 1 – 35.00r – us Hoover Inst Photo [960]

AMERICAS – 1- 1949- – 1,5,6,9 – us UMI [970]

AMERICAS – (1976- 5,6,9) – (Spanish ed.) v1-1949- – 1 – us UMI [970]

AMERICA'S MENACE, OR, THE ENEMY WITHIN : (AN EPITOME): INCLUDING "AMERICA, MY AMERICA", THE MOST POWERFULLY APPEALING PATRIOTIC POEM EVER PENNED: A CLARION CALL TO PATRIOTIC ACTION / Simmons, William Joseph – Atlanta, GA: Bureau of Patriotic Books, c1926 – us Res Libr [355]

AMERICA'S MIDDLE EAST POLICY : KISSINGER, CARTER AND THE FUTURE / Kerr, Malcolm H – Beirut: Institute for Palestine Studies, 1980 – us Res Libr [327]

AMERICA'S NATIONAL GAME : HISTORIC FACTS CONCERNING THE BEGINNING, EVOLUTION, DEVELOPMENT AND POPULARITY OF BASEBALL, WITH PERSONAL REMINISCENCES OF ITS VICISSITUDES, ITS VICTORIES AND ITS VOTARIES / Spalding, Albert G – (Cartoons by Homer C Davenport) – New York: American Sports Publ Co, 1911 – us Res Libr [790]

AMERICA'S PROMINENT FAMILIES / Wright, G Frederick – Memorial and biographical. Cleveland: Memorial Publishing Co. Mississippi Reel 3. (The Cox Library Collection) – 5 – us Americana [978]

America's Textiles *see*
- THE KNITTER
- REPORTER-BULLETIN

AMERICAS WATCH COMMITTEE – New York. 217 docs. 1982-1991 – 156mf – 9 – ne IDC [320]

AMERICA'S WONDERLANDS: A PICTORIAL AND DESCRIPTIVE HISTORY OF OUR COUNTRY'S SCENIC MARVELS AS DELINEATED BY PEN AND CAMERA / Buel, James William – Vancouver, B.C.: J. MacGregor, 1894. 03822. (Pre-1900 Canadiana) – 9 – cn C.I.H.M. [910]

AMERICKE DELNICKE LISTY = AMERICAN WORKINGMEN'S NEWS – Cleveland, OH: Press Comm of the Bohemian Socialist Org of Cleveland, 1909-53 (jan 5 1945-46; 1951-mar 27 1953) – 1 – us Res Libr [071]

AMERICKI HRVAT – Pittsburgh, v1(1946):28 – us I.H.R.C. [071]

AMERICKI HRVATSKI GLASNIK = AMERICAN CROATIAN HERALD – Chicago: Croatian Publ Co, may 14 1947-sep 1956 – 5r – 1 – us Res Libr [071]

AMERICKI HRVATSKI GLASNIK – Chicago, IL. 28 Oct 1953-26 Sep 1956 (imperfect) – 2r – 1 – uk British Libr Newspaper [071]

AMERICKI SLOVACI / Getting, Milan – 1914-1918 – 1 reel – 1 – us I.H.R.C. [975]

AMERICKY SLOVAK : WEEKLY SLOVAK LANGUAGE NEWSPAPER – Cleveland, OH. Nov 29 1934-Sept 19 1935 – 1r – 1 – us Western Res [071]

AMERIKA – Goteborg, Sweden. 1869-72 – 2r – 1 – sw Kungliga [073]

AMERIKA – New York. N.Y. 1909 – 1 – us A.J.P.C. [071]

AMERIKA : DIE POLITISCHEN, SOCIALEN UND KIRCHLICH-RELIGIOESEN ZUSTAENDE DER VEREINIGTEN STAATEN VON NORDAMERIKA: MIT BESONDERER RUECKSICHT AUF DIE DEUTSCHEN, AUS EIGENER ANSCHAUUNG / Schaff, Philipp – Berlin: Wiegandt und Grieben, 1858 – 1mf – us A.T.L.A. [975]

AMERIKA / Providence Association – Philadelphia, 14 Apr 1920-Dec 1940 – 21r – 1 – uk British Libr Newspaper [071]

AMERIKA : EIN ROMAN / Asch, Sholem – Berlin: W Borngraeber, 1911 – 1r – 1 – us U.W. Library [830]

AMERIKA, DER AUFGANG EINER NEUEN WELT / Keyserling, Hermann Alexander – Berlin: Deutsche Verlags-Anstalt, 1931. 475p – 1 – us U.W. Library [975]

AMERIKA IR AMERIKOS LIETUVIAI / Gineitis, Kazys – Kaunas, 1925 – 1r – 1 – us I.H.R.C. [947]

AMERIKA SAMOA : OFFICIAL GOVERNMENT PERIODICAL / American Samoa. Office of Samoan Information – Pago Pago: Office of Samoan Information. v1-2 no 1. Jun 1973-Jul 1974 – 3mf – 9 – $4.50 – LLMC 82-100C Title 17 – us L.L.M.C. [324]

AMERIKA TEEKAIJA = THE AMERICAN PILGRIM – V1-6. New York, 1918-1923. Estonian. 1,186p – 1 – $47.86 – us Baptist [240]

AMERIKABLADET – Orebro, Sweden. 1869-70 – 1 – sw Kungliga [072]

AMERIKAI MAGYAR VILAG = AMERICAN HUNGARIAN WORLD – Cleveland, OH: Assoc Hungarian Press, oct 8 1972-apr 16 1978 – 5r – 1 – us Res Libr [071]
AMERIKAI MAGYAR VILAG = HUNGARIAN DAILY WORLD – New York, oct 25 1937-mar 8 1938 – 1 – us Res Libr [071]
DER AMERIKA-MUEDE : AMERIKANISCHES KULTURBILD / Kuernberger, Ferdinand – Frankfurt a.M.: Meidinger, 1855 – 1r – 1 – us U.W. Library [306]
AMERIKANA SANEDESA – Bombay, India. 7 Apr 1951-26 Dec 1952 – 1r – 1 – us L of C Photodup [072]
AMERIKANA VARTAHARA – Bombay, India. 7 Apr 1951-26 Dec 1952 – 1r – 1 – us L of C Photodup [072]
DER AMERIKANER = AMERICAN FAMILY MAGAZINE – New York City, NY. v19 no 40, v34 no 37. 1919-1936 – 1r – Can$25.00 – cn Can Microfilming [073]
DER AMERIKANER – New York, N.Y. 1904-62. Yiddish – 1 – 1294.00 – us L of C Photodup [071]
AMERIKANISCH DEUTSCHE ENCYCLOPAEDIE (AEL, ABT 1;13) / ed by Prescott, Thomas H – Columbus, 1860 (mf ed 1996) – 12mf – 9 – DM150.00 – 3-89131-099-4 – gw Fischer [030]
Die Amerikanische Armee *see*
– HESSISCHE POST
– KOELNISCHER KURIER
AMERIKANISCHE GEDICHTE *see* VERMISCHTE SCHRIFTEN, UND, AMERIKANISCHE GEDICHTE
DIE AMERIKANISCHE NORDPOL-EXPEDITION / Bessels, Emil – BN-122 2 1879 – 8 – ne IDC [910]
DIE AMERIKANISCHE NORDPOL-EXPEDITION: MIT ZAHLREICHEN ILLUSTRATIONEN IN HOLZCHNITT, DIAGRAMMEN UND EINER KARTE IN FARBENDRUCK / Bessels, Emil – Leipzig, Engelmann, 1879. 03579. (Pre-1900 Canadiana) – 9 – cn C.I.H.M. [910]
AMERIKANISCHE REISEBILDER MIT BESONDERER BERUEKSICHTIGUNG DER RELIGIOESEN UND KIRCHLICHEN ZUSTAENDE DER VEREINIGTEN STAATEN / Pfleiderer, Joh Gottlob – 1882 – 1 – us A.T.L.A. [240]
DER AMERIKANISCHE ROMAN IM SPANISCHEN BUERGERKRIEG : 'FOR WHOM THE BELL TOLLS' IM SPIEGEL POLITISCHER FIKTIONEN / Scheiding, Oliver – 1993 – 2mf – 9 – DM80.00 – 3-89349-810-9 – gw Hänsel [420]
AMERIKANISCHE SCHULZEITUNG – Louisville, KY: Henry Knofel, 1870-75. NS: v1-2 n8 oct 1873-may 1875 – us Res Libr [370]
Der Amerikanischen 12. Heeresgruppe fuer die deutsche Zivilbevoelkerung *see* FRANKFURTER PRESSE
DIE AMERIKANISCHEN ANTITRUST-GESETZE, EINE UNTERSUCHUNG IHRES WESENS UND ZWECKES IN DER MODERNEN AMERIKANISCHEN MARKTWIRTSCHAFT / Jenny, Hans Heinrich – Affoltern am Albis, 1952. 182 p. LL-592 – 1 – us L of C Photodup [340]
AMERIKANISCHES SKIZZEBUECHELCHE : EINE EPISTEL IN VERSEN / Asmus, Georg – (Missing t.p. supplied) – 2. Aufl. New York: Willmer & Rogers News Co, American News Co, 1874 – 1r – 1 – us U.W. Library [810]
AMERIKANISCHES SKIZZEBUECHELCHE : ZWEITE EPISTEL IN VERSEN / Asmus, Georg – Coeln: E H Mayer, 1885 – 1r – 1 – us U.W. Library [810]
AMERIKANISMUS, FORTSCHRITT, REFORM : IHR ZUSAMMENHANG, ZWECK, UND VERLAUF IN AMERIKA, FRANKREICH, ENGLAND, UND DEUTSCHLAND / Braun, Carl – Wuerzburg: Goebel & Scherer, 1904 – 1mf – us A.T.L.A. [240]
AMERIKANSKI SLOVENEC – Chicago, 1891-1946 – 33r – 1 – us I.H.R.C. [975]
AMERIKANSKIE IZVESTII A (NEW YORK, N.Y.) – (Includes c.1: 1921:Dec.21-1924:Dec.3) – New York: Directorate of Russian Trade, 1917 – 3r – 1 – CSUXANR0889-S – us Hoover Inst Photo [380]
AMERIKANSKIE IZVESTIIA : ORGAN ROSSIIKIKH RABOCHIKH ORGANIZATSII SOEDINENNYKH SHTATOV I KANADY – New York, 1922: mar 22, may 17, jul 5-19, aug 16-30, sep 20-27, oct 11-25, nov 1-15, dec 6-27. 1923: jan 10-oct 3, oct 17, nov 21-dec 26. 1924: jan 3-feb 13, feb 27-jun 11, jul 2-aug13 – us Res Libr [071]
AMERIKANSKII PRAVOSLAVNYI VIESTNIK = RUSSIAN ORTHODOX AMERICAN MESSENGER – New York [etc]: Pravoslavnaia amerikanskaia missiia, sep 1 1896-aug 27 1897; 1897-1930 – us Res Libr [071]
AMERIKANSKIJ RUSSKIJ SOKOL SOJEDINENIJA = AMERICAN RUSSIAN FALCON – Homestead, PA: Greek Catholic Union of USA, 1926-36 – 1 – us Res Libr [073]
AMERIKANSKO SLOVENSKE NOVINY – Pittsburgh, PA. 1893-1904 – 3r – 1 – us I.H.R.C. [978]
AMERIKANSKO-RUSSKII KALENDAR – Filadelfiia, Izd. Obshchestva russkikh bratstv v Soedinennykh Shtatakh Sievernoi Ameriki, 1911, 1940, 1950 – 1 – us Res Libr [520]
AMERIKA'S GESETZE / Lehmann, Ignaz – St. Louis, Witter 1857 176 p. LL-424 – 1 – us L of C Photodup [340]
AMERIKAS VESTNESIS – Boston: Amerikas Vestnesis Inc, aug 19 1958-jul 1966 – 2r – 1 – us Res Libr [071]
AMERIKAS ZHINA – New York. 1926-1933. Incomplete – 1 – us NY Public [073]
DIE AMERIKAWANDERUNG IN GUESSIGER BEZIRK / Graupner, Ludwig – 1949 – 1r – 1 – us I.H.R.C. [304]
AMERIKA-WOCHE – Chicago.1982-84 – 1 – gw Mikrofilm [071]
AMERIKA-WOCHE *see*
– CALIFORNIA FREIE PRESSE
– CINCINNATI-KURIER
– MILWAUKEE HEROLD
– DIE WELTPOST UND DER STAATSANZEIGER
AMERIKOS LIETUVIAI / Birziska, Mikolas – Kaunas, 1932 – 1r – 1 – us I.H.R.C. [947]
AMERIKOS LIETUVIAI 19. SIMTMETYJE, 1868-1900 / Milukas, Antanas – Philadelphia, PA, 1938 – 1r – 1 – us I.H.R.C. [978]
AMERIKOS LIETUVIS = THE LITHUANIAN OF AMERICA – Worcester, MA: M Paltanavicia, dec 13 1917-apr 3 1937 – 3r – 1 – us Res Libr [071]
AMERINDIAN : AMERICAN INDIAN REVIEW – Chicago. v1-23 n1. 1952-74 (all publ) – 23mf – 9 – $5.00f – us Ross [970]
THE AMERINDIAN – 1952-74.(American Indian Periodicals in the Princeton University Library). 11 fiches – 9 – $50.00 – us UPA [305]
L'AMERIQUE AVANT LES EUROPEENS / Desdevises du Dezert, Theophile – Caen France: F. Le Blanc-Hardel, 1878. 04283. (Pre-1900 Canadiana) – 9 – cn C.I.H.M. [971]
L'AMERIQUE DU NORD PITTORESQUE: OUVRAGE REDIGE PAR UNE REUNION D'ECRIVAINS AMERICAINS / Bryant, William C – Sous la direction de W. Cullen Bryant. Traduit, revu et augmente par Benedict Henry Revoil. Paris: A. Quantin, 1880. 00305. (Pre-l900 Canadiana) – 9 – cn C.I.H.M. [970]
AMERIQUE FRANCAISE : REVUE – Montreal, Canada. Nov 1941-64 – 3r – 1 – Can$45.00r – cn Can Microfilming [073]
L'AMERIQUE LATINE – no. 1-260. Paris. 1923-oct 1924; juil 1926-27. mq no. 49, 90, 95-183, 185-191, 193-208, 234, 237 – 1 – fr A.C.R.P.P. [073]
AMERISKA DOMOVINA – Cleveland. Ohio. 1907-1939 – 1 – us UMI [071]
AMERISKA DOMOVINA : WEEKLY SLOVENIAN LANGUAGE NEWSPAPER – Cleveland, Cuyahoga, OH. 3 Jan-19 Dec 1991 – 1r – 1 – us Western Res [071]
Ameron, Jean d' *see* HISTOIRE VERITABLE ET PRODIGIEUSE SUR LA VIE, MORT ET PUNITION D'UN HOMME QUI A ESTE CONDAMNE PAR ARREST A ESTRE PENDU ESTRANGLE, PUIS BRUSLE
Amersbach, Karl *see* ABERGLAUBE, SAGE UND MAERCHEN BEI GRIMMELSHAUSEN
AMERYKA ECHO – (Sunday issue only) – Toledo, OH: A A Paryski, dec 1917-oct 24 1922 (10r); jan 1 1922-dec 25 1927 (7r); mar 22 1931; may 3-24 1931 – 1 – us Res Libr [071]
AMERYKA ECHO – Toledo, Ohio. 1889-1971. Variant frequency editions – 121r – 1 – $32.50r – us Archival [071]
Ames, A H *see*
– THE REVELATION OF ST. JOHN THE DIVINE
– REVELATION OF ST JOHN THE DIVINE
Ames, Daniel T *see* AMES ON FORGERY.
Ames, Edward Scribner *see*
– THE DIVINITY OF CHRIST
– THE PSYCHOLOGY OF RELIGIOUS EXPERIENCE
Ames, Herbert Brown *see*
– CANADIAN POLITICAL HISTORY: OUTLINES OF A COURSE OF TEN LECTURES... YOUNG MEN'S CHRISTIAN ASSOCIATION...1894
– "THE CITY BELOW THE HILL": A SOCIOLOGICAL STUDY OF A PORTION OF THE CITY OF MONTREAL, CANADA
Ames, James Barr *see*
– A SELECTION OF CASES IN EQUITY JURISDICTION.
– A SELECTION OF CASES ON PLEADING, WITH REFERENCES AND CITATIONS
– A SELECTION OF CASES ON THE LAW OF TORTS
AMES ON FORGERY. / Ames, Daniel T – Boston, Boston Book, 1901. 293 p. LL-285 – 1 – us L of C Photodup [340]
AMES PRIMITIVES : CONTRIBUTION A L'ETUDE DU SENTIMENT RELIGIEUX CHEZ LES PAIENS ANIMISTES / Burnier, Theophile – Paris: Societe des missions evangeliques, 1922 – 1 – us Res Libr [290]
AMESBURY 1685-1849 – (Mf 1T: Marriages 1686-89. Mf 1T-2T: Births 1685-1723. Mf 2T-3T: Deaths 1686-1737. Mf 3T: Marriages 1728-42. Mf 3T-7T: Births 1700-83. Mf 5T: Deaths 1729-70. Mf 7T-8T: Marriages 1701-62; Intentions 1700-27; Mf 8T: Births, Deaths 1718-81; Intentions 1760-84. Mf 8T-12T: Births 1742-1847. Mf 12T: Marriages 1700-1821; Intentions 1700-06. Mf 12T-15T: Intentions 1784-1849. Mf 14T: Deaths 1774-1846. Mf 15T-16T: Marriages 1820-44. Mf 16T: Marriages 1726-42; Out-Town Marriages 1696-1799. Mf 16T-18T: Births 1843-49. Mf 18T: Marriages 1843-49. Mf 19T: Deaths 1843-49) – (mf ed 1994) – 19mf – 9 – 0-87623-199-7 – us Holbrook [920]
AMETHYST – 1832-34 – 13mf – 9 – £110.00 – uk Chadwyck [800]
Amfilokhii, Archimandrite *see*
– OPISANIE IUR'EVSKAGO EVANGELIIA 1118-1128 G
– OPISANIE VOSKRESENSKOI NOVOIERUSALEMSKOI BIBLIOTEKI S PRILOZHENIEM SNIMKOV SO VSEKH PERGAMENNYKH RUKOPISEI I NEKOTORYKH PISANNYKH NA BUMAGE
Amfiteatrov, Aleksandr *see*
– GORESTNYI A ZAMIETY
– KROVAVYI TSAR
Amfiteatrov, G N *see* OSNOVNYE CHERTY ZHKONOPROEKTA O DOGOVORAKH
AMHCA JOURNAL / American Mental Health Counselors Association (AMHCA) – (Cont by: Journal of Mental Health Counseling) – Washington. cum index 1-3 1979-81; v1-9 jan 1979-apr 1987 1,5; v1-9 jan/jul 1979-jan/apr 1987 9 – 1,5,9 – D11726 – us UMI [360]
AMHERST 1747-1891 – (Mf 1-5: Genealogical Records: B,M,D 1747-1843. Mf 6-8: Births, Marriages, Deaths 1747-1851. Mf 9-11: Births, Marriages, Deaths 1843-51. Mf 12-18: Births 1851-91, Vol 3. Mf 19-23: Marriages 1851-91, Vol 4. Mf 24-28: Deaths 1851-91, Vol 5) – (mf ed 1987) – 28mf – 9 – 0-87623-012-5 – us Holbrook [920]
AMHERST ANNOUNCER (NEWSLETTER) AND BULLETINS / Tonawanda. New York. Amherst Baptist Church – 1964-86. Newsletter, Aug 1964-Jul 1986. Bulletins, Aug 1964-Jul 1986 – 1 – $45.18 – us Baptist [240]
AMHERST BOROUGH RATES – 1859-1876 – 1r – 1 – at Corangamite [910]
Amherst College. Amherst, MA *see* CATALOG
AMHERST GAZETTE – Amherst, Nova Scotia. v10 n23. 3 sep 1875 – 1r – 1 – Can$25.00 – cn Can Microfilming [072]
Amherst, Jeffery *see* OFFICIAL PAPERS OF SIR JEFFERY AMHERST
Amherst, Massachusetts. First Baptist Church *see* RECORDS
L'AMI COMMUN / Dickens, Charles – Our Mutual Friend. In French. Paris: Hachette, 1873. 2v. 9 fiches. (Literature Collection) – 9 – 22.00 – fr Bibl Nationale [830]
L'AMI DE LA JEUNESSE OU PLAN DE REFORME DANS LES PENSIONS / Gratieux, L – Paris. 1791 – 9 – fr Hachette [360]
L'AMI DE LA PATRIE – ou Journal de la liberte francaise. Paris. avr 1796-mars 1798. (fragm., 107 no. entre no. 54-725) – 1 – fr A.C.R.P.P. [073]
L'AMI DE LA RELIGION ET DE LA PATRIE – Quebec, Canada. 18 dec 1847-11 mar 1850? – 2r – 1 – Can$40.00 – cn Can Microfilming [072]
L'AMI DE LA RELIGION ET DU ROI – Trois-Rivieres [Quebec]: L Duvernay, [1820-182-?] – 9 – cn C.I.H.M. [971]
L'AMI DE LA RELIGION ET DU ROY / ed by Duvernay, Ludger – Trois-Rivieres, Canada. 1 jun-1 nov 1820 – 1r – 1 – Can$30.00 – cn Can Microfilming [073]
L'AMI DE L'OUVRIER – Quebec, Canada. 11-18 mars 1911 – 1r – 1 – Can$25.00 – cn Can Microfilming [072]
UN AMI DE VOLTAIRE A M. D'EPREMESNIL AU SUJET D'UN PLAIDOYER, OU L'ON OUTRAGE GRATUITEMENT LE MEMOIRE DE M. VOLTAIRE / Condorcet, Marie Jean Antoine Nicolas de – Londres, Paris: l'Esprit, 1780 – 9 – fr Hachette [920]
L'AMI DES ANIMAUX – Montreal, Canada. jun 1869 – 1r – 1 – Can$25.00 – cn Can Microfilming [636]
L'AMI DES ARTS OU JUSTIFICATION DE PLUSIERS GRANDS HOMMES... / Decroix, J -J-M – Amsterdam & Paris: Les marchands de nouveautes, 1776 – 5mf – 9 – us Sibley [780]
L'AMI DES CAMPAGNES : HEBDO DU NOUVELLISTE – Quebec, Canada. 12 jan, 2 mar 1883-v2 n6. 11 avr 1884 – 1r – 1 – Can$25.00 – cn Can Microfilming [072]
L'AMI DES CAMPAGNES – Sorel, Canada. 22-jun; v1 n2. 30 jun 1859 – 1r – 1 – Can$25.00 – cn Can Microfilming [072]
L'AMI DES CITOYENS – no. 5, 9-10, 20-21, 36, 57-59, 61-63. Paris. aout 1791-janv 1793 – 1 – fr A.C.R.P.P. [073]
L'AMI DES FOYERS CHRETIENS : DEUTSCH-FRANZOESISCHE ZEITUNG – Metz, France. 1972-78 – 1 – gw Mikrofilm [072]
L'AMI DES LOIS / Laya – (French Theatre Series). Paris. Maradan et Lepetit. 1793 – 9 – fr Hachette [820]
AMI DES MONUMENTS ET DES ARTS PARISIENS ET FRANCAIS / Comite des Monuments Francais – v. 1-23. Paris. 1887-1909. BO-1208 1 – 9 – ne IDC [073]
L'AMI DU CHANTEUR : NOUVEAU RECUEIL DE ROMANCES, MELODIES, CHANSONS ET CHANSONNETTES AVEC MUSIQUE – Montreal: E. Hardy..., 1895. SEM105P58 – 3mf – 9 – Can$6.75 – cn Bibl Nat [780]
L'AMI DU COLON / ed by Denault, Amedee – (Cont by: Le Pionnier v2 n57 4 jun 1907-1 fev 1912 1r Can$50.00) – Nominingue, Canada. 8 jun 1906-31 mai 1907 – 1r – 1 – Can$30.00 – cn Can Microfilming [072]
L'AMI DU FOYER – Montreal, Canada. v4 n2. avr 1934 – 1r – 1 – Can$25.00 – cn Can Microfilming [073]
L'AMI DU LECTEUR : MENSUEL – Montreal, Canada. 15 dec 1899-15 sep 1903 – 1r – 1 – Can$40.00 – cn Can Microfilming [073]
L'AMI DU PEUPLE – Chatham, Ontario. 1 oct 1908 – 1r – 1 – Can$25.00 – cn Can Microfilming [072]
L'AMI DU PEUPLE – (Ed. du soir. janv-juin 1930. 1) – Paris. mai 1928-oct 1937; mq 1er janv-12 mars 1934 – 1 – fr A.C.R.P.P. [073]
L'AMI DU PEUPLE : FEDERATION DES OUVRIERS DU CANADA – Montreal, Canada. 23 fev 1935 – 1r – 1 – Can$25.00 – cn Can Microfilming [072]
L'AMI DU PEUPLE : FEDERATION DES OUVRIERS DU CANADA / ed by Rancourt, J-C – Montreal, 23 fev 1935 – 1r – 1 – Can$25.00 – cn Can Microfilming [072]
L'AMI DU PEUPLE / ed by Leclere, P-E – Montreal, Canada. 2 jun 1832; 21 jul 1832-18 jul 1840 – 3r – 1 – Can$55.00r – cn Can Microfilming [072]
L'AMI DU PEUPLE – Liege, Belgium. Jul 1873-Dec 1875 – 14ft – 1 – uk British Libr Newspaper [072]
L'AMI DU PEUPLE – no. 1-24. Paris. 20 juil-15 sept 1793 – 1 – fr A.C.R.P.P. [073]
L'AMI DU PEUPLE – ou Le Defenseur des patriotes persecutes. Paris. sept 1794-oct 1797 – 1 – fr A.C.R.P.P. [073]
L'AMI DU PEUPLE : OUVRIER – Quebec, Canada. 21 jun 1876 – 1r – 1 – Can$25.00 – cn Can Microfilming [072]
L'AMI DU PEUPLE / ed by Saint-Jean, J-M – Joliette, Canada. 29 nov 1889-28 mar 1890 – 1r – 1 – Can$30.00 – cn Can Microfilming [072]
L'AMI DU PEUPLE – Trois-Rivieres, Canada. 21 fev 1901 – 1r – 1 – Can$25.00 – cn Can Microfilming [072]
L'AMI DU PEUPLE-DER VOLKSFREUND : DEUTSCH-FRANZOESISCHE ZEITUNG – Strasbourg, France. 1972-79 – 1 – gw Mikrofilm [072]

L'AMI DU PROLETAIRE. ENTRETIENS FAMILIERS SUR DIFFERENTS SUJETS DE MORALE, DE POLITIQUE, D'ECONOMIE, D'INDUSTRIE / Biard, Gustave – Bruxelles, Hoart, 2 livraisons, 36 p. Les Saint-Simoniens, 1825-1834. 6894 – 9 – fr Hachette [335]

L'AMI DU ROI – Toulouse. aout 1815-juin 1819 – 1 – fr A.C.R.P.P. [073]

L'AMI DU ROI, DES FRANCAIS, DE L'ORDRE ET SURTOUT DE LA VERITE – Paris. Quot. juin 1790-aout 1792 – 1 – fr A.C.R.P.P. [073]

Ami, Henry Marc *see*
- A BRIEF BIOGRAPHICAL SKETCH OF SIR JOHN WILLIAM DAWSON
- A CLASSIFIED LIST OF CAMBRO-SILURIAN AND POST-TERTIARY FOSSILS, FROM OTTAWA AND VICINITY
- FLORA TEMISCOUATENSIS
- NOTES ON, AND THE PRECISE GEOLOGICAL HORIZON OF SIPHONOTRETA SCOTICA, DAVIDSON
- ON A NEW OR HITHERTO UNRECOGNIZED GEOLOGICAL HORIZON IN THE GAS AND OIL REGION OF WESTERN ONTARIO
- ON THE OCCURRENCE OF SCOLITHUS IN ROCKS OF THE CHAZY FORMATION ABOUT OTTAWA, ONTARIO
- REPORT OF THE STATE OF THE PRINCIPAL MUSEUMS IN CANADA AND NEWFOUNDLAND
- SIR JOHN WILLIAM DAWSON: A BRIEF BIOGRAPHICAL SKETCH
- SYNOPSIS OF THE GEOLOGY OF MONTREAL
- THE UTICA SLATE FORMATION: WITH SPECIAL REFERENCE TO THE EXPOSURES OF THAT FORMATION AT AND NEAR OTTAWA CITY

AMIABLE BAPTIST CHURCH. GLENMORA, LOUISIANA : CHURCH RECORDS – 1829-1977 – 1 – 63.90 – us Baptist [240]

AMIABLE BAPTIST CHURCH. RAPIDES PARISH. LOUISIANA : CHURCH RECORDS – 1829-1904 – 1 – 13.59 – us Baptist [240]

AMICA – 1988-1995 – 3r per y – 5,6 – Sfr936.00 – sz Infoprint [072]

Amicus *see*
- AN AUTHENTIC HISTORY OF THE PRAYER BOOK, ITS FIVE REVISIONS AND THE PERIODS AT WHICH THEY WERE MADE:..
- CELINE, OU, UNE AUTRE MAGDELEINE A L'ASILE DU BON PASTEUR DE QUEBEC

AMICUS JOURNAL – (1985-86-. 1,5,6) – 1979-80- – 9 – us UMI [073]

AMID-I SEVDA – Nos [1]-6. – 1325 [1907] – 2mf – 9 – $35.00 – us MEDOC [949]

Amiet, R *see* THE BENEDICTONALS OF FREISING

AMIGAWORLD – 1985- – 1,5,6,9 – us UMI [510]

O AMIGO DA VERDADE – S. Joao d'el-Rei, 8 May-30 Oct 1829 – 1,5,6 – bl Biblioteca [072]

O AMIGO DAS LETRAS – Sao Paulo, 4 Apr-29 Sep 1830 – 1,5,6 – bl Biblioteca [072]

EL AMIGO DE LAS LEYES – Ano 1812, (2-XI/1-XII) – 2mf – 9 – sp Cultura [946]

EL AMIGO DE LAS LEYES – Ano 1814, (15-II/3-V) – 2mf – 9 – sp Cultura [946]

O AMIGO DO HOMEM – '(s.l.')-Sao Luis, Brazil. 16 Jul 1825; Jan-Dec 1827 – 1,5,6 – bl Biblioteca [072]

Amigo y Bertran, L *see*
- APOLOGIA...DEL AGUA DE LA VIDA...EN QUE SE HACE EXAMEN Y JUICIO DE LOS PAPELES...
- RESPUESTA DE ANDRES DAVILA...A LA APOLOGIA EN DEFENSA DE LA MEDICINA SUBSTANCIAL

AMIGOS DE LA ROMERIA DE SAN PEDRO 1975 / Torrejoncillo. Ayuntamiento – Caceres: Imp. La Minerva, 1975 – 1 – sp Bibl Santa Ana [946]

AMIGOS DE LA ROMERIA DE SAN PEDRO 1977 / Torrejoncillo. Ayuntamiento – Caceres: Tip. Extremadura, 1977 – 1 – sp Bibl Santa Ana [946]

AMIGOS DE LA ROMERIA DE SAN PEDRO, 1978 / Torrejoncillo. Ayuntamiento – Tip. Extremadura, 1978 – sp Bibl Santa Ana [060]

AMILEC, OU LA GRAINE D'HOMMES QUI SERT A PEUPLER LES PLANETES PAR L'A.D.P / Tiphaigne de la Roche, Charles-Francois – (Utopias in the Enlightenment series). 1754 – 9 – fr Hachette [830]

Amin, M *see* SEDJARAH NABI IBRAHIM

AMINO ACID AND PROTEIN GEOCHEMISTRY IN MOLLUSK SHELLS(DISS.). Z-225/2. 1966 / Mitterer, R M – 8 – ne IDC [580]

AMINO-ACID CONTENT OF FOODS AND BIOLOGICAL DATA ON PROTEIN – 3rd printing 1981 – 285p – it F.A.O. [630]

Aminova, I et al *see* SOVETSKAIA UGOLOVNAIA REPRESSIIA

Amiot, J J M *see* DICTIONNAIRE TARTARE-MANTCHOU FRANCOIS...

Amir *see* KEMENANGAN 2 SOSIALISME DI BULGARIA: TJATATAN 2 PENINDJAUAN DI BULGARIA

Amir Hamzah Wirjosukarto *see* PENDIDIKAN DAN PENGADJARAN MUHAMMADIJAH DALAM MASA PEMBANGUNAN SEMESTA

Amira, K von *see* DER STAB IN DER GERMANISCHEN RECHTSSYMBOLIK

LES AMIS DE COLLEGE OU L'HOMME OISIF ET L'ARTISAN / Picard – (French Theatre Series). Paris. Huet, an IV. 1795 – 9 – fr Hachette [820]

LES AMIS DE DIEU AU QUATORZIEME SIECLE / Jundt, Auguste – Paris: Sandoz et Fischbacher, 1879 – 2mf – us A.T.L.A. [240]

LES AMIS DE RABELAIS ET DE LA DEVINIERE – Tours. 1951-72 – 5 – fr A.C.R.P.P. [440]

AMIS DU VIN – v1-12 1964-75. Continued as: Friends of Wine – 1 – us UMI [640]

Amis du XVIe siecle et de la Pleiade *see* REVUE DE LA RENAISSANCE

LA AMISTAD ANGLO-ARGENTINA : DISCURSO PRONUNCIADO EL 6 DE OCTUBRE DE 1942 / Carcano, Miguel Angel – Buenos Aires: Comisi on Pro-Aliados, 1942? – 1 – CSUXADM8389-B – us Hoover Inst Photo [320]

AMITY STANDARD – Amity, OR. -w. 7 Apr 1910-5 Jun 1975. 22 rolls – 1 – us U.O. Library [071]

AMJ : AGRICULTURAL MACHINERY JOURNAL – (Absorbed by: Power Farming n1325 1987) – Wallington. v1-29 1947-75*; v30-41 jan 1976-oct 1987 1; v30-31 jan 1976-dec 1977*; v32 jan-dec 1978; v33-41 jan 1979-oct 1987* 5; v30-41 jan 1976-oct 1987 – 1,5,9 – inquire – D11285 – us UMI [630]

AMLETO-HAMLET / Shakespeare, William – In Italian. Testo riveduto, con versione a fronte, introduzione e commento a cura di Raffaello Piccoli. Firenze: G.C. Sansoni, 1927. xxxii,313p. Introd. and commentary in Italian. Text in English and Italian – 1 – us U.W. Library [820]

Amman, J *see*
- ICONES LIVIANAE
- KUENSTLICHE UND WOLGERISSENE FIGUREN, DER FUERNEMSTEN EVANGELIEN
- KUNSTBUECHLEIN
- THE TALKING DEAF MAN

AMMAN VALLEY TIMES – Ammanford, Wales, 15 May-24 Dec 1909 – 1/2r – 1 – uk British Libr Newspaper [072]

Ammann, Johann Josef *see* VOLKSSCHAUSPIELE AUS DEM BOEHMERWALDE

THE AMMASSALIK ESKIMO / Thalbitzer, W – BN 414 2. 1914 – 8 – ne IDC [305]

AMMISCA FILE: THE MAGRUDER MISSION TO CHINA / U.S. Army – v. 1-7. 11 Jul 1941-Jun 1942 – 1 – 34.00 – us L of C Photodup [950]

AMMSA *see* WINDSPEAKER

AMMSA: ABORIGINAL MULTI-MEDIA SOCIETY OF ALBERTA – v1-. 1983- – 1 – us UMI [306]

AMMUDEI HA-AVODAH / Landshuth, L E – v. 1-2. Berlin. 1856-62. BJ-421-10 1 – 9 – ne IDC [470]

Ammundsen, Valdemar *see* DEN UNGE LUTHER

Amner, J *see* SACRED HYMNES OF 3, 4, 5, AND 6 PARTS FOR VOICES AND VIOLS

AMNESTY ACTION – NY City, NY. 1981-1982 – 1r – 1 – $50.00 – R04919 – us Library Micro [071]

Amnesty International *see* PUBLISHED AND UNPUBLISHED RESEARCH MATERIAL

AMNESTY INTERNATIONAL (A.I.) – (Section A: Country Dossiers 1975-1991 851mf Dfl8,200.00. Section B: Publications 1962-1991 343mf Dfl3,580.00. 30% of the price goes to AI. updated annually) – 9 – ne IDC [340]

AMNESTY INTERNATIONAL NEWSLETTER – London. Amnesty International. v7-10, 1977-80. Quarterly; monthly – 1 – us U.W. Library [073]

Amo y Mora, M del *see* FLORA FANEROGAMICA DE LA PENINSULA IBERICA

AMOENITATES ACADEMICAE / Linnaeus, Carl – 158 2. v. 1-10. 1749-1790 – 8 – ne IDC [580]

AMOENITATES ACADEMICAE / Linnaeus, Carl – Holmiae, etc., 1749-1769. 7v – 87mf – 9 – ne IDC [610]

AMOK : A STORY / Zweig, Stefan – New York: Viking Press, 1931 – 1r – 1 – us U.W. Library [830]

Amon, J A *see*
- OUATOUR POUR FLUTE,...OP. 84
- QUATOURS CONCERTANS, OBOE AND STRINGS, OP. 92
- TROIS QUATOURS CONCERTANS, OP. 15
- TROIS QUATOURS POUR FLUTE...OP. 42
- TROIS QUATUORS POUR FLUTE...OP. 42
- TROIS SONATES POUR LE FORTE-PIANO ACCOMP. D'UN VIOLON
- TROIS SONATES POUR LE PIANO-FORTE AVEC ACCOMPAGNEMENT DE VIOLON ET VIOLONCELLE OBLIGES
- TROIS SONATES POUR LE PIANOFORTE AVEC ACCOMPAGT. DE FLUTE ET VIOLONCELLE OBLIGES, OP. 48
- TROIS TRIOS CONCERTANS POUR VIOLON, ALTO ET BASSE...OP. 8

AMONG DJIWA, SADURAN / Dwidjasusana, R I W – SE-5059 1. 1962 – 9 – ne IDC [950]

AMONG INDIA'S STUDENTS / Wilder, Robert Parmelee – New York: Fleming H Revell, c1899 – 1mf – 9 – 0-8370-6798-7 – 1986-0798 – us A.T.L.A. [240]

AMONG OURSELVES / South Dakota. Agricultural Extension Service. State College of Agriculture and Mechanic Arts – v.1-6. 1925-32 – 1,5,6 – us Spaulding [630]

AMONG THE BURMANS : A RECORD OF FIFTEEN YEARS OF WORK AND ITS FRUITAGE / Cochrane, Henry Park – New York: F.H. Revell, c1904 – 1mf – us A.T.L.A. [240]

AMONG THE CANNIBALS OF NEW GUINEA : BEING THE STORY OF THE NEW GUINEA MISSION OF THE LONDON MISSIONARY SOCIETY / McFarlane, Samuel – Philadelphia: Presbyterian Board of Publ & Sabbath-School Work, [1888?] – 1mf – 9 – 0-8370-6280-2 – 1986-0280 – us A.T.L.A. [240]

"AMONG THE CLOUDS" : MOUNT WASHINGTON'S NEWSPAPER DURING THE PERIOD 1877-1917 – 14r – 1 – $140.00 set – us Dartmouth [978]

AMONG THE CLOUDS, 1877-1917 – (Mount Washington, NH. Complete run of Mount Washington's most famous daily newspaper) – Dartmouth College Library Collections – 10r – 1 – $700.00 – us UMI [071]

AMONG THE ESKIMOS OF LABRADOR / Hutton, S K – 1912 – 8 – BN 265 2 – ne IDC [306]

AMONG THE FOREST TREES, OR, HOW THE BUSHMAN FAMILY GOT THEIR HOMES: BEING A BOOK OF FACTS AND INCIDENTS OF PIONEER LIFE IN UPPER CANADA.. / Hilts, Joseph Henry – Toronto: W. Briggs, 1888. 05620. (Pre-1900 Canadiana) – 9 – cn C.I.H.M. [971]

AMONG THE HUTS IN EGYPT, SCENES FROM REAL LIFE / Whately, Mary Louisa – 2nd ed. London: Seeley, Jackson, and Halliday, 1872. 344p. illus – 1 – us U.W. Library [960]

AMONG THE PIMAS : OR, THE MISSION TO THE PIMA AND MARICOPA INDIANS – Albany, NY: Ladies' Union Mission School Association, 1893 – 1mf – 9 – 0-8370-6612-3 – 1986-0612 – us A.T.L.A. [240]

AMONG THE PRIMITIVE-BAKONGO : A RECORD OF 30 YEARS' CLOSE INTERCOURSE WITH THE BAKONGO AND OTHER TRIBES OF EQUATORIAL AFRICA... / Weeks, John H – London: Seeley, Service, 1914 – 1 – us Res Libr [301]

AMONG THE THEOLOGIES / Orcutt, Hiram – new ed + suppl. Boston: De Wolfe, Fiske, 1892, c1888 – 1mf – 9 – 0-8370-3935-5 – 1985-1935 – us A.T.L.A. [210]

AMONG THE WILD NGONI : BEING SOME CHAPTERS IN THE HISTORY OF THE LIVINGSTONIA MISSION IN BRITISH CENTRAL AFRICA / Elmslie, Walter Angus – (Includes index and list of personnel at the Livingstonia Mission) – New York: Fleming H Revell, 1899 – 1mf – 9 – 0-8370-6571-2 – 1986-0571 – us A.T.L.A. [240]

AMONG THE WILD TRIBES OF THE AFGHAN FRONTIER : A RECORD OF SIXTEEN YEARS' CLOSE INTERCOURSE WITH THE NATIVES OF THE INDIAN MARCHES / Pennell, T L – London: Seeley, Service, 1912 – 1mf – us A.T.L.A. [956]

AMONG THE WORLD'S PEACEMAKERS;... / ed by Davis, H – New York, 1907 – 5mf – 1 – ILM-475/1 – ne IDC [327]

AMONG UNKNOWN ESKIMO / Bilby, J W – BN 124 2. 1923 – 8 – ne IDC [970]

AMOR : ORGAO LITTERARIO, CRITICO E NOTICIARIO – Manaos, Amazonas. 11 Abr 1910 – 1,5,6 – bl Biblioteca [072]

EL AMOR AL LIBRO... / Redonet y Lopez, Doriga; ed by Bayle, Constantino – Madrid: Razon y Fe, 1928 – 9 – sp Bibl Santa Ana [946]

AMOR ALOS ENEMIGOS EN EL ANTIGUO TESTAMENTO / Fernandez Fernandez, Juan – Madrid: R.E.E.B., 1928 – 1 – sp Bibl Santa Ana [946]

AMOR DE LA PATRIA / Forner Segarra, Juan Pablo – 1794 – 9 – 1.50f – sp Bibl Santa Ana [946]

AMOR DEI INTELLECTUALIS: EINE RELIGIONS-PHILOSOPHISCHE STUDIE / Wyneken, Gustav Adolf – Greifswald, J. Abel, 1898. 68p. Film Mas 8133 – 1 – us H.U. Library [140]

EL AMOR FAMILIAR...POESIAS / Sainz y Gomez, Manuel – 1828 – 9 – 1.50f – sp Bibl Santa Ana [810]

AMOR Y FLORES / Sanchez Arjona, Vicente – Sevilla: Imprenta Zambrano, 1955 – 1 – sp Bibl Santa Ana [830]

AMOR Y MARTIRIO / Hurtado de Mendoza, Publio – 1874 – 9 – 1.50f – sp Bibl Santa Ana [946]

LOS AMORES DE PERON / Uriarte, Roberto F – [Buenos Aires?: distribuidor en Capital, J. Vidal, 197-?] – 1 – CSUXAHZ5313-B – us Hoover Inst Photo [920]

Amores Gonzalez, Meliton *see*
- ANGEL RODRIGUEZ (ALIAS) ER PERIODISTA...
- MIS AMORES

Amoretti, Giovanni Vittorio *see* SAGGI CRITICI

AMORIS DIVINI EMBLEMATA / Veen, O van – O 790 1. 1660 – 9 – ne IDC [740]

AMORIS DIVINI ET HUMANI ANTIPATHIA – Antwerpen, 1655 – 5mf – 9 – ne IDC [700]

AMORIS DIVINI ET HUMANI ANTIPATHIA SIVE EFFECTUS VARII – Ed. 2. O-542. 1629 – 9 – ne IDC [240]

Amort, E *see*
- PHILOSOPHIA POLLINGANA AD NORMAM BURGUNDICAE
- VETUS DISCIPLINA CANONICORUM REGULARIUM ET SAECULARIUM

AMORUM EMBLEMATA / Veen, O van – O 447. 1608 – 9 – ne IDC [740]

AMORUM EMBLEMATA, FIGURIS AENEIS INCISA STUDIO OTHONIS VAENI BATAVO-LUGDUNENSIS / Vaenius, O – Antwerpen, 1608 – 3mf – 9 – ne IDC [700]

Amory, Thomas Coffin *see* THE LIFE OF ADMIRAL SIR ISAAC COFFIN, BARONET: HIS ENGLISH AND AMERICAN ANCESTORS

AMOS: AN ESSAY IN EXEGESIS / Mitchell, Hinckley Gilbert – Boston: N.J. Bartlett, 1893. 1 fiche – 9 – us A.T.L.A. [240]

AMOS OVERSAT OG FORTOLKET / Michelet, S – (In Norwegian) – Kristiania [Oslo]:H. Aschehoug, 1893 – 1mf – 9 – 0-8370-4425-1 – 1985-2425 – us A.T.L.A. [220]

AMOS: OVERSAT OG FORTOLKET / Michelet, S – Oslo: H. Aschehoug, 1893. 1 fiche – 9 – us A.T.L.A. [240]

Amos, Sheldon *see*
- AN ENGLISH CODE
- THE SCIENCE OF LAW
- A SYSTEMATIC VIEW OF THE SCIENCE OF JURISPRUDENCE

AMOS UND HOSEA : EIN KAPITEL AUS DER GESCHICHTE DER ISRAELITISCHEN RELIGION / Valeton, Josue Jean Philippe – (In German. Includes bibliographical references) – Giessen: J Ricker, 1898 – 1mf – 9 – 0-8370-5612-8 – 1985-3612 – us A.T.L.A. [220]

AMOS UND HOSEA: EIN KAPITEL AUS DER GESCHICHTE DER ISRAELITISCHEN RELIGION / Valeton, Jozua J P – Giessen: J. Ricker, 1898. 1 fiche – 9 – us A.T.L.A. [270]

L'AMOUR A PARIS, NOUVEAUX MEMOIRES / Goron, Marie Francois – (v1 L'Amour criminel 371p 4mf; v2 Les Industries de l'Amour 410p 5mf; v3 Les Parias de l'Amour 337p 4mf; v4 Le Marche aux Femmes 306p 4mf) – Paris: Flammarion, 1899. (Les Femmes Collection) – 9 – fr Bibl Nationale [360]

AMOUR A TOUS – Journal de la religion Saint-Simonienne. Toulon, bureau: rue du Pradel, no. 7. Typo. de Canquoin, rue Neuve, no. 1. 20 numeros de 4 pages in-4, du 4 aout 1833 au 15 decembre 1833. Le no. 12 manque, pagination continue: 80 p. Les Saint-Simoniens, 1825-1834. 6941 – 9 – fr Hachette [073]

L'AMOUR ET LA GUERRE / Perret, Paul – Paris: Ollendorff, 1892. viii,313p. (Les Femmes Collection) – 4mf – 9 – $10.00 – fr Bibl Nationale [306]

Amour, Jean d' *see* REMARQUES ET SUGGESTIONS SUR LA REORGANISATION DES TRIBUNAUX: ET AMENDEMENTS PROPOSES AU CODE DE PROCEDURE CIVILE

L'AMOUR, LE MARIAGE, LA JUSTICE SELON LE KORAN / Bachir, Ali – Paris: Nilsson, 1914. 122p. (Les Femmes Collection) – 2mf – 9 – $6.00 – fr Bibl Nationale [270]

L'AMOUR SALTINBANQUE / Campra, A – Paris: Ballard, 1710 – 1 – us Sibley [780]

AMOURS CONGOLAISES / Raulin, G de [pseud] – Paris: A Michel, 1881 – 1 – us Res Libr [360]

AMOURS ET AVENTURES DE CASANOVA / Casanova di Seingalt, Giacomo G – Paris: Simon, 1890-91. 10v. (Les Femmes Collection) – 30mf – 9 – $74.00 – fr Bibl Nationale [920]

Amouzou-Medina, M *see* DEVELOPPEMENT DU CHONDROCRANE ET DES VAISSEAUX SANGUINS CEPHALIQUES CHEZ LE BROCHET, ESOX LUCIUS L

AMPELIS / Thunberg, C P – Uppsala. 1823. B-1336 2 – 8 – ne IDC [580]

AMPERA : MADJALAH BULANAN PERUSAHAAN DAERAH SUMATRA UTARA – (Monthly) – Medan. v1(1-2). 1967 – 2mf – 9 – SE-1312/1 – ne IDC [950]

AMPHILOCHIUS VON IKONIUM : IN SEINEM VERHAELTNIS ZU DEN GROSSEN KAPPADOZIERN / Holl, Karl – Tuebingen: J.C.B. Mohr, 1904 – 1mf – us A.T.L.A. [240]

THE AMPHION – v1-11. 1874-85 – 1 – 625.00 – us Opus [073]

AMPHIOXUS AND ASCIDIAN: OUR GELATINOUS ANCESTORS: HOW THE MISSING LINKS WERE DISCOVERED AND MADE KNOWN / Agorastes, Phil – Toronto: s.n., 1878. 00778. (Pre-1900 Canadiana) – 9 – cn C.I.H.M. [575]

AMPHITHEATRUM SAPIENTIAE AETERNAE, SOLIUS, VERAE / Khunrath, Heinrich – Hamburg?, 1595? – 1 – us U.W. Library [190]

AMPHITRYON : EIN LUSTSPIEL NACH MOLIERE / Kleist, Heinrich von – [Wien]: Phaidon Verlag, 1924 – 1 – us U.W. Library [820]

AMPHITRYON / Purcell, Henry – Libretto and music. 1690-91 – 2 – us Sibley [780]

AMPHON ANGELICUS. A WORK OF MANY COMPOSITIONS FOR ONE, TWO, THREE AND FOUR VOICES: WITH SEVERAL ACCOMPAGNEMENTS OF INSTRUMENTAL MUSICK; AND A THOROW-BASS TO EACH SONG; FIGUR'D FOR AN ORGAN, HARPSICHORD, OR THEORBOE-LUTE... / Blow, John – London: Printed by W Pearson for the author, 1700 – 1 – us Sibley [780]

Amphoux, Henri *see*
- ESSAI SUR LA DOCTRINE SOCINIENNE
- ESSAI SUR L'HISTOIRE DU PROTESTANTISME AU HAVRE ET DANS SES ENVIRONS
- MICHEL DE L'HOPITAL ET LA LIBERTE DE CONSCIENCE AU XVIE SIECLE

AMPLA DIMOSTRAZIONE DEGLI ARMONIALI MUSICALE.. / Calegari, Francesco A – Manuscript copy believed to be in the hand of G. S. Mayr of Bergamo. 1732 – 9 – us Sibley [780]

AMPLE DISCOVRS, ET ADVIS DE L'ESTAT ET ASSIETTE DES ARMEES CHRESTIENNES ET TURQUESQUES: ... – Paris, 1572 – 1mf – 9 – H-8188/1 – ne IDC [956]

AMPLIACION DE LOS DERECHOS DE LAS REPUBLICAS DE LA UNION SOVIETICA – [Mexico: Publicados po la Embajada de la Union de Republicas Sovieticas Socialistas, 1944] – 1 – CSUX91-B269 – us Hoover Inst Photo [320]

AMPLIACIONES...HISTORIA DE MERIDA DE MORENO...FERNANDEZ / Plano y Garcia, Pedro – 1894 – 9 – 1.50f – sp Bibl Santa Ana [946]

AMRITA BAZAR PATRIKA – Calcutta, India. 1962-95 – 147r – 1 – us L of C Photodup [072]

Amrullah, Abdul Malik Karim *see*
- 1001 SOAL-SOAL HIDUP
- DARI PERBENDAHARAAN LAMA
- DIDJEMPUT MAMAKNJA
- ISLAM DAN DEMOKRASI
- ISLAM DI SOEMATERA. OLEH HAMKA
- LEMBAGA HIDUP
- MERDEKA
- "MERDEKA."SE-11,743/1. 1945
- PENUNTUN DJIWA
- REVOLUSI AGAMA

AMSBLATT – German Baptist, 1914-45. 142p – 1 – 5.00 – us Baptist [240]

Amsdorff, N von *see*
- ANTWORT, GLAUB VND BEKENTNIS AUFF DAS SCHOENE VND LIEBLICHE INTERIM
- BEKENTNIS VNTERRICHT VND VERMANUNG DER PFARRHERN VND PREDIGER DER CHRISTLICHEN KIRCHEN ZU MAGDEBURGK
- CONFESSIO ET APOLOGIA PASTORUM...
- DAS DOCTOR MARTINUS KEIN ADIAPHORIST GEWESEN I..
- DAS DOCTOR POMER VND DOCTOR MAIOR MIT IREN ADIAPHORISTEN ERGERNIS VNND ZURTRENNUNG ANGERICHT VNND DEN KIRCHEN CHRISTI VNUEBERWINTLICHEN SCHADEN GETHAN HABEN
- EIN KURTZER VNTERRICHT AUFF D. GEORGEN MAIORS ANTWORT...
- DAS DIE PROPOSITIO "GUTE WERCK SIND ZUR SELIGKEIT SCHEDLICH" EIN RECHTE WARE CHRISTLICHE PROPOSITION SEY...

Amse, Corina *see*
- BIBLIOGRAPHIE DER ARBEITEN VON PROF. DR. HELMUT BREUER UND DR. MARIA WEUFFEN, SOWIE ANDERER MITGLIEDER DER FORSCHUNGSGRUPPE "PROPHYLAKTISCHE DIAGNOSTIK" AN DER ERNST-MORITZ-ARNDT UNIVERSITAET GREIFSWALD
- KOEDUKTION ODER MAEDCHENBILDUNG?

AMSERAU *see* YR AMSERAU

AMSTERDAM NEWS – New York. N.Y. 1962- – 1 – us UMI [071]

AMSTERODAMUM MONOGRAMMON / Plemp, CG – (Contains: Quisequiliae. Seu elegiarum liber unus. Emblemata quinquaginta) – Amsterdam, 1616 – 2mf – 9 – ne IDC [700]

AMT EVENTS – (Cont in pt: Journal of the American Medical Technologists n8705) – Park Ridge. v1-5 jan 1984-dec 1988*; v6-8 jan 1989-dec 1991; v9-11 jan 1992-oct 1994*; v12 1995; v13 1996; v14 1997+ – 1 – inquire – D13914 – us UMI [073]

AMT EVENTS *see* JOURNAL OF THE AMERICAN MEDICAL TECHNOLOGISTS

AMT UND GEMEINDE – 1961-89 (complete) – 3r – 1 – ATLA S0679 – us A.T.L.A. [073]

AMTLICHE BEKANNTMACHUNGEN – (Cont by: Amtliche Bekanntmachungen fuer die Stadt Altena, Aemter Luedenscheid, Nachrodt und Neuenrade, oct 31 1947. Amtliche Bekanntmachungen fuer den Kreis Altena, nov 20 1948) – Altena, aug 25 1945-oct 26 1949 – 1 – Dist. gw Mikrofilm – gw Misc Inst [350]

AMTLICHE BEKANNTMACHUNGEN DER STADT FRIEDBERG – Friedberg. apr 3, 1945-jul 23, 1949 – 1 – gw Mikrofilm [350]

AMTLICHE BEKANNTMACHUNGEN FUER DEN KREIS ALTENA *see* AMTLICHE BEKANNTMACHUNGEN

AMTLICHE BEKANNTMACHUNGEN FUER DIE STADT ALTENA, AEMTER LUEDENSCHEID, NACHRODT UND NEUENRADE *see* AMTLICHE BEKANNTMACHUNGEN

AMTLICHE MITTEILUNGEN – (Cont: Heimatnachrichten aus dem Kreis Altoetting, -jul 3 1945) – Burghausen, jun 30 1945-aug 27 1949 – 1 – Inquire at Mikrofilmarchiv for details – gw Misc Inst [943]

AMTLICHE NACHRICHTEN / Austria. (Lower) – Vienna. 1959-1966 – 1 – us NY Public [324]

AMTLICHER BERICHT UEBER DIE 50. VERSAMMLUNG DEUTSCHER NATURFORSCHER UND AERZTE / Engler, A – Muenchen, 1877 – 5mf – 9 – 8837/1 – ne IDC [920]

AMTLICHES KREISBLATT FUER DEN KREIS WOLMIRSTEDT – Wolmirstedt, Germany. 1870-79 – 1 – gw Mikrofilm [073]

AMTLICHES KURSBLATT DER WIENER BOERSE – Vienna, 15 Nov 1948-Oct 1968 – 24r – 1 – uk British Libr Newspaper [072]

AMTLICHES NACHRICHTENBLATT FUER DEN KREIS ALTENA – (Cont by: Altenaer Kreisblatt. Amtliches Nachrichtenblatt, jul 7 1945) – Altena, jul 1-aug 18 1945 – 1 – Dist. gw Mikrofilm – gw Misc Inst [350]

AMTLICHES VERORDNUNGS- UND ANZEIGENBLATT FUER DEN KREIS ROTENBURG IN HANNOVER *see* ROTENBURGER ANZEIGER

AMTS- UND ANZEIGEBLATT DER STADT BURGHAUSEN – Burghausen, jan 10-dec 29 1920 – 1 – Inquire at Mikrofilmarchiv for details – gw Misc Inst [943]

AMTS- UND INTELLIGENZBLATT FUER DAS OBERAMT BALINGEN *see* DER VOLKSFREUND

AMTS- UND INTELLIGENZBLATT FUER DEN OBERAMTSBEZIRK BIBERACH *see* ANZEIGER VOM OBERLAND

DAS AMTSBLATT – (German language newspaper produced in Rabaul) – v1-6. Jan 1909-June 15 1914 – 1r – 1 – PMB Doc402 – at Pacific Mss [072]

AMTSBLATT DER KOENIGLICHEN REGIERUNG ZU ALLENSTEIN – Allenstein, 1913 – 1 – Dist. gw Mikrofilm – gw Misc Inst [350]

AMTSBLATT DER KOENIGLICHEN REGIERUNG ZU DANZIG / Danzig. Regierungsbezirk – Danzig. 1868-1918. (Scattered issues wanting) – 1 – 646.00 – us L of C Photodup [943]

AMTSBLATT DER KOENIGLICHEN REGIERUNG ZU WIESBADEN / Wiesbaden. Regierungsbezirk – Wiesbaden. 1869-1928 – 1 – 437.00 – us L of C Photodup [943]

AMTSBLATT DER KOENIGLICHEN REGIERUNG ZUR ALLENSTEIN – Allenstein (Olsztyn), Poland. 1913 – 1 – gw Mikrofilm [943]

AMTSBLATT DER PREUSSISCHEN REGIERUNG ZU KOENIGSBERG / Koenigsberg. Regierungsbezirk – v. 55-126. Koenigsberg. 1865-1936. (Wanting scattered issues) – 1 – 101.00 – us L of C Photodup [943]

AMTSBLATT DER REGIERUNG ZU COELN / Cologne. Regierungsbezirk – Coeln. 1874-1943. (Scattered issues wanting) – 1 – 231.00 – us L of C Photodup [943]

AMTSBLATT DER REGIERUNG ZU SCHLESWIG / Schleswig. Regierungsbezirk – Schleswig. 1869-1943. (Wanting 1870, no. 1-5, 7, 11-12, 44; 1917, no. 24; 1941) – 1 – 589.00 – us L of C Photodup [943]

AMTSBLATT DER STADT STUTTGART – June 1, 1945-1968- – 1 – us NY Public [324]

AMTSBLATT DES KANTONS AARGAU – (Switzerland, Aargau), 1958-67 – 3r – 1 – us Ross [324]

AMTSBLATT DES KOENIGLICHEN BEZIRKSAMTES ALTOETTING UND DER KOENIGLICHEN LANDGERICHTE ALTOETTING UND BURGHAUSEN *see* OETTINGER UND BURGHAUSER ANZEIGER

AMTSBLATT DES REGIERUNGSPRAESIDENTEN IN HOHENSALZA – Hohensalza (Inowroclaw), Poland.1940-41 – 1 – gw Mikrofilm [943]

AMTSBLATT DES REICHSKOMMISSARS FUER DIE BESETZEN RHEINISCHEN GEBIETE – Koblenz, Germany. 1920-No.15, 1923 – 1r – 1 – gw Mikrofilm [073]

AMTSBLATT DES REICHSKOMMISSARS FUER DIE BESETZTEN RHEINISCHEN GEBIETE – Koblenz, 1920-23 no 15 – 1r – 1 – DM75.00 – gw Mikro Press [072]

AMTSBLATT DES SAARLANDES / Saarland – Saarbrucken. Dec 1947-1969- – 1 – us NY Public [324]

DER AMTSBOTE AM INN, AN DER ROTT UND SALZACH *see* OETTINGER UND BURGHAUSER ANZEIGER

AMULET – 1826-36 – 35mf – 9 – £295.00 – uk Chadwyck [800]

L'AMULETTE / Meyer, Conrad Ferdinand – Geneve: H Robert, 1898 – 1r – 1 – us U.W. Library [830]

Amunategui Solar, Domingo *see*
- LAS ENCOMIENDAS DE INDIJENAS EN CHILE...
- FORMACION DE LA NACIONALIDADCCHILENA. SANTIAGO DE CHILE, 1943
- HISTORIA SOCIAL DE CHILE

Amundsen, R *see* NORDVESTPASSAGEN

AMUR – Irkutsk. 1860-62. Lacking: (37, 40, 47) 1860; (59-60, 71-72) 1861. BR-1509 2 – 8 – ne IDC [073]

AMURSKAI A GAZETA : POLITICHESKI I, OBSHCHESTVENNY I I LITERATURNY I ORGAN – (Library has: Jan. 1, 3-4, June 16, 1902; 1 page of no. 35[1905?]) – Blagovi eshchensk: "Amurskai a gazeta", 1895-1906. 1v – 1 – CSUX87-S191 – us Hoover Inst Photo [320]

AMUS NEWSLETTER / Alpha Micro Users Society – (Cont by: AMUS.log) – Boulder, 1985* – 1 – D22431 – us UMI [073]

AMUSEMENT PHILOSOPHIQUE SUR LE LANGAGE DES BESTES / Bougeant, Le P G H – 1739 – 9 – fr I.C.S. [190]

AMUSEMENT PHILOSOPHIQUE SUR LE LANGAGE DES BETES / Bougeant, R PG H – (Linguistics series). 1739 – 9 – fr Hachette [400]

AMUSEMENTS IN THE POTTERIES – Stoke-on-Trent, England. 31 Oct 1910-4 Sep 1911 – 55ft – 1 – uk British Libr Newspaper [072]

AMUS.LOG – (Cont: Alpha Micro Users Society – AMUS Newsletter) – Boulder, aug 1985-94* 1; 1995-97+ 1,5,9 – 1,5,9 – D2243.01 – us UMI [073]

AMUS.LOG *see* AMUS NEWSLETTER

Amyot, Charles Jean Baptiste *see* HISTOIRE NATURELLE DES INSECTES, HEMIPTERES

Amyot, Guillaume *see*
- ADDRESSE A MM. LES ELECTEURS DU COMTE DE LOTBINIERE: SUIVIE DE DIVERS DOCUMENTS
- DEUXIEME LETTRE AUX ELECTEURS DU COMTE DE LOTBINIERE
- DISCOURS PRONONCE PAR M.G. AMYOT, DEPUTE DE BELLECHASSE AUX COMMUNES DU CANADA: EN REPONSE A CELUI DE DR. RINFRET...LE 3 AVRIL 1883..
- LA PROTECTION AU CANADA: CONFERENCE LE 14 MARS 1895 AUX SALLES DU CLUB CARTIER-MACDONALD

Amyot, Michel *see* BIBLIOGRAPHIE ANALYTIQUE DE L'ILEAUX-COUDRES

AN DEN CHRISTLICHEN ADEL DEUTSCHER NATION VON DES CHRISTLICHEN STANDES BESSERUNG / Luther, Martin – Halle: Verein fuer Reformationsgeschichte, 1884. ([Schriften des Vereins fuer Reformationsgeschichte; Bd.4]) – 1mf – us A.T.L.A. [943]

AN DEN FRUHLING, OP. 43, NO. 6 / Grieg, E & LeMare, E H – (Arranged for organ) – [19–] – 1 – us Sibley [780]

L'AN DEUX MILLE QUATRE CENT QUARANTE, REVE S'IL EN FUT JAMAIS, SUIVI DE L'HOMME DE FER, SONGE / Mercier, Louis-Sebastien – (Utopias in the Enlightenment series). 1786 – 9 – fr Hachette [830]

AN DIE SOUVERAINE DER RHEINISCHEN KONFOEDERATION / Frey, F A – Bamberg, Wuerzburg, 1813 – 1mf – DM48.00 – 3-8267-3024-0 – gw Hänsel [240]

AN EINEN JUENGLING IM FELDE : DREI BRIEFE / Johannsen, Christa – Leipzig: P List, c1943 – 1r – 1 – us U.W. Library [830]

AN HA NHU'T BAO – puis An ha bao. Cantho. 20 sept 1917-16 nov 1933 – 1 – fr A.C.R.P.P. [073]

AN NAM TAP CHI – no. 1-48. 1er juil 1926-1er juin 1931; N.S., no. 1-9. 16 janv 1932-1er mars 1933 – 1 – fr A.C.R.P.P. [073]

An, Todjin *see* PEDANG KILAT DARI GUNUNG THIAN SAN;..

ANA DE JESUS Y LA HERENCIA TERESIANA... ROMA, 1968 / Moriones, Ildefonso – Madrid: Graf. Calleja, 1968 – 1 – sp Bibl Santa Ana [946]

ANA IN ACTION – American Nurses' Association. v1-3. 1969-71 – 1 – us UMI [073]

ANABAPTISM : FROM ITS RISE AT ZWICKAU TO ITS FALL AT MUENSTER 1521-36 / Heath, Richard – (Includes bibliographies) – London: Alexander and Shepheard, 1895 – 1mf – 9 – 0-8370-8908-5 – 1986-2908 – us A.T.L.A. [240]

ANABAPTISM FROM ITS RISE AT ZWICKAU TO ITS FALL AT MUNSTER / Heath, Richard – 1521-36 – 1 – 7.84 – us Baptist [240]

ANABAPTISMUS. CONTRA REBAPTIZANTES. CONFUTATIO EORUM QUAE LUTHERUS SCRIPSIT IN REBAPTIZANTES / Arnold de Vsingen, B – Coloniae, Joh. Gymnicus. 1529. BME-97 1 – 9 – ne IDC [240]

ANABAPTISTICAE HAERESEOS CONFVTATIO, ET VERE CHRISTIANI BAPTISMI / Duncanus, M – Antverpiae, J. Grauius. 1549. BME-193 1 – 9 – ne IDC [240]

ANABAPTISTICUM ET ENTHUSIASTICUM PANTHEON GEISTLICHES RUST-HAUSS WIDER DIE ALTEN QUACKER – 1702. Zurich. Switzerland – 1 – 28.00 – us Baptist [240]

ANABASEARUM REVISIO / Bunge, A A von – (Mem. Ac. Imp. Sc. Spb.). S. 7. v. 4. 1862. B-46 2 – 8 – ne IDC [580]

ANABOLIC STEROIDS : KNOWLEDGE, ATTITUDE, AND BEHAVIOR IN COLLEGE AGE STUDENTS / Munro, R – 1991 – 2mf – 9 – $8.00 – us Microform Publ [150]
ANACALYPSIS : AN ATTEMPT TO DRAW ASIDE THE VEIL OF THE SAITIC ISIS, OR, AN INQUIRY INTO THE ORIGINS OF LANGUAGES, NATIONS, AND RELIGIONS / Higgins, Godfrey – London: Longman, Rees, Orme etc, 1836 – 1 – us Res Libr [290]
Anacker, Heinrich *see*
- DER AUFBAU
- EINKEHR
- DIE FANFARE
- LIEDER AUS STILLE UND STUERMEN
- DIE TROMMEL
- UEBER DIE MAAS, UEBER SCHELDE UND RHEIN!
- EIN VOLK – EIN REICH – EIN FUEHRER!
- WIR WACHSEN IN DAS REICH HINEIN

ANACONDA STANDARD – Anaconda, Mont. 1889-1928 – 1 – us UMI [071]
ANADOLU – Izmir, 1912-1928 – 9 – $20.00 – us MEDOC [956]
ANADOLU TIB MECMUASI – Ankara: Yeni Guen Matbaasi, 1921-1922 – 9 – $20.00 – us MEDOC [956]
ANADOLU'DA KALEM – Ankara, 1921 – 9 – $20.00 – us MEDOC [956]
ANADOLU'DA ORTODOKSLUK SADASI – Kayseri, 1922-1923 – 9 – $20.00 – us MEDOC [956]
ANADOLU'DA PEYAM-I SABAH – Ankara: Yeniguen Matbaasi, OEgud Matbaasi, 1920-1922 – 9 – $20.00 – us MEDOC [956]
ANADOLU'DA TANIN / Serif, Ahmet – Istanbul: Tanin Matbaasi, 1325 [1909] – $45.00 – us MEDOC [956]
DER ANAESTHESIST – v. 1-29. 1952-80 – 1,5,9 – 2936.00 – us UMI [617]
ANAFOR – Istanbul: Ahmediye Matbaasi, 1918-?; Sahib-i Imtiyaz: Kemal Ibrahim, No 1. – 5 Kanunievvel 1334 [1918] – 1mf – 9 – $12.00 – us MEDOC [949]
ANAHEIM CITY DIRECTORIES – Orange Co, CA. 1908; 1913-1917; 1926-1927 – 5r – 1 – $250.00 – D068 – us Library Micro [910]
ANAHEIM HILLS NEWS – Anaheim Hills, CA. 1992 – 10+ r – 1 – $500.00 ($250.00y) – R04004 – us Library Micro [071]
ANAHEIM INDEPENDENT – Anaheim, CA. 1980 – 1r – 1 – $50.00 – R04000 – us Library Micro [071]
ANAHEIM NEWS PROGRESS – Anaheim, CA. 1963 – 1r – 1 – $50.00 – R04001 – us Library Micro [071]
ANALECTA AD FLORAM CAPENSEM / Schrader, H A – I. Cyperaceae. Goettingae. 1832. B-5160 2 – 8 – ne IDC [580]
ANALECTA ALGOLOGICA / Agardh, J G – Lund. 1892-99. B-5217 2 – 8 – ne IDC [580]
ANALECTA ANTE-NICAENA / Bunsen, Christian Charles Josias – London: Longman, Brown, Green, and Longmans, 1854. (Christianity and mankind. Philological section / by Christian Charles Josias Bunsen; v5-7) – 4mf – us A.T.L.A. [240]
ANALECTA AUGUSTINIANA – 1(1905) – 23(1954) – 247mf – 8 – Dfl3.50ea – ne Slangenburg [240]
ANALECTA AUGUSTINIANA DIVO PARENTI AUGUSTINO DICATA – Rome. v1-23. 1905-1954 – 247mf – 9 – ne IDC [240]
ANALECTA BOLLANDIANA – 1(1882)-60(1940) – 568mf – 9 – Dfl1,700.00 – ne Slangenburg [073]
ANALECTA BOLLANDIANA – Brussels. v1-60. 1882-1940 – 568mf – 9 – ne IDC [240]
ANALECTA BOTANICA / Schott, H W & Nyman, CF & Kotschy, T – Vindobonae. 1854. B-699 2 – 8 – ne IDC [580]
ANALECTA ENTOMOLOGICA / Schaum, H R – Halis Saxonum, 1841. iv,49p. 1 pl. Z-1599/2 – 8 – ne IDC [590]
ANALECTA HIEROSOLYMITIKES STACHYOLOGIAS / Papadopoulos-Kerameoos, A – St. Petersburg. Tomus 1-5. 1891-1898 – 72mf – 8 – ne Slangenburg [240]
ANALECTA HYMNICA MEDII AEVI / Dreves, G M & -Blume, J – Leipzig. v1-55. 1886-1922 – 265mf – 9 – Dfl928.00 – ne Slangenburg [240]
ANALECTA MONUMENTORUM OMNIS AEVI VINDOBONENSIA / Kollarius, AF – Vindobonae. Tom 1-2. 1761-1762 – Dfl228.00 – ne Slangenburg [240]
ANALECTA NOVISSIMA SPICILEGIO SOLESMENSI PARATA / Pitra, J -B – (Tomus 1 21mf. Tomus 2 18mf) – Tusculi, 1885-1888 – 9 – ne Slangenburg [240]
ANALECTA ORNITHOLOGICA / Nilsson, S – Z-1872 2. 1814 – 8 – ne IDC [590]
ANALECTA PRAEMONSTRATENSIA – Tongerloo. v1-21. 1925-1945 – 162mf – 9 – ne IDC [240]
ANALECTA PREMONSTRATENSIA – 1(1925)-21(1945) – 162mf – 9 – Dfl567.00 – ne Slangenburg [073]
ANALECTA PTERIDOGRAPHICA / Kunze, G – Lipsiae. 1837. B-7209 1 – 9 – ne IDC [580]
ANALECTA SACRA SPICILEGIO SOLESMENSI PARATA / Pitra, J B – Monte Casino. Tomus 3. Sanctae Hildegardis Opera. 1882 – 21mf – 8 – ne Slangenburg [240]
ANALECTA SACRA SPICILEGIO SOLESMENSI PARATA / Pitra, J -B – (Tomus 1 26 mf. Tomus 2 23mf. Tomus 3 21mf. Tomus 4 18mf. Tomus 5 19mf. Tomus 6 17mf) – 1876-1891 – 9 – ne Slangenburg [240]
ANALECTA SACRI ORDINIS FRATRUM PRAEDICATORUM – Rome. v1-10. 1893-1902 – 169mf – 9 – ne IDC [240]
ANALECTA SACRI ORDINIS FRATRUM PRAEDICATORUM : SEU VETERA ORDINIS MONUMENTA RECENTIORAQUE ACTA – 1(1893)-10(1902) – 169mf – 9 – Dfl592.00 – ne Slangenburg [073]
ANALECTA ZUR AELTESTEN GESCHICHTE DES CHRISTENTUMS IN ROM (T.U.U. 2-28/2B) / Harnack, Adolf von – Leipzig, 1905 – 1mf – 9 – ne Slangenburg [240]
ANALECTA ZUR SEPTUAGINTA, HEXAPLA UND PATRISTIK / Klostermann, Erich – 1895 – 1 – us A.T.L.A. [240]
ANALECTES : POUR SERVIR A L'HISTOIRE ECCLES. DE LA BELGIQUE. IE SECTION – (2e section 1(1894)-7(1905) Dfl60.00) – 1(1864)-40(1914) – 9 – Dfl239.00 – ne Slangenburg [073]
ANALECTES DE L'ORDRE DE PREMONTRE – 1(1905)-10(1914) – 56mf – 9 – Dfl196.00 – ne Slangenburg [073]
ANALECTES DE L'ORDRE DE PREMONTRE – Tongerloo. v1-10. 1905-1914 – 56mf – 9 – ne IDC [240]
ANALECTES POUR SERVIR A L'HISTOIRE ECCLESIASTIQUE DE LA BELGIQUE – Louvain. v1-40. 1864-1914; N.S. v1-7., 1894-1905 – 371mf – 9 – ne IDC [240]
ANALEKTA HIEROSOLYMITIKES STACHYOLOGIAS / Papadopoulos-Kerameoos, A – (v1 St Petersburg 1891 15mf. v2 St Petersburg 1894 14mf) – 9 – ne Slangenburg [240]
ANALEKTEN FUER DAS STUDIUM DER EXEGETISCHEN UND SYSTEMATISCHEN THEOLOGIE – Leipzig. Bd 1-4. 1813-1822 – 26mf – 9 – Dfl84.00 – ne Slangenburg [073]
ANALEKTEN ZUR TEXTKRITIK DES ALTEN TESTAMENTS / Perles, Felix – Muenchen: Theodor Ackermann, 1895. 1 fiche – 9 – us A.T.L.A. [240]
ANALES / Colombia. Senado – Bogota. 1903-13 Aug 1945 Session Extraordinary.Incomplete – 1 – us NY Public [972]
ANALES / Sociedad rural Argentina. Buenos Aires – v.1-82. 1866-1948. LC lacks v.10-14, 16, 78 & scattered issues – 1 – 380.00 – us L of C Photodup [630]
ANALES / Venezuela. Universidad Central. Caracas – 1-41. 1900-July 1956 – 1 – 184.00 – us L of C Photodup [025]
ANALES. 1959 / Colegio Oficial de Farmaceuticos. Caceres – Caceres, 1960 – 1 – sp Bibl Santa Ana [615]
ANALES BIOGRAFICAS – Madrid: Tip. Pasejo del Comercio 8, 1914 – 1 – sp Bibl Santa Ana [920]
ANALES DE CIENCIAS NATURALES – Madrid, 1799-1804. v.1-7. & plates – 3 – us Readex [574]
ANALES DE LA LITERATURA ESPANOLA CONTEMPORANEA – v.6-. 1981- – 1,5,6,9 – us UMI [440]
ANALES DE LA NARRATIVA ESPANOLA CONTEMPORANEA – v.4-. 1979- – 1 – us UMI [440]
ANALES DE LA NOVELA DE POSQUERRA – v.1-. 1976- – 1 – us UMI [440]
ANALES DEL MUSEO NACIONAL DE BUENOS AIRES – Buenos Aires: Impr de Juan A Alsina, 1991; ser 3 n5 1905 – 1r – 1 – us Res Libr [060]
ANALES DEL PARAISO / Sanchez Arjona, Vicente – Sevilla: Imprenta Alvarez, Tomo 1-8. 1955, 1956 – 1 – sp Bibl Santa Ana [946]
ANALES ECLESIASTICOS VENEZOLANOS. CARACAS, 1929 / Navarro, Nicolas E – Madrid: Razon y Fe, 1930 – 1 – sp Bibl Santa Ana [240]
ANALES ESTADISTICOS DE LA REPUBLICA DE GUATEMALA 1882-1883, TOMO 1-2 – Guatemala, 1883-1884 – 9mf – 9 – sp Cultura [310]
ANALES MINORUM...TOMUS 32 (1671-1680). ROMA, 1964 / Pandzic, Basilio – Madrid: Graf. Calleja, 1966 – 1 – sp Bibl Santa Ana [946]
ANALES...MEDICINA...Y BIOGRAFICO / Chinchilla, Anastasio – v3. 1848 – 9 – 1.50f – sp Bibl Santa Ana [920]
ANALISI DEL QUARESIMALE DEL PADRE PAOLO SEGNERI / Malmusi, Giuseppe – Torino: Giacinto Marietti, 1879 – 1mf – 9 – 0-8370-6917-3 – 1986-0917 – us A.T.L.A. [240]
ANALISIS – Buenos Aires, Argentina. Dec 1965-Dec 1969 – 16r – 1 – uk British Libr Newspaper [072]
ANALISIS DE LA CONTESTACION DEL DIPUTADO DE PROVINCIA DON ANTONIO CONCHA Y DEL LIBELO INFORMATIVO...D. JOAQUIN RODRIGUEZ LEAL... / Ceresoles, Mauricio – Caceres: Imp. D. Lucas de Burgos, 1839 – 1 – sp Bibl Santa Ana [946]
ANALISIS DE LA CONTESTACION DEL DIPUTADO...D. JOAQUIN RODRIGUEZ LEAL. / Ceresoles, Mauricio – 1839 – 9 – 1.50f – sp Bibl Santa Ana [946]
ANALISIS DE PAISAJE VEGETAL : NORTE DE LA PROVINCIA DE GUADALAJARA / Fidalgo Hijano, Concepcion – 4mf – 9 – Pta2,500.00 – 84-85422-67-8 – sp Pentalfa [630]
ANALIZ OTCHETNOSTI PROMYSLOVYKH I PROMYSLOVO-KREDITNYKH KOOPERATIVOV / Simonovich, Ia.A – M., 1930 – 2mf – 9 – COR-446/1 – ne IDC [334]
ANALOG SCIENCE FACT-SCIENCE FICTION – (1972- . 5,6. 1975- . 9) – v. 66-. 1960- – 1 – us UMI [500]
DIE ANALOGIE VON NATUR UND GEIST ALS STILPRINZIP IN NOVALIS' DICHTUNG / Feng, Chih – (Includes bibliographical references) – Heidelberg: A Lippl, 1935 – 1r – 1 – us U.W. Library [430]
THE ANALOGIES OF BEING AS EMBODIED IN AND UPON THIS ORB : SHEWN TO BE THE ONLY INDUCTIVE BASE OF DIVINE REVELATION... / Wood, Joseph – London:Frederick Farrah, 1867 – 1mf – 9 – 0-8370-5899-6 – 1985-3899 – us A.T.L.A. [210]
THE ANALOGY OF EXISTENCES AND CHRISTIANITY / Wallace, Charles J – London: Hodder & Stoughton, 1892. 1 fiche – 9 – us A.T.L.A. [240]
ANALOGY OF RELIGION NATURAL AND REVEALED / Butler, Joseph – London: J.M. Dent, (19??). 1 fiche – 9 – us A.T.L.A. [240]
THE ANALOGY OF RELIGION NATURAL AND REVEALED / Butler, Joseph – London:J M Dent; New York:E P Dutton, [19–] – 1mf – 9 – 0-8370-2558-3 – 1985-0558 – us A.T.L.A. [210]
ANALYSE BIBLIOGRAPHIQUE DE REVERENDE MERE SAINTE-LOUISE-DE-MARILLAC... / Neiges, Marie-des – 1962. SEM105P4 – 1mf – 9 – cn Bibl Nat [616]
ANALYSE CHRONOLOGIQUE RELATIVE A LA CONCESSION DU 25 FEVRIER 1661, APPELEE LA SEIGNEURIE DE L'ISLE AUX OEUFS / Bouchette, Joseph – Quebec: L'Evenement, 1868. 02533. (Pre-1900 Canadiana) – 9 – cn C.I.H.M. [971]
ANALYSE DE LA GESTION DES COOPERATIVES MAROCAINES AGRICOLES ET SOCIETES COOPERATIVES AGRICOLES MAROCAINES / Morocco. Ministere de l'Agriculture – 12 v. 1957-69. BNE-3063 1 – 9 – ne IDC [630]
ANALYSE DE LA NATURE OU TABLEAU DE L'UNIVERS ET DES CORPS ORGANISES / Rafinesque-Schmaltz, Constantine S – Palerme. 1815. B-8098 1 – 9 – ne IDC [580]
ANALYSE DE LA RELIGION CHRETIENNE / Dumarsais, Cesar-Chesneau – (D'Holbach series) – 9 – fr Hachette [240]
ANALYSE DE L'EVOLUTION DE LA TRADITION CERAMIQUE DE METEPEC, VILLAGE DE L'ETAT DE MEXICO / Duclot, C – 9 – F80.00 – fr Ethnologie [306]
ANALYSE DER FETALEN HERZFREQUENZ MIT METHODEN DER CHAOSTHEORIE / Maris, Bartolomeus – 1994 – 1mf – DM60.00 – 3-8267-2053-9 – gw Hänsel [612]
ANALYSE DER OFFENBARUNG JOHANNIS / Wellhausen, Julius – (Includes bibliographical references) – Berlin: Weidmann, 1907 – 1mf – 9 – 0-8370-5768-X – 1985-3768 – us A.T.L.A. [220]
ANALYSE DES FAMILLES DES PLANTES / Dumortier, B C J – Tournay. 1829. B-5273 2 – 8 – ne IDC [580]
L'ANALYSE DES JUGEMENTS RECENTS – La Malbaie, Canada. 16 dec 1935-v1 n31. 28 dec 1936 – 1r – 1 – Can$35.00 – cn Can Microfilming [072]
ANALYSE DU KANDJOUR : RECUEIL DES LIVRES SACRES AU TIBET / Csoma, Alexandre, de Koros – Paris: E Leroux, 1881 – 1 – us Res Libr [950]
ANALYSE D'UN ENTRETIEN SUR LA CONSERVATION DES ETABLISSEMENS DU BAS-CANADA / Viger, Denis Benjamin – Montreal: J Lane, 1826. SEM16P90 – 1r – 5 – Can$9.00 – cn Bibl Nat [971]
ANALYSE D'UNE NOUVELLE ORNITHOLOGIE ELEMENTAIRE / Vieillot, L J P – 2116 2. 1816 – 8 – ne IDC [590]
ANALYSE QUANTITATIVE DE L'ENCEPHALE DES TELEOSTEENS: CARACTERES EVOLUTIFS ET ADAPTATIFS DE L'ENCEPHALISATION / Ridet, J M – 9 – F130.00 – fr Ethnologie [590]
ANALYSE STYLISTIQUE DE QUELQUES OEUVRES DU PAYS DOGON SUIVIE D'UN ESSAI D'ANALYSE SEMANTIQUE / Jones, F & Michel, P A – 9 – F30.00 – fr Ethnologie [490]
ANALYSES ET CRITIQUES DES OUVRAGES DE M. DE VOLTAIRE / Serpe, C T – Avec plusieurs anecdotes interessantes et peu connues qui le concernent, depuis 1762 jusqu'a sa mort, arrivee en 1778. Kell. 1789 – 9 – fr Hachette [440]
ANALYSES OF ANCIENT GLASSES : 1790-1957 / Caley, Earle R – 1962. 118p. 3 fiche. Fiche no. 973 – 9 – $6.25 – us Corning Mus [740]
ANALYSING AND PROJECTING SCHOOL ENROLLMENT IN DEVELOPING COUNTRIES : A MANUAL OF METHODOLOGY / Thonstad, Tore – 1981 – 112p – 9 – 92-3-101719-5 – fr UNESCO [370]
ANALYSIS – (v39- 1978- 5,6,9) – v1- 1933- – 1 – us UMI [100]
THE ANALYSIS AND DECISION OF SUMMARY JUDGEMENT MOTIONS : A MONOGRAPH ON RULE 56 OF THE FEDERAL RULES OF CIVIL PROCEDURE / Schwarzer, William W et al – Washington: FJC, 1991 – 2mf – 9 – $3.00 – LLMC 95-382 – us L.L.M.C. [340]
AN ANALYSIS AND EVALUATION OF THE COURSES IN ELEMENTARY SCHOOL SUPERVISION OFFERED IN COLLLEGES, NORMAL SCHOOLS AND UNIVERSITIES / Selke, Erich – Minnesota, 1933 – 1mf – DM48.00 – 3-8267-3090-9 – gw Hänsel [370]
ANALYSIS FIDEI CATHOLICAE, HOC EST RATIO METHODICA EAM IN UNIVERSUM FIDEM... / Gregorius de Valencia – Ingolstadii, 1585 – 5mf – 9 – CA-75/1 – ne IDC [240]
ANALYSIS MATHEMATICA – v6- 1980- – 5,6,9 – us UMI [510]
ANALYSIS OF A SOCIAL SITUATION IN MODERN ZULULAND / Gluckman, M – 1 – uk Microform Academic [960]
AN ANALYSIS OF ASSOCIATION BETWEEN RESPIRATION RATE AND FINGER TEMPERATURE IN NORMALS AND RAYNAUD'S SUBJECTS GIVEN THERMAL BIOFEEDBACK / Spalding, Thomas W – 1982 – 3mf – 9 – $12.00 – us Microform Publ [610]
AN ANALYSIS OF BLACKSTONE'S COMMENTARIES ON THE LAWS OF ENGLAND / Bailey, Henry – 1822. 28 fiches – 9 – us South Carolina Historical [340]
ANALYSIS OF BUDGETED EXPENDITURE ON EDUCATION 1980-1981 TO 1982-1983 / India. Department of Education – New Delhi, 1983 – 5mf – 9 – DE-538/1 – ne IDC [370]

AN ANALYSIS OF BUTLER'S ANALOGY OF RELIGION : AND THREE SERMONS ON HUMAN NATURE / Angus, Joseph – London: Religious Tract Society, [1882?] – 1mf – us A.T.L.A. [240]

ANALYSIS OF DECISIONS / New York. State Labor Relations Board – No1-36, 1937-72. 63 fiches. (Harvard Law School Library Collection.) – 9 – $1.50f – us H.U. Law [330]

ANALYSIS OF DOCUMENTARY EVIDENCE / Supreme Commander for the Allied Powers. International Prosecution Section – Tokyo. On film: Doc. 1-3379, 3500-3517, 4001-4097; 1946-48. LL-023 – 1 – us L of C Photodup [340]

THE ANALYSIS OF ENROLLMENT PATTERNS AND STUDENT PROVILE CHARACTERISTICS AT A SMALL RURAL NEW ENGLAND UNIVERSITY 1978-1988 / Holmes, ML – 1990 – 5mf – 9 – $20.00 – us Microform Publ [370]

ANALYSIS OF FOOD CONSUMPTION SURVEY DATA FOR DEVELOPING COUNTRIES – 1980 – 146p – it F.A.O. [640]

ANALYSIS OF FOOTE'S ... / Bellot, Hugh Hale L – London, 1925 – 1mf – 9 – ILM-428/1 – ne IDC [327]

ANALYSIS OF IN-VIVO MENISCAL KINEMATIC MOTION OF THE NON-INJURED KNEE / Porter, Scott T – 1994 – 1mf – $4.00 – us Microform Publ [612]

AN ANALYSIS OF JOHANN LYDWIG KREBS' EIGHT CHORALE PRELUDES FOR ORGAN WITH TRUMPET OR OBOE / Pedde, Dennis R – 1981 – 1 – $5.00 – us Baptist [240]

AN ANALYSIS OF NATIONAL ATHLETIC TRAINING ASSOCIATION ACCREDITED EDUCATION PROGRAM FACILITIES FOR THE ATHLETIC TRAINER / Sabo, James M – 1994 – 5mf – $20.00 – us Microform Publ [370]

AN ANALYSIS OF NEW TESTAMENT HISTORY / Pinnock, William Henry – Cambridge: J. Hall, 1869. 1 fiche – 9 – us A.T.L.A. [240]

ANALYSIS OF REPORTS FILED BY CONSUMER FINANCE AND CONSUMER IN STALLMENT LOAN COMPANIES / Illinois. Consumer Credit Division – 1930-79. 14 fiches. (Harvard Law School Library Collection.) – 9 – $1.50f – us H.U. Law [336]

ANALYSIS OF SCHOOL CERTIFICATE EXAMINATION ACHIEVEMENT OF INPUTS TO SELECTED TERTIARY INSTITUTIONS 1972 / Papua New Guinea. Manpower Planning Unit – Port Moresby, 1972 – 1mf – 9 – DE-232/1 – ne IDC [370]

AN ANALYSIS OF SCRIPTURE HISTORY / Pinnock, William Henry – Cambridge: J. Hall, 1871. 1 fiche – 9 – us A.T.L.A. [240]

AN ANALYSIS OF SELECTED ATTENDANCE FACTORS IN THE WORLD LEAGUE OF AMERICAN FOOTBALL / Bryan, Carlton H Jr. & Billing, John E – 1992 – 1mf – 9 – $4.00 – us Microform Publ [790]

ANALYSIS OF SOURCES OF INFORMATION ON THE POPULATION OF THE NAVAHO / Johnston, Denis Foster – 1966 – 5mf – 9 – $5.00f – us Ross [970]

AN ANALYSIS OF SWIMMING ECONOMY AS ASSESSED BY A COMPARISON BETWEEN VO2 VALUES AND ARM STROKE INDEX / Sharar, Brian D – 1989 – 63p 1mf – 9 – $4.00 – us Microform Publ [612]

AN ANALYSIS OF THE BERNOULLI LIFT EFFECT AS A PROPULSIVE COMPONENT OF SWIMMING STROKES / Ferrell, M D – 1991 – 1mf – 9 – $4.00 – us Microform Publ [790]

ANALYSIS OF THE BOOK OF ISAIAH : PART FIRST. INTRODUCTION / Lord, Eleazar – (No more published) – New York:John A Gray, 1861 – 1mf – 9 – 0-8370-4178-3 – 1985-2178 – us A.T.L.A. [220]

ANALYSIS OF THE BOOK OF ISAIAH: PART FIRST: INTRODUCTION / Lord, Eleazar – New York: John A. Gray, 1861. 1 fiche – 9 – us A.T.L.A. [240]

AN ANALYSIS OF THE BRITISH FERNS AND THEIR ALLIES / Francis, G W – London. 1837. B-7186 2 – 8 – ne IDC [580]

ANALYSIS OF THE DIATOMACEOUS GENUS CAMPYLODISCUS / Deby, J – London. 1891. B-6354 2 – 8 – ne IDC [580]

ANALYSIS OF THE DRAFT COMPACT OF ASSOCIATION : PREPARED FOR THE MEMBERS OF THE MICRONESIAN INDEPENDENCE COMMISSION / Uludong, F T – (Typescript) – n.p, n.d, submitted to the Congress of Micronesia on aug 25, 1972 – 1mf – 9 – $1.50 – LLMC 82-100F, Title 46 – us L.L.M.C. [323]

AN ANALYSIS OF THE GALIC LANGUAGE / Shaw, William – 1778. 192p. (English Linguistics Series 1500-1800) – 9 – us UMI [490]

AN ANALYSIS OF THE HERMENEUTIC OF THE SOUTHERN BAPTIST CONVENTION SERMON IN SELECTED PERIODS OF BIBLICAL CONTROVERSY: 1925, 1963, 1970 / Dortch, John Douglas – 1982 – 1 – 5.92 – us Baptist [240]

ANALYSIS OF THE INSTRUCTIONAL ECOLOGY IN TUTORIAL TENNIS SETTINGS / England, Kathleen M & Tannenhill, Deborah – 1993 – 4mf – $16.00 – us Microform Publ [790]

ANALYSIS OF THE LATE CORRESPONDENCE BETWEEN OUR ADMINISTRATION AND GREAT BRITAIN AND FRANCE – Boston, n.d. – 1mf – 9 – ILM-2831/1 – ne IDC [340]

AN ANALYSIS OF THE LAWS OF ENGLAND : ENGLISH, IRISH AND FRENCH EDITIONS / Blackstone, William – 21mf – 9 – LLMC 82-800 Titles 217-224 – us L.L.M.C. [340]

AN ANALYSIS OF THE MOTIVATIONAL IMPACT OF A HEALTH RISK APPRAISAL AND A COLLEGE HEALTH EDUCATION COURSE UTILIZING A LIFESTYLE THEME ON SELECTED HEALTH BEHAVIORS / Cottrell, Randall R – 1982 – 3mf – 9 – $12.00 – us Microform Publ [790]

ANALYSIS OF THE NATURE OF CAPITAL AND INTEREST / Bilgram, Hugo – 1908. 24p – 9 – 1.00f – at Libertarian Micro [335]

ANALYSIS OF THE POPULATION STATISTICS OF JORDAN / Jordan. Department of Statistics – 1v. 1966. BNE-9765 1 – 9 – ne IDC [310]

AN ANALYSIS OF THE PRINCIPLES OF EQUITY PLEADING. / Lube, Denis George – San Francisco, Bancroft-Whitney, 1886. 283 p. L.C. copy imperfect: p. 3-4, 11-12 wanting. LL-117 – 1 – us L of C Photodup [340]

ANALYSIS OF THE PROPOSED CONSTITUTION OF THE FEDERATED STATES OF MICRONESIA / ed by Political Status Commission of the Marshall Islands – (Draft; unpag) – 1976? – 5mf – 9 – $7.50 – LLMC 82-100F, Title 97 – us L.L.M.C. [323]

ANALYSIS OF THE RESULTS OF THE GENERAL POPULATION CENSUS 1964: TEACHING IN LIBYA / Libya. Ministry of Economy and Trade. Census and Statistical Department – BNE-512 1 – 9 – ne IDC [304]

ANALYSIS OF THE RESULTS OF THE GENERAL POPULATION CENSUS 1964: THE SUPPLY OF LABOUR IN LIBYA / Libya. Ministry of Economy and Commerce. Census and Statistical Department – BNE-514 1 – 9 – ne IDC [304]

ANALYSIS OF THE RESULTS OF THE GENERAL POPULATION CENSUS OF 1964: THE DISABLED CITIZENS IN LIBYA / Libya. Ministry of Economy and Commerce. Census and Statistical Department – BNE-513 1 – 9 – ne IDC [304]

AN ANALYSIS OF THE VALUE OF IMPORTS OF THE KINGDOM OF LIBYA, 1955-1966 / Libya. Ministry of Economy and Trade. Census and Statistical Department – Tripoli. Jul 1967. BNE-609 1 – 9 – ne IDC [380]

AN ANALYSIS OF VISUAL REACTION TIME, DYNAMIC REACTION ACTIVITY, AND DEPTH PERCEPTION OF MALES WEARING COLOR EYE SHIELDS / Wilson, J E – 1991 – 1mf – 9 – $4.00 – us Microform Publ [150]

ANALYSIS OF ZIONISM / Yaari, M – New York. 1936. BJ-28-24 1 – 9 – ne IDC [270]

AN ANALYSIUS OF RELIGIOUS BELIEF / Amberley, John Russell – New York: D. M. Bennett. 1878. 745 p. "From the late London Edition. Complete." includes index. 1 reel – 1 – us U.W. Library [210]

ANALYST – (1976- . 5,6,9) – v. 1-. 1877- – 1 – us UMI [540]

ANALYST – v1-80. 1876-1955 – 1,5,6 – us Princeton Micro [540]

THE ANALYST: A QUARTERLY JOURNAL OF SCIENCE, LITERATURE, NATURAL HISTORY, AND THE FINE ARTS – London, 1834 – 3 – us Readex [500]

ANALYTIC PSYCHOLOGY / Stout, George Frederick – London: S. Sonnenschein; New York: Macmillan, 1896. 2v – 1 – us U.W. Library [150]

ANALYTICA CHIMICA ACTA – v1-166. 1947-84 – 1,5,6,13 – sz Elsevier [073]

ANALYTICA CHIMICA ACTA *see* VIBRATIONAL SPECTROSCOPY

ANALYTICAL ABSTRACTS – (1976- . 5,6,9) – v. 1-. 1954- – 1 – us UMI [540]

ANALYTICAL ABSTRACTS – Royal Society of Chemistry, Great Britain. 1956-84 (1956-68, 35mm only). Available to current subscribers to the equivalent printed editions – 1 – us UMI [073]

ANALYTICAL ABSTRACTS – v.1-27. 1954-74 – 1,5,6 – 22300.00 – us Princeton Micro [540]

ANALYTICAL AND QUANTITATIVE CYTOLOGY – (1983-. 1,5,6,9) – v1-. 1979- – 1 – us UMI [073]

ANALYTICAL AND QUANTITATIVE CYTOLOGY – v1-8. 1979-86 – 1,5,6 – us Princeton Micro [574]

ANALYTICAL CHEMISTRY – v1- 1929- – 1,5,6,9 – us A.C.S. [540]

ANALYTICAL DRAWINGS OF AUSTRALIAN MOSSES / Mueller, Ferdinand Jakob Heinrich von – Fasc. 1. Melbourne. 1864. B-8041 1 – 9 – ne IDC [580]

AN ANALYTICAL HISTORY OF THE PATENT POLICY OF THE DEPARTMENT OF HEALTH, EDUCATION, AND WELFARE / U.S. Department of Health, Education and Welfare – Washington, Govt. Print. Off., 1961. 93 p. LL-2306 – 1 – us L of C Photodup [340]

ANALYTICAL INDEX AND LIST OF PUBLICATIONS / Virginia. Agricultural Experiment Station. Blacksburg – 1888-1938. 2 fiches – 9 – us Spaulding [630]

ANALYTICAL INDEX TO THE CIVIL CODE OF LOWER CANADA – Ottawa: G E Desbarats, 1867. SEM105P432 – 2mf – 9 – Can$4.50 – cn Bibl Nat [340]

ANALYTICAL INSTRUMENTATION – v13-. 1984- – 1,5,6,9 – us UMI [073]

ANALYTICAL LETTERS – (1984-. 5,6,9) – Oct 1967- – 1 – us UMI [073]

ANALYTICAL PROCEEDINGS – Royal Society of Chemistry, Great Britain. 1964-84 (1964-68, 35mm only). Available to current subscribers to the equivalent printed editions – 1 – us UMI [073]

ANALYTICAL PROCEEDINGS – v17-. 1980- – 1,5,6,9 – us UMI [073]

AN ANALYTICAL SYNOPSIS OF THE CRIMINAL CODE OF THE CANADA EVIDENCE ACT / Crankshaw, James – Montreal: Theoret, 1899. 00096. (Pre-1900 Canadiana) – 9 – cn C.I.H.M. [971]

ANALYZED NEW YORK DECISIONS AND CITATIONS, 1914-1917, COVERING DUPLICATE REPORTS / Kreidler, Charles Ray – Rochester, Williamson Law Book Co., 1916. 832 p. LL-269 – 1 – us L of C Photodup [340]

ANALYZING THE PRIVATE CONTRIBUTIONS AMONG COLLEGIATE LETTERWINNERS / Yablunosky, Matthew S – University of North Carolina at Chapel Hill, 1995 – 1mf – 9 – $4.00 – PE3625 – us Microform Publ [790]

ANAMNESIS SIVE COMMEMORATIO / Tamayo de Salazar, Juan – (v5, 1658. v6, 1659) – v1-2. 1651. v3, 1655 – 9 – 1.50f – sp Bibl Santa Ana [946]

ANANASY V SHAMPANSKOM. POEZY / Severianin, I – M. 1915. BR-1024 2 – 8 – ne IDC [460]

ANANDA – A handy guide for Java, Madura and Bali. SE-3529 1. 1962 – 9 – ne IDC [950]

ANANDA BAZAR PATRIKA – Calcutta, India. Apr 1944-85 – 201r – 1 – us L of C Photodup [072]

ANANLES DE TAJO LISBOA / Coronado, Carolina – Lisboa, 1875. 8p – 1 – us U.W. Library [946]

Ananov, I N *see* OCHERKI FEDERAL'NOGO UPRAVLENIIA SSSR

Anantha Krishna Iyer, L K *see* THE MYSORE TRIBES AND CASTES.

ANAP / Asociacion nacional de Agricultores pequenos. Havana – v1, no.1-v3, no.12. Jan 1961-63. Missing: v2, no.2, Feb 1962; v3, no. 9, Sept 1963 – 1 – 35.00r – us Hoover Inst Photo [630]

THE ANAPHORA OR GREAT EUCHARISTIC PRAYER / Frere, Walter H – London, 1938 – 4mf – 8 – Dfl19.00 – ne Slangenburg [240]

THE ANAPHORAS OF THE ETHIOPIC LITURGY / Harden, J M – London, 1928 – 3mf – 8 – Dfl13.00 – ne Slangenburg [960]

ANAPLASIS – Athens, 15 May 1922-25 Mar 1937 – 7r – 1 – uk British Libr Newspaper [072]

L'ANARCHIA – New York, NY, 1918 – 2mf or 1r – 1,9 – us I.H.R.C. [978]

L'ANARCHICO – New York, NY, 1888 – 2mf or 1r – 1,9 – us I.H.R.C. [978]

L'ANARCHIE – no. 1-484. Paris. 13 avr 1905-16, juil 1914. mq no. 204, 272, 275, 291, 295, 307, 339, 373, 376, 387, 390, 402, 407, 413, 415-469, 475, 482 – 1 – fr A.C.R.P.P. [073]

DIE ANARCHIE / Reclus, Elisee – 1fiche (29x) – 9 – 1.00f – at Libertarian Micro [320]

L'ANARCHIE MEDICINALE OU LA MEDECINE CONSIDEREE COMME NUISIBLE A LA SOCIETE / Gilibert, Jean Emmanuel – Neuchatel, 1772.3v. 14 fiches. (Statistics Series: Medical Studies) – 9 – 35.00 – fr Bibl Nationale [310]

ANARCHISM / Eltzbacher, Paul – 1900. 253p. 1 fiche (24x) – 9 – 1.00f – at Libertarian Micro [320]

ANARCHISM / Zenker, E V – 1898. 279p. 1 fiche (24x) – 9 – 1.00f – at Libertarian Micro [320]

ANARCHISM AND CRIME / Zube, John – An open letter. 1 fiche (29x) – 9 – 1.00f – at Libertarian Micro [320]

ANARCHISM AND LEGAL RULES / Descallar, R – 1980. 11p – 9 – 1.00f – at Libertarian Micro [335]

DER ANARCHISMUS / Eltzbacher, Paul – 1900, 305p – 9 – 1.00f – at Libertarian Micro [335]

ANARCHISMUS UND PAEDAGOGIK / Baumann, Herbert – 6p – 9 – 1.00f – at Libertarian Micro [335]

DER ANARCHIST – Berlin: Verlag & Red des "Anarchist". v1-5 n7. mar 1903-oct 1907 – 1 – us Res Libr [073]

DER ANARCHIST : ORGAN ZUR PROPAGANDA DES ANARCHISMUS UND SOZIALISMUS – (Literarisches Beiblatt: v5 n5 apr 1913) – Leipzig. v1-3. oct 2 1909-dec 1911 – 1 – us Res Libr [335]

THE ANARCHIST – Glasgow, Scotland. -w. 3 May 1912-17 Jan 1913. 26 ft – 1 – uk British Libr Newspaper [072]

ANARCHIST COMMUNIST ALLIANCE – An anarchist manifesto. London: Metropolitan Printing Works, 1895. 15p – 1 – us U.W. Library [335]

ANARCHIST PAMPHLETS, 1830-1985 – (With free printed list of titles) – Labadie Collection, University of Michigan and the Library of Congress – 2,601mf – £8,930.00 – uk Chadwyck [977]

THE ANARCHIST PRESS IN BRITAIN – Freedom Press, 1928-76 – 1 – us Primary [320]

THE ANARCHISTS / MacKay, John Henry – Also: Proudhon and his bank of the people by Charles A. Dana. 4 fiches – 9 – 1.00f – at Libertarian Micro [320]

ANARCHISTS, ANARCHISM AND OTHER IMPEDIMENTS TO ANARCHY / Black, Bob – 1935. 2p – 9 – 1.00f – at Libertarian Micro [335]

ANARCHISTS IN FILMS / Ferrua, Pietro – 1980 – 9 – 1.00f – at Libertarian Micro [335]

ANARCHISTS SEEN BY PAINTERS / Ferrua, Pietro – Listing only of paintings. 1980 – 9 – 1.00f – at Libertarian Micro [335]

(ANARGHARAGHAVA....) / Murari – 1937. 395p. Title page in English. 1 reel. 1283 – 1 – us U.W. Library [280]

ANARKHICHESKII VESTNIK – v. 1-7. Berlin. 1923-24. BR-3484 2 – 8 – ne IDC [073]

ANARKHIST – Ezhenedel'nik. Organ Lefortovskoi rationnoi organizatii anarkhistov. 1918. v.2. BR-1511 2 – 8 – ne IDC [335]

ANARKHIST – Organ russkikh anarkhistov-kommunistov. Paris. 1907-09. v.1-4. BR-3504 2 – 8 – ne IDC [335]

EL ANARQUISMO MILITANTE Y LA REALIDAD ESPANOLA / Montseny, Frederica – Barcelona? 1937? Fiche W 1059. (Blodgett Collection of Spanish Civil War Pamphlets) – 9 – us H.U. College Libr [946]

Anasagasti, Pedro de *see* FRANCISCO DE ASIS BUSCA AL HOMBRE...

Anashkin, G *see* FREEDOM OF THE INDIVIDUAL IN THE USSR

Anastasevich, V G *see*
– REESTR KNIGAM KNIZHNAGO MAGAZINA A. SMIRDINIA. (SYNA), 1856. 148P. BR-5860/2
– REESTR RUSSKIM KNIGAM, PRODAIUSHCHIMSIA V KNIZHNOM MAGAZINE

Anastasius Bibliothecaris *see*
- HISTORIA DE VITIS ROMANORUM PONTIFICUM (CBH 19,2)
- HISTORIA ECCLESIASTICA SIVE CHRONOGRAPHIA TRIPERTITA (CBH 19,1)

ANASTASIUS GRUEN : VERSCHOLLENES UND VERGILBTES AUS DESSEN LEBEN UND WIRKEN / ed by Radics, P v – (Includes bibliographical references) – Leipzig: H Foltz, 1879 – 1 – us U.W. Library [920]

ANASTASIUS GRUEN'S GESAMMELTE WERKE / Gruen, Anastasius; ed by Frankl, Ludwig August – Berlin: G Grote, 1907 – 1r – 1 – us U.W. Library [800]

Anastassopoulou, Itheoni *see* CAUSALITE ET CREATION

Anatolev, P *see* DEVIATOE IANVARI A 1905-1925

ANATOLIA AND THE AEGEAN IN THE THIRD MILLENNIUM B.C. / French, D S – Cambridge, 1969 – 9 – ne IDC [956]

ANATOLIA THROUGH THE AGES / Schmidt, Eric F – 1931 – 9 – $10.00 – us I.R.C. [930]

ANATOMIA CLINICA – v.1-3, 1978-81. ISSN: 0343-6098 – 1,5,6,9,13 – 123.00v – us UMI [073]

ANATOMIA HEPATIS / Glisson, F – M-200. 1654 – 9 – ne IDC [580]

ANATOMICAL DRAWINGS / Royal Library. Windsor Castle – (84 drawings, 224 details; 14 black and white images including 7 in ultra-violet. Fully indexed) – 8 colour 1 bw mf – 15,9 – $260.00 – 0-907716-02-4 – uk Mindata [740]

THE ANATOMICAL HISTORY / Bartholin, T – M 300. 1653 – 9 – ne IDC [611]

ANATOMICAL RECORD – Baltimore, 1906-1931. V.1-48 – 403mf – 9 – ne IDC [611]

ANATOMICAL RECORD – v. 1-159. 1906-1967 – 1,5,6 – us Princeton Micro [590]

ANATOMIE DE L'ARREST RENDU PAR LE PARLEMENT DE PROVENCE LE DIX OCT 1731, SUR L'AFFAIRE DE LA DEMOISELLE CADIERE, DU R.P.J.B. GIRARD – 9 – fr Hachette [360]

L'ANATOMIE DU CALVINISME... / Gaultier, J – Lyon, 1621 – 9mf – 9 – CA-100/1 – ne IDC [240]

ANATOMIE GENERALE APPLIQUEE A LA PHYSIOLOGIE ET LA MEDICINE / Bichat, M F X. – 4v. M-188. 1801 – 9 – ne IDC [611]

ANATOMISCHER ANZEIGER – v. 1-95. 1886-1945 – 1,5,6 – us Princeton Micro [590]

ANATOMY AND EMBRYOLOGY – v. 70-160. 1923-80 – 1,5,9 – 13,514.00 – us UMI [073]

ANATOMY AND HISTOLOGY OF CHANNEL CATFISH / Auburn University. Agricultural Experiment Station – 1976. 1 reel – 1, 5 – us Spaulding [639]

THE ANATOMY AND SURGICAL TREATMENT OF INGUINAL AND CONGENITAL HERNIA / Cooper, A P – 2pts. M-49 2. 1804-1807 – 8 – ne IDC [617]

THE ANATOMY OF A HORSE / Snape, A – M 407 2. 1686 – 8 – ne IDC [590]

ANATOMY OF APARTHEID / ed by Randall, Peter – Johannesburg: Study Project on Christianity in Apartheid Soc, 1970 – us Res Libr [320]

THE ANATOMY OF HUMANE BODIES / Gibson, T – M 356. 1682 – 9 – ne IDC [611]

THE ANATOMY OF HUMANE BODIES WITH FIGURES DRAWN AFTER THE LIFE / Cowper, William – M-329 2. 1698 – 32mf – 8 – ne IDC [760]

THE ANATOMY OF HUMANE BODIES: WITH FIGURES DRAWN AFTER THE LIFE...AND CURIOUSLY ENGRAVEN.. / Cowper, William – Oxford: Printed at the Theater, for Sam. Smith and Benj. Walford, London, 1698. 1v. illus. With: Les Oeuvres de Jean Baptiste van Helmont. Lyons, 1671 – 1 – us U.W. Library [611]

THE ANATOMY OF NEGATION / Saltus, Edgar – New York: Brentano, [1886?] – 1mf – 9 – 0-8370-6364-7 – 1986-0364 – us A.T.L.A. [210]

THE ANATOMY OF PLANTS / Grew, N – 6493. 1682 – 9 – ne IDC [580]

THE ANATOMY OF SOUTH AFRICAN MISERY / Kiewiet, C W de – London, New York: Oxford UP, 1956 – us Res Libr [320]

THE ANATOMY OF THE BRAIN / Ridley, H – M 395. 1695 – 9 – ne IDC [611]

THE ANATOMY OF THE HUMANE BODY / Keill, J – M 373. 1698 – 9 – ne IDC [611]

THE ANATOMY OF VEGETABLES BEGUN / Grew, N – M 360. 1672 – 9 – ne IDC [580]

Anaya, Laureano Orencio *see* EL EJERCITO

ANBAR MANAGEMENT ABSTRACTS – 1961-85.Continued annually – 5 – PS250.00 – uk World [650]

ANBRUCH OESTERREICHISCHE ZEITSCHRIFT F. MUSIK – Vienna. v. 1-19. 1919-1937 – 1 – us Schnase [780]

ANBRUCH; OESTERREICHISCHE ZEITSCHRIFT FUER MUSIK – v. 1-19. 1919-37 – 1 – 75.00 – us L of C Photodup [780]

Anceaux, Johannes Cornelis *see* THE NIMBORAN LANGUAGE: PHONOLOGY AND MORPHOLOGY

Ancelet-Hustache, J *see*
- MECHTILDE DE MAGDEBOURG (1207-1282)
- LA VIE MYSTIQUE D'UN MONASTERE DE DOMINICAINES AU MOYEN AGE D'APRES LA CHRONIQUE DE TOESS

Ancelle, J *see* LES EXPLORATIONS AU SENEGAL ET DANS LES CONTREES VOISINES DEPUIS L'ANTIQUITE JUSQU'A NOS JOURS

Ancelot, Francois *see* SIX MOIS EN RUSSIE. LETTRES ECRITES A M.X.B. SAINTINE EN 1826 A L'EPOQUE DU COURONNEMENT DE S.M. L'EMPEREUR

ANCESTOR-WORSHIP AND JAPANESE LAW / Hozumi, Nobushige – 6th ed. rev. by Shigato Hozumi. Tokyo: The Hokuseido Press, 1940. xxxi,205p – 1 – us U.W. Library [290]

ANCESTRAL CHARTS OF GEORGE ADDISON THROOP, DEBORAH GOLDSMITH : MANY HISTORICALLY INTERESTING LETTERS FROM THE OLD TRAVELLING BAG / Smith, Olive Cole; ed by Throop, James Addison – East St Louis: Throop & Son, 1934 – 1r – 1 – us Western Res [920]

ANCESTRAL NOTES FROM CHEDWATO – v8,no.4-6, 1961.2 fiches. F-0938 – 9 – us A.G.L.L. [073]

ANCESTRAL NOTES FROM CHEDWATO & SUPPLEMENT – v14, 1967. 6 fiches. F-1606 – 9 – us A.G.L.L. [073]

ANCESTRAL ROOTS OF SIXTY COLONISTS WHO CAME TO NEW ENGLAND BETWEEN 1623 AND 1650 / Weis, Frederick Lewis – 1850. Lineage of Alfred the Great, Charlemagne, Malcom of Scotland, Robert the Strong and some of their descendants. Indexed, 151p. SW16-0009 – 5 – us A.G.L.L. [920]

ANCESTRAL STORIES AND TRADITIONS OF GREAT FAMILIES ILLUSTRATIVE OF ENGLISH HISTORY / Timbs, John – London: Griffith and Farran, 1869. xvi,428p – 1 – us U.W. Library [305]

THE ANCESTRY OF OUR ENGLISH BIBLE... VERSIONS, TEXTS, AND MANUSCRIPTS / Price, Ira Maurice – Philadelphia: Sun. Sch. Times, 1907. 1 fiche – 9 – us A.T.L.A. [240]

ANCESTRY; QUARTERLY BULLETIN OF THE PALM BEACH COUNTY GENEALOGICAL SOCIETY – v1-4, 1966-69. F-1288 to F-1291 – 9 – us A.G.L.L. [920]

L'ANCETRE AMERICAIN DU DROIT COMPARE; LA DOCTRINE DU JUGE STORY / Lambert, Edouard – Paris, Recueil Sirey, 1947. 350 p. LL-4076 – 1 – us L of C Photodup [340]

Ancey, G *see*
- BEOUMI. EXPLOITATION MANUELLE DE L'ENQUETE DEMOGRAPHIQUE. RESULTATS PARTIELS
- LES CENTRES DE PRODUCTIVITE DE BOUNDA ET DE SAMINIRKO
- DABALAKA. RECENSEMENT DEMOGRAPHIQUE
- ETUDE COMPARATIVE DE CINQ STRATES D'EXPLOITATIONS DE LA ZONE RURALE DE BROBO. EVALUATION 1961-1967
- ETUDE DE LA ZONE RURALE DE BROBO
- EXPLOITATIONS AGRICOLES EN PAYS DIAMALA-DJIMINI
- NOTES SUR LES ZONES DE DEVELOPPEMENT DE BROBO ET DE BIABO
- LES NOTIONS D'ACTIVITIES ET D'ACTIFS A L'INTERIEUR D'UNE EXPLOITATION AGRICOLE
- RECENSEMENT D'AGBOVILLE. EXPLOITATION MECANOGRAPHIQUE
- SAKASSO, EXPLOITATION MANUELLE DE L'ENQUETE DEMOGRAPHIQUE. RESULTATS PARTIELS
- LA ZONE RURALE DE BROBO VUE A TRAVERS SON MARCHE HEBDOMADAIRE

Ancharova, Mariia *see*
- EVREISKOE BEZPRAVIE I EGO PLODY
- ZHENSHCHINA I VYBORY V UCHREDITELNOE SOBRANIE

AN-CH'I HSIEN-CHIH – 1673, 12. BCH-564 2 – 8 – ne IDC [030]

ANCHOR – Northwood. Iowa. -w. 1960 – 1 – us UMI [071]

Anchorena de Acevedo, Ines *see* ABRAMOS LOS OJOS

Anciaux, Leon *see*
- LE LINGALA VEHICULAIRE
- LA PARTICIPATION DES BELGES A L'OEUVRE COLONIALE DES HOLLANDAIS AUX INDES ORIENTALES

Ancien Colon *see* LA COLONISATION BIEN FAITE PAR LES OUVRIERS ET LES TRAVAILLEURS

ANCIEN JAPON / Appert, Georges – Tokio. 1888 – 9 – 7.50 – fr Orientalistes [950]

L'ANCIEN QUEBEC, DESCRIPTIONS, NOS ARCHIVES, ETC / Bechard, Auguste – Quebec, Belleau, 1890. 03535. (Pre-1900 Canadiana) – 9 – cn C.I.H.M. [971]

ANCIEN REGIME IN TURMOIL? COMMERCE, POLITICS AND SOCIETY IN FRANCE, C 1682-1793 : THE GAZETTE MANUSCRITE, 1775-1793, AND RELATED SOURCES FROM THE JOHN RYLANDS UNIVERSITY LIBRARY OF MANCHESTER – Marlborough: Adam Matthew Publications, 1991 – 9r – 1 – $990.00 – uk Matthew [944]

L'ANCIEN ROYAUME DE DAHOMEY / Le Herisse, A – 1911. BA-392 2 – 8 – ne IDC [960]

L'ANCIENNE LITURGIE ROMAINE : LE RITE LYONNAIS / Buenner, D – Paris-Lyon, 1934 – 5mf – 8 – Dfl22.00 – ne Slangenburg [240]

ANCIENNE REFORMATION DE LA NOBLESSE DE BRETAGNE (1427 A 1429) : EVECHES DE CORNOUAILLES, DOL, LEON, NANTES, RENNES / Bretagne, Noblesse – 15th cent. 5v – 1 – F872,10 – fr Armell [920]

L'ANCIENNE VERSION LATINE DES QUESTIONS SUR LA GENESE DE PHILON D'ALEXANDRIE : 1. ED. CRITIQUE (T.U.U. 5-113) / Petit, F – Berlin, 1973 – 2mf – 9 – ne Slangenburg [240]

L'ANCIENNE VERSION LATINE DES QUESTIONS SUR LA GENESE DE PHILON D'ALEXANDRIE : 2. COMMENTAIRE (T.U.U. 5-114) / Petit, F – Berlin, 1973 – 4mf – 9 – ne Slangenburg [240]

LES ANCIENNES CORPORATIONS D'ARTS ET METIERS DE LA VILLE D'ARRAS / Parenty, Auguste – Arras. 1868. (La Condition Ouvriere. Part Two.) – 9 – 5.00 – fr Bibl Nationale [360]

ANCIENNES COUTUMES CLAUSTRALES / Gougaud, L – Liguge, 1930 – 2mf – 8 – Dfl9.00 – ne Slangenburg [240]

LES ANCIENNES LITURGIES 2. L'ANCIEN SACRAMENTAIRE DE L'EGLISE 1 / Grancolas, M J – Paris, 1699 – 16mf – 8 – Dfl56.00 – ne Slangenburg [240]

LES ANCIENNES LITURGIES 3. L'ANCIEN SACRAMENTAIRE DE L'EGLISE 2 / Grancolas, M J – Paris, 1699 – 8mf – 8 – Dfl30.00 – ne Slangenburg [240]

ANCIENNES REFORMATIONS DE LA NOBLESSE DE BRETAGNE (15E ET 16E S.) : EVECHES DE RENNES, NANTES, SAINT-MALO, DOL, VANNES, SAINT-BRIEUC, QUIMPER-CORENTIN, TREGUIER, SAINT-POL-DE-LEON / Bretagne, Noblesse – 18th cent. 3v – 1 – F627.00 – fr Armell [920]

LES ANCIENS CANADIENS / Aubert de Gaspe, Philippe – Quebec: Desbarats et Derbishire, 1863. SEM16P98 – 1r – 5 – Can$9.00 – cn Bibl Nat [440]

LES ANCIENS MINERALOGISTES DU ROYAUME DE FRANCE / Gobet, Nicholas – Paris, 1779, 2v., xxviii, 910p., 2p. (Histoire des Sciences XVIIe-XIXe Siecles) – 9 – fr Hachette [540]

LES ANCIENS MISSIONNAIRES DE L'ACADIE DEVANT L'HISTOIRE / Bourgeois, Phileas Frederic – Shediac: des Presses du Moniteur Acadien, 1910?. SEM105P930 – 2mf – 9 – Can$4.50 – cn Bibl Nat [240]

ANCIENT AMERICA, IN NOTES ON AMERICAN ARCHEOLOGY / Baldwin, John Dennison – New York: Harper, 1872. 02482. (Pre-1900 Canadiana) – 9 – cn C.I.H.M. [930]

THE ANCIENT AND MODERN SCOTS SONGS, HEROIC BALLADS, AND C. : NOW FIRST COLLECTED INTO ONE BODY, FROM THE VARIOUS MISCELLANIES WHEREIN THEY FORMERLY LAY DISPERSED... / Herd, David – Edinburgh: Printed by and for Martin & Wotherspoon, 1769 – 1 roll – 1 – 1-55879-448-4 – uk Libr Preservation [810]

"ANCIENT BABYLONIAN TABLETS" / Poebel, Arno – University of Pennsylvania Museum Journal: June 1913 – 9 – $10.00 – us I.R.C. [930]

ANCIENT BRITISH AND IRISH CHURCHES / Cathcart, William – 1894 – 1 – 13.51 – us Baptist [240]

THE ANCIENT BRITISH AND IRISH CHURCHES : INCLUDING THE LIFE AND LABORS OF ST. PATRICK / Cathcart, William – Philadelphia: American Baptist Publication Society, 1894 – 1mf – us A.T.L.A. [240]

THE ANCIENT CATHOLIC CHURCH : FROM THE ACCESSIONS OF TRAJAN TO THE FOURTH GENERAL COUNCIL (A.D. 98-451) / Rainy, Robert – New York: C. Scribner, 1902 (International theological library) – 2mf – us A.T.L.A. [240]

ANCIENT CEYLON: AN ACCOUNT OF THE ABORIGINES AND OF THE EARLY CIVILISATION / Parker, H – London. 1909. BI-979 2 – 8 – ne IDC [950]

THE ANCIENT CHURCH : ITS HISTORY, DOCTRINE, WORKSHIP, AND CONSTITUTION, TRACED FOR THE FIRST THREE HUNDRED YEARS / Killen, W D – New York: A.D.F. Randolph, c1883 – 2mf – us A.T.L.A. [240]

ANCIENT CITIES AND EMPIRES : THEIR PROPHETIC DOOM READ IN THE LIGHT OF HISTORY AND MODERN RESEARCH / Gillett, E H – Philadelphia: Presbyterian Publication Committee; New York: A.D.F. Randolph, c1867 – 1mf – us A.T.L.A. [930]

ANCIENT CITY – St. Augustine. Fl. Jan. 1850-Dec. 1854 – 1 – us P.K. Yonge [071]

THE ANCIENT CITY OF QUEBEC – 18th ed. Canadian Pacific Railway Co. 1894. 04011. (Pre-1900 Canadiana) – 9 – cn C.I.H.M. [971]

ANCIENT COLLECTS AND OTHER PRAYERS / Bright, William – Oxford: J.H.& Jas. Parker, 1862 – 1mf – us A.T.L.A. [240]

THE ANCIENT EAST / ed by Hutchison, J – London, David Nutt, no.1-6, 1901-03. -irr. No more published. Includes bibliographies. – 1 – us U.W. Library [956]

ANCIENT EGYPTIAN DANCES. / Lexova, Irena – Tr. by K. Haltmar. Praha: Oriental Institute, 1935. illus – 1 – us U.W. Library [390]

ANCIENT FACTS AND FICTIONS CONCERNING CHURCHES AND TITHES / Selborne, Roundell Palmer, Earl of – London, New York: Macmillan, 1892 – 1mf – us A.T.L.A. [240]

ANCIENT FAMILIES OF BOHEMIA MANOR; THEIR HOMES AND THEIR GRAVES – By Charles Payson Mallery, 1888.Papers of the Historical Society of Delaware no.7.2 fiches. F-1575 – 9 – us A.G.L.L. [978]

ANCIENT GAZA / Petrie, William Matthew Flinders – BSA, 1933 – 9 – $10.00 – us I.R.C. [930]

ANCIENT GAZA: I / Petrie, William Matthew Flinders – BSA, 1931 – 9 – $10.00 – us I.R.C. [930]

ANCIENT GREECE – 34p – 9 – 92-3-102596-1 – Co-published with Childrens Press, Chicago, who have exclusive sales rights in the USA and Canada – fr UNESCO [930]

ANCIENT HEBREW AND SOLOMONIC BUILDING CONSTRUCTION / Griffin, H J – 1984. 2 fiches – 9 – £25.00 – uk Mansell Publ [930]

ANCIENT HEBREW NAMES : NOTES ON THEIR SIGNIFICANCE AND HISTORIC VALUE / Jeffreys, Letitia D – (Includes index) – London: James Nisbet, 1906 – 1mf – 9 – 0-8370-3776-X – 1985-1776 – us A.T.L.A. [220]

ANCIENT HISTORY FOR COLLEGES AND HIGH SCHOOLS / Myers, Philip Van Ness – Part I: The Eastern Nations and Greece. Boston: Ginn & Co., 1890, c1888.viii,369p. ill. maps, ports.Includes index – 1 – us U.W. Library [900]

ANCIENT JERUSALEM / Merrill, Selah – F.H. Revell, 1908 – 9 – $15.00 – us I.R.C. [270]

ANCIENT KAURAWA FLAGS : WITH APOLOGIES TO A CERTAIN "NOTE" TO REBUT IGNORANT CALUMNIES, AND IN THE INTERESTS OF CEYLON HISTORY / De Soysa, A H T – Colombo: Ceylon Examiner Press, 1930 – 1 – us Res Libr [950]

ANCIENT LAWS AND INSTITUTES OF ENGLAND : MONUMENTA ECCLESIASTICA ANGLICANA – (Ancient Latin version of the Ango-Saxon laws) – London, 1840 – Dfl95.00 – ne Slangenburg [240]

ANCIENT LAWS AND INSTITUTES OF ENGLAND / Thorpe, B – 1 reel – 1 – $50.00 – us Trans-Media [941]
ANCIENT LAWS AND INSTITUTES OF WALES / Owen, Anevrin – 1 reel – 1 – $50.00 – us Trans-Media [941]
ANCIENT LAWS AND INSTITUTES OF WALES – (With an English translation of the Welsh text) – London, 1841 – Dfl154.00 – ne Slangenburg [240]
ANCIENT LAWS OF IRELAND / Ireland – Translations of 5th and 6th century laws. v1-6. 1865-1901 – 1 – $200.00 – 0-89093-027-9 – us UPA [941]
THE ANCIENT MONUMENTS, TEMPLES AND SCULPTURES OF INDIA / Burgess, J – v. 1-2. London. 1897. BI-1050 2 – 8 – ne IDC [930]
Ancient Order of United Workmen. Delphos Lodge No. 129 *see* MINUTE BOOKS
ANCIENT ORIENTAL CYLINDER AND OTHER SEALS : WITH A DESCRIPTION OF THE COLLECTION OF MRS. WILLIAM H. MOORE / Eisen, Gustavus A – 1940 – 9 – $6.00f – 0-226-19527-9 – us U.C. Orient [930]
ANCIENT POEMS, BALLADS AND SONGS OF THE PEASANTRY OF ENGLAND – 1857 – 1 – us I.U. Libraries [810]
ANCIENT RELIGION AND MODERN THOUGHT / Lilly, William Samuel – London: Chapman and Hall, 1884. 1 fiche – 9 – us A.T.L.A. [290]
ANCIENT ROME / Lanciani, Rodolfo – Houghton, Mifflin. 1890 – 9 – $15.00 – us I.R.C. [930]
ANCIENT SCIENCE, OR, SECRETS OF PYRAMIDS, WALLS AND TEMPLES / MacDonald, Dugald – Montreal: Gazette Printing Co, 1901. SEM105P463 – 1mf – 9 – Can$2.25 – cn Bibl Nat [150]
ANCIENT SHIPS / Torr, Cecil – Cambridge: University Press, 1894. xii,139p. illus – 1 – us U.W. Library [623]
ANCIENT SLAVIC MANUSCRIPTS FROM THE MOSCOW STATE UNIVERSITY LIBRARY – (Coll contains 21 ancient mss from the early 1200's to the early 1500's. Enquire for individual listings. Comes with printed guide) – 183mf coll – 9 – $1,500.00 coll – us Ross [090]
ANCIENT SYRIAC DOCUMENTS RELATIVE TO THE EARLIEST ESTABLISHMENT OF CHRISTIANITY IN EDESSA AND THE NEIGHBOURING COUNTRIES : FROM THE YEAR AFTER OUR LORD'S ASCENSION TO THE BEGINNING OF THE FOURTH CENTURY / Cureton, William – London: Williams and Norgate, 1864 – 1mf – us A.T.L.A. [240]
Ancient, William Johnson *see* THE CROSS: BEING A COURSE OF SERMONS PREACHED IN HOLY TRINITY CHURCH, HALIFAX, ON THE SUNDAY EVENINGS IN LENT, 1879
ANCIENT-BABYLONIAN TEMPLE RECORDS IN THE COLUMBIA UNIVERSITY LIBRARY / ed by Arnold, William R – (Text in Akkadian. Introduction in English) – New York: [s.n.], 1896 – 1mf – 9 – 0-8370-8480-6 – 1986-2480 – us A.T.L.A. [470]
L'Ancre, Pierre de *see* TABLEAU DE L'INCONSTANCE DES MAUVAIS ANGES ET DEMONS OU IL EST AMPLEMENT TRAICTE DES SORCIERS ET DE SORCELERIE
"AND ALL THAT JAZZ" – Sacramento, CA. 1977-1989 – 2r – 1 – $100.00 – B06051 – us Library Micro [780]
A AND C ADULT AND CHILD *see* A AND C MEDICAL CHALLENGE
A AND C MEDICAL CHALLENGE *see* A AND C ADULT AND CHILD
Anda, Diane de *see* JOURNAL OF MULTICULTURAL SOCIAL WORK
ANDACHTS-BUECHLEIN ZU EHREN DER ELF MARTYRER-SCHAAREN AUS DER GESELLSCHAFT JESU : DIE PIUS 9. AM ST. PETRUSTAGE 1867 SELIG GESPROCHEN / Weninger, Francis Xavier – Cincinnati, OH: Benziger, 1868 – 1mf – 9 – 0-8370-6848-7 – 1986-0848 – us A.T.L.A. [240]
ANDACHTSBUECHLEIN ZU EHREN DER SECHSUNDZWANZIG [SIC] JAPANESISCHEN MARTYRER / Weninger, Francis Xavier – Cincinnati: Fredewest & Donnerberger, 1863 – 1mf – 9 – 0-8370-6850-9 – 1986-0850 – us A.T.L.A. [240]
ANDACHTSBUECHLEIN ZU EHREN DER SELIGEN VIERZIG MARTIRER DER GESELLSCHAFT JESU, IGNATIUS AZEVEDO UND SEINER GEFAEHRTEN / Weninger, Francis Xavier – Cincinnati: "Wahrheitsfreundes", 1855 – 1mf – 9 – 0-8370-6849-5 – 1986-0849 – us A.T.L.A. [240]
ANDACHTSBUECHLEIN ZU EHREN DER ZWEI SELIGEN, JOHANNES UND ANDREAS : PRIESTER UND MAERTYRER DER GESELLSCHAFT JESU / Weninger, Francis Xavier – St Louis, MO: "Tageschronik", 1854 – 1mf – 9 – 0-8370-6851-7 – 1986-0851 – us A.T.L.A. [240]
ANDACHTSBUECHLEIN ZU EHREN DES SELIGEN PETER CLAVER : PRIESTER DER GESELLSCHAFT JESU UND APOSTEL VON CENTRAL-AMERIKA / Weninger, Francis Xavier – Cincinnati: "Wahrheits-Freundes", 1852 – 1mf – 9 – 0-8370-6852-5 – 1986-0852 – us A.T.L.A. [240]
ANDANZAS DE HERNAN CORTES / Valle-Arizpe, Artemio del – Mexico: Editorial Diana, 1978 – sp Bibl Santa Ana [910]
ANDEAN AIR MAIL AND PERUVIAN TIMES – (See also: Andean Times) – v31. 1972 – 1 – us UMI [073]
ANDEAN TIMES – (See also: Andean Air Mail and Peruvian Times) – v33. 1973-74 – 1 – us UMI [073]
Andelson, Robert V *see*
– CRITICS OF HENRY GEORGE
– NEO-GEORGISM: A PANEL DISCUSSION
Anderdon, William Henry *see* FASTI APOSTOLICI
DAS ANDERE DEUTSCHLAND – Hagen/Berlin. 1930-mar 4, 1933 – 1r – 1 – gw Mikrofilm [943]
DAS ANDERE DEUTSCHLAND : LA OTRA ALEMANIA – (Because of prohibition publ in Montevideo, Uruguay, dec 15 1943-apr 25 1944) – Buenos Aires, may 1938-jan 10 1949 – 1 – Inquire at Mikrofilmarchiv for details – gw Misc Inst [972]
DAS ANDERE DEUTSCHLAND-LA OTRA ALEMANIA – Buenos Aires.Jan 1939-Nov 1948 – 2r – 1 – gw Mikrofilm [072]
DAS ANDERE SYSTEM / Rittershausen, Heinrich – 2Fassung. 1948. Mit spaeteren Anmerkungen. With: Am Tage Nach dem Zusammenbruch, 1931; Die Valorisierung des Goldes als Waehrungs- u. Aussenhandelsproblem; Kreditwirtschaftliche Forderungen an eine Kimmende Nationale Bau$ u. Arbeitsbeschaffungspolitik; Modellverwendung bei Wahrungspolitischen Aussagen. 1 fiche (29x) – 9 – 1.00f – at Libertarian Micro [320]
ANDERNACHER BUERGERBLATT – Neuwied, jan 5-jun 26 1837, 1855-62 – 1 – Dist. gw Mikrofilm – gw Misc Inst [943]
Anders, Artur *see* WIEN
Andersen, Hans Christian *see*
– L'IMPROVISATION OU LA VIE EN ITALIE
– IN SPAIN
Andersen, Steven J *see* THE EFFECTS OF ACQUAINTANCE RAPE PREVENTION PROGRAMMING ON MALE ATHLETES' SEXUAL AND DATING ATTITUDES
Anderson, A W *see* THE EXTINCTION IN PERPETUITY...
Anderson, Alexander *see*
– A BRIEF ACCOUNT OF THE PROVINCE OF BRITISH COLUMBIA; ITS CLIMATE AND RESOURCES; AN APPENDIX TO THE BRITISH COLUMBIA DIRECTORY
– NOTEBOOKS
– NOTES ON NORTH-WESTERN AMERICA
Anderson, Amy *see* THE EFFECT OF A WILDERNESS THERAPY PROGRAM ON YOUTH-AT-RISK, AS MEASURED BY LOCUS OF CONTROL AND SELF-CONCEPT
ANDERSON BAPTIST CHURCH. TEXAS : CHURCH RECORDS – 1844-1911 – 1 – 53.55 – us Baptist [240]
Anderson Bros. Charlottesville, Va *see* LAW EXAMINATIONS, EMBRACING EXAMINATION PAPERS FROM THE YEAR 1869 TO 1894
Anderson, Chandler P *see* DIARIES
Anderson, Charles *see* NEW READINGS OF OLD PARABLES
ANDERSON COUNTY NEWS – Clinton. Tenn. 1905-1939 – 1 – us UMI [071]
ANDERSON COUNTY. SOUTH CAROLINA. HOPEWELL BAPTIST CHURCH – Church Records. 1868-1890, 1963-1988. WMU 1906-1926, Sunday School 1958-1960, History 1803-1981, Scrapbooks 1893-1987, 1,457p – 1 – $65.57 – us Baptist [240]
Anderson, D R *see* RADIOACTIVE WASTE MANAGEMENT AND ENVIRONMENTAL RESTORATION
Anderson, Daphne L *see* THE ROLE OF EXTERNAL NON-RIGID ANKLE BRACING IN THE PREVENTION OF INVERSION INJURIES
Anderson, David R *see* THE OMBUNDSMAN
Anderson, Don *see* INTEGRATION, COMPETITION AND THE AUSTRALIAN ACCOUNTING INDUSTRY
Anderson, Duncan *see*
– LAYS OF CANADA AND OTHER POEMS
– THE NEWER DISTRICTS OF ONTARIO: INFORMATION FOR PROSPECTIVE SETTLERS: RAINY RIVER VALLEY, WABIGOON COUNTRY, TEMISCAMINGUE, ALGOMA/ REPORT OF INPECTION.
Anderson, F M *see*
– CATTLE HERD DYNAMICS
– RESEARCH ON FARM AND LIVESTOCK PRODUCTIVITY IN THE CENTRAL ETHIOPIAN HIGHLANDS
Anderson Family *see* ANDERSON FAMILY PAPERS
ANDERSON FAMILY PAPERS / Anderson Family – 1802-1905. In Kansas State Historical Society. Guide – 1 – us KS Hist [920]
ANDERSON FIRST BAPTIST CHURCH. ANDERSON COUNTY. SOUTH CAROLINA : CHURCH RECORDS – 1869-1990 (incomplete). Misc. documents. 1,637p – 1 – $73.67 – us Baptist [240]
ANDERSON FIRST BAPTIST CHURCH. ANDERSON, MISSOURI : CHURCH RECORDS – 1852-1907, 1924-32, Apr 1950-61 – 1 – 29.07 – us Baptist [240]
Anderson, Gene *see* RAILROAD CAR DESIGN AND PULLMAN CAR DATA
Anderson, George B *see* LAND MARKS OF RENSSELAER COUNTY
Anderson, Grace M *see* NETWORKS OF CONTACT
Anderson, J *see*
– ACHEEN, AND THE PORTS ON THE NORTH AND EAST COASTS OF SUMATRA
– ENGLISH INTERCOURSE WITH SIAM IN THE SEVENTEENTH CENTURY
– MISSION TO THE EAST COAST OF SUMATRA, IN 1823
– NACHRICHTEN VON ISLAND, GROENLAND UND DER STRASSE DAVIS
– OBSERVATIONS ON THE MEANS OF EXCITING A SPIRIT OF NATIONAL INDUSTRY...
Anderson, Jack *see* TEN HUMAN RIGHTS POINTS FROM THEIR 1971 WORK, A CONSTITUTION FOR A MORAL GOVERNMENT
Anderson, James *see*
– THE HISTORY OF THE CHURCH OF ENGLAND IN THE COLONIES AND FOREIGN DEPENDENCIES OF THE BRITISH EMPIRE
– THE IMPROVEMENT OF AGRICULTURE, AND THE ELEVATION IN THE SOCIAL SCALE OF BOTH HUSBANDMAN AND OPERATIVE
Anderson, John George Clark *see* STUDIA PONTICA
Anderson, John Jacob *see* DID THE LOUISIANA PURCHASE EXTEND TO THE PACIFIC OCEAN? AND OUR TITLE TO OREGON
Anderson, Joseph *see* THE TOWN AND CITY OF WATERBURY FROM THE ABORIGINAL PERIOD TO THE YEAR 1895
Anderson, K J *see* BALLADE ET DANSE DES SYLPHES...OP. 5
Anderson, L *see* EL GOBIERNO DE FACTO
Anderson, Lynn S *see* THE EFFECTS OF A MINIUMUM IMPACT CAMPING SLIDE-TAPE PROGRAM ON WILDERNESS VISITORS' AWARENESS OF MINIMUM IMPACT CAMPING
Anderson, M H *see* THE NAVY AND PRIZE
Anderson, Martin *see* AN ECONOMIC BILL OF RIGHTS
Anderson, Mary B *see* RISING FROM THE ASHES
Anderson, Paula *see* UNIVERSITY OF WISCONSIN-LA CROSSE ADULT FITNESS/ CARDIAC REHABILITATION GRADUATE PROGRAM ASSESSMENT
Anderson, R P *see* THE STORY OF CHRISTIAN ENDEAVOR
Anderson, Rasmus Bjorn *see* VIKING TALES OF THE NORTH
Anderson, Robert *see*
– THE BIBLE AND MODERN CRITICISM
– THE BUDDHA OF CHRISTENDOM
– CHRISTIANIZED RATIONALISM AND THE HIGHER CRITICISM
– DANIEL IN THE CRITIC'S DEN
– A DOUBTER'S DOUBTS ABOUT SCIENCE AND RELIGION
– DOUBTER'S DOUBTS ABOUT SCIENCE AND RELIGION
– FIGHTING THE MILL CREEKS
– THE GOSPEL AND ITS MINISTRY
– KIRK FOLK
– PSEUDO-CRITICISM
– THE SILENCE OF GOD
Anderson, Rufus *see*
– FOREIGN MISSIONS
– HISTORY OF THE MISSION OF THE AMERICAN BOARD OF COMMISSIONERS FOR FOREIGN MISSIONS TO THE SANDWICH ISLANDS
– HISTORY OF THE MISSIONS OF THE AMERICAN BOARD OF COMMISSIONERS FOR FOREIGN MISSIONS IN INDIA
– HISTORY OF THE MISSIONS OF THE AMERICAN BOARD OF COMMISSIONERS FOR FOREIGN MISSIONS TO THE ORIENTAL CHURCHES
– OBSERVATIONS UPON THE PELOPONNESUS AND GREEK ISLANDS
Anderson, Samuel G *see* WOMAN'S SPHERE AND INFLUENCE
Anderson, T *see* CATALOGUE OF PLANTS CULTIVATED IN THE ROYAL BOTANIC GARDENS CALCUTTA...
Anderson, Thomas F *see* NOVA SCOTIA, THE LAND OF EVANGELINE AND THE TOURIST'S PARADISE:..
Anderson, W *see* THE SCOTTISH NATION
Anderson, Wayne F *see* INCOME TAX ADMINISTRATION IN THE STATE OF ISRAEL
Anderson, William *see* REGENERATION
Anderson, William B *see* FAR NORTH IN INDIA
Anderson, William G *see*
– THE ENROLLMENT AND PERSISTENCE OF AFRICAN-AMERICAN DOCTORAL STUDENTS IN PHYSICAL EDUCATION AND RELATED DISCIPLINES
– A MULTI-CASE STUDY OF FIRST YEAR ATHLETIC TRAINERS AT THE HIGH SCHOOL LEVEL
Anderson, William Henry *see* LUTHER
Anderson, William James *see*
– CANADIAN HISTORY: THE SIEGE AND BLOCKADE OF QUEBEC BY GENERALS MONTGOMERY AND ARNOLD IN 1775-6
– THE LIFE OF F. M., H. R. H. EDWARD, DUKE OF KENT: ILLUSTRATED BY HIS CORRESPONDENCE WITH THE DE SALABERRY FAMILY, NEVER BEFORE PUBLISHED, EXTENDING FROM 1791 TO 1814
– THE LOWER ST LAWRENCE: ITS SCENERY, NAVIGATION AND COMMERCE, FORMING A COMPLETE TOURIST'S GUIDE
– MILITARY OPERATIONS AT QUEBEC: FROM THE CAPITULATION BY DE RAMEZAY, ON THE 18TH SEPTEMBER, 1759 TO THE RAISING OF THE SIEGE BY DE LEVIS, BETWEEN THE NIGHT OF THE 17TH AND THE MORNING OF THE 18TH MAY, 1760
ANDERSON'S DICTIONARY – (Judicial definitions, words, phrases, maxims, principles of law comprising a dictionary and compendium of American and English jurisprudence) – 12mf – 9 – $18.00 – LLMC 87-301 – us L.L.M.C. [340]
ANDERSONVILLE BAPTIST CHURCH. ANDERSON COUNTY. SOUTH CAROLINA : CHURCH RECORDS – 1968-82.306p – 1 – 13.77 – us Baptist [240]
Andersson, L G *see* LIST OF REPTILES AND BATRACHIANS COLLECTED BY THE SWEDISH ZOOLOGICAL EXPEDITION TO EGYPT, THE SUDAN AND THE SINAITIC PENINSULA
Andersson, N J *see* SALICES BOREALI-AMERICANAE
Anderton, Paul *see* DRUG ABUSE: APPEARANCE, REALITY AND TREATMENT
ANDERTON'S MANCHESTER CHRONICLE – Manchester, Great Britain. 13 July 1762-28 Dec. 1762 – 1 – uk Manchester Libr [072]
Andhra Historical Research Society *see* QUARTERLY JOURNAL OF THE ANDHRA HISTORICAL RESEARCH SOCIETY
ANDHRA JANATHA – (In Telugu language) – Hyderabad, India. 1962-Jun 1973 – 24r – 1 – us L of C Photodup [072]
ANDHRA JYOTI – (In Telugu language) – Vijayawada, India. Jul-Sept 1966 – 1r – 1 – us L of C Photodup [072]
ANDHRA PATRIKA – (Telugu language) – Madras, India. 26 Apr 1944-Aug 1983; May 1991 – 128r – 1 – us L of C Photodup [072]
ANDHRA PRABHA – (Telugu language) – Madras, India. 18 Aug 1950-1958 – 18r – 1 – us L of C Photodup [072]
ANDHRA PRABHA – (Telugu language) – Vijayawada, India. Oct 1964-1976; May 1977-1990 – 96r – 1 – us L of C Photodup [072]
Andino, Armando Walter *see* LA RESPUESTA PERONISTA

ANDISHAH – Tehran. Shumarah-'i 1-5 (Farvardin 1358-Urdibihish 1359 [Mar 1979-Apr 1980] – 1r – 1 – $50.00 – us MEDOC [950]

ANDISHAH-'I AZAD – Tehran: Kanun-i Nivisandagan-i Iran, [1980-]. Dawrah-'i jadid, sal-i 1, shumarah-'i 1-6 (30 Bahman 1358-15 Khurdad 1359 [19 Feb 1980-30 May 1980] – 1 reel – 1 – $25.00 – us MEDOC [950]

Andorra *see* CONSEJO GENERAL. LA CUESTION DE ANDORRA...

Andosilla Salazar, V *see* LIBRO...EN QUE SE PRUEBA...CON CLARIDAD EL MAL...QUE CORRE POR ESPANA...SER NUEVO

ANDOVER 1647-1849 – (Mf 1T-2T: Births 1651-1704. Mf 2T: Deaths 1650-1700; Marriages 1647-1700. Mf 3T-6T: Births 1704-57. Mf 6T-8T: Deaths 1701-64. Mf 8T-10T: Marriages 1701-99. Mf 10T-11T: Intentions 1704-38. Mf 11T-14T: Births 1757-1801. Mf 14T: Deaths 1764-99. Mf 14T-16T: Intentions 1738-1800. Mf 17T-19T: Births 1800-44. Mf 19T-21T: Deaths 1800-44. Mf 21T-23T: Marriages 1800-43. Mf 23T-25T: Intentions 1800-49. Mf 25T-27T: Births 1843-49. Mf 27T-28T: Marriages 1844-49; Mf 28T-29T: Deaths 1844-49. Mf 30T: Out-of-Town Marriages 1674-1799; Births 1766-1843; Marriages 1827-1841; Deaths 1839) – (mf ed 1994) – 30mf – 9 – 0-87623-200-4 – us Holbrook [920]

ANDOVER 1647-1905 – (Mf 1-9: Births & Index 1649-1844. Mf 10-14: Marriages & Index 1647-1844. Mf 15-19: Deaths & Index 1650-1844. Mf 20-32: Vital Records: 1647-1803. Mf 33-34: Out-of-Town Marriges 1668-1799; Mf 35-46: Births 1649-1844. Mf 40,46-47: Deaths 1701-1844. Mf 48-53,58: Births & Deaths 1800-44. Mf 54-61: Marriages & Intentions 1701-1850. Mf 62-83: Land Records 1667-1824. Mf 84-85: Town Records 1660-1707. Mf 86-116: Town Meetings 1709-1855. Mf 117-165: Tax Assessments 1679-1851. Mf 166-168: Warnings Out 1790-93. Mf 169-171: Pew Deeds 1793-1827. Mf 172-193: Pauper Records 1815-1916. Mf 193-194: Voters 1877-84. Mf 195-201: Marriage Intentions 1850-98. Mf 201-203: Intentions Index 1850-98. Mf 204-208: Vital Records 1843-55. Mf 209-216: Births 1843-81. Mf 217-223: Marriages 1853-96. Mf 224-233: Deaths 1844-1914. Mf 234-237: Births 1882-1905. Mf 238-241: Intentions & Index 1898-1908. Mf 241-242: Marriages 1897-1905, 1812-15) – (mf ed 1998) – 242mf – 9 – 0-87623-397-3 – us Holbrook [920]

ANDOVER ADVERTISER – England, 1862; 1889; Jan-Nov 1917; 1950; 1986- – 25+ r – 1 – uk British Libr Newspaper [072]

THE ANDOVER HERESY : IN THE MATTER OF THE COMPLAINT AGAINST EGBERT C. SMYTH AND OTHERS, PROFESSORS OF THE THEOLOGICAL INSTITUTION IN PHILLIPS ACADEMY, ANDOVER / Smyth, Egbert Coffin – Boston: Cupples, Upham, 1887 – 1mf – us A.T.L.A. [240]

THE ANDOVER REVIEW – v1-19. 1884-93 (complete) – 10r – 1 – ATLA S0162 – us A.T.L.A. [073]

Andrade, V de P *see* BIBLIOGRAFIA MEXICANA DEL SAGRADO CORAZON DE JESUS

Andrae, W *see* FLUSSSLAGGENRECHT UND STROMINTERNATIONALISIERUNG

Andre de Ligneville, Jean-Francois *see* ENTRETIENS DE ZERBES, ROI DE LYDIE ET DE SON MINISTRE SUR LA SITUATION DES AFFAIRES DE SON ROYAUME. QUESTIONS SOUMISES A L'EXAMEN DES CABINETS POLITIQUES

Andre, Frederic *see* LES POETES ILLUSTRES DE XIXE SIECLE: LEMARTINE-VICTOR HUGO: ESQUISSES BIOGRAPHIQUES, NOTICES LITTERAIRES, MORCEAUX CHOISIS, RECUEILLIS ET ANNOTES.

Andre, J *see* DIE WEIBER VON WEISBER

Andre, Louis Edouard Tony *see*
- LES APOCRYPHES DE L'ANCIEN TESTAMENT
- LE PROPHETE AGGE

Andre, Louis Edward Tony *see* ETAT CRITIQUE DU TEXTE D'AGEE

Andre, Valere *see* SYNOPSIS JURIS CANONICI PER EROTEMATA DIGESTI ET ENUCLEATI.

Andre, Yves-Marie *see* VERSUCH UEBER DAS SCHOENE, DA MAN UNTERSUCHT...UND IN DER MUSIK BESTEHE..

ANDREA COSTA AND THE RISE OF SOCIALISM IN THE ROMAGNA, 1871-1892 / Gonzales, Manuel G – Hoover Institution Press, 1976. Manuscript in Microfilm Series 2+4. 581 pp – 1 – 35.00r – us Hoover Inst Photo [335]

ANDREA DELFIN : NOVELLE / Heyse, Paul – Leipzig: Insel-Verlag, [19–?] – 1r – 1 – us U.W. Library [830]

Andreae d.A E, J *see*
- ACTA COLLOQUIJ MONTIS BELLIGARTENSIS...
- ACTA ET SCRIPTA THEOLOGORVM VVIRTEMBERGENSIVM, ET PATRIARCHAE CONSTANTINOPOLITANI D. HIEREMIAE...
- BERICHT VON DER VBIQUITET,...
- EIN CHRISTLICHE PREDIGT, VON CHRISTLICHER EINIGKEIT DER THEOLOGEN AUGSPUERGISCHER CONFESSION,...
- COLLOQUIUM DE PECCATO ORIGINIS. INTER D. IACOBUM ANDREAE, ET. M. MATTHIAM FLACCIVM ILLYRICUM...
- DREY VND DREISSIG PREDIGEN VON DEN FUERNEMBSTEN SPALTUNGEN IN DER CHRISTLICHEN RELIGION...
- EPITOME COLLOQVII MONTISBELGARTENSIS INTER D. IACOBVM ANDREAE, ET D. THEODORUM BEZAM,...
- FUENFF PREDIGEN: VON DEM WERCKE DER CONCORDIEN,...
- GRUENDTLICHER BERICHT...AUFF JOHANN STURMIJ...
- GRUENDTLICHER WARHAFFTIGER VND BESTENDIGER BERICHT: VON CHRISTLICHER EINIGKEIT DER THEOLOGEN VND PREDICANTEN...
- METHODVS CONCIONANDI...
- PASSIONAL BUECHLEIN...
- SECHS CHRISTLICHER PREDIG UEBER DEN EIN VNND FUENFFZIGSTEN PSALMEN DAUIDS...
- SECHS CHRISTLICHER PREDIG VON DEN SPALTUNGEN...
- VIER CHRISTLICHE PREDIGTEN VOM WUCHER, DARINNEN NEBEN DER SUMMARISCHEN AUSSLEGUNG ETTLICHER EUANGELIEN IM ADUENT...
- ZEHEN PREDIG VON DEN SECHS HAUPTSTUCKEN CHRISTLICHER LEHR...

Andreas, A T *see*
- HISTORY OF CHICAGO
- HISTORY OF COOK COUNTY
- HISTORY OF THE STATE OF KANSAS

ANDREAS, A.T. AND CO *see* HISTORY OF ST CLAIR COUNTY

Andreas, F C *see* THE BOOK OF THE MAINYO-I-KHARD, ALSO ON OLD FRAGMENT OF THE BUNDEHESH, BOTH IN THE ORIGINAL PAHLAVI BEING A FASCIMILE OF A MANUSCRIPT...

Andreas, Fred *see* DAS VOLLKOMMENE VERBRECHEN

ANDREAS GRYPHIUS UND SEINE HERODES-EPEN : EIN BEITRAG ZUR CHARAKTERISTIK DES BAROCKSTILS / Gnerich, Ernst – (Includes bibliographical references) – Leipzig: M Hesse, 1906 – 1 – us U.W. Library [430]

ANDREAS HOFER PAMPHLET COLLECTION – 1926 – 1 – CSUXANQ3113-B – us Hoover Inst Photo [943]

ANDREAS HVYGELMVMZOON BERNARDUS KIRCHEN – Wederlegginghe, vande grove onbeschaemde vnde tastelicke Logenen van Vbbo Emmen. tegen het leven vnde leere van Dauid Iorissoon. 1600. BME-411 1 – 9 – ne IDC [240]

ANDREAS OSANG : ERZAEHLUNG / Leppa, Karl Franz – Karlsbad: Kraft, 1943 – 1r – 1 – us U.W. Library [830]

Andreas-Salome, Lou *see*
- IM ZWISCHENLAND
- MA
- MENSCHENKINDER
- RUTH

Andree, Fritz *see* WIRKUNGS- UND ERINNERUNGSSTAETTEN DES DICHTERS HOFFMANN VON FALLERSLEBEN IN WORT UND BILD

ANDREE HOFER : GESCHICHTLICHES TRAUERSPIEL IN FUENF AUFZUEGEN / Auerbach, Berthold – Leipzig: G Wigand, 1850 – 1r – 1 – us U.W. Library [820]

Andree, J *see* DREY UND DREISSIG PREDIGEN VON DEN FUERNEMMSTEN SPALTUNGEN IN DER CHRISTLICHEN RELIGION

Andree, Richard *see* DIE FLUTSAGEN

ANDREES WORLD ATLAS 1912 / ed by Scobel, A – 5th rev enl ed – 8mf – 9 – A$35.00 – 0-7241-9751-6 – at State Libr Vic [910]

Andreev, A I *see*
- PETR VELIKII
- TERMINOLOGICHESKII SLOVAR' CHASTNYKH AKTOV MOSKOVSKOGO GOSUDARSTVA

Andreev, I E et al *see* ENTSIKLOPEDICHESKII SLOVAR'

Andreev, I I *see* KHIMICHESKII SOSTAVI FIZICHESKIIA SVOISTVA I ADOVITYKH VESHCHESTV, PRIMI ENI AEMYKH DLIA BOEVYKH TSIELEI

Andreev, N N *see* SBORNIK ZAKONOV I RASPORIAZHENII OTNOSIASHCHIKHSIA K VODNOMU TRANSPORTU

Andreevskii, I *see*
- O NAMESTNIKAKH, VOEVODAKH I GUBERNATORAKH
- O PRAVAKH INOSTRANTSEV V ROSSII DO VSTUPLENIIA IOANA 3 VASIL'EVICHA NA PRESTOL VELIKOGO KNIAZHESTVA MOSKOVSKAGO

Andreevsky, Alexander von *see* DER WEG ZUM GRAL

ANDREI BELYI / Mochul'skii, K – Paris. 1955. BR-1443 2 – 8 – ne IDC [460]

Andreianov, M A *see* OPISANIE KOLLEKTSII PEDAGOGICHESKAGO MUZEIA VOENNO-UCHEBNYKH ZAVEDENII., 1. ISTORIIA

Andres, J *see*
- CONFVSION DE LA SECTE DE MVHAMED
- OPERA CHIAMATA CONFVSIONE DELLA SETTA MACHVMETANA, ...

Andres Marcos, Teodoro *see* VITORIA Y CARLOS 5TH EN LA SOBERANIA HISPANOAMERICANA. SALAMANCA, 1937

Andres Martinez, Gregorio *see* CARTA DE PEDRO PONCE DE LEON, OBISPO DE PLASENCIA, A FELIPE 2, SOBRE LAS RELIQUIAS Y LIBRERIAS DE SU OBISPADO Y SUS ACTIVIDADES LITERARIAS

Andres, Stefan Paul *see*
- GAESTE IM PARADIES
- DER GEFRORENE DIONYSUS
- DIE HOCHZEIT DER FEINDE
- DIE LIEBESSCHAUKEL
- REQUIEM FUER EIN KIND
- DIE SINTFLUT
- WIR SIND UTOPIA

Andresen, Carl *see* DIE LEHRE VON DER WIEDERGEBURT AUF THEISTISCHER GRUNDLAGE

Andreski, Stanislav *see* COMMUNISM AND THE IMPORTATION OF ADVANCED TECHNOLOGY: THE CASE OF POLAND

Andrew, A L *see* THE SAMOAN SETTLEMENT OF 1899

ANDREW CASTAGNE, OR, ADVENTURE OF AN OLD MARINER OF THE BRIGANTINE SWORDFISH WRECKED IN THE GULF OF ST LAWRENCE IN 1867 – Montreal: C. Chapleau, 1882. 00015. (Pre-1900 Canadiana) – 9 – cn C.I.H.M. [910]

ANDREW DICKSON WHITE PAPERS, 1832-1918 / White, Andrew Dickson – (Diplomat and co-founder and first president of Cornell University. Ca 100,000 items) – 149r – 1 – $9355.00 – us UMI [920]

ANDREW JACKSON 2 ACCOUNTS *see* JACKSON, ANDREW, 2, ACCOUNTS, MS 1880

ANDREW JACKSON PAPERS – 78r – 1 – $2,730.00 – Dist. us Scholarly Res – us L of C Photodup [975]

Andrew, John A *see* PAPERS OF JOHN A. ANDREW, 1772-1895

ANDREW JOHNSON PAPERS – (With guide) – 55r – 1 – $1,925.00 – Dist. us Scholarly Res – us L of C Photodup [975]

Andrew, Lucy Brett *see* PRACTICAL PATENT PROCEDURE

ANDREW PETERSON PAPERS / Peterson, Andrew – (Includes filmed inventory) – 1854-98 – 3r – 1 – $90.00 – us M.H.S. [920]

Andrews, C C *see* HISTORY OF ST PAUL

Andrews, Caesar *see* FIELD DIARY

Andrews, CF *see* NORTH INDIA

Andrews, Charles *see*
- AMERICAN JURISPRUDENCE.
- GUIDE TO THE MANUSCRIPT MATERIALS FOR THE HISTORY OF THE UNITED STATES TO 1783 IN THE BRITISH MUSEUM, MINOR LONDON ARCHIVES AND THE LIBRARIES OF OXFORD AND CAMBRIDGE
- GUIDE TO THE MANUSCRIPT MATERIALS FOR THE HISTORY OF THE UNITED STATES TO 1793, IN THE BRITISH MUSEUM, IN MINOR LONDON ARCHIVES, AND IN THE LIBRARIES OF OXFORD AND CAMBRIDGE
- GUIDE TO THE MATERIALS FOR AMERICAN HISTORY TO 1783 IN THE PUBLIC RECORD OFFICE, LONDON
- GUIDE TO THE MATERIALS FOR AMERICAN HISTORY, TO 1783, IN THE PUBLIC RECORD OFFICE OF GREAT BRITAIN

Andrews, Elisha Benjamin *see* THE HISTORY OF THE LAST QUARTER-CENTURY IN THE UNITED STATES, 1870-1895

Andrews, Emerson *see* LIVING LIFE, OR, AUTOBIOGRAPHY OF REV. EMERSON ANDREWS

Andrews, Frank M *see* SCIENTIFIC PRODUCTIVITY

Andrews, H C *see*
- BOTANISTS REPOSITORY
- BOTANISTS REPOSITORY,...
- COLOURED ENGRAVINGS OF HEATHS
- GERANIUMS
- ROSES: OR A MONOGRAPH OF THE GENUS ROSA

Andrews, Horace *see* MANUAL OF THE LAWS AND COURTS OF THE UNITED STATES.

Andrews, J A *see* WHAT IS COMMUNISM? AND OTHER ANARCHIST ESSAYS

Andrews, J N *see* HISTORY OF THE SABBATH AND FIRST DAY OF THE WEEK

Andrews, J R *see* ALONE IN THE WIDE, WIDE WORLD: A MUSICALLY ILLUSTRATED SERVICE

Andrews, James Bruyn *see* CONTES LIGURES, TRADITIONS DE LA RIVIERE: RECUEILLIS ENTRE MENTON ET GENES

Andrews, James deWitt *see* AMERICAN LAW.

Andrews, L F *see* PIONEERS OF POLK COUNTRY

Andrews, Martin R *see* HISTORY OF MARIETTA AND WASHINGTON COUNTY

Andrews, Matthew T *see* COMRADES OF THE ROAD, N.D

Andrews, Samuel James *see* GOD'S REVELATIONS OF HIMSELF TO MEN

Andrews, Stephen Pearl *see*
- THE LABOR DOLLAR
- THE SCIENCE OF SOCIETY
- DIE WISSENSCHAFT VON DER GESELLSCHAFT

ANDREWS' VALUATION TABLES AT COMPOUND INTEREST / Andrews, Walter S – Toronto: Hunter, Rose. 1884. 00802. (Pre-1900 Canadiana) – 9 – cn C.I.H.M. [332]

Andrews, Walter S *see* ANDREWS' VALUATION TABLES AT COMPOUND INTEREST

Andrews, William *see*
- LEGAL LORE
- THE LIFEBOAT AND OTHER POEMS
- SWIMMING AND LIFE-SAVING

Andriamananjara, R *see* LABOR MOBILIZATION; THE MOROCCAN EXPERIENCE

Andriessen, A J *see* PLEGTIGE INHULDIGING VAN. WILLEM KAREL HENDRIK FRISO. ALS MARKGRAAF VAN VERE

Andrieu, M *see*
- IMMIXTIO ET CONSECRATIO
- LES ORDINES ROMANI DU H.M.A

Andrieux *see* LE TRESOR

Androsov, V *see* STATISTICHESKAIA ZAPISKA O MOSKVE

Androuet du Cerceau, Jacques *see*
- LECONS DE PERSPECTIVE POSITIVE
- LIVRE D'ARCHITECTURE
- SECOND LIVRE D'ARCHITECTURE

Androutsos, Chrestos *see* THE VALIDITY OF ENGLISH ORDINATIONS FROM AN ORTHODOX CATHOLIC POINT OF VIEW

Andry de Boisregard, N *see* REFLEXIONS SUR L'USAGE PRESENT DE LA LANGUE FRANCOISE

LOS ANDZSHELESER TEGLICHE TSAYT = THE JEWISH TIMES – Los Angeles, CA.1921 – 1 – us A.J.P.C. [071]

L'ANE D'OR: RECUEIL SATIRIQUE / Texier, Edmond Auguste – Paris: Lavigne, 1842. 128p. 2 fiches. (Literature Collection) – 9 – 6.00 – fr Bibl Nationale [830]

ANECDOTA AMBROSIANA / Muratori, Lodovico A – Mediolani-Patavii. Tom 1-4. 1697-1713 – 23mf – 9 – Dfl81.00 – ne Slangenburg [945]

ANECDOTA AMBROSIANA / Muratori, Lodovico A – Mediolani/Patavii. v1-4. 1697-1713 – Dfl81.00 – ne Slangenburg [240]

ANECDOTA MAREDSOLANA : VOLS 1, 2 EN 3 / Morin, G – 37mf – 8 – ne Slangenburg [240]

ANECDOTA OXONIENSA – (Missing: v4) – Semitics Series. Oxford. v1-12. 1882-1913 – 94mf – 9 – ne IDC [240]

ANECDOTA OXONIENSIA *see* A COMMENTARY ON THE BOOK OF DANIEL

ANECDOTA OXONIENSIS, SEMITIC SERIES *see* MEDIEVAL JEWISH CHRONICLES, VOL 2

ANECDOTA SACRA ET PROFANA EX ORIENTE ET OCCIDENTE ALLATA, SIVE, NOTITIA CODICUM GRAECORUM, ARABICORUM, SYRIACORUM, COPTICORUM, HEBRAICORUM, AETHIOPICORUM, LATINORUM : CUM EXCERPTIS MULTIS MAXIMAM PARTEM GRAECIS ET TRIGINTA QUINQUE SCRIPTURARUM ANTIQUISSIMARUM EXEMPLIS / Tischendorf, Constantin von – (In Greek and Latin. Includes index) – Lipsiae: Sumptibus Hermanni Fries, 1861 – 1mf – 9 – 0-8370-9319-8 – 1986-3319 – us A.T.L.A. [220]

ANECDOTA SYRIACA / Land, J P N – Lugd. Batavorum. Tom 1-4. 1862-1875 – 54mf – 9 – Dfl189.00 – ne Slangenburg [470]

ANECDOTAL LIFE OF SIR JOHN MACDONALD / Biggar, Emerson Bristol – Montreal: J. Lovell, 1891. 00133. (Pre-1900 Canadiana) – 9 – cn C.I.H.M. [320]

ANECDOTAS MISIONALES... / Corredor Garcia, Antonio – Madrid: Arch. Ibero Americano, 1965 – 1 – sp Bibl Santa Ana [240]

ANECDOTE LIVES OF WITS AND HUMOURISTS / Timbs, John – London: R. Bentley, 1872. 2v – 1 – us U.W. Library [920]

ANECDOTES AFRICAINES, DEPUIS L'ORIGINE OU LA DECOUVERTE DES DIFFERENTS ROYAUMES QUI COMPOSENT L'AFRIQUE, JUSQU'A NOS JOURS / Dubois Fontanelle, J G – Paris, Vincent. 1775 – 9 – 20.00 – fr Orientalistes [960]

ANECDOTES DRAMATIQUES / Clement, J M B & DeLaporte, J – 3v. Paris. 1775. BP-214 1 – 9 – ne IDC [780]

ANECDOTES OF A LIFE ON THE OCEAN: BEING A PORTION OF THE EXPERIENCES OF TWENTY-SEVEN YEARS' SERVICE IN MANY PARTS OF THE WORLD / Cowans, David – s.l.: s.n., 1871 (Montreal: J. Lovell). 00265. (Pre-1900 Canadiana) – 9 – cn C.I.H.M. [910]

ANECDOTES OF EMINENT PAINTERS IN SPAIN, DURING THE 16TH AND 17TH CENTURIES / Cumberland, R – O-991 1. 2 v. 1782 – 9 – ne IDC [870]

ANECDOTES OF EMINENT PAINTERS IN SPAIN, DURING THE SIXTEENTH AND SEVENTEENTH CENTURIES... / Cumberland, R – London. 2v. 1782 – 4mf – ne IDC [700]

ANECDOTES OF PAINTING IN ENGLAND. STRAWBERRY HILL / Walpole, H – O 1079 1. 4 v – 9 – ne IDC [870]

ANECDOTES OF THE WESLEYS: ILLUSTRATIVE OF THEIR CHARACTER AND PERSONAL HISTORY / Wakeley, Joseph Beaumont – Introd. by Rev. J. M'Clintock. New York: Carlton & Lanahan, 1869. 391p – 1 – us U.W. Library [920]

ANEKA OLAH RAGA – Djakarta. (incomplete) SE-871 1. 1950-1966 – 9 – ne IDC [073]

ANEKDOTY PRO TSARIA NIKOLAIA DIKARIA NA ZLOBU DNIA – Petrograd: [s.n.], 1918 – 1 – CSUX89-B3178 – us Hoover Inst Photo [947]

Anemueller, Susann *see* AKTUELLE FRAUENARBEITSSCHUTZPOLITIK

Anene, J C O *see* THE ESTABLISHMENT AND CONSOLIDATION OF IMPERIAL GOVERNMENT IN SOUTHERN NIGERIA, 1891-1904

Aner, Karl *see* DER AUFKLAERER, FRIEDRICH NICOLAI

Anerio, G F *see* ANTIPHONAE, SEV SACRAE CANTIONES, QUAE IN TOTIVS ANNI...

ANESTHESIA AND ANALGESIA – (1983-. 1,5,6,9) – v36-. 1957- – 1 – us UMI [073]

ANESTHESIA AND ANALGESIA – v76-83. 1993-1996 – 1,5,6,9 – $110.00r – us Williams [617]

ANESTHESIA AND ANALGESIA: CURRENT RESEARCHES – (Formerly: CURRENT RESEARCHES IN ANESTHESIA AND ANALGESIA). v. 6-40. 1927-1961 – 1,5,6 – us Princeton Micro [617]

ANESTHESIOLOGY – (1967- 5,6. 1970- 9) – v. 1- 1940- – 1 – us UMI [610]

ANEXO AL PLAN DE DESARROLLO. 1964/67 / Spain. Comisaria del Plan de Desarrollo Economico y Social. Comercio Exterior – Madrid. 1964. BD-134 1 – 9 – ne IDC [338]

ANEXO AL PLAN DE DESARROLLO ECONOMICO Y SOCIAL, ANOS 1964-1967 / Spanish Guinea. (Spain). Comisaria del Plan de Desarrollo Economico y Social Guinea Ecuatorial – D 1479 1. 1964 – 9 – ne IDC [338]

ANEXOS AL PLAN / Spain. Comisaria del Plan de Desarrollo Economico y Social. Turismo y Servicios de Informacion – Madrid. 1963 – 9 – ne IDC [338]

ANF LIHIM NG ISANG PULO: NOBELANG TAGALOG. / Aguilar, Faustino – Manila. 1958 – 1 – us Res Libr [490]

DIE ANFAENGE DER BEGINEN : EIN BEITRAG ZUR GESCHICHTE DER VOLKSFROEMMIGKEIT UND DES ORDENSWESENS IM HOCHMITTELALTER / Greven, Joseph – Muenster i.W.: Aschendorff, 1912 – 1mf – us A.T.L.A. [240]

DIE ANFAENGE DER GEGENREFORMATION IN DEN NIEDERLANDEN / Kalkoff, Paul – Halle a.S.: Verein fuer Reformationsgeschichte, 1903 (Schriften des Vereins fuer Reformationsgeschichte; 21. Jahrg., Schrift 79, 81) – 1mf – us A.T.L.A. [240]

DIE ANFAENGE DER TUEBINGER THEOL. QUARTALSCHRIFT – Rottenburg, 1938 – Dfl9.00 – ne Slangenburg [240]

DIE ANFAENGE DES ERASMUS : HUMANISMUS UND "DEVOTIO MODERNA" / Mestwerdt, P – Leipzig, 1917 – 10mf – 8 – ne Slangenburg [140]

DIE ANFAENGE DES HEILIGENKULTS IN DER CHRISTLICHEN KIRCHE / Lucius, Paul Ernst; ed by Anrich, Gustav – Tuebingen: Mohr, 1904 – 2mf – us A.T.L.A. [240]

DIE ANFAENGE DES NATIONALEN JAHWEGLAUBENS : EIN BEITRAG ZUR ISRAELITISCHEN RELIGIONGESCHICHTE / Bewer, Julius August – Gotha: F A Perthes, [ca 1904] – 1mf – 9 – 0-8370-2323-8 – 1985-0323 – us A.T.L.A. [270]

DIE ANFAENGE UNSERER RELIGION / Wernle, Paul – Tuebingen: J.C.B. Mohr, 1904. 2 fiches – 9 – us A.T.L.A. [240]

ANFANGGRUNDE DER NATURLEHRE / Erxleben, Johann Christian Polykarp – Gottingen: J. C. Dietrich, 1787 – 1 – us U.W. Library [530]

ANFANGSGRUENDE DER CHEMIE / Erxleben, Johann Christian Polykarp – Goettingen, 1775 – 1 – us U.W. Library [540]

ANFANGSGRUENDE DER THEORETISCHEN MUSIK / Marpurg, Friedrich Wilhelm – 1757 – 9 – us Sibley [780]

ANFANGS-GRUENDE DES GENERAL-BASSES / Mizler, L C – 1739 – 9 – us Sibley [780]

ANFANGSGRUNDE DER OKONOMISCHEN UND TECHNISCHEN CHYMIE / Suckow, Georg Adolph – Leipzig, 1784 – 1 – us U.W. Library [540]

ANFITEATRO / Alvarez Saenz de Buruaga, Jose – Merida: Imp. Rodriguez, s.a. – 1 – sp Bibl Santa Ana [820]

EL ANFITEATRO ROMANO DE MERIDA. MEMORIA (1916 A 1918) / Melida, Jose Ramon – Madrid, 1919 – 1 – sp Bibl Santa Ana [946]

EL ANFITEATRO Y EL CIRCO ROMANOS DE MERIDA. MEMORIA / Melida, Jose Ramon – Madrid: Rev. Arch. Bibl. Mus, 1921 – 1 – sp Bibl Santa Ana [946]

Anfossi, P *see* NITTETI: DEH VIEN MECO AMATO

ANG ATONG KABILIN – Siyudad sa Sugbu: [s.n.], nov 11 1930-dec 25 1934 – reel 8 – 1 – us Res Libr [072]

ANG CAMATUORAN – Sugbu, Philippines: [s.n.], jan 2 1894-dec 27 1911 – us Res Libr [950]

Ang, Giok Goen *see* READINGS IN BUSINESS ADMINISTRATION

ANG MAIKLING KATHANG TAGALOG / Abadilla, A G – Quezon City: Bede's Publishing House, 1967. c1954. viii,307p. Tagalog fiction-history and criticism – 1 – us U.W. Library [390]

Angarov, Aleksei Ivanovich *see* KLASSOVAIA BORBA V SOVETSKOI DEREVNE

Angarskii, Nikolai Semenovich *see* MOSKOVSKI I SOVET V DVUKH REVOLIUTSII AKH

DER ANGEBLICHE EVANGELIENKOMMENTAR DES THEOPHILIUS VON ANTIOCHIEN (T.U.U. 1-1/4B) / Harnack, Adolf von – Leipzig, 1883 – 2mf – 9 – ne Slangenburg [240]

ANGEL POLICIANO-SILVAE NUTRITIA / Poliziano, Angelo; ed by Sanchez de las Brozas, Francisco – 1596 – 9 – 1.50f – sp Bibl Santa Ana [450]

ANGEL RODRIGUEZ (ALIAS) ER PERIODISTA... / Amores Gonzalez, Meliton – Astorga: Imp. y Lit. de Sierra, 1925 – 1 – sp Bibl Santa Ana [946]

ANGEL SMERTI / Odoevsteva, I – Roman. Ed. 2. Paris. 1928. BR-1222 2 – 8 – ne IDC [460]

ANGELA : TIROLER NOVELLE / Achleitner, Arthur – Leipzig: Hesse & Becker, [19–] – 1r – 1 – us U.W. Library [830]

ANGELA BORGIA : NOVELLE / Meyer, Conrad Ferdinand – 12. Aufl. Leipzig: H Haessel, 1900 – 1r – 1 – us U.W. Library [830]

THE ANGELA DAVIS TRIAL WITH INDEX / Meiklejohn Civil Liberties Institute – 13 reels – 1 – $500.00 – us Trans-Media [340]

Angeleri, G M *see* MESSE QVATTRO. OPERA SECONDA

Angelerius, Q T *see* EPIDEMIOLOGIA, SIVE TRACTATUS DE PESTE AD REGNI SARDINIAE...

Los Angeles County Pioneer Society *see* HISTORICAL RECORD AND SOUVENIR

Angelia Mangano, E de *see* DELIBAZIONE

Angelica. Presbytery (Pres. Ch. in the U.S.A.) *see* MINUTES, 1828-1856

ANGELICUM – Rome. v.13-20, 1936-43. Incomplete – 1 – 23.00 – us L of C Photodup [240]

ANGELICUM AC DIUINUM OPUS MUSICE FRANCHINI GAFURII LAUDENSIS REGII MUSICI / Gaffurius, F – Mediolani. 1508. BP-677 – 9 – ne IDC [780]

ANGELICUM AC DIVINUM OPUS MUSICE.. / Gaffurio, Franchino – 1508 – 9 – us Sibley [780]

Angelini, C A *see* FAVORITE SOLO[S] FOR THE VIOLIN AND HARPSICHORD BKS 1-2

Angelini, Marc A *see* AEROBIC RESPONSES TO 12 WEEKS OF TRAINING ON VARIOUS MODES OF HOME EXERCISE EQUIPMENT IN SEDENTARY ADULTS

ANGELIQUE ARNAULD : ABBESS OF PORT ROYAL / Martin, Frances – 2nd ed. London: Macmillan, 1873 – 1mf – 9 – 0-8370-8696-5 – 1986-2696 – us A.T.L.A. [920]

Angelis, Pedro de *see*
- BASILICAE VETERIS VATICANAE DESCRIPTIO
- COLECCION DE OBRAS Y DOCUMENTOS RELATIVOS A LA HISTORIA ANTIGUA Y MODERNA DE LAS PROVINCIAS DEL RIO DE LA PLATA
- DE LA NAVIGATION DE L'AMAZONE...

Angell, J B *see* LECTURES ON PUBLIC INTERNATIONAL LAW

Angell, Joseph Kinnicut *see* A TREATISE ON THE RIGHT OF PROPERTY IN TIDE WATERS AND IN THE SOIL AND SHORES THREROF

Angeloni, B [ps. of J Shebbeare] *see* LETTERS ON THE ENGLISH NATION

Angeloni, V *see*
- LA CAMBIALE E IL VAGLIA CAMBIARIO

ANGELOS : ARCHIV FUER NEUTESTAMENTLICHE ZEITGESCHICHTE UND KULTURKUNDE – 1(1925)-4(1932) – 21mf – 9 – Dfl74.00 – ne Slangenburg [073]

Angelov, Vasil G *see* DOBRI VESTI

ANGELS AND DEMONS ACCORDING TO LACTANTIUS / Schneweis, E – 1944 – 4mf – 9 – ne Slangenburg [240]

ANGELS OF THE BATTLEFIELD : A HISTORY OF THE LABORS OF THE CATHOLIC SISTERHOODS IN THE LATE CIVIL WAR / Barton, George – Philadelphia, Pa.: Catholic Art, 1897 – 1mf – us A.T.L.A. [240]

Angelus *see* PRIMERA ANTOLOGIA DE POETAS PACENSES

ANGELUS SILESIUS UND SEINE MYSTIK / Seltmann, C – (Includes bibliographical references) – Breslau: G P Aderholz, 1896 – 1r – 1 – us U.W. Library [430]

Angely, Louis *see* NEUESTES KOMISCHES THEATER

ANGENEHME STUNDEN – nos1-13. 1887 (complete) – 1r – 1 – ATLA 1993-S000 – us A.T.L.A. [073]

Anger, D *see*
- LES DEPENDANCES DE L'ABBAYE DE SAINT-GERMAIN-DES-PRES

Anger, Rudolf *see*
- RATIO QUA LOCI VETERIS TESTAMENTI IN EVANGELIO MATTHAEI LAUDANTUR
- VORLESUNGEN UEBER DIE GESCHICHTE DER MESSIANISCHEN IDEE

Anger, William Henry *see*
- BE YOUR OWN LAWYER: A BUSINESS MANUAL CONTAINING A SYNOPSIS OF THE MERCANTILE, OR BUSINESS LAWS OF ONTARIO: THE TECHNICAL POINTS AND MAIN FEATURES OF THE LAW.
- BUSINESS MANUAL: COMPRISING TWENTY-FIVE CHAPTERS ON BUSINESS LAW; ALSO VARIOUS FORMS OF LEGAL AND BUSINESS DOCUMENTS, TOGETHER WITH A SYSTEM OF FARM ACCOUNTS.

ANGERBURGER KREIS-BLATT – Angerburg, feb 10 1855-aug 26 1865, feb 10 1866-dec 21 1867, feb 11 1868-feb 16 1872, oct 4 1882-85, 1888-89, 1892-1903, 1906-07 (all incomplete) – 10r – 1 – Dist. gw Mikrofilm – gw Misc Inst [943]

ANGERBURGER KREISZEITUNG – Angerburg, 1939-may 31 1941 (incomplete) – 5r – 1 – Dist. gw Mikrofilm – gw Misc Inst [943]

ANGERMANLANDS NYHETER HAERNOESANDSPOSTEN – Haernoesand, Stockholm, Sweden. 1951-53 – 1 – sw Kungliga [072]

Angermayer, Fred A *see* FLIEG, ROTER ADLER VON TIROL!

ANGERMUENDER TAGEBLATT – Angermuende, 1938, 1941-jun 1944 – 1 – Dist. gw Mikrofilm – gw Misc Inst [943]

ANGERMUENDER ZEITUNG UND KREISBLATT – Angermuende, jan-mar, oct-dec 1929 – 1 – Dist. gw Mikrofilm – gw Misc Inst [943]

Angers, Auguste Real *see*
- ASSEMBLEE LEGISLATIVE DE QUEBEC: SEANCE DU 13 DECEMBRE 1876
- LE COUP D'ETAT, OU, LE RENVOI DU CABINET DE BOUCHERVILLE:..
- DISCOURS DE L'HON. SOLLICITEUR-GENERAL ANGERS: EXPOSANT LA POLITIQUE DU GOUVERNEMENT RELATIVE A LA CONSTRUCTION D'UN CHEMIN DE FER PROVINCIAL SUR LA RIVE NORD DU SAINT-LAURENT: SEANCE DU 10 DECEMBRE 1875

Angers. France. Cathedrale *see* CARTULAIRE NOIR DE LA CATHEDRALE D'ANGERS.

Angers. France. St. Laud (Church) *see* CARTULAIRE DU CHAPITRE DE SAINT-LAUD D'ANGERS.

Anges, Marie des *see*
- ARCHIVES DE L'HOTEL-DIEU SAINT-MICHEL DE ROBERVAL 1917-1922
- BIBLIOGRAPHIE ANALYTIQUE
- BIBLIOGRAPHIE DE L'OEUVRE DE JEANNE D'AIGLE (DAIGLE), MEMBRE DE LA SOCIETE DES ECRIVAINS CANADIENS...
- BIBLIOGRAPHIE DE MONSIEUR L'ABBE PAUL-EMILE GOSSELIN, PROFESSEUR DE PHILOSOPHIE AU SEMINAIRE DE QUEBEC, SECRETAIRE GENERAL DU COMITE DE LA SURVIVANCE FRANCAISE EN AMERIQUE

DIE ANGESTELLTEN-BEWEGUNG / Allgemeiner Freier Angestelltenbund – 1921-25; 1928 31. Berlin. (Serial publications of German trade unions in the Memorial Library, University of Wisconsin-Madison) – 1 – us U.W. Library [331]

ANGESTELLTEN-ZEITUNG – Teplitz-Schoenau (Teplice Lazne), Czechoslovakia. 1921-24 – 1r – 1 – gw Mikrofilm [072]

Angeville, A d' *see* ESSAI SUR LA STATISTIQUE DE LA POPULATION FRANCAISE, 1836

ANGEWANDTE BOTANIK – (v1-4. Dfl70.00v; v5. Dfl35.00; v6-25. Dfl100.00v) – Berlin. v1-25. 1919-43 – 5,9 – Dfl2,315.00 – ne Swets [580]

ANGEWANDTE CHEMIE : INCLUDING "CHEMISTRY – A EUROPEAN JOURNAL" – v1-108. 1887-1996 – 1,5,6,13 – us V.C.H. [540]

ANGEWANDTE CHEMIE : INTERNATIONAL EDITION IN ENGLISH. INCLUDING "CHEMISTRY – A EUROPEAN JOURNAL" – v1-35. 1962-96 – 1,5,6,13 – us V.C.H. [540]

ANGEWANDTE CHEMIE – Weinheim, Germany. v5-54. 1887-1941 – 31r – 5 – us Ross [540]

ANGGARAN DASAR DAN ANGGARAN RUMAH TANGGA B.T.I / Barisan Tani Indonesia – SE-4402 1. 1963 – 9 – ne IDC [950]

ANGGARAN DASAR ("S.B.T.P.") / Sarikat Buruh Technik dan Perindustrian – SE 4842 1. 1950 – 9 – ne IDC [950]

ANGGARAN KEUANGAN DAERAH ISTIMEWA JOGJAKARTA / Jogjakarta. Indonesia – Jogjakarta, 1957. v1-2.TEN 1143. BSE-1717/1 – 9 – ne IDC [950]

Anghiera, Pietro Martire d' *see* PETRI MARTYRIS AB ANGLIERA(...)DE REBUS OCEANICIS ET ORBO NOVO DECADES TRES(...)

ANGKASA – Djakarta. (incomplete) SE-581 1. 1950-1971 – 9 – ne IDC [073]

ANGKATAN BERSENDJATA – Djakarta, Indonesia: Edisi Pusat, 1965-1993 – 78r – 1 – us L of C Photodup [072]

UNE ANGLAISE INTELLECTUELLE EN FRANCE SOUS LA RESTAURATION: MISS MARY CLARK / Smith, Marion Elmina – Paris: Champion, 1927. 145p. (Les Femmes Collection) – 2mf – 9 – $6.00 – fr Bibl Nationale [920]

Anglebert, Jean H d' *see* PIECES DE CLAVECIN...AVEC LA MANIERE DE LES JOUER...ET AUTRES AIRS DE MONSIEUR DE LULLY..
Angleria, Fra. C *see* LA REGOLA DEL CONTRAPONTO, E DELLA MUSICAL COMPOSITIONE
Angleria, Pedro Martir *see*
- DE ORBE NOVO
- DE REBUS OCEANICIS & ORBE NOVO DECADA TRES
- FUENTES HISTORICAS SOBRE COLON Y AMERICA
- PREMIERE DECADE DU ORBE NOVO

THE ANGLER'S GUIDE TO EASTERN CANADA: SHOWING WHERE, WHEN AND HOW TO FISH FOR SALMON, BASS, OUANANICHE AND TROUT / Chambers, Edward Thomas Davies – Quebec: "Morning Chronicle", 1898. 02148. (Pre-1900 Canadiana) – 9 – cn C.I.H.M. [790]
L'ANGLETERRE CHRETIENNE AVANT LES NORMANDS / Cabrol, Fernand – Paris: V Lecoffre, 1909 – 1mf – us A.T.L.A. [240]
ANGLETON FIRST BAPTIST CHURCH. ANGLETON, TEXAS : CHURCH RECORDS – 1908-38 – 1 – 18.09 – us Baptist [240]
ANGLIA REDIVIVA: ENGLANDS RECOVERY / Sprigg, Joshua – 1647 – 9 – 20.00 – us Scholars' Facs [941]
ANGLIA SACRA / Wharton, Hy – H 1280 2. 2 pts. 1691 – 8 – ne IDC [240]
ANGLICAN CAREER OF CARDINAL NEWMAN / Abbott, Edwin Abbott – London, New York: Macmillan, 1892 – 3mf – us A.T.L.A. [240]
THE ANGLICAN CHURCH IN CANADA / Champion, Thomas Edward – Toronto: Hunter, Rose, 1898. 00551. (Pre-1900 Canadiana) – 9 – cn C.I.H.M. [240]
THE ANGLICAN CHURCH IN SOUTH AMERICA / Every, E F – London: S.P.C.K., 1915 – 1mf – us A.T.L.A. [240]
Anglican Church of Canada. Diocese of Nova Scotia. Bishop *see* A CHARGE DELIVERED TO THE CLERGY AT THE VISITATION HELD IN THE CATHEDRAL CHURCH OF ST LUKE, AT HALIFAX, ON THE 6TH DAY OF JULY, 1870
THE ANGLICAN EPISCOPATE AND THE AMERICAN COLONIES / Cross, Arthur Lyon – New York: Longmans, Green, 1902. (Harvard historical studies; v9) – 1mf – us A.T.L.A. [240]
ANGLICAN JOURNAL *see* CANADIAN CHURCHMAN
ANGLICAN JOURNAL/JOURNAL ANGLICAN – (Cont: Canadian Churchman. 1989 vol entitled Anglican Journal/Journal Episcopal) – Toronto. v115- 1989- – 9 – cn Micromedia [240]
ANGLICAN JOURNAL/JOURNAL EPISCOPAL *see* ANGLICAN JOURNAL/ JOURNAL ANGLICAN
THE ANGLICAN MINISTRY : ITS NATURE AND VALUE IN RELATION TO THE CATHOLIC PRIESTHOOD : AN ESSAY / Hutton, Arthur Wollaston – London: C. Kegan Paul, 1879 – 2mf – us A.T.L.A. [240]
THE ANGLICAN REFORMATION / Clark, William – New York: Christian Literature, 1897. 05259. (Pre-1900 Canadiana) – 9 – cn C.I.H.M. [240]
THE ANGLICAN REVIVAL / Overton, John H – London: Blackie, 1897 (The Victorian era series) – 1mf – us A.T.L.A. [240]
ANGLICAN THEOLOGICAL REVIEW – 12(1929-1930)-34(1952) – 141mf – 9 – Dfl494.00 – ne Slangenburg [073]
ANGLICAN THEOLOGICAL REVIEW – (Missing: 1917-1928. v1-11) – New York. v1-34. 1917-1952 – 141mf – 9 – ne IDC [240]
ANGLICISMES ET CANADIANISMES / Buies, Arthur – Quebec: C. Darveau, 1888. 00336. (Pre-1900 Canadiana) – 9 – cn C.I.H.M. [971]
ANGLICISMES ET CANADIANISMES / Buies, Arthur – Quebec: C Darveau, 1888. SEM105P19 – 2mf – 9 – Can$4.50 – cn Bibl Nat [440]
Anglim, John *see* PALAU'S STRATEGIC POSITION PLACES DEMOCRACY AT RISK
Anglin, Francis Alexander *see* LIMITATIONS OF ACTIONS AGAINST TRUSTEES AND RELIEF FROM LIABILITY FOR TECHNICAL BREACHES OF TRU
ANGLO AFRICAN – Grahamstown, South Africa. 4 Jan 1855-31 Dec 1870. 10 reels. Incorporated into: Eastern Star – 1, 16 diazo available at reduced price – sa SA Libr [072]
ANGLO FRENCH STAGE CHRONICLE (FRENCH EDITION) – (Chronique 29 Jul 1899) – London, UK. 23 Jun, 14 Jul 1899 – 1 – uk British Libr Newspaper [072]
ANGLO GERMAN FRIENDSHIP GAZETTE : DEUTSCH-ENGLISCHE FREUNDSCHAFTS ZEITUNG – London, UK. 2 May 1911 – 1 – uk British Libr Newspaper [072]
THE ANGLO-AFRICAN – Lagos. Nigeria. - w. Jun-Dec 1863, Jul 1864-Dec 1865. (Imperfect). (37 ft) – 1 – uk British Libr Newspaper [072]
ANGLO-AFRICAN MAGAZINE – New York. v1. 1859 – 1r – 1 – us Ross [960]
Anglo-American Association *see* REPORT ON THE QUESTIONS BETWEEN GREAT BRITAIN AND THE UNITED STATES WITH RESPECT TO THE NORTH AMERICAN FISHERIES
ANGLO-AMERICAN BIBLE REVISION – (Includes indexes) – New York: American Sunday School Union, 1879 – 1mf – 9 – 0-8370-2084-0 – 1985-0084 – us A.T.L.A. [220]
ANGLO-AMERICAN MAGAZINE – v1-7. July 1852-1855 – 1 – cn Precision [073]
THE ANGLO-AMERICAN MAGAZINE – Toronto: T MacLear, 1852-[1855] – 9 – cn C.I.H.M. [970]
THE ANGLO-AMERICAN MATRIMONIAL JOURNAL – Toronto?: s.n., 1886-18– or 19– – 9 – cn C.I.H.M. [306]
ANGLO-AMERICAN TIMES – London, 27 Oct 1865-7 Nov 1896 – 35r – 1 – uk British Libr Newspaper [072]
THE ANGLO-ARGENTINE CONNECTION, 1900-1939 / Gravil, Roger – Boulder: Westview Press, 1985 – 1 – CSUXAHZ6128-B – us Hoover Inst Photo [972]
ANGLO-BOER WAR – 1 – uk Microform Academic [941]
ANGLO-CANADIAN COPYRIGHTS / Clayton, Henry R – London; New York, 1889? 03053. (Pre-1900 Canadiana) – 9 – cn C.I.H.M. [070]
ANGLO-CELT – 1846-1980 – ca 110r – 1 – ie Microforms [941]
ANGLO-CELT – Cavan, Ireland. -d. 1846-1986.136 reels – 1 – PS27.50r – ie European Micro [072]
THE ANGLO-COLORADO MINING AND MILLING GUIDE – Feb 1898-May 1905 – 1 – £160.00 – uk World [977]
THE ANGLO-EGYPTIAN SUDAN / Great Britain. War Office. General Staff. Geographical Section – Rev. Dec. 1921. London, 1921 – 1 – us Res Libr [910]
THE ANGLO-EGYPTIAN SUDAN FROM WITHIN / ed by Hamilton, J A de C – 1935 – 9 – A-310 – ne IDC [960]
ANGLO-EGYPTIAN SUDAN HANDBOOK SERIES – London: H M Stationery Off. Monographic series. No 2 – 1 – us Res Libr [910]
ANGLO-GERMAN NAVAL OPERATIONS DURING WORLD WAR 2 PAMPHLET COLLECTION – 1940-1945 – 1 – CSUXANM9180-B – us Hoover Inst Photo [335]
ANGLO-INDONESIAN PLANTATIONS / Daukes, Wilfred H – SE-2256 1. 1954 – 9 – ne IDC [630]
THE ANGLO-ISRAEL ENSIGN – Truro, N.S.: J Ross, [1880-188-?] – 9 – cn C.I.H.M. [920]
ANGLO-LATIN SATIRICAL POETS AND EPIGRAMMATISTS OF THE TWELFTH CENTURY (RS59) / ed by Wright, T – (v1 1872 Dfl30.00. v2 1872 Dfl35.00) – ne Slangenburg [410]
DAS ANGLONORMANNISCHE ERBFOLGESYSTEM / Brunner, Heinrich – Leipzig, Duncker & Humblot, 1869. 88 p. LL-105 – 1 – us L of C Photodup [340]
ANGLO-PORTUGUESE NEWS – Lisbon, Portugal. 1937-92 – 17r – 1 – us L of C Photodup [072]
THE ANGLO-RUSSIAN – London. -m. Jul 1897-Jul 1914. (2 reels) – 1 – uk British Libr Newspaper [072]
ANGLO-RUSSKII SEL'SKOKHOZIAIST VENNYI SLOVAR' / Geminova, N V et al – M., 1944 – 7mf – 9 – 1384/2 – ne IDC [580]
ANGLO-SAXON – (1889, 1899 imperfect) – Ottawa, Dec 1887-Jan 1900 – 1 1/2r – 1 – uk British Libr Newspaper [072]
THE ANGLO-SAXON : DEVOTED TO THE INTERESTS OF ENGLISHMEN AND THEIR DESCENDANTS – Ottawa, Ontariio. v12 n4. fev 1899 – 1r – 1 – Can$25.00 – cn Can Microfilming [072]
THE ANGLO-SAXON – Ottawa: [s.n., 1887-1900?] – 9 – cn C.I.H.M. [941]
THE ANGLO-SAXON AND MEDIAEVAL MANUSCRIPT COLLECTION / Corpus Christi College, Cambridge – (Collection consists of manuscripts deposited by Archbishop Parker on his death in 1575. Includes the Canterbury Gospels, the Peterborough Psalter, Chaucer's Troilus and Criseyde, the Anglo-Saxon Chronicles, the Dover Bible and the Bury Bible) – 155r – 1 – uk World [090]
ANGLO-SAXON BISHOPS, KINGS AND NOBLES / Searle, W G – H 1167 2. 1899 – 8 – ne IDC [025]
ANGLO-SAXON CHRONICLE (RS23) : ACCORDING TO THE SEVERAL ORIGINAL AUTHORITIES / ed by Thorpe, B – 2v. 1861 – Dfl49.00 – ne Slangenburg [941]
THE ANGLO-SAXON CHURCH : ITS HISTORY, REVENUES, AND GENERAL CHARACTER / Soames, Henry – London: J.W. Parker, 1856 – 1mf – us A.T.L.A. [240]
Anglo-Saxon Gold Mining Company *see* PROSPECTUS...WITH REPORTS UPON THEIR PROPERTY SITUATED IN MADOC, ONTARIO
ANGLO-SAXON GOSPELS : ANGLO-SAXON MANUSCRIPTS IN MICROFICHE FACSIMILE, VOL 3 / ed by Liuzza, Roy M & Doane, A N – Binghamton, NY. 1995 – 37mf – 8 – $120.00 ($96.00 if part of subsc) – 0-86698-183-7 – Dist. us Pegasus – us MRTS [090]
ANGLO-SAXON MAGIC / Storms, G – 's-Gravenhage, 1948 – 6mf – 8 – ne Slangenburg [130]
ANGLO-SAXON MANUSCRIPTS IN MICROFICHE FACSIMILE, VOL 1 : BOOKS OF PRAYER AND HEALING / ed by Doane, A N – Binhamton, NY. 1994 – 38mf – 8 – $120.00 ($96.00 if part of subsc) – 0-86698-141-1 – Dist. us Pegasus – us MRTS [090]
ANGLO-SAXON MANUSCRIPTS IN MICROFICHE FACSIMILE, VOL 2 : PSALTERS 1 / ed by Pulsiano, Phillip – Binghamton, NY. 1994 – 50mf – 8 – $120.00 ($96.00 if part of subsc) – 0-86698-146-2 – Dist. us Pegasus – us MRTS [090]
ANGLO-SAXON MANUSCRIPTS IN MICROFICHE FACSIMILE, VOL 4 : GLOSSED TEXTS, ALDHELMIANA, PSALMS / ed by Pulsiano, Philip – Binghamton, NY. 1996 – 43mf – 8 – $120.00 ($96.00 if part of subsc) – 0-86698-210-8 – Dist. us Pegasus – us MRTS [090]
THE ANGLO-TELUGU PRIMER / Narasayya, Maddali Lakshmi – 2nd ed. Madras: Higginbotham, 1869 – 1 – us Res Libr [490]
Angly, Edward *see* OH YEAH?
ANGOLA : ANUARIO ESTATISTICO 1933-1973 / Angola. Reparticao de Estatistica Geral – (Coll title: African Official Statistical Serials, 1867-1982) – 147mf – 9 – £925.00 – uk Chadwyck [960]
Angola *see* BOLETIM OFICIAL
ANGOLA AND THE RIVER CONGO / Monteiro, J J – 2v. London. 1875. BA-342 2 – 8 – ne IDC [960]
Angola. Conselho Legislativo *see*
- ACTA DA SESSAO
- ACTAS DE SESSAO

Angola. Ministerios da. Economia e do Ultramar *see* PLANO DE FOMENTO
Angola. Presidencia do Conselho *see* PLANO INTERCALAR DE FOMENTO PARA 1965-1967
Angola. Reparticao de Estatistica Geral *see*
- ANGOLA
- ANUVARIO ESTATISTICO DE ANGOLA

Angot, Joseph *see* 6 BROCHURES, LA PLUPART EXTRAITES DE "REVUE DE BRETAGNE"
Angoulvant, Gabriel Louis *see* LA PACIFICATION DE LA COTE D'IVOIRE, 1908-1915.
Angove, John *see* IN THE EARLY DAYS
DER ANGRIFF – Berlin, 1933-1945 – 42r – 1 – DM3,990.00 – gw Mikro Press [072]
DER ANGRIFF – Berlin, 3 Apr 1934-31 May 1940 (imperfect) – 64r – 1 – uk British Libr Newspaper [072]
DER ANGRIFF – Berlin, jul 4 1927-apr 21 1945 (incomplete) – 1 – Dist. gw Mikrofilm – gw Misc Inst [943]
DIE ANGST IN DEN INTERPRETATIONEN DER EXISTENZPHILOSOPHIE UND DER TIEFENPSYCHOLOGIE / Streck, Friedrich Karl – Frankfurt a.M., 1978 – 2mf – 9 – DM62.00 – 3-89349-377-8 – gw Hänsel [120]
Anguita Valdivia, Jose *see* APUNTES BIOGRAFICOS DE DON JUAN CARRILLO SANCHEZ
Angulo, D *see*
- HISTORIA DEL ARTE HISPANOAMERICANO. TOMO 1. BARCELONA, 1945
- LA ORDEN DE SANTO DOMINGO EN EL PERU

Angulo y Puente-Arnao, J *see*
- HISTORIA DE LOS LIMITES DEL PERU
- NUESTRA CUESTION DE LIMITES CON LAS REPUBLICAS DEL ECUADOR Y COLOMBIA
- NUESTROS LIMITES CON LA REPUBLICA DEL ECUADOR

Angus, J *see* THE METHODS OF METHODISM
Angus, Joseph *see* AN ANALYSIS OF BUTLER'S ANALOGY OF RELIGION
ANGUS JOURNAL *see* ABERDEEN-ANGUS JOURNAL
Angus, Scotland *see* PARISH CHURCH RECORDS
Angus, William *see* A PRONOUNCING VOCABULARY OF THE ENGLISH LANGUAGE
ANHANG ZUM HANDBUCHE BEY DEM GENERALBASSE UND DER COMPOSITION / Marpurg, Friedrich Wilhelm – P 711. 1760 – 9 – ne IDC [780]
LOS ANHELOS DE DOS PUEBLOS HERMANOS EN LA PALABRA DE PERON E IBANEZ / Peron, Juan – Buenos Aires: La Presidencia, 1953 – 1 – CSUXADH9645-B – us Hoover Inst Photo [320]
Anhorn, Roland *see* SOZIALSTRUKTUR UND DISZIPLINARINDIVIDUUM
AN-HUI JIH-PAO – Hofei, Anhwei. June 1, 1952-Oct 14 1962. 3 reels. Incomplete – 1 – 48.75 – us Chinese Res [072]
ANHUI RIBAO – China. Anhui Daily. 1983-. M D81 – 1 – $55.00r – cc Microforms [072]
'ANI UND 'ANAV IN DEN PSALMEN / Rahlfs, Alfred – Goettingen: Dieterich, 1892 – 9 – us A.T.L.A. [240]
Anichkov, E *see* LITERATURNYI OBRAZY I MNENIIA 1903 G
Anikst, Abram *see*
- ORGANIZATSIIA RABOCHEI SILY V 1920 GODU
- ORGANIZATSIIA RASPREDELENIIA RABOCHEI SILY
- ORGANIZATSIIA RYNKA TRUDA ZA DVA GODA SOVETSKOI VLASTI

L'ANILLE : JOURNAL DE L'ARRONDISSEMENT DE SAINT-CALAIS (SARTHE) – (Numerous missing numbers) – Hebd., Saint-Calais, avril 1843-juin 1915 (nombreux no. manq.) – 14r – 1 – F7551,60 – fr Armell [073]
L'ANILLE *see* JOURNAL HEBDOMADAIRE DE L'ARRONDISSEMENT DE SAINT-CALAIS (SARTHE)
ANIMA POET : FROM THE UNPUBLISHED NOTE-BOOKS OF SAMUEL TAYLOR COLERIDGE / Coleridge, Samuel Taylor; ed by Coleridge, Ernest Hartley – Boston, New York: Houghton, Mifflin and Company; Cambridge: Riverside Press, 1895 – 1 roll – 1 – 1-55879-628-2 – uk Libr Preservation [810]
ANIMADVERSIONES...ACERCA DE LA RECETA DEL UNGUENTO DE MERCURIO / Jimenez Guillen, F – Sevilla, 1626 – 1mf – 9 – sp Cultura [610]
ANIMADVERSIONUM BOTANICARUM SPECIMEN. SPECIMEN ALTERUM / Arduino, P – Batavii. 1759 – 8 – ne IDC [580]
ANIMAL BEHAVIOR – v. 8-20. 1960-1972 – 1,5,6 – us Princeton Micro [590]
ANIMAL BEHAVIOR ABSTRACTS – Quarterly – 9 – us C.S.A. [636]
ANIMAL BLOOD : PROCESSING AND UTILIZATION – 1982 – 107p – it F.A.O. [636]
ANIMAL BONES IN ARCHAEOLOGY / Ryder, M L – 1. 12.00; ; 7 – uk Microform Academic [930]
ANIMAL BREEDING : SELECTED ARTICLES FROM THE WORLD ANIMAL REVIEW – 1977 – 137p – it F.A.O. [636]
ANIMAL BY-PRODUCTS : PROCESSING AND UTILIZATION / Mann, I – 3rd printing 1978 – 246p – it F.A.O. [631]
ANIMAL ENERGY IN AGRICULTURE IN AFRICA AND ASIA – 1984 – 148p – it F.A.O. [636]
ANIMAL FEED SCIENCE AND TECHNOLOGY – v1-11. 1976-84 – 1,5,6,13 – sz Elsevier [073]
ANIMAL GENETIC RESOURCES : A GLOBAL PROGRAMME FOR SUSTAINABLE DEVELOPMENT – 1990 – 318p – it F.A.O. [636]
ANIMAL GENETIC RESOURCES : STRATEGIES FOR IMPROVED USE AND CONSERVATION – 1987 – 332p – it F.A.O. [636]

ANIMAL GENETIC RESOURCES CONSERVATION AND MANAGEMENT – 1981 – 399p – it F.A.O. [636]
ANIMAL GENETIC RESOURCES DATA BANKS – it F.A.O. [636]
ANIMAL GENETIC RESOURCES OF THE USSR – 1989 – 531p – it F.A.O. [636]
ANIMAL HEALTH YEARBOOK – it F.A.O. [636]
ANIMAL HOSPITAL *see* JOURNAL OF THE AMERICAN ANIMAL HOSPITAL ASSOCIATION
ANIMAL HUSBANDRY PAMPHLET / South Dakota. State University. Agricultural Experiment Station – nos.1-3. 1969 – 1,5,6 – us Spaulding [636]
ANIMAL HUSBANDRY RESEARCH SUMMARY / Virginia. Agricultural Experiment Station. Blacksburg – Aug 1950, 1 fiche – 9 – us Spaulding [636]
ANIMAL HUSBANDRY: VETERINARY SCIENCE PROGRESS REPORTS / Tennessee. University. Agricultural Experiment Station – 1955-58; 1960-64 – 1,5 – us Spaulding [636]
ANIMAL INTELLIGENCE; EXPERIMENTAL STUDIES / Thorndike, Edward Lee – New York: Macmillan, 1911. viii,297p. illus – 1 – us U.W. Library [150]
ANIMAL KINGDOM – 1975- – 9 – us UMI [590]
ANIMAL NUTRITION AND HEALTH – (v39-. 1984-. 5,6,9) – v20-. May 1965- – 1 – us UMI [636]
ANIMAL REMAINS / Ewart, J – 1911 – 1 – uk Microform Academic [560]
ANIMAL REPRODUCTION SCIENCE – v1-7. 1977-84 – 1,5,6,13 – sz Elsevier [073]
ANIMAL SCIENCE RESEARCH REPORT / Oklahoma State University. Agricultural Experiment Station – 1970-82 – 1,5 – us Spaulding [636]
ANIMAL SCIENCE RESEARCH SERIES / Clemson University. Agricultural Experiment Station – No.20-68. 1970-82. 1 reel – 1,5 – us Spaulding [630]
ANIMAL SCIENCE RESEARCH SERIES / South Carolina. Agricultural Experiment Station. Clemson – n.1-19. 1955-69 – 1,5 – us Spaulding [636]
ANIMAL SHELTER SHOPTALK *see* AMERICAN HUMANE MAGAZINE
ANIMAL SYMBOLISM IN ECCLESIASTICAL ARCHITECTURE / Evans, E P – New York: Henry Holt, 1896 – 1mf – us A.T.L.A. [720]
ANIMAL SYMBOLISM IN ECCLESIASTICAL ARCHITECTURE / Evens, E P – O-1243 1. 1896 – 9 – ne IDC [240]
ANIMAL TRACTION : AN ANNOTATED BIBLIOGRAPHIC DATABASE / Starkey, P H et al – 1991 – 9 – $24.00 – 92-9053-106-1 – et ILRI [636]
ANIMALCULA INFUSORIA FLUVIATILIA ET MARINA / Mueller, Otto Frederik – 2179 2. 1786 – 8 – ne IDC [590]
ANIMALS' AGENDA *see* AGENDA
ANIMALS IN WORLD WAR 1 PAMPHLET COLLECTION – 1915-19?? – 1 – CSUXANL3604-B – us Hoover Inst Photo [350]
AN ANIMATED MOLECULE AND ITS NEAREST RELATIVE: AN ESSAY READ BEFORE THE AMERICAN ASSOCIATION OF MEDICAL SUPERINTENDENTS OF ASYLUMS FOR THE INSANE, AT WASHINGTON, D.C., ON THE 10TH OF MAY, 1878 / Clark, Daniel – Toronto, 1878, (Utica, NY: E. Roberts). 00660. (Pre-1900 Canadiana) – 9 – cn C.I.H.M. [616]
LES ANIMAUX DOMESTIQUES ET SAUVAGES EN FRANCE DU NEOLITHIQUE AU GALLO-ROMAIN / Poulain-Josien, Th. – Etude d'ethnozoologie a partir de vestiges osseux. Equides, suides, bovides – 9 – F100.00 – fr Ethnologie [306]
LES ANIMAUX VERTICAUX ET RENVERSES DANS LES REPRESENTATIONS PARIETALES PALEOLITHIQUES / Ricol, D – 9 – F50.00 – fr Ethnologie [700]
Aniq Filali, Rabea *see* DEUX MODES SATIRIQUES OU LE CHOIX FAIT PAR BUTLER DANS HUDIBRAS ET SWIFT DANS A TALE OF A TUB (LE CONTE DU TONNEAU)
Anishev, A *see* OCHERKI ISTORII GRAZHDANKSOI VOINY 1917-1920
Anisimov, M *see* SNABZHENIE DEREVNI SREDSTVAMI PROIZVODSTVA I SEL'SKOKHOZIAISTVENNAIA KOOPERATSIIA
Anisimov, Sergei Sergeevich *see* DELO O VOSSTANII NA EKATERININSKO I ZH. D
Anizan, Felix *see* LE DIEU AU COEUR QUI RAYONNE. PARIS, 1928
L'ANJOU – (10 missing numbers) – Angers (Maine-et-Loire), Sept. 1883 – Dec. 1903 – 21r – fr Armell [944]
Anjou, Gustave *see* PROBATE RECORDS-ULSTER COUNTY
ANJOU JOURNAL – Ville d'Anjou, Canada. 16 avr 1960-v2 n17. 23 mar 1962 – 1r – 1 – Can$25.00 – cn Can Microfilming [072]
ANJUMAN – Tabriz. Sal-i 1, shumarah-i 38-108 (17 Zu'l Hijjah 1324-26 Jumada al-avval 1325 [1 February 1907-7 July 1907] and Sal-i 2, shumarah-i 8 (22 Ramazan 1326 [18 October 1908] – 1 reel – 1 – $110.00 – us MEDOC [950]
ANJUMAN (CONSOLIDATED HOLDINGS) – (Includes index) – Tabriz, Gilan, Yazd, Isfahan, [1907-1911] – 2r – 1 – $25.00 – us MEDOC [950]
ANKARA EDITION FRANCAISE HEBDOMADAIRE DU "HAKIMIYETI MILLIYE" – Ankara, 22 Mar 1934-6 Jan 1938; 15 Sep 1938-6 Jun 1940 – 4r – 1 – uk British Libr Newspaper [072]
ANKER GESCHLIPPT : GESCHICHTE EINES MARINEOFFIZIERS / Dincklage-Campe, Friedrich, Freiherr von – Leipzig: Max Hesse, [18-?] – 1 – us U.W. Library [830]
Anketell, Cyrus P *see* A PRONOUNCING ENGLISH-TAMIL DICTIONARY WITH ABBREVIATIONS
ANKING NEWSLETTER / American Episcopal Diocese. Anking – v18-22, no. 1. n.s. 2, v21-22, no. 2. Autumn 1937-Oct 1941. n.s. 1945 (?)-Jun 1948 – 1 reel – 1 – $60.00 – us UPA [240]
Anklesaria, E T D *see* THE BUNDAHISHN
THE ANKOLE AGREEMENT, 1962 – Endagaano y'Ankole eya 1962. Entebbe, Uganda Protectorate, 1962. 34 p. LL-2291 – 1 – us L of C Photodup [960]
ANLEITUNG DIE IM MAEHRISCHEN GOUVERNEMENT WILD WACHSENDEN UND AM HAEUFIGSTEN CULTIVIRTEN PHANEROGAMEN PFLANZEN / Schlosser, J C – Brunn. 1843. B-1058 2 – 8 – ne IDC [580]
ANLEITUNG SO VIEL ENGL. CONTRE-DAENZE, MIT ZWEI WUERFELN ZU COMPONIEREN, SO VIEL MAN WILL / Mozart, Wolfgang Amadeus – p731 – 9 – ne IDC [780]
ANLEITUNG ZU DER MUSIKALISCHEN GELAHRTHEIT....1758 / Adlung, Jacob – 2 – us Sibley [780]
ANLEITUNG ZUM CLAVIERSPIELEN DER SCHOENERN AUSUEBUNG DER HEUTIGEN ZEIT GEMAESZ / Marpurg, Friedrich Wilhelm – P 391. 1765 – 9 – ne IDC [780]
ANLEITUNG ZUM GENERALBASS UND ZUR COMPOSITION / Sorge, G A – Mit Anmerkungen von Friedrich Wilhelm Marpurg. Nebst vier Kupfertafeln. 1760 – 9 – us Sibley [780]
ANLEITUNG ZUR ERFINDUNG DER MELODIE UND IHRER FORTSETZUNG...ERSTER [ZWEYTER] THEIL / Daube, J F – Wien: Christian Gottlob Taeubel, 1797-1798 – 3mf – 9 – us Sibley [780]
ANLEITUNG ZUR GRIECHISCHEN PALAEOGRAPHIE / Wattenbach, W – H 113 2. 1895 – 8 – ne IDC [450]
ANLEITUNG ZUR KENNTNISS DER GEWAA5CHSE / Sprengel, K P J – Halle, 1802-1804. 3 vols. 421; 367; 374 pp. B-5229 2 – 8 – ne IDC [580]
ANLEITUNG ZUR MUSIK UEBERHAUPT / Marpurg, Friedrich Wilhelm – 1763 – 9 – us Sibley [780]
ANLEITUNG ZUR MUSIKALISCHEN GELAHRTHEIT....1783 / Adlung, Jacob – 2 – us Sibley [780]
ANLEITUNG ZUR PRACTISCHEN MUSIK / Petri, Johann S – 1767 – 9 – us Sibley [780]
ANLEITUNG ZUR PRACTISCHEN MUSIK.. / Petri, Johann S – 1782 – 2 – us Sibley [780]
ANLEITUNG ZUR SICHERN ERZIEHUNG UND ZWECKMAESSIGEN ANPFLANZUNG DER EINHEIMISCHEN UND FREMDEN HOLZARTEN / Burgsdorf, F A L von – 2v. Berlin. 1787. B610 2 – 8 – ne IDC [580]
ANLEITUNG ZUR SINGCOMPOSITION / Marpurg, Friedrich Wilhelm – 1758 – 9 – us Sibley [780]
ANLEITUNG ZUR SINGEKOMPOSITION / Kirnberger, Johann P – 1782 – 9 – us Sibley [780]
ANLEITUNG ZUR SINGKUN. / Tosi, Pierfrancesco – 1757 – 2 – us Sibley [780]
Anliker, P *see* DIE ERBRECHTLICHEN VERHAELTNISSE DER SCHWEIZER IM AUSLAND
ANMAERKNINGER OVER FRANKRIGES OG ENGELLANDS FORDEELE OG MANGELERI HENSEENDE TIL HANDELEN OG ANDRE KILDER TIL LANDES MAGT OG STYRKE: OVERSATTE AF DET FRANSKE MED NOGLE FAA AF OVERSAETTEREN TILLAGDE NOTER / Plumard de Dangeul – Kiobenhavn: Lillie, 1756 – 1 – us U.W. Library [941]
ANN H. JUDSON: A MEMORIAL / Judson, Ann H – By Waler Newton Wyeth. 1888 – 9 – us A.T.L.A. [920]
Anna A *see* WHAT FRANCES E. WILLARD SAID
ANNA AKHMATOVA / Eikhenbaum, B – Opyt analiza. Spb. 1923. BR-2053 2 – 8 – ne IDC [460]
ANNA AKHMATOVA / Nedobrovo, N V – Russkaia Mysl'. nr. 7. M. 1915. BR-3685 2 – 8 – ne IDC [460]
THE ANNA ELIZABETH DICKINSON COLLECTION – 25r – 1 – $875.00 – Dist. us Scholarly Res – us L of C Photodup [976]
ANNA FIRST BAPTIST CHURCH. ANNA, ILLINOIS : CHURCH RECORDS – Aug 1910-Nov 1988 – 1 – 163.71 – us Baptist [240]
Anna. Illinois. First Baptist Church *see* DEACONS' AND TRUSTEES' MINUTES
ANNA JOURNAL – (Cont: AANNT Journal) – Pitman. v11-20 jun 1984-93* 1; v21 apr 1994*. v22-24 feb 1995-1997+ 1,5,9 – 1,5,9 – D21622.02 – us UMI [610]
ANNA JOURNAL *see* AANNT JOURNAL
ANNA MARIA VAN SCHURMAN / Schotel, G D J – 's-Hertogenbosch: Muller, 1853 – 1mf – us A.T.L.A. [240]
ANNAE COMMENAE ALEXIADIS LIBRI 15 (CSHB 38) : GRAECA AD CODD. FIDEM NUNC PRIMUM RECENSUIT, NOVAM INTERPRETATIONEM LATINAM SUBIECIT, C. DUGANGII COMMENTARIOS SUASQUE ANNOTATIONES ADDIDIT LUD. SCHOPENUS – Bonnae, 1839 – Dfl32.00 – ne Slangenburg [240]
ANNAE COMMENAE PORPHYROGENITAE CAESARISSAE ALEXIAS SIVE DE REBUS AB ALEXIO IMPERATORE VEL EJUS TEMPORE GESTIS (CBH 10) / ed by Possinus, P – Parisiis, 1651 – Dfl88.00 – ne Slangenburg [240]
ANNAES DA ASSEMBLEA LEGISLATIVA PROVINCIAL DA BAHIA – [s.l.]. Mar-Maio 1873; Jan-Jun 1874; Jan-Dez 1875; Abr-Jul 1876; Abr 1877-Set 1878; Jan-Jun 1879; Abr-Jun, Out-Dez 1880; Abr-Jun 1881; Abr-Jun 1882; Jan-Dez 1883; Jan 1886-Mar 1887 – 1,5,6 – bl Biblioteca [072]
ANNAES DA CAMARA DOS SENHORES DEPUTADOS DO ESTADO FEDERADO DA BAHIA – [s.l.]. 1894-96 – 1,5,6 – bl Biblioteca [072]
ANNAES FLUMINENSE DE SCIENCIAS, ARTES E LITERATURA – Rio de Janeiro, Jan 1822 – 1,5,6 – bl Biblioteca [073]
ANNAIS DAS BIBLIOTECAS E ARQUIVOS – Lisboa, Portugal: Biblioteca nacional. -q. 1920-24. Title varies slightly – 1 – us U.W. Library [020]
ANNAL OF MATHEMATICAL STATISTICS *see* ANNALS OF STATISTICS
ANNALEN / Vienna. Naturhistorisches Museum – v1-55 1886-1947. Scattered issues lacking. 11 reels – 1 – 225.00 – us L of C Photodup [580]
ANNALEN DER DEUTSCHEN LITERATUR : GESCHICHTE DER DEUTSCHEN LITERATUR VON DEN ANFAENGEN BIS ZUR GEGENWART: EINE GEMEINSCHAFTSARBEIT ZAHLREICHER FACHGELEHRTER / Burger, Heinz Otto – (Includes index) – Stuttgart: J B Metzler, 1952 – 1 – us U.W. Library [430]
ANNALEN DER JUDEN IN DEN PREUSSISCHEN STAATEN, BESONDERS IN DER MARK BRANDENBURG / Koenig, A B – Berlin. 1790. BJ-23-115 1 – 9 – ne IDC [943]
ANNALEN DER PHYSIK – (1972- . 5,6,9) – 1799- – 1 – us UMI [530]
ANNALEN DER PHYSIK – Series 1-5. 1799-1940 – 1,5,6 – us Princeton Micro [530]
Annalen der Physik *see*
– JOURNAL DER PHYSIK
– NEUES JOURNAL DER PHYSIK
ANNALEN DER PHYSIK: BEIBLAETTER – v. 1-43. 1877-1919 – 1,5,6 – us Princeton Micro [530]
ANNALEN DER PHYSIK - INDEXES – v. 1-150. 1824-1873. 1874-1925 – 1,5,6 – us Princeton Micro [530]
ANNALEN DER PHYSIK: INDEXES – Vollstaendiges Register, ueber Gren's Neues Journal der Physik. Leipzig, 1800 – 3 – us Readex [530]
ANNALEN DER ST. JOSEPH'S CONGREGATIE VAN MILL HILL – (Issues for nov 1920-dec 1923 filmed with: Annalen van het Missiehuis te Roosendaal en het Studiehuis te Tilburg, aug 1919-oct 1920. Issues for 1933-may 1935 filmed with: St Joseph's Congregatie van Mill Hill, jul 1935 and: Mill Hill, aug 1935-nov 1936) – Roosendaal: St Joseph's Missiehuis. v31 n7-v46 n4. nov 1920-jun 1935 – 1 – us Res Libr [240]
ANNALEN DES HISTORISCHEN VEREINS FUER DEN NIEDERRHEIN – Heft 1(1855)-Heft 140(1942) – 588mf – 9 – Dfl158.00 – ne Slangenburg [073]
ANNALEN DES K.K. NATURHISTORISCHEN HOFMUSEUMS – Wien, 1885/86-1939. v1-49 – 605mf – 9 – 2288/2 – ne IDC [500]
ANNALEN DES WIENER MUSEUMS DER NATURGESCHICHTE – Wien, 1836-1840. 2v – 11mf – 9 – 8776/1 – ne IDC [500]
ANNALEN FUER METEOROLOGIE, ERDMAGNETISMUS UND VERWANDTE GEGENSTAENDE – Munich, 1842-44. v.1-12 – 3 – us Readex [550]
ANNALEN VAN HET MISSIEHUIS TE ROZENDAAL – (Issues for may 1914-dec 1915 filmed with: Annalen van het Missiehuis te Roosendaal en het Studiehuis te Tilburg, 1916-jul 1919) – Rozendaal: Het Missiehuis. v1-26 n8. [may 1890-1915] – 1 – us Res Libr [240]
ANNALES / France. Assemblee Nationale – (Comptes rendus in extenso des elections des Presidents de la Republique. 1871-1953. 1) – juin 1916-oct 1917; 9 fevr, 19 mars, 19 avr 1940 – 1 – fr A.C.R.P.P. [323]
ANNALES / Institut Fourier – v1-12. 1950-62 – 1 – us Princeton Micro [510]
ANNALES / Institut Pasteur. Paris – v. 1-123. 1887-1972 – 1,5,6 – us Princeton Micro [500]
ANNALES / Institut Technique du Batiment et des Travaux Public – no. 205-312. Paris. 1965-73 – 5 – fr A.C.R.P.P. [073]
ANNALES / Missions de la Societe de Marie – Lyon. Puis: De l'Oceanie. 1875-1921 – 1 – fr A.C.R.P.P. [073]
ANNALES / Museum National d'Histoire Naturelle. Paris – 1802-13 – 3 – us Readex [580]
ANNALES / Paris. Universite. Institut Henri Poincare – v. 1-18. 1930-1964 – 5,6 – us UMI [530]
ANNALES / Societe Entomologique de France – 1832-80 – 1,5,6 – us Princeton Micro [590]
ANNALES / La Societe Jean-Jacques Rousseau – Geneve. v1-38 1905-1969/71 – 5 – fr A.C.R.P.P. [190]
ANNALES / Societe Royale d'Entomologie de Belgique – v14-42 1870-98 – 1,5,6 – $22,144.00 – us Princeton Micro [590]
ANNALES, 1960-63 / Congo. Senat – 14v. BA-661/1 – 9 – ne IDC [960]
ANNALES A MUNDI EXORDIO USQUE AD OBITUM ALEXII COMMENI IMPER. (CBH 9) / Glycae, Michaelis; ed by Labbe, Ph – Parisiis, 1660 – Dfl70.00 – ne Slangenburg [930]
ANNALES ABBATIAE : SANCTI PETRI BLANDINIENSIS / ed by Putte, F van de – Gandavi, 1842 – Dfl35.00 – ne Slangenburg [240]
ANNALES AEVI CAROLINI ET SAXONICI (MGH 5: 4.BD) : CHRONICA ET GESTA AEVI SAXONICI. HISTORIAE AEVI CAROLINI ET SAXONICI – 1841 – Dfl81.00 – ne Slangenburg [240]
ANNALES AEVI SUEVICI (MGH 5: 16.BD) – 1859 – Dfl74.00 – ne Slangenburg [240]
ANNALES AEVI SUEVICI (MGH 5: 17.BD) – 1861 – Dfl84.00 – ne Slangenburg [240]
ANNALES AEVI SUEVICI (MGH 5: 19.BD) – 1866 – Dfl74.00 – ne Slangenburg [240]
ANNALES AEVI SUEVICI (MGH 5: 24.BD) : SUPPL. TOM. 16 ET 17 – (Chronica Minora Saec. 12 Et 13. Gesta Saec. 12 Et 13. 1880) – 1879 – Dfl84.00 – ne Slangenburg [240]
ANNALES ALTHAHENSES MAIORES (MGH 7: 4.BD) – Ed 2a. 1891 – Dfl13.00 – ne Slangenburg [240]

ANNALES ARCHEOLOGIQUES – Paris. 1844-81. v1-28. (1873-1880 not published) O-1209 1 – 232mf – 9 – ne IDC [930]

ANNALES ARTISTIQUES ET LITTERAIRES – Paris. mars 1888-90 – 1 – fr A.C.R.P.P. [700]

ANNALES BERTINIANI (MGH 7: 5.BD) – 1883 – Dfl19.00 – ne Slangenburg [240]

ANNALES BOTANICES SYSTEMATICAE / ed by Walpers, W G – Lipsiae, 1848-1871. 7v. 1534/2 – 135mf – 8 – ne IDC [580]

ANNALES BRYOLOGICI : A YEARBOOK DEVOTED TO THE STUDY OF MOSSES AND HEPATICS – The Hague, 1928-1932. v1-5 – 20mf – 9 – 8557/1 – ne IDC [580]

ANNALES CAMALDULENSES O.S.B. / Mittarelli, J B & Costadoni, A – Venetiis. v1-9. 1750-1773 – 289mf – 9 – Dfl1,012.00 – ne Slangenburg [240]

ANNALES CAMBRIAE (A.D. 444-1288) (RS20) / ed by Ab Ithel, J Williams – 1860 – Dfl19.00 – ne Slangenburg [240]

ANNALES (CBH 22) / Zonarae, Joannis; ed by Cange, C du – (Tom. 2: Parisiis 1687 Dfl88.00) – Parisiis. Tom. 1. 1686 – Dfl102.00 – ne Slangenburg [930]

ANNALES, CHRONICA, GENEALOGIAE, CATALOGI (SUPPL. TOM. 1-12, PARS 1) (MGH 5: 13.BD) : GESTA AEVI CAROLINI ET SAXONICI (SUPPL. TOM. 2 ET 4) – 1881 – Dfl77.00 – ne Slangenburg [240]

ANNALES CHRONOLOGIQUES, LITTERAIRES, ET HISTORIQUES DE LA MACONNERIE DES PAYS-BAS – Brussel, 1822-1828. 6v – 41mf – 9 – VR-24.1/1 – ne IDC [900]

ANNALES CISTERCIENSIUM / Manrique, Angel – Lyon. Tome 1-2. 1642; Lyon. Tome 3-4. 1649 – v1 29mf; v2 32mf; v3 33mf; v4 40mf – 8 – Dfl469.00 – ne Slangenburg [240]

LES ANNALES COLONIALES – Paris. 1914-juil 1917; avr 1921; 1924 – 1 – fr A.C.R.P.P. [073]

LES ANNALES COLONIALES – Paris. v32-40, Jan 1931-June 1940 – 1 – 92.00 – us L of C Photodup [944]

ANNALES CRIMINELLES CANADIENNES – Montreal: La Societe de Publication des Annales Criminelles Canadiennes, 1896-[189- ou 19–] – 9 – cn C.I.H.M. [971]

ANNALES (CSHB 27) / Glycae, Michaelis; ed by Bekkeri, Imm – Bonnae, 1836 – Dfl42.00 – ne Slangenburg [240]

ANNALES (CSHB 42, 43) / Zonarae, Joannis; ed by Pinderi, MauR – Bonnae. v1-2. 1841-1844 – Dfl77.00 – ne Slangenburg [930]

ANNALES DE BIBLIOGRAPHIE THEOLOGIQUE – v6-20. 1898-1912 (complete) – 3r – 1 – ATLA S0516 – us A.T.L.A. [012]

ANNALES DE CHIMIE – Series 9-12. 1914-1955 – 1,5,6 – us Princeton Micro [540]

ANNALES DE CHIMIE APPLIQUEE – puis et Revue de chimie analytique reunies. Paris. 1896-1957 – 1 – fr A.C.R.P.P. [073]

ANNALES DE CHIMIE ET DE PHYSIQUE – Paris, 1789-1815. Annals (journals) of chemistry and physics – 3 – us Readex [530]

ANNALES DE CHIMIE ET DE PHYSIQUE – Series 1-8. 1789-1913 – 1,5,6 – us Princeton Micro [540]

ANNALES DE DROIT COMMERCIAL (ET INDUSTRIEL) FRANCAIS, ETRANGER ET INTERNATIONAL – Paris, 1886-1939. v1-48 – 262mf – 9 – IL-1/1 – ne IDC [340]

ANNALES DE LA BONNE STE. ANNE DE BEAUPRE – Cap Rouge [Quebec]: N A Leclerc; (Quebec: L. Brousseau) – 9 – cn C.I.H.M. [240]

ANNALES DE LA CONFEDERATION UNIVERSELLE DES AMIS DE LA VERITE – Paris. Imprimerie du Cercle Social. 1791. (Supplement a la Bouche de Fer) – 9 – fr Hachette [321]

ANNALES DE LA FACULTE DES SCIENCES DE MARSEILLE – (Missing: 1913. v22) – Marseille, Paris, 1891-1920. v1-24 – 106mf – 9 – 7470/1 – ne IDC [500]

ANNALES DE LA LITTERATURE ET DES ARTS – Paris. 1820-29 (I-XXXIV) – 1 – fr A.C.R.P.P. [410]

ANNALES DE LA MUSIQUE OU ALMANACH MUSICAL PAR UN AMATEUR – v. 1-2. 1819-1820 – 1 – us Schnase [780]

ANNALES DE LA PATRIE FRANCAISE – Paris. no. 1-125. mai 1900-juil 1905 – 1 – fr A.C.R.P.P. [073]

ANNALES DE LA PROPAGATION DE LA FOI POUR LA PROVINCE DE QUEBEC – [Montreal?: s.n.], 1877-1886; (Montreal: J A Plinguet) – 9 – cn C.I.H.M. [240]

ANNALES DE LA PROPAGATION DE LA FOI POUR LA PROVINCE DE QUEBEC ET DE MONTREAL – Montreal: Gebhardt-Berthiaume, 1886-[1923] – 9 – cn C.I.H.M. [240]

ANNALES DE LA PROPAGATION DE LA FOI POUR LE DIOCESE DE MONTREAL – [Montreal: L'Oeuvre], 1874-1876 – 9 – cn C.I.H.M. [240]

ANNALES DE LA PROPAGATION...POUR LES PROVINCES DE QUEBEC ET MONTREAL / Society for the Propagation of the Faith – 1877-1923. (American Indian Periodicals in the Princeton University Library). 160 fiches – 9 – $650.00 – us UPA [240]

ANNALES DE LA RELIGION – Memoires pour servir a l'histoire du XVIIIe SIECLE. Paris. 1795-1803 (I-XVIII) – 1 – fr A.C.R.P.P. [073]

ANNALES DE LA SOCIETE BOTANIQUE DE LYON – Lyon, 1889-1909. v16-34 – 55mf – 9 – 8589/1 – ne IDC [580]

ANNALES DE LA SOCIETE ENTOMOLOGIQUE DE BELGIQUE – Bruxelles, 1857-1924. v1-64 – 477mf – 9 – Z-918/2 – ne IDC [590]

ANNALES DE LA SOCIETE ENTOMOLOGIQUE DE FRANCE – S.1-6. Paris, 1832-1899. v1-68 – 1,009mf – 9 – Z-919/2 – ne IDC [590]

ANNALES DE LA SOCIETE HISTORIQUE ET ARCHEOLOGIQUE A MAESTRICHT – Tome 1 + 2 (1854-1858) – 14mf – 9 – Dfl49.003.50ea – ne Slangenburg [073]

ANNALES DE LA SOCIETE MALACOLOGIQUE DE BELGIQUE – (Cont. as: Annales de Societe Zoologique et Malacologique. Bruxelles, 1903-1925. v38-56; Cont. as: Annales de la Societe Zoologieque. 1926-1941. v57-72) – Bruxelles, 1863/1865-1875. v1-10; 1876-1902. v11-15[S.2, v1-5]; v16-20[S.3, v1-5]; v21-27[S.4, v1-7]; v28-37 – 423mf – 9 – Z-889c/2 – ne IDC [590]

ANNALES DE LA SOCIETE (ROYALE) ACADEMIQUE DE NANTES ET DE LA LOIRE-INFERIEURE – Nantes (Loire-Inferieure), 1830-1920 – 39r – fr Armell [910]

ANNALES DE L'ASSOCIATION DES PRETRES-ADORATEURS / Association des Pretres-Adorateurs – Montreal: L'Association, 1898-1936 – 9 – cn C.I.H.M. [360]

ANNALES DE L'EXTREME ORIENT ET DE L'AFRIQUE – v. 1-15. 1878-91 – 1 – 38.00 – us L of C Photodup [950]

ANNALES DE L'INSTITUT D'ETUDES ORIENTALES – Paris, Alger, 1934-1962. v1-20 – 109mf – 9 – NE-102/2 – ne IDC [950]

ANNALES DE L'INSTITUT D'ETUDES ORIENTALES / L'Universite d'Alger – Alger. 1934-62, 1964 (I-XX, n.s. I) – 1 – fr A.C.R.P.P. [370]

ANNALES DE L'OBSERVATOIRE DE MOSCOU – M., 1874-1884. v1-10; N.S. 1886-1890. v1-2 – 119mf – 9 – R-1648/2 – ne IDC [520]

ANNALES DE MARIE – Lyon. 1925-juil 1940 – 1 – fr A.C.R.P.P. [073]

ANNALES DE MICROBIOLOGIE / Institut Pasteur. Paris – v. 124 A,B – 127 A,B. 1973-1976 – 1,5,6 – us Princeton Micro [576]

ANNALES DE NORMANDIE – Caen. 1951-71. tb: 1951-71 – 5 – fr A.C.R.P.P. [073]

ANNALES DE PALEONTOLOGIE. INVERTEBRES – v.65-. 1979- – 1,5,6,9 – us UMI [560]

ANNALES DE PHILOSOPHIE CHRETIENNE – (Lacking: 99,104,110-120,144) – Paris, 1(1830)-166(1913) – 9 – Dfl5,226.00 – ne Slangenburg [073]

ANNALES DE PHILOSOPHIE CHRETIENNE – Paris. oct 1905-juin 1913 – 1 – fr A.C.R.P.P. [073]

ANNALES DE PHILOSOPHIE CHRETIENNE; RECUEIL PERIODIQUE... – (Missing: 1861, v62; 1879-1880, v97-98; 1882, v104(p. 227-295), v109-112; 1887-1888, v115-116; 1889-1890, v118-119; 1907, v153; 1909, v158) – Paris, 1830-1912/1913. v1-165 – 1,523mf – 9 – 5512/2 – ne IDC [100]

ANNALES DE PHYSIQUE – Series 9-13. 1914-60 – 1,5,6 – us Princeton Micro [530]

ANNALES DE RECHERCHES VETERINAIRES – ANNALS OF VETERINARY RESEARCH *see* VETERINARY RESEARCH

ANNALES DE SOEUR MORIN (1697-1730) / Hotel-Dieu de Montreal. Archives – Montreal, Canada – 1r – 1 – cn Can Microfilming [025]

ANNALES DE STATISTIQUE – Par J. P. Ballois. Paris. Valade, an X-an XI; Annales de Statistique Francaise et Etrangere; Annales de Statistiques. Redigees par Alexandre de Ferriere – 9 – fr Hachette [944]

ANNALES DES EMPEREURS DU JAPON – 1835. Nippon Dai Ichi Ran – 1 – uk Microform Academic [900]

ANNALES DES PONTS ET CHAUSSEES : MEMOIRES ET DOCUMENTS RELATIFS A L'ART DES CONSTRUCTIONS ET AU SERVICES DE L'INGENIEUR – Paris. Lts. 1-2. Tables generales; Series 1-11 1831-1941 – 1 – us NY Public [624]

ANNALES DES POSTES, TELEGRAPHES ET TELEPHONES – v. 1-28. 1910-39 – 1,5,6 – us Princeton Micro [380]

ANNALES DES SACRES-COEURS / Congregation des Sacres-Coeurs et de l'Adoration – Paris. 1928, 1936-mai 1940 – 1 – fr A.C.R.P.P. [073]

ANNALES DES SCIENCES GEOLOGIQUES – Paris. 1843 – 3 – us Readex [550]

ANNALES DES SCIENCES GEOLOGIQUES – Paris, 1869-89 – 3 – us Readex [550]

ANNALES DES SCIENCES NATURELLES : BOTANIQUE – (S.1, 1824-1830, v1-30; S.2, 1830-1843, v1-20; S.3, 1844-1853, v1-20; S.4, 1854-1863, v1-20; S.5, 1864-1874, v1-20; S.6, 1875-1885, v1-20; S.7, 1885-1895, v1-20) – S.1-7. Paris, 1824-1895 – 1,244mf – 9 – 1525/2 – ne IDC [580]

ANNALES DES SCIENCES NATURELLES – Paris, 1824-33 – 3 – us Readex [574]

ANNALES DES SCIENCES NATURELLES : ZOOLOGY – (S.2, 1834-1843, v1-20; S.3, 1844-1853, v1-20; S.4, 1854-1863, v1-20; S.5, 1864-1874, v1-20; S.6, 1875-1885 v1-20; S.7, 1886-1895, v1-20; S.8, 1896-1904, v1-20; S.9, 1905-1915, v1-20; S.10, 1916-1937, v1-20) – S.2-10. Paris, 1834-1937 – 1,395mf – 9 – Z-192a-j/2 – ne IDC [590]

ANNALES D'HISTOCHEMIE *see* CELLULAR AND MOLECULAR BIOLOGY

ANNALES D'HISTORIE ECONOMIQUE ET SOCIALE – 1929-38.Devenu: Annales d'Histoire sociale. 1939-45. Devenu: Annales Economies, Societes, Civilisations. 1946- . Paris. 1929-78, 1985-93; tb: 1929-51, 1949-68 – 5 – fr A.C.R.P.P. [073]

ANNALES D'HORTICULTURE ET DE BOTANIQUE; OU, FLORE DES JARDINS DU ROYAUME DES PAYS-BAS, ET HISTOIRE DES PLANTES. – Leiden, 1858-62. 5v. 7344 – 31mf – 8 – us Readex [631]

ANNALES D'IMMUNOLOGIE / Institut Pasteur. Paris – v. 124 C-127C. 1973-1976 – 1,5,6 – us Princeton Micro [610]

ANNALES DU CABINET DE LECTURE PAROISSIAL DE MONTREAL – Montreal: [s.n.], 1857 – 9 – cn C.I.H.M. [971]

ANNALES DU JARDIN BOTANIQUE DE BUITENZORG – Batavia, Leiden, 1876-1918. v1-30. Leiden, 1897-1918. Suppl. v1-4. 7716 – 143mf – 9 – ne IDC [580]

ANNALES DU MAGNETISME ANIMAL – Paris, 1814-1816. 4v – 28mf – 9 – VR-23.1/1 – ne IDC [590]

ANNALES DU MONASTERE DE NOTRE-DAME DU BON PASTEUR D'ANGER, DIT ASILE SAINTE DARIE A MONTREAL 1870-1900 / Asile Sainte Darie. Montreal, Quebec – Montreal: 1900? 00897. (Pre-1900 Canadiana) – 9 – cn C.I.H.M. [240]

ANNALES DU MUSEE GUIMET TOME 1-17 – (Tome 20, 22, 24 are missing; Tome 1, Paris, 1880. 13mf; Tome 2, Paris, 1881. 19mf; Tome 3, Paris, 1881: Schlagintweit, Emile de: Le Bouddhisme au Tibet. 14mf; Tome 4, Paris, 1882. 11mf; Tome 5, Paris, 1883: Fragments Extraits du Kandjour, Traduits du Tibetain par M. Leon Feer. 19mf; Tome 6, Paris, 1884: La Lalita Vistara, traduit du Sanskrit par PH. Ed. Foucaux. Premiere Partie: Traduction Francaise. 14mf; Tome 7, Paris, 1884. 17mf; Tome 8, Paris, 1885: LE YI: KING ou Livre des Changements de la Dynastie des Tsheou. Traduit par P.L.F.'Philastre. Premiere Partie. 16mf; Tome 9, Paris, 1886: M.E. Lefebure, Les Hypogees Royaux de Thebes. Premiere Division: Le Tombeau de Seti Ier. 11mf; Tome 10, Paris, 1887. 21mf; Tome 11, Paris, 1886: J.J.M. de Groot, Les Fetes Annuellement celebrees a Emoui. Ie Partie. 15mf; Tome 12, Paris, 1886: J.J.M. de Groot, Les Fetes Annuellement celebrees a Emoui. 2e Partie. 15mf; Tome 13, Paris, 1888: Ch. Schoebel, LE RAYAMANA au point de vue religieux, philosophique et moral. 8mf; Tome 14, Paris, 1887: M.E. Amelineau, Essai sur le Gnosticisme Egyptien. 11mf; Tome 15, Paris, 1887: La SIAO HIO ou Morale de la Jeunesse avec le Commentaire de Tchen. Siuen, trad. du Chinois par C. de Harlez. 12mf; Tome 16, Paris, 1889: M.E. Lefebure, Les Hypogees de Thebes. Seconde Division. Notices des Hypogees. Troisieme Division, Tombeau de Ramses 4. 16mf; Tome 17, Paris, 1889: E. Amelineau, Histoire de Saint Pakhome et de ses communautes. 26mf) – 426mf in the entire 32v set – 8 – ne Slangenburg [100]

ANNALES DU MUSEE GUIMET TOME 18-32 – (Tome 18, Paris,1891: AVADANA-CATAKA, Cent Legendes (Bouddhiques) traduites duk Sanskrit par Leon Feer. 17mf; Tome 19, Paris, 1892: LE LALITA VISTARA, 2e Partie. Traduit du Sanskrit par Ph. Ed. Foucaux. 8mf; Tome 20, Paris, 1891: Textes Taoistes traduits des originaux chinois et commentes par C. De Harlez. 13mf; Tome 23, Paris, 1893: LE YI: KING, 2e Partie, traduit du Chinois par P.L.F. 'Philastre; Tome 25, Paris, 1894: E. Amelineau, Histoire des Monasteres de la Basse-Egypte... Vies des Saints Paul, etc. 16mf; Tome 26, 1e Partie, Paris, 1894: LA COREE ou TCHOSEN par M. le Colonel Chaille-Long-Bey. 3mf; Tome 26, 3e Partie, Paris 1897: A. Gayet, L'Exploration des ruines d'Antinoe et la decouverte d'un temple de Ramses 2. 4mf; Tome 26, 4e Partie, Paris, 1900: P. Lefevre-Pontalis, Recueil de Talismans Laotiens. 2mf; Tome 27, 1e Partie, Paris, 1895: L. Fourneau, Le Siam Ancien. 16mf; Tome 28, Paris, 1896: E. Amelineau, Histoire de la sepulture et des funerailles dans l'ancienne Egypte. 14mf; Tome 29, Paris, 1896: E. Amelineau, Histoire de la sepulture et des funerailles dans l'ancienne Egypte. Vol 2. 19mf; Tome 30, Paris, 1902: G. Legrain et E. Naville, L'Alle nord du pylone d'Amenophis 3. 10mf; Tome 31, 1e Partie, Paris, 1907: E. Fossagrives, SI-LING. Etude sur les tombeaux de l'Ouest de la dynastie des Ts'ing. 7mf; Tome 31, 2e Partie, Paris, 1908: L. Founerau, Le Siam Ancien. 8mf; Tome 32, Paris, 1909: Catalogue du Musee Guimet. Galerie Egyptienne. 11mf) – 09 – ne Slangenburg [100]

ANNALES DU MUSEE ROYAL D'HISTOIRE NATURELLE DE BELGIQUE – Bruxelles, 1877-1887. v1-14 – 215mf – 9 – 2517/2 – ne IDC [500]

ANNALES DU MUSEUM NATIONAL D'HISTOIRE NATURELLE – Paris, 1802-1813. v1-20 – 266mf – 9 – 6226/2 – ne IDC [500]

ANNALES DU SERVICE DES ANTIQUITES DE L'EGYPTE – (Index included) – Le Caire, 1900-1925. v1-25 – 120mf – 9 – H-389/1 – ne IDC [930]

ANNALES DU SERVICE DES EPIPHYTIES – Paris, 1913-1920. v1-7 – 54mf – 9 – 7463/1 – ne IDC [630]

LES ANNALES DU T.S. ROSAIRE – Cap-de-la Magdeleine, Quebec: s.n., 1892?-1918 – 9 – cn C.I.H.M. [971]

ANNALES ECCLESIASTICI / Baronius, Caesar; ed by Theiner, A – Barri-Ducis/Parisiis. 37v. 1864-1883 – 577mf – 8 – Dfl2,020.00 – ne Slangenburg [240]

ANNALES ENCYCLOPEDIQUE *see* REVUE ENCYCLOPEDIQUE

ANNALES ET CHRONICA AEVI CAROLINI (MGH 5: 1.BD) – 1826 – Dfl63.00 – ne Slangenburg [240]

ANNALES ET CHRONICA AEVI SALICI (MGH 5: 5.BD) – 1844 – Dfl56.00 – ne Slangenburg [240]

ANNALES ET CHRONICA AEVI SALICI (MGH 5: 10.BD) : VITAE AEVI CAROLINI ET SAXONICI – 1852 – Dfl60.00 – ne Slangenburg [240]

ANNALES ET CRONICA ITALICA AEVI SUEVICI (MGH 5: 31.BD) – 1903 – Dfl74.00 – ne Slangenburg [240]

ANNALES ET HISTORIAE DE REBUS BELGICIS / Grotius, H – Amstelaedami, 1657 – Dfl91.00 – ne Slangenburg [240]

ANNALES FERDINANDEI : ODER KAISER FERDINANDS 2. LEBEN UND DENKWUERDIGEN GESCHICHTEN / Khevenhiller, FChr. – Leipzig. Tom 1-14. 1721-22 – 354mf – 8 – Dfl1,239.00 – ne Slangenburg [920]

ANNALES FULDENSES SIVE ANNALES REGNI FRANCORUM ORIENTALIS (MGH 7: 7.BD) – 1891 – Dfl29.00 – ne Slangenburg [240]

ANNALES GAULOISES – Paris-Besancon. mars 1889-sept 1892 – 1 – fr A.C.R.P.P. [073]

ANNALES GENERALES DES SCIENCES PHYSIQUES – Par MM. Bory de St.Vincent, Drapiez et Van Mons. Bruxelles. 1819-21 – 3 – us Readex [530]

ANNALES HEREMI DEIPARAE MATRIS MONASTERII IN HELVETIA / Hartmann, Christ. – Freiburg Br., 1612 – 13mf – 8 – Dfl46.00 – ne Slangenburg [240]

ANNALES HILDESHEIMENSES (MGH 7: 8.BD) – 1878 – Dfl9.00 – ne Slangenburg [240]

ANNALES HISTORIQUES DE LA REVOLUTION FRANCAISE – Paris. v18-53. 1946-81 – 1 – fr A.C.R.P.P. [073]

ANNALES HYDROGRAPHIQUES – Paris. 1848-1968 – 1 – fr A.C.R.P.P. [550]

ANNALES IMPERII OCCIDENTIS BRUNSVICENSES (768-1005) / Leibniz, Gottfried Wilhelm von; ed by Pertz, G H – Hannoverae. Tom 1-3. 1843-1846 – Dfl144.00 – ne Slangenburg [240]

ANNALES ITALICI AEVI SUEVICI (MGH 5: 18.BD) – 1863 – Dfl81.00 – ne Slangenburg [240]

ANNALES MARBACENSES QUI DICUNTUR (MGH 7: 9.BD) : ACCEDUNT ANNALES ALSATICI BREVIORES – (Cronica Hohenburgensis Cum Continuatione Et Additamentis Neoburgensibus) – 1907 – Dfl13.00 – ne Slangenburg [240]

ANNALES MATHEMATICA / Academiae Scientiarum Fennicae – 1941- 1; 1974- 5,6; 1975- 9 – us UMI [510]

ANNALES METTENSES PRIORES (MGH 7: 10.BD) : ACCEDUNT ADDIT. ANNALIUM METTENSIUM POSTERIORUM – 1905 – Dfl13.00 – ne Slangenburg [240]

ANNALES MINORES AEVI SAXONICI (MGH 5: 3.BD) : CHRONICA MINORA AEVI SAXONICI. ANNALES, CHRONICA, HISTORIAE AEVI SAXONICI – 1839 – Dfl84.00 – ne Slangenburg [240]

ANNALES MONASTERII S. ALBANI (CHRONIA..5) / Johannes Amundesham – (v1 1870 Dfl35.00. v2 1871 Dfl39.00) – ne Slangenburg [240]

ANNALES MONASTICI (RS36) / ed by Luard, H R – (v1: De Margam, Theokesberia (Tewkesbury) Et Burton 1864 Dfl35.00. v2: De Wintonia (Winchester) Et Waverleia (Waverly) 1864 Dfl32.00. v3: De Dunstaplia (Dunstable) Et Bermundeseia (Bermondsey) 1866 Dfl35.00. v4: De Osneneia (Osney), Chronicon Thomas Wykes, Et De Wigornia (Worcester) 1869 Dfl42.00. v5: Index And Glossary 1869 Dfl32.00) – ne Slangenburg [240]

ANNALES MUSEI BOTANICI LUGDUNO BATAVI / London. Botanical Museum – 1863-69 – 1 – uk Microform Academic [580]

ANNALES MUSEI BOTANICI LUGDUNO-BATAVI / Miquel, F A W – Amstelodami, 1863-1869. 4 vols. B-6076 1 – 9 – ne IDC [580]

ANNALES MYCOLOGICI EDITI INMOTITIAM SCIENTIAE MYCOLOGICAE UNIVERSALIS – Berlin, 1903-1941. v1-39 – 376mf – 9 – 1208c/2 – ne IDC [580]

ANNALES ORDINIS CARTUSIENSIS : TOMUS 1. COMPLECTENS EA QUAE AD INSTITUTIONEM, DISCIPLINAM ET OBSERVANTIAS ORDINIS SPECTANT – Correriae, 1687 – Dfl63.00 – ne Slangenburg [240]

ANNALES ORDINIS CARTUSIENSIS AB ANNO 1084 AD ANNUM 1429 AUCTORE D. CAROLO LE COUTEUX O. CART – Monstrolii. 8v. 1888-1891 – 77mf – 8 – Dfl270.00 – ne Slangenburg [240]

ANNALES ORDINIS S. BENEDICTI / Mabillon, Jean – Lutetiae Parisorum. v1-6. 1703-1733 – 289mf – 8 – Dfl1,012.00 – ne Slangenburg [240]

ANNALES PADERBORNENSES / Schaten, N S J – Ed Altera. Monast. Westphalorum, 1774-1775 – Dfl168.00 – ne Slangenburg [240]

ANNALES PARLEMENTAIRES : CHAMBRE DES REPRESENTANTS DU CONGO – 1e Legislation, 1960-1963; 2e Legislation, 1965-1966 – 108mf – 9 – A-663/1 – ne IDC [324]

ANNALES PARLEMENTAIRES DU SENAT DU CONGO – 1960-1963. v1-14 – 113mf – 9 – A-661/1 – ne IDC [324]

ANNALES PATRIOTIQUES ET LITTERAIRES DE LA FRANCE, ET AFFAIRES POLITIQUES DE L'EUROPE, JOURNAL LIBRE – Paris. oct 1789-94 – 1 – fr A.C.R.P.P. [073]

LES ANNALES POLITIQUES ET LITTERAIRES – Paris. -w 7 Jan 1900-27 Dec 1903; 10 Nov 1907-29 March 1908; 7 Jan 1912-26 Jul 1914; 27 Dec 1914-31 Dec 1922. Imperfect. 25 reels – 1 – uk British Libr Newspaper [072]

ANNALES POLITIQUES, MORALES ET LITTERAIRES – Paris. No.1-1277. 16 dec 1815-15 juin 1819. mq no. 1089, 1091, 1201 – 1 – fr A.C.R.P.P. [073]

ANNALES POLONIAE (MGH 7: 11.BD) – 1866 – Dfl13.00 – ne Slangenburg [240]

ANNALES REGNI FRANCORUM INDE AB A. 741 USQUE AD A. 829 (MGH 7: 6.BD) : QUI DICUNTUR ANNALES LAURISSENSES MAIORES ET EINHARDI – 1895 – Dfl19.00 – ne Slangenburg [240]

ANNALES SCIENTIFIQUES / Ecole Normale Superieure. Paris – 1864-1966 – 1,5,6 – us Princeton Micro [500]

ANNALES SCIENTIFIQUES / Paris. Ecole Normale Superieure – s. 1-4. 1864-1977 – 5,6 – us UMI [500]

ANNALES SCIENTIFIQUES, LITTERAIRES ET INDUSTRIELLES DE L'AUVERGNE. – Clermont-Ferrand, 1828-58 – 3 – us Readex [500]

ANNALES. SECTION A: PHYSIQUE THEORETIQUE / Paris. Universite. Institut Henri Poincare – v. 1-25. 1964-1977 – 5,6 – us UMI [530]

ANNALES. SECTION B: CALCUL DES PROBABILITES ET STATISTIQUES / Paris. Universite. Institut Henri Poincare – v. 1-13. 1964-1977 – 5,6 – us UMI [310]

ANNALES SVLTANORVM OTHMANIDARVM, A TVRCIS SVA LINGVA SCRIPTI / Leunclavius, J – Ed 2. Francofvrdi, 1596 – 6mf – 9 – H-8388/1 – ne IDC [956]

ANNALES TELEGRAPHIQUES – Series 2. 1-8. 1858-65; Series 3. 1-25. 1874-99 – 1,5,6 – us Princeton Micro [380]

LES ANNALES TERESIENNES – Montreal: Beauchemin & Valois, [1880-19–] – 9 – cn C.I.H.M. [971]

ANNALES TYPOGRAPHICI COLONIENSES : HANDSCHRIFT AUS DER ERSTEN HAELFTE DES 19. JAHRHUNDERTS / Buellingen, Ludwig von – Koeln. 5 Bde. 1. Haelfte 19. Jh. (mf ed 1997) – 42mf – 9 – DM720.00 – 3-89131-242-3 – gw Fischer [090]

ANNALES XANTENSES ET ANNALES VEDASTINI (MGH 7: 12.BD) – 1909 – Dfl9.00 – ne Slangenburg [240]

ANNALI / Museo Pitre – v1-14/15, 1950-63/64 – 1 – us I.U. Libraries [390]

ANNALI A MAGAZINE OF FINANCE, COMMERCE AND ECONOMICS – v1-56. 1913-40 – 1 – us Princeton Micro [332]

ANNALI DELL'ISLAM, 1-10 / ed by Caetani, L – (Index) – Milano, 1905-1926. v1-10 – 122mf – 9 – NE-307/1 – ne IDC [260]

ANNALI DI FISICA, CHIMICA E MATHEMATICHE – Milano. v1-28; 2nd series, v1-4. 1841-50 – 3 – us Readex [530]

ANNALI DI FRENIATRIA E SCIENZE AFFIN – (1975- . 5,6,9) – 1888- – 1 – us UMI [610]

ANNALI DI MATEMATICA PURA ED APPLICATA – Series 4, v. 1-96. 1924-1973 – 1,5,6 – us Princeton Micro [510]

ANNALI DI SCIENZE MATEMATICHE E FISICHE – Rome, 1850-57 – 3 – us Readex [510]

ANNALI DI STATISTICA / Italy. Istituto Centrale di Statistica – ser. 1, v. 1-10-ser. 6, v. 1-38. 1871-1936. (scattered volumes wanting) – 1 – 367.00 – us L of C Photodup [945]

ANNALI D'ITALIA DAL PRINCIPIO DELL'ERA VOLGARE SINO ALL'ANNO 1749 / Muratori, Lodovico A – Milano. Tom 1-4. 1744-1749 – 170mf – 9 – Dfl595.00 – ne Slangenburg [945]

ANNALI. R. ISTITUTO [SUPERIORE] ORIENTALE DI NAPOLI – Old Series. Napoli, 1929-1937/1938. v1-10. N.S. Roma, 1940. v1 – 65mf – 9 – I-492c/2 – ne IDC [950]

ANNALI TIPOGRAFICI DEI SONCINO; PARTE SECONDA... NEL SECOLO 16... / Manzoni, G – Bologna. v1(2). 1883 – 6mf – ne IDC [270]

THE ANNALIST – New York. v1-56. 1913-40 – 36r – 1 – us Ross [073]

THE ANNALIST; A MAGAZINE OF FINANCE, COMMERCE AND ECONOMICS – New York. v. 1-56. Jan 20 1913-Oct 24 1940 – 1 – us NY Public [330]

ANNALS / Adorers of the Blood of Christ. Wichita, KS – 1901-1985 – 1 – us KS Hist [240]

ANNALS / American Academy of Political and Social Science – v. 1-235. 1890-1944 – 1 – us Princeton Micro [320]

ANNALS / American Academy of Political and Social Science. Philadelphia – v1-28. 1890-1906 – 15r – 1 – us Ross [320]

ANNALS / Association of American Geographers – v. 1-55. 1911-1965 – 1 – us Princeton Micro [550]

ANNALS / Entomological Society of America – v1- 1908- 1; v62- 5,6; v70- 9 – us UMI [580]

ANNALS / Entomological Society of America – v1-48. 1908-55 – 1,5,6 – us Princeton Micro [590]

ANNALS / Organization of American States – v. 1-10. 1949-58 – 1 – us UMI [972]

ANNALS / Royal College of Surgeons of England – v1- 1947- 1; v38- 5,6; v58- 9 – us UMI [616]

ANNALS / Swiss Chiropractors' Association – v1- . 1962- – 1,5,6,9 – us UMI [073]

ANNALS AND FAMILIES OF CABELL COUNTY / Wallace, George S – Richmond: Garret and Massie Publisher, 1935. West Virginia Reel 3. (The Cox Library Collection) – 5 – us Americana [920]

THE ANNALS AND MAGAZINE OF NATURAL HISTORY, INCLUDING ZOOLOGY, BOTANY AND GEOLOGY *see* MAGAZINE OF ZOOLOGY AND BOTANY

ANNALS OF ALLERGY – (Cont by: Annals of Allergy, Asthma, and Immunology) – Arlington Heights. v1-73 jul 1943-dec 1994 1; v25-73 jan 1967- dec 1994 5; v28-73 jan 1970-dec 1994 9 – 1,5,9 – D2442 – us UMI [616]

ANNALS OF ALLERGY *see* ANNALS OF ALLERGY, ASTHMA, AND IMMUNOLOGY

ANNALS OF ALLERGY, ASTHMA, AND IMMUNOLOGY – (Cont: Annals of Allergy) – Arlington Heights. v74-79. jan-dec 1995- – 1,5,9 – D2442.01 – us UMI [616]

ANNALS OF ALLERGY, ASTHMA, AND IMMUNOLOGY *see* ANNALS OF ALLERGY

ANNALS OF AMERICAN HISTORY : ABSTRACTS OF CLEVELAND, OHIO NEWSPAPERS – (Vol 1: 1818-1839. $195.00; Vol 2: 1840-1849. $195.00; Vol 3: 1850-1857. $195.00; Vol 4: 1858-1865. $195.00; Vol 5: 1866-1869. $195.00; Vol 6: 1870-1873. $195.00; Vol 7: 1874-1876. $195.00) – 1818-1876 – 9 – $1,195.00 set – us Bloch [950]

ANNALS OF ANATOMY AND PHYSIOLOGY – Edinburgh, 1851-53. Nos. 1-3 – 3 – us Readex [611]

ANNALS OF AND RECOLLECTIONS OF ONEIDA COUNTY / Jones, Pomroy – Rome, 1851. New York Reel 24. (The Cox Library Collection) – 5 – us Americana [978]

ANNALS OF APPLIED PROBABILITY – Hayward. 1991-* 1; 1995- 5,9 – 1,5,9 – D21339 – us UMI [510]

ANNALS OF ARKANSAS – Ed. by Dallas T. Herndon. 1947.4v. F0005-F0008 – 9 – us A.G.L.L. [978]

ANNALS OF ATHENS, GEORGIA, 1801-1901 / Hull, Augustus Longstreet – 1906. Biog. and hist. sketches.8 fiches. F-0676 – 9 – us A.G.L.L. [920]

ANNALS OF AUGUSTA COUNTY 1726-1871 / Waddell, Joseph A – Staunton, C. R. Caldwell Publishing Co., 1902. Virginia Reel 2. (The Cox Library Collection) – 5 – us Americana [978]

ANNALS OF BENEFICENCE – (Ceased publ) – Philadelphia. v1-2. oct-oct 1823* – 1 – D4417 – us UMI [080]

ANNALS OF BIOMEDICAL ENGINEERING – v1- 1977- – 5,6,9 – us UMI [610]

ANNALS OF BIOMEDICAL ENGINEERING – New York. v1-25 sep 1972-* 1; v20-25 1992- 5*, 9 – 1,5,9 – D21492 – us UMI [610]

ANNALS OF BOTANY / ed by Koenig, K D E & Sims, J – London, [1804-]1805-1806. 2v – 23mf – 9 – 5986/2 – ne IDC [580]

ANNALS OF BOTANY – London, 1887/88-1936. v1-50 – 734mf – 9 – 7121/2 – ne IDC [580]

ANNALS OF BOTANY – o.s. v. 1-50. 1887-1936. n.s. v. 1-20. 1937-57 – 1,5,6 – us Princeton Micro [580]

ANNALS OF BROWN COUNTY / Harrington, Grant W – From earliest records to 1 Jan 1900. Hiawatha: 1903. Kansas Reel 6. (The Cox Library Collection) – 5 – us Americana [978]

THE ANNALS OF CHEMICAL PHILOSOPHY – London, 1828-29. Nos. 1-3 – 3 – us Readex [073]

ANNALS OF CLEVELAND / U.S. Work Projects Administration. Ohio – (v2. 1840-49. $210.00 (diazo); $255.00 (silver halide). v3. 1850-57. $210.00 (diazo); $255.00 (silver halide). v4. 1858-65. $210.00 (diazo); $255.00 (silver halide). v5. 1866-69. $210.00 (diazo); $255.00 (silver halide). v6. 1870-73. $210.00 (diazo); $255.00 (silver halide). v7. 1874-76. $210.00 (diazo); $255.00 (silver halide). v8. Court Records, 1837-76. $210.00 (diazo); $255.00 (silver halide)) – Cleveland newspaper abstracts including name and subject index. v1. 1818-39. 4200p – 9 – $185.00d; $235.00s – us Bloch [324]

ANNALS OF CLINICAL BIOCHEMISTRY – (Former titles: Association of Clinical Biochemists. Proceedings (1961-1968)) – London. v1-34 1961- 1*; v12-34 jan 1975- 5*, 9 – 1,5,9 – D10690 – us UMI [616]

ANNALS OF CLINICAL PSYCHIATRY – New York. v1-9. mar 1989-* – 1,5,9 – D42444 – us UMI [616]

ANNALS OF CLINICAL RESEARCH – (Ceased publ. Merged with: Medical Biology, to form: Annals of Medicine) – Helsinki. v1-20 may 1969-1988* 1; v3-20 feb 1971-1988* 5; v6-20 feb 1974-1988* 9 – 1,5,9 – D5976 – us UMI [616]

ANNALS OF CLINICAL RESEARCH *see* ANNALS OF MEDICINE

ANNALS OF COLLECTIVE ECONOMY – (Cont by: Annals of Public and Co-operative Economy) – Geneva. v1. 1925-63* – 1 – D21837 – us UMI [334]

ANNALS OF COLLECTIVE ECONOMY *see* ANNALS OF PUBLIC AND CO-OPERATIVE ECONOMY

ANNALS OF COMMUNITY-ORIENTED EDUCATION – (Cont by: Education for Health) – Maastricht. v1. 1988-1995* – 1 – D23986 – us UMI [370]

ANNALS OF CONGRESS / U.S. Congress – 1789-1824 – 1 – us Princeton Micro [324]

ANNALS OF CONGRESS, 1789-1824 / U.S. Congress – 1st to 18th Cong., 1st Sess., 42 books. All published. Followed by Congressional Debates.80-033 – 9 – 228.00 – us L.L.M.C. [323]

ANNALS OF DISCRETE MATHEMATICS – v1-10. 1977-81 – 1,5,6,13 – sz Elsevier [073]

ANNALS OF DISCRETE MATHEMATICS – (Ceased publ) – Amsterdam. v1-10. 1977-1981 – 1,5 – D42014 – us UMI [510]

ANNALS OF DYSLEXIA : AN INTERDISCIPLINARY JOURNAL OF THE ORTON DYSLEXIA SOCIETY / Orton Dyslexia Society – (Cont: Bulletin of the Orton Society) – Baltimore. v32-47 1982- – 1,5*,9 – D12837.01 – us UMI [616]

ANNALS OF ECONOMIC AND SOCIAL MEASUREMENT – (1977-78. 5,6,9) – v. 1-7. 1972-78 – 1 – us UMI [300]

ANNALS OF ECONOMIC AND SOCIAL MEASUREMENT – (Ceased publ) – New York. v1-6. jan 1972-Spr 1978 – 1,5,9 – D11430 – us UMI [300]

ANNALS OF ELECTRICITY, MAGNETISM, AND CHEMISTRY – and Guardian of Experimental Science. v.1-10. 1836-43 – 1,5,6 – 2269.00 – us Princeton Micro [530]

THE ANNALS OF ELECTRICITY, MAGNETISM, & CHEMISTRY; AND GUARDIAN OF EXPERIMENTAL SCIENCE – London. 1837-43 – 3 – us Readex [530]

ANNALS OF EMERGENCY MEDICINE – v.9-. 1980- – 1,5,6,9 – us UMI [073]

ANNALS OF EMERGENCY MEDICINE – (Cont: JACEP) – Lansing. v9-30. jan 1980- – 1,5,9 – D12584.01 – us UMI [610]

ANNALS OF EPIDEMIOLOGY – New York. v1-7. oct 1990- – 1,5*,9 – D42680 – us UMI [616]

ANNALS OF EUGENICS – (Cont by: Annals of Human Genetics) – London. v1-18. oct 1925-mar 1954* – 1 – D16516 – us UMI [573]

ANNALS OF EUGENICS *see* ANNALS OF HUMAN GENETICS

ANNALS OF EVANGELICAL NONCONFORMITY IN THE COUNTY OF ESSEX / Davids, Thomas William – 1863 – 1 – us A.T.L.A. [240]

ANNALS OF GEORGIA: IMPORTANT EARLY RECORDS OF THE STATE – v1, comp. by Caroline Price Wilson, 1928. Liberty County Records & a state revolutionary pay roll. 4 fiches. F-0095 – 9 – us A.G.L.L. [920]

ANNALS OF GEORGIA: IMPORTANT EARLY RECORDS OF THE STATE – v2, comp. by Caroline Price Wilson, 1933. Effingham County records & connecting links in other counties. 3 fiches.F-0096 – 9 – us A.G.L.L. [920]

THE ANNALS OF HAYWOOD COUNTY / Allen, W C – Publication made possible by sponsors, 1935. North Carolina Reel 1. (The Cox Library Collection) – 5 – us Americana [978]

ANNALS OF HEMATOLOGY – (Cont: Blut) – Berlin. v62-75. feb 1991- – 1* – D13107.01 – us UMI [616]

ANNALS OF HUMAN BIOLOGY – v.1-23. 1950-72 – 9 – 2418.00; 249.00v – uk Dawson [611]

ANNALS OF HUMAN BIOLOGY – London. v1-24. 1974-* – 1 – D17279 – us UMI [611]

ANNALS OF HUMAN GENETICS – (Cont: Annals of Eugenics) – London. v19-61. 1954-* – 1 – D16516.01 – us UMI [573]

ANNALS OF HUMAN GENETICS *see* ANNALS OF EUGENICS

ANNALS OF INDIAN ADMINISTRATION – Serampore. 1857-75. v1-19. I-273 – 182mf – 8 – ne IDC [321]

ANNALS OF INTERNAL MEDICINE – (1965-5,6. 1970- 9) – 1- 1927- – 1 – us UMI [610]

ANNALS OF INTERNAL MEDICINE – v. 1-57. 1927-1962 – 1,5,6 – us Princeton Micro [616]

ANNALS OF INTERNAL MEDICINE – Philadelpia. v1-127 1927- 1; 62-127 jan 1965- 5; 66-127 jan-dec 1967- 9 – 1,5,9 – D360 – us UMI [610]

ANNALS OF IOWA – (1977- . 5,6,9) – 1863- – 1 – us UMI [978]

ANNALS OF IOWA – Des Moines. 1863-1974* v43-55 Sum 1975- 1; v44-56 Sum 1977-* 5,9 – 1,5,9 – D10422 – us UMI [978]

ANNALS OF LLOYD'S REGISTER: BEING A SKETCH OF THE ORIGIN, CONSTITUTION, AND PROGRESS OF LLOYD'S REGISTER OF BRITISH & FOREIGN SHIPPING / Lloyd's Register of Shipping – London: Wyman and Sons, 1884. x,165p – 1 – us U.W. Library [380]

ANNALS OF LOCH CE (RS54) : A CHRONICLE OF IRISH AFFAIRS FROM A D 1014-1590 / ed by Hennessy, W M – v1,2 1871 – Dfl42.00v – ne Slangenburg [941]

ANNALS OF MATHEMATICAL LOGIC *see* ANNALS OF PURE AND APPLIED LOGIC

ANNALS OF MATHEMATICAL STATISTICS – (1965-72. 5,6) – 1-43. 1930-72 – 1 – us UMI [310]

ANNALS OF MATHEMATICAL STATISTICS – (Ceased publ. Cont in pt by: Annals of Probability, and: Annals of Statistics) – Baltimore. cum index v1-20 1930-1949. v1-43 1930-dec 1972 1; v36-43 feb 1965-dec 1972 5 – 1,5 – D763 – us UMI [510]

ANNALS OF MATHEMATICS – (1966- . 5,6. 1977- . 9) – 1- 1884- – 1 – us UMI [510]

ANNALS OF MATHEMATICS – v. 1-12. 1884-99. Series 2, v. 1-46. 1899-1945 – 1,5,6 – us Princeton Micro [510]

ANNALS OF MATHEMATICS – Princeton. cum index v13-72 1911-1960; v1-12 mar 1884-jun 1899; 2s v1-146 jan 1911- 1; 2s v83-146 jan 1966- 5; 2s 105- jan 1977 9 – 1,5,9 – D232 – us UMI [510]

ANNALS OF MEDICINE – (Formed by the union of: Annals of Clinical Research, and: Medical Biology) – Helsinki. v21-29. feb 1989 – 1,5,9 – D17073 – us UMI [610]

ANNALS OF MEDICINE *see* ANNALS OF CLINICAL RESEARCH

ANNALS OF NATURAL HISTORY *see* MAGAZINE OF ZOOLOGY AND BOTANY

ANNALS OF NATURE / Rafinesque-Schmaltz, Constantine S – or Annual Synopsis of New Genera and Species. B-7651 1.1820 – 9 – ne IDC [580]

ANNALS OF NATURE : OR, ANNUAL SYNOPSIS OF NEW GENERA AND SPECIES OF ANIMALS IN NORTH AMERICA – (Ceased publ) – Lexington. v1. 1820 – 1 – D3551 – us UMI [590]

ANNALS OF NEUROLOGY – Boston. v1-42. jan 1977- – 1,5,9 – D13447 – us UMI [616]

ANNALS OF NEWBERRY COUNTY / O'Neall & Chapman – Newberry, Aull and Houseal, 1892. South Carolina Reel 3. (The Cox Library Collection) – 5 – us Americana [978]

ANNALS OF NUCLEAR ENERGY – (Cont: Annals of Nuclear Science and Engineering) – Elmsford. .v2-24. 1975- – 1,5,9 – D49010.02 – us UMI [621]

ANNALS OF NUCLEAR ENERGY *see* ANNALS OF NUCLEAR SCIENCE AND ENGINEERING

ANNALS OF NUCLEAR SCIENCE AND ENGINEERING – (Cont: Journal of Nuclear Energy. Cont by: Annals of Nuclear Energy) – Elmsford. v1. 1974 – 1,5,9 – D49010.01 – us UMI [621]

ANNALS OF NUCLEAR SCIENCE AND ENGINEERING *see* ANNALS OF NUCLEAR ENERGY

ANNALS OF NUTRITION AND METABOLISM – v18-. 1975- – 1,5,9 – us UMI [073]

ANNALS OF OCCUPATIONAL HYGIENE – Oxford. v1-41. 1959- – 1,5,9 – D49011 – us UMI [360]

ANNALS OF ONCOLOGY – Dordrecht. v1-8. 1990-* – 1,5,9 – D18595 – us UMI [616]

ANNALS OF ORIENTAL RESEARCH / Madras. University – v. 1-19. 1937-64. Lacking: 1945, v. 7. BI-241 2 – 8 – ne IDC [950]

ANNALS OF OTOLOGY, RHINOLOGY AND LARYGOLOGY *see* ANNALS OF OTOLOGY, RHINOLOGY AND LARYNGOLOGY

ANNALS OF OTOLOGY, RHINOLOGY AND LARYNGOLOGY – (Included: Annals of Otology, Rhinology and Laryngology. Suppl (1971, 1973-75, 1977-79, 1981). Former titles: Annals of Otology, Rhinology and Laryngology (jan 1892-oct 1896)) – St Louis. cum index v43-52 1934-1943; v1-106 jan 1892- 1;v80-106 feb 1971- 5; v85-106 jan 1976- 9 – 1,5,9 – D3184 – us UMI [617]

ANNALS OF OTOLOGY, RHINOLOGY AND LARYNGOLOGY. SUPPLEMENT *see* ANNALS OF OTOLOGY, RHINOLOGY AND LARYNGOLOGY

ANNALS OF PHARMACOTHERAPY – (Cont: DICP) – Cincinnati. v26-31. jan 1992- – 1,5,9 – D6492.02 – us UMI [615]

ANNALS OF PHILADELPHIA, AND PENNSYLVANIA IN THE OLDEN TIME / Watson, John F – Being a collection of memoirs, anecdotes, and incidents of the city and its inhabitants. Philadelphia, Edwin S. Stuart, 1897. Vols. 1-3. Pennsylvania Reel 36. (The Cox Library Collection) – 5 – us Americana [978]

ANNALS OF PHILOSOPHY; OR, MAGAZINE OF CHEMISTRY, MINERALOGY, MECHANICS, NATURAL HISTORY, AGRICULTURE AND THE ARTS – London. 1813-20. New Series, 1821-26 – 3 – us Readex [500]

ANNALS OF PLASTIC SURGERY – Boston. v1-39. jan 1978- – 1,5,9 – D12497 – us UMI [617]

ANNALS OF PLATTE COUNTY / Paxton, W M – From exploration to June 1, 1897, with genealogies of families and sketches of its pioneers. Kansas City: Hudson-Kimberly Publ. Co., 1897. Missouri Reel 27. (The Cox Library Collection) – 5 – us Americana [978]

ANNALS OF POLK COUNTY AND THE CITY OF DES MOINES / Porter, Will – Des Moines: Geo. A. Miller Printing Co., 1898. Iowa Reel 34. (The Cox Library Collection) – 5 – us Americana [978]

ANNALS OF PROBABILITY *see* ANNALS OF MATHEMATICAL STATISTICS

ANNALS OF PUBLIC AND CO-OPERATIVE ECONOMY = ANNALES DE L'ECONOMIE COLLECTIVE – ANNALEN DER GEMEINWIRTSCHAFT – (Cont: Annals of Collective Economy) – Liege. v35-68 1964-* 1; v66-68 1995- 5,9 – 1,5,9 – D21837.01 – us UMI [334]

ANNALS OF PUBLIC AND CO-OPERATIVE ECONOMY *see* ANNALS OF COLLECTIVE ECONOMY

ANNALS OF PURE AND APPLIED LOGIC – v1-27. 1969-84 – 1,5,6,13 – sz Elsevier [073]

ANNALS OF PURE AND APPLIED LOGIC – (Former titles: Annals of Mathematical Logic (jan 1970-dec 1982)) – Amsterdam. v1-88 1970- 1,5; v37-88 jan-dec 1988- – 1,5,9 – D42108 – us UMI [160]

ANNALS OF REGIONAL SCIENCE – Belligham. v23-31. may 1989- – 1,5*,9 – D17113 – us UMI [500]

THE ANNALS OF SAN FRANCISCO / Soute, Gihon & Nesbet – San Francisco: D. Appleton & Co., 1854. California Reel 27. (The Cox Library Collection) – 5 – us Americana [978]

ANNALS OF SCIENCE – (v.30-32. 1973-75. 2413.00v; 9) – v.1-29. With index v.1-25. 1939-72 – 9 – 24265.00; 248.00v – uk Dawson [500]

ANNALS OF SCIENCE – London. v1-54. 1936- – 1*,5*,9 – D17314 – us UMI [500]

THE ANNALS OF SCOTTISH NATURAL HISTORY *see* THE SCOTTISH NATURALIST

ANNALS OF SENAT *see* ANNALS OF ULSTER OTHERWISE ANNALS OF SENAT

ANNALS OF SOUTH WEST VIRGINIA / Summers, Lewis P – Abingdon, 1929. Virginia Reel 1. (The Cox Library Collection) – 5 – us Americana [978]

ANNALS OF SOUTHWESTERN PENNSYLVANIA / Walkenshaw, Lewis C – New York, Lewis Historical Publ. Co. Vols. 1-3, Pennsylvania Reel 2; Vol. 4, Pennsylvania Reel 3. (The Cox Library Collection) – 5 – us Americana [978]

ANNALS OF SPORTING AND FANCY GAZETTE – A Magazine Entirely Appropriate to Sporting Subjects and Fancy Pursuits... v1-13 (all publ). Jan 1822-Jun 1828 – 2r – 1 – $325.00 – us UPA [970]

ANNALS OF SPORTING, AND FANCY GAZETTE – London, 1822-28 – 7r – 1 – uk British Libr Newspaper [072]

ANNALS OF ST ANNE DE BEAUPRE – Quebec: The Directors of Levis College, [1876?]-1902; (Quebec: L. Brousseau) – 9 – cn C.I.H.M. [240]

ANNALS OF ST LOUIS: IN ITS EARLY DAYS UNDER THE FRENCH AND SPANISH DOMINATIONS / Billon, Frederic Louis – Comp. by F. L. Billon from authentic data. St. Louis, MO: Nixon-Jones, 1886. 00427. (Pre-1900 Canadiana) – 9 – cn C.I.H.M. [978]

ANNALS OF STATISTICS – (Cont in part: Annals of Mathematical Statistics) – Haward. v1-25 jan 1973- 1,5; v3-25 jan 1975- 9 – 1,5,9 – D6929 – us UMI [310]

ANNALS OF STATISTICS *see* ANNALS OF MATHEMATICAL STATISTICS

ANNALS OF SURGERY – v. 25-130. 1897-1949 – 1,5,6 – us Princeton Micro [617]

ANNALS OF SURGERY – Philadelphia. cum index v1-100 jan 1885-dec 1934; v1-226 jan 1885- 1; v161-226 jan 1965- 5; v171-226 jan 1970- 9 – 1,5,9 – D1568 – us UMI [617]

ANNALS OF SURGICAL ONCOLOGY – New York. v1-4. jan-nov 1994-* – 1,5,9 – D20675 – us UMI [617]

ANNALS OF THE AMERICAN ACADEMY OF POLITICAL AND SOCIAL SCIENCE / American Academy of Political and Social Science – Philadelphia. 1890-1941, v1-218. Lacking: 1890-97, v1-10. 1910, v35-38. 1917/18, v75-76, 78. 1919, v86. 1921, v93, 96-97. 1922/23, v103-104. H-181c – 809mf – 9 – ne IDC [300]

ANNALS OF THE AMERICAN ACADEMY OF POLITICAL SCIENCE / American Academy of Political and Social Science – Thousand Oaks. cum index 1-272 1890-jul 1950. v1554 jul 1890-nov 1997+ 1; v363-554 jan 1966-nov 1997+ 5; v387-554 jan 1970-nov 1997+ 9. Shipped yrly or qrtly – 1,5,9 – D757 – us UMI [320]

ANNALS OF THE AMERICAN PULPIT – v. 1-9. (Complete) – 1 – 254.17 – us Baptist [240]

ANNALS OF THE BHANDARKAR ORIENTAL INSTITUTE / Bhandarkar Oriental Research Institute – Poona, 1918-60. v1-41. Index 1919-52, v1-33. I-130 – 276mf – 8 – ne IDC [950]

ANNALS OF THE DISRUPTION : WITH EXTRACTS FROM THE NARRATIVES OF MINISTERS WHO LEFT THE SCOTTISH ESTABLISHMENT IN 1843 / Brown, Thomas – Edinburg: Macniven & Wallace, 1884 – 2mf – us A.T.L.A. [240]

ANNALS OF THE EARLY CALIPHATE, FROM THE ORIGINAL SOURCES / Muir, William – 1883 – 1 – us A.T.L.A. [260]

ANNALS OF THE EMPEROR CHARLES 5TH / Lopez de Gomara, Francisco; ed by Merriman, Roger Bigelow – Oxford: Clarendon Press, 1912 – sp Bibl Santa Ana [940]

ANNALS OF THE EMPEROR CHARLES 5TH / Lopez de Gomara, Francisco – Spanish text and English trans. ed., with introd. and notes by Roger Bigelow Merriman. Oxford: Clarendon, 1912. lv, 302p – 1 – us U.W. Library [946]

ANNALS OF THE HISTORY OF COMPUTING – (Cont by: IEEE Annals of the History of Computing) – New York. v1-13 jul 1979-1991* 1,5; v11-13 1989-1991 9 – 1,5,9 – D16975 – us UMI [000]

ANNALS OF THE ICRP – Oxford. v1-27. 1977- – 1*,5,9 – D49080 – us UMI [080]

ANNALS OF THE INTERNATIONAL GEOPHYSICAL YEAR – London. v1-48 – 1,5 – D49012 – us UMI [550]

ANNALS OF THE "LOW-CHURCH" PARTY IN ENGLAND : DOWN TO THE DEATH OF ARCHBISHOP TAIT / Proby, William Henry Baptist – London: J.T. Hayes, 1888 – 3mf – us A.T.L.A. [240]

ANNALS OF THE LYCEUM OF NATURAL HISTORY OF NEW YORK – New York, 1824-1876. v1-11 – 62mf – 9 – 8625/1 – ne IDC [500]

ANNALS OF THE MISSOURI BOTANICAL GARDEN / Missouri Botanical Garden – St. Louis, MO. 1914-32. v1-19. 8558 – 107mf – 9 – ne IDC [580]

ANNALS OF THE PROPAGATION OF FAITH – Ireland. v58-63. 1895-1900 (incomplete) – 1r – 1 – ATLA S0663B – us A.T.L.A. [073]

ANNALS OF THE PROPAGATION OF FAITH – Quebec. v1 no 6-13. 1879-83 (incomplete) – 1r – 1 – ATLA S0663A – us A.T.L.A. [073]

ANNALS OF THE PROPAGATION OF THE FAITH – Three-Rivers [Quebec]: Published for the Institution, c1877- – 9 – cn C.I.H.M. [240]

ANNALS OF THE PROPAGATION OF THE FAITH *see* ANNALES DE LA PROPAGATION DE LA FOI POUR LA PROVINCE DE QUEBEC

ANNALS OF THE RHEUMATIC DISEASES – (Former titles: Rheumatic Diseases (jan 1939)) – London. v1-56 1939- 1; v25-56 jan 1966- 5; v35-56 feb 1976- 9 – 1,5,9 – D1330 – us UMI [616]

ANNALS OF THE ROYAL BOTANIC GARDEN – Calcutta, 1887-1931. v1-13 – 164mf – 9 – 8559/1 – ne IDC [580]

ANNALS OF THE ROYAL BOTANIC GARDENS – Peradeniya. Colombo, London, 1901-1932. v1-11 – 62mf – 9 – 7478/1 – ne IDC [580]

ANNALS OF THE ROYAL COLLEGE OF PHYSICIANS, 1518-1915 – Marlborough: Adam Matthew Publications, 1991 – 417mf – 9 – $2,950.00 – uk Matthew [610]

ANNALS OF THE ROYAL COLLEGE OF SURGEONS OF ENGLAND – London. v 1-58 1947-nov 1976* 1; v38-58 jan 1966-nov 1976 5 – 1,5 – D5324 – us UMI [617]

THE ANNALS OF THE RUSSIAN ACADEMY OF SCIENCE / Akademiia Nauk. SSSR – 1922-1924 – 3 – us Readex [500]

THE ANNALS OF THE TOWN OF GUELPH, 1827-1877 / Burrows, Charles Acton – Comp. under the direction of C. Acton Burrows. Guelph, Ont.: Herald Stream Print. House, 1877. 03827. (Pre-1900 Canadiana) – 9 – cn C.I.H.M. [971]

ANNALS OF THE UNITED STATES CHRISTIAN COMMISSION / Moss, Lemuel – 1868 – 1 – $50.00 – us Presbyterian [240]

ANNALS OF THORACIC SURGERY – (Cont: Annals of Thoracic Surgery) – Boston. v47-64. jan 1989- – 1,5,9 – D42585 – us UMI [617]

ANNALS OF THORACIC SURGERY – (Cont by: Annals of Thoracic Surgery) – Lausanne. v1-46. jan 1965-dec 1988 – 1,5,9 – D10966 – us UMI [617]

ANNALS OF THORACIC SURGERY *see* – ANNALS OF THORACIC SURGERY

ANNALS OF TOURISM RESEARCH – New York. v1-24 1973- 1; v1-24 1973- 5; v9-24 1982- 9 – 1,5,9 – D49410 – us UMI [338]

THE ANNALS OF TRINITY COUNTY / Cox, Isaac – Eugene, OR: John Henry Nash, 1940. California Reel 35. (The Cox Library Collection) – 5 – us Americana [978]

ANNALS OF TROPICAL MEDICINE AND PARASITOLOGY – v43-53. 1949-59 – 1,5,6 – us Princeton Micro [073]

ANNALS OF TROPICAL PAEDIATRICS : INTERNATIONAL CHILD HEALTH – 1992- 13v – £172.00 – 0272-4936 – uk Carfax [618]

ANNALS OF ULSTER OTHERWISE ANNALS OF SENAT : A CHRONICLE OF IRISH AFFAIRS FROM AD. 431, TO A.D. 1540 / ed by Hennesy, William M & MacCarthy, B – Dublin. 4v. 1887-1901 – 43mf – 8 – Dfl151.00 – ne Slangenburg [240]

ANNALS OF WITCHCRAFT IN NEW ENGLAND : AND ELSEWHERE IN THE UNITED STATES, FROM THEIR FIRST SETTLEMENT / Drake, Samuel G – Boston: W. Elliot Woodward, 1869 – 1mf – us A.T.L.A. [130]
ANNALY – Zhurnal vseobshchei istorii. v. 1-4. Spb. 1922-24. BR-1650 2 – 8 – ne IDC [073]
ANNALY BIOLOGII – (Summary in English) – M., 1959. v1 – 8mf – 9 – R-1649/2 – ne IDC [574]
ANNALY INSTITUTA IM. N.P. KONDAKOVA – Prague, Beograd, 1937-1940. v9-11 – 17mf – 9 – R-3387/2 – ne IDC [073]
L'ANNAM – no. 63-182. Saigon. mai 1926-fevr 1928 – 1 – fr A.C.R.P.P. [073]
L'ANNAM NOUVEAU – Hanoi. 1931-avr 1942 – 1 – fr A.C.R.P.P. [073]
ANNAMAIG : EINE DORFGESCHICHTE AUS DEM BAIREUTHER LAND / Raithel, Hans – 3. Aufl. Leipzig: C F Amelang, 1920 – 1r – 1 – us U.W. Library [430]
L'ANNAMITE, MERE DES LANGUES: COMMUNAUTE D'ORIGINE DES RACES CELTIQUES, SEMITIQUES, SOUDANAISES ET DE L'INDO-CHINE;.. / Frey, Henri Nicolas – Paris: Hachette et Cie., 1892. xvi,248p. 3 maps – 1 – us U.W. Library [572]
Annan, Robert *see* EXPOSITION AND DEFENSE OF THE WESTMINSTER ASSEMBLY'S CONFESSION
Annan, William *see* HIGH CHURCH EPISCOPACY
Annand, Edward *see*
- ANNEE DE LA PREMIERE COMMUNION, OU, GUIDE DES ENFANTS DURANT L'ANNEE DE LA PREMIERE COMMUNION.
- CHRISTIAN BAPTISM: A LECTURE IN REPLY TO A SERMON BY REV. D. M. WILSON

Annand, William *see* LETTER FROM HON. WILLIAM ANNAND TO THE ELECTORS OF HANTS
Annapolis, Maryland *see* THE MARYLAND GAZETTE, 1745-1839
AN-NASIH : EN NACIH. LE VERIDIQUE. JOURNAL POLITIQUE, LITTERAIRE, ECONOMIQUE ET SOCIAL FRANCO-ARABE – Alger ? n1-28. juil 1921-oct 1922 – 1 – fr A.C.R.P.P. [073]
AN-NASIH : ORGANE DES INTERETS MUSULMANS – Alger, 1899-mai 1902 – 1 – fr A.C.R.P.P. [073]
Annau, Zoltan *see* ACCOUNTABILITY IN RESEARCH
ANNE HEREFORD / Wood, Ellen – British Fiction Archive: Unit 1 – 9 – uk Bell [830]
Annear, S *see* THE PHYSIOLOGY OF TEETOTALISM: A LECTURE DELIVERED IN THE VESTRY OF THE FREE BAPTIST CHURCH, FREDERICTON, FEBRUARY 23RD, 1883
ANNEE 1907. LA DEUXIEME CONFERENCE DE LA HAYE / Groupe Parlementaire francais de l'Arbitage International – Paris, 1907 – 2mf – 1 – ILM-4100/1 – ne IDC [327]
L'ANNEE BENEDICTINE / Blemur, R M J de – Paris, 1667 – Dfl263.00 – ne Slangenburg [240]
L'ANNEE BIOLOGIQUE; COMPTES RENDUS DES TRAVAUX DE BIOLOGIE GENERALE – Paris. 1921 22-1925 26 – 1 – 23.00 – us L of C Photodup [574]
ANNEE DE LA PREMIERE COMMUNION, OU, GUIDE DES ENFANTS DURANT L'ANNEE DE LA PREMIERE COMMUNION. / Annand, Edward – Montreal: Granger, 1898. 04109. (Pre-1900 Canadiana) – 9 – cn C.I.H.M. [240]
UNE ANNEE DE REVOLUTION SOCIALISTE, 1962 / Algeria. Ministere de l'Orientation Nationale – 1964? BNE-8661 1 – 9 – ne IDC [320]
L'ANNEE LITTERAIRE – Paris. 1754-90 – 1 – fr A.C.R.P.P. [410]
L'ANNEE LITTERAIRE – Paris. 1849 – 1 – fr A.C.R.P.P. [410]
ANNEE LITTERAIRE – (Ceased publ) – Amsterdam. v1-292. 1754-1790* – 1 – D3358 – us UMI [400]
L'ANNEE LITTERAIRE ET DRAMATIQUE – Paris, 1859-1869. 11v – 102mf – 9 – H-1375/2 – ne IDC [400]
L'ANNEE LITURGIQUE / Gueranger, Prosper – 15 v. 1871-1901 – 1 – us A.T.L.A. [240]
L'ANNEE M.DCC.LXXXIX OU LES TRIBUNS DU PEUPLE / Bonneville, Nicolas de – De l'imprimerie du Cercle Social. s.d – 9 – fr Hachette [321]
L'ANNEE MISSIONAIRE, 1931 / Lesourd, Paul – Madrid: Razon y Fe, 1932 – 1 – sp Bibl Santa Ana [240]
L'ANNEE MUSICALE – Partis, 1912-13.-v1-2 – 17mf – 9 – P-556/1 – ne IDC [780]
ANNEE MUSICALE – Paris. v. 1-3. 1911-1913 – 1 – us NY Public [780]
ANNEE MUSICALE – Paris. v1-3. 1911-13 – 1r – 1 – us Ross [780]
L'ANNEE POLITIQUE ET ETRANGERE – no. 1-60. 1925-juin 1940. devenu: L'Annee politique economique et cooperative. no. 80-93. nov dec 1947-fevr 1950 sic. devenu: L'Annee politique et economique. no. 94-230. Paris. mars 1950-72 – 1 – fr A.C.R.P.P. [327]
L'ANNEE SOCIOLOGIQUE – Paris. 13v. (Scattered issues lacking) – 1 – 80.00 – us L of C Photodup [300]
LES ANNEES DE FORMATION DE F. H. JACOBI, D'APRES SES LETTRES INEDITES A M. M. REY (1763-1771) AVEC "LE NOBLE" DE MME. DE CHARRIERE / Booy, J T de & Mortier, Roland – (Studies on Voltaire and the eighteenth century, v45) – Oxford. 1966 – 9 – $27.00 – 0-7294-0131-6 – uk Voltaire [900]
ANNEES DE PELERINAGE : DEUXIEME ANNEE. COMPOSITIONS POUR PIANO / Liszt, F – Mayence: B. Schott's Sohne, [185-] – 1 – us Sibley [780]
ANNEES DE PELERINAGE : PREMIERE ANNEE. COMPOSITIONS POUR PIANO / Liszt, F – Mayence: B Schott's Soehne, [185-] – 1 – us Sibley [780]
ANNEES DE PELERINAGE : TROISEME ANNEE. COMPOSITIONS POUR PIANO / Liszt, Franz – Mayence: B Schott's Soehne [185-] – 1 – us Sibley [780]
LES ANNEES DE PIE IX, DE 1846 A 1878: SOUVENIR – Montreal, E. Senecal, 1878. 02194. (Pre-1900 Canadiana) – 9 – cn C.I.H.M. [240]
Annenkov, I *see* VOSPOMINANIIA OB ALEKSANDRE BLOKE
Annenkov, N *see* BOTANICHESKII SLOVAR'
Annenkov, P V *see* P.V. ANNENKOV I EGO DRUZ'IA
Annenskii, I F *see*
- FAMIRA-KIFARED. VAKKHICHESKAIA DRAMA
- KNIGA OTRAZHENII I VTORAIA KNIGA OTRAZHENII
- KNIGA OTRAZHENII. PROBLEMA GOGOLEVSKAGO IUMORA. DOSTOEVSKII DO KATASTROFY
- MELANIPPA-FILOSOF. TRAGEDIIA
- STIKHOTVORENIIA
- STIKHOTVORENIIA I TRAGEDII
- TSAR' IKSION. TRAGEDIIA V PIATI DEISTVIIAKH

Annesley, Alexander *see* A COMPENDIUM OF THE LAW OF MARINE INSURANCE
Annesley, G *see* VOYAGES AND TRAVELS TO INDIA
ANNETTE, THE METIS SPY: A HEROINE OF THE N. W. REBELLION / Collins, Joseph Edmund – Toronto: Rose, 1886. 02152. (Pre-1900 Canadiana) – 9 – cn C.I.H.M. [920]
ANNETTE VON DROSTE-HUELSHOFF ALS WESTFAELISCHE DICHTERIN / Scholz, Wilhelm von – 1995 – 1mf – 9 – DM48.00 – 3-8267-3135-2 – gw Hänsel [430]
ANNETTE VON DROSTE-HUELSHOFF IM SPIEGEL DER ZEITGENOESSISCHEN KRITIK / Raab, Karl – Muenster, 1933 – viii/147p – 9 – DM48.00 – 3-89349-100-7 – gw Hänsel [943]
ANNETTE VON DROSTE-HUESLHOFF : IHRE DICHTERISCHE ENTWICKLUNG UND IHR VERHAELTNIS ZUR ENGLISCHEN LITERATUR / Badt-Strauss, Bertha – (Includes bibliographical references) – Leipzig: Quelle & Meyer, 1909 – 1 – us U.W. Library [410]
Annexation Association of Montreal *see* THE ANNEXATION MANIFESTO OF 1849: REPRINTED FROM THE ORIGINAL PAMPHLET, WITH THE NAMES OF THE SIGNERS
THE ANNEXATION MANIFESTO OF 1849: REPRINTED FROM THE ORIGINAL PAMPHLET, WITH THE NAMES OF THE SIGNERS / Annexation Association of Montreal – Montreal: D. English, 1881. 02403. (Pre-1900 Canadiana) – 9 – cn C.I.H.M. [971]
ANNEXATION: THE IDEAS OF THE LATE WILLIAM H. SEWARD / Glen, Francis Wayland – s.l., s.n., 1893?. 04374. (Pre-1900 Canadiana) – 9 – cn C.I.H.M. [971]
ANNEXES / UN – (10th-14th sess: 1950-52 mf: E.28 F.29; 15th-55th sess: 1952-73 mf: E.192 F.211 S.206; After 55th Session, no further Annexes to the Official Records of the Council have been issued; 1st-5th Session included in the Summary Records) – 6th-9th sess. 1948-49 – E/F.24 – 9 – us U.N. Pubs [340]
ANNEXION: CONFERENCE: L'UNION CONTINENTALE / Rouilliard, Jean-Baptiste – 1893?. 03740. (Pre-1900 Canadiana) – 9 – cn C.I.H.M. [971]
L'ANNEXION DU CONGO... / Brunet, R – Bruxelles, 1911 – 4mf – 1 – ILM-823/1 – ne IDC [327]
L'ANNEXION DU CONGO A LA BELGIQUE ET LE DROIT INTERNATIONAL / Brunet, Roger – Paris, Jouve et Cie., 1911. 334 p. LL-12009 – 1 – us L of C Photodup [340]
L'ANNEXIONNISTE – Montreal, Canada. v1 n7. 21 nov 1891; 5, 19 dec 1891 – 1r – 1 – Can$31.25 – cn Can Microfilming [072]
ANNIBAL LE CARTHAGINOIS – Limoges. 1880. 63p. (HistoricaL Studies Series) – 9 – 6.00 – fr Bibl Nationale [900]
ANNIE ADAMS FIELD PAPERS, 1852-1912 / Fields, Annie Adams – Massachusetts Historical Society – 3r – 1 – $225.00 – us UMI [920]
THE ANNIE HORNIMAN COLLECTION – (With printed guide) – 77mf – 9 – $266.00 – 1-869934-30-X – uk Emmett [790]
Annis, Daniel G *see* VITAL RECORDS OF LONDONDERRY
L'ANNIVERSAIRE OU LA FETE DE LA SOUVERAINETE / Cuvelier de Trie et Mittie – French Theatre Series. Paris. Barba, an VI. 1798 – 9 – fr Hachette [820]
ANNIVERSARIES OF THE RUSSIAN REVOLUTION PAMPHLET COLLECTION – 1927-1972 – 1 – CSUXANS8017-B – us Hoover Inst Photo [350]
ANNIVERSARIES OF WORLD WAR 2 PAMPHLET COLLECTION – 1945-1985 – 1 – CSUXANP1570-B – us Hoover Inst Photo [350]
ANNIVERSARY – 1829 – 4mf – 9 – £35.00 – uk Chadwyck [800]
ANNIVERSARY NUMBER OF THE CHIGNECTO POST AND BORDERER – Sackville, N.B., 1895. 05880. (Pre-1900 Canadiana) – 9 – cn C.I.H.M. [971]
ANNIVERSARY SERMON, 1889: PREACHED...IN ST ANDREW'S CHURCH, SUNDAY EVENING, DEC 1ST / Herridge, William Thomas – Ottawa: St. Andrew's Society of Ottawa, 1889. 05556. (Pre-1900 Canadiana) – 9 – cn C.I.H.M. [971]
ANNIVERSARY SERMON PREACHED IN KNOX CHURCH, NOVEMBER 30TH, 1890 / Farries, Francis Wallace – s.l.: s.n., 1891?. 02952. (Pre-1900 Canadiana) – 9 – cn C.I.H.M. [971]
ANNO DOMINI 1921 STIKHI / Akhmatova, A – Spb. 1922. BR-1086 2 – 8 – ne IDC [460]
ANNO DOMINI 1921. STIKHOTVORENIIA / Akhmatova, A – Ed. 2. V. 3. Spb., Berlin. 1923. BR-1087 2 – 8 – ne IDC [460]
ANNO MUNDI ARDENTIS 1915 / Voloshin, M – Stikhotvoreniia. M. 1916. BR-891 2 – 8 – ne IDC [460]
ANNONCES, AFFICHES ET AVIS DIVERS – 3mai 1752-25 fevr 1761. devenu: Affiches, annonces et avis divers puis ou Journal general de France. 4 mars 1761-84. devenu: Journal general de France. 1785-10 aout 1792. voir aussi: Supplement au Journal general de France – 1 – fr A.C.R.P.P. [073]
ANNONCES, AFFICHES, NOUVELLES ET AVIS DIVERS POUR LA VILLE LA VILLE DE NANTES – (The year 1762 is missing) – Hebd., Nantes, janv. 1760-dec. 1764 (annee 1762 manq.) – 1r – 1 – F313,10 – fr Armell [073]
L'ANNONCEUR – Joliette, Canada. 23 jul 1898 – 1r – 1 – Can$25.00 – cn Can Microfilming [072]
L'ANNONCEUR – [Quebec]: L Recio, [1880] – 9 – cn C.I.H.M. [971]
ANNOTACIONES IN GALENI INTERPRETES QUIBUS VARII LOCIS, IN QUOS HACTENUS IMPEGERUNT... / Laguna, A de – Venecia, 1548 – 2mf – 9 – sp Cultura [610]
ANNOTATED BIBLIOGRAPHY OF AQUACULTURE BOOKS FOR LIBRARIES OF DEVELOPING COUNTRIES – 1990 – 130p – it F.A.O. [639]
AN ANNOTATED BIBLIOGRAPHY ON METHODS FOR NON-LINEAR LEAST SQUARES COMPUTATIONS INCLUDING TEST PROBLEMS / Nash, John C – 1976 – 9 – Can$15.00 – 0-88769-000-9 – cn Nash Info [310]
ANNOTATED BIBLIOGRAPHY ON RODENT RESEARCH IN LATIN AMERICA : 1960-1985 – 1989 – 351p – it F.A.O. [590]
AN ANNOTATED BIBLIOGRAPHY ON THE FAMILY AND RELATED TOPICS, PART 2 : ABSTRACTS OF SOCIOLOGICAL LITERATURE / Israel. Szold Institute – 1973. Ron Lahav: Jerusalem, 1975. 99, 18p (Publication no 550) – 9 – $3.00 – is I.T.T.I. [306]
AN ANNOTATED BIBLIOGRAPHY ON THE FAMILY AND RELATED TOPICS, PART 4 : ABSTRACTS OF SOCIOLOGICAL LITERATURE / Israel. Szold Institute – 1972. Ron Lahav: Jerusalem, 1977. 350p (Publication no 568) – 9 – $6.00 – is I.T.T.I. [306]
ANNOTATED CASES – AMERICAN AND ENGLISH – New York, San Francisco: Thompson Co, Bancroft-Whitney. v1916C-1918E (13v). 1916-18 (all publ) – 185mf – 9 – LLMC 84-695C – us L.L.M.C. [340]
ANNOTATED CASES – AMERICAN AND ENGLISH *see*
- AMERICAN ANNOTATED CASES
- DIGEST OF THE AMERICAN AND ENGLISH ANNOTATED CASES
- GREEN'S DIGEST OF ANNOTATED CASES
- KREIDER'S INDEX OF NOTES IN THE ANNOTATED CASES

THE ANNOTATED CORPORATION LAWS OF ALL THE STATES, GENERALLY APPLICABLE TO STOCK CORPORATIONS / Cumming, Robert Cushing – Albany, Lyon, 1899-1903. 5 v. LL-1442 – 1 – us L of C Photodup [340]
THE ANNOTATED SCOTTISH COMMUNION OFFICE : AN HISTORICAL ACCOUNT OF THE SCOTTISH COMMUNION OFFICE AND OF THE COMMUNION OFFICE OF THE PROTESTANT EPISCOPAL CHURCH OF THE UNITED STATES OF AMERICA... / Dowden, John – Edinburgh: R. Grant; New York: T. Whittaker, 1884 – 1mf – us A.T.L.A. [240]
ANNOTATED STATUTES AND RULES OF TRIAL PRACTICE AND APPELLATE PROCEDURE IN SOUTH DAKOTA AND NORTH DAKOTA. / Deland, Charles Edmund – Pierre, Carter, 1896. 581 p. LL-680 – 1 – us L of C Photodup [340]
ANNOTATED TIME TABLE: WITH INFORMATION AS TO C.P.R. TRANSCONTINENTAL ROUTES / Canadian Pacific Railway Company – Montreal?: C.P.R., 1898? 00442. (Pre-1900 Canadiana) – 9 – cn C.I.H.M. [380]
ANNOTATION OF THE CODE OF THE TRUST TERRITORY OF THE PACIFIC ISLANDS (TTPI), 1952 – n.p.,n.d. – 1mf – 9 – $1.50 – LLMC 82-100F Title 87 – us L.L.M.C. [340]
ANNOTATIONES IN L. II DE CAPTIVES, ET POSTLIMINIO REVERSIS / Baif, L de – Parisiis, 1536 – 5mf – 9 – ILM-335/1 – ne IDC [340]
ANNOTATIONES IN NOVUM TESTAMENTUM / Osiander, Lucas – Tuebingen, 1592 – 36mf – 8 – ne Slangenburg [220]
ANNOTATIONES IN PEDACII DIOSCORIDIS ANAZARBEI DE MATERIA MEDICA... / Cordus, V – Argentorati, 1561 – 17mf – 9 – ne IDC [615]
ANNOTATIONES IN PEDACII DIOSCORIDIS ANAZARBEIDE DE MEDICA MATERIA / Cordus, V – Argentorati. 1561. B-7389 2 – 8 – ne IDC [580]
ANNOTATIONES IO. BVGENHAGIJ POMERANI IN EPISTOLAS PAULI,... / Bugenhagen, J – Basilae, 1525 – 4mf – 9 – ne IDC [240]
ANNOTATIONES IVSTI IONAE, IN ACTA APOSTOLORVM. CVM INDICE / Jonas, J – Basileae, 1525 – 2mf – ne IDC [240]
ANNOTATIONS ON THE MUTINY ACT... : WITH SOME OBSERVATIONS ON THE PRACTICE OF COURTS-MARTIAL / M'Naghten, Captain – London: Stevens & Sons, 1828 – 3mf – 9 – $4.50 – LLMC 89-027 – us L.L.M.C. [340]
ANNOTATIONVM SCHOLASTICARVM LVCAE LOSSII LVNEBVRGENSIS IN NOVVM TESTAMENTVM IESV CHRISTI NAZARENI,... / Lossius, L – Franc., 1562. V.5 – 7mf – ne IDC [240]

ANNOTIROVANNOE OPISANIE PISEM A.P. CHEKHOVU / Arkhiv A P Chekhova; ed by Leitnekker, E E – Moscow, 1939-41.2v. Describes Chekhov letters in the MS division of the Lenin Library. BR-11,010/1 – 9 – ne IDC [460]
ANNOUNCEMENT / Virginia. Agricultural Experiment Station. Blacksburg – 1889. 1 fiche – 9 – us Spaulding [630]
ANNOUNCEMENT OF THE RUSSIAN MISSIONARY SOCIETY, INC. WITH "FACTS ABOUT REV. WILLIAM FETLER" : A REPLY TO THE BOOKLET ENTITLED, "PASTOR W. FETLER'S REPLY TO REV. E.E. SHIELDS" – Chicago, 1930. Publ. No. 2204-4 f. One item of several on a reel – 1 – us Baptist [240]
ANNOUNCEMENTS / Native American Rights Fund – 1972-82. (American Indian Periodicals in the Princeton University Library) – 6mf – 9 – $45.00 – us UPA [305]
ANNUAIRE / French Guiana – juin 1873-1908 – 1 – fr A.C.R.P.P. [073]
ANNUAIRE DE LA NOBLESSE DE FRANCE ET D'EUROPE – v. 50-72. 1894-1922. (v. 59 wanting) – 1 – 73.00 – us L of C Photodup [920]
ANNUAIRE DE LA VENERIE FRANCAISE – Paris. 1891-94, 1897, 1901 – 1 – fr A.C.R.P.P. [073]
ANNUAIRE DE LEGISLATION FRANCAISE ET ETRANGERE – Paris. Title Varies: 1870 71-1955, Annuaires de legislation etrangere. On film: v1-62, 1870-1936. LL-0283 – 1 – us L of C Photodup [350]
ANNUAIRE DE L'INSTITUT DE DROIT INTERNATIONAL. 1873-1919 – (Index 1873-1914) – Paris, 1877-1919. v1-27 – 114mf – 9 – H-930/1 – ne IDC [340]
ANNUAIRE DE L'INSTITUT DE PHILOLOGIE ET D'HISTOIRE ORIENTALES – Tome 2 (1934). Melanges Bidez T1+2 – 20mf – 9 – Dfl70.00 – ne Slangenburg [950]
ANNUAIRE DES ARCHIVES ISRAELITES – Paris. sept 1884-sept 1925 – 1 – fr A.C.R.P.P. [270]
ANNUAIRE DES ASSOCIATIONS INTERNATIONALES POUR LA PAIX ET LA SOCIETE DES NATIONS – Dole, Juin 1924 – 2mf – 9 – ILM-4063/1 – ne IDC [340]
ANNUAIRE DES JOURNAUX – 1881-82, 1884, 1886-87, 1890, 1892, 1894, 1896-98, 1900, 1906, 1910, 1912, 1914. Suppl. 1889-1913 – 1 – fr A.C.R.P.P. [073]
ANNUAIRE DES POSTES DE L'EMPIRE FRANCAISE – 1859-79 – 1 – 38.00 – us L of C Photodup [944]
ANNUAIRE DES STATISTIQUES 1986/87-1988/89 / Central African Republic. Ministere de l'Education Nationale – Bangui, 1987 – 10mf – 9 – DE-642/1 – ne IDC [370]
ANNUAIRE DES STATISTIQUES DU TRAVAIL 1935-36 A 1995 – (Egalement disponibles separement: 1935-36 a 1964: F65.00 le volume; 1965 a 1988: F80.00; 1989 a 1991: F120.00; A partir de 1993: F210.00 (vendu avec sources et methodes: statistiques du travail) – 54v – F2,800.00 – 92-2-010211-0 – sz I.L.O. [331]
ANNUAIRE DIPOLOMATIQUE DE L'EMPIRE DE RUSSIE – (Missing: v7-8) – 1861-1916. 43v – 253mf – 9 – R-9312/1 – ne IDC [320]
ANNUAIRE DU BUREAU D'HYGIENE DE LA VILLE DE GRENOBLE: 1897 / ed by Berlioz, Fernand – Grenoble, Baratier et Dardelet, 1898. 45 p. 1 fiche. (Statistics: Medical Studies Series) – 9 – 6.00 – fr Bibl Nationale [610]
ANNUAIRE DU CANADA = CANADA YEARBOOK / Canada – Ottawa, 1887- – 9 – Can$37.00y – cn Micromedia [971]
ANNUAIRE DU CANADA *see* CANADA YEARBOOK
ANNUAIRE DU DEPARTEMENT DES ARDENNES POUR L'AN HUIT / Ardennes. France (Department) – an VIII – 9 – fr Hachette [944]
ANNUAIRE DU MOUVEMENT PACIFISTE 1913 – Berne, n.d. – 4mf – 9 – ILM-4017/1 – ne IDC [340]
ANNUAIRE DU SENEGAL ET DEPENDENCES – 1872-89, 1891-1910 – 11r – 1 – $434.50 – us African Imprint [960]
L'ANNUAIRE ECONOMIQUE DE L'ALGERIE / Algeria. Chambre de Commerce et d'Industrie d'Alger – 1965. BNE-8620 1 – 9 – ne IDC [338]
ANNUAIRE GENERAL DE L'INDOCHINE FRANCAISE – Hanoi, 1887-1933 – 14r – 1 – us Ross [324]
ANNUAIRE METEOROLOGIQUE DE LA FRANCE POUR 1849-52 / France – Paris, 1848-53 – 3 – us Readex [550]
ANNUAIRE ORIENTAL DU COMMERCE DE L'INDUSTRIE, DE L'ADMINISTRATION ET DE LA MAGISTRATURE 9ME ANNEE 1889-1890 / Cervati, Raphael C – Encres d'Imprimerie Ch. Lorilleaux & Cie, Paris; Typographie et Lithographie J Pallamary, Constantinople – 9 – $90.00 – us MEDOC [380]
ANNUAIRE STATISTIQUE / Egypt. Maslahat al-Ihsa wa-al-Ta'dad – 1937-38 – .1 – us Res Libr [324]
ANNUAIRE STATISTIQUE / Egypt. Statistical Department – 24 v. (in 19). 1921-62. Available: 1955-62. BNE-4679 1 – 9 – ne IDC [310]
ANNUAIRE STATISTIQUE / Quebec. (Province). Secretariat provincial. Bureau de Statistiques – Quebec: E E Cinq-Mars, 1914. SEM105P893 – 6mf – 9 – Can$13.50 – cn Bibl Nat [304]
L'ANNUAIRE STATISTIQUE DE L'AFRIQUE OCCIDENTALE FRANCAISE – 1949-57 – 2r – 1 – $79.00 – us African Imprint [960]
ANNUAIRE STATISTIQUE DE L'ALGERIE / Algeria. Direction Generale du Plan et des Etudes Economiques – 2v. 1963 64-1967. BNE-8633 1 – 9 – ne IDC [324]
ANNUAIRE STATISTIQUE DE L'ALGERIE / Algeria. Service de la Statistique Generale – 13 v. 1939 47-1961. BNE-8665 1 – 9 – ne IDC [310]
ANNUAIRE STATISTIQUE DE L'ALGERIE / Algeria. Service de Statistique Generale – 1926-37 – 1 – 69.00 – us L of C Photodup [310]
L'ANNUAIRE STATISTIQUE DE L'A.O.F – (French West Africa), 1950-59 – 2r – 1 – $99.00 – us African Imprint [960]
ANNUAIRE STATISTIQUE DU DEPARTEMENT DE LA DORDOGNE POUR L'AN XII DE LA REPUBLIQUE / Delfau, Guillaume – 9 – fr Hachette [944]
ANNUAIRE STATISTIQUE DU DEPARTEMENT DES HAUTES-PYRENEES, CONTENANT L'INTRODUCTION DU GRAND MEMOIRE STATISTIQUE POUR L'AN IX. 1801 / Labouliniere, Pierre – 1807 – 9 – fr Hachette [944]
ANNUAIRE STATISTIQUE DU MAROC / Morocco. Secretariat d'Etat charge du Plan – 1947-76. BNE-3093 1 – 9 – ne IDC [330]
ANNUAIRE-ALMANACH DU COMMERCE DE L'INDUSTRIE, DE L'ADMINISTRATION ET DE LA MAGISTRATURE 4ME ANNEE 1883 / Cervati, Raphael C – Constantinople: J. Pallamary, 1883 – 9 – $75.00 – us MEDOC [380]
ANNUAIRES OFFICIELS, 1973 AND 1974 / Union Douaniere et Economique de l'Afrique Centrale – 1r – 1 – $49.50 – us African Imprint [337]
ANNUAL / Baptist Associations – (Baptist Associations. Landmark Missionary Baptist Associational Minutes of the Pacific Coast: Cooperative of Calif., 1952-1972; Northern Calif., 1952-1960; Costal Cooperative, 1961-1972; Valley, 1961-1970; Central Valley, 1952-1972; Costal Area, 1958-1961, 1968-1969, 1972; Cooperative of Oregon, 1960-1963, 1969, 1971, 1972 (A.W.W.), 1965-1968 (Scott), 1970 (Albany), 1963-1971, Washington) – 1 – us Baptist [240]
ANNUAL / Baptist Associations – (Baptist Associations. Landmark Missionary Baptist Associational Minutes of the Pacific Coast Direct Mission: California, 1932, 1934-1941, 1944, 1946-1971; Northern California, 1940-1954, 1961-1971; Central California, 1951-1958, 1960-1965; Missionary Baptist Churches of Southern Calif., 1940-1941, 1943-1970) – 1 – 105.56 – us Baptist [240]
ANNUAL / Baptist Associations. Alabama – 1815-1958 – 1 – us Baptist [240]
ANNUAL / Baptist Associations. Arizona – 1950-72 – 1 – us Baptist [240]
ANNUAL / Baptist Associations. Arkansas – 1854-1964 – 1 – us Baptist [240]
ANNUAL / Baptist Associations. California – 1944-66 – 1 – us Baptist [240]
ANNUAL / Baptist Associations. Colorado, Southeastern, Arkansas Valley – 1953, 1957, 1959, 1960 – 1 – 5.00 – us Baptist [240]
ANNUAL / Baptist Associations. Florida – 1843-1964 – 1 – us Baptist [240]
ANNUAL / Baptist Associations. Georgia – 1880-1957 – 1 – us Baptist [240]
ANNUAL / Baptist Associations. Illinois – 1844-1990 – 1 – us Baptist [240]
ANNUAL / Baptist Associations. Illinois, Chicago Southern Baptist – 1957-65. (Includes Associational Minutes, Minutes of: Executive Committee, Missions Committee, The Chicago Baptist Banner present newsletter of the CSBA, 1958-1965) – 1 – 69.30 – us Baptist [240]
ANNUAL / Baptist Associations. Indiana, Brownstown – 1836, 1839-42, 1844-46, 1849, 1850-63, 1865-68, 1874, 1879-1905 – 1 – 23.20 – us Baptist [240]
ANNUAL / Baptist Associations. Kentucky – 1785-1958 – 1 – us Baptist [240]
ANNUAL / Baptist Associations. Kentucky, Laurel River – 1959-66 – 1 – 11.90 – us Baptist [240]
ANNUAL / Baptist Associations. Louisiana – 1842-1987 – 1 – 51.28 – us Baptist [240]
ANNUAL / Baptist Associations. Maryland – 1934-69 – 1 – us Baptist [240]
ANNUAL / Baptist Associations. Michigan, Motor Cities – Jul 1951-Aug 1957 – 1 – 5.53 – us Baptist [240]
ANNUAL / Baptist Associations. Mississippi – 1811-1952 – 1 – us Baptist [240]
ANNUAL / Baptist Associations. Missouri – 1824-1957 – 1 – us Baptist [240]
ANNUAL / Baptist Associations. Missouri, Bethel Association, United Baptist – 1816-1941 – 1 – 17.22 – us Baptist [240]
ANNUAL / Baptist Associations. Missouri, Meramec Landmark Baptist Association – 1922-82 – 1 – 60.55 – us Baptist [240]
ANNUAL / Baptist Associations. Missouri, Mineral Area – 1958-81. Formerly Franklin Association, 1969 – 1 – 49.07 – us Baptist [240]
ANNUAL / Baptist Associations. New Mexico – 1871-1970 – 1 – us Baptist [240]
ANNUAL / Baptist Associations. New Mexico – (Southwestern 1942, 1944. Pecos Valley, 1944, 1947. Rio Grande 1944, 1947. Plains 1944, 1948. Lincoln 1906, 1910. Southeastern 1941, 1944-45. Central 1927. Portales 1930, 1943-45. Estanica Valley 1939-41, 1946. Organization 1939) – 1927-48, Miscellaneous Reel – 1 – 20.16 – us Baptist [240]
ANNUAL / Baptist Associations. New Mexico, Santa Fe – 1948-70. (Formerly: Atomic, name change 1956) – 1 – 20.30 – us Baptist [240]
ANNUAL / Baptist Associations. New York and Vermont. Miscellaneous Associations – 1832-40 – 1 – 11.20 – us Baptist [240]
ANNUAL / Baptist Associations. North Carolina – 1806-1949 – 1 – us Baptist [240]
ANNUAL / Baptist Associations. North Carolina, Chowan Association – 1884-90. Manuscript Minutes – 1 – 6.48 – us Baptist [240]
ANNUAL / Baptist Associations. North Carolina, Eastern Association – 1869-86. Manuscript Minutes – 1 – 5.68 – us Baptist [240]
ANNUAL / Baptist Associations. North Carolina, Flat River Association – 1828-59. Manuscript Minutes – 1 – 7.44 – us Baptist [240]
ANNUAL / Baptist Associations. North Carolina, Tar River Association – 1831-90. Manuscript minutes – 1 – 42.08 – us Baptist [240]
ANNUAL / Baptist Associations. Ohio – 1950-75 – 1 – us Baptist [240]
ANNUAL / Baptist Associations. Oklahoma – 1890-1957 – 1 – us Baptist [240]
ANNUAL / Baptist Associations. Pennsylvania, Philadelphia Baptist Association – 1707-1965 – 1 – 450.00 – us Baptist [240]
ANNUAL / Baptist Associations. Primitive: Alabama, 1848-1955 – 1 – us Baptist [240]
ANNUAL / Baptist Associations. Primitive: Arkansas, California, Arizona, Delaware, 1844-1950 – 1 – us Baptist [240]
ANNUAL / Baptist Associations. Primitive: Florida, 1874-1949 – 1 – us Baptist [240]
ANNUAL / Baptist Associations. Primitive: Georgia, 1810-1952 – 1 – us Baptist [240]
ANNUAL / Baptist Associations. Primitive: Illinois, Iowa, Indiana, Kansas, 1845-1951 (Incomplete) – 1 – us Baptist [240]
ANNUAL / Baptist Associations. Primitive: Kentucky – 1 – us Baptist [240]
ANNUAL / Baptist Associations. Primitive: Louisiana, Maine, Maryland, Michigan, Mississippi, Missouri, New York, Nebraska – 1 – us Baptist [240]
ANNUAL / Baptist Associations. Primitive: North Carolina – 1 – us Baptist [240]
ANNUAL / Baptist Associations. Primitive: Ohio, Oklahoma, Pennsylvania, South Carolina – 1 – us Baptist [240]
ANNUAL / Baptist Associations. Primitive: Tennessee – 1 – us Baptist [240]
ANNUAL / Baptist Associations. Primitive: Texas – 1 – us Baptist [240]
ANNUAL / Baptist Associations. Primitive: Virginia, West Virginia – 1 – us Baptist [240]
ANNUAL / Baptist Associations. South Carolina – 1775-1970 – 1 – us Baptist [240]
ANNUAL / Baptist Associations. South Carolina, Edgefield, Quarterly Meetings – 1877-86 – 1 – 5.00 – us Baptist [240]
ANNUAL / Baptist Associations. Tennessee – 1786-1972 – 1 – us Baptist [240]
ANNUAL / Baptist Associations. Texas – 1843-1954 – 1 – us Baptist [240]
ANNUAL / Baptist Associations. Texas, Liberty – 1883-1981 – 1 – 60.06 – us Baptist [240]
ANNUAL / Baptist Associations. Virginia – 1787-1959 – 1 – us Baptist [240]
ANNUAL / Baptist Associations. Washington, Mount Pleasant – 1904 – 1 – 5.00 – us Baptist [240]
ANNUAL / Baptist Associations. Washington, Puget Sound – 1871-88. Lacking 1874, 1875 – 1 – 15.05 – us Baptist [240]
ANNUAL / Baptist State Conventions. (American Baptist). Connecticut – 1824, 1829-1975 – 1 – 543.97 – us Baptist [240]
ANNUAL / Baptist State Conventions. (American Baptist). Pennsylvania – 1826-1975 – 1 – 650.09 – us Baptist [240]
ANNUAL / Baptist State Conventions. Kentucky – 1981 – 1 – 22.12 – us Baptist [240]
ANNUAL / Baptist State Conventions. Louisiana – 1958-81 – 1 – 220.92 – us Baptist [240]
ANNUAL / Baptist State Conventions. (Southern Baptist). Alabama – 1823-1958 – 1 – 645.22 – us Baptist [240]
ANNUAL / Baptist State Conventions. (Southern Baptist). Alaska – 1946-62. Lacking 1950 – 1 – 29.82 – us Baptist [240]
ANNUAL / Baptist State Conventions. (Southern Baptist). Arizona – 1928-72 – 1 – 134.40 – us Baptist [240]
ANNUAL / Baptist State Conventions. (Southern Baptist). Arkansas – 1848-1964 – 1 – 360.36 – us Baptist [240]
ANNUAL / Baptist State Conventions. (Southern Baptist). California – 1941-67 – 1 – 146.72 – us Baptist [240]
ANNUAL / Baptist State Conventions. (Southern Baptist). District of Columbia – 1876-1969 – 1 – 321.37 – us Baptist [240]
ANNUAL / Baptist State Conventions. (Southern Baptist). Florida – 1854-1990 – 1 – $1144.08 – us Baptist [240]
ANNUAL / Baptist State Conventions. (Southern Baptist). Georgia – 1822-1981 – 1 – 1116.43 – us Baptist [240]
ANNUAL / Baptist State Conventions. (Southern Baptist). Illinois – 1834-44, 1847-1901 – 1 – 39.83 – us Baptist [240]
ANNUAL / Baptist State Conventions. (Southern Baptist). Illinois – 1907-53 – 1 – 236.81 – us Baptist [240]
ANNUAL / Baptist State Conventions. (Southern Baptist). Kentucky – 1837-1981 – 1 – 867.02 – us Baptist [240]
ANNUAL / Baptist State Conventions. (Southern Baptist). Louisiana – 1850-1980 – 1 – 582.40 – us Baptist [240]
ANNUAL / Baptist State Conventions. (Southern Baptist). Maryland – 1836-1958 – 1 – 296.10 – us Baptist [240]
ANNUAL / Baptist State Conventions. (Southern Baptist). Mississippi – 1836-1951 – 1 – 407.40 – us Baptist [240]
ANNUAL / Baptist State Conventions. (Southern Baptist). Missouri – 1834-1952 – 1 – 611.31 – us Baptist [240]
ANNUAL / Baptist State Conventions. (Southern Baptist). New Mexico – 1914-54. (With proceedings of meetings of New Mexico Baptist Convention, 1900-1909, and the organization of the Baptist General Convention of New Mexico, 1910) – 1 – 168.28 – us Baptist [240]
ANNUAL / Baptist State Conventions. (Southern Baptist). North Carolina – 1830-1955 – 1 – 596.96 – us Baptist [240]
ANNUAL / Baptist State Conventions. (Southern Baptist). Ohio – 1954-75 – 1 – 93.66 – us Baptist [240]

ANNUAL / Baptist State Conventions. (Southern Baptist). Oklahoma – 1905-52 – 1 – 316.26 – us Baptist [240]

ANNUAL / Baptist State Conventions. (Southern Baptist). South Carolina – 1821-1970 – 1 – 732.26 – us Baptist [240]

ANNUAL / Baptist State Conventions. (Southern Baptist). Tennessee – 1875-1972 – 1 – 790.23 – us Baptist [240]

ANNUAL / Baptist State Conventions. (Southern Baptist). Texas – 1848-1987 – 1 – 1018.01 – us Baptist [240]

ANNUAL / Baptist State Conventions. (Southern Baptist). Virginia – 1824-1955 – 1 – 604.66 – us Baptist [240]

ANNUAL / Baptist Woman's Missionary Union. Kentucky – 1929-65 – 1 – 66.43 – us Baptist [240]

ANNUAL / Baptist Woman's Missionary Union. Louisiana – 1899-1957 – 1 – 114.24 – us Baptist [240]

ANNUAL / Baptist Woman's Missionary Union. Mississippi – 1878-1960 – 1 – 112.35 – us Baptist [240]

ANNUAL / Baptist Woman's Missionary Union. South Carolina – 1882-1975 – 1 – 230.86 – us Baptist [240]

ANNUAL / Baptist Woman's Missionary Union. Texas, Henderson County – 1922-47 – 1 – 5.00 – us Baptist [240]

ANNUAL / German Baptist Convention – 1849-1960 – 1 – 154.00 – us Baptist [240]

ANNUAL ABSTRACT OF STATISTICS 1928-1977 – (Coll title: British Government Publications...1801-1977, General) – 191mf – 9 – £1,200.00 – uk Chadwyck [310]

ANNUAL ABSTRACT OF STATISTICS OF THE U.K / Great Britain – 1840-to date – 1 – uk Microform Academic [324]

ANNUAL ADMINISTRATION REPORT FOR THE YEARS 1940/41 / Gwalior. India (State). Archaeological Department – Quinquennial adm. report. 1942 46. Gwalior. 1925-49. BI-785 2 – 8 – ne IDC [930]

ANNUAL ADVERTISER – Reno, NV. 25 Dec 1878 – 1r – 1 – $50.00 – U04657 – us Library Micro [071]

ANNUAL AND QUARTERLY CORPORATE REPORTS / U.S. Securities and Exchange Commission – 9 – us Disclosure [332]

ANNUAL APPROPRIATION RECORDS / Hancock County. Ohio. Biglick Township. Township Clerk – 1927-1942 – 1r – 1 – $32.50r – us Archival [324]

ANNUAL BIBLIOGRAPHY OF ENGLISH LANGUAGE AND LITERATURE – (v. 1-29. /34.50v; 9. v. 30-33. 2410.50v; WDS; 9) – v. 1-33. 1920-1957 58. London – 9 – 24170.00 – uk Dawson [420]

ANNUAL BIBLIOGRAPHY OF MODERN ART 1987 : THE MUSEUM OF MODERN ART LIBRARY, NEW YORK – 1988 – 1 reel – 1 – $190.00 export $220.00 – 0-8161-1564-8 – uk Hall [700]

THE ANNUAL BIOGRAPHY AND OBITUARY FOR THE YEAR. – v1, 1817-v21, 1837. London: Longman, Hurst, Rees, Orme, and Brown, 1817- . 21v. illus – 1 – us U.W. Library [920]

ANNUAL BUDGETS / Hancock County. Ohio. Biglick Township. Township Clerk – 1945-1989 gaps in holdings – 1r – 1 – $32.50r – us Archival [978]

ANNUAL BUDGETS / Ottawa County. Ohio. Carroll Township. Board of Trustees – 1912-1980 – 1r – 1 – $32.50r – us Archival [324]

ANNUAL BULLETIN / Alumnae Association of the Baptist WMU Training School. Louisville, Ky – 1916-Mar 1965 – 1 – 60.34 – us Baptist [240]

ANNUAL BULLETIN OF FOREIGN TRADE, 1964-1969 / Egypt. U.A.R. Central Agency for Public Mobilisation and Statistics – (lacking 1968). BNE-4611 1 – 9 – ne IDC [310]

ANNUAL CATALOGUES OF BRITISH OFFICIAL AND PARLIAMENTARY PUBLICATIONS, 1894-1909 / Great Britain. Stationery Office – 1895-1910 – 12mf – 9 – £95.00 – 0-85964-016-7 – uk Chadwyck [324]

ANNUAL CATALOGUES OF BRITISH OFFICIAL AND PARLIAMENTARY PUBLICATIONS, 1910-1919 / Great Britain. Stationery Office – 1911-20 – 8mf – 9 – £64.00 – 0-85964-017-5 – uk Chadwyck [324]

ANNUAL CONFERENCE / Auburn University. Extension Service – 1944, 60, 62, 64, 67. 1 reel – 1, 5 – us Spaulding [630]

ANNUAL CONFERENCE PROCEEDINGS / Advertising Research Foundation – (Ceased publ. Vols 1-3 were not publ) – New York. v4-23 1958-77 1*; v21-23 1975-77 5,9* – 1,5,9 – D10340 – us UMI [650]

ANNUAL CONGRESS ON CORRECTION PROCEEDINGS / American Correctional Association – 1870-1946 – 11r – 1 – us Ross [360]

Annual Convention of the Christian Association for Psychological Studies *see* PROCEEDINGS

ANNUAL DEMONSTRATION OF CROP IMPROVEMENT TRIALS, 1956 / Libya. Administration of Tripolitania. Dept. of Agriculture – BNE-1023 1 – 9 – ne IDC [630]

ANNUAL DEPARTMENTAL REPORTS / Gambia – 1881-1965 – 1 – uk Microform Academic [960]

ANNUAL DEPARTMENTAL REPORTS / Gold Coast and British Togoland – 1843-1956 – 1 – uk Microform Academic [960]

ANNUAL DEPARTMENTAL REPORTS / Kenya and E.A.H.C – 1903-4 to 1963 – 1 – uk Microform Academic [960]

ANNUAL DEPARTMENTAL REPORTS / Nigeria and British Cameroons – 1887-1961 – 1 – uk Microform Academic [960]

ANNUAL DEPARTMENTAL REPORTS / Nyasaland – 1 – uk Microform Academic [960]

ANNUAL DEPARTMENTAL REPORTS / Rhodesia. Southern – 1 – uk Microform Academic [960]

ANNUAL DEPARTMENTAL REPORTS / Sierra Leone – 1893-1961 – 1 – uk Microform Academic [960]

ANNUAL DEPARTMENTAL REPORTS / Uganda – 1903-61 – 1 – uk Microform Academic [960]

ANNUAL DEVELOPMENT PROGRAMME 1990/91 / Bangladesh. Planning Commission – Dhaka, 1990 – 6mf – 9 – ne IDC [338]

ANNUAL DEVELOPMENT PROGRAMME OF THE FEDERAL GOVERNMENT 1972-73 / Pakistan. Planning Commission – Islamabad. Jun 1972. BD-1726 1 – 9 – ne IDC [338]

ANNUAL DIGEST OF EDUCATION STATISTICS... / Nigeria. Oyo State. Ministry of Economic Planning. Statistics Division – 6mf – 9 – DE-121/1 – ne IDC [370]

ANNUAL FEED CIRCULAR / Rhode Island. Agricultural Experiment Station – 1919-69 – 1,5,6 – us Spaulding [636]

ANNUAL FERTILIZER CIRCULAR / Rhode Island. Agricultural Experiment Station – 1919-69 – 1,5,6 – us Spaulding [631]

ANNUAL FERTILIZER REVIEW – it F.A.O. [631]

ANNUAL FINANCIAL REPORTS / Fulton County. Ohio. Board of Education – 1927-1930 – 1r – 1 – $32.50r – us Archival [324]

ANNUAL FINANCIAL REPORTS / Fulton County. Ohio. County Home – 1908-1911 – 1r – 1 – $32.50r – us Archival [324]

ANNUAL FINANCIAL REPORTS / Hancock County. Ohio. Biglick Township. Board of Education – 1867-1897 – 1r – 1 – $32.50r – us Archival [324]

ANNUAL FINANCIAL REPORTS / Hancock County. Ohio. Biglick Township. Township Clerk – 1926-1973 – 1r – 1 – $32.50r – us Archival [324]

ANNUAL FORESTRY SYMPOSIUM / Louisiana State University. Agricultural Experiment Station. School of Forestry and Wildlife Management – no.19-31. 1970-82 – 1,5 – us Spaulding [634]

ANNUAL GUIDANCE INDEX – (Former titles: Vocational Guide (dec 1938-may 1946); Guidance Index (sep 1946-1954)) – Chicago. v12-19. 1949-57 – 1 – D357 – us UMI [030]

ANNUAL INSTITUTE ON SECURITIES REGULATION – (v10-. 1978- ;5,6,9) – v1-. 1969- – 1 – us UMI [073]

ANNUAL INVENTORIES / Hancock County. Ohio. Biglick Township. Township Clerk – 1945-1988 gaps in holdings – 1r – 1 – $32.50r – us Archival [324]

ANNUAL LAW REGISTER OF THE UNITED STATES – (Ceased publ) – Burlington. v3-4. 1821-22 – 1 – D4418 – us UMI [340]

ANNUAL LISTS AND GENERAL INDEX TO THE PARLIAMENTARY PAPERS RELATING TO THE EAST INDIES, 1801-1907 / India – London. 1909. BI-328 2 – 8 – ne IDC [324]

ANNUAL MEDICAL REPORT – Nairobi, 1912-19; 1920-22 – 1 – us Res Libr [610]

ANNUAL MEETING / American Institute of Instruction – (Ceased publ) – Boston. cum index 1830-50; 1830-1908 – 1 – D2774 – us UMI [073]

ANNUAL MEETING (2ND: 1871: TORONTO, ONT.) / Beaver and Toronto Mutual Fire Insurance Company – Proceedings.... 1871. 07073. (Pre-1900 Canadiana) – 9 – cn C.I.H.M. [336]

ANNUAL MEETING ACSM / American Congress on Surveying and Mapping. Meeting Technical Papers – (Ceased publ. Cont by: Meeting Technical Papers of the American Congress of Surveying and Mapping; Annual Meeting of the American Congress on Surveying and Mapping) – Falls Church. v45. 1985* – 1 – D12486.04 – us UMI [520]

ANNUAL MEETING OF THE AMERICAN CONGRESS ON SURVEYING AND MAPPING / American Congress on Surveying and Mapping. Meeting Technical Papers – (Comprises one of two parts of the proceedings of the annual ACSM-ASP Convention, the other part issued as: American Society of Photogrammetry. Cont by: Technical papers of the American Congress on Surveying and Mapping; Meeting Technical Papers of the Annual Meeting ACSM) – Falls Church. v43-44. 1983-1984* – 1 – D12486.03 – us UMI [520]

ANNUAL MEETING OF THE AMERICAN CONGRESS ON SURVEYING AND MAPPING *see* ANNUAL MEETING ACSM

ANNUAL MEETING OF THE ROYAL COLLEGE OF DENTAL SURGEONS, ONTARIO: ADDRESS / Beers, William George – 1890?. 02976. (Pre-1900 Canadiana) – 9 – cn C.I.H.M. [617]

ANNUAL OF THE PALESTINE EXPLORATION FUND – London, 1914-1915 – 5mf – 9 – H-2502/1 – ne IDC [910]

ANNUAL OPERATION OF A COASTAL GROUNDWATER BASIN AT A PRESCRIBED RELIABILITY LEVEL / Israel. Ministry of Agriculture. Water Commissioner – By Y. Bachmat. Jerusalem, Aug 1975. 34 p. (Report no. 2). Diagr – 9 – 2.00 – is I.T.T.I. [550]

ANNUAL (OR PROGRESS) REPORT ON EPIGRAPHICAL WORK, ACCOMPLISHED FROM 1887 TO 1917 – 64mf – 9 – I-579/2 – ne IDC [410]

ANNUAL PLAN 1966-67 / India. Planning Commission – Delhi. 1966 – 9 – ne IDC [338]

ANNUAL PLAN 1967-68 / India. Planning Commission – Delhi. 1967. BD-706 1 – 9 – ne IDC [338]

ANNUAL PLAN 1968-69 / India. Planning Commission – Delhi. 1968 – 9 – ne IDC [338]

ANNUAL PLAN, 1968/69 / Pakistan. Planning Commission – Karachi. 1968 – 9 – ne IDC [338]

ANNUAL PLAN 1969-70 / India. Planning Commission – Delhi. 1969. BD-1330 1 – 9 – ne IDC [338]

ANNUAL PLAN, 1969-70 / Pakistan. Planning Commission – n.p. n.d. BD-1147 1 – 9 – ne IDC [338]

ANNUAL PLAN 1970-1971 / India. Planning Commission – New Delhi. 1971. BD-1551 1 – 9 – ne IDC [338]

ANNUAL PLAN 1971-72 / India. Planning Commission – Delhi. 1971. BD-1668 1 – 9 – ne IDC [338]

ANNUAL PLAN 1972-73 / Bangladesh. Planning Commission – Dacca. Jun 1972. BD-1613 1 – 9 – ne IDC [338]

ANNUAL PLAN 1972-73 / India. Planning Commission – New Delhi. 1972 – 9 – ne IDC [338]

ANNUAL PLAN 1973-1974 / Bangladesh. Planning Commission – Dacca. 1973. BD-2006 1 – 9 – ne IDC [338]

ANNUAL PLAN, 1975-1976 / Pakistan. Planning Commission – BD-1852 1 – 9 – ne IDC [338]

ANNUAL PLAN 1993/94 / India. Planning Commission – New Delhi, 1993 – 11mf – 9 – ne IDC [338]

THE ANNUAL PLAN FOR 1972-73 / Tanzania – Dar es Salaam. 1972. BD-1755 1 – 9 – ne IDC [330]

ANNUAL PLAN FOR THE THIRD YEAR (1971) UNDER THE FIFTH FOUR-YEAR ECONOMIC DEVELOPMENT / China. Republic. Council for International Economic Cooperation and Development – Taipei. n.d. BD-1633/1 – 9 – ne IDC [338]

ANNUAL PROGRAMME / Arabian Gulf Emirates. Abu-Dhabi. Planning Board – 4v. in 1. 1970-73. BNE-10,006 1 – 9 – ne IDC [336]

ANNUAL PROGRESS REPORT / Louisiana State University. Agricultural Experiment Station. Northeast Experiment Station – 1970-83 – 1,5 – us Spaulding [630]

ANNUAL PROGRESS REPORT (ABRIDGED) OF THE SUPERINTENDENT, MUHAMMADAN AND BRITISH MONUMENTS, ARCHAEOLOGICAL SURVEY OF INDIA, NORTHERN CIRCLE... – Allahabad, United Provinces: Govt Press, 1917-18 – 1r – 1 – us Res Libr [930]

ANNUAL PROGRESS REPORT. ..BI- NO.62-74. 1970-82 / Louisiana State University. Agricultural Experiment Station. Rice Experiment Station – 1,5 – us Spaulding [630]

ANNUAL PROGRESS REPORT OF THE SUPERINTENDENT, HINDU AND BUDDHIST MONUMENTS, NORTHERN CIRCLE... – Lahore, Punjab: Supt Govt Printing, 1919-21 – 1r – 1 – us Res Libr [930]

ANNUAL PROGRESS REPORT OF THE SUPERINTENDENT...FOR THE YEAR ENDING... / Archaeological Survey of India. Northern Circle. Muhammadan and British Monuments – Allahabad, United Provinces: Govt Press, 1911-16 – 1r – 1 – us Res Libr [930]

ANNUAL REGISTER / India – Calcutta. 1920-47. Lacking: 1925, v. 1. BI-110 2 – 8 – ne IDC [324]

ANNUAL REGISTER : A VIEW OF THE HISTORY, POLITICS, AND LITERATURE – 1758-1760. 6th ed. London, 1777-1781. 2v. 1777-1778. 2nd ed. London, 1781. 2v. 1779-1787. London, 1780-1789. 10v – 256mf – 9 – H-909/2 – ne IDC [900]

ANNUAL REGISTER – Years: 1758-1974 – 1,5,6 – us Princeton Micro [334]

THE ANNUAL REGISTER OF THE BAPTIST DENOMINATION IN NORTH AMERICA, 1790-1794 / Asplund, John – 1 – 6.16 – us Baptist [240]

ANNUAL REPORT / American Anti-Slavery Society – Nos. 1-28 (nos. 8-21 never publ.). 1834-1860 – 1 reel – 1 – $65.00 – us UPA [976]

ANNUAL REPORT / American Historical Association – (1977- 1,5,6,9) – v1- 1884- – 1 – us UMI [975]

ANNUAL REPORT / American Missionary Association – 1847-1950 – 1 – $125.00 – us Amistad [240]

ANNUAL REPORT / Auburn University. Extension Service – 1946-48. 1 fiche – 9 – us Spaulding [630]

ANNUAL REPORT / Bahrain – 16v in 4. 1955-70. (lacking 1962). BNE-10.008 1 – 9 – ne IDC [956]

ANNUAL REPORT / Canada. Department of Indian Affairs – 1880-1936 – 1 – $220.00 – us L of C Photodup [360]

ANNUAL REPORT / Ceylon. Archaeological Survey; ed by Bell, H C P – 1892-1902. Reports 8-15 and Parts 16-20 unnumbered. Plans and plates. Colombo. 1914. BI-567 2 – 8 – ne IDC [930]

ANNUAL REPORT / Chicago. Board of Trade – (Formerly: Annual Statement of the Trade and Commerce of Chicago). nos. 1-83. 1858-1940 – 1 – us Princeton Micro [380]

ANNUAL REPORT / Civil Rights League. Cape Town – 1951/52-1965/66 – 1 – us Res Libr [960]

ANNUAL REPORT / Clemson University. Agricultural Experiment Station – 1970/71.1 reel – 1,5 – us Spaulding [630]

ANNUAL REPORT / Colorado. Agricultural Experiment Station. Fort Collins – 1888-1965 – 1,5,6 – us Spaulding [630]

ANNUAL REPORT / De Beers Consolidated Mines – [Kimberley, SA: De Beers Consolidated Mines?]. 1st-32nd. 1888/89-1919/20 – 1 – us Res Libr [622]

ANNUAL REPORT / Florida. Agricultural Experiment Station – 1889-1969 – 1,5,6 – us Spaulding [630]

ANNUAL REPORT / Florida. Agricultural Extension Service – 1915-69 – 1,5,6 – us Spaulding [630]

ANNUAL REPORT / India. Archaeological Survey – Frontier Circle for 1906/07-1920/21. Peshawa. 1907-20. Lacking: 1907-08; 1916-17. BI-570 2 – 8 – ne IDC [930]
ANNUAL REPORT / International Center for Aquaculture – 1971-77.1 reel – 1, 5 – us Spaulding [639]
ANNUAL REPORT / Iowa State University. Iowa Agriculture and Home Economics Experiment Station – 1958/59-1980/81 – 1r – 1,5 – us Spaulding [630]
ANNUAL REPORT / Israel. Ministry of Police – Summary of 1976. Jerusalem, Apr 1977. 70p – 9 – $2.00 – is I.T.T.I. [360]
ANNUAL REPORT / Israel. Prime Minister's Office. Atomic Energy Commission. Research Laboratories – 1960-71. Lacking: 1967-70. BJ-81-24 1 – 9 – ne IDC [530]
ANNUAL REPORT / Israel. Prime Minister's Office. Atomic Energy Commission. Research Laboratories – 1965- – 9 – 48.00; 4.00y – is I.T.T.I. [324]
ANNUAL REPORT / Jordan. Central Bank – 9v. 1964-73. Lacking: 1965 67. BNE-9755 1 – 9 – ne IDC [336]
ANNUAL REPORT / Jordan. Department of Land and Surveys – 23 v. in 8. 1948-72. Lacking: 1968; 1971. BNE-9762 1 – 9 – ne IDC [630]
ANNUAL REPORT / Kentucky. Agricultural Experiment Station – 1st-82nd v. 1888-1969 – 1,5,6 – us Spaulding [630]
ANNUAL REPORT / Kentucky. Agricultural Extension Service – 1920-67 – 1,5,6 – us Spaulding [630]
ANNUAL REPORT / Kuwait. Kuwait Foreign Trading, Contracting and Investment Company – 3v in 1. 1965/66-1976. Lacking: 1967. BNE-9019 1 – 9 – ne IDC [338]
ANNUAL REPORT / Libya. Public Development and Stabilization Agency. Economic Social Development (incl. Planning, Literacy) – 6v. 1952 53-1954 55, 1955 56-1957 58. BNE-720 1 – 9 – ne IDC [330]
ANNUAL REPORT / Lundy's Lane Historical Society – 7v. 1887-1905. Irregular numbering and dates – 1 – cn Precision [900]
ANNUAL REPORT / Massachusetts. Agricultural Experiment Station – (First Station). 1883-94 – 1,5,6 – us Spaulding [630]
ANNUAL REPORT / Massachusetts. Agricultural Experiment Station – (Second Station). 1888-1960 – 1,5,6 – us Spaulding [630]
ANNUAL REPORT / Minnesota. University. Agricultural Experiment Station. St. Paul – 1890-1963 – 1,5,6 – us Spaulding [630]
ANNUAL REPORT / Minnesota. University. State Entomologist – nos.1-19. 1895-1922 – 1,5,6 – us Spaulding [630]
ANNUAL REPORT / Mississippi. Agricultural Experiment Station. State College – v. 1-82. 1888-1969 – 1,5,6 – us Spaulding [630]
ANNUAL REPORT / Mississippi State University. Agricultural Experiment Station – No.83-89. 1970-76. 1 reel – 1,5 – us Spaulding [630]
ANNUAL REPORT / Mississippi State University. Cooperative Extension Service – 1916-69 – 1,5,6 – us Spaulding [630]
ANNUAL REPORT / Mississippi State University. Cooperative Extension Service – 1970-80.1 reel – 1,5 – us Spaulding [630]
ANNUAL REPORT / National Science Council. Taiwan – 1964-83 – 88mf – 9 – $80.00 – ch Transmission [500]
ANNUAL REPORT / North Carolina. Agricultural Experiment Station. Raleigh – n.1-72. 1879-1949 – 1,5 – us Spaulding [630]
ANNUAL REPORT / North Carolina. State University. Raleigh. Agricultural Extension Service – n.1-29. 1914-49 – 1,5 – us Spaulding [630]
ANNUAL REPORT / North Carolina. State University. Raleigh. School of Agriculture and Life Science – 1950-73 – 1,5 – us Spaulding [630]
ANNUAL REPORT / North Carolina State University.School of Agriculture and Life Sciences – 1970-82.1 reel – 1,5 – us Spaulding [630]
ANNUAL REPORT / North Dakota. Agricultural Experiment Station. Edgely – nos.1-11. 1903-13 – 1,5,6 – us Spaulding [630]
ANNUAL REPORT / North Dakota. Agricultural Experiment Station. Fargo – 1938-48 – 1,5,6 – us Spaulding [630]
ANNUAL REPORT / North Dakota. Agricultural Experiment Station. Fargo – nos.1-27. 1891-1917 – 1,5,6 – us Spaulding [630]
ANNUAL REPORT / North Dakota. Agricultural Experiment Station. Langdon – nos.1-5. 1909-13 – 1,5,6 – us Spaulding [630]
ANNUAL REPORT / North Dakota. Agricultural Experiment Station. Williston – nos.1-6. 1908-13 – 1,5,6 – us Spaulding [630]
ANNUAL REPORT / Oklahoma State University. Agricultural Experiment Station – 1970-82.1 reel – 1,5 – us Spaulding [630]
ANNUAL REPORT / Purdue University. Agricultural Experiment Station – No.1-97.1888-1984 – 1,5 – us Spaulding [630]
ANNUAL REPORT / Purdue University. Cooperative Extension Service – No.1-48.1912-61 – 1,5 – us Spaulding [630]
ANNUAL REPORT / Rhode Island. Agricultural Experiment Station – v. 1-62. 1889-1950 – 1,5 – us Spaulding [630]
ANNUAL REPORT / South African Institute of Race Relations – Johannesburg, 1930-42 – 1r – 1 – us Ross [960]
ANNUAL REPORT / South Carolina. Agricultural Experiment Station. Clemson – v.1-83. 1888-1970 – 1,5 – us Spaulding [630]
ANNUAL REPORT / South Dakota. State University. Agricultural Experiment Station – nos.1-72. 1888-1959 – 1,5,6 – us Spaulding [630]
ANNUAL REPORT / Sudan. Dept. of Agriculture – 1955 56. BNE-7608 1 – 9 – ne IDC [630]
ANNUAL REPORT / Sudan. Dept. of Cooperation – 1v. 1964 65. BNE-7610 1 – 9 – ne IDC [338]
ANNUAL REPORT / Sudan. Ministry of Irrigation and Hydroelectric Power – 10 v. in 3. 1952 65. (lacking 1956 56-1958 59). BNE-7673 1 – 9 – ne IDC [630]
ANNUAL REPORT / Tennessee. University. Agricultural Experiment Station – v.1-82. 1888-1969 – 1,5 – us Spaulding [630]
ANNUAL REPORT / Tennessee. University. Agricultural Extension Service – 1918-59 – 1,5 – us Spaulding [630]
ANNUAL REPORT / Texas A & M University. Agricultural Experiment Station – 1970-80.1 reel – 1,5 – us Spaulding [630]
ANNUAL REPORT / Texas A & M University. Agricultural Extension Service – 1970-82.11 fiches – 9 – us Spaulding [630]
ANNUAL REPORT / Texas A & M University. College of Agriculture – 1968-82.37 fiches – 9 – us Spaulding [630]
ANNUAL REPORT / U.S. Board of Indian Commissioners – 1-63. 1869-1932 – 1 – $69.00 – us L of C Photodup [305]
ANNUAL REPORT / University of Florida. Cooperative Extension Service – 1970-80.1 reel – 1, 5 – us Spaulding [630]
ANNUAL REPORT / University of Kentucky. Agricultural Experiment Station – No.83-96. 1970-83 – 1,5 – us Spaulding [630]
ANNUAL REPORT / University of Tennessee.Agricultural Experiment Station – No.83-82. 1970-79. 1 reel – 1,5 – us Spaulding [630]
ANNUAL REPORT / Vermont. Agricultural Extension Service – v. 1-29. 1915-44 – 1,5,6 – us Spaulding [630]
ANNUAL REPORT / Vermont. College of Agriculture – v.1-6. 1944-54 – 1,5 – us Spaulding [630]
ANNUAL REPORT / Virginia. Agricultural Experiment Station. Blacksburg – 1889 90-1959. 37 fiches – 9 – us Spaulding [630]
ANNUAL REPORT / Wisconsin. Agricultural Experiment Station – 1883-1969. n.1-86 – 1,5 – us Spaulding [630]
ANNUAL REPORT / Wisconsin. Agricultural Extension Service – 1916-25 – 1,5 – us Spaulding [630]
ANNUAL REPORT / Wisconsin. College of Agricultural and Life Sciences. Dept. of Forestry – 1966-69 – 1,5 – us Spaulding [630]
ANNUAL REPORT : ADVANCED DENTAL EDUCATION – Chicago, 1972-73 – 1,5 – D8936 – us UMI [617]
ANNUAL REPORT : DENTAL AUXILIARY EDUCATION – Chicago, 1967-73 – 1 – D8593 – us UMI [617]
ANNUAL REPORT : DENTAL EDUCATION – Chicago, 1973-74 – 1,5 – D8584 – us UMI [617]
ANNUAL REPORT 1980 / Papua New Guinea. Teaching Service Commission – Boroko – 1mf – 9 – DE-223/1 – ne IDC [370]
ANNUAL REPORT 1982 / Guyana. Ministry of Higher Education – Georgetown – 2mf – 9 – DE-518/1 – ne IDC [370]
ANNUAL REPORT 1984 / South Africa. Department of Education and Culture – Pretoria – 2mf – 9 – DE-465/1 – ne IDC [370]
ANNUAL REPORT 1987 (1) / India. Ministry of Human Resource Development. Department of Education – (In Hindi and English) – [New Delhi], 1987 – 6mf – 9 – DE-614/1 – ne IDC [370]
ANNUAL REPORT, 1912/13-1920/21 / India. Archaeological Survey Department. Southern Circle. Madras – Madras. 1913-21. BI-576 2 – 8 – ne IDC [930]
ANNUAL REPORT 1953/1955 / Sudan. Ministry of Agriculture – 2v. in 1. BNE-7664 1 – 9 – ne IDC [630]
ANNUAL REPORT 1955/1956-1963/1964 / Sudan. Dept. of Land Use and Rural Water Development – 8v. (lacking 1956 57). BNE-7611 1 – 9 – ne IDC [630]
ANNUAL REPORT 1955-1984/85 / Swaziland. Ministry of Education – (Missing: 1956-1959. 1961-1962. 1965. 1973. 1986) – 45mf – 9 – DE-479/1 – ne IDC [370]
ANNUAL REPORT 1959-1965 / Syria. Industrial Bank in the Syrian region – BNE-9705 1 – 9 – ne IDC [330]
ANNUAL REPORT 1964-1971 / Zambia. Ministry of Education – Lusaka – 9mf – 9 – DE-491/1 – ne IDC [370]
ANNUAL REPORT, 1966-1972 / Arabian Gulf Emirates. Qatar and Dubai Currency Board – 7v. in 1. BNE-10.024 1 – 9 – ne IDC [330]
ANNUAL REPORT 1967-1980 / Zambia. Educational and Occupational Assessment Service – (Missing: 1968-1969. 1975. 1979) – 10mf – 9 – DE-490/1 – ne IDC [370]
ANNUAL REPORT 1969/70-1976/77 / Barbados. Department of Education – (Missing: 1972/73; 1974/75-1975/76) – Bridgetown – 10mf – 9 – DE-514/1 – ne IDC [370]
ANNUAL REPORT 1970/71-1971/75 / Bahamas. Ministry of Education and Culture – Nassau – 6mf – 9 – DE-510/1 – ne IDC [370]
ANNUAL REPORT 1972-1981 / Zambia. Ministry of Education and Culture – Lusaka – 11mf – 9 – DE-494/1 – ne IDC [370]
ANNUAL REPORT ... 1974-1976 / Zambia. Department of Technical Education and Vocational Training – Lusaka – 3mf – 9 – DE-489/1 – ne IDC [370]
ANNUAL REPORT 1974-1989 / South Africa. Gazankulu. Department of Edcuation – (Missing: 1978. 1980-1984. 1988) – 16mf – 9 – DE-470/1 – ne IDC [370]
ANNUAL REPORT 1975-1977/78 / Zambia. Ministry of Education. Psychological Service – Lusaka – 3mf – 9 – DE-493/1 – ne IDC [370]
ANNUAL REPORT 1975-1981 / Mauritius. Institute of Education – (Missing: 1978-1979) – Rose Hill – 7mf – 9 – DE-452/1 – ne IDC [370]
ANNUAL REPORT 1975/76-1983/84 / Jamaica. Ministry of Education – (Missing: 1977/78-1978/79; 1980/81-1982/83) – 7mf – 9 – DE-520/1 – ne IDC [370]
ANNUAL REPORT 1976-1984 / South Africa. Lebowa. Department of Education – (Missing: 1980-1981) – 13mf – 9 – DE-473/1 – ne IDC [370]
ANNUAL REPORT 1977-1985 / South Africa. Kwa Zulu. Department of Education and Culture – Ulundi – 10mf – 9 – DE-472/1 – ne IDC [370]
ANNUAL REPORT 1979-1985 / South Africa. Venda. Department of Education – (Missing: 1982) – 16mf – 9 – DE-474/1 – ne IDC [370]
ANNUAL REPORT 1982-1988 / South Africa. Department of Education and Training – (In English and Afrikaans. Missing: 1987) – 45mf – 9 – DE-466/1 – ne IDC [370]
ANNUAL REPORT 1982-1989 / South Africa. Department of National Education – (Missing: 1984-1985. 1987-1988) – Pretoria – 15mf – 9 – DE-467/1 – ne IDC [370]
ANNUAL REPORT 1985-1988 / South Africa. Kangwane. Department of Education and Culture – (Missing. 1987) – 6mf – 9 – DE-471/1 – ne IDC [370]
ANNUAL REPORT AND ACCOUNTS / Bahrain. Bank of Bahrain – 3v. in 2. 1958-71. BNE-10.015 1 – 9 – ne IDC [956]
ANNUAL REPORT AND ACCOUNTS OF THE METHODIST MISSIONARY SOCIETY : GENERAL FUND AND WOMEN'S WORK FOR 1966-1970 – London, 1967-1971 – 11mf – 9 – H-2750/1 – ne IDC [240]
ANNUAL REPORT AND BALANCE SHEET / Jordan. Industrial Development Bank – 8v. in 2. 1966-77. BNE-9792 1 – 9 – ne IDC [338]
ANNUAL REPORT AND BALANCE SHEET, 1970-1975 / Kuwait. Gulf Bank – Lacking: 1973. BNE-9015 1 – 9 – ne IDC [324]
ANNUAL REPORT AND BULLETIN / Connecticut. Agricultural Experiment Station. New Haven – v. 1-706. 1877-1946; 1886-1969 – 1,5,6 – us Spaulding [630]
ANNUAL REPORT AND BULLETIN / Connecticut. Agricultural Experiment Station. Storrs – v. 1-20. 1888-1909; V. 1-412. 1896-1970 – 1,5,6 – us Spaulding [630]
ANNUAL REPORT AND BULLETIN / Maine. Agricultural Experiment Station – v. 1-680. 1885-37; 1889-1969 – 1,5,6 – us Spaulding [630]
ANNUAL REPORT AND BULLETIN / New Hampshire. Agricultural Experiment Station – v. 1-498. 1888-1968 – 1,5,6 – us Spaulding [630]
ANNUAL REPORT AND BULLETIN / Vermont. Agricultural Experiment Station – v. 1-57. 1887-1944; V. 1-659. 1887-1969 – 1,5,6 – us Spaulding [630]
ANNUAL REPORT AND PROCEEDINGS / Massachusetts Anti-Slavery Society – v1-24 (all publ). 1833-56 – 1 reel – 1 – $90.00 – us UPA [976]
ANNUAL REPORT AND REPORT OF THE DIRECTORS / Qatar. National Bank – 1972$76. BNE-10.025 1 – 9 – ne IDC [338]
ANNUAL REPORT AND STATEMENT OF ACCOUNTS / British Broadcasting Corporation – 1946-64 – 1 – uk Microform Academic [941]
ANNUAL REPORT AND STATEMENT OF ACCOUNTS / British Overseas Airways Corporation – 1947-65 – 1 – uk Microform Academic [941]
ANNUAL REPORT AND STATEMENT OF ACCOUNTS / Great Britain. Atomic Energy Authority – 1954-64 – 1 – uk Microform Academic [324]
ANNUAL REPORT AND STATEMENT OF ACCOUNTS / Great Britain. British Railways Board – 1963-64 – 1 – uk Microform Academic [324]
ANNUAL REPORT AND STATEMENT OF ACCOUNTS / Great Britain. British Transport Commission – 1948-62 – 1 – uk Microform Academic [324]
ANNUAL REPORT AND STATEMENT OF ACCOUNTS / Great Britain. British Waterways Board – 1963-64 – 1 – uk Microform Academic [324]
ANNUAL REPORT AND STATEMENT OF ACCOUNTS / Great Britain. Central Electricity Generating Board – 1958-64 – 1 – uk Microform Academic [324]
ANNUAL REPORT AND STATEMENT OF ACCOUNTS / Great Britain. Electricity Authority – 1947-64 – 1 – uk Microform Academic [324]
ANNUAL REPORT AND STATEMENT OF ACCOUNTS / Great Britain. Electricity Council – 1958-64 – 1 – uk Microform Academic [380]
ANNUAL REPORT AND STATEMENT OF ACCOUNTS / Great Britain. Gas Council – 1949-63 – 1 – uk Microform Academic [380]
ANNUAL REPORT AND STATEMENT OF ACCOUNTS / Great Britain. National Coal Board – 1946-64 – 1 – uk Microform Academic [324]
ANNUAL REPORT AND STATEMENT OF ACCOUNTS / Independent Television Authority. (Great Britain) – 1954-64 – 1 – uk Microform Academic [941]
ANNUAL REPORT AND STATEMENT OF ACCOUNTS / London. Transport Board – 1964 – 1 – uk Microform Academic [380]
ANNUAL REPORT AND STATEMENT OF ACCOUNTS / Scotland. North of Scotland Hydro-Electric Board – 1955-65 – 1 – uk Microform Academic [324]
ANNUAL REPORT AND STATEMENT OF ACCOUNTS / Scotland. South of Scotland Electricity Board – 1955-65 – 1 – uk Microform Academic [324]
ANNUAL REPORT AND STATEMENT OF ACCOUNTS / Sudan. Gezira Board – 11 v. 1950-64. Lacking: 1963. BNE-7642 1 – 9 – ne IDC [339]
ANNUAL REPORT AND STATEMENT OF ACCOUNTS / Transport Holding Company – 1964 – 1 – uk Microform Academic [941]
ANNUAL REPORT BY THE CHIEF ACCOUNTANT / Aden. Treasury Department – 6v. in 1. 1957-63. BNE-9608 1 – 9 – ne IDC [350]

ANNUAL REPORT CUSTOMS, EXCISE, TRADE AND INDUSTRY / Jordan. Department of Customs – Calendar year 1946-50. 5 v. in 2. BNE-9761 1 – 9 – ne IDC [380]

ANNUAL REPORT FOR 1977-1978 : PREPARED BY POLICY BRANCH, PLANNING SERVICES DIVISION, DEPARTMENT OF EDUCATION / Papua New Guinea. National Education Board – Boroko, c1979 – 3mf – 9 – DE-221/1 – ne IDC [370]

ANNUAL REPORT FOR THE YEAR ENDED...OF THE JOINT EAST AFRICAN BOARD FOR PROMOTING THE AGRICULTURAL, COMMERCIAL AND INDUSTRIAL DEVELOPMENT OF KENYA, NYASALAND, TANGANYIKA, UGANDA AND ZANZIBAR / Joint East African Board – [London]: The Board. v15 1938 – 1r – 1 – us Res Libr [338]

ANNUAL REPORT FOR THE YEARS 1886-1946 / India. Archaeological Department. Mysore – Bangalore. 1886-1947; Index. 1906-22. Lacking: 1890; 1893; 1918-20; 1922. BI-695 2 – 8 – ne IDC [930]

ANNUAL REPORT OF ECONOMIC POISONS ANALYSES / Clemson University. Agricultural Experiment Station – 1970-82.1 reel – 1,5 – us Spaulding [630]

ANNUAL REPORT OF ECONOMICS POISONS ANALYSIS / South Carolina. Agricultural Experiment Station. Clemson – 1960-69 – 1,5 – us Spaulding [630]

ANNUAL REPORT OF NEBRASKA IRRIGATION: DEVELOPMENT FARMS / Nebraska. College of Agriculture. Extension Service – no 1-17 1950-66 – 1, 5 – us Spaulding [630]

ANNUAL REPORT OF TECHNICAL SERVICE FOR ECONOMIC DEVELOPMENT AND TECHNICAL SERVICE FOR PUBLIC WORKS / Jordan. U.S. Operations Mission to Jordan – 1955 56. BNE-9819 1 – 9 – ne IDC [330]

ANNUAL REPORT OF THE ADJUTANT GENERAL, NEW YORK STATE – 1865. Vol. 1. New York Reel 1. (The Cox Library Collection) – 5 – us Americana [978]

ANNUAL REPORT OF THE ADJUTANT GENERAL OF WISCONSIN, YEAR ENDING DECEMBER 30, 1865 / Estabrook, Charles E; ed by Estabrook, Charles E – Madison: William J. Park and Co., 1912. Wisconsin Reel 22. (The Cox Library Collection) – 5 – us Americana [978]

ANNUAL REPORT OF THE AGRICULTURAL EXTENSION DIVISION / Iowa State University. Cooperative Extension Service in Agriculture and Home Economics – 1914/16-1952. 1 reel – 1,5 – us Spaulding [630]

ANNUAL REPORT OF THE AMERICAN COLONIZATION SOCIETY / American Colonization Society – 1-91 93rd (all publ). 1818-1908 10 – 3r – 1 – $220.00 – us UPA [976]

ANNUAL REPORT OF THE ARAB INVESTMENT COMPANY / Arab Investment Company. Lebanon – 7v. in 1. 1964-70. BNE-9638 1 – 9 – ne IDC [956]

ANNUAL REPORT OF THE ARCHAEOLOGICAL DEPARTMENT GWALIOR STATE FOR THE YEARS 1940/41 – Gwalior, [1925]-1949 – 53mf – 9 – I-785/2 – ne IDC [930]

ANNUAL REPORT OF THE ARCHAEOLOGICAL DEPARTMENT MYSORE FOR THE YEARS 1886-1946 – (Missing: 1890; 1893. Index 1906-1922) – Bangalore, 1886-1947 – 212mf – 9 – I-695/2 – ne IDC [930]

ANNUAL REPORT OF THE ARCHAEOLOGICAL DEPARTMENT OF HIS HIGHNESS THE NIZAM'S DOMINIONS – (Missing: 1930-1934) – Calcutta, 1940-1940 – 60mf – 9 – I-596/2 – ne IDC [930]

ANNUAL REPORT OF THE ARCHAEOLOGICAL DEPARTMENT. SOUTHERN CIRCLE. MADRAS. 1912/1913-1920/1921 – Madras, 1913-1921 – 30mf – 9 – I-576/2 – ne IDC [930]

ANNUAL REPORT OF THE ARCHAEOLOGICAL SURVEY, BENGAL CIRCLE... – Calcutta: Bengal Secretariat Press, 1905 – 1r – 1 – us Res Libr [930]

ANNUAL REPORT OF THE ARCHAEOLOGICAL SURVEY OF INDIA 1902/1903-1936/1937 – Calcutta, 1904-1940. 40v – 405mf – 9 – I-473/2 – ne IDC [930]

ANNUAL REPORT OF THE ARCHAEOLOGICAL SURVEY OF INDIA, FRONTIER CIRCLE FOR... – Peshawar, N-W Frontier Province: Govt Press, 1097-21 – 1r – 1 – us Res Libr [930]

ANNUAL REPORT OF THE ARCHAEOLOGICAL SURVEY OF INDIA. FRONTIER CIRCLE FOR 1906/1907-1920/1921 – (Missing: 1916/1917) – Peshawa, 1907-1920 – 15mf – 9 – I-570/2 – ne IDC [930]

ANNUAL REPORT OF THE BANK OF ISRAEL / Israel. Bank of Israel. Research Department – Jerusalem. 1956- – 9 – $120.00; $6.00y – is I.T.T.I. [330]

ANNUAL REPORT OF THE BOARD OF DIRECTORS / Libya. National Bank of Libya – 1-20th. 1956/57-1974/75. (lacking 1955, 1956). BNE-633/1 – 9 – ne IDC [330]

ANNUAL REPORT OF THE BOARD OF DIRECTORS AND ACCOUNTS, 1953-1977 / Kuwait. National Bank – Lacking: 1956 1957. BNE-9030 1 – 9 – ne IDC [336]

ANNUAL REPORT OF THE BOARD OF DIRECTORS. BALANCE SHEET AND PROFIT/LOSS ACCOUNT FOR THE YEARS 1947-1977 / Jordan. Arab Bank Limited – BNE-9751 1 – 9 – ne IDC [336]

ANNUAL REPORT OF THE BOARD OF INDIAN COMMISSIONERS TO THE SECRETARY OF THE INTERIOR / U.S. Board of Indian Commissioners – Washington. reports 1-63. 1869-1932 – 3r – 1 – us Ross [970]

ANNUAL REPORT OF THE CURRENCY BOARD, KUWAIT / Kuwait. Currency Board – 8v in 3. 1961/62-1969. BNE-9012 1 – 9 – ne IDC [338]

ANNUAL REPORT OF THE DEPARTMENT OF CO-OPERATIVE SOCIETIES, JORDAN / Jordan. Department of Co-operative Societies – 2v. 1953-55. BNE-9760 1 – 9 – ne IDC [956]

ANNUAL REPORT OF THE DEPARTMENT OF MIGRATION, PALESTINE / Palestine. Department of Migration – Title varies; 1940-date "The Statistics of migration and naturalization" 6v. 1939-45. BJ-28-117 1 – 9 – ne IDC [956]

ANNUAL REPORT OF THE DEVELOPMENT BOARD, JORDAN / Jordan. Development Board – 1953-54 – 9 – ne IDC [330]

ANNUAL REPORT OF THE DEVELOPMENT ORGANIZATION 1949 / Tanganyika – Dar es Salaam. 1950. BD-826 1 – 9 – ne IDC [338]

ANNUAL REPORT OF THE DEVELOPMENT ORGANIZATION 1950 / Tanganyika – Dar es Salaam. 1951 – 9 – ne IDC [338]

ANNUAL REPORT OF THE DEVELOPMENT ORGANIZATION 1951 / Tanganyika – Dar es Salaam. 1952. BD-828 1 – 9 – ne IDC [338]

ANNUAL REPORT OF THE DIRECTOR TO THE COUNCIL / Indian Institute of Science – [Bangalore: The Institute. 1st-2nd. 1908/10-1910/11 – 1 – us Res Libr [500]

ANNUAL REPORT OF THE INDIAN ARCHAEOLOGICAL DEPARTMENT / India. Archaeological Department of His Highness the Nizam's Dominions – Calcutta. 1914/15-1937 40. Lacking: 1930-34. BI-596 2 – 8 – ne IDC [930]

ANNUAL REPORT OF THE LEMBAGA GERAKAN PELAJARAN DEWASA 1970-1977/78 / Singapore. Adult Education Board – (Cont as: Singapore Vocational and Industrial Training Board: Annual report 1978/79-1985/86. Missing: 1979/80; 1982/83) – Singapore – 19mf – 9 – DE-252/1 – ne IDC [370]

ANNUAL REPORT OF THE LONDON MISSIONARY SOCIETY – (Missing: 1799-1814. Nos. 5-20) – London, 1796-1939/1940. Nos. 1-145 – 487mf – 9 – H-2142/1 – ne IDC [240]

ANNUAL REPORT OF THE MINISTRY OF LABOUR, ISRAEL / Israel. Ministry of Labour. Productivity Institute – 1956-60. BJ-81-27 1 – 9 – ne IDC [330]

ANNUAL REPORT OF THE MISSOURI BOTANICAL GARDEN – St. Louis, Mo., 1890-1912. v1-23 – 80mf – 9 – 8560/1 – ne IDC [580]

ANNUAL REPORT OF THE PRESIDENT OF THE JAVA BANK – Batavia, 1941-1951 – 18mf – 9 – ne IDC [332]

ANNUAL REPORT OF THE PROVINCIAL COMMISSIONERS / Nyasaland. Native Administration – Zomba: Govt Printer, 1945-46 – 1 – us Res Libr [960]

ANNUAL REPORT OF THE REGISTRAR GENERAL 1839-1920 – (Coll title: British Government Publications...1801-1977, Demography) – 18r – 1 (£2,110.00 demography set of 38r + 14mf) – uk Chadwyck [310]

ANNUAL REPORT OF THE SECRETARY.. / Rhodesia. Southern. Division of African Education – Salisbury: Government Printer. Illus. (-1968: C.S.R.) (1969-: Cmd. R.R.) annual. Title varies. 1252 – 1 – us U.W. Library [370]

ANNUAL REPORT OF THE SECRETARY FOR AFRICAN EDUCATION 1967-1977 / Rhodesia. Ministry of Education. Division of African Education – Salisbury – 13mf – 9 – DE-502/1 – ne IDC [370]

ANNUAL REPORT OF THE SECRETARY FOR EDUCATION 1978-1980 / Zimbabwe. Ministry of Education – Salisbury – 3mf – 9 – DE-504/1 – ne IDC [370]

ANNUAL REPORT OF THE TRADE AND COMMERCE OF CHICAGO / Chicago. Board of Trade – 1858-1940 – 16r – 1 – us Ross [380]

ANNUAL REPORT ON DEVELOPMENT 1952 / Tanganyika – Dar es Salaam. 1953 – 9 – ne IDC [338]

ANNUAL REPORT ON DEVELOPMENT 1953 / Tanganyika – Dar es Salaam. 1954. BD-830 1 – 9 – ne IDC [338]

ANNUAL REPORT ON DEVELOPMENT 1954 / Tanganyika – Dar es Salaam. 1955. BD-831 1 – 9 – ne IDC [338]

ANNUAL REPORT ON DEVELOPMENT 1955 / Tanganyika – Dar es Salaam. 1956 – 9 – ne IDC [338]

ANNUAL REPORT ON ECONOMIC CONDITIONS IN KUWAIT / Kuwait. Chamber of Commerce and Industry – 1v. 1963. BNE-9010 1 – 9 – ne IDC [380]

ANNUAL REPORT ON EDUCATION 1980 *see* ANNUAL REPORT ON EDUCATION 1974-1979

ANNUAL REPORT ON EDUCATION 1974-1979 / New Hebrides. British Service – (Cont as: Vanuatu. Ministry of Education. Annual report on education 1980) – Vila – 13mf – 9 – DE-611/1 – ne IDC [370]

ANNUAL REPORT ON EDUCATIONAL STATISTICS 1961/62-1964/65 / Iraq. Ministry of Education – Baghdad. 3v – 14mf – 9 – DE-704/1 – ne IDC [370]

ANNUAL REPORT ON OPERATIONS. 1952-1954 / Syria. Office of Foreign Exchange – 4v. (lacking 1953). BNE-9726 1 – 9 – ne IDC [330]

ANNUAL REPORT ON SOUTH INDIAN EPIGRAPHY, 1933/34-1944/45, 1955-1961 / India. Archaeological Survey – Madras, 1937-64 – 54mf – 8 – I-582/2 – ne IDC [410]

ANNUAL REPORT ON SOUTH-INDIAN EPIGRAPHY FROM 1887-1936 / India – Subject-index by C.R. Krishnamacharlu. Calcutta. 1940. BI-584 – 8 – ne IDC [410]

ANNUAL REPORT ON STATE-OWNED INSTITUTIONAL FARMS / Mississippi State University. Cooperative Extension Service – 1972-82.1 reel – 1,5 – us Spaulding [630]

ANNUAL REPORT ON THE ECONOMIC AND SOCIAL DEVELOPMENT PLAN 1960/1961 / Syria. Ministry of Planning – Damas. 1962 – 9 – ne IDC [338]

ANNUAL REPORT ON THE ECONOMIC AND SOCIAL DEVELOPMENT PLAN 1960-1961: IMPLEMENTATION REPORT ON THE FIRST FIVE-YEAR PLAN 1960-1965 / Syria. Ministry of Planning – 3v. Damascus. Lacking: 1963. BNE-9722 1 – 9 – ne IDC [338]

ANNUAL REPORT ON THE GENERAL PROGRESS OF DEVELOPMENT AND WELFARE SCHEMES, 1945-46 / Nigeria – Sessional Paper No. 10 of 1947. Lagos. 1947 – 9 – ne IDC [338]

ANNUAL REPORT ON THE WORKING OF THE RAJPUTANA MUSEUM, AJMER FOR THE YEAR ENDING 1930 / India – Calcutta. 1931. BI-1006 1 – 9 – ne IDC [060]

ANNUAL REPORT ON UNIVERSAL PRIMARY EDUCATION 1984 / Nigeria. Cross River State. Ministry of Local Government – Calabar – 2mf – 9 – DE-456/1 – ne IDC [370]

ANNUAL REPORT TO THE AGENCY FOR INTERNATIONAL DEVELOPMENT / North Carolina State University.Department of Soil Science. International Soil Fertility Evaluation and Improvement Program – 1967, 1971-74. 8 fiches – 9 – us Spaulding [630]

ANNUAL REPORT TO THE RULER OF BAHRAIN AND ITS DEPENDENCIES / Bahrain. Bahrain Petroleum Company – 13v. in 8. 1956-77. Lacking: 1958-60, 1972-73. BNE-10.010 1 – 9 – ne IDC [660]

ANNUAL REPORT...FOR THE YEAR... / Archaeological Dept. Southern Circle. Madras – Madras: Printed by the Superintendent, Govt Press, 1909/10-1911/12 – 1r – 1 – us Res Libr [930]

ANNUAL REPORT.NOS.1-6. 1909-13 / North Dakota. Agricultural Experiment Station. Dickinson – 1,5,6 – us Spaulding [630]

ANNUAL REPORTS / Baptist North America General Conference – 1851-1971. Eastern, 1851-1885; Western, 1859-1882; General, 1865-1883; Annual, 1894-1917 – 1 – $766.29 – us Baptist [240]

ANNUAL REPORTS / British and Foreign School Society. Great Britain – 1814-1900 – 9 – uk Microform Academic [370]

ANNUAL REPORTS / Canada. Public Archives – (Edition francaise 1872-1949) – Eng ed, 1872-1949 – 9 – cn Micromedia [324]

ANNUAL REPORTS / China Association – 1889-1968 – 1 – uk Microform Academic [950]

ANNUAL REPORTS / Conservative Party. Great Britain – 1867-to date – 1 – uk Microform Academic [320]

ANNUAL REPORTS / Dante Society – 1882-1896 – 1 – us UMI [440]

ANNUAL REPORTS : FINANCIAL INFORMATION ON TOP U.S. CORPORATIONS – (Base collection filmed from material in Harvard University's Baker Library. Complete backfile on microfilm (711r): Major U.S. Corporations, $43,725; microfiche backfile, 1891-1973 (5755mf), $17,450; 1974-87 complete Fortune 500 company reports (8346mf), $15,470; all reports per year, $1105; also available for specific companies) – 1,9 – us UMI [332]

ANNUAL REPORTS / Fulton County. Ohio. County Home – 1889-1916 – 1r – 1 – $32.50r – us Archival [324]

ANNUAL REPORTS / Great Northern Railway Company – 1880-1968 – 4r – 1 – $120.00; $35.50r – us M.H.S. [380]

ANNUAL REPORTS / Hancock County. Ohio. Biglick Township. Board of Education – 1868-1902 – 1r – 1 – $32.50r – us Archival [324]

ANNUAL REPORTS / Independent Labour Party. Great Britain – 1893-1932 – 1 – uk Microform Academic [320]

ANNUAL REPORTS / India. Archaeological Survey – 1904-68 – 1 – $227.00 – us L of C Photodup [930]

ANNUAL REPORTS / Indian Rights Association. Executive Committee – 1883-1934. (American Indian Periodicals in the Princeton University Library). 45 fiches – 9 – $200.00 – us UPA [340]

ANNUAL REPORTS : THE ISTHMIAN CANAL COMMISSION, 1907-1914; THE GOVERNOR OF THE PANAMA CANAL, 1915-1951; THE PANAMA CANAL COMPANY AND THE GOVERNMENT OF THE CANAL ZONE, 1952-1979 – Washington: GPO, 1907-79 (all publ) – 266mf – 9 – $399.00 – LLMC 82-100D Title 21 – us L.L.M.C. [324]

ANNUAL REPORTS / Jordan. Central Bank – 1964-1975 BNE-97 57 1 – 9 – ne IDC [332]

ANNUAL REPORTS / Lake Mohonk Conference on International Arbitration – 1895-1916 – 55mf – 9 – $220.00 – us UPA [340]

ANNUAL REPORTS / Lucas County. Ohio. Toledo, City Board of Education – 1886-1911 – 2r – 1 – $32.50r – us Archival [324]

ANNUAL REPORTS / National Advisory Committee on Aeronautics – v1-44. 1915-58 – 1,5,6 – us Princeton Micro [629]

ANNUAL REPORTS / National Association for Promotion of Technical Education. Great Britain – 1888-1894, 1897-1907. nos.1-6, 10-16 – 1 – uk Microform Academic [370]

ANNUAL REPORTS / National Liberal Federation. (Great Britain) – 1877-1936. British Political Sources – 9 – us Primary [323]

ANNUAL REPORTS / National Society. Great Britain – 1812-1900 – 7 – uk Microform Academic [941]

ANNUAL REPORTS / North American Baptist General Convention – (Eastern, 1851-85. Western, 1859-82. General, 1865-93. Annual, 1894-1917) – 1851-79.23,870p – 1 – $835.45 – us Baptist [240]

ANNUAL REPORTS / Northern Pacific Railway Company – 1870-1968 – 7r – 1 – $210.00; $35.00r – us M.H.S. [380]

ANNUAL REPORTS / Ottawa County. Ohio. Carroll Township. Township Clerk – 1925-1977 – 1r – 1 – $32.50r – us Archival [324]

ANNUAL REPORTS / Saudi Arabia. Monetary Agency – 1960-1971, 1974-77. BNE-6610 1 – 9 – ne IDC [332]

ANNUAL REPORTS / Saudi Arabia. National Commercial Bank – 9v. 1958-75. (lacking 1964 65, 1966 67, 1970 71). BNE-6611 1 – 9 – ne IDC [332]

ANNUAL REPORTS / Scottish Trades Union Congress – 1897-1979 – 1 – uk Microform Academic [331]

ANNUAL REPORTS / Sudan. Industrial Bank – 11 v. in 8. 1962-75. Lacking: 1971-72 (10, 11). 1974 – 9 – ne IDC [332]

ANNUAL REPORTS / Sudan. Survey Department – 2v. in 2. 1959-69. (lacking 1960, 1966 67). BNE-7690 1 – 9 – ne IDC [330]

ANNUAL REPORTS / Trades Union Congress (Great Britain) – 1869 to date – 1 – uk Microform Academic [331]

ANNUAL REPORTS / Unitarian Domestic Mission to the Poor. Manchester – 1833-1907 – 1 – uk Microform Academic [360]

ANNUAL REPORTS / U.S. Army. Air Force – Washington, DC. 1917-36 – 1 – us NY Public [355]

ANNUAL REPORTS / U.S. National Advisory Committee on Aeronautics – 1915-1958 – 1,5,6 – us Princeton Micro [629]

ANNUAL REPORTS / Wesleyan Education Committee. Great Britain – 1838-1901 – 7 – uk Microform Academic [370]

ANNUAL REPORTS / Women's National Indian Association – 1883-1938. (American Indian Periodicals in the Princeton University Library). 26 fiches – 9 – $100.00 – us UPA [305]

ANNUAL REPORTS / Wood County. Ohio. Bowling Green. City Mayor – 1960-1970 – 1r – 1 – $32.50r – us Archival [324]

ANNUAL REPORTS / Yemen. Central Bank of Yemen, Sana'a – 971-1976. 6 v. in 1. BNE-9609 1 – 9 – ne IDC [332]

ANNUAL REPORTS, 1817-1856 / Presbyterian Church in the U.S.A. Board of Missions – 1 – $50.00 – us Presbyterian [240]

ANNUAL REPORTS, 1818-1824 / Philadelphia Sunday and Adult School Union – 1 – $50.00 – us Presbyterian [240]

ANNUAL REPORTS, 1820-1918 / Presbyterian Church in the U.S.A. Board of Education – 1 – $100.00 – us Presbyterian [240]

ANNUAL REPORTS..., 1822-66 / U.S. Navy – RG 287. M1099. 8 rolls – 1 – us Nat'l Archives [355]

ANNUAL REPORTS, 1825-1835 / American Sunday School Union – 1 – $50.00 – us Presbyterian [240]

ANNUAL REPORTS, 1833-1958 / Presbyterian Church in the U.S.A. Board of Foreign Missions – 1 – $100.00 – us Presbyterian [240]

ANNUAL REPORTS, 1839-1923 / Presbyterian Church in the U.S.A. Board of Publication and Sabbath School Work – 1 – $50.00 – us Presbyterian [240]

ANNUAL REPORTS, 1855-1875 / Presbyterian Church in the U.S.A. General Assembly. Trustees. Committee on the Relief Fund for Disabled Ministers and the Widows and Orphans of Deceased Ministers – (Also: Board of Relief for Disabled Ministers... Annual reports, 1876-1912) – 1 – $50.00 – us Presbyterian [240]

ANNUAL REPORTS, 1855-1923 / Presbyterian Church in the U.S.A. Board of Church Erection – 1 – $150.00 – us Presbyterian [720]

ANNUAL REPORTS, 1856-1870 / Presbyterian Church in the U.S.A. Board of Church Extension (Old School) – 1 – $50.00 – us Presbyterian [240]

ANNUAL REPORTS, 1857-1870 / Presbyterian Church in the U.S.A. Board of Domestic Missions (Old School) – 1 – $50.00 – us Presbyterian [240]

ANNUAL REPORTS, 1859-1867 / African Civilization Society – 1 – $50.00 – us Presbyterian [240]

ANNUAL REPORTS, 1862-1870 / Presbyterian Church in the U.S.A. General Assembly. Committee on Home Missions (New School) – 1 – $50.00 – us Presbyterian [240]

ANNUAL REPORTS, 1866-1923 / Presbyterian Church in the U.S.A. Board of Missions for Freedmen – 1 – $150.00 – us Presbyterian [240]

ANNUAL REPORTS, 1871-1923 / Presbyterian Church in the U.S.A. Board of Home Missions – 1 – $200.00 – us Presbyterian [240]

ANNUAL REPORTS, 1871-1923 / Presbyterian Church in the U.S.A. Woman's Board of Foreign Missions – 1 – $100.00 – us Presbyterian [240]

ANNUAL REPORTS, 1872-1920 / Presbyterian Church in the U.S.A. Woman's Presbyterian Board of Missions of the Northwest – 1 – $150.00 – us Presbyterian [240]

ANNUAL REPORTS, 1872-1923 / Presbyterian Church in the U.S.A. Woman's Foreign Missionary Society – 1 – $150.00 – us Presbyterian [240]

ANNUAL REPORTS, 1876-1912 / Presbyterian Church in the U.S.A. Board of Relief for Disabled Ministers and the Widows and Orphans of Deceased Ministers – 1 – $50.00 – us Presbyterian [240]

ANNUAL REPORTS 1880-1969 / Nebraska. Agricultural Experiment Station. Lincoln – n.1-82 – 1,5 – us Spaulding [630]

ANNUAL REPORTS, 1882-1923 / Presbyterian Church in the U.S.A. Board of Temperance – 1 – $50.00 – us Presbyterian [240]

ANNUAL REPORTS, 1883-1916, 1929 / Lake Mohonk Conference of Friends of the Indians – Includes two conferences on The Negro Question. Index – 80mf – 9 – $330.00 – us UPA [305]

ANNUAL REPORTS, 1883-1920 / Presbyterian Church in the U.S.A. Woman's Presbyterian Board of Foreign Missions of the Southwest – (With Presbyterian Church in the U.S.A. Woman's North Pacific Presbyterian Board of Missions. Annual reports, 1887-1920) – 1 – $100.00 – us Presbyterian [240]

ANNUAL REPORTS, 1884-1918 / Presbyterian Church in the U.S.A. College Board – 1 – $50.00 – us Presbyterian [240]

ANNUAL REPORTS, 1887-1920 / Presbyterian Church in the U.S.A. Woman's North Pacific Presbyterian Board of Missions – (With Presbyterian Church in the U.S.A. Woman's Presbyterian Board of Foreign Mission of the Southwest. Annual reports, 1883-1920) – 1 – $100.00 – us Presbyterian [240]

ANNUAL REPORTS, 1898-1927 / Presbyterian Church in the U.S.A. Woman's Board of Home Missions – 1 – $50.00 – us Presbyterian [240]

ANNUAL REPORTS, 1913-1927 / Presbyterian Church in the U.S.A. Board of Ministerial Relief and Sustenation – (Also: Board of Pensions, Annual reports 1928-58; United Presbyterian Ch. in the U.S.A., Board of Pensions, Annual reports 1958-83) – 1 – $100.00 – us Presbyterian [240]

ANNUAL REPORTS, 1914-1946 / United Presbyterian Church of North America. Board of Education – 1 – $50.00 – us Presbyterian [240]

ANNUAL REPORTS, 1919-1923 / Presbyterian Church in the U.S.A. General Board of Education – 1 – $50.00 – us Presbyterian [240]

ANNUAL REPORTS, 1924-1957 / Presbyterian Church in the U.S.A. Board of National Missions – 1 – $200.00 – us Presbyterian [240]

ANNUAL REPORTS, 1924-1958 / Presbyterian Church in the U.S.A. Board of Christian Education – 1 – $150.00 – us Presbyterian [240]

ANNUAL REPORTS, 1936/1937 – 1972-1973 / Iraq. Agricultural Bank – Lacking: 1969 1970. BNE-2000 1 – 9 – ne IDC [332]

ANNUAL REPORTS, 1946-1958 / United Presbyterian Church of North America. Board of Christian Education – 1 – $50.00 – us Presbyterian [240]

ANNUAL REPORTS, 1958-1973 / United Presbyterian Church in the U.S.A. Board of National Missions – 1 – $100.00 – us Presbyterian [240]

ANNUAL REPORTS, 1962-1976 / Lebanon. Beirut Riyad Bank – Lacking: 1975. BNE-9648 1 – 9 – ne IDC [332]

ANNUAL REPORTS, 1962/63-1975/76 / Kuwait. Kuwait Fund for Arab Economic Development – BNE-9020 1 – 9 – ne IDC [338]

ANNUAL REPORTS 1964-68 / Wisconsin. Land Tenure Center – 1964-68 – 1,5 – us Spaulding [630]

ANNUAL REPORTS 1972-75 / North Carolina State University.Department of Soil Science. Agronomic-Economic Research on Soils of the Tropics – 10mf – 9 – us Spaulding [630]

ANNUAL REPORTS 1988-1981 / Auburn University. Agricultural Experiment Station – 1, 5 – us Spaulding [630]

ANNUAL REPORTS (A-G) / U.S. – 1870-1970. 13 reels – 1 – $35.00r – us Trans-Media [340]

ANNUAL REPORTS AND DIRECTORIES / American Baptist Home Mission Societies – 1832-1981. Single reels available – 1 – $452.60 – us A.B.H.S. [240]

ANNUAL REPORTS AND SERMONS, 1701-1845 / United Society for the Propagation of the Gospel in Foreign Parts – 1 – uk Microform Academic [240]

ANNUAL REPORTS, BULLETINS AND OCCASIONAL PAPERS, 1973-1995 – 7mf – 9 – £35.00 set £5.50 ea – uk Microform Academic [331]

ANNUAL REPORTS BY COMMON CARRIERS TO THE INTERSTATE COMMERCE COMMISSION, 1888-1914 / U.S. Interstate Commerce Commission – 1348 rolls. T913 – 5 – us Nat'l Archives [324]

ANNUAL REPORTS OF EXTENSION SERVICE FIELD REPRESENTATIVES / U.S. Federal Extension Service – (Alabama, 1909-44. 115 rolls. T845. Alaska, 1930-44. 2 rolls. T846. Arizona, 1915-44. 22 rolls. T847. Arkansas, 1909-44. 106 rolls. T848. California, 1913-44. 54 rolls. T849. Colorado, 1913-44. 77 rolls. T850. Connecticut, 1913-44. 30 rolls. T851. Delaware, 1914-44. 13 rolls. T852. District of Columbia, 1917-19. 1 roll. T853. Florida, 1909-44. 46 rolls. T854. Georgia, 1909-44. 141 rolls. T855. Hawaii, 1929-44. 7 rolls. T856. Idaho, 1913-44. 47 rolls. T857. Illinois, 1914-44. 82 rolls. T858. Indiana, 1912-44. 80 rolls. T859. Iowa, 1912-44. 195 rolls. T860. Kansas, 1913-44. 186 rolls. T861. Kentucky, 1912-44. 89 rolls. T862. Louisiana, 1909-44. 67 rolls. T863. Maine, 1915-44. 48 rolls. T864. Maryland, 1912-44. 70 rolls. T865. Massachusetts, 1914-44. 59 rolls. T866. Michigan, 1913-44. 77 rolls. T867. Minnesota, 1914-44. 105 rolls. T868. Mississippi, 1909-44. 96 rolls. T869. Missouri, 1914-44. 90 rolls. T870. Montana, 1914-44. 64 rolls. T871. Nebraska, 1913-44. 89 rolls. T872. Nevada, 1915-44. 19 rolls. T873. New Hampshire, 1914-44. 34 rolls. T874. New Jersey, 1913-44. 45 rolls. T875. New Mexico, 1914-44. 30 rolls. T876. New York, 1912-44. 90 rolls. T877. North Carolina, 1909-44. 144 rolls. T878. North Dakota, 1912-44. 68 rolls. T879. Ohio, 1915-44. 98 rolls. T880,. Oklahoma, 1909-44. 135 rolls. T881. Oregon, 1914-44. 73 rolls. T882. Pennsylvania, 1914-44. 43 rolls. T883. Puerto Rico, 1930-44. 14 rolls. T884. Rhode Island, 1914-44. 12 rolls. T885. South, 1913-14. 1 roll. T886. South Carolina, 1909-44. 91 rolls. T887. South Dakota, 1913-44. 65 rolls. T888. Tennessee, 1910-44. 64 rolls. T889. Texas, 1909-44. 182 rolls. T890. Utah, 1914-44. 30 rolls. T891. Vermont, 1912-44. 31 rolls. T892. Virginia, 1908-44. 82 rolls. T893. Washington, 1913-44. 45 rolls. T894. West Virginia, 1912-44. 47 rolls. T895. Wisconsin, 1913-44. 49 rolls. T896. Wyoming, 1914-44. 37 rolls. T897) – 5 – us Nat'l Archives [630]

ANNUAL REPORTS OF FLEETS AND TASK FORCES OF THE U.S. NAVY / U.S. Navy – 1920-41. M971 – 15r – 1 – us Nat'l Archives [355]

ANNUAL REPORTS OF THE ANGLO-CHINESE COLLEGE AT MALACCA – (Missing: 1833/1834; 1836) – Malacca, 1825-1836 – 4mf – 9 – HT-863/1 – ne IDC [370]

ANNUAL REPORTS OF THE ATTORNEY GENERAL / U.S. Department of Justice – (Includes index/digest. No report publ for 1945. Updates planned) – 1871-1988 – 416mf – 9 – $624.00 – LLMC 79-410 – us L.L.M.C. [340]

ANNUAL REPORTS OF THE DEPUTY KEEPER OF THE PUBLIC RECORDS IN IRELAND / Ireland. Public Records Office – 1869-1931. 13v.96 fiches – 9 – ie Microforms [941]

ANNUAL REPORTS OF THE ECONOMIC DEVELOPMENT ADMINISTRATION, COMMERCE DEPARTMENT – 1979-83 – 13mf – 9 – $19.50 – LLMC 95-023 – us L.L.M.C. [340]

ANNUAL REPORTS OF THE EDINBURGH MEDICAL MISSIONARY SOCIETY. THIRD, FOURTH AND FIFTH ANNUAL REPORT – Edinburgh, 1845-1849 – 2mf – 9 – ne IDC [610]

ANNUAL REPORTS OF THE FEDERAL COMMUNICATIONS COMMISSION / U.S. Federal Communications Commission – (Lacking: 1976) – 1935-84 – 14mf – 9 – $21.00 – LLMC 90-371 – us L.L.M.C. [340]

ANNUAL REPORTS OF THE FEDERAL ELECTION COMMISSION – (Lacking: 1976. Add vols planned) – 1975-84 – 14mf – 9 – $21.00 – LLMC 90-371 – us L.L.M.C. [340]

ANNUAL REPORTS OF THE GOVERNOR OF AMERICAN SAMOA TO THE SECRETARY OF THE INTERIOR : 1952/53-1981 / American Samoa – Office of the Governor, 1953-82 – 40mf – 9 – $60.00 – LLMC 82-100C Title 5 – us L.L.M.C. [324]

ANNUAL REPORTS OF THE GOVERNOR OF GUAM, 1938-1981 / Guam. (Commonwealth) – (No reports issued for 1942-50. Lacking: 1978) – 62mf – 9 – $93.00 – LLMC 82-100B Title 23 – us L.L.M.C. [324]

ANNUAL REPORTS OF THE GOVERNORS OF GUAM, 1901-41 / U.S. Navy. Office of Naval Records and Library – 3rolls. M181. Printed guide – 1 – us Nat'l Archives [324]

ANNUAL REPORTS OF THE INTERSTATE COMMERCE COMMISSION / U.S. Interstate Commerce Commission – 1st-94th. 1887-1980 – 311mf – 9 – $466.00 – LLMC 81-229 – us L.L.M.C. [380]

ANNUAL REPORTS OF THE LIBRARIAN OF CONGRESS / U.S. Library of Congress – 1866-1966 – 1 – $320.00 – us L of C Photodup [020]

ANNUAL REPORTS OF THE NATIONAL LABOR RELATIONS BOARD / U.S. National Labor Relations Board – 1st-48th. 1936-83 – 144mf – 9 – $216.00 – LLMC 81-233 – us L.L.M.C. [331]

ANNUAL REPORTS OF THE PRIMITIVE METHODIST MISSIONARY SOCIETY – (Missing: Nos. 50-66) – London, 1844-1927. Nos. 1-84, 1843-1927 – 126mf – 9 – H-2738/1 – ne IDC [240]

ANNUAL REPORTS OF THE PROGRESS OF CHEMISTRY / Chemical Society. London – v. 1-65. 1904-1968 – 1,5,6 – us Princeton Micro [540]

ANNUAL REPORTS OF THE SECRETARY OF THE NAVY, 1821-1901 / U.S. Navy. Office of the Secretary – (Includes printed guide) – 1988 – 25r – 1 – $2,125.00 – S3166 – Published in cooperation with the U.S. Naval Historical Center – us Scholarly Res [355]

ANNUAL REPORTS OF THE SECRETARY OF THE TREASURY ON THE STATE OF THE FINANCES, 1790-1974 / U.S. Treasury Department – (Part 2: 1911-74. Printed guide. ISBN 0-89093-106-2. $1,635.00) – 1982. Part 1: 1790-1910. Printed guide – 1 – $1,350.00 – 0-89093-006-6 – us UPA [339]

ANNUAL REPORTS OF THE UNITED STATES TO THE TRUSTEESHIP COUNCIL OF THE U.N. – (Reports on the US admin of the TTPI. Reports of the US Navy 1947/48-1951) – 1947-93 – 149mf – 9 – $223.00 – LLMC 82-100F title 11 – us L.L.M.C. [324]

ANNUAL REPORTS OF THE U.S. PATENT OFFICE – (Updates planned) – 1906-25; 1949-83 – 313mf – 9 – $470.00 – LLMC 94-205 – us L.L.M.C. [340]

ANNUAL REPORTS OF THE WAR DEPARTMENT / U.S. War Department – 1822-1907. 164 rolls. M997 – 1 – us Nat'l Archives [324]

ANNUAL REPORTS OF THE WESLEYAN METHODIST MISSIONARY SOCIETY – (Financial supplement 1939-1959; Missing: 1790; 1793-1803; 1807; 1810; 1932) – London, 1789-1966 – 547mf – 9 – H-2749/1 – ne IDC [240]

ANNUAL REPORTS OF THE WORLD'S CENTRAL BANKS : CURRENT COLLECTION, 1984-1993 – (1984 Base coll £820.00. Updates: 1985 £370.00. 1986 £550.00. 1987 £630.00. 1988 £525.00. 1989 £830.00. 1990 £630.00. 1991 £715.00. 1992 £775.00. 1993 £815.00. 1994 £830.00. 1995 £1,260.00. 1996 £1,030.00. 1997 £995.00. Also available by region and individual country) – 9 – uk Chadwyck [332]

ANNUAL REPORTS OF THE WORLD'S CENTRAL BANKS : RETROSPECTIVE COLLECTION, 1946-1983 – (Available as complete coll or by region. Africa 53mf £3,475. Asia 24mf £2,815. Australasia 9mf £745.00. Europe and Near East 51mf £5,340. Latin America and Caribbean 53mf £6,700. Middle East 24 mf £2,200. North

America 3mf £520.00) – 9 – £17,640.00 coll – uk Chadwyck [332]

ANNUAL REPORTS ON EPIGRAPHY, ... – [Madras], 1919-1922 – 15mf – 9 – I-581/2 – ne IDC [410]

ANNUAL REPORTS ON THE PROGRESS OF CHEMISTRY / Chemical Society. London – Section A General, Physical, and Inorganic Chemistry. v. 66-68. 1969-1971 – 1,5,6 – us Princeton Micro [540]

ANNUAL REPORTS ON THE PROGRESS OF CHEMISTRY / Chemical Society. London – Section B Organic Chemistry. v. 66-68. 1969-1971 – 1,5,6 – us Princeton Micro [540]

ANNUAL REPORTS: ROMAN CATHOLIC VOLUNTARY SCHOOLS / Catholic Poor-School Committee. Great Britain – 1848-1900 – 7 – uk Microform Academic [370]

ANNUAL REPORTS, SPECIAL REPORTS, TECHNICAL PAPERS AND RESEARCH PAPERS / Great Britain. Dept. of Scientific and Industrial Research – 7 – uk Microform Academic [324]

ANNUAL REPORTS TO THE SECRETARY OF THE INTERIOR / U.S. Bureau of Indian Affairs. Commissioner – 1870-1931. (American Indian Periodicals in the Princeton University Library). 51 fiches – 9 – $200.00 – us UPA [324]

ANNUAL RESEARCH REPORT / Louisiana State University. Agricultural Experiment Station. Department of Plant Pathology and Crop Physiology – 1982-84.1 reel – 1,5 – us Spaulding [630]

ANNUAL RESEARCH REPORT / Louisiana State University. Agricultural Experiment Station. Red River Valley Experiment Station, Bossier City – 1970-82 – 1,5 – us Spaulding [630]

ANNUAL RESEARCH REPORT / University of Florida. Institute of Food and Agricultural Science – 1970-75 – 1r – 1, 5 – us Spaulding [630]

ANNUAL REVENUE AND EXPENDITURE OF LOWER CANADA FROM ITS CONSTITUTION TO THE PERIOD OF THE UNION / Canada. Parliament. Legislative Assembly. Special Committee.. – Montreal: Lovell and Gibson, 1847. SEM105P302 – 1mf – 9 – Can$2.25 – cn Bibl Nat [336]

ANNUAL REVIEW AND HISTORY OF LITERATURE – (Ceased publ) – London. v1-7. 1802-08 – 1 – D5229 – us UMI [420]

ANNUAL REVIEW IN AUTOMATIC PROGRAMMING – v1- 1960- – 5,6,9 – us UMI [073]

ANNUAL REVIEW IN AUTOMATIC PROGRAMMING – Oxford. v1-21. 1960-* – 1,5,9 – D49013 – us UMI [000]

ANNUAL REVIEW OF ADDICTIONS RESEARCH AND TREATMENT – New York. v1-7. 1991-* – 1,5,9 – D49622 – us UMI [616]

ANNUAL REVIEW OF ASTRONOMY AND ASTROPHYSICS – Palo Alto. v3-35 1965- 1; cum index v 1-2 1963-1964; v1-35 1963-* 5; v4-35 1966- 9 – 1,5,9 – D5899 – us UMI [301]

ANNUAL REVIEW OF BANKING LAW – Boston University. v1-5. 1982-86 – 9 – $75.00 set – us Hein [340]

ANNUAL REVIEW OF BIOCHEMISTRY – Palo Alto. v1-33 1932- 1; v36-66 1967-* 5; v41-66 1972- – 1,5,9 – D230 – us UMI [574]

ANNUAL REVIEW OF BIOPHYSICS AND BIOENGINEERING – (Cont: Annual Review of Biophysics and Biophysical Chemistry) – Palo Alto. v1-13. 1972-84* – 1 – D8225 – us UMI [574]

ANNUAL REVIEW OF BIOPHYSICS AND BIOENGINEERING *see* ANNUAL REVIEW OF BIOPHYSICS AND BIOPHYSICAL CHEMISTRY

ANNUAL REVIEW OF BIOPHYSICS AND BIOMOLECULAR STRUCTURE *see* ANNUAL REVIEW OF BIOPHYSICS AND BIOPHYSICAL CHEMISTRY

ANNUAL REVIEW OF BIOPHYSICS AND BIOPHYSICAL CHEMISTRY – (Cont: Annual Review of Biophysics and Bioengineering. Cont by: Annual Review of Biophysics and Biophysical Chemistry) – Palo Alto. v14-20. 1985-91* – 1 – D8225.01 – us UMI [574]

ANNUAL REVIEW OF BIOPHYSICS AND BIOPHYSICAL CHEMISTRY *see* ANNUAL REVIEW OF BIOPHYSICS AND BIOENGINEERING

ANNUAL REVIEW OF CELL AND DEVELOPMENTAL BIOLOGY – (Cont by: Annual Review of Cell and Developmental Biology) – Palo Alto. v1-10 1985-94* 1; v1-4 1985-88 5*,9 – 1,5,9 – D14963 – us UMI [574]

ANNUAL REVIEW OF CELL AND DEVELOPMENTAL BIOLOGY *see* ANNUAL REVIEW OF CELL AND DEVELOPMENTAL BIOLOGY

ANNUAL REVIEW OF CHRONOPHARMA-COLOGY – (Ceased publ. Absorbed by: Chronobiology International (1991)) – Oxford. v1-7. 1984-90 – 1,5*,9 – D49480 – us UMI [615]

ANNUAL REVIEW OF COMPUTER SCIENCE – (Ceased publ) – Palo Alto. v1-4. 1986-90* – 1 – D16378 – us UMI [000]

ANNUAL REVIEW OF DEVELOPMENT, 1957-1958 / Somaliland – Hargeisa. 1958 – 9 – ne IDC [338]

ANNUAL REVIEW OF EARTH AND PLANETARY SCIENCE – Palo Alto. v6-25. 1978-* – 1 – D9706 – us UMI [550]

ANNUAL REVIEW OF ECOLOGY AND SYSTEMATICS – Palo Alto. v1-28 1970-* 1; v4-28 1973- 5*,9 – 1,5,9 – D11806 – us UMI [574]

ANNUAL REVIEW OF ENERGY – (Cont by: Annual Review of Energy and the Environment) – Palo Alto. v1-15 1976-90* 1; v9-15 1984-90 5*,9 – 1,5,9 – D11807 – us UMI [333]

ANNUAL REVIEW OF ENERGY AND THE ENVIRONMENT *see* ANNUAL REVIEW OF ENERGY

ANNUAL REVIEW OF ENTOMOLOGY – Palo Alto. v1-42 1956- 1; v12-42 1967-* 5; v18-42 1973-* 9 – 1,5,9 – D5094 – us UMI [590]

ANNUAL REVIEW OF FISH DISEASES – New York. v1-7. 1991-* – 1,5,9 – D49618 – us UMI [530]

ANNUAL REVIEW OF FLUID MECHANICS – Palo Alto. v1-29 1969- 1*,5; v2-29 1970- 9 – 1,5,9 – D9705 – us UMI [530]

ANNUAL REVIEW OF GENETICS – Palo Alto. v1-31 1967- 1,5*; v7-31 1973- – 1,5,9 – D7696 – us UMI [575]

ANNUAL REVIEW OF IMMUNOLOGY – Palo Alto. v1-15. 1983- – 1,5*,9 – D13391 – us UMI [616]

ANNUAL REVIEW OF JAZZ STUDIES – (Ceased publ) – New Brunswick. v1-4. 1982-88 – 1,5*,9 – D12885 – us UMI [780]

ANNUAL REVIEW OF MATERIALS SCIENCE – Palo Alto. v1-27 1971-* 1; v14-27 1984-* 5,9 – 1,5,9 – D11808 – us UMI [620]

ANNUAL REVIEW OF MEDICINE – v1-8. 1950-57 – 1,5,6 – us Princeton Micro [616]

ANNUAL REVIEW OF MEDICINE – Palo Alto. cum index 1-12 1950-1961; v1-48 1; v18-48 1967- 5; v23-48 1972- 9 – 1,5,9 – D5093 – us UMI [610]

ANNUAL REVIEW OF MICROBIOLOGY – v. 1-11. 1947-1957 – 1,5,6 – us Princeton Micro [576]

ANNUAL REVIEW OF MICROBIOLOGY – Palo Alto. v1-51 1947- 1; v21-51 1967-* 5; v26-51 1972- 9 – 1,5,9 – D5092 – us UMI [576]

ANNUAL REVIEW OF NEUROSCIENCE – Palo Alto. v1-20 1978-* 1; v7-20 1984-* 5,9 – 1,5,9 – D11809 – us UMI [612]

ANNUAL REVIEW OF NUCLEAR AND PARTICLE SCIENCE – (Cont: Annual Review of Nuclear Science) – Palo Alto. v28-47. 1978-* – 1 – D2094.01 – us UMI [530]

ANNUAL REVIEW OF NUCLEAR AND PARTICLE SCIENCE *see* ANNUAL REVIEW OF NUCLEAR SCIENCE

ANNUAL REVIEW OF NUCLEAR SCIENCE – (Cont by: Annual Review of Nuclear and Particle Science) – Palo Alto. v1-27 1952-77 1; v17-27 1967-77 5; v22-27 1972-77 9 – 1,5,9 – D2094 – us UMI [530]

ANNUAL REVIEW OF NUCLEAR SCIENCE *see* ANNUAL REVIEW OF NUCLEAR AND PARTICLE SCIENCE

ANNUAL REVIEW OF NUTRITION – Palo Alto. v1-17. 1981- – 1,5*,9 – D13358 – us UMI [612]

ANNUAL REVIEW OF PHARMACOLOGY – (Cont by: Annual Review of Pharmacology and Toxicology) – Palo Alto. cum index 1-4 1961-1964; v1-15 1961-1975 1; v7-15 1967-1975 5; v12-15 1972-1975 9 – 1,5,9 – D5091 – us UMI [615]

ANNUAL REVIEW OF PHARMACOLOGY AND TOXICOLOGY – Palo Alto. v16-37. 1976- – 1,5*,9 – D5091.01 – us UMI [615]

ANNUAL REVIEW OF PHARMACOLOGY AND TOXICOLOGY *see* ANNUAL REVIEW OF PHARMACOLOGY

ANNUAL REVIEW OF PHYSICAL CHEMISTRY – Palo Alto. cum index 8-15; v1-48 1950-* 1; v18-48 1967-* 5; v23-48 1972- 9 – 1,5,9 – D5087 – us UMI [540]

ANNUAL REVIEW OF PHYSIOLOGY – v. 1-19. 1939-1957 – 1,5,6 – us Princeton Micro [612]

ANNUAL REVIEW OF PHYSIOLOGY – Palo Alto. cum index 21-26 1959-1964; v1-59 1939- 1; v29-59 1967-* 5; v34-59 1972- 9 – 1,5,9 – D5088 – us UMI [612]

ANNUAL REVIEW OF PHYTOPATHOLOGY – Palo Alto. v1-35 1963-; v5-35 1967-* 5,9 – 1,5,9 – D5900 – us UMI [580]

ANNUAL REVIEW OF PLANT PHYSIOLOGY – v1-8. 1950-57 – 1,5,6 – us Princeton Micro [580]

ANNUAL REVIEW OF PLANT PHYSIOLOGY – (Cont by: Annual Review of Plant Physiology and Plant Molecular Biology) – Palo Alto. v1-38 1950-87 1; v18-38 1967-87* 5; v21-38 1970-87 9 – 1,5,9 – D5089 – us UMI [574]

ANNUAL REVIEW OF PLANT PHYSIOLOGY *see* ANNUAL REVIEW OF PLANT PHYSIOLOGY AND PLANT MOLECULAR BIOLOGY

ANNUAL REVIEW OF PLANT PHYSIOLOGY AND PLANT MOLECULAR BIOLOGY – (Cont: Annual Review of Plant Physiology) – Palo Alto. v39-48. 1988- – 1,5*,9 – D5089.01 – us UMI [574]

ANNUAL REVIEW OF PLANT PHYSIOLOGY AND PLANT MOLECULAR BIOLOGY *see* ANNUAL REVIEW OF PLANT PHYSIOLOGY

ANNUAL REVIEW OF PSYCHOLOGY – v1-8. 1950-57 – 1,5,6 – us Princeton Micro [073]

ANNUAL REVIEW OF PSYCHOLOGY – Palo Alto. cum index 11-15 1960-64; v1-48 1950- 1; v18-48 1967-* 5; v23-48 1972- 9 – 1,5,9 – D5090 – us UMI [150]

ANNUAL REVIEW OF PUBLIC HEALTH – Palo Alto. v1-18. 1980- – 1,5,9 – D12725 – us UMI [360]

ANNUAL REVIEW OF SOCIOLOGY – Palo Alto. v1-23. 1975- – 1,5*,9 – D11810 – us UMI [301]

ANNUAL REVIEW OF THE DEVELOPMENT PLAN, 1953 / Somaliland – Hargeisa. 1954. BD-549 1 – 9 – ne IDC [338]

ANNUAL REVIEW OF THE DEVELOPMENT PLAN, 1954 / Somaliland – Hargeisa. 1955 – 9 – ne IDC [338]

ANNUAL REVIEW OF THE FIVE YEAR DEVELOPMENT PLAN; THE DEVELOPMENT BUDGET / Sudan. Finance Department – 1v. 1947-48. BNE-7633 1 – 9 – ne IDC [336]

ANNUAL REVIEW OF THE SOCIAL SCIENCES OF RELIGION – v1-6. 1977-82. Ceased publication – 1 – us UMI [300]

ANNUAL REVIEW OF THE SOCIAL SCIENCES OF RELIGION – (Ceased publ) – The Hague. v1-6. 1977-82* – 1 – D15464 – us UMI [230]

ANNUAL RING / Louisiana State University. Agricultural Experiment Station. School of Forestry and Wildlife Management – 1973-77.1 reel – 1,5 – us Spaulding [630]

ANNUAL SCHOOL REPORTS / Ottawa County. Ohio. Auditor – 1840-1866 – 1r – 1 – $32.50r – us Archival [324]

ANNUAL SERMONS AND REPORTS / Society for the Propagation of the Gospel – 1701-1845 – 1 – uk Microform Academic [240]

ANNUAL SINGLE NUMBERS SERIES ALPHABETICAL INDEX / Genealogical Society of the Northern Territory – (File E104; Index numbers 2647-3267) – 1965-1969 – 9 – A$15.00 – item 32 – at G.S.N.T. [020]

ANNUAL SINGLE NUMBERS SERIES ALPHABETICAL INDEX / Genealogical Society of the Northern Territory – (File E104; Index numbers 3268-3681) – 1969-1976 – 9 – A$10.00 – item 33 – at G.S.N.T. [020]

ANNUAL SINGLE NUMBERS SERIES ALPHABETICAL INDEX / Genealogical Society of the Northern Territory – (File NTRS F404; Index Nos 78/001-79/233, 80/001-80/129) – 1979-1980 – 9 – A$10.00 – item 36 – at G.S.N.T. [020]

ANNUAL SINGLE NUMBERS SERIES ALPHABETICAL INDEX / Genealogical Society of the Northern Territory – (File NTRS-F404; Index No 81/001-81/083, 82/001-82/081, 83/001-83/098) – 1981-1983 – 9 – A$10.00 – item 37 – at G.S.N.T. [020]

ANNUAL SINGLE NUMBERS SERIES ALPHABETICAL INDEX / Genealogical Society of the Northern Territory – (File NTRS-F404; Index Nos 77/001-77/232, 78/001-78/217) – 1977-1978 – 9 – A$15.00 – item 35 – at G.S.N.T. [020]

ANNUAL SINGLE NUMBERS SERIES ALPHABETICAL INDEX / Genealogical Society of the Northern Territory – (Index Nos 84/001-84/105, 85/001-85/086, 86/001-86/094) – 1984-1986 – 9 – A$10.00 – item 38 – at G.S.N.T. [020]

ANNUAL SINGLE NUMBERS SERIES ALPHABETICAL INDEX, 1948-1958 : FILE E103-E104. INDEX NUMBERS 1317 TO 1980 – 1992 – A$10.00 – 0-949124-73-7 – item 30 – at G.S.N.T. [020]

ANNUAL SINGLE NUMBERS SERIES ALPHABETICAL INDEX, 1971-1976 : FILE E105 – (Index No: 71/001-71/004, 72/001-72/091, 73/001-73/195, 1974 Cyclone Tracey, 75/001-75/123, 76/001-76/200) – 1992 – A$10.00 – 0-949124-77-X – at G.S.N.T. [020]

ANNUAL SINGLE NUMBERS SERIES ALPHABETICAL INDEX, 1987-1989 – (Index Nos: 87/001-87/102, 88/001-88/112, 89/001-89/102) – 1993 – A$10.00 – 0-949124-68-0 – at G.S.N.T. [020]

ANNUAL SINGLE NUMBERS SERIES ALPHABETICAL INDEX, 1990-1991 – (Index Nos: 90/001-90/136, 91/001-91/149) – 1993 – A$10.00 – at G.S.N.T. [020]

ANNUAL STATEMENT OF FOREIGN TRADE, 1919-1961 / Egypt. Statistical Department – (lacking 1927, 1930, 1935(1), 1936(1), 1937(1), 1950 51. BNE-4677 1 – 9 – ne IDC [310]

ANNUAL STATEMENT OF THE OVERSEAS TRADE OF THE UNITED KINGDOM 1853-1975 – (Jan-june, oct-dec 1940 + 1941-43 not publ. Coll title: British Government Publications...1801-1977, Foreign Trade) – 1854/55-1979 – 95r – 1 (£15,875.00 foreign trade set of 220r + 824mf) – uk Chadwyck [380]

ANNUAL STATEMENT OF THE TRADE AND COMMERCE OF ST. LOUIS – St Louis: St Louis Merchants' Exchange etc, [1865-1923] – 1 – us Res Libr [380]

ANNUAL STATISTICAL BULLETIN / Organization of Petroleum Exporting Countries – 1966-77 – 1 – 40.00 – us L of C Photodup [330]

ANNUAL STATISTICAL REPORT / New York Produce Exchange – New York. 1902-1929 – 1 – us NY Public [073]

ANNUAL STATISTICAL REPORTS / Putnam County. Ohio. Board of Education – 1915-1928 – 1r – 1 – $32.50r – us Archival [324]

ANNUAL STATISTICAL REPORTS / Putnam County. Ohio. Common Pleas. Civil Division – 1892-1907 – 1r – 1 – $32.50r – us Archival [324]

ANNUAL STATISTICAL SURVEY OF THE ELECTRONICS INDUSTRY 1969, 1970, 1972-1974 – (Coll title: British Government Publications...1801-1977, Electronics) – 7mf – 9 – £60.00 – uk Chadwyck [338]

ANNUAL SUMMARY 1975/76-1989/90 / Hong Kong. Education Department – Hong Kong – 29mf – 9 – DE-144/1 – ne IDC [370]

ANNUAL SYNOD MINUTES AND JOURNALS : TOGETHER WITH MISCELLANEOUS CORRESPONDENCE / Australasia. Methodist Missionary Society. Fiji District – 1854-1945; 1869-99 – 4r – 1 – PMB 1138 – at Pacific Mss [240]

THE ANNUAL VOLUNTEER AND SERVICE MILITIA LIST OF CANADA / Canada. Departement de la Milice – Ottawa: Printed by G.E. Desbarats, 1866. SEM105P319 – 2mf – 9 – Can$4.50 – cn Bibl Nat [355]

ANNUAL WHEAT NEWSLETTER / Kansas. State University. Agricultural Experiment Station – nos.1-25. 1955-79 – 1,5,6 – us Spaulding [630]

ANNUALS / Arkansas Central Baptist Associations – 1919-80. Lacks 1926, 1927, 1936. 2302p – 1 – 109.00 – us Baptist [240]

ANNUALS = BAPTIST ASSOCIATION. TEXAS : DISTRICT THIRTEEN – 1954-1963 – 1r – 1 – $16.40 – us Baptist [240]

ANNUALS = BAPTIST ASSOCIATIONS. CALIFORNIA : PACIFIC – 1984-1987 – 1r – 1 – $12.40 – us Baptist [240]

ANNUALS / Baptist Associations. Flint River. Alabama – 1814-66. 352p – 1 – us Baptist [240]

ANNUALS / Baptist Associations. Illinois. Saline – 1955-1990 – 1 reel – 1 – $83.68 – us Baptist [240]

ANNUALS = BAPTIST ASSOCIATIONS. KENTUCKY : LITTLE BETHEL – 1979-1987 – 1r – 1 – $26.08 – us Baptist [240]

ANNUALS / Baptist Associations. Kentucky. Blood River – 1969-1990 – 1 reel – 1 – $57.20 – us Baptist [240]

ANNUALS / Baptist Associations. Kentucky. Greenup – 1959-1990 – 1 reel – 1 – $80.88 – us Baptist [240]

ANNUALS = BAPTIST ASSOCIATIONS. LOUISIANA : ASCENSION – 1959-1989 – 1r – 1 – $49.52 – us Baptist [240]

ANNUALS = BAPTIST ASSOCIATIONS. LOUISIANA : BAYOU MACON – 1951-1988 – 1r – 1 – $70.49 – us Baptist [240]

ANNUALS = BAPTIST ASSOCIATIONS. LOUISIANA : BEAUREGARD – 1955-1987 – 1r – 1 – $75.92 – us Baptist [240]

ANNUALS = BAPTIST ASSOCIATIONS. LOUISIANA : BIG CREEK – 1955, 1957-1987 – 1r – 1 – $64.88 – us Baptist [240]

ANNUALS = BAPTIST ASSOCIATIONS. LOUISIANA : BOSSIER – 1957-1969 – 1r – 1 – $20.32 – us Baptist [240]

ANNUALS = BAPTIST ASSOCIATIONS. LOUISIANA : CALDWELL – 1934-1991 – 1r – 1 – $84.32 – us Baptist [240]

ANNUALS = BAPTIST ASSOCIATIONS. LOUISIANA : CAREY – 1958-1989 – 1r – 1 – $86.00 – us Baptist [240]

ANNUALS = BAPTIST ASSOCIATIONS. LOUISIANA : CENTRAL LOUISIANA – 1956-1987 – 1r – 1 – $62.16 – us Baptist [240]

ANNUALS = BAPTIST ASSOCIATIONS. LOUISIANA : DEER CREEK – 1922, 1957-1991 – 1r – 1 – $79.04 – us Baptist [240]

ANNUALS = BAPTIST ASSOCIATIONS. LOUISIANA : DELTA – 1958-1991 – 1r – 1 – $55.28 – us Baptist [240]

ANNUALS = BAPTIST ASSOCIATIONS. LOUISIANA : EASTERN LOUISIANA – 1958-1990 – 1r – 1 – $56.48 – us Baptist [420]

ANNUALS = BAPTIST ASSOCIATIONS. LOUISIANA : LIBERTY – 1957-1973 – 1r – 1 – $31.84 – us Baptist [240]

ANNUALS = BAPTIST ASSOCIATIONS. LOUISIANA : LOUISIANA – 1955-1987 – 1r – 1 – $51.28 – us Baptist [240]

ANNUALS = BAPTIST ASSOCIATIONS. LOUISIANA : LUTHER RICE – 1951-1987 – 1r – 1 – $69.84 – us Baptist [240]

ANNUALS = BAPTIST ASSOCIATIONS. LOUISIANA : MADISON – 1958-1989 – 1r – 1 – $39.92 – us Baptist [240]

ANNUALS = BAPTIST ASSOCIATIONS. LOUISIANA : MOREHOUSE – 1955-1989 – 1r – 1 – $64.40 – us Baptist [240]

ANNUALS = BAPTIST ASSOCIATIONS. LOUISIANA : ST. TAMMANY – 1955, 1958-1987 – 1r – 1 – $61.84 – us Baptist [240]

ANNUALS = BAPTIST ASSOCIATIONS. LOUISIANA : VERNON – 1955-1987 – 1r – 1 – $62.72 – us Baptist [240]

ANNUALS = BAPTIST ASSOCIATIONS. LOUISIANA : WEBSTER-CLAIBORNE – 1958-1991 – 1r – 1 – $63.28 – us Baptist [240]

ANNUALS = BAPTIST ASSOCIATIONS. SOUTH CAROLINA : CHARLESTON – 1971-1986 – 1r – 1 – $45.36 – us Baptist [240]

ANNUALS = BAPTIST ASSOCIATIONS. SOUTH CAROLINA : CHARLESTON – 1987-1990 – 1r – 1 – $18.56 – us Baptist [240]

ANNUALS = BAPTIST ASSOCIATIONS. SOUTH CAROLINA : CHESTER – 1971-1991 – 1r – 1 – $153.76 – us Baptist [240]

ANNUALS = BAPTIST ASSOCIATIONS. SOUTH CAROLINA : CHESTERFIELD – 1971-1990 – 1r – 1 – $85.12 – us Baptist [240]

ANNUALS = BAPTIST ASSOCIATIONS. SOUTH CAROLINA : COLLETON – 1971-1981 – 1r – 1 – $24.24 – us Baptist [240]

ANNUALS = BAPTIST ASSOCIATIONS. SOUTH CAROLINA : COLLETON. UNION OF 1ST AND 2ND DIVISION – 1873-1878 – 1r – 1 – $5.00 – us Baptist [240]

ANNUALS / Baptist Associations. Tennesse. Sweetwater/Eastanalle – 1830-1884 – 1 reel – 1 – $16.56 – us Baptist [240]

ANNUALS / Baptist Associations. Tennessee. Big Hatchie – 1981-1987 – 1 reel – 1 – $14,64 – us Baptist [240]

ANNUALS / Baptist Associations. Tennessee. Concord – 1866, 1900, 1957-1979 – 1 reel – 1 – $58.32 – us Baptist [240]

ANNUALS = BAPTIST ASSOCIATIONS. TEXAS : DALLAS – 1980-1987 – 1r – 1 – $78.48 – us Baptist [240]

ANNUALS = BAPTIST ASSOCIATIONS. TEXAS : DISTRICT EIGHT – 1952, 1955-1963 – 1r – 1 – $58.32 – us Baptist [240]

ANNUALS = BAPTIST ASSOCIATIONS. TEXAS : DISTRICT ELEVEN – 1952, 1955-1964 – 1r – 1 – $58.40 – us Baptist [240]

ANNUALS = BAPTIST ASSOCIATIONS. TEXAS : DISTRICT FIFTEEN – 1957-1963 – 1r – 1 – $64.96 – us Baptist [240]

ANNUALS = BAPTIST ASSOCIATIONS. TEXAS : DISTRICT FIVE – 1947, 1952, 1955-1963 – 1r – 1 – $90.16 – us Baptist [240]

ANNUALS = BAPTIST ASSOCIATIONS. TEXAS : DISTRICT FOUR – 1952-1964 – 1r – 1 – $91.44 – us Baptist [240]

ANNUALS = BAPTIST ASSOCIATIONS. TEXAS : DISTRICT FOURTEEN – 1953-1963 – 1r – 1 – $86.16 – us Baptist [240]

ANNUALS = BAPTIST ASSOCIATIONS. TEXAS : DISTRICT NINE – 1955-1963 – 1r – 1 – $66.64 – us Baptist [240]

ANNUALS = BAPTIST ASSOCIATIONS. TEXAS : DISTRICT SEVEN – 1955-1962 – 1r – 1 – $24.00 – us Baptist [240]

ANNUALS = BAPTIST ASSOCIATIONS. TEXAS : DISTRICT SEVENTEEN – 1955-1964 – 1r – 1 – $11.20 – us Baptist [240]

ANNUALS = BAPTIST ASSOCIATIONS. TEXAS : DISTRICT SIX – 1951-1962 – 1r – 1 – $64.24 – us Baptist [240]

ANNUALS = BAPTIST ASSOCIATIONS. TEXAS : DISTRICT SIXTEEN – 1952, 1955-1963 – 1r – 1 – $79.20 – us Baptist [240]

ANNUALS = BAPTIST ASSOCIATIONS. TEXAS : DISTRICT TEN – 1952-1963 – 1r – 1 – $61.84 – us Baptist [240]

ANNUALS = BAPTIST ASSOCIATIONS. TEXAS : DISTRICT THREE – 1948-1964 – 1r – 1 – $21.92 – us Baptist [240]

ANNUALS = BAPTIST ASSOCIATIONS. TEXAS : DISTRICT TWO – 1956-1963 – 1r – 1 – $7.20 – us Baptist [420]

ANNUALS = BAPTIST ASSOCIATIONS. TEXAS : FRIO RIVER – 1963-1988 – 1r – 1 – $56.08 – us Baptist [240]

ANNUALS = BAPTIST ASSOCIATIONS. TEXAS 1090 DISTRICT ONE – 1952-1963 – 1r – 1 – $20.48 – us Baptist [240]

ANNUALS = BAPTIST ASSOCIATIONS. TEXAS BMA : NAVOSTA RIVER – 1970-1989 – 1r – 1 – $21.28 – us Baptist [420]

ANNUALS / Baptist Associations. Utah-Idaho, Treasure Valley – 1977-88.Continues: Boise Valley. 568p – 1 – 22.72; apply – us Baptist [073]

ANNUALS = BAPTIST STATE CONVENTIONS. (SOUTHERN BAPTIST) : DISTRICT OF COLUMBIA – Oct. 1906-Mar. 1921 – 1r – 1 – $21.68 – us Baptist [240]

ANNUALS / Baptist Woman's Missionary Union. Auxiliary to Southern Baptist Convention – 1889-1978 – 1 – 308.84 – us Baptist [240]

ANNUALS / Big Hatchie. Tennessee. Baptist Associations – 1976-80. 378p – 1 – us Baptist [240]

ANNUALS / Black Baptist Convention – ((American Baptist Missionary Convention, 1842, 1852-54, 1857-60, 1869, 1871-72, 1877, 1879; The American National Baptist Convention, 1889-91, National Baptist Educational Convention, 1892; National Baptist Convention, 1897-1905, 1907-12, 1914-15)) – 1842-1975 – 1 – 1587.00 – us Baptist [240]

ANNUALS / Florida. Baptist Associations – Chipola, 1925-79; Formerly Jackson County -name changed 1946. 2380p – 0010 1979-80. 1134p – us Baptist [240]

ANNUALS / Missouri Primitive Baptist Associations – Cuivre Siloam 1879, 1892-93, 1913; Nodway 1939; Salem 1939; Two River 1939. 790p – 1 – us Baptist [240]

ANNUALS / Montgomery. Maryland. Baptist Associations – 1969-80. 756p – 1 – us Baptist [240]

ANNUALS / National Baptist Convention – 1897-1905, 1907-12, 1914-15 – 1 – 173.95 – us Baptist [240]

ANNUALS / National Baptist Convention of America, Unincorporated – 1916-17, 1920-30, 1938, 1950, 1952-73, 1975 – 1 – 375.20 – us Baptist [240]

ANNUALS / National Baptist Convention. U.S.A., Inc – 1916-75 – 1 – 943.07 – us Baptist ·[240]

ANNUALS / New Mexico Baptist Convention – 206p – 1 – us Baptist [240]

ANNUALS / North Carolina Negro Associations – 1 – 470.12 – us Baptist [240]

ANNUALS / Oklahoma Baptist Associations – 40,944p – 1 – us Baptist [240]

ANNUALS / Southern Baptist Convention – 1845-1984. Includes index, 1845-1965 – 1 – 2456.50 – us Baptist [240]

ANNUALS / Tennessee. Baptist Associations – (Nashville, 1977-78. 264p. 1. Sweetwater, 1882-90, 1893. 158p. 1) – Jefferson County: 1971-80. 744p – 1 – us Baptist [240]

ANNUALS / Tennessee Baptist Missionary and Educational Convention – 1974-76 – 1 – 7.35 – us Baptist [240]

ANNUALS / Tennessee. Central. Baptist Associations – (Grainger County, 1972-78. 372p. 1) – 1958-78. 790p – 1 – us Baptist [240]

ANNUARIO / Conservatorio di Musica Luigi Cherubini. Florence – v1-10 1898-1913/14 – 1 – $23.00 – us L of C Photodup [780]

ANNUARIO DEL R. ISTITUTO BOTANICO DI ROMA / ed by Pirotta, R – Milano, Pisa, 1885-1901. v1-10 – 39mf – 9 – 8591/1 – ne IDC [570]

ANNUARIO DELLA R. STAZIONE DI PATOLOGIA VEGETALE DI ROMA : RICERCHE SULLE MALATTIE DELLE PIANTE / ed by Cuboni, G – Modena, 1901. v1 – 3mf – 9 – 7467/1 – ne IDC [570]

ANNUARIO DELL'AFRICA ITALIANA E DELLE ISOLE ITALIANE DELL'EGEO / Instituto fascista dell'Africa italiana. Roma – Roma: Societa an. tipografica Castaldi. v13-14. 1938/39-1940 – 1 – us Res Libr [960]

ANNUARIO DELLE COLONIE ITALIANE E DEI PAESI VICINI / Instituto coloniale fascista. Roma – Roma: Societa an. tipografica Castaldi. v3-10. 1928-35 – 1 – us Res Libr [960]

ANNUARIO DELL'IMPERO ITALIANO / Instituto coloniale fascista. Roma – Roma: Societa an. tipografica Castaldi. v12. 1937 – 1 – us Res Libr [960]

ANNUARIO STATISTICO ITALIANO / Italy. Direzione Generale Della Statistica – v. 1-22. 1878-1926. (1-2 serie) – 1 – 180.00 – us L of C Photodup [945]

ANNULUSA JAVANICA, OR AN ATTEMPT TO ILLUSTRATE THE NATURAL AFFINITIES AND ANALOGIES OF THE INSECTS COLLECTED IN JAVA BY T. HORSFIELD... / Macleay, W S – London, 1825. xii/50p. 1 pl. – 3mf – 9 – ne IDC [590]

ANNULUSA JAVANICA, OU DESCRIPTION DES INSECTES DE JAVA... / Macleay, W S – Paris, 1833 iv/163p. 5 pls. – 4mf – 9 – ne IDC [590]

O ANNUNCIADOR COMMERCIAL : ORGAO DE TODOS EM TODA PARTE – Manaos, Amazonas. 8-11 Jul 1899 – 1,5,6 – bl Biblioteca [072]

Annunzio, Gabriele d' *see* TRAGEDIE, SOGNI E MISTERI, DI GABRIELE D'ANNUNZIO

AN-NUR – En Nour. Alger. n1-78. 1931-33 – 1 – fr A.C.R.P.P. [073]

ANNUS 1-5, HISTORICO-NATURALIS / Scopoli, Giovanni Antonio – Lipsiae: C.G. Hilscheri, 1760-1762. 5v in 1. 10 fiches. (Science Collection) – 9 – $25.00 – fr Bibl Nationale [574]

ANNUS BOTANICUS / Wallroth, C F W – Halae. 1815. B-6484 2 – 8 – ne IDC [580]

ANNUS ECCLESIASTICUS GRAECORUM-SLAVICUS 1863 / Martinow, J – Bruxelles, 1963 – 14mf – 8 – Dfl49.00 – ne Slangenburg [240]

UN ANO DE ACCION SINDICAL EN LA PROVINCIA / Anton Crespo, Emilio – Badajoz: Graficas Jimenez, 1964 – sp Bibl Santa Ana [946]

UN ANO DE ACCION SINDICAL EN LA PROVINCIA DE BADAJOZ / Anton Crespo, Emilio – Imp. Inca, 1966 – sp Bibl Santa Ana [946]

UN ANO DE VIDA SERRADILLANA POR UN AMANTE DE SERRADILLA / Sanchez Rodrigo, Agustin – Serradilla (Caceres): Imp. de el Cronista, s.a. – 9 – sp Bibl Santa Ana [910]

EL ANO METEOROLOGICO 1879 / Fuertes Acevedo, Maximo – 1880 – 9 – $1.50f – sp Bibl Santa Ana [550]

EL ANO METEOROLOGICO 1881 / Fuertes Acevedo, Maximo – 1882 – 9 – $1.50f – sp Bibl Santa Ana [550]

EL ANO PEDAGOGICO HISPANOAMERICANO / Bayle, Constantino – Madrid: Razon y Fe, 1921 – 1 – sp Bibl Santa Ana [370]

Anofriev, N I *see* RUSSKAIA OKHOTNICH'IA BIBLIOTEKA

ANOKA HERALD – Anoka, NE. -w. Mar. 1903-Feb. 1909. Incomplete – 1 – us NE Hist [071]

Anokhina, A V *see* DEISTVUIUSHCHIE RASPORIAZHENIIA PO KOMMUNALNOMU KHOZIAISTVU

LES ANOMALIES CHEZ L'HOMME ET LES MAMMIFERES; PREF. PAR...CAMILLE DARESTE / Blanc, Louis – Paris: Bailliere, 1893 – 1 – F183.12 – fr Armell [574]

Anonimo *see* GRANDES DE ESPANA. PRIMERA SERIE

DER ANONIMO MORELLIANO / Frimmel, Theodor – O-517. 1888 – 9 – ne IDC [760]

ANOTHER CONSERVATIVE CATHOLIC DISAPPOINTED WITH REBELS – n.p., n.d. Fiche W 720. (Blodgett Collection of Spanish Civil War Pamphlets) – 9 – us H.U. College Libr [946]

ANOTHER MOTHER FOR PEACE – 1967-75 – 4mf – 9 – $50.00 – us UPA [320]

Anotnii *see* RAZGOVOR "PRAVOSLAVNAGO I PASHKOVTSA O SVYASHCHENNOM PISANII I PREDANIYAKH TSERKOVNYKH"

ANQ – v1-4 jan 1988-91* 1; n5-10 jan 1992-oct 1997+ 1,9; n5-7 jan 1992-oct 1994*. n8-10 Win 1995-oct 1997+ 5 – 1,5,9 – D18628 – us UMI [073]

Anquez, L *see* HISTOIRE DES ASSEMBLEES POLITIQUES DES REFORMES DE FRANCE, 1573-1622

EL ANRAH AND ABYDOS (MEES VOL 23) / Randall-Maciver, D & Mace, A C – London, 1903 – 10mf – 8 – Dfl35.00 – ne Slangenburg [930]

Anrich, Gustav *see*
- DIE ANFAENGE DES HEILIGENKULTS IN DER CHRISTLICHEN KIRCHE
- DAS ANTIKE MYSTERIENWESEN IN SEINEM EINFLUSS AUF DAS CHRISTENTUM
- MARTIN BUCER

ANS : ADVANCES IN NURSING SCIENCE – Gaithersburg. v1-20. oct 1978-jun 1998+ – 1,5,9 – D12727 – us UMI [610]

ANS (AMERICAN NUCLEAR SOCIETY) – Standards. Printed index. Updated every 60 days – 6,9 – us Info Handling [621]

Ansah, Paul et al *see* RURAL JOURNALISM IN AFRICA

Ansaldi, C F *see*
- DELLE SUCCESSIONI NEL DIRITTO INTERNAZIONALE CIVILE ITALIANO
- DELL'ESECUTORIETA IN ITALIA DELLE SENTENZE STRANIERE DI DIVORZIO

ANSARI – Delhi, India. Oct 1942-Apr 1950 – 14r – 1 – us L of C Photodup [072]

ANSBACHER MORGENBLATT – Ansbach, 1848-49 – 1 – Dist. gw Mikrofilm – gw Misc Inst [943]

DIE ANSCHAUUNG AUGUSTINS UEBER CHRISTI PERSON UND WERK : UNTER BERUECKSICHTIGUNG IHRER VERSCHIEDENEN ENTWICKLUNGSSTUFEN UND IHRER DOGMENGESCHICHTLICHEN STELLUNG / Scheel, Otto – Tuebingen: J.C.B. Mohr, 1901 – 2mf – us A.T.L.A. [240]

DIE ANSCHAUUNGEN DER PROPHETEN VON DER SITTLICHKEIT / Wiener, Max – Berlin: Mayer & Mueller, 1909. 1 fiche – 9 – us A.T.L.A. [240]

AIN ANSCHLAG WIE MAN DEM TUERCKE WIDERSTAND THUN MAG... – N.p., 1522 – 1mf – 9 – H-8137/1 – ne IDC [956]

ANSCHLUSS MOVEMENT PAMPHLET COLLECTION – 1938? – 1 – CSUXANQ2294-B – us Hoover Inst Photo [943]

Ansell, David Abraham *see* IMPERIAL FEDERATION: WELDING THE LINKS OF UNION

Anselmi Cantuar, S *see* ARCHIEPISC. OPERA OMNIA

ANSELMO ENTERPRISE – Anselmo, NE. -w. Mar. 1908-Feb. 1914; Mar. 1915-Apr. 1915; Jan. 1918-Mar. 1947 – 1 – us NE Hist [071]

ANSGAR LUTHERAN – (Merged with: Lutheran Herald to form Lutheran Standard. Lacking some pgs) – v1-33. 14 Dec 1927-1960 – 17r – 1 – ATLA S0288 – us A.T.L.A. [073]

ANSGAR LUTHERAN *see* LUTHERAN STANDARD

Anshary, Muhammed Isa *see*
- FALSAFAH PERDJUANG ISLAM
- FALSAFAH PERDUANGAN ISLAM

ANSI (AMERICAN NATIONAL STANDARDS INSTITUTE) – Only those standards written and copyrighted by ANSI are provided. 9 sections. Printed index. Updated every 60 days – 6,9 – us Info Handling [380]

ANSI. REPORTER / American National Standards Institute – (1973- . 5,6. 1975- . 9) – 1967- – 1 – us UMI [380]

ANSICHTEN UEBER AESTHETIK UND LITERATUR : SEINE BRIEFE AN CHRISTIAN GOTTFRIED KOERNER (1793-1830) / Humboldt, Wilhelm, Freiherr von; ed by Jonas, F – (Includes index) – Berlin: L Schleiermacher, 1880 – 1r – 1 – us U.W. Library [840]

ANSLEY HERALD – Ansley, NE. -w. Mar. 1892; Dec. 1892; Aug. 1895-Jan. 1898; May 1898-Dec. 1898. Incomplete; Apr. 1900-Feb. 1902. Incomplete; Aug. 1902-Apr. 1913; Jul. 1915- – 1 – us NE Hist [071]

Anson, Adelbert *see* THE CONSOLIDATION OF THE CHURCH IN CANADA: A PLEA FOR A GENERAL SYNOD WITH LEGISLATIVE POWERS, FROM THE NORTH-WEST:..

Anson, P *see* KARATELNYE EKSPEDITSII V PRIBALTIISKOM KRAEV 1905-1907 GG

Anson, Wiliam Reynell *see* BALLADS EN TERMES DE LA LEY

Anson, William *see* PRINCIPLES OF THE ENGLISH LAW OF CONTRACT AND OF AGENCY

Anspach, L *see* DES SOCIETES ANONYMES EN DROIT INTERNATIONAL PRIVE

Anspach, Ralph *see* MONETARY ASPECTS OF INDONESIA'S ECONOMIC REORGANIZATION IN 1959

ANSPRACHEN FUER CHRISTLICHE MUETTERVEREINE / Leinz, Anton – 2., verb Aufl. Freiburg i.B.: Herder, [1912?] – 1mf – 9 – 0-8370-7232-8 – 1986-1232 – us A.T.L.A. [240]

Anstadt, P *see*
- LIFE AND TIMES OF REV. S.S. SCHMUCKER
- LUTHER, ZINZENDORF, WESLEY

Ansted, David Thomas *see* STARS AND THE EARTH

Anstey, H *see* MUNIMENTA ACADEMICA

ANSTOESSE – 1954-88 (complete) – 5r – 1 – ATLA S0559 – us A.T.L.A. [073]

ANSWER OF THE GREAT CHURCH OF CONSTANTINOPLE TO THE PAPAL ENCYCLICAL ON UNION : IN THE ORIGINAL GREEK WITH AN ENGLISH TRANSLATION / ed by Metallinos, Eustathius – Constantinople (Ecumenical patriarchate). Patriarch (1895-1897 : Anthimos VII) [s.l. : s.n.], [1896?] (Oxford: Horace Hart) – 1mf – us A.T.L.A. [240]

ANSWER TO HUGH MILLER AND THEORETIC GEOLOGISTS / Davies, Thomas Alfred – New York:Rudd & Carlton, 1860 – 1mf – 9 – 0-8370-2843-4 – 1985-0843 – us A.T.L.A. [210]

ANSWER TO MR. BINNEY'S REPLY TO "REMARKS" ON HIS TREATISE ON THE HABEAS CORPUS / Wharton, George Mifflin – Philadelphia, Campbell, 1862. 8 p. LL-1646 – 1 – us L of C Photodup [340]

AN ANSWER TO RICHARD ALLEN'S ESSAY / Claridge, R – London, 1697 – 1 – us Baptist [240]

AN ANSWER TO RICHARD ALLEN'S ESSAY / Claridge, R – London. 1697 – 1 – $5.00 – us Baptist [240]

AN ANSWER TO SOME CAPITAL ERRORS CONTAINED IN MINUTES OF SOME LATE CONVERSATIONS BETWEEN THE REV. MR. WESLEY AND OTHERS PRINTED AT BRISTOL, 1770, BY JOHN WESLEY, M.A.,... / Hill, Richard – London, 1771 – 1mf – 9 – MP-472/1 – ne IDC [240]

AN ANSWER TO SOME STRICTURES IN BROWN'S SEQUEL TO CAMPBELL'S HISTORY OF YARMOUTH / Campbell, John Roy – McMillan, 1889. 02019. (Pre-1900 Canadiana) – 9 – cn C.I.H.M. [971]

AN ANSWER TO THE DECLARATION OF THE AMERICAN CONGRESS – Ed 5. London, 1776 – 2mf – 9 – ILM-877/1 – ne IDC [340]

AN ANSWER TO THE DIFFICULTIES IN BISHOP COLENSO'S BOOK ON THE PENTATEUCH / Turner, J B – 1863 – 9 – us A.T.L.A. [240]

AN ANSWER TO THE QUESTION, WHY ARE YOU A WESLEYAN METHODIST? / Peck, George – 18– – 9 – us A.T.L.A. [240]

AN ANSWER TO THE REV. MR. JOHN WESLEY'S LETTER TO WILLIAM, LORD BISHOP OF GLOUCESTER, CONCERNING THE CHARGES ALLEDGED AGAINST HIM AND HIS DOCTRINE IN A BOOK LATELY PUBLISHED ENTITLED 'THE DOCTRINE OF GRACE;... / Charndler, S – London, 1763 – 1mf – 9 – MP-423/1 – ne IDC [240]

ANSWERS TO THE QUESTIONS SUGGESTED BY THE REGENTS OF THE UNIVERSITY OF THE STATE OF NEW YORK, FOR THE EXAMINATION OF CANDIDATES FOR THE DEGREE OF BACHELOR OF LAWS. / Seabury, Samuel – New York, 1894. 36p. LL-1384 – 1 – us L of C Photodup [340]

ANSWERS TO VIRGINIA BAR EXAMINATIONS / Hairston, Samuel W – Richmond, Appeals Press, 1932 514 p. LL-895 – 1 – us L of C Photodup [340]

ANSWERS TO YOUR QUESTIONS ABOUT AMERICAN INDIANS / U.S. Bureau of Indian Affairs – 1970 – 9 – $5.00f – us Ross [970]

ANT. SAD. OPERA THEOLOGICA 1614 / Chandieu – 41mf – 8 – ne Slangenburg [290]

ANTALYA – Antalya. Sahib ve Muharriri: Mehmed Emin. No. 125 (31 Kanunisani 1339 [1923] – 9 – $20.00 – us MEDOC [956]

ANTALYA'DA ANADOLU – Antalya, 1920-19? – 9 – $20.00 – us MEDOC [956]

ANTANANVARIVO ANNUAL AND MADAGASCAR MAGAZINE – v1-6. 1875-78; v1-24. 1881-1900 (incomplete) – 1r – 1 – ATLA S0087 – us A.T.L.A. [073]

ANTANTA I VRANGEL : SBORNIK STATE I – Moskva: Gos. izd-vo, 1923- – 1 – CSUX88-B7147 – us Hoover Inst Photo [947]

ANTANTA, ROSSIIA I REVOLIUTSIIA / Bystrianskii, Vadim – Peterburg: Gos. izd-vo, 1920 – 1 – CSUX88-B5650 – us Hoover Inst Photo [947]

ANTARA – (Cologne Ed. in English). 1966- – 1 – us UMI [072]

ANTARA – Djakarta. Indonesia. (New York Edition). 1955-66 – 1 – us UMI [072]

ANTARA BERITA EKONOMI AND KEUANGAN – Djakarta. Indonesia. 1967-79 – 1 – us UMI [072]

ANTARA. ICHTISAR TAHUNAN – (Annual) – Djakarta, 1965-1969 – 74mf – 9 – SE-1314/1 – ne IDC [950]

Antara. (Indonesian National News Agency) *see* WEST IRIAN EXCERPTS FROM INDONESIAN NATIONAL NEWS AGENCY

ANTARA WEEKLY REVIEW – Djakarta. Indonesia. 1963- – 1 – us UMI [072]

ANTARCTIC JOURNAL OF THE UNITED STATES – Washington. v1-32 jan 1966-* 1; v7-32 jan 1972-* 5; v9-32 jan 1974-* 9 – 1,5,9 – D6289 – us UMI [073]

ANTE LOS OJOS DE AMERICA / Cipolletti, Emilio Domingo – Buenos Aires: Ediciones Justicia Social, [1947] – 1 – CSUXADQ2964-B – us Hoover Inst Photo [975]

ANTE TODO, ESPOSOS / Aradillas Agudo, Antonio – Madrid: Editorial La Muralla, 1969 – sp Bibl Santa Ana [240]

ANTECEDENTES DA LEGISLACAO SOCIAL ARGENTINA – [Buenos Aires?: Servico Internacional de Publica coes Argentinas, 1952] – 1 – CSUXADQ0650-B – us Hoover Inst Photo [340]

ANTECEDENTES HISPANO-MEDIOEVALES DE LA POESIA TRADICIONAL ARGENTINA / Carrizo, Juan Alfonso – 1945 – 1 – us I.U. Libraries [440]

ANTECEDENTES HISTORICOS DE LA SUBVERSION UNIVERSAL / Torrente Ballester, Gonzalo – Barcelona, 1939. Fiche W1231. (Blodgett Collection of Spanish Civil War Pamphlets) – 9 – us H.U. College Libr [946]

L'ANTECHRIST / Renan, Ernest – 3d ed. 1873 – 1 – us A.T.L.A. [240]

ANTECKNINGAR TILL EN MONOGRAFI OEFVER VAEXTFAMILJEN VALERIANEAE. 1. VALERIANELLA HALL / Krok, T OBN – (kongl. Svenska Vetenskap-Akad. Handlingar, 1864, 1866), v. 5, nr. 1). Stockholm. 1864. B-6443 2 – 8 – ne IDC [580]

THE ANTEDILUVIAN HISTORY, AND NARRATIVE OF THE FLOOD : AS SET FORTH IN THE EARLY PORTIONS OF THE BOOK OF GENESIS / Rendell, E D – (Includes bibliographical references and index) – 2nd rev ed. London: F Pitman, [1864?] – 1mf – 9 – 0-8370-4839-7 – 1985-2839 – us A.T.L.A. [220]

DER ANTEIL DES VOLKES AN DER MESSLITURGIE IM FRANKENREICHE / Nickl, Georg – Innsbruck, 1930 – 2mf – 8 – Dfl9.00 – ne Slangenburg [240]

ANTELOPE COUNTY EAGLE – Neligh, NE. -w. Jan-Jul 1881 – 1 – us NE Hist [071]

ANTELOPE HERALD – Antelope, OR. -w. 8 Jul 1892-3 Sept 1909. 1 roll – 1 – us U.O. Library [071]

ANTELOPE TRIBUNE – Neligh, NE. -w. Oct 1879-Nov 1882; Feb 1883-Mar 1897 – 1 – us NE Hist [071]

ANTELOPE VALLEY – 1992- – 3+ r – 1 – $150.00 – P00005 – us Library Micro [910]

ANTELOPE VALLEY PRESS – (Also known as: Palmdale Reporter) – Antelope Valley, CA. 1927-33; Jan-Aug 1935; 1936-38; 1940-47; 1949-66; 1966-67; 1967- – 228+ r – 1 – $11,400.00 ($250.00y) – H03269 – us Library Micro [071]

ANTELOPE VALLEY PRESS *see* LEDGER GAZETTE

Anteneh, Berhanu *see* DAIRY MARKETING IN ETHIOPIA

ANTENNA – (v72- , 1975- . 5,6,9) – v. 1-. 1928- – 1 – us UMI [380]

ANTENNES : LA REVUE QUEBECOISE DES COMMUNICATIONS / Quebec. (Province). Ministere des communications. Service des communications – Quebec. v1-6. 1976-81. SEM16P227 – 1r – 5 – Can$21.00 – cn Bibl Nat [380]

Antes, J *see* TRIOS (S VLN, VC)...OP. 3

ANTHEM COLLECTION – (Contains anthems by Blow, Humphrey, Gibbons and Purcell) – Ms, 17th century – 1 – us Sibley [780]

ANTHEMS / Wesley, Samuel – 1853 – 1 – uk Microform Academic [240]

L'ANTHICHAMBRE OU LES VALETS CHEZ EUX / Dupaty & Dalayrac, Nicolas – French Theatre Series. Paris. Mme Masson. 1808 – 9 – fr Hachette [820]

ANTHILL – (Cont: The Tongue) – Irvine, CA: UC Irvine, 1966-77 – 1r – 1 – $50.00 – R02308 – us Library Micro [370]

ANTHILL *see* THE TONGUE

THE ANTHILL *see* NEW UNIVERSITY

ANTHOLOGIA GRAECA CARMINUM CHRISTIANORUM / Christ, W & Paranikas, M – Lipsiae, 1871 – 7mf – 8 – ne Slangenburg [240]

ANTHOLOGIA GRAECA: SELECTA EPIGRAMMATA GRAECA LATINE UERSA, EX SEPTEM EPIGRAMMATUM GRAECORUM LIBRIS; ACCESSERUNT...EPIGRAMMATA, RECENS UERSA, AB ANDREA ALICIATO, OTTOMARO LUSCINIO, AC IANO CORNARIO ZUICCAUIENSI / ed by Janus Cornarius – Basilaea ex aedivs Io. Bebelii, mense, n.d. – 1 – us U.W. Library [949]

ANTHOLOGIA HIBERNICA – (Also known as: Monthly Collections of Science, Belle Lettres, and History.) v. 1-4. 1793-1794 – 1,5,6 – us Princeton Micro [500]

ANTHOLOGIE AUS DEN WERKEN VON ERNST MORITZ ARNDT : MIT DER BIBLIOGRAPHIE UND DEM PORTRAET DES VERFASSERS / Arndt, Ernst Moritz – (With: Anthologie aus den Werken von Johann Gottlieb Fichte) – Hildburghausen, New York: Verlag des Bibliographischen Instituts, [18–?] – 1r – 1 – us U.W. Library [943]

ANTHOLOGIE AUS DEN WERKEN VON JOHANN GOTTLIEB FICHTE : MIT DER BIOGRAPHIE DES VERFASSERS / Fichte, Johann Gottlieb – (With: Anthologie aus den Werken von Ernst Moritz Arndt) – Hildburghausen, New York: Verlag des Bibliographischen Instituts, 18–? – 1r – 1 – us U.W. Library [943]

L'ANTHOLOGIE DU FOLKLORE MUSICAL D'ESPAGUE / Garcia Matos, Manuel – Madrid: Hispavor, s.a., 1960 – 1 – sp Bibl Santa Ana [790]

ANTHOLOGIE FRANCOISE / Poulain, I – 1614 – 9 – fr I.C.S. [800]

ANTHOLOGIE JAPONAISE. POESIES ANCIENNES ET MODERNES DES INSULAIRES DU NIPPON / Rosny, Leon de – Traduction du japonais. Paris: Maisonneuve. 1871 – 9 – $10.00 – fr Orientalistes [800]

AN ANTHOLOGY OF MODERN ARABIC POETRY / Megally, Shafik – Zug, 1974. BNE-383/1 – 9 – ne IDC [810]

Anthonioz-Russel, S *see* L'ABRI DE SUCUPIRA: UN SITE D'ART RUPESTRE DE LA REGION DE LA SERRA DO CIPO, MINAS GERAIS, BRESIL

Anthonioz-Russel S et al *see* LES OEUVRES RUPESTRES DU MASSIF DE CERCA GRANDE, REGION DE LAGOA SANTA, MINAS GERAIS, BRESIL

Anthonioz-Russel, S et al *see* LES OEUVRES RUPESTRES DU MASSIF DE CAETANO, REGION DE LAGOA SANTA, MINAS GERAIS, BRESIL

Anthony, Alfred Williams *see*
- AN INTRODUCTION TO THE LIFE OF JESUS
- INTRODUCTION TO THE LIFE OF JESUS: AN INVESTIGATION OF THE HISTORICAL SOURCES

Anthony and Co. *see*
- DESCRIPTIVE CATALOG AND PRICE LIST OF PHOTOGRAPHIC APPARATUS
- ILLUSTRATED CATALOG OF PHOTOGRAPHIC EQUIPMENT AND MATERIALS FOR AMATEURS

ANTHONY EDEN PAMPHLET COLLECTION – 1963 – 1 – CSUXANP3032-B – us Hoover Inst Photo [940]

Anthony. Kansas. Grace Episcopal Church *see* PARISH RECORDS

Anthony, Katharine Susan *see* MOTHERS WHO MUST EARN

Anthony, Susan B *see* THE PAPERS OF ELIZABETH CADY STANTON AND SUSAN B. ANTHONY

ANTHONY WAYNE HERALD – Waterville, Ohio. 1978- – 7+r – 1 – $32.50r – us Archival [071]

ANTHONY WAYNE STANDARD – Waterville, Ohio. 1942-1981 – 11r – 1 – $32.50r – us Archival [071]

ANTHONY'S PHOTOGRAPHIC BULLETIN FOR... – New York: E & H T Anthony & Co. v1-32. feb 1870-1901 – 8r – 1 – us Res Libr [770]

ANTHOS – (v15- , 1975- . 5,6,9) – v. 1-. 1974- – 1 – us UMI [073]

AN ANTHROPOGEOGRAPHICAL STUDY OF THE ORIGIN OF THE ESKIMO CULTURE / Steensby, H P – BN 402 2. 1917 – 8 – ne IDC [306]

ANTHROPOGRAPHIA EX PROPIIS ET NOVIS OBSERVATIONIBUS COLLECTA / Riolan, Jean – Paris: H. Perrier, 1618.9 fiches. (Science Collection) – 9 – 22.00 – fr Bibl Nationale [306]

ANTHROPOLOGICA – Series 1: v1-8. Ottawa. 1955-59 – 5,9 – Dfl320.00; Dfl40.00v – ne Swets [301]

ANTHROPOLOGICA – Waterloo. v1- 1959- – 9 – Can$20.00y – cn Micromedia [301]

ANTHROPOLOGICA – Ottawa. v1-18 1959-76; ns: v19-39 1975-* – 1 – D35005 – us UMI [301]

ANTHROPOLOGICAL INDEX TO CURRENT PERIODICALS / Royal Anthropological Institute. Library – v. 1-9. 1963-71 – 1 – us UMI [301]

Anthropological Institute of Great Britain and Ireland *see* JOURNAL

ANTHROPOLOGICAL LITERATURE: INDEX – v. 1-. 1979- – 1,5,6,9 – us UMI [301]

ANTHROPOLOGICAL PAPERS OF THE AMERICAN MUSEUM OF NATURAL HISTORY – (Information formerly included in: Bulletin of the American Museum of Natural History) – New York. 1907-80; v57 1981-91; v71-72 1992-93; 1994- – 1* – D12599 – us UMI [301]

ANTHROPOLOGICAL QUARTERLY – (Former titles: Primitive Man (jan 1928-52)) – Washington. cum index v1-20 1928-1947; v1-70 jan 1928- 1; v44-70 jan 1971- 5; v48-70 jan 1975- 9 – 1,5,9 – D3296 – us UMI [301]

Anthropological Society of Bombay *see* JOURNAL OF THE ANTHROPOLOGICAL SOCIETY OF BOMBAY

Anthropological Society of London *see* MEMOIRS

ANTHROPOLOGICAL SURVEY IN ALASKA, 1928-1929 / Hrdlicka, A – BN 261 2. 1930 – 8 – ne IDC [301]

ANTHROPOLOGIE – Paris. v1-101. 1890-* – 1 – D3426 – us UMI [301]

ANTHROPOLOGIE BOLIVIENNE / Chervin, Arthur – 1907-08 – 1 – us I.U. Libraries [301]

L'ANTHROPOLOGIE CRIMINELLE ET SES RECENTS PROGRES / Lombroso, Cesare – Paris: F. Alcan, 1890. 180p. 2 fiches.(Miscellaneous Selections) – 9 – 6.00 – fr Bibl Nationale [360]

DIE ANTHROPOLOGIE DES APOSTELS PAULUS UND IHRE STELLUNG INNERHALB SEINER HEILSLEHRE : NACH DEN VIER HAUPTBRIEFEN / Luedemann, Hermann - (Includes bibliographical references) - Kiel: Universitaets-Buchhandlung, 1872 - 1mf - 9 - 0-8370-4192-9 - 1985-2192 - us A.T.L.A. [240]

ANTHROPOLOGY AND EDUCATION QUARTERLY - (Cont: Council on Anthropology and Education Quarterly) - Washington. v8-28 feb 1977-* 1; v10-28 Spr 1979- 5,9 - 1,5,9 - D12214.02 - us UMI [073]

ANTHROPOLOGY AND HUMANISM QUARTERLY - Tallahassee. v1-22 apr 1976-* 1; v16-22 mar 1991-* 5; v15-22 feb 1990-* 9 - 1,5,9 - D18229 - us UMI [301]

ANTHROPOLOGY AND THE CLASSICS : SIX LECTURES / ed by Marett, R R - Oxford: Clarendon Press; New York: H. Frowde [distributor], 1908 - 1mf - us A.T.L.A. [301]

ANTHROPOLOGY IN BRITISH COLUMBIA MEMOIR - v1-5. 1952-1964 - 1 - cn Precision [301]

ANTHROPOLOGY IN NORTH AMERICA - By Franz Boas, et al. New York: G.E. Stechert & Co., 1915. 378p. maps - 1 - us U.W. Library [301]

ANTHROPOLOGY KEBUDAJAAN UNTUK PENGADJARAN MENEGAH TINGKAT ATAS / Mariatmo, L - SE-4159 1. 1959 - 9 - ne IDC [306]

ANTHROPOLOGY TODAY - (Cont: Royal Anthropological Institute News) - London. v1-13. feb 1985- - 1,5*,9 - D15021 - us UMI [301]

ANTHROPOLOICAL REVIEW - (Ceased publ) - London. v1-8. mar 1863-apr 1870 - 1 - D2777 - us UMI [301]

ANTHROPOMETRIC DATA OF PUPILS AND STUDENTS IN SINGAPORE / Singapore. Ministry of Education. Planning and Review Division - Singapore, 1979 - 1mf - 9 - DE-255/1 - ne IDC [370]

ANTHROPOMETRY AND PHYSICAL EXAMINATION / Seaver, Jay W - 1909 - 5mf - 9 - $15.00 - us Microform Publ [790]

ANTHROPOS - Sankt Augustin. v54-92 1959-* 1; v73-92 1978- 5*,9 - 1,5,9 - D11824 - us UMI [301]

Antia, E E K *see* KARNAMAK I ARTAKHSHIR PAPAKAN

ANTI-ACHITOPHEL / ed by Jones, Harold W - 1682 - 9 - 10.00 - us Scholars' Facs [810]

ANTIAXIOMAS MORALES, MEDICOS... / Diez de Leiva, F - Madrid, 1682 - 3mf - 9 - sp Cultura [610]

DIE ANTIBOURGEOISE AESTHETIK DES JUNGEN BAUDELAIRE : UNTERSUCHUNGEN ZUM "SALON DE 1846" / Oehler, Dolf - Frankfurt a.M., 1975 - 2mf - 9 - DM62.00 - 3-89349-795-1 - gw Hänsel [440]

ANTI-BREAD TAX CIRCULAR *see* ANTI-CORN LAW CIRCULAR

L'ANTICA MUSICA RIDOTTA ALLA MODERNA PRATTICA / Vicentino, N - 1555 - 9 - us Sibley [780]

ANTI-CANCER DRUG DESIGN - v1- . 1985- - 1,5,6,9 - us UMI [073]

THE ANTI-CASTE - 1 - uk World [305]

ANTICHRIST AND OTHER SERMONS / Figgis, John Neville - London: Longmans, Green,1913 - 1mf - us A.T.L.A. [240]

DER ANTICHRIST IN DEN VORCHRISTLICHEN JUEDISCHEN QUELLEN / Friedlaender, Moriz - 1901 - 1 - us A.T.L.A. [240]

DER ANTICHRIST IN DER UEBERLIEFERUNG DES JUDENTUMS, DES NEUEN TESTAMENTS UND DER ALTEN KIRCHE / Bousset, Wilhelm - Ein Beitrag zur Auslegung der Apocalypse. 1895 - 1 - us A.T.L.A. [240]

ANTICHRIST RESISTED IN A REPLY TO A PAMPHLET WROTE BY W. MASON : INTITLED 'ANTINOMIAN HERESY EXPLODED IN AN APPEAL TO THE CHRISTIAN WORLD AGAINST THE UNSCRIPTURAL DOCTRINES AND LICENTIOUS TENETS OF MR. JAMES RELLY, ADVANCED IN HIS TREATISE OF UNION' / Relly, James - London, 1761 - 1mf - 9 - MP-411/1 - ne IDC [240]

ANTICIPATIONS OF THE REACTION OF MECHANICAL AND SCIENTIFIC PROGRESS UPON HUMAN LIFE AND THOUGHT / Wells, H G - London: Chapman & Hall, 1902 - 1 roll - 1 - 1-55879-776-9 - uk Libr Preservation [500]

UN ANTICO CATALOGO GRECO DE' ROMANI PONTEFICI INEDITO / Mercati, Giovanni - Roma: Tipografia vaticana, 1891 - 1mf - 9 - 0-8370-8362-1 - 1986-2362 - us A.T.L.A. [240]

ANTI-COMMUNIST PROPAGANDA DURING WORLD WAR 2 PAMPHLET COLLECTION - 1937?-1982? - 1 - CSUXANR3135-B - us Hoover Inst Photo [320]

THE ANTI-COMMUNIST RECORDS OF THE DJAKARTA WARUNG BOND AND OF THE HONG GIE SOEN COOPERATIVE SOCIETY OF DJAKARTA / Chung-Hsing [pseud] - In Chinese. SE-4918 1. 2 v. in 1. 1952 - 9 - ne IDC [335]

ANTI-CORN LAW CIRCULAR - Manchester, UK. 16 Apr 1839-26 Sep 1843 - 2r - 1 - uk British Libr Newspaper [072]

Anticosti Company *see* ...CONFIDENTIAL PROSPECTUS

ANTICOSTI EN 1900 / Baillairge, Charles - 1900? 02374. (Pre-1900 Canadiana) - 9 - cn C.I.H.M. [971]

L'ANTIDEMON DE MASCON OU LA RELATION PURE ET SIMPLE DES PRINCIPALES CHARGES QUI ONT ESTE FAITES PAR UN DEMON / Perrault, Francais - Geneve. 1656 - 9 - fr Hachette [360]

AN ANTIDOTARIE CHYRURGICALL / Banister, J - M 298. 1589 - 9 - ne IDC [615]

THE ANTIDOTE - Montreal: [s.n., 1892-1893] - 9 - cn C.I.H.M. [971]

THE ANTIDOTE - or Protestant Guardian. Dublin. Ireland. -w. 25 Jan 1823, 24 Jan, 14 Feb, 24 Apr, 12 Jun-9 Oct 1824, 22 Jan-2 Apr 1825. (22 ft) - 1 - uk British Libr Newspaper [072]

ANTIDOTE TO DEISM.. / Ogden, Uzal - 2v. 1795 - 1 - $50.00 - us Presbyterian [210]

ANTIDOTUM: TEGEN-GIFT VANT GEBRUYCK OF ONGEBRUYCK VANT ORGEL / Calckman, I I - P 659. 1641 - 9 - ne IDC [780]

ANTIDOTVM CONTRA IMPIVM ET BLASPHEMVM DOGMA MATTHIAE FLACII ILLYRICI,... / Hesshusen, T - Ienae, 1572 - 5mf - ne IDC [240]

Anti-dude *see* CAUSERIES: LA LIBERTE VS. LA MODE & AL, ET LA POLITIQUE

ANTI-EVOLUTION: GIRARDEAU VS WOODROW / Martin, James L - 1888. 1 fiche. 8370-4298-4 - 9 - us A.T.L.A. [240]

ANTIFASCHISTISCHE FRONT, LE FRONT ANTIFASCISTE - Kopenhagen; Paris. Mar 12-Sept 14, 1933 - 1r - 1 - gw Mikrofilm [073]

ANTIFONARIO VISIGOTICO... / Brou, Louis & Vives, D Jose - Madrid: Archivo Ibero Americano, 1960 - 1 - sp Bibl Santa Ana [946]

ANTI-FOREIGN RIOTS IN CHINA IN 1891 - 1892 - 1 - us A.T.L.A. [950]

ANTI-GALLICAN : OR STANDARD OF BRITISH LOYALTY, RELIGION AND LIBERTY - (Ceased publ) - London. v1-12. 1804 - 1 - D4608 - us UMI [073]

ANTI-GERMAN PROPAGANDA DURING WORLD WAR 1 PAMPHLET COLLECTION - 1914-1938 - 2r - 1 - CSUXANL5370-B - us Hoover Inst Photo [320]

ANTI-GERMAN PROPAGANDA PAMPHLET COLLECTION - 1933-196? - 1 - CSUXANR2684-B - us Hoover Inst Photo [320]

ANTIGONISH REVIEW - Antigonish. no1-1970/71- - 9 - Can$28.00y - cn Micromedia [420]

ANTIGONISH REVIEW - Antigonish. v1-112. 1970- - 9 - D35006 - us UMI [073]

L'ANTI-GRAMMAIRE / Pielat, B - 1673 - 9 - fr I.C.S. [400]

ANTIGUA : STATISTICAL YEARBOOK 1975-1976 - (Coll title: Latin American and Caribbean Statistical Serials, 1821-1982) - 4mf - 9 - £42.00 - uk Chadwyck [972]

Antigua *see* FIVE YEAR DRAFT PLAN, 1966-1970

ANTIGUA 1828-1887 - September 1991, M.A.P. Yorkshire - 9r - 1 - uk Microform Academic [972]

Antigua and Barbuda. Archives Committee *see* HISTORICAL NOTES ON EDUCATION IN ANTIGUA 1837-1984

Antigua and Barbuda. Ministry of Education, Health and Culture *see* REPORT ON THE EDUCATION DIVISION 1971-1973

Antigua and Barbuda. Ministry of Education, Health and Culture. *see* EDUCATIONAL STATISTICS 1974/75-1976/77

LA ANTIGUA BIBLIOTECA JESUITICA DE CORDOBA / Cabrera, Pablo - Cordoba (Argentina), 1930; Madrid: Razon y Fe, 1932 - 1 - sp Bibl Santa Ana [020]

ANTIGUA CERTA DE HERMANDAD ENTRE PLASENCIA Y TALAVERA / Berjano, Daniel Escobar - Madrid: Tip. Fortanet, 1899 - sp Bibl Santa Ana [946]

ANTIGUA DEVELOPMENT PLAN - D-939 1. 1963-66 - 9 - ne IDC [338]

ANTIGUA MAGNET - St John's, Antigua. 4 Jan 1930-31 Dec 1932; 1 Aug 1933-30 Jul 1938; 3 Jan-24 Nov 1939; 10-26 Feb 1940 - 10r - 1 - uk British Libr Newspaper [072]

ANTIGUA NEWS NOTES - St John's, Antigua. 15 Mar 1909-28 Jan 1911 - 2r - 1 - uk British Libr Newspaper [072]

ANTIGUA STAR - St John's, Antigua. 1 Apr 1937-30 Jul 1938; 4 Jan-24 Nov 1939; 10-26 Feb 1940 - 3r - 1 - uk British Libr Newspaper [072]

ANTIGUAS EPIGRAFES DE TANGER, JEREZ Y ARCOS DE LA FRONTERA (MERIDA) / Fita, Fidel - Madrid: Tip. Fortanet, 1896 - 1 - sp Bibl Santa Ana [946]

LAS ANTIGUAS FERIAS DE MEDINA DEL CAMPO / Espejo, Cristobal - Vallodolid. 1908 - 1 - us Res Libr [930]

Antiguedad, Alfredo R *see* JOSE ANTONIO EN LA CARCEL DE MADRID DEL 14 DE MARZO AL 6 DE JUNIO DE 1936

ANTIGUEDAD Y LIMITES DEL OBISPADO DE CORIA. NUEVO ESTUDIO / Escobar Prieto, Eugenio - Madrid: Tip. Fortanet, 1912. B.R.A.H. 61, pp. 314-345 - sp Bibl Santa Ana [946]

ANTIGUEDADES CACERENAS / Ramon y Fernandez, Jose - Valladolid, 1944-45 - 1 - sp Bibl Santa Ana [946]

ANTIGUEDADES DE ESPANA PROPUGNADAS EN LAS NOTICIAS DE SUS REYES Y CONDES... / Berganza, F - Madrid, 1719 - 24mf - 9 - sp Cultura [930]

ANTIGUEDADES DE EXTREMADURA / Viu, Jose de - 1852 - 9 - 1.50f - sp Bibl Santa Ana [930]

LAS ANTIGUEDADES DE LAS CIUDADES DE ESPANA. TOMO 9 / Morales, Ambrosio - Madrid: Benito Cano, 1792 - 1 - sp Bibl Santa Ana [946]

ANTIGUEDADES DE MERIDA / Forner y Segarra, Agustin F - 1893 - 9 - 1.50f - sp Bibl Santa Ana [930]

ANTIGUEDADES DE MERIDA RECIENTEMENTE REMITIDAS AL MUSEO ARQUEOLOGICO NACIONAL POR LA COMISION DE MONUMENTES DE AQUELLA CIUDAD / Rada Delgado, Juan de Dios de la - 1 - sp Bibl Santa Ana [930]

ANTIGUEDADES DE TORRECILLAS (ALCUESCAR) / Sanguino y Michel, Juan - Madrid: Fortanet, 1911. B.R.A.H. 59, 1911, pp. 439-456 - sp Bibl Santa Ana [946]

LAS ANTIGUEDADES DE...CIUDADES DE ESPANA / Morales, Antonio y otros - 1712 - 9 - $1.50f - sp Bibl Santa Ana [930]

ANTIGUEDADES EXTREMENAS. LA AUDIENCIA TERRITORIAL DE EXTREMADURA / Duarte Insua, Lino - Badajoz Tip. La Alianza, 1935 - 1 - sp Bibl Santa Ana [946]

ANTIGUEDADES ROMANAS DE ALCUESCAR / Comision de Monumentos de Caceres - Madrid: Tip. de Fortanet, 1900 - sp Bibl Santa Ana [946]

ANTIGUEDADES ROMANAS DEL CORTIJO DE LAS VIRGENES, CERCA DE BAENA / Sanguino y Michel, Juan - Madrid: Fortanet, 1913. B.R.A.H. 62, pp. 483-486 - sp Bibl Santa Ana [946]

ANTIGUEDADES Y SANTOS...DE ALCANATARA / Arias de Quintanaduenas, Jacinto - 1661 - 9 - 1.50f - sp Bibl Santa Ana [946]

ANTI-HAECKEL: EINE REPLIK NEBST BEILAGEN / Loofs, Friedrich - Halle a.S.: Max Niemeyer, 1900. 1 fiche - 9 - us A.T.L.A. [240]

ANTI-HIGHER CRITICISM : OR, THE TESTIMONY TO THE INFALLIBILITY OF THE BIBLE / Osgood, Howard et al; ed by Munhall, L W - New York: Hunt & Eaton, 1894, c1893 - 1mf - 9 - 0-8370-4540-1 - 1985-2540 - us A.T.L.A. [220]

LA ANTIHISTORIA EXTREMENA / Munoz de San Pedro, Miguel - Badajoz: Imp. de la Diputacion Provincial, 1969 - sp Bibl Santa Ana [946]

ANTI-IMPERIALISME DAN FRONT NASIONAL / Aidit, Dipa Nusantara - SE-6447 1. 1962 - 9 - ne IDC [335]

EL "ANTIIMPERIALISMO" DE PERON : LA CARTA DE FEDERICO PINEDO / Ghioldi, Americo - Montevideo, 1953 - 1 - CSUXADP9138-B - us Hoover Inst Photo [320]

ANTI-INFIDEL - (Ceased publ) - London. v1. jun-nov 1831 - 1 - D4701 - us UMI [230]

ANTI-JACOBIN : OR WEEKLY EXAMINER - (Ceased publ) - London. v1-2 nov 1797-jul 1789 - 1 - D5231 - us UMI [073]

ANTI-JACOBIN REVIEW AND MAGAZINE *see* ANTIJACOBIN REVIEW AND PROTESTANT ADVOCATE

ANTIJACOBIN REVIEW AND PROTESTANT ADVOCATE : OR, MONTHLY POLITICAL, AND LITERARY CENSOR - (Ceased publ. Former titles: Anti-Jacobin Review and Magazine, or, Monthly Political, and Literary Censor (jul 1798-apr 1810); Antijacobin Review and True Churchman's magazine, or, Monthly Political, and Literary Censor (may 1810-aug 1816); Antijacobin Review, True Churchman's Magazine and Protestant Advocate, or, Monthly, Political, and Religious Censor (sep 1816-feb 1819)) - London. v1-61. jul 1798-dec 1821 - 1 - D4200 - us UMI [073]

ANTIJACOBIN REVIEW AND TRUE CHURCHMAN'S MAGAZINE *see* ANTIJACOBIN REVIEW AND PROTESTANT ADVOCATE

ANTIJACOBIN REVIEW, TRUE CHURCHMAN'S MAGAZINE AND PROTESTANT ADVOCATE *see* ANTIJACOBIN REVIEW AND PROTESTANT ADVOCATE

L'ANTI-JUIF - Paris. 11 aout 1898-5 avr 1903, 1899-1900, inc - 1 - fr A.C.R.P.P. [270]

L'ANTIJUIF - Paris, France. 21 Aug 1898-2 Nov 1902 - 3r - 1 - uk British Libr Newspaper [072]

ANTIKE JESUS-ZEUGNISSE / Aufhauser, J B - Bonn, 1913 - 1mf - 8 - ne Slangenburg [240]

DAS ANTIKE MYSTERIENWESEN IN SEINEM EINFLUSS AUF DAS CHRISTENTUM / Anrich, Gustav - Goettingen: Vandenhoeck und Ruprecht, 1894 - 1mf - us A.T.L.A. [240]

ANTIKE UND ANTIKES LEBENSGEFUEHL IM WERKE GERHART HAUPTMANNS / Voigt, Felix Alfred - Breslau: Maruschke & Berendt, 1935 - 1r - 1 - us U.W. Library [430]

ANTIKE UND CHRISTENTUM / Doelger, Frans J - Muenster. Bd 1-6. 1930-1940/50 - 50mf - 8 - Dfl175.00 - ne Slangenburg [240]

ANTIKHRIST / Merezhkovskii, Dimitrii - Petr i Aleksei. Ed. 2. Spb. 1906. BR-749 2 - 8 - ne IDC [240]

ANTIKHRIST / Merezhkovskii, Dimitrii - Petr i Aleksei. Spb. 1905. BR-748 2 - 8 - ne IDC [240]

ANTIKOMINTERN - Berlin, 1936-39 (incomplete) - 1 - Dist. gw Mikrofilm - gw Misc Inst [072]

DIE ANTIKRIEGSAKTION - Paris, France.Aug-Sept 1933 - 1r - 1 - gw Mikrofilm [073]

ANTIKVAR - Bibliograficheskii listok. St. Petersburg, 1902-03. v.1-12. BR-4297 2 - 8 - ne IDC [010]

ANTIKVARNAIA KNIZHNAIA TORGOVLIA P. SHIBANOVA - Katalog russkikh knig, starykh i novykh, zamechatel' nykh i redkikh. Moscow, 1899. BR-5693 2 - 8 - ne IDC [010]

ANTIKVARNYI KATALOG KNIG "RUSSKAIA ZEMLIA" V ISTORICHESKOM, GEOGRAFICHESKOM, STATISTICHESKOM, MEDITSINSKOM I PR. OTNOSHENIIAKH - I.I. Bazlov. St. Petersburg, 1904. 43p. BR-5661 2 - 8 - ne IDC [010]

ANTILAICISMO. 2 VOL. BARCELONA, 1935 / Goma Tomas, Isidro - Madrid: Razon y Fe, 1935 - 1 - sp Bibl Santa Ana [946]

LES ANTILLES - St. Pierre. Martinique.1872-1901; 1962-66 - 1 - us UMI [072]

LES ANTILLES FRANCAISES, PARTICULIEREMENT LA GUADELOUPE, DEPUIS LEUR DECOUVERTE JUSQU'AU 1ER NOVEMBRE, 1825 / Peyreleau, Boyer de & Edouard, Eugene - Paris. 3v. 1825 - 1r - 1 - us Ross [972]

ANTILOGIA PAPAE: HOC EST, DE CORRUPTO ECCLESIAE STATU, AND TOTIUS CLERI PAPISTICI PERUERSITATE,... / Flacius Illyricus d.A E, M - Basileae, [1555] - 9mf - 9 - ne IDC [240]

ANTILUTHERUS..., TRES LIBROS COMPLECTENS / Clichtove, J - Parisiis, 1524 - 4mf - 9 - CA-80/1 - ne IDC [240]

ANTILYNCHING: HEARINGS:...JANUARY 29, 1920 / U.S. Congress. House. Committee on the Judiciary – Washington, Govt. Print. Off., 1920. 65 p. LL-1359 – 1 – us L of C Photodup [340]

L'ANTI-MACHIAVEL / Frederick 2nd, King of Prussia; ed by Fleischauer, C – (Studies on Voltaire and the eighteenth century, v5) – Oxford. 1958 – 9 – $45.00 – 0-7294-0063-8 – uk Voltaire [321]

ANTI-MASONIC REVIEW AND MAGAZINE – (Ceased publ) – New York. v1-2. jan 1828-dec 1830 – 1 – D3717 – us UMI [073]

ANTI-MASONIC TELEGRAPH – Norwich. N.Y. 1829-1835 – 1 – us UMI [071]

ANTI-METHODIST PUBLICATIONS ISSUED DURING THE EIGHTEENTH CENTURY... / Green, R – London, 1902 – 2mf – 9 – ne IDC [240]

ANTIMICROBIAL AGENTS AND CHEMOTHERAPY – v1-24. 1961-70, 1972-83 – 1,5,6 – us Princeton Micro [610]

ANTIMICROBIAL AGENTS AND CHEMOTHERAPY – Washington. v1-41 jan 1972- 1,5; v7-41 jan-dec 1975- 9 – 1,5,9 – D6608 – us UMI [615]

ANTI-MODERNISTENEID, FREIE FORSCHUNG UND THEOLOGISCHE FAKULTAETEN : MIT ANHANG, DER ANTI-MODERNISTENEID, LATEINISCH UND DEUTSCH, NEBST AKTENSTUECKEN / Mulert, H – Halle (Saale): Verlag des Evangelischen Bundes, 1911 – 1mf – us A.T.L.A. [240]

ANTI-MONOPOLIST – Grand Island, NE. -w. Jan-Oct 1883 – 1 – us NE Hist [071]

ANTI-NAPOLEONISCHE PAMPHLETE : POLITISCHE SCHRIFTEN AUS DEN FREIHEITSKRIEGEN 1813-15 / ed by Schoewerling, Rainer & Steinecke, Hartmut – Hildesheim, 1996 – 411mf – DM2,160.00 diazo DM2,700.00 silver – gw Olms [320]

ANTI-NAZI MOVEMENT PAMPHLET COLLECTION – 1934-198? – 1 – CSUXANS0367-B – us Hoover Inst Photo [320]

DER ANTI-NECKER J.H. MERCKS UND DER MINISTER FR. K. V. MOSER : EIN BEITRAG ZUR BEURTEILUNG J.H. MERCKS / Loebell, Richard – Darmstadt: A Klingelhoeffer, 1896 – 1r – 1 – us U.W. Library [943]

ANTINOMIANISM IN THE COLONY OF MASSACHUSETTS BAY, 1636-1638 / ed by Adams, Charles Francis – 1894 – 1 – us A.T.L.A. [240]

ANTIOCH AND PITTSBURG CITY DIRECTORIES – Contra Costa Co, CA. 1931; 1947-1950 – 3r – 1 – $150.00 – D014 – us Library Micro [910]

ANTIOCH BAPTIST CHURCH. CHEROKEE COUNTY. SOUTH CAROLINA : CHURCH RECORDS – 1815-1959 – 1 – 29.61 – us Baptist [240]

ANTIOCH BAPTIST CHURCH. DARLINGTON COUNTY. SOUTH CAROLINA : CHURCH RECORDS – (378p) – 1830-1895, 1956-1975 – 1 reel – 1 – $17.01 – us Baptist [240]

ANTIOCH BAPTIST CHURCH. EDGEFIELD COUNTY. SOUTH CAROLINA : CHURCH RECORDS – 1830-1982. Incomplete. 520p – 1 – 23.40 – us Baptist [240]

ANTIOCH BAPTIST CHURCH. ENOREE, SOUTH CAROLINA : CHURCH RECORDS – 1835-1970 – 1 – 41.49 – us Baptist [240]

ANTIOCH BAPTIST CHURCH. FAIRFIELD, TEXAS : CHURCH RECORDS – 1906-1972 – 1 – 25.56 – us Baptist [240]

ANTIOCH BAPTIST CHURCH. JOHNSON CITY, TENNESSEE : CHURCH RECORDS – 1875-1987. Minutes, 1952-87. History/other, 1875-1986 – 1 – 40.37 – us Baptist [240]

ANTIOCH BAPTIST CHURCH. LAFAYETTE, ALABAMA : CHURCH RECORDS – 1835-1951 – 1 – 42.30 – us Baptist [240]

ANTIOCH BAPTIST CHURCH. MONROE, NORTH CAROLINA : CHURCH RECORDS – Oct 1892-Nov 1916 – 1 – 7.38 – us Baptist [240]

ANTIOCH BAPTIST CHURCH OF CHRI BIBB COUNTY. ALABAMA : CHURCH RECORDS – 1833-69 – 1 – 15.03 – us Baptist [240]

ANTIOCH BAPTIST CHURCH. ORANGEBURG COUNTY. SOUTH CAROLINA : CHURCH RECORDS – 1867-80 – 1 – 11.07 – us Baptist [240]

ANTIOCH BAPTIST CHURCH. PICKENS COUNTY. SOUTH CAROLINA : CHURCH RECORDS – (188p) – 1889-1920 – 1 reel – 1 – $8.46 – us Baptist [240]

ANTIOCH MISSIONARY BAPTIST CHURCH. ROSEBUD, ILLINOIS : CHURCH RECORDS – 28 May 1864-Mar 1972 – 1 – 30.69 – us Baptist [240]

ANTIOCH REVIEW – Yellow Springs. Ohio. v. 1-5. 1941-45 – 1,5,6 – us Princeton Micro [073]

ANTIOCH REVIEW – Yellow Springs. v1-55 Spr 1941- 1; v28-55 Spr 1968- 5; v33-55 Spr 1975-9 – 1,5,9 – D1041 – us UMI [073]

ANTIOCHE PAIENNE ET CHRETIENNE / Festugiere, A J – Paris, 1959 – 14mf – 8 – ne Slangenburg [240]

ANTIOQUIA MEDICA – Medellin. v22-23. 1972-73 – 1 – D8112 – us UMI [610]

ANTIPAS, SON OF CHUZA : AND OTHERS WHOM JESUS LOVED / Houghton, Louise Seymour – New York: Anson D F Randolph, c1895 – 1mf – 9 – 0-8370-3673-9 – 1985-1673 – us A.T.L.A. [830]

EL ANTIPERONISMO COMO NEGOCIO : RADIOGRAFIA DE LA SITUACION ACTUAL, SILENCIADA POR TODA LA PRENSA / Damonte Taborda, Raul – Buenos Aires, 1957 – 1 – CSUXADJ1321-B – us Hoover Inst Photo [320]

ANTIPHONAE, SEV SACRAE CANTIONES, QUAE IN TOTIVS ANNI... / Anerio, G F – 1613 – 1 – us Sibley [780]

ANTIPHONALE MISSARUM SEXTUPLEX / ed by Hesbert, R J – Bruxelles, 1935 – 14mf – 8 – Dfl42.00 – ne Slangenburg [240]

ANTIPHONARIUM IUXTA BREVIARIUM ROMANUM, EX DECRETO SACRO-SANCTI CONCILIJ TRIDENTINI – Parisiis: Apud Ludovicum Sevestre, 1668. SEM35P291 – 1r – 1 – Can$23.00 – cn Bibl Nat [240]

ANTIPHONARIUM MOZARABICUM DE LA CATEDRAL DE LEON – Leon, 1928 – 11mf – 8 – Dfl39.00 – ne Slangenburg [240]

ANTIPHONARIUM PROPRIUM : NO[N]NULLAQ'(UE) QUORU[M]DAM SANTORU'(M) NOUA OFFICIA... – [1523] – 1 – us Sibley [780]

THE ANTIPHONARY OF BANGOR : AN EARLY IRISH MS IN THE AMBROSIAN LIBRARY AT MILAN: PART 1 / Warren, F E – 1893 – 6mf – 8 – Dfl25.00 – ne Slangenburg [240]

THE ANTIPHONARY OF BANGOR: PART 2 / Warren, G – 1895 – 6mf – 8 – Dfl25.00 – ne Slangenburg [240]

ANTIPISTORIUS, ORDER WIDERLEGUNG DES CALVINISCHEN POLITICI SIMONIS ULRICH PISTORIS IN SEUSELITZ... / Gedik, S – Leipzig, 1620 – 5mf – ne IDC [240]

ANTIPODE – Worcester. v1-29 aug 1989-* 1; v18-29 apr 1986- 5*,9 – 1,5,9 – D17385 – us UMI [073]

ANTIPOLOGIA BREVE EN QUE SE PRUEBA EL VERDADERO TEMPERAMENTO QUE LA NIEVE POSEE... / Mirez Carvajal, C – Granada, 1652 – 2mf – 9 – sp Cultura [610]

ANTIQARY : A MAGAZINE DEVOTED TO THE STUDY OF THE PAST – (Ceased publ) – London. v1-51. jan 1880-dec 1915 – 1 – D5232 – us UMI [073]

ANTIQUAE LINGUAE BRITANNICAE NUNC COMMUNITER / Davies, John – 1621. 268p. (English Linguistics Series 1500-1800) – 9 – us UMI [490]

ANTIQUAE LINGUAE BRITANNICAE, NUNC VULGO / Davies, John – 1632. 406p. (English Linguistics Series 1500-1800) – 9 – us UMI [490]

ANTIQUAE MUSICAE AUCTORES SEPTEM. GRAECE ET LATINE / Meibomius, M – 1652. 2v – 9 – us Sibley [780]

ANTIQUAE MUSICAE AUCTORES SEPTEM, GRAECE ET LATINE, MARCUS MEIBOMIUS RESTITUIT AC NOTIS EXPLICAVIT / Meibomius, M – P 400. 1652 – 9 – ne IDC [780]

ANTIQUARIAN *see* AMERICAN ARCHAEOLOGIST

ANTIQUARIAN MAGAZINE & BIBLIOGRAPHER *see* WALFORD'S ANTIQUARIAN MAGAZINE & BIBLIOGRAPHICAL REVIEW

THE ANTIQUARIAN REMAINS IN BIHAR / Patil, D R – (Historical Research Series Vol. 4). Patna. 1963. BI-1045 2 – 8 – ne IDC [930]

ANTIQUARIAN REMAINS IN HYDERABAD STATE / India – Hyderabad. 1953. BI-794 2 – 8 – ne IDC [930]

ANTIQUARIES JOURNAL – London, 1921-1941. v1-21 – 231mf – 9 – H-803c/2 – ne IDC [900]

ANTIQUARIES JOURNAL – London. cum index v1-40 1921-1960; v1-77 jan 1921- 1; v57-77 1977- 5*,9 – 1,5,9 – D1273 – us UMI [073]

ANTIQUARY : A MEDIUM OF INTERCOMMUNICATION FOR MEN OF LETTERS, THE ARCHAEOLOGIST, AND THE READING PUBLIC – (Ceased publ) – London. v 1-4. may 1871-dec 1873 – 1 – D2778 – us UMI [073]

ANTIQUE AUTOMOBILE – Hershey. v1-61 1835-* 1; v43-61 jan-dec 1979-* 5,9 – 1,5,9 – D5950 – us UMI [629]

ANTIQUE COLLECTOR – (1976- . 5,6,9) – v. 1-. 1930- – 1 – us UMI [930]

ANTIQUE MARKET REPORT – 1986- – 1,5,6,9 – us UMI [740]

ANTIQUES : ARCHITECTURE, APPLIED ARTS, STUDIO ARTS – (Individual titles not listed separately) – 15 catalogues on 21mf – 9 – £176.00 – uk Chadwyck [740]

ANTIQUES CEREMONIES DANS L'ABBAYE DE SAINT-EVROULT / Guery, Ch. – Alencon, 1916 – Dfl6.00 – ne Slangenburg [240]

ANTIQUES JOURNAL – (1977-81. 5,6,9) – v. 1-36. 1946-81 – 1 – us UMI [073]

ANTIQUES WORLD – 1978-82 – 1,5,6,9 – us UMI [740]

ANTIQUITATES ITALICAE MEDII AEVI / Muratori, Lodovico A – Mediolani. Tom 1-6. 1738-1742 – 171mf – 9 – Dfl595.00 – ne Slangenburg [945]

ANTIQUITATUM BOTANICARUM SPECIMEN PRIMUM / Sprengel, K P J – Lipsiae, 1798. 110 pp., 2 pls. B-5748 2 – 8 – ne IDC [580]

ANTIQUITE DE LA NATION ET DE LA LANGUE DES CELTES, AUTREMENT APPELLEZ GAULOIS / Pezron, P[Y] – Paris, 1703 – 6mf – 9 – ne IDC [440]

L'ANTIQUITE DE LA TERRE ET DE L'HOMME / Baillairge, Charles – Memoire lu par M. Baillairge devant la Societe royale du Canada, en mai 1899 a Ottawa. 1899?. 00084. (Pre-1900 Canadiana) – 9 – cn C.I.H.M. [900]

L'ANTIQUITE DEVOILEE PAR SES USAGES OU EXAMEN CRITIQUE DES PRINCIPALES OPINIONS, CEREMONIES ET INSTITUTIONS RELIGIEUSES ET POLITIQUES DES DIFFERENTS PEUPLES DE LA TERRE / Boulanger, Nicolas A – (D'Holbach series). 1766 – 9 – fr Hachette [300]

L'ANTIQUITE EROTIQUE / Tennodrac, M J – Paris: Editions et Publications de Lutece, 1952. 125p. (Les Femmes Collection) – 2mf – 9 – $6.00 – fr Bibl Nationale [930]

ANTIQUITES ORIENTALES. FOUILLES DE TELLO, DE SUSE ET DE SYRIE / Reunion des musees nationaux. Paris – 1930. 10 illus. 2 fiches – 9 – fr Réunion [700]

ANTIQUITIES / Caisse Nationale des Monuments Historiques et des Sites. Paris – (Large collections from the Louvre and Egyptian Museum in Cairo. Over 5,500 reproductions) – 98mf – 9 – $670.00 – 0-907006-85-X – uk Mindata [930]

ANTIQUITIES AND ART IN TURKEY PAMPHLET COLLECTION – 1918-1950? – 1 – CSUXANQ7395-B – us Hoover Inst Photo [700]

ANTIQUITIES FROM SAN THOME AND.. / Hosten, Henry – Madras: Diocese of Mylapore, 1936. xxxiii,590+46p. Plates, illus., map. 1 reel. 1263 – 1 – us U.W. Library [240]

ANTIQUITIES, HISTORICAL AND MONUMENTAL OF THE COUNTY OF CORNWALL / Borlase, William – 7 – uk Microform Academic [941]

THE ANTIQUITIES OF HERALDRY...FROM LITERATURE, COINS, GEMS, VASES, AND OTHER MONUMENTS OF PRE-CHRISTIAN AND MEDIAEVAL TIMES. / Ellis, William Smith – London: J.R. Smith, 1869. xxiv,276p – 1 – us U.W. Library [920]

ANTIQUITIES OF THE INNS OF COURT AND CHANCERY : CONTAINING HISTORICAL AND DESCRIPTIVE SKETCHES RELATIVE TO THEIR ORIGINAL FOUNDATION, CUSTOMS, CEREMONIES, BUILDINGS, GOVERNMENT, ETC... / Herbert, William – London: Vernor & Hood, 1804 – 5mf – 9 – $7.50 – LLMC 84-295 – us L.L.M.C. [340]

ANTIQUITY – (1986-. 1,5,6) – 1976- – 9 – us UMI [073]

ANTIQUITY – Cambridge, 1927-1941. v1-15 – 212mf – 9 – H-804c/2 – ne IDC [900]

ANTIQUITY – v. 1-39. H-804 2. 1927-1965 – 8 – ne IDC [073]

ANTIQUITY: A QUARTERLY REVIEW OF ARCHAEOLOGY – v.1-49. 1927-75 – 9 – 24218.00; 245.00v – uk Dawson [930]

ANTIQUITY AND SURVIVAL. VOL. 2; THE HOLY LAND: NEW LIGHT ON THE PREHISTORY AND EARLY HISTORY OF ISRAEL / ed by Ruysch, W A – Israel Exploration Society, The Hague & Jerusalem, 1957 – 9 – $10.00 – us I.R.C. [930]

ANTIQVITATUM CONVIVIALIVM LIBRI 3 IN QVIBVS HEBRAEORVM, GRAECORVM, ROMANORVM ALIARVMQVE NATIONVM ANTIQVA CONVIVIORVM GENERA... / Stucki, J W – Tigvri, Ioannes VVolph, 1582 – 9mf – 9 – PBU-503/1 – ne IDC [956]

ANTIRELIGIOZNYE STIKHI / Maiakovskii, Vladimir – M. 1940. BR-965 2 – 8 – ne IDC [240]

Anti-Saloon League of America *see* PAPERS

Anti-Saloon League of America. District of Columbia *see* PAPERS

Anti-Saloon League of America. Office of General Counsel and Legislative Superintendent *see* PAPERS

Anti-Saloon League of America. Ohio *see* PAPERS

ANTI-SEMITISM AND NATIONALISM AT THE END OF THE SOVIET ERA / Institute of Humanitarian Political Research and library of "Memorial" – (Including printed guide and plastic binder) – 138mf – 9 – ne IDC [320]

ANTI-SLAVERY ADVOCATE – London, UK. Oct 1852-May 1863 – 1 1/2r – 1 – uk British Libr Newspaper [072]

ANTI-SLAVERY BUGLE – Jan 1851-May 1861 – 1 – 74.00 – us L of C Photodup [976]

ANTI-SLAVERY BUGLE – (Ceaed publ) – Salem. v1-16. jun 1845-may 1861 – 1 – D3084 – us UMI [306]

ANTI-SLAVERY COLLECTION / Rhodes House Library. Oxford – 1795-1880 – 1 – £2,295.00 – uk World [305]

ANTI-SLAVERY COLLECTION: 18TH-19TH CENTURIES / The Society of Friends. Library – With printed index – 1 – £1,150.00 – uk World [976]

ANTI-SLAVERY EXAMINER / American Anti-Slavery Society – Nos. 1-14 (all publ). 1836-45 – 17mf – 9 – $65.00 – us UPA [976]

ANTI-SLAVERY EXAMINER – (Ceased publ) – New York. v1-14. 1836-45 – 1 – D3934 – us UMI [306]

ANTI-SLAVERY INTERNATIONAL : THE BINNS AND SUPPLEMENTARY COLLECTIONS OF ANTI-SLAVERY TRACTS, PAMPHLETS AND BOOKS, 1767 ET SEQ – 40r – 1 – £1,995.00 – 1-897955-44-8 – uk Academic [090]

Anti-Slavery International *see* ANTI-SLAVERY REPORTER 1825-1994

ANTI-SLAVERY MATERIALS, REGIONAL RECORDS AND OTHER PAMPHLETS / John Rylands University Library, Manchester – 18th-19thc. 20 reels with printed guide – £875.00 – uk World [976]

ANTI-SLAVERY MONTHLY REPORTER – London. 4v. 1827-31 – 23mf – 9 – ILM-714/1 – ne IDC [073]

ANTI-SLAVERY PAPERS / Rhodes House – BRRAM – 1 – uk Microform Academic [976]

THE ANTI-SLAVERY PROPAGANDA COLLECTION, OBERLIN COLLEGE – U.S. anti-slavery propaganda published before 1863 – 9 – us Primary [976]

ANTI-SLAVERY RECORD / American Anti-Slavery Society – v1-3 (all publ). 1835-37 – 9 – $55.00 – us UPA [976]

ANTI-SLAVERY RECORD – (Ceased publ) – New York. v1-3 jan 1835-dec 1837 – 1 – D3935 – us UMI [306]

ANTI-SLAVERY REPORTER – London. v1-5. 1825-33 – 1r – 1 – us Ross [305]

ANTI-SLAVERY REPORTER – (Ceased publ) – New York. v1. jun-nov 1833 – 1 – D3936 – us UMI [306]

ANTI-SLAVERY REPORTER *see* ANTI-SLAVERY REPORTER AND ABORIGINES' FRIEND

ANTI-SLAVERY REPORTER 1825-1994 : AND CONTINUA / Anti-Slavery International – (Formerly: Anti-Slavery Reporter and Aborigines Friend) – 18r – 1 – £950.00 – 1-897955-39-1 – uk Academic [306]

ANTI-SLAVERY REPORTER AND ABORIGINES FRIEND *see* ANTI-SLAVERY REPORTER 1825-1994

ANTI-SLAVERY REPORTER AND ABORIGINES' FRIEND – (Former titles: British and Foreign Anti-Slavery Reporter (jan 15, 1840-dec 24, 1845); Anti-Slavery Reporter (jan 1, 1846-may 1909)) – London. v1-6 jan 1840-dec 1845; ns-3s v1-20 jan 1846-nov 1877; 3s-4s v21-7 feb 1878-dec 1887; 4s v8-29 jan 1888-may 1909; 5s v1-4 oct 1909-jan 1915 – 1 – D4745 – us UMI [306]

Anti-Slavery Society *see* PAPERS: TRINIDAD

ANTI-SLAVERY SOCIETY FOR THE PROTECTION OF HUMAN RIGHTS – London. 80 docs. 1980-1991 – 41mf – 9 – ne IDC [320]

THE ANTI-SLAVERY STRUGGLE AND TRIUMPH IN THE METHODIST EPISCOPAL CHURCH / Matlack, Lucius C – New York: Phillips & Hunt; Cincinnati: Walden & Stowe, 1881 – 1mf – us A.T.L.A. [240]

ANTI-SLAVERY TRACTS / American Anti-Slavery Society – (Series 1: Nos. 1-20 (all publ). 1855-1856. Series 2: Nos. 1-25 (all and last publ). 1855-61) – 16mf – 9 – $60.00 – us UPA [976]

ANTI-SOCIALIST ORGANISATIONS IN BRITAIN – (Part 1: Anti-socialist journals, 1874-1914) – 1 – us Primary [073]

ANTISOFISMA / E CU – 1787 – 9 – 1.50f – sp Bibl Santa Ana [946]

Anti-Soviet Society *see* ARTICLES AND LEAFLETS

ANTI-STAATS-TAGE – Muenchen. 26 Sept-2 Oct 1983. 4S. Flugblatt – 9 – 1.00f – at Libertarian Micro [335]

THE ANTI-SUFFRAGE REVIEW / Women's National Anti-Suffrage League – (Missing: 1914(71, 74, p. 177-End)) – London, 1908-1918 – 41mf – 9 – W-13/1 – ne IDC [320]

THE ANTI-SWEATER – A journal devoted to the exposure of the sweating system and for the organization of the journeyman tailors and machinists. London. -m. Jul 1886-Feb 1887. (5 ft) – 1 – uk British Libr Newspaper [331]

ANTI-TEAPOT REVIEW – London. v1-19. may 1864-jan 1869 – 1 – D4709 – us UMI [073]

ANTI-TEATRO CRITICO. TOMO 1 / Maner, Salvador – 1729 – 1mf – 9 – Pta1,000.00 – 84-7848-016-1 – sp Pentalfa [440]

ANTI-TEATRO CRITICO. TOMO 2 / Maner, Salvador – 1731 – 2mf – 9 – Pta1,500.00 – 84-7848-017-X – sp Pentalfa [440]

ANTI-TEATRO CRITICO. TOMO 3 / Maner, Salvador – 1731 – 1mf – 9 – Pta1,000.00 – 84-7848-018-8 – sp Pentalfa [440]

ANTI-TIMES – London, UK. 20 Nov-11 Dec 1819 – 12ft – 1 – uk British Libr Newspaper [072]

ANTITRUST, 1890-1990 – (Guide only: $310.00) – 509mf – 9 – $3,030.00 – 1-55655-433-8 – us UPA [332]

ANTITRUST BULLETIN – (1972- . 5,6. 1975- . 9) – v. 1- 1955- – 1 – us UMI [336]

ANTITRUST LAW : MAJOR BRIEFS AND ORAL ARGUMENTS, 1955 TERM – 1975 TERM / U.S. Supreme Court – 9 – $3,125.00 – 0-89093-188-7 – us UPA [340]

ANTITRUST LAW JOURNAL – (Title varies: v1-31 1952-66 as American Bar Association. Section of Antitrust Law Proceedings) – v1-60. 1952-1991 – 9 – $665.00 set – us Hein [340]

ANTITRUST LAW JOURNAL – v1-62. 1952-94 – 1,5,6 – $900.00 – us Hein [073]

L'ANTI-VACCINATEUR – Montreal, Canada. 22 dec 1885 – 1r – 1 – Can$25.00 – cn Can Microfilming [610]

ANTIVIRAL RESEARCH – v1-4. 1981-84 – 1,5,6,13 – sz Elsevier [073]

ANTI-XENIEN : IN AUSWAHL / ed by Stammler, Wolfgang – (Includes bibliographical references) – Bonn: A Marcus/E Weber, 1911 – 1 – us U.W. Library [430]

ANTI-ZARATHUSTRA : GEDANKEN ÜBER FRIEDRICH NIETZSCHES HAUPTWERKE / Henne am Rhyn, Otto – (Includes bibliographical references and index) – Altenburg, S.-A.: Alfred Tittel, 1899 – 1r – 1 – us U.W. Library [190]

Antoine, C F *see*
- DE LA SUCCESSION LEGITIME ET TESTAMENTAIRE...

ANTOINE GOULET, DE LA SOCIETE DES POETES CANADIENS-FRANCAIS : BIO-BIBLIOGRAPHIE ANALYTIQUE / Jacques, Marthe – 1961. SEM105P4 – 1mf – 9 – cn Bibl Nat [440]

Antoine, J *see* NUNGUSIUTTUQ INUUSIQ (THE ETERNAL LIFE)

Antoine, Jean *see* TRAITE D'ARCHITECTURE OU PROPORTIONS DES TROIS ORDRES GRECS.

ANTOINE THIBAUDEAU : OEUVRES COMPLETES, MICROFILMEES ENSEMBLE / Thibaudeau, Antoine-C – 2r – 1 – F743.86 – fr Armell [350]

ANTOINETTE BOURIGNON, QUIETIST / MacEwen, Alexander R – London: Hodder and Stoughton, 1910 – 1mf – us A.T.L.A. [240]

Antokol'skii, P *see* POETY I VREMIIA. SOV. PISATEL

ANTOLOGIA DE AUTORES CLASICOS EXTRANJEROS / Tamayo Zamora, B – Badajoz: Tip. Lib. A. Arqueros, 3rd ed 1909 – 1 – sp Bibl Santa Ana [440]

ANTOLOGIA DE AUTORES LATINOS-CRISTIANOS – Toledo: Biblioteca Latina, vol 3. 1944 – 1 – sp Bibl Santa Ana [240]

ANTOLOGIA DE MIS ANTOLOGIAS DE MIS DOCE MIL SONETOS / Sanchez Arjona, Vicente – Sevilla: Imprenta Zambrano, 1959 – 1 – sp Bibl Santa Ana [810]

ANTOLOGIA DE MIS CANTARES / Sanchez Arjona, Vicente – Sevilla: Imprenta Carlos Acuna, 1944 – 1 – sp Bibl Santa Ana [780]

ANTOLOGIA DE MIS PENAS CORTAS, PENSAMIENTOS Y MADRIGALES / Sanchez Arjona, Vicente – Sevilla: Imprenta Carlos Acuna, 1945 – 1 – sp Bibl Santa Ana [800]

ANTOLOGIA DE MIS SONETOS / Sanchez Arjona, Vicente – Sevilla: Imp. Carlos A., Tomo 3. 1954. Tomo 4-10, anos 1956, 1958, 1959 – 1 – sp Bibl Santa Ana [810]

ANTOLOGIA DE MIS SONETOS / Sanchez Arjona, Vicente – Sevilla: Imprenta Carlos Acuna, Tomo 2. 1952 – 1 – sp Bibl Santa Ana [810]

ANTOLOGIA DE MIS ULTIMOS SONETOS / Sanchez Arjona, Vicente – Sevilla: Imprenta Alvarez, Tomo 7. 1959 – 1 – sp Bibl Santa Ana [810]

ANTOLOGIA ECUATORIANA – 1892 – 1 – us I.U. Libraries [390]

ANTOLOGIA LATINA / Franco y Lozano, Francisco – Badajoz: Uceda Hermanos, 1907 – 1 – sp Bibl Santa Ana [946]

ANTOLOGIIA MUSAGETA – M. 1911. BR-1828 2 – 8 – ne IDC [460]

ANTOLOGIO DE MIS -HASTA AHORA-SEISCIENTOS SONETOS / Sanchez Arjona, Vicente – Sevilla: Imprenta Carlos Acuna, 1945 – 1 – sp Bibl Santa Ana [810]

ANTON AUERSPERGS (ANASTASIUS GRUENS) POLITISCHE REDEN UND SCHRIFTEN / ed by Hock, S – Wien, 1906 – 7mf – 9 – ne IDC [943]

Anton Crespo, Emilio *see*
- UN ANO DE ACCION SINDICAL EN LA PROVINCIA
- UN ANO DE ACCION SINDICAL EN LA PROVINCIA DE BADAJOZ

Anton, Guenther K *see* GESCHICHTE DES PREUSSISCHEN TRUCKVERBOTS

Anton, Ludwig *see* WIRRWARR

ANTON WILDGANS : EIN LEBEN IN BRIEFEN / ed by Wildgans, Lilly – Wien: W Frick. 3v. 1947 – 1r – 1 – us U.W. Library [860]

Antoni, Norberto Olegario *see* LA CONSTITUCION NACIONAL (LIBERTAD, IGUALDAD Y FRATERNIDAD) Y LOS DERECHOS DEL TRABAJADOR (RAZON DE LEGITIMO AMPARO)

Antoniades, M *see* EKPHRASIS TES HAGIAS SOPHIAS

ANTONIANUM – 1(1926)-35(1960) – 465mf – 9 – Dfl631.00 – ne Slangenburg [073]

ANTONIANUM – Roma. v1-35. 1926-1960 – 465mf – 9 – ne IDC [240]

ANTONII SANDERI PRESBYTERI GANDAVUM SIVE GANDAVENSIUM RERUM LIBRI SEX / Sanderus, Antoine – Bruxellis: Apud Ioannem Pepermanum, 1627. SEM105P947 – 6mf – 9 – Can$13.00 – cn Bibl Nat [020]

THE ANTONIN GENIZAH IN THE SALTYKOV-SHCHEDRIN PUBLIC LIBRARY IN LENINGRAD / Katsh, A I – New York. 1963. R-10.882 1 – 1mf – 9 – ne IDC [025]

ANTONIN ZAPOTOCKY PAMPHLET COLLECTION – 1947 – 1 – CSUXANL4984-B – us Hoover Inst Photo [331]

Antonini *see* PRINCIPES DE LA GRAMMAIRE FRANCOISE

ANTONIO AVERLINO FILARETE'S TRACTAT UEBER DIE BAUKUNST NEBST SEINEN BUECHERN VON DER ZEICHENKUNST UND DEN BAUTEN DER MEDICI / Oettingen, W von – (Quellenschriften fuer Kunstgeschichte. n.s. v. 3, Wien, 1890). BO-517r 1 – 9 – ne IDC [700]

ANTONIO BRASIO...MONUMENTA... / Barrado Manzano, Arcangel – Madrid: Archivo Ibero-Americano, 1959 – 1 – sp Bibl Santa Ana [240]

ANTONIO DA SILVA RIEGO. DOCUMENTAO... / Barrado Manzano, Arcangel – Madrid: Archivo Ibero-Americano, 1959 – 1 – sp Bibl Santa Ana [946]

ANTONIO DE SANTA MARIA...EN CUSTODIOS Y PROVINCIALES DE LA PROVINCIA DE SAN JOSE / Perez, Lorenzo – Madrid: Archivo Ibero Americano, 1924 – 1 – sp Bibl Santa Ana [946]

Antonio de Trujillo *see* SAN MARCOS DEFENDIDO EN EL MILAGRO QUE OBRA DIOS

ANTONIO HURTADO / Blanco Garcia, Francisco – Madrid: Saenz de Jubera, 1909 – sp Bibl Santa Ana [440]

Antonio, Jorge *see*
- ARGENTINA ENVENTA
- Y AHORA QUE?

ANTONIO JOSE CAVANILLES, 1745-1804 / Royal Botanical Garden, Madrid – 279mf – 9 – ne IDC [580]

ANTONIO LABRIOLA: LA VITA E IL PENSIERO / Pane, Luigi dal – Bologna: Forni, 1968 – 1 – us U.W. Library [945]

ANTONIO LEILA DE FERMO Y LA CONDENACION DEL INDIANUM JURE... / Leturia, Pedro S – Madrid: Missionalis Hispanica, 1949 – 1 – sp Bibl Santa Ana [240]

Antonio Muratori, Ludovico *see* RERUM ITALICARUM SCRIPTORES

Antonio y Hernandez, Pedro de A *see* ARITMETICA Y SISTEMA LEGAL DE PESAS

Antoniotto, Giorgio *see* L'ARTE ARMONICA..

Antoniou, Jim *see* ISLAMIC CITIES AND CONSERVATION

ANTONIUS CORVINUS, EIN MAERTYRER DES EVANGELISCH-LUTHERISCHEN BEKENNTNISSES : VORTRAG AUF DER GENERALVERSAMMLUNG DES VEREINS FUER REFORMATIONSGESCHICHTE AM MITTWOCH NACH OSTERN, 20. APRIL 1892 / Uhlhorn, Gerhard – Halle: Verein fuer Reformationsgeschichte, 1892. ([Schriften des Vereins fuer Reformationsgeschichte; 9. Jahrg., 4. Stueck, Nr. 37]) – 1mf – us A.T.L.A. [240]

Antonov, Vladimir Pavlovich *see* POD STIAGOM PROLETARSKOI BORBY

Antonovich, M A *see* IZBRANNYE STATI. FILOSOFIIA, KRITIKA, POLEMIKA

ANTONY AND OCTAVIUS : SCENES FOR THE STUDY / Landor, Walter Savage – London: Bradbury & Evans, 1856 – 1 roll – 1 – 1-55879-748-3 – uk Libr Preservation [810]

LA ANTORCHA CATOLICA – Almendralejo, 1901 – 5 – sp Bibl Santa Ana [240]

ANTORCHA MISIONERA – 1934-40 (complete) – 1r – 1 – ATLA S0538 – us A.T.L.A. [240]

Antoshkin, Dimitrii *see* PROFESSIONALNOE DVIZHENIE SLUZHASHCHIKH 1917-1924 GG

ANTRAKT – (Cont: Artiste Russe) – Moscow, 1866-68 (weekly) – 19mf – 9 – us Ross [780]

Antram, C B *see* BUTTERFLIES OF INDIA

Antraygues, E *see* NOTIONS DE DROIT MARITIME INTERNATIONAL

ANTRIM (BELFAST), 1805 : BRITISH ISLES CENSUS DIRECTORIES PROJECT, IRELAND. VOL 9 – 1mf – 9 – A$9.00 – at Vine [941]

Antrim, Joshua *see* THE HISTORY OF CHAMPAIGN AND LOGAN COUNTIES FROM THEIR FIRST SETTLEMENT

ANTRIM (SE), BELFAST, 1860 : BRITISH ISLES CENSUS DIRECTORIES PROJECT, IRELAND. VOL 8 – 4mf – 9 – A$27.00 – at Vine [941]

Antrobus, Augustine M *see* HISTORY OF DES MOINES AND ITS PEOPLE

ANTROPOLOGIA 3ER MUNDO – (Includes c.1: v.3:no.8 1971:Sept./Oct.-v.4:no.9 (1972:Feb./Mar.); no.10 1972:June- no.12 (1973:Feb./Mar.)) – 1 – CSUXAJA8074-S – us Hoover Inst Photo [301]

ANTROPOLOGIA FILOSOFICA 1. PRELIMINARES Y CUESTIONES BASICAS / Frutos Cortes, Eugenio – Zaragoza: Facultad de Filosofia y Letras, 1971 – sp Bibl Santa Ana [100]

ANTROPOLOGIA FILOSOFICA 2. DIMENSIONES ENTITATIVAS DEL HOMBRE / Frutos Cortes, Eugenio – Zaragoza: Facultad de Filosofia y Letras, 1972 – sp Bibl Santa Ana [100]

ANTROPOLOGIIA. RICHNIK KABINETU 1927-1930 IM – F. Vovk. Kiev. 1928-31. Lacking: (2) 1929. BR-1514 2 – 8 – ne IDC [301]

ANTROPOLOGIJA : VVEDENIE K IZUCENIJU CELOVEKA I CIVILIZACII(...) / Taylor, B – S. Petersburg: Bilivina, 1882 – fr Armell [301]

Antshel, Kevin M *see* THE EFFECT OF TIME OF SEASON ON THE ATHLETIC IDENTITY IN COLLEGIATE SWIMMERS

Antsyferov, A N *see*
- KOOPERATIVNYI INSTITUT I MUZEI
- KOOPERATIVNYI KREDIT
- OCHERKI PO KOOPERATSII
- TSENTRAL'NYE BANKI KOOPERATIVNOGO KREDITA

Antunez Toribio, Manuel *see* LA CASTELLANA DE RIBERA DEL FRESNO. LEYENDA.

ANTWERP, 1477-1559, FROM THE BATTLE OF NANCY TO THE TREATY OF CATEAU CAMBRESIS / Wegg, Jervis – London: Methuen, 1916.xix,359p. plates – 1 – us U.W. Library [949]

ANTWERP ARGUS – Antwerp, Ohio. 1883-93 – 3r – 1 – $32.50r – us Archival [071]

ANTWERP BEE-ARGUS – Antwerp, Ohio, 1983- – 3r – 1 – $32.50r – us Archival [978]

Antwerp, E I Van *see* ST. AUGUSTINE, THE DIVINATION OF DEMONS AND CARE FOR THE DEAD

ANTWOORDE DER DIENAREN DES WOORTS ENDE OUDERLINGEN DER KERCKEN VAN HOLLANT, OP DE REMONSTANTIE BIJ DE OVERICHEYT VAN LEIJDEN – t' Amstelredam by N. Biestkens. 1597. BME-244 1 – 9 – ne IDC [240]

ANTWOORDE OP DE VALSCHE BESCHULDINGHEN DOOR EEN ZEKER GHESWOREN VIJANDT DER GHEREFORMEERDE RELIGIE. ONDER DEN TITEL VAN DE IUSTIFICATIE VAN LEYDEN – Rotterdam, J. v. Waesberghe. 1598. BME-245 1 – 9 – ne IDC [240]

ANTWOORT VNDE ONDERRICHT D.J. OF DER WYSEN WIJSHEYT ODER MENSCHELIJCKE GHELEERTHEYDT NIET NUTLIJCK ODER NOOTWENDICH SY VOOR DEN GHELOOUIGHEN. DIE H. GODTLIJCKE SCHRIFT TE BETH TE VERSTAEN, ALS SOMMIGHE MEENEN? / Joris, David – 1556. BME-372 1 – 9 – ne IDC [240]

ANTWOORT-LIEDT, OP EENS WEDERDOOPERS LASTER-LIEDT / Bisschop, P de – Rotterdam, J. van Waesberghen. 1600. BME-253 1 – 9 – ne IDC [240]

ANTWORDT GESCHREUEN OP EIN BRIEFF, DIE EIN DOEPER IN VRIESZLANDT, GESANDT HAT, AN MARCO / Guelich van Berch, Heindrik – Arnold Bernsen. Coa5ln, 1576. BME-261 1 – 9 – ne IDC [240]

ANTWORT AUF DIE STREITSCHRIFT D. CREMERS, ZUM KAMPF UM DAS APOSTOLIKUM / Harnack, Adolf von – Leipzig: Grunow, 1892 – 1mf – us A.T.L.A. [240]

ANTWORT AUFF D. CHRISTOPHORI PEZELII PREDIGERS ZU BREMEN FALSCH GEBRAUCHTE GRUENDE:... / Hoffmann, David – Helmstadt, 1589 – 2mf – ne IDC [240]

ANTWORT AUFF DIE WIDERLEGUNG SO CLAUSZ BREUETEL. HAT GETHAN AUFF DAS BUCH, VON DER WIDERTAUFFER VERFLUCHTEN VRSPRUNG / Fischer, Chr. A – Bruck a.d. Teya. 1604. BME-143 1 – 9 – ne IDC [240]

ANTWORT, GLAUB VND BEKENTNIS AUFF DAS SCHOENE VND LIEBLICHE INTERIM / Amsdorff, N von – [Magdeburg], 1548 – 1mf – 9 – ne IDC [240]

ANTWORT MATTHIAE FLACII ILLIRICI, AUFF DAS STENCKFELDISCHE BUECHLEIN IUDICIUM UND C. GENANT / Flacius Illyricus d.A E, M – [Nuernberg, 1555] – 1mf – 9 – ne IDC [240]

ANTZEYGUNG WIE DIE GEFALLENE CHRISTENHEIT / Reinhart, M – 1524. BME-26 1 – 9 – ne IDC [240]

ANUARIO *see* ANUARIO SOCIALISTA

ANUARIO DE ESTADISTICA DE LA CIUDAD DE BUENOS AIRES...ANO 1883-1895 – Buenos Aires, 1885-1896 – 100mf – 9 – sp Cultura [310]

ANUARIO DE ESTADISTICA DE LA PROVINCIA DE TUCUMAN...ANO 1895, TOMO 1 – Buenos Aires, 1896 – 9mf – 9 – sp Cultura [310]
ANUARIO DE ESTADISTICA DE LA PROVINCIA DE TUCUMAN...ANO 1897-1898 – Buenos Aires, 1898-1899 – 14mf – 9 – sp Cultura [310]
ANUARIO DE LA DIRECCION GENERAL DE ESTADISTICA 1894 – Buenos Aires, 1895 – 10mf – 9 – sp Cultura [310]
ANUARIO DE LA DIRECCION GENERAL DE ESTADISTICA 1897, TOMO 1-2 – Buenos Aires, 1898 – 18mf – 9 – sp Cultura [310]
ANUARIO DEPORTIVO 1969 / Junta Provincial de Educacion Fisica y Deportes – Badajoz: Graf. Nemesio Jimenez, 1970 – sp Bibl Santa Ana [946]
ANUARIO ESTADISTICO DE ESPANA / Instituto Geografico – Madrid, 1858-1867 – 76mf – 9 – sp Cultura [310]
ANUARIO ESTADISTICO DE LA REPUBLICA DE PARAGUAY, ANO 1887 – Asuncion, 1889 – 9mf – 9 – sp Cultura [310]
ANUARIO ESTADISTICO DE LA REPUBLICA ORIENTAL DE URUGUAY, ANO 1884-1896 – Montevideo, 1885-1898 – 64mf – 9 – sp Cultura [310]
ANUARIO ESTATISTICO, ANO LECTIVO 1986/87 / Sao Tome and Principe Islands. Ministerio da Educacao e Cultura. Seccao de Estatistica – Sao Tome, 1988 – 4mf – 9 – DE-630/1 – ne IDC [370]
ANUARIO GENERAL DE ESTADISTICA : COLOMBIA / Colombia. Departamento Administrativo Nacional de Estadistica – (1906-14 not publ. 1918-25, 1926-28, 1935, 1955, 1958, 1963, 1965 v4 not available.) – 1905-1969/70 – 243mf – 9 – £1,530.00 – uk Chadwyck [972]
ANUARIO LEGISLATIVO DE INSTRUCCION PUBLICA...1885-1909 – Madrid, 1890-1910 – 200mf – 9 – sp Cultura [340]
ANUARIO SOCIALISTA – (Includes c.1: 1935, 1937, 1939-1944, 1946-1948, 1951)) – 1 – CSUXADP8398-S – us Hoover Inst Photo [335]
EL ANUNCIADOR – Trinidad, Colo: La Compania Publicista de "El Anunciador". [apr 1918-nov 18 1922] – 2r – 1 – us Res Libr [071]
ANUVARIO ESTATISTICO DE ANGOLA / Angola. Reparticao de Estatistica Geral – 1 – 127.00 – us L of C Photodup [960]
THE ANVAR-I SUHAILI, OR THE LIGHTS OF CANOPUS / ed by Kashifi, Husayn Vaiz – 1854. Moral fables of Bidpai, trans. into English – 1 – us I.U. Libraries [390]
ANVIL : THE PROLETARIAN FICTION MAGAZINE – v1-3. 1933-35 – 1r – 1 – us Ross [073]
THE ANVIL: THE PROLETARIAN FICTION MAGAZINE – Moberly, Mo. etc. v. 1-3 no. 13. May 1933-Oct Nov 1935 – 1 – us NY Public [335]
Anville, J B B d' *see* NOUVEL ATLAS DE LA CHINE
Anwand, Oscar *see* BEITRAEGE ZUM STUDIUM DER GEDICHTE VON J.M.R. LENZ
Anwander, G *see* CHRISTLICHE PREDIGT VON DER VOCAL UND INSTRUMENTALISCHEN MUSIC...
Anwar, Chairul *see* THE CONTRIBUTION OF SUMATRA AND KALIMANTAN TIMBER TO THE INDONESIAN ECONOMY
Anwar, Rosihan *see* ISLAM DAN ANDA, PERTJIKAN PERMENUNGAN WAK HADJI
ANWEISUNG ZUM GENERALBASSSPIELEN HALLE / Tuerk, Daniel G – Leipzig. 1800. BP-492 1 – 9 – ne IDC [780]
DIE ANWENDUNG DES BUCHES HIOB IN DER RABBINISCHEN AGADAH : 1. THEIL, DIE TANNAITISCHE INTERPRETATION VON HILLEL BIS CHIJA NACH SCHULEN / Kaufmann, Herman Ezechiel – (Includes bibliographical references) – Frankfurt a. M: J Kauffmann, 1893 – 1mf – 9 – 0-8370-3849-9 – 1985-1849 – us A.T.L.A. [220]
ANXIETY, STRESS, AND COPING : AN INTERNATIONAL JOURNAL / ed by Hobfoll, Stevan E & Schwarzer, Ralf – 9,5,1 – us Harwood [150]
THE ANXIOUS BENCH / Nevin, John W – Chambersburg, Pa.: Printed at the publication office of the German Ref. Church, 1844 – 1mf – us A.T.L.A. [240]
ANYTHING THAT'S PEACEFUL / Read, Leonard E – 1964. Together with: Essays From "Essays On Liberty", v.IX-X. 355p total. 1 fiche (24x) – 9 – 1.00f – at Libertarian Micro [320]
ANYUAN LUKUANG GONGREN YUNDONG SHILIAO – History materials on the Workers Movements at the Anyuan Mines. Comp. by Hunan Renmin Chubanshe, 1980. 1 reel. M H134 – 5 – cc Microforms [330]
AN-YUEH HSIEN-CHIH – 1836; 1897, 16. LACKING: v. 5-12. BCH-765 2 – 8 – ne IDC [030]
Anz, Henricus *see* SUBSIDIA AD COGNOSCENDUM GRAECORUM SERMONEM VULGAREM E PENTATEUCHI VERSIONE ALEXANDRINE REPETITA
Anz, W *see* ZUR FRAGE NACH DEM URSPRUNG DES GNOSTIZISMUS (T.U.U. 1-15/4)
Anzalone, Charles *see* PAPERS
Anzano, T *see* ELEMENTOS PRELIMINARES PARA PODER FORMAR UN SYSTEMA DE GOBIERNO DEL HOSPICIO GENERAL
ANZEIGE-BLATT DER KREIS-HAUPTSTADT SPEYER – Speyer, Germany. Jan 1, 1848-Dec 29, 1849 – 1r – 1 – gw Mikrofilm [072]
ANZEIGE-BLATT FUER DEN KREIS BIEDENKOPF UND BEZIRK VOEHL *see* HINTERLAENDER ANZEIGER
ANZEIGEBLATT FUER DIE STADT GIESSEN – Giessen, Germany.1848-49 – 1r – 1 – gw Mikrofilm [072]
ANZEIGER DER BIBLIOTHEKWISSENSCHAFT *see* ANZEIGER FUER LITERATUR DER BIBLIOTHEKWISSENSCHAFT
ANZEIGER DER (KAISERLICHEN) AKADEMIE DER WISSENSCHAFTEN : MATHEMATISCH-NATURWISSENSCHAFTLICHE KLASSE – Wien, 1864-1941. v1-78 – 465mf – 9 – H-1095c/2 – ne IDC [500]
ANZEIGER DER KAISERLICHEN AKADEMIE DER WISSENSCHAFTEN : PHILOSOPHISCH-HISTORISCHE KLASSE – (Missing: 1864-1899. v1-36) – Wien, 1864-1939. v1-76 – 160mf – 9 – H-1096c/2 – ne IDC [500]
ANZEIGER DER OESTERRICHISCHEN AKADEMIE DER WISSENSCHAFTEN, MATHEMATISCH-NATURWISSENSCHAFTLICHE KLASSE – v.110-118, 1973-81. Earlier vols. quoted upon request. ISSN: 0065-535X – 1,5,6,9,13 – 80.00v – us UMI [500]
ANZEIGER DER ORNITHOLOGISCHEN GESELLSCHAFT IN BAYERN – v1-7 1919-66. Z-2003 2 – 8 – ne IDC [590]
ANZEIGER DER VERORDNUNGEN DER LANDES-VERWALTUNGEN UND GERICHTE – Bayreuth, oct 4 1808-09 (incomplete), jul 3-aug 3 1810, 1811 – 2r – 1 – Dist. gw Mikrofilm – gw Misc Inst [350]
ANZEIGER FUER BARR UND UMGEBUNG – Barr, 1900-16 – 1 – Dist. gw Mikrofilm – fr A.C.R.P.P. [944]
ANZEIGER FUER BIBLIOGRAPHIE UND BIBLIOTHELWISSENSCHAFT *see* ANZEIGER FUER LITERATUR DER BIBLIOTHEKWISSENSCHAFT
ANZEIGER FUER DEN KREIS PLESS – (Also known as: Nikolaier Anzeiger und Plesser Stadtblatt) – Pless (Pszczyna), Poland. 15 Apr-30 Dec 1923; Feb 1924-31; 10 Aug-30 Sept 1932 – 6r – 1 – gw Mikrofilm [072]
ANZEIGER FUER DEUTSCHES ALTERTUM *see* ZEITSCHRIFT FUER DEUTSCHES ALTERTUM UND DEUTSCHE LITERATUR
ANZEIGER FUER DIE ALTERTUMSWISSENSCHAFT – Vienna. v1-8. 1948-55 – 5,9 – Dfl320.00; Dfl40.00v – ne Swets [930]
DER ANZEIGER FUER HEMELINGEN UND DIE BREMER SUEDOESTLICHEN VORORTE HASTEDT, SEBALDSBRUECK UND OSTERHOLZ – Bremen, oct 1 1938-sep 30 1940 – 4r – 1 – Inquire at Mikrofilmarchiv for details – gw Misc Inst [943]
ANZEIGER FUER HOF UND UMGEGEND *see* NEUES HOEFER INTELLIGENZ-BLATT
ANZEIGER FUER KUNDE DER DEUTSCHEN VORZEIT / Organ des Germanischen Museums – (1840-1852 have not been published) – Leipzig, 1832-1839. v1-8; 1853-1883. v1-30 – 304mf – 9 – H-405/2 – ne IDC [930]
ANZEIGER FUER LITERATUR DER BIBLIOTHEKSWISSENSCHAFT : ANZEIGER FUER BIBLIOTHEKSWISSENSCHAFT. ANZEIGER FUER BIBLIOGRAPHIE UND BIBLIOTHEKWISSENSCHAFT. NEUER ANZEIGER FUER BIBLIOGRAPHIE UND BIBLIOTHEKSWISSENSCHAFT / ed by Petzoldt, Julius – (Anzeiger fuer Bibliographie und Bibliothekswissenschaft: Jahrgang 1840-43 3v v/1281p on 17mf DM100.00 diazo DM125.00 silver. Anzeiger fuer Literatur der Bibliothekswissenschaft: Jahrgang 1850-55 6v xiv/2350p on 28mf DM140.00 diazo DM168.00 silver. Neuer Anzeiger fuer Bibliographie und Bibliothekswissenschaft: Jahrgang 1856-86 31v 13,125p on 155mf DM 900.00 diazo DM1,100.00 silver) – Jahrgang 1840-86. Berlin, Dresden, Halle, Leipzig und Stuttgart, 1841-86 – 200mf – 9 – DM1,100.00 diazo DM1,300.00 silver – gw Olms [020]
ANZEIGER FUER LITERATUR DER BIBLIOTHEKWISSENSCHAFT – (Anzeiger der Bibliothekwissenschaft Dresden und Leipzig, sp. Halle 1845-49. Anzeiger fuer Bibliographie und Bibliothekwissenschaft Halle 1850-55. Neuer Anzeiger fuer Bibliographie und Bibliothekwissenschaft Dresden, sp. Berlin u. Stuttgart 1856-1886) – Dresden, Leipzig, 1840-86 (mf ed 1990) – 83mf – 9 – DM965.00 – 3-89131-034-X – gw Fischer [020]
ANZEIGER FUER OBERHESSEN *see* INTELLIGENZBLATT FUER DIE PROVINZ OBERHESSEN
ANZEIGER FUER SCHWEIZERISCHE ALTERTUMSKUNDE – 1869-1920. Zurich. 9 reels – 1 – $755.00 – us UPA [930]
DER ANZEIGER FUR GOLDINGEN UND WINDAU – Goldingen, Germany. (Kuldiga U.S.S.R.). Nov 5, 1927-29. Incomplete – 1 – gw Mikrofilm [072]
ANZEIGER VOM OBERLAND – (Cont: Nuetzliches Unterhaltungs- und Wochenblatt fuer verschiedene Leser, 1802-feb 1826; Wochenblatt fuer den Oberamtsbezirk Biberach, -sep 1831; Intelligenzblatt fuer die Oberaemter Biberach und Waldsee, -1843; Amts- und Intelligenzblatt fuer den Oberamtsbezirk Biberach, -may 17 1870. Cont by: Biberacher Tagblatt, sep 2 1935; Verbo, may 3 1940; Donau-Bodensee-Zeitung, Friedrichshafen, jan 2 1942 (Bereichsausgabe); Schwaebische Zeitung, Leutkirch, jan 3 1944 (Bereichsausgabe)) – Biberach, jul 7 1802-apr 20 1945, jul 13 1945- – 1 – Inquire at Mikrofilmarchiv for details – gw Misc Inst [943]
ANZEIGUNG WAS DER GEBRAUCH VND GEWONHAIT IN DES TUERCKEN LAND I.. – N.p., 1526 – 1mf – 9 – H-8139/1 – ne IDC [956]
ANZENGRUBER / David, Jakob Julius – Berlin: Schuster & Loeffler, [1920?] – 1r – 1 – us U.W. Library [430]
Anzengruber, Ludwig *see*
- ALLERHAND HUMORE
- ANZENGRUBERS WERKE IN VIERZEHN TEILEN
- AUS'M GEWOHNTEM G'LEIS
- BRAVE LEUT' VOM GRUND
- BRIEFE VON LUDWIG ANZENGRUBER
- EIN FAUSTSCHLAG
- GESAMMELTE WERKE
- GESAMMELTE WERKE VON LUDWIG ANZENGRUBER
- LETZTE DORFGAENGE
- DER PFARRER VON KIRCHFELD
- DER STERNSTEINHOF
- DIE TOCHTER DES WUCHERERS
- DAS VIERTE GEBOT

ANZENGRUBERS WERKE IN VIERZEHN TEILEN / Anzengruber, Ludwig; ed by Bettelheim, Anton – Berlin: Bong, [1918] – 2r – 1 – us U.W. Library [800]
ANZIEGER – Providence. R.I. 1878-1918 – 1 – us UMI [071]
Anzilotti, D *see*
- CORSO DI DIRITTO...
- IL DIRITO INTERNAZIONALE NEI GIUDIZI INTERNI
- IL RICONOSCIMENTO DELLE SENTENZE STRANIERE DI DIVORZIO...
- STUDI CRITICI...
- SUI MUTAMENTI DEL RAPPORTI PATRIMONIALI FRA CONIUGI...

AO-MEN CHI-LUEH – 1751, 2. BCH-598 2 – 8 – ne IDC [950]
AONE'S LEADERSHIP PROSPECTIVES – (Cont: Nursing Scan in Administration) – Philadelphia. v1 nov 1993-94*. v2-4 jan 1994-feb 1996 1,9; v1-2 nov 1993-dec 1994*. v3-4 jan 1995-feb 1996 5 – 1,5,9 – D20629 – us UMI [610]
AONIO PALEARIO : A CHAPTER IN THE HISTORY OF THE ITALIAN REFORMATION / Bonnet, Jules – London: Religious Tract Society, 1864 – 1mf – us A.T.L.A. [240]
AORN (Association of Operating Room Nurses) *see* JOURNAL
AOUW REPORTER – Salem OR. Jan-Feb 1901 – 1 – us U.O. Library [071]
A.P.A. del Colegio "Santisima Trinidad" de Plasencia *see* ESTATUTOS
APA MONITOR / American Psychological Association – (Only subsc to paper copy can purchase the latest 3 complete publ yrs. Does not apply to customers outside US) – Washington. v1-26 oct 1970-dec 1995; v27 1996; v28 1997+ – 1 – inquire – D6088 – us UMI [150]
THE A.P.A. MOVEMENT : A SKETCH / Desmond, Humphrey J – Washington: New Century Press, 1912 – 1mf – us A.T.L.A. [240]
APA SEBAB TERDJADI BHARATAYUDHA / Sedah, Mpu – SE 4191 1. v. 1 only. 1963 – 9 – ne IDC [950]
Apacible, G *see* TO THE AMERICAN PEOPLE
APARATO BIBLIOGRAFICO...EXTREMADURA / Barrantes Moreno, Vicente – 1875. 3 tomos – 9 – 1.50f – sp Bibl Santa Ana [946]
Aparicio Perez, Antonio *see* IMPOSICION SOBRE LA RENTA EN LA LEY DE REFORMA TRIBUTARIA DE 11-6-1964
APARTHEID AND SOCIAL RESEARCH / ed by Rex, John – 1981 – 199p – 9 – 92-3-101898-1 – fr UNESCO [305]
APARTHEID, POVERTY AND MALNUTRITION – 1982 – 106p – it F.A.O. [360]
APELACION A LA DEMOCRACIA / Saavedra, Emiliana Lopez – Buenos Aires: Editorial Redaccion, [1983] – 1 – CSUXADJ2700-B – us Hoover Inst Photo [320]
APELDOORNSCHE-BOSCHBLAADJES – (Cont. as: Boschblaadjes. Amsterdam, 1932-1940. v1-8) – Amsterdam, 1930-1931. Nos. 1-6 – 26mf – 9 – J-261-17/1 – ne IDC [073]
APENDICE A LA EDUCACION POPULAR. TOMO 1 / Rodriguez Campomanes, Pedro – 1775 – 2mf – 9 – Pta1,500.00 – 84-7848-270-9 – sp Pentalfa [370]
APENDICE A LA EDUCACION POPULAR. TOMO 2 / Rodriguez Campomanes, Pedro – 1775 – 2mf – 9 – Pta1,500.00 – 84-7848-271-7 – sp Pentalfa [370]
APENDICE A LA EDUCACION POPULAR. TOMO 3 / Rodriguez Campomanes, Pedro – 1776 – 2mf – 9 – Pta1,500.00 – 84-7848-272-5 – sp Pentalfa [370]
APENDICE A LA EDUCACION POPULAR. TOMO 4 / Rodriguez Campomanes, Pedro – 1777 – 2mf – 9 – Pta1,500.00 – 84-7848-273-3 – sp Pentalfa [370]
APENDICE ,A LA...SALIDA DE DON QUIXOTE / Habela Patino, Eugenio – 1789 – 9 – $1.50f – sp Bibl Santa Ana [830]
APENRADER TAGEBLATT – Apenrade, dec 21 1920-jan 31 1929 – 1 – Dist. gw Mikrofilm – gw Misc Inst [948]
APERCU DU PLAN D'ETUDES ET DE LA METHODE D'ENSEIGNEMENT SUIVIS AU COLLEGE D'OTTAWA / College of Ottawa – Ottawa, 1882. 00711. (Pre-1900 Canadiana) – 9 – cn C.I.H.M. [370]
APERCU GENERAL DES TROIS ROYAUMES / Sankoku, Tsuran Dzusetsu – 1832 – 1 – uk Microform Academic [900]
APERCU STATISTIQUE DE L'ARRONDISSEMENT DE LANZO DANS LE DEPARTEMENT DE L'ERIDAN FAIT EN MESSIDOR AN IX / Gregory, Gaspard de – 9 – fr Hachette [944]
APERCU STATISTIQUE SUR LA DUREE DE LA VIE / Bigeon – Toulon. Duplessis Ollivault, 1829. 60 p. 1 fiches. (Statistics Series: Medical Studies) – 9 – 6.00 – fr Bibl Nationale [310]
APERCU SUR LA CONDITION DES CLASSES OUVRIERES ET CRITIQUE DE L'OUVRAGE DE M. BURET, PAR LE PCE D.S – (Condition of 19th C. French working class series). 1844 – 9 – fr Hachette [360]
APERCU SUR QUELQUES CONTEMPORAINS – s.l., s.n., 18??. 04201. (Pre-1900 Canadiana) – 9 – cn C.I.H.M. [971]
APERCUS SUR L'ESPAGNE CHRETIENNE DU 4TH SIECLE OU LE "DE LAPSO" DE BACHIARIUS / Duhr, J – Louvain, 1934 – 3mf – 8 – ne Slangenburg [240]
APHORISMEN ZUM GELDPROBLEM = APHORISMS ON THE MONEY PROBLEM / Beckerath, Ulrich von – 1931 – 9 – 1.00f – at Libertarian Micro [335]
APHORISMI CONFESSARIORUM / Sa, E – Duaci, 1623 – 8mf – 8 – ne Slangenburg [240]
APHORISMI URBIGERANI, OR CERTAIN RULES, CLEARLY DEMONSTRATING THE THREE INFALLIBLE WAYS OF PREPARING THE GRAND ELIXIR.. / Urbigerus, Baro – London: Printed for H. Faitborne, 1690. 4 leaves, 86p – 1 – us U.W. Library [540]

APHORISMOS SACADOS DE LA HISTORIA DE P. C. TACITO / Arias Montano, Benito – 1614 – 9 – 1.50f – sp Bibl Santa Ana [450]

APHORISMS AND REFLECTIONS : CONDUCT, CULTURE AND RELIGION / Spalding, J L – Chicago: A.C. McClurg, 1901 – 1mf – us A.T.L.A. [306]

APHORISMS, SELECTED BY JULIA R. GINGELL / Spencer, Herbert – 1894. With: The Free Market and Its Enemy by Leonard E. Read. 1965. 1 fiche (24x) – 9 – $1.00f – at Libertarian Micro [320]

APHRAETES : PATROLOGIA SYRIACA 1 / ed by Graffin, B – 2v 24mf – 8 – ne Slangenburg [240]

APHRAHAT'S DES PERSISCHEN WEISEN HOMILIEN / Bert, Georg – Leipzig: J.C. Hinrichs, 1888. (Texte und Untersuchungen zur Geschichte der altchristlichen Literatur; Bd. 3, Heft 3) – 2mf – us A.T.L.A. [930]

APHRAHAT'S DES PERSISCHEN WEISEN HOMILIEN (T.U.T. 1-3/4A) / Bert, Georg – Leipzig, 1888 – 7mf – 9 – ne Slangenburg [240]

API / Lembaga Da' wah Mahasiswa Islam (HMI) Djaja – (Monthly. Ceased with 1966(4)) – Djakarta. (1-3). 1966 – 4mf – 9 – SE-1315/1 – ne IDC [950]

API ACCOUNT – (Cont: NAAPI Account) – Washington, 1978-94* 1; 1995-97+ 1,5,9 – 1,5,9 – D19025.03 – us UMI [350]

API (AMERICAN PETROLEUM INSTITUTE) – Standards. Printed index. Updated every 60 days – 6,9 – us Info Handling [660]

API KARTINI – Djakarta. (incomplete) SE-335 1. 1959-1964 – 9 – ne IDC [073]

API MARHAENISME – Sala. Se-336 1. 1963-1964. Lacking 1963(2) – 9 – ne IDC [073]

API MERDEKA – (Lacking: 1945, v1(1); 1945/1946, v3-5, p17-76; v11-12, p171-200; v15, p233-248) – Jogjakarta, Ikatan Peladjar Indonesia, 1945-1946 – 7mf – 9 – ne IDC [950]

API NEWSLETTER – (Cont: Public Interest Accounting Newsletter. Cont by: NAAPI Account) – San Francisco, 1975-76* – 1 – D19025.01 – us UMI [350]

API SERIES / North Carolina. State University. Raleigh. Agricultural Policy Institute – v.1-41. 1961-Oct 1969 – 1,5 – us Spaulding [630]

API SERIES / North Carolina State University.Agricultural Policy Institute – No.42-49. 1970-82. 1 reel – 1,5 – us Spaulding [630]

APIC / Association for Practitioners in Infection Control – (Cont: APIC Newsletter n12232. Cont by: Association for Practitioners in Infection Control (APIC) Journal) – Racine. cum index v4-5 1976-77 1,5,9; v5 mar-dec 1977 1,5*,9* – 1,5,9 – inquire – D12232.01 – us UMI [073]

APIC *see* APIC NEWSLETTER

APIC JOURNAL – Assoc. for Practitioners in Infection Control. v.8- 1980- – 1,5,6,9 – us UMI [073]

APIC JOURNAL *see*
- APIC
- AMERICAN JOURNAL OF INFECTION CONTROL

APIC NEWSLETTER / Association for Practitioners in Infection Control – (Cont by: APIC n12232.01) – Racine. v1-4. 1973-76* – 1 – inquire – D12232 – us UMI [073]

APIC NEWSLETTER *see* APIC

DER APIKOYRES = FREETHINKER – (In Yiddish) – Moscow, RU. v2 no5. May 1932 – 1r – 1 – $25.00 – cn Can Microfilming [072]

Apjohn, Lewis *see* RICHARD COBDEN AND THE FREE TRADERS

APLA QUARTERLAY JOURNAL *see* AIPLA QUARTERLY JOURNAL

APO : ORGAN OF THE AFRICAN POLITICAL ORGANISATION – (Only available as diazo) – Cape Town, South Africa, 1909-1915 – 50mf – 9 – sa SA Libr [320]

APO (AFRICAN POLITICAL ORGANISATION) – [Cape Town: The Organisation. [v1 n2-v8 n219]. jun 5 1901-apr 8 1922 – 5r – 1 – us Res Libr [073]

APOCALYPSE : ITS STRUCTURE AND PRIMARY PREDICTIONS / Brown, David – New York: Christian Literature Co, 1891 – 1mf – 9 – 0-8370-2474-9 – 1985-0474 – us A.T.L.A. [220]

THE APOCALYPSE : AN INTRODUCTORY STUDY OF THE REVELATION OF ST. JOHN THE DIVINE: BEING A PRESENTMENT OF THE STRUCTURE OF THE BOOK AND OF THE FUNDAMENTAL PRINCIPLES OF ITS INTERPRETATION / Benson, Edward White – (Includes appendix) – London: Macmillan, 1900 – 1mf – 9 – 0-8370-2275-4 – 1985-0275 – us A.T.L.A. [220]

THE APOCALYPSE : WITH A COMMENTARY AND AN INTRODUCTION ON THE REALITY OF PREDICTION, THE HISTORY OF CHRISTENDOM, THE SCHEME OF INTERPRETATION, AND THE ANTICHRIST OF ST PAUL AND ST JOHN / Huntingford, Edward – London: Kegan Paul, Trench, 1881 – 1mf – 9 – 0-8370-3696-8 – 1985-1696 – us A.T.L.A. [220]

APOCALYPSE: AN INTRODUCTORY STUDY OF THE REVELATION / Benson, Edward White – London: Macmillan, 1900.1 fiche – 9 – us A.T.L.A. [240]

L'APOCALYPSE DE JEAN / Loisy, Alfred Firmin – (Includes bibliographical references and index) – Paris: Emile Nourry, 1923 – 1mf – 9 – 0-8370-4657-2 – 1985-2657 – us A.T.L.A. [220]

THE APOCALYPSE OF BARUCH – Translated from the Syriac.... Edited, with introduction, notes and indices, by R. H. Charles. 1896 – 1 – us A.T.L.A. [220]

THE APOCALYPSE OF JESUS CHRIST: AN EXPOSITION / Mead, Willis W – New York: W.W. Mead, 1909. 1 fiche – 9 – us A.T.L.A. [240]

THE APOCALYPSE OF ST. JOHN 1-3 : THE GREEK TEXT WITH INTRODUCTION, COMMENTARY, AND ADDITIONAL NOTES / Hort, Fenton John Anthony – (Includes indexes of subjects and of Greek and Hebrew words) – London: Macmillan, 1908 – 1mf – 9 – 0-8370-3660-7 – 1985-1660 – us A.T.L.A. [220]

THE APOCALYPSE OF ST. JOHN, 1-3 / Hort, Fenton John Anthony – 1908 – 9 – $10.00 – us I.R.C. [240]

THE APOCALYPSE: VIEWED UNDER THE LIGHT OF THE DOCTRINES OF THE UNFOLDING AGES / Waller, Charles B – London: C. Kegan Paul, 1878. 1 fiche – 9 – us A.T.L.A. [240]

APOCALYPSIS ALFORDIANA, OR, FIVE LETTERS TO...H. ALFORD, DEAN OF CANTERBURY / Elliott, Edward Bishop – London: Seeley, Jackson, 1862. 1 fiche – 9 – us A.T.L.A. [240]

APOCALYPSIS SPAGYRICA ET PHILOSOPHICA / Hermogenes – Leipzig, 1739. 224p – 1 – us U.W. Library [540]

APOCALYPTICAL KEY : AN EXTRAORDINARY DISCOURSE ON THE RISE AND FALL OF PAPACY, OR, THE POURING OUT OF THE VIALS IN THE REVELATION OF ST. JOHN, CHAPTER 16 / Fleming, Robert – New York: American and Foreign Christian Union, 1855 – 1mf – 9 – 0-8370-8338-9 – 1986-2338 – us A.T.L.A. [220]

APOCRYPHA AND PSEUDEPIGRAPHA OF THE OLD TESTAMENT / Charles, R H – 1913 – 9 – $36.00 – us I.R.C. [220]

APOCRYPHA ANECDOTA : SECOND SERIES / ed by James, M R – 1897 – 5mf – 9 – ne Slangenburg [240]

APOCRYPHA ANEDOCTA / ed by James, M R – 1893 – 4mf – 9 – ne Slangenburg [240]

THE APOCRYPHA OF THE OLD TESTAMENT : WITH HISTORICAL INTRODUCTIONS, A REVISED TRANSLATION, AND NOTES CRITICAL AND EXPLANATORY / Bissell, Edwin Cone – (Includes appendixes) – New York: Charles Scribner, 1880 – 2mf – 9 – 0-8370-6723-5 – 1986-0723 – us A.T.L.A. [220]

THE APOCRYPHAL GOSPELS AND OTHER DOCUMENTS RELATING TO THE HISTORY OF CHRIST – Translated from the originals in Greek, Latin, Syriac, etc., with notes, scriptural references and prolegomena by B. Harris Cowper. 6th ed. English. 1897 – 1 – us A.T.L.A. [240]

THE APOCRYPHAL NEW TESTAMENT / James, M R – Oxford, 1924 – 9 – $21.00 – us I.R.C. [240]

THE APOCRYPHAL NEW TESTAMENT.. – London: W. Hone, 1820,1888 printing. xv,271p – 1 – us U.W. Library [240]

LES APOCRYPHES DE L'ANCIEN TESTAMENT / Andre, Louis Edouard Tony – (Includes index) – Florence: Osvaldo Paggi, 1903 – 1mf – 9 – 0-8370-2098-0 – 1985-0098 – us A.T.L.A. [220]

APOGRYPHAL ACTS OF THE APOSTLES EDITED FROM SYRIACS MSS / Wright, W – London. v1-2. 1871 – Dfl42.00 – ne Slangenburg [220]

APOKALIPSIS V RUSSKOI LITERATURE / Kruchenykh, A – M. 1923. BR-951 2 – 8 – ne IDC [460]

DIE APOKALYPSE DES ELIAS (T.U.U. 2-17/3A) / Steindorff, G – Leipzig, 1899 – 3mf – 9 – ne Slangenburg [240]

DIE APOKALYPSE UND IHRE NEUESTE KRITIK / Hirscht, Arthur – (Includes bibliographical references) – Leipzig: August Neumann, 1895 – 1mf – 9 – 0-8370-3592-9 – 1985-1592 – us A.T.L.A. [220]

APOKRIFICHESKIIA SKAZANIIA O VETKHOZAVETNYKH LITSAKH I SOBYTIIAKH PO RUKOPISIAM SOLOVETSKOI BIBLIOTEKI (SBORNIK OTDELENIIA RUSSKOGO IAZYKA I SLOVESNOSTI IMP. AK. NAUK, TOM XVII, NO. 1) / Porfir'ev, Ila – Spb. 1877. v1-101. BR-4067 2 – 1508mf – 8 – ne IDC [460]

APOKRIFY I LEHENDY Z UKRAINS'KYKH RUKOPISIV / ZIBRAV, UPORIADKOVAV I POIASNYV I. FRANKO – U L'vovi. 5v. 1896-1910 – 37mf – 9 – R-4057/2 – ne IDC [947]

APOKRIFY I LEHENDY Z UKRAINS'KYKH RUKOPISIV/ZIBRAV, UPORIADKOVAV I POIASNYV / Franko, I – U L'vovi. 5v. 1896-1910 – 37mf – 9 – ne IDC [947]

DIE APOKRYPHEN APOSTELGESCHICHTEN UND APOSTELLEGENDEN / Lipsius, Richard Adelbert – 2v. 1883-87 – 1 – us A.T.L.A. [240]

DIE APOKRYPHEN UND PSEUDEPIGRAPHEN DES ALTEN TESTAMENTS / Kautzsch, Emil F – Tuebingen, 1900. Neudr. 1921 – 28mf – 8 – ne Slangenburg [220]

APOLINEO CADUCEO...CONCORDIA ENTRE OPINIONES...SOBRE CONSULTAS DE LOS MEDICOS... / Luque, C – Sevilla, 1694 – 7mf – 9 – sp Cultura [610]

APOLLINARIOS VON LAODICEA : SEIN LEBEN UND SEINE SCHRIFTEN: NEBST EINEM ANHANG, APOLLINARII LAODICENI QUAE SUPERSUNT DOGMATICA / Draeseke, Johannes – Leipzig: J.C. Hinrichs, 1892. (Text und Untersuchungen zur Geschichte der altchristlichen Literatur; 7. Bd., Heft 3/4) – 1mf – us A.T.L.A. [240]

APOLLINARIOS VON LAODICEA (T.U.U. 1-7/3.4.) / Draeseke, J – Leipzig, 1892 – 8mf – 9 – ne Slangenburg [240]

APOLLO / Allen, Wilkes – 1790. Cover title. Manuscript collection of vocal and instrumental music in 1, 2, 3, and 4 parts, playable by solo instruments or keyboard and 1 or 2 solo instruments. Six of the tunes are the compiler's originals. MUSIC 1971 – 1 – us L of C Photodup [780]

APOLLO – Manaos, Amazonas. 28 Ago-4 Set 1882 – 1,5,6 – bl Biblioteca [072]

THE APOLLO – v1. Nov 1882-Mar 1883 – 1 – 185.00 – us Opus [073]

APOLLO BAY CEMETERY RECORDS – 1887-1993 – 4mf – 9 – at Corangamite [920]

APOLLO BAY NEWS – 1963-1964 – 1r – 1 – at Corangamite [072]

APOLLO, THE MAGAZINE OF THE ARTS – (1971- . 5,6. 1977- . 9) – 1- 1925- – 1 – us UMI [073]

APOLLON – Spb. 1909-17. B-1105 2 – 8 – ne IDC [073]

L'APOLLON MODERNE, OU LE DEVELOPPEMENT INTELLECTUEL PAR LES SONS DE LA MUSIQUE.. / Brijon, C R – 1782 – 9 – us Sibley [780]

APOLLONIOS RHODIOS: INTERPRETATIONEN ZUR ERZAEHLUNGSKUNST UND QUELLENVERWERTUNG / Stoesel, Franz – Bern, Haupt, 1941. 158 p. Film Mas 8407 – 1 – us H.U. Library [450]

APOLLONISU VON TYANA UND CHRISTUS, ODER, DAS VERHAELTNISS DES PYTHAGOREISMUS ZUM CHRISTENTHUM : EIN BEITRAG ZUR RELIGIONSGESCHICHTE DER ERSTEN JAHRHUNDERTE NACH CHRISTUS / Baur, Ferdinand Christian – Tuebingen: L.F. Fues, 1832 – 1mf – us A.T.L.A. [180]

APOLOGETIC LECTURES ON THE FUNDAMENTAL TRUTHS OF CHRISTIANITY / Luthardt, Christoph Ernst – Edinburgh: T. & T. Clark, 1888. 1 fiche – 9 – us A.T.L.A. [240]

APOLOGETIC LECTURES ON THE MORAL TRUTHS OF CHRISTIANITY / Luthardt, Christoph Ernst – 1881 – 9 – us A.T.L.A. [240]

APOLOGETIC LECTURES ON THE SAVING TRUTHS OF CHRISTIANITY / Luthardt, Christoph Ernst – 1880 – 9 – us A.T.L.A. [240]

THE APOLOGETIC OF THE NEW TESTAMENT / Scott, Ernest Findlay – (Includes index) – London: Williams & Norgate; New York: G P Putnam, 1907 – 1mf – 9 – 0-8370-5189-4 – 1985-3189 – us A.T.L.A. [230]

APOLOGETICO DISCURSO...EN QUE SE PRUEBA QUE LOS POLVOS DE QUARANGO SE DEBEN USAR... / Salado Garces de Leon, D – Sevilla, 1687 – 1mf – 9 – sp Cultura [615]

APOLOGETICS: A COURSE OF LECTURES / Smith, Henry Boynton – New York: A.C. Armstrong, 1882. 1 fiche – 9 – us A.T.L.A. [240]

APOLOGETICS, OR, THE RATIONAL VINDICATION OF CHRISTIANITY / Beattie, Francis Robert – Richmond: Pres. Comm. of Pub., 1903. 2 fiches – 9 – us A.T.L.A. [240]

APOLOGETICS: OR, THE SCIENTIFIC VINDICATION OF CHRISTIANITY / Ebrard, Johannes Heinrich August – 3v. 1886-1887 – 1 – us A.T.L.A. [240]

APOLOGETIQUE ET RAISON DANS LES PENSEES DE PASCAL / Bouchilloux, Helene – 2mf – 9 – 10064 – fr Atelier National [190]

APOLOGETISCHE VORTRAEGE : VON DEN BERNISCHEN GEISTLICHEN / Bernard, A et al – Bern: Haller, 1870 – 1mf – 9 – us A.T.L.A. [240]

APOLOGETISCHE VORTRAEGE UEBER DIE GRUNDWAHRHEITEN DES CHRISTENTHUMS / Luthardt, Christoph Ernst – Leipzig: Doerffling & Franke, 1864. 1 fiche – 9 – us A.T.L.A. [240]

APOLOGI CREATURARUM / Moerman, J – O-698 1. 1584 – 9 – ne IDC [450]

APOLOGIA : AN EXPLANATION AND DEFENCE / Abbott, Edwin Abbott – London: Adam & Charles Black, 1907 – 1mf – 9 – 0-8370-2011-5 – 1985-0011 – us A.T.L.A. [220]

APOLOGIA CATOLICA... / Sallaberry, Juan Faustino – Madrid: Razon y Fe, 1930 – 1 – sp Bibl Santa Ana [240]

APOLOGIA DANIELIS HOFMANNI, MISSA AD THEODORVM BEZAM QUA TO RETON IN VERBIS COENAE SACRAE:... / Hoffmann, David – Helmstadii, 1586 – 7mf – ne IDC [240]

APOLOGIA DE LOS BANOS DE LA MUY NOBLE Y LEAL CIUDAD DE ALHAMA / Vergara Cabezas, F – Granada, 1636 – 2mf – 9 – sp Cultura [615]

APOLOGIA DEL DOCTOR... / Luna Vega, J – Sevilla, 1605 – 1mf – 9 – sp Cultura [610]

APOLOGIA DEL TOMO 5 DE LA HISTORIA LITERARIA DE ESPANA / Rodriguez Mohedano, P & Rodriguez Mohedano R – 1789 – 1mf – 9 – Pta1,000.00 – 84-7848-161-3 – sp Pentalfa [440]

APOLOGIA M. CASPARIS AQVILAE / Adler, K – [Magdeburg], 1548 – 1mf – 9 – ne IDC [240]

APOLOGIA MATTHIAE FLACIJ ILLYRICI AD SCHOLAM VITEBERGENSEM IN ADIAPHORORUM CAUSA / Flacius Illyricus d.A E, M – [Magdeburgi, 1549] – 1mf – 9 – ne IDC [240]

APOLOGIA MEDICINALIS ACEDUNT EGREGIAE CENSURAE DE VENAE SEXTIONE IN FEBRIBUS... / Vaez, P – Barcelona, 1593 – 5mf – 9 – sp Cultura [615]

APOLOGIA ODER VERANTWORTUNG DESS CHRISTLICHEN CONCORDIEN BUCHS... / Chemnitz, Martin – Heydelberg, 1583 – 5mf – 9 – ne IDC [240]

APOLOGIA, ODER VERANTWORTUNG DESS CHRISTLICHEN CONCORDIEN BUCHS JN WELCHER DIE WAHRE CHRISTLICHE LEHRE...VERTHEYDIGET:... / Kirchner, T – Heydelberg, 1583 – 5mf – ne IDC [240]

EEN APOLOGIA OF VERANDTWOORDINGHE, OP 20. VERSHEYDEN ARTIKELEN DIE MENNO SYMONS TEGHEN HET DISPUTACY BOECXKEN VAN HET BESPRECK MET HEM OUER DE LEERE GEHOUDEN / Micron, M – Amstelredam: Jan Willemsz, 1597 – 9 – ne IDC [240]

EEN APOLOGIA OFTE VERANTWOORDINGE, DAT WY (DIE VANDER WERELT MET GROOTEN ONRECHT ANABAPTISTEN GHESCHOLDEN WORDEN) GHEEN WEEDERDOOPERS NOCH SECTEMAKERS EN SIJNT / Philips, Dirk – BME-308 1 – 9 – ne IDC [240]

APOLOGIA PRO CONSILIO MEDICINALI IN DIMINUTE VISIONES ADVERSUS DUAS EPITOLAS... / Aguiar, T – Marchena, 1621 – 6mf – 9 – sp Cultura [610]

APOLOGIA PRO PRINCIPIBUS CATHOLICIS ACALIJS ORDINIBUS IMPERIJ ADUERSUS MUCORES ET CALUMNIAS BUCERI, SUPER ACTIS COMICIORUM RATISPONAE / Eck, Johann – 1542 – 1 – us A.T.L.A. [240]

APOLOGIA PRO SANCTISSIMA VIRGINE MARIA, MATRE DOMINI / Rivetus, Andr. – Lugd. Batavorum, 1639 – 8mf – 8 – ne Slangenburg [240]

APOLOGIA...DEL AGUA DE LA VIDA...EN QUE SE HACE EXAMEN Y JUICIO DE LOS PAPELES... / Amigo y Bertran, L – Zaragoza, 1682 – 1mf – 9 – sp Cultura [610]

APOLOGIAE DUAE : GOZECHINUS – EPISTOLA AD WALCHERUM; BURCHARDUS – APOLOGIA DE BARBIS – 1985 – 5mf – 9 – Bf1,350.00 – be Brepols [240]

APOLOGIE DE VOLTAIRE / L'Hospital, J E – Londres, 1786 – 9 – fr Hachette [440]

DIE APOLOGIE DES ARISTIDES : RECENSION UND REKONSTRUKTION DES TEXTES / Hennecke, Edgar – Leipzig: J.C. Hinrichs, 1893. (Texte und Untersuchungen zur Geschichte der altchristlichen Literatur; 4. Bd., Heft 3) – 1mf – us A.T.L.A. [240]

DIE APOLOGIE DES ARISTIDES (T.U.U. 1-9/1B) / Raabe, R – Leipzig, 1892 – 2mf – 9 – ne Slangenburg [240]

APOLOGIE DES CHRISTENTHUMS / Luthardt, Christoph Ernst – 4pts. 1880-98 – 1 – us A.T.L.A. [240]

APOLOGIE DU GOUT FRANCOIS RELATIVEMENT A L'OPERA. POEME, AVEC UN DISCOURS APOLOGETIQUE, ET DES ADIEUX AUX BOUFFONS / Caux de Cappeval, N de – 1754 – 9 – us Sibley [780]

EEN APOLOGIE OF VERANDTWOORDINGHE, OP 20. VERSCHEYDEN ARTIKELEN DIE MENNO SYMONS TEGHEN HET DISPUTACY BOECXKEN VAN HET BESPRECK MET HEM OUER DE LEERE GEHOUDEN / Micron, M – Embden: G. Ctematius, 1558 – 9 – ne IDC [240]

APOLOGIE POUR LA REFORMATION, POUR LES REFORMATEURS, ET POUR LES REFORMEZ / Jurieu, P – Rotterdam, 1683 – 11mf – 9 – CA-134/1 – ne IDC [240]

APOLOGIE POUR L'AUTHEUR DE L'EXAMEN DE LA POSSESSION DES RELIGIEUSES DE LOUVIERS / Yvelin, Pierre – Rouen. 1643 – 9 – fr Hachette [360]

APOLOGIE POUR LES CATHOLIQUES CONTRE LES FAUSSETEZ ET LES CALOMNIES D'UN LIVRE INTITULE : LA POLITIQUE DU CLERGE DE FRANCE / Arnauld, Antoine – Liege. 2v. 1681-82 – 13mf – 9 – CA-114/1 – ne IDC [240]

THE APOLOGIES OF JUSTIN MARTYR. TO WHICH IS APPENDED THE EPISTLE TO DIOGNETUS / Justin the Martyr, Saint – Introd. and Notes by Basil L. Gildersleeve. New York: Harper, 1877. xli,289p. Greek or English text – 1 – us U.W. Library [240]

AN APOLOGY FOR ACTORS (1612) BY THOMAS HEYWOOD, BOUND WITH A REFUTATION OF THE APOLOGY FOR ACTORS (1615) BY I.G / Heywood, Thomas – Introds. and bibliog. notes by Richard H. Perkinson. 1941. 156p – 9 – 10.00 – us Scholars' Facs [790]

AN APOLOGY FOR GREAT BRITAIN: IN ALLUSION TO A PAMPHLET ENTITLED 'CONSIDERATIONS ETC. PAR UN CANADIEN, M.P.P.' / Cuthbert, Ross – Quebec: J. Neilson, 1809. SEM16P18 – 1r – 5 – Can$9.00 – cn Bibl Nat [941]

AN APOLOGY FOR LOLLARD DOCTRINES, ATTRIBUTED TO WYCLIFFE / Wycliffe, John – With an introduction and notes by James Henthorn Todd. 1842 – 1 – us A.T.L.A. [240]

THE APOLOGY OF ARISTIDES / Aristides – London, New York: W. Scott, 1909 – 1mf – us A.T.L.A. [240]

THE APOLOGY OF ARISTIDES ON BEHALF OF THE CHRISTIANS, FROM A SYRIAC MS : WITH AN APPENDIX BY J.A. ROBINSON / ed by Harris, J R – 1891 – 3mf – 9 – ne Slangenburg [240]

THE APOLOGY OF THE CHRISTIAN RELIGION : HISTORICALLY REGARDED WITH REFERENCE TO SUPERNATURAL REVELATION AND REDEMPTION / Macgregor, James – Edinburgh: T.& T. Clark, 1891 – 2mf – us A.T.L.A. [240]

APONSKAI A INTERVENTSII A 1918-1922 GG. V DOKUMENTAKH / Podgotovil k pechati I. Mints – Moskva: T Sentrarkhiv, 1934 – 1 – CSUX88-B8922 – us Hoover Inst Photo [947]

APONTAMENTOS PARA A HISTORIA DA ADMINISTRACAO DA DIOCESE E DA ORGANISCAO DO SEMINARIO LYCEU.. / Ferreira da Silva, Francisco, BP – Lisboa, Typ. Minerva Central, 1899. 216p. ill – 1 – us U.W. Library [240]

APONTAMENTOS PARA A HISTORIA DE GUERRA DE ZAMBEZIA, 1871-1875 / de Silva Barahona e Costa, Henrique Cesar – Lisbon: P Aurea, 1895 – 1 – us Res Libr [960]

APONTAMENTOS PHYTOGEOGRAPHICOS. ANGOLA / Welwitsch, R – (Ann. Conselho Ultramar, v. 55, 1858, Lisboa, 1859). B-5506 2 – 8 – ne IDC [580]

APOPHTEGMATA : STUDIEN ZUR GESCHICHTE DES AELTESTEN MOENCHTUMS / Bousset, Wilhelm – Tuebingen, 1923 – 9mf – 8 – Dfl32.00 – ne Slangenburg [240]

APORTACION A UN INVENTARIO DE LA CARTOGRAFIA GEOGRAFICA EN GALICIA / Mendez Martinez, Gonzalo – 2mf – 9 – Pta1,500.00 – 84-85422-68-6 – sp Pentalfa [550]

APORTACION AL ESTUDIO DE LOS ACIDOS L(-) MALICO, D(-) Y L(+) LACTICO EN MOSTOS Y VINOS DE TIERRA DE BARROS / Pinto Corraliza, Maria del Carmen – Badajoz: Universidad de Extremadura, 1980 – 1 – sp Bibl Santa Ana [946]

APORTACION AL ESTUDIO DE LOS COMPUESTOS NITROGENADOS EN MOSTOS Y VINOS DE TIERRA DE BARROS / Macias Laso, Pedro – Badajoz: Universidad de Extremadura, 1980 – 1 – sp Bibl Santa Ana [946]

APORTACION AL ESTUDIO DE LOS VINOS DE LA ZONA DE "TIERRA DE BARROS" (BADAJOZ) / Maynar Marino, Juan – Badajoz: Universidad de Extremadura. Facultad de Ciencias. Departamento de Quimica Fisica, 1975 – 1 – sp Bibl Santa Ana [550]

APORTACION AL ESTUDIO DEL FUERO DE BAYLIO / Cerro Sanchezherrera, Eduardo – Madrid: Editorial Revista de Derecho Privado, 1964 – 1 – sp Bibl Santa Ana [370]

APORTACION AL VOCABULARIO / Rodriguez Perera, Francisco – Badajoz: Imprenta de la Diputacion Provincial, 1959 – sp Bibl Santa Ana [440]

APORTACIONES AL CONOCIMIENTO DE LAS COMUNIDADES SILICICOLAS DE POA BULBOSA EN LA PROVINCIA DE LEON / Tascon Alvarez, Luis – 1980. Tesis Doctorales en Microficha no. 04 – 3mf – 9 – Pta2,000.00 – 84-85422-11-2 – sp Pentalfa [300]

APORTACIONES AL ESTUDIO DEL PROCESO DE INDUSTRIALIZACION EN ASTURIAS / Vazquez Garcia, Juan Antonio – 3mf – 9 – Pta2,000.00 – 84-85422-49-X – sp Pentalfa [338]

APORTACIONES AL LENGUAJE DE TORRES NAHARRO / Segura Covarsi, Enrique – Badajoz: Imp. Dip. Provincial, 1944 – 1 – sp Bibl Santa Ana [946]

EIN APOSTEL DER WIEDERTAEUFER / Keller, Ludwig – Leipzig: S Hirzel, 1882 – 1mf – 9 – 0-8370-8913-1 – 1986-2913 – us A.T.L.A. [240]

DER APOSTEL PAULUS: EINE MANN FUER UNSERE ZEIT: VORTRAG / Kuebel, Robert – Stuttgart: Paul Moser, 1876. 1 fiche – 9 – us A.T.L.A. [240]

DAS APOSTELDECRET NACH SEINER AUSSERCANONISCHEN TEXTGESTALT (T.U.U. 2-28/3) / Resch, A – Leipzig, 1905 – 3mf – 9 – ne Slangenburg [240]

DIE APOSTELGESCHICHTE / Belser, Johannes Evangelist – Wien: Mayer, 1905. 1 fiche – 9 – us A.T.L.A. [240]

DIE APOSTELGESCHICHTE : UNTERSUCHUNGEN / Harnack, Adolf von – Leipzig, 1908 – 4mf – 8 – ne Slangenburg [240]

DIE APOSTELGESCHICHTE: IHRE QUELLEN UND DEREN GESCHICHTLICHER WERT / Spitta, Friedrich – Halle a.S.: Waisenhauses, 1891. 1 fiche – 9 – us A.T.L.A. [240]

DIE APOSTELGESCHICHTE IM LICHTE DER NEUEREN TEXTQUELLEN / Clemen, Carl – Giessen: Alfred Toepelmann, 1905. 1 fiche – 9 – us A.T.L.A. [240]

DIE APOSTELGESCHICHTE, ODER DER ENTWICKLUNGSGANG DER KIRCHE VON JERUSALEM BIS ROM / Baumgarten M – Braunschweig 2 Baende 2. Auflage 1859 – 20mf – 8 – ne Slangenburg [240]

DIE APOSTELGESCHICHTE (T.U.U. 1-9/3.4.) / Weiss, Bernhard – Leipzig, 1893 – 5mf – 9 – ne Slangenburg [240]

DIE APOSTELGESCHICHTE UEBERSETZT UND ERKLAERT / Felten, J – Freiburg im Breisgau, 1892 – 9mf – 8 – ne Slangenburg [220]

APOSTILLAS... / Posada, Eduardo – Madrid: Razon y Fe, 1927 – 1 – sp Bibl Santa Ana [200]

THE APOSTLE OF ALASKA: THE STORY OF WILLIAM DUNCAN OF METLAKAHTLA / Arctander, Jno. W – New York: Fleming H. Revell, 1909. 395p. 1 fiche – 9 – us A.T.L.A. [240]

THE APOSTLE OF BURMA : A MISSIONARY EPIC: IN COMMEMORATION OF THE CENTENNIAL OF THE BIRTH OF ADONIRAM JUDSON / Richards, William Carey – Boston: Lee and Shepard; New York: C T Dillingham, 1889, c1888 – 1mf – 9 – 0-8370-6344-2 – 1986-0344 – us A.T.L.A. [810]

THE APOSTLE OF FREE LABOUR, THE LIFE OF WILLIAM COLLISON, FOUNDER AND GENERAL SECRETARY OF THE NATIONAL FREE LABOUR ASSOCIATION / Collison, William – Indexed – 336p – 9 – $1.00f – at Libertarian Micro [331]

THE APOSTLE OF PATIENCE AND PRACTICE:...EXPOSITION OF THE EPISTLE OF ST JAMES / Taylor, Frank Johnson – London: H.R. Allenson, 1907. 1 fiche – 9 – us A.T.L.A. [240]

AN APOSTLE OF THE NORTH : MEMOIRS OF THE RIGHT REVEREND WILLIAM CARPENTER BOMPAS, D.D., FIRST BISHOP OF ATHABASCA, 1874-1884, FIRST BISHOP OF MACKENZIE RIVER, 1884-1891, FIRST BISHOP OF SELKIRK (YUKON) 1891-1906 / Codey, H A – New York: E.P. Dutton, 1908 – 1mf – us A.T.L.A. [240]

THE APOSTLE PAUL: A SKETCH OF THE DEVELOPMENT OF HIS DOCTRINE / Sabatier, Auguste – New York: James Pott, 1896. 1 fiche – 9 – us A.T.L.A. [240]

THE APOSTLES' CREED / Harnack, Adolf von; ed by Saunders, Thomas Bailey – London: A. and C. Black, 1901 – 1mf – us A.T.L.A. [240]

THE APOSTLES' CREED : ITS ORIGIN, ITS PURPOSE, AND ITS HISTORICAL INTERPRETATION : A LECTURE, WITH CRITICAL NOTES / McGiffert, Arthur Cushman – New York: Scribner, 1902 – 1mf – us A.T.L.A. [240]

THE APOSTLES' CREED : ITS RELATION TO PRIMITIVE CHRISTIANITY / Swete, Henry Barclay – Cambridge: University Press, 1899 – 1mf – us A.T.L.A. [240]

THE APOSTLES' CREED AND THE NEW TESTAMENT / Kunze, Johannes – New York: Funk & Wagnalls, 1912 – 1mf – us A.T.L.A. [240]

APOSTLES OF MEDIAEVAL EUROPE / Maclear, George Frederick – (Includes bibliographical references) – London: Macmillan, [1869?] – 1mf – 9 – 0-8370-6148-2 – 1986-0148 – us A.T.L.A. [920]

APOSTLES OF OUR LORD / Greenhough, John Gersham – New York: A.C. Armstrong, 1904. 1 fiche – 9 – us A.T.L.A. [240]

THE APOSTLES OF OUR LORD: PRACTICAL STUDIES / Symington, Alexander MacLeod – London: Hodder & Stoughton, 1880. 1 fiche – 9 – us A.T.L.A. [240]

THE APOSTLESHIP OF PRAYER = APOSTOLAT DE LA PRIERE : A HOLY LEAGUE OF CHRISTIAN HEARTS UNITED WITH THE HEART OF JESUS / Ramiere, Henri – (In English) – Baltimore: John Murphy, 1866 – 1mf – 9 – 0-8370-7186-0 – 1986-1186 – us A.T.L.A. [240]

APOSTOL BAUTISTA EN LA PERLA ANTILLANA / Munoz, A Lopez – Biography of Dr. M.N. McCall – 1 – $14.42 – us Baptist [240]

UN APOSTOL CON TEMPLE DE MARTIN. LA BEATA FILIPINA DUCHENSE / Bayle, Constantino – Barcelona, Madrid: Razon y Fe, 1944 – 1 – sp Bibl Santa Ana [240]

EL APOSTOL DE LA MENTIRA JUAN PERON : [LAS PALABRAS Y LOS HECHOS DE UNA TIRANIA] / Dominguez, Francisco – [Buenos Aires]: Ediciones La Reja, [1956] – 1 – CSUXADP4964-B – us Hoover Inst Photo [320]

L'APOSTOLAT DE LA PRESSE: VADE MECUM DES PROPAGATEURS DE LA CROIX – Montreal: La Maison de la bonne Presse, 1894. 02481. (Pre-1900 Canadiana) – 9 – cn C.I.H.M. [240]

Apostolat des bons livres. Bibliotheque *see* CATALOGUE DE LA BIBLIOTHEQUE DE L'APOSTOLAT DES BONS LIVRES

APOSTOLAT DES OBLATS DE MARIE IMMACULEE – 1-50. 1929-79 – 1 – us Res Libr [073]

APOSTOLIC ADVOCATE *see* ADVOCATE FOR THE TESTIMONY OF GOD

THE APOSTOLIC AGE : ITS LIFE, DOCTRINE, WORSHIP AND POLITY / Bartlet, James Vernon – New York: Scribner, 1899. (Ten epochs of church history; v1) – 2mf – us A.T.L.A. [240]

THE APOSTOLIC AGE IN THE LIGHT OF MODERN CRITICISM / Ropes, James Hardy – New York: Charles Scribner, 1907. 1 fiche. 8370-4965-2 – 9 – us A.T.L.A. [240]

THE APOSTOLIC AGE OF THE CHRISTIAN CHURCH / Weizsaecker, Carl von – London: Williams and Norgate; New York: Putnam, 1907-1912. (Theological translation library; v.1, 5) – 2mf – us A.T.L.A. [240]

APOSTOLIC AND MODERN MISSIONS / Martin, Chalmers – New York: Fleming H Revell, 1898 – 1mf – 9 – 0-8370-6273-X – 1986-0273 – us A.T.L.A. [240]

APOSTOLIC CHRISTIANITY : NOTES AND INFERENCES MAINLY BASED ON S. PAUL'S EPISTLES TO THE CORINTHIANS / Henson, Hensley – London: Methuen, 1898 – 1mf – us A.T.L.A. [240]

APOSTOLIC FAITH – Portland OR. no19-no115 (no dates), Jan 1955-Dec 1965 – 1 – us U.O. Library [071]

THE APOSTOLIC FATHERS / Holland, Henry Scott – London: S.P.C.K.; New York: Pott, Young, [1878?] – 1mf – us A.T.L.A. [240]

THE APOSTOLIC FATHERS / Lightfoot, Joseph B – 2pts. in 5 v – 9 – us A.T.L.A. [240]

THE APOSTOLIC FATHERS, PART 1 : S. CLEMENT OF ROME / Lichtfoot, J – (Part 2: S. Ignatius and Polycarp) – 51mf – 8 – ne Slangenburg [240]

APOSTOLIC HYMNS / Kirkland, J V & Kirkland, R S – 1898 – 1 – 10.18 – us Baptist [240]

THE APOSTOLIC PREACHING AND ITS DEVELOPMENT / Dodd, C H – 1936 – 9 – $10.00 – us I.R.C. [240]

THE APOSTOLIC TIMES – 15 Apr 1869-24 Dec 1874 – 1 – $73.00 – us OmniSys [071]

Apostolic Union of Secular Priests *see* GENERAL RULE..

APOSTOLICAL SUCCESSION IN THE CHURCH OF ENGLAND / Haddan, Arthur West – London: Rivingtons, 1883 – 1mf – us A.T.L.A. [240]

DAS APOSTOLICUM : SEIN URSPRUNG UND SEINE BIBLISCHE BEGRUENDUNG / Werther, Richard – (Includes bibliographical references) – Rathenow: A. Haase, 1875 – 1mf – 9 – 0-8370-5799-X – 1985-3799 – us A.T.L.A. [220]

DAS APOSTOLISCHE SYMBOL : SEINE ENTSTEHUNG, SEIN GESCHICHTLICHER SINN, SEINE URSPRUENGLICHE STELLUNG IM KULTUS UND IN DER THEOLOGIE DER KIRCHE : EIN BEITRAG ZUR SYMBOLIK UND DOGMENGESCHICHTE / Kattenbusch, Ferdinand – Leipzig: J.C. Hinrichs, 1894-1900 – 4mf – us A.T.L.A. [240]

DAS APOSTOLISCHE SYMBOL IM MITTELALTER / Wiegand, F – Giessen, 1904 – 1mf – 8 – ne Slangenburg [210]

DIE APOSTOLISCHE VOLLMACHT DES PAPSTES IN GLAUBENS-ENTSCHEIDUNGEN / Weninger, Francis Xavier – (Includes bibliographical references) – Innsbruck: Felician Rauch, 1841 – 1mf – 9 – 0-8370-6853-3 – 1986-0853 – us A.T.L.A. [240]

DAS APOSTOLISCHE ZEITALTER DER CHRISTILCHEN KIRCHE / Weizsaecker, Karl Heinrich von – 1892 – 1 – us A.T.L.A. [240]

DIE APOSTOLISCHEN KONSTITUTIONEN : EINE LITTERAR-HISTORISCHE UNTERSUCHUNG / Funk, Franz Xaver – Rottenburg am Neckar: W. Bader, 1891 – 1mf – us A.T.L.A. [240]

DIE APOSTOLISCHEN VAETER : UNTERSUCHUNGEN UEBER INHALT UND URSPRUNG DER UNTER IHREM NAMEN ERHALTENEN SCHRIFTEN / Hilgenfeld, A – Halle: C.E.M. Pfeffer, 1853 – 1mf – us A.T.L.A. [220]

APOSTOLKA MILOSIERDZIA Z CHICAGO / Malak, o. Henryk Maria – London, 1962 – 1r – 1 – us I.H.R.C. [978]

APOSTOLY ANARKHII : BAKUNIN, KROPOTKIN, MAKHAEV / Berlin, Pavel Abramovich – Petrograd: "Novai a Rossii a", [1917] – 1 – CSUX89-B7297 – us Hoover Inst Photo [320]

APOTECK FUR DEN GMEYNE MAN, DER DIE ERTZET ZUERUCHE AM GUT NICHT VERMUGENS, ODER SONST IN DER NOT ALLWEGE NICHT ERRAICHEN KAN – n.p., 1529 – 1 – us U.W. Library [615]

APOTHEOSE : GRAND MARCHE SOLONELLE / Gottschalk, L M – Boston: Ditson Co, ca 1886 – 1 – us Sibley [780]

L'APOTHEOSE DU DICTIONNAIRE DE L'ACADEMIE / Chastein – 1696 – 9 – fr I.C.S. [440]

L'APOTRE PAUL : ESQUISSE D'UNE HISTOIRE DE SA PENSEE / Sabatier, Auguste – (Includes index) – 3e ed rev et augm Paris: Librairie Fischbacher, 1896 – 1mf – 9 – 0-8370-5013-8 – 1985-3013 – us A.T.L.A. [220]

App, Austin Joseph *see* THE TRUE CONCEPT OF LITERATURE; EIGHT REPRINTED AND TWO ORIGINAL ARTICLES. SAN ANTONIO: MISSION PRESS 1948. 110P. WITH: CLASSIC FRENCH PLAYS/JOYNES, EDWARD SOUTHEY

APPALACHIA – (1977- . 5,6,9) – v. 1-. 1967- – 1 – us UMI [370]

APPALACHIAN NOTES – v1-13. 1973-85 – 2r – 1 – $150.00 – us OmniSys [420]

APPANOOSE IOWEGIAN – Centerville. Iowa. 1887-1889; 1891; 1894-1895 – 1 – us UMI [071]

Appanoose Union Sunday School, Franklin County, KS *see* RECORD BOOK

APPARAAT VOOR DE STUDIE DER GESCHIEDENIS / Romein, J M – Groningen, 1960 – Dfl9.00 – ne Slangenburg [240]

APPARATUS AD HISTORIAM NATURALEM SANGUINIS HUMANI / Boyle, R – M-306. 1684 – 9 – ne IDC [612]

EIN APPARATUS CRITICUS ZUR PESITTO ZUM PROPHETEN JESAIA / Diettrich, Gustav – Giessen: Alfred Toepelmann, 1905 – 1mf – 9 – 0-8370-2913-9 – 1985-0913 – us A.T.L.A. [220]

APPARATUS HOSTIENSIS IN DECRETALES. LIBROS 3-5 (SIECLE 14) – Calahorra – 1r – 5,6 – sp Cultura [240]

APPARATUS IN LIBRIUM 6 (SIECLE 14) / Baisio, Guido de – Barcelona – 2r – 5,6 – sp Cultura [240]

APPARATUS WORK FOR BOYS AND GIRLS; A COURSE OF GRADED INSTRUCTION...IN THE USE OF HORIZONTAL BARS, PARALLEL BARS, HORSES, RINGS, LADDERS.. / Zwarg, Leopold Fredrick – Philadelphia: J.J. McVey, c1923. xix,109p. illus – 1 – us U.W. Library [790]

APPAREL MERCHANDISING – 1985- – 1,5,6,9 – us UMI [073]

APPAREL WORLD – v2- 1981- – 1,5,6,9 – us UMI [680]

APPARITIONS, OR, THE MYSTERY OF GHOSTS, HOBGOBLINS, AND HAUNTED HOUSES DEVELOPED / Taylor, Joseph – 1814 – 1 – us I.U. Libraries [390]

APPEAL – Carson City. Nev. 1865-1946 – 1 – us UMI [071]

APPEAL – Ludington. Mich. 1873-1874; 1897-1899 – 1 – us UMI [071]

APPEAL – Memphis. Tenn. -w. 1843-90 – 1 – us UMI [071]

APPEAL – Milwaukie OR. Dec 22 1911 – 1 – us U.O. Library [071]

APPEAL AVALANCHE – Memphis. Tenn. 1890-94 – 1 – us UMI [071]

APPEAL DEMOCRAT – Marysville. Calif. 1958- – 1 – us UMI [071]

APPEAL FROM TRADITION TO SCRIPTURE AND COMMON SENSE / Peck, George – 1844 – 9 – us A.T.L.A. [240]

APPEAL TO REASON – Girard, KA. 1908-10, 1915, 1917, 1919-21, 1945 (all incompl) – 1 – us Hoover Inst Photo [071]

APPEAL TO REASON – Girard. Kan. 1895-1922 – 1 – us UMI [071]

AN APPEAL TO THE BRITISH NATION, ON THE HUMANITY AND POLICY OF FORMING A NATIONAL INSTITUTION, FOR THE PRESERVATION OF LIVES AND PROPERTY FROM SHIPWRECK / Hillary, William – 5th ed. 1825 – 9 – $20.00 – uk Libr Preservation [941]

AN APPEAL TO THE BRITISH NATION ON THE TREATMENT EXPERIENCED BY NAPOLEON BUONAPARTE IN THE ISLAND OF ST HELENA / Doris, Charles, de Bourges – By M. Santini pseud.. 3rd ed. augm. with preface. London: Ridgways, 1817. 63p. French and English parallel texts – 1 – us U.W. Library [941]

AN APPEAL TO THE CANADIAN INSTITUTE ON THE RECITATION OF PARLIAMENT / Fleming, Sandford – Toronto: Copp, Clark, 1892. 03126. (Pre-1900 Canadiana) – 9 – cn C.I.H.M. [971]

APPEAL TO THE CHRISTIAN WOMEN OF THE SOUTH / Grimke, Angelina Emily – 3rd ed. 1836 – 9 – us A.T.L.A. [240]

AN APPEAL TO THE METHODIST EPISCOPAL CHURCH : CONCERNING WHAT ITS NEXT GENERAL CONFERENCE SHOULD DO ON THE QUESTION OF SLAVERY / Stevens, Abel – New York: Printed by John F. Trow, 1859 – 1mf – us A.T.L.A. [240]

AN APPEAL TO THE MONTREAL CONFERENCE AND THE METHODIST CHURCH GENERALLY: FROM A CHARGE BY REV. WILLIAM SCOTT, IN WHICH IS SHOWN HIS CHARGE TO BE INVALID, AND HIS DEFENCE OF THE SEMINARY OF ST SULPICE AGAINST THE INDIANS OF OKA TO BE BASELESS:. / Borland, John – Montreal: Witness Print. House, 1883. 00183. (Pre-1900 Canadiana) – 9 – cn C.I.H.M. [240]

AN APPEAL TO THE ORACLES OF GOD : OR, REASONS OF DISAGREEMENT FROM THE DOCTRINE OF THE REV. MR. WESLEY / Green, J – London, 1746 – 1mf – 9 – MP-332/1 – ne IDC [240]

AN APPEAL TO THE PEOPLE, ON THE CAUSES AND CONSEQUENCES OF A WAR WITH GREAT BRITAIN – Boston, 1811 – 1mf – 9 – ILM-2825/1 – ne IDC [340]

AN APPEAL TO THE PUBLIC, ON THE SUBJECT OF NATIONAL DEBT / Price, R – London, 2nd ed 1772 – 2mf – 9 – ne IDC [350]

AN APPEAL TO THE SCOTTISH BISHOPS AND CLERGY AND GENERALLY TO THE CHURCH OF THEIR COMMUNION / Palmer, William P – Edinburgh: Alex. Laurie, 1849 – 2mf – us A.T.L.A. [240]

AN APPEAL TO THE SONS OF AFRICA / Jones, Charles P – 1902 – $20.00 – us A.B.H.S. [240]

AN APPEAL TO THE UNPREJUDICED,... – London, 1739 – 1mf – 9 – ILM-2756/1 – ne IDC [340]

AN APPEAL TO THE WOMEN OF THE NOMINALLY FREE STATES / Grimke, Angelina Emily – 1838 – 9 – us A.T.L.A. [240]

AN APPEALE TO TRUTH / Webbe, Joseph – 1622. 59p. (English Linguistics Series 1500-1800) – 9 – us UMI [400]

APPEALS EXPEDITING SYSTEMS : AN EVALUATION OF 2ND AND 8TH CIRCUIT PROCEDURES / Farmer, Larry C – Washington: FJC, Sept 1981 – 1mf – 9 – $1.50 – LLMC 95-818 – us L.L.M.C. [340]

APPEARANCE AND REALITY : A METAPHYSICAL ESSAY / Bradley, Francis Herbert – London: S. Sonnenschein; New York: Macmillan, 1893 – 2mf – us A.T.L.A. [110]

APPEARANCE AND REALITY : A METAPHYSICAL ESSAY / Bradley, Francis Herbert – London: Swan Sonnenschein; New York: Macmillan, 1899 – 1 roll – 1 – 1-55879-386-0 – uk Libr Preservation [110]

APPEARANCE DOCKET / Lucas County. Ohio. Supreme Court – 1838-1855 – 1r – 1 – $32.50r – us Archival [324]

APPEARANCE DOCKETS / Crawford County. Ohio. Common Pleas. Civil Division – 1832-1853 – 1r – 1 – $32.50r – us Archival [324]

APPEARANCE DOCKETS / Huron County. Ohio. Common Pleas. Civil Division – 1818-1853 – 3r – 1 – $32.50r – us Archival [324]

APPEARANCE DOCKETS / Wood County. Ohio. Common Pleas. Civil Division – 1826-1924 – 11r – 1 – $32.50r – us Archival [324]

THE APPEARANCES OF OUR LORD AFTER THE PASSION:...EARLIEST CHRISTIAN TRADITION / Swete, Henry Barclay – London: Macmillan, 1907.1 fiche – 9 – us A.T.L.A. [240]

L'APPEL – Paris. En russe. Titre russe: Prisyv. no. 3-60. 17 oct 1915-31 mars 1917. mq no. 1-2, 7, 28, 36, 41, 45, 54, 59 – 1 – fr A.C.R.P.P. [073]

L'APPEL – Sillery, Quebec. 1 sep 1945-v3 n24. 22 avr 1948; n25. 15 avr 1948 – 1r – 1 – Can$30.00 – cn Can Microfilming [072]

L'APPEL *see* L'HORIZON

APPEL AU PARLEMENT IMPERIAL ET AUX HABITANS DES COLONIES ANGLOISES, DANS L'AMERIQUE DU NORD,. – Quebec: Flavien Vallerand, 1824. SEM105P78 – 1mf – 9 – Can$2.25 – cn Bibl Nat [971]

APPEL AU PARLEMENT IMPERIAL ET AUX HABITANTS DES COLONIES ANGLOISES, DANS L'AMERIQUE DU NORD,... / Blanchet, Francois Xavier – Quebec: Flavien Vallerand, 1824. SEM105P148 – 1mf – 9 – Can$2.25 – cn Bibl Nat [971]

L'APPEL AU PEUPLE – no. spec., no. 1-8. Tours. 20 sept-21 oct 1888 – 1 – fr A.C.R.P.P. [073]

L'APPEL AU PEUPLE: DROIT AU TRAVAIL, LES CONSERVATEURS, CRISE, FAMINE, MANDAT CONTRACTUEL / Ouvrier sans Travail – Montreal, 1875. 02480. (Pre-1900 Canadiana) – 9 – cn C.I.H.M. [971]

APPEL AUX FRANCAISES SUR LA REGENERATION DES MOEURS ET NECESITE DE L'INFLUENCE DES FEMMES DANS UN GOUVERNEMENT LIBRE / Aelders, Etta P – Paris. Imp. du Cercle Social. 1791 – 9 – fr Hachette [321]

APPEL AUX HABITANTS DE L'EUROPE SUR L'ESCLAVAGE ET LA TRAITE DES NEGRES, PAR LA SOCIETE RELIGIEUSE DES AMIS DE LA GRANDE-BRETAGNE – Paris, Didot. 1839 – 9 – 5.00 – fr Orientalistes [960]

APPEL DE L'EMPIRE *see* IMPRSKI I KLICH

APPEL D'UNE FEMME DU PEUPLE, SUR L'AFFRANCHISSEMENT DE LA FEMME / Demar, Claire – Paris, l'auteur, 1833, 16 p. Ma Loi d'avenir, par Claire Demare, 1833. Ouvrage posthume, publie par Suzanne. Paris, au bureau de la Tribune des Femmes, 1834, 75 p. Les Saint-Simoniens, 1825-1834. 6908 – 9 – fr Hachette [305]

Appel, Ernst *see* LEONE MEDIGOS LEHRE VOM WELTALL UND IHR VERHAELTNIS ZU GRIECHISCHEN UND ZEITGENOESSISCHEN ANSCHAUUNGEN

Appel, Theodore *see* LETTERS TO BOYS AND GIRLS ABOUT THE HOLY LAND AND THE FIRST CHRISTMAS AT BETHLEHEM

Appelius, Erhard W et al *see* ZUR OSTDEUTSCHEN AGRARGESCHICHTE

Appelius, Karl Theodor *see* GEISTLICHE SELBSTBEKENNTNISSE UEBER DAS WESEN UND LEBEN DER EVANGELISCH-LUTHERISCHEN KIRCHE

APPELL – Stockholm, Sweden. 1907-08, 1912-25 – 4r – 1 – sw Kungliga [073]

APPELLATE CASE FILES. 1792-1831 / U.S. Supreme Court – 96 rolls. Printed guide – 1 – M214 – us Nat'l Archives [340]

APPELLATE CASE FILES OF THE U.S. CIRCUIT COURT FOR THE SOUTHERN DISTRICT OF NEW YORK, 1793-1845 – 8r – 1 – M855 – us Nat'l Archives [340]

THE APPELLATE JURISDICTION OF THE HOUSE OF LORDS IN SCOTCH CAUSES, ILLUSTRATED BY THE LITIGATION RELATING TO THE CUSTODY OF THE MARQUIS OF BUTE / Macpherson, Norman – Edinburgh, Clark, 1861. 95 p. LL-2346 – 1 – us L of C Photodup [340]

APPELLATE OPINION WRITING : PRESENTED AT A SEMINAR FOR FEDERAL APPELLATE JUDGES, MARCH 11-14, 1975 / Re, Edward D – Washington: FJC, 1975 – 1mf – 9 – $1.50 – LLMC 95-300 – us L.L.M.C. [340]

APPELLATE PRACTICE AND PROCEDURE IN THE SUPREME COURT OF THE UNITED STATES / Robertson, Reynolds – Indianapolis: Bobbs-Merrill, 1905. 878p. LL-1495 – 1 – us L of C Photodup [340]

L'APPELLO – Cleveland, OH, 1917 – 3mf or 1r – 1,9 – us I.H.R.C. [978]

APPENDICE AU RAPPORT DU COMMISSAIRE DES TERRES DE LA COURONNE – Toronto: John Lovell, 1859. SEM105P1857 – 1mf – 9 – Can$2.25 – cn Bibl Nat [333]

APPENDICES AD NOVUM TESTAMENTUM STEPHANICUM / Sanday, William – Oxford: Clarendoniano, 1889. 1 fiche – 9 – us A.T.L.A. [240]

APPENDICES DU ONZIEME VOLUME DES JOURNAUX DE L'ASSEMBLEE LEGISLATIVE DE LA PROVINCE DU CANADA, DEPUIS LE 19 AOUT 1852...14 JUIN 1853. / Canada. (Province). Laws, Statutes, etc – 1853? SEM105P901 – 4mf – 9 – Can$9.00 – cn Bibl Nat [971]

APPENDICES, INDICES AND REPORTS IN RESPECT OF THE ROYAL COMMISSION / Great Britain. Royal Commission on the Railways of Gt. Britain and Ireland – 1867. Command No. 3844 – 1 – uk Microform Academic [380]

APPENDICES TO VOTES AND PROCEEDINGS, 1817-1890 AND REPORTS OF THE SELECT COMMITTEES ON PUBLIC PETITIONS, 1833-1900 / ed by Torrington, F W – (Includes index for 1833-1852) – 1981 – 1220mf – 9 – £4,410.00 – uk Chadwyck [324]

APPENDIX AD FLORAM PEDEMONTANAM / Bellardi, C A L – Augustae Taurinorum. 1792. B-5844 2 – 8 – ne IDC [580]

APPENDIX NO 26. TO THE HONORABLE THE PRESIDENT, AND THE HONORABLE THE MEMBERS OF THE LEGISLATIVE COUNCIL – [Quebec]: [s.n.], [1835]. SEM105P1130 – 1mf – 9 – Can$2.25 – cn Bibl Nat [340]

APPENDIX: SPECIFICATION FOR CONSTRUCTION OF DIVERSION TUNNEL AND COFFER-DAM / Indonesia. Kementerian Pekerdjaan Umum dan Tenaga – SE-11,172 1. 3 pts in 1v. 1962 – 9 – ne IDC [624]

AN APPENDIX TO COWEN'S TREATISE ON THE CIVIL JURISDICTION OF JUSTICES OF THE PEACE IN THE STATE OF NEW YORK. / Hayden, Chester – Albany: Gould, Banks and Gould, 1848. 142p. LL-646 – 1 – us L of C Photodup [340]

APPENDIX TO MEMORANDA OF JUNE, 1892, ON THE SUBJECT OF FREE TUITIONS IN THE FACULTY OF ARTS: EXEMPTIONS FROM FEES IN FAVOUR OF STUDENTS OF AFFILIATED THEOLOGICAL COLLEGES / Dawson, John William – s.l.: s.n., 1892?. 03663. (Pre-1900 Canadiana) – 9 – cn C.I.H.M. [971]

APPENDIX TO MINUTES OF EVIDENCE TAKEN BEFORE SELECT COMMITTEE OF THE HOUSE OF LORDS ON COLONIZATION FROM IRELAND – s.l., s.n. 1847. SEM105P158 – 3mf – 9 – Can$6.75 – cn Bibl Nat [324]

AN APPENDIX (TO THE BOTANICAL REGISTER) CONTAINING A TREATISE ON BULBOUS ROOTS / Herbert, W – London. 1821. B-5307 2 – 8 – ne IDC [580]

APPENDIX TO THE FIRST 23 VOLUMES OF EDWARD'S BOTANICAL REGISTER / Lindley, J – Including: Index to the present state of systematical botany and A sketch of the vegetation of the Swan River Colony. London. 1839. B-6029 2 – 8 – ne IDC [580]

APPENDIX TO THE REPORT OF THE BRITISH COMMISSIONERS APPOINTED IN JULY, 1839, TO EXPLORE AND SURVEY THE TERRITORY IN DISPUTE BETWEEN THE GOVERNMENTS OF GREAT BRITAIN AND THE UNITED STATES OF AMERICA, UNDER THE 2ND ARTICLE OF THE TREATY OF GHENT – [S.l.: s.n., 1839?]. SEM105P1385 – 1mf – 9 – Can$2.25 – cn Bibl Nat [975]

APPENDIX TO THE REPORT OF THE COMMISSIONER OF CROWN LANDS – Toronto: John Lovell, 1859. SEM105P1856 – 1mf – 9 – Can$2.25 – cn Bibl Nat [333]

Appert, B *see* RAPPORT SUR L'ETAT ACTUEL DES PRISONS, DES HOSPICES, DES ECOLES, ETC.; CONSIDERATIONS GENERALES SUR CES SORTES D'ETABLISSEMENTS

Appert, Georges *see*
- ANCIEN JAPON
- DICTIONNAIRE DES TERMES DE DROIT, D'ECONOMIE POLITIQUE ET D'ADMINISTRATION

Appier, Jean *see* RECUEIL DE PLUSIEURS MACHINES MILITAIRES ET FEUX ARTIFICIELS...

THE APPLE – London, 1920-22 – 1r – 1 – £60.00 – uk Chadwyck [760]

THE APPLE OF DISCORD, OR TEMPORAL POWER IN THE CATHOLIC CHURCH / Zurcher, George – Buffalo, N.Y.: Apple of Discord, 1905 – 2mf – us A.T.L.A. [240]

Applegate, Michael T *see* THE ECONOMIC IMPACT OF DEAN E. SMITH ACTIVITIES CENTER EVENTS ON CHAPEL HILL, NORTH CAROLINA

Applegate, Thomas *see* THE VOICE OF SACRED TRIPLES

Appleton, R J *see* TESTING THE VALIDITY OF THE NEAR INFRARED BODY COMPOSITION TECHNIQUE IN CHILDREN

APPLETON VOLKSFREUND – Appleton, WI. aug 20 1925-may 19 1932 – 1r – 1 – Dist. gw Mikrofilm – gw Misc Inst [072]

APPLETON'S GENERAL GUIDE TO THE UNITED STATES AND CANADA, 1879, 1882-1901 – 1879-1901 – 1 – 105.00 – us L of C Photodup [910]

Appleyard, J W *see* KAFIR-ENGLISH DICTIONARY

Appleyard, Reginald *see* INTERNATIONAL MIGRATION TODAY

APPLIANCE – v1- 1944- – 1,5,6,9 – us UMI [620]

APPLIANCE MANUFACTURER – (1984-. 5,6,9) – v1-. 1953- – 1 – us UMI [680]

APPLICABILITY OF INDICATORS OF SOCIO-ECONOMIC CHANGE FOR DEVELOPMENT PLANNING – 1984 – 128p – 9 – 92-3-102214-8 – fr UNESCO [338]

APPLICABLE ANALYSIS / ed by Gilbert, R P – 1971- – 1,5,9 – us Gordon [510]

L'APPLICATION DE LA LOI PENALE... / Dworzak, L W – Warszawa, 1932 – 1mf – 1 – ILM-2044/1 – ne IDC [327]

L'APPLICATION D'UN MANDAT / Feriet, R de – Paris, 1926 – 2mf – 1 – ILM-2482/1 – ne IDC [327]

AN APPLICATION OF BOWEN FAMILY SYSTEM THEORY TO THE PASTORAL MINISTRY OF THE SHARON BAPTIST CHURCH / Robertson, James Errol – 1982 – 1 – 5.36 – us Baptist [240]

THE APPLICATION OF FEDERAL LAWS IN AMERICAN SAMOA, GUAM, THE NORTHERN MARIANA ISLANDS, AND THE VIRGIN ISLANDS / American Samoa. Department of Interior – Washington: Office of the Solicitor. v1-3. Oct 1993 – 17mf – 9 – $25.50 – LLMC 95-036 – us L.L.M.C. [327]

AN APPLICATION OF ITEM RESPONSE THEORY TO THE REST OF GROSS MOTOR DEVELOPMENT / Cole, E L – 1990 – 2mf – 9 – $8.00 – us Microform Publ [150]

APPLICATION OF NITROGEN-FIXING SYSTEMS IN SOIL IMPROVEMENT AND MANAGEMENT – 1982 – 201p – it F.A.O. [631]

APPLICATION OF REMOTE SENSING TECHNOLOGY TO MARINE FISHERIES : AN INTRODUCTORY MANUAL – 1988 – 182p – it F.A.O. [639]

APPLICATION OF RESULTS FROM REPRESENTATIVE AND EXPERIMENTAL BASINS – 1982 – 477p – 9 – 92-3-101949-X – fr UNESCO [550]

APPLICATION OF THE CREDIT VALLEY RAILWAY FOR RIGHT OF WAY AND CROSSINGS AT THE CITY OF TORONTO: SECOND INTERVIEW OF THE RAILWAY DELEGATION WITH THE RAILWAY COMMITTEE OF THE PRIVY COUNCIL, OTTAWA, THURSDAY, JUNE 3RD, 1879 / Credit Valley Railway Company – Reported by A. & Geo. C. Holland. Ottawa?: s.n., 1879?. 04186. (Pre-1900 Canadiana) – 9 – cn C.I.H.M. [971]

APPLICATION OF THE TRANSTHEORETICAL MODEL TO EXERCISE ADHERENCE / Murphy, Debra & Roberts, John A – 1992 – 2mf – 9 – $8.00 – us Microform Publ [150]

APPLICATIONS / Society of Colonial Wars in South Carolina – 1908-84.95 fiches – 9 – us South Carolina Historical [978]

APPLICATIONS FOR ENROLLMENT AND ALLOTMENT OF WASHINGTON INDIANS, 1911-1919 – 6r – 1 – M1343 – us Nat'l Archives [350]

APPLICATIONS FOR ENROLLMENT OF THE COMMISSION TO THE FIVE CIVILIZED TRIBES, 1898-1914 – 468r – 1 – M1301 – us Nat'l Archives [350]

APPLICATIONS FOR RELIEF / Fulton County. Ohio. County Home – 1874-1937 – 3r – 1 – $32.50r – us Archival [324]

APPLICATIONS OF SURFACE SCIENCE – v1-22. 1978-84 – 1,5,6,13 – sz Elsevier [073]

APPLIED ACOUSTICS – v1-17. 1968-84 – 1,5,6,13 – sz Elsevier [073]

APPLIED AND ENVIRONMENTAL MICROBIOLOGY – (See also: Applied Microbiology) – v31- 1976- – 1,5,6,9 – us UMI [576]

APPLIED AND ENVIRONMENTAL MICROBIOLOGY – v1-46. 1953-83 – 1,5,6 – us Princeton Micro [576]

APPLIED AND MINOR ARTS – 93mf – $560.00 – 1-900853-10-8 – uk Mindata [700]

APPLIED ANIMAL ETHOLOGY – v1-12. 1975-84 – 1,5,6,13 – sz Elsevier [073]

APPLIED BIOCHEMISTRY AND MICROBIOLOGY – v1-30. 1965-94 – 1,5 – $90.00v – us UMI [574]

APPLIED CATALYSIS – v1-12. 1981-84 – 1,5,6,13 – sz Elsevier [073]

APPLIED CHRISTIANITY / Gladden, Washington – Moral aspects of social questions. 1886 – 1 – us A.T.L.A. [240]

APPLIED ECONOMICS – (v15-. 1983-. 5,6,9) – v13-. 1981- – 1 – us UMI [073]

APPLIED ENERGY – v1-18 1975-84 – 1,5,6,13 – sz Elsevier [621]

APPLIED ERGONOMICS – (1982-. 1,5,6,9) – v1-. 1969- – 1 – us UMI [073]

APPLIED GEOCHEMISTRY – v1- 1986- – 5,6,9 – us UMI [073]

APPLIED GEOGRAPHY AND THE HUMAN ENVIRONMENT : PROCEEDINGS OF THE FIFTH INTERNATIONAL MEETING, COMMISSION OF THE FIFTH INTERNATIONAL GEOGRAPHICAL UNION / ed by Preston, Richard E – 1973 – 397p – 9 – $8.00 set – cn Geography [910]

APPLIED LINGUISTICS – (1983-. 1,5,6,9) – v1-. 1980- – 1 – us UMI [400]

APPLIED MANAGEMENT SYSTEMS – v1-. 1982- – 1 – us UMI [650]

APPLIED MATHEMATICAL MODELLING – (1982-. 1,5,6,9) – v1-. 1976- – 1 – us UMI [073]

APPLIED MATHEMATICS AND COMPUTATION – v1-15. 1975-84 – 1,5,6,13 – sz Elsevier [073]

APPLIED MATHEMATICS AND OPTIMIZATION – v. 1-6. 1974-80 – 1,5,9 – 401.00 – us UMI [073]

APPLIED MATHEMATICS LETTERS – 1,5,69 – us UMI [510]

APPLIED MECHANICS REVIEWS – (5,6 1971- ; 9 1977-) – v1- 1948- – 1 – us UMI [621]

APPLIED MICROBIOLOGY – (1965-75. 5,6. 1970-75. 9) – v. 1-30. 1953-75 – 1 – us UMI [576]

APPLIED MICROBIOLOGY / ed by Doelle, H W & Heden, C G – (Hardback co-published with D. Reidel Publ. Co.) – 1986 – xviii/192p – 9 – 92-3-102335-7 – fr UNESCO [660]

APPLIED MICROBIOLOGY AND BIOTECHNOLOGY – v19-. 1984- – 1,5,6,9 – us UMI [073]

APPLIED OPTICS – 3 times per mth – 9,6 – $1,489.00 in US $1,540.00 outside – us Optical Soc [621]

APPLIED OPTICS / Optical Society of America – (v1-31. 1962-92. $840.00v, $35.00 per issue; v32. 1993. $910.00, $954.00 outside North America) – v1-. 1962-. Trimonthly – 9 – us Optical Soc [073]

APPLIED PHYSICS – v1-23 1973-80 – 1,5,9 – $2726.00 – us UMI [621]

APPLIED PHYSICS COMMUNICATIONS – (v4-1984- 5,6,9) – v1- 1981- – 1 – us UMI [621]

APPLIED PHYSICS LETTERS – v1- 1962- – 1,5,6,9 – us A.I.P. [621]

APPLIED POLYMER SYMPOSIA – 1965- – 1 – us UMI [073]

APPLIED PSYCHOLINGUISTICS – v1-. 1981- – 1,5,6,9 – us UMI [073]

APPLIED PSYCHOLOGICAL MEASUREMENT – (v.5-. 1981-. 5,6,9) – v.1-. 1977- – 1 – us UMI [150]

APPLIED RADIATION AND ISOTOPES – v1-1956- – 5,6,9 – us UMI [610]

APPLIED SPECTROSCOPY REVIEWS – (1984-5,6,9) – v1- 1968- – 1 – us UMI [621]

APPLIED SUPERCONDUCTIVITY – 1,5,69 – us UMI [621]

APPLIED THERAPEUTICS / ed by Luscombe, David K – 1,5,9 – us Gordon [615]

APPOINTMENT BOOK OF PRESIDENT KENNEDY (1961-1963) / Kennedy, John F – 1982. (Presidential Documents Series) – 1 – $305.00 – 0-89093-357-X – us UPA [977]

APPOINTMENT PAPERS: FLORIDA, 1849-1907 / U.S. Department of the Interior – RG 48. M1119. 6 rolls – 1 – us Nat'l Archives [978]

APPOINTMENT PAPERS: MISSOURI / U.S. Department of the Interior – 1849-1907. 9 rolls. M1058 – 1 – us Nat'l Archives [324]

APPOINTMENT PAPERS: NEVADA / U.S. Department of the Interior – 1860-1907. 3 rolls. M1033 – 1 – us Nat'l Archives [324]

APPOINTMENT PAPERS: TERRITORY OF ARIZONA / U.S. Department of the Interior – 1857-1907. 22 rolls. M576 – 1 – us Nat'l Archives [324]

APPOINTMENT PAPERS: TERRITORY OF COLOARDO / U.S. Department of Internal Revenue – 1857-1907. 13 rolls. M808 – 1 – us Nat'l Archives [324]

APPOINTMENT PAPERS: WYOMING / U.S. Department of the Interior – 1869-1907. 6 rolls. M830 – 1 – us Nat'l Archives [324]

Apponius *see* IN CANTICUM CANTICORUM EXPOSITIO

APPRAISAL AND PROSPECTS OF THE SECOND FIVE YEAR PLAN / India. Planning Commission – New Delhi. 1958 – 9 – ne IDC [330]

APPRAISAL JOURNAL – (1972- . 5,6. 1975- . 9) – v. 1- 1932- – 1 – us UMI [650]

APPRAISAL OF THE DEVELOPMENT OF KICKING BEHAVIOR OF PRESCHOOL AGE CHILDREN / Paula, E A – 1991 – 1mf – 9 – $4.00 – us Microform Publ [150]

AN APPRAISAL OF THE DEVELOPMENT OF WESTERN NIGERIA, 1959-60 / Nigeria. Western – (Sessional Paper No. 8 of 1961). Ibadan. 1961. BD-756 1 – 9 – ne IDC [338]

APPRAISING PHYSICAL STATUS; METHODS AND NORMS / McCloy, Charles H – 1938 – 10mf – 9 – $30.00 – us Microform Publ [370]

APPRAISING PHYSICAL STATUS; THE SELECTION OF MEASUREMENTS / McCloy, Charles H – 1936 – 4mf – 9 – $12.00 – us Microform Publ [370]

Apprentices Library Society. Charleston, South Carolina *see* RECORDS

L'APPRENTISSAGE DANS LES METIERS D'ART / Janneau, Guillaume – Paris. 1914. (La Condition Ouvriere. Part Two.) – 9 – 5.00 – fr Bibl Nationale [360]

THE APPROACH OF CHRIST TO MODERN INDIA / Farquhar, JN – Calcutta: Association Press, 1913 – 1mf – us A.T.L.A. [240]

APPROACH TO FOOD POPULATION PLANNING – 1977 – 70p – it F.A.O. [338]

APPROACH TO THE SECOND FIVE YEAR PLAN AND THE TENTATIVE DEVELOPMENT PROGRAMME OF VARIOUS SECTORS OF EDUCATION IN STATEMENT FORMS / Pakistan. Planning Commission. Education and Training – 1958 – 1mf – 9 – DE-576/1 – ne IDC [370]

APPROACHES TO COMMUNICATION PLANNING / ed by Middleton, John – 1980 – 300p – 9 – 92-3-101801-9 – fr UNESCO [380]

APPROACHES TO THE REGULATION OF FISHING EFFORT – 1984 – 45p – it F.A.O. [340]

APPROACHES TO THE SCIENCE OF SOCIO-ECONOMIC DEVELOPMENT / ed by Lengyel, Peter – 1971 – 383p – 9 – 92-3-100923-0 – fr UNESCO [338]

APPROACHES TO THE STUDY OF THE ENVIRONMENTAL IMPLICATIONS OF CONTEMPORARY URBANIZATION / ed by White, R & Burton, I – 1983 – 142p – 9 – 92-3-102170-2 – fr UNESCO [307]

APPROACHES TO WORLD FOOD SECURITY – 1983 – 185p – it F.A.O. [360]

APPROPRIATE FOREST INDUSTRIES – 1986 – 433p – it F.A.O. [338]

"APPROPRIATE TECHNOLOGIES" IN THE CONSERVATION OF CULTURAL PROPERTY : PROTECTION OF THE CULTURAL HERITAGE – 1981 – 9 – 92-3-101900-7 – fr UNESCO [306]

APPROPRIATE TECHNOLOGY IN FORESTRY : REPORT OF THE CONSULATION ON INTERMEDIATE TECHNOLOGY IN FORESTRY, NEW DELHI, 1981 – 1982 – 140p – it F.A.O. [634]

APPROPRIATE TECHNOLOGY MICROFICHE LIBRARY – 1000 books and documents on 1800 fiches – 9 – $895.00 – us Appropriate Tech [600]

APPROPRIATE WOOD HARVESTING IN PLANTATION FORESTS – 1987 – 282p – it F.A.O. [634]

APPROPRIATION BOOK FOR OFFICIAL NUMBERS OF BRITISH REGISTERED SHIPS, 1855-1982 / Sub-Collector of Customs, Launceston – 32166-386135 – 1 – CRS P556 – at Archives [920]

APPROPRIATIONS LEDGERS / Hancock County. Ohio. Biglick Township. Township Clerk – 1926-1988 gaps in holdings – 2r – 1 – $32.50r – us Archival [324]

APPROPRIATIONS RESOLUTIONS / Hancock County. Ohio. Biglick Township. Township Clerk – 1944-1988 gaps in holdings – 1r – 1 – $32.50r – us Archival [324]

APR – Sydney. v57-63. 1950-56 – 1,5,9 – D579 – us UMI [073]

APRAES LE CONCILE : OU, HYACINTHE ET DOELLINGER – Lyon: Denis, 1872 – 1mf – 9 – 0-8370-8375-3 – 1986-2375 – us A.T.L.A. [240]

O APRECIAVEL – San'Luiz, 1 Jan-Dec 1867; Jan-23 Dec 1876 – 1,5,6 – bl Biblioteca [072]

APRENDIZ DE LA EXERCITATION 36 / Luna Vega, J – SL, 1618 – 1mf – 9 – sp Cultura [610]

D'APRES LES PARABOLES HISTOIRES VRAIES... / Debout, Jacques; ed by Bayle, Constantino – Madrid: Razon y Fe, 1928 – 9 – sp Bibl Santa Ana [240]

APROBACION Y CONFIRMACION QUE DIO EL...AL PARECER Y ADICION QUE HIZO. FRAY JUAN DE LOS REYES... / Colegio Mayor del Conde Duque – S.l., s.i., s.a. 1640 – 1 – sp Bibl Santa Ana [240]

APROPOS SIC: AU PUBLIC DU MONTREAL POUR LES ADIEUX DE LA COMPAGNIE / Achintre, Auguste – 1867?. 06573. (Pre-1900 Canadiana) – 9 – cn C.I.H.M. [971]

APROVECHAMIENTO MAXIMO DE LOS RECURSOS NATURALES EN BENEFICIO DEL PUEBLO / Spain. Ministerio de Comunicaciones, Transportes y Obras Publicas – Barcelona, 19? Fiche W 723. (Blodgett Collection of Spanish Civil War Pamphlets) – 9 – us H.U. College Libr [946]

APROXIMACION A LA EVOLUCION SOCIO-ECONOMICA DE LA PROVINCIA DE BADAJOZ EN 1972 / Secretariado de Asuntos Economicos de Badajoz – Badajoz: Graf. Jimenez, s.a. – sp Bibl Santa Ana [330]

APROXIMACION A UN ESTUDIO DE ANTONIO HURTADO COMO POETA / Garcia Camino, Victor Gerardo & Garcia Caminos Burgos, Luis F – Badajoz: Dip. Provincial, 1958 – 1 – sp Bibl Santa Ana [440]

APS NEWS – 1,5,6,9 – us A.I.P. [530]

Aptowitzer, V *see* KAIN UND ABEL IN DER AGADA DEN APOKRYPHEN, DER HELLENISTISCHEN, CHRISTLICHEN UND MUHAMMEDANISCHE LITERATUR

APUNTACIONES PARA EL ESTUDIO DE LIMITES DEL ECUADOR CON EL PERU / Chacon, L A – Guayaquil, 1905 – 3mf – 1 – ILM-2171/1 – ne IDC [327]

APUNTACIONES PARA LA HISTORIA NATURAL DE LAS AVES..., TOMO 1-2, ASUNCION / Azara, Felix – 9mf – 9 – sp Cultura [590]

APUNTAMIENTO DE INDIAS, MS. 1568-1637 – 7mf – 9 – sp Cultura [340]

APUNTAMIENTO LEGAL DE LA O. SANTIAGO / Chaves, Bernabe de – 1 – sp Bibl Santa Ana [340]

APUNTAMIENTOS SOBRE EL ADELANTAMIENTO DE YUCATAN, DE AMALIO HUARTE Y ECHENIQUE / Beltran y Rozpide, Ricardo – Madrid: Fortanet, 1920. B.R.A.H. 76. pp. 5-6 – 1 – sp Bibl Santa Ana [946]

APUNTAMIENTOS...DE COMO SE DEBEN REFORMAR...LAS DOCTRINAS Y LA MANERA DE... / Abril, P – Madrid, 1589 – 1mf – 9 – sp Cultura [610]

APUNTE DESCRIPTIVO DE LA SERENA / Hidalgo, Juan Francisco – Castuera: Imp. La Puritana, 1924 – 1 – sp Bibl Santa Ana [946]

APUNTES BIBLIOGRAFICOS DE LA PRENSA PERIODICA DE LA BAJA EXTREMADURA. 1 Y 2 / Guerra Guerra, Arcadio – Badajoz: Imp. Dip. Provincial, 1974. Sep. REE – sp Bibl Santa Ana [073]

APUNTES BILOGICOS SOBRE EL POJO DE LAS HABAS / Moreno Marquez, Victor – Madrid: Rev. Fitopatologia, 1944 – 1 – sp Bibl Santa Ana [574]

APUNTES BIOGRAFICAS DEL M.I. SR. D. FRANCISCO DE PAULA SOTO Y MANCERA, ARCIPRESTE DE LA SANTA Y APOSTOLICA IGLESIA DE SANTIAGO DE COMPOSTELA, NATURAL DE ZAFRA, PROVINCIA DE BADAJOZ / Calderon, Cesareo – Badajoz: Uceda Hermanos, 1905 – 1 – sp Bibl Santa Ana [240]

APUNTES BIOGRAFICOS DE DON JUAN CARRILLO SANCHEZ / Anguita Valdivia, Jose – Madrid: Razon y Fe, 1929 – 1 – sp Bibl Santa Ana [920]

APUNTES DE ESPARRAGALEJO / Parejo Gonzalez, Jose – Badajoz: Tip. y Libr. Bernardo Vadillo Serrano, 1946 – 1 – sp Bibl Santa Ana [946]

APUNTES DE HERALDICA CACERENA / Rueda Sanchez Malo, Jose Miguel – Badajoz: Institucion Pedro de Valencia, 1971 – 1 – sp Bibl Santa Ana [946]

APUNTES DE HISTORIA ECLESIASTICA DE VENEZUELA. CARACAS, 1929 / Talavera y Garces, Mariano – Madrid: Razon y Fe, 1930 – 1 – sp Bibl Santa Ana [240]

APUNTES DE HISTORIA MILITAR / Peron, Juan Domingo – Buenos Aires: Ediciones de la Reconstruccion, 3rd ed 1974 – 1 – CSUXADH3660-B – us Hoover Inst Photo [355]

APUNTES DE LA SUBLEVACION FASCISTA; IMPRESIONES DE UN MILITAR REPUBLICANO / Romero, Luis – Barcelona, 1937? Fiche W1149. (Blodgett Collection of Spanish Civil War Pamphlets) – 9 – us H.U. College Libr [946]

APUNTES DE MATEMATICAS / Llinas Estevez, Jeronimo – Badajoz: La minerva extremena, s.a. – 1 – sp Bibl Santa Ana [510]

APUNTES DE ORTOGRAFIA PARA INGRESO (COLEGIO DE SAN JOSE) – Villafranca de los Barros: Imp. Rodriguez, s.a. – 1 – sp Bibl Santa Ana [946]

APUNTES DE PEDAGOGIA / Maillo, Adolfo – Caceres, s.i. 1953 – 1 – sp Bibl Santa Ana [370]

APUNTES DE PEDAGOGIA DEPORTIVA / Fernandez Santana, Ezequiel – Badajoz: Tip. Joaquin Sanchez, 1922 – sp Bibl Santa Ana [946]

APUNTES DE PSICOLOGIA Y LOGICA – Villafranca de los Barros: Tip. F. Rodriguez, 1923 – 1 – sp Bibl Santa Ana [150]

APUNTES DE RECUERDOS / Guel, Conde de (Marques de Comillas); ed by Bayle, Constantino – Madrid: Razon y Fe, 1928 – 9 – sp Bibl Santa Ana [920]

APUNTES DE TRES REVOLUCIONES : 1930, 1943, 1955 / Galindez, Bartolome – Buenos Aires, 1956 – 1 – CSUXAHZ7374-B – us Hoover Inst Photo [320]

APUNTES HISTORICOS DE LA QUE FUE SEDE ARZOBISPAL DE MERIDA DEL 507 AL 910 (403 ANOS) / Munoz Gallardo, Juan Antonio – Badajoz: Imprenta de la Diputacion Provincial, 1971. Separata Revista Estudios Extremenos – 1 – sp Bibl Santa Ana [240]

APUNTES HISTORICOS...VILLA DE FUENTE DEL MAESTRE DESDE.. / Gomez Jara y Herrera, Juan de la Cruz – 1873 – 9 – 1.50f – sp Bibl Santa Ana [946]

APUNTES PARA LA FLORA DE LAS DOS CASTILLAS / Colmeiro, D M – Madrid. 1849 – 8 – ne IDC [580]

APUNTES PARA LA HISTORIA DE SERRADILLA (CACERES) / Sanchez Rodrigo, Agustin – Serradilla (Caceres): Imprenta de Sanchez Rodrigo, 1930 – 1 – sp Bibl Santa Ana [946]

APUNTES PARA LA HISTORIA DE VILLAFRANCA DE LOS BARROS / Asensio, Jose Maria – Madrid: Fortanet, 1904. B.R.A.H. XLIV, pp. 246-249 – sp Bibl Santa Ana [946]

APUNTES PARA LA HISTORIA DE VILLAFRANCA DE LOS BARROS (BADAJOZ) / Cascales Munoz, Jose – Madrid: Est. Tip. Fortanet, 1904 – sp Bibl Santa Ana [946]

APUNTES PARA LA HISTORIA DE VILLAFRANCA DE LOS BARROS DE JOSE CASCALES MUNOZ... / Asensio, Jose Maria – Madrid: Tip. de Fortanet, 1899 – sp Bibl Santa Ana [946]

APUNTES PARA LA HISTORIA DE ZAFRA / Osuna Lara, Antonio J – Badajoz: Imp. de la Diputacion Provincial, 1976 – sp Bibl Santa Ana [946]

APUNTES PARA LA HISTORIA DEL DERECHO DE MEJICO / Esquivel Obregon, Toribio – Madrid: Missionalia Hispanica, 1945. 3v – 1 – sp Bibl Santa Ana [972]

APUNTES PARA LA HISTORIA DEL ORIGEN Y DESENVOLVIMIENTO DEL REGIO PATRONATO INDIANO HASTA 1857 / Garcia Gutierrez, Jesus – Mexico, 1941; Madrid: Missionalia Hispanica, 1944 – 1 – sp Bibl Santa Ana [240]

APUNTES PARA LA HISTORIA...PLASENCIA / Barrio y Rufo, Jose – 1851 – 9 – 1.50f – sp Bibl Santa Ana [946]

APUNTES PARA LA MILITANCIA : PERONISMO CRITICO / Cooke, John William – [Buenos Aires]: Schapire, [1972] – 1 – CSUXADL6983-B – us Hoover Inst Photo [320]

APUNTES PARA UN DICCIONARIO DE ESCRITORES DEL S. XIX / Ossorio, Bernard M – 1889 – 9 – 1.50f – sp Bibl Santa Ana [440]

APUNTES PARA...TOPOGRAFICO... BURGUILLOS / Martinez Martinez, Matias Ramon – 1884 – 9 – 1.50f – sp Bibl Santa Ana [910]

APUNTES SOBRE EL MOVIMIENTO DE POBLACION DE BUENOS AIRES DE 1879 – Buenos Aires, 1879 – 2mf – 9 – sp Cultura [310]

APUNTES SOBRE LA ESCENIFICACION DE LOS ROMANCES. MANUSCRITO / Garcia Lorca, Federico – 1mf – 9 – sp Cultura [820]

APUNTES SOBRE LA PROVINCIA MISIONAL DEL ORINOCO...CARACAS, 1933 / Bueno, Ramon – Madrid: Razon y Fe, 1934 – 1 – sp Bibl Santa Ana [946]

APUNTES SOBRE LOS SUCESOS OCURRIDOS EN...MIAJADAS – 1873 – 9 – 1.50f – sp Bibl Santa Ana [946]

APUNTES SOBRE TOPICOS INTERNACIONALES / Diez de Medina, E – La Paz, 1919 – 2mf – 1 – ILM-3134/1 – ne IDC [327]

APUNTES Y DOCUMENTOS CONTRA LA ORDEN DOMINICANA EN COLOMBIA 1680-1930. CARACAS, 1936 / Mesanza, Andres – Burgos: Razon y Fe, 1938 – 1 – sp Bibl Santa Ana [240]

APUNTES Y DOCUMENTOS... ADMINISTRATIVAS / Bravo Murillo, Juan – 1858 – 9 – 1.50f – sp Bibl Santa Ana [946]

APUNTES Y MATERIALES PARA LA BIOGRAFIA DE DON JOSE DE ESPRONCEDA / Cascales Munoz, Jose – Extrait de la Revue Hispanique. Tome 23. New York, Paris. 1910 – 1 – sp Bibl Santa Ana [920]

APUNTES...ARCHIVO GENERAL DE SIMANCAS / Romero de Castillay Perosso, Francisco – 1873 – 9 – 1.50f – sp Bibl Santa Ana [025]

APUNTES...HISTORIA...AMIGOS DEL PAIS DE BADAJOZ / Merino de Torres, Alberto – 1898 – 9 – 1.50f – sp Bibl Santa Ana [830]

APUNTES...VILLA DE GATA / Guerra Hontiveros, Marcelino – 1897 – 9 – 1.50f – sp Bibl Santa Ana [946]

Apushkin, Vladimir Aleksandrovich *see* GENERAL OT PORAZHENI I V.A. SUKHOMLINOV

AQUACHAMINE / Menominee Restoration Committee – 1974-76. (American Indian Periodicals in the Princeton University Library). 3 fiches – 9 – $45.00 – us UPA [305]

AQUACULTURE – v1-43. 1972-84 – 1,5,6,13 – sz Elsevier [639]

AQUACULTURE AND RISK MANAGEMENT – 1989 – 35p – it F.A.O. [338]

AQUACULTURE DEVELOPMENT IN CHINA : REPORT ON AN F.A.O./U.N.D.P. AQUACULTURE STUDY TOUR TO THE PEOPLE'S REPUBLIC OF CHINA (1978) – 1981 – 74p – it F.A.O. [639]

AQUACULTURE DEVELOPMENTS IN PERU / International Center for Aquaculture – Apr 1972. 1 reel – 1, 5 – us Spaulding [639]

AQUACULTURE PROJECT FORMULATION – 1990 – 140p – it F.A.O. [639]

AQUACULTURE SURVEY IN JAPAN / International Center for Aquaculture – 1972 – 1, 5 – us Spaulding [639]

AQUACULTURE SYSTEMS AND PRACTICES : A SELECTED REVIEW – 1990 – 97p – it F.A.O. [338]

AQUALERT (AN SDI SERVICE) – 1,5,69 – us UMI [360]

AQUALINE ABSTRACTS – 1,5,69 – us UMI [360]

AQUAPRENEURSHIP : CHARACTERISTICS AND BUSINESS MANAGEMENT PRACTICES OF CURRENT AND POTENTIAL SWIM SCHOOL OWNERS / Mackey, Marcia J & Parkhouse, Bonnie L – 1992 – 2mf – 9 – $8.00 – us Microform Publ [790]

L'AQUARELLE DE 1400 A 1900 / Reunion des musees nationaux. Paris – 1936. 4 illus. 1 fiche – 9 – fr Réunion [700]

AQUATIC BOTANY – v1-20. 1975-84 – 1,5,6,13 – sz Elsevier [580]

THE AQUATIC (NAIAD) STAGE OF THE BRITISH DRAGONFLIES / Lucas, W J – 1930 – 1. 20.00; ; 7 – uk Microform Academic [590]

AQUATIC SCIENCES AND FISHERIES INFORMATION SYSTEM : TAXONOMIC AUTHORITY LIST – 1988 – 472p – it F.A.O. [639]

AQUATIC TOXICOLOGY – v1-6. 1981-84 – 1,5,6,13 – sz Elsevier [574]

AQUAVIVA / Gomez Bravo, Vicente – Villafranca de los Barros (Badajoz): Imp. Bolanos Iglesias, 1941 – 1 – sp Bibl Santa Ana [946]

Aquayo Spencer, Rafael *see* DON VASCO DE QUINOGA...

AQUELLO SE LLAMO JUSTICIALISMO / Buzio, Victorio Alberto – Buenos Aires: Editorial Indice, [1958] – 1 – CSUXAHZ2313-B – us Hoover Inst Photo [320]

AQUI LA CODOSERA / Corredor Garcia, Antonio – Caceres: Ediciones Gruzada Mariana. Imp. Rodriguez, 1973 – 1 – sp Bibl Santa Ana [946]

AQUILA – Budapest, 1894-1942. v1-49 – 381mf – 9 – Z-2004c/2 – ne IDC [590]

Aquileiensis, Paulinus *see* CONTRA FELICEM

Aquilinius, C *see* DE TRIBUS HISTORICIS CONCILII TRIDENTINI

L'AQUILON – Haute-Rive, puis Baie Comeau, Canada. dec 1950-30 aut 1967 – 10r – 1 – Can$60.00r – cn Can Microfilming [072]

Aquinas, Thomas *see*
- QUAESTIONES DE DUODECIM QUODLIBET ITALIE AU 25 SIECLE
- SANCTI THOMAE AQUINATIS OPERA OMNIA
- SUMMA THEOLOGICA

AQUIS, AQUACULTURE INFORMATION SYSTEM : USERS' MANUAL – rev ed 1985 – 60p – it F.A.O. [639]

Aqus, G *see* SIX SONATAS

AR : AMERICAN REVIEW – (Former title: New American Review (sep 1967-1972)) – New York. v1-26 1967-nov 1977. cum index v1-8 1967-69 1; v22-26 1975-nov 1977 5; v24-26 apr 1976-nov 1977 9 – 1,5,9 – D8907 – us UMI [073]

AR VRO – Revue culturelle independante, bimestrielle. Concarneau, Paris. 1959-66 – 1 – fr A.C.R.P.P. [073]

ARA ROMANA DE BARCARROTA / Fita, Fidel – 1900 – 9 – 1.50f – sp Bibl Santa Ana [930]

ARA ROMANA DE BARCARROTA / Fita, Fidel – Madrid: Tip de Fortanet, 1900 – 1 – sp Bibl Santa Ana [946]

ARA Y CANTA – Badajoz, 1927-1929 – 5 – sp Bibl Santa Ana [073]

ARAB CONFEDERATION AND OTHER ISSUES, 1950-59 – Series: Confidential US State Department Central Files – 27r – $3,220.00 – 1-55655-382-X – us UPA [956]

THE ARAB CONQUESTS IN CENTRAL ASIA / Gibb, H A R – 1923 – 1 – uk Microform Academic [900]

ARAB FILOLOG O TURETSKOM IAZYKE / Melioranskii, P M – Spb. 1900. BU-358 2 – 8 – ne IDC [470]

Arab Higher Committee *see*
- THE ARAB HIGHER COMMITTEE: ITS ORIGINS, PERSONNEL AND PURPOSES
- MEMORANDUM TO THE PERMANENT MANDATES COMMISSION AND TO THE SECRETARY OF STATE FOR THE COLONIES, 23 JUL 1937
- THE PALESTINE ARAB CASE: A STATEMENT

THE ARAB HIGHER COMMITTEE: ITS ORIGINS, PERSONNEL AND PURPOSES / Arab Higher Committee – The documentary record submitted to the United Nations, May 1947. New York. 1947. BJ-28-150 1 – 9 – ne IDC [956]

Arab Investment Company. Lebanon *see* ANNUAL REPORT OF THE ARAB INVESTMENT COMPANY

ARAB LAW QUARTERLY – v1-10. 1985-1995 – 9 – $578.00 set – us Hein [340]

ARAB NEWSPAPERS – (Al-Anwar, 1960-1988 (Lebanon) 99r £6,495.00 Al-Hayat, 1950-1976 (Lebanon) 53r £3,385.00) – 1 – uk Chadwyck [072]

ARAB ORGANIZATION FOR HUMAN RIGHTS – Giza, Geneva. 32 docs. 1983-1990 – 14mf – 9 – ne IDC [320]

The Arab Palestine Office *see* COMMENTARY ON WATER DEVELOPMENT IN THE JORDAN VALLEY REGION

ARAB REPORT – Washington: Arab Information Center. v2 n1-21,23-24 dec 1975-oct 1 1976; nov 23-24 1976. v3 n1-21,23-24 dec 1976-oct 21 1977; nov 1-nov 15/dec 15 1977. v4 n1-19,21,23-24 jan-oct 1, nov 1, dec 1978). v5 (1979). v6 n1-3, 5-8 (jan-feb 1, mar-apr 1980) – 1r – 1 – us Res Libr [956]

ARAB TRADITIONAL FARMING AND THE NEED FOR REFORM / Serrag, M – 1954. BNE-1022 1 – 9 – ne IDC [630]

ARABELLE ET VASCOS OU LES JACOBINS DE GOA / Lebrun-Tossa et Lesueur – (French Theatre Series). Paris citoyenne Toubon, an III. 1794 – 9 – fr Hachette [820]

ARAB-ENGLISH DICTIONARY / Hava, J – 1915 – 9 – $33.00 – us I.R.C. [470]

ARABESKI. KNIGA STATEI / Belyi, A – 1911. BR-560 2 – 8 – ne IDC [460]

ARABIA AND THE BIBLE / Montgomery, James A – 1934 – 9 – $10.00 – us I.R.C. [220]

ARABIA, EGYPT, INDIA: A NARRATIVE OF TRAVEL / Burton, Isabel Arundell – London: W. Mullan and Son, 1879.488p. maps – 1 – us U.W. Library [910]

Arabian American Oil Company. Saudi Arabia *see* REVIEW OF OPERATION 1950-1974

ARABIAN GULF CURRENCY AGREEMENT DONE AT DUBAI 7 JUL 1965 BY THE RULERS OF BAHRAIN, ABU-DHABI, QATAR AND DUBAI / Arabian Gulf Emirates. Abu-Dhabi – 1965. BNE-10,007 1 – 9 – ne IDC [332]

Arabian Gulf Emirates. Abu-Dhabi *see*
- ARABIAN GULF CURRENCY AGREEMENT DONE AT DUBAI 7 JUL 1965 BY THE RULERS OF BAHRAIN, ABU-DHABI, QATAR AND DUBAI
- ESTIMATES OF REVENUE AND EXPENDITURE
- MINISTERIAL BUDGET ESTIMATES: ESTIMATES OF EXPENDITURE AND DETAILS OF ESTABLISHMENTS
- PETROLEUM COMPANY REVIEW

Arabian Gulf Emirates. Abu-Dhabi. Directorate General of Planning and Coordination *see* STATISTICAL ABSTRACT

Arabian Gulf Emirates. Abu-Dhabi. International Trade Centre Unctad Gatt *see* BAHRAIN, QATAR, ABU-DHABI AND DUBAI AS MARKETS FOR SELECTED MANUFACTURED PRODUCTS FROM DEVELOPING COUNTRIES

Arabian Gulf Emirates. Abu-Dhabi. Planning Board *see* ANNUAL PROGRAMME

Arabian Gulf Emirates. Dubai. Port and Customs Dept *see* STATISTICS REPORT

Arabian Gulf Emirates. Qatar and Dubai Currency Board *see* ANNUAL REPORT, 1966-1972

ARABIAN NIGHTS – Korban Sihir; Kisah 1001 Malam; Spion Kontra Spion bound in. SE-5961-1 – 9 – ne IDC [830]

ARABIAN NIGHTS – Kraton Marmer; Petikan Dongeng Sewu Satunggal Dalu. SE-3981 1. 1962 – 9 – ne IDC [830]

ARABIAN NIGHTS. ALADDIN – SE-3362 1. 1949 – 9 – ne IDC [830]

AN ARABIAN TALE : FROM AN UNPUBLISHED MANUSCRIPT: WITH NOTES CRITICAL AND EXPLANATORY / Beckford, William – London: Printed for J. Johnson, 1786 – 1 roll – 1 – 1-55879-290-2 – uk Libr Preservation [830]

ARABIC AND CHINESE TRADE IN WALRUS AND NARWHAL IVORY / Laufer, B – (T'oung Pao, v. 14). Leide. 1913. BU-523 2 – 8 – ne IDC [380]

[ARABIC MANUSCRIPTS FROM GHANA AND ADJACENT TERRITORIES] – Chicago, IL: U of Chicago, Photoduplication Dept, 1974 – 1 – us Res Libr [960]

ARABIC MANUSCRIPTS IN THE JNUL, JERUSALEM / ewish National and University Library. Jerusalem – (Includes a shelf list on microfiche) – 4,265mf – 9 – Gld27,910.00 – ne IDC [470]

ARABIC MANUSCRIPTS IN THE SOAS, LONDON / School of Oriental and African Studies, London – (Includes a printed guide by Adam Gacel) – 1,569mf – 9 – ne IDC [470]

ARABICA – Leiden. v1-36. 1954-89 – 5,9 – Dfl3,600.00; Dfl100.00v – ne Swets [470]

L'ARABIE OCCIDENTALE AVANT L'HEGIRE / Lammens, Henri – 1928 – 1 – us A.T.L.A. [260]

ARABISCH-DEUTSCHES LEXIKON ZUM SPRACHGEBRAUCH DES MAIMONIDES / Friedlaender, I – Frankfurt a.M., 1902 – 3mf – ne IDC [470]

DIE ARABISCHE LITERATUR DER JUDEN, EIN BEITRAG ZUR LITERATURGESCHICHTE DER ARABER GROSSENTEILS AUS HANDSCHRIFTLICHEN QUELLEN / Steinschneider, M – Frankfurt a.M., 1902 – 5mf – ne IDC [470]

DIE ARABISCHEN BIBELUEBERSETZUNGEN: TEXTE MIT GLOSSAR UND LITERATURUEBERSICHT / Kahle, Paul – Liepzig: J.C. Hinrichs, 1904. 1 fiche – 9 – us A.T.L.A. [220]

DIE ARABISCHEN UEBERSETZUNGEN VON ARISTOTELES' SCHRIFT DE CAEOLO / Endress, Gerhard – Frankfurt a.M., 1966 – 3mf – 9 – DM76.00 – 3-89349-667-X – gw Hänsel [180]

ARAB-ISLAMIC BIOGRAPHICAL ARCHIVE (AIBA) = ARABISCH-ISLAMISCHES BIOGRAPHISHES ARCHIV (AIBA) / Kramme, Ulrike & Muena, Zelmira Urra – 1995-1998 – ca 450mf (1:24) in 12 installments – 9 – diazo DM20,400.00 (silver DM22,000.00 ISBN: 3-598-33881-3) – 3-598-33880-5 – gw Saur [920]

ARABSKIE I PERSIDSKIE FIZIKO-MATEMATICHESKIE RUKOPISI V BIBLIOTEKAKH SOVETSKOGO SOIUZA / Rozenfel'd, B A – Sbornik statei i publikatsii. Moscow, 1966. v1, p256-289. BR-10,665/1 – 9 – ne IDC [500]

ARABSKIE ISTOCHNIKI VII-X VEKOV – Drevnie i srednevekovye istochniki po etnografii i istorii Afriki iuzhnee Sakhary. 1960. BR-2472 2 – 8 – ne IDC [960]

ARABSKIE RUKOPISI SOBRANIIA LENINGRADSKOGO GOSUDARSTVENNOGO UNIVERSITETA / Beliaev, Vl & Bulgakov, PG – Leningrad. 1958. Surveys Arabic mss in Leningrad University Library. BR-10,921/1 – 9 – ne IDC [010]

Arabyazdi, Behjat *see* DETERMINATION OF OCCUPATIONAL STRESS AND COPING STRATEGIES OF MEDIATORS UTILIZING THE DELPHI TECHNIQUE

DIE ARACHNIDEN. GETREU NACH DER NATUR / Koch, C L & Hahn, CW – Z-211 2. 16 v. 1831-1848 – 8 – ne IDC [580]

LES ARACHNIDES DE FRANCE / Simon, E – v. 1. Paris. 1874; v. 2. 1875; v. 3. 1876; v. 4. 1878; v. 5. 1881-84; v. 6. 1914-37; v. 7. 1879. BZ-2239 1 – 9 – ne IDC [590]

ARADER ZEITUNG – Arad, jan 2 1921-dec 29 1943 – 16r – 1 – Dist. gw Mikrofilm – gw Misc Inst [949]

Aradillas Agudo, Antonio *see*
- AMEN SUGERENCIAS LITURGICAS
- ANTE TODO, ESPOSOS
- BENDICENOS SENOR
- EL BESO?
- CARTAS A LA NOVIA
- COEDUCACION
- COMO ENSENAR A LOS HIJOS A VIVIR CON ALEGRIA
- CONCILIO Y VIDA CRISTIANA
- LOS CURAS
- DAVID, HOY
- EL DIALOGO SEXUAL
- DIVORCIARSE EN ESPANA MERCADO NEGRO Y CORRUPCION
- DIVORCIO EN ESPANA
- LA FAMILIA EN DIRECTO
- FIRMES
- FRAUDE NOS TRIBUNAIS ECLESIASTICOS
- GOZOY LITURGIA DE LA SANTA MISA
- IGLESIA
- IGLESIA ANO 2000
- IGREJA 2001
- IMPACTO. MEDITACIONES PARA MILITANTES
- MATRIMONIOS ROTOS
- EN LOS MATRIMONIOS ROTOS QUE HACEMOS CON LOS HIJOS?
- NOSOTROS...LIBRO DE PRECES DE LA MILITANTE DEACCION CATOLICA
- LA ORACION DE TODAS LAS NOTICIAS
- ORAD HERMANOS. MEDITACIONES SOBRE TEMAS LITURGICOS
- PAPELES PROHIBIDOS
- PROCESO A LOS TRIBUNALES
- SI, MUJER

Aragon Fernandez, Antonio *see*
- LAS ERMITAS DE CORDOBA
- LA UNIDAD ESTRUCTURAL DE LOS LAIS DE MARIE DE FRANCE

ARAGUARY – Araguary, 21 Apr-May 1894; Sep 1895; Jan 1896; Oct 1898; May 1900; Oct 1908-May 1909; Dec 1910; Jan 1911; Nov 1912; Nov 1915; Nov 1921; Mar 1925; Apr-May 1926; Apr, Nov 1932; 12 Mar 1933 – 1,5,6 – bl Biblioteca [072]

ARAH PERKEMBANGAN EKONOMI-KEUANGAN INDONESIA / Runturambi, F – SE 4561 1. 1961 – 9 – ne IDC [338]

Arakin, Vladimir D *see* INDONEZIISKIE IAZYKI

L'ARALDO DE CANADA – Montreal, Canada. v20 n6. 25 fev 1925 – 1r – 1 – Can$25.00 – cn Can Microfilming [072]

L'ARALDO. ORGANO IN LINGUA ITALIANA DEL PARTITO COMUNISTA FRANCESE (S.F.I.C.) / Communist Party. France – Paris. 4 mars 1922-1er dec 1923, inc – 1 – fr A.C.R.P.P. [073]

ARAMAEISCHE SPRICHWOERTER UND VOLKSSPRUECHE : EIN BEITRAG ZUR KENNTNIS EINES OSTARAMAEISCHEN DIALEKTS SOWIE ZUR VERGLEICHENDEN PAROEMIOLOGIE / Lewin, Moses – (Discussion in German; texts in Aramaic. Includes index) – Berlin: H Itzkowski, 1895 – 1mf – 9 – 0-8370-7302-2 – 1986-1302 – us A.T.L.A. [470]

DAS ARAMAEISCHE VERBUM IM JERUSCHALEMISCHEN TALMUD / Schlesinger, Max – Berlin. 1889. BJ-32-54 1 – 9 – ne IDC [270]

AN ARAMAIC METHOD : A CLASS BOOK FOR THE STUDY OF THE ELEMENTS OF ARAMAIC: FROM BIBLE AND TARGUMS / Brown, Charles Rufus – Chicago: American Publ Society of Hebrew, 1884-86 – 1mf – 9 – 0-8370-7047-3 – 1986-1047 – us A.T.L.A. [470]

DIE ARAMAISMEN IM ALTEN TESTAMENT UNTERSUCHT / Kautzsch, Emil F – 1902 – 1 – us A.T.L.A. [220]

Aramayo, Avelino *see* PROYECTO DE UNA NUEVA VIA ENTRE BOLIVIA Y EL OCEANO PACIFICO

Arami, M M *see* VIVE TU VIDA

THE ARAN ISLANDS / Synge, John Millington – Drawings by Jack B. Yeats. Boston, 1911 – 1 – us U.W. Library [840]

Aranda y Marzo, J *see* DESCRIPTION TRIPARTITA MEDICO-ASTRONOMICA QUE TOCA... SOBRE LA CONSTITUCION EPIDEMICA... DE ESPANA, CON ESPECIALIDAD EN LA VILLA DE ORGAZ EN 1735 Y 1737

ARANEAE SVECICAE DESCRIPTAE / Westring, N – Z 2214 2. 1861 – 8 – ne IDC [590]

Aranguez Sanz, Bibiano *see* INDUSTRIAS CARNICAS

Arantes, T C B *see* DEUS SUPER "HAMMONIA"!

LA ARANYA / Guimera, Angel – Barcelona. 1908 – 1 – us Res Libr [830]

ARAPAHOE PIONEER – Arapahoe, NE. -w. Jul. 1879-Aug. 1884; Oct. 1895-Dec. 1898; May 1899-Aug.1905; Jan. 1908-Aug. 1911 – 1 – us NE Hist [071]

ARAPAHOE PUBLIC MIRROR – Arapahoe, NE. -w. Oct. 1882; Aug. 1890; Sep. 1895-Mar. 1904; Sep. 1908- – 1 – us NE Hist [071]

ARAPAHOE ROAD BAPTIST CHURCH. LITTLETON, COLORADO : CHURCH RECORDS – 1965-75. Cherry Hills Baptist Church. Church records. 1960-65 – 1 – 39.33 – us Baptist [240]

Arapov, P *see* LETOPIS' RUSSKAGO TEATRA

ARARAT : ROMAN / Ulitz, Arnold – Muenchen: A Langen, 1920 – 1 – us U.W. Library [830]

ARARAT ADVERTISER – 1921-1945 – 21mf – 9 – at Corangamite [980]

ARATUHIPE : PERIODICO NOTICIOSO, COMMERCIAL E AGRICOLA – Aldeia (Nazareth), BA. 6 Maio, 11 Nov 1883 – 1,5,6 – bl Biblioteca [072]

ARAUCO – Santiago. Mar 1960-Jun 1967, nos. 5-89. Missing: 6-7, 21-25 – 1 – 35.00r – us Hoover Inst Photo [073]

Araujo, O *see* DICCIONARIO POPULAR DE HISTORIA DE LA REPUBLICA O. DEL URUGUAY. DESDE LA EPOCA DEL DESCUBRIMIENTO DE SU TERRITORIO, HASTA LA DE SU INDEPENDENCIA

Araus, Pedro *see*
- SEMANARIO ECONOMICO. TOMO 2
- SEMANARIO ECONOMICO. TOMO 3

ARAUTO : ORGAO DOS INTERESSES LOCAES – Itacoatiara, Amazonas. 30 Set 1906-Abr 1908; Jan 1909-Jun 1911 – 1,5,6 – bl Biblioteca [072]

O ARAUTO : ORGAO HEBDOMADARIO – Cataguazes, 21 Dec 1902 – 1,5,6 – bl Biblioteca [072]

ARAUTO DE FILOSOFIA : ORGAO DE DIVULGACAO DO 'OCENTRO DE ESTUDOS DE FILOSOFIA" DA FAFI – Manaus, Amazonas. 27 Jun, 22 Set 1964 – 1,5,6 – bl Biblioteca [072]

LES ARAWAK DE L'UCAYALI / Renard-Casevitz, F M – 9 – F90.00 – fr Ethnologie [306]

Arazola Gil, Luis Enrique *see* CONTRIBUCION A LA HISTORIA DE LA COLONIA DEL SACRAMENTO. LA EPOPEYA DE MANUEL LOBO...

ARBACES UND PANTHEA : ODER DIE GESCHWISTER: SCHAUSPIEL NACH FRANCIS BEAUMONT IN FUENF AUFZUEGEN VON LEO GREINER / Beaumont, Francis – Berlin: Reiss, [1912] – 1r – 1 – us U.W. Library [820]

ARBAI – Modern conversation in 4 lang: Indonesian, English, German, Dutch. SE-11,597 1. 1963 – 9 – ne IDC [400]

ARBAITER FRAIND BULETIN : AROISGEGEBEN FUN DER GRUPE ARBAITER FRAIND UN ANARCH – London, UK. sic Apr 1930 – 1 – uk British Libr Newspaper [072]

ARBAITER VORT = THE WORKER'S WORLD : ORGAN FUN DER IDISHER SOTSIAL-DEMOKRATISCHE – sic 28 Mar 1915-Jul 1917 – 1 – uk British Libr Newspaper [072]

ARBAJTER : ORGAN POLSKIEJ PARTYI SOCYALISTYCZNEJ – London, UK. Dec 1898; Dec 1900; Apr, Aug 1901; Jul, Nov 1902 – 1 – uk British Libr Newspaper [072]

L'ARBALETE – no. 1-13. Lyon. fevr 1940-1948 – 1 – fr A.C.R.P.P. [073]

ARBAYT-LABOR – Montreal, CN. v1 no 2. 1923 – 1r – 1 – Can$25.00 – cn Can Microfilming [072]

ARBEIDERBLADET – Oslo, 2 Jan 1939-29 Jan 1940 – 1 – us Hoover Inst Photo [331]

ARBEIDERBLAT – (Yrly reel count varies) – [Norway], 1992- – 1 – inquire – us Ross [072]

DIE ARBEIT – Eupen, Belgium. 3 Feb 1923-30 Aug 1924; 2 Jan 1926-1927; 3 Jan 1931-6 Jun 1936 – 1 – gw Mikrofilm [949]

DIE ARBEIT : GEWERKSCHAFTS-ZEITUNG – London, England. Mar-Nov 1941 – 1 – gw Mikrofilm [072]

DIE ARBEIT / ed by Leipart, Theodor – Zeitschrift fuer gewerkschaftspolitik und wirtschaftskunde.... v1-10. 1924-33. -m. (Serial publications of German trade unions in the Memorial Library, University of Wisconsin-Madison) – 1 – us U.W. Library [330]

DIE ARBEIT : ORGAN DER ZIONISTISCHEN VOLKSSOZIALISTISCHEN PARTEI HAPOEL-HAZAIR – Berlin, jan 15 1919-sep 1924, jul 1928 – 1r – 1 – Dist. gw Mikrofilm – gw Misc Inst [956]

DIE ARBEIT – Organ der zionistischen volkssozialistischen Partei Hapoel-Hazair. Berlin. v1-5. 1919-1924. 1928 (Special issue). Complete. 1 reel. B15. (Leo Baeck Institute. German-Jewish Periodicals, Pt 1) – 1 – $75.00 – us UPA [270]

DIE ARBEIT – Organ fuer die Sozialen Reformbestrebungen, hrsg. von Eduard Pfeiffer. v1, nos1-5, 7-8. 1866. Frankfurt am Main. Place of publ. varies. (Serial publications of German trade unions in the Memorial Library, University of Wisconsin-Madison) – 1 – us U.W. Library [331]

DIE ARBEIT : ZEITSCHRIFT FUER GEWERKSCHAFTSPOLITIK UND WIRTSCHAFTSKUNDE – Barmen (Wuppertal), Germany. Apr. 14, 1907-Dec. 22, 1917 – 4r – 1 – gw Mikrofilm [072]

DIE ARBEIT : ZEITSCHRIFT FUER GEWERKSCHAFTSPOLITIK UND WIRTSCHAFTSKUNDE – Barmen,1907-1917 – 4r – 1 – DM300.00 – gw Mikro Press [073]

DIE ARBEIT : ZEITSCHRIFT FUER GEWERKSCHAFTSPOLITIK UND WIRTSCHAFTSKUNDE – Berlin, 1924-32 – 3r – 1 – gw Mikro Press [330]

ARBEIT UND ARBEITSRECHT – v1-. 1946- . Title varies: Continues: Arbeit und Sozialfuersorge, v1-17, 1946-62 – 1 – us U.W. Library [331]

ARBEIT UND WEHR – Berlin, 1937 n48, 1938 (incomplete), 1940-41 (incomplete) – 1 – Dist. gw Mikrofilm – gw Misc Inst [072]

ARBEITEN / Pharmakologisches Institut zu Dorpat – v. 1-3. Dorpat. 1888-89. BM-286 2 – 8 – ne IDC [615]

ARBEITEN DER KURLAENDISCHEN GESELLSCHAFT FUER LITERATUR UND KUNST – Mitau, 1847-1851. v1-10 – 31mf – 9 – R-1654/2 – ne IDC [460]

ARBEITEN DER KURLAENDISCHEN GESELLSCHAFT FUER LITERATUR UND KUNST – Mitau. v1-10. 1847-1851 – 31mf – 9 – ne IDC [400]

ARBEITEN DES PHARMAKOLOGISCHEN INSTITUTES ZU DORPAT – Dorpat, 1888-1889.-v1-3 – 9mf – 9 – M-286/2 – ne IDC [615]

DIE ARBEITEN DES VATIKANISCHEN CONCILS / Martin, Konrad – (Includes index) – 2. unveraend Aufl. Paderborn: Ferdinand Schoeningh, 1873 – 1mf – 9 – 0-8370-8767-8 – 1986-2767 – us A.T.L.A. [240]

ARBEITEN ZU FILM UND FERNSEHEN / Boll, Uwe – 1992 – 3mf – 9 – DM98.00 – 3-89349-460-X – gw Hänsel [790]

ARBEITENDE JUGEND *see* ARBEITER-JUGEND

DIE ARBEITENDE JUGEND – (Cont by: Arbeiter-Jugend, 1909) – Berlin, 1905-feb 1933 – 1 – Dist. gw Mikrofilm – gw Misc Inst [072]

DIE ARBEITENDE JUGEND : ORGAN DES VEREINS DER LEHRLINGE UND JUGENDLICHEN ARBEITER BERLINS – (Cont by: Arbeiter-Jugend from 1909) – Berlin, 1905-08; 1909-33 – 5r – 1 – gw Mikro Press [072]

ARBEITER – Budapest, 1893-94 – 1r – 1 – Inquire at Mikrofilmarchiv for details – gw Misc Inst [072]

ARBEITER – Budapest, Hungary. 1893-94 – 1r – 1 – gw Mikrofilm [072]

DER ARBEITER – Berlin, 1919 – 1 – Dist. gw Mikrofilm – gw Misc Inst [072]

DER ARBEITER – Berlin. Vereinigung der deutschen Arbeitgeberverbaende. 1904, 1905-16, 1919, 1920, 1925-33. Title varies. (Serial publications of German trade unions in the Memorial Library, University of Wisconsin-Madison) – 1 – us U.W. Library [331]

DER ARBEITER – Muenchen, 1895-1907; 1909-18 – 12r – 1 – DM900.00 – gw Mikro Press [072]

DER ARBEITER – Muenchen, Germany. Jan. 5, 1895-1907, and 1909-Dec. 19, 1918 – 12r – 1 – gw Mikrofilm [072]

DER ARBEITER – New York. N.Y. The workman. 1904-11 – 1 – us A.J.P.C. [071]

DER ARBEITER – New York. Oct 8 1904-Aug 12 1911. Incomplete – 1 – us NY Public [071]

DER ARBEITER – New York. v. 1-11. no. 7. Sept. 15, 1927-Feb. 13, 1937 – 1 – us NY Public [073]

ARBEITER FRAIND = THE WORKER'S FRIEND – London, UK. sic 15 Jul 1885-26 Mar 1897; 14 Oct 1898-21 Jul 1916; Apr 1920-23 Dec 1923 – 1 – uk British Libr Newspaper [072]

ARBEITER ILLUSTRIERTE ZEITUNG – Berlin. 5-15 no. 33. Jan. 1926-Aug. 12, 1936. Incomplete – 1 – us NY Public [331]

Arbeiter Presse Verein *see* MITTEILUNGEN DES VEREINS ARBEITERPRESSE

ARBEITER- UND SOLDATENRAT – Sitzungsprotokolle. Bremen, 1918-19 – 1 – DM30.00 – gw Mikro Press [943]

ARBEITER UNION / Nationalen Arbeiter Union – New York. v. 1 no. 1-49. June 13 1868-May 15 1869. Weekly; v. 1-2 no. 101. May 22 1869-Sept 17 1870. Daily – 1 – us NY Public [072]

ARBEITER WELT – New York. v1. 1904 – 1r – 1 – us Ross [071]

ARBEITER ZEITUNG – New York. v1-13. 1890-1902 – 7r – 1 – us Ross [071]

ARBEITER ZEITUNG – Vienna. Oct 1909-Feb 1934; Aug 1945-Dec 1948 – 67r – 1 – us L of C Photodup [072]

ARBEITER ZEITUNG *see* SCHLESISCHE ARBEITER ZEITUNG

DIE ARBEITER ZEITUNG – New York. 1890-1902 – 1 – us NY Public [071]

DIE ARBEITER ZEITUNG – New York. N.Y. The workman's paper. 1890-1902 – 1 – us A.J.P.C. [071]

ARBEITERBEWEGUNG / Bundes der Arbeitgeber-Verbaende. Berlin – v1-2. 5 Oct 1898-27 Sept 1899. Berlin. 2v in 1. No more publ. (Serial publications of German trade unions in the Memorial Library, University of Wisconsin-Madison.) – 1 – us U.W. Library [331]

ARBEITERBEWEGUNG UND KLASSIK : AUSSTELLUNG IM GOETHE- UND SCHILLER-ARCHIV DER NATIONALEN FORSCHUNGS- UND GEDENKSTAETTEN DER KLASSISCHEN DEUTSCHEN LITERATUR IN WEIMAR, 1964-1966 / Holtzhauser, Helmut – (Includes bibliographical references) – Weimar: Aufbau-Verlag, 1964 – 1 – us U.W. Library [320]

ARBEITER-BLATT – Remscheid-Lennep, Germany.1848-49 (incomplete) – 1 – gw Mikrofilm [072]

ARBEITER-CAJTUNG – (Missing: Several issues) – Warsaw. v1-12. 1926-1937 – 3r – 1 – J-92-31/3 – ne IDC [072]

DIE ARBEITERCLASSEN-BEWEGUNG IN ENGLAND / Marx-Aveling, Eleonore – Nuernberg, 1895 – 1 – DM30.00 – gw Mikro Press [335]
DER ARBEITER-FOTOGRAF – Halle, Berlin. aug 1926-feb 1932 – 1r – 1 – gw Mikrofilm [770]
DER ARBEITER-FOTOGRAF – Halle, Berlin. aug 1926-nov 1932 – 1 – Dist. gw Mikrofilm – gw Misc Inst [770]
DIE ARBEITERFRAGE UND DAS CHRISTENTHUM / Ketteler, Wilhelm Emmanuel, Freiherr von – Mainz: F. Kirchheim, 1864 – 1mf – us A.T.L.A. [240]
ARBEITERFREUND – Berlin. 1-52. 1863-1914 – 1 – us NY Public [331]
DER ARBEITERFREUND – Berlin, 1863-1914 – 12r – 1 – DM900.00 – gw Mikro Press [072]
DER ARBEITERFREUND : ZEITSCHRIFT DES CENTRALVEREINS IN PREUSSEN FUER DAS WOHL DER ARBEITENDEN KLASSEN – Berlin, 1863-83, 1884 (incomplete), 1885-1911, 1912 (incomplete), 1913-14 – 12r – 1 – gw Mikro Press [073]
DER ARBEITERFREUND – Zeitschrift fuer die arbeiter frage....v1-52, 1863-1914. 52v in 44. illus., plates. -q. Organ of Centralverein fuer das wohl der arbeitenden Klassen. Continues Society's Zietschrift. Sub-title and imprint vary. (Serial publications of German trade unions in the Memorial Library, University of Wisconsin-Madison) – 1 – us U.W. Library [331]
ARBEITERFUNK – Berlin, no 45 1927-no 9 1932 – 1 – gw Mikrofilm [072]
ARBEITERFUNK *see* DER NEUE RUNDFUNK
ARBEITER-ILLUSTRIERTE ZEITUNG *see* SOWJETRUSSLAND IM BILD
ARBEITER-JUGEND – Berlin. v. 1-25, n.4. 1909-Apr 1933. Lacks v.25, n.3. Monatszeitschrift des Verbandes der Sozialistischen Arbeiterjugend Deutschlands. Includes 2 supplements. Die Arbeitsgemeinschaft and Kultur und Leben. Film Mas C 351 – 1 – us H.U. Library [331]
ARBEITER-JUGEND / ed by Ollenhauer, Erich – Monatsschrift der sozialistischen arbeiterjugend. Berlin, v17, 1925. illus. -m. (Serial publications of German trade unions in the Memorial Library, University of Wisconsin-Madison) – 1 – us U.W. Library [330]
ARBEITER-JUGEND : ORGAN FUER DIE GEISTIGEN UND WIRTSCHAFTLICHEN INTERESSEN DER JUNGEN ARBEITER UND ARBEITERINNEN – Berlin, 1909-Feb 1933 – 4r – 1 – DM360.00 set DM90.00r – gw Mikro Press [331]
ARBEITER-JUGEND : ORGAN FUER DIE GEISTIGEN UND WIRTSCHAFTLICHEN INTERESSEN DER JUNGEN ARBEITER UND ARBEITERINNEN – (Cont: Die Arbeitende Jugend) – Berlin, 1909-Feb 1933 – 5r – 1 – gw Mikrofilm [072]
ARBEITER-JUGEND *see*
– DIE ARBEITENDE JUGEND
Arbeiterkampf *see* ARBEITERZEITUNG DES KOMMUNISTISCHEN BUNDES
ARBEITER-LITERATUR – v1, no.1 2-12. Mar Apr 1924-Dec 1924. Wien, Verlag fuer Literatur und Politik. -m. (Serial publications of German trade unions in the Memorial Library, University of Wisconsin-Madison) – 1 – us U.W. Library [331]
ARBEITEROEFFENTLICHKEIT UND LITERATUR : ZUR THEORIE DES WERKKREISES LITERATUR DER ARBEITSWELT JUERGEN ALBERTS / Alberts, Juergen – (Includes bibliographical references) – Hamburg: VSA, 1977 – 1r – 1 – us U.W. Library [331]
ARBEITERPOLITIK – Asch, dec 1935, jan 1936, nov 1937, jan-sep 1938 (very incomplete) – 1 – Dist. gw Mikrofilm – gw Misc Inst [072]
ARBEITERPOLITIK – Prag (Praha), Czechoslovakia. Jun 22, 1929 – Aug 23, 1930 – 1r – 1 – gw Mikrofilm [072]
ARBEITERPOLITIK : WOCHENSCHRIFT FUER DEN SOZIALISMUS BREMEN – Berlin, 1917 – 1r – 1 – DM80.00 – gw Mikro Press [073]
ARBEITERPOLITIK : WOCHENSCHRIFT FUER WISSENSCHAFTLICHEN SOZIALISMUS – Bremen, 1916-19 – 1r – 1 – Inquire at Mikrofilmarchiv for details – gw Misc Inst [335]
ARBEITERPOLITIK : WOCHENSCHRIFT FUER WISSENSCHAFTLICHEN SOZIALISMUS – Bremen, Germany. 1916-19 – 1 – gw Mikrofilm [073]
DIE ARBEITERPOLITIK – Leipzig, Germany.1929-33 (incomplete) – 1 – gw Mikrofilm [072]
ARBEITERPRESSE *see*
– ARBEITER-WOCHEN-CHRONIK
DER ARBEITER-RAT : ORGAN DER ARBEITERRAETE DEUTSCHLANDS – Berlin, 1919-20 – 1r – 1 – DM100.00 – gw Mikro Press [331]
Arbeiterrat Gross-Hamburg *see*
– BERICHT UEBER DAS JAHR
– JAHRBUCH
Arbeiter-Sekretariat. Bremen *see* JAHRESBERICHT..
Arbeiter-Sekretariat. Halle *see* GESCHAEFTSBERICHT
Arbeiter-Sekretariat. Muenchen *see* JAHRESBERICHT..
Arbeiter-Sekretariat. Nuremberg *see* JAHRESBERICHT
ARBEITERSENDER – Berlin, 1928-33 – 1 – gw Mikrofilm [072]
ARBEITERSENDER *see*
– UNSER SENDER
ARBEITER-STIMME – New York. v1-4.1874-78 – 1r – 1 – us Ross [071]
ARBEITERSTIMME – Dresden, Germany.Apr 1925-1930; Jul 1931-Feb 1933 – 17r – 1 – gw Mikrofilm [072]
ARBEITERSTIMME – Wroclaw, Poland. Jul 1952-Jan 1956; Sept 1956-Apr 1958 – 7r – 1 – us L of C Photodup [072]
ARBEITERTAG FUER BRAUNSCHWEIG UND WEITERERE UMGEGEND, ABGESCHALTEN ZU BRAUNSCHWEIG / Brunswick. (City). Arbeitertag – 21 Juli 1867. 14p. (Serial publications of German trade unions in the Memorial Library, University of Wisconsin-Madison) – 1 – us U.W. Library [330]
ARBEITERTUM : BLAETTER FUER THEORIE UND PRAXIS DER NSBO – Berlin, 1931-1940 – 4r – 1 – gw Mikrofilm [072]
ARBEITERTUM : BLAETTER FUER THEORIE UND PRAXIS DER NSBO – Berlin, mar 1 1931-mar 31 1940 – 3r – 1 – DM270.00 set DM90.00r – gw Mikro Press [072]
ARBEITER-TURN- UND SPORTZEITUNG *see* ARBEITER-TURN-ZEITUNG
ARBEITER-TURN-ZEITUNG – (Cont by: Arbeiter-Turn-und-Sportzeitung 1931-) – Leipzig, 1893-1905; 1908-22 Mar 1933 – 10r – 1 – DM800.00 – gw Mikro Press [072]
ARBEITER-TURN-ZEITUNG – (Title change 1931: Arbeiter-Turn- und Sportzeitung) – Leipzig, Germany. Jul 15, 1893-1905; 1908-Mar 22, 1933 – 10r – 1 – gw Mikrofilm [072]
ARBEITER-WOCHEN-CHRONIK : SOZIALDEMOKRATISCHES VOLKSBLATT – (Cont by: Arbeiterpresse, 1891) – Budapest, 1873-94 – 6r – 1 – Inquire at Mikrofilmarchiv for details – gw Misc Inst [320]
ARBEITER-WOCHEN-CHRONIK : SOZIALDEMOKRATISCHES VOLKSBLATT – (Since 1891: Arbeiterpresse) – Budapest, Hungary. 1873-90 – 6r – 1 – gw Mikrofilm [073]
ARBEITER-WOCHEN-CHRONIK : SOZIALDEMOKRATISCHES VOLKSBLATT – (Since 1891: Arbeiterpresse) – Budapest, Hungary.1873-94 – 6r – 1 – gw Mikrofilm [072]
Arbeiterwohlfahrt Hauptausschuss *see* GESCHAEFTSBERICHT..
ARBEITER-ZEITUNG – Bern. v1-2 n1-33 jul 15 1876-oct 13 1877 – 1 – us Res Libr [072]
ARBEITER-ZEITUNG – Bremen, Germany.1927-27 Jul 1931; 6 Okt 1931-26 Feb 1933 – 1 – gw Mikrofilm [072]
ARBEITER-ZEITUNG – Chicago.1894-1910 – 30r – 1 – gw Mikrofilm [071]
ARBEITER-ZEITUNG – Essen, 1907-10; Jul-Dez 1911; Jul 1912-14; 1916-22; Apr-Jun 1923; 1924-Sept 1925; 1926; Jan-Mar, Jul-Dez 1927; Jan-Sept 1928; Jan-Sept 1929; 1930; Apr 1931-32 – 50r – 1 – DM3,570.00 – gw Mikro Press [072]
ARBEITER-ZEITUNG – Ludwigshafen, 1 Aug-30 Sept 1924; 2 Jan 1928-28 Feb 1933 – 12r – 1 – DM900.00 – gw Mikro Press [072]
ARBEITER-ZEITUNG – Ludwigshafen, Germany.Aug 1-Sept 30, 1924; Jan 2, 1928-Feb 28, 1933 – 12r – 1 – gw Mikrofilm [072]
ARBEITER-ZEITUNG – Reichenberg (Liberec), Czechoslovakia.Jul 20-Dec 28, 1929; Jan 4-Mar 1, 1930 – 1r – 1 – gw Mikrofilm [943]
ARBEITER-ZEITUNG – (Semi-monthly ed) – Bratislava, Czechoslovakia. Jun 1935-Jan 1937 – 1r – 1 – us L of C Photodup [072]
ARBEITER-ZEITUNG / Sozialdemokratische Arbeiter-partei OEsterreichs/RSOE/SPOE – Chicago, 1949- – 1 – us Res Libr [331]
ARBEITER-ZEITUNG / Sozialdemokratische Arbeiter-partei OEsterreichs/RSOE/SPOE – Vienna, 1914-25 (few missing), 1931 (incompl), 1933-34 (incompl) – 1 – us Hoover Inst Photo [331]
ARBEITER-ZEITUNG – (Title change Apr 8, 1863: Allgemeine Deutsche Arbeiter-Zeitung) – Coburg, Germany.1863-65, 1866 (incomplete) – 2r – 1 – gw Mikrofilm [072]
ARBEITER-ZEITUNG – (Title change in 1863: Allgemeine deutsche Arbeiter-Zeitung) – Coburg, 1863-65; 1866 (incomplete) – 2r – 1 – gw Mikrofilm [072]
ARBEITER-ZEITUNG – (Weekly ed. Scattered issues) – Bratislava, Czechoslovakia. Sept 1934-Jul 1936 – 1r – 1 – us L of C Photodup [072]
ARBEITER-ZEITUNG – Wien, Austria. Jan 1931-77 – 1 – gw Mikrofilm [072]
ARBEITER-ZEITUNG – Wien: R Pokorny, 1949-oct 14 1985 – 1 – us Res Libr [072]
ARBEITER-ZEITUNG *see*
– ESSENER ARBEITER-ZEITUNG
– DER KOMMUNIST
– SCHLESISCHE ARBEITER-ZEITUNG
DIE ARBEITER-ZEITUNG – (Title changes: Essener Arbeiter Zeitung, Nov 1919; Volkswacht, May 1926) – Essen, Germany. 26 Oct 1907-10; Jul-Dec 1911; Jul 1912-14; 1916-22; Apr-Jun 1923; 1924-Sept 1925; 1926-Mar 1927; Jul 1927-Sept 1928; Jan-Sept 1929; 1930; Apr 1931-32 – 51r – 1 – gw Mikrofilm [072]
ARBEITERZEITUNG DES KOMMUNISTISCHEN BUNDES / Arbeiterkampf – 1975-. Hamburg: Verlag Arbeiterkampf – 1 – us U.W. Library [073]
DER ARBEITGEBER – Archiv fuer Volkswirtschaft, patent- und gewerbe-zeitung. v5-9. (nos. 169-408; 610-1156); 1860-79. Frankfurt am Main. Subtitles varies. (Serial publications of German trade unions in the Memorial Library, University of Wisconsin-Madison) – 1 – us U.W. Library [331]
DER ARBEITGEBER – Frankfurt, 1857-1866 – 2r – 1 – DM200.00 – gw Mikro Press [072]
DER ARBEITGEBER – Frankfurt Main, Germany.1857-66 – 2r – 1 – gw Mikrofilm [331]
ARBEITSBERICHT / Verband der weiblichen Handels- und Bueroangestellten – v5. 1924 26, 1927 30. Berlin. (Serial publications of German trade unions in the Memorial Library, University of Wisconsin-Madison.) – 1 – us U.W. Library [330]
ARBEITSBESCHAFFUNG UND KREDITAUSWEITUNG / Best, Dr – 9 – 1.00f – at Libertarian Micro [335]
DER ARBEITSEINSATZ IM DEUTSCHEN REICH / Germany. Reichsarbeitsministerium. Hauptabteilung – 1927-42. 1939. No. 17-24 and 1940 wanting – 1 – $195.00 – us L of C Photodup [943]
Arbeitsgemeinschaft deutscher, oesterreicherscher und tschechoslowakischer Sozialisten *see* INFORMATIONSBRIEF
Arbeitsgruppe Deutschland *see* LIBRETTI IN DEUTSCHEN BIBLIOTHEKEN
ARBEITSLOSIGKEIT ZWISCHEN LOHN UND EFFIZIENZ : EINE DARSTELLUNG UND KRITIK DER EFFIZIENZLOHNTHEORIEN / Kaufmann, Frank – 1993 – 2mf – 9 – DM98.00 – 3-89349-656-4 – gw Hänsel [331]
ARBEITSMANN – Berlin. v. 1 no. 1-v. 7 no. 16. Oct 5 1935-Apr 19 1941. Incomplete – 1 – us NY Public [072]
DER ARBEITSMARKT – Monatsschrift des Verbandes deutscher Arbeitsnachweise. Berlin. v14-16. 1910-13. All incomplete. (Serial publications of German trade unions in the Memorial Library, University of Wisconsin-Madison) – 1 – us U.W. Library [331]
DER ARBEITSNACHWEIS IN DEUTSCHLAND – Zeitschrift des Verbandes deutscher Arbeitsnachweise. Berlin. v1-3, 1913-16. All incomplete. (Serial publications of German trade unions in the Memorial Library, University of Wisconson- Madison) – 1 – us U.W. Library [330]
Arbelaiz, M *see* LA ENSENANZA DEL DERECHO INTERNACIONAL PUBLICO
Arbelos, Carlos *see* LOS MUCHACHOS PERONISTAS
ARBEONIS EPSICOPI FRISINGENSIS VIAE SANCTORUM HAIMHRAMMI ET CORBINIANI (MGH 7: 13.BD) – 1920 – Dfl19.00 – ne Slangenburg [240]
Arber, E A N *see* CATALOGUE OF THE FOSSIL PLANTS OF THE GLOSSOPTERIS FLORA IN THE DEPARTMENT OF GEOLOGY... BRITISH MUSEUM NATURAL HISTORY
ARBETARBLADET – Gavle, Sweden. 1902-78 – 444r – 1 – sw Kungliga [072]
ARBETARBLADET – Gavle, Sweden. 1979- – 1 – sw Kungliga [072]
ARBETAREBLADET – Gaevle, 1869-88 – 9 – sw Kungliga [072]
ARBETAREN – Goeteborg, Sweden. 1868-70 – 1 – sw Kungliga [072]
ARBETAREN – Stockholm, Sweden. 1922-78 – 171r – 1 – sw Kungliga [072]
ARBETAREN – Stockholm, Sweden. 1979- – 1 – sw Kungliga [072]
ARBETARETIDNINGEN – Stockholm, Sweden. 1900-12, 1914 – 2r – 1 – sw Kungliga [072]
ARBETAREVANNEN – Lulea, Sweden. 1863-66 – 1 reel – 1 – sw Kungliga [072]
ARBETARTIDNINGEN NY DAG – Stockholm, Sweden. 1974-78 – 7r – 1 – sw Kungliga [072]
ARBETARTIDNINGEN NY DAG – Stockholm, Sweden. 1979-82 – 1 – sw Kungliga [072]
DER ARBETER STUDENT = THE STUDENT WORKER – New York City, NY. no 2. 1929 – 1r – Can$25.00 – cn Can Microfilming [071]
ARBETER TSAYTUNG = WORKER'S JOURNAL – (In Yiddish) – Lodz, PL. v5 no16 22 May 1947-v16 no71 31 Dec 1949 – 1r – 1 – $35.00 – cn Can Microfilming [073]
ARBETER TSAYTUNG = WORKERS' NEWS – (In Yiddish) – Warsaw, PL. no11 14 Mar 1930-no14 28 Apr 1939 – 1r – 1 – $25.00 – cn Can Microfilming [073]
ARBETER-FRAGN = LABOR PROBLEMS – (In Yiddish) – Warsaw, PL. (-) 15 Sep 1926 – 1r – 1 – $25.00 – cn Can Microfilming [072]
ARBETET – Malmo, Sweden. 1979- – 1 – sw Kungliga [072]
ARBETET – (Vastsv ed 1966-78 152r. Editorial pages, 1952-78 24r) – Malmo, Sweden. 1887-1978 – 79r – 1 – sw Kungliga [072]
ARBETET NYHETERNA – Malmoe, 1991- – 9 – sw Kungliga [072]
Arbie Zairany, Agus *see* DENDANG MELAJU DELI MODEREN; DIHIASI DENGAN SADJAK DAN GUBAHAN SERTA GAMBER2 PENGGEMARNJA
L'ARBITRAGE ENTRE NATIONS – Paris. 14v. 1897-1909 – 57mf – 9 – ILM-4005/1 – ne IDC [340]
ARBITRATION IN THE SCHOOLS / American Arbitration Association – New York, 1970-73 – 209mf + bd index – 9 – $5.00f – us Ross [370]
ARBITRATION INTERNATIONAL – v1-11. 1985-95 – 9 – $578.00 set – us Hein [340]
Arblay, Frances Burney *see* DIARY AND LETTERS...ED. BY HER NIECE CHARLOTTE BARRETT
Arbman, Ernst *see* RUDRA
Arbman, Per T *see* YAD AR EVANGELIUM?
Arbman, Per Theodor *see* VAD AR EVANGELIUM?
Arbo, H *see*
– CIUDADANIA Y NATURALIZACION
– DERECHO INTERNACIONAL CONVENCIONAL
ARBOG... : FOR KIRKELIG FORENING DEN INDRE MISSION I DANMARK – 1990-93 (complete) – 1r – 1 – ATLA S0900 – us A.T.L.A. [073]
ARBOGA TIDNING – Arboga, Sweden. 1851-55 – 1 reel – 1 – sw Kungliga [072]
ARBOGA TIDNING – Arboga, Sweden. 1858-80 – 9r – 1 – sw Kungliga [072]
ARBOGA TIDNING – Arboga, Sweden. 1881-1970 – 141r – 1 – sw Kungliga [072]
ARBOGA WECKOBLAD – (Nya Weckobladet i Arboga, 1853-55) – Arboga, Sweden. 1855-58 – 1r – 1 – sw Kungliga [072]
ARBOGABLADET – (Nya Arbogabladet, 1850) – Arboga, Sweden. 1848-49 – 1r – 1 – sw Kungliga [072]
ARBOK FOR DEN NORSKE KIRKE – 1952-92 (complete) – Inquire – 1 – ATLA S0605 – us A.T.L.A. [073]
ARBOL DE LAS VERAS / Lopez de Haro, Alonso – 1636 – 9 – 1.50f – sp Bibl Santa Ana [810]

ARBOL DE LAS VERAS Y...ELOGIOS / Mogroveio de Cerda, Ivan – 1636 – 9 – 1.50f – sp Bibl Santa Ana [810]
ARBOR DAY: A FEW ADVICES TO FARMERS ON THE PLANTING OF FOREST AND ORNAMENTAL TREES / Chapais, Jean Charles – Montreal: E. Senecal, 1884. 02870. (Pre-1900 Canadiana) – 9 – cn C.I.H.M. [630]
ARBOR DAY, PROVINCE OF QUEBEC: PROCLAMATIONS, ETC., INSTRUCTIONS FOR PLANTING TREES – 1883?. 02479. (Pre-1900 Canadiana) – 9 – cn C.I.H.M. [390]
ARBOR VITAE CRUCIFIXAE JESU / Ubertinus de Casali – Venetiis, 1485 – Dfl74.00 – ne Slangenburg [240]
L'ARBORE DI DIANE. DER BAUM DER DIANA. EINE COMISCHE OPER IN 2 ACTEN... / Martin y Solar, V – (Vocal score. Piano reduction by C. G. Neefe) – Bonn: Simrock, no. 27 – 1 – us Sibley [780]
Arbore-Ralli, Ekaterina Zamfirevna *see* MAT I DITIA V SOVETSKOI ROSSII
ARBORETUM SEGREZIANUM / Lavallee, P A M – Paris. 1880-85. B-6007 2 – 8 – ne IDC [580]
Arboreus, Ioan. *see* THEOSOPHIA
Arbousset, Jean Thomas *see*
- RELATION D'UN VOYAGE D'EXPLORATION AU NORD-EST DE LA COLONIE DU CAP DE BONNE-ESPERANCE
- RELATION D'UN VOYAGE D'EXPLORATION AU NORD-EST DE LA COLONIE DU CAP DU BONNE-ESPERANCE EN 1836
- VOYAGE D'EXPLORATION AUX MONTAGNES BLEUES; DECOUVERTE DU MONT-AUX-SOURCES, MARS-MAI 1836....1932

ARBRE HISTORIQUE DES DYNASTIES FRANCAISES / Soeurs de la Charite de Quebec. Academie – Levis: Mercier, 1894. 03985. (Pre-1900 Canadiana) – 9 – cn C.I.H.M. [944]
ARBROATH HERALD – 1 – £42.00r – uk Scot News [072]
ARBUCKLE AMERICAN – Arbuckle, CA. 1927; 1929-1931; 1933-1934; 1948-1965; 1967-1969 – 10r – 1 – $500.00 – B03137 – us Library Micro [071]
L'ARC – no. 1-12. Aix-en-Provence. 1958-oct 1960 – 1 – fr A.C.R.P.P. [073]
ARC : APPLYING RESEARCH TO THE CLASSROOM – Calgary. v7- 1989- – 9 – Can$20.00y – 0832-9842 – cn Micromedia [370]
ARC MAGAZINE – Ottawa, n26- 1991- – 9 – Can$20.00y – cn Micromedia [073]
ARCA NOE. THESAURUS LINGUAE SANCTAE NOVUS / Marinus, Marcus – Venetiis. Pars 1 + 2. 1593 – 71mf – 8 – ne Slangenburg [220]
ARCADIA – Montreal. 1892-93 – 1 – 45.00 – cn McLaren [800]
ARCADIA / Sannazaro, Jacopo – 15th cent. Holkham MS. 522. Holkham Hall, Norfolk, England – 1 – uk Microform Academic [810]
ARCADIA CHAMPION – Arcadia, NE. -w. May 1892-Sep. 1895. Incomplete; Oct. 1895-Dec. 1914; Dec. 1917-Sep. 1926 – 1 – us NE Hist [071]
ARCADIA CITY DIRECTORIES INCLUDING MONROVIA, DUARTE, SIERRA MADRE, TEMPLE CITY, BRADBURY AND EAST PASADENA – Los Angeles Co, CA. 1950-1992 (Fiche) – 238r – 1 – $595.00 – D054 – us Library Micro [910]
ARCADIA GUIDE – Arcadia, NE. -bw. Aug. 1948-Dec. 1971; Mar. 1972 – 1 – us NE Hist [071]
ARCADIA GUIDE – Arcadia, Valley County, NE: Apr 6, 1972-Sept 17, 1993 – us NE Hist [978]
ARCADIA TRIBUNE – Arcadia, CA. 1977-80 – 8r – 1 – $400.00 – R02020 – us Library Micro [071]
ARCADIAN – Arcadia, NE. -w. May 1937-Feb. 1943 – 1 – us NE Hist [071]
THE ARCADIAN – Arcadia. Fl. -w. 1925-26, 1931-41. 1945- – 1 – us P.K. Yonge [071]
THE ARCADIAN RHETORIKE / Fraunce, Abraham – 1588. 157p. (English Linguistics Series 1500-1800) – 9 – us UMI [400]
Arcaeus, F *see* A MOST EXCELLENT METHOD OF CURING WOUNDES
ARCAISMO Y MODERNIDAD EN LA EXPLOTACION AGRARIA DE VALDEBURON (LEON) / Martin Galindo, Jose Luis – 1 – sp Bibl Santa Ana [630]
ARCANA ENTOMOLOGICA; OR ILLUSTRATIONS OF NEW RARE, AND INTERESTING INSECTS / Westwood, J O – 2163 2. 2 v. 1841-1845 – 8 – ne IDC [590]
ARCANA HISTORIA (CBH 3,3) / Caesariensis, Procopii; ed by Maltret, C L – Parisiis, 1663 – Dfl49.00 – ne Slangenburg [930]
ARCANA OF SCIENCE AND ART ABRIDGED FROM THE TRANSACTIONS OF PUBLIC SOCIETIES, AND FROM THE SCIENTIFIC JOURNALS, BRITISH AND FOREIGN – London, 1828-1838 – 3 – us Readex [500]
ARCANA PACIS WESTPHALICAE... / Adami, A – Frankfurt, 1698 – 7mf – 9 – ILM-314/1 – ne IDC [340]
Arcand, Adrien *see*
- LE CHAMEAU
- LE FACISTE CANADIEN
- LE GOGLU
- LE MIROIR
- LE PATRIOTE

Arcangeli, G *see* COMPENDIO DELLA FLORA ITALIANA
ARCANI MUSICALI / Berardi, A – 1690 – 9 – us Sibley [780]
ARCATA COOP NEWSLETTER – Arcata, CA. 1976-1985; 1990-1991 – 2r – 1 – $100.00 – B03139 – us Library Micro [071]
ARCATA UNION *see* MCKINLEYVILLE JOURNAL
THE ARCE COLLECTION OF HISTORICAL AND LITERARY PAMPHLETS – Panama: Universidad de Panama – 8r – 1 – $480.00 – us Ross [972]
Arce, Joan C *see*
- DIFICULTADES VENCIDAS...PARA LA LIMPIEZA Y ASEO DE LAS CALLES DE ESTA CORTE
- TESTOSTERONE AND PHYSICAL ACTIVITY

Arce, Jose *see*
- NUEVAS BASES Y PRINCIPIOS PARA LA REORGANIZACION POLITICA DE LA REPUBLICA ARGENTINA, MADRID, NUEVA YORK, 1951-1953
- SEGURIDAD SOCIAL EN LA ARGENTINA

ARCEBISPO DE CANGRANOR / Meyrelles de Souto, A – 1960 – 1 – sp Bibl Santa Ana [240]
L'ARCENAL DE CHIRURGIE... / Scultet, J – Lyon, 1675 – 8mf – 9 – sp Cultura [617]
ARCHAELOGIA HUNGARICA – (Missing: v11; 12) – Budapest, 1926-1937. v1-21 – 56mf – 9 – HA-4/1 – ne IDC [930]
ARCHAEOLOGIA : OR MISCELLANEOUS TRACTS RELATING TO ANTIQUITY – (Index v1-50) – London: Oxford, 2nd ed 1779-1940.-v1-88 – 1,037mf – 9 – H-806/2 – ne IDC [930]
ARCHAEOLOGIA BRITANNICA / Lhuyd, Edward – 1707. 485p. (English Linguistics Series 1500-1800) – 9 – us UMI [420]
ARCHAEOLOGIA CORNU-BRITANNICA / Pryce, William – 1790. 296p. (English Linguistics Series 1500-1800) – 9 – us UMI [420]
ARCHAEOLOGIA OR MISCELLANEOUS TRACTS RELATING TO ANTIQUITY – v. 1-98. 1773-1961. Index, v. 1-50 – 1 – 959.00 – us L of C Photodup [930]
Archaeological Conference. Tenth. Riga *see* TRUDY DESIATOGO ARKHEOLOGICHESKOGO S"EZDA V RIGE
Archaeological Conference. Tenth. Riga. Moscow Organizing Committee *see* TRUDY MOSKOVSKOGO PREDVARITEL'NOGO KOMITETA X ARKHEOLOGICHESKOGO S'EZDA V RIGE
Archaeological Dept. Southern Circle. Madras *see* ANNUAL REPORT...FOR THE YEAR...
Archaeological Institute of America *see* BULLETIN
ARCHAEOLOGICAL INVESTIGATIONS IN THE PARITA AND SANTA MARIA ZONES OF PANAMA / Ladd, John – 1964 – 6mf – 9 – $5.00f – us Ross [930]
ARCHAEOLOGICAL JOURNAL – 1943 – 1 – uk Microform Academic [930]
ARCHAEOLOGICAL JOURNAL – London, 1844-1920. v1-77 – 1,059mf – 9 – H-806/2 – ne IDC [930]
ARCHAEOLOGICAL JOURNAL – v. 1-91. 1844-1934 – 1,5,6 – us Princeton Micro [930]
The Archaeological Museum. Naples *see* THE NATIONAL ARCHAEOLOGICAL MUSEUM, NAPLES
ARCHAEOLOGICAL NEWSLETTER – (Nos 188-216 1981-83 were titled New Series. Series 2 commences in 1984) – Toronto. no164-1979- – 9 – Can$20.00y – cn Micromedia [930]
ARCHAEOLOGICAL REPORT / Egypt Exploration Fund – London. v1-5. 1899-1905 – 1r – 1 – us Ross [930]
Archaeological Society of Delaware *see* BULLETIN
ARCHAEOLOGICAL SURVEY / India – o.s. 23 v. Calcutta. 1871-87. BI-302 2 – 8 – ne IDC [930]
THE ARCHAEOLOGICAL SURVEY – Reno, CA. University of Nevada: 1973-1983 – 2r – 1 – $100.00 – B06075 – us Library Micro [930]
ARCHAEOLOGICAL SURVEY OF CEYLON : PLANS AND PLATES FOR THE ANNUAL REPORTS, 1892-1902 / ed by Bell, H C P – Colombo, 1914 – 40mf – 9 – I-567/2 – ne IDC [930]
Archaeological Survey of Ceylon *see* EPIGRAPHIA ZEYLANICA
ARCHAEOLOGICAL SURVEY OF INDIA – Hampi ruins, described and illustrated by A.H. Longhurst. 3rd ed. Delhi: Gov't. of India, 1933. 136p. illus – 1 – us U.W. Library [720]
ARCHAEOLOGICAL SURVEY OF INDIA / India – New Imp. Series. v. 1-12, 15-54. Calcutta. Supt. Govt. Print. 1874-1937 (v. 13-14 in Epigraphia Indica. 1892-94). Lacking: 1899, v. 27-28. BI-301 2 – 8 – ne IDC [930]
ARCHAEOLOGICAL SURVEY OF INDIA / India – South Indian Inscriptions. v. 1-20. Madras. 1890-1965. Lacking: 1964 65, v. 18. BI-598 2 – 8 – ne IDC [930]
ARCHAEOLOGICAL SURVEY OF INDIA : OLD SERIES – Simla, Calcutta, 1871-1887. 23v – 124mf – 9 – I-302/2 – ne IDC [930]
Archaeological Survey of India. Northern Circle. Muhammadan and British Monuments *see* ANNUAL PROGRESS REPORT OF THE SUPERINTENDENT...FOR THE YEAR ENDING...
ARCHAEOLOGICAL SURVEY OF INDIA PHOTOGRAPHS / British Library. Oriental and Indian Office Collections – (Coll reproduces 33,800 official photographs of the architecture and monuments of South Asia taken between 1850s and 1920s) – 1993 – 232mf – 9 – $1,474.00 – 1-869934-58-X – uk Emmett [770]
ARCHAEOLOGICAL SURVEY OF MAYURABHANJA / India – v. 1 BY Nagendranth Vasu. Mayurabhanja State. Calcutta. 1911. BI-793 2 – 8 – ne IDC [930]
ARCHAEOLOGICAL SURVEY OF WESTERN INDIA / India – (2. Memorandum on the Antiquities at Dabhoi, Ahmedabad. 3. Memorandum on the Remains at Gumli, Gop) – NRS. 1-3. Memorandum on the Buddhist Caves at Junnar, by J. Burgess, and translation of three inscriptions from Badami, Pattadkal, and Aiholli, by J. F. Fleet. Bombay. 1874-75. BI-698 2 – 8 – ne IDC [930]
ARCHAEOLOGIST – Reno, NV. v1 1972; v7 1989 – 1r – 1 – $50.00 – R04884 – us Library Micro [930]
ARCHAEOLOGY : PROGRESS REPORT OF THE ARCHAEOLOGICAL SURVEY OF INDIA, WESTERN CIRCLE... – Bombay: The Survey, 1906-13 – 1r – 1 – us Res Libr [930]
ARCHAEOLOGY AND THE BIBLE / Bowden, J – 1968 – 9 – 1.00f – at Libertarian Micro [335]
ARCHAEOLOGY AND THE RELIGION OF ISRAEL / Albright, W F – Johns Hopkins Press, 1953 – 9 – $10.00 – us I.R.C. [270]
THE ARCHAEOLOGY OF PALESTINE / Albright, W F – Penguin Books, 1949 – 9 – $10.00 – us I.R.C. [930]
THE ARCHAEOLOGY OF PALESTINE AND THE BIBLE / Albright, W F – Revell, 1932 – 9 – $10.00 – us I.R.C. [930]
ARCHAEOLOGY OF THE CENTRAL ESKIMOS / Mathiassen, T – BN 315 2. 1927 – 8 – ne IDC [930]
THE ARCHAEOLOGY OF THE NAPA, CALIFORNIA REGION / Heiser, Robert F – 1953 – 1r – 1 – $50.00 – B70062 – us Library Micro [930]
ARCHAIOLOGIKE EPHEMERIS – Athens, 1837-1982. 24 reels – 1 – $1,990.00 – us UPA [930]
ARCHAISCHE TEXTE AUS URUK / Falkenstein, A – (Ausgrabungen der Deutschen Forschungsgemeinschaft in Uruk-Warka, v2). Berlin 1936 – 9 – ne IDC [490]
Archambault, Alfred *see* SERMON SUR L'AUTORITE DES EVEQUES: DONNE LE LER MAI 1894 DANS LA CATHEDRALE DE MONTREAL A L'OCCASION DU 21E ANNIVERSAIRE DE LA CONSECRATION EPISCOPALE DE MGR. EDOUARD-CHARLES FABRE.
Archambault, Horace *see* DISCOURS LE 10 JUILLET 1888, AU CONSEIL LEGISLATIF SUR LA QUESTION DES BIENS DE JESUITES
Archambault, Joseph Louis *see*
- LE BARREAU CANADIEN AU CONSEIL PRIVE: EXTRAITS D'UNE CONFERENCE PRONONCEE LE 14 MARS 1889 DEVANT LE CLUB CONSERVATEUR DE MONTREAL
- CONFERENCE SUR L'HYGIENE GENERALE
- ETUDE LEGALE, OU, REPONSE A CERTAINES QUESTIONS CONCERNANT LES SUCCURSALES DE L'UNIVERSITE LAVAL, A MONTREAL
- ETUDE POLITIQUE: LUE DEVANT L'ASSOCIATION CONSERVATRICE DE MONTREAL EN FEVRIER 1887
- JACQUES CARTIER, OU, CANADA VENGE: DRAME HISTORIQUE EN 5 ACTES (FANTASIE LITTERAIRE COMPOSEE POUR MON VILLAGE

Archambault, Louis Missael *see* GENEALOGIE DE LA FAMILLE ARCHAMBAULT, 1620-1890: TABLEAU ET NOTES HISTORIQUES
Archambault, R T et al *see* DISPLAY AND IMAGING
Archambault, Urgel Eugene *see*
- ECOLE POLYTECHNIQUE DE MONTREAL: RAPPORT DU PRINCIPAL A L'HONORABLE SURINTENDANT DE L'INSTRUCTION PUBLIQUE
- MEMOIRE SUR LA LOI 43 ET 44 VICT., CH. 22, ETABLISSANT UN FONDS DE RETRAITE ET DE SECOURS EN FAVEUR DES FONCTIONNAIRES DE L'ENSEIGNEMENT PRIMAIRE

ARCHBALD CITIZEN – (Weekly general newspaper) – Archbald, PA. apr 1-june 17, 1916 – 1r – 1 – us Western Res [071]
Archbell, James *see* A GRAMMAR OF THE BECHUANA LANGUAGE
ARCHBISHOP MACLAGAN : BEING A MEMOIR OF THE MOST REVD. THE RIGHT HONBLE. WILLIAM DALRYMPLE MACLAGAN, D.D., ARCHBISHOP OF YORK AND PRIMATE OF ENGLAND / How, Frederick Douglas – London: W. Gardner, Darton, 1911 – 2mf – us A.T.L.A. [240]
ARCHBISHOP MAKARIOS OF CYPRUS PAMPHLET COLLECTION – 1958 – 1 – CSUXANR0487-B – us Hoover Inst Photo [240]
ARCHBISHOP THOMAS BRADWARDINE : A FOURTEENTH CENTURY AUGUSTINIAN / Obermann, H A – Utrecht, 1958 – 5mf – 8 – ne Slangenburg [290]
ARCHBISHOP WAKE AND THE PROJECT OF UNION (1717-1720) BETWEEN THE GALLICAN AND ANGLICAN CHURCHES / Lupton, J H – London: G. Bell; Cambridge: Deighton; Bell, 1896 – 1mf – us A.T.L.A. [240]
ARCHBOLD BUCKEYE – Archbold, Ohio. 1983-1986 – 4r – 1 – us Archival [071]
Archdiocese of St. Paul and Minneapolis *see* PARISH QUESTIONNAIRES AND RELATED MATERIALS
Arche, Jose Vicente *see* CASTILLA AGRICOLA PARA LA ENSENANZA DE LA AGRICULTURA...CACERES
Archeological Museum of Merida *see* A BRIEF GUIDE TO THE MUSEUM
ARCHEOLOGIE DES ILES MARQUISES : CONTRIBUTION A LA CONNAISSANCE DE L'ILE DE UA POU / Ottino, P – 1985 – F180.00 – fr Ethnologie [930]
ARCHEOLOGIE PALEOCHRETIENNE ET CULTE CHRETIEN / Nedoncelle, M et al – Straszbourg, 1962 – 4mf – 8 – Dfl19.00 – ne Slangenburg [240]
ARCHEOLOGIE RELIGIEUSE DU DIOCESE DE MONTREAL, 1850 / Viger, Jacques – Montreal: Lovell et Gibson, 1850. SEM16P217 – 1r – 5 – Can$9.00 – cn Bibl Nat [240]
THE ARCHEOLOGY OF CRETE / Pendlebury, JD S – Methuen. 1939 – 9 – $15.00 – us I.R.C. [930]
ARCHEOLOGY OF ST LAWRENCE ISLAND, ALASKA / Collins, H B – BN 171 2. 1937 – 8 – ne IDC [930]
Archer, Andrew *see*
- CANADA, A SHORT HISTORY OF THE DOMINION OF CANADA
- A HISTORY OF CANADA FOR THE USE OF SCHOOLS

Archer, William *see*
- ENGLISH DRAMATISTS OF TO-DAY
- HENRY IRVING, ACTOR AND MANAGER
- POETS OF THE YOUNGER GENERATION

ARCHERY WORLD – (1975- . 5,6,9) – 1921- – 1 – us UMI [790]

Archiac, E J *see* DESCRIPTION DES ANIMAUX FOSSILES DU GROUPE NUMMULITIQUE DE L'INDE

Archibald, Adams George *see*
- ADDRESS DELIVERED ON THE 30TH DAY OF OCTOBER, A.D. 1883, ON THE OCCASION OF THE OPENING OF A LAW SCHOOL IN CONNECTION WITH DALHOUSIE COLLEGE, HALIFAX, NOVA SCOTIA
- THE INAUGURAL ADDRESSES, ETC. DELIVERED AT THE OPENING OF THE LAW SCHOOL IN CONNECTION WITH DALHOUSIE UNIVERSITY, HALIFAX, NOVA SCOTIA...1883..

Archibald, Andrew Webster *see* THE BIBLE VERIFIED

Archibald, F A *see* METHODISM AND LITERATURE

ARCHIE – Issue Nos. 11-15 Nov 1944-Aug 1945 – 5mf – 15 – $31.95 – us Comics [760]

ARCHIE – Issue Nos. 1-5 Winter 1942-Dec 1943 – 5mf – 15 – $31.95 – us Comics [760]

ARCHIE – Issue Nos. 16-20 Sept 1945-June 1946 – 5mf – 15 – $31.95 – us Comics [760]

ARCHIE – Issue Nos. 21-25 July 1946-Apr 1947 – 5mf – 15 – $31.95 – us Comics [760]

ARCHIE – Issue Nos. 26-30 May 1947-Feb 1948 – 5mf – 15 – $31.95 – us Comics [760]

ARCHIE – Issue Nos. 31-35 Mar 1948-Dec 1948 – 5mf – 15 – $31.95 – us Comics [760]

ARCHIE – Issue Nos. 36-40 Jan 1949-Oct 1949 – 5mf – 15 – $31.95 – us Comics [760]

ARCHIE – Issue Nos. 41-45 Nov 1949-Aug 1950 – 5mf – 15 – $31.95 – us Comics [760]

ARCHIE – Issue Nos. 46-50 Sept 1950-June 1951 – 5mf – 15 – $31.95 – us Comics [760]

ARCHIE – Issue Nos. 6-10 Jan 1944-Oct 1944 – 5mf – 15 – $31.95 – us Comics [760]

ARCHIEF GESCHIEDENIS AARTSBISDOM UTRECHT – 1(1875)-75(1957) – 420mf – 9 – Dfl470.00 – ne Slangenburg [025]

ARCHIEF VAN KERKELIJKE GESCHIEDENIS – (1841-1849: Nederl. Archief v. Kerkel. Gesch. 1852-1854: Nieuw Archief v. Kerkel. Gesch.) – 1(1829)-11(1840) – 54mf – 9 – Dfl89.00 – ne Slangenburg [025]

HET ARCHIEF VAN PROF. DR. W.H. DE VRIESE BETREFFENDE ZIJN ONDERZOEK NAAR DE KULTURES IN NEDERLANDS INDIE, 1857-1862 = THE ARCHIVES OF PROF. DR. W.H. DE VRIESE CONCERNING HIS INVESTIGATIONS INTO THE NETHERLANDS INDIES CULTIVATIONS / Netherlands. General State Archives – 204mf – 9 – Dfl2310.00 silver – ne MMF Publ [949]

ARCHIEF VOOR DE GESCHIEDENIS DER OUDE HOLLANDSCHE ZENDING – Utrecht. deel1-3. 1884-1886 – 16mf – 9 – Dfl56.00 – ne Slangenburg [025]

ARCHIEF VOOR DE JAVA-SUIKERINDUSTRIE – (Continues as: Archief voor de Suikerindustrie in Nederlandsch Indie.-Batavia, 1910-1934.-v18-42) – Batavia, 1893-1909.-v1-17 – 1437mf – 9 – SE-22/2 – ne IDC [338]

ARCHIEF VOOR DE KOFFIECULTUUR IN NEDERLANDSCH INDIE – (Lacking: 1947, v16 (p. 160-end.)) – Batavia, Djakarta, 1927-1950.-v1-17 – 72mf – 9 – SE-23/2 – ne IDC [338]

ARCHIEF VOOR DE RUBBERCULTUUR IN NEDERLANDSCH INDIE – Batavia, Djakarta, 1917-1958.-v1-35 – 448mf – 9 – SE-24/2 – ne IDC [338]

ARCHIEF VOOR KERKELIJKE GESCHIEDENIS, INZONDERHEID VAN NEDERLAND – v. 1-20. 1829-49 – 1 – us A.T.L.A. [073]

ARCHIEF VOOR NEDERLANDSCHE KERKGESCHIEDENIS – (1857-1866: Kerkhistorisch Archief. 1870-1880: Studien en Bijdragen op 't Gebied der Historische Theologie) – 1(1885)-7(1889) – 42mf – 9 – Dfl147.00 – ne Slangenburg [025]

ARCHIEPISC. OPERA OMNIA / Anselmi Cantuar, S – (Vol. 1 rec. Fr. S. Schmitt. Seccovii, 1938 10mf; Vol. 2 rec. Fr. S. Schmitt. Romae, 1940 10mf) – 8 – ne Slangenburg [240]

ARCHIEPISCOPATUS PARISIENSIS (GC 7) – Parisiis, 1744 – Dfl140.00 – ne Slangenburg [240]

Archimedes *see* ARCHIMEDIS OPERA NON NVLLA; A FEDERICO COMMANDINO VRBINATE; NVPER IN LATINVM CONVERSA, ET COMMENTARIIS ILLVSTRATA; QUORUM NOMINA IN SEQUENTI PAGINA LEGUNTUR

ARCHIMEDIS OPERA NON NVLLA; A FEDERICO COMMANDINO VRBINATE; NVPER IN LATINVM CONVERSA, ET COMMENTARIIS ILLVSTRATA; QUORUM NOMINA IN SEQUENTI PAGINA LEGUNTUR / Archimedes – Venetiis: Apud Paulum Manutium, 1558 – 1 – us U.W. Library [510]

L'ARCHIPEL DES COMORES / Manicacci, Jean – Tananarive: Impr Officielle, 1939 – 1 – us Res Libr [960]

L'ARCHIPEL EN FEU / Verne, Jules – Paris: J. Hetzel, 1884. 4 fiches. (Literature Collection) – 9 – 10.00 – fr Bibl Nationale [830]

ARCHIPELAGO MUNDI, AN OPEN INQUIRY INTO CLOSED SPACES / Brennan, Paul – Outline for a book. 1984, 13p – 9 – 1.00f – at Libertarian Micro [335]

ARCHITECT RECORD *see* AMERICAN ARCHITECT AND ARCHITECTURE

ARCHITECTIONICE MUSICES UNIVERSALIS / Schonsleder, W – Ingolstadii. 1634. BP-468 1 – 9 – ne IDC [780]

ARCHITECTONOGRAPHIE DES PRISONS OU PARALLELE DES DIVERS SYSTEMES DE DISTRIBUTION DONT LES PRISONS SONT SUSCEPTIBLES. / Baltard, Louis Pierre – Paris, 1829. 35p., 37 pl. (Architecture Series) – 9 – fr Hachette [720]

ARCHITECTONOGRAPHIE DES THEATRES DE PARIS OU PARALLELE HISTORIQUE ET CRITIQUE DE CES EDIFICES. / Donnet, Alexis – Paris. Dedot, 1821. 1v. 384p., un atlas in -4 fol. de 25 pl. (Architecture Series) – 9 – fr Hachette [720]

THE ARCHITECTS' AND ARTISANS' PERMANENT PRICE BOOK AND COMPENDIUM OF USEFUL TABLES AND PRACTICAL SCIENTIFIC INFORMATION: SELECTED AND COMPILED FOR THE USE OF ALL BRANCHES OF THE ARCHITECTURAL PROFESSION / Boxer, Frederick N – Montreal: Lovell Print. and Publ. Co., 1876. 00229. (Pre-1900 Canadiana) – 9 – cn C.I.H.M. [720]

THE ARCHITECTS AND BUILDERS HANDBOOKS / Kidder, Frank E – 1921 – 9 – 75.00 – us Opus [720]

ARCHITECTS' JOURNAL – v59- 1924- – 1,5,6,9 – us UMI [720]

ARCHITECTS LAW REPORTS – v1-4. 1904-08 (all publ) – 9 – LLMC 84-704 – us L.L.M.C. [340]

ARCHITECTURA / Vignola, J – SL, 1582 – 2mf – 9 – sp Cultura [720]

LA ARCHITECTURA / Alberti, L B – SL, 1575 – 7mf – 9 – sp Cultura [720]

ARCHITECTURA CIVILIS / Furttenbach, J – O-1155 1. 1628 – 9 – ne IDC [720]

ARCHITECTURA CURIOSA NOVA / Boecklern, G A – O-1147 1. 1664 – 9 – ne IDC [720]

ARCHITECTURA HYDRAULICA EN LAS FABRICAS DE PUENTES METHODO DE PROYECTARLOS Y REPARLOS / Pontones, P – SL, 1759 – 9mf – 9 – sp Cultura [620]

ARCHITECTURA MARTIALIS / Furttenbach, J – O-1140 1. 1630 – 9 – ne IDC [720]

ARCHITECTURA PRIVATA / Furttenbach, J – 1641. O-1157 1 – 9 – ne IDC [720]

ARCHITECTURA RECREATIONIS / Furttenbach, J – O-1156 1. 1640 – 9 – ne IDC [720]

ARCHITECTURA UNIVERSALIS / Furttenbach, J – O-1139 1. 1635 – 9 – ne IDC [720]

ARCHITECTURA VON AUSSTHEILUNG/ SYMMETRIA UND PROPORTION DER FUNFF SEULEN / Dietterlin, W – O-1020 1. 1598 – 9 – ne IDC [720]

ARCHITECTURAL AND DESIGN HISTORY / Pugin, A WN – (The drawings and mss. of A.W.N. Pugin from the Victoria and Albert Museum, London) – 1,14 – us Primary [720]

Architectural Association *see* JOURNAL

ARCHITECTURAL COMPONENT: (ARTIFICIAL LIGHT) – Pattee, University Park, PA. 1982 – 77p 4mf – 9 – $0.50f – us Lawrence Pub [720]

ARCHITECTURAL COMPONENT: FUNCTION – P/MS. University Park, PA. 1978 – 180p 8mf – 9 – $0.50f – us Lawrence Pub [720]

ARCHITECTURAL COMPONENT: (NATURAL) LIGHT – P/MS. University Park, PA. 1979 – 180p 8mf – 9 – $0.50f – us Lawrence Pub [720]

ARCHITECTURAL COMPONENT: SPACE – P/MS, University Park, PA. 1978 – 240p 10mf – 9 – $0.50f – us Lawrence Pub [720]

ARCHITECTURAL FORUM – (1968-74. 5,6. 1970-74. 9) – 1-140. 1892-1974 – 1 – us UMI [720]

ARCHITECTURAL HISTORY / ed by Taverne, E R M – 9 – ne IDC [720]

ARCHITECTURAL PERIODICALS AT AVERY LIBRARY, COLUMBIA UNIVERSITY – 16 titles. 286 reels. Titles available individually – 1 – $21,415.00 – us UPA [720]

ARCHITECTURAL PLANNING PARTNERSHIP / Libya. Ministry of Planning and Development – Planning 1966-67 for the development of the Muhafadahs of Gebel Ghardi and Az Zawiyah (except the Mudiriyah of Zanzur). 3 v. Gebel Gharbi and Az Zawyah. BNE-1302 1 – 9 – ne IDC [720]

ARCHITECTURAL RECORD – 1- 1891- – 1,5,6,9 – us UMI [720]

ARCHITECTURAL RECORD – New York, 1891-1920. v1-48 – 494mf – 9 – O-1228/1 – ne IDC [720]

ARCHITECTURAL RESEARCH AND TEACHING – v. 1-2. 1970-73 – 1 – us UMI [370]

ARCHITECTURAL REVIEW FOR THE ARTIST AND CRAFTSMAN – (Cont. as: Architectural Review. London, 1902-1920. v12-48) – London, 1896/1897-1902. v1-11 – 359mf – 9 – O-491/1 – ne IDC [720]

ARCHITECTURAL SCIENCE REVIEW – v1-. 1958- – 1,5,6,9 – us UMI [073]

ARCHITECTURAL TRADE CATALOGS / Columbia University. Avery Memorial Architectural Library – (General & Misc. $895.00; Sitework $560.00; Concrete $345.00; Masonry $535.00; Metals $1,350.00; Wood & Plastics $2,410.00; Thermal & Moisture Protection $415.00; Doors & Windows $2,315.00; Finishes $1,105.00; Specialties $590.00; Equipment $525.00; Furnishings $1,570.00; Special Construction $815.00; Conveying Systems $125.00; Mechanical $1,550.00; Electrical $1,510.00; Guide only $130.00) – 1760-1950 – 3,550mf – 9 – $14,920.00 set – us UPA [720]

ARCHITECTURE AND BUILDING – New York. v1-64. 1882-1932 – 30r – 1 – us Ross [720]

ARCHITECTURE AND EARLY PHOTOGRAPHY IN FRANCE / Caisse Nationale des Monuments Historiques et des Sites. Paris. Archives Photographiques – ("Architecture and Monuments in France" 137mf $725.00 ISBN: 0-907006-64-7. "Paris Views and Early Photography in France" 118mf $630.00 ISBN: 0-907006-69-8) – 255mf – 9 – $1,200.00 coll – 0-907006-74-4 – uk Mindata [700]

ARCHITECTURE AND ENVIRONMENT : ARCHITECTURE, APPLIED ARTS, STUDIO ARTS – (Individual titles not listed separately) – 53 catalogues on 64mf – 9 – £470.00 – uk Chadwyck [720]

ARCHITECTURE AND NATIVE ART (TIAM, PT 3) – (With printed catalogue ISBN: 0-914146-66-1 £30) – 21mf – 15 – £430.00 – uk Chadwyck [720]

ARCHITECTURE AND SCULPTURE COLLECTION / Victoria and Albert Museum. London – 152mf – 9 – $815.00 – 0-907006-25-6 – uk Mindata [700]

ARCHITECTURE CIVILE / Dubut, Louis Ambroise – Paris. Eberhart, 1803. 2p., 87 pl. (Architecture Series) – 9 – fr Hachette [720]

ARCHITECTURE COMMUNALE / Narjoux, Felix – Paris. Morel, 1870-80. 3v. in fol., pl. (Architecture Series) – 9 – fr Hachette [720]

L'ARCHITECTURE CONSIDEREE SOUS LE RAPPORT DE L'ART, DES MOEURS ET DE LA LEGISLATION / Ledoux, Claude Nicolas – Paris, 1804. 240p., pl. (Architecture Series) – 9 – fr Hachette [720]

L'ARCHITECTURE CONTEMPORAINE ET LE STYLE GOTHIQUE / Laviron, Gabriel – Extrait de la REVUE NOUVELLE, 1 Oct. 1846. p.46-80. (Architecture Series) – 9 – fr Hachette [720]

L'ARCHITECTURE DES VOUTES, OU L'ART DES TRAITS ET COUPE DE VOUTES. / Derand, Francois – Paris, S. Cramoisy, 1643. 453p., pl. (Architecture Series) – 9 – fr Hachette [720]

L'ARCHITECTURE ET ART DE BIEN BASTIR. / Alberti, L B – Paris. J. Kerver. 1553. 228p., illus. (Architecture Series) – 9 – fr Hachette [720]

ARCHITECTURE ET PERSPECTIVE DES FORTIFICATIONS / Perret, I – O-1144 1. 1602 – 9 – ne IDC [720]

L'ARCHITECTURE FRANCAISE – no. 1-280. Paris. nov 1940-65 – 5 – fr A.C.R.P.P. [073]

L'ARCHITECTURE FRANCAISE DES BASTIMENS PARTICULIERS / Savot, Louis – Paris. S. Cramoisy. 1624. 328p. (Architecture Series) – 9 – fr Hachette [720]

ARCHITECTURE HYDRAULIQUE OU L'ART DE CONDUIRE, D'ELEVER ET DE MENAGER LES EAUX POUR LES DIFFERENTS BESOINS DE LA VIE / Belidor, Bernard Forest de – Paris, Collot (puis) Barrot, 1782-90. 4v. in 4 fol, ill. (Architecture Series) – 9 – fr Hachette [720]

L'ARCHITECTURE MODERNE EN FRANCE / Barqui, F – Paris. Baudry, 1871. Fol., 9p., 120 pl. (Architecture Series) – 9 – fr Hachette [720]

ARCHITECTURE MODERNE, OU L'ART DE BIEN BATIR POUR TOUTES SORTES DE PERSONNES. / Briseux, C E – Paris, C. Jombert, 1728. 2v. in 4 dont un de planches. (Architecture Series) – 9 – fr Hachette [720]

ARCHITECTURE OU ART DE BIEN BASTIR / Vitruve, Marc – Tournes. J. Cologny. 1618. 391p., planches. Ill. de Jean Goujon. (Architecture Series) – 9 – fr Hachette [720]

L'ARCHITECTURE PRATIQUE. / Bullet, Pierre – Paris, E. Michallet, 1691. 14, 410p., ill. (Architecture Series) – 9 – fr Hachette [720]

L'ARCHITECTURE PRIVEE AU 19E SIECLE (SOUS NAPOLEON 3) / Daly, Cesar – Nouvelles maisons de Paris et des environs. Paris. A. Morel, 1864. 3v. in fol. (Architecture Series) – 9 – fr Hachette [720]

ARCHITECTURE RURALE THEORIQUE ET PRATIQUE. / Saint Felix Mauremont, A J M – Toulouse, Douladoure, 1820. 8 fol., xxxii, 360p., pl. (Architecture Series) – 9 – fr Hachette [720]

ARCHITECTURE SERIES *see* FRENCH ARCHITECTURAL WRITINGS: 16TH-19TH CENTURIES

ARCHITECTURE: THE AIA JOURNAL *see* AIA JOURNAL

ARCHITEKTURA SSSR – (Soviet Architecture). Moscow. U.S.S.R. 1966- – 1 – us UMI [720]

L'ARCHITETTURA / Cataneo, P – O-1007 1. 1567 – 9 – ne IDC [720]

L'ARCHITETTURA. TRADOTTA IN LINGUA FIORENTINA DA C. BARTOLI / Alberti, L B – O-1018 1. 1565 – 9 – ne IDC [720]

ARCHIV / Stader Geschichts- und Heimatverein – Stade. v1-11 1862-1886. Issued under the earlier name of the society: Verein fuer Geschichte und Alterrtuemer der Herzogtuemer Bremen und Verden und des Landes Hadeln. Film Mas C 290 – 1 – us H.U. Library [943]

ARCHIV DER EUROPAEISCHEN LEXIKOGRAPHIE *see*
- ALLGEMEINE DEUTSCHE REAL-ENCYCLOPAEDIE FUER DIE GEBILDETEN STAENDE (AEL, ABT 1; 35.17)
- ALLGEMEINE DEUTSCHE REAL-ENCYCLOPAEDIE FUER DIE GEBILDETEN STAENDE (AEL, ABT 1; 35.19)
- ALLGEMEINE DEUTSCHE REAL-ENCYCLOPAEDIE FUER DIE GEBILDETEN STAENDE (CONVERSATIONS-LEXIKON) (AEL, ABT 1; 35.8)
- ALLGEMEINE DEUTSCHE REAL-ENCYCLOPAEDIE FUER DIE GEBILDETEN STAENDE (CONVERSATIONS-LEXIKON) (AEL, ABT 1; 35.11)
- ALLGEMEINE DEUTSCHE REAL-ENCYCLOPAEDIE FUER DIE GEBILDETEN STAENDE (CONVERSATIONS-LEXIKON) (AEL, ABT 1; 35.12)
- ALLGEMEINE DEUTSCHE REAL-ENCYCLOPAEDIE FUER DIE GEBILDETEN STAENDE (CONVERSATIONS-LEXIKON) (AEL, ABT 1; 35.13)

- ALLGEMEINE DEUTSCHE REAL-ENCYCLOPAEDIE FUER DIE GEBILDETEN STAENDE (CONVERSATIONS-LEXIKON) (AEL, ABT 1; 35.14)
- ALLGEMEINE DEUTSCHE REAL-ENCYCLOPAEDIE FUER DIE GEBILDETEN STAENDE (CONVERSATIONS-LEXIKON) (AEL, ABT 1; 35.15)
- ALLGEMEINE DEUTSCHE REAL-ENCYCLOPAEDIE FUER DIE GEBILDETEN STAENDE (CONVERSATIONS-LEXIKON) (AEL, ABT. 1; 35.16)
- ALLGEMEINE DEUTSCHE REAL-ENCYCLOPAEDIE FUER DIE GEBILDETEN STAENDE (CONVERSATIONS-LEXIKON) (AEL, ABT 1; 35.18)
- ALLGEMEINE ENCYCLOPAEDIE DER WISSENSCHAFTEN UND KUENSTE (AEL, ABT 1; 33)
- ALLGEMEINE REALENCYCLOPAEDIE ODER CONVERSATIONS-LEXIKON FUER DAS KATHOLISCHE DEUTSCHLAND (AEL, ABT 1;6)
- ALLGEMEINES CONVERSTIONS-TASCHENLEXIKON (AEL, ABT 1;31)
- ALLGEMEINES DEUTSCHES SACH-WOERTERBUCH ALLER MENSCHLICHEN KENNTNISSE UND FERTIGKEITEN (AEL, ABT 1;22)
- ALLGEMEINES DEUTSCHES VOLKS-CONVERSATIONS-LEXIKON UND FREMDWOERTERBUCH (AEL, ABT 1;23)
- ALLGEMEINES, HELVETISCHES, EYDGENOESSISCHES ODER SCHWEIZERISCHES LEXICON UND SUPPLEMENT ZUM ALLGEMEINEN HELVETISCH-EIDGENOESSISCHEN LEXICON HERRN BUERGERMEISTERS LEU HERAUSGEGEBEN VON HANS JACOB HOLZHALB (AEL, ABT.1;8)
- ALLGEMEINES HISTORISCHES LEXIKON IN WELCHEM DAS LEBEN UND DIE THATEN DERER PATRIARICHEN, PROPHETEN, APOSTEL ... VORGESTELLET WERDEN (AEL, ABT 1; 37)
- AMERIKANISCH DEUTSCHE ENCYCLOPAEDIE (AEL, ABT 1;13)
- AUSFUEHRLICHE ENCYKLOPAEDIE DER GESAMMTEN STAATSARZNEIKUNDE (AEL, ABT 3;23)
- DIE "BIBLIOTHECAE" DES JEAN JACQUES MANGET (AEL, ABT 3;20)
- BILDER-CONVERSATIONS-LEXIKON FUER DAS DEUTSCHE VOLK (AEL, ABT 1;28)
- BILDNISSE DER BERUEHMTESTEN MENSCHEN ALLER VOELKER UND ZEITEN (AEL, ABT 1;25)
- DAS BROCKHAUS CONVERSATIONS-LEXIKON 1796-1898 (AEL, ABT 1; 35)
- BROCKHAUS' CONVERSATIONS-LEXIKON (AEL, ABT 1; 35.22)
- BROCKHAUS' CONVERSATIONS-LEXIKON (AEL, ABT 1; 35.23)
- BROCKHAUS' CONVERSATIONS-LEXIKON (AEL, ABT 1; 35.24)
- BROCKKHAUS' CONVERSATIONS-LEXIKON (AEL, ABT 1; 35.25)
- CASTELLUS RENOVATUS. HOC EST LEXICON MEDICUM QUONDAM A BART. CASTELLO MESSANENSI (AEL, ABT 3)
- CATHOLICON, OU DICTIONNAIRE UNIVERSEL DE LA LANGUE FRANCOISE, CATHOLICON ODER FRANZOESISCH-DEUTSCHES UNIVERSALWOERTERBUCH DER FRANZOESISCHEN SPRACHE (AEL, ABT 2;12)
- CONVERSATIONS-LEXIKON (AEL, ABT 1; 35.10)
- CONVERSATIONS-LEXIKON (AEL, ABT 1; 35.21)
- CONVERSATIONSLEXIKON MIT VORZUEGLICHER RUECKSICHT AUF DIE GEGENWAERTIGEN ZEITEN (AEL, ABT 1; 35.1)
- CONVERSATIONS-LEXIKON ODER ENCYCLOPAEDISCHES HANDWOERTERBUCH FUER GEBILDETE STAENDE (AEL, ABT 1; 35.5)
- CONVERSATIONS-LEXIKON ODER ENZYCLOPAEDISCHES HANDWOERTERBUCH FUER GEBILDETE STAENDE (AEL, ABT 1; 35.6)
- CONVERSATIONS-LEXIKON ODER HANDWOERTERBUCH FUER DIE GEBILDETEN STAENDE UEBER DIE IN DER GESELLSCHAFTLICHEN UNTERHALTUNG UND BEI DER LECTUERE VORKOMMENDEN GEGENSTAENDE, NAMEN UND BEGRIFFE... (AEL, ABT 1; 35.4)
- CONVERSATIONS-LEXIKON ODER KURZGEFASSTES HANDWOERTERBUCH FUER DIE IN DER GESELLSCHAFTLICHEN UNTERHALTUNG AUS DEN WISSENSCHAFTEN UND KUENSTEN VORKOMMENDEN GEGENSTAENDE... (AEL, ABT 1; 35.2)
- CONVERSATIONS-LEXIKON ODER KURZGEFASSTES HANDWOERTERBUCH FUER DIE IN DER GESELLSCHAFTLICHEN UNTERHALTUNG AUS DEN WISSENSCHAFTEN UND KUENSTEN VORKOMMENDEN GEGENSTAENDE... (AEL, ABT 1; 35.3)
- CYCLOPAEDIA (AEL, ABT.1;2)
- DEFINITIONUM MEDICARUM LIBRI 24 LITERIS GRAECIS DISTINCTI (AEL, ABT 3;1)
- DEUTSCH-AMERIKANISCHES CONVERSATIONS-LEXICON
- DEUTSCH-AMERIKANISCHES HAND-LEXIKON DES ALLGEMEINEN WISSENS (AEL, ABT 1;12)
- DEUTSCHE ENCYCLOPAEDIE ODER ALLGEMEINES REALWOERTERBUCH ALLER KUENSTE UND WISSENSCHAFTEN, (AEL, ABT 1;2)
- DEUTSCHE TASCHEN-ENCYKLOPAEDIE ODER HANDBIBLIOTHEK DES WISSENSWUERDIGSTEN IN HINSICHT AUF NATUR UND KUNST, STAAT UND KIRCHE, WISSENSCHAFT UND SITTE (AEL, ABT 1;21)
- DICCIONARIO MUY COPIOSO DE LA LENGUA ESPANOLA Y FRANCESA, DICTIONNAIRE TRES AMPLE DE LA LANGUE FRANCOISE ET ESPAGNOLE (AEL, ABT 2;15)
- DICTIONAIRE DES SCIENCES MEDICALES (AEL, ABT 3;16)
- DICTIONAIRE FRANCOIS ALLEMAND ET ALLEMAND FRANCOIS; DICTIONARIUM TEUTSCH FRANTZOESISCH UND FRANTZOESISCH TEUTSCH (AEL, ABT.5;5)
- DICTIONAIRE UNIVERSEL CONTENANT GENERALEMENT TOUT LES MOTS FRANCOIS TANT VIEUX QUE MODERNES, ET LES TERMES DE TOUTES LES SCIENCES ET DES ARTS (AEL, ABT 2; 17)
- A DICTIONARIE IN SPANISH AND ENGLISH
- DICTIONARIUM TEUTSCH-FRANTZOESICSH-TEUTSCH UND TEUTSCH-FRANTZOESISCHES WOERTERREGISTER UEBER KRAMERS DICTIONNAIRE (AEL, ABT.2;1)
- DICTIONARIUM MEDICUM, VEL EXPOSITIONES VOCUM MEDICINALIUM AD VERVUM EXCERPTAE ES HIPPOCRATE, ARETEO ETC. (AEL, ABT 3;21)
- DICTIONARIUM TEUTSCH-ITALIAENISCH UND ITALIAENISCH-TEUTSCH (AEL, ABT.2;7)
- A DICTIONARY ENGLISH, GERMAN AND FRENCH UND TEUTSCH-ENGLISCHES LEXICON (AEL, ABT.2;4)
- A DICTIONARY OF PRACTICAL MEDICINE (AEL, ABT 3;14)
- DICTIONNAIRE DES SCIENCES MEDICALES, PAR UNE SOCIETE DE MEDECINS ET DE CHIRURGIENS (AEL, ABT.3;5)
- DICTIONNAIRE D'HYGIENE PUBLIQUE ET DE SALUBRITE (AEL, ABT 3;24)
- DICTIONNAIRE ENCYCLOPEDIQUE DES SCIENCES MEDICALES (AEL, ABT 3;15)
- DICTIONNAIRE FRANCOIS CONTENANT LES MOTS ET LES CHOSES, VERSCH. AUSGABEN (AEL, ABT 2;16)
- DICTIONNAIRE HISTORIQUE DE LA MEDECINE ANCIENNE ET MODERNE (AEL, ABT 3; 19)
- DICTIONNAIRE HISTORIQUE DE LA MEDECINE ANCIENNE ET MODERNE (AEL, ABT 3;17)
- DICTIONNAIRE UNIVERSEL DE MEDECINE (AEL, ABT.3;3.2)
- DIZZIONARIO ITALIANO-TEDESCO
- ENCYCLOPAEDISCHES WOERTERBUCH DER MEDICINISCHEN WISSENSCHAFTEN (AEL, ABT 3;13)
- ENCYCLOPEDIE METHODIQUE
- ENCYCLOPEDIE OECONOMIQUE, OU SYSTEME GENERAL
- ENCYCLOPEDIE OU DICTIONNAIRE RAISONNE DES SCIENCES, DES ARTS ET DES METIERS (AEL, ABT 1;34)
- ENCYCLOPEDIE, OU DICTIONNAIRE UNIVERSEL RAISONNE DES CONNOISSANCES HUMAINE (AEL, ABT.1;7)
- ENCYKLOPAEDISCHES WOERTERBUCH DER WISSENSCHAFTEN, KUENSTE UND GEWERBE (AEL, ABT.1;6.1)
- ERGAENZUNGS-CONVERSATIONSLEXIKON (AEL, ABT 1;19)
- GAZOPHYLACIUM MEDICO-PHYSICUM ODER SCHATZKAMMER / MEDICINISCH- UND NATUERLICHER DINGE...(AEL, ABT.3;2)
- LA GRANDE ENCYCLOPEDIE (AEL, ABT.1;3)
- DAS GROSSE CONVERSATIONSLEXIKON FUER GEBILDETE STAENDE (AEL, ABT.1;5)
- GROSSES VOLLSTAENDIGES UNIVERSAL-LEXIKON ALLER WISSENSCHAFTEN UND KUENSTE (AEL, ABT 1;32)
- HISTORISCHES GEOGRAPHISCHES LEXIKON VON DER SCHWEIZ ODER VOLLSTAENDIGE BESCHREIBUNG ALLER IN DER GANZEN SCHWEIZERISCHEN EIDGENOSSENSCHAFT UND DEN DERSELBEN ZUGEWANDTEN ORTEN LIEGENDEN STAEDTE (AEL, ABT 1;29)
- JOHANN HUEBNERS CURIEUSES NATUR-KUNST-GEWERCK-UND HANDLUNGS-LEXICON (AEL, ABT 1;26)
- HET KONINGLYK NEDER-HOOG-DUITSCH-HOOG-NEDER-DUITSCH DICTIONARIUM (AEL, ABT.2;3)
- LEXICUM FRANTZOESISCH UND TEUTSCH (AEL, ABT 2;14)
- LE LIVRE INSTRUCTIF, OU NOUVEAU DICTIONNAIRE FRANCOIS-ESPAGNOL 1721 (AEL, ABT 2;9)
- A MEDICAL DICTIONARY, INCLUDING PHYSIC, SURGERY, ANATOMY, CHIMISTRY AND BOTANY (AEL, ABT 3;3.1)
- MEDICINISCH-CHIRURGISCHE ENCYKLOPAEDIE FUER PRAKTISCHE AERZTE (AEL, ABT.3;7)
- MEDICNISCHES SCHRIFTSTELLER-LEXIKON DER JETZT LEBENDEN AERZTE, WUNDAERZTE UND GEBURTSHELFER, APOTHEKER UND NATURFORSCHER ALLER GEBILDETEN VOELKER (AEL, ABT 3;17)
- MEDIZINISCHES REALWOERTERBUCH ZUM HANDGEBRAUCH PRACTISCHER AERZTE UND WUNDAERZTE..(AEL, ABT.3;6)
- NEUE ENCYCLOPAEDIE DER WISSENSCHAFTEN UND KUENSTE (AEL, ABT 1;24)
- NEU-VERMEHRTES HISTORISCH UND GEOGRAPHISCHES ALLGEMEINES LEXICON (AEL, ABT.1;9)
- NOUVEAU DICTIONNAIRE DE LA LANGUE ALLEMANDE ET FRANCOISE, FRANCOISE ET ALLEMANDE (AEL, ABT 2;13)
- NUCLEUS TOTIUS MEDICINAE QUINQUE PARTITUS (AEL, ABT 3;11)
- OESTERREICHISCHE NATIONAL-ENZYKLOPAEDIE ODER ALPHABETISCHE DARLEGUNG DER WISSENSWUERDIGSTEN EIGENTHUEMLICHKEITEN DES OESTERREICHISCHEN KAISERTUMS (AEL, ABT.1;10)
- ONOMASTIKON MEDICINAE (AEL, ABT 3;9)
- ONOMATOLOGIA MEDICA COMPLETA ODER MEDICINISCHES LEXICON...VON EINER GESELLSCHAFT GELEHRTER AERZTE, MIT EINER VORREDE ALBRECHT VON HALLERS (AEL, ABT.3;4)
- PETIT LAROUSSE ILLUSTRE (AEL, ABT 2;11)
- PIERER'S JAHRBUECHER DER WISSENSCHAFTEN, KUENSTE UND GEWERBE (AEL, ABT.1;6.8)
- PIERER'S KONVERSATIONS-LEXIKON (AEL, ABT.1;6.7)
- PIERER'S UNIVERSAL-CONVERSATIONS-LEXIKON
- PIERER'S UNIVERSAL-LEXIKON DER VERGANGENHEIT UND GEGENWART ODER NEUESTES ENCYCLOPAEDISCHES WOERTERBUCH DER WISSENSCHAFTEN, KUENSTE UND GEWERBE (AEL, ABT.1;6.4)
- PIERER'S UNIVERSAL-LEXIKON DER VERGANGENHEIT UND GEGENWART ODER NEUESTES ENCYCLOPAEDISCHES WOERTERBUCH DER WISSENSCHAFTEN, KUENSTE UND GEWERBE (AEL, ABT.1;6.5)
- REAL-ENCYCLOPAEDIE DER GESAMMTEN HEILKUNDE (AEL, ABT.3;8)
- RHEINISCHES CONVERSATIONS-LEXICON ODER ENCYCLOPAEDISCHES HANDWOERTERBUCH FUER GEBILDETE STAENDE (AEL, ABT 1;20)
- STAATS- UND GESELLSCHAFTS-LEXIKON (AEL, ABT 1;14)
- DAS STAATS-LEXIKON
- SUPPLEMENT ZUR ELFTEN AUFLAGE DES CONVERSATIONS-LEXIKONS (AEL, ABT 1; 35.20)
- SUPPLEMENTBAND ZUM CONVERSATIONS-LEXIKON FUER DIE BESITZER DER ERSTEN, ZWEITEN UND DRITTEN AUFLAGE (AEL, ABT 1; 35.7)
- SUPPLEMENTE ZUM CONVERSATIONS-LEXIKON FUER DIE BESITZER DER ERSTEN, ZWEITEN, DRITTEN UND VIERTEN AUFLAGE (AEL, ABT 1; 35.9)
- THEORETISCH-PRAKTISCHES HANDBUCH DER CHIRURGIE
- UNIVERSAL-LEXIKON DER GEGENWART UND VERGANGENHEIT ODER NEUESTES ENCYCLOPAEDISCHES WOERTERBUCH DER WISSENSCHAFTEN, KUENSTE UND GEWERBE (AEL, ABT.1;6.3)
- UNIVERSAL-LEXIKON DER GEGENWART UND VERGANGENHEIT ODER NEUESTES ENCYCLOPAEDISCHES WOERTERBUCH DER WISSENSCHAFTEN, KUENSTE UND GEWERBE BEARBEITET VON 220 GELEHRTEN (AEL, ABT.1;6.6)
- VOLLSTAENDIGE BESCHREIBUNG DES SCHWEIZERLANDES ODER GEOGRAPHISCH-STATISTISCHES HAND-LEXIKON UEBER ALLE IN GESAMMTER EIDSGENOSSENSCHAFT BEFINDLICHER KANTONE, BEZIRKE, KREISE, AEMTER (AEL, ABT 1;30)
- DIE WAHREN MITTEL, LAENDER UND STAATEN GLUECKLICH, IHRE BEHERRSCHER MAECHTIG UND DIE UNTERTHANEN REICH ZU MACHEN; ODER GROSSES UND VOLLSTAENDIGES OECONOMISCH- UND PHYSICALISCHES LEXIKON (AEL, ABT. 1; 36)
- WIGAND'S CONVERSATIONS-LEXIKON [UND] DIE NEUE ZEIT (ERSTER SUPPLEMENTBAND ZU WIGAND'S CONVERSATIONS-LEXIKON)(AEL, ABT 1;17)

ARCHIV DER GEGENWART – Bonn-Bad Godesberg, 1946-1993 – 47r – 1 – DM4,700.00 (Subsc DM150.00) – gw Mikro Press [943]

ARCHIV DER GESELLSCHAFT FUER AELTERE DEUTSCHE GESCHICHTSKUNDE – 1(1819-20)-12(1872) – 166mf – 9 – Dfl581.00 – ne Slangenburg [025]

ARCHIV DER GESELLSCHAFT FUER AELTERE DEUTSCHE GESCHICHTSKUNDE – Frankfurt. 12v. 1820-74 – 111mf – 9 – subsc: DM700.00 diazo DM900.00 silver – gw Olms [943]

ARCHIV DER INSECTENGESCHICHTE – Zurich & Winterthur, 1781-86 – 3 – us Readex [590]

ARCHIV DER MATHEMATIK UND PHYSIK / ed by Grunert, Johann August & Hoppe, R – Greifswald und Leipzig, 1841-84 – 455mf – 9 – subsc: DM2,500.00 diazo DM3,100.00 silver – gw Olms [510]

ARCHIV DER MATHEMATIK UND PHYSIK 1841-1920 – (Incl. Literarische Berichte, Bibliogr. Mitteilungen, Register) – Greifswald, spaeter Leipzig, 1841-1920 (mf ed 1994) – 535mf – 9 – DM5,600.00 – 3-89131-163-X – gw Fischer [510]

ARCHIV DER PHARMAZIE : AN INTERNATIONAL JOURNAL OF PHARMACEUTICAL AND MEDICINAL CHEMISTRY – v235-329. 1897-1996 – 1,5,6,13 – us V.C.H. [615]

ARCHIV DER REINEN UND ANGEWANDTEN MATHEMATIK. – Leipzig, 1795-1800. v.1-3 – 3 – us Readex [510]

ARCHIV DES HISTORISCHEN VEREINS FUER NIEDERSACHSEN – 1(1845)-5(1849) – 36mf – 9 – Dfl26.00 – ne Slangenburg [025]

ARCHIV DES HISTORISCHEN VEREINS VON UNTERFRANKEN UND ASCHAFFENBURG / Historischer Verein von Unterfranken und Aschaffenburg. Wuerzburg – Wuerzburg. v21-38 1881-96. Film Mas C 310 – 1 – us H.U. Library [943]

ARCHIV DES WIENER KONGRESSES – Nuernberg. 2pts. 1815 – 3mf – 9 – ILM-2730/1 – ne IDC [340]

ARCHIV FUER ANATOMIE, PHYSIOLOGIE UND WISSENSCHAFTLICHE MEDIZIN – Berlin, 1834-76. v. 1-43 – 3 – us Readex [611]

ARCHIV FUER ANATOMIE UND PHYSIOLOGIE – Leipzig, 1826-32 – 3 – us Readex [611]

ARCHIV FUER ASIATISCHE LITERATUR, GESCHICHTE UND SPRACHKUNDE – St Petersburg. v1. 1810 – 8mf – 8 – R-1659/2 – ne IDC [400]

ARCHIV FUER CHEMIE UND METEOROLOGIE *see* ARCHIV FUER DIE GESAMMTE NATURLEHRE 1824-1835

ARCHIV FUER DAS EISENHUETTENWESEN – v1-17. 1927-1944 – 1,5,6 – us Princeton Micro [622]

ARCHIV FUER DAS STUDIUM DER NEUEREN SPRACHEN / ed by Herrig, L & Bischoff, H – Elberfeld, 1846-1868. v1-43; 1916-1918. v134-137 – 364mf – 9 – H-399/2 – ne IDC [490]

ARCHIV FUER DERMATOLOGIE UND SYPHILIS *see* VIERTELJAHRSSCHRIFT FUER DERMATOLOGIE UND SYPHILIS

ARCHIV FUER DIE BOTANIK / Roemer, J J – Leipzig, 1796-1805.-3v – 52mf – 8 – 5681/2 – ne IDC [580]

ARCHIV FUER DIE GESAMMTE NATURLEHRE – Nuremberg, 1824-35 – 3 – us Readex [500]

ARCHIV FUER DIE GESAMMTE NATURLEHRE 1824-1835 – (Ab 19 auch unter dem Titel: Archiv fuer Chemie und Meteorologie) – Nuernberg, 1824-1830 (mf ed 1993) – 108mf – 9 – DM1,380.00 – 3-89131-161-3 – gw Fischer [500]
ARCHIV FUER DIE GESCHICHTE DER PHILOSOPHIE – 1(1888)-30(1917) – 305mf – 9 – Dfl1,068.00 – ne Slangenburg [025]
ARCHIV FUER DIE GESCHICHTE DES NIEDERRHEINS – 1(1831)-7(1870) – 57mf – 9 – Dfl200.00 – ne Slangenburg [025]
ARCHIV FUER DIE GESCHICHTE DES SOZIALISMUS UND DER ARBEITERBEWEGUNG / ed by Gruenberg, C – (Beihefte 1923-1931, v1-5) – Leipzig, 1911-1930. v1-15 – 152mf – 9 – H-134/2 – ne IDC [335]
ARCHIV FUER DIE NATURKUNDE LIV-, ESTH- UND KURLANDS – Dorpat, S.1, 1854-1935. v1-11; S.2, 1859-1930. v1-15 – 154mf – 9 – 8605/1 – ne IDC [500]
ARCHIV FUER DIE NEUESTE KIRCHENGESCHICHTE – v1-6. 1795-99 (complete) – 2r – 1 – ATLA S0118 – us A.T.L.A. [073]
ARCHIV FUER DIE PHYSIOLOGIE – D. Joh. Christ. Reil. Halle, 1795-1815 – 3 – us Readex [612]
ARCHIV FUER DIE SAECHSISCHE GESCHICHTE – Leipzig. v.1-12. 1863-73 74. Film Mas C 301. N.F. v.1-6. 1874 75-79 80. Film Mas C 156 – 1 – us H.U. Library [073]
ARCHIV FUER DIE THEOLOGIE UND IHRE NEUESTE LITERATUR – Tuebingen, 1(1815)-8(1826) – 99mf – 9 – Dfl347.00 – ne Slangenburg [025]
ARCHIV FUER ELEKTROTECHNIK – v. 1-37. 1913-1943 – 1,5,6 – us Princeton Micro [621]
ARCHIV FUER ELEKTROTECHNIK – v. 39-62. 1948-80 – 1,5,9 – 2790.00 – us UMI [073]
ARCHIV FUER EXPERIMENTELLE PATHOLOGIE UND PHARMAKOLOGIE / Naunyn, B & Schneideberg,O – 1 – uk Microform Academic [616]
ARCHIV FUER FRAUENKUNDE UND EUGENIK, 1914. ARCHIV FUER FRAUENKUNDE UND EUGENETIK, 1915-1923. ARCHIV FUER FRAUENKUNDE UND KONSTITUTIONSFORSCHUNG, 1924-1933 (HQ, 19) – 1914-1933 (mf ed 1996) – 76mf – 9 – DM1,250.00 – 3-89131-131-1 – gw Fischer [610]
ARCHIV FUER FREIMAURER UND ROSENKREUZER – Berlin, 1783-1785. 2v – 10mf – 9 – VR-35.1/1 – ne IDC [360]
ARCHIV FUER FUNKRECHT – Berlin. 1928-apr 1944; sep 1944 – 5r – 1 – gw Mikrofilm [340]
ARCHIV FUER GESCHICHTE VON OBERFRANKEN – Bayreuth. Bd. 13-18, 27-34, 1875-1941. Title varies. Film Mas C 319 – 1 – us H.U. Library [073]
ARCHIV FUER HESSISCHE GESCHICHTE UND ALTERTUMSKUNDE – Darmstadt. Neue Folge Bd. 1-22. 1894-1942. Film Mas C 410 – 1 – us H.U. Library [073]
ARCHIV FUER KATHOLISCHES KIRCHENRECHT – 1(1857)-22(1869) – 217mf – 9 – Dfl760.00 – ne Slangenburg [025]
ARCHIV FUER KATHOLISCHES KIRCHENRECHT – Mainz. v1-22. 1857-1869 – 217mf – 9 – ne IDC [240]
ARCHIV FUER KEMI – v11-31. 1957-70. See also: Chemica Scripta – 1,5,6 – us Princeton Micro [540]
ARCHIV FUER KLINISCHE MEDIZIN – v.193-216, 1947-69 – 1,5,6,9,13 – us UMI [616]
ARCHIV FUER KRIMINOLOGIE, KRIMINALANTHROPOLOGIE UND KRIMINALISTIK – Berlin, jul-aug 1932, 1933-44 – 3r – 1 – DM300.00 set DM100.00r – gw Mikro Press [350]
ARCHIV FUER LITERATUR UND KUNST *see* ALLGEMEINE DEUTSCHE THEATER-ZEITUNG
ARCHIV FUER LITERATURGESCHICHTE / ed by Gosche, Richard & Schnorr von Carolsfeld, Franz – Leipzig. 15v. 1870-87 – 92mf – 9 – subsc: DM600.00 diazo DM750.00 silver – gw Olms [410]
ARCHIV FUER LITTERATUR- UND KIRCHENGESCHICHTE DES MITTELALTERS – 1(1885)-7(1900) – 95mf – 9 – Dfl333.00 – ne Slangenburg [025]
ARCHIV FUER LITTERATUR- UND KIRCHENGESCHICHTE DES MITTELALTERS – Berlin, Freiburg. v1-7. 1885-1900 – 95mf – 9 – ne IDC [240]
ARCHIV FUER LITTERATURGESCHICHTE – Leipzig. Teubner. 1-15. Bd. 1870-87. Title varies. Film Mas C 284 – 1 – us H.U. Library [410]
ARCHIV FUER METEOROLOGIE, GEOPHYSIK UND BIOKLIMATOLOGIE – (Series B: Klimatologie, Umweltmeteorologie, Strahlungsforschung v1-29 1949-81 $42.00v 1,5,6,9,13) – Series A: Meteorologie und Geophysik v1-30, 1949-81. ISSN: 0066-6416 – 1,5,6,9,13 – $142.00v – us UMI [550]
ARCHIV FUER MIKROSKOPISCHE ANATOMIE – v. 1-44, 74-104. 1865-1895, 1909-1925 – 1 – us Princeton Micro [576]
ARCHIV FUER MINERALOGIE, GEOGNOSIE, BERGBAU UND HUETTENKUNDE – Berlin, 1829-55 – 3 – us Readex [540]
ARCHIV FUER MOLLUSKENKUNDE – Frankfurt am Main, 1920-1941. v1-22 – 134mf – 9 – 5624c/2 – ne IDC [590]
ARCHIV FUER MUSIKWISSENSCHAFT – Leipzig, 1918-27.-v1-8 – 66mf – 9 – P-559/1 – ne IDC [780]
ARCHIV FUER MUSIKWISSENSCHAFT – Trossingen. 1918-27. 2 reels – 1 – 46.00 – us L of C Photodup [780]
ARCHIV FUER OEFFENTLICHES RECHT – (Cont. as: Archiv des oeffentlichen Rechts. Tuebingen, 1911-1920. v27-39. N.F. 1921-1944. v1-34; Publication interrupted in 1944 and issued again in 1948) – Freiburg I.B., Tuebingen, 1886-1910. v1-26. Register v1-25 – 455mf – 9 – IL-2/1 – ne IDC [340]
ARCHIV FUER ORIENTFORSCHUNG, BEIBAND 1 / Oppenheim, M von – Berlin. 1933. BNE-20,055 1 – 9 – ne IDC [950]
ARCHIV FUER PATHOLOGISCHE ANATOMIE UND PHYSIOLOGIE UND FUER KLINISCHE MEDIZIN *see* VIRCHOWS ARCHIV FUER PATHOLOGISCHE ANATOMIE UND PHYSIOLOGIE UND FUER KLINISCHE MEDIZIN
ARCHIV FUER PHYSIOLOGISCHE HEILKUNDE 1. 1842-15. 1856, NEUE FOLGE 1. 1857-3. 1859 – 1842-1859 (mf ed 1994) – 62mf – 9 – DM2,100.00 – 3-89131-189-3 – gw Fischer [610]
ARCHIV FUER PSYCHIATRIE UND NERVENKRANKHEITEN – v. 118 179-229. 1947-80 – 1,5,9 – 5460.00 – us UMI [073]
ARCHIV FUER RASSEN- UND GESELLSCHAFTS-BIOLOGIE, EINSCHLIESSLICH RASSEN- UND GESELLSCHAFTS-HYGIENE – Berlin. v1-37. 1904-44 – 1 – 253.00 – us L of C Photodup [943]
ARCHIV FUER REFORMATIONSGESCHICHTE – 1(1903)-52(1961) – 297mf – 9 – Dfl1,404.00 – ne Slangenburg [025]
ARCHIV FUER REFORMATIONSGESCHICHTE – Leipzig, Berlin. v1-52. 1903/1904-1961 – 297mf – 9 – ne IDC [240]
ARCHIV FUER REFORMATIONSGESCHICHTE – v. 1-37. 1903-1940 – 1 – us Princeton Micro [240]
ARCHIV FUER RELIGIONSWISSENSCHAFT – 1(1898)-37(1941) – 317mf – 9 – Dfl1,110.00 – ne Slangenburg [025]
ARCHIV FUER RELIGIONSWISSENSCHAFT – Leipzig, Freiburg i.B. v1-37. 1898-1941 – 317mf – 9 – ne IDC [240]
ARCHIV FUER SCHWEIZERISCHE GESCHICHTE – Zuerich, 1(1843)-20(1875) – 153mf – 9 – Dfl536.00 – ne Slangenburg [025]
ARCHIV FUER SLAVISCHE PHILOLOGIE – Berlin, 1876-1929.-v1-42 – 482mf – 8 – 652/2 – ne IDC [460]
ARCHIV FUER SLAWISCHE PHILOLOGIE / ed by Berneker, Jagic – Berlin. 43v. 1876-1929 – 290mf – 9 – subsc: DM1,600 diazo DM1,900.00 silver – gw Olms [460]
ARCHIV FUER SOZIALE GESETZGEBUNG UND STATISTIK – (Cont. as: Archiv fuer Sozialwissenschaft und Sozialpolitik. Berlin, etc. 1904-1933. v19-69) – Berlin, etc., 1888-1903. v1-18 – 1,098mf – 9 – H-420/2 – ne IDC [301]
ARCHIV FUER THEATER UND LITERATUR *see* ALLGEMEINE DEUTSCHE THEATER-ZEITUNG
ARCHIV FUER URKUNDENFORSCHUNG – Leipzig, 1908-1942. v1-17 – 151mf – 9 – H-627c/2 – ne IDC [920]
ARCHIV FUER WISSENSCHAFTLICHE ERFORSCHUNG DES ALTEN TESTAMENTS – Halle, 1(1867-69) – 13mf – 9 – Dfl46.00a – ne Slangenburg [025]
ARCHIV FUER WISSENSCHAFTLICHE KUNDE VON RUSSLAND / ed by Erman, A – Berlin, 1841-1867. v1-25 – 326mf – 9 – R-1660/2 – ne IDC [500]
ARCHIV ORIENTALNI : JOURNAL OF THE CZECHOSLOVAK ORIENTAL INSTITUTE, PRAGUE – (In English, French and German) – Praha, Paris, Berlin, 1929-1941. v1-12 – 109mf – 9 – CH-872c/2 – ne IDC [950]
ARCHIVAL FINDING AIDS : INVENTORIES AND GUIDES TO DIPLOMATIC ARCHIVES – (Part1: France – Ministry of Foreign Affairs Paris 172mf Dfl1,646.00; Part2: The Netherlands – Ministry of Foreign Affairs The Hague 19mf Dfl182.00; Includes a printed guide) – 9 – ne IDC [324]
ARCHIVAL-URKUNDEN : DOCUMENTA UND PROBATIONES IN CAUSA MONASTERII AUGIAE MAJORIS – 1750 – Dfl49.00 – ne Slangenburg [240]
ARCHIVE FOR HISTORY OF EXACT SCIENCES – v.1-25, 1960-81. ISSN: 0003-9519 – 1,5,6,9,13 – 133.00v – us UMI [500]
ARCHIVE FOR RATIONAL MECHANICS AND ANALYSIS – v. 1-75. 1957-80 – 1,5,9 – 7200.00 – us UMI [073]
ARCHIVE OF FRENCH LINGUISTICS: 1500-1900 / ed by Quemada, Bernard – 405 titles comprising the most important historical works in the field. 400,000 pages of material. Special subject groups available. Individual titles available – 9 – fr I.C.S. [400]
THE ARCHIVE OF PROFESSOR DR. W.H. DE VRIESE CONCERNING HIS INVESTIGATION INTO THE NETHERLANDS INDIES CULTIVATIONS, 1857-1862 – 1857-1862 – 204mf – 9 – Dfl2,310.00 – ne MMF Publ [580]
ARCHIVE OF THE AMSTERDAM BOOKSELLERS GUILD, 1662-1812 – 1662-1812 – 141mf – 9 – Dfl2,595.00 – ne MMF Publ [070]
ARCHIVE OF THE FOURTH RUSSELL TRIBUNAL : ON THE RIGHTS OF THE INDIANS OF THE AMERICAS / ed by Vermeer, B – (Includes a printed guide and plastic binder) – 152mf – 9 – ne IDC [340]
ARCHIVE RECORDS / Trade Union Council of South Africa – Chicago, IL: Coop Africana Microform Project CRL, 1914-69 [mf ed 19–?] – 1 – us Res Libr [331]
ARCHIVES / American Committee for South Asian Art – Part 1: Kushan and Gupta art. 15,000 photographs, 173 microfiches – 9 – ne IDC [930]
ARCHIVES / American Missionary Association – 1839-82 – 1 – $5,750.00 – us Amistad [240]
ARCHIVES / Church Missionary Society. West Africa and Nigeria and Yoruba Missions – 1 – uk Microform Academic [240]
ARCHIVES / Council for World Mission – London. 1775-1940. Incorporating the London Missionary Society, Documents on Asia, Africa, Oceania and South America. Zug. 1978. BH-2132-2134 1. Collection – 9 – ne IDC [240]
ARCHIVES / Gillow & Company – "Patterns of Elegance" – 1 – £3,900.00 – uk World [025]
ARCHIVES / Honiara. Catholic Archdiocese – 1905-82 – r1-6 – 1 – PMB1120 – at Pacific Mss [980]
ARCHIVES / Inner Temple. London. Library – £2,500.00 – uk World [340]
ARCHIVES / International Missionary Council and the Conference of British Missionary Societies – London. 1910-45. Documents on Africa, Egypt and India. Zug. 1977. BH-2000 T 1. Collection – 1 – ne IDC [240]
ARCHIVES / Levers Pacific Plantations Pty Ltd / Lever Solomons Ltd – 1902-92 – r1-6 – 1 – PMB1121 – at Pacific Mss [980]
ARCHIVES – London. v1. H-801. 1949-1952 – 9 – ne IDC [941]
ARCHIVES / Maryland – v1-72. 1883-1972 – 1 – us MD Archives [324]
ARCHIVES / Mexico. Parral – 1631-1821 – 1 – us UMI [025]
ARCHIVES / National Council of Women of the United States – ca 1500mf – 9 – $4,980.00 – us UMI [360]
ARCHIVES / Papua New Guinea Trades Union Congress – 1969-95 – r1-5 – 1 – PMB1117 – at Pacific Mss [331]
ARCHIVES / Philadelphia. Pennsylvania. Old Christ Church – 1695-1976 – 1 – us UMI [240]
ARCHIVES / Plaid Cymru – 1926-93. With printed index. Continued annually – 1 – £1,895.00 – uk World [025]
ARCHIVES / Royal Literary Fund – With printed index – 1 – £5,500.00 – uk World [420]
ARCHIVES / Spanish West Florida – 1789-1816. Typescript. New Orleans, 1937-40. 7 rolls. T1116 – 1 – us Nat'l Archives [975]
ARCHIVES – (v. 1 and 2. 249.00v; 9. v. 3-10. 244.50v; WDS; 9) – v. 1-10. 1949-1971 72. London – 9 – 2450.00 – uk Dawson [025]
ARCHIVES. 1756-1806 / Moravian Church. Bristol – 1 – uk Microform Academic [025]
ARCHIVES, 1792-1914 / Baptist Missionary Society. London – Minutes, 1792-1914; Committees, 1793-1914; Home Office Correspondence, 1792-1914; Missionary Journals & Correspondence, 1792-1914. 165,931p – 1 – $6637.24 – us Baptist [240]
ARCHIVES, 1942-76 / United Church Board for Homeland Ministries. Race Relations Department – 1 – $1,500.00 – us Amistad [240]
ARCHIVES, 1962-1994 / Fiji Trades Union Congress – 16r – 1 – PMB1085 – at Pacific Mss [331]
ARCHIVES, 1987-1992 / Fiji Independent News Service – (Filming in progress) – PMB1079 – at Pacific Mss [070]
ARCHIVES ALSACIENNES D'HISTOIRE DE L'ART – All published v1-16. Strasbourg. 1922-1948 – 5,9 – Dfl720.00; Dfl45.00v – ne Swets [700]
ARCHIVES AND MANUSCRIPT COLLECTIONS : INVENTORIES – (Section I. Jewish Archives 1. The American Jewish Archives) – Cincinnati, Ohio, USA – 10mf – ne IDC [270]
ARCHIVES AND MANUSCRIPT COLLECTIONS IN THE USSR : SERIES 2: THE BALTIC COUNTRIES / ed by Grimsted, Patricia Kennedy – 385 titles – 9 – ne IDC [025]
ARCHIVES AND MANUSCRIPT COLLECTIONS IN THE USSR : SERIES 3: UKRAINE AND MOLDAVIA / ed by Grimsted, Patricia Kennedy – 450 titles – 9 – ne IDC [025]
ARCHIVES AND MANUSCRIPT REPOSITORIES IN THE USSR : SERIES 1: MOSCOW AND LENINGRAD / Grimsted, Patricia Kennedy – 631 titles – 9 – ne IDC [025]
ARCHIVES AUTHORITY : CONVICT REGISTERS ETC. – (Apply to publ for details) – 9 – at Pascoe [920]
The Archives Authority of New South Wales *see* COLONIAL SECRETARY'S PAPERS, 1788-1825
ARCHIVES BERBERES – (Missing: 1915, v1(2, p. 8-65); 1917, v2(p. 158-219); 1920, v4(p.84-End)) – Paris, 1915-1920. v1-4 – 23mf – 9 – H-617/2 – ne IDC [470]
LES ARCHIVES BERBERES / Comite d'Etudes Berberes de Rabat – Paris. 1915-20 (I-IV) – 1 – fr A.C.R.P.P. [073]
LES ARCHIVES BERBERES – Paris: Comite d'etudes berberes de Rabat [etc]. v1-4 n1/2. 1915/16-1919/20 – 1 – us Res Libr [960]
ARCHIVES BIOGRAPHIQUES FRANCAISES (ABF 1) = FRENCH BIOGRAPHICAL ARCHIVE / ed by Bradley, Susan – (Printed index 1993,ca 2400p.-ca DM1,480.00.-Free for subscribers) – 1989-1991 – 1065mf (1:24) 9 – diazo DM20,800.00 (silver DM22,800.00 ISBN:3-598-32579-7) – 3-598-32564-9 – gw Saur [920]
ARCHIVES BIOGRAPHIQUES FRANCAISES. DEUXIEME SERIE (ABF 2) = FRANZOESISCHES BIOGRAPHISCHES ARCHIV. NEUE FOLGE. FRENCH BIOGRAPHICAL ARCHIVE. SERIES II (ABF 2) / Nappo, Tommaso – 1993-1996 – 664mf (1:24) in 12 installments – 9 – diazo DM22,800.00 (silver 24,600.00 ISBN: 3-598-33568-7) – 3-598-33555-5 – gw Saur [920]
ARCHIVES CURIEUSES DE LA VILLE DE NANTES ET DES DEPARTEMENTS DE L'OUE.. / Verger, Francois-J – Nantes: Forest, 1837-1841 – 1 – F599.64 – fr Armell [910]
ARCHIVES D'ANTHROPOLOGIE CRIMINELLE DE MEDECINE LEGALE ET DE PSYCHOLOGIE NORMALE ET PATHOLOGIQUE – v. 1-29. 1886-1915 – 1 – 202.00 – us L of C Photodup [360]
ARCHIVES DE BOTANIQUE / Guillemin, J B A – 2v. Paris. 1833. B-5231 2 – 8 – ne IDC [580]
ARCHIVES DE BOTANIQUE, OU RECUEIL MENSUEL DE MEMOIRES ORIGINAUX – t.1-t.2. 1833 – 3 – us Readex [580]

ARCHIVES DE DROIT INTERNATIONAL ET DE LEGISLATION COMPAREE – Londres, Bruxelles. v1. 1874 – 6mf – 9 – ILM-3911/1 – ne IDC [340]
ARCHIVES DE FLORE; JOURNAL BOTANIQUE / Schultz, F W – 7150. 1854-1869 72 – 9 – ne IDC [580]
Archives de la Bibliotheque Juive *see*
- FONDS BRAININ
- FONDS HERZL
- FONDS HUSID
- FONDS RUBENSTEIN
- FONDS TIFERETH JERUSALEM CONGREGATION (JOURNAL)
- FONDS ZIPPER
- LIVRES DE PRIERES ET SELECTIONS DE FRAGMENTS DE L'ANCIEN TESTAMENT AVEC COMMENTAIRES, ETC

ARCHIVES DE LA FLORE DE FRANCE ET D'ALLEMAGNE / Schultz, F W – (Archives de flore. Journal botanique. Wissembourg, 1854-1869. 382p. Archives de la flore d'Europe. Recueil botanique. Wissembourg, 1872[-1874]. 32p, 4pls) – Bitche, [1842-1855]. 350p, 1pl – 9 – ne IDC [580]
ARCHIVES DE LA FRANCE MONASTIQUE – (Vols also listed individually) – Paris. v1-50 – ne Slangenburg [240]
ARCHIVES DE LA FRANCE MONASTIQUE, VOL 1 *see* RECUEIL HISTORIQUE DES ARCHEVECHES, EVECHES ET PRIEURES DE FRANCE
ARCHIVES DE LA FRANCE MONASTIQUE, VOL 2 *see* LES MOINES DE L'ANCIENNE FRANCE
ARCHIVES DE LA FRANCE MONASTIQUE, VOL 3 *see* LES DEPENDANCES DE L'ABBAYE DE SAINT-GERMAIN-DES-PRES
ARCHIVES DE LA FRANCE MONASTIQUE, VOL 4 *see* RECUEIL HISTORIQUE DES ARCHEVECHES, EVECHES, ABBAYES ET PRIEURES DE FRANCE
ARCHIVES DE LA FRANCE MONASTIQUE, VOL 6 *see* LES DEPENDANCES DE L'ABBAYE DE SAINT-GERMAIN-DES-PRES
ARCHIVES DE LA FRANCE MONASTIQUE, VOL 7 *see* RECUEIL HISTORIQUE DES ARCHEVECHES, EVECHES, ABBAYES ET PRIEURES DE FRANCE
ARCHIVES DE LA FRANCE MONASTIQUE, VOL 8 *see* LES DEPENDANCES DE L'ABBAYE DE SAINT-GERMAIN-DES-PRES
ARCHIVES DE LA FRANCE MONASTIQUE, VOL 11 *see* LES MEMOIRES DU R. P. DOM BERNARD AUDEBERT
ARCHIVES DE LA FRANCE MONASTIQUE, VOL 12 *see* ABBAYES ET PRIEURES DE L'ANCIENNE FRANCE
ARCHIVES DE LA FRANCE MONASTIQUE, VOL 13 *see* RECUEIL DE CHARTES ET DOCUMENTS DE SAINT-MARTIN-DES-CHAMPS
ARCHIVES DE LA FRANCE MONASTIQUE, VOL 14 *see* ABBAYES ET PRIEURES DE L'ANCIENNE FRANCE
ARCHIVES DE LA FRANCE MONASTIQUE, VOL 15 *see* ABBAYES ET PRIEURES DE L'ANCIENNE FRANCE
ARCHIVES DE LA FRANCE MONASTIQUE, VOL 16 *see* RECUEIL DE CHARTES ET DOCUMENTS DE SAINT-MARTIN-DES-CHAMPS
ARCHIVES DE LA FRANCE MONASTIQUE, VOL 17 *see* ABBAYES ET PRIEURES DE L'ANCIENNE FRANCE
ARCHIVES DE LA FRANCE MONASTIQUE, VOL 19 *see* ABBAUES ET PRIEURES DE L'ANCIENNE FRANCE
ARCHIVES DE LA FRANCE MONASTIQUE, VOL 20 *see* RECUEIL DE CHARTES ET DOCUMENTS DE SAINT-MARTIN-DES-CHAMPS
ARCHIVES DE LA FRANCE MONASTIQUE, VOL 21 *see* RECUEIL DE CHARTES ET DOCUMENTS DE SAINT-MARTIN-DES-CHAMPS
ARCHIVES DE LA FRANCE MONASTIQUE, VOL 22 *see* L'ABBAYE EXEMPTE DE CLUNY ET LE SAINT-SIEGE
ARCHIVES DE LA FRANCE MONASTIQUE, VOL 23 *see* LES CHARTES DE L'ORDRE DE CHALAIS (1101-1400)
ARCHIVES DE LA FRANCE MONASTIQUE, VOL 24 *see* LES CHARTES DE L'ORDRE DE CHALAIS (1101-1400)
ARCHIVES DE LA FRANCE MONASTIQUE, VOL 25 *see* LES CHARTES DE L'ORDRE DE CHALAIS (1101-1400)
ARCHIVES DE LA FRANCE MONASTIQUE, VOL 26 *see* LES ECOLES EPISCOPALES ET MONASTIQUES EN OCCIDENT
ARCHIVES DE LA FRANCE MONASTIQUE, VOL 27 *see* LA VIE DES JUSTES
ARCHIVES DE LA FRANCE MONASTIQUE, VOL 28 *see* LA VIE DES JUSTES
ARCHIVES DE LA FRANCE MONASTIQUE, VOL 29 *see* BIBLIOTHEQUE DES BENEDICTINS DE LA CONGREGATION DE SAINT-VANNE ET SAINT-HYDULPHE
ARCHIVES DE LA FRANCE MONASTIQUE, VOL 30 *see* LA VIE DES JUSTES
ARCHIVES DE LA FRANCE MONASTIQUE, VOL 31 *see* HISTOIRE DE LA CONGREGATION DE SAINT-MAUR
ARCHIVES DE LA FRANCE MONASTIQUE, VOL 32 *see* HISTOIRE DE LA CONGREGATION DE SAINT-MAUR
ARCHIVES DE LA FRANCE MONASTIQUE, VOL 33 *see* HISTOIRE DE LA CONGREGATION DE SAINT-MAUR
ARCHIVES DE LA FRANCE MONASTIQUE, VOL 34 *see* HISTOIRE DE LA CONGREGATION DE SAINT-MAUR
ARCHIVES DE LA FRANCE MONASTIQUE, VOL 35 *see* HISTOIRE DE LA CONGREGATION DE SAINT-MAUR
ARCHIVES DE LA FRANCE MONASTIQUE, VOL 36 *see* ABBAYES ET PRIEURES DE L'ANCIENNE FRANCE
ARCHIVES DE LA FRANCE MONASTIQUE, VOL 37 *see* ABBAYES ET PRIEURES DE L'ANCIENNE FRANCE
ARCHIVES DE LA FRANCE MONASTIQUE, VOL 38 *see* LE TRES ANCIEN DROIT MONASTIQUE DE L'OCCIDENT
ARCHIVES DE LA FRANCE MONASTIQUE, VOL 39 *see* LE MONACHISME CLUNISIEN DES ORIGINES AU 15E SIECLE
ARCHIVES DE LA FRANCE MONASTIQUE, VOL 40 *see* LE MONACHISME CLUNISIEN DES ORIGINES AU 15E SIECLE
ARCHIVES DE LA FRANCE MONASTIQUE, VOL 41 *see* LE TEMPOREL DE LA SITUATION FINANCIERE DES ETABLISSEMENTS DE L'ORDRE DE CLUNY DU 12E AU 14E SIECLE
ARCHIVES DE LA FRANCE MONASTIQUE, VOL 42 *see* HISTOIRE DE LA CONGREGATION DE SAINT-MAUR
ARCHIVES DE LA FRANCE MONASTIQUE, VOL 43 *see* HISTOIRE DE LA CONGREGATION DE SAINT-MAUR
ARCHIVES DE LA FRANCE MONASTIQUE, VOL 44 *see* ETUDE SUR LES PRIVILEGES D'EXEMPTION ET DE JURISDICTION ECCLESIASTIQUES DES ABBAYES NORMANDES
ARCHIVES DE LA FRANCE MONASTIQUE, VOL 45 *see* ABBAYES ET PRIEURES DE L'ANCIENNE FRANCE
ARCHIVES DE LA FRANCE MONASTIQUE, VOL 46 *see* HISTOIRE DE LA CONGREGATION DE SAINT-MAUR
ARCHIVES DE LA FRANCE MONASTIQUE, VOL 47 *see* HISTOIRE DE LA CONGREGATION DE SAINT-MAUR
ARCHIVES DE LA FRANCE MONASTIQUE, VOL 48 *see* HISTOIRE DE LA CONGREGATION DE SAINT-MAUR
ARCHIVES DE LA FRANCE MONASTIQUE, VOL 49 *see* LE "DROIT D'OBLAT"
ARCHIVES DE LA FRANCE MONASTIQUE, VOL 50 *see* THEOLOGIE DE LA VIE MONASTIQUE D'APRES QUELQUES GRANDS MOINES DES EPOQUES MODERNE ET CONTEMPORAINE
ARCHIVES DE LA LINGUISTIQUE FRANCAISE, 1500-1900 – Collection of rare works on linguistics, grammar, French language, semantics, poetics, aesthetics and literary theory. 395 titles available individually – 9 – fr I.C.S. [400]
ARCHIVES DE LA LITTERATURE RADIOPHONIQUE ET TELEVISUELLE – Montreal, 1976- Charlotte Savary 1-4. SEM16P252 – 4r – 5 – Can$150.00 – cn Bibl Nat [380]
ARCHIVES DE LA THEOLOGIE CATHOLIQUE – 1(1861)-8(1864) – 72mf – 9 – Dfl3.50ea – ne Slangenburg [025]
ARCHIVES DE L'ETAT EN POLOGNE / Manteuffel, T – Origines, organisation et etat actuel. Wydawnictwa archiwow panstwowych, nr. 14. Warszawa. 1931. BR-9826 1 – 9 – ne IDC [943]
ARCHIVES DE L'HISTOIRE DES INSECTES – Publiees en allemand par Jean Gaspar Fuessly. Winterthour, 1794 – 3 – us Readex [590]
ARCHIVES DE L'HOTEL-DIEU SAINT-MICHEL DE ROBERVAL 1917-1922 : BIBLIOGRAPHIE / Anges, Marie des – 1962. SEM105P4 – 2mf – 9 – cn Bibl Nat [360]
ARCHIVES DE L'ILLUSTRATION IN PARIS – 1843-1944 – fr Illustration [072]
ARCHIVES DE L'ORIENT LATIN – Paris, 1881-1884. 2v – 32mf – 9 – H-2503/1 – ne IDC [950]
ARCHIVES DE L'ORIENT LATIN – Paris. v1-2. 1881-84 – 1r – 1 – us Ross [025]
ARCHIVES DE PHYSIOLOGIE NORMALE ET PATHOLOGIQUE – Paris, 1868-98. 1868-73 & Series 2, 1874-82. Series 3, 1883-87; Series 4, 1888 & Series 5, 1889-98 – 3 – us Readex [612]
LES ARCHIVES DE THALIE – ou Observations sur les sciences, les arts et la litterature, publiees par Ricord aine; pour faire suite au Journal des theatres. Paris. avr 1818-fevr 1819 – 1 – fr A.C.R.P.P. [073]
ARCHIVES DE ZOOLOGIE EXPERIMENTALE ET GENERALE – Paris, 1872-1880. v1-8 – 113mf – 9 – 190/2 – ne IDC [590]
Archives des Missions scientifiques et litteraires *see* CHOIX DE RAPPORTS ET INSTRUCTIONS PUB. SOUS LES AUSPICES DU MINISTERE DE L'INSTRUCTION PUBLIQUE ET DES BEAUX-ARTS
ARCHIVES DES SCIENCES – v. 8-24. 1955-1971 – 1,5,6 – us Princeton Micro [500]
ARCHIVES DES SCIENCES – (v28- , 1975- . 5,6,9) – v. 1-. 1948- – 1 – us UMI [500]
ARCHIVES D'HISTOIRE DOCTRINALE ET LITTERAIRE DU MOYEN AGE – Paris, 1926-1939. v1-14 – 85mf – 9 – H-185/2 – ne IDC [440]
ARCHIVES D'HISTOIRE DOCTRINALE ET LITTERAIRE DU MOYEN-AGE – 1(1926)-29(1962) – 331mf – 9 – Dfl1,159.00 – ne Slangenburg [025]
ARCHIVES DIPLOMATIQUES – Series 1-4. 1861-1914 – 1 – 868.00 – us L of C Photodup [025]
ARCHIVES DU MUSEUM D'HISTOIRE NATURELLE – Paris, 1839-1858/1861. v1-10 – 188mf – 9 – 6228/2 – ne IDC [500]
ARCHIVES ET DOCUMENTS / Institut d'Ethnologie. Museum National d'Histoire Naturelle. Paris – 1971-78. Catalogues des analyses des contenus des ouvrages micro-edites – 9 – F50.00 – fr Ethnologie [306]
ARCHIVES EUROPEENNES DE SOCIOLOGIE/ EUROPEAN JOURNAL OF SOCIOLOGY/ EURAPAISCHES ARCHIV FUER SOZIOLOGIE – (v18-. 5,6,9) – v. 1-. 1960- – 1 – us UMI [300]
ARCHIVES HISTORIQUES DU POITOU : T. 4 / Poitou – Poitiers: Oudin, 1875 – 1 – F255.23 – fr Armell [944]
ARCHIVES, HISTORY, RECORDS, ANNUAL GUIDES / U.S. Volleyball Association – (Reviews (1940-80) and Official Guide (1976-80). 67 fiches. $50.00) – 1916-75. 126 fiches – 9 – $115.00 – us Microform Publ [790]
ARCHIVES IN YUGOSLAVIA PAMPHLET COLLECTION – 19?? – 1 – CSUXANL2850-B – us Hoover Inst Photo [947]
ARCHIVES INTERNATIONALES DE PHARMACODYNAMIE ET DE THERAPIE – (1977- . 5,6,9) – v. 1-. 1894- – 1 – us UMI [615]
ARCHIVES INTERNATIONALES DE PHARMACODYNAMIE ET DE THERAPIE – v. 1-200. 1895-1972 – 1,5,6 – us Princeton Micro [540]
ARCHIVES INTERNATIONALES DE PHYSIOLOGIE ET DE BIOCHIMIE – v58-85. 1950-77 – 1,5,6 – us Princeton Micro [073]
ARCHIVES ISRAELITES – Paris. 1841-1935 – 1 – fr A.C.R.P.P. [270]
ARCHIVES ISRAELITES – Paris. v. 1-98. 1840-1935. Incomplete – 1 – us NY Public [270]
ARCHIVES ISRAELITES – Paris. v1-98. 1840-1935 – 14r – 1 – us Ross [025]
LES ARCHIVES ISRAELITES DE FRANCE DE LEUR CREATION EN 1840 A FEVRIER 1848 OU UN JOURNAL JUIF SOUS LOUIS-PHILIPPE. ETUDE DE MENTALITES / Philippe, B – F80.00 – fr Ethnologie [944]
Archives judiciares des Trois-Rivieres *see* REPERTOIRES ET/OU INDEX DES NOTAIRES
ARCHIVES MAROCAINES / Mission scientifique du Maroc – Paris. 1904-34 – 1 – fr A.C.R.P.P. [073]
Archives Nationales. Ministere des Affaires culturelles *see*
- FOND BERTHIAUME-DU TREMBLAY
- FONDS MADAME SALLUSTE LAVERY

Archives Nationales, Paris *see* PLANS OF PARIS FROM THE ARCHIVES NATIONALES
ARCHIVES OF AGRONOMY AND SOIL SCIENCE / ed by Kundler, Peter – 9,5,1 – us Harwood [630]
ARCHIVES OF AMERICAN ART : COLLECTION OF EXHIBITION CATALOGS / Art Libraries Society of North America – 1979 – 1r – 1 – $100.00 – 0-8161-1531-1 – uk Hall [700]
ARCHIVES OF ANDROLOGY – (1984-. 5,6,9) – v1-. 1978- – 1 – us UMI [073]
ARCHIVES OF ANIMAL NUTRITION / ed by Bergner, Hans – 9,5,1 – us Harwood [630]
ARCHIVES OF BRITISH AND AMERICAN PUBLISHERS *see*
- ARCHIVES OF ELKIN MATTHEWS, 1811-1938
- ARCHIVES OF GEORGE ALLEN AND COMPANY, 1893-1915
- ARCHIVES OF GEORGE ROUTLEDGE AND COMPANY, 1853-1902
- ARCHIVES OF GRANT RICHARDS, 1897-1948
- ARCHIVES OF HARPER AND BROTHERS, 1817-1914
- ARCHIVES OF KEGAN PAUL, TRENCH, TRUBNER AND HENRY S. KING, 1858-1912
- ARCHIVES OF MACMILLAN AND COMPANY, 1854-1924
- ARCHIVES OF RICHARD BENTLEY AND SON, 1829-1898
- ARCHIVES OF SWAN SONNENSCHEIN AND COMPANY, 1878-1911
- ARCHIVES OF THE CAMBRIDGE UNIVERSITY PRESS, 1669-1902
- ARCHIVES OF THE HOUSE OF LONGMAN, 1794-1914

ARCHIVES OF BRITISH MEN OF SCIENCE / MacLeod, Roy M & Friday, James R – 1972. Microform original. 65 fiches – 9 – £225.00 – uk Mansell Publ [500]
ARCHIVES OF CLINICAL NEUROPSYCHOLOGY – 1,5,69 – us UMI [616]
ARCHIVES OF DERMATOLOGICAL RESEARCH – v. 186-269. 1946-80 – 1,5,9 – 13,356.00 – us UMI [616]
ARCHIVES OF DERMATOLOGY – (1965- 5,6. 1970- 9) – 1- 1920- – 1 – us UMI [616]
ARCHIVES OF ELKIN MATTHEWS, 1811-1938 – (Includes catalogue) – 1r – 1 – £68.00 – uk Chadwyck [070]
ARCHIVES OF ENTOMOLOGY, CONTAINING THE HISTORY, OR ASCERTAINING THE CHARACTERS AND CLASSES OF INSECTS NOT HITHERTO DESCRIBED. – London, 1795 – 3 – us Readex [590]
ARCHIVES OF ENVIRONMENTAL CONTAMINATION AND TOXICOLOGY – v. 1-9. 1972-80 – 1,5,9 – 1013.00 – us UMI [360]
ARCHIVES OF ENVIRONMENTAL HEALTH – (1965-82. 5,6,9) – 1-37. 1960-82 – 1 – us UMI [613]
ARCHIVES OF ENVIRONMENTAL HEALTH *see* AMA ARCHIVES OF INDUSTRIAL HEALTH
ARCHIVES OF GENERAL PSYCHIATRY – (1965- . 5,6,9) – 1- 1959- – 1 – us UMI [616]
ARCHIVES OF GEORGE ALLEN AND COMPANY, 1893-1915 – (With index 2mf £18 9) – 27r – 1 – £1,830.00 – uk Chadwyck [070]
ARCHIVES OF GEORGE ROUTLEDGE AND COMPANY, 1853-1902 – (Includes index) – 6r – 1 – £415.00 – uk Chadwyck [070]
ARCHIVES OF GRANT RICHARDS, 1897-1948 / Richards, Grant – (With index £42) – 72r – 1 – £4,515.00 – uk Chadwyck [070]
ARCHIVES OF GYNECOLOGY – v.176-232, 1948-81. Continues: Archiv fuer gynaekologie. ISSN: 0170-9925 – 1,5,6,9,13 – 138.00v – us UMI [073]
ARCHIVES OF HARPER AND BROTHERS, 1817-1914 – (With index £52) – 58r – 1 – £3,725.00 – uk Chadwyck [070]
ARCHIVES OF INDUSTRIAL HYGIENE AND OCCUPATIONAL MEDICINE *see* AMA ARCHIVES OF INDUSTRIAL HEALTH
ARCHIVES OF INTERNAL MEDICINE – (1965-5,6. 1970- 9) – 1- 1908- – 1 – us UMI [616]
ARCHIVES OF INTERNAL MEDICINE – v1-96. 1908-55 – 1,5,6 – us Princeton Micro [610]
ARCHIVES OF KEGAN PAUL, TRENCH, TRUBNER AND HENRY S. KING, 1858-1912 – (With index of authors and titles 1mf £21 9) – 27r – 1 – £1,840.00 – uk Chadwyck [070]

ARCHIVES OF MACMILLAN AND COMPANY, 1854-1924 : PARTS 1 AND 2 – (Pt 1: Readers' Report 1867-1934 8r £550. Pt 2: Publishing Records 1860-1921 65r £4,250. With printed index £68) – 73r – 1 – £4,590.00 set – uk Chadwyck [410]

ARCHIVES OF MICROBIOLOGY – v. 1-127. 1939-80 – 1,5,9 – 25,622.00 – us UMI [073]

ARCHIVES OF NATURE CONSERVATION AND LANDSCAPE RESEARCH / ed by Stoecker, Gerhard – 9,5,1 – us Harwood [333]

ARCHIVES OF NEUROLOGY AND PSYCHIATRY *see* AMA ARCHIVES OF NEUROLOGY AND PSYCHIATRY

ARCHIVES OF OLD CHRIST CHURCH, PHILADELPHIA, 1695-1976 – 51r – 1 – $3655.00 – us UMI [978]

ARCHIVES OF OPHTHALMOLOGY – (1965- 5,6. 1970- 9) – v.1- 1869- – 1 – us UMI [617]

ARCHIVES OF OPHTHAMOLOGY – v. 1-62. 1929-1959 – 1,5,6 – us Princeton Micro [617]

ARCHIVES OF ORAL BIOLOGY – v1- 1959- – 5,6,9 – us UMI [574]

ARCHIVES OF ORTHOPAEDIC AND TRAUMATIC SURGERY – v. 44-97. 1949-80 – 1,5,9 – 7007.00 – us UMI [617]

ARCHIVES OF OTOLARYNGOLOGY – (1965- 5,6. 1970- 9) – 1- 1925- – 1 – us UMI [617]

ARCHIVES OF OTO-RHINO-LARYNGOLOGY – v. 155-230. 1947-80 – 1,5,9 – 7866.00 – us UMI [073]

ARCHIVES OF PATHOLOGY – (1965-75. 5,6. 1970-75. 9) – 1-99. 1926-75 – 1 – us UMI [616]

ARCHIVES OF PATHOLOGY – American Society for Experimental Pathology. v. 1-92. 1926-1971 – 1,5,6 – us Princeton Micro [610]

ARCHIVES OF PATHOLOGY AND LABORATORY MEDICINE – v. 100- 1976- – 1,5,6,9 – aply – us UMI [616]

ARCHIVES OF PEDIATRICS AND ADOLESCENT MEDICINE *see* AMERICAN JOURNAL OF DISEASES OF CHILDREN

ARCHIVES OF PHYSICAL MEDICINE AND REHABILITATION – (1965- 5,6. 1970- 9) – 1- 1920- – 1 – us UMI [615]

ARCHIVES OF PHYTOPATHOLOGY AND PLANT PROTECTION / ed by Spaar, Dieter & Wetzel, T – 9,5,1 – us Harwood [576]

ARCHIVES OF POULTRY SCIENCE – v17-40 1953-76 – 1,5,6 – us Princeton Micro [636]

ARCHIVES OF PSYCHOLOGY – Nos. 1-300. 1906-1945 – 1,5,6 – us Princeton Micro [150]

ARCHIVES OF PSYCHOLOGY – (With printed index) – n1-300 – 9 – $5.00f – us Ross [150]

ARCHIVES OF RICHARD BENTLEY AND SON, 1829-1898 – (With index £52) – 116r – 1 – £6,645.00 – uk Chadwyck [070]

ARCHIVES OF SEXUAL BEHAVIOR – v1-23. 1971-94 – 1,5 – $90.00v – us UMI [613]

ARCHIVES OF SURGERY – (1965- 5,6. 1970- 9) – 1- 1920- – 1 – us UMI [617]

ARCHIVES OF SURGERY – v20-71. 1930-55 – 1,5,6 – us Princeton Micro [617]

ARCHIVES OF SWAN SONNENSCHEIN AND COMPANY, 1878-1911 – (With index 2mf £21 9) – 25r – 1 – £1,720.00 – uk Chadwyck [070]

ARCHIVES OF THE BRITISH CONSERVATIVE PARTY / Conservative Party. Great Britain – (Part 1: 1868-1901. Part 2: 1902-14. Part 3: 1915-25. Part 4: 1926-37. Part 5: 1938-49. Part 6: 1950-56. Part 7: 1957-63. Part 8-10: 1964-86, Pamphlets and leaflets) – National Union Gleanings, election campaign guides, party conference minutes and reports, council minutes and annual reports, pamphlets and leaflets – 1,9 – us Primary [941]

ARCHIVES OF THE BRITISH LABOUR PARTY / Labour Party. Great Britain. Archives – (Pamphlets and Leaflets, Parts 1-5. General correspondence and political records, Parts 1-8. Speeches and press statements; National Executive Committee minutes, Parts 1-9) – 9 – us Primary [941]

ARCHIVES OF THE BRITISH LIBERAL PARTY / Liberal Party. Great Britain – (Pt 1: 1885-1911. Pt 2: 1912-39. Pt 3: 1940-63. Pt 4: 1964-c1972. National Liberal Federation Annual Reports, 1877-1936. The Liberal Magazine, 1893-1950) – 1,9 – us Primary [025]

ARCHIVES OF THE BRITISH TRADES UNION CONGRESS / British Trades Union Congress – (General Council Minute Books, 1921-46. Pts 1-2: pamphlets and leaflets 1887-1972. Pts 1-4: periodicals and serials 1919-77, minutes and papers, 1922-50. Pts 1-2: records of mining crisis 1925-26) – 1,9 – us Primary [331]

ARCHIVES OF THE CAMBRIDGE UNIVERSITY PRESS, 1669-1902 – (With guide £11) – 11r – 1 – £800.00 – uk Chadwyck [070]

ARCHIVES OF THE DESTRUCTION – (15,000 photographs of the Holocaust) – 9 – us Primary [943]

ARCHIVES OF THE ENGLISH PROVINCE / Society of Jesus – 1 – uk Microform Academic [240]

ARCHIVES OF THE FABIAN SOCIETY / Fabian Society – (Pt 1: Minute Books and Records 1884-1918. Pt 2: Minutes of the Executive Committee and Lectures 1919-60. Pt 3: Correspondence of Eminent Persons and Early Material and Memorials 1881-1959. Pt 4: Papers and Records of the Finance and General Purposes Committee, of the Publications Committee and of Fabian Local Societies 1919-64, together with Earlier Documents Dating from 1884. Pt 5: Papers and Records of the Fabian Women's Group 1919-51; The Society for Socialist Inquiry and Propaganda 1931-32; The New Fabian Research Bureau 1931-39; and Other Bodies. Pt 6: Home Research Committee Minutes 1943-64, and Papers, Section A 1930-49. Pt 7: Home Research Committee Papers, Section B, 1950-64; International and Commonwealth Bureau Minutes and Papers 1940-64; London Labour Party and Fabian Regional Councils 1945-62) – 1 – us Primary [025]

ARCHIVES OF THE FEDERAL WRITERS' PROJECT – (Series One: Printed and mimeograph publications in the surviving F.W.P. files, 1933-1943. Series Two: Surveys of American Life and Culture) – 1 – us Primary [305]

ARCHIVES OF THE FELTRINELLI INSTITUTE – (Comprising Bollettino dell' Opposizione Comunista Italian (1931-33); Bollettino di Partito (1944-45); IL Domani d'Italia (1901-03); Il Domani d'Italia (1922-24); La Nostra Lotta (1943-45); L'Ordine Nuovo (1919-25); Pagine Rosse (1923-24); Politica Socialista (1933-35); Prometeo (1924); Rassegna Communista (1921-22); Il Soviet (1918-22); La Stato Operaio (1927-39); L'Unita (1924-26). Archives of the Feltrinelli Institute of Milan. Part 1. 1901-45) – 1 – us Primary [025]

ARCHIVES OF THE GERMAN EMBASSY AT WASHINGTON : AMERICAN HISTORICAL ASSOCIATION PROJECT 1 – 52r – $1,196.00 – T290 – us Nat'l Archives [327]

ARCHIVES OF THE HOUSE OF LONGMAN, 1794-1914 – (With index £52) – 73r – 1 – £4,590.00 – uk Chadwyck [070]

ARCHIVES OF THE INDEPENDENT LABOUR PARTY, SERIES 1 : PAMPHLETS AND LEAFLETS OF THE INDEPENDENT LABOUR PARTY, 1893-1975 / Independent Labour Party. Great Britain – (Pt 1: 1893-1908. Pt 2: 1909-16. Pt 3: 1917-24. Pt 4: 1925-39. Pt 5: 1940-75) – 9 – us Primary [025]

ARCHIVES OF THE INDEPENDENT LABOUR PARTY, SERIES 2 : MINUTES AND RELATED RECORDS OF THE INDEPENDENT LABOUR PARTY / Independent Labour Party. Great Britain – Pt 1: National Administrative Council and Related Records 1894-1950. Pt 2: Branch Minutes and Related Records 1892-1950 – 1 – us Primary [320]

ARCHIVES OF THE INDEPENDENT LABOUR PARTY, SERIES 3 : THE FRANCIS JOHNSON CORRESPONDENCE, 1888-1950 / Independent Labour Party. Great Britain – (Pt 1: 1888-1908. Pt 2: 1909-1950) – 1 – us Primary [025]

ARCHIVES OF THE INDEPENDENT LABOUR PARTY, SERIES 4 : ORGANISATIONAL AND REGIONAL RECORDS OF THE INDEPENDENT LABOUR PARTY / Independent Labour Party. Great Britain – 9 – us Primary [320]

ARCHIVES OF THE INTERNATIONAL INSTITUTE OF SOCIAL HISTORY – Owenite Minute Books, 1838-45 – 1 – us Primary [360]

ARCHIVES OF THE PARLIAMENTARY LABOUR PARTY / Parliamentary Labour Party. Great Britain. Archives – (Minutes and records of the Administrative Committee, 1941-45; Executive Committee, 1923-37; Liaison Committee, 1945-68; Parliamentary Committee, 1951-64; Parliamentary Labour Party, 1906-1968) – 1 – us Primary [025]

ARCHIVES OF THE SETTLEMENT MOVEMENT : SERIES ONE: RECORDS OF THE NATIONAL FEDERATION OF SETTLEMENTS AND SUCCESSORS, 1899-1958 – (Pt 1: Minutes, Reports and Proceedings of Central Policy Making Groups. Pt 2: Domestic Programs. Pt 3: National Federation of Settlements and Successors, Domestic Programs. Pt 4: International Activities of the National Federation of Settlements and Successors, c. 1920-1960. Pt 5: Major Figures of the Settlement Movement) – 1 – us Primary [975]

ARCHIVES OF THE SOVIET COMMUNIST PARTY AND SOVIET STATE, DELA SERIES *see*
- CENTRE FOR THE PRESERVATION OF CONTEMPORARY DOCUMENTATION (TSKHSD), FOND 6 COMMITTEE FOR PARTY CONTROL
- RUSSIAN CENTRE FOR THE PRESERVATION AND STUDY OF DOCUMENTS OF MOST RECENT HISTORY (RTSKHIDNI), FOND 17 CENTRAL COMMITTEE OF THE COMMUNIST PARTY OF THE USSR
- RUSSIAN CENTRE FOR THE PRESERVATION AND STUDY OF DOCUMENTS OF MOST RECENT HISTORY (RTSKHIDNI), FOND 37
- RUSSIAN CENTRE FOR THE PRESERVATION AND STUDY OF DOCUMENTS OF MOST RECENT HISTORY (RTSKHIDNI), FOND 54
- RUSSIAN CENTRE FOR THE PRESERVATION AND STUDY OF DOCUMENTS OF MOST RECENT HISTORY (RTSKHIDNI), FOND 58
- RUSSIAN CENTRE FOR THE PRESERVATION AND STUDY OF DOCUMENTS OF MOST RECENT HISTORY (RTSKHIDNI), FOND 337
- RUSSIAN CENTRE FOR THE PRESERVATION AND STUDY OF DOCUMENTS OF MOST RECENT HISTORY (RTSKHIDNI), FOND 447
- RUSSIAN CENTRE FOR THE PRESERVATION AND STUDY OF DOCUMENTS OF MOST RECENT HISTORY (RTSKHIDNI), FOND 477
- RUSSIAN CENTRE FOR THE PRESERVATION AND STUDY OF DOCUMENTS OF MOST RECENT HISTORY (RTSKHIDNI), FOND 572
- RUSSIAN CENTRE FOR THE PRESERVATION AND STUDY OF DOCUMENTS OF MOST RECENT HISTORY (RTSKHIDNI), FOND 582
- RUSSIAN CENTRE FOR THE PRESERVATION AND STUDY OF DOCUMENTS OF MOST RECENT HISTORY (RTSKHIDNI), FOND 586
- RUSSIAN CENTRE FOR THE PRESERVATION AND STUDY OF DOCUMENTS OF MOST RECENT HISTORY (RTSKHIDNI), FOND 593
- RUSSIAN CENTRE FOR THE PRESERVATION AND STUDY OF DOCUMENTS OF MOST RECENT HISTORY (RTSKHIDNI), FOND 604
- RUSSIAN CENTRE FOR THE PRESERVATION AND STUDY OF DOCUMENTS OF MOST RECENT HISTORY (RTSKHIDNI), FOND 620
- RUSSIAN CENTRE FOR THE PRESERVATION AND STUDY OF DOCUMENTS OF MOST RECENT HISTORY (RTSKHIDNI), FOND 628
- RUSSIAN CENTRE FOR THE PRESERVATION AND STUDY OF DOCUMENTS OF MOST RECENT HISTORY (RTSKHIDNI), FOND 646

ARCHIVES OF THE SOVIET COMMUNIST PARTY AND SOVIET STATE, OPISI SERIES *see*
- CENTRE FOR THE PRESERVATION OF CONTEMPORARY DOCUMENTATION (TSKHSD)
- CENTRE FOR THE PRESERVATION OF CONTEMPORARY DOCUMENTATION (TSKHSD), FOND 89

ARCHIVES OF THE SOVIET COMMUNIST PARTY AND SOVIET STATE: THE DELA SERIES : FROM THE STATE ARCHIVE OF THE RUSSIAN FEDERATION (GARF); THE RUSSIAN CENTRE FOR THE PRESERVATION AND STUDY OF DOCUMENTS OF MOST RECENT HISTORY (RTSKHIDNI); AND THE CENTRE FOR THE PRESERVATION OF CONTEMPORARY DOCUMENTATION (TSKHSD) – (Apply for other prices. Individual titles listed separately) – 4864r – 1 – £55.00r standing order complete coll – Joint publ of the State Archival Service of Russia (Rosarkhiv) and the Hoover Institution on War, Revolution and Peace – uk Chadwyck [324]

ARCHIVES OF THE SOVIET COMMUNIST PARTY AND SOVIET STATE. THE OPISI SERIES : FROM THE STATE ARCHIVE OF THE RUSSIAN FEDERATION (GARF); THE RUSSIAN CENTRE FOR THE PRESERVATION AND STUDY OF DOCUMENTS OF MOST RECENT HISTORY (RTSKHIDNI); AND THE CENTRE FOR THE PRESERVATION OF CONTEMPORARY DOCUMENTATION (TSKHSD) / ed by Pikhoia, Rudolf G et al – (Complete Opisi (Finding aids) ca 600r (£63.00r) ca £37,800.00 or in units of 100r £7,200.00 per unit. For individual orders apply for prices. Individual titles also listed separately) – 1 – £55.00r standing order for complete collection – Joint publ of the State Archival Service of Russia (Rosarkhiv) and the Hoover Institution on War, Revolution and Peace – uk Chadwyck [324]

ARCHIVES OF THE TONGAN JUDICIARY, 1905-1995 / Tonga. Ministry of Justice – 20r – 1 – PMB1088 – at Pacific Mss [340]

THE ARCHIVES OF THE U.S. GOVERNMENT: A DOCUMENTARY HISTORY, 1774-1934 / U.S. National Archives and Records Service; ed by Percy Scott Flippin – 5 rolls. T1167 – 1 – us Nat'l Archives [025]

ARCHIVES OF THE WORKS PROJECTS ADMINISTRATION AND PREDECESSORS, 1933-43 / U. S. Works Projects Administration – (Parts 1 and 2) – Series 1: The Final State Reports, 1943 – 1 – us Primary [324]

ARCHIVES OF TOXICOLOGY – v. 1-46. 1930-80 – 1,5,9 – 3726.00 – us UMI [073]

ARCHIVES OF VIROLOGY – v.1-70, 1938-81. ISSN: 0304-8608 – 1,5,6,9,13 – 129.00v – us UMI [073]

ARCHIVES PARLEMENTAIRES DE 1787-1860 / France. Chambres francaises – (Deuxieme serie, 1799-1860. 13 dec 1799-juil 1839 (I-CXXVI)) – Paris. Premiere serie, 1787-99. 4 jan 1794 (I-LXXXII bis) – 1 – fr A.C.R.P.P. [323]

ARCHIVES PHILOSOPHIQUES, POLITIQUES ET LITTERAIRES – Paris. juil. 1817-18 – 1 – fr A.C.R.P.P. [073]

ARCHIVES, RECORDS, REFERENCE MATERIAL AND CONFERENCE REPORTS / Council for National Cooperation in Aquatics – (1974-80.Biennial Conference Reports. 8 fiches. 10.00; 9) – 1951-72.32 fiches – 9 – 40.00 – us Microform Publ [790]

ARCHIVES ROYALES DE MARI – (1 Lettres. Publiees par G. Dossin. Paris 1946 5mf; 2 Lettres. Publiees par Ch. F. Jean. Paris 1941 5mf; 3 Lettres. Publiees par J.R. Kupper. Paris 1948 3mf; 4 Lettres. Publiees par G. Dossin. Paris 1951 3mf; 5 Lettres. Publiees par G. Dossin. Paris 1951 3mf; 6 Lettres. Publiees par J.R. Kupper. Paris 1953 3mf) – 8 – ne Slangenburg [240]

ARCHIVES: SERIES A / Royal Society of Arts – With printed index – 1 – £1,200.00 – uk World [700]

ARCHIVES STATISTIQUES DE LA FRANCE – Directeur: Alexandre de Ferriere. P., an XII-an XIII – 9 – fr Hachette [025]

ARCHIVES...,1789-1869 / Holland Land Company. Philadelphia, PA – (Investment and financial reports, land purchases and sales, deeds, maps, warrants, patents, legal and court papers, correspondence. Collection supplemented with additional material pertaining to land sales records in the counties of Western New York between 1830s-1860s) – 202r – 1 – us Holland [978]

ARCHIVES...(AMERICAN HISTORICAL ASSOC. PROJECT I) / Germany. Embassy. Washington, DC – 52 rolls. T290. (World War II Collection of Seized Enemy Records) – 1 – us Nat'l Archives [324]

ARCHIVIO BIOGRAFICO ITALIANO (ABI 1) = ITALIAN BIOGRAPHICAL ARCHIVE / ed by Nappo, Tommaso – (Printed index) – 1987-90 – 1046mf (1:24) – 9 – diazo DM19,800.00 (silver 22,000.00 ISBN: 3-598-31520-1) – 3-598-31540-6 – gw Saur [920]

ARCHIVIO BIOGRAFICO ITALIANO, NUOVA SERIE (ABI 2) = ITALIENISCHES BIOGRAPHISCHES ARCHIVE (ABI 2). NEUE SERIE / ed by Nappo, Tommaso – 1991-1994 – 710mf (1:24) – 9 – diazo DM22,600.00 coll DM2,260.00 per instalment (silver DM24,600.00 coll DM2,460.00 per instalment ISBN: 3-598-33154-1) – 3-598-33140-1 – gw Saur [945]

ARCHIVIO STORICO DELL' ARTE – Roma, 1888-1894. v1-7; S.2, 1895-1897. v1-3. – 157mf – 9 – O-1210/1 – ne IDC [700]

ARCHIVIO STORICO DELL'ARTE – Rome, 1888-1897 – 5r – 1 – £290.00 – uk Chadwyck [700]

ARCHIVIO STORICO DELL'ARTE – v. 1-7. Roma. 1888-94; s. 2, v. 1-3 and index. BO-1210 1 – 9 – ne IDC [700]

O ARCHIVO – Alfenas, Brazil. Dec 1914; 1915 – 1 – bl Biblioteca [072]

ARCHIVO BIOGRAFICO DE ESPANA, PORTUGAL E IBEROAMERICA 1960-1995 = SPANISCHES, PORTUGIESISCHES UND IBEROAMERIKANISCHES BIOGRAPHISCHES ARCHIV 1960-1995/SPANISH, PORTUGUESE AND LATIN-AMERICAN BIOGRAPHICAL ARCHIVE 1960-1995 / Herrero Mediavilla, Victor – 1996- – 471mf (1:24) in 12 installments – 9 – diazo DM19,800.00 (silver DM21,840.00 ISBN: 3-598-34031-1) – 3-598-34030-3 – gw Saur [920]
ARCHIVO BIOGRAFICO DE ESPANA, PORTUGAL E IBEROAMERICA (ABEPI 1) = SPANISH, PORTUGUESE AND LATIN AMERICAN BIOGRAPHICAL ARCHIVE / ed by Herrero-Mediavilla, Victor & Aguayo-Nayle, Lolita R – (Printed index) – 1986-1989 – 1,144mf (1:24) – 9 – diazo DM21,800.00 (silver 23,800.00 ISBN: 3-598-32045-0) – 3-598-32030-2 – gw Saur [920]
ARCHIVO BIOGRAFICO ITALIANO, NUOVA SERIE (ABI 2) = ITALIENISCHES BIOGRAPHISCHES ARCHIV (ABI 2). NEUE SERIE. SUPPLEMENT : SUPPLEMENTO / ed by Nappo, Tommaso – (Suppl 1: diazo DM2,260.00 ISBN: 3-598-33332-3 silver DM2,460.00 ISBN: 3-598-33334-X. Suppl 2: diazo DM2,260.00 ISBN: 3-598-33333-1 silver DM2,460.00 ISBN: 3-598-33335-8) – 1997 – 2 suppl ca 100mf (1:24) in 2 instalments – 9 – diazo DM4,520.00 set (silver DM4,920.00 set ISBN: 3-598-33331-5) – 3-598-33330-7 – gw Saur [945]
ARCHIVO CONTEMPORANEO : JORNAL ILLUSTRADO – Rio de Janeiro, 15 Sep 1872-15 Mar 1873 – 1,5,6 – bl Biblioteca [072]
ARCHIVO DE HISTORIA Y VARIEDADES / Febres Cordero, Julio – Caracas, 1930-31; Madrid: Razon y Fe, 1932. 2v – 1 – sp Bibl Santa Ana [946]
ARCHIVO DE LA NACION. CORRESPONDENCIA DE LORD STRANGFORD Y DE LA ESTACION NAVAL EN EL RIO DE LA PLATA CON EL GOBIERNO DE BUENOS AIRES. 1810-1812 / Bayle, Constantino – Madrid: Razon y Fe, 1943 – 1 – sp Bibl Santa Ana [355]
EL ARCHIVO DE LOS CONDES DE CANILLEROS / Munoz de San Pedro, Miguel – Sep de la revista Hidalguia. Enero-Marzo 1954 no 4 – sp Bibl Santa Ana [020]
ARCHIVO DEL GENERAL MIRANDA / Bayle, Constantino – Caracas, Madrid: Razon y Fe, 1931. 6v – 1 – sp Bibl Santa Ana [355]
ARCHIVO DEL GENERAL MIRANDA. REVOLUCION FRANCESA. TOMO 9 A 12 / Bayle, Constantino – Caracas, 1931-32; Madrid: Razon y Fe, 1933 – 1 – sp Bibl Santa Ana [944]
ARCHIVO EXTREMENO – v. 1-4. 1908-11 – 9 – 1.50f – sp Bibl Santa Ana [010]
Archivo Extremeno *see* DOCUMENTOS HISTORICOS REFERENTES A EXTREMADURA
EL ARCHIVO GENERAL DE INDIAS DE SEVILLA / Torre Revello, Jose – Buenos Aires, 1929; Madrid: Razon y Fe, 1931 – 1 – sp Bibl Santa Ana [305]
Archivo General de la Nacion *see* ACUERDOS DEL EXTINGUIDO CABILDO DE BUENOS AIRES
ARCHIVO GENERAL DE LA NACION. ACUERDOS DEL EXTINGUIDO CABILDO DE BUENOS AIRES. SERIE 2, TOMO 9 / Bayle, Constantino – Buenos Aires, 1931; Madrid: Razon y Fe, 1932 – 1 – sp Bibl Santa Ana [972]
ARCHIVO GENERAL DE LA NACION. UNIVERSIDAD AUTONOMA DE MEXICO. NUEVOS DOCUMENTOS RELATIVOS A LOS BIENES DE HERNANDO CORTES, 1547-1947. TOMO 2. MEXICO, 1946 / Bayle, Constantino – Madrid: Razon y Fe, 1948 – 1 – sp Bibl Santa Ana [972]
Archivo Historico Nacional *see* CONSEJO DE CASTILLA
ARCHIVO ILLUSTRADO – [s.l.]. Ago 1874; Abr-17 Jun 1875 – 1,5,6 – bl Biblioteca [072]
ARCHIVO LEONESSANO. DOCUMENTI RIGUARDANTI LA VITA E IL CULTO DI SAN GIUSEPPE DE LEONESSA. ROMA 1965 / Chiaretti, Giuseppe – Madrid: Graf. Calleja, 1966 – 1 – sp Bibl Santa Ana [240]
Archivo Ministerio de Hacienda MS. *see* EXPLICACION DE LOS ESTADOS QUE FORMAN LA BALANZA DEL COMERCIO RECIPROCO QUE HIZO ESPANA...EN 1795
Archivo Municipal, Serradilla *see* CARTA REAL POR LA QUE SE EXIME A SERRADILLA DE LA JURISDICCION DE PLASENCIA (24 DE NOVIEMBRE DE 1557)
ARCHIVO PER LE SCIENZE MEDICHE – 1876-1; 1975- 56,9 – us UMI [610]
LOS ARCHIVOS DE SALTA Y JUJUY / Olguin, Eduardo Fernandez – Madrid: Razon y Fe, 1927 – 1 – sp Bibl Santa Ana [025]
ARCHIVOS DEL FOLKLORE CUBANO – Havana. 5v. 1924-30 – 1 – 23.00 – us L of C Photodup [025]
ARCHIVOS DO JARDIM BOTANICO DO RIO DE JANEIRO – (Missing: V.2) – Rio de Janeiro, 1915-1980. v1-24 – 81mf – 9 – 8561/1 – ne IDC [580]
ARCHIVSKI FONDOMI U VOJVODINI / Mihajlovic, Velimir & Sredoje, Lalic – Novisad, 1962 – 1r – 1 – us I.H.R.C. [947]
ARCHIVUM FRANCISCANUM HISTORICUM – 1(1908)-40(1947) – 585mf – 9 – Dfl2,048.00 – ne Slangenburg [025]
ARCHIVUM IMMUNOLOGIAE ET THERAPIAE EXPERIMENTALIS – v. 13-20. 1965-72 – 1,5,6 – us Princeton Micro [610]
ARCHIVUM ROMANICUM / ed by Bertoni, G – Geneva, 1917-41.-v1-25 – 251mf – 8 – ne IDC [930]
ARCHY'S LIFE OF MEHITABEL / Marquis, Don – Garden City, NY: Doubleday, Doran & Co., 1933. viii,182p – 1 – us U.W. Library [810]
Arcieri, Giovanni P *see* THE CIRCULATION OF THE BLOOD
Arciero, Paul J *see* INFLUENCE OF AGE AND CAFFEINE ON RESTING METABOLIC RATE, BLOOD PRESSURE, AND MOOD STATE IN YOUNGER AND OLDER INDIVIDUALS
ARCILLA Y PAJARO – Caceres, 1953 – 5 – sp Bibl Santa Ana [073]
Arcimegas, German *see* LOS DEMANES EN LA CONQUISTA DE AMERICA, BUENOS AIRES, 1943
Arcin, Andre *see* LA GUINEE FRANCAISE
Arciniega, Rosa *see*
- DON PEDRO DE VALDIVIA CONQUISTADOR DE CHILE
- FRANCISCO PIZARRO. BIOGRAFIA DEL CONQUISTADOR DEL PERU
- PIZARRO BIOGRAFIA DEL CONQUISTADOR DEL PERU

Arciniegas, German *see* ENTRE LA LIBERTAD Y EL MIEDO
Arciniegas, Ismael Enrique *see* RAMANCERO DE LA CONQUISTA Y LA COLONIA...
O ARCO DA VELHA – [s.l.]. 10 Nov 1877 – 1,5,6 – bl Biblioteca [072]
D'Arco, Patrick H *see* CLINICAL, FUNCTIONAL, AND RADIOGRAPHIC ASSESSMENT OF THE CONVENTIONAL AND MODIFIED BOYD-ANDERSON SURGICAL PROCEDURES FOR REPAIR OF DISTAL BICEPS TENDON RUPTURES
O ARCO-IRIS : ORGAM INDEPENDENTE DEFENSOR DO DIREITO E DA VERDADE – Manaos, Amazonas. 4 Jul-22 Out 1927 – 1,5,6 – bl Biblioteca [072]
Arconada, Mariano *see* BENITO ARIAS MONTANO Y AUBREY F.G. BEEL
Arcos, Francisco de *see* VIDA DE LA VENERABLE MARIA DE JESUS
Arctander, Jno. W *see* THE APOSTLE OF ALASKA: THE STORY OF WILLIAM DUNCAN OF METLAKAHTLA
Arctic Club of America *see* BULLETIN
ARCTIC EXPEDITION DIARIES OF VILHJALMUR STEFANSSON / Stefansson, Vilhjalmur – 3r – 1 – $60.00 set – us Dartmouth [910]
ARCTIC EXPEDITION DIARIES OF VILHJALMUR STEFANSSON, 1878-1925 – 5r – 1 – $365.00 – us UMI [910]
ARCTIC EXPERIENCES: CONTAINING CAPT. GEORGE E. TYSON'S WONDERFUL DRIFT ON THE ICE-FLOE: A HISTORY OF THE POLARIS EXPEDITION,THE CRUISE OF THE TIGRESS AND RESCUE OF THE POLARIS SURVIVORS. – Ed. by E. Vale Blake. New York: Harper, 1874. 00172. (Pre-1900 Canadiana) – 9 – cn C.I.H.M. [910]
ARCTIC EXPLORATION, WITH INFORMATION RESPECTING SIR JOHN FRANKLIN'S MISSING PARTY / Rae, J – N 3572. 1855 – 8 – BSF 8.00 – ne IDC [910]
ARCTIC EXPLORATIONS : THE SECOND GRINNELL EXPEDITION IN SEARCH OF SIR JOHN FRANKLIN 1853, 1854, 1855 / Kane, E K – H-485. v. 1-2. 1856 – 9 – ne IDC [910]
ARCTIC LANGUAGES : AN AWAKENING / ed by Collis, Dirmid R F – 1990 – 458p – 9 – 92-3-102661-5 – fr UNESCO [490]
THE ARCTIC NEWS – 1941-76. (American Indian Perlodicals in the Princeton University Library). 13 fiches – 9 – $65.00 – us UPA [305]
THE ARCTIC PROBLEM: AND NARRATIVE OF THE PEARY RELIEF EXPEDITION OF THE ACADEMY OF NATURAL SCIENCES OF PHILADELPHIA / Heilprin, Angelo – Philadelphia: Contemporary Publ. Co., 1893. 05537. (Pre-1900 Canadiana) – 9 – cn C.I.H.M. [910]
AN ARCTIC PROVINCE / Elliot, H W – BN 201 2. 1886 – 8 – ne IDC [550]
ARCTIC SEARCHING EXPEDITION / Richardson, J – BN 369 2. v. 1-2. 1851 – 8 – ne IDC [910]
ARCTIC SEARCHING EXPEDITION: A JOURNAL OF A BOAT-VOYAGE THROUGH RUPERT'S LAND AND THE ARCTIC SEA, IN SEARCH OF THE DISCOVERY SHIPS UNDER THE COMMAND OF SIR JOHN FRANKLIN / Richardson, John – 2v. 1851 – 9 – uk Libr Preservation [910]
ARCTIC WATERS POLLUTION PREVENTION ACT AND REGULATIONS / Canada. Laws, Statutes, etc – (Amendment service. YX76-A12EM. Standing order) – Basic set. YX76-A12-1-EM – 9 – Can$5.00 – cn Communication [340]
ARCTICA – 350 titles – 8 – ne IDC [910]
ARCTURUS: A CANADIAN JOURNAL OF LITERATURE AND LIFE – 1 – 45.00 – cn McLaren [800]
Arcudius, P *see*
- DE CONCORDIA ECCLESIAE OCCID. ET ORIENTALIS
- OPUSCULA AUREA THEOLOGICA...CIRCA PROCESSIONEM SPIRITUS SANCTI

Ardagh, Alice Maud *see* TANGLED ENDS
Ardant du Picq, Charles Pierre *see* LA LANGUE SONGHAY, DIALECTE DYERMA
Ardant du Picq, Colonel Charles *see* ETUDES SUR LE COMBAT
ARDATH / Corelli, Marie – British Fiction Archive: Unit 1 – 9 – uk Bell [830]
ARDEA. TIJDSCHRIFT DER NEDERLANDSCHE ORNITHOLOGISCHE VEREENIGING. (UNIE) *see* VERSLAGEN EN MEDEDEELINGEN VAN DE NEDERLANDSCHE ORNITHOLOGISCHE VEREENIGING
Arden, A *see* BANNING AND ARDEN'S REPORTS OF PATENT CASES IN THE U.S. CIRCUIT COURTS
Ardenne de Tizac, Andree Francoise Cardine d' *see* THE FRENCH WRITER, ANDRE VIOLLIS, SPEAKS IN PARIS ABOUT THE ADMIRABLE DEFENSE OF THE SPANISH CAPITAL
ARDENNES CAMPAIGN STATISTICS, 16 DEC 1944-19 JAN 1945 / U.S. Army. Office of the Chief of Military History – 1952 – 1 – 18.00 – us L of C Photodup [977]
Ardennes. France (Department) *see* ANNUAIRE DU DEPARTEMENT DES ARDENNES POUR L'AN HUIT
Ardery, MrS W B *see*
- KENTUCKY COURT AND OTHER RECORDS, V2
- KENTUCKY RECORDS

Ardissone, F *see* LE FLORIDEE ITALICHE
Ardiwinata, Odjoh Raden *see*
- PEMELIHARAAN IKAN
- PEMELIHARAAN IKAN, DISUSUN OLEH R. O. ARDIWINATA

ARDROSSAN AND SALTCOATS HERALD – 1 – £42.00r – uk Scot News [072]
ARDROSSAN AND SALTCOATS HERALD – Ardrossan, Scotland. 1900-10; 1939-45 – 12r – 1 – uk British Libr Newspaper [072]
Arduino, M *see* IL GIUDIZIO DI DELIBAZIONE
Arduino, P *see* ANIMADVERSIONUM BOTANICARUM SPECIMEN. SPECIMEN ALTERUM
ARDUINO TERZI : MEMOIRE FRANCISCANE NELLA VALLE... / Barrado Manzano, Arcangel – Madrid: Archivo Ibero-Americano, 1959 – 1 – sp Bibl Santa Ana [240]
ARDUINO TERZI : SAN FABIANO DE LA FORESTA... / Barrado Manzano, Arcangel – Madrid: Archivo Ibero-Americano, 1959 – 1 – sp Bibl Santa Ana [240]
ARDUINO TERZI : SAN FRANCISCO D'ASSISI A ROMA... / Barrado Manzano, Arcangel – Madrid: Archivo Ibero-Americano, 1959 – 1 – sp Bibl Santa Ana [240]
ARE HEALTH EDUCATORS SOCIALIZED TO PERCEIVE ROLE MODELING AS A PROFESSIONAL RESPONSIBILITY / Scott, Lisa A – Purdue University, 1996 – 1mf – 9 – HE 570 – us Microform Publ [613]
ARE JOURNAL / Association for Research Enlightenment – Virginia Beach. v7-11 jan 1972-nov 1976; v12 jan-nov 1977*; v13-15 jan 1978-nov 1980 1; v7-8 jan 1972-nov 1973; v10-14 jan 1975-nov 1979*; v15 jan-nov 1980 5; v10-15 jan 1975-nov 1980 9 – 1,5,9 – $83.70y – D7485 – us UMI [073]
ARE MIRACLES CREDIBLE? / Lias, John James – London: Hodder & Stoughton, 1890. 1 fiche – 9 – us A.T.L.A. [240]
ARE THERE CORRUPTIONS IN THE NEW TESTAMENT / Hastings, Horace Lorenzo – Boston: Scriptural Tract Rep., 1890. 1 fiche – 9 – us A.T.L.A. [240]
ARE ZIONISM AND REFORM JUDAISM INCOMPATIBLE? – New York, 1943. BJ-28-1 1 – 9 – ne IDC [270]
AREA (AMERICAN RAILWAY ENGINEERING ASSOCIATION) – Standards. Printed index. Updated every 60 days – 6,9 – us Info Handling [625]
AREA EDITIONS: ASIA AND PACIFIC / U.S. Foreign Broadcast Information Service – 1 – us L of C Photodup [950]
AREA EDITIONS: COMMUNIST CHINA / U.S. Foreign Broadcast Information Service – 1 – us L of C Photodup [950]
AREA EDITIONS: EASTERN EUROPE / U.S. Foreign Broadcast Information Service – 1 – us L of C Photodup [949]
AREA EDITIONS: LATIN AMERICA / U.S. Foreign Broadcast Information Service – 1 – us L of C Photodup [972]
AREA EDITIONS: MIDDLE EAST AND AFRICA / U.S. Foreign Broadcast Information Service – 1 – us L of C Photodup [956]
AREA EDITIONS: SOVIET UNION / U.S. Foreign Broadcast Information Service – 1 – us L of C Photodup [947]
AREA EDITIONS: WESTERN EUROPE / U.S. Foreign Broadcast Information Service – 1 – us L of C Photodup [940]
AREA FILE OF THE NAVAL RECORDS COLLECTION, 1775-1910 / U.S. Navy. Office of Naval Records and Library – 414 rolls. M625. Printed guide – 1 – us Nat'l Archives [355]
AREA HANDBOOK FOR ARGENTINA / Weil, Thomas E et al – [Washington: For sale by the Supt. of Docs., U.S. Govt. Print. Off.], 2nd ed 1974 – 1 – CSUXADM9553-B – us Hoover Inst Photo [972]
AREA HANDBOOK FOR LIBYA / Stanford Research Institute – Prepared for the American University. Sep 1969. Publ. Dec 1969. BNE-516 1 – 9 – ne IDC [956]
AREA SHEEP DAY / South Dakota. State University. Agricultural Experiment Station – nos.1-8. 1959-67 – 1,5,6 – us Spaulding [636]
AREA STUDIES PROGRAM / Human Relations Area Files – 1980. Five major groups: Africa; the Americas; Asia; Europe and Oceania. At least 3 modules per major group – 9 – 2050.00 each – us H.R.A.F. [301]
AREA VOCATIONAL CENTRES : A BOLD NEW VENTURE IN VOCATIONAL EDUCATION / Thailand. Ministry of Education. Department of Vocational Education – 1979 – 1mf – 9 – DE-600/1 – ne IDC [370]
AREI EREZ-YISRA'EL BA-MEAH HA-16 ALPI TE'UDOT ME-HA-ARKHIYYON HA-OTHMANI / Lewis, B – v. 5. Yerushalayim. 1955. BJ-27-60 1 – 9 – ne IDC [270]
Areilza, Jose Maria de *see*
- DIARIO DE UN MINISTRO DE LA MONARQUIA
- MEMORIAS EXTERIORES, 1947-1964

ARELATENSIS EPISCOPUS, REGULA SANCTARUM VIRGINUM ALIAQUE OPUSCULA AD SANCTIMONIALES DIRECTA / Caesarius, S – Bonn, 1933 – 2mf – 8 – ne Slangenburg [240]
THE ARENA – 1889-1909 – 1 – us UMI [073]
THE ARENA – v.1-41. Dec 1889-Aug 1909 – 1 – 325.00 – us L of C Photodup [073]
Arena, Antonius *see* ...BASSAS DANSAS... AUGMENTATUS..
Arena, O *see* PER IL DOMINIO DEL MARE
Arenal de Garcia Carrasco, Concepcion *see* OBRAS COMPLETAS
Arenas, A Diaz *see* METHODS OF COMPUTATION OF LOW STREAMFLOW
Arenas Lopez, Anselmo *see*
- CURSO DE HISTORIA DE ESPANA
- CURSO DE HISTORIA DE ESPANA. TOMO 1
- CURSO DE HISTORIA GENERAL
- LA LUSITANIA CELTIBERICA
- PROGRAMA DE EXAMEN DE GEOGRAFIA
- RESUMEN DE GEOGRAFIA

- RESUMEN DE HISTORIA DE ESPANA
ARENDA TORGOVYKH PREDPRIIATII / Alfeevskii, S A – Moskva: Vseros. k-ta pomoshchi invalidam vo iny pri VT SIK Sovetov, 1923 – 1 – CSUX91-B1986 – us Hoover Inst Photo [947]
Arendt, Erich *see* HEROES: NARRACIONES PARA SOLDADOS
ARENT DE GELDER, SEIN LEBEN UND SEINE KUNST / Lilienfeld, Karl – O 518d. 1914 – 9 – ne IDC [920]
Arenz, Karl *see* DIE ENTDECKUNGSREISEN IN NORD- UND MITTEL-AFRIKA VON RICHARDSON, OVERWEG, BARTH UND VOGEL
L'AREOPAGE / Cuthbert, Ross – Quebec: J. Neilson, 1803. SEM16P19 – 1r – 5 – Can$9.00 – cn Bibl Nat [810]
Areschoug, J E *see*
- ICONOGRAPHIA PHYCOLOGICA SEU PHYCEARUM NOVARUM ET RARIORUM
- PHYCEAE CAPENSES
- PHYCEAE NOVAE ET MINUS COGNITAE IN MARIBUS EXTRAEUROPAEIS COLLECTAE
- PHYCEAE SCANDINAVICAE MARINAE SIVE FUCACEARUM
Aresi, P *see* DELLE IMPRESE SACRE. CON UTILI E DILETTEUOLI DISCORSI ACCOMPAGNATE LIBRO PRIMA
Aretin, C M von *see* BAYERNS AUSWAERTIGE VERHAELTNISSE...
ARETINO; ODER DIALOG UEBER MALEREI VON LODOVICO DOLCE. NACH DER AUSGABE VOM JAHRE 1557 AUS DEM ITALIENISCHEN UEBERSETZT VON CAJETAN CERRI / ed by Eitelberger von Edelberg, R – (Quellenschriften fuer Kunstgeschichte. v2. Wien, 1871). BO-517b 1 – 9 – ne IDC [700]
Aretinus, L *see*
- BELLUM PUNICUM, ETC
- ORATIONES
Aretinus, L et al *see* OPUSCULA, ETC
ARETS HOGTIDER – 1938 – 1 – us I.U. Libraries [390]
Arevalo, Faustino *see*
- CAELII SEDULII OPERA
- DRACONTI CARMINA
- HYMNODIA HISPANICA
- IUVENCI CARMINA
- M.AURELI CLEMENTIS PRUDENTI CARMINA
- M.AURELIO CLEMENTIS PRUDENTI CARMINA
- OPERA OMNIA...RECENSENTE
Arevalo, Rafael *see* DERECHO PENAL ISLAMICO, ESCUELA MALEKITA
AREX. DECLARACION PROGRAMATICA / Accion Regional Extremena – Caceres: Tip. Extremadura, 1977 – 1 – sp Bibl Santa Ana [946]
Arfe y Villafane, J *see* DE VARIA COMMESURACION PARA LA ESCULPTURA Y ARCHITECTURA
Argenson, Marquis *see* NOTICES SUR LES OEUVRES DE THEATRE
ARGENTERIE ORIENTALE / Smirnov, P – St. Petersburg, 1909 – 1 – uk Microform Academic [740]
L'ARGENTEUIL – Lachute, Canada. 13 mar 1952-31 jul 1992 – 33r – 1 – Can$70.00r – cn Can Microfilming [072]
ARGENTEUIL COUNTY NEWS – Lachute, Canada. v1 n17. 28 mar 1896-v1 n31. 4 jul 1896 – 1r – 1 – Can$25.00 – cn Can Microfilming [072]
ARGENTINA : DE FACTORIA AGROPECUARIA A NEODEPENDENCIA INDUSTRIAL / Aldao, Andres – [Buenos Aires]: Ediciones America, [1st ed 1971] – 1 – CSUXADJ0114-B – us Hoover Inst Photo [338]
ARGENTINA : ESTADO Y LIBERACION NACIONAL / Ceresole, Norberto – Buenos Aires: Organizacion Editorial, [1971] – 1 – CSUXAHZ2610-B – us Hoover Inst Photo [320]
ARGENTINA : EL PERONISMO / Barletta, Rafael – Caracas: Barbara, 1973 – 1 – CSUXADJ3721-B – us Hoover Inst Photo [320]
ARGENTINA : SU DESARROLLO CAPITALISTA / Fuchs, Jaime – [Buenos Aires]: Editorial Cartago, [1965] – 1 – CSUXADJ1079-B – us Hoover Inst Photo [330]
ARGENTINA : TIEMPO DE VIOLENCIA / Gonzalez Trejo, Horacio – [Buenos Aires]: C. Perez, [1969] – 1 – CSUXADJ0202-B – us Hoover Inst Photo [360]
ARGENTINA / Whitaker, Arthur Preston – Englewood Cliffs, N.J.: Prentice-Hall, [1964] – 1 – CSUXAGP8623-B – us Hoover Inst Photo [972]
LA ARGENTINA : INTRODUCCION HISTORICA A SUS PROBLEMAS ACTUALES / Ferns, Henry Stanley – Buenos Aires: Editorial Sudamericana, 2nd ed 1973 – 1 – CSUXADP4617-B – us Hoover Inst Photo [360]
ARGENTINA, 20 [I.E. VEINTE] ANOS DE LUCHAS PERONISTAS / Gonzalez Janzen, I – Mexico: Ediciones de la Patria Grande, 1st ed c1975 – 1 – CSUXADJ1077-B – us Hoover Inst Photo [320]
ARGENTINA, 1918-41 : REPORTS / U.S. Military Intelligence – 4 reels with printed guide – 1 – $420.00 – us UPA [355]
ARGENTINA, 1943-1976 : THE NATIONAL REVOLUTION AND RESISTANCE / Hodges, Donald Clark – Albuquerque: University of New Mexico Press, c1976 – 1 – CSUXADH8453-B – us Hoover Inst Photo [320]
ARGENTINA, 1946-1978 : COMO SE DESTROZA UNA ECONOMIA! / Beveraggi Allende, Walter Manuel – [Buenos Aires]: Confederacion Nacionalista Argentina, c1979 – 1 – CSUXAJA7298-B – us Hoover Inst Photo [320]
Argentina. Comision Nacional de Investigaciones *see* DOCUMENTACION, AUTORES Y COMPLICES DE LAS IRREGULARIDADES COMETIDAS DURANTE LA SEGUNDA TIRANIA
Argentina. Congreso de la Nacion. Camara de Diputados de la Nacion *see*
- EL DEBATE SOBRE LA ENSENANZA RELIGIOSA
- DIGESTO CONSTITUCIONAL DE LA NACION ARGENTINA
- EL PARLAMENTO ARGENTINO, 1854-1947
Argentina. Congreso de la Nacion et al *see* INFORME
Argentina. Congreso de la Nacion. Senado de la Nacion *see* LAS MALVINAS HANSIDO, SON Y SER AN ARGENTINAS
Argentina. Convencion Nacional Constituyente *see* DIARIO DE SESIONES
LA ARGENTINA DE AYER Y DE HOY / Benitez, Hernan – Buenos Aires, 1950 – 1 – CSUXADH2107-B – us Hoover Inst Photo [972]
Argentina Departamento Nacioanl de Agricultura *see* INFORME DEL DEPARTAMENTO NACIONAL DE AGRICULTURA
Argentina. Direccion General de Relaciones Culturales y Difusion *see*
- BUENOS AIRES EN CIFRAS
- COMO SE EDUCA UN NINO EN LA ARGENTINA
- CULTURA PARA EL PUEBLO
- LA FUNCION DEL CAPITAL EN EL JUSTICIALISMO
- LA INDUSTRIA EN LA ARGENTINA
- A JUSTICA SOCIAL E FEITA PELO POVO
- LA JUSTICE SOCIALE EST LA PIERRE ANGULAIRE DU JUSTICIALISME
- LA JUSTICIA SOCIAL ES REALIZADA POR EL PUEBLO
- EL PETROLEO EN LA ARGENTINA
- LA PROTECTION DU SAVANT ET DE L'ARTISTE
- LA VIVIENDA PROPIA, REALIDAD ARGENTINA
- LA VOLUNTAD POPULAR HACE SOBERANAS A LAS NACIONES
- WHAT IS JUSTICIALISM?
Argentina. Direccion General del Gas del Estado *see* EL GASODUCTO PRESIDENTE PERON A TRAVES DEL PERIODISMO NACIONAL Y EXTRANJERO
ARGENTINA ECONOMICA Y SOCIAL / Isacovich, Marcelo – 2 ed corr y actualizada. Buenos Aires: Editorial Quipo, 1965 – 9 – us Hoover Inst Photo [972]
ARGENTINA EN LA POST GUERRA / Cristia, Pedro Jet al – Rosario: Editorial Rosario S.A., 1946 – 1 – CSUXADH9067-B – us Hoover Inst Photo [972]
ARGENTINA EN MARCHA / Argentine Republic. Comision Nacional de Cooperacion Intelectual – Buenos Aires, [1947- – 1 – CSUXADM9532-B – us Hoover Inst Photo [972]
ARGENTINA ENVENTA : LA DESINTEGRACION DE ESTADO LIBERAL / Antonio, Jorge – [Buenos Aires]: Editorial Jorge Alverez, [1968] – 1 – CSUXAJA7177-B – us Hoover Inst Photo [320]
ARGENTINA HOY : CAPITALISMO DEPENDIENTE Y ESTRUCTURA DE CLASES / Gastiazoro, Eugenio – [Buenos Aires]: Emece, [2nd ed 1973] – 1 – CSUXAHZ2024-B – us Hoover Inst Photo [972]
ARGENTINA, HOY / Rouquie, Alain – Mexico: Siglo Veintiuno Editores, 1st ed 1982 – 1 – CSUXADJ8867-B – us Hoover Inst Photo [972]
ARGENTINA IN THE TWENTIETH CENTURY / ed by Rock, David – [Pittsburgh]: University of Pittsburgh Press, 1975 – 1 – CSUXAJA7314-B – us Hoover Inst Photo [972]
Argentina. Instituto Nacional de Prevision Social *see* BOLETIN INTERNO
A ARGENTINA JUSTICIALISTA E O MUNDO – [Buenos Aires?, 1950?] – 1 – CSUXAJA7446-B – us Hoover Inst Photo [360]
ARGENTINA LIBRE – (Includes c.1: v.8:no.289 1947:Aug. 7,; v.8:no.296 1947:Oct. 2-v.9:no.297 (1947:Oct. 9)) – 1 – CSUXAJB7782-S – us Hoover Inst Photo [972]
Argentina. Ministerio de Asistencia Social y Salud Publica *see* 2ND [I.E. SEGUNDO] PLAN QUINQUENAL
Argentina. Ministerio de Cultura y Educacion. Departamento de Estadistica *see* EGRESADOS
Argentina. Ministerio de Educacion y Justicia. Departamento de Estadistica *see* EDUCACION SUPERIOR UNIVERSITARIA
Argentina. Ministerio de Educacion y JusticiaUniversidad Nacional Cordoba *see* LA REFORMA UNIVERSITARIA 1918-1988
Argentina. Ministerio de Hacienda de la Nacion *see* MENSAJE DEL PODER EJECUTIVO E INFORME DEL MINISTERIO DE HACIENDA
Argentina. Ministerio de Obras Publicas *see* LABOR REALIZADA Y EN EJECUCION, BREVE RESENA
Argentina. Ministerio de Relaciones Exteriores y Culto *see*
- LA REPUBLICA ARGENTINA ANTE EL "LIBRO AZUL"
- TRES DISCURSOS DEL MINISTRO DE RELACIONES EXTERIORES Y CULTO DE LA REPUBLICA ARGENTINA, JUAN I. COOKE, SOBRE ASPECTOS DE LA POLITICA EXTERIOR DEL PAIS
ARGENTINA. NO. 1 (1945) : A BRIEF SUMMARY OF OFFICIAL DOCUMENTS, REVEALING THE FASCIST NATURE OF THE ARGENTINE STATE, ITS MENACE TO THE WAR AGAINST JAPAN, TO HEMISPHERE SECURITY AND WORLD PEACE / SUBMITTED TO THE COUNCIL FOR PAN AMERICAN DEMOCRACY – (To be purchased directly from the Council for Pan American Democracy) – New York, [1945] – 1 – CSUXADP7797-B – us Hoover Inst Photo [320]
LA ARGENTINA, PERON Y DESPUES / Cordoba, Tomas – Buenos Aires: Editorial Los Andes, 2nd ed 1976 – 1 – CSUXADQ2772-B – us Hoover Inst Photo [320]
Argentina. Presidencia. Subsecretaria de Informaciones *see*
- 17 DE OCTUBRE DE 1945 Y SUS EVOCACIONES EN LOS ANOS 1946, 1947, 1948, 1949 Y 1950
- LA EDUCACION PERONISTA A TRAVES DEL PENSAMIENTO DE PERON
- UNA NACION RECOBRADA
- NOBLE DEPOSITARIO DE UNA HERENCIA DE AMOR
- RESENA BIOGRAFICA DEL GENERAL JUAN PERON, PRESIDENTE DE LA NACION ARGENTINA
- EL SINDICALISMO JUSTICIALISTA A TRAVES DEL PENSAMIENTO DE PERON
Argentina. Secretaria de Industria y Comercio *see*
- ARGENTINA, TIERRA DE PAZ Y DE TRABAJO
- YACIMIENTOS PETROLIFEROS FISCALES
Argentina. Secretaria de Prensa *see*
- CONFRATERNIDAD PARAGUAYO ARGENTINA
- PERON Y EL DEPORTE
ARGENTINA, SOCIEDAD DE MASAS / Tell, Torcuato S di et al – [Buenos Aires]: Editorial Universitaria de Buenos Aires, [1965] – 1 – CSUXAHZ5808-B – us Hoover Inst Photo [972]
Argentina. Suprema Corte *see* SENTENCIA DE LA SUPREMA CORTE DE JUSTICIA DE LA NACION SOBRE LOS BIENES MAL HABIDOS DEL DICTADOR
ARGENTINA, THE LIFE STORY OF A NATION / White, John W – New York: The Viking press, 1942 – 1 – CSUXADN0117-B – us Hoover Inst Photo [972]
ARGENTINA, THE PERONIST MYTH : AN ESSAY ON THE CULTURAL DECAY IN ARGENTINA AFTER THE SECOND WORLD WAR / Aizcorbe, Roberto – Hicksville, N.Y.: Exposition Press, [1975] – 1 – CSUXADQ6601-B – us Hoover Inst Photo [306]
Argentina, Thomas d' *see* SCRIPTA SUPER 4 LIBROS SENTENTIARUM
ARGENTINA, TIERRA DE PAZ Y DE TRABAJO : PAIS SIN FRONTERAS ESPIRITUALES, ABIERTA GENEROSAMENTE A TODOS LOS HOMBRES QUE QUIERAN HABITARLA, EN OCASION DEL CUARTO CENTENARIO DE LA CIUDAD DE LA PAZ Y, CON MOTIVO DE LA EXPOSICION-FERIA INTERNACIONAL... OCTUBRE DE 1948 / Argentina. Secretaria de Industria y Comercio – [Buenos Aires, 1948] – 1 – CSUXADJ8014-B – us Hoover Inst Photo [331]
ARGENTINA UNDER PERON, 1973-76 : THE NATION'S EXPERIENCE WITH A LABOUR-BASED GOVERNMENT / Di Tella, Guido – New York: St. Martin's Press, 1983 – 1 – CSUXAJA7914-B – us Hoover Inst Photo [320]
ARGENTINA UNDER PERON, 1973-76. SPANISH PERON-PERON, 1973-1976 / Di Tella, Guido – Buenos Aires: Editorial Sudamericana, 1983 – 1 – CSUXADH8381-B – us Hoover Inst Photo [320]
ARGENTINA Y CONQUISTA DEL RIO DE LA PLATA CON OTROS ACAE CIMIENTOS DE LOS REINOS DEL PERU. TUCUMAN Y ESTADO DE BRASIL. NOTAS BIBLIOGRAFICAS Y BIOGRAFICAS DE CARLOS NAVARRO Y LAMARCA / Barco Centenera, Arcediano – Buenos Aires: Angel Estrada. Cia. Edit., 1912 – sp Bibl Santa Ana [946]
ARGENTINA Y LA U.R.S.S. / ed by Instituto Cultural Argentino-Ruso – Buenos Aires: Editorial Eslava, 1948 – 1 – CSUXAGP8417-B – us Hoover Inst Photo [337]
ARGENTINA Y SU SOMBRA / Guevara, Juan Francisco – [Buenos Aires, 1970] – 1 – CSUXADJ1061-B – us Hoover Inst Photo [972]
ARGENTINA...Y CONQUISTA DEL RIO DE LA PLATA CON OTROS ACAECIMIENTOS DE LOS REYNOS... / Barco de Centenera, M – Liboa, 1602 – 8mf – 9 – sp Cultura [972]
L'ARGENTINE DE PERON / Duquenne, Lucien & Biondini, Pierre – [Bordeaux, 1954] – 1 – CSUXADJ1860-B – us Hoover Inst Photo [320]
ARGENTINE DIARY : THE INSIDE STORY OF THE COMING OF FASCISM / Josephs, Ray – New York: Random House, [1944] – 1 – CSUXADH3574-B – us Hoover Inst Photo [320]
ARGENTINE ORNITHOLOGY / Sclater, P L & Hudson, W H – Z 1920. 2 v. 1888-1889 – 9 – ne IDC [590]
THE ARGENTINE REGIME : FACTS AND RECOMMENDATIONS TO THE UNITED NATIONS ORGANIZATION / Congress of Industrial Organizations. Committee on Latin American Affairs – [New York]: Committee on Latin American Affairs, Congress of Industrial Organizations, 1946 – 1 – CSUXADQ2807-B – us Hoover Inst Photo [320]
ARGENTINE REPUBLIC : ANUARIO DE LA DIRECCION GENERAL DE ESTADISTICA 1892-1914 / Argentine Republic. Direccion General de Estadistica – (Coll title: Latin American and Caribbean Official Statistical Serials, 1821-1982) – 215mf – 9 – £5.00f (set £1,440.00 274mf) – uk Chadwyck [972]
ARGENTINE REPUBLIC : ANUARIO ESTADISTICO 1944-1957 / Argentine Republic. Direccion Nacional de Estadistica y Censos – (1951-56 not publ. Coll title: Latin American and Caribbean Official Statistical Serials, 1821-1982) – 52mf – 9 – £5.00f (set £1,440.00 274mf) – uk Chadwyck [972]
ARGENTINE REPUBLIC : CONVENCI ON NACIONAL CONSTITUYENTE, 1949. CONSTITUCION NACIONAL JUSTICIALISTA / Convencion Nacional Constituyente – Buenos Aires: Ministerio de Educacion de la Nacion, 1953 – 1 – CSUXAHZ6016-B – us Hoover Inst Photo [340]
ARGENTINE REPUBLIC : EXTRACTO ESTADISTICO DE LA REPUBLICA ARGENTINA 1915 / Argentine Republic. Direccion General de Estadistica – (Coll title: Latin American and Caribbean Official Statistical Serials,

1821-1982) – 7mf – 9 – £7.00f (set £1,440.00 274mf) – uk Chadwyck [972]
Argentine Republic *see*
- BOLETIN OFICIAL
- BUDGET AND DEVELOPMENT PLANS
- INFORMES DE LOS CONSEJEROS LEGALES DEL PODER EJECUTIVO
- PLAN DE GOBIERNO, 1947-1951
- REGISTRO NACIONAL.
- REGISTRO NACIONAL...QUE COMPRENDE LOS DOCUMENTOS DESDE 1810 HASTA 1891

THE ARGENTINE REPUBLIC / Rennie, Ysabel (Fisk) – New York: The Macmillan company, 1945 – 1 – CSUXADH7696-B – us Hoover Inst Photo [972]
Argentine Republic. Comision Nacional de Cooperacion Intelectual *see* ARGENTINA EN MARCHA
Argentine Republic. Comision Nacional de Investigaciones *see* LIBRO NEGRO DE LA SEGUNDA TIRANIA
Argentine Republic. Comision Nacional del Antartico *see*
- LAS ISLAS MALVINAS Y EL SECTOR ANTARTICO ARGENTINO
- SOBERANIA ARGENTINA EN LA ANTARTIDA

Argentine Republic. Consejo Nacional de Desarrollo *see* PLAN NACIONAL DE DESARROLLO, 1965-1969
Argentine Republic. Consejo nacional de postguerra *see* ORDENAMIENTO ECONOMICO-SOCIAL
Argentine Republic. Contaduria General de la Nacion *see* MEMORIA
Argentine Republic. Corte Suprema de Justicia de la Nacion *see* FALLOS...: CON LA RELACION DE SUS RESPECTIVAS CAUSAS
Argentine Republic. Courts *see* BOLETIN JUDICIAL DE LA REPUBLICA ARGENTINA
Argentine Republic. Direccion de Economica Rural y Estadistica *see* DATOS ESTADISTICOS
Argentine Republic. Direccion General de Estadistica *see*
- ARGENTINE REPUBLIC

Argentine Republic. Direccion general de ferrocarriles *see* ESTADISTICA DE LOS FERROCARRILES EN EXPLOITACION
Argentine Republic. Direccion Nacional de Estadistica y Censos *see* ARGENTINE REPUBLIC
Argentine Republic. Junta de Administracion del Credito Publico Nacional *see* INFORME DEL PRESIDENTE DEL CREDITO PUBLICO NACIONAL PEDRO AGOTE SOBRE LE DEUDO PUBLICA
Argentine Republic. Laws, Statutes, etc *see*
- COLECCION COMPLETA DE LEYES NACIONALES SANCIONADAS POR EL HONORABLE CONGRESO
- LEYES NACIONALES SANCIONADAS EN EL PERIODO LEJISLATIVO DE 1883-

Argentine Republic. Ministerio de Agricultura y Ganaderia. Departamento de Bibliotecas *see* CATALOGO CENTRALIZADO DE LA BIBLIOTECA JUSTICIALISTA
Argentine Republic. Poder Ejecutivo Nacional *see* PLAN TRIENAL PARA LA RECONSTRUCCION Y LA LIBERACION NACIONAL 1974-1977
Argentine Republic. Presidencia. Coordinacion de Informaciones de Estado. Departamento "Psicologico." *see* BOLETIN DE PRENSA
Argentine Republic. Presidencia de la Nacion *see* PLAN DE GOBIERNO, 1947-1951
Argentine Republic. Presidencia. Subsecretaria de Informaciones *see*
- AYUDA MEMORIA REFERENTE A LA ORIENTACION POLITICA DEL GOBIERNO
- PERON EN 6 [I.E. SEIS] ANOS HISTORICOS
- PERON-IBANEZ
- QUE ES UN PLAN QUINQUENAL?
- LA REFORMA DE LA CONSTITUCION NACIONAL

Argentine Republic. Presidente, 1932-38 (Justo) *see* PODER EJECUTIVO NACIONAL PERIODO 1932-38
Argentine Republic. Presidente. Subsecretaria de Informaciones *see* 20 [I.E. SEGUNDO] PLAN QUINQUENAL
Argentine Republic. Secretaria de Asuntos Economicos *see* PRODUCTO E INGRESO DE LA REPUBLICA ARGENTINA EN EL PERIODO 1935-54
Argentine Republic. Secretaria de Comunicaciones *see* BOLETIN
Argentine Republic. Secretaria de Prensa *see* PERSPECTIVAS HUMANAS DE LA TERCERA POSICION
Argentine Republic. Secretaria de Prensa y Difusion *see* 20. [I.E. SEGUNDO] PLAN QUINQUENAL DE LA NACION
Argentine Republic. Secretaria de Trabajo y PrevisionInstituto Nacional de Prevision Social *see* BOLETIN MENSUAL
Argentine Republic. Secretaria del Consejo Nacional de Desarrollo. Consejo Federal de Inversiones *see* PLAN DE ACCION 1970
Argentine Republic. Servicio International Publicaciones Argentinas *see* SINTESIS HISTORICA DE LA POLITICA ARGENTINA
Argentine Republic. Subsecretaria de Informaciones *see* 2 PLAN QUINQUENAL
ARGENTINE, REVOLUTION ET CONTRE-REVOLUTIONS / Geze, Francois & Labrousse, Alain – Paris: Editions du Seuil, c1975 – 1 – CSUXAHZ2517-B – us Hoover Inst Photo [320]
ARGENTINE RIDDLE / Weil, Felix Jose – New York: The John Day Company, [1944] – 1 – CSUXADH3649-B – us Hoover Inst Photo [330]
ARGENTINE UPHEAVAL : PERON'S FALL AND THE NEW REGIME / Whitaker, Arthur Preston – New York: Praeger, [1956] – 1 – CSUXADH5432-B – us Hoover Inst Photo [320]
ARGENTINE WEEKLY – Buenos Aires, Jun 1923-Jun 1932 – 18r – 1 – uk British Libr Newspaper [072]
ARGENTINER MAGAZIN – Buenos Aires. v. 3-23. 1937-1957. Incomplete – 1 – us NY Public [073]
ARGENTINER TSIKO BLETER = ARGENTINE LITTERARY NOTES – (In Yiddish) – Buenos Aires, AG. v2 no7. Mar 1941- – 1r – 1 – $25.00 – cn Can Microfilming [072]
ARGENTINISCHES TAGEBLATT – Buenos Aires. Diario Argentino.1972-84 – 1 – gw Mikrofilm [072]
ARGENTINISCHES TAGEBLATT : DIARIO ARGENTINO – Buenos Aires, 1972- – 1 – Inquire at Mikrofilmarchiv for details – gw Misc Inst [072]
ARGENTORES: REVISTA TEATRAL – Buenos Aires. v1-31. Apr 1934-15 Aug 1946 – 1 – 115.00 – us L of C Photodup [790]
THE ARGO – West Union. Iowa. 1885-88; 1893-1902;1904-1910 – 1 – us UMI [071]
ARGONAUT – San Francisco CA. Jan 12 1878 – 1 – us U.O. Library [071]
O ARGONAUTA : PRO SERRO – Serro, 1 Nov 1921 – 1,5,6 – bl Biblioteca [072]
LOS ARGONAUTAS INGLESES DE ULTIMA HORA / Bayle, Constantino – Madrid: Razon y Fe, 1928 – 9 – sp Bibl Santa Ana [999]
LES ARGONAUTES – Paris. avr 1908-10 – 1 – fr A.C.R.P.P. [073]
DAS ARGON-RESONANZKONTINUUM IM VAKUUM-ULTRAVIOLETTEN SPEKTRALBEREICH ZWISCHEN 50 MM UND 78.7NM / Trommer, Gert F – 1995 – 2mf – 9 – DM80.00 – 3-8267-2159-4 – gw Hänsel [621]
ARGOS – Manaos, Amazonas. 21 Abr 1872 – 1,5,6 – bl Biblioteca [072]
O ARGOS – Cuiaba, 13 Jan, Apr, 18 Jul 1882 – 1,5,6 – bl Biblioteca [072]
O ARGOS : JORNAL DEMOCRATA – '(s.l.')-Sao Luis, Brazil. 16 Jul, 7-25 Sept 1897 – 1,5,6 – bl Biblioteca [072]
O ARGOS ALAGOANO – Maceio, Alagoas. 22 Jan 1852 – 1,5,6 – bl Biblioteca [072]
O ARGOS CACHOEIRANO : PERIODICO POLITICO, LITTERARIO E MORAL – Cachoeira, BA. 7 Set 1850-20 Dez 1851 – 1,5,6 – bl Biblioteca [072]
O ARGOS DA LEI – '(s.l.')-Sao Luis, Brazil. 7 Jan-10 Jul 1825 – 1,5,6 – bl Biblioteca [072]
O ARGOS SANT'AMARENSE – Santo Amaro, BA. 8 Dez 1850-6 Nov 1851 – 1,5,6 – bl Biblioteca [072]
ARGOSY – (1973-79. 5,6. 1977-79. 9) – 1882-1979 – 1 – us UMI [910]
ARGOSY – Ansley, NE. -w. Mar. 1887-Jun. 1896. Incomplete; Jul. 1896-Feb. 1905; Apr. 1905-Jul. 1914 – 1 – us NE Hist [071]
ARGOSY – Argonia. Kan. 1913-1974 – 1 – us UMI [071]
ARGOSY – London. v1-75. 1865-1901 – 12r – 1 – us Ross [830]
ARGOSY – New York. 1882-1905. (Scattered issues lacking) – 1 – 380.00 – us L of C Photodup [073]
ARGOSY ALL-STORY WEEKLY *see* ALL-STORY COMBINED WITH MUNSEY'S
THE ARGOSY. (WEEKLY ARGOSY) – Georgetown, Guyana. Jan 1887-Oct 1908.-w. 28 reels – 1 – uk British Libr Newspaper [072]
Arguello Castrillo, A *see*
- DISCURSO SOBRE EL CHARLATANISMO MEDICO Y QUIRURGICO...
- DISERTACION CHIRURGICA RELATIVA AL GOBIERNO POLITICO EN LA QUE SE PROPONEN LOS DANOS DE LA CASTRACION VULGAR SEGUN SE PRACTICA PARA CURAR NINOS QUEBRADOS
- METHODO EXEMPLAR DEL DOCTOR MEJANO PARA EL ESTUDIO DE LA MEDICINA...

DAS ARGUMENT – v. 1-13. Karlsruhe. 1959-71; Index, v. 1-11. 1959-69. Lacking: 1963, v. 5. BH-1804 1 – 9 – ne IDC [300]
THE ARGUMENT : A PRIORI, FOR THE BEING AND THE ATTRIBUTES OF THE LORD GOD, THE ABSOLUTE ONE, AND FIRST CAUSE / Gillespie, William Honyman – 6th ed. Edinburgh: T & T Clark, 1906 – 1mf – 9 – 0-8370-3288-1 – 1985-1288 – us A.T.L.A. [210]
THE ARGUMENT FROM PROPHECY / Maitland, Brownlow – 1877 – 9 – us A.T.L.A. [240]
THE ARGUMENT OF THE BOOK OF JOB UNFOLDED / Green, William Henry – New York: Robert Carter, 1874, c1873 – 1mf – 9 – 0-8370-9388-0 – 1986-3388 – us A.T.L.A. [220]
ARGUMENT OF THE REV. HENRY PRESERVED SMITH BEFORE THE PRESBYTERY OF CINCINNATI / Smith, Henry Preserved – Cincinnati: R. Clarke, 1892 – 1mf – us A.T.L.A. [240]
ARGUMENTATION AND ADVOCACY *see* JOURNAL OF THE AMERICAN FORENSIC ASSOCIATION
ARGUMENTO DE LA NUEVA ESPANA / Falange Espanola Tradicionalista y de las Juntas Ofensivas Nacional-Sindicalistas – n.p. 1937? Fiche W 869. (Blodgett Collection of Spanish Civil War Pamphlets) – 9 – us H.U. College Libr [946]
EL ARGUMENTO DE UN DRAMA / Hurtado, Antonio – 1867 – 9 – 1.50f – sp Bibl Santa Ana [830]
ARGUMENTS – no. 1-27 28. Paris. 1957-62. mq no. 16 – 1 – fr A.C.R.P.P. [073]
ARGUMENTS FOR AND AGAINST A BAPTIST THEOLOGICAL SCHOOL AT WILLIAMSBURG, VA / Jones, Scervant – 1837 – 1 – 5.00 – us Baptist [240]
ARGUMENTY I FACTY – 1 – sz Infoprint [947]
ARGUMENTY I FAKTY – (Backfile, through 1998 $85.00r) – [Russia], 1999- – 2r per y – 1 – $160.00 standing order – us Ross [320]
Argunov, Andrei Aleksandrovich *see* MEZHDU DVUMI A BOLSHEVIZMAMI
L'ARGUS : JOURNAL ELECTRONIQUE / ed by Duvernay, Ludger – Trois-Rivieres, Canada. 30 aut 1826-11 mar 1828 – 1r – 1 – Can$30.00 – cn Can Microfilming [073]
L'ARGUS / ed by Villecourt, R – Montreal, Canada. v2 n1. 6 jun 1907-v3 n8. 20 fev 1908 – 1r – 1 – Can$50.00 – cn Can Microfilming [072]
ARGUS – Adin, CA. 1882-1883; Jan 1887; Jan-Dec 1894; 1894-1915; 1934-1947 – 6r – 1 – $300.00 – B02001 – us Library Micro [071]
ARGUS – Albany. N.Y. 1813-1865 – 1 – us UMI [071]
ARGUS – Albion. Neb. 1880-81; 1887-88; 1896-1948 – 1 – us UMI [071]
ARGUS – Auburn. Wash. 1907-1913 – 1 – us UMI [071]
ARGUS / Corporation des Bibliothecaires Professionnels du QuebecCorporation of Professional Librarians of Quebec – Montreal: la Corporation, 1966-. SEM16P290 – 2r – 5 – Can$55.00 – cn Bibl Nat [073]
ARGUS – Easton. Pa. -w. 1853-1909 – 1 – us UMI [071]
ARGUS – Huntingburg. Ind. 1881-1901; 1905-1906; 1909-1913; 1915-1923; 1927-1952 – 1 – us UMI [071]
ARGUS – London, UK. 30 Jun-26 Jul 1828 – 24ft – 1 – uk British Libr Newspaper [072]
ARGUS – Melbourne, 1846-1957 – 465r – 1 – at Pascoe [072]
ARGUS – Middletown. N.Y. 1876-1918 – 1 – us UMI [071]
ARGUS – Mount Vernon. Wash. -w. 1891-1960 – 1 – us UMI [071]
ARGUS – New Philadelphia. Ohio. 1883-1885 – 1 – us UMI [071]
ARGUS – Petaluma, CA. 1861-64 – 1 – us UMI [071]
ARGUS – Racine, WI. 1880 – 1 – us UMI [071]
ARGUS – Rock Island. Ill. 1865- – 1 – us UMI [071]
ARGUS – Rock Island. Ill. and Daily Union. 1920-23 – 1 – us UMI [071]
ARGUS – Rock Island. Ill. -w. 1867-1912 – 1 – us UMI [071]
ARGUS – Seattle. Wash. 1941-1942 – 1 – us UMI [071]
ARGUS – South Sioux City, NE. -w. Nov 1891-Sep 1902, scattered issues missing – 1 – us NE Hist [071]
ARGUS – St. Louis, MO. -w. 1954-82 – 1 – us UMI [071]
ARGUS – Table Rock. Neb. 1883-1966 – 1 – us UMI [071]
ARGUS – "Vse vizhu." Ezhemesiachnyi literaturno-khudozestvennyi zhurnal. St. Petersburg, 1913-18. v.1-22. B-1216 2 – 8 – ne IDC [460]
ARGUS – Yates Center. Kansas. 1882-1885 – 1 – us UMI [071]
THE ARGUS – (Age and Argus. 1844-45) – Liverpool. England. -w. Oct 1876-Oct 1880 – 4r – 1 – uk British Libr Newspaper [072]
THE ARGUS / ed by Dalby, Henry – Montreal, Canada. 8 oct 1904-v2 n39. 30 jun 1906 – 1r – 1 – Can$45.00 – cn Can Microfilming [072]
THE ARGUS – (English Gentleman: 3 Jan-12 Sept 1846) – London, UK. 3 Feb 1839-12 Sept 1846 – 8r – 1 – uk British Libr Newspaper [072]
THE ARGUS – Fremont, CA. 1960-67; 1967- – 513+ r – 1 – $25,650.00 ($600.00y) – B02249 – us Library Micro [071]
THE ARGUS – Las Vegas, NV. 1927 – 1r – 1 – $50.00 – U04596 – us Library Micro [071]
THE ARGUS – Lovelock, NV. 1901; Mar-Dec 1904; Jan 105; Jan 1906 (scats) – 2r – 1 – $100.00 – U04619 – us Library Micro [071]
THE ARGUS – Melbourne, Australia. -d. Jan 1941-Dec 1952; Nov 1953-Dec 1956. 218 reels – 1 – uk British Libr Newspaper [072]
THE ARGUS – Monaghan, Ireland. -w. 15 Jan 1875-23 July 1881 (1875 very imperfect.) 2 1 2 reels – 1 – uk British Libr Newspaper [072]
THE ARGUS : ORGANE DE GEO. BROWN ET A.A. DORION – Montreal, Canada. v1 n27. 4 jan 1855-v4 n281. 29 sep 1858 – 1r – 1 – Can$37.50 – cn Can Microfilming [072]
THE ARGUS – Paris, Oct 1802-Sept 1803 – 1 – fr A.C.R.P.P. [073]
THE ARGUS *see* EASTERN ARGUS
ARGUS COURIER – Petaluma. Calif. 1918-50 – 1 – us UMI [071]
L'ARGUS DES REVUES – N.S. Paris, 1901-1914 – 72mf – 9 – H-1376/2 – ne IDC [073]
ARGUS GAZETTE – Bieber, CA. 1948-56 – 4r – 1 – $200.00 – C02061b – us Library Micro [071]
ARGUS HERALD – Sidney. Iowa. 1956-75 – 1 – us UMI [071]
L'ARGUS INDOCHINOIS – Hanoi. fevr 1922-juil 1930 – 1 – fr A.C.R.P.P. [073]
ARGUS JOURNAL – Montreal: la Corporation, 1975-85. SEM16P345 – 3r – 5 – Can$36.00 – cn Bibl Nat [073]
ARGUS LAW REPORTS – 83v. 1895-1973. High Court & Victorian Supreme Court (up to 1959) case reports – 1,9 – 660.00 – at Butterworths [340]
ARGUS LEADER – Sioux Falls. S.D. 1886- – 1 – us UMI [071]
L'ARGUS MUNICIPAL / ed by Doutre, A – Montreal, Canada. 20 fev 1873 – 1r – 1 – Can$25.00 – cn Can Microfilming [072]
ARGUS PRESS – Owosso. Mich. 1893- – 1 – us UMI [071]
ARGUTIAE JURIS CIVILIS THEORETICAE / Behamb, J F – 1679 – 1 – uk Microform Academic [340]
ARGYLE LIBERAL – Crookwell, Oct 13 1903-Dec 31 1907 – 9 – at Pascoe [072]
ARGYLESHIRE, 1837 : BRITISH ISLES CENSUS DIRECTORIES PROJECT, SCOTLAND. VOL 28 – 1mf – 9 – A$9.00 – at Vine [941]
Argyll, George Douglas Campbell *see* WHAT IS TRUTH?
Argyll, John Douglas Sutherland Campbell, Duke of *see*
- CANADIAN LIFE AND SCENERY
- CANADIAN PICTURES
- GUIDO AND LITA
- IMPERIAL FEDERATION
- MEMORIES OF CANADA AND SCOTLAND

- DER NORDWESTEN CANADAS
- A TRIP TO THE TROPICS AND HOME THROUGH AMERICA

ARGYLLSHIRE ADVERTISER – 1 – £42.00r – uk Scot News [072]

ARI – Buffalo, NY. 1972-86 – 1 – us A.J.P.C. [071]

ARI (AIR CONDITIONING AND REFRIGERATION INSTITUTE) – Standards. Printed index. Updated every 60 days – 6,9 – us Info Handling [621]

ARIADNE / Ouida – British Fiction Archive: Unit 3 – 9 – uk Bell [830]

ARIADNE AUF NAXOS : OPER IN EINEM AUFZUGE / Strauss, Richard & Hofmannsthal, Hugo von – Berlin, Paris: A Fuerstner, 1912 – 1r – 1 – us U.W. Library [780]

ARIADNE AUF NAXOS. PARTITUR MIT DEUTSCHEN TEXTE / Benda, Georg – 1785? – 9 – us Sibley [780]

ARIAH PARK NEWS – Temora, Apr 5 1923-Apr 28 1942 – 9 – at Pascoe [072]

THE ARIAN CONTROVERSY / Gwatkin, Henry Melvill – London: Longmans, Green, 1891 – 1mf – us A.T.L.A. [900]

THE ARIAN CONTROVERSY / Gwatkin, Henry Melvill – New York: Anson D.F. Randolph & Co., 1889. 176p – 1 – us U.W. Library [240]

THE ARIAN MOVEMENT IN ENGLAND / Colligan, J Hay – Manchester: University Press; New York: Longmans, Green [distributor], 1913. (Publications of the University of Manchester. Theological series; no. 2) (University of Manchester plublications; no. 74) – 1mf – us A.T.L.A. [240]

L'ARIANNA TRAGEDIA / Rinuccini, Ottavio – (Libretto.) 1622 – 9 – us Sibley [780]

THE ARIANS OF THE FOURTH CENTURY / Newman, John Henry – London: Basil Montague Pickering, 1876 – 2mf – us A.T.L.A. [240]

Arias, A *see* LECCIONES DE DERECHO MARITIMO...

Arias Corrales, Juan *see* CUATRO LEYENDAS CACERENAS

Arias de Quintanaduenas, Jacinto *see* ANTIGUEDADES Y SANTOS...DE ALCANATARA

ARIAS, DUETS, TRIOS, AND CHORUSES IN ITALIAN – London: ca 1790-1810 – 1 – us Sibley [780]

Arias, H *see* THE PANAMA CANAL

Arias, Juan *see* PRACTICAS ECLESIATICA PARA EL USO Y EJERCICIOS DE NOTARIOS PUBLICOS

ARIAS MONTANO / Vazquez, Jose Andr'es – Madrid: Biblioteca Nueva, 1943 – 1 – sp Bibl Santa Ana [780]

Arias Montano, Benito *see*
- APHORISMOS SACADOS DE LA HISTORIA DE P. C. TACITO
- BENITO ARIAS MONTANO (1527-1598)
- BIBLIA SACRA REGIA...
- COMENTARIO IN PROFETAS MIMOS
- COMMENTARIA IN DUODECIM PROPHETAS
- COMMENTARIA IN ISIAE PROPHETAE
- DAVIDIS REGIS...PSALMI
- DE OPTIMO IMPERIO SIVE JOSUAE
- DE VARIA REPUBLICA SIVE COMMENTARIA IN LIBRUM JUDICUM
- DICTATUM CHRISTIANUM
- ELUCIDATIONES IN OMNIA SANCTORUM APOSTOLORUM SCRIPTA
- ELUCIDATIONES IN QUATOR EVANGELIA METTHAEI, MARCI, LUCAE, IOHANNIS...
- HYMNI ET SAECULA
- HYMNI ET SECULA
- IN 31 DAVIDIS PSALMOS
- LIBER GENERATIONIS ET REGENERATIONIS ADAE SIVE DE HISTORIA
- MONUMENTOS SAGRADOS DE LA SALUD DEL HOMBRE
- PARAFRASIS DEL MAESTRO SOBRE EL CANTAR DE LOS CANTARES EN TONO PASTORIL
- Q. BIBLIA SACRA (REGIA). TOMO 1
- REY DE NUESTROS ESCRITURARIOS
- RHETORICORUM LIBRI 4

ARIAS MONTANO ESCRIBE A JUSTO LIPSIO Y A JUAN MORETO / Lopez de Toro, Jose – Madrid: Rev. de Archivos, Bibliotecas y Museos, 1954. pp. 533-543 – 1 – sp Bibl Santa Ana [780]

ARIAS MONTANO, HUMANISTA / Gonzalez de la Calle, Pedro Urbano – Badajoz: Imp. del Hospicio Provincial, 1928 – 1 – sp Bibl Santa Ana [946]

ARIAS MONTANO Y EL MONUMENTO AL DUQUE DE ALBA / Schubart, Herta – Madrid: Cruz y Raya, 1933 – 1 – sp Bibl Santa Ana [946]

ARIAS MONTANO Y LA POLITICA DE FELIPE 2, EN FLANDES POR LUIS MORALES... / Garcia Garcia, Rafael – Malaga: Revista Espanola de Estudios Biblicos, 1928 – 1 – sp Bibl Santa Ana [320]

ARIAS MONTANO Y LA POLITICA DE FELIPE 2ND EN FLANDES, POR LUIS MORALES OLIVER / Maura Gamazo, Gabriel – Madrid: Tip. R.Bib. Archivos y Museos, 1929 – 1 – sp Bibl Santa Ana [320]

ARIAS MONTANO Y LOS JESUITAS / Perez Goyena, A – Madrid: Estudios Biblicos, 1928 – 1 – sp Bibl Santa Ana [240]

ARIAS MONTANO Y SU TRATADO "DE OPTIMO IMPERIO" / Duran Ramas, Maria de los Angeles – Sevilla: Universidad, 1981 – 1 – sp Bibl Santa Ana [946]

Arias Regodon, Publio *see* NOVENA DE SAN GREGORIO OBISPO DE OSTIA PATRONO POPULAR DE LA VILLA DE RUANES POR...

ARID ZONE FORESTRY : A GUIDE FOR FIELD TECHNICIANS – 1989 – 150p – it F.A.O. [634]

ARID ZONE HYDROLOGY FOR AGRICULTURAL DEVELOPMENT – 1981 – 383p – it F.A.O. [630]

ARIEL / Israel. Ministry of Foreign Affairs. Cultural Relations Department – A review of the arts and sciences in Israel. Jerusalem, 1962-. Quarterly – 9 – 120.00; 8.00y – is I.T.T.I. [324]

ARIEL – Journal du monde elegant. no. 1-20. Paris. 2 mars-7 mai 1836. mq no. 17 – 5 – fr A.C.R.P.P. [073]

ARIEL – Stockholm, Moelnlycke. 1938-65 – 9 – sw Kungliga [072]

THE ARIEL – Natchez. Miss. 1825-1829 – 1 – us UMI [071]

ARIEL'S OFFENBARUNGEN / Arnim, Ludwig Achim, Freiherr von – (Includes bibliographical references) – Weimar: Gesellschaft der Bibliophilen, 1912 – 1r – 1 – us U.W. Library [830]

ARIETTE / Dugue, M, L'abbe – Paris: Fournier le jeune, 1765 – 1 – us Sibley [780]

Arif *see* DIVAN

Arif, Nail *see* EINE UNTERSUCHUNG UEBER WIRKUNGSUNTERSCHIEDE ZWISCHEN FERMENTIERTEN UND UNFERMENTIERTEM ISCADOR BEI HIV-POSITIVEN UND GESUNDEN PROBANDEN

ARIFAUNA Y FLORA. NOS COSTUMES, SUPERSTICOES E LENDAS BRASILEIRAS E AMERICANAS... / Teschaner, C – Madrid: Razon y Fe, 1926 – 1 – sp Bibl Santa Ana [580]

Arifin, Abudlrachman *see* STATE FINANCE ADMINISTRATION; FINANCE MANAGEMENT; ORGANIZATION OF SECOND-LEVEL AUTONOMOUS GOVERNMENT (BY SOEPARDI)

Arifin, Bey *see*
- DARI SUN YAT SEN KE MAO TZE TUNG
- RANGKAIAN TJERITA DALAM AL-QUR'AN

Arifin, Hassan Noel *see* POELAU DARAH

Arimami, tr *see* DILADANG; PILIHAN TJERPEN2 BULGARIA

ARINC (AERONAUTICAL RADIO INC.) – Standards. Printed index. Updated every 60 days – 6,9 – us Info Handling [621]

THE ARION: A CANADIAN JOURNAL OF ART – 1 – 45.00 – cn McLaren [700]

Ariosto, Lodovico *see* ORLANDO FURIOSO DI M. LODOVICO ARIOSTO,...

Aris, Reinhold *see* DIE STAATSLEHRE ADAM MUELLERS IN IHREM VERHAELTNIS ZUR DEUTSCHEN ROMANTIK

ARISE, O LORD / Hawkins – (Manuscript) – 171- – 1 – us Sibley [780]

ARIS'S BIRMINGHAM GAZETTE – England, 1824-30 – 2mqn r – 1 – uk British Libr Newspaper [072]

ARISTARCHI SAMII DE MUNDI SYSTEMATE, PARTIBUS ET MOTIBUS EJUSDEM LIBELLUS. ADJECTAE SUNT AE DE ROBERVAL / Roberval, Gilles de – Paris, 1644, pieces liminaires et 148 p. Histoire des Sciences XVIIe-XIXe Siecles. 7962 – 9 – fr Hachette [180]

O ARISTARCHO – Manaos, Amazonas. 25 Fev-3 Mar 1884 – 1,5,6 – bl Biblioteca [072]

ARISTARCHUS: OR A COMPENDIUS AND ROTATIONAL INSTITUTION OF THE LATIN TONGUE / Bowles, Thomas – 1748. 273p. (English Linguistics Series 1500-1800) – 9 – us UMI [450]

ARISTARCO...PADRE SAN FRANCISCO / Trujillo, Antonio de – (1685 ed.1.50f; 9) – 1683 – 9 – 1.50f – sp Bibl Santa Ana [240]

Aristeguieta Silva, F *see* ESPANA MOSCOVITA Y SUS CONSECUENCIAS

ARISTIDE BRIAND PAMPHLET COLLECTION – 19?? – 1 – CSUXANQ4935-B – us Hoover Inst Photo [331]

ARISTIDEAN – New York. v1. 1845 – 1r – 1 – us Ross [073]

Aristides *see*
- THE APOLOGY OF ARISTIDES
- SUPPLEMENTARY OBSERVATIONS UPON THE PROCEEDINGS OF THE HOUSE OF ASSEMBLY IN THIS PROVINCE

Aristizabal Llano, N *see* DOS TESIS Y UN CANAL

THE ARISTOCRACY, THE STATE AND THE LOCAL COMMUNITY – The Hastings Collection of mss. from the Huntington Library, San Marino, California. Part One: 1477-1701; Part Two: 1702-1828 – 1 – us Primary [975]

ARISTOCRATIC WOMEN: THE SOCIAL, POLITICAL AND CULTURAL HISTORY OF RICH AND POWERFUL WOMEN, PART 1 : THE CORRESPONDENCE OF JEMIMA, MARCHIONESS GREY (1722-97) AND HER CIRCLE – 1994 – 10r – 1 – $1,200.00 – uk Matthew [305]

ARISTOCRATIC WOMEN: THE SOCIAL, POLITICAL AND CULTURAL HISTORY OF RICH AND POWERFUL WOMEN, PART 2 : THE CORRESPONDENCE AND DIARIES OF CHARLOTTE GEORGIANA, LADY BEDINGFIELD (FORMERLY JERNINGHAM) C1780-1833, TOGETHER WITH THE LETTERS OF ANNA SEWARD C1791-5, AND LADY STAFFORD, C1774-1805, FROM BIRMINGHAM UNIVERSITY LIBRARY – (Includes guide) – Marlborough: Adam Matthews Publications, 1997 – 11r – 1 – $1,320.00 – uk Matthew [305]

L'ARISTOCRATIE EN AMERIQUE / Gaillardet, Frederic – Paris: E. Dentu, 1883. 04323. (Pre-1900 Canadiana) – 9 – cn C.I.H.M. [971]

LES ARISTOLOCHES / Planchon, LD – Montpellier, 1891 – 3mf – 9 – ne IDC [615]

Aristophanes *see* THE COMEDIES OF ARISTOPHANES

ARISTOPHANES' APOLOGY : INCLUDING A TRANSCRIPT FROM EURIPIDES BEING THE LAST ADVENTURE OF BALAUSTION / Browning, Robert – London: Smith, Elder, 1875 – 1 roll – 1 – 1-55879-832-3 – uk Libr Preservation [830]

ARISTOTELES : POLITICORUM LIBRI – Zaragoza, Barcelona SP. 1480? – 1,5 – sp Cultura [180]

Aristoteles *see* FILOSOFIA MORAL

ARISTOTLE : GREEK COMMENTATORS IN LATIN TRANSLATION / ed by Cress, Donald A – (Includes Alexander of Aphrodisias, Ammonius, Ps. Andronicus of Rhodes, Aspasius, Dexippus, Eustratius, Leo Magentinus, Michael of Ephesus, Nicephorus Blemmida, Olympiodorus, George Pachymeres, John Philoponus, Michael Psellus, Simplicius, Sophonius, Syrianus, Themistius. Printed guide includes complete title list and bibliography of studies on these commentators) – 110mf – 9 – $375.00 – us UMI [180]

Aristotle *see*
- DE ARTE DICENDI
- ETHICA, POLITICA, OECONOMICA
- FILOSOFIA MORAL
- METAPHYSICORUM LIBRICUM AVERROIS COMMENTARIIS ET EPITOME VENETIIS
- THE POLITICS..

Aristoxen der Juengere *see* GUETLIGE ZEUGNISSE UEBER DER JUENGSTE MATTHESONISCH-MUSICALISCHE KERN-SCHRIFT

Aristoxenes *see* ARISTOXENI ANTIQVISS, HARMONICORUM ELENTORUM LIBRI 3

ARISTOXENI ANTIQVISS, HARMONICORUM ELENTORUM LIBRI 3 / Aristoxenes – Venetijs. 1562. BP-131 1 – 9 – ne IDC [780]

THE ARISTOXENIAN THEORY OF MUSICAL RHYTHM / Williams, C F A – Cambridge University Press, 1911 – 1 – us Sibley [780]

ARITHMETIC TEACHER – (v16- . 5,6. v22- . 9) – 1- 1954- – 1 – us UMI [370]

ARITHMETIQUE: COURS ELEMENTAIRE: LIVRE DE L'ELEVE / Christian Brothers – Montreal, 1883? 04353. (Pre-1900 Canadiana) – 9 – cn C.I.H.M. [370]

ARITHMETISCHER TAUSENDKUNSTLER / Faulhaber, Johann – Ulm: Auf Kosten der Gaumischen Handlung, 1762 – 1 – us U.W. Library [510]

ARITMETICA / Santos Redondo, Ignacio – 1890 – 9 – 1.50f – sp Bibl Santa Ana [510]

ARITMETICA ELEMENTAL / Montero y Santaren, Eulogio – 1892 – 9 – 1.50f – sp Bibl Santa Ana [510]

ARITMETICA, LAS CUATRO OPERACIONES FUNDAMENTALES / Crespo, Nicasio – Badajoz: Tip. La Economica, 1905 – sp Bibl Santa Ana [510]

ARITMETICA PARA LOS ALUMNOS / Botello del Castillo, Carlos – 1880 – 9 – 1.50f – sp Bibl Santa Ana [510]

ARITMETICA Y SISTEMA LEGAL DE PESAS / Antonio y Hernandez, Pedro de A – 1891. Incompleto – 9 – 1.50f – sp Bibl Santa Ana [510]

Aritonang, M *see* LATIHAN KADER PERUSAHAAN (MANAGEMENT TRAINING)

A-RIVISTA ANARCHICA – Milan. r1-2 (feb 1971-nov 1972); r3 (dec 1972-73) – 1 – r1-2 $83.70; r3 $83.70y – D8536 – us UMI [073]

Ariza, A *see* BIBLIOGRAFIA DE LA PROVINCIA DOMINICANA DE COLOMBIA

ARIZONA : ARIZONA REVISED STATUTES ANNOTATED – St. Paul: West Pub Co, 1956-Mar 1996 – 9 – $1,575.00 set – us Hein [340]

ARIZONA : SESSION LAWS OF AMERICAN STATES AND TERRITORIES – 1864-1994 – 9 – $1,143.00 set – us Hein [340]

Arizona *see*
- MORTALITY SCHEDULES, 1870
- REPORTS AND OPINIONS (A-G)

ARIZONA ATTORNEY – (Cont: Arizona Bar Journal v1-23 1965-88) – v1-31. 1965-95 – 9 – $388.00 – us Hein [340]

ARIZONA ATTORNEY GENERAL REPORTS AND OPINIONS – (1915-1977 $70.00. 1978-1995 $287.50) – 1915-1995 – 9 – $357.50 set – us Hein [340]

ARIZONA BAPTIST BEACON – Phoenix, 1937-90 – 1 – $804.08 – us Baptist [240]

ARIZONA BAR JOURNAL *see* ARIZONA ATTORNEY

ARIZONA BUSINESS *see* AZB

ARIZONA EDUCATOR ADVOCATE – Phoenix, AZ. 1974-75 – 1r – 1 – $50.00 – R01501 – us Library Micro [071]

ARIZONA EDUCATOR ADVOCATE – v. 1-1974- – 1,5,6,9 – us UMI [370]

ARIZONA EDUCATOR ADVOCATE *see* AEA ADVOCATE

ARIZONA FARMER-STOCKMAN – (1985- . 5,6,9) – v1- . 1922- – 1 – us UMI [636]

Arizona. Fort Verde *see* HEADQUARTERS RECORDS

THE ARIZONA INDEX: A SUBJECT INDEX TO PERIODICALS ABOUT THE STATE / Arizona. University. Library – 1978.-26,300 entries 2 reels.-ISBN: 0-8161-1557-5 – 1 – $195.00 – uk Hall [073]

ARIZONA JOURNAL OF INTERNATIONAL AND COMPARATIVE LAW REVIEW – (None publ 1983, 1986) – 1982-88; v6-12. 1982-95 – 9 – $146.00 set – us Hein [340]

ARIZONA LAW REVIEW – (1976- . 9) – v. 1-. 1959- – 1 – us UMI [340]

ARIZONA MAPS 1 : CITIES AND TOWNS – 1886-1907. 350 maps. 29 towns. Sanborn Company Fire Insurance Maps – 1 – $53.00r – us Shkurkin [910]

ARIZONA MAPS 2 : CITIES AND TOWNS – 1908-1943. 720 maps. 52 towns. Sanborn Company Fire Insurance Maps – 1 – $80.00r – us Shkurkin [910]

Arizona. Presbytery (Pres. Church in the U.S.A.) *see* MINUTES, 1888-1906

ARIZONA QUARTERLY – (1971- . 5,6. 1977- . 9) – 1- 1945- – 1 – us UMI [073]

ARIZONA REPORTS – (Updates planned) – v1-21. 1866-1920 – 167mf – 9 – $565.00 – LLMC 84-123 – us L.L.M.C. [340]

Arizona. State Bar Association *see* PROCEEDINGS

ARIZONA STATE LAW JOURNAL – (1969-84 in reels $255.00. 1985-v26 1985-94 in mf $194.00. Title varies: 1969-74 as Law and the Social Order) – 1969-v26 1969-94 – 5,6,9 – $449.00 set – us Hein [340]

Arizona. State Water Commission *see* STATE WATER RESOURCES REPORTS

Arizona. Supreme Court *see* ARIZONA SUPREME COURT REPORTS

ARIZONA SUPREME COURT REPORTS / Arizona. Supreme Court – (No Pre-NRS vols. Add vols planned) – v1-20. 1866-1919 – 26mf (1:42) 53mf (1:24) – 9 – $196.00 – LLMC 84-123 – us L.L.M.C. [340]
Arizona. Territory. Board of Control *see* REPORT
Arizona. Territory. Prisons *see* BIENNIAL REPORT
ARIZONA THE YOUNGEST STATE / McClintock, James H – Prehistoric-aboriginal-pioneer-modern. Chicago: S.J. Clarke Publ. Co., 1916. Arizona Reel 1.(The Cox Library Collection) – 5 – us Americana [978]
ARIZONA TREND – v1- . 1986- – 1,5,6,9 – us UMI [073]
Arizona. University. Library *see* THE ARIZONA INDEX: A SUBJECT INDEX TO PERIODICALS ABOUT THE STATE
ARK – Cincinnati. 1911-23 – 1 – us A.J.P.C. [073]
ARK – v. 1-53. 1950-76 – 1 – us UMI [700]
DE ARK GODS: HET OUD-ISRAELITISCHE HEILIGDOM / Sevensma, Tietse Pieter – Amsterdam: J. Clausen, 1908. 1 fiche – 9 – us A.T.L.A. [240]
Arkad'ev, E I *see*
- SLOVAR' BIBLIOFILA
- SLOVAR' BIBLIOFILA T.E. SLOV KASAIUSHCHIKHSIA KNIZHNAGO I PECHATNAGO DELA
- VSEOBSHCHEE OBIAZATEL'NOE OBUCHENIE NARODA V ROSSII I ZA GRANITSEI

ARKADIA OSIPA MANDELSZTAMA / Przybylski, R – Slavia Orientalis. 1964. BR-3695 2 – 8 – ne IDC [460]
ARKAMISTUULED KODUMAAL = WINDS OF REVIVAL IN THE HOMELAND / Laks, Johannes – Toronto: Toronto Vabakoguduse Kirjastus (Toronto Free Church Publishing House), 1966. 137p. Publ. No. 6295 b. One item of four on reel – 1 – us Baptist [240]
ARKANSAS – 6r – 1 – $480.00 – us Scholarly Res [370]
ARKANSAS : CODE OF 1987 ANNOTATED – Charlottesville: Michie Company, 1947-Feb 1996 update – 9 – $1,980.00 – us Hein [340]
ARKANSAS : SESSION LAWS OF AMERICAN STATES AND TERRITORIES – 1818-1995 – 9 – $2,102.50 set – us Hein [340]
Arkansas *see*
- REPORTS AND OPINIONS (A-G)
- REPORTS, PRE-NRS
- STATE REPORTS, POST-NRS
- UNION LIST OF ARKANSAS NEWSPAPERS

ARKANSAS AND ITS PEOPLE / Thomas, David Y – New York: American Historical Society, Inc. 1930). Vols. 1-2. Arkansas Reel 2; Vols. 3-4. Arkansas Reel 3. (The Cox Library Collection) – 5 – us Americana [978]
ARKANSAS ATTORNEY GENERAL REPORTS AND OPINIONS – (6 1877-1943, 1953-1979 $315.00. 9 1980-1995 $469.00) – 1877-1995 – 6,9 – $784.00 set – us Hein [340]
ARKANSAS BAPTIST – 1890-1991 – 1 – $3,456.48 – us Baptist [240]
ARKANSAS BAPTIST MATERIALS – (Northwestern arkansas associations. Ben M. Bogard, An Old Landmark Made Plain. J.L. Chastain, Which of the Two Organizations, Claiming it, is Rightly Entitled to the Name, The Benton County Association?. History of Missionary Baptist Associations in Benton County, Arkansas, 1810-1940) – 76p – 1 – 5.00 – us Baptist [240]
ARKANSAS BAR ASSOCIATION REPORTS – 1900-47 (all publ) – 105mf – 9 – $157.00 – LLMC 84-404 – us L.L.M.C. [073]
Arkansas Central Baptist Association *see* MISC. NEW BULLETINS
Arkansas Central Baptist Associations *see* ANNUALS
ARKANSAS DEMOCRAT – Little Rock, AR.1947- – 1 – us UMI [071]
ARKANSAS EVANGEL – 1881-25 Mar 1886. 714p – 1 – 24.99 – us Baptist [240]
ARKANSAS FAMILY HISTORIAN – v1-2, v4, 1962-66. Some issues missing.F-1111 to F1113 – 9 – us A.G.L.L. [073]
ARKANSAS GAZETTE – Little Rock. Ark. 1891- – 1 – us UMI [071]
ARKANSAS GENEALOGICAL RESEARCH AID – Comp. by Gloria Miller Counts. 1 fiche.F-0016 – 9 – us A.G.L.L. [978]
Arkansas Historical Association *see* PUBLICATIONS
ARKANSAS HISTORICAL QUARTERLY – v9, 13-19. 1950, 1954-1960. Some issues missing. Indexed. F-1025 to F-1033 – 9 – us A.G.L.L. [073]
ARKANSAS LAW JOURNAL – Fort Smith. v1. 1877 – 1 – $40.00 – us Hein [073]
ARKANSAS LAW REVIEW – (v1-47 1946-85 in reel $392.00. v39-48 1985-95 in mf $165.00) – v1-48. 1946-95 – 5,6,9 – $557.00 set – us Hein [340]
ARKANSAS LAW REVIEW *see* THE UNIVERSITY OF ARKANSAS LAW SCHOOL BULLETIN
ARKANSAS LAWYER – v1-29. 1967-95 – 9 – $242.00 set – us Hein [340]
ARKANSAS MATERIALS / Baptist Associations – (1) Northwestern Arkansas Associations; (2) Ben M. Bogard, An old landmark made plain; (3) J. L. Chastain, Which of the two organizations, claiming it, is rightly entitled to the name, The Benton County Association?; (4) History of Missionary Baptist Associations in Benton County, Arkansas, 1810-1940 – 1 – 5.00 – us Baptist [240]
Arkansas. State Bar Association *see* PROCEEDINGS
Arkansas. Supreme Court *see* ARKANSAS SUPREME COURT REPORTS
ARKANSAS SUPREME COURT REPORTS / Arkansas. Supreme Court – (Pre-NRS: v1-46 1837-85 359mf $538.00. Updates planned) – v1-141. 1837-1919/20 – 1044mf – $1,566.00 – LLMC 82-981 – us L.L.M.C. [340]
ARKANSAS TRAVELER – Chicago.v12, no.12-v22, no.12.11 Feb 1888-12 Aug 1893 – 1 – 46.00 – us L of C Photodup [073]
Arkell, W J *see*
- PREHISTORIC SURVEY OF EGYPT AND WESTERN ASIA
- PREHISTORIC SURVEY OF EGYPT AND WESTERN ASIA, VOL 2
- PREHISTORIC SURVEY OF EGYPT AND WESTERN ASIA, VOL 3
- PREHISTORIC SURVEY OF EGYPT AND WESTERN ASIA, VOL 4

Arkhangel'skago obshchestva izucheniia Russkago Severa *see* SEVERNAGO KRAIA
Arkhangel'skh, S K *see* UKAZATEL' LITERATURY PO TELESNOMU VOSPITANIIA, RAZVITIIU I OBRAZOVANIIU
Arkhangelski i gubernski i statisticheski i otdel *see* STATISTICHESKI I SBORNIK PO ARKHANGELSKO I GUBERNII ZA...GOD
Arkhangel'skii, A S *see*
- RUSSKAIA LITERATURA 18 VEKA
- TVORENIIA OTTSOV TSERKVI V DREVNE-RUSSKOI PIS'MENNOSTI
- TVORENIIA OTTSOV TSERKVI V DREVNE-RUSSKOI PIS'MENNOSTI. OBOZRENIE RUKOPISNAGO MATERIALA. (K IZUCHENIIU DREVNE-RUSSKOI LITERATURY)

ARKHEOGRAFICHESKII EZHEGODNIK – Moscow, 1957-75. -ann. 18v. Yearbook includes archeographic studies, containing descriptions of archival fonds and manuscript collections. BR-10,754/1 – 9 – ne IDC [025]
ARKHEOLOGICHESKAIA LETOPIS' IUZHNOI ROSSII – v. 1-6. Kiev. 1899-1904. BR-3389 2 – 8 – ne IDC [930]
Arkhippov, K A *see*
- SOVETSKIE AVTONOMNYE OBLASTI I RESPUBLIKI
- ZAKON V SOVETSKOM GOSUDARSTVE

ARKHITEKTURA I STROITELSTVO – (Library has: Apr. 1946) – Moskva: Gos. arkhitekturnoe izd-vo, 1946-1950. 5v – 1 – CSUX89-S913 – us Hoover Inst Photo [720]
ARKHITEKTURA SSSR – (Library has: 1947, no. 17/18) – Moskva: Izd-vo Akademii arkhitektury SSSR, 1933- – 1 – CSUX89-S920 – us Hoover Inst Photo [720]
ARKHITEKTURNYI MUZEI IMP. AKADEMII KHUDOZHESTV – St. Petersburg, 1902-03. Lacking: v.2, 1903; v.4-10, 1903. BR-3390 2 – 8 – ne IDC [720]
ARKHITEKTURNYI VESTNIK – Zhurnal arkhitektury...St. Petersburg, 1859-60. BR-3391 2 – 8 – ne IDC [720]
Arkhiv A P Chekhova *see* ANNOTIROVANNOE OPISANIE PISEM A.P. CHEKHOVU
Arkhiv Akademii nauk SSSR *see* OBOZRENIE ARKHIVNYKH MATERIALOV
ARKHIV DIREKTSII IMPERATORSKIKH TEATROV – Part 1 (1746-1801). V.P. Pogozhev, A.E. Molchanov, and K.A. Petrov, comps.St. Petersburg, 1892. 344p. Inventories materials now located in TsGIA SSSR. BR-10,738/1 – 9 – ne IDC [790]
ARKHIV GOSUDARSTVENNAGO SOVETA / Russia. Gosudarstvennyi sovet – 1768-1826. St. Petersburg, 1869-1904 – 1 – 125.00 – us Hoover Inst Photo [324]
ARKHIV I BIBLIOTEKA SV. SINODA I KONSISTORSKIE ARKHIVY / Zdravomyslov, K Ia. – Spb. 1906. BR-9891 1 – 9 – ne IDC [240]
ARKHIV ISTORICHESKIKH I PRAKTICHESKIKH SVEDENII, OTNOSIASHCHIKHSIA DO ROSSII – St. Petersburg, 1859-1863. B-1680 2 – 8 – ne IDC [947]
ARKHIV ISTORIKO-IURIDICHESKIKH SVEDENII, OTNOSIASHCHIKHSIA DO ROSSII – (Available: 1850 v1. 1854 v2 pt2) – M. 3v. 1850-1876 – 16mf – 9 – ne IDC [947]
ARKHIV ISTORIKO-IURIDICHESKIKH SVEDENII, OTNOSIASHCHIKHSIA DO ROSSII – Moscow. 1850-76. 3v. Available: v.1 (1850); v.2, pt. 2 (1854). BR-8213 2 – 16mf – 8 – ne IDC [947]
ARKHIV KN. VORONTSOVA – Moscow, 1870-95. 40v. B-1264 2 – 8 – ne IDC [010]
ARKHIV KRASNOI ARMII / U.S.S.R. Army; ed by Bochkov, A K, et al – M. 1933. BR-10,792 1 – 9 – ne IDC [355]
ARKHIV O. A. DOBIASH-ROZHDESTVENSKOI V GOSUDARSTVENNOI PUBLICHNOI BIBLIOTEKE IMENI M. E. SALTYKOVA-SHCHEDRINA – By T. P. Voronova. (Srednie veka. Sbornik 29, 1966, p 187-90.) BR-11,114 1 – 9 – ne IDC [920]
ARKHIV PRAVITEL'STVUIUSHCHEGO SENATA – v1: Opis' imennym vysochaishim ukazam i poveleniiam tsarstvovaniia Imperatora Petra Velikogo, 1704-1725. Comp. by P. Baranov. Spb. 1872; Opis' vysochaishim ukazam i poveleniiam, khraniashchimsia v S.-Peterburgskom Senatskom arkhive za XVIII vek. v2: 1725-1740. Spb. 1875; v3: 1740-1762. Spb. 1878; Ukazateli k III tomu. Spb. 1878. BR-10,813 1 – 9 – ne IDC [947]
Arkhiv Raevskikh *see* RAEVSKIE
ARKHIV RUSSKOI ARTILLERII – D.P. Strukov, comp. v1, 1700-1718. St. Petersburg, 1889. vi,410,xxiiip.Covers material from 1700-18 now in the Military History Museum in Leningrad. BR-10,934/1 – 9 – ne IDC [947]
ARKHIV RUSSKOI REVOLIUTSII – v.1-22. Berlin. 1921-37. Br-4172 2 – 8 – ne IDC [947]
ARKHIV VENETSIANSKOGO IZDATELIA A. KALADZHERA V LENINGRADE / Bernadskaia, E V – Describes papers of D. Angelo Calogera (1699-1766) in the GPB. Moscow, 1968. BR-10,872/1 – 9 – ne IDC [920]
ARKHIV VETERINARNYKH NAUK – St. Petersburg, 1876-1917. Lacking: 1899, v.29, no.10; 1906, v.36; 1907, v.37, no.8; 1917, v.47. BR-2260 2 – 8 – ne IDC [636]
ARKHIVNA SPRAVNA – Kharkov. 1925-30. 15 issues pub. 1958 index. BR-11.293 1 – 9 – ne IDC [947]
ARKHIVNOE DELO – Moscow, 1923-41, n.1-58. Irr. (GAU). BR-10,755 1 – 9 – ne IDC [025]
ARKHIVNOE DELO – Moscow. 58v. 1923-41 – 1 – 46.00 – us L of C Photodup [025]
ARKHIVNOE DELO (ARCHIVAL WORK) – Moscow. 15 V. 1923-41 – 3 – us Readex [025]
ARKHIVNOE DELO V ROSSII / Samokvasov, D Ia – Moscow, 1902. 2v. Important survey of archival developments in Russia to the beginning of the 20th century. BR-10,769- – 9 – ne IDC [025]
ARKHIVNYE RAZYSKANIIA I ISSLEDOVANIIA / Shepelev, L E – Moscow. 1971. 144p. Basic guide for graduate students doing archival research in the USSR. BR-10,652/1 – 9 – ne IDC [025]
ARKHIVNYI FOND GLAVNOGO UPRAVLENIIA PO DELAM PECHATI. OBZOR / Polianskaia, L – BR-10,730/1 – 9 – ne IDC [025]
ARKHIVOVEDENIE UCHEBNOE POSOBIE / Shepelev, L E & Gorfein, G M – Leningrad, 1971. 85p. Introductory textbook about archival research in the USSR. BR-10,653/1 – 9 – ne IDC [025]
ARKHIVY AKADEMII NAUK SOTSIALISTICHESKIKH STRAN. BIBLIOGRAFIIA / ed by Vinogradov, I A – v1, 1917-68. Leningrad, 1971. 252p. v2, 1969-72. Leningrad, 1975. 374p. Bibliography of publ. relating to archives of the academies of science in eastern Europe, incl. Archive of Academy of Science of the USSR. v1, p109-195; v2, p101-209. BR-10,947/1 – 9 – ne IDC [500]
ARKHIVY, IKH GOSUDARSTVENNYE ZNACHENIE, SOSTAV I USTROISTVO / Kalachov, N V – (Sbornik gosudarstvennykh znanii 1877. v. 4). Spb. 1877. Also published separately. BR-11,064 1 – 9 – ne IDC [940]
Arkhivy SSSR Leningradskoe otdelenie Tsentral'nogo istoricheskogo arkhiva *see* PUTEVODITEL'PO FONDAM
ARKISYST FEASIBILITY STUDY : FINAL REPORT – 1981 – 65p – 9 – 92-3-101795-0 – fr UNESCO [650]
ARKIV FOER BOTANIK – o.s. v. 1-33. 1903-49 – 1,5,6 – us Princeton Micro [580]
ARKIV FOER BOTANIK – Stockholm, 1903-1934. v1-25 – 207mf – 9 – 8562/1 – ne IDC [580]
ARKIV FOER MATEMATIK, ASTRONOMI OCH FYSIK – (Superseded by: Arkiv foer Matematic, Arkiv foer Fysik and Arkiv foer Astronomi). v. 1-36. 1903-1949. All pub – 1,5,6 – us Princeton Micro [530]
Arkomed, S T *see* MATERIALY POISTORII OTPADENII A ZAKAVKAZI A OT ROSSII
ARKTISKE SKINDDRAGTER I EURASIEN OG AMERIKA / Hatt, G – BN 240 2. 1914 – 8 – ne IDC [306]
ARLEKIN – Zhurnal legkago i zabavnago chteniia. St. Petersburg, 1859. 400p. BR-1523 2 – 8 – ne IDC [340]
ARLEQUIN – London, UK. 19 Dec 1874 – 1 – uk British Libr Newspaper [072]
ARLEQUIN SAUVAGE / Lisle de la Drevetiere, Louis-Francois de – comedie en prose et en 3 actes. Paris. 1783 – 1 – fr A.C.R.P.P. [440]
ARLINGTON 1754-1849 – (Mf 1T: Births 1754-1834; Marriages 1838-40, 1845; Deaths 1766-1835; Intentions 1840-45. Mf 2T: Intentions 1807-40; Marriages 1807-22. Mf 3T: Marriages 1818-44. Mf 3T-4T: Births 1843-49. Mf 4T: Marriages 1844-49; Deaths 1845-49) – (mf ed 1994) – 4mf – 9 – us Holbrook [920]
ARLINGTON APPEAL – Arlington, OR. -w. 26 Feb 1903-10 Aug 1905. 1 roll – 1 – us U.O. Library [071]
ARLINGTON BULLETIN – Arlington, OR. 21 Jan 1921-7 Mar 1924. 4 rolls – 1 – us U.O. Library [071]
ARLINGTON CITIZEN – Arlington, NE. -w. Mar. 1967- – 1 – us NE Hist [071]
ARLINGTON FIRST BAPTIST CHURCH. ARLINGTON, TEXAS : CHURCH RECORDS – 1911-41 – 1 – 65.43 – us Baptist [240]
ARLINGTON RECORD – Arlington, OR. -w. 5 Oct 1900-27 Jul 1911. 2 rolls – 1 – us U.O. Library [071]
ARLINGTON TIMES – Arlington, CA. 1908-1977 – 17r – 1 – $850.00 – R03142 – us Library Micro [071]
ARLINGTON TIMES – Arlington, NE. -w. Sep. 1889-Nov. 1895. Incomplete; Nov. 1895-May 1898; Jan. 1899-Dec. 1900 – 1 – us NE Hist [071]
ARLINGTON WEEKLY NEWS – Arlington, NE. Oct. 1895-Jun. 1896. Incomplete; Aug. 1896-Jul. 1897 – 1 – us NE Hist [071]
ARLINGTONIAN – Arlington, Ohio. 1961-71 – 3r – 1 – $32.50r – us Archival [071]
ARLIS/NA NEWSLETTER / Art Libraries Society of North America – (Cont by: Art Documentation: Bulletin of the Art Libraries Society of North America n13968) – Glendale. v1-2 nov 1972-oct 1974; v3-9 dec 1974-dec 1981 – 1,5,9 – $83.70y – D10830 – us UMI [700]
Arliss, Jean *see* THE QUICK YEARS
Arlosoroff, C *see* DER JUEDISCHE VOLKSSOZIALIMUS
THE ARM CHAIR – New York. v1-5 1878-84 (wanting v3 no 134) – 1 – $47.00 – us L of C Photodup [640]
ARMA RECORDS MANAGEMENT QUARTERLY – (Microed of v11 contains a cum index for jan 1967-oct 1977. Former title: Records Management Quarterly (jan 1967-oct 1975)) – Prairie Village. v1-31 jan 1967-oct 1997+. cum index v1-5 1967-71 1; v6 jan-oct 1972. v9-31 jan 1975-oct 1997+ 5,9 – 1,5,9 – D6778 – us UMI [650]
ARMADA – Djakarta. (incomplete) SE-582 1. 1961-1969 – 9 – ne IDC [073]
ARMADA WATCHMAN – Armada, NE. -w. Aprl. 1889-Jul. 1890 – 1 – us NE Hist [071]
ARMAEISCHE PFLANZENNAMEN / Loew, L – Leipzig. 1881. BJ-32-60 1 – 9 – ne IDC [470]
ARMAES DO MUSEU PAULISTA, TOMOS 1 Y 2 / ed by Bayle, Constantino – Madrid: Razon y Fe, 1927 – 1 – sp Bibl Santa Ana [355]

ARMAGH GUARDIAN – Ireland, 3 Dec 1844-Dec 1972 – 102r – 1 – uk British Libr Newspaper [072]
ARMAMENTS, ARMS CONTROL AND DISARMAMENT : UNESCO READER FOR DISARMAMENT EDUCATION / ed by Thee, Marek – 1981 – 9 – 92-3-101920-1 – fr UNESCO [320]
ARMAN – Tehran: Sazman-i Javanan va Danishjuyan-i Dimukrat-i Iran. Dawrah-'i 2, sal-i 1: shumarah-'i 1-22 (16 Isfand 1357-17 Murdad 1358 [6 Mar 1979-8 Aug 1980]) – 1 reel – 1 – $25.00 – us MEDOC [950]
ARMANA PROUVENCAU – Avignon, 1855-1893. 39v – 117mf – 9 – H-1377/2 – ne IDC [073]
Armand, E *see* UNSERER FORDERUNGEN ALS INDIVIDUALISTISCHE ANARCHISTEN
Armand, L M *see*
- DUSHA KOOPERATSII
- KOOPERATIVNAIA CHAINAIA
- NARODNYI TEATR I KOOPERATSIIA
ARMAN-I MUSTAZ'AFIN – (Missing issues: 19-28; 30-31) – Tehran, 1979-1980. Shumarah-'i 1-32 (Apr 1979-Mar 1980) – 1 reel – 1 – $25.00 – us MEDOC [950]
Armas, Gabriel *see*
- DONOSO CORTES
- DONOSO CORTES EN LA PROBLEMATICA DE LA ESPIRITUALIDAD (ESBOZO DE BIOGRAFIA MISTICA)
- FAMA, ECLIPSE Y RESURRECCION DE DONOSO
- POR QUE VOLVEMOS A DONOSO CORTES
ARMAS I TRIUNFOS...DE LOS HIJOS DE GALICIA... / Gandara, F – Madrid, 1662 – 13mf – 9 – sp Cultura [946]
Armas Medina, Fernando *see* PIZARRO
DER ARME KONRAD – Berlin, 1896-97 (incomplete) – 1r – 1 – Dist. gw Mikrofilm – gw Misc Inst [072]
DER ARME KONRAD : KALENDER FUER DAS ARBEITENDE VOLK – Muenchen, DE. 1903; 1906 – 1r – 1 – gw Mikrofilm [072]
DER ARME TEUFEL – Berlin, 1902-04 – 1 – Dist. gw Mikrofilm – gw Misc Inst [072]
ARMED FORCES AND SOCIETY – (v5- . 5,6,9) – v. 1-. 1974- – 1 – us UMI [300]
ARMED FORCES CHEMICAL JOURNAL – v. 1-16. Oct 1946-Dec 1962 – 1 – 93.00 – us L of C Photodup [660]
Armed Forces Communications Association *see* SIGNAL
ARMED FORCES JOURNAL – (1971-72. 5,6) – 1-110. 1863-1972 – 1 – us UMI [355]
ARMED FORCES JOURNAL INTERNATIONAL – (v114- , 1976- . 9) – v110- , 1973- – 1,5,6 – us UMI [073]
ARMED FORCES MANAGEMENT – v. 1-9. Oct 1954-Sep 1963 – 1 – 134.00 – us L of C Photodup [355]
ARMEE CONGOLAISE – (Incomplete) – Leopoldville, 1959 (June 1)-1960 (Oct. 15) – 1 reel – 9 – AF-118/3 – ne IDC [355]
L'ARMEE D'AFRIQUE – no. 1-49. Alger. 1924-nov 1928 – 1 – fr A.C.R.P.P. [073]
L'ARMEE DE LA REPUBLIQUE ESPAGNOLE QUI DEFEND LA DEMOCRATIE ET LA PAIX – Paris, 1937? Fiche W 727. (Blodgett Collection of Spanish Civil War Pamphlets) – 9 – us H.U. College Libr [946]
ARMELEUTSLIEDER / Kamp, Otto – 3. durchgesehene Aufl. Frankfurt a.M.: Knauer, 1888 – 1r – 1 – us U.W. Library [810]
Armellada, Cesareo de *see* GRAMATICA Y DICCIONARIO DE LA LENGUA PEMON (AREKUNA, TAUREPAN, KAMARAKOTO) (FAMILIA CARIBE) POR EL R.P. -, MISIONERO CAPUCHINO
Armen, Eric V *see* THE CASELOAD EXPERIENCES OF THE DISTRICT COURTS FROM 1972 TO 1983
ARMENIA: SELECTED SOURCES – Ed. by J. J. S. Weitenberg. App. 80 titles per year selected from the Helsinki collection. Indexes, catalog cards and reader. Based on J. E. Eriksson, Die Armenische Buechesammlung der Univeristaetsbibliothek zu Helsinki – 9 – ne IDC [947]
ARMENIACA : ZEITSCHRIFT FUER DIE ERFORSCHUNG DER SPRACHE UND KULTUR ARMENIENS / ed by Roth, K – Leipzig, 1926-1927. v1-2 – 4mf – 9 – AR-1450/1 – ne IDC [950]
ARMENIAN ARCHITECTURE / ed by Parsegian, V L – (Includes finding aids, introductory guide, plastic binders and a printed index; Individual volumes available at Dfl1,600 per volume) – 930mf – 9 – ne IDC [720]
THE ARMENIAN AWAKENING : A HISTORY OF THE ARMENIAN CHURCH, 1820-60 / Arpee, Leon – (Includes index) – Chicago: University of Chicago Press; London: T Fisher Unwin, 1909 – 1mf – 9 – 0-8370-7601-3 – 1986-1601 – us A.T.L.A. [240]
ARMENIAN GENOCIDE IN THE U.S. ARCHIVES, 1915-1918 / U.S. National Archives and Library of Congress – (With printed index) – 396mf – 9 – £3,145.00 – uk Chadwyck [956]
THE ARMENIAN MIRROR-SPECTATOR – (V.9, no.31-v.18, no.41; v.22, no.28-v26, no.24; Ja 1942-Mr 1951; Ja 1954-D 1957; many issues missing throughout; Title varies: Armenian Spectator) – New York: Baikar Association, 19??- – 1 – CSUX86-S166 – us Hoover Inst Photo [947]
ARMENIAN SOURCES / ed by Weitenberg, J J S – 903 titles – 9 – ne IDC [947]
ARMENIAN SPECTATOR *see* THE ARMENIAN MIRROR-SPECTATOR
Armenian SSR *see*
- GRAZHDANSKII KODEKS ARMIANSKOI SOVETSKOI SOTSIALISTICHESKOI RESPUBLIKI
- GRAZHDANSKII PROTSESSUALNYI KODEKS ARMIANSKOI SOVETSKOI SOTSIALISTICHESKOI RESPUBLIKI
- KODEKS O BRAKE I SEME ARMI ANSKO I SOVETSKO I SOTSIALISTICHESKO I RESPUBLIKI
- KONSTITUTSIIA (OSNOVNO I ZAKON) ARMIANSKO I SOVETSKO I SOTSIALISTICHESKO I RESPUBLIKI
- KONSTITUTSIIA (OSNOVNO I ZAKON) ARMIANSKO I SOVETSKO I SOTSIALISTICHESKO I RESPUBLIKI
- UGOLOVNO-PROT SESSUALNYI KODEKS ARMIANSKOI SOVETSKOI SOTSIALISTICHESKOI RESPUBLIKI
- UGOLOVNYI KODEKS ARMIANSKOI SOVETSKOI SOTSIALISTICHESKOI RESPUBLIKI
- ZAKON ARMIANSKOI SOVETSKOI SOTSIALISTICHESKOI RESPUBLIKI O ZDRAVOOKHRANENII
ARMENIE – London, UK. 15 Nov 1889-1 Apr 1898 – 1 – uk British Libr Newspaper [072]
Armenini, G B *see* DE VERI PRECETTI DELLA PITTURA
ARMENISCHE IRENAEUSFRAGMENTE (T.U.U. 3-36/3) / Jordan, H – Leipzig, 1913 – 4mf – 9 – ne Slangenburg [240]
DIE ARMENISCHE KIRCHE IN IHREN BEZIEHUNGEN ZU DEN SYRISCHEN KIRCHEN BIS ZUM ENDE DES 13. JAHRHUNDERTS (T.U.U. 2-26/4) / Ter Minassiantz, E – Leipzig, 1904 – 4mf – 9 – ne Slangenburg [240]
DIE ARMENNOT; EIN SYLVESTERTRAUM; EINES SCHWEIZERS WORT / Gotthelf, Jeremias; ed by Vetter, Ferdinand – Bern: Schmid & Francke, 1899 – 1 – us U.W. Library [830]
Armenth-Brothers, Francine R *see* FRESHMEN ATHLETES' PERCEPTIONS OF ADJUSTMENT TO INTERCOLLEGIATE ATHLETICS
ARMES FOR RED SPAIN / Bayle, Constantino & Hericurt, Pierre – London, 1938; Burgos: Razon y Fe, 1938 – 1 – sp Bibl Santa Ana [946]
LES ARMES ROMAINES / Couissin, P – Paris, 1926 – Dfl39.00 – ne Slangenburg [240]
ARMIDALE EXPRESS – Australia, 8 Aug 1893-30 Jun 1922 (very imperfect) – 33r – 1 – uk British Libr Newspaper [072]
[ARMIDE] CALMA LA PENA AMARA / Mortellari, M – (Full score) – London: Longman & Broderip, 1786 – 1 – us Sibley [780]
[ARMIDE] RESTA INGRATA / Mortellari, M – (Full Score) – London: Broderip & Longman, 1786 – 1 – us Sibley [780]
Armieux, Louis Leon Cyrille *see*
- LE CHOLERA A TOULOUSE
- L'INSCRIPTION DE KASRINE, EN TUNISIE
ARMII A I REVOLIUTSII A : O TOM, KAK RAZLOZHILAS NASHA ARMIIA / Arnoldi, G M – Petrograd: Partii a narodno i svobody, 1917 – 1 – CSUX88-B6965 – us Hoover Inst Photo [320]
ARMII A NAKANUNE FEVRALSKO I REVOLIUTSII / Chaadaeva, O N – Moskva: Gos. sotsialno-ekon. izd-vo, 1935 – 1 – CSUX89-B1304 – us Hoover Inst Photo [947]
ARMII A SVOBODNO I ROSSII : PEREUSTRO ISTVO VOORUZHENYKH SIL NA DEMOKRATICHESKIKH NACHALAKH / Burskii, PD – [Moskvo: Izd-vo "1917 god"], 1917 – 1 – CSUX89-B4229 – us Hoover Inst Photo [947]
ARMIIA I FLOT : DVUKHNEDEL'NYI ILLIUSTRIRIVANNYI VOENNO-LITERATURNYI ZHURNAL – No 1-12. St. Petersburg, 1914. iv. BR-1524 2 – 8 – ne IDC [355]
THE ARMINIAN MAGAZINE : CONSISTING OF EXTRACTS AND ORIGINAL TREATISES ON UNIVERSAL REDEMPTION – (Cont. as: The Methodist Magazine. London, 1798-1821. v21-44; Cont. as: The Wesleyan-Methodist Magazine. London, 1822-1894. v45-107; Missing: 1820, v43(August, p. 561-640); 1821, v44(June/July, p. 401-560); 1856, v79(pt. 2); 1878-1891, v101-114) – London, 1778-1797. v1-20 – 1,089mf – 9 – H-2753/1 – ne IDC [240]
THE ARMINIAN MAGAZINE – London. v1-20. 1778-97 (complete) – 10r – 1 – ATLA S0825 – us A.T.L.A. [073]
THE ARMINIAN MAGAZINE, ... – (Cont. as: The Bible Christian Magazine, ... Shebbear, 1829-1850. N.S., v1-7; S.3, v1-15; Missing: 1822; v1; 1823, v2(p. 37-72); 1825, v4; 1828, v7; N.S., 1829-1832, v1-3; 1832, v4(p. 195-198); 1833, v5(p. 105-108); S.3, 1836-1838, v1-3) – Stoke-Damarel, 1822-1828. v1-7 – 100mf – 9 – MP-350/1 – ne IDC [240]
ARMINIANISM IN HISTORY, OR, THE REVOLT FROM PREDESTINATIONISM / Curtiss, George Lewis – Cincinnati: Cranston & Curts; New York: Hunt & Eaton, 1894 – 1mf – us A.T.L.A. [240]
Arminius, Jacobus *see* OPERA THEOLOGICA
Arminjon, P *see*
- DE LA NATIONALITE DANS L'EMPIRE OTTOMAN SPECIALEMENT EN EGYPTE
- OSSERVAZIONI SULLE NORME DI DIRITTO INTERNAZIONALE PRIVATO...
- LES SOCIETES ANONYMES ETRANGERES EN EGYPTE...
- TREATISE ON THE NATIONALITY OF CORPORATIONS
Armitage, E S *see* THE EARLY NORMAN CASTLES OF THE BRITISH ISLES
Armitage, James O et al *see* LEUKEMIA AND LYMPHOMA
Armitage, Thomas *see*
- A HISTORY OF THE BAPTISTS
- JESUS
- OPENING SERMON BEFORE THE HUDSON RIVER ASSOCIATION SOUTH, THE
Armitage-Smith, G *see*
- THE CITIZEN OF ENGLAND, HIS RIGHTS AND DUTIES
- THE FREE TRADE MOVEMENT AND ITS RESULTS
ARMLEY AND WORTLEY NEWS – Armley, England. 6 Sep 1889-91 – 1 1/2r – 1 – uk British Libr Newspaper [072]
ARMOISE = THE MEDICAL USES OF ARTEMISIA : MEMOIRES CONCERNANT L'HISTOIRE, LES SCIENCES...DES CHINOIS... / Cibot, P M – Paris, 1776-1783. V.5 – 1mf – 9 – ne IDC [615]
ARMONIA / Melara Berrocal, Isidro – Caceres: (Tip. El Noticiero), 1948 – 1 – sp Bibl Santa Ana [946]
ARMONIA ENTRE LA CIENCIA Y LA FE / Mir, Miguel – 1892. Libros en Microficha no 20 – 2mf – 9 – Pta1,500.00 – 84-85422-63-5 – sp Pentalfa [240]
L'ARMONICO PRATICO AL CIMBALO.... QUARTA IMPRESSIONE / Gasparini, Francesco – 1745 – 2 – us Sibley [780]
L'ARMONICO PRATICO AL CIMBALO: REGOLE, OSSERVAZIONI ED AVVERTIMENTI PER BEN SUONARE IL BASSO E ACCOMPAGNARE SOPRA IL CIMBALO SPINETTA ED ORGANI / Gasparini, Francesco – Quarta impressione. Venezia. 1745. BP-289 1 – 9 – ne IDC [780]
ARMOR – 1888- 1; 1971- 5,6; 1975- 4 x 6 in9 – us UMI [073]
Armor, Samuel *see* HISTORY OF ORANGE COUNTY
ARMORIAL DU PREMIER EMPIRE – Paris, 1894-1897. 4v – 4mf – 9 – F120.00 – fr F.F.G. [920]
ARMORIAL HISTORIQUE DE LA BRESSE, BUGEY, DOMBES / Du Mesnil – Lyon, 1872 – 3mf – 9 – F90.00 – fr F.F.G. [944]
Armour, Edward Douglas *see* A TREATISE ON THE INVESTIGATION OF TITLES TO REAL ESTATE IN ONTARIO: WITH A PRECEDENT FOR AN ABSTRACT
Armour, John M *see* ATONEMENT AND LAW, OR, REDEMPTION IN HARMONY WITH LAW AS REVEALED IN NATURE
THE ARMOUR OF LIGHT (CCC276) – (In Chinese) – 1st ed. Hong Kong: Council on Christian Literature for Overseas Chinese, 1956 – 1r – 1 – 1984-6615 – us A.T.L.A. [240]
ARMS CONTROL AND DISARMAMENT – 1964 65-1970 – 1 – $88.00 – us L of C Photodup [327]
ARMS CONTROL AND DISARMAMENT / U.S. Department of State – nos 1-11. 1963-68 (all publ) – 11mf – 9 – $16.50 – LLMC 81-912 – us L.L.M.C. [977]
ARMS CONTROL AND DISARMAMENT / U.S. Library of Congress – Library of Congress. v1-9. 1965-73 (all publ) – 65mf – 9 – $97.00 – LLMC 79-450 – us L.L.M.C. [327]
ARMS CONTROL AND DISARMAMENT BIBLIOGRAPHY – v1 no1 – v9 no2. 1964-73. Complete – 44mf – 9 – $165.00 – us UPA [327]
ARMS FOR RED SPAIN / Hericourt, Pierre – London, 1938? Fiche W 939. (Blodgett Collection of Spanish Civil War Pamphlets) – 9 – us H.U. College Libr [946]
DIE ARMSELIGEN BESENBINDER : ALTES MAERCHEN IN FUENF AKTEN / Hauptmann, Carl – Leipzig: K Wolff, 1913 – 1r – 1 – us U.W. Library [820]
Armstead, H *see* GEOTHERMAL ENERGY
Armstrong, Benjamin G *see* EARLY LIFE AMONG THE INDIANS: REMINISCENCES FROM THE LIFE OF BENJ. G. ARMSTRONG: TREATIES OF 1835, 1837, 1842, AND 1854: HABITS AND CUSTOMS OF THE RED MEN OF THE FOREST: INCIDENTS, BIOGRAPHICAL SKETCHES, BATTLES, ETC.
Armstrong, Charles Newhouse *see* CANADA AND HER RESOURCES
ARMSTRONG COUNTY: HER PEOPLE PAST AND PRESENT / J.H. Beers and Co – Chicago, 1914. v1-2. Pennsylvania Reel 9. The Cox Library Collection – 5 – us Americana [978]
Armstrong, E S *see* THE HISTORY OF THE MELANESIAN MISSION
Armstrong, George Elliot *see* TORPEDOES AND TORPEDO VESSELS
Armstrong, H F *see* REPORT ON UNITED STATES FOREIGN ASSISTANCE PROGRAMS: JORDAN, LEBANON AND IRAQ
Armstrong, J *see* LAWS OF INTESTACY IN THE DOMINION OF CANADA
Armstrong, J W *see* OUR OLD PIONEERS: A MEMORIAL ADDRESS AT THE HILLHOUSE GRAVEYARD, SUNDAY JAN 31, 1925
Armstrong, John *see*
- THE ECLECTIC ALMANAC FOR THE YEAR 1839
- REMINISCENCES
Armstrong, Joseph H *see* LYRICS, IDYLS AND FRAGMENTS
Armstrong, Louis Olivier *see* A CANOE TRIP THROUGH TEMAGAMING THE PEERLESS IN THE LAND OF HIAWATHA
Armstrong, Richard Acland *see*
- AGNOSTICISM AND THEISM IN THE NINETEENTH CENTURY; AN HISTORICAL STUDY OF RELIGIOUS THOUGHT
- GOD AND THE SOUL
- MAN'S KNOWLEDGE OF GOD
Armstrong, Robert *see* LINEAR PHONOGRAPHY: A NATURAL SYSTEM OF SHORT-HAND, FOR GENERAL USE, WITH AN EASY STENOGRAPHY FOR REPORTING PURPOSES
Armstrong, Walter *see* EL ARTE EN LA GRAN BRETANA E IRLANDA
Armstrong, William Dunwoodie *see*
- THE CHRISTIAN MINISTRY AND MODERN THOUGHT: HIGHER CRITICISM
- THE CHRISTIAN MINISTRY IN RELATION TO POLITICS AND PUBLIC QUESTIONS
- INAUGURAL ADDRESS DELIVERED BEFORE KNOX COLLEGE METAPHYSICAL AND LITERARY SOCIETY ON THE EVENING OF FRIDAY, DECEMBER 1ST, 1871
Armstrong, William Reginald *see* ESSAY ON THE TIMES: CANADA
Armstrong, Zella *see* HISTORY OF HAMILTON COUNTY AND CHATTANOOGA
ARMSTRONG'S CONTESTED ELECTION CASES / New York. (State) – 1v. 1777-1871 – 3mf – 9 – $4.50 – LLMC 80-014 – us L.L.M.C. [340]
ARMUT : EIN TRAUERSPIEL / Wildgans, Anton – Leipzig: L Staackmann, 1927, c1914 – 1r – 1 – us U.W. Library [820]

ARMY – (1969- . 5,6. 1975- . 9) – 1- 1950- – 1 – us UMI [355]
ARMY – v. 1-9. Aug 1954-Jul 1963 – 1 – 186.00 – us L of C Photodup [355]
ARMY AND NAVY JOURNAL – v. 1-83. 1863-1946 – 1 – 2,158.20 – us L of C Photodup [355]
ARMY DESERT TRAINING – Historical Archive, 1946 – 1r – 1 – $50.00 – R60010 – us Library Micro [355]
THE ARMY HISTORICAL PROGRAM IN THE EUROPEAN THEATER AND COMMAND, 8 MAY 1943-31 DEC 1950 / U.S. Army. Historical Division. European Command – v. 1-4. 1951 – 7 – 41.00 – us L of C Photodup [977]
ARMY INFORMATION DIGEST – v. 1-17. 1946-62 – 1 – 222.00 – us L of C Photodup [355]
ARMY LAWYER – (1976- . 5,6,9) – 1971- – 1 – us UMI [340]
THE ARMY LAWYER – (None publ between 1985-86. Updates planned) – v1-4. 1971-74; 1975-84; 1987-95 – 225mf – 9 – $337.00 – LLMC 84-238 – us L.L.M.C. [073]
THE ARMY LAWYER *see* THE ADVOCATE
ARMY LIST OF HER MAJESTY'S AND THE HONOURABLE COMPANY'S FORCES SERVING UNDER THE BENGAL PRESIDENCY: CORRECTED TO 31ST DECEMBER 1857 / Bengal. Armed Forces – Calcutta: Calcutta Gazette Office: Sold by Thacker Spink, B.C. Lepage. (1857?). iv,350p. With: El Pais de la Cola de Paja-M. Benedetti. 1 reel. 1257 – 1 – us U.W. Library [355]
ARMY LISTS – 1740-84. BRRAM – 9 – uk Microform Academic [975]
ARMY LOGISTICIAN *see* ALOG
ARMY MANUALS & REGULATIONS INDEX (CONSOLIDATED INDEX OF ARMY PUBLICATIONS AND BLANK FORMS) / U.S. National Technical Information Service – Quarterly. Items listed by title and Army number – 9 – us N.T.I.S. [000]
ARMY ORDERS; SOUTH AFRICA 1901-1902 / Chief Secretary's Office, Queensland – 4r – 1 – CRS B5169 – at Archives [920]
ARMY QUARTERLY AND DEFENCE JOURNAL – 1920-83 – 1 – us Primary [073]
ARMY RESERVE MAGAZINE – (1979- 5,6,9) – 1964-. Continues: Army Reservist – 1 – us UMI [073]
ARMY RESERVIST – v.1-10. Nov 1954-Feb 1964. Continued as: Army Reserve Magazine – 1 – us UMI [073]
ARMY TIMES – (1978-. 5,6,9) – 1940- – 1 – us UMI [073]
ARN JOURNAL – (Association of Rehabilitation Nurses). v1- 1975- Continues as: Rehabilitation Nursing – 1,5,6,9 – us UMI [073]
Arnason, Jon *see* ISLANDSKE FOLKESAGN OG AEVENTYR
Arnau, J *see*
– CERTAMEN PHARMACEUTICO-GALENICO IN QUO TRES CONTINENTUR DISSERTATIONES...
– OPUS NEOTERICUM MEDICUM THEORICO PRACTICUM DE LAXO ET ESTRICTO, JUSTA DIVINI. HIPPOCRATIS MENTEM
Arnaud, Camille *see* DU LIVRET D'OUVRIER
Arnaud, Enrico *see*
– INTRODUCTION A LA CHYMIE, OU A LA VRAYE PHYSIQVE
– LA TROISIEME CONFERENCE DE LA PAIX
Arnaud, Henri *see* GLORIOUS RECOVERY BY THE VAUDOIS OF THEIR VALLEYS, FROM THE ORIGINAL WITH A COMPENDIOUS HISTORY OF THAT PEOPLE, PREVIOUS AND SUBSEQUENT TO THAT EVENT, BY HUGH DYKE ACLAND
Arnaud, Jean-Claude *see* L'ECONOMIE MARAICHERE ET FRUITIERE DANS LA REGION DU CAP-VERT, GRANDE BANLIEUE DE DAKAR
Arnaud, P *see* TROIS QUATOURS, OP. 1
Arnaud, Robert *see*
– L'HOMME QUI RIT JAUNE
– L'ISLAM ET LA POLITIQUE MUSULMANE FRANCAISE EN AFRIQUE OCCIDENTALE FRANCAISE
Arnaudov, M P *see*
– BALGARSKI NARODNI PRAZDNITSI
– ISTORIIA NA SOFIISKIIA UNIVERSITET SV. KLIMENT OKHRODSKI PREZ PURVOTO MU POLUSTOLETIE, 1888-1938
– OCHERKI PO BALGARSKIIA FOLKLOR
– TVORTSI NA BALGARSKOTO VUZRAZHDANE
Arnauld, Antoine *see*
– APOLOGIE POUR LES CATHOLIQUES CONTRE LES FAUSSETEZ ET LES CALOMNIES D'UN LIVRE INTITULE
– A GENERAL AND RATIONAL GRAMMAR
– GRAMMAIRE GENERALE ET RAISONNEE
– LA LOGIQUE OU L'ART DE PENSER
– NOUVELLE METHODE POUR APPRENDRE FACILEMENT ET EN PEU DE TEMPS LA LANGUE LATINE.
– LA PERPETUITE DE LA FOY DE L'EGLISE CATHOLIQUE TOUCHANT L'EUCHARISTIE
– LE RENVERSEMENT DE LA MORALE DE JESUS-CHRIST PAR LES ERREURS DES CALVINISTES, TOUCHANT LA JUSTIFICATION
Arnault *see*
– BLANCHE ET MONTCASSIN OU LES VENITIENS
– OSCAR, FILS D'OSSIAN
Arnault, Charles *see* L'INVASION DE LA VENDEE
Arndt, Ernst Moritz *see*
– ANTHOLOGIE AUS DEN WERKEN VON ERNST MORITZ ARNDT
– DU MEIN VATERLAND
– ERNST MORITZ ARNDT
– ERNST MORITZ ARNDTS BRIEFE AN EINE FREUNDIN
– ERNST MORITZ ARNDT'S SAEMMTLICHE WERKE
– DIE FRAGE UEBER DIE NIEDERLANDE UND DIE RHEINLANDE
– FRAGMENTE UEBER MENSCHENBILDUNG
Arndt, Johann *see*
– JOHANN ARNDTS VIER BUECHER VOM WAHREN CHRISTENTHUM AUFS NEUE AUSGEFERTIGET VON JOACHIM LANGEN
– PARADISZ GAERTLEIN...
– POSTILLA...
– TRUE CHRISTIANITY
– VIER BUECHER VON WAHREM CHRISTENTHUMB...
Arndt, Theodor *see* DIE STELLUNG EZECHIELS IN DER ALTTESTAMENTLICHEN PROPHETIE
Arne, T A *see*
– ARTAXRXES
– [FROM] THE TEMPEST[:] WHERE THE BEE SUCKS...
– HARLEQUIN SORCERER, SELECTIONS, ARR. HARPSICHORD, VIOLIN ETC.
– TRIP TO PORTSMOUTH. OVERTURE AND DANCES; WITH TRANSPOSITIONS FOR THE GERMAN FLUTE AND GUITAR
Arnes Luna, Alfredo *see* ENSAYOS LITERARIOS
Arneth *see* NEUE ENCYCLOPAEDIE DER WISSENSCHAFTEN UND KUENSTE (AEL, ABT 1;24)
Arneth, A von *see*
– BRIEFE DER KAISERIN MARIA THERESIA AN IHRE KINDER UND FREUNDE
– GRAF PHILIPP COBENZL UND SEINE MEMOIREN
– JOSEPH 2 UND KATHARINA VON RUSSLAND
– JOSEPH 2 UND LEOPOLD VON TOSCANA
– MARIA THERESIA UND JOSEPH 2
Arnett, Edward John *see*
– GAZETTEER OF SOKOTO PROVINCE
– GAZETTEER OF ZARIA PROVINCE
Arnett, John Andrews *see* BIBLIOPEGIA
Arnhard, C von *see* LITURGIE ZUM TAUF-FEST DER AETHIOPISCHEN KIRCHE
Arnheim, Rudolf *see* JUGEND UND WELT
Arniches, Carlos *see* SORROW OF THE WRITER ARNICHES FOR THE RUIN OF MADRID
Arnim, Bettina von *see* BETTINA VON ARNIMS AUFRUF ZUR REVOLUTION UND ZUM VOELKERBUNDE
Arnim, H von *see*
– DIE ENTSTEHUNG DER GOTTESLEHRE DES ARISTOTELES
– EUDEMISCHE ETHIK UND METAPHYSIK
Arnim, Ludwig Achim, Freiherr von *see*
– ARIEL'S OFFENBARUNGEN
– ARNIMS TROEST EINSAMKEIT
– ARNIMS WERKE
– HOLLIN'S LIEBELEBEN
– NOVELLEN
ARNIMS TROEST EINSAMKEIT / Arnim, Ludwig Achim, Freiherr von – (Includes index) – Freiburg i.B.: J C B Mohr, 1890 – 1r – 1 – us U.W. Library [430]
ARNIMS WERKE / Arnim, Ludwig Achim, Freiherr von – Leipzig: Bibliographisches Institut, [1925?] – 1r – 1 – us U.W. Library [430]
ARNO ED AMAR MI DUOLE, FROM THE OPERA LA DISCORDIA CONJUGALE / Lazzarini, G – (Full score) – London: Skillern, Goulding, 179- – 1 – us Sibley [780]
ARNO HOLZ UND DIE DEUTSCHE PRESSE / Ress, Robert – (Includes bibliographical references) – Dresden: C Reissner, 1913 – 1r – 1 – us U.W. Library [070]
ARNO HOLZ UND DIE JUENGSTDEUTSCHE BEWEGUNG / Strobl, Karl Hans – (Includes bibliographical references) – Berlin: Gose & Tetzlaff, c1902 – 1r – 1 – us U.W. Library [430]
THE ARNO PRESS REPRINT / Sumner, Shelley et al – Together with: The Lawless State, by Karl Hess. Together, 293p. 1 fiche (29x) – 9 – $1.00f – at Libertarian Micro [320]
Arnobius iunior *see* OPERA OMNIA
Arnold, Carl Franklin *see*
– DIE AUSROTTUNG DES PROTESTANTISMUS IN SALZBURG UNTER ERZBISCHOF FIRMIAN UND SEINEN NACHFOLGERN
– CAESARIUS VON ARELATE UND DIE GALLISCHE KIRCHE SEINER ZEIT
– DIE NERONISCHE CHRISTENVERFOLGUNG
Arnold de Jesus, Frere *see* AUX HONORABLES MEMBRES DU COMITE CATHOLIQUE DU CONSEIL DE L'INSTRUCTION PUBLIQUE
Arnold de Vsingen, B *see* ANABAPTISMUS. CONTRA REBAPTIZANTES. CONFUTATIO EORUM QUAE LUTHERUS SCRIPSIT IN REBAPTIZANTES
Arnold, E Vernon *see* ROMAN STOICISM
Arnold, Edward W *see* ONE THOUSAND LEGAL FACTS.
Arnold, Edwin *see* THE LIGHT OF ASIA, OR, THE GREAT RENUNCIATION (MAHBHINISHKRAMANA)...
Arnold, F C G *see* LICHENOLOGISCHE AUSFLUEGE IN TIROL
Arnold, Gary J *see*
– THE LLOYD PAPERS
– THE WASHINGTON GLADDEN COLLECTION
Arnold, Georges-Daniel *see*
– DER PFINGSTMONTAG
Arnold, Gottfried *see*
– DIE ABWEGE, ODER IRRUNGEN UND VERSUCHUNGEN, GUTWILLIGER UND FROMMER MENSCHEN, AUS BEYSTIMMUNG DES GOTTSELIGEN ALTERTHUMS ANGEMERCKET
– AUSERLESENE SEND-SCHREIBEN DERER ALTEN....1700
– DAS EHELICHE UND UNVEREHELICHTE LEBEN DER ERSTEN CHRISTEN, NACH IHREN EIGENEN ZEUGNISSEN
– DIE GEISTLICHE GESTALT EINES EVANGELISCHEN LEHRERS, NACH DEM SINN UND EXEMPEL DER ALTEN, AUS LICHT GESTELLET
– DIE VERKLAERUNG JESU CHRISTI IN DER SEELE
Arnold, Hans *see* LEBENSDRANG UND TODESVERLANGEN IN DER DEUTSCHEN LITERATUR VON 1850-1880 IM ZUSAMMENHANG MIT DER PHILOSOPHIE SCHOPENHAUERS
Arnold, Heinz Ludwig *see* ALS SCHRIFTSTELLER LEBEN
ARNOLD HOUBRAKEN UND SEINE "GROOTE SCHOUBURGH."O 518A. 1893 / Hofstede de Groot, Cornelis – 9 – ne IDC [700]
ARNOLD HOUBRAKEN'S GROSSE SCHOUBURGH DER NIEDERLAENDISCHE MALER UND MALERINNEN / Wurzbach, A von – Wien. v14. 1880 – 7mf – ne IDC [750]
Arnold, Isaac Newton *see* THE LIFE OF BENEDICT ARNOLD: HIS PATRIOTISM AND HIS TREASON
Arnol'd, Iu. K *see* VOSPOMINANIIA
Arnold, James N *see* VITAL RECORDS OF REHOBOTH MASSACHUSETTS TO 1850
Arnold, Matthew *see*
– CIVILIZATION IN THE UNITED STATES
– DISCOURSES IN AMERICA
– EMPEDOCLES ON ETNA AND OTHER POEMS
– A FRENCH ETON, OR, MIDDLE CLASS EDUCATION AND THE STATE
– FRIENDSHIP'S GARLAN
– GOD AND THE BIBLE
– IRISH ESSAYS
– IRISH ESSAYS: AND OTHERS
– ISAIAH 40-66
– LITERATURE AND DOGMA
– MEROPE
– MIXED ESSAYS
– NEW POEMS
– PASSAGES FROM THE PROSE WRITINGS OF MATTHEW ARNOLD
– POEMS
– POEMS OF WORDSWORTH. CHOSEN AND EDITED BY MATTHEW ARNOLD
– THE POPULAR EDUCATION OF FRANCE
– ST PAUL AND PROTESTANTISM
– SCHOOLS AND UNIVERSITIES ON THE CONTINENT
– THE STRAYED REVELLER
Arnold, Paul Johannes *see* TALIB
Arnold, Robert E *see* AN INVESTIGATION INTO THE GRIEF PROCESS AND THE EMOTIONAL RESTABILIZATION OF THE DIVORCEE WITH SOME POSSIBLE IMPLICATIONS FOR THE MINISTER AS A THERAPEUTIC AGENT
Arnold, Samuel *see*
– INKLE AND YARICO
– THE SHIPWRECK
– [ZORINSKI] A PIPER O'ER THE MEADOWS
ARNOLD SENTINEL – Arnold, NE. -w. Jan. 1914-Jan. 1915. Incomplete; Feb. 1915- – 1 – us NE Hist [071]
Arnold, T *see*
– HENRICI HUNTENDUNIENSIS HISTORIA ANGLORUM (RS74)
– MEMORIALS OF ST EDMUNDS ABBEY (RS96)
– OPERA OMNIA (RS75)
Arnold, Thomas *see* SERMONS, INCLUDING AN ESSAY ON THE RIGHT INTERPRETATION AND UNDERSTANDING OF THE SCRIPTURES, AND TWO SERMONS ON THE RIGHT INTERPRETATION OF PROPHECY
Arnold, Walter *see* THE LIFE AND DEATH OF THE SUBLIME SOCIETY OF BEEF STEAKS
Arnold, William R *see* ANCIENT-BABYLONIAN TEMPLE RECORDS IN THE COLUMBIA UNIVERSITY LIBRARY
ARNOLDI CHRONICA SLAVORUM (MGH 7: 14.BD) – 1886 – Dfl25.00 – ne Slangenburg [240]
Arnoldi, G M *see* ARMII A I REVOLIUTSII A
ARNOLD'S MARCH FROM CAMBRIDGE TO QUEBEC, A CRITICAL STUDY; TOGETHER WITH A REPRINT OF ARNOLD'S JOURNAL – By Justin H. Smith, 1903. Item D. Indexed, 498p. SW16-0083 – 5 – us A.G.L.L. [975]
Arnolphus, B *see* ORATIO HABITA AD SANCTISSIMU DUM NOSTRU LEONE 10 PONT. MAX. ...
Arnon, I *see* PLANNING AND PROGRAMMING OF AGRICULTURAL RESEARCH
Arnot, Frederick Stanley *see* GARENGANZE
Arnot, JG *see* THE PRISONERS OF THE FORTY-FIVE
Arnould, A M *see*
– RESULTATS DES GUERRES, ... LA COALITION CONTRE LA FRANCE...
– SYSTEME MARITIME ET POLITIQUE DES EUROPEENS,...
Arnsperger, Walther *see* LESSINGS SEELENWANDERUNGSGEDANKE KRITISCH BELEUCHTET
ARNSTAEDTISCHE WOECHENTLICHE ANZEIGEN UND NACHRICHTEN [...] – (Cont by: Arnstaedtisches Nachrichts- und Intelligenzblatt) – Arnstadt, oct 15 1768-1904 (very incomplete) – 1 – Dist. gw Mikrofilm – gw Misc Inst [943]
Arntz, E R N *see*
– PROGRAMME DU COURS DE DROIT DES GENS...
– ...REGLEMENTS CONSULAIRES DE BELGIQUE
Arntz, W *see* AUSSENPOLITISCHE STUDIEN
AROIDEAE MAXIMILIANAE / Peyritsch, J J – Wien. 1879. B-1033 2 – 8 – ne IDC [580]
Arom, Simha *see* GUIDE FOR THE COLLECTION OF TRADITIONAL MUSICAL INSTRUMENTS
Aron, Pietro *see*
– COMPENDIOLO DI MOLTI DUBBI, SEGRETI ET SENTENZE INTORNO AL CANTO FERMO, ET FIGURATO
– LIBRI TRES DE INSTITUTIONE HARMONICA..
– TOSCANELLO IN MUSICA. CANONICO DA RIMINI. NUOVAMENTE STAMPATO CON L'AGGIUNTA DA LUI FATTA ET CON DILIGENTIA CORRETTO
– TRATTATO DELLA NATURA ET COGNITIONE DI TUTTI GLI TUONI DI CANTO FIGURATO
Aroni, Julius *see* FUTURES
Aronowsky, S S *see* DAS WECHSELINDOSSAMENT...
Aronson, Robert H *see* ATTORNEY-CLIENT FEE ARRANGEMENT
AROS – Vaesteras, Sweden. 1865-69 – 1 – sw Kungliga [072]
Arosinus, H J *see* DE LEGATIONUM JURE,...

AROSLAVSKI I SBORNIK, POSVI ASHCHENNY I GODOVSHCHINI E VELIKO I OKTI ABRSKO I REVOLIUTSII I II ULSKIM SOBYTII AM V I AROSLAVLI E / ed by Veseli, F – Aroslavl: Izd. Gub. komissii po organizatsii i ustro istvu prazdnestv godovshchiny veliko i revoliutsii, 1918 – 1 – CSUX88-B7119 – us Hoover Inst Photo [947]

Aroslavskii, Emelian *see*
- KAK RABOCHIE I KRESTIANE SBROSII TSARIA, POMESHCHIKOV I KAPITALISTOV
- PARTIIA BOLSHEVIKOV V 1917 GODU
- POCHEMU U NAS V ROSSII GOLOD I KAK S NIM BOROTSIA?
- O PRODNALOGE
- VOENNAIA RABOTA RS-DRP BOLSHEVIKOV
- VOORUZHENNOE VOSSTANIE V DEKABRE 1905 GODA
- ZHIZN I RABOTA V.I. LENINA, 23 APRELI A 1870-21 I ANVARI A 1924

Arou, Joseph *see* LA QUESTION ELECTORALE: DEUX LETTRES A PAUL DEROULEDE AVEC LA REPONSE DE CELUI-CI DE CANADA-TRANSVAAL

Aroz Pascual, L *see* TOLEDO. ARCHIVO DE LA CATEDRAL. SELLOS ECLESIASTICOS DEL ARCHIVO DE LA CATEDRAL DE TOLEDO (1099-1792)

Aroza, D *see* TESORO DE LAS EXCELENCIAS Y UTILIDADES DE LA MEDICINA Y ESPEJO DEL PRUDENTE Y SABIO MEDICO...

Arpee, Leon *see* THE ARMENIAN AWAKENING

ARPEGIOS / Lopez Ortiz de Leon, Angel – Badajoz: Arqueros, 1907 – 1 – sp Bibl Santa Ana [946]

ARQUEOLOGIA DE MAGACELA / Jimenez Navarro, E et al – Badajoz: Dip. Provincial, 1951. Sep. REE – 1 – sp Bibl Santa Ana [930]

LA ARQUEOLOGIA DE NORBA CESARINA / Callejo Serrano, Carlos – Madrid: Diana Artes Graficas, 1969 – 1 – sp Bibl Santa Ana [930]

ARQUEOLOGIA Y ANTROPOLOGIA DE LA TIERRA / Perez de Barrados, Jose – Madrid: Razon y Fe, 1940 – 1 – sp Bibl Santa Ana [930]

O ARQUIDIOCESANO : ORGAO OFICIAL DA ARQUIDIOCESE DE MARIANA – Mariana, 2 Jan 1972-Dec 1973; Jan-Feb 1974; Jan 1976-Dec 1977; Jan-Dec 1979; Jan-26 Dec 1982 – 1,5,6 – bl Biblioteca [072]

LA ARQUITECTURA NAVAL ESPANOLA (EN MADERA) – Madrid: Razon y Fe, 1926 – 1 – sp Bibl Santa Ana [355]

ARQUITECTURA RELIGIOSA DEL S. 16 DE LA TIERRA DE BARROS / Garrido Santiago, Manuel – Limanas, Tomo 1 (Aceuchal, Fuente del Maestre). Caceres: Univ. de Extremadura. Facult. de Filosofia y Letras, y Tomo 2. 1980 – 1 – sp Bibl Santa Ana [720]

ARQUITECTURA RELIGIOSA DEL S. 16 EN LA TIERRA DE BARROS / Garrido Santiago, Manuel – (Texto) – Caceres: Universidad de Extremadure. Facult. de Filosofia y L, 1980 – 1 – sp Bibl Santa Ana [720]

ARQUIVOS INDO-PORTUGUESES DE MEDICINA E HISTORIA NATURAL / Instituto Bacteriologico de Nova-Goa – Nova-Goa, 1921-27.-4v – 25mf – 8 – M-285/2 – ne IDC [580]

THE ARRAINMENT OF CHRISTENDOM / Philly, John – 1664 114p. (English Linguistics Series 1500-1800) – 9 – us UMI [400]

AN ARRANGEMENT OF BRITISH PLANTS / Withering, W – 6485. 4 V. Ed. 7. 1830 – 9 – ne IDC [580]

AN ARRANGEMENT OF BRITISH PLANTS; ACCORDING TO LATE IMPROVEMENTS OF THE LINNAEAN SYSTEM / Withering, W – 5820. 4 V. Ed. 3. 1796 – 9 – ne IDC [580]

AN ARRANGEMENT OF THE PSALMS AND SPIRITUAL SONGS OF THE REV. ISAAC WATTS, D.D / Winchell, James M – 1832 – 1 – $29.40 – us Baptist [240]

AR-RASAD – Alger. n1-56. 1938-39 – 1 – fr A.C.R.P.P. [073]

Arratibel, Juan *see* MANUAL DE LAS CUARENTA HORAS...

Arrault, Charles *see* ABREGE HISTORIQUE DE L'ESTABLISSEMENT DE L'HOPITAL DES ENFANS-TROUVES

O ARRE E IRRA – '(s.l.')-Sao Luis, Brazil. 16 Sep-7 Oct 1846 – 1,5,6 – bl Biblioteca [072]

ARREBOL : ORGAM DO GRUPO SPIRITA – "CHRISTO, DEUS E CARIDADE" – Uberaba, 1 Jul 1897 – 1,5,6 – bl Biblioteca [072]

ARREBOL : PERIODICO LITTERARIO, CRITICO E NOTICIOSO – Camaragibe, Alagoas. 7 Jul, 25 Ago 1889 – 1,5,6 – bl Biblioteca [072]

O ARREBOL – Maceio, Alagoas. 31 Out 1900 – 1,5,6 – bl Biblioteca [072]

O ARREBOL – Nazareth, BA. 24 Out 1880 – 1,5,6 – bl Biblioteca [072]

Arredondo, Martin *see*
- OBRAS DE ALBEYTERIA

ARREDONDO'S HISTORICAL PROOF OF SPAIN'S TITLE TO GEORGIA / ed by Bolton, H E – Berkeley, 1925 – 5mf – 9 – ILM-1507/1 – ne IDC [327]

ARRENDAMIENTOS RUSTICOS PROTEGIDOS (COMENTARIOS A LA LEY DE 15 DE JULIO DE 1954) / Fernandez de Soria y Villanueva, Fernando – Badajoz, 1954 – sp Bibl Santa Ana [946]

ARREST DE CONDEMNATION DE MORT CONTRE MAISTRE URBAIN GRANDIER PRESTRE CURE DE L'EGLISE SAINCT PIERRE DU MARCHE DE LOUDUN – Paris. 1634 – 9 – fr Hachette [360]

ARREST DE LA COUR DE PARLEMENT DE ROUEN CONTRE MATHURIN PICAUD ET THOMAS BOULLE – Rouen; Orleans. 1647 – 9 – fr Hachette [360]

ARREST DE LA COUR DE PARLEMENT PORTANT DEFFENCES A TOUS LES JUGES ET OFFICIERS DE JUSTICES SUBALTERNES – Paris. 1641 – 9 – fr Hachette [360]

ARREST DONNE PAR LA CHAMBRE ORDONNEE PAR LE ROY AU TEMPS DES VACATIONS CONTRE MARIE BENOIST DITE SOEUR MARIE DE LA BUCAILLE – Rouen. 1699 – 9 – fr Hachette [360]

ARREST DU CONSEIL D'ESTAT, SERVANT DE REGLEMENT POUR RESTABLIR LA REGULARITE DANS UN MONASTERE DE S. BENOI (SAINT VICTOR DE MARSEILLE) – 1668 – Dfl6.00 – ne Slangenburg [240]

ARREST LAW BULLETIN – (1982-. 1,5,6,9) – 1976- – 1 – us UMI [073]

ARRET RENDU A L'AMPHITHEATRE DE L'OPERA, SUR LA PLAINTE DU MILIEU DU PARTERRE, INTERVENANT DANS LA QUERELLE DES DEUX COINS / Holbach, Paul-Thiry d' – (D'Holbach series) – 9 – fr Hachette [790]

ARRETS DE LA CHAMBRE DES COMPTES DE PARIS / France. Ancien Regime – 1718-90 – 1 – fr A.C.R.P.P. [323]

ARRETS DE LA COUR DES AIDES / France. Ancien Regime – 1763-76 – 1 – fr A.C.R.P.P. [324]

ARRETS DE LA COUR DES MONNAIES / France. Ancien Regime – 1759-75 – 1 – fr A.C.R.P.P. [324]

ARRETS DE LA COUR DU PARLEMENT / France. Ancien Regime – 1770-71 – 1 – fr A.C.R.P.P. [324]

ARRETS DU CONSEIL D'ETAT DU ROI / France. Ancien Regime – 1703, 1770-71 – 1 – fr A.C.R.P.P. [324]

ARRETS DU GRAND CONSEIL DU ROI / France. Ancien Regime – 1748-87 – 1 – fr A.C.R.P.P. [324]

ARRETS ROYAUX / France. Ancien Regime – 1770-71 – 1 – fr A.C.R.P.P. [324]

ARRIA UND MESSALINA : TRAUERSPIEL IN FUENF AUFZUEGEN / Wilbrandt, Adolf von – 3. Aufl. Wien: Kuenast, 1895 – 1r – 1 – us U.W. Library [820]

ARRIA UND MESSALINA : TRAUERSPIEL IN FUENF AUFZUEGEN / Wilbrandt, Adolf von – Wien: L Rosner, 1874 – 1r – 1 – us U.W. Library [820]

Arriaga, Pablo Jose de *see*
- LA EXTIRPACION DE LA IDOLATRA EN EL PERU...POR HORACIO H. URTEAGA
- EXTIRPACION DE LA IDOLATRIA DEL PIRU
- HISTORIA DA REVOLUCAO PORTUGUEZE DE 1880

Arriaga, R de *see* CURSUS PHILOSOPHICUS

Arriaza, Juan Bautista *see*
- POESIAS JUVENILES. TOMO 1
- POESIAS JUVENILES. TOMO 2
- POESIAS PATRIOTICAS

ARRIBA – Madrid, 27 Mar 1940-31 Aug 1946; 16 Nov 1952-30 Dec 1956; 1 Jan 1958-31 Dec 1960 (imperfect) – 87r – 1 – uk British Libr Newspaper [072]

ARRIBA ESPANA – Pamplona, Spain. 16 Jan-13 Oct 1937; 2 Sep 1941-27 May 1945 (imperfect) – 11r – 1 – uk British Libr Newspaper [072]

Arriba. Madrid *see* SIETE EDITORIALES DE ARRIBA Y SU COMENTARIO

Arrigoni, Enrico *see*
- CAIN AND ABEL, THE UNINTENTIONAL MURDER
- GOD'S FOLLY: THE GREAT FLOOD
- THE LUNACY OF SUPERMAN & OTHER PLAYS
- THAT CHARACTER CALLED GOD
- THE TOTALITARIAN NIGHTMARE
- WHEN GOD WOKE UP FROM HIS ETERNAL SLUMBER

Arrigunaga Peon, J de *see* INDICE – RESUMEN, ALFABETICO Y CRONOLOGICO DEL ARCHIVO GENERAL DE LA ARQUIDIOCESIS DE YUCATAN

Arrillaga, Enrique de *see* UN GENERAL ESPANOL DEL SIGLO 27, DON JOSE DE GARRO

Arrington, Benjamin F *see* MUNICIPAL HISTORY OF ESSEX COUNTY IN MASSACHUSETTS

Arriu, J *see* L'UNIFICATION DU DROIT MARITIME

THE ARROW – 1904-08. (American Indian Periodicals in the Princeton University Library). 1 reel – 1 – $75.00 – us UPA [305]

THE ARROW – Bulletin of the Mackay Society. Fall 1986. 4p – 9 – 1.00f – at Libertarian Micro [335]

THE ARROW – Dublin. Oct 20 1906-Aug 25 1909; Summer 1939 – 1 – us NY Public [073]

THE ARROW – Quebec, Canada. 6 avr-31 dec 1864 – 1r – 1 – Can$35.00 – cn Can Microfilming [072]

THE ARROW – Quebec: [s.n., 1864] – 9 – cn C.I.H.M. [971]

THE ARROW – Sydney, Australia. -w. 19 March 1920-7 Jan 1922. 1 reel – 1 – uk British Libr Newspaper [072]

THE ARROW – Toronto: Crawford & Hunter, [1886] – 9 – cn C.I.H.M. [971]

THE ARROW – Worcestershire. 1889-91 – 1 – uk Microform Academic [072]

ARROW – BELTAINE – DANA : (THREE IRISH LITERARY AND DRAMATIC JOURNALS) – n1-5 + commemoration no 1906-1909; 1939. v1 1899-1900; v1 1904-1905 – 1 – us Ross [073]

ARROWOOD BAPTIST CHURCH. CHESNEE, SOUTH CAROLINA : CHURCH RECORDS – 1843-1955 – 1 – 40.41 – us Baptist [240]

ARROWS OF THE CHACE : BEING A COLLECTION OF SCATTERED LETTERS PUBLISHED CHIEFLY IN THE DAILY NEWSPAPERS, 1840-1880 / Ruskin, John – Orpington, Kent: George Allen, 1880 – 1 roll – 1 – 1-55879-962-1 – uk Libr Preservation [860]

ARROWSMITH'S DICTIONARY OF BRISTOL – 2nd ed. Bristol: J.W. Arrowsmith, 1906.447p. ill – 1 – us U.W. Library [941]

ARROYO GRANDE VALLEY HERALD RECORDER – (Cont: 5 Cities Times Press Recorder) – Arroyo Grande, CA. 1950-1969 – 14r – 1 – $700.00 – B03143 – us Library Micro [071]

ARROYO GRANDE VALLEY HERALD RECORDER *see* HERALD RECORDER

Arroyo, Leonardo *see* IGREJAS DE SAO PAULO

AR-RUH – Blida. n1-24. nov 1937-fev 1939 – 1 – fr A.C.R.P.P. [073]

ARS AMBROSIANA : COMMENTUM ANONYMUM IN DONATI PARTES MAIORES – 1982 – 5mf – 9 – Bf750.00 – 2-503-61338-1 – be Brepols [240]

ARS AMBROSIANA (CCSL 133C) – 1986 – 4mf – 9 – Bf975.00 – 2-503-71332-7 – be Brepols [240]

ARS BELLI ET PACIS / Bonbra, F D – (Missing: p99-103) – Stravbingae, 1643 – 11mf – 9 – ILM-848/1 – ne IDC [327]

ARS BREVIS / Lulle, Raymond – Paris. 1901. 101p. (Religion series) – 9 – 6.00 – fr Bibl Nationale [240]

ARS CANTANDI / Carissimi, G G – 1693 – 9 – us Sibley [780]

ARS CANTANDI: DAS IST: RICHTIGER UND AUSSFUERHLICHER WEG/DIE JUGEND AUS DEM RECHTEN GRUND IN DER SING-KUNST ZU UNTERRICHTEN / Carissimi, G G – Augsburg. 1696. BP-661 1 – 9 – ne IDC [780]

ARS CHIRURGICA / Salmon, W – London, 1699 – 13mf – 9 – ne IDC [617]

ARS CISTERCIENSI : BUCHMALEREIEN AUS MITTEL- UND OSTDEUTSCHEN KLOSTERBIBLIOTHEKEN / Libor, Reinhard Maria – (Includes bibliographical references) – Wuerzburg: Holzner Verlag, 1967 – 1 – us U.W. Library [090]

ARS (GENCLIGIN SESI) – Sahibi ve Yazi Isleri Mueduerue: Cetin Evren. Nos. 1 (10 Kasim 1949) – 9 – $20.00 – us MEDOC [956]

ARS GENERALIS ULTIMA / Lulle, Raymond – 1986 – 14mf – 9 – Bf1,550.00 – 2-503-63752-3 – be Brepols [240]

ARS GRAMATICA JAPONICAE LINGUAE / Collado, Fr. Diego – 1632 – 9 – 1.50f – sp Bibl Santa Ana [480]

ARS GRAMMATICA (CCCM 40D) / Donatus Ortigraphus – 1982 – 5mf – 9 – Bf750.00 – 2-503-60400-5 – be Brepols [240]

ARS GRAMMATICA (CCCM 40D) / Donatus Ortigraphus – 1992 – 2mf – 9 – Bf1,750.00 – be Brepols [450]

ARS IGNATIANA ANIMARUM AD DEUM PER CHRISTUM ADDUCENDORUM : QUAE LATET IN LIBRO EXERCITIORUM SPIRITUALIUM / Nonell, Iacobus – Barcinone [Barcelona]: Franciscus Rosalius, 1888 – 1mf – 9 – 0-8370-7089-9 – 1986-1089 – us A.T.L.A. [240]

ARS JOURNAL *see* AIAA JOURNAL

Arsdekin, R *see* THEOLOGIA TRIPARTITA UNIVERSA...

Arsenev, A V *see*
- SLOVAR' PISATELEI DREVNEGO PERIODA RUSSKOI LITERATURY 9-17 VEKA
- SLOVAR' PISATELEI SREDNIAGO I NOVAGO PERIODA RUSSKOI LITERATURY S KARTOI DLIA NAGLIADNAGO OBOZRENIIA

Arsenev, K K *see*
- ZA CHETVERTVEKA. (1871-94). SBORNIK STATEI
- ZAKONODATELSTVO O PECHATE (VELIKIIA REFORMY SHESTIDESIATYKH GODOV)
- ZAMETKI O RUSSKOI ADVOKATURE

ARSENIC AND TIN IN FOODS : REVIEWS AND COMMONLY USED METHODS OF ANALYSIS; JOINT F.A.O./W.H.O. EXPERT COMMITTEE ON FOOD ADDITIVES – 1979 – 114p – it F.A.O. [640]

Arsenii, Ieromonakh *see* OPISANIE SLAVIANSKIKH RUKOPISEI BIBLIOTEKI SVIATO-TROITSKOI SERGIEVOI LAVRY

Arshinov, Petr Andreevich *see* ISTORIIA MAKHNOVSKOGO DVIZHENIIA (1918-1921 GG.)

Arskii, R *see*
- PUTI RUSSKO I REVOLIUTSII, 28 FEV. 1917 G.-28 FEV. 1919[SIC] G
- REGULIROVANIE PROMYSHLENNOSTI

L'ART – no. 1-10. Paris. nov 1865-janv 1866 – 1 – fr A.C.R.P.P. [073]

L'ART – no. 1-7. Paris. mai-juin 1868 – 1 – fr A.C.R.P.P. [073]

ART / Bibliotheque Nationale – Seven 19th Century catalogues from French and Spanish museums; works by Chesnau, Clement de Ris, Cros, Galle, Havard, Lepage, MoLins, Pacheco, Perrot, Villot and Viollet-le-Duc. 14 titles on 101 fiches. Available separately – 9 – 250.00 – fr Bibl Nationale [700]

ART : REVUE HEBDOMADAIRE ILLUSTREE – Paris, 1875-1907. v1-68 – 757mf – 9 – O-1211/1 – ne IDC [700]

ART. 5 UND ART. 14 SATZ 3 DER VOELKERBUNDSATZUNG / Engel, S – Annemasse, 1936 – 2mf – 1 – ILM-4007/1 – ne IDC [327]

L'ART A NANTES AU 19E SIECLE... / Maillard, Emile – Paris: Monnier, 1888 – 1 – F184.07 – fr Armell [700]

ART ANCIEN DU TCHAD. BRONZES ET CERAMIQUES / Reunion des musees nationaux. Paris – 1962. 27 illus. 1 fiche – 9 – fr Réunion [730]

ART AND ANTIQUES – v.3-. 1980-. Continues: American Art and Antiques – 1,5,6,9 – us UMI [700]

ART AND ARTISTS OF THE CAPITOL OF THE UNITED STATES OF AMERICA / Fairman, Charles E – Washington: GPO, 1927 – 6mf – 9 – $9.00 – LLMC 96-038 – us L.L.M.C. [700]

ART AND ASIAPACIFIC / ed by Dysart, Dinah – 9,5,1 – us Gordon [700]

ART AND AUSTRALIA : QUARTERLY JOURNAL / ed by Dysart, Dinah – 9,5,1 – us Gordon [700]

THE ART AND DESIGN OF UTOPIAN AND RELIGIOUS COMMUNITIES (TIAM, PT 2) – (With printed catalogue ISBN: 0-914146-64-5 £30) – 40mf – 15 – £735.00 – uk Chadwyck [740]

ART AND HISTORY : SUBJECT COLLECTIONS – (Individual titles not listed separately) – 86 catalogues on 146mf – 9 – £920.00 – uk Chadwyck [700]

ART AND LIFE / Moore, Thomas Sturge – 8 illus. London: Methuen and Co., 1910 – xi/314p – 1 – us U.W. Library [700]

ART AND THE LAW *see* COLUMBIA-VLA JOURNAL OF LAW AND THE ARTS

ART, ARCHITECTURE AND PHOTOGRAPHY WITH ART PERIODICALS 1895-1972 (PVB 1895-1977, PT 1) – (With printed bibliography & subject index) – 276mf – 9 – £1,135.00 – uk Chadwyck [700]

Art Association of Montreal *see* FIRST EXHIBITION OF WORKS OF ART IN BLACK & WHITE, FEBRUARY, 1881: THE CATALOGUE

ART BULLETIN – (1968- . 5,6. 1977- . 9) – 1- 1913- – 1 – us UMI [700]

THE ART COLLECTOR – 1889-99 – 31mf – 9 – £175.00 – uk Chadwyck [700]

ART COM CATALOGS – (Futurist Synthetic Theater Catalog 1mf; All Xerox 1mf; West Coast Conceptual Photographers 1mf; Symbolic Reflexive, Paul Forte, producer 1mf) – 9 – us Contemporary Arts [700]

L'ART DE BATIR DES MAISONS DE CAMPAGNE / Briseux, C E – 2v. O-1161 1. 1743 – 9 – ne IDC [720]

L'ART DE BIEN PARLER FRANCOIS / Latouche, De – 1730 – 9 – fr I.C.S. [440]

L'ART DE BIEN PRONONCER / Hindret, J – 1687 – 9 – fr I.C.S. [440]

L'ART DE CHARPENTERIE. / Jousse, Mathurin – Paris. T. Moette. 1702. 6, 208p. pl. (Architecture Series) – 9 – fr Hachette [720]

L'ART DE CHARPENTERIE DE MATHURIN JOUSSE / Jousse, Mathurin – Paris: Chez Thomas Moette, 1702. SEM35P120 – 1r – 1 – Can$15.00 – cn Bibl Nat [620]

L'ART DE CONJECTURER... : 1ERE PARTIE / Bernoulli, Jacques – Caen: Le Roy, 1801 – 1 – F101.52 – fr Armell [500]

L'ART DE FAIRE L'AMOUR, OU, LA PENDULE D'AMANT – Montreal: Leprohon & Leprohon, c1897. 02464. (Pre-1900 Canadiana) – 9 – cn C.I.H.M. [830]

L'ART DE JOUER LE VIOLON. OPERA IX / Geminiani, Francesco – 1763 – 9 – us Sibley [780]

ART DE LA GUERRE PAR PRINCIPES ET PAR REGLES / Puysegur, J de Chastenet de – Paris. C. A. Jombert. 1748. 196, 244p. Portrait, maps. (Strategy of War Series) – 9 – fr Hachette [355]

L'ART DE LA MUSIQUE ENSEIGNE ET PRATIQUE / Dumas, A-J – 1753 – 9 – us Sibley [780]

L'ART DE LA POESIE FRANCOISE ET LATINE / La Croix, A P de – En Trois Parties. 1694 – 9 – us Sibley [780]

L'ART DE LA POESIE FRANCOISE ET LATINE / Lacroix, Ph. de – 1694 – 9 – fr I.C.S. [410]

L'ART DE LA POTERIE EN FRANCE DE RODIN A DUFY / Reunion des musees nationaux. Paris – 1971. 52 illus. 1 fiche – 9 – fr Réunion [730]

L'ART DE LA TEINTURE DES LAINES ET DES ETOFFES DE LAINE EN GRAND ET PETIT TEINT, AVEC UNE INSTRUCTION SUR LES DEBOUILLIS / Hellot, Jean – Paris, Vve Pissot, 1750, xx, 631 p. Histoire des Sciences XVIIe-XIXe Siecles. 7950 – 9 – fr Hachette [540]

L'ART DE PARLER ET D'ECRIRE CORRECTEMENT / Levizac, Abbe de – 1809 – 9 – fr I.C.S. [440]

L'ART DE SE PERFECTIONNER DANS LE VIOLIN. CET OUVRAGE FAIT LA SUITE DE L'ECOLE D'ORPHEE METHODE POUR LE VIOLON / Corrette, M – 1783 – 9 – us Sibley [780]

L'ART DE TOUCHER LE CLAVECIN / Couperin, Francois – 1717 – 9 – us Sibley [780]

L'ART DE VAINCRE, PRESENTE PAR LE GENERAL DRAGOMIROF / Souvorof – Paris. H. Charles. Lavauzelle. 1899. 56p. (Strategy of War Series) – 9 – fr Hachette [355]

L'ART DE VERSAILLES ET LES NOUVELLES ACQUISITIONS DU MUSEE / Reunion des musees nationaux. Paris – 1932. 26 illus. 2 fiches – 9 – fr Réunion [700]

L'ART DES EMBLEMES OU S'ENSEIGNE LA MORALE / Menestrier, Claude-Francois – O-690. 1684 – 9 – ne IDC [760]

L'ART DES JARDINS, 1730-1830 / Reunion des musees nationaux. Paris – 1934. 1 fiche – 9 – fr Réunion [700]

L'ART DES JARDINS CLASSIQUES / Reunion des musees nationaux. Paris – 1932. 1 fiche – 9 – fr Réunion [700]

L'ART D'INTRUIRE ET DE TOUCHER LES AMES DANS LE TRIBUNAL DE PENITENCE / Alletz, Pons Augustin – Paris. 1775. xv,381,362p. (Religion series) – 9 – 27.00 – fr Bibl Nationale [240]

ART DOCUMENTATION – Bulletin of the Art Libraries Society of North America. v1-. 1982- – 1,5,6,9 – us UMI [073]

ART DOCUMENTATION *see* ARLIS/NA NEWSLETTER

L'ART DU CHANT / Berard, Jean-Antoine – 1755 – 9 – us Sibley [780]

ART DU CIRIER / Duhamel du Monceau, Henri Louis – Paris: Impr. de H. L. Guerin & L. F. Delatour, 1762 – 1 – us U.W. Library [660]

ART DU COUVREUR / Duhamel du Monceau, M – [S.l.]: [s.n.], 1766 ([Paris]: de l'Imprimerie de L.F. Delatour). SEM105P1493 – 5mf – 9 – Can$11.25 – cn Bibl Nat [690]

L'ART DU FACTEUR D'ORGUES / Bedos de Celles, F – (incomplete) P 158. 1766-1778 – 9 – ne IDC [780]

L'ART DU GANDHARA ET DE L'ASIE CENTRALE / Reunion des musees nationaux. Paris – 1958. 24 illus. 1 fiche – 9 – fr Réunion [700]

L'ART DU MENUISIER / Roubo, Andre J – 4pts in 5v. Paris?: de l'imprimerie de L.F. Delatour, 1769-75. SEM35P146 – 1r – 1 – Can$66.00 – cn Bibl Nat [690]

L'ART DU PEINTRE, DOREUR ET VERNISSEUR / Watin, Jean Felix – Paris: Berlin-Leprieur, 1823. SEM16P278 – 1r – 5 – Can$9.00 – cn Bibl Nat [760]

L'ART DU PLEIN-CHANT, OU TRAITE THEORICO-PRATIQUE SUR LA FACON DE LE CHANTER – 1765 – 9 – us Sibley [780]

ART DU THEATRE : REVUE MENSUELLE – v2-6. 1902-06 – 1r – 1 – us Ross [790]

L'ART DU TUILIER ET DU BRIQUETIER / Duhamel du Monceau, M – P.[Paris]: [s.n.], 1763. SEM105P1492 – 7mf – 9 – Can$15.75 – cn Bibl Nat [690]

ART DURING WORLD WAR 2 PAMHPLET COLLECTION – 19??-1944 – 1 – CSUXANN2512-B – us Hoover Inst Photo [700]

ART EDUCATION – (1972- . 5,6. 1975- . 9) – v. 1- 1948- – 1 – us UMI [370]

ART ET CRITIQUE – no. 1-95. Paris. juin 1889-janv 1891, janv-mars 1892 – 1 – fr A.C.R.P.P. [073]

L'ART ET LA VIE – Revue mensuelle, litteraire, artisitque et sociale. Paris. 1892-97 – 1 – fr A.C.R.P.P. [073]

L'ART ET LE COMFORT DANS LA VIE MODERNE. / Havard, Henry – Paris: E. Rosveyre, 1904. 312p.4 fiches. (Art) – 9 – $10.00 – fr Bibl Nationale [700]

L'ART ET LES TECHNIQUES CULINAIRES DES INDIENS WAYAPI DE GUYANE FRANCAISE / Grenand, F – 9 – F60.00 – fr Ethnologie [306]

ART ET SCIENCE DE RHETORIQUE METRIFFIEE / Du Pont, G – 1539 – 9 – fr I.C.S. [410]

ART EXHIBITION CATALOGS SUBJECT INDEX, 1977-1990 / Santa Barbara. Arts Library at the University of California – (Former title: The Catalogs of the Art Exhibition Catalog Collection of the Arts Library, University of California at Santa Barbara) – 195mf – 9 – £990.00 – uk Chadwyck [700]

ART EXHIBITION CATALOGUES ON MICROFICHE : CATALOGUES OF MAJOR MUSEUMS AND GALLERIES; MAJOR SUBJECT COLLECTIONS; SUBJECT COLLECTIONS; ARCHITECTURE, APPLIED ARTS, STUDIO ARTS – (Some titles listed separately. Categories as provided: Catalogues of Major Museums and Galleries 3,633mf. Major Subject Collections 1,431mf. Subject Collections 3,551mf. Architecture, Applied Arts, Studio Arts 922mf) – 5,687mf – 9 – £14,000.00 coll – uk Chadwyck [700]

ART EXHIBITION CATALOGUES ON MICROFICHE *see*
- ABSTRACT AND CONSTRUCTIVIST ART
- AMERICAN FEDERATION OF ARTS CATALOGUE
- AMERICAN NINETEENTH CENTURY ART
- AMERICAN TWENTIETH CENTURY ART
- ANTIQUES
- ARCHITECTURE AND ENVIRONMENT
- ART AND HISTORY
- ART NOVEAU
- ARTS COUNCIL OF GREAT BRITAIN CATALOGUE
- BASEL. KUNSTHALLE CATALOGUE
- BERNHEIM-JEUNE ET CIE CATALOGUE
- BOOK ARTS
- BUCHHOLZ GALLERY-CURT VALENTIN CATALOGUE
- CARTOONS AND SATIRE
- CERAMICS
- COUNTY OF MUSEUM ART CATALOGUE
- CUBISM
- DRAWINGS
- ENGLISH ART
- EUROPEAN TWENTIETH CENTURY ART
- EXPRESSIONISM
- FINE ART SOCIETY CATALOGUE
- FOLK ARTS, ARTS AND CRAFTS
- FRENCH NINETEENTH CENTURY ART (INCLUDING SALON CATALOGUES)
- FURNITURE
- FUTURISM
- GALERIE CHALETTE CATALOGUE
- GALLERIA CIVICA D'ARTE MODERNA CATALOGUE
- GLASS, MOSAICS AND JEWELRY
- HAUS DER KUNST CATALOGUE
- HERWARTH WALDEN UND DIE EUROPAEISCHE AVANTGARDE
- IMPRESSIONISM
- LANDSCAPE PAINTING
- LOWE ART MUSEUM CATALOGUE. CORAL GABLES
- MEDIAEVAL ART
- METALWORK
- MINIATURES
- MURAL ART
- MUSEE DES ARTS DECORATIFS CATALOGUE
- MUSEUM OF CONTEMPORARY ART CATALOGUE
- NATIONAL MUSEUMS OF FRANCE CATALOGUES
- NINETEENTH CENTURY ART
- ORIENTAL ART
- PHOTOGRAPHY, CINEMA
- PORTRAITS
- PRINTING AND ENGRAVING
- RELIGIOUS ART
- RENAISSANCE AND BAROQUE ART
- ROYAL ACADEMY OF ARTS CATALOGUE
- SCULPTURE
- SIDNEY JANIS GALLERY CATALOGUE
- SOLOMON R GUGGENHEIM MUSEUM CATALOGUE
- SURREALISM
- SYMBOLISM
- TEXTILES, WEAVING, EMBROIDERY AND COSTUME
- THEATRE, STAGE, COSTUME
- TWENTIETH CENTURY ART
- VICTORIA AND ALBERT MUSEUM CATALOGUE
- VICTORIAN ART
- WATERCOLOURS
- WOMEN ARTISTS

L'ART FLAMAND AND HOLLANDAIS – (Missing: V.22) – Anvers, 1904-1925. v1-25 – 123mf – 9 – O-1212/1 – ne IDC [700]

L'ART FRANCAIS : REVUE HEBDOMADAIRE ILLUSTREE – n12-13.1899-1901 – 1r – 1 – us Ross [700]

"L'ART FRANCAIS" PRESENTE... [...DU NOUVEAU AVEC MARC-AURELE FORTIN, A.R.C.A.] = "L'ART FRANCAIS" PRESENTS... [SOMETHING NEW... BY MARC-AURELE FORTIN, A.R.C.A.] / Galerie L'Art francais – [Montreal: L'Art francais, 1946?]. SEM105P1895 – 1mf – 9 – Can$2.25 – cn Bibl Nat [700]

Art Gallery of Ontario *see* VERTICAL FILE COLLECTION ON CANADIAN ARTISTS

L'ART GRECO-BOUDDHIQUE DU GANDHARA / Foucher, A – Paris, 1905. v. 1. 1918. v. II, 1922, 1951. fasc. 1-3 (Publications d'Ea1cole Franca3aise d'Extrea6me-Orient. v. 5-6) – 8 – ne IDC [700]

L'ART GRECO-BOUDDHIQUE DU GRANDHARA / Ecole Francaise d'Extreme-Orient – by A. Foucher. Paris. 1905. v. 1. 1918., v. 2. 1922,1951. Fasc. 1-3. BI-586 2 – 8 – ne IDC [700]

ART GUIDES : A GUIDE TO THE PAINTING AND SCULPTURE IN THE JUSTICE BUILDING / U.S. Department of Justice – Washington: Art in Federal Buildings Inc, 1938 – 1mf – 9 – $1.50 – LLMC 91-080 – us L.L.M.C. [700]

ART HISTORY / Couprie, LD – (Titles can be purchased separately) – 48,548mf – 9 – ne IDC [700]

ART IN AMERICA – New York, 1913-1920. v1-8 – 52mf – 9 – O-1213/1 – ne IDC [700]

ART IN AMERICA – (v59- . 5,6,9) – v. 1- 1913- – 1 – us UMI [700]

Art Institute of Chicago *see*
- FRENCH DRAWINGS AND SKETCHBOOKS OF THE NINETEENTH CENTURY, VOL 1
- FRENCH DRAWINGS AND SKETCHBOOKS OF THE NINETEENTH CENTURY, VOL 2
- FRENCH DRAWINGS OF THE SIXTEENTH AND SEVENTEENTH CENTURIES
- ITALIAN DRAWINGS OF THE 18TH AND 19TH CENTURIES AND SPANISH DRAWINGS OF THE 17TH THROUGH 19TH CENTURIES
- TWENTIETH-CENTURY EUROPEAN PAINTINGS

ART INSTRUCTION *see* AMERICAN ARTIST

ART INTERCHANGE – New York. v24-25, 30-31. 1890, 1893 – 1r – 1 – us Ross [700]

ART INTERNATIONAL – (1971- . 5,6. 1975- . 9) – 1957- – 1 – us UMI [700]

ART INTERNATIONAL AUJOURD'HUI – Paris, 1929-30 – 2r – 1,14 – £165.00 – uk Chadwyck [720]

ART JOURNAL – (1968- . 5,6. 1976- . 9) – 1- 1941- – 1 – us UMI [700]

THE ART JOURNAL – 1875-87 – 65mf – 9 – £290.00 – uk Chadwyck [700]

Art Libraries Society of North America *see*
- ARCHIVES OF AMERICAN ART
- ARLIS/NA NEWSLETTER

L'ART LITTERAIRE – Bulletin d'art, de critique et bibliographie. Red. en chef Louis Lormel. no. 1-13; n.s., no. 1-12. Paris. oct 1892-1894 – 1 – fr A.C.R.P.P. [800]

L'ART MILITAIRE POUR L'INFANTERIE / Wallhausen, J J von – Franeker. U. Balck. s.d. 148p., pl. (Strategy of War Series) – 9 – fr Hachette [355]

L'ART MODERNE – Bruxelles. 1881-93; 1895-1913. Revue de critique des arts et de la litterature. Comite de redaction: Octave Maus, Edmond Picard, Emile Verhaeren – 1 – fr A.C.R.P.P. [800]

L'ART MODERNE – Paris. dec 1882-83 – 1 – fr A.C.R.P.P. [073]

L'ART MUSICAL : REVUE – Montreal, Canada. Oct 1896-jan 1899 – 1r – 1 – Can$35.00 – cn Can Microfilming [780]

ART NEWS – (1968- . 5,6,9) – 1- 1902- – 1 – us UMI [700]

ART NEWS – v1. 1897 – 1r – 1 – us Ross [700]

ART NEWS AND REVIEW : THE ARTS REVIEW – London, 12 Feb 1949-29 Dec 1962 – 5r – 1 – uk British Libr Newspaper [073]

ART NEWSLETTER – (v3- , 1977- . 5,6,9) – v. 1-. 1975- – 1 – us UMI [700]

ART NOVEAU : SUBJECT COLLECTIONS – (Individual titles not listed separately) – 18 catalogues on 28mf – 9 – £235.00 – uk Chadwyck [700]

THE ART OF ACCOMPANIAMENT / Geminiani, Francesco – or A new and well digested method to learn to perform the Thorough Bass on the Harpsichord. 2 pts. London. BP-685 1 – 9 – ne IDC [780]

THE ART OF ACCOMPANIAMENT. OPERA 11 / Geminiani, Francesco – Part the first-Second. 1756-1757 – 9 – us Sibley [780]

THE ART OF COMMUNITY / MacCallum, Spencer H – 1970. With: On Anarchism and the Newest Profession, by Paul Goodman and A. Sherman. 2 fiches (24x) – 9 – 1.00f – at Libertarian Micro [320]

THE ART OF CROSS-EXAMINATION / Wellman, Francis Lewis – New and enl. ed. New York, Macmillan, 1904. 404 p. LL-1183 – 1 – us L of C Photodup [340]

THE ART OF DELIVERING WRITTEN LANGUAGE / Cockin, William – 1775. 181p. (English Linguistics Series 1500-1800) – 9 – us UMI [400]

THE ART OF ENGLISH POETRY / Bysshe, Edward – 1702. 493p. (English Linguistics Series 1500-1800) – 9 – us UMI [420]

THE ART OF FINGERING / Heck, J C – CA.1766 – 9 – us Sibley [780]

THE ART OF FINGERING THE HARPSICHORD / Pasquali, N – CA.1758 – 9 – us Sibley [780]

THE ART OF GOOD LIVING AND GOOD DYING / Verard, A – 1 – uk Microform Academic [240]

ART OF INDIA / Victoria and Albert Museum. London – (Coll spans over 8 centuries and ranges from Bengal mss of the 12th C to work by Indian artists in 1990) – 71mf – 15 – $2,120.00 – 1-869934-47-4 – uk Emmett [700]

THE ART OF INVIGORATING AND PROLONGING LIFE, BY FOOD, CLOTHES, AIR, EXERCISE, WINE, SLEEP, ETC.: OR, THE INVALID'S ORACLE / Kitchiner, William – 6th ed. London: Printed for Geo. B. Whittaker by J. Moyes, 1828. 337p – 1 – us U.W. Library [615]

THE ART OF IRON MOULDING, IN ALL ITS VARIOUS BRANCHES – Boston, 1853 – 1 – us Res Libr [740]

THE ART OF JUDGING THE CHARACTER OF INDIVIDUALS FROM THEIR HANDWRITING AND STYLE – Edward Lumley, editor. London: John Russell Smith, 1875. viii,177p. 35 leaves of plates, facsims – 1 – us U.W. Library [150]
THE ART OF LOGICK / Spencer, Thomas – 1628. 324p. (English Linguistics Series 1500-1800) – 9 – us UMI [160]
THE ART OF LOGICK: OR THE ENTIRE BODY OF LOGICK IN ENGLISH / Coke, Zachary – 1654. 249p. (English Linguistics Series 1500-1800) – 9 – us UMI [160]
THE ART OF LOGIKE / Blundeville, Thomas – 1599. 180p. (English Linguistics Series 1500-1800) – 9 – us UMI [160]
THE ART OF MAKING DEVISES. TREATING OF HIEROGLYPHICKS, SYMBOLES, EMBLEMES / Estienne, Henri – In English. O-606. 1646 – 9 – ne IDC [760]
THE ART OF MODULATING ILLUSTRATED IN ONE GRAND LESSON, AND TWO PRELUDES FOR THE PIANOFORTE, HARPSICHORD OR ORGAN / Bemetzrieder, A – 1796 – 9 – us Sibley [780]
THE ART OF MUSICK / Lampe, J F – 1740 – 9 – us Sibley [780]
THE ART OF NAVAL WARFARE: INTRODUCTORY OBSERVATIONS / Bridge, Cyprian Arthur George – 1907 – 9 – $20.00 – uk Libr Preservation [355]
THE ART OF PLAYING ON THE VIOLIN CONTAINING ALL THE RULES NECESSARY TO ATTAIN TO A PERFECTION ON THAT INSTRUMENT / Geminiani, Francesco – London. 1751. BP-684 1 – 9 – ne IDC [780]
THE ART OF PLAYING THOROUGH BASS WITH CORRECTNESS ACCORDING TO THE TRUE PRINCIPLES OF COMPOSITION / Heck, J C – CA.1777 – 9 – us Sibley [780]
THE ART OF PREACHING (CCC8) / Chang, Chih-Chieng – (In Chinese) – [s.l: s.n], 1929 – 1r – 1 – 0-8370-1708-4 – 1984-6084 – us A.T.L.A. [240]
THE ART OF PRONUNCIATION / Robinson, Robert – 1617. 67p. (English Linguistics Series 1500-1800) – 9 – us UMI [420]
THE ART OF READING AND WRITING ENGLISH / Watts, Isaac – 1721. 184p. (English Linguistics Series 1500-1800) – 9 – us UMI [420]
THE ART OF SIMPLING / Coles, William – An introduction to the knowledge and gathering of plants. London. 1656 – 1 – us U.W. Library [631]
THE ART OF TEACHING: A MANUAL FOR THE USE OF TEACHERS AND SCHOOL COMMISSIONERS / Emberson, Frederick C – Montreal: Dawson, 1877. 02911. (Pre-1900 Canadiana) – 9 – cn C.I.H.M. [971]
THE ART OF USING THE CHINA MISSIONARY SURVEY / Clark, Sidney J W – us A.T.L.A. [240]
ART OF WATER DRAWING / D'Acres, R – 1659-60. (1930) – 7 – uk Microform Academic [550]
L'ART, OU LES PRINCIPES PHILOSOPHIQUES DU CHANT / Blanchet, J – Deuxieme ed., Corrigee et Augmentee. 1756 – 9 – us Sibley [780]
L'ART PAIEN SOUS LES EMPEREURS CHRETIENS / Allard, Paul – Paris: Didier, 1879 – 1mf – us A.T.L.A. [240]
ART PAPERS – 1981- – 9 – us UMI [700]
ART PERIODICALS COLLECTION AT VICTORIA AND ALBERT MUSEUM : PART THREE: ART AND DECORATION / National Art Library – 1750-1920. 28 reels (3 of colour) with printed index – £1,425.00 – uk World [700]
ART PERIODICALS ON MICROFORM – (Individual titles also listed sparately) – 1 – uk Chadwyck [700]
ART PERIODICALS ON MICROFORM *see*
- ALTE UND MODERNE KUNST
- THE APPLE
- ARCHIVIO STORICO DELL'ARTE
- ART INTERNATIONAL AUJOURD'HUI
- L'ART VIVANT
- L'ARTE
- L'ARTE NAIVE
- ARTITUDES INTERNATIONAL
- ARTS ET METIERS GRAPHIQUES
- LE CIEL BLEU
- ECRITS POUR L'ART
- EIDOS
- FORM
- GAZETTE DU BON TON
- GENIUS
- THE GOLDEN HIND
- ILLUSTRATIONS 63
- L'IMAGE
- THE JOURNAL OF INDIAN ART AND INDUSTRY
- KOKKA
- LIVING ARTS
- LONDON BULLETIN
- LES MAITRES DE L'AFFICHE
- MUSEUMJOURNAAL
- THE NEOLITH
- OTTAGONO
- THE PAGEANT
- THE PAINTER AND THE SCULPTOR
- PAN
- LE POINT
- THE POSTER
- THE QUARTO
- DER QUERSCHNITT
- LA REVOLUTION SURREALISTE
- SIGNATURE
- LE SURREALISME AU SERVICE DE LA REVOLUTION
- SYN
- THE VENTURE
- WENDINGEN

L'ART POETIQUE / Colletet, G – 1658 – 9 – fr I.C.S. [440]
L'ART POETIQUE / Peletier du Mans, J – 1555 – 9 – fr I.C.S. [440]
L'ART POETIQUE ABREGE DE CLAUDE DE BOISSIERE / ed by Gaiffe, F – 1554 – 9 – fr I.C.S. [410]
L'ART POETIQUE FRANCOIS / Laudun D'Aigaliers, P de – 1598 – 9 – fr I.C.S. [440]
ART POETIQUE FRANCOIS / Sebillet, Th – 1910 – 9 – fr I.C.S. [440]
ART POETIQUE FRANCOIS / Vauquelin de la Fresnaye, J – 1885 – 9 – fr I.C.S. [440]
THE ART PRESS / Victoria and Albert Museum. London – (Includes index) – 1976 – 21mf – 9 – £75.00 – uk Chadwyck [760]
L'ART PRIMITIF / Luquet, Georges-H – Paris: Doin, 1930 – 1 – F158.45 – fr Armell [700]
ART PSYCHOTHERAPY – v.1-6. 1973-79 – 5,6,9 – us UMI [150]
ART QUARTERLY – (1971-74. 5,6) – v. 1-37. 1938-74 – 1 – us UMI [700]
THE ART QUARTERLY – Detroit, 1938-1943. v1-6 – 42mf – 9 – O-493c/1 – ne IDC [700]
ART REFERENCE SERVICES QUARTERLY / ed by Teague, Edward H – v2 n1. 1996- – 1,9 – $75.00 in US $105.00 outside hardcopy subsc – us Haworth [700]
L'ART RUPESTRE DE LA LAPA DO VEADO, JANUARIA, MONTALVANIA, BRESIL / Leite, N & Lima, M A – 9 – F210.00 – fr Ethnologie [306]
L'ART RUPESTRE DE LA PEDRA PINTADA DE COCAIS, MINAS GERAIS, BRESIL / Siqueira, A de et al – F350.00 – fr Ethnologie [306]
ART SALES CATALOGUES, 1600-1825 – (A Fuji RFP2 microfiche reader (value Dfl750.00) is given free to purchasers of the complete collection) – 1992 – 3,261mf – 9 – ne IDC [700]
ART SALES CATALOGUES, 1600-1825 : SUPPLEMENT – (Includes a printed guide) – 1994. 890 catalogues from libraries in London – 274mf – 9 – ne IDC [700]
ART SUISSE CONTEMPORAIN DEPUIS HODLER. PEINTURE ET SCULPTURE / Reunion des musees nationaux. Paris – 1934. 36 illus. 1 fiche – 9 – fr Réunion [750]
THE ART TEACHING OF JOHN RUSKIN / Collingwood, WG – London: Percival, 1891 – 1 roll – 1 – 1-55879-380-1 – uk Libr Preservation [110]
L'ART VIVANT – Paris, 1925-39 – 10r – 1 – £575.00 – uk Chadwyck [740]
ART WORK OF BRITISH COLUMBIA, CANADA / Carre, William H – 1900. 02463. (Pre-1900 Canadiana) – 9 – cn C.I.H.M. [700]
ART WORK ON HAMILTON, CANADA / Carre, William H – 1899. 00025. (Pre-1900 Canadiana) – 9 – cn C.I.H.M. [700]
ART WORK ON MONTREAL, CANADA / Carre, William H – Text by Arthur Weir. 1898. 00027. (Pre-1900 Canadiana) – 9 – cn C.I.H.M. [700]
ART WORK ON OTTAWA, CANADA / Carre, William H – 1898. 00029. (Pre-1900 Canadiana) – 9 – cn C.I.H.M. [700]
ART WORK – QUEBEC, CANADA / Carre, William H – 18?? 02500. (Pre-1900 Canadiana) – 9 – cn C.I.H.M. [700]
ART XPRESS – v.1-. 1981- – 1,5,6,9 – us UMI [073]
Artana, Nestor *see* LA AUTENTICA REBELION
L'ARTASERSE : DRAMA IN TRE ATTI DI PIETRO METASTASIO / Vinci, L – (From the library of the Earl of Aylesford) – Ms, 175- – 12mf – 9 – us Sibley [780]
Artaud, Adrien Jean Marie *see* LA QUESTION DE L'EMPLOYE EN FRANCE: ETUDE SOCIALE ET PROFESSIONNELLE
Artaud (ou Furetiere) *see* LE DICTIONNAIRE DES HALLES
ARTAXRXES : THE SOLDIER TIR'D / Arne, T A – London: between 1804 & 1812 – 1 – us Sibley [780]
L'ARTE : (GIA ARCHIVIO STORICO DELL'ARTE) – Romae, etc., 1898-1941. v1-44 – 482mf – 9 – O-494c/1 – ne IDC [700]
L'ARTE – Rome, 1898-1971 – 22r – 1 – £1,155.00 – uk Chadwyck [700]
A ARTE : ORGAO DA ESCOLA DE DESENHO E PINTURA – Curitiba, 4 Mar 1888; Jan-15 Jun 1895 – 1,5,6 – bl Biblioteca [072]
L'ARTE ARMONICA.. / Antoniotto, Giorgio – 1760 – 9 – us Sibley [780]
ARTE DE CANTO-LLANO EN COMPENDIO BREVE. / Ramoneda, Ignacio – 1778 – 2 – us Sibley [780]
ARTE DE HABLAR...VERSO / Gomez Hermosilla, Jose – 1876 – 9 – 1.50f – sp Bibl Santa Ana [810]
ARTE DE LA LENGUA GUARANI, O' MAS BIEN TUPI / Ruiz de Montoya, Antonio – Viena: Faesy y Frick; Paris: Maisonneuve, 1876 – fr Armell [400]
ARTE DE LA LENGUA HILIGUAYNA DE LA ISLA DE PANAY. / Mentrida, Alonso de – Manila. 1818 – 1 – us Res Libr [490]
ARTE DE LA LENGUA PAMPANGA. : DEDICALE AL M.R.P.P. FR. FRANCISCO ZENZANO / Bergano, Diego – [Manila]: Impr de la Compania de Jesus por S L Sabino, 1729 – 1 – us Res Libr [490]
ARTE DE LA LENGUA TAGALA; Y, MANUAL TAGALOG : PARA LA ADMINISTRACION DE LOS SANTOS SACRAMENTOS / de Totanes, Sebastian – Manila: Estab tip del Colegio de Sto Tomas, 1850 – 1 – us Res Libr [490]
ARTE DE LA PINTURA, SU ANTIGUEDAD Y GRANDEZAS. / Pacheco, Francisco – Seville: S. Faxardo, 1649. 7 fiches. (Art) – 9 – $17.00 – fr Bibl Nationale [750]
ARTE DEL BARBERO-PELUQUERO-BANERO, QUE CONTIENE EL MODO DE HACER LA BARBA, CONSTRUCCION DE PELUCAS... MODOS DE PEINADOS / Garsault – Madrid, 1771 – 5mf – 9 – sp Cultura [640]
L'ARTE DEL CONTRAPONTO RIDOTTA IN TAVOLE. / Artusi, Giovanni M – 2v. Also contains: Seconda parte dell'arte del contraponto....1589. 1586 – 9 – us Sibley [780]
L'ARTE DEL NAVEGAR / Medina, Pedro de – Venitia: Aurelio Pincio, 1554. SEM105P877 – 4mf – 9 – Can$9.00 – cn Bibl Nat [355]
L'ARTE DEL NAVEGAR, IN LAQVAL SI CONTENGONO LE REGOLE, DECHIARATIONI, SECRETI, AND AUISI, ALLA BONA NAUEGATION NECESSARIJ / Medina, Pedro de – Vinetia: G. Pedrezato, 1554. SEM105P877 – 4mf – 9 – Can$9.00 – cn Bibl Nat [355]
L'ARTE D'INCENTER A L'IMPROVISTE DES FANTASIES ET CADENCES POUR LE VIOLON FORMENT UN RECUEIL DE 246 PIECES AMUSANTS ET UTILES EN TOUS MAJEURS ET MINEURS...OEUV 17 / Campagnoli, B – Leipzig: chez Breitkopf & Hartel, No. 1691 – 1 – us Sibley [780]
EL ARTE DRAMATICO EN LIMA DURANTE EL VIRREINATO. MADRID, 1945 / Lohmann Villena, Guillermo – Madrid: Razon y Fe, 1946 – 1 – sp Bibl Santa Ana [790]
ARTE EN AMERICA Y FILIPINAS. CUADERNO 1. SEVILLA, 1935 / Bayle, Constantino – Madrid: Razon y Fe, 1936 – 1 – sp Bibl Santa Ana [700]
EL ARTE EN LA GRAN BRETANA E IRLANDA / Diez Canedo, Enrique & Armstrong, Walter – Madrid: Libreria Gutenberg de Jose Ruiz, 1909 – sp Bibl Santa Ana [700]
EL ARTE EN LA REVOLUCION; CONFERENCIA PRONUNCIADA EN EL CINE COLISEUM DE BARCELONA, EL DIA 21 DE MARZO DE 1937 / Noja Ruiz, Higinio – Barcelona? 1937? Fiche W 1079. (Blodgett Collection of Spanish Civil War Pamphlets) – 9 – us H.U. College Libr [946]
ARTE ESPAGNOL : REVISTA DE LA SOCIEDAD DE AMIGOS DEL ARTE – Madrid, 1912-1920. v1-5 – 45mf – 9 – O-1214/1 – ne IDC [700]
EL ARTE EXPLICADO Y GRAMATICO / Marquez de Medina, Marcos – 1804 – 9 – 1.50f – sp Bibl Santa Ana [700]
EL ARTE EXTREMENO ACTUAL / Martin Gil, Thomas – Caceres: Tip. Extremadura, 1929 – 1 – sp Bibl Santa Ana [700]
ARTE LEGAL PARA ESTUDIAR JURISPRUDENCIA CON LA PARATITLA Y EXPOSICION... / Bermudez de Pedraza, F – Salamanca, 1612 – 5mf – 9 – sp Cultura [340]
L'ARTE MUSICALE IN ITALIA / Torchi, Luigi – Milan. 1897. 7v – 1 – 69.00 – us L of C Photodup [780]
L'ARTE NAIVE – Reggio Emilia, 1974-75 – 1r – 1 – £60.00 – uk Chadwyck [700]
ARTE, O COMPENDIO GENERAL DEL CANTO-LLANO.. / Marcos y Navas, Francisco – 1777 – 2 – us Sibley [780]
THE ARTE OF ENGLISH POESIE / Puttenham, George – 1589. 268p. (English Linguistics Series 1500-1800) – 9 – us UMI [420]
THE ARTE OF REASON / Lever, Ralph – 1573. 268p. (English Linguistics Series 1500-1800) – 9 – us UMI [160]
THE ARTE OF RHETORIQUE / Wilson, Thomas – 1553 – 9 – 15.00 – us Scholars' Facs [410]
ARTE PRATICA DI CONTRAPPUNTO / Paolucci, G – 1765-72.3v – 9 – us Sibley [780]
ARTE PRATTICA ET POETICA / Herbst, Johannes A – 1653 – 2 – us Sibley [780]
ARTE PRECOLOMBINO EN MEXICO Y EN LA AMERICA CENTRAL / Toscano, Salvador – Madrid: Missionalia Hispanica, 1948 – 1 – sp Bibl Santa Ana [700]
EL ARTE Y LA PINTURA DE ADELARDO COVARSI / Vaca Morales, Francisco – Badajoz: Diputacion Provincial, 1944 – 1 – sp Bibl Santa Ana [750]
ARTE Y USO DE ARCHITECTURA... / Lorenzo de San Nicolas, Fray – SL, SA – 6mf – 9 – sp Cultura [700]
ARTE Y USO DE LA ARQUITECTURA. CON EL PRIMER LIBRO DE EUCLIDES... / Lorenzo de San Nicolas, Fray – Madrid, 1796 – 13mf – 9 – sp Cultura [700]
Arteaga, Esteban *see* LA BELLEZA IDEAL
Arteaga, Stefano *see*
- GESCHICHTE DER ITALIAENISCHEN OPER
- LE RIVOLUZIONI DEL TEATRO MUSICALE ITALIANO
- LE RIVOLUZIONI DEL TEATRO MUSICALE ITALIANO DALLA SUA ORIGINE FINO AL PRESENTE

Arteau, Jean-Marie *see* BIO-BIBLIOGRAPHIE DE MONSIEUR CARL FAESSLER, PROFESSEUR TITULAIRE DE MINERALOGIE, FACULTE DES SCIENCES
ARTELI RABOCHIKH DLIA OSNOVANIIA FABRIK ILI MASTERSKIKH : ASSOTSIATSII / Miloradovich, L – Spb., 1962 – 1mf – 9 – COR-75/1 – ne IDC [334]
ARTELI V DREVNEI I NYNESHNEI ROSSII / Kalachov, N V – Spb., 1864 – 2mf – 9 – COR-41/1 – ne IDC [334]
ARTELI V ROSSII / Isaev, A A – Iaroslavl', 1881 – 4mf – 9 – COR-35/1 – ne IDC [334]
ARTEL'NOE DELO / ed by Izd Obshchestva dlia sodeistviia arte l'nomu delo v Rossii – (Cont by: Trudovoe edinenie. Petrograd, 1918-19 n2. Missing: 1916: n10; 1918: n10-12.) – Petrograd, 1916-17 n10 – 12mf – 9 – COR-546/1 – ne IDC [334]
ARTEL'NOE DELO / ed by Izd Soiuza soiuzov promyslovoi i proizvoditel'no-trudovoi koop. Sev. r-na "Artel'trudsoiuza" – Petrograd, 1921-24 – 13mf – 9 – COR-547/1 – ne IDC [334]
ARTEL'NYI MIR – St Petersburg, 1913-14 – 9mf – 9 – COR-548/1 – ne IDC [334]
ARTEMAS WARD PAPERS, 1721-1953 / Ward, Artemas – Massachusetts Historical Society – 5r – 1 – $385.00 – us UMI [920]
Artemev, A I *see*
- KRATKOE NACHERTANIE RIMSKIKH.
- OPISANIE RUKOPISEI, KHRANIASHCHIKHSIA V BIBLIOTEKE IMP. KAZANSKAGO UNIVERSITETA

Artemev, E A *see* SPUTNIK KUSTARIA I REMESLENNIKA
L'ARTEMISIA L'ANNO 1801 A VENEZIA / Cimarosa, D – Ms, 180? – 1 – us Sibley [780]
DIE ARTEN DER GATTUNG ALISMA / Samuelsson, A – 7 – uk Microform Academic [580]

DIE ARTEN, UNTERARTEN, VARIETAETEN UND HYBRIDEN DER SECTION PTARMICA DES GENUS ACHILLEA / Heimerl, A – Wien. 1884. B-1012 2 – 8 – ne IDC [580]

ARTERIAL HYPOXEMIA AND PERFORMANCE DURING INTENSE EXERCISE / Koskolou, Maria D & McKenzie, Donald C – 1991 – 1mf – 9 – $4.00 – us Microform Publ [613]

ARTERIOSCLEROSIS / American Heart Association, Inc – v1-. 1981- – 1,5,6,9 – us UMI [073]

ARTERY – v1-10. 1974-82 – 1,5,6 – us Princeton Micro [616]

ARTES PRAEDICANDI : CONTRIBUTION A L'HISTOIRE DE LA RHETORIQUE AU MOYEN AGE / Charland, T -M – Paris, 1936 – 7mf – 8 – ne Slangenburg [440]

ARTHRITIS AND RHEUMATISM – (v19- , 1976- . 9) – v. 1-. 1934- – 1 – us UMI [616]

THE ARTHUR A. SCHOMBURG PAPERS, 1724-1938 – (With printed guide. Col title: Manuscript Collections from the Schomburg Centre for Research in Black Culture, the New York Public Library) – 12r – 1 – $1,390.00 – 1-55655-376-5 – us UPA [305]

ARTHUR A. SHURCLIFF COLLECTION OF GLASS LANTERN SLIDES – (879 glass lantern slides illustrating 19th- and early 20th-century urban and landscape planning in Boston area) – Massachusetts Historical Society – 2r – 1 – $155.00 – us UMI [710]

ARTHUR BREED REAL ESTATE SCRAPBOOK – 1r – 1 – $50.00 – B03368 – us Library Micro [333]

Arthur, Chester A *see* PAPERS

ARTHUR ENTERPRISE – Arthur, NE. -w. Mar. 1911-Sep. 1913. Incomplete; Dec. 1915-Jun. 1917; Feb. 1920- – 1 – us NE Hist [071]

ARTHUR FITGER : SEIN LEBEN UND SCHAFFEN / Wocke, Helmut – (Includes bibliographical references) – Stuttgart: Metzler, 1913 – 1 – us U.W. Library [430]

Arthur H *see* PAPERS AND ADDRESSES...: IMPERIAL FEDERATION AND COLONISATION, FROM 1880 TO 1894

Arthur, John P *see* WESTERN NORTH CAROLINA-A HISTORY 1730-1913

Arthur, William *see*
- ON THE DIFFERENCE BETWEEN PHYSICAL AND MORAL LAW
- TONGUE OF FIRE: THE TRUE POWER OF CHRISTIANITY

ARTHUR YOUNG'S TOUR IN IRELAND (1776-1779) / Young, Arthur – Ed. with introd. and notes by Arthur Wollaston Hutton. Bibliog. by John P. Anderson. London, New York: G. Bell & Sons, 1892. 2v. map – 1 – us U.W. Library [910]

ARTI DAN TUDJUAN DEMOGRAFI / Tan, Goan Tiang – SE 5674 1. 1965 – 9 – ne IDC [310]

ARTIBUS ASIAE – Hellerau, Dresden, 1925-37.- v1-7 – 49mf – 8 – CH-857c/2 – ne IDC [073]

ARTICLE 19 – London. 61 docs. 1986-1991 – 45mf – 9 – ne IDC [320]

THE ARTICLE, BIBLE, IN THE ENCYCLOPAEDIA BRITANNICA / Smith, William Robertson – The Daily Review, 21 Jun 1876, p6 – 9 – us A.T.L.A. [220]

THE ARTICLED CLERK'S JOURNAL AND EXAMINER – London. v1-3. 1879-81 (all publ) – 4mf – 9 – $6.00 – LLMC 84-406 – us L.L.M.C. [073]

ARTICLES ACCORDEZ ENTRE LE ... ROY DE FRANCE ET LE ... ROY DE LA GRANDE BRETAIGNE – Paris, 1623 – 1mf – 9 – ILM-1243/1 – ne IDC [340]

THE ARTICLES AND CONDITIONS OF THE PERPETUAL PEACE... – Rotterdam, London, 1648 – 1mf – 9 – ILM-1165/1 – ne IDC [340]

ARTICLES AND LEAFLETS / Anti-Soviet Society – The Real Lessons of Vietnam; To Fight Communism: Why and How? Don't Blame the Russian People; Victory; Strategies That Will Win; The Real Peace Movement? The Vital Nuclear Deterrent; Sergei Soldatov Speaks; Worse Than the Tsars; Getting at the Red Army. 22p – 9 – 1.00f – at Libertarian Micro [335]

ARTICLES D'ANDRE LAURENDEAU – Montreal, 1947-1967 – 1r – 1 – cn Can Microfilming [072]

ARTICLES DE LA PAIX D'HONGRIE,... – Rouen, 1607 – 1mf – 9 – ILM-881/1 – ne IDC [340]

ARTICLES ENACTED IN THE ACT INTITULED "AN ACT TO REPEAL A CERTAIN ACT THEREIN-MENTIONED, AND TO PROVIDE FOR THE POLICE OF THE BOROUGH OF WILLIAM-HENRY,... / Bas-Canada. Laws, Statutes etc – Quebec: P.E. Desbarats, 1824. SEM105P1221 – 1mf – 9 – Can$2.25 – cn Bibl Nat [360]

ARTICLES, LETTERS AND MISCELLANEOUS PAPERS, 1873-1907 / Fison, Lorimer – 1r – at Pacific Mss [306]

ARTICLES OF PEACE AND ALLIANCE,... – [London], 1667 – 1mf – 9 – ILM-847/1 – ne IDC [340]

ARTICLES OF PEACE, ENTERCOURSE, AND COMMERCE,... – London, 1630 – 1mf – 9 – ILM-660/1 – ne IDC [340]

ARTICLES OF THE TREATY SIGNED AT SEVILLE IN SPAIN,... – London, 1729 – 1mf – 9 – ILM-2754/1 – ne IDC [340]

THE ARTICLES OF WAR : HISTORICAL TEXTS – repr of appendix to 2nd ed 1896, of William Winthrop's classic treatise on military law. Washington: GPO, 1920 – 2mf – 9 – $3.00 – LLMC 88-029 – us L.L.M.C. [340]

ARTICLES ON MODERN ART / Dimes, Louis Thomas – SE-3146 1. 1960 – 9 – ne IDC [700]

ARTICLES SUR L'HEREDITE DE LA PROPRIETE / Fournel, Henri – Paris, Le Globle, 1831, 30 p. Les Saint-Simoniens, 1825-1834. 6869 – 9 – fr Hachette [335]

ARTICLES TOUCHING NAVIGATION AND COMMERCE,... – N.p., 1668 – 1mf – 9 – ILM-1164/1 – ne IDC [340]

ARTICULI ECCLESIAE ANGLICANAE = THIRTY-NINE ARTICLES : OR, THE SEVERAL EDITIONS OF THE ARTICLES OF THE CHURCH OF ENGLAND: AS AGREED UPON IN CONVOCATION, AND SET FORTH BY ROYAL AUTHORITY, DURING THE REIGNS OF KING EDWARD 6TH AND QUEEN ELIZABETH / ed by Davey, William Harrison – (Preface in English; texts in English and Latin) – Oxford: J H & Jas Parker, 1861 – 1mf – 9 – 0-8370-8801-1 – 1986-2801 – us A.T.L.A. [240]

ARTICULOS DE COSTUMBRES / Cavanillas y Munoz, Juan Alonso – 1879 – 9 – 1.50f – sp Bibl Santa Ana [390]

ARTICVLVS DE LIBERO ARBITRIO, SEV HVMANI ARBITRII VIRIBVS, EX SCRIPTVRAE / Hunnius, A – Francofvrti ad Moenvm, 1597 – 2mf – ne IDC [240]

ARTICVLVS DE PERSONA CHRISTI: DVARVM IN EA NATVRARVM VNIONE HYPOSTATICA... / Hunnius, A – [Vrsellis, 1585] – 6mf – ne IDC [240]

LES ARTIFICES DES HERETIQUES / Rapin, R – Paris, 1681 – 5mf – 9 – CA-143/1 – ne IDC [240]

ARTIFICIAL INTELLIGENCE – v1-24. 1970-84 – 1,5,6,13 – sz Elsevier [000]

ARTIFICIAL INTELLIGENCE AND THE LAW – v1-3. 1922-1994 – 9 – us Hein [340]

ARTIFICIAL INTELLIGENCE REVIEW – v1- . 1987- – 1,5,6,9 – us UMI [073]

ARTIFICIAL KEY TO THE ORCHID GENERA OF THE NETHERLANDS EAST INDIES,... / Smith, J J – Leiden, 1934 – 1mf – 9 – 13,665/1 – ne IDC [580]

ARTIFICIAL RAINFALL : NEWSLETTER / Center of Scientific and Technological Information – (Missing: 1971(2)) – Tel Aviv, 1970-1979. Nos. 1-37 – 15mf – 9 – J-81-25/1 – ne IDC [621]

Artigas, Miguel *see* LAS CIEN MEJORES POESIAS (LIRICAS) DE LA LENGUA CASTELLANA

ARTIKEL DAN PIDATO PADA ULANGTAHUN2 REVOLUSI OKTOBER / Lenin, Vladimir Ilyich – SE-10,819 1. 1961 – 9 – ne IDC [335]

L'ARTILLERIE AU MAROC : CAMPAGNES EN CHAOUFA / Feline, Marie Charles – Paris: Berger-Levrault, 1912 – 1 – us Res Libr [960]

ARTILLERY FOR THE U.S. LAND SERVICE WITH PLATES, BY BREVET MAJOR ALFRED MORDECAI (WASHINGTON 1848-49) / U.S. War Department. Adjutant General's Office – T1104 – 1r – 1 – us Nat'l Archives [324]

ARTILLERY TRENDS – (See also: Tactical and Technial Trends in Artillery for Instruction and Field Artilleryman) – n. 6-42. 1958-1968 – 1 – us UMI [355]

ARTIS CHEMICAE PRINCIPES, AVICENNA ATQVE GEBER, HOC VOLUMINE CONTINENTUR – Basileae, 1572 – 1 – us U.W. Library [540]

ARTIS LOGICAE COMPENDIUM / Aldrich, Henry – Oxoninae, 1696 – 1 – us U.W. Library [160]

ARTIS MUSICAE LEGIBUS LOGICIS METHODICE INFORMATAE LIBRI DUO...REVISI ET RECOGNITI, MULTISQUE IN LOCIS EMENDATI ET CORRECTI, AB AUCTORE.. / Magirus, Johann – 1611 – 5,9 – us Sibley [780]

L'ARTISAN / ed by Huston, J & Aubin, Napoleon – Quebec, Canada. 10 oct 1842-26 sep 1844 – 1r – 1 – Can$30.00 – cn Can Microfilming [073]

L'ARTISAN – Journal de la classe ouvriere. prosp., no. 1-4. Paris. sept-oct 1830 – 1 – fr A.C.R.P.P. [073]

L'ARTISAN : JOURNAL OUVRIER – Quebec, Canada. 5 jan 1888-v1 n104. 9 mai 1888 – 1r – 1 – Can$50.00 – cn Can Microfilming [073]

L'ARTISAN – Repentigny, Canada. 3 avr 1968-30 dec 1970 – 2r – 1 – Can$50.00r – cn Can Microfilming [072]

L'ARTISAN – Riviere-du-Loup, Canada. 1 aut 1961; v1 n11. 17 oct 1961 – 1r – 1 – Can$25.00 – cn Can Microfilming [072]

L'ARTISAN – Saint-Hyacinthe, Canada. 31 jul 1890-11 jun 1891 – 1r – 1 – Can$25.00 – cn Can Microfilming [072]

L'ARTISAN : SOCIETE DES ARTISANS – Montreal, Canada. v48 n1. jan 1937-v73 n2. avr 1969 – 1r – 1 – Can$35.00 – cn Can Microfilming [331]

THE ARTISAN – 1 – 50.00 – cn McLaren [971]

THE ARTISAN – Freetown. Sierra Leone. -m. May 1884-Dec 1888. (28 ft) – 1 – uk British Libr Newspaper [072]

ARTISANAL FISHERIES OF THE CHAD BASIN IN AFRICA : AN OVERVIEW OF RESEARCH AND ANNOTATED BIBLIOGRAPHY 1920-1990 – 1992 – 97p – it F.A.O. [338]

L'ARTISANAT ALGERIEN / Algeria. Chambre de Commerce et d'Industrie d'Alger – 1968. BNE-8701 1 – 9 – ne IDC [331]

L'ARTISANAT AU CANADA FRANCAIS (1900-1950) : BIBLIOGRAPHIE ANALYTIQUE / Falardeau, Edith – 1956. SEM105P4 – 656mf – 9 – Can$1,476.00 – cn Bibl Nat [740]

ARTISANATS TRADITIONNELS EN COTE D'IVOIRE / Etienne-Nugue, J – 9 – F60.00 – fr Ethnologie [740]

Artisans' Permanent Building Society. Quebec *see* BY-LAWS...15TH JANUARY 1875

THE ARTIST / ed by Hoare, Prince – v1-2. 1810 – 1r – 1 – us Ross [700]

ARTIST FILES / New York. Museum of Modern Art – (mf ed 1992 A-F) – 5697mf – 9 – £18,900.00 coll – uk Chadwyck [700]

ARTIST I SSTENA – Illiustrirovannyi dvukhnedel'nyi zhurnal dramy, operetki, farsa. Spb. 1910-12. Lacking: (9, 22-23) 1910; (6, 10, 24) 1911; (7, 12-24) 1912. BR-1525 2 – 8 – ne IDC [410]

THE ARTIST OF "ISLETA PAINTINGS" IN PUEBLO SOCIETY / Goldfrank, Esther – 1967 – 5mf – 9 – $5.00f – us Ross [750]

ARTISTA – S. Salvador, BA. 6 Maio 1876 – 1,5,6 – bl Biblioteca [072]

O ARTISTA : JORNAL DEDICADO A INDUSTRIA E PRINCIPALMENTE AS ARTES – Sao Luis, 25 May 1862-Aug 1863; Mar 1868-25 Jul 1869 – 1,5,6 – bl Biblioteca [072]

O ARTISTA – Manaos, Amazonas. 28 Set-Out 1886; 5 Jan 1887 – 1,5,6 – bl Biblioteca [072]

O ARTISTA : ORGAO DEMOCRATICO, NOTICIOSO E CRITICO – Santo Amaro, BA. 22 Nov 1877-30 Jan 1878 – 1,5,6 – bl Biblioteca [072]

LOS ARTISTAS PINTORES DE LA EXPEDICION MALASPINA. BUENOS AIRES, 1944 / Torre Revello, Jose – Madrid: Razon y Fe, 1946 – 1 – sp Bibl Santa Ana [700]

L'ARTISTE – Journal de la litterature et des beaux-arts. Dir. A. Delaunay. Paris. 1831-99, 1901, dec 1904, inc – 1 – fr A.C.R.P.P. [073]

L'ARTISTE – Montreal, Canada. 10-18 mai 1860 – 1r – 1 – Can$25.00 – cn Can Microfilming [072]

L'ARTISTE – Montreal: Imprime Pour les Proprietaires par J Lovell, 1860 – 9 – cn C.I.H.M. [700]

ARTISTE RUSSE – St Petersburg, 1846-48 (bimonthly) – 24mf – 9 – us Ross [780]

ARTISTE RUSSE *see* ANTRAKT

ARTIST-MUZYKANT – Moscow, 1918-19 (3 issues publ) – 1mf – 9 – us Ross [780]

ARTISTS' AND WRITERS' CHAP BOOK – New York. Dec 15 1933; May 3 1935 – 1 – us NY Public [420]

ARTISTS FILES / New York. Public Library – (Largest publ source of info on artists & craftspeople fr all ages & countries. File is arranged by names in alphabetical order) – 1911 (mf ed 1989) – 11,381mf + index of 81,117 artists – 9 – £19,515.00 coll – uk Chadwyck [700]

ARTIST'S MAGAZINE – (1986-. 1,5,6) – 1984- – 9 – us UMI [700]

ARTISTS SCRAPBOOKS : ANNI ALBERS TO FRANK LLOYD WRIGHT / New York. Museum of Modern Art – (126 vols on 42 artists) – 642mf – 9 – £2,975.00 coll – uk Chadwyck [700]

ARTISTS' SKETCHBOOKS IN THE BRITISH MUSEUM – Bath: Mindata, September 1996 – 12r – 1 – $1,100.00 – 1-900853-50-7 – uk Mindata [700]

ARTITUDES INTERNATIONAL – St Jeannet, 1972-74 – 1r – 1 – £60.00 – uk Chadwyck [700]

Arto-Haumacher, Rafael *see* C.F. GELLERTS BRIEFSTILREFORM

Artois, Hugues d' *see* FRANCE ET CANADA

ARTROPODOS DEL VIAJE AL PACIFICO... : INSECTOS NEUROPTEROS Y ORTOPTEROS / Bolivar de Urrutia, Ignacio – Madrid: Ginesta, 1884 – 1 – F69.26 – fr Armell [590]

ARTS – Beaux-arts, litterature, spectacles. Paris. G. Wildenstein, Dir. 31 janv 1945-aout 1966 – 1 – fr A.C.R.P.P. [073]

ARTS ANCIENS DE FLANDRE – Bruges, 1905-13.-v1-6 – 48mf – 9 – O-1215/1 – ne IDC [700]

ARTS AND ACTIVITIES – (1971- . 5,6. 1975- . 9) – 1- 1939- – 1 – us UMI [073]

ARTS AND ANTIQUES *see* AMERICAN ART AND ANTIQUES

ARTS AND ARCHITECTURE – (1983-. 1,5,6,9) – NSv1-. 1981- – 1 – us UMI [073]

ARTS AND CRAFTS IN INDONESIA / Indonesia. Kementerian Penerangan – SE-10,096 1. 3d ed. 1960 – 9 – ne IDC [740]

ARTS AND ENTERTAINMENT – Mendocino, CA. v11 no11/12 1986-v15 no12 1990 – 2r – 1 – $100.00 – B06036 – us Library Micro [071]

ARTS COUNCIL OF GREAT BRITAIN CATALOGUE – (Individual titles not listed separately) – London, 1942-1978 – 892 catalogues on 1022mf – 9 – £5,365.00 – uk Chadwyck [700]

LES ARTS EN PORTUGAL / Raczynski, A – O$1058 1. 1846 – 9 – ne IDC [700]

ARTS ET METIERS / Societe des Anciens Eleves des Ecoles nationales d'Arts et Metiers – Paris. oct 1920-41 – 1 – fr A.C.R.P.P. [740]

ARTS ET METIERS GRAPHIQUES – Paris, 1927-39 – 6r – 1 – £345.00 – uk Chadwyck [760]

ARTS IN PSYCHOTHERAPY – v7- 1980- – 1,5,6,9 – us UMI [615]

ARTS IN SOCIETY – (1971- . 5,6. 1976- . 9) – v. 1-13. 1958-76 – 1 – us UMI [700]

LES ARTS INCOHERENTS : PREMIERE EXPOSITION A NANTES DU 17 FEVRIER AU 30 MARS 1887 – Nantes: Imp. du Commerce, 1887 – fr Armell [700]

THE ARTS OF THE HAUSA : AN ASPECT OF ISLAMIC CULTURE IN NORTHERN NIGERIA / Commonwealth Institute – (62p accompanying text) – 1977 – 2 color mf – 15 – $36.00f – 0-226-68899-2 – us Chicago [700]

ARTS SIGNORUM / Dalgarno, George – 1661. 147p. (English Linguistics Series 1500-1800) – 9 – us UMI [400]

ARTS WEST MAGAZINE – (Ceased: v9 1984) – v1-9. 1975-84 – 9 – Can$20.00y – cn Micromedia [700]

ARTSATLANTIC – (1977-84 Can$100.00) – Charlottetown. v1- 1977- – 5 – Can$50.00y – cn Micromedia [700]

ARTSCANADA – (Ceased: v38 1982) – Toronto. v1-38. 1943-1982 – 1,9 – Price varies with yr – cn Micromedia [073]

ARTSCANADA – (v28-39, no.1. Feb 1971-Nov 1982. 5,6. v32-39, no.1. Mar 1975-Nov 1982. 9) – v1-39, no.1. Oct 1943-Nov 1982 – 1 – us UMI [073]

Artsikhovskii, A V *see*
- NOVGORODSKIE GRAMOTY NA BERESTE (IZ RASKOPOK 1952 G.)
- NOVGORODSKIE GRAMOTY NA BERESTE (IZ RASKOPOK 1953-54 GG.)

- NOVGORODSKIE GRAMOTY NA BERESTE (IZ RASKOPOK 1956-57 GG.)
- NOVGORODSKIE GRAMOTY NA BERESTE (IZ RASKOPOK 1958-1961 GG.)
- NOVGORODSKIE GRAMOTY NA BERESTE (IZ RASPOKOK 1955 G.)
- NOVOGORODSKIE GRAMOTY NA BERESTE (IZ RASKOPOK 1951 G.)

Artsybushev, U K *see* "DIKTATURA PROLETARIATA" V ROSSII

Artus, Gaston Andre *see* GIJIG-ANANG MEKATEOKONAIE, S.J. O GAGIKWEWINAN

Artusi, Giovanni M *see*
- L'ARTE DEL CONTRAPONTO RIDOTTA IN TAVOLE.
- L'ARTUSI OVERO DELLE IMPERFETTIONI' DELLA MODERNA MUSICA RAGIONAMENTI DUI

L'ARTUSI OVERO DELLE IMPERFETTIONI' DELLA MODERNA MUSICA RAGIONAMENTI DUI / Artusi, Giovanni M – 1600. Contains also: Seconda Parte. 1589 – 9 – us Sibley [780]

ARTVIEWS – (Ceased: v15 1989) – Toronto. v1-15. 1974-89 – 9 – Can$20.00y – cn Micromedia [700]

ARTVIN VILAYETI HAKKINDA MALUMAT-I UMUMIYE / Zeki, Muvahhid – [Istanbul]: Sikret-i Mertebiye Matbaasi, 1927 – 9 – $50.00 – us MEDOC [956]

ARUANNE = REPORT / Estonian Baptist Union – 1922, 19th Report; 1939, 36th Report. 62p – 1 – 5.00 – us Baptist [240]

Aruba. (Netherlands) *see* ONTWIKKELINGSPLAN

ARUCHAS BAS-AMMI: ISRAELS HEILUNG / Ruelf, I – Frankfurt a.M. 1883. BJ-28-60 1 – 9 – ne IDC [956]

ARUK. DICTIONARIVM CHALDAICUM,... / Muenster, S – Basileae, 1527 – 5mf – ne IDC [470]

ARUK HAS-SORASOT. DICTIONARIVM HEBRAICVM,... / Muenster, S – Basel, 1523 – 6mf – ne IDC [470]

ARUN GAZETTE *see* LITTLEHAMPTON GAZETTE

Arundell, John Francis *see* SCIENTIFIC VALUE OF TRADITION: A CORRESPONDENCE

Arvatov, B *see* SOTSIOLOGICHESKAIA POETIKA

Arvieux, Laurent d' *see* VOYAGE FAIT PAR ORDRE DU ROY LOUIS 14TH DANS LA PALESTINE AVEC LA DESCRIPTION GENERALE DE L'ARABIE FAITE PAR LE SULTAN ISMAEL ABULFEDA, TRADUITE EN FRANCAIS SUR LES MEILLEURS MANUSCRITS PAR M.D.L.R. (DE LA ROQUE)

ARVIKA ALLEHANDA – Arvika, 1890-94 – 9 – sw Kungliga [072]

ARVIKA NYHETER – Arvika, Sweden. 1895- – 1 – sw Kungliga [072]

ARVORE NOVA – Rio de Janeiro, Sep-Oct 1922; Jan 1923. – 1,5,6 – bl Biblioteca [072]

Arx, Walther von *see* GOTTFRIED KELLER

ARYAN PATH – Bombay, 1930-1965. v1-36 – 438mf – 9 – I-370/2 – ne IDC [073]

ARYAVARTA – Patna, India. 2 May 1949-1951; Jul 1952-1987 – 113r – 1 – us L of C Photodup [072]

ARZNEIBUCH 'MACER' *see* HERBAR : ARZNEIBUCH 'MACER'

Arzt, Frederick Karl *see* HISTORY AND OUTLINE OF LAWS RELATING TO VESSEL INSPECTION

A.S. FALARDEAU ET A.E. AUBRY / Casgrain, Henri-Raymond – 1912. SEM105P715 – 2mf – 9 – Can$4.50 – cn Bibl Nat [920]

AS GAVETAS DA TORRE FOMBO 4, LISBOA 1964 / Barrado Manzano, Arcangel – Madrid: Graf. Calleja, 1967 – 1 – sp Bibl Santa Ana [946]

AS I LAY DYING – Concordance to the novel – 5mf – 9 – us UMI [420]

"AS I REMEMBER KANSAS CITY FROM MY BOYHOOD AND ITS TOWNHOOD DAYS." / Hymer, Julian B – ("Reminiscence of 64 years of Railroading." 1) – 1 – us KS Hist [978]

AS MISSOES... / Silva Rego, Antonio da – Madrid: Archivo Ibero Americano, 1960 – 1 – sp Bibl Santa Ana [240]

AS MOEDAS VISIGODAS DA LUSITANIA / Elias Garcia, A – Guimaraes, 1950 – 1 – sp Bibl Santa Ana [946]

AS OTHERS SAW HIM : A RETROSPECT, A.D. 54: WITH INTRODUCTION, AFTERWORDS, AND NOTES / Jacobs, Joseph – (First published anonymously in 1895. Account of Holy Week from a Jewish standpoint. Includes explanatory references) – New York: Funk & Wagnalls, 1903 – 1mf – 9 – 0-8370-3745-X – 1985-1745 – us A.T.L.A. [920]

AS OTHERS SEE US : A STUDY OF PROGRESS IN THE UNITED STATES / Brooks, John Graham – New York: Macmillan, 1908 – 1mf – us A.T.L.A. [240]

A.S. Pratt and Sons. Washington, D.C *see* DUTIES, POWERS, AND LIABILITY OF NATIONAL BANK DIRECTORS

AS REALIZACOES ARGENTINAS NO CAMPO POLITICO – [Buenos Aires?: Servico Internacional de Publicacoes Argentinas, 195-?] – 1 – CSUXADJ1068-B – us Hoover Inst Photo [320]

AS- SIDDIQ – no. 1-54. Alger. aout 1920-mars 1922. mq no. 11 – 1 – fr A.C.R.P.P. [073]

AS SIRAT – Organe de l'Association des Ulamas Musulmans Algeriens. no. 1-15. Constantine. sept-dec 1933 – 1 – fr A.C.R.P.P. [073]

AS TO ROGER WILLIAMS AND HIS 'BANISHMENT' FROM THE MASSACHUSETTS PLANTATION : WITH A FEW FURTHER WORDS CONCERNING THE BAPTISTS, THE QUAKERS, AND RELIGIOUS LIBERTY: A MONOGRAPH / Dexter, Henry Martyn – Boston: Congregational Pub. Society, 1876 – 1mf – us A.T.L.A. [978]

ASA (ACOUSTICAL SOCIETY OF AMERICA) – Printed index. Updated every 60 days – 6,9 – us Info Handling [600]

ASA TURNER : A HOME MISSIONARY PATRIARCH AND HIS TIMES / Magoun, George F – Boston: Congregational Sunday-School and Pub. Society, c1889 – 1mf – us A.T.L.A. [240]

Asad Sulayman Abduh *see* BAD AWJUH AL-IKHTILAF FI RASM ISM AL-MAKAN AL-WAHID BI-HURUF AL-LUGHAH AL ARABIYAH FI AL-MAMLAKAH AL-ARABIYAH AL-SAUDIYAH

Asadov, A *see* SEMEINOE PRAVO

ASAE (AMERICAN SOCIETY OF AGRICULTURAL ENGINEERS) – Standards. Printed index. Updated every 60 days – 6,9 – us Info Handling [630]

ASAHI EVENING NEWS – January 1954-December 1994 – 260r – 1 – Y2,666,000 – ja Japan Micro [072]

ASAHI EVENING NEWS – [Japan], 1954- – 1 – inquire – us Ross [072]

ASAHI EVENING NEWS – Tokyo, Jul 1965-Dec 1970 – 23r – 1 – uk British Libr Newspaper [072]

ASAHI SHIMBUN – 1 – F12,486.00 – sz Infoprint [072]

ASAHI SHIMBUN – 1818 – 1 – F917.00 – sz Infoprint [072]

ASAHI SHIMBUN – 1889-1920 – 1 – F3,056.00 – sz Infoprint [072]

ASAHI SHIMBUN – 1921-1940 – 1 – F4,453.00 – sz Infoprint [072]

ASAHI SHIMBUN – 1941-1943 – 1 – F2,969.00 – sz Infoprint [072]

ASAHI SHIMBUN – 1944-1948 – 1 – F1,484.00 – sz Infoprint [072]

ASAHI SHIMBUN – 1949-1951 – 1 – F1,484.00 – sz Infoprint [072]

ASAHI SHIMBUN – 1952 – 1 – F2,969.00 – sz Infoprint [072]

ASAHI SHIMBUN – 1953-1962 – 1 – F5,937.00 – sz Infoprint [072]

ASAHI SHIMBUN – 1963-1987 – 1 – F9,779.00 – sz Infoprint [072]

ASAHI SHIMBUN – 1988-1993 – 1 – F11,874.00 – sz Infoprint [072]

ASAHI SHIMBUN – (Over 100 Years of Japanese Newspaper Reporting) – Japan, 1888- – 1 – us Primary [072]

ASAHI SHIMBUN – (Tokyo Edition July 1888-December 1988 1,228r Y13,365,000 1989-36r per yr Y310,000 $1,060.00; Osaka Edition January 1879-December 1990 1 460r Y14,489,000 1991- .24r per year Y289,000; Nagoya Edition, February 1950-December 1994 902r Y9,308,000; Jiyuto/Tomoshibi/ Mesamashi (Asahi's antecedents) May 1884-July 1888 12r Y120,000) – 1 – ja Japan Micro [072]

ASAHI SHIMBUN – (Yrly reel count varies) – Nagoya, 1950- – 1 – us Ross [072]

ASAHI SHIMBUN – (Yrly reel count varies) – Osaka, 1879- – 1 – us Ross [072]

ASAHI SHIMBUN – (Yrly reel count varies) – Tokyo, 1888- – 1 – us Ross [072]

ASAIO JOURNAL – (Cont: ASAIO Transactions) – Hagerstown. v38-43 jan 1992-dec 1997+ 1,5,9; v38 1992* 5 – 1,5,9 – D16011.02 – us UMI [073]

ASAIO JOURNAL *see* ASAIO TRANSACTIONS

ASAIO TRANSACTIONS / American Society for Artificial Internal Organs – (Cont by: ASAIO Journal n16011.02) – Hagerstown. v32-37 jul 1986-dec 1991 1; v32-36 jul 1986-dec 1990. v37 1991* 5; v32-37 jul 1986-dec 1991 9 – 1,5,9 – $195.00y – D16011.01 – us UMI [500]

ASAIO TRANSACTIONS *see* ASAIO JOURNAL

ASAL USUL KAPITALIS INDUSTRI. BAB 31 "KAPITAL" DJILIK I KARL MARX / Marx, Karl – SE-10,693 1. 1965 – 9 – ne IDC [335]

ASAM BANI – (Assamese language) – Gauhati, India. 1962-Jun 1965 – 4r – 1 – us L of C Photodup [072]

ASAMBLEA ASISTENCIAL DE LA C.N.S. DE CACERES : PLAN ASISTENCIAL PROVINCIAL EN SU ALCANCE GLOBAL / Central Nacional Sindicalista. Caceres – Caceres: Tip. El Noticiero, 1948 – sp Bibl Santa Ana [330]

ASAMBLEA FILIPINA – Manila, Philippines. 18 Oct-11 Nov 1907; 27 Jul-26 Sep 1908 – 38ft – 1 – uk British Libr Newspaper [072]

ASAMBLEA PERMANENTE DE DERECHOS HUMANOS DE BOLIVIA – La Paz. 82 docs. 1980-1990 – 23mf – 9 – ne IDC [320]

ASAMBLEA PERMANENTE POR LOS DERECHOS HUMANOS (APDH) = PERMANENT ASSEMBLY FOR HUMAN RIGHTS – Buenos Aires. 138 docs. 1980-1991 – 56mf – 9 – 504.00 – ne IDC [320]

ASAMBLEA PLENARIA DEL CONSEJO ECONOMICO PROVINCIAL / Wulff Martin, Enrique – Caceres, s.i., 1953 – sp Bibl Santa Ana [330]

ASAMBLEA PLENARIA DEL CONSEJO ECONOMICO SINDICAL / Solano Pedrero, Carlos – Caceres, s.i., 1947 – sp Bibl Santa Ana [330]

ASAMBLEAS CONSTITUYENTES ARGENTINAS... / Raviguani, Emilio – Madrid: Razon y Fe, 1940 – 1 – sp Bibl Santa Ana [972]

DIE ASAPH-PSALMEN : HISTORISCH-KRITISCH UNTERSUCHT / Kopfstein, Marcus – (Includes bibliographical references) – Marburg: In Commission von Oscar Ehrhardt's Universitaets-Buchhandlung, 1881 – 1mf – 9 – 0-8370-3984-3 – 1985-1984 – us A.T.L.A. [220]

ASAR-I HAMIDE-I AKLAM – Osman Rasih, 1290 [1873] – $10.00 – us MEDOC [956]

ASAR-I ZIVER PASA – Bursa – 6mf – 9 – $36.00 – us MEDOC [949]

ASAS-ASAS HUKUM PERDATA INTERNASIONAL / Wirjono, Prodjodikoro – SE 4080 1. 1961 – 9 – ne IDC [950]

ASATIR – Samaritan Book of the Secrets of Moses. M. Gaster, Translator.1927 – 1 – uk Microform Academic [470]

ASB BULLETIN / Association of Southeastern Biologists – (1974- . 5,6. 1977- . 9) – 1954- – 1 – us UMI [574]

ASBAREZ – Glendale, CA. 1974- – 48+ r – 1 – $2,400.00 ($160.00y) – C02368 – us Library Micro [071]

Asbeck, F M van *see* ONDERZOEK NAAR DEN JURIDISCHEN WERELDBOUW

Asbeck, Wilhelm Ernst *see* DER GEHEIMNISVOLLE HOF

L'ASBESTOS / ed by Poirier, O – (Cont by and filmed with: Le Citoyen 4 avr 1950-30 dec 1986) – Asbestos, Canada. 20 mar 1941-28 mar 1950 – 31r – 1 – Can$65.00r – cn Can Microfilming [072]

L'ASBESTOS *see* LE CITOYEN

ASBESTOS – v64, no.8-. Feb 1983- – 1,5,6,9 – us UMI [073]

ASBESTOS CASE MANAGEMENT : PRETRIAL AND TRIAL PROCEDURES / Willging, Thomas E – Washington: FJC, 1985 – 1mf – 9 – $1.50 – LLMC 95-321 – us L.L.M.C. [340]

Asbjornsen, Peter Christen *see* ROUND THE YULE LOG

ASBURY AND HIS COADJUTORS / Larrabee, William Clark – 1853 – 9 – us A.T.L.A. [240]

ASC / University of Kentucky. Department of Animal Sciences – No.1-103. 1973-79. 7 fiches – 9 – us Spaulding [630]

ASCAP IN ACTION – (American Society of Composers, Authors and Publishers). 1979- – 1,5,6,9 – us UMI [780]

ASCE (AMERICAN SOCIETY OF CIVIL ENGINEERS) – Standards. Printed index. Updated every 60 days – 6,9 – us Info Handling [624]

ASCE (American Society of Civil Engineers). Technical Councils *see* JOURNAL

ASCE (American Society of Civil Engineers.) Water Resources Planning and Management Division *see* JOURNAL

LA ASCENDENCIA ESPANOLA EL INCA GARCILASO DE LA VEGA PRECISIONES GENEALOGICAS / Lohmann Villena, Guillermo – Madrid, s.i. 1958 – 1 – sp Bibl Santa Ana [920]

ASCENDIENTES Y DESCENDIENTES DE HERNANDO CORTES : LINEA DE MEDINA-SIDONIA Y OTROS / Valgoma y Diaz-Varela, Dalmiro de la – Madrid: Cultura Hispanica, 1951 – 1 – sp Bibl Santa Ana [920]

THE ASCENSION: A SACRED ORATORIO / Hook, James – 1776. Copyist's manuscript in ink with holograph corrections. Vocal score. MUSIC 1873, Item 1 – 1 – us L of C Photodup [780]

THE ASCENSION AND HEAVENLY PRIESTHOOD OF OUR LORD / Milligan, William – (Includes bibliographical references and indexes) – London; New York:Macmillan, 1892 – 1mf – 9 – 0-8370-4438-3 – 1985-2438 – us A.T.L.A. [240]

THE ASCENSION OF ISAIAH; TRANSLATED FROM (SEVERAL VERSIONS). EDITED WITH INTRODUCTION, NOTES, AND INDICES BY R. H. CHARLES. 1900 – 1 – us A.T.L.A. [270]

ASCENSO Y CAIDA DEL PERONISMO / Gonzalez, Ernesto – [Buenos Aires: Ediciones Antidoto, c1986] – 1 – CSUXADH4324-B – us Hoover Inst Photo [320]

ASCENT OF FAITH, OR, THE GROUNDS OF CERTAINTY IN SCIENCE AND RELIGION / Harrison, Alexander James – New York: Thomas Whittaker, 1894. 1 fiche – 9 – us A.T.L.A. [240]

THE ASCENT OF THE MATTERHORN / Whymper, Edward – London: J. Murray, 1880 – 1 roll – 1 – 1-55879-828-5 – uk Libr Preservation [910]

THE ASCENT OF THE SOUL / Bradford, Amory Howe – New York: Outlook, 1903.1 fiche – 9 – us A.T.L.A. [240]

L'ASCESA DEL PROLETARIO – Wilkes-Barre, PA, Oct. 1, 1908-Sep. 15, 1910 – 1r – 1 – us I.H.R.C. [978]

Asch, Sholem *see*
- AMERIKA
- PETERSBURG

Asch van Wijk, H A M van *see* DE DELICTIS EXTRA REGNI TERRITORIUM ADMISSIS

ASCHAFFENBURGER ZEITUNG – Aschaffenburg, 1848-49 – 2r – 1 – Dist. gw Mikrofilm – gw Misc Inst [943]

Ascham, Roger *see* THE SCHOOLMASTER, OR PLAINE AND PERFITE WAY OF TEACHING CHILDREN THE LATIN TONG

Aschenbrenner, Michael *see* LEHRBUCH DER METAPHYSIK

Ascher, Francois *see* TOURISM

Ascher, S *see*
- BEMERKUNGEN UEBER DIE BUERGERLICHE VERBESSERUNG DER JUDEN VERANLASZT BEI DER FRAGE: SOLL DER JUDE SOLDAT WERDEN?
- EISENMENGER DER ZWEITE
- DIE GERMANOMANIE

ASCHER TAGESBOTE *see* ASCHER ZEITUNG

ASCHER ZEITUNG – (Cont by: Ascher Tagesbote, 1933-34. Ascher Zeitung, 1935. dec 1 1933-feb 5 1934: weekly ed) – Asch, apr 16 1929-38 – 22r – 1 – Dist. gw Mikrofilm – gw Misc Inst [943]

Ascherson, P F A *see*
- FLORA DER PROVINZ BRANDENBURG, DER ALTMARK
- SYNOPSIS DER MITTELEUROPAEISCHEN FLORA

Aschoff, Wiebke *see* STUDIEN ZU NICCOLO TRIBOLO

ASCI JOURNAL OF MANAGEMENT / Administrative Staff College of India – v. 8-. 1978- – 1,5,6,9 – us UMI [650]

Asconius *see* IN ORATIONES QUASDAM CICERONIS ETC

Asdonk, Ben *see* ZUM VERHAELTNIS VON RELIGION UND MODERNER SCHULE

ASEAN ECONOMIC BULLETIN – Singapore. v1-9 jul 1984-92* 1; v10-11 jul 1993-mar 1995*. v12-14 1995-97+ 1,5,9 – 1,5,9 – D19169 – us UMI [330]

Ased y Latorre, A *see*
- HISTORIA DE LA EPIDEMIA...DE BARBASTRO EN EL ANO DE 1748...
- MEMORIA INSTRUCTIVA DE LOS MEDIOS DE PRECAVER LOS MALES RESULTAS DE UN TEMPORAL EXCESIVA MENTE HUMEDO

ASEDIO DE HUESCA; 18 JULIO 1936, 25 MARZO 1938 / Gode, Antonio – Huesca, 1938? Fiche W921. (Blodgett Collection of Spanish Civil War Pamphlets) – 9 – us H.U. College Libr [946]
ASEE PRISM – Washington. v2 sep1991-92* 1. v3-7 sep 1993-jun 1998+ 1,9; v3-4 sep 1993-jun 1995*. v5-7 sep 1995-jun 1998+ 5 – 1,5,9 – D20931 – us UMI [073]
Aseev, N *see*
– BOL'SHOI CHITATEL'. STIKHI
– DNEVNIK POETA
– IZBRANNOE
– IZBRANNYE PROIZVEDENIIA V DVUKH TOMAKH
– IZBRANNYE STIKHI
– IZBRANNYE STIKHOTVORENIIA I POEMY
– PAMIATI LET. SBORNIK STIKHOTVORENII 1912-1955
– RAZDUM'IA. STIKHOTVORENIIA
– RAZNOLET'E. STIKHI
– RUSSKII DRAMATICHESKII TEATR 17-18 VEKOV
– SOBRANIE SOCHINENII V 5 TOMAKH, TOM I
– SOBRANIE STIKHOTVORENII
– STIKHI
– STIKHOTVORENIIA I POEMY
– ZACHEM I KOMU NUZHNA POEZIIA
ASEGURAR UN REGIMEN DE LIBERTAD Y DEMOCRACIA / Spain. Ministerio de Gobernacion – Barcelona, 19?? Fiche W730. (Blodgett Collection of Spanish Civil War Pamphlets) – 9 – us H.U. College Libr [946]
Asencio, Jose Maria *see* CRONISTAS FRANCISCANOS
Asensio, Jose Maria *see*
– APUNTES PARA LA HISTORIA DE VILLAFRANCA DE LOS BARROS
– APUNTES PARA LA HISTORIA DE VILLAFRANCA DE LOS BARROS DE JOSE CASCALES MUNOZ...
Asenso, Antonio *see* LA PRENSA MADRILENA A TRAVES DE LOS SIGLOS
EL ASESINATO DE DON FRANCISCO PIZARRO / Fernandez-Davila, Guillermo – Lima: Imp. Lux, 1945 – sp Bibl Santa Ana [350]
EL ASESINATO DEL CONQUISTADOR DEL PERU : DON FRANCISCO PIZARRO (26 DE JUNIO DE 1541 / Fernandez-Davila, Guillermo – Lima: Imp. Lux. de L.E. Castro, 1941 – sp Bibl Santa Ana [350]
EL ASESINATO DEL REGATO DE LOS AVELLANOS / Ibarrola, Jose – Caceres: Tip. El Noticiero, s.a. – 1 – sp Bibl Santa Ana [946]
ASESINOS DE ESPANA ESTA ES VUESTRA OBRA – Madrid? 193? Fiche W 731. (Blodgett Collection of Spanish Civil War Pamphlets) – 9 – us H.U. College Libr [946]
THE ASG REPORT : AN OFFICIAL GOVERNMENT PERIODICAL / American Samoa. Government – Pago Pago: Govt of American Samoa, 28 Jul 1986-20 May 1988 – 6mf – 9 – $9.00 – LLMC 82-100C Title 48 – us L.L.M.C. [324]
ASGHAR AGA – (Continues: Taghut (shumarah-'i 22). Sal-i 1, shumarah-'i 23-Sal-i 4, shumarah-'i 122 (22 Day 1358-30 Murdad, 1361[12 Jan 1980-21 Aug 1982])) – London, 1980 – 1 reel – 1 – us MEDOC [950]
ASH – Portland OR. June 7 Oct 11 Dec 6 1968, Mar 28 May 9 Aug 29 Oct 24 1969, Dec 5 1969, Jan 2 Mar 6 27 1970, July 1970 – 1 – us U.O. Library [071]
Ash, John *see* GRAMMATICAL INSTITUTES
ASHA – v.21-. 1979-. Continues: ASHA (American Speech and Hearing Association) – 1,5,6,9 – us UMI [073]
ASHANTEE AND THE GOLD COAST / Beecham, J – London. 1841. BA-277 2 – 8 – ne IDC [960]
ASHANTI AND THE GOLD COAST : AND WHAT WE KNOW OF IT / Hay, John Charles Dalrymple – London: E Stanford, 1874 – 1 – us Res Libr [960]
ASHANTI PIONEER – Kumasi, Ghana. Dec 1951-Oct 1952 – 21r – 1 – uk British Libr Newspaper [072]
ASHANTI TIMES – Obuasi, Ghana. Jul 1951-Sep 1952; Dec 1953-54 – 2r – 1 – uk British Libr Newspaper [072]
Asharina, Nina et al *see* RUSSIAN GLASS OF THE 17TH-20TH CENTURIES
Ashburner, John *see* NOTES AND STUDIES IN THE PHILOSOPHY OF ANIMAL MAGNETISM AND SPIRITUALISM
Ashburner, W *see* THE RHODIAN SEA-LAW
ASHBURNHAM 1735-1900 – (Mf 1-3: Proprietors 1735-1801. Mf 4-18: Town Records 1801-56. Mf 19-20: Births 1750-1847. Mf 20: Marriages 1800-43. Mf 21: Deaths 1760-99. Mf 22-28: Town Records 1765-1801. Mf 25: Intentions 1765-69. Mf 25-26: Births 1752-1800. Mf 27: Deaths 1767-99. Mf 28: Marriages & Intents 1768-1801. Mf 29,31: Intentions 1801-1847. Mf 29-31: Births 1775-1847. Mf 30-34: Town Records 1797-1846. Mf 31: Deaths 1784-1844. Mf 31-34: Marriages 1800-43. Mf 35,37: Militia 1847-62. Mf 35-36: Intentions 1847-77. Mf 36-38: Town Records 1844-76. Mf 38: Dog Licenses 1859-76. Mf 39-40: Birth Index 1843-1900. Mf 40-41: Marriage Index 1843-1900. Mf 42-43: Death Index 1843-1900. Mf 44-45: Vital Records 1843-50. Mf 46-48: Births 1850-1900. Mf 48-51: Marriages 1851-1900. Mf 51-53: Deaths 1850-1900) – (mf ed 1993) – 53mf – 9 – 0-87623-176-8 – us Holbrook [920]
ASHBURNHAM 1752-1849 – (Mf 1T: Intentions 1765-69; Births 1752-1800. Mf 2T: Births 1755-1800; Deaths 1767-99. Mf 2T-3T: Marriages & Intentions 1769-1802. Mf 3T-4T: Intentions 1801-39. Mf 4T-5T: Births 1783-1847. Mf 6T: Intentions of Marrige 1839-47; Deaths 1784-1844; Births 1834-41. Mf 6T-7T: Marriages 1800-43. Mf 7T: Out-of-Town Marriages 1756-99. Mf 7T-8T: Births 1843-49. Mf 9T: Marriages 1843-49. Mf 10T: Deaths 1843-49) – (mf ed 1994) – 10mf – 9 – 0-87623-202-0 – us Holbrook [920]
ASHBY 1754-1891 – (Mf 1-4: Births 1754-1876. Mf 5-8: Marriages 1768-1859. Mf 9-11: Deaths 1755-1862. Mf 12-14: Births 1754-1876. Mf 15-16: Marriages 1768-1859. Mf 17: Town Records 1795-1821. Mf 18-19: Deaths 1755-1862. Mf 20-22: Marriages 1768-1859. Mf 23-25: Deaths 1851-91) – (mf ed 1983) – 25mf – 9 – 0-931248-42-6 – us Holbrook [920]
Ashby, Clifford *see* PERFORMANCE SITES OF THE ANCIENT WORLD
Ashcraft Family *see* MATERIALS FROM THE SCRAPBOOK OF THE ASHCRAFT FAMILY
ASHFIELD 1740-1849 – (Mf 1T: Marriages & Intentions 1762-64. Mf 1T-2T: Births 1750-1847. Mf 2T: Deaths 1763-1843. Mf 2T-5T: Marriages 1762-1843. Mf 3T-4T: Intentions 1787-1849. Mf 5T: Out-of-Town Marriages 1768-1799. Mf 5T-6T: Births & Deaths 1740-1849. Mf 6T-7T: Births 1843-49. Mf 7T: Marriages 1844-49; Deaths 1843-49) – (mf ed 1994) – 7mf – 9 – 0-87623-203-9 – us Holbrook [920]
ASHFIELD 1750-1895 – (Mf 1-3: Index: Birth 1750-1895; Marriage, Death 1843-95. Mf 4: Index to Deaths 1750-1895. Mf 5: Index to Births 1896-1911. Mf 6: Index to Marriages 1896-1911. Mf 7: Index to Deaths 1896-1911. Mf 8-11: Index: Births, Marriages, Deaths 1912-60. Mf 12-15: Town & Vital Records 1750-1857. Mf 16-18: Town & Vital Records 1763-1876. Mf 19-20: Births, Marriages, Deaths 1843-56. Mf 21-26: Births, Marriages, Deaths 1857-95) – (mf ed 1987) – 26mf – 9 – us Holbrook [920]
ASHFORD ADVERTISER – Ashford, Kent. 9 Dec 1967-76 – 12r – 1 – uk British Libr Newspaper [072]
ASHFORD AND ALFRED NEWS – (Missing: 1896, 1897) – England, 17 Jul 1855-Dec 1973 – 147r – 1 – uk British Libr Newspaper [072]
ASHLAND 1840-1895 – (Mf 1-2: Index to Births 1840-95. Mf 2-3: Index to Marriages 1846-97. Mf 3-4: Index to Deaths 1846-97. Mf 5-7: Births 1840-95. Mf 7-9: Marriages 1846-97. Mf 10-11: Deaths 1846-97. Mf 12-13: Index to Deaths 1898-1949. Mf 14-15: Index to Marriages 1898-1949. Mf 16-17: Index to Births 1896-1949) – (mf ed 1989) – 17mf – 9 – 0-87623-101-6 – us Holbrook [920]
ASHLAND ADVERTISER – Ashland, OR. 12 June 1895-28 Dec 1898. 1 roll – 1 – us U.O. Library [071]
ASHLAND ADVOCATE – Ashland, PA. -w 1889-1901; 1902-1907 – 13 – $25.00r – us I.M.R. [071]
Ashland County & Wayne County. Ohio *see* DEEDS, MS 3193
ASHLAND DAILY TIDINGS – Ashland, OR. 1924-52 – 1 – 1025.00 – us Oregon Hist [071]
ASHLAND DAILY TIDINGS – Ashland, OR. 2 Jan 1953-7 Mar 1979+. 69 rolls – 1 – us U.O. Library [071]
ASHLAND GAZETTE – Ashland, NE. -w. Mar. 1879-Apr. 1888. Incomplete; Dec. 1892-Sep. 1917; Nov. 1917-May 1918. Incomplete; Jun. 1918- – 1 – us NE Hist [071]
ASHLAND JOURNAL – Ashland, NE. -w. Mar. 1897-Mar. 1907 – 1 – us NE Hist [071]
Ashland, Maine. Baptist Church *see* RECORDS
ASHLAND NEWS – Ashland, NE. -w. Nov. 1894-Sep. 1896 – 1 – us NE Hist [071]
ASHLAND TIDINGS – Ashland, OR. -sw. 7 Oct 1876-27 May 1912. 4 rolls – 1 – us U.O. Library [071]
ASHLAND TIDINGS – Ashland, OR. -w. -sw. 1890-1924 – 1 – 168.00 – us Oregon Hist [071]
Ashland University *see* RECORDS
ASHLEY / Wood, Ellen – British Fiction Archive: Unit 1 – 9 – uk Bell [830]
Ashley, Barnas Freeman *see* DICK AND JANE'S ADVENTURES ON SABLE ISLAND
THE ASHLEY LIBRARY : A CATALOGUE OF PRINTED BOOKS, MANUSCRIPTS AND AUTOGRAPH LETTERS. COLLECTED BY THOMAS JAMES WISE / Wise, Thomas James – London: Printed for private circulation only, 1922-1936 – 6 rolls – 1 – 1-55879-799-8 – uk Libr Preservation [010]
ASHLEY RIVER BAPTIST CHURCH. CHARLESTON, SOUTH CAROLINA : CHURCH RECORDS – 1736-69, 1943-59, 1962-72 – 1 – 26.65 – us Baptist [240]
Ashley, William James *see*
– NINE LECTURES ON THE EARLIER CONSTITUTIONAL HISTORY OF CANADA DELIVERED BEFORE THE UNIVERSITY OF TORONTO IN EASTER TERM, 1899
– WHAT IS POLITICAL SCIENCE?
Ashman, Louis S *see* LAW AND FORMS OF PRAYERS AND INSTRUCTIONS
Ashmead, Henry G *see* HISTORY OF DELAWARE COUNTY
Ashmead, William Harris *see* A MONOGRAPH OF THE NORTH AMERICAN PROCTOTRYPIDAE
THE ASHMOLE BESTIARY / Ashmolean Museum – 13th century. (Ms 1511) – 14 – uk Microform Academic [240]
Ashmole, E *see* MEMOIRS OF THE LIFE OF THAT LEARNED ANTIQUARY...
Ashmolean Museum *see*
– THE ASHMOLE BESTIARY
– KNOSSOS NOTEBOOKS FROM THE ASHMOLEAN MUSEUM
Ashmolean Museum. *see* THE DRAWINGS OF RAPHAEL IN THE ASHMOLEAN MUSEUM
Ashmun, Jehudi *see* HISTORY OF THE AMERICAN COLONY IN LIBERIA, 1821-1823
Ashpitel, Francis *see* THE INCREASE OF THE ISRAELITES IN EGYPT
ASHRAE (AMERICAN SOCIETY OF HEATING, REFRIGERATING AND AIR-CONDITIONING ENGINEERS) – Standards. Printed index. Updated every 60 days – 6,9 – us Info Handling [621]
ASHRAE (American Society of Heating, Refrigerating and Air-Conditioning Engineers) *see*
– JOURNAL
– TRANSACTIONS
ASHRAE JOURNAL – New York. v1-39 mar 1959-dec 1997+ 1; v13-39 jan 1971-dec 1997+ 5; v17-39 jan 1975-dec 1997+ 9 – 1,5,9 – D1523 – us UMI [690]
ASHRAE TRANSACTIONS – (Former titles: American Society of Heating and Ventilating Engineers – Transactions (1895-1954); Transactions – American Society of Heating and Air-Conditioning Engineers (1955-58); American Society of Heating, Refrigerating and Air-Conditioning Engineers – Transactions (1959-79)) – New York. v1-103 1895-1997+ 1; v78-103 jan 1972-97+ 5; v80-103 feb 1974-97+ 9 – 1,5,9 – D6587 – us UMI [690]
Ashshiddiqy, Muhammad Hasbi *see* PEDOMAN PUASA
ASHTABULA SENTINEL – (Issues for aug 16 1877-oct 17 1878 filmed with: Semi-Weekly Ashtabula Sentinel, oct 23 1878-apr 24 1880) – Ashtabula, OH: O H Fitch, jan 21 1832-oct 17 1878 – 13r – 1 – us Res Libr [071]
Ashton *see* A HANDBOOK OF IOWA
ASHTON AND EAST BIRMINGHAM NEWS – England, 1898; 1901; 1904 – 3r – 1 – uk British Libr Newspaper [072]
ASHTON AND STALYBRIDGE REPORTER *see* ASHTON WEEKLY REPORTER AND STALYBRIDGE AND DUKINFIELD CHRONICLE
ASHTON HERALD – Ashton, NE. -w. Feb. 1925-Nov. 1934 – 1 – us NE Hist [071]
Ashton, Hugh *see* PROBLEM TERRITORIES OF SOUTHERN AFRICA
ASHTON WEEKLY REPORTER AND STALYBRIDGE AND DUKINFIELD CHRONICLE – (Also known as: Ashton and Stalybridge Reporter; High Peak Reporter) – 1857; 1859; 1861; 1872-73; 1877-78; 1888-89; 1928-45; 1948; 1950; 1955; 1970-96 – 120 1/2r – 9 – uk British Libr Newspaper [072]
Ashukin, N *see*
– ALEKSANDER BLOK. SINKHRONICHESKIE TABOLTSY ZHIZNI I TVORCHESTVA 1880-1921
– VALERII BRIUSOV V AUTOBIOGRAFICHESKIKH ZAPISIAKH, PIS'MAKH, VOSPOMINANIIAKH SOVREMENNIKOV I OTZYVAKH KRITIKI
Ashurbanipal, King of Assyria *see* HISTORY OF ASSURBANIPAL
Ashwell, A R *see* LIFE OF THE RIGHT REVEREND SAMUEL WILBERFORCE
ASHWOOD PROSPECTOR – Ashwood, OR. -w. 18 Aug 1903-4 Apr 1905. 1 roll – 1 – us U.O. Library [071]
Ashworth, Robert A *see* THE UNION OF CHRISTIAN FORCES IN AMERICA
ASI ERA EL HERMANO AGUSTIN. UN JESUITA DESCONOCIDO. CINCUENTA ANOS DE HEROISMO CORONADOS POR EL MOCTIVIO. VIDA HEROICA DE AGUSTIN MARIA DIAZ ZAPATA...1869-1936 / Mateos, Francisco & Stachlin, Carlos Maria – Madrid: Razon y Fe, 1944 – 1 – sp Bibl Santa Ana [240]
ASI ES LA SELVA. ESTUDIO GEOGRAFICO Y ETNOLOGIA DE LA PROVINCIA DE BAJO AMAZONAS. LIMA, 1943 / Villarejo, Avencio – Madrid: Razon y Fe, 1947 – 1 – sp Bibl Santa Ana [900]
ASI MICROFICHE LIBRARY : RETROSPECTIVE / U.S. Government – 1960s-1996 – 9 – Apply for prices – us CIS [324]
ASI MURIO EL INSIGNE BIBLIOGRAFO DON BARTOLOME J. GALLARDO / Martinez, Ildefonso – Badajoz: La Alianza, 1935 – 1 – sp Bibl Santa Ana [946]
ASI PAGA EL DIABLO... / Trigo, Felipe – Madrid: Renacimiento, 1911 – sp Bibl Santa Ana [946]
ASI SEGESTO LA DICTADURA / Guemes, Gontrande – Buenos Aires: Ediciones Rex, [1956] – 1 – CSUXADM8781-B – us Hoover Inst Photo [972]
ASIA : (AMERICAN MAGAZINE ON THE ORIENT) – (Missing: 1932-1939. v32-39) – New York, 1923-1940 – 281mf – 9 – CH-995c/2 – ne IDC [950]
ASIA – v6, no.4-. Nov-Dec 1983- – 1,5,6,9 – us UMI [073]
ASIA, 1980-94 : SPECIAL STUDIES SERIES / ed by Kesaris, Paul – (1980-82: 5r $550.00 ISBN 0-89093-434-7; 1982-85: 12r $1,320.00 ISBN 0-89093-643-9; 1985-88: 12r $1,320.00 ISBN 1-55655-112-6; 1989-91: 9r $990.00 ISBN 1-55655-427-3; 1992-94: 12r $1,430.00 ISBN 1-55655-535-0) – Supplements. With printed guides – 1 – us UPA [320]
ASIA AFRIKA BERSATU / Sudharnoto – For voice and piano. SE 5754 1. 1961 – 9 – ne IDC [780]
ASIA FOCUS – 1969-74.Continued by: C.C.A. News – 1 – uk World [240]
Asia Institute. New York *see* INDONESIAN ART
ASIA MONITOR RESOURCE CENTER – Kowloon. 45 docs. 1980-1991 – 40 mf – 9 – ne IDC [320]
ASIA PACIFIC BUSINESS – (Incorporated within BC Business 1988) – Burnaby. v1-3. 1985-1987 – 9 – Can$20.00y – cn Micromedia [380]
ASIA PACIFIC BUSINESS *see* BC BUSINESS
ASIA PARTNERSHIP FOR HUMAN DEVELOPMENT – Kowloon. 35 docs. 1980-1991 – 14mf – 9 – ne IDC [320]
ASIA RESOURCE CENTER – (Formerly Southeast Asia Resource Center) – Berkeley. 42 docs. 1980-1991 – 24mf – 9 – ne IDC [320]
ASIA SCENE – v1-16. 1956-71 – 1 – us UMI [073]
Asia South Pacific Bureau of Adult Education *see* ASPBAE JOURNAL
ASIA WATCH – New York, Washington DC. 98 docs. 1986-1991 – 58mf – 9 – ne IDC [950]
Asia-African Peoples' Solidarity Council *see* SIDANG DESRAA

L'ASIA...CONSIGLIERO DEL CHRISTIANISSIMO RE DI PORTOGALLO:... / Barros, J de – Venetia, 1561-1562 – 10mf – 9 – H-8299/1 – ne IDC [956]

ASIAE EVROPAE' Q ELEGANTISS. DESCRIPTIO, ... / Pius, 2nd, Pope – (Some irregular pagination) – Cologne, 1531 – 6mf – 9 – H-8239/1 – ne IDC [956]

Asiain, Niceforo *see* EL "MAYISMO" AL DESNUDO

ASIAN AFFAIRS: AN AMERICAN REVIEW – v1-9 1973-82 – 1,5,6,9 – us UMI [950]

ASIAN AGRICULTURAL RESEARCH AND DEVELOPMENT : A BIBLIOGRAPHY / Sutarti, Christina – 1983 – A$10.00 – 0-86758-134-4 – at BISA [630]

ASIAN AND AFRICAN STUDIES – (1976- . 5,6,9) – v. 1-. 1965- – 1 – us UMI [950]

Asian and Australian Trade Union Conference. Peking, 1949 (16 Nov-1 Dec) *see* VERSLAG

ASIAN BOOKS IN THE RUSSIAN LANGUAGE : FROM THE BIBLIOTEKA AKADEMII NAUK (BAN), ST. PETERSBURG / Biblioteka Akademii Nauk (BAN), St Petersburg – (China: 350mf $1,600. Japan: 200mf $900. Manchuria: 102mf $450. Mongolia: 281mf $1,300. Tibet: 89mf $400) – 697mf – 9 – $3,200.00 coll $25.00t – us Ross [480]

ASIAN BUREAU AUSTRALIA *see* UNIYA

ASIAN CULTURAL FORUM ON DEVELOPMENT – Bangkok. 71 docs. 1980-1991 – 30mf – 9 – ne IDC [320]

ASIAN DEVELOPMENT BANK ACT. RELEASE NO. 1, DEC. 18, 1967 / U.S. Securities and Exchange Commission – 9 – us UMI [336]

ASIAN DEVELOPMENT BANK RELEASE – no1. 18 Dec 1967 (all publ) – 1mf – 9 – $1.50 – LLMC 89-007 – us L.L.M.C. [340]

ASIAN ECONOMIC HISTORY – (Series One: The Opium Trade & the United Nations Commission on Narcotic Drugs, 1945-1948. – Public Record Office Class FO 371/50647-50654, 57020-57024, 67641-67644, 72907-72915) – Marlborough: Adam Matthew Publications, 1991 – 4r – 1 – $490.00 – uk Matthew [338]

ASIAN PACIFIC QUARTERLY OF CULTURAL AND SOCIAL STUDIES *see* ASPAC QUARTERLY OF CULTURAL AND SOCIAL AFFAIRS

ASIAN PERIODICALS – (Eleven periodicals detailing Asian culture and reactions of both western observers and Asians to that culture) – 1845-1948 – 1 – us Primary [950]

ASIAN PHILOSOPHY – 1992- 3v – 9 – £92.50 – 0955-2367 – uk Carfax [180]

ASIAN PROBLEMS SOLVED BY ASIANS / Sukarno, Pres. Indonesia – SE 11,622 1. Address 4 March 1965 – 9 – ne IDC [324]

ASIAN REVIEW – v. 1-43. 1913-1947 – 1 – us Princeton Micro [950]

ASIAN STUDIES CONFERENCE PAPERS – 1988- – 23mf – 9 – $105.00 – us UMI [950]

ASIAN SURVEY – (1961- 5,6. 1976- 9) – v1-1971- – 1 – us UMI [320]

ASIAN SURVEY *see* FAR EASTERN SURVEY

ASIAN WALL STREET JOURNAL – 1979- . -w – 1 – us UMI [072]

ASIAN WEEK – San Francisco, CA. 1979 – 18+ r – 1 – $900.00 ($00.00y) B03471 – us Library Micro [071]

Asian-African Conference. First Executive Command, 10th Anniversary *see*
- INDONESIA LEAVES THE UNITED NATIONS
- THE REVOLUTIONARY FLAME OF BANDUNG

Asian-African Women's Conferences, 1958 *see* WOMEN AND CITIZENSHIP IN INDONESIA

ASIA-RAYA : OENTOEK MEMPERINGATI ENAM BOELAN BALATENTARA DAI-NIPPON MELINDOENGI INDONESIA – Djakarta, 2602, 1942 – 8-12mf – 9 – ne IDC [950]

ASIATIC AND COLONIAL QUARTERLY JOURNAL – London: James Madden. v1-6 n1-12 [dec ? 1846-sep 1849] – 1 – us Res Libr [950]

ASIATIC ANNUAL REGISTER, 1799-1811 – London, 1801-12.-v1-12 – 172mf – 8 – I-201/2 – ne IDC [950]

ASIATIC EXCLUSION LEAGUE, SAN FRANCISCO : PROCEEDINGS – San Francisco, 1907-13 – 1r – 1 – $50.00 – C63000 – us Library Micro [978]

ASIATIC JOURNAL AND MONTHLY REVIEW – London, 1816-1829. v1-28; N.S. 1830-1843. v1-40; S.3, 1843-1845. v1-4 – 900mf – 9 – I-202/2 – ne IDC [950]

THE ASIATIC QUARTERLY REVIEW – (Cont as: The Imperial and Asiatic Quarterly Review. S.2. London 1891-1895 v1-10. S.3. Woking 1896-1912 v1-34. Cont as: The Asiatic Quarterly Review N.S. Woking 1913 v1-2. Cont as: The Asiatic Review N.S. London 1914-1941 v3-37.) – London. 1886-1890. v1-10 – 903mf – 9 – ne IDC [950]

ASIATIC RESEARCHES – (Index V.1-18) – Calcutta, 1788-1836 – 404mf – 9 – I-102/2 – ne IDC [950]

ASIATIC SOCIETY MONOGRAPHS OF THE ROYAL ASIATIC SOCIETY OF GREAT BRITAIN AND IRELAND / Royal Asiatic Society of Great Britain and Ireland – (Missing 1904, v6) – London, 1899-1909.-v1-9 – 48mf – 8 – I-544/2 – ne IDC [950]

Asiatic Society of Bengal *see*
- A CATALOGUE OF THE ARABIC BOOKS AND MANUSCRIPTS
- JOURNAL AND LETTERS OF THE ASIATIC SOCIETY OF BENGAL
- MEMOIRS OF THE ASIATIC SOCIETY OF BENGAL
- PROCEEDINGS OF THE ASIATIC SOCIETY OF BENGAL

Asiatic Society of Pakistan *see* JOURNAL OF THE ASIATIC SOCIETY OF PAKISTAN

ASIATIC(K) MISCELLANY : ...EXTRACTS FROM CURIOUS PUBLICATIONS – Calcutta, 1785-1786. v1-2 – 12mf – 9 – I-1169/1 – ne IDC [950]

DAS ASIATISCHE MUSEUM DER KAISERLICHEN AKADEMIE DER WISSENSCHAFTEN ZU ST PETERSBURG / Dorn, B A – St. Petersburg, 1846. 776p. BR-10,829/1 – 9 – ne IDC [950]

ASIAWEEK : ENGLISH-LANGUAGE WEEKLY NEWS MAGAZINE – (1975-77 $50.00y; 1978-82 $75.00y; 1983-85 $85.00y; 1986-88 $90.00; 1989-93 $100.00y) – Hong Kong – 1 – us Asia Libr [072]

L'ASIE CENTRALE AUX XVII-XVIII SIECLES. EMPIRE KLAMOUK OU EMPIRE MANTCHOUX / Courant, M – Paris, 1912. 151p. BU-717/2 – 8 – ne IDC [900]

L'ASIE FRANCAISE / Comite de l'Asie francaise – Bulletin mensuel. Apr. 1901-Apr. 1940 – 1 – 35.00r – us Hoover Inst Photo [073]

L'ASIE FRANCAISE – v. 1-40. 1901-40 – 1 – 268.00 – us L of C Photodup [944]

ASIE FRANCAISE / Comite de l'Asie francaise – no. 1-378. Paris. avr 1901-avr 1940 – 1 – fr A.C.R.P.P. [073]

L'ASIE INCONNUE A TRAVERS LE TIBET / Bonvalot, Gabriel – Paris: Flammarion, [1896] – 1 – F197.35 – fr Armell [910]

ASIEN / Hamburger, M – (Ha-Maggid, Lyck, 11th Tishri 5628). 1867-68. BJ-27-215 1 – 9 – ne IDC [380]

ASIEN, AFRIKA, LATEINAMERIKA – 1973-1989 – 411mf – 1 – DM2,342.70 – gw Mikro Press [073]

ASIEN, AFRIKA, LATEINAMERIKA / ed by Robbe, Martin – 9,5,1 – us Harwood [301]

Asik Oemer *see* DIVAN

ASIKANE / Rauf, Mehmet – Istanbul: Hilal Matbaasi, 1325 [1909] – $45.00 – us MEDOC [470]

Asikin Widjaja Kusumah, D *see* RADEN, DIAGNOSA-KIMIA DAN TAFSIR-KLINIKNJA. OLEH R.D. ASIKIN W.K. DAN AHMAD RAMALI

Asikpasazade *see*
- TEVARIH-I AL-I OSMAN [ASIKPASAZADE TARIHI]

ASILE (HOSPICE) ST JEAN DE DIEU, LONGUE-POINTE, P.Q., CANADA – Montreal, 1892. 00035. (Pre-1900 Canadiana) – 9 – cn C.I.H.M. [610]

Asile Sainte Darie. Montreal, Quebec *see* ANNALES DU MONASTERE DE NOTRE-DAME DU BON PASTEUR D'ANGER, DIT ASILE SAINTE DARIE A MONTREAL 1870-1900

ASILS INTERNATIONAL LAW JOURNAL *see* ILSA JOURNAL OF INTERNATIONAL LAW

Asim, Salih *see* UESKUB TARIHI VE CIVARI

ASIM TARIHI / Efendi, Ahmed Asim – Istanbul: Ceride-i Havadis Matba'asi, 1274 [1857] – 30mf – 9 – $150.00 – us MEDOC [949]

Asin Palacios, Miguel *see* COMENTARIOS DE DON GARCIA DE SILVA Y FIGUEROA DE LA EMBAJADA QUE DE PARTE DEL REY DE ESPANA DON FELIPE 3RD HIZO AL REY XA ABAS DE PERSIA

L'ASINO – New York, NY. Jul 5 1908-Feb 27 1910 – us I.H.R.C. [071]

Asins, Manuel *see* MONOLOGO EN PROSA. MUSICA DE DON JOAQUIN PEREZ

Asinus *see* DYNAMITE FOR A DOUBTING CASTLE, THE NECESSITY FOR THE TIMES, OR, IS THE JESUITE SIC RIGHT?

ASIO JOURNAL / American Society for Artificial Internal Organs – v. 1-. 1978- – 1,5,6,9 – us UMI [610]

ASIR [YENI ASIR] – Selanik: Asir Matbaasi, Yeni Asir Matbaasi. Sahib-i Imtiyaz: Abdurrahman Nafiz, 1895-1928 – 9 – $25.00 – us MEDOC [956]

LA ASISTENCIA SOCIAL JUSTICIALISTA – [Buenos Aires?]: Servicio Internacional Publicaciones Argentinas, [1952?] – 1 – CSUXADH4526-B – us Hoover Inst Photo [360]

ASIYAN – Istanbul, 1-2. sene, nu 1-26. – 28 Agustos 1324-29 Subat 1325 [28 Aug 1906-27 Feb 1907] – 13mf – 9 – $125.00 – us MEDOC [949]

ASJ-SJU'LLAH : BEBERAPA PENGGALAN DARI SEDJARAH PERDJOEANGAN OEMMAT ISLAM. NOMOR-PERINGATAN SETAHOEN "ASJ-SJOE'LAH" – Djakarta, Gunseikanbu Syumubu, 2605. 93p – 20mf – 9 – ne IDC [950]

ASKA WEINT : EINE MYTHE AUS URFERNEN TAGEN / Lettenmair, Josef Guenther – Berlin: Nordland Verlag, [c1942] – 1r – 1 – us U.W. Library [830]

Askariants, A V *see* OPISANIE RUKOPISEI A.I. GERTSENA

Askarkhanov, S S *see* ADMINISTRATIVNOE ZAKONODATEL'STVO

Askenazy, S *see* LE PRINCE JOSEPH PONIATOWSKI. MARECHAL DE FRANCE (1763-1813)

ASKERSUNDS TIDNING – Askersund, Sweden. 1857-68; 1956-58 – 5r – 1 – sw Kungliga [072]

Askew, E *see*
- HAND-BOOK OF THE UNITED METHODIST FREE CHURCHES

Askey, J B *see* PROS AND CONS, A GUIDE TO THE CONTROVERSIES OF THE DAY

Askim, Karen L *see* VALIDITY OF WHOLE-BODY BIOELECTRICAL IMPEDANCE ANALYSIS IN THE PREDICTION OF PERCENT BODY FAT IN WOMEN

Asknazii, F M *see* SOVETSKOE UGOLOVNOE PRAVO: BIBLIOGRAFIIA (1917-60)

Asknazii, S I *see* OCHERKI KHOZIAISTVENNOGO PRAVA SSSR

Askwith, Edward Harrison *see* THE CHRISTIAN CONCEPTION OF HOLINESS

ASLE TRANSACTIONS / American Society of Lubrication Engineers – v1- 1958- – 1,5,6 – us UMI [621]

Aslib Library *see* BIBLIOGRAPHY OF MONO- AND MULTILINGUAL VOCABULARIES, THESAURI, SUBJECT HEADINGS AND CLASSIFICATION SCHEMES IN THE SOCIAL SCIENCES

A.S.M. DEL REY DON ALFONSO 13, RECUERDO DE SUMPASO REGIO POR EXTREMADURA...SERENATA DEL PRIMER CUARTETO / Mora, Angel – Transcrita...por A.Voadmirll. Merida J. Joaquin Soler Segura, 1905 – 1 – sp Bibl Santa Ana [946]

ASME (AMERICAN SOCIETY OF MECHANICAL ENGINEERS) – Standards. Printed index. Updated every 60 days – 6,9 – us Info Handling [620]

ASME – AMERICAN SOCIETY OF MECHANICAL ENGINEERS *see*
- JOURNAL OF APPLIED MECHANICS
- JOURNAL OF ENGINEERING FOR INDUSTRY
- JOURNAL OF ENGINEERING FOR POWER
- JOURNAL OF HEAT TRANSFER

ASME: TRANSACTIONS, SERIES E, JOURNAL OF APPLIED MECHANICS – v1-17. 1933-50 – 1,5,6 – us Princeton Micro [073]

ASMODEE – (Lacking: 1862, 1863, 1875, 1876) – Amsterdam, 3 May 1854-27 Dec 1877 – 5r – 1 – uk British Libr Newspaper [072]

ASMONEAN – New York. 1849-58 – 1 – us A.J.P.C. [073]

Asmus, Georg *see*
- AMERIKANISCHES SKIZZEBUECHELCHE
- GEDICHTBUECHELCHEN

Asmuss, H M *see* MONSTROSITATES COLEOPTERORUM...

Asmusson, Erling *see* BODY TEMPERATURE AND CAPACITY FOR WORK

Asmuth, J D *see* DE IURE BELLI...

ASNAD-I TARIKHI-I JUBNISH-I KARGARI, SUSIYAL-DIMUKRASI VA KUMUNISTI-I IRAN / ed by Chaqueri, Cosroe – $200.00 – us MEDOC [320]

ASNAD-I TARIKHI-I JUNBISH-I KARGARI, SUSIYAL-DIMUKRASI VA KUMUNISTI IRAN / ed by Chaqueri, Cosroe – Bi-kushish-i Khursraw Shakiri – 2r – 9 – us MEDOC [320]

ASNAD-I TARIKHI-I JUNBISH-I KARGARI, SUSIYAL-DIMUKRASI VA KUMUNISTI-I IRAN = HISTORICAL DOCUMENTS OF THE WORKERS', SOCIAL-DEMOCRATIC, AND COMMUNIST MOVEMENT IN IRAN / ed by Chaqueri, Cosroe – 22v – 9 – $165.00 (vols 1-21 $90.00 vol 22) – us MEDOC [320]

Asnash, S M *see* OPISANIE PUSHKINSKAGO MUZEIA IMP

EL ASNO ERUDITO / Forner Segarra, Juan Pablo – Valencia: Editorial Castalia, 1948 – sp Bibl Santa Ana [946]

ASNT (AMERICAN SOCIETY FOR NONDESTRUCTIVE TESTING) – Printed index. Updated every 60 days – 6,9 – us Info Handling [670]

ASOCIACION ABUELAS DE PLAZA DE MAYO = ASSOCIATION OF GRANDMOTHERS OF PLAZA DE MAYO – Buenos Aires. 48 docs. 1983-1991 – 27mf – 9 – ne IDC [320]

Asociacion Amigos de Guadalupe *see*
- EXTREMADURA Y EL MAR
- MEMORIA Y ACTAS DE LAS REUNIONES PRO-HISPANIDAD CELEBRADAS EN EL REAL MONASTERIO DE GUADALUPE...MAYO DE 1948

Asociacion Benefica Ntra. Sra. de la Luz. Malpartida de Plasencia *see* ALA SANTISIMA VIRGEN DE LA LUZ 1978

Asociacion Cultural Chambra *see* FIESTAS DEL RISCO 1979

Asociacion Cultural "Pedro de Trejo" *see* FERIAS Y FIESTAS 1973

Asociacion Cultural Placentina Pedro de Trejo *see* FERIAS Y FIESTAS DE PLASENCIA 1975

Asociacion de Amigos de Guadalupe *see* ESTATUTOS PROVISIONALES. OCTUBRE, 1946

Asociacion de Hijas de la Purisima e Inmaculada...Viregen Maria. Spain *see*
- ORACIONES

Asociacion de Medicina Extremena *see* ESTATUTOS Y REGLAMENTO

Asociacion de Padres de Alumnos y Amigos de la Esuela de E.G.B. *see* ESTATUTOS

Asociacion Empresarial de panaderos de la Provincia de Caceres *see* ESTATUTOS

Asociacion Empresarial Harino-Panadera de la provincia de Caceres *see* ESTATUTOS DE LA...

Asociacion Espanola de Hematologia y Hemoterapia, 12 Reunion *see* 1 REUNION HISPANO PORTUGUESA DE HEMATOLOGIA

Asociacion familiar "Los Alamos" Casas de Don Antonio *see* ESTATUTOS

Asociacion Geofisica de Mexico *see* BOLETIN

Asociacion Morala de Padres de Alumnos de Educ. General Basica. Navlamoral de la Mata *see* ESTATUTOS

Asociacion nacional de Agricultores pequenos. Havana *see* ANAP

Asociacion Provincial de amas de casa *see* ESTATUTOS DE LA...

Asociacion Provincial del Magisterio de Caceres *see* REGLAMENTO DE...REFORMADO EN 1940

Asociacion Santa Eulalia. Spain *see* CORONA POETICA

ASOLANDO : FANCIES AND FACTS / Browning, Robert – London: Smith, Elder, 1890 – 1 roll – 1 – 1-55879-182-5 – uk Libr Preservation [840]

ASPAC QUARTERLY OF CULTURAL AND SOCIAL AFFAIRS – (Cont by: Asian Pacific Quarterly of Cultural and Social Studies) – Seoul. v1-2. Sum 1969-Spr 1971* – 1 – D17727 – us UMI [950]

ASP-ACSM (AMERICAN CONGRESS ON SURVEYING AND MAPPING) TECHNICAL PAPERS : FALL TECHNICAL MEETING – (Merged with: American Society of Photogrammetry Technical Papers to form: ACSM-ASP Fall Convention Technical Papers. Cont: Technical Papers of the American Congress on Surveying and Mapping Fall Technical Meeting) – Falls Church. sep 1981* – 1 – D16421.01 – us UMI [520]

ASP-ACSM FALL TECHNICAL MEETING. TECHNICAL PAPERS OF THE AMERICAN CONGRESS ON SURVEYING AND MAPPING *see* TECHNICAL PAPERS

ASPBAE JOURNAL / Asia South Pacific Bureau of Adult Education – New Delhi. v1-9. 1966-74*. v10 aug-nov 1975 1,5*,9* – 1,5,9 – inquire – D10327 – us UMI [370]
ASPECT RELIGIEUX DE LA DANSE DANS LES CIVILISATIONS ARCHAIQUES DE L'AFRIQUE DU SUD-EST / Leynaud, E – 9 – F50.00 – fr Ethnologie [960]
ASPECTOS ECONOMICOS DE NUESTRA REVOLUCION / Cardona Rossell, Mariano – Barcelona, 1937. Fiche W 773. (Blodgett Collection of Spanish Civil War Pamphlets) – 9 – us H.U. College Libr [946]
ASPECTS – Toronto. v1-29. 1970-1980 – 9 – Can$73.00 – cn Micromedia [336]
ASPECTS ARTICULATOIRES DE LA LABIALE VOCALIQUE EN FRANCAIS. CONTRIBUTION A LA MODELISATION A PARTIR DE LABIOPHOTOGRAPHIES : LABIOFILMS ET FILMS RADIOLOGIQUES. ETUDE STATIQUE, DYNAMIQUE ET CONTRASTIVE / Zerling, Jean Pierre – 2mf – 9 – 10218 – fr Atelier National [440]
ASPECTS DE LA FRANCE – Paris. 10 juin 1947-86 – 1 – fr A.C.R.P.P. [073]
ASPECTS DE L'HABITAT DANS LES CENTRES MINIERS DE LA REGION DE GAFSA / Zarka, Ch. – 9 – F50.00 – fr Ethnologie [305]
ASPECTS DE L'UNIVERS MYSTIQUE DES RWANDAIS AU TEMPS DE LA ROYAUTE NYIGINYA / Gasarabwe, E – Le partage de l'espace – 9 – F60.00 – fr Ethnologie [306]
ASPECTS LINGUISTIQUES DE L'ACCULTURATION DES ACADIENS (PROVINCES MARITIMES DU CANADA) / Fontaine, P – 9 – F50.00 – fr Ethnologie [440]
ASPECTS MECONNUS DE L'ART POPULAIRE RUSSE AU XIXEME SIECLE / Ehrenbourg-Mannati, N – 9 – F60.00 – fr Ethnologie [700]
ASPECTS OF ADJUDICATION / Warden, Robert Bruce – Washington, Ernest Institute, 1886. 22 p. LL-1368 – 1 – us L of C Photodup [340]
ASPECTS OF ALGERIAN CULTURAL POLICY / Baghli, Sid-Ahmed – 1978 – 9 – 92-3-101474-9 – fr UNESCO [960]
ASPECTS OF BRACKISH WATER FISH AND CRUSTACEAN CULTURE IN THE MEDITERRANEAN – 1980 – 135p – it F.A.O. [639]
ASPECTS OF CANADIAN CULTURAL POLICY / Schafer, Paul D – 1976 – 9 – 92-3-101405-6 – fr UNESCO [971]
ASPECTS OF INTER-REGIONAL INDUSTRIAL DEVELOPMENT, WITH SPECIAL REFERENCE TO INDONESIA / Sadli, Mohammad – SE 6346 1. 1957 – 9 – ne IDC [600]
ASPECTS OF IRAQI CULTURAL POLICY / El-Basri, Abdel-Gawad Daoud – 1980 – 9 – 92-3-101745-4 – fr UNESCO [956]
ASPECTS OF PEACE DURING WORLD WAR 1 PAMPHLET COLLECTION – 1914-1940 – 1 – CSUXANL3012-B – us Hoover Inst Photo [320]
ASPECTS OF PRIMARY EDUCATION IN THAILAND : AN INTRODUCTION / Thailand. National Primary Education Commission – Bangkok, 1984 – 1mf – 9 – DE-597/1 – ne IDC [370]
ASPECTS OF SCEPTICISM: WITH SPECIAL REFERENCE TO THE PRESENT TIME / Fordyce, John – New York: T. Whittaker, 1884. 274p. With: Meteor S.N. Behrman. Includes bibliog. references – 1 – us U.W. Library [140]
ASPECTS OF THE ALGERIAN OIL POLICY 1965-1970 / Algeria. Ministry of Industry and Power – 1970. BNE-8662 1 – 9 – ne IDC [660]
ASPECTS OF THE BEHAVIOUR AND ECOLOGY OF THE WHITE COCKATOO AND GALAH IN CROPLANDS IN NORTH-EASTERN NEW SOUTH WALES / Noske, S – (MSc Thesis) – 1980 – 9 – A$15.00 – at R.A.O.U. [590]
ASPECTS OF THE PHYSIOLOGICAL AND BEHAVIOURAL ECOLOGY OF THE WHITE-BROWED SCRUBWREN, SERICORNIS FRONTALIS (ACANTHIZIDAE) IN WESTERN AUSTRALIA / Ambrose, Stephen J – (PhD Thesis) – 1985 – 9 – A$15.00 – at R.A.O.U. [590]
ASPECTS OF THE SPIRITUAL / Brierley, Jonathan – New York: Thomas Whittaker, 1909. 1 fiche – 9 – us A.T.L.A. [240]
ASPECTS OF THE WORLD FEED ECONOMY : STRUCTURAL CHANGES, PROSPECTS AND ISSUES – 1989 – 53p – it F.A.O. [338]
ASPECTS OF THEISM / Knight, William – London: Macmillan, 1893.1 fiche – 9 – us A.T.L.A. [240]
ASPECTS PSYCHOLOGIQUES DE L'ACCULTURATION DES JUIFS MAROCAINS / Cohen, Margalit – 1975 – 9 – fr Orientalistes [150]
ASPECTS SOCIO-DEMOGRAPHIQUES DU VILLAGE DE MACAYE: INTRODUCTION A L'ETUDE ANTHROPO-BIOLOGIQUE / Ducros, J.Ducros, A. – 9 – F20.00 – fr Ethnologie [304]
Aspe-Fleurimont, Lucien Auguste *see* LA GUINEE FRANCAISE, CONAKRY ET RIVIERES DU SUD
ASPEKTE / Wachsmann, Konrad – Wiesbaden: Krausskopf, 1961. (14)p. (44) leaves of plates. Illus. 1 reel. 965 – 1 – us U.W. Library [760]
ASPEKTE DER SELBSTBESTIMMUNGSPROB-LEMATIK IN DEN VEREINTEN NATIONEN : FALLSTUDIEN ZU ZYPERN UND PUERTO RICO / Nikitopoulos, Ingeborg – Heidelberg, 1970 – 6mf – 9 – DM118.00 – 3-89349-759-5 – gw Hänsel [320]
ASPEKTE DES PERSONALMANAGEMENTS BEI DER EINFUEHRUNG UND DURCHSETZUNG VON GANZHEITLICH ORIENTIERTEN QUALITAETSSICHERUNGSSYSTEMEN NACH DIN ISO 9000FF / Natschke, Birgit – 1994 – 1mf – DM60.00 – 3-8267-2010-5 – gw Hänsel [650]
ASPEKTE EINER PROVOKATIVEN TSCHECHISCHEN GERMANISTIK / Preisner, Rio – (Includes bibliographical references) – Wuerzburg: Jal-Verlag, 1977-1981 – 1r – 1 – us U.W. Library [430]
ASPHALT PAVING TECHNOLOGY – v40- 1971- – 1,5,6,9 – us UMI [625]
ASPHODEL / Braddon, Mary Elizabeth – British Fiction Archive: Unit 5 – 9 – uk Bell [830]
Aspiazu, A *see* DOGMAS DEL DERECHO...
Aspillera, Paraluman S *see* IMPROVE YOUR TAGALOG
ASPINALL'S MARITIME LAW CASES – 1870-1940. Case reports from U.K., Commonwealth and U.S.A. – 122mf – 9 – $321.00 – uk Butterworth Law [340]
Aspinion, Robert *see* CONTRIBUTION A L'ETUDE DU DROIT COUTUMIER BERBERE MAROCAIN
ASPIRATIONS OF NATURE / Hecker, Isaac Thomas – (Includes bibliographical references) – 4th ed. New York: Catholic Publ House, 1869, c1857 – 1mf – 9 – 0-8370-6981-5 – 1986-0981 – us A.T.L.A. [230]
ASPLENII SPECIES EUROPAEAE / Heufler, L R von – Verhandl. Zool. Bot. Ver. v. 6. Wien. Wien. 1856. B-7194 2 – 8 – ne IDC [580]
Asplund, John *see* THE ANNUAL REGISTER OF THE BAPTIST DENOMINATION IN NORTH AMERICA, 1790-1794
ASQC (AMERICAN SOCIETY FOR QUALITY CONTROL) – Standards. Printed index. Updated every 60 days – 6,9 – us Info Handling [650]
'ASR-I 'AMAL – West Germany: Intisharat-i Asr-i 'Amal. Shumarah-'i 1-7 – 1 reel – 1 – $25.00 – us MEDOC [950]
L'ASSABA; ESSAI MONOGRAPHIQUE / Munier, Pierre Marie – Saint-Louis, Senegal. 1952 – 1 – us Res Libr [306]
Assabghy, A *see* LES QUESTIONS DE NATIONALITE EN EGYPTE
Assaf, S *see* YAVNEH
ASSAM : REPORT OF THE STUDY OF ADMINISTRATION OF ELEMENTARY EDUCATION IN RELATION TO THE PROGRAMME OF UNIVERSALISATION 1979 / India. Assam. Directorate of Elementary Education – Khahilipara – 6mf – 9 – DE-548/1 – ne IDC [370]
Assam *see* LEGISLATIVE COUNCIL DEBATES, 1918-1921
THE ASSAM GAZETTE / Assam. India – 1963-1966. Incomplete – 1 – us NY Public [324]
Assam. India *see* THE ASSAM GAZETTE
Assam. India (State). Legislative Assembly *see* DEBATES, 1937-1947
Assam. India (State). Legislative Council *see* DEBATES
ASSAM TRIBUNE – Gauhati, India. May 1944-Dec 1994 – 146r – 1 – us L of C Photodup [072]
Assante, A *see* PER LA PACE MONDIALE
L'ASSASSINAT DE ANDRES NIN: SES CAUSES, SES AUTEURS – Paris, 1939. Fiche W 732. (Blodgett Collection of Spanish Civil War Pamphlets) – 9 – us H.U. College Libr [946]
ASSASSINATION ATTEMPT ON ADOLF HITLER ON JULY 20, 1944 PAMPHLET COLLECTION – 1944-1964 – 1 – CSUXANS0376-B – us Hoover Inst Photo [360]
ASSASSINATION OF CATHOLIC PRIESTS IN THE DIOCESE OF BARCELONA, SPAIN, UNDER THE SO-CALLED SPANISH REPUBLIC, NOW THE SPANISH REPUBLIC IN EXILE / Spain. Embajada. United States – Washington, DC, 1946? Fiche W733. (Blodgett Collection of Spanish Civil War Pamphlets) – 9 – us H.U. College Libr [946]
ASSASSINATION OF LINCOLN – (American History Vignettes) – 1 – us Ross [976]
L'ASSAULT / Front national-syndicaliste – no. 1-3. Paris. mai 1933-mars 1934 – 1 – fr A.C.R.P.P. [073]
ASSAULT ON THE LARGEST UNKNOWN : THE INTERNATIONAL INDIAN OCEAN EXPEDITION 1959-1965 / Behrman, Daniel – 1981 – 96p – 9 – 92-3-401917-2 – fr UNESCO [550]
THE ASSAY OF GOLD AND SILVER WARES / Ryland, Arthur – London: Smith, Elder, 1852. 212p. LL-4084 – 1 – us L of C Photodup [540]
Assbit, Abdul-Rahman *see* CULTURAL POLICY IN THE KINGDOM OF SAUDI ARABIA
Asscher, B E *see* DE VERJARING IN HET INTERNATIONAAL PRIVAATRECHT
ASSE (AMERICAN SOCIETY OF SANITARY ENGINEERING) – Printed index. Updated every 60 days – 6,9 – us Info Handling [628]
ASSE JOURNAL / American Society of Safety Engineers – v1-19. 1956-1974 – 1 – us UMI [620]
Asselin, Olivar *see*
– L'ACTION
– LE NATIONALISTE
– LA RENAISSANCE
– LA RENTE
Assemani, E *see* BIBLIOTHECAE MEDICEAE LAURENTIANAE ET PALATINAE CODICUM MMS
Assemani, J S *see* BIBLIOTHECA ORIENTALIS-CLEMENTINO-VATICANA
Assemanus, J A *see* CODEX LITURGICUS ECCLESIAE UNIVERSAE
Assemanus, J S *see* BIBLIOTHECA ORIENTALIS CLEMENTINO-VATICANA
Assemanus-S E Assemanus *see* BIBLIOTHECAE APOSTOLICAE VATICANAE CODICUM MANUSCRIPTORUM CATALOGUS
L'ASSEMBLEE DE FAMILLE / Ribouttе – (French Theatre Series). Paris. J. N. Barba. 1808 – 9 – fr Hachette [820]
ASSEMBLEE GENERAL ORDINAIRE. RAPPORT DU CONSEIL D'ADMINISTRATION, RAPPORT DU COMMITTEE DE CENSURE, RAPPORTS DE MM. LES COMMISSAIRES, RESOLUTIONS DE L'ASSEMBLEE / Algeria. Credit Foncier d'Algerie et de Tunisie – 16 v. in 5. 1947-62. BNE-8627 1 – 9 – ne IDC [324]
ASSEMBLEE GENERALE DES ACTIONNAIRES; REUNION: 1955-4 JUL 1958 / Egypt. Compagnie Universelle du Canal Maritime de Suez – 5v. BNE-4618 1 – 9 – ne IDC [332]
ASSEMBLEE GENERALE ORDINAIRE / Algeria. Caisse Centrale Algerienne du Credit Populaire – 1v. in 1. 1960. BNE-8613 1 – 9 – ne IDC [330]
ASSEMBLEE GENERALE ORDINAIRE / Morocco. Banque d'Etat du Maroc – 16 v. 1937-60. (lacking 1938-45, 1948). BNE-3010 1 – 9 – ne IDC [330]
ASSEMBLEE GENERALE ORDINAIRE / Morocco. Caisse Marocaine des Marches – v. 1-3. 3 v. 1961-62. BNE-3021 1 – 9 – ne IDC [330]
ASSEMBLEE GENERALE ORDINAIRE DES ACTIONNAIRES / Morocco. Caisse de Prets Immobiliers du Maroc – 6v. 1960-66. (lacking 1964). BNE-3020 1 – 9 – ne IDC [330]
ASSEMBLEE LEGISLATIVE DE QUEBEC: SEANCE DU 13 DECEMBRE 1876 / Angers, Auguste Real – S.s.n. 1876? 00818. (Pre-1900 Canadiana) – 9 – cn C.I.H.M. [971]
L'ASSEMBLEE NATIONALE – Paris. Red. en chef, Adrien de la Valette. 1849-50, 1852-53 – 1 – fr A.C.R.P.P. [323]
ASSEMBLEE NATIONALE : EDITION DE LONDRES – London, UK. 31 Dec 1870; Jan 1871 – 1 – uk British Libr Newspaper [072]
Assemblee Nationale *see* COLLECTIONS DE DECRETS DE L'ASSEMBLEE NATIONALE(...)ENREGISTRES AU GREFFE DU DEPARTEMENT DE LA LOIRE-INFERIEURE
LES ASSEMBLEES DU CLERGUE ET LE JANSENISME / Bourlon, I – (Includes bibliographical references) – Paris: Bloud, 1909 – 1mf – 9 – 0-8370-8407-5 – 1986-2407 – us A.T.L.A. [240]
LES ASSEMBLEES PRIMAIRES OU LES ELECTIONS / Martainville – (French Theatre Series). Paris. Corbaux, an V. 1797 – 9 – fr Hachette [820]
ASSEMBLY. MINUTES... / Wesleyan Methodist Association – (Coll title: The People Called Methodists, Phase 3: Primary Sources, 1801-1850) – London, 1836-1857 – 15mf – 9 – MP-351/1 – ne IDC [240]
THE ASSEMBLY ORDER BOOKS / Sutton's Hospital. Charterhouse – 1613-1982. With printed list – 1 – £375.00 – uk World [025]
Asser, Bishop of Sherborne *see* ASSER'S LIFE OF KING ALFRED, TOGETHER WITH THE ANNALS OF ST. NEOTS
Asser, T M C *see*
– BUITENLANDSCHE VONNISSEN
– ELEMENTS DE DROIT INTERNATIONAL PRIVE OU DU CONFLIT DES LOIS
– LES SOCIETES ANONYMES ETABLIES A L'ETRANGER
ASSER'S LIFE OF KING ALFRED, TOGETHER WITH THE ANNALS OF ST. NEOTS / Asser, Bishop of Sherborne – Introduction and commentary by William Henry Stevenson. Oxford: Clarendon Press, 1904. cxxx/386p facsim. Trans. of Res Gestae Alfredi – 1 – us U.W. Library [941]
ASSERTA APHORISTICA ET CHIRURGICA EX LIBRIS... / Gasco y Navarro, J M – Valencia, 1745 – 1mf – 9 – sp Cultura [617]
ASSERTA THEO-SUBTITULIA...EFFICACIA / Gil Becerra, Benito – 1737. 2v – 9 – 1.50f – sp Bibl Santa Ana [240]
ASSERTIO SANAE ET ORTHODOXAE DOCTRINAE DE PERSONA ET MAIESTATE DOMINI NOSTRI IESV CHRISTI,... / Hunnius, A – Francofvrti ad Moenvm, 1592 – 5mf – ne IDC [240]
ASSERTIO SEPTEM SACRAMENTORUM, OR, DEFENCE OF THE SEVEN SACRAMENTS / Henry 8, King – New York: Benziger, 1908 – 2mf – us A.T.L.A. [240]
ASSESSING FOOD AID REQUIREMENTS : A REVISED APPROACH – 1984 – 25p – it F.A.O. [360]
ASSESSING LEARNING ACHIEVEMENT / Izard, John – 1992 – 47p – 9 – 92-3-102793-X – fr UNESCO [370]
ASSESSING THE EFFECTS OF CHANGES IN EXPLOITATION PATTERN USING LENGTH COMPOSITION DATA – 1984 – 128p – it F.A.O. [639]
ASSESSMENT AND COLLECTION OF DATA ON POST-HARVEST FOODGRAIN LOSSES – 1980 – 76p – it F.A.O. [630]
ASSESSMENT AND COLLECTION OF DATA ON PRE-HARVEST FOODGRAIN LOSSES – 1983 – 130p – it F.A.O. [630]
ASSESSMENT AND EVALUATION IN HIGHER EDUCATION – 1981- 18v – 9 – £153.00 – 0260-2938 – uk Carfax [370]
ASSESSMENT AND MITIGATION OF EARTHQUAKE RISK – 1978 – 341p – 9 – 92-3-101451-X – fr UNESCO [550]
ASSESSMENT IN EDUCATION : PRINCIPLES, POLICY AND PRACTICE – 1995, Vol 2 – £166.00 – uk Carfax [370]
ASSESSMENT IN HIGHER EDUCATION – v.1-5. 1975-79 – 1 – us UMI [370]
ASSESSMENT LIST : MOSCOW / Ottawa County. Ohio. Auditor – 1842 – 1r – 1 – $32.50r – us Archival [324]
ASSESSMENT LISTS / Putnam County. Ohio. Auditor – 1880 – 1r – 1 – $32.50r – us Archival [324]
ASSESSMENT LISTS / U.S. Internal Revenue Service – (Arkansas. 1867-74. 4 rolls. T1208. Territory of Idaho. 1867-74. 1 roll. T1209) – 1 – us Nat'l Archives [336]
ASSESSMENT LISTS FOR IOWA / U.S. Department of Internal Revenue – 1862-66. 16 rolls. M766 – 1 – us Nat'l Archives [324]

ASSESSMENT LISTS FOR KANSAS / U.S. Department of Internal Revenue – 1862-66. 3 rolls. M767 – 1 – us Nat'l Archives [324]
ASSESSMENT LISTS FOR KENTUCKY / U.S. Department of Internal Revenue – 1862-66. 24 rolls. M768 – 1 – us Nat'l Archives [324]
ASSESSMENT LISTS FOR LOUISIANA / U.S. Department of Internal Revenue – 1863-66. 10 rolls. M769 – 1 – us Nat'l Archives [324]
ASSESSMENT LISTS FOR MAINE / U.S. Department of Internal Revenue – 1862-66. 15 rolls. M770 – 1 – us Nat'l Archives [324]
ASSESSMENT LISTS FOR MARYLAND / U.S. Department of Internal Revenue – 1862-66. 21 rolls. M771 – 1 – us Nat'l Archives [324]
ASSESSMENT LISTS FOR MICHIGAN / U.S. Department of Internal Revenue – 1862-66. 15 rolls. M773 – 1 – us Nat'l Archives [324]
ASSESSMENT LISTS FOR MISSISSIPPI / U.S. Department of Internal Revenue – 1865-66. 3 rolls. M775 – 1 – us Nat'l Archives [324]
ASSESSMENT LISTS FOR MONTANA / U.S. Department of Internal Revenue – 1864-72. 1 roll. M777 – 1 – us Nat'l Archives [324]
ASSESSMENT LISTS FOR NEVADA / U.S. Department of Internal Revenue – 1863-66. 2 roll. M779 – 1 – us Nat'l Archives [324]
ASSESSMENT LISTS FOR NEW HAMPSHIRE / U.S. Department of Internal Revenue – 1862-66. 10 rolls. M780 – 1 – us Nat'l Archives [324]
ASSESSMENT LISTS FOR NORTH CAROLINA / U.S. Department of Internal Revenue – 1864-66. 2 rolls. M784 – 1 – us Nat'l Archives [324]
ASSESSMENT LISTS FOR PENNSYLVANIA / U.S. Department of Internal Revenue – 1862-66. 107 rolls. M787 – 1 – us Nat'l Archives [324]
ASSESSMENT LISTS FOR RHODE ISLAND / U.S. Department of Internal Revenue – 1862-66. 10 rolls. M788 – 1 – us Nat'l Archives [336]
ASSESSMENT LISTS FOR SOUTH CAROLINA / U.S. Department of Internal Revenue – 1864-66. 2 rolls. M789 – 1 – us Nat'l Archives [336]
ASSESSMENT LISTS FOR TEXAS / U.S. Department of Internal Revenue – 1865-66. 2 rolls. M791 – 1 – us Nat'l Archives [336]
ASSESSMENT LISTS FOR THE TERRITORY OF NEW MEXICO / U.S. Department of Internal Revenue – 1862-70; 1872-74. 1 roll. M782 – 1 – us Nat'l Archives [336]
ASSESSMENT LISTS FOR VERMONT / U.S. Department of Internal Revenue – 1862-66. 7 rolls. M792 – 1 – us Nat'l Archives [336]
ASSESSMENT LISTS FOR VIRGINIA / U.S. Department of Internal Revenue – 1862-66. 6 rolls. M793 – 1 – us Nat'l Archives [336]
ASSESSMENT LISTS FOR WEST VIRGINIA / U.S. Department of Internal Revenue – 1862-66. 4 rolls. M795 – 1 – us Nat'l Archives [336]
THE ASSESSMENT OF DESTINATION AWARENESS OF INDIANA'S TOURISM POTENTIAL / Yen, J – 1990 – 1mf – 9 – $4.00 – us Microform Publ [338]
AN ASSESSMENT OF SELECTED RISK MANAGEMENT PRACTICES IN LOCAL INDIANA PARK AND RECREATION DEPARTMENTS / Mukundan, V – 1991 – 2mf – 9 – $8.00 – us Microform Publ [650]
AN ASSESSMENT OF THE EFFECTIVENESS OF THE COOL CAPE ON THE RAPID REDUCTION OF EXERCISE-INDUCED, ELEVATED BODY CORE TEMPERATURE / Peterson, Paul A & Prentice, William E – 1992 – 1mf – 9 – $4.00 – us Microform Publ [613]
AN ASSESSMENT OF THE FACTOR VALIDITY OF THE PRECOMPETITIVE STRESS INVENTORY / Finch, Laura M – 1988 – 143p 2mf – 9 – $8.00 – us Microform Publ [150]
AN ASSESSMENT OF THE HEALTH HABITS AND COUNSELING PRACTICES OF PHYSICIANS / Kelley, Kristi S – University of North Carolina at Charlotte, 1996 – 2mf – 9 – $8.00 – HE 566 – us Microform Publ [613]
ASSESSMENT OF THE NEED FOR CERTIFIED ATHLETIC TRAINERS IN NEW YORK STATE HIGH SCHOOLS / Koabel-Bagley, Patricia – 1994 – 1mf – $4.00 – us Microform Publ [617]
AN ASSESSMENT OF THE PERFORMANCE OF THE FIRST PLAN FOR THE FORMULATION OF THE SECOND FIVE YEAR PLAN (EDUCATION AND TRAINING) / Pakistan. Planning Commission. Education and Training – 1959 – 1mf – 9 – DE-577/1 – ne IDC [370]
ASSESSMENT OF THE PLANNING AND IMPLEMENTATION PROCESS OF WORKSITE HEALTH PROMOTION PROGRAMS / Underwood, Lisa S – 1994 – 1mf – $4.00 – us Microform Publ [613]
AN ASSESSMENT OF THE POSSESSED QUALIFICATIONS AND IMPORTANT QUALIFICATIONS OF AQUATIC ADMINISTRATORS / Wydan, Mary E – 1989 – 73p 1mf – 9 – $4.00 – us Microform Publ [370]
ASSESSMENT ROLLS / Monroe County. Mich, Bedford Township. Township Treasurer – 1839-1882 – 1r – 1 – $32.50r – us Archival [324]
ASSESSMENT TOOLS USED BY ELEMENTARY LEVEL ADAPTED PHYSICAL EDUCATORS IN WISCONSIN / Steinbrunner, Pamela J – University of Wisconsin-La Crosse, 1995 – 1mf – 9 – $4.00 – PE3620 – us Microform Publ [370]
THE ASSESSOR'S GUIDE, A MANUAL OF THE DUTIES OF ASSESSORS PURSUANT TO THE STATUTES OF THE LEGISLATURE OF ONTARIO RELATING THERETO:.. – Comp. by George Bell. Toronto: N. Ure. 1882. 06698. (Pre-1900 Canadiana) – 9 – cn C.I.H.M. [380]
ASSESSORS RECORDERS / Nye. Nevada – Official records – 1 – us Library Micro [310]
ASSESSORS RECORDERS / Ormsby. Nevada – Official records – 1 – us Library Micro [310]
Assfalg, J *see* DIE ORDNUNG DES PRIESTERTUMS
ASSIGNMENT CHILDREN = CARNETS DE L'ENFANCE / U. N. Children's Fund – Paris. n1-29. 1963-72 – 82mf – 9 – $5.00f – us Ross [305]
ASSIMILATION-REGENERATION DES SELS NUTRITIFS DANS L'OCEAN AUSTRAL: CARACTERISATION ET RELATION AVEC LA STRUCTURE HYDROLOGIQUE DANS LE BASSIN DE WEDDELL-ENDERBY / Simon, V – 9 – F60.00 – fr Ethnologie [574]
ASSIMILATON DES LOIS CONCERNANT LA LETTRE DE CHANGE... / Barclay, T – Paris, Bruxelles, 1888 – 1mf – 9 – ILM-3534/1 – ne IDC [340]
ASSINIBOIA TODAY – Assiniboia, 1990 – 2r – 1 – cn Preston [971]
L'ASSISTANCE A PARIS SOUS L'ANCIEN REGIME ET PENDANT LA REVOLUTION / Parturier, Louis – Paris. 1897. (La Condition Ouvriere. Part Two.) – 9 – 7.50 – fr Bibl Nationale [360]
L'ASSISTANCE ETRANGERE FACE AU DEVELOPPEMENT ECONOMIQUE DU MAROC / Qualalou, F – Casablanca. 1969. BNE-3226 1 – 9 – ne IDC [338]
ASSISTANT SECRETARY FOR LABOR-MANAGEMENT RELATIONS DECISIONS / U.S. Department of Labor – (With index 1970-80) – v1-8. 1970-78 – 101mf – 9 – $151.00 – LLMC 82-602 – us L.L.M.C. [340]
ASSISTED REPRODUCTION REVIEWS – v1-6. 1991-1996 – 6r – 1,5,6,9 – $90.00r – us Williams [618]
Assmann, Elisabeth *see* DIE ENTWICKLUNG DES LYRISCHEN STILS BEI DETLEV VON LILIENCRON
Asso y Del Rio, I J de *see* SYNOPSIS STIRPIUM INDIGENARUM ARAGONIAE
THE ASSOCIATE CREED OF ANDOVER THEOLOGICAL SEMINARY / Park, Edwards Amasa – Boston: Franklin Press, 1883 – 1mf – us A.T.L.A. [240]
Associate Presbyterian Church of North America *see* BOOK OF DISCIPLINE
Associate Reformed Church in North America. General Synod *see* MINUTES, 1782-1822
ASSOCIATE REFORMED PRESBYTERIAN – 1966-86 (complete) – 10r – 1 – ATLA S0739 – us A.T.L.A. [073]
ASSOCIATE REFORMED PRESBYTERIAN – (1986- . 5,6,9) – v1- . 1976- – 1 – us UMI [073]
Associate Synod of North America *see* MINUTES, 1801-1821
ASSOCIATED CHURCHES OF CHRIST IN NEW ZEALAND – 1965-85 (complete) – 2r – 1 – ATLA S0763 – us A.T.L.A. [073]
The Associated Negro Press *see*
– THE CLAUDE A. BARNETT PAPERS, PART 1
– THE CLAUDE A. BARNETT PAPERS, PART 2
– THE CLAUDE A. BARNETT PAPERS, PART 3
ASSOCIATED PRESS CLIPPING FILE – (1977- . 5,6,9) – 1937-. Now available as a collection – 1 – us UMI [071]
Association Canada-Normandie. Section de Montreal *see* CANADA-NORMANDIE
ASSOCIATION CANADIENNE DES BIBLIOTHECAIRES DE LANGUE FRANÇAISE *see* DOCUMENTATION ET BIBLIOTHEQUES
Association Canado-Americaine *see* LE CANADO-AMERICAIN
L'ASSOCIATION C.M.B.A – Quebec, Canada. 10 mai-6 dec 1890 – 1r – 1 – Can$25.00 – cn Can Microfilming [073]
ASSOCIATION COCCINELLE – 1982 leaflet. 1p – 9 – 1.00f – at Libertarian Micro [335]
ASSOCIATION CONCORDIA OF JAPAN : REPORT – no 1-2. 1913-14; no 15 (complete) – 1r – 1 – ATLA B0141 – us A.T.L.A. [950]
Association de la propagation de la foi (Diocese de Montreal) *see* RAPPORT DE L'ASSOCIATION DE LA PROPAGATION DE LA FOI POUR LE DIOCESE DE MONTREAL
Association de l'Adoration Perpetuelle du Tres Saint Sacrement *see* REGLES...ET SOMMAIRES DES INDULGENCES
Association de Tir de Montmagny-L'Islet *see* REGLEMENTS
Association des Amis de Romain Rolland *see* BULLETIN
Association des denturologistes du Quebec *see*
– LE DENTURO
Association des Instituteurs de la Circonscription de l'Ecole Normale Jacques Cartier *see* CONSTITUTION ET REGLEMENTS....AMENDES...31 MAI 1878
Association des Instituteurs de la Circonscription de l'Ecole Normale Jacques-Cartier *see* COMPTES-RENDUS DES CONFERENCES.
Association des Libraires-Editeurs, Imprimeurs et Relieurs de la Province de Quebec *see* REPONSE AU DERNIER RAPPORT DE L'HON. SURINTENDANT DE L'INSTRUCTION PUBLIQUE DE LA PROVINCE DE QUEBEC
Association des Pretres-Adorateurs *see* ANNALES DE L'ASSOCIATION DES PRETRES-ADORATEURS
Association des recherches sur les sciences religieuses et profanes au Canada *see* CULTURE
Association for a Free Russia *see* IS THERE AN UNDERGROUND OPPOSITION IN THE SOVIET UNION?
Association for Asian Studies *see* CUMULATIVE BIBLIOGRAPHY OF ASIAN STUDIES, 1966-70
Association for Canadian Studies in the United States *see* ACSUS NEWSLETTER
Association for Communication Administration *see* ACA BULLETIN
Association for Computing Machinery *see*
– ACM COMPUTING SURVEYS
– ACM TRANSACTIONS ON DATABASE SYSTEMS
– ACM TRANSACTIONS ON MATHEMATICAL SOFTWARE
Association for Educational Data Systems *see*
– AEDS JOURNAL
– AEDS MONITOR
The Association for Good Government *see* REVENUE BASED ON LAND VALUES
ASSOCIATION FOR INFORMATION AND IMAGE MANAGEMENT *see* AIIM (ASSOCIATION FOR INFORMATION AND IMAGE MANAGEMENT)
Association for Information and Image Management *see*
– AIIM INDEX
– AIIM STANDARDS SET
Association for Practitioners in Infection Control *see*
– APIC
– APIC NEWSLETTER
Association for Promoting University Consolidation *see* A SHORT STATEMENT OF THE ADVANTAGES OF UNIVERSITY CONSOLIDATION:..
Association for Research Enlightenment *see* ARE JOURNAL
ASSOCIATION FOR RURAL ADVANCEMENT – Pietermaritzburg. 65 docs. 1980-1991 – 13mf – 9 – ne IDC [360]
Association for Science Education *see* BULLETIN
ASSOCIATION FOR THE RELEASE AND AMNESTY OF DETAINEES IN THE PHILIPPINES *see* KAPATID/ASSOCIATION FOR THE RELEASE AND AMNESTY OF DETAINEES IN THE PHILIPPINES
Association for the Sociological Study of Jewry *see* NEWSLETTER
L'Association francaise de regulation et d'automatisme *see* AUTOMATISME
L' Association Generale des Etudiants Socialistes. Flenu, Jupille, Liege, etc *see* L'ETUDIANT SOCIALISTE
Association international des Travailleurs. Section de la Suisse Romande *see* JOURNAL
Association Internationale de Droit Penal *see* PROJET DE STATUT D'UNE COUR DE JUSTICE CRIMINELLE INTERNATIONALE
ASSOCIATION INTERNATIONALE DES JURISTES DEMOCRATES = INTERNATIONAL ASSOCIATION OF DEMOCRATIC LAWYERS – Brussels. 178 docs. 1980-1990 – 159mf – 9 – ne IDC [320]
L'Association internationale des Travailleurs. La Federation jurassienne *see* BULLETIN DE LA FEDERATION JURASSIENNE DE L'ASSOCIATION INTERNATIONALE DES TRAVAILLEURS
Association internationale du Haut-Congo. Vivi Station *see* RECORDS OF THE VIVI STATION, 1881-1885
L'ASSOCIATION JOURNAL D'ECONOMIE SOCIALE – Quebec: L'Association, [1890-1891] – 9 – cn C.I.H.M. [300]
ASSOCIATION MANAGEMENT – (v.32-. 1980-5,6,9) – v.15-. 1963- – 1 – us UMI [650]
Association of African Universities *see* BULLETIN
Association of American Geographers *see*
– AAG NEWSLETTER
– ANNALS
Association of American Indian Affairs *see* WE SHAKE HANDS
ASSOCIATION OF AMERICAN LAW SCHOOLS : HANDBOOK AND PROCEEDINGS OF THE ANNUAL MEETINGS – (Lacking: 1906) – 1st to 63rd. 1902-63 – 152mf – 9 – $228.00 – LLMC 84-407 – us L.L.M.C. [370]
Association of American Law Schools *see* SELECT ESSAYS IN ANGLO-AMERICAN LEGAL HISTORY
Association of American Railroads. Telegraph and Telephone Section *see* PROCEEDINGS
Association of Canadian Etchers *see* CATALOGUE OF THE FIRST ANNUAL EXHIBITION OF THE ASSOCIATION OF CANADIAN ETCHERS
Association of Casualty and Surety Companies. Law Department *see* CHART ANALYSIS OF THE AUTOMOBILE LIABILITY SECURITY LAWS OF THE UNITED STATES AND CANADA.
ASSOCIATION OF CLINICAL BIOCHEMISTS. PROCEEDINGS *see* ANNALS OF CLINICAL BIOCHEMISTRY
Association of Departments and Administrators in Speech Communications *see* BULLETIN
Association of Departments of English *see* ADE BULLETIN
Association of Dominion Land Surveyors *see* MEMORANDUM TO CONSIDER THE QUESTION OF A TRIGONOMETRICAL SURVEY OF THE DOMINION
Association of Food and Drug Officials *see* QUARTERLY BULLETIN
Association of Governing Boards of Universities and Colleges *see* AGB REPORTS
Association of Libertarian Feminists *see* NINE LEAFLETS
ASSOCIATION OF LIFE INSURANCE COUNSEL PAPERS – (Lacking: v3 p350-399. v12. After 1949 were called: Proceedings) – v1-13. 1913-57 – 110mf – 9 – $165.00 – LLMC 84-401 – us L.L.M.C. [073]
ASSOCIATION OF LIFE INSURANCE COUNSEL PROCEEDINGS *see* ASSOCIATION OF LIFE INSURANCE COUNSEL PAPERS

Association of Military Surgeons of the National Guard of the U.S *see* TRANSACTIONS

Association of Military Surgeons of the United States. Annual Meeting *see* PROCEEDINGS

Association of Municipal Corporations. London *see* MUNICIPAL REVIEW

Association of Official Analytical Chemists *see* JOURNAL

Association of Ontario Land Surveyers. Committee on Topographical Surveying *see* REPORT

ASSOCIATION OF PRACTITIONERS BEFORE THE ICC : REPORTS OF ANNUAL MEETINGS – v1-3. 1930-32 (all publ) – 9 – LLMC 84-410 – us L.L.M.C. [340]

ASSOCIATION OF PROTESTANT TEACHERS OF THE PROVINCE OF QUEBEC: MONTREAL MEETING, 1886 / Dawson, John William – Address of the president, Sir. Wm. Dawson. Montreal?: s.n., 1886?. 03662. (Pre-1900 Canadiana) – 9 – cn C.I.H.M. [971]

Association of Research Libraries. Foreign Newspaper Microfilm Project *see* CIRCULAR LETTER

Association of Southeastern Biologists *see* ASB BULLETIN

ASSOCIATION OF SOUTHERN WOMEN FOR THE PREVENTION OF LYNCHING, 1930-1942 – (Inclusive price if purchased together with Southern Regional Council Papers, 1944-1968 and Commission on Interracial Cooperation, 1919-1944: $18,985) – 8r – 1 – $585.00 – us UMI [360]

Association of Teachers of Japanese *see* JOURNAL

ASSOCIATION OF THE BAR OF THE CITY – 1920-23 – 9 – $10.00 set – us Hein [340]

Association of the Bar of the City of New York *see*
- BULLETIN
- YEARBOOKS-ANNUAL REPORTS

ASSOCIATION OF THE BAR OF THE CITY OF NEW YORK ANNUAL REPORTS *see* ASSOCIATION OF THE BAR OF THE CITY OF NEW YORK YEARBOOKS

ASSOCIATION OF THE BAR OF THE CITY OF NEW YORK YEARBOOKS – (Lacking: 1976. Before 1909 were called: Annual Reports) – 1870-1977 – 127mf – 9 – $190.00 – LLMC 84-408 – us L.L.M.C. [340]

Association of the Laity of the Church of England. Toronto *see* EVIDENCE AND OPINIONS ON THE HOUSE OF LAYMEN IN ALLIANCE WITH THE SYNOD OF TORONTO SUBMITTED TO THE LAITY OF THE CHURCH OF ENGLAND

ASSOCIATION OF TRIAL LAWYERS OF AMERICA NEWSLETTER – v.15-19. Dec. 1972-Dec 1976. Continued as yA T L A Law Reporter – 1 – us UMI [073]

Association of United Ukrainian Canadians *see* ZVIT I REZOLIUTSII Z' IZDU

Association of University Professors *see* ACADEME

Association of University Programs In Health Administration *see* PROGRAM NOTES

Association on American Indian Affairs *see*
- THE AMERICAN INDIAN
- INDIAN AFFAIRS
- INDIAN FAMILY DEFENSE

ASSOCIATION PARISIENNE DES ANCIENS ELEVES DU LYCEE DE NANTES [AVEC DES NOTES MANUSCR. DE P. EUDEL DANS LES MARGES/ WITH HANDWR. NOTES BY P.E. IN THE MARGINS] / Eudel, Paul – 19th c. – fr Armell [370]

Association pour l'Avancement des Sciences et des Techniques de la Documentation *see* DOCUMENTATION ET BIBLIOTHEQUES

Association Professionnelle des Industriels. Congres Patronal (2e: 1946: Montreal, Quebec) *see* ORGANISATION ET REFORME DE L'INDUSTRIE MODERNE

Association Professionnelle des Industriels. Congres Patronal (4e: 1949: Montreal, Quebec) *see* OU VA L'INDUSTRIE?

ASSOCIATION PROGRESS = CH'ING-NIEN CHIN-PU – (In Chinese. Lacking: nos1-13) – nos14-150. 1918-32 – 4r – 1 – ATLA S0300 – us A.T.L.A. [073]

Association Quebecoise des Professeurs de Francais *see* QUEBEC-FRANCAIS

ASSOCIATION RECORD – Montreal: Young Men's Christian Association of Montreal, [18–?-18– or 19–] – 9 – cn C.I.H.M. [360]

Association Saint Antoine de Montreal *see* CONSTITUTION ET REGLEMENTS

ASSOCIATION SUD-AMERICAINE POUR LA PAIX UNIVERSELLE – Buenos Aires, 1910 – 2mf – 9 – ILM-4065/1 – ne IDC [340]

ASSOCIATION ZAIROISE DE DEFENSE DES DROITS DE L'HOMME = ZAIRIAN ASSOCIATON FOR THE DEFENSE OF HUMAN RIGHTS – Kinshasa. 1 doc. 1991 – 1mf – 9 – ne IDC [320]

ASSOCIATIONS – Disponibles Depuis 1983 – F280.00y – fr Journal Officiel [944]

LES ASSOCIATIONS COOPERATIVES EN FRANCE ET A L'ETRANGER / Hubert-Valleroux, P – (Condition of 19th C. French working class series). 1884 – 9 – fr Hachette [360]

DES ASSOCIATIONS ETRANGERES EN FRANCE / Cazeau, R – Paris, 1920 – 3mf – 1 – ILM-3410/1 – ne IDC [327]

DES ASSOCIATIONS OUVRIERES / Villerme, Louis Rene – Paris. 1850. (La Condition Ouvriere. Part Two.) – 9 – 2.50 – fr Bibl Nationale [360]

DES ASSOCIATIONS OUVRIERES DE LA COLLECTION DES 'PETITS TRAITES PUBLIES PAR L'ACADEMIE DES SCIENCES MORALES ET POLITIQUES.' (CONDITION OF 19TH C. FRENCH / Villerme, Louis Rene – (Condition of 19th c. French working class series). 1849 – 9 – fr Hachette [944]

LES ASSOCIATIONS OUVRIERES. ETUDES SUR LEUR PASSE, LEUR PRESENT, LEURS CONDITIONS DE PROGRES / Rougier, J C Paul – (Condition of 19th C. French working class series). 1864 – 9 – fr Hachette [331]

LES ASSOCIATIONS POPULAIRES DE CONSOMMATION, DE PRODUCTION ET DE CREDIT / Walras, L – (Condition of 19th C. French working class series). 1865 – 9 – fr Hachette [336]

LES ASSOCIATIONS PROFESSIONNELLES OUVRIERES / France. Ministere du Commerce, de l'Industrie, des Postes et des Telegraphes. Office du Travail – (Condition of 19th C. French working class series). 1899-1904 – 9 – fr Hachette [380]

ASSOCIATIVE THESAURUS OF ENGLISH – 5 – uk Microform Academic [420]

L'ASSOCIAZIONE – Nice & London. Sep 1889-Jan 1890 – 1r – 1 – uk British Libr Newspaper [072]

L'ASSOLEMENT SIDERAL DE M. G. VILLE ET LA BETTERAVE A SUCRE AU CANADA: PETIT PRECIS D'AGRICULTURE PRATIQUE A L'USAGE SPECIAL DE LA PROVINCE DE QUEBEC / Des Etangs, G – Montreal: Bibliotheque du Syndicat Central des Agriculteurs de Canada, 1893. 02682. (Pre-1900 Canadiana) – 9 – cn C.I.H.M. [338]

l'Assomption, Marie de *see* BIBLIOGRAPHIE D'OUVRAGES ANCIENS DE MEDECINE GARDES A L'HOPITAL GENERAL (1669-1874)

ASSORTED MATERIALS DEALING WITH INDIA = FILMED AT THE BRITISH MUSEUM – London: British Museum Photographic Service, [19–] – 1 – us Res Libr [950]

ASSORTED RHODESIAN AND SOUTH AFRICAN PAMPHLETS / Boston University. African Studies Library – Boston: [The Library, 197-] – 1 – us Res Libr [960]

ASSOZIATIONSVERSUCHE MIT JUGENDLICHEN RAUCHERN UND NICHTRAUCHERN / Vockrodt-Scholz, Viola – 1995 – 5mf – 9 – DM118.00 – 3-8267-2205-1 – gw Hänsel [150]

THE ASSUMPTION OF MOSES – translated (and) edited with introduction, notes, and indices by R. H. Charles. 1897 – 1 – us A.T.L.A. [240]

ASSUNTA LEONI : SCHAUSPIEL IN FUENF AUFZUEGEN / Wilbrandt, Adolf von – Wien: L Rosner, 1883 – 1r – 1 – us U.W. Library [820]

L'ASSUNTA NELL'ODIERNA TEOLOGIA CATTOLICA : STUDIO PUBBLICATO SUL PERIODICO LA SCUOLA CATTOLICA, ORGANO DELLA FACOLT A TEOLOGICA PONTIFICIA DI MILANO / Crosta, Clino – Monza: Artigianelli, 1903 – 1mf – 9 – 0-8370-8415-6 – 1986-2415 – us A.T.L.A. [240]

L'ASSURANCE CONTRE LE CHOMAGE / Denjean, Georges – Toulouse, 1899. (La Condition Ouvriere. Part Two.) – 9 – 15.00 – fr Bibl Nationale [360]

THE ASSURANCE OF IMMORTALITY / Fosdick, Harry Emerson – New York: Macmillan, 1913 – 1mf – us A.T.L.A. [240]

ASSURBANIPAL UND DIE LETZTEN ASSYRISCHEN KOENIGE / Streck, M – Leipzig. 1916. BNE-412 1 – 9 – ne IDC [930]

ASSYRIACA : EINE NACHLESE AUF DEM GEBIETE DER ASSYRIOLOGIE / Hilprecht, Hermann Vollrat – (No more published) – Boston: Ginn; Halle (Saale): Max Niemeyer, 1894 – 1mf – 9 – 0-8370-8434-2 – 1986-2434 – us A.T.L.A. [470]

ASSYRIAN AND BABYLONIAN LITERATURE : SELECTED TRANSLATIONS WITH A CRITICAL INTRODUCTION / Harper, Robert Francis – New York: D Appleton, 1904 – 2mf – 9 – 0-8370-8823-2 – 1986-2823 – us A.T.L.A. [470]

ASSYRIAN AND BABYLONIAN RELIGIOUS TEXTS / Craig, J A – (Assyriologische Bibliothek. v. 13). v. 1-2. Leipzig. 1895-97. BNE-427 1 – 9 – ne IDC [200]

THE ASSYRIAN LAWS / Driver, G R – 1935 – 9 – $18.00 – us I.R.C. [340]

AN ASSYRIAN MANUAL : FOR THE USE OF BEGINNERS IN THE STUDY OF THE ASSYRIAN LANGUAGE / Lyon, David Gordon – (Grammar in English. Texts in Akkadian) – Chicago: American Publ Society of Hebrew, 1886 – 1mf – 9 – 0-8370-8447-4 – 1986-2447 – us A.T.L.A. [470]

THE ASSYRIAN MONUMENTS ILLUSTRATING THE SERMONS OF ISAIAH / Kellner, Maximilian – Boston: Damrell & Upham, 1900 – 1mf – 9 – 0-8370-3872-3 – 1985-1872 – us A.T.L.A. [220]

ASSYRIAN TEXTS : BEING EXTRACTS FROM THE ANNALS OF SHALMANESER 2., SENNACHERIB, AND ASSUR-BANI-PAL: WITH PHILOLOGICAL NOTES / Budge, Ernest Alfred Wallis – London: Truebner: Samuel Bagster, 1880 – 1mf – 9 – 0-8370-7048-1 – 1986-1048 – us A.T.L.A. [470]

ASSYRIOLOGY / EGYPTOLOGY – 14,408mf – 9 – ne IDC [930]

ASSYRISCH-BABYLONISCHE BRIEFE : RELIGIOESEN INHALTS AUS DER SARGONIDENZEIT / Behrens, Emil – (In Akkadian and German) – Leipzig: August Pries, 1905 – 1mf – 9 – 0-8370-7442-8 – 1986-1442 – us A.T.L.A. [470]

ASSYRISCH-BABYLONISCHE MYTHEN UND EPEN / Jensen, P – (Keilinschriftliche Bibliothek). Berlin. 1889-1900. BNE-400 1 – 9 – ne IDC [930]

DIE ASSYRISCH-BABYLONISCHEN KEILINSCHRIFTEN : KRITISCHE UNTERSUCHUNG DER GRUNDLAGEN IHRER ENTZIFFERUNG: NEBST DEM BABYLONISCHEN TEXTE DER TRILINGUEN INSCHRIFTEN IN TRANSCRIPTION SAMMT UEBERSETZUNG UND GLOSSAR / Schrader, Eberhard – (Texts in Akkadian and German. Includes bibliographical references) – Leipzig: In Commission bei F A Brockhaus, 1872 – 1mf – 9 – 0-8370-8381-8 – 1986-2381 – us A.T.L.A. [470]

DIE ASSYRISCHE BESCHWOERUNGSSAMMLUNG MAQLU / Meier, G – (Archiv Orientforschung, Beiheft 2). Berlin. 1937. BNE-468 1 – 9 – ne IDC [290]

ASSYRISCHE GEBETE AN DEN SONNENGOTT. AUS DER ZEIT ASARHADDONS / Knudtzon, J A – 2v. Leipzig. 1893. BNE-20,013 1 – 9 – ne IDC [290]

ASSYRISCHE GEBETE AN DEN SONNENGOTT FUER STAAT UND KOENIGLICHES HAUS : AUS DER ZEIT ASARHADDONS UND ASURBANIPALS / ed by Knudtzon, J A – (Includes bibliographical references and glossary) – Leipzig. 2v. Eduard Pfeiffer, 1893 – 2mf – 9 – 0-8370-7074-0 – 1986-1074 – us A.T.L.A. [470]

DER ASSYRISCHE GOTT / Tallgvist, K – (Studia Orientalia. v. 4. Helsingforsiae. 1932). BNE-410 1 – 9 – ne IDC [290]

ASSYRISCHE GRAMMATIK : MIT UEBUNGSSTUECKEN UND KURZER LITERATUR-UEBERSICHT / Delitzsch, Friedrich – (Discussion in German;exercises in Akkadian) – 2. durchgesehene Aufl. Berlin: Reuther & Reichard; New York: Lemcke & Buechner, 1906 – 1mf – 9 – 0-8370-8498-9 – 1986-2498 – us A.T.L.A. [470]

DIE ASSYRISCHE VERBTAFEL : DIE ASSYRISCHE ZEICHENORDNUNG AUF GRUND VON SA UND V. RAWL. 45 / Peiser, Felix Ernst – Muenchen: F Straub, 1886 – 1mf – 9 – 0-8370-8850-X – 1986-2850 – us A.T.L.A. [470]

DAS ASSYRISCHE WELTREICH IM URTEIL DER PROPHETEN / Staerk, Willy – Goettingen: Vandenhoeck & Rup., 1908. 1 fiche – 9 – us A.T.L.A. [240]

ASSYRISCHES BEAMTENTUM NACH BRIEFEN AUS DER SARGONIDENZEIT / Klauber, E G – (Leipziger semitistischen studien. v. 5, pt. 3. Leipzig. 1914). 1910. BNE-20,117 1 – 9 – ne IDC [930]

ASSYRISCHES HANDWOERTERBUCH / Delitzsch, Franz – Leipzig. 1896. BNE-473 1 – 9 – ne IDC [470]

ASSYRISCHES SYLLABAR : FUER DEN GEBRAUCH IN SEINEN VORLESUNGEN / ed by Schrader, Eberhard – (In German and Akkadian) – Berlin: Buchdr der koenigl Akademie der Wissenschaften, 1880 – 1mf – 9 – 0-8370-8616-7 – 1986-2616 – us A.T.L.A. [470]

ASSYRISCHES UND TALMUDISCHES: KULTURGESCHICHTLICHE UND LEXIKALISCHE NOTIZEN / Pick, Hermann – Berlin: S. Calvary, 1903. 1 fiche – 8mf – 9 – us A.T.L.A. [270]

ASTA TRAVEL NEWS – v39. 1970 – 22mf – 9 – $5.00f – us Ross [910]

Astakhova, A M *see* MEL'TS, M.IA. RUSSKII FOL'KLOR

Astatke, Abiye et al *see* BUILDING PONDS WITH ANIMAL POWER IN THE ETHIOPIAN HIGHLANDS

ASTED *see* DOCUMENTATION ET BIBLIOTHEQUES

O ASTEROIDE : ORGAM DE PROPAGANDA ABOLICIONISTA – Cidade da Cachoeira, BA. 23 Set 1887-13 Maio 1889 – 1,5,6 – bl Biblioteca [072]

Astesano, Eduardo *see*
- ENSAYO SOBRE EL JUSTICIALISMO A LA LUZ DEL MATERIALISMO HISTORICO
- MANUAL DE LA MILITANCIA POLITICA

THE ASTHMATIC ATHLETE : METABOLIC AND VENTILATORY RESPONSES DURING EXERCISE WITH AND WITHOUT PRE-EXERCISE MEDICATION / Ienna, Tiziana M – 1994 – 2mf – $8.00 – us Microform Publ [612]

ASTI – Anarchistische Studenten Initiative. Leaflet, 2p – 9 – 1.00f – at Libertarian Micro [335]

ASTIANATTE / Jomelli, N – Ms, [178-?] – 1 – us Sibley [780]

Astie, J F *see*
- LES DEUX THEOLOGIES NOUVELLES DANS LE SEIN DU PORTESTANTISME FRANCAIS
- HISTOIRE DE LA REPUBLIQUE DES ETATS-UNIS DEPUIS L'ETABLISSEMENT DES PREMIERES COLONIES JUSQU'A L'ELECTION DU PRESIDENT LINCOLN (1620-1860)

Astley, Hugh John Dukinfield *see* PREHISTORIC ARCHAEOLOGY AND THE OLD TESTAMENT

Astley, T *see* A NEW GENERAL COLLECTION OF VOYAGES AND TRAVELS

ASTM (AMERICAN SOCIETY FOR TESTING AND MATERIALS) – Standards. Printed index. Updated every 60 days – 6,9 – us Info Handling [620]

ASTM BULLETIN – (Cont by: Materials Research and Standards. Former title: American Society for Testing Materials Bulletin (apr 1 1921-aug 1937)) – Philadelphia. v1-250. apr 1921-dec 1960. – 1 – D976 – us UMI [600]

ASTON'S EXCHANGE HERALD – Manchester, Great Britain. 1809-1826 – 1 – uk Manchester Libr [330]

Astor, J *see* DROIT ROMAIN

ASTORIA DAILY NEWS – Astoria, OR. 25 May 1901-30 Nov 1903. 3 rolls – 1 – us U.O. Library [071]

ASTORIA (EVENING) DAILY BUDGET – Astoria, OR. 18 Feb 1893-31 Aug 1930. 57 rolls – 1 – us U.O. Library [071]

ASTORIA HERALD – Astoria, OR. -w. 22 Jan 1893-19 Aug 1905. 2 rolls – 1 – us U.O. Library [071]

ASTORIA TRANSCRIPT – Astoria, OR. -w 1886-89 – 1 – 17.00 – us Oregon Hist [071]

ASTORIAN EVENING BUDGET – Astoria, OR. -d. 1 Sept 1930-24 Jan 1961. 75 rolls – 1 – us U.O. Library [071]

ASTORPSPOSTEN SKANE-SMALAND – Angelholm, Sweden. 1899-1901 – 2r – 1 – sw Kungliga [072]

ASTOUNDING SCIENCE FICTION – (See also: Analog Science Fact-Science Fiction) – v1-65 1930-60 – 1 – us UMI [830]

ASTRAEA : TASCHENBUCH FUER FREIMAURER... – (Available: 1824-1825, v1-2; 1846-1856, v12-18) – Ilmenau, 1824-1856 – 38mf – 9 – VR-32.1/1 – ne IDC [360]
ASTRAGALOGIA / Candolle, A P de – Paris. 1802. B-5107 2 – 8 – ne IDC [580]
ASTRAKHANSKOE RYBOLOVSTVO : DVUKHNEDI ELNY I ZHURNAL KOMISSARIATA PO VODNO-LOVET SKIM DI ELAM ASTRAKHANSKAGO KRAI A – (Includes c.1: no.3/4 1918:July-no.5/6 (1918:Aug.)) – Astrakhan: Komissar-iat, 1918 – 1 – CSUXAKY6555-S – us Hoover Inst Photo [947]
Astrakhantseva, I F et al *see* DOKUMENTY I MATERIALY PO ISTORII VELIKOI OKTIABRSKOI SOTSIAL-ISTICHESKOI REVOLIUTSII
Astrakhova, A M *see* RUSSKII FOLKLOR
ASTRAY – Toronto: W. Chewitt, 18–. 02454. (Pre-1900 Canadiana) – 9 – cn C.I.H.M. [971]
ASTREA – Rio de Janeiro, 17 Jun 1826-18 Aug 1832 – 1,5,6 – bl Biblioteca [072]
ASTREE / Urfe, Honore d' – Paris: C. Barbin, 1678. 2pts. in 1 vol.2 fiches. (Literature Collection) – 9 – 6.00 – fr Bibl Nationale [810]
O ASTRO : ORGAM DE LITTERATURA, INDUSTRIA, NOTICIAS, COMMERCIO E LAVOURA, DEDICADO ESPECIALMENTE AOS INTERESSES DO PROFESSORADO MINEIRO – Sanct'Anna do Jacare, 20 Jun 1897 – 1,5,6 – bl Biblioteca [072]
ASTRODYNAMICS 1983 – (Suppl to v54, Advances) – 1984 – 13mf – 9 – $40.00 – 0-87703-192-4 – us Univelt [629]
ASTRODYNAMICS 1985 – (Suppl to vol 58, Advances) – 1986 – 22mf – 9 – $60.00 – 0-87703-247-5 – us Univelt [629]
ASTRODYNAMICS 1987 – (Suppl to vol 65, Advances) – 1988 – 20mf – 9 – $70.00 – 0-87703-287-4 – us Univelt [629]
ASTRODYNAMICS 1989 – (Suppl to vol 71, Advances) – 1990 – 12mf – 9 – $50.00 – 0-87703-319-6 – us Univelt [629]
ASTRODYNAMICS 1991 – (Suppl to vol 76, Advances) – 1992 – 14mf – 9 – $75.00 – 0-87703-348-X – us Univelt [629]
ASTRODYNAMICS 1993 – (Suppl to vol 85, Advances) – 1994 – 5mf – $30.00 – 0-87703-381-1 – us Univelt [629]
ASTRODYNAMICS 1995 – (Suppl to vol 90, Advances) – 1996 – 4mf – $15.00 – 0-87703-408-7 – us Univelt [629]
ASTRODYNAMICS SPECIALIST CONFERENCE – 1968 – 21mf – 9 – $30.00 – 0-87703-227-0 – us Univelt [629]
ASTRODYNAMICS SPECIALIST CONFERENCE – 1971 – 66mf – 9 – $70.00 – 0-87703-237-8 – us Univelt [629]
ASTROLOGISCHE BIBLIOTHEK – Leipzig. v1-21, 1919-27. Film Mas C 640 – 1 – us H.U. Library [073]
ASTROLOGY AND RELIGION AMONG THE GREEKS AND ROMANS / Cumont, Franz – New York: G.P. Putnam, 1912. (American lectures on the history of religions; series of 1911-1912) – 1mf – us A.T.L.A. [250]
ASTROLOGY NOW – (v3- , 1977- . 5,6,9) – v. 1-. 1975- – 1 – us UMI [150]
THE ASTROLOGY OF PERSONALITY / Rudhyar, Dane – A reformulation of astrological concepts and ideals, in terms of contemporary psychology and philosophy. Garden City, NY: (Doubleday, 1970). xviii,500p. illus – 1 – us U.W. Library [150]
ASTROLOGY-YOUR DAILY HOROSCOPE – (v148- , 1974- . 5,6. v160- , 1976- . apply 9) – v. 148-. 1974- – 1 – us UMI [150]
ASTRONAUTICA ACTA *see* ACTA ASTRONAUTICA
ASTRONAUTICS *see* AEROSPACE ENGINEERING
ASTRONAUTICS AND AERONAUTICS – (1965- 5,6. 1970- 9) – v. 1- 1963- – 1 – us UMI [629]
ASTRONAUTICS AND AERONAUTICS *see*
– AIAA BULLETIN
– AEROSPACE AMERICA
ASTRONAUTICS AND AEROSPACE ENGINEERING, ASTRONAUTICS AND AERONAUTICS *see* AEROSPACE ENGINEERING
ASTRONAUTICS INTERNATIONAL – 1968 – 10mf – 9 – $15.00 – 0-87703-226-2 – us Univelt [629]
ASTRONOMICAL AND ASTROPHYSICAL TRANSACTIONS / ed by Bochkarev, Nikolai G – 1,5,9 – us Gordon [520]
ASTRONOMICAL BOOKS FROM SHROPSHIRE COUNTY LIBRARY, 17TH AND EARLY 18TH CENTURIES / Shropshire County Library – Galileo, Gassendi, etc. – 1 – uk Microform Academic [520]
THE ASTRONOMICAL JOURNAL – v1-. 1849- – 1,5,6 – us A.I.P. [520]
ASTRONOMISCHES AUS BABYLON : ODER, DAS WISSEN DER CHALDAEER UEBER DEN GESTIRNTEN HIMMEL / Epping, Joseph – (Includes bibliographical references) – Freiburg i.B.; St Louis: Herder, 1889 – 1mf – 9 – 0-8370-7060-0 – 1986-1060 – us A.T.L.A. [520]
ASTRONOMY – v1- 1973- 1; 1977- 5,6,9 – us UMI [073]
ASTRONOMY AND ASTROPHYSICS – Board of Directors, European Southern Observatory (ESO). v.1-105, 1969-81. ISSN: 0004-6361 – 1,5,6,9,13 – 81.00v – us UMI [520]
ASTRONOMY AND METEOROLOGY – Montreal: W H Smith, 1887 – 9 – cn C.I.H.M. [520]
ASTRONOMY IN THE OLD TESTAMENT / Schiaparelli, Giovani Virginio – Oxford: Clarendon Press, 1905. 1 fiche – 9 – us A.T.L.A. [520]
ASTRONOMY LETTERS – v1- 1975- – 1,5,6 – us A.I.P. [520]
ASTRONOMY OF THE BIBLE / Mitchel, Ormsby MacKnight – New York: Blakeman and Mason, 1863. 1 fiche – 9 – us A.T.L.A. [240]
THE ASTRONOMY OF THE BIBLE / Mitchel, Ormsby MacKnight – New York:Blakeman and Mason, 1863 – 1mf – 9 – 0-8370-4450-2 – 1985-2450 – us A.T.L.A. [210]
ASTRONOMY QUARTERLY – 1984- – 1,5,6,9 – us UMI [520]
ASTRONOMY QUARTERLY *see* VISTAS IN ASTRONOMY
ASTROPHYSICAL JOURNAL – (1965- . 5,6. 1977- . 9) – 1- 1895- – 1 – us UMI [520]
ASTROPHYSICAL JOURNAL – v. 1-118. 1895-1953 – 1,5,6 – us Princeton Micro [520]
ASTROPHYSICAL LETTERS / ed by Palumbo, G et al – 1967- – 1,5,9 – us Gordon [530]
ASTROPHYSICS – v. 1-. 1965- – 1,5,6 – us UMI [520]
ASTROPHYSICS – v1-36. 1965-93 – 1,5 – $65.00v – us UMI [530]
ASTROPHYSICS AND SPACE PHYSICS REVIEWS / ed by Syunyaev, R A – 9,5,1 – us Harwood [520]
ASTROPHYSICS AND SPACE SCIENCE – (1984-. 5,6,9) – v1-. 1968- – 1 – us UMI [073]
Astruc, Jean *see* DE MORBIS VENEREIS LIBRI SEX
ASTRUM ALBERTI – Belleville [Ont.]: Students of Albert College, [1883?-18– or 19–] – 9 – cn C.I.H.M. [370]
Astrup, E *see* BLANDT NORDPOLENS NABOER
Astuni, D *see* SE POSSA CONCEDERSI "L'EXEQUATUR"...
ASUNCION DEL MANDO CONSTITUCIONAL : 4 DE JUNIO 1946 / REPUBLICA ARGENTINA – [Buenos Aires?: S.n., 1946?]. 1v – 1 – CSUXADJ2666-B – us Hoover Inst Photo [340]
EL ASUNTO DE PLASENCIA / Diaz de la Cruz, Felipe – 1888 – 9 – 1.50f – sp Bibl Santa Ana [946]
ASURANSI PENGANGKUTAN / Kaihatu, J E – In Dutch, English or Indonesian. SE-4539 1. c1959 – 9 – ne IDC [950]
Asylbekov, M K *see* ZHELEZNODOROZHNIKI KAZAKHSTANA V PERVOI RUSSKOI REVOLIUTSII 1905-1907 GG
DAS ASYLRECHT UND DIE AUSLIEFERUNG FLUCHTIGER VERBRECHER... / Bulmerincq, A von – Dorpat, 1853 – 2mf – 1 – ILM-135/1 – ne IDC [327]
AT AND T BELL LABORATORIES TECHNICAL JOURNAL : A JOURNAL OF THE AT AND T COMPANIES – (Cont: Bell System Technical Journal. Cont by: AT and T Technical Journal) – New York. v63. jan-dec 1984 – 1,5,9 – D58.01 – us UMI [380]
AT AND T BELL LABORATORIES TECHNICAL JOURNAL *see* AT AND T TECHNICAL JOURNAL
AT AND T MAGAZINE – (Cont: Bell Telephone Magazine. Ceased publ) – New York. v1-2. 1984-1985* – 1 – D17802 – us UMI [380]
AT AND T -SELECTED COMMISSION DECISIONS : I.C.C. ACTIVITIES AFFECTING TELECOMMUNICATIONS – American Telephone and Telegraph Co.-Legal department. nos 1-254 46 bks. 1912-16 (all publ) – 230mf – 9 – $1,035.00 – LLMC 84-403 – us L.L.M.C. [073]
AT AND T TECHNICAL JOURNAL – (Cont: AT and T Bell Laboratories Technical Journal) – New York. v64-76. jan 1985-dec 1997+. shipped annually or quarterly – 1,5,9 – D58.02 – us UMI [380]
AT AND T TECHNICAL JOURNAL *see* AT AND T BELL LABORATORIES TECHNICAL JOURNAL
AT AND T TECHNOLOGY – (Cont: Record. AT & T Bell Laboratories n787.01) – New York. v1-10. 1986-win 1996 – 1,5,9 – $75.00y – D15465 – us UMI [073]
A.T. Andreas and Co *see* HISTORY OF ST CLAIR COUNTY
AT HOME AND ABROAD : A MAGAZINE OF HOME AND FOREIGN MISSIONS FOR YOUNG HELPERS IN THE WORK – (Cont. as: Window. London, 1974 (Autumn)-1976; Missing 1879, v1; 1941; 1946) – London, 1879-1974 (Spring-summer) – 194mf – 9 – H-2755/1 – ne IDC [240]
AT HOME AND ABROAD – v1-8. Nov 1891-Oct 1895 – 1 – 375.00 – us Opus [073]
AT HOME WITH GOD : PRIEDIEU PAPERS ON SPIRITUAL SUBJECTS / Russell, Matthew – London; New York: Longmans, Green, 1910 – 1mf – 9 – 0-8370-7013-9 – 1986-1013 – us A.T.L.A. [240]
AT HOME WITH THE PATAGONIANS; A YEAR'S WANDERINGS OVER UNTRODDEN GROUND FROM THE STRAITS OF MAGELLAN TO THE RIO NEGRO / Musters, George Chaworth – London: John Murray, 1871. xx,322p. illus., maps – 1 – us U.W. Library [305]
At, Jean Antoine *see* LA LOI
AT MICHAELMAS: A LYRIC / Carman, Bliss – Wolfville, N.S.: "Acadian" Press, 1895. 00472. (Pre-1900 Canadiana) – 9 – cn C.I.H.M. [240]
...AT NIAGARA FALLS, AUGUST 21ST, 1897 / British Association for the Advancement of Science. Canada – Local Committee. Niagara Falls: The Association, 1897. 00282. (Pre-1900 Canadiana) – 9 – cn C.I.H.M. [971]
AT OUR OWN DOOR: A STUDY OF HOME MISSIONS / Morris, Samuel Leslie – New York: Fleming H. Revell, 1904. 258p. 1 fiche – 9 – us A.T.L.A. [240]
AT THE CONVERSATION TABLE / Blume, Mary – Lily Szenasi at table, 1984. 1p – 9 – 1.00f – at Libertarian Micro [335]
ATA MAGAZINE / Alberta Teachers' Alliance – Edmonton. v1-78 jun 1920-jun 1998+ 1; v1-58 jun 1920-may 1978*. v59-61 nov 1978-may 1981. v62 nov 1981-may 1982*. v63-66 nov 1982-jun 1986. v67-75 nov 1986-jun 1995*. v76-78 fall 1995-sum 1998 5; v1-55 jun 1920-jun 1975*. v57-78 nov 1976-jun 1998+ 9 – 1,5,9 – inquire – D10092 – us UMI [370]
ATA MAGAZINE – Edmonton. v40- 1959- – 5,9 – Can$20.00y – cn Micromedia [073]
ATA NEWS / Alberta Teachers Association – v. 1-. 1967- – 1 – us UMI [370]
ATA NEWS – (v19-22 1984-88 Can$60.00) – Edmonton. v19- 1984- – 1 – Can$60.00y – cn Micromedia [073]
ATA NEWS / Alberta Teachers' Association – Edmonton. v1-. 1967-* – 1 – D10093 – us UMI [370]
Ata, Tayyarzade Ahmed *see* TARIH-I 'ATA
Atabeyoglu, Salahattin Enis *see* SARA
ATACC JOURNAL – Edmonton. v7- 1989- – 9 – Can$20.00y – cn Micromedia [073]
ATAHUALPA. TRAGEDIA / Cortes, Cristobal Maria – 1784 – 1mf – 9 – Pta1,000.00 – 84-7848-164-8 – sp Pentalfa [440]
ATAIDE, ANTONIO DE : VIAJENS DO REINO PARA A INDIA... / Alvarez, Arturo – Madrid: Archivo Ibero Americano, 1961 – 1 – sp Bibl Santa Ana [950]
Atakhodshaev, F M *see* VAZNIKNOVENIE RAZVITIIA SOVETSKOGO ZAKONODATEL'STVA O ZAKLIUCHENIE I RASTORZHENII BRAKA V UZBEKISTANE
ATAKTA BOTANIKA / Endlicher, S L – Nova genera et species plantarum descripta et iconibus illustrata. Vindonae. 1833-35. B-807 2 – 8 – ne IDC [580]
ATALAIA : PERIODICO NOTICIOSO, LITTERARIO, RELIGIOSO E COMMERCIAL – [s.l.]. 30 Jul 1887 – 1,5,6 – bl Biblioteca [072]
ATALAIA – Rio de Janeiro, 31 May-2 Sep 1823 – 1,5,6 – bl Biblioteca [072]
O ATALAIA – San Luis de Caceres, 13 Mar, Jul 1887; Feb-Mar 1888; 17 Nov 1889 – 1,5,6 – bl Biblioteca [072]
ATALAIA DA LIBERDADE – Rio de Janeiro, 4 Feb-17 Mar 1826 – 1,5,6 – bl Biblioteca [072]
EL ATALAYA BAUTISTA – 1908-24. Name changes: El Atalaya Bautista, 1908 – May 1910; El Bautista, May 1910 – Dec 1912; El Foro Cristiana, Jan 1915 – May 1915; El Alalaya Bautista, Dec 1917-24 – 1 – 322.00 – us Baptist [240]
ATALAYA DE LA MANCHA – Ano 1813-1815 (16-VII/26-IV) – 53mf – 9 – sp Cultura [946]
Atanasov, P *see* NACHALO NA BALGARSKOTO KNIGO PETCHATANE
ATASCADERO NEWS – Atascadero, CA. 1916-24; 1928- – 122+ r – 1 BC02024 – $6,100.00 ($240.00y) – us Library Micro [071]
ATASCADERO TIMES *see* TEMPLETON TIMES
ATBILDE = A REPLY: "AGAINST THE SECT OF THE BAPTISTS" : "PRET BAPTISTU SEKTI" – Riga: Aleksander Stahl, 1882. Publ. No. 6298 d. One of five items on a reel – 1 – us Baptist [240]
Atcheson, N *see* AMERICAN ENCROACHMENTS ON BRITISH RIGHTS
Atchison County. Kansas *see* STATE CENSUS
Atchison County. Kansas. School District 9 *see* MINUTES OF THE ANNUAL MEETINGS OF THE BOARD OF TRUSTEES. 1861-70
Atchison. Kansas. Trinity Episcopal Church *see* RECORDS
Atchison, Topeka and Santa Fe Railroad Company *see*
– CORRESPONDENCE
– DAILY CONSTRUCTION JOURNAL
– LIST OF BUILDINGS OF AT AND SF RR AND LEASED LINES
– PAYROLL RECORDS
– RECORDS AND CORRESPONDENCE
– SANTA FE RATE SCHEDULES
Atchison, Topeka and Santa Fe Railway Company *see*
– RECORDS
– "SPLINTERS."
Atchley, E G *see* ESSAYS ON CEREMONIAL BY VARIOUS AUTHORS
Atchley, F *see* A HISTORY OF THE USE OF INCENSE IN THE DIVINE WORSHIP
Atchoarena, David *see* EDUCATIONAL STRATEGIES FOR SMALL ISLAND STATES
THE ATCOPS REPORTER – Jul, Sept 1972; Jan, Apr, Oct 1973; Jan, Apr 1974; Apr 1976; May 1977. 18p – 9 – 1.00f – at Libertarian Micro [335]
ATEISTICHESKAIA RABOTA B KLUBE / Romanov, I N – (Trade Union publication. Essay on the contribution of trade unions in the USSR to workers' political education against religious practice) – M., 1985 – 2mf – 9 – DE-143/1 – ne IDC [331]
ATEITIS – Pittsburgh, PA, 1900-1901 – 1r – 1 – us I.H.R.C. [978]
ATEITIS – South Boston, MA: Leidzia Ateities Kooperacijos Draugija, Ink., Petnyciomis, jan-apr 1918 – 15 – 1 – us Res Libr [071]
L'ATELIER – Hebdomadaire syndicaliste. Dir. Leon Jouhaux. Paris. mars 1920-23 – 1 – fr A.C.R.P.P. [073]
L'ATELIER – Paris. dec 1940-aout 1944 – 1 – fr A.C.R.P.P. [073]
L'ATELIER – Paris. sept 1840-juil 1850 – 1 – fr A.C.R.P.P. [073]
ATELIER NATIONAL DE REPRODUCTION DES THESES DE LILLE – (All French Dissertations Literature, Human Science, Law, Politics, Sociality, Economics. Write to publisher for catalogs) – 1971- – 24,500 titles – 9 – F60.00mf – ISSN: 0294 – fr Atelier National [370]
L'ATELIER POUR LE PLAN / Confederation Generale du Travail – no. 1-31. Paris. mai 1935-37. mq no. 9-12, 16 – 1 – fr A.C.R.P.P. [330]
ATELIERS ET TAUDIS DE LA BANLIEU DE PARIS / Valdour, Jacques – Paris. 1923. (La Condition Ouvriere. Part Two.) – 9 – $7.50 – fr Bibl Nationale [360]
Aten, A *see*
– DATES
– FLAYING AND CURING OF HIDES AND SKINS AS A RURAL INDUSTRY
ATENCION! – (Includes c.1: v.1:no.1 1955:Nov. 15) – 1 – CSUXAJA8053-S – us Hoover Inst Photo [946]
ATENEA: REVISTA MENSUAL DE CIENCIAS, LETRAS Y ARTES – Santiago. Issued by Universidad de Concepcion, Chile. v. 1-92. Apr 1924-Mar 1949 – 1 – 295.00 – us L of C Photodup [800]

ATENEI : ISTORIKO-LITERATURNYI VREMENNIK – v1-3. 1924-26 – 1r – 1 – us Ross [460]

ATENEI – Zhurnal kritiki, sovremennoi istorii i literatury. M. 1858-59. B-1204 2 – 8 – ne IDC [947]

ATENEI: ISTORIKO-LITERATURNYI VREMENNIK – Leningrad. v. 1-3. 1924-1926 – 1 – us NY Public [947]

Ateneo *see*
- CERVANTES EN EL ATENEO DE BADAJOZ
- PRIMER CONCURSO FOTOGRAFICO CATALOGO MAYO 1927

ATENTADOS POLITICOS EN LA ARGENTINA / Juarez, Roberto – [1. ed. Buenos Aires]: A. Pena Lillo [1970] – us Hoover Inst Photo [972]

ATERET ZEVI. JUBELSCHRIFT ZUM SIEBZIGSTEN GEBURTSTAGE / Graetz, H – Breslau. 1887. BJ-100-38 1 – 9 – ne IDC [900]

Atget, Eugene *see* OEUVRE

ATHABASKA UNIVERSITY MAGAZINE *see* AURORA

ATHABASKA UNIVERSITY MAGAZINE (ATHABASKA) – (Cont by: Aurora v11 1987/88-) – Athabaska. v7-10. 1982-87 – 9 – Can$20.00y – cn Micromedia [370]

THE ATHANASIAN CREED : BY WHOM WRITTEN AND BY WHOM PUBLISHED: WITH OTHER ENQUIRIES ON CREEDS IN GENERAL / Ffoulkes, Edmund S – London: J.T. Hayes, 1871? – 1mf – us A.T.L.A. [240]

THE ATHANASIAN CREED AND ITS EARLY COMMENTARIES / Burn, A E – 1986 – 3mf – 9 – ne Slangenburg [240]

THE ATHANASIAN ORIGIN OF THE ATHANASIAN CREED / Brewer, J S – London: Rivingtons, 1872 – 1mf – us A.T.L.A. [240]

ATHANASIANA (T.U.U. 2-19/4) / Stuelcken, A – Leipzig, 1899 – 3mf – 9 – ne Slangenburg [240]

ATHANASIUS / Goerres, J – Regensburg: G.J. Manz, 1838 – 1mf – us A.T.L.A. [240]

ATHANASIUS : HIS LIFE AND LIFE-WORK / Reynolds, Henry Robert – London: Religious Tract Society, 1889. (The Church history series; 5) – 1mf – us A.T.L.A. [240]

ATHANASIUS DER GROSSE UND DIE KIRCHE SEINER ZEIT : BESONDERS IM KAMPFE MIT DEN ARIANISMUS: IN SECHS BUECHERN / Moehler, Johann Adam – Mainz: F. Kupferberg, 1844 – 2mf – us A.T.L.A. [240]

Athanasius, Patriarch of Alexandria *see*
- THE CANONS OF ATHANASIUS OF ALEXANDRIA
- A DISCOURSE

ATHEISM AND ARITHMETIC : MATHEMATICAL LAW IN NATURE: ARITHMETIC IN PLANTS AND PLANETS, MATHEMATICS IN MUSICAL SCIENCE, NUMBER IN VITAL ACTION / Hastings, Horace Lorenzo – Boston, MA: H L Hastings; London: S Bagster, 1885 – 1mf – 9 – 0-8370-7386-3 – 1986-1386 – us A.T.L.A. [210]

ATHEISM IN RUSSIA PAMPHLET COLLECTION – 1907 – 1 – CSUXANR0953-B – us Hoover Inst Photo [210]

ATHEISM IN THE SOVIET UNION PAMPHLET COLLECTION – 1946-1980 – 1 – CSUXANR0945-B – us Hoover Inst Photo [210]

ATHENA PRESS – Athena, OR. -w. 9 Jun 1893-30 Dec 1976+. 12 rolls – 1 – us U.O. Library [071]

ATHENAEUM – A journal of literature, science, the fine arts, music and the drama. 1828-1921 – 1 – us UMI [073]

ATHENAEUM : PHILOSOPHISCHE ZEITSCHRIFT / ed by Frohschammer, J – Bd 1-3(1862-1864) – 36mf – 9 – Dfl126.00 – ne Slangenburg [073]

ATHENAEUM : EINE ZEITSCHRIFT / ed by Schlegel, August Wilhelm & Schlegel, Friedrich – Berlin, 1798-1800. Hildesheim, 1977 – 13mf – 9 – DM110.00 diazo DM130.00 silver – gw Olms [400]

THE ATHENAEUM – Madras, India. Athenaeum & Statesman Athenaeum & Daily News. -w, -d. Jan 1844-Aug 1885. 136 reels – 1 – uk British Libr Newspaper [072]

THE ATHENAEUM – Morgantown. West Virginia. (W. Va. Univ.). 1888- – 1 – us UMI [071]

L'ATHENAEUM FRANCAIS : JOURNAL UNIVERSEL DE LA LITTERATURE, DE LA SCIENCE ET DES BEAUX-ARTS – Paris, 1852-1856 – 152mf – 9 – H-1378/2 – ne IDC [500]

The Athenaeum of Philadelphia *see* BIOGRAPHICAL DICTIONARY OF PHILADELPHIA ARCHITECTS: 1700-1930

ATHENAEUM OVERLAND – (Lacking: Sep-Dec 1887) – Madras, India. Jan 1875-Aug 1885 – 20r – 1 – uk British Libr Newspaper [072]

ATHENAEUM. PHILISOPHISCHE ZEITSCHRIFT / ed by Frohschammer, J – Muenchen. v1-3. 1862-1864 – 36mf – 9 – ne IDC [100]

ATHENAGORAE LIBELLUS PRO CHRISTIANIS; ORATIO DE RESURRECTIONE CADAVERUM / Schwartz, Eduard – Leipzig: J.C. Hinrichs, 1891 – 1mf – us A.T.L.A. [240]

ATHENAGORAE LIBELLUS PRO CHRISTIANIS RECENSUIT E. SCHWARTZ (T.U.U.-1-4/2) / Schwartz, Eduard – Leipzig, 1891 – 3mf – 9 – ne Slangenburg [240]

ATHENAI – Athens, 9 Feb 1917-12 Feb 1919 (imperfect) – 3r – 1 – uk British Libr Newspaper [072]

O ATHENEO : PERIODICO SCIENTIFICO E LITTERARIO – [s.l.]. 1 Abr 1849-15 Abr 1850 – 1,5,6 – bl Biblioteca [072]

ATHENEO BAHIANO – Bahia, BA. 9 Abr 1878-Jul 1879 – 1,5,6 – bl Biblioteca [072]

ATHENES ANCIENNE ET NOUVELLE ET L'ESTAT PRESENT DE L'EMPIRE DES TURCS, CONTENANT LA VIE DU SULTAN MAHOMET 4; LE MINISTRE DE COPROGLI, ACHMET PACHA, GRAND VIZIR AVEC LE PLAN DE LA VILLE D'ATHENES, PAR LE SR. DE LA GUILLETIERE / Guillet de Saint-George, Georges – Paris, E. Michallet, 1675. xxii/456-34p French Voyagers in the Mediterranean 16th to 18th Centuries. 5967 – 9 – fr Hachette [949]

THE ATHENEUM – Toronto: T Bengough, [1883-18– or 19–] – 9 – cn C.I.H.M. [971]

THE ATHENEUM OR SPIRIT OF THE ENGLISH MAGAZINE – Boston. v. 1-32. 1817-33 – 1 – 127.00 – us L of C Photodup [073]

O ATHENIENSE : ORGAO LITTERARIO, CRITICO E NOTICIOSO – [s.l.] 29 Dez 1907-Jan 1908; 12 Set 1909 – 1,5,6 – bl Biblioteca [072]

O ATHENIENSE – [s.l.]. 7 Set 1888 – 1,5,6 – bl Biblioteca [072]

ATHENIENSIS HISTORIARUM LIBRI 10 (CSHB 45) / Chalcocondylae, Laonici; ed by Bekkeri, Imm – Bonnae, 1843 – Dfl35.00 – ne Slangenburg [930]

ATHENS BLADE – Athens, GA. v1.1879-80 – 1r – 1 – us Ross [071]

THE ATHENS DAILY NEWS – Sayre, PA., 1889-1890 – 13 – $25.00r – us I.M.R. [071]

ATHENS FIRST BAPTIST CHURCH. ATHENS, TENNESSEE : CHURCH RECORDS – (250p) – 1871-1904 – 1 reel – 1 – $11.25 – us Baptist [240]

ATHENS FIRST BAPTIST CHURCH. ATHENS, TEXAS : CHURCH RECORDS – 1887-1945, 1966-77 – 1 – 45.45 – us Baptist [240]

THE ATHENS NEWS – Sayre, PA., 1889-1890 – 13 – $25.00r – us I.M.R. [071]

Athens, Ohio *see* MISCELLANEOUS EARLY NEWSPAPERS

Athens. Presbytery (Cum. Pres. Ch.) *see* MINUTES, 1854-1907

ATHEROSCLEROSIS – v1-53. 1961-84.Continues: Journal of Atherosclerosis Research – 1,5,6,13 – sz Elsevier [616]

ATHERSTONE OBSERVER – Nuneaton, UK. Jul-Dec 1963; Aug 1965-1966 – 4r – 1 – uk British Libr Newspaper [072]

Atherton, Gertrude *see* AMERICAN WIVES AND ENGLISH HUSBANDS: A NOVEL

Atherton, Pauline *see* HANDBOOK FOR INFORMATION SYSTEMS AND SERVICES

Athey, Irene *see* LANGUAGE, READING AND DEAFNESS

ATHIPAT : THAI-LANGUAGE DAILY NEWSPAPER – Bangkok, Thailand. Dec 1975-76 – 1 – $50.00y – us Asia Libr [072]

ATHIT : THAI-LANGUAGE DAILY NEWSPAPER – Bangkok, Thailand. Dec 1975-Dec 1976 – 1 – $50.00y – us Asia Libr [072]

O ATHLETA : ORGAM DOS INTERESSES GERAES – Cidade do Para, 1 Mar-May, Jul-Dec 1896; 17 Jan 1897 – 1,5,6 – bl Biblioteca [072]

O ATHLETA : PERIODICO LITTERARIO E NOTICIOSO – Pilar, Alagoas. 25 Maio, Out 1902; Fev 1903; Set-20 Dez 1908 – 1,5,6 – bl Biblioteca [072]

ATHLETIC DIRECTORS' PERCEIVED PREVALENCE OF NORTH CAROLINA HIGH SCHOOL ATHLETES' DRUG AND SUBSTANCE USE / Moose, Karen S – University of North Carolina at Chapel Hill, 1995 – 1mf – 9 – $4.00 – HE557 – us Microform Publ [360]

ATHLETIC FUND-RAISING : EXPLORING THE MOTIVES BEHIND PRIVATE DONATIONS / Smith, Joseph C, Jr. – 1989 – 91p 1mf – 9 – $4.00 – us Microform Publ [790]

ATHLETIC JOURNAL – (1971- 5,6. 1975- 9) – 1- 1921- – 1 – us UMI [790]

ATHLETIC LEAVES – Montreal: [Montreal Amateur Athletic Association, 1888-188-?] – 9 – cn C.I.H.M. [790]

ATHLETIC NEWS – Manchester, UK. 1882; 1888-95; 1901-08 – 17r – 1 – uk British Libr Newspaper [073]

THE ATHLETIC ORGANIZATIONAL STRUCTURE AND ADMINISTRATIVE VIEWS OF UNIVERSITY AND ATHLETIC GOVERNING PERSONNEL IN THE SOUTHWEST CONFERENCE / Cheatham, Tina R & Myers, Bettye – 1992 – 3mf – $12.00 – us Microform Publ [790]

ATHLETIC TRAINING – (v10- . 5,6. v11- . 9) – v. 1-. 1956- – 1 – us UMI [790]

ATHLETICS – (Vols 1976-80/81 publ as Ontario Atheletics) – Willowdale, 1976- – 9 – Can$20.00y – cn Micromedia [073]

ATHLONE CONSERVATIVE ADVOCATE – Ireland, 1 Jun-28 Sep 1837 – 14ft – 1 – uk British Libr Newspaper [072]

ATHLONE INDEPENDENT – Ireland, 6 Nov 1833-9 Nov 1836 – 1r – 1 – uk British Libr Newspaper [072]

ATHLONE MIRROR – Ireland, 18 Sep 1841-16 Jul 1842 – 28ft – 1 – uk British Libr Newspaper [072]

ATHOL 1737-1849 – (Mf 1-4T: Births & Deaths 1737-1847. Mf 4T: Intentions 1762-93. Mf 4T-6T: Marriages 1750-1843. Mf 6T-7T: Intentions 1793-1836. Mf 7T: Births 1843-46. Mf 8T: Deaths 1845-49) – (mf ed 1994) – 8mf – 9 – 0-87623-204-7 – us Holbrook [920]

Atholl, Katharine Marjory *see*
- MY IMPRESSIONS OF SPAIN
- REPORT OF OUR VISIT TO SPAIN

ATIEKWA. UN VILLAGE DE COTE D'IVOIRE / Ferrari, Antoine & Thoret, Jacques – Africa series. 1970 – 9 – fr Hachette [960]

Atienza, Loretta J *see* VTR WORKSHOP

Atif, Mehmet *see* NAZAR-I SERIATTE KUVVET-I BERIYE VE BAHRIYE'NIN EHEMMIYET VE VUECUBU

ATIKOTH / Israel. Ministry of Education and Culture. Antiquities Division – Journal of the Antiquities Division. Jerusalem, Institute of Archeology, Hebrew Univ. 1955-71. (Bibliogr. supplement 1973, last issue) – 9 – 30.00 – is I.T.T.I. [930]

ATILLA-ORGAAN – Groningen, 1936-1939. 6 nos – 1mf – 9 – J-261-10/1 – ne IDC [073]

ATIQOT / Israel. Ministry of Education and Culture – v. 1-10. 1955-73. BJ-81-10 1 – 9 – ne IDC [370]

ATJARA MALAM KESENIAN – Djakarta, 1955. BSEM-13380 1 – 9 – ne IDC [700]

Atjtje, Syarfuddin *see* PACIFIC REFERENCE SOURCES

ATJUNG – Bunga, menanam dan memeliharanja. Djakarta: Balai Pustaka, 1959. 104p. BSEM-9650-1651 1 – 9 – ne IDC [580]

Atkeson, W O *see* HISTORY OF BATES COUNTY

Atkins, Frederick A *see* BIBLE DIFFICULTIES AND HOW TO MEET THEM

Atkins, Gaius Glenn *see* PILGRIMS OF THE LONELY ROAD

Atkins, Henry Gibson *see* GERMAN LITERATURE THROUGH NAZI EYES

Atkins, James *see*
- THE KINGDOM IN THE CRADLE
- A VOYAGE TO GUINEA, BRASIL AND THE WEST-INDIES

Atkins, Thomas *see* REMINISCENCES OF TWELVE YEARS' RESIDENCE IN TASMANIA AND NEW SOUTH WALES, NORFOLK ISLAND AND MORETON BAY, CALCUTTA, MADRAS, AND CAPE TOWN,..

Atkins, W *see* A DISCOURSE SHEWING THE NATURE OF THE GOUT

Atkinson *see* PROMINENT MEN OF WEST VIRGINIA

Atkinson, David *see* THE LIBRARIES OF PATRU AND BOILEAU

Atkinson, Edward *see* COMMERCIAL UNION BETWEEN THE UNITED STATES AND CANADA: TWO LETTERS FROM EDWARD ATKINSON, ESQ., OF BOSTON, IN RESPONSE TO RESOLUTIONS OF THE NEW YORK CHAMBER OF COMMERCE

Atkinson, Ernest Edwin *see* A SELECTED BIBLIOGRAPHY OF HISPANIC BAPTIST HISTORY

Atkinson, G *see*
- INTERNATIONAL MORALITY; OR,...
- LES NOUVEAUX HORIZONS DE LA RENAISSANCE FRANCAISE

Atkinson, George M *see* THE OGAM INSCRIBED MONUMENTS OF THE GAEDHIL IN THE BRITISH ISLAND; WITH A DISSERTATION ON THE OGAM CHARACTER, ETC

ATKINSON GRAPHIC – Atkinson, NE. -w. Sep. 1882-Nov. 1893. Incomplete; Dec. 1893-Nov. 1901; Dec. 1901-Sep. 1902. Incomplete; Jan. 1908-Jun. 1914; Jan. 1918- – 1 – us NE Hist [071]

Atkinson, Henry A *see* THE CHURCH AND THE PEOPLE'S PLAY

Atkinson, J C *see*
- BRITISH BIRDS' EGGS AND NESTS
- A COMPENDIUM OF THE ORNITHOLOGY OF GREAT BRITAIN, WITH REFERENCE TO ANATOMY AND PHYSIOLOGY OF BIRDS

Atkinson, John *see*
- THE BEGINNINGS OF THE WESLEYAN MOVEMENT IN AMERICA AND THE ESTABLISHMENT THEREIN OF METHODISM
- CENTENNIAL HISTORY OF AMERICAN METHODISM
- THE CLASS LEADER: HIS WORK AND HOW TO DO IT, WITH ILLUSTRATIONS OF PRINCIPLES, DEEDS, METHODS AND RESULTS

ATKINSON PLAIN DEALER – Atkinson, NE. -w. Jan. 1895-Jun. 1897. Incomplete – 1 – us NE Hist [071]

Atkinson, R *see* THE IRISH LIBER HYMNORUM

Atkinson, William Walker *see* NEW THOUGHT, ITS HISTORY AND PRINCIPLES, OR, THE MESSAGE OF THE NEW THOUGHT

ATLA LAW REPORTER – (v.22- 1979- 5,6,9) – Assoc. of Trial Lawyers of America. v.20-. 1977- – 1 – us UMI [073]

ATLA LAW REPORTER *see* LAW REPORTER (ATLA)

ATLANTA AND ITS BUILDERS, A COMPREHENSIVE HISTORY OF THE GATE CITY OF THE SOUTH / Martin, Thomas H – 2v, 1902. Biog. and hist. sketches. 22 fiches.F-0677/F-0678 – 9 – us A.G.L.L. [920]

THE ATLANTA CONSTITUTION – Atlanta. Ga. (Georgia Index, 1971-79). 1868- – 1 – Apply – us UMI [071]

ATLANTA JOURNAL – Atlanta. Ga. 1883- – 1 – us UMI [071]

ATLANTA MAGAZINE – 1976-79 – 9 – us UMI [073]

Atlanta University *see* PUBLICATIONS

ATLANTES EXTREMENOS? / Roso de Luna, Mario – Caceres: Tip. Enc. y Lib. Jimenez, 1905 – 1 – sp Bibl Santa Ana [946]

L'ATLANTIADE OU LA THEOGONIE NEWTONIENNE: POEME EN SIX CHANTS / Lemercier, Nepomucene – Paris: Pichard, 1812. 4 fiches.(Literature Collection) – 9 – 10.00 – fr Bibl Nationale [810]

ATLANTIC ADVOCATE – v47-58. 1956-1968 – 1 – cn Precision [073]

ATLANTIC BUSINESS – Halifax. v1-8. 1982-89 – 9 – Can$20.00y – cn Micromedia [380]

THE ATLANTIC CABLES: A REVIEW OF RECENT TELEGRAPHIC LEGISLATION IN CANADA / Chesson, Frederick William – London: E. Wilson, 1875. 00601. (Pre-1900 Canadiana) – 9 – cn C.I.H.M. [340]

ATLANTIC COMMUNITY QUARTERLY – (1970- . 5,6. 1976- . 9) – 1- 1963- – 1 – us UMI [073]

THE ATLANTIC EXPRESS AND THE FUTURE BRITISH PORT OF ARRIVAL – 1893? 02203. (Pre-1900 Canadiana) – 9 – cn C.I.H.M. [380]

ATLANTIC GUARDIAN – v8-13. Jan. 1951-Dec. 1956 – 1 – cn Precision [073]

ATLANTIC INSIGHT – Halifax. v1-11. 1979-89 – 9 – Can$28.00y – cn Micromedia [073]

THE ATLANTIC ISLANDS AS RESORTS OF HEALTH AND PLEASURE / Benjamin, Samuel Greene Wheeler – New York: Harper, 1878. 06708. (Pre-1900 Canadiana) – 9 – cn C.I.H.M. [910]

ATLANTIC JOURNAL, AND FRIEND OF KNOWLEDGE / Rafinesque-Schmaltz, Constantine S – NRS. 1-8. Philadelphia. 1832-33. B-8100 1 – 9 – ne IDC [970]
ATLANTIC MONTHLY – (1967- 5,6. 1970- 9) – 1857- – 1 – us UMI [073]
ATLANTIC MONTHLY – Boston. v1-98. 1857-1906 – 50r – 1 – us Ross [073]
ATLANTIC MONTHLY – v1-202. 1857-1958 – 1 – us Princeton Micro [073]
ATLANTIC NEWS-TELEGRAPH – Iowa. 1912-1938; 1941-1943; 1965- – 1 – us UMI [071]
ATLANTIC PROVINCES ECONOMIC COUNCIL NEWSLETTER – (Cont by: Atlantic Review 1994) – Halifax. v1-38. 1957-94 – 9 – Can$20.00y – cn Micromedia [330]
ATLANTIC PROVINCES ECONOMIC COUNCIL NEWSLETTER *see* ATLANTIC REVIEW
ATLANTIC REPORT – Halifax. v1-30. 1966-95 – 9 – Can$20.00y – cn Micromedia [073]
ATLANTIC REPORTER – (Add vols planned) – 1st series: v1-106. 1885-1919 – 1346mf – 9 – $2,019.00 – LLMC 79-404C – us L.L.M.C. [340]
ATLANTIC REVIEW – (Cont: Atlantic Provinces Economic Council Newsletter at v1 no 1 March/April 1994) – v1- 1994- – 9 – Can$20.00y – cn Micromedia [971]
ATLANTIC REVIEW *see* ATLANTIC PROVINCES ECONOMIC COUNCIL NEWSLETTER
ATLANTIDE = ATLANTIDA – Port-au-Prince: Impr Nemours Telhomme. v1 n1-7. oct 1932-apr 1933 – 5 sheets – us Res Libr [072]
L'ATLANTIDE OU LE GEANT DE LA MONTAGNE BLEUE: POEME EN QUATRE CHANTS / Baour-Lormian, Pierre Marie Francois Louis – Paris: Brunot Labbe, s.d. 304p.4 fiches. (Literature Collection) – 9 – 10.00 – fr Bibl Nationale [810]
DIE ATLANTIK VOKHENBLATT – Atlantic City. N.J. 1922-23 – 1 – us A.J.P.C. [071]
L'ATLANTIQUE, PARIS ET QUEBEC : REVUE POUR LES DELEGUES AUX FETES DU 400E ANNIVERSAIRE DE LA DECOUVERTE DE CANADA – Quebec, Paris. 19 aut 1934-26 aut 1934 – 1r – 1 – Can$35.00 – cn Can Microfilming [072]
ATLANTIS – (In Greek) – New York, 2 Mar 1895-Dec 1932 (imperfect) – 128r – 1 – uk British Libr Newspaper [071]
ATLANTIS : WOMEN'S STUDIES JOURNAL – Halifax. v1- 1975- – 9 – Can$20.00y – cn Micromedia [073]
THE ATLANTIS: A REGISTER OF LITERATURE AND SCIENCE – v. 1-5. 1858-70 – 3 – us Readex [500]
THE ATLANTIS NEWS – 1968-72.340p – 9 – 1.00f – at Libertarian Micro [335]
DER ATLANTISCHE SKLAVENHANDEL VON DAHOMEY (1740-1797) : EINE UNTERSUCHUNG ZUR WIRTSCHAFTS- UND SOZIALGESCHICHTE AFRIKAS UND WIRTSCHAFTSANTHROPOLOGIE / Peukert, Werner – Frankfurt, 1975 – 1mf – 9 – DM48.00 – 3-89349-380-8 – gw Hänsel [380]
ATLAS – Agrupacion trabajadores Latinoamericanos Sindicalistas. Buenos Aires. v15-28, 30-45. 1954-55 – 1 – us U.W. Library [330]
ATLAS : CONSISTING OF 43 MAPS OF THE COUNTIES OF LOWER CANADA AND 42 MAPS OF UPPER CANADA / Devine, Thomas – Montreal. SEM35P90 – 1r – 1 – Can$15.00 – cn Bibl Nat [910]
ATLAS / Newson. Spencer County.Kentucky – 1882. 36p – 1 – 5.00 – us Baptist [910]
ATLAS – (v.17-21.1969-72. 5,6) – v.1-21. 1961-72 – 1 – us UMI [073]
ATLAS *see* AGRICULTURAL AND FOREST METEOROLOGY
THE ATLAS – (Englishman: 1862-65) – London, UK. 21 May 1826-22 Jan 1869 – 40r – 1 – uk British Libr Newspaper [072]
THE ATLAS – Sydney, Australia. -w. 1844-46. 2 reels – 1 – uk British Libr Newspaper [072]
ATLAS BOTANIQUE,... / Lefebure, LF H – [Paris, 1817] – 3mf – ne IDC [580]
ATLAS DA CAMARA DA CIDADE DE SAO PAULO / Sao Paulo. Divisao do Arquivo Historico do Departamento de Cultura – [v1-72. 1562/96-1886] – 1 – us Res Libr [972]
ATLAS DE SANSON / Sanson, Guillaume – (s.1.) (s.n.) (s.d.). SEM35P173 – 1r – 1 – Can$15.00 – cn Bibl Nat [910]
ATLAS DER BAUMARTEN VON JAVA... / Koorders, SH & Valenton, T – Leiden, 1913-1918. 4v – 20mf – 9 – ne IDC [580]
ATLAS DER DIATOMACEEN-KUNDE / ed by Schmidt, A W F – Leipzig, 1874-1927.- v1-10 – 70mf – 9 – 5384/2 – ne IDC [580]
ATLAS DER EVANGELISCHEN MISSIONS-GESELLSCHAFT ZU BASEL / Josenhans, Joseph – 2. Aufl. 1859 – 1 – us A.T.L.A. [240]
ATLAS DER KRANKHEITEN UND BESCHAEDIGUNGEN / Kirchner, O & Bolthauser, H – S. 1-6. Stuttgart. 1896-1902. B-7458 1 – 9 – ne IDC [616]
ATLAS DER OFFICINELLEN PFLANZEN... / Schmidt, C F & Berg, O C – Leipzig. v4. 1891-1902 – 17mf – ne IDC [580]
ATLAS DER PFLANZENGEOGRAPHIE... / Rudolph, L – Berlin, 1852 – 2mf – ne IDC [580]
ATLAS DES ALGUES MARINES... / Hariot, P A – Paris, 1892 – 2mf – ne IDC [580]
ATLAS DES BOIS DE L'INDOCHINE / Lecomte, [P] H – Paris, [1919] – 3mf – ne IDC [580]
ATLAS DES PLANTES DE FRANCE... / Masclef, A – Paris. 3v. [1890-]1893 – 14mf – ne IDC [580]
ATLAS DEUTSCHER MEERESALGEN / Reinke, J – Berlin, 1889-1892 – 9mf – ne IDC [574]
ATLAS ELECTORAL DE LA GIRONDE / Restier-Melleray, C – F140.00 – fr Ethnologie [320]
ATLAS GAMBAR-GAMBAR TERMASUK BILANGAN BUKU FUNGSI MAKANAN / Sastroamidjojo, Achmad Seno – SE 3936 1. 1953 – 9 – ne IDC [950]
ATLAS GEOGRAPHIQUE / L'Isle, Guillaume de – Paris, 169?-1715? – 1r – 1 – Can$16.00 – SEM35P123 – cn Bibl Nat [910]
ATLAS ICHTHYOLOGIQUE DES INDES ORIENTALES NEERLANDAISES / ed by Blecker, P – Amsterdam. v9. 1862-1878 – 104mf – ne IDC [590]
ATLAS INDONESIA / Indonesia – SE-4649 1. 1953 – 9 – ne IDC [910]
ATLAS LINGUISTIQUE DE COTE D'IVOIRE / Dumestre, G – (Africa series). 1971 – 9 – fr Hachette [960]
ATLAS LINGUISTIQUE DE LA FRANCE / ed by Gillieron, J & Edmont, E – Paris, 1902-1920. Fasc. 1-35 – 346mf – 9 – 22/2 – ne IDC [440]
Atlas, M S *see* NATSIONALIZATSIIA BANKOV V SSSR
ATLAS OF LOGAN COUNTY AND THE STATE OF ILLINOIS – Chicago: 1873. Illinois Reel 10. (The Cox Library Collection) – 5 – us Americana [978]
ATLAS OF THE CITY AND ISLAND OF MONTREAL / Hopkins, Henry W – Montreal: Provincial Surveying and Pub Co, 1879. SEM35P50 – 1r – 1 – Can$15.00 – cn Bibl Nat [910]
ATLAS OF THE CITY OF MONTREAL – rev ed. Montreal. 2v. 1890 – 1r – 1 – Can$15.00 – SEM35P49 – cn Bibl Nat [910]
ATLAS OF THE CITY OF MONTREAL AND VICINITY – Montreal. 4v. 1912-14 – 1r – 1 – Can$23.00 – SEM35P48 – cn Bibl Nat [910]
ATLAS OF THE FISHERIES OF THE WESTERN CENTRAL MEDITERRANEAN – 1985 – 32p – it F.A.O. [630]
ATLAS OF THE ISLAND AND CITY OF MONTREAL AND ILE BIZARD / Pinsoneault, A R – The Atlas Publishing Co, ca 1907. SEM35P122 – 1r – 1 – Can$15.00 – cn Bibl Nat [910]
ATLAS OF THE LIVING RESOURCES OF THE SEAS – 1975 – 170p – it F.A.O. [630]
ATLAS OF THE TOWN OF SAINT JOHNS AND SOREL / Hopkins, Henry W – Montreal, Canada. 1v. 1880 – 1r – 1 – Can$35.00 – cn Can Microfilming [910]
ATLAS OF THE TOWN OF SOREL AND COUNTY OF RICHELIEU, PROVINCE OF QUEBEC / Hopkins, Henry W – Quebec: Provincial Surveying and Pub, 1880. SEM35P197 – 1r – 1 – Can$15.00 – cn Bibl Nat [910]
ATLAS OF ZOOGEOGRAPHY / Bartholomew, John George et al – Edinburgh, 1911 – 17mf – ne IDC [590]
ATLAS POUR SERVIR AU VOYAGE DU SENEGAL / Durand, Jean-Baptiste-Leonard – Paris, Dentu. 1807 – 9 – 5.00 – fr Orientalistes [910]
ATLAS SEDJARAH / Yamin, Muhammad – SE 823 1. 1956 – 9 – ne IDC [910]
ATLAS TO ACCOMPANY THE OFFICIAL RECORDS OF THE UNION AND CONFEDERATE ARMIES – 1r – 1 – $50.00 – B40145 – us Library Micro [976]
ATLAS WORLD PRESS REVIEW – (See also: Atlas) – v21- 1974- 1,5,6; 1975- 9 – us UMI [072]
Atlaw, Amekalech *see* ILCA IN PRINT
O ATLHETA : JORNAL IMPARCIAL – Cuiaba, 16 May-21 Jul 1884 – 1,5,6 – bl Biblioteca [072]
Atmadi, Endang T *see* INDONESIA, GENERAL INFORMATION AND TOURISM
ATMODA = AWAKENING – 1988 + 89 – 1 reel – 1 – Sfr120.00 – sz Infoprint [947]
ATMODA = AWAKENING – 1990 + 91 – 1 reel – 1 – Sfr120.00 – sz Infoprint [947]
ATMODA = AWAKENING – (Only backfile available) – [Latvia], oct 1988-jun 1992 – 4r – 1 – $340.00 – us Ross [072]
ATMODA = AWAKENING – (Standing order available from De 1994 +. 2r per year. Sfr225.00y) – De 1992 a 1993 – 2r – 1 – Sfr240.00 – sz Infoprint [947]
ATMODA – Riga, USSR. 1989-1990; Apr 25 1991-Dec 1992 – 3r – 1 – us L of C Photodup [072]
Atmore, C *see*
– A CHRONOLOGICAL LIST OF THE ITINERANT PREACHERS IN THE CONNEXION OF THE LATE REV. JOHN WESLEY, DECEASED, ARRANGED IN ALPHABETICAL ORDER
– THE METHODIST MEMORIAL
THE ATMOSPHERE-OCEAN SYSTEM / ed by Katsaros, Kristina – 9,5,1 – us Gordon [550]
ATMOSPHERIC ENVIRONMENT – 9 – £1,297.00y – uk Elsevier Sci [550]
ATMOSPHERIC ENVIRONMENT – v1- 1967- – 5,6,9 – us UMI [574]
ATMOSPHERIC ENVIRONMENT *see* AIR AND WATER POLLUTION
ATNATANAS: NATIVES OF COPPER RIVER, ALASKA / Allen, H T – N-100. 1886 – 9 – ne IDC [305]
THE ATOM – Bombay: R K Karanjia, feb 1 1950-sep 20 1950 – 1r – 1 – us Res Libr [072]
THE ATOM – Bombay: R K Karanjia, feb 1-sep 21 1950; jan 10 1951-aug 27 1952 – 3r – 1 – us Res Libr [950]
THE ATOM – Bombay: R K Karanjia, jan 10 1951-aug 27 1952 – 2r – 1 – us Res Libr [072]
ATOM UND STROM – (1974- . 5,6. 1975- . 9) – 1955- – 1 – us UMI [621]
ATOMIC BOMB SCIENTISTS : MEMOIRS, 1939-1945 / ed by Ermenc, Joseph J – (Memoirs of nine eminent scientists directly involved in the development of nuclear energy during the war years 1939-45) – 6mf – 9 – $120.00 – us UPA [530]
ATOMIC ENERGY – v1-77. 1956-94 – 1,5 – $65.00v – us UMI [530]
ATOMIC ENERGY ACT OF 1954 : LEGISLATIVE HISTORY / U.S. Atomic Energy Commission – Washington: GPO. 3v. 1955 – 45mf – 9 – $67.00 – LLMC 81-104 – us L.L.M.C. [340]
ATOMIC ENERGY COMMISSION ANNUAL REPORTS / U.S. Nuclear Regulatory Commission – (Lacking: 1956-58) – 1956-74 (all publ) – 82mf – 9 – $123.00 – LLMC 80-500 – us L.L.M.C. [324]
ATOMIC ENERGY COMMISSION ANNUAL REPORTS *see* ATOMIC ENERGY COMMISSION REPORTS
ATOMIC ENERGY COMMISSION REPORTS / U.S. Nuclear Regulatory Commission – (Cont by: Atomic Energy Commission Annual Reports) – v1-8. 1956-75 (all publ) – 91mf – 9 – $136.00 – LLMC 80-499 – us L.L.M.C. [340]
ATOMIC ENERGY COMMISSION REPORTS *see* ATOMIC ENERGY COMMISSION ANNUAL REPORTS
ATOMIC ENERGY REVIEW – 1957-60 – 1 – uk Microform Academic [621]
Atomic Industrial Forum *see* COMMITTEE REPORTS, SURVEYS AND OTHER MISCELLANEOUS PUBLICATIONS
ATOMISM: DR. TYNDALL'S ATOMIC THEORY OF THE UNIVERSE / Watts, Robert – Belfast: William Mullan, 1874 – 1mf – 9 – us A.T.L.A. [530]
ATOMOS QUE NUEVAMENTE SE HAN DESCUBIERTO CON LAS LUCES DE APOLO, EN LA CONTROVERSIA... / Tenorio de Leon, A – SL, SA – 2mf – 9 – sp Cultura [610]
THE ATONEMENT / Bowne, Borden Parker – Cincinnati: Curts & Jennings, 1900. 1 fiche – 9 – us A.T.L.A. [240]
THE ATONEMENT / Hodge, Archibald Alexander – (Includes bibliographical references and index) – Philadelphia:Presbyterian Board of Publication, c1867 – 1mf – 9 – 0-8370-4511-8 – 1985-2511 – us A.T.L.A. [240]
THE ATONEMENT / Stalker, James – (Includes bibliographical references) – NY: A C Armstrong, 1909 – 1mf – 9 – 0-8370-5524-5 – 1985-3524 – us A.T.L.A. [240]
THE ATONEMENT : VIEWED AS ASSUMED DIVINE RESPONSIBILITY, TRACED AS THE FACT ATTESTED IN DIVINE REVELATION... / Samson, George Whitefield – (Includes index) – Philadelphia: J B Lippincott, 1878 – 1mf – 9 – 0-8370-5397-8 – 1985-3397 – us A.T.L.A. [240]
ATONEMENT AND LAW, OR, REDEMPTION IN HARMONY WITH LAW AS REVEALED IN NATURE / Armour, John M – Philadelphia: Chr. Statesman Pub., 1886.1 fiche – 9 – us A.T.L.A. [240]
THE ATONEMENT IN MODERN RELIGIOUS THOUGHT – 1902 – 9 – us A.T.L.A. [240]
THE ATONEMENT OF CHRIST : SIX LECTURES DELIVERED IN HEREFORD CATHEDRAL DURING HOLY WEEK, 1871 / Barry, Alfred – London, NY: Macmillan, 1871 – 1mf – 9 – 0-8370-5605-5 – 1985-3605 – us A.T.L.A. [220]
ATORIE-SEIKATSUBIJUTSU 1924-1941 – 50r – 1 – Y750,000 – ja Yushodo [700]
ATORNEY GENERAL OPINIONS : FROM THE TERRITORY TO DATE / Hawaii – (Vols after 1994 planned) – 1904-94 – 180mf – 9 – $270.00 – LLMC 77-104 – us L.L.M.C. [340]
ATP MAINTENANCE LIBRARY FOR AVIONICS – (Includes navigation, communication, radar and electronic equipment for Bendix, King, Collins, Foster Airdata, Global Wulfsberg, Narco, Avionic Instruments, 3-M Stormscope, Flite-Tronics and Bonzer. 32 sublibraries available separately. Biweekly Revision Service.) – 9 – us Aircraft Tech [600]
ATP MAINTENANCE LIBRARY FOR HELICOPTERS – (Service and maintenance including Aerospatiale, Robinson, Sikorsky Agusta, Bell, MBB, Enstrom, Hiller, McDonnell Douglas Eurocopter France, Allison Gas Turbine, Textron Lycoming, Pratt & Whitney of Canada, Turbomeca. Service manuals, parts catalogs & service information. With 12-months revision service. 62 sub-libraries available. Biweekly Revision Service separately) – 9 – us Aircraft Tech [629]
ATP MAINTENANCE LIBRARY FOR JET AIRCRAFT OVER 12,500 LBS – (Includes Avions Marcel Dassault Falcon Jet, Beechjet, British Aerospace, Cessna Citation, Learjet, Gulfstream, Raytheon Hawker, Lockheed Jetstar, Mitsubishi, Sabreliner, Garrett, General Electric, Rolls Royce, Pratt & Whitney of Canada and Pratt & Whitney with thrust reversers and APUs. 54 sublibraries available. Biweekly Revision Service.) – 9 – us Aircraft Tech [600]
ATP MAINTENANCE LIBRARY FOR PROPELLER AIRCRAFT – (Non-jet, fixed wing under 12,500 lbs. Airframes, engines and propellers. Contains maintenance manuals, wiring diagrams, overhaul manuals, parts catalogs, parts price lists, structural repair manuals, service information and airworthiness directives. 110 sub-libraries available separately. Biweekly Revision Service.) – 9 – us Aircraft Tech [629]
ATQ. THE AMERICAN TRANSCENDENTAL QUARTERLY – 1978- – 1,5,6,9 – us UMI [100]
ATR (AUSTRALIAN TELECOMMUNICATION RESEARCH) – Melbourne. v11. 1977 1*,5,9 – 1,5,9 – $83.70y – D10490 – us UMI [621]
ATRAS HAY DIOS / Palomino, Martin Alfonso – Caceres, 1973 – 1 – sp Bibl Santa Ana [946]
ATRAS LOS INVASORES / Hernandez, Jesus – Barcelona, 1938? Fiche W941. (Blodgett Collection of Spanish Civil War Pamphlets) – 9 – us H.U. College Libr [946]
ATRAVES DO SERTAO DO BRASIL / Roosevelt, Theodore – Sao Paulo, 1944 – 8mf – 8 – ne Slangenburg [972]

ATROCITIES DURING WORLD WAR 1 PAMPHLET COLLECTION – 1914-1920 – 2r – 1 – CSUXANL3507-B – us Hoover Inst Photo [360]

ATROCITIES FROM WORLD WAR 2 PAMPHLET COLLECTION – 1940-1956 – 1 – CSUXANQ3136-B – us Hoover Inst Photo [360]

Atsarkin, Aleksandr Nikolaevich *see* IUNOSHESKOE DVIZHENIE V MOSKVE 1917 GOD

Atsenko, I I *see* LESA SEVERA I ELEKTRIFIKATSIIA LESNOGO KHOZIA ISTVA

Atsuk, N A *see* POMOSHCH AVIATSII DEISTVIIAM PARTIZANOV

Atsumaro, Konoe, Prince *see* DIARY

ATTACHMENTS TO RECREATION SETTINGS : THE CASE OF RAIL-TRAIL USERS / Moore, R L – 1991 – 2mf – 9 – $8.00 – us Microform Publ [790]

ATTAH – Madison, WI. 1971-77 – 1 – us A.J.P.C. [071]

ATTAKADDOUM – Alger. mai 1923-juil 1931 – 1 – fr A.C.R.P.P. [073]

Attaliotae, Michaelis *see* HISTORIA (CSHB 48)

L'ATTAQUE : HUMORISTIQUE ET POLITIQUE (CARICATURES) – Montreal, Canada. 18 nov 1938-19 avr 1940 – 1r – 1 – Can$40.00 – cn Can Microfilming [072]

Atta-ur-Rahman *see* NATURAL PRODUCT LETTERS

L'ATTAWADOD D'ABOU NADDARA – Paris. 1888-89, avr 1894-nov 1898 – 1 – fr A.C.R.P.P. [073]

AN ATTEMPT TO DISENTANGLE SPACE- AND MOMENTUM COORDINATES / Schmidt, Michael – 1991 – 96p – DM98.00 – 3-89349-444-8 – gw Hänsel [530]

AN ATTEMPT TO REMOVE ERROR, DESIGNED AS A LETTER TO A FRIEND ON THE IMPORTANT SUBJECT OF THE SABBATH / Stillman, William – 1 – 5.00 – us Baptist [240]

AN ATTEMPT TO RENDER THE PRONUNCIATION OF THE ENGLISH LANGUAGE MORE EASY TO FOREIGNERS / Smith, William – 1795. 488p. (English Linguistics Series 1500-1800) – 9 – us UMI [420]

Attenberger, Toni *see* DER ENDLOSE WALD

ATTENTION IN YOUNG SOCCER PLAYERS : THE DEVELOPMENT OF AN ATTENTIONAL FOCUS TRAINING PROGRAM / Papanikolaou, Zissis & Oglesby, Carole – 1992 – 2mf – 9 – $8.00 – us Microform Publ [150]

Atteridge, Andrew Hilliard *see* FAMOUS MODERN BATTLES

L'ATTESA – no. 1-17. Agen. 21 nov 1926-16 mars 1927. mq no. 16 – 1 – fr A.C.R.P.P. [073]

ATTESTATION DE MESSIEURS LES COMMISSAIRES ENVOYEZ PAR SA MAJESTE POUR PRENDRE CONNAISSANCE – S. 1. 1643 – 9 – fr Hachette [360]

ATTESTATIONS DE SIX CURES, AU SUJET DE LA CONDUITE EN 1837-38, DU COLONEL GUGY – 187?. 02204. (Pre-1900 Canadiana) – 9 – cn C.I.H.M. [971]

ATTESTED COPIES OF THREE SEVERAL DEPOSITIONS,... / Great Britain. -Court of Chancery – London, 1794 – 1mf – 9 – MP-586/1 – ne IDC [240]

Atthill, Lombe *see* MANUEL DES MALADIES DES FEMMES: LECONS CLINIQUES

ATTI / Accademia nazionale Luigi Cherubini di Musica. Lettere e Arti figurative – 1 30, 1863-92; 39-50, 1911-13; 61, 1941 – 1 – $23.00 – us L of C Photodup [780]

ATTI – Venezia. v50. 1891/92 – us Res Libr [072]

GLI ATTI DEI SS. MONTANO : LUCIO E COMPAGNI / Cavalieri, Pio Franchi de – Roma, 1898 – Dfl13.00 – ne Slangenburg [240]

ATTI DEL TERZO CONGRESSO DI STUDI COLONIALI : FIRENZE-ROMA, 12-17 APRILE 1937-15 – Firenze 1937 – us Res Libr [945]

ATTI DELLA PONTIFICIA ACCADEMIA ROMANA DI ARCHEOLOGIA / Accademia Romana di Archeologia. Rome – (Dissertazioni della Pontificia...Roma, S.1, 1835-64.-v5-15; S.2, 1881-1921.-v1-15) – 317mf – 9 – O-1205/1 – ne IDC [930]

ATTI DELLA SOCIETA ITALIANA DI SCIENZE NATURALI – Milano: La Societa 1860-1895. v11. 1868. – 1r – us Res Libr [500]

ATTI DELLA SOCIETA TOSCANA DI SCIENZE NATURALI : MEMORIE – Pisa, 1875-1942. v1-50 – 311mf – 9 – Z-246c/2 – ne IDC [500]

ATTI E MEMORIE INEDITE E NOTIZIE ANEDDOTE DEI PROGRESSI DELLE SCIENZE IN TOSCANA...COMINCIANDO DA GALILEO GALILEI, FINO A FRANCESCO REDI ED A VINCENZO VIVIANI INCLUSIVE / Accademia del Cimento. Florence – Firenze, 1780 – 3 – us Readex [500]

ATTI PARLAMENTARI / Italy. Parlamento. Legislatura – 1870-1943 – 1 – 3,006.00 – us L of C Photodup [945]

THE ATTIC THEATRE / Haigh, Arthur Elam – Oxford, 1889. 13 plus 341p. Illus. Plates. With: Occult Japan by P. Lowell. 1 reel. 1305 – apply; – us U.W. Library [000]

ATTICA HUB – Attica, Ohio. 1975- – 5r – 1 – $32.50r – us Archival [071]

Attica. Ohio. First Baptist Church of Attica *see* CHURCH RECORDS

ATTILA : HISTORISCHER ROMAN AUS DER VOELKERWANDERUNG / Dahn, Felix – Philadelphia: Morwitz, [18–?] – 1 – us U.W. Library [830]

ATTILIO REGOLO [DRAMMA PER MUSICA SI] SIG. GIO. ADOLFO HASSE [LA POESIA E DEL SIG. ABBATE PIETRO METASTASIO / Hasse, J A – (Manuscript) – 175-? – 1 – us Sibley [780]

THE ATTIS OF CAIUS VALERIUS CATALLUS: TRANSLATED INTO ENGLISH VERSE.. / Allen, Grant – London: D. Nutt, 1892. 03848. (Pre-1900 Canadiana) – 9 – cn C.I.H.M. [450]

L'ATTITUDE INTERNATIONALE – Madrid, 1936? Fiche W 736. (Blodgett Collection of Spanish Civil War Pamphlets) – 9 – us H.U. College Libr [946]

ATTITUDE OF AMERICAN COURTS IN LABOR CASES; A STUDY IN SOCIAL LEGISLATION / Groat, George Gorham – New York, Longmans, Green, 1911. 400 p. LL-1054 – 1 – us L of C Photodup [340]

THE ATTITUDE OF PHYSICAL EDUCATION TEACHERS IN IRELAND TOWARD THE ASSESSMENT IN SECOND LEVEL TEACHING PROGRAM / Murphy, G – 1990 – 2mf – 9 – $8.00 – us Microform Publ [150]

L'ATTITUDE RELIGIEUSE DES LYCEENS DANS UNE VILLE DU WEST-CAMEROON, 1967-72. LE COMPARTIMENTAGE DES LANGUES ET LA FORMATION D'UNE LANGUE CULTUELLE / Stumpf, R K P – 9 – F160.00 – fr Ethnologie [306]

ATTITUDES ASSOCIATED WITH COMPETITIVE AGE-GROUP SWIMMING / Lauber, Russell L – 1980 – 1mf – 9 – $4.00 – us Microform Publ [790]

ATTITUDES OF CHILDREN IN INTEGRATED AND SEGREGATED PHYSICAL EDUCATION PROGRAMS TOWARD PEERS WITH DISABLING CONDITIONS / Tripp, April – 1989 – 136p 2mf – 9 – $8.00 – us Microform Publ [360]

ATTITUDES OF KOREAN NATIONAL ATHLETES AND COACHES TOWARD ATHLETICS PARTICIPATION / Cho, Kwang M et al – 1990 – 2mf – 9 – $8.00 – us Microform Publ [150]

ATTITUDES OF OLYMPIC SPORT STUDENT-ATHLETES AND COACHES TOWARD NCAA RESTRICTIONS ON PRACTICE TIME-IN SEASON / Whitfield, Davis – University of North Carolina at Chapel Hill, 1995 – 2mf – 9 – $8.00 – PSY1873 – us Microform Publ [370]

ATTITUDES OF THERAPEUTIC RECREATION PROFESSIONALS TOWARD PERSONS WITH AIDS AND THE RELATIONSHIP OF THEIR ATTITUDE TO THEIR KNOWLEDGE OF AIDS / Glenn, Cherie A & Datillo, John P – 1992 – 2mf – 9 – $8.00 – us Microform Publ [150]

ATTITUDES, PERCEPTIONS AND COPING SKILLS OF LONG-TERM BREAST CANCER SURVIVORS / Baskerville, LF – 1990 – 3mf – 9 – $12.00 – us Microform Publ [150]

THE ATTITUDES TOWARD MORMONISM IN ILLINOIS AS RECORDED BY THE PRESS / Snider, Cecil A – 1831-1849. Warsaw, Illinois. Collected 1933-1934 – 1 – us NY Public [240]

THE ATTITUDES TOWARD MORMONISM IN ILLINOIS AS RECORDED BY THE PRESS FOR THE PERIOD OF 1831 THROUGH 1849 / Snider, Cecil A – Warsaw, IL. 1933-34 – 2r – 1 – us Ross [070]

ATTITUDES TOWARD PHYSICAL ACTIVITY OF OBESE AND NON-OBESE CHILDREN AND THEIR PARENTS / Steininger, Wanda K – 1982 – 2mf – 9 – $8.00 – us Microform Publ [790]

ATTITUDES TOWARDS PHYSICAL ACTIVITY AMONG AMERICAN AND GERMAN SENIOR CITIZENS / Eckl, C – 1990 – 2mf – 9 – $8.00 – us Microform Publ [150]

ATTLEBORO 1692-1849 – (Mf 1T-4T: Vitals 1692-1796. Mf 4T: Marriages 1741-56; Marriages 1741-56. Mf 5T-9T: Intentions 1797-1849. Mf 9T-10T: Vitals 1732-1837. Mf 11T: Deaths 1753-1835; Marriages 1778-1805. Mf 11T-14T: Vitals 1709-1858. Mf 14T-16T: Marriages 1695-1845. Mf 16T-19T: Intentions 1724-97. Mf 19T-20T: Births 1843-49. Mf 21T: Marriages 1695-1799; Marriages 1843-49. Mf 22T: Deaths 1843-49) – (mf ed 1994) – 22mf – 9 – 0-87623-205-5 – us Holbrook [920]

ATTLEBORO 1694-1890 – (Mf 1-13: Births, Marriages, Deaths 1694-1844. Mf 14-17: Vital Statistics 1715-1803. Mf 18-23: Town Meeting Records 1723-34. Mf 24-27: Bounds of Lands 1735-95. Mf 28-34: Precinct Records 1745-70. Mf 35-42: Town Meeting Records 1757-78. Mf 43-49: Town Records 1782-91. Mf 50-54: Births, Marriages, Deaths 1844-70. Mf 55: Index to B,M,D 1844-70. Mf 56-64: Births 1856-90. Mf 65-72: Index to Births 1844-1910. Mf 73-80: Marriages 1856-90. Mf 81-87: Index to Marriages 1844-1910. Mf 88-93: Deaths 1856-90. Mf 94-99: Index to Deaths 1844-1904) – (mf ed 1986) – 99mf – 9 – 0-87623-008-7 – us Holbrook [920]

Attlmayr, F von *see*
– DIE ELEMENTE DES INTERNATIONALEN SEERECHTES UND SAMMLUNG VON VERTRAEGEN
– DAS INTERNATIONALE SEERECHT

ATTORNEY FEE PETITIONS : SUGGESTIONS FOR ADMINISTRATION AND MANAGEMENT / Willging, Thomas E & Weeks, Nancy – 2mf – 9 – $3.00 – LLMC 95-322 – us L.L.M.C. [340]

ATTORNEY GENERAL. OFFICIAL OPINIONS OF... U.S. DEPARTMENT OF JUSTICE – (6 v1-41 digest 1-3 $455.00. 9 v42 + digest 4 $21.00. Annual reports 1980-1994 $39.00) – v1-42. Digest 1-4 + Annual Reports 1980-1993 – 6,9 – $515.50 set – us Hein [340]

THE ATTORNEY GENERAL'S COMMITTEE ON ADMINISTRATIVE PROCEDURE : MONOGRAPHS / U.S. Department of Justice – 28pts. 1940-41 (all publ) – 56mf – 9 – $84.00 – LLMC 81-214 – us L.L.M.C. [340]

THE ATTORNEY GENERAL'S SURVEY ON RELEASE PROCEDURES / U.S. Department of Justice – 5v. 1939-40 (all publ) – 36mf – 9 – $54.00 – LLMC 81-213 – us L.L.M.C. [340]

ATTORNEY ROLLS, 1790-1951 / U.S. Supreme Court – 4rolls. Printed guide – 1 – M217 – us Nat'l Archives [340]

ATTORNEY-CLIENT FEE ARRANGEMENT : REGULATION AND REVIEW / Aronson, Robert H – Washington: n.p., 1980? – 2mf – 9 – $3.00 – LLMC 95-305 – us L.L.M.C. [340]

ATTORNEYS' ETHICS COLLECTION : PUBLICATIONS OF THE OFFICE OF DISCIPLINARY COUNSEL AND THE DISCIPLINARY BOARD OF THE HAWAII SUPREME COURT; COMPRISING THE FORMAL AND INFORMAL OPINIONS OF THE BOARD / Hawaii – (With index. Also summaries for 1857-1983 and an index. Includes text of all decisions dealing with attorney ethics between 1857- 1983) – 1974-83 – 24mf – 9 – $36.00 – LLMC 81-110 – us L.L.M.C. [340]

ATTORNEYS' FEES IN CLASS ACTIONS : A REPORT TO THE FEDERAL JUDICIAL CENTER / Miller, Arthur R – Washington: FJC, July 1980 – 5mf – 9 – $7.50 – LLMC 95-824 – us L.L.M.C. [340]

The Attorneys' Mutual Association *see* LIST OF SELECTED DOMESTIC AND FOREIGN ATTORNEYS, AND A TELEGRAPHIC CODE.

ATTORNEY'S RECORD / Leavenworth County. Kansas. District Court – 1855-1976 – 1 – us KS Hist [324]

ATTORNEYS' VIEWS OF LOCAL RULES LIMITING INTERROGATORIES / Shapard, John & Seron, Carroll – Washington: FJC, 1986 – 1mf – 9 – $1.50 – LLMC 95-329 – us L.L.M.C. [340]

ATTRACTING FISH WITH LIGHT – it F.A.O. [636]

THE ATTRACTIVE CHRIST : AND OTHER SERMONS / MacArthur, Robert Stuart – Philadelphia: American Baptist Publ Society, 1898 – 1mf – 9 – 0-8370-7484-3 – 1986-1484 – us A.T.L.A. [240]

ATTRAVERSO IL BENADIR / Carletti, Tomaso – Viterbo: Agnesotti, 1910 – 1 – us Res Libr [910]

DIE ATTRIBUTE DER HEILIGEN / Pfleiderer, R – O-1255 1. 1920 – 9 – ne IDC [240]

THE ATTRIBUTES OF CHRIST : OR, CHRIST THE WONDERFUL, THE COUNSELLOR, GOD THE MIGHTY, THE FATHER OF THE WORLD TO COME, THE PRINCE OF PEACE / Gasparini, Joseph – New York: P O'Shea, 1870 – 1mf – 9 – 0-8370-7461-4 – 1986-1461 – us A.T.L.A. [240]

THE ATTTORNEY GENERAL'S INVESTIGATION OF GOVERNMENT PATENT PRACTICES AND POLICIES / U.S. Department of Justice – Washington, DC: GPO. v1-3. 1947 (all publ) – 12mf – 9 – $18.00 – LLMC 81-215 – us L.L.M.C. [340]

Attwood, P H *see* A FEW PRACTICAL HINTS TO THE OFFICERS, N.C. OFFICERS AND MEN OF THE 26TH BATTALION: RELATIVE TO THEIR DUTIES IN CAMP

Attwood, T *see* THE ADOPTED CHILD

ATUAGAGDLIUTIT NALINGINARNIK TUSARUMINASASSUNIK UNIVKAT – Nungme. 1861-65. BH-463 2 – 8 – ne IDC [999]

ATUALIZACAO : REVISTA E DIVULGACAO TEOLOGICA PARA O CRISTAO DE HOJE – Belo Horizonte: Editora "O Lutador". v1 n1-v21 n240. dec 1969-nov/dec 1992 – 8r – us Res Libr [200]

Atwater, Albert William *see* DISCOURS DE L'HONORABLE A.W. ATWATER...ET DE FELIX CARBRAY...SUR LE BUDGET

ATWATER'S NEW TIMES – Atwater, CA. 1979- – 10+ r – 1 – $500.00 ($50.00y) – B02026 – us Library Micro [071]

Atwell, H W *see* WESTERN SHORE GAZETTEER AND COMMERCIAL DIRECTORY FOR CALIFORNIA

Atwell, William Erskine *see* PAULINE THEORY OF THE INSPIRATION OF HOLY SCRIPTURE

Atwood *see* MEMORIAL RECORD OF THE FATHERS OF WISCONSIN

Atwood, A *see* GLIMPSES IN PIONEER LIFE ON PUGET SOUND

Atwood, A C *see* GEOGRAPHICAL GUIDE TO FLORAS OF THE WORLD

Atwood, Harry F *see* BACK TO THE REPUBLIC

Atwood, Isaac Morgan *see* REVELATION

Atwood, Jerry L *see* SUPRAMOLECULAR CHEMISTRY

Atzberger, Leonhard *see*
– DIE LOGOSLEHRE DES HL. ATHANASIUS
– DIE UNSUENDLICHKEIT CHRISTI

AU BAS-NIGER / Viard, Edouard – Paris: L. Guerinet et Cie., 1885 – 9 – 10.00 – fr Orientalistes [960]

AU COEUR DE L'AFRIQUE / Villelune, E de – Paris: G Beauchesne, 1909 – 1 – us Res Libr [960]

AU COEUR DE L'AFRIQUE, 1868-1871 / Schweinfurth, Georg A – Voyages et decouvertes dans les regions inexplorees de l'Afrique centrale. Paris, Hachette. 1875 – 9 – 27.00 – fr Orientalistes [910]

AU COEUR DE L'AFRIQUE, 1868-1871. VOYAGES ET DECOUVERTES DANS LES REGIONS INEXPLOREES DE L'AFRIQUE CENTRALE / Schweinfurth, Georg A – (African Library). Paris. Hachette. 1875 – 9 – fr Hachette [960]

AU COIN DU FEU / Marjolaine – Montreal: Librairie d'Action canadienne-francaise, limitee, 1931. SEM105P1333 – 2mf – 9 – Can$4.50 – cn Bibl Nat [971]

AU COIN DU FEU = TRAEUMEREIEN AN FRANZOESISCHEN KAMINEN : CONTES / Volkmann, Richard von – (French translation from German) – Paris: Librairie Fischbacher, 1889 – 1 – us U.W. Library [430]

AU CONGO : COMMENT LES NOIRS TRAVAILLENT / Lemaire, Charles Francois Alexandre – Bruxelles: Impr Ch Bulens, 1895 – 1 – us Res Libr [960]

AU CONGO BELGE : AVEC DES NOTES ET DOCUMENTS RECENTS RELATIFS AU CONGO FRANCAIS / Mille, Pierre – Paris: Colin, 1899 – 1 – us Res Libr [960]

AU COURANT – Ottawa. v1-13. 1980-92 – 9 – Can$20.00y – cn Micromedia [073]

AU DAHOMEY, 1892 / Masse, Daniel – from La revue de Paris. Paris. 1899 – 1 – us Res Libr [960]

AU GRAND SOLEIL D'AFRIQUE / Gouzy, Rene – Geneve: A Jullien, 1923 – 1 – us Res Libr [960]

AU MAROC, 1911-1914 : SOUVENIRS D'UN AFRICAIN / Goureaud, P H – Paris: Plon, [1949] – 1 – us Res Libr [960]

AU NIGER : RECITS DE CAMPAGNES 1891-1892 / Peroz, Marie Etienne – Paris: C Levy, 1895 – 1 – us Res Libr [960]

AU NOM DE DIEU, PERE ET MERE DE TOUS LES HOMMES ET DE TOUTES LES FEMMES / Barrault, Emile – Lyon, impr. de Perret (fevrier 1833), 1 p. Colin, Auguste. Aux femmes juives et a toutes celles qui liront cette parole. Lyon, Durval, juillet 1833, 20 p. Justus, Pol. Liberte, FemmesLyon, Durval, 1833, 16 p. Terson, Jean. Un Saint-Simonien au peuple de Lyon a l'occasion des evenements d'avril 1834. Lyon, Durval, 1834, 15 p. Les Saint-Simoniens, 1825-1834. 6929 – 9 – fr Hachette [335]

AU NORD: BROCHURE ACCOMPAGNEE D'UNE CARTE GEOGRAPHIQUE DES CANTONS A COLONISER DANS LES VALLEES DE LA RIVIERE ROUGE ET DU LIEVRE ET DANS LARTIE DES VALLEES DE LA MATTAWIN ET DE LA GATINEAU – Saint Jerome, Quebec, 1883. 00037. (Pre-1900 Canadiana) – 9 – cn C.I.H.M. [910]

AU PAYS DE L'ESCLAVAGE : MOEURS ET COUTUMES DE L'AFRIQUE CENTRALE D'APRES DES NOTES RECUEILLIES / Behagle, Ferdinand de – Paris: J Maisonneuve, 1900 – 1 – us Res Libr [305]

AU PAYS DES CH'TITS GAS. / Guillaumin, Emile – Nevers. 1912. (La Condition Ouvriere. Part Two.) – 9 – 5.00 – fr Bibl Nationale [360]

AU PAYS DES FETICHES / Vigne d'Octon, Paul – Paris: A Lemerre, 1891 – 1 – us Res Libr [960]

AU PAYS DES PARDONS – 191? – 1 – us I.U. Libraries [390]

AU PAYS DU SOLEIL ET DE L'OR / Mevil, Andre – Paris: Didot, [1897?] – 1 – us Res Libr [960]

AU PAYS TSIMIHETY / Rusillon, Henri – Feuilles de route d'un missionaire. 1923 – 1 – us A.T.L.A. [240]

AU PEUPLE / Vidal, Edmond – Beziers, impr. Mariage et Vve Bory, 1833, 8 p. Les Saint-Simoniens, 1825-1834. 6917 – 9 – fr Hachette [335]

AU PORTIQUE DES LAURENTIDES; UNE PAROISSE MODERNE; LE CURE LABELLE / Buies, Arthur – Quebec: C Darveau, 1891. SEM105P74 – 1mf – 9 – Can$2.25 – cn Bibl Nat [830]

AU PORTIQUES DES LAURENTIDES: UNE PAROISSE MODERNE: LE CURE LABELLE / Buies, Arthur – Quebec: C. Darveau, 1891. 00338. (Pre-1900 Canadiana) – 9 – cn C.I.H.M. [971]

AU ROI / Fournel, Henri – S. 1. n. d., pp. 75-81 (tire a part). Les Saint-Simoniens, 1825-1834. 6882 – 9 – fr Hachette [321]

AU RUANDA SUR LES BORDS DU LAC KIVU (CONGO BELGE) : UN ROYAUME HAMITE AU CENTRE DE L'AFRIQUE / Pages, G – Bruxelles: G van Campenhout 1933 – us Res Libr [960]

AU TCHAD : TROIS ANS CHEZ LES SENOUSSISTES, LES OUADDAIENS ET LES KIRDIS / Cornet, Charles Joseph Alexandre – 2. ed. Paris: Plon-Nourrit, 1910 – 1 – us Res Libr [910]

AUA: NOVELA NEGRA / Duarte, Fausto – Lisbon, 1945 – 1 – us Res Libr [830]

AUAA JOURNAL – (Cont by: Urologic Nursing) – Portland. v1-8. jun 1980-jun 1988* – 1 – D19495 – us UMI [610]

L'AUBE – Journal quotidien du matin. Puis Organe du Mouvement republicain populaire. Paris. 20 janv 1932-10 juin 1940, 23 aout 1944-20 oct 1951 – 1 – fr A.C.R.P.P. [073]

L'AUBE – Paris. Apr. 1948-May 1949 – 1 – 35.00r – us Hoover Inst Photo [370]

Aube, Benjamin *see*
- LES CHRETIENS DANS L'EMPIRE ROMAIN
- DE CONSTANTINO IMPERATORE, PONTIFICO MAXIMO
- L'EGLISE ET L'ETAT DANS LA SECONDE MOITIE DU 3E SIECLE (249-284)
- HISTOIRE DES PERSECUTIONS DE L'EGLISE, LA POLEMIQUE PAIENNE A LA FIN DU IIE SIECLE

L'AUBE (DES TEMPS MEILLEURS) : SOCIALISTE – Montreal, Canada. 11 nov-18 nov 1908 – 1r – 1 – Can$25.00 – cn Can Microfilming [072]

Aube. France (Department) *see* PROJET DE BUDGET DES RECETTES ET DES DEPENSES DEPARTEMENTALES AND DECISION MODIFICATIVE

Auber, D F E *see*
- FRA DIAVOLO, ODER GASTHAUS VON TERRACINO... VOLLSTANDISH AUSZUG FUR DAS PIANOFORTE AUF 4 HANDS
- LA PART DU DIABLE

Auber, Jacques *see*
- FRANCAIS, MALGACHES, BANTOUS, ARABES, TURCS, CHINOIS, CANAQUES...PARLONS-NOUS UNE MEME LANGUE?
- LA LANGUE MALGACHE EN 30 FAMILLES DE MOTS

Auber, P *see* CHINA, AN OUTLINE OF ITS GOVERNMENT, LAWS AND POLICY

Auberlen, Carl August et al *see* THE FOUNDATIONS OF OUR FAITH

Aubert de Gaspe, Philippe *see* LES ANCIENS CANADIENS

Aubert de la Chesnaye des Bois, Fr. A *see* DICTIONNAIRE UNIVERSEL D'AGRICULTURE ET DE JARDINAGE

Aubert de la Rue, Edgar *see* LA SOMALIE FRANCAISE

Aubert de Vitry, Francois J P *see* J.J. ROUSSEAU A L'ASSEMBLEE NATIONALE

Aubert, Georges *see*
- L'AFRIQUE DU SUD
- L'HISTOIRE DES GVERRES FAICTES PAR LES CHRESTIENS CONTRE LES TVRCS, SOVS LA CONDUICTE DE GODEFROY DE BOUILLON, DUC DE LORRAINE, POUR LE RECOUUREMENT DE LA TERRE SAINCTE

Aubert, Hermann *see* GRUNDZUEGE DER PHYSIOLOGISCHEN OPTIK

Aubert, Martin *see* ELEMENTS DE BIBLIOGRAPHIE DES ETUDES ARABES

Aubert, Theodore William *see* RIECH OBERA, PROIZNESENNAIA V ZASHCHITU POLUNINA PERED SUDOM PRISIAZHNYKH V LOZANNI E PO DIELU OB UBIISTVI E VOROVSKAGO

Aubertin, John James *see* A FIGHT WITH DISTANCES: THE STATES, THE HAWAIIAN ISLANDS, CANADA, BRITISH COLUMBIA, CUBA, THE BAHAMAS

Aubery, Antoine *see* DE JUSTES PRETENTIONS DU ROY SUR L'EMPIRE

Aubignac, Francois Hedelin *see* DISSERTATION SVR LA CONDEMNATION DES THEATRES

Aubin, Napoleon *see*
- L'ARTISAN
- LE CANADIEN INDEPENDENT
- LE CASTOR
- LA CHIMIE AGRICOLE MISE A LA PORTEE DE TOUT LE MONDE
- LE FANTASQUE
- THE STANDARD

Aublet, Edouard Edmond *see* LA GUERRE AU DAHOMEY, 1888-1893

Aublet, J B C F *see*
- HERBARIUM
- HISTOIRE DES PLANTES DE LA GUIANE FRANCAISE

Aubry, E *see*
- L'INCAPACITE DE LA FEMME MARIEE...

Aubry, Roch *see* ROCH AUBRY, B.A., B.P., COMMANDEUR DE L'ORDRE DU MERITE SCOLAIRE DE LA PROVINCE DE QUEBEC, 1895-1949

AUBURN – 1992- – 3+ r – 1 – $150.00 – P00006 – us Library Micro [910]

AUBURN 1704-1900 – (Mf 1-4: Vital Records 1753-1844. Mf 5-6: Births & Deaths 1824-45. Mf 7-9: Births & Deaths 1704-1844. Mf 10-11: Intentions 1804-48. Mf 11: Marriages 1803-43. Mf 12-15: Town Records 1773-86. Mf 15: Intentions 1778. Mf 16-20: Tax Lists 1786-1800. Mf 20-24: Accounts 1783-1812. Mf 25-30: Town Records 1786-1802. Mf 31-36: Town Meetings 1802-23. Mf 37-40: Mortgages 1832-49. Mf 41: Intentions Index: 1848-99. Mf 42-44: Intentions 1848-99. Mf 44: Women Voters 1914-15. Mf 45-46: Birth Index 1844-1909. Mf 46-47: Marriage I ndex 1844-1909. Mf 47-48: Death Index 1844-1909. Mf 49-50: Births 1844-74. Mf 50: Marriages 1843-66. Mf 50: Out-Town Marriages 1778-96. Mf 51: Deaths 1843-66. Mf 52: Births 1873-1902. Mf 53: Marriages 1867-1902. Mf 54: Deaths 1867-1903) – (mf ed 1994) – 54mf – 9 – 0-87623-375-2 – us Holbrook [920]

AUBURN BAPTIST CHURCH. AUBURN, KENTUCKY : CHURCH RECORDS – 1929-59 – 1 – 23.76 – us Baptist [240]

AUBURN DAILY TRIBUNE – Auburn, NE. Aug. 1951-Jan. 1954 – 1 – us NE Hist [071]

AUBURN JOURNAL – Auburn, NE. irreg. Oct. 1934-Dec. 1937. Incomplete – 1 – us NE Hist [071]

AUBURN PRESS-TRIBUNE – Auburn, NE. - w. Sep. 1883-Jan. 1884. Incomplete; Aug. 1884-Jun. 1888; Jul. 1892- – 1 – us NE Hist [071]

AUBURN SEMINARY RECORD – v1-27. 1905-32 (complete) – 7r – 1 – ATLA 1993-S508 – us A.T.L.A. [073]

Auburn University. Agricultural Experiment Station *see*
- AGRICULTURAL ECONOMICS SERIES
- AGRICULTURAL ENGINEERING DEPARTMENTAL SERIES
- AGRICULTURAL WEATHER SERIES
- ANATOMY AND HISTOLOGY OF CHANNEL CATFISH
- ANNUAL REPORTS 1988-1981
- BOTANY AND PLANT PATHOLOGY DEPARTMENTAL SERIES
- BULLETIN
- CIRCULAR
- DEPARTMENTAL SERIES
- ENTOMOLOGY
- ENVIRONMENTAL STUDIES SERVICE CENTER. SPECIAL REPORT
- FORESTRY DEPARTMENTAL SERIES
- FRESHWATER FISHES OF ALABAMA
- HIGHLIGHTS OF AGRICULTURAL RESEARCH
- A HISTORY OF THE ALABAMA AGRICULTURAL EXPERIMENT STATION, 1883-1983. 1985. 1 REEL
- HORTICULTURE SERIES
- ICA COMMUNICAE
- LEAFLET
- MARKETING OF FISHERIES PRODUCTS BY MUNICIPAL FISHERMEN IN PANGUIL BAY, PHILLIPPINES
- PROGRESS REPORTS
- RURAL SOCIOLOGY SERIES
- WATER QUALITY IN WARMWATER FISH PONDS

Auburn University. Agricultural Experiment Station. Zoology-Entomology Departmental Series *see* WILDLIFE RESEARCH SERIES

Auburn University. Cooperative Extension Service *see*
- ALABAMA AGRIBUSINESS
- CIRCULAR
- CIRCULAR CRD
- CIRCULAR HE
- CIRCULAR M
- CIRCULAR P

Auburn University. Extension Service *see*
- ALABAMA AGRIBUSINESS
- ANNUAL CONFERENCE
- ANNUAL REPORT
- CIRCULAR
- CIRCULAR A
- CIRCULAR (A-EX)
- CIRCULAR ANR
- CIRCULAR EX
- CIRCULAR HE
- CIRCULAR M
- CIRCULAR P
- CIRCULAR R
- CIRCULAR SR
- COUNTY LONG-TIME EXTENSION PROGRAM SUMMARY
- DAIRY PRODUCT TESTING ANNUAL SUMMARY
- FARM BUSINESS ANALYSIS BY FARMING AREAS
- FARM BUSINESS ANALYSIS BY TYPES OF FARMS
- FARM LEAFLET: REDUCTION OF ACREAGE COTTON IN 1915
- GENERAL PUBLICATIONS
- HOME DEMONSTRATION SERIES
- KATIE NEWSLETTER
- LEAFLET 4H
- LEAFLET (L-YPH)
- LEAFLET YANR
- LEAFLET YE
- LEAFLET YEX
- LEAFLET YF
- LEAFLET YHE
- LEAFLET YM
- LEAFLET YR
- PROCEEDINGS OF THE ANNUAL CONFERENCE
- PROJECT ANNUAL REPORT
- PUBLICATIONS LIST
- RECOMMENDATIONS FOR INSECT CONTROL IN ALABAMA
- RESOURCE DEVELOPMENT REPORT
- STAT. REPORT OF STATE AND COUNTY EXTENSION WORKERS
- SUGGESTIONS FOR COUNTY PLAN OF WORK
- SURVEY OF WOOD RESIDUE IN ALABAMA

Auburn University. Service *see* CIRCULAR E

AUCHINCLOSS' CHRONOLOGY OF THE HOLY BIBLE / Auchincloss, William Stuart – (Includes chronological index) – New York: D van Nostrand, 1909 – 1mf – 9 – 0-8370-2125-1 – 1985-0125 – us A.T.L.A. [220]

Auchincloss, William Stuart *see*
- AUCHINCLOSS' CHRONOLOGY OF THE HOLY BIBLE
- BIBLE CHRONOLOGY FROM ABRAHAM TO THE CHRISTIAN ERA
- BOOK OF DANIEL UNLOCKED
- THE BOOK OF DANIEL UNLOCKED
- HOW TO READ JOSEPHUS
- THE ONLY KEY TO DANIEL'S PROPHECIES

AUCKLAND CHRONICLE – England, 6 Jan 1866-9 Jul 1869 – 1 1/2r – 1 – uk British Libr Newspaper [072]

AUCKLAND PAPERS: MATERIAL RELATING TO THE AMERICAN REVOLUTION – 1744-1814. BRRAM – 1 – uk Microform Academic [975]

AUCKLAND WEEKLY NEWS – (Lacking: Jun 1940-Jan 1941) – New Zealand, 1930-51 – 79r – 1 – uk British Libr Newspaper [072]

Auclair, Joseph *see*
- LE CONGRES DE LA BAIE SAINT PAUL
- LE CONGRES: POEMES
- LES DANSES DT LES BALS: SERMONS, NOTES ET DOCUMENTS

AUCTARIUM CHARTULARII UNIVERSITATIS PARISIENSIS / Denifle, Heinrich – Parisiis. v1-5. 1937-1942 – 102mf – 8 – Dfl357.00 – ne Slangenburg [240]

AUCTARIUM CHARTULARII UNIVERSITATIS PARISIENSIS / ed by Denifle, Heinrich & Chatelain, A – Parisiis, 1894-1897. 2v – 37mf – 9 – H-449/2 – ne IDC [370]

AUCTARIUM D.C. DE VISCH AD BIBLIOTHECAM SCRIPTORUM S.O. CISTERCIENSIS / Visch, C de; ed by Canivez, J-M – 2mf – 8 – ne Slangenburg [240]

AUCTION CATALOGUE / American Numismatic Society. New York – (First Supplement. 1967, 1962-1967. 17,100 cards. $120.00 export $150.00. – ISBN 0-8161-0788-2; Available on microfilm by request; Second Supplement, 1973. 17,300 cards 1 reel. $110.00 export $135.00. – ISBN 0-8161-1427-7; Third Supplement, 1978. 29,100 cards 4 reels. $205.00 export $245.00. – ISBN 0-8161-1375-0) – 15,300 cards on 1 reel – 1 – $100.00 export $120.00 – 0-8161-1426-9 – uk Hall [730]

AUCTION REGISTER AND LAW CHRONICLE – (Law Chronicle and Estate Advertiser 1817-19; Law Chronicle, Commericial and Bankruptcy Register 1821-47) – London, UK. 1813-19; 1821-47 – 18r – 1 – uk British Libr Newspaper [073]

AUCTOR VETUS DE BENEFICIIS (MGH LEGES 3: 2.BD. PARS 1A) : TEXTUS LATINI – 1964 – Dfl19.00 – ne Slangenburg [240]

AUCTOR VETUS DE BENEFICIIS (MGH LEGES 3: 2.BD. PARS 2A) : ARCHETYPUS UND GOERLITZER RECHTSBUCH – 1966 – Dfl22.00 – ne Slangenburg [240]

AUCTUARIUM AD FLORAM PEDEMONTANAM CUM NOTIS ET EMENDATIONIBUS / Allioni, C – Augustae Taurinorum. 1789. B-5533 2 – 8 – ne IDC [580]

L'AUDACE LITTERAIRE – no. 1-17. Paris. 1909-mai juin 1911 – 1 – fr A.C.R.P.P. [800]

Aude, Flan *see* CADET ROUSSEL MISANTHROPE ET MANON REPENTANTE

Aude, Hapde *see* CADET ROUSSEL MISANTHROPE ET MANON REPENTANTE

Aude, Joseph *see* MADAME ANGOT AU SERAIL DE CONSTANTINOPLE

AUDENSHAW PAPERS – nos 14-137. 1969-91 (incomplete) – 2r – 1 – ATLA S0407 – us A.T.L.A. [240]

Audet, Diane *see* METABOLIC COST OF DOWNHILL SKI ERGOMETRY IN MALES

Audet, Francis Joseph *see* HISTORIQUE DES JOURNAUX D'OTTAWA

Audet, M-R *see* BIBLIOGRAPHIE ANALYTIQUE DU DOCTEUR EMILE GAUMOND CHEF DU SERVICE DE DERMATO-SYPHILIGRAPHIE, HOTEL-DIEU, QUEBEC...

Audette, Louis Arthur *see* ALMANACH JUDICIAIRE DE LA PROVINCE DE QUEBEC

L'AUDIENCE – Paris. 10 oct 1873-24 aout 1884, 1883 inc., mq no. 28, 1884 inc., mq no. 15-16 – 1 – fr A.C.R.P.P. [072]

AUDIENCE REACTIONS TO THE PORTRAYAL OF BLACKS IN ATHLETIC APPAREL COMMERCIALS / Wilson, Brian – University of British Columbia, 1995 – 2mf – 9 – $8.00 – PSY1875 – us Microform Publ [302]
AUDIENCIA CASA DE CONTRATACION : JUICIOS DE RESIDENCIA – Sevilla, SP. 1544-45 – 1,5 – sp Cultura [340]
AUDIENCIA DE CANARIAS : JUICIOS DE RESIDENCIA – Sevilla, SP. 1567-1573 – 1,5 – sp Cultura [340]
AUDIENCIA DE CHARCAS : JUICIOS DE RESIDENCIA – Sevilla, SP. 1564-80 – 1,5 – sp Cultura [340]
AUDIENCIA DE MEJICO : JUICIOS DE RESIDENCIA – Sevilla, SP. 1529-1675 – 1,5 – sp Cultura [340]
Audiganne, A *see*
- MEMOIRES D'UN OUVRIER DE PARIS, 1871-1872
- LES OUVRIERS D'A PRESENT ET LA NOUVELLE ECONOMIE DU TRAVAIL
- LES OUVRIERS EN FAMILLE
- LES POPULATIONS OUVRIERES ET LES INDUSTRIES DE LA FRANCE. ETUDES COMPARATIVES SUR LE REGIME ET LES RESSOURCES DES DIFFERENTES INDUSTRIES, SUR L'ETAT MORAL ET MATERIEL DES OUVRIERS DANS CHAQUE BRANCHE DU TRAVAIL ET LES INSTITUTIONS QUI LES CONCERNENT
- LE TRAVAIL ET LES OUVRIERS SOUS LA IIIE

Audinet, E L A *see* PRINCIPES ELEMENTAIRES...
Audinet-Serville, J G *see* HISTOIRE NATURELLE DES INSECTES, HEMIPTERES
AUDIO – (1971- . 5,6. 1976- . 9) – v. 2-61. 1920- – 1 – us UMI [621]
AUDIO VIDEO CANADA – v18-19, no.11. Jul 1981-Nov 1982 – 1,5,6,9 – us UMI [073]
AUDIO VISUAL COMMUNICATION REVIEW *see* AV COMMUNICATION REVIEW
AUDIO VISUAL COMMUNICATIONS *see*
- AVC DEVELOPMENT AND DELIVERY
- AVC PRESENTATION, TECHNOLOGY AND APPLICATIONS

AUDIO VISUAL DIRECTIONS *see* AV VIDEO
AUDIO VISUAL PRODUCT NEWS – 1978-80.Continued as: Audiovisual Directions – 1,5,6,9 – us UMI [621]
AUDIOLOGY AND NEURO-OTOLOGY – v1-1996- – 1,5,9 – us UMI [073]
AUDIOSCENE CANADA – (v12- , 1975- . 5,6,9) – v. 1-. 1964- – 1 – us UMI [621]
AUDIO-VISUAL AIDS FOR COOPERATIVE EDUCATION AND TRAINING / Botham, C N – 1975 – 99p – it F.A.O. [370]
AUDIO-VISUAL COMMUNICATIONS *see* AVC PRESENTATION, TECHNOLOGY AND APPLICATIONS
AUDIOVISUAL DIRECTIONS – v.3-. 1981-. Continues: Audio Visual Product News – 1,5,6,9 – us UMI [621]
AUDIOVISUAL INSTRUCTION – (1968-78. 5,6. 1975-78. 9) – 1-23. 1956-78 – 1 – us UMI [370]
AUDIOVISUAL INSTRUCTION WITH INSTRUCTIONAL RESOURCES – v.23-24. 1978-79 – 1,5,6,9 – us UMI [073]
THE AUDIOVISUAL LIBRARIAN – (1984-. 5,6,9) – v1-. Spring 1973- – 1 – us UMI [073]
AUDIOVISUAL MATERIALS / U.S. Library of Congress – (Quinquennia: 1953-57; 1958-62; 1963-67; 1968-72) – 9 – us Advanced Libr [010]
AUDIOVISUAL MATERIALS. INDEXES. REGISTERS / U.S. Library of Congress – (1997 current subscription includes registers and fully cumulated indexes.) – 1972-96. Registers only – 9 – us Advanced Libr [010]
Audisio, G *see* IURIS NATURAE ET GENTIUM...
AUDIT BOOKS / Holkham Hall. Norfolk. England – 1707-1853 – 1 – uk Microform Academic [650]
AUDIT BUREAU OF CIRCULATIONS – London, UK. Apr 1937-Sep 1939; 1948-49; Jul 1976-Jun 1983 – 4r – 1 – uk British Libr Newspaper [073]
AUDIT REPORTS / Hancock County. Ohio. Biglick Township. Township Clerk – 1920-1988 gaps in holdings – 1r – 1 – $32.50r – us Archival [324]
AUDITING IN THE ELECTRONIC ENVIRONMENT: THEORY, PRACTICE AND LITERATURE / Cornick, Delroy L – 1981. 316p. ISBN: 0-912338-24-5 – 9 – 14.75 – us Lomond [336]
AUDITING THEORY AND PRACTICE / Montgomery, Robert H – New York: The Ronald Press, 1913 – 8mf – 9 – $12.00 – LLMC 92-184 – us L.L.M.C. [340]
AUDOBON FIELD NOTES *see* AMERICAN BIRDS
AUDOBON MAGAZINE *see* AMERICAN BIRDS
Audouin, J V *see* CATALOGUE DES LIVRES D'HISTOIRE NATURELLE ET PRINCIPALEMENTS D'ENTOMOLOGIE COMPOSANT LA BIBLIOTHEQUE DE...
Audouys *see* RECHERCHES GENEALOGIQUES SUR LES FAMILLES D'ANJOU
Audouze, F *see* CONTRIBUTION A LA TYPOLOGIE DES EPINGLES DE L'AGE DU BRONZE
Audrein, Yves-Marie *see* MEMOIRE SUR L'EDUCATION NATIONALE FRANCAISE, SUIVI D'UN PROJET DE DECRET PAR M. L'ABBE AUDREIN
Audry, L *see* LA REVISION DE LA SENTENCE ARBITRALE
AUDUBON – (1968- 5,6. 1970- 9) – 1- 1899- – 1 – us UMI [590]
Audubon, Jean-Jacques *see* SCENES DE LA NATURE DANS LES ETATS-UNIS...
Audubon, John James *see*
- THE BIRDS OF AMERICA FROM ORIGINAL DRAWING
- THE QUADRUPEDS OF NORTH AMERICA
- SCENES DE LA NATURE DANS LES ETATS UNIS ET LE NORD DE L'AMERIQUE
- A SYNOPSIS OF THE BIRDS OF NORTH AMERICA

AUDUBON MAGAZINE – v. 1-47. 1899-1945 – 1 – us Princeton Micro [590]
Auenbrugger, L *see* INVENTUM NOVUM EX PERCUSSIONE THORACIS HUMANI
Auer, J *see* DIE MENSCHLICHE WILLENSFREIHEIT IM LEHRSYSTEM DES THOMAS VON AQUIN UND JOHANNES DUNS SCOTUS
Auerbach, Berthold *see*
- ANDREE HOFER
- AUF WACHE
- BRIGITTA
- LA DIPLOMATIE FRANCAISE...
- DRAMATISCHE EINDRUECKE
- HA-ZOFEH AL DARKHEI HA-MISHNAH
- ON THE HEIGHTS
- SAEMMTLICHE SCHWARZWAELDER DORFGESCHICHTEN
- SPINOZA
- STORBONDEN OG HAND SØNNER

Auerbach, Devoira *see* RURAL AND REGIONAL DEVELOPMENT
Auerbach, Guenter *see* SACHGEHALT UND WAHRHEITSGEHALT IN SHAKESPEARES "THE TEMPEST"
Auernheimer, Raoul *see*
- CASANOVA IN WIEN
- DIE DAME MIT DER MASKE

Auerswald, Annmarie von *see*
- DIE EWIGE ORDNUNG
- HERESGAST
- KAMPF UM IRLAND
- SONNWILL

Auerswald, Hans von *see* STAATSWIRTSCHAFT
AUF, AUF IHR CHRISTEN / Abraham a Sancta Clara – Wien: C Konegen, 1883 – 1r – 1 – us U.W. Library [240]
AUF BIEGEN UND BRECHEN : DEN WELTKRIEG BEGREIFEN HEISST ERLEBEN UND REIFEN / Zindler, Erwin – Leipzig: K F Koehler, c1929 – 1 – us U.W. Library [890]
AUF DEM SCHLACHTFELDE VON CUSTOZZA / Spindler, William – [S.l.: s.n.], 1870 – 1 – us U.W. Library [810]
AUF DEM SCHNITTPUNKT ZWEIER GATTUNGEN : DRAMATISIERUNGEN ENGLISCHER ROMANE DES 18. JAHRHUNDERTS / Sebastian, Astrid – 1994 – 3mf – 9 – DM98.00 – 3-89349-856-7 – gw Hänsel [790]
AUF DEN KARGEN HUEGELN DER NEUMARK : ZUR GESCHICHTE EINES SCHAEFER- UND BAUERNGESCHLECHTS IM WARTHEBRUCH / Kuenkel, Hans – Wurzburg: Holzner Verlag, 1962 – 10r – 1 – us U.W. Library [430]
DER AUF DEN PARNASS VERSETZTE GRUENE HUT / Klemm, Christian Gottlob – Wien: C Konegen, 1883 – 1r – 1 – us U.W. Library [943]
AUF DER HOEHE *see* ON THE HEIGHTS
AUF DER MAERCHENSUCHE : DIE ENTSTEHUNG MEINER MAERCHENSAMMLUNG / Wisser, Wilhelm – Hamburg: Hanseatische Verlagsanstalt, [1926] – 1r – 1 – us U.W. Library [390]
AUF DER WALZ VOR FUENFZIG JAHREN / Krebs, Werner – Bern: Verein fuer Verbreitung guter Schriften, 1927 – 1r – 1 – us U.W. Library [390]
AUF GUT DEUTSCH – Muenchen, DE. 1918-19 – 1r – 1 – gw Mikrofilm [072]
AUF GUT DEUTSCH – Munich. Wochenschrift fua5r Ordnung und Recht. Dec. 7, 1918-May 17, 1921 – 1 – 35.00r – us Hoover Inst Photo [072]
AUF LEBEN UND TOD : ZWEI NOVELLEN / Storm, Theodor – Bayreuth: Der Gauverlag, 1944 – 1 – us U.W. Library [830]
AUF SPUREN DES JUNGEN GOETHE : BILDER AUS DEM ALTEN FRANKFURT / ed by Ernst, Otto – Frankfurt (Main): [Niemeyer], 1932 – 1 – us U.W. Library [750]
AUF STILLEN WEGEN : DICHTUNGEN / Hammer, Julius – 3. Aufl. Leipzig: F A Brockhaus, 1878 – 1r – 1 – us U.W. Library [810]
AUF VORPOSTEN – Berlin, 1912-25 – 1r – 5 – Dist. gw Mikrofilm – gw Misc Inst [072]
AUF WACHE : NOVELLE / Auerbach, Berthold – (Includes glossaries) – New York: H Holt, [18–?] – 1r – 1 – us U.W. Library [830]
AUF ZUM WERK. (TO THE WORK) – Moundridge, Kansas. Aug 1921-Jan 1923. Organ of the Mennonite Russian Bible Society – 1 – 10.78 – us Baptist [240]
AUF ZUR WOLGA : SCHICKSALE DEUTSCHER AUSWANDERER / Ponten, Josef – Koeln: H Schaffstein, 1944 – 1r – 1 – us U.W. Library [430]
AUFBAU – New York. 1934-46 – 5r – 1 – gw Mikrofilm [071]
AUFBAU – New York. v1-48. 1934-82 – 48r – 1 – us Ross [071]
DER AUFBAU : GEDICHTE / Anacker, Heinrich – Muenchen: Zentralverlag der NSDAP, F Eher, 1936 – 1r – 1 – us U.W. Library [810]
DER AUFBAU – (Lacking some pages) – v1-69. 1919-88 – 21r – 1 – ATLA S0334 – us A.T.L.A. [240]
AUFBAU, AUFGABEN UND ERGEBNISSE DER INTERNATIONALEN ARBEITSORGANISATION / Dietz, Theodor – 1995 – 1mf – 9 – DM48.00 – 3-8267-3172-7 – gw Hänsel [340]
DER AUFBAU DER AMOSREDEN / Baumann, Eberhard – Giessen: J. Ricker (Toepelmann), 1903. 1 fiche – 9 – us A.T.L.A. [240]
AUFBEREITUNG UND INTERPRETATION VON ERGEBNISSEN EXTERNER QUALITAETSSICHERUNGSMASSNAHMEN ALS EINSTIEG IN DIE INTERVENTIONEN VON QUALITAETSPROBLEMEN : KONZEPTE UND LOESUNGSVORSCHLAEGE AM BEISPIEL DER EXTERNEN QUALITAETSSICHERUNG IN KRANKENHAEUSERN SCHLESWIG-HOLSTEINS / Niemann, Frank-Michael – 1995 – 2mf – 9 – DM80.00 – 3-8267-2184-5 – gw Hänsel [360]
DER AUFBRUCH : KAMPFBLATT IM SINNE DES LEUTNANT A D SCHERINGER. ZEITSCHRIFT FUER WEHRFRAGEN, KRIEGSPROBLEME UND KAMPF GEGEN DEN FASCHISMUS – Berlin, 1931-33 n1 – 1r – 1 – Dist. gw Mikrofilm – gw Misc Inst [355]
DER AUFBRUCH – Lodz, Poland. 2 May-21 Dec 1935 – 2r – 1 – gw Mikrofilm [072]
DER AUFBRUCH : STIMMEN JUNGER DEUTSCHER – Kattowitz (Katowice), Poland. 11 Mar 1933-29 Sept 1934; 1936; Apr-Dec 1937 – 1 – gw Mikrofilm [072]
DIE AUFERSTEHUNG CHRISTI : DIE BERICHTE UEBER AUFERSTEHUNG, HIMMELFAHRT UND PFINGSTEN:IHRE ENTSTEHUNG, IHR GESCHICHTLICHER HINTERGRUND UND IHRE RELIGIOESE BEDEUTUNG / Meyer, Arnold – Tuebingen:J C B Mohr (Paul Siebeck), 1905 – 1mf – 9 – 0-8370-4399-9 – 1985-2399 – us A.T.L.A. [240]
DIE AUFERSTEHUNG JESU IN IHRER BEDEUTUNG FUER DEN CHRISTLICHEN GLAUBEN / Krueger, Wilhelm – (Includes bibliographical references) – Bremen: C Ed Mueller, 1867 – 1mf – 9 – 0-8370-4005-1 – 1985-2005 – us A.T.L.A. [240]
DIE AUFERSTEHUNG UND IHRE NEUESTE BESTREITUNG : VORTRAG GEHALTEN ZU STETTIN DEN 24. JANUAR 1865 / Beyschlag, Willibald – Berlin: Ludwig Rauh, [1865] – 1mf – 9 – 0-8370-5986-0 – 1985-3986 – us A.T.L.A. [240]
AUFFAHRT : NEUE GEDICHTE / Pulver, Max – Leipzig: Insel-Verlag, 1919 – 1r – 1 – us U.W. Library [810]
DIE AUFFASSUNG DES HOHENLIEDES BEI DEN ABESSINIERN / Euringer, Sebastian – Leipzig: J.C. Hinrichs, 1900. 1 fiche – 9 – us A.T.L.A. [240]
DIE AUFFASSUNG DES JUNGEN HERDER VOM MITTELALTER : EIN BEITRAG ZUR GESCHICHTE DER AUFKLAERUNG / Stolpe, Heinz – (Includes bibliographical references and index) – Weimar: H Boehlaus Nachfolger, 1955 – 1 – us U.W. Library [430]
AUFFGEDECKTE LARVE DAVIDIS GEORGII / Jessenius, F – Kiel, J. Reuman. 1670. BME-414 1 – 9 – ne IDC [240]
DIE AUFGABE DES RICHTERS ... / Bosshard, W – Waedenswil, [1929] – 2mf – 9 – ILM-2248/1 – ne IDC [327]
AUFGABEN AUS "DIE JUNGFRAU VON ORLEANS" / Schroeder, W – 6., verm. Aufl. Leipzig: W Engelmann, 1908 – 1r – 1 – us U.W. Library [430]
AUFGABEN AUS "MARIA STUART" / Heinze, Hermann – (Includes bibliographical references) – 3., umgearb. Aufl. Leipzig: W Engelmann, 1905 – 1r – 1 – us U.W. Library [430]
AUFGABEN AUS WALLENSTEIN / Heinze, Hermann – (Includes bibliographical references) – 6. verbess. Ausg. Leipzig: W Engelmann, 1907 – 1r – 1 – us U.W. Library [430]
DIE AUFGABEN DER NEUTESTAMENTLICHEN FORSCHUNG IN DER GEGENWART / Fiebig, Paul – Leipzig: J.C. Hinrichs, 1909. 1 fiche – 9 – us A.T.L.A. [240]
DIE AUFGABEN DER NEUTESTAMENTLICHEN WISSENSCHAFT IN DER GEGENWART / Weiss, Johannes – Goettingen: Vandenhoeck und Ruprecht, 1908 – 1mf – 9 – 0-8370-6454-6 – 1986-0454 – us A.T.L.A. [220]
AUFGABEN DER PROTESTANTISCHEN THEOLOGIE / Roehm, Johann Baptist – (Includes bibliographical references) – Augsburg: Max Huttler, 1882 – 1mf – 9 – 0-8370-4946-6 – 1985-2946 – us A.T.L.A. [240]
AUFGANG = THE RISE – (In Yiddish) – Sighet, RM. v1 no1 May/Jun 1933-v1 no37 Jan 1938 – 1r – 1 – $35.00 – cn Can Microfilming [072]
Aufhauser, J B *see* ANTIKE JESUS-ZEUGNISSE
DIE AUFHEBUNG DES EDIKTES VON NANTES IM OKTOBER 1685 / Schott, Theodor – Halle: Verein fuer Reformationsgeschichte, 1885. ([Schriften des Vereins fuer Reformationsgeschichte; Bd. 10]) – 1mf – us A.T.L.A. [240]
DER AUFKLAERER, FRIEDRICH NICOLAI / Aner, Karl – Giessen: A. Toepelmann, 1912. (Studien zur Geschichte des neueren Protestantismus; 6. Heft) – 1mf – us A.T.L.A. [240]
DIE AUFNAHMEN DER ALKOHOLPSYCHOSEN AN DER UNIV.-NERVENKLINIK IN FRANKFURT/MAIN FUER DIE JAHRE 1922-1950 / Mies, Theodor – Frankfurt a.M., 1951 – 1mf – 9 – DM48.00 – 3-89349-848-6 – gw Hänsel [616]
DER AUFRICHTIGE UND WOHLERFAHRENE SCHWEIZER BOTE – Aarau, 1798-1800, 1805 – 1 – Dist. gw Mikrofilm – gw Misc Inst [949]
DER AUFRICHTIGE UND WOHLERFAHRENE SCHWEIZER-BOTE – Aarau, Switzerland. 1798-1800 – 1 – gw Mikrofilm [949]
AUFRUF : STREITSCHRIFT FUER MENSCHENRECHTE – Prag (Praha), Czechoslovakia. 15 Apr 1933-15 Sept 1934 – 1r – 1 – gw Mikrofilm [073]
DER AUFRUHR UM DEN JUNKER ERNST : ERZAEHLUNG / Wassermann, Jakob – 1. bis 15. Aufl. Berlin: S Fischer, c1926 – 1r – 1 – us U.W. Library [430]
AUFSAETZE UND VORTRAEGE / Reischle, Max – Tuebingen: J.C.B. Mohr, 1906. xlvii,198p. 1 fiche – 9 – us A.T.L.A. [240]
AUFSAETZE ZUR DEUTSCHEN LITERATURGESCHICHTE / Mehring, Franz; ed by Koch, Hans – (Includes bibliographical references and index) – Leipzig: P Reclam, 1966 – 1r – 1 – us U.W. Library [430]
AUFSTAND DER FISCHER VON ST BARBARA / Seghers, Anna – Berlin: G Kiepenheuer, 1929 – 1r – 1 – us U.W. Library [943]
AUFSTIEG – Reval, Eesti, (Tallinn U.S.S.R.). Mar 20, 1932-Dec 3, 1933 – 1r – 1 – gw Mikrofilm [072]
DER AUFSTIEG – Berlin, Wien. 1930-32 – 1r – 1 – Dist. gw Mikrofilm – gw Misc Inst [072]

DER AUFSTIEG : EINE JUEDISCHE MONATSSCHRIFT – Berlin, Vienna. v1. 1930-32. Complete. 1 reel, B22. (Leo Baeck Institute. German-Jewish Periodicals, Pt 2) – 1 – $75.00 – us UPA [270]
DER AUFSTIEG DER MUTTERSPRACHE IM DEUTSCHEN DENKEN DES 15. UND 16. JAHRHUNDERTS / Daube, Anna – (Includes bibliographical references) – Frankfurt am Main: M Diesterweg, 1940 – 1r – 1 – us U.W. Library [430]
AUFTAKT – Moderne Musikblaetter. Prague. v. 1-18. 1920-1938 – 1 – us Schnase [780]
DER AUFTAKT; MUSIKBLAETTER – v. 1-18, no. 3 4. 1920-38 – 1 – 50.00 – us L of C Photodup [780]
DER AUFTRAG – v1-10 nos 1-22. 1956-88 (complete) – 8r – 1 – ATLA S0637 – us A.T.L.A. [240]
AUFWAERTS – Bielefeld, jan 15 1919-jun 30 1920, 1922-apr 30 1936 – 1 – Inquire at Mikrofilmarchiv for details – gw Misc Inst [072]
AUFWAERTS : JUGENDZEITSCHRIFT DES DGB (MONATLICH) – Koeln, 16 Jun 1948-15 Dec 1966; 15 Mar 1968; 15 Jan-15 Nov 1969 – 6r – DM450.00 – gw Mikro Press [073]
AUFZEICHNUNGEN DES GRAFEN WILLIAM BENTINCK UEBER MARIA THERESIA / ed by Beer, A – Wien, 1871 – 4mf – 9 – ne IDC [943]
Augar, F *see* DIE FRAU IM ROEMISCHEN CHRISTENPROCESS (T.U.U. 2-28/4C)
Augarde, L *see* JOURNAL DE NAVIGATION DE L'INFERNET DANS LE PACIFIQUE, 1874-76
Auge, Claude *see* PETIT LAROUSSE ILLUSTRE (AEL, ABT 2;11)
EL AUGE DEL IMPERIO ESPANOL EN AMERICA / Madariaga, Salvador – Buenos Aires: Editorial Sudamerica, 1955. 527p. illus – 1 – us U.W. Library [972]
Auge, M *see* LIVES OF THE EMINENT DEAD AND BIOGRAPHICAL NOTICES OF LIVING CITIZENS
DIE AUGEN DES EWIGEN BRUDERS : EINE LEGENDE / Zweig, Stefan – Leipzig: Insel-Verlag, [1933] – 1r – 1 – us U.W. Library [890]
Auger, Athanase *see*
- ORGANISATION DES ECOLES NATIONALES
- SUR LES GOUVERNEMENTS EN GENERAL ET EN PARTICULIER SUR CELUI QUI NOUS CONVIENT

Auger, Joseph Cyrille *see*
- COMPILATION ET RECUEIL DES LOIS STATUTAIRES TOUCHANT L'ENREGISTREMENT DES DROITS REEL ET DES PRIVILEGES ET HYPOTHEQUES.
- INFORMATIONS PRECISES ET OFFICIELLES TOUCHANT L'ENREGISTREMENT ET L'IMPOT

Augias, Carlo *see* ELEMENTI SCIENTIFICI DI ETICA CIVILE E DIRITTO.
Augier, Ernest *see* DU TAC AU TAC: REPONSES AUX OBJECTIONS MODERNES CONTRE LA RELIGION
THE AUGSBURG CONFESSION : AN INTRODUCTION TO ITS STUDY AND AN EXPOSITION OF ITS CONTENTS / Loy, M – Columbus, Ohio: Lutheran Book Concern,1908 – 3mf – us A.T.L.A. [240]
AUGSBURG: PAMPHLET COLLECTION – 1928-19?? – 1 – CSUXANS9163-B – us Hoover Inst Photo [943]
AUGSBURGER ABENDZEITUNG – Augsburg, Germany. 1858-Sept 1875; Apr 1882-Jun 1884; Apr-Jun 1895; 1901-Sept 1912 – 46r – 1 – us L of C Photodup [072]
AUGSBURGER ABENDZEITUNG – (Cont: Augspurger Ordinari-Zeitung, jan 5 1735. Augspurgische Ordinari-Zeitung, jan 12 1735. Augspurger Ordinari-Zeitung, 1743. Augspurgische Ordinari-Zeitung, 1746. Augspurger Ordinaere Zeitung, 1784. Augsp(b)urgische Ordinaere Zeitung, 1796. Augsburgische Ordinari(naere) Zeitung, 1800. Augsburgische Ordinaere deutsche Zeitung, 1802. Augsburgische politische Zeitung, jan 2 1809. Augsburger politische Abendzeitung, jan 2 1818-jun 30 1826. Cont by: Muenchen-Augsburger Abendzeitung, sep 2 1912) – Augsburg, jan 29 1742, 1771, 1773-85, 1792-jun 30 1798, 1801-07, feb 22 1810-12, 1814-17, 1819-25, 1827-28, jul 1-dec 31 1829, jan 2-nov 10 1832, 1835-1934 – 1 – Dist. gw Mikrofilm – gw Misc Inst [943]
AUGSBURGER ALLGEMEINE – (Cont: Schwaebische Landeszeitung, oct 31 1945-oct 30 1959) – Augsburg, oct 31 1945- – 1 – Dist. gw Mikrofilm – gw Misc Inst [072]
AUGSBURGER ORDINARI POSTZEITUNG *see* AUGSPURGISCHE ORDINARI-POST-ZEITUNG
DER AUGSBURGER PATRICIERS PHILIPP HAINHOFER REISEN NACH INNSBRUCK UND DRESDEN / Doering, O – (Quellenschriften fuer kunstgeschichte. n.s. v. 10. Wien. 1901). BO-517y 1 – 9 – ne IDC [700]
AUGSBURGER POLITISCHE ABENDZEITUNG *see* AUGSBURGER ABENDZEITUNG
AUGSBURGER POSTZEITUNG – (Mit literarischer Beilage, 1917-21) – Augsburg, 1918-21 – 7r – 1 – DM525.00 – gw Mikro Press [072]
AUGSBURGER POSTZEITUNG *see* AUGSPURGISCHE ORDINARI-POST-ZEITUNG
AUGSBURGER TAGBLATT – Augsburg, 1848-49 – 2r – 1 – Dist. gw Mikrofilm – gw Misc Inst [943]
AUGSBURGER VOLKSZEITUNG *see*
- SCHWAEBISCHE VOLKSZEITUNG
- DER VOLKSWILLE

AUGSBURGISCHE ORDINAERE DEUTSCHE ZEITUNG *see* AUGSBURGER ABENDZEITUNG
AUGSBURGISCHE ORDINARI POSTZEITUNG *see* AUGSPURGISCHE ORDINARI-POST-ZEITUNG
AUGSBURGISCHE ORDINARI(NAERE) ZEITUNG *see* AUGSBURGER ABENDZEITUNG
AUGSBURGISCHE POLITISCHE ZEITUNG *see* AUGSBURGER ABENDZEITUNG
AUGSBURGISCHES INTELLIGENZ-BLATT – Augsburg, 1784-85 (incomplete) – 1 – Dist. gw Mikrofilm – gw Misc Inst [943]
AUGSBURGISCH-WOCHENTLICHER KERN DER CURIOSITAETEN – Augsburg, Germany. 1702 – 1r – 1 – gw Mikrofilm [072]
AUGSP(B)URGISCHE ORDINAERE ZEITUNG *see* AUGSBURGER ABENDZEITUNG
AUGSPURGER ORDINAERE ZEITUNG *see* AUGSBURGER ABENDZEITUNG
AUGSPURGER ORDINARI-ZEITUNG *see* AUGSBURGER ABENDZEITUNG
AUGSPURGISCHE ORDINARI-POST-ZEITUNG – (Cont by: Augsburgische Ordinari Postzeitung, 1797. Augsburger Ordinari Postzeitung, may 7 1827. Augsburger Postzeitung, jan 1 1833. Postzeitung, nov 2 1934) – Augsburg, aug 21 1702, apr 11 1703, jan 3 1707, aug 15, 1709, jan 10 1711, aug 18 1712, nov 15 1713, may 9 1720, jan 30-jul 7 1723 (very incomplete), may 23-nov 11 1740 (very incomplete), jan 16-jul 14 1741, may 8-oct 24 1742 (very incomplete), oct 7-dec 28 1743 (very incomplete), sep 7 1746, nov 13 1751, aug 13 1757, jun 8-dec 30 1758 (very incomplete), 1759-63 (incomplete), 1765 (very incomplete), jan 6 1766-67 (very incomplete), 1768 (incomplete), 1769 (very incomplete), 1770 (incomplete), 1774-oct 5 1775 (very incomplete), feb 24 1776, jul 25-dec 31 1777 (incomplete), 1778 (very incomplete), 1779-80 (incomplete), jan 1-jul 27 1781, 1782 (incomplete), 1783, 1784 (almost complete), 1785, 1786-87 (very incomplete), 1788 (incomplete), 1789 (very incomplete), 1790, 1791 (almost complete), 1792 (incomplete), 1793 (almost complete), 1794 (incomplete), 1795, 1796-97 (almost complete), 1798 (incomplete), 1799-1800, 1801 (almost complete), 1802-04, 1805 (almost complete), 1806-08, 1813-16, 1817-20 (incomplete), 1821-1916, 1922-aug 11 1935 – 1 – Dist. gw Mikrofilm – gw Misc Inst [943]
AUGSPURGISCHE ORDINARI-ZEITUNG *see* AUGSBURGER ABENDZEITUNG
AUGSPURGISCH-WOCHENTLICHER KERN DER CURIOSITAETEN – Augsburg, jan 4-apr 26 1702 – 1r – 1 – Dist. gw Mikrofilm – gw Misc Inst [943]
THE AUGUST 1983 AMENDMENTS TO THE FEDERAL RULES OF CIVIL PROCEDURE : PROMOTING EFFECTIVE CASE MANAGEMENT AND LAWYER RESPONSIBILITY / Miller, Arthur R – Washington: FJC, 1984 – 1mf – 9 – $1.50 – LLMC 95-810 – us L.L.M.C. [340]
AUGUST GOTTLIEB SPANGENBERG : BISCHOF DER BRUEDERKIRCHE / Reichel, Gerhard – Tuebingen: J.C.B. Mohr, 1906 – 1mf – us A.T.L.A. [240]
AUGUST GRAF VON PLATENS SAEMTLICHE WERKE IN ZWOELF BAENDEN = WORKS : HISTORISCH-KRITISCHE AUSGABE MIT EINSCHLUSS DES HANDSCHRIFTLICHEN NACHLASSES / ed by Koch, Max & Petzet, Erich – (Includes bibliographical references & index) – Leipzig: Max Hesse, [1909?] – 1 – us U.W. Library [800]
AUGUST GRAF VON PLATENS WERKE / Platen, August, Graf von; ed by Redlich, Christian – Berlin: G Hempel, [1883?] – 1r – 1 – us U.W. Library [430]
AUGUST HERMANN FRANCKE : EIN LEBENSBILD / Kramer, Gustav – Halle a.S.: Buchh. des Waisenhauses, 1880-1882 – 2mf – us A.T.L.A. [240]
AUGUST VON PLATEN IN ITALIA E GIOSUE CARDUCCI / Saracco, Maria – (Includes bibliographical references) – Torino: Cesare Valentino, 1930 – 1r – 1 – us U.W. Library [920]
AUGUST WILHELM IFFLANDS SCHAUSPIELKUNST BIS ZUM ABSCHLUß DER MANNHEIMER ZEIT (1796) / David, Siegfried – Heidelberg, 1933 – 1mf – DM48.00 – 3-8267-3011-9 – gw Hänsel [790]
AUGUST WILHELM SCHLEGEL ALS LYRIKER : KAPITEL 1: FRUEHZEIT / Wulf, Erich – 1995 – 1mf – 9 – DM48.00 – 3-8267-3118-2 – gw Hänsel [430]
AUGUST ZALESKI PAMPHLET COLLECTION – 1962-1964 – 1 – CSUXANL6761-B – us Hoover Inst Photo [335]
AUGUSTA BAPTIST CHURCH. AUGUSTA, KENTUCKY : CHURCH RECORDS – 1907-62 – 1 – 24.84 – us Baptist [240]
AUGUSTA COUNTY ARGUS – Staunton. Va. 1901-1902 – 1 – us UMI [071]
AUGUSTA FIRST BAPTIST CHURCH. AUGUSTA, GEORGIA : CHURCH RECORDS – Newsletter, Vols 1-5, March 1887-Jan 1893 – 1 reel – 1 – $9.81 – us Baptist [240]
AUGUSTANA – (Lacking some pages) – v1-102. Jul 1856-1956 – 76r – 1 – ATLA S0123 – us A.T.L.A. [073]
AUGUSTANA *see* LUTHERAN COMPANION
AUGUSTANA EVANGELICAL LUTHERAN CHURCH : MINNESOTA CONFERENCE MINUTES – (Title varies) – v1-21. 1858-1962 (complete) – 10r – 1 – ATLA S0216 – us A.T.L.A. [240]
AUGUSTANA EVANGELICAL LUTHERAN CHURCH : REPORT OF THE SYNOD – (Lacking: some pages) – nos 1-103. 1860-1962 (complete) – 10r – 1 – ATLA S0093 – us A.T.L.A. [240]
AUGUSTANA QUARTERLY : THE CHURCH QUARTERLY OF THE AUGUSTANA LUTHERAN CHURCH – v1-27. 1922-48 (complete) – 7r – 1 – ATLA S0021 – us A.T.L.A. [073]
AUGUSTANA THEOLOGICAL QUARTERLY *see* TIDSKRIFT FOER TEOLOGI OCH KIRKLIGA FRAGOR
AUGUSTIN / Hertling, Georg Freiherr von – Mainz: F. Kirchheim, 1902 – 1mf – us A.T.L.A. [240]
Augustin, Catherine *see* DEIXIS
AUGUSTINE AND HIS COMPANIONS : FOUR LECTURES / DELIVERED AT ST. PAUL'S IN JANUARY, 1895 / Browne, G F – London: S.P.C.K., 1906 – 1mf – us A.T.L.A. [240]
AUGUSTINE OF CANTERBURY / Cutts, Edward L – London: Methuen, 1895. (Leaders of religion) – 1mf – us A.T.L.A. [240]
Augustine, St, Bishop of Hippo *see* SELECTIONS
Augustine, Saint, Bishop of Hippo *see*
- THE CONFESSIONS OF ST AUGUSTINE, BISHOP OF HIPPO
- SELECT ANTI-PELAGIAN TREATISES OF ST AUGUSTINE
- SELECTIONS
- THE SOLILOQUIES OF ST AUGUSTINE

DES AUGUSTINERPROPSTES IOANNES BUSCH : CHRONICON WINDESHEMENSE UND LIBER DE REFORMATIONE MONASTERIORUM / Busch, Ioannes; ed by Grube, K – Halle, 1886 – Dfl53.00 – ne Slangenburg [240]
THE AUGUSTINIAN REVOLUTION IN THEOLOGY : ILLUSTRATED BY A COMPARISON WITH THE TEACHING OF THE ANTIOCHENE DIVINES OF THE FOURTH AND FIFTH CENTURIES / Allin, Thomas; ed by Lias, John James – London: J. Clarke, 1911 – 1mf – us A.T.L.A. [240]
Augustinis, Aemilius M de *see* THE TRUE FAITH OF OUR FOREFATHERS
AUGUSTINS LEHRE VON DER EINHEIT UND DREIEINHEIT IN IHRER BEDEUTUNG FUER SEIN UND ERKENNEN / Mueller, Eberhard Johannes – 1929 – 1 – us A.T.L.A. [240]
Augustinus du Paz *see* HISTOIRE GENEALOGIQUE DE PLUSIEURS MAISONS ILLUSTRES DE BRETAGNE
AUGUSTINUS LIBER SOLILOQUIORUM – Col. Agr., 1639 – 1mf – 8 – ne Slangenburg [240]
Augustinus, St *see*
- CONFESSIONES
- CONTRA ADVERSARIUM LEGIS ET PROPHETARUM – CONTRA PRISCILLIANISTAS ET ORIGENISTAS; OROSIUS – DE ERRORE PRISCILLIANISTARUM ET ORIGENISTARUM
- DE DOCTRINA CHRISTIANA
- IN PSALMOS (SIECLE 7)
- RETRACTATIONES

AUGUSTINUS: SEIN THEOLOGISCHES SYSTEM / Dorner, Isaak August – 1873 – 1 – us A.T.L.A. [240]
AUGUSTINUS SEU DOCTRINA SANCTI AUGUSTINI DE HUMANAE NATURAE SANITATE / Jansenius, Corn. – Rothomagi. Tomus 1-3. 1652 – 56mf – 8 – ne Slangenburg [240]
AUGUSTINUS-BLATT – Duesseldorf, Germany. 1918-34 – 2r – 1 – gw Mikrofilm [072]
Augustiny, Waldemar *see*
- DIE TOCHTER TROMSEES
- DIE WIEDERKEHR DES NOVALIS

AUGUSTUS BOHSE GENANNT TALANDER : EIN BEITRAG ZUR GESCHICHTE DER GALANTEN ZEIT IN DEUTSCHLAND / Schubert, Ernst – (Includes bibliographical references) – Breslau: F Hirt, 1911 – 1 – us U.W. Library [430]
AUGUSTUS CAESAR AND THE ORGANIZATION OF THE EMPIRE OF ROME / Firth, John B – New York: G.P. Putnam, 1903, c1902 – 1mf – us A.T.L.A. [240]
AUJOURD'HUI – Paris, 9 Mar 1942-17 Jul 1944 – 4r – 1 – uk British Libr Newspaper [072]
AUJOURD'HUI-QUEBEC – Mensuel d'Idees et d'Information. v1-3. 1965-67. SEM16P274 – 1r – 5 – Can$27.00 – cn Bibl Nat [971]
AUK – (1969- . 5,6. 1975- . 9) – v. 1-1884- – 1 – us UMI [590]
AUK (AMERICAN ORNITHOLOGIST UNION) – o.s.v1-8. New series v1-71. 1876-1883; 1884-1954 – 1 – us Princeton Micro [073]
AUK (AMERICAN ORNITHOLOGIST'S UNION) – Old series. v. 1-8. 1876-1883. New series. v. 1-71. 1884-1954 – 1 – us Princeton Micro [590]
Aul, Joachim *see*
- SCHOPENHAUER BIBLIOGRAPHIE
- SCHOPENHAUERS BEGRUENDUNGSTHEORIE IM LICHTE DER ERGEBNISSE DER MODERNEN WISSENSCHAFTSTHEORIE

Aulard, Francois Victor Alphonse *see* LES ORATEURS DE LA REVOLUTION: LA LEGISLATIVE ET LA CONVENTION
THE AULD KIRKYARD, FERGUS: IN IT, AND ABOUT IT / Fordyce, Alexander Dingwall – s.l.: s.n., 1882?. 05582. (Pre-1900 Canadiana) – 9 – cn C.I.H.M. [971]
AULD LICHT IDYLLS / Barrie, James Matthew – London: Hodder and Stoughton, 1888 – 1 roll – 1 – 1-55879-597-9 – uk Libr Preservation [830]
Aulen, Gustaf *see*
- H. REUTERDAHLS TEOLOGISKA ASKADNING
- DEN KRISTNA TANKENS TOLKNING AF JESU PERSON
- SYNDERNAS FOERLATELSE
- TILL BELYSNING AF DEN LUTHERSKA KYRKOIDEN

AULIA : "MAKANAN JANG SEHAT" DAN BEBERAPA ICHTIAR JANG LAIN BOEAT MEMELIHARAKAN KESEHATAN DAN MENOLONG MENJEMBOEHKAN PENJAKIT. TJETAKAN KEDOEA. DITERBITKAN DENGA IZIN HODOHAN – Djakarta, Djawa Goenseikanboe: Balai Poestaka, 2603. 44p (B.P.no.1519) – 21mf – 9 – ne IDC [360]
AULIO PERSIO FLACO-SATURNAE...ET SCHOLIIS (SIC) / Sanchez de las Brozas, Francisco – 1599 – 9 – 1.50f – sp Bibl Santa Ana [450]
THE AULNEAU COLLECTION, 1734-45 / ed by Jones, Arthur E – Montreal: Archives of St. Mary's College. 1893. 00064. (Pre-1900 Canadiana) – 9 – cn C.I.H.M. [971]
Aulnoy, Marie-Catherine d' *see* CONTES DES FEES
AUMSVILLE STAR – Aumsville, OR. -w. 5 Feb 1915-25 Dec 1930. 3 rolls. Incl. Weekly Record (Aumsville) – 1 – us U.O. Library [071]
Aunos y Perez, E *see* EL RENACIMIENTO Y PROBLEMAS DE DERECHO INTERNACIONAL...
AURA : CRITICO – LITERARIO – Manaos, Amazonas. 19 Nov 1909 – 1,5,6 – bl Biblioteca [072]

AURAS DE ARGEME / Villalobos Bote, Rufino – Coria: Edit. Fernandez, 1953 – 1 – sp Bibl Santa Ana [946]

AURELIA OU ORLEANS DELIVRE: POEME TRADUIT EN FRANCAIS / Roussy, Jean de – Paris: Merigot, Vve. Delatour, Prault fils, 1738. x,389p. 5 fiches. (Literature Collection) – 9 – 12.00 – fr Bibl Nationale [810]

Aurelius, Marcus *see* THE MEDITATIONS

AURICULAR CONFESSION IN THE PROTESTANT EPISCOPAL CHURCH / Hawks, Francis L – New York: Geo. P. Putnam, 1850 – 1mf – us A.T.L.A. [240]

O AURIFERO : ORGAO NOTICIOSO E INDEPENDENTE – Lagoa Dourada, 16 Aug-Sep 1932; Dec 1933 – 1,5,6 – bl Biblioteca [072]

L'AURORA – Paterson, NJ, Sep. 15, 1899-May 1930 – 1r – 1 – us I.H.R.C. [978]

L'AURORA – (Title varies: The New Aurora) – 1918-41 (complete) – 3r – 1 – ATLA R0145 – us A.T.L.A. [240]

L'AURORA – Utica, NY, 1928-1929 – 24mf or 1r – 1,9 – us I.H.R.C. [978]

A AURORA : PERIODICO LITTERARIO E CHISTOSO – Pao d'Assucar, Alagoas. 9 Set 1883 – 1,5,6 – bl Biblioteca [072]

A AURORA : PERIODICO LITTERARIO, NOTICIOSO E COMMERCIAL – Valenca, BA. 12 Jul 1883 – 1,5,6 – bl Biblioteca [072]

A AURORA – S. Salvador, BA. Dez 1867 – 1,5,6 – bl Biblioteca [072]

AURORA – (Continues Athabaska University Magazine) – Athabaska. v11-15. 1987/88-91 – 9 – Can$20.00y – cn Micromedia [073]

AURORA – Enterprise, OR. -w. 15 Dec 1893-15 May 1896. 1 roll – 1 – us U.O. Library [071]

AURORA – Manaus, Amazonas. 19 Fev-25 Mar 1908 – 1,5,6 – bl Biblioteca [072]

AURORA – Philadelphia. Pa. and predecessor. 1790-1812 – 1 – us UMI [071]

AURORA – Ystad, Sweden. 1927-57.Ystadsbladet Aurora, 1899-1927 – 178r – 1 – sw Kungliga [072]

AURORA – Zanesville. Ohio. 1838-1843 – 1 – us UMI [071]

AURORA *see* ATHABASKA UNIVERSITY MAGAZINE (ATHABASKA)

LA AURORA – Albuquerque, NM. v. 1-14. 1900-1915. (incomplete file) – 1 – $50.00 – us Presbyterian [071]

LA AURORA – [Habana]: Imprenta de la viuda Barcina y compa. v1 n1-v3 n1. oct 22 1865-may 3 1868 – us Res Libr [072]

THE AURORA – Antigonish, Nova Scotia. v1 n6. 12 jan 1882-v7 n174. 6 mai 1885 – 1r – 1 – Can$30.00 – cn Can Microfilming [072]

THE AURORA – Freetown, Sierra Leone. -w. 16 April-31 Dec 1921. 1 reel – 1 – uk British Libr Newspaper [072]

THE AURORA – Middle Church, Man.: Rupert's Land Industrial School, [1893?-189- or 19–] – 9 – cn C.I.H.M. [971]

AURORA ATHENIENSE – S. Salvador, BA. Out 1880 – 1,5,6 – bl Biblioteca [072]

AURORA BANNER – Ontario, CN. 1900-75 – 49r – 1 – cn Commonwealth Micro [072]

AURORA BOREALIS – 1833 – 4mf – 9 – £35.00 – uk Chadwyck [800]

AURORA BOREALIS – Aurora, OR. -w. 21 May 1908-31 Dec 1908. 1 roll – 1 – us U.O. Library [071]

AURORA BOREALIS – London, UK. 25 Mar 1821-29 Dec 1822 – 1r – 1 – uk British Libr Newspaper [072]

AURORA DA BAHIA : FOLHA POLITICA, E COMMERICAL – '(s.l.')-BA, Brazil. 3 out 1838; 11 mar 1839 – 1,5,6 – bl Biblioteca [072]

AURORA DAILY TIMES – Aurora, NV. 27-28 Nov and 12 Dec 1863 (3 issues only) – 1r – 1 – $50.00 – U04400 – us Library Micro [071]

AURORA EN COPACAVANA, LA / Calderon de la Barca, Pedro – Madrid: Rivadeneyra, 1850 – 1 – sp Bibl Santa Ana [946]

AURORA FLOYD / Braddon, Mary Elizabeth – British Fiction Archive: Unit 5 – 9 – uk Bell [830]

AURORA FLUMINENSE : JORNAL POLITICO E LITTERARIO – Rio de Janeiro, 21 Dec 1827-Dec 1835; May-30 Jul 1839 – 1,5,6 – bl Biblioteca [072]

AURORA LEIGH / Browning, Elizabeth Barrett – London: Chapman and Hall, 5th ed 1860 – 1 roll – 1 – 1-55879-348-8 – uk Libr Preservation [810]

AURORA NEWS – Aurora, NE. -w. Apr. 1877-Jun. 1887 – 1 – us NE Hist [071]

AURORA NEWS – Aurora, NE. -w. Apr. 1929-Nov. 1942 – 1 – us NE Hist [071]

AURORA NEWS-REGISTER – Aurora, NE. -w. Nov. 1942- – 1 – us NE Hist [071]

AURORA OBSERVER – (North Marion County Observer (Aurora)) – Aurora, OR. -w 27 Jun 1912-25 July 1941. – 4r – 1 – us U.O. Library [071]

AURORA OF THE VALLEY – Newbury, Vermont. Jan 1850-Dec 1868 – 13r – 1 – uk British Libr Newspaper [071]

Aurora Snow Shoe Club *see* CONSTITUTION AND BY-LAWS

AURORA SUN – Aurora, NE. -w. Aug. 1885-Jan. 1887; Mar. 1887-Nov. 1889; Feb. 1890-Nov. 1890. Incomplete; Jan. 1891-Dec. 1902; Mar. 1903-Jan. 1929 – 1 – us NE Hist [071]

AURORA SUN – Aurora. Neb. 1885-1929 – 1 – us UMI [071]

AURORA TRADE GUIDE AND ADVERTISER! – [Aurora, Ont.?]: J R Beden, [1865-18– or 19–] – 9 – cn C.I.H.M. [380]

AURORA UND CHRISTLICHE WOCHE – Buffalo, NY. oct 28 1921-dec 25 1936 (incomplete) – 5r – 1 – Inquire at Mikrofilmarchiv for details – gw Misc Inst [240]

AURORA VOLKSFREUND – Aurora, IL: Peter Klein, jul 2 1917-jun 16 1922 – 10r – 1 – us Res Libr [071]

L'AURORE / ed by Bibaud, Michel – Montreal, Canada. 10 mar 1817-4 sep 1819 – 1r – 1 – Can$35.00 – cn Can Microfilming [072]

L'AURORE – Fort-de-France. nov 1932-avr 1935 – 1 – fr A.C.R.P.P. [072]

L'AURORE – Paris. 1er oct 1897-2 aout 1914 – 1 – fr A.C.R.P.P. [072]

L'AURORE – Paris. sept 1944-1986 – 1 – fr A.C.R.P.P. [073]

L'AURORE : PROTESTANT – Montreal, Canada. v5 n39. 30 sep 1870; v7 n46. 15 nov 1872-v86 n21. 1 dec 1952 – 2r – 1 – Can$45.00r – cn Can Microfilming [072]

L'AURORE DE LA REPUBLIQUE – Vaugirard [Paris]: Impr de Moncheny. n1. feb 27 1848 – 1r – 1 – us Res Libr [072]

L'AURORE DES CANADAS / ed by Cinq-Mars, F – Montreal, Canada. 15 jan 1839-23 mar 1849 – 4r – 1 – Can$50.00r – cn Can Microfilming [072]

A AURORE MACAENSE – Macao: [Typographia Armenia, jan 14 1843-feb 3 1844 – 1r – 1 – us Res Libr [072]

AUS DANTES VERBANNUNG : LITERARHISTORISCHE STUDIEN / Scheffer-Boichorst, Paul – Straßburg, 1882 – 2mf – 9 – 3-89349-066-3 – gw Hänsel [450]

AUS DEM BOEHMERWALDE / Rank, Josef – 1917 – 1 – us I.U. Libraries [390]

AUS DEM FELDE / Wolff, Julius – Berlin: G Grote, 1895 – 1r – 1 – us U.W. Library [810]

AUS DEM LEBEN DER JUDEN DEUTSCHLANDS IM MITTELALTER / Berliner, Abraham; ed by Ellbogen, Ismar – 1996 – 2mf – 9 – DM62.00 – 3-8267-3195-6 – gw Hänsel [270]

AUS DEM LEBEN EINES DORPATER UNIVERSITAETSLEHRERS : ERINNERUNGEN DES MEDIZINERS PROF. DR. FRIEDRICH V. BIDDER, 1810-1894 – (Includes bibliographical references and index) – Wuerzburg: Holzner-Verlag, 1959, c1958 – 1 – us U.W. Library [370]

AUS DEM NACHLASS VARNHAGEN'S VON ENSE *see* TAGEBUECHER

AUS DEM NACHLASSE DES GRAFEN PROKESCH-OSTEN : BRIEFWECHSEL MIT HERRN VON GENTZ UND FUERSTEN METTERNICH – Wien. 2v. 1881 – 10mf – 9 – ne IDC [943]

AUS DEM NACHLASSE FRIEDRICHS VON GENTZ / ed by Prokesch von Osten, A – Wien. 2v. 1867-1868 – 8mf – 9 – ne IDC [943]

AUS DEM OSTLANDE: POSENER LAND UND WEICHSELGAU – Lissa i. P. v1-13, 1906-1918. Lacks v2. Includes Supp. Title varies. Film Mas C 705 – 1 – us H.U. Library [073]

AUS DEM PERSOENLICHEN VERKEHRE MIT FRANZ GRILLPARZER / Littrow-Bischoff, Auguste von – Wien: L Rosner, 1873 – 1r – 1 – us U.W. Library [920]

AUS DEM SOWJETLANDE : INFORMATIONSBULLETIN DER GESELLSCHAFT FUER KULTURELLE VERBINDUNG DER SOWJETUNION MIT DEM AUSLANDE – (Available: v1, 1931 (p.1-24)) – Moscow, 1931.-v1-5 – 1mf – 8 – BR-8116 2 – ne IDC [947]

AUS DEM TAGEBUCHE ERZHERZOG JOHANNS VON OESTERREICH 1810-1815 / ed by Krones, F von – Innsbruck, 1891 – 3mf – 9 – ne IDC [943]

AUS DEM TAGEWERK EINES ASSYRISCHEN ZAUBERPRIESTERS / Ebeling, Erich – (Mitteilungen der altorientalischen gesellschaft. v. 5, pt. 3). Leipzig. 1931. BNE-20,104 1 – 9 – ne IDC [290]

AUS DEN ARCHIVEN DES BELGISCHEN KOLONIALMINISTERIUMS BERLIN, 1916 / Belgium. Ministere des Colonies – 1Folge. Berlin, 1918 – 1 – us Res Libr [960]

AUS DEN TAGEBUECHERN DES GRAFEN PROKESCH VON OSTEN...1830-1834 / ed by Prokesch von Osten, A – Wien, 1909 – 3mf – 9 – ne IDC [943]

AUS DEN VORBERGEN : NOVELLEN / Heyse, Paul – 2. Aufl. Berlin: W Hertz, 1893 – 1 – us U.W. Library [830]

AUS DER BRIEFMAPPE EINES BURGTHEATERDIREKTORS / Dingelstedt, Franz, Freiherr von – (Includes bibliographical references and indexes) – Wien: Schroll, 1925 – 1 – us U.W. Library [860]

AUS DER BURSCHENZEIT : EIN IDYLL / Leander, Richard – Halle a/S: M Niemeyer, 1876 – 1r – 1 – us U.W. Library [810]

AUS DER ECKE : SIEBEN NEUE NOVELLEN / Riehl, Wilhelm Heinrich – Bielefeld: Velhagen und Klasing, 1874 – 1r – 1 – us U.W. Library [830]

AUS DER FERNE. ARIE FUR SINGSTIMME UND PIANOFORTE / Righini, V – Berlin: Concha, 180- – 1 – us Sibley [780]

AUS DER GESCHICHTE DER DEUTSCH-ISRAELITISCHEN GEMEINDE IN HAMBURG / Haarbleicher, M M – Ed. 2. Hamburg. 1886. BJ-23-111 1 – 9 – ne IDC [943]

AUS DER HEIMAT : NEUE GEDICHTE / Prutz, Robert Eduard – Leipzig: F A Brockhaus, 1858 – 1r – 1 – us U.W. Library [810]

AUS DER JUGENDZEIT: LEBENSERINNERUNGEN / Stahr, Adolf Wilhelm Theodor – Schwerin i. M., U. Hildebrand, 1870-77. 2 v. in l. (His Lebenserrinnerungen, I.) Film Mas 8405 – 1 – us H.U. Library [920]

AUS DER RECHTSGESCHICHTE BENEDIKTINISCHER VERBAENDE / Molitor, R – Muenster i.W. v1-3. 1928-33 – 37mf – 8 – Dfl130.00 – ne Slangenburg [240]

AUS DER WAFFENKAMMER DES SOZIALISMUS – Frankfurt, 1903-1910 – 1r – 1 – DM140.00 – gw Mikro Press [072]

AUS DER WAFFENKAMMER DES SOZIALISMUS – Frankfurt Main, Germany. 1903-10 – 1r – 1 – gw Mikrofilm [073]

AUS DER WERDEZEIT DES CHRISTENTUMS : STUDIEN UND CHARAKTERISTIKEN / Geffcken, Johannes – Leipzig: B.G. Teubner, 1909 (Aus Natur und Geisteswelt; 54. Bdchen) – 1mf – us A.T.L.A. [240]

AUS DER ZEIT : RIGASCHE ZUSTAENDE – 1845(1) – 1mf – 9 – ne IDC [947]

AUS DEUTSCHEN BUSSBUECHERN : EIN BEITRAG ZUR DEUTSCHEN CULTURGESCHICHTE / Friedberg, Emil – Halle: Verlag der Buchh. des Waisenhauses, 1868 – 1mf – us A.T.L.A. [306]

AUS EIGENER KRAFT / Hillern, Wilhelmine von – 2. Aufl. Leipzig: E Keil's Nachfolger. 3v. [189-?] – 1 – us U.W. Library [830]

AUS EINER GANZ KLEINEN GARNISON : A NOVEL – Dresden-Niedersedlitz: H G Muenchmeyer, [18–?] – 1r – 1 – us U.W. Library [830]

AUS FRIEDRICH HEBBELS WERDEZEIT / Neumann, Alfred – (Includes bibliographical references) – Zittau: M Boehme, 1899 – 1 – us U.W. Library [430]

AUS FRIEDRICHS HEBBELS KORRESPONDENZ : UNGEDRUCKTE BRIEFE VON UND AN DEN DICHTER NEBST BEITRAEGEN ZUR TEXTKRITIK EINZELNER WERKE / ed by Hirth, Friedrich – Muenchen, Leipzig, 1913 – 2mf – DM62.00 – 3-8267-3021-6 – gw Hänsel [860]

AUS GOETHE'S FREUNDESKREISE : DARSTELLUNGEN AUS DEM LEBEN DES DICHTERS / Duentzer, Heinrich – (Includes bibliographical references) – Braunschweig: F Vieweg, 1868 – 1r – 1 – us U.W. Library [430]

AUS GOETHES LEBENSKREIS : DREI ESSAYS / Kahn-Wallerstein, Carmen – Bern: A Francke, 1946 – 1r – 1 – us U.W. Library [430]

AUS GROSSEN HOEHEN : ALPENROMAN / Ompteda, Georg, Freiherr von – Berlin: F Fontane, 1903 – 1r – 1 – us U.W. Library [830]

AUS HELLAS, ROM UND THULE : CULTUR- UND LITTERATURBILDER / Poestion, J C (Josef Calasanz) – 2. Aufl. Leipzig: W Friedrich, [1884] – 1r – 1 – us U.W. Library [410]

AUS HERDERS NACHLASS / Herder, Johann Gottfried; ed by Duentzer, Heinrich & Herder, Ferdinand Gottfried von – (Includes bibliographical references) – Frankfurt a.M.: Meidinger, 1856-57 – 1r – 1 – us U.W. Library [430]

AUS KAMPFGEWUEHL UND EINSAMKEIT : GEDICHTE / Seidel, Robert – Stuttgart: J H W Dietz, 1895 – 1r – 1 – us U.W. Library [810]

AUS KLASSISCHER ZEIT : WIELAND UND REINHOLD: ORIGINAL-MITTHEILUNGEN ALS BEITRAEGE ZUR GESCHICHTE DES DEUTSCHEN GEISTESLEBENS IM 18. JAHRHUNDERT / Keil, Robert – (Includes index) – Leipzig: W Friedrich, [1890] – 1r – 1 – us U.W. Library [430]

AUS KUNST UND LEBEN / Keppler, Paul Wilhelm von – 2., unver Aufl. Freiburg i.B.; St Louis, MO: Herder, 1905 – 1mf – 9 – 0-8370-6818-5 – 1986-0818 – us A.T.L.A. [700]

AUS LAVATERS BRIEFTASCHE : UNGEDRUCKTE HANDSCHRIFTE NEBST LAVATER-ERINNERUNGEN MIT FACSIMILES / Lavater, Johann Caspar; ed by Mueller, Gustav Adolf – Muenchen: Seitz & Schauer, 1897 – 1r – 1 – us U.W. Library [800]

AUS LEBEN UND ARBEIT / Schuchhardt, Karl – Berlin: W. de Gruyter, 1944. xiv,392p. illus. maps. 51 numbered plates – 1 – us U.W. Library [930]

AUS LUISE HENSELS JUGENDZEIT : NEUE BRIEFE UND GEDICHTE, ZUM JAHRHUNDERTTAG IHRER KONVERSION (8. DEZEMBER 1818) / Cardauns, Hermann – (Includes bibliographical references) – Freiburg i.B.: Herder, 1918 – 1r – 1 – us U.W. Library [920]

AUS MASORAH UND TALMUDKRITIK: EXEGETISCHEN STUDIEN / Koenigsberger, Bernhard – Berlin: Mayer & Mueller, 1892. 1 fiche – 9 – us A.T.L.A. [270]

AUS MEINEM LEBEN : SELBSTBIOGRAPHIE / Bretschneider, Karl Gottlieb – Gotha: J.G. Mueller, 1852 – 1mf – us A.T.L.A. [240]

AUS MEINER JUGEND : AUTOBIOGRAPHIE / Lazarus, Moritz – 1996 – 2mf – 9 – DM62.00 – 3-8267-3188-3 – gw Hänsel [920]

AUS MEINER LIEDERMAPPE : GEDICHTE / Zeise, Heinrich – Hannover: A Weichelt, 1883 – 1r – 1 – us U.W. Library [810]

AUS POLITIK UND ZEITGESCHICHTE – Bonn: Bundeszentrale fuer politische Bildung, etc. -w. "Beilage zur Wochen Zeitung, das Parlament". 1945- – 1 – us U.W. Library [073]

AUS SIBIRIEN. LOZE BLAETTER AUS DEM TAGEBUCHE EINES REISENDE LINGUISTEN / [Radlov, V V] – Leipzig, 1884 – v1-2. 534, 486p – 8 – ne IDC [400]

AUS VERGANGENHEIT UND GEGENWART DER JUDEN. IN DEN POSENER LANDEN / Heppner, A & Herzberg, I – 2v. Koschmin. omberg. 1909. BJ-23-112 1 – 9 – ne IDC [943]

AUS VIELER ZEUGEN MUND – (Lacking: 1955-56) – 1910-92 – 8r – 1 – ATLA S0551 – us A.T.L.A. [073]

Ausbourg, A d' *see* LES SUCCESSIONS EN DROIT INTERNATIONAL PRIVE...

AUSCHWITZ TRIAL OF 1963-1965 PAMPHLET COLLECTION – 1963 – 1 – CSUXANS1144-B – us Hoover Inst Photo [340]

AUSDRUCKSBEWEGUNGEN IN HEINRICH VON KLEISTS WERK / Blau, Georg – 1995 – 7mf – 9 – DM130.00 – 3-8267-2093-8 – gw Hänsel [430]

DIE AUSEINANDERSETZUNG MIT DER FRANZOESISCHEN REVOLUTION IN DER GESCHICHTSSCHREIBUNG DER "KLEINDEUTSCHEN" SCHULE / Voelker, Monika – Frankfurt a.M., 1978 – 3mf – 9 – DM76.00 – 3-89349-382-4 – gw Hänsel [370]

AUSERLESENE ANMERCKUNGEN UEBER ALLERHAND WICHTIGE MATERIEN UND SCHRIFTEN / ed by Thomasius, Christian – Frankfurt, Leipzig. bd 1-5. 1704-1707 (mf ed 1993) – 9mf – 9 – DM260.00 – 3-89131-093-5 – gw Fischer [073]

AUSERLESENE SEND-SCHREIBEN DERER ALTEN....1700 / Arnold, Gottfried – 1 – us A.T.L.A. [240]

DAS AUSERWAHLTE VOLK – May 1937-May 1938 (complete) – 1r – 1 – ATLA S0664A – us A.T.L.A. [073]

AUSFAHRT UND LANDUNG : FESTGABE FUER BIBLIOTHEKSDIREKTOR WOLFGANG VAN DER BRIELE, ZUM 65. GEBURTSTAG AM 16. MAI 1959 – (Includes bibliographical references) – Wuppertal: J H Born, 1960 – 1 – us U.W. Library [020]

EIN AUSFLUG NACH COMACCHIO / Jacoby, Leopold – Triest: J Dase, 1881 – 1r – 1 – us U.W. Library [800]

AUSFUEHRLICHE BESCHREIBUNG DES MEISSNISCHEN OBER-ERTZGEBUERGES / Lehmann, Christian – Leipzig: Bey Friedrich Lanckischens Erben, 1747. 26, 1005, 35 p. Film Mas 8986 – 1 – us H.U. Library [910]

AUSFUEHRLICHE ENCYKLOPAEDIE DER GESAMMTEN STAATSARZNEIKUNDE (AEL, ABT 3;23) / Most, Georg Friedrich – Leipzig. 2 bde + 1 suppl bd. 1838, 1840 (mf ed 1995) – 29mf – 9 – DM410.00 – 3-89131-219-9 – gw Fischer [610]

AUSFUEHRLICHER BERICHT VON ALLERHAND NEUEN BUECHERN UND ANDEREN DINGEN SO ZUR HEUTIGEN HISTORIE DER BELEHRSAMKEIT GEHOERIG / ed by Woltereck, C et al – Frankfurt, Leipzig, 1708-1710 (mf ed 1993) – 5mf – 9 – DM220.00 – 3-89131-088-9 – gw Fischer [943]

AUSFUHRLICHE VOLKS-GEWERBSLEHRE ODER ALLGEMEINE UND BESONDERE TECHNOLOGIE / Poppe, G H M von – Stuttgart 1859 – 1 – DM40.00 – gw Mikro Press [600]

AUSFUHRLICHE VOLKS-GEWERBSLEHRE; ODER, ALLGEMEINE UND BESONDERE TECHNOLOGIE ZUR BELEHRUNG UND ZUM NUTZEN FUR ALLE STENDE / Poppe, Johann Heinrich Moritz von – 1833-34 – 1 – us U.W. Library [380]

AUSFUHRLICHER BERICHT UEBER DIE VERHANDLUNGEN.. / Deutscher Webertag. 1st. Glauchau – Crimmitschau. 1871. 68p. (Serial publications of German trade unions in the Memorial Library, University of Wisconsin-Madison.) – 1 – us U.W. Library [330]

AUSG. NUERNBERG – 1933, 19.4.-31.5. – 1 – DM75.00 – gw Mikro Press [943]

Ausgabe O (Gummersbach) der Koelnischen Rundschau *see* OBERBERGISCHE VOLKS-ZEITUNG

AUSGANGSPUNKT UND ZIEL DER EVANGELISCHEN DOGMATIK / Kirn, Otto – Leipzig: Doerffling & Franke, 1896. 1 fiche – 9 – us A.T.L.A. [240]

AUSGEBURTEN DES MENSCHENWAHNS IM SPIEGEL DER HEXENPROZESSE UND DER AUTO DA FES / Koenig, B(runo) Emil – Rudolstadt: A. Bock, (1893). 811p. ill., plates – 1 – us U.W. Library [150]

AUSGEWAEHLT WERKE / Rosegger, Peter – Wien, A. Hartleben, 1888-91. 6 v. Film Mas C 568 – 1 – us H.U. Library [080]

AUSGEWAEHLTE ASPEKTE RECHNERGESTUETZTER INFORMATIONS- UND KOMMUNIKATIONSTECHNOLOGIEN / Schoop, Michael – 1994 – 1mf – DM60.00 – 3-8267-2021-0 – gw Hänsel [000]

AUSGEWAEHLTE BRIEFE = CORRESPONDENCE. SELECTIONS / Winckelmann, Johann Joachim; ed by Uhde-Bernays, Hermann – Leipzig: Insel-Verlag, 1925 – 1r – 1 – us U.W. Library [700]

AUSGEWAEHLTE DICHTUNGEN / Klopstock, Friedrich Gottlieb; ed by Heinemann, K – (Includes bibliographical references) – Bielefeld: Velhagen & Klasing, 1912 – 1 – us U.W. Library [810]

AUSGEWAEHLTE DICHTUNGEN / Vierordt, Heinrich – Heidelberg: C Winter, 1906 – 1r – 1 – us U.W. Library [810]

AUSGEWAEHLTE ERZAEHLUNGEN / Keller, Gottfried – Wien: W Frick, 1945 – 1 – us U.W. Library [830]

AUSGEWAEHLTE FABELN UND GEDICHTE / Pfeffel, Gottlieb Konrad – Stuttgart: Kroener, [18–?] – 1r – 1 – us U.W. Library [810]

AUSGEWAEHLTE GEDICHTE / Hesse, Hermann – 1.-5. Aufl. Berlin: S Fischer, 1921 – 1r – 1 – us U.W. Library [810]

AUSGEWAEHLTE KAPITEL ZU EINER HANS-SACHS-GRAMMATIK / Albrecht, Julius – 1995 – 1mf – 9 – DM48.00 – 3-8267-3141-7 – gw Hänsel [430]

AUSGEWAEHLTE KLEINE SCHRIFTEN / Gelzer, Heinrich – Leipzig: B.G. Teubner, 1907 – 1mf – us A.T.L.A. [240]

AUSGEWAEHLTE KRITISCHE SCHRIFTEN = SELECTIONS. 1975 / Tieck, Ludwig – (Includes bibliographical references. Includes index) – Tuebingen: M. Niemeyer, c1975 – 1r – 1 – us U.W. Library [430]

AUSGEWAEHLTE NOVELLEN / Storm, Theodor – Weimar: Alexander Duncker, [1919?] – 1 – us U.W. Library [830]

AUSGEWAEHLTE NOVELLEN / Zschokke, Heinrich – Leipzig, M. Hesse, 1904. 6 v. in 2. Film Mas 8640 – 1 – us H.U. Library [830]

AUSGEWAEHLTE PREDIGTEN UND REDEN / Einhorn, David – New York: E. Steiger, 1880. viii,399p. With: Gandhi and Anarchy by C. Sankaran Nair. 1 reel. 1247 – 1 – us U.W. Library [290]

AUSGEWAEHLTE PSALMEN / Gunkel, Hermann – (Includes index) – 4. verb. Aufl. Gottingen: Vandenhoeck & Ruprecht, 1917 – 1mf – 9 – 0-8370-3420-5 – 1985-1420 – us A.T.L.A. [220]

AUSGEWAEHLTE PSALMEN / Gunkel, Hermann – (Includes index) – Goettingen: Vandenhoeck und Ruprecht, 1904 – 1mf – 9 – 0-8370-9784-3 – 1986-3784 – us A.T.L.A. [220]

AUSGEWAEHLTE SCHRIFTEN / Carl, Erzherzog von Oesterreich – Wien, Leipzig. 7v. 1893-1894 – 39mf – 9 – ne IDC [920]

AUSGEWAEHLTE SCHRIFTEN / Mueller, Otto – Gera, C. G. Griesbach, 18-?. 12 v. in 6. (Title taken from cover) Film Mas 8547 – 1 – us H.U. Library [080]

AUSGEWAEHLTE SCHRIFTEN / Saphir, Moritz Gottlieb – 4Aufl. Bruenn, etc., F. Karafiat, 1870. 10 v. in 5. (Half-title: M. G. Saphir's Schriften. Cabinets-Ausgabe.) Film Mas 8494 – 1 – us H.U. Library [800]

AUSGEWAEHLTE SCHRIFTEN = SELECTIONS / Saphir, Moritz Gottlieb – 6. Aufl. Bruenn: Fr Karafiat, 1871 – 1 – us U.W. Library [800]

AUSGEWAEHLTE SCHRIFTEN / Speidel, Ludwig; ed by Radecki, Sigismund von – 1. Aufl. Wedel in Holstein: Alster Verlag C Brauns, 1947 – 1r – 1 – us U.W. Library [430]

AUSGEWAEHLTE SCHRIFTEN DES HEILIGEN GREGORIUS DES GROSSEN, PAPSTES UND KIRCHENLEHRERS = SELECTIONS / Gregory 1, Pope – (In German. Translated from Latin) – Kempten: Jos Koesel. 2v. 1873-74 – 4mf – 9 – 0-8370-8514-4 – 1986-2514 – us A.T.L.A. [240]

AUSGEWAEHLTE SCHRIFTEN UND BRIEFE = SELECTIONS. 1948 / Winckelmann, Johann Joachim; ed by Rehm, Walter – (Includes bibliographical references and indexes) – Wiesbaden: Dieterich, 1948 – 1r – 1 – us U.W. Library [700]

AUSGEWAEHLTE SCHRIFTEN VON COLUMBAN, ALKUIN, DODANA, JONAS, HRABANUS MAURUS, NOTKER BALBULUS, HUGO VON SANKT VIKTOR UND PERALDUS. EINL. U. UEBERS. P. GABRIEL MEIER / Meier, P Gabriel – Freiburg, 1890 – 6mf – 8 – Dfl25.00 – ne Slangenburg [240]

AUSGEWAEHLTE VOLKSWIRTSCHAFTLICHE UND POLITISCHE SCHRIFTEN / Bastiat, Frederic – 1859, uebersetzt von Karl Julius Bergius, 1859, 2v – 9 – 1.00f – at Libertarian Micro [335]

AUSGEWAEHLTE WERKE / Bjornson, Bjornstjerne; ed by Schaefer, Thomas – Berlin: P.J. Oestergaard, (1910). 3v – 1 – us U.W. Library [430]

AUSGEWAEHLTE WERKE / Brachvogel, Albert Emil – Neue, vom Verfasser revidierte Ausg. Berlin, O. Janke 1872-74? 4 v. Film Mas 8279 – 1 – us H.U. Library [430]

AUSGEWAEHLTE WERKE / Hoelderlin, Friedrich; ed by Schwab, Christoph Theodor – (Includes bibliographical references) – Stuttgart: J G Cotta, 1874 – 1 – us U.W. Library [800]

AUSGEWAEHLTE WERKE / Vischer, Friedrich Theodor; ed by Keyssner, Gustav – Stuttgart: Deutsche Verlags-Anstalt, 1918 – 1r – 1 – us U.W. Library [800]

AUSGEWAEHLTE WERKE / Vischer, Friedrich Theodor; ed by Keyssner, Gustav – Stuttgart: Deutsche Verlags-Anstalt. 3v. 1918 – 1 – us U.W. Library [890]

AUSGEWAEHLTE WERKE / Weerth, Georg; ed by Kaiser, Bruno – (Includes bibliographical references and index) – Berlin: Verlag Volk und Welt, 1948 – 1 – us U.W. Library [800]

AUSGEWAHLTE AKADEMISCHE REDEN UND ABHANDLUNGEN / Stade, Bernhard – (Includes bibliographical references) – Giessen:J Ricker, 1899 – 9 – 0-8370-5353-6 – 1985-3353 – us A.T.L.A. [220]

AUSGEWAHLTE SONATEN. SONATA 1, 2, 3, 4, 5, 6, PER FLAUTO TRAVERSO CON CEMBALO O CON BASSO / Quantz, Johann Joachim – Leipzig. 1921. 7v – 1 – 23.00 – us L of C Photodup [780]

DER AUSLAENDER VOR DEM STANDESAMT / Bergmann, A – Berlin, 1926 – 2mf – 9 – ILM-3328/1 – ne IDC [327]

DAS AUSLAND: UEBERSCHAU DER NEUESTEN FORSCHUNGEN AUF DEM GEBIETE DER NATUR-, ERD-, UND VOELKERKUNDE – Stuttgart. v49-66. 1876-93 – 1 – 391.00 – us L of C Photodup [910]

AUSLEGUNG DER EPISTEL S. PAULI AN DIE EPHESER IN ZEHEN PREDIGT DEN DOERFFPFARHERRN VND HAUSVETERN ZU DIENST EINFELTIGLICH VERFASSEL / Major, G – Wittemberg, 1559 – 9mf – ne IDC [240]

AUSLEGUNG DES 129TH PSALMEN DAUIDS AUFF GEGENWERTIGEN ZUSTAND DER KIRCHEN ZU WITTENBERG... / Huber, S – Wittemberg, 1593 – 1mf – ne IDC [240]

DIE AUSLEGUNG DES HOHENLIEDES IN DER JUEDISCHEN GEMEINDE UND DER GRIECHISCHEN KIRCHE / Riedel, Wilhelm – (Includes bibliographical references and index) – Leipzig: A Deichert (Georg Boehme), 1898 – 1mf – 9 – 0-8370-4896-6 – 1985-2896 – us A.T.L.A. [220]

AUSLEGUNG VON SCHRIFTABSCHNITTEN ZUM ZWECK DES HOEHEREN SCHULUNTERRICHTS / Lange, H – Breslau: Grass, Barth, 1867 – 1mf – 9 – 0-8370-8586-1 – 1986-2586 – us A.T.L.A. [220]

AUS'M GEWOHNTEM G'LEIS : POSSE MIT GESANG IN FUENF ABTHEILUNGEN / Anzengruber, Ludwig – Stuttgart: J G Cotta, [1879] – 1r – 1 – us U.W. Library [820]

AUSRININKAS (HY. JONAS SLIUPA) / Girdvainis, J V – Kaunas, 1934 – 1r – 1 – us I.H.R.C. [947]

DIE AUSROTTUNG DES PROTESTANTISMUS IN SALZBURG UNTER ERZBISCHOF FIRMIAN UND SEINEN NACHFOLGERN : EIN BEITRAG ZUR KIRCHENGESCHICHTE DES ACHTZEHNTEN JAHRHUNDERTS / Arnold, Carl Franklin – Halle: Verein fuer Reformationsgeschichte, 1900-1901. ([Schriften des Vereins fuer Reformationsgeschichte; Bd. 67, 69]) – 1mf – us A.T.L.A. [240]

AUSS GLAREANI MUSICK EIN USSZUG / Glarean, Heinrich – 1559 – 9 – us Sibley [780]

AUSSAAT UND ERNTE : GEDICHTE / Wills, Franz Hermann – Berlin: E Schmidt, 1946 – 1r – 1 – us U.W. Library [810]

AUSSENOHRCHARAKTERISTIK BEI VERSCHIEDENEN NAGERN / Blaheta, Roman – 1994 – 2mf – DM80.00 – 3-8267-2076-8 – gw Hänsel [574]

AUSSENPOLITIK : ZEITSCHRIFT FUER INTERNATIONALE FRAGEN – Stuttgart, 1950-71. v1-22. BH-1810 1 – 9 – ne IDC [327]

AUSSENPOLITIK ZWISCHEN MACHTPOLITIK UND DOGMA : DIE DEUTSCH-ITALIENISCHEN BEZIEHUNGEN VON DER JAHRESWENDE 1932/33 BIS ZUR STRESA-KONFERENZ / Poulain, Marc – Frankfurt a.M., 1971 – 2mf – DM62.00 – 3-89349-997-0 – gw Hänsel [320]

AUSSENPOLITISCHE STUDIEN : FESTGABE FUER OTTO KOEBNER / ed by Arntz, W – Stuttgart, 1930 – 5mf – 9 – ILM-3365/1 – ne IDC [340]

DIE AUSSEREUROPAEISCHEN LAUBMOOSE / Roth, G – Dresden. 1911. BZ-195 2 – 8 – ne IDC [580]

AUSSERORDENTLICHER INTERNATIONALER SOZIALISTEN-KONGRESS ZU BASEL AM NOV. 24 UND 25, 1912 / International Socialist Congress. 9th. 1912 – Berlin, 1912 – 1 – $35.00r – us Hoover Inst Photo [335]

AUSSIGER TAGBLATT – Aussig, nov 2 1928-38, nov 1 1939-aug 30 1941 – 1 – Dist. gw Mikrofilm – gw Misc Inst [943]

AUSSLEGUNG DER EUANGELIEN VON DEN FUERNEMBSTEN FESTEN VOM ADVENT BISS AUFF OSTERN. [3 AND 4] / Mathesius, Johannes – Nuernberg, 1571 – 10mf – ne IDC [240]

Austin, Alfred *see*
- ENGLISH LYRICS
- THE HUMAN TRAGEDY
- THE POETRY OF THE PERIOD
- PRINCE LUCIFER

AUSTIN AMERICAN-STATESMAN – Austin. Texas. 1 Dec 1973- – 1 – us UMI [071]

Austin, Benjamin Fish *see*
- THE JESUITS: THEIR ORIGIN, HISTORY, AIMS, PRINCIPLES, IMMORAL TEACHINGS..
- POPULAR SINS: A SERIES OF SERMONS AGAINST THE SINS OF THE TIMES

Austin, C F *see* MUSCI APPALACHIANI

AUSTIN CITY GAZETTE – Austin, TX. 1839-42 – 1r – 1 – us Ross [071]

AUSTIN ELLIOT / Kingsley, Henry – British Fiction Archive: Unit 2 – 9 – uk Bell [830]

AUSTIN, LINUS, JOURNAL, MS P.P. – 1872-1905 – 1r – 1 – us Western Res [338]

AUSTIN NEWS – Chicago. Ill. 1953-1965 – 1 – us UMI [071]

Austin. Texas. Highland Park Baptist Church *see* MINUTES

Austin, Thomas *see* TWO FIFTEENTH CENTURY COOKERY-BOOKS

THE AUSTINIAN THEORY OF LAW : BEING AN EDITION OF LECTURES 1, 5 AND 6 OF AUSTIN'S "JURISPRUDENCE" AND OF AUSTIN'S "ESSAY ON THE USES OF THE STUDY OF JURISPRUDENCE" WITH CRITICAL NOTES AND EXCURSUS / Brown, W Jethro – (LLMC's copy lacks 135-136p & 335-336p) – London: John Murray, 1906 – 5mf – 9 – $7.50 – LLMC 95-188 – us L.L.M.C. [340]

AUSTRAL AVIAN RECORD / ed by Mathews, G M – London, 1912-1927. v1-5 – 20mf – 9 – Z-2006/2 – ne IDC [073]

AUSTRALASIA AND THE WORLD'S EVANGELISATION : ADDRESSES DELIVERED AT THE STUDENT CONFERENCES ON HOME AND FOREIGN MISSIONS, MELBOURNE, AUSTRALIA, APR 10-12 1903, AND CHRISTCHURCH, NEW ZEALAND, MAY 2-3 1903 – Sydney: Australasian Student Union, [1903?] – 1mf – 9 – 0-8370-7194-1 – 1986-1194 – us A.T.L.A. [240]

Australasia. Methodist Missionary Society. Fiji District *see* ANNUAL SYNOD MINUTES AND JOURNALS

AUSTRALASIAN BIOGRAPHICAL ARCHIVE (ANZO-BA) : SUPPLEMENT / ed by Mediavilla, Victor Herrero – 1995 – 119mf – 9 – diazo DM4,800.00 (silver DM5,400.00 ISBN: 3-598-32925-3) – 3-598-32924-5 – gw Saur [920]

AUSTRALASIAN DECORATOR AND PAINTER – Sydney, Melbourne, Australia. Oct 1908-Dec 1946 – 22mqn r – 1 – uk British Libr Newspaper [073]

AUSTRALASIAN ENGINEER – Sydney, 31 Jul 1925-Oct 1972 – 58r – 1 – uk British Libr Newspaper [073]

THE AUSTRALASIAN HEBREW – Sydney. v. 1, no. 1-2, no. 26. 22 Nov 1895-13 Nov 1896 – 1 – us NY Public [073]

AUSTRALASIAN INSURANCE AND BANKING RECORD – Melbourne, 1886-1921 – 68r – 1 – uk British Libr Newspaper [073]

AUSTRALASIAN MANUFACTURER – Sydney, 15 Nov 1919-24 Jun 1922; 21 Jun 1924-14 Jan 1967 – 158r – 1 – uk British Libr Newspaper [073]

AUSTRALASIAN PASTORALISTS' REVIEW – Melbourne, 16 Mar 1891-16 Feb 1939 – 1 – uk British Libr Newspaper [073]

AUSTRALASIAN SKETCHER – (Lacking: Jul-Dec 1881; 1883) – Melbourne, Apr 1873-Dec 1889 – 4r – 1 – uk British Libr Newspaper [072]

AUSTRALASIAN TRAVELLER – (Missing: Sep-Nov 1913) – Melbourne, 5 Jul 1913-6 Dec 1921 – 7mqn r – 1 – uk British Libr Newspaper [072]

AUSTRALIA : LAND OF NATURAL WONDERS – 1995 – 36p – 9 – 92-3-102688-7 – fr UNESCO [574]

AUSTRALIA : SESSION LAWS OF AUSTRALIA – 1980-93 – 9 – $974.00 set – us Hein [340]
Australia *see* MISCELLANEOUS NEWSPAPERS
AUSTRALIA AND ASEAN IN PERSPECTIVE : A SELECT BIBLIOGRAPHY (1974-1984) / Encarnacion, Violeta V – 1985 – A$10.00 – 0-86758-181-6 – at BISA [950]
AUSTRALIA AND NEW ZEALAND BULLETIN / London Missionary Society – Auckland, jan 1952-jul 1970 – 1r – 1 – PMB Doc413 – at Pacific Mss [980]
AUSTRALIA AND NEW ZEALAND JOURNAL OF CRIMINOLOGY – v1-12 – 9 – 120.00 – at Butterworths [340]
AUSTRALIA AND THE LEAGUE OF NATIONS / Ellis, A D – Melbourne, 1922 – 1mf – 1 – ILM-4097/1 – ne IDC [327]
Australia. Army. Military Court *see* PROCEEDINGS OF A MILITARY COURT HELD AT MANUS ISLAND, JUNE 1950-APRIL 1951
Australia. Dept. of External Affairs, Treaties, etc *see* INDONESIA, AUG. 18, 1967. EXCHANGE OF NOTES BETWEEN AUSTRALIA AND INDONESIA, CONSTITUTING AN AGREEMENT FOR THE FURTHER EXTENSION OF THE OPERATION OF THE TRADE AGREEMENT OF 17 DEC. 1959
Australia. Federal Council for Aboriginal Advancement. Sub-committee on Legislative Reform *see* GOVERNMENT LEGISLATION AND THE ABORIGINES
Australia. Northern Territory *see* GOVERNMENT GAZETTE
Australia. South *see* SOUTH AUSTRALIAN GOVERNMENT GAZETTE
Australia. Western *see* GOVERNMENT GAZETTE
AUSTRALIAN – 1 – F3,660.00 – sz Infoprint [072]
AUSTRALIAN – 1964- – 24r per yr – 1 – inquire – us Ross [072]
AUSTRALIAN – Canberra, 1964-96 – 373r – 1 – at Pascoe [072]
AUSTRALIAN – Sydney, 1824-48 – 10r – 1 – A$332.00 silver A$288.00 vesicular – at Pascoe [072]
AUSTRALIAN – Sydney, AT. 1971-1975 – 46r – $2,300.00 – R04161 – us Library Micro [072]
THE AUSTRALIAN – Big Brother Has His Eye on the Teachers.1965, 2p – 9 – 1.00f – at Libertarian Micro [335]
THE AUSTRALIAN – Canberra, Australia. -d. 15 July 1964-Dec 1971. 84 reels – 1 – uk British Libr Newspaper [072]
THE AUSTRALIAN – Singapore Blazes Trail Towards a Cashless Society. 21 Jan 1986 clipping. 1p – 9 – 1.00f – at Libertarian Micro [335]
THE AUSTRALIAN – Sydney, Australia. -w. Oct 1824-Jan 1829; Aug 1838-June 1848. 3 reels – 1 – uk British Libr Newspaper [072]
Australian and New Zealand Association for the Advancement of Science *see* CONGRESS PAPERS
AUSTRALIAN AND NEW ZEALAND GAZETTE – London, UK. 19 Oct 1850-17 Dec 1870; 1871-8 Feb 1873; 17 May 1873-Sep 1882 – 40r – 1 – uk British Libr Newspaper [072]
AUSTRALIAN ANNUAL REPORT FILE 1993 : THE TOP 500 PUBLIC COMPANIES / ed by McDonel, Mary – (1950-80. 14,568 reports A$3,000.00; 1981-89. 4,446 reports A$3,500.00; 1990-91. 1,000 reports A$3,500.00; 1992. 500 reports A$1,900.00; 1993 500 reports A$2,100.00. 1994. 500 reports on CD-ROM A$2,000.00) – Sydney, Australia: Australian Graduate School of Management, University of New South Wales, 1950- – 500mf per yr – 9 – A$2,100.00y subsc A$15.00f – at A.G.S.M. [650]
AUSTRALIAN ARCHITECTURAL PERIODICALS INDEX : STANTON LIBRARY – (Apply to publ for details) – 9 – at Pascoe [720]
AUSTRALIAN ASSOCIATION OF MATHS TEACHERS : JOURNAL – (Apply to publ for details) – 9 – at Pascoe [073]
AUSTRALIAN BAPTISTS, MISC. HISTORICAL ITEMS, 1868, 1870-71 – 38p – 1 – 5.00 – us Baptist [240]
AUSTRALIAN BIBLICAL REVIEW – 1951-92 (complete) – 3r – 1 – ATLA S0658 – us A.T.L.A. [073]
AUSTRALIAN BIOGRAPHIES : PART 1 – 28mf – 9 – A$80.00 – at State Libr Vic [920]
AUSTRALIAN BOARD OF MISSIONS : REVIEW BOOK – (Apply to publ for details) – 1910-72 – 9 – at Pascoe [030]
AUSTRALIAN BOOKS IN PRINT ON MICROFICHE – (1981-. By author and title. Lists all in-print Australian books and Australian publishers, personnel and tel. nos. Also lists all overseas publishers with Australian representatives as well as distribution details for Australian publishers. Monthly updates A$320.00y) – 9 – Monthly 1997 11 issues A$320.00 Annual single issue A$190.00 – at Thorpe Mf [010]
AUSTRALIAN BREWERS' JOURNAL – Melbourne, 20 Oct 1882; 20 Dec 1910-20 Dec 1921 – 11r – 1 – uk British Libr Newspaper [073]
AUSTRALIAN BREWING AND WINE JOURNAL *see* AUSTRALIAN BREWERS' JOURNAL
Australian Bureau of Statistics *see*
- COLONIAL MICROFICHE
- HISTORICAL MICROFICHE SERIES (1990). ANNUAL SUPPLEMENT
- HISTORICAL MICROFICHE SERIES (1901-84)
- HISTORICAL MICROFICHE SERIES (1986-1989). UPDATES

AUSTRALIAN BUSINESS – 1980-June 1995 – 9 – at Pascoe [073]
AUSTRALIAN CHURCHMAN – Sydney, 1867-70 – 1r – 1 – A$35.00 silver A$30.00 vesicular – at Pascoe [072]
AUSTRALIAN COUNCIL FOR OVERSEAS AID – Canberra. 80 docs. 1980-1991 – 36mf – 9 – ne IDC [320]
AUSTRALIAN ECONOMIC HISTORY REVIEW – (1977- . 5,6,9) – v. 2-. 1962- – 1 – us UMI [980]
AUSTRALIAN FIELD – Australia, Jan 1901-Feb 1912 – 12 1/2r – 1 – uk British Libr Newspaper [072]
AUSTRALIAN FINANCIAL REVIEW – 1 – F3,141.00 – sz Infoprint [072]
AUSTRALIAN FINANCIAL REVIEW – 1951- – 12r per yr – 1 – inquire – us Ross [072]
AUSTRALIAN FINANCIAL REVIEW – (Available on subsc. Apply for details) – 1982- – 9 – at Pascoe [073]
AUSTRALIAN FINANCIAL REVIEW – Sydney, 1951-96 – 360r – 1 – at Pascoe [073]
AUSTRALIAN FINANCIAL REVIEW – Sydney, 2 Jun 1971-28 Dec 1973 – 29r – 1 – uk British Libr Newspaper [072]
AUSTRALIAN FRIEND – (Lacking: some pgs) – 1962; 1977-86 – 1r – 1 – ATLA S0863 – us A.T.L.A. [073]
AUSTRALIAN GOVERNMENT GAZETTE – (Includes ed: General and Public Service) – Canberra, jul 2 1973-jun 1977 – 16r – 1 – us Res Libr [072]
AUSTRALIAN GOVERNMENT PUBLISHING SERVICE CATALOGUE ON MICROFICHE *see* AGPS CATALOGUE ON MICROFICHE
AUSTRALIAN GRASSES AND PASTURE PLANTS / Turner, F – 6479.N 1921 – 9 – ne IDC [580]
Australian Institute of Agricultural Science *see* JOURNAL
THE AUSTRALIAN ISRAELITE – Melbourne. v. 1, no. 1-4, no. 44. 30 Jun 1871-7 May 1875. Incomplete – 1 – us NY Public [073]
AUSTRALIAN JAZZ QUARTERLY : A MAGAZINE FOR THE CONNOISSEUR OF HOT MUSIC – Nos.1-31 (all publ). May 1946-Apr 1957. (Jazz Periodicals) – 1 reel – 1 – $75.00 – us UPA [780]
AUSTRALIAN JEWISH FORUM – Sydney. v. 1-9. no. 77. Feb 1941-Sept 1949 – 1 – us NY Public [270]
AUSTRALIAN JEWISH TIMES – 1953-77 – 15r – 1 – at Pascoe [072]
AUSTRALIAN JOURNAL – Sydney, 1865-1921 – 30r – 1 – A$930.00 silver A$810.00 vesicular – at Pascoe [072]
AUSTRALIAN JOURNAL FOR HEALTH, PHYSICAL EDUCATION AND RECREATION – (v75- . 1977- . 5,6,9) – v. 67-. 1975- – 1 – us UMI [610]
AUSTRALIAN JOURNAL FOR HEALTH, PHYSICAL EDUCATION AND RECREATION (AJHPER) *see* ACHPER NATIONAL JOURNAL
AUSTRALIAN JOURNAL OF AGRICULTURAL RESEARCH – (v28- . 1977- . 5,6) – v. 1-. 1950- – 1 – us UMI [630]
AUSTRALIAN JOURNAL OF BIOLOGICAL SCIENCES – v. 6-25. 1953-72 – 1,5,6 – us Princeton Micro [574]
AUSTRALIAN JOURNAL OF BIOLOGICAL SCIENCES – (v30- . 1977- . 5,6) – v1- . 1948- – 1 – us UMI [574]
AUSTRALIAN JOURNAL OF BOTANY – (v25- . 1977- . 5,6) – v. 1-. 1953- – 1 – us UMI [580]
AUSTRALIAN JOURNAL OF CHEMISTRY – v. 1-27. 1948-74 – 1,5,6 – us Princeton Micro [540]
AUSTRALIAN JOURNAL OF CHEMISTRY – (v30- . 1977- . 5,6) – v. 6-. 1953- – 1 – us UMI [540]
AUSTRALIAN JOURNAL OF EARLY CHILDHOOD – (v.6-. 1981-. 5,6,9) – v.1- . 1976- – 1 – us UMI [150]
AUSTRALIAN JOURNAL OF EDUCATION – Sydney, 1 Jul 1903-15 Dec 1911 – 2r – 1 – uk British Libr Newspaper [073]
THE AUSTRALIAN JOURNAL OF EDUCATION – (1983-. 1,5,6,9) – v1-. 1957- – 1 – us UMI [073]
AUSTRALIAN JOURNAL OF EXPERIMENTAL AGRICULTURE AND ANIMAL HUSBANDRY – v. 1-8. 7708. 1961-1968 – 9 – ne IDC [630]
AUSTRALIAN JOURNAL OF EXPERIMENTAL AGRICULTURE AND ANIMAL HUSBANDRY – (v.19-. 1979- 5,6) – v.1-. 1961- – 1 – us UMI [630]
AUSTRALIAN JOURNAL OF EXPERIMENTAL BIOLOGY AND MEDICAL SCIENCE – v.27-55. 1949-77 – 1,5,6 – 22276.00 – us Princeton Micro [574]
AUSTRALIAN JOURNAL OF MARINE AND FRESH WATER RESEARCH – (v28- . 1977- . 5,6) – v. 1-. 1950- – 1 – us UMI [550]
AUSTRALIAN JOURNAL OF MENTAL RETARDATION – v. 1-. 1970- – 1 – us UMI [610]
AUSTRALIAN JOURNAL OF MUSIC EDUCATION / Australian Society for Music Education – n1-13. 1967-73 – 26mf – 9 – $5.00f – us Ross [780]
AUSTRALIAN JOURNAL OF PHYSICS – v. 1-27. 1948-1974 – 1,5,6 – us Princeton Micro [530]
AUSTRALIAN JOURNAL OF PHYSICS – (v30- . 1977- . 5,6) – v. 6-. 1953- – 1 – us UMI [530]
AUSTRALIAN JOURNAL OF PLANT PHYSIOLOGY – (v4- . 1977- . 5,6) – v. 1-. 1974- – 1 – us UMI [630]
AUSTRALIAN JOURNAL OF READING – (1983-. 1,5,6,9) – v1-. 1978- – 1 – us UMI [073]
AUSTRALIAN JOURNAL OF SOIL RESEARCH – (v15- . 1977- . 5,6) – v. 1-. 1963- – 1 – us UMI [631]
AUSTRALIAN JOURNAL OF STATISTICS – (v1-12. Dfl80.00v; v13-22. Dfl100.00v) – Canberra. v1-22. 1959-80 – 5,9 – Dfl1,960.00 – ne Swets [310]
AUSTRALIAN JOURNAL OF ZOOLOGY – (v25- . 1977- . 5,6) – v. 1-. 1953- – 1 – us UMI [590]
AUSTRALIAN LAW LIBRARIAN – (Cont: Australian Law Librarians Group Newsletter) – v1-3. 1993-93 – 9 – $45.00set – us Hein [340]
AUSTRALIAN LAW LIBRARIAN *see* AUSTRALIAN LAW LIBRARIANS' GROUP NEWSLETTER
AUSTRALIAN LAW LIBRARIANS GROUP NEWSLETTER *see* AUSTRALIAN LAW LIBRARIAN
AUSTRALIAN LAW LIBRARIANS' GROUP NEWSLETTER – (Cumulative index 1973-90. Cont by: Australian Law Librarian) – v1-3 nos 1-113. 1973-95 – 9 – $60.00 set – us Hein [020]
AUSTRALIAN LAW THESES AND SEMINAR PAPERS – 9 – 165.00 – at Butterworths [340]
AUSTRALIAN LEATHER JOURNAL – Melbourne, 15 Dec 1910-15 Jul 1915; 15 Jan 1916-15 Dec 1921 – 10r – 1 – uk British Libr Newspaper [073]
AUSTRALIAN LEPIDOPTERA, AND THEIR TRANSFORMATIONS / Scott, A W – London, 1864-98.2v. Z-1621/2 – 8 – ne IDC [590]
AUSTRALIAN MACWORLD – v1-. 1985- – 1,5,6,9 – us UMI [510]
AUSTRALIAN MAIL – London, UK. 17 May 1859-70 – 3 1/2r – 1 – uk British Libr Newspaper [072]
Australian Mathematical Society *see* JOURNAL
AUSTRALIAN MINING – v10-23. 1917-1931 – 1,5,6 – us Princeton Micro [622]
AUSTRALIAN MINING AND ENGINEERING REVIEW – Melbourne, Dec 1908-Sep 1917 (very imperfect – 7r – 1 – uk British Libr Newspaper [073]
AUSTRALIAN MINING STANDARD – Sydney, Melbourne, Australia, 12 Mar 1890-13 Sep 1900; 1 Jan 1901-28 Dec 1916; 15 Oct 1932-15 Feb 1933 – 66r – 1 – uk British Libr Newspaper [073]
AUSTRALIAN MONTHLY AND COLONIAL MONTHLY – Sydney, 1865-71 – 3r – 1 – A$94.00 silver A$81.00 vesicular – at Pascoe [073]
AUSTRALIAN NATIVE POLICY, ITS HISTORY ESPECIALLY IN VICTORIA / Foxcroft, Edmund John Buchanan – Melbourne, London: Melbourne University Press in assoc. with Oxford University Press, 1941. 168p – 1 – us U.W. Library [360]
AUSTRALIAN PC WORLD – 1984- – 1 – us UMI [510]
AUSTRALIAN PLAYBOY – 1979- – 9 – at Pascoe [073]
AUSTRALIAN PRESBYTERIAN LIFE – (Lacking: Jan 1982) – 1960-89 – Inquire – 1 – ATLA S0756 – us A.T.L.A. [073]
AUSTRALIAN PRIVATE DOCTOR – v1-. 1985- – 1,5,6,9 – us UMI [616]
Australian Railways Union *see* RAILROAD
AUSTRALIAN RAIN-FOREST TREES / Francis, W D – Brisbane, 1929 – xi/347p – 8 – ne IDC [580]
The Australian Rights Movement (Georgist) *see* PRINCIPLES AND POLICIES
AUSTRALIAN SCIENCE TEACHERS JOURNAL – (v22- . 1976- . 9) – v. 1-. 1955- – 1 – us UMI [370]
Australian Society for Music Education *see* AUSTRALIAN JOURNAL OF MUSIC EDUCATION
THE AUSTRALIAN SPECTRUM – 1986 directory by Archives Project. 48p – 9 – 1.00f – at Libertarian Micro [335]
AUSTRALIAN SPIRITUALIST – Brisbane, 9 Mar-9 Apr 1881 – 3ft – 1 – uk British Libr Newspaper [072]
AUSTRALIAN STAR – Sydney, Feb 24 1900 – 9 – at Pascoe [072]
AUSTRALIAN STATE SESSION LAWS – Backfile 1980-1996 update v2 – 9 – $4,900.00 set – 0-89941-414-1 – us Hein [323]
AUSTRALIAN STATESMAN AND MINING STANDARD *see* AUSTRALIAN MINING STANDARD
AUSTRALIAN STOCK EXCHANGE INTELLIGENCE – Melbourne, Aug 1895-Jul 1912 – 3mqn r – 1 – uk British Libr Newspaper [072]
THE AUSTRALIAN STOCKBROKING CARTEL / Ray Ball – 1984. 20p – 9 – 1.00f – at Libertarian Micro [335]
AUSTRALIAN SUGAR JOURNAL – (Missing: Nov-Dec 1915) – Brisbane, Jul 1910-Dec 1921 – 11r – 1 – uk British Libr Newspaper [073]
AUSTRALIAN TAKEOVERS: THE EVIDENCE / Bishop, Steven & Dodd, Peter & Officer, R R – 1972-85, CIS, 1987, 81p – 9 – 1.00f – at Libertarian Micro [335]
Australian Teachers Federation *see* CHARTER OF THE RIGHTS OF THE CHILD
AUSTRALIAN TOWN AND COUNTRY JOURNAL – Sydney, 1870-1919 – 95r – 1 – at Pascoe [073]
AUSTRALIAN TOWN AND COUNTY JOURNAL – Sydney, Aug 1874-Jun 1919 – 105r – 1 – uk British Libr Newspaper [072]
AUSTRALIAN VAUXHALL NEWS – 1977-1992 – 1r – 5 – at Corangamite [980]
AUSTRALIAN, WINDSOR RICHMOND AND HAWKESBURY ADVERTISER – Sep 27 1873-Aug 29 1874; Sep 9 1876-Mar 31 1877; Sep 18 1880-Sep 8 1883; Jul 2 1896 – 9 – at Pascoe [072]
AUSTRALIAN WOMENS WEEKLY – 1933-96 – 162r – 1 – at Pascoe [072]
AUSTRALIAN WOMENS WEEKLY – 1982- – 9 – at Pascoe [073]
AUSTRALIAN WOMEN'S WORK : CATALOGUE AND PROGRAMME OF THE FIRST EXHIBITION OF WOMEN'S WORK, MELBOURNE, 1907 – 6mf – 9 – A$36.00 – at State Libr Vic [980]
AUSTRALIAN WORKER – Sydney, 1895-1955 – 51r – 1 – at Pascoe [073]
AUSTRALIAN WORKER – Sydney, 3 Jun 1915-13 Apr 1960 – 43mqn r – 1 – uk British Libr Newspaper [072]
AUSTRALIAN WORKMAN – Sydney, 1890-91; 1895; 1897 – 1r – 1 – A$35.00 silver A$30.00 vesicular – at Pascoe [073]
AUSTRALIAN YEAR BOOK OF INTERNATIONAL LAW – v1-15. 165-1995 – 9 – us Hein [340]

AUSTRALIA'S FIRST PREACHER : THE REV. RICHARD JOHNSON, FIRST CHAPLAIN OF NEW SOUTH WALES – London: Sampson Low, Marston,1898 – 1mf – us A.T.L.A. [240]
THE AUSTRALIASIAN – Melbourne, Australia. Australasian Post New Australasian Post. -w. Oct 1864-26 June 1869; 7 Jan 1871-24 April 1880; 5 Jan 1884-21 Oct 1939; 4 Jan 1941-30 March 1946; 6 June 1946-31 Jan 1952; 17 July-23 Oct 1952. 219 reels – 1 – uk British Libr Newspaper [072]
AUSTREY, BRAILSFORD, CHURCH BROUGHTON, ETWALL, LONGSFORD, MARSTON MONTGOMERY PARISH REGISTERS / Staffordshire – 1 – uk Microform Academic [941]
AUSTRIA : OESTERREICHISCHES STATISTISCHES HANDBUCH 1882-1917 / Austria. Statistische Zentralkommission – (Coll title: European Official Statistical Serials, 1841-1984) – 153mf – 9 – £5.00f (set £2,800.00 534mf) – uk Chadwyck [943]
AUSTRIA : STATISTISCHES HANDBUCH FUER DIE REPUBLIK OESTERREICH 1920-1938, 1950-1965 / Austria. Statistisches Zentralamt – (Coll title: European Official Statistical Serials, 1841-1984) – 126mf – 9 – £5.00f (set £2,800 534mf) – uk Chadwyck [943]
AUSTRIA : STATISTISCHES JAHRBUCH DER OESTERREICHISCHEN MONARCHIE 1863-1881 / Austria. Statistische Zentralkommission – (Coll title: European Official Statistical Serials, 1841-1984) – 175mf – 9 – £5.00f (set £2,800.00 534mf) – uk Chadwyck [943]
AUSTRIA : TAFELN ZUR STATISTIK DER OESTERREICHISCHEN MONARCHIE 1842-59 / Austria. Statistische Zentralkommission – (Coll title: European Official Statistical Serials, 1841-1984) – 80mf – 9 – £6.00f (set £2,800.00 534mf) – uk Chadwyck [943]
Austria *see* LANGFRISTIGES INVESTITIONSPROGRAMM DES BUNDES
AUSTRIA. ALLGEMEINES – Austria, 1910-1913 – 1r – 1 – us I.H.R.C. [940]
AUSTRIA AND THE CAUSES AND ORIGINS OF WORLD WAR 1 PAMPHLET COLLECTION – 1914-1954 – 2r – 1 – CSUXAML2946-B – us Hoover Inst Photo [355]
Austria. Bundesministerium fuer Finanzen *see* DER KOREN PLAN. DAS WIRTSCHAFTSPOLITISCHE KONZEPT DER BUNDESREGIERUNG
Austria. Bundesministerium fuer Land-und Forstwirtschaft *see* LONG-TERM-PROGRAMM
Austria. Bundesministerium fuer Vermoegenssicherung und Wirtschaftsplanung *see* METALLINDUSTRIEPLAN
Austria. Bundespolizeidirektion, Vienna *see* FAHNDUNGSVERZEICHNIS ZU DEM ZENTRALPOLIZEIBLATTE, DEM WIENER, GRAZER UND INNSBRUCKER TAEGLICHEN FAHNDUNGSBLATTE
Austria. Finanz-Ministerium *see* STAATS-VORANSCHLAG FUER DIE IM REICHSRATHE VERTRETENEN KOENIGREICHE UND LAENDER
Austria. Herrenhaus *see* STENOGRAPHISCHE PROTOKOLLE UEBER DIE SITZUNGEN DES OESTERREICHISCHEN REICHSRATHES
Austria. (Lower) *see* AMTLICHE NACHRICHTEN
Austria. Lower. Lantag *see* STENOGRAPHISCHE PROTOKOLLE.
Austria. Reichsrat. Abgeordnetenhaus *see* STENOGRAPHISCHE PROTOKOLLE DES ABGEORDNETENHAUSES DES REICHSRATHES
AUSTRIA – STAATSARCHIV – Austria, 1848-1919 – 32r – 1 – us I.H.R.C. [940]
Austria. Statistische Zentralkommission *see* – AUSTRIA
Austria. Statistisches Zentralamt *see* AUSTRIA
Austria.Bundesministerium fuer Unterricht *see* VERORDNUNGSBLATT
AUSTRIAN ALMANACS PAMPHLET COLLECTION – 1930 – 1 – CSUXAMJ3155-B – us Hoover Inst Photo [030]
THE AUSTRIAN COURT FROM WITHIN / Radziwill, Ekaterina Rzewuska kniagina – New York: Frederick A. Stokes, 1916. 235p. illus – 1 – us U.W. Library [943]
AUSTRIAN CULTURE AND CIVILIZATION PAMPHLET COLLECTION – 1941-1965 – 1 – CSUXANQ2250-B – us Hoover Inst Photo [306]
AUSTRIAN ETHNOLOGY PAMPHLET COLLECTION – 19?? – 1 – CSUXANQ2256-B – us Hoover Inst Photo [301]
AUSTRIAN FOREIGN RELATIONS PAMPHLET COLLECTION – 1970-1978 – 1 – CSUXANQ2269-B – us Hoover Inst Photo [320]
AUSTRIAN HABSBURG HISTORY : PRINTED SOURCES 16TH-19TH CENTURIES – (Individual titles available. Also listed separately) – 1,008mf – 9 – ne IDC [943]
AUSTRIAN HISTORY PAMPHLET COLLECTION – 19??-1950 – 1 – CSUXANQ2264-B – us Hoover Inst Photo [943]
AUSTRIAN HISTORY, POLITICS, AND GOVERNMENT–1848 TO 1918–PAMPHLET COLLECTION – 1883-1918 – 2r – 1 – CSUXANQ2276-B – us Hoover Inst Photo [320]
AUSTRIAN HISTORY, POLITICS, AND GOVERNMENT–1918 TO 1938–PAMPHLET COLLECTION – 1918-1984 – 3r – 1 – CSUXANQ2289-B – us Hoover Inst Photo [320]
AUSTRIAN HISTORY, POLITICS, AND GOVERNMENT–1938 TO 1945–PAMPHLET COLLECTION – 1942-1988 – 1 – CSUXANQ3107-B – us Hoover Inst Photo [320]
AUSTRIAN IMPERIAL HYMN: "GOTT ERHALTE UNSEREN KAISER" : ARRANGED FOR VIOLIN AND PIANO / Kreisler, F – New York: C Fisher, ca 1915 – 1 – us Sibley [780]
AUSTRIAN NATIONAL LIBRARY, VIENNA. MUSIC COLLECTION *see* DIE BACH-DRUCKE DER HOBOKEN-SAMMLUNG MUSIKALISCHER ERST- UND FRUEHDRUECKE
AUSTRIAN TYROL PAMPHLET COLLECTION – 1916-19?? – 1 – CSUXANQ3114-B – us Hoover Inst Photo [943]
DER AUSTRITT DEUTSCHLANDS AUS DEM VOLKERBUND, SEINE VORGESCHICHTE UND SEINE NACHWIRKUNGEN / Fraser, Christine – Bonn, 1969 – 1 – DM30.00 – gw Mikro Press [943]
AUSTRO AMERICAN TRIBUNE *see* FORUM UND TRIBUNE
Austro-Hungarian Monarchy *see* VORANSCHLAG
Austro-Hungarian Monarchy. Ministerium des K. und K. Hauses und des aussern *see* OESTERREICH-UNGARNS AUSSENPOLITIK
Austro-Hungarian Monarchy. Reichskriegsministerium *see* VERORDNUNGSBLATT FUER DAS K. U. K. HEER
DIE AUSUBUNG DES VERORDNUNGSRECHTS IM FREISTAATE HESSEN SEIT DER REVOLUTION / Schmahl, Ludwig – Giessen 1921 – 1 – DM30.00 – gw Mikro Press [943]
AUSWAERTIGE POLITIK – Berlin, 1939 n7-1944 n4 – 1 – Dist. gw Mikrofilm – gw Misc Inst [327]
AUSWAHL / Herder, Johann Gottfried; ed by Kuehnemann, Eugen – 3. Aufl. Leipzig: Duerr, 1910 – 1r – 1 – us U.W. Library [800]
AUSWANDERUNG UND AUSWANDERUNGSPOLITIK IN OESTERREICH / Caro, Leopold – Leipzig, 1909 – 1r – 1 – us I.H.R.C. [320]
AUSWANDERUNG UND AUSWANDERUNGSPOLITIK IN OESTERREICH / Caro, Leopold – Leipzig, 1909 – 1r – 1 – us I.H.R.C. [320]
"DAS AUSWANDERUNGSPROBLEM UND DIE REGELUNG DES AUSWANDERUNGSWESENS IN OESTERREICH" / Buzek, Jozef – 1901 – 1r – 1 – us I.H.R.C. [320]
DIE AUSWIRKUNGEN DER FABRIKARBEIT AUF DAS TRADITIONALE ROLLENVERHALTEN DER FRAU IN MEGARA, GRIECHENLAND : EINE VERGLEICHENDE UNTERSUCHUNG / Kalfelis, Petros – Heidelberg, 1974 – 4mf – 9 – DM90.00 – 3-89349-755-2 – gw Hänsel [331]
DIE AUSWIRKUNGEN DES BILINGUALISMUS IN ALGERIEN (FRANZOESISCH/ARABISCH) AUF DAS ERLERNEN DES DEUTSCHEN ALS FREMDSPRACHE / Boudaa, Azzedine – 1992 – 217p – 9 – DM98.00 – 3-89349-598-3 – gw Hänsel [430]
DIE AUSWIRKUNGEN DES EUROPAEISCHEN BINNENMARKTES AUF DIE WIRTSCHAFTSBEZIEHUNGEN ZUR DRITTEN WELT / Pennekamp, Markus – 1995 – 1mf – 9 – DM60.00 – 3-8267-2274-4 – gw Hänsel [337]
DIE AUSWIRKUNGEN DES INTRAFAMILIALEN SEXUELLEN MISSBRAUCHS VON MAEDCHEN AUF DIE PERSOENLICHKEITSENTWICKLUNG DER OPFER / Schneider, Doris – 1993 – 2mf – 9 – DM98.00 – 3-89349-636-X – gw Hänsel [150]
AUSZUG DER NEUESTEN WELTGESCHICHTE *see* CHRISTIAN-ERLANGISCHER ZEITUNGS-EXTRACT
AUSZUG (KURTZER), VON DES BERUFFENEN KETZERS DAV. GEORGI ODER JORIS LEHR UND LEBEN – 1704. BME-417 1 – 9 – ne IDC [240]
AUSZUG VND KURTZER BERICHT: VON DER GERECHTIGKEIT DER CHRISTEN FUR GOTT AUS EINER PREDIG VBER DIE WORT JOHANNIS / Funck, J – Kuenigsberg, 1552 – 1mf – 9 – ne IDC [240]
O AUTAENSE : ORGAM DO SYNDICATO AGROPECUARIO AUTAENSE – Rio Autaz, Amazonas. 18 Ago 1924-Set 1925; Mar-Ago 1932 – 1,5,6 – bl Biblioteca [072]
LA AUTENTICA REBELION / Artana, Nestor – Santa Fe, Argentina: Libreria y Editorial Castellvi, [1973] – 1 – CSUXAJL9688-B – us Hoover Inst Photo [320]
EL AUTENTICO ESPRONCEDA PORNOGRAFICO Y EL APOCRIFO EN GENERAL / Cascales Munoz, Jose – Toledo, 1932 – 1 – sp Bibl Santa Ana [946]
LES AUTEURS HINDOUSTANIS ET LEURS OUVRAGES : D'APRES LES BIOGRAPHIES ORIGINALES / Tassy, M Garcin de – 2. ed. Paris: E Thorin 1868 – us Res Libr [920]
AUTHENTIC ANECDOTES OF GEOGE LUKINS, THE YATTON DOEMONIAC, WITH A VIEW OF THE CONTROVERSY AND A FULL REFUTATION OF THE IMPOSTURE / Norman, S – Bristol, [1788] – 1mf – 9 – MP-560/1 – ne IDC [240]
AUTHENTIC COPIES OF THE PAPERS RELATIVE TO THE COMMENCEMENT OF NEGOTIATIONS FOR PEACE WITH FRANCE – London, 1800 – 1mf – 9 – ILM-716/1 – ne IDC [340]
AN AUTHENTIC HISTORY OF THE MISSIONS UNDER THE CARE OF THE MISSIONARY SOCIETY OF THE METHODIST EPISCOPAL CHURCH / Bangs, Nathan – New York: J. Emory and B. Waugh, for the Methodist Episcopal Church, 1832 – 1mf – us A.T.L.A. [240]
AN AUTHENTIC HISTORY OF THE PRAYER BOOK, ITS FIVE REVISIONS AND THE PERIODS AT WHICH THEY WERE MADE:.. / Amicus – Montreal: J. Starke, 1874. 05841. (Pre-1900 Canadiana) – 9 – cn C.I.H.M. [240]
AUTHENTIC LIST OF ALL LAND LOTTERY GRANTS MADE TO VETERANS OF THE REVOLUTIONARY WAR BY THE STATE OF GEORGIA / Hitz, Alex M – 1966. From records in the Surveyor-General Dept. in Georgia Dept. of Archives & History. F-1286 or SW16-0065 – 5,9 – us A.G.L.L. [920]
THE AUTHENTICITY AND MESSIANIC INTERPRETATION OF THE PROPHECIES OF ISAIAH VINDICATED IN A COURSE OF SERMONS PREACHED BEFORE THE UNIVERSITY OF OXFORD / Payne-Smith, Robert – 1862 – 1 – us A.T.L.A. [240]
THE AUTHENTICITY OF THE GOSPEL OF ST LUKE : ITS BEARING UPON THE EVIDENCES OF THE TRUTH OF CHRISTIANITY / Hervey, Arthur Charles – 2nd ed. London: SPCK; New York: E & J B Young, 1892 – 1mf – 9 – 0-8370-3576-7 – 1985-1576 – us A.T.L.A. [220]
Authier, Henri *see* L'ABITIBI
THE AUTHOR / The Society of Authors – (Playwright and Composer). 1890-1960 – 1 – uk Microform Academic [800]
AUTHOR AND CLASSIFIED CATALOGUES OF THE ROYAL BOTANIC GARDENS LIBRARY : AUTHOR CATALOGUE / Royal Botanic Gardens Library. Kew – (Available on microfilm by request) – 1974 – 103,000 cards – 9 – $495.00 export $598.00 – uk Hall [580]
AUTHOR AND CLASSIFIED CATALOGUES OF THE ROYAL BOTANIC GARDENS LIBRARY : CLASSIFIED CATALOGUE / Royal Botanic Gardens Library. Kew – 1974 – 8r – 1 – $500.00 – 0-8161-1380-7 – uk Hall [580]
AUTHOR AND SUBJECT CATALOGS / Harvard University. Peabody Museum of Archaeology and Ethnology. Tozzer Library – (1st Suppl 1970 131,000 cards 24 r $1775.00 ISBN: 0-8161-1367-X; 2nd Suppl 1971 61,700 cards 8r $920.00 ISBN: 0-8161-1231-2; 3rd Suppl 1975 90,300 cards 14r $1060.00 ISBN: 0-8161-1377-7; 4th Suppl 1979 93,600 cards 7r $1080.00 ISBN: 0-8161-1400-5) – 1963 – 51r – 1 – $6,410.00 – 0-8161-1230-4 – uk Hall [930]
AUTHOR AND SUBJECT CATALOGS OF THE TOZZER LIBRARY, 2ND ENLARGED EDITION ON MICROFICHE / Peabody Museum of Archaeology and Ethnology, Harvard University – Boston: G.K. Hall & Co., 1988 – est. 1.34 cards on 1116 1200-frame mf – 9 – $6,600.00 export $7,260.00 – 0-8161-1731-4 – uk Hall [301]
AUTHOR AND TITLE CATALOGUE OF TRANSMITTED DRAMA AND FEATURES, 1936-1975 : WITH CHRONOLOGICAL LIST OF TRANSMITTED PLAYS (TELEVISION) / BBC (British Broadcasting Corporation) Television – 63mf – 9 – £260.00 – uk Chadwyck [790]
AUTHOR AND TITLE CATALOGUE OF TRANSMITTED DRAMA, POETRY AND FEATURES 1929-1975 / BBC (British Broadcasting Corporation) Radio – 125mf – 9 – £500.00 – uk Chadwyck [700]
AUTHOR CATALOG / New York Academy of Medicine. Library – (First Suppl., 1974.-72,900 cards 8 reels. $545.00 ISBN: 0-8161-1364-5) – 1969.-805,000 cards 36 reels.-ISBN: 0-8161-1388-2 – 1 – $4290.00 – uk Hall [610]
AUTHOR CATALOG OF THE LIBRARY OF THE NEW YORK ACADEMY OF MEDICINE / New York Academy of Medicine – (First Supplement, 1974. 72,900 cards 8 reels. $495.00 export $598.00. ISBN 0-8161-1389-0) – 1969. 805,000 cards on 86 reels – 1 – $3,900.00 export $4,720.00 – 0-8161-1388-2 – uk Hall [610]
AUTHOR HEADINGS FOR THE OFFICIAL PUBLICATIONS OF OKLAHOMA / Cramer, Rose Fulton – (Filmed with: Author Headings for the Official Publications of the State of Wisconsin by Ruth Lillian Whitlock) – 1944 – us Res Libr [324]
AUTHOR HEADINGS FOR THE OFFICIAL PUBLICATIONS OF THE STATE OF WISCONSIN 101=WHITLOCK, RUTH LILLIAN – (Filmed with: Author Headings for the Official Publications of Oklahoma by Rose Fulton Cramer) – 1941 – us Res Libr [324]
AUTHOR INDEX OF BYZANTINE STUDIES : BASED ON BYZANTINISCHE ZEITSCHRIFT / ed by Allen, Jelisaveta Stanojevich – (Includes binder) – Dumbarton Oaks, Washington, DC: Centre for Byzantine Studies. 2pts – 267mf – 9 – O-2079/1 – ne IDC [020]
AUTHOR INDEX OF BYZANTINE STUDIES 2 / ed by Allen, Jeslisaveta Stanojevich – Dumbarton Oaks, Washington DC: Center for Byzantine Studies – 97mf – 9 – ne IDC [020]
AUTHOR INDEX TO PSYCHOLOGICAL INDEX, 1894 TO 1935, AND PSYCHOLOGICAL ABSTRACTS, 1927 TO 1958 / Columbia University. Psychology Library – (Second Supplement, 1964-1968, 1970. 77,600 entries 4 reels. $290.00 export $350.00. – ISBN 0-8161-1355-6) – 1 – uk Hall [150]
Author of Heaven our home *see* TABOR'S TEACHINGS
AUTHOR TITLE CATALOG OF THE FRANCIS A. COUNTWAY LIBRARY OF MEDICINE FOR IMPRINTS THROUGH 1959 / Francis A. Countway Library of Medicine – (Available on microfilm by request) – 1973. 275.000 cards – 9 – $1,595.00 export $1,930.00 – uk Hall [610]
AUTHORITARIAN AND LIBERTARIAN VIEWS OF SOCIETY / Van Dun, Frank – 1986, LA Political Notes, no.7, 4p – 9 – 1.00f – at Libertarian Micro [335]
AUTHORITARIANISM TODAY / Ray, J J – 1978 MS. 3 fiches (29x) – 9 – 1.00f – at Libertarian Micro [320]
AUTHORITATIVE CHRISTIANITY : THE FIRST ECUMENICAL COUNCIL, THAT IS, THE FIRST COUNCIL OF THE WHOLE CHRISTIAN WORLD, WHICH WAS HELD A.D. 325 AT NICAEA IN BITHYNIA / Chrystal, James – Jersey City, N.J., U.S.A.: J. Chrystal, 1891 – 2mf – us A.T.L.A. [240]
AUTHORITIES, DEDUCTIONS AND NOTES IN CONTRACTS / Pattee, William Sullivan – Minneapolis: University, 1900. 171p. LL-999 – 1 – us L of C Photodup [340]
AUTHORITIES, DEDUCTIONS AND NOTES IN REAL PROPERTY / Pattee, William Sullivan – Minneapolis: University, 1902. 148p. LL-1036 – 1 – us L of C Photodup [340]

AUTHORITIES, DEDUCTIONS, AND NOTES IN THE ELEMENTS OF EQUITY / Pattee, William Sullivan – Minneapolis: University, 1900. 131p. LL-1016 – 1 – us L of C Photodup [340]

AUTHORITY : OR, A PLAIN REASON FOR JOINING THE CHURCH OF ROME / Rivington, Luke – 7th rev ed. London: Catholic Truth Society, 1897 – 1mf – 9 – 0-8370-8465-2 – 1986-2465 – us A.T.L.A. [240]

AUTHORITY AND THE LIGHT WITHIN / Grubb, Edward – London: James Clarke, 1908 – 9 – us A.T.L.A. [240]

AUTHORITY IN RELIGION / Leckie, Joseph H – Edinburgh: T. & T. Clark, 1909. 1 fiche – 9 – us A.T.L.A. [240]

AUTHORITY IN THE CHURCH / Strong, Thomas Banks – London, New York: Longmans, Green, 1903 – 1mf – 9 – 0-8370-5456-7 – 1985-3456 – us A.T.L.A. [240]

THE AUTHORITY OF CHRIST / Forrest, David W – Edinburgh: T. & T. Clark, 1906 – 2mf – us A.T.L.A. [240]

THE AUTHORITY OF HOLY SCRIPTURES: AN INAUGURAL ADDRESS / Briggs, Charles Augustus – 2nd ed., 1891 – 9 – us A.T.L.A. [240]

THE AUTHORIZED EDITION OF THE ENGLISH BIBLE (1611) : ITS SUBSEQUENT REPRINTS AND MODERN REPRESENTATIVES / Scrivener, Frederick Henry Ambrose – (Includes bibliographical references and index of persons and subjects) – Cambridge: University Press, 1884 – 1mf – 9 – 0-8370-5199-1 – 1985-3199 – us A.T.L.A. [220]

THE AUTHORIZED VERSION OF THE BIBLE AND ITS INFLUENCE / Cook, Albert Stanburrough – New York: G P Putnam, 1910 – 1mf – 9 – 0-8370-9214-0 – 1986-3214 – us A.T.L.A. [220]

AUTHORS AND THEIR PUBLIC IN ANCIENT TIMES : A SKETCH OF LITERARY CONDITIONS AND OF THE RELATIONS WITH THE PUBLIC OF LITERARY PRODUCERS, FROM THE EARLIEST TIMES TO THE INVENTION OF PRINTING / Putnam, George Haven – New York: Putnam, 1894 – 1mf – us A.T.L.A. [400]

AUTHOR'S APOLOGY FOR PROTESTING AGAINST THE METHODIST EPISCOPAL GOVERNMENT / O'Kelly, James – 1798 – 1 – us A.T.L.A. [240]

THE AUTHORSHIP AND HISTORICAL CHARACTER OF THE FOURTH GOSPEL / Sanday, William – London: Macmillan, 1872.1 fiche – 9 – us A.T.L.A. [240]

THE AUTHORSHIP OF THE BOOK OF DEUTERONOMY / McGarvey, John William – Cincinnati: Standard Pub., 1902.1 fiche. 8370-4354-9 – 9 – us A.T.L.A. [240]

THE AUTHORSHIP OF THE DE IMITATIONE CHRISTI : WITH MANY INTERESTING PARTICULARS ABOUT THE BOOK / Kettlewell, Samuel – London: Rivingtons, 1877 – 1mf – us A.T.L.A. [240]

THE AUTHORSHIP OF THE FOURTH GOSPEL : AND OTHER CRITICAL ESSAYS / Abbot, Ezra; ed by Thayer, J H – (Includes indexes) – Boston: G H Ellis, 1888 – 2mf – 9 – 0-8370-2004-2 – 1985-0004 – us A.T.L.A. [220]

THE AUTHORSHIP OF THE FOURTH GOSPEL : EXTERNAL EVIDENCE / Abbot, Ezra – Boston: G H Ellis, 1880 – 1mf – 9 – 0-8370-2005-0 – 1985-0005 – us A.T.L.A. [220]

THE AUTHORSHIP OF THE WEST SAXON GOSPELS / Drake, Allison Emery – New York: E Scott, 1894 – 1mf – 9 – 0-8370-2961-9 – 1985-0961 – us A.T.L.A. [220]

AUTHOR/SUBJECT CATALOGUES / Harvard University. Peabody Museum of Archaeology and Ethnology. Tozzer Library – 2nd enl ed 1988 – 1,116mf – 9 – $6000.00 – uk Hall [930]

AUTHOR-TITLE AND SUBJECT CATALOGS / California. University of Southern California. Los Angeles. Ethel Percy Andrus Gerontology Center – 1976 – 4r – 1 – $140.00 – 0-8161-1249-5 – uk Hall [616]

AUTHOR-TITLE AND SUBJECT CATALOGS OF THE BAKER LIBRARY. 1971 : AUTHOR-TITLE CATALOG / Harvard University. Graduate School of Business Administration. Baker Library – 22r – 1 – $2,995.00 – 0-8161-1438-2 – uk Hall [650]

AUTHOR-TITLE AND SUBJECT CATALOGS OF THE BAKER LIBRARY. 1971 : FIRST SUPPLEMENT / Harvard University. Graduate School of Business Administration. Baker Library – 1974 – 4r – 1 – $290.00 – 0-8161-1439-0 – uk Hall [650]

AUTHOR-TITLE AND SUBJECT CATALOGS OF THE BAKER LIBRARY. 1971 : SUBJECT CATALOG / Harvard University. Graduate School of Business Administration. Baker Library – 10r – 1 – $1,290.00 – 0-8161-1228-2 – uk Hall [650]

AUTHOR-TITLE CATALOG / California. University. Berkeley. East Asiatic Library – (First Suppl., 1973. 22,700 cards. 2 reels. $265.00 ISBN 0-8161-1359-9) – 1968. 200,000 cards. 13 reels. ISBN 0-8161-1397-1 – 1 – $1415.00 – uk Hall [950]

AUTHOR-TITLE CATALOG / Harvard University. Baker Library – (First suppl., 1974.-45,300 cards 4 reels. $240.00 ISBN: 0-8161-1438-2) – 1971.-348,000 cards 22 reels – 1 – $2720.00 – uk Hall [010]

AUTHOR-TITLE CATALOG / Wisconsin. The State Historical Society, Madison. Library – 600mf – 9 – $2,220.00 – us UPA [018]

AUTHOR/TITLE CATALOG / California. University. San Diego. Scripps Institution of Oceanography – (First Suppl., 1973.-44,100 cards 6 reels.-1. $245.00 ISBN: 0-8161-1261-4) – uk Hall [580]

AUTHOR-TITLE CATALOG OF THE DEPARTMENT LIBRARY / U.S. Department of Health, Education and Welfare. Library. Washington D.C. – (First Suppl., 1973. 109,000 cards. 14 reels. $575.00 ISBN 0-8161-1232-0) – 1965. 540,000 cards – 1 – uk Hall [310]

AUTHOR-TITLE CHINESE CATALOG / University of Chicago. Far Eastern Library – 1973. 130,000 cards. 16 reels. ISBN 0-8161-1332-7 – 1 – $1080.00 – uk Hall [950]

AUTHOR-TITLE JAPANESE CATALOG / University of Chicago. Far Eastern Library – 1973. 68,100 cards. 8 reels. ISBN 0-8161-1321-1 – 1 – $590.00 – uk Hall [950]

Autichamp, Charles, Cte d' *see* PROCES DE M. LE COMTE CH. D'AUTICHAMP ET DE M. L'ABBE LEGAULT

AUTIKON BOTANIKON / Rafinesque-Schmaltz, Constantine S – Philadelphia. 1815-40. B-8101 1 – 9 – ne IDC [580]

Autio, Wesley R *see* JOURNAL OF TREE FRUIT PRODUCTION

Autissiodorensis, Heiricus *see* HOMILIAE PER CIRCULUM ANNI

AUTO AGE DEALER BUSINESS *see* WARD'S DEALER BUSINESS

AUTO DE FE AND JEW / Adler, Elkan Nathan – London, New York: Oxford University Press, 1908 – 1mf – us A.T.L.A. [240]

AUTO DEL NUNCIO CONTRA UNA ASSERTA SENTENCIA IMPRESSA... / Fachenetti, Cesar – S.l., s.i., s.a. 1642 – 1 – sp Bibl Santa Ana [946]

AUTO DRIVER – 1942-58 – 1,5,6 – us Princeton Micro [073]

AUTO RACING DIGEST – (v5- . 1977- . 5,6,9) – v. 1-. 1973- – 1 – us UMI [790]

AUTO REPAIR BOOKS: DOMESTIC AND IMPORTED CAR, LIGHT TRUCK AND VAN – (Annual update. $449.00; $597.00 in Canada) – Over 100,000 pages. Fully indexed. Over 700mf. Sections available separately – 9 – $1,777.00; $2,363.00 in Canada – us Mitchell Int'l [629]

AUTO REPAIR BOOKS: DOMESTIC CAR REPAIR – (Annual update: $180.00; $239.00 in Canada) – 10 years of domestic car model information – 9 – $750.00; $998.00 in Canada – us Mitchell Int'l [629]

AUTO REPAIR BOOKS: DOMESTIC LIGHT TRUCK AND VAN REPAIR – (Annual update: $125.00; $166.00 in Canada) – 10 years of domestic light truck and van information – 9 – $500.00; $665.00 in Canada – us Mitchell Int'l [629]

AUTO REPAIR BOOKS: IMPORTED CAR AND LIGHT TRUCK REPAIR – (Annual update: $195.00; $259.00 in Canada) – 10 years of imported car and light truck service and repair information – 9 – $800.00; $1,064.00 in Canada – us Mitchell Int'l [629]

AUTO REPAIR BOOKS: TECHNICAL SERVICE BULLETINS – Published yearly – 9 – $50.00; $67.00 in Canada – us Mitchell Int'l [629]

AUTO WORKER – Flint. Mich. 1936-1939 – 1 – us UMI [331]

AUTO WORKERS NEWS : 1927-1934 – (Coll title: Labor Union Periodicals, Pt 1) – 1r – 1 – $135.00 – 1-55655-228-9 – us UPA [331]

AUTO WORKER/THE SPARK PLUG : 1919-24 – (Coll title: Labor Union Periodicals, Pt 1) – 1r – 1 – $135.00 – 1-55655-227-0 – us UPA [331]

AUTO Y SENTENCIA EN FAVOR DEL R. PADRE FR. SEBASTIAN DE MORATILLA VICARIO PATERNO DEL MONATERIO DE GUADALUPE... / Nunciatura Apostolica – S.l., s.i., s.a. 1641 – 1 – sp Bibl Santa Ana [946]

AUTOAGGRESSION UND PATHOLOGISCHE INFORMATIONSVERARBEITUNG BEI GEISTIGBEHINDERTEN MIT AUTISTISCHEN ZUEGEN / Elbing, Ulrich – 1992 – 3mf – 9 – DM98.00 – 3-89349-468-5 – gw Hänsel [616]

AUTOBIOGRAFIA Y SELECCION DE POESIAS / Guido y Spano, Carlos – Buenos Aires, Argentina: Hemisferio, 1954 – 1 – us U.W. Library [920]

AUTOBIOGRAPHICAL MATERIAL, MISS WILLIE KELLEY / Barton, L E – 148p – 1 – 5.18 – us Baptist [920]

AUTOBIOGRAPHICAL MEMOIRS, 1821-52 / Orchard, George Herbert – 96p – 1 – $5.00 – us Baptist [240]

AUTOBIOGRAPHICAL NOTES / Clark, Marona M (Still) – undated, Miscellaneous titles – 1 – us KS Hist [920]

AUTOBIOGRAPHICAL NOTES ON THE LIFE OF WILLIAM BELL SCOTT : AND NOTICES OF HIS ARTISTIC AND POETIC CIRCLE OF FRIENDS, 1830 TO 1882 / Scott, William Bell; ed by Minto, W – London: Osgood, McIlvaine, 1892 – 1 roll – 1 – 1-55879-211-2 – uk Libr Preservation [420]

AUTOBIOGRAPHICAL RECOLLECTIONS / Leslie, Charles Robert; ed by Taylor, Tom – London: John Murray, 1860 – 1 roll – 1 – 1-55879-272-4 – uk Libr Preservation [920]

AUTOBIOGRAPHICAL RECOLLECTIONS. WITH A BRIEF MEMOIR BY LEWIS B. BOWRING / Bowring, J – London. 1877. BCH-819 2 – 8 – ne IDC [920]

AUTOBIOGRAPHIE, 1785 / Bosanquet, M – (Coll title: The People Called Methodists, Phase 2: Primary Sources 1738-1800) – 4mf – 9 – MP-618/1 – ne IDC [240]

AN AUTOBIOGRAPHY / Spencer, Herbert – New York: D. Appleton, 1904 – 2 rolls – 1 – 1-55879-800-5 – uk Libr Preservation [920]

AUTOBIOGRAPHY / Dole, Artemus Wood – 1856-67 – 1 – us KS Hist [920]

AUTOBIOGRAPHY / Harris, Joseph S – 1 – $50.00 – us Presbyterian [920]

AUTOBIOGRAPHY / Rennolds, Edwin Hansford – Also clippings, pictures and paper, ythe Baptist Reaper, Paris, Tennessee, 2 Sep 1897 containing picture of grandfather Asa Cox. 104p – 1 – 5.00 – us Baptist [240]

AUTOBIOGRAPHY / Schwarz, Conrad Herman Alfred – 1 – us KS Hist [978]

AUTOBIOGRAPHY / Simons, Robert Bentham – 1963. Rear Admiral, U.S.N. 2 fiches – 9 – us South Carolina Historical [920]

AUTOBIOGRAPHY / Sinclair, Addie M – 1 – us KS Hist [978]

AUTOBIOGRAPHY : TEXTS A, B AND C, 1845, 1849, 1850-1851 / Bourne, H – (Coll title: The People Called Methodists, Phase 3: Primary Sources, 1801-1850) – 12mf – 9 – MP-683/1 – ne IDC [240]

AUTOBIOGRAPHY / Tresco, Carlo – 1r – 1 – us I.H.R.C. [920]

AUTOBIOGRAPHY / Wilkes, Charles – 1798-1877 – 1 – $59.00 – us L of C Photodup [920]

THE AUTOBIOGRAPHY : A CRITICAL AND COMPARATIVE STUDY / Burr, Anna Robeson – Boston: Houghton Mifflin, 1909 – 2mf – us A.T.L.A. [920]

AUTOBIOGRAPHY, 1855 / Bartlett, J – (Coll title: The People Called Methodists, Phase 3: Primary Sources, 1801-1850) – 4mf – 9 – MP-692/1 – ne IDC [240]

AUTOBIOGRAPHY, 1870 / Lea, W – (Coll title: The People Called Methodists, Phase 3: Primary Sources, 1801-1850) – 5mf – 9 – MP-687/1 – ne IDC [240]

AUTOBIOGRAPHY, 1880-1945 / King, Spencer B – 166p – 1 – 5.81 – us Baptist [240]

AUTOBIOGRAPHY AND CORRESPONDENCE / Nassau, Robert Hamill – 1 – $100.00 – us Presbyterian [920]

AUTOBIOGRAPHY AND DIARY OF SAMUEL DAVIDSON, WITH AN ACCURATE ACCOUNT OF THE CONTROVERSY OF 1857 / Davidson, Samuel – 1899 – 9 – us A.T.L.A. [240]

AUTOBIOGRAPHY AND JEFFERSON LODGE MINUTES / Steele, Oliver Hazard Perry – undated, Records of the lodge in Franklin County, Ohio, and lengthy autobiography of Steele, a resident of Columbus, Ohio, and Ogle County, Illinois – 1 – us KS Hist [920]

AUTOBIOGRAPHY AND JOURNALS OF ADMIRAL LORD CLARENCE E. PAGET, G.C.B / Paget, Clarence Edward; ed by Otway, A – 1896 – 9 – $20.00 – uk Libr Preservation [920]

AUTOBIOGRAPHY AND OTHER MATERIALS BY HIM / Dagg, John L – 1 – 60.90 – us Baptist [240]

AUTOBIOGRAPHY AND PERSONAL RECOLLECTIONS OF JOHN B. GOUGH : WITH TWENTY-SIX YEARS' EXPERIENCE AS A PUBLIC SPEAKER / Gough, John B – Springfield, Mass.: Bill, Nichols; Chicago, Ill.: Bill & Heron, 1870, c1869 – 2mf – us A.T.L.A. [240]

AUTOBIOGRAPHY, CORRESPONDENCE, ETC., OF LYMAN BEECHER, D.D / Beecher, Lyman – Ed. by Charles Beecher. 1865 – 9 – us A.T.L.A. [240]

THE AUTOBIOGRAPHY, LONGTIME MISSIONARY TO BRAZIL / Bratcher, Lewis M – 1888-1953 – 1 – 5.67 – us Baptist [240]

AUTOBIOGRAPHY OF A SHAKER : AND REVELATION OF THE APOCALYPSE / Evans, F W – Glasgow: United Publishing Co.; New York: American News Co., 1888 – 1mf – us A.T.L.A. [920]

THE AUTOBIOGRAPHY OF A THIEF (ETC.) / Reade, Charles L – British Fiction Archive: Unit 2 – 9 – uk Bell [830]

AUTOBIOGRAPHY OF ADIN BALLOU, 1803-1890 : CONTAINING AN ELABORATE RECORD AND NARRATIVE OF HIS LIFE FROM INFANCY TO OLD AGE: WITH APPENDIXES / Ballou, Adin; ed by Heywood, William S – Lowell, Mass.: Vox Populi Press, 1896 – 2mf – us A.T.L.A. [240]

THE AUTOBIOGRAPHY OF ARCHBISHOP ULLATHORNE : WITH SELECTIONS FROM HIS LETTERS – London: Burns & Oates; New York: Benziger, [1892?] – 1mf – us A.T.L.A. [240]

AUTOBIOGRAPHY OF DEAN MERIVALE : WITH SELECTIONS FROM HIS CORRESPONDENCE / ed by Merivale, Judith Anne – London: E. Arnold, 1899 – 1mf – us A.T.L.A. [240]

AUTOBIOGRAPHY OF DEAN MERIVALE, WITH SELECTIONS FROM HIS CORRESPONDENCE / Merivale, Charles – Ed. by his daughter, J.A. Merivale. London: E. Arnold, 1899. 368p. Geneal. table – 1 – us U.W. Library [920]

AUTOBIOGRAPHY OF ELDER JACOB KNAPP / Knapp, Jacob – 1868 – 9 – us A.T.L.A. [240]

AUTOBIOGRAPHY OF HOLLINGTON K. TONG (CCC302) : CHINESE CHRISTIAN MONOGRAPH / Tong, Hollington Kong – (In Chinese) – [s.l: s.n, 1973] – 1r – 1 – 1984-6641 – us A.T.L.A. [920]

THE AUTOBIOGRAPHY OF JUDAS ISCARIOT : A CHARACTER STUDY / Hart, James W T – London: Kegan Paul, Trench, 1884 – 1mf – 9 – 0-8370-3504-X – 1985-1504 – us A.T.L.A. [830]

AUTOBIOGRAPHY OF LYDIA SEXTON / Sexton, Lydia – Dayton, OH: United Brethern Publishing House, 1882 – 1r – 1 – us Western Res [240]

THE AUTOBIOGRAPHY OF MARK RUTHERFORD : DISSENTING MINISTER. EDITED BY HIS FRIEND, REUBEN SHAPCOTT / White, William Hale – New York: G.P. Putnam's Sons, 1881 – 1 roll – 1 – 1-55879-407-7 – uk Libr Preservation [240]

AUTOBIOGRAPHY OF PETER CARTWRIGHT : THE BACKWOODS PREACHER / Cartwright, Peter; ed by Strickland, W P – New York: Carlton & Porter, 1857, c1856 – 2mf – us A.T.L.A. [240]

AUTOBIOGRAPHY OF REV. JAMES B. FINLEY, OR, PIONEER LIFE IN THE WEST / Finley, James B; ed by Strickland, W P – Cincinnati : Printed at the Methodist Book Concern for the author, 1853 – 2mf – us A.T.L.A. [240]

AUTOBIOGRAPHY OF THE LATE DONALD FRASER, D.D.: AND A SELECTION FROM HIS SERMONS / Fraser, Donald – With a preface by J. Oswald Dykes. London: James Nisbet & Co., 1892. 03175. (Pre-1900 Canadiana) – 9 – cn C.I.H.M. [971]

THE AUTOBIOGRAPHY OF THE REV. CHARLES FRESHMAN, LATE RABBI OF THE JEWISH SYNAGOGUE AT QUEBEC, AND GRADUATE OF THE JEWISH THEOLOGICAL SEMINARY AT PRAGUE, AT PRESENT GERMAN WESLEYAN MINISTER AT PRESTON, ONTARIO / Freshman, Charles – Toronto: S. Rose, 1868. 03258. (Pre-1900 Canadiana) – 9 – cn C.I.H.M. [971]

THE AUTOBIOGRAPHY OF THE REV. ENOCH POND, D.D. : FOR FIFTY YEARS PROFESSOR IN BANGOR THEOLOGICAL SEMINARY: A MEMORIAL OF HIS CHARACTER, WORK, AND LAST YEARS / Pond, Enoch – Boston: Congregational Sunday-School and Publishing Society, c1883 – 1mf – us A.T.L.A. [240]

AUTOBIOGRAPHY OF THE REV. LUTHER LEE / Lee, Luther – 1882 – 9 – us A.T.L.A. [920]

THE AUTOBIOGRAPHY OF THE REV. WILLIAM JAY / Jay, William – New York, 1856, c1854. 2v in 1 with index – 9 – us A.T.L.A. [920]

AN AUTOBIOGRAPHY: THE STORY OF THE LORD'S DEALINGS WITH MRS. AMANDA SMITH, THE COLORED EVANGELIST / Smith, Amanda Berry – 1893 – 9 – us A.T.L.A. [240]

AUTOBIOGRAPHY...INCLUDING HIS VOYAGES, TRAVELS, ADVENTURES / Buckingham, James Silk – London: Longman, Brown, Green and Longmans, 1855. 2v – 1 – us U.W. Library [920]

AUTOCAR – v90-123.1945-65 – 1,5,6 – us Princeton Micro [073]

AUTOCRATIC RUSSE / Golovine, Ivan G – (Russia – 19th C. series). 1860 – 9 – fr Hachette [321]

AUTO-EMANCIPATION / Pinsker, L – Ed. by A. S. Eban. London. 1936. BJ-28-19 1 – 9 – ne IDC [956]

UNOS AUTOGRAFOS DE DON BARTOLOME JOSE GALLARDO / Llanos y Torrigua, Felix de – Madrid: Tip. Revista de Arch. Bibliot. y Museos, 1924 – 1 – sp Bibl Santa Ana [920]

AUTOIMMUNITY / ed by Wilkin, Terence J – 1,5,9 – us Gordon [616]

L'AUTO-JOURNAL – (Also available on CD-ROM) – 1988-1995 – 2r per y – 5,6 – F2,700.00y – sz Infoprint [380]

AUTOMATED PAYMENTS UPDATE *see* PAYMENTS SYSTEMS REPORT

AUTOMATIC DATA PROCESSING – 1960 – 1 – uk Microform Academic [073]

AUTOMATIC TELEPHONE – v. 7-19. 1919-31 – 1,5,6 – us Princeton Micro [380]

AUTOMATICA : INTERNATIONAL JOURNAL ON AUTOMATIC CONTROL AND AUTOMATION – v1- 1963- – 5,6,9 – us UMI [073]

AUTOMATION – (1968-76 5,6. 1976- 9. See also: Production Engineering) – 1-23. 1954-76 – 1 – us UMI [621]

AUTOMATION AND REMOTE CONTROL – v17-55. 1956-94 – 1,5 – $220.00v – us UMI [629]

AUTOMATION COMMITTEE / UN Economic Commission for Europe (ECE) – 1975-81 – E/F.3 E.76 F.69 R.67 – 9 – us U.N. Pubs [340]

AUTOMATION PRODUCTS AND TECHNOLOGY – (Continued by Automation Systems v5 1990-) – Mississauga. v1-4. 1986-1989 – 9 – Can$20.00y – cn Micromedia [620]

AUTOMATION PRODUCTS AND TECHNOLOGY *see* AUTOMATION SYSTEMS

AUTOMATION SYSTEMS – (Cont: Automation Products and Technology. Cont by: Manufacturing and Process Automation v8 1993/94. 1992/93 Can$60.00y 1) – Mississauga. v5-7. 1990-93 – 9,1 – Can$20.00y – cn Micromedia [670]

AUTOMATION SYSTEMS *see*
- AUTOMATION PRODUCTS AND TECHNOLOGY
- MANUFACTURING AND PROCESS AUTOMATION

AUTOMATISME / L'Association francaise de regulation et d'automatisme – Paris. 1956-72 – 5 – fr A.C.R.P.P. [073]

AUTOMEDICA / ed by Hyndman, B et al – 1974- – 1,5,9 – us Gordon [610]

AUTOMOBILE ENGINEER – v16-58. 1926-68 – 1,5,6 – us Princeton Micro [073]

AUTOMOTIVE CHAIN STORE – (v31-. 1983-. 1,5,6,9) – v1-30. 1953-82 – 1 – us UMI [073]

AUTOMOTIVE CHAIN STORE *see* ACS MAGAZINE

AUTOMOTIVE ELECTRONICS JOURNAL – New York – $175.00y – us Fairchild Micro [629]

AUTOMOTIVE ENGINEER – (See also: JAE: The Journal of Automotive Engineering) – v1-. 1976- – 1,5,6,9 – us UMI [629]

AUTOMOTIVE ENGINEERING – (1967-. 5,6. 1976-. 9) – v. 1- 1917- – 1 – us UMI [629]

AUTOMOTIVE EXECUTIVE – (Cont: Cars and Trucks) – McLean. v1-69. jan 1979-dec 1997+* – 1 – D12284 – us UMI [650]

THE AUTOMOTIVE HISTORY COLLECTION OF THE DETROIT PUBLIC LIBRARY : A SIMPLIFIED GUIDE TO ITS HOLDINGS / Detroit Public Library – 1966. 22,900 cards on 2 reels – 1 – $200.00 export $240.00 – 0-8161-1446-3 – uk Hall [380]

AUTOMOTIVE INDUSTRIES – (1965-1975. 5,6. 1970-1975. 9) – v.1-153. 1899-1975 – 1 – us UMI [380]

AUTOMOTIVE INDUSTRIES – v42-113.1920-55 – 1,5,6 – us Princeton Micro [073]

AUTOMOTIVE MARKETING – v. 1-. 1971- 1; 1979- 5,6,9 – us UMI [650]

AUTOMOTIVE NEWS – 1925- – 1 – us UMI [629]

L'AUTONOMIE : ORGANE BI-MENSUEL DU COMITE POUR L'AUTONOMIE DE LA MACEDOINE ET DE L'ALBANIE – London, 10 May-15 Jul 1902 – 20ft – 1 – uk British Libr Newspaper [073]

AUTONOMIE – London. v1-8 n212. nov 6 1886-apr 22 1893 – 1 – us Res Libr [073]

O AUTONOMISTA : ORGAO IMPARCIAL – Rio Branco, Acre. 1 Jun-Out 1914; Fev-Abr, Jun, Set 1915; Fev-18 Mar 1916 – 1,5,6 – bl Biblioteca [072]

AUTONOMO : HEBDOMADARIO REPUBLICANO – Queluz de Minas, 2 Jun 1900-Dec 1901; Jan-May, Sep, 27 Nov 1902 – 1,5,6 – bl Biblioteca [072]

AUTOPORTRAITS DE COURBET / Reunion des musees nationaux. Paris – 1973. 50 illus. 1 fiche – 9 – fr Réunion [700]

AUTOPRODUCTS *see* AD AND D, AUTOMOTIVE DESIGN AND DEVELOPMENT

AUTORES E LIVROS – (Suppl to: A Manha) – Rio de Janeiro, 10 Aug 1941-Mar 1945; Jun 1948-Dec 1950 – 1,5,6 – bl Biblioteca [073]

AUTORES GERMANOS EN EL PERU : FLORILEGIO DE LA POESIA ALEMANA EN VERSIONES PERUANAS / Estuardo, Nunez – Lima: Ministerio de Educacion Publica, 1953 – 1r – 1 – us U.W. Library [430]

LA AUTORIDAD DOCTRINAL DE LA IGLESIA CATOLICA Y LA LIBERTAD DE PENSAMIENTO / Vazquez Camarasa, Enrique – Madrid: Imprenta del Asilo de Hurfanos del S.C. de Jesus, 1916 – 1 – sp Bibl Santa Ana [240]

DIE AUTORITAET DER HLG. SCHRIFT UND DIE KRITIK : NACH DER SCHRIFT UND DEN GRUNDSAETZEN LUTHERS / Haug, Karl – Strassburg: Strassburger Druckerei & Verlagsanstalt, 1891 – 1mf – 9 – 0-8370-3523-6 – 1985-1523 – us A.T.L.A. [220]

L'AUTORITE : HEBDO / ed by Larue, Gilbert – Montreal, Canada. 28 dec 1913-2 avr 1955 – 8r – 1 – Can$65.00r – cn Can Microfilming [072]

L'AUTORITE – Paris. 25 fev 1886-6 sept 1914, 24 mars-19 sept 1928, 16 fevr-14 sept 1929 – 1 – fr A.C.R.P.P. [073]

L'AUTORITE – Paris: Schneider, may 1849 – reel 1 item 15 – 1 – us Res Libr [072]

L'AUTORITE DE JESUS:...SES DISCIPLES IMMEDIATS D'APRES LE TEMOIGNAGE... SYNOPTIQUES / Wuarin, Louis – Geneve: B. Soullier, 1875. 1 fiche – 9 – us A.T.L.A. [240]

L'AUTOSACRIFICE DANS LE TONALAMATL DU CODEX BORBONICUS / Beligand, N – 15 – F150.00 – fr Ethnologie [306]

AUTO-SPORT : ORGANE DE L'A.O.A. – Montreal. v2 n10. jun 1926-v3 n2. nov 1926 – 1r – 1 – Can$25.00 – cn Can Microfilming [790]

AUTOUR DE KITA : ETUDE SOUDANAISE / Tellier, G – Paris: H Chales-Lavauzell, [1898] – 1 – us Res Libr [960]

AUTOUR DE MANDERA; NOTES SUR L'OUZIGOUA, L'OUKWERE ET L'OUDOE / Picarda, R P – In Missions Catholiques. Lyons. 1886 – 1 – us Res Libr [306]

AUTOUR DE MELFI. LES IAL-NAS / Derendinger, L – Paris, Imprimerie-librairie militaire universelle, L. Fournier – 9 – 5.00 – fr Orientalistes [960]

AUTOUR DE NOIRT: REVUE MENSUELLE – v.1, nos. 1-24. 1895-96 – 9 – us Sibley [780]

AUTOUR DU PROCES DE P. O. U. M.: DES REVOLUTIONNAIRES EN DANGER DE MORT – Paris?, 1938. Fiche W 737. (Blodgett Collection of Spanish Civil War Pamphlets) – 9 – us H.U. College Libr [946]

AUTOUR D'UNE CARRIERE POLITIQUE: JOSEPH ISRAEL TARTE, 1880-97, DIX-SEPT ANS DE CONTRADICTION – Montreal: 1897? 00068. (Pre-1900 Canadiana) – 9 – cn C.I.H.M. [971]

AUTOUR D'UNE FEMME SOUS LES TROPIQUES / Poulet, Georges – Paris: Albin Michel, 1927. 254p. (Les Femmes Collection) – 3mf – 9 – $8.00 – fr Bibl Nationale [305]

L'AUTO-VELO – puis L'Auto. Paris. 16 oct 1900-17 Aout 1944 – 1 – fr A.C.R.P.P. [073]

AUTOWEEK – (1986-. 1,5,6) – 1982- – 9 – us UMI [629]

Autran, F C *see*
- CODE INTERNATIONAL DE L'ABORDAGE, DE L'ASSISTANCE...
- CODE INTERNATIONAL DE L'ABORDAGE MARITIME...
- PAPER ON LA RESPONSIBILITE DES PROPRIETAIRES DE NAVIRES...

Autremont, P d' *see* LE SAINT-SIEGE EN DROIT INTERNATIONAL

L'AUTRICHE SLAVE ET ROUMAINE – Journal politique hebdomadaire paraissant le mercredi. no. 1-29. Paris. 8 nov 1887-30 mai 1888 – 1 – fr A.C.R.P.P. [073]

Auvard, Aldred *see* HYGIENE INFANTILE ET MODERNE

Auvillain, L *see* LES OUVRIERS ETRANGERS...

Auvray, Louis M *see* STATISTIQUE DU DEPARTEMENT DE LA SARTHE

AUX ARTISTES. DU PASSE ET DE L'AVENIR DES BEAUX-ARTS / Barrault, Emile – Paris, 1830 – 1 – us U.W. Library [700]

AUX ARTISTES, DU PASSE ET DE L'AVENIR DES BEAUXARTS. DOCTRINE DE SAINT-SIMON / Barrault, Emile – Paris, A. Mesnier. 1830. 84 p. Les Saint-Simoniens, 1825-1834. 6850 – 9 – fr Hachette [335]

AUX BAMBINS CANADIENS / Marjolaine – Montreal: Editions Albert Levesque, 1934. SEM105P1332 – 2mf – 9 – Can$4.50 – cn Bibl Nat [971]

AUX CHARPENTIERS DE PARIS, MAITRES ET OUVRIERS / Le Noble, Jean Pierre F – Paris. 1845. (La Condition Ouvriere. Part Two.) – 9 – 2.50 – fr Bibl Nationale [360]

AUX CHRETIENS / Duveyrier, Charles – Paris, Pillet. s.d. 19 p. (suivi de) Extrait de l'Organisateur. Correspondance. Paris, Everat. 1830. 14 p. Les Saint-Simoniens, 1825-1834. 6857 – 9 – fr Hachette [240]

AUX DIRECTEURS DE LA COMPAGNIE DU CHEMIN DE FER DE PHILLIPSBURG, FARNHAM ET YAMASKA / Foster, John – s.l.: s.n., 1872?. 04334. (Pre-1900 Canadiana) – 9 – cn C.I.H.M. [971]

AUX ECOUTES – Paris. 1925-aout 1940 – 1 – fr A.C.R.P.P. [073]

AUX ELECTEURS DU COMTE DE LAPRAIRIE ET NAPIERVILLE: DOCUMENTS ET FAITS – 1896? 00843. (Pre-1900 Canadiana) – 9 – cn C.I.H.M. [971]

AUX ELECTEURS DU COMTE DE L'ASSOMPTION: DOCUMENTS ET FAITS – 1896? 00816. (Pre-1900 Canadiana) – 9 – cn C.I.H.M. [971]

AUX ELECTEURS DU COMTE DE L'ASSOMPTION: UNE AUTRE VOIX EPISCOPALE: CATEGORIQUES DECLARATIONS DE MGR. CAMERON: LETTRE CIRCULAIRE AU CLERGE D'ANTIGONISH – 1896? 04087. (Pre-1900 Canadiana) – 9 – cn C.I.H.M. [971]

AUX FEDERES, PAR DES CITOYENS AMIS DE LA CONSTITUTION / Robespierre, Maximilien de – Paris: Impr. du Patriote francais, 1792.4p. 1 fiche. (Political Science Collection) – 9 – 6.00 – fr Bibl Nationale [323]

AUX FEMMES / Jacob – (signe: Jeanne Victoire). s.d. (aout 1832), 3 p. Les Saint-Simoniens, 1825-1834. 6910 – 9 – fr Hachette [305]

AUX FILLETTES CANADIENNES / Marjolaine – Montreal: Editions Albert Levesque, 1933. SEM105P1820 – 1mf – 9 – Can$2.25 – cn Bibl Nat [971]

AUX FILLETTES CANADIENNES / Marjolaine – Montreal: Editions Albert Levesque, 1936. SEM105P1819 – 2mf – 9 – Can$4.50 – cn Bibl Nat [971]

AUX HONORABLES CHEVALIERS, CITOYENS ET BOURGEOIS, LES COMMUNES DU ROYAUME-UNI DE LA GRANDE-BRETAGNE ET D'IRLANDE, ASSEMBLEES EN PARLEMENT / Papineau, Louis Joseph – [Quebec]: [Chambre d'Assemblee], [1834] – 1mf – 9 – Can$2.25 – cn Bibl Nat [971]

AUX HONORABLES MEMBRES DU COMITE CATHOLIQUE DU CONSEIL DE L'INSTRUCTION PUBLIQUE / Arnold de Jesus, Frere – Montreal, 1884. 02200. (Pre-1900 Canadiana) – 9 – cn C.I.H.M. [370]

AUX INDUSTRIELS / Decourdemanche, A – Lettres sur la legislation dans ses rapports avec l'industrie et la propriete. Paris, Guiraudet, 1831, 47 et 114 p. Les Saint-Simoniens, 1825-1834. 6873 – 9 – fr Hachette [335]

AUX JEUNES GENS QUI VEULENT REUSSIR / Clement, Alex – Montreal?, 1898. 00682. (Pre-1900 Canadiana) – 9 – cn C.I.H.M. [300]

AUX MARSEILLAIS, UN COMPAGNON DE LA FEMME PARTANT POUR L'ORIENT / Colin, Auguste – Marseille, impr. de Mille et Senes, 1833, 8 p. Les Saint-Simoniens, 1825-1834. 6931 – 9 – fr Hachette [335]

AUX MINES D'OR DU KLONDIKE: DU LAC BENNETT A DAWSON CITY / Boillet, Leon – Paris: Hachette, 1899. 00163. (Pre-1900 Canadiana) – 9 – cn C.I.H.M. [550]

AUX ORIGINES DE LA SORBONNE : 1: ROBERT DE SORBON / Glorieux, P – (2: Le Cartulaire. Paris, 1965 46.00) – Paris, 1966 – Dfl28.00 – ne Slangenburg [240]

AUX OUVRIERS EN BATIMENT. UN MOT SUR LA CRISE ACTUELLE / Le Noble, Jean Pierre F – Paris. 1840. (La Condition Ouvriere. Part Two.) – 9 – 2.50 – fr Bibl Nationale [360]

AUX RUINES DES GRANDES CITES SOUDANAISES / Peyrissac, Leon – Paris: A Challamel, 1910 – 1 – us Res Libr [930]

AUX SAINT-SIMONIENS / Lechevalier, J – Lettre sur la division survenue dans l'association Saint-Simonienne. Paris, Everat, 1831, 56 p. DECLARATION DE JULES LECHEVALIER AUX SAINT-SIMONIENS, le 28 nov. 1831, Ibid., 4 p. Les Saint-Simoniens, 1825-1834. 6949 – 9 – fr Hachette [335]

AUX SAINT-SIMONIENS ET AUX SAINT-SIMONIENNES. SUR LA NECESSITE ET LA POSSIBILITE DE RALLIER LA DOCTRINE DE SAINT-SIMON A LA FOI CHRETIENNE ET AU CHRISTIANISME TEMPOREL / Bougeois, CF – Paris, Everat, 1837, xxiii-33 p. Les Saint-Simoniens, 1825-1834. 7007 – 9 – fr Hachette [335]

AUX TRAVAILLEURS DE FRANCE / Parti ouvrier francais. Conseil national – Paris. 1910. (La Condition Ouvriere. Part Two.) – 9 – 5.00 – fr Bibl Nationale [360]

O AUXILIADOR DA INDUSTRIA NACIONAL – Rio de Janeiro, 15 Jan 1833-31 Dec 1892 – 1,5,6 – bl Biblioteca [072]

AUXILIARY – Fairfield. Neb. 1914-1965 – 1 – us UMI [071]

AUXILIARY LEADER *see* VOLUNTEER LEADER

EL AUXILIO DE AMERICA PARA LA RECONSTRUCCION DE ESPANA; TEXTO TAQUIGRAFICO DE LA CONFERENCIA PRONUNCIADA EN LA SALA STUDIUM DE BARCELONA, EL DIA 9 DE OCTUBRE DE 1938 / Prieto, Indalecio – Barcelona, 1938. Fiche W1117. (Blodgett Collection of Spanish Civil War Pamphlets) – 9 – us H.U. College Libr [946]

AUXILIO SOCIAL – Spain. Valladolid, 1937? Fiche W 738. (Blodgett Collection of Spanish Civil War Pamphlets) – 9 – us H.U. College Libr [946]

Auxilio Social *see* NORMAS DE FUNCIONAMIENTO EN LOS CENTROS DE ALIMENTACION INFANTIL

Auzary, Bernadette *see* FLUCTUAT NEC MERGITUR. LA PREVOTE DES MARCHANDS ET L'URBANISME PARISIEN AU 15 SIECLE D'APRES LA JURISPRUDENCE DU PARLEMENT (1380-1500)

Auzillon, C *see* LA PROPRIETE PRIVEE...

AV COMMUNICATION REVIEW – (Cont by: ECTJ – Educational and Technology Journal n1466.01. Former title: Audio Visual Communication Review) – Washington. v1-25 win 1953-win 1977 1; v17-25 spr 1969-win 1977 5,9 – 1,5,9 – inquire – D1466 – us UMI [370]
AV GUIDE – (Former titles: Educational Screen; Educational Screen & Audio-Visual Guide) – Des Plaines. v1-76 jan 1922-dec 1997+ 1; v47-76 jan-dec 1997+ 5; v54-76 jan 1975-dec 1997+ 9 – 1,5,9 – inquire – us UMI [370]
AV VIDEO – (Cont: Audio Visual Directions. Cont by: New Directions in AV Video) – Torrance. v6-8. feb 1984-sep 1986* – 1,5,9 – D12771.02 – us UMI [073]
AV VIDEO – (Cont: New Directions in AV Video) – Torrance. v-9-19. apr 1987-dec 1997+ – 1,5*,9 – D12771.04 – us UMI [073]
AVADANA KALPALATA, A COLLECTION OF LEGENDARY STORIES ABOUT THE BODHISATTVAS; WITH ITS TIBETAN VERSION / Ksmendra – Calcutta, W. Carey, 1888-1913. 2v. By Sarat Chandra Das and Hari Mohan Vidyabushana – 1 – us U.W. Library [280]
AVALANCHE – Memphis. Tenn. -w. 1879-95 – 1 – us UMI [071]
AVALANCHE – New York, NY. 1970-76 – 1r – 1 – $50.00 – R04902 – us Library Micro [071]
AVALANCHE ATLAS : ILLUSTRATED INTERNATIONAL AVALANCHE CLASSIFICATION / International Commission on Snow and Ice of the International Assoc. of Hydrological Sciences – (English/French/ Spanish/Russian/German) – 1981 – 267p – 9 – 92-3-001696-9 – fr UNESCO [900]
AVALANCHE CONTROL – 1985 – 248p – it F.A.O. [550]
Avaliani, S *see* ZEMEL'NYI VOPOS V ROSSII I KOOPERATSIIA
Avalle, Ernest *see* NOTICES SUR LES COLONIES ANGLAISES
Avalon, A *see* THE SERPENT POWER: BEING THE SHATCHAKRA-NIRUPANA AND PADUKA-PANCHAKA
Avalov, Pavel Mikhailovich *see* V BORBIE S BOLSHEVIZMOM
O AVANCA : ORGAO DO CLUB PESSOAL DO AVANCA – Itacoatiara, Amazonas. 13 Jun-4 Jul 1907 – 1,5,6 – bl Biblioteca [072]
AVANCE – Plasencia, 1935 – 5 – sp Bibl Santa Ana [073]
EL AVANCE – (Lacking: some issues) – 1942-50 – 1r – 1 – ATLA S0665A – us A.T.L.A. [073]
AVANCE PARA LA BIBLIOGRAFIA DE OBRAS IMPRESAS DEL D. BENITO ARIAS MONTANO / Morales Oliver, Luis – Badajoz: Imprenta del Hospicio Princial, 1928. Separata R.C.Est.Ex. – 1 – sp Bibl Santa Ana [010]
AVANCES ARQUEOLOGICOS EN SANTA AMALIA / Roso de Luna, Mario – Madrid: Fortanet, 1912. B.R.A.H. 60, p. 260 – sp Bibl Santa Ana [930]
EN AVANT : BULLETIN OFFICIEL DE L'ARMEE DU SALUT – Montreal, Canada. n41. 1sep 1888 – 1r – 1 – Can$25.00 – cn Can Microfilming [073]
EN AVANT / ed by Grignon, C-Henri – St-Hyacinthe, Canada. 15 jan 1937-8 dec 1939 – 1r – 1 – Can$40.00 – cn Can Microfilming [072]
L'AVANT GARDE : ORGANE DE L'UNION MAROCAINE DU TRAVAIL – Casablanca: L'Union, 1963-feb 19 1971 – 4r – 1 – us Res Libr [072]
AVANT GARDENER – 1984- – 1,5,6,9 – us UMI [631]
AVANT PROJECT DU PLAN QUINQUENNAL 1960-1964 / Morocco. Conseil Superieur du Plan – 1960? BNE-3025 1 – 9 – ne IDC [330]
L'AVANT-COUREUR – Lachute, Canada. 15 mar 1965- – 1r – 1 – Can$20.00 – cn Can Microfilming [072]
L'AVANT-COUREUR – Red. Meusnier de Querlon. Paris. 1760-1773. Suite de: La Feuille necessaire voir a ce titre – 1 – fr A.C.R.P.P. [073]
AVANTE : JORNAL DEFENSOR DOS INTERESSES COLETIVOS – Manaus, Amazonas. 1 Dez 1945 – 1,5,6 – bl Biblioteca [072]
L'AVANT-GARDE : INDEPENDANCE, PATRIOTISME – Montreal, Canada. 10 oct 1908-v1 n8. 5 dec 1908 – 1r – 1 – Can$35.00 – cn Can Microfilming [072]
L'AVANT-GARDE – no 1- 1966- Irr. SEM35P160 – 1r – 1 – Can$15.00 – cn Bibl Nat [073]
L'AVANT-GARDE – Paris. avr 1905-mars 1906 – 1 – fr A.C.R.P.P. [073]
L'AVANT-GARDE – Paris. Dec. 22, 1944-Jan. 6, 1948 – 1 – 35.00r – us Hoover Inst Photo [072]
L'AVANT-GARDE – Quebec, Canada. 5 dec 1896-26 avr 1898 – 1r – 1 – Can$40.00 – cn Can Microfilming [072]
L'AVANT-GARDE – Quebec, Canada. v1 n2. 25 jun 1932 – 1r – 1 – Can$25.00 – cn Can Microfilming [072]
L'AVANT-GARDE – Roberval, Quebec. 13 mai 1916 – 1r – 1 – Can$25.00 – cn Can Microfilming [072]
L'AVANT-GARDE – Victoriaville, Canada. v1 n6. 6 mar 1924 – 1r – 1 – Can$25.00 – cn Can Microfilming [072]
L'AVANT-GARDE – (Filmed as pt of: Commune de Paris newspapers. Newspapers on these reels are filmed chronologically, not alphabetically) – Paris: Imp A Vallee, mar 26-31, apr 1-3,5-7,9,11-12,14-15,17-23,25-30, may 1-11,13-19,21-22 – 2r – 1 – us Res Libr [072]
L'AVANT-GARDE – Port-au-Prince: Impr de l'Oeil, 1ere annee n1-2e annee n77. 12 janv 1882-28 juin 1883 – 6 sheets – us Res Libr [072]
AVANT-GARDE AND ARCHITECTURE IN CZECHOSLOVAKIA 1909-1938 / ed by Macel, O – 11 titles – 9 – ne IDC [720]
L'AVANT-GARDE DE NORMANDIE – Rouen. 1913-14 – 1 – fr A.C.R.P.P. [073]
L'AVANT-GARDE OUVRIERE ET COMMUNISTE – puis Ouvriere et paysanne; Organe de defense des jeunes travailleurs. no. 1-687. Paris. sept 1920-36 – 1 – fr A.C.R.P.P. [073]
L'AVANT-GARDE REPUBLICAINE ET SOCIALISTE – Toulouse. sept 1891-juin 1892 – 1 – fr A.C.R.P.P. [073]
L'AVANT-GARDE VOLTAIQUE : ORGANE DE LA JEUNESSE VOLTAIQUE, RDA – [Ouagadougou: s.n. v1 n1 (undated). v1 n2 jul 22 1958 – us Res Libr [072]
L'AVANTI! – Chicago, [oct 1918-oct 1 1921] – 1 – us Res Libr [071]
AVANTI – 1945- – 2r per yr – 5 – inquiure – us Ross [072]
AVANTI – Milan, 28 Dec 1914-8 Aug 1919 (imperfect) – 10r – 1 – uk British Libr Newspaper [072]
AVANTI : QUOTIDIANO DEL PARTIDO SOCIALISTA ITALIANO – Roma, 1896-1926, 1935 (incompl) – 1 – us Hoover Inst Photo [335]
AVANTI *see* JOURNAUX DIVERS
AVANTI! – 1945-1995 – 2r per y – 5,6 – Sfr936.00 – sz Infoprint [335]
AVANTI! : BULLETIN PSI – Paris-Milan, 1922-24, 1926, 1939, 1947 (all incompl), 1948-60 (Milan ed only) – 1 – us Hoover Inst Photo [072]
AVANTI! : BULLETIN PSI / Partito Socialisto Italiano – Paris, Milan, 1956- – 1 – us Res Libr [072]
AVANTI! : ORGAN OF THE ITALIAN SOCIALIST PARTY / Italian Socialist Party – Rome, 1896-1955 – 55r – 1 – $4,160.00 – us UPA [335]
AVANTI! – Roma: Typ de l'Avanti, [1896-dec 25 1896-1991] – 1 – us Res Libr [072]
AVANTI URY KERENSKAGO I KO / E K– v – Izd. 2. Novorossi isk: Izd. Initsiativno i gruppy "Vpered", 1919 – 1 – CSUX88-B3745 – us Hoover Inst Photo [072]
L'AVANT-POSTE – Revue de litterature et de critique. no. 1-3. Paris. juin-oct nov 1933 – 1 – fr A.C.R.P.P. [800]
L'AVANT-POSTE GASPESIEN *see* LA VOIX DE LA VALLEE
AVANT-POSTES DE CAVALERIE LEGERE: SOUVENIRS / Brack, Fortune de – Paris. Anselin. 1831. 556p. fig. (Strategy of War Series) – 9 – fr Hachette [355]
L'AVANT-SCENE – Theatre. suite de: Opera. Hebdomadaire du theatre, du cinema des lettres et des arts. no. 1-327. Paris. mars 1949-fevr 1965 – 1 – fr A.C.R.P.P. [820]
AVANT-SCENE – Theatre, litterature, beaux-arts, modes. Red. en chef Charles de Sarlat. 43 no. Paris. 25 janv 1867-28 mai 1872 – 1 – fr A.C.R.P.P. [800]
EL AVARO / Moreno Torrado, Luis – Badajoz: Tipografia y Encuadernacion La Minerva Extremena, 1907 – 1 – sp Bibl Santa Ana [810]
AVC DEVELOPMENT AND DELIVERY – (Cont: Audio Visual Communications. Cont by: AVC Presentation Development and Delivery) – Melville. v25. jul-oct 1991 – 1,5,9 – D2396.03 – us UMI [380]
AVC DEVELOPMENT AND DELIVERY *see* AVC PRESENTATION DEVELOPMENT AND DELIVERY
AVC PRESENTATION – (Absorbed by: Advanced Imaging. Cont: AVC Presentation Development and Delivery. Ceased publ) – Melville. v26-27. jul 1992-jul 1993 – 1,5,9 – D2396.05 – us UMI [073]
AVC PRESENTATION *see*
- ADVANCED IMAGING
- AVC PRESENTATION DEVELOPMENT AND DELIVERY

AVC PRESENTATION DEVELOPMENT AND DELIVERY – (Cont: AVC Development and Delivery. Cont by: AVC Presentation) – Melville. v25-26. nov 1991-jun 1992 – 1,5,9 – D 2396.04 – us UMI [073]
AVC PRESENTATION DEVELOPMENT AND DELIVERY *see*
- AVC DEVELOPMENT AND DELIVERY
- AVC PRESENTATION

AVC PRESENTATION, TECHNOLOGY AND APPLICATIONS – (Cont: Audio-Visual Communications. Cont by: Audio Visual Communications) – Woodbury. v23. jul-nov 1989 – 1,5,9 – D2396.01 – us UMI [073]
Avdeev, Petr Nikolaevich *see* TRUDOVYE KONFLIKTY V SSSR
AVE EVA : ERZAEHLUNG / Johst, Hanns – Muenchen: A Langen, 1932 – 1r – 1 – us U.W. Library [830]
AVE MARIA. CUARESMA / Gil Becerra, Benito – 1733 – 9 – 1.50f – sp Bibl Santa Ana [240]
AVE MARIA. PARAISO / Gil Becerra, Benito – 1739 – 9 – 1.50f – sp Bibl Santa Ana [240]
AVE MARIA. PARAISO DE ORACIONES SAGRADAS EN... / Gil Becerra, Benito – Madrid: Thomas Rodriguez Frias, s.a. – 1 – sp Bibl Santa Ana [240]
Avebury, Lord *see* FREE TRADE
Avedisian, Lori-Ann *see* THE EFFECT OF SELECTED BUFFERING AGENTS ON PERFORMANCE IN THE COMPETITIVE 1600 METER RUN
AVENAL PROGRESS – Avenal, CA. 1986 – 3+ r – 1 – $150.00 ($50.00y) – B03582 – us Library Micro [071]
AVENAL TIMES – Avenal, CA. 1980-Jun 1982 – 3r – 1 – $150.00 – B02036 – us Library Micro [071]
Avenant, C d' *see* ESSAYS UPON PEACE AT HOME...
Avenarius, Ferdinand *see* BAAL
Avenarius, Richard *see* UEBER DIE BEIDEN ERSTEN PHASEN DES SPINOZISCHEN PANTHEISMUS
AVENCEBROLIS (IBN GEBIROL) FONS VITAE : BGPHMA 1/2-4 / Baeumker, C – Muenster, 1892/95 – 10mf – 9 – ne Slangenburg [240]
Avenel, Henri *see* CHANSONS ET CHANSONNIERS
L'AVENEMENT DU PEUPLE – Paris. No.1-75.19 sept-1 dec 1851. Suite de: L'Evenement. Voir a ce titre – 1 – fr A.C.R.P.P. [073]
L'AVENIR – Gatineau, Canada. 25 oct 1951-v3 n21. 27 mai 1954 – 1r – 1 – Can$25.00 – cn Can Microfilming [072]
L'AVENIR – Guadeloupe. French West Indies. With ommissions. 1907-1912 – 1 – us UMI [072]
L'AVENIR – Journal politique, litteraire. no. 1-32. Londres. 5 oct-16 nov 1872 – 1 – fr A.C.R.P.P. [073]
L'AVENIR : JOURNAL REPUBLICAIN, PUBLIE DANS LES INTERETS POPULAIRES – (2nd ed: v3 n11 12 oct 1849-v4 n20 29 jan 1851 1r Can$35.00) – Montreal, Canada. 16 jul 1847-v8 n23. 22 dec 1857 – 3r – 1 – Can$50.00r – cn Can Microfilming [073]
L'AVENIR / ed by Langelier, J-Francois – Quebec, Canada. 27 mai-12 jul 1893 – 1r – 1 – Can$30.00 – cn Can Microfilming [072]
L'AVENIR – Magog, Canada. v1 n4. 3 mar 1936 – 1r – 1 – Can$25.00 – cn Can Microfilming [072]
L'AVENIR – Montreal, Canada. 1847-57 – 3r – 1 – $204.00 – cn Library Assoc [971]
L'AVENIR – Revue politique, litteraire et des modes. Red. en chef H. Bonnelier. Paris. dec 1841-mars 1842 – 1 – fr A.C.R.P.P. [073]
L'AVENIR – Yarmouth, Nova Scotia. v1 n14. 1 dec 1880 – 1r – 1 – Can$25.00 – cn Can Microfilming [072]
L'AVENIR *see*
- OUI (L'AVENIR)
- LE SAUVAGE
- LES VRAIS DEBATS

L'AVENIR – Leopoldville: [s.n.], jun 20, jul 7 1960 – us Res Libr [072]
L'AVENIR – Port-au-Prince, Haiti: [s.n.] 1 annee n1-27. 30 dec 1899-7 juil 1900 – us Res Libr [072]
L'AVENIR *see* SEPT-ILES JOURNAL
L'AVENIR CANADIEN – Manchester, NH. v3 n34. 11 jun 1891-v3 n40. 23 jul 1891 – 1r – 1 – Can$25.00 – cn Can Microfilming [071]
L'AVENIR DE BEAUHARNOIS *see* LE COURRIER DE BEAUHARNOIS
L'AVENIR DE BROME MISSISQUOI – Farmham, Canada. 8 dec 1965-v8 n15. 30 aut 1972 – 3r – 1 – Can$60.00r – cn Can Microfilming [072]
L'AVENIR DE JONQUIERE – Jonquiere, Canada. 18 mai 1911-v2 n2. 21 jun 1912 – 1r – 1 – Can$35.00 – cn Can Microfilming [072]
L'AVENIR DE LA BRETAGNE – Journal national breton et federaliste europeen. Dir. Pierre Loquet. Brest. 1958-juin 1972 – 1 – fr A.C.R.P.P. [073]
L'AVENIR DE LA FRANCE – [Paris]: E Briere, aug 1 1848 – us Res Libr [072]
L'AVENIR DE LA MAURICIE – Cap-de-la-Madeleine, Canada. v12 n37. 8 jan 1947-v19 n23. 7 nov 1953 – 3r – 1 – Can$65.00r – cn Can Microfilming [072]
L'AVENIR DE LA VALLEE DE L'ORNE – Journal republicain. no. 412-488. Joeuf. 1932-juin 1933 – 1 – fr A.C.R.P.P. [073]
L'AVENIR DE L'EST / ed by Lafontaine, L-B – Montreal, Canada. v4 n26. 23 mai 1908 – 1r – 1 – Can$25.00 – cn Can Microfilming [072]
L'AVENIR DE L'EST – Pointe-aux-Trembles, Canada. v4 n33. 17 aut 1960-31 dec 1969; 7 jan1986- 31 dec 1986 – 4r – 1 – Can$120.00r – cn Can Microfilming [072]
L'AVENIR DE L'OUEST – Winnipeg, Canada. v1 n3. 13 sep 1905 – 1r – 1 – Can$25.00 – cn Can Microfilming [072]
L'AVENIR DE MAISONNEUVE – Montreal, Canada. numero unique. 6 jun 1896 – 1r – 1 – Can$25.00 – cn Can Microfilming [072]
L'AVENIR DE PARIS – Toutes les informations en toute independance. Paris. janv-juin 1919, janv-juin 1920, 1923, janv-juin 1926, juil 1927-juin 1928 – 1 – fr A.C.R.P.P. [073]
L'AVENIR DES MINORITES FRANCAISES AU CANADA / Roy, Camille – Quebec: l'Action catholique, 1938. SEM105P1744 – 1mf – 9 – Can$2.25 – cn Bibl Nat [305]
L'AVENIR DU CANADA : JOURNAL D'AGRICULTURE ILLUSTRE – Montreal, Canada. 8 avr-v1 n11. 17 jun 1910 – 1r – 1 – Can$35.00 – cn Can Microfilming [630]
L'AVENIR DU CANADA: DISCOURS PRONONCE AU PARC SOHMER A MONTREAL, LE 4 AVRIL 1893 / Mercier, Honore – Montreal: Cie d'impr. et de lithographie Gebhardt-Berthiaume, 1893. SEM16P184 – 1r – 5 – Can$9.00 – cn Bibl Nat [971]
L'AVENIR DU CITOYEN – Grand-Mere, Canada. 18 dec 1968 – 1r – 1 – Can$25.00 – cn Can Microfilming [072]
L'AVENIR DU CONGO – Leopoldville, 1959 (Dec. 31)-1960 (July 12) – 4r – 9 – AF-102/3 – ne IDC [073]
L'AVENIR DU HAUT-RICHELIEU – St Jean, Canada. v1 n39. 17 jul 1973 – 1r – 1 – Can$25.00 – cn Can Microfilming [072]
L'AVENIR DU KATANGA – (Issues for jun 19-30 1961 filmed as pt of: Herbert C Weiss collection on the Belgian Congo jun 19-30 1960) – Elisabethville: V Nawezi – us Res Libr [072]
L'AVENIR DU NORD / ed by Prevost, J-E & Prevost, Pierre – St Jerome, Canada. 3 jan 1897-22 mai 1969 – 21r – 1 – Can$50.00r – cn Can Microfilming [072]
L'AVENIR DU PEUPLE CANADIEN-FRANCAIS / Nevers, Edmond de – Paris: H. Jouve, 1896. SEM16P189 – 1r – 5 – Can$9.00 – cn Bibl Nat [971]
L'AVENIR DU TONKIN – Paraissant le mercredi et le samedi. Hanoi. oct 1886-1907, 1910-15, 1922-juin 1941 – 1 – fr A.C.R.P.P. [073]
L'AVENIR DU TRAVAILLEUR – Organe du Parti ouvrier de la region Nord. Tourcoing-Roubaix. fevr-juil 1887 – 1 – fr A.C.R.P.P. [073]

L'AVENIR ET SEPT-ILES JOURNAL *see* SEPT-ILES JOURNAL

L'AVENIR (LES VRAI DEBATS) – Montreal, Canada. 1900-01 – 1 reel – 1 – $68.00 – cn Library Assoc [971]

L'AVENIR LIBERAL – (Filmed as pt of: Commune de Paris newspapers. Newspapers on these reels are filmed chronologically, not alphabetically) – Ed. su Soir. Paris: Impr de l'Avenir liberal, mar 24 1871 – us Res Libr [072]

L'AVENIR NATIONAL – Manchester, NH. v28 n27. 23 oct 1916; v46 n245. 29 jun 1935; v54 n216. 25 jun 1943 – 1r – 1 – Can$30.00 – cn Can Microfilming [071]

L'AVENIR NATIONAL – Red. A. Peyrat. Paris. 10 janv 1865-26 oct 1873 – 1 – fr A.C.R.P.P. [073]

AVENIR NATIONAL – Red. en chef Paul Feval. Paris. 4 juil-4 sept 1848 – 1 – fr A.C.R.P.P. [073]

L'AVENIR SAGUENEEN – Chicoutimi, Canada. 12 dec 1949-26 oct 1950 – 1r – 1 – Can$65.00 – cn Can Microfilming [072]

L'AVENIR SOCIALISTE – Paris. 1933-avr 1939 – 1 – fr A.C.R.P.P. [073]

L'AVENIR SYNDICAL / Organe de la Confederation Nationale du Travail et des Unions et Federations des Syndicats Nationaux de France – no. 70-225. Paris. 29 sept 1917-1er dec 1924 – 1 – fr A.C.R.P.P. [073]

L'AVENIR WEEK-END – Sept-Iles, Canada. 1 fev 1975-3 mar 1979 – 6r – 1 – Can$70.00 – cn Can Microfilming [072]

AVENIRS – Paris. 1947-72 – 5 – fr A.C.R.P.P. [073]

AVENTURA 77 / Delegacion de la Juventud – Caceres: Imp. Sergio Dorado, 1977 – 1 – sp Bibl Santa Ana [946]

AVENTURAS DE GIL BLAS DE SANTILLANA. TOMO 1 / Lesage, Alano Renato – 1787 – 1mf – 9 – Pta1,000.00 – 84-7848-249-0 – sp Pentalfa [920]

AVENTURAS DE GIL BLAS DE SANTILLANA. TOMO 2 / Lesage, Alano Renato – 1787 – 1mf – 9 – Pta1,000.00 – 84-7848-251-2 – sp Pentalfa [920]

AVENTURAS DE GIL BLAS DE SANTILLANA. TOMO 3 / Lesage, Alano Renato – 1788 – 1mf – 9 – Pta1,000.00 – 84-7848-252-0 – sp Pentalfa [920]

AVENTURAS DE GIL BLAS DE SANTILLANA. TOMO 4 / Lesage, Alano Renato – 1788 – 1mf – 9 – Pta1,000.00 – 84-7848-253-9 – sp Pentalfa [920]

AVENTURAS DE GIL BLAS DE SANTILLANA. TOMO 5 / Lesage, Alano Renato – 1791 – 1mf – 9 – Pta1,000.00 – 84-7848-254-7 – sp Pentalfa [920]

AVENTURAS Y DESVENTURAS DEL TERCER DIEGO GARCIA DE PAREDES / Munoz de San Pedro, Miguel – Badajoz: Imp. de la Diputacion Prov., 1957. Rev. Est. Ex – sp Bibl Santa Ana [830]

L'AVENTURE – no. 5-9, fragm. Paris. juil 1927-mars 1929 – 1 – fr A.C.R.P.P. [073]

AVENTURES DE COW-BOYS – 726 nos. 1948-1962. SEM16P319 – 8r – 5 – Can$219.00 – cn Bibl Nat [800]

LES AVENTURES DE JACQUES SADEUR DANS LA DECOUVERTE ET LE VOYAGE DE LA TERRE AUSTRALE CONTENANT LES COUTUMES ET LES MOEURS DES AUSTRALIENS, LEUR RELIGION, LEURS EXERCICES, LEURS ETUDES, LEURS GUERRES / Foigny, Gabriel de – (Utopias in Enlightment series). 1692 – 9 – fr Hachette [910]

LES AVENTURES DE TELEMAQUE, FILS D'ULYSSE / Fenelon, Francois de Salignac de La Mothe – Paris: F. Delaulne, 1717. 7 fiches. (Literature Collection) – 9 – 17.00 – fr Bibl Nationale [810]

LES AVENTURES ETRANGES DE L'AGENT 9E-13 : L'AS DES ESPIONS CANADIENS / Daigneault, Pierre – nos 1-970. 1947-66. SEM16P249 – 8r – 5 – Can$278.00 – cn Bibl Nat [073]

LES AVENTURES EXTRAORDINAIRES DE GUY VERCHERES : L'ARSENE LUPIN CANADIEN-FRANCAIS – nos 1-883. 8 oct 1948-27 janv 1965. SEM16P326 – 9r – 5 – Can$285.00 – cn Bibl Nat [800]

AVENTURES POLICIERES D'ALBERT BRIEN. – 970 nos. 1948-1966. SEM16P321 – 11r – 5 – Can$358.00 – cn Bibl Nat [800]

Averbakh, O I *see* ZAKONODATEL'NYE AKTY VYZVANNYE VOINOI 1914-1917 GG; ZAKONY, MANIFESTY, RESKRIPTY...

Averchenko, Arkadii *see* DIUZHINA NOZHEI V SPINU REVOLIUTSII

Averill, A M *see* BAPTIST LANDMARKISM TESTED BY LOGIC, HISTORY AND SCRIPTURE

Averill, James P *see* FORT MEIGS: A CONDENSED HISTORY OF THE MOST IMPORTANT MILITARY POINT IN THE NORTHWEST, TOGETHER WITH SCENES AND INCIDENTS CONNECTED WITH THE SIEGES OF 1813 AND MINUTE DESCRIPTION OF THE OLD FORT AND ITS SURROUNDINGS, AS THEY NOW APPEAR

Averin, D D *see* PROTSESSUAL'NYE VOPROSY SOTRUDNICHESTVA ORGANOV IUSTITSII SOTSIALISTICHESKIKH.

Averley, G *see* BIBLIOGRAPHY OF EIGHTEENTH-CENTURY LEGAL LITERATURE

Aversa, R *see*
- LOGICA INSTITUTIONIBUS PRAEVIIS QUAESTIONIBUS CONTEXTA
- PHILOSOPHIA METAPHYSICAM PHYSICAMQUE COMPLECTENS QUESTIONIBUS CONTEXTA

AVERTISSEMENT SUR LES DISPUTES ET LE PROCEDE DES MISSIONNAIRES / Drelincourt, C – (Missing: Title page) – Charenton, 1654 – 3mf – 9 – CA-110/1 – ne IDC [240]

Avery, Asahel George *see* OUR DISRESPECT FOR LAW

Avery, E *see* LAWS APPLICABLE TO IMMIGRATION AND NATURALIZATION, 1953

Avery, Elroy M *see* HISTORY OF CLEVELAND AND ITS ENVIRONS

AVERY INDEX TO ARCHITECTURAL PERIODICALS, SECOND EDITION / Columbia University. Avery Memorial Architectural Library – (First Suppl., 1975.-26,300 cards 2 reels.$160.00.-ISBN 0-8161-1290-8; or 24mf.$160.00.-ISBN 0-8161-1737-3; Second Suppl., 1977.-29,900 cards 2 reels.$160.00.-ISBN 0-8161-1291-6; or 25mf.$145.00.-ISBN 0-8161-1738-1; Third Suppl., 1979.-23,900 cards 2 reels.-1.$160.00.-ISBN 0-8161-1292-4; Fourth Suppl, 1979-82.-1985.-47,250 entries 4 reels.$325.00.-ISBN 0-8161-1509-5; or 84mf.-1.$325.00.-ISBN 0-8161-1777-2; Fifth Suppl., 1983-84.-1985.-2,500p 4 reels.-1.$410.00.-ISBN 0-8161-1543-5; Sixth Suppl., 1985.-1986.-50,000 cards 4 reels.-1.$410.00.-ISBN 0-8161-1544-3; Seventh Suppl., 1987.-50,00 entries 4 reels.-1.$410.00.-ISBN 0-8161-1545-1; Ninth Suppl.-4 reels.$410.00 export $470.00.-ISBN 0-8161-1573-7; Tenth Suppl., 1989.-4 reels.$395.00 export $420.00.-ISBN 0-8161-1574-5) – 1973.-392,000 entries 30 reels.-ISBN: 0-8161-1278-9; 321mf.-ISBN: 0-8161-1735-7 – 1,9 – $1635.00 – uk Hall [720]

AVERY OBITUARY INDEX OF ARCHITECTS / Columbia University. Avery Memorial Architectural Library – Second expanded ed., 1980.-15,800 entries 1 reel.- ISBN: 0-8161-1425-0 – 1 – $85.00 – uk Hall [720]

Avery, R V *see* CALIFORNIA GOLD BOOK

Avery, Rachel Foster *see* TRANSACTIONS

AVES DE LA ISLA DE CUBA / Lembeye, J – Z 1827. 1850 – 9 – ne IDC [590]

AVES NEERLANDICAE / Albarda, J H – Leeuwarden, 1897 – 3mf – ne IDC [590]

AVES NEERLANDICAE / Albarda, J H – Z-325. 1897 – 9 – ne IDC [590]

AVESTA, DIE HEILIGEN SCHRIFTEN DER PARSEN...SAMMT DER HUZVARESCH-UEBERSETZUNG / Spiegel, F – Wien, 1853-1858. 2v – 13mf – NE-20153/1 – ne IDC [490]

AVESTA TIDNING – Sala, Sweden. 1882-1978 – 184r – 1 – sw Kungliga [072]

AVESTA TIDNING – Sala, Sweden. 1979- – 1 – sw Kungliga [072]

AVESTAPOSTEN – Vasteras, Hedemora, Sweden. 1897-1900 – 2r – 1 – sw Kungliga [072]

L'AVEUGLE – Montreal: [s.n.], 1912. SEM105P1575 – 1mf – 9 – Can$2.25 – cn Bibl Nat [301]

Avezac, d' *see* VOCABULAIRES GUIOLOF, MANDINGUE, FOULE, SARACOLE, SERAIRE, BAGNON ET FLOUPE, RECUEILLIS A LA COTE D'AFRIQUE

Avezac-Macaya, Armand d' *see*
- NOTICE SUR LE PAYS ET LE PEUPLE DES YEBOUS EN AFRIQUE
- VOCABULAIRES GUIOLOF, MANDINGUE, FOULE, SARACOLE, SERAIRE, BAGNON ET FLOUPE, RECUEILLIS A LA COTE D'AFRIQUE

AVIAN PATHOLOGY – 1992- 22v – 9 – £131.00 – 0307-9457 – uk Carfax [590]

AVIAT SII A I KOSMONAVTIKA – (Includes: July-Dec. 1964; Jan. 1965-June 1970) – Moskva: Izd-vo "Krasnai a zvezda", 1962 – 1 – CSUX90-S455 – us Hoover Inst Photo [947]

AVIATION AND AEROSPACE – (Cont: Canadian Aviation at v63 1990. Cont by: Canadian Aviation and Aerospace for Sale v66 1994) – Toronto. v63-66. 1990-93 – 9 – Can$20.00y – cn Micromedia [629]

AVIATION AND AEROSPACE *see*
- CANADIAN AVIATION
- CANADIAN AVIATION AND AIRCRAFT FOR SALE

AVIATION AND MARINE ENFORCEMENT DECISIONS / National Transportation Safety Board's – v1-7. 1967-91 – 9 – $310.00 set – us Hein [380]

AVIATION AS AFFECTING...1910 / Gregory, C N – N.p., n.d. – 1mf – 1 – ILM-1673/1 – ne IDC [327]

AVIATION LAW DIGEST QUARTERLY SUPPLEMENT – v1-7. Jun 1941-Sep 1947 (all publ) – 7mf – 9 – $10.50 – LLMC 84-411 – us L.L.M.C. [073]

AVIATION MAINTENANCE – Dec 1943-Nov 1948 – 1 – 202.00 – us L of C Photodup [629]

AVIATION MEDICINE *see* AEROSPACE MEDICINE AND BIOLOGY

AVIATION PSYCHOLOGY PROGRAM RESEARCH REPORTS / U.S. Army Air Forces – n1-19. 1947-48 – 1 – us Ross [150]

AVIATION SPACE AND ENVIRONMENTAL MEDICINE *see* AEROSPACE MEDICINE

AVIATION, SPACE AND ENVIRONMENTAL MEDICINE – v. 46-. 1975- – 1,5,6,9 – us UMI [610]

AVIATION WEEK AND SPACE TECHNOLOGY – (1965- 5,6. 1970- 9) – 1- 1916- – 1 – us UMI [380]

AVIATION/SPACE – (See also: Journal of Aerospace Education) – v5-. 1978- – 1,5,6,9 – us UMI [629]

Avicenna *see*
- METAHYPSICES COMPENDIUM
- METAPHYSICA SIVE PRIMA PHILOSOPHIA

AVICENNA ON THEOLOGY / Alberry, A J – London, 1952 – 1mf – 9 – ne Slangenburg [240]

AVICENNA ON THEOLOGY / Alberry, A J – London, 1952 – 1mf – 8 – ne Slangenburg [180]

Avida (Zlotnick), Yehuda L *see* MINNAH LI-YEHUDAH. YEHUDAH ZLOTNICK

AVI'EZER / Guenzburg, M A – Vilna, 1864 – 3mf – 9 – ne IDC [947]

AVI'EZER / Guenzburg, M A – Vilna. 1864. BJ-422-20 1 – 9 – ne IDC [920]

THE AVIFAUNA OF LAYSAN / Rothschild, L W – Z 1893. 1893-1900 – 9 – ne IDC [590]

DE AVIFAUNA VAN TJIBODAS EN OMGEVING, INCLUSIEF HET NATUURMONUMENT TJIBODAS-GN. GEDE, WEST-JAVA / Hoogerwerf, A – SE-4670 1. 1949 – 9 – ne IDC [950]

DIE AVIGNONESISCHEN PAEPSTE, IHRE MACHTFUELLE UND IHR UNTERGANG : VORTRAG / Hoefler, C – Wien: Aus der K.K. Hof- und Staatsdruckerei, in Commission bei Karl Gerold, 1871 – 1mf – us A.T.L.A. [940]

AVILA CONTRA BURGOS Y SUS PUEBLOS (ANNO 1670) – Avila – 1r – 5,6 – sp Cultura [946]

Avila, G G d' *see* TEATRO DE LAS GRANDEZAS DE LA VILLA DE MADRID

Aviler, A *see* DICTIONNAIRE D'ARCHITECTURE CIVILE

Avilier, Augustin Charles d' *see* COURS D'ARCHITECTURE QUI COMPREND LES ORDRES DE VIGNOLE.

Avinery, Y *see* MILLON HIDDUSHEI RASHI

Avinovitskii, I Akov Lazarevich *see* SOVETSKIE VOENNO-UCHEBNYE ZAVEDENIIA ZA CHETYRE GODA 1918-1922

AVIONES SOBRE EL PUEBLO / Montenegro, Carlos – La Habana, 1937. Fiche W 1055. (Blodgett Collection of Spanish Civil War Pamphlets) – 9 – us H.U. College Libr [946]

AVIS AU PEUPLE ARTESIAN / Robespierre, Maximilien de – Paris: Imp. L. Potier de Lille, c1789. 7 fiches. (Political Science Collection) – 9 – 17.00 – fr Bibl Nationale [320]

AVIS DU CONSEIL COLONIAL DE BOURBON SURDIVERSES PROPOSITIONS CONCERNANT L'ESCLAVAGE / Conseil Colonial de Bourbon – (Slave Trade and Abolitionism in France Series). 1939 – 9 – fr Hachette [025]

AVIS ET RAPPORTS / France. Conseil Economique – juin 1947-86 – 1 – fr A.C.R.P.P. [330]

AVIS EXPRIMES SUR LES PRINCIPALES QUESTIONS SOUMISES A SON EXAMEN PENDANT LES ANNEES 1870 A 1872: ABROGATION DE LA LOI DU 25 MAI 1864 SUR LES COALITIONS / Chambre de Commerce de Paris – (Condition of 19th C. French working class series). 1873 – 9 – fr Hachette [025]

El Avisador *see* POR QUE NO VAS A LA CONFERENCIA?

EL AVISADOR – Badajoz, 1888-1891. Numeros sueltos – 5 – sp Bibl Santa Ana [073]

AVISADOR DE BADAJOZ – Badajoz.1862-66 – 9 – 1.50f – sp Bibl Santa Ana [072]

EL AVISADOR DE BADAJOZ – Badajoz, 1882 y 1885-1887. Numeros sueltos – 5 – sp Bibl Santa Ana [073]

AVISI PARTICULARI, ULTIMAMENTE MANDATI DAL MAGNIFICO M. ANTONIO EGIPTIO MAGGIOR DOMO DELL ILLUSTRISSIMO ET ECCELLENTISSIMO SIGNOR PAULO GIORDANO / Egiptio, A – N.p., [1572] – 1mf – 9 – H-8337/1 – ne IDC [956]

AVISO – Halifax. v1- 1986- – 9 – Can$20.00y – cn Micromedia [060]

AVISO DE SANIDAD QUE TRATA DE TODOS LOS GENEROS DE ALIMENTOS Y DEL REGIMIENTO... / Nunez de Coria, F – Madrid, 1572 – 13mf – 9 – sp Cultura [610]

Avison, K *see* VERSUCH UEBER DEN MUSIKALISCHEN AUSDRUCK

AVISOS Y DOCUMENTOS PARA LA PRESERVACIN Y CURA DE LA PESTE / Diez Daza, A – Sevilla, 1599 – 1mf – 9 – sp Cultura [616]

Avity, Pierre d' *see*
- DESCRIPTION GENERALE DE L'AFRIQUE..
- DESCRIPTION GENERALE DE L'AFRIQUE SECONDE PARTIE DU MONDE, AVEC TOUS SES EMPIRES, ROYAUMES, ETATS ET REPUBLIQUE. OU SONT DEDUITS ET TRAITES PAR ORDRE LEURS NOMS, ASSIETTE, CONFINS MOEURS, RICHESSES, FORCES, GOUVERNEMENTS ET RELIGION

AVIUM GENERA / Moehring, P H G – 2106 2. 1752 – 8 – ne IDC [956]

AVIUM SPECIES NOVAE, QUAS IN ITINERE PER BRASILIAM / Spix, J B von – Z 1936. 2 v. 1824-1825 – 9 – ne IDC [590]

Avi-Yizhak *see* MIKHTAV MI-YERUSHALAYIM

AVKAT ROKHEL TAYTSH APTEYK – Amsterdam. 1647. BJ-43-1 1 – 9 – ne IDC [490]

Avni *see* DIVAN

AVOCA MAIL – (1869 missing) – 1863-1868 – 1r – 1 – at Corangamite [072]

AVOCA MAIL – 1870-1920 – 25r – 1 – at Corangamite [072]

L'AVOCAT / Roger, Jean-Francois – (French Theatre Series). Paris. Migneret. 1806 – 9 – fr Hachette [820]

Avolio, J *see* SIX AIR CONNUS, MIS EN VARIATIONS POUR LE VIOLON AVEC ACCOMPAGNEMENT DE BASS...OP. V

AVON ADVERTISER – England, 1986- – 25+r – 1 – uk British Libr Newspaper [072]

AVON BAPTIST CHURCH. MASSACHUSETTS : CHURCH RECORDS – 1780-1827. Society Book 1785-1844 (Randolph, Braintree, Stoughton). 274p – 1 – 12.33 – us Baptist [240]

AVON DEANERY MAGAZINE – (Cont: Parish Magazine) – Windsor, N.S.?: s.n, 1893-189- or 19– (Windsor [N.S.]: J.J. Anslow) – 9 – cn C.I.H.M. [240]

AVONMOUTH MAIL – England, 1912-23 – 5 1/2r – 1 – uk British Libr Newspaper [072]

L'AVOUERIE DE L'ABBAYE DE SAINT-ARMAND EN PEVELE : MEMOIRES ET TRAVAUX FAC. CATHOLIQUE DE LILLE / Naz, R – Fasc. 32. Lille, 1927 – Dfl6.00 – ne Slangenburg [240]

Avraamov, A *see* "VOPLOSHCHENIE."

Avrakh, Ia. S *see* O NEKOTORYKH VOPROSAKH UCHASTII OBSHCHESTVENNOSTI.

Avram, Duke of *see* REPORTS ON...ROYAL BANK OF AVRAM

Avramoff, D *see* LE PRESIDENT DU CONSEIL DE LA SOCIETE DES NATIONS

Avramov, Vasil *see* VOINATA MEZHDU VIZANTIIA I BULGARIIA V 986 GODINA I OBSADATA NA SOFIIA OT IMPERATORA VASILII 2 BULGAROUBIETS
AVREA ET VERE THEOLOGICA COMMENTATIO D. DANIELIS HOFMANNI... / Hoffmann, David – Magdebvrgi, 1600 – 1mf – ne IDC [240]
Avrekh, A I *see* STOLYPIN I TRET'IA DUMA
AV-REPORT – Berlin. jun 9-dec 30, 1978 – 1r – 1 – gw Mikrofilm [073]
Avril, Adolphe d' *see* DOCUMENTS RELATIFS AUX EGLISES DE L'ORIENT ET A LEURS RAPPORTS AVEC ROME
Avril, Chantal *see* LA COUR D'APPEL DE DIJON – AN HUIT – MILLE HUIT CENT CINQUANTE DEUX
Avril de Saint-Croix, Mme. Ghenia *see* LE FEMINISME
Avril, P *see* TRAVELS INTO...EUROPE AND ASIA,..
AVRORA – St Petersburg, 1875-78 – 34mf – 9 – $230.00 coll – us Ross [073]
Avrorin, V A *see* GRAMMATIKA NANAISKOGO JAZYKA
Avsieenko, Vasilii G E *see* MALOROSIYA V GODU 1767
Avsov, I et al *see* MORSKOE PRAVO SSSR
AVTOGRAFY MUZYKANTOV V IMPERATORSKOI PUBLICHNOI BIBLIOTEKE / Stasov, Vladimir Vasil'evich – (In Sobranie sochinenii V.V. Stasova 1847-86. Spb., v. 3, 1894). BR-9894 1 – 9 – ne IDC [780]
AVTOGRAFY P.I. CHAIKOVSKOGO V FONDAKH GOSUDARSTVENNOGO TSENTRAL'NOGO MUZEIA MUZYKAL'NOI KUL'TURY IMENI M.I. GLINKI – Katalog-Spravochnik. Moscow, 1956. 78p. BR-11,027/1 – 9 – ne IDC [780]
AVTOMOBIL' I VOZDUKHOPLAVANIE – M. 1911-12. Lacking: (5-24) 1912. BR-2325 2 – 8 – ne IDC [600]
AVTORSKOE PRAVO NA LITERATURNYE PROIZVEDENIIA: SBORNIK OFITSIAL'NYKH MATERIALOV / Azov, L M & Shatsillos, S A – Moscow, 1953. 134p. BR-8429 1 – 9 – ne IDC [340]
AVTRE VERITABLE DISCOVRS DE LA VICTOIRE DES CHRESTIENS CONTRE LES TURCS, EN LA BATAILLE NAUALE PRES LEPANTHO, ... 1571 – Paris, 1571 – 1mf – 9 – H-8173/1 – ne IDC [956]
L'AVVENIRE – New York, Feb. 16, 1917 – 3r – 1 – us I.H.R.C. [978]
L'AVVENIRE – Sleubenville, OH, 1910 – 2mf or 1r – 1 – us I.H.R.C. [978]
L'AVVENIRE – Utica, NJ, Oct. 5, 1900-Dec. 9, 1905 – 2r – 1 – us I.H.R.C. [978]
AVVENIRE – 1987-1995 – 2r per y – 5,6 – Sfr936.00 – sz Infoprint [900]
L'AVVENIRE D'ITALIA – Bologna, Italy. 30 Jan 1941-8 Sep 1943 (imperfect) – 6r – 1 – uk British Libr Newspaper [072]
A.W. Bowen and Co *see*
- BIOGRAPHICAL MEMOIRS OF GRANT COUNTY
- THE CITY OF GRAND RAPIDS AND KENT COUNTY
- HISTORY OF MONTGOMERY COUNTY
- PORTRAIT AND BIOGRAPHICAL RECORD OF ALLEN AND VAN WERT COUNTIES
- PORTRAIT AND BIOGRAPHICAL RECORD OF BOONE, CLINTON AND HENDRICKS COUNTIES
- PORTRAIT AND BIOGRAPHICAL RECORD OF DELAWARE AND RANDOLPH COUNTIES
- PORTRAIT AND BIOGRAPHICAL RECORD OF PORTAGE AND SUMMIT COUNTIES
- PROGRESSIVE MEN OF THE STATE OF MONTANA
- PROGRESSIVE MEN OF THE STATE OF WYOMING
- PROGRESSIVE MEN OF WESTERN COLORADO

AWAKE FOR FREEDOM'S SAKE / Read, Leonard E – Together with: Essays From "Essays On Liberty", v. VI-VIII. 356p total. 1 fiche (24x) – 9 – 1.00f – at Libertarian Micro [320]
AWAKENER *see* EYE-OPENER
AWAKENER (NEW YORK, N.Y.) : A NATIONAL ORGAN OF UNCENSORED OPINION – New York: Awakener Publishing Co., 1933-1936 – 1 – CSUX86-S13 – us Hoover Inst Photo [978]
THE AWAKENING OF SCOTLAND : A HISTORY FROM 1747 TO 1797 / Mathieson, William Law – Glasgow: J. Maclehose, 1910 – 1mf – us A.T.L.A. [240]
THE AWAKENING OF SCOTLAND, A HISTORY FROM 1747 TO 1797 / Mathieson, William Law – Glasgow: J. Maclehose, 1910. xiv,303p – 1 – us U.W. Library [941]
THE AWAKENING OF SPRING, A TRAGEDY OF CHILDHOOD / Wedekind, Frank – Trans. from the German by Francis J. Ziegler. 2nd ed. Philadelphia: Brown Brothers, 1910. xvii,23+161+(1)p. 1 reel. 1248 – 1 – us U.W. Library [820]
AWASSI SHEEP, WITH SPECIAL REFERENCE TO THE IMPROVED DAIRY TYPE – 1985 – 294p – it F.A.O. [636]
Awde, James *see* DOGMA AND DUTY
Awde, Robert *see* JUBILEE, PATRIOTIC AND OTHER POEMS
Awgerian, Y *see*
- A DICTIONARY ENGLISH-ARMENIAN AND ARMENIAN-ENGLISH
- DICTIONNAIRE FRANCAIS-ARMENIEN-TURC

AWHONN'S CLINICAL ISSUES IN PERINATAL AND WOMEN'S HEALTH NURSING – (Cont: NAACOG's Clinical Issues in Perinatal and Women's Health Nursing. Absorbed by: Journal of Obstetric, Gynecolgic, and Neonatal Nursing. Ceased publ) – Philadelphia. v4. 1993* – 1 – D19708.01 – us UMI [618]
AWOTS = THE SPRING – Riga, 1905-July 21, 1915. 6, 144p – 1 – $245.76 – us Baptist [240]
AWRAQ MUASSASAT AL-DIRASAT AL-FILASTINIYAH – Bayrut: Muassasat al-Dirasat al-Filastiniyah. n2,5-6,11-13,15-21. 1979-1983 – us Res Libr [072]
AWS (AMERICAN WELDING SOCIETY) – Standards. Printed index. Updated every 60 days – 6,9 – us Info Handling [670]
AWWA (AMERICAN WATER WORKS ASSOCIATION) – Standards. Printed index. Updated every 60 days – 6,9 – us Info Handling [628]
THE AX LAID TO THE ROOT : OR, A PRESERVATIVE AGAINST THE ERRONEOUS DOCTRINES OF THE METHODISTS, CANDIDLY OFFERED TO THE CONSIDERATION OF ALL CHRISTIANS, IN THREE DISCOURSES / Walder, J – London, 1763 – 1mf – 9 – MP-425/1 – ne IDC [240]
AXBRIDGE AND CHEDDAR GAZETTE – England, 12 Jan 1866-29 Nov 1867 – 1r – 1 – uk British Libr Newspaper [072]
THE AXE : A JOURNAL OF ACTION AGAINST REACTION / ed by Roberts, John H – Montreal, 1922-. SEM35P13 – 1r – 1 – Can$53.00 – cn Bibl Nat [360]
Axerio, E *see* SUL MATRIMONIO...
AXICON UND RINGPUPILLE ALS BILDFORMENDE ELEMENTE / Bickel, Gerhard – 1995 – 2mf – 9 – DM80.00 – 3-8267-2086-5 – gw Hänsel [530]
AXIOM – Halifax. v1-3. 1974-77 – 9 – Can$37.00 – cn Micromedia [073]
AXIOMATA EX COMMENTARIIS EJUS / Coke, Edward – 17th cent. Holkham ms. 253. Holkham Hall, Norfolk, England – 1 – uk Microform Academic [340]
THE AXIOMS OF RELIGION : A NEW INTERPRETATION OF THE BAPTIST FAITH / Mullins, Edgar Young – (Includes index) – Philadelphia: American Baptist Publ Society, 1908 – 1mf – 9 – 0-8370-8926-3 – 1986-2926 – us A.T.L.A. [240]
AXTELL REPUBLICAN – Axtell, NE. -w. Oct. 1889-Jan. 1896 – 1 – us NE Hist [071]
AXTELL TIMES – Axtell, NE. -w. May. 1896-Jul. 1902; May 1937-Sep. 1953 – 1 – us NE Hist [071]
AYALA / Solsona y Baselga, Conrado – 1891 – 9 – 1.50f – sp Bibl Santa Ana [830]
Ayala, B *see*
- DE JURE ET OFFICIIS BELLICIS,...
- DE JURE ET OFFICIIS BELLICIS,...

Ayala, Balthazar *see*
- DE IURE ET OFFICIIS BELLICIS ET DISCIPLINA MILITARI
- DE JURE ET OFFICIIS BELLICIS ET DISCIPLINA MILITARI, LIBRI 3

Ayala, Manuel Jose de *see* DICCIONARIO DE GOBIERNO Y LEGISALCION DE INDIAS... TOMO 4, VOL 1
AYANDIGAN – (Missing issues: 3256, 3279, 3287-3288, 3330, 3354-3355, 3397-3399, 3403) – Tehran. Shumarah-'i 3251-3419 (6 Aban 1357-16 Murdad 1358 [28 Oct 1978-7 Aug 1979]) – 2r – 1 – $75.00 – us MEDOC [950]
Ayape, Eugenio *see* LA CALZADA DE OROPESA, SU SANTO CRISTO Y SUS MONJAS
AYDEDE – Nos 1-90. – 1338 [1922] – 7mf – 9 – $35.00 – us MEDOC [949]
AYDIN – Izmir: Vilayet Matbaasi; Yayimliyan: Aydin Valiligi, 1897-?. – No 2111 [22 Aug 1910] – 1mf – 9 – $10.00 – us MEDOC [949]
AYDINLIK – (Subtitled: Ictimai, terbiyevi, edebi aylik mecmuadir) – Istanbul. Islamiye Mataasi, Amedi Matbaasi, Cihan Biraderler Matbaasi, 1921-1925 – $75.00 – us MEDOC [956]
Aye, Agnes *see* CHANTS ET CHANSONS EN PAYS AKYE
AYER 1871-1900 – (Mf 1-15: Town Records 1871-1907. Mf 16-18: Births 1871-92. Mf 19-20: Marriages 1871-92. Mf 21-22: Deaths 1871-92. Mf 23: Deaths 1892-1901. Mf 24: Marriages 1892-1900. Mf 25-26: Births 1892-1900) – (mf ed 1995) – 26mf – 9 – 0-87623-376-0 – us Holbrook [920]
Ayer, Albert Azro *see* HISTORICAL SKETCH OF THE GRANDE LIGNE MISSION
Ayer, Joseph Cullen *see*
- THE RISE AND DEVELOPMENT OF CHRISTIAN ARCHITECTURE
- A SOURCE BOOK FOR ANCIENT CHURCH HISTORY
- VERSUCH EINER DARSTELLUNG DER ETHIK JOSEPH BUTLERS

Ayers, S G *see* HISTORY OF THE ENGLISH BIBLE
AYIN TARIHI – History of the Month. Ankara, Istanbul. Jan. 1934-Aug. 1957. Missing: nos. 189-225 – 1 – 35.00r – us Hoover Inst Photo [956]
AYINE – Sene 1-2, nu 1-72. – 1337-1339 [1921-1923] – 5mf – 9 – $90.00 – us MEDOC [949]
AYLESFORD MANUSCRIPTS / Handel, George Frederic – 368v. 67 reels. From the Newman Flower Collection in the Henry Watson Music Library, Manchester (England) Public Libraries – 1 – 30.00r – uk Manchester Libr [780]
THE AYLESFORD UNION – Aylesford, N.S.: B.Y.P.U. of the Upper Aylesford Baptist Church, v1 no 1 (Mar 1897)- – 9 – cn C.I.H.M. [240]
Ayllon Laynez, Juan *see* ADDITIONES AD VARIAS RESOLUTIONES.
AYLMER GAZETTE – Aylmer, Canada. v2 n27. 1 mai 1895 – 1r – 1 – Can$25.00 – cn Can Microfilming [072]
AYLMER TIMES – Aylmer, Canada. v11 n29. 22 aut 1866-v18 n49. 10 avr 1872; ns: v1 n27. 22 avr 1874 – 1r – 1 – Can$25.00 – cn Can Microfilming [072]
Aymard, M et al *see* FOOD AND FOODWAYS
Aynard, Joseph *see* LA MAIN, L'OUTIL ET LA MACHINE
Ayni *see* DIVAN
Ayo, C *see* LAS EXCELENCIAS...Y... PROPIEDADES DEL TABACO...
Ayotte, Alfred *see* L'OEIL
Ayoub, C *see* LES MANDATS ORIENTAUX
AYR ADVERTISER – 1 – £42.00r – uk Scot News [072]
AYR AND DISTRICT LEADER – 1 – £42.00r – uk Scot News [072]
AYR NEWS – (1904-1992.-52r) – Ayr, 1993 – 1r – 1 – cn Preston [971]
Ayrault, Roger *see* HEINRICH VON KLEIST
Ayres, Anne *see* THE LIFE AND WORK OF WILLIAM AUGUSTUS MUHLENBERG
Ayres, Ebenezer *see* CLEVELAND, OHIO, TAXES, MS V.F. O
Ayres, Leonard Porter *see* LAGGARDS IN OUR SCHOOLS; A STUDY OF RETARDATION AND ELIMINATION IN CITY SCHOOL SYSTEMS
Ayres, P *see* EMBLEMATA AMATORIA
Ayres, Samuel Gardiner *see* COMPLETE INDEX TO THE EXPOSITOR'S BIBLE: TOPICAL AND TEXTUAL
AYRSHIRE, 1837 : BRITISH ISLES CENSUS DIRECTORIES PROJECT, SCOTLAND. VOL 29 – 1mf – 9 – A$9.00 – at Vine [941]
AYRSHIRE (PART), 1820 : BRITISH ISLES CENSUS DIRECTORIES PROJECT, SCOTLAND. VOL 60 – 1mf – 9 – A$9.00 – at Vine [941]
AYRSHIRE POST – 1 – £42.00r – uk Scot News [072]
Ayrshire, Scotland. Newmilns Old Cemetery *see* REGISTER OF BURIALS
AYRSHIRE WORLD (SOUTH EDITION) – 1 – £42.00r – uk Scot News [072]
Ayrton, Edward R *see*
- PRE-DYNASTIC CEMETARY AT EL-MAHASNA
- PRE-DYNASTIC CEMETERY AT AL MAHASNA (MEES VOL 31)

Ayrton, Edward R et al *see* ABYDOS (MEES VOL 25)
Aytoun, Robert Alexander *see* CITY CENTRES OF EARLY CHRISTIANITY
Aytoun, William Edmondstoune *see* FIRMILIAN: OR, THE STUDENT OF BADAJOZ
AYUDA MEMORIA REFERENTE A LA ORIENTACION POLITICA DEL GOBIERNO / Argentine Republic. Presidencia. Subsecretaria de Informaciones – [Buenos Aires: ARPSI], 2nd ed 1949 – 1 – CSUXAGP8758-B – us Hoover Inst Photo [350]
AYURDHARMA : LAW OF LIFE – Bombay: Rajinder Mohan Sharma, Honorary Secretary of the Indian Ayurvedic Aid Society. v1 n1 jan 1965 – us Res Libr [615]
AYYALAH SHELUHAH – Cracow. 1593-95. Cowley. BJ-43-2 1 – 9 – ne IDC [760]
AYYILDIZ – Iskenderun: Ayyildiz Matbaasi, [mar 28 1951-aug 29 1953] – 1r – us Res Libr [072]
THE 'AYYUB AND MAMLUK SULTANS / Sell, Edward – London: Church Missionary Society, 1929.84p. Bibliog. footnotes – 1 – us U.W. Library [956]
AZ – Wien: Neue AZ Zeitungsverlagsgesellschaft mbH & Co KG, [1989-dec 12 1989-aug 1991 – us Res Libr [072]
AZ 1948. I.E. EZERKILENCSZAZNEGYVEN-NYOLCADIK EVI AMNESZTIA. / Hungary. Laws, Statutes, etc – Hirlap-, Szaklap- es Konyvkiado 194-. 124p. LL-4008 – 1 – us L of C Photodup [340]
AZ 1848-49-IKI MAGYAR SZABADSAGHARZ TOERTENETE / Gracza, Gyorgy – 5v. 1894-98. BR-5284 2 – 8 – ne IDC [940]
AZ AM ABEND *see* ALLGEMEINE ZEITUNG
AZ AM MORGEN *see* ALLGEMEINE ZEITUNG
AZ EGYETEMES EUROPAI JOGTORTENETNEK ROVID VAZLATA / Wenzel, Gusztav – Budapest, Pfeifer Ferdinand, 1877. 219 p. LL-4058 – 1 – us L of C Photodup [340]
AZ EST – Budapest, 24 June 1914-14 May 1919; 28 Sep 1919-29 Jun 1924 – 30r – 1 – uk British Libr Newspaper [072]
AZ EST – Budapest, Hungary. Dec 1914-Feb 1917; Mar 1920-Apr 1921 – 4r – 1 – us L of C Photodup [072]
AZ IGAZOLO ELJARASOK ZSEBKONYVE / Hungary. Laws, Statutes, etc – Budapest Franklin-Tarsulat 1945?. 90p. LL-4052 – 1 – us L of C Photodup [340]
AZ IRAS = HUNGARIAN NEWS – Chicago: Az Iras, sep 1938-dec 22 1944; 1946-may 6 1949 – us Res Libr [071]
AZ UJ NEPBIROSAGI TORVENY (1947: 34. T.-C.) EGYSEGES SZERKEZETBEN A HATALYOS NEPBIROSAGI RENDELETEKKEL / Hungary. Laws, Statutes, etc – Budapest: Gergely, 1948 – 1 – LL-4053 – us L of C Photodup [340]
AZ UJSAG – Budapest, 28 Jun 1914-29 Jun 1924 – 42r – 1 – uk British Libr Newspaper [072]
AZ UT – Budapest, 2 Aug-18 Oct 1952; 9 Jan-25 Dec 1954; 16 Jul 1955-27 Oct 1956 – 1r – 1 – uk British Libr Newspaper [072]
AZAD – Banaras, India. Jun 1950-Jul 1953 – 1r – 1 – us L of C Photodup [072]
Azad, 'Abd al-Rahman Sayf *see* IRAN-I BASTAN
AZAD HINDUSTAN – Rangoon, Burma. 1943-44 – 1r – 1 – us L of C Photodup [072]
AZADI – (Missing issues: 22-23) – [Tehran]: Jibhah-'i Dimukratik-i Milli-i Iran. Shumarah-'i 1-36 (8 Farvardin 1358-15 Bahman 1358 [29 Mar 1979-4 Feb 1980]) – 1 reel – 1 – $25.00 – us MEDOC [950]
AZADLIG – Baku, USSR. Aug 25 1990-June 27 1992 – 1r – 1 – us L of C Photodup [072]
Azadovskii, M K *see* RUSSKAIA SKAZKA. IZBRANNYE MASSHERA
Azais, P H *see* 12 SONATES POUR LE VIOLONCELLE ET BASSE CONTINUE
Azana, Manuel *see*
- EXTRACT FROM PRES. AZANA'S SPEECH AT VALENCIA UNIVERSITY, JULY 18, 1937
- EXTRACTS FROM A SPEECH DELIVERED BY THE PRES. OF THE SPANISH REPUBLIC, JANUARY 21, 1937
- IMPORTANT DECREE ISSUED BY THE PRESIDENT OF THE CABINET
- TEXTO INTEGRO DEL DISCURSO PRONUNCIADO POR DON MANUEL AZANA DIAZ EL DIA 21 DE ENERO DE 1937 EN EL SALON DE SESIONES DEL AYUNTAMIENTO DE VALENCIA

AZANIA NEWS – Dar-es-Salaam: Dept of Publicity & Info, Pan Africanist Congress. [v1-13. 1966-78] – 1 – us Res Libr [072]

Azara, Felix *see*
- APUNTACIONES PARA LA HISTORIA NATURAL DE LAS AVES..., TOMO 1-2, ASUNCION
- DESCRIPCION E HISTORIA DEL PARAGUAY. TOMO 2
- DESCRIPTION E HISTORIA DEL PARAGUAY, TOMO 1
- VIAJES POR LA AMERICA MERIDIONAL

Azara, Jose Nicolas *see* OBRAS DE ANTONIO RAFAEL MENGS

AZARAKHSH – London, Shumarah-'i 1, 3, 5-6 (Tir 1355-Aban 2536 (1356) [Jun/Jul 1976-Oct 1977]) – 1 reel – 1 – $50.00 – us MEDOC [950]

AZARBA IJAN NEFT T AS ARR UFATY *see* AZERBA IDZHANSKOE NEFTI ANOE KHOZI A ISTVO

AZARBAIJAN SSR K AND, G AS A BA Z AH M ATKESH DEPUTATLARY SOVETI H AGGYNDA AZARBAIJAN SOVET SOSIALIST RESPUBLIKASYNYN GANUNU *see* ZAKON AZERBAIDZHANSKO I SOVETSKOI SOTSIALISTICHESKOI RESPUBLIKI O SELSKOM, POSELKOVOM SOVETE DEPUTATOV TRUDI ASHCHIKHSIA AZERBA IDZHANSKOI SSR

AZARBAIJAN SSR K AND, G AS AB A Z AH M ATKESH DEPUTATLARY SOVETI H AGGYNDA AZARBAIJAN SOVET SOSIALIST RESPUBLIKASYNYN GANUNU *see* ZAKON AZERBA IDZHANSKO I SOVETSKO I SOTSIALISTICHESKO I RESPUBLIKI O SELSKOM, POSELKOVOM SOVETE DEPUTATOV TRUDI ASHCHIKHSI A AZERBA IDZHANSKO I SSR

AZARBAYCAN (INCLUDES MAKTAB AND ZIYA-YI KAFKASIYAH) – Tehran – 1r – 1 – $75.00 – us MEDOC [949]

Azard, M M *see* L'OCCUPATION DU SOL ET LE PEUPLEMENT FRANCAIS DES TERRES ATLANTIQUES DU CANADA AUX 17E ET 19E SIECLES A PARTIR DES CARTES NAUTIQUES MANUSCRITES FRANCAISES

Azarenko, A *see* MOLODYE OPRICHNIKI BUZHUAZII

Azarenko, E K *see* MIROVOZZRENIE M. V. LOMONOSOVA

Azarola Saint, Jose Luis *see* OCHO SEMANAS EN LOS CALABOZOS PERONISTAS

AZB : ARIZONA BUSINESS WEEK – (Cont: Arizona Business) – Tempe. v42-44. jan 1995-dec 1997+ – 1,5,9 – D6383.01 – us UMI [380]

Azbi *see* DIVAN

AZBUKA KOMMUNIZMA : POPULI ARNOE OBI ASNENIE PROGRAMMY ROSSI ISKO I KOMMUNISTICHESKO I PARTII / Bukharin, Nikolai Ivanovich & Preobrazhenskii, E – Izd. 3-e, dop. Odessa: Gos. izd-vo Ukrainy, 1923 – 1 – CSUX89-B3876 – us Hoover Inst Photo [320]

AZBUKA KOMMUNIZMA : POPULI ARNOE OBI ASNENIE PROGRAMMY ROSSI ISKO I KOMMUNISTICHESKO I PARTII BOLSHEVIKOV / Bukharin, Nikolai Ivanovich & Preobrazhenskii, E – 1 – CSUX89-B3834 – us Hoover Inst Photo [320]

AZBUKA KOMMUNIZMA : POPULI ARNOE OBI ASNENIE PROGRAMMY ROSSI ISKO I KOMMUNISTICHESKO I PARTII BOLSHEVIKOV / Bukharin, Nikolai Ivanovich & Preobrazhenskii, E – Moskva: Gos. izd-vo, 1920 – 1 – CSUX89-B3822 – us Hoover Inst Photo [320]

AZBUKA KOMMUNIZMA : POPULI ARNOE OBI ASNENIE PROGRAMMY ROSSII ISKO I KOMMUNSTICHESKO I PARTII BOLSHEVIKOV / Bukharin, Nikolai Ivanovich & Preobrazhenskii, E – Peterburg: Gos. izd-vo, 1920 – 1 – CSUX89-B4618 – us Hoover Inst Photo [320]

AZBUKA KOMMUNIZMA : POPULI ARNY I VYKLAD PROGRAMY ROSSI ISKO I KOMMUNISTYCHNO I PARTII BILSHOVYKIV / Bukharin, Nikolai Ivanovich – Kyiv: Vseukra inske derzh. vyd-vo, 1920 – 1 – CSUX89-B4590 – us Hoover Inst Photo [320]

AZBUKA KOMMUNIZMA. UKRAINIAN *see* AZBUKA KOMMUNIZMA

Azcarate y Corral, Patricio de *see* EXPOSICION HISTORICO CRITICA DE LOS SISTEMAS FILOSOFICOS MODERNOS Y PRINCIPIOS DE LA CIENCA

Azcarate y Florez, Pablo de *see*
- THE COMMUNIST PLOT IN SPAIN
- SPAIN, PAST AND FUTURE: AN ADDRESS TO THE COSMOS SOCIETY, OXFORD, ON 15 MAY 1945

Azedo de la Berrueza, Gabriel *see* AMENIDADES...DE LA VERA ALTA Y BAXA

AZEF I LENIN / Burtsev, Vladimir Lvovich – [S.l.: s.n., 19–] – 1 – CSUX89-B7301 – us Hoover Inst Photo [947]

Azemard, E *see* ETUDE SUR LES ISRAELITES DE MONTPELLIER AU MOYEN AGE

AZERBA IDZHANSKOE NEFTI ANOE KHOZI A ISTVO – (Includes Jan. 1922, Oct. 1925, Mar.-Dec. 1926, Apr. 1927, Jan.-Apr., June/July 1928) – Baku: Azerneftneshr, 1921 – 1 – CSUX89-S841 – us Hoover Inst Photo [947]

AZERBAIDZHAN, BAKU-BAKINSKY RABOCHY – 1955-1967 – 1 – us UMI [072]

Azerbaijan S.S.R. *see*
- GRAZHADANKII KODEKS AZERBAIDZHANSKOI SSR
- GRAZHDANSKII KODEKS AZERBA IDZHANSKOI SSR
- GRAZHDANSKII PROTSESSUALNYI KODEKS AZERBAIDZHANSKOI SSR
- KONSTITUTSIIA (OSNOVNO I ZAKON) AZERBA IDZHANSKO I SOVETSKO I SOTSIALISTICHESKO I RESPUBLIKI
- KONSTITUTSIIA (OSNOVNO I ZAKON) AZERBAIDHANSKO I SOVETSKO I SOTSIALISTICHESKO I RESPUBLIKI
- POLOZHENIE O TOVARISHCHESKIKH SUDAKH
- SBORNIK ZAKONOV AZERBA IDZHANSKO I SSR I UKAZOV PREZIDIUMA VERKHOVNOGO SOVETA AZERBA IDZHANSKO I SSR, 1938-1966 GG
- UGOLOVNYI KODEKS AZERBAIDZHANSKOI SSR
- ZAKON AZERBA IDZHANSKO I SOVETSKO I SOTSIALISTICHESKO I RESPUBLIKI O SELSKOM, POSELKOVOM SOVETE DEPUTATOV TRUDI ASHCHIKHSI A AZERBA IDZHANSKO I SSR
- ZAKON AZERBAIDZHANSKO I SOVETSKOI SOTSIALISTICHESKOI RESPUBLIKI O SELSKOM, POSELKOVOM SOVETE DEPUTATOV TRUDI ASHCHIKHSIA AZERBA IDZHANSKOI SSR

AZERBAYCAN CUMHURIYET KEYFIYETI TESEKKUELUE VE SIMDIKI VAZIYETI / Emin, Resulzade Mehmet – Istanbul: Evkaf-i Islamiye Matbaasi, 1339M, 1341H [1923] – $21.00 – us MEDOC [956]

Azevedo, Aluizio *see*
- O CORTICO
- EMMANUELE

AZG – Boston, MA: Azk Publ Co, [nov 1917-oct 15 1921] – 7r – us Res Libr [071]

AZG-PAHAK = AZK-BAHAG – Boston, MA: Azk-Bahag Publ Co, oct 19 1921-1922 – 4r – us Res Libr [071]

AZIA I AFRIKA SEVODNYA – (Asia and Africa Today). Moscow. U.S.S.R. 1961-74 – 1 – us UMI [950]

AZIATSKII MUZEI LENINGRADSKOE OTDELENIE INSTITUTA VOSTOKOVEDENIIA AN SSR / ed by Baziiants, A P, et al – Moscow, 1972. Br-11,094 1 – 596p – 9 – ne IDC [950]

AZIATSKII VESTNIK – Spb. 1825-27. B-1683 2 – 8 – ne IDC [073]

AZII ATSKAI A POLITIKA BOLSHEVIKOV : POLITIKO- EKONOMICHESKI I OCHERK / Glonti, Fedor Zurabovich – Tiflis: [s.n.], 1920 – 1 – CSUX88-B4806 – us Hoover Inst Photo [320]

AZIIA – 1992-1995 – 1 – sz Infoprint [072]

AZIIA – (Comes in Russian) – 1992- – 1 – sz Infoprint [947]

Azikiwe, Nnamdi *see* LIBERIA IN WORLD POLITICS

L'AZIONE COLONIALE – Rome, Italy. 10 Jan 1936-6 Feb 1939; 8 May 1941-26 Aug 1943 (1941-43 very imperfect) – 4r – 1 – uk British Libr Newspaper [072]

AZIZAH DE NIAMKOKO / Crouzat, Henri – Paris, Presses de la cite [1959] – us Res Libr [944]

AZKARAH, LE-MISHMAT AVRAHAM YIZHAK HA-KONEN KOOK / Kook, A J – pts. 1-5. Jerusalem. 1937. BJ-100-70 1 – 9 – ne IDC [270]

Azopardi, F *see* LE MUSICIEN PRATIQUE

THE AZOREAN FIGHT FOR FREEDOM / Phoenix Foundation – 1fiche (29x) – 9 – 1.00f – at Libertarian Micro [320]

O AZORRAGUE – [s.l.]. 3 Out 1891 – 1,5,6 – bl Biblioteca [072]

O AZORRAQUE : ORGAO IMPARCIAL – [s.l.]. 3 Jul 1878 – 1,5,6 – bl Biblioteca [072]

Azourua, Ramon *see* BIOGRAFIAS DE HOMBRES NOTABLES DE HISPANO-AMERICA

Azov, L M *see* AVTORSKOE PRAVO NA LITERATURNYE PROIZVEDENIIA: SBORNIK OFITSIAL'NYKH MATERIALOV

Azpiazu, J *see* MARQUEZ, GABINO. LAS ENCICLICAS "RERUM NOVARUM", "QUADRAGESIMO ANNO" Y "DIVINI REDEMPTORIO" CONTRA EL COMUNISMO, AL ALCANCE DE TODOS. TOLEDO, 1938

AZTEC RUINS NATIONAL MONUMENT, NEW MEXICO / Corbett, John Maxwell – 1963 – 2mf – 9 – $5.00f – us Ross [930]

AZTLAN CHICANO JOURNAL – 1970-1974 – 1r – 1 – $50.00 – R03280 – us Library Micro [073]

AZTLAN-CHICANO JOURNAL OF THE SOCIAL SCIENCES AND THE ARTS – v. 1-5. 1971-1974 – 1 – us UMI [300]

AZTLAN-INTERNATIONAL JOURNAL OF CHICANO STUDIES RESEARCH – (v7- . 1976- . 5,6,9) – v. 6-. 1975- – 1 – us UMI [300]

Azuaga. Spain *see* ORDENANZAS MUNICIPALES

Azuar, Antonio *see* MEDALLA BATIDA POR LA VILLA DE ALCANTARA, EN HONOR DEL CORONEL MAINE

AZUL – Curitiba, 4 Mar-29 Oct 1900 – 1,5,6 – bl Biblioteca [072]

Azulai, H J D *see* MA'AGAL TOV HA-SHALEM

Azuni, D A *see*
- DROIT MARITIME DE L'EUROPE
- ORIGINE ET PROGRES DU DROIT ET DE LA LEGISLATION MARITIME,...

Azurara de Gomes Eannes *see* THE CHRONICLE OF THE DISCOVERY AND CONQUEST OF GUINEA

Azurduy, Victoria *see* EL CASO ARGENTINO

Azvitskii, Valeriiloilovich *see*
- CHTO TAKOE SAMODERZHAVIE I POCHEMU ONO PALO
- KAK NAROD DOBILSIA SVOIKH PRAV; KAK ZAKRIEPIT SVOBODU

Azzo *see* SUMMA SUPER CODICEM

THE A B C OF TAXATION : WITH BOSTON OBJECT LESSONS, PRIVATE PROPERTY IN LAND, AND OTHER ESSAYS AND ADDRESSES / Fillebrown, C B – (Concerned with taxation on real property) – Garden City, NY: Doubleday, Page & Co, 1916 – 3mf – 9 – $4.50 – LLMC 92-157 – us L.L.M.C. [336]

B NOTES / Colorado. Agricultural Experiment Station. Fort Collins. – 1950-69 – 1,5,6 – us Spaulding [630]

Ba, Amadou Hampate *see* L'EMPIRE PEUL DU MACINA.

LES BA DE LA KAMTSHA / Mertens, Joseph – Brussels. 1935-39. 3v – 1 – us Res Libr [960]

BA DER MAIN-POST *see* LOHRER ZEITUNG

BA DER WETZLARER NEUEN ZEITUNG *see* HINTERLAENDER ANZEIGER

BA HASHIYAH VA BI HASHIYAH – (Title added on title page: Asnad-i Nahat-i Azadi-i Iran. Shumarah-'i 1-4 (Aban 1341-Day 1341[Oct 1962-Dec 1962])) – [Tehran]: Nahzat-i Azadi-i Iran – 1 reel – 1 – $25.00 – us MEDOC [950]

BA IKAL – (Includes June 1, 1897-Dec. 20,1898; June 25, 1904; Mar.9, 1905; missing five issues, some issues slighty mutilated) – Ki akhta: "Ba ikal", 1897- – 1 – CSUX87-S123 – us Hoover Inst Photo [947]

BA UNDZ = WITH US – Toronto, CN, 1931 – 1r – 1 – Can$25.00 – cn Can Microfilming [072]

Baader, Clemens Alois *see* LEXIKON VERSTORBENER BAIERISCHER SCHRIFTSTELLER DES 18. UND 19. JAHRHUNDERTS

Baader, Franz von *see*
- FERMENTA COGNITIONIS
- UEBER DAS DURCH DIE FRANZOESISCHE REVOLUTION HERBEIGEFUEHRTE BEDUERFNISS EINER NEUERN UND INNIGERN VERBINDUNG DER RELIGION MIT DER POLITIK

Baak, J M J *see* DE RECHTSGEVOLGEN VAN HET HUWELIJK...

BAAL / Brecht, Bertolt – Potsdam 1922 – 1 – us U.W. Library [820]

BAAL : EIN SPIEL / Avenarius, Ferdinand – Muenchen: G D W Callwey, c1920 – 1r – 1 – us U.W. Library [820]

BAAL IN THE RAS SHAMRA TEXTS / Kapelrud, Arvid S – G.E.C. Gad, 1952 – 9 – $10.00 – us I.R.C. [290]

Baar, A H van den *see* SLAVIC PALAEOGRAPHY

Baar, Carl *see* JUDGESHIP CREATION IN THE FEDERAL COURTS

Baar, Herman *see* ADDRESSES ON HOMELY AND RELIGIOUS SUBJECTS

Baardt, P *see*
- DEUGDEN-SPOOR
- DEUGDEN-SPOOR; IN DE ON-DEUGHDEN DES WERELTS AFF-GEBEELDT

Baars, A *see* HET PROCES SNEEVLIET. DE SOCIAAL-DEMOCRATIE IN NEDERLANDSCH-INDIE

Baart, Peter A *see* THE ROMAN COURT

Baas, H *see* SEDIKIT TENTANG ADMINISTRASI KEUANGAN DAN STATISTIK GEREDJA

Baath, Albert Ulrik *see* WAGNERS SAGOR

Bab, Julius *see*
- DURCH DAS DRAMA HAUPTMANNS
- GOETHES LEBEN IN SEINEN BRIEFEN
- UEBER DEN TAG HINAUS

BABA SHAMAL – (Issues No 139 is missing) – Tehran. Dawrah-'i 2, shumarah-'i 124-148 (29 Murdad 1326-6 Isfand 1326 [20 Aug 1947-23 Mar 1947]) – 1 reel – 1 – $25.00 – us MEDOC [950]

Babaev, G V *see* MAIAKOVSKII V AZERBAIDZHANE

Babakhan, N *see* SOVETY 1905 G

BABALIK – Konya: Babalik Matbaasi, 1910-1928 – 9 – $20.00 – us MEDOC [956]

THE BABAR-NAMA...NOW REPRODUCED IN FACSIMILE... / Beveridge, A S – (E.J.W. Gibb Memorial Series). Leyden, London, 1905 – 8 – ne IDC [947]

Babatunde Somade, H M *see* CHEMICAL PROBLEMS ASSOCIATED WITH THE CONTROL OF PESTS IN STORED GROUNDNIUTS IN WEST AFRICA

Babcock, Charles A *see* VENANGO COUNTY-HER PIONEERS AND PEOPLE

Babcock, Garth J *see* A SINGLE STAGE SUBMAXIMAL TREADMILL JOG TEST TO ESTIMATE VO2 MAX IN SUBJECTS AGES 30 TO 39 YEARS

Babcock, Louis L *see* THE SIEGE OF FORT ERIE: AN EPISODE IN THE WAR OF 1812

Babcock, Rufus *see* MEMOIRS OF JOHN MASON PECK, D.D., 1864

Babcock, Willoughby Maynard 2 *see* NEWSPAPER TRANSCRIPTS INDEX

THE BABE OF BETHLEHEM: FROM THE CRADLE TO THE CROSS / Parmly, Eleazar – New York: Thomas Holman, 1861. 1 fiche.8370-4670-X – 9 – us A.T.L.A. [240]

Babeau, Albert *see* LA POPULATION DE TROYES AU DIX-HUITIEME SIECLE

BABEL – (1982-. 1,5,6,9) – v1-. 1956- – 1 – us UMI [073]

BABEL AND BIBLE = BABEL UND BIBEL : A LECTURE ON THE SIGNIFICANCE OF ASSYRIOLOGICAL RESEARCH FOR RELIGION: DELIVERED BEFORE THE GERMAN EMPEROR / Delitzsch, Friedrich – (In English) – Chicago: Open Court; London: Kegan Paul, Trench, Truebner [distributor], 1902 – 1mf – 9 – 0-8370-9376-7 – 1986-3376 – us A.T.L.A. [220]

Babel, Eugen *see* GRAF ADOLF FRIEDRICH VON SCHACK

Babell, C *see* RECUEIL DE PIECES CHOISIES A UNE ET DEUX FLUTES

BABEUF AND BABOUVISM – Rare writings of Babeuf and his contemporaries, plus historical analyses. Albert Soboul, ed 82 titles. Printed Guide – 9 – fr Hachette [321]

Babey, C M P *see* FLORA JURASSIENNE

BABIALI – Siyasi, Mesleki, Mizah Mecmua. Matbaa Teknisyenlerinin Mesleki Mecmuasi. Sahibi: Aziz Uctay. Teknik Sekreter: Ibrahim Guezelce. Nos. 1, 3-9, 13 (1 Nisan 1949-Mart 1950 – 9 – $45.00 – us MEDOC [956]

LE BABILLARD DU PALAIS-ROYAL – no. 1-139. Paris. juin-oct 1791 – 1 – fr A.C.R.P.P. [073]

LA BABILLARDE – Journal gaulois, extravagant, mondain, litteraire, anti-melancolique, artistique et joyeux. no. 3, 6-9. Paris. 11 oct-22 nov 1884 – 1 – fr A.C.R.P.P. [073]

Babin, Basile J *see* BIBLIOGRAPHIE ANALYTIQUE DES EVEQUES ET DE QUELQUES PERES EUDISTES AU CANADA

Babin, N *see* FREEDOM OF THE INDIVIDUAL IN THE USSR

Babington, C *see* THE REPRESSOR OF OVERMUCH BLAMING OF THE CLERGY (RS19)

Babington, C (v1-2) *see* POLYCHRONICON RANULPHI HIGDEN MONACHI CESTRENSIS (RS41)

Babington, William Dalton *see* FALLACIES OF RACE THEORIES AS APPLIED TO NATIONAL CHARACTERISTICS
BABOCHKA – St. Petersburg, 1829-31. BR-1526 2 – 8 – ne IDC [073]
Babonneau, F M *see* LE PERE LACORDAIRE ET LES JEUNES GENS: LECTURE FAITE AU CERCLE VILLE MARIE DE MONTREAL
Babushkina, A P *see* ISTORIIA RUSSKOI DETSKOI LITERATURY
BABUSHKINY STARINY / Krivopolena, Maria Dmitrievna; ed by Ozarovskaia, O E – 1922. Russian folk literature – 1 – us I.U. Libraries [390]
Babut, E C *see*
- LE CONCIL DE TURIN
- LE CONCILE DE TURIN
- LA PLUS ANCIENNE DECRETALE
- PRISCILLIEN ET LE PRISCILLIANISME
- ST. MARTIN DE TOURS
- SAINT MARTIN DE TOURS

THE BABY AND THE BATHWATER / Black, Bob – His conflict with PW – 9 – 1.00f – at Libertarian Micro [335]
BABY CARE – (Absorbed: Baby Care Manual) – New York. v1-9. 1970-Fall 1979* – 1 – D10358 – us UMI [618]
BABY CARE MANUAL *see* BABY CARE
BABY FAE COLLECTION / Loma Linda University Heritage Room – (Special compilation of newspapers) – Riverside Co – 1r – 1 – $50.00 – R40290 – us Library Micro [978]
BABY FAE NEWS CLIPPINGS – Loma Linda, CA. 1984 – 1r – 1 – $50.00 – R03278 – us Library Micro [071]
Baby, Georges *see*
- CHATEAUGUAY: QUI EST "TEMOIN OCULAIRE" ET SA DESCRIPTION DE LA BATAILLE EST-ELLE CORRECTE?
- L'EXODE DES CLASSES DIRIGEANTES A LA CESSION DU CANADA

Baby, William Lewis *see* SOUVENIRS OF THE PAST WITH ILLUSTRATIONS: AN INSTRUCTIVE AND AMUSING WORK, GIVING A CORRECT ACCOUNT OF THE CUSTOMS AND HABITS OF THE PIONEERS OF CANADA AND THE SURROUNDING COUNTRY.
BABYLON AND THE OLD TESTAMENT / Parrot, Andre – S.C.M. Press, 1958 – 9 – $10.00 – us I.R.C. [220]
THE BABYLONIAN AND ORIENTAL RECORD – (Lacking: 7(1893)) – London, 1(1886)-9(1901) – 36mf – 9 – Dfl126.00 – ne Slangenburg [073]
THE BABYLONIAN AND THE HEBREW GENESIS / Zimmern, Heinrich – London: David Nutt, 1901. 1 fiche – 9 – us A.T.L.A. [220]
BABYLONIAN CONTRACT TABLETS IN THE METROPOLITAN MUSEUM OF ART / ed by Moldenke, Alfred B – (Includes indexes) – 1893 – 1mf – 9 – 0-8370-7569-6 – 1986-1569 – us A.T.L.A. [470]
THE BABYLONIAN GENESIS, THE STORY OF CREATION / Heidel, Alexander – U. of C. Press, 1942 – 9 – $10.00 – us I.R.C. [290]
BABYLONIAN LAWS / Driver, G R – Oxford. 1954 – 9 – $15.00 – us I.R.C. [900]
BABYLONIAN LITERATURE : LECTURES / Sayce, Archibald Henry – (Includes bibliographical references) – London: Samuel Bagster, [1877] – 1mf – 9 – 0-8370-8378-8 – 1986-2378 – us A.T.L.A. [470]
BABYLONIAN LITURGIES / Langdon, S – Sumerian texts from the early period and from the library of Ashurbanipal, with introduction and index. Paris. 1913. BNE-423 1 – 9 – ne IDC [200]
BABYLONIAN MAGIC AND SORCERY / King, L W – London. 1896. BNE-380 1 – 9 – ne IDC [290]
BABYLONIAN RECORDS IN THE LIBRARY OF J. PIERPONT MORGAN : PT 4: EPICS, HYMNS, OMENS AND OTHER TEXTS / Clay, A T – New Haven, 1923. BNE-421 1 – 3mf – 9 – ne IDC [930]
BABYLONISCH-ASSYRISCHE TEXTE : I. DIE SCHOEPFUNGSLEGENDE – Bonn: A Marcus und E Weber, 1904 – 1mf – 9 – 0-8370-7526-2 – 1986-1526 – us A.T.L.A. [470]
DIE BABYLONISCH-ASSYRISCHEN VORSTELLUNGEN VOM LEBEN NACH DEM TODE : NACH DEN QUELLEN MIT BERUECKSICHTIGUNG DER ALTTESTAMENTLICHEN PARALLELEN / Jeremias, Alfred – (In German and Akkadian. Includes bibliographical references) – Leipzig: J C Hinrichs, 1887 – 1mf – 9 – 0-8370-7224-7 – 1986-1224 – us A.T.L.A. [230]
BABYLONISCH-ASTRALES IM WELTBILDE DES THALMUD UND MIDRASCH / Bischoff, Erich – Leipzig: J.C. Hinrichs, 1907. 1 fiche – 9 – us A.T.L.A. [270]
BABYLONISCHE BESCHWOERUNGRELIEFS. EIN BEITRAG ZUR ERKLAERUNG DER SOG. HADESRELIEFS / Frank, K – (Leipziger semitistische studien. v. 3, pt. 3. Leipzig. 1920). Leipzig. 1908. BNE-20.113 1 – 9 – ne IDC [930]
BABYLONISCHE BUSSPSALMEN / Zimmern, Heinrich – (Assyrische Bibl. v. 6). Leipzig. 1885. BNE-20,042 1 – 9 – ne IDC [930]
BABYLONISCHE BUSSPSALMEN / Zimmern, Heinrich – (Includes bibliographical references and indexes) – Leipzig: J C Hinrichs, 1885 – 1mf – 9 – 0-8370-7118-6 – 1986-1118 – us A.T.L.A. [470]
DIE BABYLONISCHE FABEL UND IHRE BEDEUTUNG FUER DIE LITERATURGESCHICHTE / Ebeling, Erich – (Mitteilungen der altorientalischen gesellschaft. v. 2, pt. 3). Leipzig. 1927. BNE-20,107 1 – 9 – ne IDC [470]
DIE BABYLONISCHE GEBETS-BESCHWOERUNG / Kunstmann, Walter G – Graefenhainichen, 1930 – 2mf – 9 – DM62.00 – 3-89349-322-0 – gw Hänsel [290]
DIE BABYLONISCHE GEBETS-BESCHWOERUNG / Kunstmann, Walter G – (Semitistische Studien, n.s. v. 2). Leipzig. 1932. BNE-20,035 1 – 9 – ne IDC [290]
BABYLONISCHE HYMNEN UND GEBETE / Zimmern, Heinrich – (Der Alte Orient, VII, v. 3). Leipzig. 1905. BNE-20,058 1 – 9 – ne IDC [290]
BABYLONISCHE HYMNEN UND GEBETE / Zimmern, Heinrich – (Der Alte Orient, XIII, v. 1). Leipzig. 1911. BNE-20,026 1 – 9 – ne IDC [290]
BABYLONISCHE SUEHNRITEN BESONDERS MIT RUECKSICHT AUF PRIESTER UND BUESSER / Schrank, W – (Leipziger semitistische studien. v. 3, pt. 1. Leipzig. 1920). Leipzig. 1908. BNE-20,112 1 – 9 – ne IDC [290]
BABYLONISCHE TALMUD, HEBRAEISCH UND DEUTSCH MIT EINSCHLUSS DER VOLLSTAENDIGE MISNAH / ed by Goldschmidt, L – Berlin. v1-9. 1925 – Dfl1,502.00 – ne Slangenburg [220]
DIE BABYLONISCHEN BUSSPSALMEN UND DAS ALTE TESTAMENT / Bahr, Johannes – Berlin: Weidmann, 1903 – 1mf – 9 – 0-8370-7361-8 – 1986-1361 – us A.T.L.A. [230]
BABYLONISCHES IM NEUEN TESTAMENT / Jeremias, Alfred – (Includes bibliographical references, general index and index of biblical and extra-biblical texts cited) – Leipzig: J C Hinrichs, 1905 – 1mf – 9 – 0-8370-3781-6 – 1985-1781 – us A.T.L.A. [220]
BACCALAUREATE SERMONS / Peabody, Andrew Preston – 1885 – 9 – us A.T.L.A. [240]
THE BACCHAE. / Euripides – Trans. into English rhyming verse with explan. notes by Gilbert Murray. 12th thousand.New York: Longman's Green, 1915. 94p – 1 – us U.W. Library [450]
Bacchinus, B D *see* BENEDICTI BACCHINI DE SISTRIS, EORUMQUE FIGURIS AC DIFFERENTIA. DISSERTATIO
Bacchus, Francis *see* ESSAYS
BACCHUS MARSH EXPRESS – Australia, 7 Jan 1911-26 Aug 1916 (imperfect) – 2r – 1 – uk British Libr Newspaper [072]
Bacchus, MK *see* EDUCATION FOR DEVELOPMENT OR UNDERDEVELOPMENT?
Baccus, Joseph H *see* SELECTED ARTICLES ON MINIMUM WAGES AND MAXIMUM HOURS
Bach, Adolf *see* LOF DER REINSTER VROWEN
Bach, C P B *see* VERSUCH UEBER SIE WAHRE ART DAS CLAVIER ZU SPIELEN...
Bach, C P E *see*
- CARL PHILIPP EMANUEL BACHS VERSUCH UEBER DIE WAHRE ART DAS CLAVIER ZU SPIELEN
- EXEMPEL NEBST ACHTZEHN PROBE-STUECKEN IN SECHS SONATEN ZU CARL PHILIPP EMANUEL BACHS VERSUCHE UEBER DIE WAHRE ART DAS CLAVIER ZU SPIELEN
- A FAVORITE SOLO FOR THE VIOLIN AND HARPSICHORD...
- HEILIG, MIT ZWEY CHOEREN UND EINER ARIETTE ZUR EINLEITUNG...
- HERRN PROF. GELLERTS GEISTLICHE ODEN UND LIEDER
- DIE ISRAELITEN IN DER WUESTE
- KURZE UN LEICHTE KLAVIERSTUCKE, W. 113, NO. 1, 2, 3, 10, 11
- MUSIKLAISCHES VIERLERLEY HRSG. VON HERRN CARL PHILIP EMANUEL BACH
- PASSIONS CANTATE, GROSZE, [DU GOTTSLICHER WARUMBIST DU SO IN DES TODES SCHMERZ VERSUNKEN?] IN MUSIK GESETZT VON KARL PHILIPP EMANUEL BACH...
- PETITES PIECES POUR LE CLAVECIN DE C.P.E. BACH
- SECHS LEICHTE CLAVIER SONATEN
- SECHS SONATEN FUER CLAVIER MIT VERAENDERTEN REPRISEN
- SECHS SONATEN: VERSUCH UEBER DIE WAHRE ART DAS KLAVIER ZU SPIELEN... THEIL 1
- SIX FUGES POUR LE FORTEPIANO [W. 119]
- SONATAS, HARPSICHORD, W. 49
- TREULICHER UNTERRICHT IM GENERAL-BASS
- VERSUCH UEBER DIE WAHRTE ART DAS CLAVIER ZU SPIELEN MIT EXEMPELN

THE BACH FAMILY : KEYBOARD COMPOSITIONS – 53mf – 9 – MS-h – ne IDC [780]
BACH JAHRBUCH – Leipzig. 1904-50. 2 reels – 1 – 46.00 – us L of C Photodup [780]
Bach, Johann Christian *see*
- A 3RD SET OF SIX CONCERTOS FOR THE HARPSICHORD... OP. 13
- 4 SONATAS AND TWO DUETTS FOR THE HARPSICHORD OR PIANOFORTE WITH AN ACCOMPANYMENT FOR A GERMAN FLUTE OR VIOLIN, OPERA 18
- QUATTRO SONATE NOTTURNE...A 2 VIOLINI, 2 BASSO, A PIU TOSTO VIOLA. OP. 4, NO 1-4
- SIX CONCERTS POUR LE CLAVECIN
- SONATAS, VIOLIN AND PIANO, OP 16, WITH AN ACCOMPANYMENT FOR THE VIOLIN OR GERMAN FLUTE
- THREE FAVORITE SYMPHONIES

Bach, Johann M *see* KURZE UND SYSTEMATISCHE ANLEITUNG ZUM GENERAL-BASS, UND DER TONKUNST UEBERHAUPT, MIT EXEMPELN ERLAEUTERT
Bach, Johann Sebastian *see*
- 6 SUITEES POUR LE CLAVECIN, S. 812-817
- 371 VERSTIMMEGE CHORALGESANG. DRITTE AUFLAGE
- CHORALBUCH, 4 STIMMIGES.
- CHROMATISCHE FANTASIE UND FUGE
- LE CLAVECIN BIEN TEMPERE: OU PRELUDES ET FUGUES DANS TOUS LES TONS ET DEMINTONS DU MODE MAJEUR ET MINEUR
- CLAVIERUEBUNG BESTEHEND IN EINER ARIA MIT VERSCHIEDENEN VERAENDERUNGEN VORS CLAVICIMBAL MIT 2 MANUALEN. DENEN LIEBHABERN ZUR GEMUETHSERGETZUNG VERFERTIGT VON...
- DRITTER THEIL DER CLAVIER UEBUNG BESTEHEND IN VERSCHIEDENEN VORSPIELEN UEBER DIE CATECHISMUS-UND ANDERE GESAENGE, VOR DIE ORGEL...
- FANTASIE AND FUGE, HARPSICHORD, S. 906 IN C MINOR
- INVENTIONS, 2-PART, HARPSICHORD
- INVENTIONS, 3-PART, HARPSICHORD
- JOHANNES PASSION. SELECTIONS
- DIE KUNST DER FUGUE DURCH HERRN JOHANN SEBASTIAN BACH...HERAUSGEBEN VON MARPURG
- MINN VON UNS, HERR... S. 101
- MUSIKALISCHES OPFER SR. KOENIGLICHEN MAJESTAET IN PREUSSEN UND C. ALLERUNTERTHAENIGST GEWIDMET...
- SIX PRELUDES A L'USAGE DES COMMENCANTS POUR LE CLAVECIN
- TOCCATA, HARPSICHORD, S. 913, D MINOR
- WERKE
- DAS WOHLTEMPERIETE CLAVIER. 24 PRELUDES UND FUGUES

Bach, Joseph *see* DIE DOGMENGESCHICHTE DES MITTELALTERS VON CHRISTOLOGISCHE STANDPUNKTE, ODER, DIE MITTELALTERLICHE CHRISTOLOGIE VOM ACHTEN BIS SECHZEHNTEN JAHRHUNDERT
Bach, Robert *see*
- DIE ERWAEHLUNG ISRAELS IN DER WUESTE
- THE POPULATION OF ISRAEL

Bachand, P *see* SPEECH ON THE BUDGET BY THE HON. P. BACHAND, TREASURER OF THE PROVINCE OF QUEBEC: DELIVERED IN THE LEGISLATIVE ASSEMBLY, QUEBEC, 18TH JUNE 1878
DIE BACH-DRUCKE DER HOBOKEN-SAMMLUNG MUSIKALISCHER ERST-UND FRUEHDRUECKE / Oesterreichische Nationalbibliothek Wien. Musiksammlung – Hildesheim, 1987 – 178mf – 9 – DM1,900.00 diazo DM2,200.00 silver – gw Olms [780]
Bache, Kent *see* LETTER TO THE REV. SAMUEL DAVIDSON: IN ANSWER TO HIS ESSAY AGAINST THE JOHANNINE AUTHOR
Bache, Kentish *see* A LETTER TO THE REV. SAMUEL DAVIDSON, D.D., LL. D
BACHELOR OF DIVINITY AND MASTER OF THEOLOGY THESES, 1968-1993 / Pacific Theological College – Suva, Fiji – 33r – 1 – PMB1084 – at Pacific Mss [370]
Bacher, Wilhelm *see*
- DIE AELTESTE TERMINOLOGIE DER JUEDISCHEN SCHRIFTAUSLEGUNG
- DIE AGADA DER BABYLONISCHEN AMORAEER
- DIE AGADA DER PALAESTINENSISCHEN AMORAEER
- DIE AGADA DER TANAITEN
- DIE AGADA DER TANNAITEN
- DIE AGADA DER TANNAITEN UND AMORAEER
- DIE BIBELEXEGESE DER JUEDISCHEN RELIGIONSPHILOSOPHEN DES MITTELALTERS VOR MAIMUNI
- DIE BIBELEXEGESE MOSES MAIMUNIS
- DIE EXEGETISCHE TERMINOLOGIE DER JUEDISCHEN TRADITIONSLITERATUR
- DIE HEBRAEISCHE SPRACHWISSENSCHAFT VOM 10. BIS ZUM 16. JAHRHUNDERT
- DIE JUEDISCHE BIBELEXEGESE
- DIE PROOEMIEN DES ALTEN JUEDISCHEN HOMILIE
- TRADITION UND TRADENTEN IN DEN SCHULEN PALAESTINAS UND BABYLONIENS

Bachiller Cantaclaro *see* HILVANES Y ZURZIDOS. LO QUE SE LLAMA PERDER EL TIEMPO. ENSAYOS POETICOS
Bachiller Reganadientes *see* DEMOSTRACTIONES PALMARIAS..
Bachir, Ali *see* L'AMOUR, LE MARIAGE, LA JUSTICE SELON LE KORAN
BACH-JAHRBUCH – v1-45, 47-51. 1904-1958, 1960-1965 – 1 – us Schnase [780]
Bachler, Levi R *see* AN EMG STUDY OF FOUR ELASTIC TUBING CLOSED KINETIC CHAIN EXERCISES
Bachman, John *see*
- THE QUADRUPEDS OF NORTH AMERICA
- SERMONS

Bachman, Kate *see* PAPERS OF KATE BACHMAN
Bachmann, Adolf *see* BOEHMEN UND SEINE NACHBARLAENDER UNTER GEORG VON PODIEBRAD, 1458-61, UND DES KOENIGS BEWERBUNG UM DIE DEUTSCHE KRONE
Bachmann, Albert *see* MITTELHOCHDEUTSCHES LESEBUCH: MIT GRAMMATIK UND WOERTERBUCH
Bachmann, Johannes *see* ALTTESTAMENTLICHEN UNTERSUCHUNGEN, 1. BUCH
Bachmann, Philipp *see*
- GRUNDLINIEN DER SYSTEMATISCHEN THEOLOGIE
- GRUNDLINIEN DER SYSTEMATISCHEN THEOLOGIE: ZUM GEBRAUCHE BEI VORLESUNGEN
- DIE PERSOENLICHE HEILSERFAHRUNG DES CHRISTEN UND IHRE BEDUETUNG FUER DEN GLAUBEN NACH DEM ZEUGNISSE DER APOSTEL
- DER ZWEITE BRIEF DES PAULUS AN DIE KORINTHER

Bachofen, Charles *see* ESSAI SUR L'ECCLESIOLOGIE DE ZWINGLE
Bachofen, J C *see* MUSICALISCHES HALLELUJA, ODER SCHONE UND GEISTREICHE GESANGE
Bachoff von Echt, J F *see* DE EO QUOD IUSTUM E..
Bachoffner, George Henry *see* CHEMISTRY AS APPLIED TO THE FINE ARTS
Bachor, Oskar-Wilhelm *see* DER KREIS GERDAUEN
Bachtiar Djamily *see* JANG BERONTAK DAN JANG MENJERAH
Bacilly, B de *see* REMARQUES CURIEUSES SUR L'ART DE BIEN CHANTER
Back, Claus *see* DER WEG NACH ROM
THE BACK HANDSPRING : COMPARISON OF KINEMATIC VARIABLES OF THE CENTER OF GRAVITY FOLLOWING THREE DIFFERENT HAND PLACEMENTS / Yuen, Garry E – 1988 – 86p 1mf – 9 – $4.00 – us Microform Publ [612]

BACK OF THE SPANISH REBELLION / Fernsworth, Lawrence A – NY, 1936? Fiche W 883. (Blodgett Collection of Spanish Civil War Pamphlets) – 9 – us H.U. College Libr [946]
BACK OF THE SPANISH REBELLION / Fernsworth, Lawrence A – Washington, DC. 1936? Fiche W 882. (Blodgett Collection of Spanish Civil War Pamphlets) – 9 – us H.U. College Libr [946]
BACK STAGE – (Has suppls: Business Screen, 1977; and Business and Home TV Screen, 1978. Beginning with 1979, Business and Home TV Screen is incl in the micro-ed as Pt 2) – New York. v1-17 dec 1960-76*. v18-38 jan 1977-jan 1998+ 1; v20-26 jan 1979-dec 1985. v27-35 jan 1986-95*. v36-38 jan 1995-1998+ 5; v20-38 jan 1979-98+ – 1 – D11170 – us UMI [790]
BACK TO CHRIST : SOME MODERN FORMS OF RELIGIOUS THOUGHT / Spence, Walter – Chicago: A C McClurg, 1900 – 1mf – 9 – 0-8370-5505-9 – 1985-3505 – us A.T.L.A. [240]
BACK TO THE REPUBLIC : THE GOLDEN MEAN, THE STANDARD FORM OF GOVERNMENT / Atwood, Harry F – Chicago: Laird & Lee, 1918 – 2mf – 9 – $3.00 – LLMC 92-182 – us L.L.M.C. [323]
Backer, C A *see*
– FLORA VAN BATAVIA
– GEILLUSTREERD HANDBOEK DER JAVAANSCHE THEEONKRUIDEN EN HUNNE BETEEKENIS VOOR DE CULTUUR
– HANDBOEK VOOR DE FLORA VAN JAVA
– ONKRUIDFLORA DER JAVASCHE SUIKERRIETGRONDEN
– THE PROBLEM OF KRAKATAO AS SEEN BY A BOTANI..
– SCHOOLFLORA VOOR JAVA (RANUNCULACEAS – MYRTACEAE)
– VARENFLORA VOOR JAVA...
– VERKLAREND WOORDENBOEK DER WETENSCHAPPELIJKE NAMEN VAN DE IN NEDERLAND EN NEDERLANDSCH INDIE IN HET WILD GROEIENDE EN IN TUINEN EN PARKEN GEKWEEKTE VARENS EN HOGERE PLANTEN
BACKGROUND AND HISTORY OF THE GENERAL ASSOCIATION OF REGULAR BAPTIST CHURCHES / Stowell, Joseph M – 3rd ed. 1949 – 1 – 5.00 – us Baptist [240]
BACKGROUND MATERIALS RELATING TO RAILROAD RETIREMENT / U.S. Congress. Senate. Committee on Labor and Public Welfare. Subcommittee on Retirement – Washington, Govt. Print. Off., 1973. 99 p. LL-2240 – 1 – us L of C Photodup [340]
BACKGROUND MATERIALS RELATING TO THE EXERCISE OF CRIMINAL JURISDICTION OVER U.S. FORCES IN JAPAN UNDER ARTICLE 17 OF THE JAPAN -UNITED STATES ADMINISTRATIVE AGREEMENT : COMPILED BY THE OFFICE OF THE JUDGE ADVOCATE, HQ. AFFE78A (REAR) APO 343 – Army-AG Admin Cen-Japan-150, 1962? – 1mf – 9 – $1.50 – LLMC 96-074 – us L.L.M.C. [340]
THE BACKGROUND OF SACRED STORY : LIFE LESSONS FROM THE LESS-KNOWN CHARACTERS OF THE BIBLE / Hastings, Frederick – London: Religious Tract Society, 1886 – 1mf – 9 – 0-8370-3519-8 – 1985-1519 – us A.T.L.A. [220]
Backhaus, Werner *see*
– COLOR VISION IN BEES
– COLOR VISION IN HONEYBEES AND OTHER INSECTS
Backhouse, Edward *see*
– BIOGRAPHICAL MEMOIRS
– EARLY CHURCH HISTORY
BACKNANGER KREISZEITUNG : MURRTAL-BOTE – Backnang, 1987- – 6r per yr – 1 – Dist. gw Mikrofilm – gw Misc Inst [072]
BACKSTAGE – New York, NY. 1978-80 – 12r – 1 – $600.00 – R04903 – us Library Micro [790]
Backus, Isaac *see*
– A HISTORY OF NEW ENGLAND
– A HISTORY OF NEW ENGLAND WITH PARTICULAR REFERENCE TO THE DENOMINATION OF CHRISTIANS CALLED BAPTISTS
– MISC. MATERIALS
– MISCELLANEOUS PRINTED PUBLICATIONS; ALSO SERMONS BY 38 OTHER NEW ENGLAND WRITERS, 1746-1800
– TEN DIARIES AND OTHER UNPUBLISHED WORKS IN MANUSCRIPT.
BACKUS, ISSAC, PAPERS, MS 71 – 1719-1805 – 1r – 1 – us Western Res [240]
Backus, James *see* JAMES BACKUS PAPERS, MS 1548
BACKUS MEMORIAL BAPTIST CHURCH. NORTH MIDDLEBORO, MASSACHUSETTS : CHURCH RECORDS – 1756-1894 – 1 – 18.45 – us Baptist [240]
THE BACKWASH OF WAR : THE HUMAN WRECKAGE OF THE BATTLEFIELD AS WITNESSED BY AN AMERICAN HOSPITAL NURSE / La Motte, Ellen Newbold – New York, London: G P Putnam's Sons, 1916 – 1r – 1 – us U.W. Library [920]
Bacon, Anthony *see* PAPERS
Bacon, Benjamin Wisner *see*
– CHRISTIANITY OLD AND NEW
– COMMENTARY ON THE EPISTLE OF PAUL TO THE GALATIANS
– THE GENESIS OF GENESIS: A STUDY OF THE DOCUMENTARY SOURCES
– SERMON ON THE MOUNT: ITS LITERARY STRUCTURE
– STORY OF ST PAUL: COMPARISON OF ACTS & EPISTLES
– THEODORE THORNTON MUNGER
– TRIPLE TRADITION OF THE EXODUS
Bacon, Charles W *see* THE AMERICAN PLAN OF GOVERNMENT
Bacon, Francis *see*
– BACONIANA
– INSTAURATIO MAGNA
– LA NOUVELLE ATLANTIDE
– OF THE ADVANCEMENT OF LEARNING
– OPUSCULA VARIA POSTHUMA
– THE PHILOSOPHICAL WORKS OF FRANCIS BACON, BARON OF VERULAM, VISCOUNT ST ALBANS.
– RESUSCITATIO
– SYLVA SYLVARUM
– THE TVVOO BOOKES OF FRANCIS BACON OF THE PROFICIENCE AND ADUANCEMENT OF LEARNING, DIUINE AND HUMANE
Bacon, Grace Mabel *see* THE PERSONAL AND LITERARY RELATIONS OF HEINRICH HEINE TO KARL IMMERMANN
Bacon Hilda *see* EFFECTS OF AEROBIC EXERCISE ON THE LIPID PROFILE LEVELS OF PATIENTS WITH MODERATE TO SEVERE BURN INJURY
Bacon, J *see* THE LIFE OF EDUARD JENNER
Bacon, Leonard *see*
– THE GENESIS OF THE NEW ENGLAND CHURCHES
– A HISTORY OF AMERICAN CHRISTIANITY
– IRENICS AND POLEMICS
– THE SABBATH QUESTION
– SLAVERY DISCUSSED IN OCCASIONAL ESSAYS
Bacon, Leonard et al *see* MEMORIAL OF NATHANIEL W. TAYLOR, D.D.
Bacon, Leonard Woolsey *see* AN INSIDE VIEW OF THE VATICAN COUNCIL
Bacon, R *see* FOR BETTER RELATIONS WITH OUR LATIN AMERICAN NEIGHBORS
Bacon, R H *see* BENIN, THE CITY OF BLOOD
Bacon, Roger *see*
– DE ARTE CHYMIAE SCRIPTA. CVI ACCESSERVNT OPUSCULA ALIA EIUSDEM AUTHORIS
– THE GREEK GRAMMAR OF ROGER BACON AND A FRAGMENT OF HIS HEBREW GRAMMAR
– ROGERI BACON OPERA QUAEDAM HACTENUS INEDITA (RS15)
Bacon, Thomas *see*
– THE QUEEN'S BIRTH-DAY IN MONTREAL, 24TH MAY, 1879: ORDERS FOR THE MILITARY REVIEW AND SHAM-FIGHT.
– THE TOWNSHIP BONDS OF MISSOURI, UNDER THE ACT OF MARCH 23RD, 1868
Bacon, Thomas Scott *see* IT IS WRITTEN: A CAREFUL STUDY OF THE GOSPELS
BACONIANA / Bacon, Francis – London, 1679 – 7mf – ne IDC [610]
BACONIANA / Bacon, Francis – M-292 2. 1679 – 8 – ne IDC [420]
BACONS' COMPLETE PRECEPTOR FOR THE CLARINET, WITH A SELECTION OF AIRS, MARCHES, &C – Philadelphia: A. Bacon, 181-. Includes: Hail to the Chief and Washington's March. Music-778, item 3 – 1 – us L of C Photodup [780]
BACON'S JUDICIAL REPOSITORY *see* NEW YORK JUDICIAL REPOSITORY
Bacot, Thomas W *see* LETTERBOOK
Bacquart, A *see* UNE COLONIE DE COMMERCE...
BACS-BODROGER ZEITUNG – Apatin, Yugoslavia. Apr 1923-May 1925 – 1r – 1 – us L of C Photodup [072]
BACTERIOLOGICAL REVIEWS – (Cont by: Microbiological Reviews) – Baltimore. cum index 1-10 1937-46; cum index 11-12 1947-58. v1-41 1937-dec 1977 1; v29-41 mar 1965-dec 1977 5; v34-41 mar 1970-dec 1977 9 – 1,5,9 – D92 – us UMI [576]
EL BACULO DE SAN PEDRO DE ALCANTARA / Munoz de San Pedro, Miguel – Badajoz: Dip. Prov., 1966 – 1 – sp Bibl Santa Ana [240]
BAD AWJUH AL-IKHTILAF FI RASM ISM AL-MAKAN AL-WAHID BI-HURUF AL-LUGHAH AL ARABIYAH FI AL-MAMLAKAH AL-ARABIYAH AL-SAUDIYAH / Asad Sulayman Abduh – al-Kuwayt: Qism al-Jughrafiya bi-Jamiat al-Kuwayt wa-al-Jamiyah al-Jughrafiya al-Kuwaytiyah, [1985] – us Res Libr [956]
BAD LAUTERBERGER ZEITUNG *see* HARZ-KURIER
BADAJOZ / Hispanicus – London, 1937. Fiche W946. (Blodgett Collection of Spanish Civil War Pamphlets) – 9 – us H.U. College Libr [946]
Badajoz *see*
– CENTANERIO DE COLON Y FERIAS
– CUENTA QUE EL ALCALDE...DE 1850
– EJERCICIO DE 1931. PRESUPUESTO ORDINARIO FORMADO PARA EL REFERIDO EJERCICIO POR LA COMISION PERMANENTE Y APROBADO POR EL AYUNTAMIENTE PLENO Y E ILMO. SR.DELEGADO DE HACIENDA
– FERIAS Y FIESTAS DE SAN JUAN. 1946
– FERIAS Y FIESTAS DE SAN JUAN. GUIA DE ESPECTACULOS 1953
– FIESTAS DE SAN JOSE. 1971
– FIESTAS DE SAN JUAN 1971
– FIESTAS DE SAN JUAN 1972
– FIESTAS DE SAN JUAN 1975
– FIESTAS EN HONOR DE SAN ROQUE 1945
– FIESTAS Y FERIA DE LA BARRIADA DE SAN ROQUE...1971
– JUSTAS LITERARIAS DE SAN JUAN ORGANIZADAS POR EL EXCELENTISIMO AYUNTAMIENTO DE BADAJOZ
– MEMORIA PRESENTADA POR LA JUNTA DIRECTIVA A LA ASAMBLEA GENERAL
– MEMORIA REGLAMENTARIA DE SECRETARIA GENERAL 1967
– ORDENANZAS
– ORDENANZAS MUNICIPALES
– ORDO DIVINI OFICCI...1828
– PRESUPUESTO ORDINARIO DE GASTOS E INGRESOS EJERCICIO DE 1961
– PRESUPUESTO ORDINARIO DEL INTERIOR CORRESPONDIENTE AL ANO 1951...BADAJOZ
– PROGRAMA OFICIAL DE FESTJOS QUE...CON MOTIVO DE LAS FIESTAS DE SAN JUAN 1969
– PROGRAMA OFICIAL DE LAS FIESTAS DE SAN JUAN QUE...SE CELEBRARAN...1968
– PROGRAMA OFICIAL DE LAS FIESTAS DE SAN JUAN...1973
– PROPIUM FESTORUM QUAE IN...PACENSIS
– REGLAMENTO DE CORO DE LA SANTA CATEDRAL DE BADAJOZ
– REGLAMENTO PARA LA ESCUELA NORMAL... BADAJOZ
– REVISTA OFICIAL DE LAS FIESTAS DE SAN JUAN 1979
– TARIFAS Y ORDENANZAS PARA LA EXACCION DE ARBITRIOS E IMPUESTOS MUNICIPALES, APROBADAS PARA EL EJERCICIO ECONOMICO DE 1924-25
BADAJOZ APUNTE ESTRUCTURAL Y GENETICO / Rubio Recio, Jose Manuel – Badajoz: Imp. Diputacion Provincial, 1962 – sp Bibl Santa Ana [946]
Badajoz, Cruz Roja *see* ACTUACION DE LA JUNTA DE SENORAS DE LA CRUZ ROJA DE BADAJOZ DURANTE LA CAMPANA DE AFRICA DE 1921 Y 1922
BADAJOZ. DATOS INFORMATIVOS / Subsecretaria de Turismo – sp Bibl Santa Ana [338]
EL BADAJOZ DEL SIGLO 16 / Guerra Guerra, Arcadio – Badajoz: Imp. Diputacion Provincial, 1964. Sep. REE – sp Bibl Santa Ana [946]
Badajoz, Delegacion Provincial de Informacion y Turismo *see* CONVOCATORIA Y REGLAMENTO DE LA 1ST ASAMBLEA PROVINCIAL DE CULTURA POPULAR
Badajoz. Diocesis *see*
– LA DIOCESIS DE BADAJOZ. ESTADISTICA DE 1970
– ORDO DIVINI OFICCI...PROANNO...1943
Badajoz. Diputacion Provincial *see* REGLAMENTO GENERAL DE FUNCINARIOS PROVINCIALES
Badajoz. Espana en Paz *see* CHRONICA DE 25 ANOS
BADAJOZ. FIESTA ESCOLAR. 1912 – Revista Semanal de la Escuela Nacional – 1 – sp Bibl Santa Ana [370]
Badajoz. Junta de Cofradias de Penitencia *see* SEMANA SANTA BADAJOZ. 1971. PROGRAMA OFICIAL
Badajoz. Junta Diocesana *see*
– OBRA DE LA PROPAGACION DE LA FE
Badajoz. Santa Infancia *see* OBRA PONTIFICIA DE LA SANTA INFANCIA
Badajoz. Spain *see* ORDENANZAS DE 1892
Badajoz. Spain. Diputacion Provincial *see* MEMORIA..
BADAJOZ TAURINO / Cabanas Ventura, Felipe – Apuntes para la historia del toreo en Extremadura. 1896 – 9 – 1.50f – sp Bibl Santa Ana [790]
Badajoz. Tribunal Provincial de lo Contencioso-Administrativo de Badajoz *see* PLEITO CELEBRE. ANTECEDENTES. INFORMES. SENTENCIA DICTADA...EN EL PLEITO PROMOVIDO POR DON SATURNINO SUDON CONTRA LA RESOLUCION DEL GOBERNADOR CIVIL CONFIRMANDO UN ACUERDO DEL AYUNTAMIENTO DE ALBURQUERQUE...
BADAJOZ-71 / Agenda Sindical – Madrid: Edita Ediciones Publicaciones Populares, 1971 – 1 – sp Bibl Santa Ana [946]
BADAN PEKERDJA : RISALAH / Komite Nasional Pusat – Djakarta, Oct. 1945-Aug. 1950 – 8mf – 9 – ne IDC [950]
BADAN TURISME. YOUR GUIDE IN JOGJAKARTA / Indonesia. Jogjakarta – SE-4537 1. 1960 – 9 – ne IDC [910]
Badanelli, Pedro *see*
– COMUNISMO O JUSTICIALISMO
– PERON, LA IGLESIA Y UN CURA
Badaro, F *see* L'EGLISE AU BRESIL PENDANT L'EMPIRE ET PENDANT LA REPUBLIQUE
Badaruttamam Akasah *see* DASAR2 BAHASA DJEPANG
Badeaux, Jean Baptiste *see* JOURNAL DES OPERATIONS DE L'ARMEE LORS DE L'INVASION DU CANADA EN 1775-76
BADEKUREN : NOVELLE; KLEINES GEFLUEGEL: NOVELLETTEN / Bluethgen, Viktor – Anklam: H Wolter, [190-?] – 1 – us U.W. Library [830]
Baden. Statistisches Landesamt *see* STATISTISCHES JAHRBUCH FUER DAS LAND BADEN
BADEN-BADENER ZEITUNG – Baden-Baden, apr 22 1952-apr 30 1955 – 1 – Dist. gw Mikrofilm – gw Misc Inst [072]
Badenhoop, W *see* GRENZEN DER DEUTSCHEN GEBIETSHOHEIT...
Baden-Powell, Baden Henry *see* A SHORT ACCOUNT OF THE LAND REVENUE AND ITS ADMINISTRATION IN INDIA: WITH A SKETCH OF THE LAND TENURES
Baden-Powell, R S S *see* SWAZILAND EXPEDITION, 1888-90 ; ZULULAND CAMPAIGN, 1888-90
Bader, Clarisse *see* LA FEMME BIBLIQUE
Bader, Karl Siegfried *see* JOSEPH VON LASSBERG
BADERECH = ON THE WAY – (Hebrew weekly) – Warsaw, PL. v2 no49 15 Dec 1933-v4 no2(121) 11 Jan 1935 – 1r – 1 – $25.00 – cn Can Microfilming [072]
BADERECH – 's-Gravenhage, 1925-1938. v1-14 – 26mf – 9 – J-261-11/1 – ne IDC [073]
BA-DEREKH – Warsaw. v1-6. 1932-1937 – 2r – 1 – J-291-37/3 – ne IDC [072]
BADEWOCHENBLATT FUER DIE GROSSHERZOGLICHE STADT BADEN-BADEN – (Cont by: Badeblatt) – Baden-Baden, 1812, 1813-19 (incomplete), 1825-28, 1829-81/82 (incomplete) – 1 – Dist. gw Mikrofilm – gw Misc Inst [790]
Badger, A *see* AN ILLUSTRATED HISTORY OF THE FLUTE, AND SKETCH OF THE SUCCESSIVE IMPROVEMENTS MADE IN THE FLUTE, AND A STATEMENT OF THE PRINCIPLES UPON WHICH FLUTES...
BADGER CHESS – 1982- – 1 – us U.W. Library [073]
Badger, George Percy *see*
– THE NESTORIANS AND THEIR RITUALS
BADGER HERALD / University of Wisconsin – Madison, WI. 12-16 Jan 1981- – 1 – us U.W. Library [071]
Badger, Joseph *see*
– A MEMOIR
– A MEMOIR OF REV. JOSEPH BADGER
Badgley, Erastus Irvine *see* FAITH VS. KNOWLEDGE
Badin, Adolphe *see* JEAN-BAPTISTE BLANCHARD AU DAHOMEY.

BADIN BAPTIST CHURCH. NORTH CAROLINA : CHURCH RECORDS – Apr 1836-Sep 1947 – 1 – 39.15 – us Baptist [240]
BADIN BAPTIST CHURCH WOMAN'S MISSIONARY UNION. NORTH CAROLINA : CHURCH RECORDS – Jul 1917-6 Oct 1939 – 1 – 11.25 – us Baptist [240]
BADISCHE ABENDZEITUNG – (Cont by: Badische Allgemeine Zeitung, apr 1 1951. Also available: AUSGABE LAND, oct 1 1954-sep 30 1959; AUSGABE HARDT, jul 1 1958-sep 30 1959. Also Bereichsausgaben available: BRETTEN, feb 6 1950-jun 30 1951; BRUCHSAL, feb 28 1950-jun 30 1951; ETTLINGEN, feb 6-jun 10 1950; PFORZHEIM, sep 2 1949-mar 31 1953) – Karlsruhe, jul 23 1949-jun 30 1967 – 1 – Inquire at Mikrofilmarchiv for details – gw Misc Inst [072]
BADISCHE ALLGEMEINE ZEITUNG *see* BADISCHE ABENDZEITUNG
DER BADISCHE GEWERKSCHAFTLER : MITTEILUNGSBLATT FUER DIE GEWERKSCHAFTEN IN DER FRANZ. BESETZTEN ZONE BADEN – Freiburg, West Germany. June 1946-1947 and 1949 (incomplete) – 1r – 1 – gw Mikrofilm [072]
DER BADISCHE GEWERKSCHAFTLER : MITTEILUNGSBLATT FUER DIE GEWERKSCHAFTEN IN DER FRANZOESISCH BESETZTEN ZONE – Baden Freibug/B, 1946-47; 1949 – 1r – 1 – DM75.00 – gw Mikro Press [072]
BADISCHE NEUESTE NACHRICHTEN – Karlsruhe, West-Germany. Jul 1954- – ca 9r per yr – 1 – gw Mikrofilm [072]
BADISCHE NEUESTE NACHRICHTEN *see*
- ACHER- UND BUEHLER BOTE
- BRUCHSALER RUNDSCHAU
- WOECHENTLICHES FRAG- UND KUNDSCHAFFTS-BLATH

BADISCHE VOLKS-ZEITUNG *see* WOECHENTLICHES FRAG- UND KUNDSCHAFFTS-BLATH
BADISCHE ZEITUNG – Freiburg Br., West Germany. 1968- – ca 12r per yr – 1 – gw Mikrofilm [072]
BADISCHE ZEITUNG – Freiburg im Breisgau, Germany. 1971-Oct 1973 – 17r – 1 – us L of C Photodup [072]
BADISCHE ZEITUNG *see* MANNHEIMER MORGENBLATT
BADISCHER MERKUR *see*
- MANNHEIMER ABENDZEITUNG

BADISCHES MAGAZIN – Mannheim, aug 1 1811-may 30 1812, jan 1-jun 30 1813 – 1r – 1 – gw Mikrofilm [943]
Badjaranputera *see* DEWI ANGGRAENI: WANITA BERNASIB MALANG
Badmaev, Petr Aleksandrovich *see* ROSSII A I KITA I
Badon-Pascal, E *see* SOCIETES A L'ETRANGER
Badreux, Jean *see* RECTIFICATION DU VOCABULAIRE
Badrin, N *see* V KOGTIAKH U BOLSHEVIKOV
BADSHAH NAMAH / Abd Al-Hamid Lahawri; ed by Lees, W N – (Bibliotheca Indica. v. 56). 2 v. Calcutta. 1867-72. BI-749 2 – 8 – ne IDC [890]
Badstueber, Hubert *see* FRIEDRICH VON HAGEDORNS JUGENDGEDICHTE
Badstuebner, Frank *see* NETZWERKANALYSE ZUR GENERIERUNG DER ZUSTANDSGLEICHUNGEN
Badsworth. Yorkshire *see* PARISH REGISTERS
Badt, Benno Guilelmus *see* DE ORACULIS SIBYLLINIS A IUDAEIS COMPOSITIS, PARS 1
Badt-Strauss, Bertha *see* ANNETTE VON DROSTE-HUESLHOFF
Baeck, Samuel *see* DIE GESCHICHTE DES JUEDISCHEN VOLKES UND SEINER LITERATUR VOM BABYLONISCHEN EXILE BIS AUF DIE GEGENWART MIT EINEM ANHANGE
Baedeker, F W J *see* DIE EIER DER EUROPAEISCHEN VOEGEL
Baedeker, K *see* PALESTINE ET SYRIE
BAEDEKER'S HANDBOOK(S) FOR TRAVELLERS – (Special Collection) – Complete collection of 266 editions published in English prior to World War II. With printed bibliography – 1,898mf – 9 – $4,690.00 – us UPA [900]
BAEDEKER'S HANDBOOK(S) FOR TRAVELLERS: AUSTRIA – Series No. 1. 1896, 1900, 1929 – 26mf – 9 – $130.00 – us UPA [900]
BAEDEKER'S HANDBOOK(S) FOR TRAVELLERS: AUSTRIA-HUNGARY – Series No. 2. 1905, 1911 – 20mf – 9 – $110.00 – us UPA [900]
BAEDEKER'S HANDBOOK(S) FOR TRAVELLERS: BELGIUM AND HOLLAND – Series No. 3. 1869, 1871, 1874, 1875, 1878, 1881, 1884, 1885, 1888, 1891, 1894, 1897, 1901, 1905, 1910 – 95mf – 9 – $335.00 – us UPA [910]
BAEDEKER'S HANDBOOK(S) FOR TRAVELLERS: BELGIUM AND LUXEMBOURG – Series No. 4. 1931 – 7mf – 9 – $50.00 – us UPA [910]
BAEDEKER'S HANDBOOK(S) FOR TRAVELLERS: BERLIN AND ITS ENVIRONS – Series No. 16. 1903, 1905, 1908, 1910, 1912, 1923 – 24mf – 9 – $130.00 – us UPA [900]
BAEDEKER'S HANDBOOK(S) FOR TRAVELLERS: CENTRAL ITALY – Series no. 21. 1867, 1869, 1872, 1875, 1877, 1879, 1881, 1883, 1886, 1890, 1893, 1897, 1900, 1904, 1909, 1930 – 101mf – 9 – $330.00 – us UPA [900]
BAEDEKER'S HANDBOOK(S) FOR TRAVELLERS: EASTERN ALPS – Series no. 6. 1879, 1883, 1888, 1891, 1895, 1899, 1903, 1907, 1911, 1927 – 86mf – 9 – $305.00 – us UPA [910]
BAEDEKER'S HANDBOOK(S) FOR TRAVELLERS: EGYPT – Series no. 7. Upper Egypt. 1892. Lower Egypt. 1873, 1885, 1895. Egypt. 1898, 1902. Egypt and Sudan. 1908, 1914, 1929 – 66mf – 9 – $285.00 – us UPA [910]
BAEDEKER'S HANDBOOK(S) FOR TRAVELLERS: GERMANY – Series no. 14. 1936 – 9mf – 9 – $60.00 – us UPA [910]
BAEDEKER'S HANDBOOK(S) FOR TRAVELLERS: GREAT BRITAIN – Series no. 17. 1887, 1890, 1894, 1897, 1901, 1906, 1910, 1927, 1937 – 85mf – 9 – $305.00 – us UPA [910]
BAEDEKER'S HANDBOOK(S) FOR TRAVELLERS: GREECE – Series no. 19. 1889, 1894, 1905, 1909 – 28mf – 9 – $125.00 – us UPA [910]
BAEDEKER'S HANDBOOK(S) FOR TRAVELLERS: ITALY – Series no. 23. 1904, 1909, 1928 – 22mf – 9 – $115.00 – us UPA [910]
BAEDEKER'S HANDBOOK(S) FOR TRAVELLERS: LONDON – Series no. 18. 1878, 1879, 1881, 1883, 1885, 1887, 1889, 1892, 1894, 1896, 1898, 1900, 1902, 1905, 1908, 1911, 1915, 1923, 1930 – 113mf – 9 – $345.00 – us UPA [910]
BAEDEKER'S HANDBOOK(S) FOR TRAVELLERS: MADEIRA – Series no. 24. 1939 – 2mf – 9 – $45.00 – us UPA [910]
BAEDEKER'S HANDBOOK(S) FOR TRAVELLERS: MEDITERRANEAN SEAPORTS AND SEA ROUTES – Series no. 31. 1911 – 9mf – 9 – $60.00 – us UPA [910]
BAEDEKER'S HANDBOOK(S) FOR TRAVELLERS: NORTHERN FRANCE – Series no. 8. 1889, 1894, 1899, 1905, 1909 – 36mf – 9 – $160.00 – us UPA [910]
BAEDEKER'S HANDBOOK(S) FOR TRAVELLERS: NORTHERN GERMANY – Series no. 12. 1870, 1873, 1878, 1881, 1884, 1886, 1890, 1893, 1897, 1900, 1904, 1910, 1913, 1925 – 98mf – 9 – $330.00 – us UPA [910]
BAEDEKER'S HANDBOOK(S) FOR TRAVELLERS: NORTHERN ITALY – Series no. 20. 1868, 1870, 1874, 1877, 1879, 1882, 1886, 1889, 1892, 1895, 1899, 1903, 1906, 1913, 1930 – 121mf – 9 – $370.00 – us UPA [910]
BAEDEKER'S HANDBOOK(S) FOR TRAVELLERS: NORWAY AND SWEDEN – Series no. 25. 1879, 1882, 1885, 1889, 1892, 1895, 1899, 1903, 1909, 1912 – 74mf – 9 – $295.00 – us UPA [910]
BAEDEKER'S HANDBOOK(S) FOR TRAVELLERS: PALESTINE AND SYRIA – Series no. 26. 1876, 1894, 1898, 1906, 1912 – 37mf – 9 – $160.00 – us UPA [910]
BAEDEKER'S HANDBOOK(S) FOR TRAVELLERS: PARIS – Series no. 11. 1865, 1867, 1872, 1874, 1876, 1878, 1881, 1884, 1888, 1891, 1894, 1896, 1898, 1900, 1904, 1907, 1910, 1913, 1924, 1932 – 136mf – 9 – $425.00 – us UPA [910]
BAEDEKER'S HANDBOOK(S) FOR TRAVELLERS: RUSSIA – Series no. 27. 1914 – 9mf – 9 – $60.00 – us UPA [910]
BAEDEKER'S HANDBOOK(S) FOR TRAVELLERS: SOUTHERN FRANCE – Series no. 9. 1891, 1895, 1898, 1902, 1907, 1914 – 56mf – 9 – $220.00 – us UPA [910]
BAEDEKER'S HANDBOOK(S) FOR TRAVELLERS: SOUTHERN GERMANY – Series no. 13. 1868, 1871, 1873, 1880, 1883, 1887, 1891, 1895, 1902, 1907, 1910, 1914, 1929. (See Austria, Germany, and the Eastern Alps) – 87mf – 9 – $310.00 – us UPA [910]
BAEDEKER'S HANDBOOK(S) FOR TRAVELLERS: SOUTHERN ITALY – Series no. 22. 1867, 1869, 1872, 1874, 1875, 1877, 1880, 1885, 1887, 1890, 1893, 1896, 1900, 1903, 1908, 1912, 1930 – 98mf – 9 – $325.00 – us UPA [910]
BAEDEKER'S HANDBOOK(S) FOR TRAVELLERS: SPAIN AND PORTUGAL – Series no. 28. 1898, 1901, 1908, 1913 – 36mf – 1 – $160.00 – us UPA [910]
BAEDEKER'S HANDBOOK(S) FOR TRAVELLERS: SWITZERLAND – Series no. 29. 1863, 1864, 1867, 1869, 1872, 1873, 1877, 1879, 1881, 1883, 1885, 1887, 1889, 1891, 1893, 1895, 1897, 1899, 1901, 1903, 1905, 1907, 1909, 1911, 1913, 1922, 1928, 1938 – 224mf – 9 – $590.00 – us UPA [910]
BAEDEKER'S HANDBOOK(S) FOR TRAVELLERS: THE DOMINION OF CANADA – Series no. 5. 1894, 1900, 1907, 1922 – 20mf – 9 – $110.00 – us UPA [900]
BAEDEKER'S HANDBOOK(S) FOR TRAVELLERS: THE RHINE – Series no. 15. 1861, 1864, 1868, 1870, 1873, 1878, 1880, 1882, 1884, 1886, 1889, 1892, 1896, 1900, 1903, 1906, 1911, 1926 – 119mf – 9 – $360.00 – us UPA [910]
BAEDEKER'S HANDBOOK(S) FOR TRAVELLERS: THE RIVIERA AND SOUTH EASTERN FRANCE – Series no. 10. 1931 – 9mf – 9 – $60.00 – us UPA [910]
BAEDEKER'S HANDBOOK(S) FOR TRAVELLERS: THE UNITED STATES – Series no. 30. 1893, 1899, 1904, 1909 – 38mf – 9 – $170.00 – us UPA [910]
Baegetr, Juan Jacobo *see* NOTICIAS DE LA PENINSULA AMERICANA DE CALIFORNIA. INTRODUCION Y NOTAS POR PAUL KIRCHHOFF...
Baehler, Eduard *see*
- ERLEBNISSE EINES SCHULDENBAUERS
- DER GELDSTAG
- LEIDEN UND FREUDEN EINES SCHULMEISTERS
- NIKOLAUS ZURKINDEN VON BERN, 1506-1588

Baehnisch, Alfred *see* DIE DEUTSCHEN PERSONENNAMEN
Baehr, H A *see* COMMERCIAL PRECEDENTS
Baehr, Karl Christian Wilhelm Felix *see* BUECHER DER KOENIGE
Baehrens, WA *see* UEBERLIEFERUNG UND TEXTGESCHICHTE DER LATEINISCHEN ORIGENESHOMILIEN ZUM ALTEN TESTAMENT (T.U.U. 3-42/1)
Baehring, Bernhard *see*
- JOHANNES TAULER UND DIE GOTTESFREUNDE
- THOMAS VON KEMPEN, DER PREDIGER DER NACHFOLGE CHRISTI

Baentsch, Bruno *see*
- ALTORIENTALISCHER UND ISRAELITISCHER MONOTHEISMUS
- DAS BUNDESBUCH, EX XX,22-XXII,33: SEINE URSPRUENGLICHE GESTALT
- EXODUS-LEVITICUS-NUMERI
- DAS HEILIGKEITS-GESETZ, LEV. 17-26

BAEPRIAN KHONG KRASUANG SUKSATHIKAN NANGSU AN PHASA THAI RUANG / Vajirevudh, King of Siam – 1958. 226p In Thai – 1 – us U.W. Library [290]
Baer, A *see* DER WELTKRIEG
DER BAER: BERLINISCHE BLAETTER FUER VATERLAENDISCHER GESCHICHTE UND ALTERTUMSKUNDE – Berlin. v1-26, 1875-1900. Film Mas C 275 – 1 – us H.U. Library [073]
Baer, Joseph *see* FRANKFURTER BUECHERFREUND 1.1900-11.1913, NEUE FOLGE 1. (12) 1914-19 BIS 4. (15) 1922
Baer, Julius Bernard *see* COMMODITY EXCHANGES
Baerwald, M *see* WIEDERVERHEIRATUNG...
Baerwolf, Walther *see* DER GRAF VON ESSEX IM DEUTSCHEN DRAMA
Baesecke, Georg *see*
- FESTGABE PHILIPP STRAUCH ZUM 80. GEBURTSTAGE AM 23. SEPTEMBER 1932 DARGEBRACHT VON FACHKOLLEGEN UND SCHUELERN
- DIE SPRACHE DER OPITZISCHEN GEDICHTSAMMLUNGEN VON 1624 UND 1625

BAESSLER-ARCHIV – Leipzig, 1911-1937. v1-20 – 134mf – 9 – H-514/2 – ne IDC [073]
Baete, Ludwig *see* JOHANN GOTTFRIED HERDER
Baeteman, J *see* DICTIONNAIRE AMARIGNA-FRANCAIS, SUIVI D'UN VOCABULAIRE FRANCAIS-AMARIGNA
Baethgen, F *see* CRONICA JOHANNIS VITODURANI (MGH 6: 3.BD)
Baethgen, Friedrich *see*
- MEDIAEVALIA (MGH SCHRIFTEN..: 17.BD)
- DIE PSALMEN
- DIE PSALMEN: UEBERSETZT UND ERKLAERT

Baets, Maurice de *see* MGR SEGHERS, L'APOTRE DE L'ALASKA
Baeumer, Gertrud *see*
- DIE FRAU (HQ 1)
- HANDBUCH DER FRAUENBEWEGUNG (HQ 26)
- RICARDA HUCH

Baeumker, C *see*
- AVENCEBROLIS (IBN GEBIROL) FONS VITAE
- DIE IMPOSSIBILIA DES SIGER VON BRABANT
- WITELO, EIN PHILOSOPH UND NATURFORSCHER DES 12. JAHRHUNDERTS
- WITELO, EIN PHILOSOPH UND NATURFORSCHER DES 12. JHT.

Baeumker, C Avencebrolis *see* FONS VITAE
Baevskii, IL *see* DEISTVUIUSHCHEE ZAKONODATELSTVO PO SOTSIALNOMU STRAKHOVANIIU (S KOMMENTARII AMI)
Baevskii, S I *see* OPISANIE TADZHIKSHIKH I PERSIDSKIKH RUKOPISEI INSTITUTA VOSTOKOVEDENIIA
Baez, C *see* THE PARAGUAYAN CHACO;...
Baffin, W *see* THE VOYAGES OF. 1612-1622
BAFRAJUNG = FREEDOM – (In Yiddish) – Munich, DE. v1 no3 21 Feb 1947-v1 no97 15 Feb 1949 – 1r – 1 – $35.00 – cn Can Microfilming [072]
BAFRAYTE ARBET = LIBERATED WORD – (In Hebrew) – Warsaw, PL. no1 1949 – 1r – 1 – $25.00 – cn Can Microfilming [072]
BAFRAYUNG = LIBERTY – (In Yiddish) – Warsaw, PL. v7 no87 21 Apr 1923 – 1r – 1 – $25.00 – cn Can Microfilming [072]
BAGAIMANA MENGETAHUI SERANGGA2 PERTANIAN / Dresner, Edgar – (Disusun dalam bahasa Inggeris). SE-10,464 1. 1954 – 9 – ne IDC [950]
BAGATELLES POUR UN MASSACRE / Celine, Louis-Ferdinand – Paris: Denoel 1937 – us Res Libr [944]
Bagatta, J B *see* ADMIRANDA ORBIS CHRISTIANI
Bagby, Alfred *see* HISTORY OF KING AND QUEEN COUNTY
BAGCE – Selanik: Asir Matbaasi. Mueduer ve Mueessisi: Abdurrahman Mehdi; Sahib-i Imtiyaz: Necib Necati, 1908-1910 – 9 – $25.00 – us MEDOC [956]
Bagehot, Eliza Wilson *see* JOURNAL OF ELIZA WILSON BAGEHOT, 1850-1921
Bagehot, Walter *see*
- BIOGRAPHICAL STUDIES
- ECONOMIC STUDIES
- ESTIMATES OF SOME ENGLISHMEN AND SCOTCHMEN
- LOMBARD STREET
- PHYSICS AND POLITICS, OR, THOUGHTS ON THE APPLICATION OF THE PRINCIPLES OF "NATURAL SELECTION" AND "INHERITANCE" TO POLITICAL SOCIETY

Bagellardo, Paolo *see* OPUSCULUM RECENS NATVM DE MORBIS PVERORVM CUM APPENICIBUS MAGISTRI PETRI TOLETI
THE BAGESU AND OTHER TRIBES OF THE UGANDA PROTECTORATE / Roscoe, J – Cambridge. 1924. BA-381 2 – 8 – ne IDC [960]
Bagg, M M *see*
- MEMORIAL HISTORY OF UTICA
- PIONEERS OF UTICA

Bagg, Stanley Clark *see* CONTINENTAL NOTES FOR PRIVATE CIRCULATION
BAGGAGE AND BOOKS; OR SMITH'S FIRST PEEP AT AMERICA: AN INSTRUCTIVE TALE OF TRAVEL AND ADVENTURE – A.B. London, Sunday School Union. 1883. 00078. (Pre-1900 Canadiana) – 9 – cn C.I.H.M. [830]
Baggaly, W *see*
- A DIGEST OF THE MINUTES, INSTITUTIONS, POLITY, DOCTRINES, ORDINANCES AND LITERATURE OF THE METHODIST NEW CONNEXION

Bagge, Oskar *see* DAS PRINZIP DES MYTHUS IM DIENST DER CHRISTLICHEN POSITION

BAGHDAD NEWS – Baghdad: Asia Print & Publ Co, jul 14 1964-dec 3 1967 – 10r – 1 – us Res Libr [072]

THE BAGHDAD OBSERVER – [Baghdad]: General Establishment for Press & Printing, dec 7 1967-jan/apr 1990; sep/dec 1990; may-aug-sep/dec 1992 – 1 – us Res Libr [072]

BAGHDAD PRESS EXTRACTS – Baghdad: British Embassy Info Dept, [aug 10 1951-aug 28 1953]; [jan 25-sep 25 1954] – us Res Libr [070]

BAGHDAD TIMES – Iraq. -d. 3 May 1921-26 Feb 1923. Imperfect. 3 reels – 1 – uk British Libr Newspaper [072]

Baghli, Sid-Ahmed *see* ASPECTS OF ALGERIAN CULTURAL POLICY

BAGINEN = DAWN – (In Yiddish. Monthly) – Vilnius, LT. no1 Jan-no5 May/Jun 1934 – 1r – 1 – $25.00 – cn Can Microfilming [072]

Bagley, Clarence B *see* HISTORY OF SEATTLE

Baglione, G *see*
- LE VITE DE' PITTORI, SCULTORI, ARCHITETTI, ED INTAGLIATORI 1572-1642
- LE VITE DE' PITTORI, SCULTORI ET ARCHITETTI 1572-1642

Baglivi, Georgii *see* OPERA OMNIA MEDICO-PRATICA ET ANATOMICA HAC SEXTA EDITIONE, POST ULTIMAN ULTRAJECTINAM AUCTA, NOVISQUE LOCUPLETATA DISSERTATIONIBUS EPISTOLIS AND PRAEFATIONE QUAE SYSTEMATIS BAGLIVIANI USUM APERIT, ADVERSARIORUMQUE DILUIT OBJECTIONES

BAG-O-BAHAR – Poeme hindoustani traduit en francais par Garcin de Tassy. 1878 – 9 – fr Orientalistes [810]

BAGONG AKLAT SA PILIPINO: AKLAT-SANAYAN / Del Rosario, Marissa E – c1969 – 1 – us U.W. Library [490]

THE BAGOTVILLE BEACON – (Also: Bagotville Phare/Beacon 30 mar 1970-23 dec 1970) – Bagotville, Canada. v3 n17. 15 sep 1964-15 mar 1970 – 1r – 1 – Can$75.00 – cn Can Microfilming [072]

BAGOTVILLE PHARE/BEACON *see* THE BAGOTVILLE BEACON

Bagrii, A V *see* RUSSKAIA LITERATURA 19 I PERVOI CHETVERTI 20 V

Bagrov, L S *see* ISTORIIA GEOGRAFICHESKOI KARTY. OCHERK I UKAZATEL' LITERATURY

Bagrow, L *see* THE ORIGIN OF PTOLEMY'S GEOGRAPHIA

Bagshawe, John B *see* THE CREDENTIALS OF THE CATHOLIC CHURCH

Baguenault de Puchesse, M Fernand *see* HISTOIRE DU CONCILE DE TRENTE

Baguer y Oliver, J *see* FLORESTA DE DISERTACIONES HISTORICO-MEDICAS...

Bagwell, N D *see* WALDO

BAHA'I INTERNATIONAL COMMUNITY – New York, Geneva. 110 docs. 1980-1991 – 18mf – 9 – ne IDC [320]

BAHAMA ARGUS – Bahamas. -sw. 1831-35 – 1 – us UMI [072]

BAHAMA GAZETTE – Nassau. Bahamas. 1784-1819 – 1 – us UMI [072]

BAHAMA HERALD – Nassau. Bahamas. 1849-1863 – 1 – us UMI [072]

BAHAMAS : SESSION LAWS OF BAHAMAS – 1968-94 – 9 – $92.00 set – us Hein [340]

BAHAMAS : STATISTICAL ABSTRACT 1969-1975 / Bahamas. Department of Statistics – (1971 not available. Coll title: Latin American and Caribbean Official Statistical Serials, 1821-1982) – 15mf – 9 – £125.00 – uk Chadwyck [972]

Bahamas. Department of Statistics *see* BAHAMAS

Bahamas. Ministry of Education and Culture *see*
- ANNUAL REPORT 1970/71-1971/75
- DIRECTORY OF SCHOOLS 1974-1975
- EDUCATION STATISTICS 1975-1976
- FOCUS ON THE FUTURE

BAHAR – Tehran. Sal-i 1, shumarah-i 1-12 (10 Rabi al-Sani 1328-25 Zu'l Qa'dah 1329 [21 April 1970-17 November 1911]). Sal-i 2, shumarah-i 1-12 (Sh'aban 1339-Jumada al-Avval 1341 [April 1921-December 1922]) – 1 reel – 1 – $325.00 – us MEDOC [950]

EL BAHAR – Djakarta. Indonesia. 1967-1972 – 1 – us UMI [072]

Bahar Mattaliu *see* ROMAN REVOLUSI: PERAHU LAJAR "MAPPASIKUWAE."SE-4512/1. 1963

BAHASA DAN KESUSASTERAAN / Direktorat Bahasa dan Kesusasteraan, DitDjen Kebudajaan, Departmen P. dan K. – (Bi-monthly. Missing: 1967 v1(6); 1970 v3(2-4); 1971 v4(3-4)) – Djakarta. v5(1). 1967-1972 – 23mf – 9 – SE-1325/1 – ne IDC [490]

BAHASA INDONESIA; AN ELEMENTARY TEXTBOOK OF THE INDONESIAN LANGUAGE, ADAPTED FOR THE USE OF ENGLISH SPEAKING STUDENTS / Molen, S. van der – SE-3713 1. 4th ed. 1961 – 9 – ne IDC [490]

BAHASA INDONESIA; EENVOUDIGE LEEPGANG VOOR DE INDONESISCHE TAAL / Rambitan, M H – SE-8527 1. 2 v. 1950 – 9 – ne IDC [950]

BAHASA INDONESIA FOR BEGINNERS / Danusugondo, Purwanto – SE-5343 1. v. 1 only. 1966 – 9 – ne IDC [490]

BAHASA INDONESIA. UCEBNICE INDONESTINY. INDONESIAN LANGUAGE / Oplt, Miroslav – SE-5876 1. 1966 – 9 – ne IDC [490]

A BAHIA – [s.l.]. 30 Ago 1881 – 1,5,6 – bl Biblioteca [072]

BAHIA ILLUSTRADA – [s.l.]-BA, Brazil. 1867 – 1,5,6 – bl Biblioteca [072]

BAHIA LITTERARIA – [s.l.]-BA, Brazil. 7 Abr 1870 – 1,5,6 – bl Biblioteca [072]

O BAHIANO : PELA CONSTITUICAO E PELA LEI – '(s.l.')-BA, Brazil. 2 maio, dez 1828; fev, maio-jul, set 1829; jun 1830; 12 apr 1831 – 1,5,6 – bl Biblioteca [072]

Bahlcke, H *see* DIE STELLUNG DER PHILANTHROPISTEN ZUM RELIGIONSUNTERRICHT

Bahlke, William A *see* CHATTEL MORTGAGE

Bahlmann, Paul *see* DIE WIEDERTAEUFER ZU MUENSTER

Bahlow, F *see* JOHANN KNIPSTRO

Bahmer, William J *see* CENTENNIAL HISTORY OF COSHOCTON COUNTY

DIE BAHN SWAKOPMUND-WINDHOEK / Gerding – Berlin: 1902. 406p. illus. maps – 1 – us U.W. Library [380]

DIE BAHN UND DER RECHTE WEG DES LAO-TSE (: TAO-TE-KING) : DER CHINESISCHEN URSCHRIFT NACHGEDACHT VON ALEXANDER ULAR / Lao-tse – Leipzig, 1921 – 2mf – 9 – DM62.00 – 3-89349-305-0 – gw Hänsel [180]

DER BAHNBRECHER: JOHN HENRY MACKAY / Solneman, K H Z – 304p. 1mf (29x) – 9 – 1.00f – at Libertarian Micro [320]

BAHNWAERTER THIEL : NOVELLISTISCHE STUDIE / Hauptmann, Gerhart – Leipzig: P Reclam, 1941 – 1r – 1 – us U.W. Library [830]

LES BAHOLOHOLO (CONGO BELGE) / Schmitz, Robert – Bruxelles, A DeWit [etc] 1912 – us Res Libr [960]

BAHOSI – Mandalay, Burma. 1959-1964 – 24r – 1 – us L of C Photodup [072]

Bahr, Alice Harrison *see* COLLEGE AND UNDERGRADUATE LIBRARIES

Bahr, Hermann *see*
- FIN DE SIECLE
- "O MENSCH"
- REZENSIONEN
- SPIELEREI
- THEATER
- UM GOETHE

Bahr, Johannes *see* DIE BABYLONISCHEN BUSSPSALMEN UND DAS ALTE TESTAMENT

Bahrain *see* ANNUAL REPORT

Bahrain. Bahrain Petroleum Company *see* ANNUAL REPORT TO THE RULER OF BAHRAIN AND ITS DEPENDENCIES

Bahrain. Bank of Bahrain *see* ANNUAL REPORT AND ACCOUNTS

Bahrain. Currency Board *see* REPORTS

Bahrain. Educational Documentation Section *see* DEVELOPMENT OF EDUCATION IN BAHRAIN DURING 1983/84-1985/86

BAHRAIN IMPORTS AND EXPORTS, CLASSIFIED ACCORDING TO SITC / Bahrain. Statistical Bureau – Revised. 2 v. 1970-77. BNE-10.011 1 – 9 – ne IDC [310]

BAHRAIN, QATAR, ABU-DHABI AND DUBAI AS MARKETS FOR SELECTED MANUFACTURED PRODUCTS FROM DEVELOPING COUNTRIES / Arabian Gulf Emirates. Abu-Dhabi. International Trade Centre Unctad Gatt – 1970. BNE-10,020 1 – 9 – ne IDC [380]

Bahrain. Statistical Bureau *see*
- BAHRAIN IMPORTS AND EXPORTS, CLASSIFIED ACCORDING TO SITC
- THE FOURTH POPULATION CENSUS OF BAHRAIN: A BRIEF ANALYTICAL AND COMPARATIVE STUDY
- STATISTICAL ABSTRACT 1967-1972
- STATISTICS OF THE POPULATION CENSUS, 1971

BAHR-I SEFID VE SIYAH BOGAZLARILE MARMARA VE KARA DENIZIN TA'RIFATI – Muetercim: Faik Bey, 1294 [1878] – 9 – $50.00 – us MEDOC [380]

BAHRIYE SALNAMESI – (1319[1901]. – 4mf. $31.50; 1326[1908]. – 4mf. $70.00; 1330[1914]. – 5mf. $75.00; 1340[1924]. – 2mf. $25.00) – 9 – us MEDOC [949]

BAIAN – Khudozhestvenno-istoricheskii zhurnal. v. 1-10. M. 1914. BR-1528 2 – 8 – ne IDC [073]

BAIAN – Khudozhestvenno-literaturnyi ezhemesiachnyi zhurnal. Spb. 1905-12. Lacking: (1-12) 1905-07; (2, 7-12) 1908; (7) 1909. BR-1527 2 – 8 – ne IDC [460]

BAIAN – Tambov, 1907-09 (monthly) – 16mf – 9 – us Ross [780]

Baicoiano, C J *see* HANDELSPOLITISCHE BESTREBUNGEN ENGLANDS...

Baicoianu, Cl *see* LE DANUBE

Baidak, Andrei Artemevich *see* UCHASTIE BIELGORODSKIKH ULAN V GRAZHDANSKOI VOINIE

Baie des Chaleurs Railway Company *see* REPONSE DE LA COMPAGNIE...AU RAPPORT DU COMMISSAIRE SPECIAL..

THE BAIE DES CHALEURS: SUMMARY OF THE EVIDENCE BEFORE THE ROYAL COMMISSION : GUILT OF THE GOVERNMENT – Bl. -1892?. (Pre-1900 Canadiana) – 9 – cn C.I.H.M. [971]

LA BAIE D'HUDSON: EXPLOITATION PROPOSEE DE SES RESSOURCES DE TERRE ET DE MER:.. / Baillairge, Charles – 189-?. 00088. (Pre-1900 Canadiana) – 9 – cn C.I.H.M. [333]

Baie, E *see* LE DROIT DES NATIONALITES

BAIE VERTE CANAL: NOTES RESPECTING UNDERGROUND FOREST, ETC.: ALSO SYNOPSIS OF REPORTS ON BAIE VERTE CANAL FROM 1822 TO 1874 – 1872. 02213. (Pre-1900 Canadiana) – 9 – cn C.I.H.M. [971]

Baier, A H *see* SYMBOLIK DER ROEMISCH-KATHOLISCHEN KIRCHE

DER BAIERISCHE LANDBOT – Muenchen, DE. 1790-91 – 2r – 1 – gw Mikrofilm [072]

DER BAIERISCHE LANDBOTE – (Title changes: 1825 der Bayersche Landbote. 1827 Der Bayer'sche Landbote. 1832 der Bayerische Landbote. 1891 publ in Regensburg) – Muenchen, DE. Jan 1825-1933 – 1 – gw Mikrofilm [072]

BAIERISCHE NATIONAL ZEITUNG – Muenchen, DE. 1807-19 – 14r – 1 – gw Mikrofilm [072]

Baierland, Ortolf von *see* HERBAR : ARZNEIBUCH 'MACER'

BAIERSCHE FLORA / Schrank, F von & Paula, A von – 2v. Muenchen. 1789. B-5727 2 – 8 – ne IDC [580]

Baif, L de *see* ANNOTATIONES IN L. II DE CAPTIVES, ET POSTLIMINIO REVERSIS

Baigger, Hans-Christoph *see* ZUR WISSENSCHAFTSKRITIK BILDUNGSPOLITISCHER ANALYSEN – UNTER BESONDERER BERUECKSICHTIGUNG DES VERHAELTNISSES VON KRITISCH-FUNKTIONALISTISCHER UND HISTORISCH-MATERIALISTISCHER THEORIEBILDUNG

BAIHUA – The Vernacular. Aug 1904. 1 fiche. F C29 – 9 – $4.50 – cc Microforms [073]

THE BAIL REFORM ACT OF 1984 / Golash, Deirdre – Washington: FJC, 1987 – 1mf – 9 – $1.50 – LLMC 95-350 – us L.L.M.C. [340]

Bailacq, Charles Jules *see* LE PLACEMENT DES TRAVAILLEURS

Baildon, W P *see* LINCOLN'S INN

Baildon, W Paley *see* THE COUCHER BOOK OF THE CISTERCIAN ABBEY OF KIRKSTALL

Bailey, Dana R *see* HISTORY OF MINNEHAHA COUNTY

Bailey, Emory E *see* WHO'S WHO IN TEXAS

Bailey, F M *see*
- LITHOGRAMS OF THE FERNS OF QUEENSLAND
- A SYNOPSIS OF THE QUEENSLAND FLORA

Bailey, Henry *see* AN ANALYSIS OF BLACKSTONE'S COMMENTARIES ON THE LAWS OF ENGLAND

Bailey, J D *see* REVERENDS PHILIP MULKEY AND JAMES FOWLER

Bailey, James *see* HISTORY OF THE SEVENTH DAY BAPTISTS, 1802-1865

Bailey, James F *see*
- FEDERAL RULES OF EVIDENCE
- IMMIGRATION AND NATIONALITY ACTS

Bailey, John Read *see* MACKINAC, FORMERLY MICHILIMACKINAC

Bailey, John W *see* DOES HELLENISM CONTRIBUTE CONSTITUENT ELEMENTS TO PAUL'S CHRISTOLOGY

Bailey, Joseph Whitman *see* THE ST JOHN RIVER IN MAINE, QUEBEC, AND NEW BRUNSWICK

Bailey, Lawrence D *see* COLLECTION

Bailey, Loring Woart *see*
- DR. JAMES ROBB: THE FIRST PROFESSOR OF CHEMISTRY AND NATURAL HISTORY IN KING'S COLLEGE, FREDERICTON: A SKETCH OF HIS LIFE AND LABOURS
- ELEMENTARY NATURAL HISTORY: AN INTRODUCTION TO THE STUDY OF MINERALS, PLANTS AND ANIMALS, WITH SPECIAL REFERENCE TO THOSE OF NEW BRUNSWICK
- THE MINERAL RESOURCES OF THE PROVINCE OF NEW BRUNSWICK
- NOTES ON THE GEOLOGY AND BOTANY OF DIGBY NECK
- REPORT OF EXPLORATIONS AND SURVEYS IN PORTIONS OF THE COUNTIES OF CARLETON, VICTORIA, YORK AND NORTHUMBERLAND, NEW BRUNSWICK, 1885
- REPORT ON THE PRE-SILURIAN (HURONIAN) AND CAMBRIAN OR PRIMORDIAL SILURIAN ROCKS: OF SOUTHERN NEW BRUNSWICK, 1877-1878
- SOME NOVA SCOTIAN ILLUSTRATIONS OF DYNAMICAL GEOLOGY

Bailey, Mark L *see* CAFFEINE

Bailey, Philip James *see* FESTUS

Bailey, Robert E *see* THE MARGARET CROSS NORTON WORKING PAPERS, 1924-1958

Bailey, Rufus W *see* DOMESTIC DUTIES OF THE FAMILY

Bailey, Samuel Wordswoth *see* HOMAGE OF EMINENT PERSONS TO THE BOOK

Bailey, T G *see*
- KANAURI VOCABULARY
- THE LANGUAGES OF THE NORTHERN HIMALAYAS

Bailey, W *see* TWO TREATISES CONCERNING THE PRESERVATION OF EYESIGHT

BAILEY, WALTER K., PAPERS, MS 4665 – (Family history, genealogy, and biographical information) – 1898-1970 – 1r – 1 – us Western Res [920]

BAILEY'S CASES IN EQUITY / South Carolina. Supreme Court – (A Pre-NRS title) – 1v. 1830-1831 (all publ) – 7mf – 9 – $10.50 – LLMC 94-029 – us L.L.M.C. [340]

BAILEY'S LAW REPORTS / South Carolina. Supreme Court – (A Pre-NRS title) – v1-2. 1828-1832 (all publ) – 16mf – 9 – $24.00 – LLMC 94-016 – us L.L.M.C. [340]

Bailie, William *see* JOSIAH WARREN: THE FIRST AMERICAN ANARCHIST

Baillairge, Charles *see*
- ADRESSE DE BIENVENUE PAR M. BAILLAIRGE A LA SECTION DE MONTREAL DES ARCHITECTES DU CANADA:...LE 2 OCTOBRE, 1895
- ANTICOSTI EN 1900
- L'ANTIQUITE DE LA TERRE ET DE L'HOMME
- LA BAIE D'HUDSON: EXPLOITATION PROPOSEE DE SES RESSOURCES DE TERRE ET DE MER:..
- CLEF SYNOPTIQUE, OU, ABREGEE DU TABLEAU STEREOMETRIQUE BAILLAIRGE
- LE COMMUNISME
- DIVERS, OU, LES ENSEIGNEMENTS DE LA VIE
- EDUCATIONAL WORD LESSONS
- THE FREE AND LIBERAL VENTILATION OF SEWERS IN ITS RELATION TO THE SANITATION OF OUR BUILDINGS
- GEOMETRIE, TOISE ET LE TABLEAU STEREOMETRIQUE: LECTURE FAITE...DU QUEBEC 20 MARS 1872
- GEOMETRY, MENSURATION AND THE STEREOMETRICAL TABLEAU: LECTURE READ...20TH MARCH 1872
- LE GREC, LE LATIN: LEUR UTILITE POUR APPRECIER LA SIGNIFICATION DES MOTS ACTUELS DE LA LANGUE..
- HUDSON BAY: PROPOSED UTILIZATION OF ITS LAND AND WATER RESOURCES: A NEW COLONY, A RAILWAY TO REACH IT
- KEY TO BAILLAIRGE'S STEREOMETRICAL TABLEAU: NEW SYSTEM OF MEASURING ALL BODIES...BY ONE AND THE SAME RULE
- LETTRE AU MAIRE DU QUEBEC
- MEMOIRES LUS DEVANT LA SOCIETE ROYALE DU CANADA 1882 & 1883
- MR. BAILLAIRGE'S ADDRESS OF WELCOME TO THE MONTREAL SECTION OF CANADIAN ARCHITECTS:...OCT 2, 1895
- THE MUNICIPAL SITUATION

- ON THE NECESSITY OF A SCHOOL OF ARTS FOR THE DOMINION: A PAPER READ BEFORE THE CANADIAN SOCIETY OF CIVIL ENGINEERS...26TH MAY 1887
- LES PROGRES DU XIXE SIECLE
- THE QUEBEC LAND SLIDE OF 1889
- QUEBEC PASSE SIC, PRESENT, FUTUR
- RAPPORT DE L'EX-INGENIEUR DE LA CITE, DES TRAVAUX FAITS SOUS LE MAIRE...ET DURANT LE DERNIER TIERS DE SIECLE, 1866 A 1899
- RAPPORT DE M. BAILLAIRGE, INGENIEUR DE LA CITE SUR LA 5EME SECTION DU CHEMIN DE FER QUEBEC & LAC ST JEAN... 18 DECEMBRE 1885
- RAPPORT DE M. BAILLAIRGE, INGENIEUR DU NOUVEL AQUEDUC DE QUEBEC...30 OCT 1885
- RAPPORT DE M. BAILLAIRGE SUR LA 3EME SECTION DU CHEMIN DE FER DE QUEBEC & LAC ST JEAN...24 SEPT 1885
- REPORT OF THE CITY ENGINEER: QUEBEC, ON THE PROPOSED DRY DOCK IN THE MOUTH OF THE RIVER ST CHARLES
- LE STEREOMETRICON: CUBAGE DE TOUS LES CORPS PAR UNE SEULE ET MEME REGLE
- THE STEREOMETRICON: MEASUREMENT OF ALL SOLIDS BY ONE AND THE SAME RULE: UNIVERSAL APPLICATION OF THE PRISMOIDAL FORMULA
- THE STEREOMETRICON: SOLID GEOMETRY: STEREOMETRY, STEREOTOMY
- A SUMMARY OF PAPERS READ AT DIFFERENT TIMES...ROYAL SOCIETY OF CANADA, CANADIAN ASSOCIATION OF CIVIL ENGINEERS: AND ARCHITECTS, AND LITERARY AND SCIENTIFIC SOCIETIES..
- SUPPLEMENTARY REPORT OF THE QUEBEC CORPORATION ENGINEER OF THE NORTH SHORE RAILWAY
- TECHNICAL EDUCATION OF THE PEOPLE IN UNTECHNICAL LANGUAGE
- LA VENTILATION LIBRE DES EGOUTS EN RAPPORT AVEC L'HYGIENE DE L'HABITATION
- LA VIE, L'EVOLUTION, LE MATERIALISME: MEMOIRE LU...DEVANT LA SOCIETE ROYALE DU CANADA...23 MAI 1899
- VINGT ANS APRES: LE CLUB DES 21 EN 1879: COURTE BIOGRAPHIE DE CHACUN DE SES MEMBRES
- VOCABULAIRE DES HOMONYMES SIMPLES DE LA LANGUE FRANCAISE
- VOCABULARY OF ENGLISH HOMONYMS

Baillairge, Frederic Alexandre *see*
- A SON EXCELLENCE MGR. DOM HENRI SMEULDERS A JOLIETTE: COMPTE-RENDU
- CA ET LA
- COUPS DE CRAYON
- LA DEUXIEME ANNEE DE GEOGRAPHIE, PREMIER QUARTIER, NOTIONS PRELIMINAIRES, OU, LA TERRE A VOL D'OISEAU
- DICTIONNAIRE DES VERBES IRREGULIERS ET DEFECTIFS DE LA LANGUE FRANCAISE
- LA LITTERATURE AU CANADA EN 1890
- LA NATURE, LA RACE, LA SANTE: DANS LEURS RAPPORTS AVEC LA PRODUCTIVITE DU TRAVAIL:..
- LA PAROISSE, OU, GEOGRAPHIE LOCALE: SAINT HUBERT (CO. DE CHAMBLY)
- TRAITE CLASSIQUE D'ECONOMIE POLITIQUE: SELON LA DOCTRINE DE LEON XIII: AVEC APPLICATIONS AU CANADA

Baillairge, George F *see*
- ALPHABETICAL RECORD: ENGINEERS AND SUPERINTENDENTS, ETC., AND THE PRINCIPAL PUBLIC WORKS ON WHICH THEY HAVE REPORTED OR BEEN EMPLOYED: CANADA, 1779 TO 1891
- CANADA ET TERRENEUVE, ETC.: CHRONOLOGIE: DIOCESES, VICARIATS, APOSTOLIQUES, PREFECTURES APOSTOLIQUES, CARDINALS, ARCHEVEQUES, EVEQUES: GOUVERNEURS, LIEUTENANTS-GOURVERNEURS ET ADMINISTRATEURS, DECOUVERTES ET FONDATIONS
- CANADA FROM THE ATLANTIC TO THE PACIFIC AND ARCTIC OCEANS, ARCTIC VOYAGES OF DISCOVERY IN THE NORTH AND PUBLIC WORKS, ETC, ETC
- LE DETROIT ET LA BAIE D'HUDSON

Baillairge, Maurice *see* DERNIERS ADIEUX DE GRAZIELLA: SUIVIS DE QUELQUES AUTRES POESIES DETACHEES

Baillargeon, Cecile *see* BIBLIOGRAPHIE ANALYTIQUE DU RHUMATISME ARTICULAIRE AIGU D'APRES LA DOCUMENTATION DE LA BIBLIOTHEQUE MEDICALE DE L'HOPITAL DU ST SACREMENT...

Baillaud, Emile *see* SUR LES ROUTES DU SUDAN

Bailleul, Louis *see* LES CHASSEURS DE FOURRURES

BAILLIAGE / Societe royale d'Agriculture et d'Horticulture – St. Peter Port. 5 Jan 1889-28 Jun 1902 – 1 – uk British Libr Newspaper [630]

LE BAILLIAGE DE DIJON APRES LA BATAILLE DE ROCROY / Rossignol, Claude – Dijon. 1857. 240p. (Historical Studies Series) – 9 – 12.00 – fr Bibl Nationale [900]

Baillie, Laureen *see* AMERICAN BIOGRAPHICAL ARCHIVE (ABA 2)

Baillie, M *see* THE MORBID ANATOMY OF SOME OF THE MOST IMPORTANT PARTS OF THE HUMAN BODY

Baillie-Grohman, William Adolph *see* CAMPS IN THE ROCKIES: BEING A NARRATIVE OF LIFE ON THE FRONTIER, AND SPORT IN THE ROCKY MOUNTAINS, WITH AN ACCOUNT OF THE CATTLE RANCHES OF THE WEST

BAILLIERE'S OFFICIAL POST OFFICE DIRECTORIES OF VICTORIA 1868 TO 1881 – (Directories for 1868, 1869, 1870, 1871-72, 1875, 1880-81) – 6v – 49mf and hard copy contents list – 9 – A$60.00 – at State Libr Vic [380]

BAILLIERE'S VICTORIAN GAZETTEERS – 1865, 1870, 1879, 3v – 19mf – 9 – A$30.00 – at State Libr Vic [980]

Baillon, D *see*
- DIRECTION DES ETUDES DE DEVELOPPEMENT. POPULATION RURALE ET URBAINE PAR DEPARTEMENT ET PAR SOUSPREFECTURE
- ERREURS SYSTEMATIQUES DE RECENSEMENT EN MILIEU RURAL TRADITIONNEL
- NOTES DE SYNTHESE SUR L'ECONOMIE DE LA VILLE DE BOUAKE

Baillon, H E *see*
- DICTIONNAIRE DE BOTANIQUE
- ETUDE GENERALE DU GROUPE DES EUPHORBIACEES
- HISTOIRE DES PLANTES
- HISTOIRE NATURELLE DES PLANTES
- TRAITE DE BOTANIQUE MEDICALE PHANEROGAMIQUE

Bailly, J B *see* ORNITHOLOGIE DE LA SAVOIE

Bailly, L *see* ESSAI D'UNE THEORIE...

Bails, B *see* LECCIONES DE CLAVE Y PRINCIPIOS DE HARMONIA

Baily, Samuel L *see*
- THE DURABILITY OF PERONISM
- LABOR, NATIONALISM, AND POLITICS IN ARGENTINA

Bain, Alexander *see*
- THE EMOTIONS AND THE WILL
- JOHN STUART MILL
- MORAL SCIENCE
- ON THE STUDY OF CHARACTER
- THE SENSES AND THE INTELLECT

Bain, Francis *see*
- BIRDS OF PRINCE EDWARD ISLAND: THEIR HABITS AND CHARACTERISTICS
- THE NATURAL HISTORY OF PRINCE EDWARD ISLAND

Bain, James *see* SKETCH OF THE HISTORY OF ST ANDREW'S LODGE OF ANCIENT, FREE AND ACCEPTED MASONS, NO. 16, G.R.C., TORONTO

Bain, John A *see* THE NEW REFORMATION

LE BAIN JURCS D'INGRES / Reunion des Musees Nationaux. Paris – 1971 – 9 – fr Réunion [750]

Baine, Thomas *see* VOYAGE DANS LE SUD-OUEST DE L'AFRIQUE ON RECITS D'EXPLORATIONS FAITES EN 1861 ET 1862 DEPUIS LA BAIE DE VALFICH JUSQU'AUX CHUTES VICTORIA

Baines, KC *see* FITNESS LEVELS OF CHILDREN IN NORTH CAROLINA

Baines, Thomas *see* HISTORY OF THE COMMERCE AND TOWN OF LIVERPOOL, AND OF THE RISE OF THE MANUFACTURING INDUSTRY IN THE ADJOINING COUNTIES

Bainton, R H *see* DAVID JORIS. WIEDERTAEUFER UND KAEMPFER FUER TOLERANZ IM 16. JAHRHUNDERT

Baiov, A K *see*
- GRAF DMITRII ALEKSEVICH MILIUTIN
- ISTORIIA VOENNAGO ISKUSSTVA, KAK NAUKA
- KURS ISTORII RUSSKOGO VOENNOGO ISKUSSTVA

Baird, Andrew et al *see* GROWTH FACTORS

Baird, Annie Laurie Adams *see* DAYBREAK IN KOREA

Baird, Charles Washington *see*
- HISTOIRE DES REFUGIES HUGUENOTS EN AMERIQUE
- HISTORY OF THE HUGUENOT EMIGRATION TO AMERICA

Baird, Frank *see* A SHORT HISTORY OF THE PRESBYTERIAN CHURCH IN THE PARISH OF CHIPMAN: CONTAINING ALSO BRIEF REFERENCES TO THE GROWTH OF THE PARISH

Baird, George W *see* PAPERS

Baird, Henry Carey *see*
- THE BRITISH CREDIT SYSTEM: INFLATED BANK CREDIT AS A SUBSTITUTE FOR CURRENT MONEY OF THE REALM
- CRITICISMS ON THE RECENT FINANCIAL POLICIES OF THE UNITED STATES AND FRANCE: INCLUDING AN ATTEMPT TO EXPLAIN THE CAUSE OF THE PRESENT PROSTRATE CONDITION OF THE SOUTHERN STATES
- THE NECESSARY FOUNDATIONS OF INDIVIDUAL AND NATIONAL WELL-BEING, AND OF CIVILIZATION
- REAL CAUSE OF BUSINESS STAGNATION IN THE UNITED STATES: A REPLY TO AN ARTICLE IN SAINT JOHN TELEGRAPH, JULY 24TH, 1878

Baird, Henry M *see* MODERN GREECE

Baird, Henry Martyn *see*
- HISTORY OF THE RISE OF THE HUGUENOTS OF FRANCE
- THE HUGUENOTS AND HENRY OF NAVARRE
- THE HUGUENOTS AND THE REVOCATION OF THE EDICT OF NANTES
- THE LIFE OF THE REV. ROBERT BAIRD, D.D.
- THEODORE BEZA

Baird, Robert *see*
- GREEK-ENGLISH WORD-LIST
- IMPRESSIONS AND EXPERIENCES OF THE WEST INDIES AND NORTH AMERICA IN 1849
- THE PROGRESS AND PROSPECTS OF CHRISTIANITY IN THE UNITED STATES OF AMERICA
- RELIGION IN AMERICA, OR, AN ACCOUNT OF THE ORIGIN, RELATION TO THE STATE, AND PRESENT CONDITION OF THE EVANGELICAL CHURCHES IN THE UNITED STATES

Baird, Samuel J *see* A HISTORY OF THE NEW SCHOOL

Baird, Spencer Fullerton *see*
- A HISTORY OF THE NORTH AMERICAN BIRDS
- THE WATER BIRDS OF NORTH AMERICA

Baird, Spencer Fullerton et al *see* THE BIRDS OF NORTH AMERICA

Baird, W *see* THE NATURAL HISTORY OF THE BRITISH ENTOMOSTRACA

Baird, William Thomas *see* SEVENTY YEARS OF NEW BRUNSWICK LIFE: AUTO-BIOGRAPHICAL SKETCHES

BAIRNSDALE ADVERTISER – 1911-1940. BAA1-27 – 27r – 1 – at Corangamite [072]

Baisio, Guido de *see* APPARATUS IN LIBRIUM 6 (SIECLE 14)

Baja California Sur. (Territory) *see* BOLETIN OFICIAL

BAJO EL TIEMPO DIFICIL / Primo de Rivera, Jose Antonio – Madrid, 1938. Fiche W722. (Blodgett Collection of Spanish Civil War Pamphlets) – 9 – us H.U. College Libr [946]

BAJO LOS AUSTRIAS. LA MUJER ESPANOLA EN LA MINERVA LITERARIA CASTELLANA / Perez de Guzman, Juan – Madrid: Escuela Tipografica Salesiana, 1923 – 1 – sp Bibl Santa Ana [440]

Bajracharya, M B *see* BUDDHIST SANSKRIT MANUSCRIPTS

Bake, R W JC *see*
- BESCHOUWINGEN OVER DEN STATENBOND EN...
- DOORGRAVING DER LANDENGTE VAN SUEZ,...

Baker *see* HISTORY OF COLORADO

Baker, Alyson et al *see* NEW ZEALAND SERIALS

Baker, Benjamin *see* THE FORTH BRIDGE

Baker, Charlotte Alice *see* TRUE STORIES OF NEW ENGLAND CAPTIVES CARRIED TO CANADA DURING THE OLD FRENCH AND INDIAN WARS

BAKER CITY WEEKLY HERALD – Baker City, OR. 4 Nov 1874-12 Aug 1875. 1 roll – 1 – us U.O. Library [071]

BAKER COUNTY PRESS – MacClenny. Fl. -w. 1946- – 1 – us P.K. Yonge [071]

BAKER COUNTY REVEILLE – (Also known as Baker City. Weekly Reveille) – Baker City, OR. 10 Nov 1880-21 Dec 1887. – 1r – 1 – us U.O. Library [071]

Baker, D W C *see* A TEXAS SCRAP BOOK

BAKER DAILY RECORD – Baker, OR. 19 May 1927-17 May 1931. 2 rolls – 1 – us U.O. Library [071]

Baker, E C S *see* INDIAN PIGEONS AND DOVES

Baker, E F *see* HENRY WHEATON, 1785-1848

Baker, E G *see* THE LEGUMINOSAE OF TROPICAL AFRICA

Baker, Frances J *see*
- FIRST WOMEN PHYSICIANS TO THE ORIENT
- THE STORY OF THE WOMAN'S FOREIGN MISSIONARY SOCIETY OF THE METHODIST EPISCOPAL CHURCH, 1869-1895

Baker, George E *see* THE WORKS OF WILLIAM H SEWARD

Baker, George Pierce *see* THE PRINCIPLES OF ARGUMENTATION

Baker, Henry Edwin *see* THE COLORED INVENTOR

BAKER HERALD – Baker, OR. -d. 1 Jan 1918-31 Jan 1929. 18 rolls – 1 – us U.O. Library [071]

BAKER HERALD – Baker, OR. -d. 1901-04, 1906-17 – 1 – 720.00 – us Oregon Hist [071]

Baker, J G *see*
- HANDBOOK OF THE BROMELIACEAE
- A SUMMARY OF THE NEW FERNS WHICH HAVE BEEN DISCOVERED OR DESCRIBED SINCE 1874

Baker, J H *see*
- THE ENGLISH LEGAL MANUSCRIPTS PROJECT
- ENGLISH LEGAL SOURCES

Baker, J R *see*
- JULIAN HUXLEY
- THE LAWS OF LAND WARFARE...

Baker, James *see* INTERNATIONAL BIMETALLISM: SPEECH...LEGISLATIVE ASSEMBLY OF BRITISH COLUMBIA: JANUARY 24TH, 1894

Baker, James Heaton *see* THE SOURCES OF THE MISSISSIPPI: THEIR DISCOVERIES, REAL AND PRETENDED: A REPORT READ BEFORE THE MINNESOTA HISTORICAL SOCIETY, FEBRUARY 8, 1887

Baker, JG *see* SYNOPSIS FILICUM

Baker, John Earl *see* FIGHTING CHINA'S FAMINES

Baker, Joseph E *see* PAST AND PRESENT OF ALAMEDA COUNTY, CALIFORNIA

Baker, Judith A *see* AN EVALUATION OF THE EFFECTS OF A SMOKING PREVENTION PROGRAM ON MIDDLE SCHOOL STUDENTS' KNOWLEDGE AND ATTITUDES CONCERNING CIGARETTE SMOKING

Baker, Maude E *see* PEN SYMPHONIES

Baker, Merl *see* 1962 REVIEW OF THE AGENCY FOR INTERNATIONAL DEVELOPMENT AND UNIVERSITY OF KENTUCKY COOPERATIVE PROGRAM AT BANDUNG INSTITUTE OF TECHNOLOGY, BANDUNG

Baker, Paul *see* HUMAN POPULATION PROBLEMS IN THE BIOSPHERE

Baker, R *see* CURSUS OSTEOLOGICUS; BEING A COMPLEAT DOCTRINE OF THE BONES

Baker, Ray Stannard *see* PAPERS

Baker, Robert *see* REFLECTIONS ON THE ENGLISH LANGUAGE

Baker, Samuel White *see*
- EXPLORATION OF THE NILE TRIBUTARIES OF ABYSSINIA. THE SOURCES, SUPPLY, AND OVERFLOW OF THE NILE..
- ISMAILIA; A NARRATIVE OF THE EXPEDITION TO CENTRAL AFRICA FOR THE SUPPRESSION OF THE SLAVE TRADE, ORGANIZED BY ISMAIL, KHEDIVE OF EGYPT
- THE NILE TRIBUTARIES OF ABYSSINIA

BAKER SENTINEL – Baker. Mont. 1912-1928 – 1 – us UMI [071]

Baker, Thomas E *see* A PRIMER ON THE JURISDICTION THE U.S. COURTS OF APPEALS

Baker, William M *see* TEN THEOPHANIES: THE APPEARANCES OF OUR LORD TO MEN BEFORE HIS BIRTH

Baker, William Mumford *see* THE LIFE AND LABOURS OF THE REV. DANIEL BAKER, D.D.

Baker-Gabb, David *see* COMPARATIVE ECOLOGY AND BEHAVIOUR OF SWAMP HARRIERS AND SPOTTED HARRIERS AND OTHER RAPTORS IN AUSTRALIA AND NEW ZEALAND

BAKERS' AND CONFECTIONERS' JOURNAL : 1888-1972 / Bakery and Confectionery Workers' International Union of America - (Coll title: Labor Union Periodicals, Pt 3) - 1996 - 23r - 1 - $3,105.00 - 1-55655-608-X - us UPA [331]
BAKER'S JOURNAL - Port Credit. v40- 1980- - 9 - Can$28.00y - cn Micromedia [073]
BAKERS' JOURNAL - New York: [s.n.] v11 n1-4 may 4-25 1895 - us Res Libr [073]
BAKERS' JOURNAL AND DEUTSCH-AMERIKANISCHE BACKER-ZEITUNG - Brooklyn, NY: [s.n.], 1895- [v21 n1-55] aug 13 1904-aug 26 1905. v29 n41-51 may 22-jul 31 1915 - us Res Libr [073]
BAKERSFIELD - 1920-33; 1992- - 16+ r - 1 - $800.00 - P00007 - us Library Micro [910]
THE BAKERSFIELD CALIFORNIAN - Bakersfield, CA. 1945-1950- - 78+ r - 1 - $3,900.00 ($1,500.00y) - C02040 - us Library Micro [071]
Bakery and Confectionery Workers' International Union of America *see* BAKERS' AND CONFECTIONERS' JOURNAL
BAKERY PRODUCTION AND MARKETING - Newton. v1-15 sep 1966-dec 1980* 1; v16-26 jan 1981-dec 1991. v30-32 jan 1995-dec 1997+ 1,5,9 - 1,5,9 - D12973 - us UMI [660]
Bakh, MG *see* POLITIKO-EKONOMICHESKIE VZAIMOOTNOSHENII A MEZHDU SSSR I PRIBALTIKO I ZA DESI AT LET 1917-1927
Bakhchisaraitsev, Khr. *see* GRAZHDANSKIE KODEKSY SOIUZNYKH RESPUBLIK
BAKHTAR - Isfahan. Sal-i 1, shumarah-i 1-6 (Azar 1312-Mihr va Aban 1313 [November 1933-September and October 1934]). Sal-i 2, shumarah-i 1-11 (Azar 1313-Mihr 1314 [November 1934-September 1935]) - 1 reel - 1 - $395.00 - us MEDOC [950]
BAKHTAR-I IMRUZ - (Dawrah-'i jadid, sal-i 1-2: shumarah-'i 2-3, 5-30, 32, 34-35, dawrah-'i 3: shumarah-'i 1, 3-5, 7-17, 20 (15 Farvardin 1340-Aban 1345[4 Apr 1961-Nov 1966])) - [Tehran:] Jabhah-'i Milli-i Iranyan-i muqim-i kharijah - 1 reel - 1 - $25.00 - us MEDOC [950]
Bakhtiarov, A A *see* ISTORIIA KNIGI NA RUSI
Baki *see* DIVAN
BAKING INDUSTRIES JOURNAL - (Cont: Biscuit Maker) - Croydon. v1-12 jul 1968-apr 1980* 1; v4-12 jul 1971-apr 1980 5; v11-12 jul 1978-apr 1980 - 1,5,9 - D10263 - us UMI [660]
BAKI'NIN ES'AR-I MUENTEHABESI - Istanbul, 1317 - 2mf - 9 - $12.00 - us MEDOC [949]
BAKINSKAIA STACHKA V DEKABRIE - 1904 - 1 - us U.W. Library [947]
BAKINSKI RABOCHII - Baku. 1955-1960. Incomplete - 1 - us NY Public [999]
BAKINSKY RABOCHY - (Baku). Azerbaidzhan. U.S.S.R. 1955- - 1 - us UMI [330]
BAKIUSKII RABOCHI - Bakusk, USSR. 1961-1981 - 21r - $1,050.00 - B63586 - us Library Micro [072]
Bakke, P Q *see* DEVELOPMENT AND EVALUATION OF AN INTERPRETIVE NINETEENTH CENTURY AMERICAN CHILDREN'S GAMES PROGRAM
Bakken, Douglas A *see* NEBRASKA FARMERS' ALLIANCE PAPERS
Bakker, Debra L *see* RELIGIOUS PRACTICES AND HIGH-RISK BEHAVIORS OF COLLEGE STUDENT ATHLETES AND NONATHLETES
Bakker, FL *see* JEZUS IN DE ISLAM
Bakoenoen, Semarang *see* BUKU PETUNDJUK ALAMAT DAGANG DAN TOURIS DJAWA-TENGAH
LES BAKONGO DANS LEURS LEGENDES / Struyf, Ivon - Bruxelles: G van Campenout, 1936 - 1 - us Res Libr [390]
Bakounine, M A *see* A MES AMIS RUSSES ET POLONAIS
Bakr, Yahya Abu et al *see* DEVELOPMENT OF COMMUNICATION IN THE ARAB STATES
Bakri, Abd Allah ibn' Abd al-Aziz, Abu Ubaid, al *see* DESCRIPTION DE L'AFRIQUE SEPTENTRIONALE
Baksh, Ahmad *see* CORRESPONDENCE 1914-1918
DIE BAKUNISTEN AN DER ARBEIT / Engels, Friedrich - Leipzig - 1 - DM30.00 - gw Mikro Press [335]
LE BAL / Campra, A - Paris: Ballard, 1710 - 1 - us Sibley [780]
Balabanoff, Angelica *see*
- NESKOLKO SLOV OB AGITATSII
- OT RABSTVA K SVOBODE

Balabanov, MS *see*
- ISTORIIA RABOCHEI KOOPERATSII V ROSSII
- OBSHCHEE UCHENIE O KOOPERATSII

BALABISH (MEES VOL 37) / Wainright, G A - London, 1920 - 6mf - 8 - Dfl25.00 - ne Slangenburg [930]
BALADAS ESPANOLAS / Barrantes Moreno, Vicente - 1865 - 9 - 1.50f - sp Bibl Santa Ana [946]
Balaguer, G *see* EPIDEMIA DE TERCIANAS... EN VARIOS PUEBLOS DE URGEL...EN 1785
BALAI KURSUS TERTULIS GANACO / MASA BARU - (Available:[196?] v1(1-2); v3(1-2)) - Bandung, [196?] - 2mf - 9 - SE-343/1 - ne IDC [950]
BALAI PENDIDIKAN MASJARAKAT DESA; B.P.M.D. VILLAGE EDUCATIONAL CENTER / Suwardjo - SE 1151 1. 1953 - 9 - ne IDC [370]
BALAI PENELITIAN BATIK / Jogjakarta. Indonesia - Album illustrating the manufacture of batik. Jogjakarta, 196?. 10,1p. BSEM-12783/1 - 9 - ne IDC [740]
Balai Pustaka, Djakarta *see* SRI POESTAKA
Balan, George *see* WHY PEOPLE MOVE
Balan, Pietro *see* MONUMENTA REFORMATIONIS LUTHERANAE EX TABULARIIS SECRETIORIBUS S. SEDIS, 1521-1525
A BALANCA - [s.l.]. 11 Nov 1878-13 Jan 1879 - 1,5,6 - bl Biblioteca [072]
BALANCE - Albany. N.Y. 1809-1811 - 1,3 - us Readex [071]
BALANCE : THE FUNDAMENTAL VERITY / Smith, Orlando Jay - (Includes index) - Boston: Houghton, Mifflin, 1904 - 1mf - 9 - 0-8370-6385-X - 1986-0385 - us A.T.L.A. [210]
BALANCE - Hudson. N.Y. 1801-1808. Wasp. 1802-1803. Sold as one unit - 3 - us Readex [071]
THE BALANCE OF EXTERNAL PAYMENTS OF THE GOLD COAST FOR THE FISCAL YEARS 1936/37 TO 1938/39 - [Bristol, 1942] - us Res Libr [336]
BALANCE OF PAYMENTS / Jordan. Currency Control - 6v. in 1. 1958-63. BNE-9759 1 - 9 - ne IDC [336]
BALANCE OF PAYMENTS / Libya. Central Statistics Office. Ministry of National Economy - 1954-75. (lacking 1969). BNE-620 1 - 9 - ne IDC [310]
BALANCE OF PAYMENTS, 1964-1976 / Jordan. Central Bank - Lacking: 1968-73. BNE-9755 1 - 9 - ne IDC [956]
BALANCE OF PAYMENTS, AUSTRALIA : HISTORICAL SERIES - 9 - at Statistics [336]
BALANCE OF PAYMENTS, AUSTRALIA : REGIONAL SERIES - 9 - at Statistics [336]
BALANCE OF PAYMENTS FOR THE YEAR 1962, 1964-1968 / Libya. Ministry of National Economy - Tripoli. BNE-620 1 - 9 - ne IDC [956]
BALANCE SHEET - Cincinnati. cum index v1-10 1919-28. v1-74 oct 1919-Win 1993 1; v53-74 sep 1971-Win 1993 5,9 - 1,5,9 - D1774 - us UMI [380]
BALANCE SHEET / Egypt. Banque du Caire - 8v. in 7. 1953-70. (lacking 1960-68). BNE-4604 1 - 9 - ne IDC [336]
BALANCES DES PAIEMENTS DU MAROC / Morocco. Office des Changes - 1955-73. (lacking 1959, 1960, 1962-66). BNE-3087 1 - 9 - ne IDC [339]
Balandier, G *see* SOCIOLOGIE DES BRAZZAVILLES NOIRES
BALANSERAD EXPANSION. BETANKANDE AVGIVET AV 1955 ARS LANGTIDSUTREDNING / Sweden. Finansdepartementet - (Balanced Expansion. Report submitted by the 1955 Long-Term Planning Commission). 2 v. Stockholm. 1956 and 1957. BD-1751 1 - 9 - ne IDC [336]
BALANZA DEL COMERCIO EXTERIOR DE ESPANA CON LAS POTENCIAS EXTRANGERAS EN 1792 - Madrid, 1803 - 7mf - 9 - sp Cultura [380]
BALANZA DEL COMERCIO EXTERIOR DE ESPANA CON LAS POTENCIAS EXTRANGERAS EN 1792 - Madrid, 1805 - 3mf - 9 - sp Cultura [380]
BALANZA DEL COMERCIO EXTERIOR DE ESPANA CON LAS POTENCIAS EXTRANGERAS EN 1826 - Madrid, 1828 - 3mf - 9 - sp Cultura [380]
O BALAO - S. Salvador, BA. 15 Jun 1980 - 1,5,6 - bl Biblioteca [072]
Balasko, A *see* LE DROIT INTERNATIONAL DE L'ACCES AUX MARCHES MONDIAUX
Balassa, Jozsef *see* A MAGYAR NYELVJARASOK OSZTALYOZASA ES JELLEMZESE
BALAUSTION'S ADVENTURE : INCLUDING A TRANSCRIPT FROM EURIPIDES / Browning, Robert - London: Smith, Elder, 1871 - 1 roll - 1 - 1-55879-173-6 - uk Libr Preservation [830]
Balazs, Bela *see* DER MANTEL DER TRAEUME
Balazs, S *see* BEITRAEGE ZUR WIRTSCHAFTSGESCHICHTE DER T'ANG-ZEIT (618-906)
Balbi, G *see*
- DE CIUILI ET BELLICA FORTITUDINE LIBER, EX MYSERIIS POETAE VERGILII NEUNE PRIMUM DEPROMPTUS...
- DE REBVS TVRCICIS LIBER
- ORATIO HABITA CORA CLEMETE 7 DE CONFOEDERATIONE NUPER INITA, PACEQUE UNIUERSALI, ATQUE EXPEDITIONE ADUERSUS TURCAS SUSPICIENDA

Balbian, Joost van *see* TRACTATVS SEPTEM DE LAPIDE PHILOSOPHICO
Balbian Verster, Jan Francois Leopold de *see* ONS MOOI INDIE BATAVIA: OUD EN NIEUW
Balbis, G B *see*
- ELENCO DELLE PLANTE CRESCENTI NEL CONTORNI DI TORINO
- FLORE LYONNAISE OU DESCRIPTION DES PLANTES QUI CROISSENT DANS LES ENVIRONS DE LYON ET SUR LE MONT-PILAT
- SYNOPSIS PLANTARUM HORTI BOTANICI TAURINENSIS

BALBOA, DESCUBRIDOR DEL PACIFICO / Bayle, Constantino & Cabal, Juan - Madrid: Razon y Fe, 1944 - 1 - sp Bibl Santa Ana [946]
BALBOA TIMES, COSTA MESA HERALD, NEWPORT BALBOA TIMES, NEWPORT NEWS - Orange Co, CA. 1919-1936 - 5r - 1 - $250.00 - H04034 - us Library Micro [071]
Balbulus *see* TROPI CARMINUM : LIBER HYMNORUM
BALCANIA / L'Institut d'etudes et recherches balkaniques - Bucarest. 1938-45 - 1 - fr A.C.R.P.P. [073]
Balcer, Georges *see* THE CITY OF THREE RIVERS AS A SEA-PORT: AND HER NET-WORK OF RAIL-ROADS
Balch, Emily Greene *see* THE PAPERS OF EMILY GREENE BALCH, 1875-1961
Balch, George Thacher *see* METHODS OF TEACHING PATRIOTISM IN THE PUBLIC SCHOOLS: BEING AN EXTRACT FROM AN ADDRESS...JUNE 28, 1889
Balch, T W *see* INTERNATIONAL COURTS OF ARBITRATION
Balch, William Monroe *see* CHRISTIANITY AND THE LABOR MOVEMENT
Balcikonis, J *see* LIETUVIU KALBOS ZODYNAS
Baldaeus, P *see*
- BESCHREIBUNG DER OST-INDISCHEN KUSTEN MALABAR UND COROMANDEL. DER KAISERREICHS ZEYLON, BENEBENST DER ABGOTTEREY DER OST-INDISCHEN HEYDEN
- NAAUWKEURIGE BESCHRYVINGE VAN MALABAR EN CHOROMANDEL, DERZELVER AANGRENZENDE KONINCKRIJCKEN. NEVENS DE AFGODERIJE DER OOST-INDISCHE HEYDENEN

Baldassarre, Pedro B *see*
- EL EQUILIBRIO UNIVERSAL PARA UN MUNDO DE PAZ
- EL JUSTICIALISMO FRENTE AL COMUNISMO

Baldassarri, A *see*
- LA CAPACITA PATRIMONIALE DELLA DONNA MARITATA...
- IL DIRITTO PENALE INTERNAZIONALE...
- SU ALCUNE IMPORTANTI QUESTIONI DI DIRITTO PENALE INTERNAZIONALE

Baldenecker, U *see* SIX TRIOS A UN VIOLON, TAILE ET VIOLONCELLO CONCERTANS, OP. 1
Baldensberger, Wilhelm *see*
- DER PROLOG DES VIERTEN EVANGELIUMS
- DAS SELBSTBEWUSSTSEIN JESU IM LICHTE DER MESSIANISCHEN HOFFNUNG SEINER ZEIT

Baldinger, E G *see* INDEX PLANTARUM HORTI ET AGRI JENENSIS
Baldinucci, Filippo *see*
- COMINCIAMENTO E PROGRESSO DELL' ARTE DELL' INTAGLIARE IN RAME, COLLE VITE DI MOLTI DE' PIU ECCELLENTI MAESTRI DELLA STESSA PROFESSIONE
- NOTIZIE DE' PROFESSORI DEL DISEGNO DA CIMABUE IN QUA, PER LE QUALI SI DIMOSTRA COME, E PER CHI LE BELL' ARTI DI PITTURA, SCULTURE, E ARCHITETTURA LASCIATA LA ROZZEZZA DELLE MANIERE GRECA, E GOTTICA...
- VITA DEL CAVALIERE GIO. LORENZO BERNINO
- VOCABOLARIO TOSCANO DELL'ARTE DEL DISEGNO...
- VOCABOLARIO TOSCANO DELL'ARTE DEL DISEGNO...CON LA NOTIZIA DE'NOMI E QUAL TA DELLE GIOIE, METALLI, PIETRE DURE..

Baldivia Galdo, Jose Maria *see* LA TRADICION PORTUENSE DE BOLIVIA
Baldoni, C *see* IL MARE TERRITORIALE...
BALDURS TOD : EIN MAIFESTSPIEL / Pannwitz, Rudolf - Nuernberg: H Carl, 1919 - 1r - 1 - us U.W. Library [820]
Baldwin, Charles Stealey *see* EXPECTATIONS OF LUTHERAN MILITARY PERSONNEL AS FACTORS IN SHAPING CHAPLAIN MINISTRY
Baldwin City Cemetery Company *see* OAKWOOD CEMETERY RECORDS
Baldwin, Elmer *see* HISTORY OF LA SALLE COUNTY
Baldwin, Father Bernard MSC *see* PAPUAN NOTES AND TROBRIAND ISLANDS LINGUISTIC MATERIAL 1940S
Baldwin, George Colfax *see*
- REPRESENTATIVE MEN OF THE NEW TESTAMENT
- REPRESENTATIVE WOMEN: FROM EVE, THE WIFE OF THE FIRST, TO MARY, THE MOTHER OF THE SECOND ADAM

Baldwin, H *see* BALDWIN'S REPORTS OF CASES IN THE THIRD CIRCUIT, 1828-1833
Baldwin, J F *see* THE KING'S COUNCIL IN ENGLAND DURING THE MIDDLE AGES
Baldwin, J H *see* THE LARGE AND SMALL GAME OF BENGAL AND THE NORTH-WESTERN PROVINCES OF INDIA
Baldwin, James Mark *see*
- DARWIN AND THE HUMANITIES
- DEVELOPMENT AND EVOLUTION
- FRAGMENTS IN PHILOSOPHY AND SCIENCE
- GENETIC THEORY OF REALITY
- HISTORY OF PSYCHOLOGY
- SOCIAL AND ETHICAL INTERPRETATIONS IN MENTAL DEVELOPMENT

Baldwin, John Dennison *see* ANCIENT AMERICA, IN NOTES ON AMERICAN ARCHEOLOGY
Baldwin, Judith *see* ACCOUNTABILITY IN RESEARCH
THE BALDWIN LECTURES *see* WITNESSES TO CHRIST
Baldwin, Maurice Scollard *see*
- A BREAK IN THE OCEAN CABLE
- CHRISTIAN EDUCATION: A SERMON PREACHED IN CHRIST CHURCH CATHEDRAL, SUNDAY, JANUARY 22, 1871
- LIFE IN A LOOK

BALDWIN PARK AND EL MONTE HERALD PRESS - Baldwin Park, CA. Jun 1990- - 4+ r - 1 - $200.00 ($100.00y) - R02044 - us Library Micro [071]
BALDWIN PARK BULLETIN - Baldwin Park, CA. 1982-90 - 17r - 1 RC02043 - $850.00 - us Library Micro [073]
Baldwin, Sara M *see*
- WHO'S WHO IN LINCOLN COUNTY
- WHO'S WHO IN OMAHA 1928

Baldwin, Stephen Livingstone *see* FOREIGN MISSIONS OF THE PROTESTANT CHURCHES
Baldwin, Susan *see* AN EVALUATION OF THE PHYSICAL FITNESS EFFECTS OF A HIGH SCHOOL AEROBIC DANCE CURRICULUM
BALDWIN'S LONDON WEEKLY JOURNAL - London, UK. 25 Jan, 11 Oct, 29 Nov 1817; 3 Jan 1818-36.-w. 7 reels - 1 - uk British Libr Newspaper [072]
BALDWIN'S REPORTS OF CASES IN THE THIRD CIRCUIT, 1828-1833 / Baldwin, H - Philadelphia: J Kay. 1v. 1837 (all publ) - 7mf - 9 - $10.50 - LLMC 81-429 - us L.L.M.C. [340]
Baldwyn, E *see* REMARKS ON THE OATH, DECLARATIONS AND CONDUCT OF JOHNSON ATKINSON BUSFIELD, ESQ.,...
Bale, J *see* SCRIPTORUM ILLUSTRIUM MAIORIS BRYTANNIAE
BALES BAPTIST CHURCH - Kansas City, Missouri. Scrapbook, 1891-1958; Minutes, Dec 1936-61; Letters, 1923-40; Membership and account books, 1892-1936 - 1 - $149.99 - us Baptist [240]
Balesteros Gaibrais, Manuel *see* RECUERDO Y PRESENCIA DE FRANCISCO PIZARRO
Balfe, MW *see* THE TALISMAN, A GRAND OPERA IN THREE ACTS...LIB A. MATTHISON

Balfet, H *see* CERAMIQUE ANCIENNE EN PROCHE-ORIENT, ISRAEL ET LIBAN, VI-IIIE MILLENAIRE
Balfet, H et al *see* POUR LA NORMALISATION DE LA DESCRIPTION DES POTERIES. ESSAI DE NOMENCLATURE DES FORMES
Balfet, H. et al *see* LES TECHNIQUES DE DECOR CERAMIQUE
Balfour, Arthur James *see*
- DEFENSE OF PHILOSOPHIC DOUBT
- FOUNDATIONS OF BELIEF
- THE RELIGION OF HUMANITY
Balfour, Clara Lucas Liddell *see* WORKING WOMEN OF THIS CENTURY; THE LESSON OF THEIR LIVES
Balfour, I B *see* BOTANY OF SOCOTRA
Balfour, Robert Gordon *see*
- CENTRAL TRUTHS AND SIDE ISSUES
- PRESBYTERIANISM IN THE COLONIES
Balfour, Thomas Alexander Goldie *see* GOD'S TWO BOOKS
BALGARSKA LIRIKA / Dinekov, P – Antologiia. Sofiia. 1940. BR-3957 2 – 8 – ne IDC [460]
BALGARSKI NARODNI PESNI / Dozon, A – Chansons populaires bulgares inedites. Paris. 1875. BR-3950 2 – 8 – ne IDC [460]
BALGARSKI NARODNI PRAZDNITSI / Arnaudov, M P – Khemus, 1943, 162p. BR-3946 2 – 8 – ne IDC [305]
BALGARSKI STARINI – v. 1-14. Sofiia. 1906-45. BR-3816 2 – 8 – ne IDC [940]
Balguerie *see* TABLEAU STATISTIQUE DU DEPARTEMENT DU GERS
BALI, AN EARTHLY VALLEY OF PEACE / Sukawati, Tjokorde Gde Rake – SE 6140 1. 1953? – 9 – ne IDC [950]
BALI BERDJUANG / Pendit, Njoman Suwandi – SE-10,958 1. 1954 – 9 – ne IDC [950]
BALI, CULTS AND CUSTOMS / Goris, R – In Indonesian and English. SE-3999 1 – 9 – ne IDC [390]
BALI POST – Denpasar, Indonesia. Oct 1971-1993 – 65r – 1 – us L of C Photodup [072]
BALI, THE ISLE OF THE GODS / Indonesia – SE-5372 1. 1957 – 9 – ne IDC [950]
BALI; WHERE, WHAT, WHEN, HOW / Indonesia – SE-2188 1. 1958 – 9 – ne IDC [950]
BALIKESIR – Balikesir. Sahib-i Imtiyaz ve Mueduer-i Mesul: Emin Vedad. No. 1 (8 Eyluel 1338 [1922] – 9 – $20.00 – us MEDOC [956]
BALINESE ARTS AND CULTURE / Murdowo, Raden – Indonesian and English. SE-4552 1. 2nd ed 1963 – 9 – ne IDC [700]
BALINGER HEIMATBLATT *see* DER VOLKSFREUND
BALI-TATUA; WRITINGS ON BALINESE HISTORY AND TRADITIONS / Maron, Ida Bagus Putu – Comp. from various lontar inscriptions. SE-5735 1. 6 v. 1967 – 9 – ne IDC [950]
Baljon, Johannes Marinus Simon *see* COMMENTAAR OP DE BRIEVEN VAN PAULUS AAN DE THESSALONIKERS, EFEZIERS, KOLOSSERS IN AAN FILEMON
BALKAN – Filibe. Sahib ve Muharriri: Ethem Ruhi, 1906-1911 – 9 – $25.00 – us MEDOC [956]
THE BALKAN CONFERENCES AND THE BALKAN ENTENTE, 1930-1935 / Kerner, R J & Howard, H N – Berkeley. 1936. BR-3881 2 – 8 – ne IDC [949]
BALKAN HERALD – Belgrade, Yugoslavia. -m. Oct 1934; June 1935-June 1940. 1 reel – 1 – uk British Libr Newspaper [949]
BALKAN WARS OF 1912 AND 1913 PAMPHLET COLLECTION – 1912-1935 – 1 – CSUXANL7356-B – us Hoover Inst Photo [355]
BALKANSKO ZNAME – Gabrovo, Bulgaria. Jul 1955-87 – 23r – 1 – us L of C Photodup [072]
Balke, Martina *see* A MULTI-CHASE STUDY OF PHYSICAL EDUCATION RESOURCE TEACHERS
Balke, W et al *see* REFORMED PROTESTANTISM
BALKSKI SVIJET = BALKAN WORLD – Chicago: J R Palandech, sep 1917-mar 6 1919 – 1r – 1 – us Res Libr [071]
BALL AND ROLLER BEARING ENGINEERING – 1963- 1; 1977- 5,6,9 – us UMI [620]
BALL BEARING JOURNAL – v1- 1926- 1; 1976- 5,6,9 – us UMI [621]
BALL CAMP BAPTIST CHURCH. KNOXVILLE, TENNESSEE : CHURCH RECORDS – 1818-Apr 1966 – 1 – 39.74 – us Baptist [240]
Ball, Charles James *see* PROPHECIES OF JEREMIAH
Ball, Eli *see* THE MANUAL OF THE SACRED CHOIR
Ball, Elias, 14th *see* FAMILY PAPERS
Ball Family *see* PAPERS
Ball, Hugo *see*
- FLAMETTI, ODER, VOM DANDYSMUS DER ARMEN
- DIE FOLGEN DER REFORMATION
Ball, Kurt Herwarth *see*
- GUENTER UND CHRISTIANE
- IM SOMMER DANACH
Ball, Louis, Jr *see* MUSIC IN THE RELIGIOUS EDUCATION OF PRIMARY CHILDREN
Ball, Mary C *see* A STUDY OF SOUTHERN BAPTIST VACATION BIBLE SCHOOL MUSIC AND ITS CORRELATION WITH EDUCATIONAL ORGANIZATION
Ball, Ray *see* THE RESOURCE RENT TAX: A PENALTY ON RISK-TAKING
Ball, Sidney *see* INDIVIDUALISM AND SOCIALISM
BALL STATE TEACHERS COLLEGE FORUM *see* BALL STATE UNIVERSITY FORUM
BALL STATE UNIVERSITY FORUM – (Former title(s): Ball State Teachers College Forum (spring 1960-winter 1965)) – Muncie. cum index 1-10. v1-30 Spr 1960-Aut 1989 1; v13-30 Win 1972-Aut 1989* 5; v17-30 Win 1976-Aut 1989 9 – 1,5,9 – D6926 – us UMI [370]
Ball, T H *see*
- ENCYCLOPEDIA OF GENEALOGY AND BIOGRAPHY OF LAKE COUNTY
- LAKE COUNTY FROM 1834-1872
- NORTHWESTERN INDIANA 1800-1900
Ball, Thomas *see* THE LIFE OF THE RENOWNED DOCTOR PRESTON
Ball, Thomas C *see* THE EFFECTS OF A CARBOHYDRATE-ELECTROLYTE REPLACEMENT DRINK TAKEN DURING HIGH INTENSITY EXERCISE ON SPRINT CAPACITY AT THE END OF EXERCISE
Ball, Wayland Dalrymple *see* EVOLUTION IN SCIENCE AND REVOLUTION IN RELIGION: WITH OTHER ADDRESSES
Ball, William Edmund *see* ST. PAUL AND THE ROMAN LAW
Ball, WV *see* THE ENFORCEMENT OF FOREIGN JUDGMENTS
A BALLAD BOOK, OR, POPULAR AND ROMANTIC BALLADS AND SONGS.. – 1883 – 1 – us I.U. Libraries [390]
A BALLAD OF FOUR RELIGIONS (CCC222) / Liu, Chiao-fei – (In Chinese) – 1st ed. Shanghai: Christian Literature Society, 1923 – 1r – 1 – 1984-B500 – us A.T.L.A. [200]
THE BALLAD OF READING GOAL / Wilde, Oscar – repr by Boston: John W Luce & Co, n.d. – 1mf – 9 – $1.50 – LLMC 92-229 – us L.L.M.C. [810]
BALLADE ET DANSE DES SYLPHES...OP. 5 / Anderson, K J – Paris: C Joubert, [188-] – 1 – us Sibley [780]
DIE BALLADE IN AFRIKAANS / Vos, Willem Hermanus – 1955 – 1 – us I.U. Libraries [390]
BALLADEN / Stucken, Eduard – 2., veraenderte Aufl. Berlin: E Reiss, 1920 – 1r – 1 – us U.W. Library [780]
DIE BALLADEN SCHILLERS IM ZUSAMMENHANG SEINER LYRISCHEN DICHTUNG / Berger, Kurt – (Includes bibliographical references) – Berlin: Junker und Duennhaupt, 1939 – 2r – 1 – us U.W. Library [430]
DIE BALLADEN UND RITTERLICHEN LIEDER DES FREIHERRN BOERRIES VON MUENCHHAUSEN / Muenchhausen, Boerries, Freiherr von – 3. Aufl. Berlin: E Fleischel, 1908 – 1r – 1 – us U.W. Library [780]
BALLADEN VOM GEIST / Hohlbaum, Robert – Berlin: K H Bischoff, 1943 – 1r – 1 – us U.W. Library [810]
BALLADES AND VERSES VAIN / Lang, Andrew – New York: C. Scribner's Sons, 1884 – 1 roll – 1 – 1-55879-714-9 – uk Libr Preservation [810]
BALLADS AND LYRICAL PIECES / Scott, Walter – London: Longman, Hurst, Rees, and Orme; Edinburgh: Archibald Constable, 1806 – 1 roll – 1 – 1-55879-645-2 – uk Libr Preservation [810]
BALLADS AND LYRICS / Tynan, Katharine – London: Kegan Paul, Trench, Trbner, 1891 – 1 roll – 1 – 1-55879-807-2 – uk Libr Preservation [810]
BALLADS AND SONGS : A COLLECTION OF BOOKS – 1869-88 – 1r – 1 – us Ross [780]
BALLADS AND SONGS / Davidson, John – London: John Lane; Boston: Copeland & Day, 1894 – 1 roll – 1 – 1-55879-803-X – uk Libr Preservation [810]
BALLADS AND SONNETS / Rossetti, Dante Gabriel – London: Ellis and White, 1881 – 1 roll – 1 – 1-55879-888-9 – uk Libr Preservation [810]
BALLADS EN TERMES DE LA LEY : ORIGINALLY WRITTEN FOR THE EXCLUSIVE USE OF THE TRINITY LAWYERS AND OTHER VERSES / Anson, Wiliam Reynell – Oxford: printed private circulation by Horace Hart, 1914? – 1mf – 9 – $1.50 – LLMC 91-501 – us L.L.M.C. [810]
BALLADS OF LOST HAVEN: A BOOK OF THE SEA / Carman, Bliss – Boston: Lamson, Wolffe, 1897. 00482. (Pre-1900 Canadiana) – 9 – cn C.I.H.M. [830]
Ballantine, William *see* A TREATISE ON THE STATUTE OF LIMITATIONS
Ballantyne, Robert Michael *see*
- THE CORAL ISLAND
- THE DOG CRUSOE: A TALE OF THE WESTERN PRAIRIES
- HUDSON'S BAY
- THE IRON HORSE
- THE LONELY ISLAND, OR, THE REFUGE OF THE MUTINEERS
- PERSONAL REMINISCENCES IN BOOK-MAKING
- THE PRAIRIE CHIEF: A TALE
- SILVER LAKE, OR, LOST IN THE SNOW
- TWICE BOUGHT, A TALE OF THE OREGON GOLD FIELDS
- UNGAVA, A TALE OF ESQUIMAUX-LANDS
THE BALLANTYNE-HUMBUG HANDLED : IN A LETTER TO SIR ADAM FERGUSSON. BY THE AUTHOR OF MEMOIRS OF THE LIFE OF SIR WALTER SCOTT / Lockhart, JG – Edinburgh: Robert Cadell; London: John Murray, Whittaker & Co, 1839 – 1r – 1 – 1-55879-353-4 – uk Libr Preservation [920]
BALLARAT : PEOPLE AND PLACES – 26mf – 9 – A$60.00 – at State Libr Vic [072]
BALLARAT COURIER – 1922-1944 – 92mf – 9 – at Corangamite [980]
BALLARAT COURIER. (COURIER) – Australia. 6 Nov 1913-18 May 1920; 10 Nov 1920-30 Jun 1922; 4 Aug 1951-19 Jul 1952 (imperfect).-w – 37r – 1 – uk British Libr Newspaper [072]
BALLARAT SCHOOL OF MINES – 1870-1989. Minute Books. BSM1-7 – 7r – 1 – at Corangamite [370]
BALLARAT SCHOOL OF MINES – 1982-1988. Student Ledger – 54mf – 9 – at Corangamite [370]
Ballard, A *see*
- THE DOMESDAY BOROUGHS
- THE DOMESDAY INQUEST
Ballard, Addison *see* FROM TALK TO TEXT
Ballard, Frank *see*
- HAECKEL'S MONISM FALSE
- THE MIRACLES OF UNBELIEF
- MIRACLES OF UNBELIEF
- THEOMONISM TRUE
- THE TRUE GOD
- TRUE GOD: A MODERN SUMMARY OF THE RELATIONS OF THEISM TO NATURALISM... PANTHEISM
IL BALLARINO DI M. FABRITO CAROSO DA SERMONETA, DIUISO IN DU TRATTATI... / Caroso, Fabrito – Ventia: Appresso Francesco Ziletti, 1581 – 1 – us Sibley [780]
IL BALLARINO. DIVISO IN DUE TRATTATI / Caroso, Fabrito – 1581. P 204 – 9 – ne IDC [790]
Ballat, Paul C *see* EFFECTS OF SELECTED CURRICULUM MATERIALS AND TEACHING EXPERIENCE ON THE PREACTIVE PLANNING OF PHYSICAL EDUCATORS
Balleine, G R *see* A HISTORY OF THE EVANGELICAL PARTY IN THE CHURCH OF ENGLAND
Ballerini, G *see* IL PROBLEMA DELLA PACE PERPETUA
Ballerini, Raffaele *see* LE PRIME PAGINE DEL PONTIFICATO DI PAPA PIO 9
Ballester, Eliel C *see* DERECHO DE PRENSA
Ballesteros Beretta, Antonio *see*
- CRISTOBAL COLON Y EL DESCUBRIMIENTO DE AMERICA. 2 VOL. BARCELONA, 1945
- PREMIO A LA VIRTUD
Ballesteros, Francisco A *see* RELACION DEL FALLECIMIENTO...MOLINA
Ballesteros, Gaibrois *see* MANUEL BREVIARIOS DEL PENSAMIENTO ESPANOL...
Ballesteros Morientes, Alfredo *see* REGLAMENTO PARA EL REGIMEN Y ADMINISTRACION DE LA COFRADIA DE LA SANTISIMA VIRGEN DE NAVELONGA, PATRON MUY QUERIDO DE CILLEROS DE LA DIOCESIS DE CORIA-CACERES
BALLET NEWS – New York. v1-7 may 1979-mar 1986 – 1,5,9 – D11849 – us UMI [790]
DES BALLETS ANCIENS ET MODERNES SELON LES REGLES DU THEATRE / Menestrier, Claude-Francois – 1682 – 9 – us Sibley [780]
Ballier *see* DE L'EDUCATION PHYSIQUE ET MORALE DES ENFANTS DES DEUX SEXES
BALLILA – Lynn, MA, 1912 – 3mf or 1r – 1,9 – us I.H.R.C. [978]
BALLINA ADVERTISER – Ireland. -w. 10 Jan 1840-10 Nov 1843. (2 reels) – 1 – uk British Libr Newspaper [072]
BALLINA HERALD – Ireland.1927-62. 15 reels – 1 – PS27.50r – ie European Micro [072]
BALLINA IMPARTIAL – Ireland. -w. 13 Jan 1823-16 Nov 1835. (Wanting 1826). (4 reels) – 1 – uk British Libr Newspaper [072]
BALLINA JOURNAL – Ireland.13 Nov 1882-11 Mar 1895. -w. 5 reels – 1 – uk British Libr Newspaper [072]
BALLINSROBE CHRONICLE – Ireland.22 Sept 1866-7 Dec 1867; 11 Apr 1868-Dec 1872; 1875-77; 1879; 1882-84; 1886-88; 1892. -w. 9 reels – 1 – uk British Libr Newspaper [072]
THE BALLOON NEWSPAPER EPOCH – Santa Cruz, CA. – 1r – 1 – $50.00 – B02949 – us Library Micro [071]
BALLOT – London, UK. 2 Jan 1831-4 Nov 1832. -w.1 reel – 1 – uk British Libr Newspaper [072]
THE BALLOT BOX – Fallon, NV. 1911-13 – 1r – 1 – $50.00 – U04520 – us Library Micro [071]
Ballou, Adin *see* AUTOBIOGRAPHY OF ADIN BALLOU, 1803-1890
Ballou, Maturin M *see* BIOGRAPHY OF REV. HOSEA BALLOU
BALLOU'S PICTORIAL DRAWING-ROOM COMPANION – Boston. v. 1-17. May 1851-Dec 1859. Incomplete – 1 – us NY Public [073]
BALLOU'S PICTORIAL DRAWING-ROOM COMPANION – Boston. v1-17. 1851-59 – 4r – 1 – us Ross [073]
Ballow, Henry *see* A TREATISE OF EQUITY
BALLSTON SPA GAZETTE – Ballston Spa, NY. 1821-25 – 1,3 – us Readex [071]
BALLWIN BAPTIST CHURCH AND MISSION. MISSOURI : CHURCH RECORDS – 1952-61 – 1 – 22.40 – us Baptist [240]
Ballyclare. Northern Ireland. Presbyterian Church *see* REGISTERS
BALLYMENA ADVERTISER – Ireland. -w. 7 Jun 1873-16 Jul 1892. (14 reels) – 1 – uk British Libr Newspaper [072]
BALLYMENA CHRONICLE – Ireland.1973-80. -d. 16 reels – 1 – uk British Libr Newspaper [072]
BALLYMENA GUARDIAN – Ireland, 22 Oct 1970- – 75+ r – 1 – uk British Libr Newspaper [072]
BALLYMENA OBSERVER – (Lacking: Nov, Dec 1869. Jan 1875-Mar 1876) – Ireland, 22 Aug 1857- Dec 1976 – 116r – 1 – uk British Libr Newspaper [072]
BALLYMENA TIMES – Northern Irland, May 1966-Aug 1970; May 1985- – 30+ r – 1 – uk British Libr Newspaper [072]
BALLYMENA WEEKLY TELEGRAPH – Ireland, 2 Jun 1894-29 Dec 1966 – 62r – 1 – uk British Libr Newspaper [072]
BALLYMONEY FREE PRESS – Ireland, 15 May 1873-1 Nov 1934 – 25r – 1 – uk British Libr Newspaper [072]
Balmaceda, Julian C *see* FILIPINO LANGUAGE LEXICON
Balmaceda, Rodolfo *see* CONDICION OBRERA Y DESPILFARRO OLIG ARQUICO
BALMAIN OBSERVER – (1901 very imperfect) – Australia, Sep 1892-Nov 1893; Apr 1896-Jun 1898; 1899-1903 – 4r – 1 – uk British Libr Newspaper [072]
DER BALMELOCKE = L'ARTISAN – (In Yiddish) – Paris, FR. v1 no1. Mar 1939 – 1r – 1 – $25.00 – cn Can Microfilming [072]
Balmer, Hans *see* ALBERT BITZIUS
BALMES EN LA ENCRUCIJADA FILOSOFICA / Frutos Cortes, Eugenio – Zaragoza: Tip. La Academica, 1949 – sp Bibl Santa Ana [100]

Balmes, Jaime Luciano *see* EUROPEAN CIVILIZATION
Bal'mont, K D *see*
- GAMAIUN. IZBRANNYE STIKHI
- GDE MOI DOM? OCHERKI (1920-1923)
- GORIASHCHIIA ZDANIIA. LIRIKA SOVREMENNOI DUSHI
- GORNYIA VERSHINY. SBORNIK STATEI
- ISPANSKIIA NARODNYIA PESNI. LIUBOV I NENAVIST
- IZ CHUZHEZEMNYKH POETOV
- IZ MIROVOI POEZII
- JASEN'. VIDENIE DREVA. (STIKHI)
- KRAI OZIRISA. EGIPETSKIE OCHERKI
- LITURGIIA KRASOTY. STIKHIINYE GIMNY
- MAREVO
- MOE-EI. ROSSIIA
- MORSKOE SVECHENIE
- PESNI MSTITELIA
- POD NOVYM SERPOM. ROMAN
- PTITSY V VOZDYKHE. STROKI NAPEVNYIA
- SEVERNOE SIIANIE. STIKHI O LITVE I RUSI
- SLOVO O MUZYKE
- SOBRANIE LIRIKI
- SOBRANIE STIKHOV
- SOLNECHNAIA PRIAZHA. IZBORNIK 1890-1918
- SONETY SOLNTSA, MEDA I LUNY PESNIA MIROV
- SONETY SOLNTSA, MEDA I LUNY. PESNIA MIROV
- SVETLYI CHAS. IZBRANNYE STIKHI
- TOL'KO LIUBOV'
- TOL'KO LIUBOV'. SEMITSVETNIK
- TRI RASTSVETA. DRAMA
- V RAZDVINUTOI DALI. POEMA O ROSSII
- VOZDUSHNYI PUT'. RAZSKAZY
- ZELENYI VERTOGRAD. SLOVA POTSELUINYIA. STIKHI
- ZHAR-PTITSA. SVIREL' SLAVIANINA
- ZLYIA CHARY
- ZMEINYE TSVETY. PUTEVYIA PIS'MA IZ MEKSIKI
- ZOLOTOI SNOP BOLGARSKOI POEZII. NARODNYIA PESNI.
- ZOVY DREVNOSTI..
- ZVEN'IA. IZBRANNYE STIKHI. 1890-1912

Balmoral Hotel. Montreal, Quebec *see* DOWN THE ST LAWRENCE & GULF
BALNEARIO DE ALANGE – Madrid: Imprenta Cosano – 1 – sp Bibl Santa Ana [946]
Balogh, A de *see* LA PROTECTION INTERNATIONALE DES MINORITES
Balough, Elemer *see* THE BRITISH EMPIRE
Balsamo, G G *see* PRODROMUS BRYOLOGIAE MEDIOLANENSIS
Balsillie, David *see* AN EXAMINATION OF PROFESSOR BERGSON'S PHILOSOPHY
Baltard, Louis Pierre *see* ARCHITECTONOGRAPHIE DES PRISONS OU PARALLELE DES DIVERS SYSTEMES DE DISTRIBUTION DONT LES PRISONS SONT SUSCEPTIBLES.
BALTASAR CUARTERO Y HUERTA Y ANTONIO VARGAS ZUNIGA Y MONTERO DE ESPINOSA. MARQUES DE SIETE IGLESIAS. INDICE... / Castro, Manuel – Madrid: Archivo Ibero-Americano, 1959 – 1 – sp Bibl Santa Ana [946]
BALTHASAR HUEBMAIER : THE LEADER OF THE ANABAPTISTS / Vedder, Henry Clay – (Includes index) – New York: G P Putnam, 1905 – 1mf – 9 – 0-8370-9193-4 – 1986-3193 – us A.T.L.A. [920]
BALTHAZAR SPRINGERS INDIENFAHRT 1505/06 / Schulze, Franz – Strassburg: Heitz, 1902 – 1 – F79.70 – fr Armell [910]
THE BALTIC AND CAUCASIAN STATES. – Boston, New York: Houghton Mifflin Co., 1923. xx,269p. maps. Prepared under the care of Major-General Lord Edward Gleichen. Bibliographies – 1 – us U.W. Library [947]
THE BALTIC AND WHITE SEA CONFERENCE : ANNUAL REPORTS – Copenhagen, 1905-1977 – 59mf – 9 – ne IDC [320]
THE BALTIC AND WHITE SEA CONFERENCE : ANNUAL REPORTS – Copenhagen, 1905-1977 – 59mf – 9 – ILM-3888/1 – ne IDC [320]
THE BALTIC CHRONICLE – Tilza, Latvia. Bi-monthly Organ of the Baltic Evangelical Mission. v1, 2, 19-39, incomplete. Publ. No. 6350b. One of two items on reel. 398p – 1 – us Baptist [240]
THE BALTIC INDEPENDENT – (Backfile 1990-98 $85r) – Estonia, 1999- – 1r per y – 1 – $80.00 standing order – us Ross [072]
THE BALTIC OBSERVER – 1992 – 1 reel – 1 – Sfr120.00 – sz Infoprint [947]
THE BALTIC OBSERVER – (1992 1r $85. 1993-98 2r per y $170y) – Latvia, 1999- – 2r per y – 1 – $160.00 standing order – us Ross [072]
THE BALTIC OBSERVER – (Standing order available from 1994. 2r per year. Sfr225.00y) – 1993 – 2r – 1 – Sfr240.00 – sz Infoprint [947]
BALTIC REPUBLICS – 133 titles – 9 – ne IDC [947]
BALTIISKII AL'MANAKH : EZHEMESIACHNIK LITERATURY, ISKUSSTVA I EKONOMIKI – Kovno. v1-2. 1923-1924 – 9mf – 9 – ne IDC [073]
BALTIJAS BAPTISTI UN BUNDE, JEB BALTIJAS BAPTISTU TAGADEJS STAHSOKLIS = THE BALTIC BAPTISTS AND THE UNION, OR THE CURRENT CONDITION OF THE BALTIC BAPTISTS / Frey, J A – Riga, 1887. Publ. No. 6347b. One of three items on reel. 146p – 1 – us Baptist [240]
THE BALTIMORE BAPTIST – (Continues: The Baptist, 1894. The Evangel, 1895-97) – 1883-97 – 5576p – 1 – $278.80 – us Baptist [240]
BALTIMORE CITY REPORTS / Maryland. Supreme Court – v1-4. 1888-1928 (all publ) – 31mf – 9 – $46.50 – LLMC 84-152 – us L.L.M.C. [340]
BALTIMORE CLIPPER *see* BALTIMORE DAILY COMMERCIAL
BALTIMORE COMMERCIAL JOURNAL AND LYFORD'S PRICE-CURRENT – Baltimore, Maryland. Jan 23 1847-Dec 8 1849 – 1r – 1 – us L of C Photodup [073]
BALTIMORE CORRESPONDENT – (dec 2 1935-jun 6 1941: Taeglicher Baltimore Correspondent) – Baltimore, MD. jul 3 1923-sep 30 1937, 1972-75 – 1 – Dist. gw Mikrofilm – gw Misc Inst [071]
BALTIMORE DAILY CLIPPER *see* AMERICAN REPUBLICAN, AND BALTIMORE DAILY CLIPPER
BALTIMORE DAILY COMMERCIAL – (Cont: Baltimore Clipper) – Baltimore, Maryland. Oct 1965-Oct 1966 – 3r – 1 – us L of C Photodup [071]
BALTIMORE DAILY GAZETTE – Baltimore, Maryland. 1862-80 – 1 – us MD Archives [071]
BALTIMORE DAILY INTELLIGENCER – Baltimore, MD. 1793-94 – 1,3 – us Readex [071]
BALTIMORE DAILY RECORD / Baltimore, MD. v4-149, Jan 1890-Dec 1962. Incomplete. LL-02 – 1 – us L of C Photodup [340]
BALTIMORE EVENING NEWS – Baltimore, Maryland. 1897-1918 – 1 – us MD Archives [071]
BALTIMORE EVENING POST – Baltimore, MD. 1792-93 – 1,3 – us Readex [071]
BALTIMORE FIRST BAPTIST CHURCH. BALTIMORE, MARYLAND : SCRAPBOOK – 1773-1968 – 1 – $28.53 – us Baptist [240]
THE BALTIMORE JEWISH AMERICAN – Baltimore. Md. 1908-09 – 1 – us A.J.P.C. [071]
Baltimore Museum of Art *see* AMERICAN PRINTS, 1870-1950
Baltimore. Presbytery (Pres. Ch. in the U.S.A.) *see* MINUTES, 1786-1906
BALTIMORE REPUBLICAN AND DAILY ARGUS – Baltimore, Maryland. 1842-61 – 1 – us MD Archives [071]
BALTISCHE BIBLIOGRAPHIE / Thomson, Erik – (Includes indexes) – Wuerzburg: Holzner-Verlag, 1957-1962 – 1 – us U.W. Library [947]
BALTISCHE MEER DAS IST HISTORISCHE AUSFUEHRUNG...1638 – N.p., n.d. – 1mf – 9 – ILM-1200/1 – ne IDC [947]
BALTISCHE MONATSSCHRIFT – Riga, 1859-1931. v1-62 – 594mf – 9 – R-11289/1 – ne IDC [073]
BALTISCHE POST – Pernau, Eesti (Paernu, U.S.S.R.). 1927-Aug 1928 – 1r – 1 – gw Mikrofilm [947]
BALTISCHE PRESSE – Danzig, Poland. Okt 1923-27 Jun 1931 – 14r – 1 – gw Mikrofilm [947]
BALTISCHE STIMMEN : WOCHENZEITUNG FUER STADT UND LAND – Riga, Latvija, USSR. 15 Dec 1927-27 Apr 1929 – 1r – 1 – gw Mikrofilm [072]
BALTISCHE STUDIEN – (NF: 6(1002)-14(1910). 46mf. Dfl161.00) – 15(1843)-40(1890) – 184mf – 9 – Dfl644.00 – ne Slangenburg [073]
BALTISCHE TEXTE DER FRUHZEIT / Mackensen, Lutz – Riga: Ernst Plates, 1936 – 1 – us U.W. Library [460]
DIE BALTISCHE TRAGOEDIE : EINE ROMANTRILOGIE / Vegesack, Siegfried von – (Each work also publ separately) – Bremen: C Schuenemann, 1935 – 1r – 1 – us U.W. Library [830]
DIE BALTISCHEN STAATEN UND DAS VOELKERRECHT / Rutenberg, G – Riga, 1928 – 2mf – 9 – ILM-1548/1 – ne IDC [320]
Baltrushaitis, Iu *see*
- GORNAIA TROPA. VTORAIA KNIGA STIKHOV
- LILIIA I SERP. TRET'IA KNIGA STIKHOV
- ZEMNYIA STUPENI. ELEGII, PESNI, POEMY

BALTU VALODU SKANAS UN FORMAS / Endzelin, J – Riga, 1948 – 5mf – 9 – ne IDC [460]
Baltz, Johanna *see* FLEURS DES ALPES
Baltzer, Otto *see*
- BEITRAEGE ZUR GESCHICHTE DER CHRISTOLOGISCHEN DOGMAS IM 11TEN UND 12TEN JAHRHUNDERT
- JUDITH IN DER DEUTSCHEN LITERATUR
- DIE SENTENZEN DES PETRUS LOMBARDUS

LES BALUBA (CONGO BELGE) / Colle, R P – Bruxelles: Dewit 1913 – us Res Libr [960]
BALUCHISTAN, 1901 (ADMINISTRATIVE REPORT) – Delhi, 1941 – 1 – us Res Libr [310]
BALUJUN JUNZHENG ZAZHI – Military and Political Journal of the Eighth Route Army. Jan 1939-Mar 1942. M C23. In Chinese – 1 – $180.00 – cc Microforms [073]
Baluzius, Stephanus *see*
- CONCILIA GALLIAE NARBONENSIS
- MISCELLANEORUM LIBRI 7, HOC EST COLLECTIO VETERUM MONUMENTORUM QUAE HACTENUS LATUERANT IN VARIIS CODICIBUS AC BIBLIOTHECIS
- VITAE PAPARUM AVENIONENSIUM

Balzac, Honore de *see* SCENES DE LA VIE DE CAMPAGNE. LES PAYSANS.
Balzani, Ugo *see* ITALY
Balzli, Ernst *see* ZWUESCHE TUER U ANGLE
BAMA KHIT – Rangoon, Burma. Oct 1959-Mar 1960 – 3r – 1 – us L of C Photodup [072]
BA-MAAVAK = THE STRUGGLE – (In Hebrew) – Antwerp, BE. no4/5. 6 Sep 1948 – 1r – 1 – $25.00 – cn Can Microfilming [072]
Bamberg, Elma L *see* "MY HOME ON THE SMOKY"
Bamberg, Felix *see* UEBER DEN EINFLUSS DER WELTZUSTAENDE AUF DIE RICHTUNGEN DER KUNST
Bamberger, F *see*
- DIE LEHREN DES JUDENTUMS NACH DEN QUELLEN

BAMBERGER NEUESTE NACHRICHTEN – Bamberg, jul 1 1860-sep 14 1923 – 1 – Dist. gw Mikrofilm – gw Misc Inst [943]
Bamberger, Richard *see* PROMOTING THE READING HABIT
Bamberger, Selig *see* SIRAEJ. HALLAH
BAMBERGER TAGBLATT – Bamberg, 1926-36 – 32r – 1 – DM2,400.00 – gw Mikro Press [072]
BAMBERGER TAGBLATT – (Cont: Taeglicher Anzeiger, -1834; Tagsblatt der Stadt Bamberg, jan 28 1835; Tagblatt der Stadt Bamberg, dec 19 1865. Cont by: Fraenkisches Volk, jul 29 1933; Bayerische Ostmark, Bereichsausgabe, oct 1 1934; Bamberger Tagblatt, aug 1 1942) – Bamberg, oct 28 1834-99, 1926-36 – 1 – Dist. gw Mikrofilm – gw Misc Inst [943]
BAMBERGER VOLKSBLATT – Bamberg, 1926-36 – 29r – 1 – DM2,175.00 – gw Mikro Press [943]
BAMBERGER VOLKSBLATT – Bamberg, dec 22 1871-dec 19 1873, jan 16 1874-aug 28 1908 – 1 – Dist. gw Mikrofilm – gw Misc Inst [943]
BAMBERGER VOLKSBLATT – Bamberg, feb 1-jun 9 1849 – 1 – Dist. gw Mikrofilm – gw Misc Inst [943]
BAMBERGER VOLKSBLATT *see* BAMBERGER VOLKSBLATT FUER STADT UND LAND
BAMBERGER VOLKSBLATT FUER STADT UND LAND – (Cont by: Bamberger Volksblatt) – Bamberg, dec 6 1852-mar 29 1856 – 1 – Dist. gw Mikrofilm – gw Misc Inst [943]
BAMBERGER ZEITUNG – Bamberg, sep 1 1848-50, 1852-nov 30 1865 – 1 – Dist. gw Mikrofilm – gw Misc Inst [943]
BAMBERGER ZEITUNG *see* FRAENKISCHER MERKUR
Bambill, Benjamin A M *see* HACIA LA REALIZACION DE UNA DEMOCRACIA RESPONSABLE
IL BAMBINO NELL'ARTE ATTRAVERSO I SECOLI / Maccone, Luigi – Bergamo. 1923 – 1 – us Res Libr [700]
BAMBOULA, DANSE DE NEGRES / Gottschalk, L M – Boston: Ditscon Co, 18– – 1 – us Sibley [780]
BAMBUSEAE OF BRITISH INDIA / Gamble, J S – 1896 – 1 – uk Microform Academic [580]
BAMDAD – (Shumarah-'i 76-336 (15 Murdad 1358-30 Tir 1359[6 Aug 1979-21 Jul 1980]); Missing issues: 145, 147, 150, 257, 287, 154, 293, 314, 325-330) – Tehran, 1979-1980 – 2r – 1 – $150.00 – us MEDOC [950]
Bamford, Michael J *see* DYNAMICS OF SMALL VERTEBRATES IN RELATION TO FIRE IN BANKSIA WOODLAND NEAR PERTH, WESTERN AUSTRALIA
BAMIDGEH / Israel. Ministry of Agriculture Fisheries Division – Bulletin of fish culture in Israel. Tel Aviv. 1951-. -m – 9 – 54.00; 2.00y – is I.T.T.I. [324]
Bampfield, Francis *see* ALL IN ONE: ALL USEFUL SCIENCE AND PROFITABLE ARTS IN ONE BOOK OF JEHOVAH AELOHIM
Bampfield, S J *see* NEW SOUTH (BEAUFORT, SOUTH CAROLINA), MARCH 7, 1895
Bampflyde, C A *see* REPORT ON THE BIRD'S NEST CAVES OF GOMANTON
THE BAMPTON LECTURES, 1876 *see* THE WITNESS OF THE PSALMS TO CHRIST AND CHRISTIANITY
Ban, J A *see*
- JOANNIS ALBERTI BANNI DISSERTATIO EPISTOLICA, DE MUSICAE NATURA, ORIGINE, PROGRESSU AND DENIQUE STUDIO BENE INSTITUENDO. LUGDUNI BATAVORUM, EX OFFICINA ISAACI
- KORT SANGH-BERICHT OP ZYNE ZIELROERENDE ZANGEN

BAN MUANG – Bangkok, Thailand. 1974-76; 1982-94 – 123r – 1 – us L of C Photodup [072]
THE BAN OF THE BORI; DEMONS AND DEMON-DANCING IN WEST AND NORTH AFRICA / Tremearne, Arthur John Newman – London: Heath, Cranton & Ouseley, 1914. 504p.illus.plates – 1 – us U.W. Library [290]
BANA, THE HARSA-CARITA – 1897 – 1 – uk Microform Academic [490]
BANATER BEOBACHTER – Zrenjanin, Yugoslavia. Jun 1942-Jun 1943 – 1r – 1 – us L of C Photodup [072]
BANATER RUNDSCHAU – Zrenjanin, Yugoslavia. Oct 1935-Apr 1939 – 2r – 1 – us L of C Photodup [072]
BANBRIDGE CHRONICLE – Ireland, Sep 1874-Dec 1984; 1986- – 125+ r – 1 – uk British Libr Newspaper [072]
BANBURY ADVERTISER – (Lacking: 1897) – Banbury, England. 5 July 1855-Dec 1947 – 50r – 1 – uk British Libr Newspaper [072]
BANBURY BEACON – (Lacking: Jan-Feb 1901) – Banbury, England. 5 Jun 1868-30 Sep 1905 – 32r – 1 – uk British Libr Newspaper [072]
BANBURY CAKE – England, 1986- – 19+ r – 1 – uk British Libr Newspaper [072]
BANBURY EVENING NEWS – Banbury, England. 1 Jan-31 Dec 1877 – 1r – 1 – uk British Libr Newspaper [072]
BANBURY GUARDIAN – (Lacking: 1872) – Banbury, England. 1843- – 200+ r – 1 – uk British Libr Newspaper [072]
BANBURY HERALD – Banbury, England. 10 Jan 1861-24 Dec 1863; 27 Jun 1867-27 Feb 1869 – 4r – 1 – uk British Libr Newspaper [072]
BANBURY TELEGRAPH AND FARMERS' CHRONICLE – Banbury, England. 2 Mar 1893-9 May 1895 – 1 1/2r – 1 – uk British Libr Newspaper [072]
BANC DE LA REINE *see* RAPPORTS JUDICIAIRES DE QUEBEC
Banca Sanchez S.A. *see* ESTATUTOS
Bancal Des Issarts, Jean Henri *see* HENRI BANCAL, DEPUTE A LA CONVENTION, A ANACHARSIS CLOOTZ, SON COLLEGUE
Bancal Des Issarts, Jean-Henri *see* DU NOUVEL ORDRE SOCIAL
Banchieri, A *see*
- CARTELLA MUSICALE NEL CANTO FIGURATO FERMO, ET CONTRAPUNTO. NOVAMENTE IN QUESTA TERZA IMPRESSIONE RIDOTTA DALL'ANTICA ALLA MODERNA PRATICA
- DIRETTORIO MONASTICO DI CANTO FERMO
- LA NOBILISSIMA, ANZI ASINISSIMA COMPAGNIA DELLI BRIGANTI DELLA BASTINA... COMPOSITIONE DI CAMILLO SCAGLIERI DALLA FRATTA

- ORGANO SUONARINO DEL P. D. ADRIANO BANCHIERI BOLOGNESE ABBATE BENEMERITO OLIVETANO. OPERA 33
- L'ORGANO SUONARINO DI ADRIANO BANCHIERI BOLOGNESE

Banco de Guatemala *see* BOLETIN ESTADISTICO

Banco de la Nacion Argentina. Buenos Aires *see* REVISTA

Banco di Roma *see* VADEMECUM ECONOMICO PER L'AOI

Banco Nacional de Mexico *see* EXAMEN DE LA SITUACION ECONOMICA DE MEXICO

BANCROFT BLADE – Bancroft, NE, -w. Jun. 1892-Mar. 1901. Incomplete; May 1901-Jun. 1954 – 1 – us NE Hist [071]

BANCROFT BUGLE – Bancroft, NE. -w. Apr. 1971-May 1974 – 1 – us NE Hist [071]

Bancroft, Charles *see* THE FOOTPRINTS OF TIME

Bancroft Co *see* SAN FRANCISCO BLUE BOOK AND PACIFIC COAST ELITE DIRECTORY

BANCROFT ENTERPRISE – Bancroft, NE. -w. Jun. 1895-May 1896 – 1 – us NE Hist [071]

Bancroft, George *see*
- GEORGE BANCROFT PAPERS
- HISTORY OF THE BATTLE OF LAKE ERIE AND MISCELLANEOUS PAPERS
- HISTORY OF THE FORMATION OF THE CONSTITUTION
- A PLEA FOR THE CONSTITUTION OF THE UNITED STATES, WOUNDED IN THE HOUSE OF ITS GUARDIANS

Bancroft, Hubert Howe *see*
- HISTORY OF THE PACIFIC STATES-NORTH AMERICA
- HISTORY OF UTAH 1540-1887
- WORKS

THE BANCROFT LIBRARY, UNIVERSITY OF CALIFORNIA, BERKELEY : CATALOG OF PRINTED BOOKS / University of California at Berkeley – 1964. 364,000 cards on 44 reels – 1 – $1,980.00 export $2,400.00 – 0-8161-1393-9 – uk Hall [978]

THE BANCROFT LIBRARY, UNIVERSITY OF CALIFORNIA, BERKELEY : FIRST SUPPLEMENT / University of California at Berkeley – 1969. 86,700 cards on 6 reels – 1 – $660.00 export $798.00 – 0-8161-1517-6 – uk Hall [978]

THE BANCROFT LIBRARY, UNIVERSITY OF CALIFORNIA, BERKELEY : INDEX TO PRINTED MAPS / University of California at Berkeley. The Bancroft Library – 1964 – 1 reel – 1 – $79.00 export $95.00 – 0-8161-1550-8 – uk Hall [910]

THE BANCROFT LIBRARY, UNIVERSITY OF CALIFORNIA, BERKELEY : SECOND SUPPLEMENT / University of California at Berkeley – 1974. 92,600 cards on 6 reels – 1 – $720.00 export $870.00 – 0-8161-1394-7 – uk Hall [978]

THE BANCROFT LIBRARY, UNIVERSITY OF CALIFORNIA, BERKELEY : THIRD SUPPLEMENT / University of California at Berkeley – 1979. 69,500 cards on 5 reels – 1 – $830.00 export $1,005.00 – 0-8161-1163-4 – uk Hall [978]

Bancroft, R J *see* HISTORY OF CLERMONT COUNTY

Bancroft, W D et al *see* JOURNAL OF PHYSICAL CHEMISTRY

EEN BAND MET TRACTATEN VAN DAVID JORIS / Rogge, Hendrik Cornelis – 's-Gravenhage. 1887-94. BME-424 1 – 9 – ne IDC [240]

BAND OF HOPE RITUAL : WITH RESPONSIVE READINGS AND TEMPERANCE HYMNS / ed by Cowie, J S – Moncton, N.B.: Office of the Telephone, 1884. 06036. (Pre-1900 Canadiana) – 9 – cn C.I.H.M. [240]

DE BAND TUSSEN AMBON EN NEDERLAND : 1. HISTORISCH GEZIEN; 2. MEER CULTUREEL GEZIEN / Graaf, H J de – 's-Gravenhage, 1969 – 1mf – 9 – ne IDC [943]

Banda, Hastings K *see* SPEECHES OF DR HASTINGS KAMUZU BANDA, PRESIDENT OF MALAWI

Banda, Ismail *see* PENGAKOEAN MESIR DAN POLITIK ARAB LEAGUE

BANDANA BAPTIST CHURCH. BANDANA, KENTUCKY : CHURCH RECORDS – (1,318p) – 1900-May 1990 – 1 reel – 1 – $59.31 – us Baptist [240]

Bandanelli, Pedro *see* PERON NO EST A EXCOMULGADO

BANDAOTI XUEBAO – (1980-82 $4.50f; 1983-84 $3.50f) – Chinese Journal of Semi-Conductor. In Chinese but English abstracts to the main articles. F p139 – 9 – cc Microforms [073]

Bandaranaike, S W R D *see* HAND BOOK OF THE CEYLON NATIONAL CONGRESS, 1919-1928

LA BANDE JOYEUSE – Port-au-Prince: A Gouraige & Co. [1ere annee n10-n26]. (14 janv.-26 aout 1886) – 1 sheet – us Res Libr [072]

O BANDEIRANTE : ACREANISTA – Rio Branco, Acre. Ago 1953 – 1,5,6 – bl Biblioteca [072]

O BANDEIRANTE : JORNAL MENSAL DA LOJA MACONICA – Xapuri, Acre. Jul, Out 1984 – 1,5,6 – bl Biblioteca [072]

O BANDEIRANTE – Uberlandia, Brazil. Sept-Oct 1937 – 1 – bl Biblioteca [072]

BANDELIER NATIONAL MONUMENT, NEW MEXICO / Wing, Kittridge A – 1955 – 9 – $5.00f – us Ross [975]

LA BANDERA REGIONAL – Plasencia, 1900. Various numeros – 5 – sp Bibl Santa Ana [073]

BANDIERA ROSSA – Milano. Organ of the Gruppi comunisti rivoluzionari. illus. semimonthly – 1 – us U.W. Library [073]

Bandinel, B *see* MONASTICON ANGLICANUM

Bandinel, J *see* SOME ACCOUNT OF THE TRADE IN SLAVES FROM AFRICA...

BANDOENG : THE MOUNTAIN CITY OF THE NEDERLANDS INDIA / Reitsma, S A – Weltevreden, Batavia, ca 1932 – 1mf – 9 – SE-1440/1 – ne IDC [910]

EL BANDOLERISMO / Zugasti, Julian de – v1, 1876; v2, 1876; v4, 1877; v6, 1877 – 9 – 1.50f – sp Bibl Santa Ana [800]

EL BANDOLERISMO...TOMO 4. PARTE PRIMERA. ORIGENES DEL BANDOLERISMO / Zugasti, Julian de – Madrid: Fortanet, Tomo 1. 2nd ed 1877 – 1 – sp Bibl Santa Ana [946]

BANDON RECORDER – Bandon, OR. -w. 1901-16 – 1 – 113.00 – us Oregon Hist [071]

BANDON RECORDER – Bandon, OR. -w. 3 Jan 1890-25 Jul 1913. 7 rolls – 1 – us U.O. Library [071]

THE BANDUNG CONFERENCE FROM THE HISTORICAL POINT OF VIEW / Supomo – SE 6249 1. Address at Islamic Cultural Centre, London, on Aug 6 1955 – 9 – ne IDC [950]

Bandung, Indonesia *see*
- LEMBAGA PENJELIDIKAN MASALAH BANGUNAN
- UNIVERSITAS PADJADJARAN. BALAI PENELITIAN PENDIDIKAN. WARTA BHALAI

BANDUNG LAUTAN API / Amar, Djen – SE-4240 1. 1963 – 9 – ne IDC [950]

BANDUNG MAKES HISTORY AGAIN; FOURTH ANNIVERSARY OF A.A. CONFERENCE / Ruslan, Abdulgani – SE 6893 1. 1959 – 9 – ne IDC [300]

BANDUNG SPIRIT; MOVING ON THE TIDE OF HISTORY / Ruslan, Abdulgani – SE 10,713 1. 1964 – 9 – ne IDC [320]

Banduri, A *see*
- IMPERIUM ORIENTALE SIVE ANTIQUITATES CONSTANTINOPOLITANI (CBH 24,1)
- IMPERIUM ORIENTALE SIVE ANTIQUITATES CONSTANTINOPOLITANI (CBH 24,2)

A BANDURRA – '(s.l.')-Sao Luiz, Brazil. 15 Jan-31 Dec 1828 – 1,5,6 – bl Biblioteca [072]

BANDWIDTH KNOWLEDGE OF RESULTS IN MOTOR SKILL PERFORMANCE AND LEARNING / Goodwin, Jeff E – Texas Woman's University, 1994 – 3mf – 9 – $12.00 – PSY 1888 – us Microform Publ [150]

Bandy de Naleche, Louis *see* LES MACONS DE LA CREUSE

Banegas, Fortunato *see* SINDICALISMO Y JUSTICIA SOCIAL

Banerji, Rakhal Das *see* HISTORY OF ORISSA, FROM THE EARLIEST TIMES TO THE BRITISH PERIOD

Banerji, Santi Kumar *see*
- A COMPARATIVE STUDY OF THE SOCIAL BACKGROUND OF ADULT EDUCATION PROBLEMS IN AFRICA AND INDIA

Banes, Dom *see*
- COMMENTARIOS INEDITOS A LA TERCERA PARTE DE SANTO TOMAE, T1-2
- SCHOLASTICA COMMENTARIA IN PRIMAM PARTEM ANGELICI DOCTORIS S. THOMAE
- SCHOLASTICA COMMENTARIA IN PRIMAM PARTEM ANGELICI DOCTORIS S. THOMAE USQUE AD 63 QUAESTIONEM COMPLECTENTIA
- SCHOLASTICA COMMENTARIA IN PRIMAM PARTEM, SUMMAE THEOLOGICAE S. THOMAE AQUINATIS
- SCHOLASTICA COMMENTARIA IN SECUNDAM SECUNDAE ANGELICI DOCTORIS S. THOMAE

BANET SUAD SERHI / Esad – Hicaz: Hicaz Vilayeti Matbaasi, 1314 [1897] – $55.00 – us MEDOC [470]

BANFFSHIRE, 1837 : BRITISH ISLES CENSUS DIRECTORIES PROJECT, SCOTLAND. VOL 30 – 1mf – 9 – A$9.00 – at Vine [941]

BANFFSHIRE, 1915 : BRITISH ISLES CENSUS DIRECTORIES PROJECT, SCOTLAND. VOL 13 – 1mf – 9 – A$9.00 – at Vine [941]

BANFFSHIRE ADVERTISER – 1 – £42.00r – uk Scot News [072]

BANFFSHIRE ADVERTISER – Buckie, Scotland. 1881-1902; 1905-24; 1953-59; 1964-66.-w. 37mqn reels – 1 – uk British Libr Newspaper [072]

BANFFSHIRE HERALD – 1 – £42.00r – uk Scot News [072]

BANFFSHIRE HERALD – Keith, Scotland. Dec 1893-Dec 1978.-w. 69 reels – 1 – uk British Libr Newspaper [072]

BANFFSHIRE JOURNAL – Banff, Scotland. -w. 1876-1978. 97 reels – 1 – uk British Libr Newspaper [072]

BANFFSHIRE JOURNAL AND NORTHERN FARMER – 1 – £42.00r – uk Scot News [072]

Bang, A C *see*
- HANS NIELSEN HAUGE OG HANS SAMTID
- DEN NORSKE KIRKES GEISTLIGHED 1 REFORMATIONS-AARHUNDREDET (1536-1600)

Bang, Herman *see* GEDANKEN ZUM SEXUALPROBLEM MIT EINEM GELEITWORT VON DR. PLACZEK

Bang, Hermann Joachim *see* DIE TAENZERIN UND ANDERE ERZAEHLUNGEN

Bang, W *see* MATERIALIEN ZUR KUNDE DES AELTEREN ENGLISCHEN DRAMAS

LES BANGALA ST (ETAT IND. DU CONGO) / Overbergh, Cyr. van – Bruxelles, A DeWit [etc] 1907 – us Res Libr [960]

LES BANGALA...AVEC LA COLLAB. DE ED. DE JONGHE... : T. 1 / Van Overbergh, Cyrille – (T.2: Les Mayombe. 1907. F227,21; T.3: Les Basonge. 1908. F275,15; T.4: Les Mangbetu. 1909. F284,64; T.5: (Delhaise, Charles G.) Les Warega; 1909. F194,50; T.6: (Van den Plas, Joseph). Les Kukus... 1910. F208,74; T.7: (Halkin, Joseph). Les Ababua... 1911. F294,13; T.8: (Gaud, Fernand). Les Mandjas... 1911. F289,38; T.9: (Schmitz, Robert). Les Baholoholo... 1912. F313,10; T.10-11: (Colle, R.P. Pierre). Les Baluba...; T.1,2. Bruxelles: Van Campenhout, 1913. F920,34) – 1907 – 2r – 1 – F222,97 – fr Armell [305]

BANGALORE EXAMINER – India. -w. 1877-1886. 19 reels – 1 – uk British Libr Newspaper [072]

BANGALORE THEOLOGICAL FORUM – (1986- . 5,6,9) – v1- . 1967- – 1 – us UMI [073]

BANGALORE THEOLOGICAL FORUM – v1-19. 1967-87 (complete) – 5r – 1 – ATLA S0448 – us A.T.L.A. [240]

BANGKOK : SUMMARY OF THE THAI AND CHINESE PRESS – Bangkok, Thailand. 1972-Jun 1986 – 1 – $50.00y – us Asia Libr [072]

BANGKOK CHRONICLE – Bangkok. Thailand. 1939-41 – 9r – 1 – us L of C Photodup [072]

BANGKOK POST – 1 – F8,120.00 – sz Infoprint [072]

BANGKOK POST – 1975-1993 – 1 – F8,644.00 – sz Infoprint [072]

THE BANGKOK POST – Bangkok: Alexander MacDonald, 1953-88 – 1 – us Res Libr [072]

THE BANGKOK POST – Bangkok, Thailand. 1975- – 1 – us Primary [072]

BANGKOK REVIEW – Bangkok: Bangkok Review. v1-3 n3. nov 14 1934-feb 1 1936 – 2r – 1 – us Res Libr [072]

BANGKOK THAI AND CHINESE PRESS – Thailand. Bangkok. 1965- – 1 – us UMI [072]

BANGKOK TIMES – Bangkok, Thailand. 1941-42 – 1r – 1 – us L of C Photodup [072]

Bangla Congress *see* ELECTION MANIFESTO AND IMMEDIATE PROGRAMME

Bangladesh *see* BANGLADESH GAZETTE

Bangladesh. Bureau of Statistics *see*
- BANGLADESH EDUCATION IN STATISTICS
- MANPOWER SITUATION IN CONTEMPORARY BANGLADESH

Bangladesh. Committee on Nonformal Education *see* NONFORMAL EDUCATION IN BANGLADESH

Bangladesh. Education Directorate *see* EDUCATION IN BANGLADESH

BANGLADESH EDUCATION IN STATISTICS / Bangladesh. Bureau of Statistics – Dacca, 1985 – 5mf – 9 – DE-528/1 – ne IDC [370]

BANGLADESH GAZETTE / Bangladesh – 1967- – 1 – 250.00y – us L of C Photodup [950]

BANGLADESH JOURNAL OF GERIATRICS – (See also: Pakistan Journal of Geriatrics/ Pakistan Probin Hitaishi; Probin Hitaishi Bagladesh/Journal of Geriatrics) – 1975- – 1,5,6,9 – us UMI [618]

Bangladesh. Ministry of Education *see* STATISTICAL PROFILE OF EDUCATION IN BANGLADESH

Bangladesh. National Foundation for Research on Human Resource Development *see*
- ROLE OF EDUCATION PROJECTIONS IN EDUCATIONAL PLANNING IN BANGLADESH
- TECHNICAL EDUCATION IN BANGLADESH

BANGLADESH OBSERVER – Dacca, Bangladesh. 1962-94 – 137r – 1 – us L of C Photodup [072]

Bangladesh. Planning Commission *see*
- ANNUAL DEVELOPMENT PROGRAMME 1990/91
- ANNUAL PLAN 1972-73
- ANNUAL PLAN 1973-1974
- THE FIRST FIVE YEAR PLAN, 1973-1978

BANGOR COMMERCIAL – Bangor, ME. nov 27 1949-jan 16 1954 – 1 – us Res Libr [071]

BANGOR DAILY COMMERCIAL – Bangor, ME: Marcellus Emery, 1872-nov 25 1949 – 1 – us Res Libr [071]

BANGOR DAILY NEWS – Bangor. Maine. 1970- – 1 – us UMI [071]

THE BANGOR DAILY NEWS – Bangor, ME: [Bangor Pub Co], 1900-sep 1970 – 1 – us Res Libr [071]

Bangor. Maine. Public Library *see* BIBLIOGRAPHY OF THE STATE OF MAINE

BANGOR THEOLOGICAL SEMINARY – 1956-80 (complete) – 3r – 1 – ATLA S0656 – us A.T.L.A. [073]

Bangs, Nathan *see*
- AN AUTHENTIC HISTORY OF THE MISSIONS UNDER THE CARE OF THE MISSIONARY SOCIETY OF THE METHODIST EPISCOPAL CHURCH
- A DISCOURSE ON OCCASION OF THE DEATH OF THE REVEREND WILBUR FISK
- THE ERRORS OF HOPKINSIANISM
- AN EXAMINATION OF THE DOCTRINE OF PREDESTINATION
- LETTERS TO YOUNG MINISTERS OF THE GOSPEL
- THE LIFE OF JAMES ARMINIUS
- THE NECESSITY, NATURE, AND FRUITS, OF SANCTIFICATION
- THE PRESENT STATE, PROSPECTS, AND RESPONSIBILITIES OF THE METHODIST EPISCOPAL CHURCH
- THE REFORMER REFORMED
- THE REVIEWER ANSWERED
- A VINDICATION OF THE METHODIST EPISCOPACY

BANGSA DAN KEBANGSAAN / Sastroamidjojo, Ali – SE 2139 1. 1947 – 9 – ne IDC [950]

Banier, Antoine *see* EXPLICATION HISTORIQUE DES FABLES

THE BANISHED BRITON – Toronto, 1839; ns: n4. 27 fev 1840 – 1r – 1 – Can$25.00 – cn Can Microfilming [072]

Banister, Eric *see* SPORTS MEDICINE, TRAINING AND REHABILITATION

Banister, J *see* AN ANTIDOTARIE CHYRURGICALL

Banister, R *see* A TREATISE OF ONE HUNDRED AND THIRTEENE DISEASES OF THE EYES AND EYE-LIDDES

BANK AND QUOTATION RECORD – (1979-. 5,6,9) – 1- 1928- – 1 – us UMI [336]

THE BANK AND THE PRESS / Dalam, Jusuf Muda – SE-6854 1. 1960 – 9 – ne IDC [336]

BANK CANADIAN NATIONAL MONTHLY LETTER – Montreal. v1- 1970- – 9 – Can$20.00y – cn Micromedia [073]

BANK CASES. 1878 / Moses, Raphel Jacob – New York: American Bankers' and Merchants' Agency, 1879. 148p. LL-2299 – 1 – us L of C Photodup [340]
BANK COMPLIANCE *see* ABA BANK COMPLIANCE
BANK DALAM ISLAM / Chotib, A – Tjetakan 1. Djakarta, Bulan Bintang. 1962. 104p. (Seri fiqih, no.12). SEM-2829 2830 – 9 – ne IDC [260]
BANK INDONESIA : BULLETIN – (Quarterly. Missing: 1953(1); 1956(12)) – Djakarta, 1953-1960(1-20) – 30mf – 9 – SE-260/1 – ne IDC [332]
Bank Indonesia. Djakarta *see* REPORT
BANK INSURANCE AND PROTECTION BULLETIN *see* ABA BANK SECURITY AND FRAUD PREVENTION
BANK LETTERS, BULLETINS AND REVIEWS – 1976 (77mf); 1976-77 (140mf); 1977-78 (125mf) – 9 – $5.00f – us Ross [336]
BANK MANAGEMENT *see* BANKERS MONTHLY
Bank Negara. Indonesia *see* PELAPOERAN. LAPORAN
BANK NEGARA INDONESIA UNIT 3 / Laporan Perkembangan – (Annual) – Djakarta, 1968-1969 – 3mf – 9 – SE-1335/1 – ne IDC [332]
BANK OF INDIA (LIBYA): A BRIEF HISTORY OF ITS FIRST DECADE, 1956-1966 – BNE-631 1 – 9 – ne IDC [332]
Bank of Montreal *see*
– BUSINESS REVIEW
– LIST OF STOCKHOLDERS...OF 31ST MAY, 1897
BANK OF MONTREAL BUSINESS REVIEW – (Cont by: Business Review 1984. 1948-79 Can$440.00 5) – Montreal, 1948-83 – 5,9 – Can$20.00y – cn Micromedia [338]
BANK OF MONTREAL BUSINESS REVIEW *see* BUSINESS REVIEW
Bank of Nova Scotia *see*
– MONTHLY REVIEW
BANK OF NOVA SCOTIA MONTHLY REVIEW – (Cont by: Business and Finance Report 1983) – Toronto, 1980-1982 – 5 – Can$50.00 – cn Micromedia [332]
BANK OF NOVA SCOTIA MONTHLY REVIEW *see* BUSINESS AND FINANCE REPORT
Bank of Taiwan. Economic Research Bureau *see* TAIWAN DOCUMENTS SERIES
BANK PEMBANGUNAN-DAERAH DJAWA-TIMUR / Laporan. Sekretariat D.P.R.D.G.R. – (Annual) – Surabaja, 1962-1969 – 2mf – 9 – SE-1336/1 – ne IDC [332]
BANK PROTECTION BULLETIN *see* PROTECTIVE BULLETIN
Bank Tabungan. Djakarta *see* POS. REPORT
Bank Umum Nasional *see* PERKEMBANGAN BANK UMUM NASIONAL DALAM TAHUN...
BANKER – London. v1-147 jan 1926-dec 1997+ 1; v121-147 jan 1971-dec 1997+ 5; v122-147 jan 1972-dec 1997+ 9 – 1,5,9 – D2978 – us UMI [332]
BANKERS' CIRCULAR – (Circular to Bankers). London. -w. 25 Jul 1828-25 Dec 1858. (16 reels) – 1 – uk British Libr Newspaper [073]
THE BANKERS' JOURNAL AND FINANCIAL REVIEW – Toronto: F. Weir, [1889?-189- or 19–] – 9 – cn C.I.H.M. [332]
BANKERS MAGAZINE – (Absorbed by: Banking Law Journal after June 1943; resumed independent publ with v147 1964. Cont: Bankers Weekly Circular and Statistical Record. Former title(s): Bankers Magazine and State Financial Register (jul 1846-jun 1849); Bankers Magazine and Statistical Register (jul 1849-nov 1894); Bankers Magazine (dec 1894-jun 1895); Rhodes' Journal of Banking and the Bankers' Magazine Consolidated (jul-dec 1895); Bankers Magazine (jun 1896-jun 1943)) – Boston. v1-180 jul 1846-dec 1997+ 1; v 152-180 Win 1969-dec 1997+ 5; v158-180 Win 1975-dec 1997+ 9 – 1,5,9 – D3483 – us UMI [332]
BANKERS MAGAZINE *see* BANKERS MAGAZINE
THE BANKERS' MAGAZINE – v. 1-102. 1844-1916. V. 2-3, 9, 16, 19, 94 wanting – 1 – 848.00 – us L of C Photodup [332]
BANKERS MAGAZINE AND STATE FINANCIAL REGISTER *see* BANKERS MAGAZINE
BANKERS MAGAZINE AND STATISTICAL REGISTER *see* BANKERS MAGAZINE
BANKERS MONTHLY – (Vols for 1884-97 not available for filming. Absorbed by: Bank Management. Former title(s): Rand McNally Banker's Monthly (jan 1884-mar 1917)) – New York. v15-41 jan 1898-dec 1910; ns: v28-110 jan 1911-jan 1993 1; v92-110 jan 1975-jan 1993 5,9 – 1,5,9 – D10484 – us UMI [332]
BANKERS' WEEKLY CIRCULAR AND STATISTICAL RECORD *see* BANKERS MAGAZINE
Bankes, Henry *see* HENRY BANKES'S TREATISE ON LITHOGRAPHY
BANKFREIHEIT = FREE BANKING / Horn, J E – 1867. 1 fiche (29x) – 9 – 1.00f – at Libertarian Micro [320]
BANKING – (v.65-71. 1972-79. 5,6. v.67-71. 1975-79. 9) – v.1-71. 1908-79 – 1 – us UMI [073]
BANKING *see* ABA BANKING JOURNAL
BANKING ACT OF 1809 / Mississippi Legislature – 1v (all publ) – 1mf – 9 – $1.50 – LLMC 91-069 – us L.L.M.C. [340]
BANKING AND COMMERCIAL GUIDE / Harcourt, Guy M – Houston: Dealy & Baker, 1891. 41 2, 21p. LL-417 – 1 – us L of C Photodup [340]
BANKING AND FINANCE IN RUSSIA, PART 1 : PRE-REVOLUTIONARY RUSSIA, 1860-1917 / ed by Petrov, Yuri A – (Pt 2: Post-Revolutionary Russia and the NEP Period, 1917-30) – 1995 – 2pts 147 titles – ne IDC [332]
BANKING AND INVESTMENT, 1789-1990 – (Guide only: $325.00) – 606mf – 9 – $3,605.00 – 1-55655-434-6 – us UPA [332]
BANKING CASES ANNOTATED / ed by Michie, Thomas J – (A collection of all cases affecting banks decided by the Courts of Last Resort in the US) – Charlottesville: Michie Co.. v1-5. 1898-1903 (all publ) – 9 – LLMC 84-705 – us L.L.M.C. [336]
BANKING CONTROVERSIES IN 1825 / Bowen, Ian – 1938, 21p – 9 – 1.00f – at Libertarian Micro [335]
BANKING LAW JOURNAL – (1971- . 5,6. 1975- . 9) – 1- 1889- – 1 – us UMI [336]
BANKING LAW JOURNAL – (Updates planned) – v1-25. 1889-1908 – 202mf – 9 – $303.00 – LLMC 84-412 – us L.L.M.C. [336]
BANKING LAW JOURNAL – v1-77. 1889-1960 – 9 – $1,550.00 set – us Hein [340]
THE BANKING OF CANADA AS CONNECTED WITH ITS TRADE AND COMMERCE:...31ST MARCH 1897 / Hague, George – Ottawa: Thoburn, 1897?. 05142. (Pre-1900 Canadiana) – 9 – cn C.I.H.M. [336]
BANKNOTEN, GELDUMLAUF UND DEVISENFRAGE / Rittershausen, Heinrich – 1936. Inflation, Hortung u. Wertbestaendige Rechnung, 1942. 143p. 1 fiche (29x) – 9 – 1.00f – at Libertarian Micro [320]
BANKNOTEN SIND TYPISIERTE WECHSEL UND IHRE SICHERUNG GEGEN INFLATION / Beckerath, Ulrich von – 9 – 1.00f – at Libertarian Micro [335]
BANKOVYE KOMISSIONNYE OPERATSII V SEL'SKO-KHOZIAISTVENNYKH KREDITNYKH TOVARISHCHESTVAKH / Vasys', I M – M., L., 1928 – 2mf – 9 – COR-373/1 – ne IDC [334]
BANKROTSTVO ANTIPROLETARSKIKH PARTII V GRUZII / Dzhangveladze, G A – Tbilisi, 1981. 231p – 3mf – 9 – ne IDC [320]
BANKROTSTVO BURZHUAZNYKH I MELKOBURZHUAZNYKH PARTII ROSSII V PERIOD PODGOTOVKI I POBEDY VELIKOI OKTIABR'SKOI SOTSIALISTICHESKOI REVOLIUTSII / Komin, V V – M., 1965. 644p – 7mf – 9 – ne IDC [320]
BANKROTSTVO MELKOBURZHUAZNYKH PARTII NA DONU / Sergeev, V N – Rostov n/D., 1979. 152p – 2mf – 9 – ne IDC [320]
THE BANKRUPT REGISTER – (Covers US District Courts. Cont by: National Bankruptcy Register Reports) – New York: George T Deller. v1-2 + suppl. 1867-69 (all publ) – 23mf – 9 – $34.50 – LLMC 89-201 – us L.L.M.C. [332]
THE BANKRUPT REGISTER *see* NATIONAL BANKRUPTCY REGISTER
BANKRUPTCY DEVELOPMENTS JOURNAL – Emory University. v1-11. 1984-1995 – 9 – $202.00 set – us Hein [340]
THE BANKRUPTCY MAGAZINE – (Lacking: Sep 1897) – v1 nos 1-12. Jun 1897-May 1898 (all publ) – 11mf – 9 – $16.50 – LLMC 84-413 – us L.L.M.C. [336]
BANKRUPTCY REFORM ACT OF 1978 : A LEGISLATIVE HISTORY / ed by Resnick, Alan N & Wypyski, Eugene M – (A collection of Federal legislation documents concerned with the policies and legislation intent underlying the new Act) – 17v. 1979 – 9 – $415.00 set – us Hein [340]
BANKS AND BANKING : CASE LAW AND INDEX – (A complete series of condensed reports, federal, state and English, including Canadian, Australian, New Zealand and Hawaiian reports) – New York: Case Law & Co. 1v + index vol. 1903 (all publ) – 9 – LLMC 95-120 – us L.L.M.C. [340]
Banks, Charles Edward *see*
– THE PLANTERS OF THE COMMONWEALTH: A STUDY OF THE EMIGRANTS AND EMIGRATION IN COLONIAL TIMES, 1620-1640
– THE WINTHROP FLEET OF 1630
Banks, Charles W *see*
– DIARIES, 1892, 1899, 1900, 1904
– DIARIES, 1897-1898
Banks, Edgar J *see* JONAH IN FACT AND FANCY
Banks, Florence Aiken *see* COINS OF BIBLE DAYS
BANKS HERALD – Banks, OR. -w. 1910-23 – 1 – 72.00 – us Oregon Hist [071]
BANKS HERALD – Banks, OR. -w. 21 Jan 1926-22 Dec 1927. 1 roll – 1 – us U.O. Library [071]
Banks, John Shaw *see*
– THE DEVELOPMENT OF DOCTRINE FROM THE EARLY MIDDLE AGES TO THE REFORMATION
– THE DEVELOPMENT OF DOCTRINE IN THE EARLY CHURCH
– A MANUAL OF CHRISTIAN DOCTRINE
– MARTIN LUTHER, THE PROPHET OF GERMANY
– THE TENDENCIES OF MODERN THEOLOGY
Banks, Jonathan *see* JANUAE CLAVIS: OR, LILLY'S SYNTAX EXPLAINED
Banks, Joseph *see* CORRESPONDENCE
Banks, Louis Albert *see* T. DE WITT TALMAGE
Banks, Martha Burr *see* HEROES OF THE SOUTH SEAS
Banks, N *see* CATALOGUE OF NEARCTIC SPIDERS
BANKURA DARPANA – Bankura: [s.n., feb 1892-oct 1 1893; [jun 8 1903-mar 8 1943]; apr 16 1943-apr 8 1945; may 1 1956; [jun 8 1956-sep 16 1959] – us Res Libr [071]
LE BANLIEUSARD – Ste-Foy, Canada. 4 avr 1963-v4 n32. 17 aut 1966 – 2r – 1 – Can$45.00r – cn Can Microfilming [072]
Bannantyne, William *see* POEMS AND SONGS ON VARIOUS SUBJECTS
Bannatyne, Andrew *see* JUDICIAL STATISTICS.
Banneker, Benjamin *see* A SELECTION OF WORKS BY AND ABOUT BENJAMIN BANNEKER
BANNER – Belzoni. Miss. 1919-1932 – 1 – us UMI [071]
BANNER – Bluffton. Ind. -w. 1881-82; 1900 – 1 – us UMI [071]
BANNER – Bonneville. Miss. 1915-1924 – 1 – us UMI [071]
BANNER – Cambridge. Md. 1975- – 1 – us UMI [071]
BANNER – Circle. Mont. and McCone County Sentinel. 1920-49, 1956-59, 1966-67 – 1 – us UMI [071]
BANNER – Clarksdale. Miss. 1902-1910 – 1 – us UMI [071]
BANNER – Cleveland. Tenn. 1865-83 – 1 – us UMI [071]
BANNER – Fort Scott. Kan. 1882-1884 – 1 – us UMI [071]
BANNER – Hastings. Mich. 1909-72 – 1 – us UMI [071]
BANNER – Logan. West Virginia. 1896- – 1 – us UMI [071]
BANNER – Pearl River. Miss. 1837-1859 – 1 – us UMI [071]
BANNER – Rio Vista, CA. 1919-20; 1923-24; 1926-30 – 3r – 1 BC02702 – $150.00 – us Library Micro [071]
THE BANNER – Richmond, Canada. v1 n1. 21 nov 1946 – 1r – 1 – Can$ 25.00 – cn Can Microfilming [072]
THE BANNER – Sonora, CA. 1885-95; 1898-1937 (broken file); 1936-53 – 31r – 1 BC02999 – $1,550.00 – us Library Micro [071]
BANNER COUNTY NEWS – Harrisburg, NE. -w. Nov 1894-Jul 1955 – 1 – us NE Hist [071]
BANNER COUNTY REPUBLICAN – Harrisburg, NE. -w. Nov 1895-Nov 1896, scattered issues missing – 1 – us NE Hist [071]
BANNER COURIER – Oregon City, OR. 1919-36 – 1 – 192.00 – us Oregon Hist [071]
BANNER OF ISRAEL – (Lacking: some issues and pgs) – v1-37. 1877-1913 – 16r – 1 – ATLA S0750 – us A.T.L.A. [073]
BANNER OF TRUTH – (1985-. 5,6,9) – v1-. 1935- – 1 – us UMI [240]
BANNER OF ULSTER – Belfast, Ireland. Jun 1842-Aug 1869.-w. 27 reels – 1 – uk British Libr Newspaper [072]
BANNER PRESS – David City. Neb. 1895-1961 – 1 – us UMI [071]
BANNER VON BERKS, UND WOCHENBLATT DER READING POST – (In German) – Reading, PA. 1864-1888 – 14r – 1 – $1,190.00 – D3385 – us Scholarly Res [071]
BANNER-COURIER – Oregon City, OR. -d. 4 Dec 1936 – 28 Feb 1950. 19 rolls – 1 – us U.O. Library [071]
Bannerman, Frances *see* MILESTONES: A COLLECTION OF VERSES
BANNER-PRESS – David City, NE. -w. Jan. 1895-Aug. 1897. Incomplete; Dec. 1897- – 1 – us NE Hist [071]
LA BANNIERE DE MARIE IMMACULEE – Ottawa: Peres oblats de Marie Immaculee, Juniorat du Sacrecoceur, 1893-1968 – 5r – 1 – us Res Libr [073]
BANNING AND ARDEN'S REPORTS OF PATENT CASES IN THE U.S. CIRCUIT COURTS / Banning, H A & Arden, A New York: L K Strouse. v1-5. 1874-81 (all publ) – 40mf – 9 – $60.00 – LLMC 81-430 – us L.L.M.C. [340]
Banning, Emile Theodore *see* AFRICA AND THE BRUSSELS GEOGRAPHICAL CONFERENCE
Banning, H A *see* BANNING AND ARDEN'S REPORTS OF PATENT CASES IN THE U.S. CIRCUIT COURTS
Bannister, H *see* MISSALE GOTHICUM
Bannister, J V *see* LIFE CHEMISTRY REPORTS
BANOS DE BANOS / Diaz Perez, Nicolas – 1881 – 9 – 1.50f – sp Bibl Santa Ana [810]
BANOS DE MONTEMAYOR. PUERTA DE EXTREMADURA. APUNTES 1971 / Hernandez Diaz, Erasmo – Caceres: Edit. Extremadura, 1971 – 1 – sp Bibl Santa Ana [946]
BANQUE – 1988-1995 – 2 times per yr – 6 – F2,200.00 – sz Infoprint [072]
LA BANQUE DE FRANCE EXPROPRIEE, LIQUIDEE POUR CAUSE D'UTILITE PUBLIQUE. / Gosset, P – Paris: Dubuisson, 1863. 287p. 4 fiches. (Economics Collection) – 9 – 10.00 – fr Bibl Nationale [332]
Banque d'epargne de la cite et du district de Montreal *see* CINQUANTENAIRE DE LA BANQUE D'EPARGNE..
LA BANQUE LIBRE / Courcelle-Seneuil, Jean Gustave – 1867. 359p. Together with: Was Ist Eigentliche Anarchie? (Verlag Freie Gesellschaft). 165p. 2 fiches (24x) – 9 – 1.00f – at Libertarian Micro [320]
BANQUE MAROCAINE DU COMMERCE EXTERIEUR, 1959/1969; DIX ANNEES DE DEVELOPPEMENT ECONOMIQUE / Morocco. Banque Marocaine du Commerce exterieur – 1970. BNE-3005 1 – 9 – ne IDC [332]
LA BANQUE MONDIALE ET L'EDUCATION AU MAROC / Morocco. Ministere de l'Education Nationale – 1969. BNE-3076 1 – 9 – ne IDC [324]
BANQUES ET DROIT – 1988-1995 – 2r per y – 6 – Sfr642.00 – sz Infoprint [332]
LES BANQUES ETRANGERES EN FRANCE / Dufourq-Lagelouse, L – Paris, 1922 – 2mf – 1 – ILM-3294/1 – ne IDC [327]
LE BANQUET DONNE A SIR JOHN A. MACDONALD A QUEBEC, LE 15 OCTOBRE 1879/DISCOURS. / Chapleau, Joseph Adolphe – 1879? 02570. (Pre-1900 Canadiana) – 9 – cn C.I.H.M. [971]
BANQUET OFFERT A SIR HECTOR L. LANGEVIN, MINISTRE DES TRAVAUX PUBLICS: FAR (SIC) LES CITOYENS DE MONTREAL:...LE JEUDI, 18 OCTOBRE, 1883 – Montreal: Impr. de la Minerve, 1883. 02505. (Pre-1900 Canadiana) – 9 – cn C.I.H.M. [971]
BANQUET TO GRADUATES OF MCGILL, FRIDAY, APRIL 2ND, 1880 – Montreal?, 1880?. 00914. (Pre-1900 Canadiana) – 9 – cn C.I.H.M. [370]

BANQUET TO THE HONORABLE F. N. BLAKE, AMERICAN CONSUL – Royal Hotel, Hamilton, 1st August, 1873. 02091. (Pre-1900 Canadiana) – 9 – cn C.I.H.M. [971]
BANQUETE DE CAVALLEROS Y ORDEN DE VIVIR, ANSI EN TIEMPO DE LA SANIDAD COMO EN... / Lobera de Avila, L – Alcala, 1542 – 9 – sp Cultura [615]
BANQUETE DE NOBLES CABALLEROS...E MODO DE BIVIR DESDE QUE SE LEVANTAN HASTA QUE SE ACUESTAN E TRAYA DEL REGIMIENTO CURATIVO Y PRESERVATIVO DE LAS FIEBRES PESTILENCIALES E DE LA PESTILENCIA / Lobera de Avila, L – Augsburg, 1530 – 4mf – 9 – sp Cultura [615]
Banta, D D *see* A HISTORICAL SKETCH OF JOHNSON COUNTY, INDIANA
BANTAM BUGLE – Chester, CA. 13 Nov 1963 – 1r – 1 – $50.00 – B02105 – us Library Micro [071]
BANTENG – (Lacking: 1946 v1(1-6, 8-9, 11-12, 14-17, 23)) – Solo, 1946-1947 – 7mf – 9 – ne IDC [950]
BANTER – Halifax, N.S.: Morton's News Agency, [1874-18–] – 9 – cn C.I.H.M. [072]
THE BANTU ARE COMING : PHASES OF SOUTH AFRICA'S RACE PROBLEM / Phillips, Ray Edmund – [2nd ed.] London: Student Christian Movt Press, [1930] – 1 – us Res Libr [960]
THE BANTU IN SOUTH AFRICAN LIFE / Brooks, Edgar Harry – Johannesburg: S A Institute of Race Relations, 1943 – 1 – us Res Libr [305]
BANTU MIRROR – Bulawayo. Rhodesia. Mar 1952-Jan 1962. gaps – 1 – 35.00r – us Hoover Inst Photo [072]
BANTU MIRROR – (Issues filmed as pt of: St Clair Drake Coll of Africana) – Bulawayo, Rhodesia, jul 21 1956 – us Res Libr [072]
BANTU STUDIES AND GENERAL SOUTH AFRICAN ANTHROPOLOGY / ed by Rheinallt Jones, J D – Johannesburg, 1921-1939.- v1-13 – 94mf – 8 – A-416/2 – ne IDC [306]
BANTU TALES / Price, Pattie – New York: E P Dutton, 1938 – us Res Libr [390]
BANTU WORLD – (Cont as: World. Absorbed by: Post (Transvaal). Suspended: 4 Nov 1944-2 Feb 1945) – Johannesburg, South Africa. 9 Apr 1932-28 Dec 1946 – 22r – 1, 16 diazo available at reduced price – sa SA Libr [072]
BANTUSTAN : A STUDY IN PRACTICAL APARTHEID / Kruger, J D L – Queenstown, South Africa: Daily Representative, 1951 – 1 – us Res Libr [960]
Bantysh-Kamenskii, N *see*
- DEIANIIA ZNAMENITYKH POLKOVODTSEV I MINISTROV SLUZHIVSHIKH V TSARSTVOVANIE GOSUDARIA IMPERATORA PETRA VELIKOGO
- OBZOR VNESHNIKH SNOCHENII ROSSII (PO 1800 GOD.)

Banu, CG *see* EXECUTAREA HOTARIRILOR STRAINE...
Banvard, John *see* FAMILY PAPERS
Banville, Th. de *see* PETIT TRAITE DE POESIE FRANCAISE
THE BANYANKOLE / Roscoe, J – Cambridge. 1923. BA-368 2 – 8 – ne IDC [960]
BANYARWANDA ET BARUNDI / Bourgeois, R – [Bruxelles, 1954-58] v3 – us Res Libr [960]
BAO DONG PHAP – Grand journal quotidien d'information en langue annamite. Dir. Ngo-Van-Phu. no. 3-2144. Hanoi. 12 janv 1925-32 – 1 – fr A.C.R.P.P. [072]
BAOESASTRA INDONESIA-DJAWI. TJAP-TJAPAN KAPING TIGA / Poerwadarminta, W J S – (Microfiche Nos 133-135) – Djakarta: Gunseikanbu Kokumin Tosyokyoku (Balai Poestaka), 2605 – 3mf – 9 – SE-2002/1 – ne IDC [950]
BAOTOU RIBAO = BAOTOU DAILY – China. Apr 1932-Sept 1948. M/B10 – 12r – 1 – $600.00 – cc Microforms [072]
Baour-Lormian *see* MAHOMET 2
Baour-Lormian, Pierre Marie Francois Louis *see*
- L'ATLANTIDE OU LE GEANT DE LA MONTAGNE BLEUE: POEME EN QUATRE CHANTS
- LE CLASSIQUE ET LE ROMANTIQUE: DIALOGUE

BAPARETZ = IN THE BREACH – (Hebrew-Underground) – Moscow, RU. Jul/Aug 1925 – 1r – 1 – $25.00 – cn Can Microfilming [072]
BAPTISM : WITH REFERENCE TO ITS IMPORT AND MODES / Beecher, Edward – New York: John Wiley, 1849, c1848 – 1mf – 9 – 0-8370-9363-5 – 1986-3363 – us A.T.L.A. [240]
BAPTISM AND THE REMISSION OF SINS / Mullins, E Y – 1906. A. E. Dickenson. What Baptist principles are worth to the world. 1889 – 1 – 5.00 – us Baptist [240]
BAPTISM: HOW AND FOR WHOM? / Colpitts, W W – Toronto: W. Briggs; Montreal: C. W. Coates; Halifax: S. F. Huestis, 1896. 00720. (Pre-1900 Canadiana) – 9 – cn C.I.H.M. [240]
THE BAPTISM OF FIRE : AND OTHER SERMONS / Johnston, J Wesley – Toronto: William Briggs, 1888 – 1mf – 9 – 0-8370-7296-4 – 1986-1296 – us A.T.L.A. [240]
THE BAPTISM OF ROGER WILLIAMS : A REVIEW OF REV. DR. W.H. WHITSITT'S INFERENCE / King, Henry Melville – Providence: Preston & Rounds, 1897 – 1mf – us A.T.L.A. [240]
THE BAPTISM OF THE AGES AND OF THE NATIONS / Cathcart, William – Philadelphia: American Baptist Publication Society, c1878 – 1mf – us A.T.L.A. [240]
THE BAPTISM OF THE HOLY GHOST / Mahan, Asa – New York: W.C. Palmer, jr., (c1870). viii,215p – 1 – us U.W. Library [240]
THE BAPTISMAL REMISSION THEORY / Lofton, George A – 1 – 5.00 – us Baptist [240]
THE BAPTIST – Chicago. v1-14 no 1. 1920-33 (complete) – 12r – 1 – ATLA R0142 – us A.T.L.A. [240]
THE BAPTIST – London, 1877-1905 (complete) – 10r – 1 – ATLA R0143 – us A.T.L.A. [240]
THE BAPTIST *see* THE BALTIMORE BAPTIST
BAPTIST ADULT UNION QUARTERLY – 1930-61 – 1 – 269.22 – us Baptist [240]
THE BAPTIST ADVOCATE – v1-7. May 1839-Jun 1845 (complete) – 2r – 1 – ATLA R0115 – us A.T.L.A. [240]
BAPTIST AND COMMONER – Little Rock. Arkansas. 23 Jul 1914-15 Feb 1939 – 1 – 432.33 – us Baptist [240]
BAPTIST AND REFLECTOR – Tennessee. 1835-1991 – 1 – $4,045.48 – us Baptist [240]
THE BAPTIST AND SLAVERY / Putnam, Mary B – 1840-45 – 1 – 5.00 – us Baptist [240]
BAPTIST ANNALS OF OREGON / Mattoon, C H – v. 1 and 2. 1844-1910 – 1 – 35.00 – us Baptist [240]
BAPTIST ANNUAL REGISTER / Rippon, John – 4v. 1790-1802. (Complete) – 1 – 92.68 – us Baptist [240]
BAPTIST ANNUAL REGISTER / ed by Rippon, John – London, UK. 1790-1802 – 1 – 54.15 – us A.B.H.S. [240]
BAPTIST ARGUS – Louisville. Ky. 1897-Apr 1908. and Baptist World. May 1908-19 – 1 – 966.73 – us Baptist [240]
Baptist Association *see*
- BAPTIST MESSAGES FROM RADIO HOUR AND TELEVISION
- CONFESSION OF FAITH ADOPTED BY THE BAPTIST ASSOCIATION MET AT PHILADELPHIA, A, 25 SEP 1742
- SKETCHES OF HISTORY OF THE BAPTIST CHURCHES WITHIN THE LIMITS OF THE RAPPAHANNOCK ASSOCIATIONS IN VIRGINIA
- SUMMARY OF CHURCH DISCIPLINE; DRAWN UP BY THE DIRECTION OF THE DOVER BAPTIST ASSOCIATION, VA

Baptist Association. Charleston, South Carolina *see* AN ADDRESS FROM THE CHARLESTON ASSOCIATION...CALLING FOR THE ORGANIZATION OF THE THE STATE BAPTIST CONVENTION OF SOUTH CAROLINA
Baptist Association. Connecticut *see* SECOND REPORT OF THE CONNECTICUT SOCIETY, AUXILIARY TO THE BAPTIST BOARD OF FOREIGN MISSIONS
Baptist Association. Louisiana *see*
- LUTHER RICE
- VERNON

Baptist Association. Louisiana. *see* PAPERS
Baptist Association. Rhode Island *see* SIX PRINCIPLE BAPTISTS
Baptist Association. Texas *see* DALLAS
Baptist Associations *see*
- ANNUAL
- ARKANSAS MATERIALS
- INDEX TO REGULAR AND PRIMITIVE BAPTIST ASSOCIATIONS' ANNUALS
- MISC. ANNUALS

Baptist Associations. Alabama *see* ANNUAL
Baptist Associations. Arizona *see* ANNUAL
Baptist Associations. Arkansas *see* ANNUAL
Baptist Associations. California *see* ANNUAL
Baptist Associations. Colorado, Southeastern, Arkansas Valley *see* ANNUAL
Baptist Associations. Flint River. Alabama *see* ANNUALS
Baptist Associations. Florida *see* ANNUAL
Baptist Associations. Georgia *see* ANNUAL
Baptist Associations. Illinois *see*
- ALTON INDUSTRIAL-WILLIAMSON COUNTY
- ANNUAL
- OLNEY

Baptist Associations. Illinois, Chicago Southern Baptist *see* ANNUAL
Baptist Associations. Illinois. Saline *see* ANNUALS
Baptist Associations. Indiana, Brownstown *see* ANNUAL
Baptist Associations. Kentucky *see* ANNUAL
Baptist Associations. Kentucky. Blood River *see* ANNUALS
Baptist Associations. Kentucky. Greenup *see* ANNUALS
Baptist Associations. Kentucky, Laurel River *see* ANNUAL
Baptist Associations. Louisiana *see* ANNUAL
Baptist Associations, Maine. Androscroggin Free Will Baptist and United Baptist Annual Meetings *see* MINUTES
Baptist Associations, Maine. Androscroggin Free Will Baptist Quarterly Meeting *see* RECORDS
Baptist Associations, Maine. Anson Free Will Baptist Quarterly Meeting *see* RECORDS
Baptist Associations, Maine. Bowdoinham Free Will Baptist Quarterly Meeting *see*
- MINUTES
- RECORDS

Baptist Associations, Maine. Bowdoinham Free Will Baptist Yearly Meeting *see* RECORDS
Baptist Associations, Maine. Cumberland Baptist Association. *see*
- RECORDS

Baptist Associations, Maine. Eastern Free Will Baptist Quarterly Conference *see* RECORDS
Baptist Associations, Maine. Eastern Maine Baptist Association. Bible and Religious Tract Society *see* MINUTES
Baptist Associations, Maine. Ellsworth Free Will Baptist Quarterly Meeting *see* RECORDS
Baptist Associations, Maine. Exeter Free Will Baptist Quarterly Meeting *see* RECORDS
Baptist Associations, Maine. Hancock Baptist Association *see* RECORDS
Baptist Associations, Maine. Kennebec Baptist Association. Woman's Baptist Foreign Missionary Society *see* RECORDS
Baptist Associations, Maine. Kennebec Free Will Baptist Yearly Meeting *see* MINUTES
Baptist Associations, Maine. Lincoln Baptist Association *see* MINUTES
Baptist Associations, Maine. Lincoln Baptist Association. *see* RECORDS
Baptist Associations, Maine. Maine Central Free Will Baptist Yearly Meeting *see* RECORDS
Baptist Associations, Maine. Maine Eastern Free Will Baptist Yearly Meeting *see* RECORDS
Baptist Associations, Maine. Maine Free Baptist Association. Annual Meeting *see* MINUTES
Baptist Associations, Maine. Oxford Free Will Baptist Quarterly Meeting *see* RECORDS
Baptist Associations, Maine. Oxford Free Will Baptist Yearly Meeting *see* RECORDS
Baptist Associations, Maine. Parsonfield Free Will Baptist Quarterly Meeting *see* RECORDS
Baptist Associations, Maine. Penobscot Baptist Association. Female Missionary Society *see* RECORDS
Baptist Associations, Maine. Penobscot Free Will Baptist Yearly Meeting *see* RECORDS
Baptist Associations, Maine. Penobscot Free Will Baptist Yearly Meeting. Ministers' Conference *see* RECORDS
Baptist Associations, Maine. South Aroostook Free Will Baptist Quarterly Meeting *see* RECORDS
Baptist Associations, Maine. Waterville Free Will Baptist Quarterly Meeting *see* RECORDS
Baptist Associations, Maine. Western Free Will Baptist Quarterly Conference *see* RECORDS
Baptist Associations. Maryland *see* ANNUAL
Baptist Associations. Michigan, Motor Cities *see* ANNUAL
Baptist Associations. Mississippi *see* ANNUAL
Baptist Associations. Missouri *see*
- ANNUAL
- ELEVEN POINTS RIVER, SHANNON COUNTY

Baptist Associations. Missouri, Bethel Association, United Baptist *see* ANNUAL
Baptist Associations. Missouri, Meramec Landmark Baptist Association *see* ANNUAL
Baptist Associations. Missouri, Mineral Area *see* ANNUAL
Baptist Associations, New Hampshire. Belknap Association of Free Will Baptist Churches *see* RECORDS
Baptist Associations, New Hampshire. Belknap Association of Free Will Baptist Churches. Woman's Missionary Society *see* RECORDS
Baptist Associations, New Hampshire. Belknap Free Will Baptist Quarterly Meeting *see* RECORDS
Baptist Associations, New Hampshire. Portsmouth Baptist Association *see* RECORDS
Baptist Associations, New Hampshire. Sandwich Free Will Baptist Quarterly Meeting. Ministers Conference *see* RECORDS
Baptist Associations. New Mexico *see*
- ANNUAL

Baptist Associations. New Mexico, Santa Fe *see* ANNUAL
Baptist Associations. New York and Vermont. Miscellaneous Associations *see* ANNUAL
Baptist Associations. North Carolina *see* ANNUAL
Baptist Associations. North Carolina, Chowan Association *see* ANNUAL
Baptist Associations. North Carolina, Eastern Association *see* ANNUAL
Baptist Associations. North Carolina, Flat River Association *see* ANNUAL
Baptist Associations. North Carolina, Tar River Association *see* ANNUAL
Baptist Associations. Ohio *see* ANNUAL
Baptist Associations. Oklahoma *see* ANNUAL
Baptist Associations, Pennsylvania. Beaver Baptist Association *see* MANUSCRIPT MINUTES
Baptist Associations. Pennsylvania, Philadelphia Baptist Association *see* ANNUAL
Baptist Associations, Pennsylvania. Redstone Baptist Association *see* MANUSCRIPT MINUTES
Baptist Associations. Primitive: Alabama, 1848-1955 *see* ANNUAL
Baptist Associations. Primitive: Arkansas, California, Arizona, Delaware, 1844-1950 *see* ANNUAL
Baptist Associations. Primitive: Florida, 1874-1949 *see* ANNUAL
Baptist Associations. Primitive: Georgia, 1810-1952 *see* ANNUAL
Baptist Associations. Primitive: Illinois, Iowa, Indiana, Kansas, 1845-1951 (Incomplete) *see* ANNUAL
Baptist Associations. Primitive: Kentucky *see* ANNUAL
Baptist Associations. Primitive: Louisiana, Maine, Maryland, Michigan, Mississippi, Missouri, New York, Nebraska *see* ANNUAL
Baptist Associations. Primitive: North Carolina *see* ANNUAL
Baptist Associations. Primitive: Ohio, Oklahoma, Pennsylvania, South Carolina *see* ANNUAL
Baptist Associations. Primitive: Tennessee *see* ANNUAL
Baptist Associations. Primitive: Texas *see* ANNUAL
Baptist Associations. Primitive: Virginia, West Virginia *see* ANNUAL
Baptist Associations. South Carolina *see* ANNUAL
Baptist Associations. South Carolina, Edgefield, Quarterly Meetings *see* ANNUAL
Baptist Associations. Tennesse. Sweetwater/Eastanalle *see* ANNUALS
BAPTIST ASSOCIATIONS. TENNESSEE = CONCORD – (1909-56. 32.48; 1) – 1812-1908 – 1 – 32.48 – us Baptist [240]
Baptist Associations. Tennessee *see* ANNUAL

Baptist Associations. Tennessee. Big Hatchie *see* ANNUALS
Baptist Associations. Tennessee. Concord *see* ANNUALS
Baptist Associations. Texas *see*
- ANNUAL
- RED FORK, SALT FORK, AND WICHITA-ARCHER-CLAY BAPTIST ASSOCIATIONS. TEXAS

Baptist Associations. Texas, Liberty *see* ANNUAL
Baptist Associations. Utah-Idaho, Treasure Valley *see* ANNUALS
Baptist Associations. Virginia *see* ANNUAL
Baptist Associations. Washington, Mount Pleasant *see* ANNUAL
Baptist Associations. Washington, Puget Sound *see* ANNUAL
BAPTIST BANNER – Atlanta/Augusta, GA. By James N. Ells. Dec 1862-Feb 1865. Scattered issues – 1 – 16.15 – us A.B.H.S. [073]
BAPTIST BANNER – Huntington, WV. Baptist General Association of West Virginia. 1891, 1893-97, 1898/99. Single reels available – 1 – 200.00 – us A.B.H.S. [073]
BAPTIST BANNER – Illinois. 1877-79, 1887-88 – 1 – 132.05 – us Baptist [240]
BAPTIST BANNER AND WESTERN PIONEER – v4-12. 1838-45 (incomplete) – 2r – 1 – ATLA R0128 – us A.T.L.A. [240]
BAPTIST BASKET – Louisville, Kentucky. v.9-15. 1881-94. v.15 incomplete – 1 – us Baptist [240]
BAPTIST BEACON – Vinita. Oklahoma. Sep, Apr 1949, Jan, Apr 1950 – 1 – 5.00 – us Baptist [240]
THE BAPTIST BEACON – Salem, Albany, McMinnville, Oregon. 1877-79. 33,710pp – 1 – 1179.85 – us Baptist [240]
A BAPTIST BIBLIOGRAPHY / Whitely, W T – v. 1 and 2. 1526-1837 – 1 – 18.20 – us Baptist [240]
BAPTIST BIOGRAPHY, BIBLICAL RECORDER, OBITUARY NOTICES, 1835-1904 – 607p – 1 – 21.24 – us Baptist [240]
BAPTIST BOYS AND GIRLS – 1904-22 – 1 – 136.92 – us Baptist [240]
Baptist Brazilian Convention *see* PROCEEDINGS
BAPTIST BUILDERS IN LOUISIANA / ed by Durham, John Pinckney & Ramond, John S – (448p) – Shreveport: Durham-Ramond, 1934 – 1 reel – 1 – $17.92 – us Baptist [240]
BAPTIST BULLETIN – Grand Rapids. Michigan. v. 1. 1933-May 1967 – 1 – 377.23 – us Baptist [240]
A BAPTIST CENTURY AROUND THE ALAMO / San Antonio Baptist Association – 1858-1958. 212p – 1 – 7.42 – us Baptist [240]
BAPTIST CHALLENGE – Little Rock. Arkansas. v. 1-7. 1961-Mar 1967 – 1 – 7.49 – us Baptist [240]
BAPTIST CHORALS – Published by Lorenz Publication. 1888 – 1 – 5.00 – us Baptist [240]
BAPTIST CHRONICLE – Louisiana. 1888-1919; Baptist Message. 1920-82 – 1 – 1,975.08 – us Baptist [240]
BAPTIST CHRONICLE AND LITERARY REGISTER – Ky. v. 1-3. 1830-32 – 1 – 33.60 – us Baptist [240]
BAPTIST CHURCH AND ASSOCIATIONS. MAINE : CHURCH RECORDS – 10 reels. 9455p – 1 – us Baptist [240]
BAPTIST CHURCH DISCIPLINE, BROADMAN PRESS, NASHVILLE, TENNESSEE / Garrett, James L, Jr – 1 – 5.00 – us Baptist [240]
BAPTIST CHURCH IN THE GREAT VALLEY. VALLEY FORGE, PENNSYLVANIA : CHURCH RECORDS – 1720-1942 – 1 – 102.96 – us Baptist [240]
BAPTIST CHURCH OF CHRIST AT BERRYVILLE. CLARK COUNTY. BERRYVILLE, VIRGINIA : CHURCH RECORDS – 1841-60 – 1 – 9.72 – us Baptist [240]
THE BAPTIST CHURCH OF CHRIST AT WOODBURY. WOODBURY, TENNESSEE : CHURCH RECORDS – Oct 1844-Feb 1888 – 1 – $11.52 – us Baptist [240]
THE BAPTIST CHURCH OF CHRIST CALLED PROVIDENCE ON BIG RIVER. WASHINGTON, MISSOURI : CHURCH RECORDS – 11 Sep 1831-Feb 1894 – 1 – $13.23 – us Baptist [240]
BAPTIST CHURCH OF JESUS CHRI LOUISVILLE, KENTUCKY : CHURCH RECORDS – 24 Oct 1830-Mar 1840. Later became Walnut Street Baptist Church – 1 – 5.00 – us Baptist [240]
BAPTIST CHURCH OF NASHVILLE (THE OLD SCHOOL BAPTISTS). NASHVILLE, TENNESSEE : CHURCH RECORDS – 3 May 1838, Jun 1839-22, Feb 1878 – 1 – $10.62 – us Baptist [240]
BAPTIST CHURCH POLITY, DOCTRINES, CONFESSION OF FAITH – 1853-90.Ten tracts – 1 – 16.31 – us Baptist [240]
BAPTIST CHURCH, POLITY, DOCTRINES, CONFESSION OF FAITH – 1845-75.Nine authors – 1 – 16.24 – us Baptist [240]
BAPTIST CHURCHES OF EAST TENNESSEE : CHURCH GENEALOGY, TABULAR FORM / Toomey, Glenn – 5r – 1 – $278.91 – us Baptist [240]
BAPTIST CONFESSIONS OF FAITH / McGlothlin, William Joseph – 1911 – 1 – 13.72 – us Baptist [240]
BAPTIST CONGRESS : PROCEEDINGS / Baptist Congress – 1882-1913 (complete) – 3r – 1 – ATLA R0116 – us A.T.L.A. [240]
Baptist Congress *see*
- BAPTIST CONGRESS
- PROCEEDINGS

BAPTIST COUNCILS IN AMERICA : A HISTORICAL STUDY OF THEIR ORIGIN AND THE PRINCIPLES OF THEIR DEVELOPMENT / Allison, William Henry – Chicago: G.K. Hazlitt,1906 – 1mf – us A.T.L.A. [240]
BAPTIST COURIER – South Carolina. 1869-1991. The Working Christian: 1869-77 – 1 – $4,284.60 – us Baptist [240]
THE BAPTIST COURIER – 1869-1914 (complete)) – 7r – 1 – ATLA R0140 – us A.T.L.A. [240]
BAPTIST DIGEST – Kansas. 3 Dec 1945-1991 – 1 – $447.36 – us Baptist [240]
BAPTIST DISHONESTY: MISQUOTATIONS AND OTHER GROSS MISREPRESENTATIONS IN THE RECENT PAMPHLET ON BAPTISM OF THE BAPTIST MINISTER, REV. A. A. CAMERON, OF OTTAWA / Bethune, John – Ottawa: J. Durie, 1876? 00103. (Pre-1900 Canadiana) – 9 – cn C.I.H.M. [240]
Baptist, Edward *see*
- DIARY
- LETTERS TO THE PAMPHLETEER

Baptist Faith and Message Committee *see* FILES
BAPTIST FAMILY IN GLOBAL VILLAGE – 180p – 1 – 6.30 – us Baptist [240]
BAPTIST FAMILY IN GLOBAL VILLAGE / ed by Langley, Thelma – 180p – 1 – 6.30 – us Baptist [240]
BAPTIST FAMILY MAGAZINE – (Ceased publ: Apr 1861) – 1857-Apr 1861 (complete) – 1r – 1 – ATLA R0101 – us A.T.L.A. [240]
BAPTIST FIDELITY – Published by Conservative Baptists. Jan, Mar, May, Jul 1948 – 1 – 5.00 – us Baptist [240]
Baptist General Association. Kentucky. Executive Board *see* MINUTES
THE BAPTIST GENERAL CONVENTION AND ITS WORK / Gambrell, James Bruton – 1918. 18p – 1 – 5.00 – us Baptist [240]
Baptist General Missionary Convention. Board of Foreign Missions *see*
- MINUTES OF THE TRIENNIAL CONVENTION
- MINUTES OF TRIENNIAL CONVENTION
- PROCEEDINGS OF TRIENNIAL CONVENTION

THE BAPTIST HARMONY / Burdett, Staunton S – 1834 – 1 – 15.96 – us Baptist [240]
THE BAPTIST HARMONY / Burdett, Staunton S – 1842 – 1 – 5.00 – us Baptist [240]
THE BAPTIST HARP / American Baptist Publication Society – 1849 – 1 – us Baptist [240]
THE BAPTIST HERALD – Cleveland, Ohio. 1923-72. 24,928p – 1 – 872.48 – us Baptist [240]
BAPTIST HISTORY / Wamble, Hugh – Research cards. 2740p – 5 – us Baptist [240]
THE BAPTIST HISTORY OF SOUTH DAKOTA / Shanafelt, T M – South Dakota Baptist Convention, 1899. South Dakota Reel 5. (The Cox Library Collection) – 5 – us Americana [978]
BAPTIST HOME MISSION MONTHLY *see* AMERICAN BAPTIST
THE BAPTIST HOME MISSION MONTHLY – v1-31. 1878-1909 (complete) – 7r – 1 – ATLA R0134 – us A.T.L.A. [240]
BAPTIST HOME MISSIONS IN NORTH AMERICA : INCLUDING A FULL REPORT OF THE PROCEEDINGS AND ADDRESSES OF THE JUBILEE MEETING... – New York: Baptist Home Mission Rooms, 1883 – 2mf – 9 – 0-8370-6153-9 – 1986-0153 – us A.T.L.A. [240]
BAPTIST HORIZON AND BULLETINS ON CANADIAN SOUTHERN BAPTISTS – Vancouver. British Columbia. Oct 1954-56; Bulletins. 1957, 1959 – 1 – $5.00 – us Baptist [240]
BAPTIST HOUR MESSAGES FROM RADIO AND TELEVISION – 1941-53. Fort Worth, Texas. 3470p – 1 – 254.38 – us Baptist [240]
BAPTIST HYMN AND TUNE BOOK – Plymouth collection, New York. 1868 – 1 – $22.47 – us Baptist [780]
THE BAPTIST HYMN BOOK / Biddle, William P & Newborn, William – 694p – 1 – $24.29 – us Baptist [780]
THE BAPTIST HYMN BOOK / Buck, William Calmes – Original and selected in two parts – 1 – $24.67 – us Baptist [780]
BAPTIST HYMN COLLECTION – (Includes: Broadus, Andrew. Collections of Sacred Ballads. 1790. Fuller, Richard and Jeter, J.B. The Psalmist with Supplement. 1847; The Psalmist, with Music...1860) – From the New Orleans Baptist Theological Seminary. 1790-1877 – 6168p – 1 – $154.20 – us Baptist [780]
BAPTIST HYMN WRITERS AND THEIR HYMNS / Burrage, Henry S – Portland, Me.: Brown Thurston, c1888 – 2mf – us A.T.L.A. [780]
BAPTIST HYMNODY IN THE UNITED STATES COLLECTION – 1616-1901 – 9 – ne IDC [240]
BAPTIST HYMNODY IN THE U.S. : SELECTED TITLES FROM THE HYMNAL COLLECTION OF SOUTHERN BAPTIST THEOLOGICAL SEMINARY – (14,480p) – 1616-1905 – 10r – 1 – $651.60 – us Baptist [240]
THE BAPTIST INFORMER, BULLETIN / Fairmont. North Carolina. First Baptist Church – 1935-69.5034p – 1 – 226.53 – us Baptist [240]
BAPTIST INTERMEDIATE UNION QUARTERLY 1 AND 2 – Intermediate B.Y.P.U. Quarterly. 1922-39. Baptist Intermediate Union Quarterly. 1940-51. Baptist Intermediate Union Quarterly, 1 and 2. 1952-61. – 1 – $299.81 – us Baptist [240]
The Baptist Joint Committee on Public Affairs *see* REPORT FROM THE CAPITAL
THE BAPTIST JUBILEE MEMORIAL / Winks, Joseph F – 1842 – 1 – 5.00 – us Baptist [240]
BAPTIST LANDMARKISM TESTED BY LOGIC, HISTORY AND SCRIPTURE / Averill, A M – 1880 – 1 – 5.00 – us Baptist [240]
BAPTIST LEADER – v1-30. 1939-69 (complete) – 30r – 1 – ATLA S0177 – us A.T.L.A. [073]
BAPTIST MANUSCRIPTS FOR THE MENNONITE SEMINARY LIBRARY – Amsterdam. 20 letters and documents from the Seventeenth Century. 156p – 1 – 5.46 – us Baptist [240]
BAPTIST MANUSCRIPTS FROM THE MENNONITE SEMINARY LIBRARY, AMSTERDAM – 20 letters and documents. 156p – 1 – us Baptist [240]
BAPTIST MARRIED YOUNG PEOPLE – Oct 1956-61 – 1 – 57.40 – us Baptist [240]
BAPTIST MEMORIAL AND MONTHLY CHRONICLE – Baptist Memorial and Monthly Record/ American Baptist Memorial. New York, 1842-56.Single reels available – 1 – 160.20 – us A.B.H.S. [073]
BAPTIST MESSAGE – Alexandria. La. -w. 1957-63 – 1 – us UMI [071]
THE BAPTIST MESSAGE – Louisiana. 1888-1991. Continues: The Baptist Chronicle, 1888-1919. 62,529p – 1 – $2,501.16 – us Baptist [240]
BAPTIST MESSAGES FROM RADIO HOUR AND TELEVISION / Baptist Association – 1954-1977 – 1 – 132.93 – us Baptist [240]
BAPTIST MESSENGER – Oklahoma. May 1912-91 – 1 – $2,688.40 – us Baptist [240]
Baptist Missionary and Educational Convention. Indian Territory *see* PAPERS
Baptist Missionary and Educational Convention. Oklahoma and Indian Territories *see* PAPERS
BAPTIST MISSIONARY ASSOCIATION OF AMERICA DIRECTORY AND HANDBOOK – 1961-92 – 1 – $204.80 – us Baptist [240]
BAPTIST MISSIONARY ASSOCIATION OF AMERICA YEARBOOK – Jacksonville, TX, 1950-1991 – 1 – $529.11 – us Baptist [240]
Baptist Missionary Association. Texas *see* PAPERS
BAPTIST MISSIONARY MAGAZINE *see* AMERICAN BAPTIST
Baptist Missionary Society. Archives. London *see*
- AMALGAMATION OF THE GENERAL AND PARTICULAR BAPTIST IN ENGLAND
- HANSERD KNOLLYS SOCIETY MATERIALS
- LONDON BAPTIST ASSOCIATION

BAPTIST MISSIONARY SOCIETY ARCHIVES. LONDON. INVENTORY (MS) TO ARCHIVES. ZUG, 1978 – 7mf – 9 – ne IDC [240]
Baptist Missionary Society. London *see*
- ARCHIVES, 1792-1914
- INDEX TO ARCHIVES
- REPORTS

BAPTIST MONITOR AND POLITICAL COMPILER – Ky. 1823-24 – 1 – 5.00 – us Baptist [240]
BAPTIST NEW MEXICAN – 1909-11; 15 Feb 1919-1991 – 1 – $1,668.48 – us Baptist [240]
BAPTIST NEWS – Illinois. 1895-1902 – 1 – 96.91 – us Baptist [240]
Baptist North America General Conference *see* ANNUAL REPORTS
BAPTIST OBSERVER – Indianapolis and Greensburg/Seymour. Indiana Baptist Convention. Sept 1902-1968. Single reels available – 1 – 907.80 – us A.B.H.S. [073]
BAPTIST PAMPHLETS – St. Louis. Mo. Mercantile Library. v. 1-9 – 1 – 158.96 – us Baptist [240]
BAPTIST PEACEMAKER – Louisville, KY. v1-5. 1980-Spring 1992 – 1 – $24.40 – us Baptist [071]
BAPTIST PRESS NEWS RELEASES – 1954-64. 4958p – 1 – us Baptist [240]
BAPTIST PROGRAM – 1923-1952-1970 – 1 – 317.17 – us Baptist [240]
THE BAPTIST PSALMODY / Manly, Basil Jr. & Manly, Basil Sr. – (1855 ed. $27.09. 1859 ed. $27.09) – 1850 – 1 – $27.09 – us Baptist [240]
BAPTIST RECORD – 1836-49 (complete) – 2r – 1 – ATLA R0111 – us A.T.L.A. [240]
BAPTIST RECORD – Mississippi. Feb 1877-1991 – 1 – $2,627.68 – us Baptist [240]
BAPTIST REFORMATION REVIEW – Nashville, TN. v2-5, 1973-76 – 1 – us A.B.H.S. [073]
BAPTIST REFORMATION REVIEW – v1-11. 1972-82 – 1 – us UMI [240]
THE BAPTIST REPORTER – London, Ont.: [s.n., 1893?-189- or 19–] – 9 – cn C.I.H.M. [240]
BAPTIST REVIEW – 1836-92. (Christian Review. 1836-63. Bibliotheca Sacra. 1863-66. Baptist Quarterly. 1867-77. Baptist Review. 1879-92) – 1 – 1194.20 – us Baptist [240]
BAPTIST SENTINEL – Dayton, Washington and Dallas, Oregon 1894 (Dec. 27, only) 1899 – 1 – 83.72 – us Baptist [240]
BAPTIST SENTINEL – Louisville. Ky. v. 1-2. 1870-71 – 1 – 31.50 – us Baptist [240]
BAPTIST SONGSTER OR DIVINE SONGS – Comp. by R. Winchell. 1829 – 1 – 8.05 – us Baptist [240]
Baptist Southern Convention *see*
- BULLETINS
- INDEX
- MINUTES

BAPTIST STANDARD – Nashville. Tenn. 1858-60 – 1 – 13.86 – us Baptist [240]
BAPTIST STANDARD – Texas. 1892-1990 – 1 – $4100.40 – us Baptist [240]
Baptist State Conventions (American Baptist). Connecticut *see* RECORDS
Baptist State Conventions. (American Baptist). Connecticut *see* ANNUAL
Baptist State Conventions (American Baptist). Maine *see*
- RECORDS
- SCRAPBOOK

Baptist State Conventions (American Baptist). New Hampshire. Board of Promotion *see* RECORDS
Baptist State Conventions (American Baptist). Oregon. Baptist Convention of the North Pacific Coast and Oregon Baptist Convention *see* MINUTES, MISSION BOARD
Baptist State Conventions. (American Baptist). Pennsylvania *see* ANNUAL
Baptist State Conventions (American Baptist). South Dakota *see* RECORDS
Baptist State Conventions (American Baptist). Vermont *see* BOARD OF TRUSTEES, RECORDS
Baptist State Conventions. Kentucky *see* ANNUAL
Baptist State Conventions. Louisiana *see* ANNUAL
Baptist State Conventions. (Southern Baptist). Alabama *see* ANNUAL

Baptist State Conventions. (Southern Baptist). Alaska *see* ANNUAL

Baptist State Conventions. (Southern Baptist). Arizona *see* ANNUAL

Baptist State Conventions. (Southern Baptist). Arkansas *see* ANNUAL

Baptist State Conventions. (Southern Baptist). California *see* ANNUAL

Baptist State Conventions. (Southern Baptist). District of Columbia *see* ANNUAL

Baptist State Conventions. (Southern Baptist). Florida *see* ANNUAL

Baptist State Conventions. (Southern Baptist). Georgia *see* ANNUAL

Baptist State Conventions. (Southern Baptist). Illinois *see*
- ANNUAL

Baptist State Conventions. (Southern Baptist). Kentucky *see* ANNUAL

Baptist State Conventions. (Southern Baptist). Louisiana *see* ANNUAL

Baptist State Conventions. (Southern Baptist). Maryland *see* ANNUAL

Baptist State Conventions. (Southern Baptist). Mississippi *see* ANNUAL

Baptist State Conventions. (Southern Baptist). Missouri *see* ANNUAL

Baptist State Conventions. (Southern Baptist). New Mexico *see* ANNUAL

Baptist State Conventions. (Southern Baptist). North Carolina *see* ANNUAL

Baptist State Conventions. (Southern Baptist). Ohio *see* ANNUAL

Baptist State Conventions. (Southern Baptist). Oklahoma *see* ANNUAL

Baptist State Conventions. (Southern Baptist). South Carolina *see* ANNUAL

Baptist State Conventions. (Southern Baptist). Tennessee *see*
- ANNUAL
- PROCEEDINGS

Baptist State Conventions. (Southern Baptist). Texas *see* ANNUAL

Baptist State Conventions. (Southern Baptist). Virginia *see*
- ANNUAL
- CORRESPONDENCE

BAPTIST STUDENT – 1922-61 – 1 – 487.06 – us Baptist [240]

BAPTIST SUNDAY SCHOOL CONVENTION / Union County. South Carolina – 1887-92. 114p – 1 – 5.00 – us Baptist [240]

BAPTIST TIMES – London. 1857-1950 – 1. 2835.00; ; 1 – 47.25r – us Baptist [240]

THE BAPTIST TIMES – Journal of the Baptist Movement 1871-1992 continued annually 92 reels – £3,950.00 – uk World [240]

BAPTIST TRAINING UNION MAGAZINE – 1926-61 – 1 – 689.08 – us Baptist [240]

BAPTIST TRIBUNE – Texas. 8 Jan 1903-18 Apr 1907 – 1 – 62.79 – us Baptist [240]

Baptist Triennial Convention *see* PROCEEDINGS

Baptist Triennial Convention. Board of Foreign Missions of the Baptist General Missionary Convention *see* MINUTES

BAPTIST TRUE UNION – Columbia, MD. 1917-91. Continues: Maryland Baptist Church Life, 1917-34; Maryland Baptist, 1935-84 – 1 – $874.96 – us Baptist [240]

BAPTIST TRUMPET – 1895-1940 (broken file) – 1 – 13.79 – us Baptist [240]

BAPTIST TRUMPET – Killeen/Maud, TX. Old School or Primitive Baptist. 1937-71. Single reels available. Incomplete – 1 – 170.20 – us A.B.H.S. [073]

BAPTIST UNION HANDBOOK – 1877-1963. Pub. by T. H. Crocott, Johannesburg, Africa – 1 – 218.89 – us Baptist [240]

BAPTIST VISITOR – Newton and Dover, MD. 1866-77. Incomplete. 96p – 1 – us Baptist [240]

BAPTIST VISITOR *see* THE CANADIAN MISSIONARY LINK

Baptist Woman's Missionary Union. Auxiliary to Southern Baptist Convention *see*
- ANNUALS
- YEARBOOKS

Baptist Woman's Missionary Union. Kentucky *see* ANNUAL

Baptist Woman's Missionary Union. Louisiana *see* ANNUAL

Baptist Woman's Missionary Union. Mississippi *see* ANNUAL

Baptist Woman's Missionary Union. South Carolina *see* ANNUAL

Baptist Woman's Missionary Union. Spartan Woman's Missionary Union, Auxiliary to Spartan Baptist Association *see* MINUTES

Baptist Woman's Missionary Union. Texas, Henderson County *see* ANNUAL

BAPTIST WORLD ALLIANCE : PROCEEDINGS / Baptist World Alliance – 1905-75 (complete) – 3r – 1 – ATLA R0117 – us A.T.L.A. [240]

Baptist World Alliance *see*
- BAPTIST WORLD ALLIANCE
- RELIEF LEDGERS
- STUDY PAPERS

Baptist World Alliance. Administrative and Executive Committees *see* MINUTES

Baptist World Alliance. Advisory Committee *see* MINUTES

Baptist World Alliance. Committee on Relief and Development *see* MINUTES

Baptist World Alliance. Continental Committee *see* MINUTES

Baptist World Alliance, Fifth Congress, Berlin *see* PAPERS

Baptist World Alliance. North American Baptist Fellowship *see* MINUTES

BAPTIST YOUNG PEOPLE – 1904-61. (B.Y.P.U. Quarterly. 1904-28. Senior B.Y.P.U. Quarterly. 1929-39. Baptist Young People's Quarterly. 1940-55. Baptist Young People. 1956-.) – 1 – 457.80 – us Baptist [240]

O BAPTISTA AMAZONENSE : ORGAM DE PROPAGANDA DA PRIMEIRA EGREJA BAPTISTA – Manaus, Amazonas. 1 Jun 1919-Set 1920; 7 Set 1922 – 1,5,6 – bl Biblioteca [072]

O BAPTISTA AMAZONICO : ORGAO OFFICIAL DA CONVENCAO BAPTISTA DA AMAZONIA – Manaos, Amazonas. Mar-Abr, Out 1928; Set-Out 1933 – 1,5,6 – bl Biblioteca [072]

BAPTISTERNES UGEBLAD – (Danish Baptist). 1851-1961 – 1 – 1228.50 – us Baptist [240]

BAPTISTI USUUGINGU (KOGUDUSE) POHIKIRI = STATUTES OF THE BAPTIST UNION (CHURCH) – (One part of a two-part item) – Keilas, Estonia: "Kulwaja" trukk, 1926 – 1r – 1 – $5.00 – us Baptist [240]

THE BAPTISTS / Rumble, L – 1 – 5.00 – us Baptist [240]

THE BAPTISTS : THEIR ORIGIN, CONTINUITY, PRINCIPLES, SPIRIT, POLITY, POSITION, AND INFLUENCE : A VINDICATION / Jones, T G – Philadelphia: American Baptist Publication Society, [1860?] – 1mf – us A.T.L.A. [240]

THE BAPTISTS AND THE AMERICAN REVOLUTION / Cathcart, William – Philadelphia: S.A. George, 1876 – 1mf – us A.T.L.A. [976]

THE BAPTISTS AND THE NATIONAL CENTENARY : A RECORD OF CHRISTIAN WORK, 1776-1876 / Weston, David; ed by Moss, Lemuel – Philadelphia: American Baptist Publication Society, 1876 – 1mf – us A.T.L.A. [240]

THE BAPTISTS IN AMERICA / Cox, F A & Hoby, J – 1836 – 1 – 17.01 – us Baptist [240]

BAPTISTS IN ROMANIA PAMPHLET COLLECTION – 1973 – 1 – CSUXANL2849-B – us Hoover Inst Photo [240]

THE BAPTISTS OF CANADA : A HISTORY OF THEIR PROGRESS AND ACHIEVEMENTS / ed by Fitch, E R – Toronto: Standard, c1911. (Mission study text book; no. 1) – 1mf – us A.T.L.A. [240]

BAPTISTS, THE ONLY THOROUGH RELIGIOUS REFORMERS / Adams, John Quincy – rev enl ed. New York: Sheldon, 1876 – 1mf – 9 – 0-8370-8880-1 – 1986-2880 – us A.T.L.A. [240]

BAPTISTS, THOROUGH RELIGIOUS REFORMERS / Adams, John Quincy – 1857 – 1 – 5.88 – us Baptist [240]

BAPTISTS TODAY – Decatur, GA. 1983-91. 2,392p. Formerly: SBC Today – 1 – $95.68 – us Baptist [073]

BAPTISTS' WHY AND WHY NOT / Frost, J M et al – 1900 – 1 – $16.03 – us Baptist [240]

BAPTISTU ZIHNAS LIHDSEKTI : ATBILDE KRIMULDAS LUTERANU MAHZITAJAM J. EHRMANA KUNGAM / Inkins, J – Riga: J.A. Freij, 1910. Publ. No. 6298 e. One of five items on a reel – 1 – us Baptist [240]

BAPTISTY (SHTUNDISTY) NA KAVKAZE = BAPTISTS (STUNDISTS) IN THE CAUCASUS – Kiev, 1885 – 1 – 5.00 – us Baptist [240]

BAPTIZING AND TEACHING: EVANS' NEW EXPOSITION OF RITUAL BAPTISM AND OF BAPTISM WITH THE HOLY SPIRIT, AS SEEN WHEN SET BACK IN THEIR RIGHT PLACES IN THE GREAT SYSTEM OF REVEALED TRUTH.. / Evans, John Swanton – Toronto: W. Briggs; Montreal: C. Coates: Halifax N.S.: S. Heustis, 1887. 02925. (Pre-1900 Canadiana) – 9 – cn C.I.H.M. [971]

Baquerizas, Jose Manuel *see* POR QUE SE CREY O EN PERON

Baquol *see* DICTIONNAIRE TOPOGRAPHIQUE, HISTORIQUE ET STATISTIQUE DU HAUT ET DU BAS RHIN

THE BAR *see* WEST VIRGINIA LAW REVIEW

THE BAR *see*
- WEST VIRGINIA LAW REVIEW

THE BAR AND LEGAL WORLD – no 12. 1903 (all publ) – 1mf – 9 – $1.50 – LLMC 84-414 – us L.L.M.C. [073]

BAR BRIEFS *see* NORTH DAKOTA LAW REVIEW

BAR BULLETIN – Boston. no 1-167. 1924-40; v12-27. 1941-56 – 9 – $150.00 – us Hein [340]

BAR BULLETIN : STATE BAR OF NEW MEXICO – (Title varies: v1-18 as State Bar of New Mexico Bulletin and Advance Opinions; v19-26 no 10 as New Mexico's News and Views) – v5-34. 1967-95 – 9 – $1,116.00 set – us Hein [340]

THE BAR BULLETIN – (Lacking: v13) – Boston Bar Association. v1-27. 1924-56 (all publ) – 35mf – 9 – $52.00 – LLMC 84-415 – us L.L.M.C. [073]

BAR BUSINESS – 1985- – 1,5,6,9 – us UMI [640]

BAR CODE QUARTERLY – (Filmed as a supplement within Materials Management and Distribution) – Toronto. v3-8. 1987-92 – 9 – cn Micromedia [380]

BAR CODE QUARTERLY *see* MATERIALS MANAGEMENT AND DISTRIBUTION

BAR EXAMINATION ANNUAL *see* THE BAR EXAMINATION JOURNAL

THE BAR EXAMINATION JOURNAL – (Cont as: The Bar Examination Annual in 1893) – 12v. 1871-94 (all publ) – 47mf – 9 – $70.00 – LLMC 84-416 – us L.L.M.C. [073]

BAR EXAMINER – v1-64. 1931-95 – 9 – $460.00 set – us Hein [340]

THE BAR EXAMINER – (Lacking: v50. Updates planned) – National Conference of Bar Examiners. v1-55. 1931-86 – 42mf – 9 – $189.00 – LLMC 84-417 – us L.L.M.C. [073]

BAR HARBOR RECORD – Bar Harbor, ME: Bar Harbor Press Co, feb 17 1887-feb 9 1916 – 1 – us Res Libr [071]

THE BAR HARBOR TIMES – (Issues for apr 9-dec 1924 filmed with: Bar Harbor Times and Bar Harbor Record, jan -apr 2 1924) – Bar Harbor, ME: Sherman Pub Co, apr 9 1924-jul 4 1968 – 1 – us Res Libr [071]

THE BAR HARBOR TIMES – (Issues for jan-aug 19 1916 filmed with: Bar Harbor Times and Bar Harbor Record, aug 26-dec 1916) – Bar Harbor, ME: W H Sherman, jul 11 1914-aug 19 1916 – us Res Libr [071]

THE BAR HARBOR TIMES *see* THE BAR HARBOR TIMES AND BAR HARBOR RECORD

THE BAR HARBOR TIMES AND BAR HARBOR RECORD – (Issues for aug 26-dec 1916, and for jan-apr 2 1924 filmed with: Bar Harbor Times) – Bar Harbor, ME: W H Sherman, aug 26 1916-apr 2 1924 – us Res Libr [071]

THE BAR HARBOR TIMES AND BAR HARBOR RECORD *see* THE BAR HARBOR TIMES

BAR KOCHBA : BLAETTER FUER DIE HERANWACHSENDE JUEDISCHE JUGEND – Berlin. v1-2. 1919-21. Complete. 1 reel, B25. (Leo Baeck Institute. German-Jewish Periodicals, Pt 2) – 1 – $75.00 – us UPA [270]

Bar, L von *see* DER BURENKRIEG,...

THE BAR LEADER – (Updates available. Lacking: v2) – American Bar Assoc. v1-11 nos 1-3 1975-85 – 25mf – 9 – $37.50 – LLMC 84-419 – us L.L.M.C. [073]

BAR LEADER (ABA) – v1-20. 1975-96 – 9 – $188.00 set – us Hein [340]

THE BAR REPORTS : CONTAINING ALL THE CASES ARGUED AND DETERMINED IN PARLIAMENT, THE HOUSE OF LORDS, THE PRIVY COUNCIL, THE COURT OF APPEAL IN CHANCERY, THE ROLLS, V.C., QUEEN'S BENCH,.... / Great Britain. England – London: Horace Cox Co. v1-12. 1865-71 (all publ) – 114mf – 9 – $171.00 – LLMC 95-225 – us L.L.M.C. [324]

Barabanshchikova, V *see* KOZA, KORMLENIE I UKHOD ZA NEI U

BARABBAS / Corelli, Marie – British Fiction Archive: Unit 1 – 9 – uk Bell [830]

BARABUDUR : ESQUISSE D'UNE HISTOIRE DU BOUDDHISME, FONDEE SUR LA CRITIQUE ARCHEOLOGIQUE DES TEXTES / Mus, Paul – Hanoi: Impr d'Extreme-Orient, 1935 – 1 – us Res Libr [950]

Barach, C S *see* BERNARDI SILVESTRIS

Barado, Francisco *see*
- LA ELOCUENCIA MILITAR
- LA HISTORIA MILITAR DE ESPANA
- LITERATURA MILITAR ESPANOLA
- MIS ESTUDIOS HISTORICOS..
- MUSEO MILITAR HISTORIA. INDUMENTARI..
- LA PINTURA MILITAR
- SITIO DE AMBERES 1584-85
- EL SITIO DE BALER, DE SATURNINO MARTIN CEREZO
- LA VIDA MILITAR EN ESDANA

Barag, Dan *see* GLASS AND GLASSMAKING IN ANCIENT MESOPOTAMIA

Barager, Joseph R *see* WHY PERON CAME TO POWER

Barajas Salas, Eduardo *see* SAQUEO E INCENDIO DE VALENCIA DE MOMBUEY EN 1641 Y UN CURIOSO DOCUMENTO DE 1693 SOBRE ESTE PUEBLO

Barandon, P *see*
- DAS KRIEGSVERHUETUNGSRECHT DES VOELKERBUNDES
- LE SYSTEME JURIDIQUE DE LA SOCIETE DES NATIONS POUR LA PREVENTION DE LA GUERRE

Baranov, A A *see*
- SBORNIK DEISTVUIUSHCHIKH ZAKONOPOLOZHENII, POSTANOVLENII, INSTRUKTSII I TSIRKULIAROV PO POTREBITEL'SKOI KOOPERATSII
- USTAV POTREBITEL'SKOGO OBSHCHESTVA, UPRAVLIAEMOGO OBSHCHIM SOBRANIEM EGO CHLENOV

Baranson, Jack *see*
- NORTH-SOUTH TECHNOLOGY TRANSFER: FINANCING AND INSTITUTION BUILDING
- ROBOTS IN MANUFACTURING: KEY TO INTERNATIONAL COMPETITIVENESS
- SOVIET AUTOMATION: PERSPECTIVES AND PROSPECTS

Barante, Claude I B de *see*
- ESSAI SUR LE DEPARTEMENT DE L'AUDE, ADRESSE AU MINISTRE DE L'INTERIEUR
- OBSERVATIONS SUR LES ETATS DE SITUATION DU DEPARTEMENT DE L'AUBE

Barante, Guillaume-Prosper de *see* NOTES SUR LA RUSSIE, 1835-1840

Barantsov, MS *see* KAK RABOTAT' REVIZIONNOI KOMISSII SEL'SKO-KHOZIAISTVENNOGO KREDITNOGO TOVARISHCHESTVA

BARAO DEMACAHUBAS : PERIODICO SCIENTIFICO, LITTERARIO E NOTICIOSO – [s.l.]. 21 Abr 1886; 9 Set 1888 – 1,5,6 – bl Biblioteca [072]

Baratier, Albert Ernest Augustin *see* SOUVENIRS DE LA MISSION MARCHAND

Baratoux, J *see* DE LA DELIMITATION DU DOMAINE PUBLIC MARITIME...

Baratov, Boris *see*
- BUDEM TVERDY DO KONTSA
- KOMMUNISTU-OTPUSKNIKU NAKAZ
- NA IUG! NA IUG!

Baratta, Joseph Preston *see*
- THE WORLD FEDERALIST MOVEMENT
- WORLD FEDERALIST MOVEMENT

BARAZA – [Dar es Salaam: s.n., aug 21/30-oct 18/24 1993; nov 1/7 1993-jan 17/23 1994; mar 7/13, jul 18/24-25/31, aug 15/21 1994; feb 21/27, feb 28/mar 6, jul 4/10-11/17, aug 8/14, 22/28, aug 30/sep 4, dec 15/18, 23/25 1994 – us Res Libr [072]

BARAZA – (Issues filmed as pt of: St Clair Drake Coll of Africana jun 9 1956) – Nairobi, Kenya: Baraza Ltd, 1979 – us Res Libr [072]

Barazzetti, P *see* LE REGIME DES BANQUES ETRANGERES DANS LES PRINCIPALES LEGISLATIONS

Barba, Alvaro Alonso *see* TRAITE DE L'ART METALIQUE

BARBA AZUL. OPERA / Hurtado, Antonio – 1869 – 9 – 1.50f – sp Bibl Santa Ana [890]

Barba, P *see* BREVE RESUMPTA Y TRATADO DE LA ESENCIA, CAUSAS, PRONOSTICO..., Y CURACION DE LA PESTE

BARBADIAN – Barbados. 1822-1861 – 1 – us UMI [072]

BARBADOS : ABSTRACT OF STATISTICS 1956-1969 / Barbados. Statistical Service – (Coll title: Latin American and Caribbean Official Statistical Serials, 1821-1982) – 12mf – 9 – £100.00 – uk Chadwyck [972]

Barbados *see*
- DEVELOPMENT PLAN, 1955-1960
- DEVELOPMENT PLAN, 1960-1965
- DEVELOPMENT PLAN, 1962-65
- DEVELOPMENT PLAN, 1965-68
- DEVELOPMENT PLAN, 1969-1972
- FIVE YEAR DEVELOPMENT PLAN, 1960-1964
- FIVE-YEAR PLAN OF DEVELOPMENT AND TAXATION
- TEN-YEAR DEVELOPMENT PLAN; 1946-1956

BARBADOS ADVOCATE – Barbados. British West Indies. Apr 1950-May 1962 – 1 – us UMI [072]

BARBADOS ADVOCATE – Bridgetown, Barbados. 21 Jan 1926-21 May 1940; 15 Feb 1941-Jun 1961.-d. 267 reels – 1 – uk British Libr Newspaper [072]

BARBADOS ADVOCATE NEWS – Bridgetown. Barbados. 1950-May 1963, 1966$ – 1 – us UMI [072]

BARBADOS AGRICULTURAL REPORTER – Bridgetown, Barbados. Jan 1887-Dec 1888; Jan 1896-June 1922. (imperfect).-d. 54 reels – 1 – uk British Libr Newspaper [630]

Barbados. Department of Education *see* ANNUAL REPORT 1969/70-1976/77

BARBADOS GLOBE – Bridgetown, Barbados. Jan 1888-19 May 1926.-tw. 35 reels – 1 – uk British Libr Newspaper [072]

THE BARBADOS HERALD – Bridgetown. Barbados. Apr. 6, 13, 27; May 11, 1940 – 1 – us NY Public [072]

Barbados. Ministry of Education and Culture *see* REPORT ON EDUCATION IN BARBADOS FOR THE PERIOD 1978-1982

BARBADOS RECORDER – Bridgetown. Barbados. -w. 3 Oct 1951-29 Apr 1953, 4 Jan 1958-30 Dec 1959. (8 reels) – 1 – uk British Libr Newspaper [072]

BARBADOS STANDARD – Bridgetown, Barbados. 29 Apr 1911-31 Dec 1921. (very imperfect; week-end editions only from 17 Feb 1912-31 Dec 1921).-d. 12 reels – 1 – uk British Libr Newspaper [072]

Barbados. Statistical Service *see* BARBADOS

BARBADOS TIMES – Barbados. 1863-74; 1877; 1884-95 – 1 – us UMI [072]

BARBADOS TIMES – Bridgetown, Barbados. 10 Jan 1920-17 Aug 1921 (imperfect) – 1r – 1 – uk British Libr Newspaper [072]

BARBARA BLOMBERG : EIN STUECK IN DREI AKTEN MIT VORSPIEL UND EPILOG / Zuckmayer, Carl – Amsterdam: Bermann-Fischer, 1949 – 1r – 1 – us U.W. Library [820]

THE BARBARIAN INVASIONS OF ITALY / Villari, Pasquale – London: Unwin, 1913 – 2mf – us A.T.L.A. [945]

Barbarina, P *see* DE LA COMPETENCE DES TRIBUNAUX FRANCAIS EN MATIERE DE SUCCESSION

Barbaro, D *see* LA PRATICA DELLA PERSPETTIVA

BARBAROSSA : A TRAGEDY / Brown, J – London, 1795 – 1mf – 9 – ne IDC [820]

Barbauld, Anna Letitia *see* THE WORKS OF ANNA LAETITIA BARBAULD

Barbay, G *see* LES SURESTARIES...

Barbeau, Raymond *see* LAURENTIE

Barbeau, Victor *see* LE COOPERATEUR

Barbella, E *see*
- SIX DUETTOS FOR THE VIOLIN AND VIOLONCELLO
- TRIO SONATAS, OP 1

Barber *see* HISTORICAL COLLECTIONS OF THE STATE OF NEW YORK

Barber, B A *see* A METHODIST PAGEANT

Barber, C R *see* THE ALEXANDRIA FUTURES MARKET (ALEXANDRIA COTTON EXPORTERS' ASSOCIATION)

BARBER COUNTY INDEX – Medicine Lodge. Kan. 1880-1964 – 1 – us UMI [071]

Barber, G L *see* CHICAGO LAW JOURNAL

Barber, Gershom Morse *see* A GUIDE FOR NOTARIES PUBLIC AND COMMISSIONERS.

Barber, Heather *see* AN EXAMINATION OF THE SOURCES AND LEVELS OF PERCEIVED COMPETENCE IN MALE AND FEMALE INTERSCHOLASTIC COACHES

Barber, John W *see* HISTORICAL COLLECTIONS–RELATING TO THE HISTORY AND ANTIQUITIES OF EVERY TOWN IN MASSACHUSETTS

Barber, R of N *see*
- SIX SONATAS FOR PIANO FORTE OR HARPSICHORD WITH AN ACCOMPANIMENT FOR A VIOLIN AND VIOLONCELLO
- THOMPSON'S HYMN TO THE SEASONS

Barber, Thomas Walter *see* SCIENTIFIC THEOLOGY

Barberet, J *see*
- LES GREVES ET LA LOI SUR LES COALITIONS
- LE TRAVAIL EN FRANCE. MONOGRAPHIES PROFESSIONNELLES

Barberi, A *see* BULLARII ROMANI CONTINUATIO

Barberino, Andrea da *see*
- GUERINO DETTO IL MESCHINO; STORIA DELLE GRANDI IMPRESE E VITTORIE DE LUI RIPORTATE CONTRO I TURCHI DURANTE IL REGNO DI CARLO MAGNO..
- GUERINO IL MESCHINO; ROMANZO CAVALLERESCO DI ANDREA DA BARBERINO,.

BARBERTON HERALD – Barberton. South Africa. 1886-92 – 1 – sa State Libr [072]

Barberton. Ohio *see* CITY DIRECTORY

Barbet, I *see* LIVRE D'ARCHITECTURE D'AUTELS ET DE CHEMINEES

Barbet, Jean *see* LIVRE D'ARCHITECTURE, D'AUTELS ET DE CHEMINEES.

Barbeu-Dubourg, Jacques *see* PETIT CODE DE RAISON HUMAINE: OU, EXPOSITION SUCCINTE DE CE QUE LA RAISON DICTE A TOUS LES HOMMES, POUR ECLAIRER LEUR CONDUITE ET ASSURER LEUR BONHEUR

Barbey, A *see* DE L'APPLICATION INTERNATIONALE DE LA REGLE "NON BIS IN IDEM"...

Barbey, C *see* HERBORISATIONS AU LEVANT

Barbey, W *see* HERBORISATIONS AU LEVANT

Barbezieux, Alexis de *see*
- HISTOIRE DE LA PROVINCE ECCLESIASTIQUE D'OTTAWA ET DE LA COLONISATION DANS LA VALLEE DE L'OTTAWA. V2
- PREMIERE RETRAITE SOUS LES AUSPICES DU CERCLE VILLE-MARIE: DANS L'EGLISE DE NOTRE-DAME DE BONSECOURS

Barbier, Alfred *see* UN MUNITIONNAIRE DU ROI A LA NOUVELLE FRANCE, JOSEPH CADET (1756-1781)

Barbier d'Aucour, J *see* SENTIMENTS DE CLEANTE SUR LES ENTRETIENS D'ARISTE ET D'EUGENE

Barbier de Montault, X. *see* TRAITE D'ICONOGRAPHIE CHRETIENNE

[IL BARBIERE DI SEVIGLIA] AH CHI SA / Paisiello, G – (In Process) – London: Birchall, 17– – 1 – us Sibley [780]

[IL BARBIERE FI SEVIGLIA] O CHE UMOR / Paisiello, G – (In Process) – London: Birchall, 17– – 1 – us Sibley [780]

THE BARBONE PARLIAMENT : FIRST PARLIAMENT OF THE COMMONWEALTH OF ENGLAND, 1653: AND THE RELIGIOUS MOVEMENTS OF THE SEVENTEENTH CENTURY CULMINATING IN THE PROTECTORATE SYSTEM OF CHURCH GOVERNMENT / Glass, Henry Alexander – London: J. Clarke, 1899 – 1mf – us A.T.L.A. [941]

Barbonius, J *see* 57 TH. MORALE SINNE-BEELDEN, AEN SIJNE HOOGHEYDT, DEN DOORLUCHTIGEN ENDE HOOGH-GHE BOREN VORST FREDRICK HENDRICK PRINCE VAN ORANGIEN...

Barbosa Rodrigues, Joao *see* O MUYRAKYTA E OS IDOLOS SYMBOLICOS...

Barbosa Rodrigues, Joao *see* HORTUS FLUMINENSIS

Barbot, J *see* A DESCRIPTION OF THE COASTS OF NORTH AND SOUTH GUINEA

Barbou, Alfred *see* HISTOIRE DE LA GUERRE AU DAHOMEY

Barbour, Dorothy Dickinson *see*
- CHRISTIAN HOME EDUCATION (CCC2)
- PRINCIPLES IN CHILD TRAINING (CCC3)

BARBOUR ENVIRONMENTAL HEALTH, FIRE AND SAFETY MICROFILE – Printed and bound index. Updated 6 times per year. 129,000p – 9 – £720.00y – uk Barbour [628]

BARBOUR ENVIRONMENTAL HEALTH MICROFILE – Printed and bound index.Updated 6 times per year. 120,000p – 9 – £576.00y – uk Barbour [628]

BARBOUR FIRE AND SAFETY MICROFILE – Printed and bound index. Updated 6 times per year. 105,000p – 9 – £596.00y – uk Barbour [360]

Barbour, G F *see*
- THE ETHICAL APPROACH TO THEISM
- A PHILOSOPHICAL STUDY OF CHRISTIAN ETHICS

BARBOUR HEALTH AND SAFETY MICROFILE – Printed and bound index.Updated 6 times per year. 96,000p – 9 – £452.00y – uk Barbour [610]

BARBOUR PRODUCT MICROFILE – Printed and bound index. Updated 3 times per year. 58,616p – 9 – £394.00y – uk Barbour [720]

BARBOUR PROPERTY AND ESTATE MANAGEMENT MICROFILE – Printed and bound index. Updated 3 times per year. 48,873p – 9 – £660.00y – uk Barbour [650]

BARBOUR TECHNICAL MICROFILE – Printed and bound index. Updated 3 times per year. 144,985p – 9 – £921.00y – uk Barbour [720]

BARBOUR'S CHANCERY APPEALS REPORTS – New York. v1-3. 1845-48 (all publ) – 24mf – 9 – $36.00 – LLMC 80-016 – us L.L.M.C. [340]

BARBOUR'S SUPREME COURT CASES / New York. (State). Supreme Court – v1-67. 1847-77 (all publ) – 536mf – 9 – $804.00 – LLMC 80-009 – us L.L.M.C. [340]

BARBOURVILLE FIRST BAPTIST CHURCH. BARBOURVILLE, KENTUCKY : CHURCH RECORDS – 1804-77 – 1 – 10.53 – us Baptist [240]

Barboza du Bocage, J V *see* ORNITHOLOGIE D'ANGOLA

Barboza, Emiliano M *see* DOCTRINA DE LA REVOLUCION DEL 4 DE JUNIO

BARBURGER, BOLSTANDIGES / Luther, Martin – The hymn book for the practice of godliness in 649 Christian and Protestant Psalms and hymns.... Printed by Christopher Saur, 1762 – 1 – 23.45 – us Baptist [240]

Barbut, J *see* THE GENERA VERMIUM OF LINNAEUS EXEMPLIFIED BY VARIOUS SPECIMENS OF THE ANIMALS

Barcarrota *see*
- FERIAS Y FIESTAS DE SEPTIEMBRE 1970
- FERIAS Y FIESTAS EN BARCARROTA. SEPTIEMBRE DE 1946
- FERIAS Y FIESTAS PATRONALES EN HONOR DE LA VIRGEN DEL SOTERRANO. 1980
- ORDENANZAS MUNICIPALES

O BARCELENSE : SEMANARIO REGIONALISTA – Barcelos, Amazonas. 20 Out 1962 – 1,5,6 – bl Biblioteca [072]

O BARCELLENSE – Barcellos, Amazonas. 3 Ago-Out 1909; Fev-4 Jul 1912 – 1,5,6 – bl Biblioteca [072]

Barcelona *see* USATAGES DE BARCELONA I COMMEMORACIONS DE PERE ALBERT, A CURA DE JOSEP ROVIRA I ERMENGOL

BARCELONA, 1933 / Alvarez, Jose Ma. Leyendas & Japon, Cuentas del – Madrid: Razon y Fe, 1934 – 1 – sp Bibl Santa Ana [946]

BARCELONA. ARCHIVO DE LA CORONA DE ARAGON GUIA HISTORICA Y DESCRIPTIVA... / Udina Martorell, F – Madrid, 1986 – 9 – sp Cultura [946]

Barcelona. (City). Ayuntamiento *see*
- ESTADISTICA MUNICIPAL

Barchwitz-Krauser, O von *see* SIX YEARS WITH WILLIAM TAYLOR IN SOUTH AMERICA

Barclay, John *see*
- A CIRCULAR LETTER SUGGESTING A PETITION TO PARLIAMENT FOR THE PROTECTION OF THE TEMPORALITIES FUND
- THE SEPULCHRE IN THE GARDEN: A SERMON PREACHED ON THE 13TH OCTOBER, 1867, IN ST ANDREW'S CHURCH, TORONTO, AFTER THE FUNERAL OF THE LATE JOHN CAMERON, ESQ..

Barclay, T *see*
- ASSIMILATON DES LOIS CONCERNANT LA LETTRE DE CHANGE...
- STUDIEN ZUR LEHRE VON DER STAATENSUKZESSION

Barclay, Thomas *see* SELECTIONS FROM THE CORRESPONDENCE OF THOMAS BARCLAY, FORMERLY BRITISH CONSUL-GENERAL AT NEW YORK

Barco Centenera, Arcediano *see* ARGENTINA Y CONQUISTA DEL RIO DE LA PLATA CON OTROS ACAE CIMIENTOS DE LOS REINOS DEL PERU. TUCUMAN Y ESTADO DE BRASIL. NOTAS BIBLIOGRAFICAS Y BIOGRAFICAS DE CARLOS NAVARRO Y LAMARCA

Barco de Centenera, M *see* ARGENTINA...Y CONQUISTA DEL RIO DE LA PLATA CON OTROS ACAECIMIENTOS DE LOS REYNOS...

Barco Perez, Paulina *see* DECIMAS EN HONOR...DE LA VIRGEN

Barco, Ricardo del. *see* EL REGIMEN PERONISTA, 1946-1955

THE BARD OF WAR IN TWO VOLUMES / Dixon, George – Saint John, N.B.: s.n., 1868 (Saint John, N.B.: H. Chubb). 02727. (Pre-1900 Canadiana) – 9 – cn C.I.H.M. [830]

Bardaji y Buitrago, A *see* CONTRIBUCIONES. IMPUESTOS, ARANCELES Y GRAVAMENES

Bardenhewer, Otto *see*
- DES H. HIPPOLYTUS VON ROM COMMENTAR ZUM BUCHE DANIEL
- DES HEILIGEN HIPPOLYTUS VON ROM COMMENTAR ZUM BUCHE DANIEL
- GESCHICHTE DER ALTKIRCHLICHEN LITTERATUR
- PATROLOGY
- POLYCHRONIUS

BARDESANES, DER LETZTE GNOSTIKER / Hilgenfeld, A – Leipzig: T.O. Weigel, 1864 – 1mf – us A.T.L.A. [240]

BARDESANES GNOSTICUS SYRORUM PRIMUS HYMNOLOGUS : COMMENTATIO HISTORICO-THEOLOGICA / Hahn, Augustus – Lipsiae: Sumtibus F.C.G. Vogelii, 1819 – 1mf – us A.T.L.A. [240]

Bardill, Donald R *see* JOURNAL OF FAMILY SOCIAL WORK

Bardin, A V *see* FOL'KLOR CHKALOVSKOI OBLASTI

Bardossy, Laszlo *see* A BARDOSSY PER. A MAGYAR ORSZAGOS TUDOSITO ES A MAGYAR TAVIRATI IRODA HIVATALOS KIADASAIBOL SZERK

A BARDOSSY PER. A MAGYAR ORSZAGOS TUDOSITO ES A MAGYAR TAVIRATI IRODA HIVATALOS KIADASAIBOL SZERK / Bardossy, Laszlo – Budapest, Hirado Konyvtar, 1945. 2 v. in 1. LL-4028 – 1 – us L of C Photodup [340]

Bardoux, Jacques *see*
- LE CHAOS ESPAGNOL, EVITERNONS-NOUS LA CONTAGION?
- CHAOS IN SPAIN
- STALINE CONTRE L'EUROPE

Bardsley, C W *see* A DICTIONARY OF ENGLISH AND WELSH SURNAMES

Bardsley, S *see* JOURNAL, 1765-1766, AND LETTER-BOOKS, 1772-1776

Bardy, Gustave *see* DIDYME L'AVEUGLE

Bare *see* AN ILLUSTRATED HISTORY OF LINCOLN COUNTY AND HER PEOPLE

O BARE – [s.l.] 1 Maio 1928 – 1,5,6 – bl Biblioteca [072]

BARE ALBERTE, ROMAN CORA SANDEL / Fabricius, Sara – Oslo: Gyldendal, 1939. 364p – 1 – us U.W. Library [830]

Barea, Arturo *see*
- LA RAIZ ROTA
- UNAMUNO

Bareel, Louis *see* VOYAGE D'ETUDE AU CANADA

BARELLAN LEADER – Jan 5 1928-Dec 19 1929 – 9 – at Pascoe [072]

O BARES : JORNAL LITTERARIO E NOTICIOSO – Manaos, Amazonas. 13 Maio 1900 – 1,5,6 – bl Biblioteca [072]

Bares, Enrique *see* SCALABRINI ORTIZ

Bargas, Luis de *see* PETICION ESCRITO DE CONCLUSIONES AL NUNCIO POR EL P. CACERES CON EL P. JUAN DE LA SERENA Y OTROS

Bargiel, Woldemar *see*
- 2TES TRIO FUER PIANO, VIOLINE UND VIOLONCELLE, OP. 20
- ERSTES TRIO, IN F DUR, PIANOFORTE, VIOLINE UND VIOLONCELLE. NEUE REV AUSG.
- TRIO NR. 3, B DUR

BARGSLAGSBLADET – Koping, Sweden. 1890-1907 – 15r – 1 – sw Kungliga [072]

BARGSLAGSBLADET – Koping, Sweden. 1979-. Arboga Tidning – 1 – sw Kungliga [072]

BARGTEHEIDER ZEITUNG – Bargteheide, 1932-37 – 16r – 1 – Dist. gw Mikrofilm – gw Misc Inst [943]

Bargy, Henry *see* LA RELIGION DANS LA SOCIETE AUX ETATS-UNIS

BARID AL GAZA'IRI *see* AL-BARID AL-GAZA'IRI

Barine, Arvede *see* NEVROSES

Baring, A *see* AN INQUIRY INTO CAUSES AND CONSEQUENCES...

Baring-Gould, Sabine *see*
- THE CHURCH IN GERMANY
- THE CHURCH REVIVAL
- ENGLISH MINSTRELSIE
- LEGENDS OF THE PATRIARCHS AND PROPHETS
- THE PASSION OF JESUS (FIRST SERIES)
- POST-MEDIAEVAL PREACHERS

BARISA – Addis Ababa: Dabata gazeta barisa, mar 12, apr 21, may 1,21 1976; mar 17-24, apr 7,21, may 12-jun 2 1977 – 1r – 1 – us Res Libr [072]
BARISAL HITAISHI – Bengal, India. Dec 1938-1939 – 1r – 1 – us L of C Photodup [072]
Barisan Propaganda *see* PEMIMPIN BAHASA NIPPON
Barisan Tani Indonesia *see* ANGGARAN DASAR DAN ANGGARAN RUMAH TANGGA B.T.I
THE BARK CANOES AND SKIN BOATS OF NORTH AMERICA / Adney, Edwin Tappan & Chapelle, Howard Irving – 1964 – 5mf – 9 – $5.00f – us Ross [390]
BARKAI – Johannesburg, South Africa. 1938-44, 1947-49 – 1 – sa State Libr [073]
Barker, Edmund Henry *see* LITERARY ANECDOTES AND CONTEMPORARY REMINISCENCES OF PROFESSOR PORSON AND OTHERS
Barker, George Stanley *see* AN HISTORICAL SURVEY OF BLACK BAPTIST HYMNODY IN AMERICA
Barker, J *see* CORRESPONDENCE RELATING TO THE JOSEPH BARKER CASE, 1838-1869
Barker, John Marshall *see* THE SALOON PROBLEM AND SOCIAL REFORM
Barker, Matthew Henry *see* GREENWICH HOSPITAL, A SERIES OF NAVAL SKETCHES, DESCRIPTIVE OF THE LIFE OF A MAN-OF-WAR'S MAN
Barker, S G *see* WOOL QUALITY
Barker, Wharton *see* SURPLUS REVENUES AND CANADIAN RELATIONS
BARKER'S CANADIAN MONTHLY MAGAZINE – Kingston [Ont.]: E.J. Barker, [1846]-1847 – 9 – cn C.I.H.M. [971]
BARKER'S CREEK BAPTIST CHURCH. ANDERSON COUNTY. SOUTH CAROLINA : CHURCH RECORDS – 1821-65, 1979-82. 272p – 1 – 12.24 – us Baptist [240]
BARKING AND DAGENHAM ADVERTISER – London, 1970-81 – 34r – 1 – uk British Libr Newspaper [072]
BARKING AND DAGENHAM CITIZEN *see* BARKING CITIZEN
BARKING AND DAGENHAM POST – London, 1970- – 75+ r – 1 – uk British Libr Newspaper [072]
BARKING AND DAGENHAM RECORDER – (Also known as: Barking and East Ham Advertiser) – England, Oct 1888-1964; 1970- – 141+ r – 1 – uk British Libr Newspaper [072]
BARKING AND EAST HAM ADVERTISER – (Also known as: Barking, East Ham and Ilford Advertiser) – London, 1888-1964 – 38r – 1 – uk British Libr Newspaper [072]
BARKING AND EAST HAM ADVERTISER *see* BARKING AND DAGENHAM RECORDER
BARKING AND EAST HAM STANDARD – London, UK. 6 Sep 1895-24 Oct 1902 – 3r – 1 – us British Libr Newspaper [072]
BARKING CITIZEN – (Barking & Dagenham Citizen, 1983-84) – London, UK. Dec 1972-1984 – 3/4r – 1 – uk British Libr Newspaper [072]
BARKING, EAST HAM AND ILFORD ADVERTISER *see* BARKING AND EAST HAM ADVERTISER
THE BARKLY AND DIGGER'S NEWS – Barkly West, South Africa. 2 Apr 1898-30 Sept 1899. 1 reel – 1, 16 diazo available at reduced price – sa SA Libr [072]
Barkov, I S *see* SOCHINENIIA I' PEREVODY
Barlach, Ernst *see* DER TOTE TAG
Barletius, M *see*
- DE VITA MORIBVS AC REBVS PRAECIPVE ADVERSVS TVRCAS, ...
- HISTORIA DEL MAGNANIMO, ET VALOROSO SIGNOR GEORGIO CASTRIOTO, DETTO SCANDERBEGO, DIGNISSIMO PRINCIPE DE GLI ALBANI

Barlett, S C *see* SKETCHES OF THE MISSIONS OF THE AMERICAN BOARD
Barletta, Rafael *see* ARGENTINA
Barlow, Alfred Ernest *see* ON SOME DYKES CONTAINING HURONITE
BARMEDMAN BANNER – Jan 1 1917-Dec 13 1918 – 9 – at Pascoe [072]
BARMER BUERGERBLATT *see* BARMER ZEITUNG
BARMER ZEITUNG – (Title change: Barmer Buergerblatt, 1852-60) – Barmen (Wuppertal), Germany. 1847-Jun 1850 – 4r – 1 – gw Mikrofilm [072]
Barnabe, G *see* CONTRIBUTION A LA CONNAISSANCE DE LA BIOLOGIE DU LOUP, DICENTRARCHUS LABRAX (L)
Barnabe, Michele *see* BIBLIOGRAPHIE ANALYTIQUE DE L'ILE D'ANTICOSTI (REINE DU GOLFE)
Barnaby, Nathaniel *see* NAVAL DEVELOPMENT IN THE 19TH CENTURY
BARNARD BULLETIN – New York. 1901-85 – 1 – us UMI [073]
Barnard, Edouard Andre *see*
- L'AGRICULTURE AU POINT DE VUE DE L'EMIGRATION: LECTURE DEVANT "L'UNION CATHOLIQUE", LE 27 OCTOBRE 1872
- UNE LECON D'AGRICULTURE: CAUSERIES AGRICOLES
- PETIT TRAITE SUR LE DESSECHEMENT ET LE DRAINAGE DES TERRES, POUVANT SERVIR DE TEXTE AUX CONFERENCES DES CERCLES AGRICOLES

Barnard, Eric A *see* RECEPTORS AND CHANNELS
Barnard, K H *see* CONTRIBUTIONS TO THE KNOWLEDGE OF SOUTH AFRICAN MARINE MOLLUSCA
Barnard, P M *see*
- BIBLICAL TEXT OF CLEMENT OF ALEXANDRIA IN THE FOUR GOSPELS AND THE ACTS OF THE APOSTLES
- CLEMENT OF ALEXANDRIA, QUIS DIVES SALVETUR

Barnaud, Nicolas *see* LE MIROIR DES FRANCOIS, COMPRIS EN TROIS LIVRES
Barnave, A P J M *see*
- RAPPORT SUR LES AFFAIRES DE SAINT-DOMINGUE FAIT LES 11 ET 12 OCTOBRE
- RAPPORT SUR LES COLONIES, ET DECRET RENDU SUR CETTE AFFAIRE. LE 28 SEPTEMBRE

Barneaud, Charles *see* ORIGINES ET PROGRES DE L'EDUCATION EN AMERIQUE: ETUDE HISTORIQUE ET CRITIQUE: LES ETATS PRIMITIFS
Barneby, William Henry *see* THE NEW FAR WEST AND THE OLD FAR EAST: BEING NOTES OF A TOUR IN NORTH AMERICA, JAPAN, CEYLON ETC
Barnes *see* THE TERRANIAN NATIONAL CONSTITUTION
Barnes, Albert *see*
- HOME MISSIONS
- MISCELLANEOUS ESSAYS AND REVIEWS
- NOTES, EXPLANATORY AND PRACTICAL ON THE ACTS OF THE APOSTLES
- NOTES, EXPLANATORY AND PRACTICAL, ON THE FIRST EPISTLE OF PAUL TO THE CORINTHIANS
- THE WAY OF SALVATION: A SERMON DELIVERED AT MORRISTOWN, NEW JERSEY, 8 FEB 1829

Barnes, Arthur Stapylton *see*
- BLESSED JOAN THE MAID
- THE EARLY CHURCH IN THE LIGHT OF THE MONUMENTS
- ST. PETER IN ROME AND HIS TOMB ON VATICAN HILL
- THE WITNESS OF THE GOSPELS

Barnes, Carolyn M *see* EFFECTS OF A CREATIVE DANCE PROGRAM ON THE PERCEPTUAL MOTOR PERFORMANCE OF TRAINABLE MENTALLY RETARDED CHILDREN
Barnes, Francis *see* THE STORY OF HOULTON: FROM THE PUBLIC RECORDS AND FROM THE EXPERIENCES OF ITS FOUNDERS, THEIR DESCENDANTS AND ASSOCIATES TO THE PRESENT TIME: ALSO ANNOUNCEMENTS OF ALL THE PROMINENT MERCHANTS AND MANUFACTURING INTERESTS
Barnes, H E *see* HANDBOOKS TO THE BIRDS OF THE BOMBAY PRESIDENCY
Barnes, Harry Elmer *see* THE STORY OF PUNISHMENT; A RECORD OF MAN'S INHUMANITY TO MAN
Barnes, Herbert *see* NYANJA-ENGLISH VOCABULARY
Barnes, J *see* TWENTY CHARGES AGAINST THE METHODISTS ANSWERED BY THE WORD OF GOD, FOR THEIR ENCOURAGEMENT AND CONVICTION OF THEIR ENEMIES
Barnes, James *see* NAVAL ACTIONS OF THE WAR OF 1812
Barnes, James N *see* LET'S SAVE ANTARCTICA
Barnes, John *see* EVITA, FIRST LADY
Barnes, Lela *see* RAILROAD COLLECTION
Barnes, Lemuel Call *see* TWO THOUSAND YEARS OF MISSIONS BEFORE CAREY
Barnes, Ralph *see* LIBER PONTIFICALIS OF EDMUND LACY, BISHOP OF EXETER
Barnes, William *see*
- HWOMELY RHYMES
- SELECT POEMS OF WILLIAM BARNES

Barnes, William Emery *see*
- BOOKS OF CHRONICLES: MAPS, NOTES, INTRODUCTION
- CANONICAL AND UNCANONICAL GOSPELS
- HAGGAI AND ZECHARIAH
- MALACHI
- THE TWO BOOKS OF THE KINGS

Barnes, William S *see* MAXIMAL POWER OUTPUT ON THE BICYCLE ERGOMETER
Barnes, William W *see* THE SOUTHERN BAPTIST CONVENTION, 1845-1953
BARNESBORSKY OROL = THE BARNESBORO EAGLE – Barnesboro, PA: A J Antos-ovi synovia, dec 1917-aug 5 1920 – 1r – 1 – us Res Libr [071]
BARNESTON STAR – Barneston, NE. -w. Nov. 1895-Nov. 1897. Incomplete; Sep. 1898-May 1903; Aug. 1905-Feb. 1907 – 1 – us NE Hist [071]
Barnesville. Georgia. Mount Zion Baptist Church *see* MINUTES
BARNET AND FINCHLEY PRESS *see* BARNET PRESS
BARNET AND POTTERS BAR TIMES *see* BARNET BOROUGM TIMES
BARNET BOROUGM TIMES – (Also known as: Barnet and Potters Bar Times) – England, 1985- – 73+ r – 1 – uk British Libr Newspaper [072]
BARNET INDEPENDENT – London, UK. 18 Jun 1982-1983 – 1r – 1 – uk British Libr Newspaper [072]
BARNET PRESS – (1862-79 imperfect) – London, 28 Dec 1861-21 Jun 1862; 6 Feb 1869-24 Jun 1871; 4 Jan 1873-30 Dec 1876; 12 Jan 1878- – 167+ r – 1 – uk British Libr Newspaper [072]
Barnett, Canon Samuel Augustus *see* TOWARDS SOCIAL REFORM
Barnett, George E *see* MEDIATION, INVESTIGATION AND ARBITRATION IN INDUSTRIAL DISPUTES
Barnett, Henrietta *see* PRACTICABLE SOCIALISM
Barnett, John *see* WHY A TWO-THOUSAND DOLLAR CAR COSTS FIFTEEN THOUSAND DOLLARS
Barnett, Samuel *see* PRACTICABLE SOCIALISM
Barnett, William T *see* DIARY
Barnette, Henlee H *see* CLARENCE JORDAN: A PROPHET IN BLUE JEANS
BARNEWELL AND ADOLPHUS' REPORTS : REPORTS OF CASES ARGUED AND DETERMINED IN THE COURT OF KING'S BENCH... / Barnewell, Richard V & Adolphus, John L – v1-5. 1831-34. London: Saunders & Benning, 1831-35 (all publ) – 56mf – 9 – $84.00 – LLMC 95-246 – us L.L.M.C. [324]
BARNEWELL AND ALDERSON'S REPORTS : REPORTS OF CASES ARGUED AND DETERMINED IN THE COURT OF KING'S BENCH... / Barnewell, Richard V & Alderson, Edward H – v1-5. 1817-22. London: J Butterworth & Son, 1818-22 (all publ) 84-744 – 37mf – 9 – $55.00 – LLMC 84-744 – us L.L.M.C. [324]
BARNEWELL AND CRESSWELL'S REPORTS : REPORTS OF CASES ARGUED AND DETERMINED IN THE COURT OF KING'S BENCH... / Barnewell, Richard V & Creswell, Creswell – v1-10. 1822-30. London: A Strahan, 1823- (all publ) – 102mf – 9 – $153.00 – LLMC 84-745 – us L.L.M.C. [324]
Barnewell, Richard V *see*
- BARNEWELL AND ADOLPHUS' REPORTS
- BARNEWELL AND ALDERSON'S REPORTS
- BARNEWELL AND CRESSWELL'S REPORTS

Barney, William L *see* NINETEENTH CENTURY POLITICAL LEADERS
Barnhill, J B *see* DO YOU THINK YOU CAN GOVERN YOURSELF CHEAPER THAN YOU CAN HIRE IT DONE?
Barni, C *see*
- AIR VARIE POUR VIOLON ET VIOLONCELLE
- TROIS TRIOS, OP. 6

Barnoldswick. Yorkshire *see* PARISH REGISTERS
BARNSLEY CHRONICLE – England, 16 Oct 1858-Dec 1865 – 5r – 1 – uk British Libr Newspaper [072]
BARNSLEY ECHO – England, Sep 1869-Dec 1871; Jan-Dec 1874 – 1r – 1 – uk British Libr Newspaper [072]
BARNSLEY EXPRESS – Barnsley, England. -w. 3 Oct 1903-16 Sept 1904. 1 reel – 1 – uk British Libr Newspaper [072]
BARNSLEY EXPRESS – Barnsley, England. -w. 6 Dec 1935-15 Sept 1939. 2 1 2 reels – 1 – uk British Libr Newspaper [072]
BARNSLEY HERALD – England. -w. Jan 1860-24 Jan 1866. (4 reels) – 1 – uk British Libr Newspaper [072]
BARNSLEY LABOUR BULLETIN – Barnsley, England. Nov 1936-Nov 1938. 3 ft – 1 – uk British Libr Newspaper [941]
BARNSLEY NEWS – Barnsley, England. -w. 22 Nov 1922-14 Aug 1926. 1 1 2 reels – 1 – uk British Libr Newspaper [072]
BARNSLEY RECORD – England. -w. 9 Oct 1858-24 Nov 1866. (4 reels) – 1 – uk British Libr Newspaper [072]
BARNSLEY SPORTING NEWS. (BARNSLEY DAILY ARGUS AND SPORTING NEWS) – England. 9 Jul 1894-7 Mar 1903 (missing 1897).-d. 4 reels – 1 – uk British Libr Newspaper [072]
BARNSLEY TELEGRAPH – England. -w. 3 Jul-25 Dec 1852. (39 ft) – 1 – uk British Libr Newspaper [072]
BARNSLEY TIMES – England. -w. 7 Apr 1855-30 Dec 1882. (Wanting 1872). (15 reels) – 1 – uk British Libr Newspaper [072]
BARNSTABLE 1643-1892 – (Mf 1-6: Births, Marriages, Deaths 1643-1714. Mf 7-11: Transcript of Records 1643-1714. Mf 12-13: Index to Transcripts 1643-1714. Mf 14-17: Town Records 1713 -81. Mf 18-22: Transcript of Records 1731-81. Mf 23-26: Index to Transcripts 1713-81. Mf 27-30: Town Records 1765-92. Mf 31-34: Town Records 1793-1816. Mf 35-39: Transcript of Records 1793-1816. Mf 40-42: Index to Transcripts 1793-1816. Mf 43-46: Births, Marriages, Deaths 1816-75. Mf 47-48: Index to Marriages 1816-75. Mf 49-52: Town Records 1844-80. Mf 53-56: Family Records 1861-90. Mf 57-59: Births, Marriages, Deaths 1844-64. Mf 60-62: Births 1865-91. Mf 63-64: Index to Births 1865-91. Mf 65: Index to Births 1844-91. Mf 66-68: Marriages 1853-92. Mf 69-70: Index to Marriages 1853-92. Mf 71-72: Deaths 1865-91, Vol 27. Mf 73: Index to Deaths 1844-91) – (mf ed 1987) – 73mf – 9 – 0-931248-93-0 – us Holbrook [920]
Barnstead, New Hampshire. First Free Will Baptist Church *see* RECORDS
Barnston, George *see* THE OREGON TREATY AND THE HUDSON'S BAY COMPANY
Barnum, F *see* GRAMMATICAL FUNDAMENTS OF THE INNUIT LANGUAGE AS SPOKEN BY THE ESKIMO OF THE WESTERN COAST OF ALASKA
Barnum, Samuel Weed *see*
- ROMANISM AS IT IS
- ROMANISM AS IT IS: AN EXPOSITION OF THE ROMAN CATHOLIC SYSTEM..

BARNWELL FIRST BAPTIST CHURCH. BARNWELL, SOUTH CAROLINA : CHURCH RECORDS – 1812-1912, 1923-72 – 1 – 48.15 – us Baptist [240]
Barny, Roger *see* ROUSSEAUISM: 1788-1797
Baro, B Fr. Joan *see* DUNS SCOTUS... PER UNIVERSAM PHILOSOPHIAM,...CONTRA ADVERSANTES DEFENSUS
DER BAROCKE GESCHICHTSBERGRIFF BEI ANDREAS GRYPHIUS / Kappler, Helmut – (Includes bibliographical references) – Frankfurt am Main: M Diesterweg, 1936 – 1r – 1 – us U.W. Library [430]
DAS BAROCKE GESCHICHTSBILD IN LOHENSTEINS ARMINIUS / Wehrli, Max – (Includes bibliographical references (p.[100]-109)) – Frauenfeld/Leipzig: Huber, 1938 – 1r – 1 – us U.W. Library [430]
BARODA STATE, 1901 – (1911 Administrative vol) – Baroda. pt 4. 1921 (mf ed 1941) – 1 – us Res Libr [310]
Baroja, P *see* PARADOX REY
BAROMETERN – Kalmar, Sweden. 1979-. Oskarshamnstidningen – 1 – sw Kungliga [072]
BAROMETERN – (Oskarshamnstidningen ed, 1868-78) – Kalmar, Sweden. 1841-1978 – 543r – 1 – sw Kungliga [072]
EL BARON / Fernandez de Moratin, Leandro – 1803 – 1mf – 9 – Pta1,000.00 – 84-7848-191-5 – sp Pentalfa [946]
Baron Castro, Rodolfo *see* ESPANOLISMO Y ANTIESPANOLISMO EN LA AMERICA HISPANA. LA POBLACION HISPANOAMERICANA A PARTIR DE LA INDEPENDENCIA. MADRID, 1945
THE BARON DE ST CASTIN / Brooks, Ivan – 1883? 00290. (Pre-1900 Canadiana) – 9 – cn C.I.H.M. [830]
Baron, E G *see* HISTORISCH-THEORETISCH UND PRAKTISCHE UNTERSUCHUNG DES INSTRUMENTS DER LAUTEN

BARON FRIEDRICH AUGUST MARSCHALL VON BIEBERSTEIN, 1768-1826 / Komarov Botanical Institute, St. Petersburg – (This detailed Includes printed guide) – 219mf – 9 – ne IDC [580]
BARON GERHARD VON MAYDELL'S TUNGUSISCHE SPRACHPROBEN / Schiefner, A – (Melanges Asiatiques 1873-1876). Spb. 1876. BU-453 2 – 8 – ne IDC [490]
Baron, J see
- THE LIFE OF EDWARD JENNER
- PEREGRINENRECHT UND IUS GENTIUM

Baron, S see DIE JUDENFRAGE AUF DEM WIENER KONGRESS
LE BARON, WILLIAM AND CO see
- HISTORY OF MCLEAN COUNTY
- HISTORY OF WILL COUNTY
- PAST AND PRESENT OF LAKE COUNTY
- PAST AND PRESENT OF WOODFORD COUNTY

Baronian, S see CATALOGUE OF THE ARMENIAN MSS IN THE BODLEIAN LIBRARY
Baronius, C see GENERALE KERCKELYCKE HISTORIE VAN DEN GHEBOORTE ONZES H. IESU CHRISTI TOT HET IAER 1624. H. ROSWEYDUS
Baronius, Caesar see ANNALES ECCLESIASTICI
Barou, Noah see KOOPERATSIIA S.S.S.R. NA VNESHNEM RYNKE V 1925 G. (V T SIFRAKH)
Barozzi, Francesco see OPVSCVLVN, IN QUO VNA ORATION, & DUAE QUESTIONES ALTERA DE CERTITUDINE, & ALTERA DE MEDIETATE MATHEMATICARUM CONTINENTUR
BARQ see AL-BARQ
Barqui, F see L'ARCHITECTURE MODERNE EN FRANCE
Barr see HISTORY OF HALL COUNTY
Barr, Eleanor M see RECORDS OF THE WOMEN'S INTERNATIONAL LEAGUE FOR PEACE AND FREEDOM, US SECTION, 1919-59
Barr, John see EARLY RELIGIOUS HISTORY OF
Barr, John O see NEURAL VERSUS MUSCULAR RESPONSES TO ISOMETRIC STRENGTH TRAINING OF THE TRICEPS BRACHII
Barr, Robert see
- THE FACE AND THE MASK
- FROM WHOSE BOURNE, ETC
- IN THE MIDST OF ALARMS
- THE MUTABLE MANY: A NOVEL
- ONE DAY'S COURTSHIP : THE HERALDS OF FAME
- REVENGED
- THE UNCHANGING EAST
- A WOMAN INTERVENES

BARRACK-ROOM BALLADS AND OTHER VERSES / Kipling, Rudyard – London: Methuen, 1892 – 1 roll – 1 – 1-55879-685-1 – uk Libr Preservation [810]
Barraco Aguirre, Rodolfo see DETRAS DE LA CRISIS
Barradas, S see COMMENTARIA IN CONCORDIAM ET HISTORIAM EVANGELICAM
Barrado, Angel see LA CASA DONDE NACIO SAN FRANCISCO DE ASIS, PATRONATO DEL ESTADO ESPANOL
Barrado Font, Francisco see
- DOMINACION Y GUERRAS DE ESPANA EN LOS PAISES BAJOS
- INTRODUCCION A UNA OBRA HISTORICA

Barrado Manzano, Arcangel see
- ALGUNAS ACTAS CAPITULARES DE LA PROVINCIA DE SAN GABRIEL AL PRINCIPIO DEL SIGLO 17 (ANOS 1601-1608)
- ANTONIO BRASIO...MONUMENTA...
- ANTONIO DA SILVA RIEGO. DOCUMENTAO...
- ARDUINO TERZI
- AS GAVETAS DA TORRE FOMBO 4, LISBOA 1964
- BASILIO DE SA. ARTURO
- BIBLIOGRAFIA MISSIONARIA ANNO 21 (1957) Y ANNO 12 (1958)...
- BIBLIOGRAFIA MISSIONARIA. ANNO 23
- BIBLIOGRAFIA MISSIONARIA. ANNO 28
- LA BULA "INTER GRAVIORES CURAS" DE PIO 7 EN LA ORDEN FRANCISCANA Y ULTERIOR REGIMEN GENERAL DE LA ORDEN EN ESPANA (1804-1904)
- CONGRESO DE ESPIRITUALIDAD FRANCISCANA
- CONSTITUCIONES DE LA PROVINCIA DE SAN GABRIEL (1580)
- EL CONSULADO DE BUENOS AIRES Y SUS PROYECCIONES EN LA HISTORIA DEL RIO DE LA PLATA. BUENOS AIRES, 1962
- DIRECCION GENERAL DE ARCHIVOS Y BIBLIOTECAS
- DIVISION BIPARTITA DE LA PROVINCIA FRANCISCANA DE SAN MIGUEL DE EXTREMADURA
- DOCTORIS SUBTILIS ET MARIANI JOANNIS DURIS SCOTI (OFM). OPERA OMNIA...
- DOCTORIS...JOANNIS DIUS SCOTI...OPERA OMNIA
- DOMINGO CRESI...
- DOS MISIONEROS FRANCISCANOS HERMANOS EN EL COLEGIO DE CHILLAN (CHILE)
- EPHREM LOUGPRE MYSTIQUE FRANCISCAIN
- FUNDACION Y FABRICA DEL CONVENTO DE SAN ANTONIO DE PADUA DE ALMENDRALEJO EN LA PROVINCIA FRANCISCANA DE SAN GABRIEL
- HISTORIA MISSIONORUM ORDINIS FRATRUM MINORIS 3. AMERICA SEPTENTRIONALIS. ROMA, 1968
- HISTORIA MISSIONUM ORDINIS FRATUM MINORUM 1. ASIA-CENTRO ORIENTALIS ET OCEANIA. ROMA, 1967
- JOSE LOPEZ DE TORO Y RAMON PAZ REMOLAR
- JOSEPH JORTZ
- LIBROS CATOLICOS DE ESPANA...
- MANUSCRITOS FRANCISCANOS DE LA BIBLIOTECA DE VICENTE BARRANTES
- MAURICE GRAFEWSKI O.F.M. THE SUPREME...
- MAYO DOCUMENTAL, ADVERTENCIA Y PROLOGO DE R. CAILLET-BOIS. 12 TOMOS. BUENOS AIRES. 1961-1966
- MONUMENTA HENRICINA, VOL. 8. (1443-1445) Y 9 (1445-1448)
- NECROLOGICA
- NUEVAS ACTAS CAPITULARES DE LA PROVINCIA DES CALZA DE SAN GABRIEL (1621-1644)
- LA PROVINCIA DESCALZA DE SAN GABRIEL Y SUS LIBROS DE PATENTES (1722-1746)
- LA PROVINCIA DESCALZA DE SAN GABRIEL Y SUS LIBROS DE PATENTES (1824-1835)
- LA PROVINCIA FRANCISCANA DE SAN MIGUEL INFRA TAGUM (1774-1815)
- SOTO, DE IUSTITIA ET IURE. 1. 1967 Y SUAREZ, TRATADO DE LEYES...2, 1967
- TERCER CENTENARIO DE LA CANONIZACION DE SAN PEDRO DE ALCANTARA (1669-28 DE ABRIL-1969)

BARRADO MANZANO, P. ARCANGEL O.F.M. LAS MISIONES FRANCISCANAS EN BOLIVIA CONFERENCIAS... / Lejarza, Fidel de – Madrid: Missionalia Hispanica, 1949 – 1 – sp Bibl Santa Ana [240]
LE BARRAGE DE L'ESCAUT ORIENTAL / [Fokker, G A] – La Haye, 1867 – 1mf – 1 – ILM-2872/1 – ne IDC [327]
Barrande, J see SYSTEME SILURIEN DU CENTRE DE LA BOHEME
Barrantes Maldonado, Francisco see RELACION DE LA CALIFICACION Y MILAGROS DEL SANTO CRUCIFIJO DE GALAMEA...DIVIDIDA EN DOS LIBROS
Barrantes Molina, Luis see DESDE MI TONEL
Barrantes Moreno, Vicente see
- APARATO BIBLIOGRAFICO...EXTREMADURA
- BALADAS ESPANOLAS
- BARROS EMERITENSES
- CATALOGO RAZONADO Y CRITICO...EXTREMADURA
- DIAS SIN SOL
- DISCURSO...ACADEMIA DE LA HISTORIA
- DISCURSOS LEIDOS ANTE LA REAL ACADEMIA DE LA HISTORIA EN LA RECEPCION...EL 14 DE ENERO DE 1872 CON UN BIOGRAFIA DE ESTE
- DISCURSOS...ACADEMIA ESPANOLA
- DISCURSOS...ACADEMIA...MANUEL DE LO PALACIO
- EPISTOLA RELIGIOSA...CEFERINO GONZALEZ..
- ESTADO DE EXTREMADURA...ISABEL LA CATOLICA
- ESTUDIOS SOBRE LOS RESTOS DE CERAMICA ROMANA
- GUERRAS PIRATICAS DE FILIPINAS
- HISTORIA GENERAL DE FILIPINAS, POR DON JOSE MONTERO Y VIDAL. INFORME
- UN HISTORIADOR MODERNO DE LA TIERRA DE LA SERENA (D. NICOLAS PEREZ JIMENEZ)
- INDICE DE LA BIBLIOTECA EXTREMENA..
- INFORME SOBRE
- INFORME (SOBRE) LETTRES INTIMES DE J.M. ALBERONI...
- LA INSTRUCCION PRIMARIA EN FILIPINAS. DESDE 1596 HASTA 1868
- JUAN DE PADILLA
- LAS JURDES Y SU LEYENDAS
- NARRACIONES EXTREMENAS. LA IMPRENTA EN EXTREMADURA
- NARRACIONES EXTREMENAS. LA SERRANA DE LA VERA..
- NOTICIA NECROLOGICA DE DON FELIPE-LEON GUERRA
- NOTICIAS SOBRE SU OBRA. "EL TEATRO TAGALO"
- LAS SIETE CENTURIAS DE LA CIUDAD DE PLASENCIA. INFORME DE ALEJANDRO MATIAS GIL
- SOBRE EL DERRIBO DE UNA CAMPANA HISTORICA EN BADAJOZ
- EL TEATRO TAGALO
- VIAJE ELECTORAL HECHO CON LA BOLSA A CUESTAS Y EL CUERPO MOLIDA A PALOS POR A LOS INFIERNOS DEL SUFRAGIO UNIVERSAL

Barras de Aragon, Francisco de las see EXCURSION A FREGENAL DE LA SIERRA Y LOS JARALES...
BAR'RASI – Qum: Mu'assasah-'i Ihya' va Nashr-i Miras-i Islami. Shumarah-'i 11, 15-18 (4 Tir 1358-Shahrivar 1358 [25 Jun 1979-Aug 1979]) – 1 reel – 1 – $25.00 – us MEDOC [950]
Barrass, Edward see
- A GALLERY OF DISTINGUISHED MEN
- MISSIONARY SCENES IN MANY LANDS
- SMILES AND TEARS, OR, SKETCHES FROM REAL LIFE

BARRATRY. ITS ORIGIN, HISTORY AND MEANING IN THE MARITIME LAWS / New York. (City). Court of Common Pleas – New York: Baker & Godwin, 1872. 30p. LL-218 – 1 – us L of C Photodup [340]
Barrau, Miguel Angel see HISTORIA DEL REGRESO
Barraud, P see DROIT CIVIL INTERNATIONAL DU MARIAGE...
Barrault, Emile see
- 1833 OU L'ANNEE DE LA MERE
- AU NOM DE DIEU, PERE ET MERE DE TOUS LES HOMMES ET DE TOUTES LES FEMMES
- AUX ARTISTES. DU PASSE ET DE L'AVENIR DES BEAUX-ARTS
- AUX ARTISTES, DU PASSE ET DE L'AVENIR DES BEAUXARTS. DOCTRINE DE SAINT-SIMON
- BARRIERE DU TRONE, 15 DECEMBRE 1832. A PARIS, ADIEU
- GUERRE OU PAIX EN ORIENT
- OCCIDENT ET ORIENT. ETUDES POLITIQUES, MORALES ET RELIGIEUSES PENDANT 1833-1834 DE L'ERE CHRETIENNE, 1249-1250 DE L'HEGYRE

Barre see PREMIER LIVRE DE PIECES POUR LA FLUTE TRAVERSIERE AVEC LA BASSE CONTINUE
BARRE 1718-1849 – (Mf 1T-2T: Vital Records 1747-1809. Mf 2T: Marriages 1755-91. Mf 2T-5T: Births 1745-1854. Mf 5T-6T: Marriages 1781-1854. Mf 6T-7T: Deaths 1757-1845. Mf 8T-10T: Intentions 1792-1849. Mf 10T: Out-of-Town Marriages 1749-98. Mf 10T-11T: Births 1844-49. Mf 11T-12T: Marriages 1844-49. Mf 12T: Deaths 1844-49) – (mf ed 1995) – 12mf – 9 – 0-87623-206-3 – us Holbrook [920]
BARRE 1718-1895 – (Mf 1-3: Births, Marriages, Deaths 1718-1810. Mf 4-8: Births, Marriages, Deaths 1752-1854. Mf 9-16: Index to B,M,D, Prior to 1845. Mf 17-19: Births, Marriages, Deaths 1844-55. Mf 20-28: Births, Marriages, Deaths 1855-95. Mf 29-32: Index to B,M, D, 1844-95) – (mf ed 1987) – 32mf – 9 – 0-87623-023-0 – us Holbrook [920]
BARRE GAZETTE – Barre, MA. 1835-66 – 1 – us Readex [071]
Barre, L see COMPLEMENT DU DICTIONNAIRE DE L'ACADEMIE FRANCAISE
BARRE PATRIOT – Barre, MA. 1844-45 – 1 – us Readex [071]
Barre, Radet, Desfontaines, Bourgueil, Maurice et Dupaty see LA GIROUETTE DE SAINT-CLOUD
Barre, Radet, Desfontaines et Bourgueil see
- CONRAD GESSNER
- MONSIEUR GUILLAUME OU LE VOYAGEUR INCONNUE

Barre, Radet et Desfontaines see ABUZAR OU LA FAMILLE EXTRAVAGANTE
Barre, SM see
- CREAM RAISING BY THE CENTRIFUGAL AND OTHER SYSTEMS:..
- ESSAY ON MR. W.H. LYNCH'S PAMPHLET ENTITLED SCIENTIFIC BUTTER MAKING
- RAPPORT SUR LA FABRICATION DU BEURRE:..

Barre, Vatry de la see DISSERTATIONS SUR LE POEME EPIQUE
LE BARREAU CANADIEN AU CONSEIL PRIVE: EXTRAITS D'UNE CONFERENCE PRONONCEE LE 14 MARS 1889 DEVANT LE CLUB CONSERVATEUR DE MONTREAL / Archambault, Joseph Louis – Montreal: A. Periard, 1889. 02197. (Pre-1900 Canadiana) – 9 – cn C.I.H.M. [340]
Barreca, Regina see LIT
BARRED AND DISALLOWED CASE FILES OF THE SOUTHERN CLAIMS COMMISSION, 1871-1880 – 4,829mf – 1 – M1407 – us Nat'l Archives [324]
Barreda, Ernesto Maria see
- UN CAMINO EN LA SELVA
- LUCHA DE ALAS
- UNA MUJER

Barrell see DNA SEQUENCE
THE BARREN GROUND OF NORTHERN CANADA / Pike, W – BN 347 2 ix, 300p., maps, index – 8 – ne IDC [970]
BARREN RUN BAPTIST CHURCH. SONORA, KENTUCKY : CHURCH RECORDS – Nov 1859-1928 – 1 reel – 1 – $29.16 – us Baptist [240]
Barrenechea, Raul Porras see CUADERNOS DE HISTORIA DEL PERU...
BARRER KANTONS-BLATT – (Cont by: Journal de Barr) – Barr, 1882-nov 9 1918, 1919, 1921-40, 1950-51, 1954 (all incomplete) – 1 – Dist. gw Mikrofilm – fr A.C.R.P.P. [944]
Barrere, P see
- ESSAI SUR L'HISTOIRE NATURELLE DE LA FRANCE EQUINOXIALE
- ORNITHOLOGIAE SPECIMEN NOVUM

Barres, Maurice see
- CONTRE LES ETRANGERS: ETUDE POUR LA PROTECTION DES OUVRIERS FRANCAIS
- THE FAITH OF FRANCE; STUDIES IN SPIRITUAL DIFFERENCES & UNITY

Barret, D see LES ILES DE L'OCEAN INDIEN OCCIDENTAL ET LE BATEAU
Barret, M l'Abbe see CARTULAIRE DE MARMOUTIER POUR LE PERCHE
Barrett, A C see COMPANION TO THE GREEK TESTAMENT
Barrett, Benjamin Fiske see LETTERS ON THE DIVINE TRINITY
Barrett, CG see THE LEPIDOPTERA OF THE BRITISH ISLANDS
Barrett, Charlotte see DIARY AND LETTERS... ED. BY HER NIECE CHARLOTTE BARRETT
Barrett, F see THE LIVES OF ALCHEMYSTICAL PHILOSOPHERS
Barrett, George Slatyer see THE TEMPTATION OF CHRIST
Barrett, George Slayter see OBJECTIONS TO ANARCHISM
Barrett, Kate R see AN INTERPRETIVE INQUIRY OF PRESERVICE TEACHERS' REFLECTIONS AND DEVELOPMENT DURING A FIELD-BASED ELEMENTARY PHYSICAL EDUCATION METHODS COURSE
Barrett, S A see THE ETHNO-GEOGRAPHY OF THE POMO AND NEIGHBORING INDIANS
Barrett, Thomas Squire see EXAMINATION OF GILLESPIE
LAS BARRIADAS DE...HONRAR AL ESPIRITU SANTO CON LOS SIGUIENTES FESTEJOS... 1976 / Parroquia del Espiritu Santo – Caceres: Tip. Rodriguez, 1976 – 1 – sp Bibl Santa Ana [946]
LAS BARRIADAS...HONRAN AL ESPIRITU SANTO CON LOS SIGUIENTES FESTEJOS. 1975 / Parroquia del Espiritu Santo – Caceres: Imp. Rodriguez, 1975 – 1 – sp Bibl Santa Ana [240]
BARRICADA – (Includes c.1: v.1:no.1 1959:Mar.3) – Buenos Aires – 1 – CSUXADN3454-S – us Hoover Inst Photo [972]
BARRICADA – Managua, NQ. 1979-1993 – 2r – $100.00 – R04227 – us Library Micro [320]
BARRICADA : OFFICIAL ORGAN / Frente Sandinista de Liberacion Nacional. Nicaragua – Nicaragua: Frente Sandinista de Liberacion Nacional, Jul 25 1979-Dec 1991 – 56r – 1 – us L of C Photodup [072]
BARRICADA INTERNACIONAL / Sandinista National Liberation Front – (1985-. 5,6,9) – 1982- – 1 – us UMI [320]
Barrichina, P see THESES IN CATHEDRAE HIPPOCRATIS CONCURSU...
Barrie, James Matthew see
- AULD LICHT IDYLLS
- BETTER DEAD
- THE LITTLE WHITE BIRD
- MARGARET OGILVY
- MY LADY NICOTINE
- SENTIMENTAL TOMMY

- TOMMY AND GRIZEL
- WHEN A MAN'S SINGLE
- A WINDOW IN THRUMS
Barrientos, Gaspar *see* CHOROGRAFIA
Barrientos Lavin, Oscar *see* ESTUDIO COMPARATIVO DE LA HIPOTECA MINERA Y LA HIPOTECA COMUN.
BARRIER COLLECTION OF SOUTH ASIAN POLITICAL TRACTS / Barrier, Norman Gerald – 1 – us Res Libr [950]
BARRIER MINER – Broken Hill, Jan 2 1907-Dec 31 1914 – 9 – at Pascoe [072]
Barrier, N G *see* POLITICAL RECORDS FILMED SPRING 1969
Barrier, Norman Gerald *see* BARRIER COLLECTION OF SOUTH ASIAN POLITICAL TRACTS
BARRIERE D'ITALIE, 15 DECEMBRE 1832, A PARIS – Avignon, impr. Chambeau, 8 p. Les Saint-Simoniens, 1825-1834. 6915 – 9 – fr Hachette [335]
BARRIERE DU TRONE, 15 DECEMBRE 1832. A PARIS, ADIEU / Barrault, Emile – Paris, impr. Duverger, s.d., 7 p. Les Saint-Simoniens, 1825-1834. 6963 – 9 – fr Hachette [335]
Barriere, Theodore *see* SCHOEN, LIEBER JOSEPH!
THE BARRIER-TREATY VINDICATED – Ed 2. London, 1712 – 3mf – 9 – ILM-2935/1 – ne IDC [340]
BARRIGA PRETA : UM POR TODOS, TODOS POR UM – Manaus, Amazonas. Abr-Dez 1949 – 1,5,6 – bl Biblioteca [072]
Barriga, Victor *see* LOS MERCEDARIOS EN EL PERU EN EL SIGLO 16. DOCUMENTOS INEDITOS DEL ARCHIVO GENERAL DE INDIAS. TOMO 1. ROMA, 1933
Barrington, New Hampshire. First Baptist Church *see* RECORDS
Barrio, Inocencio *see* HORA ARGENTINA Y TEMAS ANALITICOS RACIONLISTAS
Barrio y Rufo, Jose *see* APUNTES PARA LA HISTORIA...PLASENCIA
Barrionuevo, G *see* TRATADO SOBRE EL LAUDANO OPIATO...
Barrios, Americo *see*
- ADONDE VAMOS?
- CON PERON EN EL EXILIO
- PERON VISTO POR UN PERIODISTA
Barrios, D L de *see* TRIUMPHO DEL GOVIERNO POPULAR, Y DE LA ANTIGUEDAD HOLANDESA
Barrios, George F *see* HISTORY OF MADISON TOWNSHIP, INCLUDING GROVEPORT AND CANAL WINCHESTER, FRANKLIN COUNTY, OHIO
LA BARRIQUE : REVUE MENSUELLE – Montreal, avr 1972-nov 1984 – 2r – 1 – cn Can Microfilming [072]
THE BARRISTER : BEING ANECDOTES OF THE LATE TOM NOLAN OF THE NEW YORK BAR / Stansbury, Charles F – New York: Mab Press, 1902 – 3mf – 9 – $4.50 – LLMC 95-166 – us L.L.M.C. [340]
THE BARRISTER – (Lacking: no 2) – London: W Jenkinson. v1 nos 1,3,4. 1824 (all publ) – 1mf – 9 – $1.50 – LLMC 84-419 – us L.L.M.C. [073]
THE BARRISTER – Toronto: Law Pub Co, [1894-1897] – 9 – cn C.I.H.M. [340]
THE BARRISTER – Toronto. v1-3. 1894-97 (all publ) – 13mf – 9 – $19.50 – LLMC 84-420 – us L.L.M.C. [073]
BARRISTER (ABA) – v1-22. 1974-96 – 9 – $211.00 set – us Hein [340]
Barrit, J *see* JOURNAL, 1773-1819
Barro, M *see* CONTRIBUTION A L'ETUDE DE LA BIOLOGIE ET DE LA DYNAMIQUE DES POPULATIONS DE BRACHYDEUTERUS AURITUS VAL. 1831 (TELEOSTEEN, POMADASIIDAE) AU LARGE DE LA COTE D'IVOIRE
Barrois, T *see* ROLE DES INSECTES DANS LA FECONDATION DES VEGETAUX
BARRON'S – New York, NY. 1921- . -w. Indexed 1975- – 1 – us UMI [330]
BARRON'S INDEX – New York, NY. 1975- – 1 – us UMI [330]
BARRON'S NATIONAL BUSINESS AND FINANCIAL WEEKLY – New York. v1-19. 1921-39 – 16r – 1 – us Ross [336]
BARRON'S WEEKLY – NY City, NY. 1963-1973 – 28r – 1 – $1,400.00 – R04149 – us Library Micro [071]
Barros Arana, Diego *see*
- HISTORIA GENERAL DE CHILE
- PROCESO DE PEDRO DE VALDIVIA Y..
BARROS EMERITENSES / Barrantes Moreno, Vicente – 1877 – 9 – 1.50f – sp Bibl Santa Ana [946]
BARROS EMERITENSES / Barrantes Moreno, Vicente – S.L. s.i.s.a. – 1 – sp Bibl Santa Ana [946]
Barros, J de *see* L'ASIA...CONSIGLIERO DEL CHRISTIANISSIMO RE DI PORTOGALLO:...
Barroso, Gustavo *see* HISTORIA MILITAR DO BRASIL
Barroux, R *see* DAGOBERT
Barrow, David *see* INVOLUNTARY, UNMERITED, PERPETUAL, ABSOLUTE, HEREDITARY SLAVERY EXAMINED, 1753-1819
Barrow, J *see* A VOYAGE TO COCHINCHINA, IN THE YEARS 1792 AND 1793
Barrow, John *see*
- LIFE AND CORRESPONDENCE OF SIR WILLIAM SIDNEY SMITH
- THE LIFE OF RICHARD EARL HOWE, K.G., ADMIRAL OF THE FLEET AND GENERAL OF MARINES
- NOUVEAU VOYAGE DANS LA PARTIE MERIDIONALE DE L'AFRIQUE
- VOYAGE DANS LA PARTIE MERIDIONALE DE L'AFRIQUE
Barrows, Charles H *see* PERSONALITY OF JESUS
Barrows, Charles Henry *see* THE PERSONALITY OF JESUS
Barrows, E C *see*
- DIARY
- DIARY OF JOHN COMER
Barrows, Elijah Porter *see* COMPANION TO THE BIBLE
Barrows, Frederick I *see* HISTORY OF FAYETTE COUNTY
Barrows, H D *see* A MEMORIAL AND BIOGRAPHICAL HISTORY OF THE COAST COUNTIES OF CENTRAL CALIFORNIA
Barrows, Isabel C *see* CONFERENCE IN THE INTEREST OF PHYSICAL TRAINING, BOSTON, 1889
Barrows, John Henry *see*
- THE CHRISTIAN CONQUEST OF ASIA
- CHRISTIANITY, THE WORLD-RELIGION
- HENRY WARD BEECHER
- I BELIEVE IN GOD THE FATHER ALMIGHTY
- SEVEN LECTURES ON THE CREDIBILITY OF THE GOSPEL HISTORIES
Barrows, Samuel June *see* JESUS AS A PENOLOGIST
Barruel, Etienne *see* PLAN D'EDUCATION NATIONALE CONSIDEREE SOUS LE RAPPORT DES LIVRES ELEMENTAIRES
Barruel-Beauvert, Antoine-Joseph Comte de *see* VIE DE J.-J. ROUSSEAU, PRECEDEE DE QUELQUES LETTRES RELATIVES AU MEME SUJET
Barry, Alfred *see*
- THE ATONEMENT OF CHRIST
- THE ECCLESIASTICAL EXPANSION OF ENGLAND: IN THE GROWTH OF THE ANGLICAN COMMUNION
- MANIFOLD WITNESS FOR CHRIST
- MASTERS IN ENGLISH THEOLOGY
- WHAT IS NATURAL THEOLOGY?
BARRY AND DISTRICT NEWS – Wales, 1950; 1986- – 20+ r – 1 – uk British Libr Newspaper [072]
Barry, Dawn M *see* ENERGY EXPENDITURE OF STEP TRAINING VS. LOW IMPACT AEROBICS USING THREE COMMON MOVEMENT PATTERNS
Barry, E *see* BARRYMORE
Barry, James *see* CUSTOMS TARIFF, EXCISE AND EXPORT DUTIES, REGULATIONS, ETC..
Barry, John S *see* THE HISTORY OF MASSACHUSETTS
Barry, Phillips *see* FOLK MUSIC IN AMERICA
Barry, Robertine *see* JOURNAL DE FRANCOISE
Barry, William Francis *see*
- ERNEST RENAN
- HERALDS OF REVOLT; STUDIES IN MODERN LITERATURE AND DOGMA
- NEWMAN
- THE PAPACY AND MODERN TIMES
- THE PAPACY AND MODERN TIMES; A POLITICAL SKETCH, 1303-1870
- THE PAPAL MONARCHY
BARRYMORE / Barry, E – Cork: Guy & Co, 1902 – 1r – 1 – us Western Res [920]
Barsanti, F *see*
- SIX SONATAS FOR 2 VIOLINS AND A BASS, OP. 6
- SONATAS (1-6) 2VLNS, VC, THOROUGH-BASS; OUT OF GEMINIANIS SOLOS
Barsegiants, O B *see* REKVIZITSII A I KONFISKATSII A PO ZAKONODATELSTVU R.S.F.S.R.
Barsegiants, OB *see*
- ALFAVITNO-PREDMETNYI UKAZATEL K DEKRETAM, POSTANOVLENIIAM I RASPORI AZHENIIAM
- ALFAVITNO-PREDMETNYI UKAZATEL K POSTANOVLENIIAM I RASPORI AZHENIIAM MOSKOVSKOGO SOVETA R., K. I K.D. I EGO OTDELOV, OPUBLIKOVANNYKH V GAZETE "KOMMUNISTICHESKI I TRUD"
- ALFAVITNO-PREDMETNYI UKAZATEL ZA IANVAR 1922 G. K DEKRETAM, POSTANOVLENIIAM, RASPORIAZHENIIAM I PRIKAZAM
Barskov, I L *see* PEREPISKA MOSKOVSKIKH MASONOV XVIII VEKA. 1780-92 GG
BARSTOW COLLEGE STUDENT PAPER – Barstow, CA. 1961-79 – 1r – 1 – $50.00 – R02046 – us Library Micro [071]
BARSTOW PRINTERS REVIEW – Barstow, CA. Jun 1943-Oct 1958 – 17r – 1 – $850.00 – C02047 – us Library Micro [073]
Barsukov, A P *see* RASSKAZY IZ RUSSKOI ISTORII XVIII VEKA
Bart *see* DNA SEQUENCE
Bart des Boullais, Leonard *see* RECUEIL DES ANTIQUITEZ DU PERCHE
BARTAS: HIS DEVINE WEEKES AND WORKES / Du Bartas, Guillaume de Salluste – 1605 – 9 – 35.00 – us Scholars' Facs [810]
Bartell, Laura B *see* LAW CLERK HANDBOOK
Bartels, Adolf *see*
- BAUERNSPIEGEL
- FRIEDRICH HEBBEL UND OTTO LUDWIG
- GESCHICHTE DER DEUTSCHEN LITERATUR
- JEREMIAS GOTTHELF
- KLAUS GROTH
Bartels, Petrus *see* JOHANNES A LASCO
Bartels, Rudolf *see* ZU SCHILLERS "DAS IDEAL UND DAS LEBEN"
Barth, Auguste *see*
- BIBLIOGRAPHIE ET INDEX GENERALE DES OEUVRES DE AUGUSTE BARTH
- OEUVRES
- OEUVRES DE AUGUSTE BARTH
Barth, C *see* DIE INTERPRETATION DES NEUEN TESTAMENTS IN DER VALENTINIANISCHEN GNOSIS (T.U.U. 3-37/3)
Barth Family *see* PAPERS
Barth, Fritz *see*
- GOSPEL OF ST JOHN AND THE SYNOPTIC GOSPELS
- THE GOSPEL OF ST. JOHN AND THE SYNOPTIC GOSPELS
Barth, Hans *see* ROEMISCHE ASCHE
Barth, Heinrich *see*
- TRAVELS AND DISCOVERIES IN NORTH AND CENTRAL AFRICA
- VOYAGES ET DECOUVERTES DANS L'AFRIQUE SEPTENTRIONALE ET CENTRALE PENDANT LES ANNEES 1849 A 1855
Barth, Jakob *see*
- BEITRAEGE ZUR ERKLAERUNG DES JESAIA
- ETYMOLOGISCHE STUDIEN ZUM SEMITISCHEN
- SPRACHWISSENSCHAFTLICHE UNTERSUCHUNGEN ZUM SEMITISCHEN
- WURZELUNTERSUCHUNGEN ZUM HEBRAEISCHEN UND ARAMAEISCHEN LEXIKON
Barth, Karl *see* DER ROEMERBRIEF
Barthe, Georges Isidore *see*
- DRAMES DE LA VIE REELE
- DRAMES DE LA VIE REELLE: ROMAN CANADIEN
Barthe, Joseph Guillaume *see* SOUVENIRS D'UN DEMI-SIECLE OU MEMOIRES POUR SERVIR A L'HISTOIRE CONTEMPORAINE
Barthe, Ulrich *see*
- JOURNAL DE L'EXPOSITION
- LA VIGIE
Barthel, Max *see* REVOLUTIONAERE GEDICHTE
Barthelemy, P *see* L'OMNIBUS DU LANGAGE
Barthelemy-Lapommeraye, C J *see* RICHESSES ORNITHOLOGIQUES DU MIDI DE LA FRANCE
Barthelmon, M *see* SIX SONATAS FOR HARPSICHORD OR PIANOFORTE WITH AN ACCOMPANYMENT FOR VIOLIN
Barthelmy, M P *see* BIOGRAPHIE ET GALERIE HISTORIQUE DES CONTEMPORAINS...
Barthold, W *see*
- NACHRICHTEN UEBER DEN ARAL SEE UND DEN UNTEREN LAUF DES AMU-DARJA VON DEN AELTESTEN ZEITEN BIS ZU 17. JAHRHUNDERT
- TURKESTAN DOWN TO THE MONGOL INVASION
- ZUR GESCHICHTE DES CHRISTENTUMS IN MITTEL-ASIEN BIS ZUR MONGOLISCHEN EROBERUNG
Bartholin, Rasmus *see* ERASMI BARTHOLINI DE NATURAE MIRABILIBUS QUAESTIONES ACADEMICAE
Bartholin, T *see*
- THE ANATOMICAL HISTORY
- DE LACTEIS THORACICIS IN HOMINE BRUTISQUE NUPERRIME OBSERVATIS,...
Bartholin, Thomas *see* THOMAE BARTHOLINI ACTA MEDICA ET PHILOSOPHICA HAFNIENSIA
Bartholino, Tomas *see* EL INCENDIO DE LA BIBLIOTECA
Bartholinus, C *see* CASP. BARTHOLINI THOM. FIL. DE TIBIIS VETERUM ET EARUM ANTIQUO USU LIBRI TRES
Bartholmess, Christian *see* HUET, EVEQUE D'AVRANCHES, OU, LE SCEPTICISME THEOLOGIQUE
Bartholomaeus, A *see* DE PROPRIETATIBUS RERUM
Bartholomaeus, G *see*
- DE AFFLICTIONE TAM CAPTIVORVM QUAM ETIAM SUB TURCAE TRIBUTO VIUENTIUM CHRISTIANORUM,...
- DE TURCARUM RITV ET CAEREMONIIS,...
- DE TVRCARVM MORIBVS EPITOME
- LIBELLVS VERE CHRISTIANA...
- PROFETIA DE I TVRCHI, DELLA LORO ROUINA, O LA CONUERSIONE ALLA FEDE DI CHRISTO PER FORZA DELLA SPADA CHRSTIANA
- PROPHETIA DE MAOMETANI, ET ALTRE COSE TURCHESCHE, ...
Bartholomeus de Cotton *see* HISTORIA ANGLICANA (A.D. 449-1298) (RS16)
Bartholomew, Elam *see* DIARIES
Bartholomew, John George *see* THE POCKET ATLAS AND GAZETTEER OF THE DOMINION OF CANADA
Bartholomew, John George et al *see* ATLAS OF ZOOGEOGRAPHY
Bartholomin, Mr *see* PIZARRO O LA CONQUISTA DEL PERU
Bartin, E *see*
- ETUDES DE DROIT INTERNATIONAL PRIVE
- ETUDES SUR LES EFFETS INTERNATIONAUX DES JUGEMENTS
BARTLESVILLE FIRST BAPTIST CHURCH. BARTLESVILLE, OKLAHOMA : CHURCH RECORDS – 1904-54 – 1 – 63.63 – us Baptist [240]
Bartlet, James Vernon *see*
- ACTS: INTRODUCTION, AV, RV, WITH NOTES, INDEX
- THE APOSTOLIC AGE
Bartlett *see* HISTORY OF MORROW COUNTY
Bartlett, Caroline J *see* WOMAN'S CALL TO THE MINISTRY
Bartlett, Charles Lafayette *see* TRIAL BY JURY IN CONTEMPT PROCEEDINGS
Bartlett, D W *see* BARTLETT'S DIGEST, ELECTION CASES IN THE HOUSE OF REPRESENTATIVES
Bartlett, E *see* A MONOGRAPH OF THE WEAVER-BIRDS
Bartlett, IS *see* HISTORY OF WYOMING
Bartlett, J *see* AUTOBIOGRAPHY, 1855
Bartlett, James Herbert *see*
- THE MANUFACTURE, CONSUMPTION AND PRODUCTION OF IRON, STEEL, AND COAL IN THE DOMINION OF CANADA: WITH SOME NOTES OF THE MANUFACTURE OF IRON, AND ON THE IRON TRADE, IN OTHER COUNTRIES
- THE MANUFACTURE OF IRON IN CANADA
Bartlett, Josiah *see*
- FAMILY PAPERS
- THE PAPERS OF JOSIAH BARTLETT
- PAPERS OF JOSIAH BARTLETT
Bartlett, S T *see* THE JUNIOR LEAGUE HAND-BOOK
Bartlett, Samuel Colcord *see*
- THE DUTY AND THE LIMITATIONS OF CIVIL DISOBEDIENCE
- SOURCES OF HISTORY IN THE PENTATEUCH: SIX LECTURES
Bartlett, Vernon *see* I ACCUSE
BARTLETT'S DIGEST, ELECTION CASES IN THE HOUSE OF REPRESENTATIVES : 1865-1871 / Bartlett, D W – Washington: GPO. 41st Congress 2nd session. 1871? – 9 – LLMC 95-123 – us L.L.M.C. [340]
Bartley, E T *see* LILIAN'S RETROSPECT
BARTLEY INTER-OCEAN – Bartley, NE. -w. May 1888-Dec. 1896. Incomplete; Mar. 1899-Jan. 1901; Apr. 1901-Jun. 1901; Aug. 1901-Apr. 1902. Incomplete; Aug. 1908-Dec. 1909; Feb. 1910-Mar. 1947 – 1 – us NE Hist [071]

Bartling, F G *see* ORDINES NATURALES PLANTARUM CORUMQUE CHARACTERES ET AFFINITATES ADJECTA GENERUM ENUMERATIONE
Bartling, FG *see* BEITRAEGE ZUR BOTANIK
Bartlow et al *see* CENTENNIAL HISTORY OF BUTLER COUNTY
Bartmann, Bernard *see* NEUE BILDUNGSWEGE
Bartoche, M *see* EXPOSE...NOTAMMENT DU DROIT INTERNATIONAL COMMERCIAL...
Bartok, Bela *see*
- MAGYAR NEPDAL
- SERBO-CROATIAN FOLK SONGS
Bartol, Cyrus Augustus *see*
- IN REMEMBRANCE-ADDRESS ON OCCASION OF THE DEATH OF CHARLES GREELY LORING.
- RADICAL PROBLEMS
- THE RISING FAITH
Bartoli, D *see* DELL ISTORIA DELLA COMPAENIA DI GESU. L'ASIA. PARTES PRIMA ET SECUNDA
Bartoli, Giorgio *see* THE PRIMITIVE CHURCH AND THE PRIMACY OF ROME
Bartolo, P S *see* COLUMNA ANTONINIANA MARCI AURELII ANTONINI AUGUSTI. CUM NOTIS EXCERPTIS EX DECLARATIONIBUS J. P. BELLORII
Bartolo, Salvatore di *see* LES CRITERES THEOLOGIQUES
BARTOLOME JOSE GALLARDO... / Blanco Garcia, Francisco – Madrid: Saenz de Jubera, 1909 – 1 – sp Bibl Santa Ana [440]
Bartolt, P *see* ADMIRANDA ROMANARUM ANTIQUITATUM AC VETERIS SCULPTURAE VESTIGIA
Bartolus, A *see* THEATRI MACHINARUM
Bartolus, de Saxoferrato *see* ON THE CONFLICTS...
Barton *see* PAST AND PRESENT OF ADAMS COUNTY
Barton, Charles *see* MODERN PRECEDENTS IN CONVEYANCING.
BARTON COUNTY DEMOCRAT – Great Bend. Kan. 1915-18 – 1 – us UMI [071]
BARTON COUNTY DEMOCRAT – Great Bend. Kan. -w. 1886-1915 – 1 – us UMI [071]
Barton, Dunbar P *see* THE STORY OF THE INNS OF COURT
Barton, E S *see* THE GENUS HALIMEDA
Barton, G A *see* MISCELLANEOUS BABYLONIAN INSCRIPTIONS
Barton, George *see* ANGELS OF THE BATTLEFIELD
Barton, George A *see* HILPRECHT'S FRAGMENT OF THE BABYLONIAN DELUGE STORY
Barton, George Aaron *see* A CRITICAL AND EXEGETICAL COMMENTARY ON THE BOOK OF ECCLESIASTES
Barton, James Levi *see*
- EDUCATIONAL MISSIONS
- HUMAN PROGRESS THROUGH MISSIONS
- THE MISSIONARY AND HIS CRITICS
- THE UNFINISHED TASK OF THE CHRISTIAN CHURCH
Barton, John *see* A NEW ITALIAN GRAMMAR: OR, A GUIDE TO THE ITALIAN TONGUE
Barton, L E *see* AUTOBIOGRAPHICAL MATERIAL, MISS WILLIE KELLEY
Barton, Samuel *see* THE BATTLE OF THE SWASH AND THE CAPTURE OF CANADA
Barton, W P C *see*
- COMPENDIUM FLORAE PHILADELPHICAE
- A FLORA OF NORTH AMERICA
- VEGETABLE MATERIA MEDICA OF THE UNITED STATES OR, MEDICAL BOTANY
Barton, William E *see*
- THE BOOK OF ENLIGHTENMENT FOR THE INSTRUCTION OF THE INQUIRER
- OLD PLANTATION HYMNS
Bartoszewicz, J von *see* DIE ERBSCHAFTSSTEUER IM INTERNATIONALEN RECHTE
Bartram, W *see* TRAVELS THROUGH NORTH AND SOUTH CAROLINA, GEORGIA, EAST AND WEST FLORIDA
BART'S JOURNAL – 1975- – 1,5,6,9 – us UMI [610]
Bartsch, Gerhard N *see* WIRTSCHAFTS- UND SOZIALGEOGRAPHISCHE UNTERSUCHUNGEN IN SAN CARLOS (NICARAGUA) UNTER BESONDERER BERUECKSICHTIGUNG DES INFORMELLEN SEKTORS
Bartsch, Karl *see* DIE DEUTSCHE TREUE IN SAGE UND POESIE
Bartsch Karl et al *see* GERMANIA
Bartsch, P *see* A MONOGRAPH OF WEST AMERICAN PYRAMIDELLID MOLLUSKS
Bartsch, Rudolf Hans *see*
- ALS OESTERREICH ZERFIEL
- EWIGES ARKADIEN!
- DER FALKE VOM MONS REGIUS
- UNERFUELLTE GESCHICHTEN
Bartuska, V *see* LES LITUANIENS D'AMERIQUE
Baruch, Amy R *see* EFFECTS OF CAFFEINE ON CENTRAL ON PERIPHERAL HEMODYNAMICS AT REST AND DURING EXERCISE
Baruffaldi, G *see* VITE DE' PITTORI E SCULTORI FERRARESE...
Barvo y Bravo Fernando *see* BIMILENARIO DE LA FUNDACION DE LA COLONIA NORBA CAESERINA
BARWON EXPRESS – Walgett, Jun 29 1901-Jun 3 1905 – 9 – at Pascoe [072]
Bary, Erwin de *see* LE DERNIER RAPPORT D'UN EUROPEEN SUR GHAT ET LES TOUAREG DE L'AIR
Bary, H A de *see*
- COMPARATIVE MORPHOLOGY AND BIOLOGY OF THE FUNGI, MYCETOZOA AND BACTERIA
- UEBER DIE FRUCHTENTWICKLUNG DER ASCOMYCETEN
Bary, R *see*
- LA RHETORIQUE FRANCOISE
- LES SECRETS DE NOSTRE LANGUE
BARYKADA – (Filmed with: Miecz i Plug) – [Poland], 1942-44 – 1r – 1 – $85.00 – us Ross [072]
BARYKADA *see* MIECZ I PLUG
Baryphonus, H *see* HENRICI BARYPHONI PLEJADES MUSICAE QUAE FUNDAMENTA MUSICAE THEORETICAE EX PRINCIPIIS MATHEMATICIS QUA
Barz, Andre *see* PSYCHOLOGISCHE ASPEKTE DES DARSTELLENDEN SPIELS
BARZGAR – (Missing issues: 19, 21, 33, 43, 45, 85, 87, 91, 111, 115, 130, 144, 190, 218, 220, 258, 306, 352, 358) – Nashriyah-'i Haftigi-i Kishavarzi va Damdari. No. 18-409/410 (20 Urdibihisht 1359-22 Isfand 1366) – 3r – 1 – $60.00 – us MEDOC [950]
A BAS LA CALOTTE OU LES DEPRETRISES / Rousseau, Thomas – (French Theatre Series). Paris. Toubon. 1794 – 9 – fr Hachette [820]
BASA FIELD NOTES / Schwab, George – [Evanston, 1965] – us Res Libr [500]
BASA SUNDA / Nataprawira, P – SE-5578 1. 5 v. 1956 – 9 – ne IDC [950]
BASAKABAKA BE BUGANDA / Kagwa, Apolo – [s.l: s.n, 19–?] – 1 – us Res Libr [960]
Basar, Suekuefe Nihal *see* RENKSIZ ISTIRAB
BASARI – Manisa: Basari Murettiphanesi, [jul 9 1951-feb 22 1952] – 1r – 1 – us Res Libr [072]
Basari, Moh *see* SETJARIK PELANGI DI RICHTINGWIJZER
BASATIN AL-SALATIN / Ghulam Murtada – Hyderabad. Bl-775 2 – 8 – ne IDC [490]
Bas-Canada *see*
- COPY OF THE CHARTER OF THE CORPORATION OF SAINT NICOLET IN LOWER CANADA, WITH INSTRUCTIONS OF LORD BATHURST ON THE SUBJECT
- PUBLIC ACCOUNTS FOR... COMPTES PUBLICS POUR...
- STATEMENT OF THE PUBLIC REVENUE AND EXPENDITURE OF LOWER CANADA FOR THE YEAR...
LE BAS-CANADA : AUTONOMISTE – Montreal, Canada. 8 mar 1919-v1 n4. 19 avr 1919 – 1r – 1 – Can$30.00 – cn Can Microfilming [072]
LE BAS-CANADA – Trois-Rivieres, Canada. 22 avr-14 nov 1856 – 1r – 1 – Can$30.00 – cn Can Microfilming [072]
Bas-Canada. Chambre d'Assemblee. Comite Permanent des Griefs *see* SECOND RAPPORT DU COMITE PERMANENT DE GRIEFS : SECOND...
Bas-Canada. Commissaires pour explorer le Saguenay *see* REPORT OF THE COMMISSIONERS FOR EXPLORING THE SAGUENAY
Bas-Canada. Commissaires Pour les Chemins et Autres Communications Interieures *see* REPORTS OF COMMISSIONERS FOR ROADS AND OTHER INTERNAL COMMUNICATIONS : RAPPORTS DES...
Bas-Canada. Cour du Banc du Roi *see*
- REPORTS OF CASES ARGUED AND DETERMINED IN THE COURTS OF KING'S BENCH AND IN THE PROVINCIAL COURT OF APPEALS OF LOWER CANADA...
- TABLE OF FEES
Bas-Canada. Gouverneur *see*
- MESSAGE FROM HIS EXCELLENCY THE GOVERNOR IN CHIEF, RELATING TO THE EXPULSION OF MR. CHRISTIE
- MESSAGE FROM HIS EXCELLENCY THE GOVERNOR IN CHIEF, RELATING TO THE SUPPLY BILL FOR THE YEAR 1833. RECEIVED 13TH JANUARY, 1834 MESSAGE DE...
Bas-Canada. Laws, Statutes etc *see*
- AN ACT TO MAKE TEMPORARY PROVISION FOR THE GOVERNMENT OF LOWER CANADA
- ARTICLES ENACTED IN THE ACT INTITULED "AN ACT TO REPEAL A CERTAIN ACT THEREIN-MENTIONED, AND TO PROVIDE FOR THE POLICE OF THE BOROUGH OF WILLIAM-HENRY,...
Bas-Canada. Parlement *see*
- PROVINCIAL PARLIAMENT OF LOWER-CANADA
- RAPPORT DU COMITE SPECIAL DE LA CHAMBRE D'ASSEMBLEE DU BAS-CANADA, NOMME POUR S'ENQUERIR DE L'ETAT ACTUEL DE L'EDUCATION DANS LA PROVINCE DU BAS-CANADA
- REPORT OF A SPECIAL COMMITTEE OF THE HOUSE OF ASSEMBLY APPOINTED TO ENQUIRE INTO THE STATE OF EDUCATION IN THIS PROVINCE
Bas-Canada. Parlement. Chambre d'assemblee *see*
- ENQUETE DEVANT LA CHAMBRE D'ASSEMBLEE DU BAS-CANADA SUR LES EVENEMENTS DU 21 MAI 1832 A MONTREAL
- RAPPORT DU COMITE SPECIAL AUQUEL A ETE REFERE CETTE PARTIE DE LA HARANGUE DE SON EXCELLENCE RELATIVE A L'ORGANIZATION [SIC] DE LA MILICE
- REPORT OF THE SPECIAL COMMITTEE TO WHOM WAS REFERRED THAT PART OF HIS EXCELLENCY'S SPEECH WHICH REFERRED TO THE ORGANIZATION OF THE MILITIA
Bas-Canada. Parlement. Chambre d'Assemblee. Comite Auquel ont ete Renvoyees la Petition des Universalistes du Bas-Canada *see* REPORT OF THE COMMITTEE TO WHOM HAVE BEEN REFERRED THE PETITION OF THE UNIVERSALISTS OF LOWER CANADA : RAPPORT...
Bas-Canada. Parlement. Chambre d'Assemblee. Comite Permanent des Griefs *see*
- COPY OF THE FOURTH REPORT OF THE STANDING COMMITTEE OF THE GRIEVANCES...
- FOURTH REPORT OF THE STANDING COMMITTEE OF GRIEVANCES
- THIRD REPORT OF THE STANDING COMMITTEE OF GRIEVANCES...
- TROISIEME RAPPORT DU COMITE PERMANENT DES GRIEFS...
Bas-Canada. Parlement. Chambre d'assemblee. Comite permanent sur l'education et des ecoles *see* REPORT OF THE STANDING COMMITTEE OF EDUCATION AND SCHOOLS
Bas-Canada. Parlement. Chambre d'assemblee. Comite permanent sur les chemins et ameliorations publiques *see* STANDING COMMITTEE ON ROADS AND PUBLIC IMPROVEMENTS, 1831-1832
Bas-Canada. Parlement. Chambre d'Assemblee. Comite Special sur Diverses Communications... *see*
- SECOND RAPPORT DU COMITE SPECIAL SUR DIVERSES COMMUNICATIONS DE SON EXCELLENCE LE GOUVERNEUR EN CHEF LORD AYLMER, SUR LE SUJET DES FINANCES DE LA PROVINCE DU BAS-CANADA
- SECOND REPORT FROM THE SPECIAL COMMITTEE ON VARIOUS COMMUNICATIONS FROM HIS EXCELLENCY...
Bas-Canada. Parlement. Chambre d'Assemblee. Comite Special sur les Chemins et Autres Communications Interieures *see* REPORTS FROM THE SPECIAL COMMITTEE ON ROADS AND OTHER INTERNAL COMUNICATIONS
Bas-Canada. Parlement. Chambre d'Assemblee. Comite special sur les comptes publics de la Province *see* REPORT OF THE SELECT COMMITEE, ON THE PUBLIC ACCOUNTS OF THE PROVINCE, FROM THE COMMENCEMENT OF THE CONSTITUTION IN 1791, UNTIL 1822, INCLUSIVE
Bas-Canada. Parlement. Chambre d'Assemblee. Comite sur Cette Partie... *see* FIRST REPORT OF THE COMMITTEE OF THE HOUSE OF ASSEMBLY ON THAT PART OF THE SPEECH OF HIS EXCELLENCY...
Bas-Canada. Parlement. Chambre d'assemblee. Comite sur Cette Partie... *see*
- THE "CREDIT FONCIER"
- FIRST REPORT OF THE COMMITTEE OF THE HOUSE OF ASSEMBLY...
Bas-Canada. Parlement...Comite Special sur... *see* PREMIER RAPPORT DU COMITE SPECIAL SUR LES COMMUNICATIONS INTERIEURES
Bas-Canada. Parliament. House of Assembly *see*
- MINUTES OF EVIDENCE AND REPORT OF THE SPECIAL COMMITTEE OF THE HOUSE OF ASSEMBLY OF LOWER CANADA...
- PROCEEDINGS IN THE ASSEMBLY OF LOWER-CANADA, ON THE ACCUSATIONS AGAINST PIERRE BEDARD, ESQ. PROVINCIAL JUDGE FOR THE DISTRICT OF THREE-RIVERS
Basch, Johannes *see* GESAMMT-VERLAGS-KATALOG DES DEUTSCHEN BUCHHANDELS UND DES MIT IHM IM DIREKTEN VERKEHR STEHENDEN AUSLANDES
BASCHKAER ZEITUNG – Apatin, 1930, 1932, 1935, 1938-40 – 2r – 1 – Dist. gw Mikrofilm – gw Misc Inst [949]
Bascom, John *see*
- COMPARATIVE PSYCHOLOGY; OR, THE GROWTH AND GRADES OF INTELLIGENCE
- ETHICS
- EVOLUTION AND RELIGION, OR, FAITH AS A PART OF A COMPLETE COSMIC SYSTEM
- THE GOODNESS OF GOD
- THE INTERESTS OF THE FARMER INDEFINITELY POSTPONED
- NATURAL THEOLOGY
- THE NEW THEOLOGY
- PHILOSOPHY OF RHETORIC
- SCIENCE, PHILOSOPHY AND RELIGION
- SERMONS AND ADDRESSES
- SOCIAL THEORY
- THE WORDS OF CHRIST AS PRINCIPLES OF PERSONAL AND SOCIAL GROWTH
BASCOM, WILLIAM AND BERTA, THE YORUBA COLLECTION OF – 560mf – 9 – $3,000.00 – us Ross [060]
LE BAS-CONGO, ETAT RELIGIEUX ET SOCIAL / Philippart, Leon – Louvain: Saint-Alphonse, 1929 – 1 – us Res Libr [306]
BASDAN (1948-49) AND YENI BASDAN (1950) – Istanbul: Aziz Nesin; Rifat Ilgaz – 4mf – 9 – $36.75 – us MEDOC [949]
Basdevant, J *see*
- LA REVOLUTION FRANCAISE...
- TRAITES ET CONVENTIONS EN VIGUEUR ENTRE LA FRANCE ET LES PUISSANCES ETRANGERES
BASE BALL TRIBUNE – New York. v1 n1-18. 1887 – 1r – 1 – us Ross [790]
BASEBALL PLAYERS CHRONICLE. AMERICAN CHRONICLE OF SPORTS AND PASTIMES – New York, NY. 1867, 1868 – 1r – 1 – $40.00r – us U.N.D. Archives [790]
BASEBALL SCRAPBOOKS – ca 1853-82(-1912) – 1r – 1 – $40.00r – us U.N.D. Archives [790]
Basecke, M *see* THE RELATIONSHIPS AMONG EXERCISE BLOOD LACTATE RESPONSE, MUSCLE BLOOD FLOW, AND OXIDATIVE ADAPTATION TO ENDURANCE TRAINING IN THE RAT
Basedow, A *see* DIE INCLUSEN IN DEUTSCHLAND VORNEHMLICH IN DER GEGEND DES NIEDERRHEINS UM DIE WENDE DES 12. UND 13. JAHRHUNDERTS
Basedow, Johann Bernhard *see* PHILALETHIE
BASEL. KUNSTHALLE CATALOGUE – (Individual titles not listed separately) – uk Chadwyck [700]
The Basel Mission *see* GHANA ARCHIVE
Baselt, Randall *see* JOURNAL OF ANALYTICAL TOXICOLOGY
LAS BASES – (Includes c.1: v1:no1 1971: Nov-v3:no133 (1975:Feb.); v3:no136 1975: Mar.-v3:no154 (1975:July)) – 1 – CSUXAGP9535-S – us Hoover Inst Photo [073]
BASES DE LA 1ST EXPOSICION DE FOTOGRAFIAS... / Obra Sindical de Educacion y Descanso – Caceres: Tip. El Noticiero, s.a. – 1 – sp Bibl Santa Ana [770]

BASES DE LA PEDAGOGIA CONSTITUCIONAL / Ghioldi, Americo – Buenos Aires: [Talleres de la editorial "La Vanguardia"], 1944 – 1 – CSUXAGP8692-B – us Hoover Inst Photo [370]
BASES ET PRIORITES DES PROGRAMMES SECTORIELS. PERIODE QUINQUENNALE 1971-76 / Haiti. Conseil National de Developpement et de Planification – (Bases and priorities of sectoral programs for the five year period 1971-76) – 9 – ne IDC [338]
BASES FONDAMENTALES DE L'INSTRUCTION PUBLIQUE / Lanthenas, Francois X. – Paris. Imp. du Cercle Social. Mars 1793 – 9 – fr Hachette [321]
BASES FONDAMENTALES DE L'INSTRUCTION PUBLIQUE ET DE TOUTE CONSTITUTION LIBRE / Lanthenas, Francois X. – Seconde edition que la tyrannie de Robespierre a empechee de paraitre. Paris. l'auteur. 1793 – 9 – fr Hachette [321]
BASES OF BELIEF: AN EXAMINATION OF CHRISTIANITY AS A DIVINE REVELATION / Miall, Edward – London: Arthur Hall, Virtue, 1853. 1 fiche – 9 – us A.T.L.A. [240]
BASES OF RELIGIOUS BELIEF : HISTORIC AND IDEAL: AN OUTLINE OF RELIGIOUS STUDY / Tyler, Charles Mellen – (Includes index) – NY: G P Putnam, 1897 – 1mf – 9 – 0-8370-5591-I – 1985-3591 – us A.T.L.A. [210]
BASES ORIENTADORAS PARA LA FIJACION DE HONORARIOS APROBADOS POR LA JUNTA GENERAL DE ESTE ILUSTRE COLEGIO, EL 31 DE MARZO DE 1961 / Colegio Provincial de Abogados de Badajoz – Badajoz: Tip. Clasica, 1965 – sp Bibl Santa Ana [946]
BASES PARA LA ALIANZA CONSTITUYENTE DE LA NUEVA ARGENTINA – [Buenos Aires]: Cuadernos peronistas, 1982 – 1 – CSUXADJ0073-B – us Hoover Inst Photo [972]
BASES PARA UNA PROPUESTA PROGRAMATICA JUSTICIALISTA / Convocatoria Peronista – Corrientes, Argentina: La Convocatoria, [1983?] – 1 – CSUXAJA8010-B – us Hoover Inst Photo [320]
BASES SOCIALES DE LA CONSTITUCION JUSTICIALISTA / Ganduglia, Santiago – Buenos Aires: Presidencia de la Nacion, Secretaria de Prensa y Difusion, [1949?] – 1 – CSUXADP3965-B – us Hoover Inst Photo [340]
BASES Y DIRECTIVAS PARA PROGRAMMAR EL DESARROLLO ECONOMICO (1955-1965) / Ecuador. Junta Nacional de Planificacion y Coordinacion Economica – D-1288 1. 1958 – 9 – ne IDC [338]
BASES Y REGLAMENTOS...CIRCULO CONCORDIA / Belmonte, Francisco – 1896 – 9 – 1.50f – sp Bibl Santa Ana [240]
Basetti-Sani, Julio *see* MOHAMMED ET SAINT FRANCOIS...
Basevi, A *see*
- INTRODUCTION A UN NOUVEAU SYSTEME D'HARMONIE PAR ABRAMO BASEVI...
- INTRODUZIONE AD UN NOUVE SISTEMA D'ARMONIA
- STUDJ SULL'ARMONIA

BASHAQRA AREA SETTLEMENTS 1963; A CASE STUDY IN VILLAGE DEVELOPMENT IN THE GEZIRA SCHEME / Brausch, G & Crooke, P & Shaw, J – 1964. BNE-7603 1 – 9 – ne IDC [338]
BASHEYDN = MODEST – Toronto, CN, 1930 – 1r – 1 – Can$25.00 – cn Can Microfilming [072]
Bashford, James Whitford *see*
- CHINA AND METHODISM
- GOD'S MISSIONARY PLAN FOR THE WORLD
- WESLEY AND GOETHE

Bashkatovym, A *see* GEOGRAFICHESKII LEKSIKON
BASHKIMI – 1976-1995 – 1 – sz Infoprint [072]
BASHKIMI – Tirana, Albania. Nov 1943-Dec 1976 – 45r – 1 – us L of C Photodup [072]
BASHKIMI – Tirane, 1976-1991ff – 16r – 1 – DM1,200.00 – gw Mikro Press [947]
BASHKIMI – [Tirane, Albania], 1976- – ca 1r per y – 1 – $70.00r – us Ross [072]
Bashmakov, A A *see*
- OCHERKI PRAVA RODOVOGO, NASLEDSTVENNOGO I OBYCHNOGO
- ZA SMUTNYE GODY

LA BASI DI UN CODICE PENALE INTERNAZIONALE... / Cosentini, F – Milano, 1937 – 1mf – 1 – ILM-2475/1 – ne IDC [327]
BASIC DATA ON STUDENT ENROLMENT IN MALDIVES, FEBRUARY 1990 / Maldives. Ministry of Education – Male, 1990 – 1mf – 9 – DE-673/1 – ne IDC [370]
BASIC DESIGN PROCESS AND VISUAL COMMUNICATION PRODUCTS / Kopease, State College, PA – 1974 – 189p 90+ illus 4mf – 9 – $0.50f – us Lawrence Pub [720]
BASIC DOCUMENTS OF THE LEAGUE OF ARAB STATES – New York: The Arab Info Center, 1955 – us Res Libr [327]
BASIC EDUCATION AND LITERACY PROGRAMME / Maldives. Ministry of Education – [Male], 1990 – 1mf – 9 – DE-671/1 – ne IDC [370]
BASIC EDUCATION STATISTICS / Ethiopia. Ministry of Education – Addis Ababa, 1988 – 1mf – 9 – DE-621/1 – ne IDC [370]
BASIC EDUCATION STATISTICS 1980 EC : SELECTED REGIONAL TABLES / Ethiopia. Ministry of Education. Planning and External Relations Service – Addis Ababa, 1988 – 2mf – 9 – DE-622/1 – ne IDC [370]
BASIC EDUCATION STATISTICS IN TANZANIA (BEST) 1981-1985 / Tanzania. Ministry of Education – Dar es Salaam, 1986 – 1mf – 9 – DE-626/1 – ne IDC [370]
BASIC ELEMENTS OF THE CHRISTIAN FAITH (CCC321) / Wei, Chuo-ming – (In Chinese) – Shanghai: Association Press of China, 1950 – 1r – 1 – 1984-6660 – us A.T.L.A. [240]
BASIC LAWS ON THE STRUCTURE OF THE SOVIET STATE / ed by Berman, Harold J & Quigley, John B – Cambridge, Mass.: Harvard University Press, 1969 – 1 – CSUX90-B2254 – us Hoover Inst Photo [340]
BASIC PLAN FOR ECONOMIC SOCIETY 1973-1977 / Japan. Economic Planning Agency – Tokyo. Feb 1973. BD-1679 1 – 9 – ne IDC [338]
BASIC PRINCIPLES OF REVISIONISM – London. 1929. BJ-28-20 1 – 9 – ne IDC [320]
BASIC STATISTICS, 1964 / United Arab Republic. Central Agency for Public Mobilisation and Statistics – Cairo. 1965. BNE-4685 1 – 9 – ne IDC [310]
BASIC STATISTICS ON UNIVERSITY EDUCATION IN SRI LANKA 1981-1982 / Sri Lanka. University Grants Commission – Colombo – 9mf – 9 – DE-585/1 – ne IDC [370]
BASIC SWIMMING ANALYZED / Harris, Marjorie M – Boston: Allyn and Bacon, (1969).vii,150p. illus – 1 – us U.W. Library [790]
BASIC TECHNOLOGY IN FOREST OPERATIONS – 1982 – 137p – it F.A.O. [634]
BASIC TEXTS 1984 – 1984 – 2v 241p – it F.A.O. [630]
THE BASIL DEAN COLLECTION – (With printed guide) – 99mf – 9 – $266.00 – 1-869934-31-8 – uk Emmett [790]
Basil the Great, Saint *see* THE BOOK OF SAINT BASIL THE GREAT, BISHOP OF CAESAREA IN CAPPADOCIA, ON THE HOLY SPIRIT
Basil, V *see* HIS TRIUMPHANT CHARIOT OF ANTIMONY
Basilesco, N *see* DROIT ROMAIN
Basili, A *see* MUSICA UNIVERSALE ARMONICO PRATICA DETTATA DALL'ISTINTO. E PER I SUONATORI DI GRAVE CEMBALO, ED ORGANO ESPOSTA IN VENTIQUATTRO ESERCIZI
BASILICA / Kistler, R – O-954 1. 1712 – 9 – ne IDC [700]
BASILICA DEL SIGLO 7 EN BURGUILLOS / Martinez Martinez, Matias Ramon – Madrid: Tip. de Fortanet, 1898 – sp Bibl Santa Ana [946]
BASILICAE VETERIS VATICANAE DESCRIPTIO / Angelis, Pedro de – O-1045 1. 1646 – 9 – ne IDC [240]
BASILIDES AM AUSGANGE DES APOSTOLISCHEN ZEITALTERS ALS ERSTER ZEUGE FUER ALTER UND AUTORITAET NEUTESTAMENTLICHER SCHRIFTEN : INSBESONDERE DES JOHANNESEVANGELIUMS: IN VERBINDUNG MIT ANDERN ZEUGEN BIS ZUR MITTE DES ZWEITEN JAHRHUNDERTS / Hofstede de Groot, P – Leipzig: J.C. Hinrichs, 1868 – 1mf – us A.T.L.A. [220]
DAS BASILIDIANISCHE SYSTEM : MIT BESONDERER RUECKSICHT AUF DIE ANGABEN DES HIPPOLYTUS / Uhlhorn, Gerhard – Goettingen: Dieterich, 1855 – 1mf – us A.T.L.A. [240]
BASILIO DE SA. ARTURO : DOCUMENTACAO... / Barrado Manzano, Arcangel – Madrid: Archivo Ibero-Americano, 1959 – 1 – sp Bibl Santa Ana [240]
Basilius, Valentinus *see* THE LAST WILL AND TESTAMENT; TO WHICH IS ADDED TWO TREATISES NEVER BEFORE PUBLISHED IN ENGLISH
BASIN OPPORTUNITIES – Klamath Falls OR. Mar 25 1953 – 1 – us U.O. Library [071]
BASIN RESEARCH – v1- . 1987- – 1,5,6,9 – us UMI [574]
BASINGSTOKE AND HAMPSHIRE BUSINESS GAZETTE – (Also known as: Hampshire Business Gazette. Discontinued) – Oct 1984-Mar 1996 – 5 3/4r – 1 – uk British Libr Newspaper [072]
BASINGSTOKE AND NORTH HAMPSHIRE BUSINESS GAZETTE – England.Oct 1984-1985.-w. 1 reel – 1 – uk British Libr Newspaper [072]
BASINGSTOKE AND NORTH HANTS GAZETTE – Basingstoke, North Hants, England. 1981- – 89+ r – 1 – uk British Libr Newspaper [072]
BASINGSTOKE AND NORTH HANTS GAZETTE (WEEKEND ED.) – England.1985. -w. 4 reels – 1 – uk British Libr Newspaper [072]
BASINGSTOKE GAZETTE EXTRA – Basingstoke, England. Aug 1980- – 35+ r – 1 – uk British Libr Newspaper [072]
BASINGSTOKE MIDWEEK GAZETTE – Basingstoke, England. 27 Feb 1973-Dec 1980 – 13 1/2r – 1 – uk British Libr Newspaper [072]
BASIS – Jogjakarta. (incomplete) SE-874 1. 1951-1967 – 9 – ne IDC [073]
THE BASIS OF MORALITY / Besant, Anne Wood – Madras. 1915. 40 p. 1 reel – 1 – us U.W. Library [140]
BASIS OF RELIGION / Momerie, Alfred Williams – Edinburgh: William Blackwood, 1890. 1 fiche – 9 – us A.T.L.A. [240]
BASIVAVA (NY) – Tananarive. 1907-2 avr 1909. (no.17-133). mq no.98-99 – 1 – fr A.C.R.P.P. [073]
Baskakov, N A *see* UIGURSKORUSSKII SLOVAR'
Baskerville, LF *see* ATTITUDES, PERCEPTIONS AND COPING SKILLS OF LONG-TERM BREAST CANCER SURVIVORS
Baskes, M I *see* MODELLING AND SIMULATION IN MATERIALS SCIENCE AND ENGINEERING
BASKETBALL / Naismith, James – 1894 – 1mf – 9 – $3.00 – us Microform Publ [790]
BASKETBALL DIGEST – (v5- . 1977- . 5,6,9) – v. 1-. 1973- – 1 – us UMI [790]
Baskin and Battey Historical Publishing Co *see*
- HISTORY OF CRAWFORD COUNTY
- HISTORY OF MEDINA COUNTY

Baskin, G I *see* SOSTOIANIE PROIZVODITELNYKH SIL I TENDENTSI I IKH RAZVITIIA V RAZNYKH OTRASLIAKH NARODNAGO KHOZIAISTVA SAMARSKOI GUBERNII
BASKIN, O.L. AND CO *see*
- HISTORY OF CLEAR CREEK AND BOULDER VALLEYS
- HISTORY OF DELAWARE COUNTY
- HISTORY OF GRUNDY COUNTY
- HISTORY OF MENARD AND MASON COUNTIES
- HISTORY OF MORROW COUNTY
- HISTORY OF POTTAWATTAMIE COUNTY
- HISTORY OF THE ARKANSAS VALLEY, COLORADO
- HISTORY OF THE CITY OF DENVER AND ARAPAHOE COUNTY AND COLORADO

DAS BASLER KONZIL : SEINE BERUFUNG UND LEITUNG, SEINE GLIEDERUNG UND SEINE BEHOERDENORGANISATION / Lazarus, Paul – Berlin: E. Ebering, 1912 – 1mf – us A.T.L.A. [240]
BASLER NACHRICHTEN – Basel, nov-dec 1931, 1950-90 – 1r – 1 – Dist. gw Mikrofilm – gw Misc Inst [949]
BASLER NACHRICHTEN – Basel, oct 18 1914-aug 10 1919; aug 31 1939-apr 16 1940; 1941-dec 23 1942; feb 11 1943-46; feb 2-dec 1956 – 87r – 1 – uk British Libr Newspaper [949]
BASLER VORWAERTS – (A Social-democrat daily till 20.2.1921; then Communist daily subtitled: "Kommunistische Tageszeitung") – Basel, 1946 (incompl) – 1 – us Hoover Inst Photo [335]
BASLER ZEITSCHRIFT : FUER GESCHICHTE UND ALTERTUMSKUNDE – 1(1902)-44(1945) – 303mf – 9 – Dfl1,060.00 – ne Slangenburg [073]
BASLER ZEITUNG – 12-14r per y – 1 – inquire – us Ross [072]
BASLER ZEITUNG – 1980-1994 – 9 – Sfr750.00 – sz Infoprint [072]
BASLER ZEITUNG – 1995-1996 – 35 – Sfr1,200.00 – sz Infoprint [072]
Basolo, Fred *see* COMMENTS ON INORGANIC CHEMISTRY
Basombrio y Echenique, C *see* LA ACTUACION INTERNACIONAL DE LAS SOCIEDADES
LES BASONGE (ETAT IND. DU CONGO) / Overbergh, Cyr. van – Bruxelles, A DeWit [etc] 1908 – us Res Libr [960]
THE BASQUE PRIESTS PERSECUTED BY THE FASCIST FORCES – n.p. 193? Fiche W 749. (Blodgett Collection of Spanish Civil War Pamphlets) – 9 – us H.U. College Libr [946]
BASQUE STUDIES PROGRAM NEWSLETTER – Reno, CA. University of Nevada: 1968-1993 – 1r – 1 – $50.00 – B06076 – us Library Micro [370]
BASQUE-AMERICANS AND SEQUENTIAL THEORY OF MIGRATION AND ADAPTATION / McCall, Grant Erwin – 1r – 1 – $50.00 – C603005 – us Library Micro [304]
LES BASQUES ET LEUR EMIGRATION EN AMERIQUE / Etcheverry, Louis – Reprod. de l'extr. de "La Reforme Sociale." 2eme series. v.1, 1st sem., 1886. p.491-515. (Historical Studies Series) – 9 – 3.00 – fr Bibl Nationale [900]
Basra, Amarjit S *see* JOURNAL OF CROP PRODUCTION
LES BAS-RELIEFS DES BATIMENTS ROYAUX D'ABOMEY (DAHOMEY) / Waterlot, E G – Paris: Institut d'ethnologie, 1926 – 1 – F50.00 – fr Armell [305]
Bass, E *see* DIE MERKMALE DER ISRAELITISCHEN PROPHETIE NACH DER TRADITIONELLEN AUFFASSUNG DES TALMUD
Bass, H Royce *see* THE HISTORY OF BRAINTREE, VERMONT
Bass, Lawrence W *see* MANAGEMENT BY TASK FORCES: A MANUAL ON THE OPERATION OF INTERDISCIPLINARY TEAMS
Bass, Scott A *see* JOURNAL OF AGING AND SOCIAL POLICY
EL BASSAIR – Alger. mars 1936-39, 1947-mars 1956 – 1 – fr A.C.R.P.P. [073]
Bassano, F da. *see* VOCABOLARIO TIGRAY-ITALIANO E REPERTORIO ITALIANO-TIGRAY
...BASSAS DANSAS...AUGMENTATUS.. / Arena, Antonius – Contains also: Poema Macaronicum Huguenotico. Nova novorum novissima, sive poemata...revisitata...per Bartholomeum Bollam.... 1670 – 9 – us Sibley [780]
LA BASSE CONTINUE RENDUE AISEE / Pasquali, N – Rev. par J. G. Lustig. Amsterdam. 1763. BP-425 1 – 9 – ne IDC [780]
Basserman-Jordan, F *see* GESCHICHTE DES WEINBAUS UNTER BESONDERER BERUECKSICHTIGUNG DER BAYERISCHEN RHEINPFALZ
Bassermann, Heinrich *see* DER GLAUBE AN JESUS CHRISTUS
Basset, Andre *see*
- LE BERBERE A L'ECOLE NATIONALE DES LANGUES ORIENTALES VIVANTES
- QUATRE ETUDES DE LINGUISTIQUE BERBERE

Basset, Henri *see* ESSAI SUR LA LITTERATURE DES BERBERES
Basset, Rene *see* CONTES POPULAIRES D'AFRIQUE
Bassett, D K *see* BRITISH TRADE AND POLICY IN INDONESIA AND MALAYSIA IN THE LATE EIGHTEENTH CENTURY
Bassett, James *see*
- CRIMINAL PLEADING AND PRACTICE.
- PERSIA, EASTERN MISSION

Bassett, Samuel C *see* HISTORY OF BUFFALO COUNTY AND ITS PEOPLE
Bassetti-Sani, Julio *see* LA VIERGE INMACULEE ET LE PROBLEME DE L'APOSTOLAT MUSULMAN...
BASSETT'S DAILY CHRONICLE – Limerick, Ireland. 16 Oct 1875-1884. -d. 17 1/2 reels – 1 – uk British Libr Newspaper [072]

DER BASSGEIGER : DAS VERHEXTE BUCH: ZWEI BERLINER GESCHICHTEN / Kretzer, Max – Leipzig: P Reclam, [1910?] – 1r – 1 – us U.W. Library [830]
Bassi, M *see* DISPARERI IN MATERIA D'ARCHITETTURA ET PERSPETTIVA
LES BASSINS DU NIGER : ETUDE DE GEOGRAPHIE PHYSIQUE ET DE PALEOGRAPHIE... / Urvoy, Y – Paris: Larose, 1942 – us Res Libr [960]
BASSIR *see* AL-BASSIR
LES BASSOUTOS OU VINGT-TROIS ANNEES DE SEJOUR ET D'OBSERVATIONS AU SUD DE L'AFRIQUE / Casalis, Eugene – (African Library). Paris. Lib. de Ch. Meyrueis. 1859 – 9 – fr Hachette [960]
Basta, Susan M *see* PRESSURE SORE PREVENTION SELF-EFFICACY AND OUTCOME EXPECTATIONS IN THE SPINAL CORD-INJURED
Bastable, CF *see* THE THEORY OF INTERNATIONAL TRADE
BASTADS TIDNING – AEngelholm, 1894-97 – 9 – sw Kungliga [072]
Baster, J *see* NATUURKUNDIGE UITSPANNINGEN...
BASTERIA : TIJDSCHRIFT VAN DE NEDERLANDSCHE MALACOLOGISCHE VEREENIGING – Lisse, 1936-1941. v1-6 – 8mf – 9 – 5621c/2 – ne IDC [590]
Basterra, Ramon de *see* UNA EMPRESA EL SIGLO 18
Bastgen, Hubert *see*
- BAYERN UND DER HEILIGE STUHL IN DER ERSTEN HAELFTE DES 19. JAHRHUNDERTS
- DIE BESETZUNG DER BISCHOFSSITZE IN PREUSSEN IN DER ERSTEN HAELFTE DES 19. JAHRHUNDERTS
- DER HEILIGE STUHL UND DIE HEIRAT DER PRINZESSIN ELISABETH VON BAYERN MIT DEM KRONPRINZEN FRIEDRICH WILHELM VON PREUSSEN
- DAS HERZOGSPAAR FERDINAND UND JULIE VON ANHALT-KOETHEN, DIE ANFAENGE DER KATHOLISCHEN PFARREI KOETHEN UND DER HEILIGE STUHL
- SAEMTLICHE AUFSAETZE UND MISZELLEN

Bastian, C Don *see* THE DE SOYSA CHARITAYA
Bastian, Henry *see* BRAIN AS ORGAN OF THE MIND
Bastiat, Frederic *see*
- AUSGEWAEHLTE VOLKSWIRTSCHAFTLICHE UND POLITISCHE SCHRIFTEN
- CAPITAL AND INTEREST
- CE QU'ON VOIT ET CE QU'ON NE VOIT PAS
- ECONOMIC SOPHISMS
- ESSAYS ON POLITICAL ECONOMY
- OEUVRES COMPLETES
- POPULAR FALLACIES, ADAPTION FROM SOPHISMES ECONOMIQUES
- SOMETHING ELSE

Bastide, Jean Francois de *see* LETTRE A M. ROUSSEAU, AU SUJET DE SA LETTRE A M. D'ALEMBERT
Bastide, Roger *see* A POESIA AFRO-BRASILEIRA
Bastier, Paul *see* L'ESOTERISME DE HEBBEL
BASTILIIA I EE ARKHIV / Liublinskaia, A D – BR-10,866/1 – 9 – ne IDC [947]
THE BASTILLE / Bingham, D – New York: Scribner & Welford. 2v. 1888 – 12mf – 9 – $18.00 – LLMC 92-124 – us L.L.M.C. [340]
Bastin, Georges *see* LA NOTION D'ADAPTATION EN TRADUCTION
LE BASTION – (Becomes: Le Bastion/Le Nouveau Quebec 14 avr 1965) – Sept-Iles, Canada. v1 n7. 16 dec 1964-v1 n11. 17 fev 1965 – 1r – 1 – Can$65.00 – cn Can Microfilming [072]
LE BASTION *see*
- LE BASTION (LE NOUVEAU QUEBEC)
- LE NOUVEAU QUEBEC

LE BASTION (LE NOUVEAU QUEBEC) – (Also: Le Bastion 15 sep 1965-3 nov 1965) – Sept-Iles, Canada. 14 avr 1965-29 jul 1965 – 1r – 1 – Can$65.00 – cn Can Microfilming [072]
LE BASTION/LE NOUVEAU QUEBEC *see* LE BASTION
DER BASTLER *see*
- BAYERISCHE RADIO-ZEITUNG UND BAYERNFUNK
- FUNKSCHAU

Baston, G A R *see* VOLTAIRIMEROS
Basu, BD *see* INDIAN MEDICINAL PLANTS
Basuki Abdullah *see* EXHIBITION OF PAINTINGS,15-24 JAN., 1960, BANGKOK. SE-2195/1. 1960
Basuki, Sulistyo *see* MEMBAKAR MATAHARI
BASUTO OF BASUTOLAND / Dutton, E – London. Cape. 1923. BA-362 2 – 8 – ne IDC [305]
THE BASUTOLAND GENERAL ELECTION 1965 : REPORT / Sanders, P B – [S.l: s.n. 1965?] – us Res Libr [960]
Basutoland. National Council. Maseru *see*
- LEGISLATIVE COUNCIL DEBATES
- PROCEEDINGS

Bat', A G *see*
- SBORNIK DEISTVUIUSHCHIKH ZAKONOPOLOZHENII, POSTANOVLENII, INSTRUKTSII I TSIRKULIAROV PO POTREBITEL'SKOI KOOPERATSII
- USTAV POTREBITEL'SKOGO OBSHCHESTVA, UPRAVLIAEMOGO OBSHCHIM SOBRANIEM EGO CHLENOV

Bataafsch Genootschap der Proefondervindelijke Wijsbegeerte, Rotterdam *see* NIEUWE VERHANDELINGEN
Bataafsch Genootschap der Proefondervindelijke Wijsbegeerte. Rotterdam *see* VERHANDELINGEN
LA BATAILLE / Federation du Nord du Parti Socialiste – S.F.I.O. Dir. politique Augustin Laurent. Lille. 1936-mai 1940 – 1 – fr A.C.R.P.P. [073]
LA BATAILLE – (Le Rouge et le noir). Paris. France. -w. 7 Dec 1944-22 Dec 1950. (6 reels) – 1 – uk British Libr Newspaper [072]
LA BATAILLE – L'Hebdomadaire independant, politique et litteraire. devenu: Le Rouge et le noir. La Bataille. Paris. 30 nov 1944 1950 – 1 – fr A.C.R.P.P. [073]
LA BATAILLE : NATIONALISTE / ed by Paquin, Ubald & LaFerriere, Ph – (Incluant la caricature censuree par le gouvernement federal) – Montreal, Canada. 12 oct 1916-14 dec 1916 – 1r – 1 – Can$35.00 – cn Can Microfilming [072]
LA BATAILLE – Paris. 10 mai-15 oct 1882, 28 mai 1883-25 janv 1886, 13 janv 1889-1906, 1897-1906. Contient: Le Courrier quotidien de l'Exposition de 1889. no.1-95. 6 mai-7 aout 1889 – 1 – fr A.C.R.P.P. [073]
LA BATAILLE – Paris. (La Marseillaise) -w 13 Jan 1889-30 Jun 1893. 9 reels – 1 – uk British Libr Newspaper [072]
LA BATAILLE – Paris. Nov. 30, 1944-June 30, 1948 – 1 – 35.00r – us Hoover Inst Photo [072]
LA BATAILLE – Quebec, Canada. 23 aut 1935-v1 n14. 20 sep 1935 – 1r – 1 – Can$35.00 – cn Can Microfilming [072]
LA BATAILLE – Quebec, Canada. 26 nov-28 nov 1906 – 1r – 1 – Can$25.00 – cn Can Microfilming [072]
LA BATAILLE / ed by Sauvalle, Marc – Montreal, Canada. 14 dec 1895-10 mar 1896 – 1r – 1 – Can$30.00 – cn Can Microfilming [072]
LA BATAILLE – Port-au-Prince, Haiti: [s.n.]. [1ere annee n4-n23]. (14 juin-13 dec 1902) – 2 sheets – us Res Libr [072]
LA BATAILLE ECONOMIQUE, SOCIALE OUVRIERE – puis Syndicale et sociale. Paris. fevr 1921-mars 1938 – 1 – fr A.C.R.P.P. [073]
Bataille, M-C *see* LES RITES DE NAISSANCE CHEZ LES INDIENS MAYA DES CUCHUMATANES-GUATEMALA ET LE PROFESSIONALISME DES SAGES-FEMMES
LA BATAILLE SOCIALISTE – no. 21-78. Paris. juil 1929-avr 1934. mq no. 22-27, 29, 47, 50, 52, 55, 62, 65 – 1 – fr A.C.R.P.P. [073]
LA BATAILLE SYNDICALISTE / C G T – no. 1-45. Paris. 1er mai 1922-25 oct 1925. mq no. 41 – 1 – fr A.C.R.P.P. [073]
LA BATAILLE SYNDICALISTE – Paris. 27 avr 1911-15 dec 1920 – 1 – fr A.C.R.P.P. [073]
BATALHADOR : ORGAO IMPARCIAL CIDADE DA UNIAO – Maceio, Alagoas. 8 Mar 1893; Abr 1895; 29 Jan 1896 – 1,5,6 – bl Biblioteca [072]
LA BATALLA – Barcelona: Impr Myria, may 23-sep 6. sep 19, oct 17-dec 11 1930; feb 12, mar 5, apr 2-may 28. jun 11-18. jul 9, 23, aug 13-20, sep 3 1931 – 1r – 1 – us Res Libr [072]
LA BATALLA DE LA ALBUERA / Blake, Joaquin – 1811 – 9 – 1.50f – sp Bibl Santa Ana [946]
LA BATALLA DE ZALACA. EPISODIO HISTORICO-EXTREMENO / Hurtado de Mendoza, Publio – Caceres: Tip. Enc. y Lib. de L. Jimenez, 1909 – 1 – sp Bibl Santa Ana [946]
LA BATALLA (PARIS, FRANCE) – (Library wants: no. 20-22, 24, 28-29, 30-31, 33-41, 43-49, 51-52, 54-59, 107-109, 131-132, 138-150, 152-175) – Paris: [P.O.U.M.], 1945-71 – 1 – CSUX86-S18 – us Hoover Inst Photo [944]
Batang, Indonesia (Kabupaten) *see* DEWAN PERWAKILAN RAKJAT DAERAH GOTONG ROJONG. LAPORAN HASIL SIDANG SEKSI A.
LE BATAVE – ou Le Nouvelliste etranger. puis Ou le Sansculotte. devenu: Le Sans-culotte. no. 1-500. Paris. fevr 1793-juin 1794 – 1 – fr A.C.R.P.P. [073]
DIE BATAVER : HISTORISCHER ROMAN AUS DER VOELKERWANDERUNG / Dahn, Felix – Leipzig: Breitkopf und Haertel, 1898 – 1 – us U.W. Library [830]
BATAVIA IN POST-WAR DAYS / Batavia Municipality. Indonesia – SE-6278 1. 1948 – 9 – ne IDC [950]
Batavia Municipality. Indonesia *see* BATAVIA IN POST-WAR DAYS
BATAVIA SACRA OF KERKELIJKE HISTORIE EN OUDHEDEN / Heussen, H F van – Antwerpen. v1-3. 1715-1716 – Dfl112.00 – ne Slangenburg [240]
BATAVIA SACRA OF KERKELIJKE HISTORIE EN OUDHEDEN VAN BATAVIA – Antwerpen, 1715-1716; Aanhangsel op.Utrecht, 1744 – Dfl158.00 – ne Slangenburg [240]
BATAVIAASCH NIEUWSBLAD : VIJFTIG JAAR – 1885-1935. Batavia, 1935 – 3mf – 9 – ne IDC [072]
BATAVIAASCH NIEUWSBLAD, 1885-1926 / Netherlands. Royal Library. The Hague. Newspaper Department – (1885-89.-175mf.Dfl1095.00; 1890-94.-250mf.Dfl1560.00; 1895-99.-313mf.Dfl1960.00; 1900-04.-455mf.Dfl2845.00; 1905-09.-450mf.Dfl2810.00; 1910-14.-401mf.Dfl2505.00; 1915-19.-343mf.Dfl2145.00; 1920-24.-242mf.Dfl1510.00; 1925-26.-117mf.Dfl730.00) – KB005 – 2746mf – 9 – Dfl17,710.00 set silver – ne MMF Publ [072]
BATAVIASCH KOLONIALE COURANT, 1810-11 / Netherlands. Royal Library. The Hague. Newspaper Department – (Continued by the Java Courant, 1812-1816; Continued by the Bataviasche Courant, 1816-1827) – Official gazettes of the Batavian Republic Government, the British Interim Government and the Dutch East Indies Government, respectively. KB001 – 145mf – 9 – Dfl880.00 silver – ne MMF Publ [324]
BATAVIASCHE STUDENTEN ALMANAK VOOR HET JAAR 1931 – Batavia, 1931 – 6mf – 9 – ne IDC [080]
BATAYANG AKLAT SA WIKA / Manalastas Laraya, Consorcia – Quezon City, Philippines: Bustamente Press, 1960. xi,346p. Tagalog Language-reader – 1 – us U.W. Library [490]
Bate, Fanny *see* GEMS OF HOPE: IN MEMORY OF THE FAITHFUL DEPARTED
Bate, J *see* METHODISM DISPLAYED
Bate, J P *see* AN ELEMENTARY ACCOUNT...
LE BATEAU A VAPEUR... *see* GUIDE DU VOYAGEUR A NANTES ET AUX ENVIRONS...
LE BATEAU A VAPEUR ET LES BAINS DE MER – (Microfilmed with Promenade de Nantes...and Guide du voyageur...) – Nantes: V. Forest, 1844 – fr Armell [910]
Bateman et al *see*
- HISTORICAL ENCYCLOPEDIA OF ILLINOIS
- HISTORICAL ENCYCLOPEDIA OF ILLINOIS AND HISTORY OF CASS COUNTY

Bateman, F Foster *see*
- REPLY TO THE MONTREAL HARBOUR ENGINEER'S REPORT ON THE ST LAWRENCE BRIDGE AND MANUFACTURING SCHEME
- ST. LAWRENCE BRIDGE AND MANUFACTURING SCHEME: ENGINEER'S REPORT, 18TH JANUARY 1882

Bateman, H *see* LA DETERMINATION DE LA LOI APPLICABLE AU REGIME MATRIMONIAL
Bateman, J *see*
- A MONOGRAPH OF ODONTOGLOSSUM
- THE ORCHIDACEAE OF MEXICO AND GUATEMALA

Bateman, N *see*
- HISTORICAL ENCYCLOPEDIA OF ILLINOIS AND HISTORY OF ROCK ISLAND COUNTY
- HISTORICAL ENCYCLOPEDIA OF ILLINOIS AND HISTORY OF WARREN COUNTY

BATEMAN, WARNER M., PAPERS, MS 2900 – (Correspondence, ledgers, accounts, court records, notebooks, clippings, and other records of this Cincinnati attorney, U.S. Attorney for Southern Ohio, 1869-77, and John Sherman's Presidential campaign manager, 1880) – 1837-1897 – 39r – 1 – us Western Res [340]
Bateman, William *see* LORD BATEMAN'S PLEA FOR LIMITED PROTECTION OR FOR RECIPROCITY IN FREE TRADE
Bater, James *see* POLITICAL GEOGRAPHY AND THE CYPRUS CONFLICT
Bates, Chrisenberry Lee *see* FEDERAL PROCEDURE AT LAW.
Bates, F *see* HISTORY AND BIOGRAPHICAL REMINISCENCES OF DENTON COUNTY
Bates, Henry Walter *see*
- CONTRIBUTIONS TO AN INSECT FAUNA OF THE AMAZON VALLEY
- O NATURALISTA NO RIO AMAZONAS, VOL. 1

Bates, J C *see* HISTORY OF THE BENCH AND BAR OF CALIFORNIA
Bates, LT *see* THE DIVORCE AND SEPARATION OF ALIENS IN FRANCE
Bates, Miner Searle *see* CHRISTIANITY AND COMMUNISM (CCC4)
Bates, MK *see* EFFECT OF PEER GROUP PRESENCE ON THE GROSS MOTOR PERFORMANCE OF YOUNG CHILDREN
Bates, O *see* THE EASTERN LIBYANS: AN ESSAY
Bates, Ralph *see* EN LA ESPANA LEAL HA NACIDO UN EJERCITO
Bates, Samuel P *see*
- HISTORY OF GREENE COUNTY
- OUR COUNTY AND ITS PEOPLE

Bates, W C *see* EXPONENTIAL OUTLINE WITH DEFINITIONS OF BLACKSTONE'S COMMENTARIES.
Bates, Walter *see* KINGSTON AND THE LOYALISTS OF THE SPRING FLEET OF A.D. 1783: WITH REMINISCENCES OF EARLY DAYS IN CONNECTICUT..
Bates, William Henry *see* ALLEGED DISCREPANCIES OF THE BIBLE
Bateson, T *see* THE 2ND SET OF BATESON'S MADRIGALS
Bateson, W *see* JOURNAL OF GENETICS
BATESVILLE FIRST BAPTIST CHURCH. BATESVILLE, ARKANSAS : CHURCH RECORDS – Jun 1883-1930, 1937-Aug 1942, Mar 1946-1977 – 1 – 87.93 – us Baptist [240]
Bath and West and Southern Counties Society *see*
- JOURNAL
- LETTERS AND PAPERS ON AGRICULTURE, PLANTING, & C. SELECTED FROM THE CORRESPONDENCE OF THE BATH AND WEST OF ENGLAND SOCIETY, FOR THE ENCOURAGEMENT OF AGRICULTURE, ARTS, MANUFACTURERS, AND COMMERCE

Bath. Archives (Marquess). Longleat *see*
- CARTERET PAPERS, FROM THE ARCHIVES OF THE MARQUESS OF BATH
- CATALOGUE AND INDEX TO THE MISCELLANEOUS MANUSCRIPTS IN THE ARCHIVES OF THE MARQUESS OF BATH
- CATALOGUE OF MISCELLANEOUS MSS. AND APPENDICES TO THE COVENTRY, SEYMOUR AND PORTLAND PAPERS
- COVENTRY PAPERS
- COVENTRY PAPERS: CATALOGUE AND INDEX
- DEVEREUX PAPERS
- DUDLEY PAPERS
- MISCELLANEOUS MSS IN THE ARCHIVES OF THE MARQUESS OF BATH
- MS. 38
- MSS. 29, 30 AND 32
- PORTLAND PAPERS
- SEYMOUR PAPERS. BOXES 1-18, VOLS. 1-23, PLUS INDEX
- THYNNE PAPERS
- THYNNE PAPERS: INDEX
- WHITELOCKE PAPERS

BATH FIGARO – Bath, England. Penny Figaro. -w. 15 Sept 1838-10 Aug 1839. 19 ft – 1 – uk British Libr Newspaper [072]
BATH GUARDIAN – Bath, England. Bath & Devizes Guardian. -w. 1 Feb 1834-27 July 1839. 2 reels – 1 – uk British Libr Newspaper [072]
BATH JOURNAL – England.1801-02. -w. 1 reel – 1 – uk British Libr Newspaper [072]
Bath. Presbytery (Pres. Ch. in the U.S.A.) *see* MINUTES, 1817-1862
Bathe, Johannes Clemens *see* DIE BEWEGUNGEN UND HALTUNGEN DES MENSCHLICHEN KOERPERS IN HEINRICH VON KLEISTS ERZAEHLUNGEN
BATHURST COURIER *see* PERTH COURIER
BATHURST TIMES – Jan 2-Dec 31 1918 – 9 – at Pascoe [072]

Baticle, Y *see*
- ETUDE COMPAREE DES FETES DE LA MOISSON ET DES COUTUMES DU PREMIER MAI
- ETUDE SEMIOLOGIQUE DE LA REPRESENTATION DU PERSONNAGE DE L'ENSEIGNANT DANS LES OEUVRES DE FICTION AU CINEMA ET A LA TELEVISION

BATIENDO LA ESPERANZA / Rodriguez Rubio, Inocencia – Madrid: Graf. Saldana, 1973 – 1 – sp Bibl Santa Ana [946]

Batiffol, H *see* LES CONFLITS DE LOIS EN MATIERE DE CONTRATS

Batiffol, Pierre *see*
- HISTOIRE DU BREVIAIRE ROMAIN
- LA LITTERATURE GRECQUE
- LA PAIX CONSTANTINIENNE ET LE CATHOLICISME
- SIX LECONS SUR LES EVANGILES

Batik *see* ALBUM ILLUSTRATING THE MANUFACTURE OF BATIK

Batik. Nomor Hari Kooperasi *see* PERINGATAN HARI KO-OPERASI KE-VIII,12 DJULI 1958. SE-2625/1. 1958

BATILO. EGLOGA / Melendez Valdes, Juan – 1780 – 9 – 1.50f – sp Bibl Santa Ana [810]

BATIMENT – (Microform available only to v66 no 3 1991) – Toronto. v65- 1990- – 9 – Can$20.00y – cn Micromedia [624]

LE BATIMENT – Journal des travaux publics et particuliers. Paris. 1907-21 – 1 – fr A.C.R.P.P. [073]

BATIMENTS DE CHEMINS DE FER: EMBARCADERES, PLANS DE GARES, STATIONS, ABRIS / Chabat, Pierre – Paris. A. Morel, 1862-66. 2v. in fol., pl. (Architecture Series) – 9 – fr Hachette [720]

BATIR AL NAZI-PERONISMO PARA ABRIR UNA ERA DE LIBERTAD Y PROGRESO / Codovilla, Victorio – Buenos Aires: Editorial Anteo, 1946 – 1 – CSUXADH9252-B – us Hoover Inst Photo [320]

LE BATISSEUR – Montreal, Canada. v4 n1. jul 1969 – 1r – 1 – Can$25.00 – cn Can Microfilming [072]

BATJAAN POKOK TUNTUK AKUNTANSI KETATALAKSANAAN / Tan, Hian Kie – 1963 – 9 – SE-4223 1 – ne IDC [950]

Batjeck, A *see* L'EVOLUTION DE L'ENSEIGNEMENT DU PREMIER ET DU SECOND DEGRE DANS L'ANCIEN CAMEROUN ORIENTAL DEPUIS L'INDEPENDANCE

BATKIVSHCHINA – Toronto, Canada. Oct 1955-Dec 1975.-w. 8 reels – 1 – uk British Libr Newspaper [072]

BATKO MAKHNO : MEMUARY BELOGVARDE IT SA / Gerasimenko, N V; ed by Shchegoleva, P E – Moskva: Gos. izd-vo, 1928 – 1 – CSUX88-B9695 – us Hoover Inst Photo [999]

BATLEY EXAMINER – England. -w. 21 Jul 1893-26 Oct 1895. (2 reels) – 1 – uk British Libr Newspaper [072]

BATLEY FREE PRESS – England. -w. 23 Apr-10 Sep 1870. (24 ft) – 1 – uk British Libr Newspaper [072]

BATLEY NEWS – England. -w. 6 Jan 1883-Dec 1907. (25 reels) – 1 – uk British Libr Newspaper [072]

BATLEY NEWS – Yorkshire. 1908-75 – 1 – uk Microform Academic [072]

BATLEY REPORTER – Yorkshire. 1898-1959 – 1 – uk Microform Academic [072]

BATLEY REPORTER AND GUARDIAN – England. -w. 17 Jul 1869-Dec 1907. (Wanting 1898). (38 reels) – 1 – uk British Libr Newspaper [072]

BATLEY SENTINEL – Yorkshire. 1867 – 1 – uk Microform Academic [072]

Batllori, M *see* BIBLIOGRAFIA DE SERAFIM LEITE S.J.

BATMAN – Issue Nos. 11-15 Jun 1942-Mar 1943 – 5mf – 15 – $31,95 – us Comics [760]

BATMAN – Issue Nos. 1-5 Spring 40-Spring 41 – 5mf – 15 – $31,95 – us Comics [760]

BATMAN – Issue Nos. 16-20 Apr 1943-Jan 1944 – 5mf – 15 – $31,95 – us Comics [760]

BATMAN – Issue Nos. 21-25 Feb 1944-Nov 1944 – 5mf – 15 – $31,95 – us Comics [760]

BATMAN – Issue Nos. 26-30 Dec 1944-Sept 1945 – 5mf – 15 – $31,95 – us Comics [760]

BATMAN – Issue Nos. 31-35 Oct 1945-Jul 1946 – 5mf – 15 – $31,95 – us Comics [760]

BATMAN – Issue Nos. 36-40 Aug 1946-May 1947 – 5mf – 15 – $31,95 – us Comics [760]

BATMAN – Issue Nos. 41-45 Jun 1947-Mar 1948 – 5mf – 15 – $31,95 – us Comics [760]

BATMAN – Issue Nos. 46-50 Apr 1948-Jan 1949 – 5mf – 15 – $31,95 – us Comics [760]

BATMAN – Issue Nos. 51-55 Feb-Mar 49-Oct-Nov 49 – 5mf – 15 – $31.95 – us Comics [760]

BATMAN – Issue Nos. 56-60 Dec 49-Jan 50-Aug-Sept 50 – 5mf – 15 – $31.95 – us Comics [760]

BATMAN – Issue Nos. 6-10 Aug 1941-May 1942 – 5mf – 15 – $31,95 – us Comics [760]

BATMAN – Issue Nos. 61-65 Oct-Nov 50-Jun-Jul 51 – 5mf – 15 – $31.95 – us Comics [760]

BATMAN – Issue Nos. 66-70 Aug-Sep 51-Apr-May 52 – 5mf – 15 – $31.95 – us Comics [760]

BATMAN – Issue Nos. 71-75 Jun-Jul 52-Feb-Mar 53 – 5mf – 15 – $31.95 – us Comics [760]

BATMAN – Issue Nos. 76-80 Apr-May 53-Dec 53-Jan 54 – 5mf – 15 – $31.95 – us Comics [760]

BATMAN – Issue Nos. 81-85 Feb 1954-Aug 1954 – 5mf – 15 – $31,95 – us Comics [760]

BATMAN – Issue Nos. 86-90 Sept 1954-Mar 1955 – 5mf – 15 – $31,95 – us Comics [760]

BATMAN – Issue Nos. 91-95 Apr 1955-Oct 1955 – 5mf – 15 – $31,95 – us Comics [760]

BATMAN – Issue Nos. 96-100 Dec 1955-Jun 1956 – 5mf – 15 – $31,95 – us Comics [760]

THE BATON – (Coll title: Nineteenth Century American Music Periodicals) – Richmond, 1878-88 – 1 – £60.00 – uk Chadwyck [780]

Batsch, A J G C *see*
- BOTANISCHE BEMERKUNGEN
- ELENCHUS FUNGORUM. CONTINUATIO 1 ET 2: 1786-1789
- TABULA AFFINITATUM REGNI VEGETABILIS

BATSCHKAER ZEITUNG – Apatin, Rumaenien. 1930, 1932, 1935, 1938-40 – 2r – 1 – gw Mikrofilm [949]

BATSCHKAER ZEITUNG – Apatin, Yugoslavia. 1931; 1933-38; 1941-43 – 7r – 1 – us L of C Photodup [072]

BATSKAUSHCHUINA – Munich, DE. 2 Nov 1952; 25 Jan, 22 Feb 1953-Dec 1966 – 5r – 1 – uk British Libr Newspaper [072]

Battaglia, A G *see* L'ESTRATERRITORIALITA DELLE PERSONE GIURIDICHE

BATTAGLIONE GARIBALDI, OTTOBRE 1936-APRILE 1937 / Vita, A de – Parigi, 1937. Fiche W1248. (Blodgett Collection of Spanish Civil War Pamphlets) – 9 – us H.U. College Libr [946]

Battarra, G A *see* FUNGORUM AGRI ARIMINENSIS HISTORIA

LA BATTE – Gazette satirique. Paraissant tous les quinze jours. Red. en chef Alex Tisserand. no. 1-15. Paris. mars-oct 1888 – 1 – fr A.C.R.P.P. [073]

BATTELLE TECHNICAL REVIEW – v. 1-14. 1952-1965 – 1,5,6 – us Princeton Micro [600]

Batten, Loring Woart *see*
- HEBREW PROPHET
- OLD TESTAMENT FROM THE MODERN POINT OF VIEW

BATTERED WOMEN : ISSUES OF PUBLIC POLICY / U.S. Commission on Civil Rights – Washington: GPO, Jan 30-31 1978. LLMC 94-330 – 8mf – 9 – $12.00 – us L.L.M.C. [360]

Battersby, Hannah S *see* HOME LYRICS, A BOOK OF POEMS

Battersby, W J *see*
- THE COMPLETE CATHOLIC DIRECTORY, ALMANACK AND REGISTRY...
- A COMPLETE CATHOLIC REGISTRY, DIRECTORY AND ALMANACK...

BATTERSBY'S DOMINION POCKET RAILWAY AND TRAVELLERS GUIDE – With map. no. 107, Jan., 1885. Montreal: D. Battersby, 1885? 02999. (Pre-1900 Canadiana) – 9 – cn C.I.H.M. [910]

Battesti, T *see* LE SANCTUAIRE DE L'EMAM REZA, MASHAD, IRAN

Batteux, Charles *see* LES BEAUX ARTS REDUITS A UN MEME PRINCIPE

BATTEY, F.A. AND CO *see*
- BIOGRAPHICAL SOUVENIR OF THE COUNTIES OF BUFFALO, KEARNEY AND PHELPS
- BIOGRAPHICAL SOUVENIR OF THE COUNTIES OF BUFFALO, KEARNEY, PHELPS, HARLAN AND FRANKLIN
- BIOGRAPHICAL SOUVENIR OF THE STATE OF TEXAS
- COUNTIES OF LAGRANGE AND NOBLE
- COUNTIES OF WARREN, BENTON, JASPER AND NEWTON
- COUNTIES OF WHITE AND PULASKI

Battie, William *see* A TREATISE ON MADNESS

Battihill, J *see* SIX ANTHEMS AND TEN CHANTS

Battin *see* PAST AND PRESENT OF MARSHALL COUNTY

Battistella, Antonio *see* IL S. OFFICIO E LA RIFORMA RELIGIOSA IN FRIULI

BATTLE CREEK BLADE – Battle Creek, NE. -w. Apr. 1885-Oct. 1885. Incomplete – 1 – us NE Hist [071]

BATTLE CREEK ENTERPRISE – Battle Creek, NE. -w. Apr. 1888-Aug. 1908. Incomplete; Sep. 1908- – 1 – us NE Hist [071]

BATTLE CREEK REPUBLICAN – Battle Creek, NE. -w. Oct 1895-Oct. 1903 – 1 – us NE Hist [071]

THE BATTLE FOR BUENOS AIRES / Bradford, Saxtone E – New York Harcourt, Brace and company, [1943] – 1 – CSUXAJB7831-B – us Hoover Inst Photo [355]

Battle, J H *see*
- HISTORY OF BUCKS COUNTY
- HISTORY OF COLUMBIA AND MONTEUR COUNTIES

BATTLE MOUNTAIN BUGLE – Battle Mountain, NV. 1957-1962; 1976- – 27+ r – 1 – $1,350.00 ($90.00y) – N04406 – us Library Micro [071]

BATTLE OF CASSINO PAMPHLET COLLECTION – 194?-1952 – 1 – CSUXANM8176-B – us Hoover Inst Photo [355]

BATTLE OF DUNKERQUE PAMPHLET COLLECTION – 1940-1943 – 1 – CSUXANM8187-B – us Hoover Inst Photo [355]

THE BATTLE OF LIFE : A LOVE STORY / Dickens, Charles – London: Bradbury & Evans, 1846 – 1 roll – 1 – 1-55879-856-0 – uk Libr Preservation [830]

THE BATTLE OF LUNDY'S LANE, 1814: AN ADDRESS DELIVERED BEFORE THE LUNDY'S LANE HISTORICAL SOCIETY, OCTOBER 16TH, 1888 / Cruikshank, Ernest Alexander – Welland, Ont.: s.n., 1888? (Welland Ont.: W. Sawle). 02227. (Pre-1900 Canadiana) – 9 – cn C.I.H.M. [971]

THE BATTLE OF MISSISSINEWA, 1812 – 1969. The Mississinewa portion of the diary of William B. Northcutt; an extract from Pentland's Notes of Service; Muster rolls &/or payrolls of all military units participating in the battle. 1 fiche. F-0630 – 9 – us A.G.L.L. [976]

BATTLE OF STALINGRAD PAMPHLET COLLECTION – 1942-1943? – 1 – CSUXANR2653-B – us Hoover Inst Photo [355]

THE BATTLE OF STANDPOINTS / Cave, Alfred – 1890 – 9 – us A.T.L.A. [240]

BATTLE OF THE ARDENNES PAMPHLET COLLECTION – 1984 – 1 – CSUXANM8171-B – us Hoover Inst Photo [355]

THE BATTLE OF THE SWASH AND THE CAPTURE OF CANADA / Barton, Samuel – Montreal: J. Robinson, 1888?. 03005. (Pre-1900 Canadiana) – 9 – cn C.I.H.M. [971]

THE BATTLE OF TRENTON / Hewitt, James – A sonata for the piano-forte dedicated to General George Washington. New York: James Hewitt 1797. MUSIC 282 – 1 – us L of C Photodup [780]

BATTLE OF WESTERPLATTE PAMPHLET COLLECTION – 1987 – 1 – CSUXANL7278-B – us Hoover Inst Photo [355]

THE BATTLEAXE, OR GAZETTE OF THE CHURCH ARMY – London. 2 Apr 1883-30 Jan 1886. -f. 47 feet – 1 – uk British Libr Newspaper [073]

A BATTLE-DOOR FOR TEACHERS AND PROFESSORS TO LEARN SINGULAR AND PLURAL / Fox, George et al – 1660. 229p. (English Linguistics Series 1500-1800) – 9 – us UMI [420]

BATTLE-PIECES AND ASPECTS OF THE WAR / Melville, William – 1866 – 9 – 15.00 – us Scholars' Facs [890]

BATTLES OF THE AMERICAN REVOLUTION, 1775-1781: HISTORICAL AND MILITARY CRITICISM WITH TOPOGRAPHICAL ILLUSTRATION / Carrington, Henry Beebee – New York: A. S. Barnes, 1876. 02553. (Pre-1900 Canadiana) – 9 – cn C.I.H.M. [975]

BATTLESHIP BISMARK PAMPHLET COLLECTION – 1941? – 1 – CSUXANM9184-B – us Hoover Inst Photo [355]

BATTLESHIP TIRPITZ PAMPHLET COLLECTION – 1945-1954 – 1 – CSUXANM9201-B – us Hoover Inst Photo [355]

Batts, H Lewis *see* HISTORY OF THE FIRST BAPTIST CHURCH OF CHRIST AT MACON (MACON, GA), 1826-1968

Batty, Beatrice *see* FORTY-TWO YEARS AMONGST THE INDIANS AND ESKIMO: PICTURES FROM THE LIFE OF THE RIGHT REVEREND JOHN HORDEN, FIRST BISHOP OF MOOSONEE

LES BATUECAS Y LAS JURDES / Beauchet, Ludovico – 1895 – 9 – 1.50f – sp Bibl Santa Ana [946]

Baty, T *see*
- THE CANONS OF INTERNATIONAL LAW
- INTERNATIONAL LAW IN SOUTH AFRICA
- POLARIZED LAW

DER BAU : DER KAMPF UM EIN WERK: ROMAN / Seidl, Florian – Braunschweig: G Westermann, c1937 – 1r – 1 – us U.W. Library [830]

BAU EINER KALIBRIERSTATION FUER THERMOKOPPEL UND WAERMELEITFAEHIGKEIT VON KUNSTSTOFFEN / Wolfrum, Renate – 1995 – 1mf – 9 – DM60.00 – 3-8267-2214-0 – gw Hänsel [660]

BAU EINES RUNDLAUFTHERMOSTATEN FUER DAS FESTKOERPERDILATOMETER UND MESSUNG DES AUSDEHNUNGSVERHALTENS UND DER VOLUMENRELAXATION VON POLYMEREN / Kreuzer, Wolfgang – 1995 – 1mf – 9 – DM60.00 – 3-8267-2213-2 – gw Hänsel [660]

BAU UND LEBEN DER SPINNEN / Lebert, H – Z-2180 2. 1878 – 8 – ne IDC [590]

Baucke, Florian *see* MEMORIAS DEL P. FLORIAN PAUCKE: 1748 A 1767

Baud, C *see* OBSERVATIONS SUR LES CORDES A INSTRUMENTS DE MUSIQUE TANT DE BOYAU QUE SOIE; SUIVIES D'UNE LETTRE DU C. GOSSEC AU C. BAUD; ET DE L'EXTRAIT PROCES, VERBAL DE L'INSTITUT NATIONAL, RELATIF A CE RAPPORT

Baud-Bovy, Samuel *see* CHANSONS DU DODECANESE

Baudet-Lafarge, M J *see* ESSAI SUR L'ENTOMOLOGIE DU DEPARTEMENT DU PUY-DE-DOME

BAUDHAYANA S'RAUTA SUTRA / ed by Caland, W – 3 v. Calcutta. 1904-23. BI-503 2 – 8 – ne IDC [280]

Baudi di Selve, F *see* STUDI ENTOMOLOGICI

Baudier, M *see* THE HISTORY OF THE COURT OF THE KING OF CHINA

Baudin Hesmo, Manuel *see* EL OBISPO DE QUITO DON ALONSO DE LA PENA MONTENEGRO

Baudin, L *see* L'EMPIRE SOCIALISTE DES INKA

Baudin, P *see* FETICHISM AND FETICH WORSHIPERS

Baudissin, Eva Fanny Bernhardine Tuerk, Graefin von *see* DIE GROSSE WOGE

Baudissin, Ida, Graefin *see* DURCH STURM UND NOT

Baudissin, Wolf Ernst Hugo Emil, Graf von *see* DER KLEINE GERD

Baudissin, Wolf Wilhelm, Graf *see*
- EINLEITUNG IN DIE BUECHER DES ALTEN TESTAMENTES
- DIE GESCHICHTE DES ALTTESTAMENTLICHEN PRIESTERTUMS

Bauditz, Sophus Gustav *see* FRA POL TIL POL;.

Baudoncourt, Jacques de *see*
- LE CURE LABELLE (1833-1891)
- HISTOIRE POPULAIRE DU CANADA, D'APRES LES DOCUMENTS FRANCAIS ET AMERICAINS

Baudot, Jules *see*
- HYMNES LATINES ET HYMNAIRES
- THE LECTIONARY

Baudouin, J *see* RECUEIL D'EMBLEMES DIVERS

Baudouin, L *see* CONTRIBUTION A L'ETUDE DE LA SOCIETE DE FAIT...

Baudouin, Philibert *see* INDEX DES CORPS PUBLICS ET INCORPORES ET DU DROIT PRIVE ET LOCAL..
Baudoux, P *see* LES SPATULES ET LES LISSOIRS AU PALEOLITHIQUE SUPERIEUR
Baudri *see* DER ERZBISCHOF VON KOELN JOHANNES CARDINAL VON GEISSEL UND SEINE ZEIT
Baudrillart, Alfred *see*
- THE CATHOLIC CHURCH, THE RENAISSANCE AND PROTESTANTISM
- VIE DE MGR. D'HULST

Baudry, P *see* MORT, VIOLENCE ET SACRE DANS LA SOCIETE MODERNE
DER BAUER – Herbestahl, Germany. 7 Jan-23 Dez 1933; 6 Jan-29 Dez 1934; 3 Jan 1937-1939 – 1 – gw Mikrofilm [072]
Bauer, Adolf *see*
- DIE CHRONIK DES HIPPOLYTOS IM MATRITENSIS GRAECUS 121
- DIE CHRONIK DES HIPPOLYTOS IN MATRITENSIS GRAECUS 121 (T.U.U. 2-29/1)

Bauer, Bruno *see*
- KRITIK DER EVANGELIEN UND GESCHICHTE IHRES UHRSPRUNGS
- KRITIK DER EVANGELISCHEN GESCHICHTE
- KRITIK DER PAULINISCHEN BRIEFE

Bauer, F *see* GENERA FILICUM
Bauer, F A *see* DELINEATIONS OF EXOTICK PLANTS CULTIVATED IN THE ROYAL GARDEN AT KEW
Bauer, F L *see* ILLUSTRATIONES FLORAE NOVAE HOLLANDIAE
Bauer, FC *see* PAULUS DER APOSTEL JESUS CHRISTI...
Bauer, Franz *see* GEORG BUECHNER
Bauer, Friedrich *see* STERNE'SCHER HUMOR IN IMMERMANNS "MUENCHHAUSEN"
Bauer, Hugo *see* DER BURGGRAF VON NUERNBERG, ODER, DER HOHENZOLLERN WELTGESCHICHTLICHER BERUF
DER BAUER IM DEUTSCHEN LIEDE – 1890 – 1 – us I.U. Libraries [390]
Bauer, Ina *see* FRAUEN IM MANAGEMENT
Bauer, Josef Martin *see*
- AM ANDEREN MORGEN
- DER SONNTAGSLUEGNER

Bauer, Louis *see* LECTURES ON CAUSES, PATHOLOGY AND TREATMENT OF JOINT DISEASES:..
Bauer, Martin *see*
- HERSTELLUNG UND SPEKTROSKOPISCHE CHARAKTERISIERUNG MATRIX-ISOLIERTER SILBERCLUSTER
- PHOTOTHERMISCHE UNTERSUCHUNGEN AN KLEINEN SILBERPARTIKELN

Bauer, O *see* DIE NATIONALITAETENFRAGE UND DIE SOZIALDEMOKRATIE
Bauer, Shari R *see* COMPARISON OF HYDROSTATIC WEIGHING TO BIOELECTRICAL IMPEDANCE ANALYSIS IN WOMEN GREATER THAN THIRTY PERCENT BODY FAT
Bauer, Yehuda *see* GUIDE TO UNPUBLISHED MATERIALS OF THE HOLOCAUST PERIOD
Bauerhorst, Kurt *see* BIBLIOGRAPHIE DER STOFF- UND MOTIVGESCHICHTE DER DEUTSCHEN LITERATUR
Bauerman, Hilary *see* REPORT ON THE GEOLOGY OF THE COUNTRY NEAR THE FORTY-NINTH PARALLEL OF NORTH LATITUDE WEST OF THE ROCKY MOUNTAINS: FROM OBSERVATIONS MADE IN 1859-1861
BAUERN-ECHO : AUSGABE DRESDEN – Berlin, DE. Jul 1948-90 – 70r – 1 – gw Mikrofilm [072]
BAUERN-ECHO : AUSGABE POTSDAM, BERLIN, COTTBUS, FRANKFURT/ODER – Berlin, jul 18 1948-jul 31 1992 – 1 – Dist. gw Mikrofilm – gw Misc Inst [630]
BAUERN-ECHO – Berlin, 18 Jul 1948-31 Dec 1954 – 9r – 1 – DM675.00 – gw Mikro Press [072]
BAUERN-ECHO – Berlin, Germany. 1962-76 – 27r – 1 – us L of C Photodup [072]
Bauernfeind, O *see* DER ROEMERBRIEFTEXT DES ORIGENES (T.U.U. 3-44/3)
Bauernfeld, Eduard von *see*
- ALKIBIADES
- FORTUNAT
- DIE REPUBLIK DER THIERE
- DER VATER
- DIE VERLASSENEN
- ZWEI FAMILIEN

DER BAUERNFUERST : ROMAN / Schuecking, Levin – Leipzig: F A Brockhaus, 1851 – 1r – 1 – us U.W. Library [830]
DER BAUERNGENERAL : EIN MITKAEMPFER ERZAEHLT VON DER TRAGIK DEUTSCHEN KAEMPFERTUMS AUF AMERIKANISCHER ERDE, ROMAN / Weyland, Hans – Muenchen: F Eher, 1939 – 1r – 1 – us U.W. Library [830]
DAS BAUERNHAUS IN PALAESTINA : MIT RUECKSICHT AUF DAS BIBLISCHE WOHNHAUS / Jaeger, Karl – Goettingen: Vandenhoeck & Ruprecht, 1912 – 1mf – 9 – 0-8370-3756-5 – 1985-1756 – us A.T.L.A. [230]
DER BAUERNKANZLER / Kath, Lydia – Berlin: Junge Generation Verlag, [1944] – 1r – 1 – us U.W. Library [830]
BAUERNSCHRITT : ERZAEHLUNG / Zierer, Maria Steinmueller – Stuttgart: J G Cotta, 1943 – 1r – 1 – us U.W. Library [830]
BAUERNSCHRITT / Steinmueller Zierer, Maria – Stuttgart: J G Cotta, 1943 – 1 – us U.W. Library [830]
BAUERNSPIEGEL : ODER, LEBENSGESCHICHTE DES JEREMIAS GOTTHELF, VON IHM SELBST BESCHRIEBEN / Gotthelf, Jeremias; ed by Bartels, Adolf – Leipzig: M Hesses, [190-?] – 1 – us U.W. Library [920]
DER BAUERN-SPIEGEL : ODER, LEBENSGESCHICHTE DES JEREMIAS GOTTHELF, VON IHM SELBST GESCHRIEBEN / Gotthelf, Jeremias; ed by Mueller, Ernst – (Includes bibliographical references) – Erlenbach, Zuerich: E Rentsch, 1921 – 1 – us U.W. Library [920]
DER BAUERN-SPIEGEL, ODER, LEBENSGESCHICHTE DES JEREMIAS GOTTHELF : VON IHM SELBST BESCHRIEBEN / Gotthelf, Jeremias; ed by Vetter, Ferdinand – Bern: Schmid & Francke, 1898 – 1 – us U.W. Library [920]
DER BAUERN-SPIEGEL, ODER, LEBENSGESCHICHTE DES JEREMIAS GOTTHELF : VON IHM SELBST GESCHRIEBEN / Gotthelf, Jeremias; ed by Mueller, Ernst – (Includes bibliographical references) – Erlenbach, Zuerich: E Rentsch, 1921 – 1 – us U.W. Library [920]
BAUERNSTOLZ : DORFGESCHICHTEN AUS DEM WESERLANDE / Strauss und Torney, Lulu von – Berlin: E Fleischel, 1921 – 1r – 1 – us U.W. Library [430]
DAS BAUERNTUM IM GRENZ- UND VOLKSDEUTSCHEN ROMAN DER GEGENWART / Luis, Werner – (Includes bibliographical references) – Berlin: Junker und Duennhaupt, 1940 – 1 – us U.W. Library [430]
DER BAUERNZORN : EINE ERZAEHLUNG AUS DEM GROSSEN BAUERNKRIEG / Zacharias, Alfred – Dresden: W Heyne, [194-?] – 1r – 1 – us U.W. Library [830]
Baughman, A J *see*
- A CENTENNIAL BIOGRAPHICAL HISTORY OF RICHLAND COUNTY
- HISTORY OF ASHLAND COUNTY
- HISTORY OF HURON COUNTY
- HISTORY OF MORROW COUNTY
- HISTORY OF RICHLAND COUNTY

Baughman, Robert Williamson *see* POST OFFICES
Baugy, Louis Henri *see* JOURNAL D'UNE EXPEDITION CONTRE LES IROQUOIS EN 1687: LETTRES ET PIECES RELATIVES AU FORT SAINT-LOUIS DES ILLINOIS
BAUHAUS / Reunion des Musees Nationaux. Paris – 1969 – 9 – fr Réunion [700]
BAUHAUS LECTURE NOTES 1930-1933 / ed by Bax, Marty – (The book, Bauhaus Lecture Notes, comes free with the microfiches, but can also be purchased separately) – 14mf – 9 – ne IDC [720]
Bauhin, C *see* PINAX THEATRI BOTANICI
Bauhin, J *see* HISTORIA PLANTARUM UNIVERSALIS
DER BAUINGENIEUR – v24-55 1949-80 – 1,5,9 – $2880.00 – us UMI [624]
BAULAENDER BOTE UND BOXBERGER ANZEIGER – Adelsheim, jul 27 1914-sep 21 1918 – 1 – Dist. gw Mikrofilm – gw Misc Inst [943]
Baulin, A G *see* PARTIIA O PROMYSLOVOI KOOPERATSII I KUSTARNOI PROMYSHLENNOSTI
Baulois, A *see* LES SAGAIES DECOREES DU PALEOLITHIQUE SUPERIEUR DANS LA ZONE FRANCO-CANTABRIQUE
Baum, H *see* KUNENE-SAMBESI EXPEDITION
EIN BAUM IM ODENWALD : NOVELLE / Roquette, Otto – Breslau: S Schottlaender, 1884 – 1r – 1 – us U.W. Library [830]
Baum, J C *see* PREMIERE LITURGIE DES EGLISES REFORMEES DE FRANCE
Baum, Johann Wilhelm *see*
- CAPITO UND BUTZER, STRASSBURGS REFORMATOREN
- FRANZ LAMBERT VON AVIGNON
- THEODOR BEZA

Bauman, K Ia. *see* KHLEBNAIA SEL'SKOKHOZIAISTVENNAIA KOOPERATSIIA I SOTSIALISTICHESKOE PEREUSTROISTVO KREST'IANSKOGO KHOZIAISTVA
Baumann, C *see* L'EVOLUTION DU "JUS SOLI"...
Baumann, Eberhard *see* DER AUFBAU DER AMOSREDEN
Baumann, Frank *see* FLAMM-PUNKTSBERECHNUNG VON KOHLENWASSERSTOFFGEMISCHEN
Baumann, Herbert *see* ANARCHISMUS UND PAEDAGOGIK
Baumann, Johannes *see* MATHEMATISCHE VERFAHREN ZUR BEWERTUNG VON STANDORT- UND AUSLIEFERUNGSALTERNATIVEN IM HANDEL
Baumann, Julius *see* DIE GEMUTSART JESU
Baumann, Klaus-Dieter *see*
- INTEGRATIVE FACHTEXTSORTENSTILISTIK
- SOZIO-SEMANTISCHE BESONDERHEITEN HISTORIOGRAPHISCHER FACHTEXTE DES ENGLISCHEN

Baumann, Simone *see*
- DIE ENTWICKLUNG DER DERMATO-VENEROLOGIE AN DER FAKULTAET/DEM BEREICH MEDIZIN DER KARL-MARX-UNIVERSITAET VON 1945 BIS 1975
- DIE WIRKSAMKEIT WALTER KRUSES ALS DIREKTOR DES HYGIENINSTITUTES AN DER LEIPZIGER UNIVERSITAET VON 1913-1933/34

Baumannn, Frank *see* ROENTGEN- UDN PHOTOELEKTRONENSPEKTROSKOPISCHE UNTERSUCHUNGEN VON VERBINDUNGEN DER 3D-UEBERGANGSMETALLE UND DEM 5D-UEBERGANGSMETALL PLATIN
Baumbach, F *see* DOUZE ROMANCES AVEC ACCOMP. DU PIANO
Baumbach, J C *see* SAMMLUNG VON KLAVIER UND SING-STUCKEN VERSCHIEDENER VERFERTIGER ZUSAMMENGETRAGEN VON J.C. BAUMBACH
Baumbach, Rudolf *see*
- ES WAR EINMAL
- KRUG UND TINTENFASS

Baume, Antoine *see* DISSERTATION SUR L'AETHER, DANS LAQUELLE ON EXAMINE LES DIFFERENS PRODUITS DU MELANGE DE L'ESPRIT DE VIN AVEC LES ACIDES MINERAUX
Baumes, Jean Baptiste Theodore *see* MEMOIRE...SUR LA QUESTION PROPOSEE EN CES TERMES "DETERMINER PAR L'OBSERVATION QUELLES SONT LES MALADIES QUI RESULTENT DES EMANATIONS DES EAUX STAGNANTES.
Baumgaertner, Karl Heinrich *see* KRANKEN-PHYSIOGNOMIK
Baumgard, Otto Wilhelm Gustav *see* GUTZKOWS DRAMATURGISCHE TAETIGKEIT AM DRESDENER HOFTHEATER
Baumgart, Wolfgang *see* DER WALD IN DER DEUTSCHEN DICHTUNG
Baumgarten, Dietrich *see* DEUTSCHE FINANZPOLITIK
Baumgarten, Franz Ferdinand *see* DAS WERK CONRAD FERDINAND MEYERS
Baumgarten, Hermann *see* KARL 5. UND DIE DEUTSCHE REFORMATION
Baumgarten, J C G *see*
- ENUMERATIO STIRPIUM MAGNO TRANSSILVANIAE PRINCIPATUI
- FLORA LIPSIENSIS
- SERTUM LIPSICUM SEU STIRPES OMNES. CIRCA URBEM. PLANTATAS

Baumgarten M *see* DIE APOSTELGESCHICHTE, ODER DER ENTWICKLUNGSGANG DER KIRCHE VON JERUSALEM BIS ROM
Baumgarten, O et al *see* UNSERE RELIGIOESEN ERZIEHER
Baumgarten, Otto *see*
- NEUE BAHNEN
- VOLKSSCHULE UND KIRCHE

Baumgarten, S I *see* DE HEBRAEA ET ADFINIBVS ORIENTIS LINGVIS A GRAECA DERIVANDIS
Baumgartner, Alexander *see* CALDERON
Baumgartner, Antoine Jean *see* ETUDE CRITIQUE SUR L'ETAT DU TEXTE DU LIVRE DES PROVERBES
Baumgartner, F G *see* POLITISCHE BETRACHTUNGEN UEBER DIE GROSSEN VORTHEILE
Baumgartner, M *see*
- DIE ERKENNTNISLEHRE DES WILHELM VON AUVERGNE
- DIE PHILOSOPHIE DES ALANUS DE INSULIS

Baumgartner, Ted A *see*
- DESCRIPTIVE AND PREDICTIVE DISCRIMINANT ANALYSIS OF THE GOLF ABILITY OF COLLEGE MALES
- PHYSICAL ACTIVITY PATTERNS AND CHARACTERISTICS OF HIGH SCHOOL STUDENTS IN A GOVERNOR'S HONORS PROGRAM

Baumhoegger, M *see* DIE RECHTLICHE NATUR DER NATURALISATION
Baumier *see* CODE DE LA PATRIE ET DE L'HUMANITE
Baumkoller, A *see* LE MANDAT SUR LA PALESTINE
Baumstark, Anton *see*
- ABENDLAENDISCHE PALAESTINAPILGER DES ERSTEN JAHRTAUSENDS UND IHRE BERICHTE
- DIE CHRISTLICHEN LITERATUREN DES ORIENTS
- DENKMAELER DER ENTSTEHUNGS-GESCHICHTE DES BYZANTINISCHEN RITUS
- FESTBREVIER UND KIRCHENJAHR DER SYRISCHEN JAKOBITEN
- DIE PETRUS- UND PAULUSACTEN IN DER LITTERARISCHEN UEBERLIEFERUNG DER SYRISCHEN KIRCHE

Baunard, Louis *see*
- HISTOIRE DE MME. DUCHESNE: RELIGIEUSE DE LA SOCIETE DU SACRE-COEUR DE JESUS ET FONDATRICE DES PREMIERES MAISONS DE CETTE SOCIETE EN AMERIQUE
- THEODULFE

Baunard, Louis, Abbe *see* THE LIFE OF MOTHER DUCHESNE
Baur et le Roy, (Pere) *see* A TRAVERS LE ZANZIBAR, VOYAGE DANS L'OUDOE, L'OUZIGOUA, L'OUKWERE, L'OUKAMI ET L'OUSAGARA
Baur, Ferdinand Christian *see*
- APOLLONISU VON TYANA UND CHRISTUS, ODER, DAS VERHAELTNISS DES PYTHAGOREISMUS ZUM CHRISTENTHUM
- DAS CHRISTENTUM UND DIE CHRISTLICHE KIRCHE DER DREI ERSTEN JAHRHUNDERTE
- DAS CHRISTLICHE DES PLATONISMUS, ODER, SOKRATES UND CHRISTUS
- DIE CHRISTLICHE KIRCHE DES MITTELALTERS IN DEN HAUPTMOMENTEN IHRER ENTWICKLUNG
- DIE CHRISTLICHE LEHRE VON DER VERSOEHNUNG
- THE CHURCH HISTORY OF THE FIRST THREE CENTURIES
- DAS DOGMA DER ALTEN KIRCHE
- DAS DOGMA DER NEUEREN ZEIT
- DAS DOGMA DES MITTELALTERS
- DREI ABHANDLUNGEN ZUR GESCHICHTE DER ALTEN PHILOSOPHIE UND IHRES VERHAELTNISSES ZUM CHRISTENTUM
- DIE EPOCHEN DER KIRCHLICHEN GESCHICHTSCHREIBUNG
- DER GEGENSATZ DES KATHOLICISMUS UND PROTESTANTISMUS
- LEHRBUCH DER CHRISTLICHEN DOGMENGESCHICHTE
- DAS MANICHAEISCHE RELIGIONSSYSTEM
- DIE TUEBINGER SCHULE UND IHRE STELLUNG ZUR GEGENWART
- UEBER DEN URSPRUNG DES EPISCOPATS IN DER CHRISTLICHEN KIRCHE
- VORLESUNGEN UEBER NEUTESTAMENTLICHE THEOLOGIE

Baur, Gustav *see*
- DIE BERECHTIGUNG DER THEOLOGIE ALS EINES NOTHWENDIGEN GLIEDES IM GESAMTORGANISMUS DER WISSENSCHAFT
- GESCHICHTE DER ALTTESTAMENTLICHEN WEISSAGUNG, THEILE 1

Baur, Johannes *see* GIOVANNI GENTILES PHILOSOPHIE UND PAEDAGOGIK
Baur, L *see* GUNDISSALINUS' DE DIVISIONE PHILOSOPHIAE
Baur, Thorsten *see* COST BENCHMARKING ALS INSTRUMENT DES KOSTENMANAGEMENTS
Baur, Tobias *see* DIEMENSIONEN DER ALTERUNG IM SOZIALSTAAT
Baur, William *see* RELIGIOUS LIFE IN GERMANY DURING THE WARS OF INDEPENDENCE
Bausman, Joseph H *see* HISTORY OF BEAVER COUNTY CENTENNIAL CELEBRATION
Bausset-Roquefort, J BG F *see* ETUDE SUR LE MOUVEMENT DE LA POPULATION EN FRANCE DEPUIS LE COMMENCEMENT DUE XIXE SIECLE
BAUSTEINE FUER DIE EINHEIT DER CHRISTEN – 1961-93 (complete) – Inquire – 1 – ATLA S0621 – us A.T.L.A. [073]

BAUSTEINE ZUR DEUTSCHEN LITERATURGESCHICHTE : AELTERE DEUTSCHE DICHTUNG / Becker, Hendrik – ("Tafel 1-76" (literary selections)) – Halle (Saale): M. Niemeyer, 1957 – 1 – us U.W. Library [430]

EINER BAUT EINEN DOM : FREIHEITSGEDICHTE / Holzapfel, Karl Maria – Berlin: W Heyer, 1934 – 1 – us U.W. Library [810]

EL BAUTISMO : RENOVACION DEL RITO... / Bautismo, El – Caceres: Tip. Extremadura, 1978 – sp Bibl Santa Ana [920]

BAUTISMO DE LOS FETOS ABORTIVOS... CESAREA / Riva, Juan Antonio de la – 1817 – 9 – 1.50f – sp Bibl Santa Ana [240]

Bautismo, El *see* EL BAUTISMO

BAUTZENER NACHRICHTEN – (Cont: Budissinische woechentliche Nachrichten, 1782-1808. Budissinische Nachrichten, jan 7 1809-27. Budissiner Nachrichten, jan 5 1828-jun 1868. Cont by: Der Freiheitskampf, aug 1 1934. NS-Tageszeitung fuer Bautzen, jan 2 1935) – Bautzen, 1921-40 – ca 50r – 1 – Dist. gw Mikrofilm – gw Misc Inst [943]

BAUTZENER TAGEBLATT – Bautzen, jan 3 1898-apr 18 1945 – 90r – 1 – Dist. gw Mikrofilm – gw Misc Inst [943]

LE BAVARD – (Filmed with: Le Vrai Bavard 13 avr 1882-25 mai 1882) – Quebec, Canada. 16 fev-6 avr 1882 – 1r – 1 – Can$35.00 – cn Can Microfilming [072]

LE BAVARD / ed by Menard, Adjutor – Montreal, Canada. 2 nov 1940-23 mar 1946 – 2r – 1 – Can$45.00r – cn Can Microfilming [072]

LES BAVARDS – Port-au-Prince: Paulin Andreoli. [1ere annee n1-2e annee n14]. (21 dec 1876-22 mars 1877) – 1 sheet – us Res Libr [072]

Bavaria. Laws, Statutes, etc *see* GESETZ UBER DIE VERWALTUNGSGERICHTSBARKEIT IN BAYERN, WURTTEMBERG-BADEN UND HESSEN, MIT KOMMENTAR VON PAULUS VAN HUSEN

BAVARIA: PAMPHLET COLLECTION – 19?? – 1 – CSUXANS6072-B – us Hoover Inst Photo [943]

Bavaria. Statistisches Landesamt *see*
- BEITRAEGE ZUR STATISTIK BAYERNS
- STATISTISCHES JAHRBUCH FUR DAS KOENIGREICH BAYERN

BAVARIAN ALPS: PAMPHLET COLLECTION – 192?-19?? – 1 – CSUXANS6071-B – us Hoover Inst Photo [910]

BAVARIAN POLITICS AND GOVERNMENT: PAMPHLET COLLECTION – 1988 – 1 – CSUXANS6074-B – us Hoover Inst Photo [320]

THE BAVIAD, AND MAEVIAD / Gifford, William – London: Printed for J Wright, rev ed 1797 – 1r – 1 – 1-55879-745-9 – uk Libr Preservation [999]

Bavinck, Herman *see*
- DE ETHIEK VAN ULRICH ZWINGLI
- THE PHILOSOPHY OF REVELATION
- DE WELSPREKENDHEID

Bawa, K *see* REPRODUCTIVE ECOLOGY OF TROPICAL FOREST PLANTS

Bax, C *see* KROPOTKIN ON LAW

Bax, Ernest Belfort *see*
- JEAN PAUL MARAT, THE PEOPLE'S FRIEND
- THE PEASANTS WAR IN GERMANY, 1525-1526

Bax, Marty *see* BAUHAUS LECTURE NOTES 1930-1933

Baxter County. Arkansas *see* INVENTORY OF THE COUNTY ARCHIVES OF ARKANSAS: BAXTER

Baxter, James Phinney *see*
- THE BRITISH INVASION FROM THE NORTH: THE CAMPAIGNS OF GENERALS CARLETON AND BURGOYNE FROM CANADA, 1776-77: WITH THE JOURNAL OF LIEUT. WILLIAM DIGBY OF THE 53RD, OR SHROPSHIRE REGIMENT OF FOOT
- THE PIONEERS OF NEW FRANCE IN NEW ENGLAND: WITH CONTEMPORARY LETTERS AND DOCUMENTS

Baxter, Richard *see* THE REFORMED PASTOR

Baxter, Robert *see* IRVINGISM

Baxter, Samuel John *see* THE DEVELOPMENT OF A MINISTRY AT THE IMMANUEL BAPTIST CHURCH, TORONTO, CANADA, TO INTEGRATE MULTICULTURAL PEOPLES, WITH SPECIAL REFERENCE TO WEST INDIAN IMMIGRANTS

BAXTER'S CONTESTED ELECTION CASES / New York. (State) – 1v. 1777-1899 (all publ) – 9mf – 9 – $13.50 – LLMC 80-017 – us L.L.M.C. [340]

BAY CITY CHRONICLE – Bay City, OR. -w. 1 May 1924-14 Aug 1924. 1 roll – 1 – us U.O. Library [071]

BAY CITY TRIBUNE – Bay City, OR. -w. 29 Jun 1891-19 Nov 1891. 1 roll – 1 – us U.O. Library [071]

BAY CITY TRIBUNE WEEKLY – Bay City. Mich. -w. 1896-1904 – 1 – us UMI [071]

Bay, J C *see*
- BIBLIOGRAPHIES OF BOTANY

BAY LEAF – San Francisco, CA: San Francisco State University, 1928-1931 – 1r – 1 – $50.00 – B03664 – us Library Micro [071]

BAY LEAF *see* GOLDEN GATOR

THE BAY OF SAN FRANCISCO – Chicago, 1892. v1, California Reel 27. v2, California Reel 28.(The Cox Library Collection) – 5 – us Americana [978]

BAY PILOT – St. Andrews, Canada. 1878-89 – 4r – 1 – $260.00 – cn Library Assoc [971]

THE BAY REPORTER – Coos Bay, OR. -w. 22 Nov 1978-17 Oct 1979+. 1 roll – 1 – us U.O. Library [071]

Bayalovitch, L *see* L'UNIFICATION DU DROIT DU CHANGE

LE BAYARD – San Francisco, CA. Jan 1888-Dec 1889 – 1r – 1 – $50.00 – B02833 – us Library Micro [071]

Bayard, Henri *see* MEMOIRE SUR LA TOPOGRAPHIE MEDICALE DU 4 ARRONDISSEMENT DE LA VILLE DE PARIS

Bayard, James A *see* PAPERS

Bayard, Richard H *see* PAPERS

THE BAYARD RUSTIN PAPERS – 22r – 1 – $2,115.00 – 1-55655-064-2 – us UPA [320]

BAYARD TRANSCRIPT – Bayard, NE. -w. May 1892-Sep. 1902. Incomplete; Oct. 1908-Oct. 1909; Feb. 1910- – 1 – us NE Hist [071]

Bayard, William *see*
- AN ADDRESS UPON THE USE AND ABUSE OF ALCOHOLIC DRINKS
- HISTORY OF THE GENERAL PUBLIC HOSPITAL IN THE CITY OF SAINT JOHN, N.B
- PRESIDENTIAL ADDRESS AT THE MEETING OF THE MARITIME MEDICAL ASSOCIATION: HELD IN ST JOHN, N.B., JULY 22ND AND 23RD 1891

Bayer, E *see* O ROSTLINSTVU VRSTEV BREZENSKYCH

Bayer, J *see* A MAGYAR DRAMAIRODALOM TOERTENETE

Bayer, Robert von *see* DER WEG ZUM GLUECK

BAYERISCH LAND UND VOLK – Muenchen etc., Braun etc. v1-3, 1890-92. Lacks v1., no. 19-30, v2, no. 20-30. Film Mas C 331 – 1 – us H.U. Library [910]

Bayerische Akademie der Wissenschaften *see* SITZUNGSBERICHTE.

BAYERISCHE ARBEITER-ZEITUNG *see* DIE PERSPEKTIVE

BAYERISCHE BIBLIOTHEK – Bamberg, etc. v1-28/29. 1890-92. Film Mas C 280 – 1 – us H.U. Library [073]

DER BAYERISCHE EILBOTE – Muenchen, DE. 1848-49 – 1r – 1 – gw Mikrofilm [072]

BAYERISCHE ISRAELITISCHE GEMEINDEZEITUNG – 1 – $475.00 – us UPA [260]

BAYERISCHE LANDBOETIN – Muenchen, DE. 1848-49 – 1r – 1 – gw Mikrofilm [072]

BAYERISCHE LANDBOTE *see* DER BAIERISCHE LANDBOTE

BAYERISCHE LANDESZEITUNG – (Title changes to: Muenchener Allgemeine from Jan 28 1951) – Muenchen, DE. 21 Jan 1949-Jun 1951 – 1 – gw Mikrofilm [072]

BAYERISCHE LANDESZEITUNG *see* MUENCHNER POLITISCHE ZEITUNG

BAYERISCHE OSTMARK *see*
- BAMBERGER TAGBLATT
- FRAENKISCHES VOLK

BAYERISCHE OSTWACHT *see*
- FRAENKISCHES VOLK

DIE BAYERISCHE PRESSE – Wuerzburg, Germany. Dec 1849-8 Feb 1851 – 2r – 1 – gw Mikrofilm [072]

BAYERISCHE RADIOZEITUNG *see* BAYERISCHE RADIO-ZEITUNG UND BAYERNFUNK

BAYERISCHE RADIO-ZEITUNG UND BAYERNFUNK – (Incl the following suppl: Der Bastler. Europaeische Senderprogramme. Funkschau. Cont by: Sueddeutscher Rundfunk. Ausgabe A: Muenchen, jan 1 1925. Bayerische Radiozeitung, may 1 1928) – Muenchen, aug 3 1924-dec 22 1940 – 24r – 1 – gw Mikrofilm [790]

BAYERISCHE RUNDSCHAU – Kulmbach, West-Germany. 1977- – 1 – gw Mikrofilm [072]

BAYERISCHE STAATSZEITUNG – Muenchen, jan 30 1914, jun 29 1914-16, jun 17, jul 12 1924 – 7r – 1 – gw Mikrofilm [350]

DAS BAYERISCHE VATERLAND – Muenchen, DE. 1869-Sep 1934 – 1 – gw Mikrofilm [072]

DER BAYERISCHE VOLKSFREUND – Muenchen, DE. 1848-49 – 1r – 1 – gw Mikrofilm [072]

BAYERISCHE VOLKSPARTEIKORRESPONDENZ – Muenchen, 30 May 1921-18 Nov 1923 – 5r – 1 – DM400.00 set DM80.00r – gw Mikro Press [072]

BAYERISCHE WOCHENSCHRIFT – Muenchen, DE. 2 Apr-24 Sep 1859 – 1r – 1 – gw Mikrofilm [072]

BAYERISCHE ZEITUNG *see* MUENCHNER POLITISCHE ZEITUNG

BAYERISCHER KURIER – Muenchen, 1918-21 – 8r – 1 – DM640.00 set DM80.00r – gw Mikro Press [072]

BAYERISCHER KURIER – Munich, DE. 3 Sept 1916-1922 – 1 – uk British Libr Newspaper [072]

BAYERISCHES JAHRBUCH FUER VOLKSKUNDE – 1950-51; 1953-69 – 1 – us I.U. Libraries [300]

BAYERISCHES VOLKSBLATT – Stadtamhof, Germany. Mar-Dec 1849 – 1 – gw Mikrofilm [072]

DAS BAYERLAND – Muenchen. v.1-37, 1890-1926. Lacks v. 30, n. 24. Film Mas C 333 – 1 – app – us H.U. Library [073]

Bayerle, Bernard Gustav *see*
- DAS CHRISTLICHE ALTERTHUM
- EIN VOLLSTAENDIGES LEBEN JESU, SEINER HEILIGEN MUTTER MARIA, UND DER UEBRIGEN HEILIGEN SEINER ZEIT

BAYERN UND DER HEILIGE STUHL IN DER ERSTEN HAELFTE DES 19. JAHRHUNDERTS / Bastgen, Hubert – Muenchen, 1940 – 2v xxiv/1071p – 9 – DM300.00 – 3-89349-253-4 – gw Hänsel [240]

BAYERN-2. PARTEITAG / Sozialdemokratische Partei Deutschlands – Muenchen, 30 Sept-1 Oct 1894 – 1 – DM80.00 – gw Mikro Press [335]

BAYERN-3. PARTEITAG / Sozialdemokratische Partei Deutschlands – Nuernberg, 12-13 Jul 1896 – 1 – DM80.00 – gw Mikro Press [335]

BAYERN-4. PARTEITAG / Sozialdemokratische Partei Deutschlands – Wuerzburg, 30-31 Oct 1898 – 1 – DM80.00 – gw Mikro Press [335]

BAYERN-7. PARTEITAG / Sozialdemokratische Partei Deutschlands – Augsburg, 26-27 Jun 1904 – 1 – DM80.00 – gw Mikro Press [335]

BAYERN-8. PARTEITAG / Sozialdemokratische Partei Deutschlands – Schweinfurt, 4-5 Mar 1906 – 1 – DM80.00 – gw Mikro Press [335]

BAYERN-13. PARTEITAG / Sozialdemokratische Partei Deutschlands – Neustadt a.H., 18-20 Jul 1914 – 1 – DM80.00 – gw Mikro Press [335]

BAYERNKURIER – 1979- – 9 – inquire – us Ross [072]

BAYERNKURIER – Muenchen, DE. 3 Jun 1950- – 1 – gw Mikro Press [072]

BAYERNKURIER – Muenchen, DE. Jan 1979- – ca 55mf per yr – gw Alpha Com [072]

BAYERNKURIER – Muenchen, jan 4-nov 29 1975 – 1r – 1 – gw Mikrofilm [072]

BAYERNS AUSWAERTIGE VERHAELTNISSE... / Aretin, C M von – Passau, 1839 – 9mf – 9 – ILM-2544/1 – ne IDC [340]

BAYER'SCHE LANDBOTE *see* DER BAIERISCHE LANDBOTE

BAYERSCHE LANDBOTE *see* DER BAIERISCHE LANDBOTE

BAYERWALD-BOTE : BA DER PASSAUER NEUEN PRESSE – Regen, Germany. 1 Jun 1983- – ca 9r per yr – 1 – gw Mikrofilm [072]

BAYERWALD-ECHO : BA FUER CHAM UND UMGEBUNG DER MITTELBAYERISCHEN ZEITUNG, REGENSBURG – Cham, West-Germany. 1977- – ca 12r per yr – 1 – gw Mikrofilm [072]

Bayet, Albert *see* LA MORALE LAIQUE ET SES ADVERSAIRES

BAYETE : CRONICAS AFRICANAS DO ATLANTICO AO INDICO / Rocha, Hugo – (Filmed with: Barahona e Costa, Henrique Cesar da Silva: Apontamentos para a historia de guerra de Zambezia 1871-75 et al) – [O Porto?: Oficinas Graficas do Comercio do Porto] 1933 – 1 – us Res Libr [960]

Bayfield, Henry Wolsey *see* DIRECTIONS DE NAVIGATION POUR L'ILE DE TERRENEUVE ET LA COTE DU LABRADOR ET POUR LE GOLFE ET LE FLEUVE ST LAURENT

Bayle, Constantino *see*
- 2ND CONGRESO DE GEOGRAFIA E HISTORIA HISPANO-AMERICANAS
- EL 4 CENTENARIO DEL DESCUBRIMIENTO DE CALIFORNIA
- EL 4TH CENTENARIO DE LA FUNDACION DE LIMA
- EL 26TH CONGRESO INTERNACIONAL DE AMERICANISTAS
- A CAZA DE TESTAMENTOS. UNA PIEZA MAYOR
- A LOS LECTORES ANTIGUOS Y NUEVOS DE "RAZON Y FE"
- A ORILLAS DEL ORINOCO Y A ORILLAS DEL TAMESIS
- ABOLICION OFICIAL DEL LAICISMO EN LAS ESCUELAS
- ACTAS DEL CABILDO DE CARACAS. TOMO 1. CARACAS, 1943
- ACUERDOS DEL EXTINGUIDO CABILDO DE BUENOS AIRES. SERIE 2, TOMO 4 (1719 A 1722). BUENOS AIRES, 1927
- ACUERDOS DEL EXTINGUIDO CABILDO DE BUENOS AIRES. SERIE 2, TOMO 9 Y SERIE 3, TOMO 9
- ADICION A LA RELACION DESCRIPTIVA DE LOS MAPAS PLANOS...ARCHIVO GENERAL DE INDIAS
- ALGO MAS SOBRE LAS BULAS ALEJANDRINAS
- ALGUNOS PUNTOS DE HISTORIA ACERCA DE LA HISTORIA DEL COLONIAJE EN EL ECUADOR
- EL ALMA CRISTIANA DE CORTES. EN EL CENTENARIO DE SU MUERTE
- AMERICA EN TIEMPO DE FELIPE 2 SEGUN EL COSMOGRAFO CRONISTA JUAN LOPEZ DE VELASCO. EL TERRITORIO ESPANOL DE IFNI
- EL AMOR AL LIBRO...
- EL ANO PEDAGOGICO HISPANOAMERICANO
- UN APOSTOL CON TEMPLE DE MARTIN. LA BEATA FILIPINA DUCHENSE
- D'APRES LES PARABOLES HISTOIRES VRAIES...
- APUNTES DE RECUERDOS
- ARCHIVO DE LA NACION. CORRESPONDENCIA DE LORD STRANGFORD Y DE LA ESTACION NAVAL EN EL RIO DE LA PLATA CON EL GOBIERNO DE BUENOS AIRES. 1810-1812
- ARCHIVO DEL GENERAL MIRANDA
- ARCHIVO DEL GENERAL MIRANDA. REVOLUCION FRANCESA. TOMO 9 A 12
- ARCHIVO GENERAL DE LA NACION. ACUERDOS DEL EXTINGUIDO CABILDO DE BUENOS AIRES. SERIE 2, TOMO 9
- ARCHIVO GENERAL DE LA NACION. UNIVERSIDAD AUTONOMA DE MEXICO. NUEVOS DOCUMENTOS RELATIVOS A LOS BIENES DE HERNANDO CORTES, 1547-1947. TOMO 2. MEXICO, 1946
- LOS ARGONAUTAS INGLESES DE ULTIMA HORA
- ARMAES DO MUSEU PAULISTA, TOMOS 1 Y 2
- ARMES FOR RED SPAIN
- ARTE EN AMERICA Y FILIPINAS. CUADERNO 1. SEVILLA, 1935
- BALBOA, DESCUBRIDOR DEL PACIFICO
- BELISARIO PENA
- BIBLIOGRAFIA. HISTORIAS DEL IMPERIO LUSITANO
- BIBLIOGRAFIA JESUISTICA DE MAINAS
- BIBLIOGRAFIA SOBRE LAS MISIONES DE MAINAS. UN MISIONERO MISIONOLOGO
- BIBLIOTECA GOATHEMALA DE LA SOCIEDAD DE GEOGRAFIA E HISTORIA...
- BIOGRAFIA DOCUMENTADA
- BIOGRAFIAS. ANTONIO MAURA, DE TAXONERA, LA EMPERATRIZ EUGENIA, DE CABAL Y PEDRO DE ALVARADO, DE BARON CASTRO
- BOLETIN DE HISTORIA AMERICANA
- BOLETIN DE HISTORIAS AMERICANAS
- LAS BORRACHERAS Y EL PROBLEMA DE LAS CONVERSACIONES EN INDIAS
- BREVE HISTORIA DE MEXICO

- BROWNE, KNIGHT AND A DAY. LEIPZIG 1928
- LAS BULAS ALEJANDRINAS DE 1493 REFERENTES A LAS INDIAS
- EL CABALLO DE BATALLA DE LOS NUEVOS CRUZADOS EN LA AMERICA ESPANOLA
- CABILDOS DE INDIOS EN LA AMERICA ESPANOLA
- CABRERA, PABLO...
- CAMPANA DEL BRASIL. ANTECEDENTES COLONIALES. TOMO 1
- LA CAMPANA PROTESTANTE EN AMERICA
- CAMPANA REAUNDADA
- CAMPANAS EN EL RIF Y GEBALA, DEL GENERAL BERENGUER
- CAMPO PROPIO DEL SACERDOTE SECULAR EN LA EVANGELIZACION AMERICANA, EL
- EL CAOS DE RELIGIONES NUEVAS
- CARABELAS DE ESPANA...PINZON, JUAN DE LA COSA, DIAZ DE SOLIS JUAN SEBASTIAN ELCANO
- EL CARACTER. DEFINICION, IMPORTANCIA, IDEAL, ORIGENES...
- LA CARCEL DE MUJERES DE MADRID
- CARDENAL ANTONIO CAGGIANO, OBISPO DE ROSARIO. LA FIGURA DE SAN FRANCISCO SOLANO Y SU ACTUACION EN EL LOCUMAN...
- UN CASO CURIOSO DE DERECHO Y DE ANATOMIA MINERAL
- LAS CASTAS DEL MEXICO COLONIAL...1924
- LOS CATALANES EN GRECIA...
- CATALOGO DE DOCUMENTOS RELATIVOS A LAS ISLAS FILIPINAS EXISTENTES EN EL ARCHIVO DE INDIAS DE SEVILLA
- CATALOGO DE LOS DOCUMENTOS RELATIVO A LAS ISLAS FILIPINAS EXISTENTES EN EL ARCHIVO DE INDIAS DE SEVILLA. TOMO 7
- CATALOGO DE LOS DOCUMENTOS RELATIVOS A LAS ISLAS FILIPINAS...
- CATALOGO DE LOS FONDOS AMERICANOS DEL ARCHIVO DE PROTOCOLOS DE SEVILLA...
- CATALOGO DE PASAJEROS A INDIAS DURANTE LOS SIGLOS 16, 17 Y 18. VOL 2 (1535-1538)
- CENTENARIO DE DON FRAY JUAN DE ZUMARRAGA, EL 4TH
- EL CENTENARIO DE MAGALLANES
- THE CHURCH IN SPAIN
- CIRIACO PEREZ BUSTAMANTE, LA FUNDACION DE UN IMPERIO...
- LOS CLERIGOS Y LA EXTIRPACION DE LA IDOLATRIA ENTRE LOS NEOFITOS AMERICANOS
- EL CLERO SECULAR Y LA EVANGELIZACION DE AMERICA
- COLECCION DE DIARIOS Y RELACIONES PARA LA HISTORIA DE LOS VIAJES Y DESCUBRIMIENTOS. VOL 1...VOL 2...MADRID, 1943
- COLECCION DE DOCUMENTOS INEDITOS PARA LA HISTORIA DE IBEROAMERICA
- COLECCION DE DOCUMENTOS RELATIVOS AL ADELANTADO CAPITAN DON SEBASTIAN DE BELALCAZAR 1535-1560
- COLECCION GENERAL DE DOCUMENTOS RELATIVOS A LAS ISLAS FILIPINAS
- COLON ITALIANO? COLON ESPANOL?
- EL COLONIAJE Y SUS DETRACTORES. EL PASO, 1927
- COMMUNIST ATTACK IN GREAT BRITAIN, LONDON 1938
- COMO SE ALHAJABAN CASAS E IGLESIAS EN MAYNAS
- COMPANIA FUNDIDORA DE FIERRO Y ACERO DE MONTERREY, S.A. ...
- UN COMPLOT TERRORISTA EN EL SIGLO 15TH. MADRID, 1927
- LA COMUNION ENTRE LOS INDIOS AMERICANOS
- LAS COMUNIONES EN LA ESPANA ROJA
- EL COMUNISMO EN ESPANA. CINCO ANOS EN EL PARTIDO
- LA CONFERENCIA DE LAUSANA SOBRE FE Y DISCIPLINA
- CONGRESO EUCARISTICO DE DUBLIN
- EL CONGRESO MARIANO DE SEVILLA
- EL CONGRESO Y EXPOSICION. MISIONALES DE BARCELONA
- EL CONVENTO DE TEPOTZOTLAN...1924
- CORONA FUNEBRE, A LA MEMORIA DE LA VIRTUOSA SENORA MARIA CRISTINA ROJAS DE HERDOCIA
- LA CORONACION DE LA VIRGEN DE GUADALUPE
- EL CORPUS DE LOS NEOFITOS AMERICANOS
- UN CORRESPONSAL EXTRANJERO Y UNAS TEORIAS
- CORTES Y LA EVANGELIZACION DE NUEVA ESPANA
- CRISTOBAL COLON
- CRONICA DEL CONGRESO EUCARISTICO NACIONAL
- LA CRUZ EN LA CONQUISTA DE AMERICA
- CUANDO Y DONDE SE ORDENO BARTOLOME DE LAS CASAS
- LA CUESTION RELIGIOSA EN AMERICA
- LA CUESTION ROMANA Y EL MARQUES DE COMILLAS
- EL CULTO A LA EUCARISTIA EN LA ESPANA ROJA
- EL CURA DE SANTA CRUZ. SAN SEBASTIAN, 1928
- EL CURA SANTA CRUZ
- CURA Y MIL VECES CURA. BARCELONA, 1928
- DAMASO DE LA PRESENTACION. VIDA DEL P. JOSE MA DEL MONTECARMELO
- DE HISTORIAS AMERICANAS
- LOS DEMANES EN LA CONQUISTA DE AMERICA, BUENOS AIRES, 1943
- DESCUBRIDORES JESUITAS DEL AMAZONAS
- DESCUBRIDORES JESUITAS DEL AMAZONAS, BREVE DESCRIPCION
- DOCUMENTOS HISTORICOS COLECCIONADOS PO...SECCION GEOGRAFIA...
- DOCUMENTOS PARA LA HISTORIA ARGENTINA
- DOCUMENTOS PARA LA HISTORIA ARGENTINA. TOMO 20, IGLESIA. CARTAS ANTIGUAS DE LA PROVINCIA DEL PARAGUAY, AVILA Y TUCUMAN DE LA COMPANIA DE JESUS (1609-1614). BUENOS AIRES, 1927
- DON BOSCO
- DON CONSTITUYENTES DEL ANO 1824. BIOGRAFIAS DE DON MIGUEL RAMOS ARIZPE Y D. LORENZO ZAVALA, MEXICO. MUSEO NACIONAL DE ARQUEOLOGIA, 1925
- DON PEDRO DE ALVARADO, CONQUISTADOR DEL REINO DE GUATEMALA. MADRID, 1927
- DON PEDRO DE VALDIVIA...BADAJOZ, 1928
- LOS DORADOS INGLESES
- DOS TESTIGOS ABRUMADORES CONTRA LOS NACIONALES
- DUCHAUSSOIS, ROSE DU CANADA...
- EDUARDO POSADA. SECRETAIRE PERPETUEL DE L'ACADEMIE NATIONALE...COLOMBIE
- EDUCACION DE LA MUJER EN AMERICA
- EL DORADO FANTASMA
- ELEMENTOS GRIEGOS Y LATINOS QUE ENTRAN EN LA COMPOSICION DE NUMEROSOS TECNICISMOS ESPANOLES, FRANCESES E INGLESES. MADRID, 1929
- EL EMMO CARDENAL GOMA
- EN EL PAIS DE LOS ETERNOS HIELOS
- EN LA CATEDRAL DE TOLEDO
- EN PLEIN CONFICT
- ENSAYO POLITICO SOBRE EL REINO DE LA NUEVA ESPANA
- ENSAYOS HISTORICOS. PUBLICACION DE HOMENAJE
- LA ENSENANZA DE LENGUAS CIVILIZADAS A LOS BARBAROS. UN CASO DE TEOLOGIA PASTORAL MISIONERA
- ENTRE DOS FILOS. MANAGUA, 1927
- ERNESTO PINTO. EL SANTO DEL SIGLO
- ESPANA ANTE LA INDEPENDENCIA DE LOS ESTADOS UNIDOS POR EL DR. JUAN F...
- ESPANA EN INDIAS
- ESPANA EN TRENTO. 2. EL CONCILIO DE TRENTO EN LAS INDIAS ESPANOLAS
- ESPANA. LA ABORTADA REPUBLICA
- ESPANA. PRIMERA ASAMBLEA DE ACCION CATOLICA
- ESPANA Y EL CLERO INDIGENA DE AMERICA
- LOS ESPANOLES Y MAGALLANES EN LA EXPEDICION DEL ESTRECHO
- EL ESPIRITU DE SANTA TERESA Y EL DE SAN IGNACIO
- EL ESPIRITU GENUINO DE FALANGE ESPANOLA. ES CATOLICO?
- ESPISTOLARIO DE NUEVA ESPANA 1505-1812 RECOPILADO POR FRANCISCO DEL PASO Y TRONCOSO, TOMO 16, MEJICO, 1942
- ESTADISTICA DE SANGRE Y DE GLORIA
- ESTADISTICAS SANGRIENTAS
- ESTADO GENERAL DE LAS FUNDACIONES HECHAS POR DON JOSE ESCANDON... TOMOS 1, 2 Y 3
- ESTADOS UNIDOS MEXICANOS...
- LA ESTELA DE UN CAMPESINO
- EL ESTRECHO DE MAGALLANES. LO QUE ERA Y LO QUE ES
- EL EVANGELIO COMENTADO CONFERENCIAS POR RADIO
- EXCURSION POR EL CAMPO TEOSOFICO
- EXCURSION POR EL CAMPO TEOSOFICO. 2
- LA EXPOSICION INTERNACIONAL DE BARCELONA
- LA EXPOSICION MISIONAL DEL VATICANO
- LA EXTIRPACION DE LA IDOLATRIA EN EL PERU DEL P. PABLO JOSEPH DE ARRIAGA
- FACULTAD DE FILOSOFIA Y LETRAS. UNIVERSIDAD DE BUENOS AIRES. PUBLICACIONES HISTORICAS
- FELIPE 2ND Y LA EVANGELIZACION DE AMERICA
- FIGUEIREDO DE ESTUDIOS DE HISTORIA AMERICANA
- FILANTROPIA SOSPECHOSA
- LA FIN DE L'EMPIRE ESPAGNOL D'AMERIQUE PAR MARINS ANDRE
- FIRST EXPEDITION OF VARGAS INTO NEW MEXICO, 1692
- FTO VIDA Y VIRTUDES DEL VENERABLE SIERVO DE DIOS MARCELINO CHAMPAGNAT. BARCELONA, FTO. 1929
- LOS FUNDADORES DE BOGOTA
- GALLIONS REACH. LEIPZIG, 1928
- GARCIA MORENO
- GARCIA MORENO Y LA INSTRUCCION PUBLICA POR JULIO TOBAR DONOSO
- GEOGRAFIA DE ESPANA...
- GEOGRAFIA ECONOMICA
- GESNALDA DELLO SPIRITO SANCTO. SANTA GEMA GALGANI
- GUADALUPE DE EXTREMADURA EN INDIAS
- HACIA ALLA Y PARA ACA...
- HERNANDEZ MARCIAL
- OS HEROIS DE COARO E PIRAPO
- LE HERPEUR, M.L'ORATOIR DE FRANCE
- LOS HIJOS DE LUTERO ENTRE LOS HIJOS DEL SOL
- HISTOIRE DE NOTRE DAME DE LOURDES
- HISTOIRE DU CURE SANTA CRUZ. PARIS, 1928
- HISTORIA DE AMERICA ESPANOLA 1920-1925
- HISTORIA DE LA REPUBLICA DE EL SALVADOR...
- HISTORIA DE MEXICO, DE FRANCISCO BENEGAS GALVAN
- HISTORIA DE NUESTRA SENORA DE GUADALUPE...
- HISTORIA PEREGRINA DE UN INCA ANDALUZ
- HISTORIA VERDADERA DE LA CONQUISTA DE LA NUEVA ESPANA
- LAS HISTORIAS DEL ORIGEN DE LAS INDIAS DE ESTA PROVINCIA DE GUATEMALA
- HISTORICAL RECORDS AND STUDIES THOMAS F. MECHAN
- HISTORICAL RECORDS AND STUDIES...NEW YORK, CATHOLIC HISTORICAL SOCIETY. 1929
- IDEALES MISIONEROS DE LOS REYES CATOLICOS
- LA IGLESIA Y LA EDUCACION POPULAR EN INDIAS
- LA IGLESIA Y LA MASONERIA EN VENEZUELA...
- EL ILUSTRISIMO FRAY HIPOLITO SANCHEZ RANGEL, PRIMER OBISPO DE MAYNAS
- IMPEDIMIENTOS DE MISIONEROS
- LOS IMPERIALISMOS DE JUAN GINES DE SEPULVEDA EN SU
- IN SPAIN WITH THE INTERNATIONAL BRIGADE
- INSTITUTO HISTORICO E GEOGRAPHICO BRASILEIRO...
- INTERFERENCIAS
- ISAGOGE HISTORICA APOLOGETICA DE LAS INDIAS OCCIDENTALES Y ESPECIAL DE LA PROVINCIA DE SAN VICENTE DE CHIAPA Y GUATEMALA, DE LA ORDEN DE PREDICADORES. GUATEMALA, 1935
- UN JESUITA "A PALOS", JERONIMO DEL PORTILLO
- LOS JESUITAS EN LA PROVINCIA DE QUITO DE 1570 A 1774
- JM NUNEZ PONTE. QUIEN A SIDO ALGUIEN EN VENEZUELA?. NUESTRO GRAN APOSTOL
- JORGE RICARDO BEJARANO NARINO, SU VIDA SUS INFORTUNIOS, SU TALLA HISTORICA
- JUEGOS ANTIGUOS EN AMERICA
- LA JUNTA PARA AMPLIACION DE ESTUDIOS. RECTIFICACION Y COMENTARIOS
- JUSTIFICACIONES HISTORICAS
- LANCE CURIOSO EN VISITA PASTORAL, MISSIONALIA HISPANICA, 1948
- LECTURAS DE HISTORIA NACIONAL RELACIONADAS CON EL SANTISIMO SACRAMENTO. SANTIAGO DE CHILE, 1928
- LEGISLACION SOBRE INDIOS DEL RIO DE LA PLATA EN EL SIGLO 16TH. MADRID. 1928
- LETRADOS Y POLITICOS
- LETTURE DI FILOSOFIA...
- LIBRO PRIMERO DE CABILDOS DE LA VILLA DE SAN MIGUEL DE IBARRA 1606-1617
- LOS LIBROS DEL CABILDO DE QUITO
- LITERATURA ECLESIASTICA, CRONICA DE LA SEMANA PRO SEMINARIO CELEBRADA EN TOLEDO LOS D'IAS 4-10 DE NOVIEMBRE DE 1935...
- LA LOCA DEL SACRAMENTO
- LUCIA IN LONDON. LEIPZIG 1928
- MAGALLANES EN 1925...POR MANUEL ZORRILLA
- MANUEL JIMENEZ FERNANDEZ...
- MANUEL VICENTE VILLARAN, EX RECTOR DE LA UNIVERSIDAD. LA UNIVERSIDAD DE SAN MARCOS, DE LIMA...
- EL MARISCAL DE BERWICK
- LA MEDICINA Y LAS MISIONES
- MEDITACIONES DE LA VIDA DE CRISTO...
- MEJICO.-LA ERA DE LOS MARTIRES
- MINISTERIO DE TRABAJO Y PREVISION. APORTACION DE LOS COLONIZADORES ESPANOLES A LA PROSPERIDAD DE AMERICA (1493-16...)
- MINISTERIO DE TRABAJO Y PREVISION. CATALOGO PASAJEROS A INDIAS...VOL 1 (1509-1533)
- MINISTERIO DE TRABAJO Y PREVISION. DISPOSICIONES COMPLEMENTARIAS DE LAS LEYES DE INDIAS. TRES TOMOS
- MINISTERIO DE TRABAJO Y PREVISION. SELECCION DE LAS LEYES DE INDIAS...
- UN MISIONERO Y MISIONOLOGO DESCONOCIDO
- MISIONES DE MAINAS HACIA LA MITAD DEL SIGLO 16
- LAS MISIONES, DEFENSA DE LAS FRONTERAS MAINAS
- LOS MODERNOS EVANGELIZADORES EN LA TIERRA DE LA SANTA CRUZ
- MONUMENTA HISTOTICA SOCIETATIS JESU... ROMAE, 1946
- MOTOLINIA'S HISTORY OF THE INDIANS OF NEM SPAIN
- EL MUNDO CATOLICO Y LA CARTA COLECTIVA DEL EPISCOPADO ESPANOL
- LOS MUNICIPIOS Y LOS INDIOS
- MUSEO DE AMERICA. SUS PRECURSORES EN EL SIGLO 16
- MUSEO INTELECTUAL. VANGUARDIA. MEXICO, 1928
- MUSEO NACIONAL DE ARQUEOLOGIA
- NACIONES DE LENGUA ESPANOLA
- NATURISMO Y AFINES
- THE NIGGER OF THE "NARCISSUS"
- LOS NINOS INDIGENAS EN LA CRISTIANIZACION DE AMERICA UNA PAGINA CONMOVEDORA EN LA HISTORIA
- NOTAS ACERCA DEL TEATRO RELIGIOSO EN LA AMERICA COLONIAL
- NOTAS Y TEXTOS. INFORME SOBRE LOS NATURALES DE LA DIOCESIS DE CEBU
- NOTAS Y TEXTOS. PLANES ANTIGUOS DE SEMINARIOS DE MISIONES Y DE RECLUTAR CLERO SECULAR PARA LA EVANGELIZACION DE AMERICA
- NOTICIA DE UN LIBRO VIEJO Y DE UNA GLORIA OLVIDADA
- NOTICIAS BIBLIOGRAFICAS
- NOTICIAS GENERALES
- NUESTRA SENORA DE LOURDES
- LA NUEVA CONQUISTA DE LA AMERICA ESPANOLA
- NUEVA FASE DE LA COMPANA
- NUEVA FASE DE UNA CAMPANA
- LOS NUEVOS BEATOS MARTIRES DEL PARAGUAY, SIMIENTE DE LAS REDENCIONES
- LOS NUEVOS SANTOS INGLESES
- ORDENES RELIGIOSAS NO MISIONERAS EN INDIAS
- P. ANTONIO MARIA DE BARCELONA. O.M. MARTIRI DELLA RIVOLUTIONE MAXISTA NELLA SPANA...
- P. FR. TOMAS DE SAN RAFAEL, CARMELITA DESCALZO
- P. SILVERIO DE SANTA TERESA, C.D. OBRAS DE SANTA TERESA DE JESUS
- UNA PAGINA DE GEOGRAFIA ANEJA
- PAPELES DEL ARCHIVO. PUBLICACIONES DEL ARCHIVO GENERAL DE LA NACION
- PASTELERIAS EN LIMA PRIMITIVA
- LA PATRIA DEL ALMIRANTE...
- EL PATRONATO ESPANOL EN EL VIRREYNO DEL PERU DURANTE EL SIGLO 16
- PATZCUARO. TEXTO DE MANUEL TOUSSAINT. MEXICO, 1942
- EL PETROLEO DE COLOMBIA
- UN PINTOR QUITENO Y UN CUADRO ADMIRABLE DEL SIGLO 16 EN EL MUSEO ARQUEOLOGICO NACIONAL, 1929
- LA PLAGA SOCIAL DE LA BLASFEMIA
- EL POETA VERDAGUER Y EL MARQUES DE COMILLAS

- OS PORTUGUESES NO MUNDO. AGRANDES TRAVESSIA AFRICANA DE CAPELO E IVERIS POR...
- POSTRERA VOLUNTAD Y TESTAMENTO DE HERNANDO CORTES
- POUR LE PAPE...
- LOS PRECURSORES DEL CONGRESO EUCARISTICO DE BUENOS AIRES. LA DEVOCION AL SANTISIMO DE LOS CONQUISTADORES Y POBLADORES DE AMERICA
- LOS PRECURSORES IDEOLOGICOS DE LA GUERRA DE LA INDEPENDENCIA 1789-1794
- LA PREDICACION SAGRADA SEGUN LOS DOCUMENTOS PONTIFICIOS Y DOCTRINA DE LOS SANTOS PADRES
- LA PRIMAVERA DE LA VIDA
- LOS PRINCIPES DE LA LITERATURA...
- EL PROBLEMA RELIGIOSO EN AMERICA
- LA PROPAGANDA PROTESTANTE EN LA AMERICA ESPANOLA
- EL PROTECTOR DE INDIOS
- EL PROTESTANTISMO EN LA AMERICA ESPANOLA
- EL PROXIMO CONGRESO DE LAS JUVENTUDES HISPANO-AMERICANAS
- QUE PASA EN ESPANA? A LOS CATOLICOS DE MUNDO
- QUE PASA EN ESPANA? A LOS CATOLICOS DEL MUNDO
- QUE PASA EN MEJICO
- QUE PASA EN MEJICO?
- LO QUE QUIEREN LOS ESPANOLES DE BUENA VOLUNTAD...
- RAIMUNDO RIVA. LECTURAS HISTORICAS
- RAMON L. GOMEZ. LOS PRIVILEGIOS DE LA AMERICA LATINA EN SU PARTE HISTORICO-CRONOLOGICA
- LA RECIENTE ENCICLICA DEL PAPA SOBRE LA UNIDAD RELIGIOSA
- RELACION DE LA VISITA GENERAL QUE EN LA DIOCESIS DE CARACAS Y VENEZUELA HIZO EL ILMO. SR. D. MARIANO MARTI, DEL CONSEJO DE S.M. 1771-1784
- RENE BAZIN
- LA REPRESION DE LA BLASFEMIA
- RESPUESTA A UNA PREGUNTA INTERESANTE
- EL RESTABLECIMIENTO DEL CULTO EN LA ESPANA ROJA
- RETIRO ESPIRITUAL PARA COMUNIDADES RELIGIOSAS...
- LA RUTA DE LO DESCONOCIDO...
- UN SACERDOTE CAUTIVO DE LOS ARAUCANOS
- SAGRADA BIBLIA
- LA SALUD DE LA AMERICA ESPANOLA. PARIS, 1926
- SAN EULOGIO DE CORDOBA
- SAN EULOGIO DE CORDOBA. MADRID, 1928
- SAN FRANCISCO JAVIER. EL HOMBRE Y EL SANTO
- SANGRE EN LOS TAPEHUANES
- SANTA MARIA EN INDIAS
- LA S.C. DE PROPAGANDA FIDE E LE MISSIONI DEL GINPPANE (1622-1838)
- SEMBLANZA DE SANTA TERESA DE JESUS
- SEPTEMBRE 1792. HISTOIRE POLITIQUE DES MASSACRES...
- EL SIGLO JEROGLIFICO AZTECA...1897
- LOS SIN-DIOS. LA CAMPANA DE NUESTROS DIAS
- SOBRE LA "ESCUELA NUEVA"
- LA SUPRESION DEL JUEGO
- EL TAUMATURGO CATALAN BEATO SALVADOR DE HORTA
- EL TEATRO INDIGENA DE AMERICA
- EL TEOSOFISMO. BARCELONA, 1928
- LA TORMENTA QUE VIENE DE ORIENTE
- TRES CONQUISTADORES Y POBLADORES DE LA NUEVA ESPANA
- UNE. CONSIGNAS APROBADAS POR EL PRIMER CONGRESO NACIONAL UNCISTA REUNIDO EN CARACAS...
- UNITED NATIONS ESTADO MISIONERO
- VALLEE-POUSIN, LOUIS DE LA NIRVANA...
- VARIEDADES
- UNA VICTIMA DE AMOR DIVINO
- VIDA DE LA SIERVA DE DIOS SOR MARIA DE LOS DOLORES Y PATROCINIO, POR LA R.M. SOR MARIA ISABEL DE JESUS...
- VIDA DE SAN BERNARDO ABAD DE CLARAVAL
- VIDA DEL BEATO JUAN DE AVILA, POR UN SACERDOTE. MADRID, 1928
- VIDA DEL SEGOVIANO RODRIGO DE CONTRERAS, DEL MARQUES DE LOZOYA Y COLECCION DE LAS MEMORIAS...DE LOS VIRREYES DEL PERU DE RICARDO BELTRAN ROZPIDE
- LA VIDA SOCIAL EN LA COLONIA SEGUN LOS "LIBROS DEL CABILDO DE QUITO"
- VIDA Y OBRAS DE SANTA MARIA MARGARITA DE ALOCOQUE, 3 TOMOS. EXAMEN DE LIBROS
- LA VIRGEN DEL PILAR Y AMERICA
- THE WOMAN WHO STOLE EVERYTHING. LEIPZIG, 1928
- Y GROSSO
- YELA UTRILLA, JUAN F. CATEDRATICO Y DOCTOR EN CIENCIAS HISTORICAS...

BAYLE, CONSTANTINO. EL PROTECTOR DE INDIOS. SEVILLA, 1944 / Saenz de Santa Maria, C – Madrid: Razon y Fe, 1946 – 1 – sp Bibl Santa Ana [946]

Bayle, Francois *see* RELATION DE L'ETAT DE QUELQUES PERSONNES PRETENDUES POSSEDEES

Bayle, G L *see* RECHERCHES SUR LA PHTHISIE PULMONAIRE

Bayle, P *see*
- DICTIONNAIRE HISTORIQUE ET CRITIQUE
- PROJETS ET FRAGMENTS D'UN DICTIONNAIRE CRITIQUE

Bayle, Pierre Georges *see* LA SAISIE ET LA VENTE JUDICIAIRE DES FONDS DE COMMERCE.

Bayles, Richard M *see* HISTORY OF WINDHAM COUNTY

Bayley, Arthur Rutter *see* THE GREAT CIVIL WAR IN DORSET, 1642-1660

Bayley, W A *see* MITCHELL LIBRARY TOWN AND COUNTRY INDEX

Bayley, WA *see* MITCHELL LIBRARY SYDNEY MAIL INDEX

Baylis, Samuel Mathewson *see* CAMP AND LAMP: RAMBLES IN REALMS OF SPORT, STORY, SONG

Bayliss, Edward E *see* THE GIPSY SMITH MISSIONS IN AMERICA..

BAYLOR LAW REVIEW – (v1-36 1948-84 in reel $384.00. v37-47 1985-95 in mf $281.00) – v1-47. 1948-95 – 5,6,9 – $675.00 set – us Hein [340]

Baylor University College of Medicine. Houston, Texas *see* CATALOGS AND COLLEGE RECORDS

Bayly, Anselm *see*
- AN INTRODUCTION TO LANGUAGES, LITERARY AND PHILOSOPHICAL
- A PLAIN AND COMPLETE GRAMMAR OF THE ENGLISH LANGUAGE
- A PRACTICAL TREATISE ON SINGING AND PLAYING WITH JUST EXPRESSION AND REAL ELEGANCE..

Bayly, Mary *see*
- STORY OF OUR ENGLISH BIBLE AND WHAT IT COST
- THE STORY OF OUR ENGLISH BIBLE AND WHAT IT COST

Bayne, Peter *see*
- THE CHIEF ACTORS IN THE PURITAN REVOLUTION
- THE FREE CHURCH OF SCOTLAND
- MARTIN LUTHER
- MARTIN LUTHER, HIS LIFE AND WORK
- THE TESTIMONY OF CHRIST TO CHRISTIANITY
- TESTIMONY OF CHRIST TO CHRISTIANITY

Baynes, Arthur Hamilton *see* MY DIOCESE DURING THE WAR

Baynes, O'Hara *see* OVER THE BORDER

Baynes, Paul *see* ENTIRE COMMENTARY UPON THE WHOLE EPISTLE OF ST PAUL TO THE EPHESIANS

Baynton, Morgan *see* PAPERS

Baynton, Wharton *see* PAPERS

BAYNTON, WHARTON, AND MORGAN PAPERS, 1757-1787 / Pennsylvania Historical and Museum Commission – (Includes printed guide) – 10r – 1 – $850.00 – D3294 – Dist. us Scholarly Res – us Penn Hist [978]

Bayol, Jean *see* VOYAGE EN SENEGAMBIE

Bayonne, New Jersey *see* MISCELLANEOUS EARLY NEWSPAPERS

Bayony Posada, Nicolas *see* ESCRITAS LITERARIOS DE RUFINO JOSE CUERVO

BAYOU DAIRYMAN / Louisiana State University. Agricultural Experiment Station. Dairy Science Club – 1970/71-1980/81.1 reel – 1,5 – us Spaulding [636]

BAYREUTHER BLAETTER – Bayreuth, 1878-1905.-v1-28 – 161mf – 9 – P-562/1 – ne IDC [072]

BAYREUTHER BLAETTER. DEUTSCHE ZEITSCHRIFT IM GEISTE RICHARD WAGNERS – v. 1-61. 1878-1938 – 1 – 194.00 – us L of C Photodup [780]

BAYREUTHER INTELLIGENZ-ZEITUNG – Bayreuth, 1769, 1773-sep 1781, 1782-90, jul-dec 1793, 1795, 1797 (incomplete), 1798-1803, 1804-06 (incomplete), 1807-jul 1808 – 10r – 1 – Dist. gw Mikrofilm – gw Misc Inst [943]

BAYREUTHER ZEITUNG – (Cont by: Neue Bayreuther Zeitung, 1863) – Bayreuth, 1752-55, 1758-78, 1779 (incomplete), 1780-1800, 1802, 1804-05, 1807, 1813-19, 1848-49 – 49r – 1 – Dist. gw Mikrofilm – gw Misc Inst [943]

Bayrische Vereinsbank *see* ZEITTAFEL DES GELDES

Bayro, P *see* ...DE MEDENDIS HUMANI CORPORIS. ENCHIRIDION VULGO VENI MECUM...

BAY'S LAW REPORTS / South Carolina. Supreme Court – (A Pre-NRS title) – v1-2. 1783-1804 (all publ) – 13mf – 9 – $19.50 – LLMC 94-009 – us L.L.M.C. [340]

Baysius, L *see* DE CAPTIVIS, ET POSTLIMINIO REVERSIS

Bayssat, F *see* DE L'UNIFICATION...

BAYSWATER CHRONICLE. (PADDINGTON, KENSINGTON & BAYSWATER CHRONICLE) – London. 20 Jun 1860-22 Nov 1873; 9 Jan 1875-8 Sep 1939. 62mqn reels – 1 – uk British Libr Newspaper [072]

BAYWOOD PRESS – Point Reyes Station, CA. 1948-53 – 2r – 1 – $100.00 – C02638 – us Library Micro [071]

Baz, I *see* POCHEMU MY POBEDILI V GRAZHDANSKOI VOINE

BAZAAR – Reno, NV. Dec 1822 – 1r – 1 – $50.00 – U04658 – us Library Micro [071]

THE BAZAAR – Rodney, Ont: Bazaar Print Co, v1 no 1 (Jan 1887) – 9 – cn C.I.H.M. [073]

BAZAAR GAZET – New York, NY. The Daily Gazette of the Bazaar for the Jewish War Sufferers. 1916 – 1 – us A.J.P.C. [071]

Bazaine, Achille Francois *see*
- PIECES ANNEXES AU RAPPORT SUR L'AFFAIRE DU MARECHAL BAZAINE.
- PROCES BAZAINE.

LE BAZAR : JOURNAL MANUSCRIT – Fraserville (Riviere-du-Loup), Canada. v1 n5. 20 jul 1888 – 1r – 1 – Can$25.00 – cn Can Microfilming [073]

LE BAZAR : POUR LA CATHEDRALE DE MONTREAL. HEBDO ET QUOTIDIEN – Montreal, Canada. 7 aut-20 nov 1886 – 1r – 1 – Can$34.50 – cn Can Microfilming [240]

LE BAZAR – [Sorel, Quebec?]: J.A. Chenevert, v1 no 1 (1er dec. 1888)- – 9 – cn C.I.H.M. [971]

THE BAZAR BOOK OF DECORUM: THE CARE OF THE PERSON, MANNERS, ETIQUETTE, AND CEREMONIALS – New York: Harper & Brothers, 1871. 278p. Includes index – 1 – us U.W. Library [390]

Bazard, Palmyre *see* LA RELIGION SAINT SIMONIENNE

Bazard, Saint-Amand et Barthelemy-Prosper Enfantin *see* RELIGION SAINT-SIMONIENNE

BAZAZZAGA – (Filmed with: Zaruma and other Hausa newspapers) – Zaria: Gaskiya Corp, [dec 1956-sep 4 1958] – 1r – 1 – us Res Libr [960]

Bazelaire de Rupierre, OP de *see* CONSIDERATIONS GENERALES APPLICABLES A L'ARCHITECTURE EOLIENNE...

Bazett, L Margery *see* AFTER-DEATH COMMUNICATIONS

Bazhanov, V M et al *see* BLIZHAISHII A PERSPEKTIVY TORGOVYKH OTNOSHENII ROSSII S UKRAINOI

Baziiants, A P, et al *see* AZIATSKII MUZEI LENINGRADSKOE OTDELENIE INSTITUTA VOSTOKOVEDENIIA AN SSR

Bazilevich, K V *see*
- OCHERKI PO ISTORII PROFESSIONALNOGO DVIZHENIIA RABOTNIKOV SVIAZI 1905-1906
- PROFESSIONALNOE DVIZHENIE RABOTNIKOV SVIAZI, 1917-18

Bazin, Louis *see* LES CALENDRIERS TURCS ANCIENS ET MEDIEVAUX

BAZU-YI INQILAB – (Sal-i 1, shumarah-'i 1-32 (13 Murdad 1359-5 Aban 1359[4 Aug 1980-28 Oct 1980])) – Tehran: Junbish-i Kargaran-i Musalman, 1980 – 1 reel – 1 – $25.00 – us MEDOC [950]

Bazy, Jean Pierre Antoine *see* DE L'EPOPEE ANCIENNE ET MODERNE

BBC (British Broadcasting Corporation) Home Service *see* NINE O'CLOCK NEWS, 1939-1945

BBC (British Broadcasting Corporation) Radio *see* AUTHOR AND TITLE CATALOGUE OF TRANSMITTED DRAMA, POETRY AND FEATURES 1929-1975

BBC (British Broadcasting Corporation) Television *see* AUTHOR AND TITLE CATALOGUE OF TRANSMITTED DRAMA AND FEATURES, 1936-1975

BBC SUMMARY OF WORLD BROADCASTS / British Broadcasting Corporation – (Updated quarterly. Complete backfile Aug 1939-Dec 1972 758r $43,585. Complete coll of Monitoring Reports 1977-95 609mf $2090.75: Monitoring Reports 1972-96 $184y: Individual geographic sections 1972-96 $529. The USSR and former USSR Coll 19772-95 3044mf $10,502. Eastern Europe Coll 1972-93, Central Europe 1993-95 3049mf $10,522.50. The Far East/East Asia Coll 1972-93, Asia Pacific 1993-95 3637mf $12,546.50. The Middle East 1972-95 (including Africa & Latin America 1972-93) 1972-95 2858mf $10,453.50. Africa, Latin America & the Caribbean 1993-95 349mf $772.75) – 1972-95 (base coll) – 13,120mf – 9,1 – $45,264.00 coll (Individual yrs, all pts 1972-96 $2,029.75ea) – us UMI [380]

B.C. BUSINESS *see* BC BUSINESS MAGAZINE

BC BUSINESS – (Cont: B.C. Business Magazine. Incorporates Asia Pacific Business 1988) – Burnaby. v13- 1985- – 9 – Can$37.00y – cn Micromedia [380]

BC BUSINESS *see* ASIA PACIFIC BUSINESS

B.C. BUSINESS MAGAZINE *see* BC BUSINESS

BC BUSINESS MAGAZINE – (Cont by: B.C. Business v13 1985) – Burnaby. v1-12. 1973-84 – 9 – Can$28.00y – cn Micromedia [380]

BC GAZETTE – Victoria. v1- 1863- – 1,5,9 – Price varies with yr – cn Micromedia [971]

BC GOOD TEMPLAR / Independent Order of Good Templars, Grand Lodge of British Columbia – New Westminster: v1 no 1 (Oct 16 1893)- – 9 – cn C.I.H.M. [360]

BC GUIDE – Vancouver: [s.n., 1899?-19–] – 9 – cn C.I.H.M. [910]

BC JOURNAL OF SPECIAL EDUCATION – Vancouver. v12- 1988- – 9 – Can$20.00y – cn Micromedia [370]

BC MINING EXCHANGE – Vancouver, Jun 1899-Sep 1917 – 7r – 1 – uk British Libr Newspaper [073]

B.C. MINING EXCHANGE AND INVESTORS' GUIDE *see*
- BRITISH COLUMBIA MINING PROSPECTORS' EXCHANGE AND INVESTORS' GUIDE
- MINING TIT-BITS

THE B.C. MINING EXCHANGE AND INVESTORS' GUIDE – (Cont by: Mining Tit-Bits (ID 04027)) – Vancouver: [s.n., 1899] (Vancouver: Timms Print) – 9 – cn C.I.H.M. [622]

B.C. MINING EXCHANGE AND INVESTORS' GUIDE AND MINING TIT-BITS *see* MINING TIT-BITS

THE B.C. MINING EXCHANGE AND INVESTOR'S GUIDE AND MINING TIT-BITS – Vancouver: [s.n., 1899-1906?] – 9 – cn C.I.H.M. [622]

BC OUTDOORS – Vancouver. v43- 1987- – 9 – Can$28.00y – cn Micromedia [790]

BC STUDIES – (1975-1993, Index Can$20.00y) – Vancouver, v1- 1968- – 9 – Can$28.00y – cn Micromedia [073]

B.C. TEACHER *see* TEACHER (BC)

BC TEACHER – (Cont by: Teacher (BC) 1988-89) – Vancouver. v40-67. 1960-87 – 9 – Price varies with yr – cn Micromedia [073]

BCD BUSINESS CONDITIONS DIGEST / U. Bureau of Economics Analysis – (Cont: Business Cycle Developments) – Washington, DC: series ES. n65-1/72-12 jan 1965-dec 1972 – 6r – 1 – us Ross [073]

BE IN HARMONY WITH THE WILL OF GOD / Sukarno, Pres. Indonesia – SE 6194 1. Speech on 17 Aug. 1954 – 9 – ne IDC [324]

BE YOUR OWN LAWYER: A BUSINESS MANUAL CONTAINING A SYNOPSIS OF THE MERCANTILE, OR BUSINESS LAWS OF ONTARIO: THE TECHNICAL POINTS AND MAIN FEATURES OF THE LAW. / Anger, William Henry – Rev. by W. K. Pattison and including a practical system of farm accounts. Toronto: Printed for the author. 1895. 02407. (Pre-1900 Canadiana) – 9 – cn C.I.H.M. [340]

Beach, Abijah Ives *see* PAPERS

Beach, Charles Fisk *see*
- COMMENTARIES ON THE LAW OF RECEIVERS.
- INDIVIDUAL EVANGELISM
- A TREATISE ON THE MODERN LAW OF CONTRACTS.

BEACH CITIES LABOR JOURNAL – Santa Monica, CA. 1943-63 – 7r – 1 – $350.00 – C02967 – us Library Micro [331]

Beach, David Nelson *see* THE NEWER RELIGIOUS THINKING

Beach, Harlan P *see* A GEOGRAPHY AND ATLAS OF PROTESTANT MISSIONS. VOLUME I, GEOGRAPHY

Beach, Harlan Page *see*
- THE CROSS IN THE LAND OF THE TRIDENT
- DAWN ON THE HILLS OF T'ANG
- INDIA AND CHRISTIAN OPPORTUNITY
- PRINCELY MEN IN THE HEAVENLY KINGDOM

Beach, Harlan Page et al *see* PROTESTANT MISSIONS IN SOUTH AMERICA

BEACH JOURNAL – Daytona Beach. Fl. 1925-27 – 1 – us UMI [071]

A BEACHCOMBER IN THE ORIENT / Foster, Harry La Tourette – New York: Blue Ribbon Books, 1923. 395p. map – 1 – us U.W. Library [950]

BEACON – Canada. v1-6. 1924-1930 – 1 – cn Precision [971]

BEACON – Macon. Miss. 1938-1954 – 1 – us UMI [071]

BEACON – North Baltimore, Ohio. 1888-1942 – 20r – 1 – $32.50r – us Archival [071]

BEACON – North Baltimore. Ohio. -w. 1884-1942 – 1 – us UMI [071]

BEACON – Portland OR. Oct 8 15 1937 – 1 – us U.O. Library [071]

BEACON – Red Bluff, CA. 1857-64 – 2r – 1 – $100.00 – B02655 – us Library Micro [071]

BEACON – St. Louis. Mo. 1829-32 – 1 – us UMI [071]

BEACON – Warwick. R.I. -w. 1954- – 1 – us UMI [071]

THE BEACON – 1933-1973 – 6r – 1 – us I.H.R.C. [073]

THE BEACON – Cleveland, OH. 1933 – us I.H.R.C. [071]

THE BEACON – Montreal, Canada. v6. 5 oct 1934-20 fev 1942 Filmed with: The Canadian Register (Quebec ed) 28 fev 1942-23 oct 1948 – 6r – 1 – Can$115.00r – cn Can Microfilming [072]

THE BEACON = YMHA – Montreal, 1926-1983 – 3r – 1 – Can$60.00r – cn Can Microfilming [072]

THE BEACON *see* THE CANADIAN REGISTER

THE BEACON (B'NAI B'RITH) = UPPER CANADA LOGE – Toronto, CN. v6 no 47,48. 1953 – 1r – 1 – Can$20.00 – cn Can Microfilming [072]

BEACON DAILY – Stratford, 1887-1923 – 72r – 1 – cn Preston [971]

BEACON HERALD – (1923-1992.-451r) – Stratford, 1993 – 8r – 1 – cn Preston [971]

BEACON HILL BAPTIST CHURCH. SOMERSET, KENTUCKY : CHURCH RECORDS – Nov 1967-5 Jan 1983 – 1 – 16.11 – us Baptist [240]

BEACON LIGHT – Vale, OR. -w. 22 Mar 1912-5 Jul 1912. 1 roll – 1 – us U.O. Library [071]

BEACON NEWS – Aurora. Ill. 1848- – 1 – us UMI [071]

BEACON NEWS – Marengo. Ill. 1970- – 1 – us UMI [071]

BEACON NEWS – Newburgh. N.Y. 1959-1960 – 1 – us UMI [071]

BEACON NEWS – Paris. Ill. 1946- – 1 – us UMI [071]

THE BEACON OF THE TRUTH : OR TESTIMONY OF THE CORAN OF THE CHRISTIAN RELIGION – (Transl. from the Arabic by Sir William Muir) – London, 1894 – Dfl13.00 – ne Slangenburg [230]

BEACON WEEKLY – Stratford, 1855-1896 – 11r – 1 – cn Preston [971]

THE BEACON/LE PHARE *see* THE NORTHERN BEACON – THE BEACON/LE PHARE – LE PHARE DU NORD

BEACON-OBSERVER – Elm Creek, NE. -w. Mar 1906- .Scattered issues missing – 1 – us NE Hist [071]

BEACON-RECORD – Ashtabula. Ohio. 1900-1915 – 1 – us UMI [071]

Beadle, Delos White *see*
- THE AMERICAN LAWYER AND BUSINESSMAN'S FORMBOOK...
- CANADIAN FRUIT, FLOWER, AND KITCHEN GARDENER:..

BEADLE'S DIME LIBRARY – 1878-98. 967 issues – 1 – 214.00 – us L of C Photodup [830]

BEADLE'S HALF DIME SINGER'S LIBRARY. – .New York. 2nd ed. no. 12. 1878 – 1 – us NY Public [073]

BEADLE'S HALF-DIME LIBRARY – 1877-1905. 826 issues – 1 – 163.00 – us L of C Photodup [830]

Beakes, Samuel W *see* PAST AND PRESENT OF WASHTENAW COUNTY

Beal, William James *see*
- GRASSES OF NORTH AMERICA
- GRASSES OF NORTH AMERICA, V1:... PHYSIOLOGY, COMPOSITION, SELECTION, IMPROVING AND CULTIVATION ..
- GRASSES OF NORTH AMERICA, V2: THE GRASSES CLASSIFIED, DESCRIBED AND EACH GENUS ILLUSTRATED..
- MICHIGAN FLORA

Beale, J F *see* LIVES AND LABORS OF EMINENT DIVINES

Beale, Joseph H, Jr *see* BEALE'S CASES ON CONFLICT OF LAWS

Beale, Joseph H, Jr. *see*
- A SELECTION OF CASES ON THE LAW OF CARRIERS
- SELECTIONS FROM A TREATISE ON THE CONFLICT OF LAWS

BEALE'S CASES ON CONFLICT OF LAWS / Beale, Joseph H, Jr – Cambridge, MA: Harvard University Press. 2v. 1907 (all publ) – 18mf – 9 – $27.00 – LLMC 95-047 – us L.L.M.C. [340]

BEAM – Fort Worth. Texas. 1954-61 – 1 – 116.76 – us Baptist [240]

THE BEAM – Fresno, Oct 1943-Apr 1944 – 1r – 1 – $50.00 – B06087 – us Library Micro [978]

Beaman, Middleton G *see* INDEX-ANALYSIS OF THE FEDERAL STATUTES, 1789-1907

BEAMS OF LIGHT – v4-45. 1909-50 (gaps) – 5r – 1 – ATLA 1994-S010 – us A.T.L.A. [073]

DER BEAMTENBUND – Bonn-Bad Godesberg, 1961-88 – 1 – Inquire at Mikrofilmarchiv for details – gw Misc Inst [331]

DER BEAMTENBUND – Bonn-Bad Godesberg, West-Germany. 1961-75 – 1 – gw Mikrofilm [072]

DER BEAMTENBUND *see* DIE GEMEINSCHAFT

Bean, Edwin F *see* BEANS HISTORY AND DIRECTORY OF NEVADA COUNTY

Bean, T H *see*
- OCEANIC ICHTHYOLOGY

Bean, Theodore W *see* HISTORY OF MONTGOMERY COUNTY

BEANS HISTORY AND DIRECTORY OF NEVADA COUNTY / Bean, Edwin F – Nevada Co, CA. 1867 – 1r – 1 – $50.00 – B40246 – us Library Micro [978]

BEAR CREEK BAPTIST CHURCH. DECATUR COUNTY. PARSONS, TENNESSEE : CHURCH RECORDS – 1842-Feb 1929 – 1 – 15.57 – us Baptist [240]

Bear, James E *see* THE MISSION WORK OF THE PRESBYTERIAN CHURCH IN THE UNITED STATES IN CHINA, 1867-1952

BEAR LAKE RECORD – Bear Lake, PA. -w 1895-1896 – 13 – $25.00r – us I.M.R. [071]

BEAR RIVER NEWS *see* WHEATLAND NEWSPAPERS

BEAR SPRINGS BAPTIST CHURCH. STEWART COUNTY. DOVER, TENNESSEE : CHURCH RECORDS – 1960-Jul 1968 – 1 – 7.36 – us Baptist [240]

DIE BEARBEITUNGEN DES "VERBRECHERS AUS VERLORENER EHRE" : MIT BENUTZUNG UNGEDRUCKTER BRIEFE VON UND AN HERM. KURZ / Stoess, Willi – (Includes bibliografical references) – Stuttgart: Metzler, 1913 – 1r – 1 – us U.W. Library [430]

DIE BEARBEITUNGEN DES "VERBRECHERS AUS VERLORENER EHRE" : MIT BENUTZUNG UNGEDRUCKTER BRIEFE VON UND AN HERM. KURZ / Stoess, Willi – (Includes bibliografical references) – Stuttgart: Metzler, 1913 – 1 – us U.W. Library [430]

Beard, Augustus Field *see*
- A CRUSADE OF BROTHERHOOD
- A CRUSADE OF BROTHERHOOD: A HISTORY OF THE AMERICAN MISSIONARY ASSOCIATION
- THE STORY OF JOHN FREDERIC OBERLIN

Beard, Charles *see*
- MARTIN LUTHER AND THE REFORMATION IN GERMANY
- PORT ROYAL
- THE REFORMATION OF THE SIXTEENTH CENTURY IN ITS RELATION TO MODERN THOUGHT AND KNOWLEDGE

Beard, Charles A *see*
- AMERICAN GOVERNMENT AND POLITICS
- ECONOMIC ORIGINS OF JEFFERSONIAN DEMOCRACY

Beard, Frances B *see* WYOMING FROM TERRITORIAL DAYS TO THE PRESENT

Beard, Glenn C *see* THE EFFECT OF CARBONATED SOLUTIONS ON GASTRIC EMPTYING DURING PROLONGED CYCLING

Beard, Michael *see* EDEBIYAT

Bearden, Thomas E *see* FER-DE-LANCE BRIEFING: SOVIET SCALAR ELECTROMAGNETIC WEAPONS

Beardslee, Clark S *see* CHRIST'S ESTIMATE OF HIMSELF

Beardslee, John Walter *see*
- THE BIBLE AMONG THE NATIONS 1
- BIBLE AMONG THE NATIONS: THE GREAT TRANSLATIONS
- OUTLINES OF AN INTRODUCTION TO THE OLD TESTAMENT

Beardsley, D B *see* HISTORY OF HANCOCK COUNTY

Beardsley, E Edwards *see* LIFE AND CORRESPONDENCE OF SAMUEL JOHNSON, D.D.

Beardsley, Frank Grenville *see*
- CHRISTIAN ACHIEVEMENT IN AMERICA
- A HISTORY OF AMERICAN REVIVALS

THE BEARINGS OF MODERN COMMERCE ON THE PROGRESS OF MODERN MISSIONS : THE ANNUAL SERMON BEFORE THE BISHOPS, CLERGY AND LAITY CONSTITUTING THE BOARD OF MISSIONS OF THE PROTESTANT EPISCOPAL CHURCH IN THE UNITED STATES / Stone, John S – New York: William Osborn, 1839 – 1mf – us A.T.L.A. [240]

Bearn, Georges *see* LA DECADA PERONISTE

Beart, Charles *see* JEUX ET JOUETS DE L'OUEST AFRICAIN

Beasley, Ruth *see* CATALOG OF PERIODICAL LITERATURE IN THE SOCIAL AND BEHAVIORAL SCIENCES SECTION, INCLUDING SUPPLEMENT TO MONOGRAPHS, 1973-75

LA BEATIFICACION DEL VENERABLE SEBASTIAN DE APARICIO. MEXICO, 1934 / Ocaranza, Fernando – Madrid: Razon y Fe, 1935 – 1 – sp Bibl Santa Ana [972]

BEATITUDES OF CHRIST / Johnston, Howard Agnew – Chicago: Winona, 1905. 1 fiche – 9 – us A.T.L.A. [240]

THE BEATITUDES OF CHRIST : A STUDY OF THE WAY OF THE BLESSED LIFE / Johnston, Howard Agnew – Chicago:Winona, 1905 – 1mf – 9 – 0-8370-3789-1 – 1985-1789 – us A.T.L.A. [220]

BEATITUDES OF THE KINGDOM / Dykes, James Oswald – London: James Nisbet, 1873. 1 fiche – 9 – us A.T.L.A. [240]

BEATRICE COURIER – Beatrice, NE. -w. May. 1875-Nov. 1876; Feb. 1877-Nov. 1879, incomplete – 1 – us NE Hist [071]

BEATRICE DAILY EXPRESS – Beatrice, NE. Mar. 1886-Jun. 1895. Incomplete; Aug. 1895-Apr. 1924 – 1 – us NE Hist [071]

BEATRICE DAILY SUN – Beatrice, NE. Jul. 1902- – 1 – us NE Hist [071]

BEATRICE EVENING TIMES – Beatrice, NE. -d. Jul. 1892-Jan. 1894; Sep. 1895-Oct. 1896; Dec. 1896-Jan. 1901; Mar. 1901-Oct. 1902 – 1 – us NE Hist [071]

BEATRICE NEWS – Beatrice, NE. -w. Jun. 1926-Aug. 1949 – 1 – us NE Hist [071]

BEATRICE REPUBLICAN – Beatrice, NE. -w. Jan. 1886-Jun. 1892 – 1 – us NE Hist [071]

BEATRICE TIMES – Beatrice, NE. -d. Apr. 1942-Nov. 1952 – 1 – us NE Hist [071]

BEATRICE WEEKLY EXPRESS – Beatrice, NE. Jul. 1868-Jun. 1890. Incomplete; Sep. 1891-Jun. 1906; Nov. 1906-Mar. 1912 – 1 – us NE Hist [071]

BEATRICE WEEKLY TIMES – Beatrice, NE. Dec. 1892-Sep. 1898. Incomplete; Feb. 1900-Feb. 1909 – 1 – us NE Hist [071]

BEATRICHE V ADU / Otsup, N – Roman. Paris. 1939. BR-1213 2 – 8 – ne IDC [460]

Beatson, Robert *see* A POLITICAL INDEX TO THE HISTORIES OF GREAT BRITAIN & IRELAND: OR, A COMPLETE REGISTER OF THE HEREDITARY HONOURS, PUBLIC OFFICES, AND PERSONS IN OFFICE, FROM THE EARLIEST PERIODS TO THE PRESENT TIME

Beattie, Francis Robert *see*
- APOLOGETICS, OR, THE RATIONAL VINDICATION OF CHRISTIANITY
- THE METHODS OF THEISM
- THE METHODS OF THEISM: AN ESSAY
- METHODS OF THEISM: AN ESSAY

Beattie, J *see* ESSAYS: ON POETRY AND MUSIC, AS THEY AFFECT THE MIND

Beattie, James *see*
- HISTORY OF THE CHURCH OF SCOTLAND DURING THE COMMONWEALTH
- THE THEORY OF LANGUAGE

Beattie, William *see*
- LIFE AND LETTERS OF THOMAS CAMPBELL
- WALDENSES, OR PROTESTANT VALLEYS OF PIEDMONT AND DAUPHINY

Beatty, Charles C *see* RECORD OF THE FAMILY OF CHARLES BEATTY WHO EMIGRATED FROM IRELAND TO AMERICA IN 1792

Beatty, William Henry *see* THE BOARDS OF TRADE GENERAL ARBITRATIONS ACT (1894).

Beaty, Arthur *see* WILLIAM WORDSWORTH, HIS DOCTRINE AND ART IN THEIR HISTORICAL RELATIONS

BEAU MONT – Beloeil, Canada. 29 oct 1959 – 1r – 1 – Can$20.00 – cn Can Microfilming [072]

LE BEAU NAVIRE – Revue de la poesie. Dir. Maurice Chapelan. no. 1-9. Paris. nov 1934-juin 1939 – 1 – fr A.C.R.P.P. [410]

BEAUBIEN : CHRONIQUES JUDICAIRES / Canada. Quebec. (Province) – (Correspondances judicaires publie£1es sous forme de "chroniques" dans le journal "Le Soleil") – 1v. 1905-06 – 4mf – 9 – $6.00 – LLMC 81-068 – us L.L.M.C. [340]

Beaubien, Charles Philippe *see*
- LES AMEN DE MONSABRE: LECTURE FAITE AU CERCLE VILLE-MARIE DE MONTREAL
- LE SAULT-AU-RECOLLET: SES RAPPORTS AVEC LES PREMIERS TEMPS DE LA COLONIE: MISSION-PAROISSE

Beaubien, Louis *see*
- DISCOURS DE L'HON. M. BEAUBIEN A L'INAUGURATION DE L'ECOLE D'INDUSTRIE LAITIERE DE ST HYACINTHE, LE 11 MARS 1893
- DISCOURS DE L'HONORABLE L. BEAUBIEN, COMMISSAIRE DE L'AGRICULTURE..., PRONONCE A L'ASSEMBLEE LEGISLATIVE LE 26 DECEMBRE 1893:..
- DISCOURS PRONONCE A LA SEANCE DU 3 JUIN 1892 DE L'ASSEMBLEE LEGISLATIVE DE LA PROVINCE DE QUEBEC
- DISCOURS PRONONCE A NICOLET LE 4 OCTOBRE 1896
- A L'HONORABLE CHARLES FITZPATRICK
- LE SILO ET LE PATURAGE: CONFERENCE DE L'HONORABLE LOUIS BEAUBIEN...A ST HYACINTHE, LE 13 JANVIER 1886
- A SPEECH DELIVERED AT THE SESSION OF JUNE 3RD, 1892, OF THE LEGISLATIVE ASSEMBLY OF THE PROVINCE OF QUEBEC

LA BEAUCE – Ste-Marie, Canada. 19 dec 1891; v1 n1. 31 dec 1891 – 1r – 1 – Can$25.00 – cn Can Microfilming [072]

BEAUCE NOUVELLE – (Merged with: L'Eclaireur-Progres) – St Georges-de-Beauce, Canada. 12 mar 1968-18 oct 1988 – 25r – 1 – Can$75.00r – cn Can Microfilming [072]

Beauchamp, A de *see* THE LIFE OF ALI PACHA, OF JANNINA, LATE VIZIER OF EPIRUS, SURNAMED ASLAN, OR THE LION

Beauchamp, Claude *see* LES AFFAIRES

Beauchamp, Joseph *see*
- GUIDE INDISPENSABLE AU PEUPLE: CONTENANT D'ADRESSE SIC DES PRINCIPALES MAISONS DE COMMERCE, LISTE DE MEMBRES DU CONSEIL DE VILLE ET DES COMITES... TELEGRAPHE D'ALARMES, NOMS DES SOCIETES ET LEURS OFFICIERS, ETC., ETC
- REPERTOIRE GENERAL DE JURISPRUDENCE CANADIENNE...1770-1913 AND SUPPLEMENT 1913-23

Beauchamp, William M *see* THE IROQUOIS TRAIL, OR, FOOTPRINTS OF THE SIX NATIONS: IN CUSTOMS, TRADITIONS AND HISTORY

Beauchemin, Neree *see* LES FLORAISONS MATUTINALES

Beauchet, Ludovico *see* LES BATUECAS Y LAS JURDES

Beauclerk, Charles *see* LITHOGRAPHIC VIEWS OF MILITARY OPERATIONS IN CANADA UNDER HIS EXCELLENCY SIR JOHN COLBORNE...DURING THE LATE INSURRECTION
BEAUCOUP BAPTIST CHURCH. PINCKNEYVILLE, ILLINOIS : CHURCH RECORDS – 15 Apr 1915-72 – 1 – 50.31 – us Baptist [240]
Beaud, M *see* LE COMMERCE EXTERIEUR DU MAROC
Beaudet, Louis *see* RECENSEMENT DE LA VILLE DE QUEBEC POUR 1716
Beaudiquez, Marcelle *see* BIBLIOGRAPHICAL SERVICES THROUGHOUT THE WORLD
Beaudoin, Gilles *see* BIO-BIBLIOGRAPHIE DU REVEREND PERE GONZALVE POULIN, O.F.M., D.SC.SS., DIRECTEUR DE L'ECOLE SOCIALE POPULAIRE, UNIVERSITE LAVAL
Beaudoin, Jean *see* JOURNAL D'UNE EXPEDITION DE D'IBERVILLE
Beaudry, Edouard Alexis *see* LE QUESTIONNAIRE ANNOTE DU CODE CIVIL DU BAS-CANADA
Beaudry, Joseph Ubald *see* CODE DES CURES, MARGUILLIERS ET PAROISSIENS: ACCOMPAGNE DE NOTES HISTORIQUES ET CRITIQUES
Beaudry, Louis Napoleon *see*
- FACE A FACE, OU, LUTTES MENTALES D'UN CATHOLIQUE ROMAN
- SPIRITUAL STRUGGLES OF A ROMAN CATHOLIC

Beaudry, Pauline *see* BIBLIOGRAPHIE ANALYTIQUE DE BAIE COMEAU SUR LA COTE-NORD DU SAINT-LAURENT
Beaudry, R et al *see* LE PROGRES DE MAGOG
Beaufils, G *see* LA VIE DE LA VENERABLE MERE JEANNE DE LESTONAC
BEAUFORT BAPTIST CHURCH. BEAUFORT COUNTY. SOUTH CAROLINA : CHURCH RECORDS – 1840-1965, September 1969-84. Deacons' Meetings 1962-84 – 1 – $80.78 – us Baptist [240]
Beaufort County. North Carolina. First Baptist Church *see* WASHINGTON CHURCH BOOK
Beaufort, Secretaire de Legation *see* TABLEAU STATISTIQUE DE L'EUROPE
Beaufort. South Carolina. St. Helena's (Episcopal) Church *see* RECORDS
Beaufort. South Carolina. St. Helena's Episcopal Church *see* RECORDS
Beaugrand, Honore *see*
- ACROSS THE CONTINENT VIA THE CANADIAN PACIFIC RAILWAY: A LECTURE DELIVERED...23RD MARCH, 1887
- LA CHASSE GALERIE AND OTHER CANADIAN STORIES
- LE FARCEUR
- JEANNE LA FILEUSE: EPISODE DE L'EMIGRATION FRANCO-CANADIENNE AUX ETATS-UNIS
- LETTRES DE VOYAGE: FRANCE, ITALIE, SICILE, MALTE, TUNISIE, ALGERIE, ESPAGNE
- MELANGES: TROIS CONFERENCES
- SIX MOIS DANS LES MONTAGNES-ROCHEUSES: COLORADO, UTAH, NOUVEAU-MEXIQUE
- LE SOIR

Beaujeu, Monongahela de *see* LE HEROS DE LA MONONGAHELA: ESQUISSE HISTORIQUE
Beaujour, Louis Auguste Felix de *see* TABLEAU DU COMMERCE DE LA GRECE, FORME D'APRES UNE ANNEE MOYENNE, DEPUIS 1787 JUSQU'EN 1797, PAR FELIX-BEAUJOUR, EX-CONSUL EN GRECE
Beaulieu, Paul Leroy *see*
- COLLECTIVISM, A STUDY OF THE LEADING SOCIAL QUESTIONS OF THE DAY
- THE MODERN STATE

BEAUMARIS NEWSLETTER – 1949-1977 – 3r – 1 – at Corangamite [072]
BEAUMONT ENTERPRISE – Beaumont. Texas. 1936- – 1 – us UMI [071]
BEAUMONT ENTERPRISE AND JOURNAL – Beaumont. Texas. 1880-1935 – 1 – us UMI [071]
Beaumont, Francis *see* ARBACES UND PANTHEA
BEAUMONT JOURNAL – Beaumont. Texas. 1936- – 1 – us UMI [071]
Beaumont – Les-Tours, monastere *see* REGLE DU MONASTERE (DE BEAUMONT-LES-TOURS)
THE BEAUMONT LIBRARY CATALOGUES – 3mf – 9 – $57.50 – us UMI [020]
Beaumont, Pierre de *see* CONTES AFRICAINS
Beaumont, R C de *see* SOUVENIR DU BANQUET LAURIER, BOSTON, MASS, HOTEL VENDOME MARDI, 17 NOVEMBRE 1891:... LES DISCOURS DES ORATEURS, LEURS PORTRAITS
Beaumont, W *see* EXPERIMENTS AND OBSERVATIONS IN THE GASTRIC JUICES
Beaunier, Dom. *see*
- ABBAUES ET PRIEURES DE L'ANCIENNE FRANCE
- ABBAYES ET PRIEURES DE L'ANCIENNE FRANCE
- ABBAYES ET PRIEURES DE L'ANCIENNE FRANCE
- ABBAYES ET PRIEURES DE L'ANCIENNE FRANCE. PROVINCES ECCLESIASTIQUES D'AUCH ET DE BORDEAUX
- RECUEIL HISTORIQUE DES ARCHEVECHES, EVECHES, ABBAYES ET PRIEURES DE FRANCE
- RECUEIL HISTORIQUE DES ARCHEVECHES, EVECHES ET PRIEURES DE FRANCE

Beauregard, H *see* LES INSECTES VESICANTS
Beaurepaire, Charles de Robillard de *see* NOTES SUR LES JUGES ET LES ASSESSEURS DU PROCES DE CONDEMNATION DE JEANNE D'ARC
Beausobre, M de *see* HISTOIRE CRITIQUE DE MANICHEE ET DU MANICHEISME
Beausoleil, CleO *see* LE BIEN PUBLIC
Beausoleil, Cleophas *see*
- ADDRESSE DE M. C. BEAUSOLEIL, CANDIDAT NATIONAL, AUX ELECTEURS DU COMTE BERTHIER
- LA LOI DE FAILLITE
- SYSTEME PROTECTEUR

Beausoleil, Joseph Maxime *see*
- LE DERNIER CHANT DES SERINS SIC DE LAVAL
- ENTRE NOUS
- LA TROMPETTE DE LA METEMPSYCOSE UNIVERSITAIRE

LA BEAUTE DES FEMMES / Prato, Stanislau – 1888 – 1 – us I.U. Libraries [390]
BEAUTIES OF PRIESTERCRAFT : OR, A SHORT HISTORY OF SHAKERISM / Whitbey, John – (Printed for the author at the office of the gazette; from Historical & Philosophical Society of Ohio) – New Harmony, IN: New Harmony Gazette, 1826 – 1r – 1 – us Western Res [240]
THE BEAUTIFUL GLEANER : A HEBREW PASTORAL STORY: BEING FAMILIAR EXPOSITIONS OF THE BOOK OF RUTH / Braden, William – 2nd ed. London: James Clarke, 1872 – 1mf – 9 – 0-8370-2432-3 – 1985-0432 – us A.T.L.A. [220]
THE BEAUTIFUL LIFE OF FRANCIS E. WILLARD / Gordon, Anna Adams – 1898 – 9 – us A.T.L.A. [240]
BEAUTIFUL SANTA CRUZ COUNTY / Francis, Phil – Santa Cruz Co, CA. 1896 – 1r – 1 – $50.00 – B40265 – us Library Micro [978]
THE BEAUTIFUL WRETCH / Black, William – British Fiction Archive: Unit 4 – 9 – uk Bell [830]
Beauvais, Vincent de *see* BIBLIOTHECA MUNDI, VINCENTI BURGUNDI.
Beauvau, Henri *see* RELATION IOURNALIERE DU VOYAGE DU LEVANT PAR HAUT ET PUISSANT SEIGNEUR HENRY DE BEAUVAU
Beauvoir *see* PEKIN, YEDDO, SAN FRANCISCO. VOYAGE AUTOUR DU MONDE
Beauvois, E *see* LA NATIONALITE DU SLESVIG
Beauvois, Eugene *see*
- LES COLONIES EUROPEENNES DU MARKLAND ET DE L'ESCORILAND (DOMINATION CANADIENNE) AU XIVE SIECLE ET LES VESTIGES QUI EN SUBSISTERENT JUSQU'AUX XVIE ET XVIIE SIECLES
- LES GALLOIS EN AMERIQUE AU XIIE SIECLE
- LA NORAMBEGUE: DECOUVERTE D'UNE QUATRIEME COLONIE PRECOLOMBIENNE DANS LE NOUVEAU MONDE, AVEC DES PREUVES DE SON ORIGINE SCANDINAVE FOURNIES PAR LA LANGUE, LES INSTITUTIONS ET LES CROYANCES DES INDIGENES DE L'ACADIE
- ORIGINES ET FONDATION DU PLUS ANCIEN EVECHE DU NOUVEAU MONDE: LE DIOCESE DE GARDHS EN GROENLAND: 986-1126
- LES PAPAS DU NOUVEAU-MONDE RATTACHES A CEUX DES ILES BRITANNIQUES ET NORDATLANTIQUES

LES BEAUX ARTS REDUITS A UN MEME PRINCIPE / Batteux, Charles – Paris: Durand, 1746 – 1 – us Sibley [780]
BEAUX YEUX, AND JEUNES COEURS SOYEZ FIDELLES. THE FAVORITE FRENCH AIR AND GAVOTTE / Storace, S – (Full Score) – London: Birchall & Andrews for S Storace, [1788] – 1 – us Sibley [780]
BEAUX-ARTS – Chronique des arts et de la curiosite. Dir. G. Wildenstein. Paris. 1923-juin 1940 – 1 – fr A.C.R.P.P. [073]
LES BEAUX-ARTS / ed by Boucher, J-A & Smith, Gustave – Montreal, Canada. 1 avr 1863-v2 n2. 25 mai 1864 – 1r – 1 – Can$30.00 – cn Can Microfilming [700]
LES BEAUX-ARTS REDUITS A UN MEME PRINCIPE / Le Batteux – 1746 – 9 – fr I.C.S. [700]
Beauzee, N *see* GRAMMAIRE GENERALE
Beavan, Charles *see* BEAVAN'S REPORTS
BEAVAN'S REPORTS : REPORTS OF CASES ARGUED AND DETERMINED IN ROLLS COURT / Beavan, Charles – v1-36. 1838-66. London: Saunders & Benning/Stevens & Norton, 1840-69 (all publ) – 276mf – 9 – $414.00 – LLMC 95-283 – us L.L.M.C. [324]
Beaven, James *see* AN ACCOUNT OF THE LIFE AND WRITINGS OF S. IRENAEUS, BISHOP OF LYONS AND MARTYR
BEAVER – (1920-82 Can$60.00 1. 1986-96 Can$20.00y 9) – Winnipeg. v1- 1920- – 1,9 – Can$20.00y – cn Micromedia [073]
Beaver and Toronto Mutual Fire Insurance Company *see* ANNUAL MEETING (2ND: 1871: TORONTO, ONT.)
BEAVER ARGUS AND RADICAL – Beaver, PA. -w 1896-1912 – 13 – $25.00r – us I.M.R. [071]
BEAVER BAPTIST CHURCH. CYNTHIANA, KENTUCKY : CHURCH RECORDS – May 1809-Nov 1896; 1905-Jul 1910; Nov 1919-1920. WMU Records, 1919-55 – 1 – 47.25 – us Baptist [240]
Beaver City Times-Tribune *see* PIONEER STORIES OF FURNAS COUNTY, NEBRASKA
THE BEAVER CITY TIMES-TRIBUNE – Beaver City. Furnas County, Nebraska. Oct 2, 1903-Sept 9, 1965 – 1 – us NE Hist [071]
BEAVER COUNTY TIMES – Beaver. Pa. 1960- – 1 – us UMI [071]
Beaver Creek Baptist Church. Henry County, Virginia *see* HISTORY OF BEAVER CREEK BAPTIST CHURCH
BEAVER CREEK BAPTIST CHURCH. KERSHAW COUNTY. SOUTH CAROLINA : CHURCH RECORDS – 1868-83 – 1 – 5.00 – us Baptist [240]
BEAVER CREEK CEMETERY RECORD / Wood County. Ohio. Grand Rapids Twp Board of Trustees – 1812-1986 – 1r – 1 – $32.50r – us Archival [324]
BEAVER CROSSING BUGLE – Beaver Crossing, NE. -w. Apr. 1887-Jul. 1889 – 1 – us NE Hist [071]
BEAVER CROSSING TIMES – Beaver Crossing, NE. -w. May 1892-Jul. 1897; Dec. 1897-Apr. 1900. Incomplete; Jan. 1901-Dec. 1904; Mar. 1905-Jun. 1909; Oct. 1911-Dec. 1930; Jan. 1932-May 1968 – 1 – us NE Hist [071]
BEAVER DAM BAPTIST CHURCH. BEAUFORT COUNTY. SOUTH CAROLINA : CHURCH RECORDS – 1834-Oct 1968 – 1 – 43.56 – us Baptist [240]
BEAVER DAM BAPTIST CHURCH. FOUNTAIN CITY, TENNESSEE : CHURCH RECORDS – 1802-1959. Sunday School records. Jan 1900-12 – 1 – 63.90 – us Baptist [240]
BEAVER DAM BAPTIST CHURCH. FOUNTAIN CITY, TENNESSEE : CHURCH RECORDS – By Mary Sue Beggs. 1959 – 1 – 5.00 – us Baptist [240]
BEAVER DAM BAPTIST CHURCH. SHELBY, NORTH CAROLINA : CHURCH RECORDS – 1850-1950 – 1 – 5.00 – us Baptist [240]
Beaver, Kathryn L *see* IMPACT OF THE ACQUIRED IMMUNODEFICIENCY SYNDROME (AIDS)
Beaver, P *see* AFRICAN MEMORANDA
Beaver. Presbytery (Pres. Ch. in the U.S.A.) *see* MINUTES, 1833-1870
THE BEAVER RADICAL – Beaver, PA. Dec 11 1868-Dec 24 1869; Jan 7 1870; Dec 15 1871; March 15 1872 – 2r – 1 – us L of C Photodup [071]
BEAVER STATE HERALD – Gresham OR. July 27 1906-Aug 18 1911 – 1 – us U.O. Library [071]
BEAVER STATE HERALD – Lents OR. Aug 25 1911-Feb 12 1914 – 1 – us U.O. Library [071]
BEAVER STATE NEWS – Hubbard, OR. -w. 19 Sept 1907-23 May 1912. 2 rolls – 1 – us U.O. Library [071]
BEAVER VALLEY MERCURY – Danbury, NE. -w. Nov. 1936-Dec. 1939 – 1 – us NE Hist [071]
BEAVER VALLEY TIMES – Beaver. Pa. 1947-1959 – 1 – us UMI [071]
BEAVER VALLEY TRIBUNE – Beaver City. Furnas County, Nebraska. Apr 17, 1890-Aug 27, 1897 – 1 – us NE Hist [071]
BEAVER VALLEY TRIBUNE – Beaver City, NE. -w. Jun 1892-Aug 1893. Incomplete; Oct 1895-Jan 1902 – 1 – us NE Hist [071]
BEAVERDAM BAPTIST CHURCH. ASHEVILLE, NORTH CAROLINA : CHURCH RECORDS – 1952-75 – 1 – 53.37 – us Baptist [240]
BEAVERDAM BAPTIST CHURCH. FAIR PLAY, SOUTH CAROLINA : CHURCH RECORDS – 1868-1963 – 1 – 38.07 – us Baptist [240]
BEAVERDAM BAPTIST CHURCH. WILKES COUNTY. GEORGIA : CHURCH RECORDS – 1836-1923 – 1 – 32.99 – us Baptist [240]
BEAVERTON ENTERPRISE – Beaverton, OR. -w. 17 Mar 1927-26 Jan 1951. 6 rolls – 1 – us U.O. Library [071]
BEAVERTON EXPRESS – Beaverton, 1882-1959 – 29r – 1 – cn Preston [971]
BEAVERTON EXPRESS – Ontario, CN. 1940-79 – 18r – 1 – cn Commonwealth Micro [072]
BEAVERTON REVIEW – Beaverton, OR. -w. 28 Dec 1923-18 Apr 1941. 3 rolls – 1 – us U.O. Library [071]
BEAVERTON TIMES – Beaverton, OR. -w. 19 Aug 1915-9 Jun 1922. 1 roll – 1 – us U.O. Library [071]
Beazley, Charles Raymond *see* JOHN AND SEBASTIAN CABOT: THE DISCOVERY OF NORTH AMERICA
BEBBLY : OR, THE VICTORIOUS PREACHER / Walker, Thomas – Gainesville, FL. 1910 – 1r – 1 – us Ross [975]
Bebel, A *see* GEGEN DEN MILITARISMUS UND GEGEN DIE NEUEN STEUERN
Bebel, Auguste *see*
- LA FEMME ET LE SOCIALISME
- MASSOVAIA POLITICHESKAIA STACHKA I SOTSIALDEMOKRATIIA

Bebel, Heinrich *see* FACETIEN DREI BUECHER
BEBERAPA FASAL EKONOMI. DJALAN KE EKONOMI DAN KOOPERASI / Hatta, M – Djakarta, Oesaha Baroe "Penjiar" (2602). 133p – 189-190mf – 9 – ne IDC [330]
BEBERAPA HAL TENTANG KESUSILAAN DALAM PRAKTEK KEDOKTERAN / Wahab – SE 4583 1. 1960 – 9 – ne IDC [950]
BEBERAPA SEGI DASAR KEDJAHATAN / Sujunus, R M – SE 5202 1. 1962 – 9 – ne IDC [950]
BEBERAPA SEGI PATOLOGI TUMOR GANAS NASOPHARYNX DI DJAWA-TIMUR / Muljono, Djojopranoto – Summary in English. SE-4447 1. 1960 – 9 – ne IDC [950]
Bebermeyer, Gustav *see*
- FACETIEN DREI BUECHER
- HERMANN FLAYDERS AUSGEWAEHLTE WERKE

BEBRAER NACHRICHTEN : SONTRAER ANZEIGER MIT DEN MITTEILUNGEN DES KREISES ROTENBURG A F – OBERSUHLER ZEITUNG – Bebra, 1933-jun 29 1935 – 6r – 1 – Dist. gw Mikrofilm – gw Misc Inst [943]
BEBRAER TAGEBLATT *see* BEBRAER TAGESZEITUNG
BEBRAER TAGESZEITUNG – (Incl suppl. Cont: Bebraer Tageblatt, -1913. Cont by: NS-Tageblatt fuer den Kreis Rotenburg a F und Nachbargebiete; NS-Tageblatt fuer Ostkurhessen und Nachbargebiete, aug 15 1942) – Bebra, 1903-08, apr 1909-44 – 58r – 1 – Dist. gw Mikrofilm – gw Misc Inst [943]
BEBRAER ZEITUNG – (Incl suppl) – Cassel/Kassel, 1902-sep 29 1912 – 14r – 1 – Dist. gw Mikrofilm – gw Misc Inst [943]
BEBRAER ZEITUNG UND EISENBAHN-ANZEIGER – (Incl suppl) – Bebra, jan 4-apr 28 1896 – 1r – 1 – Dist. gw Mikrofilm – gw Misc Inst [943]
THE BEC MISSAL / Hughes, A – 1963 – 6mf – 8 – ne Slangenburg [240]
Becarud, J *see* LA DEUXIEME REPUBLIQUE ESPAGNOLE 1931-1936
BECCLES AND BUNGAY JOURNAL – England. -w. 1978-81. 8 reels – 1 – uk British Libr Newspaper [072]
Becerra, Hasperue *see* MENSAJE DE AMISTAD A LA NACION MEXICANA
Becerra y Valcarzel, Diego *see*
- CARTA PASTORAL
- DE IURE SACRORUM

Becerro de Bengoa, Ricardo *see*
- CARTILLA POLITICA DONOSIANA
- ENSAYO PARA UNA TEORIA DE EXTREMADURA
- HACIA LA UNION DE LOS PUEBLOS LATINOS
- LA HERMANDAD DE ALFERECES Y EL DESTINO DE ESPANA
- LA IDEA TRADICIONAL. DESTINO DE ESPANA POR
- EL MOVIMIENTO DE UNION LATINA EN EXTREMADURA
- EL MUNO HISPANICO Y SU REITEGRACION HISTORICA BAJO EL SIGNO DE GUADALUPE
- NACIONAL-INTEGRISMO
- PROGRAMACION IDEOLOGICA DEL BIMILENARIO DE MERIDA
- REORGANIZACION DEL FRENTE NACIONAL DE EXCOMBATIENTES

Bech, Birger *see*
- FIVE YEARS IN A SAILOR'S LIFE
- THE UNKNOWN

Bechard, Auguste *see*
- L'ANCIEN QUEBEC, DESCRIPTIONS, NOS ARCHIVES, ETC
- BIOGRAPHIE DE M. FRANCOIS VEZINA, CAISSIER DE LA BANQUE NATIONALE
- HISTOIRE DE LA BANQUE NATIONALE
- L'HONORABLE A.-N. MORIN
- MONOGRAPHIES: GOUVERNEURS, INTENDANTS ET EVEQUES DE LA NOUVELLE-FRANCE
- LA VOIX DU PEUPLE

Bechard, Henri *see* KATERI, LYS DES AGNIERS

Becher, Hubert *see*
- DER DEUTSCHE PRIMAS
- ERNST JUENGER

Bechervaise, John *see* THIRTY-SIX YEARS OF A SEAFARING LIFE

BECHERWAHRSAGUNG BEI DEN BABYLONIERN / Hunger, J – (Leipziger semitistische studien. v. 1, pt.1. 1904). Leipzig. 1903. BNE-20,109 1 – 9 – ne IDC [930]

BECHERWAHRSAGUNG BEI DEN BABYLONIERN : NACH ZWEI KEILSCHRIFTTEXTEN AUS DER HAMMURABI-ZEIT / Hunger, Johannes – (Includes bibliographical references) – Leipzig: J C Hinrichs, 1903 – 1mf – 9 – 0-8370-7068-6 – 1986-1068 – us A.T.L.A. [470]

Bechery, Louis *see* LE CHARIVARI

Bechet, Eugene *see* CINQ ANS DE SEJOUR AU SOUDAN FRANCAIS

Bechstein, Ludwig *see*
- EIN DUNKLES LOOS
- THUERINGENS KOENIGSHAUS

Bechtel, Christine *see* MUSIKDIDAKTISCHE AUFGABEN IM KINDERCHOR (1984)

Bechter, Barbara *see* DER GARTEN VON VAUX-LE-VICOMTE

Bechtold, O *see* DER "RUF NACH SYNODE" ALS KIRCHENPOLITISCHE ERSCHEINUNG IM JUNGEN ERZBISTUM FREIBURG (1827-1860)

THE BECHUANA OF SOUTH AFRICA / Crisp, William – London: Society for Promoting Christian Knowledge, 1896 – 1 – us Res Libr [960]

BECHUANALAND DAILY NEWS – Gaborone: Bechuanaland Govt Info Service, sep 1 1965-sep 16 1966 – us Res Libr [072]

Bechuanaland Protectorate *see* DRAFT DEVELOPMENT PLAN, 1963-1968

Bechuanaland Protectorate. African Advisory Council *see* MINUTES OF THE...SESSION OF THE AFRICAN ADVISORY COUNCIL

Beck, Aaron N *see* CIVIL WAR DIARY

Beck, Belinda R *see* AN INVESTIGATION OF ANATOMICAL STRUCTURES ASSOCIATED WITH THE SITE OF MEDIAL TIBIAL STRESS SYNDROME, OFTEN REFERRED TO AS "SHIN SPLINTS"

Beck, Dietrich *see* DIE KIRCHLICHEN SIMULTANVERHAELTNISSE DER RHEINPROVINZ UNTER BESONDERER BERUECKSICHTIGUNG DES RYSWICKER FRIEDENS

Beck, George Fairley *see* DAYBREAK: A POEM

Beck, Henry *see* FLUTE BOOK

Beck, Herbert *see* MITTELALTERLICHE SKULPTUREN IN BAROCKALTAEREN

Beck, Hermann *see* KASPAR KLEE VON GEROLZHOFEN

Beck, James M *see* THE EVIDENCE IN THE CASE

Beck, Johann Tobias *see*
- ERKLAERUNG DER BRIEFE PETRI
- ERKLAERUNG DER OFFENBARUNG JOHANNES, CAP. 1-12
- ERKLAERUNG DER PROPHETEN MICHA UND JOEL
- ERKLAERUNG DER PROPHETEN NAHUM UND ZEPHANJA
- ERKLARUNG DER PROPHETEN NAHUM UND ZEPHANJA
- DIE ETHISCHE ERSCHEINUNG DES CHRISTLICHEN LEBENS
- DIE GENETISCHE ANLAGE DES CHRISTLICHEN LEBENS
- OUTLINES OF BIBLICAL PSYCHOLOGY
- DIE PAEDAGOGISCHE ENTWICKLUNG DES CHRISTLICHEN LEBENS
- VORLESUNGEN UEBER CHRISTLICHE GLAUBENSLEHRE

Beck, Karl *see*
- NAECHTE
- TAEUBCHEN IM NEST, 1860

Beck, L C *see* BOTANY OF THE NORTHERN AND MIDLAND STATES

Beck, Lester Ford *see* MANUSIA: KEDJADIAN, PERTUMBUHAN, PERKEMBANGAN DJASMANI (DAN) ROHANI

Beck, W C A *see* DER PANAMAKANAL...

Becker, A *see* PAPST URBAN 2 (1088-1099) (MGH SCHRIFTEN..: 19.BD. 1.TEIL)

Becker, Bernard Henry *see* DISTURBED IRELAND; BEING THE LETTERS WRITTEN DURING THE WINTER OF 1880-81

Becker, Bernhard *see*
- BRONNEN TOT DE KENNIS VAN HET LEVEN EN DE WERKEN VAN D.V. COORNHERT
- ZINZENDORF UND SEIN CHRISTENTUM

Becker, Frank Silvester *see* THE EXCISE AND HOTEL LAWS OF THE STATE OF NEW YORK.

Becker, Hendrik *see* BAUSTEINE ZUR DEUTSCHEN LITERATURGESCHICHTE

Becker, Henrietta K *see* KLEIST AND HEBBEL

Becker, J *see* FLORA DER GEGEND UM FRANKFURT AM MAIN

Becker, Jerome *see*
- LA TROISIEME EXPEDITION BELGE AU PAYS NOIR
- LA VIE EN AFRIQUE OU TROIS ANS DANS L'AFRIQUE CENTRALE

Becker, Jeronimo *see* CARTA Y OTROS DOCUMENTOS DE HERNANDO CORTES

Becker, Nicolaus *see* GEDICHTE

Becker, P *see* DER VOELKERRECHTLICHE SCHUTZ...AUF HOHER SEE

Becker, P W *see* DE REBUS INTER IOANNEM ET...

Becker, Philipp August *see* DER SUEDFRANZOESISCHE SAGENKREIS UND SEINE PROBLEME

Becker, Rudolf *see* CHRISTIAN WEISES ROMANE UND IHRE NACHWIRKUNG

Becker, Susan L *see* AN EXAMINATION OF THE RELATIONSHIP AMONG TARGET STRUCTURES, TEAM MOTIVATIONAL CLIMATE, AND ACHIEVEMENT GOAL ORIENTATION

Becker, T *see* OUTLINE OF INTERNATIONAL LAW

Becker, Werner *see*
- SPORTUNTERRICHT UND HOCHSCHULSPORT IN FRANKREICH
- UNTERSUCHUNGEN ZUR VERAENDERUNG DER INFORMATIONSVERARBEITUNGSFAEHIGKEIT VON 9 BIS 12JAEHRIGEN KINDERN IM VERLAUF VON LERNPROZESSEN UNTERSCHIEDLICHER MODALITAETSPRAEFERENZEN

Beckerath, Ulrich von *see*
- APHORISMEN ZUM GELDPROBLEM
- BANKNOTEN SIND TYPISIERTE WECHSEL UND IHRE SICHERUNG GEGEN INFLATION
- CHINESISCHE SOLDATEN BESTIMMTEN DIE GRENZEN DES MILITAERISCHEN GEHORSAMS
- ECONOMIC AND HUMAN RIGHTS ASPECTS IGNORED BY MODERN AUTHORS
- EINIGE VON DER UN NICHT KODIFIZIERTE RECHTE DES MENSCHEN UND BUERGERS
- ENTWURF ZU EINER ARBEITSBESCHAFFUNGSBANK
- ERKLAERUNG UEBER DAS RECHT SICH ARBEIT ZU BESCHAFFEN
- FREIER GOLDMARKT VERSUS EINLOESUNG
- DIE GEWAEHRUNG LANGFRISTIGER KREDITE NACH DEM VERRECHNUNGSPRINZIP
- DAS GOLD ALS WERTMESSER, ALS ZAHLUNGSMMITTEL UND ALS KAPITAL
- GRUNDSAETZE EINER EUROPAEISCHENARMEE GEGENUEBER DEN GEZWUNGENERMASSEN AUF RUSSISCHER SEITE KAEMPFENDEN
- LETTER AND STATEMENT TO HENRY MEULEN ON THEIR DIFFERENCES/MONETARY FREEDOM
- MUST FULL EMPLOYMENT COST MONEY?
- EINE NEUE NOTVERORDNUNG ZUR BEHEBUNG DER KRISE
- THE PRACTICAL REALIZATION OF THE MILHAUD PROPOSALS
- A PROGRAMME FOR THE IMMEDIATE ABOLITION OF UNEMPLOYMENT
- PUBLIC INSURANCE AND COMPENSATION MONEY
- DIE SICHERUNG DER GOLDWAEHRUNG; DIE AUFHEBUNG DER GELDENTWERTUNGSKLAUSEL; AUFRECHNUNG UNTER FRIEDRICH DEM GROSSEN
- EIN SOFORTPROGRAMM ZUR BEHEBUNG DER ARBEITSLOSIGKEIT
- SOME LETTERS, NOTES AND DRAFTS ON HUMAN RIGHTS
- SOME TECHNICAL DETAILS OF THE STATUTES OF AN EMPLOYMENT BANK
- A SUMMARY OF THE GERMAN MONETARY FREEDOM SCHOOL
- UEBER ANARCHIE UND ANARCHISMUS
- UEBER DAS GELDPRINZIP DER MODERNEN, TOTALITAEREN STAATEN
- UEBER DEFLATION
- UEBER DEN NAMEN ANARCHISMUS
- DER ZINS UND DAS RECHT AUF DEN VOLLEN ARBEITSERTRAG
- ZUR FREIHEIT, ZUM FRIEDEN UND ZUR GERECHTIGKEIT AND JUSTICE

Beckerath, Ulrich von et al *see*
- BERLIN PROGRAMME
- UEBER EINE SCHECKBANK (VERRECHUNGSBANK)
- UEBER KANADISCHES GELDWESEN
- UEBER STEUERFUNDATION

BECKET 1765-1900 – (Mf 1-9: Town Records 1765-1835. Mf 10-14: Proprietors Records 1737-71. Mf 15-23: Towen Records 1836-56. Mf 24-27: Index to Births, Marriages, Deaths 1850-58. Mf 28-29: Births, Marriages, Deaths 1844-58. Mf 30-35: Births, Marriages, Deaths 1859-1900) – (mf ed 1988) – 35mf – 9 – 0-87623-068-0 – us Holbrook [920]

BECKET, ARCHBISHOP OF CANTERBURY : A BIOGRAPHY / Robertson, James Craigie – London: J. Murray, 1859 – 1mf – us A.T.L.A. [240]

Becket, Hugh W *see* RECORD OF WINTER SPORTS, 1883-84: SNOWSHOE AND SKATING RACES, HOCKEY AND CURLING MATCHES

BECKETT 1753-1849 – (Mf 1T-3T: Marriages & Intentions 1765-1849; Births & Deaths 1753-1841. Mf 4T: B,M,D 1844-49) – (mf ed 1995) – 4mf – 9 – 0-87623-207-1 – us Holbrook [920]

Beckford, James A *see* NEW RELIGIOUS MOVEMENTS AND RAPID SOCIAL CHANGE

Beckford, William *see* AN ARABIAN TALE

Beckherrn, Richard *see* M. OPITZ, P. RONSARD UND D. HEINSIUS

BECKLEY HEIGHTS BAPTIST CHURCH. DALLAS, TEXAS : CHURCH RECORDS – 22 Apr 1953-12 Feb 1964 – 1 – 17.82 – us Baptist [240]

Beckman, J *see*
- DIE KIRCHLICHE ORDNUNG DER TAUFE
- QUELLEN ZUR GESCHICHTE DES CHRISTLICHEN GOTTESDIENSTES

Beckman, S *see* DIE GOTTESANREDE IM ANTE-SANCTUS

Beckmann, Johann *see*
- LITTERATUR DER AELTEREN REISEBESCHREIBUNGEN...
- PHYSIKALISCH-OEKONOMISCHE BIBLIOTHEK
- VORBEREITUNG ZUR WAARENKUNDE ODER ZUR KENNTNIS DE VORNEHMSTEN AUSLAENDISCHEN WAAREN

Beckmann, Petr *see* FORT FREEDOM

BECK'S JOURNAL OF DECORATIVE ART – 1886-88 – 18mf – 9 – £100.00 – uk Chadwyck [740]

Beckwith, Albert C *see* HISTORY OF WALWORTH COUNTY

Beckwith, Clarence Augustine *see* REALITIES OF CHRISTIAN THEOLOGY

Beckwith, H W *see*
- HISTORY OF FOUNTAIN COUNTY
- HISTORY OF IROQUOIS COUNTY
- HISTORY OF MONTGOMERY COUNTY
- HISTORY OF VERMILION COUNTY
- VIGO AND PARKE COUNTIES

Beckwourth, James P *see* THE LIFE AND ADVENTURES OF JAMES P. BECKWOURTH: MOUNTAINEER, SCOUT, PIONEER, AND CHIEF OF THE CROW NATION OF INDIANS: WRITTEN FROM HIS OWN DICTATION

BECOMING AWARE : HUMAN RIGHTS AND THE FAMILY / Gallagher, Margaret – 1984 – 9 – 92-3-102178-8 – fr UNESCO [306]

BECONTREE, CHADWELL HEATH AND DAGENHAM CITIZEN – London. -m. Apr 1930-Aug 1939. (1 reel) – 1 – uk British Libr Newspaper [072]

BECONTREE GUARDIAN – London. 23 Mar-21 Dec 1923; 7 Mar-26 Dec 1924; Jan-Dec 1927.-w. 2mqn reels – 1 – uk British Libr Newspaper [072]

Becot, Joseph *see* DE L'ORGANISATION DE LA JUSTICE REPRESSIVE AUX PRINCIPALES EPOQUES HISTORIQUES

Becq de Fouquieres, L *see* TRAITE GENERAL DE VERSIFICATION FRANCAISE

Becque, E *see* L'INTERNATIONALISATION DES CAPITAUX...

BECSI MAGYAR UJAAG – v2-5. 1920-23 – 2r – 1 – us Ross [073]

Becvarovsky, A *see* TROIS SONATES POUR PIANOFORTE AVEC VIOLON ET VIOLONCELL OBLIGES

Beda Venerabilis *see*
- EXPOSITIO ACTUUM APOSTOLORUM – RETRACTATIO IN ACTUS APOSTOLORUM – NOMINA REGIONUM ATQUE LOCORUM DE ACTIBUS APOSTOLORUM – IN EPISTULAS 7 CATHOLICAS
- IN TOBIAM. IN PROVERBIA. IN CANTICA CANTICORUM. IN HABACUC

Bedard, Denyse *see* BIO-BIBLIOGRAPHIE DE JULES-S. LESAGE

Bedard, J Alphonse *see* LE GUIDE COMMERCIAL POUR LA VILLE DE DETROIT ET SES ENVIRONS: CONTENANT L'HISTOIRE DE DETROIT, MONTREAL ET QUEBEC: AVEC LES NOMS DE LEURS FONDATEURS

Bedard, J -E *see* L'IVROGNERIE ET LA LOI DES LICENCES

Bedard, MH *see* LE JEUNE HOMME ET LA LITTERATURE: LECTURE FAITE AU CERCLE VILLE-MARIE DE MONTREAL

Bedard, P J *see* ETUDES ET RECITS

Bedard, Suzanne *see* BIBLIOGRAPHIE ANALYTIQUE DE L'OEUVRE DE CHARLOTTE SAVARY

Bedard, Theophile Pierre *see*
- HISTOIRE DE CINQUANTE ANS (1791-1841): ANNALES PARLEMENTAIRES ET POLITIQUES DU BAS CANADA DEPUIS LA CONSTITUTION JUSQU'A L'UNION
- NOS ARCHIVES: LES STATISTIQUES

BEDARF ES EINER BESONDEREN INSPIRATIONSLEHRE? : VORTRAG GEHALTEN AUF DER THEOLOGISCHEN KONFERENZ IN KIEL AM 7. JULI 1891 / Kier, P O – Kiel: Ernst Homann, 1891 – 1mf – 9 – 0-8370-3895-2 – 1985-1895 – us A.T.L.A. [220]

BEDAVA GAZETE [AKBABA' NIN ILAVESI] – Istanbul: Sabah Matbaasi; Mueduer-i Mesul: Yusuf Ziya [Ortac], 1925. – Nos 1-5. – 24 Mart-9 Nisan 1341 [1925] – 1mf – 9 – $13.50 – us MEDOC [949]

Beddoes, Thomas Lovell *see*
- THE BRIDE'S TRAGEDY
- THE POETICAL WORKS OF THOMAS LOVELL BEDDOES

Beddome, R H *see*
- THE FERNS OF SOUTHERN INDIA
- HANDBOOK OF THE FERNS OF BRITISH INDIA, CEYLON AND MALAYA PENINSULAR
- HANDBOOK OF THE FERNS OF BRITISH INDIA, CEYLON AND THE MALAY PENINSULA

Bedel, J *see* LA VIE DU R.P. PIERE FOURIER

BEDERKESAER NACHRICHTEN UND ANZEIGER FUER DEN VORMALIGEN AMTSBEZIRK BEDERKESA – Bederkesa, nov 29 1903-mar 29 1940 (incomplete) – 1 – Dist. gw Mikrofilm – gw Misc Inst [943]

DIE BEDEUTENDSTEN ROMANE PHILIPPS VON ZESEN UND IHRE LITERARGESCHICHTLICHE STELLUNG / Gartenhof, Kaspar – (Includes bibliographical references) – Nuernberg: G P J Bieling-Dietz, 1912 – 1r – 1 – us U.W. Library [430]

DIE BEDEUTUNG DER IM ART. 119 I 2 DER REICHSVERFASSUNG AUSGESPROCHENEN GLEICHBERECHTIGUNG DER GESCHLECHTER DE LEGE FERENDA FUER DIE PERSONENRECHTLICHE STELLUNG DER EHEFRAU / Keßler, Aloys Wilhelm – 1995 – 1mf – 9 – DM48.00 – gw Hänsel [340]

DIE BEDEUTUNG DER REFORMIERTEN THEOLOGIE FUER DIE RELIGIOESE LAGE DER GEGENWART : VORTRAG AUF DER HAUPTVERSAMMLUNG DES REFORMIERTEN BUNDES, HERFORD, 30. AUGUST 1905 / Lang, August – Neukirchen, Kreis Moers: Verlag der Buchh. des Erziehungsvereins, [1905?] – 1mf – us A.T.L.A. [240]

DIE BEDEUTUNG DER SOMATOTROPEN ACHSE FUER MUSKELWACHSTUM UND REPRODUKTION BEI LANDWIRTSCHAFTLICHEN NUTZTIEREN / Sauerwein, Helga – 1994 – 3mf – DM98.00 – 3-8267-2014-8 – gw Hänsel [630]
DIE BEDEUTUNG DER WERTURTEILE FUER DAS RELIGIOESE ERKENNEN / Scheibe, Max – (Includes bibliographical references) – Halle a. S:Max Niemeyer, 1893 – 1mf – 9 – 0-8370-5080-4 – 1985-3080 – us A.T.L.A. [200]
DIE BEDEUTUNG DER WIRTSCHAFTLICHEN KOOPERATION FUER DIE WIRTSCHAFTSENTWICKLUNG CHINAS AM BEISPIEL JOINT VENTURES / Chen, Xinhua – 1995 – 2mf – 9 – DM80.00 – 3-8267-2189-6 – gw Hänsel [337]
DIE BEDEUTUNG DER WORTSIPPE KVD IM HEBRAEISCHEN / Caspari, Wilhelm – (Includes bibliographical references and index) – Leipzig: A Deichert, 1908 – 1mf – 9 – 0-8370-9213-2 – 1986-3213 – us A.T.L.A. [470]
DIE BEDEUTUNG DES GESCHICHTLICHEN IN DER RELIGION / Hase, Karl Alfred von – Leipzig: Breitkopf und Haertel, 1874 – 1mf – us A.T.L.A. [200]
DIE BEDEUTUNG DES LEBENDIGEN CHRISTUS FUER DIE RECHTFERTIGUNG NACH PAULUS / Schaeder, Erich – Guetersloh: C. Bertelsmann, 1893. 1 fiche – 9 – us A.T.L.A. [240]
DIE BEDEUTUNG DES MUSIKALISCHEN UND AKUSTISCHEN IN E.T.A. HOFFMANNS LITERARISCHEM SCHAFFEN / Schaeffer, Carl – (Includes bibliographical references (3rd prelim. page)) – Marburg a.L.: N G Elwert, 1909 – 1r – 1 – us U.W. Library [430]
DIE BEDEUTUNG DES NIBLUNGENLIEDER FUER DIE DEUTSCHE NATION / Bergmann, Anton – Karlsruhe i. Baden, 1924. 24p – 1 – us U.W. Library [390]
DIE BEDEUTUNG DES VERGELTUNGS-GEDANKENS FUER DIE ETHIK JESU, DARGESTELLT IM ANSCHLUSS AN DIE SYNOPTISCHEN EVANGELIEN / Karner, Friedrich Karl – Oedenburg-Sopron, 1927 – 2mf – 9 – DM62.00 – 3-89349-325-5 – gw Hänsel [240]
DIE BEDEUTUNG FUNKTIONALER PROBLEME FUER DIE MEDIZINISCHE VERSORGUNG AELTERER MENSCHEN : DAS VERSORGUNGSKONZEPT DES GERIATRISCHEN ASSESSMENT / Pientka, Ludger – 1995 – 6mf – 9 – DM125.00 – 3-8267-2168-3 – gw Hänsel [360]
DIE BEDEUTUNG VON GRUPPEN- UND MINDERHEITENRECHTEN FUER DIE SUEDAFRIKANISCHE VERFASSUNGSENTWICKLUNG / Weber, Rolf – 1993 – 3mf – 9 – DM98.00 – 3-89349-738-2 – gw Hänsel [340]
DIE BEDEUTUNGEN DER WORTSIPPE "KBD" IM HEBRAEISCHEN / Caspari, W – Leipzig. 1908. BNE-485 1 – 9 – ne IDC [470]
BEDFORD 1693-1849 – (Mf 1T-4T: Vital Records 1693-1887. Mf 3T-4T: Marriages 1810-43. Mf 4T: Out-of-Town Marriages 1731-99; Births 1840-42. Mf 5T: Births 1836-49; Marriages & Deaths 1843-49) – (mf ed 1995) – 5mf – 9 – 0-87623-208-X – us Holbrook [920]
Bedford, A *see* THE GREAT ABUSE OF MUSICK
BEDFORD ADVERTISER – Bedford, South Africa: 12 July 1878-25 Dec 1885 – 4r – 1 (diazo also available at reduced price) – sa SA Libr [072]
BEDFORD COUNTY PRESS – Bedford, PA., 1868-1984 – 13 – $25.00r – us I.M.R. [071]
BEDFORD COUNTY PRESS – Everett, PA., 1875-1959 – 13 – $25.00r – us I.M.R. [071]
BEDFORD ENTERPRISE – Bedford, South Africa: 4 Aug 1885-29 Dec 1899 – 9r – 1 (diazo also available at reduced price) – sa SA Libr [072]
BEDFORD GAZETTE – Bedford, PA. -w 1832-1847 – 13 – $25.00r – us I.M.R. [071]
BEDFORD GUARDIAN – Bedford, South Africa. 1881-1884 – 2r – 1, 16 diazo available – sa SA Libr [960]
BEDFORD INQUIRER – Bedford, PA. -w 1902-1930 – 13 – $25.00r – us I.M.R. [071]
Bedford, New Hampshire. Bedford Baptist Church *see* RECORDS
BEDFORD NEWS – Bedford, Canada. v2 n8. 6 oct 1899-v94 n12. 19 fev 1942 – 1r – 1 – Can$50.00 – cn Can Microfilming [072]
Bedford, Ohio *see* BEDFORD TIMES-REGISTER
Bedford, Thomas *see* A TREATISE OF THE SACRAMENTS
BEDFORD TIMES – Bedford & St-John, Canada. v4 n33. 6 Jan 1882-v20 n40. 14 apr 1898 – 1r – 1 – Can$50.00 – cn Can Microfilming [072]
BEDFORD TIMES-REGISTER : WEEKLY CLEVELAND SUBURBAN NEWSPAPER / Bedford, Ohio – 12 Apr 1973-24 Nov 1988 – 15r – 1 – us Western Res [071]
Bedford-Jones, T *see*
- THE CHARITY THAT COVERS A MULTITUDE OF SINS: A SERMON PREACHED ON SUNDAY, FEBRUARY 23RD, 1879,..., IN THE CHURCH OF ST ALBAN, THE MARTYR, OTTAWA
- NEW YEAR'S SERMON, LORD, WHAT WILT THOU HAVE ME TO DO?: ...CHURCH OF ST ALBAN, THE MARTYR, OTTAWA, SUNDAY, JANUARY 2, 1881

BEDFORD-SACKVILLE NEWS – Halifax, No1983-1984Oc – 1r – 1 – cn Preston [971]
BEDFORDSHIRE, 1823 : BRITISH ISLES CENSUS DIRECTORIES PROJECT, ENGLAND. VOL 238 – 1mf – 9 – A$9.00 – at Vine [941]
BEDFORDSHIRE, 1830 : BRITSH ISLES CENSUS DIRECTORIES PROJECT, ENGLAND – at Vine [941]
BEDFORDSHIRE, 1839 : BRITISH ISLES CENSUS DIRECTORIES PROJECT, ENGLAND. VOL 18 – 2mf – 9 – A$15.00 – at Vine [941]
BEDFORDSHIRE, 1850 : BRITISH ISLES CENSUS DIRECTORIES PROJECT, ENGLAND. VOL 40 – 1mf – 9 – A$9.00 – at Vine [941]
BEDFORDSHIRE, 1864 : BRITISH ISLES CENSUS DIRECTORIES PROJECT, ENGLAND. VOL 123 – 4mf – 9 – A$27.00 – at Vine [941]
BEDFORDSHIRE, 1877 : BRITISH ISLES CENSUS DIRECTORIES PROJECT, ENGLAND – at Vine [941]
BEDFORDSHIRE, 1894 : BRITISH ISLES CENSUS DIRECTORIES PROJECT, ENGLAND. VOL 29 – 4mf – 9 – A$27.00 – at Vine [941]
BEDFORDSHIRE, 1898 : BRITISH ISLES CENSUS DIRECTORIES PROJECT, ENGLAND. VOL 74 – 4mf – 9 – A$27.00 – at Vine [941]
BEDFORDSHIRE ADVERTISER *see* LUTON TIMES ETC
BEDFORDSHIRE HISTORICAL RECORD SOCIETY – (Coll title: Publications of the English Record Societies, 1835-72...) – v1-46. 1913-67 – 133mf – 9 – £840.00 – uk Chadwyck [941]
Bedier, Joseph *see* LES CHANSONS DE COLIN MUSET
Bedingfield, Christopher *see* ABSTRACT BY...OF COKE ESTATE DEEDS
Bedjan, Paul *see* LE LIVRE D'HERACLIDE DE DAMAS
Bedjaoui, Mohammed *see*
- INTERNATIONAL LAW
- TOWARDS A NEW INTERNATIONAL ECONOMIC ORDER

BEDMINSTER KNOWLE & BRISLINGTON RECORD – (South Birmingham News. 1889-92) – Bristol, England. Jun 1909-Jan 1931. -w – 8r – 1 – uk British Libr Newspaper [072]
Bednarczyk, Janet H *see* THE EFFECT OF MASS ON THE KINEMATICS OF STEADY STATE WHEELCHAIR PROPULSION IN ADULTS AND CHILDREN WITH SPINAL CORD INJURY
Bednyi, Demian *see*
- BEZ OTKAZU
- PO KONIU I PO OGLOBLIAM
- PROZEMLIU, PRO VOLIU, PRO RABOCHUIU DOLIU
- VKLAD

Bedos de Celles, F *see* L'ART DU FACTEUR D'ORGUES
Bedoya, Juan Manuel *see* ORACION FUNEBRE
BEDRIFTS/OKONOMEN – (1975- . 5,6,9) – 1938- – 1 – us UMI [330]
BEDROCK DEMOCRAT – Baker City, OR. -w. 18 May 1870-11 Oct 1897. 6 rolls – 1 – us U.O. Library [071]
DIE BEDUDINGHE NADEN SINNE VAN SUNTE AUGUSTIJNS REGULE / ed by Flou, Karel de – Gent, 1901 – 6mf – 8 – Dfl25.00 – ne Slangenburg [240]
Bedwell, Cyril E A *see* A BRIEF HISTORY OF THE MIDDLE TEMPLE
BEDWORTH ECHO – England, Sep 1979- – 29+ r – 1 – uk British Libr Newspaper [072]
BEDWORTH NEWS – (Bedworth and Foleshill News). England. -w. 1957-65. (6 reels) – 1 – uk British Libr Newspaper [072]
Bedworth, Thomas *see* THE POWER OF CONSCIENCE EXEMPLIFIED IN THE GENUINE AND EXTRAORDINARY CONFESSION OF THOMAS BEDWORTH.
BEDWORTH TIMES – Bedworth, England. -w. 16 Jan 1875-5 Feb 1876. 35 ft – 1 – uk British Libr Newspaper [072]
BEE – (1975-. 5,6,9) – Bulletin of Environmental Education. v. 1-. 1971- – 1 – us UMI [580]
BEE – Canastota. N.Y. 1903-1921 – 1 – us UMI [071]
BEE – Chehalis. Wash. -w, sw. 1884-98 – 1 – us UMI [071]
BEE – Danville. Va. 1922- – 1 – us UMI [071]
BEE – New Orleans. La. 1827-1923 – 1 – us UMI [071]
BEE – (Set incl. Sellwood-Mooreland Bee) – Portland, OR. -w. 21 Feb 1952-30 Dec 1976+. – 1 – us U.O. Library [071]
BEE – South Riverside, CA. 1887-96 – 1 – us UMI [071]
BEE – Toledo. Ohio. 1899-1903 – 1 – us UMI [071]
BEE – Tygh Valley, OR. -w. 19 apr 1906-16 May 1907. 1 roll – 1 – us U.O. Library [071]
THE BEE – (Cont by: Mechanic and Farmer) – [Pictou, N.S.?]: J. Dawson, 1836-1838 – 9 – cn C.I.H.M. [630]
THE BEE – Hillsburg [Ont.]: G.A. Lacey, [1881-18–?] – 9 – cn C.I.H.M. [073]
THE BEE – Jefferson. Iowa. -w. 1951-71 – 1 – us UMI [071]
BEE GEE NEWS – Bowling Green, Ohio. 1920-51 – 6r – 1 – $32.50r – us Archival [071]
BEE JOURNAL – Canastota. N.Y. -w. 1921-26; 1966- – 1 – us UMI [071]
BEE NEWS – Omaha. Neb. (evening). 1872-92 – 1 – us UMI [071]
BEE NEWS – Omaha. Neb. (morning). 1930-37 – 1 – us UMI [071]
BEE NUGGET – Chehalis. Wash. -w. 1898-1938 – 1 – us UMI [071]
Bee Publishing Co *see* NEBRASKANS 1854-1904
Bee, T *see* BEE'S REPORTS OF CASES IN THE DISTRICT COURT OF SOUTH CAROLINA, 1792-1805
Beebe *see* HISTORY OF SULLIVAN COUNTY
BEECH BRANCH BAPTIST CHURCH. LURAY, SOUTH CAROLINA : CHURCH RECORDS – 1918-75 – 1 – 5.31 – us Baptist [240]
BEECH ISLAND BAPTIST CHURCH. AIKEN COUNTY. SOUTH CAROLINA : CHURCH RECORDS – 1953-67 – 1 – 10.62 – us Baptist [240]
Beech, Mervyn Worcester Howard *see* THE SUK
Beecham, J *see* ASHANTEE AND THE GOLD COAST
Beecher, C E *see* STUDIES IN EVOLUTION
Beecher, Charles *see*
- EDEN TABLEAU, OR, BIBLE OBJECT-TEACHING
- THE EDEN TABLEAU, OR, BIBLE OBJECT-TEACHING
- THE METRONOME: OR MUSIC-TEACHER'S ASSISTANT

Beecher, Edward *see*
- BAPTISM
- THE CONFLICT OF AGES: OR, THE GREAT DEBATE ON THE MORAL RELATIONS OF GOD AND MAN
- THE PAPAL CONSPIRACY EXPOSED, AND PROTESTANTISM DEFENDED, IN THE LIGHT OF REASON, HISTORY, AND SCRIPTURE

Beecher, Henry Ward *see*
- BIBLE STUDIES
- A CONCORDANCE TO THE PLYMOUTH COLLECTION OF HYMNS AND TUNES
- EVOLUTION AND RELIGION
- THE LIFE OF JESUS THE CHRIST
- LIFE OF JESUS THE CHRIST
- OVERTURE OF ANGELS
- PATRIOTIC ADDRESSES
- REPORT OF A SERMON...CHARLOTTETOWN, SABBATH MORNING, AUG. 10TH, 1879
- TWELVE LECTURES TO YOUNG MEN, ON VARIOUS IMPORTANT SUBJECTS

Beecher, Lyman *see*
- AUTOBIOGRAPHY, CORRESPONDENCE, ETC., OF LYMAN BEECHER, D.D
- THE FAITH ONCE DELIVERED TO THE SAINTS: A SERMON, DELIVERED AT WORCESTER, MASS., 15 OCT. 1823
- LECTURES ON POLITICAL ATHEISM AND KINDRED SUBJECTS
- LETTERS OF THE REV. DR. BEECHER AND REV. MR. NETTLETON ON THE "NEW MEASURES" IN CONDUCTING REVIVALS OF RELIGION
- SERMONS
- VIEWS OF THEOLOGY

Beecher, Willis Judson *see*
- THE DATED EVENTS OF THE OLD TESTAMENT
- DATED EVENTS OF THE OLD TESTAMENT
- FARMER TOMKINS AND HIS BIBLES
- INDEX OF THE PRESBYTERIAN MINISTERS
- PROPHETS AND THE PROMISE
- THE TEACHING OF JESUS CONCERNING THE FUTURE LIFE
- TEACHING OF JESUS CONCERNING THE FUTURE LIFE

Beechey, Frederick William *see*
- NARRATIVE OF A VOYAGE TO THE PACIFIC AND BERING'S STRAIT
- A VOYAGE OF DISCOVERY TOWARDS THE NORTH POLE...IN HIS MAJESTY'S SHIPS DOROTHEA AND TRENT, UNDER THE COMMAND OF CAPTAIN DAVID BUCHAN, R.N., 1818..

BEECHMONT BAPTIST CHURCH. LOUISVILLE, KENTUCKY : CHURCH RECORDS – 7May 1911-69 – 1 – 58.41 – us Baptist [240]
BEECHRIDGE BAPTIST CHURCH. HATTON, KENTUCKY : CHURCH RECORDS – Feb 1914-Oct 1940 – 1 – 9.72 – us Baptist [240]
Beechwood Cemetery Company. Ottawa, Ont *see* BY-LAWS, RULES AND REGULATIONS..
BEE-DEMOCRAT – (Cont by: San Bruno Herald) – Brisbane, CA. Sep 1961-1980 – 16r – 1 – $800.00 – B02078 – us Library Micro [071]
BEEF – (1985- 1,5,6) – v19- 1982- – 9 – us UMI [640]
BEEF CATTLE DAY (PROCEEDINGS) / Washington. Agricultural College Experiment Station. Dep't. of Animal Science – nos.1-12. 1955-69 – 1,5,6 – us Spaulding [636]
BEEF CATTLE PRODUCTION FROM TROPICAL PASTURES : A DESCRIPTIVE BIBLIOGRAPHY / Butterworth, MH et al – 1985 – 9 – $20.00 – 92-9053-151-7 – et ILRI [636]
THE BEE-HIVE – London: Publ by George Potter for the Trades' Newspaper Co, jul 4-dec 1868; 1869-76 – us Res Libr [072]
THE BEE-HIVE – (The Penny Bee-Hive The Industrial Review, Social and Political). London. -w. Oct 1862-Dec 1878. (16 reels) – 1 – uk British Libr Newspaper [330]
THE BEEHIVE – 1862-1878 – 1 – uk Microform Academic [072]
THE BEEHIVE – Toronto: Pub. for the Proprietor by Rogers & Larminie, v1 no 1 (Sept – 9 26, 1874)- – cn C.I.H.M. [072]
THE BEE-HIVE NEWSPAPER – London: Publ by George Potter for the Trades' Newspaper Co, jan 1863-jun 1868 – us Res Libr [072]
Beehler, William Henry *see* THE CRUISE OF THE BROOKLYN. A JOURNAL OF THE PRINCIPAL EVENTS OF A THREE YEARS' CRUISE...IN THE SOUTH ATLANTIC STATION
BEEKEEPING IN AFRICA – 1990 – 140p – it F.A.O. [636]
BEEKEEPING IN ASIA – 1987 – 121p – it F.A.O. [636]
Beekers, L M *see* HUWELIJKEN VAN NEDERLANDERS IN HET BUITENLAND...
Beekman, A A *see* NEDERLANDSCH OF BELGISCH?
BEELD – Johannesburg, South Africa. 16 Sept. 1974- – 1 – sa Microfile [960]
Beemer, J J *see* LETTER FROM THE PRESIDENT, PONTIAC PACIFIC JUNCTION RAILWAY CO., OTTAWA, DEC. 15TH, 1893
BEEMER TIMES – Beemer, NE. -w. Mar. 1886-Sep. 1902. Incomplete; Jan. 1906-Jun. 1911. Incomplete; Aug. 1911-Aug. 1918; Jan. 1920-Jan. 1947 – 1 – us NE Hist [071]
BEE-MORNING – Modesto, CA. 1936-38 – 9r – 1 – $450.00 – B02468 – us Library Micro [071]

Beer, A *see*
- AUFZEICHNUNGEN DES GRAFEN WILLIAM BENTINCK UEBER MARIA THERESIA
- LEOPOLD 2, FRANZ 2 UND CATHARINA

Beer, Bernhard *see* LEBEN MOSES

Beer, Georg *see* DER TEXT DES BUCHES HIOB: ERSTES HEFT-KAPITEL I-XIV

Beer, J B *see* MUSICALISCHE DISCURZE DURCH DIE PRINCIPIA DEDUCIRT, UND IN GEWISSE CAPITEL EINGETHEILT

Beer, M *see* THE LEAGUE ON TRIAL

BE'ER MOSHEH – Prague. 1604-05. Cowley. BJ-43-4 1 – 9 – ne IDC [270]

BE'ER MOSHEH – Prague. 1612. BJ-43-5 1 – 9 – ne IDC [270]

Beer, Oskar *see* HEBBELS JUDITH UND MARIA MAGDALENA IM URTEIL SEINER ZEITGENOSSEN

Beer Poortugael, J C C den *see*
- L'ESCAUT ET LA NEUTRALITE PERMANENTE DE LA BELGIQUE...
- HET INTERNATIONAAL MARITIEM RECHT
- LA NEUTRALITE SUR L'ESCAUT

Beer, Sir Gavin de *see* VOLTAIRE'S BRITISH VISITORS

Beer-Hofmann, Richard *see* DER GRAF VON CHAROLAIS

Beers, F W *see* GAZETTEER AND BIOGRAPHICAL RECORD OF GENESEE COUNTY 1788-1890

BEERS, F.W. AND CO *see*
- HISTORY OF HERKIMER COUNTY
- HISTORY OF MONTGOMERY AND FULTON COUNTIES
- HISTORY OF WYOMING COUNTY

BEERS, J.B. AND CO *see* HISTORY OF GREENE COUNTY

BEERS, J.H. AND CO *see*
- ARMSTRONG COUNTY: HER PEOPLE PAST AND PRESENT
- BIOGRAPHICAL ANNALS OF LANCASTER COUNTY
- BIOGRAPHICAL ANNALS OF LEBANON COUNTY
- BIOGRAPHICAL MEMOIRS OF GRATIOT COUNTY
- COMMEMORATIVE BIOGRAPHICAL RECORD OF CENTRE, CLINTON, UNION AND SNYDER COUNTIES
- COMMEMORATIVE BIOGRAPHICAL RECORD OF DUTCHESS COUNTY
- COMMEMORATIVE BIOGRAPHICAL RECORD OF HARTFORD COUNTY, CONNECTICUT
- COMMEMORATIVE BIOGRAPHICAL RECORD OF NORTHEASTERN PENNSYLVANIA
- COMMEMORATIVE BIOGRAPHICAL RECORD OF ROCK, GREEN, GRANT, IOWA AND LAFAYETTE COUNTIES
- COMMEMORATIVE BIOGRAPHICAL RECORD OF THE COUNTIES OF SANDUSKY AND OTTAWA
- COMMEMORATIVE BIOGRAPHICAL RECORD OF THE UPPER LAKE REGION
- COMMEMORATIVE BIOGRAPHICAL RECORD OF THE UPPER WISCONSIN
- COMMEMORATIVE BIOGRAPHICAL RECORD OF THE WEST SHORE OF GREEN BAY
- COMMEMORATIVE BIOGRAPHICAL RECORD OF WASHINGTON COUNTY
- COMMEMORATIVE BIOGRAPHICAL RECORD OF WAYNE AND HOLMES COUNTIES
- COMMEMORATIVE BIOGRAPHICAL RECORDS OF THE COUNTIES OF HURON AND LORAIN
- COMMEMORATIVE BIOGRAPHICAL RECORDS OF ULSTER COUNTY
- COMMEMORATIVE HISTORICAL AND BIOGRAPHICAL RECORD OF WOOD COUNTY
- GENEALOGICAL AND BIOGRAPHICAL RECORD OF NEW LONDON COUNTY, CONNECTICUT
- GENEALOGICAL FAMILY HISTORY OF AND BIOGRAPHY OF SCHUYLKILL COUNTY
- HISTORY OF BERKSHIRE COUNTY
- HISTORY OF HARRISON AND CARROLL COUNTIES
- HISTORY OF MCKEAN, ELK, CAMERON AND POTTER COUNTIES
- HISTORY OF THE GREAT LAKES
- UPPER LAKE REGION

Beers, Leggett and Co *see*
- COMMEMORATIVE BIOGRAPHICAL AND HISTORICAL RECORD OF KANE COUNTY
- PORTRAIT AND BIOGRAPHICAL RECORD OF KANE AND KENDALL COUNTIES

BEERS, W.H. AND CO *see*
- HISTORY OF BROWN COUNTY
- HISTORY OF CHAMPAIGN COUNTY
- HISTORY OF CLARK COUNTY
- HISTORY OF CLINTON COUNTY
- HISTORY OF DARKE COUNTY
- HISTORY OF MADISON COUNTY
- HISTORY OF MIAMI COUNTY
- HISTORY OF MONTGOMERY COUNTY
- HISTORY OF WARREN COUNTY

Beers, William George *see*
- ANNUAL MEETING OF THE ROYAL COLLEGE OF DENTAL SURGEONS, ONTARIO: ADDRESS
- LACROSSE: THE NATIONAL GAME OF CANADA
- OVER THE SNOW, OR, THE MONTREAL CARNIVAL
- PATRIOTIC SPEECH: IN REPLY TO THE TOAST OF PROFESSIONAL ANNEXATION BEFORE THE DENTAL SOCIETIES OF THE STATE OF NEW YORK AT SYRACUSE, NY ON OCTOBER 25, 1888
- YOUNG CANADA'S REPLY TO ANNEXATION

Beery, Lawrence A *see*
- FIELD TRIP TO WEST BORNEO, FEB. 20 MAR. 7, 1959
- SMALLHOLDER RUBBER IN INDONESIA

BEE'S REPORTS OF CASES IN THE DISTRICT COURT OF SOUTH CAROLINA, 1792-1805 / Bee, T – Philadelphia: Farrand. 1v. 1810 (all publ) – 6mf – 9 – $9.00 – LLMC 81-431 – us L.L.M.C. [340]

Beesly, Augustus Henry *see* SIR JOHN FRANKLIN

Beeson, Luana J *see* HEALTH KNOWLEDGE COMPETENCIES AND ESSENTIAL HEALTH SKILLS OF ENTRY LEVEL COLLEGE FRESHMEN ENROLLED IN OREGON'S RESEARCH UNIVERSITIES

Beet, Joseph Agar *see*
- A COMMENTARY ON ST PAUL'S EPISTLE TO THE GALATIANS
- A COMMENTARY ON ST PAUL'S EPISTLE TO THE ROMANS
- A COMMENTARY ON ST PAUL'S EPISTLES TO THE EPHESIANS, PHILIPPIANS, COLOSSIANS, AND TO PHILEMON
- THE CREDENTIALS OF THE GOSPEL
- THE FIRM FOUNDATION OF THE CHRISTIAN FAITH
- HOLINESS: AS UNDERSTOOD BY THE WRITERS OF THE BIBLE
- HOLINESS SYMBOLIC AND REAL
- THE IMMORTALITY OF THE SOUL
- NATURE AND CHRIST
- NEW TESTAMENT: ITS AUTHORSHIP, DATE AND WORTH
- A SHORTER MANUAL OF THEOLOGY
- THROUGH CHRIST TO GOD

Beet, William Ernest *see*
- THE EARLY ROMAN EPISCOPATE TO A.D. 384
- THE MEDIEVAL PAPACY

Beethoven, Ludwig van *see*
- MISSA SOLEMNIS, OP. 132. [SKETCHES OF PORTIONS OF "QUONIAM TU SOLUS SANCTUS" PARTICULARLY "IN GLORIA DEI PATRIS, AMEN."
- WERKE

BEETHOVEN. SUGESTIONES / Hindos, Jose de – Ensayo intimo.Caceres.Imp.Mod. 1927 – 1 – sp Bibl Santa Ana [780]

BEETHOVEN, TEOSOFO, UN CAPITULO DE LA OBRA EL...DRAMA LIRICO DE... / Roso de Luna, Mario – Pontevedra: Tip. Vda. e Hijos de Antunez, 1915 – 1 – sp Bibl Santa Ana [780]

BEETHOVEN-FORSCHUNG – Wien, 1911-1925. v1-10 – 5mf – 9 – P-563/1 – ne IDC [780]

BEETHOVENJAHRBUCH – Muenchen, 1908-1909. v1-2 – 8mf – 9 – P-564/1 – ne IDC [780]

DER BEFEHL DES GEWISSENS : EIN ROMAN VON DEN WIRREN DER NACHKRIEGSZEIT UND DER ERSTEN ERHEBUNG / Zoeberlein, Hans – 17. Aufl. Muenchen: Zentralverlag der NSDAP, F Eher, c1937 – 1 – us U.W. Library [830]

BEFEHL IST BEFEHL : ERZAEHLUNGEN / Klucke, Walther Gottfried – Berlin: Bong, 1941 – 1r – 1 – us U.W. Library [830]

LE BEFFROI : Art et litterature modernes Dir. Leon Bocquet. no. 64-104. Roubaix. avr mai 1906-sept oct 1913 – 1 – fr A.C.R.P.P. [800]

LE BEFFROI : ARTS, HERALDIQUE, ARCHEOLOGIE – Bruges, 1863-1876. v1-4 – 28mf – 9 – O-1216/1 – ne IDC [700]

BEFINDLICHKEITSVERAENDERUNGEN DURCH MUSIK : EIN VERGLEICH ZWISCHEN PSYCHOTISCH KRANKEN UND PSYCHISCH GESUNDEN / Leuwer, Martin – 1995 – 2mf – 9 – DM80.00 – 3-8267-2190-X – gw Hänsel [616]

BEFOLKNING I OLDTIDEN – 1936 – 1 – us I.U. Libraries [390]

BEFOLKNING UNDER MEDELTIDEN – 1938 – 1 – us I.U. Libraries [390]

BEFORE THE COMING OF THE LOYALISTS / Haight, Canniff – Toronto: Haight, 1897. 05145. (Pre-1900 Canadiana) – 9 – cn C.I.H.M. [971]

BEFORE THE GREAT PILLAGE : WITH OTHER MISCELLANIES / Jessopp, Augustus – London: T.F. Unwin, 1901 – 1mf – us A.T.L.A. [240]

BEFORE THE MAST AND BEHIND THE PULPIT / Allan, Alexander M – 1 – us A.T.L.A. [240]

BEFORE THE MILITARY COMMISSION CONVENED BY THE COMMANDING GENERAL, UNITED STATES ARMY FORCES, WESTERN PACIFIC. PROCEEDINGS / Yamashita, Tomoyuki – (Exhibits. Manila. On film: v1-4, 1945. LL-030. 1) – Manila. On film: v1-34, 1945. LL-030 – 1 – us L of C Photodup [340]

Beg, Leskofceli Galib *see* DIVAN

Begaks, A I *see* PRAKTIKA ARBITRAZHNOI KOMISSII VSNKH SSSR I RSFSR

BEGEGNUNG – (Some pgs missing) – v70-100. 1982-87/88 – 1r – 1 – ATLA S0873 – us A.T.L.A. [073]

DIE BEGEGNUNG AUF DEM RIESENGEBIRGE : NOVELLE / Kolbenheyer, Erwin Guido – Muenchen: A Langen/G Mueller, 1934, c1932 – 1r – 1 – us U.W. Library [830]

BEGEGNUNGEN MIT MENSCHEN, BUECHERN, STAEDTEN / Zweig, Stefan – Wien: H Reichner, c1937 – 1r – 1 – us U.W. Library [430]

BEGEGNUNGEN UND WUERDIGUNGEN : LITERARISCHE PORTRAETS VON CARL SPITTELER BIS KLAUS MANN / ed by Goldammer, Peter – (Includes bibliographical references) – Rostock: Hinstorff, 1984 – 1r – 1 – us U.W. Library [430]

Beger, Kai-Uwe *see* ZUR GESELLSCHAFTLICHEN PRODUKTION VON ARMUT

Begg, Alexander *see* NOTES ON VANCOUVER ISLAND

BEGG AND LYNCH'S HAND-BOOK AND GENERAL GUIDE TO BRITISH COLUMBIA – (Cont by: Begg's Monthly and General Guide to British Columbia) – Victoria, B.C. Guide Pub Co, [1893] – 9 – cn C.I.H.M. [910]

LES BEGGARA DU ZOR / Naffakh, R – Societe traditionnelle. Changements techno-economiques et sociaux – 9 – F70.00 – fr Ethnologie [305]

THE BEGGARS OF HOLLAND AND THE GRANDEES OF SPAIN : A HISTORY OF THE REFORMATION IN THE NETHERLANDS, FROM A.D. 1200 TO 1578 / Mears, John – Philadelphia: Presbyterian Publication Committee, c1867 – 2mf – us A.T.L.A. [240]

THE BEGGAR'S OPERA / Pepusch, J C – With the additional alterations by Dr. Arne. 181-? – 9 – us Sibley [780]

THE BEGGERS APE / Niccols, Richard – 1627 – 9 – 5.00 – us Scholars' Facs [810]

BEGG'S MONTHLY AND GENERAL GUIDE TO BRITISH COLUMBIA – (Cont by: Hand-book to British Columbia) – Victoria, B.C: A. Begg, v1 no 4 (July 1893)- – 9 – cn C.I.H.M. [910]

Begin, Louis Nazaire *see*
- CHRONOLOGIE DE L'HISTOIRE DES ETATS UNIS D'AMERIQUE
- CHRONOLOGIE DE L'HISTOIRE DU CANADA
- LE CULTE CATHOLIQUE, OU, EXPOSITION DE LA FOI DE L'EGLISE ROMAINE:..
- LA PRIMAUTE ET L'INFAILLIBILITE DES SOUVERAINS PONTIFES: LECONS D'HISTOIRE DONNEES A L'UNIVERSITE LAVAL
- LA SAINTE ECRITURE ET LA REGLE DE FOI

BEGINILAH TJARA BERISTERI / Abbas, Hassan – SE-5323 1. 1965 – 9 – ne IDC [950]

A BEGINNER: A NOVEL / Broughton, Rhoda – British Fiction Archive: Unit 4 – 9 – uk Bell [830]

BEGINNER TEACHER – Nashville. Tenn. 1931-62 – 1 – 254.73 – us Baptist [240]

BEGINNER TEACHER AND PUPIL BOOK, YEARS 1-2 – 1928, 1928-33; Better Home. 1935-46 – 1 – 57.68 – us Baptist [240]

THE BEGINNERS OF A NATION : A HISTORY OF THE SOURCE AND RISE OF THE EARLIEST ENGLISH SETTLEMENTS IN AMERICA, WITH SPECIAL REFERENCE TO THE LIFE AND CHARACTER OF THE PEOPLE / Eggleston, Edward – New York: D. Appleton, 1896 – 1mf – us A.T.L.A. [971]

BEGINNING AT JERUSALEM : STUDIES IN HISTORIC COMMUNIONS OF CHRISTENDOM / Lacey, Thomas James – New York: Edwin S Gorham, c1909 – 1mf – 9 – 0-8370-8687-6 – 1986-2687 – us A.T.L.A. [240]

BEGINNING SOMALI HISTORY / Gilbert, Paul S ET A L – Afgoi: National Teacher Educ Center Press, 1967 – us Res Libr [960]

THE BEGINNINGS OF CHRISTIANITY: WITH A VIEW OF THE STATE OF THE ROMAN WORLD AT THE BIRTH OF CHRIST / Fisher, George Park – 1901 – 9 – us A.T.L.A. [240]

THE BEGINNINGS OF ENGLISH CHRISTIANITY : WITH SPECIAL REFERENCE TO THE COMING OF ST. AUGUSTINE / Collins, William Edward – London: Methuen, 1898. (The Churchman's library) – 1mf – us A.T.L.A. [240]

THE BEGINNINGS OF ENGLISH UTILITARIANISM / Albee, Ernest – Boston: Ginn, 1897. iv,101p – 1 – us U.W. Library [320]

THE BEGINNINGS OF GNOSTIC CHRISTIANITY / Rylands, Louis Gordon – London: Watts, 1940. viii,300p – 1 – us U.W. Library [240]

THE BEGINNINGS OF HISTORY ACCORDING TO THE BIBLE AND THE TRADITIONS OF ORIENTAL PEOPLES = ORIGINES DE L'HISTOIRE D'APRES LA BIBLE ET LES TRADITIONS DES PEUPLES ORIENTAUX : FROM THE CREATION OF MAN TO THE DELUGE / Lonormant, Francois – (In English. Includes bibliographical references) – New York: Charles Scribner, 1883, c1881 – 2mf – 9 – 0-8370-6995-5 – 1986-0995 – us A.T.L.A. [930]

THE BEGINNINGS OF LIBRARIES / Richardson, Ernest Cushing – Princeton: Princeton University Press, 1914 – 1mf – us A.T.L.A. [020]

THE BEGINNINGS OF QUAKERISM / Braithwaite, William C – London: Macmillan, 1912 – 2mf – us A.T.L.A. [240]

THE BEGINNINGS OF THE TEMPORAL SOVEREIGNTY OF THE POPES, A.D. 754-1073 / Cuchesne, L – London: Kegan Paul, Trench, Truebner, 1908. (The International Catholic library; v11) – 1mf – us A.T.L.A. [240]

THE BEGINNINGS OF THE WESLEYAN MOVEMENT IN AMERICA AND THE ESTABLISHMENT THEREIN OF METHODISM / Atkinson, John – New York: Hunt & Eaton, Cincinnati: Cranston & Curts, 1896 – 2mf – us A.T.L.A. [240]

BEGINNINGS OF VIJAYANAGARA HISTORY / Heras, H – Bombay, 1929; Madrid: Razon y Fe, 1931 – 1 – sp Bibl Santa Ana [950]

DE BEGINSELEN VAN GODS KONINGKRYK IN DEN MENSCH / Huygen, P – O-644 1. 1690 – 9 – ne IDC [240]

DE BEGINSELEN VAN GODS KONINKRYK IN DEN MENSCH : UYTGEDRUKT IN VERSCHEIDE ZINNE-BEELDEN, ALS MEDE EEN ALLEENSPRAAKE MET GOD, BENEVENS EENIGE STIGTELYKE RYMEN, DOOR PIETER EN JAN HUYGEN / Huygen P & Huygen, J – Amsterdam, 1738 – 5mf – 9 – O-3233/1 – ne IDC [760]

BEGONIACEEN-GATTUNGEN UND ARTEN / Klotzsch, J F – (Abh. der konigl. Akad. der Wissenschaften zu Berlin. 1854). Berlin. 1854. B-7103 1 – 9 – ne IDC [580]

DIE BEGONIEN. IHRE BESCHREIBUNG, KULTUR, ZUCHTUNG UND GESCHICHTE / Fotsch, K A – Stuttgart. 1933. B-1062 2 – 8 – ne IDC [580]

DIE BEGRAEBNISARTEN DER AMERIKANER UND NORDOSTASIATEN / Preuss, Th – BN 352. 2. 1894 – 8 – ne IDC [306]

DER BEGRIFF DER BEKEHRUNG : IM LICHTE DER HEILIGEN SCHRIFT, DER KIRCHENGESCHICHTE UND DER FORDERUNGEN DES HEUTIGEN LEBENS: EINE UNTERSUCHUNG / Herzog, Johannes – (Includes bibliographical references) – Giessen: J Ricker (Alfred Toepelmann), 1903 – 1mf – 9 – 0-8370-4883-4 – 1985-2883 – us A.T.L.A. [240]

DER BEGRIFF DER HEILIGKEIT IM NEUEN TESTAMENT : EINE VON DER HAAGER GESELLSCHAFT ZUR VERTEIDIGUNG DER CHRISTLICHEN RELIGION GEKROENTE PREISSCHRIFT / Issel, Ernst – (Includes bibliographical references and list of biblical passages cited) – Leiden: E J Brill, 1887 – 1mf – 9 – 0-8370-3733-6 – 1985-1733 – us A.T.L.A. [220]

DER BEGRIFF DES BETRIEBES / Lostorf, Edmund Willi – Bern, 1938 – 1 – DM30.00 – gw Mikro Press [650]

DER BEGRIFF DES KUNSTWERKS IN GOETHES AUFSATZ VON DEUTSCHER BAUKUNST (1772) UND IN SCHILLERS AESTHETIK : VORTRAG GEHALTEN AUF DER 46. VERSAMMLUNG DEUTSCHER PHILOLOGEN UND SCHULMAENNER ZU STRASSBURG I.E. / Gneisse, Karl – Strassburg: Heitz, 1901 – 1r – 1 – us U.W. Library [430]

DER BEGRIFF DES VOLKSGEISTES IN ERNST MORITZ ARNDTS GESCHICHTSANSCHAUUNG : EIN BEITRAG ZUR GESCHICHTE DER GESCHICHTSWISSENSCHAFT VORGELEGT VON RUDOLF KRUEGEL / Kruegel, Rudolf – (Includes vita) – Langensalza: H Beyer, 1914 – 1r – 1 – us U.W. Library [943]

DER BEGRIFF "EDEL" BEI GOETHE / Liederwald, Carl – Greifswald, 1913 – 1mf – DM48.00 – 3-8267-3082-8 – gw Hänsel [430]

DER BEGRIFF KLASSISCH BEI HERDER / Oelsner, Werner – (Includes bibliographical references) – Wuerzburg: K Triltsch, 1939 – 1r – 1 – us U.W. Library [430]

BEGRIFF UND AUFGABE DER DOGMENGESCHICHTE / Haase, Felix – Breslau: Goerlich & Coch, 1911 – 1mf – us A.T.L.A. [240]

BEGRIFF UND BEDEUTUNG DER GEBIETSHOHEIT / Guenther, W W – Heidelberg, 1899 – 1mf – 1 – ILM-1/1 – ne IDC [327]

DIE BEGRIFFE GEIST UND LEBEN BEI PAULUS : IN IHREN BEZIEHUNGEN ZU EINANDER: EINE EXEGETISCH-RELIGIONSGESCHICHTLICHE UNTERSUCHUNG / Sokolowski, Emil – (Includes bibliographical references and index) – Goettingen: Vandenhoeck & Ruprecht, 1903 – 1mf – 9 – 0-8370-6410-4 – 1986-0410 – us A.T.L.A. [220]

BEGROOTING VAN DE GEWONE EN BUITENGEWONE UITGAVEN EN ONTVANGSTEN VAN DE GEMEENTE MEDAN – (Lacking: 1926; 1928) – 1916-1940 – 54mf – 9 – ne IDC [950]

BEGROOTING VAN DE STADSGEMEENTE PEMATANGSIANTAR – 1923-1925, 1932, 1934-1938, 1940 – 40mf – 9 – ne IDC [950]

BEGROOTING VAN NEDERLANDSCH INDIE. INDISCH ONTWERP – Batavia, 1912-1920 – 119mf – 9 – ne IDC [950]

BEGROOTING VOOR DEN DIENST VOOR DE GEMEENTE TANDJOENGBALAI – Medan, 1925, 1930-1932 – 4mf – 9 – ne IDC [950]

DIE BEGRUENDUNG UNSERER SITTLICH-RELIGIOESEN UEBERZEUGUNG / Koestlin, Julius – Berlin: Reuther & Reichard, 1893 – 1mf – 9 – 0-8370-3981-9 – 1985-1981 – us A.T.L.A. [240]

Beguin, Albert *see* L'AME ROMANTIQUE ET LE REVE

Beguin, P *see* THESAURUS FRATRIS SALIMBENE DE ADAM

Beguinot, Francesco *see* IL BERBERO NEFUSI DI FASSATO

Behagel, W *see* DIE EHELICHEN GUETERVERHAELTNISSE DER AUSLAENDER, ...

Behagle, Ferdinand de *see* AU PAYS DE L'ESCLAVAGE

Behamb, J F *see* ARGUTIAE JURIS CIVILIS THEORETICAE

DIE BEHANDLUNG DES SITTLICHEN PROBLEMS IN SCHILLERS "KAMPF MIT DEM DRACHEN", DER ERZAEHLUNG BEI LIVIUS 8, 7, KLEISTS "PRINZ VON HOMBURG" UND SOPHOKLES' "ANTIGONE" / Seiler, Friedrich – (Includes bibliographical references) – Eisenberg: P Kaltenbach, 1890 – 1r – 1 – us U.W. Library [430]

BEHAR PROVERBS / Christian, John – 1891 – 1 – us I.U. Libraries [390]

BEHAUPTUNG DER HIMMLISCHEN MUSIK AUS DEN GRUENDEN DER VERNUNFT, KIRCHEN-LEHRE UND HEILGEN SCHRIFT / Mattheson, J – 1747 – 9 – us Sibley [780]

BEHAVIOR – v.14-21, 1959-63; v.23-40, 1964-71; v.44-66, n.1,2 1973-78 – 1,5,6 – 22242.00 – us Princeton Micro [150]

BEHAVIOR GENETICS – v1-24. 1970-94 – 1,5 – $100.00v – us UMI [573]

BEHAVIOR MODIFICATION – (1983-. 1,5,6,9) – v1-. 1977- – 1 – us UMI [073]

BEHAVIOR RESEARCH AND THERAPY – v.1-. 1963- – 5,6,9 – us UMI [073]

BEHAVIORAL AND SOCIAL SCIENCE TEACHER – v. 1-2. 1973-74 – 1 – us UMI [300]

BEHAVIORAL AND SOCIAL SCIENCES LIBRARIAN / ed by Lonergan, David – v1- 1979- – 1, 9 ($90.00 in US $126.00 outside hardcopy subsc) – us Haworth [020]

BEHAVIORAL ASSESSMENT – v1- 1979- – 5,6,9 – us UMI [150]

BEHAVIORAL BRAIN PROCESSES – v1-9. 1976-84 – 1,5,6,13 – sz Elsevier [073]

BEHAVIORAL BRAIN RESEARCH – v1-14. 1980-84 – . 1.5,6,13 – sz Elsevier [073]

BEHAVIORAL COUNSELING QUARTERLY – 1980- – 1,5,6,9 – us UMI [150]

BEHAVIORAL DISORDERS – (v.7-. 1981-. 5,6,9) – v.1-. 1976- – 1 – us UMI [150]

BEHAVIORAL ECOLOGY AND SOCIOBIOLOGY – v.1-9, 1976-81. ISSN: 0340-5443 – 1,5,6,9,13 – 163.00v – us UMI [574]

BEHAVIORAL HEALTH MANAGEMENT *see* ADDICTION AND RECOVERY

BEHAVIORAL NEUROSCIENCE – v97. 1983 – 1,5,6 – us Princeton Micro [073]

BEHAVIORAL SCIENCE – (1969- . 5,6. 1970- . 9) – 1- 1956- – 1 – us UMI [150]

BEHAVIORIAL AND BRAIN SCIENCES – (1981-. 1,5,6,9) – v1-. 1978- – 1 – us UMI [073]

BEHAVIORIAL MEDICINE ABSTRACTS – (1983-. 1,5,6,9) – v1-. 1980- – 1 – us UMI [073]

BEHAVIORIAL NEUROSCIENCE – v97-. 1983- – 1,5,6,9 – us UMI [073]

BEHAVIORIAL RESIDENTIAL TREATMENT – 1984- – 1,5,6,9 – us UMI [073]

BEHAVIORIAL SCIENCES AND THE LAW – 1983- – 1,5,6,9 – us UMI [073]

BEHAVIORISM – (v.8-. 1980-. 5,6,9) – v.1-. 1972- – 1 – us UMI [150]

BEHAVIOUR AND FEEDING ECOLOGY OF THE NEW HOLLAND HONEYEATER PHYLIDONYRIS NOVAEHOLLANDIAE IN VICTORIA / Paton, David C – (PhD Thesis) – 1979 – 9 – A$15.00 – at R.A.O.U. [590]

BEHAVIOUR RESEARCH AND THERAPY – (Back issues of journal available from UMI) – Incorporating Behavioural Assessment. 8 issues/y. v31. 1993 – 9 – £255.00y – uk Elsevier Sci [610]

BEHAVIOUR RESEARCH AND THERAPY – v1-1963- – 5,6,9 – us UMI [610]

BEHAVIOURAL STRATEGIES OF A SILVEREYE POPULATION IN RELATION TO FOOD RESOURCES ON A CORAL CAY ISLAND / Catterall, Carla – (PhD Thesis) – 1978 – microfiche – A$15.00 – at R.A.O.U. [590]

Beheim-Schwarzbach, Eberhard *see* DRAMENFORMEN DES BAROCK

Behety, Luis Ortiz *see* CULTURA CIUDADANA

BEHIND THE SCENES AT THE FRONT / Adam, George Jefferys – London: Chatto & Windus, 1915 – 1r – 1 – us U.W. Library [940]

BEHIND THE VEIL: A POEM / De Mille, James – Halifax, N.S.: T. Allen, 1893. 02706. (Pre-1900 Canadiana) – 9 – cn C.I.H.M. [810]

Behl, CF W *see* GERHART HAUPTMANN

Behn, Aphra *see* ORONOKO

Behn, Wolfgang *see*
- THE DISSIDENT PRESS OF REVOLUTIONARY IRAN
- IRANIAN OPPOSITION TO THE SHAH

Behourt, J *see* THRESOR DE L'ELOQUENCE FRANCOYSE

Behr, H *see* DIE VOELKERRECHTLICHE ANERKENNUNG VON MANDSCHUKUO

Behramjee, P *see* DINKARD

Behrend, C *see* DIE WIRKUNG DER AUFHEBUNG DER GOLDKLAUSELN

Behrend, Erich *see* THEODOR FONTANES ROMAN "DER STECHLIN"

Behrend, G *see* DER BESTAND DER FREIEN STADT DANZIG ...

Behrends, Adolphus Julius Frederick *see*
- THE OLD TESTAMENT UNDER FIRE
- SOCIALISM AND CHRISTIANITY
- THE WORLD FOR CHRIST

Behrens, C E *see* HISTORICO-IURIDICA DE MODERNO USU CONSTITUTIONIS PACIS PUBLICAE ...

Behrens, Emil *see* ASSYRISCH-BABYLONISCHE BRIEFE

Behrens, G *see* DAS FRUEHCHRISTLICHE UND MEROWINGISCHE MAINS NACH DEN BODENFUNDEN DARGESTELLT

THE BEHRING SEA ARBITRATION : LETTERS TO THE TIMES BY ITS SPECIAL CORRESPONDENT, TOGETHER WITH THE AWARD: REPRINTED BY PERMISSION OF THE PROPRIETORS / Blowitz, Henri Stephan de – London: W. Clowes; Toronto: Carswell; Victoria, B.C.: T. Hibben, 1893. 00825. (Pre-1900 Canadiana) – 9 – cn C.I.H.M. [340]

Behrman, Daniel *see*
- ASSAULT ON THE LARGEST UNKNOWN
- SCIENCE AND TECHNOLOGY IN DEVELOPMENT

BEI DEN ESKIMOS IN WEST-GROENLAND / Trebitsch, R – BN 425 2. 1910 – 8 – ne IDC [306]

BEI GOETHE ZU GASTE : NEUES VON GOETHE, AUS SEINEM FREUNDES- UND GESELLSCHAFTSKREISE / Gaedertz, Karl Theodor – Leipzig: G Wigand, 1900 – 1r – 1 – us U.W. Library [430]

BEI JING DA XUE XUE SHEN ZHOU KAN – Jan-May 1920. 5 ill. DL67f – 9 – 30.00 – cc Globe [073]

BEI PING JIE FANG BAO – Apr-Jul 1949 – 9 – cc Globe [950]

BEIBLATT ZUR D.A.Z., BREMEN *see* DEUTSCHE AUSWANDERER-ZEITUNG

BEIBLATT ZUR DEUTSCHEN AUSWANDERER ZEITUNG – Bremen, Germany.1856-58 – 1r – 1 – gw Mikrofilm [072]

DIE BEICHT NACH CAESARIUS VON HEISTERBACH / Koeniger, Albert Michael – Muenchen: Lentner, 1906 – 1mf – us A.T.L.A. [240]

DIE BEIDEN FASSUNGEN VON GOETHES DIE LEIDEN DES JUNGEN WERTHERS : EINE STILPSYCHOLOGISCHE UNTERSUCHUNG / Riess, Gertrud – (Includes bibliographical references) – Breslau: Trewendt & Granier, 1924 – 1r – 1 – us U.W. Library [430]

DIE BEIDEN FASSUNGEN VON SCHILLERS ABHANDLUNG "UEBER NAIVE UND SENTIMENTALISCHE DICHTUNG" : EIN BEITRAG ZUR AESTHETIK SCHILLERS / Krancke, Adolf – (Includes bibliographical references) – Goettingen: L Hofer, 1911 – 1r – 1 – us U.W. Library [430]

DIE BEIDEN GEWOEHNLICHEN AETHIOPISCHEN GREGORIUS-ANAPHOREN / Loefgren, O – Roma, 1933 – 2mf – 8 – Dfl9.00 – ne Slangenburg [960]

DIE BEIDEN GRIECHISCHEN KLEMENTINEN-EPITOMEN UND IHRE ANHAENGE (T.U.U. 5-90) / Paschke, F – Berlin, 1966 – 6mf – 9 – ne Slangenburg [240]

DIE BEIDEN LETZTEN LEBENSJAHRE VON JOHANNES CALVIN / Zahn, Adolph – Stuttgart: Union deutsche Verlagsgesellschaft, 1898 – 1mf – us A.T.L.A. [240]

DIE BEIDEN TUBUS / Kurz, Hermann – Stuttgart: K Mayer, 1946 – 1r – 1 – us U.W. Library [830]

Beidleman, B A *see* ENERGY BALANCE AND THE COMPONENTS OF TOTAL DAILY ENERGY EXPENDITURE IN ENDURANCE TRAINED AND UNTRAINED WOMEN

Beierwaltes, Andreas *see* DIE "COMMUNITARIANS"

BEIFANG DIQU GONGREN YUNDONG ZILIAO XUANBIAN (1921-23) – Selected materials on the Labour Movement in Northern China, 1921-23. Comp. by the Museum of the Chinese Revolution.14 fiches. F/H133 – 9 – $49.00 – cc Microforms [330]

BEIFANG LUNCONG – (Northern Tribune-Journal of Harbin Teacher's University.In Chinese but Table of Contents in English in each issue. F p221 – 9 – $3.50f – cc Microforms [073]

BEIHEFTE : REPERTORIUM SPECIERUM NOVARUM REGNI VEGETABILIS / ed by Fedde, F – (Missing: 1939. v118(2-3)) – 1914-1941. v1-124 – 598mf – 746c/2 – ne IDC [073]

BEIHEFTE ZUM BOTANISCHEN CENTRALBLATT – Cassel, Abt. 1-2, 1891-1915. v1-33; Abt. 2, 1916-1932. v34-49 – 530mf – 5627/1-2 – ne IDC [580]

BEIHEFTE ZUR ZEITSCHRIFT FUER DIE ALTTESTAMENTLICHE WISSENSCHAFT 3 *see* ALTISRAELITISCHE KULTSTAETTEN

BEIJA-FLOR : ANNAES BRASILEIRO DE SCIENCIA, POLITICA, LITTERATURA – Rio de Janeiro, Jan-Aug 1830 – 1,5,6 – bl Biblioteca [072]

O BEIJA-FLOR : JORNAL JOCO-SERIO E NOTICIOSO – Maceio, Alagoas. 25 Abr-Dez 1869; Mar, Nov-10 Dez 1870 – 1,5,6 – bl Biblioteca [072]

BEIJIN DAXUE XUEBAO – Acta Scientiarum Naturalium Universitatis Pekinensis. In Chinese but English abstracts to the main articles. F p181 – 9 – $4.50f – cc Microforms [073]

BEIJING DAXUE XUESHENG ZHOUKAN – La Studentaro De La S'tata Pekin-Universitato. Jan 1920-May 1920; 1925. F C8. In Chinese – 9 – $13.50 – cc Microforms [073]

BEIJING QINGNIAN BAO – Beijing Youth Gazette. 2 issues a week. 1983-. M D35 – 1 reel/y – 1 – $28.00r – cc Microforms [072]

BEIJING REVIEW – 1977-1995 – 9 – F742.00 – sz Infoprint [072]

BEIJING REVIEW – (1982. 1) – China. 1971-81. -w. In English, French, German, Japanese or Spanish. Quarterly delivery. F E2 – 1 – $4.50r – cc Microforms [072]

BEIJING REVIEW – Beijing, CC. 1979- – 21+ r – $1,050.00 ($70.00y) – R04158 – us Library Micro [072]

BEIJING RIBAO – (1979-90. 1 reel/y; 1991- . 2 reels/y) – Beijing Daily. China. In Chinese. Current subscription. Annual delivery. Backfiles supplied on request. M D12 – 1 – $55.00r – cc Microforms [072]

BEIJING RIBAO – (Yrly reel count varies) – 1979- – 1 – inquire – us Ross [072]

BEIJING SHIFAN DAXUE XUEBAO – Ziran Kexuebao. Journal of Natural Science of Beijing Normal University. In Chinese but English abstracts to the main articles. F p182 – 9 – $4.50f – cc Microforms [073]

BEIJING SHIYUAN XUEBAO – Journal of the Beijing Teacher's College. In Chinese but Table of Contents in English in each issue. F p222 – 9 – $3.50f – cc Microforms [073]

BEIJING TUSHUGUAN GUANCANG BAOZHI MULU – A checklist of newspapers in the Beijing Library. Comp. by the Beijing Library. 4 fiches. F J46 – 9 – $18.00 – cc Microforms [072]

BEIJING WANBAO – Beijing Evening Paper. 1980-87, 1 reel/y; 1988- , 2 reels/y. M/D26 – 1 – $55.00r – cc Microforms [072]

BEIJING YIXUEYUAN XUEBAO – Journal of Beijing Medical College. In Chinese but English abstracts to the main articles. F p162 – 9 – 4.00 – cc Microforms [073]

BEIJING ZHONGYI XUEYUAN XUEBAO – Journal Beijing Traditional Chinese Med. Coll. In prep.F/P 306 – 9 – 4.00f – cc Microforms [073]

O BEIJO – Manaos, Amazonas. 1896; Maio-Jul, Out 1897; Abr 1898 – 1,5,6 – bl Biblioteca [072]

Beik, Kazimir *see* ZUR ENTSTEHUNGSGESCHICHTE VON GOETHES TORQUATO TASSO

BEILAGE – Filmed on separate reels from 1891-1907 – 1 – us NY Public [072]

BEILAGEN *see* DIES BLATT GEHOERT DER HAUSFRAU

Beilby, R *see* A HISTORY OF BRITISH BIRDS

Beilin, A *see* BELI-MAH

BEIM LAMPENLICHT : ERZAEHLUNGEN / Wildermuth, Ottilie; ed by Willms, Agnes – Stuttgart: Gebrueder Kroener, 1878 – 1r – 1 – us U.W. Library [830]

BEIN HA-ZEMANIM / Weisbrem, I – Warsaw. 1888. BJ-422-94 1 – 9 – ne IDC [470]

THE BEING OF GOD : MORAL GOVERNMENT AND THESES IN THEOLOGY / Squier, Miles Powell; ed by Boyd, James Robert – (Includes bibliographical references) – Rochester, NY: E Darrow & Kempshall, 1868 – 1mf – 9 – 0-8370-5511-3 – 1985-3511 – us A.T.L.A. [210]

THE BEING OF GOD AS UNITY AND TRINITY / Steenstra, Peter Henry – (Includes bibliographical references) – Boston: Houghton, Mifflin; Cambridge: Riverside Press, 1891 – 1mf – 9 – 0-8370-2369-6 – 1985-0369 – us A.T.L.A. [210]

BEING-BLACK-IN-THE-WORLD / Manganyi, N C – [Johannesburg]: SPRO-CAS/Raven, [1973] – us Res Libr [305]

BEING-GONG XUEBAO – Acta Armamentarii. In Chinese but English abstracts to the main articles. F p81 – 9 – $4.50f – cc Microforms [073]

BEIRA NEWS – Mozambique. Noticias da Beira. -sw. 4 Sept 1917-30 Dec 1921; 2 April 1930-Dec 1932. 7 reels – 1 – uk British Libr Newspaper [072]

BEIRA POST – Beira. Mozambique. -w. 23 Mar 1898-25 Aug 1917. (Imperfect). (8 reels) – 1 – uk British Libr Newspaper [072]

BEIRAK AL AHMAR *see* AL-BEIRAK-AL-AHMAR

BEIRUT TIMES – Los Angeles, CA. 1985 – 9+ r – 1 – $450.00 ($50.00y) – H04045 – us Library Micro [071]

Beis, N *see* HIPPOLYTS SCHRIFT UEBER DIE SEGNUNGEN JAKOBS (T.U.U. 3-38/1A)

Beissel, Stephan *see*
- BILDER AUS DER GESCHICHTE DER ALTCHRISTLICHEN KUNST UND LITURGIE IN ITALIEN
- ENTSTEHUNG DER PERIKOPEN DER ROEMISCHEN MESZBUECHER
- DIE VEREHRUNG DER HEILIGEN UND IHRER RELIQUIEN IN DEUTSCHLAND BIS ZUM BEGINNE DES 13. JAHRHUNDERTS
- DIE VEREHRUNG DER HEILIGEN UND IHRER RELIQUIEN IN DEUTSCHLAND WAEHREND DER ZWEITEN HAELFTE DES MITTELALTERS
- WALLFAHRTEN ZU UNSERER LIEBEN FRAU IN LEGENDE UND GESCHICHTE

Beissner, Friedrich *see* HOELDERLIN

BEIT OZAR HA-SAFRUT – v. 1-6. Jerusalem. Przemysl. Cracow. 1887-96, 1902. BJ-100-147 1 – 9 – ne IDC [073]

DER BEITCH – New York. 1908 – 1 – us A.J.P.C. [073]

BEITIA, EUGENIO. APOSTOLADO DE LOS SEGLARES 2ND EDICION. MADRID, 1939 / Guerrero, E – Madrid: Razon y Fe, 1943 – 1 – sp Bibl Santa Ana [946]

BEITRAAGE ZUR ALGENKUNDE. VRATISLAVIAE, BONNAE, 1841 / Suhr, J N von – (Novorum Auctorum Academiae Caesar. Leopold.-Carolinae Naturae Curiosorum, v. 18, p. 275-288, 3 pls.) B-6216 2 – 8 – ne IDC [580]

BEITRAEGE ZU DER INSEKTEN-GESCHICHTE – Frankfurt am Main. 1790-93 – 3 – us Readex [590]

BEITRAEGE ZU EINER CHEMISCHEN MONOGRAPHIE DER CLADONIACEEN / Zopf, W – (Ber. Deutschen Bot. Ges., v. 26, 1907). B-6175 2 – 8 – ne IDC [580]

BEITRAEGE ZU EINER MALACOZOOLOGIA ROSSICA / Middendorff, A T von – Z-658 2. 3 pts. 1847-1849 – 8 – ne IDC [590]

BEITRAEGE ZU EINER MONOGRAPHIE DER GATTUNG PERONOSPORA CORDA / Gaeumann, E – (Beitraege zur Kryptogamenflora der Schweiz, v. 5 (4). Zuerich. 1923). B-8325 1 – 9 – ne IDC [580]

BEITRAEGE ZU EINER ORCHIDEENKUNDE CENTRAL-AMERIKA'S / Reichenbach, Heinrich G L – Hamburg. 1866. B-5028 2 – 8 – ne IDC [580]

BEITRAEGE ZU KLOPSTOCKS ZEITMESSUNG : TONAUSDRUCK, ZEITAUSDRUCK, TONVERHALT / Pawel, Jaro – S.l.: s.n., 1903 – 1r – 1 – us U.W. Library [430]

BEITRAEGE ZU LUTHERS LITURGISCHEN REFORMEN : 1. LUTHERS LATEINISCHE UND DEUTSCHE LITANEI VON 1529, 2. LUTHERS DEUTSCHE VERSIKEL UND KOLLEKTEN / Drews, Paul – Tuebingen: J.C.B. Mohr, 1910 – 1mf – us A.T.L.A. [240]

BEITRAEGE ZU LUTHERS LITURGISCHEN REFORMEN / Drews, Paul – Tuebingen, 1910 – 2mf – 8 – Dfl9.00 – ne Slangenburg [240]

BEITRAEGE ZU PAUL HEYSES NOVELLENTECHNIK / Klein, John Frederick – (Includes bibliographical references) – S.l.: s.n., 1920 – 1r – 1 – us U.W. Library [430]

BEITRAEGE ZU UHLAND : UHLANDS JUGENDDICHTUNG / Naegele, Eugen – (Includes a number of unpublished early poems. Includes bibliographical references) – Tuebingen: W Armbruster & O Riecker, 1893 – 1r – 1 – us U.W. Library [430]

BEITRAEGE ZUM RECHT DER LUFTSCHIFFAHRT / Grote, F von – Borna, Leipzig, 1907 – 1mf – 1 – ILM-1626/1 – ne IDC [327]

BEITRAEGE ZUM STUDIUM DER GEDICHTE VON J.M.R. LENZ / Anwand, Oscar – 1995 – 1mf – 9 – DM48.00 – 3-8267-3129-8 – gw Hänsel [430]

BEITRAEGE ZUR ABENDMAHLSLEHRE TERTULLIANS / Leimbach, Carl L – Gotha: F.A. Perthes, 1874 – 1mf – us A.T.L.A. [240]

BEITRAEGE ZUR AELTESTEN EXEGESE DES BUCHES THRENI / Caro, Hermann Isaak – Berlin: H. Itzkowski, 1893. 1 fiche – 9 – us A.T.L.A. [240]

BEITRAEGE ZUR ALTERTUMSKUNDE DES ORIENTS / Landau, Wilh, Freiherr von – (Includes bibliographic references) – Leipzig: Eduard Pfeiffer, 1893-1906 – 1mf – 9 – 0-8370-7301-4 – 1986-1301 – us A.T.L.A. [470]

BEITRAEGE ZUR ASKANISCHEN VOLKSKUNDE / Stephan, Oskar – 1925 – 1 – us I.U. Libraries [390]

BEITRAEGE ZUR ASSYRIOLOGIE UND VERGLEICHENDEN SEMITISCHEN SPRACHWISSENSCHAFT / ed by Delitzsch, Franz & Haupt, P – v. 1-10. Leipzig. 1890-1927 – 67mf – 9 – ne IDC [470]

BEITRAEGE ZUR AUSLEGUNG VON RICHARD WAGNERS "RING DES NIBELUNGEN" / Grisson, Rudolf Hermann Rulemann – (Includes bibliographical references) – Leipzig: A Klein, 1934 – 1 – us U.W. Library [780]

BEITRAEGE ZUR BAYERISCHEN KIRCHENGESCHICHTE – 1(1894)-26(1919) – 132mf – 9 – Dfl462.00 – ne Slangenburg [240]

BEITRAEGE ZUR BELEHRUNG UND ERHOLUNG – Osnabrueck, Germany. 20 May 1848-49 – 1r – 1 – gw Mikrofilm [072]

BEITRAEGE ZUR BESCHREIBUNG VON SCHLESIEN – Brieg, 1783 n1-4, 1784 n3, 1785 n4, 1786 n6, 1789 n9, 1791 n10, 1796 n13 – 1 – Inquire at Mikrofilmarchiv for details – gw Misc Inst [943]

BEITRAEGE ZUR BEURTHEILUNG DER SEPTUAGINTA: EINE WUERDIGUNG WELLHAUSENSCHER TEXTKRITIK / Jahn, Gustav – Kirchhain: Max Schmersow, 1902. 1 fiche – 9 – us A.T.L.A. [240]

BEITRAEGE ZUR BEURTHEILUNG G E LESSING'S / Mayr, Richard – (Includes bibliographical references) – Wien: A Hoelder, 1880 – 1 – us U.W. Library [430]

BEITRAEGE ZUR BIBLISCHEN LANDES- UND ALTERTUMSKUNDE – v68. 1949-51 (complete) – Inquire – 1 – ATLA 1994-S505 – us A.T.L.A. [073]

BEITRAEGE ZUR BIOLOGIE DER PFLANZEN – Breslau, 1870-1939. v1-26 – 220mf – 7673/1 – ne IDC [580]

BEITRAEGE ZUR BIOLOGIE UND ANATOMIE DER LIANEN, IM BESONDEREN DER IN BRASILIEN EINHEIMISCHEN ARTEN / Schenk, H – (Botanische Mittheilungen aus den Tropen, Heft 4-5. Schimper, A. F. W., ed. v. 1. Jena. 1892; v. 2. Jena. 1893. B-5378 2 – 8 – ne IDC [580]

BEITRAEGE ZUR BOTANIK / Bartling, FG & Wendland, H L – Heft 1. Goettingen. 1824; Heft 2. Goettingen. 1825. B-500 2 – 6mf – 8 – ne IDC [580]

BEITRAEGE ZUR BOTANIK / Roth, A W – 2v. Bremen. 1782-83. B-5690 2 – 8 – ne IDC [580]

BEITRAEGE ZUR CARITATIVEN TAETIGKEIT DES GALLITZINKREISES / Plugge, Heinrich – (Muenster, 1934) – 2mf – 9 – DM48.00 – 3-89349-145-7 – gw Hänsel [060]

BEITRAEGE ZUR DESKRIPTIVEN POETIK IN DEN MITTELHOCHDEUTSCHEN VOLKSEPEN UND IN DER THIDREKSSAGA / Huennerkopf, Richard – Heidelberg, 1914 – 1mf – DM48.00 – 3-8267-3104-2 – gw Hänsel [430]

BEITRAEGE ZUR DEUTSCHEN LITERATURWISSENSCHAFT : NR 1 (1907)-NR 40 (1931) – Marburg: N G Elwert. 40v. 1907-31 – 1 – us U.W. Library [430]

BEITRAEGE ZUR EINER FLORA DES ORIENTS / Koch, K H E – (Linnaea v. 21-22). Halle. 1848. B-792 2 – 8 – ne IDC [580]

BEITRAEGE ZUR ENTWICKLUNG RELIGIONSSYSTEMATISCHEN DENKENS IM JUDENTUM DES 19. JAHRHUNDERTS / Schoeps, Hans-Joachim – Dresden, 1934 – 9 – DM48.00 – 3-89349-258-5 – gw Hänsel [270]

BEITRAEGE ZUR ENTWICKLUNGSGESCHICHTE DER FARN-SPORANGIEN / Luerssen, C – Leipzig, 1872. 32p. 3 pls. B-7218 1 – 9 – ne IDC [580]

BEITRAEGE ZUR ERKLAERUNG DES BUCHES DANIEL HEFT I, DAN. 2-6 / Meinhold, Johannes – (No more published? Includes bibliographical references) – Leipzig: Doerffling & Franke, 1888 – 1mf – 9 – 0-8370-4376-X – 1985-2376 – us A.T.L.A. [220]

BEITRAEGE ZUR ERKLAERUNG DES JESAIA / Barth, Jakob – Karlsruhe: H Reuther, 1885 – 1mf – 9 – 0-8370-2195-2 – 1985-0195 – us A.T.L.A. [220]

BEITRAEGE ZUR FLORA VON ABYSSINIEN / Fresenius, J BG W – Frankfurt am Main. 1837-45. B-5126 2 – 8 – ne IDC [580]

BEITRAEGE ZUR FLORA VON AEGYPTEN UND ARABIEN / Fresenius, J BG W – Frankfurt am Main. 1834. B-5127 2 – 8 – ne IDC [580]

BEITRAEGE ZUR FRAUENBIOLOGIE : DIE JUEDISCHEN RITUELLEN SEXUALVORSCHRIFTEN / Weissenberg, S – Berlin, Koeln, 1927 – 1mf – 9 – DM48.00 – 3-89349-357-3 – gw Hänsel [270]

BEITRAEGE ZUR GEOGNOSTISCHEN KENNTNISS DES ERZGEBIRGES – Freiberg, 1845-69. Pts. 1-3 – 3 – us Readex [550]

BEITRAEGE ZUR GEOGRAPHIE UND ETHNOGRAPHIE BABYLONIENS IM TALMUD UND MIDRASCH / Berliner, Abraham – Berlin: Gorzelanczyk, 1884. 1 fiche – 9 – us A.T.L.A. [305]

BEITRAEGE ZUR GEOPHYSIK, (GERLANDS) – v. 44-61. G-164 2. 1935-1950 – 8 – ne IDC [550]

BEITRAEGE ZUR GESCHICHTE DER ARBEITERBEWEGUNG – 1959-1978, 1981-1989 – 690mf – 1 – DM3,933.00 – gw Mikro Press [335]

BEITRAEGE ZUR GESCHICHTE DER ARBEITERBEWEGUNG DES NIEDERRHEINISCH-WESTFAELISCHEN BERGBAUES / Velsen, Wilhelm von – Essen 1940 – 1 – DM30.00 – gw Mikro Press [943]

BEITRAEGE ZUR GESCHICHTE DER ARBEITERBEWEGUNG IM RHEINISCH-WESTFAELISCHEN INDUSTRIEGEBIET / Umbreit, Robert – Dortmund 1932 – 1 – DM30.00 – gw Mikro Press [331]

BEITRAEGE ZUR GESCHICHTE DER CHRISTOLOGISCHEN DOGMAS IM 11TEN UND 12TEN JAHRHUNDERT / Baltzer, Otto – Leipzig: A. Deichert, 1898 – 1mf – us A.T.L.A. [240]

BEITRAEGE ZUR GESCHICHTE DER DEUTSCHEN SPRACHE UND LITERATUR – Halle, 1874-1920. v1-44 – 291mf – H-10025/1 – ne IDC [430]

BEITRAEGE ZUR GESCHICHTE DER EVANGELISCHEN KIRCHE IN RUSSLAND / Dalton, Hermann – 4v. in 3. 1887-1905 – 1 – us A.T.L.A. [240]

BEITRAEGE ZUR GESCHICHTE DER HEBRAEISCHEN UND ARAMAEISCHEN STUDIEN / Perles, Joseph – Muenchen. 1884. BJ-32-55 1 – 9 – ne IDC [470]

BEITRAEGE ZUR GESCHICHTE DER HEBRAEISCHEN UND ARAMAEISCHEN STUDIEN / Perles, Joseph – Muenchen: Theodor Ackermann, 1884. 1 fiche – 9 – us A.T.L.A. [270]

BEITRAEGE ZUR GESCHICHTE DER LEHRE VOM PARALLELISMUS DER INDIVIDUAL- UND DER GESAMTENTWICKLUNG / Kleinsorge, John Arnold – Jena, 1899 – 1mf – DM38.00 – 3-8267-3078-X – gw Hänsel [120]

BEITRAEGE ZUR GESCHICHTE DER MYSTIK IN DER REFORMATIONSZEIT / Hegler, Alfred; ed by Koehler, Walther E – Berlin: C.A. Schwetschke, 1906 – 1mf – us A.T.L.A. [200]

BEITRAEGE ZUR GESCHICHTE DER PHILOSOPHIE DES MITTELALTERS – Muenster, 1891-1941. v1-36 – 354mf – 28/1 – ne IDC [180]

BEITRAEGE ZUR GESCHICHTE DER PHILOSOPHIE DES MITTELALTERS : SUPPLEMENTHEFTE – Muenster, 1913. v1-2; 1935. v3(1-2) – 41mf – 29/2 – ne IDC [180]

BEITRAEGE ZUR GESCHICHTE DER PHILOSOPHIE UND THEOLOGIE DES MITTELALTERS *see*
- AVENCEBROLIS (IBN GEBIROL) FONS VITAE
- AVICENNA ON THEOLOGY
- DIE DEM BOETHIUS...ZUGESCHRIEBENE ABHANDLUNG DES DOM. GUNDISALVI DE UNITATE
- DAS CHALCIDIUS KOMMENTAR ZU PLATOS TIMAEUS
- DES DOM. GUNDISSALINUS SCHRIFT 'VON DER UNSTERBLICHKEIT DER SEELE'
- GESCH. D. GOTTES BEWEISE IM MA BIS Z. AUSGANG D. HOCHSCHOLASTIK
- GUNDISSALINUS' DE DIVISIONE PHILOSOPHIAE
- DIE IMPOSSIBILIA DES SIGER VON BRABANT
- IN 12 ARISTOTELIS METAPH
- IST DUNS SCOTUS INDETERMINIST?
- DIE LEHRE VON DER ANFANGSLOSIGKEIT D. WELT BEI DEN MITTELALT. ARAB. PHILOSOPHEN
- MEISTER DIETRICH, SEIN LEBEN, SEINE WERKE, SEINE WISSENSCHAFT
- DIE PHILOS. ABHANDLUNGEN DES JA'QUB BEN ISHAG AL-KINDI
- DIE PHILOSOPHIE DES ALANUS DE INSULIS
- DIE PHILOSOPHIE DES JOSEF (IBN) ZADDIK
- DIE PHILOSOPHIE DES PETRUS LOMBARDUS
- DIE PSYCHOLOGIE DES HUGO VON S. VIKTOR
- DIE PSYCHOLOGIE DES NEMESIUS
- DIE REL. PHIL. LEHRE SAADJA GAONS UEBER DIE HL. SCHRIFT
- DIE STELLUNG DES THOMAS VON AQ. ZU AVENCEBROL
- THOMAS BRADWARDINUS U. SEINE LEHRE V. D. MENSCHL. WILLENSFREIHEIT
- WITELO, EIN PHILOSOPH UND NATURFORSCHER DES 12. JHT.
- ZUR STELLUNG AVENCEBROLS IM ENTWICKLUNGSGANGE D. ARAB. PHILOSOPHIE

BEITRAEGE ZUR GESCHICHTE DER TECHNIK UND INDUSTRIE : JAHRBUCH DES VEREINS DEUTSCHER INGENIEURE / ed by Matschoss, Conrad – (Cont as: Technik-Geschichte 1933-42) – Berlin. 30v. 1909-32 – 75mf – 9 – subsc: DM550.00 diazo DM650.00 silver – gw Olms [600]

BEITRAEGE ZUR GESCHICHTE DER THEOLOGISCHEN FACULTAET IN FREIBURG / Koenig, Joseph – Freiburg i. B.: H.M. Poppen, 1884 – 1mf – us A.T.L.A. [240]

BEITRAEGE ZUR GESCHICHTE DES JESUITEN-ORDENS / Friedrich, Johann – Muenchen: Verlag der k. Akademie in Commission bei G. Franz: Akademische Buchdruckerei von F. Straub, 1881 – 1mf – us A.T.L.A. [240]

BEITRAEGE ZUR GESCHICHTE DES JESUITENORDENS / Reusch, Franz Heinrich – Muenchen: C.H. Beck, 1894 – 1mf – us A.T.L.A. [240]

BEITRAEGE ZUR GESCHICHTE DES RUNDFUNKS – (Incl index 1967-73) – Berlin, 1967 n2-1986 n1, 1987-89 n3 – 1 – Dist. gw Mikrofilm – gw Misc Inst [790]

BEITRAEGE ZUR GESCHICHTE DORTMUNDS UND DER GRAFSCHAFT MARK – Dortmund. v. 1-32, 1875-1925. Film Mas C 358 – 1 – us H.U. Library [073]

BEITRAEGE ZUR GESCHICHTE UND ZUM VERSTAENDNIS DES MASSBEGRIFFS / Winterscheidt, Heinrich – Bonn, 1909 – 2mf – DM62.00 – 3-8267-3056-9 – gw Hänsel [100]

BEITRAEGE ZUR JESAIAKRITIK : NEBST EINER STUDIE UEBER PROPHETISCHE SCHRIFTSTELLEREI / Giesebrecht, Friedrich – (Includes appendix on the concepts of condemnation and promise in the Prophets) – Goettingen: Vandenhoeck & Ruprecht, 1890 – 1mf – 9 – 0-8370-3269-5 – 1985-1269 – us A.T.L.A. [220]

BEITRAEGE ZUR KENNTNIS DER BABYLONISCHEN RELIGION / Zimmern, Heinrich – 3tle. Leipzig. 1896-1901. BNE-471 1 – 9 – ne IDC [290]

BEITRAEGE ZUR KENNTNIS DER BABYLONISCHEN RELIGION / Zimmern, Heinrich – (Includes bibliographical references and glossaries) – Leipzig: J C Hinrichs, 1896-1901 – 1mf – 9 – 0-8370-7119-4 – 1986-1119 – us A.T.L.A. [230]

BEITRAEGE ZUR KENNTNIS DER BYZANTINISCHEN LITURGIE : TEXTE UND STUDIEN / ed by Engdahl, Richard – Berlin: Trowitzsch, 1908 – 1mf – us A.T.L.A. [240]

BEITRAEGE ZUR KENNTNIS DER ECTOCARPUS-ARTEN DES KIELER FOEHRDE / Kuckuck, P – Kiel. 1891. B-1349 2 – 8 – ne IDC [580]

BEITRAEGE ZUR KENNTNIS DER GATTUNG ERYTHROXYLON / Martius, Karl Friedrich Philipp von – Muenchen. 1840. 130p. 10 pls. B-6458 2 – 8 – ne IDC [580]

BEITRAEGE ZUR KENNTNIS DER LILIACEEN DER KAUKASUS-LAENDER. I. TRANSKAUKASISCHE BELLEVALIA ARTEN / Woronow, G N – (Bull. Jardin Principal Bot. U.S.S.R., 1927). B-228 2 – 8 – ne IDC [580]

BEITRAEGE ZUR KENNTNIS DER RELIGIONSPHILOSOPHISCHEN ANSCHAUUNGEN DES FLAVIUS JOSEPHUS / Lewinsky, Abraham – (Includes bibliographical references) – Breslau: Preuss & Juenger, 1887 – 1mf – 9 – 0-8370-4099-X – 1985-2099 – us A.T.L.A. [270]

BEITRAEGE ZUR KENNTNIS VON KLINGERS SPRACHE UND STIL IN SEINEN JUGEND-DRAMEN / Philipp, Richard – (Includes bibliographical references) – Freiburg i.Br.: U Hochreuther, 1909 – 1r – 1 – us U.W. Library [430]

BEITRAEGE ZUR KENNTNISS DER ANATOMIE UND SYSTEMATIK DER GLOEOLICHENEN / Forsell, K B J – (Nov. Act. R. Soc.). v. 13. Uppsala. 1887. B-548 2 – 8 – ne IDC [580]

BEITRAEGE ZUR KENNTNISS DER NECTARIEN / Stadler, S – Berlin, 1886. 88p. 8 pls. B-603 2 – 8 – ne IDC [580]

BEITRAEGE ZUR KENNTNISS DER RUSSISCHEN REICHES UND DER ANGRAENZENDEN LAENDER ASIENS – Spb. 1839-96. Lacking: 1839 (1, 2); 1844 (7-8). – 325mf – 8 – ne IDC [947]

BEITRAEGE ZUR KIRCHENGESCHICHTE, ARCHAEOLOGIE UND LITURGIK / Hefele, Carl Joseph – Tuebingen: H. Laupp, 1864 – 3mf – us A.T.L.A. [240]

BEITRAEGE ZUR KRITISCHEN WUERDIGUNG DER DRAMATISCHEN DICHTUNGEN THEODOR KOERNERS / Struker, Johannes – (Includes bibliographical references) – [S.l.: s.n.] 1910 (Muenster i.W.: Druck der Westfaelischen Vereinsdruckerei) – 1r – 1 – us U.W. Library [430]

BEITRAEGE ZUR KULTUR EXOTISCHER GEWAECHSE / Medikus, F K – Mannheim. 1806. B-8144 1 – 9 – ne IDC [580]

BEITRAEGE ZUR KUNDE DER INDOGERMANISCHEN SPRACHEN – Goettingen, 1877-1907. v1-30. Register – 213mf – H-1379/2 – ne IDC [430]

BEITRAEGE ZUR KUNDE EHST-, LIV- UND KURLANDS – Reval, 1868/1873-1915. v1-8 – 68mf – R-1668/2 – ne IDC [947]

BEITRAEGE ZUR LANDESKUNDE VON SUEDWESTAFRIKA / Jaeger, Fritz & Waibel, Leo – Berlin: E S Mittler, 1920-21 – 1 – us Res Libr [960]

BEITRAEGE ZUR LEHRE VOM EINHEITLICHEN WECHSELRECHT / Cohn, G – Heidelberg, 1880 – 2mf – 1 – ILM-3457/1 – ne IDC [327]

BEITRAEGE ZUR LITERATURGESCHICHTE UND – METHODOLOGIE : GEMEINSAMER STUDIENBAND VON GERMANISTEN DER FRIEDRICH-SCHILLER-UNIVERSITAET JENA UND DER ALEXANDRU-ION-CUZA-UNIVERSITAET IASI / ed by Fassel, Hort & Hammer, Klaus – (Includes bibliographical references) – Jena: Die Universitaet, 1982 – 1 – us U.W. Library [430]

BEITRAEGE ZUR MANDJURISCHEN BIBLIOGRAPHIE UND LITERATUR / Fuchs, W – (Mitt. der Deutschen Ges. fuer Natur- und Voelkerkunde Ostasiens, Supplementband XIV). Tokyo. 1936. Illus. BU-494 2 – 8 – ne IDC [480]

BEITRAEGE ZUR MORPHOLOGIE DER LEPIDOPTEREN / Petersen, W – (Mem. Acad. Imp. Sci., St. Petersburg, 1900, 144p., 4 pls.). Z-1545/2 – 8 – ne IDC [590]

BEITRAEGE ZUR MORPHOLOGIE DER MEERES-ALGEN / Pringsheim, N – Berlin. 1863. B-6397 2 – 8 – ne IDC [580]

BEITRAEGE ZUR MORPHOLOGIE, GRUPPIERUNG UND GEOGRAPHISCHEN VERBREITUNG DER VALERIANACEEN / Hoeck, F – Leipzig. 1882. B-802 2 – 8 – ne IDC [580]

BEITRAEGE ZUR MYKOLOGIE / Fresenius, J BG W – Heft 1-3. Frankfurt. 1850-63. B-1527 2 – 8 – ne IDC [580]

BEITRAEGE ZUR NATURGESCHICHTE ALS FORTSETZUNG DES NATURALIENTAUSCH / Opiz, P M – (Naturalientausch, nr. 12, 1828). Prag. 1828. B-1071 2 – 8 – ne IDC [580]

BEITRAEGE ZUR NATURKUNDE UND DEN DAMIT VERWANDTEN WISSENSCHAFTEN / Ehrhart, F – 7v. Hannover. 1787-92. B-684 2 – 8 – ne IDC [580]

BEITRAEGE ZUR ORNITHOLOGIE SUEDAFRIKAS / Holub, E & Pelzeln, A von – Z 1805. 1882 – 9 – ne IDC [590]

BEITRAEGE ZUR PETREFACTEN-KUNDE / Muenster, G von – 5351 2. Ed. 2. 1839-1846 – 8 – ne IDC [560]

BEITRAEGE ZUR PFLANZENANATOMIE, PFLANZENPHYSIOLOGIE UND EINER NEUEN CHARAKTERISTIK DER BAEUME UND STRAEUCHER / Medikus, F K – Leipzig, 1799-1801. 531, 3 pp. B-616 2 – 8 – ne IDC [580]

BEITRAEGE ZUR PSYCHOLOGIE ALBERTS DES GROSSEN / Schneider, A – Muenster, 1903/1906 – 11mf – 8 – ne Slangenburg [100]

BEITRAEGE ZUR RABBINISCHEN SPRACH- UND ALTERTHUMSKUNDE / Eisler, Leopold – (Includes index) – Wien: Herzfeld & Bauer, 1872 – 1mf – 9 – 0-8370-9141-1 – 1986-3141 – us A.T.L.A. [470]

BEITRAEGE ZUR RICHTIGEN WUERDIGUNG DER EVANGELIEN UND DER EVANGELISCHEN GESCHICHTE / Wieseler, Karl – (Includes bibliographical references and indexes) – Gotha: Friedrich Andreas Perthes, 1869 – 1mf – 9 – 0-8370-9278-7 – 1986-3278 – us A.T.L.A. [220]

BEITRAEGE ZUR SCHOENEN GARTENKUNST / Medikus, F K – Mannheim. 1782. B-8132 1 – 9 – ne IDC [631]

BEITRAEGE ZUR SEKTENGESCHICHTE DES MITTELALTERS / Doellinger, Ignaz von – (1. Theil: Geschichte Der Gnostisch-Manichaeischen Sekten Muenchen, 1890 Dfl22.00. 2. Theil: Dokumente Vornehmlich zur Geschichte der Valdesier und Katharer, Muenchen, 1890 Dfl46.00) – ne Slangenburg [290]

BEITRAEGE ZUR SEMITISCHEN SPRACHWISSENSCHAFT / Noeldeke, T – Strassburg. 1904. BNE-480 1 – 9 – ne IDC [470]

BEITRAEGE ZUR SEMITISCHEN SPRACHWISSENSCHAFT / Noeldeke, Theodor – (Includes bibliographical references) – Strassburg: Karl J Truebner, 1904 – 1mf – 9 – 0-8370-8365-6 – 1986-2365 – us A.T.L.A. [470]

BEITRAEGE ZUR SEMITISCHEN SPRACHWISSENSCHAFT / Noldeke, T – Strassburg, 1904 – 3mf – 8 – ne Slangenburg [470]

BEITRAEGE ZUR STATISTIK BAYERNS / Bavaria. Statistisches Landesamt – v. 1-207. 1853-1958. Scattered volumes wanting – 1 – 616.00 – us L of C Photodup [943]

BEITRAEGE ZUR STATISTIK DER STADT FRANKFURT – v. 1-5. 1858-90 – 1 – 82.00 – us L of C Photodup [943]

BEITRAEGE ZUR STATISTIK MECKLENBURGS / Mecklenburg-Schwerin. Statistisches Landesamt – v. 1-16. 1856-1910. V. 16 Wanting – 1 – 108.00 – us L of C Photodup [943]

BEITRAEGE ZUR STILISTIK VON HOELDERLIN "TOD DES EMPEDOKLES" / Schmidt, Wolfgang – (Includes bibliographical references) – Marburg a.L.: N G Elwert, 1927 – 1r – 1 – us U.W. Library [430]

BEITRAEGE ZUR TECHNIK IN HEBBELS TAGEBUCH / Hoestermann, Emilie – (Includes bibliographical references) – Bonn: H Ludwig, 1917 – 1r – 1 – us U.W. Library [430]

BEITRAEGE ZUR TEXT- UND LITERARKRITIK SOWIE ZUR ERKLAERUNG DER BUECHER SAMUEL / Peters, Norbert – Freiburg i.B.: Herder, 1899. 1 fiche – 9 – us A.T.L.A. [240]

BEITRAEGE ZUR TEXTKRITIK VON ORIGENES' JOHANNESCOMMENTAR (T.U.U. 2-28/2A) / Koetschau, Paul – Leipzig, 1905 – 2mf – 9 – ne Slangenburg [240]

BEITRAEGE ZUR UKRAINEKUNDE – Berlin, 1932-1941. v1-7 – 7mf – H-447/2 – ne IDC [947]

BEITRAEGE ZUR VERSTAENDIGUNG UEBER BEGRIFF UND WESEN DER SITTLICH-RELIGIOESEN ERFAHRUNG / Petran, Ernst – (Includes bibiographical references) – Guetersloh:C. Bertelsmann, 1898 – 1mf – 9 – 0-8370-4718-8 – 1985-2718 – us A.T.L.A. [240]

BEITRAEGE ZUR WEITERENTWICKLUNG DER CHRISTLICHEN RELIGION / Deissmann, Gustav Adolf – Muenchen: J.F. Lehmann, 1905 – 1mf – 9 – us A.T.L.A. [240]

BEITRAEGE ZUR WIELAND-BIOGRAPHIE / Wieland, Christoph Martin; ed by Funck, Heinrich – Freiburg i. B: J C B Mohr, 1882 – 1 – us U.W. Library [430]

BEITRAEGE ZUR WIRTSCHAFTSGESCHICHTE DER T'ANG-ZEIT (618-906) / Balazs, S – (Mitt. Sem. Orient. Sprachen Berlin, 1931, 1933). BH-172 2 – 8 – ne IDC [330]

BEITRAEGE ZUR WUERDIGUNG VON KARL GUTZKOW ALS LUSTSPIELDICHTER : MIT EINEM EINLEITENDEN TEIL UEBER EIN UNBEKANNTES TAGEBUCH / Mueller, Peter – (Includes bibliographical references) – Marburg a.L.: N G Elwert, 1910 – 1 – us U.W. Library [430]

EIN BEITRAG ZU THEODOR STORM'S STIMMUNGSKUNST / Stamm, Hermann – (Includes Bibliographical References) – Eckernfoerde: C Heldt, 1914 – 1 – us U.W. Library [430]

EIN BEITRAG ZUM ENTWURF VON ZEITREIHENREGLERN / Fux, Manfred – 1995 – 2mf – 9 – DM80.00 – 3-8267-2140-3 – gw Hänsel [621]

EIN BEITRAG ZUM UNGARISCHEN STAATSRECHT / Deak, F von – Pest. 1865. BR-5321 2 – 8 – ne IDC [943]

BEITRAG ZUR BESTIMMUNG DER PARAMETER UND ZUR DETEKTION DER STRUKTUR VON ZWEIPHASENSTROEMUNGEN MITTELS ULTRASCHALL / Hofmann, Bernd & Rockstroh, Manfred – 1993 – 1mf – 9 – DM60.00 – 3-89349-746-3 – gw Hänsel [621]

EIN BEITRAG ZUR CHRISTOLOGIE DES ALTEN TESTAMENTES : MIT BERUECKSICHTIGUNG / Schaffnit, K – (Includes bibliographical references) – Duesseldorf: C Schaffnit, [1892?] – 1mf – 9 – 0-8370-5073-1 – 1985-3073 – us A.T.L.A. [220]

EIN BEITRAG ZUR DREIDIMENSIONALEN FINITE-ELEMENTE-BERECHNUNG VON GESCHICHTETEN VERBUNDWERKSTOFFEN / Meyer, Ralf I – 1995 – v/160p – 9 – DM52.00 – 3-8267-1058-4 – gw Hänsel [620]

BEITRAG ZUR FLORA AETHIOPIENS / Schweinfurth, Georg A – Berlin. 1867. B-320 2 – 9 – ne IDC [580]

BEITRAG ZUR FLORA BRASILIENS / Nees von Esenbeck, CG D & Martius, CF P von – (Nova Acta Physico-Medica Acad. Caesareae Leopoldino-Carolinae Naturae Curiosorum, 1824, v. 12, pt. 1, 54 pp., 8 pls.) B-5446 2 – 8 – ne IDC [580]

BEITRAG ZUR GEOLOGIE DES "MASSIF DE CEZE", OESTLICHER TEIL, GARD (FRANKREICH) / Breyer, Ralf – 1992 – xi/179p – DM98.00 – 3-89349-476-6 – gw Hänsel [550]

BEITRAG ZUR GESCHICHTE DES RUNDFUNKS – Berlin, 1967-1972 – 1r – 1 – DM100.00 – gw Mikro Press [380]

BEITRAG ZUR GESCHICHTE UND SOZIOLOGIE DES RUHRAUFSTANDES VOM MARZ-APRIL 1920 / Colm, Gerhard – Essen a. d. R., 1921 – 1 – DM30.00 – gw Mikro Press [300]

BEITRAG ZUR KENNTNIS DER FLORA RUSSLANDS UND DER STEPPEN CENTRAL ASIENS / Bunge, A A von – (Mem. Ac. Imp. Sc. spb., v. 7, 1854). B-5867 2 – 8 – ne IDC [580]

EIN BEITRAG ZUR KENNTNIS DER GENSTRUKTUR DER PHOSPHOENOLPYRUVAT-CARBOXYLASE HOEHERER PFLANZEN : PSILOTUM NUDUM, WELWITSCHIA MRABILIS UND TILLANDSIA USNEOIDES / Glasow, Catharina von – 1995 – 1mf – 9 – DM60.00 – 3-8267-2186-1 – gw Hänsel [574]

EIN BEITRAG ZUR KENNTNIS DES SPRACHGEBRAUCHS KLOPSTOCKS / Wuerfl, Christoph – (Includes bibliographical references) – Bruenn: C Winiker, 1883 – 1r – 1 – us U.W. Library [430]

BEITRAG ZUR KENNTNISS DER ORNITHOLOGISCHEN FAUNA AN DER NORDSEITE DES KAUKASUS / Lorentz, Th – Moskau. 1887. Z-1843 2 – 8 – ne IDC [590]

EIN BEITRAG ZUR KRITIK VON LESSINGS LAOKOON / Brill, Bernhard – S.l.: s.n., 18–? – 1r – 1 – us U.W. Library [430]

BEITRAG ZUR NAEHEREN KENNTNISS UND VERBREITUNG DER ALGEN / Rabenhorst, G L – Leipzig. 1863. B-2784 2 – 8 – ne IDC [580]

BEITRAG ZUR VERGLEICHENDEN ANATOMIE DER CYPRIPEDILINAE / Faber, F C von – Stuttgart. 1904. B-1007 2 – 8 – ne IDC [580]

BEITRAG ZUR VORGESCHICHTE DER AUFLOESUNG DER KLOESTER IN ENGLAND UND WALES SPECIELL UNTER DER REGIERUNG HEINRICHS 8 / Wilson, Gilbert B – Halle, 1900 – 1mf – 9 – DM48.00 – 3-89349-306-9 – gw Hänsel [941]

BEITRAGE ZU EINFACH-PRAKTISCHEN PRUFUNGEN VERSCHIEDENER HANDELSWAREN / Suepke, H F W – Braunschweig, 1842 – 1 – DM40.00 – gw Mikro Press [380]

BEIYANG JUNFA SHILIAO XUANJI – Selection of historical materials on the northern warlords. Comp. by Du Chunhe and others. 9 fiches. F H192 – 9 – $36.00 – cc Microforms [950]

Bejar, Duque de *see* NUEVA DISPOSICION Y REGIMEN QUE SU EXCELENCIA HA DADO PARA LOS COLEGIOS DE NINAS POBRES. HUERFANAS DE SU VILLA Y TIERRA DE BEJAR EN ESTE ANO DEL SENOR DE MIL SETECIENTOS Y VEINTICINCO

Bejarano y Sanchez, Eloy *see*
- AGUAS AZOADAS..
- LA EDUCACION INTEGRAL
- LA EDUCACION MEDICA INTEGRAL
- MEMORIA PRESENTADA EN EL 14TH CONGRESO INTERNACIONAL DE MEDICINA POR...

DIE BEKAEMPFUNG DES CHRISTENTUMS DURCH DEN ROEMISCHEN STAAT : BIS ZUM TODE DES KAISERS JULIAN, 363 / Linsenmayer, A – Muenchen: J.J. Lentner, 1905 – 1mf – us A.T.L.A. [240]

BEKANNTE UND UNBEKANNTE GROSSEN: SKIZZEN UND NOVELLETTEN AUS DER KUNST-UND THEATERWELT / Haffner, Karl – Wien: Selbstverlag der Witwe des Verfassers Fran Elise Haffner: in Commission be: H. Engel, 1884 – 1 – us U.W. Library [830]

BEKANTNUS / Muentzer, T – 1525. BME-28 1 – 9 – ne IDC [240]

BEKANTNUSS VOM HEYLIGEN ABENDMAL... IN SECHTZEHEN PREDIGT GETHEYLET / Mathesius, Johannes – Nuernberg, 1567 – 5mf – ne IDC [240]

BEKEHIRNOK : A BAPTISTA AGYHAZ LAPJA – v10-35. 1966-91 (incomplete) – Inquire – 1 – ATLA S0335 – us A.T.L.A. [240]

DIE BEKEHRUNG JOHANNES CALVINS / Lang, August – Leipzig: A. Deichert, 1897 – 1mf – us A.T.L.A. [240]

BEKENDTNIS DOCTORIS TILEMANNI HESHVSII VON DER PERSOENLICHEN VND IN ALLE EWIGKEIT VNZERTRENLICHEN VEREINIGUNG BEYDER NATUREN IN JHESU CHRISTO... / Hesshusen, T – [Eisleben], 1585 – 1mf – ne IDC [240]

BEKENNTENISSE. WAER MEDE HY VERCLAERT, SIJN PREDICKAMPT SONDER WETTELICKE BEROEPINGHE GEBRUYCKT TE HEBBEN BECLAECHT HEM DIES / Philipsz, Obbe – Amstelredam, Corn. Claesz. 1584. BME-319 1 – 9 – ne IDC [240]

EIN BEKENNTNIS : NOVELLE / Storm, Theodor – Berlin: Gebrueder Paetel, 1888 – 1r – 1 – us U.W. Library [830]

DAS "BEKENNTNISBUCH OESTERREICHISCHER DICHTER HERAUSGEGEBEN VOM BUND DEUTSCHER SCHRIFTSTELLER OESTERREICHS" / Boehner, Claus-Peter – 1938 repr 1992 – 127p – 9 – DM98.00 – 3-89349-502-9 – gw Hänsel [430]

DIE BEKENNTNISSE UND DIE WICHTIGSTEN GLAUBENSZEUGNISSE DER GRIECHISCH-ORIENTALISCHEN KIRCHE : IM ORIGINALTEXT, NEBST EINLEITENDEN BEMERKUNGEN – (In Greek and German. Includes bibliographies) – Leipzig: J C Hinrichs, 1904 – 1mf – 9 – 0-8370-7489-4 – 1986-1489 – us A.T.L.A. [240]

BEKENTNIS D. GEORGIJ MAIORIS VON DEM ARTICKEL DER IUSTIFICATION... / Major, G – Wittemberg, 1558 – 1mf – ne IDC [240]

BEKENTNIS VNTERRICHT VND VERMANUNG DER PFARRHERN VND PREDIGER DER CHRISTLICHEN KIRCHEN ZU MAGDEBURGK / Amsdorff, N von – [Magdeburg, 1550] – 2mf – 9 – ne IDC [240]

BEKENTNISS VNND ERKLERUNG AUFFS INTERIM DURCH DER ERBARN STEDTE... / Aepinus, J – Magdeburg, [1548] – 3mf – 9 – ne IDC [240]

BEKENTNISSE VAN BEYDEN SACRAMENTEN. DOPE VNDE NACHTMAELE DER PREDICANTEN THO MUNSTER / Rothmann, B. et al – 1533. BME-147 1 – 9 – ne IDC [240]

BEKENTNIS...VON SEINEM GLAUBEN VND LERE/GESCHRIEBEN AN EYNEN WIDDERTEUFFER / Bugenhagen, J – Wittenberg, 1529 – 1mf – 9 – ne IDC [240]

Beker, Gabriele *see* ZUMUTBARKEIT VON KERNENERGIERISIKEN

Beker, Jerome *see* CHILD AND YOUTH SERVICES

BEKES MEGYEI NEPUJSAG – Bekescsaba, Hungary. 1962-90 – 58r – 1 – us L of C Photodup [072]

Beketova, M *see* ALEKSANDER BLOK I EGO MAT'

Bekker, E I *see*
- UEBER DIE COUPONSPROCESSE ...
- DAS VOELKERRECHT DER ZUKUNFT

Bekkeri, Imm *see*
- ANNALES (CSHB 27)
- ATHENIENSIS HISTORIARUM LIBRI 10 (CSHB 45)
- CHRONOGRAPHIA (CSHB 44)
- CODINI CUROPALATAE (CSHB 37)
- CORPUS SCRIPTORUM HISTORIAE BYZANTINAE (CSHB 30)
- CORPUS SCRIPTORUM HISTORIAE BYZANTINAE (CSHB 31)
- CORPUS SCRIPTORUM HISTORIAE BYZANTINAE (CSHB 33)
- CORPUS SCRIPTORUM HISTORIAE BYZANTINAE (CSHB 36)
- CORPUS SCRIPTORUM HISTORIAE BYZANTINAE (CSHB 41)
- EXCERPTA DE ANTIQUITATIBUS CONSTANTINOPOLITANI (CSHB 46)
- HISTORIA (CSHB 23)
- HISTORIARUM QUAE SUPERSUNT (CSHB 14)

Bekkerus, Imm *see*
- BREVIARIUM HISTORIAE METRICUM (CSHB 29)
- CORPUS SCRIPTORUM HISTORIAE BYZANTINAE (CSHB 28)
- DE MICHAEL ET ANDROICO PALAEOLOGIS LIBRI 13 (CSHB 24, 25)
- DESCRIPTIO TEMPLI SANCTAE SOPHIAE (CSHB 32)
- HISTORIA (CSHB 48)
- HISTORIA POLITICA ET PATRIARCHICA (CSHB 47)
- HISTORIARUM LIBRI 8 (CSHB 22)

Bekki, A *see* GEOPOLITIEK ASIA TIMOER RAJA; KOETIPAN PIDATO

BEKNOPTE GESCHIEDENIS VAN DE VEREENIGING "AMBONSCH STUDIEFONDS" (1909-1917) MET EEN KORTE TOESPRAAK TOT HET AMBONSCHE VOLK / Manusama, A T – Weltevreden, 1917 – 1mf – 9 – ne IDC [950]

BEK'S DJAKARTA DIGEST – (Missing: 1970(1, 183); 1971(347, 366). Irregular) – Djakarta. nos 1-367. 1970-1971 – 91mf – 9 – SE-1321/1 – ne IDC [910]

Bekure, Solomon et al *see* MAASAI HERDING

Bel, J H van *see* HET BUITENLANDSCH STRAFVONNIS

BELA-CRKVAER VOLKSBLATT – Bela Crkva, Yugoslavia. Oct 1923-1939 – 4r – 1 – us L of C Photodup [072]

BELAIA PECHAT', EE IDEOLOGIIA, ROL' ZNACHENIE I DEIATEL'NOST' / Belov, V – Petrograd, 1922 – 1 – 35.00r – us Hoover Inst Photo [335]

BELAIA STAIA / Akhmatova, A – Kniga 2. ed. 4. v. 2. Spb. 1923. BR-1089 2 – 8 – ne IDC [460]

BELAIA STAIA. STIKHOTVORENIIA / Akhmatova, A – Petrograd. 1917. BR-1088 2 – 8 – ne IDC [460]

Belair, Louis *see* LE FOYER DE L'INDUSTRIE

Belaney, Robert *see* THE KINGDOM OF GOD ON EARTH

Belanger, C *see* VOYAGE AUX INDES ORIENTALES PENDANT LES ANNEES 1825-1829

Belanger, Fernand *see* LE PROPRIETAIRE DE LAVAL

Belanger, Florent *see* LE SOUVENIR

Belanger, Jean Amable *see* MES VERS

Belanger, L A *see* LE PROGRES DE L'EST

Belanger, Louis Charles *see*
- MANUAL OF THE DUTIES OF ROAD AND RURAL INSPECTORS, UNDER THE MUNICIPAL CODE OF THE PROVINCE OF QUEBEC
- LE PROGRES
- LE PROGRES DE L'EST

Belanger, Pauline *see* LES MINISTRES DE LA COURONNE DU QUEBEC, 1867-1964

Belanger, Pierrette *see* BIBLIOGRAPHIE ANALYTIQUE DE L'OEUVRE DE MONSIEUR AUGUSTE VIATTE

BELARUS' – 1963-73. Monthly review. BR-10,383 1 – 9 – ne IDC [073]

BELARUSIAN PARLIAMENTARY PAPERS 1990-1995 = PARLAMENTSKIE DAKUMENTI BELARUSI : MINUTES OF THE 12TH CONGRESSIONAL SESSION OF THE SUPREME SOVIET OF THE REPUBLIC OF BELARUS – 937mf coll – 9 – $5,600.00 coll – us Ross [324]

BELARUSKI ARKHIU – v. 1-3. Mensk. 1927-30. Lacking: v. 2, 1928; v. 3 1930. BR-1670 2 – 8 – ne IDC [073]

BELARUSKI GOLAS – Toronto, Canada. -m. March 1956-Dec 1975. 3 reels – 1 – uk British Libr Newspaper [072]

Belaunde, Victor Andres *see*
- EL DEBATE CONSTITUCIONAL. DISCURSOS EN LA ASAMBLEA 1931-1933. LIMA 1933
- MEDITACIONES PERUANAS. LIMA, 1933

"BELAUSCHT!" : GEDICHTE UND SPRUECHE / Hubel, Henni – 2. Aufl. New York: A Baeumer, 1908 – 1r – 1 – us U.W. Library [810]

Belaval, Y *see* JOURNAL DES SCAVANS

Belcher, Alexander Emerson *see* WHAT I KNOW ABOUT COMMERCIAL TRAVELLING: WHO WE ARE, WHAT WE ARE, WHAT WE DO AND HOW WE DO IT

Belcher, E *see*
- NARRATIVE OF THE VOYAGE OF H.M.S. SAMARANG, DURING THE YEARS 1843-46
- THE SAILOR'S WORD-BOOK

THE BELCHER ISLANDS OF HUDSON BAY / Flaherty, R J – BN 210 2. 1918 – 8 – ne IDC [910]

Belcher, Jonathan *see* GOVERNOR JONATHAN BELCHER LETTERBOOKS, 1723-1754

Belcher, Joseph *see*
- GEORGE WHITEFIELD
- MEMORIALS OF BAPTIST MARTYRS
- ROBERT RAIKES
- WILLIAM CAREY

BELCHERTOWN 1765-1893 – (Mf 1-6: B,M,D & I 1773-1841. Mf 7: Index: Births by Families 1765-1849. Mf 8-15: Births by Families 1765-1849. Mf 16-17: Index: B,M,D 1843-57 Bk A. Mf 18-19: B,M,D 1844-57. Mf 20-22: Index to Births 1857-92 Vol B. Mf 23-24: Births 1857-92 Vol B. Mf 25-27: Index to Marriages 1857-93 Vol B. Mf 28-29: Marriages 1857-93 Vol B. Mf 30-32: Index to Deaths 1857-92 Vol B. Mf 33-35: Deaths 1857-92 Vol B) – (mf ed 1986) – 35mf – 9 – 0-87623-036-2 – us Holbrook [920]

Bel'chikov, N F *see* PUTI I NAVYKI LITERATUROVEDCHESKOGO TRUDA

BELDEN PROGRESS – Belden, NE. -w. Dec. 1911-Apr. 1914; Jun. 1914-Aug. 1914; Mar. 1922-Aug. 1942 – 1 – us NE Hist [071]

Belding, Albert Martin *see*
- A HEART-BROKEN CORONER AND OTHER WONDERS
- SIR JOHN THOMPSON

A BELEAGUERED CITY : BEING A NARRATIVE OF CERTAIN RECENT EVENTS IN THE CITY OF SEMUR... / Oliphant, Margaret – London: Macmillan, 1880 – 1 roll – 1 – 1-55879-699-1 – uk Libr Preservation [830]

BELEDIYE BUETCELERI (1930 SENESI MAHSUS OLARAK BELEDIYE MECLISLERI TARAFINDAN TANZIM OLUNUP TASDIKA IKTIRAN EDEN) – Istanbul: Matbaacilik ve Nesriyat Tuerk Anomim Sirketi, 1932 – 9 – $350.00 – us MEDOC [350]

DIE BELEGSCHAFT DER BERGWERKE UND SALINEN IM OBERAMTSBEZIRK DORTMUND NACH DER ZAHLUNG VOM 16. 12. 1893 / Taeglichsbeck, D – Dortmund 1895 – 1 – DM40.00 – gw Mikro Press [331]

BELEHRENDE UNTERHALTUNGEN [...] – Breslau, feb-nov 1797, 1798-sep 1799 – 1 – Inquire at Mikrofilmarchiv for details – gw Misc Inst [072]

Belenkogo, B S et al *see* ENTSIKLOPEDIIA SOVETSKOGO EKSPORTA

BELEP, SYNTHESE HISTORIQUE D'APRES LES TRADITIONS / Dubois, M J – 9 – F60.00 – fr Ethnologie [490]

Beletskii, S P *see* GRIGORII RASPUTIN

Beleze, G *see* DICTIONNAIRE DES NOMS DE BAPTEME

BELFAST ADVERTISER AND LITERARY GAZETTE – Ireland. -w. 5 Nov-31 Dec 1847. (7 ft) – 1 – uk British Libr Newspaper [072]

BELFAST CHARITABLE INSTITUTION BURYING GROUND – Belfast, Northern Ireland – 1 – uk Microform Academic [920]

BELFAST ELECTION – Ireland. -w. 30 Sep-18 Nov 1868. (5 ft) – 1 – uk British Libr Newspaper [072]

BELFAST EVENING TELEGRAPH – Ireland.20 Mar 1871-1881; 1883-85. -d. 39 reels – 1 – uk British Libr Newspaper [072]

BELFAST GAZETTE / Northern Ireland – 1921-73. 15 reels – 1 – $500.00 – us Trans-Media [324]

THE BELFAST GAZETTE / Northern Ireland – 1957-1968- – 1 – us NY Public [941]

BELFAST LABOUR CHRONICLE – Ireland.Nov 1904-2 Jun 1906 – 1 – ie Microforms [072]

BELFAST MERCURY AND EVENING POST – Belfast, Ireland. 1786-87. 2 reels – 1 – ie Microforms [072]

BELFAST MORNING NEWS – Ireland. -d. Nov. 1857- Aug. 1892. (96 1 2 reels) – 1 – uk British Libr Newspaper [072]

THE BELFAST NEWSLETTER – Belfast, Ireland. 1738-1925 – 236mf – 1 – Ir£5,600.00 – ie Microforms [072]

THE BELFAST NEWSLETTER, 1738-1800 – (The Belfast Newsletter Index 51mf $287.50) – 45r – 1,9 – $3,881.25 + index on mf – us UMI [072]

BELFAST SHIRE COUNCIL MINUTES – 1854-1980. 1864-76 Lost. SOB1-8 – 8r – 1 – at Corangamite [910]

BELFAST SHIRE RATE BOOKS – 1876-1954. SOBR1-2 – 2r – 1 – at Corangamite [910]

BELFAST STANDARD AND ULSTER FARMERS' JOURNAL – Ireland. -w. 18 Feb-30 Sep 1837. (21 ft) – 1 – uk British Libr Newspaper [072]

BELFAST STRIKE BULLETIN – Ireland.28 Jan-19 Feb 1919 – 1 – ie Microforms [072]

BELFAST TELEGRAPH – 1976 – 1 – F9,430.00 – sz Infoprint [072]

BELFAST TELEGRAPH – 1977 – 1 – F6,505.00 – sz Infoprint [072]

BELFAST TELEGRAPH – Belfast: Belfast Telegraph, 1956-apr 1977 – 200r – 1 – us Res Libr [072]

THE BELFAST TELEGRAPH – Belfast, Northern Ireland. 1976- – 1 – us Primary [072]

BELFAST WEEKLY ADVERTISER – Ireland.1882-Feb 1886.-w. 1 1/2 reels – 1 – uk British Libr Newspaper [072]

BELFAST WEEKLY TELEGRAPH – Ireland.15 Aug 1874-1890; 1892-93; 1895-96. -w. 20 1/4 reels – 1 – uk British Libr Newspaper [072]

Belford, Michele L *see* THE EFFECT OF ARM AND LEG VERSUS LEGS ALONE EXERCISE ON THE STAIRMASTER 4000PT IN FEMALES

BELFORD'S MONTHLY MAGAZINE – Incomplete. v. 1-3. Dec. 1876-May 1878 – 9 – fr Hachette [073]

BELFORD'S MONTHLY MAGAZINE – v1-3. Dec. 1876-May 1878 – 1 – cn Precision [073]

BELFORD'S MONTHLY MAGAZINE *see* THE CANADIAN MONTHLY AND NATIONAL REVIEW

Belfort Bax, Ernest *see* SOCIALISM AND INDIVIDUALISM

LES BELGES AU CANADA / Verbist, P J – Turnhout, Belgium: A. Van Genechten, 1872. 02289. (Pre-1900 Canadiana) – 9 – cn C.I.H.M. [971]

LES BELGES AU GUATEMALA, 1840-1845 / Fabri, Joseph – Bruxelles, 1955 – 1 – us Res Libr [972]

Belgian Congo. Secretariat general *see*
- BULLETIN ADMINISTRATIF
- BULLETIN ADMINISTRATIF ET COMMERCIAL

BELGIAN NEWS & CONTINENTAL ADVERTISER – Brussels, Belgium. -w. 30 Dec 1893-25 Sept 1896. 3 reels – 1 – uk British Libr Newspaper [949]

THE BELGIAN UNDERGROUND PRESS IN WORLD WAR 2 – $3,100.00 – us UPA [070]

BELGICA. (SHIP) *see* VOYAGE DU S.Y. BELGICA EN 1897-1898-1899

BELGIQUE – Paris. devenu: Paris-Bruxelles puis Paris-mondial. 29 aout 1944-45 – 1 – fr A.C.R.P.P. [072]

LA BELGIQUE COLONIALE – Brussels, Belgium. La Belgique maritime et coloniale. -w. 1895-1932. 27 reels – 1 – uk British Libr Newspaper [949]

LA BELGIQUE ET L'ARBITRAGE OBLIGATOIRE A LA DEUXIEME CONFERENCE DE LA PAIX – Bruxelles, 1908 – 1mf – 9 – ILM-4070/1 – ne IDC [327]

BELGIQUE HORTICOLE : JOURNAL DES JARDINS DES SERRES ET DES VERGERS / ed by Morren, C – La Haye, Liege, 1851-1885. v1-35. Index 1851-1870 – 301mf – 7302/1 – ne IDC [580]

Belgische WerkliedenpartijParti ouvrier belge *see* VOORUIT

BELGISCH-NEDERLANDS TIJDSCHRIFT VOOR OPPERVLAKTETECHNIEKEN VAN METALEN – v16-24. May 1972-Dec 1980 – 1,5,6,9 – us UMI [670]

BELGISHE BLETER = FEUILLES BELGES – (In Yiddish) – Antwerp, BE. v3 no4 Oct 1937-v4 no1-2 Feb/Mar 1938 – 1r – 1 – $25.00 – cn Can Microfilming [072]

BELGIUM : ANNUAIRE STATISTIQUE DE LA BELGE 1870-1962 / Belgium. Ministere des Affaires Economiques et des Classes MoyennesInstitut National de Statistique – (1946; 1952-54; 1956-57; 1963-65 not reproduced. Coll title: European Official Statistical Serials, 1841-1984) – 398mf – 9 – £4.00f (set £2.395.00 456mf) – uk Chadwyck [949]

BELGIUM : STATISTIQUE GENERALE DE LA BELGIQUE. EXPOSE DE LA SITUATION DU ROYAUME 1841-1900 / Belgium. Commission Centrale de Statistique – (Coll title: European Official Statistical Serials, 1841-1984) – 58mf – 9 – £6.00f (set £2,395.00 456mf) – uk Chadwyck [949]

Belgium *see*
- MONITEUR BELGE
- PROGRAMME QUINQUENNAL D'EXPANSION ECONOMIQUE
- PROGRAMME QUINQUENNAL D'EXPANSION ECONOMIQUE, 1961-1965
- PROJECT DE LOI PORTANT APPROB. DU 1ER PROGR. D'EXP. ECONOMIQUE
- RAPPORT. SUR L'EXEC. DU PROGR. D'EXP. ECON. 1963. PREV. 1964
- VOCATIONAL TRAINING AND JOB CREATION SCHEMES IN BELGIUM

BELGIUM AND THE CAUSES AND ORIGINS OF WORLD WAR 1 PAMPHLET COLLECTION – 1916 – 1 – CSUXAML2973-B – us Hoover Inst Photo [355]

Belgium. (before 1830) *see* LE PARTI LIBERAL ET LE GROS BON SENS

Belgium. Bureau de Programmation Economique *see*
- DEUXIEME PROGRAMME D'EXPANSION ECONOMIQUE, 1966-1970 LES SECTEURS DE PRODUCTION
- LES LIGNES DE FORCE DU PLAN 1971-1975

Belgium. Commission Centrale de Statistique *see* BELGIUM

Belgium. Commission Economique Interministerielle. Groupe d'Etude des Investissements Publics *see*
- INVESTISSEMENTS PUBLICS ET PARAETATIQUES BELGES. REALISATIONS 1948-1953 ET PROGRAMME 1954-1957
- INVESTISSEMENTS PUBLICS ET PARAETATIQUES BELGES. REALISATIONS 1948-1954 ET PROGRAMME 1955-1957
- INVESTISSEMENTS PUBLICS ET PARAETATIQUES BELGES. REALISATIONS 1948-1955 ET PROGRAMME 1956-1958

Belgium. Commission Gouvernementale pour l'Etude des Problemes de Financement de l'Expansion Economique *see* RAPPORT

Belgium. Ministere de la Coordination Economique et du Reequipement National *see* PROGRAMME DECENNAL DES INVESTISSEMENTS PUBLICS, 1948-1957

Belgium. Ministere de l'Interieur *see*
- BULLETIN DES COMMISSIONS ROYALES D'ART ET D'ARCHEOLOGIE
- ENQUETE SUR LA CONDITION DES CLASSES OUVRIERES ET SUR LE TRAVAIL DES ENFANTS

Belgium. Ministere des Affaires Economiques *see*
- DEUXIEME PROGRAMME D'EXPANSION ECONOMIQUE PROGRAMME GENERAL DE CADRE 1966-1970
- ECONOMISCH EXPANSIEPROGRAMMA, 1961-1965
- PROGRAMME D'EXPANSION ECONOMIQUE, 1962-1965

Belgium. Ministere des Affaires Economiques et des Classes MoyennesInstitut National de Statistique *see* BELGIUM

Belgium. Ministere des Colonies *see*
- AUS DEN ARCHIVEN DES BELGISCHEN KOLONIALMINISTERIUMS BERLIN, 1916
- PLAN DECENNAL POUR LE DEVELOPPEMENT ECONOMIQUE ET SOCIAL
- RENSEIGNEMENTS DE L'OFFICE COLONIAL

Belgium. Ministry of Foreign Affairs *see*
- GIFT FROM THE MINISTRY OF FOREIGN AFFAIRS AND EXTERNAL COMMERCE OF BELGIUM. (RECORDS RELATING TO THE U.S.)
- RECORDS RELATING TO NORTH AMERICA, 1834-99..

Belgium. Office Belge du Commerce Exterieur *see* LE MAROC: MONOGRAPHIE ECONOMIQUE

Belgium.Office du Tourisme du Congo belge et du Ruanda-Urundi *see* TRAVELLER'S GUIDE TO THE BELGIAN CONGO AND RUANDA-URUNDI
BELGRADE HERALD – Belgrade, NE. -w. Oct. 1900-Oct. 1902; Oct. 1903-Aug. 1945 – 1 – us NE Hist [071]
BELGRADER NACHRICHTEN – Belgrad, dec 15 1915-jun 30 1917, jan 1-oct 27 1918 – 1 – Dist. gw Mikrofilm – gw Misc Inst [949]
BELGRADER ZEITUNG – Belgrade, Yugoslavia. Nov 1924-Mar 1926 – 4r – 1 – us L of C Photodup [072]
Belgrano, Mario *see*
- LA FRANCIA Y LA MONARQUIA EN EL PLATA (1818-1820). LA POLITICA DEL DUQUE DE RICHELIEU. MISIONES...BUENOS AIRES, 1933
- RIVODAVIA Y SUS GESTIONES DIPLOMATICAS CON ESPANA. (1815-1820). 2ND ED. BUENOS AIRES, 1934

BELI TEKUMAH / Singer, A – St. Petersburg. 1902. BJ-422-85 1 – 9 – ne IDC [470]
Beliaev, IS *see* PRAKTICHESKII KURS IZUCHENIIA DREVNEI RUSSKOI SKOROPISI DLIA CHTENIIA RUKOPISEI XV-XVIII STOLETII
Beliaev, V *see* ISPOVIED KOMISSARA
Beliaev, V N *see* KAK ORGANIZOVAT' SEL'SKOKHOZIAISTVENNOE KREDITNOE TOVARISHCHESTVO
Beliaev, VI *see* ARABSKIE RUKOPISI SOBRANIIA LENINGRADSKOGO GOSUDARSTVENNOGO UNIVERSITETA
Belic, Aleksandar *see* LA MACEDOINE: ETUDES ETHNOGRAPHIQUES ET POLITIQUES
Belidor, Bernard Forest de *see*
- ARCHITECTURE HYDRAULIQUE OU L'ART DE CONDUIRE, D'ELEVER ET DE MENAGER LES EAUX POUR LES DIFFERENTS BESOINS DE LA VIE
- DICTIONNAIRE PORTATIF DE L'INGENIEUR ET DE L'ARTILLEUR
- LA SCIENCE INGENIEURS DANS LA CONDUITE DES TRAVAUX DE FORTIFICATION ET D'ARCHITECTURE CIVILE

BELIEF / Chaney, George Leonhard – Boston: Roberts, 1889 – 1mf – 9 – 0-8370-3213-X – 1985-1213 – us A.T.L.A. [210]
BELIEF IN GOD : ITS ORIGIN, NATURE, AND BASIS / Schurman, Jacob Gould – New York: Charles Scribner, 1907 – 1mf – 9 – us A.T.L.A. [210]
BELIEF IN GOD: AN EXAMINATION OF SOME FUNDAMENTAL THEISTIC PROBLEMS / Savage, Minot Judson – Boston: Geo. H. Ellis, 1881. 1 fiche – 9 – us A.T.L.A. [240]
BELIEF IN MENTAL IMAGERY IN FREE THROW PERFORMANCE / Nordeen, Lisa M – Springfield College, 1994 – 1mf – 9 – $4.00 – PSY1857 – us Microform Publ [611]
BELIEF IN THE DIVINITY OF JESUS CHRIST / Didon, H – London: K. Paul, Trench, Truebner; New York: Benziger, 1894 – 1mf – us A.T.L.A. [240]
BELIEFS ABOUT THE BIBLE / Savage, Minot Judson – Boston: Geo. H. Ellis, 1900. 1 fiche – 9 – us A.T.L.A. [240]
BELIEFS OF UNBELIEF / Fitchett, William Henry – New York: Eaton & Mains, 1907. 1 fiche – 9 – us A.T.L.A. [240]
THE BELIEFS OF UNBELIEF : STUDIES IN THE ALTERNATIVES TO FAITH / Fitchett, William Henry – New York: Eaton & Mains, c1907 – 1mf – 9 – 0-8370-3152-4 – 1985-1152 – us A.T.L.A. [210]
LE BELIER : CARICATURES / ed by Blanchard, J T – Montreal, Canada. 23 jul 1921 – 1r – 1 – Can$25.00 – cn Can Microfilming [072]
LE BELIER – Montreal, Canada. v1 n3. mai 1967 – 1r – 1 – Can$25.00 – cn Can Microfilming [072]
THE BELIEVER BORN OF ALMIGHTY GRACE / Dabney, Robert Lewis – 9 – $50.00 – us Presbyterian [240]
Believers' Meeting for Bible Study (12th: 1888: Niagara-on-the-Lake) *see* REPORT..
Belig *see* DIVAN
Beligand, N *see* L'AUTOSACRIFICE DANS LE TONALAMATL DU CODEX BORBONICUS
BELI-MAH / Beilin, A – London. 1918. BJ-422-6 1 – 9 – ne IDC [400]
Belimov, I T *see* ZHELEZNODOROZHNYI PROLETARIAT SIBIRI V REVOLIUTSII 1905-1907 GG
Belin, W *see* DIE NATIONALITAET DER HANDELSGESELLSCHAFTEN WAEHREND DES KRIEGES.
BELINDA: A NOVEL / Broughton, Rhoda – British Fiction Archive: Unit 4 – 9 – uk Bell [830]
Belinfante, I *see* AN EIGHTEENTH CENTURY BIBLIOPHILE
Belinfante, M C *see* BIJDRAGEN BETREKKELIJK DE VERBETERING VAN DEN MAATSCHAPPELIJKEN STAAT DER JODEN
Belinksii, VE *see* RUSSKII GERAL'DICHESKII SLOVAR
BELINSKII I RUSSKAIA LITERATURA 18 VEKA / Orishin, A D – L'vov. 1954. BR-7739 2 – 8 – ne IDC [460]
BELISARIO PENA / Bayle, Constantino – Buenos Aires: R. Herrando y Cia, Impresores, 1915. Sep. Rev. Estudios – 1 – sp Bibl Santa Ana [240]
Belisle, Louis-Alexandre *see* LE RECUEIL
Beliutin, E *see* PEDAGOGICHESKAIA SISTEMA AKADEMII KHUDOZHESTV 18 VEKA
BELIZE : ABSTRACT OF STATISTICS 1961-1970/72 / Belize. Central Planning Unit – (1964 not publ. 1961, 1963, 1967 not available. Coll title: Latin American and Caribbean Official Statistical Serials, 1821-1982) – 11mf – 9 – £92.00 – uk Chadwyck [972]
BELIZE BILLBOARD – Belize. -d. 1 Jan 1957-16 May 71. (35 reels) – 1 – uk British Libr Newspaper [072]
Belize. Central Planning Unit *see* BELIZE
BELIZE INDEPENDENT – British Honduras. -w. 1 Jan 1930-27 Jul 1938; 4 Jan 1939-8 Dec 1943, 14 Jun-20 Sep 1944, 7 Feb-28 Mar 1945. (15 reels) – 1 – uk British Libr Newspaper [072]
BELIZE TIMES – Belize. -d. 1 Jan 1959-22 Nov 1972. 30 reels – 1 – uk British Libr Newspaper [072]
BELIZEAN SEVEN YEAR DEVELOPMENT PLAN, 1964-1970 / Honduras. British – Belize. 1964. BD-125 1 – 9 – ne IDC [338]
Belkaid, M see LE PARLER ARABE DE TENES, ALGERIE
Belknap, Paul A *see* THE THINGS I AM FOR
BELL – El Reno. Okl. 1900-02 – 1 – us UMI [071]
Bell *see* HISTORY OF THE CITY OF OMAHA AND SOUTH OMAHA
THE BELL – 1940-54.17v. 131 pts.114 fiches – 9 – Ir£100.00 – ie Microforms [073]
THE BELL – Newsletter of the Association for a Free Russia. July, 1984. 12p. Sample copy – 9 – $1.00f – at Libertarian Micro [335]
THE BELL – No.1, 1982. 12p. Sample copy – 9 – $1.00f – at Libertarian Micro [335]
Bell, Alexander Melville *see* EXPLANATORY LECTURE ON VISIBLE SPEECH, THE SCIENCE OF UNIVERSAL ALPHABETICS...FEB. 9, 1870
Bell, Aubrey FG *see*
- FRANCISCO SANCHEZ EL BROCENSE
- STUDIES IN PORTUGUESE LITERATURE

Bell, B *see* A TREATISE ON GONORRHOEA VIRULENTA AND LUES VENEREA
Bell, Charles Dent *see* HENRY MARTYN
Bell, Charles Napier *see* TANGWEERS: LIFE AND ADVENTURE AMONG GENTLE SAVAGES
Bell, Clark, 1832-1918 *see* CRIMINAL ABORTION AND THE NEW ENGLISH CRIMINAL EVIDENCE ACT
Bell, Earl S *see* EVANGELICAL BEGINNINGS IN THE ARIZONA TERRITORY
Bell, Edward *see* SELECTED PROSE WORKS
Bell, Evans *see* RETROSPECTS AND PROSPECTS OF INDIAN POLICY
BELL GARDENS REVIEW – Bell Gardens, CA. 1974-1981 – 11r – 1 – $550.00 – H03152 – us Library Micro [071]
Bell, George *see*
- ROUGH NOTES BY AN OLD SOLDIER, DURING FIFTY YEARS' SERVICE, FROM ENSIGN G.B. TO MAJOR-GENERAL G.B
- SUNDAY-SCHOOL CONVENTIONS: THEIR OBJECTS AND IMPORTANCE, AND THE BEST METHODS OF CONDUCTING THEM. TWO PRIZE ESSAYS

Bell, H C *see* HISTORICAL ENCYCLOPEDIA OF ILLINOIS AND HISTORY OF CLARK COUNTY
Bell, H C P *see*
- ANNUAL REPORT
- ARCHAEOLOGICAL SURVEY OF CEYLON

Bell, Heaketh *see* FOREIGN COLONIAL ADMINISTRATION IN THE FAR EAST
Bell, Herbert C *see* HISTORY OF NORTHUMBERLAND COUNTY
Bell, John *see* PAPERS
Bell, John Allison *see* CHEBUCTO AND OTHER POEMS
Bell, John H *see* WESTERN SKIES: A NARRATIVE OF AMERICAN TRAVEL IN 1868
BELL JOURNAL OF ECONOMICS – v. 6-. 1975- – 1,5,6,9 – us UMI [330]
BELL JOURNAL OF ECONOMICS AND MANAGEMENT SCIENCE – v. 1-5. 1970-1974 – 5,6 – us UMI [330]
Bell, Kenneth Ray *see* THE DEVELOPMENT OF A PROGRAM OF STUDENT FINANCIAL ASSISTANCE FOR EAST COAST BIBLE COLLEGE
BELL LABORATORIES RECORD – (1965- 5,6. 1970- 9) – 1- 1925- – 1 – us UMI [621]
BELL LABORATORIES RECORD – v. 1-28. 1925-1950 – 1,5,6 – us Princeton Micro [621]
Bell, Lallah *see* PRINCESS & POET
Bell, Leon G *see* REPORT...ON THE EXPLORATION MADE OF THE ROUTE OF THE HURON AND OTTAWA RAILWAY FROM OTTAWA CITY TO PARRY SOUND
Bell, M S *see* CHINA BEING A MILITARY REPORT. AN ACCOUNT OF CHINA CIVIL, NAVAL, AND MILITARY ADMINISTRATION
Bell, Mackenzie *see* CHRISTINA ROSSETTI
Bell, R *see* THE ORGAN OF ISLAM IN ITS CHRISTIAN ENVIRONMENT
Bell, Robert *see*
- ALEXANDER MURRAY, F.G.S., F.R.S.C., C.M.G
- FOREST FIRES IN NORTHERN CANADA
- THE FORESTS OF CANADA
- THE GEOLOGICAL HISTORY OF LAKE SUPERIOR
- THE LAURENTIAN AND HURONIAN SYSTEMS IN THE REGION NORTH OF LAKE HURON
- MARBLE ISLAND AND THE NORTH-WEST COAST OF HUDSON'S BAY
- THE MINERAL RESOURCES OF THE HUDSON'S BAY TERRITORIES
- ON THE COMMERCIAL IMPORTANCE OF HUDSON'S BAY: WITH REMARKS ON RECENT SURVEYS AND INVESTIGATIONS
- ON THE OCCURRENCE OF MAMMOTH AND MASTODON REMAINS AROUND HUDSON'S BAY
- THE ORIGIN OF GNEISS AND SOME OTHER PRIMITIVE ROCKS
- A PLEA FOR PIONEERS
- PRE-PALEOZOIC DECAY OF CRYSTALLINE ROCKS NORTH OF LAKE HURON
- RECENT EXPLORATIONS TO THE SOUTH OF HUDSON BAY
- RISING OF THE LAND AROUND HUDSON BAY

BELL STREET CHAPEL DISCOURSES : CONTAINING SELECTIONS FROM THE WRITINGS OF JAMES EDDY, PROVIDENCE, RHODE ISLAND, 1889-1899 / Spencer, Anna Garlin – Providence, RI: Journal of Commerce, [1899?] – 1mf – 9 – 0-8370-5508-3 – 1985-3508 – us A.T.L.A. [240]
BELL SYSTEM TECHNICAL JOURNAL – (1967-5,6. 1970- 9) – 1- 1922- – 1 – us UMI [621]
BELL SYSTEM TECHNICAL JOURNAL – v1-34. 1922-55 – 1,5,6 – us Princeton Micro [621]
BELL SYSTEM TECHNICAL JOURNAL *see* AT AND T BELL LABORATORIES TECHNICAL JOURNAL
Bell, T P *see* CORRESPONDENCE FILES OF CORRESPONDING SECRETARIES, BAPTIST SUNDAY SCHOOL BOARD
BELL TELEPHONE MAGAZINE *see* AT AND T MAGAZINE
Bell, William Melvin *see* THE LOVE OF GOD
[LA BELLA PESCATRICE] AL SUON SOAVE / Gugliemi, P – (Full score) – London: Skillern, Goulding, 179- – 1 – us Sibley [780]
BELLAIRE BAPTIST CHURCH. BERMOTT, ARKANSAS : CHURCH RECORDS – 1940-75 – 1 – 27.45 – us Baptist [240]
Bellairs, N *see* HARDY FERNS: HOW I COLLECTED AND CULTIVATED THEM
Bellamy, Joseph *see* LETTERS AND OTHER PAPERS OF JOSEPH BELLAMY
Bellardi, C A L *see*
- APPENDIX AD FLORAM PEDEMONTANAM
- OSSERVAZIONI BOTANICHE CON UN SAGGIO D'APPENDICE ALLA FLORA PEDEMONTANA

Bellardi, L *see* I MOLLUSCHI DEI TERRENI TERZIARI DEL PIEMONTE E DELLA LIGURIA
Bellarmin, R *see* DISPUTATIONES DE CONTROVERSIIS CHRISTIANAE FIDEI, ADVERSUS HUIUS TEMPORIS HAERETICOS...
LAS BELLAS ARTES PLASTICAS EN SEVILLA / Cascales Munoz, Jose – Toledo: Tip. Colegio de Huerfanos, Tomo 1. 1928 – 1 – sp Bibl Santa Ana [730]
LAS BELLAS ARTES PLASTICAS EN SEVILLA...DESDE EL SIGLO 13 HASTA NUESTROS DIAS... / Cascales Munoz, Jose – Toledo: Imp. Colegio de Huerfanos, Tomo 2. 1929 – 1 – sp Bibl Santa Ana [730]
Bellay, A *see*
- L'ENSEIGNEMENT DES JESUITES AU CANADA: COLLEGE SAINTE-MARIE DE MONTREAL
- HOSPICE -JEAN DE DIEU, ASILE DE LA LONGUE-POINTE
- PENSIONNAT MONT SAINT-LOUIS

LA BELLE HELENE : OPERETTE IN 3 ACTES / Offenbach, J – Partitur. 3v. 1886? MS – 1 – us Sibley [780]
Belle, Manfred *see* DER ENTWICKLUNGSPOLITISCHE RUNDE TISCH IN DER DDR UND IM VEREINIGTEN DEUTSCHLAND
LA BELLE PROVINCE : MENSUELLE. REVUE DU CLUB DES HABITANTS – Quebec, Canada. v1 n1. jul 1946-v4 n5. oct-nov 1950 – 1r – 1 – Can$50.00 – cn Can Microfilming [072]
Belle Springs Creamery. Abilene, Kansas *see* JOURNAL AND INVENTORIES
Bellefeuille, Edouard Lefebvre de *see* LE CANADA ET LES ZOUAVES PONTIFICAUX:... L'EXPEDITION...A ROME...1868
BELLEFONTE GAZETTE – Bellefonte, PA. -w 1889-1912 – 13 – $25.00r – us I.M.R. [071]
BELLEFONTE REPUBLICAN – Bellefonte, PA. -w 1889-1931 – 13 – $25.00r – us I.M.R. [071]
Bellegotti, L *see*
- NOZIONI ELEMENTARI DI DIRITTO PENALE INTERNAZIONALE E DELLE PROCEDURE AD ESSO ATTINENTI
- LE SUCCESSIONI SECONDO IL DIRITTO INTERNAZIONALE PRIVATO ITALIANO

Belleli, Lazare *see* INTERPRETATIONS ERRONEES ET FAUX MONUMENTS
Bellemo, Vincenzo *see* I VIAGGI DI NICOLO DE CONTI.
Beller, W et al *see* SUSTAINABLE DEVELOPMENT AND ENVIRONMENTAL MANAGEMENT OF SMALL ISLANDS
Bellermann, H *see* DIE GROSSE DER MUSIKALISCHE INTERVALLE ALS GRUNDLAGE DER HARMONIE
Bellermann, Ludwig *see* SCHILLERS WERKE
BELLEROPHON, OF LUST TOT WIJSHEYD : DOOR SINNE-BEELDEN LEERLIJCK VERTOONT / Pers, DP – Amsterdam, 1638 – 4mf – 9 – ne IDC [700]
BELLEROPHON OF LUST TOT WYSHEYD / Pers, DP – O 712. 1614 – 9 – ne IDC [760]
BELLEROPHON, OF LUST TOT WYSHEYT : DOOR SINNE-BEELDEN LEERLIJCK VERTOONT / Pers, DP – Amsterdam, 1648 – 8mf – 9 – ne IDC [700]
BELLEROPHON, OF LUST TOT WYSHEYT : DOOR SINNE-BEELDEN LEERLIJCK VERTOONT / Pers, DP – Amsterdam, 1656-1662 – 8mf – 9 – ne IDC [700]
Bellerose, Joseph Hyacinthe *see*
- LETTRE A SES ANCIENS CONSTITUANTS DU COMTE DE LAVAL
- L'ORANGISME ET LE CATHOLICISME: SIR GEORGE E. CARTIER, LE GRAND CHEF DU BAS-CANADA CONTRE SIR JOHN A. MACDONALD, L'ENNEMI DES CATHOLIQUES ET DES CANADIENS-FRANCAIS

Bellerose, L H *see* PETIT MANUEL D'AGRICULTURE A L'USAGE DES ECOLES
Bellesheim, Alphons *see*
- GESCHICHTE DER KATHOLISCHEN KIRCHE IN SCHOTTLAND
- HISTORY OF THE CATHOLIC CHURCH IN SCOTLAND
- WILHELM CARDINAL ALLEN (1532-1594) UND DIE ENGLISCHEN SEMINARE AUF DEM FESTLANDE

Bellet, D *see* LA NOUVELLE VOIE MARITIME LE CANAL DE PANAMA
Bellett, John Crosthwaite *see* GOD'S WITNESS IN PROPHECY AND HISTORY
Bellett, John Gifford *see*
- EPISTLE TO THE EPHESIANS
- THE EPISTLE TO THE EPHESIANS
- THE EVANGELISTS

Belleval *see* NOBILIAIRE DU PONTHIEU DE DU VIMEU
BELLEVIEW BAPTIST CHURCH. BOONE COUNTY. KENTUCKY : CHURCH RECORDS – 1803-1914. Formerly Cedar Creek Baptist Church. Name changed Sept 12, 1885. 932p – 1 – 41.94 – us Baptist [240]

BELLEVILLE INTELLIGENCER – Belleville, Canada. 1862-73 – 11r – 1 – $715.00 – cn Library Assoc [971]
BELLEVILLER POST UND ZEITUNG – Belleville, IL. mar 2 1922-jan 4 1923 – 1r – 1 – Dist. gw Mikrofilm – gw Misc Inst [072]
BELLEVUE BAPTIST CHURCH. OWENSBORO, KENTUCKY : CHURCH RECORDS – Dec 1958-67 – 1 – 14.22 – us Baptist [240]
BELLEVUE BROADCASTER – Bellevue, NE. -w. Aug. 1932-May 1933 – 1 – us NE Hist [071]
BELLEVUE GAZETTE – Bellevue, NE. -w. Mar. 1906-Apr. 1910 – 1 – us NE Hist [071]
BELLEVUE GAZETTE – Bellevue, NE. -w. Oct. 1856-Sep. 1858 – 1 – us NE Hist [071]
BELLEVUE GUIDE – Bellevue, NE. -w. Mar. 1970-Sep. 1970 – 1 – us NE Hist [071]
Bellevue, Jean *see* UNE VISITE CHEZ LE CAPITAINE B..
Bellevue,. Ohio. Methodist Episcopal Church *see* CHURCH RECORDS, MS 2041
Bellevue. Ohio.Zion United Church of Christ *see* RECORDS
BELLEVUE PRESS – Bellevue, NE. -w. Dec. 1945-Apr. 1951; Oct. 1952- – 1 – us NE Hist [071]
LA BELLEZA IDEAL / Arteaga, Esteban – 1789 – 1mf – 9 – Pta1,000.00 – 84-7848-162-1 – sp Pentalfa [946]
BELLEZAS DEL ALMA: LA CARIDAD / Rodriguez Marcos, Antonio – 1885 – 9 – 1.50f – sp Bibl Santa Ana [240]
LE BELLEZZE DELLA CITTA DI FIRENZE / Bocchi, F – O-960 1. 1677 – 9 – ne IDC [945]
Belli, L V *see* DISSERTAZIONE SOPRA LI PREGGI DEL CANTO GREGORIANO
BELLI MONASTERIENSIS CONTRA ANABAPTISTICA MONSTRA / Kerssenbrock, H – Coloniae, M. Gymnicus. 1545. BME-164 1 – 9 – ne IDC [240]
Belli, Piero *see* DE RE MILITARI ET BELLO TRACTATUS
Bellin, Jacques N *see* LE PETIT ATLAS MARITIME
Belling, Laura R *see* THE RELATIONSHIP BETWEEN SOCIAL PHYSIQUE ANXIETY AND PHYSICAL ACTIVITY
BELLINGHAM 1698-1849 – (Mf 1T-3T: Births & Deaths 1698-1844. Mf 2T-3T: Marriages 1752-1827. Mf 3T-4T: Intentions 1739-1827. Mf 4T: marriages 1739-70. Mf 5T: Intentions & Marriages 1827-49. Mf 6T: Births & Deaths 1814-46. Mf 7T: B,M,D 1844-49) – (mf ed 1995) – 7mf – 9 – 0-87623-209-8 – us Holbrook [920]
Bellingham, Sydney *see* REASONS WHY BRITISH CONSERVATIVES VOTED AGAINST THE BOUCHERVILLE MINISTRY
Bellman, C *see* FREDMANS EPISTIAR
[Bello, A] *see* PRINCIPIOS ...
BELLO SEXO : PERIODICO RELIGIOSO, DE INSTRUCCAO E RECREIO, NOTICIOSO E CRITICO MODERADO – Rio de Janeiro, 21 Aug-28 Sep 1862 – 1,5,6 – bl Biblioteca [072]
Belloc, Hilaire *see*
- ECONOMICS FOR HEALTH
- TOURCOING

Bellogin Garcia, Andres *see* VIDA Y HAZANAS DE ALVAR NUNEZ CABEZA DE VACA. MADRID, 1928
Bellon de Saint-Quentin *see* DISSERTATION SUR LA TRAITE ET LE COMMERCE DES NEGRES
Belloni, Alberto *see*
- DEL ANARQUISMO AL PERONISMO
- PERONISMO Y SOCIALISMO NACIONAL

Bellori, Giovanni Pietro *see*
- DESCRIZZIONE DELLE IMMAGINI DIPINTE DA RAFAELLE D'URBINO NELLE CAMERE DEL PALAZZO APOSTOLICO VATICANO
- RITRATTI DI ALCUNI CELEBRI PITTORI DEL SECOLO 17. CON LE VITE DE'MEDESIMI
- VETERES ARCUS AUGUSTORUM TRIUMPHIS INSIGNES
- LE VITA DE' PITTORI, SCULTORI ET ARCHITETTI MODERNI
- LE VITE DE' PITTORI, SCULTORI, ET ARCHITETTI MODERNI
- LE VITE DE' PITTORI, SCULTORI ET ARCHITETTI MODERNI...
- LE VITE DE PITTORI, SCVLTORI ET ARCHITETTI MODERNI, SCRITTE DA GIO

Belloso Rodriguez, Pedro *see*
- CON LO QUE TENGO A BORDO (MECANOGRAFIADO)
- MILLONARIO DE POBREZA (MECANOGRAFIADO)
- EL NOMBRE NUESTRO DE CADA DIA. (MECANOGRAFIADO)
- LOS OTROS, EL PAISAJE Y YO (MECANOGRAFIADO)
- POEMAS
- POEMAS DE CAMPO Y PUEBLO (MECANOGRAFIADO)
- SALTERIO DE MIS HORAS (MECANOGRAFIADO)

Bellot, Hugh Hale L *see*
- ANALYSIS OF FOOTE'S ...
- GRAY'S INN AND LINCOLN'S INN
- THE INNER AND MIDDLE TEMPLE
- IRELAND AND CANADA: STUDIES IN COMPARATIVE CONSTITUTIONAL LAW AND POLITICS

Bellot, James *see*
- FAMILIAR DIALOGUES
- THE FRENCHE METHODE
- LE MAISTRE D'ESCOLE ANGLOIS. THE ENGLISHE SCHOLEMAISTER

Bellot, Joseph Rene *see* VOYAGE AUX MERS POLAIRES A LA RECHERCHE DE SIR JOHN FRANKLIN
Bellows, Henry Whitney *see* THE OLD THEOLOGY AND THE NEW
BELL'S DICTIONARY : A DICTIONARY OF THE LAW OF SCOTLAND – Edinburgh. 2v. 1816 – 11mf – 9 – $16.50 – LLMC 95-409 – us L.L.M.C. [340]
BELL'S LIFE IN LONDON AND SPORTING CHRONICLE – London. -w. 3 Mar 1822-29 May 1886. (67 reels) – 1 – uk British Libr Newspaper [073]
BELLS LIFE IN SYDNEY – Sydney, 1845-70 – 5r – 1 – A$176.00 silver A$152.00 vesicular – at Pascoe [073]
BELL'S NEW WEEKLY MESSENGER – London, UK. 1832-25 Mar 1855. -w. 23 1/4 reels – 1 – uk British Libr Newspaper [072]
THE BELLS OF ENGLAND / Raven, J J – H 1351 2. 1906 – 8 – ne IDC [780]
THE BELLS OF IS : OR, VOICES OF HUMAN NEED AND SORROW: ECHOES FROM MY EARLY PASTORATE / Meyer, Frederick Brotherton – New York: Fleming H Revell, c1894 – 1mf – 9 – 0-8370-6335-3 – 1986-0335 – us A.T.L.A. [920]
BELLSHILL SPEAKER – 1 – £42.00r – uk Scot News [072]
Bell-Smith, Frederick Marlett *see* A FULL DESCRIPTION OF THE TWO HISTORICAL PAINTINGS OF THE FUNERAL OF THE LATE SIR JOHN S.D. THOMPSON, K.M.G., M.P., ETC
Belluco, Bartolome *see*
- DE SACRA PRAEDICATIONES IN O.F.M...
- LEGISLATIO (OFM) DE MUSICA SACRA. STUDIUM HISTORICO-IURIDICUM

Belluga Moncada, Luis *see* CONTRA LOS TRAJES Y ADORNOS PROFANOS
BELLUM GRAMMATICALE:OR, THE GRAMMATICAL BATTEL ROYAL – Anon. 1712. 76p. (English Linguistics Series 1500-1800) – 9 – us UMI [420]
BELLUM JUDAICUM / Josephus, Flavius – 16th cent. Holkham ms. 454. Holkham Hall, Norfolk, England – 1 – uk Microform Academic [760]
BELLUM MUSICALE.. / Sebastiani, Claudio – 1563 – 2 – us Sibley [780]
BELLUM PUNICUM, ETC / Aretinus, L – 15th century. Holkham mss. 478, 488. Holkham Hall, Norfolk, England – 1 – uk Microform Academic [900]
BELLVIEW BAPTIST CHURCH. SPARTANBURG COUNTY. SOUTH CAROLINA : CHURCH RECORDS – 1891-1973 – 1 – 39.11 – us Baptist [240]
BELLWOOD GAZETTE – Bellwood, NE. -w. Jun 1892-Sep. 1902. Incomplete; Nov. 1935-Dec. 1939 – 1 – us NE Hist [071]
Belmont, August *see* PAPERS OF AUGUST BELMONT, JR., 1827-1965
THE BELMONT CIRCLE – Belmont College.Nashville, TN.1957-85 – 1 – 36.40 – us Baptist [240]
BELMONT CITIZEN – Portland OR. Sep 6-Nov 29 1951 – 1 – us U.O. Library [071]
Belmont College. Nashville *see* THE BELMONT VISION
BELMONT COURIER – Belmont, CA. 1936-1944 – 3r – 1 – $150.00 – C03154 – us Library Micro [071]
BELMONT COURIER BULLETIN – Belmont, CA. 1953-54; 1961- – 21r – 1 – $1,050.00 – B02051 – us Library Micro [073]
BELMONT ENTERPRISE – Belmont, CA. 1960 – 1r – 1 – $50.00 – H04002 – us Library Micro [071]
BELMONT HEIGHTS BAPTIST CHURCH. NASHVILLE, TENNESSEE : CHURCH RECORDS – 1909-79 – 1 – 356.27 – us Baptist [240]
THE BELMONT VISION / Belmont College. Nashville – TN alumni magazine. 1953-May 1985 – 9 – ne IDC [240]
Belmonte, Francisco *see*
- BASES Y REGLAMENTOS...CIRCULO CONCORDIA
- MEMORIA DEL JURADO...DONA ISABEL 2

O BELO VALE : ORGAO DO POVO – Belo Vale, 26 Nov 1932-31 Dec 1933 – 1,5,6 – bl Biblioteca [072]
BELOE DELO – Letopis' beloi voiny. v. 1-7. Berlin. 1926-33. BR-2310 2 – 8 – ne IDC [073]
BELOE REPORT / Great Britain. Secondary School Examinations Council on Secondary School Examinations other than G. C. E – 1958 – 9 – uk Microform Academic [324]
Belokonskii, Ivan *see*
- ZEMSKOE DVIZHENIE
- ZEMSTVO I KONSTITUTSIIA

Belokurov, Ivan Nikolaevich *see* IZ ZAPISOK AGRARNIKA
Belokurov, N G *see* INSTRUKTSIIA O PORIADKE KRATKO-SROCHNOGO KREDITOVANIIA KUSTARNO-PROMYSLOVOI KOOPERATSII I OPERATIVNYI UCHET
Belokurov, S A *see* O BIBLIOTEKE MOSKOVSKIKH GOSUDAREI V 16. STOLETTII
Belon, P *see*
- DE AQUATILIBUS LIBRI DUO
- LA NATURE ET DIVERSITE DES POISSONS
- LES OBSERVATIONS DE PLVSIEVRS SINGVLARITEZ ET CHOSES MEMORABLES, TROUUEES EN GRECE, ASIE, IUDEE, EGYPTE, ARABIE, ET AUTRES PAYS ESTRANGES, ...

Belon, Pierre *see*
- LES OBSERVATIONS DE PLUSIEURS SINGULARITEZ ET CHOSES MEMORABLES, TROUVEES EN GRECE, ASIE, IUDEE, EGYPTE, ARABIE, ET AUTRES PAYS ESTRANGES
- PORTRAITS D'OYSEAUX, ANIMAUX, SERPENTS, HERBES, ARBRES, HOMMES ET FEMMES, D'ARABIE ET D'EGYPTE PLUS Y EST ADIOUSTE LA CARTE DU MONT ATTOS ET DU MONT SINAY, POUR L'INTELLIGENCE DE LEUR RELIGION

HET BELOOFDE LAND – Amsterdam, 1922-1940. v1-18 – 120mf – J-261-12/1 – ne IDC [943]
BELORONG IMPERIALISME / Sukarno, Pres. Indonesia – SE 5319 1. 1949 – 9 – ne IDC [324]
BELORUSSKII KOOPERATOR – Minsk, 1922 – 1mf – 9 – COR-549/1 – ne IDC [334]
BELORUSSKII RYNOK – (Backfile through 1998 $85r) – Belarus, 1999- – 2r per y standing order – 1 – us Ross [072]
BELORUSY. IAZYKH BELORUSSKOGO NARODA / Karskii, E F – Moscow, 1955. v1. BR-10,334/1 – 9 – ne IDC [340]
Beloselsky, A *see* DE LA MUSIQUE EN ITALIE PAR LE PRINCE DE BELOSELSKY, DE L'INSTITUT DE BOLOGNE
Belotsvetov, N N *see* KOMMUNA PROLETARSKIKH MISSIONEROV
Belousov, I A *see* LITERATURNAIA MOSKVA
Belousov, Semen Nikitich *see* KHRESTOMATIIA PO ISTORII PERVOI RUSSKOI REVOLIUTSII 1905 G
Belov, V *see* BELAIA PECHAT', EE IDEOLOGIIA, ROL' ZNACHENIE I DEIATEL'NOST'
THE BELOVED : AN IOWA BOY IN THE JUNGLES OF AFRICA: CHARLES WARNER MCCLEARY, HIS LIFE, LETTERS AND WORK / Halsey, A W et al; ed by Hinkhouse, John Frederick – (Includes index) – Fairfield, IA: Publ by Friends, 1909 – 1mf – 9 – 0-8370-6586-0 – 1986-0586 – us A.T.L.A. [920]
THE BELOVED PHYSICIAN OF TSANG CHOU : LIFE-WORK AND LETTERS OF DR ARTHUR D PEILL, FRCSE / ed by Peill, J – London: Headley Bros, [19–] – 1mf – 9 – 0-8370-6300-0 – 1985-0300 – us A.T.L.A. [920]
BELPER, ALLSTREE AND DUFFIELD NEWS – England, Jun 1896-97; 1899-1937; 1950; 1955-57; 1986- – 62+ r – 1 – uk British Libr Newspaper [072]
Belser, Johannes Evangelist *see*
- DIE APOSTELGESCHICHTE
- DER EPHESERBRIEF DES APOSTELS PAULUS

Belsham, William *see* ESSAYS PHILOSOPHICAL AND MORAL, HISTORICAL AND LITERARY
BELSHAZZAR : A DRAMATIC POEM / Milman, Henry Hart – London: J. Murray, 1822 – 1 roll – 1 – 1-55879-329-1 – uk Libr Preservation [810]
Belsterling, Charles S *see* BELSTERLING'S DIGEST OF DECISIONS OF THE FEDERAL COURTS AND THE I.C.C. IN THE MATTER OF TRANSIT PRIVILEGES
BELSTERLING'S DIGEST OF DECISIONS OF THE FEDERAL COURTS AND THE I.C.C. IN THE MATTER OF TRANSIT PRIVILEGES / Belsterling, Charles S – Pittsburgh: C S Belsterling. 1v. 1913 – 9 – LLMC 95-119 – us L.L.M.C. [340]
BELT MOUNTAIN MINER – Baker. Mont. 1891-1893 – 1 – us UMI [071]
BELTAINE: THE ORGAN OF THE IRISH LITERARY THEATRE. LONDON. V. 1 NO. 1-3. MAY 1899-APR 1900 – 1 – us NY Public [420]
BELTON FIRST BAPTIST CHURCH. BELTON, SOUTH CAROLINA : CHURCH RECORDS – 11 Oct 1861-16 Apr 1911 – 1 – 27.81 – us Baptist [240]
Beltrami, G *see* LA CHIESA GALDEA NEL SECOLO DELL' UNIONE
Beltran y Rozpide, Ricardo *see*
- AMERICA EN TIEMPO DE FELIPE 2 SEGUN EL COSMOGRAFO CRONISTA JUAN LOPEZ DE VELASCO. EL TERRITORIO ESPANOL DE IFNI
- APUNTAMIENTOS SOBRE EL ADELANTAMIENTO DE YUCATAN, DE AMALIO HUARTE Y ECHENIQUE
- GEOGRAFIA

Belu, C *see* DES COLONIES ET DE LA TRAITE DES NEGRES
BELUSTIGUNGEN DES VERSTANDES UND DES WITZES / ed by Schwabe, Johann Joachim – Leipzig, 1741-45. Hildesheim, 1977 – 55mf – 9 – DM420.00 diazo DM520.00 silver – gw Olms [400]
BELUY KIDAN (OLD TESTAMENT), HADDIS KIDAN (NEW TESTAMENT) – The Bible in Ethiopic (Ge'ez). v. 1-5. 1934. BJ-411-1 1 – 9 – ne IDC [240]
Belvacensis, Vincentius *see*
- DE MORALI PRINCIPIS INSTITUTIONE
- SPECULUM MAIUS

BELVEDERE CITIZEN – Los Angeles. Calif. -w. 1934-67 – 1 – us UMI [071]
BELVEDERE CITIZEN & EAST SIDE JOURNAL – Los Angeles, CA. 1968-72 – 1 – us UMI [071]
BELVEDERE FIRST BAPTIST CHURCH. AIKEN COUNTY. BELVEDERE, SOUTH CAROLINA : CHURCH RECORDS – 1955-83. 812p – 1 – $36.54 – us Baptist [240]
BELVIDERE NEWS – Belvidere, NE. -w. Sep. 1891; Jun. 1893 – 1 – us NE Hist [071]
Belvis Trejo, A *see* SUPLICA GENERAL Y ULTIMA QUE INSINUA A LA...VILLA DE MADRID...(SOBRE LA LIMONA)
Belvoir Literary Society *see* RECORDS OF THE MEETINGS
Belyi, A *see*
- ARABESKI. KNIGA STATEI
- GLOSSOLALIIA
- O KHUDOZHESTVENNOI PROZE. GORN
- KOROLEVNA I RYTSARI
- KOTIK LETAEV. ROMAN
- KRESHCHENYI KITAETS
- KUBOK METELEI
- LUG ZELENYI. KNIGA STATEI
- MASTERSTVO GOGOLIA
- MEZHDU DVUKH REVOLIUTSII
- MOSKVA
- MOSKVA POD UDAROM
- NA RUBEZHE DVUKH STOLETII
- NACHALO VEKA. VOSPOMINANIIA
- PEPEL
- PERVOE SVIDANIE. POEMA
- PETERBURG
- POEZIIA SLOVA
- PUTEVYE ZAMETKI
- RITM KAK DEALEKTIKA I "MEDNYI VSADNIK"
- RUDOL'F STEINER I GETE
- SEREBRIANNYI GOLUB'
- SEREBRIANNYI GOLUB'. POVEST V SEMI GLAVAKH
- SIMVOLIZM. KNIGA STATEI
- SIRIN UCHENOGO VARVARSTVA
- SOBRANIE EPICHESKIKH POEM
- STIKHI O ROSSII
- STIKHOTVORENIIA
- TRAGEDIIA TVORCHESTVA. DOSTOEVSKII I TOLSTOI
- VETER S KAVKAZA
- VOZVRASHCHENIE NA RODINU
- VOZVRAT. TRET'IA SIMFONIIA. POVEST'
- ZAPISKI CHUDAKA. 1-2
- ZOLOTO V LAZURI

BELYI ARKHIV – Sbornik materialov po istorii i literature voiny, revoliutsii, belago dvizheniia. nr. 1-3. Paris. 1926-28. BR-3509 2 – 8 – ne IDC [920]

BELYI KAMEN' – Khudozhestvennyi zhurnal. v. 1. M. 1908. BR-3392 2 – 8 – ne IDC [947]
BELYIA NOCHI – Peterburgskii al'manakh. Spb., 1907 236, (4) pp. BR-1831 2 – 8 – ne IDC [030]
Belzer, Edwin G *see* THE NATURE AND STATUS OF HEALTH-PROMOTION PROGRAMS IN NOVA SCOTIAN GOODS-PRODUCING INDUSTRIES
Belzer, Edwin G Jr. *see* PALLIATIVE CARE
Belzile, Marie-Paule *see* BIO-BIBLIOGRAPHIE DU DOCTEUR PHILIPPE HAMEL
Belzoni, Giovanni Battista *see* VOYAGES EN EGYPTE ET EN NUBIE, CONTENANT LE RECIT DES RECHERCHES ET DECOUVERTES ARCHEOLOGIQUES FAITES DANS LES PYRAMIDES, TEMPLES, RUINES ET TOMBES DE CES PAYS
O BEM DA ORDEM – Rio de Janeiro, 1821 – 1,5,6 – bl Biblioteca [072]
O BEM PUBLICO – Ouro Preto, 23 Jul-31 Dec 1860 – 1,5,6 – bl Biblioteca [072]
O BEM TEVI – '(s.l.')-Sao Luis, Brazil. 30 Jun-Oct 1838. Jul 1847- Apr 1848. May, Jul, Oct 1849. Nov-20 Dec 1853 – 1,5,6 – bl Biblioteca [072]
BEMA *see* TO BEMA
THE BEMA – Saint Martins, N.B.: Union Baptist Seminary, [189–1893?] – 9 – cn C.I.H.M. [240]
THE BEMA *see* THE SEMINARY BEMA
Beman, Nathan S S *see* EPISCOPACY EXCLUSIVE
BEMBA MARRIAGE AND PRESENT ECONOMIC CONDITIONS / Richards, A – 7 – uk Microform Academic [960]
BEMERKUNGEN EINER REISE IM RUSSISCHEN REICH IM JAHRE 1772 / Georgi, I G – Spb. 1775. B-5551 2 – 8 – ne IDC [910]
BEMERKUNGEN UEBER DAS STUDIUM DER CRYPTOGAMISCHEN WASSERGEWAECHSE / Roth, A W – Hannover. 1797. B-5691 2 – 8 – ne IDC [580]
BEMERKUNGEN UEBER DEN EVANGELISCHEN RELIGIONSUNTERRICHT AN HOEHEREN LEHRANSTALTEN / Ubbelohde, Wilh. – Oldenburg: Gerhard Stalling, 1877 – 1mf – 9 – 0-8370-7594-7 – 1986-1594 – us A.T.L.A. [370]
BEMERKUNGEN UEBER DIE BUERGERLICHE VERBESSERUNG DER JUDEN VERANLASZT BEI DER FRAGE: SOLL DER JUDE SOLDAT WERDEN? / Ascher, S – Frankfurt a.O. 1788. BJ-23-101 1 – 9 – ne IDC [943]
Bemetzrieder, A *see*
- THE ART OF MODULATING ILLUSTRATED IN ONE GRAND LESSON, AND TWO PRELUDES FOR THE PIANOFORTE, HARPSICHORD OR ORGAN
- GENERAL INSTRUCTIONS IN MUSIC, CONTAINING PRECEPTS AND EXAMPLES IN EVERY BRANCH OF THE SCIENCE
- LECONS DE CLAVECIN, ET PRINCIPES D'HARMONIE
- METHODE ET REFLEXIONS SUR LES LECONS DE MUSIQUE
- MUSIC MADE EASY TO EVERY CAPACITY, IN A SERIES OF DIALOGUES
- NOUVELLES LECONS DE CLAVECIN OU INSTRUCTIONS GENERALES SUR LA MUSIQUE VOCALE ET INSTRUMENTALE, SUR LA MELODIE ET L'HARMONIE
- REFLEXIONS SUR LES LECONS DE MUSIQUE
- TRAITE DE MUSIQUE, CONCERNANT LES TONS, LES HARMONIES, LES ACCORDS ET LE DISCOURS MUSICAL
- TRAITE DE MUSIQUE CONCERNANT LES TONS, LES HARMONIES, LES ACCORDS ET LE DISCOURS MUSICAL

Bemies, Charles O *see* THE CHURCH IN THE COUNTRY TOWN
Bemister, George *see* MR. BEMISTER'S REPORT OF THE FLOOD AT BERTHIER IN THE MONTHS OF APRIL AND MAY, 1876
Bemmelen, J F van *see* OVER DEN BOUW DER SCHELPEN VAN BRACHIOPODEN EN CHITONEN
O BEM-TE-VI : ORGAO IMPARCIAL, CRITICO, LITTERARIO E NOTICIOSO – Barbacena, 20 Mar 1932 – 1,5,6 – bl Biblioteca [072]
O BEMTIVI : ORGAO DA SAFADEZA – Manaos, Amazonas. 19 Maio-6 Jun 1910 – 1,5,6 – bl Biblioteca [072]
BEN ABUYAH / Letteris, M H – Vienna. 1865. BJ-422-43 1 – 9 – ne IDC [470]
BEN JONSONS VOLPONE : EINE LIEBLOSE KOMOEDIE IN DREI AKTEN / Zweig, Stefan – Potsdam: G Kiepenheuer, 1926, c1925 – 1r – 1 – us U.W. Library [410]
BEN OWEN: A LANCASHIRE STORY / Perrett, Jennie – Toronto: W. Briggs, 1881. 00763. (Pre-1900 Canadiana) – 9 – cn C.I.H.M. [830]
BEN SIRA – Prague or Cracow. c.1650. BJ-43-7 1 – 9 – ne IDC [956]
Benabides Checa, Jose *see* NOTAS PARA SUS BIOGRAFIAS Y PARA LA HISTORIA DOCUMENTAL DE LA SANTA IGLESIA CATEDRAL Y CIUDAD DE PLASENCIA
Benacci, V *see* DESCRITTIONE DE GLI APPARATI FATTI IN BOLOGNA PER LA VENUTA DI N.S. PAPA CLEMENTE VIII
IL BENADIR / Mantegazza, Vico – Milan: Fratelli Treves, 1908 – us Res Libr [945]
IL BENADIR / Montegazza, Vico – Milan. 1908 – 1 – us Res Libr [960]
BENAMING, GETAL EN TRAKTEMENTEN DER INLANDSE HOOFDEN OP JAVA – 1839. Arch. Kol. no.4315. BSD-111/1 mf. 1 – 9 – ne IDC [950]
DER BENANBRIEF : EINE MODERNE LEBEN-JESU-FAELSCHUNG DES HERRN ERNST EDLER VON DER PLANITZ (T.U.U. 3-44/1) / Schmidt, Carl – Leipzig, 1921 – 2mf – 9 – ne Slangenburg [240]
Benattar, S C *see* LE BLED EN LUMIERE, FOLKLORE TUNISIEN
Benavente, Ana *see* EXPERIMENTS IN POPULAR EDUCATION IN PORTUGAL 1974-1976
Benavente, Juan Alfonso de *see* TRACTATUS DE PENITENTIIS (I. 1500)
Benavides Checa, Jose *see* EL FUERO DE PLASENCIA
Benavides Llorente, Daniel *see* REALIZACION DEL FUERO DEL TRABAJO 1 CONFERENCIA...18 DE ENERO DE 1950. PRECEDE AL TITULO JEFATURA PROVINCIAL DE FET Y DE LAS JONS
Ben-Avigdor *see* SIFREI AGORAH
Benayahu, M *see*
- HALIFAT IGGAROT BEIN HA-KEHILLAH HA-ASHKENAZIT BI-YERUSHALAYIM VE-RABBI DAVID OPPENHEIM
- IGGEROT RABBI SHEMUEL ABOHAB VE-RABBI MOSHEH ZAKKUT
- LE-TOLEDOT BATTE HA-MIDRASH BI-YERUSHALAYIM BA-MEAH HA-17
- TE'UDAH MIN HA-DOR HA-RISHON SHEL MEGORESHEI SEFARAD BI-ZEFAT

Benazet, Alexandre *see* LE THEATRE AU JAPON
BENCH AND BAR – Chicago. v1-2. 1869-71. NS: v1-3. 1871-74 – 1,5,6 – $40.00 – us Hein [073]
BENCH AND BAR : A COMPLETE DIGEST OF THE WIT, HUMOR, ASPERITIES, AND AMENITIES OF THE LAW / Bigelow, L J – New York: Harper & Bros, 1871 – 6mf – 9 – $9.00 – LLMC 91-062 – us L.L.M.C. [870]
BENCH AND BAR / Lawyers Club of Detroit – (Lacking: v1 no3. v2 nos 7-8) – Lawyers Club of Detroit. v1-6. 1921-26 (all publ) – 11mf – 9 – $16.50 – LLMC 84-424 – us L.L.M.C. [073]
BENCH AND BAR : A MONTHLY MAGAZINE FOR LAWYERS – (Lacking: os v25-27. ns v5-8) – New York: Bench & Bar Co. os: v1-28. 1906-12; ns: v1-15. 1912-20 (all publ) – 54mf – 9 – $81.00 – LLMC 84-422 – us L.L.M.C. [073]
THE BENCH AND BAR / Lawyers' Association of the 8th Judicial Circuit of Missouri – v1-7. 1935-42 – 4mf – 9 – $6.00 – LLMC 84-423 – us L.L.M.C. [073]
BENCH AND BAR OF CALIFORNIA / Taylor, Charles W – San Francisco: Knight Counihan Co., 1937. California Reel 3. (The Cox Library Collection) – 5 – us Americana [978]
BENCH AND BAR OF CHICAGO – Chicago, 1883. Illinois Reel 19. (The Cox Library Collection) – 5 – us Americana [978]
THE BENCH AND BAR OF CLEVELAND / Kennedy, James Henry – Cleveland, Cleveland Printing and Publishing Co., 1889. 358 p. LL-636 – 1 – us L of C Photodup [340]
BENCH AND BAR OF COLORADO / Lewis and Stackelbeck – Denver: Bench and Bar Publ. Co., 1917. Colorado reel 2.(Cox Library Collection) – 5 – us Americana [978]
THE BENCH AND BAR OF GEORGIA: MEMOIRS AND SKETCHES / Miller, Stephen Franks – Philadelphia: Lippincott, 1858. 2v. LL-316 – 1 – us L of C Photodup [340]
BENCH AND BAR OF ILLINOIS / Palmer, John M – Chicago: Lewis Publ. Co., 1899. Vols. 1-2. Illinois Reel 7. (The Cox Library Collection) – 5 – us Americana [978]
BENCH AND BAR OF ILLINOIS – 1920 / Hennessey & Lucas & Foy & Callahan – Chicago: Bench and Bar Publ. Co., 1920. (The Cox Library Collection) – 5 – us Americana [978]
THE BENCH AND BAR OF INDIANA / Taylor, Charles W – Indianapolis: Bench and Bar Publ. Co., 1895. Indiana Reel 2. (The Cox Library Collection) – 5 – us Americana [978]
BENCH AND BAR OF MINNESOTA – v1-52. 1934-95 – 9 – $950.00 set – us Hein [340]
THE BENCH AND BAR OF MINNESOTA – v1-23. 1943-66 – 205mf – 9 – $307.00 – LLMC 84-421 – us L.L.M.C. [073]
BENCH AND BAR OF NEW YORK / Proctor, Lucien Brock – New York, Diossy and Co., 1870. New York Reel 1. (The Cox Library Collection) – 5 – us Americana [978]
THE BENCH AND BAR OF NEW YORK / Proctor, Lucien Brock – New York: Diossy & Co, 1870 – 9mf – 9 – $13.50 – LLMC 91-009 – us L.L.M.C. [340]
THE BENCH AND BAR OF ST. LOUIS, KANSAS CITY, JEFFERSON CITY AND OTHERS – St. Louis, 1884. Missouri Reel 2. (The Cox Library Collection) – 5 – us Americana [978]
THE BENCH AND BAR OF SARATOGA COUNTY. / Mann, Enos R – Ballston, N.Y.: Waterbury & Inman, 1876. 391p. LL-628 – 1 – us L of C Photodup [340]
BENCH AND BAR OF TEXAS / Lynch, James D – St. Louis: Nixon-Jones Printing Co., 1885. Texas Reel 6. (The Cox Library Collection) – 5 – us Americana [978]
BENCH AND BAR OF WISCONSIN / Reed, Parker McCobb – Historical and biographical. Milwaukee: P. M. Reed, 1882. Wisconsin Reel 2. (The Cox Library Collection) – 5 – us Americana [978]
BEN-CHANANJA : MONATSSCHRIFT FUER JUEDISCHE THEOLOGIE / ed by Loew, Leopold – Szegedin, 1858-67. Hildesheim, 1993 – 86mf – 9 – DM600.00 diazo DM700.00 silver – gw Olms [270]
BEN-CHANANJA – Monatsschrift fuer Juedische Theologie und fuer Juedisches Leben in Gemeinde, Synagoge und Schule. v1-10. 1858-1867. Complete. 3 reels. B27. (Leo Baeck Institute. German-Jewish Periodicals, Pt 1) – 1 – $205.00 – us UPA [270]
BENCHMARK : QUARTERLY REVIEW OF THE CONSTITUTION AND THE COURTS – (None publ 1989, 1992. Ceased with v5 no 2) – v1-5. 1985-1993 – 9 – $61.00 set – us Hein [340]
BEND PILOT – Bend, OR. -w. 19 Jul 1940-25 Jun 1950. 6 rolls – 1 – us U.O. Library [071]
Benda, G *see* CONERTINO PER IL CEMBALO
Benda, Georg *see* ARIADNE AUF NAXOS. PARTITUR MIT DEUTSCHEN TEXTE
Bendahman, Jadwiga *see* DER REDUPLIZIERTE AORIST IN DEN INDOGERMANISCHEN SPRACHEN
Bendavid, Isaac Besht *see* GOLDWIN SMITH AND THE JEWS
Bendavid, L *see* ETWAS ZU CHARAKTERISTICK DER JUDEN
BENDE RANTJAGE / Djurusan Bahasa dan Sastra Sunda Fakultas Keguruan – (Missing: 1968(1)) – Bandung, 1968-1969 – 2mf – 9 – SE-1347/1 – ne IDC [950]
Bendeler, J Ph *see* ORGANOPOEIA, ODER UNTEWEIZUNG WIE EIN ORGEL. ZU ERBAUEN
Bender, E P *see* REPORT OF SURVEY OF FRENCH RIVER, GEORGIAN BAY, LAKE HURON: MADE FOR THE DEPARTMENT OF RAILWAYS AND CANALS IN 1879
Bender, Heinrich *see* HEBBELS DITHMARSCHENFRAGMENT
Bender, Henry Richard *see* TWENTIETH CENTURY INTERPRETATION OF PAUL'S EPISTLE TO THE EPHESIANS
Bender, M O *see* KATALOG VOENNO-UCHENOGO ARKHIVA GLAVNOGO SHTABA
Bender, Prosper *see*
- CANADA'S ACTUAL CONDITION
- THE DISINTEGRATION OF CANADA
- HOLIDAYS OF THE FRENCH CANADIANS
- LITERARY SHEAVES, OR LA LITTERATURE AU CANADA FRANCAIS: THE DRAMA, HISTORY, ROMANCE, POETRY, LECTURES, SKETCHES, ETC
- A NEW FRANCE IN NEW ENGLAND
- OLD AND NEW CANADA, 1753-1844: HISTORIC SCENES AND SOCIAL PICTURES, OR, THE LIFE OF JOSEPH FRANCOIS PERRAULT
- A REJOINDER TO DR. HUGHES

BENDER'S CORPORATION MANUAL, STATE OF NEW YORK. / Rosbrook, Alden Ivan – Albany: Bender, 1923. 463p. LL-1428 – 1 – us L of C Photodup [340]
BENDICENOS SENOR / Aradillas Agudo, Antonio – Madrid: Editado por PPC y el Secretariado del Apostolado Rural de los HH de A.C., 1960 – sp Bibl Santa Ana [240]
Bendig, Helmut *see* DIE ROLLE ITALIENS BEI DER ENTSTEHUNG DER EUROPAEISCHEN WIRTSCHAFTSGEMEINSCHAFT BIS 1958
BENDIGO : PEOPLE AND PLACES – 12mf – 9 – A$50.00 – at State Libr Vic [072]
BENDIGO ADVERTISER – Australia. Aug 1854-Jun 1922 (missing 1860).-w,d. 228 reels – 1 – uk British Libr Newspaper [072]
BENDIGO HOME AND HOSPITAL FOR AGED – 1875-1977. Newsclippings. BHHA1-2 – 2r – 1 – at Corangamite [360]
BENDIGO MERCURY – Australia. -w. 9, 25 June, 28 Aug 1958; 12, 22 Jan, 7, 14 April, 20 May, 1 July, 13, 22 Aug 1859. 9 ft – 1 – uk British Libr Newspaper [072]
BENEATH THE SURFACE, OR, PHYSICAL TRUTHS...SHOWN TO BE LATENT IN...HOLY SCRIPTURES / Duke, Edward – London: Hatchards, 1881.1 fiche – 9 – us A.T.L.A. [240]
Benedetti, Antonio *see* PERON Y EVA
Benedetti, Mario *see* EL PAIS DE LA COLA DE PAJA
Benedetto, L F *see* MARCO POLO/IL MILIONE
Benedetto, LF *see* MARCO POLO/IL MILIONE
BENEDICITE, OR, THE SONG OF THE THREE CHILDREN / Child, George Chaplin – New York: E.P. Dutton, 1899. 1 fiche – 9 – us A.T.L.A. [240]
BENEDICT BROADCASTER – Benedict, NE. -w. Aug. 1936-Jun. 1941 – 1 – us NE Hist [071]
Benedict, David *see*
- FIFTY YEARS AMONG THE BAPTISTS
- A GENERAL HISTORY OF THE BAPTIST DENOMINATION IN AMERICA AND OTHER PARTS OF THE WORLD
- A HISTORY OF ALL RELIGIONS
- HISTORY OF THE DONATISTS

Benedict, F *see* ORBIS LATINUS ODER VERZEICHNIS DER WICHTIGSTEN LATEINISCHEN ORTS- UND LAENDERNAMEN. ED. 3
Benedict, G G *see* VERMONT IN THE CIVIL WAR
BENEDICT HERALD – Benedict, NE. -w. Jul. 1900-Dec. 1900. Incomplete; Apr. 1901-Jun. 1902 – 1 – us NE Hist [071]
Benedict, John D *see* MUSKOGEE AND NORTHEASTERN OKLAHOMA
Benedict, Michael A *see* RELIABILITY IN THE MEASUREMENT OF MUSCLE FIBER COMPOSITION AND THE HISTOCHEMICAL STAINING FOR GLYCOGEN
BENEDICT NEWS-HERALD – Benedict, NE. -w. Jul. 1902-Dec. 1903; Jan. 1908-Jun. 1910 – 1 – us NE Hist [071]
Benedict, R D *see* BENEDICT'S REPORTS OF CASES IN THE DISTRICT COURTS OF THE U.S. (2ND CIRCUIT), 1865-1879
BENEDICTI 14 BULLARUM – T. 29 t/m T. 32, Romae, 1760-1762 – 55mf – 8 – ne Slangenburg [240]
BENEDICTI BACCHINI DE SISTRIS, EORUMQUE FIGURIS AC DIFFERENTIA. DISSERTATIO / Bacchinus, B D – Jacobus Tollius dissertatiunculam et notulas adjecit. Trajecti ad Rhenum. 1696. BP-139 1 – 9 – ne IDC [780]
Benedicti, Le P Jean *see* LA TRIOMPHANTE VICTOIRE DE LA VIERGE MARIE SUR SEPT MALINS ESPRITS
BENEDICTI PERERII VALENTINI, E SOCIETATE JESU COMMENTARIORUM ET DISPUTATIONUM IN GENESIM / Pererius, B – 2188 2. 1500-1600 – 8 – ne IDC [240]
BENEDICTI PERERII VALENTINI, E SOCIETATE JESU COMMENTARIORUM ET DISPUTATIONUM IN GENESIM / Pererius, B – v. 1-4. Lyon. 1590-1600. B-2188 2 – 8 – ne IDC [240]
BENEDICTI REGULA MONACHORUM / Linderbauer, BS – 1922 – 8mf – 8 – ne Slangenburg [240]
BENEDICTI REGULA MONACHORUM / ed by Woelffin, E – Lipsiae, 1795 – 3mf – 8 – ne Slangenburg [240]
BENEDICTI REGULA MONASTERIORUM, SANCTI / ed by Cuthbertus Butler, D OSB – Ed 3a. Friburgi Brisg., 1935 – Dfl22.00 – ne Slangenburg [240]

BENEDICTINES – (v31- . 1976- . 5,6,9) – v1- . 1946- – 1 – us UMI [240]
BENEDICTION DU NOUVEAU SEMINAIRE DE ST GERMAIN DE RIMOUSKI – Rimouski: A. Dion, 1878?. 02319. (Pre-1900 Canadiana) – 9 – cn C.I.H.M. [240]
BENEDICTION DU NOUVEAU SEMINAIRE DE STE.-THERESE, LE 26 JUIN 1883 – Montreal: Beauchemin & Valois, 1883. 02318. (Pre-1900 Canadiana) – 9 – cn C.I.H.M. [240]
BENEDICTION SOLENNELLE DU T. R. P. DOM M. ANTOINE: ABBE DE NOTRE DAME DU LAC DES DEUX MONTAGNES D'OKA – A l'eglise de Notre Dame de Montreal, le 29 juin 1892. Montreal: Arbour & Laperle, 1892. 04043. (Pre-1900 Canadiana) – 9 – cn C.I.H.M. [240]
THE BENEDICTIONAL / Ethelwold, Saint – 10th cent. British Library Add. Ms. 49598 – 14 – uk Microform Academic [240]
THE BENEDICTIONAL OF ARCHBISHOP ROBERT / Wilson, H Austin – 1903 – 4mf – 8 – Dfl19.00 – ne Slangenburg [240]
THE BENEDICTIONAL OF JOHN LONGLONDE / Woolley, R M – 1927 – 2mf – 8 – ne Slangenburg [240]
DAS BENEDICTIONALE DES DIOZESE MEISSEN VON 1512 / ed by Schoenfelder, A – Paderborn, 1904 – 2mf – 8 – Dfl9.00 – ne Slangenburg [240]
BENEDICTIONS / Cumming, John – 1858 – 9 – us A.T.L.A. [240]
Benedictis, J B *see* PHILOSOPHIA PERIPATETICA
THE BENEDICTONALS OF FREISING / Amiet, R – 3mf – 8 – ne Slangenburg [240]
BENEDICT'S REPORTS OF CASES IN THE DISTRICT COURTS OF THE U.S. (2ND CIRCUIT), 1865-1879 / Benedict, R D – New York: Baker. v1-10. 1869-82 (all publ) – 71mf – 9 – $106.00 – LLMC 81-432 – us L.L.M.C. [324]
BENEDICTUS ILLUSTRATUS SIVE DISQUISITIONUM MONASTICARUM. LIBRI 12 / Haeften, Benedictus van – Antverpiae. v1-2. 1644 – 36mf – 8 – Dfl214.00 – ne Slangenburg [240]
Benedictus van Canfield, Ofmcap *see* DEN REGEL DER VOLMAECTHEYT
BENEDIKT VAN ANIANE : WERK UND PERSOENLICHKEIT (BGAMBO 17) / Narberhaus, Jozef – Muenster, 1930 – 2mf – 8 – Dfl25.00 – ne Slangenburg [240]
BENEDIKTINER MONNIK DER ABTDYE TE EGMONT, MET TAAL- EN HISTORIKUNDIGE AANTEEKENINGEN OPGEHELDERD DOOR MR. GERARD VAN LOON / Rymchronyk van Klaas Kolyn – 's-Graavenhaage, 1745 – Dfl74.00 – ne Slangenburg [240]
DER BENEDIKTINISCHE ABT / Hegglin, P – St. Ottilien, 1961 – 3mf – 8 – ne Slangenburg [240]
BENEDIKTINISCHES ORDENSRECHT / Mayer, P H S – Beuron. v1-4. 1929 – 17mf – 8 – Dfl60.00 – ne Slangenburg [240]
Benedix, Roderich *see* NEIN
BENEFITS CANADA – Toronto. v1- 1977- – 9 – Can$28.00y – cn Micromedia [073]
BENEFITS CANADA – (v.3-. 1979- 5,6,9) – 1976- – 1 – us UMI [073]
BENEFITS LAW JOURNAL – v1-6. 1988-94 – 9 – $198.00 set – us Hein [340]
BENEI HO-AGOEDO – Rotterdam, 1933-1935. v1-2 – 3mf – J-261-13/1 – ne IDC [943]
BENEI MOSHEH U-TEKUFATAM / Tchernovitz, H – Warsaw. 1914. BJ-290-4 1 – 9 – ne IDC [940]
BENEI TEIMON – Amsterdam, 1923-1925. v1-2 – 2mf – J-261-14/1 – ne IDC [943]
Beneshevich, V N *see* OPISANIE GRECHESKIKH RUKOPISEI MONASTYRIA SVIATOI EKATERINY NA SINAE. 1, 3: 1
Benet, Stephen Vincent *see* A TREATISE ON MILITARY LAW AND THE PRACTICE OF COURTS-MARTIAL
BENEVOLENCE BAPTIST CHURCH. FORT VALLEY, GEORGIA = FORT VALLEY, GEORGIA. BENEVOLENCE BAPTIST CHURCH : CHURCH RECORDS – (790p) – Oct 1941-Nov 1980 – 1 reel – 1 – us Baptist [240]
BENEVOLENCE VERSUS ALTRUISM; THE STOLEN CONCEPT / Branden, Nathaniel – 7p – 9 – 1.00f – at Libertarian Micro [335]
BENEVOLENT ASYLUM BENDIGO : MINUTES – 1876-1957 – 3r – 5 – at Corangamite [060]
Beneze, Emil *see* DAS TRAUMMOTIV IN ALTDEUTSCHER DICHTUNG
Ben-Ezra, Victor *see* THE EFFECT OF SWIM TRAINING ON PLASMA SOMATOMEDIN-C LEVELS IN 8- TO 10-YEAR-OLD CHILDREN
Benfante, G *see* L'URTO DI NAVI ...
LOS BENFICIOS DEL TELEFONO / Garcia Garcia, Juan – Caceres: Tall. El Noticiero, 1953 – 1 – sp Bibl Santa Ana [820]
BENGAL ACTS – Calcutta. 1877-1947. – 155mf – 8 – ne IDC [073]
Bengal. Armed Forces *see* ARMY LIST OF HER MAJESTY'S AND THE HONOURABLE COMPANY'S FORCES SERVING UNDER THE BENGAL PRESIDENCY: CORRECTED TO 31ST DECEMBER 1857
THE BENGAL DISPENSATORY: CHIEFLY COMPILED FROM THE WORKS OF ROXBURGH, WALLICH, AINSLIE, WIGHT, ARNOT, ROYLE, PEREIRA, LINDLEY, RICHARD AND FEE / O'Shaughnessy, William Brooke – Calcutta: W. Thacker, St. Andrew's Library, 1842. xxiii,794p. plates – 1 – us U.W. Library [950]
Bengal Govt. Department of Agriculture, Forest and Fisheries *see* AGRICULTURAL STATISTICS BY PLOT TO PLOT ENUMERATION IN BENGAL, 1944-45
BENGAL HURKARU – Dacca, Bangladesh. 1822-1866 – 1 – uk Microform Academic [072]
Bengal. India (State) *see*
- (LAW OF LANDLORD AND TENANT)
- LAW REPORTS

Bengal. India (State). Legislative Council *see* DEBATES, 1937-1943
Bengal. India (State). Public Works Department *see* LISTS OF STATUES, MONUMENTS AND BUSTS IN CALCUTTA OF HISTORICAL INTEREST
BENGAL LAW REPORTS – Calcutta, 1868-1875. 15v – 238mf – I-667/2 – ne IDC [340]
BENGAL LEGISLATIVE ASSEMBLY PROCEEDINGS – Alipore, 1937-1944. v50-67 – 495mf – I-22/2 – ne IDC [340]
BENGAL LEGISLATIVE COUNCIL PROCEEDINGS – Calcutta, 1921-1937. v1-49 – 713mf – I-21/2 – ne IDC [320]
BENGAL LEGISLATIVE COUNCIL PROCEEDINGS – (Missing: 1940, v1-3; 1941, v1-2) – Alipore, 1937-1944 – 133mf – I-23/2 – ne IDC [320]
BENGAL MAGAZINE / ed by Day, Lal Behari – Calcutta. 1872-82. Lacking: 1878 (6, p. 1-46); 1881 (9, p. 161-196). – 94mf – 8 – ne IDC [073]
BENGAL PLANTS: A LIST OF THE PHANEROGAMS, FERNS AND FERN ALLIES / Prain, D – 2v. Calcutta. 1903. B-7317 1 – 9 – ne IDC [580]
Bengal Relief Committee *see* CORRESPONDENCE, 1943-1947
BENGAL TENANCY BILL : A SPEECH DELIVERED ON MOVING FOR LEAVE TO INTRODUCE THE BILL INTO THE LEGISLATIVE COUNCIL OF THE GOVERNOR GENERAL / Ilbert, Peregrine – (Filmed with: A Historical Sketch of Fyzabad Tehsil by P Carnegy, Lucknow, 1870) – Simla: Govt Central Branch Press, 1883 – us Res Libr [323]
BENGAL TIMES – Dacca, Bangladesh. 1876-1908 – 1 – uk Microform Academic [072]
BENGALEE – Calcutta, India. 1907-Aug 1932 – 71r – 1 – us L of C Photodup [072]
THE BENGALEE – Calcutta, India. -w. 1886-89; 1900-06, 1917. 34 reels – 1 – uk British Libr Newspaper [072]
Bengel, Johann Albrecht *see* GNOMEN OF THE NEW TESTAMENT
Bengesco, G *see* ESSAI D'UNE BIBLIOGRAPHIE SUR LA QUESTION D'ORIENT
Bengoechea, I(OC D) *see* LA VIRGEN MARIA EN LA VIDA Y EN LA OBRA DE BENITO ARIAS MONTANO
Bengough, John Wilson *see*
- BUNTHORNE ABROAD, OR, THE LASS THAT LOVED A PIRATE
- CARTOON OF THE CAMPAIGN: DOMINION OF CANADA GENERAL ELECTIONS, 1900
- THE GRIP CARTOONS, FROM MAY 1873 TO MAY 1874
- THE HUMOUROUS SIDE OF CANADIAN HISTORY
- MOTLEY: VERSES GRAVE AND GAY
- THE UP-TO-DATE PRIMER: A FIRST BOOK OF LESSONS FOR LITTLE POLITICAL ECONOMISTS: IN WORDS OF ONE SYLLABLE WITH PICTURES

BENGOUGH'S COSMOPOLITAN SHORTHAND WRITER – Toronto: T.Bengough, [1881?-1883] – 9 – cn C.I.H.M. [650]
BENGOUGH'S ILLUSTRATED MONTHLY – Toronto: W.Bengough, v1 no 1 (Feb 1885)- – 9 – cn C.I.H.M. [073]
BENGOUGH'S POPULAR READINGS – Toronto: Bengough, Moore & Bengough, 1882 – 9 – cn C.I.H.M. [420]
BENGTSFORSTIDNINGEN DALSLANNINGEN – Bengtsfors, Sweden. 1979- – 1 – sw Kungliga [072]
O BENGUELLA – Benguella: Tavares & Co, feb 5 1910 – us Res Libr [072]
Benharrat, K M *see* RECHERCHE D'UNE DIFFERENCIATION GENETIQUE AU SEIN DE POPULATIONS ICHTHYIQUES MARINES ET LAGUNAIRES DU GOLFE DU LION
Benhazera, Maurice *see* SIX MOIS CHEZ LES TOUAREGS DU AHAGGAR
Ben-hur, Ehud et al *see* LASERS IN THE LIFE SCIENCES
BENI HASAN: PART 2 / Newberry, Percy E – 1893 – 9 – $10.00 – us I.R.C. [930]
BENICIA-VALLEJO – 1921-31; 1933-45; 1992- – 13+ r – 1 – $650.00 – P00139 – us Library Micro [910]
Benigno de Canet de Mar, Padre *see* RELACIONES INTERESANTES Y DATOS HISTORICOS SOBRE LAS MISIONES CATOLICAS DEL CALQUETA Y PUTOMAYO DESDE EL ANO 1632 HASTA EL PRESENTE
Benigno-Boriko, L *see* UN VILLAGE SOUS L'EQUATEUR
BENI-HASAN, 4: ZOOLOGICAL AND OTHER DETAILS / Griffith, FL – 1900 – 9 – $10.00 – us I.R.C. [930]
BENIN : ANNUAIRE STATISTIQUE 1965-1975 / Benin. Institut nationale de l'Analyse Economique – (1966, 1968, 1970-72, 1974 not available. Coll title: African Official Statistical Serials, 1867-1982) – 16mf – 9 – £135.00 – uk Chadwyck [960]
BENIN GAMES AND SPORTS / Egharevba, Jacob U – Special ed. Sapele: Central Press, 1951 – 1 – us Res Libr [790]
Benin. Institut nationale de l'Analyse Economique *see* BENIN
BENIN LAW AND CUSTOM / Egharevba, Jacob U – 3rd ed. [Benin City: J U Egharevba, 1949] – 1 – us Res Libr [390]
THE BENIN MASSACRE / Boisragon, Alan – 2nd ed. London: Metheun, 1898 – 1 – us Res Libr [960]
BENIN, THE CITY OF BLOOD / Bacon, R H – (Filmed with: Notes africaines, apr 1942-oct 1946) – London, New York: E Arnold, 189[7] – 1 – us Res Libr [960]
Benisch, A *see* BISHOP COLENSO'S OBJECTIONS TO THE HISTORICAL CHARACTER OF THE PENTATEUCH & JOSHUA
Benisch-Darlang, Eugenie *see* MIT GOETHE DURCH DIE SCHWEIZ
Benites, J E *see* DERECHO INTERNACIONAL MARITIMO
Benitez, Hernan *see* LA ARGENTINA DE AYER Y DE HOY
Benitez, Juan J *see* LA REVOLUCION DEL 4 DE JUNIO Y LOS PARTIDOS POLITICOS
BENITO ARIAS MONTANO (1527-1598) / Arias Montano, Benito & Rekers, Bernard – Amsterdam, 1961 – 1 – sp Bibl Santa Ana [920]
BENITO ARIAS MONTANO (1527-1598) / Rekers, Bernard – London: Warburg Institute, 1972 – 1 – sp Bibl Santa Ana [240]
BENITO ARIAS MONTANO. DATOS BIOGRAFICOS / Lujan Garcia, Jose – Malaga: Revista Espanola de Estudios Biblicos, 1928 – 1 – sp Bibl Santa Ana [780]
BENITO ARIAS MONTANO. EXTRACTOS DE SU VIDA / Doetsch, Carlos – Madrid: Imp. de Blass y Cia, 1920 – 1 – sp Bibl Santa Ana [780]
BENITO ARIAS MONTANO, PADRE DE LA ARQUEOLOGIA BIBLICA / Santos Olivera, Balbino – Malaga: Revista Espanola de Estudios Biblicos, 1928 – 1 – sp Bibl Santa Ana [240]
BENITO ARIAS MONTANO, "POETA LAUREATUS" / Lopez de Toro, Jose – Madrid: Revista de Archivos, Bibliotecas y Museos, 1954. pp. 167-188 – 1 – sp Bibl Santa Ana [810]
BENITO ARIAS MONTANO Y AUBREY F.G. BEEL / Arconada, Mariano – Malaga: Revista Espanola de Estudios Biblicos, 1928 – 1 – sp Bibl Santa Ana [240]
Benitoy Endara, L *see* LA CONFERENCIA INTERNACIONAL DE DERECHO MARITIMO DE BRUSELAS – 1922
LOS BENIVERMAN EN MERIDA Y BADAJOZ / Codera, Francisco – Zaragoza: Mariano Escar, 1904 – 1 – sp Bibl Santa Ana [946]
BENJAMIN C. YANCEY PAPERS / Yancey, Benjamin C – 1800-1931. University of North Carolina Library. Guide – 1 – $288.00 – us U.N.C. Southern Hist [920]
BENJAMIN F. PERRY PAPERS / Perry, Benjamin F – 1822-1933. University of North Carolina Library. Guide – 1 – $36.00 – us U.N.C. Southern Hist [976]
BENJAMIN F. STICKNEY PAPERS *see* STICKNEY, BENJAMIN F., PAPERS, MS 3450
BENJAMIN FRANKLIN'S ACCOUNT BOOKS : 1713-1874 / Franklin, Benjamin – (Includes printed guide) – 1977 – 3r – 1 – $255.00 – S1851 – us Scholarly Res [920]
BENJAMIN HARRISON PAPERS – (With guide) – 151r – 1 – $5,285.00 – Dist. us Scholarly Res – us L of C Photodup [975]
BENJAMIN LINCOLN PAPERS, 1635-1964 / Lincoln, Benjamin – Massachusetts Historical Society – 13r – 1 – $995.00 – us UMI [920]
BENJAMIN MORSE PAPERS, MS V.F. M / Morse, Benjamin – (Morse's Justice of the Peace Docket book) – 1805-09 – 1r – 1 – us Western Res [920]
Benjamin, Samuel Greene Wheeler *see*
- THE ATLANTIC ISLANDS AS RESORTS OF HEALTH AND PLEASURE
- THE CRUISE OF THE ALICE MAY IN THE GULF OF ST LAWRENCE AND ADJACENT WATERS
- THE TURK AND THE GREEK; OR, CREEDS, RACES, SOCIETY AND SCENERY IN TURKEY, GREECE, AND THE ISLES OF GREECE

BENJAMIN TAPPAN PAPERS / Tappan, Benjamin; ed by Duckett, Kenneth W – 1795-1873. Related Guide. Book included in purchase of set of 2 rolls; may be purchased separately from publisher – 1 – us Ohio Hist [975]
BENJOELOEH TANI – Landbouw-voorlichtingsdienst, Pematangsiantar, 1937-1940. Jrg. 1, No 1. Jrg. 4, No 3 – 10mf – 9 – ne IDC [350]
Benkard, Christian *see* UNTER DEUTSCHEN PALMEN
Benkartek, Dietmar *see* EIN INTERPRETIERENDES WOERTERBUCH DER NOMINALABSTRAKTA IM "NARRENSCHIFF" SEBASTIANS BRANTS VON ABENTEUER BIS ZWIETRACHT
Benke, Bertha *see* DIARIES AND PAPERS OF BERTHA AND HERMAN BENKE
Benke, Herman C *see* DIARIES AND PAPERS OF BERTHA AND HERMAN BENKE
BENKELMAN CHRONICLE – Benkelman, NE. -w. Sep. 1897-Aug. 1904; Nov. 1904-May. 1906 – 1 – us NE Hist [071]
BENKELMAN POST – Benkelman, NE. -w. Jan. 1920-Apr. 1922 – 1 – us NE Hist [071]
BENKELMAN POST AND NEWS-CHRONICLE – Benkelman, NE. -w. Mar. 1899-Oct. 1902. Incomplete; May 1906- – 1 – us NE Hist [071]
BENLIU – The Current. -m. Jun 1928-Aug 1929. 3 reels. M C41 – 1 – $135.00 – cc Microforms [073]
Benn, Alfred William *see*
- THE HISTORY OF ENGLISH RATIONALISM IN THE NINETEENTH CENTURY
- REVALUATIONS: HISTORICAL AND IDEAL

Benn, Ernest J P *see*
- BENN'S PROTEST
- THE CASE OF BENN VS. MAXTON, A CORRESPONDENCE ON CAPITALISM AND SOCIALISM
- THE CONFESSION OF A CAPITALIST
- PRODUCER VS. CONSUMER
- THE STATE THE ENEMY

Bennasar, P Guillermo *see* DICCIONARIO TIRURAY-ESPANOL
Benndorf, Alex *see* FUER BANKFREIHEIT, 1870
Benner, Enos *see* ABHANDLUNG UEBER DIE RECHENKUNST ODER PRACTISCHE ARITHMETIK ZUM GEBRAUCH FUER SCHULEN
Benner, Samuel *see* BENNER'S PROPHECIES OF FUTURE UPS AND DOWNS IN PRICES: WHAT YEARS TO MAKE MONEY ON PIG-IRON, HOGS, CORN, AND PROVISIONS

BENNER'S PROPHECIES OF FUTURE UPS AND DOWNS IN PRICES: WHAT YEARS TO MAKE MONEY ON PIG-IRON, HOGS, CORN, AND PROVISIONS / Benner, Samuel – Toronto: Belford Bros., 1877. 00906. (Pre-1900 Canadiana) – 9 – cn C.I.H.M. [332]
Bennet, F *see* THE STORY OF W.J.E. BENNETT
Bennet, J *see*
– DIARIES, 1742-1744 [FRAGMENTS], 1747-1754
– LETTER-BOOK, 1748-1754, AND SERMONS
– LIFE, BY HIMSELF
Bennet, James Risdon *see* DISEASES OF THE BIBLE
Bennet, L *see* LE DOMICILE DES ETRANGERS EN FRANCE
Bennet, R *see* HISTORY OF CORN MILLING
BENNET UNION – Bennet, NE. -w. Nov. 1892; Feb. 1895-Jun. 1900 – 1 – us NE Hist [071]
Bennett, Arnold *see* THE WOMAN WHO STOLE EVERYTHING. LEIPZIG, 1928
Bennett, Charles W *see* CHRISTIAN ARCHAEOLOGY
Bennett, Edmund H *see* BENNETT'S FIRE INSURANCE CASES, 1729-1875
Bennett, Edmund Hatch *see*
– FOUR GOSPELS FROM A LAWYER'S STANDPOINT
– THE FOUR GOSPELS FROM A LAWYER'S STANDPOINT
– A SELECTION OF LEADING CASES IN CRIMINAL LAW
Bennett, F D *see* NARRATIVE OF A WHALING VOYAGE AROUND THE GLOBE FROM 1833 TO 1836
Bennett, J J *see* PLANTAE JAVANICAE RARIORES..
Bennett, J L *see* OUTLINES OF TRIAL PROCEDURE
Bennett, J W *see* A SELECTION OF RARE AND CURIOUS FISHES FOUND UPON THE COAST OF CEYLON
Bennett, John *see*
– THE TREASURE OF PEYRE GAILLARD
– YOUR RIGHTS
Bennett, Susan B *see* CREDENTIALS OF CARDIAC REHABILITATION PERSONNEL
Bennett, Thomas *see* TERMS OF COMMUNION AGREED UPON BY THE SCOTS METHODISTS, BUT GENERALLY KNOWN BY THE SPECIOUS DENOMINATION OF THE PRESBYTERY OF RELIEF, THEIR OWN EXPLANATION OF SAID TERMS, WITH REMARKS UPON BOTH;...
Bennett, W J E *see*
– ON ANABAPTISM, THE INDEPENDENTS, AND QUAKERISM
– ON METHODISM AND THE SWEDENBORGIANS
– ON PRESBYTERIANISM AND IRVINGISM
– ON ROMANISM
Bennett, William Henry *see*
– THE BOOK OF JEREMIAH
– BOOK OF JEREMIAH: CHAPTERS 21-52
– THE BOOKS OF CHRONICLES
– THE GENERAL EPISTLES
– GENERAL EPISTLES: JAMES, PETER, JOHN AND JUDE
– LIFE OF CHRIST ACCORDING TO ST MARK
– RELIGION OF THE POST-EXILIC PROPHETS
BENNETT'S FIRE INSURANCE CASES, 1729-1875 : U.S. AND GREAT BRITAIN / Bennett, Edmund H – New York: Hurd & Houghton. v1-5. 1872-1877 (all publ) – 9 – LLMC 95-131 – us L.L.M.C. [340]
Bennewitz, Fritz *see* DIE SUENDE IM ALTEN ISRAEL
Benni, T et al *see* GRAMATYKA JEZYKA POLSKIEGO
Bennigsen, Ingrid *see* LEBENSBILDER UND LANDSCHAFT
BENNINGTON HERALD – Bennington, NE. -w. Jan. 1908-Jan. 1917; Mar. 1917-Jul. 1927 – 1 – us NE Hist [071]
BENNO PAPENTRIGK'S SCHUETTELREIME : WIE ER SIE SEINER FREUNDSCHAFT AUF DEN OSTERTISCH ZU LEGEN PFLEGTE – [S.l.: s.n.], 1946 (Ansbach: Druck der Fraenkischen Landeszeitung) – 1 – us U.W. Library [430]
BENN'S PROTEST / Benn, Ernest J P – 1945. 1 fiche (29x) – 9 – 1.00f – at Libertarian Micro [320]
Benny, Philip Berger *see* CRIMINAL CODE OF THE JEWS ACCORDING TO THE TALMUD
Benois, A *see* KHUDOZHESTVENNYE SOKROVISHCHA ROSSII
Benoist, Charles *see*
– LES OUVRIERES DE L'AIGUILLE A PARIS
– LES OUVRIERS DE L'AIGUILLE A PARIS
Benoiston de Chateauneuf *see* RECHERCHES SUR LES CONSOMMATIONS DE TOUT GENRE DE LA VILLE DE PARIS; COMPAREES A CE QU'ELLES ETAIENT EN 1789
Benoit, Alphonse *see* SAINT GREGOIRE DE NAZIANZE
BENOIT DE CANFIELD (1562-1610) : SA VIE, SA DOCTRINE ET SON INFLUENCE / Veghel, Optat de – Romae, 1949 – 14mf – 8 – ne Slangenburg [290]
Benoit, Emmanuel P *see* LA FEMME AUPRES DU MALADE A NOTRE EPOQUE: CONFERENCE..
Benoit, F *see* A L'ABBAYE DE MONTMAJOUR
Benoit, L *see* ORNITHOLOGIA SICILIANA
Benoit, Samuel *see* LA CHARLOIADE, OU, LE MENTEUR DEMASQUE: POEME HEROI-COMIQUE
Benough, John Wilson *see* A CARICATURE HISTORY OF CANADIAN POLITICS: EVENTS FROM THE UNION OF 1841..
Benrath, Karl *see*
– GESCHICHTE DER REFORMATION IN VENEDIG
– JULIA GONZAGA
– LUTHER IM KLOSTER, 1505-1525
Bensa, A *see* INTRODUCTION A L'ETUDE DES CULTES POPULAIRES DANS LE PERCHE
Bensen *see* NEUE ENCYCLOPAEDIE DER WISSENSCHAFTEN UND KUENSTE (AEL, ABT 1;24)
Ben-Shachar, C *see* ECONOMIC STRUCTURE AND DEVELOPMENT PROSPECTS OF THE WEST BANK AND THE GAZA STRIP
Bension, A *see* SAR SHALOM SHARABI
Bensley, A A *see* DIARY
Bensley, Robert L *see* MISSING FRAGMENT OF THE LATIN TRANSLATION OF THE FOURTH BOOK OF EZRA
Bensly, Robert L *see*
– EPISTLE TO THE HEBREWS
– THE FOURTH BOOK OF EZRA, THE LATIN VERSION FROM THE MSS
Benson, Arthur Christopher *see*
– ESSAYS
– THE LIFE OF EDWARD WHITE BENSON
– WILLIAM LAUD
Benson, C *see* AN ACCOUNT OF THE KURNOOL DISTRICT
Benson, David P *see* CHURCH MUSIC IN THEORY AND PRACTICE IN SELECTED BAPTIST CHURCHES, AN EXPLORATORY STUDY
Benson, E F *see* LUCIA IN LONDON. LEIPZIG 1928
Benson, Edward White *see*
– THE APOCALYPSE
– APOCALYPSE: AN INTRODUCTORY STUDY OF THE REVELATION
– THE CATHEDRAL
– CYPRIAN
Benson, Elizabeth P *see* PRE-COLUMBIAN ART
Benson, J *see* OUT-LETTERS, 1766-1820
Benson, Jane *see* QUAKER PIONEERS IN RUSSIA
Benson, L *see* THE BOOK OF REMARKABLE TRIALS AND NOTORIOUS CHARACTERS
Benson, Lawrence Sluter *see*
– CREATION: MAN'S FALL EXPLAINED IN THE LIGHT OF MODERN SCIENCE
– DARWINISM
Benson, Louis F *see*
– THE ENGLISH HYMN
– STUDIES OF FAMILIAR HYMNS
Benson, Margaret *see* VENTURE OF RATIONAL FAITH
Benson, Richard Meux *see* LIFE OF FATHER GOREH
Benson, Robert Hugh *see*
– THE LIGHT INVISIBLE
– A MYSTERY PLAY
BENSON SUN – Omaha, NE. -w. Jan 1907-Dec 1938; Jun 1950 to date – 1 – us NE Hist [071]
Benson, Wilson *see* LIFE AND ADVENTURES OF WILSON BENSON
Bensow, Oscar *see*
– DIE LEHRE VON DER KENOSE
– DIE LEHRE VON DER VERSOEHNUNG
Bent, Charles *see* HISTORY OF WHITESIDE COUNTY
Bent, Samuel Arthur *see* WHY WAS LOUISBURG TWICE BESEIGED?: A PAPER READ BEFORE THE SOCIETY OF COLONIAL WARS IN THE COMMONWEALTH OF MASSACHUSETTS AT BOSTON, APRIL 30, 1895
BENTARA – Ende, Flores. 1949-1957. (incomplete) SE-983 1 – 9 – ne IDC [073]
Bentham, Edward *see* AN INTRODUCTION TO LOGICK, SCHOLASTICK AND RATIONAL
Bentham, G *see*
– THE BOTANY OF THE VOYAGE OF H. M. S. SULPHUR
– CATALOGUE DES PLANTES INDIGENES DES PYRENEES ET DU BAS LANGUEDOC
– COMMENTATIONES DE LEGUMINOSARUM GENERIBUS
– ENUMERATIO PLANTARUM QUAS IN NOVAE HOLLANDIAE
– FLORA AUSTRALIENSIS
– GENERA PLANTARUM
– LABIATARUM GENERA ET SPECIES
– PLANTAS HARTWEGIANAS IMPRIMIS MEXICANAS
– SYNOPSIS OF THE DALBERGIAE, A TRIBE OF THE LEGUMINOSAE
Bentham, J *see* THREE TRACTS RELATIVE TO SPANISH AND PORTUGUEZE AFFAIRS ...
Bentham, Maria Sophia *see* THE LIFE OF BRIGADIER-GENERAL SIR SAMUEL BENTHAM
Bentham, Samuel *see* NAVAL ESSAYS; OR, ESSAYS ON THE MANAGEMENT OF PUBLIC CONCERNS AS EXEMPLIFIED IN THE NAVAL DEPARTMENT, CONSIDERED AS A BRANCH OF THE BUSINESS OF WARFARE. ESSAY 1: EFFICIENCY OF THE MATERIEL. PART 1
Bentley *see* MEDICINAL PLANTS
Bentley, Eliza *see* PRECIOUS STONES FOR ZION'S WALLS: A RECORD OF PERSONAL EXPERIENCE IN THINGS CONNECTED WITH THE KINGDOM OF GOD ON EARTH
Bentley, OH *see* HISTORY OF WICHITA AND SEDGWICK COUNTIES
Bentley, W Darley *see* DIRECT TRADE BETWEEN THE DOMINION OF CANADA AND THE EMPIRE OF BRAZIL, ETC
Bentley, William Preston *see* ILLUSTRIOUS CHINESE CHRISTIANS
Bentley-Taylor, David *see* THE GREAT VOLCANO
Benton County. Arkansas *see* INVENTORY OF THE COUNTY ARCHIVES OF ARKANSAS: BENTON
BENTON COUNTY COURIER – Corvallis, OR. -w. 1915-24 – 1 – 72.00 – us Oregon Hist [071]
BENTON COUNTY HERALD – Corvallis, OR. -w. 4 Aug 1932-25 Dec 1975+. 15 rolls – 1 – us U.O. Library [071]
THE BENTON COUNTY PIONEER – v1-5, 1956-60. Biog. and hist. sketches. F-0025 to F-0029 – 9 – us A.G.L.L. [978]
BENTON COUNTY REPUBLICAN – Corvallis, OR. -w. 11 Oct 1906-11 Mar 1915. 2 rolls – 1 – us U.O. Library [071]
BENTON COUNTY REVIEW – Philomath, Or. -w. 2 Nov 1907-13 Aug 1964. 13 rolls – 1 – us U.O. Library [071]
BENTON DEMOCRAT – Corvallis, OR. -w. 4 May 1871-29 Nov 1878. 2 rolls – 1 – us U.O. Library [071]
Benton, E J *see* INTERNATIONAL LAW AND DIPLOMACY OF ...
BENTON FIRST BAPTIST CHURCH. BENTON, TENNESSEE : CHURCH RECORDS – 1836-Aug 1946 – 1 – 40.95 – us Baptist [240]
BENTON INDEPENDENT – Corvallis, OR. -w. 1924-32 – 1 – 72.00 – us Oregon Hist [071]
BENTON INDEPENDENT – Corvallis, OR. -w. 31 Oct 1929-4 Mar 1932. 1 roll – 1 – us U.O. Library [071]
Benton, Nathaniel S *see* A HISTORY OF HERKIMER COUNTY, INCLUDING THE UPPER MOHAWK VALLEY
Bentwich, N *see*
– THE LAW OF DOMICILE IN ITS RELATION TO SUCCESSION ...
– THE MANDATES SYSTEM
Bentz, Paul A *see* CANAL ZONE CODE, 1934
DIE BENUETZUNG DER ANTIKE IN WIELANDS MORALISCHEN BRIEFEN : BEITRAG ZUR ENTWICKLUNGS-GESCHICHTE DER DEUTSCHEN LITERATUR IM 18. JAHRHUNDERT / Doell, M – (Includes bibliographical references) – Eichstaett: Ph Broenner, 1903 – 1 – us U.W. Library [430]
DIE BENUTZUNG DER PFLANZENWELT IN DER ALTTESTAMENTLICHEN RELIGION / Lundgreen, Friedrich – Giessen: Alfred Toepelmann, 1908. 1 fiche – 9 – us A.T.L.A. [240]
Benvenutus V Venraai *see* HANDLEIDING DER PATROLOGIE
Ben-Yami, M *see*
– FINDING FISH WITH ECHO-SOUNDERS
– PURSE-SEINING WITH SMALL BOATS
Ben-Yehuda, E *see*
– MIKHTAV MI-ZAREFAT
– SHE'ELAH NIKHBADAH
Benyon, B G *see* JOURNAL, MS 1236
Benz, E *see*
– MARIUS VICTORINUS UND DIE ENTWICKLUNG DER ABENDLAENDISCHEN WILLENSMETAPHYSIK
– ZUR UEBERLIEFERUNG DER MATTHAEUSERKLAERUNG DES ORIGENES (T.U.U. 4-47/2)
Benz, Richard *see*
– DER GESTIEFELTE KATER – DAS ROTKAEPPCHEN
– JEAN PAUL
Benzin, Vasilii M *see* MOTORNAI A VSPASHKA, KAK SREDSTVO V BORBI E S GOLODOM V ROSSII
Benzinger, Immanuel *see* DIE BUECHER DER KOENIGE
Ben-Zvi, I *see* MASSA'OT EREZ-YISRA'EL LE-RABBI MOSHEH BASOLA
BEOBACHTER – Rochester. N.Y. 1864-1865; 1867-1882 – 1 – us UMI [071]
DER BEOBACHTER – Stuttgart, Germany. Jun 1-Dec 31, 1849 – 1r – 1 – gw Mikrofilm [072]
DER BEOBACHTER – Zary, Poland. Dec 1934-Oct 1935 – 4r – 1 – us L of C Photodup [072]
BEOGRADSKA NEDELJA – Belgrade, Yugoslavia. Sept 1961-Nov 1962 – 1r – 1 – us L of C Photodup [949]
THE BEOTHUCKS OR RED INDIANS / Howley, J P – BN 259 2. 1915 – 8 – ne IDC [306]
BEOTHUK AND MICMAC. INDIAN NOTES AND MONOGRAPHS / Speck, F G – BN 392 2. 1922 – 8 – ne IDC [305]
BEOUMI. ETUDE ECONOMIQUE D'UN CENTRE SEMI URBAIN / Chevassu, J – (Africa series). 1968 – 9 – fr Hachette [338]
BEOUMI. EXPLOITATION MANUELLE DE L'ENQUETE DEMOGRAPHIQUE. RESULTATS PARTIELS / Ancey, G – (Africa series). 1967 – 9 – fr Hachette [310]
Berab, J *see* ZIMRAT HA-AREZ
BERABER – Nos 1-9. – 1952-1953 – 1mf – 9 – $10.50 – us MEDOC [949]
BERAETTELSE OM DE INHEMSKA VAEXTER, SOM I BRIST AF SAD KUNNA ANVAENDAS TILL BROED-OCH MATREDNING / Linnaeus, Carl – Stockholm. 1757. B-6142 2 – 8 – ne IDC [580]
Beran, M A *see* HYDROLOGICAL ASPECTS OF DROUGHT
Beranger, Charles *see* PETITION D'UN PROLETAIRE A LA CHAMBRE DES DEPUTES
Beranger, Pierre Jean de *see*
– MUSIQUE DES CHANSONS DE BERANGER
– SONGS FROM BERANGER
Berar. India (State). Superintendent of Census Operations *see* MISCELLANY
Berard, Jean-Antoine *see* L'ART DU CHANT
Berardi, A *see*
– ARCANI MUSICALI
– DOCUMENTI ARMONICI
– MISCELLANEA MUSICALE
– IL PERCHE MUSICALE
– RAGIONAMENTI MUSICALI COMPOSTI DAL SIG D. ANGELO BERARDI
Berardini, Lorenzo *see* FRATE ANGELO DA CHIARINO...OSIMO 1964
Beraud *see* ADONIS OU LE BON NEGRE
Berault-Bercastel, Antoine Henri de *see* LA CONQUETE DE LA TERRE PROMISE
Berben, Abdon *see* AGUAS BICARBONATADAS CALCICAS DE ALANGE
Berber, G *see* DE JURE SOCIETATIS ARMORUM ...
LE BERBERE A L'ECOLE NATIONALE DES LANGUES ORIENTALES VIVANTES / Basset, Andre – Paris: Impr Nationale de France, 1948 – 1 – us Res Libr [470]
LES BERBERES MAROCAINS ET LA PACIFICATION DE L'ATLAS CENTRAL : 1912-1933 / Guillaume, Gal A – Paris: Julliard, 1946 – 1 – F263.77 – fr Armell [960]
IL BERBERO NEFUSI DI FASSATO : GRAMMATICA, TESTI RACCOLTI DALLA VIVA VOCE, VOCABOLARIETTI / Beguinot, Francesco – 2. rev miglio. ed. Roma: Instituto per l'Oriente, 1942 – us Res Libr [470]
Berberova, N N *see* ALEXANDER BLOK ET SON TEMPS
Berchoux, J de *see* VOLTAIRE OU LE TRIOMPHE DE LA PHILOSOPHIE MODERNE

BERCHTESGADENER ANZEIGER – Berchtesgaden, may 1976- – ca 4r per yr – 1 – Dist. gw Mikrofilm – gw Misc Inst [072]
Berchtold, Joseph *see* DIE UNVEREINBARKEIT DER NEUEN PAEPSTLICHEN GLAUBENSDEKRETE MIT DER BAYERISCHEN STAATSVERFASSUNG
Berdiaev, N A *see*
- ALEKSEI STEPANOVICH KHOMIAKOV
- DEKADENSTVO I MISTICHESKII REALIZM
- KHRISTIANSTVO I AKTIVNOST' CHELOVEKA
- KRIZIS ISKUSSTVA
- REVOLIUTSIIA I KUL'TURA
- SAMOPOZNANIE
- O SAMOUBIISTVIE
- SEREBRIANNYI GOLUB' BELOGO. RETSENZIIA
- SLAVERY AND FREEDOM
- SUDBA ROSSII
- VLAD. SOLOV'EV I MY. SOVREMENNYE ZAPISKI

Berdichevskii, N G *see*
- DEISTVUIUSHCHEE KOOPERATIVNOE ZAKONODATEL'STVO
- DEISTVUIUSHCHEE KOOPERATIVNOE ZAKONODATELSTVO
- DEISTVUIUSHCHEE ZAKONODATEL'STVO O POTREBITEL'SKOI KOOPERATSII
- DEKRET O POTREBITEL'SKOI KOOPERATSII, 20 MAIA 1924 G.
- ZAKON O ZHILISHCHNOI KOOPERATSII

Berdnikov, Aleksandr Ivanovich *see* OCHEREDNYE ZADACHI MAKSIMALIZMA
Berdrow, Otto *see* RAHEL VARNHAGEN
BEREA BAPTIST CHURCH. BEREA, KENTUCKY : CHURCH RECORDS – Feb 1896-Sept 1985. Lacking: 1902-07, 1909, Aug 1911-Aug 1912, Oct 1912-Mar 1913 – 1 – 96.21 – us Baptist [240]
BEREA BAPTIST CHURCH. EDGEFIELD COUNTY. SOUTH CAROLINA : CHURCH RECORDS – 1954-76.36p – 1 – 5.00 – us Baptist [240]
Berea College *see* BEREA COLLEGE NEWS
BEREA COLLEGE NEWS / Berea College – Berea. Ky. 1906-08 – 1 – us UMI [370]
THE BEREAN : ANGLICAN – Quebec, Canada. 4 avr 1844-22 mar 1849 – 1r – 1 – Can$50.00 – cn Can Microfilming [240]
BERECHNUNG UND DIMENSIONIERUNG PERMANENTERREGTER GLEICHSTROMLINEARANTRIEBE DER FEINWERKTECHNIK / Roemer, Olaf – 1994 – 2mf – DM80.00 – 3-89349-883-4 – gw Hänsel [620]
DIE BERECHTIGUNG DER THEOLOGIE ALS EINES NOTHWENDIGEN GLIEDES IM GESAMTORGANISMUS DER WISSENSCHAFT : VORTRAG AUF DER CONFERENZ ZU MEISSEN AM 10. JUNI 1874 / Baur, Gustav – Gotha:Friedrich Andreas Perthes, 1875 – 1mf – 9 – 0-8370-2215-0 – 1985-0215 – us A.T.L.A. [210]
BERECHTIGUNG UND PRAKTISCHE ANWENDUNG DES VERBOTS DER WERBUNG MIT SONDERANGEBOTEN BEI MENGENMAESSIG BESCHRAENKTER ABGABE : EINE KRITISCHE BETRACHTUNG DES PARAGRAPHEN 6 D ABS. 1 NR. 2 UWG / Conrad, Christine – 1993 – 3mf – 9 – DM98.00 – 3-89349-820-6 – gw Hänsel [340]
DIE BEREDSAMKEIT J. ENOCH POWELLS / Lang, Hartmut – Frankfurt a.M., 1972 – 3mf – 9 – DM76.00 – 3-89349-749-8 – gw Hänsel [943]
Beremant, Gordon et al *see* THE CASES OF THE U.S. COURT OF APPEALS FOR THE D.C. CIRCUIT
Berend, Julia Z *see* INFLUENCE OF DIET AND THE MENSTRUAL CYCLE ON LACTATE CONCENTRATION DURING INCREASING EXERCISE INTENSITIES
Berendsohn, Walter Arthur *see*
- GRUNDFORMEN VOLKSTUEMLICHER ERZAEHLERKUNST IN DEN KINDER- UND HAUSMAERCHEN DER BRUEDER GRIMM
- DER IMPRESSIONISMUS HOFMANNSTHALS ALS ZEITERSCHEINUNG

Berendt, G C *see* DIE INSEKTEN IM BERNSTEIN
Berendts Alexander *see* VOM JUEDISCHEN KRIEGE
Berendts, Alexander *see*
- DIE HANDSCHRIFTLICHE UEBERLIEFERUNG DER ZACHARIAS- UND JOHANNES-APOKRYPHEN (T.U.U. 2-26/3A)
- STUDIEN UEBER ZACHARIAS-APOKRYPHEN UND ZACHARIAS-LEGENDEN
- UEBER DIE BIBLIOTHEKEN DER METEORISCHEN UND OSSA-OLYMPISCHEN KLOESTER (T.U.U. 2-26/3B)
- DAS VERHAELTNIS DER ROEMISCHEN KIRCHE ZU DEN KLEINASIATISCHEN VOR DEM NICAENISCHEN KONZIL
- DIE ZEUGNISSE VOM CHRISTENTUM IM SLAVISCHEN "DE BELLO JUDAICO" DES JOSEPHUS
- DIE ZEUGNISSE VOM CHRISTENTUM IM SLAVISCHEN "DE BELLO JUDAICO" DES JOSEPHUS (T.U.U. 2-29/4)

BERENGARIUS TURONENSIS, ODER, EINE SAMMLUNG IHN BETREFFENDER BRIEFE / Sudendorf, Hans – Hamburg: F. und A. Perthes, 1850 – 1mf – us A.T.L.A. [240]
Berenger-Feraud, Laurent Jean Baptiste *see*
- CONTES POPULAIRES DES PROVENCAUX DE L'ANTIQUITE ET DU MOYEN-AGE
- LES PEUPLADES DE LA SENEGAMBIE
- RECUEIL DE CONTES POPULAIRES DE LA SENEGAMBIE

Berenguer, F *see* EL HISPANO-AMERICANISMO
Berenhorst, Georg Heinrich von *see* BETRACHTUNGER UEBER DIE KRIEGSKUNST, UEBER IRHE FORTSCHRITTE, IHRE WIDERSPRUECHE UND IHRE ZUVERLAESSIGHEIT
Berens, Lewis H *see* DICTATOR-DEMOCRAT
Berenshtam, Vladimir *see* VOGNI E ZASHCHITY
Berenson, Senda *see* LINE BASKETBALL, OR BASKETBALL FOR WOMEN
Beresford, Charles William DelaPoer *see* THE BETRAYAL: BEING A RECORD OF FACTS CONCERNING NAVAL POLICY AND ADMINISTRATION FROM THE YEAR 1902 TO THE PRESENT TIME
Beresford, John *see* CORRESPONDENCE
EL BERESH I: THE TOMB OF TEHUTI-HETEP / Newberry, Percy E – 9 – $10.00 – us I.R.C. [930]
EL BERESH, PART 2 / Griffith, Fl & Newberry, Percy E – 9 – $10.00 – us I.R.C. [930]
Beresteyn, E A van *see* ICONOGRAPHIE VAN HUGO GROTIUS
LE BERET : JOURNAL DES ETUDIANTS DE L'ETUDIANTS DE L'UNIVERSITE DE LAVAL – Quebec, Canada. v5 n9. 20 nov 1931-v5 n13. 17 dec 1931. 4 nos – 1r – 1 – Can$25.00 – cn Can Microfilming [072]
Beretty, D W *see* VAN 13 MOMENTEN UIT EEN 13-JARIG BESTAAN
Berezin, M M *see* PLANIROVANIE KHOZIAISTVENNOI DEIATEL'NOSTI SOIUZOV I NIZOVOI SETI PROMYSLOVOI KOOPERATSII
Berezin, N I *see* MATERIALY PO VOPROSU O VYVOZE IZ Z. SIBIRI PISHCHEVYKH PRODUKTOV
Berezin, V *see* OPISANIE RUKOPISEI POCHAEVSKOI LAVRY
Berg, C *see* CONTRIBUCION AL ESTUDIO DE LA FAUNA ENTOMOLOGICA DE PATAGONIA
Berg, E de *see* ADDITAMENTA AD THESAURUM LITERATURAE BOTANICAE
BERG FREI! : ORGAN DES TOURISTENVEREINS "DIE NATURFREUNDE" – Aussig, 1930 n3-1936 n4 – 1r – 1 – Dist. gw Mikrofilm – gw Misc Inst [790]
Berg, J Frederic *see* INFLUENCE OF THE SEPTUAGINT UPON THE PESHITTA PSALTER
Berg, J van den *see* CONSTRAINED BY JESUS' LOVE
Berg, Joseph Frederic *see* THE INFLUENCE OF THE SEPTUAGINT UPON THE PESITTAA PSALTER
Berg, O C *see* ATLAS DER OFFICINELLEN PFLANZEN...
Berg, Richard K *see* GOVERNMENT IN THE SUNSHINE ACT
BERG- UND HUETTENMAENNISCHE RUNDSCHAU – Katowice, Poland. 5 Oct 1904-20 Mar 1921 – 412r – 1 – uk British Libr Newspaper [622]
BERG- UND HUETTENMAENNISCHE ZEITUNG – Freiberg, Germany. Jan 1851-Dec 1852.-w. 1 reel – 1 – uk British Libr Newspaper [072]
BERG- UND HUETTENMAENNISCHE ZEITUNG – Leipzig, Germany. 1853-1904.-w. 29 reels – 1 – uk British Libr Newspaper [072]
BERG- UND HUETTENMAENNISCHE ZEITUNG – Nordhausen, Germany. Jan-Dec 1842.-w. mqn reel – 1 – uk British Libr Newspaper [072]
Berga, A *see* UN PREDICATEUR DE LA COUR DE POLOGNE SOUS SIGISMOND 3, PIERRE SKARGA (1536-1612)
Bergamin, Jose *see* MARANON'S BETRAYAL
Bergano, Diego *see* ARTE DE LA LENGUA PAMPANGA.
Berganza, F *see* ANTIGUEDADES DE ESPANA PROPUGNADAS EN LAS NOTICIAS DE SUS REYES Y CONDES...
BERGARBEITER : SCHAUSPIEL IN EINEM AKT / Maerten, Lu – Stuttgart: J H W Dietz, 1909 – 1r – 1 – us U.W. Library [820]
DER BERGARBEITERAUSSTAND UND DIE TECHN. GRUBENBEAMTEN GELSENKIRCHEN 1905 / Bertenburg, Carl – 1 – DM30.00 – gw Mikro Press [330]
BERGARBEITER-STREIK IM RUHRGEBIET IM FRUEHJAHR 1912 – Coeln o. J – 1 – DM30.00 – gw Mikro Press [331]
DER BERGARBEITERSTREIK UND DIE UNTERSUCHUNGSKOMMISSIONEN – Bochum 1905 – 1 – DM30.00 – gw Mikro Press [331]
DER BERGARBEITERSTREIK VOM MAI 1889 IM RHEINISCH-WESTFALISCHEN INDUSTRIEGEBIET UNTER BESONDERER BERUECKSICHTIGUNG DER STELLUNG KAISER WILHELM 2. UND FURST / Hahn, Wilhelm – 1 – DM30.00 – gw Mikro Press [943]
DIE BERGARBEITER-VERHAELTNISSE IN GROSSBRITANNIEN / Hasse, R & Kruemmer, G – Saarbruecken, 1891 – 1 – DM40.00 – gw Mikro Press [331]
BERGARBEITER-ZEITUNG *see*
- DEUTSCHE BERG- UND HUETTENARBEITER-ZEITUNG
- DEUTSCHE BERG- UND HUETTEN-ARBIETER-ZEITUNG
- GLUECKAUF!
- GLUECKAUF

DIE BERGBAU- INDUSTRIE *see* DEUTSCHE BERG- UND HUETTEN-ARBIETER-ZEITUNG
DIE BERGBAU-INDUSTRIE *see*
- DEUTSCHE BERG- UND HUETTENARBEITER-ZEITUNG
- GLUECKAUF!
- GLUECKAUF

Bergbohm, C *see*
- DIE BEWAFFNETE NEUTRALITAET 1780-1783 ...
- STAATSVERTRAEGE ...

Bergbohm, K *see* THEORIE DES VOELKERRECHTS
BERGCULTURES – (Continues as: Menara Perkebunan) – Djakarta, 1926-1942, 1948-1957. v1-26. Lacking: 1965, v34(9); 1969, v38(1-2 , 11-12); 1970, v39(3-...) – 662mf – 9 – ne IDC [306]
BERGE IN FLAMMEN : EIN ROMAN AUS DEN SCHICKSALSTAGEN SUEDTIROLS / Trenker, Luis – Berlin: Neufeld & Henius, c1931 – 1r – 1 – us U.W. Library [830]
BERGEDORFER ZEITUNG – Hamburg-Bergedorf, West-Germany. May 1, 1976- – 1 – gw Mikrofilm [072]
Bergel, Joseph *see*
- DER HIMMEL UND SEINE WUNDER
- STUDIEN UEBER DIE NATURWISSENSCHAFTLICHEN KENNTNISSE DER TALMUDISTEN

Bergen, C A von *see* CLASSES CONCHYLIORUM
Bergen, John Tallmadge *see* EVIDENCES OF CHRISTIANITY
Bergengruen, Werner *see* E.T.A. HOFFMANN
BERGENS TIDENDE – 1991- – 24r per yr – 1 – inquire – us Ross [072]
Berger, Arnold Erich *see*
- DER JUNGE HERDER UND WINCKELMANN
- KLOPSTOCKS SENDUNG

Berger, Berta *see* DER MODERNE DEUTSCHE BILDUNGSROMAN
Berger, Daniel *see* HISTORY OF THE CHURCH OF THE UNITED BRETHREN IN CHRIST
Berger, Johann *see*
- LEBEN UND WIRKEN DES HOCHSELIGEN JOHANNES NEP. NEUMANN
- LIFE OF RIGHT REV. JOHN N. NEUMANN, D.D.

Berger, Karl *see*
- SCHILLER
- THEODOR KOERNER

Berger, Kurt *see*
- DIE BALLADEN SCHILLERS IM ZUSAMMENHANG SEINER LYRISCHEN DICHTUNG
- RAINER MARIA RILKES FRUEHE LYRIK

Berger, P *see*
- BIBLIOGRAFIA DO RIO DE JANEIRO DE VIAJANTES E AUTORES ESTRANGEIROS, 1531-1900
- BIBLIOGRAFIA DO RIO DE JANEIRO DE VIAJANTES E ESTRANGEIROS 1531-1900

Berger, Philippe *see* M. ERNEST RENAN ET LA CHAIRE D'HEBREU AU COLLEGE DE FRANCE
Berger, Richard A *see*
- AN EVALUATION OF A HOME-BASED EXERCISE PROGRAM INVOLVING NON-EXERTIONAL HYPOXEMIC AND EXERTIONAL HYPOXEMIC CHRONIC OBSTRUCTIVE PULMONARY DISEASED PATIENTS
- PHYSIOLOGICAL RESPONSE OF TRAINED CYCLISTS TO VARIOUS CYCLING HANDLEBAR POSTURES

Bergeron, Helene *see* BIO-BIBLIOGRAPHIE ANALYTIQUE DE RENE OUVRARD
Bergeron, Jules *see* RAPPORT SUR LA STATISTIQUE DES DECES DU TROISIEME ARRONDISSEMENT DE PARIS PENDANT LE PERIODE QUINQUENNALE 1853-57
Bergeron, Juliana *see* CHANOINE JEAN BERGERON, 1868-1956
Bergeron, Pierre *see* LES VOYAGES FAMEUX DU SIEUR VINCENT LE BLANC MARSEILLAIS, QU'IL A FAIT DEPUIS L'AGE DE DOUZE ANS JUSQU'A SOIXANTE AUX QUATRE PARTIES DU MONDE
Bergerson, Mark *see* A COMPARISON OF THE EFFECTS OF A WRESTLING PRACTICE AND A WEIGHTLIFTING WORKOUT ON THE BODY FAT PERCENT OF WRESTLERS
Berges, W *see* DIE FUERSTENSPIEGEL DES HOHEN UND SPAETEN MITTELALTERS (MGH SCHRIFTEN..: 2.BD)
Bergfeld, E *see* DIE FRANZOESISCHEN MANDATSGEBIETE KAMERUN UND TOGO
DER BERGGEIST – Cologne, Germany. 1 Jul 1856-28 Dec 1860; 2 Jan 1866-29 Dec 1885.-w. 13mqn reels – 1 – uk British Libr Newspaper [072]
BERGGESCHICHTEN / Achleitner, Arthur – Stuttgart: Adolf Bonz, 1905 – 1r – 1 – us U.W. Library [830]
Berggren, S *see* STUDIER OEFVER MOSSORNAS BYGGNAD OCH UTVECKLING
Bergh, Christine E *see* THE RELATIONSHIP BETWEEN SEX-ROLE CLASSIFICATION AND ACTIVITY, AND TRAIT AND STATE ANXIETY
Bergh, G van den *see*
- ONDERZOEK NAAR DE ECHTHEID VAN CLEMENS' EERSTEN BRIEF AAN DE CORINTHIERS
- DER PESSIMISMUS BEI THOMAS HARDY, G. CRABBE UND J. SWIFT

Bergh, I L C van den *see* HISTORIAM NOVARUM LEGUM DE FLUMINUM COMMUNIUM NAVIGATIONE
Berghaeuser, Wilhelm *see* DIE DARSTELLUNG DES WAHNSINNS IM ENGLISCHEN DRAMA BIS ZUM ENDE DES 18. JAHRHUNDERTS
Berghe, Wouter Van den *see* ENGINEERING MANPOWER
Bergholtz, Gustav Fredric *see* THE LORD'S PRAYER IN THE PRINCIPAL LANGUAGES, DIALECTS AND VERSIONS OF THE WORLD, PRINTED IN THE TYPE AND VERNACULARS OF THE DIFFERENT NATIONS
Bergholz, Harry *see* UEBER DEN TAG HINAUS
Bergien, Angelika *see* SYNCHRONISCH-DIACHRONISCHE UNTERSUCHUNGEN ZUR ZEICHENSETZUNG IN ENGLISCHEN TEXTEN
Bergier, [N S] *see* LES ELEMENS PRIMITIFS DES LANGUES...
Bergin, Darby *see* THE CORNWALL CANAL: ITS LOCATION AND CONSTRUCTION, BREAKS AND PRESENT CONDITION
BERGISCHE ARBEITERSTIMME – Solingen, 1901-1933 – 67r – 1 – DM5,025.00 – gw Mikro Press [072]
BERGISCHE ARBEITERSTIMME – Solingen, Germany. 1901-Jun 1920; 1921-Feb 20, 1933 – 67r – 1 – gw Mikrofilm [072]
BERGISCHE VOLKSSTIMME – Barmen (Wuppertal), Germany. 1877-Oct 1878 – 4r – 1 – gw Mikrofilm [072]
BERGISCHES VOLKSBLATT – (Title change: Solinger Zeitung, 1 Jul 1868) – Solingen, Germany. Jun 29-Dec 28, 1849 – 1r – 1 – gw Mikrofilm [072]
BERGISCH-GLADBACHER VOLKSZEITUNG *see* VOLKSBLATT FUER BERGISCH GLADBACH UND UMGEBUNG
Bergius, P J *see* DESCRIPTIONES PLANTARUM EX CAPITE BONAE SPEI
DER BERGKNAPPE : ZEITSCHRIFT FUER CHRISTLICHE BERGLEUTE – Essen, 1896-1932 – 9r – 1 – DM675.00 – gw Mikro Press [073]
DER BERGKNAPPE : ZEITSCHRIFT FUER CHRISTLICHE BERGLEUTE – Essen, Germany. 1896-1932 – 9r – 1 – gw Mikrofilm [072]

BERGKRISTALLE: NOVELLEN UND ERZAEHLUNGEN AUS DER SCHWEIZ – (v.1-15. Novellen und Erzaehlungen von Arthur Bitter. 1. v.16-20. Novellen und Erzaehlungen von J.J. Romang. Film Mas 8366. 1) – Bern, B.F. Haller, 1876-79. 20v. in 7v – 1 – us H.U. Library [830]

BERGLIEDERBUECHLEIN : HISTORISCH-KRITISCHE AUSGABE / ed by Mincoff-Marriage, Elizabeth – (Without music. Includes bibliographical references) – Leipzig: K W Hiersemann, 1936 – 1 – us U.W. Library [810]

Bergman, Genrikh *see* ROSSI ISKAI A SOTSIALISTICHESKAI A ARMII A

Bergmann, A *see*
- DER AUSLAENDER VOR DEM STANDESAMT
- INTERNATIONALES EHE- UND KINDSCHAFTSRECHT

Bergmann, Anton *see* DIE BEDEUTUNG DES NIBLUNGENLIEDER FUER DIE DEUTSCHE NATION

Bergmann, B *see* NOMADISCHE STREIFEREIEN UNTER DEN KALMUEKEN

Bergmann, E *see* HIERATISCHE UND HIERATISCH-DEMOTISCHE TEXTE DER SAMMLUNG AEGYPTISCHER ALTERTHUEMER DES ALLERHOECHSTEN KAISERHAUSES

Bergna, Costanzo *see* TRIPOLI DAL 1510 AL 1850

Bergner, Hans *see* ARCHIVES OF ANIMAL NUTRITION

Bergobzoomer, Johann Baptist *see* IN DER NOTH LERNET MAN DIE FREUNDE KENNEN

DIE BERGPREDIGT / Weinel, Heinrich – ihr Aufbau, ihr urspruenglicher Sinn und ihre Echtheit, ihre Stellung in der Religionsgeschichte und ihre Bedeutung fuer die Gegenwart. 1920 – 1 – us A.T.L.A. [240]

DIE BERGPREDIGT JESU CHRISTI / Stockmeyer, Immanuel – Basel: R. Reich, 1891. 1 fiche – 9 – us A.T.L.A. [240]

DIE BERGPREDIGT (MATTH. 5-7, LUK. 6, 20-49) / Heinrici, Carl Friedrich Georg – (Includes bibliographical references) – Leipzig: Alexander Edelmann, 1905 – 1mf – 9 – 0-8370-3549-X – 1985-1549 – us A.T.L.A. [220]

BERGPREDIGTEN : GEHALTEN AUF DER HOEHE DER ZEIT UNTER FREIEM HIMMEL UND ZU SCHIMPF UND SPOTT UNSEREN FEINDEN DEN SCHWAECHEN, LASTERN UND IRRTHUEMERN DER CULTUR GEWIDMET / Rosegger, Peter – Wien: A Hartleben, 1885 – 1r – 1 – us U.W. Library [840]

BERGPSALMEN : DICHTUNG / Scheffel, Joseph Viktor von – (Within red line borders) – 6. Aufl. Stuttgart. A Bonz, 1895 – 1r – 1 – us U.W. Library [810]

BERGSLAGSKURIREN *see* OREBROKURIREN

BERGSLAGSPOSTEN – Lindesberg, Sweden. 1979- – 1 – sw Kungliga [072]

Bergsland, K *see* ESKIMO LANGUAGE

Bergsma, W B *see* EINDRESUME VAN HET GOEVERNEMENTSBESLUIT DD. 10/6/1867 NO. 2 BEVOLEN ONDERZOEK NAAR DE RECHTEN VAN DEN INLANDER OP DEN GROND OP JAVA EN MADOERA

Bergson, Henri *see*
- DREAMS
- THE INTRODUCTION TO A NEW PHILOSOPHY
- LAUGHTER
- TIME AND FREE WILL

BERGSTRAESSER ANZEIGEBLATT – Bensheim, jan 1-jun 30 1937, 1940-jun 30 1941, 1942-jun 30 1943, jul 1-dec 30 1944, aug 17 1945-may 15 1946, 1949-59 (incomplete) – 1 – Dist. gw Mikrofilm – gw Misc Inst [943]

BERGSTRAESSER ANZEIGER – Bensheim, 1973- – 1 – Dist. gw Mikrofilm – gw Misc Inst [072]

Bergstraesser, G *see* NICHTKANONISCHE KORANLESARTEN IM MUHTASAB DES IBN GINNI

Berguizas, Francisco P *see* OBRAS POETICASIDE PINDARO..

DIE BERGUNG : EINE ERZAEHLUNG / Leip, Hans – Stuttgart: J G Cotta, 1944, c1939 – 1r – 1 – us U.W. Library [830]

BERGWERKS- UND INDUSTRIE ANZEIGER – Berlin, Jan 1859-Nov 1865 – 1r – 1 – uk British Libr Newspaper [072]

BERGWERKS- UND INDUSTRIEANZEIGER – Berlin, jan 4 1859-nov 7 1865 – 1r – 1 – uk British Libr Newspaper [622]

Beria, G B *see*
- CONCERTI MUSICALI A DUE, TRE, W QUATTRO VOCI, CON UNA MESSA A QUATTRO CONCERTATA, ET INTROITI, PANGE LINGUA A QUATTRO DA CAPELLA
- MOTTETI A DUE, TRE, E QUATTRO VOCI CO'L, TE DEUM, LE LETANIE DELLA B. VERGINE CONCERTTATI, ET IL PASIJ DELLA DOMENICA DELLE PALME, ET DEL VENERDI SANCTO CO'L, TAMTUM ERGO SACRAMENTUM; VENI CREATOR...

BERICHT / Akademie der Wissenschaften. Berlin – 20v 1836-55 – 1 – us Schnase [500]

BERICHT / Allgemeiner deutscher Gewerkschaftsbund. Ortsausschuss Halle – Halle. 1929. Continues: Halle. Arbeiter-Sekretariat. Bericht? (Serial publications of German trade unions in the Memorial Library, University of Wisconsin-Madison.) – 1 – us U.W. Library [073]

BERICHT / Centralverband der Handlungsgehulfen und Gehulfinnen Deutschlands – Hamburg, 1904-05. (Serial publications of German trade unions in the Memorial Library, University of Wisconsin-Madison.) – 1 – us U.W. Library [330]

BERICHT / Deutscher Landarbeiter-Verband – Berlin. 1926-28. Sometimes includes Niederschrift der Generalversammlung. (Serial publications of German trade unions in the Memorial Library, University of Wisconsin-Madison.) – 1 – us U.W. Library [330]

BERICHT / Evangelische Kirche in Deutschland. Kirchenkanzlei – 1948-85.Lacks: 1953, 1959, 1962, 1964, 1969. 12 reels – 1 – us A.T.L.A. [073]

BERICHT / Gerwerkschaftsbund der Angestellten – Berlin. 1925-29, 1931. (Serial publications of German trade unions in the Memorial Library, University of Wisconsin-Madison.) – 1 – us U.W. Library [330]

BERICHT / Hamburger Gewerkschaftskartell – v7-12. 1903-08. Includes Bericht des Arbeiter Sekretariats Hamburg with different numbering. (Serial publications of German trade unions in the Memorial Library, University of Wisconsin-Madison.) – 1 – us U.W. Library [330]

BERICHT / Historischer Verein. Bamberg – Bamberg. Bd. 29-91; 1865 66-1951. Title varies. Name of issuing body varies. Film Mas C 362 – 1 – us H.U. Library [073]

BERICHT / Naturforschende Gesellschaft. Bamberg – Bamberg: J.M. Reindl. -irr. Continues: Ueber das Bestehen und Wirken der Naturforschenden Gesellschaft – 1 – us U.W. Library [500]

BERICHT / Zentralverband christlicher Lederarbeiter Deutschlands – 1925 26. n.p. 1925 26 includes Niederschrift ueber die verhandlungen der 11. Verbandsgeneralversammlung. 1927. (Serial publications of German trade unions in the Memorial Library, University of Wisconsin-Madison.) – 1 – us U.W. Library [330]

BERICHT.. / Allgemeiner deutscher Gewerkschaftsbund. Ortsausschuss Berlin – Berlin. 1923 24. Distinctive Title: Unsere Arbeit, 1923 24. (Serial publications of German trade unions in the Memorial Library, University of Wisconsin-Madison) – 1 – us U.W. Library [073]

BERICHT.. / Saechsischer Berg- und Huettenarbeiter Deligiertentag. Bergmanns Fluch – Zwickau. 20 Sept 1874. 60p. (Serial publications of German trade unions in the Memorial Library, University of Wisconsin-Madison.) – 1 – us U.W. Library [330]

BERICHT AUSZ DER HEYLIGEN GESCHRIFT VON DER RECHT GOTTSELIGEN ANSTELLUNG VND HAUSZHALTUNG CHRISTLICHER GEMEYN, EYNASTZUNG DER DIENER DES WORTS, HALTUNG VND BRAUCH DER HEYLIGEN SACRAMENTEN – Straszburg, M. Apiarius. 1534. BME-149 1 – 9 – ne IDC [240]

BERICHT DER.. / Deutscher Gewerkschaftsbund. (British Zone). Zonen jugendkonferenz – v1, May 1948. (Serial publications of German trade unions in the Memorial Library, University of Wisconsin-Madison.) – 1 – us U.W. Library [330]

BERICHT DER BEZIRKSVERWALTUNG FUER DAS JAHR.../BEZIRK 6, SITZ BERLIN / Zentralverband der Schuhmacher Deutschlands. Bezirk 6 – 1928-29. Caption title. Description based on: 1928. (Serial publications of German trade unions in the Memorial Library, University of Wisconsin-Madison.) – 1 – us U.W. Library [330]

BERICHT DER HAUPTVERWALTUNG / Zentralverband der Hotel-, Restaurant-, und Cafeangestellten – Berlin. 1928. (Serial publications of German trade unions in the Memorial Library, University of Wisconsin-Madison.) – 1 – us U.W. Library [330]

BERICHT DES NATURHISTORISCHEN VEREINS IN AUGSBURG – (Continued as: Bericht des Naturwissenschaftlichen Vereins fuer Schwaben und Neuburg. Augsburg, 1887-1928. v29-46; Missing: 1848/1849. v1-2) – Augsburg, 1848/1849-1885. v1-28 – 185mf – 7645/2 – ne IDC [060]

BERICHT DES OBERGERICHTS VON SCHAFFHAUSEN AN DEN GROSSEN RATH DES KANTONS SCHAFFHAUSEN UEBER DIE GESCHAFTSFUHRUNG SAMMTLICHER GERICHTSSTELLEN UND DEN ZUSTAND DES GERICHTSWESENS IN DEM AMTSJAHRE VOM 1. JUNI 1871 BIS UND MIT DEM 31. MAI 1872 / Schaffhausen. (Canton). Obergericht – Schaffhausen: Gelzer, 1873. 24p. LL-4021 – 1 – us L of C Photodup [340]

BERICHT DES OBERGERICHTS VON SCHAFFHAUSEN AN DEN GROSSEN RATH DES KANTONS SCHAFFHAUSEN UEBER DIE GESCHAFTSFUHRUNG SAMMTLICHER GERICHTSSTELLEN UND DEN ZUSTAND DES GERICHTSWESENS VOM 1. JUNI 1873 BIS UND MIT DEM 31. MAI 1874 / Schaffhausen. (Canton). Obergericht – Schaffhausen: Gelzer, 1875. 27p. LL-4020 – 1 – us L of C Photodup [340]

BERICHT DES REICHSKOHLENRATES UEBER DIE KOHLENWIRTSCHAFT – Berlin, 1921-38 – 2r – 1 – DM180.00 – gw Mikro Press [072]

BERICHT OB MAN ON DIE TAUFFE VND EMPFAHUNGEN DES LEIBS VND BLUTS CHRISTI ALLEIN DURCH DEN GLAUBEN KUENNE SELIG WERDEN... / Corvinus, A – [Magdeburgk], 1538 – 1mf – 9 – ne IDC [240]

BERICHT OVER DE PADI-GEWASSEN, DOOR SURA WINATA, 1694 – 9mf – 9 – ne IDC [580]

BERICHT UBER DIE VERHANDLUNGEN DES ORDENTLICHEN PARTEITAGES / Deutsche Demokratische Partei – Berlin. n1-5. 1919-24 – 1r – 1 – us Ross [324]

BERICHT UEBER ARCHAEOLOGISCHE ARBEITEN IN IDIKUTSCHARI UND UMGEBUNG, IM WINTER 1902-1903 / Gruenwedel, A – ABAW. XXIV. 1909. BU-625 2 – 8 – ne IDC [930]

BERICHT UEBER DAS GESCHAFTSJAHR / Allgemeiner freier Angestelltenbund. Bezirkskartell Brandenburg. Ortskartell Berlin – Berlin. 1926-31. (Serial publications of German trade unions in the Memorial Library, University of Wisconsin-Madison) – 1 – us U.W. Library [338]

BERICHT UEBER DAS GESCHAFTSJAHR.. / Verband der landwirtschaftlichen Genossenschaften im Koenigreiche Sachsen – v23,25. 1913-16. Dresden. tables. (Serial publications of German trade unions in the Memorial Library, University of Wisconsin-Madison.) – 1 – us U.W. Library [330]

BERICHT UEBER DAS JAHR / Arbeiterrat Gross-Hamburg – Hamburg. 1923 24, 1925 26. Title varies: Jahresbericht. (Serial publications of German trade unions in the Memorial Library, University of Wisconsin-Madison) – 1 – us U.W. Library [330]

BERICHT UEBER DEN ERSTEN KONGRESS, ROM, 5.-10. SEPTEMBER 1955 / ed by Internationale Vereinigung fuer Germanische Sprach- und Literaturwissenschaft – [S.l.]: Die Vereinigung, 1958 – 1 – us U.W. Library [430]

BERICHT UEBER DEN PARTEITAG / Communist Party. Germany – Berlin. no. 1-12, 15. 1918-1929, 1946 – 1 – us NY Public [335]

BERICHT UEBER DIE 32. ORDENTLICHE HAUPTVERSAMMLUNG....MITTWOCH. 6 OCT 1926. 68P. ILLUS. (SERIAL PUBLICATIONS OF GERMAN TRADE UNIONS IN THE MEMORIAL LIBRARY, UNIVERSITY OF WISCONSIN-MADISON.) / Verein ostdeutscher Holzhaendler und Saegewerke. Berlin – 1 – us U.W. Library [331]

BERICHT UEBER DIE LAGE IN DEUTSCHLAND – Prag (Praha), Czechoslovakia. Oct 1933-Sept 1936 – 1r – 1 – gw Mikrofilm [073]

BERICHT UEBER DIE VERHANDLUNGEN / Communist Party. Germany – Berlin. des 1-12 Parteitages der Kommunisticschen Partei Deutschlands (Sektion der Kommunistischen Internationale) hrsg. von der Zentrale der Kommunistischen Partei Deutschlands – 1 – $35.00r – us Hoover Inst Photo [335]

BERICHT UEBER DIE VERHANDLUNGEN. / Naturforschende Gesellschaft in Basel – Basel, 1835-52 – 3 – us Readex [500]

BERICHT UEBER DIE VERHANDLUNGEN.. / Deutscher Arbeiter-Kongress – 1st. v2-4. 1907-17. (Serial publications of German trade unions in the Memorial Library, University of Wisconsin-Madison.) – 1 – us U.W. Library [330]

BERICHT UEBER DIE VERHANDLUNGEN.. / Deutscher Arbeitverein – v2,5. 1864-68. v3, 1865. (Serial publications of German trade unions in the Memorial Library, University of Wisconsin-Madison.) – 1 – us U.W. Library [330]

BERICHT UND ABRECHNUNG / Zentralkommission der Maschinensetzer Deutschlands – Berlin. 1929. Zentralkommission der Maschinensetzer Deutschlands is a subgroup of the Verband der Deutschen Buchdrucker. Some vols. contain "Kurze Berichten der Gauvereine." (Serial publications of German trade unions in the Memorial Library, University of Wisconsin-Madison.) – 1 – us U.W. Library [330]

BERICHT VON DEM EXORCISMO BEY DER TAUFFE... / Coler, J – [Magdeburgk], 1590 – 1mf – 9 – ne IDC [240]

BERICHT VON DER VBIQUITET,... / Andreae d.A E, J – Tuebingen, 1589 – 1mf – 9 – ne IDC [240]

BERICHT (WAIRHAFTIGER) DER WUNDERBARLICHENN HANDLUNG, DER DEUFFER ZU MUENSTER ETC – Coellen, S. Lupus. BME-157 1 – 9 – ne IDC [240]

BERICHT...AN DEN ORDENTLICHEN VERBANDSTAG / Verband der Fabrik-, Land-, Hilfsarbeiter und Arbeiterinnen Deutschlands – Hannover. v9. 1908. (Serial publications of German trade unions in the Memorial Library, University of Wisconsin-Madison.) – 1 – us U.W. Library [330]

BERICHTE / Deutsche Pharmazeutsche Gesellschaft – v.7-33, 1897-1923 – 1,5,6 – 22206.00 – us Princeton Micro [615]

BERICHTE AUS PARIS AN DIE "NEUE FREIE PRESSE" IN WIEN, 1891-1895 / Herzl, T – An original microfiche ed. Zug. 1977. BJ-72-102 1 – 9 – ne IDC [956]

BERICHTE BIOCHEMIE UND BIOLOGIE – v. 1-521. 1926-80 – 1,5,9 – 61,348.00 – us UMI [073]

BERICHTE DER BUNSEN-GESELLSCHAFT : PHYSICAL CHEMISTRY, CHEMICAL PHYSICS – v1-100 1894-1996 – 1,5,6,13 – us V.C.H. [540]

BERICHTE DER DEUTSCHEN BOTANISCHEN GESELLSCHAFT – Berlin, 1883-1943. v1-61 – 831mf – 6152/1 – ne IDC [060]

BERICHTE DER DEUTSCHEN CHEMISCHEN GESELLSCHAFT – Leipzig, Weimheim, 1868-1941. v1-74 – 4,437mf – 32c/2 – ne IDC [060]

BERICHTE DER DEUTSCHEN PHARMAZEUTISCHEN GESELLSCHAFT – v7-33. 1897-1923 – 1,5,6 – us Princeton Micro [073]

BERICHTE DER RHEINISCHEN MISSION – Barmen. Germany. 1830-1964 – 1 – sa State Libr [072]

BERICHTE DER SCHWEIZERISCHEN BOTANISCHEN GESELLSCHAFT – Basel, Genf, 1891-1929. v1-38 – 85mf – 8563/1 – ne IDC [060]

BERICHTE PHYSIOLOGIE, PHYSIOLOGISCHE CHEMIE UND PHARMAKOLOGIE – v. 1-382. 1920-80 – 1,5,9 – 31,806.00 – us UMI [073]

BERICHTE UEBER DIE ALLGEMEINE UND SPEZIELLE PATHOLOGIE – v. 1-96. 1948-80 – 1,5,9 – us UMI [073]

BERICHTE UEBER DIE GESAMTE GYNAEKOLOGIE UND GEBURTSHILFE – v. 47-116. 1952-80 – 1,5,9 – us UMI [618]

BERICHTE UEBER DIE GESAMTE PHYSIOLOGIE UND EXPERIMENTELLE PHARMAKOLOGIE – v. 1-134. 1920-1943 – 1,5,6 – us Princeton Micro [612]

BERICHTE UEBER DIE MITTEILUNGEN VON FREUNDEN DER NATURWISSENSCHAFTEN IN WIEN – Vienna, 1847-51. v.1-7 – 3 – us Readex [500]

BERICHTE UEBER DIE VERHANDLUNGEN DER NATURFORSCHENDEN GESELLSCHAFT ZU FREIBURG I. B – (Cont. as BERICHTE DER NATURFORSCHENDEN GESELLSCHAFT ZU FREIBURG I. B., 1886-1935. v1-34) – Freiburg i. B., 1858-1882. v1-8 – 188mf – 1 – ne IDC [500]

BERICHTE UEBER DIE ZUR BEKANNTMACHUNG GEEIGNETEN VERHANDLUNGEN DER KOENIGL. PREUSS. AKADEMIE DER WISSENSCHAFTEN ZU BERLIN – (Continued as: Monatsberichte der Koeniglich Preussischen Akademie der Wissenschaften zu Berlin. Berlin, 1856-1881. v1-46. Register 1836-1873; Continued as: Sitzungsberichte der Koeniglich Preussischen Akademie der Wissenschaften zu Berlin. Berlin, 1882-1938) – Berlin, 1836-1855. v1-20 – 2,554mf – H-411/2 – ne IDC [943]

BERICHTE UND PROTOKOLL.. / Verband der Lithographen, Steindrucker und verwandten Berufe – 1925. Berlin. At head of title: Deutscher Senefelderbund. (Serial publications of German trade unions in the Memorial Library, University of Wisconsin-Madison.) – 1 – us U.W. Library [330]

BERICHTE WESTPREUSSISCHEN BOTANISCH-ZOOLOGISCHEN VEREINS ZU DANZIG – Danzig, 1878-1931. v1-54 – 90mf – 8629/1 – ne IDC [060]

BERICHTE ZUR RAUMFORSCHUNG UND RAUMPLANUNG – vs.17, 1973; 19-25, 1975-81. Vols. 1-8 pub. as berichte zur landes forschung und landesplanung. ISSN:0005-9102 – 1,5,6,9,13 – 45.00v – us UMI [333]

BERICHTEN UITGEGEVEN DOOR HET UTRECHTSCHE : STUNDENTEN SENDINGGEZELSCHAP – 1896-1908 (complete) – 3r – 1 – ATLA S0741 – us A.T.L.A. [073]

BERICHTEN VAN DE DIENST VAN ECONOMISCHE ZAKEN – (Missing: 1961(1, 4-5, 9); 1962(13-15, 18-19, 24-25, 28-31)) – Hollandia, 1961-1962(1-34) – 9mf – SE-1843/1 – ne IDC [060]

DIE BERICHTIGTE LUTHERBIBEL: REKTORATSREDE MIT ANMERKUNGEN / Kamphausen, Adolf – Berlin: Reuther & Reichard, 1894. 1 fiche – 9 – us A.T.L.A. [240]

BERIGTSCHRIFT VAN...TER VERVAARDOJING VAN EEN ONTWERP VOOR EEN VIEUW RUSSISCH WETBOEK / Catherine 2, Empress of Russia – Delft, 1794. 132p. Last Dutch ed. of Catherine II's Nakaz. BR-9083/1 – 9 – ne IDC [947]

BERING'S VOYAGES / ed by Golder, F A – N 224. 2 v. 1922-25 – 9 – ne IDC [910]

Berington, Joseph *see* THE LITERARY HISTORY OF THE MIDDLE AGES

Berington, Simon *see* MEMOIRES DE GAUDENTIO DI LUCCA, OU IL REND COMPTE AUX PERES DE L'INQUISITION DE BOLOGNE QUI L'ONT FAIT ARRETER, DE TOUT CE QUI LUI EST ARRIVE DE PLUS REMARQUABLE...

BERITA ANTROPOLOGI / Djurusan Antropologi, Fakultas Sastra, Universitas Indonesia – (Bi-monthly) – Djakarta, 1969-1972 – 9mf – 9 – SE-1348/1 – ne IDC [301]

BERITA BIBLIOGRAFI – (Annual) – Djakarta, 1956-1961 – 21mf – 9 – SE-627/1 – ne IDC [950]

BERITA BIBLIOGRAFI – (Monthly, quarterly, bimonthly) – Djakarta, 1963-1966 – 14mf – 9 – SE-628/1 – ne IDC [950]

BERITA BUANA – Djakarta, Indonesia. Feb 1976-Dec 1993 – 77r – 1 – us L of C Photodup [072]

BERITA EKONOMI – Djakarta. SE-274 1. 1952 53-1958 59 – 9 – ne IDC [330]

BERITA FAKTA INDONESIA AND INTERNASIONAL / Jajasan Penerbit Pantjasila – (Bi-weekly) – Djakarta, 1966-1967 – 16mf – 9 – SE-1349/1 – ne IDC [950]

BERITA HARIAN AND MINGGU – Kuala Lumpur. Malaysia.1962- – 1 – us UMI [072]

BERITA INDONESIA – Indonesia. Djakarta. 1961-1964 – 1 – us UMI [072]

BERITA INDUSTRI / Departemen Perindustrian – (Weekly. Irregular. Missing: 1968 v1(1)) – Djakarta. v1-5(4/5). 1968-1972 – 70mf – 9 – SE-1350/1 – ne IDC [338]

BERITA MAPIE – (incomplete) SE-704 1. 1951-1958 – 9 – ne IDC [073]

BERITA MINGGU – Indonesia. Djakarta. 1958-1965 – 1 – us UMI [072]

BERITA PADJAK / Direktorat Pembinaan Wilajah Direktorat Djendral Padjak – (Weekly. Missing: 1967 v1(1); 1968 v1(36); 1968 v2(56,64)) – Djakarta. v1-3. 1967-1970 – 56mf – 9 – SE-1353/1 – ne IDC [630]

BERITA PERIKANAN / Djawatan Perikanan Darat/Laut – (Monthly. Missing: Several vols) – Djakarta. v1-14(4/6). 1949-1962 – 31mf – 9 – SE-1355/1 – ne IDC [630]

BERITA REPOEBLIK INDONESIA – (Lacking: 1946, V.2(8, 12-14)) – Djakarta: Departement Penerangan, 1945-1946 – 9mf – 9 – ne IDC [950]

BERITA YUDHA – Djakarta, Indonesia: Edisi Pusat, 1965-1993 – 87r – 1 – us L of C Photodup [072]

BERITA-NEGARA REPUBLIK INDONESIA – Djakarta, 1950-68 – 44r – 1 – us Ross [950]

BERITH CHALOETSIM DATMI'IM BEHOLLAND – Amsterdam, 1935-1939. v1-7 – 9mf – J-261-15/1 – ne IDC [943]

Berjano, Daniel Escobar *see*
- ANTIGUA CERTA DE HERMANDAD ENTRE PLASENCIA Y TALAVERA
- NOTAS EPIGRAFICAS. CACERES

Berjano Escobar, Daniel *see* EXTREMADURA EN LAS OBRAS DE CERVANTES

BERKALA BERITA / Corps Bukit Barisan – (Semi-annual) – Medan. v1(1). 1968 – 2mf – 9 – SE-1397/1 – ne IDC [950]

BERKELA "SEDJARAH MILITER" / Sedjarah Militer Angkatan Darat, Semdam 2, Burit Barisan – (Quarterly. Missing: 1958-1961 v1-4; 1962 v5(2-End)) – Medan, 1958-1963(3) – 3mf – 9 – SE-1357/1 – ne IDC [355]

BERKELEY AND SPIRITUAL REALISM / Fraser, Alexander Campbell – London: A. Constable, 1908 – 1mf – us A.T.L.A. [140]

BERKELEY CITIZEN – Berkeley, CA. 1966-67 – 1r – 1 – $50.00 – C02055 – us Library Micro [071]

Berkeley County. South Carolina. St. John's Parish *see* RECEIPTS

Berkeley County. South Carolina. St. Stephen's and St. John's Parishes *see* REGISTER

Berkeley County. South Carolina. St. Stephen's (Episcopal) Church *see* RECORDS

BERKELEY DAILY GAZETTE – (Also known as: North East Bay Independent and Gazette) – Berkeley, CA. 1894-1912; 1946-1983 – 372r – 1 BC02057 – $18,600.00 – us Library Micro [071]

BERKELEY DAILY TIMES *see* BERKELEY TIMES

Berkeley, G H F *see* LETTER BOOKS, 1847-8

Berkeley, George *see* THE WORKS

BERKELEY JOURNAL OF EMPLOYMENT AND LABOR LAW – v1-16. 1976-95 – 1,5,6 – $225.00 – us Hein [073]

BERKELEY JOURNAL OF SOCIOLOGY – v5,no1.- . 1959- . Graduate students, Dept. of Sociology and Social Institutions, University of Calif., Berkeley. -ann – 1 – us U.W. Library [073]

Berkeley, M J *see*
- HANDBOOK OF BRITISH MOSSES: COMPRISING ALL THAT ARE KNOWN TO BE NATIVES OF THE BRITISH ISLES
- NOTICES OF BRITISH FUNGI
- OUTLINES OF BRITISH FUNGOLOGY

THE BERKELEY MONTHLY – Berkeley, CA. v9 no 8 May 1979 – v18 no 2 Nov 1987 – 8r – 1 – $400.00 – B06012 – us Library Micro [071]

BERKELEY POST – (Cont: Tri City Post) – Berkeley, CA. 1979-Aug 1980; 1981; Jan-Jul 1985 (incomplete) – 9r – 1 – $450.00 – B02058 – us Library Micro [071]

BERKELEY POST *see* THE BERKELEY/TRI-CITY POST

BERKELEY TIMES – (Also known as: Berkeley Daily Times) – Berkeley, CA. 1920-1922; 1984-1985 – 4r – 1 – $200.00 – C03158 – us Library Micro [071]

BERKELEY TRIBE – Berkeley, CA. 1969-72 – 4r – 1 – $200.00 – B02059 – us Library Micro [071]

BERKELEY WOMEN'S LAW JOURNAL – v1-11. 1985-1996 – 9 – $163.00 set – us Hein [340]

THE BERKELEY/TRI-CITY POST – (Cont: The Berkeley Post) – Berkeley, CA. 1985- – 19+ r – 1 – $950.00 ($90.00y) – B03159 – us Library Micro [071]

Berkenkamp, F *see* VERMAAKLYK LUSTHOF VAN ZEDE – EN ZINNEBEELDEN WAAR IN VOORKOMEN LEERZAAME...

BERKHAMPSTEAD & DISTRICT GAZETTE – Hemel Hempstead, England. 1985.-w. 4 reels – 1 – uk British Libr Newspaper [072]

BERKHAMSTEAD GAZETTE – Berkhamstead, England. -w. 1980-81. 7 1 2 reels – 1 – uk British Libr Newspaper [072]

BERKLEY 1670-1900 – (Mf 1-5: Town Records 1670-1824. Mf 6-12: Town Records 1735-1834. Mf 13-22: Town Records 1748-1838. Mf 23-25: Vital Records 1737-1887. Mf 26-27: Vital Records 1844-59. Mf 28: Marriages 1860-1900. Mf 29-30: Births 1860-1900. Mf 31-32: Deaths 1860-1902) – (mf ed 1991) – 32mf – 9 – 0-87623-139-3 – us Holbrook [920]

Berkoff, David C *see* CHLOROFORM EXPOSURE AND DOSE DETERMINATION ASSOCIATED WITH COMPETITIVE SWIMMERS DURING A TWO-HOUR SWIM PRACTICE

Berkov, P N *see*
- ISTORIIA RUSSKOI ZHURNALISTIKI 18 VEKA
- RUSSKAIA NARODNAIA DRAMA 17-20 VEKOV
- V.I. LUKIN, 1737-1794
- V.V. KAPNIST (1757-1823)

Berkovskii, N I *see* TEKUSHCHAIA LITERATURA

BERKS AND OXON ADVERTISER – Wallingford, England. -w. June 1889-Dec 1941. Lacking 1896-98, Aug-Dec 1911. 45 reels – 1 – uk British Libr Newspaper [072]

BERKS COUNTY DEMOCRAT – Boyertown, PA. 1902-29. 10 rolls – 13 – $25.00r – us I.M.R. [071]

BERKS COUNTY DEMOCRAT – Reading, PA., 1858-1859 – 13 – $25.00r – us I.M.R. [071]

BERKSHIRE, 1823 : BRITISH ISLES CENSUS DIRECTORIES PROJECT, ENGLAND. VOL 226 – 1mf – 9 – A$9.00 – at Vine [941]

BERKSHIRE, 1830 : BRITISH ISLES CENSUS DIRECTORIES PROJECT, ENGLAND – at Vine [941]

BERKSHIRE, 1844 : BRITISH ISLES CENSUS DIRECTORIES PROJECT, ENGLAND. VOL 267 – 3mf – 9 – at Vine [941]

BERKSHIRE, 1848 : BRITISH ISLES CENSUS DIRECTORIES PROJECT, ENGLAND – at Vine [941]

BERKSHIRE, 1852 : BRITISH ISLES CENSUS DIRECTORIES PROJECT, ENGLAND. VOL 150 – 3mf – 9 – A$21.00 – at Vine [941]

BERKSHIRE, 1864 : BRITISH ISLES CENSUS DIRECTORIES PROJECT, ENGLAND. VOL 130 – 4mf – 9 – A$27.00 – at Vine [941]

BERKSHIRE, 1877 : BRITISH ISLES CENSUS DIRECTORIES PROJECT, ENGLAND – at Vine [941]

BERKSHIRE, 1891 : BRITISH ISLES CENSUS DIRECTORIES PROJECT, ENGLAND. VOL 26 – 4mf – 9 – A$27.00 – at Vine [941]

BERKSHIRE, 1915 : BRITISH ISLES CENSUS DIRECTORIES PROJECT, ENGLAND – (In prep) – at Vine [941]

BERKSHIRE, 1920 : BRITISH ISLES CENSUS DIRECTORIES PROJECT, ENGLAND – (In prep) – at Vine [941]

BERKSHIRE, 1931 : BRITISH ISLES CENSUS DIRECTORIES PROJECT, ENGLAND – (In prep) – at Vine [941]

BERKSHIRE CHRONICLE *see*
- BERKSHIRE CHRONICLE, WINDSOR HERALD
- READING CHRONICLE

BERKSHIRE CHRONICLE, WINDSOR HERALD – (Berkshire Chronicle, 1905. Berkshire Daily Chronicle, 1912-) – Reading, England. 1825-1959 – 190r – 1 – uk British Libr Newspaper [072]

BERKSHIRE DAILY CHRONICLE *see* BERKSHIRE CHRONICLE, WINDSOR HERALD

BERKSHIRE STAR – Stockbridge. Mass. 1815-1820 – 1,3 – us Readex [071]

BERKSHIRE TIMES – Faringdon, England. -w. 1 June-30 June; Nov 1866. 20 ft – 1 – uk British Libr Newspaper [072]

Berla, Alois *see* FRATER THOMERL

Berland, R *see* DES MARCHES A TERME SUR DEVISES ETRANGERES

Berle, Adolf A *see* DIARY

Berlepsch, H A *see* CONCORDANZ DER DEUTSCHEN NATIONAL-LITERATUR

Berlese *see* ACARI, MYRIPODA ET SCORPIONES HUCUSQUE IN ITALIA REPERTA

Berlese, Adolf A *see* GLI INSETTI: LORO ORGANIZZAZIONE SVILUPPO, ABITUDINI E RAPPORTI COLL'UOMO

Berliere, Ursmer *see* DOCUMENTS INEDITS POUR SERVIR A L'HISTOIRE ECCLESIASTIQUE DE LA BELGIQUE

BERLIN – Filmed with Nanking Theological Seminary. 1 reel – 1 – us A.T.L.A. [073]

BERLIN AM MITTAG – Berlin, feb 4 1947-feb 21 1948 – 1r – 1 – Dist. gw Mikrofilm – gw Misc Inst [072]

BERLIN AM MORGEN – (Between mar 15-apr 19 1929 known as: Die Welt am Morgen) – Berlin, mar 15 1929-feb 12 1933 (incomplete) – 14r – 1 – Dist. gw Mikrofilm – gw Misc Inst [943]

BERLIN BAPTIST CHURCH DOCUMENTS 1837-41 / Oncken Archives. Hamburg, Germany – 60p – 1 – us Baptist [240]

BERLIN BLOCKADE, 1948-1949: PAMPHLET COLLECTION – 1949-1963 – 1 – CSUXANS9156-B – us Hoover Inst Photo [355]

BERLIN CALL – Berlin Heights, Ohio. 1912-58 – 14r – 1 – $32.50r – us Archival [071]

Berlin, Charles *see* HEBREW BOOKS FROM THE HARVARD COLLEGE LIBRARY

THE BERLIN CRISIS, 1958-1962 – (With 2-vol printed guide & index £630.00) – 460mf – 9 – £2,940.00 – uk Chadwyck [327]

BERLIN CULTURE: PAMPHLET COLLECTION – 1964-1992 – 1 – CSUXANS9137-B – us Hoover Inst Photo [306]

Berlin. Germany. Deutsches Institut fur Wirtschaftsforschung *see* STATISTISCHES KOMPENDIUM UBER DIE SOWJETISCHE BESATZUNGSZONE

BERLIN GUIDEBOOKS: PAMPHLET COLLECTION – 192?-1965 – 1 – CSUXANS8678-B – us Hoover Inst Photo [910]

Berlin Heights, OH. Lorain County 1858 *see* AGE OF FREEDOM

Berlin. Institut fuer Marxismus-Leninismus *see* GESCHICHTE DER DEUTSCHEN ARBEITSBEWEGUNG IN 15 KAPITELN

Berlin, Pavel Abramovich *see*
- APOSTOLY ANARKHII
- KARL MARKS I EGO VREMI A
- RUSSKAIA BURZHUAZIIA V STAROE I NOVOE VREMIA

BERLIN PROGRAMME / Beckerath, Ulrich von et al – Also, unemployment as a problem of turnover credits and the supply of means of payment, by Heinrich Ritterhausen; Circulation charts for shop foundation money and On financing Defence by John Zube. 1 fiche – 9 – 1.00f – at Libertarian Micro [320]

THE BERLIN RECORD : THE PREDECESSOR OF THE KITCHENER WATERLOO RECORD, IS NOW AVAILABLE IN 21 REELS FROM JAN 1907-DEC 1916 – (Cont by: Kitchener-Waterloo Record) – Ontario, CN. Jan 1907-Dec 1916 – 21r – 1 – cn Commonwealth Micro [072]

Berlin. Staatliche Museen *see* HERWARTH WALDEN UND DIE EUROPAEISCHE AVANTGARDE

Berlin. Staatliche Museen. Museum fuer Voelkerkunde *see* FUEHRER DURCH DIE SAMMLUNGEN DES MUSEUMS FUER VOELKERKUNDE

Berlin. Statistisches amt *see* STATISTICHES JAHRBUCH DER STADT BERLIN

Berlin. Universitaet. Seminar fuer Orientalische Sprachen *see* MITTHEILUNGEN

BERLIN WALL: PAMPHLET COLLECTION – 1961-1988 – 1 – CSUXANS9161-B – us Hoover Inst Photo [943]

THE BERLIN WEST AFRICAN CONFERENCE, 1884-1885 / Crowe, S E – (Pub. for the Royal Empire Society). London. 1942. BA-408 2 – 8 – ne IDC [960]

DER BERLINER – Berlin, 2 Aug 1945-Dec 1954 – 46r – 1 – uk British Libr Newspaper [072]

DER BERLINER – (Cont by: Telegraf, may 1 1946) – Berlin, aug 2 1945-jun 30 1972 – 1 – Dist. gw Mikrofilm – gw Misc Inst [072]

DER BERLINER – (Vorlaeufer des Telegraf) – Berlin, Aug 1945-Jun 1972 – 1r – 1 – DM80.00 – gw Mikro Press [072]

DER BERLINER *see*
- TELEGRAF

Berliner, Abraham *see*
- AUS DEM LEBEN DER JUDEN DEUTSCHLANDS IM MITTELALTER
- BEITRAEGE ZUR GEOGRAPHIE UND ETHNOGRAPHIE BABYLONIENS IM TALMUD UND MIDRASCH
- FESTSCHRIFT
- GESAMMELTE SCHRIFTEN

BERLINER ADRESSBUCH – 1891-1941. Scattered volumes wanting – 1 – 2,486.00 – us L of C Photodup [943]

BERLINER ADRESSBUCH = BERLIN DIRECTORY / ed by Umlauf, Konrad – 1919-32.Adressbuch fuer Berlin und seine Vororte. 1984 – 981 fiches (1:24) – 9 – silver DM5,600.00 – 3-598-30284-3 – gw Saur [943]

BERLINER ALLGEMEINE MUSIKALISCHE ZEITUNG – Berlin, 1824-29. v1-6. – 52mf – 9 – us Sibley [780]

BERLINER ALLGEMEINE MUSIKALISCHE ZEITUNG 1824-1830 – (Silver DM2,980.00. ISBN: 3-598-33805-8) – 1994 – 37 fiches (1:24) – 9 – diazo DM2,400.00 – 3-598-33804-X – gw Saur [780]

BERLINER ALLGEMEINE ZEITUNG – Berlin, dec 14 1861-63 – 6r – 1 – Dist. gw Mikrofilm – gw Misc Inst [943]

BERLINER ARBEITER-ZEITUNG – Berlin, 1890-1901; Jan 9 1927-Dec 20 1930 – 2r – 1 – gw Mikrofilm [072]

BERLINER ARBEITER-ZEITUNG – Berlin, jan 9 1927-dec 20 1930 – 2r – 1 – DM150.00 – gw Mikro Press [943]

BERLINER ASTRONOMISCHES JAHRBUCH / Akademie der Wissenschaften. Berlin – Berlin, Heidelberg, 1776-1920 – 1096mf – 9 – ne IDC [520]

DER BERLINER BAER – Berlin, jan-jun 1930 – 2r – 1 – Dist. gw Mikrofilm – gw Misc Inst [072]

BERLINER BLATT – Berlin, jan.mar 1907 – 1r – 1 – Dist. gw Mikrofilm – gw Misc Inst [072]

BERLINER BOERSEN-COURIER – Berlin, apr 1 1895-1933 – 253r – 1 – Dist. gw Mikrofilm – gw Misc Inst [943]

BERLINER BOERSEN-COURIER – Berlin, jul-dec 1878, apr-dec 1879, apr, may, aug-dec 1880, may 1885, sep-oct 1921, jun, jul, oct 1924, jan, may, jun, aug 1925, aug 1926 – 13r – 1 – Dist. gw Mikrofilm – gw Misc Inst [943]

BERLINER BOERSEN-ZEITUNG – Berlin, 1856-63, apr 1864-aug 1884, oct 1884-aug 1944 – 796r – 1 – Dist. gw Mikrofilm – gw Misc Inst [943]

BERLINER BOERSEN-ZEITUNG – Berlin. 1926-27. jun-nov 1941 (incomplete) – 14r – 1 – gw Mikrofilm [072]

BERLINER BORSEN-ZEITUNG – Berlin, Germany. Jun 1934-Aug 1944 – 83r – 1 – us L of C Photodup [072]

BERLINER CARICATUREN UND SILHOUETTEN : DIE NICHTDEMOKRATISCHE PRESSE BERLINS – Bremen, 1850 – 1 – Dist. gw Mikrofilm – gw Misc Inst [760]

Berliner, Emile *see* CONCLUSIONS

BERLINER ENTOMOLOGISCHE ZEITSCHRIFT – (Continued as DEUTSCHE ENTOMOLOGISCHE ZEITSCHRIFT. Berlin, 1875-1880. v.25-58. Continued as BERLINER ENTOMOLOGISCHE ZEITSCHRIFT. Berlin, 1881-1913. v.25-58. Index 1857-1906. v1.51) – Berlin, 1857-1874. v.1-18 – 504mf – 9 – ne IDC [590]

DIE BERLINER ESTAFETTE – Berlin, jul 10-dec 31 1827 – 1r – 1 – Dist. gw Mikrofilm – gw Misc Inst [072]

BERLINER EXTRA-DIENST – -sw. 1970-73, 1975-79. Berlin: Verlag & Druck Informdienst GmbH Westberlin – 1 – us U.W. Library [072]

DER BERLINER FIGARO – Berlin, 1835 – 2r – 1 – Dist. gw Mikrofilm – gw Misc Inst [072]

BERLINER FLIEGENDE BLAETTER : BEILAGE ZUM NEUEN BERLINER TAGEBLATT – Berlin, 1875-1876 – 1 – gw Mikrofilm [072]

BERLINER FLIEGENDE BLAETTER : BEILAGE ZUM NEUEN BERLINER TAGEBLATT – Berlin, sep 19 1875-jun 22 1876 – 1r – 1 – DM75.00 – gw Mikro Press [072]

BERLINER FREIE PRESSE – Berlin, dec 21 1875, 1876 (incomplete), jan-oct 1878 (incomplete) – 1 – Dist. gw Mikrofilm – gw Misc Inst [943]

DIE BERLINER HANDSCHRIFT DER SAHIDISCHEN APOSTELGESCHICHTE (T.U.U. 5-109) / Hintze, F & Schenke, H M – Berlin, 1970 – 3mf – 9 – ne Slangenburg [240]

BERLINER ILLUSTRIERTE NACHTAUSGABE – Berlin, 1922-44 (incomplete) – 74r – 1 – gw Mikrofilm [072]

BERLINER ILLUSTRIERTE NACHTAUSGABE *see* NACHTAUSGABE-DER TAG

BERLINER ILLUSTRIERTE ZEITUNG – Berlin. aug 18-dec 30, 1894. 1905. 1909. 1911-14. 1920-23. jul 6-dec 28, 1924. jul 5, 1925-26. dec 31, 1927-28. 1938. jul 6, 1944-apr 29, 1945 – 10r – 1 – gw Mikrofilm [072]

BERLINER ILLUSTRIERTE ZEITUNG – Berlin, dec 14 1891-apr 29 1945 (incomplete) – 1 – Dist. gw Mikrofilm – gw Misc Inst [943]

Berliner Industrie Und Handeskammer *see* WIRTSCHAFTBLATT

BERLINER INTELLIGENZBLATT – (Also suppl available: Besondere Beylage, 1802-06, 2r; and: Gemeinnuetziger Anzeiger, jul-dec 1810, jul-dec 1811, 1816, 1818, 1819, 1821, 3r) – Berlin, oct-dec 1788, jul-dec 1792, 1807-09, 1811-12, 1816-1910, 1912-22 – 498r – 1 – Dist. gw Mikrofilm – gw Misc Inst [943]

BERLINER JOURNAL – Kitchener, Canada. 1859-79 – 6r – 1 – $390.00 – cn Library Assoc [971]

BERLINER KINDER-WOCHENBLATT – Berlin, 1832-35 – 1 – Dist. gw Mikrofilm – gw Misc Inst [640]

BERLINER KIRCHEN BRIEFE – 1961-85 (incomplete) – 3r – 1 – ATLA S0842 – us A.T.L.A. [073]

BERLINER KURIER *see*
– BERLINER KURIER AM ABEND

BERLINER KURIER AM ABEND – (Cont by: Berliner Kurier, aug 1 1992) – Berlin, 1992- – ca 2r per yr – 1 – Dist. gw Mikrofilm – gw Misc Inst [072]

BERLINER KURIER AM ABEND – (Cont by: Berliner Kurier, aug 1 1992) – Berlin, nov 12 1945-49, apr 22 1970-jul 17 1971, 1992-96 – 1 – Dist. gw Mikrofilm – gw Misc Inst [072]

BERLINER KURIER AM MORGEN – Berlin, 1992- – ca 2r per yr – 1 – Dist. gw Mikrofilm – gw Misc Inst [072]

BERLINER LOKAL-ANZEIGER : BEILAGE: BILDER VOM TAGE – Berlin. jul 1910-dec 1912. jan 1914-dec 1917. jan-apr 20, 1919 – 1 – gw Mikrofilm [072]

BERLINER LOKAL-ANZEIGER : BEILAGE: DIE WEITE WELT – Berlin. 1925-26. nov 22, 1931-sep 24, 1933 – 1r – 1 – gw Mikrofilm [072]

BERLINER LOKAL-ANZEIGER – Berlin: A Scherl, 19288 (r1-12); jan-mar 1933 (r13-15) – 15r – 1 – us Res Libr [072]

BERLINER LOKAL-ANZEIGER – Berlin, nov 4 1883-aug 31 1944 – 1 – Dist. gw Mikrofilm – gw Misc Inst [943]

BERLINER LOKAL-ANZEIGER – Berlin. v32-38.1914-20 – 8r – 1 – us Ross [072]

Berliner, M W *see*
– VEREINBARUNGEN UEBER DEN GERICHTSSTAND IM INTERNATIONALEN RECHTSVERKEHR

BERLINER MISSIONSBERICHTE – Berlin, Germany. 1836-1939 – 544mf – 9 – sa State Libr [072]

DER BERLINER MITTAG – Berlin, jan-jun 18 1928 – 2r – 1 – Dist. gw Mikrofilm – gw Misc Inst [943]

BERLINER MITTAGSZEITUNG – Berlin, nov 19 1918-19 – 1r – 1 – Dist. gw Mikrofilm – gw Misc Inst [943]

BERLINER MODENSPIEGEL – Berlin, 1838-46, 1848 – 6r – 1 – Dist. gw Mikrofilm – gw Misc Inst [640]

BERLINER MONATSHEFTE – v1-6 under title: Kriegsschuldfrage; v7-9 under title: Berliner Monatshefte fuer Internationale Aufklarung; v3-19 1925-1941. All pub – 1,5,6 – us Princeton Micro [943]

BERLINER MONTAG – Berlin, jul 26 1948-52 – 2r – 1 – Dist. gw Mikrofilm – gw Misc Inst [072]

BERLINER MONTAGS ECHO – Berlin. Germany. -d. 3 Jan 1948-30 Dec 1957. (7 reels) – 1 – uk British Libr Newspaper [072]

BERLINER MONTAGS-ECHO : ORGAN DER LIBERAL-DEMOKRATISCHEN PARTEI (LDP) – (Cont: Montags-Echo, -jan 3 1948) – Berlin, jan 3 1948-57 – 7r – 1 – uk British Libr Newspaper [072]

BERLINER MONTAGS-POST – Berlin, dec 25 1854-64 – 3r – 1 – Dist. gw Mikrofilm – gw Misc Inst [943]

BERLINER MONTAGSPOST – Berlin, may 10 1920-38 (incomplete), 1940-dec 28 1942 (incomplete) – 14r – 1 – Dist. gw Mikrofilm – gw Misc Inst [943]

BERLINER MONTAGS-ZEITUNG – Berlin, jan 7 1861-feb 11 1884 – 8r – 1 – uk British Libr Newspaper [943]

BERLINER MORGENPOST – Berlin, 1907-mar 1908, jul 1908-aug 1909, nov 1909-jun 1920, oct 1920-23, apr 1924-aug 1926, nov 1926-jan 1929, mar 1929-jun 1934, sep 1934-feb 1939, apr 1939-feb 1941, may 1941-jun 1942, oct 1942-sep 1944 – 239r – 1 – Dist. gw Mikrofilm – gw Misc Inst [943]

BERLINER MORGENPOST – Berlin. aug 3, 1971-96 – 126r – 1 – gw Mikrofilm [072]

BERLINER MORGENPOST – Berlin, Germany. 13 Jan 1923-1939 – 164r – 1 – us L of C Photodup [072]

BERLINER MORGENPOST – Berlin, Sep 1916-Jul 1919; Jan 1965-Dec 1968 – 64r – 1 – uk British Libr Newspaper [072]

BERLINER MORGENPOST – Berlin, sep 26 1952- – 1 – Dist. gw Mikrofilm – gw Misc Inst [072]

BERLINER MORGENZEITUNG – Berlin, 1891, jul-sep 1892, jul 1893-1903, apr 1904-mar 1907, jul 1907-19, may 1920-23, apr 1924-mar 1928, jul 1928-feb 15 1939 – 124r – 1 – Dist. gw Mikrofilm – gw Misc Inst [943]

BERLINER NACHTAUSGABE *see* NACHTAUSGABE-DER TAG

BERLINER NEUESTE NACHRICHTEN – Berlin, 1889-jun 30 1919 (incomplete) – 130r – 1 – Dist. gw Mikrofilm – gw Misc Inst [943]

BERLINER NEUESTE NACHRICHTEN – Berlin, 25 Jul 1914-Jun, 30 Sept-Dec 1915; Apr 1916-Mar 1917; Jul-Dec 1917; Apr-Nov 1918 – 10r – 1 – DM750.00 – gw Mikro Press [072]

BERLINER NEUSTE NACHRICHTEN – Berlin. July 5, 1914-May 31, 1919. Missing: July 6-22, 1914 + 6 scattered issues – 1 – 35.00r – us Hoover Inst Photo [072]

BERLINER PAEDAGOGISCHE ZEITUNG – (Also available: Rechtsbeilage, 1898-1919) – Berlin, oct 5 1872-dec 26 1918 – 1 – Dist. gw Mikrofilm – gw Misc Inst [370]

BERLINER PFENNIG-BLAETTER – Berlin, 1847 – 1r – 1 – Dist. gw Mikrofilm – gw Misc Inst [072]

BERLINER POLITISCHES WOCHENBLATT – Berlin. 11v. 1831-41 – 37mf – 9 – DM184.00 – gw Olms [072]

BERLINER SKIZZEN / Kretzer, Max – Berlin: C. Duncker, 1898 – 1 – us U.W. Library [943]

BERLINER SONTAGSBLATT: DIE KIRCHE – v26-42, 1971-87 – 1 – us A.T.L.A. [240]

BERLINER SOZIALDEMOKRAT *see* SOZIALDEMOKRAT

BERLINER STADTBLATT *see* SOZIALDEMOKRAT

BERLINER STIMME – Berlin, 20 Oct 1951-1967 – 8r – 1 – DM600.00 – gw Mikro Press [072]

BERLINER STIMME – West-Berlin, Germany. Oct 20, 1951-67. Sozialdemokratische Wochenzeitung. Forts von: Der Sozialdemokrat. West-Berlin – 1 – gw Mikrofilm [072]

BERLINER STIMME *see* SOZIALDEMOKRAT

BERLINER STIMMEN – Berlin, 1926-31 – 1 – Dist. gw Mikrofilm – gw Misc Inst [072]

BERLINER TAGEBLATT : ABEND- UND MORGEN-AUSGABE – 1906-37 n51 – 1 – Dist. gw Mikrofilm – gw Misc Inst [943]

BERLINER TAGEBLATT : ABEND-AUSGABE – Berlin, 1895-1906 – 1 – Dist. gw Mikrofilm – gw Misc Inst [943]

BERLINER TAGEBLATT – Berlin, 1872-jan 31 1939 – 1 – Dist. gw Mikrofilm – gw Misc Inst [943]

BERLINER TAGEBLATT – Berlin, 1914-31 Jan 1939 – 153r – 1 – DM11,475.00 – gw Mikro Press [072]

BERLINER TAGEBLATT – Berlin, Germany. Dec 1899-Jan 1939 – 215r – 1 – us L of C Photodup [072]

BERLINER TAGEBLATT : GROSSE AUSGABE – Berlin, 1937 n 152-1939 n30/31 – 1 – Dist. gw Mikrofilm – gw Misc Inst [943]

BERLINER TAGEBLATT : MORGEN-AUSGABE – Berlin, 1895-1906 – 1 – Dist. gw Mikrofilm – gw Misc Inst [943]

BERLINER TAGEBLATT : PARLAMENTS-AUSGABE – Berlin, 1899-1908 – 1 – Dist. gw Mikrofilm – gw Misc Inst [943]

BERLINER TAGEBLATT : WOCHENENDAUSGABE FUER AUSLAND UND UEBERSEE – Berlin, 1914-30 (incomplete) – 11r – 1 – Dist. gw Mikrofilm – gw Misc Inst [943]

BERLINER TAGEBLATT – LITERARISCHE RUNDSCHAU – Berlin, 11 Dec 1898-1900; 1903-07 (incomplete) – 4r – 1 – gw Mikrofilm [072]

BERLINER THEATER-ZEITUNG – Berlin, 1837-40 – 1r – 1 – Dist. gw Mikrofilm – gw Misc Inst [790]

BERLINER VEREINSBOTE – (Title varies) – Berlin. 1895-96. 2v. Lacking: 1895, v1; 1896, v2 (1) – 10mf – 9 – ne IDC [920]

BERLINER VOLKSBLATT – Berlin, 1884-1933 – 171r – 1 – gw Mikro Press [072]

BERLINER VOLKSBLATT – (Cont by: Vorwaerts, jan 1 1891. Neuer Vorwaerts, Karlsbad, jun 18 1933. Also suppl available: Die Neue Welt, 1876-77, 1881-84, 1892-1913, 1914 n31, 1916 n24-46, 1918 n1-42. Volk und Zeit, Bilder zum Vorwaerts, 1919-33, 4r) – Berlin, apr 1 1884-feb 28 1933 – 168r – 1 – Dist. gw Mikrofilm – gw Mikro Press [943]

BERLINER VOLKS-ZEITUNG *see* VOLKS-ZEITUNG

BERLINER VOLKSZEITUNG *see* VOLKS-ZEITUNG

BERLINER VOLKS-ZIETUNG *see* VOLKS-ZEITUNG (URWAEHLER-ZEITUNG)

BERLINER WESPEN – Berlin, jan 23 1874-75, jan-nov 26 1880, 1881-82 – 3r – 1 – Dist. gw Mikrofilm – gw Misc Inst [073]

DER BERLINER WESTEN *see* BERLIN-WILMERSDORFER ZEITUNG

BERLINER ZEITUNG – 1945-1994 – 9 times per yr – 1 – DM540.00 – sz Infoprint [072]

BERLINER ZEITUNG – (1981-1993 71r DM5,325.00. 1995 subsc DM700.00) – Berlin, 21 Mai 1945- 1980 – 86r – 1 – DM6,450.00 – gw Mikro Press [072]

BERLINER ZEITUNG – Berlin, 1883-aug 1886, jan-aug 1887, 1888, may-dec 1889, may 1890-mar 1892, jul 1893-jun 1898, oct 1898-mar 1899, jul-dec 1899, apr-jun 1900, oct 1900-mar 1901, jul-sep 1901, jul 1902-03, jul-sep 1904, jan-mar 1905 – 1 – Dist. gw Mikrofilm – gw Misc Inst [943]

BERLINER ZEITUNG – Berlin, Germany. Jul 1946-Sept 1947; 1962-Apr 1973 – 39r – 1 – us L of C Photodup [072]

BERLINER ZEITUNG – (Suppl "Die Woche im Bild" available from other sources, inquire Mikrofilmarchiv Dortmund) – Berlin, may 21 1945- – 1 – Dist. gw Mikrofilm – gw Misc Inst [072]

BERLINER ZEITUNG – (Yrly reel count varies) – 1945- – 1 – us Ross [072]

BERLINER ZEITUNGS-HALLE – Berlin, oct 1846-48 – 5r – 1 – Dist. gw Mikrofilm – gw Misc Inst [072]

Berlingieri, F *see*
– NOTES ON THE HAGUE RULES, 1921
– LA POLIZZA DI CARICO ...
– VERSO L'UNIFICAZIONE DEL DIRITTO DEL MARE

BERLINGSKE TIDENDE – Kobenhavn: Interessentskabet Berlingske Tidende, jul 1938-55 – 204r – 1 – us Res Libr [072]

BERLINGSKE TIDENDE – (Yrly reel count varies) – 1992- – 1 – inquire – us Ross [072]

Berlinguet, Francois Xavier *see*
– IN THE EXCHEQUER COURT OF CANADA:..
– RAPPORT ET PLANS SUR DES AMELIORATIONS GENERALES DANS LE HAVRE DE QUEBEC..

BERLINISCHE MONATSCHRIFT – Berlin, 1783-1790. v1-16 – 136mf – H-574/2 – ne IDC [943]

BERLINISCHE MONATSSCHRIFT 1783-96; BERLINISCHE BLAETTER 1797-98; NEUE BERLINISCHE MONATSSCHRIFT 1799-1811 / ed by Gedike, Friedrich & Biester, Johann Erich – Berlin und Stettin, 1783-1811. Hildesheim 1992 – 370mf – 9 – DM2,400.00 diazo DM3,000.00 silver – gw Olms [943]

BERLINISCHE NACHRICHTEN VON STAATS- UND GELEHRTEN SACHEN – (Also known as: Hofzeitung; Haudesche Zeitung. Cont by: Spenersche Zeitung, jun 4 1872) – Berlin, jun 30 1740-jun 29 1811, 1812-oct 31 1874 – 150r – 1 – Dist. gw Mikrofilm – gw Misc Inst [943]

BERLINISCHE NACHRICHTEN VON STAATS- UND GELEHRTEN SACHEN – Berlin, 1806-11; 1840-42; 1850-59 – 41r – 1 – uk British Libr Newspaper [072]

BERLINISCHE PRIVILEGIRTE ZEITUNG – (Publ 1721-78. Cont newspapers known under different titles since 1617. Issues available from that former period: 1618 (incomplete), 1619-24, 1658-59 (many issues missing), 1666 (many issues missing), 1676 (incomplete), dec 1677, 1681 (incomplete), jun 1686, jan 1691. Cont by: Koeniglich Berlinische privilegirte Staats- und gelehrte Zeitung, 1779-1911) – Berlin, 1724, 1725 (many issues missing), 1735-36 (incomplete), 1737, 1738 (incomplete), 1739, 1740-43 (incomplete), 1745 (incomplete), 1750, 1755, 1758 (many issues missing), 1759, 1766-67, 1771, 1773, 1777-78 – 1 – Inquire at Mikrofilmarchiv for details – gw Misc Inst [943]

BERLINISCHE PRIVILEGIRTE ZEITUNG *see* KOENIGLICH BERLINISCHE PRIVILEGIRTE STAATS- UND GELEHRTE ZEITUNG

BERLINISCHE ZEITUNG – Berlin, Jan 1816-Dec 1850 – 157r – 1 – uk British Libr Newspaper [072]

BERLIN'S 750TH ANNIVERSARY: PAMPHLET COLLECTION – 1987 – 1 – CSUXANS9142-B – us Hoover Inst Photo [943]

BERLIN-WILMERSDORFER ZEITUNG – (Cont: Wilmersdorfer Zeitung. Cont by: Der Berliner Westen, may 3 1920. Der Westen, jan 1 1933) – Berlin, may 9 1908-18, jul 1919-jun 1925, sep 1925-mar 1926, jul 1926-mar 1931, jul 1931-32, jan-apr 1934, jul 1934-apr 1938, jul 1939-jun 1944 – 87r – 1 – Dist. gw Mikrofilm – gw Misc Inst [943]

Berlioux, Etienne-Felix *see* LA TRAITE ORIENTALE

BERLIOZ ET LE MOUVEMENT DE L'ART CONTEMPORAIN / Noufflard, Georges – Florence, 1883. 110p. 2 fiches. (Music Collection) – 9 – 6.00 – fr Bibl Nationale [780]

Berlioz, Fernand *see* ANNUAIRE DU BUREAU D'HYGIENE DE LA VILLE DE GRENOBLE: 1897

Berlioz, H *see* L'IMPERIALE. CANTATA FOR THE PARIS EXHIBITION... OP. 26

Berlioz, Hector *see* WERKE

Berlyn, Graeme P *see* JOURNAL OF SUSTAINABLE FORESTRY

Berman, Harold J *see*
- BASIC LAWS ON THE STRUCTURE OF THE SOVIET STATE
- DOCUMENTS ON SOVIET MILITARY LAW AND ADMINISTRATION

Bermann, Gregorio *see* LA CRISIS ARGENTINA

Bermant, George et al *see* PROTRACTED CIVIL TRIALS

Bermant, Gordon *see*
- ALTERNATIVE DISPUTE RESOLUTION IN A BANKRUPTCY COURT
- CONDUCT OF THE VOIR DIRE EXAMINATION
- JURY SELECTION PROCEDURES IN U.S. DISTRICT COURTS
- PREPARING A U.S. COURT FOR AUTOMATION
- THE QUALITY OF ADVOCACY IN THE FEDERAL COURTS
- THE VOIR DIRE EXAMINATION, JUROR CHALLENGES, AND ADVERSARY ADVOCACY

Bermejo Larrea, Esperanza *see* NARRATIVA BREVE EN EL SIGLO 13 FRANCES

Bermejo, Vladimiro *see* VIDA Y HECHOS DEL CONQUISTADOR DEL PERU

BERMONDSEY AND ROTHERHITHE ADVERTISER. (SOUTHWARK RECORDER) – London. 23 May 1868-31 Mar 1933.-w. 61 reels – 1 – uk British Libr Newspaper [072]

BERMONDSEY REVIEW AND SOUTH LONDON RECORD – London, UK. 25 Jul 1855-15 Jan 1857. -f. 20 feet – 1 – uk British Libr Newspaper [072]

BERMUDA : BERMUDA DIGEST OF STATISTICS 1973-1974 / Bermuda. Statistical Office – (Coll title: Latin American and Caribbean Official Statistical Serials, 1821-1982) – 2mf – 9 – £17.00 – uk Chadwyck [972]

Bermuda *see* ROYAL GAZETTE

BERMUDA BAPTIST CHURCH. DILLON COUNTY. SOUTH CAROLINA : CHURCH RECORDS – 1944-45, 1957-72 – 1 – 5.04 – us Baptist [240]

BERMUDA: BLUE BOOKS – 1836-1950 – 25r – 1 – uk Microform Academic [972]

BERMUDA COLONIST – Hamilton, Bermuda. 5 Jan 1887-21 Dec 1920 (missing 1889-94; Apr-Jul 1920).-d. 41 reels – 1 – uk British Libr Newspaper [072]

BERMUDA MID-OCEAN NEWS – Hamilton, Bermuda. 2 Jan 1958-8 Aug 1970.-d. 53 reels – 1 – uk British Libr Newspaper [072]

BERMUDA NEWS PICTORIAL – Hamilton. Bermuda. -w. 31 Jan 1960-18 Nov 1961. (1 reel) – 1 – uk British Libr Newspaper [072]

BERMUDA OFFICIAL GAZETTE – 1967-69 – 1r – 1 – us Ross [972]

BERMUDA RECORDER – Hamilton, Bermuda. 3 Jan 1959-5 May 1967; 13 Apr 1968-3 Jan 1969.-w. 15 reels – 1 – uk British Libr Newspaper [072]

Bermuda. Statistical Office *see* BERMUDA

BERMUDA SUN – Hamilton, Bermuda. Oct 1 1993-June 24 1994; July 1-Dec 30 1994; 1995 – 5r – 1 – us L of C Photodup [072]

BERMUDA SUN WEEKLY – Hamilton, Bermuda. 24 Oct 1964-31 Dec 1966.-w. 5 reels – 1 – uk British Libr Newspaper [072]

THE BERMUDA TIMES – Hamilton, Bermuda. Mar 4 1987-Dec 15 1989; 1990-June 1994; Aug 5 1994-1995 – 9r – 1 – us L of C Photodup [072]

Bermudez de Pedraza, F *see* ARTE LEGAL PARA ESTUDIAR JURISPRUDENCIA CON LA PARATITLA Y EXPOSICION...

Bermudez Plata, C *see* SEVILLA. ARCHIVO GENERAL DE INDIAS. SECCION DE CONTRATACION. CATALOGO DE PASAJEROS DE INDIAS...(1509-1599)

Bermudez Plata, Cristobal *see* CATALOGO DE PASAJEROS A INDIAS DURANTE LOS SIGLOS 16, 17 Y 18. VOL 2 (1535-1538)

BERMUDIAN : A COMMERCIAL, LITERARY AND POLITICAL SEMI-WEEKLY JOURNAL – Hamilton. v2-6. 1835-39 – 1r – 1 – us Ross [072]

Bermudo, J *see* COMIENCA EL LIBRO PRIMERO DELA D'CLARACIO DE INSTRUMETOS, DIRIGIDO AL ELEMENTISSIMO Y MUY PODEROSE DON JOAN TERCERO DESTE NOMBRE

BERMUNKAS = WAGE WORKER – Chicago: General Exec Board of Industrial Workers of the World, 1923- ; 1948-feb 1952 – 2r – 1 – us Res Libr [331]

Bernab y Thomas, Alfred *see* AFTER CORONADO. SPANISH EXPLORATION NORTHEAST OF NEW MEXICO, 1696-1727...

Bernadskaia, E V *see*
- ARKHIV VENETSIANSKOGO IZDATELIA A. KALADZHERA V LENINGRADE
- ITAL'IANSKAIA RUKOPISNAIA KNIGA V SOBRANII GOSUDARSTVENNOI PUBLICHNOI BIBLIOTEKI..

Bernaldez, Andres *see*
- HISTORIA DE LOS REYES CATOLICOS
- HISTORIA DE LOS...DON FERNANDO Y..

Bernaldez, Fernando *see* RESENA SOBRE LA TRAIDA DE AGUAS A BADAJOZ

Bernard, A *see* RECUEIL DES CHARTES DE L'ABBAYE DE CLUNY

Bernard, A et al *see* APOLOGETISCHE VORTRAEGE

Bernard, Auguste Joseph *see* HISTOIRE TERRITORIALE DU DEPARTEMENT DE RHONE-ET-LOIRE

Bernard, C *see* LECONS SUR LA PHYSIOLOGIE ET LA PATHOLOGIE DU SYSTEME NERVEUX

Bernard, David *see* LIGHT ON MASONRY

BERNARD DE MONTFAUCON ET LES BERNARDINS 1715-1750 / Broglie, E de. – Paris. v1-2. 1891 – Dfl46.00 – ne Slangenburg [240]

BERNARD DELICIEUX ET L'INQUISITION ALBIGEOISE (1300-1320) / Haureau, B – Paris: Hachette, 1877 – 1mf – us A.T.L.A. [240]

Bernard, Edward *see* CATALOGUE OF BOOKS AND MSS IN ENGLISH AND IRISH COLLECTIONS, WITH ALPHABETICAL INDEX

Bernard, H *see* THE SHADE OF THE BALKANS: A COLLECTION OF BULGARIAN FOLKSONGS AND PROVERBS

Bernard, Henry Norris *see* THE MENTAL CHARACTERISTICS OF THE LORD JESUS CHRIST

Bernard, J *see* THE IRISH LIBER HYMNORUM

Bernard, J H *see* THE ODES OF SOLOMAN

Bernard, John *see* RETROSPECTIONS OF AMERICA, 1797-1911

Bernard, Marc *see* EN HYDRAVION AU-DESSUS DU CONTINENT NOIR

Bernard, Marius (de Cannes) *see* DE L'ORIENT A TOULON SUR MER ET SUR TERRE

BERNARD OF CLAIRVAUX : THE TIMES, THE MAN, AND HIS WORK: AN HISTORICAL STUDY IN EIGHT LECTURES / Storrs, Richard Salter – New York: Scribner, 1892 – 2mf – us A.T.L.A. [240]

Bernard of Trevisano *see* VON DER HERMETISCHENN PHILOSOPHIA. ITEM, DICTA ALANI. EXLIBRIS HENRICI VUOLFFIJ. IETZ VON NEWEN WIDERUMB MIT FLEISS CORRIGIRT, VND VBERSEHEN

Bernard, P *see*
- EXPLICATION DE L'EDICT DE NANTES PAR LES AUTRES EDICTS DE PACIFICATION, DECLARATIONS ET ARRESTS DE REGLEMENT
- TRAITE ... DE L'EXTRADITION ...

Bernard, Richard *see* RUTH'S RECOMPENCE

BERNARD SHAW : WITH FOUR PORTRAITS / Jackson, Holbrook – Philadelphia: G.W. Jacobs; London: E. Grant Richards, 1907 – 1 roll – 1 – 1-55879-694-0 – uk Libr Preservation [420]

BERNARD SHAW: THE DIARIES, 1885-1897 / ed by Weintraub, Stanley – With earlier and later diary fragments from 1875 to 1917. Over 1200p. 2v. Facsim. of the original mss – 9 – $100.00 – us Penn State [420]

Bernard, Thomas D *see* CENTRAL TEACHING OF JESUS CHRI..JOHN XIII TO XVII INCLUSIVE

Bernard, Thomas Dehany *see*
- THE CENTRAL TEACHING OF JESUS CHRIST
- THE PROGRESS OF DOCTRINE IN THE NEW TESTAMENT

Bernard-Duquenet, N *see* LE FRONT POPULAIRE ET LE SENEGAL

Bernardi Abbatis Casinensis *see* IN REGULAM S. BENEDICTI EXPOSITIO

BERNARDI SILVESTRIS / De Mundi Universitate libri duc, sive Megacosmus et microcosmus; ed by Barach, C S & Wrobel, J – Innsbruck, 1876 – 8 – ne Slangenburg [210]

Bernardino, S *see* TRACTATUS DE SEPTEM DONIS SPIRITUS SANCTI 15TH

BERNARDO PEREIRA DE VASCONCELLOS E SEU TEMP / Sousa, Octavio Tarquinio de – Rio de Janeiro. 1937 – 1 – us Res Libr [920]

BERNARDSTON 1735-1897 – (Mf 1-4: Town & Vital Records 1762-86. Mf 5-9: Town & Vital Records 1786-1815. Mf 10-11: Vital Records 1747-1815. Mf 12-18: Proprietors Records 1735-1819. Mf 19: Proprietors Records 1819-55. Mf 20-21: B,M,D 1844-60. Mf 22-25: B,M,D 1861-97) – (mf ed 1987) – 25mf – 9 – 0-87623-055-9 – us Holbrook [920]

BERNARDUS GUTOLFI MONACHI : SEU VITA SANCTISSIMI P.N. BERNARDI PER MONACHUM GUTOLPHI / ed by Heimb, TheopH – Nerimbergae. v1-2. 1743-1746 – v1 22mf; v2 27mf – 8 – Dfl172.00 – ne Slangenburg [240]

Bernatz, Johann Martin *see* SCENES IN ETHIOPIA

Bernays, Edward L *see* PROPAGANDA

Bernays, J *see* L'ACTION DIRECTE EXERCEE PAR LA VICTIME D'UN ACCIDENT ...

Berndt, Inge *see* WAS HALTET IHR VON JESUS?

Berneisen, Ewald *see* HOFFMANN VON FALLERSLEBEN ALS VORKAEMPFER UND ERFORSCHER DER NIEDERLAENDISCH-VLAEMISCHEN LITERATUR

Berneker, E *see* SLAVISCHES ETYMOLOGISCHES WOERTERBUCH

Berneker, Jagic *see* ARCHIV FUER SLAWISCHE PHILOLOGIE

Berner, A F *see* WIRKUNGSKREIS DES STRAFGESETZES, ...

DIE BERNER TAEUFER BIS 1532 / McGlothlin, William Joseph – Berlin: E. Ebering, 1902 – 1mf – us A.T.L.A. [240]

BERNER TAGWACHT / Sozialdemokratische Partei der Schweiz – Bern, 1914-54 (incompl) – 1 – $35.00r – us Hoover Inst Photo [072]

Bernes, J *see* PAPEL QUE RESPONDE A...DAMIAN DE MAYORGA Y GUZMAN, MEDICO...SOBRE...LA CALENTURA MALIGNA

Bernetti, Jorge Luis *see* EL PERONISMO DE LA VICTORIA

Berney, J *see* DE LA PROCEDURE SUIVIE ...

Bernfeld, Simon *see*
- DIE RELIGIOESE POESIE DER JUDEN IN SPANIEN, BERLIN, 1845
- DER TALMUD

Bernfield, Simon *see*
- DIE LEHREN DES JUDENTUMS NACH DEN QUELLEN

Bernhard, E *see* JEHUDA HALEVI: EIN DIWAN

BERNHARD PANKOK : DAS GEBRAUCHSGRAPHISCHE WERK / Heinen, Mechthild – 1993 – 6mf – 9 – DM125.00 – 3-89349-706-4 – gw Hänsel [700]

BERNHARD VOGEL: PAMPHLET COLLECTION – 1972-1983 – 1 – CSUXANS3229-B – us Hoover Inst Photo [943]

BERNHARD VON BREYDENBACH AND HIS JOURNEY TO THE HOLY LAND, 1843-4 : A BIBLIOGRAPHY / Davies, H W – 4mf – ne IDC [910]

Bernhardi, J J *see* SYSTEMATISCHES VERZEICHNISS DER PFLANZEN WELCHE IN DER GEGEND UM ERFURT GEFUNDEN WERDEN

Bernhardi, Theodor von *see* VOLKSMAEHRCHEN UND EPISCHE DICHTUNG

Bernhardt, G de *see*
- HANDBOOK OF COMMERCIAL TREATIES AND C., BETWEEN GREAT BRITAIN AND FOREIGN POWERS
- HANDBOOK OF TREATIES, ... COMMERCE AND NAVIGATION BETWEEN GREAT BRITAIN AND FOREIGN POWERS, ... 1907

Bernhardt, Peter *see* ZUR IDENTIFIKATION KONTINUIERLICHER ZERKLEINERUNGSPROZESSE IM LABORBETRIEB

Bernhardt, Wilhelm *see* LUDWIG UHLANDS POLITISCHE BETAETIGUNGEN UDN ANSCHAUUNGEN

Bernhardy, Gottfried *see*
- GRUNDRISS DER GRIECHISCHEN LITTERATUR

Bernhart, Joseph *see* VOM PAPSTE

Bernheim, Ernst *see*
- LEHRBUCH DER HISTORISCHEN METHODE UND DER GESCHICHTSPHILOSOPHIE
- DAS WORMSER KONKORDAT UND SEIN VORURKUNDEN

Bernheim, Hippolyte *see* HYPNOTISME, SUGGESTION, PSYCHOTHERAPIE. ETUDES NOUVELLES. V. V. V

BERNHEIM-JEUNE ET CIE CATALOGUE – (Individual titles not listed separately) – Paris – uk Chadwyck [700]

BERNICE FIRST BAPTIST CHURCH. BERNICE, LOUISIANA : CHURCH RECORDS – 1900-17 – 1 – 7.56 – us Baptist [240]

Bernice P. Bishop Museum. Honolulu *see*
- DICTIONARY CATALOG
- DICTIONARY CATALOG OF THE LIBRARY OF THE BERNICE P. BISHOP MUSEUM

Bernier, Bernard *see*
- MEMOIRES CONCERNANT LE FONCTIONNEMENT DES LOIS QUI REGISSENT LES ECOLES DE REFORME ET D'INDUSTRIE
- MEMORIALS RESPECTING THE WORKING OF THE LAWS GOVERNING REFORMATORY AND INDUSTRIAL SCHOOLS
- REPONSE A QUELQUES OBSERVATIONS FORMULEES PAR L'HONORABLE L. P. PELLETIER, SECRETAIRE PROVINCIAL DANS L'AUDIENCE DU 29 MARS 1893

Bernier, C-E *see* LE DEFRICHEUR DU LAC ST-JEAN

Bernieres de Louvigny, Jean de *see* DEN INWENDIGHEN CHRISTENEN

Bernier-Lesieur, Raymond *see* BIBLIOGRAPHIE ANALYTIQUE DES ETUDES PEDOLOGIQUES DES SOLS DES COMTES DANS LA PROVINCE DE QUEBEC

Bernikov, Ilya Stepanovich (1839-1915) *see* KRATKII KURS TSERKOVNAGO PRAVA PRAVOSLAVNOI TSERKVI

BERNKASTELER ZEITUNG – (Cont: Gemeinnuetziges Wochenblatt, -1846; Bernkast'ler Wochenblatt, -jun 1850; Bernkast'ler Zeitung, -1884) – Bernkastel, apr 2 1835-dec 18 1944 – 1 – Inquire at Mikrofilmarchiv for details – gw Misc Inst [943]

BERNKASTELER ZEITUNG *see* GEMEINNUETZIGES WOCHENBLATT

BERNKAST'LER TAGEBLATT *see* GEMEINNUETZIGES WOCHENBLATT

BERNKAST'LER WOCHENBLATT *see* BERNKASTELER ZEITUNG

BERNKAST'LER ZEITUNG *see* BERNKASTELER ZEITUNG

Berno, K A *see* AN EXAMINATION OF RIDER AROUSAL IN THE THREE PHASES OF AN EQUESTRIAN COMBINED TRAINING EVENT

Bernouilli, J *see* DE MOTU MUSCULORUM...

Bernoulli, Carl Albrecht *see*
- DAS KONZIL VON NICAEA
- DIE WISSENSCHAFTLICHE UND DIE KIRCHLICHE METHODE IN DER THEOLOGIE

Bernoulli, Jacques *see* L'ART DE CONJECTURER...

BERZANDJI TERDJEMAH BAHASA BUGIS / Abdul Rahman daeng Matamman – (In Buginese script). SE-4590 1. 1962 – 9 – ne IDC [950]

Berzelius, Jons Jakob *see*
- LEERBOEK DER SCHEIKUNDE
- NOUVEAU SYSTEME DE MINERALOGIE

Besancenet, Etienne de *see* PAUVRETE, SILHOUETTES PARISIENNES

BESANCON AUX 17EME ET 18EME SIECLES – (Textes et documents extraits des Archives du Genie conserves au Chateau de Vincennes) – 1979 – 2mf – 15 – F60.00 – fr C.R.D.P. [944]

Besant, Anne Wood *see*
- THE BASIS OF MORALITY
- FOR INDIA'S UPLIFT; A COLLECTION OF SPEECHES AND WRITINGS ON INDIAN QUESTIONS
- MY PATH TO ATHEISM
- OUR CORNER
- THE STORY OF THE GREAT WAR: SOME LESSONS FROM THE MAHABHARATA FOR THE USE OF HINDU STUDENTS IN THE SCHOOLS OF INDIA
- VEGETARIANISM IN THE LIGHT OF THEOSOPHY: A LECTURE

BESCHAEFTIGUNGEN DER BERLINISCHEN GESELLSCHAFT NATURFORSCHENDER FREUNDE – (Continued as: Schriften der Berlinischen Gesellschaft Naturforschender Freunde. Berlin, 1780-1794. v1-11; Continued as: Neue Schriften der Gesellschaft Naturforschender Freunde. Berlin, 1795-1803. v1-4; Continued as: Magazin der Gesellschaft Naturforschender Freunde. Berlin, 1807-1818. v1-8; Continued as: Verhandlungen der Gesellschaft Naturforschender Freunde. Berlin, 1829; Continued as: Sitzungsberichte der Gesellschaft Naturforschender Freunde zu Berlin. Berlin, 1839-1933. v1-63) – Berlin, 1775-1779. v1-4 – 380mf – 8608/1 – ne IDC [060]

BESCHEIDEN AANGAANDE DE KERKHERVORMING IN VLAANDEREN (DE WERKEN..3,3) / ed by Janssen, H Q – Utrecht, 1877 – Dfl9.00 – ne Slangenburg [240]

Bescherelle, E *see*
- CONTRIBUTION A LA FLORE BRYOLOGIQUE DU TONKIN
- MUSCI YUNNANENSES
- NOUVEAUX DOCUMENTS POUR LA FLORE BRYOLOGIQUE DU JAPON

Bescherelle, LN *see* DICTIONNAIRE NATIONAL DE LA LANGUE FRANCAISE

Beschi, Constantino Giuseppe *see* A GRAMMAR OF HIGH TAMIL

BESCHOUWING DER WERELD / Luiken, J – O 350. 1708 – 9 – ne IDC [760]

BESCHOUWINGEN OVER DEN STATENBOND EN... / Bake, R W JC – Amsterdam, 1881 – 3mf – 9 – ILM-1680/1 – ne IDC [340]

BESCHREIBUNG ALLER NATIONEN DES RUSSISCHEN REICHES / Georgi, I G – U 773. v. 1-4. 1776-1780 – 9 – ne IDC [947]

BESCHREIBUNG DER AEGYPTISCHEN SAMMLUNG DES NIEDERLAENDISCHEN REICHSMUSEUMS DER ALTERTUEMER IN LEIDEN / Boeser, P A A – Haag, 1909-1910 – 10mf – 9 – ne IDC [930]

BESCHREIBUNG DER AEGYPTISCHEN SAMMLUNG DES NIEDERLAENDISCHEN REICHSMUSEUMS DER ALTERTUEMER IN LEIDEN / Boeser, P A A – Haag, 1911-1932 – 27mf – 9 – ne IDC [930]

BESCHREIBUNG DER GRAESER / Schreber, J C D von – Leipzig. 1769-1810. B-233 2 – 8 – ne IDC [580]

BESCHREIBUNG DER LAENDER ZWISCHEN DEN FLUESSEN TEREK UND KAR AM CASPISCHEN MEERE / Bieberstein, Friedrich August Marschall von – Frankfurt am Main, 1800. 211 pp. B-793 2 – 8 – ne IDC [910]

BESCHREIBUNG DER LAENDER ZWISCHEN DEN FLUESSEN TEREK UND KUR AM CASPISCHEN MEERE – Frankfurt am Main, 1800 – 7mf – 9 – ne IDC [574]

BESCHREIBUNG DER LAGERSTROEMIA INDICA / Medikus, F K – Historia et Commentationes Academiae. v. 4. Theodoro-Palatinae. 1780. B-8130 1 – 9 – ne IDC [580]

BESCHREIBUNG DER OST-INDISCHEN KUSTEN MALABAR UND COROMANDEL. DER KAISERREICHS ZEYLON, BENEBENST DER ABGOTTEREY DER OST-INDISCHEN HEYDEN / Baldaeus, P – Amsterdam. 1672. B-507 2 – 8 – ne IDC [240]

BESCHREIBUNG UND ABBILDUNG DES ESSBAREN UND GIFTIGEN SCHWAEMME, WELCHE IN DEUTSCHLAND UND FRANKREICH WACHSEN / Cordier, F S – Quedlinburg, Leipzig. 1838 – 8 – ne IDC [580]

BESCHREIBUNG UND ABBILDUNG. RIEDGRAESERN / Schkuhr, C – Wittenberg. 1801; Nachtrag. 1806. B-5187 2 – 8 – ne IDC [580]

BESCHREIBUNGEN VON ALLERLEY INSECTEN IN DEUTSCHLAND / Frisch, J L – Berlin, (1720) 1730(-38). 13pts. Z/1263/2 – 8 – ne IDC [590]

BESCHRIJVENDE CATALOGUS DER PAMFLETTEN-VERZAMELING VAN DE BOEKERIJ DER REMONSTRANTSCHE KERK TE AMSTERDAM / Rogge, Hendrik Cornelis – Five parts. 1862-65 – 1 – us A.T.L.A. [240]

BESCHRIJVING DER HANDSCHRIFTEN VAN JAN VAN RUUSBROEC'S WERKEN / Vreese, W de – Gent, 1900-1902 – 13mf – 8 – ne Slangenburg [290]

BESCHRIJVING DER NEDERLANDSCHE BEZITTINGEN IN OOST-INDIE / Aa, Abraham Jacob von der – Amsterdam: J.F. Schleijer, 1846.illus.Imprint varies. Bibliographic foo – 1 – us U.W. Library [950]

BESCHRIJVING DER VERZAMELINGEN VAN HET GROOT-OOSTEN DER NEDERLANDEN – 's-Gravenhage. 7v. 1880-1912 – 19mf – ne IDC [780]

BESCHRIJVING VAN DE EGYPTISCHE VERZAMELING IN HET RIJSMUSEUM VAN OUDHEDEN TE LEIDEN / Boeser, P A A – Leiden, 1905 – 6mf – 9 – ne IDC [930]

BESCHRIJVING VAN DE KRATON VAN GROOT-ATJEH ZIJNE VERDEDEGINGSKRACHT EN BEWAPENING : MERKWAARDIGHEDEN ER IN AANGETROFFEN – Batavia, 1874 – 1mf – 9 – ne IDC [950]

DAS BESCHUETZTE ORCHESTRE, ODER DESSELBEN ZWEYTE EROEFFNUNG / Mattheson, J – 1717 – 9 – us Sibley [780]

BESEDA – Izdanie russkikh Evangel'skikh khristian. v. 4-6:2. Stockholm. 1894-96. BR-1671 2 – 8 – ne IDC [073]

BESEDA – no. 1-7. 1923-25 – 1 – 25.00 – us L of C Photodup [460]

BESEDA – Zhurnal uchenyi, literaturnyi i politicheskii. M. 1871-72. B-1685 2 – 8 – ne IDC [073]

BESEDUYUSHCHII GRAZHDANIN – St. Petersburg. 1789. v. 1-3 – 1 – us NY Public [999]

BESEDY PO RUSSKOMU RASKOLU I SEKTANTSTVU = DISCUSSIONS ON THE RUSSINA SCHISM AND SECTARIANISM / Flegmatov, Andrei – (One of three items on reel by same author: Poucheniya i besedy po Russkomu i Sektantstvu. – Exhortations and Idscussions on the Russian Schism and Sectarianism. – 3rd ed 1899; Poucheniya i besedy po Russkomu Raskolu i Sektantstvu. – Exhortations and Discussions on the Russian Schism and Sectariansim. – 2nd ed 1897) – Tsaritsyn, 1892 – 1r – 1 – $52.84 set – us Baptist [240]

BESER – Sahibi ve Nesriyat Mueduerue: Abidin Nesimi. No. 1 (1 Ocak 1949) – 9 – $20.00 – us MEDOC [956]

DIE BESETZUNG DER BISCHOFSSITZE IN PREUSSEN IN DER ERSTEN HAELFTE DES 19. JAHRHUNDERTS / Bastgen, Hubert – Paderborn, 1941 – 556p – 9 – DM148.00 – 3-89349-254-2 – gw Hänsel [240]

DIE BESETZUNG DES PAEPSTLICHEN STUHLS UNTER DEN KAISERN HEINRICH 3. UND HEINRICH 4. / Martens, Wilhelm – Freiburg i.B.: J C B Mohr, 1887 – 1mf – 9 – 0-8370-7648-X – 1986-1648 – us A.T.L.A. [240]

BESIDE THE BOWERY / Denison, John Hopkins – New York: Dodd,Mead, 1914 – 1mf – us A.T.L.A. [240]

BESIDE THE FIRE : A COLLECTION OF IRISH GAELIC FOLK STORIES / Hyde, Douglas – London: David Nutt, 1890 – 1 roll – 1 – 1-55879-498-0 – uk Libr Preservation [390]

BESITZEN WIR DEN URSPRUENGLICHEN TEXT DER HEILIGEN SCHRIFT? / Muehlau, Ferdinand – Dorpat: E.J. Karow, 1884. 1 fiche – 9 – us A.T.L.A. [240]

BESKIDENLAENDISCHE DEUTSCHE ZEITUNG *see*
- BIELITZ-BIALER DEUTSCHE ZEITUNG

Beskov, Gustaf E *see* DEN SVENSKA MISSIONEN I OST-AFRIKA

BESKRIVELSE AV GUINEISKA PLANTER / Schumacher, H C F – Kjobenhavn. 1828-29. B-5279 2 – 8 – ne IDC [580]

Besler, Samuel *see*
- GAUDIJ PASCHALES IESV CHRISTI REDIVIVI, IN GLORIOSISSIMAE RESURRECTIONIS EJUS LAETAM CELEBRATIONEM RELATIO HISTORIA, A QVATUOR EVANGELISTIS CONSIGNATA, ET MELODIA HARMONICA ADORNATA
- HYMNOR[UM] ET THRENDORIARVM SANCTAE CRVCIS IN SALVTAREM PASSIONIS IESU CHRI..
- HYMNOR'(UM] ET THRENODIARVM SANCTAE CRVCIS IN DEVOTAM PASSIONIS IESU CHRISTI DEI...
- THRENODIARVM SANCTAE CRVCIS SALUTIFERAM PASSIONIS D.N.I.C. RECORDATIONEM, CONTINVATIO HISTORICA...

BESLUITEN DER EERSTE KAMER VAN HET VERTEGENWOORDIGEND LICHAAM DES BATAAFSCHEN VOLKS : DECREETEN VAN DE ALGEMEENE VERGADERING VAN HET VERTEGENWOORDIGEND LICHAAM DES BATAFFSCHEN VOLKS – (Missing: 1800. v21(Apr. 15-30); Index. 38v) – Den Haag, augustus 1798-18 september 1801 – 631mf – H-2566/1 – ne IDC [943]

BESLUITEN VAN DE TWEEDE KAMER EN DECRETEN VAN HET VERTEGENWOORDIGEND LICHAAM DES BATAAFSCHEN VOLKS – (Index. 38v) – Den Haag, 4 mei 1798-18 september 1801 – 275mf – H-2567/1 – ne IDC [943]

Besnier, Pierre *see*
- DISCOURS SUR LA SCIENCE DES ETYMOLOGIES
- A PHILOSOPHICAL ESSAY FOR THE REUNION OF THE LANGUAGES

BESNOVATYE. SAVVA GRUDTSYN I SOLOMONIIA / Remizov, A – Paris, 1951. 93, (2)p. BR-815 2 – 8 – ne IDC [460]

EL BESO? / Aradillas Agudo, Antonio – Madrid: Ediciones Studium, 1960 – sp Bibl Santa Ana [946]

BESOF MAARAV – Los Angeles, CA. Spring 1981-Fall/Winter 1982 – 1 – us A.J.P.C. [071]

Besold, C *see* DE NATURA POPULORUM...

Besoldus, C *see* DE FOEDERUM JURE: ...

LOS BESOS BAJO TIERRA (POEMAS DEL AMOR Y DEL DESAMOS) / Camino Burgos, Luis G – Caceres: Talleres Extremadura – 1 – sp Bibl Santa Ana [946]

O BESOURO : PERIODICO CRITICO, NOTICIOSO E LITTERARIO – Maceio, Alagoas. 19 Jan, Abr-3 Maio 1880 – 1 – bl Biblioteca [440]

Bess, B *see* UNSERE RELIGIOESEN ERZIEHER

[BESS OF BEDIAM] MAD BESS / Purcell, Henry – London: Birchall, 179- – 1 – us Sibley [780]

BESSARABSKOE SLOVO – (Includes c.1: 1927:Mar.25-27) – Kishenev: Tip. akt s. o-va "Unzer Zeit" – 1 reel – 1 – CSUXANRO261-S – us Hoover Inst Photo [947]

Bessarion, Ioannes *see* QUAE HOC IN VOLUMINE TRUCTANTUR

BESSARIONE : PUBBLICAZIONE PERIODICA DI STUDI ORIENTALI – (Serie 3: v9(1912) 7mf. v34(1918) 6mf. Dfl25.00) – 1(1896)-9(1901) – 107mf – 9 – Dfl375.00 – ne Slangenburg [073]

BESSARIONE; PUBBLICAZIONE PERIODICA DI STUDI ORIENTALI – Roma, 1896-1922 – 200mf – AR-1775/1 – ne IDC [950]

Besse, Dom J M *see*
- ABBAYES ET PRIEURES DE L'ANCIENNE FRANCE. PROVINCES ECCLESIASTIQUES D'AUCH ET DE BORDEAUX
- LES MOINES DE L'AFRIQUE ROMAINE. (4TH ET 5TH SIECLE.)
- LES MOINES DE L'ANCIENNE FRANCE
- LES MOINES D'ORIENT ANTERIEURS AU CONCILE DE CHALCEDOINE (451)

Besse, Henry T *see*
- BIBLICAL CHRONOLOGY
- JEWISH CALENDAR

Besse, J et al *see* ABBAYES ET PRIEURES DE L'ANCIENNE FRANCE

Bessels, Emil *see*
- DIE AMERIKANISCHE NORDPOL-EXPEDITION
- DIE AMERIKANISCHE NORDPOL-EXPEDITION: MIT ZAHLREICHEN ILLUSTRATIONEN IN HOLZSCHNITT, DIAGRAMMEN UND EINER KARTE IN FARBENDRUCK
- EINIGE WORTE UEBER DIE INNUIT (ESKIMO) DES SMITH SUNDES NEBST BEMERKUNGEN UEBER INNUIT SCHAEDEL
- THE NORTHERNMOST INHABITANTS OF THE EARTH

Besser, A A *see* BORBA ZA UROZHA I

Besser, W S JG von *see*
- CATALOGUE DES PLANTES DU JARDIN BOTANIQUE DU GYMNASE DE VOLHYNIE A KRZEMIENIEC
- CATALOGUS PLANTARUM IN HORTO BOTANICO GYMNASII VOLHYNIENSIS CREMENECI CULTARUM
- PRIMITIAE FLORAE GALICIAE AUSTRIACAE

Besser, Wilhelm Friedrich *see*
- PAULUS
- ST. PAUL THE APOSTLE: A BIBLICAL PORTRAIT

Bessey, W E *see* EVIDENCES OF ANCIENT CIVILIZATION IN AMERICA: CONSTITUTING A LECTURE DELIVERED ON BEHALF OF THE MECHANICS' INSTITUTE ON TUESDAY, 1ST OF MARCH, 1870

Bessie Beatty Home Printing Co *see* WHO'S WHO IN NEVADA

Bessieres, A *see* POUR LE PAPE...

Bessieux *see* CATECHISMUS HISTORICUS MINOR

Bessler, Johann Ernst Elias *see* DAS TRIUMPHIRENDE PERPETUUM MOBILE ORFFYREANUM

Bessodes, Maurice *see* SAINT ROCH. HISTOIRE ET LEGENDES

Besson, Antonin *see* LE PROJET DE REFORME DE LA PROCEDURE PENALE, RAPPORT

Besson, J M *see* HIGH PRESSURE RESEARCH

Besson, Paul *see*
- CONSULTATION DES TROIS EVEQUES SUR LES MOYENS DE SOUTENIR L'EGLISE ROMAINE PRESENTEE AU PAPE JULES 3 EN 1553
- ETUDES SUR LE THEATRE CONTEMPORAIN EN ALLEMAGNE

Bessonnet, Rene *see* ESSAI SUR LES HALLUCINATIONS CONSCIENTES

BESSY RANE / Wood, Ellen – British Fiction Archive: Unit 1 – 9 – uk Bell [830]

BEST AND SMITH'S REPORTS : REPORTS OF CASES ARGUED AND DETERMINED IN THE COURT OF QUEEN'S BENCH AND THE COURT OF EXCHEQUER CHAMBER ON APPEAL... / Best, William M & Smith, George J P – v1-20. 1863-70. London: H Sweet, 1863-71 (all publ) – 110mf – 9 – $165.00 – LLMC 84-748 – us L.L.M.C. [324]

BEST (Baptist Education Study Task) *see* CORRESPONDENCE, 1964-67

Best, Dr *see*
- ARBEITSBESCHAFFUNG UND KREDITAUSWEITUNG
- UEBER DIE VIER GESETZENTWUERFE
- WAEHRUNGSFRAGEN
- ZUR FRAGE DER GOLDWAEHRUNG

Best, Henry *see* THE FARMING AND ACCOUNTS BOOKS OF 1641

BEST IDEAS, A DIRECTORY OF SOCIAL INVENTIONS / ed by Albery, Nicholas & Mills, Christine – 1986. 156p – 9 – 1.00f – at Libertarian Micro [320]

THE BEST METHODS OF COUNTERACTING MODERN INFIDELITY = BESTEN METHODEN DER BEKAEMPFUNG DES MODERNEN UNGLAUBENS : A PAPER READ BEFORE THE GENERAL CONFERENCE OF THE EVANGELICAL ALLIANCE, NEW YORK, OCTOBER 6, 1873 / Christlieb, Theodor – (In English) – New York: Harper, 1874, c1873 – 1mf – 9 – 0-8370-2660-1 – 1985-0660 – us A.T.L.A. [230]

Best, Nolan Rice *see* BEYOND THE NATURAL ORDER: ESSAYS ON PRAYER, MIRACLES AND THE INCARNATION

Best, R *see* THE MARYROLOGY OF TALLAGHT

Best, Randolph B *see* PAPERS OF THE MARYLAND STATE COLONIZATION SOCIETY, 1817-1902

Best, William M *see* BEST AND SMITH'S REPORTS

DER BESTAND DER FREIEN STADT DANZIG ... / Behrend, G – Breslau, 1933 – 1mf – 9 – ILM-966/1 – ne IDC [327]

DER BESTAND PREUSSISCHE AKADEMIE DER KUENSTE - KAISERREICH, WEIMARER REPUBLIK, NATIONALSOZIALISMUS, NACHKRIEGSZEIT (1871-1955) TEIL 1 : DIE SEKTIONEN FUER DIE BILDENDEN KUENSTE, FUER MUSIK UND FUER DICHTKUNST / ed by Stiftung Archiv der Akademie der Kuenste Berlin – (1 findbuch 1994 DM48.00 ISBN: 3-598-33712-4. Free with set) – (mf ed 1994) – 1218mf (1:24) – 9 – diazo DM10,800.00 silver DM13,800.00 – 3-598-33704-3 – silver ISBN: 3-598-33705-1 – gw Saur [370]

DER BESTAND PREUSSISCHE AKADEMIE DER KUENSTE - KAISERREICH, WEIMARER REPUBLIK, NATIONALSOZIALISMUS, NACHKRIEGSZEIT (1871-1955), TEIL 2 : PRAESIDENT, MITGLIEDER, STAENDIGE SEKRETAERE STATUTEN UND SENATSPROTOKOLLE – (1 findbuch 1996 DM48.00 ISBN: 3-598-33722-1. Free with set) – (mf ed 1995) – 969mf (1:24) – 9 – diazo DM10,800.00 silver DM13,800.00 – 3-598-33714-0 – silver ISBN: 3-598-33719-9 – gw Saur [370]

DER BESTAND PREUSSISCHE AKADEMIE DER KUENSTE - KAISERREICH, WEIMARER REPUBLIK, NATIONALSOZIALISMUS, NACHKRIEGSZEIT (1871-1955), TEIL 3 : AUSTELLUNGEN UND KUNSTPREISE – (1 findbuch 1997 ca DM48.00 ISBN: 3-598-33732-9. Free with set) – (mf ed 1998) – 1150mf (1:24) – 9 – diazo DM10,800.00 silver DM13,800.00 – 3-598-33724-8 – silver ISBN: 3-598-33725-6 – gw Saur [370]

Bestaux, E *see* BIBLIOGRAPHIE TCHEQUE

Beste, Konrad *see* GRILLPARZERS VERHAELTNIS ZUR POLITISCHEN TENDENZLITERATUR SEINER ZEIT

BESTENDIGE BEKANTNUS D. SAMUEL HUBERS. OB GOTT DURCH SEINEN LIEBEN SON JESUM CHRISTUM NUR ALLEIN ETLICH WENIG MENSCHEN ORDER ZUMAL ALLE MENSCHEN...VOM TODE ALLESAMPT ERLOE..HABE / Huber, S – N.p., 1598 – 1mf – ne IDC [240]

BESTENDIGE ENTDECKUNG DES CALUINISCHEN GEISTS WELCHER SICH VNTERSTEHE DAS LEIDEN JHESU CHRISTI FUER VNSERE SUENDE ZU VERLAEUGNEN VND AUFFZUHEBEN / Huber, S – Wittemberg, 1593 – 3mf – ne IDC [240]

Besterman, Theodore *see*
- LE THEATRE DE VOLTAIRE
- VOLTAIRE ON SHAKESPEARE

BESTIMMUNG DER RENALEN CLEARANCE IM RAHMEN DER NUKLEARMEDIZINISCHEN NIERENDIAGNOSTIK / Mende, Traute – 1993 – 9 – DM48.00 – 3-89349-453-7 – gw Hänsel [616]

DIE BESTIMMUNG DES FACHLICHKEITSGRADES VON TEXTEN DER INDUSTRIESOZIOLOGIE DES ENGLISCHEN UND DEUTSCHEN / Dohms, Evelyn – 1995 – 1mf – 9 – DM60.00 – 3-8267-2177-2 – gw Hänsel [400]

BESTIMMUNG VON HLA KLASSE 1 AN ZUR AUTOVACCINATION BESTIMMTEN, EPITHELMARKER-CHARAKTERISIERTEN TUMORZELLEN / Kleef, Rald – 1994 – 1mf – DM48.00 – 3-89349-890-7 – gw Hänsel [611]

BESTIMMUNGSGRUENDE UND PROBLEME STAATLICHER UND INSTITUTIONELLER FAMILIENPOLITIK AM BEISPIEL DER BUNDESREPUBLIK DEUTSCHLAND / Schluchter, Wolfgang – Heidelberg, 1973 – 2mf – 9 – DM62.00 – 3-89349-723-4 – gw Hänsel [320]

DER BESTIRNTE HIMMEL UEBER MIR : EIN KANT-ROMAN / Treptow, Alfred – Berlin: Steuben Verlag P G Esser, c1939 – 1r – 1 – us U.W. Library [830]

Beston, Henry *see* THE BOOK OF GALLANT VAGABONDS

DIE BESTRAFUNG DER BOEHMISCHEN REBELLION, INSBESONDERE DIE CORRESPONDENZ FERDINAND 2 MIT DEM FUERSTEN LIECHTENSTEIN / ed by D'Elvert, C – Bruenn, 1868 – 4mf – 9 – ne IDC [943]

BEST'S REVIEW-LIFE/HEALTH INSURANCE EDITION – (1971- . 5,6. 1976- . 9) – 1-1906- – 1 – us UMI [336]

BEST'S REVIEW-PROPERTY/CASUALTY INSURANCE EDITION – v. 77-. 1976- – 1,5,6,9 – us UMI [336]

BEST'S REVIEW-PROPERTY/LIABILITY INSURANCE EDITION – (1971-76. 5,6. 1975-76. 9) – v. 39-76. 1938-76 – 1 – us UMI [336]

Beszler, M *see* EINFELTIGER BERICHT AUSZ GOTTES WORT VOM EIDSCHWEREN

BET RABBI / Kunitzer, M – Vienna. 1805. BJ-422-39 1 – 9 – ne IDC [470]

BET TZEDEK NEWS – Los Angeles, CA.1980-84 – 1 – us A.J.P.C. [071]

BET YEHUDAH / Levinsohn, I B – Vilna, 1839 – 7mf – 9 – ne IDC [270]

BET YEHUDAH / Levinsohn, I B – Vilna. 1839. BJ-422-47 1 – 9 – ne IDC [270]

LE BETAIL TRYPANOTOLERANT D'AFRIQUE OCCIDENTALE ET CENTRALE : TOME 3. BILAN D'UNE DECENNIE / Hoste, C H et al – 1991 – 9 – Gratuit – 92-9053-228-9 – et ILRI [636]

LA BETE NOIRE – no. 1-4. Paris. mai-juil 1935 – 1 – fr A.C.R.P.P. [073]

DIE BETEILIGUNG DER CHRISTEN AM OEFFENTLICHEN LEBEN IN VORCONSTANTINISCHER ZEIT : EIN BEITRAG ZUR AELTESTEN KIRCHENGESCHICHTE / Bigelmair, Andreas – Muenchen: J.J. Lentner, 1902. (Veroeffentlichungen aus dem Kirchenhistorischen Seminar Muenchen; Nr. 8) – 1mf – us A.T.L.A. [240]

DIE BETEILIGUNG DER RELIGIONSGESELLSCHAFTEN AN STAATLICHEN AUFGABEN : GEGENUEBERSTELLUNG DER VEHAELTNISSE VOR UND NACH DEM JAHRE 1918 / Jung, Hermann – 1995 – 1mf – 9 – DM48.00 – 3-8267-3183-2 – gw Hänsel [340]

DE BETEKENIS VAN HET WOORD SOLITUDO IN DE COLL. VAN CASSIANUS / Kabel, Michael – 1959 – 4mf – 8 – ne Slangenburg [240]

DIE BETEKENIS VAN WALVISBAAI AS HAWE VIR SUIDWES-AFRICA / Smit, Phillipus – [Stellenbosch] Universiteit van Stellenbosch 1962 – us Res Libr [960]

Betencourt *see* NOMS FEODAUX OU NOMS DE CEUX QUI ONT TENU FIEFS EN FRANCE DEPUIS LE XIIE JUSQU'AU MILIEU DU XVIIIE

DER BETENDE GERECHTE DER PSALMEN : HISTORISCHKRITISCHE UNTERSUCHUNG ALS BEITRAG ZU EINER EINLEITUNG IN DEN PSALTER / Engert, Thaddaeus – Wuerzburg:Goebel & Scherer, 1902 – 1mf – 9 – 0-8370-3062-5 – 1985-1062 – us A.T.L.A. [220]

BETERNAK LEBAH / Suparma, Satiadiredja – SE 4218 1. 1948 – 9 – ne IDC [950]

Beth, Karl *see*
- DIE ENTWICKLUNG DES CHRISTENTUMS ZUR UNIVERSAL-RELIGION
- DER ENTWICKLUNGSGEDANKE UND DAS CHRISTENTUM
- MIRACLES OF JESUS
- DIE MODERNE UND DIE PRINZIPIEN DER THEOLOGIE
- DIE ORIENTALISCHE CHRISTENHEIT DER MITTELMEERLAENDER

BETH SIFRENU – (New York). 1920 – 1 – us A.J.P.C. [073]

BETH VAAD LA'CHACHOMIM – (New York). 1903 – 1 – us A.J.P.C. [073]

BETHABARA, SOUTH CAROLINA : CHURCH RECORDS – Bethabara. Laurens County. South Carolina – 1 – 16.65 – us Baptist [240]

BETHADA NAEM NERENN = LIVES OF IRISH SAINTS / Plummer, Ch – Oxford. 2v. 1922 – Dfl60.00 – ne Slangenburg [240]

BETHAL TRIAL – 4r – 1 – sa Microfile [960]

THE BETHAL TRIAL: STATE VS. Z. MOTHOPENG AND 17 OTHERS, IN THE SUPREME COURT OF SOUTH AFRICA, SOUTHEASTERN LOCAL DIVISION / Mothopeng, Zephania – 1978 – 1 – us Res Libr [960]

BETHANY ADVERTISER – Bethany, PA., 1841 – 13 – $25.00r – us I.M.R. [071]

BETHANY BAPTIST CHURCH. BURNT CORN, ALABAMA : CHURCH RECORDS – 1821-1956 – 1 – 20.70 – us Baptist [240]

BETHANY BAPTIST CHURCH. FLAT RIVER ASSOCIATION. NORTH CAROLINA : CHURCH RECORDS – 1883-98 – 1 – 5.04 – us Baptist [240]

Bethany Baptist Church, Hunter, KS *see* UNIVERSAL CHURCH RECORD AND CLERK'S BOOKS

BETHANY BAPTIST CHURCH. JEFFERSON DAVIS COUNTY. MISSISSIPPI : CHURCH RECORDS – 1820-1949 – 1 – 36.90 – us Baptist [240]

BETHANY BAPTIST CHURCH. KINGS MOUNTAIN ASSOCIATION. GROVER, NORTH CAROLINA : CHURCH RECORDS – 1947-63 – 1 – 6.93 – us Baptist [240]

BETHANY BAPTIST CHURCH. MCCORMICK COUNTY. SOUTH CAROLINA : CHURCH RECORDS – 1956-83.142p – 1 – 6.39 – us Baptist [240]

BETHANY BAPTIST CHURCH. MILAM, TEXAS : CHURCH RECORDS – 1892-1978. Lacks Apr 1918-Jan 1921. 718p – 1 – 32.31 – us Baptist [240]

BETHANY BAPTIST CHURCH. NESHOBA COUNTY. MISSISSIPPI : CHURCH RECORDS – Aug 1884-91 – 1 – 5.00 – us Baptist [240]

BETHANY BAPTIST CHURCH. WILLIAMSBURG COUNTY. SOUTH CAROLINA : CHURCH RECORDS – 1890-1921 – 1 – 5.00 – us Baptist [240]

BETHCAR BAPTIST CHURCH. AIKEN COUNTY. SOUTH CAROLINA : CHURCH RECORDS – 1863-76, 1894-34. 380p – 1 – 17.10 – us Baptist [978]

EL BETHEL BAPTIST CHURCH. CHEROKEE COUNTY. SOUTH CAROLINA : CHURCH RECORDS – 1803-1950 – 1 – 38.88 – us Baptist [240]

BETHEL BAPTIST CHURCH. HEARD COUNTY. GEORGIA : CHURCH RECORDS – 1828-1901 – 1 – 14.40 – us Baptist [240]

BETHEL BAPTIST CHURCH. JASPER COUNTY. GEORGIA : CHURCH RECORDS – 1853-1900 – 1 – 14.40 – us Baptist [240]

BETHEL BAPTIST CHURCH. MORRISTOWN, TENNESSEE : CHURCH RECORDS – Feb 1874-Aug 1889; Apr 1893-Apr 1896; Jan 1938-Sept 1975; Financial Records, 1894-1906; 1917-19; 1960-64. 1422p – 1 – 63.99 – us Baptist [240]

BETHEL BAPTIST CHURCH. NEW DESIGN, ILLINOIS : CHURCH RECORDS – 1806-1951. Church history on front of film – 1 – 6.57 – us Baptist [240]

BETHEL BAPTIST CHURCH. OCONEE COUNTY. SOUTH CAROLINA : CHURCH RECORDS – 1934-Oct 1989 – 1 – $80.96 – us Baptist [240]

BETHEL BAPTIST CHURCH. PITT COUNTY. NORTH CAROLINA : CHURCH RECORDS – By Mrs. W. W. Taylor. 1887-1953 – 1 – 5.00 – us Baptist [240]

BETHEL BAPTIST CHURCH. SALUDA COUNTY. SOUTH CAROLINA : CHURCH RECORDS – 1853-69 – 1 – 13.37 – us Baptist [240]

BETHEL BAPTIST CHURCH. SHELBY, NORTH CAROLINA : CHURCH RECORDS – 1940-63 – 1 – 11.48 – us Baptist [240]

BETHEL BAPTIST CHURCH. TAMPA, FLORIDA : CHURCH RECORDS – 1902-Mar 1971 – 1 – 115.65 – us Baptist [240]

BETHEL BAPTIST CHURCH. TOWNSEND, TENNESSEE : CHURCH RECORDS – 1840-1924, 24 Aug 1947-Nov 1963 – 1 – 31.50 – us Baptist [240]

Bethel, Maine. Free Will Baptist Church *see* RECORDS

BETHEL, POLK COUNTY OF OREGON / Smith, John E – 1941. (Cox Library Collection) – 5 – us Americana [978]

Bethel Township. Ohio. Honey Creek Baptist Church *see* CHURCH RECORDS, MS 670

BETHESDA BAPTIST CHURCH. HINDS COUNTY. MISSISSIPPI : CHURCH RECORDS – 1846-1937 – 1 – 43.02 – us Baptist [240]

Bethizy, J -L de *see*
- EFFETS DE L'AIR SUR LE CORPS HUMAIN.
- EXPOSITION DE LA THEORIE ET DE LA PRATIQUE DE LA MUSIQUE SUIVANT LES NOUVELLES DECOUVERTES
- EXPOSITION DE LA THEORIE ET DE LA PRATIQUE DE LA MUSIQUE, SUIVANT LES NOUVELLES DECOUVERTES

Bethke, T *see* EFFECTS OF RELATIONSHIP STATUS, SETTING AND SEX OF PERPETRATOR ON COLLEGE STUDENT EVALUATIONS OF DATING VIOLENCE

BETHLEHEM BAPTIST CHURCH. COLLETON COUNTY. SOUTH CAROLINA : CHURCH RECORDS – 1911-1924, 1954-1989. B.Y.P.U. 1925-1929 – 1 reel – 1 – $22.59 – us Baptist [240]

BETHLEHEM BAPTIST CHURCH. KINGS MOUNTAIN, NORTH CAROLINA : CHURCH RECORDS – 1854-1963 – 1 – 65.88 – us Baptist [240]

BETHLEHEM BAPTIST CHURCH. LOUISVILLE, KENTUCKY : CHURCH RECORDS – 1960-65 – 1 – 25.74 – us Baptist [240]

BETHLEHEM BAPTIST CHURCH. OCILLA, GEORGIA : CHURCH RECORDS – (635p) – Oct 1969-Sept 1989 – 1 reel – 1 – $28.58 – us Baptist [240]

BETHLEHEM BAPTIST CHURCH. ROUND-O, SOUTH CAROLINA : CHURCH RECORDS – 1913-80.Minutes scattered 1942-53, 1954-79, only May of 1980 – 1 – 13.68 – us Baptist [240]

BETHLEHEM BAPTIST CHURCH. SANDY CREEK ASSOCIATION. NORTH CAROLINA : CHURCH RECORDS – 1834-1919. 200p – 1 – $9.00 – us Baptist [240]

BETHLEHEM BAPTIST CHURCH. WASHINGTON COUNTY. GEORGIA : CHURCH RECORDS – 1791-1812. Washington County. Georgia. Darren Baptist Church. Church records. 1791-1856 – 1 – 64.80 – us Baptist [240]

BETHLEHEM BAPTIST CHURCH. WINONA, MISSISSIPPI : CHURCH RECORDS 1846-1953 – 1849-1866. Historical Sketches. 116p – 1 – $5.22 – us Baptist [240]

BETHLEHEM CHURCH. SANDY CREEK ASSOCIATION. NORTH CAROLINA : CHURCH RECORDS – 1834-1914 – 1 – 9.00 – us Baptist [240]

Bethmann, Johann Philipp *see* WARNUNG AN ALLE

BETHNAL GREEN TIMES – London, England. -w. 4 Jan 1862-10 July 1869. 5 reels – 1 – uk British Libr Newspaper [072]

BETHSAIDA BAPTIST CHURCH. FAYETTE COUNTY, GEORGIA : CHURCH RECORDS – 1830-1913 – 1 – 29.16 – us Baptist [240]

"BETHSHEAN" / Fisher, Clarence S – University of Pennsylvania Museum Journal: Dec 1923 – 9 – $10.00 – us I.R.C. [930]

BETHUEL BAPTIST CHURCH. GREENVILLE COUNTY. GREENVILLE, SOUTH CAROLINA : CHURCH RECORDS – 1949-1977 – 1 – 18.09 – us Baptist [240]

Bethune, Alexander Neil *see*
- MEMOIR OF THE RIGHT REVEREND JOHN STRACHAN, D.D., LL. D.
- MEMOIR OF THE RIGHT REVEREND JOHN STRACHAN, D.D.L., L.D.: FIRST BISHOP OF TORONTO
- A SERMON PREACHED IN THE CHURCH OF ST GEORGE THE MARTYR, TORONTO, ON SUNDAY, NOVEMBER 19, 1876, ON THE OCCASION OF THE DEATH OF THE HONORABLE JOHN HILLYARD CAMERON, Q. C., LATE CHANCELLOR OF THE DIOCESE OF TORONTO

Bethune, Anne B de *see*
- EXERCICES POUR LES NOVICES [DE L'ABBAYE DE BEAUMONT-LES-TOURS]
- EXERCICES POUR LES NOVICES (DE L'ABBAYE DE BEAUMONT-LES-TOURS)

Bethune, Joanne *see* BIOGRAPHICAL SKETCH OF JOANNE BETHUNE

Bethune, John *see* BAPTIST DISHONESTY: MISQUOTATIONS AND OTHER GROSS MISREPRESENTATIONS IN THE RECENT PAMPHLET ON BAPTISM OF THE BAPTIST MINISTER, REV. A. A. CAMERON, OF OTTAWA

Bethune, Mary McLeod *see* MARY MCLEOD BETHUNE PAPERS

Bethune, Norman *see*
- THE CRIME ON THE ROAD MALAGA-ALMERIA
- EL CRIMEN DEL CAMINO MALAGA-ALMERIA

Bethune, Thomas Greene *see* A COLLECTION OF PUBLISHED MUSIC INCLUDING 17 PIANO PIECES AND 3 VOCAL SELECTIONS

Bethune-Baker, James Franklin *see*
- INFLUENCE OF CHRISTIANITY ON WAR
- AN INTRODUCTION TO THE EARLY HISTORY OF CHRISTIAN DOCTRINE
- THE MEANING OF HOMOOUSIOS IN THE "CONSTANTINOPOLITAN" CREED
- THE MEANING OF HOMOOUSIOS IN THE 'CONSTANTINOPOLITAN CREED'
- NESTORIUS AND HIS TEACHING
- THE OLD FAITH AND THE NEW LEARNING

Bethusy-Huc, Valeska von Reiswitz-Kaderzin, Graefin von *see* DER AELTESTE SOHN

BETI CUMULATION 4 / Librarians of Institutes and Schools of Education (LISE) – British Education Theses Index. 1950-83. 1986. Education and relevant titles in psychology, sociology and linguistics. Over 8500 British and Irish theses produced for higher degrees. By subject and author. 11 fiches – 9 – £50.00; £20.00 existing subscribers – uk L.I.S.E. [370]

DER BETLER = THE BEGGAR – Philadelphia, PA. 1908 – 1 – us A.J.P.C. [830]

BETON ARME – no. 1-71. Paris. 1957-mai 1967 – 5 – fr A.C.R.P.P. [073]

BETRACHTUNGEN UEBER DIE VERHAELTNISSE DER KATHOLISCHEN KIRCHE IM UMFANGE DES DEUTSCHEN BUNDES / Wessenberg, Ignaz Heinrich, Freiherr von – O.O., 1818 – 155p – 9 – DM48.00 – 3-89349-080-9 – gw Hänsel [240]

BETRACHTUNGER UEBER DIE KRIEGSKUNST, UEBER IRHE FORTSCHRITTE, IHRE WIDERSPRUECHE UND IHRE ZUVERLAESSIGHEIT / Berenhorst, Georg Heinrich von – Leipzig. G. Fleischer. 1827. vi, 562p (Strategy of War Series) – 9 – fr Hachette [355]

THE BETRAYAL: BEING A RECORD OF FACTS CONCERNING NAVAL POLICY AND ADMINISTRATION FROM THE YEAR 1902 TO THE PRESENT TIME / Beresford, Charles William DelaPoer – 1912 – 9 – $20.00 – uk Libr Preservation [355]

BETRIEBSRAETE : ZEITSCHRIFT FUER FUNKTIONAERE DER METALLINDUSTRIE – 15 Apr 1920-22 Dec 1923 – 2r – 1 – DM140.00 set DM70.00r – gw Mikro Press [331]

BETRIEBSRAETE-SCHRIFTEN...ADGB UND AFA – v1, 3-4, 6-7, 9-12. 1919-22. (Serial publications of German trade unions in the Memorial Library, University of Wisconsin-Madison) – 1 – us U.W. Library [331]

BETRIEBSRAETE-SCHRIFTEN...AFA – no.1-3, 5-8. 1919-20. (Serial publications of German trade unions in the Memorial Library, University of Wisconsin-Madison) – 1 – us U.W. Library [331]

DER BETRIEBSRAT IN DER HOLZINDUSTRIE – Berlin, Aug 1920-Jul 1923; 1924-27 – 1 – gw Mikrofilm [072]

BETRIEBSRATEPOST / Deutscher Gewerkschaftsbund – Essen. v2-3. 1921-22. -m. illus. (Serial publications of German trade unions in the Memorial Library, University of Wisconsin-Madison.) – 1 – us U.W. Library [330]

BETRIEBSRATEZEITUNG DES ALLGEMEINEN DEUTSCHEN GEWERKSCHAFTSBUNDES UND DES ALLGEMEINEN FREIE ANGESTELLTENBUNDES – Berlin. v3, 1923. (Serial publications of German trade unions in the Memorial Library, University of Wisconsin-Madison) – 1 – us U.W. Library [331]

DIE BETRIEBSRECHNUNG / Kaefer, Karl – Zurich, 1943 – 1 – DM30.00 – gw Mikro Press [943]

DIE BETRIEBSSTEUER : EINE ALTERNATIVE ZUR DERZEITIGEN UNTERNEHMENSBESTEUERUNG / Boeer, Bjoern – 1994 – 1mf – 9 – DM60.00 – 3-8267-2025-3 – gw Hänsel [336]

BETRIEBSZEITUNG DER BREMER STRASSENBAHN A.G. UND BREMER VORORTBAHNEN G.M.B.H. – Bremen, Germany. 1936-39 – 1r – 1 – gw Mikrofilm [072]

BETRIEBSZEITUNG DER BREMER STRASSENBAHN AG UND BREMER VORORTBAHNEN GMBH – Bremen, 1936-39 – 1r – 1 – Inquire at Mikrofilmarchiv for details – gw Misc Inst [331]

Bett, A *see* CHANGING ATTITUDES TOWARD PHYSICALLY DISABLED PERSONS USING A VIDEOTAPE SPORT INTERVENTION

Bettelheim, Anton *see*
- ANZENGRUBERS WERKE IN VIERZEHN TEILEN
- LUDWIG ANZENGRUBER

Bettelheim, Anton et al *see* GESAMMELTE WERKE VON LUDWIG ANZENGRUBER

Bettelheim, Ch. *see* UNE VILLE FRANCAISE MODERNE

Bettelheim, E *see* DAS INTERNATIONALE WECHSELRECHT OESTERREICHS

Bettencourt Vasconcellos Corte Real do Canto, Vital de *see* DESCRIPCAO HISTORICA, TOPOGRAPHICA E ETHNOGRAPHICA DO DISTRICTO DE S. JOAO BAPTISTA D'AJUDIA E DO REINO DE DAHOME NA COSTA DA MINA

BETTER DEAD / Barrie, James Matthew – London: S. Sonnenschein, Lovrey, and Co., 1888 – 1 roll – 1 – 1-55879-782-3 – uk Libr Preservation [890]

BETTER FARMING SERIES – it F.A.O. [630]

BETTER FRESHWATER FISH FARMING : RAISING FISH IN PENS AND CAGES – 1990 – 83p – it F.A.O. [639]

BETTER HEALTH FOR RURAL INDONESIA / Indonesia. Health Education Section, KMD, Bekasi – SE-10,875 1. 1960? – 9 – ne IDC [610]

BETTER HOMES AND GARDENS – 1- 1922-1; 1969- 5,6; 1970- 4 x 6 in9 – us UMI [720]

BETTER INVESTING – (1970- 5,6. 1977- 9) – 1- 1951- – 1 – us UMI [336]

BETTER JOURNALS FOR THE LIBRARY PROFESSION / Borchardt, DH – ED 244-647 – 9 – 0.91 – us EDRS [020]

BETTER NUTRITION – (1983-. 1,5,6,9) – v1-. 1938- – 1 – us UMI [613]

BETTER RURAL LIFE / Rhode Island. Agricultural Extension Service – v. 1-15. 1940-54 – 1,5,6 – us Spaulding [307]

BETTER UTILIZATION OF CROP RESIDUES AND BY-PRODUCTS IN ANIMAL FEEDING : RESEARCH GUIDELINES – it F.A.O. [636]

Betteridge, Harold T *see* DIE ALPEN

Bettex, Frederic *see*
- MIRACLE
- NATURSTUDIUM UND CHRISTENTUM
- LA RELIGION ET LES SCIENCES DE LA NATURE
- SCIENCE AND CHRISTIANITY
- WUNDER
- ZWEIFEL?

BETTINA / Seidel, Ina – Stuttgart: J G Cotta, 1944 – 1r – 1 – us U.W. Library [430]

BETTINA VON ARNIM : EIN ERINNERUNGSBLATT ZU IHREM HUNDERTSTEN GEBURTSTAGE / Alberti, Conrad – Leipzig: O Wigand, 1885 – 1r – 1 – us U.W. Library [943]

BETTINA VON ARNIMS AUFRUF ZUR REVOLUTION UND ZUM VOELKERBUNDE : GESPRAECHE MIT DAEMONEN / Arnim, Bettina von – Muenchen: H Schmidt, [1919] – 1r – 1 – us U.W. Library [943]

DER BETTLER IN DER SCHOTTISCHEN DICHTUNG / Raske, Karl – Berlin, 1908 – 2mf – DM62.00 – 3-8267-3059-3 – gw Hänsel [420]

BETTY O'NEAL CONCENTRATOR – NV, Jun 1924 – 1r – 1 – $50.00 – U04420 – us Library Micro [071]

BETULAT BAT YEHUDAH / Luzzatto, S D – Prague. 1840. BJ-421-52 1 – 9 – ne IDC [470]

BETWEEN HEATHENISM AND CHRISTIANITY : BEING A TRANSLATION OF SENECA'S DE PROVIDENTIA, AND PLUTARCH'S DE SERA NUMINIS VINDICTA: TOGETHER WITH NOTES, ADDITIONAL EXTRACTS FROM THESE WRITERS AND TWO ESSAYS ON GRAECO-ROMAN LIFE IN THE FIRST CENTURY AFTER CHRIST / Super, Charles William – (In English. Includes bibliographies) – Chicago: Fleming H Revell, 1899 – 1mf – 9 – 0-8370-6418-X – 1986-0418 – us A.T.L.A. [230]

BETWEEN TWO STOOLS / Broughton, Rhoda – British Fiction Archive: Unit 4 – 9 – uk Bell [830]

BETWEEN YOU AND ME / Nefertiti, pseud – SE-5313 1. 1960 – 9 – ne IDC [999]

Betz, H D: *see* LUKIAN VON SAMOSATA UND DAS NEUE TESTAMENT

Betzendoerfer, W *see* GLAUBEN UND WISSEN BEI DEN GROSSEN DENKERN DES MITTELALTERS

Betzendoerfer, Walter *see* HOELDERLINS STUDIENJAHRE IM TUEBINGER STIFT

BETZI OU L'AMOUR COMME IL EST: ROMAN QUI N'EN EST PAS UN – Paris: Remouard, 1801. 375p. (Les Femmes Collection) – 4mf – 9 – $10.00 – fr Bibl Nationale [830]

BEULAH BAPTIST CHURCH. ABBEVILLE COUNTY. SOUTH CAROLINA : CHURCH RECORDS – 1960-72 – 1 – 5.00 – us Baptist [240]

BEULAH BAPTIST CHURCH. FLORENCE COUNTY. SOUTH CAROLINA : CHURCH RECORDS – 1872-1924. History of Church. 1872-1966 – 1 – 9.36 – us Baptist [240]

BEULAH BAPTIST CHURCH. RICHLAND COUNTY. SOUTH CAROLINA : CHURCH RECORDS – 1806-83.208p – 1 – 9.36 – us Baptist [240]

BEULAH BAPTIST CHURCH. TIPPAH COUNTY. MISSISSIPPI : CHURCH RECORDS – 1848-Jun 1885 – 1 – 11.88 – us Baptist [240]

BEULAH BAPTIST CHURCH. UNION COUNTY. SOUTH CAROLINA : CHURCH RECORDS – 1881-Feb 1973 – 1 – 20.70 – us Baptist [240]

BEULAH CHRISTIAN – 1888, 1890-1902, 1903-15 – 1 – us A.T.L.A. [240]

BEULAH STANDARD – 1916-1936. BES1-4 – 4r – 1 – at Corangamite [072]

BEULAH STAR – 1949-1957. BEST1-2 – 2r – 1 – at Corangamite [072]

Beumelburg, Werner *see* KAMPF UM SPANIEN: DIE GESCHICHTE DER LEGION CONDOR. BEARB. IM AUFTRAG DES REICHSLUFTFAHRTMINISTERIUMS; MIT 16 BILDTAFELN UND 5 KARTEN. 41.-60. TAUSEND. OLDENBURG I.O

BEUORDERING VAN WETENSKAP VAN DIE SUID-AFRIKANSE : VERENIGUNG – v4-16. 1966-68 (complete) – 1r – 1 – ATLA S0676 – us A.T.L.A. [073]

Beurden, AF van *see* HET MISSALE VAN DE KERK TE WIJK BIJ HEUSDEN

Beurhusius, Friedrich *see* MUSICAE EROTEMATUM LIBRI DUO...CUM PRAEFATIONE D. JOANNIS FREIGII

Beurmann, M von *see* VOCABULARY OF THE TIGRE LANGUAGE

BEURS-EN NIEUWSBERICHTEN – Curacao. Netherlands West Indies. 1935-62; 1970 – 1 – us UMI [072]

Beus, Alexei A *see* GEOLOGY OF TUNGSTEN

DAS BEUTERECHT ... / Bluntschli, J K – Noerdlingen, 1878 – 2mf – 9 – ILM-126/1 – ne IDC [327]

BEUTHENER ZEITUNG *see* OSTDEUTSCHE MORGENPOST

Bevan, Anthony Ashley *see*
- THE HYMN OF THE SOUL, CONTAINED IN THE SYRIAC ACTS OF ST THOMAS
- A SHORT COMMENTARY ON THE BOOK OF DANIEL FOR THE USE OF STUDENTS

BEVAN'S TREATIES : TREATIES AND OTHER INTERNATIONAL AGREEMENTS OF THE UNITED STATES, 1776-1949 / U.S. Department of State – (Includes index) – v1-13 (all publ) – 160mf – 9 – $240.00 – LLMC 79-440 – us L.L.M.C. [975]

Beveraggi Allende, Walter Manuel *see* ARGENTINA, 1946-1978

Beveregio, G *see* SYNODICON SIVE PANDECTAE CANONUM APOSTOLORUM ET CONCILIORUM AB ECCLESIA GRAECA RECEPTORUM

Beveridge, A S *see* THE BABAR-NAMA...NOW REPRODUCED IN FACSIMILE...

Beveridge, Albert J *see* THE LIFE OF JOHN MARSHALL

Beveridge, Henry *see* THE TRIAL OF MAHARAJA NANDA KUMAR

Beveridge, James A *see* SCRIPTWRITING FOR SHORT FILMS

Beverland, Adriaan *see* DE FORNICATIONE CAVENDA ADMONITIO...1698. VWITH

BEVERLEY GUARDIAN – England, 1860; 1862; 1877; 1889; 1894; 1910; 1950; 1986- – 28+ r – 1 – uk British Libr Newspaper [072]

BEVERLEY INDEPENDENT – Beverley, England. -w. 14 April 1888-25 March 1911. 15 reels – 1 – uk British Libr Newspaper [072]

BEVERLEY WEEKLY RECORDER – Beverley, England. Beverley Recorder – Beverley & East Riding Recorder – East Riding County Recorder. -w. 7 July 1855-7 May 1921. Lacking 1879, 1896, 1897. 50 reels – 1 – uk British Libr Newspaper [072]

BEVERLY 1650-1849 – (Mf 1T-2T: Births 1650-1704. Mf 1T: Deaths 1660-1704. Mf 2T: Marriages: 1666-1704. Mf 2T-3T: Intentions 1695-1722. Mf 3T-4T: Intentions 1771-72. Mf 3T-10T: Births 1670-1779. Mf 7T-9T: Marriages 1689-1766. Mf 9T-11T: Intentions 1716-67. Mf 9T-10T: Deaths 1686-1795. Mf 11T-15T: Births 1750-1854. Mf 12T-17T: Deaths 1772-1872. Mf 18T-21T. Intentions 1772-1813. Mf 21T-23T: Marriages 1771-1833. Mf 23T-25T: Intentions 1813-33. Mf 25T-27T: Deaths 1770-1857. Mf 27T-29T: Intentions 1834-49. Mf 27T-30T: Marriages 1834-43. Mf 30T: Births & Deaths 1811-49. Mf 31T: Vital Records 1813-49. Mf 31T-34T: Births 1844-49. Mf 34T-35T: Marriages 1843-49. Mf 35T-37T: Deaths 1843-49. Mf 37T: Births 1818-45. Mf 38T: Out-of-Town Marrs 1683-1799) – (mf ed 1995) – 38mf – 9 – 0-87623-210-1 – us Holbrook [920]

BEVERLY 1653-1907 – (Mf 1-35: Vital Records 1653-1850. Mf 36-41: Town Records 1685-1711. Mf 42-45: Proprietors 1698-1817. Mf46-56: Births & Deaths 1750-1845. Mf 57: Out-of-Town Marriages 1683-1798. Mf 58-61: Index: Marriages 1723-1813. Mf 62-74: Marriages & Intentions 1770-1853. Mf 75-77: Index: Vital Records 1843-50. Mf 78-81: Vital Records 1843-50. Mf 82-83: Index: Deaths 1851-82. Mf 84-90: Deaths 1851-82. Mf 91-92: Index: Deaths 1883-92. Mf 93-94: Deaths 1883-92. Mf 95-97: Index: Deaths 1893-1907. Mf 98-102: Deaths 1893- 1907. Mf 103-105: Index: Marriages 1851-86. Mf 106-112: Marriages 1837-86. Mf 113-114: Index: Marriages 1887-92. Mf 115-116: Marriages 1887- 92. Mf 117-119: Index: Marriages 1893-1907. Mf 120-124: Marriages 1893-1907. Mf 125-134: Marriage Intentions 1873-97. Mf 135-136: Index: Births 1851-79. Mf 137- 143: Births 1851-79. Mf 144-145: Index: Births 1880-92. Mf 146-48: Births 1880-92. Mf 149-151: Index: Births 1893-1907. Mf 152-56: Births 1893-1907) – (mf ed 1989) – 151mf – 9 – 0-87623-102-4 – us Holbrook [920]

BEVERLY HILLS – 1945-50; 1977-87; 1989-92 – 26r – 1 – $1,300.00 – P00008 – us Library Micro [910]

BEVERLY HILLS BAR ASSOCIATION JOURNAL – (Title varies: v1-11 1967-80 as Journal of the Beverly Hills Bar Association) – v1-28. 1967-94 – 9 – $298.00 set – us Hein [340]

BEVERLY HILLS INDEPENDENT – Santa Monica, CA. 1957 – 269+ r – 1 – $13,450.00 ($365.00y) – R03519 – us Library Micro [071]

BEVERLY HILLS/SANTA MONICA – 1993- – 3+ r – 1 – $150.00 – P00009 – us Library Micro [910]

Beverovicius, Joh. *see* EPISTOLICA QUAESTIO DE VITAE TERMINO..FATALI, AN MOBILI?

Bevervoorde, W F E van *see* MONOGRAFIE DER SOLOSCHE ENCLAVES PASARGEDE EN IMAGIRI

DIE BEVOELKERUNGS-UND BERUFSVERHAELTNISSE DER JUDEN IM DEUTSCHEN REICH / Silbergleit, H – v. 1 (no more published). Berlin. 1930. BJ-23-118 1 – 9 – ne IDC [310]

BEWAEHRUNG : GEDICHTE / Marteau, Eugen Henrik – [Bayreuth]: Gauverlag Bayreuth, 1943 – 1r – 1 – us U.W. Library [810]

BEWAEHRUNG DER HERZEN : NOVELLE / Wittek, Erhard – Feldausg. Guetersloh: C Bertelsmann, [1943] – 1r – 1 – us U.W. Library [830]

BEWAEHRUNGS- UND ENTLASSENENHILFE IN EINEM WIEDERVEREINIGTEN DEUTSCHLAND / Lohner, Wolfgang – 1991 – 190p – 9 – DM98.00 – 3-89349-412-X – gw Hänsel [360]

BEWAERUNG VND ERKLAERUNG DES VRALTEN GEMEYNEN SPRUECHWORTS: DIE GELEHRTEN DIE VERKEHRTEN / Fischart, J – Strassburg. 1584. BME-83 1 – 9 – ne IDC [240]

DIE BEWAFFNETE NEUTRALITAET 1780-1783 ... / Bergbohm, C – Berlin, 1884 – 4mf – 9 – ILM-124/1 – ne IDC [327]

BEWARE: THE INDONESIAN FASCIST REGIME USES REACTIONARY JOURNALISTS TO DECEIVE PEOPLE AND TO SPLIT AFRO-ASIAN SOLIDARITY / Indonesia. Progressive Indonesian Journalists – SE-6191 1. 1966 – 9 – ne IDC [950]

DIE BEWEGUNGEN UND HALTUNGEN DES MENSCHLICHEN KOERPERS IN HEINRICH VON KLEISTS ERZAEHLUNGEN / Bathe, Johannes Clemens – (Includes bibliographical references) – Tuebingen: H Laupp, 1917 – 1r – 1 – us U.W. Library [430]

Bewer, Julius A *see*
- GE'ULLAH IN THE BOOK OF RUTH
- THE HISTORY OF THE NEW TESTAMENT CANON IN THE SYRIAN CHURCH

Bewer, Julius August *see*
- DIE ANFAENGE DES NATIONALEN JAHWEGLAUBENS
- THE STORY OF HOSEA'S MARRIAGE

BEWERTUNG DER TV-SERIE AUF EMPIRISCHER GRUNDLAGE / Boll, Uwe – 1994 – 2mf – DM80.00 – 3-8267-2043-1 – gw Hänsel [790]

BEWIJSINGHE (EEN GANTSCH CLAER GRONDIGHE) ENDE ONDERRECHTINGHE VAN DER DOOPE – 1581. BME-214 1 – 9 – ne IDC [240]

BEXAR ARCHIVES: 1717-1836 / Texas. University of Texas at Austin. Barker Texas History Center – (1717-1803: 31r. 1-55655-042-1. $2,985.00; 1804-1821: 37r. 1-55655-043-X. $3,660.00; 1822-1836: 102r. 1-55655-044-8. $9,915.00; Translations: 1-55655-046-4. $2,510.00) – 1 – $18,105.00 – us UPA [975]

Bey, Alican Serif *see* HARFLERIMIZIN MUEDAFAASI

Bey, E Colombani *see* LES QUESTIONS DE NATIONALITE EN EGYPTE

Bey, Feridun *see* MECMU'A-I MUENSEAT-I SELATIN

Bey, Mehmet Ata *see* GUEFT UE SENID

Bey, Mustafa Koci *see* KOECI BEY RISALESI

Bey, Sait *see* HIZIRAGAZADE ARIF AGA'NIN MAHDUMU SAIT BEY DIVANI

BEYAN UEL-HAK – Istanbul: Yeni Ikdam Matbaasi, Mahmud Bey Matbaasi, 1906-1910 – 9 – $325.00 – us MEDOC [956]
Beyen, Petrus *see* KORTE VERHANDELING OVER HET ZINGEN EN SPEELEN IN DE HERVORMDE KERK VAN NEDERLAND..
Beyer, Henry Otley *see* POPULATION OF THE PHILIPPINE ISLANDS IN 1916
Beyer, Konrad *see* FRIEDRICH RUECKERT
Beyer, Roberta *see* MOTOR PROFICIENCY OF MALES WITH ATTENTION DEFICIT HYPERACTIVE DISORDER AND MALES WITH LEARNING DISABILITIES
Beyer, Walter Frederick *see* DEEDS OF VALOR
Beyerhaus, Gisbert *see* STUDIEN ZUR STAATSANSCHAUUNG CALVINS
Beyerus, G *see* DELINEATIO IURIS DIVINI, ...
Beyne, Pierre *see* MANUAL DE L'EMPRUNTEUR SUR WARRANTS COMMERCIAUX ET SUR WARRANTS AGRICOLES
THE BEYNON MANUSCRIPT – (Includes guide which appears on Reel 4) – 4r – 1 – $368.00 – us UMI [090]
BEYOGLU ALEMI – Sahibi ve Muedueruе: M. Nizamettin. No. 3 (3 Temmuz 1930) – 9 – $20.00 – us MEDOC [956]
THE BEYOND THAT IS WITHIN, AND OTHER ADDRESSES / Boutroux, Emile – London: Duckworth, 1912 – 1mf – us A.T.L.A. [240]
BEYOND THE HILL OF DREAMS / Campbell, Wilfred – Boston; New York: Houghton, Mifflin, 1899. 00405. (Pre-1900 Canadiana) – 9 – cn C.I.H.M. [830]
BEYOND THE NATURAL ORDER: ESSAYS ON PRAYER, MIRACLES AND THE INCARNATION / Best, Nolan Rice – New York: Fleming H. Revell, 1908. 1 fiche – 9 – us A.T.L.A. [240]
BEYOND THE PLEASURE PRINCIPLE / Freud, Sigmund – Authorized trans. from the 2nd German ed by C.J.M. Hubback. London, Vienna: The International Psycho-Analytical Press, 1922. 90p – 1 – us U.W. Library [150]
BEYOND THE RHINE: MEMORIES OF ART AND LIFE IN GERMANY BEFORE THE WAR / Henry, Marc – London: Constable and Company, Ltd., 1918. viii,248p. "Authorized translation" – 1 – us U.W. Library [390]
BEYOND THESE VOICES / Braddon, Mary Elizabeth – British Fiction Archive: Unit 5 – 9 – uk Bell [830]
Beyschlag, Willibald *see*
- DIE AUFERSTEHUNG UND IHRE NEUESTE BESTREITUNG
- DER BRIEF DES JACOBUS
- DIE CHRISTOLOGIE DES NEUEN TESTAMENTS
- UEBER DAS "LEBEN JESU" VON RENAN
- ZUR DEUTSCH-CHRISTLICHEN BILDUNG
- ZUR JOHANNEISCHEN FRAGE
- ZUR VERSTAENDIGUNG UEBER DEN CHRISTLICHEN VORSEHUNGSGLAUBEN

Beyssac, J *see* ABBAYES ET PRIEURES DE L'ANCIENNE FRANCE
BEYTRAEGE ZUR CRITISCHEN HISTORIE DER DEUTSCHEN SPRACHE, POESIE UND BEREDSAMKEIT / ed by Gottsched, Johann Christoph & Lotter, Johann Gottfried – Leipzig, 1732-44. Hildesheim, 1977 – 74mf – 9 – DM620.00 diazo DM720.00 silver – gw Olms [073]
BEYTRAEGE ZUR GESCHICHTE DER MUSIK, BESONDERS IN DEUTSCHLAND; NEBST FREYMUETHIGEN ANMERKUNGEN UEBER DIE KUNST / Boecklin von Boecklins, F F S A – Freyburg im Breisgau. 1790. BP-641 1 – 9 – ne IDC [780]
BEYTRAEGE ZUR GESCHICHTE DER VOEGEL / Jacquin, J F – 2092 2. 1784 – 8 – ne IDC [590]
BEYTRAEGE ZUR LITTERATUR DER MUSIK HERAUSGEGEBEN VON JOHANN SIGMUND GRUBER / ed by Gruber, Johann Sigmund – Nuernberg. 1785. BP-689 1 – 9 – ne IDC [780]
BEYTRAEGE ZUR PFLANZEN-ANATOMIE, PFLANZEN-PHYSIOLOGIE / Medikus, F K – Leipzig. 1799-1801. B-8139 1 – 9 – ne IDC [580]
BEYTRAEGE...STAATS- UND VOELKERRECHTE,... / Breme, E D – N.p., 1766 – 1mf – 1 – ILM-648/1 – ne IDC [327]
BEZ OTKAZU / Bednyi, Demian; ed by Efremina, A – Moskva: Gos. izd-vo, khudozh. lit-ra, 1934 – 1 – CSUX88-B5118 – us Hoover Inst Photo [999]
Beza, Theodor *see* TRACTATIONES THEOLOGICAE...
BEZAE CODEX CANTABRIGIENSIS – Edited with a critical introduction. by Frederick H. Scrivener. 1864 – 1 – us A.T.L.A. [240]
Bezard-Falgas, J *see* TRAITE DE LA PERTE ET DE LA RESTITUTION DES TITRES AU PORTEUR ...
Bezauzee, N *see* GRAMMAIRE GENERALE, OU EXPOSITION RAISONNEE DES ELEMENTS NECESSAIRES DU LANGAGE
BEZBOZHIE POBEDIT = ATHEISM TRIUMPHS / Tikhomirov, P – Simferopol, 1930. One of 13 titles by Soviet authors on reel – 1 – 74.32 – us Baptist [240]
BEZBOZHNIK U STANKA – M. 1923-31. Lacking: (1, 2, 4, 6, 7) 1923; (4, 12) 1924; (1, 5) 1926. BR-5854 2 – 8 – ne IDC [073]
Beze, Th. de *see*
- DE FRANCISCAE LINGUAE RECTA PRONUNTATIONE
- LES VRAIS POURTRAITS DES HOMMES ILLUSTRES...

Bezerov, Rodion Mikhailovich *see* O CHEM SHEPCHET DEREVNIA
Bezerra Tanco, Luis *see* FELICIDAD DE MEXICO...GUADALUPE EXTREMUROS
DIE BEZIEHUNGEN DER NICHTISRAELITEN ZU JAHVE / Peisker, Martin – Giessen: Alfred Toepelmann, 1907. 1 fiche – 9 – us A.T.L.A. [240]
DIE BEZIEHUNGEN DER STAATEN DER T'O-PA UND DER SHA-T' O ZUM AUSLAND / Eberhard, W – In: Annales de l'Universite d'Ankara, 1947-48. v. 2. Ankara. 1948. BU-565 2 – 8 – ne IDC [947]
DIE BEZIEHUNGEN DES DRAMATIKERS ACHIM VON ARNIM ZUR ALTDEUTSCHEN LITERATUR / Bottermann, Walther – 1995 – 1mf – 9 – DM48.00 – 3-8267-3121-2 – gw Hänsel [430]
DIE BEZIEHUNGEN DES DRAMATIKERS ACHIM VON ARNIM ZUR ALTDEUTSCHEN LITTERATUR / Bottermann, Walther – (Includes bibliographical references) – Goettingen: Druck der Dieterich'schen Univ.-Buchdruckerei, 1895 – 1r – 1 – us U.W. Library [430]
DIE BEZIEHUNGEN DES SUMERISCHEN ZUM BASKISCHEN WESTKAUSISCHEN UND TIBETISCHEN / Bouda, K – (Mitteilungen der altorientalischen gesellschaft. v. 12, pt. 3). Leipzig. 1938. BNE-20,106 1 – 9 – ne IDC [400]
BEZIEHUNGEN ZWISCHEN DEN SYMBIOSEPARTNERN IN DER ORCHIDEEN-MYCORRHIZA / Rohm, Eva Maria – 1993 – 5mf – 9 – DM125.00 – 3-89349-718-8 – gw Hänsel [574]
BEZNACHALIE – Izdanie Anarkhistov-Kommunistov (Vyp. 1-3). Paris-Geneve. 1905. BR-3485 2 – 8 – ne IDC [335]
Bezobrazov, P V *see* O SNOSHENIIAKH ROSSII S FRANTSIEI
BEZOEK AAN EEN NEDERLANDSCHE STAD IN DE XIVE EEUW / Telting, A – (Deventer). Den Haag, 1906 – Dfl13.00 – ne Slangenburg [240]
Bezold, C *see* DIE SCHATZHOEHLE "ME'ARATH GAZZE"
Bezold, Carl *see*
- KURZGEFASSTER UEBERBLICK UEBER DIE BABYLONISCHASSYRISCHE LITERATUR
- ORIENTAL DIPLOMACY

Bezold, Friedrich von *see* ZUR GESCHICHTE DES HUSITENTUMS
Bezold, G von *see* DIE KIRCHLICHE BAUKUNST DES ABENDLANDES, HISTORISCH UND SYSTEMATISCH DARGESTELLT
Bezpalov, Vasilii F *see* TEATRY V DNI REVOLIUTSII 1917
Bezrabotnyi, I *see* PRAVDA OB II ULSKIKH DNI AKH
Bezsonov, I Urii Dmitrievich *see* DVADTSATSHESTTI UREM I POBIEG S SOLOVKOV
Bezymenskii, Aleksandr *see* KOMSOMOLII A
B.F. Bowen and Co *see*
- BINKERHOFF'S HISTORY OF MARION COUNTY
- BIOGRAPHICAL AND REMINISCENT HISTORY OF RICHLAND, CLAY AND MARION COUNTIES
- BIOGRAPHICAL HISTORY OF GENESEE COUNTY
- BIOGRAPHICAL MEMOIRS OF WYANDOT COUNTY
- BIOGRAPHICAL RECORD OF BARTHOLOMEW COUNTY
- HISTORY OF DEKALB COUNTY
- HISTORY OF FAYETTE COUNTY
- HISTORY OF HENDRICKS COUNTY
- HISTORY OF LAWRENCE AND MONROE COUNTIES
- HISTORY OF WAYNE COUNTY
- PAST AND PRESENT OF FAYETTE COUNTY

BG NEWS – Bowling Green, Ohio. 1951- – 31r – 1 – $32.50r – us Archival [071]
Bhadrabahu *see* THE KALPA-SUTRA AND NAVA TATVA
BHAGANAGAR STRUGGLE : A BRIEF HISTORY OF THE MOVEMENT LED BY HINDU MAHA SABHA IN HYDERABAD IN 1938-39 / Date, S R – Pune: Date, [1940?] – 1 – us Res Libr [950]
THE "BHAGAVAD GITA" / Chatterji, M M – or "The Lord's Lay" with commentary and notes, as well as references to the Christian scriptures. Calcutta. 1887. BI-1069 1 – 9 – ne IDC [280]
THE BHAGAVADGITA, WITH THE SANATSUGATIYA AND THE ANUGITA / ed by Mueller, Friedrich Max – (Translated by Kashinath Trimbak Telang) – 1882 – 8mf – 8 – ne Slangenburg [280]
BHAKTI; MADJALAH BULANAN TENTANG PENDIDIKAN DALAM KELUARGA / Jajasan Penerbitan "Djiwa Baru" – (Monthly. Missing: 1953-1956 v1-4(1,7)) – Jogjakarta, 1953-1956 – 6mf – 9 – SE-1358/1 – ne IDC [950]
Bhandarkar Oriental Research Institute *see* ANNALS OF THE BHANDARKAR ORIENTAL INSTITUTE
Bhaneman, Carl P *see* A SURVEY OF DIVISION 2 ATHLETIC AND PHYSICAL EDUCATION FISCAL TRENDS FOR THE NEXT TWENTY YEARS
BHARAT – Allahabad, India. 3 Sept 1946-Aug 1966 – 58r – 1 – us L of C Photodup [072]
THE BHARAT JYOTI – Bombay, India. 1962-64 – 3r – 1 – us L of C Photodup [072]
BHARATA; BERKALA SENI DAN BUDAYA. JAJASAN "PANTJA MURTI" – (Monthly. Ceased publication with v2 no2. Missing: 1968 v2(1)) – Djakarta. v1-2(2). 1967-1968 – 2mf – 9 – SE-1359/1 – ne IDC [950]
BHARATA KA RAJAPATRA / India – 1967- – 1 – 600.00y – us L of C Photodup [950]
BHARATIYA SAMACHAR – New Delhi, India. 8 Mar 1941-15 Dec 1943; 1944-May 1945 – 2r – 1 – us L of C Photodup [072]
Bharucha, Sheriarji Dadabhai *see* A BRIEF SKETCH OF THE ZOROASTRIAN RELIGION AND CUSTOMS..
Bhatta, Jitandra Nath *see*
- AN ESTIMATE OF FERTILITY LEVEL OF THE POPULATION OF DJAKARTA BY POLYNOMIAL FUNCTION
- THE FUTURE CENSUS(OCTOBER 1961)
- OBSERVATIONS ON THE MUSLIM SETTLEMENTS OF MINAHASA
- SOCIAL SCIENCE BIBLIOGRAPHY OF INDONESIA
- SOURCE AND RELIABILITY OF DEMOGRAPHIC DATA IN INDONESIA

Bhattacharya, J N *see* HINDU CASTES AND SECTS
BHATTAGOPINATHADIKSITAVIRACITA SAMSKARARATNAMALA / Gopinatha, Diksita, Bhatta – Punyakhyapattane: Anandasramamudrapalaye, 1899 – 1 – us U.W. Library [280]
BHAVNAGAR STATE CENSUS – Bhavnagar. pts1-2. 1931 – 1 – us Res Libr [310]
Bheme, Herman *see* UEBER DAS VERHAELTNIS HEINRICH VON KLEISTS ZU C.M. WIELAND
"BHM" BERG- UND HUETTENMAENNISCHE MONATSHEFTE – Combined with Montan-Rundschau. v77, 1929; 85, 1937; 92-105, 1947-60; 107-126, 1962-81. Former vols. incomplete; prices quoted upon request. ISSN: 0005-8912 – 1,5,6,9,13 – $90.00v – us UMI [622]
BHMA (BUILDERS HARDWARE MANUFACTURERS ASSOCIATION INC.) – Printed index. Updated every 60 days – 6,9 – us Info Handling [690]
Bhola, H S *see*
- SOURCEBOOK FOR LITERACY WORK
- WORLD TRENDS AND ISSUES IN ADULT EDUCATION

Bhumirat, C *see* THE DROP-OUT PROBLEM IN THAILAND
Bhutan. Planning Commission *see* SEVENTH FIVE YEAR PLAN (1992/93-1996/97)
BI UDZHET GORODA ASHKHABADA NA...GOD – (Includes c.1: 1929/1930) – Ashkhabad: Ashkhabadski i gorodsko i sovet – 1 – CSUXAKY9952-S – us Hoover Inst Photo [947]
BI UDZHETY GORODSKOGO NASELENII A SIBIRI ZA 1928-29 I 1929-30 G.G. / Sektor narodno-khozi a istvennogo ucheta Zapsibkra iplana – Novosibirsk: [Sektor], 1931 – 1 – CSUX91-B676 – us Hoover Inst Photo [999]
BI UDZHETY KRESTI AN KHARKOVSKO I GUBERNII V 1922-23 GODU / Kharkovskoe gubernskoe statisticheskoe bi uro – Kharkov: [Bi uro], 1924-1925. 3v – 1 – CSUX91-B1374 – us Hoover Inst Photo [999]
BI UDZHETY KRESTI AN SIBIRSKOGO KRAI A V...GODU – (Includes c.1: 1923/1924) – Novo-Nikolaevsk: [Bi uro], 1925- – 1 – CSUXAKZ1393-S – us Hoover Inst Photo [947]
BI UDZHETY LENINGRADSKIKH RABOCHIKH I SLUZHASHCHIKH V 1922-1926 G.G. / R.S.F.S.R. T Sentralnoe statisticheskoe upravlenie, Leningradski i gubernski i otdel statistiki – Leningrad: Orgotdel Leningradskogo gubispolkoma, 1927 – 1 – CSUX91-B2645 – us Hoover Inst Photo [999]
BI UDZHETY RABOCHIKH I SLUZHASHCHIKH / T Sentralnoe statisticheskoe upravlenie SSSR, Sektor statistiki truda, Sekt sii a obshche i statistiki – Moskva: Statisticheskoe izd-vo TSSU, 1929. 3v – 1 – CSUX91-B572 – us Hoover Inst Photo [999]
BI ULET EN T SENTRALNAE STATYSTYCHNAE UPRAVY – (Includes c.1: v.4 1925:Aug./Dec) – Minsk: Upravlenie, 1925 – 1 – CSUXAKY6445-S – us Hoover Inst Photo [947]
BI ULETEN BOROTBY Z SHKIDNYKAMY SILSKO-HOSPODARSKYKH ROSLYN – (c.1: no.2/3 1924: Jan./Feb.-no.4/5 (1924:Mar./Apr.)) – Kharkiv; Kyiv: Redaktsi ino-vidavniche bi uro Komitetu, -1924. 5v – 1 – CSUXAKZ1760-S – us Hoover Inst Photo [947]
BI ULLETEN LENINGRADSKOGO GUBSTATOTDELA *see* BIULLETEN LENINGRADSKOGO GUBERNSKOGO OTDELA STATISTIKI
BI ULLETEN T SENTRALNOGO STATISTICHESKOGO UPRAVLENII *see* BI ULET EN T SENTRALNAE STATYSTYCHNAE UPRAVY
Biach, Adolf *see* BIBLISCHE SPRACHE UND BIBLISCHE MOTIVE IN WIELANDS OBERON
Bialik, H N *see* SEFER BIALIK
BIALYSTOKER ZEITUNG – Bialystok, jul 3-sep 30 1917 – 1 – Inquire at Mikrofilmarchiv for details – gw Misc Inst [947]
BIALYSTOKER ZEITUNG – Bialystok, Poland. Feb-Sept 1916 – 1r – 1 – us L of C Photodup [072]
Biana, J *see* TRATADO DE PESTE, SUS CAUSAS Y CURACION...
Bianchi, Lorenzo *see*
- DER JUNGE JOSEF GOERRES UND FRIEDRICH HOELDERLINS HYPERION
- STUDIEN ZUR BEURTEILUNG DES ABRAHAM A SANTA CLARA

Bianchini, F *see*
- DE TRIBUS GENERIBUS INSTRUMENTORUM MUSICAE VETERUM ORGANICAE DISSERTATIO
- [INES DE CASTRO] SELECTIONS

Biancolelli, Pierre-Francois *see* AGNES DE CHAILLOT
BIANNUAL REPORT 1979/80 / Papua New Guinea. National Education Board – Boroko – 2mf – 9 – DE-608/1 – ne IDC [370]
Bianquis, Genevieve *see* HENRI HEINE
Bianquis, Jean *see* L'OEUVRE DES MISSIONS PROTESTANTES A MADAGASCAR
Biard, Gustave *see*
- A MES SOEURS ET FRERES DE PARIS, DE LYON, DE GRENOBLE
- A TOUS ET A TOUTES
- L'AMI DU PROLETAIRE. ENTRETIENS FAMILIERS SUR DIFFERENTS SUJETS DE MORALE, DE POLITIQUE, D'ECONOMIE, D'INDUSTRIE

Biard, Pierre *see* RELATION DE LA NOUVELLE FRANCE, DE SES TERRES, NATUREL DU PAIS, ET DE SES HABITANTS: ITEM, DU VOYAGE DES PERES JESUITES AUSDICTES CONTREES, ET DE CE QU'ILS Y ONT FAICT JUSQUES A LEUR PRINCE PAR LES ANGLOIS
Biart, Lucien *see*
- A TRAVERS L'AMERIQUE: NOUVELLES ET RECITS
- MY RAMBLES IN THE NEW WORLD

Biaynia-Cho odecki, Jozef *see* WSPOMNIENIA Z LAT NIEDOLI I NIEWOLI, 1914-1918

EL BIB: GOD AND MAN BY THE LIGHT OF NATURE: A SKETCH IN OUTLINE – Chicago: Meyers & Chandler, 1868. 1 fiche – 9 – us A.T.L.A. [240]

Bibaud, Francois Marie Uncas Maximilien *see*
- MEMORIAL DES HONNEURS ETRANGERS CONFERES A DES CANADIENS OU DOMICILIES DE LA PUISSANCE DU CANADA
- LE MEMORIAL DES VICISSITUDES ET DES PROGRES DE LA LANGUE FRANCAISE EN CANADA

Bibaud, Michel *see*
- L'AURORE
- BIBLIOTHEQUE CANADIENNE
- LE COURRIER DU BAS-CANADA
- L'ENCYCLOPEDIE CANADIENNE

Bibbesworth, Walter de *see* LE TRAITE DE WALTER DE BIBBESWORTH SUR LA LANGUE FRANCAISE

DIE BIBEL ALS KANON: DREI VORTRAEGE / Volck, Wilhelm – Tartu, Estonia: E.J. Karow, 1885. 1 fiche – 9 – us A.T.L.A. [240]

DIE BIBEL BERNHARD OVERBERGS / Kruchen, Gottfried – Muenster, 1956 – 386p – 9 – DM98.00 – 3-89349-242-9 – gw Hänsel [240]

BIBEL UND GEMEINDE – 1957-92 (incomplete) – Inquire – 1 – ATLA S0676 – us A.T.L.A. [073]

BIBEL UND KIND – (Lacking some pages) – v2-5. 1955-58 – 1r – 1 – ATLA S0729 – us A.T.L.A. [073]

BIBEL UND KIRCHE – 1947-88 (complete) – 5r – 1 – ATLA S0674 – us A.T.L.A. [073]

BIBEL UND NATUR IN DER HARMONIE IHRER OFFENBARUNGEN / Zollmann, Theodor – Hamburg: Agentur des Rauhen Hauses, 1869 – 1mf – 9 – 0-8370-9358-9 – 1986-3358 – us A.T.L.A. [210]

BIBEL UND NATUR; VORLESUNGEN UEBER DIE MOSAISCHE URGESCHICHTE UND IHR VERHAELTNISS ZU DEN ERGEBNISSEN DER NATURFORSCHUNG / Reusch, Franz Heinrich – 1876 – 1 – us A.T.L.A. [240]

BIBEL UND PFLUG – (Lacking some issues) – 1954-67; 1970-89 – 8r – 1 – ATLA S0431 – us A.T.L.A. [240]

BIBEL UND WISSENSCHAFT : GRUNDSAETZE UND DEREN ANWENDUNG AUF DIE PROBLEME DER BIBLISCHEN URGESCHICHTE, HEXAEMERON, SINTFLUT, VOELKERTAFEL, SPRACHVERWIRRUNG... / Schoepfer, Aemilian – (Includes bibliographical references) – Brixen:Buchh. des Katholisch-Politischen Pressvereins, 1896 – 1mf – 9 – 0-8370-5133-9 – 1985-3133 – us A.T.L.A. [220]

DIE BIBELEXEGESE DER JUEDISCHEN RELIGIONSPHILOSOPHEN DES MITTELALTERS VOR MAIMUNI / Bacher, Wilhelm – Budapest, 1892 – 4mf – 8 – ne Slangenburg [220]

DIE BIBELEXEGESE DER JUEDISCHEN RELIGIONSPHILOSOPHEN DES MITTELALTERS VOR MAIMUNI / Bacher, Wilhelm – Strassburg. 1892. BJ-33-6 1 – 9 – ne IDC [270]

DIE BIBELEXEGESE MOSES MAIMUNIS / Bacher, Wilhelm – Budapest, 1896 – 4mf – 8 – ne Slangenburg [220]

DIE BIBELFRAGE IN DER GEGENWART: FUENF VORTRAEGE / Klostermann, D et al – Berlin: Fr. Zillesen, 1905. 1mf – 9 – us A.T.L.A. [240]

BIBELOT – (Reprint of poetry and prose). v. 1-21. 1895-1925. All pub – 1,5,6 – us Princeton Micro [800]

DER BIBEL'SCHE ORIENT : EINE ZEITSCHRIFT IN ZWANGLOSEN HEFTEN – 1 – $95.00 – us UPA [260]

BIBELSTUDIEN : BEITRAEGE, ZUMEIST AUS DEN PAPYRI UND INSCHRIFTEN, ZUR GESCHICHTE DER SPRACHE, DES SCHRIFTTUMS UND DER RELIGION DES HELLENISTISCHEN JUDENTUMS UND DES URCHRISTENTUMS / Deissmann, Gustav Adolf – (Includes bibliographical references and index) – Marburg: N G Elwert, 1895 – 1mf – 9 – 0-8370-9373-2 – 1986-3373 – us A.T.L.A. [220]

BIBELWORT UND BIBELWISSENSCHAFT / Walther, Ernst – Berlin: Ernst Sieg. Mittler, 1903. 1 fiche – 9 – us A.T.L.A. [240]

BIBERACHER TAGBLATT *see* ANZEIGER VOM OBERLAND

BIBERACHER UNTERHALTUNGSBLATT – Biberach, 1863-1921 – 5r – 1 – Inquire at Mikrofilmarchiv for details – gw Misc Inst [072]

BIBLE : DEREK HA-QODESH SIUE BIBLIA SACRA – (In Hebrew) – Hamburg. 3pts. 1587 – 28mf – 9 – H-8433/1 – ne IDC [220]

BIBLE – Dutch. 1560. Inhoudende dat Oude ende Nieuwe Testament. Emden, Nic. Biestkens v. Diest. 1560. BME-326 1 – 9 – ne IDC [240]

BIBLE – Dutch. 1568. Inhoudende dat Oude ende Nieuwe Testament. Emden, Nic. Biestkens van Diest. 1568. BME-327 1 – 9 – ne IDC [240]

BIBLE – Dutch. 1579. Inhoudende dat Oude ende Nieuwe Testament. Harlingen, P. v. Putten, na de Copie v. Nic. Biestkens van Diest. 1579. BME-357 1 – 9 – ne IDC [240]

BIBLE – Dutch. 1582. Inhoudende dat Oude ende Nieuwe Testament. Haerlinghen, P. v. Putten. 1582. BME-358 1 – 9 – ne IDC [240]

BIBLE – Dutch. 1598. Dat is De Boecken der heyligher Schriftuer, uytten oirspronckelijcken Hebreuschen ende Grieckschen ghetrouwelick verduytschet. Schotlandt bij Danswijck, Krijn Vermeulen, de jonghe. 1598. BME-329 1 – 9 – ne IDC [240]

BIBLE – Dutch. 1598. Inhoudende dat Oude ende Nieuwe Testament. Harlingen, P. Sebastiaenzs. 1598. BME-328 1 – 9 – ne IDC [240]

BIBLE – Indonesian. Alkitab. 1960. SE-3479-1 – 9 – ne IDC [220]

BIBLE – Javanese. Kitab sutji. 1961. SE-4913-1 – 9 – ne IDC [220]

BIBLE – N. T. English. 1865. "A Baptist Translation" (the Common English Version). Publ. by the American Bible Union. 490p – 1 – us Baptist [240]

BIBLE : NEW TESTAMENT. GALATIANS. EPISTOLA PAVLI AD GALATAS, ITEM SEX PRIMARIA CAPITA CHRISTIANAE... – Heidelbergae, 1583 – 1mf – 9 – H-8438/1 – ne IDC [220]

BIBLE – N.T. Student's chronological New Testament – 1 – 13.58 – us Baptist [240]

BIBLE / Smith, William Robertson – (The Encyclopaedia Britannica, v. 3, 1878, p. 634-648) – 9 – us A.T.L.A. [220]

BIBLE – Tae'. Sura' Madatu. 1960. SE-11,256-1 – 9 – ne IDC [220]

BIBLE : YITHBARAK HA-ME'IR ME-'ISHON, ... BIBLIA RABBINICA, WITH TARGUMS AND COMMENTARIES BY RASHI, IBN EZRA, KIMHI ET OTHERS – Venice. 4v. 1548 – 54mf – 9 – H-8406/1 – ne IDC [220]

THE BIBLE : A MISSIONARY BOOK / Horton, Robert Forman – Edinburgh: Oliphant Anderson & Ferrier; New York: Pilgrim Press [distributor, 1908?] – 1mf – 9 – 0-8370-6066-4 – 1986-0066 – us A.T.L.A. [220]

THE BIBLE : A SCIENTIFIC REVELATION / Adams, Charles Coffin – (Spine title: The Bible scientific. Includes index) – New York: James Pott, 1882 – 1mf – 9 – 0-8370-2040-9 – 1985-0040 – us A.T.L.A. [220]

BIBLE: A SCIENTIFIC REVELATION / Adams, Charles Coffin – New York: James Pott, 1882. 1 fiche – 9 – us A.T.L.A. [240]

BIBLE ADVOCATE – v. 1-4. 1846-1848 – 1 – us UMI [240]

THE BIBLE ADVOCATE – Montreal: Montreal Auxiliary Bible Society, 1837-1838 – 9 – cn C.I.H.M. [220]

THE BIBLE AMONG THE NATIONS 1 : A STUDY OF THE GREAT TRANSLATIONS / Beardslee, John Walter – Chicago: Fleming H Revell, 1899 – 1mf – 9 – 0-8370-2221-5 – 1985-0221 – us A.T.L.A. [220]

BIBLE AMONG THE NATIONS: THE GREAT TRANSLATIONS / Beardslee, John Walter – Chicago: Revell, 1899. 1 fiche – 9 – us A.T.L.A. [220]

THE BIBLE: AN OUTGROWTH OF THEOCRATIC LIFE / Simon, David Worthington – Edinburgh: T.&T. Clark, 1886. 1 fiche – 9 – us A.T.L.A. [240]

THE BIBLE AND CRITICISM : FOUR LECTURES / Rainy, Robert – London: Hodder & Stoughton, 1878 – 1mf – 9 – 0-8370-4828-1 – 1985-2828 – us A.T.L.A. [220]

BIBLE AND FILIAL PIETY (CCC194) = SHENG-CHING YU CHUNG-KUO HSIAO-TAO / Hsu, Sung-shih – (In Chinese) – Hong Kong: Baptist Press, 1970 – 1r – 1 – 1984-B500 – us A.T.L.A. [220]

THE BIBLE AND ITS LITERATURE / Robinson, Edward – 1841 – 9 – us A.T.L.A. [240]

THE BIBLE AND MEN OF LEARNING / Mathews, James McFarlane – New York: Daniel Fanshaw, 1855. 1 fiche – 9 – us A.T.L.A. [240]

THE BIBLE AND MODERN CRITICISM / Anderson, Robert – 5th ed. 1905 – 9 – us A.T.L.A. [240]

THE BIBLE AND MODERN INVESTIGATION: THREE LECTURES DELIVERED TO CLERGY AT THE REQUEST OF THE BISHOP; WITH AN ADDRESS ON THE AUTHORITY OF HOLY SCRIPTURES / Wace, Henry – 1903 – 9 – us A.T.L.A. [240]

BIBLE AND MODERN THOUGHT / Birks, Thomas Rawson – Cincinnati: Poe & Hitchcock, 1867. 1 fiche – 9 – us A.T.L.A. [240]

BIBLE AND SCIENCE : THE BIBLE AND OTHER ANCIENT LITERATURE IN THE NINETEENTH CENTURY / Townsend, Luther Tracy – (Originally issued in 1874 under title: The Bible and science, and in 1883 under title: The Bible in the light of modern science) – New York: Chautauqua Press, C L S C Dept, 1889, c1884 – 1mf – 9 – 0-8370-5657-8 – 1985-3657 – us A.T.L.A. [210]

BIBLE AND SCIENCE / Brunton, Thomas Lauder – London: Macmillan, 1881.1 fiche – 9 – us A.T.L.A. [240]

THE BIBLE AND SLAVERY : IN WHICH THE ABRAHAMIC AND MOSAIC DISCIPLINE IS CONSIDERED IN CONNECTION WITH THE MOST ANCIENT FORMS OF SLAVERY, AND THE PAULINE CODE ON SLAVERY AS RELATED TO ROMAN SLAVERY AND THE DISCIPLINE OF THE APOSTOLIC CHURCHES / Elliott, Charles – Cincinnati: L. Swormstedt & A. Poe for the Methodist Episcopal Church, 1857 – 1mf – us A.T.L.A. [220]

THE BIBLE AND THE PRAYER BOOK: MISTRANSLATIONS, MUTILATIONS AND ERRORS WITH REFERENCES TO PAGANISM / Dixon, Benjamin Homer – Toronto: Toronto Willard Tract Depository, 1895. 02644. (Pre-1900 Canadiana) – 9 – cn C.I.H.M. [971]

"THE BIBLE AND THE SQUARE": BEING A MASONIC MIRROR AND GUIDE, CONTAINING SCRIPTURAL AND MASONIC TEACHINGS, TO WHICH IS ADDED A SYMBOLIC CHART, WITH FULL EXPLANATIONS: A VALUABLE HANDBOOK TO THE CRAFT / Akerman, William – Printed and pub. by Wm. Akerman, Montreal, 1875. 03243. (Pre-1900 Canadiana) – 9 – cn C.I.H.M. [360]

THE BIBLE AND WOMAN: A CRITICAL AND COMPREHENSIVE EXAMINATION OF THE TEACHING OF THE SCRIPTURES CONCERNING THE POSITION AND SPHERE OF WOMAN / Hayden, M P – 1902 – 9 – us A.T.L.A. [240]

THE BIBLE AND WOMAN SUFFRAGE / Hooker, John – 1874 – 9 – us A.T.L.A. [240]

THE BIBLE AS LITERATURE / Moulton, Richard Green et al – (Includes bibliographical references) – New York:Thomas Y. Crowell, c1896 – 1mf – 9 – 0-8370-3445-0 – 1985-1445 – us A.T.L.A. [220]

THE BIBLE BY COVERDALE 1805 : REMARKS ON THE TITLES, THE YEAR OF PUBLICATION, THE PRELIMINARY, THE WATER-MARKS, ETC WITH FACSIMILES / Fry, Francis – (Includes bibliographical references) – London: Willis & Sotheran; Bristol: Lasbury, 1867 – 1mf – 9 – 0-8370-9469-0 – 1986-3469 – us A.T.L.A. [220]

BIBLE (CCC289) / Surdam, T Janet – (In Chinese) – 1st ed. Hong Kong: Council on Christian Literature for Overseas Chinese, 1960 – 1r – 1 – 1984-6628 – us A.T.L.A. [220]

BIBLE CHARACTERS / Reade, Charles L – New York: Harper, 1889. 1 fiche – 9 – us A.T.L.A. [240]

BIBLE CHARACTERS. AHITHOPHEL TO NEHEMIAH / Whyte, Alexander – New York: Fleming H Revell, 1899 – 1mf – 9 – 0-8370-9670-7 – 1986-3670 – us A.T.L.A. [220]

THE BIBLE CHRISTIAN : MONTREAL UNITARIAN SOCIETY – Montreal, Canada. v2 n2. jan 1845-v5 n12. dec 1848 – 1r – 1 – Can$40.00 – cn Can Microfilming [240]

BIBLE CHRISTIAN MAGAZINE : THE ARMINIAN MAGAZINE... – (Cont. as: The Bible Christian Magazine...Shebbear, 1829-1850. N.S., V.1-7; S.III, V.1-15; Missing: 1822, V.1; 1823, V.2(p. 37-72); 1825, V.4; 1828, V.7; N.S., 1829-1832, V.1-3; 1832, V.4(p. 195-198); 1833, V.5(p. 105-108); S.III, 1826-1838, V.1-3) – Stoke-Damarel, 1822-1828. V.1-7 – 96mf – 9 – MP-350/1 – ne IDC [240]

THE BIBLE CHRISTIAN MAGAZINE *see* THE ARMINIAN MAGAZINE, ...

Bible Christians *see*
- CONFERENCE. MINUTES ... 1819-1850
- A DIGEST OF THE RULES, REGULATIONS AND USAGES OF THE PEOPLE DENOMINATED BIBLE CHRISTIANS,...

THE BIBLE CHRISTIANS : THEIR ORIGIN AND HISTORY (1815-1900) / Bourne, FW – London, 1905. vii/568p – 7mf – 9 – ne IDC [240]

BIBLE CHRONOLOGY CAREFULLY UNFOLDED... / Goodenow, Smith Bartlett – New York: Fleming H Revell, 1896 – 1mf – 9 – 0-8370-3336-5 – 1985-1336 – us A.T.L.A. [220]

BIBLE CHRONOLOGY FROM ABRAHAM TO THE CHRISTIAN ERA / Auchincloss, William Stuart – New York: D van Nostrand, 1905 – 1mf – 9 – 0-8370-2126-X – 1985-0126 – us A.T.L.A. [220]

BIBLE CHRONOLOGY VINDICATED BY ITS OWN INTERNAL EVIDENCE : DATES TABULATED / Brown, Oliver May – (Includes chronological tables) – Cleveland: Christian Messenger Publ Co, c1901 – 1mf – 9 – 0-8370-2479-X – 1985-0479 – us A.T.L.A. [220]

THE BIBLE COLLECTOR – v1-20. 1965-84 (complete) – 1r – 1 – ATLA S0385 – us A.T.L.A. [240]

BIBLE CRITICISM AND THE AVERAGE MAN / Johnston, Howard Agnew – (Includes index) – New York: Fleming H Revell, 1902 – 1mf – 9 – 0-8370-3790-5 – 1985-1790 – us A.T.L.A. [220]

BIBLE DIFFICULTIES AND HOW TO MEET THEM / Atkins, Frederick A – New York: Revell, 1891. 1 fiche – 9 – us A.T.L.A. [220]

BIBLE DIFFICULTIES AND THEIR ALLEVIATIVE INTERPRETATION / MacArthur, Robert Stuart – New York: E.B. Treat, 1899. 1 fiche – 9 – us A.T.L.A. [240]

BIBLE DOCTRINE OF INSPIRATION EXPLAINED / Manly, Basil – New York: A.C. Armstrong, 1888. 1 fiche – 9 – us A.T.L.A. [240]

THE BIBLE DOCTRINE OF MAN, OR, THE ANTHROPOLOGY AND PSYCHOLOGY OF SCRIPTURE / Laidlow, John – Edinburgh: T. & T. Clark, 1895. 1 fiche – 9 – us A.T.L.A. [240]

THE BIBLE DOCTRINE OF THE SOUL : AN ANSWER TO THE QUESTION, IS THE POPULAR CONCEPTION OF THE SOUL THAT OF HOLY SCRIPTURE? / Ives, Charles Linnaeus – (Includes index and appendix containing biblical citations) – New Haven, CT: Judd & White, 1873 – 1mf – 9 – 0-8370-3738-7 – 1985-1738 – us A.T.L.A. [220]

THE BIBLE DOCTRINE OF THE SOUL : OR, MAN'S NATURE AND DESTINY AS REVEALED / Ives, Charles Linnaeus – (Includes appendixes of biblical references) – [rev ed]. Philadelphia: Claxton, Remsen, & Haffelfinger, 1878, c1877 – 1mf – 9 – 0-8370-3739-5 – 1985-1739 – us A.T.L.A. [220]

BIBLE DOCTRINE OF THE SOUL, OR, MAN'S NATURE AND DESTINY AS REVEALED / Ives, Charles L – Philadelphia: Claxton, Rem. and Haf., 1878. 1 fiche – 9 – us A.T.L.A. [240]

LA BIBLE EN FRANCE : OU, LES TRADUCTIONS FRANCAISES DES SAINTES ECRITURES / Petavel, Emmanuel – (Includes bibliographical references & index) – Paris: Librairie Francais et Etrangere, 1864 – 1mf – 9 – 0-8370-4714-5 – 1985-2714 – us A.T.L.A. [220]

BIBLE ENGLISH / Davies, Thomas Lewis Owen – Chapters on old and disused expressions in the Authorized version of the Scriptures and the Book of Common Prayer. 1875 – 1 – us A.T.L.A. [240]

BIBLE ENGLISH: CHAPTERS ON OLD AND DISUSED EXPRESSIONS IN THE AV / Davies, J Lewis O – London: George Bell, 1875. 1 fiche – 9 – us A.T.L.A. [240]

BIBLE ET TERRE SAINTE – 1(1957)-166(1974) – 221mf – 9 – Dfl774.00 – ne Slangenburg [073]

BIBLE ET VIE CHRETIENNE – 1(1953)-83(1968) – 170mf – 9 – Dfl595.00 – ne Slangenburg [073]

BIBLE EXAMINER – 1843 – 1 – us UMI [240]

BIBLE EXAMINER – (Lacking: v1-2. v16-19) – v3-23. 1848-63; 1876-80 – 2r – 1 – ATLA S0327 – us A.T.L.A. [240]

A BIBLE HAND-BOOK, THEOLOGICALLY ARRANGED / Holliday, Fernandes C – 1869 – 9 – us A.T.L.A. [240]

BIBLE HERALD *see* BRITISH HERALD

BIBLE HISTORY / Spalding, Benedict Joseph – New York: Schwartz, Kirwin, 1883. 1 fiche – 9 – us A.T.L.A. [240]

BIBLE HISTORY OF THE NEGRO / Morrisey, Richard Alburtus – Nashville, 1915 – 1r – 1 – us Ross [975]

THE BIBLE IN BRAZIL : COLPORTER EXPERIENCES / Tucker, Hugh Clarence – (Includes index) – New York: Young People's Missionary Movt of the US and Canada, c1902 – 1mf – 9 – 0-8370-6708-1 – 1986-0708 – us A.T.L.A. [240]

THE BIBLE IN OUR PUBLIC SCHOOLS : A SERMON PREACHED BEFORE THE PRESBYTERY OF LYONS, N.Y. SEP 13, 1870 IN WHICH IS FOUND A BRIEF REPLY TO DR. SPEAR'S ARGUMENT FOR EXCLUDING THE BIBLE FROM OUR PUBLIC SCHOOLS / Rudd, George R – Lyons, NY: Office of the Republican, 1870 – 1mf – 9 – 0-8370-7579-3 – 1986-1579 – us A.T.L.A. [370]

THE BIBLE IN PUBLIC SCHOOLS : ADDRESS UPON A RESOLUTION TO PETITION THE BOARD OF EDUCATION TO EXCLUDE THE BIBLE FROM PUBLIC SCHOOLS / Kilgore, Damon Y – 2nd ed. Philadelphia: The League, [ca 1875] – 1mf – 9 – 0-8370-7552-1 – 1986-1552 – us A.T.L.A. [370]

THE BIBLE IN PUBLIC SCHOOLS : A SERMON / Spear, Samuel Thayer – New York: Wm C Martin, 1870 – 1mf – 9 – 0-8370-7589-0 – 1986-1589 – us A.T.L.A. [370]

THE BIBLE IN SPAIN : OR, THE JOURNEYS, ADVENTURES, AND IMPRISONMENTS OF AN ENGLISHMAN IN AN ATTEMPT TO CIRCULATE THE SCRIPTURES IN THE PENINSULA / Borrow, George Henry – (Includes bibliographical references, appendix, glossary and index) – New York: G P Putnam, 1899 – 2mf – 9 – 0-8370-6164-4 – 1986-0164 – us A.T.L.A. [910]

THE BIBLE IN THE CHURCH / Westcott, Brooke Foss – London: Macmillan, 1885.1 fiche – 9 – us A.T.L.A. [240]

THE BIBLE IN THE COMMON SCHOOLS : SUPERIOR COURT OF CINCINNATI IN GENERAL TERM, FEBRUARY, 1870: JOHN D. MINOR ET ALS. VERSUS THE BOARD OF EDUCATION OF THE CITY OF CINCINNATI ET ALS. / Storer, Bellamy – Cincinnati: Robert Clarke, 1870 – 1mf – 9 – 0-8370-8791-0 – 1986-2791 – us A.T.L.A. [370]

BIBLE IN THE LIGHT OF NATURE, OF MAN, AND OF GOD / Chisholm, Alexander – Inverness: A. Chisholm, 1891. 1 fiche – 9 – us A.T.L.A. [240]

THE BIBLE IN THE LIGHT OF NATURE, OF MAN, AND OF GOD : VOL 1: TO THE CALL OF ABRAHAM ALSO IN ITS ESSENTIAL RELATIONS TO THE RELIGIONS OF THE WORLD / Chisholm, Alexander – (No more published) – Inverness: A Chisholm, 1891 – 1mf – 9 – 0-8370-2654-7 – 1985-0654 – us A.T.L.A. [220]

THE BIBLE IN THE NINETEENTH CENTURY / Carpenter, Joseph Estlin – 1903 – 9 – us A.T.L.A. [240]

THE BIBLE IN THE PUBLIC SCHOOLS : OPINIONS OF INDIVIDUALS AND OF THE PRESS, AND JUDICIAL DECISIONS – New York: J W Schermerhorn, 1870 – 1mf – 9 – 0-8370-8543-8 – 1986-2543 – us A.T.L.A. [370]

THE BIBLE IN THE WORLD'S EDUCATION / Warren, Henry White – New York: Hunt & Eaton, 1893. 1 fiche – 9 – us A.T.L.A. [240]

BIBLE INDEX AND CHRISTIAN SENTINEL – Toronto: [s.n., 1881?-188- or 19–] – 9 – cn C.I.H.M. [220]

THE BIBLE INDICATOR – Owen Sound, Ont.: [s.n., 1868?-18– or 19–] – 9 – cn C.I.H.M. [220]

THE BIBLE: ITS EVIDENCES, CHARACTERISTICS, AND EFFECTS: A LECTURE / Perry, Charles – Oxford: Clarendon Press, 1873. 1 fiche – 9 – us A.T.L.A. [240]

BIBLE: ITS MEANING AND SUPREMACY / Farrar, Frederic William – New York: Longmans, Green, 1899.1 fiche – 9 – us A.T.L.A. [240]

THE BIBLE, ITS ORIGIN AND NATURE : SEVEN LECTURES / Dods, Marcus – New York: Charles Scribner, 1905 – 1mf – 9 – 0-8370-9463-1 – 1986-3463 – us A.T.L.A. [220]

THE BIBLE: ITS REVELATION, INSPIRATION AND EVIDENCE / Robson, John – London: Hodder & Stoughton, 1883. 1 fiche – 9 – us A.T.L.A. [240]

BIBLE LEAGUE ESSAYS IN BIBLE DEFENCE AND EXPOSITION / Leavitt, John McDowell – New York: Bible League Book Co, 1909, c1908 – 1mf – 9 – 0-8370-4369-7 – 1985-2369 – us A.T.L.A. [220]

BIBLE LORE / Gray, James Comper – New York: Dodd & Mead, 1870. 1 fiche – 9 – us A.T.L.A. [240]

BIBLE MANNERS AND CUSTOMS / Mackie, George M – New York: Fleming H. Revell, (1888). 1 fiche – 9 – us A.T.L.A. [240]

BIBLE MINIATURES: CHARACTER SKETCHES OF...HEROES AND HEROINES OF HOLY WRIT / Wells, Amos Russell – New York: Fleming H. Revell, 1909. 1 fiche. 8370-5777-9 – 9 – us A.T.L.A. [240]

BIBLE MONTHS, OR, THE SEASONS IN PALESTINE: AS ILLUSTRATIVE OF SCRIPTURE / Groser, William H – London: Sunday School Union, 1864. 1 fiche – 9 – us A.T.L.A. [240]

BIBLE MORALISEE – (Bodley Mss, Mss 270b. Sc 2937 Folios 1v-224v c.1250- French) – 14 – uk Microform Academic [240]

BIBLE. N.T – Batak (Karo). Padan si mbaru e me kap kitab kerina si nurikentja kerna Tuhanta Jesus Kristus. 1961. SE-3780-1 – 9 – ne IDC [220]

BIBLE. N.T – Batak (Toba). Padan na Imbaru. 1961. SE-4914-1 – 9 – ne IDC [220]

BIBLE. N.T – Dutch. Testament (Dat nieuwe) ons Heeren Jesu Christi,beschreuen door dat ingheuen des heyligen Gheest. 1559. BME-331-1 – 9 – ne IDC [240]

BIBLE. N.T – Dutch. Testament (Dat nieuwe) ons liefs Heeren Jesu Christi, dwelck hy wt den hoogen Hemel hier beneden ghebracht heeft. Gedr. na de copye van Mattheus Jacobszoon. 1558. BME-330-1 – 9 – ne IDC [240]

BIBLE. N.T – Dutch. Testament (Dat nieuwe) ons liefs Heeren Jesu Christi. Gedr. na de copie v. Nic. Biestkens, 1579. BME-335-1 – 9 – ne IDC [240]

BIBLE. N.T – Dutch. Testament (Dat nieuwe) ons liefs Heeren Jesu Christi. Haerlinghen, P. v. Putte, 1583. BME-336-1 – 9 – ne IDC [240]

BIBLE. N.T – Dutch. Testament (Dat nieuwe) ons liefs Heeren Jesu Christi, het welcke hy wt den hoogen Heemel. Gheprent int Jaer ons Heeren MDLX. BME-332-1 – 9 – ne IDC [240]

BIBLE. N.T – Dutch. Testament (Dat nieuwe) ons liefs Heeren Jesu Christi. Nu op't nieu. Ouersien, gecorrigeert, ende verbetert.Gedr. na de copie v. Nic. Biestkens. 1577. BME-334-1 – 9 – ne IDC [240]

BIBLE. N.T – Javanese. Kitab Sutji, Perdjandjian Anjar. 1960. SE-4916-1 – 9 – ne IDC [220]

BIBLE. N.T – Oloh Ngadju. 1955. SE-5044-1 – 9 – ne IDC [220]

BIBLE. N.T – Sundanese. Na Parandingu Bidi. 1961. SE-3685-1 – 9 – ne IDC [220]

BIBLE. N.T – Sundanese. Perdjangdjian Anjar.1962. SE-4091-1 – 9 – ne IDC [220]

BIBLE. N.T – Timor. 1961. SE-3987-1 – 9 – ne IDC [220]

BIBLE. N.T. ACTS – Indonesian. Kitab kissah Rasulrasul. 1959. SE-3435-1 – 9 – ne IDC [220]

THE BIBLE OF ST. MARK : ST. MARK'S CHURCH, THE ALTAR AND THRONE OF VENICE / Robertson, Alexander – London: G. Allen, 1898 – 2mf – us A.T.L.A. [220]

THE BIBLE OF THE REFORMATION : ITS TRANSLATORS AND THEIR WORK / Heaton, William James – (Includes bibliographical references) – London: Francis Griffiths, 1910 – 1mf – 9 – 0-8370-9154-3 – 1986-3154 – us A.T.L.A. [220]

THE BIBLE ON WOMEN'S PUBLIC SPEAKING / Eaton, Thomas Treadwell – 1895. 50p – 1 – $5.00 – us Baptist [400]

THE BIBLE ON WOMEN'S PUBLIC SPEAKING / Eaton, Thomas Treadwell – c.1895 – 9 – us A.T.L.A. [400]

BIBLE. O.T – Indonesian. Selections.1960. SE-10,864-1 – 9 – ne IDC [220]

BIBLE. O.T. ESTHER – (In Dutch) – Amsterdam, 1649 – 9 – BJ-43-43-1 – ne IDC [220]

BIBLE. O.T. ESTHER – Indonesian. 1959. SE-3480-1 – 9 – ne IDC [220]

BIBLE. O.T. EXODUS – Indonesian. 1959. SE-3504-1 – 9 – ne IDC [220]

BIBLE. O.T. EXODUS 1-15 – Indonesian. 1963. SE-10,452-1 – 9 – ne IDC [220]

BIBLE. O.T. JUDGES – Indonesian. Para Hakim; para pembebas umat Allah. 1959. SE-3222-1 – 9 – ne IDC [220]

BIBLE. O.T. MINOR PROPHETS. ENGLISH – With commentary, explanatory and practical. By Rev. E.E. Pusey.New York: Funk & Wagnalls, 1885. 2v – 1 – us U.W. Library [220]

BIBLE. O.T. PSALMS – Indonesian. 1947. SE-6061-1 – 9 – ne IDC [220]

BIBLE. O.T. PSALMS – Indonesian. Kitab Mazmur; njanjian pudji2an orang Israel. 1960. SE-3436-1 – 9 – ne IDC [220]

BIBLE. O.T. PSALMS – Indonesian. Kitab Sutji kitab Mazmur. 1960. SE-3877-1 – 9 – ne IDC [220]

BIBLE. O.T. RUTH – Indonesian. 1959. SE-2994-1 – 9 – ne IDC [220]

BIBLE OUTLINES : COMPREHENSIVE EPITOMES OF THE LEADING FEATURES OF THE BOOKS OF THE OLD AND NEW TESTAMENTS / Scott, W – London:Alfred Holness; Glasgow:R.L. Allan, [1879] – 1mf – 9 – 0-8370-5196-7 – 1985-3196 – us A.T.L.A. [220]

BIBLE PICTURE BOOK / Holkham Hall. Norfolk. England – 14th century. Holkham Ms 666 – 14 – uk Microform Academic [240]

Bible Presbyterian Church. General Synod *see* MINUTES, 1938-1955

Bible Presbyterian Church. General Synod. Collingswood *see* MINUTES, 1956-1985

Bible Presbyterian Church. General Synod. Columbus *see* MINUTES, 1956-1960

BIBLE PROBLEMS AND THE NEW MATERIAL FOR THEIR SOLUTION : A PLEA FOR THOROUGHNESS OF INVESTIGATION ADDRESSED TO CHURCHMEN AND SCHOLARS / Cheyne, Thomas Kelly – New York: Putnam's, 1904 – 1mf – 9 – 0-8370-2641-5 – 1985-0641 – us A.T.L.A. [220]

BIBLE READERS GUIDE – 1955-61 – 1 – 17.22 – us Baptist [240]

THE BIBLE READERS' MANUAL, OR, AIDS TO BIBLICAL STUDY FOR STUDENTS OF THE HOLY SCRIPTURES / ed by Wright, Charles Henry Hamilton – (Includes indexes) – London: William Collins; New York: International Bible Agency, [1892?] – 1mf – 9 – 0-8370-9755-X – 1986-3755 – us A.T.L.A. [220]

BIBLE, SCIENCE, AND FAITH / Zahm, John Augustine – Baltimore: John Murphy, 1894. 1 fiche – 9 – us A.T.L.A. [240]

BIBLE SOCIETIES AND THE BAPTISTS / Bitting, C C – 1897 – 1 – 5.00 – us Baptist [240]

BIBLE SOCIETY RECORDER – Toronto: Upper Canada Bible Society, [1870?-1892] – 9 – cn C.I.H.M. [220]

BIBLE STUDENT – Beamsville, CN. 1904-13 – 1r – 1 – cn Commonwealth Micro [073]

BIBLE STUDIES = BIBELSTUDIEN : CONTRIBUTIONS CHIEFLY FROM PAPYRI AND INSCRIPTIONS TO THE HISTORY OF THE LANGUAGE, THE LITERATURE, AND THE RELIGION OF HELLENISTIC JUDAISM AND PRIMITIVE CHRISTIANITY / Deissmann, Gustav Adolf – (Includes bibliographical references and indexes) – Edinburgh: T & T Clark, 1901 – 1mf – 9 – 0-8370-9372-4 – 1986-3372 – us A.T.L.A. [220]

BIBLE STUDIES : READINGS IN THE EARLY BOOKS OF THE OLD TESTAMENT, WITH A FAMILIAR COMMENT / Beecher, Henry Ward; ed by Howard, John R – New York: Fords, Howard, & Hulbert, 1893 – 1mf – 9 – 0-8370-2234-7 – 1985-0234 – us A.T.L.A. [220]

BIBLE TEACHINGS IN NATURE / Macmillan, Hugh – London; New York: Macmillan, 1867 – 1mf – 9 – 0-8370-9295-7 – 1986-3295 – us A.T.L.A. [210]

THE BIBLE, THE BAPTIST AND THE BOARD SYSTEM / Scarboro, J A – 1904 – 1 – 16.24 – us Baptist [240]

THE BIBLE, THE CHURCH, AND THE REASON / Briggs, Charles Augustus – New York: Scribner's, 1892. 1 fiche – 9 – us A.T.L.A. [240]

THE BIBLE, THE MISSAL, AND THE BREVIARY, OR, RITUALISM SELF-ILLUSTRATED / Lewis, George – Edinburgh: T. & T. Clark, 1853. viii,809p. 2 fiches – 9 – us A.T.L.A. [240]

BIBLE THEOLOGY AND MODERN THOUGHT / Townsend, Luther Tracy – Boston: Lee & Shephard; New York: Charles T Dillingham, 1883, c1882 – 1mf – 9 – 0-8370-5604-7 – 1985-3604 – us A.T.L.A. [210]

BIBLE TRANSLATING / Nida, E – London, 1961 – 8mf – 8 – ne Slangenburg [220]

THE BIBLE UNDER TRIAL: IN VIEW OF PRESENT-DAY ASSAULTS ON HOLY SCRIPTURE / Orr, James – New York: A.C. Armstrong, 1907. 1 fiche – 9 – us A.T.L.A. [240]

THE BIBLE VERIFIED / Archibald, Andrew Webster – Philadelphia: Presbyterian Bd of Publ & Sabbath-School Work, c1890 – 1mf – 9 – 0-8370-2111-1 – 1985-0111 – us A.T.L.A. [220]

THE BIBLE VERSUS INFIDELITY / Adams, Henry – St. John, N.B.: E.J. Armstrong, 1895. 06152. (Pre-1900 Canadiana) – 9 – cn C.I.H.M. [240]

THE BIBLE, WHO WROTE IT? / Pendleton, CS – v1; The English Bible, how did we get it?, v1; The English Bible; how did we get it?, v2. 308p – 1 – $10.78 – us Baptist [240]

BIBLE WORK IN BIBLE LANDS : OR, EVENTS IN THE HISTORY OF THE SYRIA MISSION / Bird, Isaac – Philadelphia: Presbyterian Board of Publ, c1872 – 1mf – 9 – 0-8370-6019-2 – 1986-0019 – us A.T.L.A. [240]

BIBLE'S AUTHORITY SUPPORTED BY THE BIBLE'S HISTORY / Gauss, J H – St. Louis: Buxton & Skinner, 1896. 1 fiche – 9 – us A.T.L.A. [240]

THE BIBLE'S AUTHORITY SUPPORTED BY THE BIBLE'S HISTORY : IN FOUR CHAPTERS / Gauss, J H – St Louis: Buxton & Skinner, 1896 – 1mf – 9 – 0-8370-3234-2 – 1985-1234 – us A.T.L.A. [220]

THE BIBLES OF ENGLAND : A PLAIN ACCOUNT FOR PLAIN PEOPLE OF THE PRINCIPAL VERSIONS OF THE BIBLE IN ENGLISH / Edgar, Andrew – (Includes appendixes on Scottish versions, theocracy and the word mass) – London: Alexander Gardner, 1889 – 1mf – 9 – 0-8370-3027-7 – 1985-1027 – us A.T.L.A. [220]

BIBLES OF ENGLAND: A PLAIN ACCOUNT FOR PLAIN PEOPLE / Edgar, Andrew – London: Alexander Gardner, 1889.1 fiche – 9 – us A.T.L.A. [240]

BIBLES, PRAYER-BOOKS, AND DEVOTIONS FOR SOLDIERS DURING WORLD WAR 1 PAMPHLET COLLECTION – 1914-1919 – 10r – 1 – CSUXANL5346-B – us Hoover Inst Photo [200]

THE BIBLE-WHENCE AND WHAT? / Westbrook, Richard Brodhead – Philadelphia: J.B. Lippincott, 1882. 1 fiche – 9 – us A.T.L.A. [240]

BIBLIA *see* AMERICAN ANTIQUARIAN AND ORIENTAL JOURNAL

BIBLIA. A.T. (SIECLE 13) – Calahorra – 1r – 5,6 – sp Cultura [220]

LA BIBLIA DE GUADALUPE. UN INTERESANTE CODICE DESCONOCIDO (1) / Zamora, Hermenegildo – Madrid: CSIC, 1967 – 1 – sp Bibl Santa Ana [020]

BIBLIA FILIPINA : PRIMERA PIEDRA PARA UN GENESIS CIENTIFICO EXPUESTO SEGUN LAS RECTIFICACIONES DE JESUS / Aglipay y Labayan, Gregorio – (No more published?) – Barcelona: Antonio Virgili, 1908 – 1mf – 9 – 0-8370-9361-9 – 1986-3361 – us A.T.L.A. [210]

BIBLIA HOJE – Rio de Janeiro: Publicacao de Tempo e Presenca Editora LTDA, n4 (1971); n32,36 (feb, nov 1975); n37 (feb 1976); n40-46 (jul 1976-may 1978); n48-52 (sep 1978-mar 1979) – 1r – us Res Libr [072]

BIBLIA LATINA CUM GLOSSA ORDINARIA – Strassburg: Adolph Rusch, c1480 – 137mf – 8 – ne Slangenburg [220]

BIBLIA LATINA DE GUTENBERG (I. MAGUNTIAE, J. GUTENBERG ANNO 1455) – Burgos – 1r – 5,6 – sp Cultura [220]

BIBLIA NATURAE; SIVE HISTORIA INSECTORUM / Swammerdam, Jan – Latin and Dutch in parallel colums. Z 219 2. 2 v. 1737-1738 – 8 – ne IDC [590]

BIBLIA RABBINICA CUM TARGUM ET COMMENTARIS RABBINORUM – Amsterdam v1-4 s.a. – 127mf – 8 – ne Slangenburg [270]

BIBLIA ROMANICA DE SAN PEDRO DE CARDENA (SIECLE 12) – Burgos – 1r – 5,6 – sp Cultura [220]
BIBLIA SACRA CUM GLOSSA ET EXPOSITIONIBUS / Lyra, Nicolaus de – (Tom 5: Matthaeus – Johannes. 45mf) – Lugduni, 1545 – 8 – ne Slangenburg [220]
BIBLIA SACRA CUM GLOSSA ET EXPOSITIONIBUS / Lyra, Nicolaus de – (Tom. 6: ad Romanos-Apocalypsis. 32mf) – Lugduni, 1545 – 8 – ne Slangenburg [220]
BIBLIA SACRA CUM GLOSSA ORDINARIA ET EXPOSITIONIBUS / Lyra, Nicolaus de – (Tom. 4: ISAIAS – Machabaeroum Libros. 54mf) – Lugduni, 1545 – 8 – ne Slangenburg [220]
BIBLIA SACRA CUM GLOSSA ORDINARIA ET POSTILLA / Lyra, Nicolaus de – (Tom. 3: Iob – Eccles. 49mf) – Lugduni, 1545 – 8 – ne Slangenburg [220]
BIBLIA SACRA CUM GLOSSIS, INTERLINEARI ET ORDINIARIA / Lyra, Nicolaus de – (Tom. 1. Pentateuch: 42mf; Tom. 2. – et expositionibus : Iosue-Esther: 36mf) – Lugduni, 1545 – 8 – ne Slangenburg [220]
BIBLIA SACRA CUM UNIVERSIS FRANC. : VATABLI ET VARIORUM INTERPRETUM ANNOTATIONIBUS – Parisiss. v.1-2. 1729-1745 – 92mf – 8 – ne Slangenburg [220]
BIBLIA SACRA HEBRAICE, CHALDAICE, GRAECE, LATINE / ed by Montanus, A – Antverpiae. v1-8. 1572 – 99mf – 8 – ne Slangenburg [220]
BIBLIA SACRA POLYGLOTTA / Brian Walton – (Vol. 1 t/m Vol. 6) – Londini, 1653-1657 – 328mf – 8 – ne Slangenburg [220]
BIBLIA SACRA REGIA... / Arias Montano, Benito – Amberes: Christof Plantinus, 1569 – 1 – sp Bibl Santa Ana [240]
BIBLIA SACRA VULG. ED. : ...CUM SCHOLIIS..J.MARIANAE, ET NOTATIONIBUS E. SA. – Antverpiae. v1-2. 1624 – 91mf – 8 – ne Slangenburg [220]
[BIBLIA SANCTI PETRI RODENSIS] – 10th-11th cent – us Res Libr [999]
BIBLIA (SIECLE 14) – Calahorra – 1r – 5,6 – sp Cultura [220]
BIBLIA (SIECLE 15) – Barcelona – 1r – 5,6 – sp Cultura [220]
BIBLIA VULGATA Y VETUS LATINA (SIECLE 9-10). DESPUES DE SU RESTAURACION – Madrid – 1r – 5,6 – sp Cultura [220]
Bibliander *see* DE RATIONE COMMUNI OMNIUM LINGUARUM ET LITTERARUM COMMENTARIUS
BIBLICA – 1(1920)-27(1946) – 214mf – 9 – Dfl749.00 – ne Slangenburg [073]
BIBLICA – Rome. v1-27. 1920-1946 – 214mf – 9 – ne IDC [220]
BIBLICAL AND LITERARY ESSAYS / Davidson, Andrew Bruce – 2nd ed. 1903 – 9 – us A.T.L.A. [240]
BIBLICAL AND LITERARY ESSAYS / Davidson, Andrew Bruce – New York: A.C. Armstrong, 1902. 1 fiche – 9 – us A.T.L.A. [220]
BIBLICAL AND PATRISTIC RELICS OF THE PALESTINIAN SYRIAC LITERATURE – Oxford v1-pt 9 1896 – 4mf – 8 – ne Slangenburg [220]
BIBLICAL AND SEMITIC STUDIES : CRITICAL AND HISTORICAL ESSAYS – New York: Scribner's, 1901 – 1mf – 9 – 0-8370-2334-3 – 1985-0334 – us A.T.L.A. [220]
BIBLICAL APOCALYPTICS / Terry, Milton Spenser – New York: Eaton & Mains, 1898. 513p. 2 fiches – 9 – us A.T.L.A. [240]
BIBLICAL CHRONOLOGY / Besse, Henry T – Syracuse: Wesleyan Methodist Publishing House, 1895. 1 fiche – 9 – us A.T.L.A. [220]
BIBLICAL COMMENTARY ON ST PAUL'S EPISTLES TO THE GALATIANS, EPHESIANS, COLOSSIANS, AND THESSALONIANS / Olshausen, Hermann – 1851 – 1 – us A.T.L.A. [240]
BIBLICAL CRITICISM AND MODERN THOUGHT : OR, THE PLACE OF THE OLD TESTAMENT DOCUMENTS IN THE LIFE OF TODAY / Jordan, William George – (Based on the Chancellor's Lectureship of Queen's University for 1906-1907. Includes bibliographical references and index) – Edinburgh: T & T Clark, 1909 – 1mf – 9 – 0-8370-3800-6 – 1985-1800 – us A.T.L.A. [220]
BIBLICAL EPOCHS / Hart, Burdett – Philadelphia: Presbyterian Board of Publ, 1896 – 1mf – 9 – 0-8370-3503-1 – 1985-1503 – us A.T.L.A. [220]
BIBLICAL ESCHATOLOGY / Hovey, Alvah – (Includes appendix & indexes) – Philadelphia: American Baptist Publ Soc, c1888 – 1mf – 9 – 0-8370-3677-1 – 1985-1677 – us A.T.L.A. [220]
BIBLICAL ESSAYS / Lightfoot, Joseph Barber – (Includes bibliographical references and indexes) – London; New York: Publ by the Trustees of the Lightfoot Fund: Macmillan, 1893 – 2mf – 9 – 0-8370-9400-3 – 1986-3400 – us A.T.L.A. [220]
BIBLICAL ESSAYS: EXEGETICAL STUDIES ON JOB, JONAH, EZEKIEL, PETER, APOCALYPSE / Wright, Charles Henry Hamilton – Edinburgh: T. & T. Clark, 1886. 1 fiche – 9 – us A.T.L.A. [220]
BIBLICAL FRAGMENTS FROM MOUNT SINAI / ed by Harris, James Rendel – (Text in Greek and Syriac; introduction in English) – London: C J Clay, 1890 – 1mf – 9 – 0-8370-9153-5 – 1986-3153 – us A.T.L.A. [220]
BIBLICAL HERMENEUTICS / Cellerier, Jacob Elisee – New York: Randolph, 1881. 1 fiche – 9 – us A.T.L.A. [240]
BIBLICAL INSPIRATION AND CHRIST / Vincent, Marvin Richardson – New York: A.D.F. Randolph, 1894.1 fiche – 9 – us A.T.L.A. [240]
BIBLICAL LITERATURE AND ITS BACKGROUNDS / Macarthur, John Robertson – New York, London: D. Appleton-Century Company, c1936. xix,528p. illus.maps. facsims – 1 – us U.W. Library [220]
BIBLICAL PSYCHOLOGY : IN FOUR PARTS / Forster, Jonathan Langstaff; ed by Forster, Henry L – (Includes index) – London:Longmans, Green, 1873 – 1mf – 9 – 0-8370-3165-6 – 1985-1165 – us A.T.L.A. [220]
BIBLICAL RECORDER – North Carolina. 1834-1991 – 1 – $3,798.92 – us Baptist [240]
BIBLICAL RECORDER AND SOUTHERN WATCHMAN – South Carolina. 3 Mar 1838-26 Dec 1840 – 1 – 13.65 – us Baptist [240]
BIBLICAL REPERTORY : A COLLECTION OF TRACTS IN BIBLICAL LITERATURE – v1-4. 1825-28 (complete) – 2r – 1 – ATLA S0205 – us A.T.L.A. [240]
BIBLICAL REPERTORY AND PRINCETON REVIEW – (Lacking some pages) – v1-43. 1829-71 – 13r – 1 – ATLA S0210 – us A.T.L.A. [240]
THE BIBLICAL REPERTORY AND PRINCETON REVIEW : INDEX – 1825-68 (complete) – 1r – 1 – ATLA S0209 – us A.T.L.A. [240]
BIBLICAL REPOSITORY AND CLASSICAL REVIEW – v1 no 1-12; v2 no 1-12; v3 no 1-6. 1831-50 (complete) – 9r – 1 – ATLA S0219 – us A.T.L.A. [240]
BIBLICAL RESEARCHES IN PALESTINE / Robinson, Edward – 3v. 1874 – 9 – us A.T.L.A. [240]
THE BIBLICAL REVIEW – v1-17. 1916-32 (complete) – Inquire – 1 – ATLA 1993-S511 – us A.T.L.A. [073]
BIBLICAL STANDPOINT : VIEWS OF THE SONSHIP OF CHRIST, THE COMFORTER, AND TRINITY / Wilbur, Asa – (Includes appendix) – 2nd rev enl ed. Boston: A Williams, 1875 – 1mf – 9 – 0-8370-2972-4 – 1985-0972 – us A.T.L.A. [240]
BIBLICAL STUDY: ITS PRINCIPLES, METHODS, AND HISTORY / Briggs, Charles Augustus – 1883 – 9 – us A.T.L.A. [240]
BIBLICAL STUDY: ITS PRINCIPLES, METHODS, AND HISTORY / Briggs, Charles Augustus – New York: Charles Scribner, 1894. xv,506p. 2 fiches – 9 – us A.T.L.A. [240]
BIBLICAL TEXT OF CLEMENT OF ALEXANDRIA IN THE FOUR GOSPELS AND THE ACTS OF THE APOSTLES : WITH AN INTRODUCTION BY F.C. BURKITT / ed by Barnard, P M – 1899 – 2mf – 9 – ne Slangenburg [220]
BIBLICAL THEOLOGY BULLETIN – (1977-. 5,6,9) – v. 1-. 1971- – 1 – us UMI [240]
BIBLICAL THEOLOGY BULLETIN – v1-6. 1971-76 – 1 – £475.00 – uk World [240]
BIBLICAL THEOLOGY OF THE NEW TESTAMENT / Gould, Ezra P – New York: Macmillan, 1901 – 9 – us A.T.L.A. [240]
BIBLICAL THINGS NOT GENERALLY KNOWN – London: Elliot, Stock, 1879. 1 fiche – 9 – us A.T.L.A. [240]
THE BIBLICAL VIEW OF MARRIAGE (CCC88) = SHENG CHING CHIH HUN YIN KUAN / ed by Ch'en, Chien-hsun – (In Chinese) – Hankow: Lutheran Board of Publication, 1932 – 1r – 1 – 1984-B500 – us A.T.L.A. [240]
BIBLICAL VIEWPOINT – (1985-. 5,6,9) – v1-. 1967- – 1 – us UMI [240]
BIBLICAL WORLD – v. 1-54. 1893-1920 – 1 – us Princeton Micro [240]
BIBLICAL WORLD *see* AMERICAN JOURNAL OF THEOLOGY
BIBLIGRAPHIE ANALYTIQUE DES TRAVAUX DE JOSEPH RISI, B.A., B.SC., D.SC., M.S.R.C. / Lacroix, Celine – 1959. SEM105P4 – 1mf – 9 – cn Bibl Nat [010]
BIBLIOFILIA SENTIMENTAL / Castaneda, Vicente – Valencia: Editorial Castalia, 1949 – sp Bibl Santa Ana [020]
BIBLIOGRAF – Kritiko-bibliograficheskii zhurnal. v. 1-3. Spb. 1869. BR-3500 2 – 8 – ne IDC [019]
BIBLIOGRAF – Vestnik literatury, nauki i iskusstva. Cont. as: Zhurnal istoriko-literaturnyi i bibliograficheskii. Spb. 1885-95. B-1687 2 – 8 – ne IDC [073]
BIBLIOGRAFA COLONIAL, CONTRIBUCION A UN INDICE DE PUBLICATIONES AFRICANAS / Fontan Lobe, J – (Direccion general de Marruecos y colonias). Madrid. 1946. BA-407 2 – 8 – ne IDC [960]
BIBLIOGRAFI NASIONAL INDONESIA – SE-629 1. 1945-1963 – 9 – ne IDC [010]
BIBLIOGRAFI NASIONAL INDONESIA, KUMULASI 1945-1963 / Indonesia. Biro Perpustakaan – SE-10,671 1. 2 v. 1965 – 9 – ne IDC [010]
BIBLIOGRAFIA AFROVENEZOLANA *see* PANORAMA DE ESTUDIOS AFROAMERICANOS
BIBLIOGRAFIA BIOGRAFICA MEXICANA / Iguiniz, J B – Mexico: UNAM, Instituto de Investigaciones historicas, 1969 – 5mf – 9 – ne IDC [972]
BIBLIOGRAFIA CHILENA DE FILOSOFIA DESDE FINES DEL SIGLO 16 HASTA EL PRESENTE / Santiago de Chile, Biblioteca del Congreso – Santiago: Biblioteca del Congreso, 1979 – 4mf – 9 – ne IDC [100]
BIBLIOGRAFIA COLONIAL, CONTRIBUCION A UN INDICE DE PUBLICACIONES AFRICANAS / Fontan Lobe, J – Madrid, 1946 – 23mf – 9 – ne IDC [960]
BIBLIOGRAFIA CUBANA DE LES SIGLOS 17 Y 18 / Govin, Trelles & Manuel, Carlos – 1r – 1 – $75.00 – us OmniSys [019]
BIBLIOGRAFIA DE D. VICENTE BARRANTES. (1829-1898) / Rodriguez Monino, Antonio – Badajoz, 1946 – 1 – sp Bibl Santa Ana [920]
BIBLIOGRAFIA DE EXTREMADURA / Sanchez Loro, Domingo – Caceres: Departamento de Seminarios, 1951 – 1 – sp Bibl Santa Ana [010]
BIBLIOGRAFIA DE LA LENGUA GUARANI. BUENOS AIRES, 1930 / Medina, Jose Toribio – Madrid: Razon y Fe, 1931 – 1 – sp Bibl Santa Ana [440]
BIBLIOGRAFIA DE LA LITERATURA INDIGENA VENEZOLANA : SEMINARIO DE LITERATURA INDIGENA VENEZOLANA / Cardozo, L – Merida, 1970 – 2mf – 9 – ne IDC [490]
BIBLIOGRAFIA DE LA PROVINCIA DOMINICANA DE COLOMBIA / Mesanza, Andres – Caracas, 1929; Madrid: Razon y Fe, 1931 – 1 – sp Bibl Santa Ana [972]
BIBLIOGRAFIA DE LA PROVINCIA DOMINICANA DE COLOMBIA / Mesanza, Andres & Ariza, A – Caracas: UCAB, Inst. Invest. Historicas, 1981 – 4mf – 9 – ne IDC [972]
BIBLIOGRAFIA DE LAS PUBLICACIONES / Munoz de San Pedro, Miguel – Valencia: Artes Graficas Solers, 1966 – 1 – sp Bibl Santa Ana [070]
BIBLIOGRAFIA DE LOS ESCRITORES DE LA PROVINCIA MEXICANA DE LA COMPANIA DE JESUS, DESDE SU RESTAURACION EN 1816 HASTA NUESTROS DIAS / Iguiniz, J B – Mexico, Buena Prensa, [1945] – 6mf – 9 – ne IDC [972]
BIBLIOGRAFIA DE R. FOULCHE-DELBOSC NEW YORK / Foulche Delbosc, Isabel & Puyol, Julio – 1933. Extrait de la revue Hispanique. Tome 91 – 1 – sp Bibl Santa Ana [010]
BIBLIOGRAFIA DE SERAFIM LEITE S.J. / Batllori, M – Roma, Inst. Hist. S.J., 1962 – 2mf – 9 – ne IDC [970]
BIBLIOGRAFIA DEL PLAN NACIONAL DE INTEGRACION DE LA POBLACION ABORIGEN (PNIPA) / Peru. Ministerio de Trabajo y Comunidades. Instituto Indigenista Peruano – v. 3. Lima. 1966. BD-1845 1 – 9 – ne IDC [310]
BIBLIOGRAFIA DO RIO DE JANEIRO DE VIAJANTES E AUTORES ESTRANGEIROS, 1531-1900 / Berger, P – Rio de Janeiro: SEEC, 1980 – 6mf – 9 – ne IDC [910]
BIBLIOGRAFIA DO RIO DE JANEIRO DE VIAJANTES E ESTRANGEIROS 1531-1900 / Berger, P – Rio de Janeiro: Livr. Sao Jose, 1964 – 4mf – 9 – ne IDC [910]
BIBLIOGRAFIA ECLESIASTICA CHILENA / Universidad Catolica de Chile, Biblioteca Central – Santiago: Univ. Catolica, 1959 – 5mf – 9 – ne IDC [240]
BIBLIOGRAFIA ETIOPICA : CATALOGO DESCRITTIVO E RAGIONATO DEGLI SCRITTI PUBBLICATI DALLA INVENZIONE DELLA STAMPA FINO A TUTTO IL 1891, INTORNO ALLA ETIOPIA E REGIONI LIMITROFE / Fumagalli, Guiseppe – Milan: U Hoepli, 1893 – 1 – us Res Libr [960]
BIBLIOGRAFIA ETIOPICA : IN CONTINUAZIONE ALLA "BIBLIOGRAFIA ETIOPICA" DI G. FUMAGALLI / Zanutto, Silvio – Roma: a cura del Ministero delle colonie, Sindicato italiano arti grafiche, 1932-36. 2v – 1 – us Res Libr [960]
BIBLIOGRAFIA GERAL DE MOCAMBIQUE / Costa, M A da – Lisbon. 1946. BA-485 2 – 8 – ne IDC [960]
BIBLIOGRAFIA GERAL DE MOCAMBIQUE... / Costa, M A da – (Index) – Lisbon, 1946 – 7mf – 9 – ne IDC [960]
BIBLIOGRAFIA GIURIDICA COLONIALE (ITALIA) – Rome: Edizione de 'Il Codice tributario dell' Africa italiana", 1943 – 1 – us Res Libr [340]
BIBLIOGRAFIA. HISTORIAS DEL IMPERIO LUSITANO / Bayle, Constantino – Madrid: Razon y Fe, 1946 – 1 – sp Bibl Santa Ana [019]
BIBLIOGRAFIA HISTORII POLSKIEJ / Finkel, L – 3v. Lviv Krakow. 1891-1906; Suppl. 2. Krakow. 1914. BR-9820 1 – 9 – ne IDC [943]
BIBLIOGRAFIA JESUISTICA DE MAINAS / Bayle, Constantino – Madrid: Missionalia Hispanica, 1949 – 1 – sp Bibl Santa Ana [240]
BIBLIOGRAFIA MANCHEGA. BIBLIOGRAFIA DE LAS PROVINCIAS DE ALBACETE, CIUDAD REAL, CUENCA Y TOLEDO / Cotta y Marquez de Prado, Fernando de – Madrid, 1961. Sep. Rev. Estudios Regionales La Mancha – sp Bibl Santa Ana [946]
BIBLIOGRAFIA MEXICANA DEL SAGRADO CORAZON DE JESUS / Andrade, V de P – Mexico: "El Tiempo", 1906 – 1mf – 9 – ne IDC [972]
BIBLIOGRAFIA MISSIONARIA ANNO 21 (1957) Y ANNO 12 (1958)... / Barrado Manzano, Arcangel – Madrid: Archivo Ibero Americano, 1959 – 1 – sp Bibl Santa Ana [012]
BIBLIOGRAFIA MISSIONARIA. ANNO 23 / Barrado Manzano, Arcangel – Madrid: Arch. Ibero Americano, 1961 – 1 – sp Bibl Santa Ana [240]
BIBLIOGRAFIA MISSIONARIA. ANNO 28 / Barrado Manzano, Arcangel – Madrid: Arch. Ibero Americano, 1964 – 1 – sp Bibl Santa Ana [240]
BIBLIOGRAFIA MISSIONARIA ANNO 30, 1966. ROMA, 1967 / Rommeiskichen, Giovanni – Madrid: Graf. Calleja, 1967 – 1 – sp Bibl Santa Ana [240]
BIBLIOGRAFIA MISSIONARIA ANNO 39, 1965. ROMA, 1966 / Rommerskichen, Giovanni – Madrid: Graf. Calleja, 1966 – 1 – sp Bibl Santa Ana [240]
BIBLIOGRAFIA PISOMNICTVA SLOVENSKEHO NA SPONSOB SLOVNIKA OD NAJSTARSICH CIAS DO KONCA R. 1900 / Rizner, L – v. 1-6. Turciansky sv. Martin. 1929-34. BR-5018 2 – 8 – ne IDC [460]
BIBLIOGRAFIA PUERTORRIQUENA (1493-1930). MADRID, 1932 / Pedreira, Antonio S – Madrid: Razon y Fe, 1935 – 1 – sp Bibl Santa Ana [920]
BIBLIOGRAFIA PUERTORRIQUENA, ESCRITA EN 1892-1894 / Geigle y Zenon, J & Ferrer, Morales A – Barcelona: Araluce, 1934 – 6mf – 9 – ne IDC [972]
BIBLIOGRAFIA SOBRE LAS MISIONES DE MAINAS. UN MISIONERO MISIONOLOGO / Bayle, Constantino – Madrid: Ediciones Jura, 1949 – 1 – sp Bibl Santa Ana [240]
BIBLIOGRAFIA SOBRE LOS MIXTECAS (1719-1991) : ANTROPOLOGIA FISICA, ANTROPOLOGIA SOCIAL Y APLICADA, ARQUEOLOGIA, HISTORIA, CODIECES Y LINGUISTICA / Dittmar, Manuela – 1994 – 1mf – DM60.00 – 3-8267-2057-1 – gw Hänsel [574]
BIBLIOGRAFIA...ANNO 28, 1964 / Rommerskichen, Giovanni – Roma, 1965; Madrid: Graf Calleja, 1966 – 1 – sp Bibl Santa Ana [946]

BIBLIOGRAFICHESKAIA LETOPIS' – v. 1-3. Spb. 1914-17. BR-3501 2 – 8 – ne IDC [073]

BIBLIOGRAFICHESKI YEZHEGODNIK – Moscow. v. 1-8. 1911-1914, 1921 22-1924 – 1 – us NY Public [010]

BIBLIOGRAFICHESKIE MATERIALY PO ISTORII NOVOROSSII. UKAZATEL' / Ribas, L M de – Odessa. 1914. BR-7235 – 8 – ne IDC [947]

BIBLIOGRAFICHESKII DESIATIGODNIK PO KOOPERATSII : KOMMUNISTICHESKAIA KOOPERATIVNAIA LITERATURA 1917-1927 GG – Moscow, 1928 – 2mf – 9 – COR-527/1 – ne IDC [334]

BIBLIOGRAFICHESKII EZHEGODNIK, VYPUSK 4 / Vladislavlev, I V – Sistematicheskii ukazatel' literatury za 1914 g. M. 1915. BR-3592 2 – 8 – ne IDC [460]

BIBLIOGRAFICHESKII OBZOR APOKRIFOV V IUZHNOSLAVIANSKOI I RUSSKOI PIS'MENNOSTI (SPISKI PAMIATNIKOV) / Iatsimirskii, A I – Vyp I: Apokrity vetkhozavetnye. Petrograd. 1921. BR-175 2 – 8 – ne IDC [460]

BIBLIOGRAFICHESKII OCHERK ARMIANSKOI ISTORICHESKOI LITERATURY / Patkanov, K P – Spb. 1879. BR-7203 2 – 8 – ne IDC [460]

BIBLIOGRAFICHESKII SLOVAR' I TSERKOVNYE K NEMU MATERIALY / Stroev, P M – St. Petersburg, 1882. 532p. BR-7280/2 – 8 – ne IDC [947]

BIBLIOGRAFICHESKII SLOVAR' PISATELEI, UCHENYKH I KHUDOZHNIKOV UROZHENTSEV (PREIMUSHCHESTVENNO) RIAZANSKOI GUBERNII / Dobroliubov, IV & Iakhontov, SD – Riazan'. 1910. BR-5870 2 – 8 – ne IDC [460]

BIBLIOGRAFICHESKII SLOVAR' RUSSKIKH PISATEL'NITS / Golitsyn, N N – Spb. 1889. BR-5901 2 – 8 – ne IDC [460]

BIBLIOGRAFICHESKII SPISOK LITERATURNYKH TRUDOV KIEVSKAGO MITROPOLITA EVGENIIA BOLKHOVITINOVA. 1 / Shmurlo, E F – Spb. 1888. BR-7270 2 – 8 – ne IDC [240]

BIBLIOGRAFICHESKII SPISOK SOCHINENII I IZDANII I.I. SREZNEVSKAGO – St. Petersburg, 1879. 38p BR-5877/2 – 8 – ne IDC [460]

BIBLIOGRAFICHESKII UKAZATEL' / Biblioteka Akademii Nauk S SS R, 1714-1964 – Leningrad, 1964.308p. Lists publications about mss., p106-140 and p215-236. BR-10,951/1 – 9 – ne IDC [010]

BIBLIOGRAFICHESKII UKAZATEL' KNIG BROSHIUR, ZHURNAL'NYKH STATEI ZAMETOK PO ISTORII RUSSKOGO TEATRA / Adariukov, V Ia – Spb. 1904. BR-7048 2 – 8 – ne IDC [790]

BIBLIOGRAFICHESKII UKAZATEL' KNIG I STATEI I ZHIZNI I SOCHINENIIAKH EGO. 1816-1852 / Mezhov, VI & Aksakov, ST – Spb. 1888. BR-7163 2 – 8 – ne IDC [010]

BIBLIOGRAFICHESKII UKAZATEL' KNIG I STATEI, OTNOSIASHCHIKHSIA DO OBSHCHESTV, OSNOVANNYKH NA NACHALAKH VZAIMNOSTI, ARTELEI, POLOZHENIIA RABOCHEGO SOSLOVIIA I MELKOI KUSTARNOI PROMYSHLENNOSTI V ROSSII / Mezhov, V I – St Petersburg. v1-6. Suppl 1-5. 1872-89 – 5mf – 9 – COR-535/1 – ne IDC [334]

BIBLIOGRAFICHESKII UKAZATEL' KNIG I STATEI PO NARODNOMU OBRAZOVANIIU ZA 1894 GOD / Kudriavtsev, V A & Charnoluskaia, E M – Spb. 1895. BR-5958 2 – 8 – ne IDC [460]

BIBLIOGRAFICHESKII UKAZATEL' KNIG I ZAKLIUCHAIUSHCHIKHSIA V NIKH STATEI... / Mezhov, VI – Sp. iv. 1983 – 3mf – 9 – ne IDC [947]

BIBLIOGRAFICHESKII UKAZATEL' KNIG I ZAKLIUCHAIUSHCHIKHSIA V NIKH STATEI OBNIMAIUSHCHII DEIATEL'NOST' STATISTICHESKII KOMITETOV S SAMAGO NACHALA IKH UCHREZHDENII VPLOT' DO 1873 G / Mezhov, VI – Spb. 1873. BR-7152 2 – 3mf – 8 – ne IDC [310]

BIBLIOGRAFICHESKII UKAZATEL' KNIG I ZAKLIUCHAIUSHCHIKHSIA V NIKH STATEI OBNIMAIUSHCHII DEIATEL'NOST' STATISTICHESKIKH KOMITETOV S SAMOGO NACHALA IKH UCHREZHDENIIA VPLOT' DO 1873 G / Mezhov, VI – Spb., 1873 – 3mf – 9 – R-7152/2 – ne IDC [947]

BIBLIOGRAFICHESKII UKAZATEL' KOOPERATIVNOI LITERATURY ZA 1927 G / Brovkin, T M – Moscow, 1929 – 2mf – 9 – COR-529/1 – ne IDC [334]

BIBLIOGRAFICHESKII UKAZATEL' LITERATURY O BASHKIRAKH / Nikol'skii, D P – M. 1900. BR-7179 2 – 8 – ne IDC [460]

BIBLIOGRAFICHESKII UKAZATEL' PECHATANNYM NA RUSSKOM IAZYKE SOCHINENIIAM I STAT'IAM O VOENNYKH DEISTVIIAKH RUSSKIKH VOISK NA KAVKAZE / Gizetti, A – Spb. 1901. BR-5925 2 – 8 – ne IDC [460]

BIBLIOGRAFICHESKII UKAZATEL PO ISTORII, GERALDIKE I RODOSLOVIIU ROSSIISKAGO DVORIANSTVA / Savelov, L M – Ed.2, Ostrogozhsk, 1897.266p. BR-7250/2 – 8 – ne IDC [947]

BIBLIOGRAFICHESKII UKAZATEL RABOT NAUCHNYKH SOTRUDNIKOV INSTITUTA VYSOKOMOLEKULIARNYKH SOEDINENII AN SSSR / Akademiia nauk SSSR, Institut vysokomolekuliarnykh soedinenii i Biblioteka Akademii nauk SSSR – Leningrad: Biblioteka 1961-1977/79 – us Res Libr [947]

BIBLIOGRAFICHESKII UKAZATEL' RUSSKIKH DISSERTATII PO MEDITSINE I VETERINATII / Petrov, N P – Ed. 2. Spb. 1892. BR-7211 2 – 8 – ne IDC [610]

BIBLIOGRAFICHESKII UKAZATEL' RUSSKOI ETNOGRAFICHESKOI LITERATURY O VNESHNEM BYTE NARODOV ROSSII. 1700-1910 GG / Zelenin, D K – Spb. 1913. BR-7021 2 – 8 – ne IDC [305]

BIBLIOGRAFICHESKII UKAZATEL' RUSSKOI I INOSTRANNOI LITERATURY PO VZRYVCHATYM VESHCHESTVAM S 1529 PO 1882 G / Gekkel', A – Spb. 1886. BR-7104 2 – 8 – ne IDC [460]

BIBLIOGRAFICHESKII UKAZATEL' STATEI, OTNOSIASHCHIKHSIA K PSKOVSKOI GUBERNII, 1517-1887 G / Vasil'ev, I I – Pskov. 1891. BR-7015 2 – 8 – ne IDC [010]

BIBLIOGRAFICHESKII UKAZATEL'LITERATURY PO RUSSKOI NUMISMATIKE / Gromachevskii, S G – Zhitomir, 1904. BR/5926/2 – 8 – ne IDC [730]

BIBLIOGRAFICHESKII UKAZATEL'SOCHINENII I PROIZVEDENII ISKUSSTVA OTNOSIASHCHIKHSIA K ZHIZNI I DEIATEL'NOSTI F. M. DOSTOEVSKOGO 1846-1903 / Dostoevskaia, A – Spb. 1906. BR-5888 2 – 8 – ne IDC [460]

BIBLIOGRAFICHESKIIA IZVESTIIA O REDNIKH KNIGAKH. NO. 2 / Kartavov,D A – Saint Petersburg, 1898. 176p. BR-4660/2 – 8 – ne IDC [010]

BIBLIOGRAFICHESKIIA ZAMETKI O STARO-SLAVIANSKIKH PECHATNYKH IZDANIIAKH 1491-1730 / Karataev, I – Saint Petersburg, 1872. 52p. BR-4677/2 – 8 – ne IDC [460]

BIBLIOGRAFICHY PREHLED CESKYCH NARODNICH PISNI / Zibrt, C – Praha. 1895. BR-5171 2 – 8 – ne IDC [010]

BIBLIOGRAFIE CESKE HISTORIE / Zibrt, C – 5v. Praha. 1900-12. B-1277 2 – 8 – ne IDC [943]

BIBLIOGRAFIIA / Komovskii, V D – Spisok vsekh knig, vyshedshikh v Rossii v 1829 godu. Moskovskii Vestnik. pt. 4-5. M. 1830. BR-4355 2 – 8 – ne IDC [460]

BIBLIOGRAFIIA / Lisovskii, N M – Obzor trudov bibliograficheskago soderzhaniia. Spb. 1900. BR-4651 2 – 8 – ne IDC [010]

BIBLIOGRAFIIA AZII, VSIA AZIIA, ISKLIUCHAIA SIBIRI UKAZATEL' KNIG I STATEI OB AZII NA RUSSKOM IAZYKE I ODNEKH TOL'KO KNIG NA INOSTRANNYKH IAZYKAKH, KASAIUSHCHIKHSIA OTNOSHENII ROSSII K AZIATSKIM GOSUDARSTVAM / Mezhov, VI – v. 1-3. Spb. 1891-94. BR-5619 2 – 8 – ne IDC [950]

BIBLIOGRAFIIA DISSERTATSII. 1941-1945 / Gosudarstvennaia Biblioteka SSSR im V.I. Lenina. Moscow – 1 – us UMI [010]

BIBLIOGRAFIIA FINANSOV PROMYSHLENNOSTI I TORGOVLI:SO VREMEN PETRA VELIKOGO PO NASTOIASHCHEE VREMIA (S 1714 PO 1879 G, VKL.) / Karataev, S – Spb. 1880. BR-7115 2: 375p – 5mf – 8 – COR-532/1 – ne IDC [336]

BIBLIOGRAFIIA IAKUTII / Gribanovskii, N N – v. 1. Leningrad. 1932; v. 2 (1). Leningrad. 1934; v. 2 (2). Leningrad. 1935. BU-338 2 – 8 – ne IDC [010]

BIBLIOGRAFIIA IUGO-VOSTOCHNOI AZII – Dorevoliutsionnaia i sovetskaia literatura na russkom iazyke, original'naia i perevodnaia. (Sostavila A. M. Grishtna i dr.). M. 1960. BR-7705 2 – 8 – ne IDC [460]

BIBLIOGRAFIIA OBSHCHESTVENNOI-POLITICHESKOI LITERATURY / Levin, LA & Savitskaia, R M & Kortunov, OP – M. 1958. BR-5717 2 – 8 – ne IDC [320]

BIBLIOGRAFIIA PO ISTORII RIMSKOI LITERATURY V ROSSII S 1709 PO 1889 GOD / Naguevskii, D I – Kazan'. 1889. BR-7173 2 – 8 – ne IDC [460]

BIBLIOGRAFIIA PO VOPROSU OB ALKOGOLIZME / Viazemskii, T K – Moscow, 1909. 62p. BR-7042/2 – 8 – ne IDC [073]

BIBLIOGRAFIIA SOCHINENII A. P. CHEKHOVA / Masanov, I F – M. 1906. BR-7146 2 – 8 – ne IDC [460]

BIBLIOGRAFIIA SPORTA I FIZICHESKAGO RAZVITIIA / Diuperron, G A – Sistematicheskaia rospis' vsekh knig, broshiur, zhurnalov, vyshedsikh v Rossii po 1913 god vkl. Petrograd. 1915. BR-7093 2 – 8 – ne IDC [790]

BIBLIOGRAFIIA TURKESTANA 1 / Gorodetskii, V D – Tashkent. 1913. BR-7106 2 – 8 – ne IDC [950]

BIBLIOGRAFIIA VLADIMIRSKOI GUBERNII / Masanov, I F – v. 1. Vladimir. 1905. BR-5921 2 – 8 – ne IDC [460]

BIBLIOGRAFIIA VOSTOKA – Moscow, Leningrad, 1932-36. 10 nos. in 6 issues. Includes bibliog. articles and descriptions of oriental ms. holdings in the USSR. BR-1677/2 – 8 – ne IDC [010]

BIBLIOGRAFIIA ZA 1856 I 1857 GG. ILI UKAZATEL' KNIG, SOSTAVLENNYI NA OSNOVANII ISTOCHNIKOV, DOSTAVLENNYKH IZ IMP. PUBLICHNOI BIBLIOTEKI V.I.M / Mezhov, VI – M. 1859. BR-5634 2 – 8 – ne IDC [370]

BIBLIOGRAFIJA EDVARDA KARDELJA / Bulovec, Stefka – Ljubljana: Komunist, 1980. 254p. Introd. in English, Albanian, Hungarian, Macedonian, Russian and Serbo-Croatian. Includes indexes – 1 – us U.W. Library [010]

BIBLIOGRAFISKI PREGLED NA SLAVIANSKITE KIRILSKI IZTOCHNISTSI ZA ZHIVOTA I DEINOSTTA NA KIRILA I METODIIA / Popruzhenko, M & Romanski, S – Sofiia, 1935. 68p. BR-8108/2 – 8 – ne IDC [460]

BIBLIOGRAFIYA PERIODIKI – Moscow. v. 1-4. 1923 – 1 – us NY Public [010]

BIBLIOGRAFSKI ISTOCHNITSI ZA ISTORIIATA NA TURTSIIA I BALGARIIA / Mikhov, N V – v. 1-4. Sofiia. 1914-34. BR-3893 2 – 8 – ne IDC [949]

BIBLIOGRAPHIA AMERICANA HISTORICO-NATURALIS... FOR 1851 / Girard, CF – Washington, 1852 – 2mf – ne IDC [590]

BIBLIOGRAPHIA BOTANICA / Junk, W – Berlin, 1909. Supplementum. Berlin, 1916 – 22mf – ne IDC [580]

BIBLIOGRAPHIA BOTANICA / Krueger, MS – Berlin. 1841. B-6496 2 – 9mf – 8 – ne IDC [580]

BIBLIOGRAPHIA CAUCASICA ET TRANSCAUCASICA / Miansarov, M – Spb. 1874-75. BR-7170 2 – 8 – ne IDC [010]

BIBLIOGRAPHIA GEOGRAPHICA PALAESTINAE / Tobler, T – Leipzig, 1867 – 3mf – 9 – ne IDC [956]

BIBLIOGRAPHIA KABBALISTICA, VERZEICHNIS DER GEDRUCKTEN; DIE JUEDISCHE MYSTIK (GNOSIS, KABBALA...) VON REUCHLIN BIS ZUR GEGENWART / Scholem, G – Leipzig, 1927 – 3mf – ne IDC [270]

BIBLIOGRAPHIA LINGUA TUPI OU GUARANI : TAMBEM CHAMADA LINGUA GERAL DO BRAZIL / Cabral, A do Valle – Rio de Janeiro: Typ. Nacional, 1880 – 1mf – 9 – ne IDC [440]

BIBLIOGRAPHIA ZOOLOGIAE ET GEOLOGIAE / Agassiz, Louis – Ray Society. 1848-54 – 1. 208.00; ; 7 – uk Microform Academic [550]

BIBLIOGRAPHIA ZOOLOGIAE ET GEOLOGIAE : A GENERAL CATALOGUE OF ALL BOOKS... / Agassiz, J L R – London. 4v. 1848-1854 – 42mf – 9 – ne IDC [015]

BIBLIOGRAPHIC GUIDE TO STUDIES ON THE STATUS OF WOMEN, DEVELOPMENT AND POPULATION TRENDS : WOMEN IN A WORLD PERSPECTIVE – 1983 – 9 – 92-3-102122-2 – fr UNESCO [305]

BIBLIOGRAPHICAL INDEX TO NORTH AMERICAN BOTANY;... / Watson, S – Washington, 1878 – 6mf – ne IDC [580]

BIBLIOGRAPHICAL SERVICES THROUGHOUT THE WORLD / Beaudiquez, Marcelle – 9 – fr UNESCO [020]

Bibliographical Society of America *see* PAPERS

BIBLIOGRAPHICAL SURVEY OF JEWISH PRAGUE / Muneles, O – Prague, 1952 – 6mf – ne IDC [943]

BIBLIOGRAPHIE : CINQUANTE OUVRAGES TRAITANT DE L'ADOLESCENCE / Houle, Alphonse – 1964. SEM105P4 – 3mf – 9 – cn Bibl Nat [305]

BIBLIOGRAPHIE : LES MONUMENTS HISTORIQUES DE QUEBEC, 1854-1901 / St-Roger, Soeur – 1963. SEM105P4 – 1mf – 9 – cn Bibl Nat [720]

BIBLIOGRAPHIE : LES MONUMENTS HISTORIQUES DE QUEBEC, 1901-1920 / Ste-Martine, Soeur – 1963. SEM105P4 – 2mf – 9 – cn Bibl Nat [720]

BIBLIOGRAPHIE (1915 A 1940) DU DR GEORGES MAHEUX, ENTOMOLOGISTE, MEMBRE DE LA SOCIETE ROYALE DU CANADA / Naud, Denise – 1963. SEM105P4 – 2mf – 9 – cn Bibl Nat [590]

BIBLIOGRAPHIE 1950-1958 DE LA BIENHEUREUSE MARGUERITE D'YOUVILLE, FONDATRICE DES SOEURS DE LA CHARITE (SOEURS GRISES) DE MONTREAL / Sainte-Fernande, Soeur – 1963. SEM105P4 – 1mf – 9 – cn Bibl Nat [240]

BIBLIOGRAPHIE ANALYTIQUE : ECRITS DES PERES OBLATS DE MARIE-IMMACULEE SUR LA SAINTE-VIERGE DANS LES ANNALES DE NOTRE-DAME DU CAP, 1902-1962 / Anges, Marie des – 1963. SEM105P4 – 4mf – 9 – cn Bibl Nat [240]

BIBLIOGRAPHIE ANALYTIQUE DE ALAIN GRANDBOIS / Gagnon, Huguette – 1964. SEM105P4 – 2mf – 9 – cn Bibl Nat [010]

BIBLIOGRAPHIE ANALYTIQUE DE BAIE COMEAU SUR LA COTE-NORD DU SAINT-LAURENT / Beaudry, Pauline – 1959. SEM105P4 – 1mf – 9 – cn Bibl Nat [971]

BIBLIOGRAPHIE ANALYTIQUE DE C.-J. MAGNAN / Laberge, Raymond-Marie – 1953. SEM105P4 – 1mf – 9 – cn Bibl Nat [010]

BIBLIOGRAPHIE ANALYTIQUE DE ERNEST PALLASCIO-MORIN, JOURNALISTE, AUTEUR DRAMATIQUE, CONFERENCIER / Lys, Marie-des – 1961. SEM105P4 – 2mf – 9 – cn Bibl Nat [070]

BIBLIOGRAPHIE ANALYTIQUE DE FRANCOISE L.-ROY, JOURNALISTE, VICE-PRESIDENTE DU CERCLE DES FEMMES JOURNALISTES DE MONTREAL, MEMBRE DE LA SOCIETE DES ECRIVAINS CANADIENS / Saint-Jean-Marie, Soeur – 1964. SEM105P4 – 2mf – 9 – cn Bibl Nat [070]

BIBLIOGRAPHIE ANALYTIQUE DE JACQUES DE MONLEON / Vachon, Madeleine E – 1963. SEM105P4 – 1mf – 9 – cn Bibl Nat [010]

BIBLIOGRAPHIE ANALYTIQUE DE JOSEPH-THOMAS LEBLANC / Blouin, Gisele – 1950. SEM105P4 – 2mf – 9 – cn Bibl Nat [971]

BIBLIOGRAPHIE ANALYTIQUE DE LA CHANSON DE FOLKLORE : OUVRAGES PARUS AU CANADA DE 1950 A 1962 / Dupuis, Monique – 1964. SEM105P4 – 1mf – 9 – cn Bibl Nat [780]

BIBLIOGRAPHIE ANALYTIQUE DE LA DELINQUANCE JUVENILE OU DE L'INADAPTATION FAMILIALE ET SOCIALE DES MAL-AIMES... / Chapdelaine, Cecile – 1966. SEM105P4 – 8mf – 9 – cn Bibl Nat [360]

BIBLIOGRAPHIE ANALYTIQUE DE LA FEDERATION DES GUIDES CATHOLIQUES DE LA PROVINCE DE QUEBEC / Drolet, Bernadette – 1963. SEM105P4 – 1mf – 9 – cn Bibl Nat [240]

BIBLIOGRAPHIE ANALYTIQUE DE LA GENEALOGIE DANS LES COMTES DE SAINT-MAURICE, MASKINONGE, CHAMPLAIN / Lemay, Leona – 1964. SEM105P4 – 2mf – 9 – cn Bibl Nat [920]

BIBLIOGRAPHIE ANALYTIQUE DE LA LITTERATURE MUSICALE CANADIENNE FRANCAISE / Laflamme, Claire – 1950. SEM105P4 – 1mf – 9 – cn Bibl Nat [780]

BIBLIOGRAPHIE ANALYTIQUE DE LA LITTERATURE PEDAGOGIQUE CANADIENNE FRANCAISE DE 1790 A 1900 / Gagnon, Gilberte – 1951. SEM105P4 – 1mf – 9 – cn Bibl Nat [440]

BIBLIOGRAPHIE ANALYTIQUE DE LA LITTERATURE PEDAGOGIQUE CANADIENNE-FRANCAISE DEPUIS 1900 / Ratte, Alice – 1951. SEM105P4 – 2mf – 9 – cn Bibl Nat [440]

BIBLIOGRAPHIE ANALYTIQUE DE LA PSYCHOLOGIE INFANTILE, 1948 A 1952 / Dumas, Rollande – 1952. SEM105P4 – 1mf – 9 – cn Bibl Nat [150]

BIBLIOGRAPHIE ANALYTIQUE DE LA RELIURE AU CANADA FRANCAIS / Desrochers-Leduc, Lucienne – 1953. SEM105P4 – 1mf – 9 – cn Bibl Nat [680]

BIBLIOGRAPHIE ANALYTIQUE DE LA VALLEE DE LA MATAPEDIA / Saint-Joseph-Jean, Marie de – 1964. SEM105P4 – 2mf – 9 – cn Bibl Nat [910]

BIBLIOGRAPHIE ANALYTIQUE DE LA VIE PERSONNELLE DE L'INFIRMIERE D'APRES LA DOCUMENTATION DES REVUES D'INFIRMIERES... / Munger, Angele – 1962. SEM105P4 – 1mf – 9 – cn Bibl Nat [360]

BIBLIOGRAPHIE ANALYTIQUE DE L'ABBE ANSELME LONGPRE, PH.L., TH.L., B.D.C. DU DIOCESE DE SAINT-HYACINTHE, PREMIERE PARTIE (1927-1947) / Joseph-Marie, Soeur – 1963. SEM105P4 – 2mf – 9 – cn Bibl Nat [240]

BIBLIOGRAPHIE ANALYTIQUE DE L'ABBE HENRI-RAYMOND CASGRAIN / Sainte-Thecle, Soeur – 1955. SEM105P4 – 2mf – 9 – cn Bibl Nat [240]

BIBLIOGRAPHIE ANALYTIQUE DE L'AMIANTE DU CANADA / Marcoux, Lucile – 1953. SEM105P4 – 1mf – 9 – cn Bibl Nat [622]

BIBLIOGRAPHIE ANALYTIQUE DE L'HISTOIRE D'ACADIE / Corrivault, Blaise – 1950. SEM105P4 – 1mf – 9 – cn Bibl Nat [971]

BIBLIOGRAPHIE ANALYTIQUE DE L'HONORABLE JUGE SIR ADOLPHE-BASILE ROUTHIER, HOMME DE LETTRES / Sainte-Janviere, Soeur – 1952. SEM105P4 – 1mf – 9 – cn Bibl Nat [340]

BIBLIOGRAPHIE ANALYTIQUE DE L'ILE D'ANTICOSTI (REINE DU GOLFE) / Barnabe, Michele – 1959. SEM105P4 – 1mf – 9 – cn Bibl Nat [910]

BIBLIOGRAPHIE ANALYTIQUE DE L'ILEAUX-COUDRES / Amyot, Michel – 1952. SEM105P4 – 1mf – 9 – cn Bibl Nat [910]

BIBLIOGRAPHIE ANALYTIQUE DE L'OEUVRE, 1941-1960, DE MONSIEUR PIERRE-PAUL TURGEON, NOTAIRE / Pelletier, Carmen – 1964. SEM105P4 – 1mf – 9 – cn Bibl Nat [340]

BIBLIOGRAPHIE ANALYTIQUE DE L'OEUVRE DE BERAUD DE SAINT MAURICE (MERE CLOTILDE-ANGELE DE JESUS, O.S.U., URSULINE DE TROIS-RIVIERES) / Sainte-Hildegarde, Mere – 1963. SEM105P4 – 1mf – 9 – cn Bibl Nat [240]

BIBLIOGRAPHIE ANALYTIQUE DE L'OEUVRE DE BERTRAND VAC / Guilbault, Renee – 1963. SEM105P4 – 1mf – 9 – cn Bibl Nat [010]

BIBLIOGRAPHIE ANALYTIQUE DE L'OEUVRE DE BRUNO LAFLEUR / Laki, Georgette – 1964. SEM105P4 – 1mf – 9 – cn Bibl Nat [010]

BIBLIOGRAPHIE ANALYTIQUE DE L'OEUVRE DE CHARLOTTE SAVARY / Bedard, Suzanne – 1951. SEM105P4 – 1mf – 9 – cn Bibl Nat [971]

BIBLIOGRAPHIE ANALYTIQUE DE L'OEUVRE DE DOM ALBERT JAMET DE L'ABBAYE BENEDICTINE DE SOLESMES / Sainte Therese-de-l'Enfant-Jesus, Mere – 1960. SEM105P4 – 1mf – 9 – cn Bibl Nat [240]

BIBLIOGRAPHIE ANALYTIQUE DE L'OEUVRE DE GERARD MORISSET, N.P., DE LA SOCIETE ROYALE DU CANADA... / Mercure, Henri – 1947. SEM105P4 – 1mf – 9 – cn Bibl Nat [060]

BIBLIOGRAPHIE ANALYTIQUE DE L'OEUVRE DE I.-W. JONES, GEOLOGUE, DIRECTEUR DES SERVICES GEOLOGIQUES, MINISTERE DES RICHESSES NATURELLES / Fortier, Marie-Marthe – 1962. SEM105P4 – 1mf – 9 – cn Bibl Nat [550]

BIBLIOGRAPHIE ANALYTIQUE DE L'OEUVRE DE JEAN-PAUL LEGARE, JOURNALISTE DE RIMOUSKI, PRESIDENT DU JOURNAL L'ECHO DU BAS ST-LAURENT, 1945-1961 / Sainte-Madeleine-du-Calvaire, Soeur – 1964. SEM105P4 – 4mf – 9 – cn Bibl Nat [070]

BIBLIOGRAPHIE ANALYTIQUE DE L'OEUVRE DE L'ABBE ARTHUR MAHEUX POUR LES ANNEES 1942, 1943, 1944 / Nadeau, Marie-Marthe – 1947. SEM105P4 – 1mf – 9 – cn Bibl Nat [240]

BIBLIOGRAPHIE ANALYTIQUE DE L'OEUVRE DE L'ABBE JEAN HOLMES, UN DES FONDATEURS DE L'UNIVERSITE LAVAL / Lefaivre, Louise – 1964. SEM105P4 – 1mf – 9 – cn Bibl Nat [370]

BIBLIOGRAPHIE ANALYTIQUE DE L'OEUVRE DE L'ABBE ROCH DUVAL, LICENCIE EN ORIENTATION, DEBUT A SEPTEMBRE 1964 / Pouliot, Aline – 1964. SEM105P4 – 1mf – 9 – cn Bibl Nat [240]

BIBLIOGRAPHIE ANALYTIQUE DE L'OEUVRE DE LEOPOLD LAMONTAGNE DE LA SOCIETE ROYALE DU CANADA, DOYEN DE LA FACULTE DES LETTRES A L'UNIVERSITE LAVAL / Roy, Reina L – 1963 [i.e. 1964]. SEM105P4 – 2mf – 9 – cn Bibl Nat [400]

BIBLIOGRAPHIE ANALYTIQUE DE L'OEUVRE DE L'HONORABLE SENATEUR CYRILLE VAILLANCOURT... / Boutin, Rose-Anne – 1961. SEM105P4 – 3mf – 9 – cn Bibl Nat [350]

BIBLIOGRAPHIE ANALYTIQUE DE L'OEUVRE DE LOUIS-PHILIPPE ROY, M.D., COMMANDEUR DE L'ORDRE DE SAINT-GREGOIRE LE GRAND... / Sainte-Marie-Cleophas, Soeur – 1964. SEM105P4 – 10mf – 9 – cn Bibl Nat [240]

BIBLIOGRAPHIE ANALYTIQUE DE L'OEUVRE DE LOUIS-PHILIPPE ROY, M.D., DIRECTEUR DE L'ACTION, 1920-1948 / Saint-Majella, Soeur – 1964. SEM105P4 – 6mf – 9 – cn Bibl Nat [070]

BIBLIOGRAPHIE ANALYTIQUE DE L'OEUVRE DE M. ALBERT RIOUX, AGRONOME... / Carbonneau, Leopold – 1952. SEM105P4 – 2mf – 9 – cn Bibl Nat [630]

BIBLIOGRAPHIE ANALYTIQUE DE L'OEUVRE DE M. AVILA BEDARD, I.F.M.F., SOUSMINISTRE DES TERRES ET FORETS DANS LE CABINET PROVINCIAL / Houde, Marguerite A – 1958. SEM105P4 – 3mf – 9 – cn Bibl Nat [333]

BIBLIOGRAPHIE ANALYTIQUE DE L'OEUVRE DE M. EMILE CASTONGUAY / Daigle, Louise – 1964. SEM105P4 – 2mf – 9 – cn Bibl Nat [010]

BIBLIOGRAPHIE ANALYTIQUE DE L'OEUVRE DE M. EUGENE L'HEUREUX, JOURNALISTE, MEMBRE DE LA SOCIETE ROYALE DU CANADA, 1918-1929 / Sainte-Daniella, Soeur – 1962. SEM105P4 – 2mf – 9 – cn Bibl Nat [070]

BIBLIOGRAPHIE ANALYTIQUE DE L'OEUVRE DE M. L'ABBE ARTHUR MAHEUX DE LA SOCIETE ROYALE DU CANADA, ARCHIVISTE DU SEMINAIRE DE QUEBEC / Pelletier, Jacqueline – [1956]. SEM105P4 – 1mf – 9 – cn Bibl Nat [240]

BIBLIOGRAPHIE ANALYTIQUE DE L'OEUVRE DE M. L'ABBE LOUIS O'NEILL, AUMONIER A L'ACADEMIE DE QUEBEC, PROFESSEUR DE MORALE SOCIALE / Morin, Romuald – 1962. SEM105P4 – 1mf – 9 – cn Bibl Nat [300]

BIBLIOGRAPHIE ANALYTIQUE DE L'OEUVRE DE M. LOUIS-PHILIPPE ROBIDOUX DE LA SOCIETE ROYALE DU CANADA, REDACTEUR EN CHEF DE LA TRIBUNE DE SHERBROOKE / Saint-Fidele, Soeur – 1964. SEM105P4 – 4mf – 9 – cn Bibl Nat [070]

BIBLIOGRAPHIE ANALYTIQUE DE L'OEUVRE DE MADAME MARCELLE LEPAGE-THIBAUDEAU, LICENCIEE EN SCIENCES NATURELLES, LICENCIEE EN PHYCHOLOGIE ET PSYCHOTHERAPIE / Cantin, Louise – 1964. SEM105P4 – 2mf – 9 – cn Bibl Nat [500]

BIBLIOGRAPHIE ANALYTIQUE DE L'OEUVRE DE MADEMOISELLE GERTIE KATHLEEN HART, DIPLOMEE DE L'UNIVERSITE LAVAL, DE L'UNIVERSITE D'OXFORD, DE LA FACULTE DES LETTRES DE LA SORBONNE / Marie-de-la-Charite, Soeur – 1962. SEM105P4 – 1mf – 9 – cn Bibl Nat [370]

BIBLIOGRAPHIE ANALYTIQUE DE L'OEUVRE DE MAITRE EUGENE L'HEUREUX, JOURNALISTE, 1950-1960, BIBLIOTHECAIRE-ADJOINT AU PARLEMENT / Salette, Marie-de-la – 1964. SEM105P4 – 6mf – 9 – cn Bibl Nat [070]

BIBLIOGRAPHIE ANALYTIQUE DE L'OEUVRE DE MAITRE EUGENE L'HEUREUX, MEMBRE DE LA SOCIETE ROYALE DU CANADA ET DE L'ACADEMIE CANADIENNE, REDACTEUR EN CHEF DU PROGRES DU SAGUENAY ET DE L'ACTION CATHOLIQUE, 1929-1940 / Miracles, Marie-des – 3mf – 1964. SEM105P4 – cn Bibl Nat [240]

BIBLIOGRAPHIE ANALYTIQUE DE L'OEUVRE DE MARCEL CLEMENT, LICENCIE ES LETTRES, DIPLOME D'ETUDES SUPERIEURES DE PHILOSOPHIE (SORBONNE)... / Joly, Monique – 1950. SEM105P4 – 1mf – 9 – cn Bibl Nat [320]

BIBLIOGRAPHIE ANALYTIQUE DE L'OEUVRE DE MARCEL DUBE / Laforest, Marthe – 1964. SEM105P4 – 2mf – 9 – cn Bibl Nat [010]

BIBLIOGRAPHIE ANALYTIQUE DE L'OEUVRE DE ME EUGENE L'HEUREUX, JOURNALISTE, MEMBRE DE LA SOCIETE ROYALE DU CANADA ET DE L'ACADEMIE CANADIENNE, 1940-1949 / Saint-Louis-Daniel, Soeur – 1964. SEM105P4 – 6mf – 9 – cn Bibl Nat [070]

BIBLIOGRAPHIE ANALYTIQUE DE L'OEUVRE DE MGR ARTHUR MAHEUX, P.D., ARCHIVISTE DU SEMINAIRE DE QUEBEC, MEMBRE DE LA SOCIETE ROYALE DU CANADA / Thibault, Priscille – 1964. SEM105P4 – 2mf – 9 – cn Bibl Nat [240]

BIBLIOGRAPHIE ANALYTIQUE DE L'OEUVRE DE MONSEIGNEUR ALBERT TESSIER, P.D. DE LA SOCIETE ROYALE DU CANADA, DE LA SOCIETE DES DIX, VISITEUR EN CHEF DES INSTITUTS FAMILIAUX... / Elisabeth-de-la-Trinite, Soeur – 1962. SEM105P4 – 2mf – 9 – cn Bibl Nat [971]

BIBLIOGRAPHIE ANALYTIQUE DE L'OEUVRE DE MONSEIGNEUR ARTHUR MAHEUX DE LA SOCIETE ROYALE DU CANADA, ARCHIVISTE AU SEMINAIRE DE QUEBEC / Bois, Jacqueline – 1964. SEM105P4 – 1mf – 9 – cn Bibl Nat [240]

BIBLIOGRAPHIE ANALYTIQUE DE L'OEUVRE DE MONSEIGNEUR VICTORIN GERMAIN, P.D., D.TH., L.PH., O.B.E., DIRECTEUR-ADMINISTRATEUR DE LA SAUVEGARDE DE L'ENFANCE / Marie-Liberatrice, Soeur – 1962 [i.e. 1963]. SEM105P4 – 3mf – 9 – cn Bibl Nat [360]

BIBLIOGRAPHIE ANALYTIQUE DE L'OEUVRE DE MONSIEUR AUGUSTE VIATTE / Belanger, Pierrette – 1948. SEM105P4 – 1mf – 9 – cn Bibl Nat [440]

BIBLIOGRAPHIE ANALYTIQUE DE L'OEUVRE DE MONSIEUR CHARLES-MARIE BOISSONNAULT, HISTORIEN, POETE, CRITIQUE ET PUBLICISTE / Lapointe, Madeleine – 1959. SEM105P4 – 1mf – 9 – cn Bibl Nat [971]

BIBLIOGRAPHIE ANALYTIQUE DE L'OEUVRE DE MONSIEUR CHARLES-MARIE BOISSONNAULT, HISTORIEN, POETE ET CRITIQUE / Guire, Juliette de – 1950. SEM105P4 – 1mf – 9 – cn Bibl Nat [971]

BIBLIOGRAPHIE ANALYTIQUE DE L'OEUVRE DE MONSIEUR L'ABBE JEAN-BAPTISTE GAUVIN, L.PH., D.TH., PRINCIPAL DE L'ECOLE NORMALE DE MONT-JOLI / Cherubins, Marie des – 1963. SEM105P4 – 2mf – 9 – cn Bibl Nat [370]

BIBLIOGRAPHIE ANALYTIQUE DE L'OEUVRE DE MONSIEUR LE CHANOINE GEORGES PANNETON, TROIS-RIVIERES / Saint-Alphonse-de-Jesus – 1963 [i.e. 1964]. SEM105P4 – 2mf – 9 – cn Bibl Nat [240]

BIBLIOGRAPHIE ANALYTIQUE DE L'OEUVRE DE MONSIEUR LE CHANOINE PAUL-EMILE CREPEAULT, 1944-1964 / Gingras, Jean-Jules – 1965. SEM105P4 – 1mf – 9 – cn Bibl Nat [240]

BIBLIOGRAPHIE ANALYTIQUE DE L'OEUVRE DE MONSIEUR PIERRE-H. RUEL, DOYEN, FACULTE DES SCIENCES DE L'EDUCATION, UNIVERSITE DE SHERBROOKE / Saint-Raymond-du-Sauveur, Soeur – 1964. SEM105P4 – 2mf – 9 – cn Bibl Nat [370]

BIBLIOGRAPHIE ANALYTIQUE DE L'OEUVRE DE MONSIEUR RENE POMERLEAU, DOCTEUR ES SCIENCES DE LA SOCIETE ROYALE DU CANADA, PATHOLOGISTE FORESTIER, LABORATOIRE DES RECHERCHES FORESTIERES, GOUVERNEMENT DU CANADA, QUEBEC / Maheux, Laura – 1964. SEM105P4 – 2mf – 9 – cn Bibl Nat [611]

BIBLIOGRAPHIE ANALYTIQUE DE L'OEUVRE DE ODILON ARTEAU, REDACTEUR A L'ACTION CATHOLIQUE / Sainte-Anne-de-Marie, Soeur – 1964. SEM105P4 – 6mf – 9 – cn Bibl Nat [070]

BIBLIOGRAPHIE ANALYTIQUE DE L'OEUVRE DE OLIVETTE LAMONTAGNE / Gagnon, Jacques Etiennette – 1957. SEM105P4 – 1mf – 9 – cn Bibl Nat [010]

BIBLIOGRAPHIE ANALYTIQUE DE L'OEUVRE DE REVERENDE SOEUR SAINTE-CLAIRE-DE-RIMINI (1887-), SOEUR DE LA CHARITE DE QUEBEC / Sainte-Apollonie, Soeur – 1962. SEM105P4 – 1mf – 9 – cn Bibl Nat [240]

BIBLIOGRAPHIE ANALYTIQUE DE L'OEUVRE DE SOEUR MARIE-EMMANUEL, RELIGIEUSE URSULINE, PROFESSEUR DE LITTERATURE FRANCAISE AU COLLEGE DES URSULINES DE QUEBEC / Sainte-Madeleine, Soeur – 1955. SEM105P4 – 1mf – 9 – cn Bibl Nat [240]

BIBLIOGRAPHIE ANALYTIQUE DE L'OEUVRE DE SON EXCELLENCE REV'ME MGR NAPOLEON-ALEXANDRE LABRIE, C.J.M.,.... / Guilbault, Germaine – 1964. SEM105P4 – 2mf – 9 – cn Bibl Nat [240]

BIBLIOGRAPHIE ANALYTIQUE DE L'OEUVRE DU DOCTEUR DE LA BROQUERIE FORTIER, M.D. F.A.A.P., PROFESSEUR TITULAIRE DE CLINIQUE PEDIATRIQUE... / Paul de Rome, Soeur – 1962. SEM105P4 – 2mf – 9 – cn Bibl Nat [618]

BIBLIOGRAPHIE ANALYTIQUE DE L'OEUVRE DU DOCTEUR JEAN-BAPTISTE JOBIN, PRESIDENT DU COLLEGE DES MEDECINS ET CHIRURGIENS DE LA PROVINCE DE QUEBEC / Desjardins, Jeannette – 1963. SEM105P4 – 2mf – 9 – cn Bibl Nat [610]

BIBLIOGRAPHIE ANALYTIQUE DE L'OEUVRE DU DOCTEUR JEAN-CHARLES MILLER, MEDECIN-PSYCHIATRE A L'ECOLE LA JEMMERAIS, 1898-1952 / Montciel, Marie-de – 1963. SEM105P4 – 3mf – 9 – cn Bibl Nat [616]

BIBLIOGRAPHIE ANALYTIQUE DE L'OEUVRE DU DOCTEUR LOUIS-EDMOND HAMELIN, PROFESSEUR TITULAIRE DE GEOGRAPHIE A L'UNIVERSITE LAVAL... / Saint-Alphonse-de-Liguori, Marie de – 1962 [i.e. 1963]. SEM105P4 – 2mf – 9 – cn Bibl Nat [900]

BIBLIOGRAPHIE ANALYTIQUE DE L'OEUVRE DU DOCTEUR MARCEL LANGLOIS, PROFESSEUR TITULAIRE A L'UNIVERSITE LAVAL, CERTIFIE DU COLLEGE ROYAL EN PEDIATRIE... / Marie Gemma, Soeur – 1961. SEM105P4 – 1mf – 9 – cn Bibl Nat [618]

BIBLIOGRAPHIE ANALYTIQUE DE L'OEUVRE DU DOCTEUR PIERRE JOBIN... / Christine-Marie, Soeur – 1964. SEM105P4 – 2mf – 9 – cn Bibl Nat [611]

BIBLIOGRAPHIE ANALYTIQUE DE L'OEUVRE DU DOCTEUR ROLAND DESMEULES, M.D. / Sainte-Veronique, Soeur – 1964. SEM105P4 – 2mf – 9 – cn Bibl Nat [616]

BIBLIOGRAPHIE ANALYTIQUE DE L'OEUVRE DU R. PERE PHILIAS F. BOURGEOIS DE LA CONGREGATION DE SAINTE-CROIX, PROFESSEUR DE LITTERATURE ET D'HISTOIRE A L'UNIVERSITE SAINT-JOSEPH / Saint-Marc, Mere – 1964. SEM105P4 – 2mf – 9 – cn Bibl Nat [400]

BIBLIOGRAPHIE ANALYTIQUE DE L'OEUVRE DU REVEREND PERE ALEXIS DE BARBEZIEUX, CAPUCIN / Dumas, Gabriel-Marie – 1956. SEM105P4 – 1mf – 9 – cn Bibl Nat [240]

BIBLIOGRAPHIE ANALYTIQUE DE L'OEUVRE DU REVEREND PERE EDMOND GAUDRON, O.F.M., D.PH. (LOUVAIN), PROFESSEUR D'HISTOIRE DE LA PHILOSOPHIE ANCIENNE A LA FACULTE DE PHILOSOPHIE DE L'UNIVERSITE LAVAL DE QUEBEC / Saint-Jean-de-Brebeuf-Hudon, Mere – 1956. SEM105P4 – 1mf – 9 – cn Bibl Nat [100]

BIBLIOGRAPHIE ANALYTIQUE DE L'OEUVRE DU REVEREND PERE EUGENE LEFEBVRE... / Roy, Jean – 1960. SEM105P4 – 1mf – 9 – cn Bibl Nat [240]

BIBLIOGRAPHIE ANALYTIQUE DE L'OEUVRE DU REVEREND PERE JEAN BOUSQUET, O.P., LECTEUR EN THEOLOGIE / Marie-Helene-de Rome, Soeur – 1964. SEM105P4 – 1mf – 9 – cn Bibl Nat [240]

BIBLIOGRAPHIE ANALYTIQUE DE L'OEUVRE DU R.P. J.-HERMANN POISSON / Saint-Damase-Marie, Soeur – 1962. SEM105P4 – 1mf – 9 – cn Bibl Nat [010]

BIBLIOGRAPHIE ANALYTIQUE DE L'OEUVRE DU R.P. MARCEL DUBOIS, C.SS.R. / Marcotte, Beatrice – 1957. SEM105P4 – 1mf – 9 – cn Bibl Nat [010]

BIBLIOGRAPHIE ANALYTIQUE DE L'OEUVRE D'UN GRAND CHRONIQUEUR LOUIS-PHILIPPE AUDET, DR PED., MEMBRE DE LA SOCIETE DES ECRIVAINS CANADIENS... / Louis-Ernest, Soeur – 1963. SEM105P4 – 3mf – 9 – cn Bibl Nat [400]

BIBLIOGRAPHIE ANALYTIQUE DE LOUIS HEMON / Carpentier, Denyse – 1962 [i.e. 1963]. SEM105P4 – 1mf – 9 – cn Bibl Nat [010]

BIBLIOGRAPHIE ANALYTIQUE DE LOUIS-ALEXANDRE BELISLE, AUTEUR ET EDITEUR / Blouin, Gervaise – 1953. SEM105P4 – 1mf – 9 – cn Bibl Nat [700]

BIBLIOGRAPHIE ANALYTIQUE DE LUC LACOURCIERE, TITULAIRE DE LA CHAIRE DE FOLKLORE, UNIVERSITE LAVAL, QUEBEC / Couture, Marguerite – 1950. SEM105P4 – 1mf – 9 – cn Bibl Nat [390]

BIBLIOGRAPHIE ANALYTIQUE DE M. JEAN-CHARLES FALARDEAU, SOCIOLOGUE, DIRECTEUR DU DEPARTEMENT DE SOCIOLOGIE A LA FACULTE DES SCIENCES SOCIALES DE L'UNIVERSITE LAVAL / Legare, Claire – 1953. SEM105P4 – 1mf – 9 – cn Bibl Nat [301]

BIBLIOGRAPHIE ANALYTIQUE DE MADAME HELENE B. BEAUSEJOUR / Gagnon, Marcelle – 1964. SEM105P4 – 1mf – 9 – cn Bibl Nat [010]

BIBLIOGRAPHIE ANALYTIQUE DE MADAME YOLANDE CHENE / Morissette, Rachel – 1963. SEM105P4 – 1mf – 9 – cn Bibl Nat [010]

BIBLIOGRAPHIE ANALYTIQUE DE MADEMOISELLE SIMONE PARE, M.S.S., PROFESSEUR A L'ECOLE DE SERVICE SOCIAL, FACULTE DES SCIENCES SOCIALES, UNIVERSITE LAVAL / Gignac, Francoise – 1958. SEM105P4 – 2mf – 9 – cn Bibl Nat [300]

BIBLIOGRAPHIE ANALYTIQUE DE MARIE-THERESE 1944-1961 (MLLE MARIE-THERESE CHEVALIER) RESPONSABLE DU SERVICE MARIAL DE MONTREAL ET REDACTRICE DU DIGESTE MARIAL DE 1948 A 1961 / Recouvrance, Marie de la – 1962. SEM105P4 – 2mf – 9 – cn Bibl Nat [360]

BIBLIOGRAPHIE ANALYTIQUE DE MAXINE, MEMBRE DE LA SOCIETE DES ECRIVAINS CANADIENS ET DE LA SOCIETE DES ECRIVAINS POUR LA JEUNESSE / Lemay, Clotilde – 1950. SEM105P4 – 1mf – 9 – cn Bibl Nat [400]

BIBLIOGRAPHIE ANALYTIQUE DE MGR LOUIS-JOSEPH AUBIN, P.D., PRINCIPAL DE L'ECOLE NORMALE N.-D. DU BON-CONSEIL, CHICOUTIMI / Croix, Madeleine-de-la – 1961. SEM105P4 – 2mf – 9 – cn Bibl Nat [370]

BIBLIOGRAPHIE ANALYTIQUE DE MME PAULE DEVELUY, MEMBRE DE LA SOCIETE DES ECRIVAINS CANADIENS, ECRIVAIN CONSEIL... / Brulotte, Marie-Berthe – 1964. SEM105P4 – 2mf – 9 – cn Bibl Nat [400]

BIBLIOGRAPHIE ANALYTIQUE DE MONSEIGNEUR FELIX-ANTOINE SAVARD, PROFESSEUR DE POESIE FRANCAISE A L'UNIVERSITE LAVAL / Therese du Carmel, Soeur – 1964. SEM105P4 – 3mf – 9 – cn Bibl Nat [440]

BIBLIOGRAPHIE ANALYTIQUE DE MONSIEUR ALPHONSE DESILETS / Gresley, J -E Le – 1950. SEM105P4 – 1mf – 9 – cn Bibl Nat [010]

BIBLIOGRAPHIE ANALYTIQUE DE MONSIEUR ANDRE GIROUX, PUBLICISTE AU MINISTERE DE L'INDUSTRIE ET DU COMMERCE / Giroux, Yvette – 1948. SEM105P4 – 1mf – 9 – cn Bibl Nat [380]

BIBLIOGRAPHIE ANALYTIQUE DE MONSIEUR FRANCIS DESROCHES / Pouliot, Ghislaine – 1959. SEM105P4 – 1mf – 9 – cn Bibl Nat [010]

BIBLIOGRAPHIE ANALYTIQUE DE MONSIEUR L'ABBE ARMAND DUBE, CURE DE KAMOURASKA / Perusse, Claire – 1957. SEM105P4 – 1mf – 9 – cn Bibl Nat [240]

BIBLIOGRAPHIE ANALYTIQUE DE MONSIEUR L'ABBE ROLAND DUFOUR, DIRECTEUR DE LA REVUE TEMOIGNAGES, AUMONIER A L'INSTITUT FAMILIAL N.-D. DU BON-CONSEIL, CHICOUTIMI / Sainte-Candide, Soeur – 1962. SEM105P4 – 2mf – 9 – cn Bibl Nat [350]

BIBLIOGRAPHIE ANALYTIQUE DE MONSIEUR YVON THERIAULT, CONSEILLER EN RELATIONS PUBLIQUES / Defoy, Louisa – 1960. SEM105P4 – 1mf – 9 – cn Bibl Nat [650]

BIBLIOGRAPHIE ANALYTIQUE DE OEUVRES DE M. JEAN-MARIE LAURENCE, DIRECTEUR LINGUISTIQUE ET CHEF DES SERVICES D'ANNONCEURS DES RESEAUX FRANCAIS DE RADIO-CANADA / Clarence, Frere – 1964. SEM105P4 – 2mf – 9 – cn Bibl Nat [440]

BIBLIOGRAPHIE ANALYTIQUE DE PAUL LEGENDRE, REALISATEUR A RADIO-CANADA, MEMBRE DE LA "SOCIETE DES ECRIVAINS CANADIENS" / Roland, Jacqueline – 1953. SEM105P4 – 1mf – 9 – cn Bibl Nat [380]

BIBLIOGRAPHIE ANALYTIQUE DE REINE MALOUIN, MEMBRE DE LA SOCIETE DES ECRIVAINS CANADIENS, DIRECTRICE DE LA SOCIETE DES POETES DU CANADA ET SOCIETAIRE DE L'ACADEMIE DE LA BALLADE FRANCAISE / Levasseur, Carmelle – 1950. SEM105P4 – 1mf – 9 – cn Bibl Nat [440]

BIBLIOGRAPHIE ANALYTIQUE DE RENEE DES ORMES / Talbot, Bernadette – 1947. SEM105P4 – 1mf – 9 – cn Bibl Nat [010]

BIBLIOGRAPHIE ANALYTIQUE DE SIMONE BUSSIERES / Gagnon, Francoise – 1963. SEM105P4 – 1mf – 9 – cn Bibl Nat [010]

BIBLIOGRAPHIE ANALYTIQUE DE SON EXCELLENCE MONSEIGNEUR JEAN-MARIE FORTIER, EVEQUE DE GASPE / Galilee, Madeleine-de – 1965. SEM105P4 – 3mf – 9 – cn Bibl Nat [240]

BIBLIOGRAPHIE ANALYTIQUE DES ECRITS CANADIENS SUR L'OEUVRE ET LA PERSONNALITE DE CORNELIUS KRIEGHOFF / Cimon, Constance – 1964. SEM105P4 – 1mf – 9 – cn Bibl Nat [400]

BIBLIOGRAPHIE ANALYTIQUE DES ECRITS DE JEAN HUBERT, EDITORIALISTE A L'ACTION / Labrie, Jean-Marc – 1964. SEM105P4 – 4mf – 9 – cn Bibl Nat [070]

BIBLIOGRAPHIE ANALYTIQUE DES ECRITS PUBLIES AU CANADA FRANCAIS DE 1930 A 1960 SUR LA PEINTURE RELIGIEUSE / Sainte-Jeanne-de-Domremy, Marie de – 1964. SEM105P4 – 3mf – 9 – cn Bibl Nat [750]

BIBLIOGRAPHIE ANALYTIQUE DES ECRITS PUBLIES PAR LES SOEURS DE LA CHARITE DE QUEBEC, 1942-1961 / Varennes, Marguerite-de – 1964. SEM105P4 – 2mf – 9 – cn Bibl Nat [240]

BIBLIOGRAPHIE ANALYTIQUE DES ETUDES PEDOLOGIQUES DES SOLS DES COMTES DANS LA PROVINCE DE QUEBEC / Bernier-Lesieur, Raymond – 1956. SEM105P4 – 3mf – 9 – cn Bibl Nat [618]

BIBLIOGRAPHIE ANALYTIQUE DES EVEQUES ET DE QUELQUES PERES EUDISTES AU CANADA / Babin, Basile J – 1949. SEM105P4 – 2mf – 9 – cn Bibl Nat [240]

BIBLIOGRAPHIE ANALYTIQUE DES ILES-DE-LA-MADELEINE / Harvey, Leonise – 1964. SEM105P4 – 3mf – 9 – cn Bibl Nat [910]

BIBLIOGRAPHIE ANALYTIQUE DES NOTICES BIOGRAPHIQUES ET DES ECRITS DES SOEURS DE LA CHARITE DE QUEBEC DECEDEES, 1851-1917 / Sainte-Heliene-de-Marie, Soeur – 1963. SEM105P4 – 2mf – 9 – cn Bibl Nat [240]

BIBLIOGRAPHIE ANALYTIQUE DES NOTICES BIOGRAPHIQUES ET DES ECRITS DES SOEURS DE LA CHARITE DE QUEBEC DECEDEES, 1918-1938 / Sainte-Mariette, Soeur – 1963. SEM105P4 – 2mf – 9 – cn Bibl Nat [240]

BIBLIOGRAPHIE ANALYTIQUE DES NOTICES BIOGRAPHIQUES ET DES ECRITS DES SOEURS DE LA CHARITE DE QUEBEC DECEDEES, 1939-1959 / Sainte-Therese-de-l'Enfant-Jesus, Soeur – 1964. SEM105P4 – 3mf – 9 – cn Bibl Nat [240]

BIBLIOGRAPHIE ANALYTIQUE DES OUVRAGES DE LANGUE FRANCAISE SUR L'HISTOIRE DE LA VILLE DE QUEBEC AU 19E SIECLE / Cote, Athanase – 1964. SEM105P4 – 2mf – 9 – cn Bibl Nat [910]

BIBLIOGRAPHIE ANALYTIQUE DES OUVRAGES EDITES PAR LES PRESSES UNIVERSITAIRES LAVAL, 1950 A 1957 / Pare, Richard – 1959. SEM105P4 – 1mf – 9 – cn Bibl Nat [070]

BIBLIOGRAPHIE ANALYTIQUE DES RECUEILS BIOGRAPHIQUES CANADIENS, FRANCAIS ET ANGLAIS / Rainville, Lucie – 1964. SEM105P4 – 2mf – 9 – cn Bibl Nat [920]

BIBLIOGRAPHIE ANALYTIQUE DES TRAVAUX DE PAUL-ANTOINE GIGUERE, DIRECTEUR DU DEPARTEMENT DE CHIMIE, FACULTE DES SCIENCES, UNIVERSITE LAVAL / Tanguay, Marthe – 1959. SEM105P4 – 1mf – 9 – cn Bibl Nat [540]

BIBLIOGRAPHIE ANALYTIQUE DES TRAVAUX DE PAUL-EDOUARD GAGNON... / Fortin, Isabelle – 1958. SEM105P4 – 1mf – 9 – cn Bibl Nat [010]

BIBLIOGRAPHIE ANALYTIQUE DU BASSON / Laberge, Gaetan – 1954. SEM105P4 – 1mf – 9 – cn Bibl Nat [780]

BIBLIOGRAPHIE ANALYTIQUE DU DOCTEUR EMILE GAUMOND CHEF DU SERVICE DE DERMATO-SYPHILIGRAPHIE, HOTEL-DIEU, QUEBEC... / Audet, M-R – 1953. SEM105P4 – 1mf – 9 – cn Bibl Nat [616]

BIBLIOGRAPHIE ANALYTIQUE DU DOCTEUR LOUIS-GEORGES GODIN (1897-1932) / Giroux, Pauline – 1964. SEM105P4 – 2mf – 9 – cn Bibl Nat [610]

BIBLIOGRAPHIE ANALYTIQUE DU MAJOR LOUIS-ALEXANDRE PLANTE / Plante, Therese – 1953. SEM105P4 – 1mf – 9 – cn Bibl Nat [355]

BIBLIOGRAPHIE ANALYTIQUE DU REVEREND PERE PHILIPPE DESCHAMPS, C.S.V., PROVESSEUR AGREGE A LA FACULTE DE PEDAGOGIE ET D'ORIENTATION DE L'UNIVERSITE LAVAL / Charlotin, Marie-Joseph – 1950. SEM105P4 – 1mf – 9 – cn Bibl Nat [370]

BIBLIOGRAPHIE ANALYTIQUE DU RHUMATISME ARTICULAIRE AIGU D'APRES LA DOCUMENTATION DE LA BIBLIOTHEQUE MEDICALE DE L'HOPITAL DU ST SACREMENT... / Baillargeon, Cecile – 1954. SEM105P4 – 1mf – 9 – cn Bibl Nat [610]

BIBLIOGRAPHIE ANALYTIQUE DU SUJET PEDAGOGIQUE : L'ECOLE ACTIVE EN GENERAL A L'ECOLE PRIMAIRE ELEMENTAIRE / Roy, Marguerite – 1960. SEM105P4 – 1mf – 9 – cn Bibl Nat [370]

BIBLIOGRAPHIE ANALYTIQUE PARTIELLE DE LA COTE-NORD / Coulombe, Marie-Anne – 1950. SEM105P4 – 2mf – 9 – cn Bibl Nat [971]

BIBLIOGRAPHIE ANALYTIQUE "POUR MIEUX SERVIR", DE 1956 A 1960 / Monique-Madeleine, Soeur – 1962. SEM105P4 – 1mf – 9 – cn Bibl Nat [240]

BIBLIOGRAPHIE ANALYTIQUE, PRECEDEE D'UNE BIOGRAPHIE DE MONSEIGNEUR ALPHONSE-MARIE PARENT... / l'Aeropagite, Marie-de-Saint-Denis – 1964. SEM105P4 – 2mf – 9 – cn Bibl Nat [370]

BIBLIOGRAPHIE ANALYTIQUE, PRECEDEE D'UNE BIOGRAPHIE, DE MONSIEUR L'ABBE ALEXANDRE PARADIS, P.M.E., AUMONIER AU FOYER VILLA-MARIA, SAINT-ALEXANDRE, KAMOURASKA / Sainte-Rachel-Therese, Soeur – 1964. SEM105P4 – 3mf – 9 – cn Bibl Nat [240]

BIBLIOGRAPHIE ANALYTIQUE, PRECEDEE D'UNE BIOGRAPHIE, DU REV. PERE FLORIAN LARIVIERE, S.J., RECTEUR DU COLLEGE DES JESUITES, QUEBEC, 1943-1962 / Sainte-Agilberte, Soeur – 1963. SEM105P4 – 1mf – 9 – cn Bibl Nat [370]

BIBLIOGRAPHIE ANALYTIQUE PRECEDEE D'UNE BIOGRAPHIE DU REV. PERE JEAN-PAUL DALLAIRE, S.J. COLLEGE DES JESUITES, QUEBEC / Sion, Marie-de – 1960. SEM105P4 – 2mf – 9 – cn Bibl Nat [240]

BIBLIOGRAPHIE ANALYTIQUE, PRECEDEE D'UNE BIOGRAPHIE, DU REVEREND PERE FRANCIS GOYER, CONGREGATION DES PERES DU TRES SAINT-SACREMENT, QUEBEC, 1948-1962 / Saint-Donat-Joseph, Soeur – 1963. SEM105P4 – 1mf – 9 – cn Bibl Nat [240]

BIBLIOGRAPHIE ANALYTIQUE, PRECEDEE D'UNE BIOGRAPHIE, DU R.P. HENRI-MARIE GUINDON, S.M.M., DOCTEUR EN THEOLOGIE DE LA SOCIETE CANADIENNE D'ETUDES MARIALES / Saint-Antoine-de-Padoue, Soeur – 1962. SEM105P4 – 2mf – 9 – cn Bibl Nat [240]

BIBLIOGRAPHIE ANALYTIQUE SUR LA METHODOLOGIE DE L'HISTOIRE DU CANADA (1950-1962) / Gabriel-de-l'Annonciation, Soeur – 1963. SEM105P4 – 1mf – 9 – cn Bibl Nat [971]

BIBLIOGRAPHIE ANALYTIQUE SUR L'ARTISANAT CANADIEN / Saint-Achillas, Soeur – 1962. SEM105P4 – 2mf – 9 – cn Bibl Nat [740]

BIBLIOGRAPHIE ANALYTIQUE SUR LE FORUM CATHOLIQUE DE MONTREAL (CATHOLIC INQUIRY FORUM) 1952-1962 / Sacre-Coeur, Florence-du – 1963. SEM105P4 – 2mf – 9 – cn Bibl Nat [240]

BIBLIOGRAPHIE ANALYTIQUE SUR L'HYGIENE MENTALE PREVENTIVE DES JEUNES DE LA PROVINCE DE QUEBEC, 1925-1955 / Marie-Patricia, Soeur – 1963. SEM105P4 – 1mf – 9 – cn Bibl Nat [616]

BIBLIOGRAPHIE ANNOTEE D'OUVRAGES GENEALOGIQUES A LA BIBLIOTHEQUE DU PARLEMENT / Varennes, Kathleen M de – Ottawa: Bibliotheque du Parlement, 1963. SEM16P270 – 1r – 5 – Can$9.00 – cn Bibl Nat [920]

BIBLIOGRAPHIE CANADIENNE DE L'ACCREDITATION DES HOPITAUX, 1955-1962 / Sainte-Anne-du-Sauveur, Soeur – 1962. SEM105P4 – 2mf – 9 – cn Bibl Nat [360]

BIBLIOGRAPHIE CANADIENNE DES ARCHIVES MEDICALES D'UN HOPITAL, 1944-1950 / Ste-Antonie, Soeur – 1960. SEM105P4 – 1mf – 9 – cn Bibl Nat [610]

BIBLIOGRAPHIE CANADIENNE DES ARCHIVES MEDICALES D'UN HOPITAL, 1951-1956 / Saint-Pierre, Jeanne-M – 1961. SEM105P4 – 2mf – 9 – cn Bibl Nat [610]

BIBLIOGRAPHIE COLLECTIVE DES AUTEURS DE LA REGION DU SAGUENAY / St-Pierre, Jacqueline – 1964. SEM105P4 – 2mf – 9 – cn Bibl Nat [400]

BIBLIOGRAPHIE COREENNE / Courant, Maurice – 1890 – 9 – fr Orientalistes [010]

BIBLIOGRAPHIE COURANTE D'ARTICLES DE PERIODIQUES POSTERIEURS A 1944 SUR LES PROBLEMES POLITIQUES, ECONOMIQUES ET SOCIAUX / Fondation nationale des Sciences politiques. Paris – (First Suppl.-1969.-25,100 cards 2 reels.$225.00 export 270.00.-ISBN 0-8161-1484-6; Second Suppl.-1970.-26,700 cards 2 reels.$225.00 export $270.00.-ISBN 0-8161-1485-4; Third Suppl.-1971.-28,200 cards 2 reels.$225.00 export $270.00.-ISBN 0-8161-1486-2; Fourth Suppl.-1972.-26,500 cards 4 reels.$225.00 export $270.00.-ISBN 0-8161-1241-X; Fifth Suppl.-1973.-24,300 cards 4 reels.$225.00 export $270.00.-ISBN 0-8161-1242-8; Sixth Suppl.-1974.-21,300 cards 4 reels.$225.00 export $270.00.-ISBN 0-8161-1243-6; Seventh Suppl.-1976.-23,800 cards 2 reels.$225.00 export $270.00.-ISBN 0-8161-1244-4; Eighth Suppl.-1977.-26,300 cards 2 reels.$225.00 export $270.00.-ISBN 0-8161-1505-2; Ninth Suppl.-1978.-20,800 cards 2 reels.$240.00 export $290.00.-ISBN 0-8161-1534-6; Tenth Suppl.-1979.-21,600 cards 2 reels.$290.00 export $350.00.-ISBN 0-8161-1487-0; Eleventh Suppl.-1981.-27,000 cards 2 reels.$290.00 export $350.00.-ISBN 0-8161-1535-4) – 1 – uk Hall [320]

BIBLIOGRAPHIE CRITIQUE ET ETAT DES CONNAISSANCES SUR LA PATAGONIE ARGENTINE / Guffroy, J – 9 – F100.00 – fr Ethnologie [972]

BIBLIOGRAPHIE DE CERTAINS MARISTES (PERES, EVEQUES ET MISSIONNAIRES) AMERICAINS ET NEO-ZELANDAIS / Bisson, Fernand – 1953. SEM105P4 – 3mf – 9 – cn Bibl Nat [240]

BIBLIOGRAPHIE DE JOSEPH BELLEAU / Vallee, Camille – 1951. SEM105P4 – 1mf – 9 – cn Bibl Nat [010]

BIBLIOGRAPHIE DE JOSEPH-EDMOND ROY / Verret, Madeleine – 1947. SEM105P4 – 1mf – 9 – cn Bibl Nat [010]

BIBLIOGRAPHIE DE LA CROISADE EUCHARISTIQUE, MOUVEMENT D'"ACTION CATHOLIQUE DES ENFANTS" (PIE 12) / Helene de la Presentation, Soeur – 1964. SEM105P4 – 2mf – 9 – cn Bibl Nat [240]

BIBLIOGRAPHIE DE LA FRANCE – Bibliographie. Complete Collection Includes all Sections and Indexes: 3890.00. v. 1-160. 1811-1971 – 1,5,6 – us Princeton Micro [010]

BIBLIOGRAPHIE DE LA FRANCE – Chronique. v. 1-160. 1811-1971 – 1,5,6 – us Princeton Micro [010]

BIBLIOGRAPHIE DE LA FRANCE – Indexes. v. 86-160. 1898-1971 – 1,5,6 – us Princeton Micro [010]

BIBLIOGRAPHIE DE LA FRANCE. ANNONCES – v1-160. 1811-1971 – 1,5,6 – us Princeton Micro [073]

BIBLIOGRAPHIE DE LA NOUVELLE-CALEDONIE / O'Reilly, P – 9 – F100.00 – fr Ethnologie [980]

BIBLIOGRAPHIE DE LA PEINTURE AU CANADA / Charbonneau, Jeannine – 1952. SEM105P4 – 1mf – 9 – cn Bibl Nat [750]

BIBLIOGRAPHIE DE LA POESIE CANADIENNE-FRANCAISE 1935-1958 / Fortier, Suzanne – 1960. SEM105P4 – 1mf – 9 – cn Bibl Nat [018]

BIBLIOGRAPHIE DE LA PSYCHOLOGIE RATIONNELLE AU CANADA FRANCAIS, 1945-1963 / Germaine-Marie, Soeur – 1964. SEM105P4 – 1mf – 9 – cn Bibl Nat [150]

BIBLIOGRAPHIE DE L'AFRIQUE EQUATORIALE FRANCAISE / Bruel, Georges – Paris, 1914 – 6mf – 9 – ne IDC [440]

BIBLIOGRAPHIE DE L'AFRIQUE EQUATORIALE FRANCAISE / Bruel, Georges – Paris: E Larose, 1914 – 1 – us Res Libr [010]

BIBLIOGRAPHIE DE L'AFRIQUE OCCIDENTALE FRANCAISE / Joucla, E – (Societe d'Editions Geographiques Maritimes et Coloniales). Paris. 1912. Paris. 1937. BA-384 2 – 14mf – 8 – ne IDC [960]

BIBLIOGRAPHIE DE L'HISTOIRE DE FRANCE : CATALOGUE METHODIQUE ET CHRONOLOGIQUE DES SOURCES ET DES OUVRAGES RELATIFS A L'HISTOIRE DE FRANCE DEPUIS LES ORIGINES JUSQU'EN, 1789 / Monod, G – Paris, 1888 – 5mf – ne IDC [944]

BIBLIOGRAPHIE DE L'HOTEL-DIEU D'ALMA / Sept-Douleurs, Marie-des – 1960 [i.e. 1961]. SEM105P4 – 1mf – 9 – cn Bibl Nat [360]

BIBLIOGRAPHIE DE L'HOTEL-DIEU ST-VALLIER DE CHICOUTIMI, 1879-1889 / Grace, Marie de la – 1962. SEM105P4 – 1mf – 9 – cn Bibl Nat [360]

BIBLIOGRAPHIE DE L'ILE D'ORLEANS / Leclerc, Marcel – 1950. SEM105P4 – 1mf – 9 – cn Bibl Nat [910]

BIBLIOGRAPHIE DE L'OEUVRE DE GEORGES DUHAMEL DE L'ACADEMIE FRANCAISE, PRESIDENT DE L'ALLIANCE FRANCAISE UNIVERSELLE... / Lizotte, Marguerite – 1947. SEM105P4 – 1mf – 9 – cn Bibl Nat [370]

BIBLIOGRAPHIE DE L'OEUVRE DE GERARD TREMBLAY, S.-MIN., MINISTERE DU TRAVAIL, GOUV. PROV., ANCIEN PROFESSEUR A L'UNIVERSITE LAVAL / Bourgoing, Andre – 1963. SEM105P4 – 1mf – 9 – cn Bibl Nat [370]

BIBLIOGRAPHIE DE L'OEUVRE DE JEANNE D'AIGLE (DAIGLE), MEMBRE DE LA SOCIETE DES ECRIVAINS CANADIENS... / Anges, Marie des – 1961. SEM105P4 – 2mf – 9 – cn Bibl Nat [400]

BIBLIOGRAPHIE DE L'OEUVRE DE LA VENERABLE ANNE-MARIE RIVIER, UNE FEMME-APOTRE, 1768-1838 / Saint-Jean-Eudes, Marie – 1964. SEM105P4 – 1mf – 9 – cn Bibl Nat [240]

BIBLIOGRAPHIE DE L'OEUVRE DE L'ABBE ANSELME LONGPRE, LICENCIE EN PHILOSOPHIE, LICENCIE EN THEOLOGIE, BACHELIER EN DROIT CANON, 1947-1964 / Sainte-Angele, Soeur – 1964. SEM105P4 – 2mf – 9 – cn Bibl Nat [100]

BIBLIOGRAPHIE DE L'OEUVRE DE LOUIS BERUBE... / Levesque, Ginette – 1962 [i.e. 1963]. SEM105P4 – 1mf – 9 – cn Bibl Nat [010]

BIBLIOGRAPHIE DE L'OEUVRE DE LOUIS-PHILIPPE AUDET, D. PED. / Chandonnet, Gemma – 1954. SEM105P4 – 2mf – 9 – cn Bibl Nat [010]

BIBLIOGRAPHIE DE L'OEUVRE DE LOUIS-PHILIPPE AUDET, L. SC. DE LA SOCIETE DES ECRIVAINS CANADIENS, PROFESSEUR A L'UNIVERSITE LAVAL / Cossette, Angele – 1948. SEM105P4 – 1mf – 9 – cn Bibl Nat [370]

BIBLIOGRAPHIE DE L'OEUVRE DE M. JEAN-BAPTISTE CAOUETTE, POETE CANADIEN / Legare, Helene – 1964. SEM105P4 – 1mf – 9 – cn Bibl Nat [440]

BIBLIOGRAPHIE DE L'OEUVRE DE MADAME FRANCOISE GAUDET-SMET DE LA SOCIETE DES ECRIVAINS CANADIENS ET DU CERCLE DE FEMMES JOURNALISTES, ECRIVAIN DE PRESSE, RADIO ET T.V., SPECIALISTE EN ARTS DOMESTIQUES / St-Gilles, Marie de – 1963. SEM105P4 – 3mf – 9 – cn Bibl Nat [070]

BIBLIOGRAPHIE DE L'OEUVRE DE MAURICE LEBEL, SECRETAIRE A LA FACULTE DES LETTRES ET PROFESSEUR DE LITTERATURE GRECQUE A L'UNIVERSITE LAVAL / Pare, Rosario – 1947. SEM105P4 – 1mf – 9 – cn Bibl Nat [400]

BIBLIOGRAPHIE DE L'OEUVRE DE MONSIEUR GERARD MORISSET, MEMBRE DE LA SOCIETE ROYALE DU CANADA, 1950-1962 / Garneau, Marthe – 1964. SEM105P4 – 1mf – 9 – cn Bibl Nat [010]

BIBLIOGRAPHIE DE L'OEUVRE DE MONSIEUR L'ABBE ADRIEN BOUFFARD, PTRE, SECRETAIRE NATIONAL DE L'UNION PONTIFICALE MISSIONNAIRE DU CLERGE... / Pierre-de-la-Croix, Soeur – 1962. SEM105P4 – 2mf – 9 – cn Bibl Nat [240]

BIBLIOGRAPHIE DE L'OEUVRE DE MONSIEUR L'ABBE ANDRE JOBIN, L. TH., PRINCIPAL DE L'ECOLE NORMALE NOTRE-DAME, ST-ROCH, QUEBEC, PROFESSEUR AU COLLEGE UNIVERSITAIRE GARNEAU, QUEBEC... / Celine-de-la-Presentation, Soeur – 1964. SEM105P4 – 2mf – 9 – cn Bibl Nat [240]

BIBLIOGRAPHIE DE L'OEUVRE DE MONSIEUR ROLLAND DUMAIS, CONSEILLER PEDAGOGIQUE EN SCIENCES NATURELLES... / Garneau, Robert – 1964. SEM105P4 – 2mf – 9 – cn Bibl Nat [500]

BIBLIOGRAPHIE DE L'OEUVRE DE MONSIEUR ROLLAND DUMAIS, CONSEILLER PEDAGOGIQUE EN SCIENCES NATURELLES A LA COMMISSION DES ECOLES CATHOLIQUES DE QUEBEC, DIRECTEUR-FONDATEUR DU CAMP MARIE-VICTORIN / Morin, Jacques – 1964. SEM105P4 – 2mf – 9 – cn Bibl Nat [500]

BIBLIOGRAPHIE DE L'OEUVRE DE SA GRANDEUR MONSEIGNEUR PAUL-EUGENE ROY, 1859-1926, DIX-HUITIEME EVEQUE ET HUITIEME ARCHEVEQUE DE QUEBEC / Perpetuel-Secours, Marie-du – 1964. SEM105P4 – 3mf – 9 – cn Bibl Nat [240]

BIBLIOGRAPHIE DE L'OEUVRE DU DOCTEUR ALBERT JOBIN, M.D., 1867 A 1952 / Raymond-Marie, Soeur – 1964. SEM105P4 – 2mf – 9 – cn Bibl Nat [610]

BIBLIOGRAPHIE DE L'OEUVRE DU DOCTEUR MARCEL LAPOINTE (PSEUDONYME: MARCEL PORTAL / Saint-Leonce, Soeur – 1962. SEM105P4 – 3mf – 9 – cn Bibl Nat [610]

BIBLIOGRAPHIE DE L'OEUVRE DU REVEREND PERE GASTON CARRIERE, O.M.I., PROFESSEUR DE PHILOSOPHIE A L'UNIVERSITE D'OTTAWA ET HISTORIEN DE LA CONGREGATION / Louis-Bernard, Soeur – 1963. SEM105P4 – 2mf – 9 – cn Bibl Nat [100]

BIBLIOGRAPHIE DE L'OEUVRE DU REVEREND PERE HECTOR-L. BERTRAND, S.J., FONDATEUR DU COMITE DES HOPITAUX DU QUEBEC... / Deschenes, Jean-Claude – 1963. SEM105P4 – 2mf – 9 – cn Bibl Nat [360]

BIBLIOGRAPHIE DE L'OEUVRE MUSICALE DU FRERE BARNABE, S.C., DOCTEUR EN MUSIQUE, MEMBRE DE LA SOCIETE DES COMPOSITEURS CANADIENS / Traversy, Paul – 1963. SEM105P4 – 1mf – 9 – cn Bibl Nat [780]

BIBLIOGRAPHIE DE LOTBINIERE / Couture, Suzanne – 1959. SEM105P4 – 1mf – 9 – cn Bibl Nat [010]

BIBLIOGRAPHIE DE M. JEAN-PAUL GELINAS, B.A., M.D. / Marie Simeon, Soeur – 1962. SEM105P4 – 1mf – 9 – cn Bibl Nat [240]

BIBLIOGRAPHIE DE MADAGASCAR / Grandidier, Guillaume – Paris: Comite de Madagascar, 1906 [i.e. 1905]-57 – 1 – us Res Libr [960]

BIBLIOGRAPHIE DE MADAGASCAR 1904-1933 / Grandidier, Guillaume – (Societe d'Editions Geographiques, Maritimes et Coloniales). Paris. 1935. BA-383 2 – 11mf – 8 – ne IDC [960]

BIBLIOGRAPHIE DE MADAME ELLA CHARLAND-OSTIGUY / Ostiguy, Flore-Ella – 1950. SEM105P4 – 1mf – 9 – cn Bibl Nat [010]

BIBLIOGRAPHIE DE MADAME EMMA BOIVIN-VAILLANCOURT / Lockwell, Huguette – [1954]. SEM105P4 – 1mf – 9 – cn Bibl Nat [010]

BIBLIOGRAPHIE DE MADAME GABRIELLE ROY / Gauthier, Georges – 1960. SEM105P4 – 2mf – 9 – cn Bibl Nat [010]

BIBLIOGRAPHIE DE MERE ISABELLE SORMANY, DITE LADAUVERSIERE, RELIGIEUSE HOSPITALIERE DE SAINT-JOSEPH, PREMIERE SUPERIEURE GENERALE 1897-1957... / Albert, Maria – 1962. SEM105P4 – 3mf – 9 – cn Bibl Nat [010]

BIBLIOGRAPHIE DE MME MARTHE LEMAIRE-DUGUAY / Dery, Marie-Claire – 1962. SEM105P4 – 2mf – 9 – cn Bibl Nat [971]

BIBLIOGRAPHIE DE MONSIEUR L'ABBE EMILE BEGIN, PROFESSEUR A L'UNIVERSITE LAVAL / Sainte-Enfance, Marie-de-la – 1963. SEM105P4 – 2mf – 9 – cn Bibl Nat [370]

BIBLIOGRAPHIE DE MONSIEUR L'ABBE HENRI GRENIER, DOCTEUR EN PHILOSOPHIE, DOCTEUR EN THEOLOGIE, DOCTEUR EN DROIT CANON / St-Didier, Marie de – 1948. SEM105P4 – 1mf – 9 – cn Bibl Nat [240]

BIBLIOGRAPHIE DE MONSIEUR L'ABBE HONORIUS PROVOST, L.TH., L.PH., DU SEMINAIRE DE QUEBEC, ARCHIVISTE A L'UNIVERSITE LAVAL / Labbe, Edith – 1962. SEM105P4 – 1mf – 9 – cn Bibl Nat [240]

BIBLIOGRAPHIE DE MONSIEUR L'ABBE J.-ALFRED TREMBLAY / Marie-de-la-Croix, Soeur – 1961. SEM105P4 – 1mf – 9 – cn Bibl Nat [240]

BIBLIOGRAPHIE DE MONSIEUR L'ABBE J.W. LAVERDIERE, GEOLOGUE-PRETRE / Chaperon, Elisee – 1957. SEM105P4 – 2mf – 9 – cn Bibl Nat [550]

BIBLIOGRAPHIE DE MONSIEUR L'ABBE PAUL-EMILE GOSSELIN, PROFESSEUR DE PHILOSOPHIE AU SEMINAIRE DE QUEBEC, SECRETAIRE GENERAL DU COMITE DE LA SURVIVANCE FRANCAISE EN AMERIQUE / Anges, Marie des – 1948. SEM105P4 – 1mf – 9 – cn Bibl Nat [100]

BIBLIOGRAPHIE DE MONSIEUR LE CURE L. BOISSEAU, CURE DE NEW CARLISLE / Alberta-Marie, Soeur – 1961. SEM105P4 – 1mf – 9 – cn Bibl Nat [010]

BIBLIOGRAPHIE DE MONSIEUR RICHARD JOLY, 1955 A 1963 / Larrivee, Pierrette – 1964. SEM105P4 – 1mf – 9 – cn Bibl Nat [010]

BIBLIOGRAPHIE DE NOS GRANDS PRIX DE LA PROVINCE, 1944-1954 / Saint-Hilaire, Alphonse – 1955. SEM105P4 – 3mf – 9 – cn Bibl Nat [971]

BIBLIOGRAPHIE DE PAUL-ANDRE LAMONTAGNE / Guay, Marcel – 1956. SEM105P4 – 1mf – 9 – cn Bibl Nat [010]

BIBLIOGRAPHIE DE [SES] OUEVRES / Goldziher, I & Heller, B – Paris, 1927 – 3mf – ne IDC [270]

BIBLIOGRAPHIE DE SOEUR MARIE DE SAINT-PAUL-DE-LA-CROIX, S.C.I.M. (GEORGIANNA JUNEAU) (1873-1940) / Saint-Joseph-du-Redempteur, Marie de – 1962. SEM105P4 – 2mf – 9 – cn Bibl Nat [240]

BIBLIOGRAPHIE DE STANISLAS VACHON : SES OEUVRES, SES ECRITS / Legare, Denise – 1955. SEM105P4 – 1mf – 9 – cn Bibl Nat [010]

BIBLIOGRAPHIE DER ARBEITEN VON PROF. DR. HELMUT BREUER UND DR. MARIA WEUFFEN, SOWIE ANDERER MITGLIEDER DER FORSCHUNGSGRUPPE "PROPHYLAKTISCHE DIAGNOSTIK" AN DER ERNST-MORITZ-ARNDT UNIVERSITAET GREIFSWALD / Amse, Corina – 1995 – 1mf – 9 – DM60.00 – 3-8267-2156-X – gw Hänsel [370]

BIBLIOGRAPHIE DER DEUTSCHEN UNIVERSITAETEN. SYSTEMATISCH GEORDNETES VERZEICHNIS DER BIS ENDE 1899 GEDRUCKTEN BUECHER UND AUFSAETZE UEBER DAS DEUTSCHE UNIVERSITAETSWESEN . DRITTER TEIL, REGISTER UND NACHTRAEGE ENTHALTEND – Leipzig, Berlin, 1905 – 2mf – 9 – DM100.00 – 3-89349-324-7 – gw Hänsel [370]

BIBLIOGRAPHIE DER DEUTSCHEN UNIVERSITAETEN. SYSTEMATISCH GEORDNETES VERZEICHNIS DER BIS ENDE 1899 GEDRUCKTEN BUECHER UND AUFSAETZE UEBER DAS DEUTSCHE UNIVERSITAETSWESEN : ERSTER ALLGEMEINER TEIL / ed by Erman, Wilhelm & Horn, Ewald – Leipzig, Berlin 1904 – 9mf – 9 – DM220.00 – 3-89349-223-2 – gw Hänsel [370]

BIBLIOGRAPHIE DER DEUTSCHEN UNIVERSITAETEN. SYSTEMATISCH GEORDNETES VERZEICHNIS DER BIS ENDE 1899 GEDRUCKTEN BUECHER UND AUFSAETZE UEBER DAS DEUTSCHE UNIVERSITAETSWESEN : ZWEITER, BESONDERER TEIL – Leipzig, Berlin, 1904 – 13mf – 9 – DM280.00 – 3-89349-323-9 – gw Hänsel [370]

BIBLIOGRAPHIE DER FREIMAUREREI... / Kloss, G – Frankfurt am Main, 1844 – 5mf – ne IDC [360]

BIBLIOGRAPHIE DER KLINISCHEN ENTOMOLOGIE / Huber, J C – Jena, 1899-1900.4pts.,Suppl. Z/1359/2 – 3mf – 8 – ne IDC [590]

BIBLIOGRAPHIE DER MUSIK-WERKE IN DER RATSSCHULBIBLIOTHEK ZU ZWICKAU / Volhardt, R – Leipzig: Breitkopf & Haertel, 1896 – 1 – us Sibley [780]

BIBLIOGRAPHIE DER SCHRIFTEN WILHELM BACHERS NEBST EINEM HEBRAEISCHEN SACH- UND ORTSNAMENREGISTER / Guttman, M & Klein, S; ed by Blau, L L – Frankfort a.M., 1910 – 1mf – ne IDC [470]

BIBLIOGRAPHIE DER STOFF- UND MOTIVGESCHICHTE DER DEUTSCHEN LITERATUR / Bauerhorst, Kurt – Berlin: W de Gruyter & Co, 1932 – 2r – 1 – us U.W. Library [430]

BIBLIOGRAPHIE DES BIOGRAPHIES DES RELIGIEUSES AUGUSTINES HOSPITALIERES DE LA MISERICORDE DE JESUS / Marie-de-la-Portectin, Soeur – 1962. SEM105P4 – 3mf – 9 – cn Bibl Nat [360]

BIBLIOGRAPHIE DES BIOGRAPHIES DES RELIGIEUSES DECEDEES A L'HOTEL-DIEU DU SACRE-COEUR DE JESUS DE QUEBEC : 1825-1960 / Saint-Augustin, Catherine-de – 1961. SEM105P4 – 1mf – 9 – cn Bibl Nat [240]

BIBLIOGRAPHIE DES BIOGRAPHIES DES RELIGIEUSES DECEDEES A L'HOTEL-DIEU DU SACRE-COEUR DE JESUS DE QUEBEC, 1879-1925 / Sainte-Monique, Soeur – 1961. SEM105P4 – 1mf – 9 – cn Bibl Nat [910]

BIBLIOGRAPHIE DES BIOGRAPHIES DES RELIGIEUSES DECEDEES A L'HOTEL-DIEU SAINT-VALLIER DE CHICOUTIMI (1884-1959) / Sainte Marie-Madeleine, Soeur – 1961. SEM105P4 – 1mf – 9 – cn Bibl Nat [910]

BIBLIOGRAPHIE DES ECRITS DU TRES REV. PERE PASCAL D'OTTAWA, EX-PROV. DE L'ORDRE DES FRERES MINEURS CAPUCINS, EX-PROF. DE PATROLOGIE ET D'HISTOIRE SAINTE / Bourdages, J – 1962. SEM105P4 – 2mf – 9 – cn Bibl Nat [240]

BIBLIOGRAPHIE DES JOURNAUX DE QUEBEC, 1889-1940 / Pettigrew, Renee – 1952. SEM105P4 – 1mf – 9 – cn Bibl Nat [070]

BIBLIOGRAPHIE DES MEMELLANDES / Szameitat, Max – (Includes index) – Wuerzburg: Holzner-Verlag, 1957 – 10r – 1 – us U.W. Library [943]

BIBLIOGRAPHIE DES OEUVRES DU TRES REVEREND PERE FREDERIC JANSSOONE DE GHYVELDE, APOTRE DE PALESTINE ET DE NOTRE-DAME DU CAP, FONDATEUR DU COMMISSARIAT DE TERRE SAINTE AU CANADA, 1838-1916 / Salvy, S F A – 1963. SEM105P4 – 2mf – 9 – cn Bibl Nat [240]

BIBLIOGRAPHIE DES OEUVRES LITTERAIRES PUBLIEES AU CANADA DE ROBERT RUMILLY, ECRIVAIN, MEMBRE DE L'ACADEMIE CANADIENNE-FRANCAISE, TRADUCTEUR AU SENAT CANADIEN A OTTAWA / Desautels, Adrien – 1947. SEM105P4 – 1mf – 9 – cn Bibl Nat [440]

BIBLIOGRAPHIE DES OUVRAGES RELATIFS A LA SENEGAMBIE ET AU SOUDAN OCCIDENTAL / Colzel, M – Paris, C Delagrave 1891 – us Res Libr [960]

BIBLIOGRAPHIE DES QUOTIDIENS DE LANGUE FRANCAISE PARUS DANS LA PROVINCE DE QUEBEC DEPUIS 1867 / Boucher, Louis – 1957. SEM105P4 – 1mf – 9 – cn Bibl Nat [440]

BIBLIOGRAPHIE DES REVUES ET JOURNAUX LITTERAIRES DES 19E ET 20E SIECLES / Place, Jean-Michel & Vasseur, Andre – (ACCORDS. Cahiers mensuels de litterature. Dir. Andre Desson, Andre Harlaire. Paris. mai-oct; nov 1924 (no. 1-3; 4) 1. ACTION. Cahiers individualistes de philosophie et d'art. Dir. Florent Fels. Paris. fevr 1920-mars; avr 1922 (no. 1-12) 1. AVENTURE. Dir. Marcel Arland, Rene Crevel, Georges Limbour, Roger Vitrac. Paris. nov 1921-janv 1922 (no. 1-3) suivi de: DES. Dir. Marcel Arland. Paris. avr 1922 (no. 1) 1. LES CAHIERS IDEALISTES FRANCAIS. Dir. Edouard Dujardin. Paris. fevr 1917-juin 1920 (no. 1-37. fevr 1921-fevr 1928 (n.s. no. 1-16) 1. INTENTIONS. Revue mensuelle. Dir. Pierre-Andre May. Paris. 1922-24 (no. 1-28; 30) 1. INTERVENTIONS. Gazette internationale des lettres et des arts modernes. Dir. Paul Dermee. Paris. dec 1923-janv 1924 (no. 1-2) suivi de: LE MOUVEMENT ACCELERE. Organe accelerateur de la revolution artistique et litteraire. Dir. Paul Dermee. Paris. nov 1924 (no. 1) 1. INVERSIONS. Paris. 15 nov 1924-1er mars 1925 (no. 1-4) suivi de: L'AMITIE. Paris. avr 1925 (no. 1) 1. LE MOUTON BLANC. Revue mensuelle. Dir. Jean Hytier. Lyon. sept 1922-nov 1924 (no. 1-7) 1. L'OEUF DUR. dir. Gerard Rosenthal. Paris. mars 1921-ete 1924 (no. 1-16) 1. LA REVUE EUROPEENNE. Dir. Edmond Jaloux, Valery Larbaud, Andre Germain, Philippe Soupault. Paris. 1er mars 1923-juil 1931 (no. 1-101) 1. SIC. Sons, idees, couleurs, formes. Dir. Pierre Albert-Birot. Paris. 1916-19 (no. 1-54) suivi de: PARIS. Dir. Pierre Albert-Birot. Paris. nov 1924 (no. 1) 1. SURREALISME. Revue mensuelle. Dir. Ivan Goll. Paris. oct 1924 (no. 1) 1) – v3 – 1 – fr A.C.R.P.P. [800]

BIBLIOGRAPHIE DES REVUES ET JOURNAUX LITTERAIRES DES 19E ET 20E SIECLES / Place, Jean-Michel & Vasseur, Andre – (CABARET VOLTAIRE. Dir. Hugo Ball. Zurich. juin 1916 (no. 1) 1. CANNIBALE. Dir. Francis Picabia. Paris. 25 avr-25 mai 1920 (no. 1-2) 1. LE COEUR A BARBE. Journal transparent. Dir. Paul Eluard, Georges Ribemont-Dessaignes, Tristan Tzara. Paris. avr 1922 (no. 1) 1. DADA. Dir. Tristan Tzara. Zurich, Paris. juil 1917-sept 1921 (no. 1-8) 1. DER ZELTWEG. Dir. Otto Flake, Walter Serner, Tristan Tzara. Zurich. nov 1919 (no. 1) 1. LITTERATURE. Dir. Louis Aragon, Andre Breton, Philippe Soupault. Paris. mars 1919-aout 1921 (no. 1-20). 1er mars 1922-juin 1924 (n.s. no. 1-13) 1. MANOMETRE. Dir. Emile Malespine. Lyon. juil 1922-janv 1928 (no. 1-9) 1. LA POMME DE PINS. Dir. Francis Picabia. Saint-Raphael. 25 fevr 1922 (no. 1) 1. PROJECTEUR. Dir. Celine Arnuald. Paris. 21 mai 1920 (no. 1) 1. 391. Dir. Francis

Picabia. Barcelone, New York, Zurich, Paris. 25 janv 1917-oct 1924 (no. 1-19) 1. Z. Dir. Paul Dermee. Paris. mars 1920 (no. 1-2) 1) – v4 – 1 – fr A.C.R.P.P. [800]

BIBLIOGRAPHIE DES REVUES ET JOURNAUX LITTERAIRES DES 19E ET 20E SIECLES / Place, Jean-Michel & Vasseur, Andre – (L'ACADEMIE FRANCAISE: Revue d'art et de litterature, ed. Saint-Georges de Bouhelier. Paris, Feb-Mar 1893 (nos 1-2); L'ASSOMPTION: Essais d'art catholique, ed. Saint-Georges de Bouhelier. Paris, 10 Mar-Apr 1893 (nos 1-2); L'ANNONCIATION: Livet de reve et d'amour, ed. Saint-Georges de Bouhelier. Paris, 10 Jun-1 Oct 1894 (nos 1-5); LES AGAPES, ed. Paul d'Orsay. Paris, 10 Nov-14 Dec 1840 (nos 1-2); LA COUPE: Recueil mensuel d'art et d'ethique, ed. Joseph Loubet, Richard Wemau. Montpellier, May 1895-Jun 1898 (nos 1-15); LE COURRIER SOCIAL ILLUSTRE: Philosophie, art, science, ed. Andre Ibels. Paris, 1 Nov-31 Dec 1894 (nos 1-4); LE FOU: Journal litteraire, ed. Edouard Guillaumet. Paris, 26 Feb-4 Jun 1883 (nos 1-12); LES GRIMACES: Pamphlet hebdomadaire, ed. Octave Mirbeau. Paris, 21 Jul 1883-12 Jan 1884 (nos 1-26); LES IBIS: Revue litteraire et artistique, ed. Henri Degron, Tristan Klingsor. Paris, Apr-Dec 1894 (nos 1-4); LA RENAISSANCE LITTERAIRE ET ARTISTIQUE, ed. Jean Aicard, Emile Blemont. Paris, 27 Apr 1872-3 May 1874 (nos 1-99); LE REVEIL, ed. Adolphe Granier de Cassagnac. Paris, 2 Jan 1858-16 Apr 1859 (nos 1-68); LE SAINT-GRAAL: Cahiers d'art et d'esthetique, ed. Emmanuel Signoret. Paris, etc., 25 Jan 1892-Feb 1899 (nos 1-20); LA SYRINX, ed. Joachim Gasquet, Paul Souchon. Aix-en-Provence, Jan 1892-Feb 1894 (nos 1-13); LA VARIETE: Revue litteraire, ed. Leconte de Lisle. Rennes, 1 Apr 1840-1 Mar 1841 (nos 1-12)) – v1 – 1 – fr A.C.R.P.P. [800]

BIBLIOGRAPHIE DES REVUES ET JOURNAUX LITTERAIRES DES 19E ET 20E SIECLES / Place, Jean-Michel & Vasseur, Andre – (LE BANQUET: Publication mensuelle, ed. Fernand Gregh. Paris, Mar 1892-Mar 1893 (nos 1-8); LES CAHIERS OCCITANS, ed. Comite d'Action de la Ligue Occitane. Paris, Feb-Aug 1899 (nos 1-2); LES CHRONIQUES: Revue litteraire et artistique, ed. Charles Le Goffic, Maurice Barres. Paris, 1 Nov 1886-Oct; Nov 1887 (nos 1-12); LA CONQUE, ed. Pierre Louys. Paris, 15 Mar 1891-Jan 1892 (nos 1-11); LES CONTEMPORAINS: Journal hebdomadaire, ed. Alfred Le Petit, Felicien Champsaur. Paris, Dec 1880-7 Dec 1881 (nos 1-43); L'ENCLOS: Arts, dits et faits, pour le mieux, ed. Louis Lumet. Paris, Apr 1894-Jan, Feb 1899 (nos 1-36; 37); LES FEMMES DU JOUR. Paris, Apr 1886-1892 (nos 1-11); LES HOMMES D'AUJOURD'HUI, ed. Cinqualbre, later Vanier. Paris, 13 Sep 1878-Jan 1899 (nos 1-469); L'IDEE LIBRE: Revue mensuelle de litterature et d'art, ed. Emile Besnus. Paris, Apr 1892-95 (nos 1-36) (combines with LE REVE ET L'IDEE: Documents sur le naturisme, to form: DOCUMENTS SUR LE NATURISME, q.v.); LA REVE ET L'IDEE, ed. Maurice Le Blond. Paris, May 1894-May 1895 (nos 1-5), continued as: DOCUMENTS SUR LE NATURISME, ed. Maurice Le Blond. Paris, Nov 1895-11 Sep 1896 (nos 1-11), continued as: LA REVUE NATURISTE, ed. Maurice Le Blond. Paris, Mar 1897-Nov 1901 (nos 1-35); LA REVUE ROUGE DE LITTERATURE ET D'ART, ed. Gustave Langlet, later F. Hache. Paris, 1896-Apr 1898 (nos 1-8); LES TACHES D'ENCRE: Gazette mensuelle, ed. Maurice Barres. Paris, 5 Nov 1884-Feb 1885 (nos 1-4); LA TREVE-DIEU: Revue d'art et de litterature, ed. Yves Berthou. Le Havre, 1897 (nos 1-12); LA VIE LITTERAIRE, ed. Albert Collignon. Paris, 28 Oct 1875-26 Sep 1878 (nos 1-153)) – v2 – 1 – fr A.C.R.P.P. [800]

BIBLIOGRAPHIE DES REVUES ET JOURNAUX LITTERAIRES DES XIXE ET XXE SIECLES / Place, Jean-MichelVasseur, Andre – Tome I-IV – 1 – fr A.C.R.P.P. [440]

BIBLIOGRAPHIE D'OUVRAGES ANCIENS DE MEDECINE GARDES A L'HOPITAL GENERAL (1669-1874) / l'Assomption, Marie de – 1961. SEM105P4 – 1mf – 9 – cn Bibl Nat [610]

BIBLIOGRAPHIE D'OUVRAGES AYANT TRAIT A L'AFRIQUE EN GENERAL DANS SES RAPPORTS AVEC L'EXPLORATION AND LA CIVILISATION DE SES CONTREES... / Kayser, Gabriel – Bruxelles, 1887 – 1 – us Res Libr [960]

BIBLIOGRAPHIE D'OUVRAGES AYANT TRAIT A L'AFRIQUE EN GENERAL DANS SES RAPPORTS AVEC L'EXPLORATION, ET LA CIVILISATION DE CES CONTREES / Kayser, Gabriel – Bruxelles. 1887. BA-251 2 – 8 – ne IDC [960]

BIBLIOGRAPHIE DU COMTE DE LOTBINIERE / Tousignant, J Laureat – 1961. SEM105P4 – 1mf – 9 – cn Bibl Nat [010]

BIBLIOGRAPHIE DU CONGO, 1880-1895 : CATALOGUE METHODIQUE DE 3,800 OUVRAGES,... / Wauters, Alphonse Jules – Bruxelles, 1895 – 5mf – 9 – ILM-1153/1 – ne IDC [960]

BIBLIOGRAPHIE DU CONGO, 1880-1895.. / Wauters, Alphonse Jules – Brussels. 1895 – 1 – us Res Libr [960]

BIBLIOGRAPHIE DU CONGO BELGE ET DU RUANDA-URUNDI : REGIME FONCIER / Heyse, Theodore – Bruxelles: G van Campenhout, 1947 – 1 – us Res Libr [960]

BIBLIOGRAPHIE DU DROIT INTERNATIONAL / Olivart, R de – Paris. 2v. 1905-1910 – 14mf – ne IDC [270]

LA BIBLIOGRAPHIE DU DROIT NATUREL DANS LA PHILOSOPHIE CHRETIENNE DU COMMENCEMENT DE L'EPOQUE JUSQU'AU DIXSEPTIEME SIECLE / Laupacis, Benedict – 1952. SEM105P4 – 1mf – 9 – cn Bibl Nat [240]

BIBLIOGRAPHIE DU QUEBEC : INDEX.... / Bibliotheque Nationale. Quebec – Montreal: La Bibliotheque, 1968-1988. SEM105P415 – 110mf – 9 – Can$247.50 – cn Bibl Nat [971]

BIBLIOGRAPHIE DU QUEBEC: LISTE DES PUBLICATIONS QUEBECOISES OU RELATIVES AU QUEBEC, ETABLIE PAR LA BIBLIOTHEQUE NATIONALE DU QUEBEC / Bibliotheque Nationale. Quebec – 1968-1988. SEM105P414 – 62mf – 9 – Can$326.25 – cn Bibl Nat [971]

BIBLIOGRAPHIE DU REV. F. ELOI-GERARD, MARISTE, GENEALOGISTE, HISTORIEN, PEDAGOGUE / Savard, Leo – 1955. SEM105P4 – 2mf – 9 – cn Bibl Nat [920]

BIBLIOGRAPHIE DU REVEREND FRERE M.-CYRILLE COTE DES ECOLES CHRETIENNES / Lefebvre, Gerard – 1965. SEM105P4 – 2mf – 9 – cn Bibl Nat [240]

BIBLIOGRAPHIE DU REVEREND FRERE ROBERT, E.C., D.SC. / Marie-Elie, Frere – 1962. SEM105P4 – 1mf – 9 – cn Bibl Nat [240]

BIBLIOGRAPHIE DU ROCHER DE GRAND-MERE / Lord, Marcel A – 1964. SEM105P4 – 1mf – 9 – cn Bibl Nat [010]

BIBLIOGRAPHIE DU R.P. ARCADE-M. MONETTE / Paradis, Andre – 1964. SEM105P4 – 1mf – 9 – cn Bibl Nat [010]

BIBLIOGRAPHIE DU THEATRE CANADIEN-FRANCAIS AVANT 1900 / Ouellet, Therese – 1949. SEM105P4 – 1mf – 9 – cn Bibl Nat [790]

BIBLIOGRAPHIE DU THEATRE CANADIEN-FRANCAIS DE 1900-1955 / Bilodeau, Francoise – 1956. SEM105P4 – 1mf – 9 – cn Bibl Nat [790]

BIBLIOGRAPHIE EN HISTORIE / Seeligmann, S – Amsterdam, 1927 – 1mf – ne IDC [949]

BIBLIOGRAPHIE ENTOMOLOGIQUE, COMPRENANT L'INDICATION PAR ORDRE ALPHABETIQUE DE NOMS D'AUTEURS... / Percheron, A R – Paris, Londres. 2v. 1837 – 13mf – ne IDC [590]

BIBLIOGRAPHIE ET INDEX GENERALE DES OEUVRES DE AUGUSTE BARTH / Barth, Auguste – Paris, 1927 – 2mf – 9 – ne IDC [240]

BIBLIOGRAPHIE ETHNOGRAPHIQUE DE L'AFRIQUE EQUATORIALE FRANCAISE, 1914-48 – Paris: Impr nationale, 1949 – 1 – us Res Libr [305]

BIBLIOGRAPHIE ETHNOGRAPHIQUE DU CONGO BELGE ET DES REGIONS AVOISINANTES / Musee du Congo Belge. Brussels – 1931-40 – 1 – us Ross [305]

BIBLIOGRAPHIE GENERALE ET METHODIQUE D'HAITI / Duvivier, U – Port-au-Prince: Impr. de l'Etat. 2v. 1941 – 8mf – 9 – ne IDC [972]

BIBLIOGRAPHIE GEOGRAPHIQUE DE L'EGYPTE / Lorin, Henri – Cairo: Impr de l'Institut francais d'archeologie orientale du Caire. 2v. 1928-29 – 1 – us Res Libr [910]

BIBLIOGRAPHIE JAPONAISE / Pages, Leon – Catalogue des ouvrages relatifs au Japon qui ont ete publie depuis le XVe jusqu'a nos jours. Paris, Benjamin Duprat. 1859 – 9 – 5.00 – fr Orientalistes [010]

BIBLIOGRAPHIE METHODIQUE, ANALYTIQUE ET CRITIQUE DES ILES WALLIS ET FUTUNA / O'Reilly, P – 9 – F50.00 – fr Ethnologie [010]

BIBLIOGRAPHIE NECROLOGIQUE DES RELIGIEUSES HOSPITALIERES DE SAINT-JOSEPH, PROVINCE DE NOTRE-DAME DE L'ASSOMPTION, VALLEE-LOURDES, N.B. / Duplessis, T – 1962. SEM105P4 – 2mf – 9 – cn Bibl Nat [240]

BIBLIOGRAPHIE RAISONEE DES OUVRAGES CONCERNANT LE DAHOMEY / Pawlowski, Auguste – Paris: L Baudoin, 1895 – 1 – us Res Libr [010]

BIBLIOGRAPHIE RELATIVE A L'HISTOIRE DE LA NOUVELLE-FRANCE, 1516-1700 / Lavoie, Amedee – 1949. SEM105P4 – 1mf – 9 – cn Bibl Nat [971]

BIBLIOGRAPHIE SAINT-SIMONIENNE / Fournel, Henri – Paris, A. Johanneau, 1833, 130 p. Les Saint-Simoniens, 1825-1834. 6899 – 9 – fr Hachette [335]

BIBLIOGRAPHIE SUR LA DEVOTION AU SACRE-COEUR CHEZ LES MISSIONNAIRES DU SACRE-COEUR FRANCAIS ET CANADIENS / Robert, Lionel – 1962 [i.e.] 1963. SEM105P4 – 1mf – 9 – cn Bibl Nat [240]

BIBLIOGRAPHIE SUR LA METHODOLOGIE DE LA LECTURE / Marie-Paul, Frere – 1947. SEM105P4 – 1mf – 9 – cn Bibl Nat [370]

BIBLIOGRAPHIE SUR LA METHODOLOGIE DU CATECHISME / Pierre, Frere – 1948. SEM105P4 – 1mf – 9 – cn Bibl Nat [240]

BIBLIOGRAPHIE SUR LE CENTRE DE SERVICE SOCIAL DU DIOCESE DES TROIS-RIVIERES / DeRouyn, Solange – 1962 [i.e. 1963]. SEM105P4 – 2mf – 9 – cn Bibl Nat [360]

BIBLIOGRAPHIE SUR LE CINEMA : ESSAI DE BIBLIOGRAPHIE DES PUBLICATIONS CANADIENNES-FRANCAISES SUR LE CINEMA DE 1940 A 1960 / Roy, Jean-Luc – 1963. SEM105P4 – 2mf – 9 – cn Bibl Nat [790]

BIBLIOGRAPHIE SUR LE SCOUTISME CATHOLIQUE DANS LA PROVINCE DE QUEBEC / Hamel, Andre – 1948. SEM105P4 – 1mf – 9 – cn Bibl Nat [240]

BIBLIOGRAPHIE SUR L'OPHTALMO-OTORHINO-LARYNGOLOGIE : TRAVAUX PUBLIES DE 1940 A 1950... / Ste-Therese de Lisieux, Soeur – 1950. SEM105P4 – 1mf – 9 – cn Bibl Nat [617]

BIBLIOGRAPHIE TCHEQUE : CONTENANT UN CERTAIN NOMBRE D'OUVRAGES... EN LANGUES DIVERSES... FASC. 1 / Bestaux, E – (Index) – Prague, 1920 – 2mf – 9 – ne IDC [460]

BIBLIOGRAPHIE TRIMESTRIELLE DE DROIT INTERNATIONAL – Paris. 3v. 1913-1915 – 5mf – ILM-2871/1 – ne IDC [340]

BIBLIOGRAPHIE ZUR JUEDISCH-HELLENISTISCHEN UND INTERTESTAMENTARISCHEN LITERATUR 1900-1965 (T.U.U. 5-106) / Delling, G – 3mf – 9 – ne Slangenburg [240]

BIBLIOGRAPHIE ZUR VOLKSKUNDE DER DONAUSCHWABEN / Rez, Heinrich – 1935 – 1 – us I.U. Libraries [390]

BIBLIOGRAPHIES BY MEDINA RELATING TO LATIN AMERICA AND THE PHILIPPINES / Medina, Jose Toribio – Approx. 15,300 pp – 3 – us Readex [010]

LES BIBLIOGRAPHIES DU COURS DE BIBLIOTHECONOMIE / Universite Laval. Quebec, Canada – 1947-1966. A collection of 389 bibliographies. SEM105P4 – 656mf – 9 – Can$1,476.00 – cn Bibl Nat [020]

LES BIBLIOGRAPHIES DU COURS DE BIBLIOTHECONOMIE DE L'UNIVERSITE LAVAL, 1947-1966 : [INDEX] / Universite Laval. Quebec, Canada – SEM105P4 – 1mf – 9 – cn Bibl Nat [020]

BIBLIOGRAPHIES (NATIONAL) – Cuba. 8022 p. (Medina, Trelles y Govin) – 3 – us Readex [010]

BIBLIOGRAPHIES (NATIONAL) – Latin America, general. 4724 p. (Medina's, Biblioteca hispano-americana, and, La imprenta en Rio de la Plata) – 3 – us Readex [010]

BIBLIOGRAPHIES (NATIONAL) – Mexico and Guatemala. 12,011 p. (Medina, Andrade, Beristain de Souza, Garcia Icazbalceta, Leon) – 3 – us Readex [010]

BIBLIOGRAPHIES (NATIONAL) – Philippines. 4501 p. (Medina, Perez, Retana y Gamboa) – 3 – us Readex [010]

BIBLIOGRAPHIES (NATIONAL) – Portugal. 9009 p. (Barbosa Machado, Pinto de Mattos, Silva) – 3 – us Readex [010]

BIBLIOGRAPHIES (NATIONAL) – South America. 10,776 p. (Gutierrez, Rene-Moreno, Sacramento Blake, Briseno, Medina, Estrada, Sanchez) – 3 – us Readex [010]

BIBLIOGRAPHIES (NATIONAL) – Spain. 4408 p. (Antonio, Salva Y Perez) – 3 – us Readex [010]

BIBLIOGRAPHIES (NATIONAL) – Spanish and Portuguese. The major national bibliographies of the Spanish and Portuguese-speaking countries published prior to 1900, with emphasis on J. T. Medina. Also sold in units – 3 – us Readex [010]

BIBLIOGRAPHIES OF BOTANY / Bay, J C – A contribution toward a bibliotheca bibliographica. (J. P. Lotsy, Progressus Rei Botanicae, v. 3). 1909 – 9 – ne IDC [580]

BIBLIOGRAPHIES OF BOTANY : A CONTRIBUTION TOWARD A BIBLIOTHECA BIBLIOGRAPHICA / Bay, J C – J.P.Lotsy. Progressus Rei Botanicae. v3. 1909 – 3mf – ne IDC [580]

BIBLIOGRAPHISCHE MITTEILUNGEN UEBER DIE RECHTSSTELLUNG DER FRAU IM DEUTSCHEN REICH UND IN OESTERREICH (HQ 2) : GESETZGEBUNG – RECHTSPRECHUNG – SCHRIFTTUM – 1991. v1-21. 1935-41 (mf ed 1991) – 3mf – 9 – DM45.00 – 3-89131-043-9 – gw Fischer [305]

BIBLIOGRAPHISCHER VIERTELJAHRESBERICHT FUER DIE JUEDISCHE LITERATUR – 1 – $95.00 – us UPA [470]

BIBLIOGRAPHY / National Advisory Committee on Aeronautics – 1909-32 – 1,5,6 – us Princeton Micro [629]

BIBLIOGRAPHY / U.S. National Advisory Committee on Aeronautics – 1909-1932 – 1,5,6 – us Princeton Micro [629]

BIBLIOGRAPHY AND REFERENCE LIST OF THE HISTORY AND LITERATURE : RELATING TO THE ADOPTION OF THE CONSTITUTION OF THE UNITED STATES / Ford, Paul L – Brooklyn, 1896 – 1mf – 9 – $1.50 – LLMC 84-808 – us L.L.M.C. [340]

BIBLIOGRAPHY IN CHRISTIAN EDUCATION FOR SEMINARY AND COLLEGE LIBRARIES / Wyckoff, DeWitt Campbell – 1960-73 – 1 – us A.T.L.A. [012]

BIBLIOGRAPHY OF AFRICAN CHRISTIAN LITERATURE / Conference of Missionary Societies in Great Britain and Ireland – 1923 – 1 – us A.T.L.A. [012]

BIBLIOGRAPHY OF AFRICAN CHRISTIAN LITERATURE / Conference of Missionary Societies in Great Britain and Ireland – London, 1923 – 1 – us Res Libr [240]

BIBLIOGRAPHY OF AFRICAN FRESHWATER FISH. SUPPLEMENT 1 (1968-1975) – 1976 – 52p – it F.A.O. [590]

BIBLIOGRAPHY OF AFRICAN STATISTICAL PUBLICATIONS 1966-1973 / Africa. Economic Commission for Africa – Addis Abeba. 1973. BD-1800 1 – 9 – ne IDC [960]

BIBLIOGRAPHY OF AGRICULTURAL BIBLIOGRAPHIES, 1960-1977 / ed by Agricultural Library, Wageningen, Netherlands – Zug, 1972, 1977 – 222mf – ne IDC [630]

BIBLIOGRAPHY OF AGRICULTURE – (1970-. 5,6,9) – v. 1- 1942- – 1 – us UMI [630]

BIBLIOGRAPHY OF AGRICULTURE / U.S. National Agricultural Library – (v43-46. 1979-82. $298.50y in North America, $308.50y elsewhere; v47-48. 1983-84. $505.00 in North America, $515.00 elsewhere) – v34-42. 1970-78. Annual updates & cumulated index – 9 – $1,559.00 in North America, $1,575.00 elsewhere – us Oryx [630]

BIBLIOGRAPHY OF AGRICULTURE – v1-41. 1942-77 – 1,5,6 – us Princeton Micro [630]

BIBLIOGRAPHY OF AGRICULTURE ANNUAL CUMULATION – (1976-. 9) – v. 39- 1975- – 1,5,6 – us UMI [630]

A BIBLIOGRAPHY OF AMERICAN NATURAL HISTORY / Meisel, M – New York. 3v. 1924-1929 – 19mf – 9 – ne IDC [015]

BIBLIOGRAPHY OF AMERICAN WOMEN / Marlow, H Carleton – 1 – us Primary [305]

BIBLIOGRAPHY OF ARTICLES ON COLONIES APPEARING IN AMERICAN GEOGRAPHICAL AND KINDRED JOURNALS THROUGH 1934 / Ragatz, Lowell J – Washington. 1935. BA-259 2 – 8 – ne IDC [900]

BIBLIOGRAPHY OF ARTICLES... ON COLONIES... APPEARING IN AMERICAN GEOGRAPHICAL AND KINDRED JOURNALS THROUGH 1934 / Ragatz, Lowell J – Washington, 1935 – 4mf – 9 – ne IDC [960]

BIBLIOGRAPHY OF BASIC DESIGN PROCESS AND VISUAL COMMUNICATION PRODUCTS – (1982. 12,000 refs. 24mf. $0.50f) – Management Services, University Park, PA. 5000 refs. 1975 – 514p 9mf – 9 – $0.50f – us Lawrence Pub [720]

A BIBLIOGRAPHY OF BRITISH ORNITHOLOGY... / Mullens, W H & Swann, H K – (Supplement) – London. 6pts. 1916-1917 – 14mf – ne IDC [590]

A BIBLIOGRAPHY OF BRITISH SOMALILAND / Viney, N M – London, 1937 – 1mf – 9 – ne IDC [960]

THE BIBLIOGRAPHY OF CARTOGRAPHY / U.S. Library of Congress. Geography and Map Division – (First Suppl., 1980.-21,500 entries 2 reels. $285.00 ISBN: 0-8161-1526-5) – 1973.-91,600 entries 10 reels.-ISBN: 0-8161-1294-0 – 1 – $615.000 – uk Hall [910]

A BIBLIOGRAPHY OF CEYLON / Goonetileke, H A I – A systematic guide to the literature on the land, people, history and culture, published in Western languages from the sixteenth century to the present day. (Bibliotheca Asiatica. v.5.). v. 1-2. Zug. 1970; (Bibliotheca Asiatica. v.14). v. 3. 1976. BI-1058 1 – 9 – ne IDC [950]

A BIBLIOGRAPHY OF CONGO LANGUAGES / Starr, Frederick – (University of Chicago, Dept. of Anthropology. Bulletin V). Chicago. 1908 – 1 – us Res Libr [490]

BIBLIOGRAPHY OF CONGO LANGUAGES / Starr, Frederick – (Univ. of Chicago, Dept. of Anthrop., Bull. 5). Chicago. 1908. BA-261 2 – 3mf – 8 – ne IDC [490]

BIBLIOGRAPHY OF DISSERTATIONS / Moscow. Gosudarstvennaia Biblioteka SSSR im V.I. Lenina. (V.I. Lenin state library of the U.S.S.R.) – 1941-1945 – 3 – us Readex [010]

BIBLIOGRAPHY OF EIGHTEENTH-CENTURY LEGAL LITERATURE / Adams, J N & Averley, G – 1982 – 6mf – 9 – uk Chadwyck [340]

BIBLIOGRAPHY OF FISHERIES AND LIMNOLOGY FOR LAKE TANGANYIKA – 1982 – 52p – it F.A.O. [639]

A BIBLIOGRAPHY OF FISHES / Dean, B & Eastman, C R – 2124 2. 3 v. 1916-1923 – 8 – ne IDC [590]

A BIBLIOGRAPHY OF FISHES... / Dean, B & Eastman, C R – New York. 3v. 1916-1923 – 61mf – ne IDC [590]

BIBLIOGRAPHY OF FOOD AND AGRICULTURAL MARKETING IN THE DEVELOPING COUNTRIES – 1985 – 151p – it F.A.O. [650]

BIBLIOGRAPHY OF FOOD CONSUMPTION SURVEYS – 1981 rev ed 1987 – 94p – it F.A.O. [338]

BIBLIOGRAPHY OF INDIVIDUALIST LIBERTARIAN ANARCHIST WRITINGS – A preliminary compilation, inviting collaboration. 4 fiches (24x) – 9 – 1.00f – at Libertarian Micro [320]

BIBLIOGRAPHY OF INDO-MOSLEM HISTORY / Hasan, BMZ – Calcutta, 1932 – 1mf – 9 – ne IDC [260]

THE BIBLIOGRAPHY OF INTERNATIONAL LAW... / Borchard, Edwin Montefiore – Washington, 1913 – 1mf – ne IDC [340]

THE BIBLIOGRAPHY OF INTERNATIONAL LAW AND ... / Borchard, E M – Washington, 1913 – 1mf – 9 – ILM-1769/1 – ne IDC [327]

BIBLIOGRAPHY OF LENIN'S LIFE PAMPHLET COLLECTION – 1970 – 2r – 1 – CSUXANS8508-B – us Hoover Inst Photo [320]

BIBLIOGRAPHY OF MASSACHUSETTS VITAL RECORDS 1620-1905 / Holbrook, Jay Mack – (Mf 1: Abington to Groton. Mf 2: Halifax to Norton. Mf 3: Oakham to Yarmouth. This ed annotates 389 microfiche colls that provide vital and other public records for 313 towns. Also catalogues 194 towns (290mf) included in the old printed series of Massachusetts Vital Records to 1850) – 7th ed 1999 – 3mf – 9 – 0-87623-404-X – us Holbrook [019]

BIBLIOGRAPHY OF MAURITIUS, (1502-1954) / Toussaint, A – Port Louis, 1956 – 19mf – 9 – ne IDC [960]

BIBLIOGRAPHY OF MONO- AND MULTILINGUAL VOCABULARIES, THESAURI, SUBJECT HEADINGS AND CLASSIFICATION SCHEMES IN THE SOCIAL SCIENCES / Aitchison, Jean & Allen, G G – 1983 – 101p – 9 – 92-3-102072-2 – fr UNESCO [020]

A BIBLIOGRAPHY OF MUGHAL INDIA, 1526-1707 / Sharma, R – Bombay, 1939 – 4mf – 9 – I-356/2 – ne IDC [019]

A BIBLIOGRAPHY OF NIGERIAN HISTORY / Jenkins, George – [s.l.]: Microsystems Inc, 1962 – us Res Libr [960]

A BIBLIOGRAPHY OF NIGERIAN HISTORY : PRELIMINARY DRAFT / Oni-Orisan, B A – 1968 – us Res Libr [960]

A BIBLIOGRAPHY OF NINETEENTH-CENTURY LEGAL LITERATURE / Adams, J N & Davies, M J – (Subject catalogue on diazo mf and CD-ROM edition) – 3v. 1992-95 – 9 – £1,200.00 – 0-907977-42-1 – uk Chadwyck [340]

BIBLIOGRAPHY OF NORTH AMERICAN GEOLOGY – (All published. Formerly: Geologic Literature on North America.) Years: 1785-1969 – 1,5,6 – us Princeton Micro [550]

BIBLIOGRAPHY OF PUBLICATIONS ISSUED BY UNESCO OR UNDER ITS AUSPICES : THE FIRST TWENTY-FIVE YEARS 1946-1971 – 1973 – 385p – 9 – 92-3-001037-5 – fr UNESCO [060]

BIBLIOGRAPHY OF RESIDUES OF AGRICULTURE, FISHERIES, FORESTRY AND RELATED INDUSTRIES – 1978 – 125p – it F.A.O. [630]

A BIBLIOGRAPHY OF SHIP PASSENGER LISTS, 1538-1825 / Lancour, Harold – Item D. Guide to published lists of early immigrants to North America. 137p. SW16-0054 – 5 – us A.G.L.L. [920]

A BIBLIOGRAPHY OF SIERRA LEONE, PRECEDED BY AN ESSAY ON THE ORIGIN, CHARACTER AND PEOPLES OF THE COLONY AND PROTECTORATE / Lukach, H C – Oxford, 1910 – 3mf – 9 – ne IDC [960]

BIBLIOGRAPHY OF SOCIAL ASPECTS OF AGRICULTURE IN BALI / Tirtayasa, I G N – Sydney: BISA, 1988 – 1mf – 9 – A$10.00 – 0-86758-271-5 – at BISA [630]

BIBLIOGRAPHY OF THE CRIOLLO CATTLE OF THE AMERICAS – 1980 – 71p – it F.A.O. [636]

A BIBLIOGRAPHY OF THE FINE AND APPLIED ARTS – (Complete author catalogue of the National Art Library, Victoria and Albert Museum, London) – 9 – us Primary [700]

A BIBLIOGRAPHY OF THE HISTORY OF CALIFORNIA, 1510-1930 / Cowen, Robert Ernest & Cowen, Robert Grainess – Four vols. in one. 1 roll – 1 – 25.00 – uk Libr Preservation [978]

BIBLIOGRAPHY OF THE ICJ / UN International Court of Justice – nos 19-41 – E/F.43 – 9 – us U.N. Pubs [340]

A BIBLIOGRAPHY OF THE LITERATURE...THE CENTRAL INDIA AGENCY / Eckford Luard, C – London, 1908. BI-1054 2 – 2mf – 8 – ne IDC [010]

BIBLIOGRAPHY OF THE NEGRO IN AFRICA AND AMERICA / Work, M N – New York. Wilson. 1928. BA-403 2 – 19mf – 8 – ne IDC [960]

BIBLIOGRAPHY OF THE NEW HEBRIDES ISLANDS / Ferguson, J A – 1610-1942 – 1r – 1 – PMB 1126 – at Pacific Mss [019]

BIBLIOGRAPHY OF THE SEMITIC LANGUAGES OF ETHIOPIA / Leslau, W – New York. 1946. BA-253 2 – 2mf – 8 – ne IDC [470]

BIBLIOGRAPHY OF THE SPANISH CIVIL WAR 1936-1939 / Institute of History of the Spanish Civil War – 1r – 1 – $40.00 – B50562 – us Library Micro [946]

BIBLIOGRAPHY OF THE STATE OF MAINE / Bangor. Maine. Public Library – 1962.-16,800 cards 1 reel.-ISBN: 0-8161-1559-1 – 1 – $110.00 – uk Hall [978]

BIBLIOGRAPHY OF THE TSWANA LANGUAGE – Pretoria State Library, 1982. Updated regularly at R2.50f – 1310mf – 9 – sa State Libr [490]

BIBLIOGRAPHY ON AGRICULTURAL EMPLOYMENT – it F.A.O. [331]

A BIBLIOGRAPHY ON DEVELOPMENT PLANNING IN NIGERIA, 1955-1968 / Akinyotu, Adetunji – Ibadan: Nigerian ISER, 1968 – us Res Libr [013]

BIBLIOGRAPHY ON ECONOMIC AND SOCIAL PLANNING AND PROJECTIONS IN ECE COUNTRIES / United Nations – UN-EC.AD.(XI) CRP. 1. UN-ST Geneva Lib Ser.B Ref. 6. Geneva. Feb 1974. BD-1801 1 – 9 – ne IDC [338]

A BIBLIOGRAPHY ON LAND TENURE AND RELATED QUESTIONS IN LIBYA / Alwan, A S – Benghazi. Oct 1963. (FAO Land Tenure Expert). BNE-1032 1 – 1mf – 9 – ne IDC [960]

BIBLIOGRAPHY ON MANGROVE RESEARCH 1600-1975 – 1981 – 479p – 9 – 92-3-101819-1 – fr UNESCO [630]

A BIBLIOGRAPHY ON OIL PALM "ELAEIS GUINEENSIS JACQUIN"; ITS AGRONOMY, BOTANY, BREEDING AND SELECTION, DISEASES AND PESTS / Hutauruk, Bulan – SE-5077 1. 1963 – 9 – ne IDC [631]

BIBLIOGRAPHY ON SOILS, FERTILIZERS, PLANT NUTRITION AND GENERAL AGRONOMY IN ETHIOPIA / Haque, I et al – 1985 – 9 – $15.00 – 92-9053-150-9 – et ILRI [631]

BIBLIOGRAPHY ON THE NIGERIAN CIVIL WAR / Cervenka, Zdenek – Chicago, U of Chicago, Photodup Dep, [19–?] (mf ed) – us Res Libr [960]

BIBLIOGRAPHY: PUBLICATIONS IN ENGLISH (ON) INDONESIAN SOCIAL, POLITICAL ECONOMIC LIFE AND INSTITUTIONS – By Garth N. Jones. SE-11,450 1. 1960 – 9 – ne IDC [950]

BIBLIOPEGIA : OR, THE ART OF BOOKBINDING IN ALL ITS BRANCHES / Arnett, John Andrews – London: R Groombridge; New York: W Jackson, 1835 – us Res Libr [680]

LE BIBLIOPHILE CANADIEN / ed by Renault, Raoul – Quebec, Canada. aut 1895-v1 n2. sep 1895 – 1r – 1 – Can$25.00 – cn Can Microfilming [070]

LE BIBLIOPHILE CANADIEN *see* LE COURRIER DU LIVRE

BIBLIOTECA ARABICO-HISPANA. TOMO 1 / Casiri, Miguel – 1760 – 5mf – 9 – Pta3,000.00 – 84-7848-227-X – sp Pentalfa [020]

BIBLIOTECA ARABICO-HISPANA. TOMO 2 / Casiri, Miguel – 1770 – 4mf – 9 – Pta2,500.00 – 84-7848-228-8 – sp Pentalfa [020]

BIBLIOTECA ARGENTINA DE LIBROS RAROS AMERICANOS, TOMO 4 : FR. JOSEPH ANTONIO DE SAN ALBERTO... – Madrid: Razon y Fe, 1927 – 1 – sp Bibl Santa Ana [972]

BIBLIOTECA BIBLIOGRAFICO-AGUSTINIANA DEL COLEGIO DE VALLADOLID / Blanco, Antonio – Valladolid, 1909 – 13mf – 9 – ne IDC [240]

BIBLIOTECA BIOBIBLIOGRAFICA DELLA TERRA SANTA E DELL'ORIENTE FRANCESCANO / Golubovich, PG – Firenze. 5v. 1906-1927 – 72mf – 9 – ne IDC [950]

BIBLIOTECA BRASILIENSE. CATALOGO ANNOTADO DOS LIVROS SOBRE O BRASIL : PT. 1: DESCOBRIMENTO DA AMERICA: BRASIL COLONIAL, 1491-1822 / Rodrigues, Jose C – Rio de Janeiro: "Jornal do Commercio", 1907 – 8mf – 9 – ne IDC [972]

BIBLIOTECA DE CATALUNYA / Institute d'estudis Catalans. Barcelona – 1921-36. 13v – 1 – 69.00 – us L of C Photodup [800]

BIBLIOTECA DE HISTORIA NACIONAL – Bogota. n. 1-83. (wanting 68 and 70) – 1 – 881.00 – us L of C Photodup [972]

LA BIBLIOTECA DE JULES JANIN / Lacroix, Pablo – Valencia: Editorial Castalia, 1950 – sp Bibl Santa Ana [020]

BIBLIOTECA de las tradiciones Espanolas. Sevilla, Guichot y Compania *see*
- DE LOS MALEFICIOS Y LOS DEMONIOS
- EL FOLKLORE DE MADRID
- JUEGOS INFANTILES DE EXTREMADURA

LA BIBLIOTECA DE TRADICIONES POPULARES / Machado Alvarez, Antonio – (Tomo III. 1884.1.50f; 9) – Tomo II. 1884 – 9 – $1.50f – sp Bibl Santa Ana [390]

LA BIBLIOTECA DEL CAMARISTA DE CASTILLA D. FERNANDO JOSE DE VELASCO Y CEBALLOS / Escagedo Salmon, Mateo – Santander. Lib. Moderna, 1932 – 1 – sp Bibl Santa Ana [020]

BIBLIOTECA DELL' ECONOMISTA – Turin. ser. 1 v. 1-ser. 5 v. 20. 1850-1923. Incomplete – 1 – us NY Public [330]

BIBLIOTECA ESPANOLA. TOMO 1 / Rodriguez de Castro, Jose – 1781 – 7mf – 9 – Pta4,000.00 – 84-7848-354-3 – sp Pentalfa [020]

BIBLIOTECA ESPANOLA. TOMO 2 / Rodriguez de Castro, Jose – 1786 – 6mf – 9 – Pta3,500.00 – 84-7848-355-1 – sp Pentalfa [020]

BIBLIOTECA ESPANOLA-PORTUGUEZA-JUDAICA / Kayserling, M – Straszbourg. 1890. BJ-262-29 1 – 3mf – 9 – ne IDC [900]

BIBLIOTECA GOATHEMALA DE LA SOCIEDAD DE GEOGRAFIA E HISTORIA... / Bayle, Constantino – Madrid: Razon y Fe, 1939 – 1 – sp Bibl Santa Ana [972]

BIBLIOTECA HISPANO-AMERICANA (1493-1810) / Medina, Jose Toribio – 7V. 1898-1907. Sold with, Historia y bibliografia de la imprenta en...Rio de la Plata – 3 – us Readex [010]

BIBLIOTECA HISTORICA CUBANA / Govin, Trelles & Manuel, Carlos – 2r – 1 – $150.00 – us OmniSys [972]

BIBLIOTECA HISTORICO-GENEALOGICA ASTURIANA... / Alvarez de la Rivera, Senen – Madrid, Razon y Fe, 1926 – 1 – sp Bibl Santa Ana [920]

BIBLIOTECA MANUAL MEDICO-PRACTICA... / Carrion, C – Barcelona, 1745 – 7mf – 9 – sp Cultura [610]

BIBLIOTECA MILITAR ESPANOLA / Garcia de la Huerta, Vicente – 1760 – 9 – 1.50f – sp Bibl Santa Ana [355]

BIBLIOTECA NACIONAL, MADRID : THE AUTHOR CATALOGUES – (Mf ed divided into 2pts wh are also listed separately. Guide included) – set of 2 catalogues – 4982mf – 9 – £18,400.00 set – uk Chadwyck [020]

BIBLIOTECA NACIONAL, MADRID : CATALOGO DE LA COLECCION GOMEZ-IMAZ – 13mf – 9 – £90.00 – uk Chadwyck [946]

BIBLIOTECA NACIONAL, MADRID : CATALOGO DE PUBLICACIONES PERIODICAS – Madrid – 133mf – 9 – £510.00 – uk Chadwyck [946]

BIBLIOTECA NACIONAL, MADRID : CATALOGO DE VARIOS ESPECIALES – 153mf – 9 – £550.00 – uk Chadwyck [946]

BIBLIOTECA NACIONAL, MADRID: THE AUTHOR CATALOGUES *see*
- CATALOGO GENERAL DE LIBROS IMPRESOS, 1982-1987
- CATALOGO GENERAL DE LIBROS IMPRESOS, HASTA 1981

Biblioteca Nacional. Rio de Janeiro *see*
- COLECAO ESPECIAL-JORNAIS OPERARIOS, 1
- COLECAO ESPECIAL-JORNAIS OPERARIOS, 2

Biblioteca Publica Municipal *see* CATALOGO DE OBRAS QUE EXISTEN EN ESTA BIBLIOTECA EN 30 DE MARZO DE 1952

LAS BIBLIOTECAS DE ESPANA...PUBLICAS / Diaz Perez, Nicolas – 1885 – 9 – $1.50f – sp Bibl Santa Ana [020]

LAS BIBLIOTECAS DE LA ANTIGUEDAD ESTUDIO, TRADUCCION PROLOGO Y NOTAS POR JOSE LOPEZ DE TORO / Lipsio, Justo – Valencia: Editorial Castalia, 1948 – sp Bibl Santa Ana [946]

BIBLIOTECHNOE DELO V ROSSII DO 18 VEKA / Slukhovskii, M I – Moscow, 1968. 231p. Comprehensive survey of library development in Russia in the 18th century. BR-10,770/1 – 9 – ne IDC [947]

Biblioteka Akademii Nauk (BAN), St Petersburg *see* ASIAN BOOKS IN THE RUSSIAN LANGUAGE

Biblioteka Akademii Nauk S SS R, 1714-1964 *see* BIBLIOGRAFICHESKII UKAZATEL'

BIBLIOTEKA I ARKHIV MOSKOVSKIKH GOSUDAREI V 16 STOLETII / Likhachev, N P – St. Petersburg, 1894. Library and recordkeeping in 16th-century Moscow. BR-4755/2 – 8 – ne IDC [025]

BIBLIOTEKA IMP. OBSHCHESTVA ISTORII DREVNOSTEI ROSSIISKIKH – 2v. Describes Slavic mss and rare books in Lenin Library (Society of History and Russian Antiquities). Moscow, 1845. BR-4766/2 and BR-7332/2 – 8 – ne IDC [010]

BIBLIOTEKA KOMMUNISTA / Kerzhentsev, V – Sistematicheskii ukazatel' sotsialisticheskoi literatury. Ed. 4. M. 1919. BR-5713 2 – 8 – ne IDC [335]

Biblioteka Soiuza sel'skokhoziaistvennoi, kreditnoi i kustarno-promyslovoi kooperatsii *see* REKOMENDATE L'NYI SPISOK KNIG DLIA KOMPLEKTOVANIIA I POPOLNENIIA BIBLIOTEK SEL'SKOKHOZIAISTVENNOI, KUST.-PROM. KOOPERATSII I OBSHCHESTV SEL.-KHOZ. KREDITA

BIBLIOTEKA SOTSIALISTA / Nestroev, G – Sistematicheskii ukazatel' knig. M. 1906. BR-7176 2 – 8 – ne IDC [335]

BIBLIOTEKA STEFANA IAVORSKAGO / Maslov, S I – Kiev. 1914. BR-4457 2 – 8 – ne IDC [460]

BIBLIOTEKA UCHENAIA, EKONOMICHESKAIA I PROCH., IZDAVAVSHAIASIA P.P. SUMAROKOVYM V 1793-1794 GG. V TOBOL'SKE / Neustroev, A N – Spb. 1874. BR-4680 2 – 8 – ne IDC [330]

Biblioteka Vol'tera *see* KATALOG KNIG/ BIBLIOTHEQUE DE VOLTAIRE

BIBLIOTEKAR' – Zhurnal Obshchestva Bibliotekovedeniia. Petrograd. 1910-1914, nos. 1-4. Missing: nos. 1,2, 1912 – 1 – 35.00r – us Hoover Inst Photo [073]

O BIBLIOTEKE MOSKOVSKIKH GOSUDAREI V 16. STOLETTII / Belokurov, S A – Moscow, 1898. xvi,336, 528p. Study of 16th-cent. Russian libraries and ms. collections. BR-4756/2 – 8 – ne IDC [020]

BIBLIOTEKI MOSKOVSKOGO GLAVNOGO ARKHIVA MINISTERSTVA INOSTRANNYKH DEL, KATALOG DELAM I RUKOPISAM APTEKARSKOGO PRIKAZA I INYM, OTNOSIASHCHIMSIA K MEDITSINE S 15-GO STOLETIIA / Tokmakov, I F – M. 1879. BR-11,152 1 – 9 – ne IDC [615]

BIBLIOTEKI MOSKOVSKOGO GLAVNOGO ARKHIVA MINISTERSTVA INOSTRANNYKH DEL, KATALOG RUKOPISIAM, OTNOSIASCHIMSIA DO MOSKVY, MOSKOVSKOI GUBERNII, IKH TSERKVEI I MONASTYREI / Tokmakov, I F – M. 1879. PKG-B-75.71 BR-11,169 1 – 9 – ne IDC [010]

BIBLIOTEKI MOSKOVSKOGO GLAVNOGO ARKHIVA MINISTERSTVA INOSTRANNYKH DEL, KATALOG RUKOPISIAM, OTNOSIASHCHIMSIA DO TSERKOVNOI ISTORII / Tokmakov, I F – M. 1880. PKG-B-75.72 BR-11,151 1 – 9 – ne IDC [010]

BIBLIOTEKI MOSKOVSKOGO GLAVNOGO ARKHIVA MINISTERSTVA INOSTRANNYKH DEL. KATALOG RUKOPISIAM, PECHATNYM KNIGAM, GEOGRAFICHESKIM KARTAM, PLANAM I VIDAM, OTNOSIASHCHIMSIA DO VLADIMIRSKOI GUBERNII, I EE SVIATNI, S 16 STOLETIIA / Tokmakov, I F – Vladimir. 1881. BR-11,162 1 – 9 – ne IDC [947]

BIBLIOTEKI MOSKOVSKOGO GLAVNOGO ARKHIVA MINISTERSTVA INOSTRANNYKH DEL, KATALOG RUKOPISIAM PO IURISPRUDENTSII S 12 PO 19 STOLETIE / Tokmakov, I F – M. 1879. BR-11,159 1 – 9 – ne IDC [340]

BIBLIOTEKI MOSKOVSKOGO GLAVNOGO ARKHIVA MINISTERSTVA INOSTRANNYKH DEL, KATALOG RUKOPISIAM PO IURISPRUDENTSII S 12 PO 19 STOLETIE *see* BIBLIOTEKI MOSKOVSKOGO GLAVNOGO ARKHIVA MINISTERSTVA INOSTRANNYKH DEL, KATALOG RUKOPISIAM PO IURISPRUDENTSII S 12 PO 19 STOLETIE

BIBLIOTEKI RSFSR PO DANNYM PEREPISI NA 1/X 1934 GODA – Moskva: Izd. UNKhU RSFSR, 1935 – 1 – CSUX91-B350 – us Hoover Inst Photo [947]

BIBLIOTEKOVEDENIE VYSSHAGO PORIADKA V EGO OTNOSHENIIA K METODAM NAUCHNAGO ISSLEDOVANIIA I PREPODAVANIIA / Eikhler, F – Perevod s nemetskago. Spb. 1913. BR-4646 2 – 8 – ne IDC [020]

BIBLIOTHECA AEGYPTIACA : REPERTORIUM UEBER DIE BIS ZUM JAHRE 1857 IN BEZUG AUF AEGYPTEN, SEINE GEOGRAPHIE, LANDESKUNDE, NATURGESCHICHTE... / Jolowitz, Heimann – Leipzig: W Engelmann, 1858 – 1 – us Res Libr [956]

BIBLIOTHECA AETHIOPICA / Goldschmidt, L – Leipzig, 1893 – 1mf – 9 – ne IDC [960]

BIBLIOTHECA AFRICANA – Innsbruck, 1924-34 – 1 – us Res Libr [960]

BIBLIOTHECA AMERICANA / John Carter Brown Library. Providence – 1st ed. 1871-1875 – 3 – us Readex [010]

BIBLIOTHECA AMERICANA ET PHILIPPINA / Maggs Bros. London – pts1-4. 1922-25 – 1 – us Ross [020]

BIBLIOTHECA ANATOMICA / Haller, Albrecht von – M-56. 2 v. 1774-1777 – 9 – ne IDC [611]

BIBLIOTHECA ANATOMICA / Haller, Albrecht von – Tiguri. 2v. 1774-1777 – 37mf – ne IDC [611]

BIBLIOTHECA ANTI-TRINITARIORUM : COMPENDIUM HISTORIAE ECCLESIASTICAE UNITARIORUM / Sandius, C – Freistadii, 1684 – 4mf – 8 – Dfl22.00 – ne Slangenburg [290]

BIBLIOTHECA ASCETICA ANTIQUO-NOVA / Pez, Bern. – Ratisbonae. Tomus 1-10. 1723-1733 – 65mf – 8 – ne Slangenburg [240]

BIBLIOTHECA AUGUSTINIANA / Ossinger, J F O E S A – Ingolstadii, 1768 – Dfl151.00 – ne Slangenburg [240]

BIBLIOTHECA BENEDICTINO-MAURIANA / Pez, Bern. – Augustae-Vindelicorum, 1716 – 6mf – 8 – Dfl25.00 – ne Slangenburg [240]

BIBLIOTHECA BIBLIOTHECARUM MANUSCRIPTORUM NOVA : UBI, QUAE INUMERIS PENE MANUSCRIPTORUM BIBLIOTHECIS CONTINENTUR... DESCRIBENTUR ET INDICANTUR / Montfaucon, B de – Parisiis. 2v. 1739 – 32mf – 9 – AR-1686/1 – ne IDC [090]

BIBLIOTHECA BIO-BIBLIOGRAFICA DELLA TERRA-SANTA E DELL' ORIENTE FRANCESCANO / Golubovich, PG – v. 1-5. Firenze. 1906-27. BU-673 2 – 8 – ne IDC [240]

BIBLIOTHECA BOTANICA : ABHANDLUNGEN AUS DEM GESAMMTGEBIETE DER BOTANIK / ed by Luerssen, C – (Missing: v22(p. 230-278)) – Cassel, 1887-1941. v1-30 – 302mf – 9239/1 – ne IDC [580]

BIBLIOTHECA BOTANICA / Haller, Albrecht von – Tiguri. 2v. 1771-1772 – 31mf – ne IDC [580]

BIBLIOTHECA BOTANICA... / Linnaeus, Carl – Amstelodami, 1751 – 5mf – ne IDC [580]

BIBLIOTHECA BOTANICA... / Linnaeus, Carl – Lugduni Batavorum, 1736 – 4mf – ne IDC [580]

BIBLIOTHECA BOTANICA, SIVE CATALOGUS AUCTORUM... / Seguier, J F – Hagae, Comitum, 1740 – 17mf – ne IDC [580]

BIBLIOTHECA CANADENSIS – [Quebec]: O. Frechette, [1881] – 9 – cn C.I.H.M. [971]

Bibliotheca Casinensis *see* SEU CODICUM MANUSCRIPTORUM QUI IN TABULARIO CASINENSI ASSERVANTUR

BIBLIOTHECA CLUNIACENSIS / ed by Marrier, D Martin – Bruxelles-Paris, 1915 – 45mf – 8 – Dfl158.00 – ne Slangenburg [240]

BIBLIOTHECA ELIOTAE: ELIOTIS LIBRARIE / Elyot, Thomas – Augmented by Thomas Cooper, London, 1548. Reprint Delmar, 1975. Introd. by Lillian Gottesman, Bronx Community College.Latin-English dictionary widely used in Tudor times – 9 – 60.00 – us Scholars' Facs [450]

BIBLIOTHECA ENTOMOLOGICA: DIE LITERATUR UEBER DAS GANZE GEBIET DER ENTOMOLOGIE BIS ZUM JAHRE 1862 / Hagen, H A – Leipzig, 1862-63. v1-2.Z/1323/2 – 8 – ne IDC [590]

BIBLIOTHECA FRANCISCANA ASCETICA MEDII AEVI – The first 7 vols. of this series: Meditatio pauperis in solitudine auctore anonymo saec. 13 and works by Aegidius of Assisi, Conradus de Brunopoli, Francesco d'Assisi, Guibert de Tournai, Jacobus Mediolanensis, and Thomas de Papia. Also available and priced separately, under main entries – 1 – us A.T.L.A. [240]

BIBLIOTHECA FRATRUM POLONORUM – (Fausti SOCINI SENENSIS. Opera Omnia.-Tome 1 + 2.-Irenopoli, 1656.-59mf; Joh. CRELLII FRANCI. Opera Omnia. Tom. 1-4.-Eleutheropoli, 1656.-86mf; SLICHTINGII DE BUKOWIEC, J. Commentaria Posthuma in plerosque Novi Testamenti Libros.-Tomus 1.-Irenopoli, 1656.-12mf; Tomus 2.-Irenopoli, 1656.-18mf; Joh. Lud. WOLZOGENII, Opera Omnia.-Tom. 1-3.-Irenopoli, 1656.-54mf; Sam. PRZIPCOVII. Omnia Opera.-Eleutheropoli, 1692.-31mf) – 8 – ne Slangenburg [290]

BIBLIOTHECA GEOGRAPHICA PALAESTINAE, CHRONOLOGISCHES VERZEICHNIS DER AUF DIE GEOGRAPHIE DES HEILIGEN LANDES BEZUEGLICHEN LITERATUR VON 333 BIS 1878 UND VERSUCH EINER CARTOGRAPHIE / Roehricht, R – Berlin, 1890 – 8mf – 9 – ne IDC [956]

BIBLIOTHECA GRAECA : SIVE NOTITIA SCRIPTORUM VETERUM GRAECORUM / ed by Fabricius, J A – Hamburg, 3rd ed 1712-1724. 12v – 215mf – ne IDC [949]

BIBLIOTHECA HAGIOGRAPHICA ORIENTALIS – Bruxelles, 1910 – 4mf – 9 – ne IDC [200]

BIBLIOTHECA HISPANA NOVA... – Matriti. 2v. 1783-88 – 27mf – 9 – O-1734/1 – ne IDC [019]

BIBLIOTHECA HISPANA VETUS,... – Romae. 2v. 1696 – 15mf – 9 – O-1733/1 – ne IDC [019]

BIBLIOTHECA HISTORICA – Goettingen. Vandenhoeck & Ruprecht. V.10-30, n. 1, 1862-82. N.S. v.1, 1887. Film Mas C 607 – 1 – us H.U. Library [900]

BIBLIOTHECA HISTORICA MEDII AEVI : WEGWEISER DURCH DIE GESCHICHTSWERKE DES EUROP. MITTELALTERS BIS 1500 / Potthast, A – Berlin. bd1-2. 1896 – Dfl140.00 – ne Slangenburg [240]

BIBLIOTHECA HISTORICO-NATURALIS – Goettingen. v. 1-37, 1851-87. Title varies. Film Mas C 606 – 1 – us H.U. Library [500]

BIBLIOTHECA HISTORICO-PHILOLOGICO THEOLOGICA BREMENSIS – 1(1718)-8(1725). Amstelodami, 1720-1725 – 96mf – 9 – Dfl336.00 – ne Slangenburg [073]

Bibliotheca Indosinica *see* DICTIONNAIRE BIBLIOGRAPHIQUE DES OUVRAGES RELATIFS A LA PENINSULE INDOCHINOISE

BIBLIOTHECA INSTITUTA ET COLLECTA PRIMUM A CONRADO GESNERO / Simler, J – Zuerich: Christoph Froschauer, 1574 – 8mf – 9 – ne IDC [240]

BIBLIOTHECA JUDAICA ANTICHRISTIANA... / Rossi, J B de – Parmae, 1800 – 2mf – ne IDC [270]

BIBLIOTHECA LATINA MEDIAE ET INFIMAE AETATIS / ed by Fabricius, J A – Hamburg, 1734-1746. 6v – 86mf – H-123/2 – ne IDC [450]

BIBLIOTHECA LATINA MEDIAE ET INFIMAE AETATIS / Fabricius, J A; ed by Mansi, J D – Hamburg. 6v. 1754 – 45mf – ne IDC [450]

BIBLIOTHECA LIVONIAE HISTORICA: SYSTEMATISCHES VERZEICHNIS DER QUELLEN UND HILFSMITTEL ZUR GESCHICHTE ESTLANDS, LIVLANDS UND KURLANDS / Wineklmann, E A – Ed. 2. Berlin. 1878. BR-9822 1 – 7mf – 9 – ne IDC [947]

BIBLIOTHECA LUTHERANA : A COMPLETE LIST OF THE PUBLICATIONS OF ALL THE LUTHERAN MINISTERS IN THE UNITED STATES / Morris, John G – Philadelphia: Lutheran Board of Publication, Lutheran Book Store, 1876, 1875 – 1mf – us A.T.L.A. [240]

BIBLIOTHECA MEDIEVALIS GRAECA / Sathas – 7v. 1872-94 – 56mf – 9 – OA-246/1 – ne IDC [019]

BIBLIOTHECA MISSIONUM / ed by Streit, R – Muenster, 1916-1934. v1-8 – 78mf – H-3050/1 – ne IDC [020]

BIBLIOTHECA MUNDI, VINCENTI BURGUNDI. / Beauvais, Vincent de – Douai: B. Belleri, 1624.75 fiches. (Miscellaneous Selections) – 9 – 186.00 – fr Bibl Nationale [020]

BIBLIOTHECA ORIENTALIS : OR A COMPLETE LIST OF BOOKS... ON THE HISTORY... OF THE EAST / Friederici, C – London, etc., 1876-1883 – 10mf – 9 – ne IDC [950]

BIBLIOTHECA ORIENTALIS CLEMENTINO VATICANA – Rome. v. 1-4. 1719-28 – 1 – us Princeton Micro [480]

BIBLIOTHECA ORIENTALIS CLEMENTINO-VATICANA / Assemanus, J S – Romae Tomi 1-3 1719-1728 – 122mf – 8 – ne Slangenburg [950]

BIBLIOTHECA ORIENTALIS-CLEMENTINO-VATICANA / Assemani, J S – 55mf – 9 – ne IDC [240]

BIBLIOTHECA OSLERIANA : A CATALOGUE OF BOOKS ILLUSTRATING THE HISTORY OF MEDICINE AND SCIENCE... / Osler, W – Oxford, 1929 – 28mf – 9 – ne IDC [610]

BIBLIOTHECA PALATINA : DRUCKSCHRIFTEN – STAMPATI PALATINI – PRINTED BOOKS / ed by Boyle, Leonard & Mittler, Elmar – (Subscribers receive a gratis copy of the 2v Heidelberg exhibition catalog) – 1989-1994 – 21,103 fiches (1:24) in 20 installments – 9 – silver DM49,800.00 – 3-598-32880-X – gw Saur [900]

BIBLIOTHECA PATRUM CISTERCIENSIUM / Tissier, Bertrandus – (Tome 1, 1660. 12mf; Tome 2, 1662. 16mf; Tome 3, 1660. 12mf; Tome 4, 1662. 14mf; Tome 5, 1662. 17mf; Tome 6, 1664. 6mf; Tome 7, 1669. 16mf; Tome 8, 1669. 13mf) – Bonofonte, 1660-69 – 106mf – 8 – Dfl371.00 – ne Slangenburg [240]

BIBLIOTHECA PHILOLOGICA CLASSICA – Leipzig. v. 1-65, 1874-1938. Film Mas C 562 – 1 – us H.U. Library [073]

BIBLIOTHECA PREMONSTRATENSIS ORDINIS / Paige, Johannis, Le – Parisiis, 1633 – 48mf – 8 – Dfl168.00 – ne Slangenburg [240]

BIBLIOTHECA RABBINICA : EINE SAMMLUNG ALTER MIDRASCHIM ZUM ERSTEN MALE INS DEUTSCHE UEBERTRAGEN / ed by Wuensche, August – Leipzig. bd1-11. 1880-1885 – Dfl217.00 – ne Slangenburg [220]

BIBLIOTHECA REALIS PHILOSOPHICA / Lipenius, Martin – HP1 6153-6154 2. 1682 – 8 – ne IDC [190]

BIBLIOTHECA REFORMATORIA NEERLANDICA / ed by Cramer, J & Pijper, F – 'S-Gravenhage. v1-10. 1903-1914 – Dfl602.00 – ne Slangenburg [240]

BIBLIOTHECA RERUM GERMANICARUM / ed by Jaffe, Ph – Berolini. v1-6. 1864-1873 – 81mf – 8 – Dfl921.00 – ne Slangenburg [943]

BIBLIOTHECA ROSENTHALIANA (HEBRAICA AND JUDAICA) – Amsterdam, 1932 – 1mf – ne IDC [270]

BIBLIOTHECA SACRA AND AMERICAN BIBLICAL REPOSITORY – 8(1851)-20(1863) – 204mf – 9 – Dfl714.00 – ne Slangenburg [073]

BIBLIOTHECA SACRA AND AMERICAN BIBLICAL REPOSITORY – (Missing: 1844-1850. v1-7) – New York. v1-20. 1844-1863 – 204mf – 9 – ne IDC [220]

BIBLIOTHECA SACRA AND THEOLOGICAL REVIEW – 1(1844)-7(1850) – 98mf – 9 – Dfl343.00 – ne Slangenburg [073]

BIBLIOTHECA SACRA DALLAS THEOLOGICAL SEMINARY – (With index: 1(1844)-30(1873) 5mf. Dfl22.00) – 21(1864)-39(1882) – 267mf – 9 – Dfl935.00 – ne Slangenburg [073]

BIBLIOTHECA SACRI ORDINIS CISTERCIENSIS / Visch, C de – Koeln, 1656 – 10mf – 8 – Dfl35.00 – ne Slangenburg [240]

BIBLIOTHECA SANCTA / Sixtus of Siena – Lyon. 2v. 1575 – 15mf – 9 – CA-60/1 – ne IDC [240]

BIBLIOTHECA SCHOLASTICA / Rider, John – 1589. 1056p. (English Linguistics Series 1500-1800) – 9 – us UMI [450]

BIBLIOTHECA SCRIPTORUM HISTORIAE NATURALIS / Boehmer, G R – Leipzig. 5v. 1785-1789 – 66mf – 9 – ne IDC [500]

BIBLIOTHECA SINICA / Cordier, Henri – 1851, 1885, 1895 – 9 – fr Orientalistes [490]

BIBLIOTHECA THERAPEUTICA,... / Waring, E J – London. 2v. 1878-1879 – 17mf – ne IDC [615]

BIBLIOTHECA UNIVERSALIS,... / Gessner, C – Tiguri: Apud Christophorum Froschoverum, 1545; 1548; 1549; 1555 – 48mf – 9 – H-2544/1 – ne IDC [010]

BIBLIOTHECA VETUSTISSIMA / Harrisse, Henry – New York. 2V. 1866. Additions. Paris. 1872 – 3 – us Readex [010]

BIBLIOTHECAE APOSTOLICAE VATICANAE CODICUM MANUSCRIPTORUM CATALOGUS / Assemanus-S E Assemanus – Romae Tomi 3 1756-1759 – 75mf – 8 – ne Slangenburg [220]

DIE "BIBLIOTHECAE" DES JEAN JACQUES MANGET (AEL, ABT 3;20) / Manget, Jean Jacques – (Contains: Bibliotheca medico-practica 1695-98 DM 740.00. Bibliotheca anatomica 1699 DM 410.00. Bibliotheca chemica (curiosa) 1702 Dm 320.00. Bibliotheca Pharmaceutico-medica 1703 DM 370.00. Bibliotheca chirurgica 1721 DM 420.00. Bibliotheca scriptorum medicorum veterum et recentiorum 1731 DM450.00) – Genf, Koeln, 1695-1731 (mf ed 1996) – 174mf – 9 – DM2,320.00 – 3-89131-216-4 – gw Fischer [610]

BIBLIOTHECAE MEDICEAE LAURENTIANAE ET PALATINAE CODICUM MMS : ORIENTALIUM CATALOGUS / Assemani, E – Florentiae, 1742 – 38mf – 8 – ne Slangenburg [240]

BIBLIOTHEK DER DEUTSCHEN LITERATUR : MIKROFICHE-GESAMTAUSGABE NACH ANGABEN DES TASCHENGOEDEKE – (A bibliography and index also available 581p DM48.00 ISBN: 3-598- 50100-5 (hb) DM20.00 ISBN: 3-598-53763-8 (sb). Free to subsc of entire work) – (mf ed 1990-98) – ca 20,660mf (1:42) – 9 – diazo set DM35,800.00 silver set DM62,800.00 – 3-598-50000-9 – silver ISBN: 3-598-50001-7 – gw Saur [430]

BIBLIOTHEK DER DEUTSCHEN LITERATUR : SUPPLEMENT / Frey, Axel – ca 700mf (1:24) – 9 – diazo ca DM3,560.00 (silver ca DM5,280.00 ISBN: 3-598-53301-2) – 3-598-53300-4 – gw Saur [430]

BIBLIOTHEK DER GESAMMTEN NATURGESCHICHTE – Frankfurt und Mainz. 1789-91 – 3 – us Readex [500]

BIBLIOTHEK DER KIRCHENVAETER. 1 REIHE – (63 Baende. Individual titles not listed. Please apply to publisher for a complete list) – 472mf – 8 – Dfl1,620.00 – ne Slangenburg [240]

BIBLIOTHEK DER KOMMUNISTISCHEN INTERNATIONALE – Hamburg. n1-40. 1920-21 – 3r – 1 – us Ross [335]

BIBLIOTHEK DER PAEDAGOGISCHEN LITERATUR – Leipzig, sep-dec 1803 – 1r – 1 – gw Mikrofilm [370]

BIBLIOTHEK DES DEUTSCHEN JUDENTUMS *see*
- BEN-CHANANJA
- JAHRBUECHER FUER JUEDISCHE GESCHICHTE UND LITERATUR
- DER JUDE
- JUEDISCHE ZEITSCHRIFT FUER WISSENSCHAFT UND LEBEN
- MENORAH, JARHON MESEWAJER LEBET HA-JEHUDI
- MITTEILUNGEN DES GESAMTARCHIVS DER DEUTSCHEN JUDEN
- DER ORIENT
- OST UND WEST
- ZEITSCHRIFT FUER DIE GESCHICHTE DER JUDEN IN DEUTSCHLAND

BIBLIOTHEK DES DEUTSCHEN MUSEUMS. MUENCHEN = LIBRARY CATALOGUE OF THE DEUTSCHE MUSEUM, MUNICH – (Alphabetischer Katalog. 313 fiches; Schlagwort Katalog . 299 fiches (1:42)) – 1981-82 – 2pts – 9 – silver DM7,800.00 – 3-598-30397-1 – gw Saur [020]

BIBLIOTHEK DES DEUTSCHEN PATENTAMTES MUENCHEN = LIBRARY OF THE GERMAN PATENT OFFICE MUNICH – 1945-74. 1983 – 167 fiches (1:42) – 9 – diazo DM3,400.00 (silver DM3,800.00 ISBN: 3-598-30453-6) – 3-598-30454-4 – gw Saur [340]

BIBLIOTHEK RUSSISCHER DENKWUERDIGKEITEN – Stuttgart, 1894-1895. v1-7 – 33mf – R-1680/2 – ne IDC [947]

BIBLIOTHEK STEIN : HISTORY OF SOCIALISM – (Microfiche edition accompanied by a printed catalogue (silver halide microfiche on request) – Wildberg: BELSER WISS. DIENST, 1992 – 3,212mf – 9 – DM24,500.00 diazo – 3-628-00100-5 – gw Belser Wiss [335]

BIBLIOTHEKA HEBRAICA PO MENDELSSOHNIANA, BIBLIOGRAPHISCHES HANDBUCH DER NEU HEBRAEISCHEN LITTERATUR... BIS ZUM JAHRE 1890 / Zeitlin, W – Leipzig. 2v. 1891-1895 – 7mf – ne IDC [470]

LA BIBLIOTHEQUE A CINQ CENTS – Montreal: Poirier, Bessette, v1 no 1 (8 avril 1886)- – 9 – cn C.I.H.M. [971]

BIBLIOTHEQUE AFRICAINE: 16TH CENTURY TO 1800 – (Following authors from this series are also listed separately in this directory:. Adanson, Michel. Alexis de Saint Lo (Le Pere). Alvarez, Francois. Bergeron, Pierre. Bosman, Willem. Brisson, P. R. de. Castilhon, L. Chenier, L. S. de. Contant d'Orville, Andre-Guillaume. Coste d'Arnobat, Pierre-Nicolas. Damberger, Chr. Fr. D'Elbee. Demanet, Abbe. Draise de Grandpierre. Follie. Frejus, Roland. Froger, Francois. Gaby, le Pere F. J. B. Gattine, N. A. de and D. de Plaisance. Golberry, Silvain-Meinrad-Xavier de. Grandpre, Comte Louis de. Isert, Paul Erdman. Jannequin, Claude, sieur de Rochefort. Labat, Jean-Baptiste. La Croix, Sieur de. Lalande, Jerome. Lamiral, D. H. Leguat, Francois. Le Maire, Jacques. Linschoten, J. H. van. Lobo, Le Pere Jerome.. Loyer, Le Pere Godefroy. Ludolf, H. Mocquet, Jean. Montauban. Norris, Robert. Radet et Barre. Sainte-Marie, Jean de. Santos, Jean Dos. Saugnier. Smith, Guillaume. Villauet, Nicolas, sieur de Bellfond) – (Series). v. 1-2: 19th century. Early reports of explorations and missionary work: geographical descriptions: studies of indigenous cultures. In French. Titles also available individually; inquire – 9 – fr Hachette [550]

BIBLIOTHEQUE ANCIENNE ET MODERNE – Amsterdam. 1714-27 (I-XXVII) – 1 – fr A.C.R.P.P. [073]

BIBLIOTHEQUE ANGLOISE – ou Histoire litteraire de la Grande-Bretagne. Amsterdam. 1717-28 (I-XV) – 1 – fr A.C.R.P.P. [420]

BIBLIOTHEQUE BRITANNIQUE – ou Histoire des ouvrages des savans de la Grande-Bretagne. La Haye. avr 1733-mars 1747 (I-XXII) – 1 – fr A.C.R.P.P. [420]

BIBLIOTHEQUE BRITANNIQUE, OU HISTOIRE DES OUVRAGES DES SAVANS DE LA GRANDE-BRETAGNE – La Haye, 1733-1747 – 3 – us Readex [000]

BIBLIOTHEQUE BRITANNIQUE, OU, RECUEIL EXTRAIT DES OUVRAGES ANGLAIS PERIODIQUES & AUTRES, DES MEMOIRES ET TRANSACTIONS DES SOCIETES ET ACADEMIES DE LA GRANDE-BRETAGNE, D'ASIE, D'AFRIQUE ET D'AMERIQUE – Geneva, 1796-1815 – 3 – us Readex [941]

BIBLIOTHEQUE CANADIENNE / ed by Bibaud, Michel – (Cont by: L'Observateur) – Montreal, Canada. jun 1825-v9 n24. 15 jun 1830 – 1r – 1 – Can$35.00 – cn Can Microfilming [073]

BIBLIOTHEQUE CANADIENNE – Levis [Quebec]: P.G. Roy, 1898- – 9 – cn C.I.H.M. [971]

LA BIBLIOTHEQUE CANADIENNE *see* L'OBSERVATEUR

LA BIBLIOTHEQUE CANADIENNE-FRANCAISE – Quebec: Societe Saint-Vincent de Paul, 1896-1897 – 9 – cn C.I.H.M. [440]

Bibliotheque de la Societe Psychanalytique de Paris *see* ALMANACH FUER DAS JAHR

BIBLIOTHEQUE DE L'ECOLE DES CHARTES – 1(1839)-116(1958) – 1,778mf – 9 – Dfl6,223.00 – ne Slangenburg [020]

BIBLIOTHEQUE DE L'ECOLE DES CHARTES – Paris, 1839-1852 – 138mf – 1 – ne IDC [010]

BIBLIOTHEQUE DES BENEDICTINS DE LA CONGREGATION DE SAINT-VANNE ET SAINT-HYDULPHE / Godefroy, J – 1925 – Dfl25.00 – ne Slangenburg [240]

LA BIBLIOTHEQUE DES BONNES LECTURES ILLUSTREES – Trois-Rivieres, Quebec: Societe de publication des bonnes lectures illustrees, [180-?-180-?] – 9 – cn C.I.H.M. [440]

BIBLIOTHEQUE DES CROISADES / Michaud, M – Paris, France. 4v. 1829 – 1r – 1 – Can$45.00 – cn Can Microfilming [020]

BIBLIOTHEQUE DES PHILOSOPHES CHIMIQUES – Paris. 4v. 1741-1754 – 28mf – ne IDC [660]

BIBLIOTHEQUE DES SCIENCES ET DES BEAUX ARTS – t.1-t.50. 1754-80 – 3 – us Readex [700]

BIBLIOTHEQUE DES SCIENCES ET DES BEAUX-ARTS – La Haye. 1754-80 (I-L) – 1 – fr A.C.R.P.P. [500]

Bibliotheque Forney. Paris *see*
- CATALOGUE D'ARTICLES DE PERIODIQUES-ARTS DECORATIFS ET BEAUX ARTS
- CATALOGUE DES CATALOGUES DE VENTES D'ART

LA BIBLIOTHEQUE FRANCAISE – Montreal: Societe des Publications Francaises, 1887-[189- ou 19–] – 9 – cn C.I.H.M. [440]

BIBLIOTHEQUE FRANCOISE – ou Histoire litteraire de la France. Amsterdam. 1723-46 – 1 – fr A.C.R.P.P. [440]

LA BIBLIOTHEQUE FRANCOISE / Sorel, Ch – 2E ED. 1667 – 9 – fr I.C.S. [020]

BIBLIOTHEQUE FRANCOISE OU HISTOIRE DE LA LITTERATURE FRANCOISE / Goujet, C P – 1741-56 – 9 – fr I.C.S. [440]

BIBLIOTHEQUE GERMANIQUE – ou Histoire litteraire de l'Allegmagne, de la Suisse et des pays du Nord. Amsterdam. 1720-41 – 1 – fr A.C.R.P.P. [430]

BIBLIOTHEQUE HISTORIQUE DE LA FRANCE : CONTENANT LE CATALOGUE DE TOUS LES OUVRAGES, TANT IMPRIMEZ QUE MANUSCRIPTS, QUI TRAITENT DE L'HISTOIRE DE CE ROIAUME, OU QUI Y ONT RAPPORT; AVEC DES NOTES CRITIQUES ET HISTORIQUES / Long, J le – Paris, 1719 – 52mf – 9 – ne IDC [944]

BIBLIOTHEQUE HISTORIQUE DE TOURAINE... / Chalmel, J L – 19th cent – 1 – F123.50 – fr Armell [944]

LA BIBLIOTHEQUE ILLUSTREE – Montreal: Patry & Peeters, [1898-19–] – 9 – cn C.I.H.M. [700]

Bibliotheque Interuniversitaire. Montpellier. Bibliotheque de la Faculte de Medecine *see* CATALOGUE DE SERVICE

Bibliotheque Juive. Montreal. Archives *see* FONDS SEGAL

BIBLIOTHEQUE LINGUISTIQUE AMERICAINE – 70mf – 9 – $215.00 – us UPA [420]

BIBLIOTHEQUE MACONNIQUE OU RECUEIL DE MATERIAUX... – Paris, 1818 – 4mf – ne IDC [360]

LA BIBLIOTHEQUE MEDICALE DE L'HOTEL-DIEU DE QUEBEC, 17-18-19E SIECLES / Langlois, Marguerite – 1961. SEM105P4 – 4mf – 9 – cn Bibl Nat [610]

Bibliotheque Municipale. Amiens *see* FONDS MASSON: CATALOGUE DES IMPRESSIONS DU XVE AU XVIIIE SIECLE

Bibliotheque Municipale. Arras *see* CATALOGUE DES BROCHURES REVOLUTIONNAIRES DE LA COLLECTION CHARPENTIER

Bibliotheque Municipale. Autun *see* FONDS DU SEMINAIRE ET DE L'EVECHE

Bibliotheque Municipale. Beaune *see* LE FONDS ANCIEN

Bibliotheque Municipale. Beauvais *see* CATALOGUE DU FONDS ANCIEN E'IMPRIMES

Bibliotheque Municipale. Carpentras *see* CATALOGUE DE L'ANCIEN FONDS DE LA BIBLIOTHEQUE INGUIMBERTINE

Bibliotheque Municipale. Dole *see* FONDS ANCIEN

Bibliotheque Municipale. Fougeres *see* CATALOGUE DU FONDS ANCIEN

Bibliotheque Municipale. Mende *see* CATALOGUE DE FONDS ROUSSEL

Bibliotheque Municipale. Rouen *see* CATALOGUE DES IMPRESSIONS DUE XVI SIECLE

Bibliotheque National. France. Dept des Imprimes *see* CATALOGUE DE L'HISTOIRE DE L'AFRIQUE

BIBLIOTHEQUE NATIONALE : THE AUTHOR CATALOGUES OF PRINTED BOOKS – (Catalogue general: Auteurs 1897-1959 1445mf £4,960. Catalogue general: Auteurs, Collectivites-Auteurs, Anonymes 1960-69 430mf £1,655. Catalogue general: Auteurs, 1897-1959 Suppl 2,890mf £9,975. Includes guide £20) – 3 catalogues 4765mf – 9 – £15,435.00 set – uk Chadwyck [020]

BIBLIOTHEQUE NATIONALE : CATALOGUE DE L'HISTOIRE DE FRANCE – (With printed guide & subject index) – 1500mf – 9 – £4,850.00 – uk Chadwyck [944]

BIBLIOTHEQUE NATIONALE : CATALOGUE GENERAL DES PERIODIQUES DES ORIGINES A 1959 – (Includes an addendum of 44mf. With printed guide) – 1344mf – 9 – £4,235.00 – uk Chadwyck [073]

BIBLIOTHEQUE NATIONALE : CATALOGUES DU DEPARTEMENT DE LA MUSIQUE – 1836mf – 9 – £7,995.00 – uk Chadwyck [780]

BIBLIOTHEQUE NATIONALE : CATALOGUES DU DEPARTEMENT DES ARTS DU SPECTACLE – 1020mf – 9 – £4,520.00 – uk Chadwyck [790]

BIBLIOTHEQUE NATIONALE : COLLECTIONS OF THE DEPARTMENT OF PRINTS AND PHOTOGRAPHS / Bibliotheque Nationale – 250,000 images currently available. Titles, collections listed individually – 1 – fr Bibl Nationale [760]

BIBLIOTHEQUE NATIONALE : L'INVENTAIRE DES CATALOGUES DES MANUSCRITS – 9 – £14,100.00 – uk Chadwyck [090]

Bibliotheque Nationale *see*
- ART
- BIBLIOTHEQUE NATIONALE
- CATALOGUE DE L'HISTOIRE D'ESPAGNE ET DU PORTUGAL
- LA CONDITION OUVRIERE
- ECONOMICS COLLECTION
- EDUCATION COLLECTION
- LES ENQUETES DES PREFETS DE L'EMPIRE, 1795-1815
- LES FEMMES
- HISTORICAL STUDIES SERIES
- LANGUAGE COLLECTION
- LAW COLLECTION
- LITERATURE COLLECTION
- MINIATURES DES PLUS ANCIENS MANUSCRITS GRECS... DU 6E AU 14E SIECLE...
- MISCELLANEOUS SELECTIONS
- MUSIC COLLECTION
- PARIS MAY '68
- PHILOSOPHY COLLECTION
- POLITICAL SCIENCE COLLECTION
- RARE BOOKS CATALOGS
- RECUEILS DOCUMENTAIRES DES ARTS DU SPECTACLE
- RELIGION
- SCIENCE COLLECTION
- SELECTED PERIODICALS
- STATISTICS: PART 2. DEMOGRAPHY
- STATISTICS: PART 3. TOPOGRAPHY
- STATISTICS: PART I. MEDICAL STUDIES
- TRAVEL

BIBLIOTHEQUE NATIONALE DEPARTEMENT DES MANUSCRITS : INVENTAIRE DES INSTRUMENTS DE RECHERCHE: MANUSCRIPTS OCCIDENTAUX / Departement des Manuscrits – 2,632mf – 9 – £9,910.00 – uk Chadwyck [090]

BIBLIOTHEQUE NATIONALE DU QUEBEC *see* ETUDE SUR LES STATISTIQUES

Bibliotheque Nationale. Paris. Dept. des Imprimes *see* CATALOGUE DE L'HISTOIRE DE L'AFRIQUE

Bibliotheque Nationale. Quebec *see*
- BIBLIOGRAPHIE DU QUEBEC
- BIBLIOGRAPHIE DU QUEBEC: LISTE DES PUBLICATIONS QUEBECOISES OU RELATIVES AU QUEBEC, ETABLIE PAR LA BIBLIOTHEQUE NATIONALE DU QUEBEC
- BULLETIN..
- PLANS D'ASSURANCES DE VILLES DU QUEBEC
- POLITIQUE DE CONSERVATION DU PATRIMOINE DOCUMENTAIRE
- RADAR

Bibliotheque Nationale. Quebec. Service de catalogage *see* FICHIER D'AUTORITE DES ORGANISMES GOUVERNEMENTAUX DU QUEBEC

BIBLIOTHEQUE ORIENTALE, OU DICTIONNAIRE UNIVERSEL,... / Herbelot de Molainville, B d' – Maestricht, 1776-1780. 2v – 36mf – 9 – ne IDC [610]

BIBLIOTHEQUE ORIENTALE, OU DICTIONNAIRE UNIVERSEL,... / Herbelot de Molainville, B d' – Maestricht. 2v. 1776-1780 – 36mf – 9 – ne IDC [950]

Bibliotheque Osler. Montreal *see* DIVERS – BIBLIOTHEQUE OSLER CATALOG NO. 107-7636

Bibliotheque paroissiale de Notre-Dame *see* CATALOGUE DE LA BIBLIOTHEQUE DE L'OEUVRE DES BONS LIVRES, ERIGEE A MONTREAL

BIBLIOTHEQUE PATRIOTIQUE ET REPUBLICAINE ILLUSTREE: LES LIVRES DU PEUPLE – J. Lermina, dir. Paris. 1837-38. (Historical Studies Series) – 9 – 63.00 – fr Bibl Nationale [900]

BIBLIOTHEQUE RAISONNEE DES OUVRAGES DES SAVANS DE L'EUROPE – Amsterdam. 1752 – 1 – fr A.C.R.P.P. [073]

BIBLIOTHEQUE SULPICIENNE OU HISTOIRE LITTERAIRE DE LA COMPAGNIE DE SAINT SULPICE / Bertrand, Louis Jacques – Paris: A. Picard, 1900. 02063. (Pre-1900 Canadiana) – 9 – cn C.I.H.M. [440]

BIBLIOTHEQUE SULPICIENNE, OU, HISTOIRE LITTERAIRE DE LA COMPAGNIE DE SAINT SULPICE / Bertrand, Louis Jacques – Paris: A. Picard, 1900. 02061. (Pre-1900 Canadiana) – 9 – cn C.I.H.M. [240]

LES BIBLIOTHEQUES PAROISSIALES : BIBLIOGRAPHIE ANALYTIQUE DE LA LITTERATURE FRANCAISE PARUE SUR LE SUJET DANS LA PROVINCE DE QUEBEC / Turcotte, Fernande – 1952. SEM105P4 – 1mf – 9 – cn Bibl Nat [440]

BIBLIOTHEQUES PUBLIQUES. LES PONTIFICAUX MANUSCRITS / ed by Leroquais, Victor – O 478. 3 v. 1937 – 9 – ne IDC [020]

DER BIBLISCHE BERICHT UEBER DIE STIFTSHUETTE...COMPOSITION UND DIASKEUE DES PENTATEUCH / Popper, Julius – Leipzig: Heinrich Hunger, 1862. 1 fiche – 9 – us A.T.L.A. [240]

DIE BIBLISCHE CHRONOLOGIE / Schaefer, Aloys – Muenster: Adolf Russel, 1879. 1 fiche – 9 – us A.T.L.A. [240]

BIBLISCHE CHRONOLOGIE BIS AUF DAS JAHR DER GEBURT JESU / Roeckerath, Peter Joseph – Muenster: Aschendorff, 1865. 1 fiche. 8370-4945-8 – 9 – us A.T.L.A. [240]

BIBLISCHE CHRONOLOGIE UND ZEITRECHNUNG DER HEBRAEER / Mahler, Eduard – Wien: Carl Konegen, 1887. 1 fiche – 9 – us A.T.L.A. [220]

BIBLISCHE GESCHICHTE: DER HEILIGEN SCHRIFT / Kurtz, Johann Heinrich – Berlin: Justus A. Wohlgemuth, 1865. 1 fiche – 9 – us A.T.L.A. [240]

BIBLISCHE KOENIGSDRAMEN IN DER FRANZOESISCHEN TRAGOEDIE DES 16. UND 17. JAHRHUNDERTS / Carlebach, David – Halberstadt, 1912 – 1mf – 9 – DM48.00 – 3-89349-331-X – gw Hänsel [440]

BIBLISCHE LIEBESLIEDER : DAS SOGENANNTE HOHELIED SALOMOS: UNTER STETER BERUECKSICHTIGUNG DER UEBERSETZUNGEN GOETHES UND HERDERS IM VERSMASSE DER URSCHRIFT / Haupt, Paul – (Includes index comapring the version of the Song of Solomon in the bk with the traditional text) – Leipzig: J C Hinrichs; Baltimore: John Hopkins, 1907 – 1mf – 9 – 0-8370-3530-9 – 1985-1530 – us A.T.L.A. [220]

DIE BIBLISCHE POESIE : BESONDERS DIE ALTTESTAMENTLICHE, UND IHRE BEHANDLUNG IN DER SCHULE / Traenckner, Chr – (Includes bibliographical references) – Gotha: C F Thienemann, 1902 – 1mf – 9 – 0-8370-8554-3 – 1986-2554 – us A.T.L.A. [470]

DER BIBLISCHE SAMSON / Zapletal, Vincenz – Freiburg (Schweiz): O Gschwend, 1906 – 1mf – 9 – 0-8370-9676-6 – 1986-3676 – us A.T.L.A. [220]

BIBLISCHE SPRACHE UND BIBLISCHE MOTIVE IN WIELANDS OBERON / Biach, Adolf – (Includes bibliographical references) – Bruex: M Herzum, 1897 – 1r – 1 – us U.W. Library [430]

DIE BIBLISCHE THEOLOGIE : EINLEITUNG IN'S ALTE UND NEUE TESTAMENT UND DARSTELLUNG DES LEHRGEHALTES DER BIBLISCHEN BUECHER NACH IHRER ENTSTEHUNG UND IHREM GESCHICHTLICHEN VERHAELTNISS: EIN HANDBUCH ZUM SELBSTUNTERRICHT / Noack, Ludwig – (Includes bibliographical references) – Halle: C E M Pfeffer, 1853 – 1mf – 9 – 0-8370-9722-3 – 1986-3722 – us A.T.L.A. [220]

DIE BIBLISCHE THEOLOGIE UND IHRE GEGNER / Myrberg, Otto Ferdinand – Guetersloh: C Bertelsmann, 1892 – 1mf – 9 – 0-8370-8847-X – 1986-2847 – us A.T.L.A. [220]

BIBLISCHE UND BABYLONISCHE URGESCHICHTE = THE BABYLONIAN AND THE HEBREW GENESIS / Zimmern, Heinrich – (In English) – London: David Nutt, 1901 – 1mf – 9 – 0-8370-5966-6 – 1985-3966 – us A.T.L.A. [220]

DIE BIBLISCHE URGESCHICHTE / Lotz, Wilhelm – Leipzig: A. Deichert, 1907. 1 fiche – 9 – us A.T.L.A. [240]

DIE BIBLISCHE URGESCHICHTE I. MOSE 1-12 GEMEINVERSTAENDLICH DARGESTELLT / Meinhold, Johannes – Bonn: A. Marcus & E. Weber, 1904. 1 fiche – 9 – us A.T.L.A. [240]

DIE BIBLISCHE ZEITRECHNUNG : VOM AUSZUGE AUS AEGYPTEN BIS ZUM BEGINNE DER BABYLONISCHEN GEFANGENSCHAFT / Lederer, Carl – (Includes bibliographical references) – Speier: In Kommission der Ferd. Kleeberger'schen Buchhandlung, [1888?] – 1mf – 9 – 0-8370-4077-9 – 1985-2077 – us A.T.L.A. [220]

BIBLISCHE ZEITSCHRIFT – 1(1903)-24(1938/39) – 191mf – 9 – Dfl669.00 – ne Slangenburg [073]

BIBLISCHE ZEITSCHRIFT – (1977-. 5,6,9) – n.s. v. 1-. 1957- – 1 – us UMI [220]

BIBLISCHE ZEITSCHRIFT – Paderborn. v1-24. 1903-1938/1939 – 191mf – 9 – ne IDC [220]

DIE BIBLISCHEN ASYLE IN TALMUDISCHEM GEWANDE / Ohlenburg, Salomon – Muenchen: F. Straub, 1895. 1 fiche – 9 – us A.T.L.A. [270]

DIE BIBLISCHEN FRAUEN DES ALTEN TESTAMENTES / Zschokke, Hermann – (Includes bibliographical references and index) – Freiburg im Breisgau; St Louis: Herder, 1882 – 2mf – 9 – 0-8370-5972-0 – 1985-3972 – us A.T.L.A. [220]

DIE BIBLISCHEN WUNDERGESCHICHTEN / Wimmer, Richard – 3. u 4. Aufl. Freiburg i.B.: J C B Mohr (Paul Siebeck), 1890 – 1mf – 9 – 0-8370-5867-8 – 1985-3867 – us A.T.L.A. [240]

DIE BIBLISCH-TALMUDISCHE GLAUBENSLEHRE...BEILAGE UEBER STAAT UND KIRCHE / Duschak, Moritz – Wien: Wilhelm Braumueller, 1873.1 fiche – 9 – us A.T.L.A. [240]

BIBLISKA STUDIER = ETUDES BIBLIQUES DEUXI EME SERIE : ANDRA DELEN, NYA TESTAMENTET / Godet, Frederic Louis – (Includes errata. Includes bibliographical references) – Upsala: W Schultz, 1878 – 1mf – 9 – 0-8370-9471-2 – 1986-3471 – us A.T.L.A. [220]

BIBLISKA STUDIER = ETUDES BIBLIQUES. PREMIERE SERIE : FOERSTA DELEN, GAMLA TESTAMENTET / Godet, Frederic Louis – (Includes errata. Includes bibliographical references) – Upsala: W Schultz, 1879 – 1mf – 9 – 0-8370-9472-0 – 1986-3472 – us A.T.L.A. [220]

Bican, Ahmed *see* ENVAR UEL-'ASIKIN

BICENTENNIAL / Tussekiah Baptist Church – 1776-1976 – 1 – 5.00 – us Baptist [240]

BICESTER ADVERTISER – Bicester, England. -w. 7 July 1855-26 Jan 1866. 5 reels – 1 – uk British Libr Newspaper [072]

BICH NARODA : LITERATURNO-NAUCHNYI ILLIUSTRIROVANNY I SBORNIK / ed by Kazakova, Iskhaka – Kazan: Izd. T Skpomgola pri Tatt sike, 1922 – 1 – CSUX89-B1659 – us Hoover Inst Photo [460]

Bichat, M F X. *see* ANATOMIE GENERALE APPLIQUEE A LA PHYSIOLOGIE ET LA MEDICINE

BICHINHO : SEMANARIO DA BICHARIA – (Suppl of: Rio Nu) – Rio de Janeiro, 1 Oct 1915-4 Jan 1917 – 1,5,6 – bl Biblioteca [072]

Bichon, S *see* LE DROIT DES ETRANGERS A LA PROPRIETE COMMERCIALE

Bickart, E *see*
- ETUDE SUR L'ACQUISITION DU DROIT DE CITE A ROME ...
- LA NATURALISATION

Bickel, Gerhard *see* AXICON UND RINGPUPILLE ALS BILDFORMENDE ELEMENTE

Bickell, Gustav *see*
- METRICES BIBLICAE REGULAE EXEMPLIS ILLUSTRATAE
- OUTLINES OF HEBREW GRAMMAR

Bickelmann, Ingeborg *see* GOETHES "WERTHER" IM URTEIL DES 19. JAHRHUNDERTS

Bickerman, Joseph *see* ROSSI ISKAIA REVOLIUTSIIA I GOSUDARSTVENNAIA DUMA

Bickerstaff, Isaac *see* THE PADLOCK

Bickersteth, Edward Henry *see*
- PRACTICAL AND EXPLANATORY COMMENTARY ON THE NEW TESTAMENT
- THE ROCK OF AGES
- THE ROCK OF AGES; OR, A SCRIPTURE TESTIMONY TO THE ONE ETERNAL GODHEAD OF THE FATHER

Bickersteth, Emily *see* EXTRACTS FROM WOMAN'S SERVICE ON THE LORD'S DAY

Bickersteth, M Cyril *see* LETTERS TO A GODSON: HOW TO READ THE OLD TESTAMENT IN THE LIGHT OF THE NEW

Bickmore, A S *see* TRAVELS IN THE EAST INDIAN ARCHIPELAGO

Bicknell, A *see* PAINTING PERSONIFIED

Bicknell, C *see* FLOWERING PLANTS AND FERNS OF THE RIVIERA AND NEIGHBOURING MOUNTAINS

Bicknell, Thomas W *see* HISTORY OF STATE OF RHODE ISLAND AND PROVIDENCE PLANTATIONS

Bickum, Bonnie D *see* THE HISTORY OF GRADED EXERCISE TESTING IN CARDIAC REHABILITATION

LE BICORNE : ORGANE DU PARTI RHINOCEROS / ed by Ferron, Jacques – Ville Jacques-Cartier (Longueuil), Canada. 6 oct 1964; ?dec 1964 – 1r – 1 – Can$25.00 – cn Can Microfilming [072]

THE BICYCLE – Hamilton [Ont.: s.n., 1882-18– or 19–] – 9 – cn C.I.H.M. [073]

BICYCLE GAZETTE – Coventry, England. -f. 15 Feb-1 Aug 1879. 25 ft – 1 – uk British Libr Newspaper [072]

BICYCLE JOURNAL – London, England. Bicycle, Swimming & Athletic Journal. -w. 18 Aug 1876-27 Nov 1878. 1 1 2 reels – 1 – uk British Libr Newspaper [072]

LA BICYCLETTE / Dorion, F. X. J – Quebec?: s.n., 1898. 04299. (Pre-1900 Canadiana) – 9 – cn C.I.H.M. [971]

BICYCLING – (1976-. 5,6,9) – v. 1- 1962- – 1 – us UMI [790]

BICZ BOZY = GOD'S WHIP – (New York-1934, bi-monthly) – Chicago, Ill. 1909-1917 – us I.H.R.C. [071]

BIDAR. ITS HISTORY AND MONUMENTS / Yazdani, G – I 1055. 1947 – 9 – ne IDC [950]

Biddle, George Washington *see* A SKETCH OF THE PROFESSIONAL AND JUDICIAL CHARACTER OF THE LATE GEORGE SHARSWOOD

Biddle, Nicholas *see* PAPERS

Biddle, William P *see* THE BAPTIST HYMN BOOK

Biddlecombe, George *see* NAVAL TACTICS, AND TRIALS OF SAILING; ALSO THE ESTABLISHED PLAN OF LIGHTS FOR STEAM-VESSELS, AND REGULATIONS TO AVOID COLLISION

Biddulph, John *see* THE PIRATES OF MALABAR; AND AN ENGLISHWOMAN IN INDIA TWO HUNDRED YEARS AGO

BIDDULPH, MS. 652: EXTRACTS – 1 – uk Microform Academic [980]

THE BIDDULPH TRAGEDY – 1880? 02301. (Pre-1900 Canadiana) – 9 – cn C.I.H.M. [971]

Bidez, J *see* LA TRADITION MANUSCRITE DE SOZOMENE (T.U.U. 3-32/2B)

Bidloo, G *see* DE PUBLIJKE INTREDE VAN WILLIAM DE 3., 5 FEBRUARIJ 1691

BIDPAI – Arabic version. Kalilah wa-Dimnah. Indonesian. Hikajat Kalilah dan Dimnah. 1948. 4 v. SE-3034 1. 1948 – 9 – ne IDC [800]

Bidpai *see* THE EARLIEST ENGLISH VERSION OF THE FABLES OF BIDPAI, THE MORALL PHILOSOPHIE OF DONI

BIDRAG TIL BESKRIVELSE OVER ST CROIX MED EN KORT UDSIGT OVER ST THOMAS, ST JEAN, TORTOLA, SPANISHTOWN OG CRABENEILAND / West, H – Kjoebenhavn. 1793. B-5807 2 – 8 – ne IDC [580]

BIDRAG TIL EN SKILDRING AF GUINEA-KYSTEN OG DENS INDBYGGERE : OG TIL EN BESKRIVELSE OVER DE DANSKE COLONIER PAA DENNE KYST, SAMLEDE UNDER MIT OPHOLD I AFRIKA I AARENE 1805 TIL 1809 / Monrad, Hans Christian – Kobenhavn: A Seidelin, 1822 – 1 – us Res Libr [960]

BIDRAG TIL KAENNEDOMEN OM SKANDINAVIENS ECTOCARPEER OCH TILOPTERIDER / Kjellman, F R – Stockholm. 1872. B-5248 2 – 8 – ne IDC [580]

BIDRAG TIL KJENDSKABET OM ESKIMOERNES HERKOMST / Holm, G – BN-251 2. 1892 – 8 – ne IDC [306]

BIDRAG TILL SPITSBERGENS MOLLUSKFAUNA / Torell, O M – Stockholm. 1859. BZ-838 2 – 8 – ne IDC [590]

Bidwell, George *see* FORGING HIS CHAINS

BIDWELL GOLD NUGGET (BIDWELL NEWS) – Fort Bidwell, CA. Jan 1907-Sept 1917 (broken file) – 3r – 1 – $150.00 – B02237 – us Library Micro [071]

Bidwell, John *see* JOHN BIDWELL, PIONEER

BIDWELL NEWS *see* BIDWELL GOLD NUGGET (BIDWELL NEWS)

Bie, C de *see*
- HET GULDEN CABINET VAN DE EDELE VRYE SCHILDERCONST ONTSLOTEN DOOR DEN LANCK GHEWENSCHTEN VREDE TUSSCHEN DE TWEE MACHTIGHE CROONEN VAN SPAIGNIEN EN VRANCKRYK
- DEN SEDIGHEN TOET-STEEN VAN DE ONVERDRAEGHELYCKE WELDE

Bieberstein, Friedrich August Marschall von *see*
- BESCHREIBUNG DER LAENDER ZWISCHEN DEN FLUESSEN TEREK UND KAR AM CASPISCHEN MEERE
- CENTURIA PLANTARUM RARIORUM ROSSIAE MERIDIONALIS....
- FLORA TAURICO-CAUCASICA
- FLORA TAURICO-CAUCASICA EXHIBENO STIRPES PHANOGAMAS, IN CHERSONESO TAURICA ET REGIONIBUS CAUCASICIS SPONTE CRESCENTES...

DAS BIECHLIN ZAIGET AN WER DER LEBENDIG SEY AUFF ERDTRICH / Storch, N ? – 1522? BME-16 1 – 9 – ne IDC [240]

Biechteler, B *see* VOX SUPREMA OLORIS PARTHENII...

Bieder, W *see* EKKLESIA UND POLIS IM NEUEN TESTAMENT UND IN DER ALTEN KIRCHE

Biedermann, Alois Emanuel *see* CHRISTLICHE DOGMATIK

Biedermann, Flodoard, Freiherr von *see* GOETHE ALS RAETSELDICHTER

Biedermann, Michael C *see* CORRELATION BETWEEN MUSCLE RELAXATION AND SARCOPLASMIC RETICULUM CA2+-ATPASE DURING FATIGUE

Biedermann, Woldemar Freiherr von *see* GOETHES BRIEFWECHSEL MIT FRIEDRICH ROCHLITZ

Biedma, C M *see* FUERZA EXTRATERRITORIAL DE LAS LEYES SUCESORIAS

BIEDNOTA : IZD. TSENTRALNOGO KOMITETA ROSSIISKOI KOMMUNISTICHESKOI PARTII (BOLSHEVIKOV) – Moskva: Komitet, [sep 8 1921-apr 5 1923] – 1r – us Res Libr [320]

Biel, G *see*
- CANONIS MISSE EXPOSITIO EDIDERUNT
- SERMONES DOMINICALES DE TEMPORE...

Bieleck, Rudolph *see*
- DER MENSCHENFEIND
- DES VATERS FLUCH

BIELEFELDER ABENDZEITUNG – Bielefeld, 1923-25 – 1 – Inquire at Mikrofilmarchiv for details – gw Misc Inst [943]

BIELEFELDER BEOBACHTER – Bielefeld, oct 11 1930-jul 27 1934 – 1 – Inquire at Mikrofilmarchiv for details – gw Misc Inst [943]

BIELEFELDER GENERALANZEIGER – (Cont by: Westfaelische Neueste Nachrichten, 1918) – Bielefeld, sep 16 1900-apr 2 1944 – 1 – Inquire at Mikrofilmarchiv for details – gw Misc Inst [943]

BIELEFELDER KREISBLATT *see* WESTFAELISCHE ZEITUNG

BIELEFELDER POST – Bielefeld, may 31 1890-92 – 1 – Inquire at Mikrofilmarchiv for details – gw Misc Inst [072]

BIELEFELDER TAGEBLATT *see* WESTFAELISCHE ZEITUNG

BIELEFELDER VOLKSZEITUNG – Bielefeld, 1902-jun 15 1909 – 1 – Inquire at Mikrofilmarchiv for details – gw Misc Inst [943]

BIELEFELDER WOCHENBLATT *see* WESTFAELISCHE ZEITUNG

Bieler, L *see* THE LIFE AND LEGEND OF ST. PATRICK

Bielfeld, Baron de *see* INSTITUCIONES POLITICAS

BIELITZ-BIALER DEUTSCHE ZEITUNG – (Cont by: Beskidenlaendische Deutsche Zeitung, sep 1930) – Bielitz-Biala, apr 16 1924-oct 1934 – 1 – Inquire at Mikrofilmarchiv for details – gw Misc Inst [947]

BIELITZ-BIALER DEUTSCHE ZEITUNG – (Title change: Sept 1930: Beskidenlaendische Deutsche Zeitung) – Bielitz-Biala (Bielsko-Biala), Poland. 16 Apr 1924-Oct 1934 – 1 – gw Mikrofilm [947]

Bielogorskii, N *see*
- CHTO-ZHE DOLZHNY MY SDIELAT?
- STRASHNYE GODY

Bielotsvietov, N A *see* PUTI ROSSII

Bielov, Vadim *see* PONOVYM VIEKHAM

Bielsa, R *see* LA NACIONALIDAD Y EL DOMICILIO

Bielykh, Grigorii *see* RESPUBLIKA BEZPRIZORNYKH (SHKID)

Biema, N H van *see* CATALOG DER REICHHALTIGEN SAMMLUNG HEBRAISCHER U. JUEDISCHER BUECHER, HANDSCHRIFTEN, PORTRAITS ETC

BIEN = THE BEE – (In Danish/Norwegian) – San Francisco, CA. Sep-Dec 1905 – 1r – 1 – $50.00 – B02789 – us Library Micro [071]

LE BIEN INFORME – Paris. Imprimerie-Librairie du Cercle Social. 1797-1800 – 9 – fr Hachette [321]

LE BIEN PUBLIC / ed by David, Laurent Oliver & Beausoleil, CleO – Montreal, Canada. 10 avr 1874-v2 n26. 19 mai 1876 – 2r – 1 – Can$60.00r – cn Can Microfilming [072]

LE BIEN PUBLIC – (Filmed as pt of: Commune de Paris newspapers. On these reels, newspapers are filmed chronologically) – Paris: Impr Dubuisson et Ce, mar 28-29,31, apr 1-3,6-8,11-14,18-19,21 1871 – us Res Libr [072]

LE BIEN PUBLIC : HEBDO – Trois-Rivieres, Canada. 8 jun 1909-dec 1978 – 30r – 1 – Can$55.00r – cn Can Microfilming [072]

LE BIEN PUBLIC – Journal politique quotidien. Red. en chef H. Vrignault. no. 1-193. Paris. 5 mars 1871-30 juin 1878, 8 juin 1882-21 janv 1883; no. 99-144. 7 janv 1883 sic-17 janv 1884; no. 1-7. 15 nov-24 dec 1891; no. 1-32. janv-9 oct 1892. mq no. 8, 24, 29; no. 1. 3 dec 1893; no. 1-2. 4 juil., 14 dec 1894 – 1 – fr A.C.R.P.P. [073]

LE BIEN PUBLIC – Red. en chef E. Pelletan. Paris. 24 mai-12 dec 1848 – 1 – fr A.C.R.P.P. [073]

LE BIEN PUBLIC DE TOURCOING – Tourcoing (Nord), May 1890 – May 1891 – 1r – fr Armell [944]

EL BIEN PUBLICO – Montevideo. Uruguay. -d. Sep 1955-Dec 1962. (Imperfect). (49 reels) – 1 – uk British Libr Newspaper [072]

DIE BIENE – (German language, labor newspaper, publ at varying frequencies) – Cleveland, OH. aug 9, 1873-dec 30, 1882 – 4r – 1 – us Western Res [071]

DIE BIENE, 1808-1810 / ed by Kotzebue, August von – 1808-10 (mf ed 1997) – 19mf – 9 – DM390.00 – 3-89131-232-6 – gw Fischer [305]

Bienert, T *see* LEPIDOPTEROLOGISCHE ERGEBNISSE EINER REISE IN PERSIEN IN...1858-1859

LE BIEN-ETRE SOCIAL – Journal politique hebdomadaire. Bruxelles. 1858-aout 1860. I.F.H.S – 1 – fr A.C.R.P.P. [949]

BIEN-ETRE SOCIAL CANADIEN – (Cont by Digest Sociale at v26 1974) – Ottawa. v1-25. 1949-73 – 5 – Can$100.00 – cn Micromedia [073]
BIEN-ETRE SOCIAL CANADIEN 1974 *see* DIGESTE SOCIAL
DE LA BIENFAISANCE PUBLIQUE / Gerando, J M de – (Condition of 19th C. French working class series). 1939 – 9 – fr Hachette [360]
LA BIENFAITEUR – Joliette [Quebec]: Comite du Monument Joliette, [1892-189- ou 19–] – 9 – cn C.I.H.M. [971]
LE BIENHEREUX MARTIN DE PORRES... **PARIS** / Fumet, Stanislas – Madrid: Razon y Fe, 1935 – 1 – sp Bibl Santa Ana [920]
BIENHEUREUSE MARGUERITE D'YOUVILLE, FONDATRICE DES SOEURS DE LA CHARITE (SOEURS GRISES) DE MONTREAL : BIBLIOGRAPHIE CANADIENNE, 1938-1949 / Saint-Hyacinthe, Soeur – 1963. SEM105P4 – 2mf – 9 – cn Bibl Nat [240]
BIENNIAL REPORT / Arizona. Territory. Prisons – Phoenix. 1891/92-97/98 – 1 – $23.00r – us L of C Photodup [360]
BIENNIAL REPORT / Kansas. State University. Agricultural Experiment Station – 1888-1976 – 1,5,6 – us Spaulding [630]
BIENNIAL REPORT OF THE SECRETARY OF STATE / Nevada. State Dept – Carson City. 1883-1884, 1889-1890 – 1 – us NY Public [978]
BIENNIAL REPORT OF THE SECRETARY OF STATE OF THE STATE OF OREGON 1897-1898 / Kincaide, H R – Salem: W.H. Leeds, 1899.Oregon reel 8.(Cox Library Collection) – 5 – us Americana [978]
BIENNIAL REPORT ON EDUCATION FOR 1978-1979 / Mauritius. Ministry of Education and Cultural Affairs – Port Louis, 1982 – 1mf – 9 – DE-451/1 – ne IDC [370]
BIENNIAL REPORTS (A-G), 1882-1936 / Alabama – Quarterly. 1935-80. 16 reels – 1 – $35.00r – us Trans-Media [340]
Biens, C P *see*
- HANDT-BOECXKEN DER CHRISTELIJCKE GEDICHTEN...
- PROFYTELYCK CABINET, VOOR DEN CHRISTELIJCKEN JONGELINGH

Bienvenida. Ayuntamiento *see*
- FIESTAS PATRONALES EN HONOR DE NTRA. SRA. DE LOS MILAGROS. 1979
- FIESTAS PATRONALES EN HONOR DE NUESTRA SENORA DE LOS MILAGROS. SEPTIEMBRE 1970

BIENVENIDO! 6 DE JULIO DE 1953 – Buenos Aires: [Sevicio Internacional Publicaciones Argentinas, 1953?] – 1 – CSUXAGP8609-B – us Hoover Inst Photo [390]
BIENVILLE FIRST BAPTIST CHURCH. BIENVILLE, LOUISIANA : CHURCH RECORDS – 1894-Apr 1969 – 1 – 43.02 – us Baptist [240]
Bierbower, Austin *see* THE VIRTUES AND THEIR REASONS
Biersack, J P *see* RADIATION EFFECTS AND DEFECTS IN SOLIOS
Bierwirth, Gerhard *see* DIE PROBLEMATIK DES ENGLISCHEN SCHAUERROMANS
EL BIERZO. NUEVAS LAPIDAS ROMANAS / Roso de Luna, Mario – Madrid: Fortanet, 1912. B.R.A.H 60, pp. 496-506 – sp Bibl Santa Ana [946]
Biesalski, E *see* SMALL FARM IMPLEMENTS
Biese, Alfred *see*
- DEUTSCHE LITERATURGESCHICHTE
- FRITZ REUTER, HEINRICH SEIDEL UND DER HUMOR IN DER NEUEREN DEUTSCHEN DICHTUNG
- HEINRICH SEIDEL UND DER DEUTSCHE HUMOR
- THEODOR STORM UND DER MODERNE REALISMUS

Biesenthal, Johannes Heinrich Raphael *see* DAS TROSTSCHREIBEN DES APOSTELS PAULUS AN DIE HEBRAEER KRITISCH WIEDERHERGESTELLT UND SPRACHLICH, ARCHAEOLOGISCH UND BIBLISCH-THEOLOGISCH ERLAEUTERT
Biester, Johann Erich *see* BERLINISCHE MONATSSCHRIFT 1783-96; BERLINISCHE BLAETTER 1797-98; NEUE BERLINISCHE MONATSSCHRIFT 1799-1811
DIE BIF : BLAETTER IDEALER FRAUENFREUNDSCHAFTEN – Berlin, 1925 n2-3 – 1r – 1 – Dist. gw Mikrofilm – gw Misc Inst [073]
BIFUR – no. 1-8. Paris. mai 1929-juin 1931 – 1 – fr A.C.R.P.P. [073]
BIG BEAR LAKE LIMELIGHT – Big Bear Lake, CA. 1848-1958 – 3r – 1 – $150.00 – C02066 – us Library Micro [071]
BIG BEAR LIFE – Big Bear, CA. Apr 1929-1959 – 1r – 1 – $50.00 – R02064 – us Library Micro [071]
BIG BEND COUNTRY / Carlysle, G Raht – Romance of Davis Mountains. El Paso: Rahtbook Co., 1919. Texas Reel 10. (The Cox Library Collection) – 5 – us Americana [978]
BIG BEND COUNTRY – Lincoln, Douglas, Adams and Franklin Counties. 1904. Washington reel 1. (Cox Library Collection) – 5 – us Americana [978]
BIG BEND EMPIRE – Waterville. Wash. -w. 1888-1921 – 1 – us UMI [071]
BIG BONE BAPTIST CHURCH. UNION CITY, KENTUCKY : CHURCH RECORDS – 1823-1948; Ladies Missionary Society and Aid Society, 1913-27. 1744p – 1 – 69.76 – us Baptist [240]
BIG COUNTRY NEWS – Alberta, CN. 1975-78 – 2r – 1 – cn Commonwealth Micro [072]
BIG CREEK BAPTIST CHURCH. ANNA, ILLINOIS : CHURCH RECORDS – 1852-1983 – 1 – 5.00 – us Baptist [240]
BIG CREEK BAPTIST CHURCH. COOLIDGE, GEORGIA : CHURCH RECORDS – Aug 1882-Sept 1982. 1440p – 1 – 64.80 – us Baptist [978]
BIG DEAL – (v3- . 1975- . 9) – v. 1-. 1973- – 1,5,6 – us UMI [073]
Big Hatchie. Tennessee. Baptist Associations *see* ANNUALS
THE BIG PINE CITIZEN – Big Pine, CA. Jan 1914-Jun 1933 – 5r – 1 – $250.00 – B02069 – us Library Micro [071]
BIG ROCK BAPTIST CHURCH. STEWART COUNTY. BIG ROCK, TENNESSEE : CHURCH RECORDS – 1938-67 – 1 – 17.19 – us Baptist [240]
THE BIG SANDY VALLEY – By William Ely. The people and the country from the earlies settlement to the present time. 1887. Includes index. 500p. SW16-0061 – 5 – us A.G.L.L. [920]
THE BIG SANDY VALLEY / Jillson, Willard R – Louisville: John P. Morton and Co., 1923. Kentucky Reel 6. (The Cox Library Collection) – 5 – us Americana [978]
THE BIG SANDY VALLEY: A HISTORY OF THE PEOPLE AND COUNTRY FROM EARLIEST SETTLEMENT TO PRESENT TIME / Ely, William – Catlettsburg: Central Methodist, 1887. KentuckyReel 6. (The Cox Library Collection) – 5 – us Americana [978]
BIG SPRING BAPTIST CHURCH. SEVERNS VALLEY ASSOCIATION. KENTUCKY : CHURCH RECORDS – 1884-1913, 1957-68 – 1 – 17.73 – us Baptist [240]
BIG SPRINGS BAPTIST CHURCH. HARDIN COUNTY. KENTUCKY : CHURCH RECORDS – 1816-1940 – 1 – 31.05 – us Baptist [240]
BIG SPRINGS ENTERPRISE – Big Springs, NE. -w. Feb. 1952- – 1 – us NE Hist [071]
BIG SPRINGS NEWS – Big Springs, NE. -w. Oct. 1935-Oct. 1936 – 1 – us NE Hist [071]
BIG STEVENS CREEK BAPTIST CHURCH. EDGEFIELD DISTRICT. SOUTH CAROLINA : CHURCH RECORDS – Jun 1803-1901 – 1 – 24.39 – us Baptist [240]
THE BIG STICK – London, England. -f. 1.15 Oct 1920. 3 ft – 1 – uk British Libr Newspaper [072]
THE BIG STICK – (New York), 1909-27 – 1 – us A.J.P.C. [073]
BIG VALLEY GAZETTE – Bieber, CA. 1893-1948 – 22r – 1 – $1,100.00 – C02062 – us Library Micro [071]
LES BIGAILLES – Port-au-Prince, (H): Impr de l'Abeille, [1901- – us Res Libr [072]
LES BIGAILLES – [Port-au-Prince]: Impr Bouchereau & Co, 1876- – us Res Libr [072]
Bigandet, Paul Ambrose, Bp *see* VOYAGE EN BIRMANIE....TRADUIT DE L'ANGLAIS ET AUGM. D'UNE INTROD. PAR ADRIEN LAUNAY. 1891
LES BIGARRURES ET TOUCHES DU SEIGNEUR DES ACCORDS. (E.T.) AVEC LES APOPHTEGMES DU SIEUR GAULARD LES ESCRAIGNES DIJONNOISES / Tabourot, Etienne – O 863. 1640 – 9 – ne IDC [880]
Bigelmair, Andreas *see* DIE BETEILIGUNG DER CHRISTEN AM OEFFENTLICHEN LEBEN IN VORCONSTANTINISCHER ZEIT
Bigelow, Harry Augustus *see* INTRODUCTION TO THE LAW OF REAL PROPERTY
Bigelow, J *see*
- AMERICAN MEDICAL BOTANY
- FLORULA BOSTONIENSIS

Bigelow, L J *see* BENCH AND BAR
Bigelow, Melville M *see*
- BIGELOW'S REPORTS OF ALL THE PUBLIC LIFE AND ACCIDENT INSURANCE CASES
- HISTORY OF PROCEDURE IN ENGLAND FROM THE NORMAN CONQUEST; THE NORMAN PERIOD 1066-1204
- AN INDEX OF THE CASES OVERRULED, REVERSED, DENIED, DOUBTED, MODIFIED, LIMITED, EXPLAINED, AND DISTINGUISHED, BY THE COURTS OF AMERICA, ENGLAND, AND IRELAND.

Bigelow, Timothy *see* JOURNAL OF A TOUR TO NIAGARA FALLS IN THE YEAR 1805
BIGELOW'S REPORTS OF ALL THE PUBLIC LIFE AND ACCIDENT INSURANCE CASES : DETERMINED IN THE AMERICAN COURTS PRIOR TO JANUARY 1871, WITH NOTES ON THE ENGLISH CASES / Bigelow, Melville M – New York: Hurd & Houghton. v1-5. 1874-77 (all publ) – 9 – LLMC 95-129 – us L.L.M.C. [340]
Bigeon *see* APERCU STATISTIQUE SUR LA DUREE DE LA VIE
Bigg, Charles *see*
- THE CHRISTIAN PLATONISTS OF ALEXANDRIA
- THE CHURCH'S TASK UNDER THE ROMAN EMPIRE
- A CRITICAL AND EXEGETICAL COMMENTARY ON THE EPISTLES OF ST PETER AND ST JUDE
- NEOPLATONISM
- THE ORIGINS OF CHRISIANITY
- THE SPIRIT OF CHRIST IN COMMON LIFE
- WAYSIDE SKETCHES IN ECCLESIASTICAL HISTORY

Biggar, Emerson Bristol *see*
- ANECDOTAL LIFE OF SIR JOHN MACDONALD
- THE BOER WAR: ITS CAUSES, AND ITS INTEREST TO CANADIANS WITH A GLOSSARY OF CAPE DUTCH AND KAFIR TERMS

Biggers, Earl Derr *see* LOVE INSURANCE
THE BIGGS ARGUS – Biggs, CA. 1888-92; 1894; 1897; 1901-02; 1905; Jun-Dec 1906; 1908; 1910-11 – 4r – 1 – $200.00 – B02067 – us Library Micro [071]
Biggs, Asa *see* PRESENTATION OF PORTRAIT OF HONORABLE ASA BIGGS TO UNITED STATES DISTRICT COURT
Biggs, C R Davey *see* RUSSIA AND REUNION
Biggs, Joseph et al *see* A CONCISE HISTORY OF KEHUKEE BAPTIST ASSOCIATION, N.C
BIGGS NEWS – Biggs, CA. Apr-Dec 1928; 1930; 1932; 1934-1935; 1936-1938; 1939-1941; 1945-1954; 1955-1990 – 35r – 1 – $1,750.00 – B03162 – us Library Micro [071]
BIGGS WEEKLY NEWS – Biggs, CA. 1924-1930 – 2r – 1 – $100.00 – C03163 – us Library Micro [071]
Bigliati, F G *see* DIRITTO INTERNAZIONALE E ...
Bignami, Enrico *see* LA PLEBE
Bignold, H B *see* IMPERIAL STATUTES IN FORCE IN NEW SOUTH WALES...
Bigot, Charles *see* DE PARIS AU NIAGARA
Bigot de Morogues, Pierre Marie Sebastien *see* MEMOIRE HISTORIQUE ET PHYSIQUE SUR LES CHUTES DES PIERRES...EPOQUES
Bigot, Francois *see* LETTRES DE L'INTENDANT BIGOT AU CHEVALIER DE LEVIS, PUBLIEES SOUS LA DIRECTION DE H. R. CASGRAIN
Bigot, J M F *see* DIPTERES NOUVEAUX OU PEU CONNUS
Bigsby, J J *see* THESAURUS DEVONICO-CARBONIFERUS. THE FLORA AND FAUNA OF THE DEVONIAN AND CARBONIFEROUS PERIODS
Bihar *see* LEGISLATIVE COUNCIL DEBATES, 1937-1939
BIHAR AND ORISSA – Patna: Supt Govt Print, Bihar and Orissa. pt 3. 1921 – us Res Libr [310]
Bihar and Orissa. India (States). Legislative Council *see* PROCEEDINGS OF THE LEGISLATIVE COUNCIL OF THE LIEUTENANT-GOVERNOR OF BIHAR AND ORISSA
THE BIHAR GAZETTE / Bihar. India. (State) – Patna. 1945-1966 – 1 – us NY Public [324]
Bihar. India. (State) *see* THE BIHAR GAZETTE
Bihar. India (State). Legislative Assembly *see* DEBATES, 1937-1939
BIHAR LEGISLATIVE COUNCIL DEBATES – Bihar, Patna, 1937-1940 v1-5 – 85mf – I-46/2 – ne IDC [320]
Bihl, Josef *see* DIE GESTALT DER WORTFORM UND DES SATZES UNTER EINWIRKUNG DES RHYTHMUS BEI CHAUCER UND GOWER
Bihlmeyer, K *see* DEUTSCHE SCHRIFTEN
BIJBLAD OP HET STAATSBLAD VAN NEDERLANDSCH INDIE – (Cont. as TAMBAHA LEMBARAN NEGARA. Djakarta, 1950-1969. v1-20. Nos 1-2979) – Batavia, 1857-1949, v1-78. Lacking: 1941-1945(14331-15011); 1961(2315); 1962(2486); 1963(2530,2544-2546,2551,2553,2556,2566-2567,2570-2571, 2617); 1964(2660-2661,2679-2680,2682,2691,2693,2698,2718);196 5(2765-2766,2768-2769 ,2784,2793-2794); 1966(2801,2808,2816-2817) – 1087mf – 9 – ne IDC [072]
BIJDRAGE TOT DE KENNIS DER SCHRIFTEN VAN DAVID JORIS / Harderwijk, I van – Leiden. 1845. BME-421 1 – 9 – ne IDC [240]
BIJDRAGE TOT DE KENNIS VAN HET FAMILIE- EN ERFRECHT DER CHINEEZEN IN NEDERLANDSCH-INDIE / Tian, Han Swie – Amsterdam, 1936 – 2mf – 9 – ILM-3798/1 – ne IDC [306]
BIJDRAGE TOT DE TEKSTKRITIEK VAN RICHTEREN 1-16 / Doornink, Adam van – Leiden: E J Brill, 1879 – 1mf – 9 – 0-8370-2950-3 – 1985-0950 – us A.T.L.A. [220]
BIJDRAGE TOT...REGELING DER SCHEEPSVOORRECHTEN / Fokker, T H – Leiden, 1907 – 3mf – 1 – ILM-3244/1 – ne IDC [327]
BIJDRAGEN BETREKKELIJK DE VERBETERING VAN DEN MAATSCHAPPELIJKEN STAAT DER JODEN / ed by Belinfante, M C – Amsterdam. 1806. BJ-262-12 1 – 9 – ne IDC [073]
BIJDRAGEN EN MEDEDELINGEN (VAN HET GENOOTSCHAP VOOR DE JOODSCHE WETENSCHAP IN NEDERLAND) – (1941-1956 have not been published; Missing: 1934-1964) – Amsterdam, 1922-1965. v1-9 – 15mf – J-261-19/1 – ne IDC [943]
BIJDRAGEN EN MEDEDELINGEN VAN HET HISTORISCH GENOOTSCHAP – Utrecht, 1(1878)-66(1948) – 522mf – 9 – Dfl1,827.00 – ne Slangenburg [900]
BIJDRAGEN TOT DE FLORA VAN NEDERLANDSCH INDIE / Blume, C L – 1825-26 – 5 – uk Microform Academic [580]
BIJDRAGEN TOT DE FLORA VAN NEDERLANDSCH INDIE / Blume, C L – Batavia, 1825-27. 1169p. B-5080/2 – 19mf – 8 – ne IDC [580]
BIJDRAGEN TOT DE GESCHIEDENIS DER PORTUGEESCHE ISRAELIETEN IN HUNNER GEMEENTEN TE 'S-GRAVENHAGE VAN PLM / Buzaglo, J H – (Jaarboek. die Haghe. 1939). 1690 tot plm. 1730. BJ-262-11 1 – 9 – ne IDC [360]
BIJDRAGEN TOT DE KENNIS DER BOOMSOORTEN VAN JAVA / Koorders, SH & Valenton, T – Batavia, 1894-1914. 13v – 61mf – 9 – ne IDC [580]
BIJDRAGEN TOT DE KENNIS DER FLORA VAN MIDDEN SUMATRA / Hasselt, A L van – Leiden, 1884 – 2mf – 9 – ne IDC [580]
BIJDRAGEN TOT DE KENNIS VAN HET HINDOEIESME OP JAVA / Brummund, Jan Frederik Gerrit – 1868 – 1 – us A.T.L.A. [240]
BIJDRAGEN TOT DE KENNIS VAN HET LEVEN EN DE WERKEN VAN JAN VAN RUUSBROEC / De Vreesse, W – Het Belfort, 1895 – 2mf – 8 – Dfl9.00 – ne Slangenburg [200]
BIJDRAGEN TOT DE NATUURKUNDIGE WETENSCHAPPEN – Amsterdam, 1826-32 – 3 – us Readex [500]
BIJDRAGEN TOT DE TAAL-, LAND- EN VOLKENKUNDE VAN NEDERLANDSCH INDIE – 's-Gravenhage, 1853-1939. v1-98. Index, 1853-1964 – 1036mf – 9 – ne IDC [950]
BIJDRAGEN VOOR DE GESCHIEDENIS VAN HET BISDOM HAARLEM – (Includes indexes) – 1(1873)-65(1958) – 405mf – 9 – Dfl1,418.00 – ne Slangenburg [073]
BIJLAGE BEHORENDE BIJ TWEEDE VIJFJARENPLAN 1972-1976 / Surinam. (Netherlands). Stichting Planbureau Suriname – (Annex to Second Five Year Plan 1972-1976). BD-1745 1 – 9 – ne IDC [338]

Bijleveld, C G *see* TENUITVOERLEGGING VAN BUITENLANDSCHE ARBITRALE VONNISSEN
BIJOU – 1828-30 – 13mf – 9 – £110.00 – uk Chadwyck [800]
LES BIJOUX DU SUD MAROCAIN: ESSAI D'INTERPRETATION DE LEURS FORMES ET DE LEURS DECORS / Rabate, M R – 9 – F130.00 – fr Ethnologie [306]
BIJVOEGSEL TOT HET STAATSBLAD VAN HET KONINKRIJK DER NEDERLANDEN – Gorinchem, 1834-1850 – 154mf – H-2032/1 – ne IDC [943]
BIJVOEGSELEN TOT DE LEVENSBESCHRIJVING VAN DAVID JORIS / Cramer, A M – Leiden. 1844. BME-420 1 – 9 – ne IDC [240]
BIKE TECH – (1984-. 5,6,9) – v1-. 1982- – 1 – us UMI [073]
BIKHER-NAYES = BOOK NEWS – (Yiddish monthly) – Warsaw, PL. v1 no1 Dec 1937-v3 no6-7 Jun/Jul 1939 – 1r – 1 – $25.00 – cn Can Microfilming [070]
BIKHER-VELT = BOOK WORLD – (In Yiddish) – Kiev, UA. v1 no4-5. Aug 1919 + v- no- – 1r – 1 – $25.00 – cn Can Microfilming [072]
BIKKUREI HA-ITTIM – Vienna. 1820-31. BJ-100-106 1 – 9 – ne IDC [470]
BIKKUREI HA-ITTIM HA-HADASHIM / ed by Regio, I S & Busch, I – Vienna. 1845. BJ-422-4 1 – 9 – ne IDC [305]
BIKKUREI RIVAL / Levinsohn, I B – Warsaw. 1900. BJ-422-50 1 – 9 – ne IDC [900]
BIKKUREI TO'ELET – Amsterdam. 1820. BJ-422-7 1 – 9 – ne IDC [470]
Biko, B S *see* BLACK VIEWPOINT
BIKO ENQUIRY – 2r – 1 – sa Microfile [960]
BIKUPAN – Malmo, Sweden. 1868-69 – 1 – sw Kungliga [072]
BILAGA TILL ELFSBORGS LANS ANNONSBLAD – Vanersborg, Sweden. 1891 – 1 – sw Kungliga [072]
BILAN : L'AGEFI SUISSE – 1989-1995 – 2r per y – 5,6 – Sfr802.00 – sz Infoprint [949]
BILAN ACTUEL DES COPEPODES PLANCTONIQUES MARINS ET DES EAUX SAUMATRES : CORRECTIONS ET COMPLEMENTS / Razouls, Claude – F60.00 – fr Ethnologie [580]
LE BILAN DE LA FRANCE, OU LA MISERE ET LE TRAVAIL / Perreymond – (Condition of 19th C. French working class series). 1849 – 9 – fr Hachette [336]
LE BILAN DE L'EXECUTION DU PREMIER PLAN QUINQUENNAL DE L'ECONOMIE NATIONAL DE L'U.R.S.S / U.S.S.R. Gosudarstvennaia Planovaia Komissiia – M. 1934. BD-782 1 – 9 – ne IDC [338]
BILAN DE L'OPERATION SECTEURS PILOTES EN MOYENNE COTE D'IVOIRE, 1959-1968 / Trouchaud, J P – 2v. 1968. (Africa Series) – 9 – fr Hachette [960]
BILAN DEMOGRAPHIQUE ET EVALUATION PERSPECTIVE DE L'EMPLOI AU LIBAN / Lebanon. University. Faculte de Droit et des Sciences Economiques. Etudes Economiques – 1968. Mazure, C. BNE-19.714 1 – 9 – ne IDC [331]
BILAN DES DEUX PREMIERS PLANS SITUATION ECONOMIQUE, SOCIALE ET FINANCIERE (EVOLUTION DEPUIS 1946) / French Equatorial Africa – 1v. Brazzaville. 1958. BD-483 1 – 9 – ne IDC [338]
BILAN DOGMATIQUE DE L'ORTHODOXIE REGNANTE *see* COLLECTED WORKS
BILAN ECONOMIQUE D'UNE ANNEE D'INDEPENDANCE / Algeria. Chambre de Commerce et d'Industrie d'Alger – 1964? BNE-8621 1 – 9 – ne IDC [338]
Bilan, V *see* NARODNA ARMIIA
BILANZ – Zurich. 1979-81 – 2232.00y; CPC; 9 – gw Alpha Com [073]
DIE BILANZRECHTLICHEN BESCHLUESSE DER GROSSEN SENATE VON RFH UND BFH / Hildebrand, Ulrich – 1992 – 160p – 9 – DM98.00 – 3-89349-596-7 – gw Hänsel [330]
BILATERAL LOWER EXTREMITY FUNCTION DURING THE SUPPORT PHASE OF RUNNING / McCaw, Steven T – 1989 – 151p 2mf – 9 – $4.00 – us Microform Publ [612]
BILATERAL STAFF CONVERSATIONS WITH LATIN AMERICAN REPUBLICS / Munden, Cecil L – New Orleans. 1947. 166p – 1 reel – 1 – $16.00 – us L of C Photodup [977]
BILBO *see* MOVEMENT
DIE BILBUNGSGESETZE DER VOGELZIER / Seidlitz, G C M von – Z 1994. 1869 – 9 – ne IDC [590]
Bilby, J W *see* AMONG UNKNOWN ESKIMO
BILD : AUSGABE WIRTSCHAFTSRAUM OESTLICHES RUHRGEBIET – (1958-oct 1960: Muenster edition) – Dortmund. jun 25, 1952-67 – 23r – 1 – gw Mikrofilm [072]
BILD – Hamburg, West Germany. 1968-. Continues: Bild-Zeitung. Ausgabe Stuttgart Esslingen: 1968-74 – 1 – gw Mikrofilm [072]
DAS BILD DES CHRISTENTUMS BEI DEN GROSSEN DEUTSCHEN IDEALISTEN : EIN BEITRAG ZUR GESCHICHTE DES CHRISTENTUMS / Luelmann, Christian – (Includes bibliographical references) – Berlin: C A Schwetschke, 1901 – 1mf – 9 – 0-8370-8693-0 – 1986-2693 – us A.T.L.A. [240]
BILD DES FUEHRERS : GEDICHTE / Vesper, Will; ed by Schmidkunz, Walter – [Muenchen]: Muenchner Buchverlag, [194-?] – 1r – 1 – us U.W. Library [810]
DAS BILD IN DER DRAMATISCHEN SPRACHE GRILLPARZERS / Cafasso, Arthur – (Includes bibliographical references) – Leoben: Im Verlage des Landes-Obergymnasiums, 1884 – 1r – 1 – us U.W. Library [430]
DAS BILD IN DIR : ROMAN / Wilhelm, Wolfgang – Berlin: W Limpert, 1942 – 1r – 1 – us U.W. Library [830]
Bildarchiv Foto Marburg *see* INDEX PHOTOGRAPHIQUE DE L'ART EN FRANCE
Bildarchiv Foto Marburg – Deutsches Dokumentationszentrum fuer Kunstgeschichte Philipps-Universitaet Marburg *see*
- AEGYPTEN-INDEX
- MARBURGER-INDEX
- SCHWEIZ-INDEX
- SPANIEN-UND PORTUGAL-INDEX

Bildarchiv Foto Marburg im Kunstgeschichtlichen Institut der Philipps Universitaet Marburg *see* MARBURGER INDEX. INVENTAR DER KUNST IN DEUTSCHLAND
BILD-ARCHIV/BILD UND SCHULE – Muenchen, 1920-21 – 1 – gw Mikrofilm [370]
BILDER AUS DEM LEBEN JESU : BIBLISCHE VORTRAEGE / Lehmann, Ernst Gottlob – Leipzig: J C Hinrichs, 1875 – 1mf – 9 – 0-8370-4083-3 – 1985-2083 – us A.T.L.A. [240]
BILDER AUS DER GESCHICHTE DER ALTCHRISTLICHEN KUNST UND LITURGIE IN ITALIEN / Beissel, Stephan – Freiburg im Breisgau, St. Louis, Mo.: Herder, 1899 – 1mf – us A.T.L.A. [700]
BILDER AUS DER SCHWEIZ : ZWEI ERZAEHLUNGEN / Gotthelf, Jeremias; ed by Braasch, Theodor & Ten Hoor, George J – (Includes bibliographical references) – New York: F S Crofts, c1937 – 1 – us U.W. Library [830]
BILDER AUS EINEM LEBEN : ERINNERUNGEN EINES OSTPREUSSISCHEN JUDEN / Rosenberg, Curt – Wuerzburg: Holzner Verlag, 1962 – 10r – 1 – us U.W. Library [920]
BILDER DER ZEIT – Leipzig, 1855 – 1r – 1 – gw Mikrofilm [072]
BILDER DES ORIENTS VON H. STEIGLITZ FUR EIN SINGSTIMME MIT BEGLEITUNG DES PIANOFORTE. OP. 140 HEFT 3 / Marschner, H – (In Process) – Leipzig: Fr Keistner, 1849 – 1 – us Sibley [780]
BILDER NACH SKULPTUREN UND GEMAELDEN DER SAMMLUNG / Zurich. Kunsthaus – 1936, 1959 – 2mf – 9 – uk Chadwyck [730]
BILDER SAAL – Leipzig, Germany. 1847-53 – 1 – gw Mikrofilm [072]
BILDER TAG – Berlin, Apr 1950-Feb 1952 – 1 – gw Mikrofilm [072]
BILDER UND SYMBOLE BABYLONISCH-ASSYRISCHER GOETTER / Frank, K – (Leipziger semitistische studien. v. 2, pt. 2. Leipzig. 1908). Leipzig. 1906. BNE-20,110 1 – 9 – ne IDC [290]
BILDER-CONVERSATIONS-LEXIKON FUER DAS DEUTSCHE VOLK (AEL, ABT 1;28) – Leipzig. 4 bde. 1837-1841 (mf ed 1995) – 32mf – 9 – DM380.00 – 3-89131-206-7 – gw Fischer [030]
BILDER-MAGAZIN FUER ALLGEMEINE WELTKUNDE – Leipzig, 1834-35 – 1r – 1 – gw Mikrofilm [072]
BILDERSAAL FUER GESCHICHTE, NATUR UND KUNST – Karlsruhe, DE. 1833-36 – 1r – 1 – gw Mikrofilm [072]
BILDERWELT – Zwickau, Germany. 1849 – 1 – gw Mikrofilm [072]
DER BILDHAUER : EIN ROMAN / Zobeltitz, Hanns von – Stuttgart: Deutsche Verlags-Anstalt, 1906 – 1r – 1 – us U.W. Library [830]
DER BILDHAUER KURT LEHMANN : DAS PLASTISCHE WERK. EIN BEITRAG ZUR BILDHAUSERKUNST DES 20. JAHRHUNDERTS / Bury, Karin – 1995 – 6mf – 9 – DM125.00 – 3-8267-2171-3 – gw Hänsel [730]
BILDJOURNALEN – Stockholm, 1954-80 – 32r – 1 – sw Kungliga [073]
DER BILDLICHE AUSDRUCK IN DER PROSA EDUARD MOERIKES / Kappenberg, Hans – (Includes bibliographical references (p.[8]-9)) – Greifswald: H Adler, 1914 – 1r – 1 – us U.W. Library [430]
BILDNISSE DER BERUEHMTESTEN MENSCHEN ALLER VOELKER UND ZEITEN (AEL, ABT 1;25) / ed by Seemann, Otmar – (Supplementband zu jedem biographischen Woerterbuch, besonders zu dem Conversations-Lexicon; 35 Hefte mit 420 Bildnissen) – Zwickau 1818-1832 (mf ed 1995) – 5mf – 9 – DM240.00 – 3-89131-192-3 – gw Fischer [030]
DIE BILDNISSE WIELANDS / Weizsaecker, Paul – (Includes bibliographical references and indexes) – Stuttgart: W Kohlhammer, 1893 – 1r – 1 – us U.W. Library [430]
DIE BILDSPIELKUNST – Berlin. aug 15, 1913 – 1 – gw Mikrofilm [790]
DIE BILDUNG DER EVANG. THEOLOGEN FUER DEN PRAKTISCHEN KIRCHENDIENST : EINE DENKSCHRIFT ZUR FUENFUNDZWANZIGJAEHRIGEN STIFTUNGSFEIER DES EVANG.-PROTESTANTISCHEN PREDIGERSEMINARS IN HEIDELBERG / Schenkel, Daniel – Heidelberg: J.C.B. Mohr, 1863 – 1mf – us A.T.L.A. [240]
DER BILDUNGSVEREIN/VOLKSBILDUNG – Berlin. 1896; 1898-1920 – 1 – DM670.00 – gw Mikro Press [072]
DER BILDUNGSVEREIN/VOLKSBILDUNG – Berlin, 1896-1920 – 1 – Dist. gw Mikrofilm – gw Mikrofilm [370]
DER BILDWART – Berlin. 1925-30. may 1931-oct 1932. feb 1935 – 3r – 1 – gw Mikrofilm [073]
BILD-ZEITUNG *see* BILD
Bilets'kyi, O I *see* UKRAJINS'KI PYS'MENNYKY
BILGI MECMUASI – Istanbul: Matbaa-i Amire, 1913-1914 – $75.00 – us MEDOC [956]
Bilgram, Hugo *see*
- ANALYSIS OF THE NATURE OF CAPITAL AND INTEREST
- A STUDY OF THE MONEY QUESTION

Bilhon, Jean F J *see* ELOGE DE J.J. ROUSSEAU
THE BILINGUAL SCHOOL : A STUDY OF BILINGUALISM IN SOUTH AFRICA / Malherbe, Ernst Gideon – Johannesburg: Central News Agency, [1943] – 1 – us Res Libr [400]
Bill, A *see* ZUR ERKLAERUNG UND TEXTKRITIK DES 1. BUCHES TERTULLIANS, "ADVERSUS MARCIONEM" (T.U.U. 3-38/2)
BILL: ACTE POUR REFONDRE LES STATUTS RELATIFS AUX MUNICIPALITES ET AUX CHEMINS DANS LE BAS-CANADA / Canada. Laws, Statutes, etc – Toronto: s.n, 1859. SEM105P197 – 2mf – 9 – Can$4.50 – cn Bibl Nat [324]
BILL: AN ACT TO CONSOLIDATE THE ACTS RESPECTING MUNICIPALITIES AND ROADS IN LOWER CANADA / Canada. Laws, Statutes, etc – Quebec: S Derbishire and G Desbarats, 1859. SEM105P196 – 2mf – 9 – Can$4.50 – cn Bibl Nat [324]
BILL: AN ACT TO REGULATE THE INSPECTION AND MEASUREMENT OF TIMBER, MASTS, SPARS,...IN THE PORTS OF QUEBEC AND MONTREAL / Canada. Laws, Statutes, etc – Kingston: R Stanton, 1841. SEM105P174 – 1mf – 9 – Can$2.25 – cn Bibl Nat [324]
BILL: AN ACT TO REPEAL CERTAIN ACTS THEREIN MENTIONED, AND TO PROVIDE FOR THE FURTHER ENCOURAGEMENT OF ELEMENTARY EDUCATION IN THIS PROVINCE / Canada. Bas-Canada. Laws, Statutes, etc – s.l. Legislative Council, 1836. SEM105P133 – 2mf – 9 – Can$4.50 – cn Bibl Nat [324]
BILL (AS AMENDED BY THE COMMITTEE) FOR UNITING THE LEGISLATURES OF LOWER AND UPPER CANADA – Quebec: Re-printed at the New Printing-Office, Free-Masons'Hall, 1822. SEM105P1146 – 1mf – 9 – Can$2.25 – cn Bibl Nat [324]
A BILL, AS AMENDED BY THE COMMITTEE, TO MAKE TEMPORARY PROVISION FOR THE GOVERNMENT OF LOWER CANADA / Grande-Bretagne. Parliament. House of Commons – [London]: [s.n.], [1838]. SEM105P1142 – 1mf – 9 – Can$2.25 – cn Bibl Nát [323]
BILL BARNES AIR TRAILS *see* AMERICAN AIRCRAFT MODELER
BILL BOOKS OF THE U.S. SENATE, 1795-1845 / U.S. Senate – 2r – 1 – M1255 – us Nat'l Archives [324]
Bill, IE *see* FIFTY YEARS WITH THE BAPTIST MINISTERS AND CHURCHES OF THE MARITIME PROVINCES OF CANADA
A BILL INTITULED AN ACT TO EXPLAIN AND AMEND THE LAWS RELATING TO LANDS HOLDEN IN FREE AND COMMON SOCCAGE IN THE PROVINCE OF LOWER CANADA – [Canada?]: [s.n.], [1831] SEM105P1141 – 1mf – 9 – Can$2.25 – cn Bibl Nat [340]
BILL INTRODUIT...POUR MIEUX REGLER LA MILICE DE CETTE PROVINCE = A BILL INTRODUCED...FOR BETTER REGULATION OF THE MILITIA OF THIS PROVINCE / Canada. Bas-Canada. Parlement. Chambre d'Assemblee – Quebec: Imprime a la nouvelle imprimerie, 1816. SEM16P300 – 1r – 5 – Can$9.00 – cn Bibl Nat [971]
BILL OF RIGHTS IN ACTION – v. 10-. 1976- – 1,5,6,9 – us UMI [321]
BILL OF RIGHTS JOURNAL – (v.12-. 1979-5,6,9) – 1968- – 1 – us UMI [073]
BILL OF RIGHTS NEWSLETTER – (v9-10. 5,6. v10. 1976. 9) – v. 1-10. 1967-1976 – 1 – us UMI [323]
BILL OF RIGHTS REVIEW – v1-2. 1940-42 – 1,5,6 – us Princeton Micro [073]
THE BILL OF RIGHTS REVIEW : A QUARTERLY – Bill of Rights Committee of the ABA. v1-2. 1940-42 (all publ) – 9mf – 9 – $13.50 – LLMC 84-425 – us L.L.M.C. [073]
BILL OF THE PLAY / Daly's Fifth Avenue Theatre. New York – 1879 1880-1896 1897 – 1 – us NY Public [790]
LE BILL SEIGNEURIAL EXPOSE SOUS SON VRAI JOUR PAR LE JOURNAL "LA PATRIE" – Montreal: Imprime par Senecal & Daniel, 1855. SEM105P276 – 1mf – 9 – Can$2.25 – cn Bibl Nat [323]
BILL TO ENFORCE THE ANCIENT LAWS OF THIS PROVINCE, COMPELLING SEIGNIORS TO CONCEDE THEIR LANDS, SUBJECT ONLY TO RENTS AND SERVICES, AND TO FACILITATE THE RE-UNION OF LANDS EN... – [S.l.]: [s.n.], [1825] SEM105P1143 – 1mf – 9 – Can$2.25 – cn Bibl Nat [340]
BILL TO PROVIDE FOR MAKING AND MAINTAINING A RAIL ROAD FROM THE RIVER ST LAWRENCE TO THE NAVIGABLE WATERS OF LAKE CHAMPLAIN BILL POUR POURVOIR A LA CONSTRUCTION... – [S.l.]: [s.n.], 1831. SEM105P1222 – 1mf – 9 – Can$2.25 – cn Bibl Nat [324]
Billard, A *see* LES TRAITES PASSES LE 28 MAI 1902 ...
Billard de Saint-Laumer, J *see* DU DROIT DE LA GUERRE SUR TERRE ...
Billard, Louis Phillip *see* DIARY
Billard, Pierre *see* LA CIRCULATION DANS LE SUD CAMEROUN
Billard-Duminceau, E *see* VOLTAIRE APPRECIE. COMEDIE
Billaud-Varenne, Jacques N *see*
- LES ELEMENTS DU REPUBLICANISME
- PRINCIPES REGENERATEURS DU SYSTEME SOCIAL

Billberg, G J *see* ENUMERATIO INSECTORUM IN MUSEO G.J. BILLBERG
BILLBOARD – v. 82- 1970- – 1 – us UMI [780]
THE BILLBOARD – Cincinnati, Ohio. v. 1-72. Nov 1 1894-Dec 31 1960 – 1 – us NY Public [071]
THE BILLBOARD – Pittsburgh. Pa. 1949-75 – 1 – us UMI [071]
Billeau, Fernand *see* RECHERCHES STATISTIQUES SUR LA POPULATION DES 485 COMMUNES DE L'YONNE PENDANT 80 ANS: 1801-81
Billeb, Hermann *see* DIE WICHTIGSTEN SAETZE DER NEUEREN ALTTESTAMENTLICHEN KRITIK
Billerberg, F de *see* EPISTOLA CONSTANTINOLOPI RECENS SCRIPTA. DE PRAESENTI TURCICI IMPERIJ STATU, ET GUBERNATORIBUS PRAECIPUIS, ET DE BELLO PERSICO

BILLERICA 1627-1849 – (Mf 1T-3T: Vital Records 1627-1814. Mf 3T: Vital Record Indexes 1627-1847. Mf 4T-8T: Vital Records 1627-1847. Mf 8T: Vital Records Index 1785-1848. Mf 8T-10T: Vital Records 1785-1847. Mf 11T: Births & Deaths 1800-48. Mf 11T-12T: Births 1843-49. Mf 12T: Marriages 1843-49; Deaths 1843-49. Mf 13T: Out-of-Town Marriages 1674-1799. Mf 14T-15T: Baptisms 1747-1838) – (mf ed 1995) – 15mf – 9 – 0-87623-211-X – us Holbrook [920]

Billeter, Gustav *see* WILHELM MEISTERS THEATRALISCHE SENDUNG

Billette, J Emile *see* LA CAUSE DES OBLIGATIONS ET PRESTATIONS

Billiard, Auguste *see* PROJET DE CODE NOIR POUR LES COLONIES FRANCAISES

Billiardiere *see* NOVAE HOLLANDIAE PLANTARUM SPECIMEN

BILLIJCKE VERANTWOORDINGE ENDE EENVOLDIGHE WEDERLEGGHINGHE OP EENEN SCHELTLASTERIGHEN BRIEF DOOR DR. HIER. WILHELMI. IN 'T JAER 1544 / Blesdijk, Nicolaas M van – Wtgegaen Anno 1547. 1610. BME-389 1 – 9 – ne IDC [240]

Billing, Einar *see* LUTHERS LAERA OM STATEN I DESS SAMBAND MED HANS REFORMATORISKA GRUNDTANKAR OCH MED TIDIGARE KYRKLIGA LAEROR

Billing, John E *see* AN ANALYSIS OF SELECTED ATTENDANCE FACTORS IN THE WORLD LEAGUE OF AMERICAN FOOTBALL

Billings, Carolyn *see* VALIDATION OF THE DELTA T MODE OF THE OMNISOUND 3000(TM)

Billings, William *see*
- THE NEW ENGLAND PSALM-SINGER: OR, AMERICAN CHORISTER
- THE SINGING MASTER'S ASSISTANT, OR A KEY TO PRACTICAL MUSIC

Billington, T *see* COLLECTION OF WORKS

BILLIONS MORE TO FEED – 1979 – 47p – it F.A.O. [630]

Billon, Frederic Louis *see* ANNALS OF ST LOUIS: IN ITS EARLY DAYS UNDER THE FRENCH AND SPANISH DOMINATIONS

Billot, F *see* L'OUVERTURE DU CANAL DE PANAMA ...

Billot, Ludovico *see* DE SACRA TRADITIONE CONTRA NOVAM HAERESIM EVOLUTIONISMI

BILLS / Canada. Parliament – Public, 1980- – 9 – cn Micromedia [324]

BILLS / Charleston Library Society. Charleston, South Carolina – 1788-1810, 1858 – 1mf – 9 – us South Carolina Historical [020]

BILLS AND RESOLUTIONS / U. S. Laws, Statutes, etc. (Bills) – Washington, DC. On film: 1st-72nd Congress; 1789-1933. LL-01 – 1 – us L of C Photodup [340]

THE BILLS OF EXCHANGE ACT, 1890: AN ACT TO CODIFY THE LAWS RELATING TO BILLS OF EXCHANGE, CHEQUES AND PROMISSORY NOTES, PASSED BY THE PARLIAMENT OF CANADA, 53 VIC., CH33, WITH NOTES AND COMMENTS / Girouard, Desire – Montreal: J. Valois, 1891. 03376. (Pre-1900 Canadiana) – 9 – cn C.I.H.M. [971]

The Billy Graham Center, Wheaton College Holdings. From Grace College and Seminary, Winona Lake, IN. *see* THE BILLY SUNDAY PAPERS, 1882-1974

THE BILLY SUNDAY PAPERS, 1882-1974 / The Billy Graham Center, Wheaton College Holdings. From Grace College and Seminary, Winona Lake, IN.; ed by Shuster, Robert – (Includes printed guide) – 1978 – 29r – 1 – $2,465.00 – D1622 – us Scholarly Res [240]

Bilodeau, Ernest *see*
- UN CANADIEN ERRANT
- L'EMULATION

Bilodeau, Francoise *see* BIBLIOGRAPHIE DU THEATRE CANADIEN-FRANCAIS DE 1900-1955

Bilodeau, J *see* SEPT CONTES SANGU DANS LEUR CONTEXTE CULTUREL ET LINGUISTIQUE, TANZANIE

BILYCHNIS – Rome. v1-36. 1912-31 (complete) – 9r – 1 – ATLA S0147 – us A.T.L.A. [240]

BIMBI / Ouida – British Fiction Archive: Unit 3 – 9 – uk Bell [830]

Bimeler, Joseph Michael *see*
- SAMMLUNG AUSERLESNER GEISTLICHER LIEDER
- DIE WAHRE SEPARATION

BIMILENARIO DE LA FUNDACION DE LA COLONIA NORBA CAESERINA / Barvo y Bravo Fernando – Caceres, 1967 – 1 – sp Bibl Santa Ana [946]

BIMILENARIO DE LA FUNDADCION ROMANA DE CACERES – Madrid: Servicio de Publicaciones del Ministerio de Informacion y Turismo, 1967 – sp Bibl Santa Ana [946]

Bimler, Kurt *see* DIE ERSTE UND ZWEITE FASSUNG VON GOETHES "WANDERJAHREN"

Binder, W *see* DAS RECHT DER STAATSANGEHOERIGKEIT ... SEIT DEM JAHRE 1870

Binder, Wilhelm *see* ALLGEMEINE REALENCYCLOPAEDIE ODER CONVERSATIONS-LEXIKON FUER DAS KATHOLISCHE DEUTSCHLAND (AEL, ABT 1;6)

Bindloss, Harold *see* A WIDE DOMINION

Bineman, IM *see* KADRY GOSUDARSTVENNOGO I KOOPERATIVNOGO APPARATA SSSR

Binet, Estienne *see* RECUEIL DES OEUVRES SPIRITUELLES DU P. ESTIENNE BINET

Binet, Vincent *see* CORRESPONDENCE WITH THE GOVERNMENT, 1926-1931 AND WITH DR CLIFFORD JAMES ON CLOTHES, 1931

BING – Dakar, Senegal. n31-93 aug 1955-oct 1960; n120-227 1963-71 – 1 – us Res Libr [073]

Bingay, George *see* THE COUNTY COURT MANUAL: BEING A COLLECTION OF THE STATUTES RELATING TO THE PRACTICE, PROCEDURE AND JURISDICTION OF THE COUNTY COURTS OF NOVA SCOTIA WITH NOTES, ETC

BING-CHUAN DONGTU – Journal of Glaciology and Cryopedology. In Chinese but English abstracts to the main articles. F p103 – 9 – 4.00f – cc Microforms [073]

Bingel, Horst *see* VERBAND DEUTSCHER SCHRIFTSTELLER. PHANTASIE UND VERANTWORTUNG

Binger, Louis Gustave *see*
- DU NIGER AU GOLFE DE GUINEE PAR LE PAYS DE KONG ET LE MOSSI (1887-1888)
- DU NIGER AU GOLFE DE GUINEE PAR LE PAYS DE KONG ET LE MOSSI, 1887-1889
- DU NIGER AU GOLFE DE GUINEE PAR LE PAYS DE KONG ET LE MOSSI PAR LE CAPITAINE BINGER (1887-1889)
- DU NIGER AU GOLFE DU GUINEE PAR LE PAYS DE KONG ET LE MOSSI
- ESCLAVAGE
- TRANSACTIONS, OBJETS DE COMMERCE

Bingham, D *see* THE BASTILLE

Bingham, Helen M *see* HISTORY OF GREEN COUNTY, WISCONSIN

Bingham, John A *see* PAPERS

Bingham, John Elliot *see* NARRATIVE OF THE EXPEDITION TO CHINA, FROM THE COMMENCEMENT OF THE WAR TO THE PRESENT PERIOD; WITH SKETCHES OF THE MANNERS AND CUSTOMS OF THAT COUNTRY

Bingham, Joseph *see* ORIGENES ECCLESIASTICAE: OR, THE ANTIQUITIES OF THE CHRISTIAN CHURCH, AND OTHER WORKS

Bingham, Peregrine *see*
- BINGHAM'S NEW CASES
- BINGHAM'S REPORTS
- BRODERIP AND BINGHAM'S REPORTS

BINGHAM'S NEW CASES : NEW CASES IN THE COURT OF COMMON PLEAS... / Bingham, Peregrine – v1-6. 1834-40. London: Saunders & Benning, 1835-41 (all publ) – 54mf – 9 – $81.00 – LLMC 84-750 – us L.L.M.C. [324]

BINGHAM'S REPORTS : REPORTS OF CASES ARGUED AND DETERMINED IN THE COURT OF COMMON PLEAS... / Bingham, Peregrine – v1-10. 1822-34. London: J Butterworth/Saunders & Benning, 1824-34 (all publ) – 77mf – 9 – $115.00 – LLMC 84-749 – us L.L.M.C. [324]

BINGKISAN / Jajasan Kebudajaan Sulawese Selatan dan Tenggara – (Monthly) – Makassar. v1-3. 1967-1970 – 26mf – 9 – SE-1360/1 – ne IDC [950]

BINH PHU TAN VAN – no. 2-29. Hue. 1er aout 1930-15 sept 1931. mq no. 11, 22, 28 – 1 – fr A.C.R.P.P. [073]

BINKERHOFF'S HISTORY OF MARION COUNTY / B.F. Bowen and Co – Biographical sketches. Indianapolis, 1909. Illinois Reel 42. The Cox Library Collection – 5 – us Americana [978]

Binmore, Charles J *see* THE CANADIAN NATIONALITY

DIE BINNENMOLLUSKEN DER NOERDLICH GEMAESSIGTEN LAENDER VON EUROPA UND ASIEN UND DER ARKTISCHEN LAENDER / Jordan, H – (Nova Acta Ac. Caesrea Leopoldino-Carolina, v. 45, no. 4). Halle. 1883. BZ-592 2 – 8 – ne IDC [590]

Binney, Amos *see* BINNEY'S THEOLOGICAL COMPEND IMPROVED

Binney, E W *see* OBSERVATIONS ON THE STRUCTURE OF FOSSIL PLANTS FOUND IN THE CARBONIFEROUS STRATA

Binney, Horace *see* OPINION OF HORACE BINNEY, ESQ., UPON THE RIGHT OF THE CITY COUNCILS TO SUBSCRIBE FOR STOCK IN THE PENNSYLVANIA RAIL-ROAD COMPANY

Binney, T *see* LIGHTS AND SHADOWS OF CHURCH-LIFE IN AUSTRALIA

Binney, Thomas *see* SIR THOMAS FOWELL BUXTON, BART.

Binney, W G *see* THE COMPLETE WRITINGS OF C.S. RAFINESQUE ON RECENT AND FOSSIL CONCHOLOGY

BINNEY'S REPORTS / Pennsylvania. Superior Court – (A Pre-NRS title) – v1-6. 1799-1814 (all publ) – 13mf – 9 – $58.00 – LLMC 84-194 – us L.L.M.C. [340]

BINNEY'S THEOLOGICAL COMPEND IMPROVED / Binney, Amos – New York: Phillips & Hunt, 1875.1 fiche – 9 – us A.T.L.A. [240]

Binnie, William *see* THE PSALMS

O BINOCULO : JORNALSATYRICO, CHISTOSO E LITTERARIO – Bahia, BA. 27 Jun, 7 Nov 1877 – 1,5,6 – bl Biblioteca [072]

O BINOCULO : LITTERARIO, NOTICIOSO E RECREATIVO – Maceio, Alagoas. 16-24 Ago 1899 – 1,5,6 – bl Biblioteca [072]

O BINOCULO – Paraopoba, Brazil. Feb-Apr 1954 – 1 – bl Biblioteca [072]

BINTANG MERAH – Djakarta. (incomplete) SE-353 1. 1945-1965 – 9 – ne IDC [073]

BINTANG TIMUR – Djakarta. Indonesia. -d. 1958-65 – 1 – us UMI [072]

Binterim, Anton Joseph *see* PRAGMATISCHE GESCHICHTE DER DEUTSCHEN CONCILIEN VOM 4. JAHRHUNDERT BIS ZUM CONCILIUM VON TRIENT

BIOASTRONAUTICS : FUNDAMENTAL AND PRACTICAL PROBLEMS – (v17, Advances) – 9 – $20.00 – us Univelt [629]

BIO-BASE 1990: MASTER CUMULATION / ed by McNeil, Barbara – (Bio-Base 1991: over 450,000 citations in a single alphabet. Includes printed bibliography of sources indexed. $195 Updated annually with master cumulation 5-yearly) – 7.5 million citations to biographical entries appearing in over 600 biographical dictionaries. Citation includes full name, birth/death dates, code indicating source of data. Printed bibliography of sources indexed – 9 – $995.00 – 0-8103-4828-4 – us Gale [920]

BIOBEHAVIORAL REVIEWS – (See also: Neuroscience and Biobehavioral Reviews) – v1. 1977 – 1,5,6,9 – us UMI [150]

BIO-BIBLIGRAPHIE ANALYTIQUE DE SOEUR SAINT-IGNACE-DE-LOYOLA, C.N.D. / Sainte-Marie-Antonin, Soeur – 1962. SEM105P4 – 1mf – 9 – cn Bibl Nat [240]

BIO-BIBLIOGRAFIA DE LOS JESUITAS EN LA VENEZUELA COLONIAL / Rey Fajardo, J del S J – Caracas: Inst. Inv. Hist., 1974 – 7mf – 9 – ne IDC [240]

BIO-BIBLIOGRAFIA ECLESIASTICA MEXICANA (1821-1943) / Valverde Tellez, E – Mexico: Jus. 3v. 1949 – 14mf – 9 – ne IDC [240]

BIO-BIBLIOGRAPHIE : LA TRES REVERENDE MERE, MARIE DE SAINT-JEAN MARTIN O.S.U., PRIEURE GENERALE DE L'U.R. / Perpetuel-Secours, Marie-du – 1955. SEM105P4 – 2mf – 9 – cn Bibl Nat [240]

BIO-BIBLIOGRAPHIE ANALYTIQUE, 1918 A 1961 INCLUSIVEMENT, DE L'ABBE ERNEST ARSENAULT, MISSIONNAIRE-COLONISATEUR / Saint-Camille-de-Jesus, Marie-de – 1963. SEM105P4 – 3mf – 9 – cn Bibl Nat [240]

BIO-BIBLIOGRAPHIE ANALYTIQUE 1917-1941 DE MONSIEUR L'ABBE PIERRE GRAVEL CURE DE BOISCHATEL / Saint-Sacrement, Beatrice-du – 1961. SEM105P4 – 2mf – 9 – cn Bibl Nat [240]

BIO-BIBLIOGRAPHIE ANALYTIQUE, 1941-1957, DE MONSIEUR L'ABBE PIERRE GRAVEL, CURE DE BOISCHATEL / Georges-Andre, Soeur – 1961. SEM105P4 – 2mf – 9 – cn Bibl Nat [240]

BIO-BIBLIOGRAPHIE ANALYTIQUE DE EDDY BOUDREAU, MEMBRE DE LA SOCIETE DES ECRIVAINS CANADIENS ET DE LA SOCIETE DES POETES / Vaillancourt, Emilienne – 1954. SEM105P4 – 1mf – 9 – cn Bibl Nat [400]

BIO-BIBLIOGRAPHIE ANALYTIQUE DE F. FITZ OSBORNE, GEOLOGUE, TITULAIRE DE LA CHAIRE DE PETROLOGIE A L'UNIVERSITE LAVAL / Champagne, Andre – 1950. SEM105P4 – 1mf – 9 – cn Bibl Nat [550]

BIO-BIBLIOGRAPHIE ANALYTIQUE DE GERARD LANGLOIS, JOURNALISTE-DIRECTEUR DES EDITIONS DU CACTUS / Prince, Madeleine – 1954. SEM105P4 – 2mf – 9 – cn Bibl Nat [070]

BIO-BIBLIOGRAPHIE ANALYTIQUE DE JEAN SIMARD / Mainguy, Louise – 1959. SEM105P4 – 1mf – 9 – cn Bibl Nat [010]

BIO-BIBLIOGRAPHIE ANALYTIQUE DE L'OEUVRE DE L'ABBE ARTHUR MAHEUX DE LA SOCIETE ROYALE DU CANADA, ARCHIVISTE ET PROFESSEUR D'HISTOIRE DE AMERIQUES A L'UNIVERSITE LAVAL / Boivin, Jean – [1954]. SEM105P4 – 2mf – 9 – cn Bibl Nat [970]

BIO-BIBLIOGRAPHIE ANALYTIQUE DE L'OEUVRE DE MARCEL TRUDEL, DOCTEUR ES LETTRES / Nive – 1959. SEM105P4 – 2mf – 9 – cn Bibl Nat [400]

BIO-BIBLIOGRAPHIE ANALYTIQUE DE L'OEUVRE DU REVEREND PERE OVILA MELANCON / Sainte-Cecile, Soeur – 1962 [i.e. 1963]. SEM105P4 – 2mf – 9 – cn Bibl Nat [240]

BIO-BIBLIOGRAPHIE ANALYTIQUE DE M. AIME PLAMONDON / Deslauriers, Francoise – 1948. SEM105P4 – 2mf – 9 – cn Bibl Nat [971]

BIO-BIBLIOGRAPHIE ANALYTIQUE DE M. ELPHEGE-J. DAIGNAULT / Bourget, Magdeleine – 1952. SEM105P4 – 1mf – 9 – cn Bibl Nat [971]

BIO-BIBLIOGRAPHIE ANALYTIQUE DE MARCEL TRUDEL / Des Rochers, Guy – 1948. SEM105P4 – 1mf – 9 – cn Bibl Nat [971]

BIO-BIBLIOGRAPHIE ANALYTIQUE DE MARTHE BERGERON-HOGUE / Bonin, Marie – 1964. SEM105P4 – 2mf – 9 – cn Bibl Nat [971]

BIO-BIBLIOGRAPHIE ANALYTIQUE DE ME JEAN-CHARLES BONENFANT, MEMBRE DE LA SOCIETE ROYALE DU CANADA, CONSERVATEUR DE LA BIBLIOTHEQUE DE LA LEGISLATURE PROVINCIALE DE QUEBEC ET PROFESSEUR A L'UNIVERSITE LAVAL / Saint-Emile, Soeur – 1964. SEM105P4 – 2mf – 9 – cn Bibl Nat [320]

BIO-BIBLIOGRAPHIE ANALYTIQUE DE ME MARIE-LOUIS BEAULIEU, AVOCAT A QUEBEC / Hache, Patricia – 1957. SEM105P4 – 1mf – 9 – cn Bibl Nat [340]

BIO-BIBLIOGRAPHIE ANALYTIQUE DE MGR LEONCE BOIVIN, P.D., B.S., L.D.C., D. TH. / Labbe, Wilfrid – 1961. SEM105P4 – 1mf – 9 – cn Bibl Nat [240]

BIO-BIBLIOGRAPHIE ANALYTIQUE DE MONSEIGNEUR JOSEPH FERLAND, P.D., V.U., CURE DE SAINT-ROCH DE QUEBEC / Saint-Joseph-de-la-Charite, Soeur – 1960. SEM105P4 – 2mf – 9 – cn Bibl Nat [240]

BIO-BIBLIOGRAPHIE ANALYTIQUE DE MONSIEUR GERALD GODIN / Charest, Pauline – 1964. SEM105P4 – 1mf – 9 – cn Bibl Nat [971]

BIO-BIBLIOGRAPHIE ANALYTIQUE DE MONSIEUR HENRI TURGEON, NOTAIRE, PROFESSEUR AGREGE A LA FACULTE DE DROIT DE QUEBEC / Cote, Berthe – 1956. SEM105P4 – 1mf – 9 – cn Bibl Nat [340]

BIO-BIBLIOGRAPHIE ANALYTIQUE DE MONSIEUR HERVE BIRON, REDACTEUR EN CHEF AU JOURNAL LE NOUVELLISTE DES TROIS-RIVIERES, PRESIDENT DE LA SOCIETE D'HISTOIRE REGIONALE DES TROIS-RIVIERES / Lemaire, Ghyslaine – [1963]. SEM105P4 – 2mf – 9 – cn Bibl Nat [070]

BIO-BIBLIOGRAPHIE ANALYTIQUE DE MONSIEUR L'ABBE PASCAL POTVIN, L.PH., L.L., PRINCIPAL DE L'ECOLE NORMALE DE LEVIS / Saint-Gerard, Soeur – 1962. SEM105P4 – 2mf – 9 – cn Bibl Nat [370]

BIO-BIBLIOGRAPHIE ANALYTIQUE DE REINE MALOUIN / Plamondon, Jocelyne – 1959. SEM105P4 – 1mf – 9 – cn Bibl Nat [971]

BIO-BIBLIOGRAPHIE ANALYTIQUE DE REINE MALOUIN, MEMBRE DE LA SOCIETE DES ECRIVAINS CANADIENS / Dubeau, Jean – 1963. SEM105P4 – 2mf – 9 – cn Bibl Nat [400]

BIO-BIBLIOGRAPHIE ANALYTIQUE DE RENE OUVRARD / Bergeron, Helene – 1957. SEM105P4 – 1mf – 9 – cn Bibl Nat [971]

BIO-BIBLIOGRAPHIE ANALYTIQUE DE RODOLPHE LAPLANTE, REGISSEUR ET SECRETAIRE-GENERAL DE L'OFFICE DU CREDIT AGRICOLE DU QUEBEC / Severien, Frere – 1955 [i.e. 1956]. SEM105P4 – 4mf – 9 – cn Bibl Nat [332]

BIO-BIBLIOGRAPHIE ANALYTIQUE DE ROGER CHARTIER, DIRECTEUR DU PERSONNEL A L'HYDRO-QUEBEC, PROFESSEUR A LA FACULTE DES SCIENCES SOCIALES DE L'UNIVERSITE LAVAL / Miko, Eugenie – 1962. SEM105P4 – 1mf – 9 – cn Bibl Nat [300]

BIO-BIBLIOGRAPHIE ANALYTIQUE DE SOEUR SAINT-DAMASE-DE-ROME, C.N.D., DIRECTRICE DU CENTRE MARGUERITE BOURGEOYS / Sainte-Marie-Gedeon, Soeur – 1963 [i.e. 1964]. SEM105P4 – 2mf – 9 – cn Bibl Nat [240]

BIO-BIBLIOGRAPHIE ANALYTIQUE DE SOEUR SAINT-FRANCOIS-DE-L'ALVERNE, C.N.D., PREFETE PROVINCIALE DES ETUDES / Sainte-Jeanne-d'Annecy, Soeur – 1963. SEM105P4 – 2mf – 9 – cn Bibl Nat [240]

BIO-BIBLIOGRAPHIE ANALYTIQUE DES DISCOURS ET CONFERENCES DE L'HONORABLE TELESPHORE-DAMIEN BOUCHARD / Morin, Maurice – 1964. SEM105P4 – 2mf – 9 – cn Bibl Nat [920]

BIO-BIBLIOGRAPHIE ANALYTIQUE DES ECRITS DU DOCTEUR WILFRID LEBLOND, PROFESSEUR TITULAIRE A L'UNIVERSITE LAVAL / Ste-Suzanne, Soeur – 1962. SEM105P4 – 2mf – 9 – cn Bibl Nat [370]

BIO-BIBLIOGRAPHIE ANALYTIQUE DES IMPRIMES DES SOEURS DE LA CONGREGATION DE NOTRE-DAME DE MONTREAL / Sainte-Marie-de-Pontmain, Soeur – 1952. SEM105P4 – 2mf – 9 – cn Bibl Nat [240]

BIO-BIBLIOGRAPHIE ANALYTIQUE DU POETE ADOLPHE POISSON / Richard, Marie-France – 1952. SEM105P4 – 1mf – 9 – cn Bibl Nat [400]

BIO-BIBLIOGRAPHIE ANALYTIQUE DU REVEREND FRERE MARIE-MAXIMIN, E.C., DIRECTEUR-ADJOINT DE LA LEGION DE MARIE, MAISON PROVINCIALE, QUEBEC / Sainte-Marie-Rita, Soeur – 1964. SEM105P4 – 2mf – 9 – cn Bibl Nat [240]

BIO-BIBLIOGRAPHIE ANALYTIQUE DU REVEREND PER PAUL-HENRI BARABE, O.M.I., SUPERIEUR DE LA PROVINCE OBLATE NOTRE-DAME-DU-TRES-SAINT-ROSAIRE, QUEBEC / Sainte-Rollande-de-l'Immaculee, Soeur – 1963. SEM105P4 – 2mf – 9 – cn Bibl Nat [240]

BIO-BIBLIOGRAPHIE ANALYTIQUE DU REVEREND PERE LAURENT TREMBLAY, O.M.I., MISSIONNAIRE ECRIVAIN... / Ste-Marthe-de-la-Trinite – 1961. SEM105P4 – 1mf – 9 – cn Bibl Nat [240]

BIO-BIBLIOGRAPHIE ANALYTIQUE D'UNE RELIGIEUSE EDUCATRICE, SOEUR SAINTE-MADELEINE-DES-ANGES DE LA CONGREGATION DE NOTRE-DAME / Sainte-Jeanne-de-Jesus, Soeur – 1952. SEM105P4 – 1mf – 9 – cn Bibl Nat [240]

BIO-BIBLIOGRAPHIE CANADIENNE DES OEUVRES DE MGR EMILE CHARTIER, P.D., 1938-1962 / Levasseur, Georgette – 1963. SEM105P4 – 2mf – 9 – cn Bibl Nat [440]

BIO-BIBLIOGRAPHIE CRITIQUE D'ANNE HEBERT / Boutet, Odina – 1950. SEM105P4 – 1mf – 9 – cn Bibl Nat [971]

BIO-BIBLIOGRAPHIE CRITIQUE DE L'AVOCAT GEORGES BELLERIVE, 1859-1935 / St-Jean, Marie de – 1950. SEM105P4 – 1mf – 9 – cn Bibl Nat [340]

BIO-BIBLIOGRAPHIE DE ALCIDE FLEURY, HISTORIEN ET JOURNALISTE / Saint-Augustin, Soeur – 1963. SEM105P4 – 2mf – 9 – cn Bibl Nat [070]

BIO-BIBLIOGRAPHIE DE BEATRICE CLEMENT / Mercier, Jeanne Mance – 1961. SEM105P4 – 2mf – 9 – cn Bibl Nat [010]

BIO-BIBLIOGRAPHIE DE DAMASE POTVIN / Treffry, Philippe – 1947. SEM105P4 – 1mf – 9 – cn Bibl Nat [240]

BIO-BIBLIOGRAPHIE DE DAMASE POTVIN, ECRIVAIN ET JOURNALISTE / Raymond, Frere – 1956. SEM105P4 – 2mf – 9 – cn Bibl Nat [070]

BIO-BIBLIOGRAPHIE DE FEU SON EMINENCE LE CARDINAL JEAN-MARIE-RODRIGUE VILLENEUVE, OBLAT DE MARIE IMMACULEE, ARCHEVEQUE DE QUEBEC / Houle, R – 1948. SEM105P4 – 1mf – 9 – cn Bibl Nat [240]

BIO-BIBLIOGRAPHIE DE GEORGINA LEFAIVRE / Cote, Antonia – 1948. SEM105P4 – 2mf – 9 – cn Bibl Nat [971]

BIO-BIBLIOGRAPHIE DE GERARD MARTIN DE LA SOCIETE DES ECRIVAINS CANADIENS / Normand, Rita – 1953. SEM105P4 – 1mf – 9 – cn Bibl Nat [400]

BIO-BIBLIOGRAPHIE DE HENRI [I.E. HECTOR] DE SAINT-DENYS GARNEAU (1953-1963) / Page, Jean-Pierre – 1964. SEM105P4 – 1mf – 9 – cn Bibl Nat [971]

BIO-BIBLIOGRAPHIE DE JULES-S. LESAGE / Bedard, Denyse – 1948. SEM105P4 – 1mf – 9 – cn Bibl Nat [971]

BIO-BIBLIOGRAPHIE DE LA R.S. GABRIEL-LALEMANT, S.G.C., B.A., B.ED., CONSEILLERE PEDAGOGIQUE AU SECRETARIAT NATIONALE DE LA J.E.C. A MONTREAL / Telmon, Soeur – 1962. SEM105P4 – 1mf – 9 – cn Bibl Nat [370]

BIO-BIBLIOGRAPHIE DE L'ABBE FELIX-ANTOINE SAVARD, PROFESSEUR A LA FACULTE DES LETTRES DE L'UNIVERSITE LAVAL, QUEBEC / Savard, Marcelle – 1947. SEM105P4 – 1mf – 9 – cn Bibl Nat [400]

BIO-BIBLIOGRAPHIE DE L'ABBE JOSEPH-WILLIAM-IVANHOE CARON, 1875-1941 / Pelletier, J -Antoine – 1947. SEM105P4 – 1mf – 9 – cn Bibl Nat [240]

BIO-BIBLIOGRAPHIE DE M. ALBERT RIOUX / Carbonneau, Leopold – 1952. SEM105P4 – 1mf – 9 – cn Bibl Nat [630]

BIO-BIBLIOGRAPHIE DE M. JEAN BRUCHESI, M.S., R.C., SOUS-SECRETAIRE ET SOUS-REGISTRAIRE DE LA PROVINCE DE QUEBEC / Boissonneault, Henri – 1948. SEM105P4 – 1mf – 9 – cn Bibl Nat [320]

BIO-BIBLIOGRAPHIE DE M. L'ABBE ANDRE LALIBERTE, PTRE, JOURNALISTE ET EDUCATEUR, 1926-32 / Sainte-Pauline, Soeur – 1961. SEM105P4 – 2mf – 9 – cn Bibl Nat [070]

BIO-BIBLIOGRAPHIE DE ME JEAN-CHARLES BONENFANT, MEMBRE DE LA SOCIETE ROYALE DU CANADA, BIBLIOTHECAIRE DE LA LEGISLATURE PROVINCIALE DE QUEBEC ET PROFESSEUR A L'UNIVERSITE LAVAL / Jacques, Colette – 1954. SEM105P4 – 2mf – 9 – cn Bibl Nat [020]

BIO-BIBLIOGRAPHIE DE MERE MARGUERITE-MARIE LASALLE, O.S.U., URSULINE DES TROIS-RIVIERES / Sainte-Catherine-de-Sienne, Mere – 1964. SEM105P4 – 1mf – 9 – cn Bibl Nat [240]

BIO-BIBLIOGRAPHIE DE MERE MARIE-BERTHE THIBAULT / Bresoles, Judith de – 1962. SEM105P4 – 1mf – 9 – cn Bibl Nat [240]

BIO-BIBLIOGRAPHIE DE MGR JOSEPH-CLOVIS K.-LAFLAMME / Trottier, Irenee – 1961. SEM105P4 – 1mf – 9 – cn Bibl Nat [240]

BIO-BIBLIOGRAPHIE DE MONSEIGNEUR ALEXANDRE VACHON / Parent, Jean-Baptiste – 1947. SEM105P4 – 1mf – 9 – cn Bibl Nat [971]

BIO-BIBLIOGRAPHIE DE MONSEIGNEUR ELIAS ROY, P.A., DIRECTEUR NATIONAL DE L'UNION MISSIONNAIRE DU CLERGE ET ANCIEN SUPERIEUR DU COLLEGE DE LEVIS / LaBrie, Hilda – 1954. SEM105P4 – 1mf – 9 – cn Bibl Nat [240]

BIO-BIBLIOGRAPHIE DE MONSEIGNEUR LOUIS-JOSEPH-ARTHUR MELANSON, PREMIER ARCHEVEQUE DE MONCTON, N.-B., 1879-1941 / Marie-Irene, Soeur – 1963. SEM105P4 – 3mf – 9 – cn Bibl Nat [240]

BIO-BIBLIOGRAPHIE DE MONSIEUR ALBERT GERVAIS / Brousseau, Vincent – 1963. SEM105P4 – 3mf – 9 – cn Bibl Nat [971]

BIO-BIBLIOGRAPHIE DE MONSIEUR CARL FAESSLER, PROFESSEUR TITULAIRE DE MINERALOGIE, FACULTE DES SCIENCES / Arteau, Jean-Marie – 1948. SEM105P4 – 1mf – 9 – cn Bibl Nat [540]

BIO-BIBLIOGRAPHIE DE MONSIEUR ELPHEGE BOIS, D.SC., DIRECTEUR DU DEPARTEMENT DE BIOCHIMIE DE LA FACULTE DES SCIENCES / Garant, J -Honorat – 1949. SEM105P4 – 1mf – 9 – cn Bibl Nat [574]

BIO-BIBLIOGRAPHIE DE MONSIEUR GERARD FILION, JOURNALISTE, CONFERENCIER, ECRIVAIN / Leveque, Isabella – 1964. SEM105P4 – 2mf – 9 – cn Bibl Nat [070]

BIO-BIBLIOGRAPHIE DE MONSIEUR GERARD FILTEAU, CONSEILLER TECHNIQUE EN PEDAGOGIE AU DEPARTEMENT DE L'INSTRUCTION PUBLIQUE / Sauveur, Maria-du – 1962. SEM105P4 – 1mf – 9 – cn Bibl Nat [370]

BIO-BIBLIOGRAPHIE DE MONSIEUR JEAN VALLERAND, B.A., LICENCIE ES LETTRES, DIPLOME DE L'UNIVERSITE DE MONTREAL EN JOURNALISME, CRITIQUE MUSICAL / Juchereau-Duchesnay, Marguerite – 1953. SEM105P4 – 1mf – 9 – cn Bibl Nat [370]

BIO-BIBLIOGRAPHIE DE MONSIEUR JEAN-CHARLES BONENFANT ATTACHE A LA BIBLIOTHEQUE DE LA LEGISLATURE PROVINCIALE, CHARGE DE COURS D'HISTOIRE POLITIQUE A L'UNIVERSITE LAVAL / Pouliot, Marcelle – 1947. SEM105P4 – 1mf – 9 – cn Bibl Nat [320]

BIO-BIBLIOGRAPHIE DE MONSIEUR LE CHANOINE VICTOR TREMBLAY, PRESIDENT DE LA SOCIETE HISTORIQUE DU SAGUENAY ET MEMBRE DE LA SOCIETE DES ECRIVAINS CANADIENS-FRANCAIS / Dandurand, Therese – 1956. SEM105P4 – 2mf – 9 – cn Bibl Nat [971]

BIO-BIBLIOGRAPHIE DE ROGER LEMELIN / Turgeon, Marguerite – 1949. SEM105P4 – 1mf – 9 – cn Bibl Nat [971]

BIO-BIBLIOGRAPHIE DE S.E. LE CARDINAL NICOLAS WISEMAN / Morissette, Lucy – 1947. SEM105P4 – 1mf – 9 – cn Bibl Nat [240]

BIO-BIBLIOGRAPHIE DE YVES LECLERC, 1953-1961 / Denoncourt, Louise – 1mf – 1964. SEM105P4 – cn Bibl Nat [010]

BIO-BIBLIOGRAPHIE DES ANCIENS ELEVES DES FRERES MARISTES / Bolduc, Marcel – 1963. SEM105P4 – 2mf – 9 – cn Bibl Nat [240]

BIO-BIBLIOGRAPHIE D'EUGENE ROUILLARD, NOTAIRE, MEMBRE DE LA SOCIETE ROYALE DU CANADA, MEMBRE FONDATEUR DE LA SOCIETE DU PARLER FRANCAIS... / Rouillard, Joseph – 1963. SEM105P4 – 2mf – 9 – cn Bibl Nat [340]

BIO-BIBLIOGRAPHIE DU CHANOINE LIONEL GROULX, D.TH., D.PH. ET PROFESSEUR A L'UNIVERSITE DE MONTREAL / Lefebvre, Marguerite – 1947. SEM105P4 – 1mf – 9 – cn Bibl Nat [370]

BIO-BIBLIOGRAPHIE DU COLONEL G.E. MARQUIS, CONSERVATEUR DE LA BIBLIOTHEQUE DE LA LEGISLATURE DU QUEBEC / Magloire, Frere – 1947. SEM105P4 – 1mf – 9 – cn Bibl Nat [320]

BIO-BIBLIOGRAPHIE DU DOCTEUR LOUIS PAUL DUGAL / Potvin, Micheline – 1950. SEM105P4 – 1mf – 9 – cn Bibl Nat [610]

BIO-BIBLIOGRAPHIE DU DOCTEUR PHILIPPE HAMEL / Belzile, Marie-Paule – 1949 [i.e. 1950]. SEM105P4 – 2mf – 9 – cn Bibl Nat [610]

BIO-BIBLIOGRAPHIE DU FRERE ROBERT, E.C., PROFESSEUR AU MONT-SAINT-LOUIS / Lippens-Giguere, Magdeleine – 1947. SEM105P4 – 1mf – 9 – cn Bibl Nat [370]

BIOBIBLIOGRAPHIE DU LIEUTENANT ERNEST PAICHARI [SIC], SOLDAT DE FRANCE / Montreuil, Madeleine – 1949. SEM105P4 – 1mf – 9 – cn Bibl Nat [355]

BIO-BIBLIOGRAPHIE DU REVEREND PERE FRANCIS GOYER, S.S.S., CONSULTEUR PROVINCIAL / Coulombe, M – 1947. SEM105P4 – 1mf – 9 – cn Bibl Nat [240]

BIO-BIBLIOGRAPHIE DU REVEREND PERE GONZALVE POULIN, O.F.M., D.SC.SS., DIRECTEUR DE L'ECOLE SOCIALE POPULAIRE, UNIVERSITE LAVAL / Beaudoin, Gilles – 1955. SEM105P4 – 2mf – 9 – cn Bibl Nat [240]

BIO-BIBLIOGRAPHIE DU REVEREND PERE JOSEPH-FRANCOIS RICHARD, S.J. / Toutant, Thomas – 1963. SEM105P4 – 2mf – 9 – cn Bibl Nat [240]

BIO-BIBLIOGRAPHIE DU REVEREND PERE PAUL-EMILE BRETON, O.M.I., JOURNALISTE ET ECRIVAIN / Durocher, Georges – 1961. SEM105P4 – 2mf – 9 – cn Bibl Nat [070]

BIO-BIBLIOGRAPHIE DU R.P. FERNAND PORTER, O.F.M. / Caron, Alfred – 1952. SEM105P4 – 1mf – 9 – cn Bibl Nat [971]

BIO-BIBLIOGRAPHIE DU T.R.P. GEORGES-HENRI LEVESQUE, O.P., DOYEN DE LA FACULTE DES SCIENCES SOCIALES DE L'UNIVERSITE LAVAL / Ubald, Frere – 1947. SEM105P4 – 1mf – 9 – cn Bibl Nat [300]

BIOCATALYSIS / ed by Leak, David – 9,5,1 – us Harwood [574]

A BIOCHEMICAL ANALYSIS OF THE EXERCISE-INDUCED DYSFUNCTION OF THE RAT GASTROCNEMIUS SARCO-PLASMIC RETICULUM CA2+-ATPASE PROTEIN / Luckin, Kristen A & Klug, Gary A – 1992 – 2mf – 9 – $8.00 – us Microform Publ [612]

BIOCHEMICAL EDUCATION – v8- 1980- – 5,6,9 – us UMI [540]

BIOCHEMICAL GENETICS – v1-32. 1967-94 – 1,5 – $80.00v – us UMI [612]

BIOCHEMICAL JOURNAL – v. 1-130. 1906-72 – 1,5,6 – us Princeton Micro [540]

BIOCHEMICAL JOURNAL – v.1-130. 1906-72 – 1 – us UMI [540]

BIOCHEMICAL JOURNAL. CELLULAR ASPECTS – (v.194-. 1981-. 5,6,9) – v.132-. 1973- – 1 – us UMI [540]

BIOCHEMICAL JOURNAL. MOLECULAR ASPECTS – (v.193-. 1981-. 5,6,9) – v.131-. 1973- – 1 – us UMI [540]

BIOCHEMICAL PHARMACOLOGY – v1- 1958- – 5,6,9 – us UMI [540]

BIOCHEMICAL SYSTEMATICS AND ECOLOGY – v1- 1973- – 5,6,9 – us UMI [574]

BIOCHEMISCHE ZEITSCHRIFT – v. 1-319. 1906-1949 – 1,5,6 – us Princeton Micro [540]

BIOCHEMISCHE ZEITSCHRIFT – v.268-346, 1934-67. Partly reprint. Former vols. incomplete – 1,5,9 – us UMI [073]

BIOCHEMISCHE ZEITSCHRIFT – Berlin, J Springer. v[310-312]. 1942 – us Res Libr [660]

BIOCHEMISCHE ZEITSCHRIFT BEITRAGE ZUR CHEMISCHEN PHYSIOLOGIE UND PATHOLOGIE – 1-318. 1906-48 – 1 – us UMI [520]

BIOCHEMISCHES HANDLEXIKON – v. 1-14. 1911-1933 – 1,5,6 – us Princeton Micro [540]

BIOCHEMISTRY – v1- 1962- – 1,5,6,9 – us A.C.S. [612]

BIOCHEMISTRY – (v41-59. 1976-94. $200.00v) – v21-40 1956-75 – 1,5 – $90.00v – us UMI [540]

BIOCHEMISTRY ABSTRACTS: PART 1: BIOLOGICAL MEMBRANES – 9 – us C.S.A. [540]

BIOCHEMISTRY ABSTRACTS: PART 2: NUCLEIC ACIDS – 9 – us C.S.A. [540]

BIOCHEMISTRY ABSTRACTS: PART 3: AMINO-ACIDS, PEPTIDES, PROTEINS – 9 – us C.S.A. [540]

BIOCHEMISTRY AND CELL BIOLOGY – (Cont: Canadian Journal of Biochemistry and Cellular Biology v64 1986) – Ottawa. v64-1986- – 9 – Price varies – cn Micromedia [073]

BIOCHEMISTRY AND CELLULAR BIOLOGY *see* CANADIAN JOURNAL OF BIOCHEMISTRY AND CELLULAR BIOLOGY

BIOCHIMICA ET BIOPHYSICA ACTA (BBA) – (General Subjects. Enzymology. Lipids and Lipid Metabolism. Nucleic Acids and Protein Synthesis. Protein Structure. Biomembranes. Bioenergetics. Reviews on Cancer. Reviews on Biomembranes. Reviews on Bioenergetics. Gene Structure and Expression. Protein Structure and Molecular Enzymology. Molecular Cell Research. Bioelectrochemistry and Bioenergetics) – v1-805. 1947-84 – 1,5,6,13 – sz Elsevier [574]

BIOCHIMIE – v1-61. 1914-79 – 1,5,6 – us Princeton Micro [073]

BIOCONJUGATE CHEMISTRY – v1- 1990- – 1,5,6,9 – us A.C.S. [660]

BIOCONTROL SCIENCE AND TECHNOLOGY – 1992- 3v – 9 – £176.00 – 0958-3157 – uk Carfax [570]

BIO-ECONOMIC MODEL OF SEQUENTIAL ARTISANAL AND INDUSTRIAL SHRIMP FISHERIES – 1985 – 56p – it F.A.O. [338]

BIOETHICS NORTHWEST – v.1. 1976-79 – 1,5,6,9 – us UMI [170]

BIOETHICS QUARTERLY – v.2-. 1980- – 1,5,6,9 – us UMI [170]

BIOFEEDBACK AND SELF REGULATION – v1-19. 1976-94 – 1,5 – $65.00v – us UMI [612]

BIOFOULING / ed by Evans, Len – 9,5,1 – us Harwood [574]

BIOGAS PROCESSES FOR SUSTAINABLE DEVELOPMENT – 1992 – 238p – it F.A.O. [660]

BIOGEOCHEMISTRY OF ESTAURINE SEDIMENTS : PROCEEDINGS OF A UNESCO/ SCOR WORKSHOP, MELREUX 1976 – 1978 – 293p – 9 – 92-3-101594-X – fr UNESCO [550]

BIOGEOGRAPHIE, BIOMETRIE ET BIOLOGIE DU SANDRE, LUCIOPERCA LUCIOPERCA (L.) OSTEICHTHYEN PERCIDE / Goubier, J – Lyon. 1975. 259p – 9 – F100.00 – fr Ethnologie [574]

BIOGRAFIA DE CACERES / Agundez Fernandez, Antonio – Villanueva de la Serena, 1957 – 1 – sp Bibl Santa Ana [920]

BIOGRAFIA DE FR. LUIS DE GRANADA...DEMUESTRA...AUTOR DEL LIBRO DE ORACION / Cuervo, Fray usto – 1896 – 9 – 1.50f – sp Bibl Santa Ana [920]

BIOGRAFIA DE LEXCMO. D. VICENTE BARRANTES / Cortijo Valdes, A – 1873 – 9 – $1.50f – sp Bibl Santa Ana [920]

BIOGRAFIA DE ROBERTO G. / Fernandez Molina, Antonio – Madrid, 1953 – 1 – sp Bibl Santa Ana [920]

BIOGRAFIA DOCUMENTADA / Lopez, Jose Maria et al; ed by Bayle, Constantino – Madrid: Razon y Fe, 1928 – 9 – sp Bibl Santa Ana [920]

BIOGRAFIA PATRIA : VISION RETROSPECTIVA Y CRITICA DEL RECIENTE PASADO ARGENTINO / Franco, Luis – Buenos Aires: Editorial Stilcograf, 1958 – 1 – CSUXADH0448-B – us Hoover Inst Photo [320]

BIOGRAFIA Y CRITICA DE D. JOSE ESPRONCEDA ISAGOGE / Munoz, Juan Antonio – Badajoz: Imprenta de la Diputacion Provincial, 1970 – sp Bibl Santa Ana [920]

BIOGRAFIAS. ANTONIO MAURA, DE TAXONERA, LA EMPERATRIZ EUGENIA, DE CABAL Y PEDRO DE ALVARADO, DE BARON CASTRO / Bayle, Constantino – Madrid: Razon y Fe, 1946 – 1 – sp Bibl Santa Ana [946]

BIOGRAFIAS BAYLE / Meseguer, Pedro – Madrid: Razon y Fe, 1944 – 1 – sp Bibl Santa Ana [920]

BIOGRAFIAS DE HOMBRES NOTABLES DE HISPANO-AMERICA / Azourua, Ramon – Caracas. 1877. 4v. (Historical Studies Series) – 9 – 6.00 – fr Bibl Nationale [900]

BIOGRAFICHESKII OCHERK V.G. ORLOVA / Orlov-Davydov, V – 2v. Spb. 1878. BR-7742 2 – 8 – ne IDC [920]

BIOGRAFICHESKII SLOVAR' STUDENTOV PERVYKH 27-MI KURSOV S.-PETERBURGSKOI DUKHOVNOI AKADEMII : K 100-LETIIU S-PETERBURGSKOI DUKHOVNOI AKADEMII – St Petersburg: Tip I V Leonteva, 1907 – 1 – us Res Libr [947]

THE BIOGRAPH – v1-2. 1914-15 – 1r – 1 – us Ross [770]

BIOGRAPHIANA. BY THE COMPILER OF ANECDOTES OF DISTINGUISHED PERSONS / Seward, William – London: Printed for J. Johnson, 1799. 2v in 1. illus – 1 – us U.W. Library [920]

BIOGRAPHIC REGISTER / U.S. Department of State – 1869 70-1910 – 1 – 38.00 – us L of C Photodup [324]

BIOGRAPHICAL AND BIBLIOGRAPHICAL DICTIONARY OF THE ITALIAN HUMANISTS AND OF THE WORLD OF CLASSICAL SCHOLARSHIP IN ITALY, 1300-1800 / Cosenza, Mario Emilio – (Suppl. vol., 1967.-5300 cards 1 reel. $120.00 ISBN: 0-8161-1490-0) – 1962.-67,900 cards 8 reels.-ISBN: 0-8161-1340-8 – 1 – $545.00 – uk Hall [920]

BIOGRAPHICAL AND BIBLIOGRAPHICAL DICTIONARY OF THE ITALIAN PRINTERS AND OF FOREIGN PRINTERS IN ITALY FROM THE INTRODUCTION OF THE ART OF PRINTING INTO ITALY TO 1800 / Cosenza, Mario Emilio – 1968.-12,200 entries 1 reel.-ISBN: 0-8161-1421-8 – 1 – $110.00 – uk Hall [010]

BIOGRAPHICAL AND DESCRIPTIVE WORKS ON THE REV. JOHN WESLEY : BIBLIOGRAPHY SUBMITTED IN PART REQUIREMENT FOR UNIVERSITY OF LONDON DIPLOMA IN LIBRARIANSHIP / Judson, S – 1963 – 3mf – 9 – ne IDC [240]

BIOGRAPHICAL AND GENEALOGICAL HISTORY OF APPANOOSE AND MONROE COUNTIES / Lewis, S Thompson – (Chicago: Lewis Publ. Co., 1903). Iowa Reel 6. (The Cox Library Collection) – 5 – us Americana [920]

BIOGRAPHICAL AND GENEALOGICAL HISTORY OF SOUTHEASTERN NEBRASKA – Chicago, n.d. 2v. Nebraska Reel 3. (The Cox Library Collection) – 5 – us Americana [978]

BIOGRAPHICAL AND GENEALOGICAL HISTORY OF THE CITY OF NEWARK AND ESSEX COUNTY – New York, 1898. Vols. 1-2. New Jersey Reel 3. (The Cox Library Collection) – 5 – us Americana [978]

BIOGRAPHICAL AND GENEALOGICAL HISTORY OF THE STATE OF DELAWARE / J.M. Runk and Co – Chambersburg, 1899. Vol 1, Delaware Reel 1; Vol 2, Delaware Reel 2. The Cox Library Collection – 5 – us Americana [978]

BIOGRAPHICAL AND GENEALOGICAL HISTORY OF WAYNE, FAYETTE, UNION AND FRANKLIN COUNTIES – Chicago, 1899. 2v. Indiana Reel 30. (The Cox Library Collection) – 5 – us Americana [920]

BIOGRAPHICAL AND GENEALOGICAL RECORD OF LA SALLE AND GRUNDY COUNTIES – Chicago, 1900. Vols. I and II (Illinois Reel 38). (The Cox Library Collection) – 5 – us Americana [978]

BIOGRAPHICAL AND GENEALOGICAL RECORD OF LA SALLE COUNTY – Chicago, 1900. Vols. I and II (Illinois Reel 37). (The Cox Library Collection) – 5 – us Americana [978]

BIOGRAPHICAL AND HISTORICAL CYCLOPEDIA OF WESTMORELAND COUNTY / John M. Gresham and Co – Philadelphia, 1890. Pennsylvania Reel 42. The Cox Library Collection – 5 – us Americana [978]

BIOGRAPHICAL AND HISTORICAL INDEX OF AMERICAN INDIANS AND PERSONS INVOLVED IN INDIAN AFFAIRS / U.S. Department of the Interior – 1966.-203,000 entries 8 reels.-ISBN: 0-8161-1548-6 – 1 – $940.00 – uk Hall [975]

BIOGRAPHICAL AND HISTORICAL MEMOIRS OF ADAMS, CLAY, HALL AND HAMILTON COUNTIES – Chicago, 1890. Nebraska Reel 5.(The Cox Library Collection) – 5 – us Americana [978]

BIOGRAPHICAL AND HISTORICAL MEMOIRS OF ADAMS, CLAY, WEBSTER AND NUCKOLLS COUNTIES – Chicago, 1890. Nebraska Reel 5.(The Cox Library Collection) – 5 – us Americana [978]

BIOGRAPHICAL AND HISTORICAL MEMOIRS OF EASTERN ARKANSAS – Chicago: 1890. Arkansas Reel 4. (The Cox Library Collection) – 5 – us Americana [978]

BIOGRAPHICAL AND HISTORICAL MEMOIRS OF ELKHART AND ST JOSEPH COUNTIES – Chicago, 1893. Indiana Reel 11. (The Cox Library Collection) – 5 – us Americana [978]

BIOGRAPHICAL AND HISTORICAL MEMOIRS OF LOUISIANA – Chicago, 1892. 2v. Louisiana Reel 1. (The Cox Library Collection) – 5 – us Americana [978]

BIOGRAPHICAL AND HISTORICAL MEMOIRS OF MUSKINGUM COUNTY – Chicago: 1892. Ohio Reel 51. (The Cox Library Collection) – 5 – us Americana [978]

BIOGRAPHICAL AND HISTORICAL MEMOIRS OF NORTHEAST ARKANSAS – 1889. History of state and each county with biog. sketches. 18 fiches. F-0012 – 9 – us A.G.L.L. [978]

BIOGRAPHICAL AND HISTORICAL MEMOIRS OF PULASKI, JEFFERSON, LONOKE, FAULKNER, GRANT, SALINE, PERRY, GARLAND AND HOT SPRINGS, ARKANSAS – Chicago: 1890. Arkansas Reel 4. (The Cox Library Collection) – 5 – us Americana [978]

BIOGRAPHICAL AND HISTORICAL MEMOIRS OF SOUTHERN ARKANSAS – Chicago: 1890. Arkansas Reel 3. (The Cox Library Collection) – 5 – us Americana [978]

BIOGRAPHICAL AND HISTORICAL RECORD OF GREENE AND CARROLL COUNTIES – Chicago: 1887. Iowa Reel 18. (The Cox Library Collection) – 5 – us Americana [978]

BIOGRAPHICAL AND HISTORICAL RECORD OF JAY AND BLACKFORD COUNTIES – Chicago, 1887. Indiana Reel 16. (The Cox Library Collection) – 5 – us Americana [978]

BIOGRAPHICAL AND HISTORICAL RECORD OF KOSCUISKO COUNTY – Chicago, 1887. Indiana Reel 18. (The Cox Library Collection) – 5 – us Americana [978]

BIOGRAPHICAL AND HISTORICAL RECORD OF PUTNAM COUNTY – Chicago, 1887. Indiana Reel 24. (The Cox Library Collection) – 5 – us Americana [920]

BIOGRAPHICAL AND HISTORICAL RECORD OF RINGGOLD AND DECATUR COUNTIES – Chicago: 1887. Iowa Reel 37. (The Cox Library Collection) – 5 – us Americana [978]

BIOGRAPHICAL AND HISTORICAL RECORD OF RINGGOLD AND UNION COUNTIES – Chicago: 1887. Iowa Reel 37. (The Cox Library Collection) – 5 – us Americana [978]

BIOGRAPHICAL AND HISTORICAL RECORD OF WAYNE AND APPANOOSE COUNTIES / Inter-State Publishing Co – Chicago, 1886. Iowa Reel 42. (The Cox Library Collection) – 5 – us Americana [978]

BIOGRAPHICAL AND HISTORICAL SKETCHES OF EARLY INDIANA / Woollen, William Wesley – Indianapolis: Hammond and Co., 1883. Indiana Reel 2. (The Cox Library Collection) – 5 – us Americana [978]

BIOGRAPHICAL AND HISTORICAL SOUVENIR FOR COUNTIES OF CLARK, CRAWFORD, HARRISON, FLOYD, JEFFERSON, JENNINGS, SCOTT AND WASHINGTON / John M. Gresham and Co – Chicago, 1889. Indiana Reel 7. The Cox Library Collection – 5 – us Americana [978]

BIOGRAPHICAL AND LITERARY NOTICES... / Carey, W – London, 1886 – 2mf – 9 – ne IDC [240]

BIOGRAPHICAL AND PICTORIAL HISTORY OF ARKANSAS / Hallien, John – (Albany: Weed, Parsons & Co., 1887). Arkansas Reel 1. (The Cox Library Collection) – 5 – us Americana [978]

BIOGRAPHICAL AND PORTRAIT CYCLOPEDIA OF CAMBRIA COUNTY – Philadelphia, 1896. Pennsylvania Reel 14. (The Cox Library Collection) – 5 – us Americana [978]

BIOGRAPHICAL AND PORTRAIT CYCLOPEDIA OF CHESTER COUNTY / Wiley, Samuel T – Philadelphia, Gresham Publ. Co., 1893. Pennsylvania Reel 16. (The Cox Library Collection) – 5 – us Americana [978]

BIOGRAPHICAL AND PORTRAIT CYCLOPEDIA OF FAYETTE COUNTY / Wiley, Samuel T – Chicago, John M. Gresham and Co., 1889. Pennsylvania Reel 22. (The Cox Library Collection) – 5 – us Americana [978]

BIOGRAPHICAL AND PORTRAIT CYCLOPEDIA OF NIAGARA COUNTY / Wiley & Garner – Philadelphia, Gresham Publ. Co., 1892. New York Reel 23. (The Cox Library Collection) – 5 – us Americana [978]

BIOGRAPHICAL AND PORTRAIT CYCLOPEDIA OF SCHUYLKILL COUNTY / Ruoff, Henry W – Philadelphia, Rush, West and Co., 1893. Pennsylvania Reel 37. (The Cox Library Collection) – 5 – us Americana [978]

BIOGRAPHICAL AND REMINISCENT HISTORY OF RICHLAND, CLAY AND MARION COUNTIES / B.F. Bowen and Co – Indianapolis, 1909. Illinois Reel 50. The Cox Library Collection – 5 – us Americana [978]

BIOGRAPHICAL ANNALS OF CUMBERLAND COUNTY / Genealogical Publishing Co – 1905. Pennsylvania Reel 18. (The Cox Library Collection) – 5 – us Americana [978]

BIOGRAPHICAL ANNALS OF LANCASTER COUNTY / J.H. Beers and Co – Chicago, 1903. Pennsylvania Reel 27. The Cox Library Collection – 5 – us Americana [978]

BIOGRAPHICAL ANNALS OF LEBANON COUNTY / J.H. Beers and Co – Chicago, 1904. Pennsylvania Reel 27. The Cox Library Collection – 5 – us Americana [978]

BIOGRAPHICAL ANNALS OF MONTGOMERY COUNTY / Roberts, Ellwood – New York, T. S. Benham and Lewis Publishing Co., 1904. Vols. 1-2. Pennsylvania Reel 33. (The Cox Library Collection) – 5 – us Americana [978]

BIOGRAPHICAL ANNALS OF OHIO – A HANDBOOK OF THE GOVERNMENT AND INSTITUTIONS OF THE STATE OF OHIO / Scobey & McElroy – 75th General Assembly, 1902-1903. Mississippi Reel 3. (The Cox Library Collection) – 5 – us Americana [978]

THE BIOGRAPHICAL CYCLOPEDIA AND PORTRAIT GALLERY WITH AN HISTORICAL SKETCH OF THE STATE OF OHIO / Western Biographical Publishing Co – Cincinnati: 1883. Vols. 1-4. Ohio Reel 2; Vols. 5-6. Ohio Reel 3. (The Cox Library Collection) – 5 – us Americana [978]

BIOGRAPHICAL CYCLOPEDIA OF MARYLAND AND DISTRICT OF COLUMBIA / National Biographical Publishing Co – Baltimore, MD, 1879. Maryland Reel 1. (The Cox Library Collection) – 5 – us Americana [978]

BIOGRAPHICAL CYCLOPEDIA OF THE COMMONWEALTH OF KENTUCKY / John M. Gresham and Co – Chicago, 1896. Kentucky Reel 5. The Cox Library Collection – 5 – us Americana [920]

BIOGRAPHICAL DATA AND ARMY RECORD OF OLD SOLDIERS WHO HAVE LIVED IN O'BRIEN CO., IOWA – Comp. by George W. Schee and O.H. Montzheimer. Survivors of the Civil War who lived in O'Brien County. 4 fiches. F-0139 – 9 – us A.G.L.L. [355]

BIOGRAPHICAL DATA FOR ELECTED OFFICERS AND MEMBERS OF BOARDS, COMMISSIONS, AND STANDING COMMITTEES / Southern Baptist Convention – Comp. by Historical Comm. in co-op. with the Public Relations Dir., SBC, Exec. Comm. Feb 1961. 1348p – 1 – us Baptist [240]

BIOGRAPHICAL DICTIONARY / Ibn Khallikan – 1842-71 – 1 – uk Microform Academic [920]

A BIOGRAPHICAL DICTIONARY OF EMINENT SCOTSMEN / Chambers, Robert – With suppl. vol. by Rev. Thomas Thomson.Edinburgh, London: Blackie and Son, 1859.5v – 1 – us U.W. Library [920]

BIOGRAPHICAL DICTIONARY OF PHILADELPHIA ARCHITECTS: 1700-1930 / Tatman, Sandra L & Moss, Roger W – 1984 – 1r – 1 – $99.50 export $120.00 – 0-8161-1561-3 – uk Hall [920]

BIOGRAPHICAL DICTIONARY OF REPRESENTATIVE MEN IN CHICAGO AND THE WORLD'S COLUMBIAN EXPOSITION – Chicago, 1892. Illinois Reel 19. (The Cox Library Collection) – 5 – us Americana [920]

BIOGRAPHICAL DIRECTORY OF THE U.S. CONGRESS, 1774-1989 : BICENTENNIAL EDITION – Washington: GPO, 1989 (all publ) – 22mf – 9 – $33.00 – LLMC 95-029 – us L.L.M.C. [323]

BIOGRAPHICAL DIRECTORY OF THE VOTERS AND TAXPAYERS OF KENDALL COUNTY, ILLINOIS / George Fisher and Co – Chicago, 1876. Illinois Reel 33. The Cox Library Collection – 5 – us Americana [978]

BIOGRAPHICAL ENCYCLOPAEDIA OF OHIO OF THE 19TH CENTURY / Galaxy Publishing Co – Cincinnati: 1876. Ohio Reel 1. (The Cox Library Collection) – 5 – us Americana [978]

THE BIOGRAPHICAL ENCYCLOPEDIA OF ILLINOIS OF THE NINETEENTH CENTURY / Galaxy Publishing Co – Philadelphia, 1875. Illinois Reel 5. (The Cox Library Collection) – 5 – us Americana [978]

BIOGRAPHICAL ENCYCLOPEDIA OF KENTUCKY / J.M. Armstrong and Company – Cincinnati, 1878. Kentucky Reel 4. The Cox Library Collection – 5 – us Americana [978]

BIOGRAPHICAL ENCYCLOPEDIA OF PENNSYLVANIA / Galaxy Publishing Co – Philadelphia, 1874. Pennsylvania Reel 5. (The Cox Library Collection) – 5 – us Americana [978]

BIOGRAPHICAL ENCYCLOPEDIA OF THE COMMONWEALTH OF KENTUCKY – Comp. by John M. Gresham. 1896.Indexed. 15 fiches. F-0152 – 9 – us A.G.L.L. [920]

BIOGRAPHICAL FILE OF AFRICAN LEADERS / Adloff, Virginia McLean – [Stanford, CA: Hoover Library, Stanford Uni, 1965?] – us Res Libr [960]

BIOGRAPHICAL HISTORY AND PORTRAIT GALLERY OF SCOTT COUNTY – Chicago: 1895. Iowa Reel 38. (The Cox Library Collection) – 5 – us Americana [978]

BIOGRAPHICAL HISTORY CLOUD COUNTY / Hollibaugh, E F – 1903. Kansas Reel 7. (The Cox Library Collection) – 5 – us Americana [978]

BIOGRAPHICAL HISTORY OF ATCHISON COUNTY / Stapel, H F – Rockport, 1905. Missouri Reel 8. (The Cox Library Collection) – 5 – us Americana [978]

BIOGRAPHICAL HISTORY OF CENTRAL KANSAS – Chicago, 1902. 2v. Kansas Reel 5. (The Cox Library Collection) – 5 – us Americana [978]

BIOGRAPHICAL HISTORY OF CHEROKEE COUNTY / W.S. Dunbar and Co – Chicago, 1889. Iowa Reel 10. The Cox Library Collection – 5 – us Americana [978]

BIOGRAPHICAL HISTORY OF CLARK AND JACKSON COUNTIES – Chicago: 1891. Wisconsin Reel 7. (The Cox Library Collection) – 5 – us Americana [978]

BIOGRAPHICAL HISTORY OF CLINTON COUNTY – Chicago, 1901. Iowa Reel 11. The Cox Library Collection – 5 – us Americana [978]

BIOGRAPHICAL HISTORY OF CRAWFORD, IDA AND SAC COUNTIES – Chicago: 1893. Iowa Reel 12. (The Cox Library Collection) – 5 – us Americana [978]

BIOGRAPHICAL HISTORY OF DARKE COUNTY – Chicago, 1900. Ohio Reel 28. (The Cox Library Collection) – 5 – us Americana [978]

A BIOGRAPHICAL HISTORY OF EMINENT & SELF-MADE MEN OF THE STATE OF INDIANA – 1880. 2v. Indexed. F-0291,0292 – 9 – us A.G.L.L. [920]

A BIOGRAPHICAL HISTORY OF FREMONT AND MILLS COUNTIES – Chicago: 1901. Iowa Reel 18. (The Cox Library Collection) – 5 – us Americana [978]

BIOGRAPHICAL HISTORY OF GENESEE COUNTY / B.F. Bowen and Co – Indianapolis. Michigan Reel 9. The Cox Library Collection – 5 – us Americana [978]

BIOGRAPHICAL HISTORY OF LA CROSSE, MONROE, AND JUNEAU COUNTIES – Chicago: 1892. Wisconsin Reel 12. (The Cox Library Collection) – 5 – us Americana [978]

BIOGRAPHICAL HISTORY OF LA CROSSE TREMPELEAN AND BUFFALO COUNTIES – Chicago: 1892. Wisconsin Reel 13. (The Cox Library Collection) – 5 – us Americana [978]

A BIOGRAPHICAL HISTORY OF NODAWAY AND ATCHISON COUNTIES – Chicago, 1901. Missouri Reel 26. (The Cox Library Collection) – 5 – us Americana [978]

BIOGRAPHICAL HISTORY OF NORTHEASTERN OHIO – Chicago, 1893. Ohio Reel 14. (The Cox Library Collection) – 5 – us Americana [978]

BIOGRAPHICAL HISTORY OF PAGE COUNTY / Lewis and Dunbar, Publishers – Chicago, 1890. Iowa Reel 32. The Cox Library Collection – 5 – us Americana [978]

BIOGRAPHICAL HISTORY OF POTTAWATAMIE COUNTY – Chicago: 1891. Iowa Reel 35. (The Cox Library Collection) – 5 – us Americana [978]

A BIOGRAPHICAL HISTORY OF PREBLE COUNTY – Chicago: 1900. Ohio Reel 54. (The Cox Library Collection) – 5 – us Americana [978]

BIOGRAPHICAL HISTORY OF PRIMITIVE OR OLD SCHOOL BAPTIST MINISTERS OF THE UNITED STATES / Pittman, R H – 1909 – 1 – 14.28 – us Baptist [240]

BIOGRAPHICAL HISTORY OF SHELBY AND AUDUBON COUNTIES / W.S. Dunbar and Co – Chicago, 1889. Iowa Reel 39. The Cox Library Collection – 5 – us Americana [978]

BIOGRAPHICAL HISTORY OF THE AMERICAN IRISH IN CHICAGO / French, Charles – Chicago: American Biographical Publ. Co., 1897. Illinois Reel 20. (The Cox Library Collection) – 5 – us Americana [978]

A BIOGRAPHICAL HISTORY OF THE EBY FAMILY: BEING A HISTORY OF THEIR MOVEMENTS IN EUROPE DURING THE REFORMATION: AND THEIR EARLY SETTLEMENT IN AMERICA: AS ALSO MUCH OTHER UNPUBLISHED HISTORICAL INFORMATION BELONGING TO THE FAMILY / Eby, Ezra E – s.l.: s.n., 1889 (Berlin, Ont.: Hett & Eby). 05213. (Pre-1900 Canadiana) – 9 – cn C.I.H.M. [971]

BIOGRAPHICAL INDEX TO THE CENTENNIAL HISTORY OF ARKANSAS – Comp. by Mrs. Leister E. Presley. Complete index to v2-3. 1 fiche. F-0011 – 9 – us A.G.L.L. [920]

BIOGRAPHICAL MAGAZINE – v. 1-7. 1852-1855 – 1,5,6 – us Princeton Micro [920]

BIOGRAPHICAL MANUAL OF THE MEMBERS AND OFFICERS OF THE 20TH LEGISLATURE OF NEBRASKA / Hall, C L – Lincoln: Journal Co., State Printers, 1887. Nebraska Reel 4. (The Cox Library Collection) – 5 – us Americana [978]

BIOGRAPHICAL MATERIALS / Buck, William Calmes – 1790-1872. 184p – 1 – 6.44 – us Baptist [920]

BIOGRAPHICAL MATERIALS, CORRESPONDENCE, SERMONS / Eaton, Thomas Treadwell – 26,338p – 1 – $921.83 – us Baptist [240]

A BIOGRAPHICAL MEMOIR OF SAMUEL HARTLIB : MILTON'S FAMILIAR FRIEND / Dircks, H – London: J.R. Smith, [1865?] – 1mf – us A.T.L.A. [240]

A BIOGRAPHICAL MEMOIR OF THE LATE SIR PETER PARKER, BARONET, CAPTAIN OF HIS MAJESTY'S SHIP MENELAUS, OF 38 GUNS, KILLED IN ACTION WHILE STORMING THE AMERICAN CAMP AT BELLAIR, NEAR BALTIMORE, ON THE THIRTY-FIRST OF AUGUST, 1814 / Dallas, George – 1815 – 9 – uk Libr Preservation [920]

BIOGRAPHICAL MEMOIRS : BEING A RECORD OF THE CHRISTIAN LIVES, EXPERIENCES, AND DEATHS OF MEMBERS OF THE RELIGIOUS SOCIETY OF FRIENDS FROM ITS RISE TO 1653 / Backhouse, Edward – London: W. and F.G. Cash, 1854 – 1mf – us A.T.L.A. [240]

BIOGRAPHICAL MEMOIRS OF GRANT COUNTY / A.W. Bowen and Co – Chicago, 1901. Indiana Reel 13. The Cox Library Collection – 5 – us Americana [978]

BIOGRAPHICAL MEMOIRS OF GRATIOT COUNTY / J.H. Beers and Co – Chicago, 1906. Michigan Reel 10. The Cox Library Collection – 5 – us Americana [978]

BIOGRAPHICAL MEMOIRS OF WYANDOT COUNTY / B.F. Bowen and Co – Logansport, 1902. Ohio Reel 69. The Cox Library Collection – 5 – us Americana [978]

BIOGRAPHICAL NOTES UPON BOTANISTS / New York Botanical Garden. Library – John Hendley Barnhart, comp., 1965.-44,700 cards 6 reels.-ISBN: 0-8161-1342-4 – 1 – $370.00 – uk Hall [580]

BIOGRAPHICAL NOTICES OF DISTINGUISHED MEN IN NEW ENGLAND: STATESMEN, PATRIOTS, PHYSICIANS, LAWYERS, CLERGMEN & MECHANICS – By Alden Bradford, 1842.Indexed. 7 fiches. F-0627 – 9 – us A.G.L.L. [978]

BIOGRAPHICAL NOTICES OF PERSIAN POETS / Ouseley, Gore – 1846 – 1 – uk Microform Academic [920]

BIOGRAPHICAL & PICTORIAL HISTORY / Hallum, John – v1, 1887. 11 fiches. F-0013 – 9 – us A.G.L.L. [978]

BIOGRAPHICAL RECORD AND PORTRAIT ALBUM OF TIPPECANOE COUNTY – Chicago, 1888. Indiana Reel 27. (The Cox Library Collection) – 5 – us Americana [920]

BIOGRAPHICAL RECORD AND PORTRAIT ALBUM OF WEBSTER AND HAMILTON COUNTIES – Chicago, 1888. Iowa Reel 42. (The Cox Library Collection) – 5 – us Americana [978]

BIOGRAPHICAL RECORD OF BARTHOLOMEW COUNTY / B.F. Bowen and Co – Including biographies of the governors and other representative citizens of Indiana. Indianapolis, 1964. Indiana Reel 5. The Cox Library Collection – 5 – us Americana [978]

THE BIOGRAPHICAL RECORD OF BUREAU, MARSHALL AND PUTNAM COUNTIES, ILLINOIS – Chicago, 1896. Illinois Reel 13. The Cox Library Collection – 5 – us Americana [978]

BIOGRAPHICAL RECORD OF CALHOUN COUNTY – Chicago, 1902. Iowa Reel 8. The Cox Library Collection – 5 – us Americana [978]

BIOGRAPHICAL RECORD OF CHAMPAIGN COUNTY – Chicago, 1900. Illinois Reel 14. The Cox Library Collection – 5 – us Americana [978]

A BIOGRAPHICAL RECORD OF CLARK COUNTY – Chicago, 1902. Ohio Reel 19. The Cox Library Collection – 5 – us Americana [978]

BIOGRAPHICAL RECORD OF COWLEY COUNTY – Chicago, 1901. Kansas Reel 7. (The Cox Library Collection) – 5 – us Americana [978]

BIOGRAPHICAL RECORD OF DE KALB COUNTY – Chicago, 1898. Illinois Reel 21. The Cox Library Collection – 5 – us Americana [978]

BIOGRAPHICAL RECORD OF DE WITT COUNTY – Chicago, 1901. Illinois Reel 23. The Cox Library Collection – 5 – us Americana [978]

BIOGRAPHICAL RECORD OF FAIRFIELD COUNTY – Chicago, 1902. Ohio Reel 30. The Cox Library Collection – 5 – us Americana [978]

BIOGRAPHICAL RECORD OF HENRY COUNTY – Chicago, 1901. Illinois Reel 27. The Cox Library Collection – 5 – us Americana [978]

BIOGRAPHICAL RECORD OF HOUGHTON, BARAGO AND MARQUETTE COUNTIES – Chicago: 1903. Michigan Reel 11. (The Cox Library Collection) – 5 – us Americana [978]

BIOGRAPHICAL RECORD OF JASPER COUNTY / McGregor, Malcolm – Chicago: Lewis Publ. Co., 1901. Missouri Reel 21. (The Cox Library Collection) – 5 – us Americana [978]

BIOGRAPHICAL RECORD OF JOHNSON, POWESHIEK AND IOWA COUNTIES – Chicago: 1895. Iowa Reel 24. (The Cox Library Collection) – 5 – us Americana [978]

BIOGRAPHICAL RECORD OF KANE COUNTY – Chicago, 1898. Illinois Reel 31. The Cox Library Collection – 5 – us Americana [978]

BIOGRAPHICAL RECORD OF KANE COUNTY – Chicago, 1898. Illinois Reel 31. The Cox Library Collection – 5 – us Americana [978]

THE BIOGRAPHICAL RECORD OF KNOX COUNTY – Chicago: 1902. Ohio Reel 41. (The Cox Library Collection) – 5 – us Americana [978]

BIOGRAPHICAL RECORD OF LINN COUNTY – Chicago, 1901. Iowa Reel 26. The Cox Library Collection – 5 – us Americana [978]

BIOGRAPHICAL RECORD OF MCLEAN COUNTY – Chicago, 1899. Illinois Reel 45. The Cox Library Collection – 5 – us Americana [978]

BIOGRAPHICAL RECORD OF OGLE COUNTY – Chicago, 1899. Illinois Reel 47. The Cox Library Collection – 5 – us Americana [978]

BIOGRAPHICAL RECORD OF ROCK ISLAND COUNTY – Chicago, 1897. Illinois Reel 51. The Cox Library Collection – 5 – us Americana [978]

BIOGRAPHICAL RECORD OF SALT LAKE CITY AND VICINITY – Chicago, 1902. Utah reel 4. (Cox Library Collection) – 5 – us Americana [978]

BIOGRAPHICAL RECORD OF SAN JOAQUIN COUNTY – San Joaquin Co, CA. 1905 – 1r – 1 – $50.00 – D089 – us Library Micro [920]

BIOGRAPHICAL RECORD OF SCHUYLER COUNTY – New York, 1903. New York Reel 34. The Cox Library Collection – 5 – us Americana [978]

BIOGRAPHICAL RECORD OF SEDGWICK COUNTY – Chicago, 1901. Kansas Reel 11. (The Cox Library Collection) – 5 – us Americana [978]

BIOGRAPHICAL RECORD OF THE CITY OF ROCHESTER AND MONROE COUNTY – New York, 1902. New York Reel 22. The Cox Library Collection – 5 – us Americana [978]

BIOGRAPHICAL RECORD OF WHITESIDE COUNTY – Chicago, 1900. Illinois Reel 60. The Cox Library Collection – 5 – us Americana [978]

BIOGRAPHICAL REGISTER OF THE OFFICERS AND GRADUATES OF THE U.S. MILITARY ACADEMY AT WEST POINT, NY FROM ITS ESTABLISHMENT IN 1802, TO 1890 / Cullum, George Washington – With the early history of the United States Military Academy. Boston and New York: Houghton, Mifflin and Co., 1891.v1-5. Military Books reel 1. (Cox Library Collection) – 5 – us Americana [920]

Biographical Research Association *see* THE BLUE BOOK OF TOPEKA, 1910

BIOGRAPHICAL REVIEW OF BELKNAP AND STRAFFORD COUNTIES – Boston, 1897. New Hampshire Reel 2. (The Cox Library Collection) – 5 – us Americana [978]

BIOGRAPHICAL REVIEW OF CALHOUN COUNTY / Hobart & Mather – Historical, biographical and genealogical sketches. Chicago, 1904. Michigan Reel 7. (The Cox Libary Collection) – 5 – us Americana [920]

BIOGRAPHICAL REVIEW OF CAMDEN AND BURLINGTON COUNTIES – Boston, 1897. New Jersey Reel 1. (The Cox Library Collection) – 5 – us Americana [978]

BIOGRAPHICAL REVIEW OF CASS, SCHUYLER AND BROWN COUNTIES – Chicago, 1892. Illinois Reel 14. (The Cox Library Collection) – 5 – us Americana [978]

BIOGRAPHICAL REVIEW OF CUMBERLAND COUNTY – Biographical sketches of leading citizens. Boston, 1896. New Jersey Reel 2. (The Cox Library Collection) – 5 – us Americana [978]

BIOGRAPHICAL REVIEW OF CUMBERLAND COUNTY – Boston, 1896. Maine Reel 3. (The Cox Library Collection) – 5 – us Americana [978]

BIOGRAPHICAL REVIEW OF DANE COUNTY – Chicago: 1893. Wisconsin Reel 9. (The Cox Library Collection) – 5 – us Americana [978]

BIOGRAPHICAL REVIEW OF DES MOINES COUNTY / Hobart Publishing Co – Chicago: 1905. Iowa Reel 14. (The Cox Library Collection) – 5 – us Americana [978]

BIOGRAPHICAL REVIEW OF ESSEX COUNTY – Life sketches of leading citizens. Boston, 1898. Massachusetts Reel 4. (The Cox Library Collection) – 5 – us Americana [978]

BIOGRAPHICAL REVIEW OF HANCOCK COUNTY / Hobart Publishing Co – Chicago, 1907. (Illinois Reel 27). (The Cox Library Collection) – 5 – us Americana [978]

BIOGRAPHICAL REVIEW OF HENRY COUNTY / Hobart Publishing Co – Chicago: 1906. Iowa Reel 20. (The Cox Library Collection) – 5 – us Americana [978]

BIOGRAPHICAL REVIEW OF LEADING CITIZENS OF CAYUGA COUNTY – Boston, 1894. New York Reel 10. (The Cox Library Collection) – 5 – us Americana [978]

BIOGRAPHICAL REVIEW OF LEADING CITIZENS OF COLUMBIA COUNTY – Boston, 1894. New York Reel 13. (The Cox Library Collection) – 5 – us Americana [978]

BIOGRAPHICAL REVIEW OF LEADING CITIZENS OF DELAWARE COUNTY – Boston, 1895. New York Reel 13. (The Cox Library Collection) – 5 – us Americana [978]

BIOGRAPHICAL REVIEW OF LEADING CITIZENS OF FRANKLIN AND OXFORD COUNTIES – Boston, 1897. Maine Reel 3. (The Cox Library Collection) – 5 – us Americana [978]

BIOGRAPHICAL REVIEW OF LIVINGSTON AND WYOMING COUNTIES – Boston, 1895. New York Reel 21. (The Cox Library Collection) – 5 – us Americana [978]

BIOGRAPHICAL REVIEW OF MERRIMACK AND SULLIVAN COUNTIES – Boston, 1897. New Hampshire Reel 6. (The Cox Library Collection) – 5 – us Americana [978]

BIOGRAPHICAL REVIEW OF OTSEGO COUNTY – Biographical sketches. Boston, 1893. New York Reel 30. (The Cox Library Collection) – 5 – us Americana [978]

BIOGRAPHICAL REVIEW OF SCHOHARIE, SCHENECTADY, AND GREENE COUNTIES – Life sketches. Boston, 1899. New York Reel 33. (The Cox Library Collection) – 5 – us Americana [978]

BIOGRAPHICAL REVIEW, YORK COUNTY, MAINE – Boston, 1896. Maine Reel 4. (The Cox Library Collection) – 5 – us Americana [978]

BIOGRAPHICAL SKETCH OF JOANNE BETHUNE / Bethune, Joanne – 1768 – 1 – 5.00 – us Baptist [240]

A BIOGRAPHICAL SKETCH OF SIR ANTHONY PANIZZI...LATE PRINCIPAL LIBRARIAN, BRITISH MUSEUM / Cowtan, Robert – London: Asher, 1873. 87p – 1 – us U.W. Library [920]

A BIOGRAPHICAL SKETCH OF SIR N. F. BELLEAU / Fry, Henry – Quebec: s.n., 1894 (Quebec: A. Cote). 03265. (Pre-1900 Canadiana) – 9 – cn C.I.H.M. [971]

BIOGRAPHICAL SKETCH OF TENNESSEE BAPTIST MINISTERS / Borum, Joseph H – 1880 – 1 – 22.54 – us Baptist [240]

BIOGRAPHICAL SKETCHES, 1852-1875 / Martineau, Harriet – London: Macmillan, 4th ed 1885 – 1 roll – 1 – 1-55879-446-8 – uk Libr Preservation [920]

BIOGRAPHICAL SKETCHES; BEING MEMORIALS OF ARTHUR PENRHYN STANLEY... HENRY ALFORD...MRS. DUNCAN STEWART, ETC / Hare, Augustus John Cuthbert – London: G. Allen; New York: Dodd, Mead, 1895. vi,209p. illus – 1 – us U.W. Library [920]

BIOGRAPHICAL SKETCHES OF CHINESE COMMUNIST MILITARY LEADERS / U.S. Office of the Chief of Military History – 1 – 18.00 – us L of C Photodup [950]

BIOGRAPHICAL SKETCHES OF LOYALISTS OF THE AMERICAN REVOLUTION : WITH AN HISTORICAL ESSAY / Lorenzo, Sabine – Boston: Little, Brown, c1864 – 3mf – us A.T.L.A. [975]

BIOGRAPHICAL SKETCHES OF OUR PULPIT / Carter, E R – 1856-88 – 1 – 10.25 – us Baptist [240]

BIOGRAPHICAL SKETCHES OF SOME OF THOSE PREACHERS WHOSE LABOURS CONTRIBUTED TO THE ORIGINATION AND EARLY EXTENSION OF THE PRIMITIVE METHODIST CONNEXION / Herod, G – London, [1855] – 6mf – 9 – ne IDC [240]

BIOGRAPHICAL SKETCHES OF THE DELEGATES FROM GEORGIA TO THE CONTINENTAL CONGRESS / Jones, Charles C, Jr – 1891. 4 fiches.F-0089 – 9 – us A.G.L.L. [920]

BIOGRAPHICAL SKETCHES OF THE FATHERS OF NEW ENGLAND / Clark, Mary – 1836 – 1 – $50.00 – us Presbyterian [920]

BIOGRAPHICAL SKETCHES OF THE FOUNDER AND PRINCIPAL ALUMNI OF THE LOG COLLEGE : TOGETHER WITH AN ACCOUNT OF THE REVIVALS OF RELIGION UNDER THEIR MINISTRY / Alexander, Archibald – Philadelphia: Presbyterian Board of Publication, c1851 – 1mf – us A.T.L.A. [240]

BIOGRAPHICAL SKETCHES OF THE LEADING MEN OF CHICAGO / Wilson & St Clair – Chicago: 1868. Illinois Reel 18. (The Cox Library Collection) – 5 – us Americana [978]

BIOGRAPHICAL SKETCHES OF THE LIVES AND PUBLIC MINISTRY OF VARIOUS HOLY WOMEN,...IN WHICH ARE INCLUDED SEVERAL LETTERS FROM THE REV. J. WESLEY NEVER BEFORE PUBLISHED / Taft, Z – London. 2v. 1825-1828 – 8mf – 9 – ne IDC [240]

BIOGRAPHICAL SOUVENIR OF THE COUNTIES OF BUFFALO, KEARNEY AND PHELPS / F.A. Battey and Co – Chicago, 1890. Nebraska Reel 5.(The Cox Library Collection) – 5 – us Americana [978]

BIOGRAPHICAL SOUVENIR OF THE COUNTIES OF BUFFALO, KEARNEY, PHELPS, HARLAN AND FRANKLIN / F.A. Battey and Co – Chicago, 1890. Nebraska Reel 6.(The Cox Library Collection) – 5 – us Americana [978]

BIOGRAPHICAL SOUVENIR OF THE STATE OF TEXAS / F.A. Battey and Co – Chicago, 1889. Texas Reel 5. (The Cox Library Collection) – 5 – us Americana [978]

BIOGRAPHICAL STORY OF THE CONSTITUTION : A STUDY OF THE GROWTH OF THE AMERICAN UNION / Elliot, Edward – New York, London: G P Putnam's Sons, 1910 – 5mf – 9 – $7.50 – LLMC 95-091 – us L.L.M.C. [323]

BIOGRAPHICAL STUDIES / Bagehot, Walter; ed by Holt Hutton, Richard – London, New York: Longmans, Green, 2nd ed 1889 – 1 roll – 1 – 1-55879-790-4 – uk Libr Preservation [920]

BIOGRAPHIE AVEC PORTRAIT DE M. L'ABBE MERCIER / David, Laurent Olivier – s.l.: s.n., 1875 (Montreal?: Le bien public). 04205. (Pre-1900 Canadiana) – 9 – cn C.I.H.M. [971]

BIOGRAPHIE D'ABDEL-KADER : CONSIDERATIONS QUI L'ONT AMENE A NOUS DECLARER LA GUERRE – [Paris?]: Service historique de l'Armee, [19–] – us Res Libr [920]

BIOGRAPHIE DE LA FAMILLE DENECHAUD – Quebec: Commerciale, 1895. 04038. (Pre-1900 Canadiana) – 9 – cn C.I.H.M. [920]

BIOGRAPHIE DE M. FRANCOIS VEZINA, CAISSIER DE LA BANQUE NATIONALE / Bechard, Auguste – St. Roche de Quebec: Ateliers du Nouvelliste, 1878. 03028. (Pre-1900 Canadiana) – 9 – cn C.I.H.M. [920]

BIOGRAPHIE DE SIR N.F. BELLEAU: CHEVALIER COMMANDEUR DE L'ORDRE DE SAINT-MICHEL ET DE SAINT-GEORGES, ET PREMIER LIEUTENANT-GOUVERNEUR DE LA PROVINCE DE QUEBEC, SOUS LA CONFEDERATION DES PROVINCES DE L'AMERIQUE DU NORD / Drapeau, Stanislas – Quebec?: s.n., 1893 (Quebec: L. Brousseau). 02759. (Pre-1900 Canadiana) – 9 – cn C.I.H.M. [971]

BIOGRAPHIE DES HOMMES VIVANTS, OU HISTOIRE PAR ORDRE ALPHABETIQUE... – Paris. 5v. 1816-19 – 31mf – H-3028/1 – ne IDC [920]

BIOGRAPHIE DU GENERAL MONTHOLON – [Paris 1849?] – us Res Libr [920]

BIOGRAPHIE ET GALERIE HISTORIQUE DES CONTEMPORAINS... / ed by Barthelmy, M P – Paris. 2v. 1822 – 12mf – 9 – H-3029/1 – ne IDC [920]

BIOGRAPHIE TOURANGELLE / Touraine – 19th cent. 2v – 1 – F419.37 – fr Armell [920]

BIOGRAPHIE UNIVERSELLE / ed by Michaud, L G – Paris. 45v. 1843-65 – 340mf – 1 – 8839/1 – ne IDC [920]

BIOGRAPHIES DE A.S. FALARDEAU ET A.E. AUBRY / Casgrain, Henri-Raymond – Montreal: Beauchemin et Valois, 1886. SEM16P10 – 1r – 5 – Can$9.00 – cn Bibl Nat [920]

BIOGRAPHIES DE A.S. FALARDEAU ET A.E. AUBRY / Casgrain, Henri-Raymond – Montreal: Beauchemin & Valois, 1886. 03021. (Pre-1900 Canadiana) – 9 – cn C.I.H.M. [920]

BIOGRAPHIES DE L'HONORABLE BARTHELEMI JOLIETTE ET DE M. LE GRAND VICAIRE A. MENSEAU / Bonin, Joseph – Montreal: E. Senecal, 1874. 02109. (Pre-1900 Canadiana) – 9 – cn C.I.H.M. [920]

LES BIOGRAPHIES DU MANHAL SAFI / Wiet, G – Cairo, 1932 – 6mf – 9 – ne IDC [956]

BIOGRAPHIES OF FELLOWS, AMERICAN ACADEMY OF PHYSICAL EDUCATION / Clarke, Henry Harrison – 1953 – 3mf – 9 – $9.00 – us Microform Publ [790]

BIOGRAPHIES OF FORMER GREENVILLE COUNTY PHYSICIANS – South Carolina. 151p – 1 – us Baptist [610]

BIOGRAPHIES OF THE STATE OFFICERS AND THIRTY-SECOND GENERAL ASSEMBLY OF ILLINOIS – Springfield, 1883. Illinois Reel 8. (The Cox Library Collection) – 5 – us Americana [978]

BIOGRAPHIES OF WEST GERMAN POLITICIANS: PAMPHLET COLLECTION – 1962-1989 – 3r – 1 – CSUXANS2516-B – us Hoover Inst Photo [320]

BIOGRAPHISCHE DENKMALE / Varnhagen von Ense, Karl August – 2. verm. und verb. Aufl. Berlin: G Reimer, 1845-1846 – 1 – us U.W. Library [943]

BIOGRAPHISCHES JAHRBUCH UND DEUTSCHER NEKROLOG – Berlin, G. Reimer. 1897-1917. v.1-18; 1896-1913. Includes index v.1-10, 1896-1905. Title varies. Film Mas C 685 – 1 – us H.U. Library [920]

BIOGRAPHISCHES LEXIKON / ed by Wurzbach, C von – Wien. v1-60. 1856-1891 – 299mf – 9 – 8762/1 – ne IDC [920]

BIOGRAPHISCHES LEXIKON DER HERVORRAGENDEN AERZTE ALLER ZEITEN UND VOELKER / ed by Gurlt, E – (Includes a supplement) – Berlin, Wien, Ed.2 1929-1935. 5v – 60mf – 9 – ne IDC [610]

BIOGRAPHISCHES LEXIKON FUER DAS GEBIET ZWISCHEN INN UND SALZACH / Fuerst, Max – Muenchen, 1901. Hildesheim, 1983 – 3mf – 9 – DM36.00 diazo DM42.00 silver – gw Olms [920]

BIOGRAPHISCH-LITERARISCHES HANDWOERTERBUCH ZUR GESCHICHTE DER EXACTEN WISSENSCHAFTEN / ed by Poggendorff, J C – Leipzig. v1-6. 1863-1940 – 101mf – 8701/1 – ne IDC [920]

BIOGRAPHISCH-LITERARISCHES LEXIKON DER KATHOLISCHEN DEUTSCHEN DICHTER, VOLKS-UND JUNGENDSCHRIFTSTELLER IM 19. JAHRHUNDERT / Kehrein, Josef – Zuerich, Stuttgart und Wuerzburg, 1868-71. Hildesheim, 1983 – 8mf – 9 – DM70.00 diazo DM80.00 silver – gw Olms [430]

BIOGRAPHY / Allston, Joseph Blyth – 1900. "Life and times of James L. Petigru." from the Sunday News of Charleston, Jan 21-June 17. 1 fiche – 9 – us South Carolina Historical [920]

BIOGRAPHY / Chang-chi-chih – (Chang-chi-chih hsien-sheng chuan-chi). Comp. by Chang-hsiao-jo. 1930. 682p. 1 reel – 1 – 32.50 – ch Transmission [920]

BIOGRAPHY INDEX – 71mf – 9 – A$320.00 – at State Libr Vic [920]

BIOGRAPHY OF BARON DEKALB GRAY / Seay, Warren Mosby – 1 – 10.78 – us Baptist [240]

THE BIOGRAPHY OF ELD. BARTON WARREN STONE / Stone, Barton W – Cincinnati: J.A. & U.P. James, 1847, c1846 – 1mf – us A.T.L.A. [240]

BIOGRAPHY OF GOSPEL SONG AND HYMN WRITERS / Hall, J H – New York: F.H. Revell, c1914 – 1mf – us A.T.L.A. [780]

BIOGRAPHY OF IOWA INDIANS OF KANSAS AND NEBRASKA FROM 1880-96 / Nuzum, George – 1 – us KS Hist [978]

BIOGRAPHY OF REV. HOSEA BALLOU / Ballou, Maturin M – Boston: A. Tompkins, 1852 – 1mf – us A.T.L.A. [240]

BIOGRAPHY OF WILLIAM SHERMAN WILEY / Derigo, G A – 1867-1935 – 1 – $5.00 – us Baptist [240]

BIOIMAGING / ed by Jovin, Tom – Bristol, UK: 10P Publishing, 1993.-v1 – 1,5,6,9 – £95.00 – uk I.O.P. [621]

BIOKHIMIIA – [Moskva]: Obedinennoe nauchno-tekhnicheskoe izd-vo. v15-16 (1950-1951). v17 n2 (1952) – us Res Libr [660]

BIOLA BROADCASTER – Biola, CA. 1961-1973 – 3r – 1 – $150.00 – R04007 – us Library Micro [071]

THE BIOLA CHIMES – Biola, CA. 1938-1990 – 7r – 1 – $350.00 – B06015 – us Library Micro [071]

BIOLAW : A LEGAL AND ETHICAL REPORTER ON MEDICINE, HEALTH CARE, AND ENGINEERING – 1986-1995 – 9 – $995.00 – us UPA [340]

BIOLOGIA CENTRALI AMERICANA : ZOOLOGY – London, 1879-1915. v1-52 – 801mf – 2423/2 – ne IDC [590]

BIOLOGICAL ABSTRACTS : REPORTS, REVIEWS, MEETINGS, FIVE YEAR COLLECTIVE INDEXES – Philadelphia: BIOSIS, 1980-1984. Vol 18-27 – 9 – $1,000.00 – us BIOSIS [574]

BIOLOGICAL ABSTRACTS FIVE-YEAR COLLECTIVE INDEXES – (Vol 79-88 (1985-89)) – Philadelphia, BIOSIS, 1985-1989 – 10r – 5,6 – us BIOSIS [574]

BIOLOGICAL ABSTRACTS IN MICROFORM – (Abstracts vol 1-92, 1927-92. $45,755.00; Indexes vol 1-33, 1927-1959. $1,000.00) – Philadelphia: BIOSIS, 1926-1992 – 5,6 – $5,350.00 vol 93-94 (1992) – us BIOSIS [574]

BIOLOGICAL BULLETIN – v1-113. 1899-1957 – 1,5,6 – us Princeton Micro [574]

BIOLOGICAL CHEMISTRY HOPPE-SEYLER – v366-. Jan 1985- – 1,5,6,9 – us UMI [073]

BIOLOGICAL CONSERVATION – v1-30. 1968-84 – 1,5,6,13 – sz Elsevier [333]

BIOLOGICAL CYBERNETICS – v. 1-38. 1961-80 – 1,5,9 – 3420.00 – us UMI [574]

BIOLOGICAL MEMBRANES / ed by Chizmadzhev – 1,5,9 – us Gordon [574]

BIOLOGICAL OCEANOGRAPHY JOURNAL – v.1-. 1981- – 1,5,6,9 – us UMI [574]

BIOLOGICAL PSYCHOLOGY – v1-19. 1973-84 – 1,5,6,13 – sz Elsevier [073]

THE BIOLOGICAL REVIEW MAGAZINE – London, 1858-59. v1, nos. 1-4 – 3 – us Readex [574]

THE BIOLOGICAL REVIEW OF ONTARIO – Toronto: Biological Society of Ontario, [1894] – 9 – cn C.I.H.M. [574]

BIOLOGICAL REVIEWS / Cambridge Philosophical Society – (1985-. 5,6,9) – v10-. 1935- – 1 – us UMI [574]

BIOLOGICAL REVIEWS : PROCEEDINGS OF THE CAMBRIDGE PHILOSOPHICAL SOCIETY – Cambridge, 1923-1941. v1-16 – 133mf – 2217c/2 – ne IDC [574]

BIOLOGICAL REVIEWS AND BIOLOGICAL PROCEEDINGS / Cambridge Philosophical Society – v2-9. 1926-34 – 1 – us UMI [574]

Biological Sciences Curriculum Study *see* JOURNAL

BIOLOGICAL SCIENCES CURRICULUM STUDY JOURNAL *see* BSCS NEWSLETTER

BIOLOGICAL SIGNALS – v2-. 1993- – us UMI [574]

BIOLOGICAL STUDY OF THE TAP WATER IN THE SCHOOL OF PRACTICAL SCIENCE, TORONTO / Acheson, George – 1883? 02386. (Pre-1900 Canadiana) – 9 – cn C.I.H.M. [628]

BIOLOGICAL WARFARE IN WORLD WAR 1 PAMPHLET COLLECTION – 1922 – 1 – CSUXANM2699-B – us Hoover Inst Photo [355]

BIOLOGICAL WASTES *see* AGRICULTURAL WASTES

BIOLOGIE DE L'ATHERINE: ATHERINA BOYERI RISSO, 1810 (POISSON-TELEOSTEEN) DANS TROIS MILIEUX SAUMATRES DU ROUSSILLON (LEUCATE, CANET, BOURDIGOU) / Marfin, J P – 9 – F70.00 – fr Ethnologie [590]

BIOLOGIE, ECOLOGIE ET DYNAMIQUE DES CREVETTES DE LA MANGROVE GUADELOUPEENNE (ANTILLES FRANCAISES): PHASE LAGUNAIRE DES PENAEIDES / Rojas-Beltran, R – 9 – F90.00 – fr Ethnologie [590]

BIOLOGISCHE VERFAHREN DES PFLANZENSCHUTZES IM ZIERPFLANZENBAU, GEZEIGT AM BEISPIEL DES EINSATZES VON RAUBMILBEN (PHYTOSEIULUS PERSIMILIS ATHIAS-HENRIOT) : ZUR BEKAEMPFUNG DER SPINNMILBE (TETRANYCHUS URTICAE KOCH) IN HAUSROSEN (ACARI-ANACTINOTRICHIDA: PHOTYSEIIDAE BERLESE) (ACARI-ACTINOTRICHIDA: TETRANYCHIDAE DONNADIEU) (1984) / Hantke, Friedrich – 1993 – 2mf – 9 – DM80.00 – 3-89349-764-1 – gw Hänsel [660]

BIOLOGISCHES ZENTRALBLATT – v. 1-71. 1881-1952 – 1,5,6 – us Princeton Micro [574]

BIOLOGIST – (v.63-. 1981-. 5,6,9) – v.1-. 1916- – 1 – us UMI [574]

BIOLOGY AND ETHICS : REFLECTIONS INSPIRED BY A UNESCO SYMPOSIUM / Ribes, Bruno – 1978 – 202p – 9 – 92-3-101568-0 – fr UNESCO [574]

BIOLOGY AND PHILOSPHY – v1-. 1986- – 1,5,6,9 – us UMI [574]

BIOLOGY BULLETIN – v1-21. 1974-94 – 1,5 – $90.00v – us UMI [574]

BIOLOGY DIGEST – v5-. 1978- – 9 – us UMI [574]

BIOLOGY OF DESERTS / ed by Cloudsey-Thompson, J L – 1954 – 7 – uk Microform Academic [574]

BIOLOGY OF THE NEONATE – v26-. 1975- – 1,5,9 – us UMI [618]

BIOLOGY OF THE SHORT-BILLED FORM OF THE WHITE-TAILED BLACK COCKATOO / Saunders, Denis – (PhD Thesis) – 1976 – microfiche – A$15.00 – at R.A.O.U. [590]

BIOMASS – v1-5. 1981-84 – 1,5,6,13 – sz Elsevier [574]

BIOMASS AND BIOENERGY – 1,5,69 – us UMI [333]

BIOMASS ENERGY PROFILES – 1983 – 144p – it F.A.O. [333]

BIOMATERIALS – (1982-. 1,5,6,9) – v1-. 1980- – 1 – us UMI [574]

BIOMATERIALS, MEDICAL DEVICES, AND ARTIFICIAL ORGANS – (1984-. 5,6,9) – v1-. 1973- – 1 – us UMI [610]

A BIOMECHANICAL ANALYSIS OF CANINE GAIT BEFORE AND AFTER UNILATERAL CEMENTED TOTAL HIP REPLACEMENT / Dogan, Selami – 1989 – 264p 3mf – 9 – $12.00 – us Microform Publ [619]

A BIOMECHANICAL ANALYSIS OF CHILDREN'S BALANCE BEHAVIOR : AN INVESTIGATION IN BALANCE THEORY / Kennedy, S O – 1991 – 3mf – 9 – $12.00 – us Microform Publ [790]

BIOMECHANICAL ANALYSIS OF FORCES AND TORQUES AT THE SUPPORT LOWER EXTREMITY DURING TWO RUNNING-IN-PLACE EXERCISES AT THREE PACES / Muniz, A E – 1990 – 4mf – 9 – $16.00 – us Microform Publ [790]

A BIOMECHANICAL ANALYSIS OF PATELLOFEMORAL STRESS SYNDROME / Moss, R I – 1989 – 2mf – 9 – $8.00 – us Microform Publ [790]

A BIOMECHANICAL ANALYSIS OF THE DEMI PLIE AND GRAND PLIE / Buday, Marie T – 1989 – 83p 1mf – 9 – $4.00 – us Microform Publ [612]

A BIOMECHANICAL ANALYSIS OF THE EFFECTS OF HAND WEIGHTS ON THE ARM-SWING WHILE WALKING AND RUNNING / Denny, Karen L – University of Wisconsin-La Crosse, 1995 – 1mf – 9 – $4.00 – PE3588 – us Microform Publ [612]

A BIOMECHANICAL ANALYSIS OF THE PROLONGED EFFECTS ON FUNCTIONAL PARAMETERS OF A TEST SEATING SYSTEM FOR MODERATELY INVOLVED CEREBRAL PALSIED CHILDREN / Boucher, George P – 1986 – 92p 1mf – 9 – $4.00 – us Microform Publ [620]

A BIOMECHANICAL ANALYSIS OF THE SINGLE ARM VERSUS THE PARALLEL DOUBLE ARM TAKEOFFS IN THE TRIPLE JUMP / Larkins, Clifford – 1987 – 158p 2mf – 9 – $8.00 – us Microform Publ [612]

A BIOMECHANICAL AND PHYSIOLOGICAL ANALYSIS OF EFFICIENCY DURING DIFFERENT RUNNING PACES / Price, Kathleen M & Wilkerson, Jerry D – 1992 – 2mf – $8.00 – us Microform Publ [612]

BIOMECHANICAL COMPARISON OF SUPPORT PROVIDED BY THE AIRSTIRRUP ANKLE TRAINING BRACE™ PRE- AND POST-EXERCISE / Money, Sharon M & Kimura, Iris F – 1993 – 1mf – $4.00 – us Microform Publ [612]

THE BIOMECHANICAL EFFECTS OF PROLOTHERAPY ON TRAUMATIZED ACHILLES TENDONS OF MALE RATS / Harrison, Maria E G – Brigham Young University, 1995 – 1mf – 9 – PE 3651 – us Microform Publ [617]

BIOMEDICAL COMMUNICATIONS – (v5- . 1977- . 5,6,9) – v. 1-. 1973- – 1 – us UMI [610]

BIOMEDICAL COMPUTING *see* INTERNATIONAL JOURNAL OF BIOMEDICAL COMPUTING

BIOMEDICAL ENGINEERING – v1-28. 1967-94 – 1,5 – $65.00v – us UMI [610]

BIOMEDICAL MASS SPECTROMETRY – (1982-. 1,5,6,9) – v1-. 1974- – 1 – us UMI [610]
BIOMEDICAL MATERIALS AND ENGINEERING – 1,5,69 – us UMI [610]
BIOMEDICAL PRODUCTS – (1983-. 1,5,6,9) – 1976- – 1 – us UMI [073]
BIOMEDICAL TECHNOLOGY AND HUMAN RIGHTS / Brody, Eugene B – 1993 – 312p – 9 – 92-3-102806-5 – Co-published with Dartmouth Publishing Co., which has exclusive sales rights in the UK and USA – fr UNESCO [619]
BIOMETRICS – v. 1-31. 1945-75 – 1,5,6 – us Princeton Micro [590]
BIOMETRIKA – v. 1-62. 1901-75 – 1,5,6 – us Princeton Micro [590]
BIOMETRIKA – (v64- . 1977- . 5,6,9) – v. 1-. 1901- – 1 – us UMI [574]
BIOMIMETICS – v1-2. 1992-94 – $65.00v – us UMI [570]
Biondini, Pierre *see* L'ARGENTINE DE PERON
BIOORGANIC AND MEDICINAL CHEMISTRY LETTERS – v1- 1991- – 5,6,9 – us UMI [540]
BIOPHYSICAL CHEMISTRY – v1-20. 1973-84 – 1,5,6,13 – sz Elsevier [073]
BIOPHYSICAL JOURNAL – (v.25-. 1979- 5,6,9) – v.1-. 1960- – apply; Um; 1 – us UMI [574]
BIOPHYSICS – v2- 1957- – 5,6,9 – us UMI [574]
BIOPHYSICS OF STRUCTURE AND MECHANISM – v. 1-7. 1974-80 – 1,5,9 – 698.00 – us UMI [073]
BIOPOLYMERS – v. 1-. 1963- – 1,5,6,9 – us UMI [660]
BIOPOLYMERS – v1-22. 1963-83 – 1,5,6 – us Princeton Micro [073]
BIOPSYCHOSOCIAL HEALTH – v. 1-. 1980- – 5,6,9 – us UMI [610]
BIOPUSO BA BASOTHO – Mafeteng, BCP Youth League. v[1]. jul 9-dec 19 1965 – us Res Libr [960]
BIORHEOLOGY – v1- 1962- – 5,6,9 – us UMI [073]
BIOSCIENCE – (1972- 9) – v. 1- 1951- – 1,5,6 – us UMI [574]
BIOSCIENCE REPORTS – v1-14. 1981-94 – 1,5 – $100.00v – us UMI [574]
THE BIOSCOPE – London. 1908-32 – 1 – £2,900.00 – uk World [790]
BIOSYSTEMS – v1-17. 1967-84.Continues: Currents in Modern Biology – 1,5,6,13 – sz Elsevier [574]
Biot, E C *see* DICTIONNAIRE DES NOMS ANCIENS ET MODERNES DES VILLES ET ARRONDISSEMENTS... DANS L'EMPIRE CHINOIS...
Biot, M *see* MEMOIRE SUR LA PROPAGATION DE LA CHALEUR
BIOTECHNIC AND HISTOCHEMISTRY – (Formerly: Stain Technology) – v28-71. 1953-96 – 1,5,6,9 – $80.00r – us Williams [540]
BIOTECHNOLOGIES AND DEVELOPMENT / Sasson, Albert – 1988 – 361p – 9 – 92-3-102426-4 – fr UNESCO [600]
BIOTECHNOLOGIES IN DEVELOPING COUNTRIES : PRESENT AND FUTURE; VOLUME 1: REGIONAL AND NATIONAL SURVEY / Sasson, Albert – 1993 – 764p – 9 – 92-3-102875-8 – fr UNESCO [660]
BIOTECHNOLOGIES IN PERSPECTIVE : SOCIO-ECONOMIC IMPLICATIONS FOR DEVELOPING COUNTRIES / ed by Sasson, Albert & Costarini, Vivien – 1991 – 166p – 9 – 92-3-102738-7 – fr UNESCO [660]
BIO/TECHNOLOGY – v1-. 1983- – 1,5,6,9 – us UMI [073]
BIOTECHNOLOGY ADVANCES – v1- 1983- – 5,6,9 – us UMI [073]
BIOTECHNOLOGY: AN INTERNATIONAL JOURNAL – 1,5,9 – us Harwood [660]
BIOTECHNOLOGY AND BIOENGINEERING – v. 1-. 1959- – 1,5,6,9 – us UMI [576]
BIOTECHNOLOGY AND BIOENGINEERING – v1-28. 1959-86 – 1,5,6 – us Princeton Micro [660]
BIOTECHNOLOGY AND BIOENGINEERING SYMPOSIUM – (1976-. 5,6,9) – n. 1-. 1969- – 1 – us UMI [660]
BIOTECHNOLOGY AND BIOENGINEERING. SYMPOSIUM – No.1-16.1969-86 – 1,5,6 – us Princeton Micro [660]
BIOTECHNOLOGY EDUCATION – 1,5,69 – us UMI [660]
BIOTECHNOLOGY PROGRESS – v1-. 1985- – 1,5,6,9 – us UMI [660]
BIOTECHNOLOGY PROGRESS – v6- 1990- – 1,5,6,9 – us A.C.S. [073]
BIOTROPICA – (v6-. 1974-. 5,6. v8-. 1976-. 9) – v. 1-. 1969- – 1 – us UMI [574]
BIP – (Some issues lacking) – v4 no 62; v6 no 66. 1969-1991 – Inquire – 1 – ATLA S0455 – us A.T.L.A. [240]
BIP - SNOP - SOP – (Some issues missing) – 1971-82; 1985-88 – Inquire – 1 – ATLA S0456 – us A.T.L.A. [073]
BIR CICEK DEMETI / Resit, Mustafa – Istanbul: Matbaa-i Ebuezziya, 1304 [1877] – $20.00 – us MEDOC [470]
Biragh, J *see* DIE LOESING VON OESTERREICHISCHEN, ... EHEN IN UNGARN
Birch, Ian *see* LAW AND EDUCATIONAL PLANNING
Birch, John Grant *see* TRAVELS IN NORTH AND CENTRAL CHINA
Birch, S *see* INSCRIPTIONS IN THE HIERATIC AND DEMOTIC CHARACTER, FROM THE COLLECTIONS OF THE BRITISH MUSEUM
Birch, Walter de Gray *see*
- CATALOGUE OF SEALS IN THE DEPARTMENT OF MANUSCRIPTS IN THE BRITISH MUSEUM
- EARLY DRAWINGS AND ILLUMINATIONS
- FASTI MONASTICI AEVI SAXONICI, OR, AN ALPHABETICAL LIST OF THE HEADS OF RELIGIOUS HOUSES IN ENGLAND PREVIOUS TO THE NORMAN CONQUEST

Bircher, Martin et al *see* DEUTSCHE DRUCKE DES BAROCK 1600-1720. MIT DEN ERGAENZUNGEN POLNISCHE DRUCKE UND POLONICA 1501-1700 SOWIE UNGARISCHE DRUCKE UND HUNGARICA 1480-1720
BIRCHIP ADVERTISER – 1919-1945. BA1-9 – 9r – 1 – at Corangamite [072]
Birch-Pfeiffer, Charlotte *see* GESAMMELTE NOVELLEN UND ERZAEHLUNGEN
Birckenstock, J *see* SONATE A VIOLINO SOLO E VIOLONCELLE A BASSO CONTINUO...OPERA PRIMO, LIBRO PRIMO
Birckholtz, J G *see* DE ARMIS ILLICITIS
Bird, George W *see* WANDERINGS IN BURMA
Bird, Isaac *see* BIBLE WORK IN BIBLE LANDS
BIRD ISLAND LIGHTHOUSE LETTERBOOK, 1852-75 – 5 fiche – 9 – sa SA Libr [960]
Bird, John *see* GROUNDS OF GRAMMER PENNED AND PUBLISHED
BIRD WATCHER'S DIGEST – 1985- – 1,5,6,9 – us UMI [590]
Bird, William Hamilton *see* THE ORIENTAL MISCELLANY
BIRD'S EYE VIEWS = LES VUES A VOL D'OISEAUX / National Archives of Canada – (Halifax, 1879; Lunenburg, 1890; Moncton, 1881; Montreal, 1889; Sherbrooke, 1881; Sorel, 1881; Brantford, 1893; Kingston, 1875; London, 1893; Ottawa, 1893; Port Arthur, 1885; Simcoe, 1881; St. Catharine, 1875; Tillsonburg, 1881; Toronto, 1876; Morris, 1880; Winnipeg, 1880; Victoria, 1878; Yukon, 1903) – 1994 – 19mf – 15 – $171.00 set $9.50f – us Comics [971]
THE BIRDS OF AFRICA / Shelley, G E & Sclater, W L – Z 1932 2. 3 v. 1896-1902 – 8 – ne IDC [590]
THE BIRDS OF AMERICA FROM ORIGINAL DRAWING / Audubon, John James – 5v. 2068 2. 1826-1840 – 8 – ne IDC [740]
THE BIRDS OF ASIA / Gould, J – London, 1850-83.7v. BZ/1777/2 – 8 – ne IDC [590]
THE BIRDS OF CELEBES AND THE NEIGHBOURING ISLANDS / Meyer, A B & Wiglesworth, L W – Berlin. Z-1855/2. 2v. 1898 – 40mf – 9 – ne IDC [590]
THE BIRDS OF EASTERN NORTH AMERICA / Cory, C B – 2v. 1899 – 8 – Z-2063 2 – ne IDC [590]
THE BIRDS OF EUROPE / Gould, J – London, (1832-) 1837. 5v. Z/1969/2 – 8 – ne IDC [590]
THE BIRDS OF GREAT BRITAIN / Gould, J – London, 1873. 5v. Z/1779/2 – 8 – ne IDC [590]
THE BIRDS OF GREAT BRITAIN AND IRELAND / Jardine, W – Z 1811. 4 v. 1838-1843 – 9 – ne IDC [590]
THE BIRDS OF INDIA / Jerdon, T C – Z-276 2. 3 v. 1862-1864 – 8 – ne IDC [590]
THE BIRDS OF JAMAICA / Gosse, P H – 1847. Lacking: Illustrations of the birds of Jamaica. Z-1768 2.. 1849 – 8 – ne IDC [590]
THE BIRDS OF NEW GUINEA / Gould, J – London, 1875-88.5v. Z/1781/2 – 8 – ne IDC [590]
THE BIRDS OF NORTH AMERICA / Baird, Spencer Fullerton et al – Z-338 2. 1860 – 8 – ne IDC [590]
THE BIRDS OF NORTH AND MIDDLE AMERICA / Ridgway, R – Z 1888 2. 8 v. 1901-1919 – 8 – ne IDC [590]
BIRDS OF PREY / Braddon, Mary Elizabeth – British Fiction Archive: Unit 5 – 9 – uk Bell [830]
BIRDS OF PRINCE EDWARD ISLAND: THEIR HABITS AND CHARACTERISTICS / Bain, Francis – Charlottetown: Haszard & Moore, 1891. 04171. (Pre-1900 Canadiana) – 9 – cn C.I.H.M. [590]
BIRDS OF THE BAHAMA ISLANDS / Cory, C B – 1880 – 8 – Z-2060 2 – ne IDC [590]
THE BIRDS OF THE WEST INDIES / Cory, C B – 1889 – 8 – Z-2061 2 – ne IDC [590]
THE BIRDS OF THE WEST OF SCOTLAND / Gray, R – Z-1785 2. 1871 – 8 – ne IDC [590]
THE BIRDS OF TIERRA DEL FUEGO / Crawshay, R – 2076 2. 1907 – 8 – ne IDC [590]
THE BIRDS OF TUNISIA / Whitaker, J I S – Z 1959. 2 v. 1905 – 9 – ne IDC [590]
BIRDS OF WESTERN AFRICA / Swainson, W – Naturalist's library v. 7 Ornithology. Z 1944 2. 2 v. 1837 – 8 – ne IDC [590]
Birdsall *see*
- HISTORY OF DAVIESS COUNTY
- HISTORY OF GRUNDY COUNTY
- HISTORY OF LINN COUNTY

A BIRD'S-EYE VIEW OF BEE-KEEPING / Clarke, William F – (Beeton, Ont.: Canadian Bee Journal), 1886. 00676. (Pre-1900 Canadiana) – 9 – cn C.I.H.M. [630]
A BIRDSEYE VIEW OF INDIAN POLICY – 1935. (American Indian Periodicals in the Princeton University Library). 1 fiche – 9 – $45.00 – us UPA [305]
BIRD'S-EYE VIEW OF LIFE INSURANCE: AND MATHEMATICAL AND LOGICAL EXPOSITION OF THE LEVEL PREMIUM PLAN / Bruce, King – Toronto: K. Bruce, 1888. 00291. (Pre-1900 Canadiana) – 9 – cn C.I.H.M. [336]
Birell, Augustine *see* OBITER DICTA
Birerdinc, E *see* LES RITES DE MARIAGE TURC A CHYPRE ET EN ANATOLIE
BIRGITTA-STUDIER / Westman, Knut B – Uppsala: Akademiska boktryckeriet, 1911 – 1mf – us A.T.L.A. [240]
BIRGYS-BARYS – Paris. Titre francais: Aigle de Paris. 1859-66. Ed. arabe no. 1-179; ed. bilingue no. 1-25 – 1 – fr A.C.R.P.P. [073]
Biria, J A J *see* HISTOIRE NATURELLE ET MEDICALE DES RENONCULES,...
O BIRIMBAU : ORGAO DE COUSA ALGUMA – Baturite-CE, Brazil. 22 Dez 1891 – 1 – bl Biblioteca [072]
Biringer Gun Shop. Leavenworth, Kansas *see* RECORDS AND HISTORY
Biringer Gun Shop. Leavenworth. Kansas *see* RECORDS AND HISTORY
Biringuccio, V *see* DE LA PIROTECHNIA LIBRI 10
BIRIUCH PETROGRADSKIKH GOSUDARSTVENNYKH TEATROV – Petrograd, 1918-19, 1919-20, 1920 – 10mf – 9 – us Ross [780]
Birk, A *see* DER SUEZKANAL
Birk, Karl *see*
- HEINRICH VON KLEIST

Birkas, G *see* DAS STAATSINTERESSE ALS GRUNDLAGE DES VOELKERRECHTS
BIRKAT HA-MAZON – Amsterdam. 1648. BJ-43-9 1 – 9 – ne IDC [470]
Birkbeck, W J *see* RUSSIA AND THE ENGLISH CHURCH DURING THE LAST FIFTY YEARS
Birkeland, Harris *see* THE LORD GUIDETH
Birkeland, Knut Bergesen *see* LIGHT IN THE DARKNESS, OR, CHRISTIANITY AND PAGANISM...AROUND THE GLOBE
BIRKENHEAD GUARDIAN – England. -w. 26 Jan 1861-3 Mar 1866. (4 reels) – 1 – uk British Libr Newspaper [072]
Birket-Smith, K *see*
- THE CARIBOU ESKIMOS
- CONTRIBUTIONS TO CHIPEWYAN ETHNOLOGY
- THE CUGACH ESKIMO
- ESKIMOERNE
- DET ESKIMOISKE SLAEGTSKABSSYSTEM
- THE ESKIMOS
- LOS ESQUIMALES
- ETHNOGRAPHY OF THE EGEDESMINDE DISTRICT
- THE EYAK INDIANS OF THE COPPER RIVER DELTA
- FIVE HUNDRED ESKIMO WORDS
- FOLK WANDERINGS AND CULTURE DRIFTS IN NORTHERN NORTH AMERICA
- FORELOBIGT BIDRAG TIL KAP FARVEL-DISTRIKTERNES KULTURHISTORIE
- A GEOGRAPHIC STUDY OF THE EARLY HISTORY OF THE ALGONQUIAN INDIANS
- THE GREENLAND BOW
- GRONLANDSBOGEN 1-2
- KOBMAND B. J. LUND'S BESKRIVELSE AF GRONLAENDERNES ISFANGST
- MOEURS ET COUTUMES DES ESKIMO
- NYE FREMSKRIDT INDEN FOR ESKIMOFORSKNINGEN
- PRELIMINARY REPORT OF THE FIFTH THULE EXPEDITION
- RECENT ACHIEVEMENTS IN ESKIMO RESEARCH
- SKRAELINGERNE I VINLAND OG ESKIMOERNES SYDOSTGRAENSE

Birkner, Siegfried *see* DIE MECHANISIERUNG DES LEBENS IM WERK JOHANN GOTTFRIED HERDERS
Birks, Herbert *see* THE LIFE AND CORRESPONDENCE OF THOMAS VALPY FRENCH
Birks, Thomas Rawson *see*
- BIBLE AND MODERN THOUGHT
- THE PENTATEUCH AND ITS ANATOMISTS
- THE SCRIPTURE DOCTRINE OF CREATION
- SUPERNATURAL REVELATION, OR, FIRST PRINCIPLES OF MORAL THEOLOGY

BIRLIK – Cankiri [Turkey]: Birlik Matbaasi, [nov 20 1950-aug 24 1953] – 4r – 1 – us Res Libr [072]
BIRLIK – Galata [Turkey]: s.n., [jan 2-aug 31 1950] – 1r – 1 – us Res Libr [072]
BIRLIK – Nicosia, Cyprus. Oct 1991-June 1992; Sept-Nov 1992 – 4r – 1 – us L of C Photodup [072]
Birlinger, Anton *see* ALEMANNIA ZEITSCHRIFT FUER SPRACHE, LITTERATUR UND VOLKSKUNDE DES ELSASSES UND OBERRHEINS
Birmann, Martin *see* GESAMMELTE SCHRIFTEN
BIRMINGHAM AND LICHFIELD CHRONICLE – England.1821-22. -w. 1 reel – 1 – uk British Libr Newspaper [072]
BIRMINGHAM CHRONICLE – England.9 Sept 1819-28 Dec 1820; 1824-19 Apr 1827. -w. 2 reels – 1 – uk British Libr Newspaper [072]
BIRMINGHAM DAILY MAIL – Birmingham, England. -d. 1875-80. 16 reels – 1 – uk British Libr Newspaper [072]
BIRMINGHAM DAILY POST – England. -d. Jan 1861-Dec 1862. (4 reels) – 1 – uk British Libr Newspaper [072]
Birmingham, G A *see* GOD'S IRON
BIRMINGHAM JOURNAL – England. -w. June 1825- Feb. 1869. (39 reels) – 1 – uk British Libr Newspaper [072]
Birmingham Ladies' Society for the Relief of Negro Slaves *see* RECORDS
BIRMINGHAM, MOSELEY AND BALSALL HEATH NEWS, ETC *see* MOSELEY AND BALSALL HEATH NEWS ETC
Birmingham Museum and Art Gallery *see* PRE-RAPHAELITE PAINTINGS AND DRAWINGS
BIRMINGHAM NEWS – Birmingham, Alabama. 1947- – 1 – us UMI [071]
BIRMINGHAM NEWS (SOUTH ED.) *see* MOSELEY AND BALSALL HEATH NEWS ETC
Birmingham, Peter *see* AMERICAN ART IN THE BARBIZON MOOD
BIRMINGHAM POST – England. 1950-53.-d. 17 reels – 1 – uk British Libr Newspaper [072]
BIRMINGHAM REFERENCE LIBRARY CATALOGUE 1879-1963 – 341mf – 9 – £1,200.00 – uk Chadwyck [020]
BIRMINGHAM SUBURBAN TIMES – England. Dec 1884-Feb 1901. 15mqn reels – 1 – uk British Libr Newspaper [072]
BIRMINGHAM SUNDAY SCHOOL UNION : CHURCH RECORDS – May 1848-Dec 1913 – 1 – 577.67 – us Baptist [240]
Birn, Raymond F *see* PIERRE ROUSSEAU AND THE PHILOSOPHES OF BOUILLON
Birnbach, Franz Bernhard *see* HEINRICH FEDERER. SEINE PERSOENLICHKEIT UND SEINE KUNSTFORM
Birnbaum, N *see*
- JUEDISCHE MODERNE
- DIE NATIONALE WIEDERGEBURT DES JUEDISCHEN VOLKES IN SEINEM LANDE ALS MITTEL ZUR LOESUNG DER JUDENFRAGE
- VOM SINN DES JUDENTUMS, SAMMELBAND

Birney, Catherine H *see* THE GRIMKE SISTERS: SARAH AND ANGELINA GRIMKE, THE FIRST AMERICAN WOMEN ADVOCATES OF ABOLITION AND WOMEN'S RIGHTS
Birney, Hoffman *see*
- BROTHERS OF DOOM. THE STORY OF THE PIZARROS OF PERU
- LOS HERMANOS DEL DESTINO (LOS PIZARROS Y LA CONQUISTA DEL PERU)

Birney, William *see* JAMES G. BIRNEY AND HIS TIMES
Biroat, Jacques *see* THE EUCHARISTIC LIFE OF JESUS CHRIST
BIROBIDZHAN / Bruk, Boris Lvovich – Izd. 2-e, ispr. Moskva: Izd. T Sentr. pravlenii a "OZETa", 1929 – 1 – CSUX89-B5614 – us Hoover Inst Photo [947]
Birolli, G *see* CATALOGUS PLANTARUM REGII HORTI BOTANICI TAURINENSIS
BIRONOVSHCHINA I KABINET MINISTROV / Stroev, V N – 2v. M. 1909-10. BR-7898 2 – 8 – ne IDC [947]
Birrell, Augustine *see* LIFE OF CHARLOTTE BRONTE
Birsen, K *see* DEVLETLER HUSUSI HUKUKU
Birt, Henry Norbert *see*
– DOWNSIDE
– THE ELIZABETHAN RELIGIOUS SETTLEMENT
Birt, Th *see* CLAUDII CLAUDIANI CARMINA (MGH 1: 10.BD)
Birt, W *see* THE DOCTRINE OF PREDESTINATION DEFENDED, IN ANSWER TO MR. JOHN WESLEY'S BOOK ENTITULED 'FREE GRACE', WHEREIN HIS SELF-CONTRADICTIONS ARE SHEWN;...
BIRTH – v9-. 1982- – 1,5,6,9 – us UMI [618]
THE BIRTH AND INFANCY OF JESUS CHRIST: ACCORDING TO THE GOSPEL NARRATIVES / Sweet, Louis Matthews – Philadelphia: Westminster Press, 1906. 1 fiche – 9 – us A.T.L.A. [240]
BIRTH AND THE FAMILY JOURNAL – v1-8 1973-81 – 1,5,6,9 – us UMI [618]
BIRTH CERTIFICATES / Putnam County, Ohio. General Health District – 1931-96 – 3r – 1 – $32.50r – us Archival [920]
BIRTH CERTIFICATES / Wood County. Ohio. General Health District – 1800s-1939 – 16r – 1 – $32.50r – us Archival [324]
BIRTH CERTIFICATES / Wood County. Ohio. Middletown Township. Township Clerk – (Incomplete) – 1908-1950 – 1r – 1 – $32.50r – us Archival [324]
THE BIRTH OF GANEFO / Indonesia. Departemen Penerangan – ((Games of the New Emerging Forces).) – SE-10,476 1. 1963 – 9 – ne IDC [790]
THE BIRTH OF JESUS CHRIST / Soltau, Wilhelm – London:A. & C. Black, 1903. 1 fiche – 9 – us A.T.L.A. [240]
THE BIRTH OF NEW INDONESIA (SIX MONTHS P.R.R.I.) COMMEMORATION MONOGRAPH GENESIS AND DEVELOPMENT OF THE REVOLUTIONARY GOVERNMENT OF THE REPUBLIC OF INDONESIA / Pemerintah Revolusioner Republik Indonesia – SE-3513 1. 1958 – 9 – ne IDC [335]
THE BIRTH OF PANTJASILA; AN OUTLINE OF FIVE PRINCIPLES OF INDONESIAN STATE / Sukarno, Pres. Indonesia – SE 2205 1. 1958 – 9 – ne IDC [324]
THE BIRTH OF THE FIRST SOUTHERN BAPTIST CHURCH OF SYRACUSE, 1957-58 – 1957-58.Formerly a mission of the Lasalle Baptist Church of Syracuse, NY. 98p – 1 – 5.00 – us Baptist [240]
BIRTH OF THE WAR GOD (KUMARASAMBHAVA) / Kalidasa – 1835 – 1 – uk Microform Academic [280]
BIRTH RECORD / Crawford County. Ohio. Galion – 1879-1889 – 1r – 1 – $32.50r – us Archival [324]
BIRTH RECORDS / Defiance County, Ohio. Probate Court – (Some issues missing) – 1856-1908 – 2r – 1 – $32.50r – us Archival [324]
BIRTH RECORDS / Hardin County, Ohio. Probate Court – 1867-1908 – 2r – 1 – $32.50r – us Archival [920]
BIRTH RECORDS / Huron County. Ohio. County Home – 1898-1922 – 1r – 1 – $32.50r – us Archival [324]
BIRTH RECORDS / Monroe County. Mich, Bedford Township. Board of Trustees – 1887-1889 – 1r – 1 – $32.50r – us Archival [324]
BIRTH RECORDS / Ottawa County. Ohio. Probate Court – 1867-1908 – 1r – 1 – $32.50r – us Archival [324]
BIRTH RECORDS / Van Wert County. Ohio. Probate Court – 1867-1908 – 2r – 1 – $32.50r – us Archival [324]
BIRTH RECORDS / Wood County. Ohio. Probate Court – 1867-1908 – 2r – 1 – $32.50r – us Archival [324]
BIRTH REGISTRATION RECORDS / Putnam County. Ohio. Probate Court – 1941-1964 – 11r – 1 – $32.50r – us Archival [324]
BIRTH REGISTRATION RECORDS / Putnam County. Ohio. Probate Court – 1941-1964 – 11r – 1 – $32.50r – us Archival [324]
BIRTH REGISTRATIONS / Wood County. Ohio. Probate Court – 1987-94 – 1r – 1 – $32.50r – us Archival [920]
BIRTH/DEATH RECORDS / Defiance County, Ohio. Probate Court – 1873-1908 – 5r – 1 – us Archival [324]
BIRTH/DEATH STATEMENTS / Defiance County, Ohio. Probate Court – 1873-1908 – 5r – 1 – $32.50r – us Archival [978]
THE BIRTHPLACE OF ANCIENT RELIGIONS AND CIVILIZATION / Campbell, John – 18?? 00412. (Pre-1900 Canadiana) – 9 – cn C.I.H.M. [900]
BIRTHS AND DEATHS REGISTERS, 1867-1973 (GAPS – MAINLY 19TH CENTURY REGISTERS) / Ministry of Justice, Tonga, Tongatapu Registry – 2r – 1 – PMB1095 – at Pacific Mss [920]
BIRTHS, BAPTISMS, MARRIAGES & DEATHS, 1703-1850 / Mansfield. Connecticut – Copied by Susan W. Dimock, 1898.Includes index. V126-0001 – 1 – us A.G.L.L. [920]
BIRTHS, DEATHS, AND MARRIAGE RECORD CARDS / Geary County, KS – undated – 1 – us KS Hist [920]
BIRTHS, MARRIAGES AND DEATHS – London, UK. 9 Oct 1871-30 Sept 1872. -w. 1 reel – 1 – uk British Libr Newspaper [072]
BIRTLEY ECHO = WEEKBLAD DER BELGISCHE KOLONIE, TE BIRTLEY-ELISABTHVILLE : JOURNAL HEBDOMADAIRE DE LA COLONIE BELGE, DE BIRTLEY-ELISABETHVILLE – (Includes no. 1, 9 (Oct. 20, 1917, Dec. 15, 1917)) – Birtley: Birtley echo, 1917- – 1 – CSUX86-S98 – us Hoover Inst Photo [943]
Biruni *see* THE CHRONOLOGY OF ANCIENT NATIONS
BIRZHEVUIYA VEDOMOSTI – Leningrad, U.S.S.R. 16, 17 Jul 1907; 1 Dec 1915; 24 Apr 1916-25 oct 1917.-d. 5 reels – 1 – uk British Libr Newspaper [072]
BIRZHEVYE VEDOMOSTI, RUSSIA – (Backfile through 1998 $85.00r) – 1999- – 1r per y – 1 – $80.00 standing order – us Ross [072]
BIRZHEVYI A IZVI EST-II A – (Includes c.1: 1914:July 21) – Vechernee izd. s.-Peterburg: I.M. En-l Ankov – 1 – CSUXANRO522-S – us Hoover Inst Photo [947]
BIRZHEVYIA VEDOMOSTI – Petrograd. Jan. 1, 1917-Oct. 22, 1917. Missing: scattered issues – 1 – 35.00r – us Hoover Inst Photo [073]
BIRZHEVYIA VIEDOMOSTI – Petrograd: [s.n], jan-dec 1916 – 1 – us Res Libr [072]
Birziska, Mikolas *see* AMERIKOS LIETUVIAI
Birziska, V *see* LIETUVIU BIBLIOGRAFIIA
BISA *see* FAR EASTERN ECONOMIC REVIEW INDEX ON MICROFICHE
BISA CATALOGUE – Oct 1985 – ISSN 0158-9997 – A$20.00 – at BISA [010]
BISA SPECIAL PROJECT NO. 2 *see* SINGAPORE-MALAYSIA CONFERENCES ON HEALTH AND RELATED SCIENCES
BISA SPECIAL PROJECT NO. 4 *see* HAMKA
BISA SPECIAL PROJECT NO. 5 *see* FAR EASTERN ECONOMIC REVIEW INDEX ON MICROFICHE
BISA SPECIAL PROJECT NO. 6 *see* CHINESE KUNGFU STORIES IN INDONESIAN
BISA SPECIAL PROJECT NO. 7 *see* MALAYSIAN SERIALS
BISA SPECIAL PROJECT NO. 8 *see* ASIAN AGRICULTURAL RESEARCH AND DEVELOPMENT
BISA SPECIAL PROJECT NO. 9 *see* PHILIPPINE ETHNOGRAPHIC SERIES
BISA SPECIAL PROJECT NO. 10 *see* VIETNAMESE COLLECTION OF THE ANU LIBRARY
BISA SPECIAL PROJECT NO. 11 *see* RESEARCH IN INDONESIAN AND REGIONAL LANGUAGES
BISA SPECIAL PROJECT NO. 12 *see* AUSTRALIA AND ASEAN IN PERSPECTIVE
BISA SPECIAL PROJECT NO. 14 *see* NUTRITION IN MALAYSIA
BISA SPECIAL PROJECT NO. 15 *see* PHILIPPINE ETHNOGRAPHIC SERIES
BISA SPECIAL PROJECT NO. 19 *see* CRIME IN INDONESIA
BISA SPECIAL PROJECT NO. 21 *see* TRADE AND INDUSTRY IN MALAYSIA
BISA SPECIAL PROJECT NO. 23 *see* MODERN INDONESIAN DRAMA
BISA SPECIAL PROJECT NO. 26 *see* PORTUGUESE EURASIANS IN MALAYSIA
BISA SPECIAL PROJECT NO. 28 *see* SINGAPOREAN EDUCATION IN PERSPECTIVE
BISA SPECIAL PROJECT NO. 29 *see* PHILIPPINE LIBERATION THEOLOGY
BISA SPECIAL REPORTS *see* 20 YEARS OF INDONESIAN FICTION 1940-1960
Bisaillon, Francois Joseph *see* JUSTICE AUX MINORITES: PROTECTION DE L'INDUSTRIE NATIONALE: PROTECTION ET DEVELOPPEMENT DE L'AGRICULTURE
BISBEE BUZZ – Orum, Washington County, NE: Jan 28, 1936-Oct 4, 1940 – us NE Hist [978]
Biscarrat, F *see* NOUVEAU MANUEL DE LA PURETE DU LANGAGE
DIE BISCHOEFLICHEN DIOEZESANBEHOERDEN, INSBESONDERE DAS BISCHOEFLICHE ORDINARIAT / Mueller, Joseph – 1995 – 2mf – 9 – DM62.00 – 3-8267-3151-4 – gw Hänsel [240]
Bischof, H *see*
– GRUNDRISS DES ... SEERECHTS
– KATECHISMUS DES VOELKERRECHTS
Bischoff *see* WOOL, WOOLLENS AND SHEEP
Bischoff, Erich *see*
– BABYLONISCH-ASTRALES IM WELTBILDE DES THALMUD UND MIDRASCH
– ERLAEUTERUNGEN ZU LESSING'S HAMBURGISCHER DRAMATURGIE
– KRITISCHE GESCHICHTE DER THALMUD-UEBERSETZUNGEN ALLER ZEITEN UND ZUNGEN
Bischoff, G W *see*
– HANDBUCH DER BOTANISCHEN TERMINOLOGIE UND SYSTEMKUNDE
– WOERTERBUCH DER BESCHREIBENDEN BOTANIK
Bischoff, H *see* ARCHIV FUER DAS STUDIUM DER NEUEREN SPRACHEN
Bischoff, Heinrich *see* NIKOLAUS LENAUS LYRIK
Bischoff, Karl *see* GEDENKSCHRIFT FUER FERDINAND JOSEF SCHNEIDER, 1879-1954
EIN BISCHOFSBRIEF VOM CONCIL UND EINE DEUTSCHE ANTWORT : EIN BEITRAG ZUR UNTERSCHEIDUNG VON KATHOLICISMUS UND JESUITISMUS / Nippold, Friedrich – Berlin: C G Luederitz, 1870 – 1mf – 9 – 0-8370-8464-4 – 1986-2464 – us A.T.L.A. [240]
DIE BISCHOFSLINIEN UND DIE APOSTOLISCHE NACHFOLGE IN DER KIRCHENGESCHICHTE DES EUSEBIUS / Overbeck, Franz – Basel: Fr. Reinhardt, 1898 – 1mf – us A.T.L.A. [240]
BISCUIT MAKER *see* BAKING INDUSTRIES JOURNAL
DIE BISHER BEKANNTEN EUROPAA5ISCHEN CHARACEEN / Sydow, P – Berlin, 1882. 104 pp. B-6408 1 – 9 – ne IDC [580]
EINE BISHER NICHT ERKANNTE SCHRIFT DES PAPSTES SIXTUS 2 (T.U.U. 1-13/1A) / Harnack, Adolf von – Leipzig, 1895 – 2mf – 9 – ne Slangenburg [240]
EINE BISHER NICHT ERKANNTE SCHRIFT NOVATIANS (T.U.U. 1-13/4B) / Harnack, Adolf von – Leipzig, 1895 – 1mf – 9 – ne Slangenburg [240]
EINE BISHER UNBEKANNTE VERSION DES ERSTEN TEILES DER "APOSTELLEHRE" (T.U.U. 1-13/1B) / Iselin, L E – Leipzig, 1895 – 1mf – 9 – ne Slangenburg [240]
BISHOP ASBURY / Lowrey, Asbury – Cincinnati: Published By the Cincinnati Annual Conference Historical Society; Curts & Jennings, [ca. 1898] – 1mf – us A.T.L.A. [240]
BISHOP CHASE'S REMINISCENCES : AN AUTOBIOGRAPHY / Chase, Philander – Boston: J.B. Dow, 1848, c1847 – 3mf – us A.T.L.A. [240]
BISHOP COLENSO'S OBJECTIONS TO THE HISTORICAL CHARACTER OF THE PENTATEUCH & JOSHUA / Benisch, A – London: Jewish Chronicle, 1863. 1 fiche – 9 – us A.T.L.A. [240]
Bishop, Cortlandt Field *see* HISTORY OF ELECTIONS IN THE AMERICAN COLONIES
BISHOP CROWTHER'S REPORT OF THE OVERLAND JOURNEY : FROM LOKAJA TO BIDA, ON THE RIVER NIGER, AND THENCE TO LAGOS, ON THE SEA COAST, FROM NOVEMBER 10TH 1871 TO FEBRUARY 8TH 1872 – London: Church Missionary House, 1872 – 1 – us Res Libr [910]
Bishop, E *see* EDWARD 6TH AND THE BOOK OF COMMON PRAYER
Bishop, Edmund *see* EDWARD 6 AND THE BOOK OF COMMON PRAYER
BISHOP GORE AND THE CATHOLIC CLAIMS / Chapman, John – (Includes bibliographical references) – London; New York: Longmans, Green, 1905 – 1mf – 9 – 0-8370-6656-5 – 1986-0656 – us A.T.L.A. [240]
BISHOP HEBER : POET AND CHIEF MISSIONARY TO THE EAST, SECOND LORD BISHOP OF CALCUTTA 1783-1826 / Smith, George Adam – London: J. Murray, 1895 – 1mf – us A.T.L.A. [240]
Bishop, IL (Bird) *see* DER GOLDENE CHERSONES
Bishop, James K *see* SAMOA COMES OF AGE
Bishop, James Lord *see* A TREATISE ON THE COMMON AND STATUTE LAW OF THE STATE OF NEW YORK RELATING TO INSOLVENT DEBTORS.
Bishop, Joel Prentiss *see*
– COMMENTARIES ON THE THE LAW OF MARRIAGE AND DIVORCE.
– COMMENTARIES ON THE WRITTEN LAWS AND THEIR INTERPRETATION
BISHOP JOHN SELWYN : A MEMOIR / How, Frederick Douglas – London: Isbister, 1899 – 1mf – us A.T.L.A. [240]
BISHOP JOSPH LONG : THE PEERLESS PREACHER OF THE EVANGELICAL ASSOCIATION / Yeakel, Reuben – Cleveland, O[hio]: Thomas & Mattill, c1897 – 1mf – us A.T.L.A. [240]
Bishop, L C *see* "MASSACRE BY INDIANS...."
Bishop, Matthew *see* THE LIFE AND ADVENTURES OF MATTHEW BISHIP OF DEDDINGTON IN OXFORDSHIRE
Bishop, Nathaniel Holmes *see*
– EN CANOT DE PAPIER DE QUEBEC AU GOLFE DU MEXIQUE: 2,500 MILLES.
– VOYAGE OF THE PAPER CANOE: A GEOGRAPHICAL JOURNEY OF 2500 MILES, FROM QUEBEC TO THE GULF OF MEXICO, DURING THE YEARS 1874-5
THE BISHOP OF EXETER'S ANSWER TO MR. J. WESELY'S LATE LETTER TO HIS LORDSHIP / Lavington, G – London, 1752 – 1mf – 9 – MP-360/1 – ne IDC [240]
THE BISHOP OF LONDON'S DOCTRINE OF JUSTIFICATION, IN HIS LATE PASTORAL LETTER,... / Warne, J – London, 1740 – 1mf – 9 – MP-278/1 – ne IDC [240]
THE BISHOP OF LONDON'S PASTORAL LETTER TO THE PEOPLE OF HIS DIOCESE,... / Gibson, E – London, 1739 – 1mf – 9 – MP-261/1 – ne IDC [240]
BISHOP PATTESON : THE MARTYR OF MELANESIA / Page, Jesse – New York: Fleming H Revell, [189-?] – 1mf – 9 – 0-8370-6591-7 – 1986-0591 – us A.T.L.A. [920]
THE BISHOP POTTER MEMORIAL HOUSE: HISTORY OF ITS ORIGIN, DESIGN, AND OPERATIONS, ILLUSTRATING WOMAN'S SPIRITUAL MISSION IN THE CHRISTIAN CHURCH – 1868 – 9 – us A.T.L.A. [240]
BISHOP SEABURY AND BISHOP PROVOOST : AN HISTORICAL FRAGMENT / Perry, William Stevens – [S.l.: s.n.], 1862 – 1mf – us A.T.L.A. [240]
BISHOP SELWYN OF NEW ZEALAND AND OF LICHFIELD : A SKETCH OF HIS LIFE AND WORK, WITH SOME FURTHER GLEANINGS FROM HIS LETTERS, SERMONS, AND SPEECHES / Curteis, G H – London: Kegan Paul, Trench, 1889 – 2mf – us A.T.L.A. [240]
Bishop, Steven *see* AUSTRALIAN TAKEOVERS: THE EVIDENCE
BISHOP ULLATHORNE : THE STORY OF HIS LIFE – London: Burns & Oates, [1886?] – 1mf – 9 – 0-8370-7015-5 – 1986-1015 – us A.T.L.A. [920]
Bishop, William H *see* HISTORY OF ROANE COUNTY
Bishop, William Samuel *see* THE DEVELOPMENT OF TRINITARIAN DOCTRINE IN THE NICENE AND ATHANASIAN CREEDS
THE BISHOPS IN THE TOWER : A RECORD OF STIRRING EVENTS AFFECTING THE CHURCH AND NONCONFORMISTS FROM THE RESTORATION TO THE REVOLUTION / Luckock, Herbert Mortimer – London: Rivingtons, 1887 – 1mf – us A.T.L.A. [240]
BISHOPS REGISTERS / Norwich. (Diocese) – 1299-1912 – 1 – uk Microform Academic [240]
BISHOP'S STORTFORD GAZETTE – England. -w. 25 Sept-25 Dec 1981. 1 reel – 1 – uk British Libr Newspaper [072]
BISHOP'S STORTFORD OBSERVER – England. -w. Jan 1980-Dec 1981. 5 reels – 1 – uk British Libr Newspaper [072]
Bishopsgate Institute. London *see*
– HOLYOAKE PAPERS
– HOLYOAKE PAPERS: INDEX

BISHOPVILLE FIRST BAPTIST CHURCH. LEE COUNTY : CHURCH RECORDS – 1848-1871 – 1 – 5.00 – us Baptist [240]
Bismarck, Herbert von see COLLECTION OF CORRESPONDENCE..., 1881-83
Bismarck, Otto, Fuerst von see DIE POLITISCHEN BERICHTE DES FUERSTEN BISMARCK AUS PETERSBURG UND PARIS (1859-1862)
BISMARCK-ERINNERUNGEN DES STAATSMINISTERS / Lucius von Ballhausen, Freiherr Robert Sigmund Maria Joseph – 3rd ed. Stuttgart, 1920. xii,589p – 1 – us U.W. Library [920]
BISMARCK-JAHRBUCH / ed by Kohl, Horst – Berlin. 1894-99. 6v. Film Mas C 682 – 1 – us H.U. Library [073]
Bismut, V see LA NATIONALITE DES SOCIETES EN TUNISIE
Bissainthe, M see DICTIONNAIRE DE BIBLIOGRAPHIE HAITIENNE
Bisschof, B see MITTELALTERLICHE STUDIEN
Bisschop, P de see
- ANTWOORT-LIEDT, OP EENS WEDERDOOPERS LASTER-LIEDT
- SPIEGHEL DER WATERLANTSCHER WEDERDOOPEREN LEUGHENKON ONTDECKENDENDE DE ONGHEGRONDE ENDE LEUGHENACHTIGE BESCHULDINGHEN

Bisschop, W R see LIMITATION OF SHIPOWNER'S LIABILITY AND ...
Bissell, Allen Page see THE LAW OF ASYLUM IN ISRAEL HISTORICALLY AND CRITICALLY EXAMINED
Bissell, Edwin Cone see
- THE APOCRYPHA OF THE OLD TESTAMENT
- GENESIS PRINTED IN COLORS
- HISTORIC ORIGIN OF THE BIBLE
- PENTATEUCH ANALYSIS
- PENTATEUCH LAWS AND THE HIGHER CRITICISM
- A PRACTICAL INTRODUCTORY HEBREW GRAMMAR

Bissell, J H see BISSELL'S REPORTS OF CASES IN THE SEVENTH CIRCUIT, 1851-1883
BISSELL'S REPORTS OF CASES IN THE SEVENTH CIRCUIT, 1851-1883 / Bissell, J H – Philadelphia: Callaghan. v1-11. 1873-83 (all publ) – 73mf – 9 – $109.00 – LLMC 81-438 – us L.L.M.C. [340]
Bissels, Thomas see ZUM ZUSAMMENHANG VON IDENTIFIKATION MIT DEM GRUPPENREPRAESENTANTEN UND REGIONALER IDENTITAET
Bissing, F W von see DIE MASTABA DES SEMNI-KAI IM VEREIN MIT A.E.P
Bissing, FW von see
- CATALOGUE GENERAL DES ANTIQUITES EGYPTIENNES DU MUSEE DE CAIRE
- CATALOGUE GENERAL DES ANTIQUITIES EGYPTIENNES DU MUSEE DE CAIRE

Bisso, Jose see CRONICA DE LA PROVINCIA DE MURCIA
Bisson, Fernand see BIBLIOGRAPHIE DE CERTAINS MARISTES (PERES, EVEQUES ET MISSIONNAIRES) AMERICAINS ET NEO-ZELANDAIS
BISSULA / Dahn, Felix – 33.-44. Aufl. Berlin: P Franke, [189-?] – 1 – us U.W. Library [830]
DAS BIST DU : EIN SPIEL IN 5 VERWANDLUNGEN / Wolf, Friedrich – Dresden: R Kaemmerer, 1920, c1919 – 1r – 1 – us U.W. Library [820]
BISTRITZER DEUTSCHE ZEITUNG – (Cont by: Siebenbuergisch-Deutsche Zeitung) – Bistritz, oct 1 1920-oct 16 1942 – 10r – 1 – Inquire at Mikrofilmarchiv for details – gw Misc Inst [949]
BISTRIZER DEUTSCHE ZEITUNG – Bistriz (Bistrita), Rumaenien. 10 Okt 1920-16 Okt 1942 – 10r – 1 – gw Mikrofilm [949]
DIE BISTUMSGRUENDUNEN HEINRICHS DES LOEWEN (MGH SCHRIFTEN..: 3.BD) : UNTERSUCHUNGEN ZUR GESCHICHTE DES OSTDEUTSCHEN KOLONISATION / Jordan, K – 1939 – Dfl19.00 – ne Slangenburg [240]
O BISTURI : LITTERARIO, CRITICO E HUMORISTICO – Manaos, Amazonas. 12 Jan 1913 – 1,5,6 – bl Biblioteca [072]
BISU-YI AZADI – London: Shumarah-'i 1-4 (Farvardin 1357-Murdad 1357 [Mar/Apr 1978-Jul/Aug 1978]) – 1 reel – 1 – $50.00 – us MEDOC [950]
BISU-YI SUSYALISM – (Shumarah-'i 1-4 (1 Murdad 1359-Bahman 1359[23 Jul 1980-Jan 1981])) – [S.l.]: Ittihad-i Mubarizan-i Kumunist, 1980-1981 – 1 reel – 1 – $25.00 – us MEDOC [950]
BITALIAN NEWS – Chicago, IL. 1977-78 – 1r – 1 – $50.00 – R04300 – us Library Micro [071]
Bitaube, Paul Jeremie see
- JOSEPH
- REFLEXIONS SUR LE MERVEILLEUX EPIQUE

BITBURGER KREIS- UND INTELLIGENZBLATT – Bitburg, 1854-67 – 1 – Inquire at Mikrofilmarchiv for details – gw Misc Inst [943]
BITLIS – 1316H/1314. Mali, [1898] – $45.00 – us MEDOC [956]
Bitovt, Iu see REDKIE RUSSKIE KNIGI I LETUCHI IZDANIIA 18 VEKA S BIBLIOGRAFICHESKIMI PRIMECHANIIAMI, UKAZANIEM STEPENI REDKOSTI I TSENAMI..
BITS OF FAMILY HISTORY : PAPER READ BEFORE THE JOHN BRADFORD CLUB, LEXINGTON, KENTUCKY, DECEMBER 8 1932 / Clay, Henrietta – [Lexington, KY: Clay Print Co, 1933] – us Res Libr [978]
Bittel, Deolindo Felipe see
- PERONISMO Y DICTADURA
- QUE ES EL PERONISMO

Bitter, G see DIE GATTUNG ACAENA
BITTER ROOT TIMES – Hamilton. Mont. 1894-1896; 1898-1899 – 1 – us UMI [071]
BITTERE WAHRHEITEN : EINE UNERWARTETE BELEUCHTUNG DER "ERNSTEN GEDANKEN" DES HERRN OBERSTLIEUTENANT V. EGIDY / Bornemann, Wilhelm – 3. unver. Aufl. Goettingen:Vandenhoeck & Ruprecht, 1891 – 1mf – 9 – 0-8370-2416-1 – 1985-0416 – us A.T.L.A. [240]
BITTERES LEIDEN : OBERAMMERGAUER PASSIONSSPIEL, TEXT VON 1750 / Rosner, Ferdinand; ed by Mausser, Otto – (Includes bibliographical references) – Leipzig: K W Hiersemann, 1934 – 1 – us U.W. Library [820]
Bitting, C C see BIBLE SOCIETIES AND THE BAPTISTS
Bittinger, Lucy Forney see GERMAN RELIGIOUS LIFE IN COLONIAL TIMES
Bittner, L see CHRONOLOGISCHES VERZEICHNIS DER OESTERREICHISCHEN STAATSVERTRAEGE
Bittremieux, Leo see LA SOCIETE SECRETE DES BAKHIMBA AU MAYOMBE
BITUMINOUS COAL DIVISION, DECISIONS AND ORDERS / U.S. Department of the Interior – 1 Oct 1940-June 30 1941 (all publ) – 9 – LLMC 84-112 – us L.L.M.C. [324]
BITZARON – (New York). 1939-54 – 1 – us A.J.P.C. [073]
THE BIU BOOK : A COLLATION AND REFERENCE BOOK ON BIU DIVISION (NORTHERN NIGERIA) / Davies, J G – Norla, Zaria: [s.n.] 1954-1956 – us Res Libr [960]
BIUDZHET KREST'IANSKOGO KHOZIAISTVA : RUKOVODSTVO PO SCHETOVODNOMU ANALIZU KREST'IANSKOGO KHOZIAIAISTVA DLIA KOOPERATOROV I AGRONOMOV / Studenskii, G A – Moscow, 1923 – 2mf – 9 – COR-518/1 – ne IDC [334]
BIUDZHETNYE ISSLEDOVANIIA : ISTORIIA I METODY / Chaianov, A V – M., 1929 – 4mf – 9 – COR-228/1 – ne IDC [334]
BIUDZHETY GORNOZAVODSKOGO NESELENIIA URALA V 1926-27 G – Sverdlovsk: Upravlenie, 1928 – 1 – CSUX91-B1746 – us Hoover Inst Photo [330]
BIULETEN NARODNOGO KOMISARIIATU IUSTYTSII / Ukraine, Narodnyi komisariat iustytsii – (Includes c.1: no.42 1926:Nov.26-no.44 (1926:Dec.9) – Kharkiv: Komisariat, 1922 – 1 – CSUXAKY5549-S – us Hoover Inst Photo [340]
BIULETENI RELIGIOZNO PEDAGOGICHESKAGO KABINETA – Paris, 1928-1929 – 1 reel – 1 – us I.H.R.C. [944]
BIULETYN / Polskie Towarzystwo Jezykoznawcze – Cracow. v. 1-13. 1927-19 – 1 – us NY Public [460]
BIULETYN / Zydowski Instytut Historyczny. Warsaw – nos 1-40 1951-1961 and index to nos 1-32 – 1 – us NY Public [947]
BIULETYN INFORMACYJNY, POLAND – 1941-44 – 1r – 1 – $85.00 – us Ross [072]
BIULLETEN 3-GO VSEROSSI ISKOGO SEZDA GUBKHIMOV. BIULLETEN TRETEGO VSEROSSI ISKOGO SEZDA GUBKHIMOV – (Library has: Oct. 11-15, 18-19, 1921) – Moskva: Glavkhim V.S.N.Kh. – 1 – CSUX89-S533 – us Hoover Inst Photo [947]
BIULLETEN 3-GO VSEROSSI ISKOGO SEZDA GUBKHIMOV I SOI UZA RABOCHIKH KHIMIKOV see BIULLETEN 3-GO VSEROSSI ISKOGO SEZDA GUBKHIMOV. BIULLETEN TRETEGO VSEROSSI ISKOGO SEZDA GUBKHIMOV
BIULLETEN 3-GO VSEROSSI ISKOGO SEZDA SOI UZA RABOCHIKH KHIMIKOV I GUBKHIMOV see BIULLETEN 3-GO VSEROSSI ISKOGO SEZDA GUBKHIMOV. BIULLETEN TRETEGO VSEROSSI ISKOGO SEZDA GUBKHIMOV
BIULLETEN (ASSOT SIAT SII A PO IZUCHENII U PROIZVODITELNYKH SIL SEVERA – (Includes c.1: v.1 1927) – Arkhangelsk: [Obshchestvo], 1927 – 1 – CSUXAKZ2486-S – us Hoover Inst Photo [947]
BIULLETEN / ASSOT SIAT SII A PO IZUCHENII U PROIZVODITELNYKH SIL SEVERA PRI ARKHANGELSKOM GUBPLANE I ARKHANGELSKOE OBSHCHESTVO KRAEVEDENII A. see BIULLETEN (ASSOT SIAT SII A PO IZUCHENII U PROIZVODITELNYKH SIL SEVERA
BIULLETEN BI URO RUSSKO I PECHATI V KONSTANTINOPOLI E – (Library has: no. 40 (30/13 okt. 1920)) – Konstantinopol: Bi uro russko i pechati – 1 – CSUX88-S467 – us Hoover Inst Photo [947]
BIULLETEN DIALEKTOLOGICHESKOGO SEKTORA INSTITUTA RUSSKOGO IAZYKA – Akad. Nauk SSSR. Moscow, Leningrad, 1947-49. v1-6. BR-1684 2 – 8 – ne IDC [947]
BIULLETEN' "DOMA PESNI" – (Parallel texts in French, German and in pt Russian) – Moscow, 1912-17 – 1mf – 9 – us Ross [780]
BIULLETEN GLAVNAUKI see BIULLETEN GLAVNOGO UPRAVLENII A NAUCHNYKH, KHUDOZHESTVENNYKH I MUZE INYKH UCHREZHDENI I AKADEMICHESKOGO T SENTRA NARKOMPROSA
BIULLETEN GLAVNOGO UPRAVLENII A NAUCHNYKH, KHUDOZHESTVENNYKH I MUZE INYKH UCHREZHDENI I AKADEMICHESKOGO T SENTRA NARKOMPROSA – (Library has: May, July, Sept./Nov. 1922) – Moskva: Glavnauka, 1922- – 1 – CSUX89-S507 – us Hoover Inst Photo [947]
BIULLETEN' GUBSOIUZA – (Cont by: Golos kooperatora. Saratov, 1922-23 n7. Cont by: Golos nizhne-volzhskogo kooperatora. Saratov, 1924-28 n1. Cont by: Golos kooperatora. Saratov, 1928 n2-1929 n21. Missing: 1921 n1-12; 1921 n14-1922 n15; 1922 n19-20, 22) – Saratov, 1921-22 n27 – 114mf – 9 – COR-578/1 – ne IDC [334]
BIULLETEN INOSTRANNO I KOMMERCHESKO I INFORMAT SII – (Includes c.1: no.3108 1968:Mar.2-no.3144 (1968:May 30)) – Moskva: Nauchno-issl. Koni unkturny i in-t, 1948 – 1 – CSUXAKY5378-S – us Hoover Inst Photo [947]
BIULLETEN INOSTRANNO I KOMMERCHESKO I INFORMAT SII. PRILOZHENIE – (Includes c.1: 1968:no.1-1968:no.2) – Moskva: NIKI, 1955 – 1 – CSUXAKZ0040-S – us Hoover Inst Photo [947]
BIULLETEN / KONTRAGENTSTVO V.T S.I.K. SOVI ETOV R., S. I KR. DEPUTATOV, INFORMAT-IONNY I OTDI EL see BIULLETEN (RUSSIAN S.F.S.R. VSEROSSI ISKI I T SENTRALNY I ISPOLNITELNY I KOMITET. KONTRAGENTSTVO. INFORMAT SIONNY I OTDEL)
BIULLETEN' KOOPERATIVNOI SEKTSII KOMINTERNA – (Cont by: Mezhdunarodnaia kooperatsiia. Moscow, 1926-30 n6. Missing: 1924 n1-10) – Moscow, 1924-25 – 36mf – 9 – COR-650/1 – ne IDC [334]
BIULLETEN KRYMSKOGO T SENTRALNOGO STATISTICHESKOGO UPRAVLENII A – (Includes c.1: no.9 1928:June) – Simferopol: Krymskoe gos. izd-vo, 1923 – 1 – CSUXAKZ1414-S – us Hoover Inst Photo [947]
BIULLETEN LENINGRADSKOGO GUBERNSKOGO OTDELA STATISTIKI : IZDANIE LENINGARDSKOGO GUBERNSKOGO EKONOMICHESKOGO SQVESHCHANII A – (Includes c.1: no.10 1924:Apr./May, no.15 (1925:Oct./1926:June)) – Leningrad: [Soveshchanie] – 1 – CSUXAKZ0565-S – us Hoover Inst Photo [947]
BIULLETEN MIROVOGO KHOZI A ISTVA – (Includes c.1: v.2:no.7/8 1926:Apr.15-; v.2:no.10/11 1926:June 15) – Moskva: Izd. T Sentr. upr. pechati VSNKh SSSR, 1924 – 1 – CSUXAKZ5988-S – us Hoover Inst Photo [947]
BIULLETEN MOSKOVSKOGO NARODNOGO KHOZI A ISTVA – (Includes c.1: v.2:no.10 1921:June 30, v.2:no.13; v.2:no.15/16-v.2:no.17; v.2:no.21/22 1921:Dec.15) – [Moskva: Sovet], 1920. 2v – 1 – CSUXAKZ2705-S – us Hoover Inst Photo [947]
BIULLETEN MOSKOVSKOGO OTDELENII A ROSSI ISKOGO PISHCHEVOGO NAUCHNO-TEKHNICHESKOGO INSTITUTA – (Library has: Apr. 1919) – Moskva: Vysshi i sovet narodnogo khozi a istva, Nauchnotekhnicheski i otdel – 1 – CSUX89-S587 – us Hoover Inst Photo [947]
BIULLETEN' NARKOMVNUTORGA SSSR – Moscow. 1935-Jun 1940. Bulletin of the USSR People's Commissariat of Internal Trade. Available: 1936-39 (1-16). BR-9564/1 – 9 – ne IDC [947]
BIULLETEN NARODNOGO KOMISSARIATA FINANSOV R.S.F.S.R. – (Library has: Jan. 15, Dec. 14, 30 1925 and Feb. 19, 1927) – Moskva: NKF RSFSR, 1924-1927. 4v – 1 – CSUX89-S510 – us Hoover Inst Photo [947]
BIULLETEN NARODNOGO KOMISSARIATA INOSTRANNYKH DEL – (Includes c.1: no.1 1920:Feb.22-no.2 (1920:Mar.10); no.7 1920:Apr.25, no.12 (1920:May 17); no.14 1920: May 29; no.16 1920: June 8-no.76 (1921:May 15); no.87 192?) – Moskva: Komissariat, [1920-1922]. 118 no – 1 – CSUXAKY5442-S – us Hoover Inst Photo [947]
BIULLETEN' NARODNOGO KOMISSARIATA IUSTITSII UKSSR – Kharkov, 1922-31. Bulletin of the Ukrainian People's Commissariat of Justice. Scattered issues available. BR-9323/1 – 9 – ne IDC [947]
BIULLETEN' NARODNOGO KOMISSARIATA PISHCHEVOI – Moscow, 1934-40. Bulletin of the People's Commissariat of the Food Industry. BR-9339/1 – 9 – ne IDC [640]
BIULLETEN NARODNOGO KOMISSARIATA PO PRODOVOLSTVII U – (Includes c.1: 1919:July 31-1920:Dec.30) – Moskva: Komissariat, 1919-1920. 104 no.; 45-59 – 1 – CSUXAKZ2558-S – us Hoover Inst Photo [947]
BIULLETEN NARODNOGO KOMISSARIATA SNABZHENIIA / Soviet Union, Narodnyi komissariat snabzheniia – (Includes c.1: 1933:no.15) – Moskva: Za pishchevuiu industriiu, 19uu – 1 – CSUXAKZ2698-S – us Hoover Inst Photo [640]
BIULLETEN' NARODNOGO KOMISSARIATA SNABZHENIIA – Moscow, 1932-34. Bulletin of the People's Commissariat of Supply. Lacking: 1932 nos 26,27. BR-9563/1 – 9 – ne IDC [335]
BIULLETEN' NARODNOGO KOMISSARIATA TRUDA – Moscow, Aug 1918-1919. Bulletin of the People's Commissariat of Labor. BR-1544/2 – 8 – ne IDC [947]
BIULLETEN NARODNOGO KOMISSARIATA ZDRAVOOKHRANENII A – (Includes c.1: 1922:no.1-no.10/11, no.22-no.24; 1924:no.1-no.9, no.11-no.24; 1925:no.2, no.7/8-1926:no.20, no.24-1927:no.6; 1927:no.8-no.24) – Moskva: Komissariat, [1922]-1927. 6v – 1 – CSUXAKZ0581-S – us Hoover Inst Photo [947]
BIULLETEN' NIZHEGORODSKOGO GUBERNSKOGO KOOPERATIVNOGO SOVETA – (Cont by: Nizhgorodskii kooperator. Nizhnyi Novgorod, 1926-31 n12. Missing: 1925 n3) – Nizhnyi Novgorod, 1925-26 n12 – 109mf – 9 – COR-656/1 – ne IDC [334]
BIULLETEN N.K.I.D. see BIULLETEN NARODNOGO KOMISSARIATA INOSTRANNYKH DEL
BIULLETEN OFFIT SIALNYKH RASPORI AZHENI I I SOOBSHCHENI I / NARKOMPROS – (Library has: March-Dec. 1921; Jan.-Apr., Dec. 1922; some issues missing) – Moskva: Narkompros, 1921-1922 – 1 – CSUX89-S544 – us Hoover Inst Photo [947]
BIULLETEN OFFIT SIALNYKH RASPORI AZHENI I I SOOBSHCHENI I NARODNOGO KOMISSARIATA PROSVESHCHENII A see BIULLETEN OFFIT SIALNYKH RASPORI AZHENI I I SOOBSHCHENI I / NARKOMPROS
BIULLETEN' OPPOZITSII – Paris. France. 1929-1941. (Rus. Lang.) – 1 – us UMI [072]
BIULLETEN OTDELA NORMIROVANII A TRUDA T SENTRALNOGO KOMITETA VSRKH ZA PERIOD... – (Includes c.1: no.1 1921:Apr./Aug.) – Moskva: Komitet, [1921- – 1 – CSUXAKY6568-S – us Hoover Inst Photo [947]

BIULLETEN' OTDELA TSK PO RABOTE SREDI ZHENSHCHIN – Moscow, 1921-25 – 11mf – 9 – $90.00 coll – us Ross [305]

BIULLETEN PETROGRADSKOGO SOVETA NARODNOGO KHOZI A ISTVA – (Includes c.1: no.1 1921) – [Petrograd]: Gos. izd-vo, 1921 – 1 – CSUXAKZ6000-S – us Hoover Inst Photo [947]

BIULLETEN' PRODOVOL'STVENNOGO OTDELA MOSKOVSKOGO SOVETA RABOCHIKH I KRASNOARMEISKIKH DEPUTATOV – (Missing: Nos. 1-139; 144; 174; 183; 246; 248; 251; 255; 257; 268) – M., (?)-1918. Nos. 1-278 – 22mf – 9 – R-2336/1 – ne IDC [947]

BIULLETEN' PROMKOOPERATSII – (Missing: 1922 n1-2; 1922 n5-1923 n1) – Moscow, 1922-23 n5 – 7mf – 9 – COR-551/1 – ne IDC [334]

BIULLETEN' RUKOPISNOGO OTDELA PUSHKINSKOGO DOMA – 1947-61. 9v. BR-10,962/1 – 9 – ne IDC [010]

BIULLETEN (RUSSIAN S.F.S.R. VSEROSSI ISKI I T SENTRALNY I ISPOLNITELNY I KOMITET. KONTRAGENTSTVO. INFORMAT SIONNY I OTDEL) – (Includes c.1: no.1 1918:Oct) – Moskva: Kontragentstvo, 1918- – 1 – CSUXAKZ6286-S – us Hoover Inst Photo [947]

BIULLETEN SAKHAROTRESTA – (Includes c.1: v.5:no.3 1927:Mar.-v.5:no.5 (1927:May); v.7:no.2/3 1929:Feb./Mar.-v.7:no.5 (1929:May)) – Moskva: Promizdat. 7v – 1 – CSUXAKZ6805-S – us Hoover Inst Photo [947]

BIULLETEN (SARATOVSKAI A GUBERNII A (R.S.F.S.R.). ZEMELNY I OTDEL. STATISTICHESKAI A SEKT SII A) – (Includes c.1: no.9) – [Saratov: Otdel] – 1 – CSUXAKZ1963-S – us Hoover Inst Photo [947]

BIULLETEN SARATOVSKOGO GUBERNSKOGO STATISTICHESKOGO BI URO – (Includes c.1: no.1 1920:Apr.26-no.2 (1920:July 1)) – [Saratov]: Bi uro, 1920- – 1 – CSUXAKZ1933-S – us Hoover Inst Photo [947]

BIULLETEN SEVERO-KAVKAZSKOGO KRAEVOGO STATISTICHESKOGO UPRAVLENII A – (Includes c.1: no.5 1926:Jan.-no.6 (1926:Feb.)) – Rostov na Donu: Upravlenie – 1 – CSUXAKZ1640-S – us Hoover Inst Photo [947]

BIULLETEN SHKOLNO-SANITARNAGO OTDELA PRI KOMISSARIATE NARODNOGO PROSVESHCHENII A – (Includes c.1: no.2 1918-no.4 (1919)) – Moskva: Otdel, [1918] – 1 – CSUXAKY9959-S – us Hoover Inst Photo [947]

BIULLETEN SHKOLNO-SANITARNNOGO OTDELA PRI KOMISSARIATE NARODNOGO PROSVESHCHENII A NO. 2-4 *see* BIULLETEN SHKOLNO-SANITARNAGO OTDELA PRI KOMISSARIATE NARODNOGO PROSVESHCHENII A

BIULLETEN SIBIRSKOGO STATISTICHESKOGO UPRAVLENII A – (Includes c.1: no.1 1924:Oct.-no.2 (1925:Mar.)) – Novonikolaevsk: [Upravlenie], 1924-1925. 2 no – 1 – CSUXAKZ2443-S – us Hoover Inst Photo [947]

BIULLETEN SMOLENSKOGO GUBERNSKOGO STATISTICHESKOGO BI URO – (Includes c.1: no.1 1924:Apr) – Smolenks: [Bi uro], 1924- – 1 – CSUXAKZ2429-S – us Hoover Inst Photo [947]

BIULLETEN' SOVIESHCHANII CHLENOV UCHREDITEL NAGO SOBRANIIA – Parizh. 1v – 1 – us U.W. Library [073]

BIULLETEN (SOVIET UNION. KOMITET PO VYSSHE I TEKHNICHESKO I SHKOLE) – (Includes c.1: no.2 1933:Apr. 15-no.7/8 (1933:Sept.)) – [Moskva: Vlast sovetov, 1933] – 1 – CSUXAKY6131-S – us Hoover Inst Photo [947]

BIULLETEN (SOVIET UNION. VSESOI UZNY I KOMITET PO VYSSHEMU TEKHNICHESKOMU OBRAZOVANII U) – (Includes c.1: no.9/10 1933:Sept./Oct.; no.13 1933:Dec.1-no.22 (1934:May 1); no.24 1934:June 15, no.25 (1934:July 1); no.28 1934:Aug.15-no.62 (1935:Dec.31)) – [Moskva: vlast sovetov, 1933- – 1 – CSUXAKY6182-S – us Hoover Inst Photo [947]

BIULLETEN / STATISTICHESKAI A SEKT SII A GUBERNSKAGO ZEMELNAGO OTDELA *see* BIULLETEN (SARATOVSKAI A GUBERNII A (R.S.F.S.R.). ZEMELNY I OTDEL. STATISTICHESKAI A SEKT SII A)

BIULLETEN T SENTRALNO I KOMISSII PO BORBE S POSLEDSTVII AMI GOLODA I TSENTRALNO I KOMISSII POMOSHCHI DETI AM PRI VUT SIKE – (Includes c.1: no.10 1923:Apr) – Kharkov: [VUT SIK], 1921 – 1 – CSUXAKZ2511-S – us Hoover Inst Photo [947]

BIULLETEN T SENTRALNOGO STATISTICHESKOGO UPRAVLENII A UZBEKISTANA – (Includes c.1: no.10 1925:Oct) – Samarkand: T SU, 1925 – 1 – CSUXAKZ1705-S – us Hoover Inst Photo [947]

BIULLETEN TAMBOVSKOGO GUBERNSKOGO STATISTICHESKOGO BI URO – (Includes c.1: no.4 1924:June, no.7 (1926:Jan.)) – [Tambov]: Bi uro – 1 – CSUXAKY6370-S – us Hoover Inst Photo [947]

BIULLETEN' TEATRA I MUZYKA – Elisavetgrad, 1912 (irregular 8 issues publ) – 1mf – 9 – us Ross [780]

BIULLETEN TRUDOVOGO FRONTA : OFIT SIALNOE IZDANIE NARODNOGO KOMISSARIATA TRUDA I GLAVKOMTRUDA – (Library has: Feb.-Dec. 1921, Feb. 28 1922; scattered issues missing) – Moskva: Komissariat, 1920-1922. 3v – 1 – CSUX89-S610 – us Hoover Inst Photo [947]

BIULLETEN URALSKOGO OBLASTNOGO STATISTICHESKOGO UPRAVLENII A – (Includes c.1: no.1 1926:Jan) – Sverdlovsk: Uralski i oblastno i ispolnitelny i komitet, 1926 – 1 – CSUXAKZ1812-S – us Hoover Inst Photo [947]

BIULLETEN' UZAKONENII I RASPORIAZHENII PO SEL'SKOMU I LESNOMU KHOZIAISTVU / Russia. (1917-R.S.F.S.R). Narodnyi Komissariat Zemledeliia – Moscow. 1928-30. On film: v1-3. LL-014 – 1 – us L of C Photodup [340]

BIULLETEN VERKHOVNOGO SUDA SSSR – (Includes 1957-. For latest issues, see Current Periodicals) – Moskva: Izvestii a, 1957 – 1 – CSUX89-S630 – us Hoover Inst Photo [947]

BIULLETEN' VERKHOVNOGO SUDA SSSR – Moscow, 1957- . Bulletin of the USSR Supreme Court; published bi-monthly since 1957.Available: 1957-70. BR-8602/1 – 9 – ne IDC [947]

BIULLETEN' VSEROSSIISKOGO KOOPERATIVNOGO BANKA – (Missing: 1924 n18-1925 n13, 16-17/1) – Moscow, 1924-26 n4 – 9mf – 9 – COR-550/1 – ne IDC [334]

BIULLETEN VSEROSSIISKOGO TSENTRALNOGO SOVETA PROFESSIONALNYKH SOIUZOV / Vserossiiskii tsentralnyi sovet professionalnykh soiuzov – (Includes c.1: no.1 1920:Aug.-no.59 (1923:July)) – Moskva: V. T S.S.P.S., 1920- – 1 – CSUXAKZ1531-S – us Hoover Inst Photo [331]

BIULLETEN / VSESOI UZNY I KOMITET PO VYSSHEMU TEKHNICHESKOMU OBRAZOVANII U PRI T SIK SSSR *see* BIULLETEN (SOVIET UNION. VSESOI UZNY I KOMITET PO VYSSHEMU TEKHNICHESKOMU OBRAZOVANII U)

BIULLETENI GLAVNAGO TORFI ANOGO KOMITETA OTDI ELA TOPLIVA VYSSHAGO SOVI ETA NARODNAGO KHOZI A ISTVA – (Library has: July 1918) – Moskva: Komitet, 1918 – 1 – CSUX89-S765 – us Hoover Inst Photo [947]

BIULLETENI GOSUDARSTVENNO I KOMISSII PO ELEKTRIFIKAT SII ROSSII – (Library has: Apr., June-July 1920) – [Moskva]: Gos. tekh. izd-vo Nauchno-tekhnicheskogo otdela Vysshego sov. nar. khozi a istva, 1920 – 1 – CSUX89-S565 – us Hoover Inst Photo [947]

BIULLETENI LITERATURY I ZHIZNI / Vokrus Dostoevskogo i Gor'kogo – Nr. 4. Polemika, 1913; nr.7, 1913; nr.10, 1914.BR-3344-2 – 8 – ne IDC [460]

BIULLETENI OBEDINENNOGO BI URO STATISTIKI TRUDA T.S.P.S., T.S.U., T.N.K.T. – (Includes c.1: no.4 1922:Dec) – Kazan: T.S.U., 1922 – 1 – CSUXAKZ0549-S – us Hoover Inst Photo [947]

BIULLETENI OTDELA NARODNOGO PROSVESHCHENII A M.S.R.D. (TRUDOVAI A SHKOLA) – (Includes c.1: no.1 1918:Sept., no.3 (1919:Mar.)) – Moskva: [Otdel], 1918- – 1 – CSUXAKZ0526-S – us Hoover Inst Photo [947]

BIULLETENI VYSSHAGO SOVI ETA NARODNAGO KHOZI A ISTVA – (Library has: 1932, no 1-2) – Moskva: Tip. Rossi isko i Federativno i Sot sialistichesko i Sovi etsko i Respubliki, 1918. 2 no – 1 – CSUX89-S614 – us Hoover Inst Photo [947]

BIULLETENI VYSSHAGO SOVI ETA NARODNAGO KHOZI A ISTVA – Moskva: Tip. Rossi isko i Federativno i Sot sialistichesko i Sovi etsko i Respubliki, 1918. 2 no – 1 – CSUX89-S612 – us Hoover Inst Photo [947]

BIULLTEN / KOMITET PO VYSSHE I TEKHNICHESKO I SHKOLE PRI T SIK SSSR *see* BIULLETEN (SOVIET UNION. KOMITET PO VYSSHE I TEKHNICHESKO I SHKOLE)

BIURO MIROVOGO KHOZI A ISTVA INO VSNKH SSSR *see* BIULLETEN MIROVOGO KHOZI A ISTVA

Bivona-Bernardi, A *see* STIRPIUM RARIORUM MINUSQUE COGNITARUM

Bivort, Jean Baptiste *see* CODE CONSTITUTIONEL DE LA BELGIQUE, OU COMMENTAIRE SUR LA CONSTITUTION, LA LOI ELECTORALE, LA LOI COMMUNALE ET LA LOI PROVINCIALE

BIWARA – (Lacking: 1946, V.1 (1-2, p.1-28, 4-7, p.45-109, 9)) – Jogjakarta, Badan Penerbit Nasional, 1946-1947 – 3mf – 9 – ne IDC [999]

BIWEEKLY INTELLIGENCE SUMMARIES, 1928-38 / U.S. Military Intelligence – 6 reels with printed guide – 1 – $620.00 – 0-89093-659-5 – us UPA [355]

Bixby, George F *see* THE FIRST BATTLE OF LAKE CHAMPLAIN

Bixby, James Thompson *see*
- THE CRISIS IN MORALS
- THE NEW WORLD AND THE NEW THOUGHT
- RELIGION AND SCIENCE AS ALLIES

BIZ – Fairfield, Jan 5 1953-Dec 19 1962 – 9 – at Pascoe [072]

BIZ – Toronto: S C Trethewey, [1893?-189- or 19–] – 9 – cn C.I.H.M. [971]

Bizari, P *see*
- CYPRIVM BELLVM, INTER VENETOS, ET SELYMVM TVRCARVM IMPERATOREM...
- HISTOIRE DE LA GVERRE QUI C'EST PASSEE, ENTRE LES VENITIENS ET LA SAINCTE LIGUE, CONTRE LES TURCS, POUR L'ISLE DE CYPRE, ES ANNEES 1570, 1571 ET 1572

Bizeul, Louis-Jacques-Marie *see*
- DU CHASTEAU-SE OU CASTRUM SEIUM...
- EXTRAITS ET COPIES PAR BIZEUL DE CHARTES RELATIVES A DIVERS MONASTERES DU DIOCESE DE NANTES...

BIZIM MECMUA – Istanbul: Sanayi-i Nefise Matbassi, Evkaf Matbaasi, 1922-1928; Mueduer-i Mes'ul: Huluesi, Mehmed Ali, Nos 1-28. – 5 Nisan-12 Tesrinievvel 1922 – 8mf – 9 – $200.00 – us MEDOC [949]

BIZIM PASA – Istanbul, vol 1. nos 1-3. – 1949 – 1mf – 9 – $10.50 – us MEDOC [949]

BIZNES – BANKI – BIRZHA – (Backfile through 1998 $85r) – Russia, 1999- – 2r per y standing order – 1 – us Ross [072]

BIZNES – BANKI – BIRZHA, RUSSIA – (Backfile through 1998 $85.00r) – 1999- – 2r per y – 1 – $160.00 standing order – us Ross [332]

BIZNES, BIRZHA, BANKI – 1991 – 1 – sz Infoprint [947]

BIZZARON – v. 1-65. New York. 1939-74. BJ-91-3 1 – 9 – ne IDC [270]

Bjoerksten, S R *see* DAS WASSERGEBIET FINNLANDS ...

BJORGVIN – 1954-85 (complete) – 4r – 1 – ATLA S0770 – us A.T.L.A. [073]

Bjornson, Bjornstjerne *see*
- AUSGEWAEHLTE WERKE
- OVIND; A STORY OF COUNTRY LIFE IN NORWAY

Bjurstrom, Per *see* DRAWINGS OF JOHAN TOBIAS SERGEL

THE BKSTS JOURNAL – British Kinematography, Sound and Television Society. v56-. 1974- – 1,5,6 – us UMI [073]

Blache, Robert *see* SPAIN'S OCTOBER

Blachere, R *see* LE CORAN

BLACK ABOLITIONIST PAPERS, 1830-1865 – (Guide available separately $55.00) – 17r – 1 – $1,466.25 – us UMI [976]

BLACK ACADEMY OF ARTS AND LETTERS RECORDS : FROM THE HOLDINGS OF THE SCHOMBURG CENTER FOR RESEARCH IN BLACK CULTURE, MANUSCRIPTS, ARCHIVES AND RARE BOOKS DIVISION: THE NEW YORK PUBLIC LIBRARY, ASTOR, LENOX AND TILDEN FOUNDATIONS – (Guide sold separately for $20.00 covers all coll under "Literature and the Arts" D3305.G6) – 1995 – ca 10r – 1 – ca $850.00 – D3305P25 – Dist. us Scholarly Res – us L of C Photodup [700]

BLACK AMERICAN LITERATURE FORUM *see* AFRICAN AMERICAN REVIEW

BLACK AMERICANS IN CONGRESS 1870-1989 / Ragsdale, Bruce A & Treese, Joel D – Washington: GPO, 1990 – 2mf – 9 – $3.50 – LLMC 95-031 – us L.L.M.C. [323]

BLACK AND THIRD WORLD PERIODICALS: SAMPLE ISSUES, 1844-1963 : FROM THE HOLDINGS OF THE SCHOMBURG CENTER FOR RESEARCH IN BLACK CULTURE, MANUSCRIPTS, ARCHIVES AND RARE BOOKS DIVISION: THE NEW YORK PUBLIC LIBRARY, ASTOR, LENOX AND TILDEN FOUNDATIONS – (Guide which covers all coll under "Black Periodicals" sold separately for $20.00 D3305.G4) – 1995 – 8r – 1 – $680.00 – D3305P14 – Dist. us Scholarly Res – us L of C Photodup [960]

BLACK AND WHITE / League of American Writers – 1-2 2+5 (all publ). 1939-1940 – 5mf – 9 – $40.00 – us UPA [335]

BLACK AND WHITE – London. -w. 6 Feb 1891-13 Jan 1912. (42 reels) – 1 – uk British Libr Newspaper [072]

BLACK AND WHITE BUDGET – London. v1-3. 1899-1900 – 1r – 1 – us Ross [975]

BLACK AND WHITE IN SOUTH EAST AFRICA : A STUDY IN SOCIOLOGY / Evans, Maurice S – London; New York: Longmans, Green, 1911 – 1mf – us A.T.L.A. [305]

BLACK AND WHITE IN THE SOUTHERN STATES : A STUDY OF THE RACE PROBLEM IN THE UNITED STATES FROM A SOUTH AFRICAN POINT OF VIEW / Evans, Maurice S – London; New York: Longmans, Green, 1915 – 1mf – us A.T.L.A. [305]

THE BLACK ARROW : A TALE OF THE TWO ROSES / Stevenson, Robert Louis – New York: Charles Scribner's Sons, 1888 – 1 roll – 1 – 1-55879-878-1 – uk Libr Preservation [830]

Black Baptist Convention *see* ANNUALS

BLACK BIOGRAPHICAL DICTIONARIES, 1790-1950 – (With printed handlist) – 1,068mf – 9 – £4,040.00 – uk Chadwyck [920]

Black, Bob *see*
- ANARCHISTS, ANARCHISM AND OTHER IMPEDIMENTS TO ANARCHY
- THE BABY AND THE BATHWATER
- LEFT RITES

BLACK BOOK OF LOCALITIES WHOSE JEWISH POPULATION WAS EXTERMINATED BY THE NAZIS – 2mf – 9 – $5.00 – us A.G.L.L. [350]

THE BLACK BOOK OF PAISLEY, AND OTHER MANUSCRIPTS OF THE SCOTICHRONICON; WITH A NOTE UPON JOHN DE BURDEUS... AND THE PESTILENCE / Murray, David – Paisley: A. Gardner, 1885 – 1 – us U.W. Library [941]

BLACK BOOK OF THE ADMIRALITY (RS55) : MONUMENTA JURIDICA / ed by Twiss, Travers – (With transl and appendix. v1 1871 Dfl35.00. v2 1873 Dfl35.00. v3 1874 Dfl49.00. v4 1876 Dfl46.00) – ne Slangenburg [340]

Black, Catherine H *see* INFLUENCING A BROADER UNDERSTANDING OF JAZZ DANCE

Black, Charles Clarke *see* PROOF AND PLEADINGS IN ACCIDENT CASES.

THE BLACK CODE OF GEORGIA, U.S.A – (manuscripts). 1900 – 1 – 20.00 – us L of C Photodup [978]

THE BLACK CODE OF THE DISTRICT OF COLUMBIA, IN FORCE SEPTEMBER 1ST, 1848 / Snethen, Worthington Garrettson – New York, Harned, 1848. 61 p. LL-204 – 1 – us L of C Photodup [340]

Black, Conrad *see* THE EASTERN TOWNSHIPS ADVERTISER

THE BLACK CONSCIOUSNESS MOVEMENT OF SOUTH AFRICA : MATERIAL FROM THE COLLECTION OF GAIL M GERHART – [Nairobi: Kenyan Photographic Supply Co] for the Cooperative Africana Microform Project, 1979 – us Res Libr [320]

BLACK CREEK BAPTIST CHURCH. DOVESVILLE (DARLINGTON), SOUTH CAROLINA : CHURCH RECORDS – 1798-1896 – 1 – 15.39 – us Baptist [240]

BLACK CREEK BAPTIST CHURCH. WALTERBORO, SOUTH CAROLINA : CHURCH RECORDS – 1842-78, 1980-89 – 1 – $31.46 – us Baptist [240]
BLACK CULTURAL LEADERS IN LITERATURE – 1 – us Ross [975]
BLACK CULTURAL LEADERS IN MUSIC – 1 – us Ross [975]
BLACK CULTURAL LEADERS IN THEATRE – 1 – us Ross [975]
BLACK CULTURE – (Includes 3v catalog ($165) and guide. Slavery in History $1638 19r. South America and the West Indies $2932.50 34r. United States $33,568.50 417r) – 471r – 1 – $37,835.00 – us UMI [305]
BLACK DEATH: SOURCES CONCERNING THE EUROPEAN PLAGUE : SERIES ONE: RARE PRINTED SOURCES FROM THE HERZOG AUGUST BIBLIOTHEK, WOLFENBUTTEL,C.1470-1822 – (Part 2: 16 reels.-$1,900.00) – Marlborough: Adam Matthew Publications, 1994 – 18r – 1 – $2,100.00 (Part 1) – uk Matthew [614]
BLACK DISPATCH – Oklahoma City. Okl. 1948-68 – 1 – us UMI [071]
BLACK DWARF – 1-12 (all publ). 1817-1824 – 101mf – 9 – $340.00 – us UPA [305]
BLACK EDUCATION IN SOUTH AFRICA / South Africa. Signatory Association. Task Force on Education – Johannesburg, [1986] – 1mf – 9 – DE-651/1 – ne IDC [370]
BLACK ENTERPRISE – (1975-. 9) – v. 1- 1970- – 1,5,6 – us UMI [380]
BLACK HAWK WAR RECORDS, 1832 / Illinois. Military Records – General and Staff, 2nd Brigade, Captain John Dement Co., Whiteside Brigade. V130-0001 – 1 – us A.G.L.L. [920]
Black, Henry Campbell *see*
- HANDBOOK ON THE CONSTRUCTION AND INTERPRETATION OF THE LAWS.
- A TREATISE ON FEDERAL TAXES.
- A TREATISE ON THE LAW OF JUDGMENTS, INCLUDING THE DOCTRINE OF RES JUDICATA
- A TREATISE ON THE LAW OF TAX TITLES.
- A TREATISE ON THE LAWS REGULATING THE MANUFACTURE AND SALE OF INTOXICATING LIQUORS

BLACK HERITAGE – v17-21. 1977-82 – 1,5,6,9 – us UMI [305]
Black, Hugh *see* FRIENDSHIP
THE BLACK INTERPRETERS : NOTES ON AFRICAN WRITING / Gordimer, Nadine – [Johannesburg] SPRO-CAS/Ravan [1973] – us Res Libr [490]
THE BLACK ISLE 1851 CENSUS INDEX : ARGYLL AND WEST SCOTLAND CENSUS INDEX, PART 12 / Maciines, John & Gibson, Peter – 1996 – 3mf – 9 – A$21.95 – 0-9586638-1-5 – at Seanachas [920]
Black, J M *see* FLORA OF SOUTH AUSTRALIA
Black, Jeremiah S *see* PAPERS
Black, John G *see* A COMPARATIVE ANALYSIS OF EQUIVALENT SUBMAXIMAL TREADMIL AND BICYCLE ERGOMETER EXERCISE
Black, John Sutherland *see* BOOK OF JOSHUA
BLACK JOURNALS: PART 2 – Periodical resources for Afro-American and African studies. Part 2. African; American Anti-Slavery Society; Annual Report; American Colonization Society: Annual Report; Freedman; Freedman's Journal; Freedman's Advocate; Massachusetts Anti-Slavery Society: Annual Report and Proceedings; National Freedman; Negro Educational Review; Negro Farmer and Messenger; Ohio Anti-Slavery Society: Report of Anniversary; Phelps-Stokes Fellowship Papers; Phelps-Stokes Fellowship Studies; Service; Tuskegee Messenger. Titles available individually; see under title for price – 1 – $1,465.00 – us UPA [073]
BLACK JOURNALS: PART I – Periodical resources for Afro-American and African studies. Part 1. African Observer; Alexander's Magazine; American Anti-Slavery Reporter; American Jubilee; Anti-Slavery Examiner; Anti-Slavery Record; Anti-Slavery Tracts; Brown American; Colored American Magazine; Color Line; Competitor; Crisis; Douglass' Monthly; Education; A Journal of Reputation; Fire!!; Half-Century Magazine; Harlem Quarterly; Messenger; National Anti-Slavery Standard; National Era; National Negro Health News; National Negro Voice; National Principia; Negro Music Journal; Negro Quarterly; Negro Story; New Challenge; The Non-Slaveholder; Quarterly Review of Higher Education Among Negroes; Race; Race Relations; Radical Abolitionist; Slavery in America; Southern Frontier; Voice of the Negro. Titles available individually; see under title for price – 1,9 – $3,590.00 – us UPA [073]
BLACK LEADERS IN AMERICAN HISTORY – 13r – 1 – us Ross [970]
BLACK LEADERS IN TECHNOLOGY – 1 – us Ross [975]
BLACK LEADERS OF THE RECONSTRUCTION ERA – 1 – us Ross [975]
BLACK LIBERATOR – 1972-78. Incomplete. London. "Theoretical and discussion journal for black liberation." – 1 – us U.W. Library [073]
BLACK LITERATURE, 1827-1940 / ed by Gates, Henry Louis Jr – (Includes cumulative index) – 200mf per y – 9 – £1,435.00y – uk Chadwyck [800]
Black, M *see* RITUALE MELCHITARUM
BLACK MALE/FEMALE RELATIONSHIPS – 1979- – 1,5,6,9 – us UMI [306]
BLACK NATIONALISM IN SOUTH AFRICA : A SHORT HISTORY / Walshe, Peter – Johannesburg, SPRO-CAS/Ravan 1973 – us Res Libr [320]
BLACK NEWSPAPER COLLECTION – (Core coll 909r + indexes $66,297.50. Core coll 1977-96 covering period of indexes only 314r $32,085. Suppl 1 343r $21,102.50. Suppl 2 162r $9,970.50. 1977-96 Indexes $762.50y) – 1,414r – 1 – $95,335.00 coll + indexes – us UMI [073]
BLACK NEWSPAPERS: SAMPLE ISSUES, 1845-1966 : FROM THE HOLDINGS OF THE SCHOMBURG CENTER FOR RESEARCH IN BLACK CULTURE, MANUSCRIPTS, ARCHIVES AND RARE BOOKS DIVISION: THE NEW YORK PUBLIC LIBRARY, ASTOR, LENOX AND TILDEN FOUNDATIONS – (Guide which covers all coll under "Black Periodicals" sold separately for $20.00 D3305.G4) – 1995 – 4r – 1 – $340.00 – D3305P12 – Dist. us Scholarly Res – us L of C Photodup [071]
BLACK ORPHEUS – Ibadan, Nigeria: General Publ Section, Ministry of Education. n1-13 (sep 1957-nov 1963) – 1r – us Res Libr [073]
BLACK PERSPECTIVE ON THE NEWS – Philadelphia, 1971 – 21mf – 9 – $5.00f – us Ross [975]
The Black Prince. (Ship) *see* THE LOG AND JOURNAL
BLACK RANGE – Chloride. N.M. 1886-89 – 1 – us UMI [071]
BLACK REVIEW 1972 – Durban, Black Community Programmes 1973 – us Res Libr [073]
BLACK RIVER BAPTIST CHURCH. BLACK, MISSOURI : CHURCH RECORDS – 1850-92 – 1 – 5.76 – us Baptist [240]
Black, Samuel *see* HISTORY OF SAN DIEGO COUNTY
BLACK SASH – Mowbray. 84 docs. 1980-1991 – 47mf – 9 – ne IDC [360]
THE BLACK SASH = DIE SWART SERP – Johannesburg, Women's Defence of the Constitution League. v1-10 n3 1956; aug/oct 1966; v9-12 1965/66-1968/69 – us Res Libr [320]
BLACK SASH PAPERS – ((Case history)) – 8r – 1 – sa Microfile [960]
Black Sash (Society) *see* [PAPER, 3RD SERIES]
BLACK SCHOLAR – (1976-. 9) – v. 1- 1969- – 1,5,6 – us UMI [305]
BLACK SOCIOLOGIST – (1979- 5,6,9) – 1977-. Continues: CBS Newsletter x(Caucus of Black Sociologists) – 1 – us UMI [073]
BLACK STUDIES RESEARCH SOURCES *see*
- PAPERS OF THE NAACP, PART 1
- PAPERS OF THE NAACP, PART 2
- PAPERS OF THE NAACP, PART 3
- PAPERS OF THE NAACP, PART 4
- PAPERS OF THE NAACP, PART 5
- PAPERS OF THE NAACP, PART 6
- PAPERS OF THE NAACP, PART 7
- PAPERS OF THE NAACP, PART 8
- PAPERS OF THE NAACP, PART 9
- PAPERS OF THE NAACP, PART 10
- PAPERS OF THE NAACP, PART 11
- PAPERS OF THE NAACP, PART 12
- PAPERS OF THE NAACP, PART 13
- PAPERS OF THE NAACP, PART 14
- PAPERS OF THE NAACP, PART 15
- PAPERS OF THE NAACP, PART 16
- PAPERS OF THE NAACP, PART 17
- PAPERS OF THE NAACP, PART 18
- PAPERS OF THE NAACP, PART 19
- PAPERS OF THE NAACP, PART 20
- PAPERS OF THE NAACP, PART 21
- PAPERS OF THE NAACP, PART 22
- PAPERS OF THE NAACP, PART 23
- RECORDS OF THE NATIONAL ASSOCIATION OF COLORED WOMEN'S CLUBS, 1895-1992
- RECORDS OF THE SOUTHERN CHRISTIAN LEADERSHIP CONFERENCE, 1954-1970
- SLAVERY IN ANTE-BELLUM SOUTHERN INDUSTRIES, SERIES C

BLACK VIEWPOINT / ed by Biko, B S – Durban, Spro-Cas Black Community Programmes, 1972 – us Res Libr [305]
BLACK VOICE – Riverside, CA. 1977-91 – 11r – 1 – $550.00 – R02714 – us Library Micro [071]
THE BLACK VOICE – v. 1-2. 1972-74 – 1 – 65.00 – cn McLaren [073]
Black, William *see*
- ADVENTURES IN THULE: THREE STORIES FOR BOYS
- THE BEAUTIFUL WRETCH
- BRISEIS
- A DAUGHTER OF HETH
- A DAUGHTER OF HETH: A NOVEL
- DONALD ROSS OF HEIMRA
- GREEN PASTURES AND PICCADILLY
- THE HANDSOME HUMES
- HIGHLAND COUSINS: A NOVEL
- IN FAR LOCHABER
- IN SILK ATTIRE: A NOVEL
- JAMES MERLE: AN AUTOBIOGRAPHY
- JUDITH SHAKESPEARE: A ROMANCE
- KILMENY
- LADY SILVERDALE'S SWEETHEART; AND OTHER TALES
- LOVE OR MARRIAGE? A NOVEL
- MACLEOD OF DARE: A NOVEL
- MADCAP VIOLET: A NOVEL
- THE MAGIC INK; AND OTHER TALES
- THE MAID OF KILLEENA; AND OTHER STORIES
- THE MONARCH OF MINCING LANE: A NOVEL
- MR. PISISTRATUS BROWN, M.P. IN THE HIGHLANDS
- THE NEW PRINCE FORTUNATUS
- THE PENANCE OF JOHN LOGAN; AND TWO OTHER TALES
- A PRINCESS OF THULE
- SABINA ZEMBRA: A NOVEL
- SHANDON BELLS: A NOVEL
- STAND FAST CRAIG-ROYSTON: A NOVEL
- THE STRANGE ADVENTURES OF A HOUSE-BOAT
- THE STRANGE ADVENTURES OF A PHAETON
- SUNRISE: A STORY OF THESE TIMES
- THREE FEATHERS: A NOVEL
- WHITE HEATHER: A NOVEL
- WHITE WINGS: A YACHTING ROMANCE
- WILD EELIN, HER ESCAPADES, ADVENTURES AND BITTER SORROWS
- THE WISE WOMAN OF INVERNESS: A TALE; AND OTHER MISCELLANIES
- WITH THE EYES OF YOUTH; AND OTHER SKETCHES
- WOLFENBERG
- YOLANDE: THE STORY OF A DAUGHTER

Black, William L *see* THE REBIRTH OF THE HISTORIC OLD HOLE-IN-THE-ROCK TRAIL AS A RECREATIONAL TRAIL
BLACK WORKERS IN THE ERA OF THE GREAT MIGRATION, 1916-29 – 25 reels. Printed guide – 1 – $2,750.00 – 0-89093-740-0 – us UPA [331]
BLACK WORLD – (1971-76. 5,6) – v. 1-25. 1942-76 – 1 – us UMI [073]
Blackbird, Andrew J *see* HISTORY OF THE OTTAWA AND CHIPPEWA INDIANS OF MICHIGAN: A GRAMMAR ON THEIR LANGUAGE, AND PERSONAL AND FAMILY HISTORY OF THE AUTHOR
BLACKBURN LABOUR JOURNAL – Lancashire. 1898-1909 – 1 – uk Microform Academic [072]
Blackburn, W M *see* THE COLLEGE DAYS OF CALVIN
Blacker, Irwir R *see* CORTES AND THE AZTEC CONQUE CONSULTENT. GORDON ECKHOLM
BLACKFORD AND GRANT COUNTIES / Shinn, Benjamin – Chronicle of people past and present with family lineage. Chicago: Lewis Publ. Co., 1914. Vols. 1-2. Indiana Reel 5. (The Cox Library Collection) – 5 – us Americana [978]
BLACKFORD BAPTIST CHURCH. HAWESVILLE, KENTUCKY : CHURCH RECORDS – Feb 1853-Apr 1984 – 1 – 52.74 – us Baptist [240]
BLACKFORD'S INDIANA REPORTS – v1-8. 1817-47 – 53mf – 9 – $79.00 – LLMC 84-133 – us L.L.M.C. [340]
BLACKFORD'S REPORTS / Indiana. Supreme Court – (A Pre-NRS title) – v1-8. 1817-1847 (all publ) – 53mf – 9 – $79.00 – LLMC 84-133 – us L.L.M.C. [340]
Blackham, Robert J *see* WIG AND GOWN
BLACKHEATH BEACON – Nov 14 1930-Mar 27 1931 – 9 – at Pascoe [072]
BLACKHEATH BULLETIN – Aug 8 1929-Nov 13 1930; Feb 5 1931 – 9 – at Pascoe [072]
BLACKHEATH GAZETTE – London, UK. 1892-97. -d. 6 reels – 1 – uk British Libr Newspaper [072]
BLACKHOOD – Issue Nos. 14-18 Spring 1945-Spring 46 – 5mf – 15 – $31.95 – us Comics [760]
BLACKHOOD – Issue Nos. 9-13 Winter 43-Winter 44-45 – 5mf – 15 – $31.95 – us Comics [760]
Blackie, John Stuart *see*
- FOUR PHASES OF MORALS: SOCRATES, ARISTOTLE, CHRISTIANITY, UTILITARIANISM
- LAY SERMONS
- NATURAL HISTORY OF ATHEISM
- ON SELF-CULTURE
- WHAT DOES HISTORY TEACH?

Black-Jewish Information Center *see* MEDIA PROJECT
Blackledge, William James *see* THE LEGION OF MARCHING MADMEN
BLACKLETTER JOURNAL *see* HARVARD BLACKLETTER JOURNAL
Blacklock, Thomas *see* AN ESSAY ON UNIVERSAL ETYMOLOGY
Blackmar, Frank W *see*
- KANSAS-A CYCLOPEDIA OF THE STATE HISTORY AND PROMINENT PERSONS
- SPANISH COLONIZATION IN THE SOUTHWEST
- SPANISH INSTITUTIONS OF THE SOUTHWEST

Blackmore, Richard Doddridge *see*
- ALICE LORRAINE
- CHRISTOWELL
- CLARA VAUGHAN
- CRADOCK NOWELL
- CRIPPS, THE CARRIER
- CRIPPS THE CARRIER
- DARIEL
- EREMA
- KIT AND KITTY
- LORNA DOONE
- THE MAID OF SKER
- MARY ANERLEY
- PERLYCROSS
- THE REMARKABLE HISTORY OF SIR THOMAS UPMORE
- SPRINGHAVEN
- TALES FROM THE TELLING HOUSE (SLAIN BY THE DOONES)

Blackpool and District Labour Representation Committee *see* LABOUR ADVOCATE
BLACK-ROBES : OR, SKETCHES OF MISSIONS AND MINISTERS IN THE WILDERNESS / Nevin, Robert Peebles – Philadelphia: J B Lippincott, 1872 – 1mf – 9 – 0-8370-6232-2 – 1986-0232 – us A.T.L.A. [240]
Blackrock. Ireland *see* DEAN'S GRANGE CEMETERY MONUMENTAL INSCRIPTIONS
BLACKS IN SELECTED NEWSPAPERS, CENSUSES AND OTHER SOURCES: AN INDEX TO NAMES AND SUBJECTS / Abajian, James de T – (First Supplement, 1985.-45,000 cards 2 reels. $330.00 ISBN: 0-8161-1525-7) – 1977.-102,000 cards 6 reels.-ISBN: 0-8161-1322-X – 1 – $370.00 – uk Hall [305]
BLACKS IN THE RAILROAD INDUSTRY, 1946-1954 : FROM THE HOLDINGS OF THE SCHOMBURG CENTER FOR RESEARCH IN BLACK CULTURE, MANUSCRIPTS, ARCHIVES AND RARE BOOKS DIVISION: THE NEW YORK PUBLIC LIBRARY, ASTOR, LENOX AND TILDEN FOUNDATIONS – (Guide which covers all coll under "African-American Organizations" sold separately for $20.00 D3305.G1) – 1995 – 1r – 1 – $85.00 – D3305P04 – Dist. us Scholarly Res – us L of C Photodup [380]
BLACKS IN THE U.S. ARMED FROCES : BASIC DOCUMENTS, 1639-1973 / ed by Nalty, Bernard C & MacGregor, Morris J – (Comes with printed guide) – 1994 – 5r – 1 – $425.00 – S3304 – Dist. us Scholarly Res – us L of C Photodup [355]

BLACKSBURG FIRST BAPTIST CHURCH. CHEROKEE COUNTY. SOUTH CAROLINA : CHURCH RECORDS – 1900-1929, 1934-1970. History. 1889 – 1 – 23.04 – us Baptist [240]
Blacksmith, A T *see* ENTHUSIASM DELINEATED
BLACKSMITH'S ACCOUNT BOOK / Mitchell, Caleb – 1842, 1844. 1 fiche – 9 – us South Carolina Historical [025]
BLACKSMITHS, DROP FORGERS AND HELPERS JOURNAL : 1901-1929 – (Coll title: Labor Union Periodicals, Pt 1) – 6r – 1 – $810.00 – 1-55655-229-7 – us UPA [331]
THE BLACKSMITHS GUIDE : VALUABLE INSTRUCTIONS ON FORGING, WELDING, HARDENING, TEMPERING, CASEHARDENING, ANNEALING, COLORING, BRAZING, AND GENERAL BLACKSMITHING / Sallows, J F – 1st ed. Brattleboro, VT: The Technical Press 1907 – us Res Libr [670]
BLACKSTICK PAPERS / Thackeray, Anne – British Fiction Archive: Unit 3 – 9 – uk Bell [830]
BLACKSTONE 1844-1903 – (Mf 1-4: Military 1861-65. Mf 5-7: Births 1844-60. Mf 8: Marriages 1845-55. Mf 8-9: Deaths 1845-57. Mf 10-14: Births 1861-82. Mf 15-19: Marriages 1856-94. Mf 20-24: Deaths 1858-93. Mf 25-29: Births 1883-1903. Mf 30: Marriages 1895-1904. Mf 31-32: Deaths 1898-1903) – (mf ed 1992) – 32mf – 9 – 0-87623-162-8 – us Holbrook [920]
Blackstone, Henry *see* H. BLACKSTONE'S REPORTS
Blackstone Institute *see* MODERN AMERICAN LAW
Blackstone, J *see* SPECIMEN BOTANICUM
BLACKSTONE QUIZZER B. / Ellis, Griffith Ogden – 2d ed. Detroit, The Collector, 1895. 46 p. LL-869 – 1 – us L of C Photodup [340]
Blackstone, William *see*
- AN ANALYSIS OF THE LAWS OF ENGLAND
- BLACKSTONE'S COMMENTARIES.
- COMMENTARIES ON THE LAWS OF ENGLAND
- COMMENTARIES ON THE LAWS OF ENGLAND; IN FOUR BOOKS
- REPORTS OF CASES DETERMINED IN THE SEVERAL COURTS OF WESTMINSTER-HALL, FROM 1746-1779
- THE STUDENT'S BLACKSTONE

BLACKSTONE'S COMMENTARIES. / Blackstone, William – Philadelphia, Birch and Small, 1803. 5 v. LL-904 – 1 – us L of C Photodup [340]
BLACKSTONE'S COMMENTARIES ON THE LAWS OF ENGLAND : (AMERICAN ABRIDGEMENTS AND EXTRACTS) – 197mf – 9 – LLMC 82-800 Titles 137-178 – us L.L.M.C. [340]
BLACKSTONE'S COMMENTARIES ON THE LAWS OF ENGLAND : (ENGLISH ABRIDGEMENTS AND EXTRACTS) – 142mf – 9 – LLMC 82-800 Titles 46-79 – us L.L.M.C. [340]
Blacktoft. Yorkshire *see* PARISH REGISTERS
Blackwall, J *see*
- A HISTORY OF THE SPIDERS OF GREAT BRITAIN AND IRELAND

Blackwell, E B *see* AN INVENTORY FOR ASSESSMENT OF ATTITUDES OF HIGH SCHOOL STUDENTS TOWARD HEALTH-REALTED PHYSICAL FITNESS
Blackwell family *see* PAPERS
Blackwell, G F *see* EARLY ADOLESCENTS' KNOWLEDGE OF AND ATTITUDES TOWARD HIV AND AIDS
Blackwell, Michael C *see* THE ETHICAL THOUGHT OF CARLYLE MARNEY
Blackwell, Thomas E *see* REPORT...OF THE GRAND TRUNK RAILWAY COMPANY OF CANADA FOR THE YEAR 1859
Blackwood, James Stevenson *see* ALMUTH: THE MESSIANIC ENIGMA OF THE XLIX PSALM
BLACKWOOD'S MAGAZINE – (1971- . 5,6. 1977- . 9) – 1- 1817- – 1 – us UMI [073]
BLACKWOOD'S MAGAZINE – Edinburgh. v. 1-270. 1817-1951 – 1,5,6 – us Princeton Micro [900]
"BLAD" VAN DEN PLAATSELIJKEN RAAD VAN HET CULTUURGEBIED DER OOSTKUST VAN SUMATRA – Medan, 1918-1933 – 61mf – 9 – ne IDC [072]
EN BLADARTIKEL / Kierkegaard, Soren – Kjobenhavn: C.A. Reitzel, 1859 – 1mf – us A.T.L.A. [190]
BLADE – Aurora. Ill. -w. 1882- – 1 – us UMI [071]
BLADE – Bancroft. Neb. 1892-1954 – 1 – us UMI [071]
BLADE – Bellingham. Wash. -tw. 1894-1901 – 1 – us UMI [071]
BLADE – Bellingham. Wash. -w. 1895-1904 – 1 – us UMI [071]
BLADE – Cheney. Kan. 1888-90 – 1 – us UMI [071]
BLADE – Concordia. Kan. 1879-1902 – 1 – us UMI [071]
BLADE – Denver. Col. -w. 1961-70 – 1 – us UMI [071]
BLADE – Irvine, CA. 1975-1989 – 1r – 1 – $50.00 – R04034 – us Library Micro [071]
BLADE – Oceanside. Calif. 1893-1900; 1902-1929 – 1 – us UMI [071]
BLADE – Speareville. Kan. 1885-1892 – 1 – us UMI [071]
BLADE – Toledo. Ohio. 1940- – 1 – us UMI [071]
BLADE – Toledo. Ohio. -w. 1871, 1874, 1879-97, 1899-1916, 1921-24 – 1 – us UMI [071]
BLADE – Walnut City. Kan. 1878-1880 – 1 – us UMI [071]
BLADE TRIBUNE – Oceanside. Calif. 1930-34; 1938; 1941-42 – 1 – us UMI [071]
BLADE-CITIZEN – Encinitas, Del Mar, CA. 1982 – 144+ r – 1 – $7,200.00 ($600.00y) – H04042 – us Library Micro [071]
BLADE-CITIZEN – La Costa, CA. 1990 – 36+ r – 1 – $1,800.00 ($300.00y) – H04044 – us Library Micro [071]
BLADE-CITIZEN – Oceanside, CA. 1988 – 72+ r – 1 – $3,600.00 ($600.00y) – H04054 – us Library Micro [071]
Bladel, G van *see* CONNAISSEMENTS ET REGLES DE LA HAYE
BLADEN ENTERPRISE – Bladen, NE. -w. Oct. 1895-Oct. 1905. Incomplete; Dec. 1905-Jul. 1911; Dec. 1911-Mar. 1936 – 1 – us NE Hist [071]
BLADEN UNION BAPTIST CHURCH. FAYETTEVILLE, NORTH CAROLINA : CHURCH RECORDS – 13 May 1956-10 Oct 1965 – 1 – 20.43 – us Baptist [240]
BLADEN UNION BAPTIST CHURCH. FAYETTEVILLE, NORTH CAROLINA : CHURCH RECORDS – 1859-1965 – 1 – 20.43 – us Baptist [240]
Blades, William *see* SHAKESPEARE AND TYPOGRAPHY; BEING AN ATTEMPT TO SHOW SHAKESPEARE'S PERSONAL CONNECTION WITH, AND TECHNICAL KNOWLEDGE OF, THE ART OF PRINTING..
BLAETTER AUS DEM WERTHER-KREIS / ed by Wolff, Eugen – Breslau: S Schottlaender, 1894 – 1r – 1 – us U.W. Library [430]
BLAETTER DER PLATEN-GESELLSCHAFT / ed by Praesidium und vom wissenschaftlichen Ausschuss der Platen-Gesellschaft e.V. – (Includes bibliographical references) – Berlin: Platen-Gesellschaft 1925-26 – 1r – 1 – us U.W. Library [430]
BLAETTER DER ZEIT – Braunschweig, 1848-mar 25 1855 – 1 – Inquire at Mikrofilmarchiv for details – gw Misc Inst [943]
BLAETTER DER ZEIT – Braunschweig, Germany. 2 Oct 1849-25 Mar 1855 – 2r – 1 – gw Mikrofilm [072]
BLAETTER DES JUEDISCHEN FRAUENBUNDES – Berlin, jul 4 1924-38 – 1 – Dist. gw Mikrofilm – gw Misc Inst [270]
BLAETTER DES OPERNTHEATERS – Vienna 1919-20. 1 reel – 1 – 17.00 – us L of C Photodup [780]
BLAETTER FUER ALLE – Berlin, 1927-mar 1933 – 3r – 1 – Dist. gw Mikrofilm – gw Misc Inst [072]
BLAETTER FUER DAS BAYERISCHE GYMNASIALSCHULWESEN – Bamberg. v. 1-71, 1864-1935. Title varies. Film Mas C 396 – 1 – us H.U. Library [073]
BLAETTER FUER DEMOGRAPHIE, STATISTIK UND WIRTSCHAFTSKUNDE DER JUDEN – Berlin, feb 1923-jun 1925 – 1r – 1 – Dist. gw Mikrofilm – gw Misc Inst [310]
BLAETTER FUER DEMOGRAPHIE, STATISTIK UND WIRTSCHAFTSKUNDE DER JUDEN – Berlin. Nos.1-5. 1923-25. In Yiddish. Complete. 1 reel. B33. (Leo Baeck Institute. German-Jewish Periodicals, Pt 1) – 1 – $75.00 – us UPA [270]
BLAETTER FUER DIE KUNST; EINE AUSLEESE AUS DEN JAHREN 1892-1909 – Berlin, 1899-1909. 3v – 12mf – H-442/2 – ne IDC [700]
BLAETTER FUER DIE LEIPZIGER WOHLFAHRTSPFLEGE – Leipzig, 1924-28 – 1r – 1 – gw Mikrofilm [072]
BLAETTER FUER GENOSSENSCHAFTSWESEN. (INNUNG DER ZUKUNFT.) – v. 20-88. 1873-1941 – 1 – 581.00 – us L of C Photodup [331]
BLAETTER FUER JUEDISCHE GESCHICHTE UND LITERATUR – Mainz. v1-5. 1899-1904. Incomplete. 1 reel. B34. (Leo Baeck Institute. German-Jewish Periodicals, Pt 2) – 1 – $60.00 – us UPA [270]
BLAETTER FUER LITERARISCHE UNTERHALTUNG – Leipzig. 1863-68. Film Mas C 628 – 1 – us H.U. Library [430]
BLAETTER FUER MENSCHENRECHT – (1928 n12 publ as Menschenrecht) – Berlin, 1923 n1-1929 n9 (very incomplete) – 1r – 1 – Dist. gw Mikrofilm – gw Misc Inst [072]
BLAETTER FUER MISSION – v1-78. Sept 1863-1940 (incomplete) – 2r – 1 – ATLA S0249 – us A.T.L.A. [240]
BLAETTER FUER POMMERSCHE VOLKSKUNDE – Stettin. J. Burmeister. v. 1-10, Oct 1892-Sept 1902. Film Mas 8368 – 1 – us H.U. Library [073]
BLAETTER FUER SUDETENDEUTSCHE SOZIALDEMOKRATEN – (Also known as: Mitteilungsblaetter fuer Sudetendeutsche Sozialdemokraten, Feb 1944-49) – Malmo, Sweden. Feb 1944-1976 – 1 – gw Mikrofilm [072]
BLAETTER FUER TAUBSTUMMENBILDUNG – Berlin, oct 1 1887-mar 15 1934 – 1 – Dist. gw Mikrofilm – gw Misc Inst [370]
Blagoj, Dmitrij *see* ALEXANDER PUSHKIN
BLAGOTVORITEL'NOST V ROSSII / Mezhov, VI – Bibliograficheskii ukazatel' knig i statei na russkom iazyke, vyshedsikh v Rossii v period tsarstvovaniia. Imperatora Aleksandra II. Spb. 1883. BR-7155 2 – 8 – ne IDC [370]
Blagoveshchenskii *see* OLONETSKI SBORNIK
BLAGOVESTNIK / ed by Fetler, Robert – (Publ. No. 3481-7d. One part of a four-part item) – Vladivostok. 1920-22. Incomplete – 1 – $124.80 – us Baptist [240]
Blaheta, Roman *see* AUSSENOHRCHARAKTER-ISTIK BEI VERSCHIEDENEN NAGERN
Blaho, P *see* CORRESPONDENCE
Blaikie, Alexander *see*
- A HISTORY OF PRESBYTERIANISM IN NEW ENGLAND
- THE PHILOSOPHY OF SECTARIANISM, OR, A CLASSIFIED VIEW OF THE CHRISTIAN SECTS IN THE UNITED STATES

Blaikie, William *see* HOW TO GET STRONG AND HOW TO STAY SO
Blaikie, William Garden *see*
- AFTER FIFTY YEARS, OR, LETTERS OF A GRANDFATHER
- THE BOOK OF JOSHUA
- THE COLLEGES AND THEOLOGICAL INSTITUTIONS OF AMERICA
- FIRST BOOK OF SAMUEL
- FOR THE WORK OF THE MINISTRY
- THE PREACHERS OF SCOTLAND
- THE PUBLIC MINISTRY AND PASTORAL METHODS OF OUR LORD
- THE SECOND BOOK OF SAMUEL
- THOMAS CHALMERS
- WILLIAM GARDEN BLAIKIE

Blaikie, William Garden et al *see* IS CHRISTIANITY TRUE?
BLAINE COUNTY BEACON – Brewster, NE. -w. Jun 1892; Aug. 1895-Jan. 1975 – 1 – us NE Hist [071]
BLAINE COUNTY BOOSTER – Dunning, NE. -w. Jun. 1914-Oct. 1953; Dec. 1953-Aug. 1955, incomplete – 1 – us NE Hist [071]
Blaine, Ephraim *see* PAPERS OF EPHRAIM BLAINE
Blaine, James G *see*
- FREE TRADE FOR SHIPPING
- PAPERS

Blaine, James Gillespie *see* TWENTY YEARS OF CONGRESS
Blainville, Charles-H de *see*
- L'ESPRIT DE L'ART MUSICAL
- HISTOIRE GENERALE, CRITIQUE ET PHILOLOGIQUE DE LA MUSIQUE
- HISTOIRE GENERALE CRITIQUE ET PHILOLOGIQUE DE LA MUSIQUE

Blair *see* HISTORY OF DODGE AND WASHINGTON COUNTIES
BLAIR AND KETCHUM'S COUNTRY JOURNAL – (1976- . 9) – 1- 1974- – 1,5,6 – us UMI [073]
Blair, Andrew George *see* THE CANADIAN CONTINGENT: AN EXTRACT FROM A SPEECH BY THE HON. MINISTER OF RAILWAYS, AT CAMPBELLTON, N. B. ON 21ST NOV., 1899
BLAIR COURIER – Blair, NE. -w. Jul. 1889-Aug. 1907 – 1 – us NE Hist [071]
Blair, Dorothy *see* A HISTORY OF GLASS IN JAPAN
Blair, Ed *see* HISTORY OF JOHNSON COUNTY
BLAIR, EMILY N., FAMILY PAPERS, MS 4342 – 1785-1972 – 17r – 1 – us Western Res [320]
THE BLAIR FAMILY PAPERS – 47r – 1 – $1,645.00 – Dist. us Scholarly Res – us L of C Photodup [975]
Blair, Lewis H *see* UNWISE LAWS (ON PROTECTING TARIFFS)
BLAIR PILOT – Blair, NE. -w., sw. Apr. 1876-Sep. 1890. Incomplete; Nov. 1890-Apr. 1902; Jul. 1902-Jan. 1929 – 1 – us NE Hist [071]
Blair, William A *see* JOURNAL OF RELIGION IN DISABILITY AND REHABILITATION
BLAIRSVILLE ENTERPRISE – Blairsville, PA. -w 1889-1912 – 13 – $25.00r – us I.M.R. [071]
Blairsville. Presbytery (Pres. Ch. in the U.S.A.) *see* MINUTES, 1830-1920
BLAIRSVILLE RECORD – Blairsville, PA., 1830 – 13 – $25.00r – us I.M.R. [071]
Blake, A V *see*
- ALVES SACRAMENTO
- DICCIONARIO BIBLIOGRAPHICO BRAZILEIRO

Blake, Buchanan *see* JOSEPH AND MOSES, THE FOUNDERS OF ISRAEL
THE BLAKE DEMONSTRATION AT THE PAVILION, HORTICULTURAL GARDENS, MONDAY EVENING SEPTEMBER 19TH, 1892 / Blake, Edward – 1892? 00873. (Pre-1900 Canadiana) – 9 – cn C.I.H.M. [360]
Blake, Edward *see*
- ADDRESS AT THE CONVOCATION OF THE UNIVERSITY OF TORONTO, JUNE 10TH, 1890
- ADDRESS DELIVERED IN BOSTON MUSIC HALL, WEDNESDAY EVENING, JANUARY 31, 1894
- THE BLAKE DEMONSTRATION AT THE PAVILION, HORTICULTURAL GARDENS, MONDAY EVENING SEPTEMBER 19TH, 1892
- CANADIAN PACIFIC RESOLUTIONS: THOROUGH SIFTING OF A GREAT SCANDAL: ASTOUNDING DISCREPANCIES IN GOVERNMENT ESTIMATES: CONVINCING ARGUMENT FOR REJECTION OF TERMS
- DISCOURS AU SUJET DE LA PROPOSITION DEMANDANT LA DEUXIEME LECTURE DU BILL CONSTITUANT EN CORPS LEGAL L'ORDRE DES ORANGISTS, 17 MARS 1884
- EXTRACTS FROM HON. EDWARD BLAKE'S FAMOUS SPEECH DELIVERED IN THE CANADIAN HOUSE OF COMMONS, APRIL 16TH, 1880
- THE IRISH QUESTION: WITH SPECIAL REFERENCE TO HOME RULE IN CANADA: SPEECHES
- THE IRISH SITUATION: SPEECH OF MR. BLAKE, M. P., AT GLASGOW, DECEMBER, 1898
- LETTER OF THE HON. EDWARD BLAKE TO THE WEST DURHAM REFORM CONVENTION: TO WHICH IS APPENDED CORRESPONDENCE AS TO THE INVERARY MEETING
- OFFICIAL REPORT OF THE SPEECH ON THE IRISH QUESTION
- THE ORANGE ASSOCIATION UNMASKED: A CRUSHING BLOW TO OATH-BOUND SECRET SOCIETIES
- THE OVER-TAXATION OF IRELAND: SPEECH IN THE HOUSE OF COMMONS, ON 29TH MARCH, 1897: WITH INTRODUCTION, INDEX AND TABLES
- REFORM GOVERNMENT IN THE DOMINION: HON. EDWARD BLAKE BEFORE HIS CONSTITUENTS OF THE SOUTH RIDING OF BRUCE: SPEECH DELIVERED BY HIM AT TEESWATER, MONDAY, SEPT. 24TH, 1877
- THE SITUATION: 'READ MARK LEARN AND INWARDLY DIGEST'
- SPEECH AT AURORA: DELIVERED OCTOBER 3RD, 1874 ON THE OCCASION OF A MEETING OF THE REFORM PARTY OF NORTH YORK
- SPEECH BY THE HON. EDWARD BLAKE, Q.C., M.P., EX-PREMIER OF ONTARIO, CANADA, IN CONNECTION WITH THE FROME DIVISION LIBERAL ASSOCIATION, AND IN SUPPORTING A RESOLUTION OF CONFIDENCE IN MR. GLADSTONE'S GOVERNMENT...JANUARY 27TH, 1893

- SPEECH OF THE HON. EDWARD BLAKE ON THE ADDRESS IN ANSWER TO THE SPEECH FROM THE THRONE: DELIVERED IN THE HOUSE OF COMMONS AT OTTAWA, ON FRIDAY, JAN. 30TH, 1885
- SPEECH OF THE HONORABLE EDWARD BLAKE, M.P.: DELIVERED IN THE HOUSE OF COMMONS OF CANADA ON THE MOTION FOR THE SECOND READING OF THE ORANGE INCORPORATION BILL, 17TH MARCH, 1884
- SPEECH ON HOME RULE FOR IRELAND
- SPEECHES: DELIVERED BY HON. EDWARD BLAKE, THE LEADER OF THE LIBERAL PARTY: AND A SYNOPSIS OF THE DEBATE ON THE HOME RULE RESOLUTIONS IN THE HOUSE OF COMMONS
- SPEECHES OF THE HON. EDWARD BLAKE, M.P., ON THE NORTH-WEST TERRITORIES ACT, TUESDAY, 6TH MAY, 1890

Blake, James Vila *see* NATURAL RELIGION IN SERMONS
Blake, Joaquin *see* LA BATALLA DE LA ALBUERA
Blake, John William *see*
- EUROPEAN BEGINNINGS IN WEST AFRICA, 1454-1578; A SURVEY OF THE FIRST CENTURY OF WHITE ENTERPRISE IN WEST AFRICA.
- EUROPEAN BEGINNINGS IN WEST AFRICA 1454-1578: A SURVEY OF THE FIRST CENTURY OF WHITE ENTERPRISE IN WEST AFRICA

Blake, Lillie Devereux *see* WOMAN'S PLACE TO-DAY
BLAKE MEMORIAL BAPTIST CHURCH. LAKE HELEN, FLORIDA : CHURCH RECORDS – 1891-Sep 1951 – 1 – 22.50 – us Baptist [240]
Blake, Nancy E *see* THE RELATIONSHIP BETWEEN LACTATE AND VENTILATORY THRESHOLDS IN MEN WITH SPINAL CORD INJURY
Blake, S F *see* GEOGRAPHICAL GUIDE TO FLORAS OF THE WORLD
Blake, S Leroy *see* THE SEPARATES, OR, STRICT CONGREGATIONALISTS OF NEW ENGLAND
Blake, Samuel Hume *see* OUR FAULTY GAOL SYSTEM: MEMORANDUM OF AN ADDRESS DELIVERED ON BEHALF OF THE PRISONERS' AID ASSOCIATION IN THE METROPOLITAN CHURCH, TORONTO
BLAKE STUDIES – v1-9 nos 1-2 Fall 1968-80 – 1 – us UMI [420]
Blake, Virgil *see* PUBLIC AND ACCESS SERVICES QUARTERLY
Blake, Warrenne *see* AN IRISH BEAUTY OF THE REGENCY
Blake, William *see*
- AMERICA, A PROPHECY
- THE BOOK OF THEL (COPY G) AND THE VISIONS OF THE DAUGHTERS OF ALBION (COPY P)
- COLOURED ENGRAVINGS TO EDWARD YOUNG'S "NIGHT THOUGHTS" FROM SIR JOHN SOANE'S MUSEUM, LONDON
- ENGRAVINGS FROM THE SMALL AND LARGE BOOKS OF DESIGNS
- EUROPE, A PROPHECY
- ILLUSTRATIONS TO BLAIR'S THE GRAVE
- ILLUSTRATIONS TO BUNYAN'S PILGRIM'S PROGRESS
- ILLUSTRATIONS TO EDWARD YOUNG'S NIGHT THOUGHTS, FROM BRITISH MUSEUM, DEPT. OF PRINTS AND DRAWINGS
- JERUSALEM
- THE SONG OF LOS (COPY A) AND MILTON (COPY A)
- SONGS OF EXPERIENCE
- SONGS OF INNOCENCE
- SONGS OF INNOCENCE AND EXPERIENCE

BLAKELY BAPTIST CHURCH. EARLY COUNTY. GEORGIA : CHURCH RECORDS – 1837-94 – 1 – 28.80 – us Baptist [240]
Blakeney, Sally *see* PARENTS, TEACHERS FIGHT OVER PLEASE-YOURSELF SCHOOL FREEDOM
Blakeslee, G H et al *see* THE JOURNAL OF RACE DEVELOPMENT
Blakey, Robert *see*
- HISTORY OF THE PHILOSOPHY OF MIND
- LIVES OF THE PRIMITIVE FATHERS

Blakney, Raymond B *see* THE LIFE AND TEACHINGS OF JESUS (CCC318)
Blamire, Susanna *see* THE POETICAL WORKS OF MISS SUSANNA BLAMIRE
Blanc, Henry *see* MA CAPTIVITE EN ABYSSINIE SOUS L'EMPEREUR THEODOROS
Blanc, Louis *see* LES ANOMALIES CHEZ L'HOMME ET LES MAMMIFERES; PREF. PAR...CAMILLE DARESTE
BLANCA DE BORBON / Espronceda, Jose de; ed by Churman, Philip H – Extrait de la Revue Hispanique. Tome 8. New York, Paris, 1907 – 1 – sp Bibl Santa Ana [946]
Blancard, S *see*
- A PHYSICAL DICTIONARY

BLANCAS Y NEGRAS (CRONICAS) / Montoto de Sedas Castor – Madrid: Razon y Fe, 1927 – 1 – sp Bibl Santa Ana [305]
Blanch e Illa, Narciso *see* CRONICA DE LA PROVINCIA DE ALBACETE
Blanchard *see*
- COUNTIES OF PORTER AND LAKE
- COUNTIES OF WHITELY AND NOBLE
- COUNTY OF WILLIAMS

Blanchard, C E *see* HISTOIRE NATURELLE DES INSECTES
Blanchard, Charles *see*
- COUNTIES OF MORGAN, MONROE AND BROWN
- HISTORICAL AND BIOGRAPHICAL RECORD OF HOWARD AND TIPTON COUNTIES

Blanchard, F M *see* PRACTICAL PUBLIC SPEAKING
Blanchard, J T *see* LE BELIER
Blanchard, Jim *see* NATIONAL COMMITTEE FOR MONETARY REFORM, SUBSCRIPTION APPEAL
Blanchard, Richard *see* CLAY AND OWEN COUNTIES
Blanchard, Rufus *see*
- THE DISCOVERY AND CONQUESTS OF THE NORTHWEST
- HISTORY OF DU PAGE COUNTY
- HISTORY OF ILLINOIS: ACCOMPANY SIC AN HISTORICAL MAP OF THE STATE

BLANCHE ET MONTCASSIN OU LES VENITIENS / Arnault – (French Theatre Series). Paris. Demonville, an VII. 1798 – 9 – fr Hachette [820]
BLANCHE, LADY FALAISE / Shorthouse, Joseph Henry – British Fiction Archive: Unit 1 – 9 – uk Bell [830]
Blanchet, Francois Xavier *see* APPEL AU PARLEMENT IMPERIAL ET AUX HABITANTS DES COLONIES ANGLOISES, DANS L'AMERIQUE DU NORD,...
Blanchet, J *see* L'ART, OU LES PRINCIPES PHILOSOPHIQUES DU CHANT
Blanchet, Jean Gervais Protais (1843-1908) *see* SPEECH BY THE HONORABLE J. BLANCHET, SECRETARY OF THE PROVINCE OF QUEBEC, ON THE AUTONOMY OF THE PROVINCES
Blanchet, L J N *see*
- CAHIERS HISTORIQUES
- CANADA-PATRIE
- L'ECHO DE LA RIVE SUD

Blanchini, J *see* OPERA OMNIA
Blanchinus, F Francisci Blanchini *see* DE TRIBUS GENERIBUS INSTRUMENTORUM MUSICAE VETERUM ORGANICAE DISSERTATIO
Blanchon, Pierre *see* JEAN GUITON ET LE SIEGE DE LA ROCHELLE
Blanck, Karl *see* DER FRANZOESISCHE EINFLUSS IM ZWEITEN TEIL VON GOTTSCHEDS CRITISCHER DICHTKUNST
Blanckenburg, Curt *see* STUDIEN UEBER DIE SPRACHE ABRAHAMS A SANTA CLARA
Blanckenburgh, G van *see* ONDERWYZINGE HOE EMEN ALLE DE TOON EN EN HALVE TOONEN, DIE MEEST GEBRUYCKELYCK ZYN, OP DE HANDTFLUYT ZAL KONNEN T'EENEMAEL ZUYVER BLAEZEN, EN HOE MEN OP YEDER, 'T GEMACKELYCKST EEN TRAMMELANT ZAL KONNEN MAKEN, HEEL DIENSTIGH VOOR DE LIEFHEBBERS
Blanco, Antonio *see*
- BIBLIOTECA BIBLIOGRAFICO-AGUSTINIANA DEL COLEGIO DE VALLADOLID
- MOSAICOS ROMANOS DE MERIDA. INVESTIGACION Y CIENCIA

Blanco, F M *see*
- FLORA DE FILIPINAS

Blanco Fombona, Horacio *see* CRIMENES DEL IMPERIALISMO NORTEAMERICANO
Blanco Garcia, Francisco *see*
- ADELARDO LOPEZ DE AYALA
- ANTONIO HURTADO
- BARTOLOME JOSE GALLARDO...
- CAROLINA CORONADO
- DONOSO CORTES
- ESPRONCEDA
- FERNANDO DE GABRIEL
- GABINO TEJADO
- JOSE MORENO NIETO
- JOSE SANCHEZ ARJONA
- JUAN JUSTINIANO Y ARRIBAS
- LEANDRO HERRERO
- NICOLAS DIAZ PEREZ
- VICENTE BARRANTES

Blanco, Indalecio *see* COLECCION...MEJORES POETAS ESPANOLES
Blanco, Jose Felix *see* DOCUMENTOS PARA LA HISTORIA DE LA VIDA PUBLICA DEL LIBERTADOR DE COLOMBIA, PERU, Y BOLIVIA
Blanco, Jose Maria *see* HISTORIA DOCUMENTADA DE LA VIDA Y GLORIOSA MUERTE DE LOS PADRES ROQUE GONZALEZ DE SANTA CRUZ, ALONSO RODRIGUEZ Y JUAN DEL CASTILLO...BUENOS AIRES, 1929
Blanco Sanchez, R *see* PARA LA HISTORIA DEL MONASTERIO DE GUADALUPE
BLANCO Y NEGRO – Revista Ilustrada. Madrid. Ano 1-46. 1891-1936. Incomplete – 1 – us NY Public [073]
Bland, Desmond S *see* EARLY RECORDS OF FURNIVAL'S INN
BLANDFORD 1737-1860 – (Mf 1-4: Index to Births 1741-1982. Mf 5-10: Index to Marriages & Deaths 1741-1842. Mf 11-19: Index to Marriages & Deaths 1843-1982. Mf 20-22: Miscellaneous Records 1737-73. Mf 23-29: Miscellanous Records 1774-1802. Mf 30-37: Records 1803-34. Mf 38-47: Records 1835-60. Mf 48-51: Cemetery Records) – (mf ed 1983) – 51mf – 9 – 0-931248-36-1 – us Holbrook [920]
BLAND'S CHANCERY REPORTS – v1-3. 1811-32 (all publ) – 9mf – 9 – $40.50 – LLMC 84-147 – us L.L.M.C. [340]
BLANDT ESKIMOERNE I LABRADOR / Lindow, H – BN 294 2. 1023-24 – 8 – ne IDC [306]
BLANDT NORDPOLENS NABOER / Astrup, E – BN-108 2. 1895 – 8 – ne IDC [910]
BLANEY BAPTIST CHURCH. ELGIN, SOUTH CAROLINA : CHURCH RECORDS – 1905-75 – 1 – 8.24 – us Baptist [240]
Blanford, H F *see* CRETACEOUS FAUNA OF SOUTHERN INDIA
Blanford, WT *see* A MANUAL OF THE GEOLOGY OF INDIA
Blank, Sally E *see* VERSACLIMBER EXERCISE ELICITS HIGHER MAXIMAL OXYGEN UPTAKE IN WOMEN ROWERS THAN DOES TREADMILL EXERCISE OR ROWING ERGOMETRY
Blankenburg, Q. van *see*
- ELEMENTA MUSICA
- ELEMENTA MUSICA OF NIEUW LICHT TOT HET WELVERSTAAN VAN DE MUSIEC EN DE BASCONTINUO

Blankenburg, Roland, Gambla, Michael *see* EINFLUESSE IMPLIZITER EIGNUNGSTHEORIEN AUF DIE BEOBACHTUNGSGENAUIGKEIT IN ASSESSMENT-CENTERN
Blankertz, Stefan *see*
- NOCH EIN TSCHERNOBYL, WENN DAS VOLK ES WHYL-EINE ANARCHISTISCHE KRITIK AN DER GRUENEN FORDERUNG NACH VOLKSENTSCHEID
- TOWARDS A LIBERTARIAN THEORY OF FASCISM

Blanpied, Peter R *see* THE COMPARISON OF ACTIVE PLANTARFLEXOR MUSCLE STIFFNESS BETWEEN YOUNG AND ELDERLY HUMAN FEMALES
Blanquart-Evrard, Louis-Desire *see*
- LA PHOTOGRAPHIE, SES ORIGINES, SES PROGRES, SES TRANSFORMATIONS

Blanqui, Adolphe *see* DES CLASSES OUVRIERES EN FRANCE PENDANT L'ANNEE 1848
Blantyre Mission *see* JOURNAL
BLAS DE LEDESMA, UN PINTOR RECIEN DESCUBIERTO / Torres Martin, Ramon – Badajoz: Imprenta Diputacion Prov., 1967 – sp Bibl Santa Ana [946]
BLASERSTUCK / Dopper, C – (Holograph) – Manuscript score, 19– – 1 – us Sibley [780]
Blashfield, De Witt Clinton *see* A TREATISE ON INSTRUCTIONS TO JURIES IN CIVIL AND CRIMINAL CASES.
BLASON DE ALMAS / Reyes Huertas, Antonio – Madrid: Editorial Paez, 1926 – 1 – sp Bibl Santa Ana [946]
BLASON POPULAIRE DE VILLEDIEU-LES-POELES, ARRONDISSEMENT D'AVRANCHES (MANCHE) / Brunet, Victor Armand – 1888 – 1 – us I.U. Libraries [390]
Blasquez y Delgado-Aquilera, Antonio *see* PREHISTORIA DE LA REGION NORTE DE MARRUECOS
Blass, Fridericus *see*
- ACTA APOSTOLORUM, SIVE, LUCAE AD THEOPHILUM LIBER ALTER
- EVANGELIUM SECUNDUM LUCAM, SIVE, LUCAE AD THEOPHILUM LIBER PRIOR

Blass, Friedrich *see* GRAMMAR OF NEW TESTAMENT GREEK
Blass, Piotr *see* ULAM QUARTERLY
EINE BLASSBLAUE FRAUENSCHRIFT / Werfel, Franz – Buenos Aires: Editorial Estrellas, c1941 – 1r – 1 – us U.W. Library [430]
BLAST – 1-2 2+5 (all publ). 1916-1917 – 3mf – 9 – $35.00 – us UPA [335]
BLAST – London. v. 1-2. June 20 1914-July 1915 – 1 – us NY Public [073]
BLAST; A MAGAZINE OF PROLETARIAN SHORT STORIES – New York. v. 1 no. 1-5. Sept 1933-Nov 1934 – 1 – us NY Public [335]
Blatch, F K *see* PERPETUAL READY REFERENCE GUIDE TO THE STATUTES OF CANADA: VIZ. THE REVISED STATUTES OF 1886, AND ALL SUBSEQUENT AMENDING, REPEALING, COGNATE AND NEW ACTS
BLATCHFORD AND HOWLAND'S REPORTS OF CASES IN THE SOUTHERN DISTRICT COURT OF NEW YORK, 1827-1837 / Blatchford, S & Howland, F – (A selection of cases decided by Judge Samuel R Betts, sometimes called "Bett's Decisions") – New York: Halsted. 1v. 1937 (all publ) – 7mf – 9 – $10.50 – us L.L.M.C. [324]
Blatchford, S *see*
- BLATCHFORD AND HOWLAND'S REPORTS OF CASES IN THE SOUTHERN DISTRICT COURT OF NEW YORK, 1827-1837
- BLATCHFORD'S PRIZE CASES IN THE SECOND CIRCUIT, 1861-1865
- BLATCHFORD'S REPORTS OF CASES IN THE SECOND CIRCUIT, 1845-1887

BLATCHFORD'S PRIZE CASES IN THE SECOND CIRCUIT, 1861-1865 / Blatchford, S – New York: Baker-Voorhis, 1v. 1866 (all publ) – 8mf – 9 – $12.00 – LLMC 81-435 – us L.L.M.C. [340]
BLATCHFORD'S REPORTS OF CASES IN THE SECOND CIRCUIT, 1845-1887 / Blatchford, S – New York: Baker-Voorhis. v1-24. 1859-88 (all publ) – 169mf – 9 – $253.00 – LLMC 81-433 – us L.L.M.C. [340]
Blatchley, J S *see* LITTLETON AND BLATCHLEY'S DIGEST OF FIRE INSURANCE DECISIONS
Blatchley, W S *see* THE COLEOPTERA OF INDIANA
Blathwayt, William *see* ACCOUNTS OF BRITISH TRADE IN AMERICA
DAS BLATT – Bogota, 1943/44-1944/45 (incomplete) – 1 – Inquire at Mikrofilmarchiv for details – gw Misc Inst [072]
DAS BLATT DER HAUSFRAU *see* DIES BLATT GEHOERT DER HAUSFRAU
DAS BLATT GEHOERT DER HAUSFRAU *see*
- DIES BLATT GEHOERT DER HAUSFRAU

Blau, Georg *see* AUSDRUCKSBEWEGUNGEN IN HEINRICH VON KLEISTS WERK
Blau, Gerda et al *see* FOOD AID FOR DEVELOPMENT
BLAU IST DAS MEER : EINE ERZAEHLUNG AUS DER DEUTSCHEN KRIEGSMARINE / Zerkaulen, Heinrich – Leipzig: Quelle & Meyer, [1936?] – 1r – 1 – us U.W. Library [830]
Blau, L L *see*
- BIBLIOGRAPHIE DER SCHRIFTEN WILHELM BACHERS NEBST EINEM HEBRAEISCHEN SACH- UND ORTSNAMENREGISTER
- PAPYRI UND TALMUD IN GEGENSEITIGER BELEUCHTUNG

BLAUE FERNEN : NEUE REISEBILDER / Hevesi, Lajos – Stuttgart: Adolf Bonz, 1897 – 1 – us U.W. Library [910]
Blaufuss, H *see*
- ABODAH ZARA. MISCHNA UND TOSEFTA
- GOETTER, BILDER UND SYMBOLE NACH DEN TRAKTATEN UEBER FREMDEN DIENST
- ROEMISCHEN FESTE UND FEIERTAGE NACH DEN TRAKTATEN UEBER FREMDEN DIENST (ABODAH ZARAH) IN MISCHNA, TOSEFTA, JERUSALEMER UND BABYLONISCHEN TALMUD

Blaurer, Th *see* WIE LUDWIG HETZER ZU CONSTANTZ MIT DEM SCHWERT GERICHT
Blaustein, Leopold *see* DAS GOTTESERLEBNIS IN HEBBELS DRAMEN
BLAUW EN WIT : MAANDBLAD VOOR PROPAGANDA DER ZIONISTISCHE BEGINSELEN – Amersfoort, 1908(1-3) – 1mf – J-261-16/1 – ne IDC [320]
BLAU-WEISS-BLAETTER – Berlin, 1916-18, 1924 (all incomplete) – 1 – Dist. gw Mikrofilm – gw Misc Inst [072]
Blaxall, Arthur William *see* TEN CAMEOS FROM DARKEST AFRICA
Blaxland, Bruce *see* THE STRUGGLE WITH PURITANISM

BLAYDON COURIER – England. -w. 1905-55. (46 reels) – 1 – uk British Libr Newspaper [072]
BLAYNEY ADVOCATE – Jan 1 1898-Dec 28 1907 – 9 – at Pascoe [072]
BLAZON OF ARMS / Hatton, Christopher – 14 – uk Microform Academic [920]
Blazquez, Antonio *see*
- EXTREMADURA EN LA GUERRA DE LA INDEPENDENCIA (INFORME DE GOMEZ VILLAFRANCA)
- INFORME RELATIVO A PARTE DE LA VIA ROMANA NUM. 25 DEL ITINERARIO DE ANTONINO
- INFORME SOBRE DECLARACION DE MONUMENTO NACIONAL DE PUENTE DE ALCANTARA
- VIA ROMANA DE MERIDA A SALAMANCA
- VIAS ROMANAS DE LA BETURIA DE LOS TURDULOS, POR DON ANGEL DELGADO

Blazquez del Barco, Juan *see*
- EXPLICACION...CONFESORES..
- (FRANCISCANO DE LA PROVINCIA DE SAN MIGUEL) EN NOTAS DE BIBLIOGRAFIA FRANCISCANA
- RELOX DEL ALMA Y ORACION MENTAL
- TROMPETA EVANGELICA..
- TROMPETA EVANGELICA, ALFANGE..

Blazquez Izquierdo, Jose *see* 1ST CONGRESO SINDICAL AGRARIO DE EXTREMADURA. PONENCIA 7. SITUACION DE LA, PRODUCCION GANADERA
Blazquez Marcos, Jose *see*
- POR LA VIEJA EXTREMADURA-PROVINCIA DE CACERES
- TRANSCENDENCIA EMOCIONAL DE LA LECTURA

Blazquez Prieto, Gabriel R *see*
- RESOLUCION DE LA INCORPORACION DE OLIVENZA..
- RESOLUCION...OLIVENZA Y LAS ALDEAS DE..
- ...SE DIRIGE A LOS CURAS..

Blazquez, Vidal *see* EPIGRAFIA ROMANA
Bleby, Henry *see* SCENES IN THE CARIBBEAN SEA
Blecker, P *see* ATLAS ICHTHYOLOGIQUE DES INDES ORIENTALES NEERLANDAISES
LE BLED EN LUMIERE, FOLKLORE TUNISIEN / Benattar, S C – Paris: J Tallandier, [c1923] – 1 – us Res Libr [390]
Bledel, Rodolfo *see*
- LA ECONOMIA ARGENTINA, 1952-1963
- LA ECONOMIA ARGENTINA (1952-1972)

Bledsoe, Albert Taylor *see* AN ESSAY ON LIBERTY AND SLAVERY
Bledsoe, Anthony Jennings *see* BUSINESS LAW FOR BUSINESS MEN, STATE OF CALIFORNIA.
BLEDY JEZYKOWE / Passendorfer, A – Lwow. 1904. BR-8017 2 – 8 – ne IDC [460]
BLEDY NASZE / Walicki, A – Wyd. 3. Krakow. 1886. BR-8016 2 – 8 – ne IDC [999]
Bleeck van Rijsewijk, FG B van *see* CATALOGUS VAN NEDERLANDSCHE HANDSCHRIFTEN, WELKE BERUSTEN IN DE KEIZERLIJKE BIBLIOTHEEK TE ST PETERSBURG
Bleek, Friedrich *see*
- DR. FRIEDRICH BLEEKS VORLESUNGEN UEBER DIE BRIEFE (KOLOSSER, PHILEMON, EPHESIER)
- EINLEITUNG IN DIE HEILIGE SCHRIFT
- VORLESUNGEN UEBER DIE APOKALYPSE

Bleek, W H I *see* THE LIBRARY OF H.E. SIR GEORGE GREY
Bleeker, Louis Hendrik Karel *see* JEREMIA'S PROFETIEEN TEGEN DIE VOLKEREN
Blegny, E de *see* L'ORTOGRAFE FRANCOISE
Blei, Franz *see* KARL HENCKELL, EIN MODERNER DICHTER
BLEIB STET! : VIERZEHN VOLKSGESCHICHTEN / Rothacker, Gottfried – Muenchen: A Langen, G Mueller, 1943, c1938 – 1r – 1 – us U.W. Library [390]
DIE BLEIBENDE BEDEUTUNG DES ALTEN TESTAMENTS : EIN KONFERENZVORTRAG / Kautzsch, Emil – 2., verm Aufl. Tuebingen: J C B Mohr, 1903 – 1mf – 9 – 0-8370-9705-3 – 1986-3705 – us A.T.L.A. [220]
DIE BLEIBENDE BEDEUTUNG DES NEUTESTAMENTLICHEN KANONS FUER DIE KIRCHE : VORTRAG AUF DER LUTHERISCHEN PASTORALKONFERENZ ZU LEIPZIG AM 2. JUNI 1898 / Zahn, Theodor – (Includes bibliographical references) – Leipzig: A Deichert, 1898 – 1mf – 9 – 0-8370-9353-8 – 1986-3353 – us A.T.L.A. [220]
Bleiberg, German *see* LA CANCION PETRARQUISTA EN LA LIRICA ESPANOLA DEL SIGLO DE ORO, DE ENRIQUE SEGURA COVARSI
Bleibtrau, Walter *see* DIE DREI ERSTEN KAPITEL DES ROEMERBRIEFS
Bleibtreu, Karl *see* GROESSENWAHN
BLEKINGE FOLKBLAD – Karlskrona, 1903-21 – 9 – sw Kungliga [072]
BLEKINGE FOLKBLAD *see* SYDOSTRA SVERIGES DAGBLAD
BLEKINGE LANS TIDNING – (Karlshamns Allehanda; Solvesborgstidningen) – Karlskrona, Sweden. 1979- – 1 – sw Kungliga [072]
BLEKINGE LANS TIDNING – (Solvesborgstidningen, 1967-78; Vaxjobladet 1967-75; Karlshamns Allehanda, 1976-78) – Karlskrona, Sweden. 1869-1978 – 534r – 1 – sw Kungliga [072]
BLEKINGEPOSTEN – Karlskrona, Sweden. 1945-78 – 32r – 1 – sw Kungliga [072]
BLEKINGEPOSTEN – Ronneby, Sweden. 1979- – 1 – sw Kungliga [072]
Blemur, R M J de *see*
- L'ANNEE BENEDICTINE
- ELOGES DE PLUSIEURS PERSONNES O.S.B.
- VIE DES SAINTS
- VIE DU R.P. PIERRE FOURNIER

BLENCO SISTEMATICO DEI COLEOTTERI FINORA RACCOLTI NELLA VALLE LAGARINA / Halbherr, B – Rovereto, 1885-98. Pt.1-10. Z/1327/2 – 8 – ne IDC [590]
Blendecq, D Charles *see* CINQ HISTOIRES ADMIRABLES
BLENDING LIGHTS : OR, THE RELATIONS OF NATURAL SCIENCE, ARCHAEOLOGY, AND HISTORY TO THE BIBLE / Fraser, William – New York:Robert Carter, 1874 – 1mf – 9 – 0-8370-3185-0 – 1985-1185 – us A.T.L.A. [210]
Blenerhasset, Thomas *see* A REVELATION OF THE TRUE MINERVA
THE BLENHEIM PAPERS: THE PAPERS OF THE FIRST DUKE OF MARLBOROUGH, SARAH, DUCHESS OF MARLBOROUGH, AND THE 3RD EARL OF SUNDERLAND – Part 1: 1st Duke of Marlborough, additional manucripts 61101-61158 and 61160-61166. Part 2: 1st Duke of Marlborough, selected from additional mss. 61167-61303. Part 3: 1st Duke of Marlborough, additional mss. 61306-61315, 61319-21, 61363-73, 61378, 61380-61402, 61408, and 61411-61413 – 1 – us Primary [920]
Blennerhassett, Charlotte, Lady *see* KARDINAL JOHN HENRY NEWMAN
Blennerhassett, Harman *see* PAPERS
Bles, Numa *see* PARIS-MONTREAL
Blesdijk, Nicolaas M van *see*
- BILLIJCKE VERANTWOORDINGE ENDE EENVOLDIGHE WEDERLEGGHINGHE OP EENEN SCHELTLASTERIGHEN BRIEF DOOR DR. HIER. WILHELMI. IN 'T JAER 1544
- CHRISTELIJCKE VERANTWOORDINGHE, ENDE BILLIJCKE NEDERLEGGINGE DES VALSCHEN ONGHEGRONDEDEN OORDEELS, LASTERENS ENDE SCHELDENS
- EENVULDIGHE VNDE CHRISTELIJCKE BERICHTINGHE OP VIJF VRAGHEN BY EENIGHE VAN MEN. SYM. GESINTHEYT VOORGHESTELT
- DIE GANTSCHE LEERINGHE VAN DAUID IORISZOEN INT CORTE BEGREPEN, TOT NUT VANDEN ONPARTYDIGHEN
- HISTORIA VITAE, DOCTRINAE, AC RERUM GESTARUM DAVIDIS GEORGII HAERESIARCHAE
- HOOFT-SOMMA VNDE GRONT VAN 'TGENE WY WT DIE LEERE DAVID IORIS HEBBEN CONNEN VERSTAEN
- WEDERANTWOORT OP ZEKEREN BRIEF BY GELLIUM ONDERTEECKENT WAER IN HY SIJNE MEYNINGE VNDE OORDEEL STELT. IN 'T JAER 1545

Bleses, Peter *see* DAS SPD-KONZEPT DER "SOZIALEN GRUNDSICHERUNG" UNTER BESONDERER BERUECKSICHTIGUNG IHRER AUSWIRKUNG AUF DIE ARBEITSLOSENVERSICHERUNG (ALS STRATEGIE GEGEN "NEUE ARMUT")
BLESSED ARE THEY, OR, THOUGHTS ON THE BEATITUDES / Gilbert, Jesse S – Paterson: Carleton M. Herrick, 1890. 1 fiche – 9 – us A.T.L.A. [240]
BLESSED JOAN THE MAID / Barnes, Arthur Stapylton – London: Burns & Oates; New York: Benziger, [1909?] – 1mf – us A.T.L.A. [240]
THE BLESSED VIRGIN IN THE FATHERS OF THE FIRST SIX CENTURIES / Livius, Thomas – London: Burns & Oates, 1893. xxvii,481p. 2 fiches – 9 – us A.T.L.A. [240]
THE BLESSED VIRGIN IN THE NINETEENTH CENTURY : APPARITIONS, REVELATIONS, GRACES / St-John, Bernard – London: Burns & Oates; New York: Benziger, [1903?] – 2mf – 9 – 0-8370-8621-3 – 1986-2621 – us A.T.L.A. [240]
Blessi, M *see* NELLA ROTTA DELL' ARMATA DE SVLTAN SELIN, VLTIMO RE DE TVRCHI
THE BLESSINGS OF LIBERTY – 1956-90 (complete) – 3r – 1 – ATLA S0587 – us A.T.L.A. [073]
Blessington, Marguerite *see* CONVERSATIONS OF LORD BYRON WITH THE COUNTESS OF BLESSINGTON
BLETCHLEY DISTRICT GAZETTE – England.1951-52; 1961.-w. 2 reels – 1 – uk British Libr Newspaper [072]
BLETCHLEY GAZETTE – (Milton Keynes Gazette, Nov 1974-) – England, Aug-Dec 1974 – 2r – 1 – uk British Libr Newspaper [072]
BLEU ET ROUGE – Port-au-Prince, Haiti: [s.n.] v2 n2-v4 n116 1916-1918. v7 n1-n38 1922 – 6 sheets – us Res Libr [972]
Bleuler, Sharon A *see* NONVERBAL BEHAVIOR OF NATIONAL FIGURE SKATING COACHES
Bleutler, Sharon A *see* IS THERE A RELATIONSHIP BETWEEN PRENATAL EXERCISE AND POSTPARTUM DEPRESSION
Blewett, George John *see*
- THE CHRISTIAN VIEW OF THE WORLD
- THE STUDY OF NATURE AND THE VISION OF GOD

Blewett, Jean *see* HEART SONGS
Bley, Buchner *see* REPORTS
EIN BLICK AUF RUSSLAND / Melissander, Friedrich – Kiel: Lipsius und Tischer, 1892 – 1r – 1 – us U.W. Library [947]
BLICK DURCH DIE WIRTSCHAFT – 1965-1994 – 2 times per yr – 1 – DM140.00 – sz Infoprint [072]
BLICK DURCH DIE WIRTSCHAFT – (1995 2r per yr DM140.00 subsc) – Frankfurt, 1965-94 – 56r – 1 – DM4,200.00 – gw Mikro Press [330]
BLICK DURCH DIE WIRTSCHAFT – Frankfurt/Main. 1974-79 – 1 – gw Mikrofilm [072]
BLICK DURCH DIE WIRTSCHAFT – Monatsregister 1959-Juni 1980 – 2r – 1 – DM150.00 – gw Mikro Press [330]
BLICK IN DIE ZEIT – Berlin, 1933-35 – 2r – 1 – Dist. gw Mikrofilm – gw Misc Inst [072]
BLICKE EINES TONKUENSTLER IN DIE MUSIK DER GEISTER / Dalberg, Johann F H von – P 667. 1787 – 9 – ne IDC [780]
BLICKE EINES TONKUENSTLERS IN DIE MUSIK DER GEISTER / Dalberg, Johann F H von – Mannheim: In der neuen Hof- und akademischen Buchhandlung, 1787 – 1 – us Sibley [780]
BLICKE IN DAS LEBEN DER GEGENWART UND IN DIE HOFFNUNG DER ZUKUNFT / Reichenbach, Heinrich G L – Dresden: Woldemar Tuerk, 1864. 1 fiche.8370-4862-1 – 9 – us A.T.L.A. [240]
BLICKE IN DIE ZEIT NACH DER SCHRIFT – Bremen, dec 25 1848-jul 14 1855 – 1r – 1 – Inquire at Mikrofilmarchiv for details – gw Misc Inst [240]
Bliemel, B *see* VERKETTUNG VON DICHTER UND WERK BEI THOMAS HARDY
Bliesener, J *see* TROIS QUATUORS
Bliff, Geo. Ripley *see* AN ADDRESS, THE PLACE OF BAPTISTS IN PROTESTANT CHRISTENDOM
Bligh, Donald A *see* METHODS AND TECHNIQUES IN POST-SECONDARY EDUCATION
Bligh, Harris Harding *see* STATUTORY ANNOTATIONS TO THE REVISED STATUTES OF CANADA, 1906, AND OTHER CANADIAN STATUTES (2D ED.) PROVIDING REFERENCES TO EVERY CHANGE MADE BY THE ANNUAL STATUTES FOR 1907, 1908, 1909, 1910, 1911, 1912, 1913 AND 1914
Bligh, Richard *see* BLIGH'S PARLIAMENTARY REPORTS
Bligh, William *see*
- THE MUTINY ON BOARD H.M.S. BOUNTY, AND THE SUBSEQUENT VOYAGE OF A PART OF THE CREW..
- A VOYAGE TO THE SOUTH SEA, UNDERTAKEN BY COMMAND OF HIS MAJESTY, FOR THE PURPOSE OF CONVEYING THE BREAD-FRUIT TREE TO THE WEST INDIES, IN HIS MAJESTY'S SHIP THE BOUNTY

BLIGH'S PARLIAMENTARY REPORTS : REPORTS OF CASES HEARD IN THE HOUSE OF LORDS ON APPEALS AND WRITS OF ERROR... / Bligh, Richard – v1-4 pt 1. 1819-21. London: J & W T Clarke and Baldwin, Cradock & Joy, 1823-? (all publ) – 26mf – 9 – $39.00 – LLMC 84-752 – us L.L.M.C. [324]
Blind, Mathilde *see* GEORGE ELIOT
BLIND RELIEF APPLICATIONS / Fulton County. Ohio. Board of County Commissioners – 1908-1936 – 1r – 1 – $32.50r – us Archival [324]
BLIND RELIEF APPLICATIONS / Wood County. Ohio. Board of County Commissioners – 1914-1942 – 1r – 1 – $32.50r – us Archival [324]
BLIND RELIEF DISBURSEMENTS / Wyandot County. Ohio. Auditor – 1904-1936 – 1r – 1 – $32.50r – us Archival [324]
BLIND RELIEF PAPERS / Wood County. Ohio. Board of County Commissioners – 1904-1936 – 3r – 1 – $32.50r – us Archival [324]
BLIND RELIEF RECORDS / Defiance County. Ohio. Auditor – 1908-1928 – 1r – 1 – $32.50r – us Archival [324]
BLIND RELIEF RECORDS / Seneca County. Ohio. Board of County Commissioners – (Incomplete) – 1904-1936 – 1r – 1 – $32.50r – us Archival [324]
BLIND RELIEF RECORDS / Van Wert County, Ohio. Board of County Commissioners – 1904-1906 – 1r – 1 – $32.50r – us Archival [324]
BLIND RELIEF RECORDS AND MINUTES / Fulton County. Ohio. Board of County Commissioners – 1908-1912 – 1r – 1 – $32.50r – us Archival [324]
DIE BLINDE GOETTIN : SCHAUSPIEL IN FUENF AKTEN / Toller, Ernst – Berlin: G Kiepenheuer, 1933 – 1r – 1 – us U.W. Library [820]
BLINDED EAGLE: A SHORT LIFE OF EDWARD IRVING / Whitely, H C – 9 – $10.00 – us I.R.C. [920]
Blinov, I A *see* OTNOSHENIIA SENATA K MESTNYM UCHREZHDENIIAM V XIX VEKE
Blinovskii, PI *see* ZEMSTVO I KOOPERATSIIA
Bliss, Edwin Munsell *see*
- THE MISSIONARY ENTERPRISE
- ORGANIZATION AND METHODS OF MISSION WORK
- TURKEY AND THE ARMENIAN ATROCITIES....WITH AN INTROD. BY MISS FRANCES E. WILLARD

Bliss, F J *see* A MOUND OF MANY CITIES (TELL EL HESY EXCAVATED)
Bliss, Frank C *see* ST. PAUL PAST AND PRESENT
Bliss, P P *see* THE CHARM OF SUNDAY SCHOOLS
Bliss, PO *see* GOSPEL HYMNS AND SACRED SONGS
Bliss, W D P *see* THE NEW ENCYCLOPAEDIA OF SOCIAL REFORM
BLITZ – 1974-. Bombay. -w. illus – 1 – us U.W. Library [073]
BLITZ – Bombay, India: Blitz Publ, [1952-61] – 10r – 1 – us Res Libr [073]
BLITZ – Hannover. oct 29, 1953-mar 16, 1954 – 1r – 1 – gw Mikrofilm [072]
BLITZ; INDIA'S GREATEST WEEKLY – Bombay. 1944-1951, 1961- – 1 – 20.00y – us L of C Photodup [073]
BLIZHAISHIE EKONOMICHESKIE ZADACHI / Miliutin, V – M., 1926 – 2mf – 9 – COR-173/1 – ne IDC [334]
BLIZHAISHII A PERSPEKTIVY TORGOVYKH OTNOSHENII ROSSII S UKRAINOI / Bazhanov, V M et al – Moskva: [s.n.], 1918 – 1 – CSUX89-B2347 – us Hoover Inst Photo [380]
"BLIZKIE TENI."VOSPOMINANIIA. PT. 1. SPB. 1909; PT. 2. M. 1916. BR-9064/1 / Elpat'evskii, S Ia – 9 – ne IDC [380]
LE BLOC – Organe de l'Association generale des fonctionnaires de la Guadeloupe et des dependances. Dir. Leon Loya. no. 1-3. Pointe-a-Pitre. avr-juin 1926 – 1 – fr A.C.R.P.P. [073]
LE BLOC / ed by Trepanier, V et al – Montreal, Canada. 12 fev 1944-12 sep 1945 – 1r – 1 – Can$40.00 – cn Can Microfilming [072]
Bloch, Armand *see* PHOENICISCHES GLOSSAR
Bloch, Ernest *see* LETTERS TO EDMOND FLEGG
Bloch, I *see* ZEITSCHRIFT FUER SEXUALWISSENSCHAFT (HQ 8)

Bloch, Joseph S *see* EINBLICKE IN DIE GESCHICHTE DER ENTSTEHUNG DER TALMUDISCHEN LITERATUR
Bloch, M E *see* ICHTHYOLOGIE OU HISTOIRE GENERALE ET PARTICULIERE DES POISSONS
Bloch, Moses *see*
- DIE CIVILPROCESS-ORDNUNG NACH MOSAISCH-RABBINISCHEM RECHTE
- DAS MOSAISCH-TALMUDISCHE POLIZEIRECHT
- SEFER HA-YOVEL. MOSHEH ARYEH BLOCH

Blochet, Edgar *see* CATALOGUE DES MANUSCRITS ARABES DES NOUVELLES ACQUISITIONS (1884-1924)
BLOCK BOOK : WESTERN ADDITION – San Francisco, 1890 – 1r – 1 – $50.00 – B03723 – us Library Micro [978]
Block, Louis *see* MEXICAN-AMERICAN REPORTS
Block, M *see* DICTIONNAIRE GENERAL DE LA POLITIQUE
DER BLOCKADEBRECHER – (Suppl available: Neue Wirtschaft, 1926. Spec issues, 1927-28. Auslandsausgabe 1925, 1927) – Bremen, sep 1924-25, jun 18-dec 18 1926, 1927-30 (incomplete), 1931 (many issues missing) – 3r – 1 – Inquire at Mikrofilmarchiv for details – gw Misc Inst [380]
LE BLOCUS PACIFIQUE,... / Falcke, H P – Leipzig, 1919 – 4mf – 1 – ILM-677/1 – ne IDC [327]
Blodget, Lorin *see*
- THE INDUSTRIES OF PHILADELPHIA
- THE REVISED STATUTES OF THE UNITED STATES

BLODGETT COLLECTION OF SPANISH CIVIL WAR PAMPHLETS *see*
- KORTFATTAD REDOGORELSE OVER ARBETET, DESS ORGANISATION OCH UTVECKLING SAMT RAPPORT FRAN KOMMITTENS REVISORER
- SEIS MESES DE SOLIDARIDAD ANTIFASCISTA

THE BLODGETT COLLECTION OF SPANISH CIVIL WAR PAMPHLETS / Harvard College. Library – 680 pamphlets published in 1936-39 in Spain, Europe, Latin America, and U.S. by agencies of the Spanish gov't., Spanish political parties, and organizations world-wide. Titles listed separately – 9 – us H.U. College Libr [080]
Blodgett, May N *see* CHARACTER STUDIES IN GENESIS
BLOEMFONTEIN POST – Bloemfontein, South Africa. 1900-1915 – 1 – sa State Libr [072]
BLOEMHOF DER DOORLUCHTIGE VOORBEELDEN : DAER IN DOOR WARE, VREEMDE EN DEFTIGE GESCHIEDENISSEN, LEERINGEN EN EYGENSCHAPPEN, ALLES DAT DE MENSCH TOT NUT EN VERMAEK VERSTREKKEN KAN, TE BEMERKEN IS / Heyns, Maria – Amsterdam, 1647 – 4mf – 9 – O-3083/1 – ne IDC [760]
BLOEMKRANS VAN CHRISTELYKE LIEFDE-EN ZEEDEDICHTEN / Willink, D – O 805. 1714 – 9 – ne IDC [240]
BLOEM-TUYNTJE / Schaep, J C – O 749. 1724 – 9 – ne IDC [700]
BLOEM-TUYNTJE, BESTAANDE IN TWEE DEELEN : HET EERSTE IN INNERLYKE BEDENKINGEN, EN GELYKENISSEN. HET TWEEDE IN EENIGE SANG- EN LEES-RYMEN / Schaep, J C – Amsterdam, 1697 – 4mf – 9 – O-3258/1 – ne IDC [760]
BLOEM-TUYNTJE, BESTAENDE IN INDERLIJCKE BEDENCKINGEN, GELIJCKENISSEN, OFTE EXEMPELEN : MIDSGADERS EENIGE SANG-RIJMEN, OFTE LIEDEKENS / Schaep, J C – 1st ed. Amsterdam, 1660 – 3mf – 9 – ne IDC [700]
BLOEM-TUYNTJE, BESTAENDE IN TWEE DEELEN : HET EERSTE IN INNERLYKE BEDENKINGEN, EN GELYKENISSEN. HET TWEEDE IN EENIGE SANG- EN LEES-RYMEN / Schaep, J C – Amsterdam, 1671 – 4mf – 9 – O-3164/1 – ne IDC [760]
Bloesch, E *see* GESCHICHTE DER SCHWEIZERISCH-REFORMIERTEN KIRCHEN
Bloesch, Hans *see*
- AM KACHELOFEN
- GELD UND GEIST
- DIE KAESEREI IN DER VEHFREUDE
- KALENDERGESCHICHTEN
- SAEMTLICHE WERKE IN 24 BAENDEN
- ULI DER PAECHTER
- ZEITGEIST UND BERNERGEIST

Bloette, J A A *see* DENATIONALITEIT VAN DE VEREENIGING ...
Blois, Charles de *see* RECUEIL DE 44 ACTES ET PIECES CONCERNANT SURTOUT
Blok, Aleksandr Aleksandrovich *see* DVENADTSAT
O BLOKE – Sbornik literaturno-issledovatel'skoi assotsiatsii Ts D R P (E.F. Nikitonoi, Red.). (Nikitinskie subbotniki). M. 1929. BR-1465 2 – 8 – ne IDC [460]
BLOKNOT AGITATORA – Moscow. Jul 1946-Dec 1957. gaps – 1 – 35.00r – us Hoover Inst Photo [947]
Blom, Abraham Herman *see*
- DE LEER VAN HET MESSIASRIJK BIJ DE EERSTE CHRISTENEN
- DE LEER VAN HET MESSIASRIJK BIJ DE EERSTE CHRISTENEN

BLOMBERGER ANZEIGER – (Cont by: Lippische Bergwarte) – Blomberg, 1900-11, 1919-28 – 9 – Inquire at Mikrofilmarchiv for details – gw Misc Inst [943]
Blomfield, Alfred *see* THE OLD TESTAMENT AND THE NEW CRITICISM
Blondeau, A *see* L'ESCAUT FLEUVE INTERNATIONAL ...
Blondel *see* MEMORIAS DE ARQUITECTURA...
Blondel, D *see* DE LA PRIMAUTE EN L'EGLISE
Blondel, Jacques Francois *see*
- COURS D'ARCHITECTURE ENSEIGNE DANS L'ACADEMIE ROYALE D'ARCHITECTURE
- COURS D'ARCHITECTURE, OU TRAITE DE LA DECORATION, DISTRIBUTION ET CONSTRUCTION DES BATIMENTS.
- DE LA DISTRIBUTION DES MAISONS DE PLAISANCE ET DE LA DECORATION DES EDIFICES EN GENERAL
- DISCOURS SUR LA NECESSITE DE L'ETUDE DE L'ARCHITECTURE.
- NOUVELLE MANIERE DE FORTIFIER LES PLACES

Blondin, J N *see* MANUEL DE LA PURETE DU LANGAGE
DIE BLONDJAEGER : EIN ROMAN VON NEGERN, WEISSEN MAEDCHEN, GENTLEMEN UND HALUNKEN / Leip, Hans – Berlin: Propylaeen-Verlag, c1929 – 1r – 1 – us U.W. Library [830]
Blonina, El *see*
- OCHEREDNYE ZADACHI PO RABOTE SREDI ZHENSHCHIN
- RABOTNITSY V INTERNATSIONALE

Blood, Benjamin *see*
- OPTIMISM
- OPTIMISM: THE LESSON OF AGES

BLOOD CELLS – v. 1-6. 1975-80 – 1,5,9 – 356.00 – us UMI [073]
BLOOD GLUTATHIONE OXIDATION DURING HUMAN EXERCISE / Viguie, Christine A – 1988 – 95p 1mf – 9 – $4.00 – us Microform Publ [612]
BLOOD LACTATE RESPONSES FOR THREE COMPETITIVE SWIMMING STROKES / Chase, Lisa A – 1988 – 46p 1mf – 9 – $4.00 – us Microform Publ [612]
THE BLOOD OF JESUS / Reid, William – Philadelphia: American Baptist Publication Society, [186-] – 1mf – 9 – 0-8370-5444-3 – 1985-3444 – us A.T.L.A. [240]
BLOOD PURIFICATION – v1-. 1983- – 1,5,9 – us UMI [073]
BLOOD VESSELS *see* JOURNAL OF VASCULAR RESEARCH
BLOODY PRECEDENT / Cowles, Fleur – New York: Random House, 1952 – 1 – CSUXAHZ7039-B – us Hoover Inst Photo [320]
BLOODY PRECEDENT : THE PERON STORY / Cowles, Fleur – London: F. Muller, [1952] – 1 – CSUXADP3214-B – us Hoover Inst Photo [320]
BLOOM CENTER LITERARY SOCIETY MINUTES – Wood County. Ohio. 1875-1876 – 1 reel – 1 – us Archival [978]
Bloom Center Literary Society (Wood County, Ohio) *see* MINUTES
Bloom, H I *see* THE ECONOMIC ACTIVITIES OF THE JEWS OF AMSTERDAM IN THE SEVENTEENTH AND EIGHTEENTH CENTURIES
Bloom, Michele L *see* PERSONALS
Bloom, Solomon *see*
- A TREATISE ON THE LAW OF MECHANICS' LIENS AND BUILDING CONTRACTS WITH ANNOTATED FORMS
- U.S. CONSTITUTION SESQUICENTENNIAL COMMISSION

Bloomdale. Ohio. Trinity United Methodist Church *see* RECORDS
Bloomdale. Ohio. United Brethren Church *see* RECORDS
DIE BLOOMFIELD GERMANIA – Bloomfield, NE. -w. Apr. 1908-May 1914 – 1 – us NE Hist [071]
BLOOMFIELD JOURNAL – Bloomfield, NE -w. Nov. 1892; Jul. 1896; Sep. 1896-Dec. 1902; Apr. 1908-Nov. 1910; May 1911-Dec. 1911; Jun. 1914-Oct. 1921 – 1 – us NE Hist [071]
Bloomfield. Kansas. Public Schools *see* TEACHERS RECORDS
BLOOMFIELD MONITOR – Bloomfield, NE. -w. Jun. 1892; Sep. 1895-Nov. 1899; Jan. 1900-Jan. 1901; Apr. 1901- – 1 – us NE Hist [071]
Bloomfield, Robert *see*
- MAY DAY WITH THE MUSES
- THE REMAINS OF ROBERT BLOOMFIELD
- RURAL TALES, BALLADS, AND SONGS
- WILD FLOWERS

Bloomfield, Susan A et al *see* SITE-SPECIFIC CHANGES IN BONE MASS AND ALTERATIONS IN CALCIOTROPIC HORMONES WITH ELECTRICAL STIMULATION EXERCISE IN INDIVIDUALS WITH CHRONIC SPINAL CORD INJURY
Bloomfield, V *see* CONFERENCE ON THE ACQUISITION OF MATERIAL FROM AFRICA
BLOOMING GROVE BAPTIST CHURCH. MCLEANSBORO, ILLINOIS : CHURCH RECORDS – 1850-68 – 1 – 34.56 – us Baptist [240]
BLOOMINGTON ARGUS – Bloomington, NE. -w. Sep. 1889-Sep. 1890 – 1 – us NE Hist [071]
THE BLOOMSBURY REVIEW – Denver, CO. ill. -bim, -m. Has also occasional unnumbered suppls – 1 – us U.W. Library [420]
BLOOMVILLE GAZETTE – Bloomville, Ohio. 1928- – 28r – 1 – $32.50r – us Archival [071]
EL BLOQUE – Caceres, 1910-1919 – 5 – sp Bibl Santa Ana [073]
BLOQUE PARLAMENTARIO DE LA UNION CIVICA RADICAL *see* EL DEBATE SOBRE EL SEGUNDO PLAN QUINQUENAL EN LA CAMERA DE DIPUTADOS DE LA NACION
BLOQUE YRIGOYENISTA "ALEM-YRIGOYEN-PER ON" *see* YRIGOYEN Y PERON
BLOSSBURG ADVERTISER – Blossburg, PA. 1889-1910 – 13 – $25.00r – us I.M.R. [071]
Blosseville, Ernest Poret *see* DICTIONNAIRE TOPOGRAPHIQUE DU DEPARTEMENT DE L'EURE
BLOTTERS OF THE OFFICE OF THE REGISTER OF THE TREASURY, 1782-1810 / U.S. Treasury Department. Bureau of Accounts – 10 rolls. T723 – 1 – us Nat'l Archives [336]
THE BLOUDY TENENT OF PERSECUTION *see* PUBLICATIONS
Blouin, Gervaise *see* BIBLIOGRAPHIE ANALYTIQUE DE LOUIS-ALEXANDRE BELISLE, AUTEUR ET EDITEUR
Blouin, Gisele *see* BIBLIOGRAPHIE ANALYTIQUE DE JOSEPH-THOMAS LEBLANC
Blount, George A *see* MATERIALS
Blount, Marie-Louise *see* OCCUPATIONAL THERAPY IN MENTAL HEALTH
Blount, P Clavell *see* LEAFLETS
Blount, Thomas *see*
- THE ACADEMIE OF ELOQUENCE
- GLOSSOGRAPHIA

Blow, John *see* AMPHON ANGELICUS. A WORK OF MANY COMPOSITIONS FOR ONE, TWO, THREE AND FOUR VOICES: WITH SEVERAL ACCOMPAGNEMENTS OF INSTRUMENTAL MUSICK; AND A THOROW-BASS TO EACH SONG; FIGUR'D FOR AN ORGAN, HARPSICHORD, OR THEORBOE-LUTE...
Blowitz, Henri Stephan de *see* THE BEHRING SEA ARBITRATION
Bludau, August *see* DE ALEXANDRINAE INTERPRETATIONIS LIBRI DANIELIS
THE BLUE AND WHITE – Athens, Ohio. 1944-Nov 1945 – 1 – us A.J.P.C. [071]
Blue, Archibald *see* RESOURCES AND PROGRESS OF THE PROVINCE OF ONTARIO: A PAPER READ BEFORE THE COMMERCIAL UNION CLUB OF ST THOMAS, NOVEMBER 22, 1887
BLUE BANNER FAITH AND LIFE – v1-34. 1946-79 (complete) – 10r – 1 – ATLA S0215 – us A.T.L.A. [073]
THE BLUE BOOK OF IOWA WOMEN / Reeves, Winona E – (Mexico, MO.: Missouri Printing and Publ., 1914). Iowa Reel 4. (The Cox Library Collection) – 5 – us Americana [978]
THE BLUE BOOK OF THE STATE OF WISCONSIN / Cunningham, Thomas J – 1891. Wisconsin Reel 23. The Cox Library Collection – 5 – us Americana [978]
THE BLUE BOOK OF TOPEKA, 1910 / Biographical Research Association – Topeka, 1910. Kansas Reel 12. (The Cox Library Collection) – 5 – us Americana [978]
BLUE BOOKS / Uganda – 1892-99 – 1 – uk Microform Academic [960]
Blue, Herbert T O *see* HISTORY OF STARK COUNTY
BLUE HILL LEADER – Blue Hill, NE. -w. Jun. 1892; Sep. 1895-Aug. 1897; Oct. 1897-Nov. 1898; Apr. 1901-Sep. 1901; Jan. 1907- – 1 – us NE Hist [071]
BLUE ISLAND SUN – Chicago, IL. 1913-14; 1918 – 1 – us UMI [071]
BLUE ISLAND SUN STANDARD – Chicago. Ill. 1919-1926; 1928-1930 – 1 – us UMI [071]
Blue, John *see* ALBERTA-PAST AND PRESENT
BLUE LAKE ADVOCATE – Blue Lake, CA. 1888-1969 – 33r – 1 BC02071 – $1,650.00 – us Library Micro [071]
BLUE LAKE ADVOCATE – Eureka, CA. 1913-1914; 1947; 1959-1969 – 6r – 1 – $300.00 – B02208 – us Library Micro [071]
BLUE MOUNTAIN AMERICAN – Sumpter, OR. -w. 13 Oct 1900-8 Nov 1917. 5 rolls – 1 – us U.O. Library [071]
Blue Mountain College. Blue Mountain, Mississippi *see* CATALOGS AND COLLEGE RECORDS
BLUE MOUNTAIN EAGLE – Canyon City, OR. -w. 1909-10, 1929-47 – 1 – 161.00 – us Oregon Hist [071]
BLUE MOUNTAIN EAGLE – Canyon City, OR. -w. 30 Nov 1900-16 Aug 1929. – 7r – 1 – us U.O. Library [071]
BLUE MOUNTAIN EAGLE – (Set incl. Grant County Blue Mountain Eagle (John Day)) – John Day, OR. 2 Jan 1948-31 Aug 1978+. – 15r – 1 – us U.O. Library [071]
BLUE MOUNTAIN TIMES – LaGrande, OR. -w. 25 Jul 1868-19 Dec 1868. 1 roll – 1 – us U.O. Library [071]
BLUE MOUNTAINS DEMOCRAT – Katoomba, Apr 19 1961 – 9 – at Pascoe [072]
BLUE MOUNTAINS ECHO – Katoomba, Mar 6 1909-Dec 28 1928; May 12-Oct 17 1939 – 9 – at Pascoe [072]
BLUE MOUNTAINS GAZETTE – Katoomba, Jan 9 1903-Dec 30 1904 – 9 – at Pascoe [072]
BLUE MOUNTAINS STAR – Katoomba, Jan 5 1929-Feb 7 1931 – 9 – at Pascoe [072]
BLUE MOUNTAINS TIMES – Katoomba, Oct 16 1931-Nov 12 1937 – 9 – at Pascoe [072]
BLUE RIBBON – Issue Nos. 1-5 Nov 1939-Jul 1940 – 5mf – 15 – $31.95 – us Comics [760]
BLUE RIBBON – Issue Nos. 6-10 Sept 1940-Mar 1941 – 5mf – 15 – $31.95 – us Comics [760]
BLUE RIVER BAPTIST CHURCH. WASHINGTON COUNTY. INDIANA : CHURCH RECORDS – 1847-1869 – 1 – 6.93 – us Baptist [240]
BLUE SKY : THE LIFE OF HARRIET CASWELL-BROAD / Clark, Joseph B – Boston: Pilgrim Press, c1911 – 1mf – us A.T.L.A. [240]
BLUE SKY NEWS – (Lacking: 1936-37. In 1947 the organization became "The National Association of Securities Administrators") – National Assoc of Securities Commissioners, 1934-46 (all publ) – 12mf – 9 – $18.00 – LLMC 84-426 – us L.L.M.C. [073]
BLUE SPRINGS BEE – Blue Springs, NE. -w. Apr. 1927-Sep. 1946 – 1 – us NE Hist [071]
BLUE VALLEY BLADE – Seward, NE. -w. Mar-Dec 1879; Feb-Dec 1880; Feb 1881-Apr 1955 – 1 – us NE Hist [071]
BLUE VALLEY BLADE – Wilber, NE. -w. Feb 1884-Feb 1886, scattered issues missing – 1 – us NE Hist [071]
BLUE VALLEY JOURNAL – McCool Junction, NE. -w. Jun 1897-Dec 1942 – 1 – us NE Hist [071]
BLUE VALLEY RECORD – Milford, NE. -w. Dec 1870-Apr 1873 – 1 – us NE Hist [071]
[BLUEBEARD] THE GRAND MARCH...FOR THE PIANOFORTE... / Kelly, M – London: Corri, Dussek & Co, 179- – 1 – us Sibley [780]
BLUEBEARD'S KEYS / Thackeray, Anne – British Fiction Archive: Unit 3 – 9 – uk Bell [830]
Bluefield College. Virginia *see* CATALOGS
BLUEFIELD FIRST BAPTIST CHURCH. BLUEFIELD, WEST VIRGINIA : CHURCH RECORDS – 1889-1903, 1912-46 – 1 – 84.69 – us Baptist [240]

BLUEFIELDS SENTINEL – Mar. 10, 1892-Mar. 28, 1894 – 1 – us NY Public [970]
BLUE-GREEN ALGAE FOR RICE PRODUCTION : A MANUAL FOR ITS PROMOTION – 1981 – 110p – it F.A.O. [338]
Bluehdorn, R *see* EINFUEHRUNG IN DAS ANGEWANDTE VOELKERRECHT
DER BLUEHENDE BAUM : ERZAEHLUNG / Sturm, Stefan – Karlsbad: A Kraft, 1944 – 1r – 1 – us U.W. Library [430]
DER BLUEHENDE STAB : NEUN GESCHICHTEN, NEUN HOLZSCHNITTE / Schaumann, Ruth – Muenchen: J Koesel & F Pustet, c1929 – 1r – 1 – us U.W. Library [430]
BLUE-JAY – v1-27. 1942/43-1969 – 1 – cn Precision [073]
Bluemel, Rudolf *see* DIE DEUTSCHE SCHALLFORM DER LETZTEN BLUETEZEIT UND IHRER AUSLAUFER IN DICHTUNG UND PROSA
Bluemml, E K *see* CAROLINE PICHLER GEBORNE VON GREINER
Bluemner, Hugo *see* WINCKELMANNS BRIEFE AN SEINE ZUERICHER FREUNDE
THE BLUENOSE – Halifax, N.S.: Imperial Pub. Co., 1900 – 9 – cn C.I.H.M. [971]
BLUES – Columbus, Miss. no. 1-9. Feb 1929-Fall 1930 – 1 – us NY Public [073]
THE BLUESHIRT – Dublin, Ireland.5 Aug 1933-15 Jun 1935 – 1 – ie Microforms [072]
DER BLUETENZWEIG : EIN AUSWAHL AUS DEN GEDICHTEN / Hesse, Hermann – Zuerich: Fretz & Wasmuth, 1945 – 1r – 1 – us U.W. Library [810]
DIE BLUETEZEIT DER DEUTSCHEN POLITISCHEN LYRIK VON 1840 BIS 1850 : EIN BEITRAG ZUR DEUTSCHEN LITERATUR UND NATIONALGESCHICHTE / Petzet, Christian – Muenchen, 1903 – 6mf – DM118.00 – 3-8267-3030-5 – gw Hänsel [430]
DIE BLUETEZEIT DER DEUTSCHEN PREDIGT IM MITTELALTER, 1100-1400 / Albert, F R – Guetersloh: C. Bertelsmann, 1896. (Die Geschichte der Predigt in Deutschland bis Luther / von F.R. Albert; 3. T.) – 1mf – us A.T.L.A. [240]
BLUETHEN DES GEFUEHLS GESPROSSEN IN MEINEN ERHOLUNGSSTUNDEN / Reindahl, E Rullmann – Bremen: [J G Heyse] 1819 – 1 – us U.W. Library [800]
BLUETHENDIAGRAMME, CONSTRUIRT UND ERLAUETERT / Eichler, A W – 2v. Leipzig. 1875-78. B-2291 2 – 8 – ne IDC [580]
BLUETHEZEIT DER ROMANTIK / Huch, Ricarda – Leipzig: H Haessel, 1899 – 1r – 1 – us U.W. Library [430]
Bluethgen, Viktor *see*
– BADEKUREN
– MAMA KOMMT!
BLUEWATER BAPTIST CHURCH. DUBLIN, GEORGIA : CHURCH RECORDS – Oct 1942-Dec 1977. 416p – 1 – 18.72 – us Baptist [240]
Bluff. (Plantation) *see* PLANTATION BOOK
Bluff Point, New York. Bluff Point Baptist Church *see* RECORDS
Bluffton General Store. Bluffton, South Carolina *see* ACCOUNT BOOK
Bluffton, Indiana *see* MISCELLANEOUS EARLY NEWSPAPERS
BLUFFTON NEWS – Bluffton, Ohio. 1915-33 – 16r – 1 – $32.50r – us Archival [071]
BLUM BAPTIST CHURCH. TEXAS : CHURCH RECORDS – 1886-1902 – 1 – 9.27 – us Baptist [240]
Blum, J Joseph et al *see* COMMENTS ON THEORETICAL BIOLOGY
Blum, J R *see* PSEUDOMORPHOSEN DES MINERALREICHS
Blum, John Morton *see* THE PRICE OF VISION
Blum, Paul Richard *see* THE CATHOLIC REFORMATION
Bluma, Daciano *see* DE VITA RECESSUOLI...
BLUMBERGSHOF... / Vegesack, Siegfried von – c1933 – 1r – 1 – us U.W. Library [943]
Blume, C L *see*
– BIJDRAGEN TOT DE FLORA VAN NEDERLANDSCH INDIE
– CATALOGUS...'S LANDS PLANTENTUIN TE BUITENZORG...
– ENUMERATIO PLANTARUM JAVAE ET INSULARUM ADJACENTIUM
– FLORA JAVAE ET INSULARUM ADJACENTIUM
– FLORA JAVAE NEC NON INSULARUM ADJACENTIUM
– MUSEUM BOTANICUM LUGDUNO-BATAVUM...
– RUMPHIA, SIVE COMMENTATIONES BOTANICAE IMPRIMIS DE PLANTIS INDIAE ORIENTALIS
– TABELLEN EN PLATEN VOOR DE JAVAANSCHE ORCHIDEEN
-Blume, J *see*
– ANALECTA HYMNICA MEDII AEVI
– EIN JAHRTAUSEND LATEINISCHER HYMNENDICHTUNG
Blume, Mary *see* AT THE CONVERSATION TABLE
Blume, Wilhelm von *see*
– DER DEUTSCHE MILITARISMUS
– DIE WUERZELN DER DEUTSCHEN VOLKSKRAFT
BLUMEA – Tijdschrift voor de Systematiek en de Geografie der Planten. Leiden, 1934-41. v1-4. – 39mf – 8 – ne IDC [073]
BLUMENAUER ZEITUNG – Blumenau, 1921-dec 2 1938 (incomplete) – 7r – 1 – Inquire at Mikrofilmarchiv for details – gw Misc Inst [072]
BLUMENLESE / Goldfaden, A – Ed. 2. Cracow. 1897. BJ-422-18 1 – 9 – ne IDC [470]
BLUMENLESE AUS DEN SAEMMTLICHEN WERKEN VON JOHANN RUDOLF WYSS DEM JUENGERN / Wyss, Johann Rudolf; ed by Greyerz, O von – Bern: K J Wyss, 1872 – 1r – 1 – us U.W. Library [430]
Blumenstein, J *see* DIE VERSCHIEDENEN EIDESARTEN NACH MOSAISCH-TALMUDISCHEN RECHTE
Blumenstiel, Alexander *see*
– AN ACT TO ESTABLISH A UNIFORM SYSTEM OF BANKRUPTCY THROUGHOUT THE UNITED STATES
– THE LAW AND PRACTICE IN BANKRUPTCY.
DER BLUMENSTRAUSS *see* GEDICHTBUECHELCHEN
Blumenthal, Harvey *see* FACTORS AFFECTING THE PERFORMANCE OF INTRAMURAL OFFICIALS IN COMPETITIVE SITUATIONS
Blumenthal, M *see* FORMEN UND MOTIVE IN DEN APOKRYPHEN APOSTELGESCHICHTEN (T.U.U. 4-48/1)
Blumenthal, Oscar *see*
– BUCH DER SPRUECHE
– LEBENSSCHWAENKE
Blumenthal, Oskar *see*
– IM WEISSEN ROESSL
– SCHERZGEDICHTE
BLUMENTHALER ZEITUNG – (Cont by: Allgemeine Blumenthaler Zeitung, aug 1 1929; Blumenthaler Zeitung, mar 10 1930; Nordwestdeutsche Landes-Zeitung, sep 30 1933) – Bremen-Blumenthal, sep 1 1913-feb 23 1917, sep 20 1924-mar 31 1940 – 38r – 1 – Inquire at Mikrofilmarchiv for details – gw Misc Inst [943]
BLUME'S UNREPORTED OPINIONS / Michigan. Supreme Court – (A Pre-NRS title) – 1v. 1836-1843 (all publ) – 3mf – 9 – $4.50 – LLMC 88-050 – us L.L.M.C. [340]
Blumhardt, Christoph *see* VON DER NACHFOLGE JESU CHRISTI..
Blumhardt, Johann Christoph *see* HANDBUCH DER MISSIONSGESCHICHTE UND MISSIONSGEOGRAPHIE
Blumhart, W F *see* LE NOUVEAU MONDE
Blundell, VH *see* LEGACY OF INFLATION AND LAND MONOPOLY
BLUNDERS AND FORGERIES : HISTORICAL ESSAYS / Bridgett, T E – (Allegations of anti-Catholic bias in the press) – London: Kegan Paul, Trench, Truebner, & Co, 1890 – 4mf – 9 – $6.00 – LLMC 92-117 – us L.L.M.C. [320]
BLUNDERS AND FORGERIES : HISTORICAL ESSAYS / Bridgett, T E – London: K. Paul, Trench, Truebner, 1890 – 1mf – us A.T.L.A. [240]
Blundeville, Thomas *see* THE ART OF LOGIKE
Blunt, John Henry *see* DICTIONARY OF DOCTRINAL AND HISTORICAL THEOLOGY
Blunt, Wilfrid Scawen *see* THE LOVE SONNETS OF PROTEUS
Bluntschli, J K *see*
– DAS BEUTERECHT ...
– LE DROIT INTERNATIONAL ...
– DAS MODERNE KRIEGSRECHT ...
– DAS MODERNE VOELKERRECHT ...
– THE THEORY OF THE STATE
Blusse van Oud-Alblas, A *see* DE HAGUE RULES IN DE BRUSSELSCHE CONVENTIE 1924
BLUT – v. 10-41. 1964-80 – 1,5,9 – 2832.00 – us UMI [073]
BLUT *see* ANNALS OF HEMATOLOGY
DER BLUTABERGLAUBE BEI CHRISTEN UND JUDEN / Strack, Hermann Leberecht – Muenchen: C.H. Beck, 1891. 1 fiche – 9 – us A.T.L.A. [240]
DER BLUTIGE ERNST – Germany. 1919, nos. 1-6 (complete) – 1 – 35.00r – us Hoover Inst Photo [072]
Bluwstein, J *see* SPINOZAS BRIEFWECHSEL U. ANDERE DOKUMENTE
BLY BULLETIN – Bly, OR. -w. 21 Mar 1930-31 Jul 1931. 1 roll – 1 – us U.O. Library [071]
Blyden, Edward Wilmot *see*
– ADDRESSES AND CORRESPONDENCE, 1857-1908
– THE PROBLEMS BEFORE LIBERIA
– A SELECTION OF WORKS BY AND ABOUT EDWARD W. BLYDEN
– WRITINGS, 1862?-1908
BLYDEN OF LIBERIA : AN ACCOUNT OF THE LIFE AND LABORS OF EDWARD WILMOT BLYDEN, LL.D., AS RECORDED IN LETTERS AND IN PRINT / Holden, Edith – 1st ed. New York: Vantage Press, [1967, c1966] – us Res Libr [920]
Blymer and Sons (Hancock County, Ohio) *see* THRESHING RECORDS
BLYTH CITIZEN – Ontario, CN. 1986 – 1r – 1 – cn Commonwealth Micro [072]
Blyth, E *see* CATALOGUE OF THE BIRDS IN THE MUSEUM ASIATIC SOCIETY
BLYTH NEWS & WANSBECK TELEGRAPH – England.10 Jan-26 Dec 1911. -w. 1/2 reel – 1 – uk British Libr Newspaper [072]
BLYTHE HERALD – Blythe, CA. 1915-1925 – 6r – 1 – $300.00 – R03164 – us Library Micro [071]
Blythe, James *see* THE DEATH OF THE GOOD MAN...REV. JOHN BROWN
Blythe, Wayne T *see* THE USE OF NOYE IN THE AUTHENTICALLY PAULINE EPISTLES
Blytheville. Arkansas *see* CEMETERY INSCRIPTIONS
BMA NEWS : PENINSULAR EDITION – Kuala Lumpur, Malaysia. 23 Jan-27 Mar 1946 – 4ft – 1 – uk British Libr Newspaper [072]
BMR COMMENT – Toronto. v101-166. 1966-77 – 9 – cn Micromedia [600]
BMR COMMENT *see* TOPIC
B'NAI B'RITH *see* ADL ON THE FRONTLINE
B'NAI B'RITH BERLIN : MONATSSCHRIFT DER BERLINER LOGEN – Berlin, 1926-33 (incomplete) – 1r – 1 – Dist. gw Mikrofilm – gw Misc Inst [072]
B'NAI B'RITH BERLIN – Monatsschrift der Berliner Logen. U.O.B.B. Berlin. v1-13? 1921-1933? Lacking: v1-5, 1921-1925 and misc. issues in v6, 8, 9, 12. 1 reel. B37. (Leo Baeck Institute. German-Jewish Periodicals, Pt 1) – 1 – $75.00 – us UPA [270]
B'NAI B'RITH COVENANT – Downsview, Ontario. Oct 1975-15 Dec 1987. Many issues missing – 1 – us A.J.P.C. [072]
B'NAI B'RITH DEUTSCHLAND – Berlin, apr 1891-1937 – 3r – 1 – Dist. gw Mikrofilm – gw Misc Inst [072]
B'NAI B'RITH DEUTSCHLAND / Der Orden Bne Briss – Mitteilungen der Grossloge fuer Deutschland VIII U.O.B.B. Berlin. 1891-1937. Lacking misc. issues. 3 reels. B40. (Leo Baeck Institute. German-Jewish Periodicals, Pt 1) – 1 – $205.00 – us UPA [270]
B'NAI B'RITH DISTRICT TWO NEWS – Cincinnati, OH. 1980-84 – 1 – us A.J.P.C. [071]
B'NAI B'RITH HILLEL RECORD – Evanston, IL. 24 Nov 1937; Dec 1940-Apr 1941 – 1 – us A.J.P.C. [071]
B'NAI B'RITH MESSENGER – (California). 1958 67 – 1 – us A.J.P.C. [073]
B'NAI B'RITH MESSENGER – v1-16. 1898-1913 – 4r – 1 – us Ross [270]
B'NAI B'RITH VOICE – San Antonio, TX.Jun 1960 – 1 – us A.J.P.C. [071]
B'NAI BRITH VOICE – San Antonio, TX.May 1976-Apr 1987. Incomplete – 1 – us A.J.P.C. [071]
BNAI ZION TRAVELER – New York, NY. Spring 1975-Spring/Summer/Fall 1985. Many issues lacking – 1 – us A.J.P.C. [071]
BNAMU-UIN SHUA5UA5KH / Sangidanzan, D – Ulan Bator, 1967. 98 pp. BR-15.017 1 – 9 – ne IDC [323]
BNDD BULLETIN / U.S. Bureau of Narcotics and Dangerous Drugs – (Lacking: v1 nos 2,4) – v1-4. 1969-73 (all publ) – 6mf – 9 – $9.00 – LLMC 81-200 – us L.L.M.C. [360]
BNDD BULLETIN *see* DRUG ENFORCEMENT
BNEI AKIVA BEHAAPALA = SONS OF AKIVA... – (In Yiddish) – Munich, DE. v2 no2-3. Jan/Feb 1948 – 1r – 1 – $25.00 – cn Can Microfilming [072]
BNMA ULSUIN ERUA5UA5GYN ERKH DEKH GEM BURUUGYN ZARIM ASUUDAL / Sovd, G – Ulan Bator, 1966. 74 pp. BR-15.021 1 – 9 – ne IDC [340]
BNQ *see* ECOLE LITTERAIRE DE MONTREAL
BO LUAT DAN-SU' VA THU'O'NG-SU' TO-TUNG / Nguyen Hung Tru'o'ng – Saigon: Khai-Tri 1973. 167p. LL-10031 – 1 – us L of C Photodup [340]
BOA ESPERANCA : ORGAM MUNICIPAL – Dores da Boa Esperanca, 21 Dec 1902 – 1,5,6 – bl Biblioteca [072]
Boa, Myrtle J *see* IDYLLS OF OUR ISLAND
BOARD OF AGRICULTURE OF LOWER CANADA, THE FARMERS' JOURNAL AND TRANSACTION OF THE BOARD OF AGRICULTURE OF LOWER CANADA *see* LOWER CANADA AGRICULTURIST, MANUFACTURING, COMMERCIAL, AND COLONIZATION INTELLIGENCER
Board of Arts and Manufactures for Lower Canada *see* QUARTERLY REPORT OF THE SUB-COMMITTEE OF THE BOARD OF ARTS AND MANUFACTURES FOR LOWER CANADA
Board of Arts and Manufactures for Upper Canada *see* JOURNAL
BOARD OF CONTRACT APPEALS DECISIONS / U.S. Department of the Interior – (v22-30 filmed in 1995) – v1-21. 1970-83 – 84mf – 9 – $126.00 – LLMC 82-202 – us L.L.M.C. [324]
BOARD OF DIRECTORS MINUTE BOOKS / Free Public Library, Ottawa, KS – 1872-1945 – 1 – us KS Hist [020]
Board of Documents, Cabinet of Japan *see* HOKI BUNRUI TAIZEN
BOARD OF EXAMINERS' MINUTES / Fulton County. Ohio. Board of Education – 1861-1900 – 1r – 1 – $32.50r – us Archival [324]
BOARD OF EXAMINERS' MINUTES / Huron County. Ohio. Board of Education – 1875-1909 – 1r – 1 – $32.50r – us Archival [324]
BOARD OF EXAMINERS' MINUTES / Wyandot County. Ohio. Board of Education – 1873-1887 – 1r – 1 – $32.50r – us Archival [324]
BOARD OF INDIAN APPEALS DECISIONS AND ORDERS / U.S. Department of the Interior – (Includes list of cases decided in v26. v1-8 part of Native American Collection. Updates available) – v1-15. 1970-86 – 77mf – 9 – $115.00 – LLMC 82-203 – us L.L.M.C. [324]
BOARD OF INDIAN COMMISSIONERS' ANNUAL REPORTS / U.S. Department of the Interior – (Lacking: Reports no 1, 18, 64) – 1869-1933 (all publ) – 97mf – 9 – $145.00 – LLMC 88-005 – us L.L.M.C. [340]
BOARD OF LAND APPEALS DECISIONS AND ORDERS / U.S. Department of the Interior – (Updates available) – v1-98. 1970-87 – 599mf – 9 – $898.00 – LLMC 82-204 – us L.L.M.C. [324]
BOARD OF MINE OPERATIONS APPEALS DECISIONS AND ORDERS / U.S. Department of the Interior – v1-8. 1970-78 (all publ) – 39mf – 9 – $58.00 – LLMC 82-205 – us L.L.M.C. [324]
Board of National Missions (United Pres. Ch. in the U.S.A.) *see* MINUTES, 1958-1972
BOARD OF PARK COMMISSIONS : MINUTES / Lucas County, Ohio. Toledo Metropolitan Park District – 1929-86 – 6r – 1 – $32.50r – us Archival [978]
BOARD OF REVIEW, JAG BRANCH, CHINA-BURMA-INDIA/INDIA-BURMA THEATER, HOLDINGS, OPINIONS AND REVIEWS / U.S. Army. Judge Advocate General. Board of Review, CBI-IBT – (Covers: CM-CBI-15 to CM-CBI-249. CM-IBT-282 to CM-IBT-762) – v1-3. 1943-45. Washington: Office of the JAG, 1946? – 12mf – 9 – $18.00 – LLMC 84-224 – us L.L.M.C. [340]
BOARD OF TAX APPEALS REPORTS – 1924-1942 – 738mf – 9 – $1,107.00 – LLMC 79-420 – us L.L.M.C. [332]
BOARD OF TAX APPEALS, REPORTS / U.S. Tax Court – (Cont as: Tax Court Reports) – v1-47. 1924-1942 – 9 – $975.00 set – us Hein [336]
BOARD OF TRADE JOURNAL – 1-199. 1886-1970 – 1 – us UMI [380]
BOARD OF TRADE NEWS – Toronto, Canada. Apr 1911-Dec 1921.-w. 2 reels – 1 – uk British Libr Newspaper [072]

BOARD OF TRADE OF METRO TORONTO BUSINESS JOURNAL – v84- 1994- – 9 – Can$20.00y – cn Micromedia [380]
BOARD OF TRADE OF METRO TORONTO BUSINESS JOURNAL *see* METROPOLITAN TORONTO BUSINESS JOURNAL
Board of Trade of the City of Toronto *see* MONTHLY RETURNS OF IMPORTS AND EXPORTS AT THE PORT OF TORONTO FOR...
BOARD OF TRUSTEES MINUTES / Putnam County District Library (Ottawa, Ohio) – 1924-1990 – 2r – 1 – $32.50r – us Archival [978]
BOARD OF TRUSTEES, RECORDS / Baptist State Conventions (American Baptist). Vermont – (Executive Committee, Records, 1964-75. Commission on Ordination, Records, 1955-62. Deeds and Wills, 1886-1961) – 1824-1975 – 1 – us A.B.H.S. [240]
BOARD RECORD / Monroe County. Mich, Bedford Township. Board of Education – 1866-1901 – 1r – 1 – $32.50r – us Archival [324]
Boardman, George Dana *see*
- DIVINE MAN: FROM THE NATIVITY TO THE TEMPTATION
- EPIPHANIES OF THE RISEN LORD
- KINGDOM (BASILEIA): AN EXEGETICAL STUDY
- STUDIES IN THE CREATIVE WEEK
- STUDIES IN THE MOUNTAIN INSTRUCTION

Boardman, George Nye *see*
- A HISTORY OF NEW ENGLAND THEOLOGY
- REGENERATION

Boardman, Henry Augustus *see*
- THE DOCTRINE OF ELECTION
- EARTHLY SUFFERING AND HEAVENLY GLORY
- THE GREAT QUESTION, WILL YOU CONSIDER THE SUBJECT OF PERSONAL RELIGION?
- THE HIGHER LIFE DOCTRINE OF SANCTIFICATION: TRIED BY THE WORD OF GOD
- A TREATISE ON THE SCRIPTURE DOCTRINE OF ORIGINAL SIN
- TWO SERMONS
- THE VANITY OF A LIFE OF FASHIONABLE PLEASURE

BOARDMAN MIRROR – Boardman, OR. -w. 11 Feb 1921-4 Sep 1925. 1 roll – 1 – us U.O. Library [071]
Boardman, William Edwin *see*
- GLADNESS IN JESUS
- IN THE POWER OF THE SPIRIT

BOARDROOM REPORTS – (1975- . 5,6,9) – 1972- – 1 – us UMI [338]
THE BOARDS OF TRADE GENERAL ARBITRATIONS ACT (1894). / Beatty, William Henry – Toronto, Hunter, Rose, 1894. 88 p. LL-2290 – 1 – us L of C Photodup [340]
Boas, Eduard *see* SCHILLER'S UND GOETHE'S XENIEN-MANUSCRIPT
Boas, Franz *see*
- THE CENTRAL ESKIMO
- CHINOOK TEXTS
- THE ESKIMO OF BAFFIN LAND AND HUDSON BAY
- ETHNOLOGICAL PROBLEMS IN CANADA
- ETHNOLOGY OF THE KWAKIUTL
- FACIAL PAINTINGS OF THE INDIANS OF NORTHERN BRITISH COLUMBIA
- HANDBOOK OF AMERICAN INDIAN LANGUAGES
- INDIANISCHE SAGEN VON DE NORD-PACIFISCHEN KUESTE AMERIKAS
- INDIANISCHE SAGEN VON DER NORD-PACIFISCHEN KUESTE AMERIKAS
- MYTHOLOGY AND FOLK-TALES OF THE NORTH AMERICAN INDIANS
- THE MYTHOLOGY OF THE BELLA COOLA INDIANS
- THE PROFESSIONAL CORRESPONDENCE OF FRANZ BOAS
- SHAKESPEARE AND HIS PREDECESSORS
- TSIMSHIAN MYTHOLOGY

O BOATA THEATRAL – Manaos, Amazonas. 30 Mar 1898 – 1,5,6 – bl Biblioteca [072]
Boateng, Ernest Amano *see* A GEOGRAPHICAL STUDY OF HUMAN SETTLEMENT IN THE EASTERN PROVINCE OF THE GOLD COAST COLONY WEST OF THE VOLTA DELTA
BOATING – (1971- . 5,6. 1976- . 9) – 1956- – 1 – us UMI [790]
BOATING INDUSTRY – 1979- – 9 – us UMI [790]
BOATING PRODUCT NEWS – (1985- . 5,6,9) – v1- . 1977- – 1 – us UMI [073]
BO'AZ VE-RUT / Ha-Cohen, I – Breslau. 1834. BJ-422-33 1 – 9 – ne IDC [470]
BOB SHULER MAGAZINE *see* THE BOB SHULER PERIODICALS, 1916-1960
THE BOB SHULER PERIODICALS, 1916-1960 : BOB SHULER'S FREE LANCE, THE BOB SHULER MAGAZINE, THE METHODIST CHALLENGE – 136mf – 9 – $595.00 – us Schnappsburg [240]
BOB SHULER'S FREE LANCE *see* THE BOB SHULER PERIODICALS, 1916-1960
THE BOBBIO MISSAL : NOTES AND STUDIES / Wilmart, Dom A et al – 1924 – 3mf – 8 – ne Slangenburg [240]
THE BOBBIO MISSAL, VOL. 1 / Lowe, E A – 1917 – 9mf – 8 – ne Slangenburg [240]
THE BOBBIO MISSAL, VOL. 2 / Lowe, E A – 1920 – 4mf – 8 – ne Slangenburg [240]
Bobertag, Felix *see* WIELANDS ROMANE
Bobo and Ray Families. South Carolina *see* GENEALOGY
Bobrik, Johannes Eduard Guenther *see* WIELANDS DON SYLVIO UND OBERON AUF DER DEUTSCHEN SINGSPIELBUEHNE
Bobrishchev-Pushkin, Aleksandr M *see* SUD I RASKOLI' NIKISEKTANTY
Bobrishchev-Pushkin, Aleksandr M Vladimirovich *see* PATRIOTY BEZ OTECHESTVA
Bobrovnikov, Nikolai *see* CHTO PROIZOSHLO V ROSSII?
Bobrowski, C *see* LA YOUGOSLAVIE SOCIALISTE
Bobzin, Hartmut *see* WAGENSEIL COLLECTION
Bocangelino, N *see* LIBRO DE LAS ENFERMEDADES MALIGNAS Y PESTILENTES, CAUSAS, PRONOSTICOS, CURACION...
O BOCAYUVA – Bocayuva, 8 Jun 1924; 23 Aug 1925 – 1,5,6 – bl Biblioteca [072]
Boccaccio G *see* DECAMERONE
Boccaccio, G *see*
- DE CERTALDO INSIGNIS OPUS DE CLARIS MULIERIBUS
- EIN SCHOENE CRONICA, ODER HYSTORIBUCH VON DEN FUER NAMLICHSTEN WEYBERN

Boccalinus, T *see* GESPRAECH UND DISCURSEN ...
Boccara, M *see* LES REVEURS D'EAU
Boccherini, K *see* SIX QUATUORS, OP. 2. G. 166, 165, 167-170
Boccherini, Luigi *see*
- MINUET IN A, TRANSCRIBED FOR THE ORGAN BY E.H. LEMARE
- QUARTET NO. 44 FOR 2 VIOLINS, VIOLA AND CELLO
- QUARTETTI, 6, OP. 6A. [G. 165-170]
- QUARTETTI CONCERTANTI, SEI, OP. 27
- QUINTETS, FLUTE AND STRINGS, "OP. 21E", G. 419-424
- [QUINTETS] OP. 20, G. 277-282
- QUINTETS, SIX. OP. 18, G. 283-288
- [QUINTETS] THIRD SET OF SIX. OP. 20, G. 277-282
- QUINTETS, THREE. OP. 36, G. 295-297
- SEI QUARTETTI...OP. 26. [G. 183-188]
- SEI QUARTETTI...OP. 33. G. 201-206
- SEI QUARTETTI...OP.26, G. 183-188
- SEI QUINTETTI PER DUE VIOLINI, ALTOS E DUE VIOLONCELLO CONCERTANTI...OPERA 23
- SEI SEXTOUR PER DUE VIOLINI, VIOLA, DUE VIOLONCELLE E FLAUTO. OP. 15, G. 461-466
- SEI SINFONIE O SIA QUARTETTI...PER DUE VIOLINI, ALTO E VIOLONCELLO OBBLIGATI
- SEI SONATE A TRE, OP. 3. G. 119-124
- SEI TRIO PER DUE VIOLINI...
- SEI TRIO PER DUS VIOLINI E VIOLONCELLO OBBLIGATO...
- SEI TRITETTI PER DUE VIOLINI ET BASSO, OP.2. G. 77-82
- SERENADE, D MAJOR, G. 501
- SIX QUARTETTI, OP. 32. G. 195-200
- SIX QUATUORS CONCERTANS, OP. 11. G. 191, 194, 192, 190, 189, 193
- SIX QUATUORS, OP. 7. G. 171-176
- SIX QUATUORS, OR DIVERTISSEMENT...OP. 8. G. 177-182
- SIX QUINTETS, OP. 13, G. 271-276
- SIX SONATES A VIOLON SEUL...ET BASSE
- SIX SONATES POUR LE CLAVECIN
- SIX TRIOS, OP. 9, G. 95-100
- TRIOS, VIOLINS AND VIOLONCELLO, G. 83-94, G. 89-94
- TRIOS, VIOLINS & VIOLONCELLO, G. 83-88

Bocchi, F *see* LE BELLEZZE DELLA CITTA DI FIRENZE
Boccone, P *see* MUSEO DI PIANTE RARE DELLA SICILIA, MALTA, CORSICA
Boch, Gustav *see* NEUE BERLINER MUSIKZEITUNG
Bocha, R *see* DEUX NOCTURNES POUR HARPE & HAUTBOIS, OEUV. 51, NO. 1
Bochartus, Sam *see* OPERA OMNIA
Boche, Holger *see* DAS PROBLEM DER ANALYTISCHEN FORTSETZBARKEIT IN DER THEORIE DER LAPLACE-TRANSFORMATION
Bochius, I *see* HISTORICA NARRATIO PROFECTIONIS ET INAUGURATIONIS SERENISSIMORUM
Bochkarev, Nikolai G *see* ASTRONOMICAL AND ASTROPHYSICAL TRANSACTIONS
Bochkov, A K, et al *see* ARKHIV KRASNOI ARMII
Bochkovskyi, Olgerd Ippolit *see* FINLIANDIIA TA FINLIANDSKE PYTANNIE
BOCHOLTER-BORKENER VOLKSBLATT – Bocholt. 1972-76 – 26r – 1 – gw Mikrofilm [072]
BOCHOLTER-BORKENER VOLKSBLATT – Bocholt, jan 3-mar 15 1972, 1977- – 1 – Inquire at Mikrofilmarchiv for details – gw Misc Inst [072]
BOCHUMER ANZEIGER – Bochum, 1914-oct 1 1944 – 1 – Inquire at Mikrofilmarchiv for details – gw Misc Inst [943]
DER BOCHUMER ARZT DR. CARL ARNOLD KORTUM, DER DICHTER DER JOBSIADE : SEIN LEBEN UND SEIN WIRKEN / Tegeler, Ernst – (Includes bibliographical references) – Jena: Gustav Fischer, 1931 – 1 – us U.W. Library [920]
BOCHUMER KREISBLATT – Bochum, Germany. 1 Jan-24 Jun 1848 – 1 – gw Mikrofilm [072]
BOCHUMER KREISBLATT – (Cont by: Bochumer Zeitung, jan 1875) – Bochum, 1863 – 1 – Inquire at Mikrofilmarchiv for details – gw Misc Inst [943]
BOCHUMER KREISBLATT – (Cont by: Maerkischer Speicher, jul 1 1848; Bochumer Zeitung, sep 18 1909) – Bochum, 1830-1915, 1925-30 – 1 – Inquire at Mikrofilmarchiv for details – gw Misc Inst [943]
BOCHUMER ZEITUNG *see*
- BOCHUMER KREISBLATT

Bock, Hieronymus *see* HIERONYMI TRAGI, DE STIRPIVM, MAXIME EARVM QVAE IN GERMANIA NOSTRA NASCVNTUR, USITATIS NOMENCLATURIS, PROPRIJSQ DIFFERENTIJS, NEQ NON TEMPERATURIS AC FACULTATIBUS, COMMENTARIORUM LIBRI TRES
Bock, Ulrich Manfred *see* HEPATITIS C BEI HAEMODIALYSEPATIENTEN
Bocker Family *see* DIARIES
Bocket, Thomas J *see* DIFFERENCES IN PHYSICAL ACTIVITY ATTITUDES AND FITNESS KNOWLEDGE BETWEEN HEALTH FITNESS STANDARD, SEX, AND GRADE GROUP
Bocklenberg, Ute *see* MODERNE BLOCKFLOETENTECHNIKEN UND IHRE VERMITTLUNG
BOCKSGESANG : IN FUENF AKTEN / Werfel, Franz – Muenchen: K Wolff, 1921 – 1r – 1 – us U.W. Library [820]
Bocquillon-Limousin, H *see* ETUDE DES PLANTES DES COLONIES FRANCAISES
Bod, Petri *see* HISTORIA HUNGARORUM ECCLESIASTICA
BODARC RECORD – Bodarc, NE. -w. Nov. 1886-Apr. 1887 – 1 – us NE Hist [071]
Bodard, Auguste *see* EXPOSITION DES FAITS ET DE LA SITUATION ACTUELLE DE LA SOCIETE DE COLONISATION DU TEMISCAMINGUE VIS-A-VIS DES ACTIONNAIRES FRANCAIS
BODAS Y OBRAS JUVENILES DE ZURBARAN / Caturla, Maria Luisa – Granada: Imp. Francisco Roman Camacho, 1948 – sp Bibl Santa Ana [946]
Boddam-Whetham, John W *see*
- ACROSS CENTRAL AMERICA
- WESTERN WANDERINGS: RECORD OF TRAVEL IN THE EVENING LAND

Bode, G H *see*
- SCRIPTORES RERUM MYTHICARUM LATINI TRES ROMAE NUPER REPERTI
- SCRIPTORES RERUM MYTHICARUM TRES ROMAE NUPER REPERTI

Bode, Johann Joachim Christoph *see* DER WANDSBECKER BOTHE
Bode, John Ernest *see* THE ABSENCE OF PRECISION IN THE FORMULARIES OF THE CHURCH OF ENGLAND SCRIPTURAL, AND SUITABLE TO A STATE OF PROBATION: IN EIGHT SERMONS
Bode, Wilhelm *see*
- GOETHE IN VERTRAULICHEN BRIEFEN SEINER ZEITGENOSSEN
- GOETHES GESUNDHEITSPFLEGE
- GOETHES LEBEN
- GOETHES LEBEN IM GARTEN AM STERN
- GOETHES PERSOENLICHKEIT
- GOETHES WEG ZUR HOEHE

Bodecker, Albert *see* REMINISCENCES OF LIFE IN BUTLER COUNTY
THE BODEGA BAY NAVIGATOR – Bodega Bay, CA. 1987- – 2+ r – 1 – $100.00 ($50.00y) – B05029 – us Library Micro [071]
THE BODEGA BAY SIGNAL – Bodega Bay, CA. 1985- – 12+ r – 1 – $600.00 ($50.00y) – B05028 – us Library Micro [071]
Bodemann, Friedrich Wilhelm *see* DER WICHTIGSTEN BEKENNTNISSCHRIFTEN DER EVANGELISCH-REFORMIRTEN KIRCHE
BODEN – Lulea, Sweden. 1899-1905 – 2r – 1 – sw Kungliga [072]
Bodenehr, H G *see* GEISTLICHE HERZENS EINBILDUNGEN INN ZWEIHUNDERT UND FUENFZIG BIBLISCHEN FIGURSPRUECHEN ANGEDEUTET
Bodenheimer, M J *see* WOHIN MIT DEN RUSSISCHEN JUDEN? HAMBURG. 1891. BJ-72-503/1
BODENNUTZUNG IN VENEZUELA : OEKOLOGISCHE UND OEKONOMISCHE ASPEKTE VON MARKT- UND SUBSISTENZPRODUKTION AM BEISPIEL DES GEMEINDELANDES VON YARITAGUA, UNTER BESONDERER BERUECKSICHTIGUNG IHRER AUSWIRKUNGEN AUF DEN BODEN / Jordan, Ronald – 1991 – 83p – 9 – DM98.00 – 3-89349-450-2 – gw Hänsel [333]
Bodenreuth, Friedrich *see*
- ALLE WASSER BOEHMENS FLIESSEN NACH DEUTSCHLAND
- DAS ENDE DER EISERNEN SCHAR

BODENS TIDNING – Boden, Sweden. 1986-88 – 1 – sw Kungliga [072]
DIE BODENSCHAETZE DER KAMPFGEBIETE IN IHRER BEDEUTUNG FUER UNS UND UNSERE FEINDE / Pompecki, Josef Felix – Tuebingen: Kloeres, 1915. 24p – 1 – us U.W. Library [943]
DER BODENSEE IM INTERNATIONALEN RECHT / Doka, C – Leipzig, 1927 – 2mf – 1 – ILM-2316/1 – ne IDC [327]
Bodenstedt, Friedrich *see* VERSCHOLLENES UND NEUES
Bodette, Derek R *see* THE PERCEPTIONS OF COLLEGE PHYSICAL EDUCATION TEACHING MAJORS WITH RESPECT TO TEACHER ENTHUSIASM
Bodge, George Madison *see* SOLDIERS IN KING PHILIP'S WAR; BEING A CRITICAL ACCOUNT OF THAT WAR,... CONCISE HISTORY OF THE INDIAN WARS OF NEW ENGLAND FROM 1620-1677
Bodhisattva, Asvaghosha *see* THE FO-SHO-HING-TSAN-KING
Bodichon, Barbara Leigh *see* A BRIEF SUMMARY, IN PLAIN LANGUAGE, OF THE MOST IMPORTANT LAWS OF ENGLAND CONCERNING WOMEN
Bodin, Jean *see* LE FLEAU DES DEMONS ET SORCIERS
Bodine and Co *see* ILLINOIS POLITICAL DIRECTORY AND SKETCHBOOK, 1898 WITH PORTRAITS OF PARTY LEADERS
Bodington, O E *see* THE FRENCH LAW OF MARRIAGE, MARRIAGE CONTRACTS AND DIVORCE ...
BODLEIAN AND GRAY'S INN : STAGES 3-4 – 574mf – 9 – H-1789-1795/1 – ne IDC [340]
Bodleian Library *see*
- BOOK PROSPECTUS
- CALENDARS OF CHARTERS AND ROLLS IN THE MANUSCRIPT COLLECTIONS OF THE BODLEIAN LIBRARY
- CATALOGUE OF THE HEBREW MANUSCRIPTS IN THE BODLEIAN LIBRARY AND IN THE COLLEGE LIBRARIES OF OXFORD: INCLUDING MSS. IN OTHER LANGUAGES WHICH ARE WRITTEN WITH HEBREW CHARACTERS, OR RELATING TO THE HEBREW LANGUAGE OR LITERATURE, AND A FEW SAMARITAN MSS
- HERBAL

BODLEIAN LIBRARY COLLECTIONS *see*
- 17TH AND 18TH CENTURY BOOK PROSPECTUSES
- DICKENS PLAYBILLS IN THE BODLEIAN LIBRARY

Bodmer, Johann Jakob *see*
- DIE DISCOURSE DER MAHLERN
- DER MAHLER DER SITTEN

BOD-MIHI-RAN DBAN = TIBETAN FREEDOM – Darjeeling, India. Jul 1965-1991 – 22r – 1 – us L of C Photodup [072]

BODMIN GUARDIAN – England.13 Jan 1911-5 Jan 1912. -w. 1 reel – 1 – uk British Libr Newspaper [072]

BODOCNOST – Milwaukee, WI, 1913 – 1mf or 1 reel – 9,1 – us I.H.R.C. [975]

Bodurtha, Arthur L *see* HISTORY OF MIAMI COUNTY

Bodwich, T E *see*
- THE BRITISH AND FRENCH EXPEDITIONS TO TEEMBO, WITH REMARKS ON CIVILIZATION IN AFRICA
- MISSION FROM CAPE COAST CASTLE TO ASHANTEE

BODY AND MIND: AN INQUIRY INTO THEIR CONNECTION AND MUTUAL INFLUENCE, SPECIALLY IN REFERENCE TO MENTAL DISORDERS: AN ENLARGED AND REVISED EDITION / Maudsley, Henry – New York: D. Appleton, 1895. 275p – 1 – us U.W. Library [150]

BODY AND SOUL : AN ENQUIRY INTO THE EFFECT OF RELIGION UPON HEALTH: WITH A DESCRIPTION OF CHRISTIAN WORKS OF HEALING FROM THE NEW TESTAMENT TO THE PRESENT DAY / Dearmer, Percy – New York: E.P. Dutton, c1909 – 1mf – us A.T.L.A. [240]

THE BODY BUILDER: ROBERT J. ROBERTS / Brink, Benjamin D – 1916 – 4mf – 9 – $12.00 – us Microform Publ [790]

Body, Charles WE *see* PERMANENT VALUE OF THE BOOK OF GENESIS

BODY COMPOSITION DETERMINATION OF OLDER MEN / Latin, Richard W – 1982 – 1mf – 9 – $4.00 – us Microform Publ [611]

THE BODY COMPOSITION OF MASTERS WOMEN ENDURANCE ATHLETES FROM 35 TO 74 YEARS OF AGE / Riggs, Donna M & Wells, Christine L – 1990 – 2mf – 9 – $8.00 – us Microform Publ [612]

BODY FASHIONS: INTIMATE APPAREL – v11-. 1984- – 1,5,6,9 – us UMI [073]

BODY FASHIONS/INTIMATE APPAREL – (v.8-. 1981-. 5,6,9) – v.1-. 1974- – 1 – us UMI [740]

BODY PART IDENTIFICATION AND COMPREHENSION OF SPATIAL PREPOSITIONS IN HANDICAPPED AND NONHANDICAPPED PRESCHOOL CHILDREN / Toon, C J – 1991 – 2mf – 9 – $8.00 – us Microform Publ [150]

THE BODY POLITIC – no.1-, Nov-Dec 1971-. -bim. Gay liberation newspaper. Continues in part: Our Image – 1 – us U.W. Library [072]

THE BODY POLITIC; GAY LIBERATION NEWSPAPER – No.1-135, 1971-87. Ceased publication – 1 – $675.00 – cn McLaren [305]

BODY TEMPERATURE AND CAPACITY FOR WORK / Asmusson, Erling & Boje, Ore – 1945 – 1mf – 9 – $3.00 – us Microform Publ [612]

BODY THERAPY REPATTERNING AND THE NEUROMOTOR SYSTEM / Honka, Rita J M – University of Oregon, 1992 – 2mf – 9 – $8.00 – PE3599 – us Microform Publ [790]

BODY-BUILD AND ITS INHERITANCE / Davenport, Charles Benedict – Washington: The Carnegie Institution of Washington, 1923. vi,176p. 9 pls., diagrs. Publication no. 239. "Paper no. 35 of the Department of Genetics" – 1 – us U.W. Library [573]

BOEAH PIKIRAN / Djamaloedin Bin Moh. Rasad, B – (In Indonesian and Dutch) – 's-Gravenhage, 1910 – 2mf – 9 – ne IDC [999]

Boece de Boodt, Anselme *see* LA PARFAICT JOALLIER, OU HISTOIRE DES PIERRERIES: OU SONT AMPLEMENT DESCRITES LEUR NAISSANCE, JUSTE PRIX, MOYEN DES LES COGNOISTRE, ET SE GARDER DES CONTREFAITES...

Boece, Hector *see* THE BUIK OF THE CHRONICLES OF SCOTLAND (RS6)

Boeck, C de *see*
- DE LA PROPRIETE PRIVEE ...
- LE DROIT INTERNATIONAL DE LA NAUFRAGE DU "TITANIC"

Boeck, F J de *see* VIER-HONDERD-JAERIG JUBILE VAN HET HOOG-WEERDIG EN ALDERHEYLIGSTE SACRAMENT VAN MIRAKEL...

Boeck, L B de *see* MANUEL DE LINGALA

Boeck, Thorvald Olaf *see* EFTERRETNINGER OM GEISTLIGE EMBEDER I NORGE

BOECK VAN RECHTEN DER STAD KAMPEN: DAT GULDEN BOECK / Kampen. Netherlands. Ordinances, Local Laws, etc – Zwolle, Willink, 1875. 279 p. LL-4009 – 1 – us L of C Photodup [340]

DIT BOECK WORDT GHENOEMT: HET OFFER DES HEEREN – Amsterdam, W. J. Buys. 1590. BME-3 1 – 9 – ne IDC [240]

DIT BOECK WORT GENAEMT – Het offer des Heeren, om het inhout van sommighe opgeofferde kinderen Gods:... Belydingen, Sendtbrieven ende Testamenten, de welcke sy met den monde beleden, ende metten bloede bezeghelt hebben, Tot troost ende versterckinge der slachschaepkens Christi... 1567. BME-2 1 – 9 – ne IDC [240]

DIT BOECK WORT GENAEMT – Het offer des Heeren, om het inhout van sommighe opgeofferde kinderen Gods:..., Tot troost ende versterckinge der slachschaepkens Christi... 1562. Een Liedtboecxken, tracterende van den Offer des Heeren,... 1563. BME-1 1 – 9 – ne IDC [240]

DIT BOECK WORT GENAEMT: HET OFFER DES HEEREN. SOMMIGE BRIEVEN OFTE BELIJDINGEN GESCHREVEN VAN JOOS DE TOLLENAER – Harlinghen, Peter Sebastiaensz. 1599. BME-4 1 – 9 – ne IDC [240]

Boeckaert, C *see* WEDERLEGGINGE EENS TRACTAETS, GHEMAECKT DOOR TWEE WATERLANTSCHE WEDERDOOPERSSCHE BISSCHOPPEN, NAMELIJCK: HANS DE RIES, ENDE JACOB JANSZ

Boecklern, G A *see* ARCHITECTURA CURIOSA NOVA

Boecklin von Boecklins, F F S A *see* BEYTRAEGE ZUR GESCHICHTE DER MUSIK, BESONDERS IN DEUTSCHLAND; NEBST FREYMUETHIGEN ANMERKUNGEN UEBER DIE KUNST

Boedder, Bernard *see* THEOLOGIA NATURALIS

Boeer, Bjoern *see* DIE BETRIEBSSTEUER

Boege, Guenther *see* NESTROY ALS BEARBEITER

BOEGINEESCH-HOLLANDSCH WOORDENBOEK, MET HOLLANDSCH-BOEGINESCHE WOORDENLIJST, EN VERKLARING VAN EEN TOT OPHELDERING BIJGEVOEGDEN ETHNOGRAPHISCHEN ATLAS. SUPPLEMENT / Matthes, B F – 's-Gravenhage, 1874. Atlas, (Amsterdam), [1874] – 21mf – 9 – ne IDC [040]

BOEGINEESCH-HOLLANDSCH WOORDENBOEK, MET HOLLANDSCH-BOEGINESCHE WOORDENLIJST, EN VERKLARING VAN EEN TOT OPHELDERING BIJGEVOIEGDEN ETHNOGRAPHISCHEN ATLAS / Matthes, B F – (Includes supplementadlatlas) – 's-Gravenhage, 1874. [Amsterdam, 1874] – 21mf – ne IDC [490]

BOEGINESCHE CHRESTOMATHIE : AANTEEKENINGEN OP DE BOEGINESCHE CHRESTOMATHIE / Matthes, B F – Makassar, 1864. v1. Amsterdam, 1872. v2 – 13mf – 9 – ne IDC [490]

Boegner, Marc *see* THE UNITY OF THE CHURCH

BOEHEIMS PHAENEROGRAMISCHE UND CRYPTOGAMISCHE GEWAECHSE / Opiz, P M – Prag. 1823. B-5200 2 – 8 – ne IDC [580]

Boehl, Eduard *see*
- DIE ALTTESTAMENTLICHEN CITATE IM NEUEN TESTAMENT
- CHRISTOLOGIE DES ALTEN TESTAMENTES
- VATICINIUM JESIAIAE: CAP. 24-27
- ZUM GESETZ UND ZUM ZEUGNISS: EINE ABWEHR WIDER DIE NEU-KRITISCHE SCHRIFTFORSCHUNG
- DIE ZWEITE HELVETISCHE CONFESSION

Boehlaus, H *see* LUTHERS WERKE

Boehle, Uta-Regina *see*
- MOLEKULARE PHYLOGENIE UND EVOLUTION DER GATTUNG ECHIUM L. (BORAGINACEAE)
- PFLANZENSOZIOLOGISCHE ANALYSE DER HALBTROCKENRASEN IM SUEDLICHEN RINGGAU (NORDHESSEN)

Boehlich, Ernst *see* GOETHES PROPYLAEEN

Boehm, F *see*
- HANDBUCH DER INTERNATIONALEN NACHLASSBEHANDLUNG ...
- ZEITSCHRIFT FUER INTERNATIONALES PRIVAT- UND STRAFRECHT (T. NIEMEYER)

Boehm, Gotthold *see* STATISTISCHE UNTERSUCHUNGEN UEBER DIE ARBEITSKAEMPFE IN BORGBAU UND HUETTENINDUSTRIE DEUTSCHLANDS IN DER NACHKRIEGSZEIT

Boehm, Wilhelm *see*
- ENGLANDS EINFLUSS AUF GEORG RUDOLF WECKHERLIN
- GESAMMELTE WERKE
- HOELDERLIN UND DIE SCHWEIZ
- IM KREUZFEUER ZWEIER REVOLUTIONEN

Boehme, Walther *see* LESSINGS MINNA VON BARNHELM

BOEHME ZEITUNG – Soltau, West Germany. 1978- – ca 5r per yr – 1 – gw Mikrofilm [072]

O BOEHMEN! : ROMAN / Watzlik, Hans – Leipzig: L Staackmann, 1923 – 1r – 1 – us U.W. Library [830]

BOEHMEN UND SEINE NACHBARLAENDER UNTER GEORG VON PODIEBRAD, 1458-61, UND DES KOENIGS BEWERBUNG UM DIE DEUTSCHE KRONE / Bachmann, Adolf – Prag: J.G. Calve, 1878. xii,309p – 1 – us U.W. Library [943]

Boehmer, E *see* ROMANISCHE STUDIEN

Boehmer, Eduard *see* FRANZISCA HERNANDEZ UND FRAI FRANZISCO ORTIZ

Boehmer, G R *see* BIBLIOTHECA SCRIPTORUM HISTORIAE NATURALIS

Boehmer, Heinrich *see*
- DIE FAELSCHUNGEN ERZBISCHOF LANFRANKS VON CANTERBURY
- LUTHER IM LICHTE DER NEUEREN FORSCHUNG
- LUTHERS ROMFAHRT
- STUDIEN ZUR GESCHICHTE DER GESELLSCHAFT JESU

Boehmer, Julius *see*
- DER ALTTESTAMENTLICHE UNTERBAU DES REICHES GOTTES
- REICH GOTTES UND MENSCHENSOHN IM BUCHE DANIEL: EIN BEITRAG
- DER RELIGIONSGESCHICHTLICHE RAHMEN DES REICHES GOTTES

BOEHMISCHE KORALLEN AUS DER GOETTERWELT / Krauss, Friedrich S – 1893 – 1 – us I.U. Libraries [390]

BOEHMISCHES WANDERBUCH : LIEDER UND GEDICHTE / Hoeller, Franz – Prag: Volk und Reich Verlag, 1943 – 1r – 1 – us U.W. Library [810]

Boehner, Claus-Peter *see*
- DIE 1920 ALS "DICHTERISCHE BEKENNTNISSE" VON ARTHUR TREBITSCH HERAUSGEGEBENE TEXTSAMMLUNG "DEUTSCHER GEIST AUS OESTERREICH"
- DAS "BEKENNTNISBUCH OESTERREICHISCHER DICHTER HERAUSGEGEBEN VOM BUND DEUTSCHER SCHRIFTSTELLER OESTERREICHS"
- EINLASSUNGEN
- KULTURPOLITIK IM STAENDESTAAT
- DIE LITERATUR OESTERREICHISCHER AUTOREN IN DER ERSTEN REPUBLIK, 1918-1938
- DAS MOTIV DER ORGANISATION UND WIRKUNG VON MACHT IN PETER WEISS' EPISCHEN STUECKEN "MARAT / SADE" UND "HOELDERLIN"

Boehnke, Frieda *see* DIE DEUTSCHE DICHTUNG IN DER SCHULE

Boehtlingk, A *see* DIE VOELKER UND DAS MEER ...

HET BOEK DER GEESTELIJKE GEZANGEN / Mechelen, Lucas van – Amsterdam: Johannes Stichter, 1688 – 9mf – 8 – ne Slangenburg [240]

Boekholt, J *see* 'T GEOPENDE, EN BEREIDWILLIGE HERTE, NA DEN HEERE JESUS...

Boeklen, Ernst *see* ADAM UND QUAIN IM LICHTE DER VERGLEICHENDEN MYTHENFORSCHUNG

Boekman, E *see* DEMOGRAFIE VAN DE JODEN IN NEDERLAND

BOEKOE PELADJARAN HOEROEF KANJI (PERMOELAAN) : MEMOEAT TJARA MENOELIS, TJARA MEMBATJA AND LATIHAN / Ling, CS – Soerakarta, 2603. 96p – 101-102mf – 9 – ne IDC [370]

BOEKOE PELADJARAN ILMOE PENJEBERANGAN LAOET / Pardi, M – Djakarta, Kaidjii Sookyoku, 2603. 54p – 126mf – 9 – ne IDC [950]

BOEKOE PELADJARAN PERMOELAAN BAHASA NIPPON – Djakarta: "Asia-Raya" 2602. 6, 255p – 25-27mf – 9 – ne IDC [480]

BOEKOE PETOENDJOEK PRAKTEK TEKNIK BAGI PEMIMPIN SEINENDAN / Java – 3rd ed Djakarta Djawa Gunseikanbu (2604). 101p – 67-68mf – 9 – ne IDC [620]

DE BOEKZAAL VAN EUROPA : TE ROTTERDAM / Slaart, Pieter van der – 1692-1670 – 113mf – 9 – Dfl396.00 – ne Slangenburg [073]

Boell, E *see* L'HYGIENE DU PAYSAN.

Boellenruecher, J *see* GEBETE UND HYMNEN AN NERGAL

Boelsche, Wilhelm *see*
- DIE MITTAGSGOETTIN
- WIELANDS AUSGEWAEHLTE WERKE

Boemus, J *see*
- RECUEIL DE DIVERSES HISTOIRES TOVCHANT LES SITVATIONS DE TOUTES REGIONS ET PAYS CONTENUZ ES TROIS PARTIES DU MONDE, AUEC LES PARTICULIERES MOEURS, LOIX ET CAEREMONIES DE TOUTES NATIONS ET PEUPLES Y HABITAS
- REPERTORIVM LIBRORVM TRIVM... DE OMNIVM GENTIVM RITIBVS

Boenisch, H *see* DIE STRAFBARKEIT EINER IN DEN KONSULARGEBIETEN BEGANGENEN BIGAMIE ...

Boenneken, Margarete *see* WILHELM RAABES ROMAN "DIE AKTEN DES VOGELSANGS"

BOENNISCHE INTELLIGENZ-NACHRICHTEN *see* BOENNISCHES INTELLIGENZBLATT

BOENNISCHER SITTEN- , STAATS- UND GESCHICHTSLEHRER – Bonn, 1772 – 1 – Inquire at Mikrofilmarchiv for details – gw Misc Inst [943]

BOENNISCHES INTELLIGENZBLATT – (Incl suppl: Annalen, jan 9-dec 25 1787 (incomplete). Cont by: Boennische Intelligenz-Nachrichten, jul 28 1795; Bonner Intelligenz-Blatt, aug 2 1795) – Bonn, jul 4 1772-dec 10 1776 (incomplete), apr 1-oct 7 1780 (incomplete), 1781 (many issues missing), jan 11 1783-92 (incomplete), mar 2 1793, jul 28 1795-jul 17 1796 – 5r – 1 – Inquire at Mikrofilmarchiv for details – gw Misc Inst [943]

BOENNISCHES WOCHENBLATT – Bonn, 1785-88 (incomplete) – 1r – 1 – Inquire at Mikrofilmarchiv for details – gw Misc Inst [943]

BOENNISCHES WOCHENBLATT *see*
- BONNER WOCHENBLATT
- WOCHENBLATT DES BOENNISCHEN BEZIRKS

Boer, H J de *see* FURTHER RESEARCHES INTO THE PHYSICAL REALITY OF SOME LONG-PERIODIC CYCLES IN THE BAROMETRIC PRESSURE OF BATAVIA

BOER WAR : MISCELLANEOUS PAMPHLETS PUBLISHED IN GREAT BRITAIN AND THE UNITED STATES., 1899-1902 – Chicago, IL: U of Chicago, Photoduplication Dept, 1972 (mf ed) – 1 – us Res Libr [960]

THE BOER WAR: ITS CAUSES, AND ITS INTEREST TO CANADIANS WITH A GLOSSARY OF CAPE DUTCH AND KAFIR TERMS / Biggar, Emerson Bristol – Toronto: Montreal: Biggar, Samuel & Co., 1899. 02110. (Pre-1900 Canadiana) – 9 – cn C.I.H.M. [960]

DER BOEREN BODE – Aliwal North, South Africa. 21 Jan 1882-29 Dec 1883. 1 reel – 1, 16 diazo available at reduced price – sa SA Libr [072]

BOEREN COURANT, DE – Colesburg, South Africa. 1 Aug 1871-28 Jun 73. 1 reel – 1, 16 diazo available at reduced price – sa SA Libr [072]

DIE BOERENUUS – Aliwal North, South Africa. 4 Jan 1922-23 Dec 1925. 2 reels – 1, 16 diazo available at reduced price – sa SA Libr [072]

Boerger, Willi *see* VOM DEUTSCHEN WESEN

Boergesen, FC E *see*
- THE MARINE ALGAE OF THE DANISH WEST INDIES, PT I-II. CHOLOROPHYCAEA-PHAEOPHYCEAE
- OM ALGEVEGETATIONEN VED FAEROERNES KYSTER

Boerhaave, H *see*
- INDEX ALTER PLANTARUM, QUAE IN HORTO ACADEMICO LUGDUNO-BATAVO ALUNTUR
- INSTITUTIONES MEDICAE

Boerlage, J G *see* HANDLEIDING TOT DE KENNIS DER FLORA VAN NEDERLANDSCH INDIE

BOERNE DER ZEITGENOSSE : EINE AUSWAHL / Boerne, Ludwig; ed by Kuh, Anton – Leipzig: Verlag der Wiener Graphischen Werkstaette, 1922 – 1 – us U.W. Library [840]

Boerne, Ludwig *see*
- BOERNE DER ZEITGENOSSE
- FRAGMENTS POLITIQUES ET LITTERAIRES
- GESAMMELTE SCHRIFTEN
- LUDWIG BOERNES GESAMMELTE SCHRIFTEN
- SCHRIFTEN ZUR DEUTSCHEN LITERATUR

BOERNE'S LEBEN / Gutzkow, Karl – Hamburg: Hoffmann und Campe, 1840 – 1 – us U.W. Library [920]

Boero, Joseph *see* THE LIFE OF THE BLESSED MARY ANN OF JESUS, DE PAREDES Y FLORES

Boersch, Charles *see* ESSAI SUR LA MORTALITE A STRASBOURG: PARTIE RETROSPECTIVE

BOERSENBLATT FUER DEN DEUTSCHEN BUCHHANDEL – Leipzig. v. 53-82. 1886-1915 – 1 – 4,293.00 – us L of C Photodup [010]

BOERSENBLATT FUER DEN DEUTSCHEN BUCHHANDEL, 1834-1945 = JOURNAL FOR THE GERMAN BOOK TRADE – 1979-1981 – 3057 fiches (1:42) – 9 – diazo DM19,900.00 – 3-598-10177-5 – gw Saur [070]

BOERSEN-HALLE *see* PRIVILIGIRTE LISTE DER BOERSENHALLE

Boeschenstein, Bernhard *see* LEUCHTTUERMEN

Boese, Karl *see* GESCHICHTE DER STADT SCHNEIDEMUEHL

Boeseken, A J *see* NEDERLANDSCHE COMMISSARISSEN AAN DE KAAP, 1657-1700

DIE BOESEN GEISTER IM ALTEN TESTAMENT / Duhm, Hans – Tuebingen: J.C.B. Mohr, 1904. 1 fiche – 9 – us A.T.L.A. [240]

Boesenberg, F W *see* DIE SPINNEN DEUTSCHLANDS

Boeser, P A A *see*
- BESCHREIBUNG DER AEGYPTISCHEN SAMMLUNG DES NIEDERLAENDISCHEN REICHSMUSEUMS DER ALTERTUEMER IN LEIDEN
- BESCHRIJVING VAN DE EGYPTISCHE VERZAMELING IN HET RIJSMUSEUM VAN OUDHEDEN TE LEIDEN
- MANUSCRITS COPTES DUMUSEE D'ANTIQUITES DES PAYS-BAS A LEYDE

BOESMANN'S TELEGRAPHISCHES BUREAU – Bremen, 1916-19 (incomplete) – 4r – 1 – Inquire at Mikrofilmarchiv for details – gw Misc Inst [072]

Boesnier *see* LE MEXIQUE CONQUIS

Boethius *see* DE CONSOLATIONE PHILOSOPHIAE

DIE DEM BOETHIUS...ZUGESCHRIEBENE ABHANDLUNG DES DOM. GUNDISALVI DE UNITATE : BGPHMA 1/1 / Correns, P – Muenster, 1891 – 2mf – 9 – ne Slangenburg [240]

DIE DEM BOETHIUS...ZUGESCHRIEBENE ABHANDLUNG DES DOM. GUNDISALVI DE UNITATE / Correns, P – Muenster, 1891 – 2mf – 8 – ne Slangenburg [100]

BOETJER BASCH : EINE GESCHICHTE / Storm, Theodor – Berlin: Gebrueder Paetel, 1887 – 1r – 1 – us U.W. Library [830]

Boettcher, Christoph *see* ELEKTRONENMIKROSKOPISCHE UNTERSUCHUNGEN ZUR STEREOSELEKTIVEN BILDUNG MIZELLARER LIPIDFASERN AUS N-ALKYLALDONAMIDEN

Boettger, F *see* INTERNATIONALE WECHSELPRAXIS

Boettger, Gustav *see* TOPOGRAPHISCH-HISTORISCH LEXICON ZU DEN SCHRIFTEN DES FLAVIUS JOSEPHUS

Boettger, O *see* HERPETOLOGISCHE MISCELLEN

Boetticher, Gotthold *see* GESCHICHTE DER DEUTSCHEN LITERATUR

Boetticher, Otto *see* DAS VERHAELTNIS DES DEUTERONOMIUMS ZU 2. KOEN: 22., 23., UND ZU PROPHETIE JEREMIA

Boetticher, Wilhelm *see* LOS VOM ULTRAMONTANISMUS

BOEUF RIVER BAPTIST CHURCH. WINNSBORO, LOUISIANA : CHURCH RECORDS – (1,668p) – May 1911-Jan 1991 – 1 reel – 1 – $75.06 – us Baptist [240]

BOEVOI SOSTAV SOVETSKOI ARMII / Military-Scientific Directorate of the Soviet General Staff – (Part 1 of 5 parts) – Minneapolis: East View Publications, 1993 – 2mf – 9 – $49.95 – us East View [355]

BOEVYE DEISTVIIA NA ZAKASPIISKOM FRONTE, 1918-1920 G.G. / Filippov, ST – Ashkhabad: Izd. T Sentr. i ubile ino i komissii pri TurmenT SIK-e po x-letii u Krasno i Armii, 1928 – 1 – CSUX88-B3852 – us Hoover Inst Photo [355]

BOEVYE DEISTVIIA VTOROOCHEREDNYKH CHASTEI V MIROVUIU VOINU / Gilchevskii, Konstantin Lukich; ed by Svechina, A – Moskva: Gos. izd-vo, Otdel voen. lit-ry, 1928 – 1 – CSUX89-B1655 – us Hoover Inst Photo [355]

BOG I BIRZHA : SBORNIK REVOLIUTSIONNYKH PES / Reisner, Mikhail Andreevich – Moskva: Gos. izdvo, 1921 – 1 – CSUX88-B7187 – us Hoover Inst Photo [947]

Bog, P (United Nations Technical Assistance Administration) *see* STATISTICS FOR ECONOMIC DEVELOPMENT PLANNING: EGYPTIAN REGION, UNITED ARAB REPUBLIC

Bogaert, A S *see* SCHYNVOETS MUNTKABINET DER ROOMSCHE KEIZERS EN KEIZERINNEN

Bogaevskii, P M *see* PRAVO I MIR V MEZHDUNARODNYKH OTNOSHENIIAKH

BOGAZICI SIRKET-I HAYRIYE TARIHCE, SALNAME – 1330 [1914] – 8mf – 9 – $70.00 – us MEDOC [949]

Bogdanov, Aleksandr I *see* UROKI PERVYKH SHAGOV REVOLIUTSII

Bogdanov, B *see* MASLODEL'NYE ARTELI V VOLOGODSKOI GUBERNII

Bogdanov, M *see* RABOCHIE DEPUTATY V I-OI GOSUDARSTVENNOI DUME

Bogdanov, N *see* SELSKO-KHOZIAISTVENNOE PROIZVODSTVO

Bogdanovich, Savva *see* MISSIONERSKAYA BESEDA SO SHTUNDISTAMI O KRESTE I O KRESTNOM ANAMENII

Boge, Justin *see* PHYSICAL SELF-ESTEEM ACROSS FOUR PHASES OF A CARDIAC REHABILITATION PROGRAM

Bogeat y Asuar, Antonio *see* GUIA DE VILLAFRANCA DE LOS BARROS

Bogert, George Gleason *see*
- THE ELEMENTS OF BUSINESS LAW
- HANDBOOK OF THE LAW OF TRUSTS

Boghitchevitch, M *see*
- HALBSOUVERAENITAET

Bogler, Wilhelm *see* HARTMUTH VON KRONBERG

Bogliolo, Romulo *see*
- CUANDO EL ESTADO GASTA
- POLITICA MONETARIA Y FINANCIERA

BOGNAR REPORT – [Accra 1962] – us Res Libr [960]

BOGNOR OBSERVER AND VISITORS' LIST – (Bognor Regis Observer). England. -w. 1890-1972. (Wanting Jan-Jul 1900). (92 reels) – 1 – uk British Libr Newspaper [072]

BOGNOR POST – (Bognor Regis Post). England. -w. 15 Mar 1924-Dec 1972; 1975-81. (70 reels) – 1 – uk British Libr Newspaper [072]

BOGNOR REGIS POST – England.1924-72; 1975-85. -w.78 reels – 1 – uk British Libr Newspaper [072]

BOGOR, CITY OF THREE MOUNTAINS AND THREE RIVERS / Indonesia – SE-5978 1 – 9 – ne IDC [950]

BOGOR; ROAD TO ASIAN-AFRICAN SOLIDARITY / Indonesia – SE-5702 1. 1955? – 9 – ne IDC [950]

Bogoras, W G *see*
- ELEMENTS OF THE CULTURE OF THE CIRCUMPOLAR ZONE
- THE ESKIMO OF SIBERIA

Bogoraz, V G *see* DICTIONNAIRE TCHOUKTCHE-RUSSE

Bogoslovskii, N *see* NOVGORODSKII SBORNIK

BOGOTA : LA LITERATURA COLOMBIANA A MEDIADOS DEL S. 19 / Gomez Restrepo, Antonio – Madrid: Razon y Fe, 1927 – 1 – sp Bibl Santa Ana [490]

BOGSAMER ZEITUNG – Bogsan, oct 25 1930-dec 27 1931 – 1r – 1 – Inquire at Mikrofilmarchiv for details – gw Misc Inst [949]

Bogue, David *see*
- E AU AKOANGA NO NGA TUMU TUATUA I KITEA I ROTO I TE TUTUA NA TE ATUA
- THE HISTORY OF DISSENTERS: FROM THE REVOLUTION TO THE YEAR 1808

Boguet, Henri *see* DISCOURS EXECRABLE DES SORCIERS: ENSEMBLE LEUR PROCEZ FAITS DEPUIS DEUX ANS EN CA EN DIVERS ENDROITS DE LA FRANCE

Boguslavskii, Mark Moiseevich *see* THE LEGAL STATUS OF FOREIGNERS IN THE U.S.S.R

BOGUSLAVSKOE OBSHCHESTVO TREZVOSTI I BOR'BA SO SHTUNDOYU / Skvortsov, Vasilii M – The Boguslav Society of Temperance and the Struggle with the Stunda. Kiev, 1895. One of 13 titles on reel – 1 – 86.44 – us Baptist [240]

BOHAI RIBAO = BOHAI DAILY – Feb 1947-Apr 1950 – 5r – $325.00 – cc Microforms [950]

Bohatec, Josef *see* ZUR NEUESTEN GESCHICHTE DES ONTOLOGISCHEN GOTTESBEWEISES

Boheman, C H *see* INSECTA CAFFRARIA ANNIS 1838-45 A J.A. WAHLBERG COLLECTA...COLEOPTERA

LA BOHEME / Leoncavallo, Ruggiero – Commedia lirica in quattro atti...Riduzione per canto e pianoforte. 1897 – 9 – us Sibley [780]

LA BOHEME BOURGEOISE / Flor O'Squarr, Charles M – Paris: L. Genonceaux, 1890. 373p. 4 fiches. (Miscellaneous Selections) – 9 – 10.00 – fr Bibl Nationale [360]

LA BOHEME DEPUIS LA MONTAGNE BLANCHE / Denis, E – 2v. Paris. 1903. BR-5088 2 – 8 – ne IDC [940]

BOHEMIA – Havana. Jan 1956-Dec 1977 – 1 – 35.00r – us Hoover Inst Photo [073]

BOHEMIA – Havana. v. 8-47. 1917-55 – 1 – 2,352.00 – us L of C Photodup [073]

BOHEMIA – Munich, DE. 28 Aug 1950-Jul 1960 – 1 – uk British Libr Newspaper [072]

BOHEMIA – Prag (Praha), CS. 1855; 1861-1938 – 361r – 1 – gw Mikrofilm [072]

BOHEMIA – Prague, CS. 31 Jan 1917-31 Dec 1918 (incomplete) – 7r – 1 – uk British Libr Newspaper [072]

BOHEMIA FROM THE EARLIEST TIMES TO THE FALL OF NATIONAL INDEPENDENCE IN 1620: WITH A SHORT SUMMARY OF LATER EVENTS / Maurice, Charles Edmund – London: T.F. Unwin, (c1896). xxvi,533p.ill.,ports.,fold. map – 1 – us U.W. Library [943]

BOHEMIA NUGGET – Cottage Grove, OR. -w. 20 Jan 1899-25 Dec 1907. 3 rolls – 1 – us U.O. Library [071]

BOHEMIA PAMPHLET COLLECTION – 1909-1919 – 1 – CSUXANL4421-B – us Hoover Inst Photo [947]

Bohemia. Zemsky Snem *see* STENOGRAPHISCHE BERICHT. STENOGRAFICKE ZPRAVY

BOHEMIAN BUGLE – Las Vegas, NV. 1986-1992 – 2r – 1 – $100.00 – U04849 – us Library Micro [071]

O BOHEMIO : NEUTRO E HUMORISTICO – Fortaleza-CE, Brazil. 14 Set-Out, 5 Dez 1900 – 1 – bl Biblioteca [072]

Bohic, Cl. O Carth. *see* CHRONICA ORDINIS CARTHUSIENSIS AB ANNO 1084 AD ANNUM 1510

Bohl de Faber, Juan N *see* TEATRO ESPANOL ANTERIOR A LOPE DE VEGA

BOHLEN LECTURES *see* FOUR LECTURES

THE BOHLEN LECTURES *see* THE FITNESS OF CHRISTIANITY TO MAN

Bohn, John A *see*
- ADMINISTRATIVE RULES AND REGULATIONS OF THE GOVERNMENT OF GUAM, 1975
- THE CIVIL AND PENAL CODES OF THE TERRITORY OF GUAM, 1953
- THE CIVIL CODE OF THE TERRITORY OF GUAM, 1970
- THE CODE OF CIVIL PROCEDURE AND PROBATE CODE OF GUAM, 1953
- THE CODE OF CIVIL PROCEDURE AND PROBATE CODE OF GUAM, 1970
- THE GOVERNMENT CODE OF GUAM, 1952
- THE GOVERNMENT CODE OF GUAM, 1961
- THE GOVERNMENT CODE OF GUAM, 1970
- THE PENAL CODE OF THE TERRITORY OF GUAM, 1970
- STATUTES AND AMENDMENTS TO THE CODES OF THE TERRITORY OF GUAM, 1951-1952

Bohnenblust, Gottfried *see* KAETHI DIE GROSSMUTTER

Bohnert, Werner *see* PLANUNG ALS DURCHSETZUNGSSTRATEGIE

Bohnsack, G *see* LAND PROBLEMS AND THEIR SOLUTION IN THE FEDERAL REPUBLIC OF GERMANY

Bohoslavskyi, Mykola *see* MAKHNOVSHCHYNA

BOHUMIL POLAN PAMPHLET COLLECTION – 1967 – 1 – CSUXANL6753-B – us Hoover Inst Photo [999]

BOHUSKORRESPONDENTEN – Marstrand, 1873-76 – 9 – sw Kungliga [072]

BOHUSKUSTEN – Uddevalla, Sweden. 1941-43 – 1 reel – 1 – sw Kungliga [072]

BOHUSLANINGEN – (Dals Dagblad, 1983) – Uddevalla, Sweden. 1979- – 1 – sw Kungliga [072]

BOHUSLANINGEN – Uddevalla, Sweden. 1878-1978 – 419r – 1 – sw Kungliga [072]

BOHUSLANS ALLEHANDA – Uddevalla, Sweden. 1887-1891 – 4r – 1 – sw Kungliga [072]

BOHUSLANS ANNONSBLAD – Uddevalla, Sweden. 1890-95 – 2r – 1 – sw Kungliga [072]

BOHUSLANS NYHETS OCH ANNONSBLAD – Uddevalla, Sweden. 1890-91 – 1 reel – 1 – sw Kungliga [072]

BOHUSLANS TIDNING – Uddevalla, Sweden. 1838-83 – 20r – 1 – sw Kungliga [072]

BOHUSLANS TIDNING UDDEVALLA – Sweden, 1904-07 – 3r – 1 – sw Kungliga [072]

BOHUSPOSTEN – Uddevalla, Sweden. 1910-52 – 100r – 1 – sw Kungliga [072]

Boiarenko, A G *see* IZBRANNYE RABOTY I STAT'I

Boidin, P *see* LES LOIS DE LA GUERRE ET LES DEUX CONFERENCES DE LA HAYE (1899-1907)

Boie, Heinrich Christian *see* DEUTSCHES MUSEUM

Boieldieu *see* MATANTE AURORE OU LE ROMAN IMPROMPTU

Boieldieu, Adrien *see* LA DAME BLANCHE: OPERA COMIQUE EN TROIS ACTES

Boieldieu, F *see* SONATAS, PIANO, VIOLIN, OP. 7

BOIGRAPHIE [I.E. BIOGRAPHIE] DE MONSIEUR L'ABBE HERMANN PLANTE, BACHELIER ES ARTS DE L'UNIVERSITE LAVAL, LICENCIE ES LETTRES DE L'UNIVERSITE DE MONTREAL, LICENCIE EN DICTION DE L'ECOLE CLASSIQUE DE MONTREAL / Virginie Marie, Soeur – 1964. SEM105P4 – 9 – cn Bibl Nat [400]

Boilat, P D *see* GRAMMAIRE DE LA LANGUE WOLOFFE

Boilat, PD *see* ESQUISSES SENEGALAISES
- PYSHIONOMIE DU PAYS – PEUPLADES
- COMMERCE – RELIGIONS – PASSE ET AVENIR – RECITS ET LEGENDES

BOILED-DOWN ESSAYS / Crouter, John Wesley – London, Ont.?: s.n., 1886 (London, Ont.: Free Press). 02224. (Pre-1900 Canadiana) – 9 – cn C.I.H.M. [971]

BOILERMAKERS-BLACKSMITHS JOURNAL : 1893-1955 – (Coll title: Labor Union Periodicals, Pt 1) – 14r – 1 – $1,890.00 – 1-55655-230-0 – us UPA [331]

BOILING SPRINGS BAPTIST CHURCH. NORTH CAROLINA : CHURCH RECORDS – 1847-1963. Bulletins. 1949-63. Miscellaneous items. 1816-1959 – 1 – 100.76 – us Baptist [240]

BOILING SPRINGS BAPTIST CHURCH. SPARTANBURG, SOUTH CAROLINA : CHURCH RECORDS – Mar 1971-Oct 1976 – 1 – 10.71 – us Baptist [240]

Boillet, Leon *see* AUX MINES D'OR DU KLONDIKE: DU LAC BENNETT A DAWSON CITY

Boillot, Joseph *see* NOUVEAUX POURTRAITZ ET FIGURES DE TERMES POUR USER EN L'ARCHITECTURE...

Boindin, N *see* OEUVRES (REMARQUES SUR LES SONS DE LA LANGUE)

Boinvilliers, J E F *see* PETIT VOCABULAIRE COMPARATIF DU BON ET DU MAUVAIS LANGAGE

BOIPUSO BA BASOTHO – [Mafeteng, Lesotho: BCP Youth League. v1 n1,5,7-13,16-23. jul 9-dec 19 1965 – 1r – us Res Libr [960]

Bois, Henri *see*
- DE LA CERTITUDE CHRETIENNE: ESSAI SUR LA THEOLOGIE DE FRANK
- LE DOGME GREC
- LA POESIE GNOMIQUE CHEZ LES HEBREUX ET CHEZ LES GRECS

Bois, Jacqueline *see* BIBLIOGRAPHIE ANALYTIQUE DE L'OEUVRE DE MONSEIGNEUR ARTHUR MAHEUX DE LA SOCIETE ROYALE DU CANADA, ARCHIVISTE AU SEMINAIRE DE QUEBEC

Bois, Louis Edouard *see*
- ETUDE BIOGRAPHIQUE SUR M. JEAN RAIMBAULT: ARCHIPRETRE, CURE DE NICOLET, ETC
- NOTICE SUR M. JOS. O. LEPROHON: ARCHIPRETRE, DIRECTEUR DU COLLEGE DE NICOLET, ETC. ETC

Bois, Patterson du *see* THE NATURAL WAY IN MORAL TRAINING

BOIS SINISTRE / Lacerte, E A Bourgeois – Montreal: Ed E Garand, c1929. SEM105P64 – 2mf – 9 – Can$4.50 – cn Bibl Nat [830]

Boisduval, J B A D de *see*
- CONSIDERATIONS SUR LES LEPIDOPTERES ENVOYES DU GUATEMALA A M. DE L'ORZA
- ESSAI SUR L'ENTOMOLOGIE HORTICOLE, COMPRENANT L'HISTOIRE DES INSECTES NUISIBLES A L'HORTICULTURE
- FAUNE ENTOMOLOGIQUE DE MADAGASCAR, BOURBON ET MAURICE
- FAUNE ENTOMOLOGIQUE DES ENVIRONS DE PARIS

- GENERA ET INDEX METHODICUS EUROPAEORUM LEPIDOPTERORUM
- HISTOIRE GENERALE ET ICONOGRAPHIE DES LEPIDOPTERES ET DES CHENILLES DE L'AMERIQUE SEPTENTRIONALE
- HISTOIRE NATURELLE DES INSECTES
- ICONES HISTORIQUES DES LEPIDOPTERES NOUVEAUX OU PEU CONNUS

Boisduval, J B A D de et al *see* COLLECTIONS ICONOGRAPHIQUES ET HISTORIQUES DES CHENILLES...D'EUROPE
Boise, James R *see* EPISTLES OF PAUL WRITTEN AFTER HE BECAME A PRISONER
Boise, James Robinson *see* NOTES CRITICAL AND EXPLANATORY ON PAUL'S EPISTLE TO THE GALATIANS GREEK TEXT OF TISCHENDORF
Boislisle, Arthur Michel de *see* MEMOIRE DES INTENDANTS SUR L'ETAT DES GENERALITES POUR L'INSTRUCTION DU DUC DE BOURGOGNE
Boisragon, Alan *see* THE BENIN MASSACRE
Boissard, J J *see*
- EMBLEMATUM LIBER
- THEATRUM VITAE HUMANAE
- VITAE ET ICONES SVLTANORVM TVRCICORVM, PRINCIPVM PERSORVM...

Boisseau, Fernand *see* DEBOUT!
Boissier, A *see* MANTIQUE BABYLONIENNE ET MANTIQUE HITTITE
Boissier de Sauvages, P A *see* DICTIONNAIRE LANGUEDOCIEN-FRANCOIS
Boissier, E P *see*
- CENTURIA EUPHORBIARUM DIAGNOSES PLANTARUM NOVARUM HISPANICARUM
- DIAGNOSES PLANTARUM ORIENTALIUM NOVARUM
- ELENCHUS PLANTARUM NOVARUM MINUSQUE COGNITARUM, QUAD IN ITINERE LEGIT
- FLORA ORIENTALIS
- ICONES EUPHORBIARUM, OU FIGURES DE CENT VING-DEUX ESPECES
- PUGILLUS PLANTARUM NOVARUM AFRICAE BOREALIS HISPANIAEQUE AUSTRALIS
- VOYAGE BOTANIQUE DANS LE MIDDE DE L'ESPAGNE
- VOYAGE BOTANIQUE DANS LE MIDI DE L'ESPAGNE

Boissier, Gaston *see*
- LA FIN DU PAGANISME
- LA RELIGION ROMAINE D'AUGUSTE AUX ANTONINS

Boissiere, Jules *see* FUMEURS D'OPIUM
Boissiere, P *see* DICTIONNAIRE ANALOGIQUE DE LA LANGUE FRANCAISE
Boissieu, Alphonse de *see* LES SAINT-SIMONIENS
Boissieu, C V de *see* FLORE D'EUROPE
BOIS-SINISTRE : ROMAN CANADIEN INEDIT / Lacerte, A B – Montreal: Ed. Edouard Garand, cop. 1929. SEM105P64 – 2mf – 9 – Can$4.50 – cn Bibl Nat [830]
Boisson, Claude *see* CONTRIBUTION A L'ETUDE BIOLOGIQUE DU LEPTOPORUS LIGNOSUS
Boissonnade, Gustave *see*
- PROJET DE CODE CIVIL POUR L'EMPIRE DU JAPON
- PROJET DE CODE DE PROCEDURE CRIMINELLE POUR L'EMPIRE DU JAPON

Boissonneault, Henri *see* BIO-BIBLIOGRAPHIE DE M. JEAN BRUCHESI, M.S., R.C., SOUS-SECRETAIRE ET SOUS-REGISTRAIRE DE LA PROVINCE DE QUEBEC
Boiste, P CV *see* DICTIONNAIRE UNIVERSEL DE LA LANGUE FRANCAISE
Boistel, A *see* NOUVELLE FLORE DES LICHENS
Boiteau, P *see*
- DICTIONNAIRE DES NOMS MALGACHES DE VEGETAUX
- INDEX DES NOMS SCIENTIFIQUES AVEC LEURS EQUIVALENTS MALGACHES
- LES TRAITES DE COMMERCE ...

Boiter, Albert *see* SOBRANIE DOKUMENTOV SAMIZDATA
Boivin, J *see* BYZANTINA HISTORIA (CBH 23)
Boivin, Jean *see* BIO-BIBLIOGRAPHIE ANALYTIQUE DE L'OEUVRE DE L'ABBE ARTHUR MAHEUX DE LA SOCIETE ROYALE DU CANADA, ARCHIVISTE ET PROFESSEUR D'HISTOIRE DE AMERIQUES A L'UNIVERSITE LAVAL
Boizard, Ricardo *see*
- ESA NOCHE DE PERON

BOJANOWOER ANZEIGER : WOCHENBLATT DER POSEN-SCHLESISCHEN GRENZE – Bojanowo, aug 7 1926-jun 30 1932 – 1 – Inquire at Mikrofilmarchiv for details – gw Misc Inst [943]
BOJANOWOER ANZEIGER – Wochenblatt der Posen-Schlesischen Grenze. Bojanowo, Poland. 7 Aug 1926-30 Jun 1932 – 1 – gw Mikrofilm [943]
Boje, Ore *see* BODY TEMPERATURE AND CAPACITY FOR WORK
Bojolali, Indonesia (Kabupaten) *see*
- HIMPUNAN SURAT – SURAT KEPUTUSAN / PERATURAN DAERAH KABUPATEN BOJOLALI TAHUN DINAS ... DAN UNTUK LANDASAN PEDOMAN KERDJA DALAM TAHUN DINAS...
- LAPORAN BUPATI TENTANG KEADAAN DAERAH KABUPATEN BOJOLALI

BOJOVNIK – Bratislava, Czechoslovakia. Jun-Oct 1945 – 1r – 1 – us L of C Photodup [072]
Bok, Marcia *see* JOURNAL OF HIV/AIDS PREVENTION AND EDUCATION FOR ADOLESCENTS AND CHILDREN
Bokanowski, M *see* LES COMMISSIONS ...
THE BOKE NAMED THE GOVERNOUR / Elyot, Thomas – 1531. 531p. (English Linguistics Series 1500-1800) – 9 – us UMI [320]
THE BOKE OF ENGLYSSHE, AND SPANYSSHE – Anon. 1554. 36p. (English Linguistics Series 1500-1800) – 9 – us UMI [420]
A BOKE OF THE PROPERTIES OF HERBES / Cary, W – M 324. 1560 – 9 – ne IDC [580]
A BOKE OR COUNSEILL AGAINST THE DISEASE CALLED THE SWEATE / Caius, John – 1522 – 9 – 10.00 – us Scholars' Facs [616]
A BOKE, OR COUNSEILL AGAINST THE DISEASE COMMONLY CALLED THE SWEATE, OR SWEATING SICKNESSE / Caius, John – M-86. 1552 – 9 – ne IDC [616]
Boker, George Henry *see* KOENIGSMARK, THE LEGEND OF THE HOUNDS AND OTHER POEMS
BOKUDU ETHNO-HISTOIRE GHETSOGHO / Gollnhofer, O – Essai sur l'histoire generale de la tribu d'apres la tradition orale – 9 – F90.00 – fr Ethnologie [306]
Bokwe, J K *see* LETTERBOOKS, 1882-9, 1894-7
A BOLA – Rio Branco, Acre. 20 Maio-Dez 1967; Mar, Maio, 6 Jul 1968 – 1,5,6 – bl Biblioteca [072]
A BOLA EM REVISTA – Rio Branco, Acre. Dez 1968 – 1,5,6 – bl Biblioteca [072]
Bolamba, Antoine Roger *see* ESANZO, CHANTS POUR MON PAYS
Bolandus, J F *see* MOTVS MONASTERIENSIS LIBRI 10
Bolanos y Noboa, P *see* COMPENDIO ... DEL DERECCHO DE GENTES NATURAL, ...
EL BOLCHEVISMO...TRAD. DE EMILIO M. MARTINEZ AMADOR. BARCELONA, 1932 / Gurian, Waldemar – Madrid: Razon y Fe, 1934 – 1 – sp Bibl Santa Ana [946]
BOLDERN BERICHT – nos 1-48. 1966-81 (complete) – 1r – 1 – ATLA S0428 – us A.T.L.A. [240]
Boldingh, I *see* CATALOGUS HERBARII PLANTARUM IN HORTO BOGORIENSI CULTARUM
Bolduc, Marcel *see* BIO-BIBLIOGRAPHIE DES ANCIENS ELEVES DES FRERES MARISTES
Boldyrev, V G *see* DIREKTORIIA, KOLCHAK I INTERVENTY; VOSPOMINANIIA (IZ TSIKLA "SHEST'LET" 1917-1922 GG)
BOLECINA RAZLIKE / Zizek, Slavoj – Maribor: Zalozba Obzorja 1972 – us Res Libr [999]
Boles, John B *see*
- THE JOHN PENDLETON KENNEDY PAPERS
- THE WILLIAM WIRT PAPERS

Bolet, Julio C *see* SAN SEBASTIAN DE LOS REYES. CARACAS, 1929
BOLETIM ANNUNCIADOR DE BENGUELLA – Benguella: O Benguella, sep 28 1910 – us Res Libr [073]
BOLETIM DA ASSOCIACAO COMERCIAL DE PASSOS : ORGAM DAS CLASSES COMERCIAIS E INDUSTRIAIS DE PASSOS – Passos, Apr 1937 – 1,5,6 – bl Biblioteca [072]
BOLETIM DA ASSOCIACAO COMERCIAL DO ACRE – Rio Branco, Acre. 6 Ago-7 Set 1967 – 1,5,6 – bl Biblioteca [072]
BOLETIM DA SOCIEDADE DE GEOGRAPHIA DE LISBOA – [Lisboa]: A Sociedade. v1-3, v5-53. dec 1876-1883,1885-1935 – 20r – us Res Libr [073]
BOLETIM DE INFORMACAO / Conferencia das Organizacoes Nacionalistas das Colonias Portuguesas (CONCP) – Rabat: Conferencia das Organizacoes Nacionalistas das Colonias Portuguesas, Secretariado Permanente. n5. nov 1962 – us Res Libr [073]
BOLETIM DE INFORMACOES – Lisboa. 1945-53 – 1 – 92.00 – us L of C Photodup [330]
BOLETIM DO MILITANTE / MPLA – [S.l.]: MPLA. n4. feb 1965 – us Res Libr [073]
BOLETIM GEOGRAFICO – v. 1-11, no. 1-117. Apr 1943-Dec 1953 – 1 – 119.00 – us L of C Photodup [910]
BOLETIM INFORMATIVO – Nanuque, Brazil. Nov 1968 – 1 – bl Biblioteca [072]
BOLETIM INTERDIOCESANO *see* A CATEDRAL
BOLETIM OFFICIAL – Manaos, Amazonas. 18 Dez 1872-22 Jul 1873 – 1,5,6 – bl Biblioteca [072]
BOLETIM OFFICIAL – Rio Branco, Acre. 11 Jul-Set, Dez 1915; Jan-Dez 1916; Jan-Maio, Nov-Dez 1917; 10, 24 Fev 1918 – 1,5,6 – bl Biblioteca [072]
BOLETIM OFICIAL / Angola – Luanda, 1935-38, 1957-70 – 24r – 1 – us Ross [324]
BOLETIM OFICIAL / Guinea-Bissau – 1963-65 – 3r – 1 – us Ross [324]
BOLETIM OFICIAL / Mozambique – 1956-70 – 38r – 1 – us Ross [324]
BOLETIM OFICIAL / Portugal. Direccao Geral das Alfandegas – 1892-1949 – 1 – 529.00 – us L of C Photodup [336]
BOLETIM OFICIAL / Saint Thomas and Principe – 1969 – 1r – 1 – us Ross [324]
BOLETIM OFICIAL AND SUPPLEMENTS / Macao – 1957-1969- – 1 – us NY Public [324]
BOLETIM OFICIAL DE CABO VERDE / Cape Verde Islands – Praia, 1959-69 – 9r – 1 – us Ross [324]
BOLETIM OFICIAL DE MACAU / Macao – 1965-69 – 5r – 1 – us Ross [324]
BOLETIM OFICIAL DE TIMOR – v66-67. 1965-66 – 1r – 1 – us Ross [324]
BOLETIM OFICIAL DILL / Timor – 1958-July 30, 1966 – 1 – us NY Public [946]
BOLETIM OFICIAL DO ESTADO DA INDIA / Goa – 1942, 1951-Dec. 14, 1961 – 1 – us NY Public [950]
BOLETIM OFICIAL DO GOVERNO GERAL DA PROVINCIA DE ANGOLA – Luanda. series 1,2,3: 1935-1938 4r; 1957-1962 13r; series 1: 1954-1956 2r 1963-nov 10 1975 15r – us Res Libr [073]
BOLETIN / Academia de la Historia. Madrid – v.1-76. Nov. 1877-June 1920 – 1 – 368.00 – us L of C Photodup [946]
BOLETIN / Argentine Republic. Secretaria de Comunicaciones – v. 1-24. 1929-52. Boletin Suplemento. N. 1-3386. 1932-48. (Scattered issues wanting) – 1 – 564.00 – us L of C Photodup [380]
BOLETIN / Asociacion Geofisica de Mexico – Mexico. v. 1-2 no. 3. July 1929-Sept 1930 – 1 – us NY Public [550]
BOLETIN / Chile. Ministerio de Hacienda – Santiago de Chile. t. 1-(27). 1888-1914. (Wanting t. 2, Jan-May 1889; t. 3-4, 1890-91; t. 6-13, 1893-1900; t. 23-24, 1910-11) – 1 – 115.00 – us L of C Photodup [360]
BOLETIN : INTERAMERICAN CHILDREN'S INSTITUTE / Interamerican Children's Institute. Montevideo – v15-30 1941-56 – 1 – $81.00 – us L of C Photodup [305]
BOLETIN / Mexico (City). Radiodifusora XELA – v. 1-12. Feb 4, 1952-Mar 4, 1963 – 1 – $46.00 – us L of C Photodup [380]
BOLETIN / Radiodifusora XELA. Mexico City – v. 1-12, N. 1-574. 4 Feb 1952-4 Mar 1963. (Scattered issues wanting) – 1 – 46.00 – us L of C Photodup [380]
EL BOLETIN CATOLICO – Cebu: [s.n.], sep 26 1918-oct 17 1929 – us Res Libr [240]
BOLETIN CULTURAL DE LA U.R.S.S. – (Includes c.1: no.2 1929:Jan.-no.5, 7-13 (1930:Jan.)) – Mexico, D.F.: [Oficina de Informaciones de la Legacion de la Union de las Republicas Sovieticas Socialistas en Mexico, 1929- – 1 – CSUXAKZ1315-S – us Hoover Inst Photo [335]
BOLETIN DE HISTORIA AMERICANA / Bayle, Constantino – Madrid: Razon y Fe, 1934 – 1 – sp Bibl Santa Ana [970]
BOLETIN DE HISTORIAS AMERICANAS / Bayle, Constantino – Madrid: Razon y Fe, 1933 – 1 – sp Bibl Santa Ana [970]
BOLETIN DE INFORMACION / Federacion Espanola de Trabajadores de la Ensenanza – Valencia, 1937. Fiche W 879. (Blodgett Collection of Spanish Civil War Pamphlets) – 9 – us H.U. College Libr [946]
BOLETIN DE LA ACADEMIA NACIONAL DE LA HISTORIA / Caracas – 1940-53; 1959-60 – 1 – us UMI [972]
BOLETIN DE LA DIRECCION GENERAL DE ARCHIVOS Y BIBLIOTECAS, INDICES DE LOS N. 1-62-99-104, 1952-1968 – 175mf – 9 – sp Cultura [020]
BOLETIN DE LA REAL ACADEMIA DE LA HISTORIA. INFORMES / Coello, Francisco – Madrid, 1889 – 1 – sp Bibl Santa Ana [946]
BOLETIN DE LA REAL ACADEMIA GALLEGA – Began in 1906?. Some issues are combined no – 1 – us U.W. Library [073]
BOLETIN DE LA SOCIEDAD ARAGONESA DE CIENCIAS NATURALES – Zaragoza: Libreria editorial de Cecilio Gasca. ill. 1902-17. Continued by: Boletin de la Sociedad Iberica de Ciencias Naturales – 1 – us U.W. Library [500]
BOLETIN DE LA SOCIEDAD IBERICA DE CIENCIAS NATURALES – v18, no.1. 1918- . ill. -m except Aug and Sept – 1 – us U.W. Library [500]
BOLETIN DE PRENSA / Argentine Republic. Presidencia. Coordinacion de Informaciones de Estado. Departamento "Psicologico." – (Includes c.1: v.1, 3, 5-14, 16-19) – 1 – CSUXADQ3930-S – us Hoover Inst Photo [972]
BOLETIN DE SANIDAD VEGETAL – v.1-3. 1941-43. Continued as: Agricultura Technica – 1 – us UMI [630]
BOLETIN DEL ARCHIVO HISTORICO – Venezuela. v1-10. 1943-55 – 1 – 23.00 – us L of C Photodup [972]
BOLETIN DEL AVUNTAMIENTO DE MADRID / Madrid. Ayuntamiento – 1956-1968 – 1 – us NY Public [946]
BOLETIN DEL AYUNTAMIENTO / Madrid. Ayuntamiento – Resumen Estadistico. 1959-1961 – 1 – us NY Public [946]
BOLETIN DEL CONSULADO GENERAL DEL PERU EN LONDRES – London, UK. March-May 1924 – 1 – uk British Libr Newspaper [072]
BOLETIN DEL GREMIO DE OBREROS – [Habana]: Imprenta la Razon. v1 n5,8. aug 5, sep 20 1886 – 1mf – 9 – us Res Libr [073]
EL BOLETIN DIPLOMATICO – Madrid. 2v. 1869-70 – 16mf – 9 – ILM-3864/1 – ne IDC [327]
BOLETIN ECLESIASTICO DE LA DIOCESIS DE CORIA – 1856-1962 – 9 – 1.50f – sp Bibl Santa Ana [072]
BOLETIN ECLESIASTICO DEL OBISPADO DE PLASENCIA – 1859-1963 – 9 – 1.50f – sp Bibl Santa Ana [072]
BOLETIN ECLESIASTICO DEL OBISPADO DEL PRIORATO DE SAN MARCOS DE LEON – 1857-73 – 9 – 1.50f – sp Bibl Santa Ana [072]
BOLETIN ESTADISTICO / Banco de Guatemala – July 1948-68 – 1 – 138.00 – us L of C Photodup [336]
BOLETIN INFORMATIVO EXTRAORDINARIO / Hermandad de Donates de Sangre – Caceres: Navidad, 1975. Caceres: Linea XXI, 1975 – 1 – sp Bibl Santa Ana [946]
BOLETIN INSTITUTO CARO Y CUERVO *see* THESAURUS
BOLETIN INTERNO : INSTITUTO NACIONAL DE PREVISION SOCIAL / Argentina. Instituto Nacional de Prevision Social – (Includes c.1: 1947:Oct.- 1948:Sept.) – Buenos Aires: El Instituto, [19–]- – 1 – CSUXAJA8101-S – us Hoover Inst Photo [060]
BOLETIN JUDICIAL DE LA REPUBLICA ARGENTINA / Argentine Republic. Courts – N. 4562-15313. Buenos Aires. 1910-39. (Wanting scattered issues and issues for Jan 1926-Jun 1937) – 1 – 2,941.00 – us L of C Photodup [972]
BOLETIN MENSUAL / Argentine Republic. Secretaria de Trabajo y PrevisionInstituto Nacional de Prevision Social – (Includes c.1: v.1-5) – 1946 – 1 – CSUXADQ5186-S – us Hoover Inst Photo [331]
BOLETIN MUNICIPAL / Lima. (City). Consejo Provincal – 1959-66 – 1 – us NY Public [972]
BOLETIN MUNICIPAL DE ZARAGOZA / Saragossa. Spain (City). Ayuntamiento – Zaragossa. 1960-1962 – 1 – us NY Public [946]
BOLETIN OFICIAL / Argentine Republic – 1893-1956; 1971-79; 1980- – 1 – us L of C Photodup [972]
BOLETIN OFICIAL / Argentine Republic – Buenos Aires. Feb. 24, 1899-1968 – 1 – us NY Public [324]

BOLETIN OFICIAL / Baja California Sur. (Territory) – La Paz. Jan 1882-Dec 1912; Jan 1929-43. LL-02014 – 1 – 69.00 – us L of C Photodup [340]

BOLETIN OFICIAL / California. (Lower). Southern territory – La Paz. 1945-1956 – 1 – us NY Public [324]

BOLETIN OFICIAL / Chile. Direccion General de Correos y Telegrafos – v. 5-32, Jan 1926-June 1, 1960 – 1 – $207.00 – us L of C Photodup [380]

BOLETIN OFICIAL / Sonora. Mexico (State) – v79-106. 1959-70 – 8r – 1 – us Ross [324]

BOLETIN OFICIAL, AND SUPPLEMENTS / Cape Verde Islands – (Praia). 1948-1967 – 1 – us NY Public [324]

BOLETIN OFICIAL DE LA PROVINCIA DE BADAJAZ – 1836-1954 – 9 – 1.50f – sp Bibl Santa Ana [946]

BOLETIN OFICIAL DE LA PROVINCIA DE CACERES – 1835-82 – 9 – 1.50f – sp Bibl Santa Ana [072]

BOLETIN OFICIAL DE LA PROVINCIA DE LA HABANA – Habana: Imp del Gobierno y Capitania General. v1. 1879 – 55 sheets – us Res Libr [073]

BOLETIN OFICIAL DE LA REPUBLICA ARGENTINA – Buenos Aires, 1968-70 – 29r – 1 – us Ross [324]

BOLETIN OFICIAL DE LA REPUBLICA ARGENTINA – (Seccion 3: feb 24 1899-1970) – Buenos Aires, jul 1 1893- – us Res Libr [972]

BOLETIN OFICIAL DE LA ZONA DE PROTECTORADO ESPANOL EN MORROCCO / Morocco. (Spanish Zone) – 1949-56 – 6r – 1 – us Ross [324]

BOLETIN OFICIAL DE LA ZONA NORTE DE MARRUECOS / Morocco – 1956-57 – 2r – 1 – us Ross [324]

BOLETIN OFICIAL DE VENTAS DE BIENES NACIONALES DE LA PROVINCIA DE BADAJAZ – Badajoz, 1870-72, 1875-1882, 1893-1899 y 1924 – 5 – sp Bibl Santa Ana [073]

BOLETIN OFICIAL DEL ESTADO / Spain – 1711-1986 5; 1984-1996 9 – 5,9 – sp Boletín [324]

BOLETIN OFICIAL DEL ESTADO – GACETA DE MADRID / Spain – Madrid, 1968-69 – 17r – 1 – us Ross [940]

BOLETIN OFICIAL DEL GOBIERNO CONSTITUCIONAL DEL ESTADO DE SONARA / Sonara. Mexico (State) – Hermosillo. On film: 1885-1955. LL-02035 – 1 – us L of C Photodup [340]

BOLETIN OFICIAL DEL OBISPADO DE BADAJAZ – 1855-1973 – 9 – 1.50f – sp Bibl Santa Ana [240]

BOLETIN OFICIAL Y JUDICIAL / Catamarca. Argentine Republic. (Province) – 1957-1968- – 1 – us NY Public [324]

BOLETIN OFICIEL DEL ESTADO / Spain – (1985- inquire) – 1711-1984 – 739r – 1 – inquire – us Ross [946]

BOLETIN PARROQUIAL DE LA DIOCESIS DE BADAJOZ – Badajoz, 1914-1918 – 5 – sp Bibl Santa Ana [240]

BOLETIN REVISTA DEL INSTITUTO DE BADAJAZ – 1881-82 – 9 – 1.50f – sp Bibl Santa Ana [072]

BOLETINES DEL EXTERIOR / Castro y Oyanguren, E – Lima, 1920 – 4mf – 1 – ILM-3173/1 – ne IDC [327]

Bolin, Luis *see* ESPANA. LOS ANOS VITALES. PROLOGO DE SIR ARTHUR BRYANT. MADRID, 1967

BOLIVAR COMMERCIAL – Cleveland. Miss. 1934-1966 – 1 – us UMI [071]

BOLIVAR COUNTY DEMOCRAT – Rosedale. Miss. 1902-1904; 1936-1952 – 1 – us UMI [071]

Bolivar de Urrutia, Ignacio *see* ARTROPODOS DEL VIAJE AL PACIFICO...

BOLIVAR FIRST BAPTIST CHURCH. BOLIVAR, TENNESSEE : CHURCH RECORDS – 1882-1937 – 1 – 28.17 – us Baptist [240]

Bolivar, Jorge *see* PATERNALISMO Y MUNDO NUEVO

BOLIVAR SECOND BAPTIST CHURCH. BOLIVAR, MISSOURI : CHURCH RECORDS – 1952-63 – 1 – 9.50 – us Baptist [240]

Bolivar, Simon *see*
- OBRAS COMPLETAS
- SIMON BOLIVAR. THE HOPE OF THE UNIVERSE

BOLIVAR Y LEON 12 / Leturia, Pedro S – Caracas, 1931; Madrid: Razon y Fe, 1931 – 1 – sp Bibl Santa Ana [946]

BOLIVIA : ANUARIO GEOGRAFICO Y ESTADISTICO DE LA REPUBLICA DE BOLIVIA 1919 / Bolivia. Direccion General de Estadistica y Estudios Geograficos – (Coll title: Latin American and Caribbean Official Statistical Serials, 1821-1982) – 8mf – 9 – £7.00f (set £185.00 22mf) – uk Chadwyck [972]

BOLIVIA : ANUARIO NACIONAL ESTADISTICO Y GEOGRAFICO DE BOLIVIA 1917 / Bolivia. Direccion General de Estadistica y Estudios Geograficos – (Coll title: Latin American and Caribbean Official Statistical Serials, 1821-1982) – 7mf – 9 – £7.00f (set £185.00 22mf) – uk Chadwyck [972]

BOLIVIA : BOLIVIA EN CIFRAS 1973 / Bolivia. Instituto Nacional de Estadistica – (Coll title: Latin American and Caribbean Official Statistical Serials, 1821-1982) – 7mf – 9 – £7.00f (set £185.00 22mf) – uk Chadwyck [972]

Bolivia *see*
- GACETA DEL GOBIERNO
- GACETA OFICIAL

Bolivia. Direccion General de Estadistica y Estudios Geograficos *see*
- BOLIVIA

Bolivia. Instituto Nacional de Estadistica *see* BOLIVIA

Bolivia. Junta Nacional de Planeamiento *see* PLAN DE DESARROLLO ECONOMICO Y SOCIAL, 1962-1971

Bolivia. Laws, Statutes, etc *see*
- CODIGO PENAL BOLIVIANO
- COLECCION OFICIAL DE LEYES, DECRETOS, ORDENES, RESOLUCIONES.

Bolivia Ministerio de Guerra *see*
- INFORME [...]

Bolivia Ministerio de Hacienda *see* INFORME DEL MINISTRO DE HACIENDA DE BOLIVIA AL CONGRESO ORDINARIO DE [...]

Bolivia. Ministerio de Hacienda *see* INFORME QUE EL OFICIAL MAYOR ENCARGADO DEL MINISTERIO DE HACIENDA PRESENTA A LA ASAMBLEA NACIONAL ORDINARIA DE [...]

Bolivia Ministerio de Hacienda e Industria *see*
- INFORME [...]
- INFORME DEL MINISTRO DE HACIENDA E INDUSTRIA A LA ASAMBLEA ORDINARIA DE [...]

Bolivia. Ministerio de Hacienda y Estadistica *see* INFORME QUE PRESENTA A LA LEGISLATURA ORDINARIA DE [...]

Bolivia Ministerio de la Guerra *see* INFORME PRESENTADO AL CONGRESO ORDINARIO DE [...]

Bolivia. Ministerio de Planificacion y Coordinacion *see* ESTRATEGIA SOCIO-ECONOMICA DEL DESARROLLO NACIONAL 1971-1991

Bolivia Ministerio de Relaciones Exteriores y Culto *see* INFORME [...]

Bolivia. Ministerio de Relaciones Exteriores y Culto *see* PLAN INMEDIATO DE POLITICA ECONOMICA DEL GOBIERNO DE LA REVOLUCION NACIONAL

Bolivia Minsterio de Relaciones Exteriores y Colonizacion *see* INFORME [...]

Bolivia. Secretaria Nacional de Planificacion y Coordinacion *see*
- PLAN BIENAL DE DESARROLLO ECONOMICO Y SOCIAL, 1963-64
- PLAN BIENAL DE DESARROLLO ECONOMICO Y SOCIAL, 1965-1966

Boll, F *see* VORLESUNGEN UND ABHANDLUNGEN

Boll, Stefan *see*
- SEGELSURFEN IM SCHULSPORT
- VERGLEICHENDE ANALYSE DER FERNSEHSPORTBERICHTERSTATTUNG DER ARD AUS DER SICHT VON KOMMUNIKATOREN UND REZIPIENTEN

Boll, Uwe *see*
- ARBEITEN ZU FILM UND FERNSEHEN
- BEWERTUNG DER TV-SERIE AUF EMPIRISCHER GRUNDLAGE
- MATERIALIEN ZUR MEDIENTHEORIE

BOLLAND EN PETRUS / Schaepman, Herman Johan Aloysius Maria – 4. druk. Utrecht: Wed J R van Rossum, 1899 – 1mf – 9 – 0-8370-7103-8 – 1986-1103 – us A.T.L.A. [240]

Bolland, Henry *see* EXPLORACIONES PRACTICADAS EN EL ALTO PARAGUAY...

Bollandus, J *see* ACTA SANCTORUM

Bollers, H J *see* HENRY J. BOLLERS FORTEPIANO BOOK

Bolles, Albert Sidney *see*
- EVERYMAN'S LAWYER...BEING A NEW EDITION...OF THE HOME LIBRARY OF LAW
- THE LAW OF THE SUSPENSION OF THE POWER OF ALIENATION IN THE STATE OF NEW YORK
- THE LAW RELATING TO BANKS AND THEIR DEPOSITORS AND TO BANK COLLECTIONS

Bolles, George S *see* BUSINESS MAN'S COMMERCIAL LAW LIBRARY

Bolles, John Augustus *see* A TREATISE ON USURY AND USURY LAWS

BOLLETINO / Societa Italiana di Biologia Superimentale – v.28-55. 1952-79 – 1,5,6 – 22780.00 – us Princeton Micro [580]

BOLLETINO UFFICIALE / Trentino-Alto Adige. Italy – Trento. 1960-1968 – 1 – us NY Public [945]

BOLLETTINO BIBLIOGRAFICO MUSICALE – Milan. v. 1-8 no. 4 5. Sept 1926-Apr May 1933 – 1 – us NY Public [780]

BOLLETTINO BIBLIOGRAFICO MUSICALE – Milano. v1-8. 1926-33 – 2r – 1 – us Ross [780]

BOLLETTINO BIBLIOGRAFICO MUSICALE – v1-8, No4-5. 1926-1933 – 1 – us Schnase [780]

BOLLETTINO DEL NEVADA – Reno, NV. 1915-19; 1926-44 – 12r – 1 – $600.00 – U04659 – us Library Micro [071]

BOLLETTINO DELLA SOCIETA ITALIANA DI FARMACIA OSPEDALIERA – (1977- . 5,6,9) – 1955- – 1 – us UMI [610]

BOLLETTINO DELLO SCIOPERO DEI SARTI – Chicago, Nov, Dec 1910 – 3r – 1 – us I.H.R.C. [978]

BOLLETTINO DI STATISTICA E LEGISLAZIONE COMPARATA / Italy. Ministero delle Finanze – Roma. Anno. 1-25. 1900-1926 1927 – 1 – us NY Public [336]

BOLLETTINO DI STUDI STORICO-RELIGIOSI – nos1-2. 1921-22 (complete) – 1r – 1 – ATLA 1994-S515 – us A.T.L.A. [073]

BOLLETTINO D'INFORMAZIONI – (v.19- 1979$ 5,6,9) – Associazione Italiana Biblioteche. v.1- 1961- – 1 – us UMI [020]

BOLLETTINO OFFICIALE *see* ORDINE FIGLI D'ITALIA IN AMERICA

BOLLETTINO SOCIALISTA-RIVOLUZIONARIO – London, UK. 6 Mar-2 May 1879 – 1 – uk British Libr Newspaper [072]

BOLLETTINO STORICO DELLA SVIZZERA ITALIANA – 25-30. 1950-1955 – 1 – us UMI [949]

BOLLETTINO UFFICIALE / Italy. Dogane e Imposte Indirette. Direzione Generale delle – Milan. v. 1-79. 1862-1939. Incomplete – 1 – us NY Public [324]

BOLLETTINO UFFICIALE / Somaliland. Italian – v1-4. 1957-60 – 1 – us Ross [324]

BOLLETTINO UFFICIALE DELLA REPUBBLICA DI SAN MARINO – 1926-68 – 3r – 1 – us Ross [324]

Bolling, Helmuth *see* A LOOK INTO THE PAST

Bollioud de Mermet, L *see* ABHANDLUNG VON DEM VERDERBEN DES GESCHMACKS IN DER FRANZOESISCHEN MUSIK

DEM BOLLME SI BOES WUCHE : LUSTSPIEL IN DREI AKTEN / Huggenberger, Alfred – Frauenfeld: Huber, 1914 – 1r – 1 – us U.W. Library [820]

BOLLSTANDIGES BARBURGER – 1762 – 1 – 23.45 – us Baptist [240]

Bolmer, William Brevoort *see* CHURCH AND THE BIBLE: AN EXPLANATION AND VINDICATION

BOL'NAIA ROSSIIA / Merezhkovskii, Dimitrii – Spb. 1910. BR-750 2 – 8 – ne IDC [460]

Bologna. Camera di Commercio ed Arti *see* SUL PROGRETTO DI UNA LEGGE INTERNAZIONALE SUL DIRITTO CAMBIARIO

Bolognetti, F *see* LA CHRISTIANA VITTORIA MARITIMA

Bolotov, P A *see*
- SBORNIK POLOZHENII I INSTRUKTSII PO BUKHGALTERSKOMU UCHETU I OTCHETNOSTI SOIUZOV KUSTARNO-PROMYSLOVOI I LESNOI KOOPERATSII
- SCHETOVODSTVO PROIZVODITEL'NO-TRUDOVYKH ARTELEI V SVIAZI S OSNOVAMI OBSHCHEGO SCHETOVODSTVA

BOL'SHAIA ENTSIKLOPEDIIA : PROSVESHCHENIE / ed by Iuzhakova, S N – Spb., [1896] 1900-1909. v1-22. Suppl – 344mf – 9 – R-8384/2 – ne IDC [030]

BOL'SHAIA SOVETSKAIA ENTSIKLOPEDIIA – Stalin dan karjanja. SE-4514 1. 1959 – 9 – ne IDC [030]

Bol'shakov, A M *see*
- OCHERKI DEREVNI SSSR, 1917-1927
- SOVREMENNAIA DEREVNIA V TSIFRAKH

BOLSHE PRAVDY, CHIEM FANTAZII : ZAPISKI BURZHUIA / G, Mark – Paris: Russkoe kn-vo v Parizhi e, [1919?] – 1 – CSUX88-B5122 – us Hoover Inst Photo [390]

BOL'SHEVIK – (Kommunist). Moscow. Apr 1924-Oct 1952. Incomplete – 1 – us NY Public [335]

BOLSHEVIKI I ARMII A V 1905-1917 GG : VOENNAI A ORGANIZAT SII A PRI PETERBURGSKOM KOMITETE RSDRP(B) I REVOLIUTSIONNOE DVIZHENIE V VO ISKAKH PETERBURGA / Akhun, Mikhail Ilich & Petrov V A – Leningrad: Krasnai a gazeta, 1929 – 1 – CSUX88-B840 – us Hoover Inst Photo [320]

BOL'SHEVIKI, MEN'SHEVIKI I REVOLIUTSIONNAIA SOTSIAL-DEMOKRATIIA / Lindov, G & Leiteizen, G D – M., 1917. 46p – 1mf – 9 – ne IDC [320]

BOLSHEVIKI U VLASTI : SOTSIALNO-POLITICHESKIE ITOGI OKTI ABRSKAGO PEREVOROTA: SBORNIK STATE I – Moskva: "Revoliutsionnai a mysl", 1918 – 1 – CSUX89-B2540 – us Hoover Inst Photo [320]

BOLSHEVIKI V ROLI ORGANIZATOROV I UPRAVITELEI – Tokio: Izd. "Russkago bi uro pechati", 1919 – 1 – CSUX88-B1249 – us Hoover Inst Photo [947]

BOLSHEVIKI V TSARITSYNIE / sostavlena Osobo i komissie i po razsli edovanii u zlodi ei an i i bolshevikov,... – Rostov: [s.n.], 1919 – 1 – CSUX88-B6459 – us Hoover Inst Photo [947]

BOL'SHEVIKI ZAPADNOI SIBIRI V PERIOD PERVOI RUSSKOI REVOLIUTSII 1905-1907 GG / Rossiiskaia Sotsial' Demokraticheskaia Rabochaia Partiia – dokumenty i materialy. Novosibirsk, 1958 – 1 – 35.00r – us Hoover Inst Photo [335]

BOL'SHEVISTSKAIA PECHAT', RUSSIA = BOLSHEVIK PRESS : PUBLICATION OF THE CENTRAL COMMITTEE OF THE COMMUNIST PARTY – Moscow, 1933-41 – 138mf – 9 – $790.00 coll – us Ross [335]

BOL'SHEVISTSKIE ORGANIZATSII SREDNEGO POVOLZH'IA V BOR'BE ZA KREST'IANSKIE MASSY V REVOLIUTSII 1905-1907 GG / Shmygin, I P – Ul'ianovsk, 1962 – 1 – 35.00r – us Hoover Inst Photo [335]

BOLSHEVISTSKIE TAINYE TIPOGRAFII V MOSKVE I MOSKOVSKOI OBLASTI 1904-1910 G.G : VOSPOMINANII A I DOKUMENTY SOBRANNYE I OBRABOTANNYE T S. ZELIKSON-BOBROVSKO I – Moskva: Gos. izd-vo, 1923 – 1 – CSUX89-B6587 – us Hoover Inst Photo [947]

BOL'SHOI CHITATEL'. STIKHI / Aseev, N – M. 1932. BR-897 2 – 8 – ne IDC [460]

Bolte, Johannes *see*
- COLIGNY – GUSTAV ADOLF – WALLENSTEIN
- DREI SCHAUSPIELE VOM STERBENDEN MENSCHEN

Bolten, Carl *see* LANDGEWINNUNGSARBEITEN IM BEREICH DER HALLIGEN AN DER SCHLESWIGSCHEN WEST KUESTE UND IHRE WIRTSCHAFTLICHE BEDEUTUNG

Bolthauser, H *see* ATLAS DER KRANKHEITEN UND BESCHAEDIGUNGEN

BOLTON 1726-1905 – (Mf 1-2,48: Accounts 1781-91, 1810-46. Mf 3-37: Town Records 1778-1872. Mf 37: New Town Residents 1788-95. Mf 37-58: Payments 1782-1837, 1865-86. Mf 59-63: Poor Farm 1827-45. Mf64-73: Mortgages 1806-62. Mf 74: Tax Valuations 1860. Mf 75,83: Civil & Revolutionary Wars. Mf 76: Church Members 1817-33. Mf 77-79: Births 1727-1849 A-W. Mf 79,83: Deaths 1823-34 A-W. Mf 80-83: Marriages 1742-1853 A-W. Mf 84-86: Births 1726-82. Mf 85-86: Deaths 1727, 1756-81. Mf 86: Marriages 1745-81. Mf 87-89: 1st Parish Vitals 1759-1852. Mf 90: Births 1743-63, 1796-1848; Deaths 1780, 1823-59. Mf 91-92: Births 1844-68 & Index. Mf 91-94: Marriages 1844-56 & Index. Mf 93-94: Deaths 1844-69 & Index. Mf 94-97: Marriages 1856-1906 & Index. Mf 98-100: Births 1864-1905 & Index. Mf 98,102: Voters 1820, 1836, 1868-76. Mf 100-102: Deaths 1869-1906 & Index. Mf 102: Non-Resident Burials 1855-1917) – (mf ed 1999) – 102mf – 9 – 0-87623-402-3 – us Holbrook [920]

BOLTON 1728-1849 – (Mf 1T-2T: Births & Deaths 1728-82. Mf 3T-7T: Births & Deaths 1743-1849. Mf 2T-6T: Marriages 1746-1844. Mf 3T-6T: Intentions 1787-1850. Mf 7T: Out-of-Town Marriages 1739-1799. Mf 8T: B,M,D 1844-49) – (mf ed 1995) – 8mf – 9 – 0-87623-212-8 – us Holbrook [920]

BOLTON AND DISTRICT INDEPENDENT LABOUR PARTY PIONEER – Bolton, England. -m. Jan-Sept 1895. 10 ft – 1 – uk British Libr Newspaper [072]
BOLTON & BURY CATHOLIC HERALD – Bolton, Bury, England. -w. Feb 1908-Dec 1909. 2 1 2 reels – 1 – uk British Libr Newspaper [072]
Bolton, C S *see* DIARY
Bolton, Charles Knowles *see*
– BOLTON'S AMERICAN ARMORY
– THE REAL FOUNDERS OF NEW ENGLAND
– SCOTCH IRISH PIONEERS IN ULSTER AND AMERICA
BOLTON CHRONICLE – Bolton, England. -w. 1831-34. 2 reels – 1 – uk British Libr Newspaper [072]
BOLTON EVENING GUARDIAN – England. 1874-76.-d. 9 reels – 1 – uk British Libr Newspaper [072]
BOLTON FREE PRESS – Bolton, England. -w. 1842; 1847. 50 ft – 1 – uk British Libr Newspaper [072]
Bolton, H E *see* ARREDONDO'S HISTORICAL PROOF OF SPAIN'S TITLE TO GEORGIA
Bolton, J *see* FILICES BRITANNICAE
BOLTON'S AMERICAN ARMORY / Bolton, Charles Knowles – 1927. Item I. Indexed with mottos at the end. 222p. SW16-0082 – 5 – us A.G.L.L. [920]
Bolton-Smith, Robin *see* PORTRAIT MINIATURES IN THE NATIONAL MUSEUM OF AMERICAN ART
BOLUR ERIKE "EINE KETTE AUS BERGKRISTALLEN", EINE MONGOLISCHE CHRONIK DER KIENLUNG-ZEIT, VON RASIPUNGSUY (1774-1775) LITERATURHISTORISCH UNTERSUCHT / Heissig, W – MS Monograph X. Peiping. 1946. BU-418 2 – 8 – ne IDC [460]
Bolus, H *see* A LIST OF THE FLOWERING PLANTS AND FERNS OF THE CAPE PENINSULA
O BOM LADRAO : PERIODICO RELIGIOSO, LITTERARIO E NOTICOSO – Marianna, 1 Oct 1873; Feb 1875; 10 May 1876 – 1,5,6 – bl Biblioteca [072]
O BOM SENSO – Ouro Preto, 1 Apr-Jul 1852; Apr-Jul 1853; Apr-Jun 1854; Jan 1855-29 Dec 1856 – 1,5,6 – bl Biblioteca [072]
O BOM SILVERIO – Mariana, Brazil. Aug, Oct-Dec 1913; Jan-Apr, Nov 1914 – 1 – bl Biblioteca [072]
O BOM SUCCESSO – Bom-Successo, 30 Apr-23 Jul 1893 – 1,5,6 – bl Biblioteca [072]
A BOMBA – '(s.l.')-Curitiba, Brazil. 12 Jun-31 Dec 1913 – 1,5,6 – bl Biblioteca [072]
LE BOMBARDEMENT DES VILLES OUVERTES – Paris, 1938? Fiche W 757. (Blodgett Collection of Spanish Civil War Pamphlets) – 9 – us H.U. College Libr [946]
BOMBARDEMENTS ET AGRESSIONS EN ESPAGNE, JUILLET 1936-JUILLET 1938 – (World Committee Against War and Fascism). Paris, 1938. Fiche W 758. (Blodgett Collection of Spanish Civil War Pamphlets) – 9 – us H.U. College Libr [946]
EL BOMBARDEO DE ALMERIA POR LA ESCUADRA ALEMANA – Madrid, 1937? Fiche W 760. (Blodgett Collection of Spanish Civil War Pamphlets) – 9 – us H.U. College Libr [946]
THE BOMBARDIER AND POCKET GUNNER / Adye, Ralph Willett – 1827. 8th ed – 9 – $20.00 – uk Libr Preservation [355]
THE BOMBARDMENT OF EGYPTIAN LEGATION IN MADRID – n.p. 1937. Fiche W 759. (Blodgett Collection of Spanish Civil War Pamphlets) – 9 – us H.U. College Libr [946]
BOMBARDMENT OF THE BRITISH EMBASSY IN MADRID / Spain. Servicio Informativo Espanol – n.p., n.d. Fiche W1512. (Blodgett Collection of Spanish Civil War Pamphlets) – 9 – us H.U. College Libr [946]
Bombay *see* BOMBAY GOVERNMENT GAZETTE
BOMBAY, 1885 TO 1890: A STUDY IN INDIAN ADMINISTRATION / Hunter, William Wilson – London: H. Frowde; Bombay: B.M. Malabari, 1892. vii,504p – 1 – us U.W. Library [950]
BOMBAY ACTS – Bombay. 1871-1934. Lacking: 1893 – 118mf – 8 – ne IDC [073]
BOMBAY CO-OPERATIVE QUARTERLY – Bombay, v. 1-28. 1917-45. Lacking: v5(2), v7(1), v8(2), v10(3-4), v11(1-4), v19(2)-v22(1), v23(1), v28(2) – 126mf – 8 – ne IDC [073]
BOMBAY COURIER – India. -w. 15 Nov 1793-Dec 1794; Jan-Dec 1837. 2 reels – 1 – uk British Libr Newspaper [072]
BOMBAY DUCKS / Dewar, D – London, New York. 1906. BZ-267 2 – 8 – ne IDC [590]
THE BOMBAY FLORA / Dalzell, N A & Gibson, A – Bombay. 1861 – 9 – ne IDC [580]
BOMBAY GAZETTE – India. Overland Summary. -w. July 1875-March 1911. 106 reels – 1 – uk British Libr Newspaper [072]
BOMBAY GAZETTE – India. -w. July 1868-March 1914. 171 reels – 1 – uk British Libr Newspaper [072]
Bombay Geographic Society *see* TRANSACTIONS OF THE BOMBAY GEOGRAPHIC SOCIETY
BOMBAY GOVERNMENT GAZETTE / Bombay – 1931-1940; Apr. 1956-1960. Incomplete – 1 – us NY Public [324]
Bombay Historical Society *see* JOURNAL OF THE BOMBAY HISTORICAL SOCIETY
Bombay. India. Legislative Assembly *see* DEBATES
Bombay. India. Legislative Council *see* DEBATES
Bombay. India. Political and Services Department *see* SECOND FIVE-YEAR PLAN (1956-57 TO 1960-61)
Bombay. India (Presidency). Educational Department *see* CATALOGUE OF NATIVE PUBLICATIONS IN THE BOMBAY PRESIDENCY UP TO 31 DEC 1864
BOMBAY LAW REPORTER – (Missing: 1899, v1; 1943, v45(1-3, 13, 22); 1957, v59(11, 19, 20); 1958, v60(3, 4, 5-8, 24); 1962, v64(9, 10, 15, 17, 24)) – Bombay, 1899-1963. v1-65 – 1,563mf – I-541/2 – ne IDC [340]
BOMBAY LEGISLATIVE ASSEMBLY DEBATES – Bombay, 1937-1939. v1-7 – 332mf – I-29/2 – ne IDC [320]
BOMBAY LEGISLATIVE COUNCIL DEBATES – Bombay, 1937-1939. v1-8 – 76mf – I-28/2 – ne IDC [320]
BOMBAY LEGISLATIVE COUNCIL DEBATES – (Index 1922-1937, v1-45) – Bombay, 1921-1936. v1-45 – 1,128mf – I-27/2 – ne IDC [320]
Bombay Literary Society *see* TRANSACTIONS OF THE BOMBAY LITERARY SOCIETY
BOMBAY QUARTERLY REVIEW – Bombay, 1855-58. v. 1-7 – 54mf – 1 – ne IDC [950]
THE BOMBAY QUARTERLY REVIEW – Bombay: Smith, Taylor; London: Smith, Elder. v1-[7] (n1-14). 1855-sep 1858 – us Res Libr [073]
BOMBAY SAMACHAR – (Cont as: Mumbai Samacara) – Bombay, India. Apr 1944-Jul 1995 – 278+ r – 1 – us L of C Photodup [072]
BOMBAY SANSKRIT AND PRAKRIT SERIES – (Missing: Nos. 32; 64-67 (partly); 68; 77; 81) – Bombay, 1868-1942. Nos 1-85 – 592mf – I-556/2 – ne IDC [490]
BOMBAY SANSKRIT SERIES *see* BOMBAY SANSKRIT AND PRAKRIT SERIES
BOMBAY STANDARD AND CHRONICLE OF WESTERN INDIA – Bombay. 1858-59. – 4r – 1 – ne IDC [072]
BOMBAY STANDARD AND WESTERN CHRONICLE – India. 1858-59. 10 reels – 1 – uk British Libr Newspaper [072]
BOMBAY TELEGRAPH AND COURIER – Bombay. 1847-56 – 13r – 1 – ne IDC [072]
BOMBAY TELEGRAPH AND COURIER – India. -w. 1847-1858. 32 reels – 1 – uk British Libr Newspaper [072]
BOMBAY TIMES AND JOURNAL OF COMMERCE – India. -w. Jan 1845-Aug 1850, 1854-59. 42 reels – 1 – uk British Libr Newspaper [072]
BOMBAY TIMES AND STANDARD – Bombay. 1838-61. Lacking: 1861, May 26(126); June 4(132) – 25r – 1 – ne IDC [072]
BOMBAY TIMES AND STANDARD – India. -w. 1860-17 May 1861. 5 reels – 1 – uk British Libr Newspaper [072]
BOMBAY URBAN INDUSTRIAL LEAGUE FOR DEVELOPMENT (BUILD) – Bombay. 41 docs. 1980-1984 – 26mf – 9 – ne IDC [338]
LA BOMBE – Montreal, Canada. 25 jul-v1 n6. dec 1909 – 1r – 1 – Can$25.00 – cn Can Microfilming [072]
LA BOMBE LIBERALE – Montreal, Canada. 16 aut 1919-v1 n3. 30 aut 1919 – 1r – 1 – Can$25.00 – cn Can Microfilming [072]
BOMBER OFFENSIVE / Harris, Arthur Travers – London: Collins, 1947. 288p. Map on lining papers – 1 – us U.W. Library [940]
Bomberger, Johann H A *see*
– REFORMED, NOT RITUALISTIC, APOSTOLIC, NOT PATRISTIC
– THE REVISED LITURGY
Bomberger, John H A *see*
– INFANT SALVATION IN ITS RELATION TO INFANT DEPRAVITY, INFANT REGENERATION AND INFANT BAPTISM
– SELECTED WORKS
BOMBS OVER BARCELONA / Medical Bureau and North American Committee to Aid Spanish Democracy – N.Y., 1938. Fiche W 1034. (Blodgett Collection of Spanish Civil War Pamphlets) – 9 – us H.U. College Libr [946]
BOM-DESPACHO – Bom Despacho, 27 Mar 1927; 18 Mar 1928 – 1,5,6 – bl Biblioteca [072]
Bommer, J E *see* MONOGRAPHIE DES FOUGERES
Bompas *see* ON THE INDIANS OF THE MACKENZIE AND YUKON RIVERS
Bompas, William Carpenter *see* NORTHERN LIGHTS ON THE BIBLE: DRAWN FROM A BISHOP'S EXPERIENCE DURING TWENTY-FIVE YEARS IN THE GREAT NORTH-WEST
Bon, A del *see* PROPRIETA TERRITORIALE
LE BON APOTRE / Soupault, Philippe – Paris: Editions du Sagittaire c1923 – 1 – us U.W. Library [830]
LE BON CINEMA / ed by Denault, Amedee – Montreal, Canada. v1 n2. oct 1927 – 1r – 1 – Can$25.00 – cn Can Microfilming [072]
LE BON COMBAT : REVUE DE L'ABBE BAILLARGE – Joliette, Canada. jan-dec 1893 – 1r – 1 – Can$40.00 – cn Can Microfilming [073]
DU BON ET DU MAUVAIS USAGE DANS LES MANIERES DE S'EXPRIMER / Callieres, F de – 3e ed. 1693 – 9 – fr I.C.S. [440]
Bon, F. et al *see* LE COMMUNISME EN FRANCE
LE BON FRANCAIS – no. 1-7. Paris. 15 fevr-15 mai 1890 – 1 – fr A.C.R.P.P. [073]
LE BON FRANCAIS – Paris. 1817-23 fevr 1818 – 1 – fr A.C.R.P.P. [073]
LE BON SECOURS / ed by Robillard, M & Duncan, John – Montreal, Canada. v1 n2. nov 1970 – 1r – 1 – Can$25.00 – cn Can Microfilming [072]
LE BON SENS = COMMON SENSE / ed by Lavery, Salluste – Montreal, Canada. 28 mar 1934-6 avr 1934 – 1r – 1 – Can$25.00 – cn Can Microfilming [072]
LE BON SENS – Port-au-Prince, Haiti: Imp H Amblard, jul 1909-apr 19 1910 – 25 sheets – us Res Libr [972]
LE BON SENS OU IDEES NATURELLES OPPOSEES AUX IDEES SURNATURELLES / Holbach, Paul-Thiry d' – (D'Holbach series). 1772 – 9 – fr Hachette [190]
LE BON SENS REPUBLICAIN – Democratique et social. Dir. Laplacette. no. 1-69. Paris. 2 aout-10 oct 1881. mq no. 28-29, 66, 68 – 1 – fr A.C.R.P.P. [073]
Bona, Constantin *see* INTERNATIONAL REVIEWS OF IMMUNOLOGY
Bona, Johannes *see* RERUM LITURGICARUM LIBRI DUO
Bonaeret, Benedictius de *see* COLOPHONS DE MANUSCRITS...
Bonafos-Lazerme, H *see* DE L'EXTRADITION
Bonafous, Louis-Abel de *see* ESPRIT DES LIBRES DEFENDUS, OU ANTILOGIES PHILOSOPHIQUES
Bonald, Louis Gabriel Ambroise, Vicomte de *see* RECHERCHES PHILOSOPHIQUES SUR LES PREMIERS OBJECTS DES CONNAISSANCES MORALES – DEMONSTRATION PHILOSOPHIQUE DU PRINCIPE CONSTITUTIF DE LA SOCIETE – MEDITATIONS POLITIQUES TIREES DE L'EVANGILE
Bonan, Jules *see* COMPTABILITE DES AFFAIRES A ENZEL ET LEURS CONSEQUENCES JURIDIQUES POUR LES COMMERCANTS
A BONANCA – Sacramento, 3 Sep 1911 – 1,5,6 – bl Biblioteca [072]
Bonanni, F *see*
– DESCRIZIONE DEGL'ISTROMENTI ARMONICI D'OGNI GENERE DEL PADRE BONANNI
– GABINETTO ARMONICO. DESCRIZIONE DEGL' ISTROMENTI ARMONICI
– GABINETTO ARMONICO PIENO D'INSTROMENTI SONORI
– GABINETTO ARMONICO PIENO D'INSTROMENTI SONORI, INDICATI, SPIEGATI, E DI NUOVO CORRETTI
BONANZA – Grantsville, NV. 7 May, 30 Jun 1881 – 1r – 1 – $50.00 – U04570 – us Library Micro [071]
BONANZA – Tonopah, NV. 1901-09; 1912-27; 7-12 Jul 1929 – 22r – 1 – $1,100.00 – U04762 – us Library Micro [071]
BONAPARTE EN EGYPTE / Reunion des musees nationaux. Paris – 1938. 4 fiches – 9 – fr Réunion [700]
Bonaparte, Guillermo *see* UN PAIS SIN JUSTICIA, UN EPISODIO DE LA RESISTENCIA
Bonaparte, Louis-Napoleon *see* EXTINCTION DU PAUPERISME
Bonaparte, Roland *see* LA LAPONIE ET LA CORSE
Bonar, A A *see* A COMMENTARY ON THE BOOK OF LEVITICUS
Bonar, Horatius *see*
– EARTH'S MORNING, OR, THOUGHTS ON GENESIS
– THE EVERLASTING RIGHTEOUSNESS, OR, HOW SHALL MEN BE JUST WITH GOD
– GOD'S WAY OF HOLINESS
– TRUTH AND ERROR, OR, LETTERS TO A FRIEND ON SOME OF THE CONTROVERSIES OF THE DAY
Bonardi, Carlo *see* ENRICO HEINE NELLA LETTERATURA ITALIANA
Bonaventura Argonensis O *see* DE OPTIMA LEGENDORUM ECCLESIAE PATRUM METHODO
Bonbra, F D *see* ARS BELLI ET PACIS
Bonch-Bruevich, Vladimir Dmitrievich *see*
– D. N. MAMIN-SIBIRIAK. RUKOPISI I PEREPISKA
– POKUSHENIE NA V.I. LENINA V MOSKVE 30-GO AVGUSTA 1918 GODA
– STRASHNOE V REVOLIUTSII
– VOLNENII A V VOISKAKH I VOENNYIA TIURMY
O BOND : HEBDOMADARIO HUMORISTICO, CRITICO E CHISTOSO – [s.l.] 15 Set-20 Out 1906 – 1,5,6 – bl Biblioteca [072]
O BOND : PERIODICO FACETO CRITICO E NOTICIOSO – Bahia, BA. 12 Jul 1876 – 1,5,6 – bl Biblioteca [072]
Bond, B *see* THE MONROE MISSION TO FRANCE 1794-96
BOND BAPTIST CHURCH. PRESTON, MISSISSIPPI : CHURCH RECORDS – 1839-1950. Formerly: New Hope Baptist Church (until 1951) – 1 – 25.29 – us Baptist [240]
Bond, Carol *see* PRACTICE AND BELIEF BARRIERS TO DIABETES MANAGEMENT IN CAMBODIAN NON-INSULIN-DEPENDENT DIABETES MELLITUS PATIENTS
Bond, E A *see* CHRONICA MONASTERII DE MELSA, A FUNDATIONE USQUE AD ANNUM 1396 (RS43)
Bond, Francis *see*
– THE CATHEDRALS OF ENGLAND AND WALES
– DEDICATIONS AND PATRON SAINTS OF ENGLISH CHURCHES: ECCLESIASTICAL SYMBOLISM
– AN INTRODUCTION TO ENGLISH CHURCH ARCHITECTURE, 11TH TO 16TH CENTURY
– AN INTRODUCTION TO ENGLISH CHURCH ARCHITECTURE FROM THE ELEVENTH TO THE SIXTEENTH CENTURY
– WOOD CARVINGS IN ENGLISH CHURCHES
Bond, George John *see* SKIPPER GEORGE NETMAN: A STORY OF OUT-PORT METHODISM IN NEWFOUNDLAND
Bond, Goerge John *see* OUR SHARE IN CHINA AND WHAT WE ARE DOING WITH IT
Bond, L H *see* BOND'S REPORTS OF CASES IN THE SIXTH CIRCUIT, 1856-1871
Bond, S *see* CHURCH MEMBERSHIP, OR, THE CONDITIONS OF NEW TESTAMENT AND METHODIST CHURCH MEMBERSHIP EXAMINED AND COMPARED
Bond, T M *see* REPUBLICATION OF THE MINUTES OF THE MISSISSIPPI BAPTIST ASSOCIATION, A, 1806-47
Bond & Weigley *see* THE LEGAL, BANK, AND REPORTING DIRECTORY.
Bondan, Molly *see* USEFUL ENGLISH
THE BONDELSWARTS REBELLION OF 1922 / Lewis, Gavin Llewellyn Mackenzie – Grahamstown: [s.n.] 1977 – us Res Libr [960]
Bondi, J H *see* DEM HEBRAEISCH-PHOENIZISCHEN SPRACHZWEIGE ANGEHOERIGE LEHNWOERTER IN HIEROGLYPHISCHEN UND HIERATISCHEN TEXTEN

BONDS AND LETTERS / Putnam County. Ohio. Probate Court – 1843-1850 – 1r – 1 – $32.50r – us Archival [324]
BONDS AND OATHS / Monroe County. Mich, Bedford Township. Township Treasurer – 1936-1972 – 1r – 1 – $32.50r – us Archival [324]
BOND'S REPORTS OF CASES IN THE SIXTH CIRCUIT, 1856-1871 / Bond, L H – Cincinnati: Clarke. v1-2. 1879 (all publ) – 13mf – 9 – $19.50 – LLMC 81-436 – us L.L.M.C. [340]
BONE – 1,5,69 – us UMI [617]
BONE DENSITY PATTERNS IN ADULT FEMALES WITH A HISTORY OF ANOREXIA NERVOSA / Siemers, Beverly J & Gench, Barbara E – 1992 – 3mf – $12.00 – us Microform Publ [612]
BONE MARROW TRANSPLANTATION – v1- . 1986- – 1,5,6,9 – us UMI [617]
BONE MINERAL AND MENSTRUAL CYCLE STATUS IN COMPETITIVE FEMALE ATHLETES : A LONGITUDINAL STUDY / Robinson, Tracey L – Oregon State University, 1994 – 3mf – 9 – $12.00 – PH 1505 – us Microform Publ [612]
Bonekemper, Johannes *see* DIARIES
Boner, Jose M *see* EL P. JUAN DE MALDONADO. TEOLOGO Y ESCRITURARIO
Boner, Ulrich *see*
– DER EDELSTEIN
Bonet-Maury, Gaston *see*
– LE CONGRES DES RELIGIONS A CHICAGO EN 1893
– EARLY SOURCES OF ENGLISH UNITARIAN CHRISTIANITY
– FRANCE
– L'ISLAMISME ET LE CHRISTIANISME EN AFRIQUE
– LA LIBERTE DE CONSCIENCE EN FRANCE DEPUIS L'EDIT DE NANTES JUSQU'A LA SEPARATION (1598-1905)
– LES PRECURSEURS DE LA REFORME ET DE LA LIBERTE DE CONSCIENCE DANS LES PAYS LATINS DU XIIE AU XVE SIECLE
– L'UNITE MORALE DES RELIGIONS
[BONFANTI COLLECTION OF MATERIALS RELATING TO THE SOUTHERN SUDAN, 1956-1971] – Chicago, IL: U of Chicago, Photoduplication Dep, 1973 (mf ed) – 1 – us Res Libr [080]
[BONFANTI COLLECTION OF MATERIALS RELATING TO THE SOUTHERN SUDAN 1956-71] – Chicago: Uni of Chicago, Photodup Dept, 1973 – us Res Libr [960]
Bonfatti, E et al *see* MOMENTI DI CULTURA TEDESCA
Bonfils, H *see* MANUEL DE DROIT ...
Bonfrere, J *see* PENTATEUCHUS MOYSIS COMMENTARIO ILLUSTRATUS
Bongers, Herman *see* ROUND THE WORLD WITH ENGLISH
Bonham, John Milton *see* SECULARISM: ITS PROGRESS AND ITS MORALS
Bonham, Milledge L *see* PAPERS
LE BONHEUR – (Filmed with: BONHEUR ET VIE jan/fev 1962-20 mar 1966) – Trois-Rivieres, Canada. avr 1941-dec 1961 – 2r – 1 – Can$50.00r – cn Can Microfilming [072]
LE BONHEUR AU FOYER DOMESTIQUE / Pietremont, Maria – Paris: Garnier, 1891. vi,376p. (Les Femmes Collection) – 4mf – 9 – $10.00 – fr Bibl Nationale [640]
BONHEUR ET VIE *see* LE BONHEUR
Bonhomme, Joseph *see* NOIR OR
LE BONHOMME RICHARD – 6avr 1832-31 aout 1833. devenu: L'Impartial. Paris. 1er sept 1833-6 oct 1836 – 1 – fr A.C.R.P.P. [970]
LE BONHOMME RICHARD – Journal de Franklin. no. 1-3. Paris. 1848 – 1 – fr A.C.R.P.P. [970]
BONIFACE / Smith, Gregory – London: S.P.C.K.; New York: E. & J.B. Young, 1896 – 1mf – us A.T.L.A. [240]
Boniface, A *see*
– GRAMMAIRE METHODIQUE ET RAISONNEE
– MANUEL DES AMATEURS DE LA LANGUE FRANCAISE
BONIFACE OF CREDITON AND HIS COMPANIONS : BASED ON LECTURES DELIVERED IN THE CATHEDRAL CHURCH OF BRISTOL IN 1906 / Browne, G F – London: S.P.C.K., 1910 – 1mf – us A.T.L.A. [240]
Bonifacino, Victor *see* CONFERENCIA BELIGERANTE
BONIFACIUS AMERBACH UND DIE REFORMATION / Burckhardt-Biedermann, T – Basel: R. Reich, 1894 – 1mf – us A.T.L.A. [240]
BONIFATIUS, DER APOSTEL DER DEUTSCHEN, UND DIE SLAVENAPOSTEL, KONSTANTINOS (CYRILLUS) UND METHODIOS : EINE HISTORISCHE PARALLELE / Hoefler, Constantin Ritter von – Prag: H. Dominicus, 1887 – 1mf – us A.T.L.A. [240]
Bonilla Samaniego, A *see* EXERCITATION MEDICA PHYLOSOPHICA SOBRE LA ESSENCIA DEL MORBO GALLICO
Bonilla y San Martin, Adolfo *see*
– FUERO DE USAGRE (SIGLO 18)
– LAS LEYENDAS DE WAGNER EN LA LITERATURA ESPANOLA
Bonin, Daniel *see* JOHANN GEORG ZIMMERMANN U. JOHANN GOTTFRIED HERDER
Bonin, Joseph *see* BIOGRAPHIES DE L'HONORABLE BARTHELEMI JOLIETTE ET DE M. LE GRAND VICAIRE A. MENSEAU
Bonin, Marie *see* BIO-BIBLIOGRAPHIE ANALYTIQUE DE MARTHE BERGERON-HOGUE
Bonivard, Francois *see* ADVIS ED DEVIS DES LENGUES; SUIVIS DE LAMARTIGENEE, CEST A DIRE DE LA SOURCE DE PECHE
BONJOUR – Hebdomadaire bilingue de grande information. Strasbourg. 1964-sept 1972 – 1 – fr A.C.R.P.P. [073]
Bonn, A *see* EIN JAHRHUNDERT RHEINISCHE MISSION
Bonnafe, P *see* LE NATIONALISME AFRICAIN
Bonnaire, Felix *see* MEMOIRE AU MINISTRE DE L'INTERIEUR SUR LA SITUATION DU DEPARTEMENT DES HAUTES-ALPES
BONNARD / Reunion des musees nationaux. Paris – 1947. 8 illus. 1 fiche – 9 – fr Réunion [700]
Bonnard du Hanlay, Sebastien-F *see* YORICK OU LE VOYAGEUR BRETON DE 1788
Bonnard, F *see* HISTOIRE DE L'ABBAYE ROYALE ET DE L'ORDRE DES CHANOINES REGULIERS DE ST VICTOR DE PARIS
BONNARD, VUILLARD ET LES NABIS, 1888-1903 / Reunion des musees nationaux. Paris – 1955. 24 illus. 2 fiches – 9 – fr Réunion [750]
Bonnassieux, Pierre *see* LES GRANDES COMPAGNIES DE COMMERCE: ETUDE POUR SERVIR A L'HISTOIRE DE LA COLONISATION
Bonnaud, Dominique *see* D'OCEAN A OCEAN: IMPRESSIONS D'AMERIQUE
LA BONNE CHANSON / Faure, Gabriel – (Holograph in ink without title or signature) – [Paris, 1891] – 1 – us Sibley [780]
LA BONNE FERMIERE : REVUE TRIMESTRIELLE D'ECONOMIE DOMESTIQUE ET D'AGRICULTURE FEMININE – Quebec: les Cercles, v1 no 1 1920-. SEM16P317 – 1r – 5 – Can$38.00 – cn Bibl Nat [640]
LA BONNE LITTERATURE FRANCAISE – Montreal: Leprohon & Leprohon, [1894?-1900?] – 9 – cn C.I.H.M. [440]
LA BONNE NOUVELLE – (And a sermon from cure E.V. Lavergne 17 nov 1935) – Quebec, Canada. 1 oct 1919-v1 n10. jul 1920; 1 oct 1924-v11 n1. 6 fev 1937 – 2r – 1 – Can$50.00r – cn Can Microfilming [240]
LA BONNE STE. ANNE : SA VIE, SES MIRACLES, SES SANCTUAIRES / Ghyvelde, Frederic de – Quebec, 1900. SEM105P533 – 5mf – 9 – Can$11.25 – cn Bibl Nat [920]
Bonneau, S *see*
– LE DRAME LYRIQUE D'ALEXANDRE BLOK
– L'UNIVERS POETIQUE D'ALEXANDRE BLOK
Bonnechose, Charles de *see* MONTCALM ET LE CANADA FRANCAIS: ESSAIS HISTORIQUE
Bonnefon, Jean de *see* LOURDES ET SES TENANCIERS
Bonnefond, Th *see* ESQUISSE BIBLIOGRAPHIQUE RECENTE EN SCIENCES HUMAINES DU DEPARTEMENT DU CENTRE DE LA COTE D'IVOIRE
Bonnefoy, G *see* LE CODE DE L'AIR; ...
BONNER AND MIDDLETON'S BRISTOL JOURNAL – Bristol, England. The Mirror – Bristol Mirror. -w. 24 Dec 1774; 7, 14 Jan, 11 March, 1 April 1775; 6, 13 Jan 1776; 19 July, 6 Sept-25 Oct, 15 Nov, 6, 20, 27 Dec 1783; 10 Jan-7, 28 Feb, 13, 20 March, 3-17 April, 24 July 1784-26 July 1788; 21 Aug 1790; 19 March 1791; 15 March 1794; 7 Jan 1797-27 Dec 1800; 2 Jan 1808-Dec 1832. 11 reels – 1 – uk British Libr Newspaper [072]
BONNER ANZEIGER – Bonn, jun 28-nov 8 1850 – 1 – Inquire at Mikrofilmarchiv for details – gw Misc Inst [943]
BONNER DEPESCHE : FUNKTIONAERORGAN DER SPD – Bonn, 1961-65 – 1r – 1 – DM100.00 – gw Mikro Press [072]
BONNER DEPESCHE : FUNKTIONAERSORGAN DER SPD – Bonn, 1961-65 – 1r – 1 – Inquire at Mikrofilmarchiv for details – gw Misc Inst [320]
BONNER DEPESCHE – Funktionaersorgan der SPD. Bonn, West Germany. 1961-65 – 1r – 1 – gw Mikrofilm [073]
Bonner, Hypatia Bradlaugh *see* PENALTIES UPON OPINION, OR, SOME RECORDS OF THE LAWS OF HERESY AND BLASPHEMY
BONNER INTELLIGENZ-BLATT *see* BOENNISCHES INTELLIGENZBLATT
BONNER JAHRBUCH – S.18-155 1895; S.54-163 1896 – 1r – 1 – DM80.00 – gw Mikro Press [943]
Bonner, John *see* AN ESSAY ON THE REGISTRY LAWS OF LOWER CANADA
BONNER NACHRICHTEN *see*
– GENERAL-ANZEIGER FUER BONN UND UMGEBUNG
BONNER NACHRICHTS- UND ANZEIGE-BLATT : FEUILLE D'AFFICHES – Bonn, 5 Jan 1812-14 Jan 1814 – 1r – 1 – DM80.00 – gw Mikro Press [072]
BONNER NACHRICHTS- UND ANZEIGEBLATT *see* WOCHENBLATT DES BOENNISCHEN BEZIRKS
Bonner, Richard I *see*
– HISTORICAL AND BIOGRAPHICAL RECORD OF LENAWEE COUNTY
– ILLUSTRATED HISTORY AND BIOGRAPHICAL RECORD OF LENAWEE COUNTY
– MEMOIRS OF LENAWEE COUNTY
BONNER RUNDSCHAU – Bonn, West Germany. Former title: 1946-Aug 1949, Koelnische Rundschau. Ausgabe Bonn-Land 19 Mar 1946-67 – 1 – gw Mikrofilm [072]
BONNER RUNDSCHAU *see* KOELNISCHE RUNDSCHAU
BONNER RUNDSCHAU, AUSGABE BONN-LAND *see* KOELNISCHE RUNDSCHAU
BONNER TAGEBLATT – Bonn, jan 3 1883-90 – 1 – Inquire at Mikrofilmarchiv for details – gw Misc Inst [943]
BONNER VOLKSBLATT – Bonn, sep 23, oct 1-nov 30 1862 – 1 – Inquire at Mikrofilmarchiv for details – gw Misc Inst [943]
BONNER VOLKSZEITUNG – Bonn, aug 3 1882-jan 22 1906 – 1 – Inquire at Mikrofilmarchiv for details – gw Misc Inst [943]
BONNER WOCHENBLATT – (Cont: Wochenblatt des Boennischen Bezirks, -1811; Feuilles d'affiches annonces et avis divers(es) de Bonn/Bonner Nachrichts- und Anzeigeblatt (zweisprachig), -jan 1814; Boennisches Wochenblatt, -jan 1816. Cont by: Bonner Zeitung verbunden mit dem Bonner Wochenblatt, sep 1 1850; Bonner Zeitung, oct 1 1850) – Bonn, feb 6 1808-jan 1 1811, jan 5 1812-sep 30 1891 – 58r – 1 – Inquire at Mikrofilmarchiv for details – gw Misc Inst [943]
BONNER WOCHENBLATT *see* WOCHENBLATT DES BOENNISCHEN BEZIRKS
BONNER ZEITSCHRIFT FUER THEOLOGIE UND SEELSORGE – 1(1924)-8(1931) – 56mf – 9 – Dfl196.00 – ne Slangenburg [073]
BONNER ZEITSCHRIFT FUER THEOLOGIE UND SEELSORGE – Duesseldorf. v1-8. 1924-1931 – 56mf – 9 – ne IDC [240]
BONNER ZEITUNG – Bonn, oct 2 1824-30 – 1 – Inquire at Mikrofilmarchiv for details – gw Misc Inst [943]
BONNER ZEITUNG – (Cont: Neue Bonner Zeitung, -dec 14 1895) – Bonn, apr 28 1892-mar 22 1923, sep 1 1924-1931, may 3 1932-mar 31 1933 – 1 – Inquire at Mikrofilmarchiv for details – gw Misc Inst [943]
BONNER ZEITUNG – (Incl suppl: Spartacus, jan 15-jul 9 1849. Cont by: Neue Bonner Zeitung, 1849) – Bonn, may 7 1848-jun 30 1850 – 2r – 1 – Inquire at Mikrofilmarchiv for details – gw Misc Inst [943]
BONNER ZEITUNG – (Title change Jan 1849: Neue Bonner Zeitung) – Bonn, Germany. 7 May 1848-30 Jun 1850 – 2r – 1 – gw Mikrofilm [072]
BONNER ZEITUNG *see*
– BONNER WOCHENBLATT
– WOCHENBLATT DES BOENNISCHEN BEZIRKS
BONNER ZEITUNG VERBUNDEN MIT DEM BONNER WOCHENBLATT *see* BONNER WOCHENBLATT
Bonnet, C *see* TRAITE D'INSECTOLOGIE...
Bonnet, Charles *see*
– CONSIDERATIONS SUR LES CORPS ORGANISES
– PALINGENESIE PHILOSOPHIQUE, OU IDEES SUR L'ETAT PASSE ET SUR L'ETAT FUTUR DES ETRES VIVANTS, OUVRAGE DESTINE A SERVIR DE SUPPLEMENT AUX DERNIERS ECRITS DE L'AUTEUR
Bonnet, Henry F A *see* L'ALIENE DEVANT LUI-MEME, L'APPRECIATION LEGALE, LA LEGISLATION, LES SYSTEMES, LA SOCIETE ET LA FAMILLE
Bonnet, J *see*
– HISTOIRE DE LA MUSIQUE, ET DE SES EFFETS
– HISTOIRE DE LA MUSIQUE ET DE SES EFFETS
Bonnet, Jules *see*
– AONIO PALEARIO
– NOTICE SUR LA VIE ET LES ECRITS DE M. MERLE D'AUBIGNE
Bonnet, Max *see* LE LATIN DE GREGOIRE DE TOURS
LE BONNET ROUGE – Paris. 1914-1916 – 1 – 35.00r – us Hoover Inst Photo [072]
LE BONNET ROUGE – Quotidien republicain du soir. Dir. Miguel Almereyda. Paris. 6 dec 1913-10 juil 1917, 18 oct, 22 nov 1922 – 1 – fr A.C.R.P.P. [073]
LE BONNET ROUGE – (Filmed as pt of: Commune de Paris newspapers. Newspapers on these reels are filmed chronologically, not alphabetically) – Paris: Impr Le Douarin, apr 10-16, 19, 22 1871 – us Res Libr [072]
LE BONNET ROUGE – [Paris]: Bonaventure et Ducessois, jun 11-15/18 1848 – us Res Libr [072]
Bonnet y Reveron, Buenoventura *see* LAS CANARIAS Y LA CONQUISTA FRANCO-NORMANDA
Bonnetain, Madame Paul *see* UNE FRANCAISE AU SOUDAN SUR LA ROUTE DE TOMBOUCTOU, DU SENEGAL AU NIGER
Bonnetain, Paul *see* DANS LE BROUSSE
Bonnetain, Paul (Madame) *see* UNE FRANCAISE AU SOUDAN SUR LA ROUTE DE TOMBOUCTOU, DU SENEGAL AU NIGER
Bonneuil, Noel et al *see* MATHEMATICAL POPULATION STUDIES
Bonneval, Rene de *see* REFLEXIONS SUR LE PREMIER AGE DE L'HOMME, SERVANT DE SUPPLEMENT AUX ELEMENTS ET PROGRES DE L'EDUCATION
BONNEVILLE DAM CHRONICLE – Hood River, OR. 6 Apr 1934-1 Sept 1939. 2 rolls – 1 – us U.O. Library [071]
Bonneville, Jean-Pierre *see*
– LA FRONTIERE
– LE PROGRES DE ROUYN-NORANDA
Bonneville, Nicolas de *see*
– L'ANNEE M.DCC.LXXXIX OU LES TRIBUNS DU PEUPLE
– DE L'ESPRIT DES RELIGIONS
– ELECTEUR DU DEPARTEMENT DE PARIS, AUX VERITABLES AMIS DE LA LIBERTE
– L'HYMNE DES COMBATS
– LES JESUITES CHASSES DE LA MACONNERIE
– LETTRE. A MR LE MARQUIS DE CONDORCET
– LE NOUVEAU CODE CONJUGAL, ETABLI SUR LES BASES DE LA CONSTITUTION
– LES POESIES
Bonney, Thomas G *see*
– CHRISTIAN DOCTRINES AND MODERN THOUGHT
– OLD TRUTHS IN MODERN LIGHTS: THE BOYLE LECTURES FOR 1890 WITH OTHER SERMONS
– THE PRESENT RELATIONS OF SCIENCE AND RELIGION
Bonney, W P *see* HISTORY OF PIERCE COUNTY
Bonnier, Gaetan *see* L'OCCUPATION DE TOMBOUCTOU
Bonniot, Joseph de *see* LE MIRACLE ET SES CONTREFACONS
THE BONNYVILLE TRIBUNE – Bonnyville, Alberta. 30 mai 1947-19 oct 1968 – 6r – 1 – Can$57.50r – cn Can Microfilming [072]
Bonolis, G *see* QUESTIONI DI DIRITTO INTERNAZIONALE ...
Bonomi, Giovanni Francesco *see* CHIRON ACHILLIS, SIVE NAVARCHUS HUMANAE VITAE
Bononcini, G M *see*
– MUSICO PRATTICO CHE BREVEMENTE DIMOSTRA IL MODO DI GIUNGERE
Bonorden, H F *see* HANDBUCH DER ALLGEMEINEN MYKOLOGIE
Bonorden, Hermann Friedrich *see* DIE ERKENNTNISS DES CHRISTENTHUMES VOM NATURWISSENSCHAFTLICHEN STANDPUNCTE

Bonpland, A J A *see*
- DESCRIPTION DES PLANTES RARES CULTIVEES A MALMAISON ET A NAVARRE
- HERBARIUM
- SYNOPSIS PLANTARUM, QUAS IN ITINERE AD PLAGAM AEQUINOCTIALEM ORBIS NOVI
- VOYAGE AUX REGIONS EQUINOCTIALES DU NOUVEAU CONTINENT
- VOYAGE AUX REGIONS EQUINOXIALES DU NOUVEAU CONTINENT
- VOYAGE AUX REGIONS EQUINOXIALES DU NOUVEAU CONTINENT, FAIT DANS LES ANNEES 1799-1804

BONPLANDIA... / ed by Seemann, W E G & Seemann, B – Hannover, London, Paris, 1853-1862. 10v – 101mf – 328/2 – ne IDC [073]

LES BONS PELERINS DE STE. ANNE – Quebec, 1878. 02840. (Pre-1900 Canadiana) – 9 – cn C.I.H.M. [240]

LES BONS ROMANS ILLUSTRES – Montreal: J H A Lamarre, [1887-18– ou 19–] – 9 – cn C.I.H.M. [700]

Bonsels, Waldemar *see* DER HUETER DER SCHWELLE

LA BONTE – Paris: Impr Ed. Proux etc, aug 24-sep 10 1849 – 1r – us Res Libr [072]

Bonte, P *see* PRODUCTION ET ECHANGES CHEZ LES TOUAREG KEL GRESS DU NIGER

Bontempi, G A A *see*
- HISTORIA MUSICA
- HISTORIA MVSICA, NELLA QUALE SI HA PIENA COGNITIONE DELLA TEORICA, E DELLA PRATICA ANTICA DELLA MVSICA HARMONICA
- NOVA QUATUOR VOCIBUS COMPONENDI METHODUS

Bonus, Alb. *see* COLLATIO CODICIS LEWISIANI RESCRIPTI EVANGELIORUM SACRORUM SYRIACORUM CUM CODICE CURETONIANO

Bonus, John *see* SHADOWS OF THE ROOD

Bonvallet des Brosses *see* RICHESSES ET RESSOURCES DE LA FRANCE.

Bonvalot, Gabriel *see* L'ASIE INCONNUE A TRAVERS LE TIBET

Bonvini, Kassim *see* TRAITS OPPOSITIONNELS ET TRAITS CONTRASTIFS EN KASSIM

Bonwetsch, G N *see*
- DIE BUECHER DER GEHEIMNISSE HENOCHS (T.U.U. 3-44/2)
- CYRILL UND METHODIUS
- DREI GEORGISCH ERHALTENE SCHRIFTEN VON HIPPOLYTUS
- DIE GESCHICHTE DES MONTANISMUS
- HIPPOLYTS KOMMENTAR ZUM HOHENLIED AUF GRUND VON N. MARRS AUSGABE DES GRUSINISCHEN TEXTES (T.U.U.2-23/2C)
- STUDIEN ZU DEN KOMMENTAREN HIPPOLYTS ZUM BUCHE DANIEL UND HOHEN LIEDE (T.U.U. 2-16/2)
- DIE UNTER HIPPOLYTS NAMEN UEBERLIEFERTE SCHRIFT UEBER DEN GLAUBEN (T.U.U. 3-31/2A)

Bonwetsch, Nathanael *see*
- DIE SCHRIFTEN TERTULLIANS NACH DER ZEIT IHRER ABFASSUNG
- DIE UNTER HIPPOLYTS NAMEN UEBERLIEFERTE SCHRIFT UEBER DEN GLAUBEN

Bonwick, James *see* THE MORMONS AND THE SILVER MINES

BONZEN UND REBELLEN : GESCHICHTE EINES UNBEKANNTEN FREIWILLIGEN DER NATION / Weller, Anton Friedrich Tuedel – Muenchen: Zentralverlag der NSDAP: F Eher Nachf, 1939 – 1 – us U.W. Library [890]

Boodberg, P A *see* MARGINALIA TO THE HISTORIES OF THE NORTHERN DYNASTIES

Boodin, John Elof *see* TRUTH AND REALITY

A BOOK ABOUT LAWYERS / Jeaffreson, John C – New York: C W Carleton & Co. 2v in 1. 1867 – 5mf – 9 – $7.50 – LLMC 91-065 – us L.L.M.C. [340]

BOOK AND ART – Hightstown, NJ. 1979 – 1r – 1 – $50.00 – R04975 – us Library Micro [071]

BOOK ART – 49mf – $280.00 – 1-900853-15-9 – uk Mindata [740]

BOOK ARTS : ARCHITECTURE, APPLIED ARTS, STUDIO ARTS – (Individual titles not listed separately) – 67 catalogues on 81mf – 9 – £595.00 – uk Chadwyck [740]

BOOK BITS – (Librarian: 3 Apr-25 Sept 1897) – London, UK. 4 Jul 1896-25 Sept 1897 – 1r – 1 – uk British Libr Newspaper [072]

THE BOOK BUYER – New York. v. 9-10; n.s. 1-2; 3rd Series 37-39. Nov 1875-Dec 1877; Sep 1878-Sep 1880; 1912-1915 – 1 – us NY Public [073]

THE BOOK BUYER : A REVIEW AND RECORD OF CURRENT LITERATURE – New York: [Charles Scribner's Sons, 1867-1903]. v7-10 n3 oct 1873-77 – 1 – us Res Libr [073]

BOOK CATALOGUE OF THE LIBRARY OF THE ROYAL SOCIETY / Royal Society – $760.00 – us UPA [015]

BOOK COLLECTOR – London. v1-12. 1952-63 – 2r – 1 – us Ross [070]

BOOK DRAFTS / Murray, Chalmers S – ca.1948. 14 fiches – 9 – us South Carolina Historical [025]

Book House Training CentreUNESCO *see* BOOK PROMOTION, SALES AND DISTRIBUTION

BOOK IN MULTILINGUAL COUNTRIES : PROCEEDINGS OF THE SYMPOSIUM ON THE PUBLICATION OF BOOKS IN THE VARIOUS LANGUAGES OF MULTILINGUAL COUNTRIES, MOSCOW-ALMA ATA SEPT. 1976 / Hasan, Abul – 1978 – 9 – 92-3-101573-7 – fr UNESCO [070]

BOOK INDEXES, BOSTON PASSENGER LISTS, 1899 / U.S. Immigration and Naturalization Service – 107 rolls. T790 – 1 – us Nat'l Archives [324]

BOOK INDEXES, NEW YORK PASSENGER LISTS, 1906-42 / U.S. Immigration and Naturalization Service – 807 rolls. T612 – 1 – us Nat'l Archives [324]

BOOK INDEXES, PHILADELPHIA PASSENGER LISTS, 1906 / U.S. Immigration and Naturalization Service – 23 rolls. T791 – 1 – us Nat'l Archives [324]

BOOK INDEXES, PORTLAND, MAINE, PASSENGER LISTS, 1907 / U.S. Immigration and Naturalization Service – 12 rolls. T793 – 1 – us Nat'l Archives [324]

BOOK INDEXES, PROVIDENCE PASSENGER LISTS, 1911 / U.S. Immigration and Naturalization Service – 15 rolls. T792 – 1 – us Nat'l Archives [324]

BOOK INDUSTRY – 1964 – 1 – us UMI [070]

THE BOOK OF AMOS / Schmoller, Otto – New York: Charles Scribner, c1874 – 1mf – 9 – 0-8370-6236-5 – 1986-0236 – us A.T.L.A. [220]

BOOK OF ANGLICAN CHANT...IN MANUSCRIPT / Carter, John – Lacking pages 59-62, 75-76. Before 1842 – 9 – us Sibley [780]

THE BOOK OF ANTELOPES / Sclater, P L & Thomas, M R O – 2063 2. 4 v. 1894-1900 – 8 – ne IDC [590]

THE BOOK OF ARDA VIRAF – Bombay, London, 1872 – 5mf – NE-20159/1 – ne IDC [490]

THE BOOK OF BALLADS / Martin, Theodore; ed by Gaultier, Bon – London: W.S. Orr, and Co., [1849] – 1 roll – 1 – 1-55879-363-1 – uk Libr Preservation [810]

BOOK OF BROME – 15th century – 1 – uk Microform Academic [941]

THE BOOK OF CLEVELANDERS / Borrows Brothers Co – Biographical dictionary of living men of the city of Cleveland. Cleveland, 1914. Ohio Reel 27. (The Cox Library Collection) – 5 – us Americana [978]

THE BOOK OF COMMON ORDER OF THE CHURCH OF SCOTLAND – London, 1962 – 4mf – 8 – Dfl19.00 – ne Slangenburg [941]

BOOK OF COMMON PRAYER / Church of England – Portuguese. 1817 – 1 – us A.T.L.A. [240]

THE BOOK OF COMMON PRAYER WITH MUSICAL NOTES : THE FIRST OFFICE BOOK OF THE REFORMATION / Marbeck, J; ed by Rimbault, E F – London: Novello, Ever & Co, 1871 – 1 – us Sibley [780]

BOOK OF COMMON WORSHIP (CCC120) – (In Chinese. With English index) – 1st ed. Hong Kong: Council on Christian Literature for Overseas Chinese, 1959 – 1r – 1 – 1984-B500 – us A.T.L.A. [240]

THE BOOK OF CONSTITUTION OF THE GRAND LODGE OF ANCIENT, FREE AND ACCEPTED MASONS OF CANADA / Freemasons. Grand Lodge (Canada) – Hamilton Ont.: s.n., 1881? (Hamilton Ont.: Times Print 6.). 03247. (Pre-1900 Canadiana) – 9 – cn C.I.H.M. [060]

THE BOOK OF CONSTITUTION OF THE GRAND LODGE OF QUEBEC, ANCIENT FREE AND ACCEPTED MASONS / Francs-Macons. Grande loge de Quebec – Montreal: C R Corneil Limited, 1922. SEM105P1637 – 2mf – 9 – Can$4.50 – cn Bibl Nat [360]

BOOK OF CRESTS / Fairbairn, J – 1892 – 1 – uk Microform Academic [920]

BOOK OF DANIEL / Farrar, Frederic William – New York: A.C. Armstrong, 1895. 1 fiche – 9 – us A.T.L.A. [240]

THE BOOK OF DANIEL : OR, THE SECOND VOLUME OF PROPHECY... / Murphy, James Gracey – Andover: Warren F Draper, 1885 – 1mf – 9 – 0-8370-4542-8 – 1985-2542 – us A.T.L.A. [220]

THE BOOK OF DANIEL : WITH INTRODUCTION AND NOTES / Driver, Samuel Rolles – (Includes appendix & index) – Cambridge: University Press, 1900 – 1mf – 9 – 0-8370-2964-3 – 1985-0964 – us A.T.L.A. [220]

BOOK OF DANIEL FROM THE CHRISTIAN STANDPOINT / Kennedy, John – London: Eyre & Spottiswoode, 1898. 1 fiche – 9 – us A.T.L.A. [240]

BOOK OF DANIEL UNLOCKED / Auchincloss, William Stuart – New York: Van Nostrand, 1905. 1 fiche – 9 – us A.T.L.A. [240]

THE BOOK OF DANIEL UNLOCKED / Auchincloss, William Stuart – (Includes explanatory notes and chronological tables) – NY: D van Nostrand, 1905 – 1mf – 9 – 0-8370-2127-8 – 1985-0127 – us A.T.L.A. [220]

THE BOOK OF DELIGHT AND OTHER PAPERS / Abrahams, Israel – Philadelphia. 1912. BJ-421-66 1 – 9 – ne IDC [400]

THE BOOK OF DETROITERS / Marquis, Albert N – Biographical Dictionary of Leading Citizens of the City of Detroit. Chicago: A. N. Marquis and Co., 1908. Michigan Reel 23. (The Cox Library Collection) – 5 – us Americana [978]

THE BOOK OF DEUTERONOMY / Harper, Andrew – (Includes bibliographical references) – New York: A C Armstrong, 1895 – 2mf – 9 – 0-8370-2291-6 – 1985-0291 – us A.T.L.A. [220]

BOOK OF DISCIPLINE / Associate Presbyterian Church of North America – 1840 – 1 – $50.00 – us Presbyterian [240]

THE BOOK OF ECCLESIASTES : WITH A NEW TRANSLATION / Cox, Samuel – New York: A C Armstrong, [1890] – 1mf – 9 – 0-8370-2760-8 – 1985-0760 – us A.T.L.A. [220]

BOOK OF ECCLESIASTES: A NEW METRICAL TRANSLATION / Haupt, Paul – Baltimore: Johns Hopkins Press, 1905. 1 fiche – 9 – us A.T.L.A. [220]

BOOK OF ECCLESIASTES: WITH A NEW TRANSLATION / Cox, Samuel – New York: A.C. Armstrong, (1890). 1 fiche – 9 – us A.T.L.A. [240]

THE BOOK OF ENLIGHTENMENT FOR THE INSTRUCTION OF THE INQUIRER / Jacob, Son of Aaron; ed by Barton, William E – Sublette, IL: Puritan Press, 1913 – 1mf – 9 – 0-8370-9795-9 – 1986-3795 – us A.T.L.A. [240]

THE BOOK OF ENOCH : WITH INTRODUCTION, NOTES, APPENDICES, AND INDICES – (translated from Professor Dillmann's Ethiopic text, amended and revised in accordance with hitherto uncollated Ethiopic mss. and with the Gizeh and other Greek and Latin fragments which are here publ in full by R H Charles) – Oxford: Clarendon Press 1893 – us Res Libr [470]

THE BOOK OF ENOCH: TRANSLATED FROM THE ETHIOPIC, WITH INTRODUCTION AND NOTES / Schodde, George H – 1882 – 1 – us A.T.L.A. [240]

A BOOK OF ESSAYS / Hirsch, S A – London: Published for the Jewish Historical Society of England by Macmillan, 1905 – 1mf – us A.T.L.A. [270]

THE BOOK OF ESTHER : ILLUSTRATIVE OF CHARACTER AND PROVIDENCE / McEwan, Thomas – Edinburgh:Andrew Elliot, 1877 – 1mf – 9 – 0-8370-4349-2 – 1985-2349 – us A.T.L.A. [220]

THE BOOK OF ESTHER: A NEW TRANSLATION / Lowell Hebrew Club – Andover: Warren F. Draper, 1885.1 fiche – 9 – us A.T.L.A. [240]

THE BOOK OF ESTHER: ITS PRACTICAL LESSONS AND DRAMATIC SCENES / Raleigh, Alexander – 9 – us A.T.L.A. [220]

BOOK OF EXODUS / Chadwick, George Alexander – New York: A.C. Armstrong, (1890). 2 fiches – 9 – us A.T.L.A. [240]

THE BOOK OF EXODUS / Driver, Samuel Rolles – 1911 – 9 – $18.00 – us I.R.C. [220]

THE BOOK OF EXODUS : IN THE REVISED VERSION: WITH INTRODUCTION AND NOTES / Driver, Samuel Rolles – (Includes bibliographical references and index) – Cambridge: University Press, 1911 – 2mf – 9 – 0-8370-6812-6 – 1986-0812 – us A.T.L.A. [220]

THE BOOK OF EZEKIEL / Skinner, John – New York: A.C. Armstrong, 1895. 2 fiches – 9 – us A.T.L.A. [240]

BOOK OF FORMS, ADAPTED TO THE CODE OF PROCEDURE / New York. (State). Commissioners of the Code – Albany: Weed, Parsons, 1861. 273p. LL-1697 – 1 – us L of C Photodup [340]

THE BOOK OF FORTUNE (LIBER FORTUNAE) / Cousin, Jean – (Drawings). O 213. 1883 – 9 – ne IDC [760]

THE BOOK OF GALLANT VAGABONDS / Beston, Henry – New York: G H Doran, [1925] – 1 – us Res Libr [960]

THE BOOK OF GENESIS / Dods, Marcus – New York: A.C. Armstrong, 1888. 2 fiches – 9 – us A.T.L.A. [240]

THE BOOK OF GENESIS / Driver, Samuel Rolles – 1904 – 9 – $18.00 – us I.R.C. [220]

THE BOOK OF GENESIS / Goodspeed, Calvin & Welton, D M – Philadelphia: American Baptist Publication Society, 1909, c1908. (An American commentary on the Old Testament) – 1mf – us A.T.L.A. [220]

THE BOOK OF GENESIS, AND PART OF THE BOOK OF EXODUS : A REVISED VERSION, WITH MARGINAL REFERENCES, AND AN EXPLANATORY COMMENTARY / Alford, Henry – London: Daldy, Isbister, 1877 – 1mf – 9 – 0-8370-2071-9 – 1985-0071 – us A.T.L.A. [220]

THE BOOK OF GILLY : FOUR MONTHS OUT OF A LIFE / Lawless, Emily – British Fiction Archive: Unit 4 – 9 – uk Bell [830]

THE BOOK OF HABAKKUK : INTRODUCTION, TRANSLATION, AND NOTES ON THE HEBREW TEXT / Stonehouse, George Gordon Vigor – (Includes index) – London: Rivingtons, 1911 – 1mf – 9 – 0-8370-9747-9 – 1986-3747 – us A.T.L.A. [220]

THE BOOK OF HABAKKUK / Kleinert, Paul – New York: Charles Scribner, 1874. 41p. 1 fiche – 9 – us A.T.L.A. [220]

THE BOOK OF HAGGAI / McCurdy, James Frederick – New York: Charles Scribner, c1874 – 1mf – 9 – 0-8370-6075-3 – 1986-0075 – us A.T.L.A. [220]

THE BOOK OF HOSEA / Schmoller, Otto – New York: Charles Scribner, c1874 – 1mf – 9 – 0-8370-6237-3 – 1986-0237 – us A.T.L.A. [220]

BOOK OF HOURS *see* HORAE

A BOOK OF INDIANA / Kin-Hubbard – Biography. Indiana Biographical Asso., 1929. Indiana Reel 3. (The Cox Library Collection) – 5 – us Americana [978]

THE BOOK OF ISAIAH / Smith, George Adam – (Includes bibliographical references & indexes) – New York: A C Armstrong, [1889]-1898 – 4mf – 9 – 0-8370-2370-X – 1985-0370 – us A.T.L.A. [220]

BOOK OF ISAIAH CHRONOLOGICALLY ARRANGED / Cheyne, Thomas Kelly – London: Macmillan, 1870.1 fiche – 9 – us A.T.L.A. [240]

THE BOOK OF JEREMIAH : CHAPTERS 21-52 / Bennett, William Henry – (Suppl: The prophecies of Jeremiah: with a sketch of his life and times by C.J. Ball. Includes index of biblical passages cited and chronological table) – NY: A C Armstrong, 1895 – 1mf – 9 – 0-8370-2267-3 – 1985-0267 – us A.T.L.A. [220]

BOOK OF JEREMIAH: CHAPTERS 21-52 / Bennett, William Henry – New York: A.C. Armstrong, 1895. 1 fiche – 9 – us A.T.L.A. [240]

BOOK OF JOB / Gibson, Edgar CS – London: Methuen, 1899. 1 fiche – 9 – us A.T.L.A. [240]

THE BOOK OF JOB = LIVRE DE JOB / Renan, Ernest – (In English. Includes bibliographical references) – London: W M Thomson, [1889?] – 1mf – 9 – 0-8370-9413-5 – 1986-3413 – us A.T.L.A. [220]

THE BOOK OF JOB : THE TEXT OF THE REVISED VERSION ADAPTED TO MODERN PRINTING, PREPARED IN CONNECTION WITH THE LECTURES OF THE PEOPLE'S INSTITUTE, CHICAGO – Chicago: Fleming H Revell, 1892 – 1mf – 9 – 0-8370-9806-8 – 1986-3806 – us A.T.L.A. [220]

THE BOOK OF JOB / Watson, Robert Alexander – New York: A.C. Armstrong, 1892. 1 fiche – 9 – us A.T.L.A. [240]

THE BOOK OF JOB IN THE REVISED VERSION : EDITED WITH INTRODUCTIONS AND BRIEF ANNOTATIONS / ed by Driver, Samuel Rolles – (Includes index) – Oxford: Clarendon Press, 1906 – 1mf – 9 – 0-8370-2965-1 – 1985-0965 – us A.T.L.A. [220]

THE BOOK OF JOEL / Schmoller, Otto – New York: Charles Scribner, c1874 – 1mf – 9 – 0-8370-6238-1 – 1986-0238 – us A.T.L.A. [220]

THE BOOK OF JONAH / Kleinert, Paul – New York: Charles Scribner, c1874 – 1mf – 9 – 0-8370-6195-4 – 1986-0195 – us A.T.L.A. [220]

THE BOOK OF JONAH : PRECEDED BY A TREATISE ON THE HEBREW AND THE STRANGER / Kalisch, Marcus Moritz – (Includes bibliography and index of authors cited) – London: Longmans, Green, 1878 – 1mf – 9 – 0-8370-3837-5 – 1985-1837 – us A.T.L.A. [220]

BOOK OF JOSHUA / Black, John Sutherland – Cambridge: University Press, 1891. 1 fiche – 9 – us A.T.L.A. [220]

BOOK OF JOSHUA / Fay, F R – New York: Scribner, Armstrong, 1876. 1 fiche – 9 – us A.T.L.A. [240]

THE BOOK OF JOSHUA / Blaikie, William Garden – New York: A C Armstrong, 1893 – 1mf – 9 – 0-8370-2360-2 – 1985-0360 – us A.T.L.A. [220]

THE BOOK OF JOSHUA / Douglas, George Cunningham Monteath – Edinburgh: T&T Clark, 1882 – 1mf – 9 – 0-8370-2954-6 – 1985-0954 – us A.T.L.A. [220]

THE BOOK OF JOSHUA : IN THE REVISED VERSION: WITH INTRODUCTION AND NOTES / Cooke, George Albert – (Includes bibliographical references and index) – Cambridge: University Press; New York: G P Putnam [distributor], 1918 – 1mf – 9 – 0-8370-6729-4 – 1986-0729 – us A.T.L.A. [220]

THE BOOK OF JOSHUA: WITH NOTES, MAPS, AND INTRODUCTION / Maclear, George Frederick – Cambridge: University Press, 1888 – 1mf – 9 – us A.T.L.A. [240]

THE BOOK OF JUBILEES OR THE LITTLE GENESIS / Charles, R H – London, 1902 – 7mf – 8 – ne Slangenburg [220]

BOOK OF JUDGES / Cassel, Paulus – New York: Scribner, Armstrong, 1876. 1 fiche – 9 – us A.T.L.A. [240]

THE BOOK OF JUDGES / Douglas, George Cunningham Monteath – Edinburgh: T&T Clark, 1881 – 1mf – 9 – 0-8370-2955-4 – 1985-0955 – us A.T.L.A. [220]

THE BOOK OF JUDGES : IN THE REVISED VERSION: WITH INTRODUCTION AND NOTES / Cooke, George Albert – (Includes bibliographical references and index) – Cambridge: University Press; New York: G P Putnam [distributor], 1913 – 1mf – 9 – 0-8370-6730-8 – 1986-0730 – us A.T.L.A. [220]

THE BOOK OF JUDGES: WITH MAPS, NOTES, AND INTRODUCTION / Lias, John James – Cambridge: University Press, 1882. 1 fiche – 9 – us A.T.L.A. [240]

THE BOOK OF LEVITICUS / Kellogg, Samuel Henry – New York: A C Armstrong, 1891 – 2mf – 9 – 0-8370-2306-8 – 1985-0306 – us A.T.L.A. [220]

THE BOOK OF LEVITICUS: ENGLISH TRANSLATION / Driver, Samuel Rolles – 1898 – 9 – $10.00 – us I.R.C. [220]

THE BOOK OF MALACHI / Packard, Joseph – New York: Charles Scribner, c1874 – 1mf – 9 – 0-8370-6076-1 – 1986-0076 – us A.T.L.A. [220]

THE BOOK OF MICAH / Kleinert, Paul – New York: Charles Scribner, c1874 – 1mf – 9 – 0-8370-6196-2 – 1986-0196 – us A.T.L.A. [220]

THE BOOK OF MINNESOTANS / Marquis, Albert N – Biographical dictionary of leading living men in Minnesota. Chicago: A.N. Marquis and Co., 1907. Minnesota Reel 2.(The Cox Library Collection) – 5 – us Americana [978]

BOOK OF MISCELLANEOUS RECORDS / Seneca County. Ohio. Bloom Township. Board of Trustees – 1824-1863 – 1r – 1 – $32.50r – us Archival [324]

THE BOOK OF MONOGRAPHS: VOID EXECUTION, JUDICIAL AND PROBATE SALES, ETC – 2d ed. St. Louis, Central Law Journal, 1877. 144, vii, 42, xvi, 105, 52 p. LL-1621 – 1 – us L of C Photodup [340]

THE BOOK OF NAHUM / Kleinert, Paul – (Includes bibliographies) – New York: Charles Scribner, c1874 – 1mf – 9 – 0-8370-6197-0 – 1986-0197 – us A.T.L.A. [220]

THE BOOK OF NATURE OR THE HISTORY OF INSECTS. / Swammerdam, Jan – London: C.G. Seyffert, 1768. 11 fiches.(Science Collection) – 9 – 27.00 – fr Bibl Nationale [590]

THE BOOK OF NOBLESSE: ADDRESSED TO KING EDWARD THE FOURTH ON HIS INVASION OF FRANCE IN 1475 / ed by Nichols, J G – H-1328 2. 1852 – 8 – ne IDC [941]

BOOK OF NUMBERS / Watson, Robert Alexander – New York: A.C. Armstrong, 1894. 1 fiche – 9 – us A.T.L.A. [240]

THE BOOK OF NUMBERS : IN THE REVISED VERSION: WITH INTRODUCTION AND NOTES / McNeile, Alan Hugh – (Includes bibliographical references and index) – Cambridge: University Press; New York: G P Putnam [distributor], 1911 – 1mf – 9 – 0-8370-6759-6 – 1986-0759 – us A.T.L.A. [220]

THE BOOK OF OBADIAH / Kleinert, Paul – New York: Charles Scribner, c1874 – 1mf – 9 – 0-8370-6198-9 – 1986-0198 – us A.T.L.A. [220]

THE BOOK OF PEACE: ... – Boston, 1845 – 6mf – 9 – ILM-708/1 – ne IDC [327]

A BOOK OF PRAYER / Levy, Joseph Leonard – Pittsburgh: Publicity Press, 1902. 1 fiche – 9 – us A.T.L.A. [210]

THE BOOK OF PROVERBS / Horton, Robert Forman – New York: A C Armstrong, 1891 – 1mf – 9 – 0-8370-3665-8 – 1985-1665 – us A.T.L.A. [220]

THE BOOK OF PROVERBS : IN AN AMENDED VERSION / Muenscher, Joseph – (With introduction & explanatory notes) – Gambier, OH: Western Episcopalian Off, 1866 – 1mf – 9 – 0-8370-4534-7 – 1985-2534 – us A.T.L.A. [220]

THE BOOK OF PSALMS / Kirkpatrick, Alexander F – Cambridge: University Press, 1891. cxii,556p. 2 fiches – 9 – us A.T.L.A. [240]

THE BOOK OF PSALMS / Perowne, J J Stewart – 8th ed. 1892 – 9 – $39.00 – us I.R.C. [220]

THE BOOK OF PSALMS : TRANSLATED FROM A REVISED TEXT WITH NOTES AND INTRODUCTION / Cheyne, Thomas Kelly – (Includes bibliographical reference and index) – London: Kegan Paul, Trench, Truebner, 1904 – 2mf – 9 – 0-8370-6035-4 – 1986-0035 – us A.T.L.A. [220]

BOOK OF PSALMS: WITH INTRODUCTION AND NOTES / Cobb, William Frederick – London: Methuen, 1905.1 fiche – 9 – us A.T.L.A. [220]

BOOK OF REFERENCE OF THE CITY OF QUEBEC AND VILLAGE OF SAINT SAUVEUR: ACCOMPANYING THE CADASTRAL PLAN / Cousin, Paul – Quebec: P. Cousin, 1875. 00257. (Pre-1900 Canadiana) – 9 – cn C.I.H.M. [971]

BOOK OF REFERENCE OF THE CITY OF QUEBEC AND VILLAGE OF SAINT SAUVEUR: ACCOMPANYING THE CADASTRAL PLAN – Quebec: Paul Cousin, 1875. 02829. (Pre-1900 Canadiana) – 9 – cn C.I.H.M. [971]

THE BOOK OF REMARKABLE TRIALS AND NOTORIOUS CHARACTERS / ed by Benson, L – From "Half-Hanged Smith," 1700, to Oxford Who Shot at the Queen, 1840.... Illus. by Phiz (pseud). London: J.C. Hotten (1871). iv, (9)/545p. With: The Germans by I.A.R. Wylie. 1 reel. 1260 – 1 – us U.W. Library [360]

BOOK OF REMEMBERANCES OF MARION COUNTY PIONEERS / Steeves, Sarah H – Portland: Berncliff Press, 1927.Oregon reel 7.(Cox Library Collection) – 5 – us Americana [978]

BOOK OF REVELATION / Milligan, William – New York: A.C. Armstrong, (1889). 1 fiche – 9 – us A.T.L.A. [240]

THE BOOK OF REVELATION : AN EXPOSITION / Warren, Israel Perkins – New York: Funk & Wagnalls, 1886 – 1mf – 9 – 0-8370-5715-9 – 1985-3715 – us A.T.L.A. [220]

THE BOOK OF REVELATION – London: Samuel Bagster, 1849 – 1mf – 9 – 0-8370-9751-7 – 1986-3751 – us A.T.L.A. [220]

THE BOOK OF REVELATION / Milligan, William – New York:A C Armstrong, [1889] – 1mf – 9 – 0-8370-4439-1 – 1985-2439 – us A.T.L.A. [220]

THE BOOK OF REVELATION: AN EXPOSITION: BASED ON...PROF. STUART'S COMMENTARY / Warren, Israel Perkins – New York: Funk & Wagnalls, 1886.1 fiche – 9 – us A.T.L.A. [240]

BOOK OF REVELATION, OR, THE LAST VOLUME OF PROPHECY / Murphy, James Gracey – London: James Nisbet, 1882. 1 fiche – 9 – us A.T.L.A. [240]

THE BOOK OF REVELATION: STUDY AND TRANSLATION OF THE SYMBOLS / Moore, Theophilus Wilson – Chicago: Fleming H. Revell, 1897. 1 fiche – 9 – us A.T.L.A. [240]

BOOK OF RUTH / Cassel, Paulus – New York: Scribner, Armstrong, 1876. 1 fiche – 9 – us A.T.L.A. [240]

THE BOOK OF RUTH : IN THE REVISED VERSION: WITH INTRODUCTION AND NOTES / Cooke, George Albert – (Includes bibliographical references and index) – Cambridge: University Press; New York: G P Putnam [distributor], 1913 – 1mf – 9 – 0-8370-6731-6 – 1986-0731 – us A.T.L.A. [220]

BOOK OF RUTH: A POPULAR EXPOSITION / Cox, Samuel – London: Religious Tract Soc., (187?). 1 fiche – 9 – us A.T.L.A. [240]

THE BOOK OF SAINT BASIL THE GREAT, BISHOP OF CAESAREA IN CAPPADOCIA, ON THE HOLY SPIRIT : WRITTEN TO AMPHILOCHIUS, BISHOP OF INCONIUM, AGAINST THE PNEUMATOMACHI: A REVISED TEXT / Basil the Great, Saint – Oxford: Clarendon, 1892 – 1mf – us A.T.L.A. [240]

THE BOOK OF SNOBS / Thackeray, William Makepeace – London: Punch Office, 1848 – 1 roll – 1 – 1-55879-728-9 – uk Libr Preservation [880]

THE BOOK OF THE BEE / ed by Budge, Ernest A Wallis – Oxford v1-pt 2 1886 – 12mf – 8 – ne Slangenburg [220]

THE BOOK OF THE BEGINNINGS : A STUDY OF GENESIS / Newton, Richard Heber – (Includes bibliographical references) – New York: G P Putnam, 1884 – 1mf – 9 – 0-8370-4580-0 – 1985-2580 – us A.T.L.A. [220]

THE BOOK OF THE BEGINNINGS; A STUDY OF GENESIS WITH AN INTRODUCTION TO THE PENTATEUCH / Newton, Richard Heber – New York, London: G.P. Putnam's sons, 1884. xv,311p. illus – 1 – us U.W. Library [240]

THE BOOK OF THE DEAD. FACSIMILES OF THE PAPYRI OF HUNEFER, ANHAI, KERASHER AND NETCHEMET, WITH SUPPLEMENTARY TEXT FROM THE PAPYRUS OF NU / Budge, E A W – London. 1899. BNE-20,015 1 – 9 – ne IDC [290]

THE BOOK OF THE GANDA CLANS / Kagwa, Apolo – (Transl of: Ekitabo kye bika bya Baganda) – [196-] – 1 – us Res Libr [960]

THE BOOK OF THE IRIS / Lynch, R I – London, 1904. 214 pp. B-736 2 – 8 – ne IDC [580]

A BOOK OF THE LAWS OF WASHINGTON RELATING TO NOTARIES PUBLIC / Skinner, Joseph Osmun – San Francisco: Bancroft Whitney, 1911. 365p. LL-1344 – 1 – us L of C Photodup [340]

THE BOOK OF THE MAINYO-I-KHARD, ALSO ON OLD FRAGMENT OF THE BUNDEHESH, BOTH IN THE ORIGINAL PAHLAVI BEING A FASCIMILE OF A MANUSCRIPT... / ed by Andreas, F C – Kiel, 1882 – 1mf – NE-20160/1 – ne IDC [490]

THE BOOK OF THE PROPHET EZEKIEL / Henderson, Ebenezer – Andover: Warren F Draper, 1870 – 1mf – 9 – 0-8370-3559-7 – 1985-1559 – us A.T.L.A. [220]

THE BOOK OF THE PROPHET EZEKIEL : WITH INTRODUCTION AND NOTES / Redpath, Henry Adeney – (Includes index) – London: Methuen, 1907 – 1mf – 9 – 0-8370-7418-5 – 1986-1418 – us A.T.L.A. [220]

THE BOOK OF THE PROPHET EZEKIEL: IN THE REVISED VERSION / Davidson, Andrew Bruce – Cambridge: University Press, 1916. lxii,403p. 2 fiches – 9 – us A.T.L.A. [240]

THE BOOK OF THE PROPHET ISAIAH, CHAPTERS 1-39 : WITH INTRODUCTION AND NOTES / Skinner, John – (Includes bibliography and index) – Stereotyped ed. Cambridge:University Press, 1896 – 1mf – 9 – 0-8370-2518-4 – 1985-0518 – us A.T.L.A. [220]

THE BOOK OF THE PROPHET ISAIAH, CHAPTERS 40-66 : IN THE REVISED VERSION / Skinner, John – (Includes index) – Cambridge:University Press, 1917 – 1mf – 9 – 0-8370-2593-1 – 1985-0593 – us A.T.L.A. [220]

BOOK OF THE PROPHET JEREMIAH / Brown, Charles Rufus – Philadelphia: Amer. Bap. Pub., 1907. 1 fiche – 9 – us A.T.L.A. [240]

THE BOOK OF THE PROPHET JEREMIAH : CRITICAL EDITION OF THE HEBREW TEXT – (Includes indexes) – Leipzig: J C Hinrichs; Baltimore: Johns Hopkins Press, 1895 – 1mf – 9 – 0-8370-9215-9 – 1986-3215 – us A.T.L.A. [220]

THE BOOK OF THE PROPHET JEREMIAH : A REVISED TRANSLATION WITH INTRODUCTIONS AND SHORT EXPLANATIONS / Driver, Samuel Rolles – (Includes bibliographical references and index) – London: Hodder & Stoughton, 1906 – 1mf – 9 – 0-8370-2966-X – 1985-0966 – us A.T.L.A. [220]

THE BOOK OF THE PROPHET JEREMIAH AND THAT OF THE LAMENTATIONS : TRANSLATED FROM THE ORIGINAL HEBREW: WITH A COMMENTARY, CRITICAL, PHILOLOGICAL, AND EXEGETICAL / Henderson, Ebenezer – Andover: Warren F Draper, 1868 – 1mf – 9 – 0-8370-4709-9 – 1985-2709 – us A.T.L.A. [220]

BOOK OF THE STATES – Chicago. v1-19. 1935-73 – 169mf – 9 – $5.00f – us Ross [336]

BOOK OF THE STATES – (With suppl) – v1-30. 1935-95 – 9 – $695.00 set – us Hein [340]

THE BOOK OF THE TWELVE PROPHETS : COMMONLY CALLED THE MINOR / Smith, George Adam – (Includes chronological tables, bibliographical references & indexes) – New York: A C Armstrong, 1896 – 2mf – 9 – 0-8370-2371-8 – 1985-0371 – us A.T.L.A. [220]

THE BOOK OF THE TWELVE PROPHETS / Smith, George Adam – Armstrong. 1903 – 9 – $33.00 – us I.R.C. [220]

BOOK OF THE VICTORIAN ERA BALL: GIVEN AT TORONTO ON THE TWENTY EIGHTH OF DECEMBER MDCCCXCVII – Toronto: Rowsell & Hutchison, 1898. 02845. (Pre-1900 Canadiana) – 9 – cn C.I.H.M. [360]

THE BOOK OF THEL (COPY G) AND THE VISIONS OF THE DAUGHTERS OF ALBION (COPY P) / Blake, William – 14 – uk Microform Academic [810]

A BOOK OF VERSES / Henley, William Ernest – London: David Nutt, 1888 – 1 roll – 1 – 1-55879-588-X – uk Libr Preservation [810]

THE BOOK OF VIRGINS AND LAYS AND LEGENDS OF THE CHURCH AND THE WORLD / Ross, William Stewart – London: W. Stewart & Co., 189-?. 224p – 1 – us U.W. Library [240]

A BOOK OF WINES / Turner, William – 1568 – 9 – 15.00 – us Scholars' Facs [640]

BOOK OF WORSHIP / Evangelical Lutheran Church in the United States of America. General Synod. Liturgy and ritual – 1881 – 1 – us A.T.L.A. [240]

THE BOOK OF ZECHARIAH / Chambers, Talbot Wilson – New York: Charles Scribner, c1874 – 1mf – 9 – 0-8370-6033-8 – 1986-0033 – us A.T.L.A. [220]

THE BOOK OF ZEPHANIAH / Kleinert, Paul – New York: Charles Scribner, c1874 – 1mf – 9 – 0-8370-6199-7 – 1986-0199 – us A.T.L.A. [220]

A BOOK ON BAPTISM / Pitts, F E – 1835 – 1 – $50.00 – us Presbyterian [240]

BOOK ON THE PHYSICIAN HIMSELF : AND THINGS THAT CONCERN HIS REPUTATION AND SUCCESS / Cathell, D W – 10th rev enl ed. Philadelphia: F A Davis Co, 1895, c1892 – us Res Libr [610]

BOOK PLATES IN THE BRITISH MUSEUM / British Museum. London – (Over 25,000 family crests and heraldic documentation, British and European) – 10r – 1 – $795.00 – 0-907006-88-4 – uk Mindata [760]

BOOK PRODUCTION INDUSTRY – (1971-77. 5,6. 1976-77. 9) – 1-53. 1925-77 – 1 – us UMI [070]

BOOK PROMOTION, SALES AND DISTRIBUTION : A MANAGEMENT TRAINING COURSE / Book House Training CentreUNESCO – 1991 – x/166p – 9 – 92-3-102730-1 – Co-published with Book House Training Centre – fr UNESCO [650]

BOOK PROSPECTUS / Bodleian Library – 17th and 18th centuries – 9 – us UMI [020]

BOOK RESEARCH QUARTERLY – v1-. 1984- – 1,5,6,9 – us UMI [073]

BOOK SALES CATALOGUES OF THE DUTCH REPUBLIC, 1599-1800 / ed by Gruys, J A – (This collection includes a printed guide) – 1993 – 2,536mf – 9 (subsc Dfl2,000 per installment) – ne IDC [020]

BOOK SELLER – White Plains, NY. no3811-3862 – 4r – 1 – $200.00 – R04153 – us Library Micro [071]

BOOK TODAY IN AFRICA / Kotei, S I A – 1981 – 210p – 9 – 92-3-101876-0 – fr UNESCO [070]

THE BOOK TRADE IN LIVERPOOL FROM 1806 TO 1850 : A DIRECTORY / Liverpool Bibliographical Society. University of Liverpool – (Text of directory on fiches 1-5. Maps and illustrations on fiches 5-6. 13 appendices with annals, statistics, charts, tables, names of printers, maps and illustrations, etc) – 1987. xxiv/403p – 11 – £8.00 UK £9.00 surface £10.50 airmail elsewhere – uk Liverpool Bib [070]

BOOK WEEK – New York, NY. 1963-67 – 4r – 1 – $200.00 – R04904 – us Library Micro [071]

BOOK WORLD – London, UK. 1 Aug 1890-4 Sept 1892; 1893; March 1894-Apr 1899. -irr. 1 reel – 1 – uk British Libr Newspaper [072]

BOOKBIRD – (1976- . 5,6,9) – v. 1- 1962- – 1 – us UMI [830]

A BOOKE CALLED THE FOUNDACION OF REHTORIKE / Rainolde, Richard – 1563. 135p. (English Linguistics Series 1500-1800) – 9 – us UMI [400]

Booker, Alfred *see* CATALOGUE DE RARETES BIBLIOGRAPHIQUES CANADIENNES: COMPRENANT 200 OUVRAGES

Booker, M *see* TWO LETTERS CONCERNING THE METHODISTS, ONE TO THE RT. REV. THE LORD B—P OF M—H, THE OTHER TO HIS LORDSHIP'S V—R G—L

BOOKER T. WASHINGTON – 1 – us Ross [920]

BOOKER T. WASHINGTON PAPERS – (With guide) – 388r – 1 – $13,580.00 – Dist. us Scholarly Res – us L of C Photodup [370]

BOOKFELLOW – Sydney, 1899-1925 – 2r – 1 – A$35.00 silver A$56.00 vesicular – at Pascoe [072]

BOOK-KEEPING BY DOUBLE AND SINGLE ENTRY: WITH AN APPENDIX ON PRECIS WRITING AND INDEXING: DESIGNED FOR SELF-INSTRUCTION AND FOR USE IN SCHOOLS AND COLLEGES. – Kingston: Dominion Business College, 1887. 02732. (Pre-1900 Canadiana) – 9 – cn C.I.H.M. [336]

BOOKLIST – (1968- . 5,6. 1975- . 9) – 1-1905- – 1 – us UMI [010]

BOOKMAN, A REVIEW OF BOOKS AND LIFE – v. 1-76. 1895-1933 – 1 – us UMI [800]

BOOKMAN: A REVIEW OF BOOKS AND LIFE – v. 1-76. 1895-1933 – 1,5,6 – us Princeton Micro [070]

BOOKMARK – Vancouver. v30- 1988/89- – 9 – Can$28.00y – 0381-6028 – cn Micromedia [370]

BOOKS 1-10 / Livy – c1470. Holkham ms. 347.Holkham Hall, Norfolk, England – 1 – uk Microform Academic [760]

BOOKS 1-10 / Livy – Late 15th cent. Holkham ms. 346. Holkham Hall, Norfolk, England – 1 – uk Microform Academic [760]

BOOKS 1-10 / Livy – With introd., historical examination, and notes by J.R. Seeley. Book I. Oxford, 1871. 6+198p. (Clarendon Press Series). 1 reel.1294 – 1 – us U.W. Library [930]

BOOKS 1-10 AND 21-22 / Livy – 15th cent. Holkham ms. 345. Holkham Hall, Norfolk, England – 1 – uk Microform Academic [760]

BOOKS 1-10 AND 21-32: ILLUMINATIONS / Livy – 14th cent. Holkham ms. 344. Holkham Hall, Norfolk, England – 14 – uk Microform Academic [760]

BOOKS 21-30 / Livy – 15th cent. Italian. Holkham mss. 351, 352. Holkham Hall, Norfolk, England – 1 – uk Microform Academic [760]

BOOKS 21-30 / Livy – Late 15th cent. Holkham ms. 350. Holkham Hall, Norfolk, England – 1 – uk Microform Academic [760]

BOOKS 31-40 / Livy – 15th cent. Italian. Holkham ms. 355. Holkham Hall, Norfolk, England – 1 – uk Microform Academic [760]

BOOKS 31-40, ETC / Livy – 14th cent. Italian. Holkham mss. 354, 364. Holkham Hall, Norfolk, England – 1 – uk Microform Academic [760]

BOOKS ABROAD – (1969-76. 5,6) – v1-50. 1927-76.Continued by: World Literature Today – 1 – us UMI [010]

BOOKS AND NOTIONS – (Contd by: Canada Bookseller and Stationer (ID 06028)) – Toronto: Bookseller's and Stationers' Association of Ontario, 1884-1895 – 9 – cn C.I.H.M. [020]

BOOKS AND NOTIONS *see* CANADA BOOKSELLER AND STATIONER

BOOKS AND NOTIONS; ORGAN OF THE BOOK, STATIONERY, AND FANCY GOODS TRADES OF CANADA – 1884-95 – 1 – 65.00 – cn McLaren [070]

BOOKS AND PAMPHLETS BY OR ABOUT JOHN LELAND / Leland, John – 1754-1841 – 1 – 63.73 – us Baptist [240]

BOOKS AT BOSTON SPA – (Annual) – 9 – £167.00 + VAT E.U. £173.00 overseas – uk British Libr Docs [020]

BOOKS AT BOSTON SPA / British Library. Document Supply Centre – Record of all English-language monographs published 1980 or later and held at Document Supply Centre – 9 – £167.00 in UK £173.00 overseas – uk British Libr Humanities [010]

BOOKS CONCERNING MUSIC PRINTED BEFORE 1800 / U.S. Library of Congress. Music Division – 1 – 5060.00 – us L of C Photodup [780]

BOOKS FOR AFRICA – (Lacks vol.5) – v1-33. 1931-63 – 2r – 1 – us A.T.L.A. [240]

BOOKS FOR LIBERTARIANS – 1972-74.Continued as: Libertarian Review – 1 – us UMI [073]

BOOKS IN CANADA – Toronto. v1- 1971- – 9 – Price varies with yr – cn Micromedia [070]

BOOKS IN CANADA; THE INDEPENDENT BOOK REVIEW MAGAZINE – v1-6, 1971-77. Includes printed index – 9 – 40.00y – cn McLaren [070]

BOOKS IN ENGLISH / British Library. National Bibliographic Service – (1971-80 cumulation. £499.00 + VAT, £550.00 overseas; 1981-85 cumulation. £325.00 + VAT, £350.00 overseas) – 1992-. Bi-monthly progressive cumulations of English-language titles – 17 – £425.00y + VAT, £549.00y overseas – uk British Libr [010]

BOOKS IN PRINT ON MICROFICHE – (Provides easy access to all US in-print and forthcoming books) – Updated mthly and quarterly – 9 – Mthly update $2,180.00 Quarterly $1,260.00 Annual $$185.00 – us Bowker [010]

BOOKS IN REVIEW – 1977- – 1,5,6,9 – us UMI [070]

BOOKS LISTED IN AALS LAW BOOKS RECOMMENDED FOR LIBRARIES : ADMIRALTY – 39v – 9 – $550.00 – us Hein [340]

BOOKS LISTED IN AALS LAW BOOKS RECOMMENDED FOR LIBRARIES : BIOGRAPHY – 321v – 9 – $3,825.00 – us Hein [340]

BOOKS LISTED IN AALS LAW BOOKS RECOMMENDED FOR LIBRARIES : CONFLICTS – 51v – 9 – $765.00 – us Hein [340]

BOOKS LISTED IN AALS LAW BOOKS RECOMMENDED FOR LIBRARIES : CONSTITUTIONAL LAW – 111v – 9 – $875.00 – us Hein [340]

BOOKS LISTED IN AALS LAW BOOKS RECOMMENDED FOR LIBRARIES : CONTRACTS – 132v – 9 – $895.00 – us Hein [340]

BOOKS LISTED IN AALS LAW BOOKS RECOMMENDED FOR LIBRARIES : CRIMINAL LAW AND PROCEDURE – 88v – 9 – $695.00 – us Hein [340]

BOOKS LISTED IN AALS LAW BOOKS RECOMMENDED FOR LIBRARIES : EVIDENCE – 37v – 9 – $495.00 – us Hein [340]

BOOKS LISTED IN AALS LAW BOOKS RECOMMENDED FOR LIBRARIES : INTELLECTUAL AND INDUSTRIAL PROPERTY – 80v – 9 – $925.00 – us Hein [340]

BOOKS LISTED IN AALS LAW BOOKS RECOMMENDED FOR LIBRARIES : JUDICIAL ADMINISTRATION (PART 1 MONOGRAPHS) – 263v – 9 – $775.00 – us Hein [340]

BOOKS LISTED IN AALS LAW BOOKS RECOMMENDED FOR LIBRARIES : JUDICIAL ADMINISTRATION, PART 2 (SERIALS) – (With 1990 Supplement) – 1327v – 9 – $4,235.00 – us Hein [340]

BOOKS LISTED IN AALS LAW BOOKS RECOMMENDED FOR LIBRARIES : JURISPRUDENCE – 71v – 9 – $750.00 – us Hein [340]

BOOKS LISTED IN AALS LAW BOOKS RECOMMENDED FOR LIBRARIES : LABOR LAW – 107v – 9 – $995.00 – us Hein [340]

BOOKS LISTED IN AALS LAW BOOKS RECOMMENDED FOR LIBRARIES : LEGAL HISTORY – 318v – 9 – $4,200.00 – us Hein [340]

BOOKS LISTED IN AALS LAW BOOKS RECOMMENDED FOR LIBRARIES : MEDICAL JURISPRUDENCE – 108v – 9 – $1,450.00 – us Hein [340]

BOOKS LISTED IN AALS LAW BOOKS RECOMMENDED FOR LIBRARIES : PROPERTY – 294v – 9 – $3,320.00 – us Hein [340]

BOOKS LISTED IN AALS LAW BOOKS RECOMMENDED FOR LIBRARIES : ROMAN LAW – 34v – 9 – $495.00 – us Hein [340]

BOOKS LISTED IN AALS LAW BOOKS RECOMMENDED FOR LIBRARIES : TORTS – 93v – 9 – $985.00 – us Hein [340]

BOOKS LISTED IN AALS LAW BOOKS RECOMMENDED FOR LIBRARIES : TRUST AND ESTATES – 42v – 9 – $950.00 – us Hein [340]

THE BOOKS OF CHRONICLES / Bennett, William Henry – (Includes bibliographical references and index) – New York: A C Armstrong, 1894 – 2mf – 9 – 0-8370-2340-8 – 1985-0340 – us A.T.L.A. [220]

BOOKS OF CHRONICLES: MAPS, NOTES, INTRODUCTION / Barnes, William Emery – Cambridge: University Press, 1899. 1 fiche – 9 – us A.T.L.A. [220]

BOOKS OF ENROLLED CERTIFICATES OF NATURALIZATION, ISSUED 1848-1858, ENROLLED 1850-1888, 1850-1889 / General Registry Office – 2r – 1 – CRS A729 – at Archives [920]

THE BOOKS OF JOEL AND AMOS : WITH AN INTRODUCTION AND NOTES / Driver, Samuel Rolles – (Includes bibliographical references and indexes) – Cambridge: University Press, 1897 – 1mf – 9 – 0-8370-6110-5 – 1986-0110 – us A.T.L.A. [220]

THE BOOKS OF NAHUM, HABAKKUK AND ZEPHANIAH : WITH INTRODUCTION AND NOTES / Davidson, Andrew Bruce – (Includes bibliographical references and index) – Cambridge: University Press; New York: Macmillan [distributor], 1896 – 1mf – 9 – 0-8370-6733-2 – 1986-0733 – us A.T.L.A. [220]

THE BOOKS OF NAHUM, HABAKKUK AND ZEPHANIAH : WITH INTRODUCTION AND NOTES / Davidson, Andrew Bruce – (Includes index) – rev ed. Cambridge: University Press, 1920 – 1mf – 9 – 0-8370-3707-7 – 1985-1707 – us A.T.L.A. [220]

BOOKS OF SERMONS / Winkler, E T – 1851-79. 528p – 1 – 18.48 – us Baptist [240]

THE BOOKS OF THE CHRONICLES / Zoeckler, Otto – New York: Scribner, Armstrong, 1876. 1 fiche – 9 – us A.T.L.A. [240]

BOOKS OF THE FAIRS – A Collection of World's Fair publications Drawn from the holdings of the Smithsonian Institution Libraries – 1 – us Primary [900]

BOOKS OF THE KINGS...HARMONY OF THE BOOKS OF SAMUEL, KINGS, AND CHRONICLES / Crockett, William D – New York: Eaton & Mains, 1897. 1 fiche – 9 – us A.T.L.A. [220]

BOOKS ON MUSIC AND SOUND RECORDINGS / U.S. Library of Congress. Music Division – (1997 current subscription) – Quinquennia: 1953-57; 1958-62; 1963-67; 1968-72; 1973-77. Triennium: 1978-80. 1981-90 Cumulation. 1991; 1992; 1993; 1994; 1995; 1996 Registers – 9 – us Advanced Libr [780]

BOOKS, PAMPHLETS AND SERIALS / Oneida Community – 1834-1972. 15 reels – 1 – us UMI [240]

BOOKS, PAMPHLETS; ESSAYS AND ARTICLES / Research Centre for Monetary and Financial Freedom – Over 60 titles – 9 – 1.00f – at Libertarian Micro [320]

BOOKS PRINTED IN THE LOW COUNTRIES BEFORE 1601 – 1967- – 524r – 1 – $32,750.00 $1,200.00y – us OmniSys [010]

THE BOOKSELLER – (1976- . 5,6,9) – 1864- – 1 – us UMI [070]

BOOKSELLER AND STATIONER – (Cont: Canada Bookseller and Stationer. Contd by: Bookseller and Stationer and Canadian Newsdealer) – Toronto: MacLean, 1897-1907 – 9 – cn C.I.H.M. [020]

BOOKSELLER AND STATIONER *see*
– BOOKSELLER AND STATIONER AND CANADIAN NEWSDEALER
– CANADA BOOKSELLER AND STATIONER

BOOKSELLER AND STATIONER AND CANADIAN NEWSDEALER – (Cont: Bookseller and Stationer. Contd by: Bookseller and Stationer and Office Equipment Journal) – Montreal: MacLean, [1908-1910] – 9 – cn C.I.H.M. [020]

BOOKSELLER AND STATIONER AND CANADIAN NEWSDEALER *see* BOOKSELLER AND STATIONER

BOOKSELLER AND STATIONER AND OFFICE EQUIPMENT JOURNAL – Toronto, Canada. Mar 1913-Sep 1916.-w. 3mqn reels – 1 – uk British Libr Newspaper [073]

BOOKSELLER AND STATIONER AND OFFICE EQUIPMENT JOURNAL *see* BOOKSELLER AND STATIONER AND CANADIAN NEWSDEALER

THE BOOKSELLER, NEWSDEALER AND STATIONER – New York: Excelsior Publ House, [1894- (v6-7 (mar 1897-feb 1898) – us Res Libr [070]

BOOKSELLER'S RECORD – London, UK. 19 Nov-31 Dec 1859.-w. 9 feet – 1 – uk British Libr Newspaper [072]

BOOKSELLERS REVIEW – London, UK. 11 Mar 1897-27 Jan 1898. -w. 1 reel – 1 – uk British Libr Newspaper [072]

Bool, Henry *see* FOR LIBERTY (LIBERTY LUMINANTS)

Boole, Mary Everest *see* THE MATHEMATICAL PSYCHOLOGY OF GRATRY AND BOOLE TRANSLATED FROM THE LANGUAGE OF THE HIGHER CALCULUS INTO THAT OF ELEMENTARY GEOMETRY

Boon, A *see* PACHOMIANA LATINA

Boon, Albertus Goswinus *see* DISSERTATIO HISTORICO-CRITICA DE DOGMATICES CHRISTIANAE FONTIBUS EORUMQUE USU PUBLICO OMNIUM EXAMINI OFFERT ALBERTUS GOSWINUS BOON

Boon, Martin James *see* THE IMMORTAL HISTORY OF SOUTH AFRICA

Boone, Charles Theodore *see* LAW OF REAL PROPERTY.

BOONE COMPANION – Albion, NE. -w. Oct. 1958-May 1963 – 1 – us NE Hist [071]

BOONE COUNTY BLADE – Albion, NE. -w. Dec. 1896-Mar. 1898. Incomplete – 1 – us NE Hist [071]

BOONE COUNTY DEMOCRAT – Boone. Iowa. 1868-1914 – 1 – us UMI [071]

BOONE COUNTY, MISSOURI DIRECTORY 1921 / Smith, Clinton – Moberly, n.d. Missouri Reel 9. (The Cox Library Collection) – 5 – us Americana [978]

BOONE COUNTY PIONEER – Boone, IA. 1921-23 – 1 – us UMI [071]

BOONE COUNTY REPUBLICAN – Boone. Iowa. 1874-1897 – 1 – us UMI [071]

BOONE ENTERPRISE – Boone, NE. -w. Mar. 1908-Dec. 1910; Dec. 1911-Jun. 1912 – 1 – us NE Hist [071]

Boone, Ilsley *see* ELEMENTS IN BAPTIST DEVELOPMENT

Boone Library School *see* WEN-HUA T'U-SHU-KUAN CHUAN-K'O-HSUEH-HSIAO CHI-K'AN

BOONE STANDARD – Boone. Iowa. 1877-1901 – 1 – us UMI [071]

Boone, William J, Bp *see* A VINDICATION OF COMMENTS ON THE TRANSLATION OF EPHESIANS I IN THE DELEGATES' VERSION OF THE NEW TESTAMENT

BOONE'S CREEK BAPTIST CHURCH (FORMERLY: BOGGS FORK BAPTIST CHURCH). LEXINGTON, KENTUCKY : CHURCH RECORDS – 1795-1900. 730p – 1 – 32.85 – us Baptist [240]

BOONE'S CREEK BAPTIST CHURCH. PICKENS COUNTY. SALEM, SOUTH CAROLINA : CHURCH RECORDS – 1912-1977 – 1 – 9.72 – us Baptist [240]

BOONESBORO BOONE COUNTY ADVOCATE – Boone. Iowa. -w. 1866-1874 – 1 – us UMI [071]

BOONESBORO DEMOCRAT – Boone. Iowa. 1857-1866 – 1 – us UMI [071]

BOONESBORO INDEX – Boone. Iowa. 1865-1867 – 1 – us UMI [071]

BOONESBORO NEWS – Boone, IA. -w. 1875-76 – 1 – us UMI [071]

BOONESBORO NEWS – Boone. Iowa. 1876-1878 – 1 – us UMI [071]

Boor, C de *see*
- CHRONOGRAPHIA
- NEUE FRAGMENTE DES PAPIAS, HEGESIPPUS UND PIERIUS (T.U.U. 1-5/2B)

Boorde, A *see*
- THE BREVIARY OF HELTHE...
- A COMPENDIOUS REGYMENT OR A DYETARY

BOORT STANDARD – 1926-1951 – 9r – 1 – at Corangamite [072]

BOOSTER – Bloom. Kan. 1916-20 – 1 – us UMI [071]

BOOSTER – Bovard, NV. Jan 1908 – 1r – 1 – $50.00 – U04426 – us Library Micro [071]

BOOSTER – Dorris, CA. 1908-11 – 1r – 1 – $50.00 – B02173 – us Library Micro [071]

THE BOOSTER – Purvis. Miss. 1915-1923; 1948-1951 – 1 – us UMI [071]

Booth, Abraham *see* THE REIGN OF GRACE: FROM ITS RISE TO ITS CONSUMMATION

Booth, Catherine Mumford *see*
- PAPERS ON GODLINESS: BEING REPORTS OF A SERIES OF ADDRESSES DELIVERED AT JAMES'S HALL, LONDON, W., DURING 1881
- THE SALVATION ARMY IN RELATION TO THE CHURCH AND STATE

Booth, Meyrick *see* COLLECTED ESSAYS OF RUDOLF EUCKEN

Booth, Tucker *see* THE LIFE OF CATHERINE BOOTH

Booth, W B *see* ILLUSTRATIONS AND DESCRIPTIONS OF THE PLANTS WHICH COMPOSE THE NATURAL ORDER CAMELLIAE

Booth, Walter Sherman *see*
- THE CONVEYANCER'S AND NOTARY'S MANUAL...IN THE STATE OF MINNESOTA
- THE CONVEYANCER'S AND NOTARY'S MANUAL...IN THE STATE OF SOUTH DAKOTA

Booth, William *see*
- THE GENERAL'S LETTERS, 1885
- IN DARKEST ENGLAND AND THE WAY OUT

Boothe, Charles Octavius *see* THE CYCLOPEDIA OF THE COLORED BAPTISTS OF ALABAMA

BOOTLE GAZETTE – Lancashire. 1887-88 – 1 – uk Microform Academic [072]

BOOTLE TIMES – England. -w. 12 Feb 1878-11 Jun 1887. (5 reels) – 1 – uk British Libr Newspaper [072]

BOOTS AND CHUTES – Sparks, NV. 1954-55 – 1r – 1 – $50.00 – U04743 – us Library Micro [071]

Boott, F *see* ILLUSTRATIONS OF THE GENUS CAREX

Booy, J T de *see*
- LES ANNEES DE FORMATION DE F. H. JACOBI, D'APRES SES LETTRES INEDITES A M. M. REY (1763-1771) AVEC "LE NOBLE" DE MME. DE CHARRIERE
- JACQUES LE FATALISTE ET LA RELIGIEUSE

Boradaevskii, S V *see* KOOPERATSIIA SREDI SLAVIAN

BORAS NYA TIDNING *see* BORAS TIDNING

BORAS NYHETER – Boras, Sweden. 1990-1992 – 1 – sw Kungliga [072]

BORAS TIDNING – (Boras Nya Tidning. 1834-35, 1837-38; Boras Tidning, 1838-1978) – Boras, Sweden – 578r – 1 – sw Kungliga [072]

BORAS TIDNING – Boras, Sweden. 1979- – 1 – sw Kungliga [072]

BORAS WECKOBLAD – Boras, Sweden. 1826-29, 1831-33 – 2r – 1 – sw Kungliga [072]

BORAX MINER – Columbus, NV. Oct 1873; 1875-77 – 2r – 1 – $100.00 – U04481 – us Library Micro [071]

BORBA – Belgrade, Yugoslavia. Jan-Jun 1955 – 2r – 1 – us L of C Photodup [072]

BORBA – Beograd, 1976-1993ff – 77r – 1 – DM5,775.00 – gw Mikro Press [949]

BORBA : ORGAN KOMUNISTICKE PARTIJE JUGOSLAVIJE – Belgrade: [s.n, nov 15 1944-75] – 1 – us Res Libr [949]

BORBA – Turnovo, Bulgaria. 1951-Dec 1986 – 32r – 1 – us L of C Photodup [072]

BORBA – Zagreb, Yugoslavia. Jul 1949-1953; Aug-Dec 1956 – 9r – 1 – us L of C Photodup [072]

BORBA *see* NASHA BORBA

BORBA : ORGAN SOCIJALISTICKI SAVEZA RADNOG NARODA JUGOSLAVIJE – Zagreb: "Borba", jan 3 1972-dec 31 1973/jan 1/2 1974 – 12r – us Res Libr [949]

BOR'BA KLASSOV – Moscow. 1931-1934 complete – 1 – 35.00r – us Hoover Inst Photo [073]

BOR'BA KLASSOV I PARTII V 1-I GOSUDARSTVENNOI DUME / Tomsinskii, S G – Rostov n/D, Krasnodar, 1924. 103p – 2mf – 9 – ne IDC [320]

BOR'BA KLASSOV I PARTII VO VTOROI GOSUDARSTVENNOI DUME / Tomsinskii, S G; ed by Pokrovksii, M M – M., 1924. 173p – 2mf – 9 – ne IDC [320]

BOR'BA NE NA ZHIVOT, A NA SMERT', S NOVYMI ISTORICHESKIMI ERESIAMI / Pogodin, M P – M. 1874. BR-8299 2 – 8 – ne IDC [947]

BOR'BA PLEKHANOVA PROTIV MODERNIZMA V ISKUSSTVE / Fomina, V – "Vorposy filosofii" no 3 1951. BR-3263 – 8 – ne IDC [100]

BOR'BA S ZAPADOM V NASHEI LITERATURE / Strakhov, N – Istoricheskie i kriticheskie ocherki. 2 v. v. 1st ed, 1 and 2; v. 2, ed. 2. Spb. 1882-90. BR-10.633 2 – 8 – ne IDC [460]

BORBA S ZASUKHOI : SBORNIK RUKOVODI ASHCHIKH MATERIALOV NARKOMZEMA PO REORGANIZATSII KRESTI ANSKIKH KHOZIAISTV V ZASUSHLIVYKH RAIONAKH / R.S.F.S.R., Narodny i komissariat zemledelii a – Moskva: "Novai a derevni a", 1926 – 1 – CSUX90-B6157 – us Hoover Inst Photo [947]

BORBA S ZASUKHOI : SBORNIK RUKOVODI ASHCHIKH MATERIALOV NARKOMZEMA PO REORGANIZATSII KRESTI ANSKIKH KHOZIAISTV V ZASUSHLIVYKH RAIONAKH / R.S.F.S.R., Narodny i komissariat zemledelii a – Moskva: "Novai a derevni a", 1926 – 1 – CSUX90-B6156 – us Hoover Inst Photo [947]

BOR'BA SO SHTUNDOI = THE STRUGGLE WITH THE STUNDA / Ol'shevskii, I – Poltava, 1902 – 1 – 5.00 – us Baptist [240]

BOR'BA TRUDIASHCHIKHSIA CHECHENOINGUSHETII V PERVOI REVOLIUTSII 1905-1907 GG / Khasbulatov, A I – Groznyi, 1966 – 1 – 35.00r – us Hoover Inst Photo [335]

BOR'BA ZA IDEALIZM / Volynskii, A L – Kriticheskie stat'l. Izd. Molostvova. Spb. 1900. BR-2213 2 – 8 – ne IDC [460]

BOR'BA ZA KACHESTVO V PROMKOOPERATSII / Kremianskii, Ia. – M., 1931 – 1mf – 9 – COR-424/1 – ne IDC [334]

BORBA ZA KRYM I RAZGROM VRANGELIA / Buiskii, A – 2-e izd. Moskva: Gos. izd-vo, Otdel voen. lit-ry, 1930 – 1 – CSUX88-B7625 – us Hoover Inst Photo [947]

BOR'BA ZA STIL' / Grossman, L – Opyty po kritike i poetike. (On Akhmatova p. 227-239). M. 1927. BR-1284 2 – 8 – ne IDC [460]

BORBA ZA UROZHA I : NAKOPLENIE I SBEREZHENIE VLAGI V POCHVE / Besser, A A – Moskva: Gos. izd-vo, 1921 – 1 – CSUX91-B1603 – us Hoover Inst Photo [947]

BORBA ZA USTANOVLENIE I UPROCHENIE SOVETSKOI VLASTI V IAKUTII : SBORNIK DOKUMENTOV I MATERIALOV / Tebekin, D A & Nikolaeva, V V – Ikutsk: Ikutskoe knizhnoe izd-vo, 1957-1962 – us Res Libr [949]

Borberg, Allan *see* CLINICAL AND GENETIC INVESTIGATIONS INTO TUBEROUS SCLEROSIS AND RECKLINGHAUSEN'S NEUROFIBROMATOSIS

A BORBOLETA : NO CLUB "CINCO DE SETEMBRO" – [s.l.] 1892 – 1,5,6 – bl Biblioteca [072]

A BORBOLETA : PERIODICO LITTERARIO, NOTICIOSO E JOCO-SERIO – Maceio, Alagoas. 10 Set, 4 Out 1876 – 1,5,6 – bl Biblioteca [072]

BORBOLETA : CRITICO E LITTERARIO – Carajas, Amazonas. 11, 15 Abr 1909 – 1,5,6 – bl Biblioteca [072]

Borbon, F *see* MEDICINA DOMESTICA...DEL MEDICO CARITATIVO...

Borchard, E M *see* THE BIBLIOGRAPHY OF INTERNATIONAL LAW AND ...

Borchard, Edwin Montefiore *see*
- THE BIBLIOGRAPHY OF INTERNATIONAL LAW...
- CONVICTING THE INNOCENT; ERRORS OF CRIMINAL JUSTICE

Borchardt, DH *see* BETTER JOURNALS FOR THE LIBRARY PROFESSION

Borchardt, L *see* DAS RE-HEILIGTUM DES KOENIGS NE-WOSER-RE (RATHURES)

Borcherdt, Hans Heinrich *see*
- DIE ERSTEN AUSGABEN VON GRIMMELSHAUSENS SIMPLICISSIMUS
- GOETHE'S BRIEFE AN CHARLOTTE VON STEIN

Borchmann, Johann Friedrich *see* BRIEFE ZUR ERINNERUNG AN MERKWUERDIGE ZEITEN, UND RUEHMLICHE PERSONEN, AUS DEM WICHTIGEN ZEITLAUFE VON 1740, BIS 1778

Borck, J B von *see* SKANDINAVIENS RATVINGADE INSEKTERS NATURAL HISTORIA

Borcke-Stargordt, Henning Graf von *see* DER OSTDEUTSCHE LANDBAU ZWISCHEN FORTSCHRITT, KRISE UND POLITIK

Borde, Charles *see*
- LE CATECHUMENE
- TABLEAU PHILOSOPHIQUE DU GENRE HUMAIN

Bordeaux. France. Chambre de Commerce *see* EXTRAITS DES PROCES-VERBAUX

Bordeaux, Henry *see* LE MARIAGE: HIER ET AUJOURD'HUI

Bordeianu-Taladoire, R *see* CATALOGUE RAISONNE DES SCULPTURES APPELEES "CHAC MOOL."

BORDER ALLIANCE – Pioneer, Ohio. 1879 – 1r – 1 – $32.50r – us Archival [071]

BORDER COUNTIES ADVERTISER – Oswestry, England. -w. 1972-78. 15 reels – 1 – uk British Libr Newspaper [072]

BORDER CROSSINGS – Winnipeg. v1-13. 1981/82-1994 – 9 – Can$20.00y – cn Micromedia [073]

THE BORDER NEWS – Canaan, VT. v11 n6. 10 jun 1926 – 1r – 1 – Can$25.00 – cn Can Microfilming [071]

BORDER RUFFIAN – Coolidge. Kan. -w. 1886-87 – 1 – us UMI [071]

BORDER STAR – Columbus. Kan. 1878-1880; 1882-1886 – 1 – us UMI [071]

BORDER TELEGRAPH – 1 – £42.00r – uk Scot News [072]

BORDERER – Sackville, Canada. 1865-70 – 1 reel – 1 – $68.00 – cn Library Assoc [971]

BORDERLAND : A QUARTERLY REVIEW AND INDEX – London. v1-4. 1893-97 – 1r – 1 – us Ross [150]

BORDER/LINES – (1984-1988/89 Can$115.00) – Toronto. v1-34. 1984-94 – 1 – Can$60.00y – cn Micromedia [073]

Bordet *see* METHODE RAISONNEE, POUR APPRENDRE LA MUSIQUE D'UNE FACON PLUS CLAIRE ET PLUS PRECISE A LAQUELLE ON JOINT L'ETENDUE DE LA FLUTE TRAVERSIERE

Bordet, Henri *see* L'OR ET L'ARGENT EN 1864

Bordier, H L *see* LIBRI MIRACULORUM ALIAQUE OPERA MINORA

Bordier, L-C *see* TRAITE DE COMPOSITION

Bordihn, F *see* DIE RECHTSVERHAELTNISSE UND DER RECHTSSCHUTZ DES AUSLANDSDEUTSCHTUMS, ...

Bordin, Ruth M *see* TEMPERANCE AND PROHIBITION PAPERS, 1830-1933

BORDON DE PEREGRINO. POEMAS / Corredor Garcia, Antonio – Caceres: Ediciones Gruzada Mariana, 1965 – 1 – sp Bibl Santa Ana [810]

Bordon, Jose Octavio *see* LA RACIONALIDAD DEL PERONISMO

BORE – Stockholm, Sweden. 1848-51 – 3r – 1 – sw Kungliga [072]

Borea, Domingo *see* LEGISLACION AGRARIA DE LA REPUBLICA ARGENTINA

BOREAL – (Cont by: Northward Journal n13 1979) – Toronto. n1-12. 1974-78 – 9 – Can$46.00 – cn Micromedia [073]

BOREAL *see* NORTHWARD JOURNAL

BOREALIS – Aurora, NV. 23 Dec 1905 – 1r – 1 – $50.00 – U04402 – us Library Micro [071]

BOREALIS MAGAZINE – v1-5. 1988/90-94 – 9 – Can$20.00y – cn Micromedia [971]

BOREAS – (1981-. 1,5,6,9) – v1-. 1972- – 1 – us UMI [550]

Boreau, A *see* SUR LES ENVELOPPES FLORALES DES VEGETAUX MONOCOTYLEDONS

BOREHAMWOOD TIMES – England, 1987- – 62+ r – 1 – uk British Libr Newspaper [072]

Borel d'Hauterive *see* REVUE HISTORIQUE DE LA NOBLESSE

Borel, F *see*
- DE L'ORIGINE ET DES FONCTIONS DES CONSULS
- FORMULAIRE DES CONSULATS

Borel, P *see*
- DICTIONNAIRE DES TERMES DU VIEUX FRANCOIS
- TRESOR DES RECHERCHES ET ANTIQUITES GAULOISES ET FRANCOISES

Borelli, Giovanni Alfonso *see* DE 6 PERCUSSIONIS LIBER

Borely, N *see* LA VIE DE MESSIRE CHRISTOPHLE D'AUTHIER DE SISGAU, EVEQUE DE BETHLEEM

Borges, M et al *see* LES OEUVRES RUPESTRES DE L'ABRI DE MALHADOR (MUNICIPIO DE JANUARIA, MINAS GERAIS, BRESIL)

Borges, Milo Adrian *see* MANUAL DE LA LEGISLATION COLOMBIANA

Borges, Pedro *see* EUGENIO SARRALBO AQUARELES, ANTONIO CORREA Y ARTURO ALVAREZ. (OFM). INVENTARIO...

Borghese, A D R *see* A NEW AND GENERAL SYSTEM OF MUSIC OR THE ART OF MUSIC

Borghini, R *see* IL RIPOSO

BORI : GENIES D'UN CULTE DE POSSESSION HAUSA DE L'ADER ET DU KURFEY (NIGER) / Echard, N – F60.00 – fr Ethnologie [306]

Boria, J de *see* EMPRESAS MORALES

Borie, Henri Jules *see* AERODOMES

Borie, Nicolas Y *see* STATISTIQUE DU DEPARTEMENT D'ILLE ET VILAINE

BORIS I. NICOLAEVSKY COLLECTION : "THE LEON TROTSKY PAPERS" – 41r – 1 – $3,075.00 – us UMI [320]

Borisov, B *see* DALNI I VOSTOK

BORIUS WICHART : ROMAN AUS DER GEGENREFORMATION / Wegner, Max – 3. Aufl. Stuttgart: G Truckenmueller, c1939 – 1r – 1 – us U.W. Library [830]

Borjon de Scellery, Charles-Emmanuel *see* TRAITE DE LA MUSETTE..

BORKENER ZEITUNG – Borken/Hessen, 1926-35 – 8r – 1 – Inquire at Mikrofilmarchiv for details – gw Misc Inst [943]

BORKENER ZEITUNG – Borken/Westfalen, 1987- – 1 – Inquire at Mikrofilmarchiv for details – gw Misc Inst [072]

Borkovskii, V I *see*
- NOVGORODSKIE GRAMOTY NA BERESTE (IZ RASKOPOK 1953-54 GG.)
- NOVGORODSKIE GRAMOTY NA BERESTE (IZ RASKOPOK 1956-57 GG.)
- NOVGORODSKIE GRAMOTY NA BERESTE (IZ RASPOKOK 1955 G.)
- PALEOGRAFICHESKII I LINGVISTICHESKII ANALIZ NOVGORODSKIKH BERESTIANYKH GRAMOT

Borland, C R *see* A DESCRIPTIVE CATALOGUE OF THE WESTERN MEDIAEVAL MANUSCRIPTS IN EDINBURGH UNIVERSITY LIBRARY

Borland, John *see*
- AN APPEAL TO THE MONTREAL CONFERENCE AND THE METHODIST CHURCH GENERALLY: FROM A CHARGE BY REV. WILLIAM SCOTT, IN WHICH IS SHOWN HIS CHARGE TO BE INVALID, AND HIS DEFENCE OF THE SEMINARY OF ST SULPICE AGAINST THE INDIANS OF OKA TO BE BASELESS:.
- LETTERS TO A MEMBER OF THE WESLEYAN METHODIST CHURCH: IN WHICH CERTAIN REFLECTIONS AGAINST PROTESTANTISM, AND VARIOUS ASSUMPTIONS IN FAVOUR OF ROMANISM, PUT FORWARD BY AN ECCLESIASTIC OF ROME, ARE EXAMINED AND REFUTED

BORLANGE TIDNING – Borlange, Sweden. 1979- – 1 – sw Kungliga [072]

BORLANGE TIDNING – Hedemora, Borlange, Sweden. 1885-1920 – 26r – 1 – sw Kungliga [072]

Borlase, William *see* ANTIQUITIES, HISTORICAL AND MONUMENTAL OF THE COUNTY OF CORNWALL

Borlenghi, Angel G *see*
- EVOLUCION DEL MOVIMIENTO OBRERO
- LA REFORMA CONSTITUCIONAL

Born, I von *see*
- INDEX RERUM NATURALIUM MUSEI CAESAREI VINDOBONENSIS, VOL 1
- TESTACEA MUSEI CAESAREI VINDOBONENSIS

BORN OF WATER AND SPIRIT : A SERIES OF ESSAYS CONCERNING REGENERATION AND THE NEW LIFE / Hough, Samuel – New York: Sheldon, 1879 – 1mf – 9 – 0-8370-4860-5 – 1985-2860 – us A.T.L.A. [240]

Bornemann, D W *see* DIE FRIEDENSFAHRT DEUTSCHER KIRCHENMAENNER NACH ENGLAND

Bornemann, F W B *see* IN INVESTIGANDA MONCHATUS ORIGINE...

Bornemann, Wilhelm *see*
- DIE ALLEGORIE IN KUNST, WISSENSCHAFT UND KIRCHE
- BITTERE WAHRHEITEN
- EINFUEHRUNG IN DIE EVANGELISCHE MISSIONSKUNDE

BORNEO BULLETIN – Kuala Belait. Brunei. -w. 1959- – 1 – us UMI [072]

Bornet, J BE *see*
- LES ALGUES DE P.K.A. SCHOUSBOE
- ETUDES PHYCOLOGIQUES
- NOTES ALGOLOGIQUES

Bornhak, K *see* EINSEITIGE ABHAENGIGKEITSVERHAELTNISSE ...

Bornhausen, Karl *see*
- DIE ETHIK PASCALS
- RELIGION IN AMERIKA

Bornmuller, J *see* ITER PERSICO-TURCICUM

Bornstedt, Louise von *see* DIE LEGENDE DER H. JUNGFRAU UND MAERTYRIN SANKT KATHARINA

Bornstein, George *see* TWO CENTURIES OF BRITISH PERIODICALS, 1732-1914

Bornstein, Paul *see* HEBBELS HERODES UND MARIAMNE

A BORNU ALMANAC FOR THE YEAR A D 1916 : (A H 1334 AND PART OF 1335) – London, NY: Oxford UP, 1916 – 1 – us Res Libr [030]

BORNU PROVINCE GAZETTEER – [Lagos: Govt Printer, 1929] – 1 – us Res Libr [960]

Borodaevskii, S V *see*
- KOOPERATSII. SVOD TRUDOV MESTNYKH KOMITETOV PO 49 GUBERNIIAM EVROPEISKOI ROSSII
- SBORNIK PO MELKOMU KREDITU

Borodkin, P A *see* REVOLIUTSIONNYE SOBYTIIA NA ALTAE V 1905-1907 GG

Borodkine, M *see* LA FINLANDE, COMME PARTIE INTEGRANTE DE L'EMPIRE RUSSE

BOROOLOOLA INQUEST BOOK, 28 DECEMBER 1889 TO 10 NOVEMBER 1930 – (Anythony's Lagoon Mortuary Book 1890-1948; Newcastle Waters Police Station Mortuary Book 1893-1951; Adelaide River Police Day Books 1946-1958; Brock's Creek Police Day Books 1926-1948; Rankine River Police Day Books (includes a ces) 1930-1934; Pine Creek Police Day Books 1882-1948) – 4mf – 9 – A$15.00 – 0-949124-67-2 – item 28 – at G.S.N.T. [920]

BOROT'BA – Vienna. 1920 – 1 – 75.00 – cn McLaren [072]

THE BOROUGH OF STOKE ON TRENT, STAFFORDSHIRE / Ward, J – 19th Century – 1 – uk Microform Academic [941]

Borough of Tamworth, Staffs *see* THE TAMWORTH COURT ROLLS

Boroughs, J *see* THE SOVEREIGNTY OF THE BRITISH SEAS

Boroughs, R Zig *see* TWO BOOKLETS RELATIVE TO THE BEGINNINGS OF SOUTHERN BAPTIST MISSIONS IN NIAGARA FALLS, NY, 1953-59

Borowski, Christian *see* FUNKTIONELLE CHARAKTERISIERUNG VON DOMAENEN DES ELONGATIONSFAKTORS G

Borowski, F *see* QUATUOR

BOROZDY I MEZHI / Ivanov, V – Opyty esteticheskie i kriticheskie. "Musaget". M. 1916. BR-732 2 – 8 – ne IDC [460]

LAS BORRACHERAS Y EL PROBLEMA DE LAS CONVERSACIONES EN INDIAS / Bayle, Constantino – Madrid: Razon y Fe, 1943 – 1 – sp Bibl Santa Ana [950]

Borrallo Salgado, Teofilo *see* RUERO DEL BAYLIO

Borrely, Jean-Alexis *see* PLAN DE REFORMATION DES ETUDES ELEMENTAIRES

Borremans, Valentina *see* THE HISTORY OF RELIGIOSITY IN LATIN AMERICA, 1880-1970

Borrichius, O *see* DE CAUSIS DIVERSITATIS LINGVARUM DISSERTATIO

Borrier, W *see* SPECIMEN OF A LICHENOGRAPHIA BRITANNICA

Borromeo, Charles N *see* REDUCTION OF SPORTS INJURY MORBIDITY WITH HYPERBARIC OXYGEN TREATMENT

Borroni, Otelo *see*
- EVA PERON
- LA VIDA DE EVA PERON

Borrow, George Henry *see*
- THE BIBLE IN SPAIN
- ROMANO LAVO-LIL
- ROMANO LAVO-LIL, WORD-BOOK OF THE ROMANY; OR, ENGLISH GYPSY LANGUAGE
- THE WORKS OF GEORGE BORROW

Borrows Brothers Co *see* THE BOOK OF CLEVELANDERS

Borsa, G *see* LA CESSAZIONE DEL MANDATO INTERNAZIONALE

BORSEN [DENMARK] – (Yrly reel count varies) – 1992- – 1 – inquire – us Ross [072]

Borshchevskii, I E *see* MATERIALY DLIA BIBLIOGRAFII RABOT O PERSIDSKIKH RUKOPISIAKH

Borsodi, Ralph *see*
- THE CONSTANT
- DECENTRALIST, MONEY- AND LAND REFORMER, FREE TRADER, PEACE LOVER AND FOUNDER OF THE SCHOOL OF LIVING
- INFLATION IS COMING
- SEVENTEEN PROBLEMS OF MAN AND SOCIETY

Borst, A *see* DIE KATHAREN (MGH SCHRIFTEN..: 12.BD)

BORSTIDNINGEN – Stockholm, Sweden. 1888-1900 – 7r – 1 – sw Kungliga [948]

Borthwick, John Douglas *see*
- EVERY MAN'S MINE OF USEFUL KNOWLEDGE, OR, A BOOK FOR ALL
- HISTORY AND BIOGRAPHICAL GAZETTEER OF MONTREAL TO THE YEAR 1892
- HISTORY OF MONTREAL: INCLUDING THE STREETS OF MONTREAL, THEIR ORIGIN AND HISTORY
- HISTORY OF THE MONTREAL PRISON FROM A. D. 1784 TO A. D. 1886
- REBELLION DE 37-38: PRECIS COMPLET DE CETTE PERIODE: ROLE D'HONNEUR, OU, LISTE COMPLETE DES PATRIOTES DETENUS DANS LES PRISONS DE MONTREAL EN 1837-39: DATE ET LIEUX DES ARRESTATIONS ET AUTRES DETAILS.

Bortnik, Ruben *see*
- BREVE HISTORIA DE LAS LUCHAS SOCIALES EN ARGENTINA
- EL EJERCITO ARGENTINO Y EL ARTE DE LO POSIBLE
- PERONISMO, GOBIERNO Y PODER (DE LA CRISIS DEL SISTEMA AL SOCIALISMO NACIONAL)

Borum, Jospeh H *see* BIOGRAPHICAL SKETCH OF TENNESSEE BAPTIST MINISTERS

Borwicz, Michal Maksymilian *see* DOKUMENTY ZBRODNI I MECZENSTWA, KOLEGIUM REDAKCYJNE

Bory de Saint-Vincent, J B C M *see*
- DICTIONNAIRE CLASSIQUE D'HISTOIRE NATURELLE
- ESSAIS SUR LES ISLES FORTUNEES ET L'ANTIQUE ATLANTIDE OU PRECIS DE L'HISTOIRE GENERALE DE L'ARCHIPEL DES CANARIES
- EXPEDITION SCIENTIFIQUE DE MOREE
- NOUVELLE FLORE DU PELOPONNESE ET DES CYCLADES
- VOYAGE DANS LES QUATRE PRINCIPALES ILES DES MERS D'AFRIQUE

Bory de Saint-Vincent, J B G M *see* VOYAGE AUX INDES ORIENTALES PENDANT LES ANNEES 1825-1829

Bory de Saint-Vincent, J BG M *see* EXPEDITION SCIENTIFIQUE DE MOREE

Borzi, A *see*
- CONTRIBUZIONO ALLA BIOLOGIA VEGETALE
- STUDI ALGOLOGICI
- STUDI SULLE MIXOFICEE

BOSANQUET AND PULLER'S NEW REPORTS : NEW REPORTS OF CASES ARGUED AND DETERMINED IN THE COURT OF COMMON PLEAS... / Bosanquet, John B & Puller, Christopher – v1-2. 1804-07. London: J Butterworth, 1806-08 (all publ) – 6mf – 9 – $27.00 – LLMC 84-754 – us L.L.M.C. [324]

BOSANQUET AND PULLER'S REPORTS : REPORTS OF CASES ARGUED AND DETERMINED IN THE COURT OF COMMON PLEAS AND EXCHEQUER CHAMBER, AND IN THE HOUSE OF LORDS ON APPEAL THEREFROM... / Bosanquet, John B & Puller, Christopher – (v1 printed for Byrne & Hudson, 1804. v2 printed for P Byrne, 1803. Both in Philadelphia) – v1-2. 1796-1801 – 15mf – 9 – $22.50 – LLMC 95-247 – us L.L.M.C. [324]

Bosanquet, Bernard *see*
- THE CIVILIZATION OF CHRISTENDOM
- THE ESSENTIALS OF LOGIC
- PSYCHOLOGY OF THE MORAL SELF
- THE VALUE AND DESTINY OF THE INDIVIDUAL

Bosanquet, John B *see*
- BOSANQUET AND PULLER'S NEW REPORTS
- BOSANQUET AND PULLER'S REPORTS

Bosanquet, M *see*
- AUTOBIOGRAPHIE, 1785
- DIARIES, 1767, 1772-1786, 1788-1791
- JOURNALS, 1764, 1783, 1785, 1788, 1792-1799
- JOURNALS, 1790, 1792, 1794-1795, 1797-1798, 1800-1806
- JOURNALS, 1807-1815

Bosbach, Heinz *see* FUERST BISMARCK UND DIE KAISERIN AUGUSTA

BOSBOGAZ – Koyu Cumhuiyetci Siyasi Gazete. Sahibi ve Muharriri: Mehmed Asaf (Borsaci). Nos. 6 (19 Haziran 1930), 10-12, 1730 (16 Tesriniewel 1930) – 9 – $30.00 – us MEDOC [956]

Bosch, B de *see* DICHTLIEVENDE VERLUSTIGINGEN, VAN BERNARDUS DE BOSCH

Bosch, J Van den *see* CAPA, BASICLICA, MONASTERIUM ET LE CULTE DE ST MARTIN DE TOURS

Bosch, R B van den *see*
- HYMENOPHYLLACEAE JAVANICAE;...
- SYNOPSIS HYMENOPHYLLA CEARUM, MONOGRAPHIAE HUJUS ORDINIS PRODROMUS

Boschan, R *see*
- HUGO GROTIUS: VON DER FREIHEIT DES MEERES
- DER STREIT UM DIE FREIHEIT DER MEERE ...

BOSCHBLAADJES *see* APELDOORNSCHE-BOSCHBLAADJES

Boschet, A *see* LE PARFAIT MISSIONNAIRE OU LA VIE DU R.P. JULIEN MAUNOIR

Boschinger, H von *see* DIE WIRTSCHAFTLICHEN VERTRAEGE DEUTSCHLANDS

Boschini, Marco *see* LA CARTA DEL NAVEGAR PITORESCO

Boschma, Anne L C *see* BREAST SUPPORT FOR THE ACTIVE WOMEN

Bosco, G *see* LE NUOVE LEGGI SUL MATRIMONIO ...

Boscovich, Nicolas *see* SOLUCIONES ARGENTINAS

Bose, George Mathias *see* RECHERCHES SUR LA CAUSE ET SUR LA VERITABLE TEORIE DE L'ELECTRICITE

Bose, H von *see* DIE NACHTEILE IM VOELKERRECHT

Bose, J C A *see* A MANUAL OF INDIAN BOTANY

Bose, Manindra Mohan *see* SAHAJIYA SAHITYA

Bose, S C *see* THE HINDOOS AS THEY ARE

Bosio, A *see*
- ROMA SOTTERANEA
- ROMA SOTTERRANEA

Boskovich, Rudzer J *see* DE CONTINUITATIS LEGE ET EJUS CONSECTARIIS PERTINENTIBUS AD PRIMA MATERIAE ELEMENTA EORUMQUE VIRES

Bosl, K *see* DIE REICHSMINISTERIALITAET DER SALIER UND STAUFER (MGH SCHRIFTEN..: 10.BD)

Bosman, Willem *see*
- DESCRIPTION OF THE COAST OF GUINEA
- NAUWKEURIGE BESCHRYVING VAN DE GUINESE GOUD-, TAND-, EN SLAVE-KUST...
- VOYAGE DE GUINEE
- VOYAGE DE GUINEE CONTENANT UNE DESCRIPTION NOUVELLE ET TRES EXACTE DE CETTE COTE OU L'ON TROUVE ET OU L'ON TRAFIQUE L'OR, LES DENTS D'ELEPHANT, ET LES ESCLAVES: DE CES PAYS ROYAUMES, ET REPUBLIQUE, DES MOEURS DES HABITANTS

LE BOSPHORE EGYPTIEN – Cairo. Egypt. -d. 3 Oct 1884-4 Jul 1886, 2 Nov-2 Dec 1894. (Imperfect). (5 reels) – 1 – uk British Libr Newspaper [072]

LE BOSPHORE ET LES DARDANELLES / Goriainow, S – Paris, 1910 – 5mf – 1 – ILM-2205/1 – ne IDC [327]

BOSQUEJO DE LA MATEMATICA ESPANOLA EN LOS SIGLOS DE LA DECADENCIA / Penalver y Bachiller, P – Sevilla, 1930 – 2mf – 9 – sp Cultura [510]

BOSQUEJO HISTORICO ACERCA DE LA VIRGEN Y MONASTERIO DE SANTA MARIA DE GUADALUPE – Avila: Cayetano Gonzalez Hernandez – 1 – sp Bibl Santa Ana [240]

BOSQUEJO HISTORICO DE LA VILLA DE CECLAVIN / Rosado, Joaquin – Caceres: Extremadura, 1927 – 1 – sp Bibl Santa Ana [946]

BOSQUEJO HISTORICO DE LAS REVOLUCIONES DE CENTRO-AMERICA. DESDE 1811 HASTA 1834 / Marure, Alejandro – 2nd ed. Guatemala, 1877-78. 2v in one – 1 – us U.W. Library [972]

BOSQUEJO PARA UN CURSO DE GIMNASIA PARA EL USO DE ORGANIZACIONES JUVENILES DE F.E.T. Y DE LAS JONS DE LA PROVINCIA DE CACERES POR... / O'Ferrall, Arturo – Caceres: Imprenta Moderna, 1938 – 1 – sp Bibl Santa Ana [946]

BOSQUEJO SOBRE EL TRABAJO Y LA SEGURIDAD SOCIAL EN EL DOMINIO DEL CANADA / Sani Poblete, Margot – Santiago?, 1951. 66, 6p. LL-2397 – 1 – us L of C Photodup [340]

BOSQUEJO...LITERATURA DE ASTURIAS.. / Fuertes Acevedo, Maximo – 1885 – 9 – 1.50f – sp Bibl Santa Ana [440]

BOSQUEJOS CIENTIFICOS / Fuertes Acevedo, Maximo – 1880 – 9 – 1.50f – sp Bibl Santa Ana [500]

Boss, Richard W *see* DOCUMENT DELIVERY IN THE UNITED STATES: A REPORT

BOSS TWEED IN COURT : A DOCUMENTARY HISTORY / Tweed, Boss – $660.00 – 1-55655-167-3 – us UPA [340]

Bossange, Gustave *see*
- IL CANADA E L'EMIGRAZIONE
- LA NOUVELLE FRANCE, LE CANADA: APPEL AUX CLASSES NECESSITEUSES DE FRANCE
- LA NUOVA FRANCIA: ANTICA COLONIA FRANCESE: APPELLO ALLE CLASSI OPERAIE

Bossard, abbe Eugene *see* GILLES DE RAIS MARECHAL DE FRANCE...

Bosse, A *see* SENTIMENS SUR LA DISTINCTION DES DIVERSES MANIERES DE PEINTURE, DESSEIN ET GRAVUEURE

Bosse, Abraham *see*
- TRAICTE DES MANIERES DE GRAVER EN TAILLE-DOUCE
- TRAITE DES MANIERES DE DESSINER LES ORDRES DE L'ARCHITECTURE ANTIQUE

Bossenbrook, William John *see* JUSTUS MOESER'S APPROACH TO HISTORY

Bossert, Adolphe *see* GOETHE ET SCHILLER

Bossert, Gustav *see*
- DAS INTERIM IN WUERTTEMBERG
- WUERTTEMBERG UND JANSSEN

Bossert, P J *see* LES SOCIETES ETRANGERES EN FRANCE ...

Bossert, Theodor Adolf *see* FRIEDRICH HEINRICH JACOBI UND DIE FRUEHROMANTIK

Bosshard, W *see* DIE AUFGABE DES RICHTERS ...

Bossi, C *see*
- LES DUES JUMELLES OU LA MEPRISE
- HYLAS ET TEMIRE
- LE MARCHAND DE SMYRNE

Bossi, Giuseppe *see* STATISTIQUE GENERALE DE LA FRANCE

Bossion, A *see* DROIT ROMAIN: DE L'ACTION DE DOL ...

Bossler, H P K *see* MUSIKALISCHE KORRESPONDENZ DER TEUTSCHEN FILARMONISCHEN GESELLESCHAFT FUER DAS JAHR JUL 1790-DEZ 1791

Bosso, John A *see* JOURNAL OF INFECTIOUS DISEASE PHARMACOTHERAPY

Bossu, N *see* TRAVELS THROUGH THAT PART OF NORTH AMERICA FORMERLY CALLED LOUISIANA

BOSSUET ET LA PROTESTANTISME : ETUDE HISTORIQUE / Crousle, L – Paris: H. Champion, 1901 – 1mf – us A.T.L.A. [240]

BOSSUET ET LES PROTESTANTS / Julien, E – Paris: G. Beauchesne, 1910 – 1mf – us A.T.L.A. [240]

Bossuet, J -B *see* EXPOSITION DE LA DOCTRINE DE L'EGLISE CATHOLIQUE SUR LES MATIERES DE CONTROVERSE

Bossuet, Jacques B *see*
- CONFERENCE AVEC M. CLAUDE...SUR LA MATIERE DE L'EGLISE
- EXPOSITION DE LA DOCTRINE DE L'EGLISE CATHOLIQUE SUR LES MATIERES DE CONTROVERSE

Bossuet, Jacques Benigne *see*
- DEVOTION TO THE BLESSED VIRGIN
- ORAISONS FUN EBRES DE BOSSUET

Bossy, A *see* DROIT ROMAIN: DETERMINATION DES ELEMENTS DU LITIGE ...

Bostelle *see* RAPPORTS A SON EXCELLENCE LE MINISTRE DE L'INTERIEUR SUR L'EMIGRATION ANNEES 1859 ET 1860

BOSTON ADVOCATE – Boston, Mass. 1905-52 – 1 – us A.J.P.C. [071]
BOSTON AND LINCOLNSHIRE STANDARD *see* BOSTON STANDARD
Boston Athenaeum Library. Boston *see* CARD CATALOG OF THE BOSTON ATHENAEUM PRINT AND PHOTOGRAPH COLLECTION
BOSTON BAR JOURNAL – v1-39. 1957-95 – 9 – $568.00 set – us Hein [340]
BOSTON BIRTHS 1849-1881 – (Mf 1-177 1849-81. Mf 178-79 1852-69. Mf 180-196: Corrections and Additions to Birth Records 1870-81. Index 1849-69: Mf 197-203: Vol A-G. Mf 204-209: Vol H-M. Mf 210-215: Vol N-Z. Index 1870-81: Mf 216-222: Vol A-G. Mf 223-228: Vol H-M. Mf 229-234: Vol N-Z) – (mf ed 1987) – 234mf – 9 – 0-931248-77-9 – us Holbrook [920]
BOSTON BIRTHS 1882-1895 – (Mf 1-267: 1882-95. Index 1882-1891: Mf 268-313 A-Z. Mf 314-325: Index 1892-1895) – (mf ed 1988) – 325mf – 9 – 0-931248-90-6 – us Holbrook [920]
Boston. Brattle square church *see* THE MANIFESTO CHURCH
BOSTON BUSINESS JOURNAL: BBJ – (1985-. 1,5,6) – 1981- – 9 – us UMI [380]
THE BOSTON CHRONICLE – Boston, Mass. 1767-70. Also: The Massachusetts Spy, 1770-75, and The Censor, 1771-72. Sold as one unit – 1,3 – us Readex [071]
THE BOSTON CHRONICLE – Boston. Mass. aug. 31, Dec. 21, 1940 – 1 – us NY Public [071]
THE BOSTON COLLECTION OF INSTRUMENTAL MUSIC – Containing marches, quicksteps, waltzes, airs, cotillions, contra-dances, hornpipes, quadrilles, arranged with figures, Scotch and Irish jigs, reels, and strathspeys, arranged for brass, wooden & stringed instruments. Boston: O. Ditson 1850?. The music is in 2, 3 and 4 parts. MUSIC 1977 – 1 – us L of C Photodup [780]
Boston College *see* ENVIRONMENTAL AFFAIRS LAW REVIEW
BOSTON COLLEGE INTERNATIONAL AND COMPARATIVE LAW JOURNAL *see* BOSTON COLLEGE INTERNATIONAL AND COMPARATIVE LAW REVIEW
BOSTON COLLEGE INTERNATIONAL AND COMPARATIVE LAW REVIEW – (v1-7 1977-84 in reel $72.00. v8-19 1985-96 in mf $148.00. Title varies: v1-2 1977-79 as Boston College International and Comparative Law Journal) – v1-19. 1977-96 – 5,6,9 – $212.00 set – us Hein [340]
BOSTON COLLEGE LAW REVIEW – v1-36. 1959-95 – 1,5,6,9 – $1,035.00 – us Hein [073]
BOSTON COLLEGE THIRD WORLD LAW JOURNAL – (v1-5 1980-85 in reel $55.00. v6-16 1986-96 in mf $123.00) – v1-16. 1980-96 – 5,6,9 – $178.00 set – us Hein [340]
BOSTON COMMONWEALTH – Boston. v1-9. 1862-71 – 2r – 1 – us Ross [071]
BOSTON DAILY ADVERTISER – Boston. Mass. 1813-1820 – 1,3 – us Readex [071]
BOSTON DAILY LAW BULLETIN – (v2 called: Boston Daily Law Reporter. Lacking: v1) – v1-2 no 38. 1876-78 – 9 – LLMC 84-427 – us L.L.M.C. [073]
BOSTON DAILY LAW REPORTER *see* BOSTON DAILY LAW BULLETIN
BOSTON DEATHS 1849-1890 – (Mf 1-274: 1849-90. Index 1849-69: Mf 275-280: Vol A-G. Mf 281-285: Vol n-Z. Index 1870-81: Mf 291-297: Vol A-G-. Mf 298-302: Vol H-M. Mf 303-307: Vol N-Z. Index: Mf 308-325: 1882-90. Mf 326: Index of Removals 1823-59. Mf 327: Deaths Out of City 1850-54. Mf 328-329: Deaths Out of City 1853-98. Mf 3320-331: Out-of-Town Index 1853-1901. Mf 332-338: Record of Deaths 1875. Mf 339-342: Record of Deaths 1876. Mf 343-348: Record of Deaths 1877. Mf 349-355: Death Index 1875-77. Mf 256-357: Record of Deaths 1878. Mf 358-359: Death Index 1878. Mf 360-363: Stillborns 1854-81. Mf 364-365: Stillborns 1882-96. Mf 366-369: Index of Still Births 1875-81) – (mf ed 1987) – 369mf – 9 – 0-931248-80-9 – us Holbrook [920]
THE BOSTON EVENING POST – Boston. Mass. 1735-1775 – 3 – us Readex [071]
THE BOSTON EVENING POST – Boston. Mass. 1781-1784. The American Herald. Boston. 1784-88; and Worcester. 1788-89. Sold as one unit – 1,3 – us Readex [071]
BOSTON EVENING TRANSCRIPT – Boston, MA: H W Dutton 1872-1941 – us Res Libr [071]
BOSTON FIRST BAPTIST CHURCH. BOSTON, MASSACHUSETTS : CHURCH RECORDS – Orig. manuscript Minutes, 1665-1797) – 1 – 8.10 – us Baptist [240]
Boston. First National Bank. Foreign Division *see* RECIPROCAL TRADE AGREEMENT BETWEEN UNITED STATES AND ARGENTINA
BOSTON GAZETTE – Boston. Mass. 1719-1798 – 1,3 – us Readex [071]
BOSTON GAZETTE – Boston, Mass. 1800-20 – 1,3 – us Readex [071]
BOSTON HEBREW OBSERVER – Boston. Mass. 1883-86 – 1 – us A.J.P.C. [071]
BOSTON HERALD AMERICAN – Boston, MA. 1973-76 – 1 – us UMI [071]
BOSTON HERALD AMERICAN AND SUNDAY ADVERTISER – Boston. Massachusetts. 1977- – 1 – us UMI [071]
Boston Historic Co *see* LAND MARKS OF MONROE COUNTY
BOSTON HISTORICAL EDITION OF THE JEWISH DAILY NEWS – New York, NY. 1915 – 1 – us A.J.P.C. [071]
Boston History Co *see* ONONDAGA'S CENTENNIAL
Boston History Publishers *see* SARATOGA COUNTY: OUR COUNTY AND ITS PEOPLE
BOSTON HOTEL GUIDE AND RAILWAY REPORTER – Boston, MA. v13 n6. 21 mar 1891 – 1r – 1 – Can$25.00 – cn Can Microfilming [071]
BOSTON INTELLIGENCER – Boston. Mass. 1816-20 – 3 – us Readex [071]
BOSTON JEWISH TIMES – Boston, MA. 1983-86 – 1 – us A.J.P.C. [071]
BOSTON LAW SCHOOL MAGAZINE – 1v. 1896-97 (all publ) – 1mf – 9 – $1.50 – LLMC 82-909 – us L.L.M.C. [073]
Boston, Lyon *see* THE U.S. AS A CREDITOR OF INSOLVENT DEBTORS
BOSTON MARRIAGES 1849-1890 – (mf ed 1986) – 310mf – 9 – 0-931248-78-7 – us Holbrook [920]
BOSTON MASSACHUSETTS BIRTHS 1700-1800 – Boston: Boston Record Commissioners 24th Report, 1894 – 1mf – 9 – us Holbrook [920]
BOSTON MASSACHUSETTS BIRTHS, BAPTISMS, MARRIAGES, DEATHS 1630-1699 – Boston: Boston Record Commissioners 9th Report, 1900 – 1mf – 9 – us Holbrook [920]
Boston, Massachusetts. First Baptist Church *see* RECORDS
BOSTON MASSACHUSETTS MARRIAGES 1700-1751 – Boston: Boston Record Commissioners 28th Report, 1898 – 2mf – 9 – us Holbrook [920]
BOSTON MIRROR – Boston, Mass. 1808-10. Also: The Satirist, 1812; Boston Scourge, 1811; The Idiot, 1817-19; Kaleidoscope, 1818-19. Sold as one unit – 3 – us Readex [071]
BOSTON MUSICAL GAZETTE – v. 1-2, no. 2. 2 May 1838-15 May 1839 – 9 – us Sibley [780]
THE BOSTON MUSICAL GAZETTE – Boston & Bellows Falls. v1-5 n9. 1846-50 – 2r – 1 – £115.00 – uk Chadwyck [780]
THE BOSTON MUSICAL GAZETTE – v1-5. Feb 1846-Nov 1848 – 1 – 495.00 – us Opus [073]
THE BOSTON MUSICAL TIMES – Boston. v1-13. 1860-71 – 3r – 1 – £165.00 – uk Chadwyck [780]
THE BOSTON MUSICAL TIMES – v1-13. Feb 1860-Oct 1871 – 1 – 600.00 – us Opus [073]
THE BOSTON MUSICAL YEARBOOK – Boston, Chicago. v1-10. 1883/84-1892/93 – 1r – 1 – £60.00 – uk Chadwyck [780]
THE BOSTON NEWS-LETTER – Boston. Mass. 1704-1776 – 1,3 – us Readex [071]
BOSTON PATRIOT – Boston. Mass. 1809-1820 – 1,3 – us Readex [071]
BOSTON PEARL AND GALAXY – v. 1-20. 10 Oct 1817-31 Dec 1836 – 1 – us UMI [073]
THE BOSTON POST-BOY – Boston. Mass. 1734-1775 – 1,3 – us Readex [071]
Boston. Presbytery *see* MINUTES
BOSTON PRICE-CURRENT – Boston, Mass. 1795-98. yRussell's Gazette. 1798-1800. Sold as one unit – 1,3 – us Readex [071]
Boston Public Library *see*
- CATALOG OF THE DEFOE COLLECTION IN THE BOSTON PUBLIC LIBRARY
- DICTIONARY CATALOG OF THE MUSIC COLLECTION
- YOUNG ADULT CATALOG OF THE BOSTON PUBLIC LIBRARY

Boston Public Library. Research Library *see* CATALOG FILE 1843-1989
BOSTON RECORDER – Boston. Mass. 1816-20 – 3 – us Readex [071]
BOSTON REVIEW – v7-. 1982- – 1,5,6,9 – us UMI [410]
BOSTON STANDARD – (Also known as: Boston and Lincolnshire Standard) – England, 1914-19; 1950; 1952; 1986- – 52+ r – 1 – uk British Libr Newspaper [072]
BOSTON SYMPHONY ORCHESTRA PROGRAM NOTES – 1881-1975 – 41r – 1 – us Ross [780]
Boston Theological Institute *see* NEWSLETTER
BOSTON THEOLOGICAL INSTITUTE (B.T.I.) NEWSLETTER – (lacks some issues) – 1968-88 – 2r – 1 – ATLA S0411 – us A.T.L.A. [073]
Boston, Thomas *see*
- PEDWAR CYFLWR DYN...WEDI EI GHFIEITHU O'R SAESONEG GAN I. PARRY
- A SOLILOQUY ON THE ART OF MAN-FISHING

THE BOSTON TIMES – Boston. Mass. feb. 24, Oct. 26, 1944 – 1 – us NY Public [071]
Boston Transcript *see* GENEALOGICAL COLUMN, 1896-1941
BOSTON UNITARIANISM, 1820-1850 : A STUDY OF THE LIFE AND WORK OF NATHANIEL LANGDON FROTHINGHAM / Frothingham, Octavius Brooks – New York: G.P. Putnam, 1890 – 1mf – us A.T.L.A. [240]
Boston University. African Studies Library *see* ASSORTED RHODESIAN AND SOUTH AFRICAN PAMPHLETS
BOSTON UNIVERSITY AFRICANA LIBRARIES NEWSLETTER – Boston: Boston University, African Studies Library. n17-33. jun 1978-nov 1982 – 1r – us Res Libr [020]
BOSTON UNIVERSITY INTERNATIONAL LAW JOURNAL – v1-13. 1982-95 – 9 – $212.00 set – us Hein [340]
BOSTON UNIVERSITY LAW REVIEW – v1-74. 1921-94 – 1,5,6,9 – $1,260.00 – us Hein [073]
Boston University. Libraries *see* CATALOG OF AFRICAN GOVERNMENT DOCUMENTS
BOSTON WEEKLY TRANSCRIPT – Boston, dec 1889-oct 1890 – us Res Libr [071]
BOSTONAS LATWEESCHU BAPTISTU DRAUDSES DARBIBAS PAHRSKATS PAR 1940, GADU = REPORT OF THE BOSTONAS LATVIAN BAPTIST CHURCH FOR 1940 – 1940. Publ. No. 6346,no. 6. One of sic items on reel. Total Pages 152 – 1 – us Baptist [240]
BOSTONER IDISHE SHTIMME = BOSTON JEWISH VOICE – Boston, MA. 1913-16 – 1 – us A.J.P.C. [071]
BOSTON-OUT-OF-TOWN MARRIAGES 1858-1895 – (Mf 1-41: 1858-95. Mf 19-22: Indexes 1857-83. Mf 32-36: Indexes 1884-92) – (mf ed 1988) – 41mf – 9 – 0-931248-88-4 – us Holbrook [920]
BOSTON'S AWAKENING : A COMPLETE ACCOUNT OF THE GREAT BOSTON REVIVAL UNDER THE LEADERSHIP OF J WILBUR CHAPMAN AND CHARLES M ALEXANDER, JANUARY 26TH TO FEBRUARY 21ST 1909 / ed by Conrad, Arcturus Zodiac – Boston, MA: King's Business Publ Co, 1909 – 1mf – 9 – 0-8370-6038-9 – 1986-0038 – us A.T.L.A. [240]
Bostroem, Christopher Jacob *see* CHR. JAC. BOSTROEMS FOERELAESNINGAR I RELIGIONSFILOSOFI
Boswell, J A C *see* A MANUAL OF THE NELLORE DISTRICT
Boswell, James *see* THE LIFE OF SAMUEL JOHNSON
BOSWORTH BAPTIST CHURCH. MISSOURI : CHURCH RECORDS – 4Dec 1915-3 Jun 1964 – 1 – 18.64 – us Baptist [240]
Bot, S Pierre Njovk *see* STUDIES ON BASA CUSTOMS
BOTAANIQUE MEDICALE,... / Richard, Achille – Paris, 1823. 2 pts – 9mf – 9 – ne IDC [615]
Botana Santamarina, A E *see* EL FRACASO DE FRONDIZI
THE BOTANIC GARDEN... / ed by Maund, B – London, 1825-1851. v1-13 – 39mf – 7358/1 – ne IDC [580]
BOTANIC GARDENS REPORT BOOK – 1898-1958 – 4mf – 9 – at Corangamite [580]
LA BOTANICA IN ITALIA / Saccardo, P A – 5705. 2 V. 1895-1901 – 9 – ne IDC [580]
BOTANICAL AND PHYSIOLOGICAL MEMOIRS / Henfrey, A – Ray Society. 1853 – 1 £56.00 7 £35.00 – uk Microform Academic [580]
BOTANICAL APPENDIX / Richardson, J – In: Narrative of a journey to the shores of the Polar Sea in 1819-1822,by J. Franklin. 5424. 1823 – 9 – ne IDC [580]
A BOTANICAL ARRANGEMENT OF ALL THE VEGETABLES NATURALLY GROWING IN GREAT BRITAIN / Withering, W – 5818. 2 V. 1776-1792 – 9 – ne IDC [580]
A BOTANICAL ARRANGEMENT OF BRITISH PLANTS / Withering, W – 5819. 3 V. Ed. 2. 1786-1792 – 9 – ne IDC [580]
BOTANICAL BULLETIN – (Continued as: Botanical Gazette. Hannover (Indiana), 1875-1940. v2-102) – Hannover (Indiana), 1874-1875. v1 – 1,011mf – 41c/2 – ne IDC [580]
BOTANICAL BULLETIN OF ACADEMIA SINICA – Shanghai, 1947-1949. 3v – 12mf – 8146/1 – ne IDC [580]
BOTANICAL CABINET... / ed by Loddiges, C – London, 1817-1833. 20v – 107mf – 5312/2 – ne IDC [580]
A BOTANICAL DESCRIPTION OF BRITISH PLANTS IN THE MIDLAND COUNTIES / Purton, T – v. 1-2. Stratford-upon-Avon. 1817; An Appendix to the Midland flora. v. 3. London. 1821. B-5090 2 – 8 – ne IDC [580]
BOTANICAL GAZETTE – (1970- . 5,6) – v. 1-1875- – 1 – us UMI [580]
BOTANICAL GAZETTE – v1-117. 1875-1955 – 1,5,6 – us Princeton Micro [580]
THE BOTANICAL GAZETTE – London, 1849-51. v1-3 – 3 – us Readex [580]
THE BOTANICAL GEOGRAPHY OF SYRIA AND PALESTINE / Post, George Edward – 1878. 1 fiche – 9 – us A.T.L.A. [580]
BOTANICAL MAGAZINE / ed by Curtis, W – London, 1793-1940. v1-163 – 742mf – 5183c/2 – ne IDC [580]
BOTANICAL MAGAZINE : THE ILLUSTRATIONS OF ROSES / ed by Curtis, W – 4mf – 7677/2 – ne IDC [580]
BOTANICAL MAGAZINE – Tokyo, 1887-1941. v1-55 – 793mf – 5588c/2 – ne IDC [580]
A BOTANICAL MATERIA MEDICA / Stokes, J – 867. 4 V. 1812 – 9 – ne IDC [580]
BOTANICAL MISCELLANY / Hooker, W J – 1883 – 7 – uk Microform Academic [580]
BOTANICAL MISCELLANY / Hooker, W J – 3v. London. 1829-33. B-1006 2 – 8 – ne IDC [580]
BOTANICAL MISCELLANY – London, 1830-1833 – 3 – us Readex [580]
BOTANICAL MONOGRAPHS – Ray Society. 18th, 19th and 20th centuries – 1,7 – uk Microform Academic [580]
BOTANICAL REGISTER / ed by Edwards, S T – (1839, appendix to v1-23) – London, 1815-1827. v1-13; N.S., 1828-1847. v1-20 – 215mf – 5422/2 – ne IDC [580]
BOTANICAL REVIEW – Lancaster, 1935-41. v. 1-7 – 83mf – 1,5,6 – ne IDC [580]
Botanical Society of Edinburgh *see*
- 1ST-8TH ANNUAL REPORT AND PROCEEDINGS...SESSION 1836/7-43/44
- LAWS, BYE-LAWS, AND REGULATIONS.

BOTANICHESKII SLOVAR' / Annenkov, N – Spb., 1878 – 13mf – 9 – 1382/2 – ne IDC [580]
BOTANICHESKII ZHURNAL / Akademiia Nauk. SSSR – Moskva, Leningrad: Izd-vo Akademii nauk SSSR. v35-37 n2 1950-mar/apr 1952. v60 n8-9 aug/sep 1975 – us Res Libr [580]
BOTANICON GALLICUM / Duby, J E – 2v. Paris. 1828-30. B-6508 2 – 8 – ne IDC [580]
BOTANICON PARISIENSE / Vaillant, S – 6481. 1723 – 9 – ne IDC [580]
BOTANICON PARISIENSE / Vaillant, S – Leiden, Amsterdam. 1727. B-8323 1 – 9 – ne IDC [580]
BOTANICON PARISIENSE / Vaillant, S – Lugduni Batavorum. 1723. B-6481 2 – 8 – ne IDC [580]
BOTANICUM MONSPELIENSI, SIVE PLANTARUM CIRCA MONSPELIUM NASCENTIUM / Magnol, P – Monspelii, 1686. 309 pp., 4 pls. B-194 2 – 8 – ne IDC [580]
BOTANICUS UNIVERSALIS ET HORTULANUS / Weston, R – 4v. Londini. 1770-77. B-950 2 – 8 – ne IDC [580]

BOTANISCHE ABHANDLUNGEN UND BEOBACHTUNGEN / Roth, A W - Nuernberg. 1787. B-297 2 - 8 - ne IDC [580]
BOTANISCHE BEMERKUNGEN / Batsch, A J G C - Halle. 1791. B-5837 2 - 8 - ne IDC [580]
BOTANISCHE BEMERKUNGEN / Presl, K B - Prag. 1844. B-260 2 - 8 - ne IDC [580]
BOTANISCHE BEMERKUNGEN UND BERICHTUNGEN / Roth, A W - Leipzig. 1807. B-5693 2 - 8 - ne IDC [580]
BOTANISCHE BEOBACHTUNGEN / Medikus, F K - Historia et Commentationes Academiae. v. 4. Theodoro-Palatinae. 1780. B-8131 1 - 9 - ne IDC [580]
BOTANISCHE BEOBACHTUNGEN DES JAHRES 1782 / Medikus, F K - Mannheim. 1783. B-8133 1 - 9 - ne IDC [580]
BOTANISCHE BEOBACHTUNGEN DES JAHRES 1783 / Medikus, F K - Mannheim. 1784. B-8134 1 - 9 - ne IDC [580]
BOTANISCHE BEOBACHTUNGEN NEBST EINIGEN NEUEN GATTUNGEN UND ARTEN / Wendland, J C - Hannover. 1798. B-446 2 - 8 - ne IDC [580]
DER BOTANISCHE GARTEN DER UNIVERSITAA5T ZU HALLE / Sprengel, K P J - Erster Nachtrag. Halle, 1801. 44 pp. B-7120 1 - 9 - ne IDC [580]
BOTANISCHE JAEHRBUCHER FUER SYSTEMATIK, PFLANZENGESCHICHTE UND PFLANZENGEOGRAPHIC / ed by Engler, A - (Generalregister. v1-30. (1881-1902). Leipzig, 1904. Generalregister. v31-66. (1901-1934). Stuttgart, 1938) - Leipzig, 1881-1941. v1-71 - 1,046mf - 5262c/2 - ne IDC [580]
BOTANISCHE ZEITUNG / ed by Hoppe, D H - Regensburg, 1802-1806. v1-5 - 31mf - 7147/2 - ne IDC [580]
BOTANISCHE ZEITUNG / ed by Schlechtendal, D F L & Mohl, H von - Leipzig, Berlin, 1843-1910. v1-68 - 1,072mf - 5590/2 - ne IDC [580]
BOTANISCHER JAHRESBERICHT / ed by Just - (1917, v45(2); 1922, v50(2); 1924, v52(2) have not been published) - Berlin, 1873-1933/1934. v1-62(2) - 1,856mf - 5421/2 - ne IDC [580]
BOTANISCHES ARCHIV : ZEITSCHRIFT FUER DIE GESAMTE BOTANIK - Koenigsberg, 1922-1934. v1-36 - 272mf - 18260/1 - ne IDC [580]
BOTANISCHES CENTRALBLATT - (Index v1-60) - Cassel, 1880-1915. v1-130 - 1,177mf - 5275/2 - ne IDC [580]
BOTANISCHES HANDBUCH DER MEHRESTEN THEILS IN DEUTSCHLAND WILD WACHSENDEN. GEWAECHSE / Schkuhr, C - ed. 2. 5 v. Leipzig. 1806-1808-14. B-5715 2 - 8 - ne IDC [580]
BOTANISCHES TASCHENBUCH AUF DAS JAHR 1807 / Weber, F & Mohr, D M H - Kiel. 1807. B-6444 2 - 8 - ne IDC [580]
BOTANISCHES TASCHENBUCH FUER DIE ANFAENGER DIESER WISSENSCHAFT UND DER APOTHEKERKUNST / ed by Hoppe, D H - (Continued as: Neues Botanisches Taschenbuch...) - Regensburg, 1790-1804; Nuernberg, Altdorf, 1805-1810 - 81mf - 9 - ne IDC [615]
BOTANISCHES ZENTRALBLATT - v. 1-176. 1880-1941 - 1 - us Princeton Micro [580]
EN BOTANISK RESA IN FINMARKEN / Fries, T M - (Botaniska Notiser, 1865). B-2339 - 8 - ne IDC [580]
BOTANISK TIDSSKRIFT - Copenhagen, 1866-1939. v 1-45 - 344mf - 9 - ne IDC [580]
BOTANISKA NOTISER : LUNDS, BOTANISKA FOERENING - (Index. 1847-1848. 1859-1862, 1869-1870 have not been published) - Lund, 1839-1941 - 566mf - 7339c/2 - ne IDC [580]
BOTANISTE - Caen, 1889-1938. v1-29 - 209mf - 6232c/2 - ne IDC [580]
LE BOTANISTE CULTIVATEUR / ed by Dumont de Courset, G L M - Paris, 1802-1805. 5 vols - 57mf - 8 - ne IDC [580]
LE BOTANISTE CULTIVATEUR OU DESCRIPTION, CULTURE ET USAGE / ed by Dumont de Courset, G L M - Ed. 2. Paris, 1811-14. 7 vols - 8 - ne IDC [580]
THE BOTANISTS OF PHILADELPHIA AND THEIR WORK / Harshberger, J W - 7553 2. 1899 - 8 - ne IDC [580]
BOTANISTS REPOSITORY / ed by Andrews, H C - London, 1797-1812(-15) 10 vols - 51mf - 8 - ne IDC [580]
BOTANISTS REPOSITORY,... / ed by Andrews, H C - London. 10v. 1797-1812[-1815] - 51mf - ne IDC [580]
BOTANOGRAPHIE BELGIQUE / Lestiboudois, T G - 2v. Paris. 1827. B-6018 2 - 8 - ne IDC [580]
BOTANY / ed by Stafleu, F A & Mink-van der Plas, Oetje de - 9 - ne IDC [580]
BOTANY AND PLANT PATHOLOGY DEPARTMENTAL SERIES / Auburn University. Agricultural Experiment Station - No.1-3. 1966-79 - 1, 5 - us Spaulding [580]
THE BOTANY OF CAPTAIN BEECHEY'S VOYAGE / Hooker, W J & Walker-Arnott, G A - London. 1830-41. B-5264 2 - 8 - ne IDC [580]
BOTANY OF CENTRAL AMERICA. BIOLOGIA CENTRALI-AMERICANA / Hemsley, W B - 5v. London. 1879-88. B-567 2 - 8 - ne IDC [580]
BOTANY OF SOCOTRA / Balfour, I B - (Trans. Roy. Soc. Edinburgh, v. 31). Edinburgh. 1887. B-437 2 - 8 - ne IDC [580]
BOTANY OF THE FORTIETH PARALLEL (U.S.A.) / Watson, S & Eaton, D C - 7638 2. 1871 - 8 - ne IDC [580]
BOTANY OF THE NORTHERN AND MIDLAND STATES / Beck, L C - Albany. 1833. B-5113 2 - 8 - ne IDC [580]
THE BOTANY OF THE SPEKE AND GRANT EXPEDITION / Grant, J A & Oliver, D - An enumeration of the plants collected during the journey from Zanzibar to Egypt. (Transact. Linn. Soc., v. 29). London. 1875. B-225 2 - 8 - ne IDC [580]
THE BOTANY OF THE VOYAGE OF H. M. S. SULPHUR / Bentham, G - 5375 2. 6 pts. 1844-1846 - 8 - ne IDC [580]
THE BOTANY OF THE VOYAGE OF H.M.S. HERALD. 1845-51 / Herald. (Ship) - Pt. 1: Flora of western Esquimaux-land. Pt. 2: Flora of the Isthmus of Panama. Pt. 3: Flora of north western Mexico. Pt. 4: Flora of Hong Kong. By B.C. Seemann. B-5739 2. 1852-1857 - 8 - ne IDC [580]
BOTANY: REPORTS AND PAPERS - 1846. Includes: I. Zuccarini, J. J. On the Morphology of the Coniferae. II. Grisebach, A. Report on Botanical Geography. III. Negali, C. Memoir on the Nuclei Formation and Growth of Vegetable Cells. IV. Link, H. F. Report on Physiological Botany - 1 - uk Microform Academic [580]
BOTATAUNG - Rangoon, Burma. 1962; 1964; 1973-88 - 45r - 1 - us L of C Photodup [072]
DER BOTE - Ein Mennonitisches Familien- und Gemeindeblatt. Saskatoon, Canada. 1972-76; 1977 (incomplete) - 1 - gw Mikrofilm [073]
DER BOTE AUS DEM EHEMALIGEN AMTE BERGEN - Bergen/Celle, jun 14 1910-may 29 1941 (very incomplete) - 1 - Dist. gw Mikrofilm - gw Misc Inst [943]
BOTE AUS DEM RIESENGEBIRGE - Hirschberg (Jelenia Gora), Poland. - 12r - 1 - gw Mikrofilm [943]
DER BOTE AUS DEN VOGESEN/PFAELZER ZEITUNG - Annweiler, apr 4-dec 29 1849 (incomplete) - 1r - 1 - Dist. gw Mikrofilm - gw Misc Inst [943]
BOTE AUS DER HEIMAT - Strasbourg, France. 1893-99 - 1 - fr A.C.R.P.P. [072]
DER BOTE AUS KURPFALZ - (Title changes: Christliches Volk Heidelberg, 1919; Christliches Volks-Blatt 1920; Sonntagsblatt des Arbeitenden Volkes in Karlsruhe, 1925; Der Religioese Sozialist in Mannheim, 1931; 1916-12 Mar 1933) - Hockenheim, Germany. - 16r - 1 - gw Mikrofilm [072]
BOTE AUS LONDON - London, UK. 27 Oct-8 Dec 1860 - 1 - uk British Libr Newspaper [072]
DER BOTE AUS THUERINGEN - Schnepfenthal (b. Gotha), 1788-1816 - 9 - gw Olms [943]
BOTE FUER STADT UND LAND - Kaiserslautern, Germany. 1848-Jun 1849 - 2r - 1 - gw Mikrofilm [072]
DER BOTE VOM GEISING UND MUEGLITZTHAL-ZEITUNG - (Incl suppl: Rund um den Geisingberg) - Altenberg, 1923-jan 1945 - 1r - 1 - Dist. gw Mikrofilm - gw Misc Inst [943]
BOTE VOM MUENSTERTAL - Munster, France.1877-1914 - 1 - fr A.C.R.P.P. [072]
DER BOTE VOM NIEDERRHEIN - Duisburg, Germany. Okt. 1865-Jun. 1866 - 1 - gw Mikrofilm [072]
DER BOTE VOM REMTSHALE *see* GEMEINNUETZIGES WOCHENBLATT
BOTE VOM UNTER-MAIN - Miltenberg, Germany. 1983- - ca 9r per yr - 1 - gw Mikrofilm [072]
DER BOTE VON AALEN - Aalen, jan 5 1848-dec 28 1849 - 1r - 1 - Dist. gw Mikrofilm - gw Misc Inst [943]
Boteler, Thomas *see* NARRATIVE OF A VOYAGE OF DISCOVERY TO AFRICA AND ARABIA
Botelho, S X. *see*
- MEMORIA ESTATISTICA SOBRE OS DOMINIOS PORTUGUEZES NA AFRICA ORIENTAL
- SEGUNDA PARTE DA MEMORIA ESTATISTICA SOBRE OS DOMINIOS PORTUQUEZES NA AFRICA ORIENTAL

Botello del Castillo, Carlos *see*
- ARITMETICA PARA LOS ALUMNOS
- COMPENDIO DE ARITMETICA..
- COMPENDIO DE GEOMETRIA Y TRIGONOMETRIA..
- ORACION...EN EL INSTITUTO PROVINCIAL DE BADAJOZ..

Botenhagen, Kim A *see* COMPARISON OF SKINFOLD MEASUREMENTS UNDER NORMALLY HYDRATED AND DEHYDRATED CONDITIONS IN FEMALES AGES TO 54
Botha, Marika G *see* THE INFLUENCE OF THE HOME ENVIRONMENT ON THE MOTOR PERFORMANCE OF PRESCHOOL CHILDREN
BOTHALIA : A RECORD OF CONTRIBUTIONS FROM THE NATIONAL HERBARIUM UNION OF SOUTH AFRICA - Pretoria, 1921-1950. v1-5 - 42mf - 8630/1 - ne IDC [580]
Botham, C N *see* AUDIO-VISUAL AIDS FOR COOPERATIVE EDUCATION AND TRAINING
Bothner, Krisanne E *see* THE DEVELOPMENT OF A VIDEO-BASED MOTION ANALYSIS SYSTEM
BOTSCHAFT UND DIENST - 1961-62; 1965-91 (complete) - Inquire - 1 - ATLA S0570 - us A.T.L.A. [073]
BOTSCHAFTER DER WAHRHEIT - (Lacking: v35 nos21, 23) - v32-56. 1931-52 - 2r - 1 - ATLA 1993-S017 - us A.T.L.A. [073]
BOTSCHAFTER DES HEILS IN CHRISTO *see*
- DIE GEMEINDE UNTERM KREUZ
- DIE KIRCHE UNTERM KREUZ

BOTSCHAFTER DES HEILS IN CHRISTO UND ZEICHEN DIESER ZEIT - (Lacking: v2 nos1-2, 4, 6. v3 no6) - v1-3. 1889-91 - 1r - 1 - ATLA 1994-S018 - us A.T.L.A. [073]
Botsford, David *see*
- AGAINST CENSORSHIP
- INDUSTRY AND STATE: MYTH AND REALITY
- THE LIBERTARIAN CHALLENGE

Botsford, Elder Edmund *see* MEMOIRS
Botsianovskii, Vladimir *see* RUSSKAIA SATIRA PERVOI REVOLIUTSII 1905-1906
BOTSWANA : STATISTICAL ABSTRACT 1966-1976 / Botswana. Central Statistics Office - (Coll title: African Official Statistical Serials, 1867-1982) - 17mf - 9 - £145.00 - uk Chadwyck [960]
BOTSWANA : 'N STUDIE IN INTERNASIONELE BETREKKINGE / Wolvaardt, Pieter Jacobus - 1968 - us Res Libr [960]
Botswana *see*
- NATIONAL DEVELOPMENT PLAN
- TRANSITIONAL PLAN FOR SOCIAL AND ECONOMIC DEVELOPMENT

BOTSWANA. CENTRAL DISTRICT : CENTRAL DISTRICT DEVELOPMENT PLAN 1989/90-1994/95 - Gaborone, 1990 - 5mf - 9 - ne IDC [338]
Botswana. Central Statistics Office *see* BOTSWANA
BOTSWANA. CHOBE DISTRICT : CHOBE DISTRICT DEVELOPMENT PLAN 1989/90-1994/95 - Gaborone, 1990 - 4mf - 9 - ne IDC [338]
BOTSWANA DAILY NEWS - [Gaborone, Botswana]: Botswana Information Service. oct 3 1966-may 11 1973; may 14 1973-sep 16 1975 - us Res Libr [072]
Botswana. Department of Education and Teacher Training *see*
- PRIMARY EDUCATION IN BOTSWANA 198?-1988(1-23)
- REPORT 1982-1983

Botswana. Educational Statistics Unit *see* EDUCATION STATISTICS 1968-1988
BOTSWANA. GHANZI DISTRICT : GHANZI DISTRICT DEVELOPMENT PLAN 1989-1995 - Gaborone, 1990 - 3mf - 9 - ne IDC [338]
Botswana. Kgalagadi District *see* KGALAGADI DISTRICT DEVELOPMENT PLAN 1989-1995
Botswana. Kgatleng District *see* KGATLENG DISTRICT DEVELOPMENT PLAN 1989-1995
Botswana. Kweneng District *see* KWENENG DISTRICT DEVELOPMENT PLAN 1989-1995
Botswana. Ministry of Education *see*
- THE AIMS AND OBJECTIVES OF EDUCATION IN BOTSWANA
- SETTING UP A PARENT-TEACHER ASSOCIATION

Botswana. Ministry of Finance and Development Planning *see*
- NATIONAL DEVELOPMENT PLAN. 1973-1978

Botswana. Ngamiland District *see* NGAMILAND DISTRICT DEVOLOPMENT PLAN 1989-1995
Botswana. North East District *see* NORTH EAST DISTRICT DEVELOPMENT PLAN 1989-1995
Botswana. South East District *see* SOUTH EAST DISTRICT DEVELOPMENT PLAN 1989-1995
Botswana. Southern District *see* SOUTHERN DISTRICT DEVLOPMENT PLAN 1989-1995
Botswana. University of Botswana. Institute of Adult Education *see* AN EVALUATION OF THE NATIONAL LITERACY PROGRAMME
Bott, Elisabeth *see* ERNST FRIES (1801-1833)
Bottalla, Paul *see* THE PAPACY AND SCHISM
Bottani, G *see* DESCRIZIONE STORICA DELLE PITTURE DEL REGIO-DUCALE PALAZZO DEL TE FUORI DELLA PORTA DI MANTOVA DETTA PUSTERLA
Bottari, G *see* VITE DE' PIU ECCELLENTI PITTORI SCULTORI E ARCHITETTI
Bottari, MN *see* IL MUSEO CAPITOLINO...
Bottego, Vittorio *see*
- L'ESPLORAZIONE DEL GUIBA
- IL GUIBA ESPLORATO
- IL GUIBA ESPORATO

Bottens, Fulg. OF M *see*
- HET GODDELYCK HERTE, OFTE DE WOONSTE GODTS IN HET HERTE
- JUDICIUM PACIFICI SALOMONIS CHRISTI DOMINI NOSTRI

Bottermann, Walther *see*
- DIE BEZIEHUNGEN DES DRAMATIKERS ACHIM VON ARNIM ZUR ALTDEUTSCHEN LITERATUR
- DIE BEZIEHUNGEN DES DRAMATIKERS ACHIM VON ARNIM ZUR ALTDEUTSCHEN LITTERATUR

Bottiglia, William F *see* VOLTAIRE'S CANDIDE: ANALYSIS OF A CLASSIC
Bottino, L *see* DEL FORO COMPETENTE PER LE AZIONI SUCCESSORIE ...
Botto, Antonio *see*
- MOTIVOS DE BELLEZA
- SONETOS
- A VERDADE E NADA MAIS

THE BOTTOM DOG - Ireland.20 Oct 1917-10 Aug 1918 - 1 - ie Microforms [072]
BOTTOM LINE - (v1-2 1985-86 1986/87-1989 Can$60.00y) - Markham. v1-2. 1985-86; 1986/87-1995 - 1 - Can$85.00y - cn Micromedia [073]
Bottome, Margaret McDonald *see* WOMEN IN THE CHURCH
Bottome, Willard B *see* THE STENOGRAPHIC EXPERT
BOTTOMLINE - v1-. Nov 1983- - 1,5,6,9 - us UMI [073]
Bottrigari, Ercole *see* IL DESIDERIO OVERO DE' CONCERTI DI VARII STRUMENTI MUSICALI..
BOTTROPER VOLKSZEITUNG - Bottrop, 1883-88, 1889 (many issues missing), 1890-91, 1893-94 - 1 - Inquire at Mikrofilmarchiv for details - gw Misc Inst [943]
BOTVIN = BATALLION "PALAFOX" - (In Yiddish) - Barcelona (Catalonia), SP. v1 no4. 12 Jun,3 Nov 1938 - 1r - 1 - $25.00 - cn Can Microfilming [072]
Botwood, Edward *see* ADDRESS DELIVERED IN ST MARY'S CHURCH, ST JOHN'S, N.F., 22ND MAY, 1898, TO LODGE DUDLEY S.O.E
Bouchage, F *see* SAINT GREGOIRE LE GRAND
Bouchard, Paul *see* LA NATION
Bouchard, T D *see*
- FEUILLES DEMOCRATIQUES
- LE HAUT-PARLEUR

Bouchaud, M A *see* ESSAI SUR LA POESIE RYTHMIQUE
Bouche *see* ELEMENTS DE GRAMMAIRE NAGO
LA BOUCHE D'ACIER AU MARAIS - [Paris]: Impr Dondey-Dupre, sep 2 1848 - us Res Libr [944]

LA BOUCHE DE FER – 1re serie: Cercle social. Lettre Ire XLVII. 1790 (t. I-II). Publ. parallelement a La Bouche de fer. 2e-3e serie: La Bouche de fer. oct 1790-juil 1791 (t. I-IV). suivi de: Annales de la Confederation universelle des amis de la verite. Supplement a La Bouche de fer. 1791 (t. V, no. 1-2). suivi de: Bulletin de La Bouche de fer. juil 1790. Paris – 1 – fr A.C.R.P.P. [073]
LA BOUCHE DE FER – no. 26-27. Paris. aout-sept 1893 – 1 – fr A.C.R.P.P. [073]
LA BOUCHE DE FER – Redacteurs: Claude Fauchet et Nicolas de Bonneville. Paris. Imprimerie du Cercle Social. 1790-91 – 9 – fr Hachette [321]
LA BOUCHE DE FER – [Paris]: J Frey, aug 24 1848 – us Res Libr [944]
Bouche, P F *see* NATURGESCHICHTE DER INSEKTEN, BESONDERS IN HINSICHT IHRER ERSTEN ZUSTAENDE ALS LARVEN UND PUPPEN
Bouche, Pierre Bertrand *see*
- LE COTE DES ESCLAVES ET LE DAHOMEY
- SEPT ANS EN AFRIQUE OCCIDENTALE.

Bouche-Leclercq, A *see* L'INTOLERANCE RELIGIEUSE ET LA POLITIQUE
BOUCHER AND PRATTE'S MUSICAL JOURNAL – Montreal: [s.n.], 1881-1882 – 9 – cn C.I.H.M. [780]
Boucher, Andre *see* A TRAVERS LES MISSIONS DU TOGO ET DU DAHOMEY
Boucher de Boucherville, George *see*
- LE CREDIT FONCIER
- UNE DE PERDUE, DEUX DE TROUVEES

Boucher de la Bruere, Pierre *see*
- DE L'EDUCATION: CONFERENCE FAITE EN FEVRIER 1881 DEVANT LE CERCLE CATHOLIQUE DE QUEBEC
- LE SAGUENAY

Boucher, George P *see* A BIOMECHANICAL ANALYSIS OF THE PROLONGED EFFECTS ON FUNCTIONAL PARAMETERS OF A TEST SEATING SYSTEM FOR MODERATELY INVOLVED CEREBRAL PALSIED CHILDREN
Boucher, J-A *see* LES BEAUX-ARTS
Boucher, John N *see* HISTORY OF WESTMORELAND COUNTY
Boucher, Louis *see* BIBLIOGRAPHIE DES QUOTIDIENS DE LANGUE FRANCAISE PARUS DANS LA PROVINCE DE QUEBEC DEPUIS 1867
Boucher, Pierre *see*
- CANADA IN THE SEVENTEENTH CENTURY
- HISTOIRE VERITABLE ET NATURELLE DES MOEURS ET PRODUCTIONS DU PAYS DE LA NOUVELLE-FRANCE, VULGAIREMENT DITE LE CANADA
- HISTOIRE VERITABLE ET NATURELLE DES MOEURS & PRODUCTIONS DU PAYS DE LA NOUVELLE FRANCE, VULGAIREMENT DITE LE CANADA

Boucherville, Georges Boucher de *see* DICTIONNAIRE DU LANGAGE DES NOMBRES...: AVEC UNE INTRODUCTION CONTENANT LES PRINCIPES D'UNE METHODE DE REDUCTION ET L'USAGE QUE L'ON EN PEUT FAIRE POUR ABREGER LES CORRESPONDANCES TELEGRAPHIQUES ET AUTRES
Boucherville, J B de *see* RAPPORTS D'UNE EXPLORATION, DEPUIS LA CHUTE AUX IROQUOIS DANS LE COMTE D'OTTAWA, JUSQU'A LA BAIE DES PERES DANS LA COMTE DE PONTIAC
Bouchette, Errol *see*
- EMPARONS-NOUS DE L'INDUSTRIE
- ETUDES SOCIALES ET ECONOMIQUES SUR LE CANADA
- L'INDEPENDANCE ECONOMIQUE DU CANADA FRANCAIS

Bouchette, Joseph *see*
- ANALYSE CHRONOLOGIQUE RELATIVE A LA CONCESSION DU 25 FEVRIER 1661, APPELEE LA SEIGNEURIE DE L'ISLE AUX OEUFS
- THE BRITISH DOMINIONS IN NORTH AMERICA.
- DESCRIPTION TOPOGRAPHIQUE DE LA PROVINCE DU BAS-CANADA
- DESCRIPTION TOPOGRAPHIQUE DE LA PROVINCE DU BAS-CANADA, AVEC DES REMARQUES SUR LE HAUT-CANADA
- TO HIS ROYAL HIGHNESS GEORGES AUGUSTUS FREDERICK,...THIS TOPOGRAPHICAL MAP OF THE PROVINCE OF LOWER CANADA
- A TOPOGRAPHICAL DICTIONARY OF THE PROVINCE OF LOWER CANADA

Bouchette, Robert Shore Milnes *see* MEMOIRES..
Bouchilloux, Helene *see* APOLOGETIQUE ET RAISON DANS LES PENSEES DE PASCAL
Boucqueau, Philippe *see* MEMOIRE STATISTIQUE DU DEPARTEMENT DE RHIN-ET-MOSELLE
Bouda, K *see* DIE BEZIEHUNGEN DES SUMERISCHEN ZUM BASKISCHEN WESTKAUSISCHEN UND TIBETISCHEN
Boudaa, Azzedine *see* DIE AUSWIRKUNGEN DES BILINGUALISMUS IN ALGERIEN (FRANZOESISCH/ARABISCH) AUF DAS ERLERNEN DES DEUTSCHEN ALS FREMDSPRACHE
BOUDDHISME CHINOIS. EXTRAITS DU TRIPITAKA, DES COMMENTAIRES, TRACTS, ETC / Wieger, Leon – 1910-13 – 1 – us A.T.L.A. [280]
Boudier, E *see* DES CHAMPIGNONS AU POINT DE VUE DE LEURS CARACTERES USUELS, CHIMIQUES ET TOXICOLOGIQUES...
Boudin, Amedee *see* HISTOIRE GENEALOGIQUE DU MUSEE DES CROISADES
Boudin, Jean Christian Marc Francois Joseph *see* TRAITE DE GEOGRAPHIE ET DE STATISTIQUE MEDICALE ET DES MALADIES ENDEMIQUES
Boudinot, Elias *see* THE MAN IN A TRANCE
Boudyck Bastiaanse, J H van *see* VOYAGE A LA COTE DE GUINEE, DANS LE GOLFE DE BIAFRA, A L'ILE DE FERNANDO-PO, L'ILE DE STE HELENE ET AUTRES ILES DANS LE PASSAGE
Bouet-Willaumez, E *see* COMMERCE ET TRAITE DES NOIRS AUX COTES OCCIDENTALES D'AFRIQUE
Boufflers, Stanislas Jean de *see* JOURNAL INEDIT DU SECOND SEJOUR AU SENEGAL (3 DECEMBRE 1786 – 25 DECEMBRE 1787)
Bougainville, L A de *see* VOYAGE AUTOUR DU MONDE, PAR LA FREGATE DU ROI LA BOUDEUSE, ET LA FLUTE L'ETOILE; EN 1766, 1767, ET 1769
Bougaud, Emile *see*
- GESCHICHTE DER HEILIGEN MONIKA
- HISTORY OF ST. VINCENT DE PAUL

Bougeant *see* HISTOIRE DES GUERRES ... TRAITE DE WESTPHALIE, ...
Bougeant, Le P G H *see* AMUSEMENT PHILOSOPHIQUE SUR LE LANGAGE DES BESTES
Bougeant, R PG H *see* AMUSEMENT PHILOSOPHIQUE SUR LE LANGAGE DES BETES
Bougeois, CF *see* AUX SAINT-SIMONIENS ET AUX SAINT-SIMONIENNES. SUR LA NECESSITE ET LA POSSIBILITE DE RALLIER LA DOCTRINE DE SAINT-SIMON A LA FOI CHRETIENNE ET AU CHRISTIANISME TEMPOREL
Bougouin, E *see*
- LA FINANCE INTERNATIONALE ET LA GUERRE D'ESPAGNE
- LA FINANZA INTERNACIONAL Y LA GUERRA DE ESPANA

Bouguer, M Pierre *see* TRAITE COMPLET DE LA NAVIGATION CONTENANT LES PROPOSITIONS ET PRATIQUES DE GEOMETRIE, UN TRAITE DE LA SPHERE ET D'ASTRONOMIE.
Bouhours, D *see*
- DOUTES SUR LA LANGUE FRANCOISE
- LES ENTRETIENS D'ARISTE ET D'EUGENE
- REMARQUES NOUVELLES SUR LA LANGUE FRANCOISE
- SUITE DES REMARQUES NOUVELLES SUR LA LANGUE FRANCOISE

Bouillard, Dom J, OSB *see* HISTOIRE DE L'ABBAYE DE SAINT-GERMAIN-DES-PREZ
Bouillet, Jean B *see* NOBILIAIRE D'AUVERGNE
Bouilly, Jean Nicolas *see*
- L'ABBE DE L'EPEE
- LES DEUX JOURNEES
- FANCHON LA VIELLEUSE
- JEAN-JACQUES ROUSSEAU, A SES DERNIERS MOMENTS: TRAIT HISTORIQUE: EN UN ACTE ET EN PROSE: REPRESENTE POUR LA PREMIERE FOIS, A PARIS, PAR LES COMEDIENS ITALIENS ORDINAIRES DU ROI, LE 31 DECEMBRE 1790
- LEONORE OU L'AMOUR CONJUGAL
- MADAME DE SEVIGNE
- RENE DESCARTES

Boujard, T *see* ETUDE DU PEUPLEMENT PISCICOLE DE PLANS D'EAU NON VIDANGEABLES
Boukhari, Mir A K *see* HISTOIRE DE L'ASIE CENTRALE
Boulaese, Jehan *see* L'ABBREGEE HISTOIRE DU GRAND MIRACLE PAR NOSTRE SAUVEUR
Boulanger, Nicolas A *see*
- L'ANTIQUITE DEVOILEE PAR SES USAGES OU EXAMEN CRITIQUE DES PRINCIPALES OPINIONS, CEREMONIES ET INSTITUTIONS RELIGIEUSES ET POLITIQUES DES DIFFERENTS PEUPLES DE LA TERRE
- RECHERCHES SUR L'ORIGINE DU DESPOTISME ORIENTAL

Boulard, Antoine Marie Henri *see* ESSAI D'UN NOUVEAU COURS DE LANGUE ALLEMANDE OU CHOIX DES MEILLEURS POEMES DE ZACHARIE, KLEIST ET HALLER
Boulay, A *see* MUSCINEES DE LA FRANCE
BOULDER CITY AGE – Boulder City, NV. May 1932; Aug 1933 – 1r – 1 – $50.00 – U04422 – us Library Micro [071]
BOULDER CITY AGE – Las Vegas, NV. 1932-1933 – 1r – 1 – $50.00 – U04597 – us Library Micro [071]
THE BOULDER CITY BULLETIN – Boulder City, NV. 1994 – 1+ r – 1 – $50.00 ($50.00y) – U04907 – us Library Micro [071]
BOULDER CITY CITIZEN – Boulder City, NV. 1951 – 1 – U04830 – us Library Micro [071]
BOULDER CITY DAILY REMINDER – Boulder City, NV. 1938-1940 – 4r – 1 – $200.00 – U4831 – us Library Micro [071]
BOULDER CITY NEWS – Boulder City, NV. 1941- – 65+ r – 1 UN04424 – $3,250.00 ($95.00y) – us Library Micro [071]
BOULDER COUNTY (COLORADO) AREA KEY – Comp. by Florence Runyan Clint. 1969. 1 fiche.F-0057 – 9 – us A.G.L.L. [920]
BOULDER DAM CHALLENGE – Las Vegas, NV. 1936 – 1r – 1 – $50.00 – U04850 – us Library Micro [071]
Boulenger, G A *see*
- CATALOGUE OF FRESHWATER FISHES OF AFRICA
- CATALOGUE OF THE FRESH-WATER FISHES OF AFRICA IN THE BRITISH MUSEUM (NATURAL HISTORY)
- REVISION DES ROSES D'ASIE
- LES ROSES D'EUROPE DE L'HERBIER CREPIN
- THE TAILLESS BATRACHIANS OF EUROPE

Boulet, J B *see* DECLARATION
LES BOULETS ROUGES : LE DU CLUB PACIFIQUE DES DROITS DE L'HOMME – [Paris]: F Malteste, jun 22-25 1848 – us Res Libr [944]
LE BOULEVARD – Paris. dec 1861-juin 1863 – 1 – fr A.C.R.P.P. [073]
O BOULEVARD : JORNAL PARA SENHORAS – Bahia, BA. 19 Out 1870 – 1,5,6 – bl Biblioteca [072]
BOULEVARD BAPTIST CHURCH. ANDERSON, SOUTH CAROLINA : CHURCH RECORDS – 1953-65 – 1 – $62.56 – us Baptist [240]
THE BOULEVARDIER – Paris. v. 1-6 no. 1. 1927-Jan 1932 – 1 – us NY Public [073]
Boulgakof, S *see*
- DU VERBE INCARNE (AGNUS DEI)
- LE PARACLET

Boulger, Demetrius Charles de Kavanagh *see* ENGLAND AND RUSSIA IN CENTRAL ASIA
Boulinier-Giraud, G *see* ETUDE MORPHOLOGIQUE DE LA PIROGUE A BALANCIER AUX COMORES ET DANS L'OUEST DE L'OCEAN INDIEN
Boullault, Mathurin-J *see* MATHURIN J. BOULLAULT
Boullay, B *see* L'ETAT ET LES COMPAGNIES ...
Boullay, G *see* DE LA CONDITION JURIDIQUE DES SOCIETES ETRANGERES EN FRANCE ...
Boullier, J *see* DE L'ASILE ACCORDE AUX VAISSEAUX DE GUERRE ...
Boulliette, Abbe *see* TRAITE DE LA MANIERE D'ENSEIGNER A LIRE
Boulogne, E A de *see* INSTRUCTION PASTORALE DE MONSEIGNEUR L'EVEQUE DE TROYES
BOULOGNE EXPRESS – London. -w. 25 Jun 1864-5 Jan 1867. (2 reels) – 1 – uk British Libr Newspaper [072]
BOULOU : CHACAL DU MYOMBE / Trautmann, Rene – Bordeaux: Editions Delmas, 1944 – 1 – us Res Libr [960]
Boulouis, J *see* ESSAI SUR LA POLITIQUE DES SUBVENTIONS ADMINISTRATIVES
Boulton, George D'Arcy *see* REPLY TO THE STATEMENTS MADE AFFECTING THE NORTHERN RAILWAY COMPANY OF CANADA IN THE PETITION OF THE CREDIT VALLEY RAILWAY FOR A RAILWAY COMMISSION
Boulton, Mathew *see* EIGHT SILVER PATTERN BOOKS
BOUND MSS IN THE A.R. WENTZ LIBRARY. (MIMEO) / Lutheran Theological Seminary – Gettysburg, PA. 1977 – 1mf – 9 – ne IDC [240]
BOUND RECORDS OF THE GENERAL LAND OFFICE RELATING TO PRIVATE LAND CLAIMS IN LOUISIANA, 1767-1892 – 8r – 1 – M1382 – us Nat'l Archives [324]
BOUND VOLUMES OF THE GENERAL RECORDS OF THE U.S. CONSULATE AT YOKOHAMA, JAPAN, 1936-1939 – 22 rolls – 9 – $506.00 – Dist. us Scholarly Res – us L of C Photodup [324]
BOUND VOLUMES OF THE GENERAL RECORDS OF THE U.S. CONSULATE AT YOKOHAMA, JAPAN, 1936-1939 – 22r – 1 – M1520 – us Nat'l Archives [324]
BOUNDARIES AND ETHNOGRAPHY OF HUNGARY PAMPHLET COLLECTION – 1918-1942 – 1 – CSUXANL5682-B – us Hoover Inst Photo [947]
BOUNDARIES BETWEEN WEST AND EAST GERMANY PAMPHLET COLLECTION – 1961-1971 – 1 – CSUXANS2485-B – us Hoover Inst Photo [306]
BOUNDARIES OF POLAND PAMPHLET COLLECTION – 1912-1970 – 1 – CSUXANL7232-B – us Hoover Inst Photo [947]
THE BOUNDARY QUESTION / Cockburn, James – Ottawa?, 1880?. 03206. (Pre-1900 Canadiana) – 9 – cn C.I.H.M. [971]
BOUNDARY-LAYER METEOROLOGY – (1984-5,6,9) – v1- Mar 1970- – 1 – us UMI [550]
Bounere, Benedictius du *see* COLEPHOUS DE MANUSCRITO
LE BOUQUET : DEDIE A LA JEUNESSE CANADIENNE / ed by Malo, J-H – Montreal, Canada. 24 dec 1881-v1 n3. 7 jan 1882 – 1r – 1 – Can$25.00 – cn Can Microfilming [072]
Bouquet, A C *see* AN INTRODUCTION TO THE STUDY OF EFFORTS AT CHRISTIAN REUNION
Bouquet, D *see* RECUEIL DES HISTORIENS DES GAULES ET DE LA FRANCE
Bouquet, Henry *see* PAPERS
Bouquet, Louis *see* LE TRAVAIL DES ENFANTS ET DES FILLES MINEURES DANS L'INDUSTRIE. LOI DU 19 MAI 1874. REGLEMENTS D'ADMINISTRATION PUBLIQUE, CIRCULAIRES, INSTRUCTIONS MINISTERIELLES, DECISIONS JUDICIARIES REUNIS ET COMMENTES
Bouquet, Martin *see* RERUM GALLICARUM ET FRANCICARUM SCRIPTORES (RGFS)
Bouquet, Martin et al *see* RECUEIL DES HISTORIENS DES GAULES ET DE LA FRANCE
Bouquie, J *see* DE LA JUSTICE ...
Bouquier et Moline (musique de Porta) *see* LA REUNION DU 10 AOUT OU L'INAUGURATION DE LA REPUBLIQUE FRANCAISE
LE BOUQUINEUR / ed by Laplace, O – Montreal, Canada. aut 1894; v1 n2. sep 1894 – 1r – 1 – Can$25.00 – cn Can Microfilming [073]
Bour, R S *see* L'INSCRIPTION DE QUIRINIUS ET LE RECENSEMENT DE S. LUC
Bourassa, Gustave *see*
- CONFERENCES ET DISCOURS
- L'HOTEL DE RAMBOUILLET: CONFERENCE FAITE A L'UNIVERSITE LAVAL
- LA JEUNESSE DE MONTALEMBERT: CONFERENCE FAITE AU CERCLE VILLE-MARIE DE MONTREAL
- M. CHAUVEAU ET L'IDEE NATIONALE: CONFERENCE FAITE DEVANT L'ASSOCIATION DES INSTITUTEURS DE LA CIRCONSCRIPTION DE L'ECOLE NORMALE JACQUES CARTIER, A L'OCCASION DE SA CENTIEME CONFERENCE, LE 24 JANVIER, 1895

Bourassa, Lucette *see* LE ROMAN AU CANADA-FRANCAIS, 1925-1949
Bourassa, Napoleon *see* NOS GRAND'MERES: DISCOURS PRONONCE DEVANT LA SOCIETE DES DAMES DE CHARITE DE MONTREAL
Bourbon County, KS. Public School *see* RECORDS
Bourbon, J de *see* LA GRANDE ET MERUEIILEUSE, ET TRESCRUELLE OPPUGNATIO DE LA NOBLE CITE DE RHODES, ...
Bourcet *see* PRINCIPES DE LA GUERRE DE MONTAGNES.
Bourchier, Lady *see* MEMOIR OF THE LIFE OF ADMIRAL SIR EDWARD CODRINGTON, WITH SELECTIONS FROM HIS PUBLIC AND PRIVATE CORRESPONDENCE

Bourdages, J *see* BIBLIOGRAPHIE DES ECRITS DU TRES REV. PERE PASCAL D'OTTAWA, EX-PROV. DE L'ORDRE DES FRERES MINEURS CAPUCINS, EX-PROF. DE PATROLOGIE ET D'HISTOIRE SAINTE
Bourdalque, Luis *see* RETIRO ESPIRITUAL PARA COMUNIDADES RELIGIOSAS...
Bourdeaux, Jean *see* LES CARRIERES FEMININES INTELLECTUELLES
BOURDELLE / Reunion des musees nationaux. Paris – 1931. 18 illus. 2 fiches – 9 – fr Réunion [700]
Bourdelles, R de *see*
- DE L'APPLICATION DU ... ENTRE LA FRANCE ET LA SARDAIGNE ...
- LE DROIT INTERNATIONAL PUBLIC MARITIME ...

LE BOURDON – St-Hyacinthe, Canada. 14 jul 1866 – 1r – 1 – Can$20.00 – cn Can Microfilming [072]
Bourdon de la Crosniere, Louis Jean Joseph Leonard *see* PLAN D'UN ESTABLISSEMENT D'EDUCATION NATIONALE
Bourdon, Hilaire *see* THE CHURCH AND THE FUTURE
Bourdon-Viane, G *see* MANUEL ELEMENTAIRE ...
Bourgain, L *see* LA CHAIRE FRANCAISE AU 12 SIECLE
Bourgeois, L *see* POUR LA SOCIETE DES NATIONS
Bourgeois, Phileas Frederic *see*
- LES ANCIENS MISSIONNAIRES DE L'ACADIE DEVANT L'HISTOIRE
- L'ECOLE AUX APPARATIONS MYSTERIEUSES
- PANEGYRIQUE DE L'ABBE JEAN MANDE SIGIGNE: MISSIONNAIRE FRANCAIS A LA BAIE STE. MARIE, N. ECOSSE DEPUIS 1799 JUSQU'EN 1844

Bourgeois, R *see* BANYARWANDA ET BARUNDI
Bourget, Ignace *see*
- DERNIERS AVIS A SES JEUNES PRETRES.
- FIORETTI VESCOVILI, OU, EXTRAITS DES MANDEMENTS, LETTRES PASTORALES ET CIRCULAIRES DE MSG. IGNACE BOURGET SECOND EVEQUE DE MONTREAL
- VIE DE SAINT VIATEUR: CONFESSEUR ET LECTEUR DE L'EGLISE DE LYON

Bourget, Joseph G *see* PASSETEMPS SUR LES CHARS: RECITS ET NOUVELLES
Bourget, Magdeleine *see* BIO-BIBLIOGRAPHIE ANALYTIQUE DE M. ELPHEGE-J. DAIGNAULT
Bourgoin, J *see* PRECIS DE L'ART ARABE
Bourgoing, Andre *see* BIBLIOGRAPHIE DE L'OEUVRE DE GERARD TREMBLAY, S.-MIN., MINISTERE DU TRAVAIL, GOUV. PROV., ANCIEN PROFESSEUR A L'UNIVERSITE LAVAL
Bourgoing, P de *see* LES GUERRES D'IDIOME ET DE NATIONALITE
Bourguignat, J R *see*
- MALACOLOGIE D'AIX-LES-BAINS
- MALACOLOGIE DE LA GRANDE CHARTREUSE
- MALACOLOGIE TERRESTRE ET FLUVIATILE DE LA BRETAGNE

Bourguignon, C *see* VIE DU PERE ROMILLION, PRETRE DEL'ORATOIRE DE JESUS. VIE DU PERE ROMILLION, PRETRE DEL'ORATOIRE DE JESUS
Bourguignon, H *see*
- TRAITE ENTOMOLOGIQUE ET PATHOLOGIQUE DE LA GALE DE L'HOMME
- TRAITE PRATIQUE D'ENTOMOLOGIE ET DE PATHOLOGIE COMPAREES DE LA PSORE

Bourinot, John George *see*
- BUILDERS OF NOVA SCOTIA: A HISTORICAL REVIEW, WITH AN APPENDIX CONTAINING COPIES OF RARE DOCUMENTS RELATING TO THE EARLY DAYS OF THE PROVINCE
- CANADA AND THE UNITED STATES: A STUDY IN COMPARATIVE POLITICS
- CANADA AND THE UNITED STATES: AN HISTORICAL RETROSPECT
- CANADA AS A HOME
- CANADA DURING THE VICTORIAN ERA: A HISTORICAL REVIEW
- CANADA UNDER BRITISH RULE: 1760-1900
- CANADA'S MARINE AND FISHERIES
- A CANADIAN MANUAL ON THE PROCEDURE AT MEETINGS OF MUNICIPAL COUNCILS, SHAREHOLDERS AND DIRECTORS OF COMPANIES, SYNODS, CONVENTIONS, SOCIETIES AND PUBLIC BODIES GENERALLY
- CANADIAN STUDIES IN COMPARATIVE POLITICS
- ELECTED OR APPOINTED OFFICIALS?: A PAPER SUBMITTED TO THE AMERICAN ACADEMY OF POLITICAL AND SOCIAL SCIENCE
- FEDERAL GOVERNMENT IN CANADA
- THE FISHERY QUESTION: ITS IMPERIAL IMPORTANCE
- HISTORICAL AND DESCRIPTIVE ACCOUNT OF THE ISLAND OF CAPE BRETON: AND OF ITS MEMORIALS OF THE FRENCH REGIME: WITH BIBLIOGRAPHICAL, HISTORICAL AND CRITICAL NOTES
- HOW CANADA IS GOVERNED: A SHORT ACCOUNT OF ITS EXECUTIVE, LEGISLATIVE, JUDICIAL AND MUNICIPAL INSTITUTIONS: WITH AN HISTORICAL OUTLINE OF THEIR ORIGIN AND DEVELOPMENT
- ILLUSTRATIONS OF THE HISTORICAL BALL: GIVEN BY THEIR EXCELLENCIES THE EARL AND COUNTESS OF ABERDEEN IN THE SENATE CHAMBER, OTTAWA, 17TH FEBRUARY, 1896
- THE INTELLECTUAL DEVELOPMENT OF THE CANADIAN PEOPLE: AN HISTORICAL REVIEW
- A MANUAL OF THE CONSTITUTIONAL HISTORY OF CANADA FROM THE EARLIEST PERIOD TO THE YEAR 1888: INCLUDING THE BRITISH NORTH AMERICA ACT, 1867, AND A DIGEST OF JUDICIAL DECISIONS ON QUESTIONS OF LEGISLATIVE JURISDICTION
- THE NATIONAL DEVELOPMENT OF CANADA
- OUR INTELLECTUAL STRENGTH AND WEAKNESS: A SHORT HISTORICAL AND CRITICAL REVIEW OF LITERATURE, ART AND EDUCATION IN CANADA
- PARLIAMENTARY GOVERNMENT IN CANADA: A CONSTITUTIONAL AND HISTORICAL STUDY
- PARLIAMENTARY PROCEDURE AND PRACTICE: WITH AN INTRODUCTORY ACCOUNT OF THE ORIGIN AND GROWTH OF PARLIAMENTARY INSTITUTIONS IN THE DOMINION OF CANADA
- SOCIAL AND ECONOMIC CONDITIONS OF THE BRITISH PROVINCES AFTER THE CANADIAN REBELLIONS 1838-40
- THE STORY OF CANADA

BOURKE BANNER – 1899-1907 – 9 – at Pascoe [072]
Bourke, John Gregory *see* DIARIES OF CAPTAIN JOHN GREGORY BOURKE
Bourke, Ulick Joseph *see*
- INEFFABILIS DEUS
- THE LIFE AND TIMES OF THE MOST REV. JOHN MACHALE

Bourlamaque, Francois Charles de *see* LETTRES AU CHEVALIER DE LEVIS...PUBLIEES SOUS LA DIRECTION DE L'ABBE H. R. CASGRAIN
Bourlon, I *see* LES ASSEMBLEES DU CLERGUE ET LE JANSENISME
Bourne, FW *see* THE BIBLE CHRISTIANS
Bourne, H *see*
- AUTOBIOGRAPHY
- JOURNALS, 1803-1804, 1808-1813, 1816-1820, 1842-1852

Bourne, Henry Richard Fox *see* THE STORY OF OUR COLONIES: WITH SKETCHES OF THEIR PRESENT CONDITIONS
Bourne, Hugh *see* THE JOURNAL OF HIS AMERICAN MISSION
Bourne, Richard *see* POLITICAL LEADERS OF LATIN AMERICA
BOURNEMOUTH DAILY ECHO – England.20 Aug 1900-1905; 1909-25. -d. 53 reels – 1 – uk British Libr Newspaper [072]
Bourneville, Desire Magloire *see* LAICISATION DE L'ASSISTANCE PUBLIQUE.
Bourquin, Theodor *see* GRAMMATIK DER ESKIMO-SPRACHE.
LES BOURREAUX DEPUIS 1837 JUSQU'A 1871: DETAILS INEDITS SUR LEUR ORIGINE, LEURS ACTES, ETC: SOURVENIRS DE L'INSURRECTION CANADIENNE EN 1837 – 1871? 00219. (Pre-1900 Canadiana) – 9 – cn C.I.H.M. [971]
BOURREAUX ET MARTYRS: CONFERENCE DONNEE A L'INSTITUT CANADIEN D'OTTAWA, LE 12 FEVRIER 1891 – 1891?. 03815. (Pre-1900 Canadiana) – 9 – cn C.I.H.M. [971]
Bourricaud, F *see* POUVOIR ET SOCIETE DANS LE PEROU CONTEMPORAIN
Bourrousse de Laffore, Pierre Jules de *see* DU PROGRES ALARMANT DE LA MORTALITE DANS LE DEPARTEMENT DE LOT-ET-GARONNE ET EN PARTICULIER DANS LA COMMUNE D'AGEN
LE BOURRU : ILLUSTRE – CARICATURES. HEBDO – Longueuil, Canada. 8 aut-12 sep 1885 – 1r – 1 – Can$31.25 – cn Can Microfilming [740]
LE BOURRU – Quebec, Canada. 1 fev 1859-28 jan 1860 – 1r – 1 – Can$35.00 – cn Can Microfilming [072]
Bourru, Henri et Ferdinand Burot *see* VARIATIONS DE LA PERSONNALITE PAR LES DOCTEURS H. BOURRU ET P. BUROT
LA BOURSE : HEBDO – Montreal, sep 1986-nov 1987 – 1r – 1 – Can$50.00 – cn Can Microfilming [072]
BOURSE DE PARIS – Copie du cours authentique. Paris. avr-dec 1881 – 1 – fr A.C.R.P.P. [073]
Bourse du travail de Paris *see* BULLETIN OFFICIEL DE LA BOURSE DU TRAVAIL DE PARIS
LA BOURSE EGYPTIENNE – Cairo, Egypt. -d. 15 June 1945-9 Aug 1946; 2 June 1952-31 Jan 1955; 2 May 1955-25 Oct 1956. 18 reels – 1 – uk British Libr Newspaper [072]
BOURSES DE VOYAGE / Verne, Jules – Paris: J. Hetzel, s.d. 313p. 4 fiches.(Literature Collection) – 9 – 10.00 – fr Bibl Nationale [830]
Bourzat, D *see* SMALL RUMINANTS IN AFRICAN AGRICULTURE
BOU-SAADA, CITE DE BONHEUR / Lehuraux, Leon – Alger, Soubiron, [1934?] – 1 – us Res Libr [960]
Bousquet, Georges *see* LE JAPON DE NOS JOURS ET LES ECHELLES DE L'EXTREME-ORIENT
Boussenard, Louis *see*
- LE CAPITAINE CASSE-COU
- CHASSEURS CANADIENS

Bousset, J B *see* IL RECUEIL D'AIRS NOUVEAUX SERIEUX ET A BOIRE
Bousset, Wilhelm *see*
- DER ANTICHRIST IN DER UEBERLIEFERUNG DES JUDENTUMS, DES NEUEN TESTAMENTS UND DER ALTEN KIRCHE
- APOPHTEGMATA
- DIE EVANGELIENCITATE JUSTIN DES MAERTYRERS IN IHREM WERT FUER DIE EVANGELIENKRITIK VON NEUEM UNTERSUCHT
- THE FAITH OF A MODERN PROTESTANT
- JESU PREDIGT IN IHREM GEGENSATZ ZUM JUDENTUM
- JESUS
- DIE JUEDISCHE APOKALYPTIK
- TEXTKRITISCHE STUDIEN ZUM NEUEN TESTAMENT (T.U.U. 1-11/4)
- UNSER GOTTESGLAUBE
- WESEN DER RELIGION
- DAS WESEN DER RELIGION
- WHAT IS RELIGION

LA BOUSSOLE : NATIONALISTE – Montreal, 18 avr 1935-6 avr 1946 – 2r – 1 – Can$35.00 – cn Can Microfilming [072]
LA BOUSSOLE *see* LE NICOLETAIN
LA BOUSSOLE MORALE ET POLITIQUE DES HOMMES, ... – Boston, 1779 – 2mf – 9 – ILM-851/1 – ne IDC [327]
Boussus, F *see* LE DIVORCE ET LA SEPARATION DE CORPS ...
Boustany, W F *see* PALESTINE MANDATE ...
Boutant, C A *see* LES MANDATS INTERNATIONAUX
Boutard, Charles *see* LAMENNAIS
Bouteiller, Ernest de *see* DICTIONNAIRE TOPOGRAPHIQUE DE L'ANCIEN DEPARTEMENT DE LA MOSELLE: COMPRENANT LES NOMS DE LIEU ANCIENS ET MODERNES
Bouteiller, J *see* DE SAINT-LOUIS A SIERRA-LEONE
Bouteron, J *see*
- DE L'UNIFICATION DU DROIT RELATIF A LA LETTRE DE CHANGE ET AU BILLET A ORDRE
- LE STATUT INTERNATIONAL DU CHEQUE

Bouterwek, Friedrich *see* GESCHICHTE DER POESIE UND BEREDSAMKEIT SEIT DEM ENDE DES 13. JAHRHUNDERTS
Boutet, Monvel De *see* LES VICTIMES CLOITREES
Boutet, Odina *see* BIO-BIBLIOGRAPHIE CRITIQUE D'ANNE HEBERT
Bouthillier Chavigny, Charles de *see*
- A TRAVERS LE NORD-OUEST CANADIEN
- A TRAVERS LE NORD-OUEST CANADIEN: DE MONTREAL AUX MONTAGNES ROCHEUSES: NOTES DE VOYAGE
- ADDRESS BEFORE THE IMPERIAL INSTITUTE OF GREAT BRITAIN ON THE 10TH OF MARCH, 1898
- JUSTICE AUX CANADIENS-FRANCAIS

Boutillier, T *see* RAPPORT DES TRAVAUX DE COLONISATION DE L'ANNEE 1855
Boutin, Rose-Anne *see* BIBLIOGRAPHIE ANALYTIQUE DE L'OEUVRE DE L'HONORABLE SENATEUR CYRILLE VAILLANCOURT...
Boutiot, Theophile *see* DICTIONNAIRE TOPOGRAPHIQUE DU DEPARTEMENT DE L'AUBE
BOUTIQUE AND VILLAGER – (Cont: Burlingame Villager) – Burlingame, CA. 1965- – 37+ r – 1 – $1,850.00 ($90.00y) – B02085 – us Library Micro [071]
BOUTIQUE AND VILLAGER – Hillsborough, CA. 1965- – 37+ r – 1 – $1,850.00 ($90.00y) – B02295 – us Library Micro [071]
Bouton, Rene *see* L'INFANTICIDE, ETUDE MORALE ET JURIDIQUE
Boutroux, Emile *see*
- THE BEYOND THAT IS WITHIN, AND OTHER ADDRESSES
- EDUCATION AND ETHICS
- HISTORICAL STUDIES IN PHILOSOPHY
- PASCAL
- SCIENCE AND RELIGION IN CONTEMPORARY PHILOSOPHY
- WILLIAM JAMES

Boutroux, Emile [et al] *see* LECTURES
Boutwell, George S *see* THE CONSTITUTION OF THE UNITED STATES AT THE END OF THE FIRST CENTURY
Bouverot, A *see* DOSSIERS D'ETHNOLOGIE PROVENCALE, NO. 1. LA CUISINE EN BASSE PROVENCE RURALE
Bouvet, J *see*
- ICON REGIA MONARCHAE SINARUM... 1699
- PORTRAIT HISTORIQUE DE L'EMPEREUR DE LA CHINE,...

Bouvier, A *see* CATALOGUE DES COLLECTIONS ORNITHOLOGIQUES
Bouvier, Ch. *see* LA COLLECTIVISATION DE L'AGRICULTURE
Bouvier, E L *see*
- DESCRIPTION DES CRUSTACES DE LA FAMILLE DES GALATHEIDES
- LES PORCELLANIDES ET DES BRACHYURES

Bouvier, Jeanne *see* LA LINGERIE ET LES LINGERES
Bouwman, M *see* VOETIUS OVER HET GEZAG DER SYNODEN
BOUWSTEENEN – Amsterdam, 1869/1872-74/1881. v 1-3 – 12mf – 1 – ne IDC [780]
Bovea, A *see* OBRA...DE LA GRANDE Y TERRIBLE MORTANDAD
Bovee, Kristin K *see* CURRENT TRENDS IN THE RECONSTRUCTION AND REHABILITATION OF THE ANTERIOR CRUCIATE LIGAMENT
Bovelles, Ch. de *see* LIBER DE DIFFERENTIA VULGARIUM LINGUARUM
BOVINE PRACTICE – v.1-3. 1980-82 – 1,5,6,9 – us UMI [073]
BOVINE PRACTICE *see* AGRI-PRACTICE
BOW AND ARROW NEWS / North American Indian Association – 1973-74. (American Indian Periodicals in the Princeton University Library) – 1mf – 9 – $45.00 – us UPA [305]
THE "B.O.W.C.": A BOOK FOR BOYS / De Mille, James – By the author of "The Dodge Club," &c. Boston: Lee and Shepard, 1869. 02705. (Pre-1900 Canadiana) – 9 – cn C.I.H.M. [830]
Bowden, Henry Sebastian *see* THE RELIGION OF SHAKESPEARE
Bowden, J *see* ARCHAEOLOGY AND THE BIBLE
Bowden, Jeanne J *see* A PRACTICAL GUIDE TO REVISION OF LOCAL COURT RULES
Bowden, Robert *see* GOVERNMENT RED TAPE COSTS PUT AT EIGHTY BILLION A YEAR
Bowdich, Thomas Edward *see* VOYAGE DANS LE PAYS D'ASCHANTIE, OU RELATION DE L'AMBASSADE ENVOYEE DANS CE ROYAUME PAR LES ANGLAIS
Bowditch, Thomas Edward *see*
- AN ACCOUNT OF THE DISCOVERIES OF THE PORTUGUESE IN THE INTERIOR OF ANGOLA AND MOZAMBIQUE
- EXCURSIONS IN AFRICA
- MISSION FROM CAPE COAST CASTLE TO ASHANTEE

Bowe, William G Jr *see* A COMPARISON OF SIX PERSONALITY FACTORS BETWEEN PROFESSIONAL, COLLEGE, AND HIGH SCHOOL BASKETBALL PLAYERS
Bowell, Mackenzie *see* SPEECH...ON THE MOIETY SYSTEM, UNDERVALUATIONS AND ADMINISTRATION OF THE CUSTOMS
Bowen, Anna Maude *see* THE SOURCES AND TEXT OF RICHARD WAGNER'S OPERA "DIE MEISTERSINGER VON NUERNBERG"
BOWEN, A.W. AND CO *see*
- BIOGRAPHICAL MEMOIRS OF GRANT COUNTY
- THE CITY OF GRAND RAPIDS AND KENT COUNTY
- HISTORY OF MONTGOMERY COUNTY

- PORTRAIT AND BIOGRAPHICAL RECORD OF ALLEN AND VAN WERT COUNTIES
- PORTRAIT AND BIOGRAPHICAL RECORD OF BOONE, CLINTON AND HENDRICKS COUNTIES
- PORTRAIT AND BIOGRAPHICAL RECORD OF DELAWARE AND RANDOLPH COUNTIES
- PORTRAIT AND BIOGRAPHICAL RECORD OF PORTAGE AND SUMMIT COUNTIES
- PROGRESSIVE MEN OF THE STATE OF MONTANA
- PROGRESSIVE MEN OF THE STATE OF WYOMING
- PROGRESSIVE MEN OF WESTERN COLORADO

BOWEN, B.F. AND CO *see*
- BINKERHOFF'S HISTORY OF MARION COUNTY
- BIOGRAPHICAL AND REMINISCENT HISTORY OF RICHLAND, CLAY AND MARION COUNTIES
- BIOGRAPHICAL HISTORY OF GENESEE COUNTY
- BIOGRAPHICAL MEMOIRS OF WYANDOT COUNTY
- BIOGRAPHICAL RECORD OF BARTHOLOMEW COUNTY
- HISTORY OF DEKALB COUNTY
- HISTORY OF FAYETTE COUNTY
- HISTORY OF HENDRICKS COUNTY
- HISTORY OF LAWRENCE AND MONROE COUNTIES
- HISTORY OF WAYNE COUNTY
- PAST AND PRESENT OF FAYETTE COUNTY

Bowen, Francis *see*
- THE DOCTRINE OF INTERNATIONAL EXCHANGES: THE LIMITS OF FREE TRADE AND THE PROTECTIVE SYSTEM
- MODERN PHILOSOPHY
- THE PRINCIPLES OF METAPHYSICAL AND ETHICAL SCIENCE
- A TREATISE ON LOGIC, OR, THE LAWS OF PURE THOUGHT

Bowen, H W *see* INTERNATIONAL LAW:...

Bowen, Ian *see* BANKING CONTROVERSIES IN 1825

Bowen, John *see*
- JOURNAL OF RESTAURANT AND FOODSERVICE MARKETING
- MEMORIALS

BOWEN OR AN EVIDENCE OF GRACE / Roberson, Cecil F – 1969. Biography of Rev. Thomas Jefferson Bowen, SBC's first missionary to Nigeria, West Africa. Nigerian Bapt. Hist. Mat. 103p – 1 – us Baptist [240]

Bowen, T J *see*
- PAPERS
- PAPERS OF T.J. BOWEN

Bowerbank, J S *see* A MONOGRAPH OF THE BRITISH SPONGIADAE

Bowerman, George Franklin *see* A SELECTED BIBLIOGRAPHY OF THE RELIGIOUS DENOMINATIONS OF THE UNITED STATES

Bowers, D N *see* SEVENTY YEARS IN NORTON COUNTY, KANSAS. 1872-1942

Bowers, John *see* THE RESOURCE RENT TAX: A PENALTY ON RISK-TAKING

Bowers, Richard *see* PLYOMETRIC TRAINING AND ITS EFFECTS ON SPEED, STRENGTH, AND POWER OF INTERCOLLEGIATE ATHLETES

Bowery, Norman G *see* PHARMACOLOGY COMMUNICATIONS

Bowes, Michelle L *see* THE DEVELOPMENT OF WEIGHT-ADJUSTED ESTIMATES OF CALORIC EXPENDITURES FOR THE NORDIC TRACK

Bowie, W Copeland *see* LIBERAL RELIGIOUS THOUGHT AT THE BEGINNING OF THE TWENTIETH CENTURY

Bowker, H C *see* THINGS TO COME

Bowker, Richard Rogers *see*
- COPYRIGHT, ITS HISTORY AND ITS LAW
- ULRICH'S ON MICROFICHE

BOWKER'S INTERNATIONAL SERIALS DATABASE ON MICROFICHE *see* ULRICH'S MICROFICHE

Bowler, Ernest Constant *see* AN ALBUM OF THE ATTORNEYS OF RHODE ISLAND, WITH A PORTRAIT AND BRIEF RECORD OF THE LIFE OF EACH

Bowles, Ada Chastina Burpee *see* WOMAN IN THE MINISTRY

Bowles, Guillermo *see* INTRODUCCION A LA HISTORIA NATURAL

Bowles, J *see* OBJECTIONS TO THE CONTINUANCE OF THE WAR...

Bowles, Samuel *see* OUR NEW WEST

BOWLES, SAMUEL AND CO *see* SPRINGFIELD COUNTY DIRECTORY 1867/68

Bowles, T G *see*
- THE DECLARATION OF PARIS OF 1856
- MARITIME WARFARE
- SEA LAW...

Bowles, Thomas *see* ARISTARCHUS: OR A COMPENDIUS AND ROTATIONAL INSTITUTION OF THE LATIN TONGUE

Bowles, Thomas Gibson *see* SEA LAW AND SEA POWER, AS THEY WOULD BE AFFECTED BY RECENT PROPOSALS; WITH REASONS AGAINST THOSE PROPOSALS

BOWLING GREEN FIRST BAPTIST CHURCH. BOWLING GREEN, KENTUCKY : CHURCH RECORDS – (1,710p) – 1833-Jan 1847 (incomplete), 1852-1946 – 2r – 1 – $76.95 – us Baptist [240]

Bowling Green. Ohio. First Presbyterian Church *see* RECORDS

Bowling Green. Ohio. Hope Lutheran Church *see* RECORDS

Bowling Green. Ohio. Plain Congregational Church *see* RECORDS

BOWLING GREEN SECOND BAPTIST CHURCH. BOWLING GREEN, MISSOURI : CHURCH RECORDS – Dec 1890-Jul 1980. 1730p – 1 – 77.85 – us Baptist [240]

Bowman, CV *see* MISSIONSVAENNERNA I AMERIKA

Bowman, F H *see* STRUCTURE OF WOOL FIBRE

Bowman, George Ernest *see* THE MAYFLOWER DESCENDANT 1620-1937

Bowman, George Ernest Bowman *see* VITAL RECORDS OF TRURO MASSACHUSETTS TO 1850

Bowman, J N *see* ADOBES IN SAN MATEO COUNTY

Bowman, Russell Keith *see* THE CONNECTIONS OF THE GESTE DES LOHERAINS WITH OTHER FRENCH EPICS AND MEDIAEVAL GENRES

Bowman, Selwyn Zadock *see* OUR TRADE WITH CANADA: ARGUMENT OF HON SELWYN Z. BOWMAN OF MASSACHUSETTS IN THE HOUSE OF REPRESENTATIVES, TUESDAY, JUNE 9, 1880

Bowman, W *see* THE IMPOSTURE OF METHODISM DISPLAY'D

Bowne, Borden Parker *see*
- THE ATONEMENT
- THE CHRISTIAN LIFE: A STUDY
- THE CHRISTIAN REVELATION
- THE ESSENCE OF RELIGION
- THE IMMANENCE OF GOD
- INTRODUCTION TO PSYCHOLOGICAL THEORY
- KANT AND SPENCER
- METAPHYSICS
- PERSONALISM
- THE PHILOSOPHY OF HERBERT SPENCER
- PHILOSOPHY OF THEISM
- THE PRINCIPLES OF ETHICS
- STUDIES IN CHRISTIANITY
- THEISM
- THEORY OF THOUGHT AND KNOWLEDGE

BOWNI ORGAAN PEGAWAI2 : DEPARTMENT'S LANDS BURGERLIJKE OPENBARE WERKEN DI HINDIA OLANDA – (Lacking: 1914(3)) – Malang, 1914-1916. v1-3 – 13mf – 9 – ne IDC [950]

Bowring, Edgar Alfred *see* THE POEMS OF HEINE, COMPLETE

BOWRING, GOBDEN AND CHINA: A MEMOIR / Lammer Moor – Edinburgh. 1857. BCH-822 2 – 8 – ne IDC [305]

Bowring, J *see*
- AUTOBIOGRAPHICAL RECOLLECTIONS. WITH A BRIEF MEMOIR BY LEWIS B. BOWRING
- THE KINGDOM AND PEOPLE OF SIAM
- A VISIT TO THE PHILIPPINE ISLANDS

Bowring, John *see* HYMNS

Box, George Herbert *see* A SHORT INTRODUCTION TO THE LITERATURE OF THE OLD TESTAMENT

BOX HILL REPORTER – 1925-1950. BHR1-14 – 14r – 1 – at Corangamite [072]

Boxberger, R *see* KLOPSTOCKS LEBEN UND WERKE / WIELANDS LEBEN UND WERKE

BOXBOARD CONTAINERS – (v.87-. 1979-5,6,9) – v.68-. 1960- – 1 – us UMI [670]

BOXBOROUGH 1767-1849 – (Mf 1T: Births & Deaths 1767-1844; Intentions 1838-49; Marriages 1841-44. Mf 2T: Intentions 1794-1844; Marriages 1790-95, 1822-40+; Births & Deaths 1786-1843. Mf 3T: Births 1843-49; Marriages 1844-49; Out-of-Town Marriages 1784-1798; Deaths 1844-49) – (mf ed 1995) – 3mf – 9 – 0-87623-213-6 – us Holbrook [920]

BOXBOROUGH 1767-1905 – (Mf 1-7: Births & Deaths 1767-1845. Mf 1,5,7: Town Records 1755-1870. Mf 5-7: Marriage Intentions 1794-1856; Marriages 1790-97, 1822-44. Mf 6-7: Church Members 1798, 1811-22. Mf 8-13: Town Meetings 1783-1834. Mf 14-27: Town Records 1835-66. Mf 28-37: Town Records 1866-96. Mf 38-44: Town Records 1896-1918. Mf 45: Births 1843-73. Mf 46: Marriages 1844-73; Out-of-Town Marriages 1778-98. Mf 46-47 Deaths 1844-1905. Mf 48-49: Marriages & Births 1874-1905) – (mf ed 1996) – 49mf – 9 – 0-87623-385-X – us Holbrook [920]

Boxer, Frederick N *see* THE ARCHITECTS' AND ARTISANS' PERMANENT PRICE BOOK AND COMPENDIUM OF USEFUL TABLES AND PRACTICAL SCIENTIFIC INFORMATION: SELECTED AND COMPILED FOR THE USE OF ALL BRANCHES OF THE ARCHITECTURAL PROFESSION

BOXFORD 1666-1849 – (Mf 1T-2T: Births & Deaths 1666-1757. Mf 1T: Marriages 1715-30. Mf 2T: Marriages & Intentions 1690-1741. Mf 3T-4T: Births 1723-1822. Mf 4T: Deaths 1838-1843; Marriages 1739-1843. Mf 4T-6T: Marriage Publishments 1741-1849. Mf 6T-7T: Out-of-Town Marriages 1690-1799. Mf 7T: Marriages 1843-49; Births 1843-49. Mf 8T: Deaths 1842-49) – (mf ed 1995) – 8mf – 9 – 0-87623-214-4 – us Holbrook [920]

Boxhorn, MZ *see*
- EMBLEMATA POLITICA, AND ORATIONES
- EPISTOLAE AND POEMATA
- ORIGINUM GALLICARUM LIBER... CUI ACCEDIT ANTIQUAE BRITTANICAE, LEXICON BRITTANNICO-LATINUM...

BOY / Corelli, Marie – British Fiction Archive: Unit 1 – 9 – uk Bell [830]

THE BOY IN GREY / Kingsley, Henry – British Fiction Archive: Unit 2 – 9 – uk Bell [830]

Boyce, G *see* A SERIOUS REPLY TO THE REV. MR. JOHN WESLEY IN PARTICULAR AND TO THE PEOPLE CALLED METHODISTS IN GENERAL,...

Boyce, James Petigru *see*
- AN INAUGURAL ADDRESS, "THREE CHANGES IN THEOLOGICAL INSTITUTIONS"
- SPECIAL PAPERS, 1850-1888

Boyce, W *see* SOLOMON. A SERENATA, IN SCORE, TAKEN FROM THE CANTICLES

Boyceau de la Barraudier, J *see* TRAITE DU JARDINAGE SELON LES RAISONS DE LA NATURE ET DE L'ART.

BOYD COUNTY REGISTER – Butte, NE. -w. Sep. 1896-Jul. 1898; Jun. 1899-Jan. 1910 – 1 – us NE Hist [071]

Boyd, David *see* A HISTORY OF GREELEY AND THE UNION COLONY OF COLORADO

Boyd, J F *see* STATE DIRECTED EMIGRATION: WITH PREFATORY LETTER FROM HIS EXCELLENCY THE RIGHT HON. THE EARL OF DUFFERIN.

Boyd, James Robert *see* THE BEING OF GOD

Boyd, Peter *see* NORTHWEST WEST VIRGINIA PANHANDLE

Boyd, Thomas Munford *see* VIRGINIA BAR EXAMINATIONS

Boydell, Cary *see* GENDER DIFFERENCES IN SPORT CENTRALITY

Boyden, Jo *see* FAMILIES

Boyden, W *see*
- HAND-BOOK OF THE UNITED METHODIST FREE CHURCHES

BOYD'S COMBINED BUSINESS DIRECTORY OF 1875-6:. – Montreal: W. Boyd, 1875. 03714. (Pre-1900 Canadiana) – 9 – cn C.I.H.M. [380]

Boy-Ed, Ida *see* DAS MARTYRIUM DER CHARLOTTE VON STEIN

Boyen, Herman von *see* PAPERS

Boyer *see* QUARTETTI, 6, OP. 6A. [G. 165-170]

Boyer, Abel *see*
- THE COMPLEAT FRENCH-MASTER, FOR LADIES AND GENTLEMEN
- THE ROYAL DICTIONARY ABRIDGED

Boyer, Adolphe *see* DE L'ETAT DES OUVRIERS ET DE SON AMELIORATION PAR L'ORGANISATION DU TRAVAIL

Boyer, Gaston *see* UN PEUPLE DE L'OUEST AFRICAIN

Boyer, Gustave *see* L'ECHO DE VAUDREUIL

Boyer, J A N *see* LE SALABERRY

Boyer, Jeanette C *see* HUMAN RESPONSE TO FROST HAZARDS IN THE ORCHARD INDUSTRY

Boyer, Pascal *see* NOUVELLES RECHERCHES SUR LE STATUS DES FORGERONS D'AFRIQUE NOIRE

DER BOYERTOWN BAUER – Boyertown, PA. 1851-1896. 1 roll – 13 – $25.00r – us I.M.R. [071]

BOYERTOWN DEMOCRAT – Boyertown, PA. -w 1868-1915 – 13 – $25.00r – us I.M.R. [071]

Boyesen, Hjalmar Hjorth *see*
- ESSAYS ON GERMAN LITERATURE
- A HISTORY OF NORWAY FROM THE EARLIEST TIMES

BOYHOOD AND LAWLESSNESS – New York: Survey Associates, 1914. xi-xix,215p. illus., plates, diagrs. (West Side Studies, v1,pt.1). At head of title: Russell Sage Foundation – 1 – us U.W. Library [360]

Boyle, C *see* ACCOUNTS

Boyle, David *see*
- HINTS AND EXPEDIENTS: A POCKET BOOK FOR YOUNG TEACHERS
- NOTES ON PRIMITIVE MAN IN ONTARIO: BEING AN APPENDIX TO THE REPORT OF THE MINISTER OF EDUCATION FOR ONTARIO
- NOTES ON THE LIFE OF DR. JOSEPH WORKMAN
- ON THE PAGANISM OF THE CIVILISED IROQUOIS OF ONTARIO
- THE TOWNSHIP OF SCARBORO 1796-1896

BOYLE GAZETTE & ROSCOMMON REPORTER – Ireland. -w. 14 Feb-25 July 1891. 19 ft – 1 – uk British Libr Newspaper [072]

Boyle, Leonard *see* BIBLIOTHECA PALATINA

Boyle, R *see*
- APPARATUS AD HISTORIAM NATURALEM SANGUINIS HUMANI
- CERTAIN PHYSIOLOGICAL ESSAYS
- EXERCITATIO DE ORIGINE ET VIRIBUS GEMMARUM
- MEDICINAL EXPERIMENTS
- MEMOIRS FOR THE NATURAL HISTORY OF HUMANE BLOOD, ESPECIALLY THE SPIRIT OF THAT LIQUOR
- OF THE RECONCILEABLENESS OF SPECIFICK MEDICINES TO THE CORPUSCULAR PHILOSOPHY
- THE SCEPTICAL CHYMIST

Boyle, Robert *see* LETTERS AND PAPERS OF ROBERT BOYLE

Boyle, Robert H et al *see* THE WATERHUSTLERS

Boyle, Roger *see* CORRESPONDENCE 1621-79

BOYLE'S COURT GUIDE – (St. Marylebone). 1838 – 1 – uk Microform Academic [340]

BOYLSTON 1742-1905 – (Mf 1: Vitals Index 1768-1843. Mf 2-3: Intentions & Marrs 1786-1835. Mf 4: Births & Deaths 1768-1843. Mf 4: Out-of-Town Marriages 1788-99. Mf 5: Deaths 1776-1856. Mf 6-7: Intentions 1835-1917; Marriages 1794-1843. Mf 5,8-10: Precinct 1742-86. Mf 11-16: Town Records 1815-35. Mf 17-24: Town Records 1835-62. Mf 25-32: Mortgages 1838-85. Mf 33-41: Store Accounts 1802-25. Mf 42-45: Taxes 1797-1812. Mf 45-51: Taxes 1812-40. Mf 52-56: Taxes 1841-59. Mf 57-61: Taxes 1860-64. Mf 62: Rebellion Rec 1861-65. Mf 63-64: Voters 1884-1939. Mf 65-78: Paupers 1846-1939. Mf 79-81: Paupers Register 1907-43. Mf 82-83: Vital Records 1844-66. Mf 84-85: Deaths 1867-1910. Mf Marriages 1867-1906. Mf 87: Births) – (mf ed 1996) – 87mf – 9 – us Holbrook [920]

Boym, M P *see* SPECIMEN MEDICINAE SINICAE,...

Boynton, B *see* THE PHYSICAL GROWTH OF GIRLS

Boynton, Charles Luther *see* NOTES ON THE CHRONOLOGICAL LIST OF MISSIONARIES TO CHINA AND THE CHINESE

Boyon, J *see* LE GHANA

Boys, Albert Du *see* CATHARINE OF ARAGON AND THE SOURCES OF THE ENGLISH REFORMATION

Boys, Ernest *see* THE SURE FOUNDATION, OR, THOUGHTS ON THE BELIEVER'S SAFETY

BOYS' LIFE – (1976-. 1,5,6,9) – v1-. 1911- – 1 – us UMI [800]

THE BOYS OWN PHILATELIST *see* THE CANADIAN PHILATELIC WEEKLY

THE BOYS' OWN PHILATELIST – (Contd by: The Canadian Philatelic Weekly) – Berlin [Kitchener], Ont.: Ontario Philatelic Co., [1897-1898] – 9 – cn C.I.H.M. [760]

A BOY'S RELIGION FROM MEMORY / Jones, Rufus M – Philadelphia: Ferris & Leach, 1902. 141p – 1 – us U.W. Library [920]

BOYS' TOWN TIMES – Omaha. Neb. 1962-75 – 1 – us UMI [071]

BOYS' WEEKLY – 1922-29 – 1 – 57.96 – us Baptist [240]

Boyton, Paul (Mrs) *see* A HEROIC PRIEST
Boyvin, J G *see* PHILOSOPHIA SCOTI A PROLIXITATE ET SUBTILITAS EJUS AB OBSCURITATE LIBERA ET VINDICATA...
Bozkurt, Mahmut *see* DIE WAEHRUNGSPOLITISCHE KOOPERATION IN DER EUROPAEISCHEN GEMEINSCHAFT
BOZNER BUERGERSPIELE : ALPENDEUTSCHE PRANG- UND KRANZFESTE / ed by Doerrer, Anton – (Includes bibliographical references) – Leipzig: K W Hiersemann, 1941- – 1 – us U.W. Library [820]
Boztepe, Halil Nihad *see* MAHITAP
Bozzoni, R *see* LA "CONSTITUTIO ANTONINIANA" ED I "DEDITICII"
BRA REVIEW / British Rheumatism and Arthritis Association – (1977- . 5,6,9) – 1950- – 1 – us UMI [610]
Braasch, Theodor *see* BILDER AUS DER SCHWEIZ
Brabourn, Theoph *see* A CONFUTATION OF THE DUTCH ARMINIAN TENET OF UNIVERSAL REDEMPTION
Bracco, B *see* LA LEGGE UNIFORME SULLA CAMBIALE
Brace, Charles Loring *see*
- GESTA CHRISTI, OR, A HISTORY OF HUMANE PROGRESS UNDER CHRISTIANITY
- THE UNKNOWN GOD, OR, INSPIRATION AMONG PRE-CHRISTIAN RACES

Brace, David K *see* MEASURING MOTOR ABILITY
BRACEBRIDGE GAZETTE – 1955-1986 – cn Commonwealth Micro [072]
BRACEBRIDGE HERALD-GAZETTE – 1956-1986 – cn Commonwealth Micro [072]
LE BRACELET DE FER. / Lacerte, E A Bourgeois – Montreal: Ed. E Garand, ca 1926. SEM105P65 – 2mf – 9 – Can$4.50 – cn Bibl Nat [830]
LES BRACELETS OGBONI: ANALYSE ICONOGRAPHIQUE ET STYLISTIQUE / Brincard, MT – 9 – F120.00 – fr Ethnologie [740]
Bracewell-Milnes, Barry *see* THE REALITY OF THE MONEY ECONOMY
Bracey, John H, Jr *see*
- THE PAPERS OF A. PHILIP RANDOLPH
- PAPERS OF THE NAACP
- PAPERS OF THE NAACP, PART 1
- PAPERS OF THE NAACP, PART 2
- PAPERS OF THE NAACP, PART 3
- PAPERS OF THE NAACP, PART 4
- PAPERS OF THE NAACP, PART 5
- PAPERS OF THE NAACP, PART 6
- PAPERS OF THE NAACP, PART 8
- PAPERS OF THE NAACP, PART 10
- PAPERS OF THE NAACP, PART 11
- PAPERS OF THE NAACP, PART 12
- PAPERS OF THE NAACP, PART 13
- PAPERS OF THE NAACP, PART 14
- PAPERS OF THE NAACP, PART 15
- PAPERS OF THE NAACP, PART 23
- RECORDS OF THE AMERICAN COMMITTEE ON AFRICA

Brachet, Jean-Louis *see* TRAITE COMPLET DE L'HYPOCHONDRIE
Brachvogel, Albert Emil *see*
- AUSGEWAEHLTE WERKE
- DER FELS VON ERZ
- LESSINGS LAOKOON
- NARCISS

Brack, Fortune de *see* AVANT-POSTES DE CAVALERIE LEGERE: SOUVENIRS
Brackenbury, Henry *see* THE RIVER COLUMN
Brackenridge, W D *see* FILICES IN CHARLES WILKES' U.S. EXPLORING EXPEDITION
Brackett, FP *see* POMONA VALLEY
BRACKNELL AND ASCOT TIMES – England, 1972-81; 1988- – 71+ r – 1 – uk British Libr Newspaper [072]
BRACKNELL NEWS – Feb 5-Dec 31 1959; 1960-Jan-Apr 1963; Oct-Dec 1972; 1986-96 – 52 1/2r – 1 – uk British Libr Newspaper [072]
Bracko, Michael R *see* TIME MOTION ANALYSIS OF THE SKATING CHARACTERISTICS OF PROFESSIONAL ICE HOCKEY PLAYERS
Bradburn, S *see*
- MEMORANDA BOOKS, 1774-1815
- OUT-LETTERS, SERMONS AND MISCELLANEOUS PAPERS, 1779-1815

Bradbury, William Batchelder *see*
- FRESH LAURELS FOR THE SUNDAY SCHOOL
- PSALMIST OR CHOIR MELODIES
- THE VICTORY: A NEW COLLECTION OF SACRED AND SECULAR MUSIC, COMPRISING A GREAT VARIETY OF TUNES, ANTHEMS, GLEES, ELEMENTARY EXERCISES AND SOCIAL SONGS...

BRADBURY'S PLEADING AND PRACTICE REPORTS / New York. (State) – v1-5. 1910-19 – 36mf – 9 – $54.00 – LLMC 80-018 – us L.L.M.C. [340]
Bradby, Eliza Dorothy *see* SHORT HISTORY OF THE FRENCH REVOLUTION, 1789-1795
Braddock, Edward *see* MAJOR GENERAL EDWARD BRADDOCK'S ORDERLY BOOKS: FROM FEBRUARY 26 TO JUNE 17, 1755
BRADDOCK TRIBUNE – Braddock, PA. -w 1889-1890; 1891-1893 – 13 – $25.00r – us I.M.R. [071]
Braddon, M E *see* DIAVOLA
Braddon, Mary Elizabeth *see*
- ALL ALONG THE RIVER
- ASPHODEL
- AURORA FLOYD
- BEYOND THESE VOICES
- BIRDS OF PREY
- THE CAPTAIN OF THE VULTURE
- CHARLOTTE'S INHERITANCE: A NOVEL
- THE CHRISTMAS HIRELINGS
- CIRCE: THREE ACTS IN THE LIFE OF AN ARTIST
- THE CLOVEN FOOT
- THE CONFLICT
- CUT BY THE COUNTY
- THE DAY WILL COME
- DEAD LOVE HAS CHAINS
- DEAD MEN'S SHOES
- DEAD SEA FRUIT
- THE DOCTOR'S WIFE
- DURING HER MAJESTY'S PLEASURE
- ELEANOR'S VICTORY
- THE FATAL THREE
- FENTON'S QUEST
- FLOWER AND WEED; AND OTHER TALES
- GERARD, OR THE WORLD, THE FLESH AND THE DEVIL
- THE GOLDEN CALF
- THE GREEN CURTAIN
- HENRY DUNBAR: THE STORY OF AN OUTCAST
- HER CONVICT
- HIS DARLING SIN
- HOSTAGES TO FORTUNE
- IN HIGH PLACES
- THE INFIDEL: A STORY OF THE GREAT REVIVAL
- ISHMAEL
- JOHN MARCHMONT'S LEGACY
- JOSHUA HAGGARD'S DAUGHTER
- JUST AS I AM
- LADY AUDLEY'S SECRET
- THE LADY LISLE
- THE LADY'S MILE
- LIKE AND UNLIKE
- LONDON PRIDE, OR WHEN THE WORLD WAS YOUNGER
- A LOST EDEN
- LOST FOR LOVE
- THE LOVELS OF ARDEN
- LUCIUS DAVOREN, OR PUBLICANS AND SINNERS
- MARY
- MILLY DARRELL; AND OTHER TALES
- MIRANDA
- MOHAWKS
- MOUNT ROYAL
- ONE LIFE, ONE LOVE
- ONE THING NEEDFUL
- ONLY A CLOD
- AN OPEN VERDICT
- OUR ADVERSARY
- PHANTOM FORTUNE
- RALPH THE BAILIFF; AND OTHER TALES
- ROBERT AINSLEIGH
- THE ROSE OF LIFE
- ROUGH JUSTICE
- RUN TO EARTH
- RUPERT GODWIN
- SIR JASPER'S TENANT
- SONS OF FIRE
- THE STORY OF BARBARA, HER SPLENDID MISERY AND HER GILDED CAGE
- A STRANGE WORLD
- STRANGERS AND PILGRIMS
- TAKEN AT THE FLOOD
- THOU ART THE MAN
- TO THE BITTER END
- THE TRAIL OF THE SERPENT, OR THE SECRET OF THE HEATH
- UNDER LOVE'S RULE
- UNDER THE RED FLAG; AND OTHER TALES
- THE VENETIANS
- VIXEN. 1879
- WEAVERS AND WEFT; AND OTHER TALES
- THE WHITE HOUSE
- WYLLARD'S WEIRD

Brade, William *see* OEDIPUS ON THE SPHINX OF THE NINETEENTH CENTURY; OR, POLITICO-POLEMICAL RIDDLES INTERPRETED
Braden *see* CENTENNIAL HISTORY OF AKRON 1825-1925
Braden, Roberta L *see* SEX ROLE PERCEPTIONS AND DEFENSE MECHANISMS OF FEMALE ATHLETES
Braden, William *see* THE BEAUTIFUL GLEANER
Bradfield, William *see* PERSONALITY AND FELLOWSHIP
BRADFORD 1669-1849 – (Mf 1T: Births 1669-78. Mf 1T-3T: Vital Records 1678-1739. Mf 4T-5T: Deaths 1736-74; Marriages 1735-68. Mf 4T-8T: Births 1684-1796. Mf 6T-8T: Marriages 1679-1795. Mf 7T-8T: Deaths 1682-1796. Mf 8T-11T: Births 1772-1844. Mf 11T-12T: Marriages 1795-1848. Mf 12T: Out-of-Town Marriages 1684-1799. Mf 12T-13T: Deaths 1788-1847. Mf 14T: Births 1843-49. Mf 15T: Marriages & Deaths 1843-49) – (mf ed 1995) – 15mf – 9 – 0-87623-215-2 – us Holbrook [920]
Bradford, Amory Howe *see*
- THE AGE OF FAITH
- THE ASCENT OF THE SOUL

BRADFORD ARGUS – Towanda, PA. -w 1861-1912 – 13 – $25.00r – us I.M.R. [071]
BRADFORD COUNTY TELEGRAPH – Starke. Fl. -w. 1887-90, 1892, 1914, 1916-to date – 1 – us P.K. Yonge [071]
BRADFORD DAILY TELEGRAPH – Bradford, England. -d. Jan-June 1898. 1 reel – 1 – uk British Libr Newspaper [072]
BRADFORD EVENING STAR AND BRADFORD DAILY RECORD – Bradford, PA. -d 1894-1903; 1928-1931; 1931-1943; 1943-1946 – 13 – $25.00r – us I.M.R. [071]
Bradford, Gamaliel *see* TYPES OF AMERICAN CHARACTER
BRADFORD HISTORICAL AND ANTIQUARIAN SOCIETY : LOCAL RECORD SERIES – (Coll title: Publications of the English Record Societies, 1835-1972...) – v1-4. 1929-59 – 9mf – 9 – £75.00 – uk Chadwyck [941]
Bradford, James C *see* PAPERS OF JOHN PAUL JONES
Bradford. New Hampshire. Christian Church *see* CHURCH RECORDS, MS 1797
BRADFORD OBSERVER – Bradford, England. -w. 1850-1880; July-Dec 1882; Jan-March 1897; July-Aug 1901. 65 1 2 reels – 1 – uk British Libr Newspaper [072]
BRADFORD PIONEER – Bradford. England. 1913-35 – 1 – uk Microform Academic [072]
Bradford, Robert *see*
- ADDRESSES DELIVERED AT AGINCOURT, APRIL 2ND AND MAY 7TH, 1878: AN ABLE EXPOSITION OF THE CAUSE OF THE HARD TIMES: THE BANKS, LOAN COMPANIES AND IMPORTING MERCHANTS CHIEFLY TO BLAME
- R. BRADFORD VS MESSRS TAYLOR AND OATES

Bradford, Saxtone E *see* THE BATTLE FOR BUENOS AIRES
Bradford, Simeon Briggs *see* PROHIBITION IN KANSAS AND THE KANSAS PROHIBITORY LAW
Bradford Springs. South Carolina. St. Philip's (Episcopal) Church *see* VESTRY MINUTES
BRADFORD STAR – Bradford, PA., 1894-1903 – 13 – $25.00r – us I.M.R. [071]
BRADFORD WEEKLY TELEGRAPH – (Illustrated Weekly Telegraph 1884-99) – England. 31 Jul 1869-18 May 1878; 13 May 1882-1896; 1898-1899; 1901-1910; 1912-Jun 1920. -w – 30r – 1 – uk British Libr Newspaper [072]
Bradford, William *see*
- HISTORY OF PLYMOUTH PLANTATION 1620-1647
- NEW YORK GAZETTE

BRADFORD'S CASES – (A Pre-NRS title) – Iowa. 1v. 1838-41 (all publ) – 2mf – 9 – $3.00 – LLMC 94-004 – us L.L.M.C. [340]
Bradish, Joseph Arno von *see*
- DER BRIEFWECHSEL HOFMANNSTHAL – WILDGANS
- GOETHE ALS ERBE SEINER AHNEN

Bradlaugh, Charles *see*
- HUMANITY'S GAIN FROM UNBELIEF
- PAPERS

Bradle, T A *see* LEVELS OF PARK SATISFACTION AMONG FLORIDA STATE PARK VISITORS AND THEIR RELATIONSHIPS TO SELECTED VISITOR CHARACTERISTICS
Bradley, A L *see* THE WINGATE TEST
Bradley, Arthur Granville *see*
- THE EMIGRATION OF GENTLEMEN'S SONS TO THE UNITED STATES AND CANADA
- WOLFE

THE BRADLEY BIBLIOGRAPHY / Rehder, A – Cambridge. 5v. 1911-1918 – 72mf – ne IDC [580]
Bradley, Carolyn G *see* THE EFFECTS OF DIET AND EXERCISE OF VARYING INTENSITIES ON THE BODY COMPOSITION OF ADULT WOMEN
Bradley, Francis Herbert *see*
- APPEARANCE AND REALITY
- ESSAYS ON TRUTH AND REALITY
- ETHICAL STUDIES
- THE PRINCIPLES OF LOGIC

Bradley, George Granville *see* LECTURES ON ECCLESIASTES DELIVERED IN WESTMINSTER ABBEY
Bradley, Henry *see* THE STORY OF THE GOTHS, FROM THE EARLIEST TIMES TO THE END OF THE GOTHIC DOMINION IN SPAIN
Bradley, James *see* THE NETTLE CREEK CHURCH CASE OR WHO ARE THE REGULAR BAPTISTS
Bradley, Kenneth *see* THE STORY OF NORTHERN RHODESIA
Bradley, Susan *see* ARCHIVES BIOGRAPHIQUES FRANCAISES (ABF 1)
O BRADO AFRICANO – Lourenco Marques: Empreza do Journal O Brado Africano, [dec 24 1918-nov 24 1956; 1966-jun 15 1974] – 25r – 1 – us Res Libr [072]
O BRADO DA COMARCA DE PORTO CALVO : JUSTICA, CONSTITUICAO EO IMPERADOR – Maceio, Alagoas. 4 Maio 1859 – 1,5,6 – bl Biblioteca [072]
O BRADO DA LIBERDADE – [s.l.]. 15 Set 1876 – 1,5,6 – bl Biblioteca [072]
BRADO FEDERAL – [s.l.]. 2 Out 1890 – 1,5,6 – bl Biblioteca [072]
O BRADO LIBERAL DA BAHIA : PERIODICO LITTERARIO E NOTICIOSO – [s.l.]. 22 Dez 1869 – 1,5,6 – bl Biblioteca [072]
Bradsby, H C *see*
- HISTORY OF BRADFORD COUNTY
- HISTORY OF BUREAU COUNTY
- HISTORY OF LUZERNE COUNTY

Bradshaw, James Daniel *see* A PLANNED PREACHING PROGRAM UTILIZING CONGREGATIONAL INVOLVEMENT AT FIRST BAPTIST CHURCH, MCDONOUGH, GEORGIA. 1982
BRADSHAW MONITOR – Bradshaw, NE. -w. Aug. 1898-Aug. 1943 – 1 – us NE Hist [071]
BRADSHAW'S RAILWAY MANUAL – Shareholders' guide & official directory. London. v. 26-75. 1874-1923 – 1 – us NY Public [380]
Bradstreet, Anne *see* THE TENTH MUSE AND FROM THE MANUSCRIPTS, MEDITATIONS DIVINE AND MORALL, TOGETHER WITH LETTERS AND OCCASIONAL PIECES
BRADSTREET'S: A JOURNAL OF TRADE, FINANCE AND PUBLIC ECONOMY – v. 1-61. 1879-1933 – 1,5,6 – us Princeton Micro [380]
Bradt, Charles Edwin *see* MEN AND THE MODERN MISSIONARY ENTERPRISE
Bradt, Joseph *see* ESSAY ON BEE KEEPING, OR, AN EASY METHOD OF MANAGING BEES IN THE MOST PROFITABLE MANNER TO THEIR OWNER: WITH INFALLIBLE RULES TO PREVENT THEIR DESTRUCTION BY THE MOTH, OR OTHERWISE
Bradwell, S *see* HELPS FOR SUDDAIN ACCIDENTS
Brady, Charles B *see* AN INDEX TO THE ARKANSAS REPORTS, VOLS 1 TO 31 INCLUSIVE, AND HEMPSTEAD'S U.S. COURT REPORTS, ALSO ALL THE ARKANSAS CASES IN WOOLWORTH'S AND DILLON'S U.S.C.C. REPORTS
Brady, Christine P *see* EFFECTS OF ACUTE RESISTIVE EXERCISE ON THE RESTING METABOLIC RATE OF WOMEN
Brady, Cyrus Townsend *see*
- AMERICAN FIGHTS AND FIGHTERS: STORIES OF THE FIRST FIVE WARS OF THE UNITED STATES FROM THE WAR OF THE REVOLUTION TO THE WAR OF 1812
- FOR THE FREEDOM OF THE SEA: A ROMANCE OF THE WAR OF 1812
- GETHSEMANE AND AFTER
- RECOLLECTIONS OF A MISSIONARY IN THE GREAT WEST

Brady, F X *see* THE GREAT SUPPER OF GOD
Brady, G S *see* A MONOGRAPH OF THE FREE AND SEMI-PARASITIC COPEPODA OF THE BRITISH ISLANDS
Brady, Gerard *see*
- L'IDEE OUVRIERE
- LE REVEIL LAURENTIEN

Brady, M J *see* A FRAUD UNMASKED: THE CAREER OF MRS. MARGARET L. SHEPERD, "EX-ROMANIST", "EX-NUN", "EX-PENITENT" AND BIGAMIST: HER OWN CONFESSIONS ATTESTED BY THE MOST RELIABLE WITNESSES
Brady, Robert Alexander *see* BUSINESS AS A SYSTEM OF POWER
BRADY STUDIO CARTE-DE-VISITE PORTRAITS / U.S. Library of Congress. Prints and Photographs Division – 193 photographs. 1 reel. P&P2822 – 1 – 23.00r – us L of C Photodup [976]
BRADY STUDIO CIVIL WAR VIEWS / U.S. Library of Congress. Prints and Photographs Division – 10,000 Civil War images. P&P1 – 1 – 23.00r – us L of C Photodup [976]
BRADY VINDICATOR – Brady, NE. -w. Aug. 1909-Oct. 1941 – 1 – us NE Hist [071]
Brady, W Maziere *see*
- THE EPISCOPAL SUCCESSION IN ENGLAND, SCOTLAND AND IRELAND, A.D. 1400 TO 1875
- ESSAYS ON THE ENGLISH STATE CHURCH IN IRELAND
- THE IRISH REFORMATION, OR, THE ALLEGED CONVERSION OF THE IRISH BISHOPS AT THE ACCESSION OF QUEEN ELIZABETH, AND THE ASSUMED DESCENT OF THE PRESENT ESTABLISHED HIERARCHY IN IRELAND, FROM THE ANCIENT IRISH CHURCH, DISPROVED
- STATE PAPERS CONCERNING THE IRISH CHURCH IN THE TIME OF QUEEN ELIZABETH

Braeker, Jakob *see* DER ERZIEHERISCHE GEHALT IN J J BREITINGERS "CRITISCHER DICHTKUNST"
Braess, Dietrich (Herausgeber der Microfiche-Edition: Martin Welke) *see* ZEITUNG FUER STAEDTE, FLECKEN UND DOERFER, INSBESONDERHEIT FUER DIE LIEBEN LANDSLEUTE JUNG UND ALT
Braeuning-Oktavio, Hermann *see* SILHOUETTEN AUS DER WERTHERZEIT
Braeutigam, Harald *see* DIE HANDELSPOLITIK POLENS SEIT ERLANGUNG DER SELBSTAENDIGKEIT BIS ZUM ABLAUF DER GENFER KONVENTION AM 15. JUNI 1925
BRAGA : VTORAIA KNIGA STIKHOV 1921-1922 / Tikhonov, Nikolai – Moskva, Peterburg: Krug 1922 – us Res Libr [947]
Bragaccia, G *see* L'AMBASCIATORE
BRAGG, BRAXTON, PAPERS, MS 2000 – 1833-1879 – 8r – 1 – us Western Res [976]
Bragg, John *see* DIARY
Bragg, Thomas *see* DIARY
Bragin, A *see* PRODOVOLSTVENNO-SEMENNOI I FURAZHNYI BIUDZHET UFIMSKOI GUBERNII NA 1921-22 GOD, PO PREDVARITELNYM DANNYM OB UROZHAE KHLEBOV I TRAV
Bragin, M *see* KOOPERATIVY
Braginskii, M et al *see* OBSHCHESTVA, TOVARISHCHESTVA, TRESTY, ARTELI, KOOPERATIVY I DRUGIE OB"EDINENIIA
Brahler, C Jayne *see* VERSACLIMBER EXERCISE ELICITS HIGHER MAXIMAL OXYGEN UPTAKE IN WOMEN ROWERS THAN DOES TREADMILL EXERCISE OR ROWING ERGOMETRY
Brahm, Otto *see*
- GOTTFRIED KELLER
- HEINRICH VON KLEIST

BRAHMAVADIN – v1-17. 1966-82 (complete) – 3r – 1 – ATLA S0462 – us A.T.L.A. [240]
Brahms, Johannes *see*
- CONCERT FUR VIOLINE; MIT BEGLEITUNG DES ORCHESTERS, OP. 77
- SAMTLICHE WERKE
- SONATA, VIOLONCELLO AND PIANO, NO. 2, OP. 99, F-DUR

Braiden, Russell W *see* THE EFFECT OF COCAINE ON MUSCLE CARBOHYDRATE METABOLISM AND ENDURANCE DURING HIGH INTENSITY EXERCISE IN RATS
BRAIDWOOD EXPRESS – Jan 3 1899-Dec 31 1907 – 9 – at Pascoe [072]
BRAILLE LISTENER – London, UK. May 1955 – 1 – uk British Libr Newspaper [072]
BRAILLE LITERARY JOURNAL – London, UK. 10 Feb 1911 – 1 – uk British Libr Newspaper [072]
BRAILLE NEWS SUMMARY – London, UK. 6 Jun 1947 – 1 – uk British Libr Newspaper [072]
Brailsford, H N *see* TOWARDS A NEW LEAGUE
BRAIN – (1966- . 5,6. 1976- . 9) – Journal of neurology. 1878- – 1 – us UMI [616]
BRAIN : A JOURNAL OF NEUROLOGY – London, 1878-1920. V.1-43. Index 1878-1900 – 336mf – 9 – ne IDC [616]
BRAIN. A JOURNAL OF NEUROLOGY – v69-98. 1946-75 – 1,5,6 – us Princeton Micro [616]
BRAIN AS ORGAN OF THE MIND / Bastian, Henry – London: Khegan Paul, Trench, Trubner & Co., 1890. 708p – 1 – us U.W. Library [150]
BRAIN, BEHAVIOR AND EVOLUTION – v1-. 1968- – 1,5,9 – us UMI [073]
Brain, Belle Marvel *see*
- THE REDEMPTION OF THE RED MAN
- THE TRANSFORMATION OF HAWAII

BRAIN RESEARCH – v1-322. 1966-84 – 1,5,6,13 – sz Elsevier [073]
BRAIN RESEARCH BULLETIN – (1978- 5,6,9) – 1976- – 1 – us UMI [616]
BRAINARD CLIPPER – Brainard, NE. -w. Jul. 1897-Mar. 1900. Incomplete; Apr. 1901-Apr. 1910. Incomplete; Jan. 1911-Mar. 1911; May 1911-Dec. 1916; Aug. 1916-Mar. 1943; Jun. 1947-Sep. 1950 – 1 – us NE Hist [071]
BRAINARD'S MUSICAL – New York City, Chicago – 3r – 1 – £165.00 – uk Chadwyck [780]
BRAINARD'S MUSICAL WORLD – Cleveland. v. 17, no. 198-v. 29, no. 347. Jun 1880-Nov 1892. Incomplete – 1 – us NY Public [073]
Brainerd, Thomas *see* THE LIFE OF JOHN BRAINERD
BRAIN/MIND BULLETIN – (1977- . 5,6,9) – v. 1-. 1975- – 1 – us UMI [150]
Braithwaite, Joseph Bevan *see*
- MEMOIRS OF JOSEPH JOHN GURNEY
- PAUL THE APOSTLE: A POEM

Braithwaite, R *see*
- THE BRITISH MOSSFLORA
- THE SPHAGNACEAE OR PEAT-MOSSES OF EUROPE AND NORTH AMERICA

Braithwaite, William C *see* THE BEGINNINGS OF QUAKERISM
Braitmaier, Friedrich *see* DIE POETISCHE THEORIE GOTTSCHED'S UND DER SCHWEIZER
BRAK, SEMIA, OPEKA; RUKOVODSTVO DLIA ZAGS / Aliakrinskii, A – Moscow, 1930. 309p. BR-9620 1 – 9 – ne IDC [947]
Brake, Wilhelm *see* NIEDER MIT DEN SOZIALDEMOKRATEN
Brakte, E *see* DAS SOGENANNTE RELIGIONSGESPRAECH AM HOF DER SASANIDEN (T.U.U. 2-19/3A)
Brambach, Wilhelm *see* UEBER DIE BETONUNGSWEISE IN DER DEUTSCHEN LYRIK
Bramble, Charles A *see* KLONDIKE
Bramham. Yorkshire *see* PARISH REGISTERS
Brammeier, Michele R *see* THE INFLUENCE OF THE MENSTRUAL CYCLE AND DIET ON METABOLISM DURING REST AND EXERCISE
BRAMPTON TIMES – (1976-1990Ap.-110r; 1867-1874.-1r) – Brampton, 1930-1975 – 85r – 1 – cn Preston [971]
Bramson, Leontii Moiseevich *see* PERVAIA DUMA I VTORAIA REVOLIUTSIIA
BRAMSTEDTER ANZEIGENBLATT *see* BRAMSTEDTER NACHRICHTEN
BRAMSTEDTER NACHRICHTEN – (Called: Bramstedter Anzeigenblatt, may 13-sep 23 1949. Later publ in Bad Segeberg) – Bad Bramstedt, 1881-99, 1902-may 2 1945, sep 24 1949-85 – 141r – 1 – Inquire at Mikrofilmarchiv for details – gw Misc Inst [943]
BRAMSTEDTER TAGEBLATT – Bad Bramstedt, 1905-06 – 2r – 1 – Inquire at Mikrofilmarchiv for details – gw Misc Inst [943]
Bramuglia, Juan Atilio *see*
- JUBILACIONES FERROVIARIAS
- EL NUEVO DERECHO SOCIAL ARGENTINO

Bran, Friedrich Alexander *see* HERDER UND DIE DEUTSCHE KULTURANSCHAUUNG
Bran, T *see* LE PIONNIER CANADIEN
Brancas-Villeneuve, Andre Francois de *see* HISTOIRE OU POLICE DU ROYAUME DE GALA
Branch, E E *see* HISTORY OF IONIA COUNTY
BRANCH MANAGER'S CORRESPONDENCE AND RELATED PAPERS / W R Carpenter & Ltd. Tulagi Branch – 1925-32 – 1r – 1 – PMB1112 – at Pacific Mss [980]
BRANCHING OUT – Edmonton. v1-7. 1974-80 – 9 – Can$20.00y – cn Micromedia [073]
BRANCOS E PETROS NA BAHIA / Pierson, Donald – Sao Paulo, 1945 – 9mf – 8 – ne Slangenburg [999]
BRAND – Stockholm, Sweden. 1898-1967 – 14r – 1 – sw Kungliga [073]
BRAND : TILLFALLIGHETSTIDNINGAR – Stockholm, Sweden. 1909-46 – 1 reel – 1 – sw Kungliga [073]
Brand, A *see* RELATION DU VOYAGE DE M. EVERT ISBRAND/ENVOYE DE SA MAJESTE SZARIENNE A L'EMPEREUR DE LA CHINE, EN 1692, 93 ET 94
Brand, C L de *see* DE HONORE GENTIUM...
Brand, Carl F *see* BRITISH LABOUR'S RISE TO POWER
Brand, R *see*
- DYNAMISME DES SYMBOLES DANS LES CULTES VODUN
- REGARDS SUR L'ART DAHOMEEN

Brand, Y *see* A DICTIONARY ENGLISH-ARMENIAN AND ARMENIAN-ENGLISH
BRANDEIS BRIEF *see* OPINION AND BRIEF IN THE CASE OF MULLER VS OREGON
Brandeis, Louis Dembitz *see*
- THE LOUIS D. BRANDIES PAPERS
- OPINION AND BRIEF IN THE CASE OF MULLER VS OREGON

Brandell, Jerrold R *see* JOURNAL OF ANALYTIC SOCIAL WORK
Branden, C van den *see*
- CATALOGUE DES COLEOPTERES CARNASSIERS AQUATIQUES...
- REVUE COLEOPTEROLOGIQUE

Branden, Nathaniel *see* BENEVOLENCE VERSUS ALTRUISM; THE STOLEN CONCEPT
Brandenburg, Edward *see* BRANDENBURG'S BANKRUPTCY DIGEST
Brandenburg, Edwin Charles *see* THE LAW OF BANKRUPTCY, INCLUDING THE NATIONAL BANKRUPTCY LAW OF 1898.
Brandenburg, Erich *see* VORTRAEGE
Brandenburg, Werner *see* DAS POETISCHE GENUS PERSONFIZIERTER SUBSTANTIVA BEI JAMES THOMSON UND EDWARD YOUNG BETRACHTET IM ZUSAMMENHANG DER GESCHICHTLICHEN ENTWICKLUNG VOM MITTEL-ENGLISCHEN BIS AUF LORD TENNYSON
BRANDENBURGER ANZEIGER *see* BRANDENBURGISCHER ANZEIGER
Brandenburger, C L *see* HISTORIA DE POLONIA
BRANDENBURGISCHE NEUESTE NACHRICHTEN – (Cont by: Potsdamer Neueste Nachrichten, Stadtausgabe Brandenburg, feb 29 1992) – Brandenburg, jul 1954-jul 2 1992 – 1 – Inquire at Mikrofilmarchiv for details – gw Misc Inst [072]
BRANDENBURGISCHE NEUESTE NACHRICHTEN – (Title change: Potsdamer Neueste Nachrichten, 29 Feb 1992) – Potsdam, East Germany. Juli 1954-1990 – 65r – 1 – gw Mikrofilm [072]
BRANDENBURGISCHER ANZEIGER – (Cont by: Brandenburgscher Anzeiger, 1823?; Brandenburger Anzeiger, jul 30 1845) – Brandenburg, dec 2 1809-10, 1812-16 (incomplete), 1817-18, 1819-21 (incomplete), 1822, 1823 (incomplete), 1824, 1825 (incomplete), 1826-33, 1834-35 (incomplete), 1836-51, 1852 (incomplete), 1853-56, 1857 (incomplete), 1858-59, 1860 (incomplete), 1861-62, 1863-84 (incomplete), jul 11 1885-jun 15 1887, 1888, jan 2-jun 30 1890, apr 1 1891-apr 23 1945 (incomplete) – 1 – Inquire at Mikrofilmarchiv for details – gw Misc Inst [943]
BRANDENBURG'S BANKRUPTCY DIGEST / Brandenburg, Edward – (Index-Digest of bankruptcy decisions containing the decisions of the Supreme Court of the US from 1800-99, and of the Federal and State Courts of Last Resort under the Act of 1867) – Chicago: Callaghan, 1899 – 6mf – 9 – $9.00 – LLMC 84-390 – us L.L.M.C. [340]
BRANDENBURGSCHER ANZEIGER *see* BRANDENBURGISCHER ANZEIGER
Brandes *see* JOHANN SAMUEL TRAUGOTT GEHLERS PHYSIKALISCHES WOERTERBUCH
Brandes, Georg M *see* LORD BEACONSFIELD
Brandes, J *see* KAWI-BALINEESCH-NEDERLANDSCH WOORDENBOEK...
Brandes, Karl *see* HEILIGE PETRUS IN ROM UND ROM OHNE PETRUM
Brandis, D *see*
- THE FOREST FLORA OF NORTH-WEST AND CENTRAL INDIA
- ILLUSTRATIONS OF THE FOREST FLORA OF NORTH-WEST AND CENTRAL INDIA
- INDIAN TREES

Brandl, Benedict *see* LESSINGS FRAGMENTENSTREIT
Brandl, J *see*
- DEUXIEME QUINTUOR POUR LA FLUTE, 2 ALTO ET VIOLONCELLE, OP. 60
- GRAND QUATOUR, OP. 18
- NOTTURNO POUR DEUX ALTOS ET VIOLONCELLE
- TROIS QUATUORS POUR LA FLUTE, VLN, VLA, VC, OP. 40

Brandl, Leopold *see* DER SCHIMMELREITER
BRANDON DAILY MAIL – Brandon, Canada. 1882-97 – 9r – 1 – $585.00 – cn Library Assoc [971]
BRANDON DAILY NEWS – Canada. 31 Dec 1912-11 Dec 1914.-d. 8 reels – 1 – uk British Libr Newspaper [072]
BRANDON SUN – Brandon, Manitoba, CN. 1959- – 12r per yr – 1 – Can$55.00r – cn Commonwealth Micro [072]
Brandon. Vermont. Brandon Seminary *see* CATALOGS AND COLLEGE RECORDS
BRANDON WEEKLY SUN – Canada. Sep 1912-Dec 1920.-w. 10mqn reels – 1 – uk British Libr Newspaper [072]
BRANDS MANADSHAFTE – Stockholm, Sweden. 1908-09, 1913, 1915-16 – 1 reel – 1 – sw Kungliga [073]
Brandstaedter, M D *see* KOL KITVEI
Brandstetter, R *see*
- AN INTRODUCTION TO INDONESIAN LINGUISTICS
- WIR MENSCHEN DER INDONESISCHEN ERDE

Brandt, A J H Wilhelm *see* DIE MANDAEISCHE RELIGION
Brandt de Galametz, Rodolphe M *see* LA TAXE DES PAUVRES A ABBEVILLE EN 1588, PRECEDEE D'UNE ETUDE SUR L'ASSISTANCE PUBLIQUE AVANT CETTE EPOQUE
Brandt, J J *see* WENLI PARTICLES
Brandt, R F *see* LEKTSII PO SLAVIANO-RUSSKOI PALEOGRAFII, CHITANNYE V MOSKOVSKOM ARKHEOLOGICHESKOM INSTITUTE V 1908, 1909 I 1910 GG
Brandt, W *see* MANDAEISCHE SCHRIFTEN
BRANDUNG : GESCHICHTEN VON DE WATERKANT / Lau, Fritz – Hamburg: M Glogau, 1921 – 1r – 1 – us U.W. Library [830]
DIE BRANDWAG – Johannesburg, South Africa. 1 Sept-29 Dec 1939.2 reels – 1, 16 diazo available at reduced price – sa SA Libr [072]
BRANDWEEK *see* ADWEEK'S MARKETING WEEK
BRANDYWINE BAPTIST CHURCH. CHADD'S FORD, PENNSYLVANIA : CHURCH RECORDS – 1699-1881(MS materials), 1791-1838, 1843-1904 – 1 – 53.55 – us Baptist [240]
BRANIGAN'S CHRONICLES AND CURIOSITIES – Hamilton, C W [Ont]: T Branigan, [1858?-1859?] – 9 – cn C.I.H.M. [971]
Brann, Henry A *see* CURIOUS QUESTIONS
Brannan, Tori L *see* A COMPARISON OF ANTERIOR TIBIAL-FEMORAL LAXITY IN FEMALE INTERCOLLEGIATE GYMNASTS TO A NORMAL POPULATION
Brannon, J D *see* HISTORY OF CISCO BAPTIST ASSOCIATION IN TEXAS
Branson, Isaac Reichelderfer *see* A DREAM: DESERTED: AND THE FROLICSOME SNOW
Branson, Sheri W *see* A STEP BY STEP GUIDE TO CONCERT PLANNING FOR DANCE IN SECONDARY EDUCATION
BRANT AGRICULTURIST AND INDIAN MAGAZINE – (Cont: The Indian Magazine) – Brantford, Ont: [s.n., 1898?-19–?] – 9 – cn C.I.H.M. [630]
BRANT AGRICULTURIST AND INDIAN MAGAZINE *see* THE INDIAN MAGAZINE
Brant and Fuller and Company *see* HISTORY OF INDIANA
BRANT COUNTY HERALD – 1857-58 – 1 – 65.00 – cn McLaren [072]
Brant, Fuller and Co *see*
- HISTORY OF BARTHOLOMEW COUNTY
- HISTORY OF HUNTINGTON COUNTY
- HISTORY OF JOHNSON COUNTY
- HISTORY OF RUSH COUNTY
- HISTORY OF SHELBY COUNTY
- HISTORY OF THE GREAT KANAUHA VALLEY
- HISTORY OF VANDERBURGH COUNTY
- MEMORIAL RECORD OF ALABAMA
- UPPER MAUMEE RIVER VALLEY

Brant, S *see*
- STULTIFERA NAVIS NARRAGONICE PROFECTIONIS NUMQUAM SATIS LAUDATA NAVIS
- VON DEM ANFANG UND WESEN DER HAILIGEN STATT JERUSALEM

Brant, Sebastian *see* SHIPS OF FOOLS

BRANT SHPIGL – Basle. 1602. BJ-43-11 1 – 9 – ne IDC [956]
BRANT SHPIGL – Hanau. 1626. BJ-43-13 1 – 9 – ne IDC [956]
BRANT SHPIGL – Prague. 1610. BJ-43-12 1 – 9 – ne IDC [956]
Branta, Crystal *see* A FIELDWORK STUDY OF HOW YOUNG CHILDREN LEARN FUNDAMENTAL MOTOR SKILLS AND HOW THEY PROGRESS IN THE DEVELOPMENT OF STRIKING
BRANTFORD EXPOSITOR – Ontario, CN. 1852- – 12r per yr – 1 – Can$53.00r – cn Commonwealth Micro [072]
Brantome, Pierre de Bourdeille *see* ILLUSTRIOUS DAMES OF THE COURT OF THE VALOIS KINGS
Brants, Victor L *see* LA PETITE INDUSTRIE CONTEMPORAINE
Brard, C P *see* HISTOIRE DES COQUILLES TERRESTRES ET FLUVIATILES QUI VIVENT AUX ENVIRONS DE PARIS
Brasavola, Antonio Musa *see* EXAMEN OMNIUM CATAPOTIORUM UEL PILULARUM. CONRADI GESNERI ENVMERATIO MEDICAMETORUM PURGANTIUM..
Brasch, Moritz *see*
- MOSES MENDELSSOHN
- RUDOLF VON GOTTSCHALL

Braseau, Alphonse Victor *see* CHICOT: COMEDIE EN UN ACTE
Brash, Richard Rolt *see* THE OGAM INSCRIBED MONUMENTS OF THE GAEDHIL IN THE BRITISH ISLAND; WITH A DISSERTATION ON THE OGAM CHARACTER, ETC
Brash, W B *see* METHODISM
Brasil *see* RELATORIOS MINISTERIAIS
O BRASIL : JORNAL CATHOLICO, LITTERARIO E NOTICIOSO – [s.l.]. 25 Jan 1863 – 1,5,6 – bl Biblioteca [072]
BRASIL ACUCAREIRO – (Cont of: Economia e Agricultura) – Rio de Janeiro, Mar 1934-Dec 1979 – 1,5,6 – bl Biblioteca [072]
BRASIL CENTRAL : ORGAM INDEPENDENTE, NOTICIOSO E LITERARIO – Uberaba, 27 Mar 1913 – 1,5,6 – bl Biblioteca [072]
BRASIL E PORTUGAL : SCIENCIAS, ARTES, COMMERCIO E INDUSTRIA – Rio de Janeiro, 1 Jun-15 Aug 1872 – 1,5,6 – bl Biblioteca [072]
BRASIL HODIERNO – (Cont of: Gazeta de Curvello) – Curvello, 17 Apr, 28 Jun 1936 – 1,5,6 – bl Biblioteca [072]
O BRASIL ILLUSTRADO : PUBLICACAO LITTERARIA – Rio de Janeiro, 14 Mar 1855-31 Dec 1856 – 1,5,6 – bl Biblioteca [072]
EL BRASIL. LA TIERRA Y EL HOMBRE, SEGUIDO DE UN ESTUDIO HISTORICO DE JOAQUINA COMAS ROS. BARCELONA / Deffontaines, Pierre – Madrid: Razon y Fe, 1946 – 1 – sp Bibl Santa Ana [946]
BRASIL MARITIMO – [s.l.]. 1 Dez 1853-Dez 1854; Mar 1855-Jan 1857; Ago 1858-31 Ago 1859 – 1,5,6 – bl Biblioteca [072]
BRASIL NOVO : QUINZENARIO NOTICIOSO E INDEPENDENTE – Cruzeiro do Sul, Acre. 16 Maio 1937 – 1 – bl Biblioteca [072]
BRASIL POST – Semanario Brasilieiro. Sao Paulo, Brazil. 1971-82; 3 Dec 1983-24 Nov 1984 – 1 – gw Mikrofilm [072]
IL BRASILE COM'E / Felici, Osea – Milano, 1923. 253p – 1 – us U.W. Library [972]
O BRASILEIRO – '(s.l.')-Sao Luis, Brazil. 8 Feb-Sep 1830. Aug-16 Nov 1832 – 1,5,6 – bl Biblioteca [072]
O BRASILEIRO IMPARCIAL – Rio de Janeiro, 2 Jan-28 Dec 1830 – 1,5,6 – bl Biblioteca [072]
THE BRASILIANS – 1978-. New York: Jota Alves Enterprises. -m. To promote the interests of Brasil in the U.S.A – 1 – us U.W. Library [972]
Brasol, Boris Leo *see* WORLD AT THE CROSS ROADS
THE BRASS BAND JOURNAL – A collection of new and beautiful marches, quicksteps, polkas, etc., arranged in an easy manner for brass bands of 6 to 12 instruments. First series. New York: Firth, Pond & Co., c1853-54. Twenty-four pieces in parts, No. 3 wanting. MUSIC 3031 – 1 – us L of C Photodup [780]
BRASS WORKER *see* MACHINISTS AND BLACKSMITHS' MONTHLY JOURNAL, 1870-1875 : THE BRASS WORKER, 1895-1896 : OFFICIAL JOURNAL, 1902-1904
Brassard, Marc F *see* THE EFFECT OF THE AIRSTIRRUP AND A CONVENTIONAL METHOD OF STRAPPING THE ANKLE ON AGILITY AND VERTICAL JUMP PERFORMANCE
Brassey, Annie *see* A CRUISE ON THE EOTHEN, 1872
Brassey, Earl *see* PAPERS AND ADDRESSES...: IMPERIAL FEDERATION AND COLONISATION, FROM 1880 TO 1894
Brassey, Thomas *see*
- THE BRITISH NAVY: ITS STRENGTH, RESOURCES AND ADMINISTRATION
- PAPERS AND ADDRESSES...: IMPERIAL FEDERATION AND COLONISATION, FROM 1880 TO 1894

BRASTVO – v1-32, 1887-1941 – 1 – us U.W. Library [073]
Braswell, O Klute *see* HISTORY OF CARROLL COUNTY, ARKANSAS
Bratcher, Lewis M *see* THE AUTOBIOGRAPHY, LONGTIME MISSIONARY TO BRAZIL
BRAT'IA LIKHUDY. (OPYT ISSLEDOVANIIA IZ ISTORII TSERKOVNOGO PROSVESHCHENIIA I TSERKOVNOI ZHIZNI KONTSA 17 I NACHALA 18 VEKOV) / Smentsovskii, M N – Spb. 1899. BR-7875 2 – 8 – ne IDC [240]
BRAT'IA LIKHUDY. (OPYT ISSLEDOVANIIA IZ ISTORII TSERKOVNOGO PROSVESHCHENIIA I TSERKOVNOI ZHIZNI KONTSA 17 I NACHALA 18 VEKOV) *see* BRAT'IA LIKHUDY. (OPYT ISSLEDOVANIIA IZ ISTORII TSERKOVNOGO PROSVESHCHENIIA I TSERKOVNOI ZHIZNI KONTSA 17 I NACHALA 18 VEKOV)
BRAT'IA LUGININY, PIONERY KREDITNOI KOOPERATSII I PERVYI KREDITNYI KOOPERATIV V ROSSII / Merkulov, A V – M., 1918 – 1mf – 9 – COR-71/1 – ne IDC [334]
Bratke, Eduard *see*
- LUTHER'S 95 THESEN UND IHRE DOGMENHISTORISCHEN VORAUSSETZUNGEN
- WEGWEISER ZUR QUELLEN- UND LITTERATURKUNDE DER KIRCHENGESCHICHTE

Bratranek, F T H *see* GOETHE'S NATURWISSENSCHAFTLICHE CORRESPONDENZ
BRATSTVO – Brotherhood. v.17-19, 1940-1942 – 1 – us Res Libr [073]
BRATSTVO – Calumet, MI. 1926 – 1mf or 1r – 9,1 – us I.H.R.C. [978]
Bratstvo svobody i pori adka *see* DOVOLNO NASILI !!!!
BRAUCHEN WIR EIN NEUES DOGMA? : VORTRAG:GEHALTEN AUF DER LEIPZIGER PASTORALKONFERENZ AM 21. MAI 1891 / Seeberg, Reinhold – Erlangen:Andr. Deichert (George Boehme), 1892 – 1mf – 9 – 0-8370-5207-6 – 1985-3207 – us A.T.L.A. [140]
Braude, M *see* SEFER HA-YOVEL LE-MORDEKHAY ZE'EV BRAUDE
Braudes, R A *see* ZEKENIM IM NE'ARIM
Brauer, Karl *see* DIE UNIONSTAETIGKEIT JOHN DURIES UNTER DEM PROTEKTORAT CROMWELLS
Braun, A C H *see*
- ALGARUM UNICELLULARUM GENERA NOVA ET MINUS COGNITA
- CONSPECTUS SYSTEMATICUS CHARACEARUM EUROPAEARUM
- FRAGMENTE EINER MONOGRAPHIE DER CHARACEEN

Braun, Antoine *see* UNE FLEUR DU CARMEL: LA PREMIERE CARMELITE CANADIENNE, MARIE-LUCIE-HERMINE FREMONT: EN RELIGION SOEUR THERESE DE JESUS
Braun, Carl *see* AMERIKANISMUS, FORTSCHRITT, REFORM
Braun, F M *see*
- JEAN LE THEOLOGIEN
- JEAN TE THEOLOGIEN ET SON EVANGILE DANS L'EGLISE ANCIENNE (ETB)

Braun, Felix *see* DEUTSCHE GEISTER
Braun, G *see* CIVITATES ORBIS TERRARVM
Braun, Hanns *see* GRILLPARZERS VERHAELTNIS ZU SHAKESPEARE
Braun, J *see*
- DER CHRISTLICHE ALTAR
- DIE LITURGISCHE GEWANDUNG IN OCCIDENT UND ORIENT
- DIE LITURGISCHE PARAMENTE IN GEGENWART UND VERGANGENHEIT

Braun, Lily *see*
- GESAMMELTE WERKE
- LE PROBLEME DE LA FEMME

Braun, Otto *see* VON WEIMAR ZU HITLER
Braune, Karl *see* DREI BRIEFE DES APOSTELS JOHANNES
BRAUNKOHLE – Halle, Germany. Apr 1902-Mar 1910. -f – 6r – 1 – uk British Libr Newspaper [622]
Braunschweig-Bevern, August Wilhelm Herzog von *see* PAPERS
BRAUNSCHWEIGER ARBEITER ZEITUNG : ORGAN DER DRITTEN INTERNATIONALE – (Cont as: Niedersaechsische Arbeiter Zeitung. Organ der Vereinigten Kommunistischen Partei Deutschlands. 1921-26. Cont as: Neue Arbeiter-Zeitung. 1927-26 Feb 1933) – Braunschweig, 13 Nov-31 Dec 1920 – 20r – 1 – DM1,500.00 – gw Mikro Press [072]
BRAUNSCHWEIGER ARBEITER-ZEITUNG – (Title changes: Niedersaechsische Arbeiterzeitung Organ der VKPD, Jan 1921; and Neue Arbeiterzeitung, 1926, no.256; 13 Nov 1920-26 Feb 1933) – Braunschweig, Germany. Organ der III Internationale. – 20r – 1 – gw Mikrofilm [072]
BRAUNSCHWEIGER ARBEITER-ZEITUNG *see* NEUE ARBEITER-ZEITUNG
BRAUNSCHWEIGER LEUCHTKUGELN – Braunschweig, Germany. 1872-78 – 1 – gw Mikrofilm [072]
Braunschweiger, Moses *see* DIE LEHRER DER MISCHNAH: IHR LEBEN UND WIRKEN
BRAUNSCHWEIGER NEUESTE NACHRICHTEN – Braunschweig, Germany. 1910-33 – 87r – 1 – gw Mikrofilm [072]
BRAUNSCHWEIGER NEUESTE NACHRICHTEN – Braunschweig. v14-37. 1910-33 – 87r – 1 – DM6,525.00 – gw Mikro Press [072]
BRAUNSCHWEIGER POST-ZEITUNG – Braunschweig, Germany. 1682-85, 1689-1701. Formerly: Eingelauffene Ordinari Postzeitung – 1 – gw Mikrofilm [072]
BRAUNSCHWEIGER TAGESZEITUNG – Braunschweig, Germany. Oct 1931-10 Apr 1945 – 1 – gw Mikrofilm [072]
BRAUNSCHWEIGER TAGESZEITUNG *see* NIEDERSAECHSISCHE TAGESZEITUNG
BRAUNSCHWEIGER VOLKSFREUND – (Cont by: Braunschweigisches Unterhaltungsblatt, nov 2 1878; Braunschweiger Volksfreund, nov 30 1890; Volksfreund, 1907. Suppl available: Braunschweiger Leuchtkugeln, 1872-oct 1878; Nach Feierabend, 1903-06; Die Neue Welt, 1892-95; Unterhaltungsblatt, 1908-16) – Braunschweig, may 15 1871-mar 2 1933 – 93r – 1 – Inquire at Mikrofilmarchiv for details – gw Misc Inst [943]
BRAUNSCHWEIGER VOLKSFREUND *see* VOLKSFREUND
BRAUNSCHWEIGER ZEITUNG – Braunschweig, 8 Jan 1946-20 Feb 1950 – 4r – 1 – DM300.00 – gw Mikro Press [072]
BRAUNSCHWEIGER ZEITUNG – Braunschweig, jan 8 1946-feb 22 1950, 1968- – 1 – Inquire at Mikrofilmarchiv for details – gw Misc Inst [072]
BRAUNSCHWEIGER ZEITUNG – Braunschweig, West Germany. 8 Jan 1946-20 Feb 1950; 1968- – 4r – 1 – gw Mikrofilm [072]
BRAUNSCHWEIGER ZEITUNG *see* NIEDERSAECHSISCHE BEOBACHTER
BRAUNSCHWEIGISCHE ANZEIGEN – (Publ started jan 2 1745. Cont by: Oeffentliche Anzeigen, feb 4 1809; Braunschweigische Anzeigen, nov 13 1813; Braunschweigische Staatszeitung (incl suppl: Braunschweigisches Magazin), oct 1 1923-jan 1 1934) – Braunschweig, 1789, 1794, 1796, 1848-49, jan 3-jun 7 1906 – 1 – Inquire at Mikrofilmarchiv for details – gw Misc Inst [943]
BRAUNSCHWEIGISCHE ANZEIGEN MIT BRAUNSCHWEIGISCHES MAGAZIN – Braunschweig, Germany. 1848-49 – 4r – 1 – gw Mikrofilm [072]
BRAUNSCHWEIGISCHE STAATSZEITUNG *see* BRAUNSCHWEIGISCHE ANZEIGEN
BRAUNSCHWEIGISCHES FRIEDHOFS- UND BESTATTUNGSRECHT / Ostmann, Hans – Leipzig, 1933 – 1 – DM48.00 – 3-8267-3026-7 – gw Hänsel [340]
BRAUNSCHWEIGISCHES UNTERHALTUNGSBLATT *see* BRAUNSCHWEIGER VOLKSFREUND
BRAUNSCHWEIGWER TAGESZEITUNG *see* NIEDERSAECHSISCHE TAGESZEITUNG
Brausch, G *see* BASHAQRA AREA SETTLEMENTS 1963; A CASE STUDY IN VILLAGE DEVELOPMENT IN THE GEZIRA SCHEME
Brauw, O G S de *see* DE JURE VICTORIS IN PERSONAM ET BONA HOSTIS,...
BRAVE LEUT' VOM GRUND : VOLKSSTUECK MIT GESANG IN DREI ABTEILUNGEN / Anzengruber, Ludwig – Stuttgart: J G Cotta, 1892 – 1r – 1 – us U.W. Library [820]
BRAVE RESENA DE LAS AGUAS SULFURADO-SODI CAS TERMALES DE MONTEMAYOR O BANOS / Crespo y Escoriaza, Benito – Trujillo: Imp. Lib. y Enc. de Benito Pena y Pena, 1902 – 1 – sp Bibl Santa Ana [946]
Bravo de Piedrahita, J *see* DE HYDROPHOBIAE NATURA, CAUSIS ATQUE MEDELA...
Bravo, Luis *see* CUANDO PINTO ZURBARAN LOS CUADROS DE LA CARTUJA DE JEREZ DE LA FRONTERA?
Bravo Murillo, Juan *see*
- APUNTES Y DOCUMENTOS... ADMINISTRATIVAS
- DE LAS DEUDAS AMORTIZABLES...CUPONES
- DISCURSOS...CONGRESO DE LOS DIPUTADOS..
- OPUSCULOS

Bravo Riesco, Agustin *see*
- DE LA LAMENTACION DE LA VIRGEN MARIA
- FLORES DE SAN BERNARDO. DE LA LAMENTACION DE LA VIRGEN MARIA

Brawer, A J *see* RESHIT HA-SHIMMUSH BI-ZEKHUT HA-KAPITULAZIYYOT AL-YEDEI YEHUDIM BE-EREZ-YISRA'EL
THE BRAWLEY NEWS – Brawley, CA. 1904- – 252+ r – 1 RC02073 – $12,600.00 ($480.00y) – us Library Micro [071]
BRAWLEY WILDCAT – Brawley, CA. 1929-1986 – 4r – 1 – $200.00 – R04008 – us Library Micro [071]
BRAXTON BRAGG PAPERS *see* BRAGG, BRAXTON, PAPERS, MS 2000
BRAXTON CENTRAL – Sutton. West Virginia. 1886- – 1 – us UMI [071]
BRAXTON DEMOCRAT – Sutton. West Virginia. -w. 1883- – 1 – us UMI [071]
Bray, Alfred James *see*
- CHURCHES OF CHRISTENDOM: LECTURES, CRITICAL AND HISTORICAL
- ENGLAND AND IRELAND: A LECTURE

Bray, Anna Eliza *see*
- COURTENAY OF WALREDDON
- DE FOIX
- A FATHER'S CURSE
- FITZ OF FITZ-FORD
- HARTLAND FOREST
- HENRY DE POMEROY
- THE PROTESTANT
- ROSETEAGUE
- THE TALBA
- TRELAWNY OF TRELAWNE
- TRIALS OF THE HEART
- WARLEIGH
- THE WHITE HOODS

BRAY GAZETTE – (Kingston and Bray Gazette etc. 3 Feb 1872) – County Wicklow, Ireland. 5 Jun 1861-29 Mar 1873. -w. – 4r – 1 – uk British Libr Newspaper [072]
BRAY HERALD – Wicklow, Ireland. 21 Oct-30 Dec 1876; 1878-96. -w. 9 reels – 1 – uk British Libr Newspaper [072]
Bray, John *see* THE INDIAN PRINCESS, OR LA BELLE SAVAGE
BRAY PEOPLE – Bray, Ireland. -d. 1979-86. 21 reels – 1 – PS27.50r – ie European Micro [072]
Bray, W *see* JOURNAL
Bray, Wayne D *see* THE CONTROVERSY OVER A NEW CANAL TREATY BETWEEN THE U.S. AND PANAMA
Braye, Alfred Thomas Townshend Verney-Cave *see* THE PRESENT STATE OF THE CHURCH IN ENGLAND
Brayer, E *see* MANUSCRITS FRANCAIS DU MOYEN AGE CONSERVES A LENINGRAD
BRAYTON'S REPORTS / Vermont. Supreme Court – (A Pre-NRS title) – 1v. 1815-1819 (all publ) – 3mf – 9 – $4.50 – LLMC 90-310 – us L.L.M.C. [340]
O BRAZ CUBAS : ORGAO DOMINICAL – Manaos, Amazonas. 17 Mar 1901 – 1,5,6 – bl Biblioteca [072]
Brazao, Eduardo *see* RELACOES EXTERNAS DE PORTUGAL: REINADO DE D. JOAO V
Brazeau, A V *see* LE PETARD
BRAZIL : ANUARIO ESTATISTICO DE BRASIL 1908/12-1969 / Brazil. Instituto Brasileiro de Geografia e Estatistica – (Coll title: Latin American and Caribbean Official Statistical Serials, 1821-1982) – 9 – £1,300.00 – uk Chadwyck [972]
Brazil *see*
- CUARTO PLANO DIRECTOR DE DESENVOLVIMENTO ECONOMICO E SOCIAL DO NORDESTE
- DIARIO OFICIAL
- FIRST NATIONAL DEVELOPMENT PLAN 1972-74
- FIRST NATIONAL DEVELOPMENT PLAN 1972/74

- PLANO BASICO DE DESENVOLVIMENTO CIENTIFIO E TECHNOLOGICO 1973-1974
- RELATORIOS DOS PRESIDENTES DAS PROVINCIAS BRASILEIRAS
- RELATORIOS MINISTERIAIS

O BRAZIL : ORGAM NOTICIOSO E COMMERCIAL, DEDICADO AOS INTERESSES DO POVO – (Cont by: Gazeta do Sul) – Corumba, 19 Oct-Nov 1902; Jan-Sep, Nov-Dec 1903; Jan-Jun 1904; Oct-Nov 1905; Jan-Apr, Sep-Dec 1907; Jan-Aug, Oct-Dec 1908; Jan-Dec 1909; Jan-Apr, Aug-13 Sep 1910 – 1,5,6 – bl Biblioteca [072]

O BRAZIL : SEMANARIO POLITICO, DE INSTRUCCAO E RECREIO – Cachoeira, BA. Jan 1885 – 1,5,6 – bl Biblioteca [072]

O BRAZIL *see* O CHRONISTA

BRAZIL ACREANO : ORGAO DO PARTIDO PROGRESSISTA – Senna Madureira, Acre. 12 Abr-Dez 1910; Jan-Fev, Abr-Jun, Ago-Out, Dez 1911; Jan-Dez 1912; Jan, Mar 1913 – 1,5,6 – bl Biblioteca [072]

BRAZIL AMERICANO – Rio de Janeiro, 7 Jul 1875-14 Mar 1876 – 1,5,6 – bl Biblioteca [072]

BRAZIL AND RIVER PLATE MAIL – (South American Journal). London. -m. 1863-1955. (123 reels) – 1 – uk British Libr Newspaper [072]

Brazil. Congresso *see* DIARIO DO CONGRESSO NACIONAL

Brazil. Conselho do Desenvolvimento *see* PROGRAMA DE METAS

Brazil. Conselho nacional de Estatistica *see* REVISTA BRASILEIRA DE ESTATISTICA

Brazil. Courts *see* DIARIO DA JUSTICA AND APENSO JURISPRUDENCIA

O BRAZIL E A EDUCACAO POPULAR / Leao, Antonio Carneiro – Rio de Janeiro: Jornal do Commercio, de Rodrigues, 1917 – 1 – us U.W. Library [972]

Brazil. Instituto Brasileiro de Geografia e Estatistica *see* BRAZIL

Brazil, Mark *see* TROPICAL HOME GARDENS

Brazil. Ministerio do Planjamento e Coordenacao Economica *see*
- PLANO DECENAL DE DESENVOLVIMENTO ECONOMICO E SOCIAL
- PROGRAMA DE ACAO ECONOMICA DO GOVERNO, 1964-1966 (SINTESE)

Brazil. Presidencia de Republica *see*
- METAS E BASES PARA ACAO DO GOVERNO
- PLANO TRIENAL DE DESENVOLVIMENTO ECONOMICO E SOCIAL, 1963-1965
- THREE YEAR PLAN FOR ECONOMIC AND SOCIAL DEVELOPMENT, 1963-65

Brazil. Sao Paulo. Departamento do Archivo do Estado *see* INVENTARIOS E TESTAMENTOS

Brazil. Superintendencia do Desenvolvimento da Fronteira Sudoeste-Sudesul *see* PRIMEIRO PLANO DIRECTOR, 1967-1969

Brazil. Superintendencia do Desenvolvimento do Nordeste *see*
- THE BRAZILIA NORTHEAST SUDENE AND ITS FIRST GUIDING PLAN
- CUARTO PLANO DIRECTOR, 1969-73
- PLANO DE APROVEITAMENTO DE CAMARATUBA, MAMANGUAPE, PARAIBA
- PLANO DE DESENVOLVIMENTO DO NORDESTE. (1972-1974)
- SEGUNDO PLANO DIRECTOR DE DESENVOLVIMENTO ECONOMICA E SOCIAL DO NORDESTE, 1963-65
- TERCERO PLANO DIRECTOR DE DESENVOLVIMENTO ECONOMICA E SOCIAL DO NORDESTE, 1966-68

THE BRAZILIA NORTHEAST SUDENE AND ITS FIRST GUIDING PLAN / Brazil. Superintendencia do Desenvolvimento do Nordeste – Recife. 1962 – 9 – ne IDC [338]

...BRAZILIAN COFFEE / Moreira, Nicolau Joaquim – New York: O Novo Mundo, 1876. 11p – 1 – us U.W. Library [972]

BRAZILIAN PERSPECTIVES ON SUSTAINABLE DEVELOPMENT OF THE AMAZON REGION – 1995 – 311p – 9 – 92-3-103053-1 – Co-publ with Parthenon/UNESCO Publishing – fr UNESCO [333]

BRAZOPOLIS – Brazopolis, Brazil. Jul-Dec 1933; 1934-35; 1937; Jan, Mar-Jul, Oct-Nov 1938; Apr-Jun, Sept 1939; Feb, May-Jun 1940; Jun 1941; Feb 1953 – 1 – bl Biblioteca [072]

Brazos. Synod (Cum. Pres. Ch.) *see* MINUTES, 1849-1887

BREA PROGRESS – (Also known as: Brea Star) – Brea, CA. 1917- – 81r – 1 – $4,050.00 ($50.00y) – R02074 – us Library Micro [071]

BREA STAR *see* BREA PROGRESS

BREACH REPAIRED IN GOD'S WORSHIP / Keach, Benjamin – or Singing of Psalms, Hymns and Spiritual Songs. London. 1691 – 1 – 6.72 – us Baptist [240]

BREAD AND FREEDOM – (Philadelphia). 1906 – 1 – us A.J.P.C. [830]

THE BREAD OF LIFE = DE SACRAMENTO ALTARIS : OR, ST. THOMAS AQUINAS ON THE ADORABLE SACRAMENT OF THE ALTAR / Rawes, Henry Augustus – New ed. London: Burns & Oates; New York: Benziger, [1879?] – 1mf – 9 – 0-8370-7028-7 – 1986-1028 – us A.T.L.A. [240]

BREAD PUDDING ENCYCLOPEDIA : 1001 PLUS VARIATIONS / Data Notes Staff – 1988 – 9 – $19.95 – us Continnuus [640]

A BREAK IN THE OCEAN CABLE / Baldwin, Maurice Scollard – Montreal: Dawson Bros., 1877. 00840. (Pre-1900 Canadiana) – 9 – cn C.I.H.M. [971]

BREAKDOWN – Klamath Falls, OR. -w. 12 Jul 1971-9 Oct 1973. 2 rolls – 1 – us U.O. Library [071]

BREAKING DOWN CHINESE WALLS : FROM A DOCTOR'S VIEWPOINT / Osgood, Elliott Irving – New York: Fleming H Revell, c1908 – 1mf – 9 – 0-8370-6590-9 – 1986-0590 – us A.T.L.A. [610]

THE BREAKING WAVES DASHED HIGH : THE PILGRIM FATHERS / Hemans, Felicia – Boston: Lee & Shepard, 1880 – 1mf – 9 – $1.50 – LLMC 91-012 – us L.L.M.C. [320]

BREAKTHROUGH – (Title varies. Lacking some pages) – 1948-83 – 2r – 1 – ATLA S0452 – us A.T.L.A. [073]

Breal, M *see* ESSAI DE SEMANTIQUE

Breard, Charles *see* LE VIEUX HONFLEUR ET SES MARINS: BIOGRAPHIES ET RECITS MARITIMES

BREAST SUPPORT FOR THE ACTIVE WOMEN : RELATIONSHIP TO 3D KINEMATICS OF RUNNING / Boschma, Anne L C – Oregon State University, 1995 – 2mf – 9 – $8.00 – PE 3632 – us Microform Publ [612]

Breasted, J H *see* ORIENTAL FORERUNNERS OF BYZANTINE PAINTING

THE BREATH OF GOD : A SKETCH: HISTORICAL, CRITICAL AND LOGICAL OF THE DOCTRINE OF INSPIRATION / Hallam, Frank – (Includes bibliographical references) – New York: Thomas Whittaker, 1895 – 1mf – 9 – 0-8370-3453-1 – 1985-1453 – us A.T.L.A. [220]

BREATH OF GOD: A SKETCH...OF THE DOCTRINE OF INSPIRATION / Hallam, Frank – New York: Thomas Whittaker, 1895. 1 fiche – 9 – us A.T.L.A. [240]

Brebisson, Alphonse de *see* STATISTIQUE DE L'ARRONDISSEMENT DE FALAISE

Brebisson, L A de *see* CONSIDERATIONS SUR LES DIATOMEES

BREBISSONIA : REVUE MENSUELLE ILLUSTREE DE BOTANIQUE. CRYPTOGAMIQUE – Paris, 1878/1880-1881. 3v – 8mf – 7413/2 – ne IDC [580]

Brechenmacher, Josef Karlmann *see* DEUTSCHE SIPPENNAMEN, ABLEITENDES WOERTERBUCH DER DEUTSCHEN FAMILIENNAMEN

BRECHIN ADVERTISER – 1 – £42.00r – uk Scot News [072]

Brecht, Bertolt *see* BAAL

Brecht, Theodor *see* PAPST LEO 13. UND DER PROTESTANTISMUS

BRECK, JOHN, FAMILY PAPERS, MS 4675 – (Correspondence, writings, financial, legal, and other documents pertaining to John Breck, founder of Brecksville, and family) – Brecksville, Cuyahoga, OH. 1782-1993 – 2r – 1 – us Western Res [920]

Breckenridge, Roeliff Morton *see*
- THE CANADIAN BANKING SYSTEM, 1817-1890
- FREE BANKING IN CANADA

Breckinridge, Robert J *see* THE KNOWLEDGE OF GOD

Brecksville. Ohio. Brecksville Congregational Church *see* CHURCH RECORDS, MS 3168

BRECON REPORTER & SOUTH WALES GENERAL ADVERTISER – Wales, UK. 12 Sept 1863-16 Nov 1867. -w. 4 reels – 1 – uk British Libr Newspaper [072]

Brecot, Jean *see* LA GRANDE GREVE DE MAI 1920

Breda, J S G van *see* GENERA ET SPECIES ORCHIDEARUM ET ASCLEPIADEARUM

Bredemeier, Brenda Jo Light *see* GOAL ORIENTATION AND MORAL ATMOSPHERE IN YOUTH SPORT

Bredenbeck, Anton *see* 1889. DIE ERSTE ERHEBUNG DER BERGARBEITER. ZUR ERINNERUNG AN DEN GROSSEN BERGARBEITERSTREIK VOR 20 JAHREN

Bredenberg, Fritz von *see* DER KREIS SENSBURG

Bredenkamp, Conrad Justus *see*
- DER PROPHET JESAIA
- DER PROPHET SACHARJA

Brederek, E *see* KONKORDANZ ZUM TARGUM ONKELOS

Brederlow, CG F *see* VORLESUNGEN UEBER DIE GESCHICHTE DER DEUTSCHEN LITERATUR

Bredius, A *see* KUENSTLER-INVENTARE. URKUNDEN ZUR GESCHICHTE DER HOLLAENDISCHE KUNST DER 16TEN, 17TEN, 18TEN JAHRHUNDERTS

Bree, C R *see* A HISTORY OF THE BIRDS OF EUROPE

Bree, M *see* THE LESCHETIZKY METHOD: AN EXPOSITION OF HIS PERSONAL VIEWS

Breed, David R *see* THE HISTORY AND USE OF HYMNS AND HYMN-TUNES

Breed, Wiliam P *see* WITHERSPOON

Breed, William P *see* PRESBYTERIANS AND THE REVOLUTION

Breed, William Pratt *see* PRESBYTERIANISM THREE HUNDRED YEARS AGO

BREEDING FOR DURABLE DISEASE AND PEST RESISTANCE – 1984 2nd print 1985 – 172p – it F.A.O. [631]

BREEDING FOR DURABLE RESISTANCE IN PERENNIAL CROPS – 1986 – 135p – it F.A.O. [631]

BREEDING FOR HORIZONTAL RESISTANCE TO WHEAT DISEASES – 1986 – 120p – it F.A.O. [631]

BREEDING PLANTS FOR RUMINANT LIVESTOCK IN THE TROPICS – 1982 – 92p – it F.A.O. [636]

BREEDING POPLARS FOR DISEASE RESISTANCE – 1985 – 72p – it F.A.O. [634]

Breer, H *see* DIE INTERZESSIONS-BESCHRAENKUNGEN FUER FRAUEN...

BREEZE – Defuniak Springs. Fla. 1936-37, 1939-41, Sep 1945-58. Continued by Defuniak Herald – 1 – us P.K. Yonge [071]

BREEZE – Gretna. Neb. 1899-1927; 1930-1965 – 1 – us UMI [071]

BREEZE – Oceanside, CA. 1990 – 8+ r – 1 – $400.00 ($100.00y) – H04058 – us Library Micro [071]

BREEZE – Wauneta. Neb. 1887-1960 – 1 – us UMI [071]

BREEZE-COURIER – Taylorville. Ill. 1946-1954; 1956- – 1 – us UMI [071]

BREF HISTOURQUE DE L'INSTRUCTION PUBLIQUE – [Buenos Aires?]: Service International Argentin de Publications, [1952?] – 1 – CSUXAGN1668-B – us Hoover Inst Photo [972]

Breganze, G *see* SULLA LIBERTA DEI MARI

Bregeault, J *see* DE L'AUDITION EN MATIERE CRIMINELLE...

Breggin, Peter R *see* PSYCHIATRIC HOLOCAUST

Brehaut, Ernest *see* AN ENCYCLOPEDIST OF THE DARK AGES

Brehier, Emile *see* LES IDEES PHILOSOPHIQUES ET RELIGIEUSES DE PHILON D'ALEXANDRIE

Brehier, Louis *see* LE SCHISME ORIENTAL DU 11E SIECLE

Brehm, C L *see*
- HANDBUCH DER NATURGESCHICHTE ALLER VOGEL DEUTSCHLANDS
- MONOGRAPHIE DER PAPAGEIEN

Breidenbach, Bernhard von *see* HERBAR : ARZNEIBUCH 'MACER'

Breimer, R F et al *see* GUIDELINES FOR SOIL SURVEY AND LAND EVALUATION IN ECOLOGICAL RESEARCH

Breitenkamp, Paul *see* KUENDER DEUTSCHER EINHEIT

Breithaupt, Christian *see* A GRAMMAR FOR LEARNING THE PRINCIPLES OF THE MALABAR LANGUAGE

Breitinger, Johann Jakob *see*
- DIE DISCOURSE DER MAHLERN
- DER MAHLER DER SITTEN

Breitkopf, C *see* TERPISCHORE. SELECTIONS. IM CLAVIERAUSZUG

Breitner, Thomas C *see* HUMAN RIGHTS IN A WORLD FEDERATION

Breitscheid, Rudolf *see* DAS FREIE VOLK

BREIZ ATAO / Parti autonomiste breton – Rennes. 1919-aout 1939 – 1 – fr A.C.R.P.P. [073]

Brembeck, Cole Speicher *see* SPEECH FOR THE MILITARY

Breme, E D *see* BEYTRAEGE...STAATS- UND VOELKERRECHTE,...

Breme, F de *see* MONOGRAPHIE DE QUELQUES GENRES DE COLEOPTERES HETEROMERES...

THE BREMEN LECTURES ON GREAT RELIGIOUS QUESTIONS OF TO-DAY – Philadelphia: Amer. Bap. Pub. Soc., 1898. 1 fiche – 9 – us A.T.L.A. [240]

BREMEN: PAMPHLET COLLECTION – 19?? – 1 – CSUXANS9167-B – us Hoover Inst Photo [943]

Bremen. Statistisches Amt *see* JAHRBUCH FUER DIE AMTLICHE STATISTIK DES BREMISCHEN STAATS

Bremen. Statistisches Landesamt *see* JAHRBUCH FUER BREMISCHE STATISTIK

BREMER ABENDBLATT FUER GEMEINNUETZIGES UND ERHEITERNDES – Bremen, dec 31 1842-mar 25 1843 – 1r – 1 – Inquire at Mikrofilmarchiv for details – gw Misc Inst [072]

BREMER ARBEITER-ZEITUNG – Bremen, dec 14 1918-sep 30 1922 – 5r – 1 – Inquire at Mikrofilmarchiv for details – gw Misc Inst [943]

BREMER ARBEITER-ZEITUNG – Bremen, Germany.1918-22 – 5r – 1 – gw Mikrofilm [072]

BREMER BEOBACHTER – Bremen, Germany.6 Jan 1911-25 Mar 1917 – 1r – 1 – gw Mikrofilm [072]

BREMER BEOBACHTER – Bremen, jan 6 1911-mar 25 1917 – 1r – 1 – Inquire at Mikrofilmarchiv for details – gw Misc Inst [943]

BREMER BLAETTER FUER JEDERMANN – Bremen, aug 1917-oct 1918 – 1r – 1 – Inquire at Mikrofilmarchiv for details – gw Misc Inst [072]

BREMER BOTE – Bremen, 1903-17 – 6r – 1 – Inquire at Mikrofilmarchiv for details – gw Misc Inst [072]

BREMER BOTE – Bremen, Germany.1903-17 – 6r – 1 – gw Mikrofilm [072]

BREMER BUERGERFREUND *see* DER BUERGERFREUND

BREMER BUERGER-ZEITUNG – Bremen, 1890-1933 – 96r – 1 – DM7,200.00 – gw Mikro Press [072]

BREMER BUERGER-ZEITUNG – Bremen, Germany. -d. 20, 21 Sept, 4, 21 Dec 1916-7 Aug 1919. Imperfect. 5 reels – 1 – uk British Libr Newspaper [072]

BREMER BUERGER-ZEITUNG – (Cont by: Bremer Volksblatt, 1919; Bremer Volkszeitung, oct 2 1922) – Bremen, may 1 1890-mar 11 1933 – 1 – Inquire at Mikrofilmarchiv for details – gw Misc Inst [943]

BREMER BUERGER-ZEITUNG – (Title change: Bremer Volkszeitung) – Bremen, Germany. Title change: 2 Oct 1922. 1 May 1890-3 Feb 1919; and 1920-12 Mar 1933 – 1 – gw Mikrofilm [072]

BREMER COURIER *see*
- DER COURIER AN DER WESER

Bremer, Franz Peter *see* FRANZ VON SICKINGENS FEHDE GEGEN TRIER

BREMER FREIE ZEITUNG – Bremen, jul 1 1876-oct 17 1878 – 2r – 1 – Inquire at Mikrofilmarchiv for details – gw Misc Inst [943]

BREMER FREMDEN- UND ANZEIGE-BLATT *see* BREMER FREMDENBLATT

BREMER FREMDENBLATT – Bremen, 1855-60 – 5r – 1 – Inquire at Mikrofilmarchiv for details – gw Misc Inst [943]

BREMER FREMDENBLATT – (Cont by: Bremer Fremden- und Anzeige-Blatt, 1875) – Bremen, jul 1 1874-feb 20 1875 – 1 – Inquire at Mikrofilmarchiv for details – gw Misc Inst [943]

BREMER GENERAL-ANZEIGER – Bremen, Germany.24 Sept 1894-1897 – 9r – 1 – gw Mikrofilm [072]

BREMER GENERAL-ANZEIGER – (Suppl available: Bremer Familienblatt, nov 10 1895-jun 20 1897) – Bremen, sep 24 1894-97 – 9r – 1 – Inquire at Mikrofilmarchiv for details – gw Misc Inst [943]

BREMER HANDELSBLATT – Bremen, 1851-83 – 1 – Inquire at Mikrofilmarchiv for details – gw Misc Inst [380]

BREMER HANDELSBLATT – Bremen, Germany. -w. 11 Oct 1851-29 Sept 1883. 17 reels – 1 – uk British Libr Newspaper [072]

BREMER HANDELS-ZEITUNG – Bremen, 1883-84 – 1r – 1 – Inquire at Mikrofilmarchiv for details – gw Misc Inst [380]

BREMER HANDELS-ZEITUNG – Bremen, Germany.1883-84 – 1r – 1 – gw Mikrofilm [072]
BREMER HAUSFRAUEN-ZEITUNG – Bremen, 1922-23, 1925-28, 1930, 1932, 1934 – 4r – 1 – Inquire at Mikrofilmarchiv for details – gw Misc Inst [640]
BREMER HAUSFRAUEN-ZEITUNG – Bremen, Germany.1922-23; 1925-28; 1930; 1932; 1934 – 4r – 1 – gw Mikrofilm [072]
BREMER ILLUSTRIERTE WOCHE – Bremen, 1931-33 – 2r – 1 – Inquire at Mikrofilmarchiv for details – gw Misc Inst [072]
BREMER ILLUSTRIERTE WOCHE – Bremen, Germany.1931-33 – 2r – 1 – gw Mikrofilm [073]
BREMER JOURNAL – Bremen, Germany.Jul 1877-17 Jun 1880 – 1r – 1 – gw Mikrofilm [073]
BREMER JOURNAL – Bremen, jul 1 1877-jun 17 1880 – 1r – 1 – Inquire at Mikrofilmarchiv for details – gw Misc Inst [072]
BREMER MONTAGSBLATT – Bremen, feb 21-may 29 1876 – 1 – Inquire at Mikrofilmarchiv for details – gw Misc Inst [072]
BREMER MONTAGSBLATT – Bremen, Germany.13 Jul 1874-28 Jun 1875; 21 Feb-29 Mai 1876 – 1 – gw Mikrofilm [073]
BREMER MONTAGSBLATT – Bremen, jul 13 1874-jun 28 1875 – 1 – Inquire at Mikrofilmarchiv for details – gw Misc Inst [072]
BREMER MORGENPOST – (Suppl available: Morgenpost fuer die Jugend, mar 29-dec 20 1868) – Bremen, sep 1 1863-66, 1867 (many issues missing), 1868-sep 13 1870 – 13r – 1 – Inquire at Mikrofilmarchiv for details – gw Misc Inst [943]
BREMER MORGENPOST – (Title change: Morgenpost, 20 Aug 1865) – Bremen, Germany.1868-1870 – 7r – 1 – gw Mikrofilm [072]
BREMER NACHRICHTEN – Bremen, West Germany. 3 Jan 1950-1977; 1 Sept 1978- – ca 10r per yr – 1 – gw Mikrofilm [072]
BREMER NACHRICHTEN – (Cont: Bremer Woechentliche Nachrichten, jan 7 1743-1853. Cont by: Bremer Nachrichten mit Weser Zeitung, sep 30 1934-aug 31 1944; Bremer Nachrichten, sep 29 1949. Also available: Sonntags-Zeitung der Bremer Nachrichten, 1909; Sonntagsblatt der Bremer Nachrichten, 1901-aug 2 1914) – Bremen, 1743, 1745, 1767, 1782 (single issues only), 1796 (incomplete), 1797-1809, 1810 (incomplete), 1811-aug 29 1944, sep 20 1949- – 1 – Inquire at Mikrofilmarchiv for details – gw Misc Inst [943]
BREMER NACHRICHTEN – Germany. -d. 1 March 1942-2 Aug 1944; 20 Sept 1949-30 Nov 1952. Imperfect. 24 reels – 1 – uk British Libr Newspaper [072]
BREMER NACHRICHTEN MIT WESER ZEITUNG *see* BREMER NACHRICHTEN
BREMER NATIONALSOZIALISTISCHE ZEITUNG – (Cont by: Bremer Zeitung, nov 1 1933) – Bremen, jan 10 1931-apr 28 1945 – 1 – Inquire at Mikrofilmarchiv for details – gw Misc Inst [943]
BREMER NATIONALSOZIALISTISCHE ZEITUNG – (Title change: Bremer Zeitung, 1 Nov 1933) – Bremen, Germany.1931-45 – 43r – 1 – gw Mikrofilm [072]
BREMER POST – Bremen, 1856 n1-7, 1857 n8-12, 1858 n1-12, 1860 n1-12 – 1 – Inquire at Mikrofilmarchiv for details – gw Misc Inst [943]
BREMER POST – Bremen, Germany.H.1-7, 1856; H.8-12, 1857; H.1-12, 1858; H.1-12, 1860 – 1 – gw Mikrofilm [072]
BREMER SONNTAGSBLATT – Bremen, Germany.8 Okt 1843-29 Dez 1844; 1853-25 Mar 1866 – 7r – 1 – gw Mikrofilm [073]
BREMER SONNTAGSBLATT – Bremen, oct 8 1843-dec 29 1844 – 1 – Inquire at Mikrofilmarchiv for details – gw Misc Inst [072]
BREMER SONNTAGSBLATT – (Suppl available: Literarischer Wegweiser, jan-mar, may-dec 1864) – Bremen, jan 2 1853-mar 25 1866 – 7r – 1 – Inquire at Mikrofilmarchiv for details – gw Misc Inst [072]
BREMER TAGEBLATT – Bremen, dec 1855-mar 1859 – 1 – Inquire at Mikrofilmarchiv for details – gw Misc Inst [943]
BREMER TAGEBLATT – Bremen, Germany.1855-59 Mar (incomplete); Nov 1895-25 Jan 1896; 21 Nov 1897-1920 31 Dec – 1 – gw Mikrofilm [072]
BREMER TAGEBLATT – Bremen, nov 24 1895-jan 25 1896 – 1 – Inquire at Mikrofilmarchiv for details – gw Misc Inst [943]
BREMER TAGEBLATT – (Suppl available: Bremer Tuermer, jul 21 1907-aug 2 1914) – Bremen, nov 21 1897-1920 – 1 – Inquire at Mikrofilmarchiv for details – gw Misc Inst [943]
BREMER TAGES-CHRONIK *see*
- TAGES-CHRONIK
BREMER TELEGRAPH – Bremen, Germany.2 Okt-29 Dez 1846; 18 Jan-25 Apr 1848 (incomplete) – 1r – 1 – gw Mikrofilm [072]
BREMER TELEGRAPH – Bremen, oct 2-dec 29 1846, dec 23 1847, jan 18-apr 25 1848 (many issues missing) – 1r – 1 – Inquire at Mikrofilmarchiv for details – gw Misc Inst [943]
BREMER TELEGRAPH *see* TELEGRAPH
BREMER TUERMER – Bremen, Germany.21 Jul 1907-2 Aug 1914 – 1 – gw Mikrofilm [072]
BREMER VOLKSBLATT – Bremen, 1875-sep 23 1878 – 4r – 1 – Inquire at Mikrofilmarchiv for details – gw Misc Inst [943]
BREMER VOLKSBLATT – Bremen, Germany.1875-23 Sept 1878 – 1r – 1 – gw Mikrofilm [072]
BREMER VOLKSBLATT *see* BREMER BUERGER-ZEITUNG
BREMER VOLKS-ZEITUNG – Bremen, apr 1-jun 10 1888 – 1r – 1 – Inquire at Mikrofilmarchiv for details – gw Misc Inst [943]
BREMER VOLKSZEITUNG *see*
- BREMER BUERGER-ZEITUNG
BREMER WESER-ZEITUNG *see*
- WESER ZEITUNG
- WESER-ZEITUNG
BREMER WOCHEN-SCHRIFT – Bremen, dec 29 1749-dec 21 1750 – 1r – 1 – Inquire at Mikrofilmarchiv for details – gw Misc Inst [072]
BREMER WOCHEN-SCHRIFT – Bremen, Germany.29 Dez 1749-21 Dez 1750 – 1r – 1 – gw Mikrofilm [073]
BREMER WOECHENTLICHE NACHRICHTEN – Bremen, Germany.1743; 1796; 1797-1809; 1810; 1811-1944; 20 Sept 1949- – 1 – gw Mikrofilm [072]
BREMER WOECHENTLICHE NACHRICHTEN *see* BREMER NACHRICHTEN
BREMER ZEITUNG – (Cont by: Norddeutsche Rundschau, sep 1 1923; Nationale Rundschau, sep 2 1924; Neue Bremer Zeitung, apr 1 1926; Bremer Zeitung, aug 1 1926. Incl suppl: Bremen im Weltverkehr, 1924; Bremer Schiffahrtszeitung, 1921-23; Buehne und Film, 1921-jun 25 1922; BZ fuer Kleinhandel und Gewerbe, 1921-jun 12 1922; Der deutsche Arbeiter, 1921-24; Der Domshof, 1921-sep 1 1923; Frauen-Zeitung, 1921-aug 13 1922; Die Helling, 1921-23; Kiekinnewelt, 1921-23; Landwirtschaftliche Rundschau, 1925-feb 8 1926; Plattdeutsche Waelte, 1922; Der praktische Ratgeber fuer Haus und Garten, 1921-23; Wahl-Ulk, 1921; Weihnachtsanzeiger, 1923-24) – Bremen, 1921-29 – 22r – 1 – Inquire at Mikrofilmarchiv for details – gw Misc Inst [943]
BREMER ZEITUNG – (Cont by: Zeitung fuer Norddeutschland) – Bremen, Germany. 1741-42; 1752; 1765; 1770; 1815-48 – 34r – 1 – gw Mikrofilm [072]
BREMER ZEITUNG – (Cont by: Zeitung fuer Norddeutschland, dec 26 1848. Since then publ in Hannover) – Bremen, 1741, 1742, 1752, 1765 (single issues only), oct 1815-jun 30 1864, 1865-71 – 1 – Inquire at Mikrofilmarchiv for details – gw Misc Inst [943]
BREMER ZEITUNG *see*
- BREMER NATIONALSOZIALISTISCHE ZEITUNG
BREMERLEHER WOECHENTLICHE ANZEIGEN *see* DER MITTHEILER AN DER UNTERWESER
BREMERTON SUN – Bremerton, WA. 1901- – 514+ r – 1 – $25,700.00 ($500.00y) – R05400 – us Library Micro [071]
BREMERVOERDER ZEITUNG – (Bereichsausgabe der Zevener Zeitung, may 3 1943-apr 16 1945) – Bremervoerde, apr 1 1911-jun 23 1923, jan 2 1924-apr 16 1945, 1978- – 1 – Inquire at Mikrofilmarchiv for details – gw Misc Inst [943]
BREMERVOERDER ZEITUNG – Bremervoerde, West Germany. 1978- – ca 5r per yr – 1 – gw Mikrofilm [072]
BREMISCHE BLAETTER – Bremen, 1835 n1-2, 1836 n3-5 – 1 – Inquire at Mikrofilmarchiv for details – gw Misc Inst [943]
BREMISCHE BLAETTER – Bremen, Germany.H.1-2, 1835; H.3-5, 1836; H.1-9, 1879 – 1 – gw Mikrofilm [073]
BREMISCHE BLAETTER FUER UNTERHALTUNG, BELEHRUNG UND WITZ – Bremen, apr 13-jun 1 1879 – 1 – Inquire at Mikrofilmarchiv for details – gw Misc Inst [072]
BREMISCHE CORRESPONDENZ – Bremen, 1916 – 1r – 1 – Inquire at Mikrofilmarchiv for details – gw Misc Inst [072]
BREMISCHE CORRESPONDENZ – Bremen, Germany.1916 – 1r – 1 – gw Mikrofilm [072]
BREMISCHE POLIZEIBEAMTEN-ZEITUNG – (Cont by: Nachrichten der NSDAP) – Bremen, Germany. 1924, Feb 1933 – 1r – 1 – gw Mikrofilm [072]
BREMISCHE POLIZEIBEAMTEN-ZEITUNG – (Cont by: Nachrichten der NSDAP, Mai? 1933) – Bremen, 1924-34 – 1 – Inquire at Mikrofilmarchiv for details – gw Misc Inst [331]
BREMISCHE VOLKSZEITUNG – Bremen, 18 Oct 1878-25 Feb 1879 – 1r – 1 – DM80.00 – gw Mikro Press [072]
BREMISCHE VOLKSZEITUNG – Bremen, 1878-79 – 1 – Inquire at Mikrofilmarchiv for details – gw Misc Inst [943]
BREMISCHE VOLKSZEITUNG – Bremen, Germany. 18 Oct 1878-25 Feb 1879 – 1r – 1 – gw Mikrofilm [072]
BREMISCHER BEOBACHTER – Bremen, 1849-55 – 2r – 1 – Inquire at Mikrofilmarchiv for details – gw Misc Inst [943]
BREMISCHER BEOBACHTER – Bremen, Germany.1849-55 – 2r – 1 – gw Mikrofilm [072]
BREMISCHER VOLKSFREUND – Bremen, Germany.23 Nov 1849-30 Nov 1852 – 1r – 1 – gw Mikrofilm [072]
BREMISCHER VOLKSFREUND – Bremen, nov 23 1849-jun 30 1852 – 1r – 1 – Inquire at Mikrofilmarchiv for details – gw Misc Inst [943]
BREMISCHES CONVERSATIONSBLATT – Bremen, 3 Mai 1838-30 Jun 1839 – 1r – 1 – gw Mikrofilm [072]
BREMISCHES CONVERSATIONSBLATT – Bremen, may 3 1831-jun 30 1839 – 1r – 1 – Inquire at Mikrofilmarchiv for details – gw Misc Inst [072]
BREMISCHES JAHRBUCH – Bremen. v. 1-29, 1864-1924; v. 41-42, 1944-47. Film Mas C 408 – 1 – us H.U. Library [943]
BREMISCHES MAGAZIN – Bremen, 1831-34 n1-12 – 1r – 1 – Inquire at Mikrofilmarchiv for details – gw Misc Inst [072]
BREMISCHES MAGAZIN – Bremen, Germany. H. 1-12, 1831-34 – 1r – 1 – gw Mikrofilm [073]
BREMISCHES MAGAZIN ZUR AUSBREITUNG DER WISSENSCHAFTEN, KUENSTE UND TUGEND; VON EINIGEN LIEBHABERN DER SELBEN MEHRENTHEILS AUS DEN ENGLISCHEN MONATSSCHRIFTEN GESAMMELT UND HERAUSGEGEBEN – Hannover, 1757-65 – 3 – us Readex [000]
BREMISCHES UND VERDISCHES THEOLOGISCHES MAGAZIN – Bremen, 1795-98 – 1r – 1 – Inquire at Mikrofilmarchiv for details – gw Misc Inst [240]
BREMISCHES UNTERHALTUNGSBLATT – Bremen, 1823-47, 1848 (single issue only), 1855-59 – 12r – 1 – Inquire at Mikrofilmarchiv for details – gw Misc Inst [072]
BREMISCHES UNTERHALTUNGSBLATT – Bremen, Germany.1855-59 – 12r – 1 – gw Mikrofilm [073]
BREMISCHES VOLKSBLATT – Bremen, Germany.1823-47; 1851; 1855-59 – 1 – gw Mikrofilm [072]
Bremner, Archie *see* CITY OF LONDON, ONTARIO, CANADA: THE PIONEER PERIOD AND THE LONDON OF TODAY
Bremond, A *see*
- BULLARIUM ORDINIS FF. PRAEDICATORUM
- HISTOIRE DU SENTIMENT RELIGIEUX EN FRANCE
Bremond, Henri *see*
- THE MYSTERY OF NEWMAN
- SIR THOMAS MORE (THE BLESSED THOMAS MORE)
Bremser, W et al *see* CARBON-13 NMR SPECTRAL DATA
BREMSSTRAHLUNG NIEDERENERGETISCHER ELEKTRONEN : EXPERIMENTELLE UNTERSUCHUNGEN UND SIMULATIONSRECHNUNGEN / Lindenstruth, Stefan – 1994 – 1mf – DM60.00 – 3-8267-2027-X – gw Hänsel [530]
Brenan, Michael John *see* AN ECCLESIASTICAL HISTORY OF IRELAND
Brenan, P *see* THE EMERALD
Brenchley, Julius L *see* THE BRENCHLEY PAPERS, 1840-1865
THE BRENCHLEY PAPERS, 1840-1865 / Brenchley, Julius L – 1r – at Pacific Mss [920]
Brenckman, Fred *see* HISTORY OF CARBON COUNTY
BRENHAM BANNER-PRESS – Brenham. Texas. 1913- – 1 – us UMI [071]
BRENHAM DAILY BANNER – Brenham. Texas. 1876-1913 – 1 – us UMI [071]
Brenil, H *see* GLANES PALEOLITHIQUES ANCIENNES DANS LE BASSIN DU GUADIANA
Brennan, Geoffrey *see*
- CHAINING AUSTRALIA. CHURCH BUREAUCRACIES AND POLITICAL ECONOMY
- THE CHRISTIAN AND THE STATE
- CONSTITUTIONAL ROUTES TO SMALLER GOVERNMENT
Brennan, J J *see* LE REVEIL LITTERAIRE
Brennan, Paul *see*
- ARCHIPELAGO MUNDI, AN OPEN INQUIRY INTO CLOSED SPACES
- THE PARAQUAT REPORT, A HIT-AND-RUN HERBICIDE
BRENNAN, SULLIVAN AND CONNELLY SCRAPBOOKS – (Photographs, clippings, programs, letters, obituaries, memorials, certificates and memorabilia of the allied Brennan, Sullivan, and Connelly families, Irish immigrants to Cleveland in the 19th Century) – Cleveland, Cuyahoga, OH. 1844-1994 – 1r – 1 – us Western Res [920]
BRENNDORFER NACHRICHTEN – Brenndorf (Horineves), Czechoslovakia. 5 Jan 1929-1937 31 Dec – 2r – 1 – gw Mikrofilm [072]
BRENNDORFER NACHRICHTEN – Brenndorf, jan 5 1929-37 – 2r – 1 – Inquire at Mikrofilmarchiv for details – gw Misc Inst [943]
Brenner, D A I *see* HISTORIA DE LAS REVOLUCIONES DE HUNGARIA
Brenner, Stefan *see* DIE ENTWICKLUNG DER FRAGE DER BUENDNISZUGEHOERIGKEIT EINES WIEDERVEREINIGTEN DEUTSCHLANDS VON DER MAUEROEFFNUNG BIS ZUM TREFFEN VON MICHAIL GORBATSCHOW UND HELMUT KOHL IN SCHELESNOWODSK UNTER BESONDERER BERUECKSICHTIGUNG DER SOWJETISCHEN POSITION
Brenner, Vl *see* SET' SEL'SKOKHOZIAISTVEN-NOI KOOPERATSII SSSR
DIE BRENNESSEL – Muenchen, Berlin. 1931-38 – 5r – 1 – gw Mikrofilm [072]
Brenning, Emil *see*
- GRAF ADOLF FRIEDRICH VON SCHACK
- WILHELM HERBSTS HILFSBUCH FUER DIE DEUTSCHE LITTERATURGESCHIHTE
BRENNUS – Berlin, 1802 – 1 – Dist. gw Mikrofilm – gw Misc Inst [072]
Brent, Charles H *see*
- ADVENTURE FOR GOD
- THE CONSOLATIONS OF THE CROSS
- THE INSPIRATION OF RESPONSIBILITY, AND OTHER PAPERS
- LEADERSHIP
- LIBERTY AND OTHER SERMONS
- PRESENCE
- PRISONERS OF HOPE AND OTHER SERMONS
- THE REVELATION OF DISCOVERY
- WITH GOD IN PRAYER
- WITH GOD IN THE WORLD
Brentano, Clemens *see*
- GOCKEL, HINKEL UND GACKELEIA
- WERKE
Brentano, Franz Clemens *see* THE ORIGIN OF THE KNOWLEDGE OF RIGHT AND WRONG
Brentano, Maria Rafaela *see* AMALIE FUERSTIN VON GALLITZIN
BRENTANOS IM RHEINGAU : AM URQUELL DER RHEINROMANTIK / Doderer, Otto – 2. Aufl. Ratingen: A Henn, 1955 – 1 – us U.W. Library [430]
BRENTANOS JUGENDDICHTUNGEN : ABSCHNITT 1: DER IDEENGEHALT DES GODWI / Kempner, Alfred – 1995 – 1mf – 9 – DM48.00 – 3-8267-3132-8 – gw Hänsel [430]
Brenton, Edward Pelham *see* LIFE AND CORRESPONDENCE OF JOHN, EARL OF ST VINCENT, G.C.B., ADMIRAL OF THE FLEET, ETC

Brenton, Jahleel *see* MEMOIR OF CAPTAIN EDWARD PELHAM BRENTON, WITH SKETCHES OF HIS PROFESSIONAL LIFE, OBSERVATIONS UPON HIS NAVAL HISTORY, AND LIFE OF THE EARL OF SAINT VINCENT

BRENTWOOD BAPTIST CHURCH. CHARLESTON COUNTY, SOUTH CAROLINA : CHURCH RECORDS – (Other minutes 1962-1988) – 1957-1988 – 2r – 1 – $103.86 – us Baptist [240]

BRENTWOOD NEWS – Brentwood, CA. 1937-56; 1969- – 32+ r – 1 BC02076 – $1,600.00 ($90.00y) – us Library Micro [071]

BRENTWOOD-WESTWOOD HILLS PRESS – Santa Monica, CA. 1957 – 269+ r – 1 – $13,450.00 ($365.00y) – R03520 – us Library Micro [071]

Brentz, J the elder *see* TUERCHEN BUCHLEIN

BRENZTAL-BOTE : BA DER SUEDWESTPRESSE – Giengen-Ulm, Germany. 2 Jan 1975- – 101r (1975-1990) – 1 – gw Mikrofilm [072]

Brerewood, E *see* SCRUTINIUM RELIGIONUM ET LINGUARUM

Bres, G de *see*
- DE WORTEL, DEN OORSPRONCK ENDE HET FONDAMENT DE WEDERDOOPEREN. ANNO 1565

Breschi, B *see* LA COMPETENZA DEI TRIBUNALI STRANIERI...

Brescia, Anthony M *see* THE LETTERS AND PAPERS OF RICHARD RUSH

Bresee, James C *see* GEOTHERMAL SCIENCE AND TECHNOLOGY

Breshko-Breshkovskaia, Ekaterina Konstantinovna *see* CHTO DIELAT V UCHREDITELNOM SOBRANII

Breshko-Breshkovsko, Ekaterina Konstantinova et al *see* TERNISTYI PUT K SVOBODIE

LE BRESIL : STRUCTURE SOCIALE ET INSTITUTIONS POLITIQUES / Lambert, J – F30.00 – fr Ethnologie [320]

LE BRESIL ET L'AFRIQUE : LES NOUVELLES FORMES DES RELATIONS INTERNATIONALES DES AMERIQUES LATINES / Martiniere, G – F180.00 – fr Ethnologie [320]

BRESLAUER ANZEIGER – (Title change: Kleine Morgenzeitung, 1853; Morgenzeitung, 1858; Breslauer Morgenzeitung, 1862) – Breslau (Wroclaw), Poland. 1854, 1856, 1857-60, 1862-73 – 17r – 1 – gw Mikrofilm [943]

BRESLAUER ANZEIGER *see* BRESLAUER MORGENZEITUNG

BRESLAUER BEITRAEGE ZUR LITERATURGESCHICHTE – Leipzig: M Hesse, 1904-19 – 1r – 1 – us U.W. Library [430]

BRESLAUER BEITRAEGE ZUR LITERATURGESCHICHTE – Leipzig: M Hesse. 48v. 1904-19 – 1 – us U.W. Library [410]

BRESLAUER FREMDENBLATT – Breslau, 1853 (incomplete), 1854-sep 1858, 1859-62 – 1 – Inquire at Mikrofilmarchiv for details – gw Misc Inst [943]

BRESLAUER GENERAL-ANZEIGER – (Title change: Breslauer Neueste Nachrichten, 15 Apr 1918) – Breslau (Wroclaw), Poland. 1 Oct 1888-29 Feb 1944 – 1 – gw Mikrofilm [943]

BRESLAUER GENERAL-ANZEIGER *see* BRESLAUER NEUESTE NACHRICHTEN

BRESLAUER GERICHTS-ZEITUNG – Breslau, apr 2 1916-mar 25 1917 – 3r – 1 – Inquire at Mikrofilmarchiv for details – gw Misc Inst [072]

BRESLAUER HANDELSBLATT – Breslau, 1854-56 (incomplete), 1861-sep 30 1863 (incomplete), jan 2-oct 31 1864, 1865, 1873, jul 2-dec 31 1874 – 12r – 1 – Inquire at Mikrofilmarchiv for details – gw Misc Inst [380]

BRESLAUER HANDELSBLATT – Breslau (Wroclaw), Poland. 1854-56, 1861-65, 1873-74 – 12r – 1 – gw Mikrofilm [943]

BRESLAUER HAUSBLAETTER *see* SCHLESISCHE VOLKSZEITUNG

BRESLAUER HAUSBLAETTER FUER DAS VOLK – Breslau, 1789-1806 – 1 – Inquire at Mikrofilmarchiv for details – gw Misc Inst [943]

BRESLAUER INTELLIGENZ-BLATT – Breslau, oct 5-dec 28 1835, jul 2-dec 24 1838 – 2r – 1 – Inquire at Mikrofilmarchiv for details – gw Misc Inst [943]

BRESLAUER JUEDISCHES GEMEINDEBLATT : AMTLICHES BLATT DER SYNAGOGENGEMEINDE BRESLAU – Breslau. v1-15. 1924-1938. Lacking misc. issues. B435 (Leo Baeck Institute. German-Jewish Periodicals, Pt 1) – 2r – 1 – $135.00 – us UPA [270]

BRESLAUER JUEDISCHES GEMEINDEBLATT – (Cont by: Juedisches Gemeindeblatt fuer die Synagogengemeinde Breslau, aug 10 1937) – Breslau, aug 8 1924-aug 25 1938 (incomplete) – 2r – 1 – Inquire at Mikrofilmarchiv for details – gw Misc Inst [943]

BRESLAUER KREISBLATT – BRESLAU, 1928 – 1 – Inquire at Mikrofilmarchiv for details – gw Misc Inst [072]

BRESLAUER KREISBLATT – Breslau (Wroclaw), Poland. 1928 – 1 – gw Mikrofilm [943]

BRESLAUER MORGENZEITUNG – (Cont: Breslauer Anzeiger, sep 29 1845-mar 28 1853; Kleine Morgenzeitung, -1857; Morgenzeitung, -sep 1862) – Breslau, 1854-60, jan 1-apr 23, jul 17-dec 31 1862, 1873 – 1 – Inquire at Mikrofilmarchiv for details – gw Misc Inst [943]

BRESLAUER MORGENZEITUNG *see* BRESLAUER ANZEIGER

BRESLAUER NEUESTE NACHRICHTEN – (Cont: Breslauer General-Anzeiger, oct 1 1888-apr 14 1918) – Breslau, apr 1-dec 1916, 1939-feb 29 1944 – 16r – 1 – Inquire at Mikrofilmarchiv for details – gw Misc Inst [943]

BRESLAUER NEUESTE NACHRICHTEN *see* BRESLAUER GENERAL-ANZEIGER

DIE BRESLAUER RITUALIEN / Jungniss, J – Breslau, 1892 – 1mf – 8 – Dfl6.00 – ne Slangenburg [240]

BRESLAUER VOLKSBLAETTER – Breslau, 1904-06 – 3r – 1 – Inquire at Mikrofilmarchiv for details – gw Misc Inst [072]

BRESLAUER VOLKSBLAETTER – Breslau (Wroclaw), Poland. 1904-06 – 2r – 1 – gw Mikrofilm [943]

BRESLAUER VOLKSSPIEGEL – Breslau (Wroclaw), Poland. 1846-47 – 2r – 1 – gw Mikrofilm [943]

BRESLAUER VOLKSSPIEGEL – (Since 1847: Volksspiegel) – Breslau, 1846-47 – 2r – 1 – Inquire at Mikrofilmarchiv for details – gw Misc Inst [072]

BRESLAUER ZEITUNG – Breslau, Germany. (Wroclaw, Poland). Jan-Sept 1848 – 2r – 1 – gw Mikrofilm [072]

BRESLAUER ZEITUNG – (Cont: Neue Breslauer Zeitung, 1820-27) – Breslau, 1820-83, 1884 (incomplete), 1885-91, oct-dec 1892, apr 1893-oct 1895, apr-jun 1898, jan-feb 1912 – 1 – Inquire at Mikrofilmarchiv for details – gw Misc Inst [943]

BRESLAUER ZEITUNG – Poland. -d. 12 Jan 1916-10 Aug 1919. Imperfect. 19 reels – 1 – uk British Libr Newspaper [943]

BRESLAUER ZEITUNG *see* NEUE BRESLAUER ZEITUNG

BRESLAUISCHER MERKURIUS – Breslau, 1701-02 (incomplete) – 1 – Inquire at Mikrofilmarchiv for details – gw Misc Inst [943]

Bresler, M *see* GENERIS ASPARAGI HISTORIA NATURALIS ATQUE MEDICA

Bresoles, Judith de *see* BIO-BIBLIOGRAPHIE DE MERE MARIE-BERTHE THIBAULT

Bressani, Francisco Giuseppe *see* LES JESUITES-MARTYRS DU CANADA

Bresslau, H *see* CHRONICA HEINRICI SURDI DE SELBACH (MGH 6: 1.BD)

BRESSLAUISCHER MERCURIUS – Breslau, Poland. 1701-02 (incomplete) – 1 – gw Mikrofilm [943]

Bressolles, P *see* LIQUIDATION DE LA COMPAGNIE DE PANAMA

Bressonnet, M *see* DE LA QUALITE...

BREST-LITOVSK PEACE CONFERENCE (1917-1918) *see* BREST-LITOVSKAI A KONFERENTSIIA

BREST-LITOVSKAI A KONFERENTSIIA : ZASEDANIIA EKONOMICHESKO I I PRAVOVO I KOMISSII / ed by Shteina, B E – Moskva: Izd. Narodnogo komissariata po inostrannym delam, 1923 – 1 – CSUX91-B540 – us Hoover Inst Photo [320]

Bretagne, Anjou *see* RECUEIL D'ACTES ET PIECES DIVERSES CONCERNANT DES SEIGNEURIES BRETONNES ET ANGEVINES

Bretagne, Noblesse *see*
- ANCIENNE REFORMATION DE LA NOBLESSE DE BRETAGNE (1427 A 1429)
- ANCIENNES REFORMATIONS DE LA NOBLESSE DE BRETAGNE (15E ET 16E S.)

LA BRETAGNE PITTORESQUE ET LEGENDAIRE / Sebillot, Paul – 1911 – 1 – us I.U. Libraries [390]

LA BRETAGNE REELLE – Merdrignac (Cotes-du-Nord). 1954-juin 1972 – 1 – fr A.C.R.P.P. [073]

Bretholz, B *see* COSMAE PRAGENSIS CHRONICA BOEMORUM (MGH 6: 2.BD)

BRETHREN EVANGELIST – Ashland. Ohio. 1885-89; 1894-1902 – 1 – us UMI [240]

THE BRETHREN JOURNAL – v65-90. 1966-91 (incomplete) – 7r – 1 – ATLA S0421 – us A.T.L.A. [240]

BRETHREN MISSIONARY HERALD AND THE BRETHREN ANNUAL – v1-38. 1939-76 (complete) – 28r – 1 – ATLA S0324 – us A.T.L.A. [240]

THE BRETHREN'S ALMANAC – 1871-79 (complete) – 1r – 1 – ATLA S0905 – us A.T.L.A. [030]

BRETHREN'S ALMANAC AND DIRECTORY – 1897-98 (complete) – 1r – 1 – ATLA 1993-S027 – us A.T.L.A. [030]

THE BRETHREN'S FAMILY ALMANAC – 1880-1917 (complete) – 2r – 1 – ATLA S0906 – us A.T.L.A. [030]

LE BRETON : POLITIQUE, INDUSTRIE ET COMMERCE (...) – (Six missing numbers) – Quotid. de Nantes, nov. 1826-avril 1855 (6 no. manq.) – 29r – 1 – F16338,94 – fr Armell [320]

Breton de la Martiniere, J B J *see* LE JAPON

Breton, Pierre Napoleon *see* HISTOIRE ILLUSTREE DES MONNAIES ET JETONS DU CANADA: DONNANT L'HISTOIRE, LA GRAVURE

Bretonne, Nicolas Edme Retif de la *see* CONFESSIONS D'UNE ROUE DE LA REGENCE

Bretschneider *see* RECHERCHES ARCHEOLOGIQUES ET HISTORIQUES SUR PEKIN ET SES ENVIRONS

Bretschneider, C G *see* CORPUS REFORMATORUM

Bretschneider, H et al *see* JANUS

Bretschneider, Karl Gottlieb *see*
- AUS MEINEM LEBEN
- A MANUAL OF RELIGION AND OF THE HISTORY OF THE CHRISTIAN CHURCH

Brett, H J *see* REPORT ON THE INDUSTRIAL AND ECONOMIC SITUATION OF CHINA IN JUNE, 1923

Brett, Henry *see* WHITE WINGS

Brett, James Warden *see* JOURNAL OF A HARPOONER ON BOARD THE WHALING SHIP MASSACHUSETTS, 1836-1840

Brett, Thomas *see* LEADING CASES IN MODERN EQUITY

Brett, W H *see* MISSION WORK AMONG THE INDIAN TRIBES IN THE FORESTS OF GUIANA

Brette, Armand *see*
- DICTIONNAIRE DES CONSTITUANTS, LISTE DES DEPUTES ET DES SUPPLEANTS ELUS A L'ASSEMBLEE CONSTITUANTE DE 1789
- LES LIMITES ET LES DIVISIONS TERRITORIALES DE LA FRANCE EN 1789

BRETTENER NACHRICHTEN – Bretten, mar 16 1949-apr 30 1953 – 1 – Inquire at Mikrofilmarchiv for details – gw Misc Inst [072]

Bretteville, Abbe de *see* L'ELOQUENCE DE LA CHAIRE ET DU BARREAU

Brettingham, Matthew *see* ACCOUNTS OF THE WORKS OF ART BOUGHT IN ROME

BRETTON WOODS AGREEMENT ACT. RELEASE NUMBER 1-2, JAN. 9, 1950-JAN. 19, 1955 / U.S. Securities and Exchange Commission – 9 – us UMI [324]

BRETTON WOODS AGREEMENT RELEASES – nos1-2. 9 Jan 1950-19 Jan 1955 (all publ) – 1mf – 9 – $1.50 – LLMC 89-004 – us L.L.M.C. [340]

Bretz, A *see* STUDIEN UND TEXTE ZU ASTERIOS VON AMASEA (T.U.U. 3-40/1)

Breuer, Joerg *see* KONZEPTE EINER ZENTRALEN EUROPAEISCHEN VERKEHRSWEGEPLANUNG

Breughel, G H van *see* CUPIDO'S LUSTHOF ENDE DER AMOUREUSE BOOGAERT BEPLANT ENDE VERCIERT MEET 22 SCHOONE COPERE FIGUIREN...

Breuning, C *see* SIX SONATAS POUR LE CLAVECIN AVEC UN VIOLON OBLIGE... OEUVRE 5

BREVARD'S LAW REPORTS / South Carolina. Supreme Court – (A Pre-NRS title) – v1-3. 1793-1816 (all publ) – 20mf – 9 – $30.00 – LLMC 94-010 – us L.L.M.C. [340]

BREVARIUM (SIECLE 15) – Valencia – 1r – 5,6 – sp Cultura [240]

Breve *see* BREVE NOTICIA DE EL ORIGEN QUE TUVO LA DEVOCION DE LA PURISIMA CONCEPCION DE NUESTRA SENORA Y DE UNA SANTA IMAGEN...

BREVE ANTIPOLOGIA AL DISCURSO NUEVO... MIGUEL FERNANDEZ DE LA PENA...DEL USO DE AGUA DE LA NIEVE EN DIA DE PURGA / Perez Merino, I – Jaen, 1641 – 2mf – 9 – sp Cultura [615]

BREVE COMPENDIO DELLA VITA DEL FAMOSO TITIANO VECELLIO DI CADORE / Titiano Vecellio – O 1072 1. 1622 – 9 – ne IDC [920]

BREVE DISCURSO EM QUE SE CONTA A CONQUISTA DO REINO DO PEGU / Mousinho, Manuel de Abreu – Barcelos: Portugalense Editora, 1936. xxii,71p.Portuguese version. 1 reel. 1189 – 1 – us U.W. Library [946]

BREVE ENSAYO SOBRE LOS NOMBRES GENTILICIOS USADO EN LA ALTA EXTREMADURA / Gutierrez Macias, Valeriano – Badajoz: Dip. Provincial, 1970 – sp Bibl Santa Ana [946]

BREVE ESTUDIO DE LA OBRA Y PERSONALIDAD DEL ESCULTOR Y ARQUITECTO DON MANUEL TOLSA. MEXICO / Escontria, Alfredo – Madrid: Razon y Fe, 1935 – 1 – sp Bibl Santa Ana [720]

BREVE GUIA DE TRUJILLO, CUNA DE CONQUISTADORES / Moreno Lazaro, J – 1973 – 1 – sp Bibl Santa Ana [946]

BREVE HISTORIA DE LAS LUCHAS SOCIALES EN ARGENTINA / Bortnik, Ruben – Buenos Aires: Corregidor, 1st ed 1974 – 1 – CSUXAHZ2940-B – us Hoover Inst Photo [335]

BREVE HISTORIA DE MEXICO / Bayle, Constantino & Vasconcelos, Jose – Madrid: Razon y Fe, 1944 – 1 – sp Bibl Santa Ana [972]

BREVE HISTORIAL DE LAS SAGRADAS RELIQUIAS QUE SE VENERAN EN LAS PARROQUIAS DE SANTA EULALIA Y STA. MARTA LA MAYOR DE MERIDA / Gonzales y Gomez de Soto, Juan Jose – Merida: Tip.Lib.y Enc.Juan F.Rivera Silva, 1916 – 1 – sp Bibl Santa Ana [240]

BREVE INFORME DE LA ACTIVIDAD DE LA OFICINA DE PRENSA Y PROPAGANDA DE LA REPRESENTACION DE ESPANA EN LA ARGENTINA DESDE EL MES DE SEPTIEMBRE DE 1937 HASTA EL DE AGOSTO DE 1938 / Spain. Embajada. Argentine Republic – Buenos Aires, 1938. Fiche W1174. (Blodgett Collection of Spanish Civil War Pamphlets) – 9 – us H.U. College Libr [946]

BREVE METODO PER FONDATAMENTE, E CON FACILITA APPRENDERE IL CANTO FERMO.. / Tettamanzi, Fabricio – 1706 – 2 – us Sibley [780]

BREVE NOTICIA DE EL ORIGEN QUE TUVO LA DEVOCION DE LA PURISIMA CONCEPCION DE NUESTRA SENORA Y DE UNA SANTA IMAGEN... / Breve – Madrid, 1706 – sp Bibl Santa Ana [946]

BREVE PUNTUAL NOTICIA DE EL MODO, SOLEMNIDAD Y CIRCUNSTANCIA CON QUE SE CELEBRO LA GLORIOSA ACLAMACION DE NUESTRO INCLITO REY Y SENOR LUIS PRIMERO...CACERES...1724 – Madrid, 1724 – 1 – sp Bibl Santa Ana [946]

BREVE RACCONTO DELLA TRANSPORTATIONE DEL CORPO DI PAPA PAOLO V. DALLA BASILICA DI S. PIETRO A'QUELLA DI S. MARIA MAGGIORE / Guidiccioni, L – O-1125 1. 1623 – 9 – ne IDC [240]

BREVE RAGGUAGLIO DELLE PRINCIPALI REGOLE DEL CANTO FERMO GREGORIANO.. / Della Gatta, Marco – 2V. 1793-1794 – 2 – us Sibley [780]

BREVE RELACION DEL PLEYTO DE ORELLANA – S.l., s.i., s.a. – 1 – sp Bibl Santa Ana [946]

Breve Resena *see* BREVE RESENA PARA GOBIERNO DE LAS QUE ASPIRAN A INGRESAR EN EL INSTITUTO DE HERMANAS DE LA CARIDAD DEL SAGRADO CORAZON DE JESUS

BREVE RESENA DE BADAJOZ / Direccion General de Turismo – Badajoz: Industrias Graficas, 1962 – sp Bibl Santa Ana [910]

BREVE RESENA DE LAS LINEAS...MALPARTIDA DE PLASENCIA A CACERES.. – 1881 – 9 – 1.50f – sp Bibl Santa Ana [946]

BREVE RESENA HISTORICA...SAN VICENTE DE PAUL – 1862 – 9 – $1.50f – sp Bibl Santa Ana [240]

BREVE RESENA PARA GOBIERNO DE LAS QUE ASPIRAN A INGRESAR EN EL INSTITUTO DE HERMANAS DE LA CARIDAD DEL SAGRADO CORAZON DE JESUS / Breve Resena – S.L.Si.s.a. – 1 – sp Bibl Santa Ana [240]

BREVE RESUMPTA Y TRATADO DE LA ESENCIA, CAUSAS, PRONOSTICO..., Y CURACION DE LA PESTE / Barba, P – Madrid, 1648 – 69mf – 9 – sp Cultura [616]

BREVE TRATADO DE PESTE CON SUS CAUSAS SENALES Y CURACION... / Perez, A – Madrid, 1589 – 2mf – 9 – sp Cultura [615]

BREVE TRATADO DE TODO GENERO DE BOBEDAS ASI REGULARES COMO IRREGULARES... / Torija, J – Madrid, 1661 – 3mf – 9 – sp Cultura [720]

BREVES ADVERTENCIAS PARA BEBER FRIO CON NIEVE... / Porres, M – Lima, 1621 – 2mf – 9 – sp Cultura [610]

BREVES DEFINICIONES DE HISTORIA GENERAL Y DE ESPANA...SUCESOS...BADAJOZ / Romero Morera, Joaquin – Badajoz: Imp. y libr. de Emilio Orduna, 1878 – 1 – sp Bibl Santa Ana [946]

BREVES NOUVELLES D'INDONESIE – (Missing:[1953], v1-1954, v2(1-23); 1955, v3(15-19, 21, 24-28?); 1956, v4(3, 10, 11, 14)) – Berne. v1-4. [1953]-1956 – 8mf – 9 – SE-1363/1 – ne IDC [950]

BREVES...AGUAS...BANOS DE MONTAMAYOR / Pesado Blanco, Sergio – (1898 ed.1.50f; 9) – 1897 – 9 – 1.50f – sp Bibl Santa Ana [890]

BREVES-GEOGRAFIA ASTRONOMICA / Guillen y Flores, Agustin – 1861 – 9 – 1.50f – sp Bibl Santa Ana [520]

BREVES...ISLA DE CUBA / Fernandez Golfin, Luis – 1866 – 9 – 1.50f – sp Bibl Santa Ana [972]

BREVE...UNIVERSI / Urbano Octavo. Papa – 1632 – 9 – 1.50f – sp Bibl Santa Ana [240]

LES BREVIAIRES : MANUSCRITS DES BIBLIOTHEQUES PUBLIQUES DE FRANCE / Leroquais, Victor – Paris. Tom 1-5, Planches. 1934 – 81mf – 8 – Dfl284.00 – ne Slangenburg [240]

LES BREVIAIRES MANUSCRITS DES BIBLIOTHEQUES PUBLIQUES DE FRANCE / France. Bibliotheques publiques; ed by Leroquais, Victor – Paris. 5v. 1934 – 54mf – 9 – O-477/1 – ne IDC [020]

BREVIARIO – Calahorra – 1r – 5,6 – sp Cultura [240]

IL BREVIARIO AMBROSIANO / Cattaneo, E – Milano, 1943 – 7mf – 8 – Dfl28.00 – ne Slangenburg [240]

BREVIARIO DE CIUDADANIA... / Migueta, Juan – Madrid: Razon y Fe, 1927 – 1 – sp Bibl Santa Ana [680]

BREVIARIO DE LA IGLESIA DE CALAHORRA (ANNO 1400) – Calahorra – 1r – 5,6 – sp Cultura [240]

BREVIARIO SENTIMENTAL / Delgado Fernandez, Rufino – Caceres: Tip. El Noticiero, 1964 – 1 – sp Bibl Santa Ana [946]

BREVIARIO (SIECLE 15) – Calahorra – 1r – 5,6 – sp Cultura [240]

BREVIARIUM AD USUM INISIGNIS ECCLESIAE EBORACENSIS, 1-2 / Lawley, M – Edinburgh, 1883 – 18mf – 8 – Dfl63.00 – ne Slangenburg [240]

BREVIARIUM ARTIS MUSICES / Leisring, V – Oder ein kurtzes band einfeltiges Musicbuechlein fuer die jungen Knaben. Jehna. 1615. BP-363 1 – 9 – ne IDC [780]

BREVIARIUM HISTORIAE METRICUM (CSHB 29) : IOELIS CHRONOGRAPHIA COMPENDIARIA.GEORGII ACROPOLITAE ANNALES / Manassis, Constantini; ed by Bekkerus, Imm – Bonnae, 1837 – Dfl46.00 – ne Slangenburg [240]

BREVIARIUM HISTORICUM (CBH 2,2) / Nicephori, S, Patriarchae Constantinopolitani; ed by Petau, D – Parisiis, 1648 – Dfl22.00 – ne Slangenburg [930]

BREVIARIUM HISTORICUM (CBH 12,1) / Manassis, Constantini; ed by Allatius, L & Fabrotus, C – Parisiis, 1655 – Dfl32.00 – ne Slangenburg [240]

BREVIARIUM PLANTARUM NOVARUM / Jordan, A & Fourreau, P J – Parisiis. 1866-68. B-5050 2 – 8 – ne IDC [580]

BREVIARIUM ROMANUM A FRANCISCO CARDINALE QUIGNONIO. ED. 1535 / Legg, J Wickham – 1e ed. Cambridge, 1888 – 5mf – 8 – Dfl22.00 – ne Slangenburg [240]

BREVIARUM LUGDUNUM – Possibly written in France, 15th century – 1 – us A.T.L.A. [240]

THE BREVIARY OF HELTHE... / Boorde, A – London, 1547 – 7mf – 9 – ne IDC [613]

Brevie, J *see* ISLAMISME CONTRE "NATURISME" AU SOUDAN FRANCAIS

BREVIER DER LEBENSKUNST / Villers, Alexander von; ed by Schirmer, Jo – Frankfurt a.M.: Siegel-Verlag, [1947] – 1r – 1 – us U.W. Library [920]

DAS BREVIER UND DER SAEKULARKLERUS / Merk, KJ – Stuttgart, 1950 – 3mf – 8 – Dfl13.00 – ne Slangenburg [240]

BREVILOQUIUM...QUATOR LIBROS...SENTENTIARUM / Ovando Mogollon de Baredes, Francisco – (1587 ed.1.50f; 9) – 1584 – 9 – 1.50f – sp Bibl Santa Ana [880]

BREVIS DESIGNATIO MEDITATIONUM DE ORIGINIBUS GENTIUM / Leibniz – Berlin. Akademie der Wissenschaften. Miscellanea Berolinensia, v1(p1-16). 1710 – 1mf – 9 – ne IDC [400]

BREVIS INTRODUCTIO IN NOTITIAM LEGUM NAUTICARUM... – Luebeck, 1713 – 2mf – 1 – ILM-712/1 – ne IDC [327]

BREVIS LINGUAE SYRIACAE GRAMMATICA, LITTERATURA, CHRESTOMATHIA CUM GLOSSARIO : IN USUM PRAELECTIONUM ET STUDIORUM PRIVATORUM / Nestle, Eberhard – (Discussion in Latin; texts in Syriac) – Carolsruhae: H Reuther, 1881 – 1mf – 9 – 0-8370-8600-0 – 1986-2600 – us A.T.L.A. [470]

BREVISSIMA RHETORICES INSTITUTIO / Evans, David – 1733. Also: Physica Compendiosa, 1737 – 1 – $50.00 – us Presbyterian [400]

BREVISSIMA RUDIMENTA MUSICAE, PRO INCIPIENTIBUS. – Anonymous. 1608 – 9 – us Sibley [780]

BREVIS...TRACTATUS DE ESSENTIA...CURATIONE ET PRAECAUTIONE FAUCIUM ET GUTTURIS... / Perez de Herrera, C – Madrid, 1615 – 3mf – 9 – sp Cultura [610]

Brewer, David J *see*
- THE U.S. A CHRISTIAN NATION
- THE WORLD'S BEST ORATIONS

Brewer, E Cobham *see* A DICTIONARY OF MIRACLES

Brewer, J S *see*
- THE ATHANASIAN ORIGIN OF THE ATHANASIAN CREED
- THE ENDOWMENTS AND ESTABLISHMENT OF THE CHURCH OF ENGLAND
- GIRALDI CAMBRENSIS OPERA, VOLS 1-4 (RS21)
- MONUMENTA FRANCISCANA (RS4)
- REGISTRUM MALMESBURIENSE (RS72)
- THE REIGN OF HENRY 8 FROM HIS ACCESSION TO THE DEATH OF WOLSEY
- ROGERI BACON OPERA QUAEDAM HACTENUS INEDITA (RS15)

Brewer, Julia R *see* CORONARY HEART DISEASE RISK FACTORS IN CHILDREN AGES 9 TO 11 YEARS

Brewer, KD *see* THE EFFECTS OF INTERMITTENT COMPRESSION AND COLD ON EDEMA IN POSTACUTE ANKLE SPRAINS

Brewer, Mandane Williamson *see* DIARIES

Brewer, T M *see*
- A HISTORY OF THE NORTH AMERICAN BIRDS
- NORTH AMERICAN OOLOGY

Brewer, W *see* ALABAMA, HER HISTORY, RESOURCES, WAR RECORD AND PUBLIC MEN

BREWER'S GUARDIAN – (1975- 5,6,9) – 1871- – 1 – us UMI [660]

BREWERY WORKER : 1886-1973 / International Union of Brewery, Flour, Cereal, Soft Drink and Distillery Workers of America – (Coll title: Labor Union Periodicals, Pt 3) – 1996 – 18r – 1 – $2,430.00 – 1-55655-615-2 – us UPA [331]

BREWSTER 1745-1900 – (Mf 1-3: Births & Deaths 1745-1838. Mf Births & Deaths 1753-1892. Mf 8,17: Militia 1841-1864. Mf 9-10: Town Records 1803-08. Mf 10-11: Marriages, Intents 1802-26. Mf 12: Vital Records 1769-1829. Mf 11-17: Town & Vital 1803-31. Mf 18-20: Deeds 1829-45. Mf 18-21: Marriages, Intents 1829-46. Mf 21: Dogs Registered 1859-89. Mf 22-28: Town Records 1829-71. Mf 29-38: Town Records 1871-1918. Mf 39-40: School 1834-69. Mf 41-47: Payments 1809-65. Mf 48-49: Poor Records 1851-81. Mf 50-57: Mortgages 1846-1932. Mf 58-60: Valuation List 1890. Mf 61: Intentions Index 1847-1904. Mf 62-65: Intentions 1847-1916. Mf 66: Birth Index 1843-1916. Mf 67: Marriage Index 1843-1916. Mf 68: Death Index 1843-1916. Mf 69-70: Vital Records 1843-51. Mf 71-72: Births 1852-1900. Mf 73-74: Marriages 1852-1900. Mf 75-76: Deaths 1852-1900) – (mf ed 1994) – 76mf – 9 – 0-87623-190-3 – us Holbrook [920]

Brewster, Chauncey B *see* THE KINGDOM OF GOD AND AMERICAN LIFE

Brewster, David *see* THE MARTYRS OF SCIENCE. LIVES OF GALILEO, TYCHO BRAHE, AND KEPLER

Brewster, Frederick Carroll *see*
- A TREATISE ON PRACTICE IN THE COURTS OF COMMON PLEAS OF PENNSYLVANIA
- A TREATISE ON PRACTICE IN THE COURTS OF PENNSYLVANIA

Brewster, William Nesbitt *see* THE EVOLUTION OF NEW CHINA

Breyer, Ralf *see* BEITRAG ZUR GEOLOGIE DES "MASSIF DE CEZE", OESTLICHER TEIL, GARD (FRANKREICH)

Brez, J *see* LA FLORE DE INSECTOPHILES PRECEDEE D'UN DISCOURS SUR L'UTILITE DES INSECTES ET DE L'ETUDE DE L'INSECTOLOGIE

Brian Walton *see* BIBLIA SACRA POLYGLOTTA

BRIAND: STATESMAN OF PEACE / Franzius, Enno – Hoover Institution Press, 1976. Manuscript in Microfilm Series 2+6. 449 pp – 1 – $35.00r – us Hoover Inst Photo [920]

Briano-Iragorry, Mario *see* LECTURAS VENEZOLANAS

Brianskii, N G *see* MOSKOVSKIE PROIZVODITEL'NO-TRUDOVYE ARTELI

BRIARCLIFF QUARTERLY – Briarcliff Manor, New York etc v. 1-3 no. 12. Jan 1944-Jan 1947 – 1 – us NY Public [370]

BRIARPATCH – Regina. v1-22. 1972/73-1993/94 – 9 – Can$20.00y – cn Micromedia [360]

BRIC-A-BRAC – Montreal: H W Robinson, [1885?-18-?] – 9 – cn C.I.H.M. [971]

Bricaire de la Dixmarie, Nicolas *see*
- LA COMETE: CONTE EN L'AIR
- LA SIBYLE GAULOISE OU LA FRANCE TELLE QU'ELLE FUT, TELLE QU'ELLE EST, TELLE, A PEU PRES, QU'ELLE POURRA ETRE

Bricaire de la Dixmerie, N *see* ELOGE DE VOLTAIRE, PRONONCE DANS DANS LA L. MACONNIQUE DES NEUFS SOEURS

Briceno-Iregorry, Mario *see* DISCURSO DE RECEPCION...EN LA ACADEMIA DE LA HISTORIA

BRICES WEEKLY JOURNAL – Exeter, England.30 Apr 1725-9 Jun 1729. 1 reel – 1 – uk British Libr Newspaper [072]

Brichford, Maynard *see* GUIDE TO THE UNIVERSITY OF ILLINOIS ARCHIVES

Bricker, Garland A *see* SOLVING THE COUNTRY CHURCH PROBLEM

BRICKLAYER AND MASON – Indianapolis. v. 1-13. 1898-1910 – 1 – us NY Public [331]

BRICKLAYER, MASON AND PLASTERER – v1-14. 1898-1911 – 2r – 1 – us Ross [690]

BRIDAL GREETINGS : A MARRIAGE GIFT / Wise, Daniel – New York, NY: Carlton & Phillips, 1854 – 1r – 1 – us Western Res [390]

A BRIDE FROM THE DESERT / Allen, Grant – New York: R. F. Fenno, c1896. 05012. (Pre-1900 Canadiana) – 9 – cn C.I.H.M. [830]

Bridel, S E de *see*
- BRYOLOGIA UNIVERSA SEU SYSTEMATICA
- MUSCOLOGIA RECENTIORUM SEU ANALYSIS

THE BRIDE'S TRAGEDY / Beddoes, Thomas Lovell – London: Printed for F.C. and J. Rivington, 1822 – 1 roll – 1 – 1-55879-635-5 – uk Libr Preservation [830]

BRIDGE AND CULVERT REPORTS / Lucas County. Ohio. Engineer – 2r – 1 – $32.50r – us Archival [324]

THE BRIDGE AND THE ABYSS / Wolfe, Bertram D – The troubled friendship of Maxim Gorky and V. I. Lenin. 1967. 180p – 1 – 35.00r – us Hoover Inst Photo [920]

BRIDGE BULLETIN – Eugene, OR. -w. 2 Jan 1963-20 Mar 1963. 1 roll – 1 – us U.O. Library [071]

Bridge, Cyprian Arthur George *see*
- THE ART OF NAVAL WARFARE: INTRODUCTORY OBSERVATIONS
- SEA-POWER, AND OTHER STUDIES

BRIDGE OF HISTORY OVER THE GULF OF TIME / Cooper, Thomas – London: Hodder & Stoughton, 1874. 1 fiche – 9 – us A.T.L.A. [240]

BRIDGEBURG REVIEW – Ontario, CN. 1930-31 – 2r – 1 – cn Commonwealth Micro [072]

BRIDGEN'S SURROGATE'S REPORTS / New York. (State). Surrogate Court – 1v. 1825 (all publ) – 3mf – 9 – $4.50 – LLMC 80-019 – us L.L.M.C. [340]

BRIDGEPORT CHRONICLE-UNION – (Cont. see Mammoth Lakes) – Bridgeport, CA. 1890-1943; 1947-86 – 53r – 1 – $2,650.00 – C02077 – us Library Micro [071]

BRIDGEPORT HERALD – Bridgeport, NE. -w. Apr. 1925-Mar. 1928; Nov. 1928-May 1919 – 1 – us NE Hist [071]

BRIDGEPORT LAW REVIEW *see* QUINNIPAC LAW REVIEW

BRIDGEPORT NEWS-BLADE – Bridgeport, NE. -w. Jan. 1901- – 1 – us NE Hist [071]

Bridgers *see* HISTORY OF EDGECOMBE COUNTY

Bridges, Charles *see* AN EXPOSITION OF THE BOOK OF ECCLESIASTES

Bridges, James *see* A LETTER TO THE RIGHT HON. ROBERT POOL, ON THE COURTS OF LAW IN SCOTLAND

Bridges, Robert Seymour *see*
- EROS AND PSYCHE
- THE FEAST OF BACCHVS

BRIDGETSTOW / Pearse, Mark Guy – 1907 – 9 – us A.T.L.A. [240]

Bridgett, T E *see*
- BLUNDERS AND FORGERIES
- A HISTORY OF THE HOLY EUCHARIST IN GREAT BRITAIN

Bridgett, T F *see* THE TRUE STORY OF THE CATHOLIC HIERARCHY DEPOSED BY QUEEN ELIZABETH

BRIDGEWATER 1608-1849 – (Mf 1T-4T: Vital Records 1645-1810. Mf 3T-5T: Marriages 1704-86. Mf 5T-11T: Vital Records 1721-1846. Mf 8T-12T: Marriage Bans 1762-1820. Mf 13T-14T: Marriages 1775-1831. Mf 14T-19T: Vital Records 1608-1896. Mf 17T-20T: Marriage Banns 1820-50. Mf 18T: Out-of-Town Marriages 1702-99; Marriages 1830-33. Mf 20T: Marriages 1759-1843; Births 1843-49. Mf 21T: Marriages & Deaths 1843-49) – (mf ed 1992) – 21mf – 9 – 0-87623-216-0 – us Holbrook [920]

BRIDGEWATER 1641-1900 – (Mf 1-39: Town & Vitals 1641-1853. Mf 40-64: Town & Vitals 1645-1881. Mf 65-74: Town & Vitals: 1645-1881. Mf 75: Marriages 1788-1815. Mf 76-77: Births, Deaths 1639-1882. Mf 78-98: Purchasers 1645-1847. Mf 99-100: Proprietors 1725-1835. Mf 101-102: School Book 1826-55. Mf 103-109: Town Record 1789-1863. Mf 110: Town Record 1703-28. Mf 111-115: Accounts 1821-59. Mf 116-118: Taxpayers 1837-49. Mf 119-122: Valuations 1840-50. Mf 123-124: Militia 1840-67. Mf 125-126: Rebellion 1861-65. Mf 127: GAR Register 1890-1914. Mf 128-131: Paupers. Mf 132-141: Intentions 1835-1929. Mf 142: Marriages 1759-1843. Mf 143-147: Birth Index 1843-1956. Mf 148-151: Marriage Index 1843-1956. Mf 152-156: Deaths Index 1843-1956. Mf 157-159: Vital Records 1843-56. Mf 160-164: Deaths 1857-1904. Mf 165-168: Marriages 1857-1901. Mf 169-173: Births 1857-1902) – (mf ed 1992) – 173mf – 9 – 0-87623-160-1 – us Holbrook [920]

BRIDGEWATER BAPTIST CHURCH. VIRGINIA : CHURCH RECORDS – 1873-1919 – 1 – 12.78 – us Baptist [240]

Bridgewater, New Hampshire. Free Will Baptist Church *see* RECORDS

Bridgewater, Thomas *see* SEVEN YEARS MILITARY LIFE IN SOUTHERN INDIA

Bridgham, Percy Albert *see* ONE THOUSAND LEGAL QUESTIONS ANSWERED BY THE PEOPLE'S LAWYER OF THE BOSTON DAILY GLOBE

Bridgman, Raymond L *see* CONCORD LECTURES ON PHILOSOPHY

BRIDGNORTH BEACON – Bridgnorth, England. -w. 1 Oct 1852-23 Dec 1854. 23 ft – 1 – uk British Libr Newspaper [072]

BRIDGNORTH JOURNAL – England. 2 Nov 1854-10 Jul 1869; 22 Oct 1887-29 Sep 1900 (missing 1897).-w. 25 reels – 1 – uk British Libr Newspaper [072]

BRIDGNORTH WEEKLY NEWS – Bridgnorth, England. -w. 31 May-5 July 1856. 10 ft – 1 – uk British Libr Newspaper [072]

THE BRIDGTON RECORD – Bridgeton, ME: Libby & Smith, nov 3 1915-sep 6 1916 – 1r – 1 – us Res Libr [071]

BRIDGWATER AND SOMERSETSHIRE HERALD – (The Alfred London Weekly Journal). England. -w. Jan 1831-Dec 1833. (3 reels) – 1 – uk British Libr Newspaper [072]

Bridwell, Arthur *see* DIARIES

Brie, S *see*
– DER BUNDESSTAAT
– THEORIE DER STAATENVERBINDUNGEN

BRIEF – (Brief, The Week's News. Jul 1880-25 Jun 1881; Weeks News. 2 Jul 1881-25 Feb 1882. -w) – London, UK. 3 Nov 1877-25 Feb 1882. -w – 8r – 1 – uk British Libr Newspaper [072]

BRIEF / ed by Phi Delta Phi – v1-72. 1887-1978 – 5,6 – $325.00 set – us Hein [340]

BRIEF : MIDDLE EAST HIGHLIGHTS – Tel Aviv: Middle East Information Media 1971-1976. n1,3-4,8,13,15-20,22-117. jan 1-15, feb, apr 16-30, jul 1-15, aug-oct 1971, nov 16-20 1971-nov1/15 1975 – 1r – us Res Libr [956]

THE BRIEF : A LEGAL MISCELLANY – (Regular updates) – Phi Delta Phi. v1-72. 1887-1976/78 – 322mf – 9 – $483.00 – LLMC 84-429 – us L.L.M.C. [073]

THE BRIEF / Mississippi. State College. Agricultural Extension Service – v. 1. 1921-22 – 1,5,6 – us Spaulding [630]

THE BRIEF : THE SOLICITORS' MONTHLY REVIEW – London, UK. v1-3. 1894-95 (all publ) – 9mf – 9 – $13.50 – LLMC 84-428 – us L.L.M.C. [073]

BRIEF AAN DEN HOOGGELEERDEN HEER.. / Hofstede, Petrus – 1775 – 9 – us Sibley [780]

THE BRIEF (ABA) – v8-24. 1978-95 – 9 – $166.00 set – us Hein [340]

BRIEF ACCOUNT OF THE EDUCATIONAL SYSTEM WITH STATISTICAL SUMMARY 1972; 1976 / Hong Kong. Education Department – Hong Kong, 1972 – 2mf – 9 – DE-166/1 – ne IDC [370]

A BRIEF ACCOUNT OF THE FENIAN RAIDS ON THE MISSISQUOI FRONTIER: IN 1886 AND 1870 – Montreal: "Witness" Steam Printing House, 1871. 02836. (Pre-1900 Canadiana) – 9 – cn C.I.H.M. [971]

A BRIEF ACCOUNT OF THE LATE PERSECUTION AND BARBAROUS USAGE OF THE METHODISTS AT EXETER,... / Coade, George – Exon, 2nd ed 1745 – 1mf – 9 – MP-321/1 – ne IDC [240]

A BRIEF ACCOUNT OF THE OCCASION, PROCESS AND ISSUE OF A LATE TRIAL AT THE ASSIZE HELD AT GLOUCESTER, MARCH 3 1743,... / Whitefield, George – London, 1744 – 1mf – 9 – MP-313/1 – ne IDC [240]

A BRIEF ACCOUNT OF THE PROVINCE OF BRITISH COLUMBIA; ITS CLIMATE AND RESOURCES; AN APPENDIX TO THE BRITISH COLUMBIA DIRECTORY / Anderson, Alexander – 1882-83. Victoria, B.C.: R. T. Williams. 1883. 00099. (Pre-1900 Canadiana) – 9 – cn C.I.H.M. [971]

A BRIEF ACCOUNT OF THE RISE OF THE SOCIETY OF FRIENDS – Philadelphia: Friends' Book Store, 1878. 57p – 1 – us U.W. Library [240]

DER BRIEF AN DER HEBRAEER / Kurtz, Johann Heinrich – Mitau: Aug. Neumann, 1869. 1 fiche – 9 – us A.T.L.A. [220]

DER BRIEF AN DIE EPHESER / Kloepper, Albert – Goettingen: Vandenhoeck & Rup., 1891. 1 fiche – 9 – us A.T.L.A. [240]

DER BRIEF AN DIE GALATER / Sieffert, Friedrich – Goettingen: Vandenhoeck & Ruprecht, 1899. 1 fiche – 9 – us A.T.L.A. [240]

BRIEF AN DIE HEBRAEER = THE EPISTLE TO THE HEBREWS / Moll, Carl Bernhard – (In English) – New York: Charles Scribner, c1868 – 1mf – 9 – 0-8370-6763-4 – 1986-0763 – us A.T.L.A. [220]

DER BRIEF AN DIE HEBRAEER / Moll, Carl Bernhard – Bielefeld: Velhagen & Klasing, 1865. 1 fiche – 9 – us A.T.L.A. [240]

DER BRIEF AN DIOGNETOS : NEBST BEITRAEGEN ZUR GESCHICHTE DES LEBENS UND DER SCHRIFTEN DES GREGORIOS VON NEOCAESAREA / Draeseke, Johannes – Leipzig: J.A. Barth, 1881 – 1mf – us A.T.L.A. [240]

A BRIEF ANALYSIS OF SALE / Landreth, Lucius Scott – Philadelphia, Welsh, 1880. 65 p. LL-386 – 1 – us L of C Photodup [340]

A BRIEF AND IMPARTIAL ACCOUNT OF THE CHARACTER AND DOCTRINES OF MR. WHITEFIELD AND MR. WESLEY, IN A LETTER FROM LONDON, SEPTEMBER 1743 – Edinburgh, 1743 – 1mf – 9 – MP-308/1 – ne IDC [240]

BRIEF ANIMADVERSIONS ON SOME PASSAGES IN THE ELEVEN LETTERS TO THE REVEREND MR. JOHN WESLEY JUST PUBLISHED UNDER THE NAME OF THE LATE REVEREND MR. JAMES HERVEY – London, 1765 – 1mf – 9 – MP-432/1 – ne IDC [240]

BRIEF BIOGRAPHICAL SKETCH OF DR. THOMAS CURTIS FOUNDER FOR LIMESTONE COLLEGE / Curtis, Thomas – Ed. by Dr. Elmer Douglas Johnson. From a MS. of Dr. R. W. Sanders. 16p – 1 – $5.00 – us Baptist [920]

A BRIEF BIOGRAPHICAL SKETCH OF SIR JOHN WILLIAM DAWSON / Ami, Henry Marc – Minneapolis, American Geologist, 1900. 00796. (Pre-1900 Canadiana) – 9 – cn C.I.H.M. [910]

BRIEF BIOGRAPHICAL SKETCHES OF BIBLE CHRISTIAN MINISTERS AND LAYMEN / Michell, W J – Jersey. 2v. 1906 – 7mf – 9 – ne IDC [240]

BRIEF CASE *see* NLADA BRIEFCASE

BRIEF COMMENT ON "HOUSING IN LIBYA" / Libya. Ministry of Planning and Development. Doxiadis Associates – From Dr. Rawle Farley, Senior Economist, to Dr. Alo Attiga. Jul 30, both 1964. BNE-1104 1 – 9 – ne IDC [360]

A BRIEF COMPEND OF BIBLE TRUTH / Alexander, Archibald – Philadelphia: Presb. Bd. of Pub., 1846. 1 fiche – 9 – us A.T.L.A. [240]

BRIEF DES AMBASSADEURS VAN FRANCKRIJCK AEN DE HEEREN STATEN GENERAEL... – [The Hague], 1619 – 1mf – 1 – ILM-953/1 – ne IDC [327]

DER BRIEF DES APOSTELS PAULUS AN DIE PHILIPPER / Kloepper, Albert – Gotha: F.A. Perthes, 1893. 1 fiche – 9 – us A.T.L.A. [240]

DER BRIEF DES JACOBUS / Beyschlag, Willibald – Goettingen: Vandenhoeck & Rup., 1897 – 9 – us A.T.L.A. [220]

DER BRIEF DES JACOBUS: IN VIERZIG PREDIGTEN / Stockmeyer, Immanuel – Basel: Felix Schneider, 1874. 1 fiche – 9 – us A.T.L.A. [240]

DER BRIEF DES JAKOBUS / Lange, Johann Peter & Oosterzee, J J van – Bielefeld: Velhagen & Klasing, 1866. 1mf – 9 – us A.T.L.A. [240]

BRIEF DIRECTIONS FOR TRUE-SPELLING / Preston, Henry – 1574. 67p. (English Linguistics Series 1500-1800) – 9 – us UMI [420]

BRIEF DISCOURSE CONCERNING SINGING IN PUBLIC WORSHIP / Marlow, Isaac – London. 1690 – 1 – 5.00 – us Baptist [240]

BRIEF DOCUMENTARY HISTORY OF THE TRANSLATION OF THE SCRIPTURES INTO THE ARABIC LANGUAGE / Smith, Eli – 1900 – 1 – us A.T.L.A. [240]

BRIEF DRAWING / Ringwalt, Ralph Curtis – New York: Longmans, Green 1929. 214p. LL-1262 – 1 – us L of C Photodup [340]

A BRIEF ENGLISH TRACT OF LOGICK / Good, Thomas – 1677. 47p. (English Linguistics Series 1500-1800) – Apply; sp; 9 – us UMI [160]

A BRIEF EXPOSITION OF GOSPEL DIFFERENCES GIVEN ACCORDING TO THE DIVINE LAW OF PROGRESSIVE INSTRUCTION / Horton, Mary B – rev ed. New York: Mary B Horton, 1892, c1891 – 1mf – 9 – 0-8370-3664-X – 1985-1664 – us A.T.L.A. [220]

A BRIEF FOR THE TRIAL OF CRIMINAL CASES / Abbott, Austin – (2nd ed., Rochester, Lawyers Co-op. Pub. Co., 1902. 814p. LL-1270) – New York, Diossy, 1889. 566p. LL-1271 – 1 – us L of C Photodup [340]

A BRIEF GUIDE TO THE MUSEUM / Archeological Museum of Merida – Caceres: Edit. Extremadura, 1975 – 1 – sp Bibl Santa Ana [060]

A BRIEF GUIDE TO THE SONO BUDOJO MUSEUM / Jogjakarta. Indonesia. Museum Sono Budojo – Jogjakarta, 196?. 3p. BSEM-11091/1 – 9 – ne IDC [060]

BRIEF HISTORICAL SKETCH OF THE WESTERN BAPTIST THEOLOGICAL INSTITUTE, IN COVINGTON, KY.: A REPLY – 1850 – 1 – 5.00 – us Baptist [240]

BRIEF HISTORIES OF U.S. ARMY COMMANDS (ARMY POSTS) AND DESCRIPTIONS OF THEIR RECORDS / U.S. Army – T912 – 1r – 1 – us Nat'l Archives [355]

BRIEF HISTORY AND TENTH ANNIVERSARY SERVICES / Truett Memorial Baptist Church – 1962 – 1 – 5.00 – us Baptist [240]

A BRIEF HISTORY FROM OFFICIAL SOURCES OF THE LEGISLATION RESPECTING SEPARATE SCHOOLS SINCE THE YEAR 1863 IN THE UNITED PROVINCE OF CANADA, AND IN THE DOMINION SINCE CONFEDERATION – 18??. 02835. (Pre-1900 Canadiana) – 9 – cn C.I.H.M. [971]

A BRIEF HISTORY OF CONGREGATION OHEB SHALOM, BALTIMORE, MD / Rosenau, William – Baltimore: Guggenheimer, Weil, 1903. 1 fiche – 9 – us A.T.L.A. [270]

A BRIEF HISTORY OF GERMAN LITERATURE / Priest, George Madison – (Includes bibliographical references and index) – New York: C Scribner's Sons, 1928, c1909 – 1r – 1 – us U.W. Library [430]

A BRIEF HISTORY OF MISSIONARY ENTERPRISE IN ANTIENT AND MODERN TIMES : LECTURE MEMORANDA WORLD MISSIONARY CONFERENCE, EDINBURGH, 1910 – (Includes index) – London; New York: Burroughs, Wellcome, [1910?] – 1mf – 9 – 0-8370-7357-X – 1986-1357 – us A.T.L.A. [240]

A BRIEF HISTORY OF NYASALAND / Morris, Martin – London, New York; Longmans, Green 1952 – us Res Libr [960]

A BRIEF HISTORY OF THE BAPTIST CHURCH, HEBDEN BRIDGE, YORKSHIRE, ENGLAND / Williams, Charles – 1877 – 1 – 5.00 – us Baptist [240]

A BRIEF HISTORY OF THE BEGINNING OF THE MISSION WORK IN NICOMEDIA BY THE AMERICAN BOARD OF FOREIGN MISSIONS / Nergararian, Garabed – Waynesboro, Pa.: Gazette Steam Printing House, 1885 – 1mf – us A.T.L.A. [240]

A BRIEF HISTORY OF THE COURT OF CUSTOMS AND PATENT APPEALS / Rich, Giles S – (Publ by authorization of the Committee on the Bicentennial of Independence and the Constitution of the Judicial Conference of the United States), 1980) – Washington: GPO, 1981 (all publ) – 3mf – 9 – $4.50 – LLMC 95-015 – us L.L.M.C. [340]

A BRIEF HISTORY OF THE FIRST 25 YEARS' HISTORY OF THE YMCA'S IN CHINA (CCC237) = CHUNG HUA CHI TU CHIAO CH'ING NIEN HUI ER SHIH WU NIEN HSIAO SHIH / Lyon, D Willard – (In Chinese) – [s.l: s.n, 1920] – 1r – 1 – 1984-6576 – us A.T.L.A. [360]

A BRIEF HISTORY OF THE G-2 SECTION, GHQ, SWPA AND AFFILIATED UNITS / U.S. Army. Far East Command – 1948 – 1 – 16.00 – us L of C Photodup [950]

A BRIEF HISTORY OF THE LUTHERAN CHURCH IN AMERICA / Neve, J L – Burlington, Iowa: German Literary Board, 1904 – 1mf – us A.T.L.A. [240]

A BRIEF HISTORY OF THE MADISON SQUARE PRESBYTERIAN CHURCH AND ITS ACTIVTIES / Parkhurst, Charles H – New York: [s.n.], 1906 (Irving Press) – 1mf – us A.T.L.A. [240]

A BRIEF HISTORY OF THE MIDDLE TEMPLE / Bedwell, Cyril E A – London: Butterworth, 1909 – 2mf – 9 – $3.00 – LLMC 84-272 – us L.L.M.C. [323]

A BRIEF HISTORY OF THE PRINCIPLES OF METHODISM,... / Tucker, J – Oxford, 1742 – 1mf – 9 – MP-297/1 – ne IDC [240]

A BRIEF HISTORY OF THE REPUBLIC OF CHINA ARMED FORCES / U.S. Office of the Chief of Military History – 1971 – 1 – 18.00 – us L of C Photodup [950]

A BRIEF HISTORY OF THE TOWN OF MAYNARD, MASSACHUSETTS / Gitteridge, William H – Published by the town of Maynard, 1921. Massachusetts Reel 6. (The Cox Library Collection) – 5 – us Americana [978]

A BRIEF INTRODUCTION TO NEW TESTAMENT GREEK : WITH VOCABULARIES AND EXERCISES / Green, Samuel Gosnell – New York: Fleming H Revell; London: Religious Tract Society, [1894?] – 1mf – 9 – 0-8370-9237-X – 1986-3237 – us A.T.L.A. [450]

A BRIEF INTRODUCTION TO THE ART OF DESCANT OR COMPOSING MUSICK IN PARTS / Campian, Th – P 200. 1687 – 9 – ne IDC [780]

A BRIEF INTRODUCTION TO THE STUDY OF THEOLOGY / Foster, Robert Verrell – (Includes index) – Chicago: Fleming H Revell, c1899 – 1mf – 9 – 0-8370-3168-0 – 1985-1168 – us A.T.L.A. [240]

BRIEF INTRODUCTION TO THE STUDY OF THEOLOGY / Foster, Robert V – Chicago: Fleming H. Revell, 1899. 1 fiche – 9 – us A.T.L.A. [240]

BRIEF JUDAE = THE EPISTLE GENERAL OF JUDE / Fronmueller, G F C – (In English) – New York: Charles Scribner, c1867 – 1mf – 9 – 0-8370-6737-5 – 1986-0737 – us A.T.L.A. [220]

A BRIEF MEMOIRE OF THE LATE HONORABLE JAMES WILLIAM JOHNSTON, FIRST JUDGE IN EQUITY OF NOVA SCOTIA / Calnek, William Arthur – Saint John, N.B., G. Knodell, 1884. 00384. (Pre-1900 Canadiana) – 9 – cn C.I.H.M. [920]

A BRIEF NARRATIVE OF AN UNSUCCESSFUL ATTEMPT TO REACH REPULSE BAY / Lyon, G F – BN-300 2. 1825 – 8 – ne IDC [910]

BRIEF NOTES ON JAVANESE CUSTOMS AND MANNERS AND WEDDING CEREMONIES / Sidik Gondowarsito – SE 4894 1. 1965 – 9 – ne IDC [390]

BRIEF NOTES ON THE ISLAND OF ANTICOSTI: IN THE GULF OF ST LAWRENCE, DOMINION OF CANADA – London: G. Smythe, 1886. 02523. (Pre-1900 Canadiana) – 9 – cn C.I.H.M. [971]

A BRIEF OF THE AUTHORITIES UPON THE LAW OF IMPEACHABLE CRIMES AND MISDEMEANORS / Lawrence, William Beach – Washington, Govt. Print. Off., 1868. 27 p. LL-183 – 1 – us L of C Photodup [340]

A BRIEF ON THE MODES OF PROVING THE FACTS MOST FREQUENTLY IN ISSUE. / Abbott, Austin – 3rd ed. Rochester, N.Y., The Lawyers' Cooperative Publishing Co., 1912. 1007 p. LL-934 – 1 – us L of C Photodup [340]

A BRIEF OUTLINE ON THE ASPECTS OF THE JAVANESE WAYANG KULIT / Josodharmodjo, S B – SE-6293 1. 1967 – 9 – ne IDC [950]

DER BRIEF PAULI AN DIE GALATER / Dalmer, Johannes – Guetersloh: Bertelsmann, 1897. 1 fiche – 9 – us A.T.L.A. [240]

DER BRIEF PAULI AN DIE GALATER / Schmoller, Otto – 2. durch. Aufl. Bielefeld: Velhagen und Klasing, 1865 – 1mf – 9 – 0-8370-5996-8 – 1985-3996 – us A.T.L.A. [220]

A BRIEF POLITICAL AND ECONOMIC SURVEY / Royal Institute of International Affairs. London – Chatham House Memoranda. May 1961. Owen, R. BNE-502 1 – 9 – ne IDC [320]

BRIEF RECIT ET SUCCINCTE NARRATION DE LA NAVIGATION FAICTE ES YLES DE CANADA, HOCHELAGA, SAGUENAY ET AUTRES / Cartier, Jacques – Paris, France. 1v. 1545 – 1r – 1 – cn Can Microfilming [910]

BRIEF REPORT CONCERNING THE SITUATION OF THE MUNICIPALITY OF BANDUNG / Indonesia. Bandung – SE-10,385 1. 1955? – 9 – ne IDC [324]

BRIEF REPORT ON THE WORK BEING DONE UNDER THE MINISTRY OF SOCIAL AFFAIRS, THE BUREAU OF NATIONAL RECONSTRUCTION, THE MINISTRY OF EDUCATION, AND THE MINISTRY OF LABOUR / Smith, P Martin – SE 3600/1. 1951 – 9 – ne IDC [360]

A BRIEF REVIEW OF CRIMINAL CASES IN THE SUPREME COURT FOR THE PAST YEAR / Green, Frederick – Urbana: University of Illinois 1913. 24p. LL-543 – 1 – us L of C Photodup [340]

A BRIEF REVIEW OF FOREIGN ASSISTANCE IN INDONESIA'S ENGLISH LANGUAGE PROGRAM / Ford Foundation. Indonesia – By Daniel S. Lev. 1961.SE-3484-1 – 9 – ne IDC [420]

A BRIEF SKETCH OF THE LIFE OF THE REV. FATHER JOSEPH HENRY TABARET: OBLATE OF MARY IMMACULATE, DOCTOR OF DIVINITY, FOUNDER AND SUPERIOR OF THE COLLEGE OF OTTAWA: DIED IN OTTAWA, 28TH FEBRUARY, 1886, AGED 58 YEARS – Ottawa: MacLean, Roger, 1886.

00868. (Pre-1900 Canadiana) – 9 – cn C.I.H.M. [240]

A BRIEF SKETCH OF THE ZOROASTRIAN RELIGION AND CUSTOMS.. / Bharucha, Sheriarji Dadabhai – Introd. by Dr. Jivanji Jamshedji Modi. 3rd ed. rev. and enl. Bombay: D.B. Taraporevala Sons, 1928. 210p – 1 – us U.W. Library [290]

BRIEF SKETCH ON THE LIFE AND TIMES OF THE LATE HON. LOUIS JOSEPH PAPINEAU / Brown, Thomas Storrow – 1872? 00971. (Pre-1900 Canadiana) – 9 – cn C.I.H.M. [340]

A BRIEF STATE OF THE CONTESTS THAT HAVE LATELY ARISEN IN THE SALISBURY CONCERT – By a subscriber. 1781 – 9 – us Sibley [780]

A BRIEF STATEMENT OF MUNICIPAL TAX EXEMPTIONS IN TORONTO FROM 1869 TO 1890 / Hallam, John – Toronto: Imrie & Graham, 1890. 05341. (Pre-1900 Canadiana) – 9 – cn C.I.H.M. [971]

A BRIEF STUDY OF CHRISTIAN SCIENCE / Sandt, G W – Philadelphia, Pa.: General Council Publication House, 1911 – 1mf – us A.T.L.A. [240]

A BRIEF SUMMARY, IN PLAIN LANGUAGE, OF THE MOST IMPORTANT LAWS OF ENGLAND CONCERNING WOMEN / Bodichon, Barbara Leigh – 3rd ed. London, Trubner, 1869. 39p. LL-1700 – 1 – us L of C Photodup [340]

A BRIEF SURVEY ABOUT THE SYPHILIS PROBLEM IN JAVA / Indonesia. Venereal Disease Research Institute – By Mas Sutopo. SE-12,134 1. 1949 – 9 – ne IDC [610]

A BRIEF SURVEY OF EQUITY JURISDICTION. / Langdell, Christopher Columbus – Cambridge, Harvard, 1904. 259 p. LL-1087 – 1 – us L of C Photodup [340]

A BRIEF TEXT-BOOK OF MORAL PHILOSOPHY / Coppens, Charles – (Includes index) – New York: Schwartz, Kirwin & Fauss, c1895 – 1mf – 9 – 0-8370-6173-3 – 1986-0173 – us A.T.L.A. [170]

BRIEF, THE WEEK'S NEWS *see* BRIEF

BRIEF TRAICTE DE LA VICTOIRE QUE LE COMPTE CHARLES DE MASFELT, ...A L'ENCONTRE DU TURC, ... L'AN 1595 – Anvers, 1595 – 1mf – 9 – H-8212/1 – ne IDC [920]

A BRIEF TREATISE ON THE CANON AND INTERPRETATION OF THE HOLY SCRIPTURES / McClelland, Alexander – New York: Robert Carter, 1860. 1 fiche – 9 – us A.T.L.A. [240]

A BRIEF UNPUBLISHED HISTORY OF THE BAPTISTS OF SOUTH CAROLINA, 1683-1937 / Allen, W C – Ms. 565p – 1 – 19.77 – us Baptist [240]

BRIEF VINDICATIONS OF AN ESSAY TO PROVE SINGING OF PSALMS, ETC / Allen, Richard – London. 1696 – 1 – us Baptist [240]

BRIEFE / Herzl, T – 1860-1904. Von der Jugendzeit bis zum Tode. An original microfiche ed. Zug. 1977. BJ-72-101 1 – 9 – ne IDC [956]

BRIEFE / Rosenzweig, F – Berlin, 1935 – 13mf – 8 – ne Slangenburg [100]

DIE BRIEFE AN DIE EPHESER, PHILIPPER, KOLOSSER / Schenkel, Daniel – Bielefeld: Velhagen & Klasing, 1867. 1 fiche – 9 – us A.T.L.A. [240]

BRIEFE AN EINE CHRISTLICHE FREUNDIN UEBER DIE GRUNDWAHRHEITEN DES JUDENTHUMS : MIT EINEM BIOGRAPHISCHEN VORWORT / Izates, Esther – Leipzig: C L Morgenstern, 1883 – 1mf – 9 – 0-8370-2130-8 – 1985-0130 – us A.T.L.A. [920]

BRIEFE AN FRIEDRICH BARON DE LA MOTTE FOUQUE VON CHAMISSO, CHEZY, COLLIN... / Karl, Freiherr de; ed by La Motte-Fouque, Albertine Baronin de – Berlin: W Adolf, 1848 – 1r – 1 – us U.W. Library [920]

BRIEFE AN LUDWIG TIECK / ed by Holtei, Karl von – (Includes index) – Breslau: E Trewendt, 1864 – 1r – 1 – us U.W. Library [860]

BRIEFE AN SEINE BRAUT / Storm, Theodor; ed by Storm, Gertrud – Braunschweig: G Westermann, 1922 – 1r – 1 – us U.W. Library [920]

BRIEFE AN SEINE FRAU / Storm, Theodor; ed by Storm, Gertrud – Berlin: G Westermann, 1915 – 1r – 1 – us U.W. Library [920]

BRIEFE AN SEINE FREUNDE HARTMUTH BRINKMANN UND WILHELM PETERSEN / Storm, Theodor; ed by Storm, Gertrud – Berlin: G Westermann, 1917 – 1r – 1 – us U.W. Library [920]

BRIEFE AN SEINE KINDER / Storm, Theodor; ed by Storm, Gertrud – Berlin: G Westermann, c1916 – 1 – us U.W. Library [920]

BRIEFE AN UND VON JOHANN HEINRICH MERCK : EINE SELBSTAENDIGE FOLGE DER IM JAHR 1835 ERSCHIENENEN BRIEFE AN J.H. MERCK / Merck, Johann Heinrich; ed by Wagner, Karl – Darmstadt: J P Diehl, 1838 – 1 – us U.W. Library [920]

A BRIEFE AND A PLAYNE INTRODUCTION, TEACHYNG HOW TO PRONOUNCE THE LETTERS IN THE BRITISH TONGUE (NOW COMMENLY CALLED WALSH) / Salesbury, William – 1550. 45p. (English Linguistics Series 1500-1800) – 9 – us UMI [490]

BRIEFE, DEPESCHEN, UND BERICHTE UEBER LUTHER VOM WORMSER REICHSTAGE 1521 / ed by Kalkoff, Paul – Halle: Verein fuer Reformationsgeschichte, 1898. (Schriften des Vereins fuer Reformationsgeschichte; 15. Jahrg., Schrift 59) – 1mf – us A.T.L.A. [240]

BRIEFE DER KAISERIN MARIA THERESIA AN IHRE KINDER UND FREUNDE / ed by Arneth, A von – Wien. 4v. 1881 – 24mf – 9 – ne IDC [943]

DIE BRIEFE DES APOSTELS PAULUS UND DIE REDEN DES HERRN JESU : EIN BLICK IN DEN ORGANISCHEN ZUSAMMENHANG DER NEUTESTAMENTLICHEN SCHRIFTEN / Roos, Friedrich – Ludwigsburg: Ad Neubert, 1887 – 1mf – 9 – 0-8370-4963-6 – 1985-2963 – us A.T.L.A. [220]

DIE BRIEFE DES BISCHOFS RATHER VON VERONA (MGH EPISTOLAE 2: 1.BD) – 1949 – Dfl22.00 – ne Slangenburg [240]

BRIEFE DES DREISTOECKIGEN HAUSBESITZERS MISTER SCHORSCH DOBBELJUH HUTZELBERGER AN DIE "MISSISSIPPI BLAETTER" : "O TEMPORA, O MORES!": GEDICHTE / Thiersch, Curt – St. Louis: Im Selbstverlag des Verfassers, 1899 – 1r – 1 – us U.W. Library [810]

BRIEFE DES GRAFEN MERCY-ARGENTEAU... : GRAFEN LOUIS STARHEMBERG (VOM 1791-1794) / Thuerheim, A – Innsbruck, 1884 – 4mf – 9 – ne IDC [943]

DIE BRIEFE DES HL. BONIFATIUS UND LULLUS (MGH EPISTOLAE 4: 1.BD) – 1916 – Dfl28.00 – ne Slangenburg [240]

DIE BRIEFE DES LIBANIUS (T.U.U. 2-30/1.2) / Seeck, Otto – Leipzig, 1906 – 8mf – 9 – ne Slangenburg [240]

DIE BRIEFE DES SEXTUS JULIUS AFRICANUS AN ARISTIDES UDN ORIGENES (T.U.U. 3-34/3) / Reichardt, W – Leipzig, 1909 – 2mf – 9 – ne Slangenburg [240]

BRIEFE DEUTSCHER PHILOSOPHEN (1750-1850) / ed by Henrichs, Norbert & Weeland, Horst – 1990 – 3141mf (1:24) – 9 – diazo DM12,000.00 (silver DM15,000.00 ISBN 3-598-33020-0) – 3-598-33010-3 – gw Saur [190]

BRIEFE DIE NEUESTE LITTERATUR BETREFFEND / ed by Lessing, Gotthold Ephraim et al – Berlin, 1759-65. Hildesheim, 1977 – 71mf – 9 – DM590.00 diazo DM690.00 silver – gw Olms [430]

BRIEFE EINES AUFMERKSAMEN REISENDEN DIE MUSIK BETREFFEND / Reichardt, Johann F – 1774-76.2v – 9 – us Sibley [780]

BRIEFE EINES AUFMERKSAMEN REISENDEN DIE MUSIK BETREFFEND / Reichardt, Johann F – 2v. Frankfurt Leipzig. 1774. Frankfurt Breslau. 1776. BP-749 1 – 9 – ne IDC [910]

BRIEFE FRIEDRICH LEOPOLDS GRAFEN ZU STOLBERG UND DER SEINIGEN AN JOHANN HEINRICH VOSS : NACH DEN ORIGINALEN DER MUENCHENER HOF- UND STAATSBIBLIOTHEK / ed by Hellinghaus, Otto – (Includes bibliographical references) – Muenster: Aschendorff, 1891 – 1 – us U.W. Library [430]

DIE BRIEFE HEINRICHS 4 (MGH DEUTSCHES..: 1.BD) – 1937 – Dfl9.00 – ne Slangenburg [240]

BRIEFE NACH DEM WESTWALL : ROMAN / Woerner, Hans – Berlin: Keil, c1939 – 1r – 1 – us U.W. Library [830]

DIE BRIEFE PETRI UND DER BRIEF JUDAE : THEOLOGISCH-HOMILETISCH BEARBEITET / Fronmueller, G F C – 2. verb. Aufl. Bielefeld: Velhagen und Klasing, 1862 – 1mf – 9 – 0-8370-3210-5 – 1985-1210 – us A.T.L.A. [220]

BRIEFE POLITISCHEN INHALTS VON UND AN FRIEDRICH VON GENTZ AUS DEN JAHREN 1799-1827 / ed by Klinkowstroem, C von – Wien, 1870 – 3mf – 9 – ne IDC [943]

BRIEFE UEBER DIE CHRISTLICHE RELIGION / Mueller, F A – Stuttgart: J.C. Koetzle, 1870. 1 fiche – 9 – us A.T.L.A. [240]

BRIEFE UEBER DIE MORALITAET DER LEIDEN DES JUNGEN WERTHERS : EINE VERLOREN GEGLAUBTE SCHRIFT DER STURM- UND DRANGPERIODE / Lenz, Jakob Michael Reinhold; ed by Schmitz-Kallenberg, L – (Includes bibliographical references) – Muenster i.W.: F Coppenrath, 1918 – 1r – 1 – us U.W. Library [430]

BRIEFE UEBER MERKWUERDIGKEITEN DER LITTERATUR / ed by Gerstenberg, Heinrich Wilhelm von et al – Schleswig/Leipzig, 1766/67 und Hamburg/Bremen, 1770. Hildesheim, 1977 – 8mf – 9 – DM80.00 diazo DM100.00 silver – gw Olms [410]

BRIEFE UND ACTEN ZUR GESCHICHTE DES DREISSIG-JAEHRIGEN KRIEGES IN DEN ZEITEN DES VORWALTENDEN EINFLUSSES DER WITTELSBACHER – (Missing: v2 p289-304) – Muenchen, v1-11. 1870-1909 – 108mf – 1 – HQC-5/1 mf1-8; 23-43; 98-176 – ne IDC [327]

BRIEFE UND ACTEN ZUR GESCHICHTE DES DREISSIGJAEHRIGEN KRIEGES IN DEN ZEITEN DES VORWALTENDEN EINFLUSSES DER WITTELSBACHER – (Missing: v2-2) – Muenchen. v1-11. 1870-1909 – 108mf – 9 – ne IDC [943]

BRIEFE UND AKTEN ZUR GESCHICHTE DES SECHZEHNTEN JAHRHUNDERTS MIT BESONDERER RUECKSICHT AUF BAYERNS FUERSTENHAUS – Muenchen, Leipzig. 6v. 1873-1913 – 53mf – 1 – HQ-6/1 – ne IDC [327]

BRIEFE UND AKTEN ZUR GESCHICHTE DES SECHZEHNTEN JAHRHUNDERTS MIT BESONDERER RUECKSICHT AUF BAYERNS FUERSTENHAUS – Muenchen, Leipzig. 6v. 1873-1913 – 53mf – 9 – ne IDC [943]

BRIEFE UND ERKLAERUNG VON J. VON DOELLINGER UEBER DIE VATICANISCHEN DECRETE, 1869-87 = DECLARATIONS AND LETTERS ON THE VATICAN DECREES, 1869-87 / Doellinger, Johann Joseph Ignaz von – New York: Charles Scribner, 1891 – 1mf – 9 – 0-8370-8502-0 – 1986-2502 – us A.T.L.A. [240]

BRIEFE UND ERKLAERUNGEN VON J. VON DOELLINGER UEBER DIE VATICANISCHEN DECRETE, 1869-87 / Doellinger, Johann Joseph Ignaz von; ed by Reusch, Franz Heinrich – (In German, French, English) – Muenchen: C H Beck, 1890 – 1mf – 9 – 0-8370-8419-9 – 1986-2419 – us A.T.L.A. [240]

BRIEFE UND GESPRAECHE VERANLASST DURCH DIE ENTFUEHRUNG UND GEFANGENSCHAFTSREISE DES HEILIGEN VATERS PIUS DES SIEBENTEN, VON ROM NACH SAWONNA IM JULI UND AUGUST 1809, GESAMMELT UND ZUR BELEHRUNG UND ERBAUUNG SEINER MITCHRISTEN / ed by Dewora, Viktor Joseph – Hadamar, Koblenz, 1816 – 2mf – 9 – DM62.00 – 3-89349-360-3 – gw Hänsel [240]

BRIEFE UND SCHRIFTEN / Niebuhr, Barthold Georg – Berlin, (1918) – 9 – DM48.00 – 3-89349-262-3 – gw Hänsel [800]

BRIEFE UND VERTRAUTE BLAETTER VON FRIEDRICH VON GENTZ / ed by Schlesier, G – Mannheim, 1838-1840 – 24mf – 9 – ne IDC [943]

BRIEFE VON ALEXANDER VON HUMBOLDT AN VARNHAGEN VON ENSE AUS DEN JAHREN 1827 BIS 1858 : NEBST AUSZUEGEN AUS VARNHAGEN'S TAGEUECHERN, UND BRIEFEN VON VARNHAGEN UND ANDERN AN HUMBOLDT / Humboldt, Alexander von – (Includes bibliographical references) – 3. Aufl. Leipzig: F A Brockhaus, 1860 – 1 – us U.W. Library [920]

BRIEFE VON ANDREAS MASIUS UND SEINEN FREUNDE 1538-1573 (PGRG 2) / ed by Lossen, Max – Leipzig, 1886 – Dfl35.00 – ne Slangenburg [920]

BRIEFE VON FRIEDRICH VON GENTZ AN BILAT / ed by Mendelssohn-Bartholody, K – Leipzig. 2v. 1868 – 11mf – 9 – ne IDC [943]

BRIEFE VON HEINRICH HEINE AN HEINRICH LAUBE / ed by Wolff, Eugen – Breslau: S Schottlaender; New York: G E Stechert, 1893 – 1r – 1 – us U.W. Library [920]

BRIEFE VON JOHANN HEINRICH VOSS : NEBST ERLAEUTERNDEN BEILAGEN / Voss, Johann Heinrich; ed by Voss, Abraham – Halberstadt: C Brueggemann. 3v. 1829-33 – 1 – us U.W. Library [860]

BRIEFE VON JOHANN PETER UZ AN EINEN FREUND : AUS DEN JAHREN 1753-82 / Uz, Johann Peter; ed by Henneberger, August – Leipzig: F A Brockhaus, 1866 – 1r – 1 – us U.W. Library [920]

BRIEFE VON LUDWIG ANZENGRUBER : MIT NEUEN BEITRAEGEN ZU SEINER BIOGRAPHIE / Anzengruber, Ludwig – Stuttgart: Cotta, 1902 – 1r – 1 – us U.W. Library [430]

BRIEFE VON STAEGEMANN, METTERNICH, HEINE UND BETTINA VON ARNIM : NEBST BRIEFEN, ANMERKUNGEN UND NOTIZEN VON VARNHAGEN VON ENSE – Leipzig: F A Brockhaus, 1865 – 1r – 1 – us U.W. Library [943]

BRIEFE VON UND AN FRIEDRICH VON GENTZ / ed by Wittichen, F C & Salzer, E – (Missing: v1) – Muenchen, Berlin. 3v. 1909-1913 – 17mf – 9 – ne IDC [943]

BRIEFE VON UND AN GOTTFRIED AUGUST BUERGER : EIN BEITRAG ZUR LITERATURGESCHICHTE SEINER ZEIT / AUS DEM NACHLASSE BUERGER'S UND ANDEREN, MEIST HANDSCHRIFTLICHEN QUELLEN / ed by Strodtmann, Adolf – (Includes bibliographical references and index) – Berlin: Gebrueder Paetel. 4v. 1874 – 1 – us U.W. Library [860]

BRIEFE VON WILHELM VON HUMBOLDT AN FRIEDRICH HEINRICH JACOBI / ed by Leitzmann, Albert – Halle a.d.S.: M Niemeyer, 1892 – 1r – 1 – us U.W. Library [920]

BRIEFE ZUR ERINNERUNG AN MERKWUERDIGE ZEITEN, UND RUEHMLICHE PERSONEN, AUS DEM WICHTIGEN ZEITLAUFE VON 1740, BIS 1778 / Borchmann, Johann Friedrich – Berlin: Gedruckt mit Spenerschen Schriften, 1778 – 1 – us Sibley [780]

BRIEFING ON INDONESIA. 'PREPARED FOR VISIT OF CONGRESSIONAL DELEGATIONS TO INDONESIA IN 1959' / U.S. Embassy. Indonesia – SE 4776/1 – 9 – ne IDC [950]

BRIEFLET – Portland OR. Nov 19 1904, Jan 14 Apr 1 May 6 1905 – 1 – us U.O. Library [071]

BRIEFLETS / Vermont. Agricultural Extension Service – v. 1-1172. 1914-70 – Inc – 1,5,6 – us Spaulding [630]

DER BRIEFLICHE UND TELEGRAPHISCHE VERTRAG... / Achenbach, E – Leipzig, 1934 – 2mf – 9 – ILM-3027/1 – ne IDC [340]

BRIEF-MAKING / Thompson, William Goodrich – Boston, Ellis Co., 1914. 25 p. LL-1103 – 1 – us L of C Photodup [340]

BRIEFS AND TRANSCRIPTS / Canada. Mackenzie Valley Pipeline Inquiry – 1975-76 – 5 – cn Micromedia [971]

BRIEFS AND TRANSCRIPTS / Canada. Royal Commission on Dominion-Provincial Relations – 1937 – 1 – cn Micromedia [971]

BRIEFS AND TRANSCRIPTS / Canada. Royal Commission on Energy – 1957 – 1 – cn Micromedia [621]

BRIEFS AND TRANSCRIPTS / Canada. Royal Commission on Taxation – 1962 – 1 – cn Micromedia [336]

BRIEFS AND TRANSCRIPTS / Canada. Royal Commission on the Economic Union and Development Prospects for Canada – 1983-84 – 5 – cn Micromedia [330]

BRIEFS AND TRANSCRIPTS OF PUBLIC HEARINGS / Canada. Royal Commission on Bilingualism and Biculturalism – 1963 – 1 – cn Micromedia [360]

BRIEFS AND TRANSCRIPTS OF PUBLIC HEARINGS / Canada. Royal Commission on Broadcasting – 1955 – 1 – cn Micromedia [380]

BRIEFS AND TRANSCRIPTS OF PUBLIC HEARINGS / Canada. Royal Commission on National Development in the Arts, Letters, and Sciences – 1949 – 1 – cn Micromedia [324]

BRIEFS AND TRANSCRIPTS OF PUBLIC HEARINGS / Canada. Royal Commission on the Status of Women – 1967 – 1 – cn Micromedia [305]
BRIEFS AND TRANSCRIPTS OF PUBLIC HEARINGS / Ontario. Commission on Metropolitan Toronto – 5 – cn Micromedia [324]
BRIEFS AND TRANSCRIPTS OF PUBLIC HEARINGS. 1969 / Canada. Commission of Inquiry into the non-medical use of drugs – 1 – cn Micromedia [324]
BRIEFS AND TRANSCRIPTS OF PUBLIC HEARINGS 1970 / Canada. Parliament. Senate. Special Committee on the Mass Media – 1 – cn Micromedia [025]
Briefs, Henry W *see* NATO IN QUEST OF COHESION
BRIEFS ON THE LAW OF INSURANCE / Cooley, Roger William – St. Paul, West, 1905-19. 7 v. LL-1440 – 1 – us L of C Photodup [340]
BRIEFS, PROPOSED FINDINGS AND EXHIBIT DIGESTS / U.S. Indian Claims Commission – (Suppl. $1,335.00) – 3000v. 1,536 fiches. With printed index – 9 – $5,005.00 – us UPA [305]
DIE BRIEFSAMMLUNG GERBERTS VON REIMS (MGH EPISTOLAE 2: 2.BD) – 1966 – Dfl30.00 – ne Slangenburg [240]
BRIEFSAMMLUNGEN DER ZEIT HEINRICHS 4 (MGH EPISTOLAE 2: 5.BD) – 1950 – Dfl32.00 – ne Slangenburg [240]
BRIEFUE DESCRIPTIO DE LA COVRT DV GRANT TVRC ET VNG SOMMAIRE DU REGNE DES OTHMANS AUEC VN ABREGE DE LEURS FOLLES SUPERSTITIONS / Geuffroy, A – Paris, 1546 – 2mf – 9 – H-8276/1 – ne IDC [956]
BRIEFVE INSTITUTION DE LA LANGUE FRANCOISE, EXPLIQUEE EN ALEMAN / Vivier, G du – 1568 – 9 – fr I.C.S. [440]
BRIEFWECHSEL DECEMBER 1522 BIS FRUELING 1523 / Adrianus 6 & Erasmus, Desiderius – Frankfurt a.M., 1849. BH.P-28 – 9 – ne IDC [190]
BRIEFWECHSEL DES GROSSHERZOGS CARL AUGUST VON SACHSEN-WEIMAR-EISENACH MIT GOETHE IN DEN JAHREN VON 1775 BIS 1828 – Weimar: Landes-Industrie-Comptoir, 1863 – 1r – 1 – us U.W. Library [920]
DER BRIEFWECHSEL HOFMANNSTHAL – WILDGANS / ed by Bradish, Joseph Arno von – (Includes bibliographical references) – Ergaenzter u. verb. Neudruck. Zuerich: Franklin Press, 1935 – 1r – 1 – us U.W. Library [920]
BRIEFWECHSEL ZWISCHEN GOETHE UND K. GOETTLING IN DEN JAHREN 1824-1831 / ed by Fischer, Kuno – Muenchen: F Bassermann, 1880 – 1r – 1 – us U.W. Library [920]
BRIEFWECHSEL ZWISCHEN GOETHE UND STAATSRATH SCHULTZ / ed by Duentzer, Heinrich – (Includes bibliographical references) – Leipzig: Dyk, 1853 – 1r – 1 – us U.W. Library [920]
BRIEFWECHSEL ZWISCHEN H. L. MARTENSEN UND J. A. DORNER, 1839-1881.. / Martensen, Hans Lassen – 2v. 1888 – 1 – us A.T.L.A. [240]
BRIEFWECHSEL ZWISCHEN JOSEPH FREIHERRN VON LASSBERG UND LUDWIG UHLAND / ed by Pfeiffer, Franz – Wien: W Braumueller, 1870 – 1r – 1 – us U.W. Library [943]
BRIEFWECHSEL ZWISCHEN JOSEPH VICTOR VON SCHEFFEL UND PAUL HEYSE / Scheffel, Joseph Viktor von; ed by Hoeser, Conrad – Karlsruhe: [s.n.] 1932 – 1r – 1 – us U.W. Library [920]
BRIEFWECHSEL ZWISCHEN SCHILLER UND GOETHE – (Includes index) – 4. Aufl. Stuttgart: J G Cotta, 1881 – 1r – 1 – us U.W. Library [920]
DER BRIEFWECHSEL ZWISCHEN THEODOR STORM UND GOTTFRIED KELLER / Storm, Theodor; ed by Koester, Albert – (Includes index) – 4. voellig umgearb. und vervollstaendigte Aufl. Berlin: Gebrueder Paetel, 1924 – 1r – 1 – us U.W. Library [920]
BRIEFWECHSEL ZWISCHEN VARNHAGEN UND RAHEL / Varnhagen von Ense, Karl August – Leipzig: F A Brockhaus, 1874-1875 – 1r – 1 – us U.W. Library [943]
BRIEF-WRITING AND ADVOCACY / Walter, Carroll Gibson – New York, Baker, Voorhis, 1931. 248 p. LL-1258 – 1 – us L of C Photodup [340]
Brieger, Auguste *see* KAIN UND ABEL IN DER DEUTSCHEN DICHTUNG
Brieger, Theodor *see* ZWEI BISHER UNBEKANNTE ENTWUERFE DES WORMSER EDIKTES GEGEN LUTHER
BRIER CREEK BAPTIST CHURCH. WILKES COUNTY. NORTH CAROLINA : CHURCH RECORDS – 1783-1955 – 1 – 23.94 – us Baptist [240]
BRIERLEY HILL ADVERTISER – (The Advertiser). England. -w. 1856-1907. (45 reels) – 1 – uk British Libr Newspaper [072]
Brierley, Jonathan *see*
– ASPECTS OF THE SPIRITUAL
– OURSELVES AND THE UNIVERSE: STUDIES IN LIFE AND RELIGION
– RELIGION AND EXPERIENCE
– ROME FROM THE INSIDE, OR, THE PRIESTS' REVOLT
Brierre de Boismont, Alexandre Jacques Francois *see*
– DES HALLUCINATIONS OU HISTOIRE RAISONNEE DES APPARITIONS, DES VISIONS, DES SONGES, DE L'EXTASE, DU MAGNETISME ET DU SOMNAMBULISME
– DU SUICIDE ET DE LA FOLIE SUICIDE CONSIDERES DANS LEURS RAPPORTS AVEC LA STATISTIQUE, LA MEDECINE ET LA PHILOSOPHIE
BRIESENER ZEITUNG *see*
– ALLGEMEINE NACHRICHTEN FUER POMMERELLEN
Brieux, Eugene *see* LA FEMME SEULE
Brieva, Matias *see*
– COLECCION DE LEYES...CIRCULARES...DE LA MESTA DESDE EL ANO 1729 AL DE 1827
– COLECCION DE LEYES...RAMO DE LA MESTA
BRIEVE HISTOIRE DE LA GVERRE DE PERSE, FAITE L'AN MIL CINQ CENS SEPTANTE HUIT / Porsius, H – [Geneva], 1583 – 1mf – 9 – H-8203/1 – ne IDC [956]
BRIEVEN UIT ONDERSCHEIDENE KERKELIJKE ARCHIEVEN (DE WERKEN..3,2) / ed by Janssen, H Q & Toorenbergen, J J van – Utrecht, 1878 – Dfl25.00 – ne Slangenburg [240]
BRIEVEN UIT ONDERSCHEIDENE KERKELIJKE ARCHIEVEN (DE WERKEN..3,4) / ed by Janssen, H Q & Toorenbergen, J J van – Utrecht, 1880 – Dfl22.00 – ne Slangenburg [240]
BRIEVEN UIT ONDERSCHEIDENE KERKELIJKE ARCHIEVEN (DE WERKEN..3,5) / ed by Toorenbergen, J J van – Utrecht, 1885 – Dfl28.00 – ne Slangenburg [240]
Brifaut, Charles *see* NINUS 2
BRIGADE MAUT / Wahjudi – (Short stories). SE 5690 1 – 9 – ne IDC [830]
Brigader, Anna *see* KVELOSA LOKA: ROMANS
LE BRIGAND / Hoffman & Kreutzer – French Theatre Series. Paris. Huet, an III. 1795 – 9 – fr Hachette [820]
LE BRIGANDAGE DE LA MUSIQUE ITALIENNE / Goudar, A – 1780 – 9 – us Sibley [780]
Brigentius, A *see* VILLA BURGHESIA VULGO PINCIANA POETICE DESCRIPTA AB A. B. PATAVINO
Briggs, Charles Augustus *see*
– AMERICAN PRESBYTERIANISM : ITS ORIGIN AND EARLY HISTORY
– THE AUTHORITY OF HOLY SCRIPTURES: AN INAUGURAL ADDRESS
– THE BIBLE, THE CHURCH, AND THE REASON
– BIBLICAL STUDY: ITS PRINCIPLES, METHODS, AND HISTORY
– CASE AGAINST PROFESSOR BRIGGS
– ETHICAL TEACHINGS OF JESUS
– THE FUNDAMENTAL CHRISTIAN FAITH
– GENERAL INTRODUCTION TO THE STUDY OF HOLY SCRIPTURE
– HISTORY OF THE STUDY OF THEOLOGY
– INCARNATION OF THE LORD: A SERIES OF SERMONS
– INSPIRATION AND INERRANCY
– MESSIAH OF THE APOSTLES
– MESSIAH OF THE GOSPELS
– MESSIANIC PROPHECY...A CRITICAL STUDY
– NEW LIGHT ON THE LIFE OF CHRIST
– ORIGIN AND HISTORY OF PREMILLENARIANISM
– PAPAL COMMISSION AND THE PENTATEUCH
– WHITHER? A THEOLOGICAL QUESTION FOR THE TIMES
Briggs, Emilie Grace *see* HISTORY OF THE STUDY OF THEOLOGY
Briggs, Horace *see* LETTERS FROM ALASKA AND THE PACIFIC COAST
Briggs, W *see* OPHTHALMO-GRAPHIA
Brigham, Johnson *see*
– DES MOINES TOGETHER WITH THE HISTORY OF POLK COUNTY
– IOWA: ITS HISTORY AND ITS FOREMOST CITIZENS
Brigham, Thomas M *see* THE L.S.D., INDONESIA'S VOLUNTARY VILLAGE LEVEL SELF-HELP PROGRAM
BRIGHAM YOUNG UNIVERSITY EDUCATION AND LAW JOURNAL – v1-4. 1992-95 – 9 – $28.00 set – us Hein [073]
BRIGHAM YOUNG UNIVERSITY LAW REVIEW – (v4- . 1978- . 5,6,9) – v. 1-. 1975- – 1 – us UMI [340]
BRIGHOUSE AND RASTRICK GAZETTE – (Brighouse Gazette etc. 1896-) – England. 28 Mar 1874-28 Jan 1899. -w – 21r – 1 – uk British Libr Newspaper [072]
BRIGHOUSE GAZETTE ETC *see* BRIGHOUSE AND RASTRICK GAZETTE
BRIGHOUSE NEWS – England.2 Jul 1870-1908; 1910-11. -w.22 1/2 reels – 1 – uk British Libr Newspaper [072]
Bright, Charles *see* SUBMARINE TELEGRAPHS: THEIR HISTORY, CONSTRUCTION AND WORKING: FOUND IN PART ON WUENSCHENDORFF'S "TRAITE DE TELEGRAPHIE SOUS-MARINE".
Bright, John *see* WOMEN'S DISABILITIES REMOVAL BILL
Bright, R *see* REPORTS ON MEDICAL CASES
Bright, T *see* HYGIEINA
Bright, William *see*
– THE AGE OF THE FATHERS
– ANCIENT COLLECTS AND OTHER PRAYERS
– THE CANONS OF THE FIRST FOUR GENERAL COUNCILS OF NICAEA, CONSTANTINOPLE, EPHESUS AND CHALCEDON
– CHAPTERS OF EARLY ENGLISH CHURCH HISTORY
– A HISTORY OF THE CHURCH
– LESSONS FROM THE LIVES OF THREE GREAT FATHERS
– THE ROMAN SEE IN THE EARLY CHURCH
– SELECT ANTI-PELAGIAN TREATISES OF ST AUGUSTINE
– SELECTED LETTERS OF WILLIAM BRIGHT
– SOME ASPECTS OF PRIMITIVE CHURCH LIFE
– WAYMARKS IN CHURCH HISTORY
BRIGHT/HUNTINGTON COLLECTION – (Letters and papers of American Revolutionary leaders up to late 1800s) – 1r – 1 – $75.00 – us UMI [976]
Brightland, John *see* A GRAMMAR OF THE ENGLISH TONGUE
Brightly, Frederick C *see* BRIGHTLY'S LEADING CASES ON THE LAW OF ELECTIONS
BRIGHTLY'S LEADING CASES ON THE LAW OF ELECTIONS / Brightly, Frederick C – Philadelphia: Kay & Brother, 1871 (all publ) – 9mf – 9 – $13.50 – LLMC 95-049 – us L.L.M.C. [340]
BRIGHTLY'S REPORTS / Pennsylvania. Nisi Prius. Supreme Court – (A Pre-NRS title) – 1v. 1809-1851 (all publ) – 6mf – 9 – $9.00 – LLMC 95-053 – us L.L.M.C. [340]
Brightman, FE *see*
– LITURGIES, EASTERN AND WESTERN
– LITURGIES EASTERN AND WESTERN
BRIGHTON 1771-1873 – (Mf 1: Marriages, Intents,...1771-1817. Mf 2-7: B,M,D 1771-1873. Mf 8-10: Index to B,M,D 1771-1873. Mf 11-20: B,M,D 1771-1874. Mf 21: Births & Deaths 1817-45. Mf 22-24: Marriages & Intentions 1817-58. Mf 25-26: B,M,D 1843-55. Mf 27-28: Births 1855-73. Mf 29-30: Marriage Intentions 1858-73. Mf 31: Marriages 1855-73. Mf 32-33: Deaths 1854-73) – (mf ed 1985) – 33mf – 9 – 0-931248-86-8 – us Holbrook [920]
BRIGHTON ENSIGN – Brighton, 1895-1957 – 32r – 1 – cn Preston [971]
BRIGHTON GAZETTE – Brighton, England. -w. 1856-71. 16 reels – 1 – uk British Libr Newspaper [072]
BRIGHTON GUARDIAN – England. -w. 1832-33; 1860-69; 1871. (18 reels) – 1 – uk British Libr Newspaper [072]
Brighton, John George *see*
– ADMIRAL OF THE FLEET: SIR PROVO W. P. WALLIS, C. C. B. ETC.: A MEMOIR
– ADMIRAL OF THE FLEET SIR PROVO W.P. WALLIS
BRIGHTON PATRIOT – England. -w. 24 Feb 1835-13 Aug 1839. (2 reels) – 1 – uk British Libr Newspaper [072]
THE BRIGHTS OF SUFFOLK, ENGLAND : DESCENDANTS IN AMERICA OF HENRY BRIGHT / Wilson, John – 1858. Massachusetts Reel 8. (The Cox Library Collection) – 5 – us Americana [978]
BRIGITTA : A TALE / Auerbach, Berthold – Louisville, KY: R H Carothers, 1902 – 1r – 1 – us U.W. Library [830]
BRIGITTA UND ANDERE ERZAEHLUNGEN / Stifter, Adalbert – Wiesbaden: Agrippina-Buecherei, [19–?] – 1r – 1 – us U.W. Library [830]
BRIGITTE – (Since 1957 n9: publ in Hamburg) – Berlin, 1953 n1-25, 1954 n1-26, 1955, n6-1956 n26/1, 1957 n2-23, 1958-dec 19 1975, 1976-feb 24 1982, mar 24 1982-dec 9 1992 – 160r – 1 – gw Mikrofilm [640]
Brignole, Dardo *see* EU DE NORTEAMERICA CONTRA LA ARGENTINA
Brigode, G and M Ducarne *see* L'ESCAUT...
Brigstocke, Frederick Hervey John *see*
– HOW ARE THE MIGHTY FALLEN: A SERMON PREACHED ON THE DEATH OF GENERAL JAMES A. GARFIELD, LATE PRESIDENT OF THE UNITED STATES, IN TRINITY CHURCH, SAINT JOHN, ON SUNDAY, SEPTEMBER 25, 1881
– A PAPER ON THE REVISED VERSION OF THE NEW TESTAMENT: AS READ BEFORE THE SUNDAY SCHOOL TEACHERS' ASSOCIATION OF THE DEANERY OF SAINT JOHN, ON OCTOBER 4TH, 1881
Brijon, C R *see* L'APOLLON MODERNE, OU LE DEVELOPPEMENT INTELLECTUEL PAR LES SONS DE LA MUSIQUE..
Brill, Bernhard *see* EIN BEITRAG ZUR KRITIK VON LESSINGS LAOKOON
Brill, Patricia A *see* PERSONALITY TRAITS, CARDIOVASCULAR FITNESS, AND MORTALITY IN MEN
Brill, Robert H *see*
– GLASS AND GLASSMAKING IN ANCIENT MESOPOTAMIA
– SCIENTIFIC INVESTIGATIONS OF ANCIENT GLASSES AND LEAD-ISOTOPE STUDIES
– SCIENTIFIC RESEARCH IN EARLY CHINESE GLASS
Brillant, Jacques *see* METRO-EXPRESS
Brilling, D *see* LE-TOLEDOT HA-YEHASIM SHEL YEHUDEI HAMBURG LE-EREZ-YISRA'EL
Brilon, Izrail *see* NA KATORGE
BRIL'S SPESHEL (BRIL'S SPECIAL) – London, UK. 9 Aug 1901-30 May 1902 – 1 – uk British Libr Newspaper [072]
BRIL'S TELEFON (BRIL'S TELEPHONE) – London, UK. 6 Aug 1901-8 Jun 1902 – 1 – uk British Libr Newspaper [072]
BRIMA ZEME – Riga, De 1919 a 1940 – 46r – 1 – $3,680.00 – sz Infoprint [947]
BRIMFIELD 1696-1849 – (Mf 1T-2T: Marriages 1726-1824. Mf 2T-5T: Births 1698-1838. Mf 5T-6T: Deaths 1730-1825. Mf 6T: Marriages 1814-46; Out-of-Town Marriages 1727-98. Mf 6T-7T: Births 1795-1849. Mf 7T: Deaths 1813-44. Mf 8T: Publishments 1826-49; Births 1844-49. Mf 9T: Marriages 1844-49; Deaths 1844-49) – (mf ed 1995) – 9mf – 9 – 0-87623-217-9 – us Holbrook [920]
BRIMFIELD 1696-1893 – (Mf 1-8: Vital Records 1696-1844. Mf 9-12: Vital Records 1700-1850. Mf 13-14: Marr & Birth 1724-1886. Mf 15: Marriage Index 1724-1886. Mf 15-26: Proprietors 1730-1824. Mf 27-41: Town Records 1730-1829: Mf 42-48: Selectmen 1766-1839. Mf 49-52: Property Lists 1798. Mf 53-59: Tax Valuations 1831-54. Mf 60-61: School Records 1825-61. Mf 62-63: Voter Register 1847-82. Mf 64: Voter Register 1877, 1889. Mf 65-66: Soldiers 1861-65. Mf 67-70: Paupers 1841-1917. Mf 71-73: Vital Records 1843-55. Mf 74-77: Vitals Index 1856-92. Mf 78-79: Births 1856-93. Mf 80: Intentions 1856-93. Mf 81: Marrs 1856-93, 1771-99. Mf 82-83: Deaths 1856-93) – (mf ed 1991) – 83mf – 9 – 0-87623-134-2 – us Holbrook [920]
Brimley, George *see* ESSAYS BY THE LATE GEORGE BRIMLEY
Brincard, MT *see* LES BRACELETS OGBONI: ANALYSE ICONOGRAPHIQUE ET STYLISTIQUE
BRINEY-TAYLOR DEBATE: "THE CHURCH OF THE NEW TESTAMENT." – 30 Mar-8 Apr 1881. Oakland Station, KY. Bowling Green District. 78p – 1 – us Baptist [240]
BRINGING CRIMINAL DEBT INTO BALANCE : IMPROVING FINE AND RESTITUTION COLLECTION – Washington: FJC, n.d. (1992?) – 1mf – 9 – $1.50 – LLMC 95-385 – us L.L.M.C. [340]
BRINGING IN SHEAVES / Earle, A B – 1869 – 9 – us A.T.L.A. [240]

Brink, Benjamin D *see* THE BODY BUILDER: ROBERT J. ROBERTS
Brink, McDonough and Co *see*
- COMBINED HISTORY OF SHELBY AND MOULTRIE COUNTIES
- HISTORY OF MACOUPIN COUNTY
- HISTORY OF ST. CLAIR COUNTY
Brink, T L *see* CLINICAL GERONTOLOGIST
BRINK, W.R. AND CO *see*
- COMBINED HISTORY OF SCHUYLER COUNTY AND BROWN COUNTY
- HISTORY OF DE WITT COUNTY
- HISTORY OF MADISON COUNTY
Brinkley, John Richard *see*
- JOHN RICHARD BRINKLEY VS. KANSAS STATE BOARD OF MEDICAL REGISTRATION AND EXAMINATION, ET AL
- JOHN RICHARD BRINKLEY VS. THE KANSAS CITY STAR
Brinsley, John *see*
- A CONSOLATION FOR OUR GRAMMAR SCHOOLES
- LUDUS LITERARIUS: OR, THE GRAMMAR SCHOOLE
- PEURILES CONFABULATIUNCULAE
- THE POSING OF THE PARTS
Brinton, Daniel Garrison *see*
- ABORIGINAL AMERICAN AUTHORS AND THEIR PRODUCTIONS: ESPECIALLY THOSE IN THE NATIVE LANGUAGES: A CHAPTER IN THE HISTORY OF LITERATURE
- AMERICAN HERO-MYTHS: A STUDY IN THE NATIVE RELIGIONS OF THE WESTERN CONTINENT
- THE AMERICAN RACE: A LINGUISTIC CLASSIFICATION AND ETHNOGRAPHIC DESCRIPTION OF THE NATIVE TRIBES OF NORTH AND SOUTH AMERICA
- GIORDANO BRUNO: PHILOSOPHER AND MARTYR
- THE MYTHS OF THE NEW WORLD: A TREATISE ON THE SYMBOLISM AND MYTHOLOGY OF THE RED RACE OF AMERICA
BRIO – (v.11-. 1974- 5,6. v.12-. 1975- 9) – v.1-. 1964- – 1 – us UMI [073]
Briones, Mariano *see* LA JUVENTUD ANARQUISTA: FACTOR DETERMINATIVO DE LA GUERRA Y DE LA REVOLUCION
Brioneus, M *see* TOTIUS TERRAE SANCTAE VRBIVMQVE ET QVICQVID IN EIS MEMORIA DIGNUM ACTUM GESTUMUE FUIT: ...
Briot, Alain *see* HISTOIRE DE LA MEDECINE JAPONAISE MODERNE
LA BRIQUE ET LA TERRE CUITE. / Chabat, Pierre – Avec Felix Monmory. Paris: Morel, 1881.2v. in fol., pl. (Architecture Series) – 9 – fr Hachette [720]
Briquet, C M *see* LES FILIGRAINES: A HISTORICAL DICTIONARY OF WATERMARKS, 1923
Briquet, Pierre de *see*
- CODE MILITAIRE OU COMPILATION DES ORDONNANCES DES ROIS DE FRANCE, CONCERNANT LES GENS DE GUERRE
- TRAITE CLINIQUE ET THERAPEUTIQUE DE L'HYSTERIE
BRIQUETTING OF AGRICULTURAL WASTES FOR FUEL – 1990 – 140p – it F.A.O. [333]
A BRISA : JORNAL LITTERARIO, CRITICO E RECREIATIVO – '(s.l.')-Sao Luiz, Brazil. Aug 1872. Incomplete – 1,5,6 – bl Biblioteca [072]
BRISBANE COURIER – Australia. -d. 21 July 1866; 26 Nov, 9 Dec 1867; 23 Feb, 23 March, 6 April, 24, 27 Nov 1869; Jan 1871-Dec 1886. 96 reels – 1 – uk British Libr Newspaper [072]
BRISBANE COURIER – Brisbane, 1846-1996 – 864r – 1 – at Pascoe [072]
BRISBANE DAILY MAIL *see* DAILY MAIL
Brisbane, William *see*
- RECEIPT BOOK
- TRAVEL ACCOUNT
BRISEIS / Black, William – British Fiction Archive: Unit 4 – 9 – uk Bell [830]
Briseux, C E *see*
- ARCHITECTURE MODERNE, OU L'ART DE BIEN BATIR POUR TOUTES SORTES DE PERSONNES.
- L'ART DE BATIR DES MAISONS DE CAMPAGNE
- TRAITE DU BEAU ESSENTIEL DANS LES ARTS AVEC UN TRAITE DES PROPORTIONS HARMONIQUES., ET LES CINQ ORDRES D'ARCHITECTURE
BRISKER VOKHENBLAT = BRISKER WEEKLY – (In Yiddish) – Brzesc, PL. v1 no1 28 May 1926-v5 no51 27 Dec 1929 – 1r – 1 – $45.00 – cn Can Microfilming [072]
Brissac, Henri *see* TRAVAIL ET PROLETARIAT
Brissaud, Jean Baptiste *see* MANUEL D'HISTOIRE DU DROIT FRANCAIS (SOURCES, DROIT PUBLIC, DROIT PRIVE) A L'USAGE DES ETUDIANTS EN LICENCE ET EN DOCTORAT
Brisset, Pierre *see* LA GRAMMAIRE LOGIQUE: RESOLVANT TOUTES LES DIFFICULTES
Brisson *see* HISTOIRE DU NAUFRAGE ET DE LA CAPTIVITE DE M. DE BRISSON
Brisson, M J *see* ORNITHOLOGIA SIVE SYNOPSIS METHODICA
BRISSON PAPERS : TAHITIAN AND OTHER MANUSCRIPTS FORMERLY IN THE POSSESSION OF CAPTAIN VICTOR BRISSON, 1862-1928 / Brisson, Victor – 1r – 1 – at Pacific Mss [980]
Brisson, PR de *see* HISTOIRE DU NAUFRAGE ET DE LA CAPTIVITE DE M. DE BRISSON, OFFICIER DE L'ADMINISTRATION DES COLONIES; AVEC LA DESCRIPTION DES DESERTS D'AFRIQUE, DEPUIS LE SENEGAL JUSQU'AU MAROC
Brisson, Roger *see* JOURNAL OF INTERNET CATALOGING
Brisson, Victor *see* BRISSON PAPERS
Brissot De Warville, Jacques-Pierre *see* A TOUS LES REPUBLICAINS DE FRANCE SUR LA SOCIETE DES JACOBINS DE PARIS
Brister, E M P *see* CENTENNIAL HISTORY OF THE CITY OF NEWARK AND LICKING COUNTY
BRISTOL ADVENTURER AND WEEKLY NEWS – England.5 May 1922-19 Oct 1923. -w. 1 reel – 1 – uk British Libr Newspaper [072]
BRISTOL ADVERTISER EVENING TELEGRAM – England.Jul 1875-Jul 1876. -d. 2 reels – 1 – uk British Libr Newspaper [072]
BRISTOL ADVOCATE – England. -w. 17 Sep 1836-11 Feb 1837. (31 ft) – 1 – uk British Libr Newspaper [072]
BRISTOL AND CLIFTON AMUSEMENTS – England.Dec 1900-1903.-w. 2 reels – 1 – uk British Libr Newspaper [072]
BRISTOL AND KINGSWOOD HERALD – (Bristol District Herald. Feb 1875-Jan 1876) – London, UK. Jul 1874-Jan 1876. -w. 8 feet – 1 – uk British Libr Newspaper [072]
BRISTOL AND WEST OF ENGLAND ADVERTISER *see* WEST OF ENGLAND ADVERTISER
BRISTOL COUNTY – No title page. Massachusetts Reel 3. (The Cox Library Collection) – 5 – us Americana [978]
BRISTOL COUNTY ITEM – Warren. R.I. 1907-1912 – 1 – us UMI [071]
BRISTOL DISTRICT HERALD *see* BRISTOL AND KINGSWOOD HERALD
BRISTOL EVENING POST – Bristol, England. -d. Jan-June 1949. 2 reels – 1 – uk British Libr Newspaper [072]
BRISTOL FIRST – England.27 Nov 1923; 5 Jan-4 Apr 1925.-w. 1/2 reel – 1 – uk British Libr Newspaper [072]
Bristol, Frank Milton *see* PROVIDENTIAL EPOCHS
BRISTOL LIBERAL AND WEST OF ENGLAND COMMERCIAL AND GENERAL ADVERTISER – England. -w. 23 Jul 1831-3 Mar 1832. (21 ft) – 1 – uk British Libr Newspaper [072]
BRISTOL MERCURY – England. 1831-32.-w. 1 reel – 1 – uk British Libr Newspaper [072]
Bristol Naturalist's Society *see* PROCEEDINGS
BRISTOL OBSERVER – England. -w. 7 Jan 1819-1 Oct 1823. (2 reels) – 1 – uk British Libr Newspaper [072]
BRISTOL PAPER – England.Feb 1932-Jan 1933. -w. 1 reel – 1 – uk British Libr Newspaper [072]
BRISTOL PRESENTMENTS – 1770-1917. BRRAM – 1 – uk Microform Academic [970]
BRISTOL RECORD SOCIETY – (Coll title: Publications of the English Record Societies, 1835-1972...) – v1-19. 1930-55 – 65mf – 9 – £480.00 – uk Chadwyck [941]
BRISTOL STANDARD – England. -w. 23 Jan 1839-27 Jan 1842. (1 reel) – 1 – uk British Libr Newspaper [072]
BRISTOL TELEGRAPH – England.Jun 1855-Jun 1856. -w. 1/2 reel – 1 – uk British Libr Newspaper [072]
BRISTOL TIMES – Bristol. England. -w. 1860-64. (10 reels) – 1 – uk British Libr Newspaper [072]
BRISTOL TIMES AND BATH ADVOCATE – England. -w. 2 Mar 1839-26 Mar 1853. (7 reels) – 1 – uk British Libr Newspaper [072]
Bristol, William W *see* BRISTOL'S COMPILATION; MECHANICS' LIEN LAW, TORRENS LAND TITLE, BUILDERS' DIRECTORY
BRISTOL'S COMPILATION; MECHANICS' LIEN LAW, TORRENS LAND TITLE, BUILDERS' DIRECTORY / Bristol, William W – Chicago, 1896. 189 p. LL-7 – 1 – us L of C Photodup [340]
BRISTOW ENTERPRISE – Bristow, NE. -w. Apr. 1908-Sep. 1918; Feb. 1919-Feb. 1932 – 1 – us NE Hist [071]
Bristow, Joseph L *see* JOSEPH L. BRISTOW PAPERS
Bristow, Lewis J *see* SCRAPBOOK, SOUTHERN BAPTIST HOSPITALS
BRITAIN AND EUROPE SINCE 1945 – 1969-1972. Basic set – 9 – us Primary [940]
BRITAIN AND EUROPE SINCE 1945 – (Comprising the publications and documents of various groups and organizations. Enlarged and updated annually) – 1969-1994 – 9 – us Primary [941]
BRITAIN AND EUROPE SINCE 1945-1973 UPDATE – (Comprising the publications and documents of 48 groups and organisations) – 1973 – 9 – us Primary [941]
BRITAIN AND EUROPE SINCE 1945-1974 UPDATE – (Comprising the publications and documents of 33 groups and organisations) – 1974 – 9 – us Primary [941]
BRITAIN AND EUROPE SINCE 1945-1975 UPDATE – (Comprising the publications and documents of 53 groups and organisations) – 1975 – 9 – us Primary [941]
BRITAIN AND EUROPE SINCE 1945-1976 UPDATE – (Comprising the publications and documents of 41 groups and organisations) – 1976 – 9 – us Primary [941]
BRITAIN AND EUROPE SINCE 1945-1977 UPDATE – (Comprising the publications and documents of 44 groups and organisations) – 1977 – 9 – us Primary [941]
BRITAIN AND EUROPE SINCE 1945-1978 UPDATE – (Publ and docs of 44 groups and organisations) – 1978 – 9 – us Primary [941]
BRITAIN AND EUROPE SINCE 1945-1979 UPDATE – (Publ and docs of 32 groups and organizations) – 1979 – 9 – us Primary [941]
BRITAIN AND EUROPE SINCE 1945-1980 UPDATE – (Publ and docs of 32 groups and organizations) – 1980 – 9 – us Primary [941]
BRITAIN AND EUROPE SINCE 1945-1981 UPDATE – (Comprising the publications and documents of 32 groups and organisations) – 1981 – 9 – us Primary [941]
BRITAIN AND EUROPE SINCE 1945-1982 UPDATE – (Comprising the publications and documents of 32 groups and organisations) – 1982 – 9 – us Primary [941]
BRITAIN AND EUROPE SINCE 1945-1983 UPDATE – (Comprising the publications and documents of 28 groups and organisations) – 1983 – 9 – us Primary [941]
BRITAIN AND EUROPE SINCE 1945-1984 UPDATE – (Comprising the publications and documents of 33 groups and organisations) – 1984 – 9 – us Primary [941]
BRITAIN AND EUROPE SINCE 1945-1985 UPDATE – (Comprising the publications and documents of 28 groups and organisations) – 1985 – 9 – us Primary [941]
BRITAIN AND EUROPE SINCE 1945-1986 UPDATE – (Comprising the publications and documents of 32 groups and organisations) – 1986 – 9 – us Primary [941]
BRITAIN AND EUROPE SINCE 1945-1987 UPDATE – (Comprising the publications and documents of 51 groups and organisations) – 1987 – 9 – us Primary [941]
BRITAIN AND EUROPE SINCE 1945-1988 UPDATE – (Comprising the publications and documents of 33 groups and organisations) – 1988 – 9 – us Primary [941]
BRITAIN AND EUROPE SINCE 1945-1989 UPDATE – (Comprising the publications and documents of 32 groups and organisations) – 1989 – 9 – us Primary [941]
BRITAIN AND EUROPE SINCE 1945-1990 UPDATE – (Comprising the publications and documents of 40 groups and organisations) – 1990 – 88mf – 9 – us Primary [941]
BRITAIN AND EUROPE SINCE 1945-1991 UPDATE – (Comprising the publications and documents of 36 groups and organisations) – 1991 – 9 – us Primary [941]
BRITAIN AND EUROPE SINCE 1945-1992 UPDATE – (Comprising the publications and documents of 38 groups and organisations) – 1992 – 9 – us Primary [941]
BRITAIN AND EUROPE SINCE 1945-1993 UPDATE – (Comprising the publications and documents of 37 groups and organizations) – 1993 – 9 – us Primary [941]
BRITAIN IN EUROPE NEWSLETTER – 1959-63.(Britain and Europe since 1945) – 9 – us Primary [940]
BRITAIN IN EUROPE QUARTERLY REVIEW – 1963-67.(Britain and Europe since 1945-1973 Update) – 9 – us Primary [940]
Britan, Ilia *see* IBO IA–BOLSHEVIK!!
BRITANNIA. 1-7. 18 OCT 1912-20 DEC 1918 / Women's Social and Political Union – 1 – 54.00 – us L of C Photodup [360]
BRITANNIA AND TRADES ADVOCATE – Hobart, 1846-55 – 5r – 1 – A$93.00 silver A$81.00 vesicular – at Pascoe [073]
BRITANNIA; OR, THE MORAL CLAIMS OF SEAMEN STATED : AN ESSAY IN THREE PARTS / Harris, John – 1837 – 9 – $20.00 – uk Libr Preservation [355]
BRITANNIA ROMANA / Horsley, J – H-1127 2 – 8 – ne IDC [941]
BRITANNIEN UND DER KRIEG / Franz, Wilhelm – Tuebingen: Kloeres, 1915. 64p – 1 – us U.W. Library [940]
Britischen Militaerbehoerde *see* NEUE RHEINISCHE ZEITUNG
BRITISCHER HOLZMARKT – London, UK. Nov 1928-Oct 1929 – 1 – uk British Libr Newspaper [072]
BRITISH 20TH CENTURY WAR ART / Imperial War Museum. London – (1500 works from First World War Collection. Over 5000 works from Second World War. Some colour fiches. Each work has caption-details of artist, title, medium, dimensions and Museum number. Sequence is alphabetical by artist. Printed index to artists included) – 122 bw 4 colour mf – 9,15 – $800.00 – 0-907006-53-1 – uk Mindata [760]
BRITISH AERIAL OPERATIONS DURING WORLD WAR 2 PAMPHLET COLLECTION – 1941-1942 – 1 – CSUXANM9822-B – us Hoover Inst Photo [355]
BRITISH AGRICULTURAL WRITERS, 1550-1820 – 443mf coll – 9 – $1,782.50 – us UMI [630]
BRITISH AID STATISTICS 1966-1973/77 – (Coll title: British Government Publications...1801-1977, Foreign Aid) – 16mf – 9 – £135.00 – uk Chadwyck [338]
BRITISH AMERICA – London: K. Paul, 1900. 00875. (Pre-1900 Canadiana) – 9 – cn C.I.H.M. [971]
BRITISH AMERICAN BOOK AND TRACT SOCIETY REPORTER – Halifax, N.S.: [The Society, 1873-187- or 18–] – 9 – cn C.I.H.M. [020]
THE BRITISH AMERICAN CIRCULAR FOR EMIGRANTS AND SETTLERS – St-John, New Brunswick. jun 1858 – 1r – 1 – Can$25.00 – cn Can Microfilming [072]
BRITISH AMERICAN CULTIVATOR *see* THE CANADA FARMER
THE BRITISH AMERICAN CULTIVATOR – Toronto: J Eastwood & W G Edmundson, 1842-[1847] – 9 – cn C.I.H.M. [630]
British American Land Company *see* LANDS FOR SALE, IN THE EASTERN TOWNSHIPS OF LOWER CANADA
BRITISH AMERICAN MAGAZINE – v1-2. May 1863-April 1864 – 1 – cn Precision [327]
BRITISH AMERICAN PRESBYTERIAN – (Contd by: The Canada Presbyterian) – Toronto: C B Robinson, [1872-1877] – 9 – cn C.I.H.M. [240]
BRITISH AMERICAN REGISTER – (Bilingual) – Quebec, Canada. 18 dec 1802; 8 jan-6 aut 1803 – 1r – 1 – Can$35.00 – cn Can Microfilming [072]

British and Colonial Emigration Fund *see* PAPERS
BRITISH AND COLONIAL WEEKLY REGISTER – London, UK. 3 Jan-25 Sept 1824.-w. 1/2 reel – 1 – uk British Libr Newspaper [072]
BRITISH AND CONTINENTAL RHETORIC AND ELOCUTION, 1500-1900 – (Reel guide available separately $15.00) – 16r coll + guide – 1 – $1,385.75 – us UMI [410]
BRITISH AND EUROPEAN BUTTERFLIES AND MOTHS (MACROLEPIDOPTERA) / Kappel, A W & Kirby, W F – London, New York, 1895. xvi,273p. 30 pls. Z-1384- – 8 – ne IDC [590]
BRITISH AND EUROPEAN COLLECTION, 1910-1919 *see* LITTLE MAGAZINES (COLLECTION)
BRITISH AND EUROPEAN COLLECTION, 1920-1929 *see* LITTLE MAGAZINES (COLLECTION)
BRITISH AND EUROPEAN COLLECTION, 1930-1940 *see* LITTLE MAGAZINES (COLLECTION)
BRITISH AND FOREIGN ANTI-SLAVERY REPORTER *see* ANTI-SLAVERY REPORTER AND ABORIGINES' FRIEND
British and Foreign Bible Society. Archives *see* MINUTES OF THE GENERAL COMMITTEE
THE BRITISH AND FOREIGN EVANGELICAL REVIEW *see* THE THEOLOGICAL MONTHLY
British and Foreign School Society. Great Britain *see* ANNUAL REPORTS
BRITISH AND FOREIGN STATE PAPERS / Great Britain. Foreign Office – (Principal documents on international affairs, 170v, 1812-1968) – 74r – 5 – $3670.00 – us UMI [941]
BRITISH AND FOREIGN STATE PAPERS – London, 1812-1920. Available: 1904-1907, v98-100; 1920, v113 – 8 – ne IDC [324]
BRITISH AND FOREIGN STATE PAPERS, 1812-1968. V1-170 – 74r – 1 – $3,000.00 – us Trans-Media [340]
THE BRITISH AND FRENCH EXPEDITIONS TO TEEMBO, WITH REMARKS ON CIVILIZATION IN AFRICA / Bodwich, T E – Paris. 1821. BA-283 2 – 8 – ne IDC [910]
BRITISH AND INDIAN OBSERVER – London, UK. 14 Dec 1823-11 Jul 1824. -w. 1/4 reel – 1 – uk British Libr Newspaper [072]
BRITISH AND IRISH BIOGRAPHIES 1840-1940 / ed by Jones, David Lewis – (6pt collection available individually by title £6.880 per part) – 14,287mf – 9 – £37,265.00 – uk Chadwyck [941]
BRITISH ANNUAL AND EPITOME OF THE PROGRESS OF SCIENCE FOR 1837-39 – London, 1837-39. v.1-3 – 3 – us Readex [500]
BRITISH ANTARCTIC EXPEDITION 1907-1909 UNDER THE COMMAND OF SIR E. H. SHACKLETON. GEOLOGY / Shackleton, E H – (V. 1: Glaciology, Physiography, Stratigraphy, and Tectonic Geology. 2823. 1914. SF 51.00; 9. v. 2: Contribution to the Palaeontology and Petrology of South Victoria Land. 2824. 1916. SF 31.00; IDC; 9) – ne IDC [910]
BRITISH ARCHITECT – 1874-1919 – 1 – uk Manchester Libr [720]
British Architectural Library *see*
- COMPREHENSIVE INDEX TO ARCHITECTURAL PERIODICALS
- MICROFILMED COLLECTION OF RARE BOOKS
- RIBA NOMINATION PAPERS 1834-1900
- UNPUBLISHED MANUSCRIPTS

BRITISH ARCHIVES OF THE INTERNATIONAL BRIGADE TO SPAIN – (Articles, journals, pamphlets, correspondence, photographs and ephemera relating to the Spanish Civil War, 1936-39, held at the Marx Memorial Library, London. With printed guide) – 390mf – 9 – $2,060.00 – 0-907006-79-5 – uk Mindata [025]
BRITISH ARMY ADMINISTRATION: A CHRONOLOGY, 1858-1938 – 1 – uk Microform Academic [941]
British Assocation for the Advancement of Science *see* JOURNAL OF SECTIONAL PROCEEDINGS
British Association for American Studies *see* BULLETIN
British Association for the Advancement of Science. Canada *see*
- ...AT NIAGARA FALLS, AUGUST 21ST, 1897
- CANADIAN ECONOMICS: BEING PAPERS PREPARED FOR READING BEFORE THE ECONOMICAL SECTION, WITH AN INTRODUCTORY REPORT: MONTREAL MEETING, 1884
- LIST OF RESIDENT AND NON-RESIDENT MEMBERS: MONDAY, 6 P.M., AUGUST 16, 1897
- REPORT ON CONVEYANCE
- SECOND LIST OF RESIDENT AND NON-RESIDENT MEMBERS AND ASSOCIATES: WEDNESDAY, 6 P.M., AUGUST 18, 1897
- SIXTY SEVENTH ANNUAL MEETING...: TORONTO MEETING: AUGUST 18-25, 1897: PROGRAMME OF LOCAL ARRANGEMENTS WITH MAP OF CITY, SHOWING STREET RAILWAY, PLAN OF UNIVERSITY GROUNDS AND QUEEN'S PARK.
- TORONTO MEETING 1897: PRELIMINARY PROGRAMME WITH MAPS AND ILLUSTRATIONS

BRITISH ATTITUDE TO GERMAN COLONIAL DEVELOPMENT, 1880-1885 / Adams, M – 1935 – us Res Libr [320]
THE BRITISH BANDSMAN AND CONTEST FIELD – London. 1907-75. A weekly newspaper devoted entirely to bands. 7 reels – 1 – 130.00 – us L of C Photodup [780]
BRITISH BANNER – London, UK. 1848-58. -irr. 13 reels – 1 – uk British Libr Newspaper [072]
BRITISH BAPTIST: 133 EARLY ENGLISH BAPTIST TITLES – Filmed from the Regent's Park College Collection, Oxford, England. (Author Index furnished by request) – 1 – 352.55 – us Baptist [240]
BRITISH BAPTIST HISTORICAL RESOURCE MATERIALS – Books, tracts, periodicals and sermons from the Libraries of English Baptist Colleges of Manchester and Regent's Park. 495 titles – 1. 2172.80; ; 1 – 47.25r – us Baptist [240]
BRITISH BAPTIST MATERIALS – (43 books and pamphlets from British Library of the British Museum, London, England) – 1 – 205.34 – us Baptist [240]
BRITISH BAPTIST MATERIALS – (80 books and pamphlets from Angus Library, Regents Park College, Oxford, England) – 1 – 270.51 – us Baptist [240]
BRITISH BAPTIST MATERIALS – Selected by faculty of Southwestern Baptist Theological Seminary from Whitley's Baptist bibliography, 1526-1837. (Title and author index furnished) – 1. 2031.75; ; 1 – 47.25r – us Baptist [240]
BRITISH BAPTIST MATERIALS – Selected by professors of Southern Baptist Seminaries from Whitley's Baptist Bibliography, 1653-1862 – 1 – 552.86 – us Baptist [240]
BRITISH BAPTIST MATERIALS FROM ANGUS LIBRARY OF REGENTS PARK COLLEGE – Oxford, England. Index. 3 reels – 1 – 191.00 – us Baptist [240]
BRITISH BAPTIST MATERIALS FROM ANGUS LIBRARY OF REGENTS PARK COLLEGE, OXFORD, ENGLAND – 17th-18th century items listed in Whitley's Baptist Bibliography. Five reels.Index available upon request – 1 – 444.78 – us Baptist [240]
BRITISH BAPTIST MATERIALS FROM THE BODLEIAN LIBRARY, OXFORD, ENGLAND – 17th-18th century selections from Whitley's Baptist Bibliography. Index available upon request – 1 – 451.35 – us Baptist [240]
BRITISH BAPTIST MATERIALS: INDEX – 5 – 5.04 – us Baptist [240]
BRITISH BAPTIST MATERIALS OF 17TH CENTURY – 1 – 303.24 – us Baptist [240]
BRITISH BEE JOURNAL – (1975- . 5,6,9) – 1873- – 1 – us UMI [630]
THE BRITISH BIRD BOOK / ed by Kirkman, F B – Z 1815. 4 v. 1911-1913 – 9 – ne IDC [590]
BRITISH BIRDS : AN ILLUSTRATED MAGAZINE – London, 1907/1908-1919/1920. v1-13 – 90mf – Z-2011/2 – ne IDC [590]
BRITISH BIRDS' EGGS AND NESTS / Atkinson, J C – Z-1968. 1861 – 9 – ne IDC [590]
BRITISH BIRTH CONTROL MATERIAL AT THE B.L.P.E.S / British Library of Political and Economic Sciences – 1800-1947. With printed index – 1 – £425.00 – uk World [360]
British Broadcasting Corporation *see*
- ANNUAL REPORT AND STATEMENT OF ACCOUNTS
- BBC SUMMARY OF WORLD BROADCASTS

British Broadcasting Corporation. Monitoring Service *see* REPORTS
BRITISH BURMA GAZETTEER / ed by Spearman, H R – Rangoon, 1879-1880. 2v – 22mf – I-1168/1 – ne IDC [073]
BRITISH CABINET RECORDS : CABINET REPORTS BY PRIME MINISTERS TO THE CROWN – (Part 1: 1837-1867. Part 2: 1868-1916) – 1 – us Primary [320]
BRITISH CALIFORNIAN – San Francisco, CA. -m. July, Sept 1903; June 1911; Jan 1913-Dec 1921. 1 reel – 1 – uk British Libr Newspaper [071]
BRITISH CAMPAIGNS DURING WORLD WAR 2 PAMPHLET COLLECTION – 194? – 1 – CSUXANM8199-B – us Hoover Inst Photo [355]
BRITISH CANADIAN CENTRAL – Brockville, Se1862-1870Au – 1r – 1 – cn Preston [971]
BRITISH CANADIAN GOLD FIELDS EXPLORATION, DEVELOPMENT AND INVESTMENT COMPANY – Toronto: The Company, 1896. 00284. (Pre-1900 Canadiana) – 9 – cn C.I.H.M. [622]
BRITISH CANADIAN REVIEW – v1. Dec. 1862-Feb. 1863 – 1 – cn Precision [971]
British Chamber of Commerce for the NEI *see* JAVA GAZETTE
BRITISH CHAMBER OF COMMERCE IN INDONESIA : GENERAL CIRCULAR – (Missing: 1959(2387, 2392, 2399, 2415-2417, 2510, 2538, 2586, 2592)) – Djakarta, 1959-1964 – 186mf – SE-673/1 – ne IDC [380]
BRITISH CHAMBER OF COMMERCE IN INDONESIA : REVIEW – Djakarta, 1959-1964 – 4mf – SE-674/1 – ne IDC [380]
BRITISH CHAMBER OF COMMERCE IN INDONESIA : WEEKLY CIRCULAR TO MEMBERS – (Missing: 1959(1-9)) – Djakarta, 1959-1964 – 92mf – SE-675/1 – ne IDC [380]
THE BRITISH CHAROPHYTA / Groves, J – Ray Society. v. 1. 1920 – 1. 20.00; ; 7 – uk Microform Academic [580]
THE BRITISH CHAROPHYTA / Groves, J & Bullock-Webster, G R – Ray Society. v. 2. 1924 – 1. 20.00; ; 7 – uk Microform Academic [580]
THE BRITISH CHARTERED COMPANIES : 1877-1900, BRITISH NORTH BORNEO, NIGERIA, BRITISH EAST AFRICA, RHODESIA 101=LUND, FRANZ EDWARD – Madison, 1944 – us Res Libr [380]
BRITISH CHRONICLE *see* HEREFORD JOURNAL
THE BRITISH CICERO : OR A SELECTION OF THE MOST ADMIRED SPEECHES IN THE ENGLISH LANGUAGE, ARRANGED UNDER THREE DISTINCT HEADS OF POPULAR, PARLIAMENTARY, AND JUDICIAL ORATORY / Browne, Thomas – Philadelphia: Birch & Small. 3v. 1810 – 18mf – 9 – $27.00 – LLMC 92-115 – us L.L.M.C. [340]
BRITISH CIVILIZATION PAMPHLETS COLLECTION – 1941-1966 – 1 – CSUXANP3010-B – us Hoover Inst Photo [941]
THE BRITISH CLAYWORKER – 1892-Aug 1973 – 1 – us UMI [073]
THE BRITISH COLEOPTERA DELINEATED: CONSISTING OF FIGURES OF ALL THE GENERA OF BRITISH BEETLES / ed by Spry, W J & Shuckard, W E – London, 1840 – VII, 83p, 94pls – 8 – ne IDC [590]
BRITISH COLONIAL MAGAZINE – v1. 1852-1853 – 1 – cn Precision [971]
BRITISH COLONIAL OFFICE : PALESTINE CORRESPONDENCE, 1927-1934 / British Colonial Office. Palestine – (1927-1930 49r $4,165.00 S0627-30. 1931-1934 103r $8,755.00 S0631-34. Registers 1927-1930 6r $510.00 S0527-30. Registers 1931-1934 6r $510.00 S0531-34. With printed guides) – C.O. 733. All of the original correspondence for Palestine during the period of the British Mandate – 1 – us Scholarly Res [941]
British Colonial Office. Palestine *see* BRITISH COLONIAL OFFICE
BRITISH COLONIES AND WORLD WAR 2 PAMPHLET COLLECTION – 1940-1944 – 1 – CSUXANM8201-B – us Hoover Inst Photo [355]
BRITISH COLONIST – Halifax, Canada. 1848-74 – 28r – 1 – $1,820.00 – cn Library Assoc [971]
BRITISH COLONIST – Stanstead, Canada. 1823-31 – 2r – 1 – $136.00 – cn Library Assoc [971]
BRITISH COLONIST – Toronto, Canada. 1838-54 – 10r – 1 – $650.00 – cn Library Assoc [971]
BRITISH COLONIST *see* DAILY COLONIST
THE BRITISH COLONIST / ed by Dickerson, S H – Stanstead, Canada. 1 mai 1823-30 jul 1829 – 1r – 1 – Can$35.00 – cn Can Microfilming [072]
THE BRITISH COLONIST IN NORTH AMERICA: A GUIDE FOR INTENDING EMIGRANTS – London: S. Sonnenschein, 1890. 00294. (Pre-1900 Canadiana) – 9 – cn C.I.H.M. [971]
BRITISH COLUMBIA / Scholefield, E OS – (v3. Canada reel 4) – From the earliest times to the present. Vancouver, Winnipeg, Montreal, Chicago: S.J. Clarke Publ. Co., 1914. v1-2. Canada reel 3. (Cox Library Collection) – 5 – us Americana [971]
British Columbia *see* LEGISLATIVE ASSEMBLY JOURNALS
British Columbia Agricultural and Horticultural Society *see* CONSTITUTION AND BY-LAWS
BRITISH COLUMBIA AND YUKON DIRECTORY *see* BRITISH COLUMBIA DIRECTORIES, 1940-1948
BRITISH COLUMBIA AND YUKON DIRECTORY, 1935-1939 – Vancouver, BC: Sun Directories, 1935-39 – 10r – 1 – Can$70.00r – cn U.B.C. Preserve [971]
British Columbia. Canada *see*
- BRITISH COLUMBIA LAW REPORTS
- BRITISH COLUMBIA STATUTES, SESSION LAWS AND REVISIONS
- FELL AND LANGLEY'S BRITISH COLUMBIA SPEAKER'S DECISIONS
- MARTIN'S MINING CASES

BRITISH COLUMBIA DIGEST – v1-23. Jan. 1945-Dec. 1967 – 1 – cn Precision [971]
BRITISH COLUMBIA DIRECTORIES, 1860-1900 – Vancouver, BC: University of British Columbia Library, Facilities and Preservation Office, 1997 – 21r – 1 – Can$75.00r – cn U.B.C. Preserve [971]
BRITISH COLUMBIA DIRECTORIES, 1900-1910 – (Includes items indexed in Young, George, 1948- Researcher's Guide to British Columbia Directories, 1901-1940) – Vancouver: University of British Columbia Library, Faculties and Preservation Officer, 1995 – 16r – 1 – Can$75.00r – cn U.B.C. Preserve [971]
BRITISH COLUMBIA DIRECTORIES, 1911-1919 – (Includes items indexed in Young, George, 1948- Researcher's guide to British Columbia directories, 1901-1940. Individual titles also listed) – Vancouver: University of British Columbia Library, Facilities and Preservation Office, 1995 – 21r – 1 – Can$75.00r – cn U.B.C. Preserve [971]
BRITISH COLUMBIA DIRECTORIES, 1920-1929 – (Includes items indexed in Young, George, 1948- Researcher's guide to British Columbia directories, 1901-1940) – Vancouver, BC: University of British Columbia Library, Facilities and Preservation Office, 1996 – 21r – 1 – Can$75.00r – cn U.B.C. Preserve [971]
BRITISH COLUMBIA DIRECTORIES, 1930-1939 – (Includes Wrigley's British Columbia Directory (Vancouver: Wrigley Directories, 1930-1932) 3v. Wrigley's Greater Vancouver and New Westminster (British Columbia) Directory (Vancouver: Wrigley Directories, 1933) 1v. Sun British Columbia Directory (Vancouver: Sun Directories, 1934) 1v. British Columbia and Yukon Directory (Vancouver: Sun Directories, 1935-1939) 5v. See individual listings for details) – Vancouver, BC: University of British Columbia Library, 1994 – 19r – 1 – Can$75.00r – cn U.B.C. Preserve [971]
BRITISH COLUMBIA DIRECTORIES, 1930-1939 *see*
- BRITISH COLUMBIA AND YUKON DIRECTORY, 1935-1939
- SUN BRITISH COLUMBIA DIRECTORY, 1934
- WRIGLEY'S BRITISH COLUMBIA DIRECTORY, 1930-1932
- WRIGLEY'S GREATER VANCOUVER AND NEW WESTMINSTER (BRITISH COLUMBIA) DIRECTORY, 1933

BRITISH COLUMBIA DIRECTORIES, 1940-1948 – (Original title: British Columbia and Yukon Directory) – Vancouver: Sun Directories. 9v. 1940-1948 – 18r – 1 – Can$75.00r – cn U.B.C. Preserve [971]
BRITISH COLUMBIA EDUCATION HISTORY ON MICROFILM – Vancouver: University of British Columbia Library, Facilities and Preservation Office, 1996-97 – 10r – 1 – Can$60.00r – cn U.B.C. Preserve [370]

BRITISH COLUMBIA FINANCIAL TIMES – Vancouver, Canada. -w. Nov 1914-Dec 1921. 3 1 2 reels – 1 – uk British Libr Newspaper [072]

BRITISH COLUMBIA FOR SETTLERS: ITS MINES, TRADE AND AGRICULTURE / Macnab, Frances – London: Chapman & Hall, 1898. 03173. (Pre-1900 Canadiana) – 9 – cn C.I.H.M. [971]

BRITISH COLUMBIA GAZETTE – Victoria. 1863-1970 – 167r – 1 – us Ross [324]

BRITISH COLUMBIA GAZETTE *see* BC GAZETTE

BRITISH COLUMBIA HISTORICAL NEWS – (Includes index) – Vancouver. v1-27. 1968-1993/94 – 9 – Can$20.00y – cn Micromedia [971]

BRITISH COLUMBIA: ITS RESOURCES AND CAPABILITIES – Montreal, 1889. 00861. (Pre-1900 Canadiana) – 9 – cn C.I.H.M. [971]

THE BRITISH COLUMBIA LAW NOTES – Victoria, B.C.?: s.n., 1894 – 9 – cn C.I.H.M. [340]

BRITISH COLUMBIA LAW REPORTS / British Columbia. Canada – (Cont by 2nd series. Not offered by LLMC) – v1-63. 1867-1947 (all publ) – 434mf – 9 – $651.00 – LLMC 81-019 – us L.L.M.C. [340]

British Columbia. Legislative Assembly *see*
- BRITISH COLUMBIA SESSIONAL CLIPPING BOOKS
- SESSIONAL PAPERS

BRITISH COLUMBIA LIBRARY ASSOCIATION BULLETIN – 1938-54 – 1r – 1 – $68.00 – cn Library Assoc [020]

BRITISH COLUMBIA LOGGING NEWS – v1-8,no.5. Feb 1974-May 1977 – 1 – us UMI [073]

BRITISH COLUMBIA LUMBERMAN – v4-53. 1920-1969 – 1 – cn Precision [634]

BRITISH COLUMBIA MAGAZINE – v1-11. 1907-1915 – 1 – cn Precision [971]

BRITISH COLUMBIA MINING AND ENGINEERING RECORD *see*
- BRITISH COLUMBIA MINING RECORD
- THE MINING RECORD

BRITISH COLUMBIA MINING CRITIC – Vancouver: British Columbia Mining Critic Print. and Pub. Co., [1897-189- or 19–] – 9 – cn C.I.H.M. [622]

BRITISH COLUMBIA MINING PROSPECTORS' EXCHANGE AND INVESTORS' GUIDE – (Contd by: B.C. Mining Exchange and Investors' Guide) – Vancouver: [s.n., 1899] (Vancouver: Timms) – 9 – cn C.I.H.M. [622]

BRITISH COLUMBIA MINING RECORD – (Cont: The Mining Record. Contd by: British Columbia Mining and Engineering Record) – Victoria, B.C: British Columbia Record, [1904-1908] – 9 – cn C.I.H.M. [622]

British Columbia. Ministry of Education *see* PROVINCIAL EXAMINATION PAPERS, 1988-95

THE BRITISH COLUMBIA MONTHLY AND MINING REVIEW – Victoria, B.C: J M Leet, [1889?-18– or 19–] – 9 – cn C.I.H.M. [622]

BRITISH COLUMBIA MONTHLY AND WESTMINSTER MAGAZINE – v1-27. June 1911-Dec. 1927 – 1 – cn Precision [971]

BRITISH COLUMBIA ODDFELLOW – Vancouver: A Mackenzie; G L Center, [1895?-189- or 19–] – 9 – cn C.I.H.M. [971]

BRITISH COLUMBIA OUTDOORS *see* BC OUTDOORS

BRITISH COLUMBIA PUBLIC SERVICE BULLETIN – v1-4. June 1925-Dec. 1928 – 1 – cn Precision [971]

BRITISH COLUMBIA REPORT – (1992/93 Can$64.00y) – v1- 1989- – 9 – Can$73.00y – cn Micromedia [971]

BRITISH COLUMBIA SESSIONAL CLIPPING BOOKS : NEWSPAPER ACCOUNTS OF THE DEBATES / ed by British Columbia. Legislative Assembly – Victoria, BC. 1890-1972 – 26r – 1 – Can$60.00r – cn U.B.C. Preserve [971]

BRITISH COLUMBIA STATUTES, SESSION LAWS AND REVISIONS / British Columbia. Canada – (Updates planned) – Revised Statutes 1871-32nd Parliament 1st sess. 1871-1979 – 889 – 9 – $1,333.00 – LLMC 90-120 – us L.L.M.C. [340]

BRITISH COLUMBIA STUDIES *see* BC STUDIES

BRITISH COLUMBIA TEACHER *see* BC TEACHER

BRITISH COLUMBIAN – New Westminster, Canada. Daily British Columbian The Columbian Daily Columbian. -d. 1864-67; Feb 1868-July 1869; June, July 1888; Sept, Oct 1898; Oct, Dec 1915. Imperfect. 4 1 2 reels – 1 – uk British Libr Newspaper [072]

BRITISH COLUMBIAN – Victoria and New Westminster. Canada. 1861-69 – 6r – 1 – $390.00 – cn Library Assoc [072]

THE BRITISH COLUMBIAN FANCIER – Nanaimo, B.C: Nanaimo Poultry Society, [1894-189- or 19–] – 9 – cn C.I.H.M. [630]

THE BRITISH COLUMBIAN MAGAZINE – Victoria, B C: Dominion Magazine Co., [1889-18– or 19–] – 9 – cn C.I.H.M. [971]

BRITISH CONFERVAE / Dillwyn, L W – 1809 – 7 – uk Microform Academic [580]

BRITISH CONFERVAE / Dillwyn, L W – London. 1802-09 – 8 – ne IDC [580]

THE BRITISH CONSULATE IN JERUSALEM IN RELATION TO THE JEWS IN PALESTINE / Hyamson, A – 2v. London. 1939-41. BJ-27-32 1 – 9 – ne IDC [956]

BRITISH CONSULS ABROAD... / Fynn, R – London, 1846 – 4mf – 1 – ILM-919/1 – ne IDC [327]

BRITISH CORROSION JOURNAL – (1985- . 5,6,9) – v1- . 1965- – 1 – us UMI [073]

THE BRITISH CREDIT SYSTEM: INFLATED BANK CREDIT AS A SUBSTITUTE FOR CURRENT MONEY OF THE REALM / Baird, Henry Carey – Philadelphia: H. Baird & Co., 1875. 00805. (Pre-1900 Canadiana) – 9 – cn C.I.H.M. [336]

BRITISH CULTURE, SERIES ONE: 18TH AND 19TH CENTURY – Includes contemporary and retrospective history, biography, criticism – 9 – us Primary [900]

BRITISH CULTURE, SERIES TWO: THEOLOGY – Titles from The New Cambridge Bibliography of English Literature, v3, 1800-1900. 1969 – 9 – us Primary [306]

BRITISH DAILY COLONIST – Victoria, B. C., Canada. Daily Colonist. -d. March 1864-June 1904; April 1911-Dec 1921. 121 reels – 1 – uk British Libr Newspaper [072]

BRITISH DEFENCE DOCUMENTS – 1973. 1v. 7 sections. Updated quarterly – 5 – uk Tech [355]

BRITISH DENTAL JOURNAL – London. v114-121. 1963-66. M-16/2 – 8 – ne IDC [073]

THE BRITISH DESMIDIEAE / Ralfs, J – London. 1848. B-6400 1 – 9 – ne IDC [580]

BRITISH DESMIDS / Cooke, M C – A supplement to British fresh-water algae. London, etc. 1887 – 8 – ne IDC [580]

BRITISH DIPLOMACY ILLUSTRATED IN THE AFFAIR OF THE "VIXEN" – Ed 2. Newcastle, 1838 – 1mf – 1 – ILM-626/1 – ne IDC [327]

BRITISH DIPLOMATIC BLUE BOOKS 1801-1899 : BRITISH HOUSE OF COMMONS PARLIAMENTARY PAPERS – ie Microforms [941]

BRITISH DIPLOMATIC BLUE BOOKS CONCERNING CENTRAL AND SOUTH AMERICA / Great Britain. Parliament. House of Commons – 1800-99. By country chronologically, with catalogue including F.O. Commercial Reports – 338mf – 9 – Ir£328.00 – ie Microforms [941]

BRITISH DOCUMENTS ON FOREIGN POLICY. SERIES C : PART 2: NORTH AMERICA, 1919-1939 – 9 – $3,240.00 – 0-89093-605-6 – us UPA [324]

BRITISH DOCUMENTS ON THE ORIGINS OF WAR – 1898-1914 – 9 – us UMI [324]

THE BRITISH DOMINIONS AS MANDATORIES / Evatt, H V – Melbourne, 1934 – 1mf – 1 – ILM-1971/1 – ne IDC [327]

THE BRITISH DOMINIONS IN NORTH AMERICA. / Bouchette, Joseph – London, 1832. 2v – 1 – us Res Libr [971]

BRITISH EAST AFRICA : PAST, PRESENT AND FUTURE / Hindlip, Charles Allsopp – London: T F Unwin, 1905 – 1 – us Res Libr [960]

British Ecological Society *see* JOURNAL OF ECOLOGY

BRITISH EDIBLE FUNGI: HOW TO DISTINGUISH AND HOW TO COOK THEM / Cooke, M C – London. 1891. B-6260 2 – 8 – ne IDC [580]

BRITISH EDUCATION THESES INDEX, NEW SERIES 2, 1984-89 / Librarians of Institutes and Schools of Education (LISE) – 8 fiches. 1990 – 9 – £20.00 – uk L.I.S.E. [370]

BRITISH EDUCATIONAL RESEARCH JOURNAL – 1975- 19v – 9 – £269.50 – 0141-1926 – uk Carfax [370]

THE BRITISH EMPIRE / Balough, Elemer – Halle (Saale) etc. Sack & Montanus, 1931-35. 2 v. LL-2326 – 1 – us L of C Photodup [340]

British Empire League *see*
- REPORT OF MEETING AT GUILDHALL, 3RD DECEMBER, 1896, AND SPEECHES DELIVERED IN THE HOUSE OF LORDS: WITH OPINIONS OF THE PRESS
- REPORT OF MEETING OF COUNCIL, JULY 12TH, 1897: TO RECEIVE A DEPUTATION FROM THE LEAGUE IN CANADA
- REPORT OF SPEECHES DELIVERED AT MEETINGS HELD DURING THE VISIT OF THE PRIME MINISTERS OF THE SELF-GOVERNING COLONIES BETWEEN JUNE 12TH AND JULY 5TH, 1897
- REPORT OF THE INAUGURAL MEETING OF THE LEAGUE: HELD ON WEDNESDAY, JANUARY 29TH, 1896, AT THE MANSION HOUSE

British Empire League. Canada *see*
- THE BRITISH EMPIRE LEAGUE IN CANADA
- CANADIAN INSOLVENCY LEGISLATION

THE BRITISH EMPIRE LEAGUE IN CANADA : ITS OFFICERS, COMMITTEES AND CONSTITUTION, INCLUDING REPORT OF ANNUAL MEETING HELD AT OTTAWA, APRIL 28TH, 1897 / British Empire League. Canada – Toronto: Carswell, 1897. 02158. (Pre-1900 Canadiana) – 9 – cn C.I.H.M. [971]

THE BRITISH EMPIRE LEAGUE IN CANADA : ITS ORIGIN, CONSTITUTION AND BY-LAWS: INCLUDING REPORT OF SPECIAL GENERAL MEETING HELD AT OTTAWA, MARCH 4TH, 1896 / British Empire League. Canada – Toronto: Carswell, 1896. 02830. (Pre-1900 Canadiana) – 9 – cn C.I.H.M. [971]

THE BRITISH EMPIRE LEAGUE IN CANADA: SPEECH DELIVERED BY THE PRESIDENT, GEORGE T. DENISON, IN MOVING THE ADOPTION OF THE ANNUAL REPORT AT THE ANNUAL MEETING OF THE LEAGUE : HELD IN THE RAILWAY COMMITTEE ROOM, HOUSE OF COMMONS, OTTAWA, ON THURSDAY, 6TH APRIL, 1899 / Denison, George Taylor – Toronto: Printed by order of the annual meeting by the Carswell Co., 1899. 02634. (Pre-1900 Canadiana) – 9 – cn C.I.H.M. [971]

BRITISH EMPLOYERS' CONFEDERATION ARCHIVE : LIST AND INDEXES / Jenkins, Deborah – (List of the BEC records, subject index and index of correspondents (primarily employers' and trade associations)) – Coventry: University of Warwick Library, 1983 – 3mf – 9 – £15.00 – Modern Records Centre, U of Warwick, Coventry – uk Microform Academic [331]

BRITISH ENTOMOLOGY / Curtis, J – London, 1824-39.769 pls. with descriptive letterpress.Lacking: pls. 195-769. Z-1160/2 – 8 – ne IDC [590]

THE BRITISH ESSAYISTS / Chalmers, Alexander – London. 45v. 1803 – 110mf – 9 – subsc: DM700.00 diazo DM800.00 silver – gw Olms [420]

BRITISH FASCISTI BULLETIN – British Fascist Bulletin The Bulletin The British Lion British Fascism. London. Jun 1930-Jun 1934 – 1r – 1 – uk British Libr Newspaper [360]

The British Federation of Film Societies *see* FILM

BRITISH FERN GAZETTE – Kendal, 1909-1939. v1-7(7) – 44mf – 7287c/2 – ne IDC [580]

THE BRITISH FERNS / Hooker, W J – or Coloured figures and descriptions of the ferns of Great Britain and Ireland. London. 1861. B-7197 2 – 8 – ne IDC [580]

BRITISH FERNS AND THEIR VARIETIES / Druery, C T – London. New York. 1911 – 9 – ne IDC [580]

BRITISH FERNS AND THEIR VARIETIES / Fraser, P N – Edinburgh. 1864. B-7187 1 – 9 – ne IDC [580]

BRITISH FICTION ARCHIVE – (Unit 1: Corelli, Ewing, Shorthouse, Wood. PS736.00; 9. Unit 2: Bray, Kingsley, Reade, Ward. PS624.00; IPL; 9. Unit 3: Blackmore, Cholmondeley, Ouida, Thackeray (Anne). PS664.00; IPL; 9. Unit 4: Black, Broughton, Lawless. PS600.00; IPL; 9. Unit 5: Braddon, Taylor. PS672.00; IPL; 9) – Major prose fiction writings of over one hundred lesser known Victorian and Edwardian novelists. Selection based on Minor Fiction noted in the New Cambridge Bibliography of English Literature, 1800-1900: v3, with important additions. Five units (411 titles). Titles (minimum 5) and units available individually – 9 – PS3082.00 – uk Bell [830]

British Film Institute *see* CINEMA PRESSBOOKS, 1920-1940

British Film Institute. London *see*
- CATALOGUE
- CATALOGUE OF THE BOOK LIBRARY OF THE BRITISH FILM INSTITUTE

BRITISH FLAG AND CHRISTIAN SENTINEL – London, UK. 1894. -w. 3 feet – 1 – uk British Libr Newspaper [072]

THE BRITISH FLORA COMPRISING THE PHAENOGAMOUS OR FLOWERING PLANTS AND THE FERNS / Hooker, W J & Walker-Arnott, G A – ed. 6. London. 1850. B-8320 1 – 9 – ne IDC [580]

THE BRITISH FLORA COMPRISING THE PHAENOGAMOUS OR FLOWERING PLANTS AND THE FERNS / Hooker, W J & Walker-Arnott, G A – ed. 8. London. 1860. B-8321 1 – 9 – ne IDC [580]

BRITISH FOREIGN AND COLONIAL JOURNAL – (Greater Britain. 1891) – London, UK. 15 Mar 1889-91. -m – 2r – 1 – uk British Libr Newspaper [072]

BRITISH FOREIGN MISSIONS, 1837-97 / Thompson, Ralph Wardlaw & Johnson, Arthur N – (Includes bibliographical references and index) – London: Blackie, 1899 – 1mf – 9 – 0-8370-6781-2 – 1986-0781 – us A.T.L.A. [941]

BRITISH FOREIGN OFFICE : US CORRESPONDENCE, 1930-48 – (1930-32: Tho Early Doprocoion 36r $3,060 S0830-32. 1933-34: FDR and the "Hundred Days" 38r $3,230 S0833-34. 1935-36: Period of Social Reform 41r $3,485 S0835-36. 1937-38: The Second New Deal 51r $4,335 S0837-38. 1939-40: The Advent of War 46r $3,910 S0839-40. 1941-44 World War 2 93r $7,905 S0841-44. 1945-46: Dissolving the Grand Alliance 49r $4,165 S0845-46. 1947-48: Onset of the Cold War 28r $2,380 S0847-48. With printed guides) – BFO file 371, 1978-81 – us Scholarly Res [320]

British Foreign Office *see*
- JAPAN CORRESPONDENCE, 1856-1905
- JAPAN CORRESPONDENCE, 1856-1948
- JAPAN CORRESPONDENCE, 1856-1951
- RUSSIA CORRESPONDENCE, 1883-1948

BRITISH FOREIGN RELATIONS ITLAY PAMPHLET COLLECTION – 1916?-1941 – 1 – CSUXANP2064-B – us Hoover Inst Photo [320]

BRITISH FOREIGN RELATIONS PAMPHLET COLLECTION – 1921-1986 – 1 – CSUXANP2027-B – us Hoover Inst Photo [320]

BRITISH FOREIGN RELATIONS WITH CHINA PAMPHLET COLLECTION – 19?? – 1 – CSUXANP2058-B – us Hoover Inst Photo [320]

BRITISH FOREIGN RELATIONS WITH EGYPT PAMPHLET COLLECTION – 1952 – 1 – CSUXANP2061-B – us Hoover Inst Photo [320]

BRITISH FOREIGN RELATIONS WITH FRANCE PAMPHLET COLLECTION – 1853?-1924 – 1 – CSUXANP2029-B – us Hoover Inst Photo [320]

BRITISH FOREIGN RELATIONS WITH GERMANY PAMPHLET COLLECTION – 1908-1954 – 1 – CSUXANP2033-B – us Hoover Inst Photo [320]

BRITISH FOREIGN RELATIONS WITH JAPAN PAMPHLET COLLECTION – 1921 – 1 – CSUXANP2068-B – us Hoover Inst Photo [320]

BRITISH FOREIGN RELATIONS WITH POLAND PAMPHLET COLLECTION – 1946? – 1 – CSUXANP2072-B – us Hoover Inst Photo [320]

BRITISH FOREIGN RELATIONS WITH SCANDINAVIA PAMPHLET COLLECTION – 1941 – 1 – CSUXANP2040-B – us Hoover Inst Photo [320]

BRITISH FOREIGN RELATIONS WITH SPAIN PAMPHLET COLLECTION – 1948?-1954 – 1 – CSUXANP2051-B – us Hoover Inst Photo [320]

BRITISH FOREIGN RELATIONS WITH THE NETHERLANDS PAMPHLET COLLECTION – 1946 – 1 – CSUXANP2036-B – us Hoover Inst Photo [320]

BRITISH FOREIGN RELATIONS WITH TURKEY PAMPHLET COLLECTION – 1915 – 1 – CSUXANP2079-B – us Hoover Inst Photo [320]

BRITISH FOUNDRYMAN – (v70- . 1977- . 5,6,9) – v49-. 1956 – 1 – us UMI [670]

BRITISH FREEHOLDER – London, UK. 5 Feb 1820-10 May 1823. -w – 2r – 1 – uk British Libr Newspaper [072]
BRITISH FRESH-WATER ALGAE / Cooke, M C – Exclusive of Desmidae and Diatomaceae. London, etc. 1882-84. B-6349 2 – 8 – ne IDC [580]
THE BRITISH FRESHWATER COPEPODA / Gurney, R – Ray Society. 1931-33 – 1. 60.00; ; 7 – uk Microform Academic [590]
BRITISH FRESH-WATER FISHES / Houghton, W – Z-2114 2. 2 v. 1879 – 8 – ne IDC [590]
BRITISH FRESH-WATER FISHES / Maxwell, H E – Z-2122 2. 1904 – 8 – ne IDC [590]
THE BRITISH FRESHWATER RHIZOPODA AND HELIOZA / Cash, J & Wailes, G H – Ray Society. v. 5. 1921 – 7 – uk Microform Academic [590]
THE BRITISH FRESHWATER RHIZOPODA AND HELIOZOA / Cash, J & Hopkinson, J – Ray Society. v. 1. 1905 – 1. 20.00; ; 7 – uk Microform Academic [590]
THE BRITISH FRESHWATER RHIZOPODA AND HELIOZOA / Cash, J & Wailes, G H – Ray Society. v. 4. 1919 – 1 £14.00 7 £35.00 – uk Microform Academic [590]
THE BRITISH FRIEND / The Society of Friends – 1843-1913 – 1 – £575.00 – uk World [240]
BRITISH GAZETTE / Great Britain – London. - d. Pub. by HMSO during the General Strike 5$13 May 1926. (7 ft.) – 1 – uk British Libr Newspaper [072]
THE BRITISH GAZETTE – (No. 1 is slightly mutilated) – [London]: H.M.S.O., 1926. 8 no – 1 – CSUX88-5441 – us Hoover Inst Photo [941]
THE BRITISH GAZETTE – (Publ during general strike) – London: H M Stationery Off, may 5-13 1926 – 1r – 1 – us Res Libr [072]
BRITISH GOVERNMENT PUBLICATIONS, 1801-1977 *see* FAMILY EXPENDITURE SURVEY 1957/59-1977
BRITISH GOVERNMENT PUBLICATIONS CONTAINING STATISTICS, 1801-1977 – (Individual titles also listed and may be purchased separately) – 362r and 1766mf – 1,9 – £22,820.00 coll – uk Chadwyck [941]
BRITISH GOVERNMENT PUBLICATIONS... 1801-1977 *see*
- ACCOUNTS RELATING TO TRADE AND NAVIGATION 1847/48-1964
- AGRICULTURAL STATISTICS
- ANNUAL ABSTRACT OF STATISTICS 1928-1977
- ANNUAL REPORT OF THE REGISTRAR GENERAL 1839-1920
- ANNUAL STATEMENT OF THE OVERSEAS TRADE OF THE UNITED KINGDOM 1853-1975
- ANNUAL STATISTICAL SURVEY OF THE ELECTRONICS INDUSTRY 1969, 1970, 1972-1974
- BRITISH AID STATISTICS 1966-1973/77
- BRITISH LABOUR STATISTICS
- CRIMINAL STATISTICS, ENGLAND AND WALES
- CRIMINAL STATISTICS, SCOTLAND
- DIGEST OF UNITED KINGDOM ENERGY STATISTICS 1948/49-1977
- EDUCATION STATISTICS FOR THE UNITED KINGDOM 1967-1975
- FINANCE ACCOUNTS OF GREAT BRITAIN FOR THE YEAR ENDED 5TH JANUARY...1801-1817
- FINANCE ACCOUNTS OF IRELAND FOR THE YEAR ENDED 5TH JANUARY 1801-1817
- FINANCE ACCOUNTS OF THE UNITED KINGDOM OF GREAT BRITAIN AND IRELAND FOR THE FINANCIAL YEAR ENDED 31ST MARCH...1818-1966
- GENERAL REPORT IN REGARD TO THE SHARE AND LOAN CAPITAL, THE TRAFFIC IN PASSENGERS AND GOODS, AND THE WORKING EXPENDITURE OF THE RAILWAY COMPANIES IN THE UNITED KINGDOM 1871-1901
- GOVERNMENT CONTROL OF RAILWAYS; ESTIMATES OF THE POOLED REVENUE, RECEIPTS AND EXPENSES AND RESULTANT NET REVENUE 1939/40-1947
- HEALTH AND PERSONAL SOCIAL SERVICES STATISTICS FOR ENGLAND
- HEALTH AND PERSONAL SOCIAL SERVICES STATISTICS FOR ENGLAND AND WALES
- HEALTH AND PERSONAL SOCIAL SERVICES STATISTICS FOR WALES 1974-1977
- HEALTH AND SAFETY, MINES AND QUARRIES 1851-1965
- NATIONAL COAL BOARD REPORTS AND ACCOUNTS 1945-1964/65
- NATIONAL DEBT
- NATIONAL INCOME AND EXPENDITURE 1938/45-1967/77
- NORTHERN IRELAND FAMILY EXPENDITURE SURVEY 1971-1977
- OVERSEAS TRADE ACCOUNTS OF THE UNITED KINGDOM 1965-1969
- OVERSEAS TRADE STATISTICS OF THE UNITED KINGDOM 1970-1977
- POPULATION PROJECTIONS (NATIONAL FIGURES) OPCS SERIES PP2 1970-1977
- REGISTRAR GENERAL'S STATISTICAL REVIEW OF ENGLAND AND WALES 1921-1973
- REPORT OF AN ENQUIRY INTO HOUSEHOLD EXPENDITURE IN 1953-1954
- REPORT OF THE COMMISSIONERS OF HER MAJESTY'S CUSTOMS AND EXCISE 1857-1978
- REPORT OF THE COMMISSIONERS OF H.M. INLAND REVENUE ON THE INLAND REVENUE 1857-1977
- THE REPORT ON THE CENSUS OF PRODUCTION 1907-1967
- RETURNS OF THE CAPITAL, TRAFFIC, RECEIPTS AND WORKING EXPENDITURE OF THE RAILWAY COMPANIES OF GREAT BRITAIN 1848-1938
- SCOTTISH HEALTH STATISTICS 1958-1977
- STATISTICS ABSTRACT FOR THE PRINCIPAL FOREIGN COUNTRIES IN EACH YEAR 1860/72-1901/12
- STATISTICS OF EDUCATION 1961-1976
- STATISTICS OF SCIENCE AND TECHNOLOGY
- STATISTICS OF TRADE THROUGHOUT U.K. PORTS 1976 AND 1977
- TRANSPORT STATISTICS GREAT BRITAIN 1964/74-1967/77
- UNITED KINGDOM BALANCE OF PAYMENTS 1946/47-1967/77
- WORLD MINERAL STATISTICS 1882-1966

BRITISH GOVERNMENTAL BLUE BOOKS OF STATISTICS – 1991 – 1 – uk Microform Academic [941]
THE BRITISH GRAMMAR / Buchanan, James – 1762. 301p. (English Linguistics Series 1500-1800) – 9 – us UMI [420]
BRITISH GUARDIAN AND PROTESTANT ADVOCATE – London, UK. 1824-22 Mar 1826. -w. 1 1/2 reels – 1 – uk British Libr Newspaper [072]
British Guiana *see*
- BRITISH OFFICIAL GAZETTE
- BULLETIN DES ACTES ADMINISTRATIFS DE LA PREFECTURE DE LA GUYANE
- DEVELOPMENT PROGRAMME, 1956-1960
- DEVELOPMENT PROGRAMME, 1960-1964
- GENERAL TEN-YEAR PLAN OF DEVELOPMENT AND WELFARE, 1947-56
- GOUVERNEMENTSBLAD VAN SURINAME
- OFFICIAL GAZETTE
- ROYAL GAZETTE

BRITISH HEART JOURNAL – (1967- . 5,6. 1975- . 9) – 1- 1939- – 1 – us UMI [616]
THE BRITISH HEMIPTERA / Douglas, J W & Scott, J – Ray Society. v. 1. 1865 – 1. 60.00; ; 7 – uk Microform Academic [580]
BRITISH HERALD – (Bible Herald. Jan-Feb 1876) – London, UK. 1861-Feb 1876. -m – 3r – 1 – uk British Libr Newspaper [072]
THE BRITISH HERBAL / Hill, J – London. 1756-58. B-5225 2 – 8 – ne IDC [616]
BRITISH HERITAGE – v.1-. 1979-. Continues: British History Illustrated – 1,5,6,9 – us UMI [073]
BRITISH HISTORY ILLUSTRATED – v1-6. 1974-79. Continued as: British Heritage – 1 – us UMI [073]
BRITISH HISTORY PAMPHLET COLLECITON – 1914-1949 – 1 – CSUXANP2022-B – us Hoover Inst Photo [941]
British Honduras *see*
- DEVELOPMENT PLAN, 1963-1970
- DEVELOPMENT PLANNING COMMITTEE REPORT, 1947-1956
- DEVELOPMENT POLICY AND INTERIM EXPENDITURE PROGRAMME 1961-1963

BRITISH HOUSING AND PLANNING REVIEW / National Housing and Town Planning Council. London, England – 1948-52. With printed Finding List – 1 – £35.00r – uk Altair [710]
THE BRITISH HYDRACARINA / Soar, C D & Williamson, W C – Ray Society. 1925 – 1 – uk Microform Academic [580]
THE BRITISH IN IOWA / Van Der Zee, Jacob – (Iowa City: State Historical Society of Iowa, 1922). Iowa Reel 2. (The Cox Library Collection) – 5 – us Americana [978]
THE BRITISH IN IRELAND / Dublin Castle. Ireland. Records, 1880-1921 – (Part 2: Royal Irish Constabulary Monthly Reports and Returns of Outrages, 1892-97; CO 904. Boxes 48-67. Part 3: Inspector Generals' and County Inspectors' Monthly Reports, 1898-1913; CO 904. Boxes 68-91. Part 4: Inspector Generals' and County Inspectors' Monthly Reports, 1914-18, and Police Reports, 1920-21. CO 904.Boxes 92-122 and 148-156A. Part 5: Public Control and Administration, 1884-1921. CO 904, Boxes 159-179. Part 6: Judicial Proceedings, Enquiries and Miscellaneous Records, 1872-1926. CO 904. Boxes 30-35, 37-39) – Part 1: Anti-Government Organisations, 1882-1921; (PRO Class CO 904). Boxes 7-23, 27-29 and 157 – 1 – us Primary [941]
BRITISH INDIA : IN ITS RELATION TO THE DECLINE OF HINDOOISM AND THE PROGRESS OF CHRISTIANITY: CONTAINING REMARKS ON THE MANNERS, CUSTOMS, AND LITERATURE OF THE PEOPLE / Campbell, William – London: John Snow, 1858 – 2mf – 9 – 0-8370-6568-2 – 1986-0568 – us A.T.L.A. [950]
BRITISH INDIAN ADVOCATE – London, UK. 1841-1 Jan 1842. 24 feet – 1 – uk British Libr Newspaper [072]
BRITISH INDUSTRY, LABOUR AND TRADE UNIONISM, 1887-1934 – Series 1: Official reports on strikes and lockouts, labour statistics, earnings and hours of labour, 1888-1934 – 1 – us Primary [331]
BRITISH INDUSTRY, LABOUR AND TRADE UNIONISM, 1887-1934 – Series 2: Official reports on trade unions, standard time rates, standard piece rates, rules of voluntary conciliation and arbitration boards and joint committees, 1887-1913 – 1 – us Primary [331]
BRITISH INTERESTS AND ACTIVITIES IN TEXAS, 1838-1846 / Adams, E D – Baltimore, 1910 – 3mf – 9 – ILM-1752/1 – ne IDC [340]
THE BRITISH INVASION FROM THE NORTH: THE CAMPAIGNS OF GENERALS CARLETON AND BURGOYNE FROM CANADA, 1776-1777, WITH THE JOURNAL OF LIEUT. WILLIAM DIGBY, OF THE 53RD, OR SHROPSHIRE REGIMENT OF FOOT / Digby, William – Illustrated with historical notes by James Phinney Baxter. Albany, N.Y.: J. Munsell's Sons, 1887. 02709. (Pre-1900 Canadiana) – 9 – cn C.I.H.M. [971]
THE BRITISH INVASION FROM THE NORTH: THE CAMPAIGNS OF GENERALS CARLETON AND BURGOYNE FROM CANADA, 1776-77: WITH THE JOURNAL OF LIEUT. WILLIAM DIGBY OF THE 53RD, OR SHROPSHIRE REGIMENT OF FOOT / Baxter, James Phinney – Illus. with historical notes by Baxter, Albany, NY: Munsell, 1887. 03506. (Pre-1900 Canadiana) – 9 – cn C.I.H.M. [971]
BRITISH INVESTMENT REVIEW – London, UK. 1897; 31 Jan-31 Mar 1899. -w. 24 feet – 1 – uk British Libr Newspaper [072]
BRITISH ISLES CENSUS DIRECTORIES PROJECT : ENGLISH SERIES; WELSH SERIES; IRISH SERIES; SCOTTISH SERIES / ed by Hall, Nick Vine – (English series: ISBN: 1-875652-00-0. Welsh series: 1-875652-31-0. Irish series: ISBN: 1-875652-52-3. Scottish series: 1-875652-34-5) – Melbourne, 1991-96 – 1361mf (increasing wkly) – 9 – $6.00f – at Vine [941]
BRITISH ISLES CENSUS DIRECTORIES PROJECT 1841-1911 – (Filming of a further 220 directories in progress, bringing the series total to 535v) – 1991- – 315v 1157mf – 9 – at Vine [941]
BRITISH ISLES GAZETTEER – (Based on 1901 census index. Includes some maps) – Bartholomew: 1904 – 8mf – 9 – NZ$32.00 – 0-908989-18-0 – nz BAB [941]
BRITISH JOURNAL FOR EIGHTEENTH-CENTURY STUDIES / ed by Hammond, Brean S – v1-4. Oxford. 1978-81 – 9 – $27.00v – uk Voltaire [410]
BRITISH JOURNAL FOR THE HISTORY OF SCIENCE – (1977- . 5,6,9) – v. 1-. 1962- – 1 – us UMI [500]
BRITISH JOURNAL OF ADDICTION – (1982- . 1,5,6,9) – v75- . 1980- – 1 – us UMI [073]
BRITISH JOURNAL OF ADDICTION *see* ADDICTION
BRITISH JOURNAL OF ADDICTION (TO ALCOHOL AND OTHER DRUGS) – v44-74. 1947-79 – 1 – us UMI [073]
THE BRITISH JOURNAL OF ANIMAL BEHAVIOUR – v. 1-5. 2447 2. 1953-1957 – 8 – ne IDC [590]
BRITISH JOURNAL OF CANCER – v. 1-12. 1947-1958 – 1,5,6 – us Princeton Micro [616]
BRITISH JOURNAL OF CLINICAL EQUIPMENT – 1975- – 1,5,6,9 – us UMI [616]
BRITISH JOURNAL OF CLINICAL PHARMACOLOGY – (1976- . 5,6,9) – v. 1- 1974- – 1 – us UMI [615]
BRITISH JOURNAL OF CLINICAL PSYCHOLOGY – (Continues: British Journal of Social and Clinical Psychology) – London. v20-29. 1981-90 – 5,9 – Dfl1,160.00; v20-27 Dfl110.00v; v28-29 Dfl140.00v – ne Swets [150]
BRITISH JOURNAL OF DENTAL SCIENCE – London, Oxford House. v2 1858-1859; v3 n37-54 1859-1860; v5 n67-68 1862; v25 n335-358 1882; v26 n359-382 1883 – us Res Libr [617]
BRITISH JOURNAL OF DEVELOPMENTAL PSYCHOLOGY – London. v1-8. 1983-90 – 5,9 – Dfl1,120.00; Dfl140.00v – ne Swets [150]
BRITISH JOURNAL OF EDUCATIONAL PSYCHOLOGY – Glasgow. v21-29, 31-47. 1951-77 – 5,9 – Dfl1,820.00; Dfl70.00v – ne Swets [370]
BRITISH JOURNAL OF EDUCATIONAL STUDIES – (1971-72. 16.00; 9) – 1953-70 – 1 – uk Microform Academic [073]
BRITISH JOURNAL OF EDUCATIONAL STUDIES – (v.25-. 1977- 5,6,9) – v21- . 1973- – 1 – us UMI [073]
THE BRITISH JOURNAL OF EXPERIMENTAL BIOLOGY – v1-6. 1923-29 – 1 – us UMI [574]
BRITISH JOURNAL OF EXPERIMENTAL PATHOLOGY – v1-36. 1920-55 – 1,5,6 – us Princeton Micro [610]
BRITISH JOURNAL OF GUIDANCE AND COUNSELLING – 1995, Vol 23 – £106.00 – uk Carfax [370]
BRITISH JOURNAL OF HAEMATOLOGY – v.1-31, 1955-75 – 1,5,6 – 22240.00 – us Princeton Micro [610]
BRITISH JOURNAL OF INEBRIETY – (Alcoholism and Drug Addiction). v1-43. 1903-46 – 1 – us UMI [073]
BRITISH JOURNAL OF LAW AND SOCIETY *see* JOURNAL OF LAW AND SOCIETY
BRITISH JOURNAL OF MATHEMATICAL AND STATISTICAL PSYCHOLOGY – London. v1-43. 1947-90 – 5,9 – Dfl3,870.00; Dfl90.00v – ne Swets [150]
BRITISH JOURNAL OF MEDICAL PSYCHOLOGY – London. v1-49. 1920-76 – 5,9 – Dfl3,430.00; Dfl70.00v – ne Swets [150]
BRITISH JOURNAL OF NEUROSURGERY – 1987- 7v – 9 – £213.50 – 0268-8697 – uk Carfax [617]
BRITISH JOURNAL OF NON-DESTRUCTIVE TESTING – (v.22-. 1980- 5,6,9) – v.1-. 1959- – 1 – us UMI [073]
BRITISH JOURNAL OF NUTRITION – (1985-. 5,6,9) – v1-. 1947- – 1 – us UMI [616]
BRITISH JOURNAL OF NUTRITION – (v1-34. Dfl80.00v; v35-44. Dfl130.00v) – London. v1-44. 1947-80 – 5,9 – Dfl4,020.00 – ne Swets [612]
BRITISH JOURNAL OF NUTRITION – v3-32 1949-74 – 1,5,6 – $22,180.00 – us Princeton Micro [612]
BRITISH JOURNAL OF OBSTETRICS AND GYNAECOLOGY – (1977- . 5,6,9) – v. 82-. 1975- – 1 – us UMI [618]
BRITISH JOURNAL OF ORAL AND MAXILLOFACIAL SURGERY – v22-. 1984- – 1,5,6,9 – us UMI [617]
BRITISH JOURNAL OF ORAL SURGERY – (1982-. 1,5,6,9) – v1-. 1963- – 1 – us UMI [617]
BRITISH JOURNAL OF ORTHODONTICS – (1982-. 1,5,6,9) – v1-. 1973- – 1 – us UMI [073]
BRITISH JOURNAL OF PHARMACOLOGY – (1965- . 5,6. 1975- . 9) – 1946- – 1 – us UMI [615]
BRITISH JOURNAL OF PHOTOGRAPHY – (Yrly reel count varies) – 1854- – 1 – inquire – us Ross [770]
THE BRITISH JOURNAL OF PHOTOGRAPHY – 1854-1993. Continued annually – 1 – £4,395.00 – uk World [700]

THE BRITISH JOURNAL OF PHOTOGRAPHY ANNUAL – 1860-1993. Continued annually. Continues: The British Journal Photographic Almanac – 1 – £2,500.00 – uk World [700]

BRITISH JOURNAL OF PLASTIC SURGERY – 1948-55 – 7 – uk Microform Academic [617]

BRITISH JOURNAL OF PLASTIC SURGERY – (1982-. 1,5,6,9) – v1-. 1948- – 1 – us UMI [617]

BRITISH JOURNAL OF POLITICAL SCIENCE – (1976- . 5,6,9) – v. 1-. 1971- – 1 – us UMI [320]

BRITISH JOURNAL OF PSYCHOLOGY – 1904-83 – 7, 9 – uk Microform Academic [073]

BRITISH JOURNAL OF PSYCHOLOGY – (v1-70. Dfl90.00v; v71-73. Dfl130.00v; v74-81. Dfl170.00v) – London. v1-81 with gen'l index, v1-20. 1904-90 – 5,9 – Dfl8,050.00 – ne Swets [150]

BRITISH JOURNAL OF RELIGIOUS EDUCATION – v. 1-. 1978- – 1,5,6,9 – us UMI [240]

BRITISH JOURNAL OF RHEUMATOLOGY – v22-. 1983- – 1,5,6,9 – us UMI [073]

BRITISH JOURNAL OF SOCIAL AND CLINICAL PSYCHOLOGY – London. v1-19. 1962-80. Continued by: British Journal of Clinical Psychology. British Journal of Social Psychology – 5,9 – Dfl1,520.00; Dfl80.00v – ne Swets [150]

BRITISH JOURNAL OF SOCIAL PSYCHOLOGY – (v20-27. Dfl110.00v; v28-29. Dfl140.00v) – London. v20-29. 1981-90. Continues: British Journal of Social and Clinical Psychology – 5,9 – Dfl1,160.00 – ne Swets [150]

BRITISH JOURNAL OF SOCIAL WORK – (v5- . 1975- . 5,6,9) – v. 1-. 1971- – 1 – us UMI [360]

BRITISH JOURNAL OF SOCIOLOGY – 1950-1993. Continued annually – £595.00 – uk World [301]

BRITISH JOURNAL OF SOCIOLOGY OF EDUCATION – 1980- 14v – 9 – £230.00 – 0142-5692 – uk Carfax [370]

BRITISH JOURNAL OF SURGERY – (1965- . 5,6. 1975- . 9) – 1- 1913- – 1 – us UMI [617]

BRITISH JOURNAL OF VENEREAL DISEASES – (v42-60. Mar 1966-Dec 1984. 5,6. v52-60. Feb 1976-Dec 1984. 9) – v40-60. Mar 1964-Dec 1984 – 1 – us UMI [616]

BRITISH JOURNAL ON ALCOHOL AND ALCOHOLISM *see* ALCOHOL AND ALCOHOLISM

BRITISH JUNGERMANNIAE: BEING A HISTORY AND DESCRIPTION WITH COLOURED FIGURES OF EACH SPECIES OF THE GENUS / Hooker, W J – London. 1816. B-5961 2 – 8 – ne IDC [580]

BRITISH KINEMATOGRAPHY, SOUND AND TELEVISION – 1938-73 – 1 – us UMI [073]

BRITISH KNITTING INDUSTRY – v1-48 1929-75 – 1 – us UMI [680]

BRITISH LABOUR HISTORY EPHEMERA – (1880-1900. With printed index. £1,850.00; 1. 1900-26. With printed index. £900.00; WMP; 1) – 1790-1880 – 1 – uk World [331]

BRITISH LABOUR STATISTICS : HISTORICAL ABSTRACT 1886-1968 – (Coll title: British Government Publications...1801-1977, Labour) – 5mf – 9 (£345.00 labour set of 41mf) – uk Chadwyck [331]

BRITISH LABOUR STATISTICS : YEARBOOK 1969-1976 – (Coll title: British Government Publications...1801-1977, Labour) – 36mf – 9 (£345.00 labour set of 41mf) – uk Chadwyck [331]

BRITISH LABOURERS' PROTECTOR AND FACTORY CHILD'S FRIEND – Nos. 1-31 (all publ). 1832-1833 – 3mf – 9 – $55.00 – us UPA [335]

BRITISH LABOUR'S RISE TO POWER / Brand, Carl F – 1941 – 1 – 35.00r – us Hoover Inst Photo [941]

THE BRITISH LANGUAGE IN ITS LUSTRE, OR A COPIOUS DICTIONARY OF WELSH AND ENGLISH / Jones, Thomas – 1688. 352p. (English Linguistics Series 15001-800) – 9 – us UMI [490]

British Library *see*
- THE BRITISH LIBRARY GENERAL CATALOGUE OF PRINTED BOOKS
- BRITISH UNION CATALOGUE OF ORCHESTRAL SETS: 2ND ED
- CALENDARS OF CHARTERS AND ROLLS IN THE MANUCRIPT COLLECTIONS OF THE BRITISH LIBRARY
- COBDEN PAPERS
- HUSKISSON PAPERS
- LINGUISTICS SPECIALIST COLLECTION
- MICROFICHE EDITION OF THE SHEL DKAR MANUSCRIPT BKA'GYUR
- NINETEENTH CENTURY BOOKS ON CHINA
- THE NINETEENTH CENTURY GENERAL COLLECTION
- THE NINETEENTH CENTURY LITERATURE SPECIALIST COLLECTION
- THE SAMAS RELIGIOUS TEXTS
- SCICAT
- SERIALS IN THE BRITISH LIBRARY
- STEVENS TRANSCRIPTS

British Library. Document Supply Centre *see*
- BOOKS AT BOSTON SPA
- INDEX OF CONFERENCE PROCEEDINGS RECEIVED, 1964-1988
- KEYWORD INDEX TO SERIAL TITLES (KIST)

THE BRITISH LIBRARY GENERAL CATALOGUE OF PRINTED BOOKS : 1976-1982 ON MICROFICHE VOLS 1 AND 2 / British Library – London, 1982 – 9 – £400.00 – uk British Libr Humanities [020]

THE BRITISH LIBRARY GENERAL CATALOGUE OF PRINTED BOOKS : SUPPLEMENT 1990-1992 ON MICROFICHE / British Library – London, Sept 1993 – 160mf – 9 – £350.00 – uk British Libr Humanities [020]

British Library. Harleian Collection *see* TUDOR AND STUART MANUSCRIPTS

British Library. Humanities and Social Sciences *see*
- EIGHTEENTH CENTURY SHORT TITLE CATALOGUE
- SERIALS IN THE BRITISH LIBRARY 1976-86
- UK PATENTS FOR INVENTION

British Library. National Bibliographic Service *see*
- BOOKS IN ENGLISH
- BRITISH NATIONAL BIBLIOGRAPHY
- FICTION ON FICHE
- NAME AUTHORITY LIST
- SERIALS IN THE BRITISH LIBRARY

British Library of Political and Economic Sciences *see* BRITISH BIRTH CONTROL MATERIAL AT THE B.L.P.E.S

British Library. Oriental and Indian Office Collections *see* ARCHAEOLOGICAL SURVEY OF INDIA PHOTOGRAPHS

BRITISH LION – London, UK. 3 Apr-12 Jun 1825; 29 Jun 1867; 9 May-11 Jul 1868. -w. 23 feet – 1 – uk British Libr Newspaper [072]

BRITISH LITERARY MANUSCRIPTS FROM CAMBRIDGE UNIVERSITY LIBRARY, SERIES 1 – (Part 2: Medieval Mss. from Mss. Gg-Ii. Part 3: Medieval Mss. from Mss. Kk-Oo and additional) – The Medieval Age, c1150-c1500. Part 1: Medieval Mss. from Mss. Dd-Ff – 1 – us Primary [090]

BRITISH LITERARY MANUSCRIPTS FROM CAMBRIDGE UNIVERSITY LIBRARY, SERIES 2 – (Part 1: Manuscripts from the Double-letter series. Part 2: Manuscripts from the Additional series, including the Sir Geoffrey Keynes Collection) – The English Renaissance, c1500-c1700 – 1 – us Primary [090]

BRITISH LITERARY MANUSCRIPTS FROM PRINCETON UNIVERSITY – (Part 1: The William Cowper Papers And Other Eighteenth Century Literary Manuscripts) – 1 – us Primary [090]

BRITISH LITERARY MANUSCRIPTS FROM THE BODLEIAN LIBRARY, OXFORD, SERIES 1 – (Part 1: Rawlinson Poetry Manuscripts; Part 2: English Poetry, English Miscellaneous and English Theology Manuscripts; Part 3: Additional, Ashmole, Aubrey, Bodleian, Cherry, Clarendon, Don, Douce, Fairfax and Firth Collections) – The English Renaissance, c1500-c1700 – 1 – us Primary [090]

BRITISH LITERARY MANUSCRIPTS FROM THE BRITISH LIBRARY, LONDON, SERIES 1 – The English Renaissance: Literature from the Tudor Period to the Restoration, c1500-c1700. Parts 1-6 – 1 – us Primary [090]

BRITISH LITERARY MANUSCRIPTS FROM THE BRITISH LIBRARY, LONDON, SERIES 2 – The Eighteenth Century, c1700-c1800. Parts 1-3 – 1 – us Primary [090]

BRITISH LITERARY MANUSCRIPTS FROM THE BRITISH LIBRARY, LONDON, SERIES 3 – The Medieval Age, c1150-c1500. Parts 1-2 – 1 – us Primary [090]

BRITISH LITERARY MANUSCRIPTS FROM THE FOLGER SHAKESPEARE LIBRARY, WASHINGTON, DC – (Part One: Folger MSS Ccl-Va 358. Part Two: Folger MSS Va 363-Bd.w. 131) – The English Renaissance: Literature from the Tudor Period to the Restoration, c1500-c1700 – 1 – us Primary [090]

BRITISH LITERARY MANUSCRIPTS FROM THE NATIONAL LIBRARY OF SCOTLAND – (Part Two: 18th cent. Literary MSS., c1700-c1800. Part Three: 19th cent. MSS., c1800-c1880, Section A. Part Four: 19th cent. MSS., c1800-c1880, Section B) – Part One: Medieval and Renaissance Literature, c1300-c1700 – 1 – us Primary [090]

BRITISH LUMINARY AND WEEKLY INTELLIGENCER – London, UK. 3 Oct 1818-30 Dec 1821. -w – 1 – uk British Libr Newspaper [072]

BRITISH MARINE CONCHOLOGY / Thorpe, C – Z 836 2. 1844 – 8 – ne IDC [590]

BRITISH MASTERS OF THE ALBUMEN PRINT : A SELECTION OF MID-NINETEENTH CENTURY VICTORIAN PHOTOGRAPHY / International Museum of Photography at George Eastman House; ed by Sobieszek, Robert A – 1976 – 3 color mf – 15 – $42.00f – 0-226-69171-3 – us Chicago [770]

British Medical Association. Joint Committee on Psychiatry and the Law *see* THE CRIMINAL LAW AND SEXUAL OFFENDERS; A REPORT

BRITISH MEDICAL JOURNAL – 1872-1955 – 1,5,6 – us Princeton Micro [610]

BRITISH MEDICAL JOURNAL – (1966- . 5,6. 1977- . 9) – 1857- – 1 – us UMI [616]

BRITISH MINER AND GENERAL NEWSMAN – (The Miner, The Miner and Workman's Advocate, The Workman's Advocate, The Commonwealth) – London, 13 Sep 1862-20 Jul 1867 – 4r – 1 – uk British Libr Newspaper [331]

BRITISH MONITOR – (English Gentleman: 1826-13 Jan 1828) – London, UK. 1818-13 Jan 1828 – 5r – 1 – uk British Libr Newspaper [072]

BRITISH MONUMENTAL INSCRIPTIONS – 1 – uk Microform Academic [410]

BRITISH MORNING NEWS – Vienna, Austria. Morning News. -d. 3, 7 Feb 1946; 22, 28 Jan 1947-19 June 1949. 4 reels – 1 – uk British Libr Newspaper [072]

THE BRITISH MOSSFLORA / Braithwaite, R – 3v. London. 1887-1905. B-6199 1 – 9 – ne IDC [580]

British Museum *see*
- EGERTON MANUSCRIPTS: PAPERS RELATING TO THE ENGLISH COLONIES IN AMERICA AND THE WEST INDIES, 1627-1699
- FROM MANET TO TOULOUSE-LAUTREC
- INDEX-CATALOGUE OF INDIAN OFFICIAL PUBLICATIONS IN THE LIBRARY OF THE BRITISH MUSEUM
- JAPANESE WOOD-BLOCK PRINTS IN THE BRITISH MUSEUM
- MATERIALS ON THE EARLY EDUCATIONAL LIFE OF THE ENGLISH BAPTISTS
- PALMERSTON PAPERS AMERICAN CORRESPONDENCE, 1835-41 AND 1846-50. ADD MSS 48495, 48575. BRRAM
- SPORTING PRINTS

BRITISH MUSEUM COLLECTIONS OF NATURAL HISTORY SPECIMENS AND DRAWINGS FROM THE "ENDEAVOUR" VOYAGE OF CAPTAIN COOK, 1768-1771 / British Museum (Natural History) – (Includes catalogues £70.00 ea) – 3pts 38 colour and 18 b/w mf – 15,9 – £1,435.00 – uk Chadwyck [574]

British Museum. Department of Prints and Drawings *see*
- THE CRACE COLLECTION OF LONDON VIEWS IN THE BRITISH MUSEUM
- HISTORICAL PRINTS IN THE BRITISH MUSEUM
- THE TURNER BEQUEST

BRITISH MUSEUM ENTOMOLOGICAL LITERATURE, 1800-1864 / British Museum (Natural History); ed by Gilbert, Pamela – (Guide included £42.00) – 6,003mf – 9 – £21,940.00 – uk Chadwyck [590]

British Museum. London *see*
- BOOK PLATES IN THE BRITISH MUSEUM
- COSTUME PRINTS IN THE BRITISH MUSEUM
- THE NATIONAL PHOTOGRAPHIC RECORD AND SURVEY
- TRADE CARDS IN THE BRITISH MUSEUM

British Museum (Natural History) *see*
- BRITISH MUSEUM COLLECTIONS OF NATURAL HISTORY SPECIMENS AND DRAWINGS FROM THE "ENDEAVOUR" VOYAGE OF CAPTAIN COOK, 1768-1771
- BRITISH MUSEUM ENTOMOLOGICAL LITERATURE, 1800-1864
- EARLY AMERICAN HERBARIA AND RELATED DRAWINGS

BRITISH NATIONAL BIBLIOGRAPHY / British Library. National Bibliographic Service – (1950-84 cumulation. £475.00 + VAT, £520.00 overseas; 1981-85 full cumulation. £275.00 + VAT, £350.00 overseas) – 1993-. Annual volume – 17 – £155.00y + VAT, £199.00y overseas – uk British Libr [010]

BRITISH NATIONAL FILM CATALOGUE – 1963-85.Continued annually – 1 – £320.00 – uk World [790]

BRITISH NAVAL OPERATIONS DURING WORLD WAR 1 PAMPHLET COLLECTION – 1915-1926 – 2r – 1 – CSUXANL2780-B – us Hoover Inst Photo [355]

THE BRITISH NAVY: ITS STRENGTH, RESOURCES AND ADMINISTRATION / Brassey, Thomas – 5v. 1882-83 – 9 – $180.00 – uk Libr Preservation [941]

BRITISH NEW GUINEA DEATHS 1888-1906 : LAND OWNERS PAPUA NEW GUINEA 1891-1906 – 1mf – 9 – A$4.00 – 0-949124-18-4 – item 6 – at G.S.N.T. [920]

THE BRITISH NEWS OF CANADA – Montreal, Toronto, London. 21 jan 1911 – 1r – 1 – Can$25.00 – cn Can Microfilming [072]

BRITISH NEWS OF CANADA. (CANADIAN & BRITISH NEWS OF CANADA.-THE CANADIAN) – Montreal, Canada. Jan 1912-Mar 1914.-w. 2 reels – 1 – uk British Libr Newspaper [072]

BRITISH NEWSREELS ISSUE SHEETS 1913-1970 ON MICROFICHE – 1984 – 275mf – 9 – £245.00 set – uk British Univ Film [941]

THE BRITISH NORTH AMERICA ACT, 1867, MADE EASY: INTENDED AS AN EASY COACH FOR CIVIL SERVICE CANDIDATES – Ottawa: Citizen Print. and Pub. Co., 1883. 00304. (Pre-1900 Canadiana) – 9 – cn C.I.H.M. [971]

BRITISH NORTH AMERICA: COPIES OR EXTRACTS OF CORRESPONDENCE RELATIVE TO THE AFFAIRS OF BRITISH NORTH AMERICA – s.l. House of Commons, 1839. SEM105P111 – 5mf – 9 – Can$11.25 – cn Bibl Nat [971]

BRITISH NORTH AMERICA: REPORTS OF PROGRESS TOGETHER WITH A PRELIMINARY AND GENERAL REPORT, ON THE ASSINNIBOINE AND SASKATCHEWAN EXPLORING EXPEDITION / Hind, Henry Youle – London: George Edward Eyre and William Spottiswoode, 1860. SEM105P285 – 3mf – 9 – Can$6.75 – cn Bibl Nat [910]

THE BRITISH NORTH AMERICAN – Quebec, 10 may 1841; v1 n4. 17 may – 1 – Can$25.00 – cn Can Microfilming [072]

THE BRITISH NORTH AMERICAN MAGAZINE AND COLONIAL JOURNAL – [Halifax, N.S.?: s.n., 1831-183-?]; (Halifax, N.S.: E Ward) – 9 – cn C.I.H.M. [971]

BRITISH NOVELISTS AND THEIR STYLES : BEING A CRITICAL SKETCH OF THE HISTORY OF BRITISH PROSE FICTION / Masson, David – Cambridge: Macmillan, 1859 – 1 roll – 1 – 1-55879-897-8 – uk Libr Preservation [420]

BRITISH NUCLIBRANCHIATE MOLLUSCA / Alder, J & Hancock, A – 1845-52 and 1910. Ray Society – 7 – uk Microform Academic [590]

BRITISH OFFICIAL GAZETTE / British Guiana – Georgetown. 1952-May 21, 1966. For later file See: Guyana. Official gazette – 1 – us NY Public [324]

BRITISH OFFICIAL PUBLICATIONS NOT PUBLISHED BY HMSO DOCUMENT DELIVERY SERVICE – (Also available by sections. Major Coll: Science and Technology 1111mf £1,300; Social Sciences 1473mf £7,485. Subject Coll: Annual Reports 151mf £250; Local Government 61mf £160; Background Briefs and Foreign Policy Documents £40; Agriculture, Forestry, Fisheries 444mf £293; Environment £797; Education 256mf £1,083; Employment and Working Conditions 259mf £299; Food 20mf £96; Health and Medicine 308mf £1,362; Health and Safety £382; Library Information Science and Bibliographies 114mf £110; Local Government £160; Scotland 19mf £465; Transport 96mf £107) – 1980 – 2 major coll + 13 subject coll – 9 – £6,360.00 coll – uk Chadwyck [324]

British Ordnance Survey *see*
- KENT STREET MAPS
- MAPS FROM THE UNITED KINGDOM
- ORDNANCE SURVEY MAPS: LANDRANGER SERIES
- SURREY STREET MAPS

BRITISH ORIBATIDAE / Michael, A D – 1884 and 1888 – 1,7 – uk Microform Academic [580]

BRITISH ORNITHOLOGY / Hunt, J – Incomplete. Z-1807 2. 3 v. 1815-1822 – 8 – ne IDC [590]

BRITISH ORNITHOLOGY: BEING THE HISTORY OF EVERY KNOWN SPECIES OF BRITISH BIRDS / Graves, G – Z-1783. 3 v. Ed. 2. 1821 – 9 – ne IDC [590]

British Overseas Airways Corporation *see* ANNUAL REPORT AND STATEMENT OF ACCOUNTS

BRITISH PAINTINGS 1500 TO 1850 – (Over 20,000 reproductions, 2,000 artists) – 235mf – $1,180.00 – 1-900853-85-X – uk Mindata [750]

BRITISH PAMPHLETS RELATING TO THE AMERICAN REVOLUTION – BRRAM – 1 – uk Microform Academic [975]

THE BRITISH PARASITIC COPEPODA / Scott, Thomas Lucas & Scott, Andrew – Ray Society. 1913 – 1 – uk Microform Academic [590]

BRITISH PERIODICALS IN THE CREATIVE ARTS (EBP 3), 1770-1930 – (Reproduces 71 periodicals. AACR1 cataloging available) – 244r (6 units) – 1 – $14,490.00 – us UMI [410]

BRITISH PLANNING HISTORY, 1900-1952 / ed by Simpson, Michael et al – Printed and archival records of the National Housing and Town Planning Council, The Town and Country Planning Association and the Royal Town Planning Institute – 38r – 1 – £35.00r – uk Altair [710]

BRITISH POETS – Riverside ed. Boston. 122 v. (lacks v. 14-17, 26, 61) – 1 – 388.00 – us L of C Photodup [810]

BRITISH POLICY IN ASIA: INDIA OFFICE MEMORANDA / Great Britain. India Office. Political and Secret Department; ed by Tuson, Penelope & Farrington, Anthony – (v2: Tibet, Burma and Indo-China, 1862-1940. 24 fiches. Printed booklet.) – 1856-1947. Full texts with editorial notes. 1980. v1: The Middle East, 1856-1947. 39 fiches. Printed booklet. – 9 – IrL£220.00 set; v1 IrL£130.00; v2 IrL£90.00 – uk Mansell Publ [324]

BRITISH POLICY IN RELATION TO THE GOLD COAST 1815-1850 / James, Philip Gilbert – [London 1935] – us Res Libr [320]

BRITISH POLICY IN THE SUDAN 1882-1902 / Shibikah, Makki – London, New York, Oxford University Press, 1952 – us Res Libr [320]

BRITISH POLITICAL AND SOCIAL CARTOONS / U.S. Library of Congress. Prints and Photographs Division – 2200 prints from 1650-1832. 4 reels. P&P12022 – 1 – 23.00r – us L of C Photodup [941]

BRITISH POLITICAL PARTY GENERAL ELECTION ADDRESSES – (Part 1: General Election Addresses, 1892-1922. Part 2: General Election Addresses, 1923-31) – The National Liberal Club Collection from Bristol University – 1 – us Primary [941]

BRITISH POLITICS AND GOVERNMENT, 1901 TO 1936, PAMPHLET COLLECTION – 1901-1934 – 1 – CSUXANP3021-B – us Hoover Inst Photo [320]

BRITISH POLITICS AND GOVERNMENT, 1936 TO 1945, PAMPHLET COLLECTION – 1939-1944 – 1 – CSUXANP3034-B – us Hoover Inst Photo [320]

BRITISH POLITICS AND GOVERNMENT, 1945 TO 1964, PAMPHLET COLLECTION – 1945-1964 – 2r – 1 – CSUXANP3040-B – us Hoover Inst Photo [320]

BRITISH POLITICS AND GOVERNMENT, 1964 TO THE PRESENT, PAMPHLET COLLECTION – 1965-1986 – 1 – CSUXANP3048-B – us Hoover Inst Photo [320]

BRITISH POSTERS 1851-1988 : IN THE VICTORIA AND ALBERT MUSEUM NATIONAL POSTER COLLECTION – (Printed index and list of sources) – 1990 – 48mf – 9 – $1,150.00 – uk Hall [760]

BRITISH POSTERS TO 1988 / Victoria and Albert Museum. London – (Over 100yrs of advertising design – from 'Bubbles' to Saatchi & Saatchi – are documented in this visual catalogue) – 47mf – 15 – $988.00 – 1-869934-16-4 – uk Emmett [760]

BRITISH POULTRY SCIENCE – 1960- 34v – 9 – £139.00 – 0007-1668 – uk Carfax [636]

BRITISH PRESS & JERSEY TIMES – St. Helier, England. -w. 1870-75. 12 reels – 1 – uk British Libr Newspaper [072]

BRITISH PRESS OR MORNING LITERARY ADVERTISER – London, UK. 26 Jan-7 Jul 1803; May 1804-1811; May 1812; 8 Jul, 5, 10, 20 Sept 1814; 11-27 May 1816; 25 Dec 1817-31 Oct 1826.-d. 32 reels – 1 – uk British Libr Newspaper [072]

BRITISH PRINTER – 1939-62 – 1 – uk Microform Academic [073]

BRITISH PROPAGANDA DURING WORLD WAR 1 PAMPHLET COLLECTION – 1915-1917 – 2r – 1 – CSUXANL9098-B – us Hoover Inst Photo [303]

THE BRITISH PROTECTORATES AND THE UNION OF SOUTH AFRICA 1930-1950 / Thayer, Ralph Noyes – Madison, 1951 – us Res Libr [320]

BRITISH PROVINCIAL NEWSPAPERS – Bedfordshire, Berkshire, Cambridgeshire, Cheshire, Cumberland, County Durham, Dorset, Essex, Glamorgan, Hampshire, Herefordshire, Huntingdonshire, Kent, Lancashire, Lincolnshire, Norfolk, Northamptonshire, Nottinghamshire, Shropshire, Somerset, Staffordshire, Suffolk, Surrey, Sussex, Warwickshire, Worcestershire, Yorkshire and others – 1 – uk Microform Academic [072]

BRITISH QUARTERLY TRADE REVIEW – London, UK. 1886-95. -q. 2 1/2 reels – 1 – uk British Libr Newspaper [072]

BRITISH RARE MILITANT 19TH CENTURY FREETHOUGHT BOOKS COLLECTION – 1 – £595.00 – uk World [210]

British Record Society Ltd *see* INDEX LIBRARY

BRITISH RECORDS RELATING TO AMERICA IN MICROFORM – Series: Theses relating to American history – 1 – uk Microform Academic [970]

BRITISH REGIONAL CHURCH CARVING (1600-1640) AND FURNITURE (1600-1800) / Museum of Early Southern Decorative Arts; ed by Rauschenberg, L – Bradford – 58mf – 9 – $63.00 – us MESDA [720]

British Rheumatism and Arthritis Association *see* BRA REVIEW

BRITISH RULING CASES / Great Britain. Courts – 1900-31.6 reels – 1 – $300.00 – us Trans-Media [340]

BRITISH SALMONIDAE / Jardine, W – Z-2116 2. Pt. 1-2. 1839-1841 – 9 – ne IDC [580]

BRITISH SCHOOL : PAINTINGS AND WATERCOLOURS / Christie's Pictorial Archive. London – 170mf – 9 – $925.00 – 0-907006-02-7 – uk Mindata [750]

BRITISH SEAFARER – Southampton, England. -m. Jan 1913-Jan 1922. Imperfect. 2 reels – 1 – uk British Libr Newspaper [072]

BRITISH SOCIALIST : A MONTHLY SOCIALIST REVIEW – v1-2 (all publ). 1912-1913 – 1 reel – 1 – $65.00 – us UPA [335]

BRITISH SOCIETY OF FRANCISCAN STUDIES – Aberdeniae, 1908-20. v 1-9 – 34mf – 8 – ne IDC [240]

British Solomon Islands *see* FIFTH DEVELOPMENT PLAN, 1968-1970

British Solomon Islands Protectorate *see* NEWS SHEET, 1955-1965

BRITISH SOMALILAND AND ITS TRIBES – [n.p.] Military Govt of British Somaliland, 1945 – 1 – us Res Libr [960]

THE BRITISH SPECIES OF ANGIOCARPUS LICHENS ELUCIDATED BY THEIR SPORIDIA / Leighton, W A – Ray Society. 1851 – 1. 16.00; ; 7 – uk Microform Academic [580]

BRITISH SPIDERS / Staveley, E F – Z 2195 2. 1866 – 8 – ne IDC [590]

BRITISH STANDARDS (BSI) MICROFILE – 1970. Microfilm 12 sections; microfiche 35 sections; updated monthly – 5,9 – uk Tech [380]

BRITISH STATESMAN – London. -w. 13 Mar 1842-21 Jan 1843. (1 reel) – 1 – uk British Libr Newspaper [072]

BRITISH STATISTICAL BLUE BOOKS – 14 titles – 9 – ne IDC [304]

BRITISH STEELMAKER – 1935-58 – 1 – uk Microform Academic [670]

BRITISH SYNONYMY / Piozzi, Hester Lynch – 1794. 2v. (English Linguistics Series 1500-1800) – 9 – us UMI [420]

BRITISH TRADE AND POLICY IN INDONESIA AND MALAYSIA IN THE LATE EIGHTEENTH CENTURY / Bassett, D K – SE-663 1. 1971 – 9 – ne IDC [380]

BRITISH TRADE UNION HISTORY COLLECTION – With printed index – 5,9 – £1,500.00r; £1,800.00mf – uk World [331]

British Trades Union Congress *see* ARCHIVES OF THE BRITISH TRADES UNION CONGRESS

BRITISH TRANSPORT COMMISSION: ANNUAL REPORT... *see* GOVERNMENT CONTROL OF RAILWAYS; ESTIMATES OF THE POOLED REVENUE, RECEIPTS AND EXPENSES AND RESULTANT NET REVENUE 1939/40-1947

BRITISH TRAVELLER – London, UK. 9 Jul-31 Dec 1821; 1823-25 May 1833. -d. 27 reels – 1 – uk British Libr Newspaper [072]

THE BRITISH TREASURY, ECONOMIC DEPRESSION, AND INTERNATIONAL FINANCE / Great Britain. Public Record Office – (Part 1: International Finance Situation and Policy, 1916-43. Part 2: Domestic, Monetary and Unemployment Policy, 1919-43, including deputations to the Chancellor of the Exchequer, 1919-41) – 1916-43. Complete files selected from PRO Treasury Class T172 – 1 – us Primary [336]

THE BRITISH TREATIES OF 1871 & 1874: LETTERS TO THE PRESIDENT OF THE UNITED STATES / Carey, Henry Charles – Philadelphia: Collins, 1874. 02066. (Pre-1900 Canadiana) – 9 – cn C.I.H.M. [971]

BRITISH TRIALS, 1660-1900 – (Available seperately for £3,035.00 per unit. Includes index and printed title listing) – Units 1-4 available – ca 800mf per y for 6 years – 9 – £2,755.00 per unit standing order – uk Chadwyck [340]

BRITISH UNDERWRITER AND INSURANCE ADVOCATE – London, UK. Oct 1906. -irr. 7 feet – 1 – uk British Libr Newspaper [072]

BRITISH UNION CATALOGUE OF LATIN AMERICANA (BUCLA) MAINTAINED AT THE INSTITUTE OF LATIN AMERICAN STUDIES, LONDON : SECTION 1: BRITISH HOLDINGS CATALOGUE – (Includes printed guide) – Zug, 1987 – 9 – LA-2/1 – ne IDC [020]

BRITISH UNION CATALOGUE OF LATIN AMERICANA (BUCLA) MAINTAINED AT THE INSTITUTE OF LATIN AMERICAN STUDIES, LONDON : SECTION 2: LIBRARY OF CONGRESS HOLDINGS CATALOGUE – (Includes printed guide) – Zug, 1987 – 123mf – 9 – LA-3/1 – ne IDC [020]

BRITISH UNION CATALOGUE OF ORCHESTRAL SETS: 2ND ED / British Library – 1988 – 9 – £15.00 in UK £19.00 overseas – uk British Libr Humanities [010]

BRITISH VETERINARY JOURNAL (LONDON) – v112-131. 1956-75. Continues: Veterinary Journal and Annals of Comparative Pathology – 1,5,6 – us Princeton Micro [636]

BRITISH VIRGIN ISLANDS : STATISTICAL ABSTRACT NUMBER 1 1974 / British Virgin Islands. Statistics Office – (Coll title: Latin American and Caribbean Official Statistical Serials, 1821-1982) – 2mf – 9 – £17.00 – uk Chadwyck [972]

British Virgin Islands. Administrator's Office *see* REVISED DEVELOPMENT PLAN, 1964-1966

British Virgin Islands. Education Department *see* REPORT FOR THE YEAR 1973-1977

British Virgin Islands. Statistics Office *see* BRITISH VIRGIN ISLANDS

BRITISH VOGUE 1916-1939 – (Available in 4 sections. 1916-23 366mf $1,570.00 ISBN: 0-907006-04-3. 1924-29 316mf $1,355.00 ISBN: 0-907006-09-4. 1930-34 332mf $1,420.00 ISBN: 0-907006-14-0. 1935-39 368mf $1,575.00 ISBN: 0-907006-19-1) – 1382mf – 9 – $5,400.00 set – 0-907006-24-8 – uk Mindata [390]

BRITISH WAR OFFICE : AMERICAN REVOLUTION, 1773-1783 – 1r – 1 – $85.00 – S1291 – us Scholarly Res [941]

BRITISH WATERCOLOURS AND DRAWINGS TO 1850 – (Over 20,000 reproductions, 2,000 artists) – 217mf – $1,190.00 – 1-900853-90-6 – uk Mindata [700]

BRITISH WEEKLY – London, UK. 1903-1939 – 45r – $2,250.00 – R63602 – us Library Micro [072]

THE BRITISH WEEKLY : A JOURNAL OF SOCIAL AND CHRISTIAN PROGESS – (Lacking some pages) – v1-157. Nov 1886-1990 – 90r – 1 – ATLA S0052 – us A.T.L.A. [073]

THE BRITISH WORKER : OFFICIAL STRIKE NEWS BULLETIN – (Library wants: no. 6 (May 10, 1926)) – London: The General Council of the Trades Union Congress, 1926. 10 no – 1 – CSUX88-S372 – us Hoover Inst Photo [331]

BRITISH WORKMAN – London, England. -m. Feb 1855-Dec 1868. 1 reel – 1 – uk British Libr Newspaper [072]

BRITISH WORLD – London, UK. Nov 1906. -irr. 8 feet – 1 – uk British Libr Newspaper [072]

BRITISH YEARBOOK OF INTERNATIONAL LAW – v1-44. 1920-70 – 1,5,6 – $360.00 – us Hein [340]

THE BRITISH-AMERICAN – Philadelphia. 10 Dec 1887-Jul 1918 (imperfect).-w,m. 30 reels – 1 – uk British Libr Newspaper [071]

Brito, Lemos *see* A GLORIOSA SOTAINA DO PRIMEIRO IMPERIO

BRITON – London, UK. 1819. -irr. 4 feet – 1 – uk British Libr Newspaper [072]

Brittain, John *see* TEACHER'S MANUAL OF NATURE LESSONS FOR THE COMMON SCHOOLS

Britten, J *see* EUROPEAN FERNS

Britton, N L *see*
- AN ILLUSTRATED FLORA OF THE NORTHERN UNITED STATES, CANADA AND THE BRITISH POSSESSIONS
- MANUAL OF THE FLORA OF THE NORTHERN STATES AND CANADA
- NORTH-AMERICAN TREES

BRITYI CHELOVEK / Mariengof, A – Berlin. 1930. BR-1077 2 – 8 – ne IDC [460]

Britzelmayr, M *see* HYMENOMYCETEN AUS SUDBAYERN, 1879-1897

Briuk, D I *see* SLAVIANSKIE KNIGI KIRILLOVSKOI PECHATI 15-18 VV

BRIUSOV I BLOK / Gol'tsev, V A – Pechat' i revoliutsiia. no. 4. 1928. BR-3264 2 – 8 – ne IDC [460]

Briusov, Valerii I *see* OPIS' DOKUMENTAL'NYKH MATERIALOV LICHNOGO FONDA NO. 56

O BRIUSOVE / Mirskii, D S – 'Sovremennye Zapiski' no 22 1924. BR-3279 2 – 8 – ne IDC [460]

BRIVA ZEME – Riga, U.S.S.R. -d. 3 Jan 1938-27 April 1940. 28 reels – 1 – uk British Libr Newspaper [947]

BRIVA ZEME, LATVIA – Riga, 1919-40 – 46r – 1 – $3,000.00 – us Ross [072]

BRIVAIS STRELNIEKS – Riga, De 1917 a 1918 – 1 reel – 1 – Sfr120.00 – sz Infoprint [947]

BRIVAIS STRELNIEKS, LATVIA – Riga, 1917-18 – 1r – 1 – $75.00 – us Ross [072]

BRIVIBA – Paris/Stockholm, 1956-93 (incompl) – 1 – us Hoover Inst Photo [072]

Brix, Fritz *see* TILSIT-RAGNIT

BRIXTON FREE PRESS – London, UK. 29 Jul 1882-1902. -w. 11 reels – 1 – uk British Libr Newspaper [072]

Broad, C D *see* PERCEPTION, PHYSICS, AND REALITY

THE BROAD CHURCH : OR, WHAT IS COMING? / Haweis, Hugh Reginald – London: Sampson Low, Marston, Searle & Rivington, 1891 – 1mf – 9 – 0-8370-5005-7 – 1985-3005 – us A.T.L.A. [240]

BROAD OUTLINES OF THE FIVE-YEAR DEVELOPMENT PLAN, 1956-1960 / Indonesia. Biro Perantjang Negara – D-1331 1. 1958 – 9 – ne IDC [338]

BROAD OUTLINES OF THE NATIONAL OVERALL DEVELOPMENT PLAN, 1961-1969 / Indonesia. Dewan Perantjang Nasional – SE-4937 1. 1960? – 9 – ne IDC [338]

BROAD RIVER BAPTIST CHURCH. CHEROKEE COUNTY. GAFFNEY, SOUTH CAROLINA : CHURCH RECORDS – 1931, 1934-39, 1953-72 – 1 – 5.00 – us Baptist [240]

BROADAXE – Manistee, Mich. -w. 1886-91 – 1 – us UMI [071]

THE BROAD-AXE – Charlottetown, P E I: [s.n., 1871] – 9 – cn C.I.H.M. [971]

BROAD-AXE TRIBUNE – Eugene, OR. -w. 24 Dec 1894-28 Feb 1900. 1 roll – 1 – us U.O. Library [071]

Broadbent, E H *see* THE PILGRIM CHURCH

Broadbent, R J *see* A HISTORY OF PANTOMIME

BROADCASTER – Barmedman, Jan 13 1923-Dec 17 1924 – 9 – at Pascoe [072]

BROADCASTING – (1968- 5,6. 1975- 9) – 1-1935- – 1 – us UMI [073]

Broaddus, Andrew *see* THE EXTRA EXAMINED

Broadhead, J R *see* DOCUMENTS RELATING TO THE COLONIAL HISTORY OF THE STATE OF NEW YORK
Broadhurst, Cyrus Napoleon *see* PERSONAL WORK
BROADMEAD CHURCH: THE RECORDS *see* PUBLICATIONS
BROADMOUTH BAPTIST CHURCH. ABBEVILLE, SOUTH CAROLINA : CHURCH RECORDS – 1837-1966 – 1 – 53.82 – us Baptist [240]
BROADSIDE : A FEMINIST REVIEW – (1979/80-1984/85 Can$115.00) – Toronto. v1-10. 1979/80-1988/89 – 1 – Can$60.00y – cn Micromedia [305]
BROADSIDE, THE NATIONAL TOPICAL SONG MAGAZINE – 1962-87.Complete. 30 fiches. Printed guide – 9 – $145.00 – us UPA [780]
BROADSTAIRS AND ST PETER'S MAIL ETC – Ramsgate, England. 1912. -w. 1 reel – 1 – uk British Libr Newspaper [072]
Broadus, Andrew *see* THE DOVER SELECTION OF SPIRITUAL SONGS
Broadus, John A *see*
- ADDRESSES, ESSAYS, LECTURES
- BUECHER SAMUELIS
- IMMERSION ESSENTIAL TO CHRISTIAN BAPTISM
- LECTURES ON THE HISTORY OF PREACHING
- MATERIALS
- MEMOIR OF JAMES PETIGRU BOYCE, D.D., LL.D.

Broadus, John Albert *see* JESUS OF NAZARETH
BROADWATER NEWS – Broadwater, NE. -w. Aug. 1914; Feb. 1920-Jan. 1958 – 1 – us NE Hist [071]
BROADWATER'S BUCKINGHAMSHIRE ADVERTISER *see* BUCKINGHAMSHIRE AND ADJACENT COUNTIES ADVERTISER
BROADWAY BAPTIST CHURCH. LOUISVILLE, KENTUCKY : CHURCH RECORDS – 1878-1975 – 1 – 240.93 – us Baptist [240]
BROADWAY BAPTIST CHURCH. MEMPHIS, TENNESSEE : CHURCH RECORDS – 1944-63 – 1 – 42.30 – us Baptist [240]
BROADWAY BAPTIST CHURCH. WOMAN'S MISSIONARY SOCIETY. LOUISVILLE, KENTUCKY : CHURCH RECORDS – 1887-1966. Lacks 1896-1900. 5046p – 1 – 258.75 – us Baptist [240]
BROADWAY EDITOR – Burlingame, CA. 1944-47 – 1r – 1 – $50.00 – C02083 – us Library Micro [071]
THE BROADWOOD ARCHIVE : THE BUSINESS RECORDS OF JOHN BROADWOOD AND SONS, PIANO-MAKERS – 1794-1901. 95 reels with printed index – £4,250.00 – uk World [680]
Brobst, Flavius J *see* MAKE WAY FOR THE KING
Broca, G de *see* UN MANUSCRIT DEL LIBRE DEL CONSOLAT DE MAR...
Broca, Paul *see* SUR LA PRETENDUE DEGENERESCENCE DE LA POPULATION FRANCAISE
EL BROCENSE : CONFERENCIA...EN LA CASA DE SALAMANCA DE MADRID EL DIA 16 DE MAYO DE 1958 / Alamillo Salgado, Ildefonso – Madrid: summ.grag, 1958 – 1 – sp Bibl Santa Ana [946]
Broch, O *see* SLAVISCHE PHONETIK
Brochard, Andre Theodore *see*
- DE LA MORTALITE DES NOURRISSONS EN FRANCE: SPECIALEMENT DANS L'ARRONDISSEMENT DE NOGENT-LE-ROTROU
- LA VERITE SUR LES ENFANTS TROUVES

Brocher, C *see* ESTUDIO SOBRE LOS CONFLICTOS DE LAS LEGISLACIONES EN MATERIA DE DERECHO PENAL
Brocher, C A *see*
- COURS DE DROIT...
- NOUVEAU TRAITE...

Brochner, H *see* OM DET RELIGIOSE I DETS ENHED MED DET HUMANE
LA BROCHURE : NAPOLEON 1 ET NAPOLEON 3 ET L'OPINION – s.l.: s.n., s.d. SEM105P443 – 1mf – 9 – Can$2.25 – cn Bibl Nat [944]
LA BROCHURE POPULAIRE MENSUELLE – Dir. Ch. Rappoport. no. 1-24. Paris. 1934-35 – 1 – fr A.C.R.P.P. [073]
BROCK BUGLE – Brock, NE. -w. Dec. 1965- – 1 – us NE Hist [071]
BROCK BULLETIN – Brock, NE. -w. May 1898-Aug. 1898. Incomplete; Oct.1899-Dec. 1902; Aug. 1909-Jan. 1927; Mar. 1927-Mar. 1944 – 1 – us NE Hist [071]
BROCK CHAMPION – Brock, NE. -w. Nov.1895-Dec. 1897 – 1 – us NE Hist [071]
BROCK EDUCATION – St. Catharines, v1-4. 1991-94 – 9 – Can$20.00y – cn Micromedia [370]
Brock, Erich *see* DAS WELTBILD ERNST JUENGERS
Brock, Isaac *see* THE CHURCH OF ENGLAND: ITS CONTINUOUS ORGANIC LIFE, AND ITS CATHOLIC RESTORATION: A LECTURE DELIVERED BEFORE THE CHURCH OF ENGLAND INSTITUTE, HALIFAX, AND SUBSEQUENTLY IN MONTREAL AND SHERBROOKE, PROVINCE OF QUEBEC, AND IN WINDSOR, NOVA SCOTIA
Brock, M J *see* HISTORY OF PLACER AND NEVADA COUNTIES
Brock, Robert Kincaid *see* NEEDHAM LAW SCHOOL, 1821-1842, CUMBERLAND COUNTY, VIRGINIA
Brock, Stephan *see*
- CAROLINE VON WOLZOGENS "AGNES VON LILIEN" (1798)

Brock, Susan *see* SHAKESPEARIANA
Brockbank, J P *see* SHAKESPEARIANA
Brockelmann, C *see*
- ALTTURKESTANISCHE VOLKSPOESIE
- MAHMUD AL-KASA7GHARIS DARSTELLUNG DES TURKISCHEN VERBALBAUS
- SEMITISCHE SPRACHWISSENSCHAFT
- VOLKSKUNDLICHES AUS ALTTURKESTAN. IN: ASIA MAJOR

Brockenbrough, J W *see* BROCKENBROUGH'S REPORTS OF CASES IN THE FOURTH CIRCUIT, 1802-1833
BROCKENBROUGH'S REPORTS OF CASES IN THE FOURTH CIRCUIT, 1802-1833 / Brockenbrough, J W – (Sometimes known as: Chief Justice Marshall's Decisions) – Philadelphia: J Kay. v1-2. 1837 (all publ) – 13mf – 9 – $19.50 – LLMC 81-437 – us L.L.M.C. [340]
Brockhaus, Clemens Friedrich *see* NICOLAI CUSANI DE CONCILII UNIVERSALIS POTESTATE SENTENTIA EXPLICATUR
DAS BROCKHAUS CONVERSATIONS-LEXIKON 1796-1898 (AEL, ABT 1; 35) : MIKROFICHE EDITION DER ERSTEN 14 AUFLAGEN UND DER DAZUGEHOERIGEN SUPPLEMENTE – 1796-1898 (mf ed 1997) – 1400mf – 9 – DM18,900.00 – 3-89131-250-4 – gw Fischer [943]
BROCKHAUS' CONVERSATIONS-LEXIKON (AEL, ABT 1; 35.22) : ALLGEMEINE DEUTSCHE REAL-ENCYCLOPAEDIE – 13. Aufl. Leipzig. 16 Bde. 1882-87 (mf ed 1997) – 161mf – 9 – DM1,490.00 – 3-89131-271-7 – gw Fischer [943]
BROCKHAUS' CONVERSATIONS-LEXIKON (AEL, ABT 1; 35.23) : ALLGEMEINE DEUTSCHE REAL-ENCYKLOPAEDIE – Supplbd zur 13. Aufl. Leipzig. 1887 (mf ed 1997) – 11mf – 9 – DM150.00 – 3-89131-272-5 – gw Fischer [943]
BROCKHAUS' CONVERSATIONS-LEXIKON (AEL, ABT 1; 35.24) – 14. Aufl. Leipzig/Berlin/Wien. 16 Bde (Supplement: Bd 17, 1897). 1892-95 (mf ed 1997) – 191mf – 9 – DM1,790.00 – 3-89131-273-3 – gw Fischer [943]
BROCKKHAUS' CONVERSATIONS-LEXIKON (AEL, ABT 1; 35.25) : REVIDIERTE JUBILAEUMSAUSGABE – 14. Aufl. Leipzig/Berlin/Wien. 17 Bde. 1898 (mf ed 1997) – 191mf – 9 – DM1,790.00 – 3-89131-274-1 – gw Fischer [943]
BROCKLEY NEWS & HATCHAM & NEW CROSS REVIEW – London, UK. 3 May 1890-1931. -w. 30 1/2 reels – 1 – uk British Libr Newspaper [072]
Brockmeyer, Gretchen A *see*
- THE CONSTRUCT VALIDITY OF A SCALE TO MEASURE TEACHER ENTHUSIASM IN SECONDARY PHYSICAL EDUCATION
- GENDER DIFFERENCES IN OVERT COACHING BEHAVIORS OF HIGH SCHOOL SOCCER COACHES
- PERCEPTIONS OF THE IMPORTANCE AND ACHIEVEMENT OF STUDENT TEACHING OBJECTIVES
- PERCEPTIONS OF "UTILITY" AND "LIKEABILITY" DIMENSIONS OF A PHYSICAL EDUCATION FITNESS CURRICULUM

Brockport, New York. Brockport Baptist Church *see* RECORDS
BROCKTON 1795-1849 – (Mf 1T: Births 1795-1850. Mf 1T-2T: Publishments 1821-49. Mf 2T-3T: Marriages 1821-47. Mf 3T-6T: Births 1843-49. Mf 6T: Marriages 1843-49. Mf 6T-7T: Deaths 1843-49) – (mf ed 1995) – 7mf – 9 – 0-87623-218-7 – us Holbrook [920]
BROCKVILLE DAILY TIMES – Brockville, 1882-1907 – 5r – 1 – cn Preston [971]
BROCKVILLE GAZETTE – Brockville, Canada. 1828-32 – 1 reel – 1 – $68.00 – cn Library Assoc [971]
BROCKVILLE GAZETTE – Brockville, Ontario. 22 aut 1828 – 1r – 1 – Can$25.00 – cn Can Microfilming [072]
BROCKVILLE RECORDER – Brockville, Canada. 1830-49 – 6r – 1 – $390.00 – cn Library Assoc [971]
THE BROCKVILLE RECORDER – Brockville, Ontario. v8 n26. 1 jul 1828-v8 n34. 26 aut 1828 – 1r – 1 – Can$30.00 – cn Can Microfilming [072]
BROCKVILLE TIMES – Brockville, 1907-1917 – 19r – 1 – cn Preston [971]
Brockway, Fenner *see* THE TRUTH ABOUT BARCELONA
Brockway, Josephus *see* MR. BROCKWAY'S APOLOGY TO THE REV. NATHAN S.A. BEMAN..
BROCKWAYVILLE WEEKLY RECORD – Brockwayville, PA. -w 1887-1973. 31 rolls – 13 – $25.00r – us I.M.R. [071]
Broderick, Francis L *see* WILLIAM EDWARD BURGHARDT DU BOIS: THE TRAIL OF HIS IDEAS
LA BRODERIE GORCY *see* MONTREAL-MODE
BRODERIP AND BINGHAM'S REPORTS : REPORTS OF CASES ARGUED AND DETERMINED IN THE COURT OF COMMON PLEAS... / Broderip, William J & Bingham, Peregrine – v1-3. 1819-22. London: A Strahan, 1820-22 (all publ) – 7mf – 9 – $31.50 – LLMC 84-755 – us L.L.M.C. [324]
Broderip, Robert *see* A SHORT INTRODUCTION TO THE ART OF PLAYING THE HARPSICHORD.
Broderip, William J *see* BRODERIP AND BINGHAM'S REPORTS
BRODERSKAP – 1968-92 (complete) – Inquire – 1 – ATLA S0437 – us A.T.L.A. [073]
BRODERSKAP – Stockholm, Sweden. 1980- – 1 – sw Kungliga [072]
Brodhull *see* THE WHITE AND BLACK BOOKS OF THE CINQUE PORTS
Brodie, P B *see* A HISTORY OF THE FOSSIL INSECTS IN THE SECONDARY ROCKS OF ENGLAND...
Brodie, William *see* THE SPRUCE-GALL LOUSE: (CHERMES ABIETIS)
Brodnitz, Kaethe *see* DER JUNGE TIECK UND SEINE MAERCHENKOMOEDIEN
Brodovich, S M *see* ADMINISTRATIVNOE ZAKONODATEL'STVO
Brodribb, William Jackson *see* CONSTANTINOPLE, A SKETCH OF ITS HISTORY FROM ITS FOUNDATION TO ITS CONQUEST BY THE TURKS IN 1453
Brodrick-Cloete, W *see* THE HISTORY OF THE GREAT BOER TREK AND THE ORIGINS OF SOUTH AFRICAN REPUBLICS
Brodruch, Karl *see* DER KAMPS UM BADAJOZ UN FRUHJAHR
Brody, Eugene B *see* BIOMEDICAL TECHNOLOGY AND HUMAN RIGHTS
Brody, H *see*
- SHA'AR HA-SHIR
- SHELOMOH DA PIERRA
- SHIRIM
- STUDIEN ZU DEN DICHTUNGEN JEHUDA HA-LEVI'S 1: UEBER DIE METRA DER VERSGEDICHTE

Brody, Heinrich *see* SHAOAR HA-SHIR
Broeckaert, Joseph *see* THE FACT DIVINE
Broehmer, Heinrich *see* DIE EINWIRKUNGEN DER REFORMATION AUF DIE ORGANISATION UND BESETZUNG DES REICHSKAMMERGERICHTS
Broek, J A van den *see* DE CHERIBONSCHE OPSTAND VAN 1806
Broekhuijse, Johan Theodorus *see* RELIGION AND WARFARE AMONG THE DANI OF BALIEM-VALLEY
Broemme, Simone *see* UNTERSUCHUNG SYNTAKTISCHER STRUKTUREN IN RECHTSSPRACHLICHEN EINZELTEXTEN AUS ZWICKAUER STADTBUECHERN DER 1. HAELFTE DES 16. JAHRHUNDERTS
Brogan, O *see* THE ROMAN FRONTIER SETTLEMENT AT GHIZA: AN INTERIM REPORT
Broglie, L'Abbe de *see* PROBLEMES ET CONCLUSIONS DE L'HISTOIRE DES RELIGIONS
Broglie, Albert, Duc de *see* ST. AMBROSE
Broglie, Albertine IG de Stael-Holstein, Duchesse de *see* LETTRES DE LA DUCHESSE DE BROGLIE: 1814-1838
Broglie, E de. *see* BERNARD DE MONTFAUCON ET LES BERNARDINS 1715-1750
Broglie, J V A de *see* L'ALLIANCE AUTRICHIENNE
Broglie, Leonce Victor *see* CHAMBRE DES PAIRS DE FRANCE. SESSION DE 1821
Broglie, Paul de *see* PREUVES PSYCHOLOGIQUES DE L'EXISTENCE DE DIEU
BROILER BUSINESS – v28. 1977. Continues: Poultry Meat. Continued by: PPM: Poultry Processing and Marketing – 1 – us UMI [636]
THE BROKE HUSTLER – Iroquois Falls, Ontario. v2 n13. 23 nov 1918; v2 n14. 30 nov 1918 – 1r – 1 – Can$25.00 – cn Can Microfilming [072]
Broke, Philipp BV *see* ADMIRAL SIR PHILIPP B.V. BROKE
BROKEN HILL AGE – Australia. Oct 1893-May 1895.-w. 3mqn reels – 1 – uk British Libr Newspaper [072]
BROKEN HILL ARGUS – Feb 20 1888-Nov 20 1888 – 9 – at Pascoe [072]
BROKEN HILL TIMES – Aug 21 1886-Feb 18 1888 – 9 – at Pascoe [072]
THE BROKEN PLEDGES OF LIBERALS: SPEECH IN REPLY TO SIR WILFRID LAURIER. BY HON. GEORGE E. FOSTER, HOUSE OF COMMONS, OTTAWA, MARCH 21ST, 1899 / Foster, George Eulas – s.l.: s.n., 1899?. 05991. (Pre-1900 Canadiana) – 9 – cn C.I.H.M. [971]
Brokhage, J D *see* FRANCIS PATRICK KENRICK'S OPINION ON SLAVERY
Brokken, R F *see* DAIRY MARKETING IN SUB-SAHARAN AFRICA
Brollo, B de Glemona *see* DICTIONNAIRE CHINOIS, FRANCAIS ET LATIN,...
Bromage, Richard Raikes *see* THE HOLY CATECHISM OF NICOLAS BULGARIS
BROMBERGER TAGEBLATT *see* DEUTSCHE RUNDSCHAU IN POLEN
Brome County Historical Society. Knowlton, Canada *see* FONDS GENERAL
BROME COUNTY REGISTER – Knowlton, Canada. v1 n10. 26 mar 1880-v1 n18. 21 mai 1880 – 1r – 1 – Can$25.00 – cn Can Microfilming [072]
BROME LAKE NEWS – Knowlton, Canada. v2 n2. Aug 1969 – 1r – 1 – Can$25.00 – cn Can Microfilming [072]
BROME-MISSISQUOI COUNTY JOURNAL – Cowansville, Canada. 15 jun; 15 jul 1936 – 1r – 1 – Can$25.00 – cn Can Microfilming [072]
BROMLEY AND BECKENHAM TIMES *see* BROMLEY TIMES
BROMLEY AND DISTRICT TIMES *see* BROMLEY TIMES
BROMLEY AND WEST KENT MERCURY *see* BROMLEY MERCURY
BROMLEY CHRONICLE – London. -w. 10 Sep 1891-2 Jun 1921. (Wanting 1897). (26 reels) – 1 – uk British Libr Newspaper [072]
BROMLEY & DISTRICT TIMES – London, UK. 1906. -w. 1/2 reel – 1 – uk British Libr Newspaper [072]
BROMLEY JOURNAL AND WEST KENT HERALD – London. -w. 21 May 1869-3 May 1912. (Wanting 1886). (31 reels) – 1 – uk British Libr Newspaper [072]
BROMLEY & KENTISH TIMES – London, UK. 1932-69. -d. 68 reels – 1 – uk British Libr Newspaper [072]
BROMLEY MERCURY – (Bromley & West Kent Mercury Jul 1934-Jun 1954. West Kent Mercury July 1955-) – London, UK. 16 May 1919-Jun 1959 – 60r – 1 – uk British Libr Newspaper [072]
BROMLEY TELEGRAPH – (Lacking: 1897) – (Bromley and West Kent Telegraph). London, 1 Feb 1868-18 Oct 1913 – 23r – 1 – uk British Libr Newspaper [072]
BROMLEY TIMES – London, UK. 1906; 1911; 1932- – 147+ r – 1 – uk British Libr Newspaper [072]
BROMMA NYHETER – Stockholm, Sweden. 1946-54 – 4r – 1 – sw Kungliga [072]
Bromwell, William J *see* A DIGEST OF THE MILITARY AND NAVAL LAWS OF THE CONFEDERATE STATES
Bronckart, J -P *see* LANGUAGE SCIENCES
Brongniart, A T *see*
- ESSAI D'UNE CLASSIFICATION NATURELLE DES CHAMPIGNONS, OU TABLEAU METHODIQUE DES GENRES RAPPORTES JUSQU'A PRESENT A CETTE FAMILLE
- HISTOIRE DES VEGETAUX FOSSILES
- MEMOIRE SUR LA FAMILLE DES RHAMNEES
- TABLEAU DES GENRES DE VEGETAUX FOSSILES

- VOYAGE PENDANT LES ANNEES 1822-1825. BOTANIQUE

Bronn, H G *see*
- KLASSEN UND ORDNUNGEN DES THIERREICHS
- SYSTEM DER URWELTLICHEN KONCHYLIEN DURCH DIAGNOSE

BRONNEN EN GRONDSLAGEN VAN HET GODSDIENSTIG GELOOF : FORMEEL GEDEELTE VAN DE GELOOFSLEER, OP HET STANDPUNT VAN DE MODERNE WETENSCHAP / Hoekstra, Sytze – Amsterdam:P.N. van Kampen, 1864 – 1mf – 9 – 0-8370-3613-5 – 1985-1613 – us A.T.L.A. [210]

BRONNEN TOT DE KENNIS VAN HET LEVEN EN DE WERKEN VAN D.V. COORNHERT / Becker, Bernhard – Den Haag, 1928 – 7mf – 8 – ne Slangenburg [100]

DE BRONNEN VAN CAREL VAN MANDER VOOR "HET LEVEN DER DOORLUCHTIGHE NEDERLANDTSCHE EN HOOGDUYTSCHE SCHILDERS" / Greve, H E – (Quellenstudien zur hoellandischen kunstgeschichte. v. 2. Haag. 1903). BO-518b 1 – 9 – ne IDC [700]

BRONNENBOEK VOOR HET NIEUWE TAALONDERWIJS IN INDIE / Nieuwenhuis, G J – Groningen, 1925 – 5mf – 9 – ne IDC [950]

Bronshteyn, Karen *see* THE 1989 USSR CENSUS

BRONSON ALCOTT'S FRUITLANDS / Sears, Clara Endicott – Boston: Houghton Mifflin, 1915 – 1mf – us A.T.L.A. [240]

Bronson, Walter C *see* HISTORY OF BROWN UNIVERSITY, 1764-1914

Bront, Anne *see* THE TENANT OF WILDFELL HALL

Bronte, Charlotte *see*
- JANE EYRE
- LEGENDS OF ANGRIA

THE BRONTE MANUSCRIPTS : LITERARY MANUSCRIPTS AND CORRESPONDENCE OF THE BRONTE FAMILY FROM THE BRONTE PARSONAGE, HAWORTH AND THE BRITISH LIBRARY, LONDON – 1 – us Primary [420]

The Bronte Society *see* TRANSACTIONS, 1893-1984

BRONTERESS NATIONAL REPORTER – London, UK. 1837 – 5r – 1 – uk British Libr Newspaper [072]

BRONTERRE'S NATIONAL REFORMER – London. 1837 – 1 – uk Microform Academic [072]

Bronw, J *see* ESSAYS ON THE CHARACTERISTICS

Bronwley, K A *see* THE EFFECTS OF MUSIC ON PSYCHOPHYSIOLOGICAL STRESS RESPONSES TO GRADED EXERCISE

BRONZE RAVEN – Toledo. Ohio. 1951-73 – 1 – us UMI [071]

BRONZE REPORTER – Flint. Mich. 1953-1963 – 1 – us UMI [071]

BRONZEMAN – Chicago.1931-33 – 1r – 1 – us Ross [975]

DER BROOK / Tuegel, Ludwig – 2. Aufl. Hamburg: Hanseatische Verlagsanstalt, 1943, c1938 – 1r – 1 – us U.W. Library [830]

BROOK FARM : ITS MEMBERS, SCHOLARS, AND VISITORS / Swift, Lindsay – New York: Macmillan, 1900 – 1mf – us A.T.L.A. [978]

Brook Farm *see* PAPERS

BROOK FARM PAPERS, 1842-1861 – (Commune whose members included Nathaniel Hawthorne, Ralph Waldo Emerson, Margaret Fuller, Charles A. Dana. Includes letters by Margaret Dwight. Includes Constitutions and Minutes, Articles of Incorporation, list of members) – Massachusetts Historical Society – 1r – 1 – $85.00 – us UMI [420]

Brook, William M *see* A HISTORY OF THE EASTERN DEFENSE COMMAND

Brookbank, Joseph *see* THE WELL-TUNED ORGAN...WHETHER OR NO INSTRUMENTAL AND ORGANICAL MUSIC BE LAWFUL IN HOLY PUBLICK ASSEMBLIES

Brooke *see* THE LIFE OF SIR PHILIP SYDNEY

Brooke, Alan E *see*
- THE FRAGMENTS OF HERACLEON
- THE OLD TESTAMENT IN GREEK

Brooke, Frances *see* THE HISTORY OF EMILY MONTAGUE

Brooke, George J *see*
- THE ALLEGRO QUMRAN COLLECTION ON MICROFICHE
- THE ALLEGRO QUMRAN PHOTOGRAPH COLLECTION

Brooke, H *see* JULIET GRENVILLE; OR, THE HISTORY OF THE HUMAN HEART

Brooke, John *see* POEMS

Brooke, John T *see* THE LEGAL PROFESSION: ITS MORAL NATURE, AND PRACTICAL CONNECTION WITH CIVIL SOCIETY

BROOKE NEWS – Wellsburg. West Virginia. -w. 1938- – 1 – us UMI [071]

Brooke, Stopford Augustus *see*
- FREEDOM IN THE CHURCH OF ENGLAND
- GOD AND CHRIST
- THE GOSPEL OF JOY
- MILTON
- THE OLD TESTAMENT AND MODERN LIFE
- THE ONWARD CRY AND OTHER SERMONS
- RELIGION IN LITERATURE
- SHORT SERMONS
- THE SPIRIT OF THE CHRISTIAN LIFE
- A STUDY OF CLOUGH, ARNOLD, ROSSETTI AND MORRIS
- THEOLOGY IN THE ENGLISH POETS

Brookes, C A *see* JOURNAL OF HARD MATERIALS

Brookes, Iveson L *see* A DISCOURSE, INVESTIGATING THE DOCTRINE OF WASHING THE SAINTS' FEET

Brookes, James Hall *see*
- GOD SPAKE ALL THESE WORDS
- IS THE BIBLE INSPIRED?
- IS THE BIBLE TRUE?
- SALVATION

Brookes, Patrick *see*
- THE FREEDOM AVALANCHE OF 1980
- OPERATION REBUTTAL

BROOKFIELD 1696-1849 – (Mf 1T,3T: Births 1701-96. Mf 1T-3T: Marriages 1718-93. Mf 3T: Deaths 1758-1806. Mf 4T-9T: Births & Deaths 1696-1814. Mf 9T: Intentions & Marriages 1766-77. Mf 9T-12T: Births & Deaths 1696-1847. Mf 12T-14T: Intents & Marriages 1792-1825. Mf 15T-16T: Marriages 1816-43. Mf 16T-17T: Intents & Marriages 1840-45. Mf 17T-18T: Births 1839-49. Mf 18T: Marriages 1842-49. Mf 19T: Deaths 1843-49. Mf 20T: Out-of-Town Marriages 1696-1799) – (mf ed 1995) – 20mf – 9 – 0-87623-219-5 – us Holbrook [920]

BROOKFIELD 1700-1895 – (Mf 1-9: Births & Deaths 1700-1818. Mf 10-14: Births & Deaths 1768-1847. Mf 15-22: Marriages, Publishments, Misc. 1793-1844. Mf 23-26: B,M,D 1844-60. Mf 23-24: Births 1843-58. Mf 25: Births 1859-60; Marriages 1843-57. Mf 26: Deaths 1843-57. Mf 27: Marriage Intentions 1845-49; Marriages 1850-72. Mf 28: Marrigaes 1873-95. Mf 29-31: Town Records 1845-1918. Mf 32-34: Births 1861-95. Mf 34-37: Marriages 1722-1895. Mf 37-39: Deaths 1857-95. Mf 40-44: Index to Vital Records 1857-1911) – (mf ed 1987) – 44mf – 9 – 0-87623-019-2 – us Holbrook [920]

Brookfield, H C *see* POPULATION-ENVIRONMENT RELATIONS IN TROPICAL ISLANDS

BROOKHILL BAPTIST CHURCH. ETOWAH, TENNESSEE : CHURCH RECORDS – Apr 1946-Dec 1982. Formerly New Hope Baptist Church, name changed to West Etowah in 1949, name changed to Brookhill in 1965 – 1 – 24.75 – us Baptist [240]

BROOKINGS HARBOR-PILOT – Brookings, OR. -w. 7 Mar 1946-20 Jul 1978+. 18 rolls – 1 – us U.O. Library [071]

BROOKLIN BULLETIN – Brooklin, 1959-1960 – 1r – 1 – cn Preston [971]

BROOKLIN PROFILE – Brooklin, 1983Oc-Mr1987 – 2r – 1 – cn Preston [971]

BROOKLINE 1655-1849 – (Mf 1T-3T: B,D,M 1683-1758. Mf 2T-4T: Births & Deaths 1707-1847. Mf 3T-4T: Publishments & Marriages 1753-1842. Mf 4T-6T: B,D,M 1680-1845. Mf 6T-7T: Out-of-Town Marriages 1655-1799. Mf 7T-8T: Marriages 1839-45. Mf 7T: Publishments 1842-46. Mf 8T: Vital Records 1772-1849. Mf 9T: Intentions 1846-49. Mf 9T-10T: Births 1844-49. Mf 10T-11T: Marriages 1844-49. Mf 11T: Deaths 1844-49) – (mf ed 1995) – 11mf – 9 – 0-87623-220-9 – us Holbrook [920]

BROOKLINE 1748-1928 – (Mf 1-3: Births 1748-1896; Deaths 1764-1921. Mf 2: Marriages 1778-1849. Mf 3-6: Marriages & Intents 1850-1923. Mf 7-16: Town and Tax Record 1769-1831. Mf 9,12: Marriages 1810-13. Mf 14: Births 1764-79. Mf 14-15: Marriages 1791-1841. Mf 17-25: Town & Tax Recs 1821-48. Mf 26-29: Town Payments 1782-1840. Mf 29-31: Militia 1827-37, 1877. Mf 32-48: Tax Invoices 1836-57. Mf 49-54: Town Rayments 1864-94. Mf 55-62: Town Records 1848-67. Mf 63-70: Town Records 1867-82. Mf 70-79: Town Records 1882-95. Mf 80,82: Deaths 1838-96. Mf 80-81: Marriages 1879, 1882-97. Mf 80-82: Births 1850-97. Mf 83-84: Marriages & Index 1897-1928. Mf 85: Births & Index 1897-1901. Mf 85-87: Deaths & Index 1897-1928) – (mf ed 1999) – 87mf – 9 – 0-87623-175-X – us Holbrook [920]

BROOKLYN BARRISTER – v1-45. 1950-94 – 9 – $340.00 set – us Hein [340]

THE BROOKLYN DAILY TIMES – Brooklyn, NY. n44. 30 apr 1901 – 1r – 1 – Can$25.00 – cn Can Microfilming [071]

BROOKLYN JEWISH EXAMINER – Brooklyn, NY. 1932-37 – 1 – us A.J.P.C. [071]

BROOKLYN JOURNAL OF INTERNATIONAL LAW – (v1-10 1975-95 in reel $80.00. v11-21 1985-96 in mf $174.00) – v1-21. 1975-96 – 5,6,9 – $254.00 set – us Hein [340]

BROOKLYN LAW REVIEW – v1-61. 1932-95 – 1,5,6 – $1,395.00 – us Hein [073]

BROOKLYN LIFE – Brooklyn. v. 1-83. 1890-1931 – 1 – 1,000.00 – us L of C Photodup [073]

Brooklyn. New York. Siloam Presbyterian Church *see* SEMI-CENTENNIAL

BROOKLYN NEWS – Portland OR. Apr 15 29 June 24 1949 – 1 – us U.O. Library [071]

Brooklyn, Presbytery (Pres. Ch. in the U.S.A.) *see* RECORDS, 1838-1918

BROOKLYN'S GUARDIANS-RECORD OF POLICE FORCE IN CITY OF HOMES / Fales, William E S – Brooklyn, 1887. New York Reel 19. (The Cox Library Collection) – 5 – us Americana [978]

Brooks, A D *see* HISTORY OF ELLIS COUNTY BAPTIST ASSOCIATION

Brooks, Annie Elston *see* THE HEIRESS OF MYRTLE GROVE: AN ENGLISH TALE FOUNDED ON FACTS

Brooks, David M *see* TAXATION IS ROBBERY

Brooks, Edgar Harry *see* THE BANTU IN SOUTH AFRICAN LIFE

Brooks, Elbridge Streeter *see* THE STORY OF THE AMERICAN INDIAN: HIS ORIGIN, DEVELOPMENT, DECLINE AND DESTINY

Brooks, George *see* INDUSTRY AND PROPERTY, A PLEA FOR TRUTH AND HONESTY IN ECONOMICS AND FOR LIBERTY AND JUSTICE IN SOCIAL REFORM

Brooks, Gladys C *see* HISTORY OF LEXINGTON BAPTIST CHURCH, OGLETHORPE COUNTY, GEORGIA, 1847-1974

Brooks, Henry M *see* OLDEN-TIME MUSIC

Brooks, Ivan *see* THE BARON DE ST CASTIN

Brooks, J *see* TWO DUETTS FOR ONE PERFORMER

Brooks, J W *see* A NEW ARRANGEMENT OF THE PROVERBS OF SOLOMON

Brooks, John Graham *see* AS OTHERS SEE US

Brooks, Joseph S *see* LAWS THE DETECTIVE SHOULD KNOW

Brooks, Michael John *see* A PROGRAM OF NEW CHURCH MEMBER ORIENTATION IN THE FAIRFAX BAPTIST CHURCH, VALLEY, ALABAMA

Brooks, Phillips *see*
- ADDRESSES
- THE CANDLE OF THE LORD AND OTHER SERMONS
- THE LAW OF GROWTH AND OTHER SERMONS
- LECTURES ON PREACHING
- NEW STARTS IN LIFE AND OTHER SERMONS
- SEEKING LIFE AND OTHER SERMONS
- SERMONS

BROOKSIANA : OR, THE CONTROVERSY BETWEEN SENATOR BROOKS AND ARCHBISHOP HUGHES: GROWING OUT OF THE RECENTLY ENACTED CHURCH PROPERTY BILL – New York: T W Strong, 1870 – 1mf – 9 – 0-8370-7128-3 – 1986-1128 – us A.T.L.A. [240]

BROOKVILLE AMERICAN – Brookville, PA. -w 1981-1982 – 13 – $25.00r – us I.M.R. [071]

BROOKVILLE AMERICAN – Jefferson, PA., 1918-1981 – 13 – $25.00r – us I.M.R. [071]

BROOKVILLE DEMOCRAT – Brookville, PA., 1879-1884 – 13 – $25.00r – us I.M.R. [071]

BROOKVILLE DEMOCRAT – Jefferson, PA., 1879-1883 – 13 – $25.00r – us I.M.R. [071]

BROOKVILLE ENQUIRER – Brookville, Ind.1819-21 – 1,3 – us Readex [071]

BROOKVILLE REPUBLICAN – Brookville, PA., 1826-1837, 1873 – 13 – $25.00r – us I.M.R. [071]

BROOKWOOD – Brookwood, Katonah, New York. v. 1-14. Mar 20 1923-July 1936. Incomplete – 1 – us NY Public [073]

BROOKWOOD REVIEW – Katonah, NY. v1-14. 1923-36 – 1r – 1 – us Ross [330]

BROOM: AN INTERNATIONAL MAGAZINE OF THE ARTS – Rome. v. 1-6 no. 1. Nov 1921-Jan 1924 – 1 – us NY Public [073]

Broome, C E *see*
- NOTICES OF BRITISH FUNGI

Broome, Gordon *see* REPORT ON THE CANADIAN PHOSPHATES: CONSIDERED WITH REFERENCE TO THEIR APPLICATION TO AGRICULTURE

Broomhall, B *see* THE EVANGELISATION OF THE WORLD

Broomhall, M *see* ROBERT MORRISON

Broomhall, Marshall *see*
- THE CHINESE EMPIRE
- THE JUBILEE STORY OF THE CHINA INLAND MISSION
- MARTYRED MISSIONARIES OF THE CHINA INLAND MISSION
- PIONEER WORK IN HUNAN BY ADAM DORWARD

Bros *see* VOLTAIRE ET SON GENIE

Brosch, Hermann Josef *see*
- DER SEINSBEGRIFF BEI BOETHIUS

Brossard, S de *see*
- DICTIONAIRE DE MUSIQUE...
- DICTIONNAIRE DE MUSIQUE
- ELEVATIONS ET MOTETS A 2 ET 3 VOIX

Brosses, Charles de *see*
- DU CULTE DES DIEUX FETICHES, OU PARALLELE DE L'ANCIENNE RELIGION DE L'EGYPTE AVEC LA RELIGION ACTUELLE DE LA NIGRITIE
- TRAITE DE LA FORMATION MECANIQUE DES LANGUES
- TRAITE DE LA FORMATION MECHANIQUE DES LANGUES
- TRAITE DE LA FORMATION MECHANIQUE DES LANGUES, ET DES PRINCIPES PHYSIQUES DE L'ETYMOLOGIE

Brosses, P de *see* LE GRAND DICTIONNAIRE FRANCOIS-LATIN

[Brosset, M] *see* LISTE DES TRAVAUX DE M. BROSSET...LE 22 AOUT (3 SEPTEMBRE) 1880

BROSUR ADAT ISTIADAT DAN TJERITERA RAKJAT. URUSAN ADAT-ISTIADAT DAN TJERITERA RAKJAT, DJAWATAN KEBUDAJAAN, DEPARTEMEN P.P. DAN K. – (Twice a year) – Jogjakarta, 1960-1962 – 9mf – 9 – SE-1364/1 – ne IDC [950]

BROT : ROMAN / Waggerl, Karl Heinrich – Leipzig: Inselverlag, 1938 – 1r – 1 – us U.W. Library [830]

BROTERIA : REVISTA DE SCIENCIAS NATURAES – Lisboa, 1902-1906. v1-5; 1907-1922. v6-20 – 77mf – 7438/1 – ne IDC [580]

Brotero, F di Avelar *see*
- FLORA LUSITANICA, SEU PLANTARUM
- PHYTOGRAPHIA LUSITANIAE
- PHYTOGRAPHIA LUSITANIAE SELECTIOR SEU NOVARUM ET ALIARUM MINUS COGNITARUM STIRPIUM

BROTHER AZARIAS : THE LIFE STORY OF AN AMERICAN MONK / Smith, John Talbot – New York: William H Young, 1897 – 1mf – 9 – 0-8370-6776-6 – 1986-0776 – us A.T.L.A. [920]

BROTHER FABIAN'S MANUSCRIPT : AND OTHER POEMS / Evans, Sebastian – London: Macmillan, 1865 – 1 roll – 1 – 1-55879-194-9 – uk Libr Preservation [810]

BROTHER JOHN'S CANAAN IN CAROLINA, 1872-1956 / Washburn, W Wyan – 1 – 11.76 – us Baptist [240]

BROTHERHOOD = BRATSTVO – Cleveland, OH: American Russian National Brotherhood, v17-18. 1940-1941; v14 1942 – us Res Libr [060]

BROTHERHOOD; A MONTHLY MAGAZINE DESIGNED TO HELP THE PEACEFUL EVOLUTION OF A JUSTER AND HAPPIER SOCIAL ORDER. LONDON – May 1895-Apr. 1900. Incomplete – 1 – us NY Public [073]

BROTHERHOOD JOURNAL – Memphis. Tenn. 1940-67 – 1 – 290.71 – us Baptist [240]

Brotherhood of Machinery MoldersUnited Sons of Vulcan *see* MACHINERY MOLDERS JOURNAL, 1888-1892 : VULCAN RECORD, 1868-1875

Brotherhood of Metal WorkersUnited Brotherhood of Weldors, Cutters and Helpers of America *see* METAL WORKERS BULLETIN, 1910-1914 : WELDORS' JOURNAL, 1938-1941

BROTHERHOOD OF THE NEW LIFE *see* THOMAS LAKE HARRIS AND THE BROTHERHOOD OF THE NEW LIFE, 1854-1942
Brothers, Barbara Jo *see* JOURNAL OF COUPLES THERAPY
BROTHERS OF DOOM. THE STORY OF THE PIZARROS OF PERU / Birney, Hoffman – New York: G.P. Potnams Sons, 1942 – sp Bibl Santa Ana [350]
BROTHERS OF PITY / Ewing, Juliana Horatia – British Fiction Archive: Unit 1 – 9 – uk Bell [830]
Brothers of the Christian Schools *see*
- COMPENDIUM OF THE HISTORY OF CANADA AND OF THE BRITISH NORTH AMERICAN PROVINCES
- COMPENDIUMS OF GENERAL HISTORY, THE HISTORY OF CANADA, AND OTHER BRITISH NORTH AMERICAN PROVINCES
- THE THIRD BOOK OF READING LESSONS

BROTTERODER ANZEIGER – Brotterode, apr 1 1911-jun 29 1937 (incomplete) – 15r – 1 – Inquire at Mikrofilmarchiv for details – gw Misc Inst [943]
Brou, L *see*
- THE MONASTIC ORDINALE OF ST VEDAST'S ABBEY ARRAS
- THE PSALTER COLLECTS – FROM 5-6TH CENTURY SOURCES

Brou, Louis *see* ANTIFONARIO VISIGOTICO...
Brouchu, Delphis *see* CONVENTION DES MEDECINS DU DISTRICT DE QUEBEC: DISCOURS PRONONCE AU BANQUET DU 25 JUIN 1900, LE JOUR DE LA SAINT JEAN BAPTISTE, A L'HOTEL CHATEAU FRONTENAC
Brouerius van Niedek, M *see*
- ZEDERYKE ZINNEBEELDEN DER TONGE, DOOR MATTHEUS BROUERIUS VAN NIEDEK

LA BROUETTE/LE BROUTTEUX : JOURNAL-PASQUILLE HEBDOMADAIRE DE TOURCOING – Hebd., Tourcoing (Nord), juil. 1882-sept. 1907. avec un index et un album-souvenir concernant son propriétaire J. Watteeuw – 9r – 1 – F3037,11 – fr Armell [072]
Brough, Joshua *see* EARLY LIFE OF OUR LORD
Brough, William *see* THE NATURAL LAW OF MONEY: THE SUCCESSIVE STEPS IN THE GROWTH OF MONEY TRACED FROM THE DAYS OF BARTER TO THE INTRODUCTION OF THE MODERN CLEARING-HOUSE, AND MONETARY PRINCIPLES EXAMINED IN THEIR RELATION TO PAST AND PRESENT LEGISLATION
Brougham, Henry *see* LIVES OF MEN OF LETTERS OF THE TIME OF GEORGE 3
Brougham, Henry Peter *see*
- A LETTER FROM THE RIGHT HON. LORD BROUGHAM TO THE RIGHT HON. SIR JAMES GRAHAM, BT., M.P., ON THE MAKING AND DIGESTING OF THE LAW
- THE LIFE AND TIMES OF HENRY, LORD BROUGHAM, WRITTEN BY HIMSELF

BROUGHTON BAPTIST CHURCH. FULTON COUNTY. ARKANSAS : CHURCH RECORDS – 1893-1915 – 1 – 11.25 – us Baptist [240]
Broughton House. Northamptonshire *see* SHREWSBURY PAPERS
Broughton, Leonard Gaston *see* THE REVIVAL OF A DEAD CHURCH
Broughton, Rhoda *see*
- ALAS: A NOVEL
- A BEGINNER: A NOVEL
- BELINDA: A NOVEL
- BETWEEN TWO STOOLS
- COMETH UP AS A FLOWER
- COMETH UP AS A FLOWER: AN AUTOBIOGRAPHY
- CONCERNING A VOW
- DEAR FAUSTINA: A NOVEL
- THE DEVIL AND THE DEEP SEA
- DOCTOR CUPID: A NOVEL
- FOES IN LAW
- A FOOL IN HER FOLLY
- THE GAME AND THE CANDLE
- GOOD-BYE SWEETHEART: A TALE
- JOAN: A TALE
- LAVINIA
- MAMMA
- MRS. BLIGH: A NOVEL
- NANCY, A NOVEL
- NANCY: A NOVEL
- NOT WISELY, BUT TOO WELL: A NOVEL
- RED AS A ROSE IS SHE
- RED AS A ROSE IS SHE: A NOVEL
- SCYLLA OR CHARYBDIS? A NOVEL
- SECOND THOUGHTS
- TALES FOR CHRISTMAS EVE
- A THORN IN THE FLESH
- A WAIF'S PROGRESS
- A WIDOWER INDEED

BROUGHTY FERRY GUIDE AND CARNOUSTIE GAZETTE – 1 – £42.00r – uk Scot News [072]
Broun, M *see* INDEX TO NORTH AMERICAN FERNS
Brouse *see* CENTENNIAL HISTORY OF AKRON 1825-1925
Brousseau, Georges *see* SOUVENIRS DE LA MISSION SAVORGNAN DE BRAZZA
Brousseau, Vincent *see* BIO-BIBLIOGRAPHIE DE MONSIEUR ALBERT GERVAIS
Broussonet, P M A *see* ELENCHUS PLANTARUM HORTI BOTANICI MONSPELIENSIS
Brouwer, A *see* IETS OVER AANVARINGEN IN VOL ZEE
Brouwer, Johannes *see*
- A FAMOUS DUTCH WRITER DENOUNCES REBEL ATROCITIES
- THE LAST DAYS OF UNOMUNO
- WORDS OF INDIGNATION AND OF TRUTH

Brovkin, T M *see* BIBLIOGRAFICHESKII UKAZATEL' KOOPERATIVNOI LITERATURY ZA 1927 G
BROWARD JEWISH WORLD – (Merged with Miami Jewish tribune and Palm Beach Jewish world to form South Florida Jewish tribune) – Boca Raton, Florida. v10 n44 (Oct 25-31 1991)-v13 n7 (Feb 25-Mar 3 1994) – 100ft – us A.J.P.C. [270]
BROWARD JEWISH WORLD *see* PALM BEACH JEWISH WORLD
Browarzik, Ulrich *see* GLAUBE, HISTORIE UND SITTLICHKEIT...
Browder, Earl *see* NEXT STEPS TO WIN THE WAR IN SPAIN
Brower, D H B *see* DANVILLE, PENNSYLVANIA
Brower, David *see* WILDERNESS
Brower, Jacob V *see*
- FIELD NOTEBOOKS
- THE MISSISSIPPI RIVER AND ITS SOURCE: A NARRATIVE AND CRITICAL HISTORY OF THE DISCOVERY OF THE RIVER AND ITS HEADWATERS, ACCOMPANIED BY THE RESULTS OF DETAILED HYDROGRAPHIC AND TOPOGRAPHIC SURVEYS

Browershaven, P C van *see* DEN SCHILT TEGHEN DIE WEDERDOOPERS
Brown *see* THE ENCYCLOPEDIA OF THE NEW WEST
Brown, A *see* AN ILLUSTRATED FLORA OF THE NORTHERN UNITED STATES, CANADA AND THE BRITISH POSSESSIONS
Brown, Albert J *see* HISTORY OF CLINTON COUNTY
Brown, Alec *see* THE JURYMAN'S HANDBOOK
BROWN AMERICAN / National Association of Negroes in American Industries – v1-5, no. 8 (all publ). 1941-1945. 1936-45 – 12mf – 9 – $115.00 – us UPA [970]
Brown and Co *see* HISTORY OF VERNON COUNTY
Brown, Antoinette L *see* EXEGESIS OF I CORINTHIANS XIV: 34,35; AND I TIMOTHY XI: 11-12
Brown, Arthur Judson *see*
- THE FOREIGN MISSIONARY; AN INCARNATION OF A WORLD MOVEMENT
- RISING CHURCHES IN NON-CHRISTIAN LANDS
- UNITY AND MISSIONS
- THE WHY AND HOW OF FOREIGN MISSIONS

Brown, B F *see* A CONCISE STATEMENT OF THE LAW OF PARTNERSHIP
BROWN BOVERI REVIEW – v. 11-44. 1924-1957 – 1,5,6 – us Princeton Micro [621]
Brown & Boyd *see* HISTORY OF SAN BERNARDINO AND RIVERSIDE COUNTIES
Brown, Brian et al *see* DIVINE OR CIVIL OBEDIENCE?
Brown, C B *see* CIVIL ENGINEERING SYSTEMS
Brown, C Campbell *see* A CHINESE ST FRANCIS, OR, THE LIFE OF BROTHER MAO
Brown, Charles *see* THE CANADIAN GAZETTE
Brown, Charles Brockden *see* THE RHAPSODIST
Brown, Charles J *see* THE DIVINE GLORY OF CHRIST
Brown, Charles Philip *see*
- ENGLISH AND TELUGU DICTIONARY
- TELUGU-ENGLISH DICTIONARY
- VAKYAVALI

Brown, Charles Reynolds *see* THE YOUNG MAN'S AFFAIRS
Brown, Charles Rufus *see*
- AN ARAMAIC METHOD
- BOOK OF THE PROPHET JEREMIAH

Brown, Clark *see* SERMON PREACHED AT WAREHAM (MASSACHUSETTS), 31 MAR 1695
BROWN COUNTY DEMOCRAT – Ainsworth, NE. -w. Aug. 1909-Jun. 1923; Jun. 1923-Jun. 1929. Incomplete; Jun. 1929-Jun. 1945 – 1 – us NE Hist [071]
BROWN COUNTY DEMOCRAT – Ainsworth. Neb. 1909-1945 – 1 – us UMI [071]
BROWN COUNTY HERALD – Hiawatha, KS. 1917-75 – 1 – us UMI [071]
BROWN COUNTY WORLD – Hiawatha. Kan. 1882-1916 – 1 – us UMI [071]
Brown, David *see*
- APOCALYPSE
- COMMENTARY ON THE EPISTLE TO THE ROMANS
- THE EPISTLE TO THE ROMANS

Brown, David S *see*
- MANAGEMENT'S HIDDEN ENEMY-AND WHAT YOU CAN DO ABOUT IT
- MANAGING THE LARGE ORGANIZATION: ISSUES, IDEAS, PRECEPTS, INNOVATIONS

Brown, DE *see* PREDICTING BLOOD PRESSURE FROM ACTIVITY, FITNESS, AND BODY COMPOSITION OF BORDERLINE HYPERTENSIVE INDIVIDUALS
Brown, Edgar G *see* THE CIVILIAN CONSERVATION CORPS AND COLORED YOUTH
Brown, Edmund Woodward *see* THE DIVINE INDWELLING
Brown, Elijah P *see* FROM NOWHERE TO BEULAHLAND
Brown, Elmer E *see* DIE STELLUNG DES STAATES ZUR KIRCHE IN BEZUG AUF DEN RELIGIONSUNTERRICHT IN DER SCHULE IN PREUSSEN, ENGLAND UND DEN VEREINIGTEN STAATEN VON NORDAMERIKA
BROWN, EPHRAIM, PAPERS, MS 1872 – 1790-1887 – 22r – 1 – us Western Res [978]
Brown, Ethan A *see* PAPERS
Brown, Fortune Charles *see* CHRIST ON THE THRONE OF POWER AND ANTICHRIST
Brown, Fred R *see* MANAGEMENT: CONCEPTS AND PRACTICE
Brown, George *see*
- GEORGE BROWN, D.D., PIONEER-MISSIONARY AND EXPLORER
- MELANESIANS AND POLYNESIANS
- SPEECH IN THE CANADIAN SENATE, MARCH 21, 1878 ON THE PUBLIC FINANCES OF THE DOMINION: THE FINANCIAL TRANSACTIONS OF THE MACKENZIE AND MACDONALD GOVERNMENTS CONTRACTED

Brown, George A *see* DIARIES AND MEMOIRS
Brown, George Stayley *see*
- YARMOUTH, NOVA SCOTIA: A SEQUEL TO CAMPBELL'S HISTORY

Brown, George W *see* THE ECONOMIC HISTORY OF LIBERIA
Brown, George William *see* THE RELATION OF THE LEGAL PROFESSION TO SOCIETY
Brown, Gordon D et al *see* A COMPARISON OF SKELETAL MUSCLE RESPONSIVENESS TO EXERCISE IN MALE AND FEMALE SPRAGUE-DAWLEY RATS TREATED WITH AN ANABOLIC STEROID
Brown, H *see* CANCER BIOCHEMISTRY BIOPHYSICS
Brown, H B *see* BROWN'S REPORTS OF ADMIRALTY AND REVENUE CASES IN THE SIXTH CIRCUIT
Brown, Henriette *see* AFFAIRE GUIBORD: QUESTION DE REFUS DE SEPULTURE
Brown, Howard Nicholson *see* LIFE OF JESUS FOR YOUNG PEOPLE
Brown, Hubert William *see* LATIN AMERICA
Brown, Isaac V *see* A HISTORICAL VINDICATION OF THE ABROGATION OF THE PLAN OF UNION BY THE PRESBYTERIAN CHURCH IN THE UNITED STATES OF AMERICA
Brown, J *see*
- BARBAROSSA
- AN ESTIMATE OF THE MANNERS AND PRINCIPLES OF THE TIMES
- THE HISTORY OF THE RISE AND PROGRESS OF POETRY THROUGH IT'S SEVERAL SPECIES

Brown, J C *see* PASTORAL DISCOURSES
Brown, J Newton *see* ENCYCLOPEDIA OF RELIGIOUS KNOWLEDGE
Brown, James *see*
- THE CANADIAN GAZETTE
- PAPERS

Brown, James Alexander Campbell *see* EVOLUSI MASJARAKAT
Brown, James Baldwin *see*
- THE CHRISTIAN POLICY OF LIFE
- THE DOCTRINE OF THE DIVINE FATHERHOOD IN RELATION TO THE ATONEMENT
- IDOLATRIES, OLD AND NEW
- POTTER AND CLAY: A SERMON PREACHED IN THE BRIXTON INDEPENDENT CHURCH, LONDON, ENGLAND
- THE SOUL'S EXODUS AND PILGRIMAGE
- STOICS AND SAINTS

Brown, James W *see* FANTI CONFEDERATION
Brown, John *see*
- COMMONWEALTH ENGLAND
- THE ENGLISH PURITANS
- FROM THE RESTORATION OF 1660 TO THE REVOLUTION OF 1688
- JOHN BROWN LETTERS
- LETTERS
- LETTERS, MANUSCRIPTS, ARTICLES, ETC
- MEMORANDUM BOOK
- PAPERS
- THE PILGRIM FATHERS OF NEW ENGLAND AND THEIR PURITAN SUCCESSORS
- PURITAN PREACHING IN ENGLAND
- SELECTED PAPERS FROM THE KSHS COLLECTION
- A SELECTION OF WORKS BY AND ABOUT JOHN BROWN

Brown, John Crombie *see* THE ETHICS OF GEORGE ELIOT'S WORKS
Brown, John Henry *see*
- HISTORY OF TEXAS
- INDIAN WARS AND PIONEERS OF TEXAS

Brown, John S *see* JOHN S. BROWN PAPERS
Brown, John T *see*
- CHURCHES OF CHRIST
- A LIST OF LEGAL FEES, FOR THE USE OF PROBATE COURTS, WITHIN THE STATE OF CONNECTICUT

Brown, Joseph D *see* THE EFFECTS OF COOPERATIVE AND INDIVIDUALISTIC GOAL STRUCTURES ON THE LEARNING DOMAINS OF BEGINNING TENNIS STUDENTS
Brown, Josiah *see*
- BROWN'S PARLIAMENTARY CASES
- REPORTS OF CASES UPON APPEALS AND WRITS OF ERROR DETERMINED IN THE HIGH COURT OF PARLIAMENT

Brown, L C *see* STATE AND SOCIETY IN INDEPENDENT NORTH AFRICA
Brown, L E G *see*
- THE HEREFORD BREVIARY, VOL. 1
- THE HEREFORD BREVIARY, VOL. 2
- THE HEREFORD BREVIARY, VOL. 3

Brown, L F *see* THE FREEDOM OF THE SEAS
Brown, Louise Fargo *see* THE POLITICAL ACTIVITIES OF THE BAPTISTS AND FIFTH MONARCHY MEN IN ENGLAND DURING THE INTERREGNUM
Brown, Lucinda White *see* DIARY, MS 4
Brown, Marc A *see* RELATION OF BODY FATNESS AND BLOOD LIPIDS AS RISK FACTORS FOR CORONARY HEART DISEASE IN AFRICAN AMERICAN WOMEN
Brown, Marianna C *see* SUNDAY-SCHOOL MOVEMENTS IN AMERICA
Brown, Marshall *see* WIT AND HUMOR OF BENCH AND BAR
Brown, Maurice Henry *see* MORTGAGES
Brown, O E *see* WOMEN PREACHERS
Brown, Oliver May *see* BIBLE CHRONOLOGY VINDICATED BY ITS OWN INTERNAL EVIDENCE
Brown, P Hume *see* JOHN KNOX
Brown, P M *see*
- FOREIGNERS IN TURKEY;...
- INTERNATIONAL REALITIES

Brown, Peter B *see* ORANGE-BELLIED PARROT RECOVERY PLAN
Brown, Peter Hume *see*
- GEORGE BUCHANAN, HUMANIST AND REFORMER..
- GEORGE BUCHANAN, HUMANIST AND REFORMER

Brown, Peter J *see* MEDICAL ANTHROPOLOGY
Brown, R *see* OBSERVATIONS ON THE ORGANS AND MODE OF FECUNDATION IN ORCHIDEAE AND ASCLEPIADEAE
Brown, R Balfour *see* DESCRIPTION OF RUNIC STONES FOUND NEAR YARMOUTH, NOVA SCOTIA
BROWN, R.C. AND CO *see*
- HISTORY OF BUTLER COUNTY
- HISTORY OF TIOGA COUNTY

Brown, Richard FGS *see*
- THE COAL FIELDS AND COAL TRADE OF THE ISLAND OF CAPE BRETON
- A HISTORY OF THE ISLAND OF CAPE BRETON: WITH SOME ACCOUNT OF THE DISCOVERY AND SETTLEMENT ON CANADA, NOVA SCOTIA AND NEWFOUNDLAND

Brown, Richard L *see* 31P METABOLIC RESPONSES TO ACTIVITY OF NONSPECIFICALLY TRAINED MUSCLE TISSUE IN ELITE ENDURANCE ATHLETES AND IN HEALTHY, SEDENTARY SUBJECTS AS OBSERVED BY 31P MAGNETIC SPECTROSCOPY

Brown, Robert *see*
- MISCELLANEOUS BOTANICAL WORKS
- THE MISCELLANEOUS BOTANICAL WORKS
- ON THE ASCLEPIADEAE
- PLANTAE JAVANICAE RARIORES..
- PRODROMUS FLORAE NOVAE HOLLANDIAE
- PRODROMUS FLORAE NOVAE HOLLANDIAE ET INSULAE VAN DIEMEN
- PROSROMUS MOLLET: SUPPLEMENT
- THE STORY OF AFRICA AND ITS EXPLORERS
- TALES AND TRADITIONS OF THE ESKIMOES

Brown, Robert Allen *see* LIST OF INDIANA LAWYERS, JUDGES AND PROSECUTORS

Brown, Robert Christopher Lundin *see* KLATSASSAN: AND OTHER REMINISCENCES OF MISSIONARY LIFE IN BRITISH COLUMBIA

Brown, Ronald Keith *see* THE USE OF SYSTEMS THEORY OF ORGANIZATION IN ANALYZING, PLANNING AND ADMINISTERING THE WORK OF FIRST BAPTIST CHURCH, COLUMBIA, TENNESSEE

Brown, Runk and Co *see*
- HISTORY OF MERCER COUNTY
- HISTORY OF VENANGO COUNTY PAST AND PRESENT

Brown, Samuel *see* LECTURES ON THE ATOMIC THEORY; AND ESSAYS SCIENTIFIC AND LITERARY

Brown, Samuel Windsor *see* THE SECULARIZATION OF AMERICAN EDUCATION AS SHOWN BY STATE LEGISLATION, STATE CONSTITUTIONAL PROVISIONS AND STATE SUPREME COURT DECISIONS

Brown, Stanley McKeown *see* WITH THE ROYAL CANADIANS

Brown, T *see*
- ILLUSTRATIONS OF THE CONCHOLOGY OF GREAT BRITAIN AND IRELAND
- ILLUSTRATIONS OF THE FOSSIL CONCHOLOGY OF GREAT BRITAIN AND IRELAND

Brown, Theron *see* THE STORY OF THE HYMNS AND TUNES

Brown, Thomas *see*
- ANNALS OF THE DISRUPTION
- CHURCH AND STATE IN SCOTLAND

Brown, Thomas Storrow *see*
- 1837: MY CONNECTION WITH IT
- BRIEF SKETCH ON THE LIFE AND TIMES OF THE LATE HON. LOUIS JOSEPH PAPINEAU
- CANADA CORRESPONDENCE
- STRONG DRINK: WHAT IT IS, AND WHAT IT DOES

Brown, Timothy *see* COMMENTARIES ON THE JURISDICTION OF COURTS

Brown, Tom *see* OIL ON ICE

Brown University. John Hay Library *see* CATALOG OF BROADSIDES OF AMERICAN VERSE IN THE HARRIS COLLECTION OF AMERICAN POETRY AND PLAYS

Brown University. Library *see* DICTIONARY CATALOG OF THE HARRIS COLLECTION OF AMERICAN POETRY AND PLAYS

Brown, W Jethro *see* THE AUSTINIAN THEORY OF LAW

Brown, W Kennedy *see* GUNETHICS, OR, THE ETHICAL STATUS OF WOMAN

Brown, Wallace *see* THE AMERICAN REVOLUTION IN CONTEXT

Brown, Walter Folger *see* WALTER FOLGER BROWN PAPERS

Brown, Walter H *see* NOTES ON THE SMELTING PROCESSES AT FREIBERG

Brown, Warren *see* HISTORY OF THE TOWN OF HAMPTON FALLS 1640-1900

Brown, William *see*
- THE HISTORY OF THE CHRISTIAN MISSIONS OF THE SIXTEENTH, SEVENTEENTH, EIGHTEENTH, AND NINETEENTH CENTURIES
- PROPOSALS FOR AN AMERICAN BIMETALLIC UNION
- PROSPECTUS OF NEW KINCARDINESHIRE COLONY OF NEW BRUNSWICK: WITH REPORTS OF DIRECTORS REGARDING SITUATION, SOIL, CLIMATE, ETC. ETC., AND A STATEMENT OF CONDITIONS CONCERNING FREE HOUSES, FREE GRANTS OF LAND, AND ASSISTED PASSAGES
- SILVER IN ITS RELATION TO INDUSTRY AND TRADE: THE DANGER OF DEMONETIZING IT: THE UNITED STATES MONETARY COMMISSION IN 1876: REVIEW OF PROF. FRANCIS BOWEN'S MINORITY REPORT
- THREE RONDOS FOR THE PIANO FORTE OR HARPSICHORD

Brown, William Adams *see*
- CHRIST THD VITALIZING PRINCIPLE OF CHRISTIAN THEOLOGY: AN ADDRESS
- THE CHRISTIAN HOPE
- THE ESSENCE OF CHRISTIANITY
- MODERN THEOLOGY AND THE PREACHING OF THE GOSPEL
- MORRIS KETCHUM JESUP

Brown, William Barrick *see* THE HISTORY OF A FAMOUS COURT HOUSE LOCATED AT CARLINVILLE, ILLINOIS

Brown, William Bryant *see* THE PROBLEM OF FINAL DESTINY

Brown, William Carlos, 1853-1924 *see* AN ADDRESS BEFORE THE COMMERCIAL EXCHANGE OF DES MOINES, IOWA, THURSDAY, DECEMBER 20, 1894

Brown, William Montgomery *see* THE LEVEL PLAN FOR CHURCH UNION

Brown, William Wells *see* A SELECTION OF WORKS

Brown, Winifred R *see* FEDERAL RULEMAKING

Brown, Wm. M, 3rd *see* SEDIMENT TRANSPORT AND TURBIDITY IN THE EEL RIVER BASIN

Brown, Wrisley *see* IMPEACHMENT: A MONOGRAPH ON THE IMPEACHMENT OF THE FEDERAL JUDICIARY

Browne, A M *see* LIST OF THE BRITISH MACRO-LEPIDOPTERA

Browne, Chad *see* MEMORIAL

Browne, E G *see* THE CHAHAR MAQALA OF NIDHAMI-I-ARUNDI-I-SAMARQANDI

Browne, Edward Harold *see*
- AN EXPOSITION OF THE THIRTY-NINE ARTICLES
- THE PENTATEUCH AND THE ELOHISTIC PSALMS

Browne, G F *see*
- ALCUIN OF YORK
- AUGUSTINE AND HIS COMPANIONS
- BONIFACE OF CREDITON AND HIS COMPANIONS
- THE CHRISTIAN CHURCH IN THESE ISLANDS BEFORE THE COMING OF AUGUSTINE
- THE RECOLLECTIONS OF A BISHOP
- ST. ALDHELM
- THEODORE AND WILFRITH

Browne, George *see* THE HISTORY OF THE BRITISH AND FOREIGN BIBLE SOCIETY

Browne, George W *see* HISTORY OF HILLSBOROUGH, 1735-1921

Browne, H *see* EVENING SONG TO THE VIRGIN

Browne, Irving *see*
- BROWNE'S INDEX/DIGEST TO THE NEW YORK COURT OF APPEALS REPORTS
- HUMOROUS PHASES OF THE LAW
- SHORT STUDIES IN EVIDENCE
- SHORT STUDIES OF GREAT LAWYERS
- A TREATISE ON THE ADMISSIBILITY OF PAROLE EVIDENCE IN RESPECT TO WRITTEN INSTRUMENTS

Browne, J Ross *see* CRUSOE'S ISLAND

Browne, John *see* SERMONS

BROWNE, KNIGHT AND A DAY. LEIPZIG 1928 / Bayle, Constantino – Madrid: Razon y Fe, 1928 – 9 – sp Bibl Santa Ana [999]

Browne, N E *see* A(MERICAN) L(IBRARY) A(SSOCIATION) PORTRAIT INDEX

Browne, P *see*
- THE CIVIL AND NATURAL HISTORY OF JAMAICA

Browne, P D *see* THE SEVENTH AND JAMES STREET BAPTIST CHURCH OF WACO, TEXAS

Browne, R *see* MEDICINA MUSICA

Browne, R H C *see* THE CANADIAN POLAR EXPEDITION, OR, WILL CANADA CLAIM HER OWN

Browne, Richard *see* THE ENGLISH-SCHOOL REFORMED

Browne, Robert *see* THE "RETRACTATION" OF ROBERT BROWNE

Browne, T *see*
- PSEUDODOXIA EPIDEMICA
- THE WORKS OF THE LEARNED T. BROWNE

Browne, Thomas *see* THE BRITISH CICERO

Browne, Thomas Gunter *see* HERMES UNMASKED

Browne, Walter Raleigh *see* INSPIRATION OF THE NEW TESTAMENT

Browne, William Hardcastle *see* FAMOUS WOMEN OF HISTORY: CONTAINING NEARLY THREE THOUSAND BRIEF BIOGRAPHIES AND OVER ONE THOUSAND FEMALE PSEUDONYMS

Browne, William Henry *see* THE CATHOLICOS OF THE EAST AND HIS PEOPLE

BROWNE'S INDEX/DIGEST TO THE NEW YORK COURT OF APPEALS REPORTS : VOLS 1-95 / Browne, Irving – Albany: Parsons. 1v. 1884 (all publ) – 7mf – 9 – $10.50 – LLMC 79-522 – us L.L.M.C. [340]

BROWNE'S NATIONAL BANK CASES *see* NATIONAL BANK CASES

BROWNFIELD BAPTIST CHURCH. GOLCONDA, ILLINOIS : CHURCH RECORDS – 1860-1950 – 1 – 23.58 – us Baptist [240]

Brownfield, J M *see* DIARY

Brownfield, Maine. Brownfield Free Will Baptist Church *see* RECORDS

BROWNHILLS AND CHASETOWN POST – Lichfield, England. 11 Feb 1888-12 Sept 1890. -w. 2 1/2 reels – 1 – uk British Libr Newspaper [072]

THE BROWNIES / Ewing, Juliana Horatia – British Fiction Archive: Unit 1 – 9 – uk Bell [830]

BROWNIES' BOOK – New York. v1-2. 1920-21 – 1r – 1 – us Ross [975]

THE BROWNIES' BOOK; A MONTHLY MAGAZINE FOR NEGRO CHILDREN / ed by DuBois, W E Burghard & Dill, Augustus – v1-2 Jan 1920-Dec 1921. New York. No 77-2 – 1r – 1 – $20.00 – us Partington [305]

Browning, Charles H *see*
- THE MAGNA CHARTA BARONS & THEIR AMERICAN DESCENDANTS.
- MAGNA CHARTA BARONS & THEIR DESCENDANTS, WITH THE STORY OF THE GREAT CHARTER OF KING JOHN.

Browning, Colin *see* CATALOGUE OF SANSKRIT MSS EXISTING ON OUDH

Browning, Elizabeth Barrett *see*
- AURORA LEIGH
- THE GREEK CHRISTIAN POETS AND THE ENGLISH POETS
- PROMETHEUS BOUND

BROWNING ENGINEERING COMPANY BULLETIN – (Serial publication advertising this Cleveland-based company's material handling products. Also included is the first issue of Hoisting Machinery March, 1912) – Cleveland, Cuyahoga, OH. 1902-12 – 1r – 1 – us Western Res [620]

Browning, Henry B *see* THE NEW THEOLOGY

Browning, Oscar *see* AN INTRODUCTION TO THE HISTORY OF EDUCATIONAL THEORIES

Browning, Robert *see*
- ARISTOPHANES' APOLOGY
- ASOLANDO
- BALAUSTION'S ADVENTURE
- CHRISTMAS-EVE AND EASTER-DAY
- DRAMATIC IDYLS
- DRAMATIS PERSONAE
- FERISHTAH'S FANCIES
- FIFINE AT THE FAIR
- THE INN ALBUM
- JOCOSERIA
- PARLEYINGS WITH CERTAIN PEOPLE OF IMPORTANCE IN THEIR DAY
- RED COTTON NIGHT-CAP COUNTRY, OR, TURF AND TOWERS
- ROBERT BROWNING AND ALFRED DOMETT
- LA SAISIAZ

Browning, Robert Franklin *see* A PROGRAM OF PREPARATION FOR MARRIAGE FOR THE YOUTH OF THE RICH POND BAPTIST CHURCH

Browning, Thomas Blair *see* CHART OF ELOCUTIONARY DRILL

Brownlee, William C *see* A CAREFUL AND FREE INQUIRY INTO THE TRUE NATURE AND TENDENCY OF THE RELIGIOUS PRINCIPLES OF THE SOCIETY OF FRIENDS, COMMONLY CALLED QUAKERS

Brownlee, William Craig *see* ROMANISM IN THE LIGHT OF PROPHECY AND HISTORY

Brownlow, Edward Burrough *see* ORPHEUS AND OTHER POEMS

Brownlow, W R *see* ROMA SOTTERRANEA, OR, SOME ACCOUNT OF THE ROMAN CATACOMBS, ESPECIALLY OF THE CEMETERY OF SAN CALLISTO

Brownrigg, Edwin Blake *see* OBADIAH RICH COLLECTION

BROWN'S BAPTIST CHURCH. TAR RIVER ASSOCIATION. WARREN COUNTY. NORTH CAROLINA : CHURCH RECORDS – 1830-84 – 1 – 6.75 – us Baptist [240]

BROWNS LITERARY OMNIBUS – Philadelphia, PA., 1838 – 13 – $25.00r – us I.M.R. [071]

BROWN'S NISI PRIUS REPORTS – Michigan. v1-2. 1869-71 (all publ) – 11mf – 9 – $16.50 – LLMC 81-305 – us L.L.M.C. [340]

BROWN'S PARLIAMENTARY CASES : REPORTS OF CASES UPON APPEALS AND WRITS OF ERROR DETERMINED IN THE HIGH COURT OF PARLIAMENT / Brown, Josiah – (With notes and additional cases brought down to 1800. First 3v completed during J Brown's lifetime. T E Tomlins was responsible for v4-8. 8th vol is called an Appendix and contains additional cases reported by Tomlins) – 2nd ed. v1-8. 1702-1800. London: J Butterworth, 1803 – 54mf – 9 – $81.00 – LLMC 84-756 – us L.L.M.C. [324]

BROWN'S REPORTS OF ADMIRALTY AND REVENUE CASES IN THE SIXTH CIRCUIT / Brown, H B – New York: Baker-Voorhis. 1v. 1876 (all publ) – 7mf – 9 – $10.50 – LLMC 81-446 – us L.L.M.C. [340]

Brownson, Henry Francis *see* ORESTES A. BROWNSON'S...LIFE

Brownson, Lydia B et al *see* GENEALOGICAL NOTES ON CAPE COD FAMILIES, 1620-1901

Brownson, Orestes A *see*
- THE AMERICAN REPUBLIC, ITS CONSTITUTION, TENDENCIES AND DESTINY
- AN ESSAY IN REFUTATION OF ATHEISM
- PAPERS ORESTES A. BROWNSON

Brownson, Orestes Augustus *see*
- CONVERSATIONS ON LIBERALISM AND THE CHURCH
- THE SPIRIT-RAPPER

Brownson, W J, et al *see* HEROIC MEN

BROWNSVILLE ADVERTISER – Brownsville, OR. -w. 31 Mar 1878-30 Jan 1879. 1 roll – 1 – us U.O. Library [071]

BROWNSVILLE CLIPPER – Brownsville, PA. -w 1889-1912 – 13 – $25.00r – us I.M.R. [071]

BROWNSVILLE TIMES – Brownsville, OR. -w. 4 Jan 1901-29 Dec 1977+. 22 rolls – 1 – us U.O. Library [071]

BROWNSVILLE WEEKLY NEWS – Flint. Mich. 1939-1941 – 1 – us UMI [071]

BROWNVILLE NEWS – Brownville, NE. -w. Sep.1889-Dec. 1890 – 1 – us NE Hist [071]

BROWNVILLE REPUBLICAN – Brownville, NE. -w. Apr. 1822-Dec. 1883 – 1 – us NE Hist [071]

BROWNVILLE SUN – Brownville, NE. -w. Dec. 1897-Feb. 1900 – 1 – us NE Hist [071]

Brownwood, David O *see* SELECTED EAST AFRICAN CASES ON COMMERCIAL LAW

BROWSE IN AFRICA = LES FOURRAGES LIGNEUX EN AFRIQUE. ETAT ACTUEL DES CONNAISSANCES : THE CURRENT STATE OF KNOWLEDGE / ed by Houerou, H N Le – 1983 – 9 – $56.00 – 92-9053-134-7 – et ILRI [636]

Broyde, I *see* LES REFLEXIONS SUR L'AME PAR BAHYA BEN JOSEPH IBN PAKOUDA

BROZAS. LA ENCOMIENDA MAYOR : CONFERENCIA PRONUNCIADA EN BROZAS CON MOTIVO DE "EL CARRO DE LA ALEGRIA". ORGANIZADO POR INFORMACION Y TURISMO EL 12 DE DICIEMBRE DE 1969 / Conde de Canilieros – Caceres: Tip. Extremadura, 1970 – sp Bibl Santa Ana [338]

Bruand D'uzelle, C T *see* CATALOGUE SYSTEMATIQUE ET SYNONYMIQUE DES LEPIDOPTERES

Bruant, Aristide *see* CHANSONS ET MONOLOGUES: PAROLES ET MUSIQUE

Bruce, A T *see* OBSERVATIONS ON THE EMBRYOLOGY OF INSECTS AND ARACHNIDS

Bruce, Alexander Balmain *see*
- THE CHIEF END OF REVELATION
- THE GALILEAN GOSPEL
- GALILEAN GOSPEL
- KINGDOM OF GOD: CHRIST'S TEACHING ACCORDING TO THE SYNOPTICAL GOSPELS
- THE MIRACULOUS ELEMENT IN THE GOSPELS
- THE MORAL ORDER OF THE WORLD
- THE PROVIDENTIAL ORDER OF THE WORLD
- ST. PAUL'S CONCEPTION OF CHRISTIANITY
- WITH OPEN FACE: JESUS MIRRORED IN MATTHEW, MARK, AND LUKE

Bruce, Charles *see* GRAPHIC SCENES IN AFRICAN STORY

Bruce, Colin *see* THE ECONOMIC DEVELOPMENT OF MALTA, A REPORT CONTAINING A REVISION OF THE 5 YEAR DEVELOPMENT PROGRAMME, 1956/57 TO 1960/61
Bruce, George *see* MORNING THOUGHTS FOR BUSY DAYS
BRUCE HERALD – Tokomairira. New Zealand. -sw. 21 Mar 1893-19 Jun 1896. (Imperfect). 3mqn reels – 1 – uk British Libr Newspaper [072]
Bruce, James *see*
- LIVES OF THE EMINENT MEN OF ABERDEEN
- LIVES OF THE EMINENT MEN OF FIFE
- SELECT SPECIMENS OF NATURAL HISTORY, COLLECTED IN TRAVELS TO DISCOVER THE SOURCE OF THE NILE, IN EGYPT, ARABIA, ABYSSINA, AND NUBIA
- THOSE PERPLEXING ARGENTINES
- TRAVELS IN ABYSSINIA AND NUBIA, 1768-1773
- TRAVELS TO DISCOVER THE SOURCE OF THE NILE, IN THE YEARS 1768-1773
- VOYAGE AUX SOURCES DU NIL, EN NUBIE ET EN ABYSSINIE

Bruce, King *see* BIRD'S-EYE VIEW OF LIFE INSURANCE: AND MATHEMATICAL AND LOGICAL EXPOSITION OF THE LEVEL PREMIUM PLAN
Bruce, Wiliam S *see* SOCIAL ASPECTS OF CHRISTIAN MORALITY
Bruce, William S *see* THE FORMATION OF CHRISTIAN CHARACTER
Bruce, William Straton *see* THE ETHICS OF THE OLD TESTAMENT
Bruch, M *see*
- PHANTASIE, 2 PIANOS, OP. 11
- PHANTASIE D MOLL, OP. 11, FUER 2 KLAVIERE ZU 4 HAENDEN
- SINFONIE, [ES DUR]...OP. 28

Bruchesi, Louis Joseph Paul Napoleon *see* DEUXIEME CENTENAIRE DE LA FONDATION DE L'INSTITUT DES FRERES DES ECOLES CHRETIENNES: SERMON PRONONCE DANS L'EGLISE ST JEAN BAPTISTE DE QUEBEC LE 20 OCTOBRE 1880
Bruchhaus, G *see* GEORGIAN ARCHITECTURE
Bruchmann, H *see*
- UEBER DIE PROTHALLIEN UND DIE KEIMPFLANZEN MEHRERER EUROPAEISCHER LYCOPODIEN
- UNTERSUCHUNGEN UEBER SELAGINELLA SPINULOSA A. BR

BRUCHSALER POST – Bruchsal, 1950-apr 30 1953 – 1 – Inquire at Mikrofilmarchiv for details – gw Misc Inst [072]
BRUCHSALER RUNDSCHAU – (Bereichsausgabe der Badischen Neuesten Nachrichten, Karlsruhe) – Bruchsal, jun 1 1983- – ca 10r per yr – 1 – Inquire at Mikrofilmarchiv for details – gw Misc Inst [072]
BRUCHSALER RUNDSCHAU – Bruchsal, Germany. 1 Jun 1983- – ca 10r per yr – 1 – gw Mikrofilm [072]
BRUCHSTUECKE DES ERSTEN CLEMENSBRIEFES : NACH DEM ACHMIMISCHEN PAPYRUS DER STRASSBURGER UNIVERSITAETS- UND LANDESBIBLIOTHEK, MIT BIBLISCHEN TEXTEN DERSELBEN HANDSCHRIFT / Clement 1st, Pope; ed by Roesch, Friedrich – Strassburg i.E.: Schlesier & Schweikhardt, 1910 – 1mf – us A.T.L.A. [240]
BRUCHSTUECKE DES EVANGELIUMS UND DER APOKALYPSE DES PETRUS (T.U.U. 1-9/2) / Harnack, Adolf von – Leipzig, 1893 – 2mf – 9 – ne Slangenburg [240]
BRUCHSTUECKE EINES TAGEBUCHES GEHALTEN IN GROENLAND / Saabye, H E – Aus Dem Daen. Uebers. von G. Fries. BN 379 2. 1817 – 8 – ne IDC [025]
Bruck, Iacobi a *see* EMBLEMATA POLITICA
DIE BRUCKE – 1959-88 (complete) – 3r – 1 – ATLA S0643 – us A.T.L.A. [073]
Bruckner, A *see* JULIAN VON ECLANUM (T.U.U. 1-15/3A)
Bruckner, Albert *see* DER ALTE WEG ZUM ALTEN GOTT
Bruckner, Ferdinand *see* ELISABETH VON ENGLAND
Bruder, K *see* DIE PHILOSOPHISCHE ELEMENTE IN DEN OPUSCULA SACRA DES BOETHIUS
BRUDER LUSTIG : FUR DIE MAERCHENSPIELE DER KUENSTLERISCHEN VOLKSBUEHNE SCHLICHT UND GETREU NACH GRIMMS MAERCHEN IN HANDLUNG UND REDE GESETZT / Guembel-Seiling, Max – Leipzig: Breitkopf & Haertel, [19–?] – 1r – 1 – us U.W. Library [820]
Brueck, Heinrich *see*
- GESCHICHTE DER KATHOLISCHEN KIRCHE IN DEUTSCHLAND IM NEUNZEHNTEN JAHRHUNDERT
- LEHRBUCH DER KIRCHENGESCHICHTE

DIE BRUECKE – Deutsche Wochenzeitschrift fuer Ostasien. Shanghai, China. 1925-Jun 1933 – 3r – 1 – gw Mikrofilm [072]
DIE BRUECKE – Frankfurt Main, West Germany. Halbmonatsschrift fuer Politik, Kultur, Wirtschaft. 1946-48 – 1 – gw Mikrofilm [073]
DIE BRUECKE : SCHAUSPIEL IN VIER AUFZUEGEN / Kolbenheyer, Erwin Guido – Muenchen: G Mueller, 1933 – 1r – 1 – us U.W. Library [820]
DIE BRUECKE – Shanghai. 1925-33. KCHF-9-3 – 1 – ne IDC [072]
DIE BRUECKE – (Title change: Deutsche Zukunft, Jan 1925) – Flensburg, Germany. 1924-33 – 1r – 1 – gw Mikrofilm [072]
DIE BRUECKEN : EINE AUSWAHL AUS SEINEM SCHAFFEN / Zerkaulen, Heinrich – Berlin: Die Heimbuecherei, 1942 – 1r – 1 – us U.W. Library [943]
BRUECKENKOPF : NOVELLE / Truestedt, Haro – Berlin: Wiking Verlag, c1944 – 1r – 1 – us U.W. Library [830]
Bruecker, Martin *see* DIE ENTSTEHUNG DER PAULINISCHEN CHRISTOLOGIE
Brueckner, Aleksander *see* DZIEJE KULTURY POLSKIEJ
Brueckner, Martin *see* DIE KOMPOSITION DES BUCHES JES. C. 28-33: EIN REKONSTRUKTIONSVERSUCH
DIE BRUEDER VON ST BERNHARD : SCHAUSPIEL IN FUENF AUFZUEGEN / Ohorn, Anton – 8. Aufl. Berlin: Vita Deutsches Verlagshaus [between 1906 and 1926?] – 1r – 1 – us U.W. Library [820]
BRUEDERBOTE : MONATSZEITSCHRIFT DES BESSARABISCHEN GEMEINSCHAFTSVERBANDES – v4-9; v18-44. 1951-55; 1964-91 (incomplete) – 6r – 1 – ATLA S0423 – us A.T.L.A. [240]
DAS BRUEDERLICHE JAHR : GEDICHTE / Moeller, Eberhard Wolfgang – Neue, verm. Aufl. Wien: Wiener Verlag, 1943, c1941 – 1r – 1 – us U.W. Library [810]
Brueders, P *see* COMMUNICATIONS OF THE INTERNATIONAL ASSOCIATION OF MARINE UNDERWRITERS...
Brueel, E *see* DIE DAENISCHE BELTSPERRE 1914-1918...
Brueggemann, Joseph *see* LUDWIG TIECK ALS UEBERSETZER MITTELHOCHDEUTSCHER DICHTUNG
Bruehl, I A *see* GESCHICHTE DER KATHOLISCHEN LITERATUR DEUTSCHLANDS VOM 17. JAHRHUNDERT BIS ZUR GEGENWART
Bruehl, P A *see* CENSUS OF INDIAN MOSSES
Bruel, A *see* RECUEIL DES CHARTES DE L'ABBAYE DE CLUNY
Bruel, Georges *see*
- BIBLIOGRAPHIE DE L'AFRIQUE EQUATORIALE FRANCAISE

Bruell, Nehemias *see* JAHRBUECHER FUER JUEDISCHE GESCHICHTE UND LITERATUR
BRUENNER MONTAGSBLATT – Bruenn (Brno), Czechoslovakia. Oct 1921-Dec 1929 – 5r – 1 – gw Mikrofilm [072]
BRUENNER MONTAGSBLATT – Bruenn, oct 1921-29 – 5r – 1 – Inquire at Mikrofilmarchiv for details – gw Misc Inst [943]
BRUENNER TAGEBLATT – Bruenn (Brno), Czechoslovakia. Oct 1926-May 1928; Jan-Apr 1942 – 5r – 1 – gw Mikrofilm [072]
BRUENNER TAGEBLATT – Bruenn, oct 1926-may 1928, dec 1 1940-jun 30 1944 – 1 – Inquire at Mikrofilmarchiv for details – gw Misc Inst [943]
BRUENNER TAGESPOST *see*
- TAGESPOST

BRUESSELER ZEITUNG – Belgium. -w. 18 Feb-21 Mar, 8 Jun, 5 Jul 1941-2 Sep 1944. (13 reels) – 1 – uk British Libr Newspaper [949]
BRUESSELER ZEITUNG – Bruessel (Bruxelles), Belgium. Jul 1940-2 Sept 1944 – 9r – 1 – gw Mikrofilm [949]
BRUESSELER ZEITUNG – Bruessel, jul 4-aug 2 1936, jul 1 1940-sep 2 1944 – 1 – Inquire at Mikrofilmarchiv for details – gw Misc Inst [949]
BRUESSELER ZEITUNG – Brussels, Jul 1940-Sept 1944 – 9r – 1 – DM675.00 – gw Mikro Press [949]
Bruestle, Wilhelm *see* KLOPSTOCK UND SCHUBART
Brueyre, B *see* DICTIONARIUM SINENSE-LATINUM SUN-KIAM A M D G 1847
Brueys, D-A *see*
- DEFENSE DU CULTE EXTERIEUR DE L'EGLISE
- REPONSE AU LIVRE DE MONSIEUR DE CONDOM

DE BRUG – Apeldoorn, 1937-1940. v1-3 – 10mf – J-261-18/1 – ne IDC [073]
DIE BRUG : TUSSEN PROTESTANT EN KATOLIEK – v16-18. 1967-69 (complete) – 1r – 1 – ATLA S0531 – us A.T.L.A. [240]
Brugensis, Galbertus Notarius *see* DE MULTRO, TRADITIONE ET OCCISIONE GLORIOSI KAROLI COMITIS FLANDRIARUM
Brugere, Lud-Fred *see*
- DE ECCLESIA CHRISTI
- DE VERA RELIGIONE

Bruggeboes, W *see* DIE FRATERHERREN IM LUECHTENHOFE ZU HILDESHEIM
Brugmans, H *see*
- DE WIELINGEN...
- GESCHIEDENIS DER JODEN IN NEDERLAND

Brugsch, H *see*
- HIEROGLYPHISCH-DÉMOTISCHES WOERTERBUCH
- THESAURUS INSCRIPTIONUM AEGYPTIACARUM
- THESAURUS INSCRIPTIONUM AEGYPTIACARUM. ALTAEGYPTISCHE INSCHRIFTEN GESAMMELT, UEBERTRAGEN, ERKLAERT UND AUTOGRAPHIERT VON HEINRICH BRUGSCH

Bruguera, O *see* NOVAE AC INFESTAE DESTILLATIONIS... QUAE CIVITATI BARCINONESIS ANNI 1562 ACCIDIT BREVIS ENARATIO
Bruhat, L *see* LE MONACHISME EN SAINTONGE ET EN AUNIS. (11 ET 12 SIECLES)
Bruhns, Carl *see* LIFE OF ALEXANDER VON HUMBOLDT
Bruin, C *see* AANMERKINGEN, OP OTTO VAN VEENS ZINNEBEELDEN DER GODDELIJKE LIEFDE
Bruin, Cornelis de *see* VOYAGE AU LEVANT, C'EST A DIRE DANS LES PRINCIPAUX ENDROITS DE L'ASIE MINEURE DE MEME QUE DANS LES PLUS CONSIDERABLES VILLES D'EGYPTE, DE SYRIE, DE LA TERRE SAINTE; ENRICHI DE PLUS DE DEUX CENS TAILLES DOUCES
BRUINGTON BAPTIST CHURCH. GASTON ASSOCIATION. GASTON COUNTY. NORTH CAROLINA : CHURCH RECORDS – 1853-72 – 1 – 5.00 – us Baptist [240]
Bruistens, J *see* DE LIBERTATE COMMERCIORUM EX STATU COMMUNIONIS PRIMAEVAE DERIVANDA
Bruk, Boris Lvovich *see* BIROBIDZHAN
BRUKLINER IDISHE SHTIMME = BROOKLYN JEWISH VOICE – Brooklyn, NY. 1932-34 – 1 – us A.J.P.C. [071]
BRULE CITIZEN – Brule, NE. -w. Jan. 1937-Apr. 1941 – 1 – us NE Hist [071]
Bruller, Jean *see* LE SILENCE DE LA MER
Brulotte, Marie-Berthe *see* BIBLIOGRAPHIE ANALYTIQUE DE MME PAULE DEVELUY, MEMBRE DE LA SOCIETE DES ECRIVAINS CANADIENS, ECRIVAIN CONSEIL...
Brum, B *see*
- LA PAIX DE L'AMERIQUE
- THE PEACE OF AMERICA

Brumbaugh, Martin Grove *see* A HISTORY OF THE GERMAN BAPTIST BRETHREN IN EUROPE AND AMERICA
Brumell, Henry Peareth H *see* ON THE GEOLOGY OF NATURAL GAS AND PETROLEUM IN SOUTHWESTERN ONTARIO: NOTES ON THE OCCURENCE OF PETROLEUM IN GASPE, QUEBEC
Brumer, Judah *see* RABBINIC MSS. CATALOG
Brummet, Stephan DH *see* DIE SPANISCHE POLITIK IM WESTSAHARA-KONFLIKT
Brummund, Jan Frederik Gerrit *see* BIJDRAGEN TOT DE KENNIS VAN HET HINDOEIESME OP JAVA
Brun, B *see* CRONICA JOHANNIS VITODURANI (MGH 6: 3.BD)
Brun, J *see* DICTIONARIUM SYRIACO-LATINUM
Brun, Jean *see* EMPEDOCLE; OU, LE PHILOSOPHE DE L'AMOUR ET DE LA HAIN
Brun, Mme., nee Maisonforte *see* ESSAY D'UN DICTIONNAIRE COMTOIS-FRANCOIS
THE BRUNDTLAND COLLECTION – 9 – Can$500.00 set – cn I.D.R.C. [630]
Brune, J de *see* EMBLEMATA OF ZINNEWERCK
Bruneau, Arthur *see* LOUIS BOURDAGES ET SON TEMPS: CONFERENCE FAITE DANS LES SALLES DE LA "PATRIE", VENDREDI, LE 22 JANVIER 1886
BRUNEHAUT OU LES SUCCESSEURS DE CLOVIS / Aighan – (French Theatre Series). Paris. Vente. 1811 – 9 – fr Hachette [820]
Brunei *see*
- FIVE-YEAR DEVELOPMENT PLAN, SUMMARY OF PROPOSALS 1954-1958
- GOVERNMENT GAZETTE
- NATIONAL DEVELOPMENT PLAN, 1962-66

Brunel, C *see* DAVID D'ASHBY AUTEUR MECONNU DES FAITS DES TARTARES
Brunel, Ismael-Matthieu *see* LE GENERAL FAIDHERBE
Brunel, J *see* LA FEMME MARIEE ET LES CHARGES DU MENAGE
Brunel, Rene *see* ESSAI SUR LA CONFRERIE RELIGIEUSE DES AISSAOUA AU MAROC...
Brunet, G *see* LES ETRANGERS EN FRANCE
Brunet, Jacques Charles *see*
- DICTIONNAIRE DE GEOGRAPHIE ANCIENNE ET MODERNE A L'USAGE DU LIBRAIRE ET DE L'AMATEUR DE LIVRES
- MANUEL DE LIBRAIRE ET DE L'AMATEUR DE LIVRES

Brunet, Jacques Louis Dubreuil *see* DE LA VACCINE ET DE SES HEREUX RESULTATS: DEMONTRES PAR DES VISITES FAITES AU DOMICILE DES INDIVIDUS DECEDES A PARIS...EN 1825
Brunet, Louis *see* DE MARSEILLE A TAMATAVE
Brunet, Louis Alexandre *see* LA FAMILLE ET SES TRADITIONS
Brunet, Ovide *see* ELEMENTS DE BOTANIQUE ET DE PHYSIOLOGIE VEGETALE: SUIVIS D'UNE PETITE FLORE SIMPLE ET FACILE POUR AIDER A DECOUVRIR LES NOMS DES PLANTES LES PLUS COMMUNES DU CANADA
Brunet, Pierre *see* LIVRE DE LA VIE ET DOCTRINE SPIRITUELLE DE SAINT ESTIENNE DE MURET...
Brunet, R *see* L'ANNEXION DU CONGO...
Brunet, Roger *see* L'ANNEXION DU CONGO A LA BELGIQUE ET LE DROIT INTERNATIONAL
Brunet, Victor Armand *see* BLASON POPULAIRE DE VILLEDIEU-LES-POELES, ARRONDISSEMENT D'AVRANCHES (MANCHE)
Brunetiere, Ferdinand *see* LES DIFFICULTES DE CROIRE
Brunetti, Gaetano *see*
- SINFONIA CON VIOLINI, OBOE, CORNI, VIOLA, FAGOTTO, E BASSO, NO. 29
- SINFONIA CON VIOLINI, OBOE, CORNI, VIOLA, FAGOTTO E BASSO. NO.25

Brunfels, Otto *see*
- ONOMASTIKON MEDICINAE
- ONOMASTIKON MEDICINAE (AEL, ABT 3;9)
- REFORMATION DER APOTECKEN WELCHE INHALTET VIL QUTER STUCK DIE EYEN YEGLICHEN FA.
- THESES SEV COMMVNES LOCI TOTIUS REI MEDICAE. ITEM, DE VSV PHARMACORUM, DEQUE ARTIFICIO SUPPRESSAM ALUUM CIENDI, LIBER

Bruni *see*
- LE MAJOR PALMER
- TOBERNE OU LE PECHEUR SUEDOIS

Bruni, A *see*
- LA PETITE CONVERSATION. SIX TRIOS POUR 2 VIOLINE, ALTO OU BASSE (AD. LIB.)
- SIX QUATUORS CONCERTANS
- SIX QUATUORS-CONCERTANS
- SIX TRIOS CONCERTANTS...OP. 34
- SIX TRIOS POUR 2 VIOLONS ET ALTO ET VIOLONCELLE

Bruni, LA *see* LIBRO DELLA GVERRA DE GHOTTI COMPOSTO DA MISSER LEONARDO ARETINO
BRUNING BOOSTER – Bruning, NE. -w. May 1914-Dec. 1916 – 1 – us NE Hist [071]
BRUNING COURIER – Bruning, NE. -w. June.1899-Dec. 1902; Jan. 1907-Apr. 1907 – 1 – us NE Hist [071]
BRUNNENRAUSCHEN : KALENDERGESCHICHTEN / Leppa, Karl Franz – Karlsbad: A Kraft, 1942 – 1r – 1 – us U.W. Library [390]
Brunner, A *see* BRUNNER'S REPORTS OF CASES IN THE CIRCUIT COURTS OF THE U.S., 1789-1879
BRUNNER ABENDBLATT – Brno, Czechoslovakia. Dec 1940-Aug 1944 – 3r – 1 – us L of C Photodup [072]
Brunner, F *see* LA DOCTRINE DE LA MATIERE CHEZ AVICEBRON
Brunner, Heinrich *see* DAS ANGLONORMANNISCHE ERBFOLGESYSTEM

Brunner, S *see* CORRESPONDANCES INTIMES DE L'EMPEREUR JOSEPH 2 AVEC SON AMI LE COMTE DE COBENZL ET SON PREMIER MINISTRE LE PRINCE DE KAUNITZ. MAYENCE
Brunner, Sebastian *see* DIE HOFSCHRANZEN DES DICHTERFUERSTEN
BRUNNER TAGBLATT – Brno, Czechoslovakia. Dec 1940-Feb 1945 – 6r – 1 – us L of C Photodup [072]
Brunner von Wattenwyl, C *see* REVISION DU SYSTEME DES ORTHOPTERES ET DESCRIPTION DES ESPECES RAPPORTEES PAR...L. FEA DE BIRMANIE
BRUNNER'S REPORTS OF CASES IN THE CIRCUIT COURTS OF THE U.S., 1789-1879 / Brunner, A – San Francisco: Sumner-Whitney. 1v. 1884 (all publ) – 8mf – 9 – $12.00 – LLMC 81-439 – us L.L.M.C. [340]
Bruno, A *see* REPORT TO THE GOVERNMENT OF THE FEDERATION OF SOUTH ARABIA ON EXISTING AND POTENTIAL CITRUS AREAS
Bruno Cartusiense *see* OPERA ET VITA...
BRUNO CHAP BOOKS – New York. v1-3 1915-1916 – 1 – us NY Public [800]
Bruno, Jacobus Pancratius *see* CASTELLUS RENOVATUS. HOC EST LEXICON MEDICUM QUONDAM A BART. CASTELLO MESSANENSI (AEL, ABT 3)
BRUNO KREISKY PAMPHLET COLLECTION – 1970-1971 – 1 – CSUXANQ2311-B – us Hoover Inst Photo [320]
Bruno, Michael S *see* JOURNAL OF MARINE ENVIRONMENTAL ENGINEERING
BRUNONIS DE BELLO SAXONICO LIBER (MGH 7: 15.BD) – 1880 – Dfl13.00 – ne Slangenburg [240]
BRUNOS BUCH VOM SACHSENKRIEG (MGH DEUTSCHES..: 2.BD) – 1937 – Dfl13.00 – ne Slangenburg [240]
BRUNO'S WEEKLY – New York. v. 1-3. July 26 1915-Dec 30 1916. Incomplete – 1 – us NY Public [800]
Brunot, F *see* LA DOCTRINE DE MALHERBE
Bruns, C G *see* GESAMMELTE SCHRIFTEN ZUR MINDERHEITENFRAGE
Bruns, Paul Jakob *see* NEUE SYSTEMATISCHE ERDBESCHREIBUNG VON AFRIKA
Brunschwig, Hieronymus *see*
- DAS BUCH ZU DISTILIEREN DIE ZUSAMEN GETHONEN DING
- HAUSS APOTECK ZU YEDEN LEIBS GEBRESTEN, FUER DEN GEMAINEN MANN, VND DAS ARM LANDUOLCK
- LIBER DE ARTE DISTILLANDI DE COMPOSITIS. DAS BUCH DER WAREN KUNST ZU DISTILLIEREN DIE COMPOSITA UND SIMPLICIA UND DAS BUCH THESAURUS PAUPERUM
- THESAVRVS PAVPERVM; EINN FURTREFLICHE VND VOLKOMNE HAUSSAPOTECK

Brunson, Alfred *see* KEY TO THE APOCALYPSE, OR, REVELATION OF JESUS CHRIST TO ST JOHN
BRUNSWICK AND COBURG LEADER – 1913-1921. BCL1-3 – 3r – 1 – at Corangamite [072]
Brunswick. (City). Arbeitertag *see* ARBEITERTAG FUER BRAUNSCHWEIG UND WEITERERE UMGEGEND, ABGESCHALTEN ZU BRAUNSCHWEIG
Brunswick, Maine. Baptist Church *see* RECORDS
BRUNSWICK TIMES-GAZETTE – Lawrenceville. Va. 1965- – 1 – us UMI [071]
Brunton, E *see* A GRAMMAR AND VOCABULARY OF THE SUSCO LANGUAGE
Brunton, Guy *see*
- LAHUN 2
- LAHUN I: THE TREASURE

Brunton, Thomas Lauder *see* BIBLE AND SCIENCE
Bruny, Chevalier de *see* LETTRE SUR J.J. ROUSSEAU
Bruschi, A F *see* REGOLE PER IL CONTRAPUNTO, E PER L'ACCOMPAGNATURA DEL BASSO CONTINUO COMPENDIATE
BRUSH AND PENCIL – 1897-1907 – 110mf – 9 – £500.00 – uk Chadwyck [700]
BRUSH CREEK BAPTIST CHURCH. TENNESSEE : CHURCH RECORDS – 1828-1984 – 1 – 75.69 – us Baptist [240]
Brush, Florence C *see* A COMPARISON OF SELECTED NEUROMUSCULAR AND KINEMATIC VARIABLES BEFORE AND AFTER LEARNING AN AIMING TASK
BRUSHY CREEK BAPTIST CHURCH. COPIAH COUNTY. MISSISSIPPI : CHURCH RECORDS – 1875-1882 – 1 – 5.00 – us Baptist [240]
BRUSHY CREEK BAPTIST CHURCH. GREENVILLE COUNTY. SOUTH CAROLINA : CHURCH RECORDS – June 1795-1969; Deacons' Minutes, 1961-72 – 1 – 77.00 – us Baptist [240]
Brusilov, Aleksei Alekseevich *see* MOI VOSPOMINANIIA
Brusina, S *see* IPSA CHIEREGHINII CONCHYLIA
Brusle de Valsuzenay, Claude L *see* TABLEAU STATISTIQUE DU DEPARTEMENT DE L'AUBE
Brussius, G *see* DE TARTARIS DIARIVM
Bruston, Charles *see*
- ETUDES SUR DANIEL ET L'APOCALYPSE
- HISTOIRE CRITIQUE DE LA LITTERATURE PROPHETIQUE DES HEBREUZ
- LA VIE FUTURE D'APRES SAINT PAUL

Bruston, Edouard *see* IGNACE D'ANTIOCHE, SES EPITRES, SA VIE, SA THEOLOGIE
BRUT Y TYWYSOGION (RS17) : OR THE CHRONICLE OF THE PRINCES OF WALES (681-1281) / ed by Ab Ithel, J Williams – 1860 – Dfl35.00 – ne Slangenburg [941]
LA BRUTA (HEROES DE AHORA) / Trigo, Felipe – Madrid: Renacimiento, 6th ed 1907 – sp Bibl Santa Ana [946]
BRUTUS : TRAUERSPIEL VON HEINRICH KRUSE / Kruse, Heinrich – 2. Aufl. Leipzig: S Hirzel, 1882 – 1r – 1 – us U.W. Library [820]
BRUUN MEMORIAL LECTURES : PRESENTED AT SESSIONS OF THE IOC ASSEMBLY, UNESCO, PARIS – 9 – fr UNESCO [550]
Bruxelles. Academie Royale des Sciences Coloniales. Classe des Sciences Morales et Politiques *see* MEMOIRES IN-80
Bruxelles. Institut Royal Colonial Belge. Section des Sciences Morales et Politiques *see* MEMOIRES
Bruyas, N *see* DE LA DECLARATION DE GUERRE;...
Bruyne, Philippe Charles Antoine de *see* HISTOIRE DE LA BELGIQUE SOUS LE REGNE DE MARIE-THERESE
Bruzen la Martiniere, Antoine A *see* INTRODUCTION A L'HISTOIRE DE L'ASIE, DE L'AFRIQUE, ET DE L'AMERIQUE
Bry, J T de *see* FLORILEGIUM NOVUM
Bry, Jean A J *see* MEMOIRE STATISTIQUE DU DEPARTEMENT DU DOUBS
Bry, Jean A J de *see* ESSAI SUR L'EDUCATION NATIONALE
BRYAN AND DARROW AT DAYTON: THE RECORD AND DOCUMENTS OF THE BIBLE-EVOLUTION TRIAL – Ed. and comp. by Leslie H. Allen. New York: A. Lee & Co., c1925. viii,218p – 1 – us U.W. Library [240]
Bryan, Carlton H Jr. *see* AN ANALYSIS OF SELECTED ATTENDANCE FACTORS IN THE WORLD LEAGUE OF AMERICAN FOOTBALL
Bryan, Chester E *see* HISTORY OF MADISON COUNTY
BRYAN DEMOCRAT – Bryan, Ohio. 1865-1926 – 14r – 1 – $32.50r – us Archival [071]
Bryan, George *see* THE IMPERIALISM OF JOHN MARSHALL: A STUDY IN EXPEDIENCY
Bryan. Ohio. First Presbyterian Church *see* RECORDS
Bryan. Ohio. Trinity Episcopal Church *see* RECORDS
Bryan. Ohio. Trinity Lutheran Church *see* RECORDS
BRYAN PRESS – Bryan, Ohio. 1869-99 – 15r – 1 – $32.50r – us Archival [071]
Bryan, R G *see* GOD'S WITNESS TO HIS OWN WORD
BRYAN UNION PRESS – Bryan, Ohio. 1862-69 – 3r – 1 – $32.50r – us Archival [071]
BRYANS CREEK BAPTIST CHURCH. LINCOLN COUNTY. MISSOURI : CHURCH RECORDS – 1831-1948. 468p – 1 – 21.06 – us Baptist [240]
Bryant, Edwin Eustace *see*
- THE CONSTITUTION OF THE UNITED STATES WITH NOTES OF THE DECISIONS OF THE SUPREME COURT THEREON.
- FORMS IN CIVIL ACTIONS AND PROCEEDINGS IN THE COURTS OF RECORD OF WISCONSIN
- A SELECTION OF FORMS TO ACCOMPANY THE VOLUME ON WISCONSIN CODE PRACTICE.

Bryant Family *see* LETTERS
Bryant, John Ebenezer *see* AGRICULTURE IN PUBLIC SCHOOLS: AN ADDRESS DELIVERED BEFORE THE MEMBERS OF THE ONTARIO TEACHER'S ASSOCIATION AT THEIR THIRTIETH ANNUAL CONVENTION HELD AT NIAGARA-ON-THE-LAKE, AUGUST, 1890
Bryant, Stratton and Odell's Business College *see* THE INDEX
Bryant, William C *see*
- L'AMERIQUE DU NORD PITTORESQUE: OUVRAGE REDIGE PAR UNE REUNION D'ECRIVAINS AMERICAINS
- THE EMBARGO

Bryant, Wm M *see* ETHICS AND THE "NEW EDUCATION"
Bryce, George *see*
- EDUCATIONAL THOUGHTS FOR THE DIAMOND JUBILEE YEAR: INAUGURAL ADDRESS DELIVERED IN CONVOCATION HALL, MANITOBA COLLEGE, WINNIPEG, NOVEMBER 19TH, 1897
- A SHORT HISTORY OF THE CANADIAN PEOPLE
- UNIVERSITY EDUCATION: INAUGURAL ADDRESS DELIVERED IN CONVOCATION HALL, MANITOBA COLLEGE, WINNIPEG, NOVEMBER 10TH, 1899

Bryce, James *see*
- THE AMERICAN COMMONWEALTH
- THE AMERICAN CORRESPONDENCE OF J. BRYCE, 1871-1922. BRRAM
- THE HOLY ROMAN EMPIRE
- MODERN DEMOCRACIES
- STUDIES IN CONTEMPORARY BIOGRAPHY
- UNIVERSITY AND HISTORICAL ADDRESSES

Bryce, Lloyd *see* ROMANCE OF AN ALTER EGO
BRYCE ON AMERICAN DEMOCRACY : SELECTIONS FROM THE AMERICAN COMMONWEALTH AND THE HINDRANCES TO GOOD CITIZENSHIP / ed by Fulton, Maurice G – New York: Macmillan, 1919 – 5mf – 9 – $7.50 – LLMC 95-086 – us L.L.M.C. [323]
Brydges, Charles John *see* REPORT BY MR. BRYDGES ON HIS INSPECTION OF THE PORTIONS OF THE INTERCOLONIAL RAILWAY NOW IN OPERATION
Brydges, S E *see* MODERN ARISTOCRACY, OR THE BARD'S RECEPTION
Bryennii, Nicephori Caesaris *see* COMMENTARII DE REBUS BYZANTINIS (CBH 3,4)
Brymner, Douglas *see*
- ENDOWMENTS OF THE CHURCH OF SCOTLAND IN CANADA: EVIDENCE OF MR. DOUGLAS BRYMNER BEFORE THE SENATE COMMITTEE ON PRIVATE BILLS, IN OPPOSITION TO THE BILLS FOR TRANSFERRING THE SAID ENDOWMENTS TO THE PRESBYTERIAN CHURCH IN CANADA, 24TH AND 26TH APRIL, 1882
- FAULTS AND FAILURES OF THE LATE PRESBYTERIAN UNION IN CANADA
- THE JAMAICA MAROONS: HOW THEY CAME TO NOVA SCOTIA: HOW THEY LEFT IT

BRYOLOGIA AUSTRIACA EXCURSORIA / Garovaglio, S – Vindobonae. 1840. B-6202 2 – 8 – ne IDC [580]
BRYOLOGIA BRITTANICA / Wilson, W – London. 1855. B-6205 2 – 8 – ne IDC [580]
BRYOLOGIA DANICA / Jensen, T – Kjobenhavn. 1856. B-5316 – 8 – ne IDC [580]
BRYOLOGIA EUROPA / Schwizerbart, E – 1836-55 – 1 – uk Microform Academic [580]
BRYOLOGIA EUROPAEA / Schimper, W P – 187 2. 6 v. 1836-1855 – 9 – ne IDC [580]
BRYOLOGIA GERMANICA / Nees von Esenbeck, CG D & Hornschuch, CF & Sturm, J – Nurnberg, Leipzig, 1823-1831. 2 vols. B-6204 1 – 9 – ne IDC [580]
BRYOLOGIA JAVANICA... / Dozy, F & Molkenboer, J H – Lugduni Batavorum, 1855-1870, v1. 1862-1870, v2 – 24mf – 9 – ne IDC [574]
BRYOLOGIA SILESIACA / Milde, J – Leipzig, 1869. 410 pp. B-5452 2 – 8 – ne IDC [580]
BRYOLOGIA UNIVERSA SEU SYSTEMATICA / Bridel, S E de – v. 1. Lipsiae. 1826; v. 2. Lipsiae. 1827. B-5191 2 – 8 – ne IDC [580]
BRYOLOGIST – New York, 1898-1941. v1-44 – 124mf – 135c/2 – ne IDC [580]
THE BRYOPHYTA OF SOUTH AFRICA / Sim, T R – Cape Town, 1926. 475 pp. (Transact. Royal Soc. South Africa, v. 15). B-6164 2 – 8 – ne IDC [580]
Brysgawer, M *see* WIE MAN CHRISTLICHER WEYSZ BEICHTEN
Bryson, Mary Isabella *see* JOHN KENNETH MACKENZIE
BS *see* SOZIALDEMOKRAT
BS. BERLINER SOZIALDEMOKRAT *see* SOZIALDEMOKRAT
BS. DAS BERLINER STADTBLATT *see* SOZIALDEMOKRAT
BSCS JOURNAL – v2-. 1979- – 1,5,6,9 – us UMI [580]
BSCS NEWSLETTER / American Institute of Biological Sciences. Biological Sciences Curriculum Study – (Ceased publ. Superseded by: Biological Sciences Curriculum Study journal) – Boulder, 1959-1971; v46-69 1972-nov 1977 1*; v46-69 1972-nov 1977 5*; v58-69 feb 1975-nov 1977 9 – 1,5,9 – D7084 – us UMI [574]
BSER AND T : BUILDING SERVICES ENGINEERING RESEARCH AND TECHNOLOGY – v1- 1980- – 1,5,6,9 – us UMI [073]
BSI (BRITISH STANDARDS INSTITUTION) – Printed index. Updates every 60 days – 6,9 – us Info Handling [380]
B'TSELEM : THE ISRAELI INFORMATION CENTER FOR HUMAN RIGHTS IN THE OCCUPIED TERRITORIES – Jersualem. 30 docs. 1989-1991 – 16mf – 9 – ne IDC [320]
BU ER SHI WEI KE – A Central Committee Party magazine begun in Oct 1927. 52 issues. 74 ill. DL53f – 9 – 350.00 – cc Globe [073]
BUANG TONDJAM / Motinggo, Busje – SE-4443 1. 1963 – 9 – ne IDC [950]
BUBASTIS (MEES VOL 8) / Naville, E – London, 1891 – 8mf – 8 – Dfl30.00 – ne Slangenburg [930]
BUBBLE GUM GAZETTE SUMMER WEEKLY READER – (v.5-. 1979- 5,6,9) – v.1-. 1975- – 1 – us UMI [800]
Buber, S *see* MIDRASCH TEHILLIM, ODER HAGGADISCHE ERKLAERUNG DER PSALMEN
Bublikov, Aleksandr Aleksandrovich *see* RUSSKAI A REVOLIUTSII A: EI A NACHALO, AREST TSARI A, PERSPEKTIVY
Bubnov, Andrei *see* OSNOVNYE MOMENTY V RAZVITII KOMMUNISTICHESKOI PARTII V ROSSII
Bubnov, N *see* SILVESTRI 2 PAPAE OPERA MATHEMATICA
Bubnov, Nikolai Mikhailovich *see* FRIEDRICH NIETZSCHES KULTURPHILOSOPHIE UND UMWERTUNGSLEHRE
Buccaeus, I *see* HET NECROLOGIUM DIOECESIS HARLEMENSIS
THE BUCCANEERS AND MAROONERS OF AMERICA / ed by Pyle, Howard – New illus. ed. London: T. Fisher Unwin; New York: Macmillan, 1891. 403p. illus – 1 – us U.W. Library [970]
Bucci, A *see* ORATIONE DELLA PACE, ET DELLA GUERRA CONTRA TURCHI, A'I PRENCIPI CHRISTIANI
Bucelini, Gabr. *see*
- MENOLOGIUM BENEDICTINUM
- SACRARIUM BENEDICTINUM

Buceta Facorro, Luis *see* EL SOCIOGRAMA DE LA ESTRUCTURA INFORMAL
DAS BUCH – Paris. Zeitschrift fua5r die unabhaa5ngige deutsche Literatur. Mar. 1938-Mar. 1940 – 1 – 35.00r – us Hoover Inst Photo [073]
DAS BUCH – Zeitschrift fUEr die unabhaengige deutsche literatur. Paris. 1938-1940 – 1 – gw Mikrofilm [430]
DAS BUCH BARUCH: GESCHICHTE UND KRITIK, UEBERSETZUNG UND ERKLAERUNG / Kneucker, Johann Jacob – Leipzig: F.A. Brockhaus, 1879. 1 fiche – 9 – us A.T.L.A. [240]
DAS BUCH BEI DEN GRIECHEN UND ROMERN / Schubart, W – 993 2. Ed. 2. 1921 – 8 – ne IDC [930]
DAS BUCH DANIEL / Kranichfeld, Rudolph – Berlin: Gustav Schlawitz, 1868. 1 fiche – 9 – us A.T.L.A. [240]
DAS BUCH DANIEL : TEXT-KRITISCHE UNTERSUCHUNG / Riessler, Paul – (Includes bibliographical references) – Stuttgart:Jos. Roth, 1899 – 1mf – 9 – 0-8370-4901-6 – 1985-2901 – us A.T.L.A. [220]
DAS BUCH DANIEL: NACH DER SEPTUAGINTA HERGESTELLT / Jahn, Gustav – Leipzig: Eduard Pfeiffer, 1904. 1 fiche – 9 – us A.T.L.A. [240]

DAS BUCH DER JUBILAEEN; ODER, DIE KLEINE GENESIS, HRSG. VON HERMANN ROENSCH. 1874 – 1 – us A.T.L.A. [240]
DAS BUCH DER MALERZECHE IN PRAG / Pangeri, Matthias – O 517m. 1878 – 9 – ne IDC [760]
DAS BUCH DER RINGSTEINE FARABIS / Horten, M – Muenster, 1906 – 10mf – 8 – ne Slangenburg [190]
BUCH DER SPRUECHE / Blumenthal, Oscar – 2. Aufl. Berlin: Concordia Deutsche Verlags-Anstalt, c1909 – 1 – us U.W. Library [810]
DAS BUCH DER VERSAMLUNG; ORDER, DAS BUCH DER HEIMLIGKEITEN MAGNI ALBERTI, VON ARTZNEY VND TUGENDEN DER KRUTER VNND EDEL GSETEIN, VND VON ETLICHE WOLBEKANTEN THIERE / Albertus Magnus – Stra., 1519 – 1 – us U.W. Library [240]
DAS BUCH DER WEISHEIT DES JESUS SIRACH (JOSUA BEN SIRA) IN SEINEM VERHAELTNISS ZU DEN SALOMONISCHEN SPRUECHEN UND SEINER HISTORISCHEN BEDEUTUNG / Seligmann, Caesar – (Includes bibliographical references) – Halle (Saale): [s.n.], 1883 (Breslau [Wroclaw]: Th Schatzky) – 1mf – 9 – 0-8370-9820-3 – 1986-3820 – us A.T.L.A. [220]
DAS BUCH DES PROPHETEN HABACKUK / Happel, Otto – Wuerzburg: Andreas Goebel, 1900 – 1mf – 9 – 0-8370-3468-X – 1985-1468 – us A.T.L.A. [220]
DAS BUCH DEUTSCHER BRIEFE / ed by Heynen, Walter – (Includes bibliographical references and index) – Wiesbaden: Insel-Verlag, 1957 – 1 – us U.W. Library [860]
DAS BUCH ESTER / Jahn, Gustav – Leiden: E.J. Brill, 1901. 1 fiche – 9 – us A.T.L.A. [240]
DAS BUCH ESTHER : AUF SEINE GESCHICHTLICHKEIT / Jampel, Sigmund – (Includes bibliographical references) – Frankfurt (Main): J Kauffmann, 1907 – 1mf – 9 – 0-8370-3767-0 – 1985-1767 – us A.T.L.A. [220]
DAS BUCH EZECHIEL / Jahn, Gustav – Leipzig: Eduard Pfeiffer, 1905. 1 fiche – 9 – us A.T.L.A. [240]
Buch, F F *see* DAS RECHT DER DONAUSCHIFFAHRT...
DAS BUCH GENESIS DER VULGATA UND DES HEBRAEISCHEN TEXTES / Neteler, Bernhard – Muenster i.W.: Theissing, 1905. 1 fiche – 9 – us A.T.L.A. [220]
DAS BUCH HABAKUK: TEXT, UEBERSETZUNG UND ERKLAERUNG / Duhm, Bernhard – Tuebingen: J.C.B. Mohr, 1906. 1 fiche – 9 – us A.T.L.A. [220]
DAS BUCH HENOCH : AETHIOPISCHER TEXT (T.U.U. 2-22/1) / Flemming, J – Leipzig, 1902 – 3mf – 9 – ne Slangenburg [240]
DAS BUCH HENOCH: AUS DEM AETHIOPISCHEN / Gollancz, Hermann – Berlin: Richard Heinrich, 1892. 1 fiche – 9 – us A.T.L.A. [240]
DAS BUCH HIOB / Duhm, Bernhard – (Includes subject index) – Freiburg i.B: J C B Mohr, 1897 – 1mf – 9 – 0-8370-2991-0 – 1985-0991 – us A.T.L.A. [220]
DAS BUCH HIOB UEBERSETZT UND AUSGELEGT / Hitzig, Ferdinand – (Includes bibliographical references and index) – Leipzig: C F Winter, 1874 – 1mf – 9 – 0-8370-3596-1 – 1985-1596 – us A.T.L.A. [220]
DAS BUCH JEREMIA / Cornill, Carl Heinrich – (Includes index) – Leipzig: Chr Herm Tauchnitz, 1905 – 2mf – 9 – 0-8370-9691-X – 1986-3691 – us A.T.L.A. [220]
DAS BUCH JEREMIA / Duhm, Bernhard – Tuebingen: J.C.B. Mohr, 1901 – 9 – us A.T.L.A. [240]
DAS BUCH JEREMIA / Giesebrecht, Friedrich – 2. völlig umgearb. Aufl. Gottingen: Vandenhoeck & Ruprecht, 1907 – 1mf – 9 – 0-8370-3271-7 – 1985-1271 – us A.T.L.A. [220]
DAS BUCH JEREMIA – Uebersetzt von Bernhard Duhm. 1903 – 1 – us A.T.L.A. [220]
DAS BUCH JOB : UEBERSETZT UND ERKLAERT / Zschokke, Hermann – Wien: Wilhelm Braumueller, 1875 – 1mf – 9 – 0-8370-5973-9 – 1985-3973 – us A.T.L.A. [220]
DAS BUCH JOSUA / Holzinger, Heinrich – (Includes subject index) – Tuebingen: J C B Mohr, 1901 – 1mf – 9 – 0-8370-3645-3 – 1985-1645 – us A.T.L.A. [220]
DAS BUCH JUDITH ALS GESCHICHTLICHE URKUNDE : VERTHEIDIGT UND ERKLAERT NEBST EINGEHENDEN UNTERSUCHUNGEN UEBER DAUER UND AUSDEHNUNG DER ASSYRISCHEN OBMACHT IN ASIEN UND AEGYPTEN, UEBER DIE HYKSOS, UEBER DIE URSITZE DER CHALDAEER UND DEREN ZUSAMMENHANG MIT DEN SKYTHEN, UEBER PHUD, LUD, ELAM, CHNA / Wolff, O – (Includes bibliographical references) – Leipzig: Doerffling und Franke, 1861 – 1mf – 9 – 0-8370-9754-1 – 1986-3754 – us A.T.L.A. [220]
DAS BUCH KOHELET...TALMUD UND MIDRASCH UND DER JUEDISCHEN ERKLAERER DES MITTELALTERS / Schiffer, Sinai – Frankfurt a.M.: J. Kauffmann, 1884. 1 fiche – 9 – us A.T.L.A. [220]
BUCH NEHEMIAH = THE BOOK OF NEHEMIAH CRITICALLY AND THEOLOGICALLY EXPOUNDED, INCLUDING THE HOMILETICAL SECTIONS OF DR. SCHULTZ / Crosby, Howard – (In English) – New York:Scribner, Armstrong, c1877 – 1mf – 9 – 0-8370-3242-3 – 1985-1242 – us A.T.L.A. [220]
Buch, Ricarda *see* DIENSTLEISTNGEN DER INFORMATIONS/AUSKUNFTSBANK
DAS BUCH RICHTER UND RUTH / Bertheau, Ernst – Leipzig: S. Hirzel, 1883. 1 fiche – 9 – us A.T.L.A. [240]
DAS BUCH RUTH IN DER MIDRASCH-LITTERATUR : EIN BEITRAG ZUR GESCHICHTE DER BIBELEXEGESE / Hartmann, David – (Includes list of abbreviations & appendix) – Leipzig: Baer & Hermann, 190! – 1mf – 9 – 0-8370-3506-6 – 1985-1506 – us A.T.L.A. [220]
DAS BUCH TOBIAS / Reusch, Franz Heinrich – (In German, Latin, and Greek) – Freiburg i.B.: Herder, 1857 – 1mf – 9 – 0-8370-9730-4 – 1986-3730 – us A.T.L.A. [220]
DAS BUCH UM ANTON WILDGANS / Soyka, Josef – Leipzig: L Staackmann, 1932 – 1 – us U.W. Library [430]
DAS BUCH VON DEN VIER QUELLEN / Wibbelt, Augustin – Warendorf: J Schnellschen Buchhandlung, 1912 – 1r – 1 – us U.W. Library [430]
Buch, Walter *see* NIEDERGANG UND AUFSTIEG DER DEUTSCHEN FAMILIE
DAS BUCH WANDERSCHAFT / Winnig, August – Hamburg: Hanseatische Verlagsanstalt, c1941 – 1r – 1 – us U.W. Library [910]
DAS BUCH WEINSBERG, BD 2 1552-1577 (PGRG 3) / ed by Hoehlbaum, K – Leipzig, 1887 – Dfl30.00 – ne Slangenburg [240]
DAS BUCH ZU DISTILIEREN DIE ZUSAMEN GETHONEN DING / Brunschwig, Hieronymus – Strassburg, 1532 – 1 – us U.W. Library [430]
BUCHAN OBSERVER – 1 – £42.00r – uk Scot News [072]
BUCHAN OBSERVER, PETERHEAD, FRASERBURGH AND GENERAL ADVERTISER – (East Aberdeenshire Observer, Peterhead, Fraserburgh & General Advertiser, 1878-93) – Peterhead, Scotland, UK. 16 Jan 1863-16 Nov 1920; 1921-81 – 113r – 1 – uk British Libr Newspaper [072]
Buchanan, A C *see*
- RAPPORT DE A.C. BUCHANAN, ECUYER, AGENT PRINCIPAL DES EMIGRES, POUR L'ANNEE 1855
- RAPPORT DE L'AGENT EN CHEF DE L'IMMIGRATION, POUR L'ANNEE 1860

Buchanan, Edgar Simmons *see* SYLLABUS OF A COURSE OF FOUR LECTURES ON THE HISTORY AND AUTHORITY OF THE HOLY SCRIPTURES IN THE CHURCH
Buchanan, Francis Hamilton *see* AN ACCOUNT OF THE DISTRICTS OF BIHAR AND PATNA IN 1811-1812
Buchanan, George *see* DE PROSODIA LIBELLUS
Buchanan, George Sir *see* MOI A MISSII A V ROSSII
Buchanan, J *see* REVISED LIST OF THE FERNS OF NATAL
Buchanan, James *see*
- THE BRITISH GRAMMAR
- LINGUAE BRITANNICAE VERA PRONUNCATIO: OR, A NEW ENGLISH DICTIONARY
- PAPERS

Buchanan, Joseph Rodes *see* MORAL EDUCATION
Buchanan, Martin L *see* STRATEGIES FOR LIBERTY
Buchanan, Robert Williams *see* A LOOK ROUND LITERATURE
Buchbinder, N *see* DI GESHIKHTE FUN YIDISHER ARBAYTER BAWEGUNG IN RUSLAND
BUCHDRUCKER WACHT – Leipzig, Germany. 1896-99; 1900-02 – 1 – gw Mikrofilm [072]
BUCHDRUCKER-ZEITUNG : 1873-1940, 1887-1940 – (Coll title: Labor Union Periodicals, Pt 2) – 5r – 1 – $675.00 – 1-55655-304-8 – us UPA [680]
Bucher Family *see* FAMILY REUNION MINUTES
THE BUCHEUM (MEES VOL 41, 2) : THE INSCRIPTIONS / Mond, R & Myers, OL – London, 1934 – 5mf – 8 – Dfl22.00 – ne Slangenburg [930]
THE BUCHEUM (MEES VOL 41, 3) : THE PLATES / Mond, R & Myers, OL – London, 1934 – 16mf – 8 – Dfl56.00 – ne Slangenburg [930]
THE BUCHEUM (MEES VOL 41,1) : THE HISTORY AND ARCHAEOLOGY OF THE SITE / Mond, R & Myers, OL – London, 1934 – 10mf – 8 – Dfl35.00 – ne Slangenburg [930]
BUCHGEMEINSCHAFTEN IN DEUTSCHLAND 1918-1933 / Scholl, Bernadette – 1994 – 4mf – 9 – DM112.00 – 3-89349-873-7 – gw Hänsel [430]
BUCHHAENDLER IM NEUEN REICH – Berlin, 1936-40 (incomplete) – 1 – Dist. gw Mikrofilm – gw Misc Inst [020]
BUCHHAENDLER PALM : EIN DEUTSCHES HELDENSCHICKSAL AUS DEM JAHRE 1806 / May, Werner – (Includes bibliographical references) – Breslau: H Handel, 1935 – 1r – 1 – us U.W. Library [920]
Buchheim, C A *see* HARZREISE
Buchheit, V *see* STUDIEN ZU METHODIOS VON OLYMPOS (T.U.U. 5-69)
Buchholtz, Arend *see* DIE GESCHICHTE DER FAMILIE LESSING
Buchholtz, H F *see* VINDICAE GROTIANI DOGMATIS DE PRAESCRIPTIONE INTER GENTES LIBERAS...
Buchholtz, Ludwig *see* DIE CHRISTLICHE LEHRE AUF HEILSGESCHICHTLICHEM GRUNDE
Buchholz, C A *see* ACTENSTUEKKE, DIE VERBESSERUNG DES BUERGERLICHE ZUSTANDES DER ISRAELITEN BETREFFEND
BUCHHOLZ GALLERY-CURT VALENTIN CATALOGUE – (Individual titles not listed separately) – New York, 1937-1955 – 144 catalogues on 145mf – 9 – £915.00 – uk Chadwyck [700]
BUCHLOER ZEITUNG – Buchloe, 1954-sep 1968 – 1 – Inquire at Mikrofilmarchiv for details – gw Misc Inst [072]
Buchmann, J *see* DIE UNFREIE UND DIE FREIE KIRCHE
Buchmann, Jacob *see*
- KIRCHLICHE AUTORITAET UND MACHT DER WISSENSCHAFT
- KRUMME WEGE ZUR UNFEHLBARKEIT
- EIN MISSIONSBISCHOF AUS LAENGST VERGANGENER ZEIT

Buchmann, Klaere *see* DER WIDERSCHEIN
Buchner, R *see* TEXTKRITISCHE UNTERSUCHUNGEN ZUR LEX RIBVARIA (MGH SCHRIFTEN..: 5.BD)
Buchori, Mochtar *see* SOME PROBLEMS PERTAINING TO THE EXAMINATION AND THE SELECTION OF PROSPECTIVE STUDENTS OF THE TEACHER TRAINING AND EDUCATIONAL SCIENCES, BANDUNG(ACADEMIC YEAR 1958/1959). SE-11,530/1. 1959
Buchotte *see* LES REGLES DU DESSIN ET DU LAVIS POUR LES PLANS PARTICULIERS DES OUVRAGES ET DES BATIMENTS.
Buchoz, P J *see*
- CATALOGUE LATIN ET FRANCOIS DES PLANTES VIVACES,...
- HISTOIRE DES INSECTES NUISIBLES A L'HOMME, AUX BESTIAUX
- MANUEL MEDICAL ET USUEL DES PLANTES,...
- PLANTES NOUVELLEMENT DECOUVERTES, RECEMMENT DENOMMEES ET CLASSEES, REPRESENTEES EN GRAVURES AVEC LEURS DESCRIPTIONS; POUR SERVIR D'INTELLIGENCE A L'HISTOIRE GENERALE ET ECONOMIQUE DES TROIS REGNES
- TRAITE HISTORIQUE DES PLANTES QUI CROISSENT DANS LA LORRAINE ET LET TROIS EVECHES, CONTENANT LEUR DESCRIPTION, LEUR FIGURE, LEUR CULTURE LEUR ANALYSE, LEURS PROPRIETES, TANT POUR LA MEDICINE, QUE POUR LES ARTS ET METIERS

Buchtenkirch, Gustav *see* KLEISTS LUSTSPIEL "DER ZERBROCHENE KRUG" AUF DER BUEHNE
Buchwald, Reinhard *see* SCHILLER UND BEETHOVEN
Buck *see* HISTORY OF HAMILTON AND CLAY COUNTIES
Buck, Adriaan de *see*
- THE EGYPTIAN COFFIN TEXTS, VOL 2
- THE EGYPTIAN COFFIN TEXTS, VOL 6

Buck, Carl Darling *see* INTRODUCTION TO THE STUDY OF THE GREEK DIALECTS
Buck, Clayton A *see* CELL ADHESION AND COMMUNICATION
BUCK CREEK BAPTIST CHURCH. CALHOUN, KENTUCKY : CHURCH RECORDS – 1824-Aug 1973 – 1 – 81.00 – us Baptist [240]
BUCK CREEK BAPTIST CHURCH. SPARTANBURG, SOUTH CAROLINA : CHURCH RECORDS – 1851-1966 – 1 – 33.12 – us Baptist [240]
Buck, Dudley *see* THE CENTENNIAL MEDITATION OF COLUMBIA
Buck, Edward *see* MASSACHUSETTS ECCLESIASTICAL LAW
Buck, Herbert *see* KASSEL UND AHNABERG
Buck, William Calmes *see*
- THE BAPTIST HYMN BOOK
- BIOGRAPHICAL MATERIALS
- THEOLOGY: THE PHILOSOPHY OF RELIGION

Bucke, Richard Maurice *see*
- ALCOHOL IN HEALTH AND DISEASE
- COSMIC CONSCIOUSNESS: A STUDY IN THE EVOLUTION OF THE HUMAN MIND
- MAN'S MORAL NATURE: AN ESSAY
- WALT WHITMAN

Buckel, A *see* DIE GOTTESBEZEICHNUNGEN IN DEN LITURGIEN DER OSTKIRCHEN
BUCKEYE – Troy. Ohio. 1886-87; 1891-1901 – 1 – us UMI [071]
BUCKEYE AMERICAN : WEEKLY KU KLUX KLAN NEWSPAPER – Warren, OH. 11 Sept 1923 – 1r – 1 – us Western Res [071]
BUCKEYE BANNER : WEEKLY TEMPERANCE NEWSPAPER – Warren, OH. 27 July and 3 Aug 1849 – 1r – 1 – us Western Res [071]
BUCKEYE FIRST SOUTHERN BAPTIST CHURCH. BUCKEYE, ARIZONA : CHURCH RECORDS – 1925-90 – 1 – $88.38 – us Baptist [240]
BUCKEYE GRANGER – Perrysburg, Ohio. 1876-78 – 1r – 1 – $32.50r – us Archival [071]
BUCKEYE SMOKE SIGNALS / North American Indian Association – Jan-Feb 1969. (American Indian Periodicals in the Princeton University Library). 1 fiche – 9 – $45.00 – us UPA [305]
BUCKEYE VIDETTE – Bryan, Ohio. 1880-81 – 1r – 1 – $32.50r – us Archival [071]
Buckham, John Wright *see*
- CHRIST AND THE ETERNAL ORDER
- PERSONALITY AND THE CHRISTIAN IDEAL

Buckingham, James Silk *see*
- AMERICA, HISTORICAL, STATISTIC, AND DESCRIPTIVE
- AUTOBIOGRAPHY...INCLUDING HIS VOYAGES, TRAVELS, ADVENTURES
- OUTLINE SKETCH OF THE VOYAGES, TRAVELS, WRITINGS, AND PUBLIC LABOURS OF JAMES SILK BUCKINGHAM.
- TRAVELS IN PALESTINE: THROUGH THE COUNTRIES OF BASHAN AND GILEAD, EAST OF THE RIVER JORDAN..

THE BUCKINGHAM POST – Buckingham, Canada. 16 mai 1895-18 oct 1978 – 23r – 1 – Can$65.00r – cn Can Microfilming [072]
Buckingham, William *see* THE HON. ALEXANDER MACKENZIE: HIS LIFE AND TIMES
BUCKINGHAMSHIRE, 1823 : BRITISH ISLES CENSUS DIRECTORIES PROJECT, ENGLAND. VOL 225 – 1mf – 9 – A$9.00 – at Vine [941]
BUCKINGHAMSHIRE, 1830 : BRITISH ISLES CENSUS DIRECTORIES PROJECT, ENGLAND – at Vine [941]
BUCKINGHAMSHIRE, 1839 : BRITISH ISLES CENSUS DIRECTORIES PROJECT, ENGLAND. VOL 30 – 2mf – 9 – A$15.00 – at Vine [941]
BUCKINGHAMSHIRE, 1844 : BRITISH ISLES CENSUS DIRECTORIES PROJECT, ENGLAND. VOL. 268 – 2mf – 9 – at Vine [941]
BUCKINGHAMSHIRE, 1853 : BRITISH ISLES CENSUS DIRECTORIES PROJECT, ENGLAND – at Vine [941]
BUCKINGHAMSHIRE, 1854 : BRITISH ISLES CENSUS DIRECTORIES PROJECT, ENGLAND – at Vine [941]

BUCKINGHAMSHIRE, 1864 : BRITISH ISLES CENSUS DIRECTORIES PROJECT, ENGLAND. VOL 124 – 4mf – 9 – A$27.00 – at Vine [941]
BUCKINGHAMSHIRE, 1877 : BRITISH ISLES CENSUS DIRECTORIES PROJECT, ENGLAND. VOL 9 – 3mf – 9 – A$21.00 – at Vine [941]
BUCKINGHAMSHIRE, 1891 : BRITISH ISLES CENSUS DIRECTORIES PROJECT, ENGLAND. VOL 67 – 4mf – 9 – A$27.00 – at Vine [941]
BUCKINGHAMSHIRE, 1899 : BRITISH ISLES CENSUS DIRECTORIES PROJECT, ENGLAND. VOL 79 – 5mf – 9 – A$33.00 – at Vine [941]
BUCKINGHAMSHIRE, 1915 : BRITISH ISLES CENSUS DIRECTORIES PROJECT, ENGLAND – at Vine [941]
BUCKINGHAMSHIRE, 1920 : BRITISH ISLES CENSUS DIRECTORIES PROJECT, ENGLAND – (In prep) – at Vine [941]
BUCKINGHAMSHIRE ADVERTISER *see* BUCKINGHAMSHIRE AND ADJACENT COUNTIES ADVERTISER
BUCKINGHAMSHIRE ADVERTISER AND COUNTY GAZETTE – Uxbridge, England. 1922-56; 1986; 1988- – 84+ r – 1 – uk British Libr Newspaper [072]
BUCKINGHAMSHIRE AND ADJACENT COUNTIES ADVERTISER – (Buckinghamshire Advertiser. Broadwater's Buckinghamshire Advertiser. Middlesex and Buckinghamshire Advertiser. Middlesex Advertiser) – Amersham and Uxbridge, England. Nov 1853-Jul 1869; Apr 1874-Dec 1960 – 116r – 1 – uk British Libr Newspaper [072]
BUCKINGHAMSHIRE RECORD SOCIETY – (Coll title: Publications of the English Record Societies, 1835-1972) – v1-11. 1937-56 – 25mf – 9 – £210.00 – uk Chadwyck [941]
BUCKLAND 1841-1849 – (Mf 1T: Births & Marriages 1843-49; Deaths 1841-49) – (mf ed 1995) – 1mf – 9 – 0-87623-221-7 – us Holbrook [920]
BUCKLAND 1873-1895 – (Mf 1: Births 1873-89. Mf 2: Births 1889-95; Marriages 1869-91. Mf 3: Marriages 1882-95. Mf 4: Deaths 1873-90. Mf 5: Deaths 1891-95) – (mf ed 1988) – 5mf – 9 – 0-87623-046-X – us Holbrook [920]
Buckland, Augustus R *see* WOMEN IN THE MISSION FIELD, PIONEERS AND MARTYRS
Buckland, C E *see* DICTIONARY OF INDIAN BIOGRAPHY
Buckland, Lawrence F *see* DATA INPUT FOR PUBLISHERS. STATE OF THE ART REPORT
Buckler, John Chessell *see* A HISTORY OF THE ARCHITECTURE OF THE ABBEY CHURCH OF ST ALBAN; WITH SPECIAL REFERENCE TO THE NORMAN STRUCTURE
Buckler, W M *see* THE LARVAE OF THE BRITISH BUTTERFLIES AND MOTHS
Buckley, Homer John *see* THE SCIENCE OF MARKETING BY MAIL
Buckley, James Monroe *see*
- AN ADDRESS ON SUPPOSED MIRACLES
- ADDRESS ON SUPPOSED MIRACLES
- CONSTITUTIONAL AND PARLIAMENTARY HISTORY OF THE METHODIST EPISCOPAL CHURCH
- FAITH-HEALING, CHRISTIAN SCIENCE AND KINDRED PHENOMENA
- FUNDAMENTALS AND THEIR CONTRASTS
- A HISTORY OF METHODISTS IN THE UNITED STATES
- WHAT METHODISM OWES TO WOMEN

Buckley, John *see* AN IMPARTIAL ACCOUNT OF A LATE DEBATE AT LYME IN THE COLONY OF CONNECTICUT
Buckley, Theodore Alois *see* A HISTORY OF THE COUNCIL OF TRENT
BUCKLEY-MATTHEW COLLECTION, 1850-56 – BRRAM – 1 – uk Microform Academic [080]
Buckminster, Joseph Stevens *see*
- GRIESBACH'S NEW TESTAMENT
- NOTICE OF GRIESBACH'S EDITION OF THE NEW TESTAMENT
- SERMON
- SERMONS, NOW FIRST PUBLISHED FROM THE AUTHOR'S MANUSCRIPTS

BUCKNELL REVIEW – (v25- . 1980- . 5,6,9) – v.5-. 1954- – 1 – us UMI [073]
BUCKNELL UNIVERSITY STUDIES – v.1-. 1941- – 1,5,6,9 – us UMI [073]
BUCKNELL WORLD – Lewisburg, PA., 1984-1987 – 13 – $25.00r – us I.M.R. [071]
BUCKNELLAN PAPER – Lewisburg, PA., 1984-1987 – 13 – $25.00r – us I.M.R. [071]
Buckner, Heike *see* LOHN- UND TARIFPOLITIK IN DER METALLINDUSTRIE 1918 BIS 1933
Bucknew, H F *see* A GRAMMAR OF THE MASKOKE, OR CREEK LANGUAGE
BUCKOWER LOKAL-ANZEIGER – Buckow, jul-dec 1936, jul-dec 1938 – 2r – 1 – Inquire at Mikrofilmarchiv for details – gw Misc Inst [943]
BUCKS ADVERTISER AND AYLESBURY NEWS – Aylesbury, England. Dec 1836-40; 1843-52; 1863-95; Feb 1897-1919; 1922; 1925-26; 1928; 1930; 1933; 1935; 1937; 1940; 1947-53; 1986- – 121+ r – 1 – uk British Libr Newspaper [072]
BUCKS COUNTY GAZETTE – New Hope. Pa. 1958-66 – 1 – us UMI [071]
BUCKS COUNTY GAZETTE – New Hope, PA. -w 1972 – 13 – $25.00r – us I.M.R. [071]
BUCKS COUNTY INTELLIGENCER – Doylestown, PA. -w 1898-1912; 1918-1927 – 13 – $25.00r – us I.M.R. [071]
Bucks County. Pennsylvania *see* TAX LISTS
BUCKS COUNTY PRESS – Levittown, PA. -w 1952-1953 – 13 – $25.00r – us I.M.R. [071]
BUCKS EXAMINER – Chesham, England. Jul 1889-1910; 1912-54; 1986- – 101+ r – 1 – uk British Libr Newspaper [072]
BUCKS GAZETTE – Aylesbury, England. 21 Feb 1829-6 Oct 1849 – 7r – 1 – uk British Libr Newspaper [072]
THE BUCKSKIN – 1970-71. (American Indian Periodicals in the Princeton University Library). 7 fiches – 9 – $45.00 – us UPA [305]
Buckton, G B *see*
- A MONOGRAPH OF THE BRITISH APHIDES
- A MONOGRAPH OF THE MEMBRACIDAE

BUCOLICA ET GEORGICA / Vergil – 15th cent. Holkham ms. 307. Holkham Hall, Norfolk, England – 14 – uk Microform Academic [760]
BUCOLICA, ETC / Siculus, Calpurnius – 15th Century. Holkham 334 – 1 – uk Microform Academic [760]
Bucquoy, E et al *see* LES MOLLUSQUES MARINS DU ROUSILLON
Bucyrus. Ohio. First Presbyterian Church *see* RECORDS
Bucyrus. Ohio. Harmony Evangelical Church *see* RECORDS
Bucyrus. Ohio. St. John's United Church of Christ *see* RECORDS
BUDAJA DJAJA; MADJALAH KEBUDAJAAN UMUM. DEWAN KESENIAN DJAKARTA – (Monthly. Missing: 1971 v4(40, p513-576)) – Djakarta. v1-5. 1968-1972 – 41mf – 9 – SE-1365/1 – ne IDC [950]
BUDAPEST SUN – 1980-1994 – 1 – sz Infoprint [072]
THE BUDAPEST SUN – 1993-1995 – sz Infoprint [072]
THE BUDAPEST SUN – (Comes in English) – 1 – sz Infoprint [947]
BUDAPESTER RUNDSCHAU – 1976-1995 – 3 times per yr – 1 – F371.00 – sz Infoprint [072]
BUDAPESTER RUNDSCHAU – Budapest, 1967-92 n1 – 16r – 1 – Inquire at Mikrofilmarchiv for details – gw Misc Inst [072]
BUDAPESTER RUNDSCHAU – Budapest, Hungary. 1972-75; 1976- – 1 – gw Mikrofilm [072]
BUDAPESTER RUNDSCHAU – Ungarn, 1976-1992 – 16r – 1 – DM1,200.00 – gw Mikro Press [943]
BUDAPESTI HIRLAP – Budapest. 1926-1930, 1935-1936, Jan-Apr 1939 – 1 – us NY Public [073]
BUDAPESTI HIRLAP – Budapest, 1926-36 – 6r – 1 – us Ross [072]
BUDAPESTI HIRLAP – (Lacking: Sept, Oct 1937) – Budapest, Hungary. Jan 1905-Apr 1939 – 206r – 1 – uk British Libr Newspaper [072]
BUDAPESTI SZEMLE – ser. 1, v. 1-ser. 3, v. 177, no. 505. 1857-1919. Incomplete – 1 – us NY Public [073]
Buday, Marie T *see* A BIOMECHANICAL ANALYSIS OF THE DEMI PLIE AND GRAND PLIE
BUDBAEREREN – (Several mergers. Lacking some pgs) – v1-49. Dec 1868-June 1917 – 26r – 1 – ATLA S0249 – us A.T.L.A. [073]
BUDBAERERREN *see* LUTHERANEREN
Budberg, Aleksei Pavlovich Baron *see* DNEVNIK ALEKSI EI A BUDBERGA
Budd, G *see* ON DISEASES OF THE LIVER
Budd, Henry *see*
- THE 39 ARTICLES OF OUR ESTABLISHED CHURCH – 1571
- LEADING CASES IN THE AMERICAN LAW OF REAL PROPERTY

Budde, Karl *see*
- DIE BUECHER RICHTER UND SAMUEL
- GESCHICHTE DER ALTHEBRAEISCHEN LITTERATUR (MIT) APOKRYPHEN UND PSEUDEPIGRAPHEN
- DER KANON DES ALTEN TESTAMENTS: EIN ABRISS
- DIE RELIGION DES VOLKES ISRAEL BIS ZUR VERBANNUNG

BUDDELMEYER-ZEITUNG – Berlin, apr 2 1849-dec 29 1851 – 1r – 1 – Dist. gw Mikrofilm – gw Misc Inst [072]
Budden, Heber *see* NEWFOUNDLAND: ITS CLIMATE, GEOGRAPHICAL POSITION, RESOURCES, ETC.: AND BENARES, THE SACRED CITY OF THE HINDUS: TWO LECTURES DELIVERED BEFORE THE Y.M.C.A
Buddensieg, Rudolf *see* JOHANN WICLIF UND SEINE ZEIT
Buddeus, I F *see* DE IURE GENTIS AUSTRIACAES IN REGNUM HISPANIAE
BUDDHA : EPISCHE DICHTUNG IN ZWANZIG GESAENGEN / Widmann, Joseph Viktor – Bern: Dalp (C. Schmid), 1869 – 1r – 1 – us U.W. Library [810]
THE BUDDHA OF CHRISTENDOM : A BOOK FOR THE PRESENT CRISIS / Anderson, Robert – (Includes indexes) – London: Hodder & Stoughton, 1899 – 1mf – 9 – 0-8370-2493-5 – 1985-0493 – us A.T.L.A. [240]
BUDDHISM AND ITS CHRISTIAN CRITICS / Carus, Paul – Chicago: The Open Court Publishing Co., 1897. 316p – 1 – us U.W. Library [280]
LE BUDDHISME AU CAMBODGE / Leclere, Adhemard – Paris: E. Leroux, 1899. xxxi,535p. front.,illus.,plates – 1 – us U.W. Library [280]
BUDDHIST AND HINDU ART OF EASTERN INDIA AND BANGLADESH : SOUTH ASIAN ART PHOTO COLLECTION PART 1: KUSHAN PERIOD, CAVES AND GUPTA PERIOD / ed by Huntington, Susan L – 187mf – 9 – ne IDC [700]
BUDDHIST AND HINDU ART OF EASTERN INDIA AND BANGLADESH : SOUTH ASIAN ART PHOTO COLLECTION PART 2: GANDHARA – 75mf – 9 – ne IDC [700]
BUDDHIST AND HINDU ART OF EASTERN INDIA AND BANGLADESH : SOUTH ASIAN ART PHOTO COLLECTION PART 3.1 / ed by Huntington, Susan L – (Bihar State 157mf Dfl1,727.00. West Bengal State 14mf Dfl154.00. Assam State 2mf Dfl22.00. Bangladesh 34mf Dfl374.00. Provenance Unknown 18mf Dfl198.00. Includes printed guide with indexes) – 225mf – 9 – ne IDC [700]
BUDDHIST AND HINDU ART OF EASTERN INDIA AND BANGLADESH : SOUTH ASIAN ART PHOTO COLLECTION PART 3.2: ISLAMIC MOUNUMENTS OF EASTERN INDIA AND BANGLADESH – (Includes printed guide) – 118mf – 9 – ne IDC [700]
BUDDHIST ECONOMICS AND THE MODERN WORLD / Jha, Hari Bansh – Kathmandu: Dharmakirti Baudha Adhyayan Gosthi, 1979 – us Res Libr [330]
BUDDHIST IDEALS (A STUDY IN COMPARATIVE RELIGION) / Saunders, Kenneth James – Madras: Christian Literature Society for India, 1912. 179p – 1 – us U.W. Library [280]
BUDDHIST SANSKRIT MANUSCRIPTS / Bajracharya, M B & George, CS – (Supplemental Manuscripts. 43 titles. 314 fiches. $900.00; Title List. 1 fiche. $1.00; Descriptive Catalog, Part 1. 6 fiches. $6.00; Descriptive Catalog, Part 2. 9 fiches. $9.00; Descriptive Catalog, Part 3. 2 fiches. $2.00; Supplemental Descriptive Catalog. 2 fiches. $2.00) – 471 titles. 1185 fiches – 9 – $3400.00 – us I.A.S.W.R. [280]
BUDDHIST SHRINES IN INDIA / Valisinha, Devapriya – Colombo: Maha Bodhi Society of Ceylon, 1948 – 1 – us U.W. Library [280]
BUDDHIST SUTTAS / ed by Mueller, Friedrich Max – (Translated from Pali by T.W. Rhys Davids) – 8 – ne Slangenburg [280]
BUDDHISTISCHE KUNST IN INDIEN / Gruenwedel, A – ed. 2. Berlin. 1900. BI-1139 1 – 9 – ne IDC [280]
DIE BUDDHISTISCHE SPAETANTIKE IN MITTELASIEN / Le Coq, A von – v. 1-7. Berlin. 1922-33. Illus. BU-623 2 – 8 – ne IDC [280]
THE BUDDHIZATION OF CHRISTIANITY (CCC10) = FU HUA CHI TU CHIAO / Chang, Chun-i – (In Chinese) – [s.l: s.n], 1924 – 1r – 1 – 0-8370-1710-6 – 1984-6093 – us A.T.L.A. [230]
BUDDIST MAHAYANA TEXTS : PART 1: THE BUDDHA-KARITA OF ASVAGHOSHA / ed by Mueller, Friedrich Max – (Translated from the Sanskrit by E.B. Cowell) – Oxford, 1894 – 4mf – 8 – ne Slangenburg [280]
BUDDIST MAHAYANA TEXTS : PART 2: THE LARGER SUKHAVATI-VYUHA... / ed by Mueller, Friedrich Max – (A General Index.- Oxford, 1910.-12mf) – Oxford, 1894 – 5mf – 8 – ne Slangenburg [280]
BUDDY'S WEEKLY READER – v54- . 1976- . Continues: My Weekly Reader – 1,5,6,9 – us UMI [370]
Bude, Eugene Guillaume Theodore de *see* LETTRES INEDITES ADRESSEES DE 1686 A 1737 A J.-A. TURRETTINI
Bude, G *see* COMMENTARII LINGUAE GRAECA
BUDEM TVERDY DO KONTSA / Baratov, Boris – Moskva: Gos. izd-vo, 1919 – 1 – CSUX88-B7676 – us Hoover Inst Photo [947]
BUDET RADOST' / Merezhkovskii, Dimitrii – P' esa v 4 deistviiakh. Petrograd. 1916. BR-751 2 – 8 – ne IDC [460]
Budge, E A W *see*
- THE BOOK OF THE DEAD. FACSIMILES OF THE PAPYRI OF HUNEFER, ANHAI, KERASHER AND NETCHEMET, WITH SUPPLEMENTARY TEXT FROM THE PAPYRUS OF NU
- FACSIMILES OF EGYPTIAN HIERATIC PAPYRI IN THE BRITISH MUSEUM
- THE GREENFIELD PAPYRUS IN THE BRITISH MUSEUM
- THE LIFE OF TAKLA HAYMANOT... AND THE MIRACLES OF TAKLA HAYMANOT, IN THE VERSION OF DABRA LIBANOS, AND THE BOOK OF THE RICHES OF KINGS
- THE LIVES OF MABA' SYON AND GABRA KRESTOS
- THE ROSETTA STONE

Budge, E A Wallis *see* THE EGYPTIAN SUDAN
Budge, Ernest A Wallis *see* THE BOOK OF THE BEE
Budge, Ernest Alfred Wallis *see* ASSYRIAN TEXTS
Budge, Sir Ernest Alfred Thompson Wallis *see* ONE HUNDRED AND TEN MIRACLES OF OUR LADY MARY, TRANSLATED FROM ETHIOPIC MANUSCRIPTS FOR THE MOST PART IN THE BRITISH MUSEUM..
Budgell, E A *see* LETTER TO THE MERCHANTS AND TRADESMEN OF GT. BRITAIN, PARTICULARLY TO THOSE OF LONDON AND BRISTOL, CONCERNING THEIR SUCCESSFUL OPPOSITION TO THE EXTENSION OF THE EXCISE LAWS 1733
BUDGET / Morocco. Empire Cherifien Protectorat Francais – 1955-62. (lacking 1956(1), 1957(1), 1958(1)). BNE-3050 1 – 9 – ne IDC [332]
THE BUDGET – (Filmed with: The Saturday Budget 17 dec 1870-4 mar 1871; 7 dec 1872-29 dec 1906; The Weekly Budget 11 mar 1871-30 nov 1872) – Quebec, Canada. 12 nov-10 dec 1870 – 12r – 1 – Can$60.00r – cn Can Microfilming [072]
THE BUDGET – Sugarcreek. Ohio. 1890-1949 – 1 – us UMI [071]
THE BUDGET – Toronto: W Campbell, [1881?-1893] – 9 – cn C.I.H.M. [971]
BUDGET AND DEVELOPMENT PLANS / Argentine Republic – (Plan General de Gobierno 1953-57. D-940-1. Plan Nacional de Desarrollo, 1965-69. 2v. D-903-1. Plan Nacional de Desarrollo, 1970-74. 7v. D-942-1. Plan Nacional de Desarrollo y Seguridad, 1971-75. D-1557-1) – 9 – ne IDC [338]
BUDGET DE CAPITAL PROGRAMME DE DEVELOPEMENT ECONOMIQUE, 1 OCT 1951-30 SEP 1956 / Haiti – (Montieur (Port-au-Prince). 29 Sep 1951 – 9 – ne IDC [350]
BUDGET DES RECETTES ET DES DEPENSES DEPARTEMENTALES / Oise. France. (Department) – Beauvais. Exercise 1945-1949 & Supplements – 1 – us NY Public [350]

BUDGET ESTIMATES, 1959/1960, 1965/1966, 1966/1967-1968/1969 / Libya. Ministry of Finance – (Arabic and English). BNE-634 1 – 9 – ne IDC [336]

BUDGET FOR THE FISCAL YEAR 1960 / Philippines. Budget Commission – Manila. 1959 – 9 – ne IDC [350]

BUDGET FOR THE UNITED SERVICE IN THE REGIONS OF SYRIA AND EGYPT / Egypt – 3v. 1958-1961. BNE-4627 1 – 9 – ne IDC [350]

BUDGET GENERAL DE L'ETAT – 1974 and 1975 – 1 – $49.50y – us African Imprint [960]

BUDGET GENERAL DE L'EXERCISE, 1970-1971 / Syria – (Recueil des lois et de la legislation financiere de la Republique arabe syrienne). 3 v. in 2. BNE-9735 1 – 9 – ne IDC [350]

BUDGET LAW / Jordan. Ministry of Finance – 1957-77. Lacking: 1957 58; 1976. BNE-9806 1 – 9 – ne IDC [336]

BUDGET OF THE EGYPTIAN REGION / Egypt. Ministry of Treasury – 14 v. 1947-62. (lacking 1952-53). BNE-4670-1 – 9 – ne IDC [336]

THE BUDGET OF THE SOVIET-UNION FOR THE FINANCIAL YEAR 1924/25 AND THE ESTIMATE FOR THE CURRENT FINANCIAL YEAR 1925/26 / The foreign General Representation of the USSR Finance-Commissariat – Berlin: The Representation, [192-] – 1 – CSUX90-B8154 – us Hoover Inst Photo [350]

BUDGET OF THE UNITED STATES GOVERNMENT / U.S. Bureau of the Budget – 1923- 1; 1967- 5,6; 1975- 4 x 6 in. 9 – us UMI [336]

BUDGET OF THE UNITED STATES GOVERNMENT / U.S. Office of Management and Budget – (1967-. 1,5,6,9) – Dept. ed. 1922- – 1 – us UMI [336]

BUDGET OF THE UNITED STATES GOVERNMENT. APPENDIX / U.S. Office of Management and Budget – Dept. ed. 1982- – 1,5,6,9 – us UMI [350]

BUDGET PLANS / Peru – (Instituto Nacional de Planificacion. Programa De Inversiones Publicas, 1964-1965. D-1425; 1. 2 v. 1964. SF 39.00; 9. Instituto Nacional de Planificacion. Programa De Inversiones Publicas, 1966. D-1426; 1. 2 v. 1965. SF 28.00; IDC; 9. Ministerio de Economia y Finanzas. Plan Economico Anual, 1970. D-918; 1. 2 v. 1970. SF 23.00; IDC; 9. Sistema Nacional de Planificacion. Plan Nacional De Desarrollo 1971-1975. D-1153; 1. 2 v. 1971. SF 14.00; IDC; 9) – ne IDC [336]

BUDGET PLANS / Philippines – (Budget Commission. Five year fiscal plan (1957-1961). D-1431; 1. 1957. SF 8.00; 9. Budget Commission. Five year fiscal plan (1960-1964). D 1434; 1. 1960. SF 8.00; IDC; 9. Budget Commission. Five year fiscal program (1964-1968). D-1438; 1. 1963. SF 8.00; IDC; 9. Four year economic program for the Philippines. 1967-1970. D-882; 1. 1966. SF 10.00; IDC; 9. Four year development plan fy 1971-74. D-1154; 1. 1970. SF 14.00; IDC; 9) – ne IDC [338]

BUDGET PLANS / Uganda – (Development plan 1947-1956. D 1508; 1. 1947. SF 12.00; 9. 1948 revision of the plan 1947-1956. D 1509; 1. 1949. SF 12.00; IDC; 9. Five year capital development plan, 1955-1960. D 1510; 1. 1954. SF 8.00; IDC; 9. Second five year plan 1966; 67-1970; 71. Project Supplement. D 1224; 1. 1969. SF 14.00; IDC; 9. Third five year development plan, 1971; 72-1975; 76. D 1541; 1. 1971. SF 18.00; IDC; 9) – ne IDC [338]

THE BUDGET REPORT / Syria. Ministry of Economy and Treasury – 2v. 1959-61. BNE-9714 1 – 9 – ne IDC [350]

THE BUDGET REPORT / United Arab Republic. Ministry of Treasury – 7v. 1954-60 – 9 – ne IDC [336]

BUDGET SPEECH DELIVERED IN THE HOUSE OF COMMONS OF CANADA ON TUESDAY, FEBRUARY 20TH, 1877 / Cartwright, Richard – Ottawa: 1877. 05710. (Pre-1900 Canadiana) – 9 – cn C.I.H.M. [971]

BUDGET STATISTICS ON EDUCATION OF THE CENTRAL AND PROVINCIAL GOVERNMENTS 1970/71 TO 1976/77 / Pakistan. Ministry of Education. Bureau of Educational Planning and Management – Islamabad, 1977 – 1mf – 9 – DE-566/1 – ne IDC [370]

THE BUDGETARY IMPACT OF POSSIBLE CHANGES IN DIVERSITY JURISDICTION / Partridge, Anthony – Washington: FJC, 1988 – 1mf – 9 – $1.50 – LLMC 95-340 – us L.L.M.C. [340]

BUDGETS / Hancock County. Ohio. Biglick Township. Township Clerk – 1928-1952 – 1r – 1 – $32.50r – us Archival [324]

LES BUDGETS DE DEVELOPPEMENT EN R.A.S., 1967-1968-1969 / Syria. Office Arabe de Presse et de Documentation – Damas. 1969. BNE-9734 1 – 9 – ne IDC [338]

BUDGETS DE L'ETAT – 1971 and 1972.-1r.$49.50; 1973 and 1974.-1r.$49.50 – 1 – us African Imprint [960]

BUDGETS DE L'EXERCISE/ESTIMATES – (In French and English) – 1976/77, 1977/78, 1979/80, 1982/83 – 1 – $49.50r – us African Imprint [324]

BUDGETS OF THE GOVERNMENT OF LIBERIA – 1974, 1975, 1976, 1977/78 – 4r – 1 – $49.50ea – us African Imprint [960]

THE BUDGET...SPEECH IN THE HOUSE OF COMMONS, IN REPLY TO THE FINANCE MINISTER'S STATEMENT: DELIVERED TUESDAY, MARCH 5, 1889 / Cartwright, Richard – 1889? 02145. (Pre-1900 Canadiana) – 9 – cn C.I.H.M. [971]

BUDI LUHUR; BUKU BATJAAN AGAMA UNTUK SEKOLAH RAKJAT OLAN MADRASAH-MADRASAH. DIHIASI OLEH M. LUBIS / Abdullah, Z – Jakarta: Firma Rada, 1954. illus. SEM-3053 – 9 – ne IDC [950]

BUDIL'NIK – St Petersburg, Moscow, 1865-1917 – 649mf – 9 – $3,800.00 – us Ross [790]

BUDISSINER NACHRICHTEN *see* BAUTZENER NACHRICHTEN

BUDISSINISCHE NACHRICHTEN *see* BAUTZENER NACHRICHTEN

BUDISSINISCHE WOECHENTLICHE NACHRICHTEN *see* BAUTZENER NACHRICHTEN

Budisteano, R *see* LA CONDITION JURIDIQUE DES MINORITES ETHNIQUES...

BUDS AND BLOSSOMS AND FRIENDLY GREETINGS – Halifax, N.S: J F Avery, [1876-188-?] – 9 – cn C.I.H.M. [971]

BUDUSHCHAIA VOINA / ed by Tukhacheskii, M N – (Part 1 of 7 parts) – Minneapolis: East View Publications, 1993 – 1mf – 9 – $39.95 – us East View [947]

BUDUSHCHEE *see* V BORBIE S BOLSHEVIKAMI I NIEMTSAMI

BUDUSHCHNOST RUSSKAGO TSARIA / Ignotus – Berlin: Izd. F. Shteinitsa, 1906 – 1 – CSUX89-B6760 – us Hoover Inst Photo [947]

BUDWEISER ZEITUNG – Budweis, aug 24 1938-oct 27 1942 – 1 – Inquire at Mikrofilmarchiv for details – gw Misc Inst [943]

BUDWEISER ZEITUNG – Budweis (Ceske Budejovice), Czechoslovakia. 24 Aug 1938-27 Oct 1942 – 1 – gw Mikrofilm [072]

DIE BUECHER DER BIBEL : 1. BAND: UEBERLIEFERUNG UND GESETZ. DAS FUENFBUCH BOSE UND DAS BUCH JOSUA / ed by Rahlwes, F – 1996 – 6mf – 9 – DM118.00 – 3-8267-3184-0 – gw Hänsel [220]

DIE BUECHER DER BIBEL : 6. BAND: DIE LIEDERDICHTUNG. DIE PSALMEN, DIE KLAGELIEDER, DAS HOHELIED / ed by Rahlwes, F – 1996 – 4mf – 9 – DM90.00 – 3-8267-3186-7 – gw Hänsel [220]

DIE BUECHER DER BIBEL : 7. BAND: DIE LEHRDICHTUNG. DIE SPRUECHE, HIOB, DER PREDIGER, RUTH, JONA, ESTHER, DANIEL / ed by Rahlwes, F – 1996 – 4mf – 9 – DM90.00 – gw Hänsel [220]

DIE BUECHER DER CHRONIK DER VULGATA UND DES HEBRAEISCHEN TEXTES / Neteler, Bernhard – Muenster i. W: Theissing, 1899 – 1mf – 9 – 0-8370-3874-X – 1985-1874 – us A.T.L.A. [220]

DIE BUECHER DER GEHEIMNISSE HENOCHS (T.U.U. 3-44/2) / Bonwetsch, G N – Leipzig, 1922 – 3mf – 9 – ne Slangenburg [240]

BUECHER DER KOENIGE = THE BOOKS OF THE KINGS / Baehr, Karl Christian Wilhelm Felix; ed by Harwood, Edwin & Sumner, William Graham – (In English) – New York: Charles Scribner, c1872 – 2mf – 9 – 0-8370-6722-7 – 1986-0722 – us A.T.L.A. [220]

DIE BUECHER DER KOENIGE : MIT NEUN ABBILDUNGEN IM TEXT, EINEM PLAN DES ALTEN JERUSALEM UND EINER GESCHICHTSTABELLE / Benzinger, Immanuel – (Includes chronological table and index) – Freiburg i. B: J C B Mohr (Paul Siebeck), 1899 – 1mf – 9 – 0-8370-2280-0 – 1985-0280 – us A.T.L.A. [220]

DIE BUECHER ESRA (A UND B) UND NEHEMJA / Jahn, Gustav – Leiden: E.J. Brill, 1909. 1 fiche – 9 – us A.T.L.A. [240]

BUECHER EXODUS, LEVITICUS, NUMERII = EXODUS OR, THE SECOND BOOK OF MOSES : BUCH DER TRILOGIE DES GESETZES / Lange, Johann Peter – (In English) – New York:Charles Scribner, c1876 – 1mf – 9 – 0-8370-5164-9 – 1985-3164 – us A.T.L.A. [220]

DIE BUECHER EXODUS UND LEVITICUS / Dillmann, August; ed by Ryssel, Victor – 3. Aufl. Leipzig: S Hirzel, 1897 – 2mf – 9 – 0-8370-9460-7 – 1986-3460 – us A.T.L.A. [220]

DIE BUECHER NUMERI, DEUTERONOMIUM UND JOSUE / Dillmann, August – Leipzig: S. Hirzel, 1886. 1 fiche – 9 – us A.T.L.A. [220]

DIE BUECHER RICHTER UND SAMUEL / Budde, Karl – Giessen: J. Ricker, 1890. 1 fiche – 9 – us A.T.L.A. [220]

BUECHER SAMUELIS = THE BOOKS OF SAMUEL / Erdmann, David; ed by Toy, C H & Broadus, John A – (Includes appendix) – New York: Charles Scribner, c1877 – 2mf – 9 – 0 8370 6735 9 – 1986-0735 – us A.T.L.A. [220]

Buecher, Wilhelm *see* GRILLPARZERS VERHAELTNIS ZUR POLITIK SEINER ZEIT

DIE BUECHER-KOMMENTARE – Vierteljahreshefte der Deutschen Kommentare. Stuttgart. 3rd quarter 1952-67 – 1 – gw Mikrofilm [430]

Buechi, R *see*
– DIE GESCHICHTE DER PAN-AMERIKANISCHEN BEWEGUNG
– DIE PAN-AMERIKANISCHEN KONFERENZEN

[BUECHLEIN DER HAUSZUCHT] / Huberinus, Caspar – Augsburg: Philipp Ulhart, 1532 – 3mf – 9 – HUB-84/1 – ne IDC [240]

Buechler *see* HISTORY OF HALL COUNTY

Buechler, A *see* TYPES OF JEWISH-PALESTINIAN PIETY FROM 70 B.C.E. TO 70 C.E.

Buechler, Adolf *see*
– DIE PRIESTER UND DER CULTUS IM LETZTEN JAHRZEHNT DES JERUSALEMISCHEN TEMPELS
– DAS SYNEDRION IN JERUSALEM UND DAS GROSSE BETH-DIN IN DER QUADERKAMMER DES JERUSALEMISCHEN TEMPELS

Buechner, Georg *see*
– DAS EHERNE GESETZ
– THE PLAYS OF GEORG BUECHNER
– SAEMMTLICHE WERKE UND HANDSCHRIFTLICHER NACHLASS
– SAEMTLICHE POETISCHE WERKE, NEBST EINER AUSWAHL SEINER BRIEFE

Buechner, Ludwig *see*
– GOTT UND DIE WISSENSCHAFT
– MATERIALISM: ITS HISTORY AND INFLUENCE ON SOCIETY

Buechner, Thomas S *see*
– CZECHOSLOVAKIAN DIARY: 1980
– FREDERICK CARDER: HIS LIFE AND WORK
– GLASS VESSELS IN DUTCH PAINTING OF THE 17TH CENTURY

BUECHNER-PREIS-REDEN, 1951-1971 – (Includes bibliographical references) – Stuttgart: P Reclam, 1972 – 1r – 1 – us U.W. Library [430]

Bueck, H W *see* GENERA, SPECIES ET SYNONYMA CANDOLLEANA ALPHABETICO ORDINE DISPOSITA, SEU INDEX GENERALIS ET SPECIALIS AD A. P. DE CANDOLLE (ET A. DE CANDOLLE)

Buehlbaecker, Alexander *see* ZUR VERWENDBARKEIT VON STUTENMILCH, KUMYSS UND ESELMILCH ALS DIAETETIKA UND HEILMITTEL UNTER BESONDERER BERUECKSICHTIGUNG DER BEDUERFNISSE DES SAEUGLINGS UND DES FRUEHGEBORENEN

Buehler, Adolph *see*
– THEOKRISIS
– THEOKRISIS: IDEEN UEBER GOTT UND WELT

BUEHLER BOTE *see* ACHER- UND BUEHLER BOTE

Buehler, G *see* THE LAWS OF MANU

BUEHLER TAGEBLATT *see* BUEHLER WOCHEN- UND UNTERHALTUNGSBLATT

BUEHLER WOCHEN- UND UNTERHALTUNGSBLATT – (Cont by: Buehler Wochenblatt, 1894?; Buehler Tageblatt, sep 18 1913) – Buehl, jan 24 1866-72, 1874-93, 1895-jun 30 1915 – 1 – Inquire at Mikrofilmarchiv for details – gw Misc Inst [072]

BUEHLER WOCHENBLATT *see* BUEHLER WOCHEN- UND UNTERHALTUNGSBLATT

DIE BUEHNENGERECHTEN EINRICHTUNGEN DER SCHILLERSCHEN DRAMEN FUER DAS KOENIGLICHE NATIONAL-THEATER ZU BERLIN / Schmieden, Alfred – (Includes bibliographical references) – Berlin: E Fleischel, 1906 – 1 – us U.W. Library [790]

Buehner, Karl Hans *see* HERMANN HESSE UND GOTTFRIED KELLER

Buel, James William *see* AMERICA'S WONDERLANDS: A PICTORIAL AND DESCRIPTIVE HISTORY OF OUR COUNTRY'S SCENIC MARVELS AS DELINEATED BY PEN AND CAMERA

Buel, Samuel *see* EUCHARISTIC PRESENCE, EUCHARISTIC SACRIFICE, AND EUCHARISTIC ADORATION

BUELL COLLECTION OF HISTORICAL DOCUMENTS RELATING TO THE CORPS OF ENGINEERS, 1801-19 / U.S. War Department. Office of the Chief of Engineers – 3 rolls. M417. Printed guide – 1 – us Nat'l Archives [355]

Buell, R L *see* THE NATIVE PROBLEM IN AFRICA

Buellingen, Ludwig von *see* ANNALES TYPOGRAPHICI COLONIENSES

Buelow, Frieda, Freiin von *see* IRDISCHE LIEBE

Buelow, G *see*
– DES DOM. GUNDISSALINUS SCHRIFT 'VON DER UNSTERBLICHKEIT DER SEELE'

Buelow, Wilhelm *see* DAS KNAPPSCHAFTSWESEN IM RUHRKOHLENBEZIRK BIS ZUM ALLGEMEINEN PREUSSISCHEN BERGGESETZ VOM 24.6.1865

BUENA PARK NEWS – Buena Park, CA. 1993-1994 – 6r – 1 – $300.00 – R04009 – us Library Micro [071]

BUENA VISTA BAPTIST CHURCH. OWENSBORO, KENTUCKY : CHURCH RECORDS – 1920-Sept 1984 – 1 – 77.85 – us Baptist [240]

Buenacasa, Manuel *see* DARK ROAD AHEAD OF LABOR

Buenaventura, San *see*
– LIBER DE PROFECTU RELIGIOSORUM
– MEDITACIONES DE LA VIDA DE CRISTO...

BUENDER GENERAL-ANZEIGER – (Cont by: Buender Zeitung, Herford) – Buende, 1938-40 – 1 – Inquire at Mikrofilmarchiv for details – gw Misc Inst [943]

BUENDER TAGEBLATT – Buende, jan 21 1901-05, 1910-11, jan 19-dec 30 1920, jan 2-dec 29 1922, 1923-24, jan 5-sep 6 1926, mar 2-nov 30 1927, 1928-apr 30 1930, jan 2-nov 30 1931, jan 2-nov 30 1932, 1933-35, apr 1 1936-mar 31 1937, feb 1-aug 31 1938, aug 1-nov 30 1942, jun 25-dec 3 1955. Also suppl available: Illustrirtes Sonntags-Blatt, 1901-05, 1910-13, 1916 (all incomplete); Wort und Bild, 1924, 1926-28 (all incomplete) – 1 – Inquire at Mikrofilmarchiv for details – gw Misc Inst [943]

BUENDER TAGEBLATT – Buende Westf., Germany. 21 Jan 1901-Dec 1905; 1910-11 – 7r – 1 – gw Mikrofilm [072]

BUENDER ZEITUNG *see* BUENDER GENERAL-ANZEIGER

DAS BUENDNIS DER PARTEIEN: HERAUSBILDUNG UND ROLLE DES MEHRPARTEIENSYSTEMS IN DER EUROPAEISCHEN SOZIOLISTISCHEN LAENDERN / Grosser, Guenther – Berlin: Buchverlag Der Morgen, 1967. 150p. Bibliog – 1 – us U.W. Library [320]

BUENDNIS UND BEKENNTNIS 1529/1530 : DER TOLERANZGEDANKE IM REFORMATIONSZEITALTER / Schubert, Hans von & Hermelink, Heinrich – Leipzig: Verein fuer Reformationsgeschichte, 1908. (Schriften des Vereins fuer Reformationsgeschichte; 26. Jahrg., Schrift 98) – 1mf – us A.T.L.A. [240]

BUENDNISPOLITIK UND REVOLUTIONAERE KRISE : ZU EINIGEN ASPEKTEN DER BRITISCH-RUSSISCHEN BEZIEHUNGEN 1917 / Maier, Lothar August – Heidelberg, 1975 – 3mf – 9 – DM76.00 – 3-89349-687-4 – gw Hänsel [327]

DIE BUENDNUESSE UND VERTRAEGE DER HELVETISCHEN NATION,... – Bern, 1737 – 3mf – 1 – ILM-974/1 – ne IDC [327]
Buenner, D *see* L'ANCIENNE LITURGIE ROMAINE
Bueno, Ramon *see* APUNTES SOBRE LA PROVINCIA MISIONAL DEL ORINOCO... CARACAS, 1933
Buenos Aires (Argentina: Province) *see* 20. PLAN QUINQUENAL
BUENOS AIRES, CAPITAL DEL JUSTICIALISMO : CONFERENCIA PLENIPOTENTIARIA INTERNACIONAL DE TELECOMUNICACIONES, BUENOS AIRES, 1952 – Buenos Aires: Presidencia de la Nacion Argentina, Subsecretaria de Informaciones, 1952 – 1 – CSUXADJ2755-B – us Hoover Inst Photo [380]
Buenos Aires. Centro de Investigacion y Accion Social *see* CIAS
BUENOS AIRES CON PERON : [SERIE DE DISCURSOS PRONUNCIADOS EN MARZO Y ABRIL DE 1954] / Aloe, Carlos – [Buenos Aires]: Gobernacion de Buenos Aires, [1954?] – 1 – CSUXAJA7434-B – us Hoover Inst Photo [320]
BUENOS AIRES EN CIFRAS / Argentina. Direccion General de Relaciones Culturales y Difusion – [Buenos Aires?, 1950?] – 1 – CSUXADJ1307-B – us Hoover Inst Photo [304]
Buenos Aires. Escuela Superior Peronista *see* PRINCIPIOS DEL PERONISMO
BUENOS AIRES HERALD : ILLUSTRATED WEEKLY EDITION – Argentina, 2 Jan 1914-27 Apr 1917 – 7r – 1 – uk British Libr Newspaper [072]
BUENOS AIRES MUSICAL – Buenos Aires. 1954-75. 3 reels – 1 – 47.00 – us L of C Photodup [780]
BUENOS AIRES MUSICAL – v25-. 1970-. illus. -irr. Title varies: BAM – 1 – us U.W. Library [073]
BUENTETOEJOG A NEMZETKOEZI JOGBAN... / Doleschall, A – Budapest – 1mf – 1 – ILM-2451/1 – ne IDC [327]
BUERENER ZEITUNG – (Since 1925 part of Der Patriot, Lippstadt) – Bueren, nov 3-30 1896, 1897, 1900, jan 4 1902-03, jul 21-dec 31 1914, 1933-44 – 1 – Inquire at Mikrofilmarchiv for details – gw Misc Inst [943]
Buerger, Gottfried August *see*
– GEDICHTE IN ZWEI TEILEN
– SAEMMTLICHE GEDICHTE
BUERGER- UND BAUERN-ZEITUNG – Potsdam, Germany. 5 Jul 1849-22 May 1850 – 1r – 1 – gw Mikrofilm [072]
BUERGERBLATT FUER DEN KREIS REES – Rees Niederrhein, Germany. 1848 – 1 – gw Mikrofilm [072]
DER BUERGERFREUND – Bremen, Germany.1816-47, 1850-1866 – 1 – gw Mikrofilm [072]
DER BUERGERFREUND – (Cont by: Bremer Buergerfreund, jan 25 1857) – Bremen, jun 1 1816-66 – 37r – 1 – Inquire at Mikrofilmarchiv for details – gw Misc Inst [943]
BUERGERLICHES LEBENSGEFUEHL IN GRILLPARZERS DRAMEN / Weissbart, Gertrud – (Includes bibliographical references) – Bonn: L Roehrscheid, 1929 – 1r – 1 – us U.W. Library [430]
BUERGERLICHES NATURGEFUEHL UND OFFIZIELLE LANDSCHAFTSMALEREI IN FRANKREICH 1753-1824 / Rosenthal, Gisela – Heidelberg – 3mf – 9 – DM76.00 – 3-89349-397-2 – gw Hänsel [750]
BUERGERNAEHE DER VERWALTUNG ALS THEMA DER AUSBILDUNG VON BEAMTEN DES GEHOBENEN NICHTTECHNISCHEN DIENSTES / Moellers, Martin – 1992 – viii/201p – 9 – DM98.00 – 3-89349-556-8 – gw Hänsel [350]
BUERGERS VERSKUNST / Zaunert, Paul – (Includes bibliographical references) – Marburg a.L.: N G Elwert, 1911 – 1r – 1 – us U.W. Library [430]
BUERGERZEITUNG *see* HAMBURG-ALTONAER VOLKSBLATT
BUERGER-ZEITUNG FUER GROSS-LICHTERFELDE UND DAHLEM *see* GENERAL-ANZEIGER FUER GROSS-LICHTERFELDE
BUERGSCHAFT UND GARANTIEVERTRAG UNTER BESONDERER BERUECKSICHTIGUNG DER BANKPRAXIS / Dudenhausen, Wolfgang – 1994 – 1mf – 9 – DM48.00 – 3-8267-3003-8 – gw Hänsel [340]
Buerki, Robert A *see*
– JOURNAL OF PHARMACY TEACHING
– PHARMACY PRACTICE – THE CHALLENGE OF ETHICS
BUEROKRATIE ALS LERNENDE ORGANISATION / Maetzing, Ortwin – 1994 – 2mf – DM80.00 – 3-8267-2035-0 – gw Hänsel [370]
Buesch, Johann Georg *see* ABHANDLUNG VON DEM GELDUMLAUF
Buesser, F *see*
– EARLY PRINTED BIBLES
– HUMANISM IN 16TH CENTURY ZURICH
– REFORMED PROTESTANTISM
– SIMLER MANUSCRIPT COLLECTION
– THESAURUS HOTTINGERIANUS
Buesser, Fritz *see* EARLY PRINTED BIBLES
Buet, Charles *see* GRANDS HOMMES EN ROBE DE CHAMBRE
BUETOWER ANZEIGER – (Incl monthly suppl: Blaetter fuer Heimatpflege im Kreise Buetow) – Buetow, apr 1926-apr 1927 – 1r – 1 – Inquire at Mikrofilmarchiv for details – gw Misc Inst [943]
BUETZOWISCHE NEBENSTUNDEN [...] – Buetzow, 1768, pt3 – 9 – Inquire at Mikrofilmarchiv for details – gw Misc Inst [072]
BUEYUEK DONANMA MUENECCIMI – 1330 M. [(1329) 1913] 4. sene – 3mf – 9 – $30.00 – us MEDOC [949]
BUEYUEK MECMU'A – (Nos 1-17. – 1919) – 9mf – 9 – $42.00 – us MEDOC [949]
BUEYUEK SALNAMESI – 1341-1342 [1925-26] – 4mf – 9 – $70.00 – us MEDOC [949]
Bufalini, F *see*
– QUESTIONI INTERNAZIONALI...
– REPERTORIO ALFABETICO...
BUFFALO BAPTIST CHURCH. CHEROKEE COUNTY. SOUTH CAROLINA : CHURCH RECORDS – 1805-1910, 1858-1917, 1919-23, 1940-41, 1945-60 – 1 – 20.21 – us Baptist [240]
BUFFALO BAPTIST CHURCH. RUTLEDGE, TENNESSEE : CHURCH RECORDS – 1859-Jul 1953 – 1 – 44.19 – us Baptist [240]
BUFFALO COUNTY BEACON – Gibbon, NE. -w. Jun 1892-Oct 1894, scattered issues missing; Jan 1896-Feb 1896; Apr-Nov 1896 – 1 – us NE Hist [071]
BUFFALO COUNTY BEACON – Gibbon. Neb. 1892-1896 – 1 – us UMI [071]
BUFFALO COUNTY JOURNAL – Kearney, NE. -w. Jul 1876-Aug 1877, scattered issues missing – 1 – us NE Hist [071]
BUFFALO COUNTY PILOT – Kearney, NE. -w. Jun 1892-Nov 1900, scattered issues missing – 1 – us NE Hist [071]
BUFFALO COURIER EXPRESS – Buffalo. New York. 1926- – 1 – us UMI [071]
THE BUFFALO CRITERION – Buffalo. N.Y. Aug. 16, Oct. 11, 1941 – 1 – us NY Public [071]
BUFFALO GROVE BAPTIST CHURCH. JEFFERSON CITY, TENNESSEE : CHURCH RECORDS – Jul 1905-Mar 1979 – 1 – 44.64 – us Baptist [240]
BUFFALO JEWISH REVIEW – Buffalo. N.Y. 1963-67 – 1 – us A.J.P.C. [071]
BUFFALO LAW REVIEW – (v1-33 1951-84 in reel $380.00. v34-43 1985-95 in mf $220.00) – v1-43. 1951-95 – 5,6,9 – $600.00 set – us Hein [340]
Buffalo. New York. Superior Court *see* SHELDON'S SUPERIOR COURT REPORTS
BUFFALO REPRODUCTION AND ARTIFICIAL INSEMINATION – 1979 – 370p – it F.A.O. [636]
BUFFALO RIDGE BAPTIST CHURCH. WASHINGTON COUNTY. TENNESSEE : CHURCH RECORDS – 1827-74 – 1 – 16.11 – us Baptist [240]
BUFFALO STUDIES – v.1-4. 1964-68 – 1 – us UMI [073]
Buffalo. Synod (Pres. Ch. in the U.S.A. Old School) *see* MINUTES, 1843-1870
BUFFALO VOLKSFREUND – Buffalo, NY. sep 1 1920-may 16 1939 (incomplete) – 30r – 1 – Inquire at Mikrofilmarchiv for details – gw Misc Inst [072]
BUFFALOER ARBEITER-ZEITUNG – Buffalo, New York. 1898-1917 (incomplete) – 1 – gw Mikrofilm [071]
BUFFALOER ARBEITER-ZEITUNG – Buffalo, NY. 1898 (incomplete), 1899-1916, 1917 (incomplete) – 11r – 1 – Inquire at Mikrofilmarchiv for details – gw Misc Inst [331]
BUFFALOES OF CHINA / Cockrill, W R – 1976 – 96p – it F.A.O. [636]
Buffet, M *see* NOUVELLES OBSERVATIONS SUR LA LANGUE FRANCOISE
Buffetaut, E *see* HISTORICAL BIOLOGY
Buffier, Cl *see*
– GRAMMAIRE FRANCOISE SUR UN PLAN NOUVEAU
– SUITE DE LA GRAMMAIRE FRANCAISE SUR UN PLAN NOUVEAU OU TRAITE PHILOSOPHIQUE ET PRATIQUE D'ELOQUENCE
– SUITE DE LA GRAMMAIRE FRANCOISE
Buffon, Georges L L *see* HISTOIRE NATURELLE GENERALE ET PARTICULIERE
BUGANDA AND KING : A ROYAL HISTORY OF BUGANDA / Zimbe, Bartolomayo Musoke – Chicago: Uni of Chicago, Photodup [19–] – us Res Libr [960]
Bugarin, Jose *see* DICCIONARIO IBANAG-ESPANOL
Bugarski, Georg M *see* DIE NATUR UND DER DETERMINISUMUS DES WILLENS BEI LEIBNIZ
Bugeaud de la Piconnerie, T R *see* OEUVRES MILITAIRES
Bugenhagen, J *see*
– DER 29TH PSALM AUSGELEGT...
– ANNOTATIONES IO. BVGENHAGIJ POMERANI IN EPISTOLAS PAULI,...
– BEKENTNIS...VON SEINEM GLAUBEN VND LERE/GESCHRIEBEN AN EYNEN WIDDERTEUFFER
– EYN CHRISTLICH VNTERRICHT EYNES GOTTSELIGEN LEBENS...
– AIN CHRISTLICHER SEDNPRIEFF AN FRAUW ANNA...
– IN 4. PRIORA CAPITA EUANGELIJ SECUNDUM MATTHAEUM
– IN IEREMIAM PROPHETAM...COMMENTARIUM...
– IN REGVM DVOS VLTIMOS LIBROS, ANNOTATIONES...POST SAMUELEM IAM PRIMU EMISSAE...
– INDICES QVIDAM IONNIS BVGENHAGIJ POMERANI IN EUANGELIA...
– IOAN
– IOANNIS BVGENHAGII POMERANI COMMENTARIUS, IN QUATUOR CAPITA PRIORIS EPISTOLAE AD CORINTHIOS,...
– IOANNIS BVGENHAGII...PUBLICA, DE SACRAMENTO CORPORIS ET SANGUINIS CHRISTI...
– IOANNIS BVGENHAGUE POMERANI ANNOTATIONES AB IPSO IAM EMISSAE. IN DEUTERONOMIUM. IN SAMUELEM PROPHETA ID EST DUOS LIBROS REGU...
– IONAS PROPHETA...
– AIN KURTZE, WOLGEGRUENDTE AUSZLEGUNG UEBER DIE ZEHEN NACHGEENDEN EPISTELN S. PAULI
– EYN SENDEBRIEFF...
– EYN SERMON VON DER EYGENSCHAFFT VND WEYSE DES SACRAMENTS DER TAUFF...
– VON DEM KONIGREYCH VND PRIESTERTHUM CHRISTI DER HUNDERT VND ZEHENDE PSALM DAUIDS
– VON DEN VNGEBORN KINDERN, VND VON DEN KINDERN, DIE WIR NICHT TEUFFEN KOENNEN
– VON DER CLOSTER KEUESCHEYT VNND CHRISTENLICHER BEICHT...
Bugge, A *see* GRONLANDSK REJSPARLOR
BUGLE CALL – Portland OR. Aug 15 1945 – 1 – us U.O. Library [071]
BUGLE CALL – Roseburg OR. Feb 6 1892 – 1 – us U.O. Library [071]
Bugler, Jeremy *see* POLLUTING BRITAIN: A REPORT
Bugnet, Nicolas *see* LA PHILOSOPHIE DE RURAVEBOHNI, PAYS DONT LA DECOUVERTE SEMBLE D'UN GRAND INTERET POUR L'HOMME, OU RECIT DIALOGUE DES MOYENS PAR LESQUELS LES RURAVEHEUXIS HABITANTS DE CE PAYS ONT ETE CONDUITS AU VRAI ET SOLIDE BONHEUR
Buhayri, Marwan *see* AL-HILF AL-ATLASI WA-AL-SHARQ AL-AWSAT
Buhl, Frants *see* DEN GAMMELTESTAMENTLIGE SKRIFTOVERLEVERING
Buhle, J G *see* VERSUCH EINER KRITISCHEN LITERATUR DER RUSSISCHEN GESCHICHTE
EL BUHO DEL RIBERO / Delgado Solis, Sebastian – Caceres: Imp. y Enc. Vda. de Floriano, 1957 – 1 – sp Bibl Santa Ana [946]
Buhre, U T *see* THE EFFECT OF A 60-MINUTE DURATION EXERCISE, AT THE INTENSITIES OF THE LACTATE AND THE INDIVIDUAL ANAEROBIC THRESHOLDS, ON THE CARDIOVASCULAR DRIFT
Buies, Arthur *see*
– ANGLICISMES ET CANADIANISMES
– AU PORTIQUE DES LAURENTIDES; UNE PAROISSE MODERNE; LE CURE LABELLE
– AU PORTIQUES DES LAURENTIDES: UNE PAROISSE MODERNE: LE CURE LABELLE
– LE CHEMIN DE FER DU LAC SAINT-JEAN
– LES COMTES DE RIMOUSKI, DE MATANE ET DE TEMISCOUATA: EXPLORATION SPECIALE
– CONFERENCES
– LE FIGARO
– L'INDEPENDANT
– THE LAKE ST JOHN REGION: THE GRANARY OF THE PROVINCE OF QUEBEC: A GUIDE FOR SETTLERS
– LA LANTERNE
– PETITES CHRONIQUES POUR 1877
– QUEBEC EN 1900: CONFERENCE DONNEE A L'ACADEMIE DE MUSIQUE DE QUEBEC, LUNDI LE 29 MAI, 1893
– RECITS DE VOYAGES
– LA REGION DU LAC SAINT-JEAN: GRENIER DE LA PROVINCE DE QUEBEC: GUIDE DES COLONS
– REPONSE A UN ORDRE DE L'ASSEMBLEE LEGISLATIVE...11 DECEMBRE 1890, POUR COPIE DES RAPPORTS DE M. ARTHUR BUIES SUR LES COMTES DE RIMOUSKI, DE MATANE, ET DE TEMISCOUATA
– LE REVEIL
– LE SAGUENAY ET LA VALLEE DU LAC SAINT-JEAN: ETUDE HISTORIQUE, GEOGRAPHIQUE, INDUSTRIELLE ET AGRICOLE
– LE SIGNAL
– SUR LE PARCOURS DU CHEMIN DE FER DU LAC SAINT-JEAN: 1ERE CONFERENCE FAITE A LA SALLE VICTORIA, LE 31 MARS, 1886
– LA VALLEE DE LA MATAPEDIA
– LA VALLEE DE LA MATAPEDIA: OUVRAGE HISTORIQUE ET DESCRIPTIF
THE BUIK OF THE CHRONICLES OF SCOTLAND (RS6) : OR: A METRICAL VERSION OF THE HISTORY OF HECTOR BOECE, BY WILLIAM STEWART / Boece, Hector; ed by Turnbull, W B – 3v. 1858 – Dfl42.00v – ne Slangenburg [941]
BUILDER – v1-2 1978-79; v4- 1981- – 1,5,6,9 – us UMI [690]
THE BUILDER – 1843-1915 – 1 – uk Manchester Libr [720]
BUILDER AND CONTRACTOR, 1893-1917 – Contains building and contracting news of the Southwest – 21r; individualr available – 1 – $525.00 – uk Libr Preservation [690]
THE BUILDER'S EXCHANGE OF MONTREAL : YEAR BOOK AND INDEX – Montreal, Canada. 1909 – 1r – 1 – Can$25.00 – cn Can Microfilming [072]
THE BUILDERS OF BABEL / M'Causland, Dominick – London: Richard Bentley, 1874. 1 fiche – 9 – us A.T.L.A. [240]
BUILDERS OF NOVA SCOTIA: A HISTORICAL REVIEW, WITH AN APPENDIX CONTAINING COPIES OF RARE DOCUMENTS RELATING TO THE EARLY DAYS OF THE PROVINCE / Bourinot, John George – 1899. 00220. (Pre-1900 Canadiana) – 9 – cn C.I.H.M. [971]
BUILDERS OF UNITED ITALY / Holland, Rupert Sargent – New York: H. Holt, 1908.349p. 8 ports., front., plates – 1 – us U.W. Library [945]
BUILDING – 1842- – 1,5,6,9 – us UMI [690]
BUILDING – (Cont: Canadian Building at v41 n3 1991) – Toronto. v41-44. 1991/92-1994 – 9 – Can$20.00y – cn Micromedia [073]
BUILDING A BRIDGE BETWEEN ATHLETICS AND ACADEMICS / Kilbourne, John R – 1994 – 2mf – $8.00 – us Microform Publ [790]
BUILDING ACTIVITY MICROFICHE SERVICE, AUSTRALIA – 9 – at Statistics [690]
BUILDING AND ENVIRONMENT – (Formerly Building Science) – v1- 1965- – 5,6,9 – us UMI [720]
BUILDING APPROVALS MICROFICHE SERVICE, AUSTRALIA – 9 – at Statistics [690]
BUILDING APPROVALS MICROFICHE SERVICE, AUSTRALIAN CAPITAL TERRITORY – 9 – at Statistics [690]
BUILDING APPROVALS MICROFICHE SERVICE, NEW SOUTH WALES – 9 – at Statistics [690]
BUILDING APPROVALS MICROFICHE SERVICE, NORTHERN TERRITORY – 9 – at Statistics [690]
BUILDING APPROVALS MICROFICHE SERVICE, QUEENSLAND – 9 – at Statistics [690]

BUILDING APPROVALS MICROFICHE SERVICE, SOUTH AUSTRALIA – 9 – at Statistics [690]
BUILDING APPROVALS MICROFICHE SERVICE, TASMANIA – 9 – at Statistics [690]
BUILDING APPROVALS MICROFICHE SERVICE, VICTORIA – 9 – at Statistics [690]
BUILDING APPROVALS MICROFICHE SERVICE, WESTERN AUSTRALIA – 9 – at Statistics [690]
BUILDING COMMENCEMENTS MICROFICHE SERVICE, NEW SOUTH WALES – 9 – at Statistics [690]
BUILDING COMMENCEMENTS MICROFICHE SERVICE, QUEENSLAND – 9 – at Statistics [690]
BUILDING COMMENCEMENTS MICROFICHE SERVICE, TASMANIA – 9 – at Statistics [690]
BUILDING COMMENCEMENTS MICROFICHE SERVICE, VICTORIA – 9 – at Statistics [690]
BUILDING COMMUNITY SCHOOLS : AN ANALYSIS OF EXPERIENCES / Kennedy, Margrit I – 1979 – 155p – 9 – 92-3-101583-4 – fr UNESCO [370]
BUILDING DESIGN – 1969- – 1,5,6,9 – us UMI [720]
BUILDING MAGAZINE *see* BUILDING RENOVATION
BUILDING NEWS *see* FREEHOLD LAND TIMES BUILDING NEWS
THE BUILDING NEWS AND ENGINEERING JOURNAL – London, 1854-1926. v. 1-130. Lacking: 1854-55. v1-2 – 1704mf – 1 – ne IDC [620]
THE BUILDING NEWS AND ENGINEERING JOURNAL – London, 1856-1926 – 1 – $10,155.00 – us UPA [620]
THE BUILDING OF CHARACTER / Miller, James Russell – New York: Thomas Y Crowell, c1894 – 1mf – 9 – 0-8370-7179-8 – 1986-1179 – us A.T.L.A. [240]
BUILDING PONDS WITH ANIMAL POWER IN THE ETHIOPIAN HIGHLANDS : A MANUAL / Astatke, Abiye et al – 1986 – 9 – $11.00 – 92-9053-145-2 – et ILRI [630]
BUILDING RECORD – (Some missing issues) – British Columbia, CN. 1912-51 – 32r – 1 – cn Commonwealth Micro [073]
BUILDING RENOVATION – (Publ temporarily suspended at v8 1991. Included as suppl within Building Magazine commencing Aug/ Sept 1991) – Toronto. v1-8. 1984-91 – 9 – Can$20.00y – cn Micromedia [640]
BUILDING SCIENCE *see* BUILDING AND ENVIRONMENT
BUILDING SPECIALTIES AND HOME IMPROVEMENTS – v1-21 1948-69. Continued as: Home Improvements – 1 – us UMI [640]
BUILDING SUPPLY & HOME CENTERS – (1984-85. 5,6,9) – v145-148. 1983-85 – 1 – us UMI [600]
BUILDING SUPPLY NEWS – v1-145. 1917-83 – 1 – us UMI [600]
BUILDING SYSTEMS DESIGN – (5,6 1970- ; 9 1976-) – v1- 1904- – 1 – us UMI [690]
BUILDING TECHNOLOGY AND MANAGEMENT – (5,6,9, 1976-) – v1- 1963- – 1 – us UMI [690]
BUILDING THE FUTURE / M'Bow, Amadou-Mahtar – 1981 – 258p – 9 – 92-3-101968-6 – fr UNESCO [303]
BUILDING WORKERS' INDUSTRIAL UNION : BUILDING WORKER – (Apply to publ for details) – 1935-85 – 9 – at Pascoe [073]
THE BUILDINGS AT SAMARIA / Crowfoot, J W – PEF. 1942 – 9 – $10.00 – us I.R.C. [930]
BUILDINGS IN THE PUNJAB / India. Preservation of National Monuments; ed by Cole, H H – Calcutta, 1884. BI-686 2 – 8 – ne IDC [720]
BUILETYN ZBRODNI HITLEROWSKICH, POLAND – (Different yrs – please inquire) – 2r – 1 – $170.00 – us Ross [073]
BUILT ENVIRONMENT – v1-4 1972-75 – 1 – us UMI [720]
Buiskii, A *see*
– BORBA ZA KRYM I RAZGROM VRANGELIA
– KRASNAIA ARMIIA NA VNUTRENNEM FRONTE
– VOENNAIA PODGOTOVKA OKTIABRIA
Buisseret, Francois *see* HISTOIRE ADMIRABLE ET VERITABLE DES CHOSES ADVENUES A L'ENDROIT D'UNE RELIGIEUSE
Buisson, Ferdinand *see* LIBRE-PENSEE ET PROTESTANTISME LIBERAL
Buisson, Paul Ulric du *see* LETTRES CRITIQUES ET POLITIQUES SUR LES COLONIES ET LE COMMERCE DES VILLES MARITIMES DE FRANCE
HET BUITENLANDSCH STRAFVONNIS / Bel, J H van – Leiden, 1884 – 2mf – 9 – ILM-2000/1 – ne IDC [327]
BUITENLANDSCHE VONNISSEN / Asser, T M C – 's-Gravenhage, 1888 – 1mf – 9 – ILM-2418/1 – ne IDC [340]
BUITENLANDSE SENDING KWARTAALBLAD VAN DIE NED. GEREF. KERK IN S.A. – Mkhoma, Nyasaland: Sending Drukkery. v1 1923; v2 n2-4 apr/jun-oct/dec 1924; v3 n2-4 apr/jun-oct/dec 1925; v4-8 1926-30 – 1r – us Res Libr [960]
BUKARESTER DEUTSCHE TAGESPOST – Bukarest, 1924-nov 15 1925 – 3r – 1 – Inquire at Mikrofilmarchiv for details – gw Misc Inst [949]
BUKARESTER DEUTSCHE TAGESPOST – Bukarest, Rumaenien. 1 Jan 1924-15 Nov 1925 – 3r – 1 – gw Mikrofilm [949]
BUKARESTER DEUTSCHES TAGEBLATT – Bukarest, oct 3 1926-mar 31 1927 – 1r – 1 – Inquire at Mikrofilmarchiv for details – gw Misc Inst [949]
BUKARESTER DEUTSCHES TAGEBLATT – Bukarest, Rumaenien. 3 Okt 1926-31 Mar 1927 – 1r – 1 – gw Mikrofilm [949]
BUKARESTER LLOYD – Bukarest, jan 2 1923-mar 8 1924 – 1 – Inquire at Mikrofilmarchiv for details – gw Misc Inst [072]
BUKARESTER LLOYD – Bukarest, Rumaenien. 1923-8 Mar 1924 – 1 – gw Mikrofilm [949]
BUKARESTER POST – Bukarest, jan 8 1933-jan 1 1940 – 5r – 1 – Inquire at Mikrofilmarchiv for details – gw Misc Inst [949]
BUKARESTER POST – Bukarest, Rumaenien. 8 Jan 1933-Jan 1940 – 5r – 1 – gw Mikrofilm [949]
BUKARESTER TAGEBLATT – Bucharest, Rumania. 1 Jul 1942-22 Aug 1944 (imperfect) – 10r – 1 – uk British Libr Newspaper [949]
BUKARESTER TAGEBLATT – Bukarest, jul 1-nov 7 1918, 1926-apr 30 1944 – 1 – Inquire at Mikrofilmarchiv for details – gw Misc Inst [949]
BUKARESTER TAGEBLATT – Bukarest, Rumaenien. 1 Jul-7 Nov 1918, 1926-43 – 30r – 1 – gw Mikrofilm [949]
Bukh, Niels E *see* FUNDAMENTAL GYMNASTICS
Bukharev, Rais Gatich *see* VEROIATNOSTNYE AVTOMATY
Bukharin, Nikolai Ivanovich *see*
– AZBUKA KOMMUNIZMA
– DOKLADNA 23RD CHREZVYCHAINOI LENINGRADSKOI GUBERNSKOI KONFERENTSII VKP(B)
– GDE NASTOIASHCHAIA SVOBODA?
– IMPERIALIZM I NAKOPLENIE KAPITALA
– K DESIATILETIIU OKTIABRSKOI REVOLIUTSII
– KLASSOVAI A BORBA I REVOLIUTSII A V ROSSII
– KLASSOVAIA BORBA I REVOLIUTSIIA V ROSSII
– MEZHDUNARODNOE POLOZHENIE I ZADACHI KOMINTERNA
– MIKROVOE KHOZI A ISTVO I IMPERIALIZM
– NA PODSTUPAKH K OKTIABRIU
– NAUKA I SSSR
– NEKOTORYE VOPROSY EKONOMICHESKO I POLITIKI
– NOVOE OTKROVENIE O SOVETSKO I EKONOMIKE II KAK MOZHNO POGUBIT RABOCHE-KRESTI ANSKI I BLOK
– OT DIKTATURY IMPERIALIZMA K DIKTATURE PROLETARIATA
– OT DIKTATURY IMPERIALIZMA K DIKTATURI E PROLETARIATA
– OT KRUSHENIIA TSARIZMA DO PADENIIA BURZHUAZII
– PROGRAMMA KOMMUNISTOV (BOLSHEVIKOV)
– PROIZVODSTVENNAI A PROPAGANDA
– PROLETARSKAI A REVOLIUTSII A I KULTURA
– PUT K SOTSIALIZMU I RABOCHE-KRESTIANSKII SOIUZ
– RABOTNITSA, K TEBE NASHE SLOVO!
– TSEZARIZM POD MASKO I REVOLIUTSII
– ZASADY REWOLUCJI SOCJALISTYCZNEJ W ROSJI
Bukhbinder, Naum Abramovich *see* ISTORIIA EVREISKOGO RABOCHEGO DVIZHENIIA V ROSSII PO NEIZDANNYM ARKHIVNYM MATERIALAM
Buki Ben Yogli (Katzenelson, J L B) *see* SHIRAT HA-ZAMIR
Bukovina. Landtag *see* STENOGRAPHISCHE PROTOKOLLE
BUKOVINA PAMPHLET COLLECTION – 1915-1931 – 1 – CSUXANL5558-B – us Hoover Inst Photo [947]
BUKU ALAMAT DAGANG – (Annual) – Surabaja, 1961 – 5mf – 9 – SE-1367/1 – ne IDC [950]
BUKU BARU = HET NIEUWE BOEK : BIBLIOGRAPHISCH TIJDSCHRIFT VOOR INDONESIE – (Missing: 1951, v1(1-6); 1952, v2(3); 1953, v3(5-6); 1954, v4(1-4); 1955, v5(1, 4-6); 1956, v6(2-6)) – Medan, 1951-1957(1) – 12mf – SE-630/1 – ne IDC [019]
BUKU KITA – Djakarta. SE-631 1. 1955-1956 – 9 – ne IDC [950]
BUKU PELADJARAN EKONOMI UMUM AND INDONESIA / Supardo – SE 4651 1. 1952 – 9 – ne IDC [330]
BUKU PELADJARAN SEDJARAH DUNIA UNTUK S.M.P. TJORAK BARU / Wiramihardja, J – SE 4079 1. Lacking: v. 1; 1962. 3 v. 1962-63 – 9 – ne IDC [950]
BUKU PENERANGAN / Jogjakarta. Indonesia. Universitas Gadjah Mada. Fakultas Ilmu Pasti dan Alam – 1957. 44p. illus. BSE-3260/1 – 9 – ne IDC [950]
BUKU PENUNTUN BATIK / Sewan Susanto, K – SE 4377 1. 1961 – 9 – ne IDC [950]
BUKU PENUNTUN SERAT NIPA / Pouw, Boen Seng – SE-4175 1. 1959? – 9 – ne IDC [950]
BUKU PENUNTUN UNTUK PEMBANTU AKUNTAN / Tjhio, Jan Seng – SE 4859 1. 1961 – 9 – ne IDC [950]
BUKU PETUNDJUK ALAMAT DAGANG DAN TOURIS DJAWA-TENGAH / Bakoenoen, Semarang – (In Indonesian or English) – 1956 – 9 – SE-4594/1 – ne IDC [950]
BUKU STATISTIK BARANG2 IMPOR; DISUSUN MENURUT NOMOR URUT 10 S/D 11660 DAN DIBAHAGI DALAM 15 KELOMPOK / Lombogia, D – SE-4811 1. 1962 – 9 – ne IDC [310]
LA BULA "INTER GRAVIORES CURAS" DE PIO 7 EN LA ORDEN FRANCISCANA Y ULTERIOR REGIMEN GENERAL DE LA ORDEN EN ESPANA (1804-1904) / Barrado Manzano, Arcangel – Madrid: Archivo Ibero-Americano, 1964 – 1 – sp Bibl Santa Ana [240]
Bulaeus (du Boulay), Caesar Egassius *see* HISTORIA UNIVERSITATIS PARISIENSIS
Bulanov, Leonid Petrovich *see* KAK MOZHNO KONCHIT VOINU I KAKOVY SPRAVEDLIVYIA USLOVIIA MIRA
LAS BULAS ALEJANDRINAS DE 1493 REFERENTES A LAS INDIAS / Bayle, Constantino – Madrid: Razon y Fe, 1945 – 1 – sp Bibl Santa Ana [950]
Bulatsel, A *see* NA RODINU IZ STANA BELYKH
BULAWAYO CHRONICLE – Zimbabwe. -w, -d. 12 Oct 1894-Dec 1949. Imperfect. 131 reels – 1 – uk British Libr Newspaper [072]
BULAWAYO EXPRESS – (Weekly ed.). Rhodesia. -w. 24 Dec 1904-25 Mar 1905. (19 ft) – 1 – uk British Libr Newspaper [072]
BULETIN – London, UK. Aroisgegeben fun dem Anarchistisher Roiter Kraits mit der hilf fun di London. Dec 1924 – 1 – uk British Libr Newspaper [072]
BULETIN – London, UK. Aroisgegeben fun der Dropotkin Grupe, London. Apr 1925 – 1 – uk British Libr Newspaper [072]
BULETIN MUSEUM / Museum Pasat – (Irregular. Missing: 1967(1-3); 1967/1968(8-12); 1968/1969(5-End)) – Djakarta, 1967-1969(2) – 7mf – 9 – SE-1368/1 – ne IDC [060]
BULETINUL OFICIAL / Romania – Bucharest. Pt. I Annul I-Pt. III Annul IV. Aug. 21, 1965-Dec. 31, 1968 – 1 – us NY Public [324]
BULETINUL OFICIAL / Romania. Marea Adunare Nationala – v6-12. 1957-63 – 2r – 1 – us Ross [324]
Bulfeta, Getachew *see* LAND AND TREE TENURE IN HUMID WEST AFRIA
Bulgakov, PG *see* ARABSKIE RUKOPISI SOBRANIIA LENINGRADSKOGO GOSUDARSTVENNOGO UNIVERSITETA
Bulgakov, Sergei Nikolaevich *see*
– NA PIRU BOGOV
– VOINA I RUSSKOE SAMOSOZNANIE
LES BULGARES DEVANT LE CONGRES DE LA PAIX / Ivanoff, J – Documents historiques, ethnographiques et diplomatiques, avec quatre cartes en couleurs. Ed. 2. Berne. 1919. BR-3873 2 – 8 – ne IDC [940]
LES BULGARES EN DOBROUDJA; APERCU HISTORIQUE ET ETHNOGRAPHIQUE / Ishirkov, A – Berne. 1919. BR-3872 2 – 8 – ne IDC [949]
BULGARIA : STATISTICKESKI GODISHNIK NA NARODNA REPUBLIKA BULGARIA 1956-1970 / Bulgaria. Darzhavno Upravlenie za Informatsiya – (1956, 1969 not available. Coll title: European Official Statistical Serials, 1841-1984) – 77mf – 9 – £6.00 (set £1,320.00 254mf) – uk Chadwyck [949]
Bulgaria *see*
– ADULT EDUCATION IN THE PEOPLE'S REPUBLIC OF BULGARIA
– MOUVEMENT DE LA POPULATION
Bulgaria. Darzhavno Upravlenie za Informatsiya *see* BULGARIA
Bulgaria. Glavna Direktsiia na Statistikata *see*
– BULGARIA. STATISTICHESKI GODISHNIK NA BULGARSKOTO TSARSTVO
– MESECHNI STATISTICHESKI IZVESTIIA
Bulgaria. Laws, Statutes, etc *see*
– LAW OF ADMINISTRATIVE PROCEDURE
– LAW OF ADMINISTRATIVE VIOLATIONS AND PUNISHMENTS
Bulgaria. Ministere des Affaires Etrangeres *see* RAPPORT SUR LE PLAN ECONOMIQUE QUINQUENNAL
Bulgaria. Ministry of Foreign Affairs *see* BULGARIA'S FIVE-YEAR PLAN REPORT
Bulgaria. Obiknoveno Narodno Subraniye *see* DNEVNITZI
BULGARIA, PAST AND PRESENT; HISTORICAL, POLITICAL, AND DESCRIPTIVE / Samuelson, James – Illus. with map of United Bulgaria. London: Truebner & Co., 1888. xiv,247p. illus., plates, ports., map – 1 – us U.W. Library [949]
BULGARIA. STATISTICHESKI GODISHNIK NA BULGARSKOTO TSARSTVO : ANNUAIRE STATISTIQUE DU ROYAUME DE BULGARIE 1909-1942 / Bulgaria. Glavna Direktsiia na Statistikata – (Coll title: European Official Statistical Serials, 1841-1984) – 174mf – 9 – £5.00f (set £1,320.00 251mf) – uk Chadwyck [949]
BULGARIAN ALMANACS PAMPHLET COLLECTION – 1955 – 1 – CSUXANL1892-B – us Hoover Inst Photo [030]
THE BULGARIAN EXARCHATE : ITS HISTORY AND THE EXTENT OF ITS AUTHORITY IN TURKEY / Mach, Richard von – London: T.F. Unwin; Neuchatel: Attinger, 1907 – 1mf – us A.T.L.A. [240]
BULGARIAN-BRITISH REVIEW – 1928-40 – 1 – 19.00 – us L of C Photodup [949]
THE BULGARIANS IN THE PAST, PAGES FROM BULGARIAN CULTURAL HISTORY / Mishev, D – Lausanne. 1919. BR-3894 2 – 8 – ne IDC [949]
BULGARIA'S FIVE-YEAR PLAN REPORT / Bulgaria. Ministry of Foreign Affairs – Terpeshev, Dobri. Sofia. 1949. BD-645 1 – 9 – ne IDC [949]
BULGARIA'S FOREIGN RELATIONS PAMPHLET COLLECTION – 1906-1985 – 1 – CSUXANL7405-B – us Hoover Inst Photo [320]
BULGARIA'S FOREIGN RELATIONS WITH YUGOSLAVIA PAMPHLET COLLECTION – 1978 – 1 – CSUXANL7421-B – us Hoover Inst Photo [320]
BULGARIE : OUVRAGES ET ARTICLES DE REVUES PARUS DE 1613 A 1937 / Kersopoulos, J G – Athenes, 1937 – 4mf – 9 – ne IDC [947]
LA BULGARIE – Sofia, Bulgaria. 1892; 1926-35 – 11r – 1 – us L of C Photodup [949]
LA BULGARIE – Sofia, Bulgaria. -d. 2 Jan 1924-27 Dec 1935. 12 reels – 1 – uk British Libr Newspaper [949]
LA BULGARIE DANS LE PASSE ET LE PRESENT; ETUDE HISTORIQUE, ETHNOGRAPHIQUE, STATISTIQUE ET MILITAIRE / Lamouche, L – Paris. 1892. BR-3806 2 – 8 – ne IDC [949]
BULGARIE: OUVRAGES ET ARTICLES DE REVUES PARUS DE 1613 A 1937 / Kersopoulos, J G – Athenes, 1937. 180p. BR-3805/2 – 8 – ne IDC [949]
BULGARIEN UND DIE WELTKRISE / Radoslavoff, V – Berlin. 1923. BR-3908 2 – 8 – ne IDC [940]
Bulgaris, Nicolas *see* THE HOLY CATECHISM OF NICOLAS BULGARIS
BULGARISCHE WIRTSCHAFTGESCHICHTE / Sakazov, I – Trans. from the Bulgarian by O. Mueller-Neudorf. Berlin, Leipzig. 1929. BR-3942 2 – 8 – ne IDC [330]

BULGARISCHE WOCHENSCHAU – Sofia, Bulgaria. Jul 1940-1942 – 1r – 1 – us L of C Photodup [072]
BULGARO-SOVETSKO EDINSTVO – Sofia, Bulgaria. 1951-54 – 1r – 1 – us L of C Photodup [949]
BULGARSKI KNIGOPIS – Sofia. v. 1-48. 1897-1945 – 1 – 93.00 – us L of C Photodup [949]
Bulger, George Ernest *see*
- EXTRACTS FROM MY SOUTH-AFRICAN JOURNAL DURING FIVE YEARS' SERVICE IN THE 2ND BATT., 10TH FOOT, FROM JANUARY 1860 TO DECEMBER 1864
- NOTES OF A TOUR FROM BANGALORE TO CALCUTTA: THENCE TO DELHI, AND SUBSEQUENTLY, TO BRITISH SIKKIM DURING THE EARLY PART OF 1867
- A WEEK IN THE NEIGHBOURHOOD OF LAKE ETCHEMIN AND QUEBEC

BULITIN-I BAHS-I DAKHILI – (March 1976-October 1977) – 1 reel – 1 – $50.00 – us MEDOC [950]
Bulkley, John *see* AN IMPARTIAL ACCOUNT OF THE LATE DEBATE AT LYME IN THE COLONY OF CONNECTICUT
Bull, Edvard *see* FOLK OG KIRKE I MIDDELALDEREN
Bull, L C *see* SURVEY OPERATIONS IN UNADMINISTRATED AREAS OF ASSAM AND BURMA, 1935-1936. REPORT
Bull, Lucien *see* LA CINEMATOGRAPHIE
Bull, P *see* A WOLF IN SHEEP'S CLOATHING
BULL SESSION / New Mexico State University. Cooperative Extension Service – 1970-82.1 reel – 1,5 – us Spaulding [630]
BULL SWAMP BAPTIST CHURCH. ORANGEBURG COUNTY. SOUTH CAROLINA : CHURCH RECORDS – (Centennial address by G.W. Garner, 1816-1916) – us Baptist [240]
Bull, W (London) *see* A RETAIL LIST OF NEW BEAUTIFUL AND RARE PLANTS,... CATALOGUES 1866-1890
BULLAE, MOTUS PROPIS AC BREVIAQUE.. – 1704 – 9 – 1.50f – sp Bibl Santa Ana [240]
Bulland, Jean *see* REGLES GENERALES D'ARCHITECTURE DES CINQ MANIERES DE COLONNES.
Bullard, J M *see* THE GROWTH HORMONE RESPONSE TO EXERCISE AT DIFFERENT TIMES OF THE DAY
BULLARII ROMANI CONTINUATIO / ed by Barberi, A & Spetia, A – T. 1-T. 19, Romae, 1835-1857 – 455mf – 8 – ne Slangenburg [240]
BULLARIUM CANONICORUM REGULARIUM CONGREGATIONIS SANCTISSIMI SALVATORIS – Romae, 1733 – Dfl105.00 – ne Slangenburg [240]
BULLARIUM CASINENSE SEU CONSTITUTIONES : PRO CONGREGATIONE CASINENSE / ed by Margarinus, G – Venetiis-Tuderti. v1-2. 1650-1670 – Dfl196.00 – ne Slangenburg [240]
BULLARIUM EQUESTRIS...IACOBI DE SPATHA / Lopez Agurleta, Jose – 1719 – 9 – 1.50f – sp Bibl Santa Ana [790]
BULLARIUM LATERANENSE : COLLECTIO PRIVILEGIORUM APOSTOLICORUM A SANCTA SEDE CANONICIS REGULARIBUS ORDINIS SANCTI AUGUSTINI CONGREGATIONIS SALVATORIS LATERANENSIS CONCESSORUM – Romae, 1727 – Dfl74.00 – ne Slangenburg [240]
BULLARIUM ORDINIS FF. PRAEDICATORUM / ed by Bremond, A – Romae. 8v. 1729-1740 – 246mf – 8 – Dfl861.00 – ne Slangenburg [240]
BULLARIUM ORDINIS RECOLLECTORUM SANCTI AUGUSTINI / Fernandez de S Corde, J – Madrid: Archivo Ibero Americano, 1963 – 1 – sp Bibl Santa Ana [240]
BULLARIUM SIVE COLLECTIO CONSTITUTIONUM / Sixtus, V – Roma, 1588 – 12mf – 8 – ne Slangenburg [240]
BULLARIUM...ALCANTARA...PEREIRO / Ortega y Cotes, Ignacio – 1759 – 9 – 1.50f – sp Bibl Santa Ana [946]
BULLARUM PRIVILEGIORUM AC DIPLOMATUM ROMANORUM PONTIFICUM AMPLISSIMA COLLECTIO – Studio Caroli Cocquelines. Tom 1-20. Romae, 1739-1762 – 388mf – 8 – Dfl1,008.00 – ne Slangenburg [240]
BULLARUM ROMANUM – Tom. 21-28. Romae, 1733-1744 – 171mf – 8 – Dfl599.00 – ne Slangenburg [240]
THE BULLDOG – Redlands, CA: U of Redlands, 1968-92 – 5r – 1 – $500.00 – R02678 – us Library Micro [370]
Bullein, W *see*
- BULLEINS BULWARKE OF DEFECE
- BULLEINS BULWARKE OF DEFENCE
- A NEWE BOKE OF PHISICKE

BULLEINS BULWARKE OF DEFECE / Bullein, W – London, 1562 – 28mf – ne IDC [610]
BULLEINS BULWARKE OF DEFENCE / Bullein, W – M 317. 1562 – 9 – ne IDC [610]
DIE BULLEN DER PAEPSTE : BIS ZUM ENDE DES ZWOELFTEN JAHRHUNDERTS / Pflug-Harttung, Julius von – Gotha: F.A. Perthes, 1901 – 1mf – us A.T.L.A. [240]
Bullen, Frank Thomas *see* THE LOG OF A SEA-WAIF: BEING RECOLLECTIONS OF THE FIRST FOUR YEARS OF MY SEA LIFE
Buller, A H R *see* RESEARCHES OF FUNGI
Buller, J *see* A REPLY TO THE REV. MR. WESLEY'S 'ADDRESS TO THE CLERGY'
Buller, James *see* FORTY YEARS IN NEW ZEALAND..
BULLET – Las Vegas, NV. 1987-1989 – 4r – 1 – $200.00 – U04851 – us Library Micro [071]
Bullet, Pierre *see* L'ARCHITECTURE PRATIQUE.
...BULLETIN / World Future Society – (1983-. 1,5,6,9) – v9-. 1975- – 1 – us UMI [073]
BULLETIN – 1 – F1,360.00 – sz Infoprint [072]
BULLETIN – 1847-1982 – 1 – us UMI [073]
BULLETIN – Aberdeen. Wash. 1902-1908 – 1 – us UMI [071]
BULLETIN / Academie Polonaise Des Sciences – Serie des Sciences de la Terre – 1953- 1; 1975- 5,6,9 – us UMI [550]
BULLETIN / Academie Polonaise Des Sciences – Serie des Sciences Mathematiques, Astronomiques, et Physiques – 1953- 1; 1975- 5,6,9 – us UMI [500]
BULLETIN / Academie Polonaise Des Sciences – Serie des Sciences Techniques – 1953- 1; 1975- 5,6,9 – us UMI [600]
BULLETIN / ADFL (Association of Departments of Foreign Languages) – v1- 1969- 1; 1976- 56,9 – us UMI [400]
BULLETIN / Adyar Library – v1-29 Madras 1937-65. Lacking: 1945, v9; 1960, v24; 1965 v29. BI-365 2 – 8 – ne IDC [100]
BULLETIN / Aeronautical Society of America – New York. Jul. 1908-Dec. 1909; July 1911 – 1 – us NY Public [073]
BULLETIN / Africa Institute – English Edition – v1- 1963- 1; v10- 6; v13- 1975- 9 – us UMI [306]
BULLETIN / AIAA (American Institute of Aeronautics and Astronautics) – v1-12 1964-75 1; 1971-75 5,6; 1975 4 x 6 in9 – us UMI [629]
BULLETIN / Alabama. Agricultural Experiment Station – 1883-1970 – 1,5,6 – us Spaulding [630]
BULLETIN / Alabama. Canebrake Agricultural Experiment Station – v. 1-29. 1888-1916 – 1,5,6 – us Spaulding [630]
BULLETIN / American Academy of Arts and Sciences – Boston, jan 1948-may 1977; v35-51 oct 1981-may 1998+ 1* – 1 – D11447 – us UMI [700]
BULLETIN / American Association of Petroleum Geologists – v5-11. 1921-27 – 1,5,6 – 510.00 – us Princeton Micro [550]
BULLETIN / American Association of University Professors – v. 23-42. 1937-1956 – 1 – us Princeton Micro [370]
BULLETIN / The American Astronomical Society – v1-. 1969- – 1,5,6 – us A.I.P. [520]
BULLETIN / American Ceramic Society – v1-34. 1922-55 – 1,5,6 – us Princeton Micro [740]
BULLETIN / American College of Surgeons – (v64- 1979- 5,6,9) – v1- 1916- – 1 – us UMI [617]
BULLETIN / American Congregational Association. Library – (1985-. 5,6,9) – 1955- – 1 – us UMI [020]
BULLETIN / American Congress on Surveying and Mapping – (Cont by: Surveying and Mapping. Former title: National Congress on Surveying and Mapping Report (oct 1941-42)) – Washington. cum index v1-5; v1-4 jun 1941-apr 1944 1,5*,9 – 1,5,9 – D12487 – us UMI [520]
BULLETIN / American Congress on Surveying and Mapping – v1- 1961- – 1,5,6,9 – us UMI [520]
BULLETIN / American Iris Society – (v56-. 1975-. 5,6,9) – v. 1-. 1920- – 1 – us UMI [580]
BULLETIN / American Iron and Steel Association – v1-46. 1886-1912 – 1 – $241.00 – us L of C Photodup [670]
BULLETIN / American Library Association – v. 1-60. 1907-1966 – 1 – us Princeton Micro [020]
BULLETIN / American Lung Association – (1974- . 9) – v59- 1973- – 1,5,6 – us UMI [616]
BULLETIN / American Mathematical Society – Series 2. v. 1-54. 1894-48 – 1,5,6 – us Princeton Micro [510]
BULLETIN / American Meteorological Society – v27-46 1946-65 – 1,5,6 – us Princeton Micro [550]
BULLETIN / American Museum of Natural History – v. 1-146. 1886-1971 – 1,5,6 – us Princeton Micro [580]
BULLETIN / American Pharmaceutical Association – (Superseded by its journal.) v. 5-6. 1910-1911. All pub – 1,5,6 – us Princeton Micro [540]
BULLETIN / The American Physical Society – Series 1. v1-30. 1925-55 – 1,5,6,9 – us A.I.P. [530]
BULLETIN / American Physical Society – Series 2. v1-. 1956- – 1,5,6,9 – us A.I.P. [530]
BULLETIN / American Society for Information Science – (v5- , 1978- . 5,6,9) – v. 1-. 1974- – 1 – us UMI [020]
BULLETIN – Anderson. Ind. 1952- – 1 – us UMI [071]
BULLETIN / Archaeological Institute of America – 1909- 1; 1976- 5,6,9 – us UMI [930]
BULLETIN / Archaeological Society of Delaware – (1975- . 5,6,9) – 1933- – 1 – us UMI [930]
BULLETIN / Arctic Club of America – New York. nos. 1-27. 1907-1911 – 1 – us NY Public [073]
BULLETIN : ASSOCIATION CANADIENNE DES PARENTS DES PRISONNIERS DE GUERRE – Montreal, 1942?-45? SEM105P798 – 1mf – 9 – Can$2.25 – cn Bibl Nat [360]
BULLETIN / Association des Amis de Romain Rolland – no. 1-102. Paris. aout 1946-72 – 1 – fr A.C.R.P.P. [440]
BULLETIN / Association for Science Education – 1962-64 – 1 – uk Microform Academic [370]
BULLETIN / Association of African Universities – (1976- . 5,6,9) – 1974- – 1 – us UMI [370]
BULLETIN / Association of Departments and Administrators in Speech Communications – (See also: ACA Bulletin) – n. 1-12. 1972-1975 – 1 – us UMI [410]
BULLETIN / Association of the Bar of the City of New York – 1914-29 – 1 – us UMI [340]
BULLETIN / Association of the Bar of the City of New York – (1980- 5,6,9) – 1930- – 1 – us UMI [340]
BULLETIN / Auburn University. Agricultural Experiment Station – No.397-546. 1970-82 – 1, 5 – us Spaulding [630]
BULLETIN – (Available on subsc. Apply for details) – 1980- – 9 – at Pascoe [073]
BULLETIN – Bayonne. N.J. 1948-49 – 1 – us UMI [071]
BULLETIN – Bedford. Va. -w. 1899-1932, 1935- – 1 – us UMI [071]
BULLETIN / British Association for American Studies – 1960-66 – 1 – uk Microform Academic [073]
BULLETIN – Cairo. Ill. 1868-84; 1904-28 – 1 – us UMI [071]
BULLETIN – California State Nurses Association. v40-55. 1944-59 – 1 – us UMI [073]
BULLETIN / Chemical Society. Japan – v1-38. 1926-65 – 1,5,6 – us Princeton Micro [540]
BULLETIN / Clemson University. Agricultural Experiment Station – No.549-644. 1970-82 – 1,5 – us Spaulding [630]
BULLETIN / College Art Association – v1. 1913-18. Continued by: The Art Bulletin. New York, 1919-28. v2-10.BOC-492/1 – 9 – ne IDC [073]
BULLETIN – Collingwood, 1886-1932 – 21r – 1 – cn Preston [971]
BULLETIN / Colorado. Agricultural Experiment Station. Fort Collins – nos.1-540-2. 1887-1969 – 1,5,6 – us Spaulding [630]
BULLETIN / Colorado. Agricultural Extension Service. Fort Collins Cooperative Extension Service – nos. 101-466A. 1915-69 – 1,5,6 – us Spaulding [630]
BULLETIN / Comite de l'Afrique francaise – devenu: L'Afrique francaise. Bulletin mensuel du Comite de l'Afrique francaise du Maroc. Paris. 1891-1940, 1952-janv mars 1960 – 1 – fr A.C.R.P.P. [960]
BULLETIN / Comite d'Etudes Historiques et Scientifiques de l'Afrique Occidentale Francaise – v1-21 1918-38 – 1 – us Res Libr [960]
BULLETIN / Committee to Restore the Constitution; ed by Roberts, Archibald E – No.291, Sept 1986. 6p. Sample copy – 9 – 1.00f – at Libertarian Micro [335]
BULLETIN / Committee to Restore the Constitution – Sept 1986 sample. 6p. Plunder, American Style, 2p leaflet – 9 – 1.00f – at Libertarian Micro [335]
BULLETIN / Council on the Study of Religion – v7- 1976- 1; v9- 1978- 5,6,9 – us UMI [290]
BULLETIN / Deccan College. Research Institute – v. 1-18. Poona. 1939-57. BI-236 2 – 8 – ne IDC [073]
BULLETIN – Des Moines. Iowa. 1870 – 1 – us UMI [071]
BULLETIN / Ecole Francaise d'Extreme-Orient – Hanoi. v1-52. 1901-52.BSEC-18-2 – 8 – ne IDC [950]
BULLETIN / Ecole Francaise d'Extreme-Orient – v. 1-51. 1901-63 – 1 – 618.00 – us L of C Photodup [950]
BULLETIN – Endicott. N.Y. 1950-1960 – 1 – us UMI [071]
BULLETIN / Essex Naturalists, Trust – 1959- 1; 1975- 5,6,9 – us UMI [630]
BULLETIN / Evangelical Theological Society – v1-11. 1958-68.Continued by: Journal – 1 – us UMI [240]
BULLETIN – Fairmont. Neb. 1876-1896 – 1 – us UMI [071]
BULLETIN / Federation radicale et radicale-socialiste de Guyane. Comite Executif – Cayenne. dec 1908-sept 1910 – 1 – fr A.C.R.P.P. [073]
BULLETIN / Florida. Agricultural Experiment Station – v. 1-733. 1888-1969 – 1,5,6 – us Spaulding [630]
BULLETIN / Florida. Agricultural Experiment Station. Southern Cooperative Series – v. 13-24 – 1,5,6 – us Spaulding [630]
BULLETIN / Florida. Agricultural Extension Service – v. 1-182. 1915-66 – 1,5,6 – us Spaulding [630]
BULLETIN / France. Agence Generale des Colonies – v. 1-27. 1908-34. (v. 16, no. 192; v. 17, no. 200, 201 wanting) – 1 – 301.00 – us L of C Photodup [944]
BULLETIN / France. Conseil Economique – 1948-52 – 1 – fr A.C.R.P.P. [330]
BULLETIN / France. Convention Nationale – Paris. 21 sept 1794-28 aout 1795 – 1 – fr A.C.R.P.P. [944]
BULLETIN / France. L'Assemblee nationale – Paris. juil 1789-janv 1790 – 1 – fr A.C.R.P.P. [324]
BULLETIN – Freeport. Ill. 1877-83 – 1 – us UMI [071]
BULLETIN – Freeport. Ill. -w. 1858-64, 1866-82 – 1 – us UMI [071]
BULLETIN / Geological Society of America – v1- 1890- 1; v86- 1975- 5,6,9 – us UMI [550]
BULLETIN / Geological Society of America – v. 1-51. 1888-1940 – 1 – us Princeton Micro [550]
BULLETIN / Georgia. Agricultural Experiment Station. Athens – n.s. v. 1-183. 1954-66 – 1,5,6 – us Spaulding [630]
BULLETIN / Georgia. Agricultural Experiment Station. Athens – v. 1-6. 1952-54 – 1,5,6 – us Spaulding [630]
BULLETIN / Georgia. Coastal Plain Experiment Station. Tifton – v. 1-54. 1921-54 – 1,5,6 – us Spaulding [630]
BULLETIN / Georgia. Experiment Station. Experiment – v. 1-286. 1888-1953 – 1,5,6 – us Spaulding [630]
BULLETIN / Georgia. University. Agricultural Extension Service – v. 1-682. 1912-69 – 1,5,6 – us Spaulding [630]
BULLETIN / Georgia. University. George Foster Peabody School of Forestry – 1943-50 – 1,5 – us Spaulding [634]
BULLETIN / Georgia. University. Southern Cooperative Series – n.1-147. 1943-69 – 1,5 – us Spaulding [630]
BULLETIN – Greenville, CA. 1886-87 (broken file) – 1r – 1 – $50.00 – B02278 – us Library Micro [071]

BULLETIN / Groupe du Bas-Languedoc de l'Association Sully – devenu: Sully. Montpellier, Nimes. dec 1933-aout 1939, 1943-juin 1944 – 1 – fr A.C.R.P.P. [073]

BULLETIN / Harvard University. Houghton Library – v. 1-. 1947- – 1. – apply; v.23-6; v.24- 1976- 9 – us UMI [020]

BULLETIN / History of Education Society – v. 1-. 1968- – 1. ; 5,6,9 – apply; v.19- – us UMI [370]

BULLETIN / IDOC (International Documentation on the Contemporary Church) Documentation Service – v. 1-. 1977- – 1,5,6,9 – us UMI [073]

BULLETIN / Illinois. Agricultural Experiment Station – n.1-736. 1888-1969 – 1, 5 – us Spaulding [630]

BULLETIN / Illinois. Department of Agricultural Economics – n.0-17. 1960-68 – 1,5 – us Spaulding [630]

BULLETIN / Indonesian Current Affairs Translation Service – (1975-. 5,6) – 1975 – 1 – us UMI [320]

BULLETIN / Institut Francais d'Afrique Noire – T. 1-15. Jan 1939-Oct 1953, and Bulletin. Series A, Sciences naturelles. T. 16-27. 1954-65 – 1 – 269.00 – us L of C Photodup [960]

BULLETIN / Institut General Psychologique. Paris – v. 1-33. 1900-33 – 1 – 93.00 – us L of C Photodup [150]

BULLETIN / Institut Pasteur. Paris – v. 1-61. 1903-1963 PLUS. Supplement 38-41. 1940-1943 – 1,5,6 – us Princeton Micro [370]

BULLETIN / Institute of Historical Research – H 788. v1 1923-1924 – 9 – ne IDC [900]

BULLETIN / Institute of Historical Research – (Special suppl. 3-8 complete. 2412.00; 9326Special suppl. 3. 244.50v; WDS; 9. Special suppl. 4-8. 241.50v; WDS; 9) – v. 1-43, NOS. 1-108. 1923-70 – 9 – 24190.00; 4.50v – uk Dawson [900]

BULLETIN / International Association of Jewish Lawyers and Jurists – 1970- – 1,5,6,9 – us UMI [340]

BULLETIN / Iowa State University. Agricultural Experiment Station – No.1-382. 1888-1957 – 1,5 – us Spaulding [630]

BULLETIN / Jewish Telegraphic Agency – New York. N.Y. 1956-67 – 1 – us A.J.P.C. [073]

BULLETIN / John Rylands Library – Manchester, 1903-28. v1-12. BHC-787 2 – 8 – ne IDC [020]

BULLETIN – Kalama. Wash. -w. 1889-1919; 1966-78 – 1 – us UMI [071]

BULLETIN / Kansas. State University. Agricultural Experiment Station – nos.1-16. 1929-47 – 1,5,6 – us Spaulding [630]

BULLETIN / Kansas. State University. Agricultural Experiment Station – nos.1-626. 1888-1978 – 1,5,6 – us Spaulding [630]

BULLETIN / Kentucky. Agricultural Experiment Station – v. 1-708. 1885-1968 – 1,5,6 – us Spaulding [630]

BULLETIN / L'Association Emile-Zola – no. 1-7. Paris. 1910-12 – 1 – fr A.C.R.P.P. [440]

BULLETIN – Latrobe. Pa. 1903- – 1 – us UMI [071]

BULLETIN / L'Ecole francaise d'Extreme-Orient – Hanoi. 1901-08, 1910-11, 1914-18 – 1 – fr A.C.R.P.P. [930]

BULLETIN / Library Association. China – Peking. v. 1-14, no. 5. June 1925-Mar Apr 1940 – 1 – us NY Public [020]

BULLETIN / L'Institut Francais d'Afrique Noire – Paris. 1939-65 – 1 – fr A.C.R.P.P. [073]

BULLETIN / L'Institut francais de sociologie – Paris. 1931-33 (I-III) – 1 – fr A.C.R.P.P. [073]

BULLETIN / Louisiana library association – 1937- 1; 1970- 5,6; 1976- 4 x 6 in. 9 – us UMI [020]

BULLETIN / Louisiana State University. Agricultural Experiment Station – No.644-759. 1970-84 – 1,5 – us Spaulding [630]

BULLETIN / Louisiana State University. Agricultural Experiment Station. Southern Cooperative Series – No.159-260. 1970-81 – 1,5 – us Spaulding [630]

BULLETIN / Lutheran Theological Seminary. Gettysburg, PA – v20-59. 1941-79 – 1 – us UMI [240]

BULLETIN / Madjelis Ilmu Pengetahuan Indonesia – Djakarta. SE-493 1. v1-12. Lacking: 1960, v1. 1960-1969 – 9 – ne IDC [073]

BULLETIN / Maine. Agricultural Experiment Station – First Series. 1885-1888 – 1,5,6 – us Spaulding [630]

BULLETIN – Manteca, CA. 1918-78 – 72r – 1 – $3,600.00 – B02416 – us Library Micro [071]

BULLETIN – Martinsville. Va. 1959- – 1 – us UMI [071]

BULLETIN / Massachusetts. Agricultural Experiment Station – (First Station). v. 1-57. 1883-1895 – 1,5,6 – us Spaulding [630]

BULLETIN / Massachusetts. Agricultural Experiment Station – (Second Station). v. 1-582. 1888-1969 – 1,5,6 – us Spaulding [630]

BULLETIN / Massachusetts. Agricultural Extension Service – v. 1-36. 1914-20 – 1,5,6 – us Spaulding [630]

BULLETIN / Medical library association – (1965- . 5,6. 1977- . 9) – 1911- – 1 – us UMI [610]

BULLETIN / Metropolitan Museum of Art – v1-1905- 1; v27- 1968- 5,6; v33- 9 – us UMI [700]

BULLETIN – Miamisburg. Ohio. 1872-94 – 1 – us UMI [071]

BULLETIN / Minneapolis Institute of Arts – v1-1905- 1; v62- 5,6,9 – us UMI [073]

BULLETIN / Minnesota. University. Agricultural Experiment Station. St. Paul – nos.1-515. 1888-1975 – 1,5,6 – us Spaulding [630]

BULLETIN / Mississippi. Agricultural Experiment Station. State College – v. 1-777. 1888-1969 – 1,5,6 – us Spaulding [630]

BULLETIN / Mississippi. State College. Agricultural Extension Service – v. 1-157. 1916-50 – 1,5,6 – us Spaulding [630]

BULLETIN / Mississippi State University. Agricultural Experiment Station – 1970. 778-779. 1 reel – 1,5 – us Spaulding [630]

BULLETIN / Mississippi State University. Agricultural Experiment Station. Agricultural and Forestry Experiment Station – No.780-910. 1970-82 – 1,5 – us Spaulding [630]

BULLETIN / Missouri Historical Society – v.1-36. 1944-80. Continued as: Gateway Heritage – 1 – us UMI [073]

BULLETIN / Montana. Agricultural Experiment Station – nos.1-630. 1894-1969 – 1,5,6 – us Spaulding [630]

BULLETIN / Montana. Agricultural Extension Service – nos.1-332. 1915-69 – 1,5,6 – us Spaulding [630]

BULLETIN / Montana. Forest and Conservation Experiment Station. Missoula – nos.1-37. 1949-69 – 1,5,6 – us Spaulding [630]

BULLETIN / Museum of Modern Art – 1933-63 – 1 – us UMI [700]

BULLETIN / N. A. S. S. P. (National Association of Secondary School Principals) – v1- 1917- 1; v55- 5,6; v59-9 – us UMI [370]

BULLETIN / National Catholic Education Association – v. 1-65. 1904-69 – 1 – us Princeton Micro [240]

BULLETIN / National Catholic Educational Association – v. 1-65. 1904-69 – 1 – us UMI [240]

BULLETIN / National Model Railroad Association – v35- 1969- 1; v39- 5,6; v41- 9 – us UMI [790]

BULLETIN / National Research Council – v. 1-123. 1919-1950 – 1,5,6 – us Princeton Micro [500]

BULLETIN / National Tuberculosis Association – See now: American Lung Association. Bulletin – us UMI [616]

BULLETIN / Nebraska. Agricultural Experiment Station. Lincoln – n.1-506. 1960-64 – 1,5 – us Spaulding [630]

BULLETIN / Nebraska. Conservation and Survey Division – n.1$17. 1916-25 – 1, 5 – us Spaulding [630]

BULLETIN / New Jersey Academy of Science – 1955- 1; 1972- 5,6; 1975- 9 – us UMI [073]

BULLETIN / New Mexico State University. Agricultural Experiment Station – No.558-695. 1970-82 – 1,5 – us Spaulding [630]

BULLETIN / New York Academy of Medicine – v1- 1925- 1; v41- 5,6; v46- 9 – us UMI [610]

BULLETIN / New York Academy of Medicine – v1-31. 1925-55 – 1,5,6 – us Princeton Micro [610]

BULLETIN / North Carolina. Agricultural Experiment Station. Raleigh – n.57-436. Jun 1888-Mar 1969 – 1,5 – us Spaulding [630]

BULLETIN / North Carolina State University.Agricultural Experiment Station – No.437-459. 1970-79. 1 reel – 1,5 – us Spaulding [630]

BULLETIN / North Carolina State University.Agricultural Research Service – No.460-464. 1979-82. 1 reel – 1,5 – us Spaulding [630]

BULLETIN / North Dakota. Agricultural Experiment Station. Fargo – nos.1-499. 1892-1975 – 1,5,6 – us Spaulding [630]

BULLETIN / Ohio Association of School Librarians – 1949-76 1; 1971-76 5,6 – us UMI [020]

BULLETIN / Oklahoma State University. Agricultural Experiment Station – B672-B764. 1970-82 – 1,5 – us Spaulding [630]

BULLETIN / Pan American Union – Washington. v1-82 1893-1948 – 1,5,6 – us Princeton Micro [970]

BULLETIN – Pembroke, 1934-1955 – 11r – 1 – cn Preston [971]

BULLETIN / Phoenix Foundation – May 1980. 1 fiche (29x) – 9 – 1.00f – at Libertarian Micro [320]

BULLETIN – Portland OR. Mar 28-Oct 18 1935, June 3 1936-May 14 1938 – 1 – us U.O. Library [071]

BULLETIN / Purdue University. Agricultural Experiment Station – No.1-652. 1885-1957 – 1,5 – us Spaulding [630]

BULLETIN / Rhode Island. Agricultural Experiment Station – v. 1-401. 1889-1969 – 1,5,6 – us Spaulding [630]

BULLETIN / Rhode Island. Agricultural Extension Service – v. 1-196. 1915-68 – 1,5,6 – us Spaulding [630]

BULLETIN / Rhode Island. Agricultural Extension Service – v. 1-5. 1911-15 – 1,5,6 – us Spaulding [630]

BULLETIN / Scottish Institute of Missionary Studies – 1967- 1; 1976- 5,6,9 – us UMI [240]

BULLETIN / Societe Belge d'Etudes Coloniales – 1906-1914, 1919-1925. Suspended 1915-1918. Missing: 1920, 1922, 1923 (nos. 1 2, 11) – 1 – 35.00r – us Hoover Inst Photo [323]

BULLETIN / Societe Chimique de France – Paris, 1858-1941 – 62r – 5 – us Ross [500]

BULLETIN / Societe Chimique de France – Series 1-5. 1858-1983 – 1,5,6 – us Princeton Micro [540]

BULLETIN / Societe de Chimie Biologique. Paris – v. 1-55. 1914-73 – 1,5,6 – us Princeton Micro [500]

BULLETIN / La Societe de Geographie d'Algier et de L'Afrique du Nord – v. 1-48 49. Jul 1896-1943 44. Missing no. 1, 1902 – 1 – 35.00r – us Hoover Inst Photo [960]

BULLETIN / Societe de l'Histoire de France – puis Annuaire-bulletin. Paris. 1834-69 – 1 – fr A.C.R.P.P. [944]

BULLETIN / Societe de l'histoire du Protestantisme Francais. Paris – v1-52, 94-98. 1852-1902, 1947-51. Lacking Oct-Dec 1948 and Jan-Jun 1951 – 1 – $368.00 – us L of C Photodup [270]

BULLETIN / Societe de Pathologie Exotique – v. 1-32. 1908-1939 – 1,5,6 – us Princeton Micro [616]

BULLETIN / Societe des Amis de Georges Bernanos – no. 1-58. Paris. dec 1949-janv 1966. mq no. 31, 49 – 1 – fr A.C.R.P.P. [073]

BULLETIN / Societe des Anciens Textes Francais. Paris – v1-62. 1875-1936. v41-45, 1915-19 never publ. List of members in each volume – 1 – us U.W. Library [440]

BULLETIN / Societe des compositeurs de musique – Paris. 1863-70 – 1 – fr A.C.R.P.P. [780]

BULLETIN / Societe des Etudes Indochinoises de Saigon – 1883-1923 – 1 – 69.00 – us L of C Photodup [950]

BULLETIN / Societe des Etudes Indochinoises de Saigon – Saigon. 1926-59 – 1 – fr A.C.R.P.P. [490]

BULLETIN / Societe des Gens de Lettres – Paris. 1847 (t. 3) – 1 – fr A.C.R.P.P. [800]

BULLETIN / Societe des sciences historiques et naturelles de la Corse. Bastia – v(1)-46/49. 1881-1929 – 1 – $119.00 – us L of C Photodup [944]

BULLETIN / Societe d'Etudes Philosophiques du Sud-Est – Marseilles, 1926-28. v1-2. Lacking: v12(3-4), 1938; v13-14, 1934/40. BHC-186/2 – 8 – ne IDC [100]

BULLETIN / Societe Ethnologique de Paris – Paris. 1846-47 – 1 – fr A.C.R.P.P. [306]

BULLETIN / Societe francaise des Electriciens – v1-9. 1931-39 – 1 – us Princeton Micro [073]

BULLETIN / Societe Historique du VIe Arondissement de Paris – Paris. v1-30 1898-1929 – 1 – us NY Public [944]

BULLETIN / Societe Jules Verne – Dir. G.-H. Guermonprez. no. 1-11 13. Paris. nov 1935-38 – 1 – fr A.C.R.P.P. [830]

BULLETIN / Societe litteraire des Amis d'Emile Zola – no. 1-24. Paris. 1922-38 – 1 – fr A.C.R.P.P. [830]

BULLETIN / Societe Mathematique de France. Paris – v85-96. 1957-68 – 1,5,6 – us Princeton Micro [073]

BULLETIN / Societe ornithologique suisse – Geneve. v1-2. 1865-70 – 3 – us Readex [590]

BULLETIN / Societe Paul Claudel – no. 1-32, no. special. Paris. 1958-68 – 1 – fr A.C.R.P.P. [810]

BULLETIN / Societe royale de Botanique de Belgique.Brussels – 1874-1961 – 1,5,6 – us Princeton Micro [580]

BULLETIN / Societe Union Musicologique – v. 1-6. 1921-1926 – 1 – us Schnase [780]

BULLETIN / Society for Applied Spectroscopy – Bound Brook, N.J. v1-6 1946-Nov 1952 – 1 – us NY Public [621]

BULLETIN / South Carolina. Agricultural Experiment Station. Clemson – n.1-548. Apr 1888-Oct 1969 – 1,5 – us Spaulding [630]

BULLETIN / South Dakota. State University. Agricultural Experiment Station – nos.1-628. 1887-1974 – 1,5,6 – us Spaulding [630]

BULLETIN / Stephen F. Austin University. School of Forestry – No.19-25. 1970-72. 1 reel – 1,5 – us Spaulding [630]

BULLETIN – Sydney, 1880-1996 – 241r – 1 – at Pascoe [073]

BULLETIN / Tennessee Nurses Association – (1983-. 5,6,9) – 1957- – 1 – us UMI [610]

BULLETIN / Tennessee State Nurses' Association – Feb 1934-56 – 1 – us UMI [610]

BULLETIN / Tennessee. University. Agricultural Experiment Station – v.1-465. 1888-1969 – 1,5 – us Spaulding [630]

BULLETIN / Texas A & M University. Agricultural Experiment Station and Agricultural Extension Service – No.90-1088. 1970-82. (Revisions of pre-1970 Bulletins); No.1092-1425 – 1,5 – us Spaulding [630]

BULLETIN / Texas Graduate Nurses Association – 1939-64 – 1 – us UMI [610]

BULLETIN / Theological Seminary of the Evangelical and Reformed Church – (Superseded in 1958 by: THEOLOGY AND LIFE). v. 1-28. 1930-1957 – 1,5,6 – us Princeton Micro [240]

BULLETIN / Tuskegee Institute. Agricultural Experiment Station – v. 1-43. 1899-1942 – 1,5,6 – us Spaulding [630]

BULLETIN / Tuskegee Normal and Industrial Institute. Experiment Station – n1-42. 1898-1936 – 1r – 1 – us Ross [975]

BULLETIN / United Bible Societies – (1985-. 5,6,9) – 1950- – 1 – us UMI [240]

BULLETIN / U.S. Bureau of Plant Industry – Nos. 1-285. 1901-1913 – 1,5,6 – us Princeton Micro [630]

BULLETIN / U.S. Department of State – v. 1-53. 1939-1965 – 1 – us Princeton Micro [323]

BULLETIN / U.S. Department of State – (v60-1969- 5,6; v62- 1970- 9) – 1- 1939- – 1 – us UMI [977]

BULLETIN / U.S. Internal Revenue Service – 1922-1972 – 1,5,6 – us Princeton Micro [323]

BULLETIN / U.S. Social Security Administration – v. 1-38. 1938-1975 – 1,5,6 – us Princeton Micro [360]

BULLETIN / U.S. Treasury Department – 1939-1973 – 1,5,6 – us Princeton Micro [336]

BULLETIN / U.S. Treasury Department. Bureau of Customs – v1-20. 1966-86.Continues: Treasury Decisions.78-234B – 9 – $132.00 – us L.L.M.C. [336]

BULLETIN / University of Florida. Agricultural Experiment Station – No.734-832. 1970-82 – 1, 5 – us Spaulding [630]

BULLETIN / University of Florida. Cooperative Extension Service – No.182-194. 1966-81. 1 reel – 1, 5 – us Spaulding [630]

BULLETIN / University of Georgia. Agricultural Extension Service – No.683-883. 1970-82. 56 fiches – 9 – us Spaulding [630]

BULLETIN / University of Kentucky. Agricultural Experiment Station – No.709-719. 1970-83. 1 reel – 1,5 – us Spaulding [630]
BULLETIN / University of Missouri. Agricultural Experiment Station – No.1-886. 1888-1970 – 1,5 – us Spaulding [630]
BULLETIN / University of Nebraska. State Museum – (v9- 1974- 5,6; v10- 1975- 9) – v1- 1965- – 1 – us UMI [700]
BULLETIN / University of Tennessee. Agricultural Experiment Station – No.466-618. 1970-83 – 1,5 – us Spaulding [630]
BULLETIN – v1-2. 1975-77 – 1 – us UMI [073]
BULLETIN / Virginia. Agricultural Experiment Station. Blacksburg – 1889-Nov 1966.n.1-577 – 1,5 – us Spaulding [630]
BULLETIN / Virginia. Polytechnic Institute. College of Agriculture. Wood Research Laboratory – v. 1-87. 1949-69 – 1,5,6 – us Spaulding [630]
BULLETIN / Virginia. Polytechnic Institute. Extension Division – n.1-310. Apr 1915-Sep 1967 – 1,5 – us Spaulding [630]
BULLETIN / Virginia. Polytechnic Institute. Research Division. Blacksburg – v. 1-50. 1967-69 – 1,5,6 – us Spaulding [630]
BULLETIN / Virginia. Truck Experiment Station. Norfolk – v. 1-116. 1909-56 – 1,5,6 – us Spaulding [630]
BULLETIN / Washington. Agricultural Experiment Station – nos.1-792. 1891-1974 – 1,5,6 – us Spaulding [630]
BULLETIN / Wisconsin. College of Agriculture. Dept. of Agricultural Journalism – n.1-37. 1929-67 – 1,5 – us Spaulding [630]
BULLETIN / World Health Organization – (Geneva). (Supersedes: League of Nations Health Organization. Also known as: WHO Bulletin.) v. 1-33. 1947-1965 – 1,5,6 – us Princeton Micro [610]
BULLETIN *see*
– LA PETITE NATION/LE BULLETIN
– LA REVUE, LE BULLETIN (HEBDOS DE L'OUTAOUAIS 1984 INC.)
BULLETIN. / Congo. Ministere des Affaires Sociales – Leopoldville, 1961-65. v1-5. BA-689/1 – 9 – ne IDC [960]
BULLETIN.. / Bibliotheque Nationale. Quebec – Montreal, v7 no 1 1973-v17 1983. SEM16P296 – 1r – 5 – Can$23.00 – cn Bibl Nat [020]
BULLETIN.. / Oxford University. Institute of Statistics – v1-24. 1939-62 – 1 – us UMI [073]
BULLETIN / American Congress on Surveying and Mapping – (Cont ACSM bulletin) – Falls Church. v1-74 nov 1961-aug 1981* – 1 – D12485 – us UMI [520]
BULLETIN / American Geographical Society of New York – (Superseded by: Geographical review. Former titles: Bulletin of the American Geographical and Statistical Society (aug 1852-jan 1857); Journal of the American Geographical and Statistical Society (jan 1859-1870); Journal of the American Geographical Society of New York (1872-1900)) – New York. cum index 1852-1915; v1-47 1852-1915 – 1 – D5214 – us UMI [975]
BULLETIN / American Mathematical Society – (Ceased publ. Superseded by: Bulletin, new series of the American Mathematical Society) – Providence. cum index v31-70 1925-1964; 2s v1-84 oct 1894-jan-nov 1978 1; 2s v1-84 oct 1894-nov 1978 9* – 1,9 – D13410 – us UMI [510]
BULLETIN / Institut de recherches scientifiques au Congo – Brazzaville, 1962-1963 – us Res Libr [073]
BULLETIN / Ligue de defense des libertes publiques (Haiti) – [Port-au-Prince]: la Ligue. n1. 29 dec 1953 – us Res Libr [073]
BULLETIN *see* AMERICAN JOURNAL OF HOSPITAL PHARMACY
LE BULLETIN – Hartford, CT. v8 n7. 13 jun 1943; v8 n8. 27 jun 1943 – 1r – 1 – Can$25.00 – cn Can Microfilming [071]
LE BULLETIN : HEBDO DU COMMERCE ET LA COLONISATION / ed by Grignon, J-J – St Jerome, Canada. 22 oct-29 oct 1892 – 1r – 1 – Can$25.00 – cn Can Microfilming [380]
LE BULLETIN : NATIONLISTE – (Called: Le Sport) – Montreal, Canada. v2 n19. 4 sep 1904-27 dec 1908; 7 jun 1914; 30 mar 1924 – 1r – 1 – Can$60.00 – cn Can Microfilming [072]
LE BULLETIN – Quebec, Canada. 18 avr 1878 – 1r – 1 – Can$25.00 – cn Can Microfilming [072]
LE BULLETIN : SOCIETE ST-JEAN BAPTISTE – (Cont by and filmed with: L'Information Nationale jan 1962-jun 1984) – Montreal. mar 1952-v10 n7. dec 1961 – 3r – 1 – Can$55.00r – cn Can Microfilming [073]
LE BULLETIN – St-Jerome [Quebec]: J J Grignon, 1892 – 9 – cn C.I.H.M. [971]
THE BULLETIN – 1880- – 4r per y – 1 – inquire – us Ross [072]
THE BULLETIN – (Also known as: The Call Bulletin) – San Francisco, CA. 1906-56 – 769r – 1 – $38,450.00 – C02791 – us Library Micro [071]
THE BULLETIN – Anaheim, CA. 1966-70; 1992- – 59+ r – 1 RC02014 – $2,950.00 ($500.00y) – us Library Micro [071]
THE BULLETIN – Chicago. Ill. 1959-1967 – 1 – us UMI [071]
THE BULLETIN – Rossland, B.C: Collins, [1900-19–] – 9 – cn C.I.H.M. [971]
THE BULLETIN – Sydney, Australia. 2 April-29 Oct 1941; 25 Feb 1942-18 Nov 1953 – 23r – 1 – uk British Libr Newspaper [980]
THE BULLETIN – Toronto: Bulletin Pub. Co., [1893-1950] – 9 – cn C.I.H.M. [971]
THE BULLETIN – Twinsburg. Ohio. -w. 1964 – 1 – us UMI [071]
BULLETIN / American College of Surgeons – Chicago. v1-63 1916-78* 1; v64- jan 1979- 1,5,9 – 1,5,9 – D12391 – us UMI [617]
BULLETIN A SES CORRESPONDANTS / Societe Philomatique de Paris – Serie originale manuscrite Paris, 1791-92 puis imprimee: Paris, Du Pont, 1792-an 51797, 192 p. plus 14 pl. BULLETIN DES SCIENCES, PAR LA SOCIETE PHILOMATIQUE DE PARIS. Premiere serie. nos. 1-96. 1791-1805. Paris, Fuchs, puis Klostermann fils. Avec six pieces annexes dont cinq propsectus, 1793-1804, 14 p. Introduction par Jonathan Mandelbaum. Histoire des Sciences XVIIe-XIXe Siecles. 7990 3 – 9 – fr Hachette [500]
BULLETIN A.C.B.L.F. *see* DOCUMENTATION ET BIBLIOTHEQUES
BULLETIN ADMINISTRATIF / Belgian Congo. Secretariat general – 1928-58. Incomplete. Semimonthly – 1 – us U.W. Library [960]
BULLETIN ADMINISTRATIF / Cambodia – 1921-23, 1927 – 1 – fr A.C.R.P.P. [950]
BULLETIN ADMINISTRATIF / Congo. Belgian – Leopoldville. Pt1: 1958-59, Pt2: 1958-59 – 1 – us NY Public [960]
BULLETIN ADMINISTRATIF / Indochina. French – 1921 – 1 – fr A.C.R.P.P. [073]
BULLETIN ADMINISTRATIF / Laos – 1919, 1921-22, 1927 – 1 – fr A.C.R.P.P. [950]
BULLETIN ADMINISTRATIF / Senegal – Paris. 1819-1829, 1845-1908. Gaps – 1 – 35.00r – us Hoover Inst Photo [324]
BULLETIN ADMINISTRATIF ET COMMERCIAL / Belgian Congo. Secretariat general – 1912-27. Incomplete. Semimonthly – 1 – us U.W. Library [960]
BULLETIN AGENCE DE PRESSE LIBRE DU QUEBEC *see* BULLETIN POPULAIRE
BULLETIN – AMERICAN ASSOCIATION FOR THE ADVANCEMENT OF SCIENCE / American Association for the Advancement of Science – (Publ suspended 1947-1960. Former title: AAAS Bulletin (mar 1942-jan 1974)) – Washington. v1-19. mar 1942-sep 1974 – 1 – D8728 – us UMI [500]
BULLETIN: AMERICAN CONGRESS ON SURVEYING AND MAPPING – v1-4. 1941-44. Continued by: Surveying and Mapping – 1 – us UMI [910]
BULLETIN: AMERICAN PROTESTANT HOSPITAL ASSOCIATION – (v.44-. 1980-. 5,6,9) – v.1-. 1936- – 1 – us UMI [610]
BULLETIN AND SPECIAL BULLETIN / U.S. Department of Labor. Women's Bureau – 1919-75; 1940-45 – 575mf – 9 – $5.00f – us Ross [330]
BULLETIN ANNEXE AU JOURNAL OFFICIEL / France – 1905-12 – 1 – fr A.C.R.P.P. [323]
BULLETIN ARCHEOLOGIQUE DU COMITE DES TRAVAUX HISTORIQUES ET SCIENTIFIQUES – Paris. 1955 56-1963 64 – 1 – fr A.C.R.P.P. [930]
BULLETIN. ASSOCIATION DES BIBLIOTHECAIRES DU QUEBEC – nos 1-34. 1950-52? – 1r – 5 – Can$11.00 – cn Bibl Nat [020]
LE BULLETIN (BUCKINGHAM, QUEBEC) : LA REVUE DE LA LIEVRE – Buckingham: '(s.n.)' v5- 1986-. SEM35P283 – 14r – 1 – Can$620.00 – cn Bibl Nat [072]
BULLETIN BULANAN INDUSTRI MINJAK DAN GAS BUMI INDONESIA / Direktorat Djenderal Minjak dan Gas Bumi – (Monthly. Missing: 1965-1969(Jan-March)) – Djakarta, 1965-1969 – 3mf – 9 – SE-1369/1 – ne IDC [338]
BULLETIN (CAJ) *see* MEDIA
BULLETIN (CENTRE FOR INVESTIGATIVE JOURNALISM) – (Incorporated in: Media v1 1994. nos 1-36 1978-88 Can$82.00) – nos 1- 1978- – 9 – Can$20.00y – cn Micromedia [070]
BULLETIN COLONIAL / Communist Party. France – Paris. oct 1933-juin 1936 – 1 – fr A.C.R.P.P. [335]
LE BULLETIN COMMERCIAL – Montreal, Canada. 22 jan 1858; v1 n2. 26 jun 1858 – 1r – 1 – Can$25.00 – cn Can Microfilming [072]
BULLETIN COMMERCIAL AGRICOLE – Paris. 27 janv-11 juil 1848 – 1 – fr A.C.R.P.P. [630]
BULLETIN COMMUNISTE / Comite de la Troisieme Internationale – Paris. mars 1920-30, 1933 – 1 – fr A.C.R.P.P. [335]
BULLETIN COMMUNISTE / Organe du Comite de la Troisieme Internationale – Paris. v1,no1-v14,no32-33. Mar 1920-Jul 1933 – 60 fiches – 9 – $145.00 – us UPA [335]
BULLETIN COMMUNISTE – Paris. v. 1-5. June 10 1920-Nov 14 1924. Incomplete – 1 – us NY Public [335]
BULLETIN: CONNECTICUT LABOR DEPARTMENT / Connecticut. Employment Security Division – v.1, n.1, Jan. 1936-78. 94 fiches. (Harvard Law School Library Collection.) – 9 – 1.50f – us H.U. Law [336]
LE BULLETIN CONTINENTAL – (Continued as BULLETIN ABOLITIONNISTE) – Geneva, 1875-1901. Lacking: 1877, v2(9); 1879, v4(2,p.9-16); 1913, (142,p.7 7-84); 1942 (67,p.1.16) – 137mf – 1 – ne IDC [305]
BULLETIN, D SERIES / Colorado. Agricultural Extension Service. Fort Collins Cooperative Extension Service – nos.1-50. 1941-44 – 1,5,6 – us Spaulding [630]
LE BULLETIN DE BUCKINGHAM – Buckingham: '(s.n.)' v1-22. 1958-79. SEM35P282 – 10r – 1 – Can$537.00 – cn Bibl Nat [971]
BULLETIN DE COLLECTE – [Quebec?]: Paroisse de St. Jean-Baptiste de Quebec, 1899-1900; (Quebec: E Vincent) – 9 – cn C.I.H.M. [971]
BULLETIN DE CORRESPONDANCE AFRICAINE – Alger. 1882, 1884-86 (I, III-V) – 1 – fr A.C.R.P.P. [960]
BULLETIN DE CORRESPONDANCE HELLENIQUE – Paris, 1877-1941. v. 1-65 – 446mf – 1 – ne IDC [930]
BULLETIN DE LA BIBLIOTHEQUE NATIONALE DU QUEBEC *see* BULLETIN..
BULLETIN DE LA BIBLIOTHEQUE SAINT-SUPLICE *see* BULLETIN..
BULLETIN DE LA BOUCHE DE FER – Paris. Imprimerie du Cercle Social. 1790 – 9 – fr Hachette [321]
BULLETIN DE LA CHAMBRE DE COMMERCE DU DISTRICT DE MONTREAL *see* COMMERCE
BULLETIN DE LA CHAMBRE DE COMMERCE FRANCAISE DE GRANDE-BRETAGNE *see* COMMUNIQUE DE LA CHAMBRE DE COMMERCE FRANCAISE DE LONDRES
BULLETIN DE LA CHAMBRE DE COMMERCE FRANCAISE DE LONDRES *see* COMMUNIQUE DE LA CHAMBRE DE COMMERCE FRANCAISE DE LONDRES
BULLETIN DE LA CLASSE HISTORICO-PHILOLOGIQUE DE L'ACADEMIE IMPERIALE DES SCIENCES DE SAINT-PETERSBOURG – Leipzig, 1844-1859. v1-16 – 129mf – R-1702/2 – ne IDC [400]
BULLETIN DE LA CLASSE PHYSICO-MATHEMATIQUE DE L'ACADEMIE IMPERIALE DES SCIENCES DE -PETERSBOURG – Leipzig, 1843-1856. v1-14 – 142mf – R-5820/2 – ne IDC [530]
BULLETIN DE LA COMMISSION DE TOPONYMIE ET DIALECTOLOGIE – Liege, 1927-1929. v1-3 – 10mf – H-10026/1 – ne IDC [410]
BULLETIN DE LA COMMISSION INTERNATIONALE PENALE ET PENITENTIAIRE / International Penal and Prison Commission – v. 1-21. 1880-1930. Publication suspended from 1906-09 and 1911-24 – 1 – 115.00 – us L of C Photodup [360]
BULLETIN DE LA FEDERATION JURASSIENNE DE L'ASSOCIATION INTERNATIONALE DES TRAVAILLEURS / L'Association internationale des Travailleurs. La Federation jurassienne – (See also series: Important Periodicals of Italian and International Socialism, 1868-1917) – Sonvillier, Locle, La Chaux-de-Fonds. v1 no 1-v7 no 12 Feb 1872-Mar 1878. Bakuninist tendencies reflected by the Anarchist International – 1r – 1 – $70.00 – us UPA [335]
LE BULLETIN DE LA FERME – Quebec. v1-24. 1913-1936. SEM35P182 – 12r – 1 – Can$487.00 – cn Bibl Nat [630]
BULLETIN DE LA MILICE CANADIENNE – Quebec: A l'Imprimerie Canadienne, [1807-18–] – 9 – cn C.I.H.M. [350]
BULLETIN DE LA SEMAINE POLITIQUE, SOCIALE ET RELIGIEUSE – Paris. 1905-aout 1914 – 1 – fr A.C.R.P.P. [944]
BULLETIN DE LA SOCIETE ARCHEOLOGIQUE DE NANTES ET DU DEPARTEMENT DE LA LOIRE-INFERIEURE – Annuel, Nantes, annees 1859-1920, plus tables – 20r – 1 – F10624,66 – fr Armell [930]
BULLETIN DE LA SOCIETE BIENVEILLANTE ST-ROCH / Societe Bienveillante St-Roch – Quebec: La Societe, [1893-1903?] – 9 – cn C.I.H.M. [360]
BULLETIN DE LA SOCIETE BOTANIQUE DE GENEVE – Geneve, 1909-1913. v1-5 – 34mf – 1010/2 – ne IDC [580]
LE BULLETIN DE LA SOCIETE COOPERATIVE AGRICOLE – (Also: Le Bulletin des agriculteurs 2 fev 1918-dec 1991) – Montreal, Canada. 26 fev 1916-26 jan 1918 – 40r – 1 – Can$75.00r – cn Can Microfilming [630]
BULLETIN DE LA SOCIETE DE PATHOLOGIE VEGETALE DE FRANCE – Paris, 1914-1920. v1-7 – 14mf – 7461/1 – ne IDC [580]
BULLETIN DE LA SOCIETE DES ARTISANS CANADIENS-FRANCAIS DE LA CITE DE MONTREAL – Montreal: La Societe, [1891-189- ou 19–] – 9 – cn C.I.H.M. [740]
BULLETIN DE LA SOCIETE DES ETUDES INDO-CHINOISES DE SAIGON – (Missing: 1930, v4; 1932, v2) – Saigon. 1883-1923. 71v; N.S. 1926-1932. 23v – 179mf – ne IDC [950]
BULLETIN DE LA SOCIETE DES RECHERCHES CONGOLAISES – Brazzaville: Impr du gouvernement general. n1-27. 1922-39 – 1 – us Res Libr [960]
BULLETIN DE LA SOCIETE D'ETUDES CAMEROUNAISES – Doula: Institut francais d'afrique noire, Centre local Cameroun. n1-19/20. dec 1935-sep/dec 1947 – 1 – us Res Libr [960]
BULLETIN DE LA SOCIETE D'ETUDES PHILOSOPHIQUES DU SUD-EST – (Missing: 1938, v12(3-4); 1939, v13; 1940, v14) – Marseille, 1926-1943/1944. v1-18 – 45mf – H-186/2 – ne IDC [100]
BULLETIN DE LA SOCIETE D'HISTOIRE ET DE GEOGRAPHIE D'HAITI – [Port-au-Prince]: Imp Cheraquit. v1 n1. may 1925 – reel 1 – us Res Libr [073]
BULLETIN DE LA SOCIETE D'INDUSTRIE LAITIERE DE LA PROVINCE DE QUEBEC / Societe d'Industrie Laitiere de la Province de Quebec – (Dairymen's Association of the Province of Quebec. Bulletin of the Dairymen's Association of the Province of Quebec) – [St-Hyacinthe, Quebec?]: La Societe, [1891?-189- ou 19–]; (St-Hyacinthe, Quebec: B de la Bruere) – 9 – cn C.I.H.M. [630]
BULLETIN DE LA SOCIETE FRANCAISE DE PHILOSOPHIE / Societe Francaise de Philosophie – Paris. 1901-71 – 5 – fr A.C.R.P.P. [100]
BULLETIN DE LA SOCIETE IMPERIALE DES NATURALISTES DE MOSCOU – (Continued as: Moskovskoe obshchestvo ispytatelei prirody. Biulleten'. Otdel biologicheskii. 1922/23-1968, v31-73) – 1829-1886(-87). v1-62; N.S., 1887-1917. v1-30 – 1,978mf – 7118/2 – ne IDC [580]
BULLETIN DE LA SOCIETE LEPIDOPTEROLOGIQUE – Geneve, 1905/1909-1918. v1-4 – 22mf – Z-928/2 – ne IDC [590]
BULLETIN DE LA SOCIETE MALACOLOGIQUE DE FRANCE – Paris, 1884-1890. v1-7 – 51mf – Z-893/2 – ne IDC [590]
BULLETIN DE LA SOCIETE MINERALOGIQUE DE FRANCE – Paris, 1878-1941. v1-64 – 447mf – 2512c/2 – ne IDC [540]
BULLETIN DE LA SOCIETE MYCOLOGIQUE – Paris, 1885-1941. v1-57 – 410mf – 5589c/2 – ne IDC [580]

BULLETIN DE LA SOCIETE ORNITHOLOGIQUE SUISSE – Geneve, Bale, 1865-1870. v1-2 – 10mf – Z-2015/2 – ne IDC [590]

BULLETIN DE LA SOCIETE ZOOLOGIQUE DE FRANCE – Paris, 1876-1920. v1-45 – 308mf – 6234/2 – ne IDC [590]

BULLETIN DE L'ABQ. ASSOCIATION DES BIBLIOTHECAIRES DU QUEBEC = QLA NEWSLETTER. QUEBEC LIBRARY ASSOCIATION – Montreal, 1971-. SEM16P350 – 1r – 5 – Can$31.00 – cn Bibl Nat [020]

BULLETIN DE L'ACADEMIE IMPERIALE DES SCIENCES DE -PETERSBOURG – 1860-1888. v1-32 – 331mf – R-5821/2 – ne IDC [500]

BULLETIN DE L'ACADEMIE IMPERIALE DES SCIENCES DE -PETERSBOURG – 1890-1894. v1-4 – 81mf – R-1701/2 – ne IDC [500]

BULLETIN DE L'ACADEMIE IMPERIALE DES SCIENCES DE -PETERSBOURG (IZVESTIIA IMPERATORSKOI, AKADEMII NAUK) – 1894-1906. v1-25 – 435mf – 1431/2 – ne IDC [500]

LE BULLETIN DE L'ART ANCIEN ET MODERNE – Suppl. de: La Revue de l'art ancien et moderne. no. 1-819. Paris. 1899-1935 – 1 – fr A.C.R.P.P. [700]

BULLETIN DE L'ECOLE FRANCAISE D'EXTREME ORIENT – Hanoi. 1901-1965. v1-52 – 918mf – 9 – ne IDC [950]

BULLETIN DE L'ECOLE POLYTECHNIQUE DE MONTREAL – v1-2. 1913-14 – 1r – 5 – Can$14.00 – cn Bibl Nat [370]

BULLETIN DE LEGISLATION ET DU JURISPRUDENCE EGYPTIENNE – Alexandria. On film: v1-8; 1941-49. (incomplete). LL-020 – 1 – us L of C Photodup [340]

BULLETIN DE L'ENSEIGNEMENT DE L'AFRIQUE OCCIDENTALE FRANCAISE – 1913-35. Became L'EDUCATION AFRICAINE, 1935-48; n.s. 1948-58. Lacks 4 issues. 8 reels – 1 – 316.00 – us African Imprint [370]

BULLETIN DE L'HERBIER BOISSIER – Geneva, 1893-1900. v. 1-8; S.2, 1901-08. v. 1-8 – 352mf – 1 – ne IDC [631]

BULLETIN DE LIAISON SAHARIENNE – no. 1-32. Alger. oct 1950-58 – 1 – fr A.C.R.P.P. [960]

BULLETIN DE L'INSTITUT BOTANIQUE DE BUITENZORG – (Continues as: Bulletin du De£1partement de l'Agricultur aux Indes Ne£1erlandaises. Buitenzorg, 1906-1911. v1-47; Continues as: Bulletin du Jardin Botanique de Buitenzorg. S.2. Buitenzorg, 1911-1918. v1-28; S.3. 1918-1949/1950. v1-18. Suppl. v1-3) – Buitenzorg, 1898-1905. v1-22 – 190mf – 9 – ne IDC [580]

BULLETIN DE L'INSTITUT FRANCAIS D'ARCHEOLOGIE ORIENTALE – Le Caire, 1901-1942. v1-41 – 173mf – NE-490/1 – ne IDC [930]

BULLETIN DE L'INSTITUT INTERMEDIAIRE INTERNATIONAL / ed by Torley Duwel, C L – Harlem, La Haye, 1919-1940. v1-42(1) – 231mf – Dfl 1.395 – ILM-3126/1 – ne IDC [073]

BULLETIN DE LITTERATURE ET DE DROIT DE L'UNIVERSITE DE CHANGHAI – (Missing: S.1, 1909-1919, v1-19; S.2, 1919, v2; 1929-1930, v18-19; 1931-1933, v22-26) – 1909-1919. v1-19; S.2, 1919-1940. v1-40; S.3, 1940-1949. v1-10 – 222mf – CH-144/2 – ne IDC [410]

BULLETIN DE L'OPPOSITION BOLCHEVIKS-LENINISTES – no. 1 2-72. Paris. juil 1929-38. mq no. 20, 33, 40-41 – 1 – fr A.C.R.P.P. [335]

BULLETIN DE L'UNION ALLET – Montreal, Canada. 25 aut 1873-dec 1883 – 1r – 1 – Can$40.00 – cn Can Microfilming [072]

BULLETIN DE L'UNION COLONIALE FRANCAISE – Paris: L'Union. v1. nov 1894-1895 – us Res Libr [073]

BULLETIN DE MADAGASCAR – (Lacks: n136 sep 1957. n145-151 jun-dec 1958. n162 nov 1959. n254-255 jul-aug 1967. n258 nov 1967. n260-261 jan-feb 1968. n266-267 jul-aug 1968) – [Tananarive: Haut Commissariat de la Republique francaise a Madagascar et dependances, Service general de l'information. n89 oct 1953; n120-121 may-jun 1956; n131-295 apr 1957-70 – 13r – 1 – us Res Libr [960]

BULLETIN DE NOUVELLES *see* ARGUS

BULLETIN DE NOUVELLES. ASSOCIATION DES BIBLIOTHECAIRES QUEBEC = NEWSLETTER. QUEBEC LIBRARY ASSOCIATION – Montreal, 1954-71. SEM16P349 – 1r – 5 – Can$16.00 – cn Bibl Nat [020]

BULLETIN DE NOUVELLES D'AFRIQUE – [oct-dec 1960] – us Res Libr [073]

BULLETIN DE NOUVELLES DU CONGO – [oct-dec 1960] – us Res Libr [073]

BULLETIN DE PARIS – Paris. 1955-57 – 1 – fr A.C.R.P.P. [944]

BULLETIN DE PHARMACIE – Montreal, Canada. avr 1902 – 1r – 1 – Can$25.00 – cn Can Microfilming [615]

BULLETIN DE PRESSE / Inforcongo. 1ere Direction. Presse et relations publiques – [Brussels]: Inforcongo, sep 10 1956-jan 21 1957; feb 1957-dec 22 1958; jan 25-sep 19 1960 – 1r – us Res Libr [070]

BULLETIN DE STE ANNE DE LA POINTE-AU-PERE – Rimouski: P Sylvain, [1882-1883] – 9 – cn C.I.H.M. [240]

BULLETIN DE STE ANNE DE LA POINTE-AU-PERE *see* LE MESSAGER DE SAINTE ANNE

BULLETIN DE THEOLOGIE ANCIENNE ET MEDIEVALE – 1(1929)-4(1945) – 45mf – 9 – ne Slangenburg [073]

BULLETIN DE THEOLOGIE ANCIENNE ET MEDIEVALE – (Missing: 1937-1940. v3(p. 189-360)) – Louvain, 1929-1940. v1-3 – 35mf – H-309c/2 – ne IDC [200]

BULLETIN DER AGITPROPABTEIL DER RGI / Gewerkschaftspropaganda und Kulturarbeit – v3. 1930. (Serial publications of German trade unions in the Memorial Library, University of Wisconsin-Madison.) – 1 – us U.W. Library [330]

BULLETIN DES 3. KONGRESSES DER KOMMUNISTISCHEN INTERNATIONALE / Communist International. Congress. 3. (1921) – Moscow. Nos.1-24, 24 Jun-20 Jul 1921 – 6mf – 9 – $45.00 – us UPA [335]

BULLETIN DES 4. KONGRESSES DER KOMMUNISTISCHEN INTERNATIONALE / Communist International. Congress. 4. (1922) – Moscow. Nos 1-31, 11 Nov-12 Dec 1922 – 9 – $45.00 – us UPA [335]

BULLETIN DES ACTES ADMINISTRATIFS DE LA PREFECTURE DE LA GUYANE / British Guiana – Cayene. 1957-July 4, 1966. Incomplete – 1 – us NY Public [324]

BULLETIN DES ACTS ET ADMINISTRATIFS / French Guiana – Aug. 1947-1956 – 1 – us UMI [324]

LE BULLETIN DES AGRICULTEURS *see* LE BULLETIN DE LA SOCIETE COOPERATIVE AGRICOLE

BULLETIN DES AMIS DE LA VERITE – no. 1-121. Paris. janv-avr 1793 – 1 – fr A.C.R.P.P. [073]

BULLETIN DES AMIS DU LAOS – Hanoi. juil 1937-aout 1940 – 1 – fr A.C.R.P.P. [950]

BULLETIN DES AMIS DU VIEUX HUE – Hanoi, Haiphong. 1914-avr juin 1944 (1-31) – 1 – fr A.C.R.P.P. [950]

BULLETIN DES ANCIENS *see* GALAS D'INAUGURATION

BULLETIN DES ANNONCES LEGALES OBLIGATOIRES (B.A.L.O.) / France – 1912-1993 – 1 – fr A.C.R.P.P. [323]

BULLETIN DES ARRETS / France. Cour de Cassation. Chambre criminelle – Paris. 1798-1816, 1818-19, 1821-40, 1943-86, tb: 1798-1986 – 1 – fr A.C.R.P.P. [960]

BULLETIN DES ARRETS / France. Cour de Cassation. Chambres civiles – Paris. 1798-1942, 1947-86, tb: 1958-86 – 1 – fr A.C.R.P.P. [960]

BULLETIN DES COMMISSIONS ROYALES D'ART ET D'ARCHEOLOGIE / Belgium. Ministere de l'Interieur – Brussels, 1862-93. 10 reels – 1 – $835.00 – us UPA [720]

BULLETIN DES CONSTRUCTEURS – Paris, 1895-99; 1904-05 – 3r – 1 – $245.00 – us UPA [690]

BULLETIN DES DENTUROLOGISTES DU QUEBEC *see* LE DENTURO

BULLETIN DES ECRIVAINS PROLETAIRES – no. 2, 4. Vincennes. avr-juin 1932 – 1 – fr A.C.R.P.P. [335]

BULLETIN DES ETUDES ARABES – (All published) – v1-12. Algiers. 1941-1952 – 5,9 – Dfl720.00; Dfl60.00v – ne Swets [260]

BULLETIN DES ETUDES FRANCAISES DE HUNTINGDON : MENSUEL – Huntingdon. v1 n1. avr 1941-v5 n5. sep-oct 1945 – 1r – 1 – cn Can Microfilming [072]

BULLETIN DES FABRICANTS DE PAPIER – Paris. Jul 1890-Jul 1914. – 11r – 1 – uk British Libr Newspaper [670]

BULLETIN DES FRERES ET AMIS – ou L'Echo de l'opinion. no. 1-19. Paris. juil 1797 – 1 – fr A.C.R.P.P. [073]

BULLETIN DES LOIS, DEA1CRETS ET DOCUMENTS OFFICIELS / Exposition Universelle 1900. Paris – Paris. v2-7 Dec 5 1895-Nov 16 1900. Incomplete – 1 – us NY Public [900]

BULLETIN DES MUSEES – Paris, 1890-93 – 1r – 1 – $85.00 – us UPA [060]

BULLETIN DES NOUVELLES – Cap-Haitien: Imp du Progres, sheets 1-3 dec 1900-jan 16,19-22, 24-feb 1,4 16-26,28 1901; sheet 4 mar 9 1901 filmed out of sequence; sheets 5-6 mar 11,16-19,29, apr 13-15,18,23 1901; sheet 5 may 2-7 1901 filmed out of sequence – us Res Libr [073]

BULLETIN DES PRESSE-INFORMATIONSAMTES.. / Germany. Federal Republic. Bundesregierung – Bonn. 27 Oct 1951-56 – 1 – gw Mikrofilm [324]

BULLETIN DES PRESSE- UND INFORMATIONSAMTES DER BUNDESREGIERUNG – Bonn, 27 Oct 1951-1956 – 5r – 1 – DM375.00 – gw Mikro Press [943]

BULLETIN DES RECHERCHES HISTORIQUES / Societe des Etudes Historiques – v1-36. 1895-1930 – 7r – 1 – us Ross [944]

BULLETIN DES SCIENCES MATHEMATIQUES – s1, v1-s2, v100.1870-1976 – 1,5,6 – us UMI [510]

BULLETIN DES SCIENCES MATHEMATIQUES – Series 1. v. 1-11. 1870-1876. Series 2. v. 1-84. 1877-1960 – 1,5,6 – us Princeton Micro [510]

BULLETIN DES SEANCES DE LA SOCIETE MALACOLOGIQUE DE BELGIQUE – (Continued as: Proces-verbaux des seances de la Societe Malacologique de Belgique. Bruxelles, 1871-1898. v1-27) – Bruxelles, 1863/1865-1875. v1-10 – 130mf – Z-892/2 – ne IDC [590]

BULLETIN DES TRAVAUX DE LA SOCIETE BOTANIQUE DE GENEVE – Geneve, 1879-1905. v1-11 – 44mf – 6447/2 – ne IDC [580]

BULLETIN D'ETUDES ORIENTALES / Institut francais de Damas – Le Caire, Paris. 1931-66 (I-XIX) – 1 – fr A.C.R.P.P. [073]

BULLETIN D'INFORMATION DE L'A.T.E.N / A T E N – Paris. 1966-73 – 5 – fr A.C.R.P.P. [073]

BULLETIN D'INFORMATION DE L'ETAT DE LEOPOLDVILLE – Leopoldville-Kalina, 1961(March)-1962(August) – 6mf – 1620P/2 – ne IDC [960]

BULLETIN D'INFORMATION DU BUREAU PERMANENT DU FRONT DE LIBERATION DE MOZAMBIQUE A ALGER – Alger: Le Bureau. n1-3 jan-apr/may 1964; n4? jul 1964; n3-5 mar/may 1965; sep 1966 – us Res Libr [320]

BULLETIN D'INFORMATION DU KATANGA – Elisabethville, 1962 – 19mf – A-691/1 – ne IDC [960]

BULLETIN D'INFORMATION OUVRIERE – no. 2-8. Paris. mars-juin 1940 – 1 – fr A.C.R.P.P. [331]

BULLETIN D'INFORMATION RELIGIEUSE – En cambodgien. Cambodge. 1932-34, 1936-42 – 1 – fr A.C.R.P.P. [240]

BULLETIN D'INFORMATIONS / Institut Francais d'Opinion Publique – devenu: Sondages. Revue francaise de l'opinion publique. Paris. oct 1944-53, 1955 – 1 – fr A.C.R.P.P. [073]

BULLETIN D'INFORMATIONS DU SECRETARIAT PERMANENT DE LA CONFERENCE DES ORGANIZATIONS NATIONALISTES DES COLONIES PORTUGAISES (CONCP) – Rabat: Le Secretariat. n1-3 dec 30 1961-may 10 1962; n6 jan 1963 – us Res Libr [320]

BULLETIN D'INFORMATIONS SOCIALES 1974-1992 / International Labour Organisation – 9 – Sfr1,000.00 – 92-2-208928-6 – sz I.L.O. [330]

BULLETIN DU BUREAU MEDICAL DU COLLEGE DES MEDECINS ET CHIRURGIENS DE LA PROVINCE DE QUEBEC / College des Medecins et Chirurgiens de la Province de Quebec. Bureau Medical – Montreal: Le College, 1894-[19-?] – 9 – cn C.I.H.M. [610]

BULLETIN DU CERCLE ERNEST RENAN – Jan 1956-Mar 1977 (complete) – 1r – 1 – ATLA S0810 – us A.T.L.A. [073]

BULLETIN DU CERCLE JUIF – Montreal, CN, 1954-1985 – 1r – 1 – cn Can Microfilming [072]

LE BULLETIN DU CLUB CARTIER – Montreal: Berthiaume & Sabourin, [1880] – 9 – cn C.I.H.M. [360]

BULLETIN DU COMITE D'ETUDES HISTORIQUES ET SCIENTIFIQUES DE L'AFRIQUE OCCIDENTALE FRANCAISE – Paris [etc]: Librairie Larose [etc]. v1-21. 1918-1938 – 11r – us Res Libr [073]

BULLETIN DU LIVRE – (1975- . 5,6,9) – 1958- – 1 – us UMI [070]

LE BULLETIN DU MARDI-GRAS – Quebec, Canada. 28 oct; 4 nov 1911 – 1r – 1 – Can$30.00 – cn Can Microfilming [390]

BULLETIN DU MINISTERE DES AFFAIRES SOCIALES – Leopoldville, 1961-1965. v1-5 – 28mf – A-689/1 – ne IDC [360]

BULLETIN DU PARLER FRANCAIS AU CANADA *see* LE CANADA-FRANCAIS

BULLETIN DU R.I.N – Montreal, Canada. mar 1961-oct/nov 1961 – 1r – 1 – Can$30.00 – cn Can Microfilming [072]

LE BULLETIN DU TRAVAIL : ORGANE DES INTERETS TEMPORELS DE L'ARTISAN ET DU LABOUREUR – Quebec: '(s.n.)' no 4 1900-. SEM105P928 – 1mf – 9 – Can$2.25 – cn Bibl Nat [331]

LE BULLETIN DU TRAVAIL – Quebec, Canada. v1 n7. 5 jan 1900-5 dec 1903 – 1r – 1 – Can$30.00 – cn Can Microfilming [072]

BULLETIN ECONOMIQUE / Madagascar – 1901-15, 1919-20 – 1 – fr A.C.R.P.P. [330]

BULLETIN ECONOMIQUE DE L'INDO-CHINE / Gouvernement General de l'Indo-Chine – (Missing: 1898(p. 1-210)) – Hanoi, Haiphong, Saigon, 1898-1929 – 1,044mf – ne IDC [330]

BULLETIN EKONOMI KEUANGAN / Djakarta, Biro Penerangan Ekonomi – (Missing: 1968, v2(102, 119, 202, 203); 1970, v3(241-246); 1972, v6(29, 40, 53, 60)) – Djakarta, 1967(July)-1972 – 650mf – SE-1370/1 – ne IDC [330]

BULLETIN EKONOMI-KEUANGAN – Djakarta. Incomplete. SE-276 1. 1962-1970 – 9 – ne IDC [330]

BULLETIN ELECTORAL – Montreal, 1 dec 1851; 3 dec 1851 – 1r – 1 – Can$20.00 – cn Can Microfilming [072]

BULLETIN ELECTORAL – Montreal, Canada. n9. 22 nov 1851; n10. 26 nov 1851 – 1r – 1 – Can$25.00 – cn Can Microfilming [072]

LE BULLETIN ET JOURNAL DES JOURNAUX, REVISEUR IMPARTIAL DU POUR ET DU CONTRE – devenu: Le Reviseur impartial et universel de tous les journaux pour et contre et Bulletin de Madame de Beaumont. Paris. 1791-juil 1792 (I-III) – 1 – fr A.C.R.P.P. [944]

BULLETIN EUCHARISTIQUE – Montreal: [s.n, 1896?-1955?] – 9 – cn C.I.H.M. [240]

BULLETIN EUROPEEN DE PHYSIOPATHOLOGIE RESPIRATOIRE – v. 15-. 1979- – 5,6,9 – us UMI [616]

BULLETIN EVANGELIQUE DE LA BASSE-BRETAGNE – Quimper: Lion, [s.d.] – fr Armell [240]

BULLETIN FAKTA-FAKTA EKONOMI DAERAH ISTIMEWA ATJAH / Darussalam, Banda Atjah, Lembaga Penjelidikan Ekonomi dan Sosial, Fakultas Ekonomi Universitas Sjiah Kuala – (Quarterly. Missing: 1986/1969 v1(3-4); 1969/1970 v2(7-8)) – Darussalam. v1-4. 1968-1971 – 14mf – 9 – SE-1371/1 – ne IDC [330]

BULLETIN: FINANCIAL PUBLIC RELATIONS ASSOCIATION – 1951-65. Continued by: Journal, Financial Public Relations Assoc – 1 – us UMI [073]

BULLETIN FROM THE MONASTIC INTERRELIGIOUS DIALOGUE – (Title varies) – 1978-94 (complete) – 1r – 1 – ATLA S0931A-E – us A.T.L.A. [073]

BULLETIN HEBDOMADAIRE DE PRESSE D'INTERET ET DE DOCUMENTATION GENERALE AU KATANGA – Elisabethville, 1960(October)-1965(December) – 60mf – 1632P/2 – ne IDC [960]

BULLETIN HEBDOMADAIRE D'INFORMATION / Congo. Ambassade. Bruxelles – Ambassade RDC a Bruxelles. 1965-66. BA-680/1 – 9 – ne IDC [960]

BULLETIN HEBDOMADAIRE D'INFORMATION DU BUREAU EUROPIENNE DE L'AGENCE CONGOLAISE DE PRESSE – Bruxelles, 1960-1963 – 47mf – A-681/2 – ne IDC [960]

BULLETIN HEBDOMADAIRE D'INFORMATION DU CONGO – 1965-1966 – 32mf – A-680/1 – ne IDC [960]

BULLETIN HISTORIQUE ET ARCHEOLOGIQUE DE VAUCLUSE ET DES DEPARTEMENTS LIMITROPHES – Avignon, 1879-83. 2 reels – 1 – $160.00 – us UPA [930]

BULLETIN INDEX : MISCELLANEOUS YEARS – 1880-1962 – 4r – 1 – A$176.00 silver A$152.00 vesicular – at Pascoe [020]
BULLETIN INDEX – Pittsburgh. Pa. 1895-1949 – 1 – us UMI [071]
BULLETIN INTERNATIONAL DE L'ELECTRICITE – Paris, France. Jan 1886-Aug 1895; Jan 1900-Dec 1910 – 4r – 1 – uk British Libr Newspaper [621]
BULLETIN INTERNATIONAL DU MOUVEMENT SYNDICALISTE – Paris, Amsterdam. 6 Oct 1907, 5 April 1908-19 July 1914 – 2r – 1 – uk British Libr Newspaper [335]
BULLETIN JOURNAL – Independence. Iowa. -w. 1951-73 – 1 – us UMI [071]
BULLETIN KOPERASI / Direktorat Djenderal Koperasi – (Semi-monthly. Missing: 1966 v1; 1967 v2(1-12, 17-20); 1968 v3(1-2, 5/6,9-20); 1969 v4(1-7/8,15); 1971 v6(7-12)-1972(1-3)) – Djakarta, 1966-1972 – 29mf – 9 – SE-1372/1 – ne IDC [337]
BULLETIN MANAGEMENT SEA – Surbaja. Indonesia. 1964-1966 – 1 – us UMI [650]
BULLETIN MENSUEL DE L'UNION PATRIOTIQUE – Port-au-Prince: Comite de Port-au-Prince. n1-2/3. dec 1920-jan/feb 1921 – 2 sheets – us Res Libr [073]
BULLETIN MENSUEL D'INFORMATION DU CONGO – Brussels, 1964-66 – 21mf – 9 – ne IDC [960]
BULLETIN MENSUEL DU CONSEIL MONETAIRE. INSTITUT D'EMISSION – Leopoldville, 1961-1967 – 41mf – A-698/1 – ne IDC [330]
LE BULLETIN MENSUEL DU TRAVAIL : ORGANE DES INTERETS TEMPORELS DE L'ARTISAN ET DU LABOUREUR – Quebec: '(s.n.)' nos 1-3 1900. SEM105P925 – 1mf – 9 – Can$2.25 – cn Bibl Nat [331]
LE BULLETIN MENSUEL DU TRAVAIL : POUR L'OUVRIER ET L'AGRICULTEUR – Quebec, Canada. 1 sep 1900-v1 n4. 15 dec 1900 – 1r – 1 – Can$30.00 – cn Can Microfilming [073]
BULLETIN MILITAIRE – Leopoldville, 1963-1964. v1(1-7) – 7mf – A-694/1 – ne IDC [355]
BULLETIN MONUMENTAL – v1-79. Indexes. 1834-1920. BO-1219 1 – 9 – ne IDC [700]
BULLETIN MUNICIPAL / Dijon – 1959-1968 – 1 – us NY Public [944]
BULLETIN MUNICIPAL OFFICIEL / Lyons. France – 1940-1968 – 1 – us NY Public [944]
BULLETIN MUNICIPAL OFFICIEL / Marseille – 1958-1968 – 1 – us NY Public [944]
BULLETIN MUNICIPAL OFFICIEL / Paris. Conseil Municipal – 1959-1968 – 1 – us NY Public [944]
BULLETIN MUNICIPAL OFFICIEL / Versailles. France – Dec. 1955-1967 – 1 – us NY Public [944]
BULLETIN, NEW SERIES / American Mathematical Society – (Supersedes: Bulletin of the American Mathematical Society) – Providence. v1-37. jan 1979-* – 1,5,9 – D13411 – us UMI [510]
BULLETIN, NEW SERIES OF THE AMERICAN MATHEMATICAL SOCIETY *see* BULLETIN
BULLETIN OF... *see* AMERICAN JOURNAL OF MEDICAL TECHNOLOGY
BULLETIN OF ALLOY PHASE DIAGRAMS – 1980- – 1,5,6,9 – us UMI [660]
BULLETIN OF APPLIED BOTANY AND PLANT BREEDING – (Supplements included) – Leningrad, 1908-1931. v1-27(5); 1957. v30(3); 1958. v33 – 648mf – 13260/1 – ne IDC [631]
BULLETIN OF ART THERAPY *see* AMERICAN JOURNAL OF ART THERAPY
BULLETIN OF BIBLIOGRAPHY AND MAGAZINE NOTES – (1970-78. 5,6. 1977-78. 9) – 1897-1978 – 1 – us UMI [010]
BULLETIN OF COLGATE ROCHESTER, BEXLEY HALL, CROZER THEOLOGICAL SEMINARY – v43-51 no4. 1970-79 (gaps) – Inquire – 1 – ATLA 1994-S527 – us A.T.L.A. [073]
BULLETIN OF COMMERCIAL LAW LEAGUE OF AMERICA *see* COMMERCIAL LAW JOURNAL
BULLETIN OF ENTOMOLOGICAL RESEARCH – London, 1910-1920. v1-10 – 136mf – Z-924/2 – ne IDC [590]
BULLETIN OF ENVIRONMENTAL CONTAMINATION AND TOXICOLOGY – v. 1-16. 1966-76 – 1,5,6 – us Princeton Micro [360]
BULLETIN OF ENVIRONMENTAL CONTAMINATION AND TOXICOLOGY – v1-25. 1966-80 – 1,5,9 – 1763.00 – us UMI [073]
BULLETIN OF EXPERIMENTAL BIOLOGY AND MEDICINE – v41-118. 1956-94 – 1,5 – $80.00v – us UMI [619]
BULLETIN OF FAR EASTERN BIBLIOGRAPHY – v. 1-5. 1936-40 – 1 – 19.00 – us L of C Photodup [950]
BULLETIN OF HYGIENE *see* ABSTRACTS ON HYGIENE
BULLETIN OF INTERNATIONAL SOCIALISM – New York. v. 1, no. 2-4, no. 11. 28 Sep 1964-19 Feb 1968. Incomplete – 1 – us NY Public [335]
BULLETIN OF JOHN RYLANDS LIBRARY – Manchester. v1-23. 1903-1939 – 228mf – 9 – H-787c/2 – ne IDC [020]
BULLETIN OF LATIN AMERICAN RESEARCH – v1- 1981- – 5,6,9 – us UMI [073]
BULLETIN OF MATHEMATICAL BIOLOGY – (Formerly Bulletin of Mathematical Biophysics) – v35- 1973- – 5,6,9 – us UMI [574]
BULLETIN OF MATHEMATICAL BIOPHYSICS *see* BULLETIN OF MATHEMATICAL BIOLOGY
BULLETIN OF MISCELLANEOUS INFORMATION / Royal Gardens Kew – London, 1887-1941 – 475mf – 5591c/2 – ne IDC [580]
BULLETIN OF PEACE PROPOSALS – (1981-. 1,5,6,9) – v1-. 1970- – 1 – us UMI [073]
BULLETIN OF PLANT INDUSTRY / U.S. Department of Agriculture – Nos.1-285. 1901-13 – 1,5,6 – us Princeton Micro [073]
BULLETIN OF PROCEEDINGS / Pan-Pacific Trade Union Conference. Hankow. 1927 – 1927. 5v in 1 – 1 – $35.00r – us Hoover Inst Photo [331]
BULLETIN OF THE 4TH ASIAN GAMES – (Ceased publ) – Djakarta. nos 1-5. 1962 – 7mf – 9 – SE-1319/1 – ne IDC [790]
BULLETIN OF THE ADYAR LIBRARY – (Missing: 1965. v29) – Madras, 1937-1965. v1-29 – 284mf – I-365/2 – ne IDC [020]
BULLETIN OF THE AMERICAN ACADEMY OF PSYCHIATRY AND THE LAW / American Academy of Psychiatry and the Law – Pittsburgh. v1-25. Aut 1972-1997+ 1,5*,9 – 1,5,9 – D12354 – us UMI [340]
BULLETIN OF THE AMERICAN ACADEMY OF PSYCHIATRY AND THE LAW – (v1-12 1973-84 in reel $125.00. v13-23 1985-95 in mf $289.00) – v1-23. 1973-95 – 5,6,9 – $414.00 set – us Hein [340]
BULLETIN OF THE AMERICAN ASSOCIATION OF PETROLEUM GEOLOGISTS *see* AAPG BULLETIN
BULLETIN OF THE AMERICAN ASSOCIATION OF UNIVERSITY PROFESSORS *see* AAUP BULLETIN
BULLETIN OF THE AMERICAN CERAMIC SOCIETY *see* AMERICAN CERAMIC SOCIETY BULLETIN
BULLETIN OF THE AMERICAN CONGREGATIONAL ASSOCIATION – v1-5. 1949-54 – 1 – us UMI [240]
BULLETIN OF THE AMERICAN GEOGRAPHICAL AND STATISTICAL SOCIETY *see* BULLETIN
BULLETIN OF THE AMERICAN LIBRARY ASSOCIATION *see* ALA BULLETIN
BULLETIN OF THE AMERICAN MATHEMATICAL SOCIETY – v1-84. 1894-1978 – 1 – us UMI [073]
BULLETIN OF THE AMERICAN MATHEMATICAL SOCIETY *see* BULLETIN, NEW SERIES
BULLETIN OF THE AMERICAN MATHEMATICAL SOCIETY, NEW SERIES – (1982-. 1,5,6,9) – nsv1-. 1979- – 1 – us UMI [073]
BULLETIN OF THE AMERICAN MUSEUM OF NATURAL HISTORY – (1980- 5,6,9) – 1881- – 1 – us UMI [574]
BULLETIN OF THE AMERICAN MUSEUM OF NATURAL HISTORY *see* ANTHROPOLOGICAL PAPERS OF THE AMERICAN MUSEUM OF NATURAL HISTORY
BULLETIN OF THE AMERICAN SOCIETY OF HOSPITAL PHARMACISTS *see* AMERICAN JOURNAL OF HOSPITAL PHARMACY
BULLETIN OF THE AMERICAN SOCIETY OF VETERINARY CLINICAL PATHOLOGISTS – v.1-5. 1972-76 – 1 – us UMI [073]
BULLETIN OF THE ASIAN-AFRICAN CONFERENCE – Djakarta, 1955 – 5mf – 9 – SE-1318/1 – ne IDC [950]
BULLETIN OF THE ASSOCIATION FOR BUSINESS COMMUNICATION – v48-. Mar 1985- – 1,5,6,9 – us UMI [073]
BULLETIN OF THE ASSOCIATION FOR BUSINESS COMMUNICATION *see* ABCA BULLETIN
BULLETIN OF THE ASSOCIATION OF DEPARTMENTS AND ADMINISTRATION *see* ACA BULLETIN
BULLETIN OF THE ATOMIC SCIENTISTS – (1965- 5,6. 1970- 9) – 1- 1945- – 1 – us UMI [530]
BULLETIN OF THE BAR ASSOCIATION OF THE DISTRICT OF COLUMBIA *see* JOURNAL OF THE BAR ASSOCIATION OF THE DISTRICT OF COLUMBIA
BULLETIN OF THE BRITISH ORNITHOLOGISTS' CLUB – (Index v16-39) – London, 1892/1893-1920. v1-40 – 126mf – Z-2012/2 – ne IDC [590]
BULLETIN OF THE BRITISH PSYCHOLOGICAL SOCIETY – London: The Society, [1953- v30 (1977) – 1r – us Res Libr [150]
BULLETIN OF THE BRITISH SCHOOL AT ATHENS – (Missing: 1894-1895. v1(p. 1-54)) – London, 1895-1920. v1-24 – 147mf – O-1217/1 – ne IDC [930]
BULLETIN OF THE BUREAU OF MINES AND THE GEOLOGICAL SURVEY IN INDONESIA / Dutch East Indies. Dienst van den Mijnbouw – Bandoeng. 1947. TEN 514. BSE-1463 1 – 9 – ne IDC [622]
BULLETIN OF THE CALIFORNIA NURSES ASSOCIATION – v59-60. 1963-64 – 1 – us UMI [073]
BULLETIN OF THE CANADIAN MANUFACTURERS' ASSOCIATION – Toronto: Canadian Manufacturer Pub.Co., [1898-189- or 19–] – 9 – cn C.I.H.M. [670]
BULLETIN OF THE CHRISTIAN INSTITUTE FOR THE STUDY OF SOCIETY – v1-4,no.2. 1954-57 – 1 – us UMI [073]
BULLETIN OF THE COLLEGE ART ASSOCIATION – (Continued as: The Art Bulletin. New York, 1919-1941. V.2-23) – 1913-1918. v1 – 239mf – O-492c/1 – ne IDC [700]
BULLETIN OF THE COMMERCIAL LAW LEAGUE – (v10 no 8 was never issued. Lacking: v1-5,14,20,21,23,27) – v1-28. 1895-1923 (all publ) – 9 – LLMC 84-4301 – us L.L.M.C. [073]
BULLETIN OF THE CONGREGATIONAL LIBRARY / American Congregational Association Library – (Cont by: Bulletin of the American Congregational Association) – Boston. 1955-Sum 1951* v43-49 Fal 1991-Sum 1998 – 1 – D1516.01 – us UMI [020]
BULLETIN OF THE COOPER ORNITHOLOGICAL CLUB – v.1. 1899. Superseded by Condor – 1 – us UMI [073]
BULLETIN OF THE COUNCIL FOR A DEMOCRATIC GERMANY – New York, Sept 1944-May 1945 – 1r – 1 – gw Mikrofilm [073]
BULLETIN OF THE DAIRYMEN'S ASSOCIATION OF THE PROVINCE OF QUEBEC / Dairymen's Association of the Province of Quebec – [S.l.]: The Association, [1891?-189- or 19–] – 9 – cn C.I.H.M. [630]
BULLETIN OF THE DAIRYMEN'S ASSOCIATION OF THE PROVINCE OF QUEBEC *see* BULLETIN DE LA SOCIETE D'INDUSTRIE LAITIERE DE LA PROVINCE DE QUEBEC
BULLETIN OF THE DECCAN COLLEGE RESEARCH INSTITUTE – Poona, 1939-1957. v1-18 – 150mf – I-236/2 – ne IDC [370]
BULLETIN OF THE EAST-AFRICAN INTER-TERRITORIAL (SWAHILI) COMMITTEE – (Continued as: Journal of the East African Swahili Committee. Arusha, 1954-1958. v24-28. (antinued as: Swahili, Arusha, 1959-1968. v29-38) – Arusha, 1953. v23 – 59mf – A-708/2 – ne IDC [960]
BULLETIN OF THE ENTOMOLOGICAL SOCIETY OF AMERICA *see* AMERICAN ENTOMOLOGIST
BULLETIN OF THE EXECUTIVE COMMITTEE OF THE COMMUNIST INTERNATIONAL / Communist International. Executive Committee – Petrograd. Nos 1-5. 8 Sept 1921-7 Jul 1922 – 2mf – 9 – $45.00 – us UPA [335]
BULLETIN OF THE FAN MEMORIAL INSTITUTE OF BIOLOGY – (Missing: 1939, v9(6); 1940, v10(6); 1941, v11(3-6)) – Peiping, 1929-1941. v1-11 – 60mf – 8147/1 – ne IDC [574]
BULLETIN OF THE HISTORICAL AND NATURAL SCIENCES / Rafinesque-Schmaltz, Constantine S – NRS. 1, 3-5, 7. Philadelphia. 1834-38. B-7418 1 – 9 – ne IDC [580]
BULLETIN OF THE HISTORY OF MEDICINE – (1972- . 5,6. 1976- . 9) – v. 1- 1933- – 1 – us UMI [610]
BULLETIN OF THE HISTORY OF MEDICINE – v. 1-32. 1933-1958 – 1,5,6 – us Princeton Micro [610]
BULLETIN OF THE INDONESIAN ORGANIZATION FOR AFRO-ASIAN PEOPLE'S SOLIDARITY – (Missing: 1967, v1; 1968, v2; 1969, v3(1-4, 9); 1970, v4(3-10?); 1971/72, v5(4-10?)) – 1967-1972. v1-6(1) – 8mf – SE-1854/1 – ne IDC [950]
BULLETIN OF THE INSTITUTE OF HISTORICAL RESEARCH – London, 1923-1924. v1 – 4mf – H-788/2 – ne IDC [900]
BULLETIN OF THE INTERNATIONAL ASSOCIATION OF ORIENTALIST LIBRARIANS *see* NEWSLETTER OF THE INTERNATIONAL ASSOCIATION OF ORIENTALIST LIBRARIANS
BULLETIN OF THE INTERNATIONAL TYPOGRAPHICAL UNION : 1912-1955 / International Typographical Union – (Coll title: Labor Union Periodicals, Pt 2) – 7r – 1 – $945.00 – 1-55655-305-6 – us UPA [680]
BULLETIN OF THE JOHN RYLANDS LIBRARY – v1-54. 1903-72 – 1 – us UMI [020]
BULLETIN OF THE JOHN RYLANDS UNIVERSITY LIBRARY OF MANCHESTER – (1985-. 5,6,9) – v55-. 1972- – 1 – us UMI [020]
BULLETIN OF THE LABOUR AND SOCIALIST INTERNATIONAL / International Socialist Congress – 1919-22 – 1r – 1 – us Ross [335]
BULLETIN OF THE LOS ANGELES NEUROLOGICAL SOCIETIES – (v44-. 1979-5,6,9) – v31-. 1966- – 1 – us UMI [616]
BULLETIN OF THE LOS ANGELES NEUROLOGICAL SOCIETY – v1-30. 1936-65 – 1 – us UMI [616]
BULLETIN OF THE NATIONAL COMMISSION ON LITURGY / Canadian Catholic Conference. National Commission on Liturgy – Nos.1-4.Apr-May 1965 – 1 – us UMI [240]
THE BULLETIN OF THE NATIONAL TAX ASSOCIATION – v1-33. 1915-47 (all publ) – 33mf – 9 – $49.50 – LLMC 84-369 – us L.L.M.C. [336]
BULLETIN OF THE NEW HEBRIDES CHAMBER OF COMMERCE, INDUSTRY AND AGRICULTURE / BULLETIN OF THE VANUATU CHAMBER OF COMMERCE / New Hebrides Chamber of Commerce & Vanuatu Chamber of Commerce – Port Vila, 1976-86 – 1r – 1 – PMB Doc425 – at Pacific Mss [338]
BULLETIN OF THE NEW YORK BOTANICAL GARDEN – New York, 1896/1900-1932. v1-14 – 124mf – 7459/1 – ne IDC [580]
BULLETIN OF THE NUTTALL ORNITHOLOGICAL CLUB / ed by Allen, J A – (Continued as: Auk. A quarterly Journal of Ornithology. Boston, etc., 1884-1920. v1-37) – Cambridge, 1876-1883. v1-8 – 392mf – Z-2014/2 – ne IDC [590]
BULLETIN OF THE ORTON SOCIETY – (v.30-. 1980-. 5,6,9) – v.1-. 1951- – 1 – us UMI [370]
BULLETIN OF THE ORTON SOCIETY *see* ANNALS OF DYSLEXIA
BULLETIN OF THE ROBERT MORRIS ASSOCIATES – v.1-49. 1918-67. Superseded by Journal of Commercial Bank Lending – 1 – us UMI [073]
BULLETIN OF THE SCHOOL COMMITTEE OF THE VAAD HAIR – Montreal, CN. v2 no 3. 1923 – 1r – 1 – Can$25.00 – cn Can Microfilming [072]
BULLETIN OF THE SCHOOL OF ORIENTAL STUDIES – London, 1917-1939. v1-9 – 160mf – A-398c/2 – ne IDC [950]
BULLETIN OF THE SOUTHWESTERN ASSOCIATION OF PETROLEUM GEOLOGISTS *see* AAPG BULLETIN
BULLETIN OF THE STATE BAR OF WISCONSIN *see* WISCONSIN LAWYER
BULLETIN OF THE TORREY BOTANICAL CLUB – New York, 1870-1941. v1-68 – 675mf – 5593c/2 – ne IDC [580]
BULLETIN OF THE TREASURY *see* TREASURY BULLETIN
BULLETIN OF THE WINDSOR JEWISH COMMUNITY COUNCIL – (Windsor, Ont.) September 1968 – June 1984 – us A.J.P.C. [270]

BULLETIN OF WHOA (WILDHORSE ORG. ASSISTANCE) – Reno, NV. 1893; 1983-1990 – 2r – 1 – $100.00 – U04878 – us Library Micro [071]

BULLETIN OFFICIAL / Morocco – (1980-. ca $85.00y) – 1970-79. (Part I-Textes legislatifs). (Part II-Annonces Legales) – 32r – 1 – $675.00; outside North America add $1.25r – us L of C Photodup [324]

BULLETIN OFFICIEL / Cambodia – Protectorat francais. 1883-86 – 1 – fr A.C.R.P.P. [950]

BULLETIN OFFICIEL / Congo. Belgian – 1885-1908. Missing: 1894, Jan. Feb., June Sept., Nov. Dec – 1 – 35.00r – us Hoover Inst Photo [324]

BULLETIN OFFICIEL / Congo. Belgian – 1910-1959. Gaps – 1 – 35.00r – us Hoover Inst Photo [324]

BULLETIN OFFICIEL / Congo. Belgian – Brussels. 1949. 1952-1959 – 1 – us NY Public [960]

BULLETIN OFFICIEL / Expedition de Cochinchine. Puis, de la Cochinchine francaise – 1862, 1864-69, 1872-79, 1881-87; TB. 1861-77 – 1 – fr A.C.R.P.P. [950]

BULLETIN OFFICIEL / Federation Nationale des Ouvriers Metallurgistes de France – Paris. 1891-1901. Continued as: L'Ouvrier Metallurgiste – 1 – fr A.C.R.P.P. [660]

BULLETIN OFFICIEL / France. Ministere des Colonies – 1914-45. Missing 1923, no. 5; 1924, no. 3; 1925, nos. 9, 10; 1926, no. 12 – 1 – 35.00r – us Hoover Inst Photo [944]

BULLETIN OFFICIEL / Gabon – 1885 – 1 – fr A.C.R.P.P. [960]

BULLETIN OFFICIEL / Indochina. French – 1887-1902, 1904-05, 1911 – 1 – fr A.C.R.P.P. [324]

BULLETIN OFFICIEL / Indochina. French. Commissariat – 1947-51 – 1 – fr A.C.R.P.P. [324]

BULLETIN OFFICIEL / Indochina. French. Commissariat – mars 1948-50 – 1 – fr A.C.R.P.P. [073]

BULLETIN OFFICIEL / Morocco – v46-59. 1957-70 – 16r – 1 – us Ross [324]

BULLETIN OFFICIEL – Ottawa: Le Bureau, [1895-189- ou 19–] – 9 – cn C.I.H.M. [971]

BULLETIN OFFICIEL / Protectorate of Annam and Tonkin – 1883-86 – 1 – fr A.C.R.P.P. [324]

BULLETIN OFFICIEL / Syndicat regional unitaire des mineurs – Federation unitaire du sous-sol. 10 no. Lille. 1927-30 ? – 1 – fr A.C.R.P.P. [331]

BULLETIN OFFICIEL DE LA BOURSE DU TRAVAIL DE PARIS / Bourse du travail de Paris – Union des syndicats du department de la Seine. no. 1-16. Paris. juil 1904-oct 1905 – 1 – fr A.C.R.P.P. [331]

BULLETIN OFFICIEL DE LA CONCURRENCE ET DE LA CONSOMMATION DEPUIS 1941 / France – (1941-1980 F800.00) – 1981-. Approx. 25 fiches per year – 9 – F110.00y – fr Journal Officiel [338]

BULLETIN OFFICIEL DE LA GUYANE FRANCAISE / French Guiana – 1827-1927 – 1 – us UMI [324]

BULLETIN OFFICIEL DE LA PROVINCE DU LUALABA – Kolwezi, 1964(January)-1965(February) – 4mf – 1634P/2 – ne IDC [960]

BULLETIN OFFICIEL DE LA SANTE – Disponible Depuis 1988 – F580.00y – fr Journal Officiel [944]

BULLETIN OFFICIEL DE L'EDUCATION NATIONALE – Suite de: Bulletin officiel du Ministere de l'Education nationale. Paris.oct 1944-64 – 1 – fr A.C.R.P.P. [370]

BULLETIN OFFICIEL DES AFFAIRES SOCIALES ET DE LA SOLIDARITE / France – 1988-Approx. 100mf per year – F580.00y – fr Journal Officiel [360]

BULLETIN OFFICIEL DES ANNONCES COMMERCIALES / France – B.O.D.A.C.. 1972 – 1 – fr A.C.R.P.P. [323]

BULLETIN OFFICIEL DES FORCES FRANCAISES LIBRES / France – no. 1. Londres. 15 aout 1940. suivi de Journal officiel du Haut Commissariat de France puis du Commandement en chef EN Afrique. no. 1-24. Alger. janv-30 mai 1943. suivi de: Journal officiel de la France libre puis de la France combattante. Londres. 20 janv 1941-16 sept 1943. suivi de: Journal officiel de la Republique francaise. Alger. 10 juin 1943-31 aout 1944 – 1 – fr A.C.R.P.P. [323]

BULLETIN OFFICIEL DU BURUNDI – Usumbura, 1962-68 – 3r – 1 – us Ross [324]

BULLETIN OFFICIEL DU DEPARTEMENT DE L'INSTRUCTION PUBLIQUE – (Scattered issues wanting) – Port-au-Prince: Imp de la jeunesse McDonald Dugue & H. Archer. sheets 1-5 [dec 1895-mar 2 1898]; sheets 5-21 [oct/nov/dec 1908/jan 1909-jan/sep 1919]; sheets 22-43 [dec/jan 1923-july/aug/sep 1931] – 43 sheets – us Res Libr [073]

BULLETIN OFFICIEL DU PARTI SOCIALISTE POLONAIS – London, UK. Jun 1895-Jul 1899 – 1 – uk British Libr Newspaper [073]

BULLETIN OFFICIEL DU SERVICE DES PRIX – Disponible Depuis 1981 – F110.00y – fr Journal Officiel [944]

BULLETIN OFFICIEL DU SERVICE DES PRIX 1941-1980 – F800.00 – fr Journal Officiel [944]

BULLETIN OFFICIEL DU TRAVAIL – 1988- – F380.00y – fr Journal Officiel [944]

BULLETIN ON NARCOTICS – (1976- . 5,6,9) – v. 1-. 1949- – 1 – us UMI [610]

BULLETIN ON NARCOTICS – v. 8-18. 1956-66 – 1,5,6 – us Princeton Micro [360]

BULLETIN P / Iowa State University. Iowa Agriculture and Home Economics Experiment Station – Nos 1-141 1939-50 – 1,5 – us Spaulding [630]

BULLETIN PERIODIQUE DE LA PRESSE ETRANGERE – Paris – 1 – 35.00r – us Hoover Inst Photo [072]

BULLETIN PERIODIQUE DES ACTES ADMINISTRATIFS / Indochina. French – juil 1921 – 1 – fr A.C.R.P.P. [950]

BULLETIN PERIODIQUE DU BUREAU SOCIALISTE INTERNATIONAL, PERIODISCHES BULLETIN DES INTERNATIONALEN SOCIALISTISCHEN BUREAU, PERIODICAL BULLETIN OF THE INTERNATIONAL SOCIALIST BUREAU – 2-3, 5-8, 10-11, Brussels: s.n., 1909-13 – 1 – us U.W. Library [073]

BULLETIN PERTAMINA / Dinas Humas Pusat – (Weekly. Missing: 1965-1968 v1-4(1-19,24-25,27-52); 1969 v5(1-7,19, 21,24,27,33-34) 1970 v6(7-9,34,50); 1971 v7(4,6-7,11,15,22-23, 25,27,31,41)) – Djakarta, 1965-1971 – 31mf – 9 – SE-1373/1 – ne IDC [950]

BULLETIN POLITIQUE : HEBDO GRAND-FORMAT – Riviere-du-loup, Canada. 17 fev 1899-15 jun 1900 – 1r – 1 – Can$37.50 – cn Can Microfilming [073]

BULLETIN POPULAIRE / Agence de Presse Libre du Quebec – 1971-76? – 2r – 1 – Can$129.00 – cn Bibl Nat [070]

BULLETIN PROVINCIAL DU KATANGA ORIENTAL / Congo – Elisabethville, 1963-65 – 7mf – 9 – ne IDC [960]

BULLETIN PROVINCIAL DU LUALABA – Kolwezi, 1964(August-December) – 4mf – 1634BP/2 – ne IDC [960]

BULLETIN PROVINCIAL DU SUD-KASAI *see* MONITEUR DU SUD-KASAI

BULLETIN QUOTIDIEN / Congo. Congo Presse – Kinshasa, 1966, v1-2; 1967, v1-5. BA-674/1 – 9 – ne IDC [960]

BULLETIN QUOTIDIEN / Congo. Congo Presse – Leopoldville, 1962. Nos.1-112. BA-673/1 – 9 – ne IDC [960]

BULLETIN QUOTIDIEN – Vientiane. Laos. 1952-1968 – 1 – us UMI [072]

BULLETIN QUOTIDIEN D'INFORMATIONS – [Ouagadougou], [mar 5 1956-1966] – us Res Libr [073]

BULLETIN. RUSSIAN ACADEMY OF SCIENCES *see* RUSSIAN CHEMICAL BULLETIN

BULLETIN SCIENTIFIQUE DE L'ACADEMIE IMPERIALE DES SCIENCES DE SAINT-PETERSBOURG – 1836-1842. v1-10 – 76mf – R-5819/2 – ne IDC [500]

BULLETIN SENTINEL – Decatur. Ill. -w. 1895-96 – 1 – us UMI [071]

BULLETIN SERIES: ANNUAL REPORT SERIES / National Museums of Canada – 9 – cn Micromedia [060]

BULLETIN SOCIALISTE – no. 125, 141-397. Paris. sept 1933, 1934-aout 1939 – 1 – fr A.C.R.P.P. [335]

BULLETIN SOCIALISTE – no. 1-373. Paris. mars 1970-71. fait suite a: Le Populaire. no. 12719. 28 fevr 1970. Remplace par: L'Unite voir a ce titre – 1 – fr A.C.R.P.P. [335]

BULLETIN SOCIALISTE VOIR A CE TITRE *see* LE POPULAIRE

BULLETIN, SPECIAL SERIES / Washington. Agricultural Experiment Station – nos.1-9. 1909-12 – 1,5,6 – us Spaulding [630]

BULLETIN STATISTIQUE – Ouagadougou. v[1-6]. 1960-1966 – us Res Libr [310]

BULLETIN STATISTIQUE (KIEVSKOE GUBERNSKOE STATISTICHESKOE BI URO) – (Includes c.1: no.3 1925:Dec) – Kiev: Bureau – 1 – CSUXAKZ1998-S – us Hoover Inst Photo [310]

BULLETIN STATISTIQUE MENSUEL *see* EZHEMESI ACHNY I STATITICHESKI I BI ULLETEN

BULLETIN SUR LES CHEMINS / Camirand, J A – Quebec?: Departement de l'agriculture, 1897 – 9 – cn C.I.H.M. [971]

BULLETIN TECHNIQUE DU BUREAU VERITAS – Paris. 1919-72; 1985-1992 – 5 – fr A.C.R.P.P. [600]

BULLETIN THOMISTE – (Lacking: 9(1932). 14(1937)-16(1939)) – Le Saulchoir, 1(1924)-33(1956) – 121mf – 9 – Dfl434.00 – ne Slangenburg [073]

BULLETIN THOMISTE – (Missing: v9 1932. v11-12 1934-1935. v14-16 1937-1939) – Paris. v1-33. 1924-1956 – 121mf – 9 – ne IDC [240]

BULLETIN THOMISTE – Paris v6-10(3) 1940-59 H-308/2 – 8 – ne IDC [240]

BULLETIN: UNITED STATES INDIAN SERVICE / U.S. Bureau of Indian Affairs – 1921-23. (American Indian Periodicals in the Princeton University Library). 3 fiches – 9 – $45.00 – us UPA [324]

BULLETIN VAN HET CENTRAAL LABORATORIUM VAN DE BLOEDTRANSFUSIEDIENST VAN HET NEDERLANDSE RODE KRUIS *see* VOX SANGUINIS

BULLETIN VOLCANOLOGIQUE – G-242 ? Series 1: v.1-8, 1924-1931. Series 2: v. 1-32, 1933-1969 – 9 – ne IDC [550]

BULLETIN-BOOSTER – Chicago. Ill. -w. 1969-70 – 1 – us UMI [071]

BULLETIN/[LITERARY AND HISTORICAL SOCIETY OF QUEBEC] / Literary and Historical Society of Quebec – (Contd by: Literary and Historical Society of Quebec. Library Bulletin ... of the Literary and Historical Society of Quebec) – S.l.: The Society?, 1900-1904 – 9 – cn C.I.H.M. [971]

BULLETIN-LOISIRS *see* LOISIRS QUEBEC (1984)

BULLETINO DEL LABORATORIO BOTANICO DELLA R. UNIVERSITA DI SIENA / ed by Tassi, F – 1897-1906. v1-8 – 29mf – 7661/2 – ne IDC [580]

BULLETINO DELLA R. SOCIETA TOSCANA DI ORTICULTURA – Firenze, 1876-1924. v1-49 – 235mf – 7465/1 – ne IDC [630]

BULLETINO DELLA SOCIETA ENTOMOLOGICA ITALIANA – Firenze, 1869-1920. v1-52 – 312mf – Z-930/2 – ne IDC [590]

BULLETINO DI ARCHEOLOGIA / ed by Rossi, Cav. Battista, Giovanni de – 1863-1894 – 147mf – 9 – Dfl515.00 – ne Slangenburg [073]

BULLETINO MALACOLOGICO ITALIANO – (Continued as: Bulletino della Societa Malacologica Italiana. Pisa, 1875-1895/1896, v1-20) – Pisa, 1868-1874. v1-7 – 133mf – Z-894/2 – ne IDC [590]

BULLETINS / American Baptist Theological Seminary – 1924-78 – 1 – $80.15 – us Baptist [240]

BULLETINS / Baptist Southern Convention – 1950-70 – 1 – $14.07 – us Baptist [240]

BULLETINS / Clemson University. Agricultural Extension Division – n.A-123. Oct 1914-Aug 1964 – 1,5 – us Spaulding [630]

BULLETINS / Queen's University. Canada. Dept. of History and Political and Economic Science – v2-59. Jan 1912-May 1930 – 1 – cn Precision [320]

BULLETINS / U.S. Bureau of Mines – Nos 1-699. 1910-76 – 1,5,6 – $22,990.00 – us Princeton Micro [622]

BULLETINS / U.S. Geological Survey – n.1-1520. 1883-1981 – 1,5,6 – us Princeton Micro [550]

BULLETINS / Wisconsin. Dept. of Revenue. Bureau of Local Financial Assistance – (Indebtedness. 1948-79. Municipal Resources Provided and Expended. 1921-78. Property Tax. 1937-78. Taxes and aids. 1920-68. Town, Village and City Taxes. 1920-78) – 76 fiches. (Harvard Law School Library Collection.) – 9 – $1.50f – us H.U. Law [336]

BULLETINS AND OTHER EPHEMERA RELATING TO THE FOURTH INTERNATIONAL, 1930-1940 – In English, French, Spanish, Dutch and German. Arranged chronologically within each language on 5 reels – 1 – £160.00 – uk Altair [335]

BULLETINS AND REVISIONS / Wisconsin. Agricultural Experiment Station – no.1-601. 1883-1970 – 1,5 – us Spaulding [630]

BULLETINS, CATALOGS AND OTHER MATERIAL / Golden Gate Baptist Theological Seminary – 1 – us Baptist [240]

BULLETINS DE LA SOCIETE ROYALE DE BOTANIQUE DE BELGIQUE – Bruxelles, 1862-1935. v1-68 – 326mf – 8565/1 – ne IDC [580]

BULLETINS DE LA SOCIETE ROYALE DE ZOOLOGIE D'ANVERS *see* ACTA ZOOLOGICA ET PATHOLOGICA ANTVERPIENSIA

[BULLETINS DE VOTE AU NOM DE LOUIS-NAPOLEON BONAPARTE] – Paris 1848 – us Res Libr [944]

BULLETINS DES SEANCES DE LA SOCIETE VAUDOISE DES SCIENCES NATURELLES – (Index 1842-1939) – Lausanne, 1842-1942. v1-62 – 668mf – Z-247c/2 – ne IDC [550]

BULLETINS ET TRAVAUX COMPTE RENDU DES SEANCES / Institut Indochinois pour l'Etude de l'Homme. Hanoi – v. 1-6. 1938-43 – 1 – $25.00 – us L of C Photodup [930]

BULLETINS OF THE UNITED STATES GEOLOGICAL SURVEY – Washington, 1883-1916. Nos 1-651 – 2,303mf – 2547/1 – ne IDC [550]

BULLETINS OF THE U.S. BUREAU OF LABOR AND THE U.S. BUREAU OF LABOR STATISTICS, 1895-1919 – (With printed guide) – 1993 – 838mf – 9 – $4,975.00 – 1-55655-460-0 – us UPA [331]

BULLETINS ON NARCOTICS / UN Commission on Narcotic Drugs – v1-36. 1949-84 – E.249 F.255 R.203 S.194 – 9 – us U.N. Pubs [340]

BULLETIN-TEXAS NURSES ASSOCIATION – 1964-73 – 1 – us UMI [610]

BULLETTINO DI ARCHEOLOGIA – (Prima Serie 1863 31mf, Seconda Serie 1870 32mf, Terza Serie 32mf, Quarta Serie 1889 32mf, Quinta Serie 1894 20mf) – 147mf – 8 – ne Slangenburg [930]

BULLETTINO SETTIMANALE DELLE LEGGI E DEI DECRETI DEL REGNO D'ITALIA / Italy. Laws, Statutes, etc – Napoli. On film: v1-19; 1894-1912. LL-0251 – 1 – us L of C Photodup [340]

BULLFROG MINER – Beatty, NV. 1905-08 – 3r – 1 – $150.00 – U04413 – us Library Micro [071]

BULLFROG MINER – Rhyolite, NV. 1907-09; 1905-07 (scats) – 2r – 1 – $100.00 – U04728 – us Library Micro [071]

BULLFROG TIMES PICAYUNE – Silver City, NV. 1987-1988 – 1 – U04898 – us Library Micro [071]

Bullialdus, IsM *see* HISTORIA BYZANTINA (CBH 15)

Bulliard, J BF *see*
- DICTIONNAIRE ELEMENTAIRE DE BOTANIQUE,...
- HISTOIRE DES PLANTES MEDICINALES,...

Bullinger, H *see*
- ADVERSUS OMNIA CATABAPTISTARVM PRAVA DOGMATA LIB. IIII. PER LEONEM JUDAE AUCTI
- COMMENTARII IN OMNES PAULI EPI ET EPI CATHOLICAS
- COMMENTARIORUM LIBRI 10 IN...EVANGELIUM SECUNDUM IOANNEM
- COMMENTARIORUM LIBRI 12 IN...EVANGELIUM SECUNDUM MATTHAEUM
- HANDLUNG ODER ACTA GEHALTNER DISPUTATION VND GESPRAECH ZU ZOFFINGEN INN BERNNER BIET MIT DEN WIDERTOEUFFERN
- IN LUCULENTUM ET SACROSANCTUM EVENGELIUM...SECUNDUM LUCAM COMMENTARIORUM LIB. 9
- IN SACROSANCTUM EVANGELIUM DOMINI NOSTRI IESU CHRISTI SEC. MARCUM COMMENTARIORUM LIB. 6

Bullinger, Heinrich *see*
- DE GRATIA DEI IUSTIFICANTE NOS PROPTER CHRISTUM, PER SOLAM FIDEM ABSQUE OPERIBUS BONIS, FIDE INTERIM EXUBERANTE IN OPERA BONA LIBRI 4....1554
- REFORMATIONSGESCHICHTE NACH DEM AUTOGRAPHON HRSG. AUF VERANSTALTUNG DER VATERLANDISCH-HISTORISCHEN GESELLSCHAFT IN ZUERICH VON J. J. HOTTINGER UND H. H. VOEGELI
- VON DEM VNUERSCHAMPTEN FRAEFEL, ERGERLICHEM VERWYRREN VNND VNWARHAFFTEM LEEREN, DER SELBSGESANDTEN WIDERTOEUFFERN

- DER WIDERTOEUFFEREN VRSPRUNG, FUERGANG, SECTEN, WAESEN, FUERNEMME VND GEMEINE JRER LEER ARTICKEL
- DER WIDERTOUFFEREN URSPRUNG/ FURGANG/SECTION/WASEN/FURNEM ME UND GEMINE JRER LEER ARTICKLE

Bullinger, W *see* THINGS TO COME

Bullingeri, Heinrichi *see* COMMENTARII IN OMNES PAULI EPISTOLAS, IN EPISTOLAM AD HEBRAEOS ET IN EPISTOLAS CANONICAS

Bullingerus, H *see* TEGHENS DE WEDERDOOPERS, SES BOECKEN, NV EERST WT DE LATIJNSCHE TALE IN NEDERDUYTSCH OUERGESTELT, D. G. NICOLAJ DIE DAER BY GHEUOECHT HEEFT DE WEDERLEGGINGHE DER LEERINGEN V. MENNO SYMONS, DIERICK PHILIPS, ADAM PASTOR, HENDRICK NICLAES

BULLION LEDGERS OF THE U.S. MINT AT PHILADELPHIA, 1794-1802 / U.S. Bureau of the Mint – T587 – 1r – 1 – us Nat'l Archives [324]

BULLLETIN QUOTIDIEN D'INFORMATIO OUAGADOUGOU, [SEP 20-NOV 8 1965] – (Filmed with: Upper Volta. Service de l'information. Bulletin quotidien d'information) – us Res Libr [073]

Bulloch County. Georgia. Macedonia Baptist Church *see* SOUVENIR PROGRAM AND 100-YEAR HISTORY

Bullock, Charles J *see* ESSAYS ON THE MONETARY HISTORY OF THE UNITED STATES

BULLOCK REPORT / Great Britain. Committee of Inquiry on A Language for Life – 1975 – 9 – uk Microform Academic [324]

Bullock-Webster, G R *see* THE BRITISH CHAROPHYTA

Bullokar, John *see* AN ENGLISH EXPOSITOR

Bullon de Mendoza, Alfonso *see* LAS ORDENES MILITARES EN LA RECONQUISTA DE LA PROVINCIA DE BADAJOZ

Bullon Ramirez, Francisco *see* CANALIZACION DEL AHORRO PROVINCIAL. CONFERENCIA. COLEGIO O. DE SECRETARIOS, INTERVENTORES Y DEPOSITARIOS DE ADMINISTRACION LOCAL DE LA PROVINCIA DE CACERES

BULLSEYE – Las Vegas, NV. 1993 – 4+ r – 1 – $200.00 ($90.00y) – U04852 – us Library Micro [071]

BULLSEYE – North Las Vegas, NV. 1974-1984 – 14r – 1 – $700.00 – N04633 – us Library Micro [071]

Bulmerincq, A von *see*
- DAS ASYLRECHT UND DIE AUSLIEFERUNG FLUCHTIGER VERBRECHER...
- PRAXIS, THEORIE...
- DIE SYSTEMATIK...
- DAS VOELKERRECHT...

Bulova, J A *see* DIE EINHEITSLEHRE (MONISMUS) ALS RELIGION

Bulovec, Stefka *see* BIBLIOGRAFIJA EDVARDA KARDELJA

Bulow, Franz Josef von *see* DEUTSCH-SUDWESTAFRIKA

Bulow, Franz von *see* IM FELDE GEGEN DIE HEREROS

Bulow, H D von *see* ESPRIT DU SYSTEME DE GUERRE MODERNE

Bulow, Heinrich von *see* DEUTSCH-SUDWESTAFRIKA SEIT DER BESITZERGREIFUNG, DIE ZUGE UND KRIEGE GEGEN DIE EINGEBORENEN

Bulter, G *see* THE DEVELOPMENT...

Bulthaupt, H et al *see* UEBER DEN EINFLUSS DES ZEITUNGSWESENS AUF LITTERATUR UND LEBEN

Bulwer, J *see*
- CHIROLOGIA
- CHIRONOMIA
- PATHOMYOTOMIA
- PHILOCOPHUS

Bulwer Lytton, Edward *see* LETTERS OF THE LATE EDWARD BULWER, LORD LYTTON, TO HIS WIFE...

BUMAGA I DREVNEISHIIA BUMAZHNYIA MEL'NITSY V MOSKOVSKOM GOSUDARSTVE / Likhachev, N P – Istoriko-arkheograficheskii ocherk. St. Petersburg, 1891. 222p. BR-4581/2 – 8 – ne IDC [460]

BUMAZHNAI A PROMYSHLENNOST : ORGAN NAUCHNO-TEKHNICHESKOGO SOVETA BUMAZHNO I PROMYSHLENNOSTI N.T.O. V.S.N.KH – (Includes c.1: v.5:no.7/8 1926:July/Aug.-v.5:no.12 (1926:Dec.)) – Moskva: [Sovet], 1922 – 1 – CSUXAKZ6910-S – us Hoover Inst Photo [600]

Bumgarner, Simeon Columbus *see* BUMGARNER'S ANNOTATED POCKET CODE OF TENNESSEE.

BUMGARNER'S ANNOTATED POCKET CODE OF TENNESSEE. / Bumgarner, Simeon Columbus – Harrisburg, Pa., United Evangelical Church, 1915. 451 p. LL-488 – 1 – us L of C Photodup [340]

Bump, Orlando Franklin *see*
- COMPOSITION IN BANKRUPTCY
- DECISIONS CONSTITUCIONALES DE LOS TRIBUNALES FEDERALES DE ESTADOS UNIDOS DESDE 1789.

Bunau-Varilla, P *see* HISTORIA...DE LA ESCANDALOSA NEGOCIACION DEL TRATADO DEL CANAL DE PANAMA

BUNAVESTIRE – Bucharest, 1940-41 – 1 – us Res Libr [072]

Bunbury, Sarah S *see* LIFE AND LETTERS OF R.C. SCONCE, FORMERLY SECRETARY TO ADMIRAL SIR JOHN THOMAS DUCKWORTH

Bunce, C R *see* CANTERBURY: CATALOGUE OF THE ARCHIVES OF THE DEAN AND CHAPTER

Bunce, Dearl Linwood I *see* COGGINS MEMORIAL BAPTIST CHURCH'S INVOLVEMENT IN A MEANINGFUL WORLD HUNGER MINISTRY

Bunce, John Thackray *see* HISTORY OF THE CORPORATION OF BIRMINGHAM; WITH A SKETCH OF THE EARLIER GOVERNMENT OF THE TOWN

DER BUND – Bern, 1940- (incomplete) – 1 – Inquire at Mikrofilmarchiv for details – gw Misc Inst [072]

DER BUND – Bern. apr 1-30, 1974 – 1r – 1 – gw Mikrofilm [949]

DER BUND – Das Gewerkschaftsblatt der britischen zone. Koeln, West Germany. 1947-49. Continues: Welt der Arbeit – 1 – gw Mikrofilm [073]

DER BUND : DAS GEWERKSCHAFTSBLATT DER BRITISCHEN ZONE – Koeln, 1947-49 – 1r – 1 – DM80.00 – gw Mikro Press [072]

Bund der Bau-, Maurer- und Zimmermeister zu Berlin *see* JAHRBUCH

Bund der technischen Angestellten und Bund der technischen Angestellten und Beamten *see* SCHRIFTEN

Bund der technisch-industriellen Beamten. Berlin *see* PROTOKOLL DES ORDENTLICHEN BUNDESTAGES

Bund Deutscher Offizier *see* EHREN-RANGLISTE DES EHEMALIGEN DEUTSCHEN HEERES..

THE BUNDAHISHN / ed by Anklesaria, E T D – Bombay, 1908 – 4mf – NE-20152/1 – ne IDC [490]

BUNDEHESH, LIBER PEHLVICUS E VETUSTISSIMO CODICE HAVNIENSI DESCRIPSIT / Westergaard, N L – Havniae, 1851 – 1mf – NE-20150/1 – ne IDC [490]

DER BUNDEHESH, ZUM ERSTEN MALE HERAUSGEGEBEN, TRANSCRIBIRT, UEBERSETZT UND MIT GLOSSAR VERSEHEN / Justi, F – Leipzig, 1868 – 6mf – NE-20151/1 – ne IDC [490]

Bundes der Arbeitgeber-Verbaende. Berlin *see* ARBEITERBEWEGUNG

BUNDES-ANZEIGER – Bonn. 1983-87 – 1 – gw Mikrofilm [340]

BUNDES-ANZEIGER – (In the beginning also called: Oeffentlicher Anzeiger fuer das Vereinigte Wirtschaftsgebiet) – Frankfurt, Bonn. 1949- – 1 – Inquire at Mikrofilmarchiv for details – gw Misc Inst [350]

BUNDESANZEIGER / Germany. Federal Republic – v1-22. 1949-70 – 70r – 1 – us Ross [324]

BUNDESBOTE – Teplitz-Schoenau (Teplice), Czechoslovakia. 1930 – 1r – 1 – gw Mikrofilm [072]

BUNDESBOTE-KALENDER – 1886-1947 (complete) – 2r – 1 – ATLA 1993-S024 – us A.T.L.A. [073]

DAS BUNDESBUCH, EX XX,22-XXII,33: SEINE URSPRUENGLICHE GESTALT / Baentsch, Bruno – Halle: Max Niemayer, 1892. 1 fiche – 9 – us A.T.L.A. [240]

BUNDESGESETZ UBER DAS VERFAHREN BEI DEM BUNDESGERICHTE IN BURGERLICHEN RECHTSSTRETIGKEITEN / Switzerland. Laws, Statutes, etc – (Vom 22. November 1850) 54 p. LL-4024 – 1 – us L of C Photodup [340]

BUNDESGESETZBLATT / Germany. Federal Republic – 1949- – 9 – inquire – us Ross [943]

BUNDESGESETZBLATT : TEIL 1, 2 AND 3 (1949-1980) – (Teil 1 und 3: ca DM2,750.00. ISBN: 3-406-08627-6; Teil 2: ca DM3,600.00. ISBN: 3-409-08628-4) – 402mf – 9 – ca DM5,750.00 set – 3-406-33516-0 – Co-published with Bundesanzeiger-Verlag, Bonn – gw Beck [340]

BUNDESGESETZBLATT, TEIL 1 – (mit Folgelieferungen zum Preis von DM 200,-/ Jahrgang) – saemtl. Jahrgaenge 1949 bis einschl. 1992 – DM5,000.00 – gw Boorberg [340]

Bundessekretariat des Deutschen Kulturbundes, Sektor Publikationen *see* HOELDERLIN, FRIEDRICH

DER BUNDESSTAAT / Brie, S – Leipzig, 1874 – 3mf – 1 – ILM-1553/1 – ne IDC [327]

DIE BUNDESVORSTELLUNG IM ALTEN TESTAMENT IN IHRER GESCHICHTLICHEN ENTWICKELUNG / Kraetzschmar, Richard – (Includes bibliographical references, appendixes on the etymology of the Hebrew word berit and words used with it and index of biblical citations) – Marburg: N G Elwert, 1896 – 1mf – 9 – 0-8370-3987-8 – 1985-1987 – us A.T.L.A. [220]

A BUNDLE OF MEMORIES / Holland, Henry Scott – London: Wells Gardner, Darton, [1915?] – 1mf – us A.T.L.A. [240]

Bundy, Charles Smith *see* THE JUSTICES' MANUAL OF STATUTE, JUDICIAL AND ELEMENTARY LAW, WITH APPROPRIATE FORMS.

Bunegin, Maksim F *see* REVOLIUTSIIA I GRAZHDANSKAIA VOINA V KRYMU, 1917-1920 GG

BUNG KARNO / Subagijo, I N – SE 10,222 1. 1952 – 9 – ne IDC [950]

BUNG KARNO DAN INDONESIA / Sabur, Moch – SE 3556 1. 1963? – 9 – ne IDC [950]

BUNG KARNO DIHADAPAN PENGADILAN KOLONIAL / ed by Notosutardjo, Achmad – SE-4554 1. 1963 – 9 – ne IDC [950]

BUNG KARNO KITA; SEBUAH SKETSA / Sukarno, Pres. Indonesia – SE 5922 1. 1964? – 9 – ne IDC [324]

BUNG KARNO MENDJAWAB / Notosutardjo, Achmad – SE-4820 1. 1964 – 9 – ne IDC [950]

BUNG KARNO, PENJAMBUNG LIDAH RAKJAT INDONESIA. (AUTOBIOGRAPHY) / Sukarno, Pres. Indonesia – SE 11,424 1. 1966 – 9 – ne IDC [920]

BUNG KARNO SEBAGAI AHLI SEDJARAH / Sumardjo – SE 11,425 1. 1964 – 9 – ne IDC [950]

BUNG KARNO: SUKARNO / Sukarno, Pres. Indonesia – SE 4746 1. 1963 – 9 – ne IDC [920]

Bunge, A A von *see*
- ANABASEARUM REVISIO
- BEITRAG ZUR KENNTNIS DER FLORA RUSSLANDS UND DER STEPPEN CENTRAL ASIENS
- DELECTUS SEMINUM IN HORTO BOTANICO. DORPATENSIS
- ENUMERATIO PLANTARUM, QUAS IN CHINA BOREALI COLLEGIT
- RELIQUIAE BOTANICAE, SIVE ENUMERATIO PLANTARUM IN. ASIAE MEDIAE, AB S
- VERZEICHNISS DER IM JAHRE 1832 IM OESTLICHEN THEILE DES ALTAI-GEBIRGES GESAMMELTEN PFLANZEN

Bunge, Alejandro Ernesto *see* UNA NUEVA ARGENTINA

Bunge, H J *see* TEXTURES AND MICROSTRUCTURES

Bungener, Felix *see*
- PAPE ET CONCILE AU 19E SIECLE
- SAINT PAUL

Bungener, Laurence Louis Felix *see* HISTORY OF THE COUNCIL OF TRENT

THE BUNHILL MEMORIALS / Jones, J A – 1849 – 1 – 14.35 – us Baptist [240]

Bunin, Ivan Alekseevich *see* TEMNYE ALLEI

Bunina, I A et al *see* "DEN PECHATI"

Bunke, O *see* STATISTICS

Bunker, Alonzo *see* SKETCHES FROM THE KAREN HILLS

BUNKYOKYOKU. DIDIKAN BOEDI PEKERTI / JAVA. (Japanese Military Administration 1942-45) – Djakarta, Gunseikanbu Kanrikojo "Kolff", 2602 – 58mf – 9 – ne IDC [350]

Bunnell, Lafayette H *see* WINONA

Bunov, L M *see* MOLECULAR MATERIALS

Bunroku, Yoshioka *see* SHO KAI-SEKI TO GENDAI SHINA

Bunsen, Christian Charles Josias *see*
- ANALECTA ANTE-NICAENA
- HIPPOLYTUS AND HIS AGE, OR, THE BEGINNINGS AND PROSPECTS OF CHRISTIANTY
- OUTLINES OF THE PHILOSOPHY OF UNIVERSAL HISTORY APPLIED TO LANGUAGE AND RELIGION
- SIGNS OF THE TIMES

Bunsen, Christian Karl Josias, Freiherr von *see* EGYPT'S PLACE IN UNIVERSAL HISTORY

Bunsen, Ernest de *see*
- KEYS OF SAINT PETER...CONNECTED WITH THE HISTORY OF SYMBOLISM AND IDOLATRY
- DIE RECONSTRUCTION DER KIRCHLICHEN AUTORITAET

Bunsen, Frances *see* A MEMOIR OF BARON BUNSEN

Bunster, Arthur *see* SPEECH ON THE BRITISH COLUMBIA TARIFF, WEDNESDAY, 7TH MARCH, 1877

BUNTE – Offenburg. 1979-81 – 9 – 22150.00y – gw Alpha Com [073]

BUNTE BLUETHEN / Steinlein, A – (Poems, chiefly in German (some in English)) – La Crosse, Wis.: J Ulrich, 1884 – 1r – 1 – us U.W. Library [810]

BUNTETOJOGI DONTVENYTAR. – Budapest. On film: v1-27; 1908-35. LC set imperfect: v25 wanting. LL-0263 – 1 – us L of C Photodup [340]

BUNTHORNE ABROAD, OR, THE LASS THAT LOVED A PIRATE / Bengough, John Wilson – 1883?. 00124. (Pre-1900 Canadiana) – 9 – cn C.I.H.M. [830]

Bunting, Thomas Percival *see* THE LIFE OF JABEZ BUNTING, D.D.

A BUNVADI PERRENDTARTAS ZSEBKONYVE, KIEGESZITVE AZ UJABB BUNVADI ELJARASI SZABALYOKKAL; IRTAK EDVI ILLES KAROLY ES VARGHA FERENC / Hungary. Laws, Statutes, etc – 7. kiad. Budapest: Grill K., 1919. 687p. LL-4106 – 1 – us L of C Photodup [340]

BUNYAN / Froude, James Anthony – London: Macmillan, 1880 – 1mf – us A.T.L.A. [240]

BUNYAN / Froude, James Anthony – New York: Harper & Brothers, 1880 – 1 – us U.W. Library [920]

Bunzel, Ulrich *see* SCHLESIEN LEBT

Buonagurio, Joseph J *see* THE RELATIONSHIP BETWEEN PERCEIVED STRESSFUL LIFE EVENTS AND OCCURRENCE OF ATHLETIC INJURY AMONG COLLEGE LEVEL GYMNASTS

Buonaiuti, Ernesto *see* THE PROGRAMME OF MODERNISM

BUONAPARTE UND DIE BOURBONS : ODER UEBER DIE NOTHWENDIGKEIT, DASS SICH FRANKREICH, ZU SEINEM EIGNEN UND GANZ EUROPA'S GLUECK, MIT SEINEN RECHTMAESSIGEN FUERSTEN WIEDER VEREINIGE / Chateaubriand, F A de – Berlin, 1814 – 9 – DM48.00 – 3-89349-121-X – gw Hänsel [944]

Buonarroti, Filippo *see* GIORNALE PATRIOTTICO DI CORSICA

Buondelmonti, Christophorus *see* LIBER INSULARUM ARCHIPELAGI

Burachek, S *see*
- MAIAK SOVREMENNOGO PROSVESHCHENIIA I OBRAZOVANNOSTI

O BURACO – Paraopeba, Brazil. Sept 1932; Oct 1933; Sept-Nov 1946; May-Aug 1949 – 1 – bl Biblioteca [072]

BURAKU LIBERATION RESEARCH INSTITUTE – Osaka. 175 docs. 1980-1991 – 173mf – 9 – ne IDC [320]

BURBANK – 1972-75 – 22r – 1 – $1,100.00 – P00010 – us Library Micro [910]

BURBANK COMMUNITY BOOK / Monroe, Lynn – Burbank: Arthur H. Cawston, 1944. California Reel 17. (The Cox Library Collection) – 5 – us Americana [978]

BURBANK DAILY REVIEW *see* BURBANK LEADER

BURBANK LEADER – (Also known as: Burbank Daily Review) – Burbank, CA. 1909; 1910-1911; 1912 (scats); 1913-1914; 1916 1923; 1927; 1927-1928; 1931-1934; 1935-1981; 1984- – 504+ r – 1 – $25,200.00 ($2,300.00y) – H03168 – us Library Micro [071]

Burbidge, FW *see* THE NARCISSUS

Burbidge, George Wheelock *see* A DIGEST OF CRIMINAL LAW OF CANADA (CRIMES AND PUNISHMENTS): FOUNDED BY PERMISSION ON SIR JAMES FITZJAMES STEPHEN'S DIGEST OF THE CRIMINAL LAW

Burbidge, Thomas *see* CLOUGH, ARTHUR H. AMBARVALIA
BURCARDI GOTTHELFFII STRUVII,...CORPUS HISTORIAE GERMANICAE. / Struve, Burkhard Gotthelf – Ienae: Sumptibus I.F. Bielckii, 1730. SEM35P322 – 1r – 1 – Can$50.00 – cn Bibl Nat [943]
BURCHARD 1. VON WORMS UND DIE DEUTSCHE KIRCHE SEINER ZEIT (1000-1025) : EIN KIRCHEN- UND SITTENGESCHICHTLICHES ZEITBILD / Koeniger, Albert Michael – Muenchen: J.J. Lentner, 1905 – 1mf – us A.T.L.A. [240]
BURCHARD NEWS – Burchard, NE. -w. Jul. 1885-Oct. 1887 – 1 – us NE Hist [071]
BURCHARD TIMES – Burchard, NE. -w. Jun. 1892-Feb. 1899. Incomplete; Oct. 1901-Mar. 1903. Incomplete; Aug. 1909-Dec. 1910; Aug. 1911-Sep. 1912 – 1 – us NE Hist [071]
Burchard, U *see* HORTULUS MUSICES PRACTICE OMIBUS DIVINO GREGORIANI COCENTUS
BURCHARDI PRAEPOSITI URSPERGENSIS CHRONICON (MGH 7: 16.BD) – Ed 2a – Dfl13.00 – ne Slangenburg [240]
Burchardt, M *see* DIE ALTKANAANAEISCHEN FREMDWORTE UND EIGENNAMEN IM AEGYPTISCHEN
Burchardus, U *see* CHRONICVM ... CONTINENS HISTORIAM RERVM MEMORABILIVM, A NINO ASSYRIORVME REGE AD TEMPORA FRIDERICI 2...
Burchell, W J *see* TRAVELS IN THE INTERIOR OF SOUTHERN AFRICA
Burchinal, Mary Cacy *see* HANS SACHS AND GOETHE
Burcio, Humberto F *see* LA CECA DE LA VILLA IMPERIAL DE POTOSI Y LA MONEDA COLONIAL BUENOS AIRES, 1945
Burck, Arthur *see* DECAYING WITH THE DINOSAURS, U.S. FUTURE IS IN NIMBLER FIRMS, NOT MERGER-CRAZED GIANTS
Burckhard, C *see* LE MANDAT FRANCAIS EN SYRIE ET AU LIBAN
Burckhardt, Jakob *see*
- GRIECHISCHE-KULTURGESCHICHTE
- DIE ZEIT CONSTANTIN'S DES GROSSEN
Burckhardt, P *see* DAVID JORIS
Burckhardt, W *see*
- GUTACHTEN...BETREFFEND DIE BESTEUERUNG VON ERBSCHAFTEN IN DER SCHWEIZ DOMIZILIERTER RUSSEN
- DIE UNVOELKOMMENHEIT DES VOELKERRECHTS
Burckhardt-Biedermann, T *see* BONIFACIUS AMERBACH UND DIE REFORMATION
Burckmeyer *see* LETTERS
Burczynski, J *see* FINDING FISH WITH ECHO-SOUNDERS
Burden, Harold Nelson *see*
- LIFE IN ALGOMA, OR, THREE YEARS OF A CLERGYMAN'S LIFE AND CHURCH WORK IN THE DIOCESE
- MANITOULIN, OR, FIVE YEARS OF CHURCH WORK AMONG OJIBWAY INDIANS AND LUMBERMEN, RESIDENT UPON THAT ISLAND OR IN ITS VICINITY
THE BURDEN OF THE LORD : ASPECTS OF JEREMIAH'S PERSONALITY, MISSION, AND AGE / Thomson, W R – London, 1919 – 5mf – 8 – ne Slangenburg [240]
Burder, Samuel *see* MEMOIRS OF EMINENTLY PIOUS WOMEN
Burdett, Staunton S *see*
- THE BAPTIST HARMONY
Burdette Co *see* HISTORICAL SKETCHES OF IOWA BAPTISTS
Burdette, Robert J *see* LOS ANGELES AND SOUTHERN CALIFORNIA
BURDETT'S OFFICIAL INTELLIGENCE, 1882-1898 – 26r – 1 – uk Microform Academic [941]
Burdick, Charles Kellog *see* CASES ON THE LAW OF PUBLIC SERVICE
Burdick, Francis Marion *see* THE LAW OF TORTS.
Burditt, B A *see*
- THE GERMANIA; A COLLECTION OF THE MOST FAVORITE OPERATIC AIRS, MARCHES, POLKAS, WALTZES, DANCES, AND MELODIES OF THE DAY
- THE NEW GERMANIA.
Burdon, J A *see* HISTORICAL NOTES ON CERTAIN EMIRATES AND TRIBES
BUREAU COUNTY REPUBLICAN – Princeton. Ill. and Record. 1961- – 1 – us UMI [071]
Bureau des commissaires d'ecoles catholiques romains de Montreal *see*
- MEMOIRE PRESENTE AU GOUVERNEMENT DE LA PROVINCE DE QUEBEC...AU SUJET DE L'ENQUETE TENUE PAR LA COMMISSION ROYALE SUR L'ADMINISTRATION DES DITS COMMISSAIRES CATHOLIQUES
- NOTICE SUR LES ECOLES RELEVANT DU BUREAU...DE LA CITE DE MONTREAL
Bureau, Helene *see* GUIDE PRATIQUE POUR LE CHOIX DES PROFESSIONS FEMININES
Bureau International permanent de la Paix *see* LISTE DES SOCIETES DE LA PAIX AU 30 OCTOBRE 1912
Bureau, Jacques *see* DISCOURS ET VOTES DE JACQUES BUREAU CONTRE LA CONSCRIPTION EN 1917
BUREAU MEMORANDUM – (1976- . 5,6,9) – v. 1-. 1959- – 1 – us UMI [370]
BUREAU OF INDIAN AFFAIRS RECORDS CREATED BY THE SANTA FE INDIAN SCHOOL, 1890-1918 – 38r – 1 – M1473 – us Nat'l Archives [350]
BUREAU OF JUSTICE STATISTICS SLIM – 1985-89. 240 documents. Justice Statistics Clearinghouse – 9 – $190.00 – us N.C.J.R.S. [360]
BUREAU OF JUSTICE STATISTICS SLIM / U.S. Justice Statistics Clearinghouse – 1971-84. 288 documents – 9 – $203.00 – us N.C.J.R.S. [360]
BUREAU OF MUNICIPAL RESEARCH : CIVIC AFFAIRS – Ottawa, v1 1978- – 9 – cn Micromedia [320]
THE BUREAU OF NATURALIZATION... / Smith, D H – Baltimore, 1926 – 2mf – 9 – ILM-3635/1 – ne IDC [327]
BUREAU OF SOCIAL HYGIENE PROJECT AND RESEARCH FILES, 1913-1940 / Rockefeller University. Archives – (With printed guide) – 1980 – 31r – 1 – $2,635.00 – S1846 – Co-publ with Rockefeller Archive Center – us Scholarly Res [360]
BUREAU OF THE BUDGET BILL REPORTS : PUBLIC LAWS, 87TH AND 88TH CONGRESSES – 9 – $2,215.00 – 0-89093-363-4 – us UPA [340]
BUREAUCRACY A LA MODE / Latimer, Joseph W – 1924-25. (American Indian Periodicals in the Princeton University Library). 1 fiche – 9 – $45.00 – us UPA [305]
BUREAUCRACY IN GHANA : THE CIVIL SERVICE / Tiger, Lionel Samuel – London, 1962 – us Res Libr [350]
BUREAUCRAT – (1976- . 5,6,9) – v. 1-. 1972- – 1 – us UMI [323]
DER BURENKRIEG,... / Bar, L von – Hannover, 1900 – 1mf – 9 – ILM-1182/1 – ne IDC [340]
Buret, Eugene *see* DE LA MISERE DES CLASSES LABORIEUSES EN ANGLETERRE ET EN FRANCE. DE LA NATURE DE LA MISERE, DE SON EXISTENCE, DE SES EFFETS, DE SES CAUSES ET DE L'INSUFFISANCE DES REMEDES QU'ON LUI A OPPOSES JUSQU'ICI
Burevii, Kost *see*
- KOLCHAKOVSHCHINA
- RASPAD, 1918-1922
Burg, H van den *see* VERZAMELING VAN UITGEKORENE ZIN-SPREUKEN
BURG NEIDECK / Riehl, Wilhelm Heinrich; ed by Jonas, J B E – (German text with introd etc in English) – Boston: D C Heath, c1907 – 1r – 1 – us U.W. Library [430]
Burgaud des Marets, J H *see* GLOSSAIRE DU PATOIS ROCHELAIS
BURGAZKI FAR – Burgas, Bulgaria. 4 Jul-15 Aug 1944 – 1r – 1 – us L of C Photodup [072]
BURGDORFER KREISBLATT – (Cont: Burgdorfer Wochenblatt, -1895) – Burgdorf/Lehrte, jan 2 1867-85, 1887-apr 4 1945, sep 1 1978-apr 30 1986 – 117r – 1 – Inquire at Mikrofilmarchiv for details – gw Misc Inst [943]
BURGDORFER KREISBLATT *see* BURGDORFER WOCHENBLATT
BURGDORFER WOCHENBLATT – (Since 1897: Burgdorfer Kreisblatt) – Burgdorf b. Lehrte, West Germany. 1 Sept 1978- – 40r – 1 – gw Mikrofilm [072]
BURGDORFER WOCHENBLATT *see* BURGDORFER KREISBLATT
Burge, W *see* COMMENTARIES ON COLONIAL AND FOREIGN LAWS GENERALLY AND IN THEIR CONFLICT WITH EACH OTHER AND WITH THE LAW OF ENGLAND
Burge, William *see* OBSERVATIONS ON THE SUPREME APPELLATE JURISDICTION OF GREAT BRITAIN.
BURGENLAND, AUSTRIA, PAMPHLET COLLECTION – 1937 – 1 – CSUXANQ3117-B – us Hoover Inst Photo [943]
DE BURGER – Bloemfontein. South Africa. 1894-97 – 1 – sa State Libr [072]
DIE BURGER – Cape Town, South Africa: Nasionale Pers, 1 Jul 1915- current – 1 (diazo also available at reduced price) – sa SA Libr [072]
DIE BURGER = OOS-KAAP UITGAWE – Port Elizabeth, South Africa, 2 Aug 1993 filmed currently – 28+ r – 1,16 diazo available – sa SA Libr [960]
DIE BURGER – Kaapstad: [Die Nasionale Pers Beperk, may 16-31 1969; jan 1,3-31 1970 – 2r – us Res Libr [072]
Burger, Dionijs H *see* SEDJARAH EKONOMIS SOSIOLOGIS INDONESIA
Burger, Heinz Otto *see*
- ANNALEN DER DEUTSCHEN LITERATUR
- "DASEIN HEISST EINE ROLLE SPIELEN"
BURGERS VRIEND *see* KIMBERLEY CITIZEN
Burgess, Ernest Watson *see* PERSONALITY AND THE SOCIAL GROUP
Burgess, G A *see* FREE BAPTIST CYCLOPAEDIA
Burgess, Henry *see* ESSAYS BIBLICAL AND ECCLESIASTICAL
Burgess, J *see*
- THE ANCIENT MONUMENTS, TEMPLES AND SCULPTURES OF INDIA
- LIST OF MONUMENTS
- LISTS OF MONUMENTS
- REVISED LISTS OF ANTIQUARIAN REMAINS IN THE BOMBAY PRESIDENCY AND THE NAT. STATES OF BARODA, PALANPUR, RADHANPUR, KATHIAWAS, KACHI, KOLHAPUR, AND THE SOUTHERN MARATHA MINOR STATES
- TAMIL AND SANSKRIT INSCRIPTIONS
Burgess, Thomas *see* GREEKS IN AMERICA
Burgess, Thomas Joseph Workman *see* HOW TO STUDY BOTANY
Burgess, Walter H *see* JOHN SMITH, THE SE-BAPTIST AND THE PILGRIM FATHERS HELWYS AND BAPTIST ORIGINS
Burgess, William *see* LAND, LABOR AND LIQUOR: A CHAPTER IN THE POLITICAL ECONOMY OF THE PRESENT DAY
DER BURGGRAF VON NUERNBERG, ODER, DER HOHENZOLLERN WELTGESCHICHTLICHER BERUF : HISTORISCHES SCHAUSPIEL IN FUENF ACTEN UND EINEM VORSPIEL / Bauer, Hugo – 6. Aufl. Berlin: H Bauer, 1888 – 1r – 1 – us U.W. Library [820]
Burgh, W de *see* THE ELEMENTS OF MARITIME...
Burghaber, A *see* THEOLOGIA POLEMICA...
Burghardt, W J *see* THE IMAGE OF GOD IN MAN ACCORDING TO CYRIL OF ALEXANDRIA
BURGHAUSER ANZEIGEBLATT FUER DEN SALZACH-, TRAUN- UND INN-BEZIRK *see* BURGHAUSER ANZEIGER
BURGHAUSER ANZEIGER – (Cont: Burghauser Anzeigeblatt fuer den Salzach-, Traun- und Inn-Bezirk, -1866; Burghauser Wochenblatt, 1867-sep 1887) – Burghausen, 1866-1935 – 1 – Inquire at Mikrofilmarchiv for details – gw Misc Inst [943]
BURGHAUSER WOCHENBLATT *see* BURGHAUSER ANZEIGER
BURGHAUSER-MUEHLDORFER WOCHENBLATT *see* OETTINGER UND BURGHAUSER ANZEIGER
BURGHAUSER-WOCHEN-BLATT *see* OETTINGER UND BURGHAUSER ANZEIGER
THE BURGHERSDORP GAZETTE – Burgersdorp, South Africa. 6 Jan 1872-27 Dec 1873. 1 reel. Absorbed by: Albert Times – 1, 16 diazo available at reduced price – sa SA Libr [072]
Burghley, William Cecil *see* THE EXECUTION OF JUSTICE IN ENGLAND
Burgin, E L *see* ADMINISTRATION OF FOREIGN ESTATES
Burgmueller, F *see* PENSEE A SON AMI SIGISMOND THALBERG...
Burgoa, Francisco de *see*
- GEOGRAFICA DESCRIPCION
- GEOGRAFICA DESCRIPCION DE LA PARTE SEPTENTRIONAL DEL POLO ARTICO DE LA AMERICA Y NUEVA IGLESIA DE LAS INDIAS OCCIDENTALES...2 VOL. MEXICO, 1934
Burgon, John William *see*
- THE CAUSES OF THE CORRUPTION OF THE TRADITIONAL TEXT OF THE HOLY GOSPELS
- LAST 12 VERSES OF THE BIBLE ACCORDING TO ST MARK VINDICATED
- LIVES OF TWELVE GOOD MEN
- PROPHECY – NOT "FORECAST"
- THE TRADITIONAL TEXT OF THE HOLY GOSPELS VINDICATED AND ESTABLISHED BY THE LATE JOHN WILLIAM BURGON
BURGOS. ARCHIVO HISTORICO PROVINCIAL. LOS PROTOCOLOS DEL ARCHIVO HISTORICO PROVINCIAL / Castro, P – Burgos, 1986 – 13mf – 9 – sp Cultura [946]
Burgoyne, Charles G *see* BURGOYNE'S DIRECTORY OF LAWYERS PRACTICING IN NEW YORK CITY, 1883
BURGOYNE'S DIRECTORY OF LAWYERS PRACTICING IN NEW YORK CITY, 1883 / Burgoyne, Charles G – New York, 1883 36 p. LL-1102 – 1 – us L of C Photodup [340]
BURGOYNE'S INVASION OF 1777: WITH AN OUTLINE SKETCH OF THE AMERICAN INVASION OF CANADA, 1775-76 / Drake, Samuel Adams – Boston: Lee and Shepard, 1889. 02755. (Pre-1900 Canadiana) – 9 – cn C.I.H.M. [971]
Burgsdorf, F A L von *see* ANLEITUNG ZUR SICHERN ERZIEHUNG UND ZWECKMAESSIGEN ANPFLANZUNG DER EINHEIMISCHEN UND FREMDEN HOLZARTEN
Burgt, Joannes Michael M van der *see* HET KRUIS GEPLANT IN EEN ONBEKEND NEGERLAND VAN MIDDEN-AFRIKA..
Burgt, Johannes Michael M van der *see* UN GRAND PEUPLE DE L'AFRIQUE EQUATORIALE
BURGUILLOS, ALDEA Y BASILICA DEL SIGLO 17 / Martinez Martinez, Matias Ramon – Caceres: Tip. Enc. y Lib. Jimenez, 1904 – 1 – sp Bibl Santa Ana [946]
Burguillos, Pedro *see* NOVENA A JESUS NAZARENO EN SU..
Burgundia, A *see* DES WERELDTS PROEF-STEEN OFTE DE YDELHEYDT DOOR DE WAERHEYD BESCHULDIGHT ENDE OVERTUYGHT VAN VALSCHEYDT
Burgy, Jules *see*
- DETRESSE DES OUVRIERS AU XIXE SIECLE
- PRESENT ET AVENIR DES OUVRIERS PAR UN TYPOGRAPHE
BURHAM-ON-SEA GAZETTE ETC – England.1948-74. -w. 62 1/2 reels – 1 – uk British Libr Newspaper [072]
Buri, Fritz *see* GOTTFRIED KELLERS GLAUBE
THE BURIAL CHAMBER OF THE TREASURER SOBK-MOSE / Hayes, William C – MMA. 1939 – 9 – $10.00 – us I.R.C. [930]
BURIAL PERMITS/TRANSIT PERMITS / Ottawa County, Ohio. Put-in-Bay, Township Clerk/Treasurer – (Some issues missing) – 1923-1935 – 1r – 1 – us Archival [324]
BURIAL RECORDS / Van Wert County. Ohio. Soldiers' Relief Commission – 1886-1926 – 2r – 1 – $32.50r – us Archival [324]
BURIAL RECORDS / Wood County. Ohio. Pemberville. Village Cemetery Association – 1931-1994 – 1r – 1 – $32.50r – us Archival [324]
BURIAL REGISTER / Sandusky County. Ohio. Woodville Township. Board of Trustees – 1906-1936 – 1r – 1 – $32.50r – us Archival [324]
BURIAL REMOVAL PERMITS / Wood County. Ohio. Middletown Township. Township Clerk – (Incomplete) – 1934-1951 – 1r – 1 – $32.50r – us Archival [324]
BURIAL TRANSIT PERMITS / Huron. County, Ohio. New London, Village Village Clerk – 1937-1957 – 1r – 1 – $32.50r – us Archival [324]
Burigny, Jean-Levesque de *see* EXAMEN CRITIQUE DES APOLOGISTES DE LA RELIGION CHRETIENNE
Burigny, M de *see* THE LIFE OF... HUGO GROTIUS
Burk, Frederic *see* FROM FUNDAMENTAL TO ACCESSORY IN THE DEVELOPMENT OF THE NERVOUS SYSTEM AND OF MOVEMENTS
Burke, Barlow *see* DISCOVERY PROBLEMS IN CIVIL CASES
Burke, Darren *see* A COMPARISON OF MANUAL AND MACHINE ASSISTED PROPRIOCEPTIVE NEUROMUSCULAR FACILITATION FLEXIBILITY TECHNIQUES
Burke, Edmund *see*
- A PHILOSOPHICAL INQUIRY INTO THE ORIGIN OF OUR IDEAS OF THE SUBLIME AND BEAUTIFUL
- A VINDICATION OF NATURAL SOCIETY: OR, A VIEW OF THE MISERIES AND EVILS ARISING TO MANKIND FROM EVERY SPECIES OF ARTIFICIAL SOCIETY
- WORKS OF EDMUND BURKE
Burke, J *see* CHANGES IN SPINAL EXCITABILITY PRECEDING A VOLUNTARY MOVEMENT IN YOUNG AND OLD ADULTS

Burke, J B *see*
- DORMANT AND EXTINCT PEERAGES
- ENCYCLOPAEDIA OF HEREDITY
- EXTINCT AND DORMANT BARONETCIES OF ENGLAND

Burke, Junius Jessel *see*
- LETTERS TO A LAW STUDENT

BURKE, J.W. AND CO *see* HISTORY OF CLINCH COUNTY

Burke, T Patrick *see*
- THE MORAL BASIS OF CAPITALISM
- WHAT IS THE MORAL STATUS OF MATERIAL POSSESSIONS? A CHRISTIAN DEFENCE OF PROPERTY RIGHTS

Burke, Thomas *see* THOMAS BURKE PAPERS

Burke, W B *see* PAPERS, 1887-1964

BURKESVILLE BAPTIST CHURCH. BURKESVILLE, KENTUCKY : CHURCH RECORDS – 1893-1966 – 1 – 22.05 – us Baptist [240]

BURKEVILLE JOURNAL – Crewe. Va. 1967$ – 1 – us UMI [071]

Burkhard, Werner *see* GRIMMELSHAUSEN, ERLOESUNG UND BAROCKER GEIST

Burkhard,H *see* SENCKENBERGISCHE BIBLIOTHEK, FRANKFURT AM MAIN

Burkhardt, C A H *see*
- HAND- UND ADRESSBUCH DER DEUTSCHEN ARCHIVE IM GEBIETE DES DEUTSCHEN REICHES, LUXEMBURGS, OESTERREICH-UNGARNS, DER RUSSISCHEN OSTSEEPROVINZEN UND DER DEUTSCHEN SCHWEIZ
- DER HISTORISCHE HANS KOHLHASE UND HEINRICH VON KLEIST'S MICHAEL KOHLHAAS

Burkill, IH *see* A DICTIONARY OF THE ECONOMIC PRODUCTS OF THE MALAY PENINSULA...

Burkitt, F C *see*
- EPHRAIM'S QUOTATIONS FROM THE GOSPEL
- THE RULES OF TYCONIUS

Burkitt, F Crawford *see*
- EARLY EASTERN CHRISTIANITY
- EVANGELION DA-MEPHARRESHE
- FRAGMENTS OF THE BOOKS OF KINGS ACCORDING TO THE TRANSLATION OF AQUILA

Burkitt, FC *see*
- EARLY CHRISTIANITY OUTSIDE THE ROMAN EMPIRE
- THE FAILURE OF LIBERAL CHRISTIANITY, AND, SOME THOUGHTS ON THE ATHANASIAN CREED
- THE OLD LATIN AND THE ITALA

Burkley, Renee L *see* THE EFFECTIVENESS OF BEHAVIORAL CONTRACTS IN PROMOTING THE MAINTENANCE OF CANCER RISK REDUCTION BEHAVIOR WHILE UTILIZED IN A COLLEGE CANCER AVOIDANCE COURSE

Burlamacchi Archive *see* INTERNATIONAL TRADE FROM THE 17TH CENTURY AMSTERDAM

Burlamaqui, J J *see*
- PRINCIPES DU DROIT DE LA NATURE ET DES GENS
- PRINCIPES DU DROIT NATUREL...

Burlaton, Louis *see* LE VENERABLE GERONIMO..

Burleigh, Bennet *see* TWO CAMPAIGNS

Burleigh, Lord Balfour of *see* AN HISTORICAL ACCOUNT OF THE RISE AND DEVELOPMENT OF PRESBYTERIANISM IN SCOTLAND

BURLEIGH, SHREWSBURY U. LEICESTER IN SCHILLERS MARIA STUART / Kennel, A (Albert) – Speyer: Dr Jaeger, 1906 – 1r – 1 – us U.W. Library [430]

Burles, Edward *see* GRAMMATICA BURLESA

BURLINGAME ADVANCE – Burlingame, CA. 1910-17; 1920-26 – 10r – 1 – $500.00 – B02081 – us Library Micro [071]

BURLINGAME ADVANCE STAR – Burlingame, CA. 1926-32; 1946; 1949-50; 1951; 1967-69 – 44r – 1 – $2,200.00 – B02082 – us Library Micro [071]

Burlingame Cemetery *see* LOT RECORD BOOK

BURLINGAME VILLAGER *see* BOUTIQUE AND VILLAGER

BURLINGTON 1752-1849 – (Mf 1T-2T: Marriages & Intentions 1799-1849; Family Births & Deaths 1752-1851. Mf 2T: Births & Deaths 1809-46; B,M,D 1843-49) – (mf ed 1995) – 9 – 0-87623-222-5 – us Holbrook [920]

BURLINGTON ADVERTISER – Burlington, NJ. 1790-91 – 1r – 1 – us Ross [071]

THE BURLINGTON ADVERTISER – Burlington, N.J. Apr 13 1790-Dec 13 1791 – 1 – us NY Public [071]

BURLINGTON COUNTY HERALD – Mount Holly. N.J. 1860; 1863- – 1 – us UMI [071]

Burlington Fine Arts Club. London *see*
- EARLY GERMAN ART
- ENGLISH MEZZOTINT PORTRAITS

THE BURLINGTON MAGAZINE – (v126-. Jan 1984-. 5,6,9) – v90-. Jan 1948- – 1 – us UMI [073]

BURLINGTON MAGAZINE FOR CONNOISSEURS – London, 1903-1920. v1-37 – 293mf – O-497/1 – ne IDC [073]

THE BURLINGTON MAGAZINE FOR CONNOISSEURS – v1-89. Mar 1903-Dec 1947 – 1 – us UMI [073]

Burlington, Vermont. Gove Hill Christian Association *see* TRUSTEES RECORDS

Burlington, Vermont. Vermont Baptist Home, Inc *see* RECORDS

BURMA / Ferrars, M & Ferrars, B – SE-199 1. 1900 – 9 – ne IDC [950]

BURMA – Rangoon: Office of the Supt Govt Printing. pt3. 1911 – 1 – us Res Libr [310]

Burma *see*
- CATALOGUE OF BOOKS
- INDEX INSCRIPTIONUM BIRMANICARUM

BURMA ACTS – Rangoon, 1898-1948 – 78mf – 9 – ne IDC [323]

Burma. Archaeological Survey. Director *see* REPORT OF THE DIRECTOR, FOR THE YEAR ENDING 1959

Burma. Archaeological Survey. Superintendent *see* REPORT OF THE SUPERINTENDENT, FOR THE YEAR ENDING 31ST MARCH, 1924

BURMA ECHO – Rangoon, Burma. -w. 18 May 1907-16 May 1908. 1 reel – 1 – uk British Libr Newspaper [072]

Burma. Economic and Social Board *see* PYIDWATHA, THE NEW BURMA: REPORT ON LONG-TERM PROGRAMME FOR ECONOMIC AND SOCIAL DEVELOPMENT 1952-1960?

Burma. Economic Planning Board *see* TWO-YEAR PLAN OF ECONOMIC DEVELOPMENT FOR BURMA

BURMA GAZETTE – (Lacks: 1924-50) – Rangoon, 1913-70 – 81r – 1 – us Ross [324]

BURMA. HISTORICAL DOCUMENTS AND MANUSCRIPTS *see* HISTORICAL DOCUMENTS AND MANUSCRIPTS

Burma. Knappen-Tippetts-Abbett Engineering Co., et al *see* PRELIMINARY REPORT ON ECONOMIC AND ENGINEERING SURVEY OF BURMA FOR BURMA ECONOMIC COUNCIL

Burma. Laws, Statutes, etc *see* THE LAND NATIONALIZATION BILL, 1948

BURMA LEGISLATIVE ABSTRACTS OF THE PROCEEDINGS OF THE COUNCIL OF THE LIEUTENANT-GOVERNOR OF BURMA... – Rangoon, 1897-1922. v1-3 – 51mf – I-38/2 – ne IDC [340]

Burma. Legislative Council *see* PROCEEDINGS

BURMA LEGISLATIVE COUNCIL PROCEEDINGS – (Index 1923-1936. v1-32) – Rangoon, 1923-1936. v1-32 – 314mf – I-39/2 – ne IDC [340]

BURMA LEGISLATIVE PROCEEDINGS OF THE FIRST SENATE – Rangoon, 1937-1940. v1-8 – 39mf – I-41/2 – ne IDC [340]

Burma. Lists of Monuments *see*
- AMENDED LIST OF ANCIENT MONUMENTS IN BURMA
- LIST OF ANCIENT MONUMENTS IN BURMA. MANDALAY DIVISION
- LIST OF OBJECTS OF ANTIQUARIAN AND ARCHAEOLOGICAL INTEREST IN BRITISH BURMA
- LIST OF OBJECTS OF ANTIQUARIAN AND ARCHAEOLOGICAL INTEREST IN UPPER BURMA

Burma. Ministry of National Planning *see*
- FOUR-YEAR PLAN OF CAPITAL EXPENDITURES 1956/57-1959/60
- SECOND FOUR-YEAR PLAN FOR THE UNION OF BURMA

BURMA NEWS – (Lacks vol.40:8) – v1-78. 1888-1965 – 7r – 1 – us A.T.L.A. [073]

BURMA, PAST AND PRESENT WITH PERSONAL REMINISCENCES OF THE COUNTRY / Fytche, A – London. 2v. 1878 – 9mf – 9 – ne IDC [950]

Burma Research Society *see* JOURNAL OF THE BURMA RESEARCH SOCIETY

BURMA RIGHTS MOVEMENT FOR ACTION – Bangkok. 8 docs. 1991 – 2mf – 9 – ne IDC [320]

Burma. Senate *see* PROCEEDINGS OF THE FIRST HOUSE OF REPRESENTATIVES BURMA LEGISLATURE

BURMA UNDER BRITISH RULE – AND BEFORE / Nisbet, J – London. 2v. 1901 – 11mf – 9 – ne IDC [950]

THE BURMAN – Rangoon, Burma. Dec 1945-Sept 1963 – 53r.00 – 1 – us L of C Photodup [072]

Burman, David *see* PEDIATRIC REVIEWS AND COMMUNICATIONS

Burman, J *see* FLORA MALABARICA

Burman, N L B *see*
- FLORA INDICA. LUGDUNI BATAVORUM, 1768
- SPECIMEN BOTANICUM DE GERANIIS

Burmann, Karl *see* IM DUNKLEN ERDTEIL

Burmeister, C H C *see*
- DE INSECTORUM SYSTEMATE NATURALI
- HANDBUCH DER ENTOMOLOGIE
- A MANUAL OF ENTOMOLOGY

Burmeister, H *see* THE ORGANIZATION OF TRILOBITES

Burmeister, J *see*
- HYPOMNEMATUM MUSICAE POETICAE
- MUSICA AUTOSCHEDIASIKOU, QUAE PER ALIQUOT ACCESSIONES IN GRATIAM PHILOMUSORUM
- MUSICAE PRACTICAE SIVE ARTIS CANENDI RATIO, QUAMVIS SUCCINCTA

THE BURMESE EMPIRE A HUNDRED YEARS AGO / Sangermano, V – Westminster, 1893 – 4mf – 9 – ne IDC [950]

THE BURMESE REVIEW AND MONDAY NEW TIMES – Rangoon: "Burmese Review" Press, [1948-1960]. [jan 9 1956-jul 25 1960] – 10r – us Res Libr [072]

Burn, A E *see*
- THE ATHANASIAN CREED AND ITS EARLY COMMENTARIES
- AN INTRODUCTION TO THE CREEDS AN TO THE TE DEUM
- NICETA OF REMESIANA

Burn, AU *see* FACSIMILES OF THE CREEDS FROM EARLY MANUSCRIPTS

Burn, John *see* A PRONOUNCING DICTIONARY OF THE ENGLISH LANGUAGE

Burn, Richard *see*
- LE JUGE A PAIX, ET OFFICIER DE PAROISSE, POUR LA PROVINCE DE QUEBEC
- A NEW LAW DICTIONARY

BURNABY ADVERTISER – Burnaby, British Columbia, CN. 1935-64 – 8r – 1 – cn Commonwealth Micro [073]

BURNABY BROADCAST – Burnaby, British Columbia, CN. 1926-35 – 2r – 1 – cn Commonwealth Micro [073]

BURNABY NEWS – British Columbia, CN. 1987- – 2r per yr – 1 – Can$57.00r – cn Commonwealth Micro [072]

BURNABY NEWS COURIER – Burnaby, British Columbia, CN. Jan 1944-Aug 1953 – 5r – 1 – cn Commonwealth Micro [072]

BURNABY POST – British Columbia, CN. May 1934-Nov 1937 – 1r – 1 – cn Commonwealth Micro [072]

BURNABY TODAY – British Columbia, CN. Oct 1979-1981 – 2r – 1 – cn Commonwealth Micro [072]

Burnakina, A A *see* ALMANAKH NA PROSHCHANIE

Burnap, George Washington *see* LECTURES ON THE SPHERE AND DUTIES OF WOMAN

Burnashev, VP *see* OPYT TERMINOLOGICHESKOGO SLOVARIA SEL'SKOGO KHOZIAISTVA...

Burnell, A C *see*
- HOBSON-JOBSON
- HOBSON-JOBSON; A GLOSSARY OF COLLOQUIAL ANGLO-INDIAN WORDS AND PHRASES

Burnes, A *see* TRAVELS INTO BOKHARA; BEING THE ACCOUNT OF A JOURNEY FROM INDIA TO CABOOL

Burnet, James Lord Monboddo *see*
- OF THE ORIGIN AND PROGRESS OF LANGUAGE
- ORIGIN AND PROGRESS OF LANGUAGE

Burnet, John *see* THE ETHICS OF ARISTOTLE

BURNETT BLADE – Burnett, NE. -w. Aug. 1884-Jan. 1887; Jun. 1888 – 1 – us NE Hist [071]

Burnett, Daniel Frederick *see* CASES ON THE LAW OF PRIVATE CORPORATIONS.

Burnett, Frances Hodgson *see* LITTLE LORD FAUNTLEROY

Burnett, James J *see* TENNESSEE PIONEER BAPTIST PREACHERS

Burnett, Madeline L *see* THE DEVELOPMENT OF AMERICAN HYMNODY, 1620-1900

BURNETT'S REPORTS / Wisconsin. Supreme Court – (For purposes of Pre-NRS coverage, all of Burnett's cases are included in Pinney) – 1v. 1839-1843 (all publ) – 3mf – 9 – $4.50 – LLMC 91-302 – us L.L.M.C. [340]

Burney, Charles *see*
- AN ACCOUNT OF THE MUSICAL PERFORMANCES IN WESTMINSTER ABBEY, AND THE PANTHEON
- AN ACCOUNT OF THE MUSICAL PERFORMANCES IN WESTMINSTER-ABBEY AND THE PANTHEON
- FOUR SONATAS OR DUETS
- FOUR SONATAS OR DUETS FOR TWO PERFORMERS ON ONE PIANO FORTE OR HARPSICHORD
- A GENERAL HISTORY OF MUSIC FROM THE EARLIEST AGES TO THE PRESENT PERIOD
- MEMOIRS OF THE LIFE AND WRITINGS OF THE ABATE METASTASIO
- DER MUSIK DOCTORS TAGEBUCH SEINER MUSIKALISCHEN REISEN
- ...NACHRICHT VON GEORG FRIEDRICH HAENDELS LEBENSUMSTAENDEN UND DER IHM ZU LONDON..
- NACHRICHT VON GEORG FRIEDRICH HAENDEL'S LEBENSUMSTAENDEN UND DER IHM ZU LONDON IN MAI UND JUNI 1784 ANGESTELLTEN GEDAECHTNISFEYER; AUS DEM ENGLISCHEN UBERZETZT VOM J. J. ESCHENBURG
- THE PRESENT STATE OF MUSIC IN FRANCE AND ITALY..
- THE PRESENT STATE OF MUSIC IN FRANCE AND ITALY
- THE PRESENT STATE OF MUSIC IN GERMANY, THE NETHERLANDS, AND UNITED PROVINCE
- THE PRESENT STATE OF MUSIC IN GERMANY, THE NETHERLANDS, AND UNITED PROVINCES..
- THE PRESENT STATE OF MUSIC IN GERMANY, THE NETHERLANDS, AND UNITED PROVINCES
- SIX CORNET PIECES, WITH AN INTRODUCTION FOR THE DIAPSONS AND A FUGUE

Burney, Charles Fox *see* OUTLINES OF OLD TESTAMENT THEOLOGY

BURNEY COLLECTION OF EARLY ENGLISH NEWSPAPERS – See also: Early English Newspapers – 1 – us Primary [072]

Burney, W *see* AN UNIVERSAL DICTIONARY OF THE MARINE: OR, A COPIOUS EXPLANATION OF THE TECHNICAL TERMS EMPLOYED IN THE CONSTRUCTION OF A SHIP. TO WHICH IS ANNEXED A TRANSLATION OF FRENCH SEA-TERMS

Burnfield, George *see* VOICES FROM THE ORIENT, OR, THE TESTIMONY OF THE MONUMENTS: OF THE RECENT HISTORICAL AND TOPOGRAPHICAL DISCOVERIES: AND OF THE CUSTOMS AND TRADITIONS OF THE PEOPLE IN THE ORIENT TO THE VERACITY OF THE SACRED RECORD

Burnham, Brian *see* VALUES EDUCATION

BURNHAM GAZETTE ETC – England. 1903-02 – 1r – 1 – uk British Libr Newspaper [072]

BURNHAM-ON-SEA GAZETTE AND HIGHBRIDGE EXPRESS – England, 1983 – 3r – 1 – uk British Libr Newspaper [072]

BURNIE ADVOCATE – Burnie, 1923-96 – 1 – at Pascoe [072]

Burnier, L *see* HISTOIRE LITTERAIRE DE L'EDUCATION MORALE ET RELIGIEUSE EN FRANCE ET DANS LA SUISSE ROMANDE

Burnier, Theophile *see* AMES PRIMITIVES

BURNING AND SHINING LIGHTS : A SOUVENIR OF PRIMITIVE METHODISTS RADIANT PERSONALITIES / Pearce, J – Halesowen, 1935. xv/104p – 2mf – 9 – ne IDC [240]

Burnouf, Emile *see* THE SCIENCE OF RELIGIONS

Burns, A *see* OBSERVATIONS ON SOME OF THE MOST FREQUENT AND IMPORTANT DISEASES OF THE HEART

Burns, A W *see* HISTORICAL RECORDS OF HILLSBOROUGH COUNTY, TAMPA, FLORIDA

Burns, Emile *see* SPAIN

Burns, John *see* A SERMON PREACHED IN THE PRESBYTERIAN CHURCH IN STAMFORD, UPPER CANADA, ON THE 3RD DAY OF JUNE, 1814: BEING THE DAY APPOINTED BY HIS HONOR THE PRESIDENT OF UPPER CANADA FOR A PROVINCIAL THANKSGIVING

Burns, Julia A *see* THE IMPACT OF THE LA CROSSE WELLNESS PROJECT ON THE HEALTH PROMOTION INVOLVEMENT OF COLLEGE STUDENTS RESIDING ON THE CAMPUS OF THE UNIVERSITY OF WISCONSIN-LA CROSSE
Burns, Martha J *see* TOURISM MARKETING ON THE WORLD WIDE WEB
Burns, Nelson *see* DIVINE GUIDANCE, OR, THE HOLY GUEST: A DISCUSSION OF THE BELIEVER'S PRIVILEGE IN CHRIST JESUS: THE HOLY SPIRIT AS GUIDE INTO ALL TRUTH: THE PENTECOSTAL BAPTISM, PHYSICAL RELIGIOUS MANIFESTATIONS, INDWELLING SIN.
BURNS NEWS – (Set incl. Harney County News (Burns)) – Burns, OR. -w. 8 May 1902-27 Dec 1929. – 3r – 1 – us U.O. Library [071]
Burns, R F *see* THE MAINE LIQUOR LAW
Burns, Robert *see*
- THE POETRY OF ROBERT BURNS
- THE SONGS OF ROBERT BURNS

BURNS TIMES-HERALD – Burns, OR. -w, -d. 22 Jul 1896-29 Dec 1977+. 33 rolls – 1 – us U.O. Library [071]
Burnside, William *see* THEORY OF GROUPS OF FINITE ORDER
BURNSVIEW BAPTIST CHURCH. SPARTANBURG COUNTY. SOUTH CAROLINA : CHURCH RECORDS – 1921-72 – 1 – 21.60 – us Baptist [240]
Buron, Edmond Joseph Pierre *see* LES RICHESSES DU CANADA
Burov, I Akov *see* CHTO OZNACHAET ZAKON O SVOBODE SOVESTII OTDELENII TSERKVI OT GOSUDARSTVA?
Burov, I Akovlosifovich *see* ORGANIZU ITE DEREVNIU!
Burque, Francois Xavier *see* PLURALITE DES MONDES HABITES CONSIDEREE AU POINT DE VUE NEGATIF
Burque, F-X. *see* ELEVATIONS POETIQUES
Burr *see* HISTORY OF HAMILTON AND CLAY COUNTIES
Burr, Aaron *see*
- THE PAPERS OF AARON BURR, 1756-1836
- REPORTS OF THE TRIALS OF COLONEL AARON BURR, (LATE VICE PRESIDENT OF THE UNITED STATES), FOR TREASON.

Burr, Agnes Rush *see* RUSSELL H. CONWELL
Burr, Anna Robeson *see*
- THE AUTOBIOGRAPHY
- RELIGIOUS CONFESSIONS AND CONFESSANTS

BURR BULLETIN – Burr, NE. -w. Sep. 1917-Sep. 1934 – 1 – us NE Hist [071]
Burr, Enoch Fitch *see* TEMPTED TO UNBELIEF
Burr, Horace *see*
- CATALOGUE AND ERRATA OF THE RECORDS OF HOLY TRINITY (OLD SWEDES) CHURCH
- THE RECORDS OF HOLY TRINITY (OLD SWEDES) CHURCH, WILMINGTON, DELAWARE 1697-1773

BURR OAK – Burr, NE. -w. Jun. 1896-Dec. 1896 – 1 – us NE Hist [071]
BURR STAR – Burr, NE. -w. Mar. 1897-Jul. 1897 – 1 – us NE Hist [071]
Burr, W K *see* LEAVES FROM MY PORTFOLIO
Burrage, Champlin *see*
- THE CHURCH CEVENANT IDEA
- THE CHURCH COVENANT IDEA
- THE EARLY ENGLISH DISSENTERS IN THE LIGHT OF RECENT RESEARCH (1550-1641)
- JOHN PENRY
- NAZARETH AND THE BEGINNINGS OF CHRISTIANITY
- NEW FACTS CONCERNING JOHN ROBINSON
- THE TRUE STORY OF ROBERT BROWNE (1550?-1633) FATHER OF CONGREGATIONALISM

Burrage, Henry S *see*
- THE ACT OF BAPTISM IN THE HISTORY OF THE CHRISTIAN CHURCH
- BAPTIST HYMN WRITERS AND THEIR HYMNS
- A HISTORY OF THE ANABAPTISTS IN SWITZERLAND
- HISTORY OF THE BAPTISTS IN MAINE
- A HISTORY OF THE BAPTISTS IN NEW ENGLAND

Burrage, Robert *see*
- A FREE MARKET IN HUMAN ORGANS
- IN DEFENCE OF COMPANIES

BURRANGONG ARGUS – Young, Jan 1 1908-Feb 8 1913 – 9 – at Pascoe [072]
Burrard, SC *see* A SKETCH OF THE GEOGRAPHY AND GEOLOGY OF THE HIMALAYA MOUNTAINS AND TIBET
THE BURRELL COLLECTION – (A visual catalogue of the complete collection of fine and applied art in the important new museum opened in 1983. 7000 captioned photographs. Printed index. Binder) – Glasgow – 104mf – 9 – $500.00 – 0-907006-48-5 – uk Mindata [700]
Burrell, David James *see* EARLY CHURCH: STUDIES IN THE ACTS OF THE APOSTLES
Burrell, Howard A *see* HISTORY OF WASHINGTON COUNTY
Burret, M *see*
- DIE AFRIKANISCHE ARTEN DER GATTUNG FICUS LINN
- MYRTACEEN STUDIEN

Burrill, Alexander *see* NEW LAW DICTIONARY
Burrill, Alexander Mansfield *see* A TREATISE ON THE LAW AND PRACTICE OF VOLUNTARY ASSIGNMENTS FOR THE BENEFIT OF CREDITORS.
BURRILLVILLE GAZETTE – Pascoag. R.I. 1880-1893 – 1 – us UMI [071]
BURRILLVILLE NEWS – Pascoag. R.I. 1892-1893 – 1 – us UMI [071]
BURRILLVILLE NEWS GAZETTE – Harrisville. R.I. 1894-1895 – 1 – us UMI [071]
Burris, F Holiday *see* THE TRINITY
Burritt, Elihu *see* CHIPS FROM MANY BLOCKS
Burroughs, Henry *see* A HISTORICAL ACCOUNT OF CHRIST CHURCH, BOSTON: AN ADDRESS, DELIVERED ON THE ONE HUNDRED AND FIFTIETH ANNIVERSARY OF THE OPENING OF THE CHURCH, DECEMBER 29TH, 1873
Burroughs, Joseph Washington *see* FARM JOURNALS
Burroughs, P E *see*
- THE CONVENTION SYSTEM OF TEACHER TRAINING
- MEET B. H. CARROLL

Burroughs, William Henry *see* A TREATISE ON THE LAW OF TAXATION AS IMPOSED BY THE STATES AND THEIR MUNICIPALITIES.
BURROUGHS WORLD – 1984- – 1,5,6,9 – us UMI [073]
Burrow, E *see* ELEMENTS OF CONCHOLOGY
Burrow, James *see* BURROW'S REPORTS
BURROWA NEWS – Jun 13 1874-Dec 19 1968 – 9 – at Pascoe [072]
Burrows, Charles Acton *see* THE ANNALS OF THE TOWN OF GUELPH, 1827-1877
Burrows, H. Lansing *see* MISCELLANEOUS MANUSCRIPT WORKS
Burrows, J L *see* A CHRISTIAN MERCHANT, A MEMOIR OF JAMES C. CRANE
Burrows, J. Lansing *see* AMERICAN BAPTIST REGISTER FOR 1852
BURROW'S REPORTS : REPORTS OF CASES ARGUED AND ADJUDGED IN THE COURT OF KIN'S BENCH DURING THE TIME OF LORD MANSFIELD... / Burrow, James – (All 5v were publ by Strahan in 1790, but v1-3 are called "4th ed corr". v4-5 are called "2nd ed corr". Title also known as: Burrow's Reports Tempore Mansfield) – 4th ed. v1-5. 1756-72. London: A Strahan, 1790 (all publ) – 33mf – 9 – $49.50 – LLMC 84-757 – us L.L.M.C. [324]
BURROW'S REPORTS TEMPORE MANSFIELD *see* BURROW'S REPORTS
BURSA MECMUASI – Bursa: Vilayet Matbaas, 1916-1920 – 9 – $35.00 – us MEDOC [956]
DES BURSCHEN HEIMKEHR : ODER, DER TOLLE HUND / Niebergall, Ernst Elias; ed by Fuchs, Georg – Darmstadt: A Bergstraesser, 1894 – 1r – 1 – us U.W. Library [820]
BURSCHEN HERAUS! : ROMAN AUS DER ZEIT UNSERER TIEFSTEN ERNIEDRIGUNG / Sperl, August – 11. Aufl. Muenchen: C H Beck, 1922 – 1 – us U.W. Library [830]
Burser, Joachim *see* HERBARIUM HORTUS SICCUS
Bursics, Zoltan *see* A MAGYAR BUNVADI ELJARASI JOG VAZLATA. 3. KIAD
Burskii, PD *see* ARMII A SVOBODNO I ROSSII
Burssens, Amaat *see*
- MANUEL DE TSHILUBA (KASAYI, CONGO BELGE)
- TONOLOGISCHE SCHETS VAN HET TSHILUBA (KAYASI, BELGISCH KONGO)

Burt, A W *see* A MANUAL OF ELEMENTARY PHONETICS
Burt, Armistead *see* LETTERS
BURT COUNTY HERALD – Tekamah, NE. -w. Jun 1892; Jan 1895-Jan 1896, scattered issues missing; Apr 1896-Oct 1897; Dec 1897-Aug 1942 – 1 – us NE Hist [071]
BURT COUNTY PLAINDEALER – Tekamah, NE. -w. Apr 1934-Nov 1948; Feb 1949 to date – 1 – us NE Hist [071]
BURT COUNTY PLAINDEALER – Tekamah. Neb. 1934-1966 – 1 – us UMI [071]
Burt, Henry Martyn *see* BURT'S ILLUSTRATED GUIDE OF THE CONNECTICUT VALLEY: CONTAINING DESCRIPTIONS OF MOUNT HOLYOKE, MOUNT MANSFIELD, WHITE MOUNTAIN, LAKE MEMPHREMAGOG, LAKE WILLOUGHBY, MONTREAL, QUEBEC, ETC
Burt, William D *see* LOCAL PROBLEMS: LIBERTARIAN SOLUTIONS
Burte, Hermann *see* SIEBEN REDEN
Burtin, Nicholas Victor *see* VIE DE CATHERINE TEKAKWITHA, VIERGE IROQUOISE: DECEDEE EN ODEUR DE SAINTETE A L'ANCIEN VILLAGE DU SAULT ST LOUIS, LE 17 AVRIL, 1680
Burtner, Patricia A *see* MECHANICAL AND MUSCLE ACTIVATION CHARACTERISTICS DURING CROUCH STANCE BALANCE IN CHILDREN WITH SPASTIC CEREBRAL PALSY
BURTON BANNER – Flint. Mich. 1945-1950 – 1 – us UMI [071]
Burton, Catherine J *see* THE HEART RATES OF ELEMENTARY CHILDREN DURING PHYSICAL EDUCATION CLASSES
BURTON CHRONICLE – England, 18 Oct 1860-Dec 1865 – 5r – 1 – uk British Libr Newspaper [072]
Burton, Clarence Monroe *see*
- THE CITY OF DETROIT, MICHIGAN 1701-1922
- IN THE FOOTSTEPS OF CADILLAC

BURTON DAILY MAIL – Burton-on-Trent, England. 1972-77 – 33r – 1 – uk British Libr Newspaper [072]
Burton, E *see* THREE PRIMERS PUT FORTH IN THE REIGN OF HENRY 8TH
Burton, E D *see* SOME PRINCIPLES OF LITERARY CRITICISM AND THEIR APPLICATION TO THE SYNOPTIC PROBLEM
Burton, Edwin H *see* THE LIFE AND TIMES OF BISHOP CHALLONER (1691-1781)
Burton, Ernest De Witt *see*
- THE LIFE OF CHRIST
- NOTES ON NEW TESTAMENT GRAMMAR
- AN OUTLINE HANDBOOK OF THE LIFE OF CHRIST
- RECORDS AND LETTERS OF THE APOSTOLIC AGE
- SHORT INTRODUCTION TO THE GOSPELS
- SYNTAX OF THE MOODS AND TENSES IN NEW TESTAMENT GREEK
- SYNTAX OF THE MOODS AND TENSES OF NEW TESTAMENT GREEK

Burton Family *see* REUNION RECORDS
Burton, H R *see* A MANUAL OF METHODISM AND OF WESLEYAN POLITY
BURTON HEIGHTS RECORD – Grand Rapids. Mich. -w. 1924-37, 1942-52 – 1 – us UMI [071]
Burton, I *see* APPROACHES TO THE STUDY OF THE ENVIRONMENTAL IMPLICATIONS OF CONTEMPORARY URBANIZATION
BURTON INDEPENDENT – Burton, NE. -w. Dec. 1911-Dec. 1912; May 1914-Aug. 1917 – 1 – us NE Hist [071]
Burton, Isabel Arundell *see* ARABIA, EGYPT, INDIA: A NARRATIVE OF TRAVEL
Burton, J B *see* LECTURES ON ENTOMOLOGY
Burton, John *see* THE FRENCH CANADIAN, IMPERIUM IN IMPERIO: A LECTURE ON OUR CREED AND RACE PROBLEM
Burton, Margaret E *see*
- THE EDUCATION OF WOMEN IN CHINA
- THE EDUCATION OF WOMEN IN JAPAN

Burton, Marion Le Roy *see* THE PROBLEM OF EVIL
Burton, Richard Francis *see*
- LETTERS FROM THE BATTLE-FIELDS OF PARAGUAY
- A MISSION TO GELELE, KING OF DAHOMEY
- VIKRAM AND THE VAMPIRE, OR, TALES OF HINDU DEVILRY
- VOYAGE AUX GRANDS LACS D'AFRIQUE ORIENTALE
- VOYAGE AUX GRANDS LACS DE L'AFRIQUE ORIENTALE
- WANDERINGS IN WEST AFRICA FROM LIVERPOOL TO FERNANDO PO

BURTON, THEODORE E., PAPERS, MS 3469 – (Personal and political correspondence, speeches and articles, campaign materials and business papers of Burton, a U.S. Congressman, U.S. Senator, attorney, and banker, and correspondence of Grace Burton, his niece) – 1870-1958 – 129r – 1 – us Western Res [920]
BURTONIAN – Tekamah, NE. -w. Jun 1874-Sept 1875; Feb 1876-Jul 1882; Sept 1883-Sept 1884; Sept 1885-Sept 1888; Oct 1892-Sept 1901 – 1 – us NE Hist [071]
BURT'S ILLUSTRATED GUIDE OF THE CONNECTICUT VALLEY: CONTAINING DESCRIPTIONS OF MOUNT HOLYOKE, MOUNT MANSFIELD, WHITE MOUNTAIN, LAKE MEMPHREMAGOG, LAKE WILLOUGHBY, MONTREAL, QUEBEC, ETC / Burt, Henry Martyn – Northampton, MA: New England Pub. Co., 1867. 05693. (Pre-1900 Canadiana) – 9 – cn C.I.H.M. [971]
Burtsev, Vladimir Lvovich *see*
- AZEF I LENIN
- IUBILEI PREDATELEI I UBI IT S, 1917-1927
- MOI VYZOV PREDATELIAMI IKH ZASHCHITNIKAM
- OTVI ETSTVENNOST TSARIA
- V BORBIE S BOLSHEVIKAMI I NIEMTSAMI

Burtt, Scott L *see* PHYSICAL ACTIVITY, CALCIUM INTAKE, BODY COMPOSITION AND STATURE AS PREDICTORS OF BONE INDICES IN COLLEGE-AGED MEN
BURUNDI : ANNUAIRE STATISTIQUE 1969-1975 / Burundi. Departement des Etudes et Statistiques – (Coll title: African Official Statistical Serials, 1867-1982) – 9mf – 9 – £75.00 – uk Chadwyck [960]
Burundi *see*
- PLAN DE DEVELOPPEMENT ECONOMIQUE ET SOCIAL
- PLAN QUINQUENNAL DE DEVELOPPEMENT ECONOMIQUE ET SOCIAL DU BURUNDI, 1968-1972

Burundi. Departement des Etudes et Statistiques *see* BURUNDI
Burwash, Nathaniel *see*
- A HANDBOOK OF THE EPISTLE OF ST PAUL TO THE ROMANS: BASED ON THE REVISED VERSION AND THE REVISER'S TEXT: FOR THE USE OF STUDENTS AND BIBLE CLASSES
- MANUAL OF CHRISTIAN THEOLOGY ON THE INDUCTIVE METHOD
- THE RELATION OF CHILDREN TO THE FALL, ATONEMENT AND THE CHURCH

Burwell, Cynthia B *see* THE RELATIONSHIP BETWEEN ADOLESCENT SMOKING BEHAVIOR AND PEER INFLUENCE
BURWELL MASCOT – Burwell, NE. Jun. 1892; Aug. 1895-Oct. 1903 – 1 – us NE Hist [071]
BURWELL TRIBUNE – Burwell, NE. -w. Feb.1899-Aug. 1902; Oct. 1903-Jan. 1904; Oct. 1908-May 1931; Jul. 1931-Feb. 1933; Jun. 1933- – 1 – us NE Hist [071]
BURY AND NORWICH POST – (Missing: 1896) – Bury St Edmunds, England. 1850-61; 1870-1901 – 35r – 1 – uk British Libr Newspaper [072]
BURY FREE PRESS – (Missing: Jan 1871-72) – Bury St Edmunds, England. Jul 1855-1901; 1911-67; 1970-75; 1977- – 224+ r – 1 – uk British Libr Newspaper [072]
Bury, J B *see*
- THE CONSTITUTION OF THE LATER ROMAN EMPIRE
- A HISTORY OF FREEDOM OF THOUGHT
- A HISTORY OF THE EASTERN ROMAN EMPIRE FROM THE FALL OF IRENE TO THE ACCESSION OF BASIL I. (A.D. 802-867)
- A HISTORY OF THE LATER ROMAN EMPIRE
- AN INAUGURAL LECTURE
- THE LIFE OF ST PATRICK AND HIS PLACE IN HISTORY

Bury, Karin *see* DER BILDHAUER KURT LEHMANN
Bury, Richard de *see* PHILOBIBLON
BURY ST EDMUNDS MERCURY – Ipswich, England. 7 Aug 1986-Jun 1991; Jul 1992- – 26+ r – 1 – uk British Libr Newspaper [072]
BURYING GROUND OF SHARON, CONNECTICUT & ANEMIA & NORTH EAST NEW YORK / Litchfield County. Connecticut – Item I. SW16-0220 – 5 – us A.G.L.L. [920]
BURZENLAENDER BOTE – Kronstadt (Brasov), Rumaenien. 20 Okt-12 Nov 1921 – 1r – 1 – gw Mikrofilm [949]

BURZHAZIIA I POMESHCHIKI V 1917 GODU : CHASTNYE SOVESHCHANIIA CHLENOV GOS. DUMY / ed by Drezen, A K – M., L., 1932. 328p – 4mf – 9 – ne IDC [320]
BURZHUAZIIA I TSARIZM V PERVOI RUSSKOI REVOLIUTSII / Chermenskii, E D – 2nd ed. M., 1970. 448p – 5mf – 9 – ne IDC [320]
BURZHUAZNYE I MELKOBURZHUAZNYE PARTII ROSII V OKTIABR'SKOI REVOLIUTSII I GRAZDANSKOI VOINE : MATERIALY SIMPOZIUMA V G. KALININE I G. TSKHALTUBO / ed by Komin, V V – M., 1980. 156p – 2mf – 9 – ne IDC [320]
BUS AND TRUCK TRANSPORT – (Cont by Truck Fleet at v63 1987) – Toronto. v46-62. 1970-86 – 9 – Can$28.00y – cn Micromedia [380]
BUS AND TRUCK TRANSPORT *see* TRUCK FLEET
Bus, N *see* MATERIALY DLIA FLORY KAVKAZA. FLORA CAUCASICA CRITICA
Busby, Richard *see* A SHORT INSTITUTION OF GRAMMAR
O BUSCAPE : ORGAM CRITICO – Manaos, Amazonas. 15-22 Out 1899 – 1,5,6 – bl Biblioteca [072]
Busch, H *see* DER PFLICHTTEIL IM DEUTSCHEN UND ENGLISCHEN RECHT
Busch, I *see* BIKKUREI HA-ITTIM HA-HADASHIM
Busch, Ioannes *see* DES AUGUSTINERPROPSTES IOANNES BUSCH
Busch, K A *see* WILLIAM JAMES ALS RELIGIONSPHILOSOPH
Busch, M *see* RIDALA ARKAMISE AJALUGU-THE HISTORY OF THE REVIVAL IN RIDALA
Buscher, Heide *see* DIE FUNKTION DER NEBENFIGUREN IN FONTANES ROMANEN
Busdugan, C N *see*
- DU MARIAGE DES ROUMAINS A L'ETRANGER...
- FORMA TESTAMENTELOR IN DREPTUL INTERNATIONAL PRIVAT

Busenbaum, H *see* THEOLOGIA MORALIS...
Busey, J L *see* CONDENSATION OF PROGRESS AND POVERTY BY HENRY GEORGE
BUSH AND QUILL – Owen Sound, 1974-1975 – 1r – 1 – cn Preston [971]
Bush, Annie Forbes *see* MEMOIRS OF THE QUEENS OF FRANCE
Bush, George *see* NOTES, CRITICAL AND PRACTICAL, ON THE BOOK OF GENESIS
Bush, George P *see*
- TECHNOLOGICAL CHANGE IN PRINTING AND PUBLISHING
- TECHNOLOGY AND COPYRIGHT
- TECHNOLOGY AND COPYRIGHT: SOURCES AND MATERIALS

BUSH NEGRO ART / Dark, Phillip John Crosskey – [New Haven] 1950 – us Res Libr [700]
Bush, P S et al *see* REPLY TO: BRIEF HISTORICAL SKETCH OF THE WESTERN BAPTIST THEOLOGICAL INSTITUTE IN COVINGTON, KENTUCKY BY THE BOARD OF TRUSTEES, P.S.BUSH, J.M. FROST AND LEWIS ROACH 1850
BUSH RIVER BAPTIST CHURCH. NEWBERRY COUNTY. SOUTH CAROLINA : CHURCH RECORDS – (History, 1771-1933. 65p) – 1 reel – 1 – $5.00 – us Baptist [240]
BUSH RIVER, SOUTH CAROLINA : CHURCH RECORDS – 1791-1945 – 1 – 32.00 – us Baptist [240]
BUSHE COMMISSION – Cmd 4623. 1937 – 1 – uk Microform Academic [960]
Bushnell, Horace *see*
- THE CHARACTER OF JESUS
- THE CHARACTER OF JESUS: FORBIDDING HIS POSSIBLE CLASSIFICATION WITH MEN
- CHRIST IN THEOLOGY
- FORGIVENESS AND LAW
- GOD IN CHRIST
- MORAL USES OF DARK THINGS
- NATURE AND THE SUPERNATURAL, AS TOGETHER CONSTITUTING THE ONE SYSTEM OF GOD
- THE VICARIOUS SACRIFICE, GROUNDED IN PRINCIPLES OF UNIVERSAL OBLIGATION
- WOMAN'S SUFFRAGE: THE REFORM AGAINST NATURE
- WORK AND PLAY; OR, LITERARY VARIETIES

BUSHNELL RECORD – Bushnell, NE. -w. Jul. 1919-Nov. 1944 – 1 – us NE Hist [071]
Busia, Kofi Abrefa *see* REPORT ON A SOCIAL SURVEY OF SEKONDI-TAKORADI
BUSINESS ADVOCATE: A U.S. CHAMBER OF COMMERCE PUBLICATION – 1984- – 1,5,6,9 – us UMI [380]
BUSINESS AMERICA – v. 1-. 1978- – 1,5,6,9 – us UMI [380]
BUSINESS AND FAMILY PAPERS RE ACTIVITIES IN THE NEW HEBRIDES / Zeitler, Adolf – 1899-1935 – 1r – 1 – PMB1091 – at Pacific Mss [920]
BUSINESS AND FINANCE REPORT – (Cont: Bank of Nova Scotia Monthly Review) – Toronto, 1983-89 – 5 – Price varies – cn Micromedia [073]
BUSINESS AND FINANCE REPORT *see* BANK OF NOVA SCOTIA MONTHLY REVIEW
BUSINESS AND FINANCIAL PAPERS, 1780-1939 : SELECTED TITLES FROM THE BODLEIAN LIBRARY, OXFORD AND THE BRITISH LIBRARY NEWSPAPER LIBRARY, COLINDALE. SERIES ONE: INTERNATIONAL TRADE / ed by Trebilcock, Clive – (Pt 1: 11 titles including Anglo-Japanese Gazette 1902-1909 30r $3,500.00. Pt 2: The African Review, 1892-1904 23r $2,700.00. With guides) – Marlborough: Adam Matthew Publications, 1991 – 1 – uk Matthew [380]
BUSINESS AND FINANCIAL PAPERS, 1780-1939 : SELECTED TITLES FROM THE BODLEIAN LIBRARY, OXFORD AND THE BRITISH LIBRARY NEWSPAPER LIBRARY, COLINDALE. SERIES THREE: INDUSTRIAL ENTERPRISE – (Pt 1: Oil News, 1912-39 24r $2,800.00. Pt 2: Building World, 1895-1918 17r $2,000.00. With guides) – Marlborough: Adam Matthew Publications, 1996 – 1 – uk Matthew [338]
BUSINESS AND FINANCIAL PAPERS, 1780-1939 : SELECTED TITLES FROM THE BODLEIAN LIBRARY, OXFORD AND THE BRITISH LIBRARY NEWSPAPER LIBRARY, COLINDALE. SERIES TWO: THE ECONOMIC IMPACT OF SCIENTIFIC AND TECHNICAL CHANGE – (Pt 1: The Mechanical Engineer, 1897-1907 22r $2,600.00. Pt 2: The Mechanical Engineer, 1908-1917 16r $1,900.00. With guides) – Marlborough: Adam Matthew Publications – 1 – uk Matthew [330]
BUSINESS AND HEALTH – (1985-. 5,6,9) – v1-. 1983- – 1 – us UMI [380]
BUSINESS AND LAW, OR THE CAREFUL MAN'S GUIDE : A COMPLETE LEGAL AND BUSINESS COMPENDIUM / Roe, E T & Loomis, Elihu G – Boston/Chicago: Hertel, Jenkins & Co, 1907 – 8mf – 9 – $12.00 – LLMC 92-192 – us L.L.M.C. [340]
BUSINESS ARCHIVES COUNCIL LIBRARY – 9 – £50.00 – uk Business [650]
BUSINESS AS A SYSTEM OF POWER / Brady, Robert Alexander – New York: Columbia University Press, 1943. xx,340p. Bibliog – 1 – us U.W. Library [380]
BUSINESS ATLANTA – (v.8- 1979- 5,6,9) – v.7-. 1978- – 1 – us UMI [073]
BUSINESS BANKRUPTCY / Warren, Elizabeth – Washington: FJC, 1993 – 2mf – 9 – $3.00 – LLMC 95-383 – us L.L.M.C. [340]
BUSINESS BOOKKEEPING AND PRACTICE / Sadler, W H & Rowe, H M – (Includes index) – Baltimore: Sadler-Rowe Co, 1894 – 3mf – 9 – $4.50 – LLMC 92-128 – us L.L.M.C. [340]
BUSINESS COMPUTER SYSTEMS – 1982- – 1,5,6,9 – us UMI [073]
BUSINESS COMPUTING – 1983- – 1,5,6,9 – us UMI [073]
BUSINESS COMPUTING *see* REFERENCE
BUSINESS COMPUTING AND COMMUNICATIONS – Nov 1983- – 1,5,6,9 – us UMI [073]
BUSINESS CONDITIONS DIGEST – (1972- . 5,6. 1975- . 9) – 1961- – 1 – us UMI [650]
THE BUSINESS CORPORATIONS LAW. / Jones, Dwight Arven – 5th ed. New York, Baker, Voorhis, 1897. 129 p. LL-1327 – 1 – us L of C Photodup [340]
THE BUSINESS CORPORATIONS LAW...AND OTHER LAWS CONCERNING BUSINESS CORPORATIONS IN THE STATE OF NEW YORK / Jones, Dwight Arven – 3rd ed. New York: Baker, Voorhis, 1893.120p. LL-689 – 1 – us L of C Photodup [340]
BUSINESS CORRESPONDENCE : ACCOUNTS AND WAGE BOOKS / Ussher, J – Nguna, New Hebrides, 1915-19; 1935-43 – 1r – 1 – PMB 1131 – at Pacific Mss [650]
BUSINESS CYCLE DEVELOPMENTS *see* BCD BUSINESS CONDITIONS DIGEST
BUSINESS DAY – Johannesburg, South Africa. 1 May 1985- – 89r – 1 – sa Microfile [072]
BUSINESS DIRECTORY OF INDONESIA 1954-1955 – Djakarta, 1955 – 15mf – SE-615/1 – ne IDC [380]
BUSINESS EDUCATION FORUM – (1970- . 5,6. 1975- . 9) – 1947- – 1 – us UMI [380]
BUSINESS EDUCATION WORLD – (1967- 5,6. 1969- 9) – 1920- – 1 – us UMI [380]
BUSINESS GAZETTE – London, UK. 22 Nov 1862-27 Jun 1863 – 1/2r – 1 – uk British Libr Newspaper [072]
BUSINESS, GOVERNMENT AND ALL OF US / Ellis, C A A – 116p. Together with: How to Reduce Taxes, 12p; How to Advance Liberty – A Learning, Not a Seeling Problem, 16p. By Leonard E. Read. 1 fiche (24x) – 9 – 1.00f – at Libertarian Micro [320]
BUSINESS GRADUATE – (1984-. 5,6,9) – v1-. 1970- – 1 – us UMI [380]
BUSINESS GUIDE BOOK TO DJAKARTA, 1969-1971 – (Annual. Missing: 1969) – 5mf – 9 – SE-1374/1 – ne IDC [380]
A BUSINESS HISTORY COLLECTION – (Information from 50 serial publications representing American economy during the 20th century) – 9 – us Primary [380]
BUSINESS HISTORY REVIEW – (1970- . 5,6. 1976- . 9) – 1- 1926- – 1 – us UMI [900]
BUSINESS HORIZONS – (1971- . 5,6. 1975- . 9) – v. 1- 1958- – 1 – us UMI [380]
BUSINESS IDEA PUBLICATIONS / Lamp Light Press Staff – 3mf – 9 – $45.00 – 0-917593-30-8 – us Continnuus [338]
BUSINESS INDEX – Monthly cumulative index of over 700 business, trade and industry periodicals, plus business-related articles from newspapers, general and legal publications – 5,17 – us I.A.C. [380]
BUSINESS JAPAN – (1982-. 1,5,6,9) – v16-. 1971- – 1 – us UMI [073]
BUSINESS LAW / Hirschl, Samuel D – Chicago: LaSalle Extension University, 1927 – 6mf – 9 – $9.00 – LLMC 96-050 – us L.L.M.C. [340]
BUSINESS LAW / Pomeroy, Dwight Abel – (Manual to accompany Business Law, 2nd ed. Cincinnati, 1939. 236p. LL-1006) – 2d ed. Cincinnati: South-Western 1939. 906p. L.C. copy imperfect: p. 93-98 wanting. LL-1006 – 1 – us L of C Photodup [340]
BUSINESS LAW CASE METHOD. / Commerce Clearing House – Chicago, 1915 7 v. LL-885 – 1 – us L of C Photodup [340]
BUSINESS LAW FOR BUSINESS MEN, STATE OF CALIFORNIA. / Bledsoe, Anthony Jennings – 9th ed. San Francisco, Business Law Publishing Co., 1912. 1021 p. LL-889 – 1 – us L of C Photodup [340]
BUSINESS LAW JOURNAL – University of Miami. v1-4. 1990-94 – 9 – $29.00 set – us Hein [340]
BUSINESS LAW REVIEW – v1-15. 1960-94 – 9 – $525.00 set – us Hein [340]
BUSINESS LAW REVIEW – (v.12-14. 1979-81. 5,6,9) – v.8-14. 1975-81 – 1 – us UMI [380]
BUSINESS LAWYER (ABA) – v1-51. 1946-96 – 1,5,6 – $1,620.00 – us Hein [073]
BUSINESS LIBRARY REVIEW : AN INTERNATIONAL JOURNAL / ed by Whitten, David O & Whitten, Bess E – 9,5,1 – us Gordon [338]
BUSINESS LIFE IN WESTERN CANADA – Edmonton. v1-11. 1973-83 – 9 – Can$20.00y – cn Micromedia [073]
BUSINESS MANAGEMENT TRAINING / Indonesia. Bandung – SE-4401 1 – 9 – ne IDC [650]
THE BUSINESS MAN'S ADVISER. / Butts, Isaac Ridler – Boston, Butts, 1854. 10, 132, vi, 120, iv, 108 p. LL-246 – 1 – us L of C Photodup [340]
BUSINESS MAN'S COMMERCIAL LAW LIBRARY / Bolles, George S – NY: Double-Day/Collier. 6v. 1924 – 18mf – 9 – $27.00 – LLMC 92-173 – us L.L.M.C. [340]
THE BUSINESS MAN'S ENCYCLOPEDIA : THE BUSINESS MAN'S BRAIN, PARTNERS, CONTRACTS, COMMERCIAL USAGE, BUSINESS LAW, FOREIGN TRADE, SAVING SYSTEMS – 16th rev ed. Chicago etc: A W Shaw Co, 1927 – 6mf – 9 – $9.00 – LLMC 96-058 – us L.L.M.C. [650]
THE BUSINESS MAN'S LAW CABINET / Butts, Isaac Ridler – v1. 1857-59 – 9 – 75.00 – us Opus [380]
BUSINESS MANUAL: COMPRISING TWENTY-FIVE CHAPTERS ON BUSINESS LAW; ALSO VARIOUS FORMS OF LEGAL AND BUSINESS DOCUMENTS, TOGETHER WITH A SYSTEM OF FARM ACCOUNTS. / Anger, William Henry – St. Catharines, Ont., 1892? 02406. (Pre-1900 Canadiana) – 9 – cn C.I.H.M. [340]
BUSINESS MARKETING *see* ADVERTISING AGE'S BUSINESS MARKETING
BUSINESS MICROWORLD – 1984- – 1,5,6,9 – us UMI [510]
BUSINESS MN – 1992 – 1 – sz Infoprint [947]
BUSINESS NEWS – Djakarta. Indonesia. (Summary in English). Jul 1958- – 1 – us UMI [072]
BUSINESS NEWS ANALISA – Djakarta. Indonesia. Aug. 1958- – 1 – us UMI [072]
BUSINESS NEWSBANK – 1985-. Monthly index with cumulations – 9 – us NewsBank [650]
BUSINESS OF BOOK PUBLISHING : A MANAGEMENT TRAINING COURSE – 1990 – xi/164p – 9 – 92-3-102636-4 – Co-published with Book House Training Centre, London – fr UNESCO [650]
THE BUSINESS OF THE SUPREME COURT: A STUDY IN THE FEDERAL JUDICIAL SYSTEM / Frankfurter, Felix – New York: Macmillan, 1927. 349p. LL-1174 – 1 – us L of C Photodup [340]
THE BUSINESS OF TRAVEL: A FIFTY YEARS' RECORD OF PROGRESS / Rae, William Fraser – 1841-Leicester to Loughborough (12 miles) 1891-all over the globe. London, New York: T. Cook and Son, 1891. History of the origin and progress of Thomas Cook and Son company, 22 July 1897 – 1 – us U.W. Library [910]
BUSINESS OWNER – v. 1-. 1977- – 1,5,6,9 – us UMI [650]
BUSINESS PRESS – Las Vegas, NV. 1984-1994 – 8r – 1 – $400.00 – B06062 – us Library Micro [071]
BUSINESS QUARTERLY – (v58 1993/94 Can$28.00y) – London. v19-59. 1954-1994/95 – 9 – Can$20.00y – cn Micromedia [380]
BUSINESS RECORDS / Clark, Gabriel Penn – 1853-1920, Relate to Platte county, Missouri, and Shawnee county, KS – 1 – us KS Hist [380]
BUSINESS REVIEW / Bank of Montreal – (Cont: Bank of Montreal Business Review) – Montreal, 1984-92 – 9 – Can$20.00y – cn Micromedia [073]
BUSINESS REVIEW *see* BANK OF MONTREAL BUSINESS REVIEW
BUSINESS REVIEW WEEKLY – 1980- – 9 – at Pascoe [073]
BUSINESS STATISTICS – (v.22-. 1979- 5,6,9) – v.1-. 1951- – 1 – us UMI [310]
BUSINESS TALKS – Tuscarora, NV. 1908 – 1r – 1 – $50.00 – U04772 – us Library Micro [071]
THE BUSINESS TAX – Ottawa, 1891?. 03022. (Pre-1900 Canadiana) – 9 – cn C.I.H.M. [336]
BUSINESS TIMES – 1 – F2,095.00 – sz Infoprint [072]
BUSINESS TIMES – 1984- – 24r per y – 1 – inquire – us Ross [072]
BUSINESS TIMES – (Continuation offered) – Kuala Lumpur, Malaysia. 1977-92 – 83r – 1 – us L of C Photodup [072]
BUSINESS TIMES – Dar es Salaam: Business Times Ltd, nov 4 1988-jul 12/18 1996 – us Res Libr [650]
BUSINESS TOPICS: A COLLECTION OF TEXTS WITH NOTES / ed by Kho, K G – SE-6499 1. v. 1 only. 1964.n – 9 – ne IDC [380]
BUSINESS WEEK – (1965- . 5,6. 1960- . 9) – v. 1- 1929- – 1 – us UMI [380]
BUSINESS WOMAN – Toronto. v. 1-4, no. 10. Nov 1926-Oct 1929. Incomplete – 1 – us NY Public [073]
BUSINESSWEEK'S GUIDE TO CAREERS – (1985- . 5,6,9) – v1- . 1983- – 1 – us UMI [073]
Busk, Hans *see* THE NAVIES OF THE WORLD
Buslaev, Fedor Ivanovich *see*
- NARODNAIA POEZIIA
- RUSSKII LITSEVOI APOKALIPSIS

Busnelli, Juan *see* MANUAL DE TEOSOFIA O BREVE ESTUDIO CRITICO DE LAS DOCTRINAS TEOSOFICAS. MEJICO, 1929
Buss *see* HISTORY OF DODGE AND WASHINGTON COUNTIES
DAS DIE BUSS REWE ODER ERKENTNIS DES ZORNS VND DER SUENDEN EIGENTLICH ALLEIN AUS DEM GESETZ... / Flacius Illyricus d.A E, M – [Jhena, 1559] – 1mf – 9 – ne IDC [240]
DIE BUSSBUECHER UND DIE BUSSDISCIPLIN DER KIRCHE / Schmitz, Hermann Joseph – (Includes index) – Mainz: Franz Kirchheim, 1883 – 2mf – 9 – 0-8370-7424-X – 1986-1424 – us A.T.L.A. [240]
Busse, Carl *see*
- NOVALIS' LYRIK
- UEBER ZEIT UND DICHTUNG

Busse, CF de *see* EXAMEN IURIS GENTIUM...

Bussell, FW *see*
- CHRISTIAN THEOLOGY AND SOCIAL PROGRESS
- MARCUS AURELIUS AND THE LATER STOICS
- THE SCHOOL OF PLATO

Busshoff, L et al *see* CURRICULA AND LIFELONG EDUCATION

A BUSSOLA : JORNAL CATHOLICO SEMANAL – Juiz de Fora, 13 Jun 1914; May, 29 Jul 1916 – 1,5,6 – bl Biblioteca [072]

Busson, H *see* LES SOURCES ET LE DEVELOPPEMENT DU RATIONALISME DANS LA LITTERATURE FRANCAISE DE LA RENAISSANCE (1533-1601)

BUSSTUFEN UND KATECHUMEN-TATSKLASSEN / Schwartz, Eduard – Strassburg: K.J. Truebner, 1911 – 1mf – us A.T.L.A. [240]

Bustamante, Carlo M de *see* HORRIBLES CRUELDADES DE LOS CONQUISTADORES DE MEXICO...

Bustamante y Sirven, A S de *see*
- EL MAR TERRITORIAL
- THE TERRITORIAL SEA

Bustamente, A S de *see* PROGRAMAS ASIGNATURAS DE DERECHO INTERNACIONAL PUBLICO...

[Bustamente, D S] *see* LOS CONFLICTOS INTERNACIONALES Y EL PANAMERICANISMO

THE BUSTAN AL-UKUL / Ibn al Fayyumi, Nathanael – New York, 1908. 1 fiche – 9 – us A.T.L.A. [290]

EL BUSTO DE ELISA / Hurtado, Antonio – 1871 – 9 – 1.50f – sp Bibl Santa Ana [830]

Buston, Thomas Fowell *see* THE AFRICAN SLAVE TRADE

Bustos de Olmedilla, G *see* EL MONSTRUO HORRIBLE DE GRECIA MORTAL ENEMIGO DEL HOMBRE. LAS SANGRIAS

BUSY BEE – Weston. West Virginia. 1890-1898 – 1 – us UMI [071]

BUSY MAN'S MAGAZINE – v1-21. 1896-1911. Continued by: MacLean's, Mar 1911- – 1 – us UMI [073]

Butcher, Bernard L *see* HISTORY OF UPPER MONONGAHELA VALLEY

Butcher, Edith Louisa *see* THE STORY OF THE CHURCH OF EGYPT

Butcher, SD *see* PIONEER HISTORY OF CUSTER COUNTY

Butcher, W W *see* W.W. BUTCHER'S CANADIAN NEWSPAPER DIRECTORY

BUTCHER WORKER : 1937-1942 / Hebrew Butcher Workers' Union – (Coll title: Labor Union Periodicals, Pt 3) – 1996 – 3r – 1 – $405.00 – 1-55655-625-X – us UPA [331]

BUTCHER WORKMAN : 1915-1960 / Amalgamated Meat Cutters and Butcher Workmen of North America – (Coll title: Labor Union Periodicals, Pt 3) – 1996 – 8r – 1 – $1,080.00 – 1-55655-620-9 – us UPA [331]

BUTE BROADSIDES IN THE HOUGHTON LIBRARY, HARVARD UNIVERSITY – 1 – us Primary [090]

BUTEMAN – 1 – £42.00r – uk Scot News [072]

UN BUTEN SINGT DE NACHTIGALL : UN ANNERE BELLER UN GESCHICHTEN UP MOENSTERLAENNSK BLATT / Wagenfeld, Karl – Essen-Ruhr: Fredebeul und Koenen, 1912 – 1r – 1 – us U.W. Library [430]

BUTESHIRE, 1837 : BRITISH ISLES CENSUS DIRECTORIES PROJECT, SCOTLAND. VOL 32 – 1mf – 9 – A$9.00 – at Vine [941]

Butin, Romain F *see* TEN NEQUDOTH OF THE TORAH...THE EXTRAORDINARY POINTS OF THE PENTATEUCH

Butler, A G *see* REVISION OF THE HETEROCEROUS LEPIDOPTERA OF THE FAMILY SPHINGIDAE

Butler, A J *see* THE CHURCHES AND MONASTERIES OF EGYPT AND SOME NEIGHBOURING COUNTRIES, ATTRIBUTED TO ABU SALIH, THE ARMENIAN

Butler, A O *see* WHAT MOSES SAW OR HEARD, OR, THE IDEA OF GOD IN THE OLD TESTAMENT

Butler, Alford Augustus *see* HOW TO STUDY THE LIFE OF CHRIST

Butler, C *see*
- THE LAUSIAC HISTORY OF PALLADIUS
- THE LIFE OF HUGO GROTIUS...

Butler, C E *see* OLD TESTAMENT WORD STUDIES

Butler, C H *see* THE TREATY-MAKING POWER OF THE UNITED STATES

Butler, Carlos A *see* THE TEMPLE IN THE TIME OF CHRIST AS RESTORED BY HEROD

Butler, Charles *see*
- THE FEMININ 'MONARCHI', OR THE HISTORI OF THE BEE'S
- THE PRINCIPLES OF MUSIK, IN SINGING AND SETTING..

Butler, Clement Moore *see*
- INNER ROME
- THE REFORMATION IN SWEDEN
- THE REFORMATION IN SWEDEN; ITS RISE, PROGRESS, AND CRISIS; AND ITS TRIUMPH UNDER CHARLES IX
- ST. PAUL IN ROME: LECTURES

BUTLER COUNTY CITIZEN – Pennsylvania. -d and -w 1876-1919 – 13 – $25.00r – us I.M.R. [071]

BUTLER COUNTY DEMOCRAT – El Dorado. Kan. 1881-91; 1913-15 – 1 – us UMI [071]

BUTLER COUNTY DEMOCRAT – Hamilton, OH. 18 Aug 1887 – 1r – 1 – us Western Res [071]

BUTLER COUNTY DEMOCRAT – Hamilton. Ohio. 1875-1891; 1894-1896-1922 – 1 – us UMI [071]

BUTLER COUNTY NEWS RECORD – Zelienople. Pa. 1942- – 1 – us UMI [071]

BUTLER COUNTY PRESS – David City, NE. -w. except -sw. 1899-1900. Sep. 1891; Jul. 1892; Sep. 1895-Dec. 1953 – 1 – us NE Hist [071]

BUTLER COUNTY REPUBLICAN – David City, NE. -w. Feb. 1897-Jun. 1898 – 1 – us NE Hist [071]

BUTLER COUNTY SIGNAL – Middletown. Ohio. 1902-1904 – 1 – us UMI [071]

BUTLER COUNTY TELEGRAPH : WEEKLY DEMOCRATIC NEWSPAPER – Hamilton, OH. 29 Apr-11 Nov 1847 – 1r – 1 – us Western Res [071]

BUTLER COUNTY'S EIGHTY YEARS 1885-1935 / Stratford, Jessie P – 1934. Kansas Reel 7. (The Cox Library Collection) – 5 – us Americana [978]

BUTLER DEMOCRATIC – Butler, PA., 1898-1901 – 13 – $25.00r – us I.M.R. [071]

Butler, E A *see* A CATALOGUE OF THE BIRDS OF THE SOUTHERN PORTION OF THE BOMBAY PRESIDENCY

Butler, E J *see* FUNGI AND DISEASE IN PLANTS

Butler, Eric D *see* COMMUNISM CAN BE DEFEATED WITHOUT A THIRD WORLD WAR

Butler, G *see* STUDIES IN STATECRAFT

Butler, G G *see* INTERNATIONAL LAW AND AUTOCRACY

BUTLER HERALD – Butler, PA., 1901-1912 – 13 – $25.00r – us I.M.R. [071]

Butler, J *see*
- SKETCH OF ASSAM, WITH SOME ACCOUNT OF THE HILL TRIBES
- TRAVELS AND ADVENTURES IN THE PROVINCE OF ASSAM, DURING A RESIDENCE OF FOURTEEN YEARS

Butler, J M *see* SCRAPBOOK

Butler, James, First Duke of OrmondeButler, James Second Duke of Ormonde *see* CORRESPONDENCE, 1610-88 AND 1665-1745

Butler, John P *see* INDEX TO THE PAPERS OF THE CONTINENTAL CONGRESS, 1774-1789

Butler, Joseph *see*
- THE ANALOGY OF RELIGION NATURAL AND REVEALED
- ANALOGY OF RELIGION NATURAL AND REVEALED

Butler, Josephine E *see*
- CATARINE OF SIENA
- THE DAWN
- SHIELD
- STORM-BELL

Butler, Josephine Elizabeth Grey *see* WOMAN'S PLACE IN CHURCH WORK

Butler, Marian *see* CANADIAN BOOKS IN PRINT

Butler, Martin *see* MAPLE LEAVES AND HEMLOCK BRANCHES: A COLLECTION OF POEMS

BUTLER PLANTATION PAPERS : THE PAPERS OF PIERCE BUTLER (1744-1822) AND SUCCESSORS, FROM THE HISTORICAL SOCIETY OF PENNSYLVANIA – (Guide included) – 1996 – 21r – 1 – $2500.00 – uk Matthew [976]

Butler, Samuel *see*
- THE FAIR HAVEN
- LIFE AND HABIT

Butler, Sharon *see* A MICROFICHE CONCORDANCE TO OLD ENGLISH

Butler, Stanley B *see* PHYSICAL EDUCATION AND NONPHYSICAL EDUCATION MAJORS

BUTLER TOWNSHIP SCHOOL DISTRICT 5, MS 908 – (Attendance and grading records of students in the Butler Township, Columbiana Co, Ohio, School District 5) – 1846-61 – 1r – 1 – us Western Res [978]

Butler, W E *see*
- COLLECTED WORKS ON SOCIALIST LEGAL SYSTEMS
- INTERNATIONAL LAW
- RUSSIAN, SOVIET, AND MONGOLIAN LAW

Butler, William *see*
- FROM BOSTON TO BAREILLY AND BACK
- THE LAND OF THE VEDA
- MEXICO IN TRANSITION

Butler, William A *see* TWO MILLIONS

Butler, William Archer *see* LETTERS ON ROMANISM

Butler, William Francis *see* FAR OUT: ROVINGS RETOLD

BUTLER'S JOURNAL – Fredericton, Canada. 1890-95; 1898-1903 – 2r – 1 – $136.00 – cn Library Assoc [971]

Butt, K L *see* FOUR MIDDLE SCHOOL PHYSICAL EDUCATION TEACHERS' EXPERIENCES DURING A COLLABORATIVE ACTION RESEARCH STAFF DEVELOPMENT PROJECT

BUTTE, COLUSA, GLENN, NEVADA, PLACER, SHASTA, SUTTER, TEHAMA AND YUBA COUNTIES – Butte Co, CA. 1892-1894 – 1r – 1 – $50.00 – D008 – us Library Micro [978]

BUTTE, COLUSA, GLENN, NEVADA, PLACER, SHASTA, SUTTER, TEHAMA AND YUBA COUNTIES – Colusa Co, CA. 1892-1894 – 1r – 1 – $50.00 – D008 – us Library Micro [978]

BUTTE, COLUSA, GLENN, NEVADA, PLACER, SHASTA, SUTTER, TEHAMA AND YUBA COUNTIES – Glenn Co, CA. 1892-1894 – 1r – 1 – $50.00 – D008 – us Library Micro [978]

BUTTE, COLUSA, GLENN, NEVADA, PLACER, SHASTA, SUTTER, TEHAMA AND YUBA COUNTIES – Nevada Co, CA. 1892-1894 – 1r – 1 – $50.00 – D008 – us Library Micro [978]

BUTTE, COLUSA, GLENN, NEVADA, PLACER, SHASTA, SUTTER, TEHAMA AND YUBA COUNTIES – Placer Co, CA. 1892-1894 – 1r – 1 – $50.00 – D008 – us Library Micro [978]

BUTTE, COLUSA, GLENN, NEVADA, PLACER, SHASTA, SUTTER, TEHAMA AND YUBA COUNTIES – Shasta Co, CA. 1892-1894 – 1r – 1 – $50.00 – D008 – us Library Micro [978]

BUTTE, COLUSA, GLENN, NEVADA, PLACER, SHASTA, SUTTER, TEHAMA AND YUBA COUNTIES – Sutter Co, CA. 1892-1894 – 1r – 1 – $50.00 – D008 – us Library Micro [978]

BUTTE, COLUSA, GLENN, NEVADA, PLACER, SHASTA, SUTTER, TEHAMA AND YUBA COUNTIES – Tehama Co, CA. 1892-1894 – 1r – 1 – $50.00 – D008 – us Library Micro [978]

BUTTE, COLUSA, GLENN, NEVADA, PLACER, SHASTA, SUTTER, TEHAMA AND YUBA COUNTIES – Yuba Co, CA. 1892-1894 – 1r – 1 – $50.00 – D008 – us Library Micro [978]

BUTTE, COLUSA, SUTTER, TEHAMA AND YUBA COUNTIES – Butte Co, CA. 1881; 1884-1885 – 4r – 1 – $200.00 – D007 – us Library Micro [978]

BUTTE, COLUSA, SUTTER, TEHAMA AND YUBA COUNTIES – Colusa Co, CA. 1881; 1884-1885 – 4r – 1 – $200.00 – D007 – us Library Micro [978]

BUTTE, COLUSA, SUTTER, TEHAMA AND YUBA COUNTIES – Sutter Co, CA. 1881; 1884-1885 – 4r – 1 – $200.00 – D007 – us Library Micro [978]

BUTTE, COLUSA, SUTTER, TEHAMA AND YUBA COUNTIES – Tehama Co, CA. 1881; 1884-1885 – 4r – 1 – $200.00 – D007 – us Library Micro [978]

BUTTE, COLUSA, SUTTER, TEHAMA AND YUBA COUNTIES – Yuba Co, CA. 1881; 1884-1885 – 4r – 1 – $200.00 – D007 – us Library Micro [978]

BUTTE COUNTY – 1992- – 2+ r – 1 – $100.00 – P00011 – us Library Micro [910]

BUTTE COUNTY HISTORICAL SOCIETY "DIGGIN'S" / McIntosh, Patricia & Parker, Virginia – v1-3. 1957-69 – 3r – 1 B40205 – $150.00 – us Library Micro [978]

THE BUTTE COUNTY SENIOR POST – Paradise, CA. 1991 – 4+ r – 1 – $200.00 ($50.00y) – B06045 – us Library Micro [071]

BUTTE DEMOCRAT – Oroville, CA. 1859-62 – 1r – 1 – $50.00 – C02568 – us Library Micro [071]

Butte, G C *see* GREAT BRITAIN AND THE PANAMA-CANAL

BUTTE GAZETTE – Butte, NE. -w. Dec. 1892-Dec. 1901. Incomplete; Feb. 1902-Jan. 1927;Mar. 1927- – 1 – us NE Hist [071]

BUTTE VALLEY STAR – Dorris, CA. 1924; 1927; 1930-39; 1983- – 9+ r – 1 – $450.00 ($50.00y) – B02174 – us Library Micro [071]

Buttenweiser, M *see* DIE HEBRAEISCHE ELIAS-APOKALYPSE UND IHR STELLUNG IN DER APOKALYPTISCHEN LITTERATUR

Buttenwieser, Moses *see* OUTLINE OF THE NEO-HEBRAIC APOCALYPTIC LITERATURE

Butterfield, Consul Willshire *see*
- HISTORY OF BRULE'S DISCOVERIES AND EXPLORATIONS, 1610-26: BEING A NARRATIVE OF THE DISCOVERY BY STEPHEN BRULE OF LAKES HURON, ONTARIO AND SUPERIOR, AND OF HIS EXPLORATIONS...OF PENNSYLVANIA AND WESTERN NEW YORK: ALSO OF THE PROVINCE OF ONTARIO
- HISTORY OF SAUK COUNTY
- HISTORY OF THE CITY OF OMAHA AND SOUTH OMAHA
- HISTORY OF THE GIRTYS: A CONCISE ACCOUNT OF THE GIRTY BROTHERS, THOMAS, SIMON, JAMES AND GEORGE, AND OF THEIR HALF-BROTHER JOHN TURNER

BUTTERFIELD EXPRESS – Sunnymead, CA. 1967-93 – 21r – 1 – $1,050.00 – R03021 – us Library Micro [071]

BUTTERFLIES AND MOTHS OF NORTH AMERICA / ed by Strecker, H – Reading, 1878 – II, 283p, 2pls – 8 – ne IDC [590]

THE BUTTERFLIES OF AUSTRALIA; A MONOGRAPH OF THE AUSTRALIAN RHOPALOCERA / Waterhouse, G A & Lyell, G – 2162 2. 1914 – 8 – ne IDC [590]

BUTTERFLIES OF HONGKONG AND SOUTH-EAST CHINA / Kershaw, J C – Z-235 2. 1907 – 8 – ne IDC [590]

BUTTERFLIES OF INDIA / Antram, C B – Z-256 2. 1924 – 8 – ne IDC [590]

THE BUTTERFLIES OF INDIA, BURMAH AND CEYLON / Marshall, G FL & Niceville, L de – Z-281 2. 3 v. 1882-1890 – 8 – ne IDC [590]

Butterworth, Benjamin *see*
- COMMERCIAL UNION BETWEEN CANADA AND THE UNITED STATES: AN ADDRESS DELIVERED BEFORE THE CANADIAN CLUB OF NEW YORK
- TRADE WITH CANADA: ADDRESS...BEFORE THE COMMITTEE ON WAYS AND MEANS, MARCH 3, 1890

Butterworth, Hezekiah *see*
- THE STORY OF THE HYMNS AND TUNES
- THE STORY OF THE HYMNS, OR, HYMNS THAT HAVE A HISTORY
- ZIGZAG JOURNEYS IN ACADIA AND NEW FRANCE: A SUMMER'S JOURNEY OF THE ZIGZAG CLUB THROUGH THE HISTORIC FIELDS OF THE EARLY FRENCH SETTLEMENTS OF AMERICA

Butterworth, John *see* A NEW CONCORDANCE TO THE HOLY SCRIPTURES

Butterworth, MH *see* A GUIDE TO CONDITION SCORING OF ZEBU CATTLE

Butterworth, MH et al *see* BEEF CATTLE PRODUCTION FROM TROPICAL PASTURES

Buttmann, Philipp Karl *see*
- DIE CHRISTLICHE HEILSLEHRE
- RECENSUS OMNIUM LECTIONUM QUIBUS CODEX SINAITICUS DISCREPAT

Button, Charles P *see* THE GENERAL LAW OF PARTNERSHIP AS APPLIED TO COMMERCIAL AND BUSINESS LIABILITIES

Butts, Isaac Ridler *see*
- THE BUSINESS MAN'S ADVISER.
- THE BUSINESS MAN'S LAW CABINET
- DIRECTIONS AND FORMS FOR THE EXECUTION AND ACKNOWLEDGEMENT OF DEEDS TO BE USED OR RECORDED IN OTHER STATES
- THE TRADER'S GUIDE, AND BUSINESS MAN'S LEGAL COMPANION, CONTAINING THE LAWS OF TRADE.

Butts, Nancy Kay *see*
- AEROBIC RESPONSES TO 12 WEEKS OF EXERSTRIDING OR WALKING TRAINING IN SEDENTARY ADULT WOMEN

- A COMPARISON OF RATING OF PERCEIVED EXERTION IN TREADMILL VS TRACK WALKING AND RUNNING
- THE ENERGY COST OF WOMEN WALKING WITH AND WITHOUT HAND WEIGHTS WHILE PERFORMING RHYTHMIC ARM MOVEMENTS
- A FIVE-MILE MOUNTAIN BICYCLE TEST TO PREDICT VO2MAX
- HANDRAIL ASSISTED VERSUS NONHANDRAIL ASSISTED STAIRMASTER GAUNTLET ERGOMETRY
- PHYSIOLOGICAL RESPONSES OBTAINED DURING EXERCISE ON THE STAIRMASTER GAUNTLET WITH AND WITHOUT THE USE OF HANDS
- PSYCHOLOGICAL PROFILES BEFORE AND AFTER 12 WEEKS OF WALKING OR EXERSTRIDER TRAINING IN ADULT WOMEN
- VALIDATION OF EQUATIONS TO PREDICT LACTATE THRESHOLD, FIXED BLOOD LACTATE CONCENTRATIONS, AND PEAK VALUES FROM A 3200 METER PERFORMANCE TIME
- A VALIDATION STUDY OF THE Q-PLEX 1 CARDIOP-ULMONARY EXERCISE SYSTEM

Buttstett, J H *see* UT, MI, SOL, RE, FA, LA, TOTA MUSICA ET HARMONIA AETERNA

BUTZBACHER ZEITUNG, WETTERAUER BOTE – Butzbach, 1988- – 6r per yr – 1 – Inquire at Mikrofilmarchiv for details – gw Misc Inst [072]

Butzer, M *see* DIE HANDELINGE VANDER OPENBAERDER DISPUTACIE, DIE GHEHOUDEN IS. TE STRAESBURCH, TEGHEN MELCHIOR HOFFMAN, DOOR DIE PREDICANTEN DERSELUER STADT

Butzlaff, Martin E *see* VERGLEICH DER GASTRALEN SAEURESEKRETION BEI DIABETIKERN MIT UND OHNE AUTONOME NEUROPATHIE

BUVEURS D'AMES / Duval, Paul Alexandre Martin – Paris: Charpentier et Fasquelle, 1893. 277p. 3 fiches.(Literature Collection) – 9 – 8.00 – fr Bibl Nationale [830]

Buwo, B *see*
- EEN VRIENDELICKE TSAMENSPRECKINGHE, VAN TWEE PERSOONEN VAN DER DOOPE DER IONGHER ONMONDIGHER KINDEREN
- EEN VRIENDELICKE TSAMENSPREKINGHE, VAN TWEE PERSOONEN, VAN DER DOOPE DER IONGHER ONMONDIGHER KINDEREN

Buxoyo, Simon Benito *see* HISTORIA DE CACERES Y SU PATRONA

Buxton, Thomas Fowell *see*
- THE AFRICAN SLAVE TRADE
- DE LA TRAITE DES ESCLAVES EN AFRIQUE ET DES MOYENS D'Y REMEDIER

Buys, Egbert *see*
- A NEW AND COMPLETE DICTIONARY OF TERMS OF ART
- A NEW AND COMPLETE DICTIONARY OF TERMS OF ART... KONSTWOORDENBOEK

Buzaglo, J H *see* BIJDRAGEN TOT DE GESCHIEDENIS DER PORTUGEESCHE ISRAELIETEN EN HUNNER GEMEENTEN TE 'S-GRAVENHAGE VAN PLM

Buzea, N T *see* REGLE DE DROIT PENAL...

Buzek, Jozef *see*
- "DAS AUSWANDERUNGSPROBLEM UND DIE REGELUNG DES AUSWANDERUNGSWESENS IN OESTERREICH"
- POGLAD NA WROST LUDNOSCI ZIEM POLSKICH W WIEKU 19-TYM
- DIE UEBERSECISCHE OESTERREICHISCHE WANDERUNG IN DEN JAHREN 1896-1898 FROM STATISTISCHE MONATSSCHRIFT

Buzio, Victorio Alberto *see* AQUELLO SE LLAMO JUSTICIALISMO

Buzy, Odette *see* LA NOTION DE CONGREGATION, SA PORTEE EN DROIT CIVIL FRANCAIS.

Buzzati, G C *see*
- LE DROIT INTERNATIONAL PRIVE...
- L'URTO DI NAVI IN MARE

Buzzati-Traverso, Adriano A *see* SCIENTIFIC ENTERPRISE, TODAY AND TOMORROW

Buzzell, John M G *see*
- THE LIFE OF ELDER BENJAMIN RANDAL
- RELIGIOUS MAGAZINE CONTAINING AN ACCOUNT OF THE UNITED CHURCHES OF CHRIST COMMONLY CALLED FREEWILL BAPTIST

BY CANOE AND DOG-TRAIN AMONG THE CREE AND SALTEAUX INDIANS / Young, E R – BN 458 2. 1894 – 8 – ne IDC [910]

BY PU. BOOSTER – Louisville. Kentucky. Oct 1920-Oct 1922. (The Reflector. Jan 1928. Junior Baptist. Aug 1922, Oct 1922). Baptist Young Adults. 1956-61 – 1 – 15.75 – us Baptist [240]

BY THE AURELIAN WALL: AND OTHER ELEGIES / Carman, Bliss – Boston: Lamson, Wolffe, 1898. 00484. (Pre-1900 Canadiana) – 9 – cn C.I.H.M. [810]

BY THE EQUATOR'S SNOWY PEAK : A RECORD OF MEDICAL MISSIONARY WORK AND TRAVEL IN BRITISH EAST AFRICA / Crawford, E May Grimes – London: Church Missionary Society, 1913 – 1 – us Res Libr [240]

BY THE IONIAN SEA : NOTES OF A RAMBLE IN SOUTHERN ITALY / Gissing, George Robert – London: Chapman and Hall, 1901 – 1 roll – 1 – 1-55879-392-5 – uk Libr Preservation [890]

BY THE RIVER CHEBAR: SOME APPLICATIONS OF EZEKIEL'S VISIONS / Lewis, Howell Elvet – London: Hodder & Stoughton, 1903. 1 fiche – 9 – us A.T.L.A. [240]

BY THE STILL WATERS : A MEDITATION ON THE TWENTY-THIRD PSALM / Miller, James Russell – New York:Thomas Y. Crowell, c1897 – 1mf – 9 – 0-8370-4430-8 – 1985-2430 – us A.T.L.A. [220]

BY WOMEN, FOR WOMEN, ABOUT WOMEN : THE SISTER-BOOKS OF FOURTEENTH-CENTURY GERMANY / Lewis, Gertrud Jaron – (The first comprehensive study of these writings by Dominican nuns in the German-speaking countries during the first half of the 14th C) – 1996 – 2mf – 9 – Can$73.00 – 0-88844-125-8 – cn Pontif [305]

A 'BY-A' OSTORPSTIDNINGEN – AEngelholm, 1898-1901 – 9 – sw Kungliga [072]

B'YACHAD – Northridge, CA. Sept 1977-Sept 1984 – 1 – us A.J.P.C. [071]

BYBEL-EN ZEDEDICHTEN, BESTAENDE IN ZINNEBEELDEN; HET ZALIGE LANTLEVEN / Schim, H – O 750. 1726 – 9 – ne IDC [760]

Bychkov, I A *see* KRATKII OBZOR SOBRANIIA RUKOPISEI, PRINADLEZHASHCHEGO PREOSVIASHCHENNOMU EPISKOPU PORFIRIIU, A NYNE KHRANIASHCHEGOSIA V IMP. PUBLICHNOI BIBLIOTEKE

THE BYE-LAWS AND REGULATIONS OF THE MARINE SOCIETY / Marine Society – 8th ed. 1849 – 9 – $20.00 – uk Libr Preservation [623]

THE BYE-LAWS AND REGULATIONS OF THE MARINE SOCIETY / Marine Society – London, 8th ed 1849 – 1mf – 9 – 1-55879-097-7 – uk Libr Preservation [340]

Byelorussian S.S.R. *see*
- KANSTYTUTSYI A (ASNO UNY ZAKON) BELARUSKAE SATSYI ALISTYCHNAE SAVETSKAE RESPUBLIKI
- KANSTYTUTSYI A (ASNO UNY ZAKON) BELARUSKAI SAVETSKAI SATSYI ALISTYCHNAI RESPUBLIKI
- KODEKS ZAKONA U ABPRAT SY BELARUSKAI SSR. RUSSIAN KODEKS ZAKONOV O TRUDE BELORUSSKOI SSR
- KRYMINALNA-PRATSESUALNY KODEKS BELARUSKAI SSR
- KRYMINALNA-PRATSESUALNY KODEKS BELARUSKAI SSR (1923). RUSSIAN UGOLOVNO-PROTSESSUALNYI KODEKS BELORUSSKOI SSR
- KRYMINALNA-PRATSESUALNY KODEKS BELARUSKAI SSR (1961). RUSSIAN UGOLOVNO-PROTSESSUALNYI KODEKS BELORUSSKOI SSR
- POLOZHENIE O VYBORAKH RAIONNYKH (GORODSKIKH) NARODNYKH SUDOV BELORUSSKOI SSR
- POLOZHENIE O VYBORAKH V OBLASTNYE, RAIONNYE, GORODSKIE, SELSKIE I POSELKOVYE SOVETY DEPUTATOV TRUDI ASHCHIKHSIA BELORUSSKOI SSR
- POLOZHENIE O VYBORAKH V VEKHOVNYI SOVET BELORUSSKOI SSR
- SBORNIK ZAKONOV BELORUSSKO I SSR I UKAZOV PREZIDIUMA VERKHOVNOGO SOVETA BELORUSSKO I SSR, 1938-1955 GG

Byelorussian S.S.R. TS entralny vykana uchny kamit et *see*
- ITOGI RABOTY PO ZEMLEUSTROISTVU TRUDI ASHCHEGOSIA EVREISKOGO NASELENIIA V BELORUSSKOI SOTSIALISTICHESKOI SOVETSKOI RESPUBLIKE
- STENOGRAFICHESKI I OTCHET...SESSII T SENTRALNOGO ISPOLNITELNOGO KOMITETA B.S.S.R...

Byelorussian S.S.R. Usebelaruski zezd saveta u rabochykh, si ali anskikh i chyrvona-arme iskikh d eputata u *see* STENAHRAFICHNAI A SPRAVAZDACHA

BYEN: JUNKER FRIKLOVER: NUTIDSROMAN / Claussen, Sophus – Kobenhavn: Det Schubotheske Forlag. 1900. 282p – 1 – us U.W. Library [830]

BYER OG BYBEBYGGELSE – 1933 – 1 – us I.U. Libraries [390]

Byers, George D *see* DIARIES

Byford, Charles T *see* PEASANTS AND PROPHETS

BYGNADSKULTUR – 1953 – 1 – us I.U. Libraries [390]

Byhan, A *see* DIE POLARVOELKER

Byington, Ezra Hoyt *see* THE PURITAN AS A COLONIST AND REFORMER

Byington & Lewis *see* HISTORY OF SAN FRANCISCO

Bykhovskii, Naum I Akovlevich *see* DLIA CHEGO NUZHNY SOVIETY KRESTIANSKIKH DEPUTATOV

BYKKYO GEIJUTSU – (Ars Buddhica). Incomplete. CH-883 2. 1948-1968 – 8 – ne IDC [073]

DE BYKORF DES GEMOEDS / Luiken, J – O 354. 1711 – 9 – ne IDC [760]

BY-LAWS AND CONSTITUTION; MINUTES / Ladies' Enterprise Association. Mound City, Kansas – 1864-69 – 1 – us KS Hist [060]

BY-LAWS OF ST FRANCIS LODGE OF ANCIENT, FREE AND ACCEPTED MASONS, NO. 24 G.R.C.: INSTITUTED A.L. 1839 AT SMITH'S FALLS, ONTARIO: APPROVED BY THE GRAND MASTER ON FEB. 21ST 1895 – Smith's Falls: s.n., 1895 (Smith's Falls: News Print). 03253. (Pre-1900 Canadiana) – 9 – cn C.I.H.M. [060]

BY-LAWS, RULES AND REGULATIONS.. / Beechwood Cemetery Company. Ottawa, Ont – Ottawa: J. Durie, 1886. 03303. (Pre-1900 Canadiana) – 9 – cn C.I.H.M. [360]

BY-LAWS...15TH JANUARY 1875 / Artisans' Permanent Building Society. Quebec – 1875. 07063. (Pre-1900 Canadiana) – 9 – cn C.I.H.M. [060]

BYLES FAMILY PAPERS, 1757-1837 – Massachusetts Historical Society – 2r – 1 – $155.00 – us UMI [920]

Byles, John Barnard *see* A TREATISE OF THE LAW OF BILLS OF EXCHANGE, PROMISSORY NOTES, BANK-NOTES AND CHECKS

BYLO I BUDET / Merezhkovskii, Dimitrii – Dnevnik 1910-1914. Petrograd. 1915. BR-752 2 – 8 – ne IDC [460]

BYLOE – Leningrad. Moscow. Jan. 1906-Oct. 1907. n.s. July 1917-26 – 1 – 35.00r – us Hoover Inst Photo [073]

Bynkershoek, C *see* TRAITE DU JUGE COMPETENT DES AMBASSADEURS,...

Bynkershoek, C van *see*
- DE FORO LEGATORUM...
- A TREATISE ON THE LAW OF WAR

Bynon, A A *see* OREGON STATE DIRECTORY 1881

BYPOSTEN – (Orders outside U.S.A. via University of Oslo, Norway) – Oslo, Norway, 1907-1909 – 1r – 1 – $12.88 – us Baptist [240]

BY-PRODUCTS OF THE STUDY OF LAW / Northwestern University. School of Law – Chicago, Ill.: School of Law 1939 14p. LL-1362 – 1 – us L of C Photodup [340]

THE B.Y.P.U. BOOSTER – Louisville, KY. Oct 1920-Oct 1922. The Reflector, Jan 1928. Junior Baptist, Aug, Oct 1922 – 1 – 15.75 – us Baptist [240]

Byrd, B J *see* THE RELATIONSHIP OF HISTORY OF STRESSORS, PERSONALITY, AND COPING RESOURCES, WITH THE INCIDENCE OF ATHLETIC INJURIES

Byrd, Marcia J *see* DRUG AND ALCOHOL USE BY FRESHMAN AT SIUSLAW HIGH SCHOOL AND THEIR OPINIONS REGARDING POTENTIALLY EFFECTIVE DRUG AND ALCOHOL EDUCATION PROGRAMS

Byrd, Simpson Lesley *see* STUDIES IN THE ADMINISTRATION OF THE INDIANS IN NEW SPAIN. BERKELEY, 1934

Byrd, W et al *see* CHINA

Byrd, William *see* MUSIC PART BOOKS

Byrne, James *see* NATURALISM AND SPIRITUALISM

Byrne, John Elliott *see* FEDERAL CRIMINAL PROCEDURE, WITH FORMS FOR THE DEFENSE.

Byrne, William *see* THE CATHOLIC DOCTRINE OF FAITH AND MORALS, GATHERED FROM SACRED SCRIPTURE; DECREES OF COUNCILS, AND APPROVED CATECHISMS

BYRNE'S EMIGRANT'S JOURNAL AND NATAL NEWS – London, England.1855 – 1 – sa State Libr [072]

Byrnes, John *see* THE RELATIONSHIP BETWEEN ELEMENTARY CLASSROOM TEACHERS' PERCEPTIONS OF SCHOOL HEALTH EDUCATION AND THEIR LEVEL OF HEALTH TEACHING

Byrnes, Michael *see* PROGRESSIVE SCHOOLS DON'T HAVE TO BE RADICAL, JUST DIFFERENT

BYRON AND ESPRONCEDA / Churchman, Philip H – Extrait de la Revue Hispanique. Tome 20. New York, Paris, 1909 – 1 – sp Bibl Santa Ana [946]

BYRON BLADE – Byron, NE. -w. Jan. 1908-Jul. 1910; May 1911-Dec. 1912 – 1 – us NE Hist [071]

Byron, George Anson *see* VOYAGE OF H.M.S. BLONDE TO THE SANDWICH ISLANDS 1824-25

Byron, George Gordon Byron *see*
- FUGITIVE PIECES AND REMINISCENCES OF LORD BYRON...
- HOURS OF IDLENESS
- LARA
- MARINO FALIERO, DOGE OF VENICE
- SARDANAPALUS
- THE SIEGE OF CORINTH

BYRON HERALD – Byron, NE. -w. Dec. 1896-Dec. 1898; Apr. 1904-Aug. 1904 – 1 – us NE Hist [071]

BYRON TIMES – Byron, CA. 1907-1935 – 13r – 1 – $650.00 – BC03169 – us Library Micro [071]

THE BYRTH OF MANKYNDE, OTHERWYS NAMED THE WOMANS BOOKE / Roesslin, E – M 398. 1565 – 9 – ne IDC [810]

THE BYRTH OF MANKYNDE, OTHERWYSE NAMED THE WOMANS BOOKE / Roesslin, E – M 163. 1545 – 9 – ne IDC [810]

THE BYRTH OF MANKYNDE, OTHERWYSE NAMED THE WOMANS BOOKE / Roesslin, E – M 397. 1560 – 9 – ne IDC [810]

Byrum, Enoch Edwin *see* DIVINE HEALING OF SOUL AND BODY

Bysshe, Edward *see* THE ART OF ENGLISH POETRY

BYSTANDER – Inquire about exact issue dates. v1-3; 1880-83. NS no. 1-12 Oct 1889-Sep 1890 – 1 – cn Precision [073]

Bystrianskii, Vadim *see*
- ANTANTA, ROSSIIA I REVOLIUTSIIA
- IZ ISTORII GRAZHDANSKOI VOINY V ROSSII
- KONTR-REVOLIUTSIIA I EE METODY
- MENSHEVIKI I ESERY V RUSSKOI REVOLIUTSII
- PARTII A KOMMUNISTOV BOLSHEVIKOV
- RABOCHE-KRESTIANSKAIA REVOLIUTSIIA V ROSSII V OTSENKE BURZHUAZNO I PUBLITSISTIKI

Bystron, J S *see*
- NAZWISKA POLSKIE
- PRZYSLOWIA POLSKIE

BYTE – v. 1-. 1975- – 1,5,6,9 – us UMI [073]

BYTOWN GAZETTE – Ottawa, Canada. 1836-45 – 3r – 1 – $204.00 – cn Library Assoc [971]

BYTOWN GAZETTE – Ottawa, Ontario. v18 n50. 6 mar 1856 – 1r – 1 – Can$25.00 – cn Can Microfilming [072]

BYULETIN FAR DI FOLKS-ATENEEN = PEOPLE'S BULLETIN – (In Yiddish) – Bucarest, RM. v- no7-8. Nov/Dec 1949 – 1r – 1 – $25.00 – cn Can Microfilming [072]

BYULETIN FUNDER ERSHTER KOOPERATIV FAR FEGNZAYTIKER HILF = BULLETIN OF THE FIRST CO-OP... – Montevideo, UY. v1 no3. Mar 1934 – 1 – cn Can Microfilming [072]

BYULLETEN INOSTRANNOIE KOMMERCHESKOIE INFORMATSY – Moscow, USSR. Jan-Dec 1955 – 2r – 1 – uk British Libr Newspaper [947]

BYVOEGSELS TOT DIE VOLKSBLAD & OOSTERLIG – South Africa. 1953-65 – 1 – sa State Libr [072]

BYZANTINA HISTORIA (CBH 23) / Gregorae, Nicephori; ed by Boivin, J – Parisiis, 1702 – Dfl137.00 – ne Slangenburg [930]

BYZANTINA HISTORIA (CSHB 6-8) : GRAECE E LATINE CUM ANNOTATIONIBUS H. WOLFII, C.DUCANGII, IO.BOIVINI ET C. CAPPERONNERII / Gregorae, Nicephori; ed by Schopeni, Lud. – (v2 Bonnae 1830 Dfl49.00. v3 Bonnae 1855 Dfl35.00) – Bonnae. v1. 1829 – Dfl42.00 – ne Slangenburg [240]

BYZANTINE BIBLIOGRAPHY, BASED ON BYZANTINOSLAVICA, PRAGUE – Zug, 1985 – 24mf – 9 – O-1768/1 – ne IDC [019]

THE BYZANTINE CATHOLIC WORLD – Pittsburgh, PA: Pittsburgh Byzantine Catholic Press Associates, 1956-74 – 1 – us Res Libr [240]

BYZANTINE GOSPELS (ILLUMINATED) – 11th and 13th cents. Holkham mss. 3, 4.Holkham Hall, Norfolk, England – 1 £35.00 14 £20.00 – uk Microform Academic [240]

BYZANTINE PORTRAITS / Diehl, Charles – Harold Bell, trans. New York: A.A. Knopf, 1927.vii,342p. Originally issued as Figures byzantines. Paris: Armand Colin, 1906 – 1 – us U.W. Library [900]

BYZANTINE STUDIES : LITERATURE IN VARIOUS BYZANTINE DISCIPLINES / ed by Allen, Jelisaveta Stanojevich – (Index in printed form included) – Dumbarton Oaks, Washington DC. – 12mf – 9 – DOB-1/1 – ne IDC [920]

BYZANTINISCHE KULTURGESCHICHTE / Gelzer, Heinrich – Tuebingen: J.C.B. Mohr, 1909 – 1mf – us A.T.L.A. [930]

BYZANTINISCHE LEGENDEN / Lietzmann, Hans – Jena: E. Diederichs, 1911 – 1mf – us A.T.L.A. [390]

BYZANTINISCHE ZEITSCHRIFT – 1(1892)-42(1943/49) – 687mf – 9 – Dfl2,405.00 – ne Slangenburg [073]

BYZANTINOSLAVICA : RECUEIL POUR L'ETUDE DES RELATIONS BYZANTINO-SLVAES – Prague, 1929-1981. 42v – 208mf – OA-248/1 – ne IDC [956]

BYZANZ UND PERSIEN IN IHREN DIPLOMATISCH-VOELKERRECHTLICHEN BEZIEHUNGEN IM ZEITALTER JUSTINIANS / Gueterbock, K – Berlin, 1906 – 2mf – 1 – AR-1894/1 – ne IDC [327]

BZ – Berlin. aug 3, 1971- – 1 – gw Mikrofilm [072]

BZ – Berlin, Germany. 1962 – 4r – 1 – us L of C Photodup [072]

BZ – Berlin, nov 19 1953- – 1 – Dist. gw Mikrofilm – gw Misc Inst [072]

BZ AM ABEND – Berlin, aug 2 1954- – 1 – Dist. gw Mikrofilm – gw Misc Inst [072]

BZ AM ABEND – Berlin, DE. Jul 1949-Jun 1950; May 1953-Jul 1954; 1962-76 – 34r – 1 – us L of C Photodup [072]

BZ AM ABEND – Pressburg (Bratislava), Czechoslovakia. Jan-Dec 1924 – 1r – 1 – gw Mikrofilm [072]

BZ AM MITTAG – Berlin, 4 Apr 1916-30 Jul 1919 (imperfect) – 6r – 1 – uk British Libr Newspaper [072]

BZ AM MITTAG – Berlin, apr 1906-08, jan-mar 1909, jul 1909-mar 1914, jul 1914-jun 1916, oct 1916-mar 1922, jul 1922-oct 1926, 1927-aug 1930, oct 1930-apr 1934, jul 1934-apr 1939, jul 1939-feb 1943 (incomplete) – 1 – Dist. gw Mikrofilm – gw Misc Inst [943]

BZ AM MITTAG – Berlin. jul 1939 – 1 – gw Mikrofilm [072]

C A RP ENTIER POSB *see* GLOSSARIUM NOVUM AD SCRIPTORES MEDII AEVI

C G T *see*
- LA BATAILLE SYNDICALISTE
- LA VOIX DU PEUPLE

C G T -F O *see* FORCE OUVRIERE

C MAGAZINE – Toronto. v1-40. 1983-1993/94 – 5 – Can$50.00y – cn Micromedia [073]

C ONE MOLECULES CHEMISTRY: AN INTERNATIONAL JOURNAL – 1,5,9 – us Harwood [540]

"C" SERIES RECORDS RELATING TO CANADA (NOVA SCOTIA) / United Society for the Propagation of the Gospel – 1722-1858. BRRAM – 1 – uk Microform Academic [240]

"C" SERIES RECORDS RELATING TO THE WEST INDIES AND "X" SERIES RELATING TO CODRINGTON COLLEGE, BARBADOS / United Society for the Propagation of the Gospel – 1710-1908. BRRAM – 1 – uk Microform Academic [240]

C Smith *see* ALTCHRISTLICHE TEXTE

C, T *see* AN HOSPITALL FOR THE DISEASED

C, W *see* REMARKS UPON THE REVEREND MR. WHITEFIELD'S LETTER TO THE VICE-CHANCELLOR OF THE UNIVERSITY OF OXFORD,...

CA *see* ACCOUNTANT'S MAGAZINE

CA CHEMISSUES – Current Chemical Abstracts on Microfiche distributed weekly plus backfile of Chemical Abstracts on 16mm microfilm casettes or microfiches – 6,9 – us Chemical [540]

CA E LA : ORGAO ESPECIAL DO "GRUPO RECREATIVO CA E LA" – Itacoatiara, Amazonas. 31 Dez 1910 – 1,5,6 – bl Biblioteca [072]

CA ET LA / Baillairge, Frederic Alexandre – Montreal: Cadieux & Derome, 1881. 00073. (Pre-1900 Canadiana) – 9 – cn C.I.H.M. [830]

CA IRA – no. 1-20. Anvers. avr 1920-janv 1923 – 1 – fr A.C.R.P.P. [073]

CA IRA; OR, DANTON IN THE FRENCH REVOLUTION; A STUDY / Gronlund, Laurence – Boston: Lee and Shepard; New York: C.T. Dillingham, 1888. vi/261p – 1 – us U.W. Library [920]

CA ON MICROFILM – v1-101. 1907 – 6 – us Chemical [540]

CAA (BRITISH CIVIL AVIATION AUTHORITY) – Printed index. Updated every 60 days – 6,9 – us Info Handling [629]

Caba, Pedro *see*
- ALGUNOS RASGOS DEL HOMBRE EXTREMENO
- LA CIENCIA, LA NATURALEZA Y EL MILAGRO
- EUGENIO NOEL
- FILOSOFIA DE LA PRESENCIA HUMANA
- LA FILOSOFIA DEL CONOCIMIENTO DE SAN AGUSTIN
- LA FILOSOFIA DEL NO-SER EN EL PENSAMIENTO GRIEGO (ANAXIMANDRO-PLATON)
- EL HOMBRE ANTE EL HOMBRE
- EL HOMBRE CONTRA LA NATURALEZA
- METAFISICA DE LOS SEXOS HUMANOS
- LA METAFISICA DEL ESPACIO
- MISTERIO Y POESIA
- NOSTALGIA DE DIOS EN AGUSTIN Y EN PASCAL
- LOS SEXOS, EL AMOR Y LA HISTORIA
- SOBRE LA VIDA Y LA MUERTE
- TIERRA Y MUJER O LAZARA LA PROFETISA

Caba, Ruben *see* IMPETU, PASION Y FUGA

Cababe, M *see* THE FREEDOM OF THE SEAS:...

Cabal, Alfonso Borrero *see* UNIVERSITY AS AN INSTITUTION TODAY

Cabal, Juan *see*
- BALBOA, DESCUBRIDOR DEL PACIFICO
- CARABELAS DE ESPANA...PINZON, JUAN DE LA COSA, DIAZ DE SOLIS JUAN SEBASTIAN ELCANO

EL CABALLERO DE LA GLORIA / Vial Solar, Javier – Santiago de Chile: Imprenta y Litografia La Ilustracion, 1916 – 1 – sp Bibl Santa Ana [946]

Caballero De Puga, Eduardo *see* RITUAL DEL MAESTRO FRANCMASON E HISTORIA DE LA MASONERIA

Caballero, Fernando *see* LA CASA EN QUE MURIO HERNAN CORTES EN CASTILLEJA DE LA CUESTA

Caballero y Tejerina, Antonio *see* MEMORIAL AJUSTADO...DEL PLEYTO...DE LA ALISEDA... CON LA PROPIA VILLA, PUEBLOS DE SU SEXMERIA Y DEL SENOR FISCAL SOBRE EXCUSION DE SORTEOS, CONTRIBUCION DE SOLDADOS...Y QUE CACERES CON SU SEXMERIA ENTREGUE...A ALISEDA

CABALLEROS CLERIGOS EXTREMENOS DEL ORDEN Y CABALLERIA DE ALCANTARA / Velo Nieto, Gervasio – Madrid: Imp. Accasor, 1953 – sp Bibl Santa Ana [240]

CABALLEROS DE ESPUELA DORADA (DESCUBRIMIENTO Y CONQUISTA DEL PERU) / Funes, Jorge Ernesto – Buenos Aires: Emece, 1980 – 1 – sp Bibl Santa Ana [972]

LOS CABALLEROS DE LAS ORDENES MILITARES EN MEXICO / Martinez Cosio, Leopoldo – Madrid: Razon y Fe, 1947 – 1 – sp Bibl Santa Ana [355]

LOS CABALLEROS DE NUESTRA SENORA DE SALOR / Munoz de San Pedro, Miguel – Madrid: Diana Artes Graficas, 1954. Hidalguia II pp. 449-460 – 1 – sp Bibl Santa Ana [946]

CABALLEROS DEL MONASTERIO DE YUSTE – Caceres: Tip. La Minerva, 1971 – 1 – sp Bibl Santa Ana [340]

EL CABALLO DE BATALLA DE LOS NUEVOS CRUZADOS EN LA AMERICA ESPANOLA / Bayle, Constantino – Madrid: Razon y Fe, 1926 – 1 – sp Bibl Santa Ana [972]

Cabanas Ventura, Felipe *see* BADAJOZ TAURINO

Cabanellas, Guillermo *see* DERECHO SINDICAL Y CORPORATIVO

Cabanis, J *see* ORNITHOLOGISCHES CENTRALBLATT

Cabannes, A *see* DE L'AUTORITE QUE POSSEDENT EN FRANCE LES JUGEMENTS ETRANGERS

Cabaton, Antoine *see* CATALOGUE SOMMAIRE DES MANUSCRITS SANSCRITS ET PALIS

Cabeen, Violet Abbott *see* CHANGES IN THE DOCUMENTS OF BRITISH INDIA CAUSED BY THE GOVERNMENT OF INDIA ACT 1935

CABELL RECORD – Milton. West Virginia. 1954- – 1 – us UMI [071]

Cabello de Balboa, Miguel *see* OBRAS

Cabello de Carbonera, Mercedes *see* SACRIFICIO Y RECOMPENSA: NOVELA

Cabeus, N *see* PHILOSOPHIA MAGNETICA...

Cabeza del Buey. Ayuntamiento *see*
- FERIA Y FIESTAS, 1947. CABEZA DEL BUEY
- FERIAS Y FIESTAS EN HONOR A SAN MIGUEL. 1979

CABILDOS DE INDIOS EN LA AMERICA ESPANOLA / Bayle, Constantino – Madrid: Missionalia Hispanica, 1951 – 1 – sp Bibl Santa Ana [972]

THE CABINET – Detroit, 1892-93 – 1 – £60.00 – uk Chadwyck [780]

LE CABINET DE L'AMOUR DE L'HOTEL LAMBERT / Réunion des Musées Nationaux. Paris – 1972 – 9 – fr Réunion [700]

LE CABINET DE LECTURE – Paris. 4 oct 1829-34, 1836-45 – 1 – fr A.C.R.P.P. [073]

LE CABINET DE TOILETTE D'UNE HONNETE FEMME / Gence, Comtesse de – Paris: Pancier, 1909. 466p. (Les Femmes Collection) – 5mf – 9 – $12.00 – fr Bibl Nationale [390]

LE CABINET DES BEAUX ARTS / Perrault – O-1085 1. 1699 – 9 – ne IDC [700]

LE CABINET DES BEAUX ARTS / Perrault – O-1086 1. 1690 – 9 – ne IDC [700]

CABINET DES SINGULARITES D'ARCHITECTURE, PEINTURE, SCULPTURE, ET GRAVEURE / Comte, Florent le – O 206.. 3 v. 1699-1700 – 9 – ne IDC [700]

LE CABINET DU ROI – With printed index – 1 – £100.00 – uk World [944]

LE CABINET DU ROI ET LES ANCIENS CABINETS DE CURIOSITES DANS LES COLLECTIONS DU MUSEE DE L'HOMME / Fardoulis-Vitart, A – 9 – F70.00 – fr Ethnologie [306]

CABINET MINUTES : (CAB 23) / Great Britain. Cabinet Office – (Subject indexes, bibliographical chronological guide. Individual years available) – 1916-39 – 58r – 1 – us Ross [324]

CABINET MINUTES AND MEMORANDA / Great Britain. Cabinet Office – (Lloyd George, Bowar Law, Ramsay MacDonald and Neville Chamberlain. Subject indexes, bibliographical chronological guide. Individual years available) – 1916-39 – 256r – 1 – us Ross [324]

CABINET NEWSPAPER – London, England. -w. 27 Nov 1858-Feb 1860. 1 reel – 1 – uk British Libr Newspaper [072]

CABINET OF LITERATURE – [Toronto?: s.n.], 1838-[18–?]; (Toronto: J Gedd) – 9 – cn C.I.H.M. [400]

CABINET PAPERS : COMPLETE CLASSES FROM THE CAB AND PREM SERIES IN THE PUBLIC RECORD OFFICE – (Series One: PREM 3 – Papers concerning defence and operational subjects, 1940-1945, Winston Churchill, Minister of Defence, Secretariat Papers 19r $2,400.00. Series Two: CAB 50 and CAB 51 – The Papers of the Committee of Imperial Defense – Papers of the Oil Board, 1925-1939 and Middle East Questions, 1930-1939 13r $1,600.00. Series Three: CAB 128 and CAB 129 – Cabinet Conclusions and Cabinet Memoranda, 1945 and following: Pt 1: The Attlee Government, Aug 1945-Oct 1951 (CAB 128/1-13 and CAB 129/1-20) 15r $1,850.00; Pt 2: The Attlee Government, Aug 1945-Oct 1951 (CAB 128/14-23 and CAB 129/21-47) 15r $1,850.00) – Marlborough: Adam Matthew Publications, 1994 – 1 – uk Matthew [324]

CABLE CAR DAYS : CLIPPINGS – San Francisco Public Lib, 1880-89 – 1r – 1 – $50.00 – B40312 – us Library Micro [978]

Cable, John Levi *see* LOSS OF CITIZENSHIP, DENATURALIZATION, THE ALIEN IN WARTIME

CABLE LOGGING SYSTEMS – 1981 – 111p – it F.A.O. [634]

CABLE TELEVISION BUSINESS – v19-. 1982- – 1,5,6,9 – us UMI [073]

CABLE TV STATION DISTRIBUTION FILE / U.S. National Technical Information Service – Lists cable TV stations (sorted by call sign) carried by different cable communities – 9 – us N.T.I.S. [000]

CABLE VISION – (1983-. 1,5,6,9) – v1-. 1975- – 1 – us UMI [073]

CABLEGRAMS EXCHANGED BETWEEN GENERAL HEADQUARTERS, AMERICAN EXPEDITIONARY FORCES, AND THE WAR DEPARTMENT / U.S. War Department. Adjutant General's Office – 1917-19. 19 rolls. M930 – 1 – us Nat'l Archives [324]

CABOS SUELTOS PARA LA HISTORIA DE CHIGUINGUIRA / Mesanza, Andres – Madrid: Razon y Fe, 1935 – 1 – sp Bibl Santa Ana [972]

Cabot, James Elliot *see* A MEMOIR OF RALPH WALDO EMERSON

Cabot, Samuel *see* PAPERS OF SAMUEL CABOT, 1713-1858

Cabral, A do Valle *see* BIBLIOGRAPHIA LINGUA TUPI OU GUARANI

Cabranes, Diego de *see* ABITO Y ARMADURA ESPIRITUAL...CON PRIVILEGIO IMPERIAL. 1544

Cabrera de la Rocha, Juan *see* ALEGATO DE BUENA PRUEBA PRESENTADO

Cabrera, F *see* REMEDIOS ESPIRITUALES Y CORPORALES PARA CURAR Y PRESERVAR DEL MAL DE PESTE...

Cabrera Moreno, Juliana *see* ESTUDIOS SOBRE EL PRISCILIANISMO EN LA GALICIA ANTIGUA

CABRERA, PABLO... / ed by Bayle, Constantino – Madrid: Razon y Fe, 1926 – 1 – sp Bibl Santa Ana [920]

Cabrera, Pablo *see*
- LOS ABORIGENES DEL PAIS DE CUYO
- LA ANTIGUA BIBLIOTECA JESUITICA DE CORDOBA
- ENSAYOS SOBRE ETNOLOGIA ARGENTINA
- INTRODUCCION A LA HISTORIA ECLESIASTICA DEL TUCUMAN, 1535 A 1590. BUENOS AIRES, 1934
- LA SEGUNDA IMPRENTA DE CORDOBA
- TESOROS DEL PASADO ARGENTINO...

Cabrol, F *see*
- DICTIONNAIRE D'ARCHEA1OLOGIE CHRETIENNE ET DE LITURGIE
- LES EGLISES DE JERUZALEM

Cabrol, Fernand *see*
- L'ANGLETERRE CHRETIENNE AVANT LES NORMANDS
- INTRODUCTION AUX ETUDES LITURGIQUES

CAC VAN KIEN PHAP LUAT PHUC VU CUOC VAN DONG NGHI QUYET 228 NQ/TW NGAY 12/1/1974 CUA BO CHINH TRI TRUNG UONG DANG / Legal Bureau of the City of Hai Phong – 1974 – 2mf – 9 SEL-114/1 – ne IDC [340]

Cacace, Giovanni Battista *see* THEATRUM OMNIUM SCIENTIARUM

CACERES / Caceres. Junta Provincial de Turismo – (Texto tambien en frances, ingles y aleman) – Madrid: Sucesos de Rivadeneyra – sp Bibl Santa Ana [910]

CACERES / Junta Provincial de Turismo – (Texto en ingles) – Vitoria: Tip. Fourner, s.a. – 1 – sp Bibl Santa Ana [338]

Caceres *see*
- COMISION ESPECIAL DE AGUAS. DICTAMEN...
- COMISION ESPECIAL DE AGUAS. DICTAMEN...6.11.1934
- CONSTITUCION DE LA CORPORACION MUNICIPAL EL 6 DE FEBRERO DE 1949
- CONSTITUCION DE LA CORPORACION MUNICIPAL EL 31 DE JULIO DE 1948
- CONSTITUIDO...2 DE FEBRERO DE 1958
- CONTADURIA. MEMORIA DEL ANO 1910
- FOLLETO INFORMATIVO SOBRE EL SERVICIO MUNICIPAL DE LIMPIEZA
- LIQUIDACION DEL PRESUPUESTO DE 1914, DEUDORES Y ACREEDORES PARA RESULTAS
- ORDENANZAS 1 AL 6. PRESUPUESTO EXTRAORDINARIO DE OBRAS, SERVICIOS Y URBANISMO, VIGENCIA INDEFINIDA DESDE 1957
- ORDENANZAS FISCALES QUE AGREGANDO O RECTIFICANDO ALGUNAS DE 1939 FORMAN, CON LAS DE ESTE, LAS DEL EJERCICIO ECONOMICO DE 1940
- ORDENANZAS FORMADAS PARA EL COBRO DE LOS IMPUESTOS Y ARBITRIOS DEL PRESUPUESTO 1915-26
- ORDENANZAS FORMADAS PARA EL COBRO DE LOS IMPUESTOS Y ARBITRIOS DEL PRESUPUESTO DE 1959
- ORDENANZAS MUNICIPALES...DE CACERES... APROBADAS EN 1912
- ORDENANZAS PARA EL COBRO DE LOS IMPUESTOS Y ARBITRIOS DEL PRESUPUESTO
- PATRONATO LOCAL DE CANTINAS ESCOLARES (REGLAMENTO)
- PRESUPUESTO DE GASTOS E INGRESOS PARA EL ANO

- PRESUPUESTO ORDINARIO DE GASTOS E INGRESOS PARA 1948. MEMORIA JUSTIFICADA ORDENANZAS Y TARIFAS NUEVAS O MODIFICADAS. BASES DE EJECUCION
- PRESUPUESTO ORDINARIO DE INGRESOS Y GASTOS ANO
- PRESUPUESTO ORDINARIO DE INGRESOS Y GASTOS PARA EL ANO
- PRESUPUESTO ORDINARIO PARA INGRESOS Y GASTOS PARA EL ANO 1910
- RECTIFICACIONES Y ADICIONES A LAS ORDENANZAS MINERAS 2, 4, 5, 8, 9, 12, 13, 14 BIS, 16 BIS, 18, 20, 24, 25-26, 28, 31, 35, 47, 48, 51, 52 Y 65 FORMULADAS PARA EL COBRO DE IMPUESTOS Y ARBITRIOS DEL PRESUPUESTO, VIGENTES PARA EL DE - 1958 Y SUCESIVAS
- REGLAMENTACION MUNICIPAL CONTRA EL PARO FORZOSO...1931
- REGLAMENTO DE LA ACADEMIA DE MUSICA Y BANDA MUNICIPAL DE CACERES (1892)
- REGLAMENTO DE LA ACADEMIA DE MUSICA Y BANDA MUNICIPAL DE CACERES (1935-1949)
- REGLAMENTO DE LA MUTUALIDAD DE PREVISION PARA FUNCIONARIOS DEL AYUNTAMIENTO DE CACERES, 1955
- REGLAMENTO DE PROCEDIMINETO ADMINISTRATIVO Y DE OBRAS Y SERVICIOS...1955
- REGLAMENTO DE REGIMEN INTERIOR DELA GUARDIA MUNICIPAL DE LA CIUDAD DE CACERES (1945)
- REGLAMENTO DE SANIDAD E HIGIENE...1959
- REGLAMENTO DEL SERVICIO MUNICIPAL DE MERCADOS 1955...
- REGLAMENTO MUNICIPAL CONTRA EL PARO FORZOSO (1931)
- REGLAMENTO PARA EL REGIMEN INTERIOR DE LAS OFICINAS DEL EXCMO
- REGLAMENTO PARA EL REGIMEN INTERIOR DE LAS OFICINAS DEL EXCMO. AYUNTAMIENTO DE CACERES
- REGLAMENTO PARA ELREGIMEN INTERIOR DEL CEMENTERIO PUBLICO MUNICIPAL DE ESTA CAPITAL
- ...REGLAMENTO...DEL MATADERO MUNICIPAL DE CACERES...1919

Caceres, 34th Asamblea de la Federacion Espanola de Centros de Iniciativas y Turismo *see* A CELEBRAR EN CACERES DEL 5 AL 11 DE OCTUBRE DE 1969

CACERES ANTE LA HISTORIA. LA CUESTION CRITICA DE LA FUNDACION Y EL NOMBRE DE CACERES / Floriano Cumbreno, Antonio C - Caceres: Imprenta, Libreria y Encuadernacion de Garcia Floriano, 1931 - sp Bibl Santa Ana [946]

Caceres, Antonio de *see* SERMONES VARIOS DE DIVERSOS ASUNTOS PANEGIRICOS

Caceres. Asociacion Cultural *see* ESTATUTOS

Caceres. Asociacion de Padres de Alumnos del Colegio San Antonio de Padua *see* ESTATUTOS DE LA...CACERES

Caceres. Asociacion Nacional de Invalidos Civiles *see* MEMORIA DE LAS ACTIVIDADES DESARROLLADAS POR LA JUNTA DIRECTIVA...

Caceres. Ayuntamiento *see*
- EXPOSICION HISTORIA DE LA FERIA DE MAYO EN CACERES (DOCUMENTACION DEL ARCHIVO MUNICIPAL) CATALOGO 1973
- FERIA DE SAN MIGUEL, 1954
- FERIA Y FIESTAS MAYO DE 1952. GUIA COMERCIAL
- FERIAS Y FIESTAS. 1973. GUIA OFICIAL
- FERIAS Y FIESTAS DE MAYO 1954
- FERIAS Y FIESTAS DE MAYO DE 1950 GUIA COMERCIAL
- FERIAS Y FIESTAS MAYO 1947
- FERIAS Y FIESTAS MAYO 1963
- FERIAS Y FIESTAS PATRONALES. SAN JORGE, 1960
- FIESTA DE SAN JORGE, 1953
- FIESTAS PATRONALES SAN JORGE, 1955
- FIESTAS PATRONALES SAN JORGE 1959
- GUIA COMERCIAL DE FERIAS Y FIESTAS MAYO, 1945
- PRESUPUESTO ORDINARIO DE GASTOS E INGRESOS PARA 1951
- REVISTA OFICIAL FERIAS Y FIESTAS 1972

Caceres. Ayuntamiento. Caceres *see* FERIAS Y FIESTAS 1952

Caceres, Ayuntamiento, Trujillo. Ayuntamiento *see* FERIA Y FIESTAS MAYO-JUNIO, 1953

CACERES BAJO LA REINA CATOLICA Y SU CAMARERO SANCHO PAREDES GOLFIN / Orti Belmonte, Miguel Angel - Badajoz: Dip. Provincial, 1955 - 1 - sp Bibl Santa Ana [240]

Caceres. Centro de Estudios Historicos *see* ESTATUTOS QUE HAN DE REGULAR EL FUNCIONAMIENT TO DE LA ASOCIACION CULTURAL CENTRO DE ESTUDIOS HISTORICOS DE CACERES

CACERES. CENTRO EXTREMENO - Caceres: Rime Publicidad, 1973 - 1 - sp Bibl Santa Ana [946]

Caceres. Club de tenis "Cabeza Rubia" *see* ESTATUTOS SOCIALES DEL...

Caceres. Comision Semana Santa *see* SEMANA SANTA EN CACERES, 1957

Caceres. Delegacion Provincial de Organizaciones del Movimiento *see* 2 JUEGOS DEPORTIVOS

Caceres. Delegacion Provincial del Ministerio, de Educacion *see* DESDE LA FORMACION PROFESIONAL A LAS FACULTADES O ESCUELAS UNIVERSITARIAS E INDUSTRIAS Y SERVICIOS

Caceres, Diego de *see*
- CARGOS QUE RESULTAN CONTRA...EL P. DIEGO DE CACERES, GENERAL DE...S. GERONIMO..
- CONCILIABULO DE BASILEA
- DILUCIDATIO IN GENERALI CAPITULO ORDINO D. HYERONYMI A..
- DIOSCORO PATRIARCHA ALEXANDRINO
- ELUCIDATIONES DE POTESTATE PAPAE
- EXPOSICION AL NUNCIO
- MEMORIAL AL REY PIDIENDOLE SE REMITA LA CAUSA AL NUNCIO Y A OTROS PRELADOS Y DA CUENTA DE SU VIDA
- PARECER DEL REVERENDO...DEBE SER CABEZA DE LA DICHA RELIGION
- SENTENCIA QUE N.R.P.M.F., GENERAL DE LA ORDEN DE N.P.S. GERONIMO, DIO Y PRONUNCIO EN EL MONASTERIO DE SAN BARTOLOME...EN 15 DIAS DEL MESDE OCTUBRE

Caceres. Diputacion Provincial *see* PRESUPUESTO ORDINARIO DE INGRESOS Y GASTOS PARA EL EJERCICIO DE 1972

CACERES EN 1828. DATOS HISTORICOS, ESTADISTICOS Y OTRAS CURIOSIDADES TOMADOS DE...INSTITUTO DE SEGUNDA ENSENANZA DE LA MISMA - 1874 - 9 - 1.50f - sp Bibl Santa Ana [946]

CACERES EN TIEMPO DE LOS ROMANOS / Huebner, Emilio - Caceres: Tip. y Lib. de N.M. Jimenez, 1899 - 1 - sp Bibl Santa Ana [946]

Caceres. Espana en Paz *see* CHRONICA DE VEINTICINCO ANOS

Caceres. Hermandad de Donantes de Sangre. San Pedro de Alcantara *see* MEMORIA 1980

Caceres. Hermandad Nacional de Alfereces Provisionales *see* RELACION ALFABETICA DE LOS ALFERECES PROVISIONALES DE LA PROVINCIA DE CACERES

CACERES. IGLESIA DEL CONVENTO DE SAN FRANCISCO... / Meseguer Fernandez, Juan - Madrid: Graf. Calleja, 1970 - 1 - sp Bibl Santa Ana [240]

Caceres. Junta Provincial de Turismo *see*
- CACERES
- CACERES. PLANO GUIA
- TRUJILLO (CACERES)

Caceres. Junta Provincial del Turismo. Caceres *see* PLANO-GUIA

CACERES. MAPA DE COMUNICACIONES DE LA PROVINCIA - Arqueros, 1950 - 1 - sp Bibl Santa Ana [380]

CACERES. MAPA GUIA TURISTICO PROVINCIAL / Junta Provincial de Informacion, Turismo y Educacion Popular - San Sebastian: Valverde S.A, 1959 - 1 - sp Bibl Santa Ana [338]

CACERES MONUMENTAL / Callejo Serrano, Carlos - Madrid: Editorial Plus Ultra, 1960 - 1 - sp Bibl Santa Ana [946]

Caceres. Mutua Aseguradora de Transportes *see* MEMORIA. EJERCICIO 1964

Caceres. Mutua Aseguradora de transportistas *see* MEMORIA. EJERCICIO 1960

Caceres. Mutua Aseguradora de Transportistas de la Provincia de Caceres *see*
- ESTATUTOS APROBADOS POR ORDEN MINISTERIAL HACIENDA DE 1960
- REGLAMENTO DEL MINISTERIO DE HACIENDA DE 17 DE JUNIO DE 1960
- REGLAMENTO DEL RAMO DE ACCIDENTES APROBADO POR ORDEN DEL MINISTERIO DE HACIENDA DE 17 DE JUNIO DE 1960

Caceres. Mutua Cerealistica *see*
- ESTATUTOS
- MEMORIA. EJERCICIO 1959

Caceres. Mutua extremena de Vehiculos *see* MEMORIA. EJERCICIO 1973

Caceres. Mutualidad General Deportiva *see* NORMAS DE PROCEDIMIENTO EN CASO DE ACCIDENTE DEPORTIVO

Caceres. Obra Sindical de Educacion y Descanso *see* NAVIDAD 74

Caceres. Parroquia de San Jose *see* IGLESIA PARROQUIAL DE SAN JOSE

Caceres. Pena. Amigos del Flamenco de Extremadura *see* ESTATUTOS...

CACERES. PLANO GUIA / Caceres. Junta Provincial de Turismo - Alicante: Graf. Gutenberg, 1948 - sp Bibl Santa Ana [910]

CACERES PRIMERA CUNA DE LA ORDEN MILITAR DE SANTIAGO / Munoz Gallardo, Juan Antonio - Badajoz: Imprenta Diputacion Provincial, 1974. Separata Rev. Estudios Extremenos - 1 - sp Bibl Santa Ana [350]

Caceres, Rafael de *see* PERJUICIOS DE LA SEPARACION DE LA MEDICINA Y LA CIRUJIA..

CACERES. RESENA DE LOS FESTEJOS CELEBRADOS EN ESTA CAPITAL PARA SOLEMNIZAR LA PROMULGACION DE LA LEY FUNDAMENTAL DEL ESTADO...EN 1869 - Caceres: Imp. Nicolas M. Jimenez, 1869 - 1 - sp Bibl Santa Ana [946]

Caceres. (Spain) *see* ORDENANZAS MUNICIPALES

Caceres. Spain *see*
- CONSEJO PROVINCIAL DE AGRICULTURA, INDUSTRIA Y ENERGIA DE CACERES
- RESENA DE LOS FESTEJOS..

Caceres. Terpresa *see* MEMORIA 1974

Caceres: Universidad Laboral Hispanoamericana *see* ORQUESTA FILARMONICA MORAVA DE OLOMONE-SINFONICA DEL ESTADO

Caceres y Sotomayor, Antonio *see*
- PARAPHASIS DE LOS PSALMOS DE DAVID... Y MODO DE HABLAR DE LA LENGUA ESPANOLA
- SERMONES Y DISCURSOS DE TIEMPO... PREDICADOS POR..
- TERCERA PARTE DE LOS SERMONES Y DISCURSOS QUE CONTIENE DESDE EL...SERMON EN LA FERIA SEGUNDA..

Cacharron, Francisco de Paula *see* OCIOS Y VERSOS

Cacici, A S *see* DE LA EXTRATERRITORIALIDAD DE LA PERSONA JURIDICA

CACTEARUM GENERA NOVA SPECIESQUE NOVAE ET OMNIUM IN HORTO MONVILLIANO CULTARUM / Lemaire, C A - Lutetiis, Parisorium. 1839. B-6014 2 - 8 - ne IDC [580]

CACTUS AND SUCCULENT JOURNAL OF GREAT BRITAIN - 1957 - 7 - uk Microform Academic [580]

CAD CAM TECHNOLOGY - v1-3, no.3. Spring 1982-Fall 1984 - 1,5,6,9 - us UMI [073]

CAD SYSTEMS - (Cont: CAD/CAM Systems at v9 1991) - Mississauga. v9- 1991/92- - 1 - Can$60.00y - cn Micromedia [000]

CAD SYSTEMS *see* CAD/CAM SYSTEMS

CADALOZ - Istanbul: Tercueman-i Hakikat Matbaasi, 1911; Sahib-i Imtiyaz ve Sermuharriri: Nureddin Ruesdi, Nos 20. - 10 Haziran 1911, 24. - 25 Haziran 1911 - 1mf - 9 - $12.00 - us MEDOC [949]

Cadalso Vazquez, Jose *see*
- CARTAS MARRUECAS
- LOS ERUDITOS A LA VIOLETA Y SUPLEMENTO
- OCIOS DE MI JUVENTUD

CADAMS PROGRESS - Cadams, NE. -w. Jun. 1916-Dec.1916 - 1 - us NE Hist [071]

CADASTRAL PLANS : CITY OF MONTREAL / Sicotte, Louis W - Montreal: Department of Public Works, ca 1874. SEM35P118 - 1r - 1 - Can$15.00 - cn Bibl Nat [910]

CADASTRE ABREGE DE LA SEIGNEURIE DE LEVRARD... / Canada (Province). Commissaire sous l'Acte seigneurial refondu - Quebec: Stewart Derbishire et George Desbarats, 1861. SEM105P1526 - 1mf - 9 - Can$2.25f - cn Bibl Nat [971]

CADASTRE ABREGE DE LA SEIGNEURIE DE ROCQUETAILLADE,... / Canada (Province). Commissaire sous l'Acte seigneurial refondu - Quebec: Stewart Derbishire et George Desbarats, 1861. SEM105P1525 - 1mf - 9 - Can$2.25 - cn Bibl Nat [971]

CADASTRE ABREGE DE LA SEIGNEURIE DE ST VALIER... / Canada (Province). Commissaire sous l'Acte seigneurial refondu - [Quebec ?: s.n., 1862 ?]. SEM105P1524 - 1mf - 9 - Can$2.25 - cn Bibl Nat [971]

CADASTRE ABREGE DU FIEF COTEAU ST LOUIS... / Canada (Province). Commissaire sous l'Acte seigneurial refondu - [Quebec: George Desbarats, 1864]. SEM105P1167 - 1mf - 9 - Can$2.25 - cn Bibl Nat [971]

CADASTRE ABREGE DU FIEF ST JOSEPH OU L'EPINAY,... / Canada (Province). Commissaire sous l'Acte seigneurial refondu - [Quebec: Stewart Derbishire et George Desbarats, 1861 [i.e. 1862 ?]. SEM105P1371 - 1mf - 9 - Can$2.25 - cn Bibl Nat [971]

CADASTRES ABREGES DES SEIGNEURIES APPARTENANT A LA COURONNE.. - Quebec: Georges Desbarats..., 1863. SEM35P226 - 1r - 1 - Can$22.00 - cn Bibl Nat [971]

CADASTRES ABREGES DES SEIGNEURIES DU DISTRICT DE MONTREAL - Montreal, Canada. 3v. 1863 - 2r - 1 - Can$50.00r - cn Can Microfilming [910]

CADASTRES ABREGES DES SEIGNEURIES DU DISTRICT DE MONTREAL.. - Quebec: Stewart Derbishire et Georges Desbarats..., 1863. SEM35P207 - 2r - 1 - Can$102.00 - cn Bibl Nat [971]

CADASTRES ABREGES DES SEIGNEURIES DU DISTRICT DE QUEBEC - Quebec, Canada. 2v. 1863 - 2r - 1 - Can$50.00r - cn Can Microfilming [910]

CADASTRES ABREGES DES SEIGNEURIES DU DISTRICT DE TROIS-RIVIERES - Montreal, Canada. 1v. 1863 - 1r - 1 - Can$50.00 - cn Can Microfilming [910]

CADASTRES ABREGES DES SEIGNEURIES DU DISTRICT DES TROIS-RIVIERES.. - Quebec: Stewart Derbishire et Georges Desbarats..., 1863. SEM35P225 - 1r - 1 - Can$37.00 - cn Bibl Nat [971]

CAD/CAM AND ROBOTICS - (Cont by: CAD/CAM Systems at v8 1990) - Mississauga, 1984-89 - 9 - Can$20.00y - cn Micromedia [000]

CAD/CAM AND ROBOTICS *see* CAD/CAM SYSTEMS

CAD-CAM INDUSTRY DIRECTORY - 1985- - 1 - us UMI [073]

CAD/CAM SYSTEMS - (Cont: CAD/CAM and Robotics at v8 1990. Cont by: CAD Systems at v9 no 4 1991) - Mississauga. v8. 1990 - 9 - Can$20.00y - cn Micromedia [000]

CAD/CAM SYSTEMS *see*
- CAD SYSTEMS
- CAD/CAM AND ROBOTICS

CAD/CAM TECHNOLOGY - 1982- - 1,5,6,9 - us UMI [073]

Caddell, Cecilia Mary *see* A HISTORY OF THE MISSIONS IN JAPAN AND PARAGUAY

Cadden, Joseph *see* SPAIN

CADENCE OF THE CLINICAL LABORATORY *see* AMERICAN JOURNAL OF MEDICAL TECHNOLOGY

THE CADENZA - Kansas City. 1894-1924. A music magazine. 7 reels - 1 - 161.00 - us L of C Photodup [780]

CADERNOS CEDI - Rio de Janeiro: Centro Ecumenico de Documentacao e Informacao, [1980?- n1 1980] - 1r - us Res Libr [972]

CADERNOS DE HORA PRESENTE - Rio de Janeiro, BL. 1939-1940 - 2r - $100.00 - R04166 - us Library Micro [073]

CADERNOS DE NOSSO TEMPO - Rio de Janeiro, BL. 1954-1956 - 1r - $50.00 - R04167 - us Library Micro [320]

CADERNOS DO CEDI - Rio de Janeiro: Centro Ecumenico de Documentacao e Informacao, [1980?- n2-20 (1980-1990) - 1r - us Res Libr [972]

CADERNOS DO POVO BRASILEIRO - Rio de Janeiro, BL. 1962-1964 - 2r - $100.00 - R04168 - us Library Micro [072]

CADES BAPTIST CHURCH. WILLIAMSBURG COUNTY. SOUTH CAROLINA : CHURCH RECORDS - (309p) - 1919-1926, 1947-1954, 1957-1958, Oct 1959, 1960-1974 incomplete - 1 reel - 1 - $13.91 - us Baptist [240]

THE CADET - Montreal: J C Becket, [1852-1854] - 9 - cn C.I.H.M. [971]

THE CADET - [Saint John, N.B.]: Grand Section [1867?] - 9 - cn C.I.H.M. [971]

Cadet, Ernest *see* LE MARIAGE EN FRANCE

CADET ROUSSEL MISANTHROPE ET MANON REPENTANTE / Aude, Hapde & Aude, Flan - French Theatre Series. Paris. Chez le libraire "Au Theatre du Vaudeville." an VII. 1799 - 9 - fr Hachette [820]

THE CADETS' TRUMPET - Windsor, N.S.: Cadets of Temperance, [1880] - 9 - cn C.I.H.M. [971]

CADILLAC MANUAL – Detroit, MI. Pts 1 + 2. 1964 – 2r – 1 – $100.00 – R04146 – us Library Micro [071]
"CADILLAC'S VILLAGE", OR, "DETROIT UNDER CADILLAC": WITH LIST OF PROPERTY OWNERS AND A HISTORY OF THE SETTLEMENT, 1701 TO 1710 – Comp. by C. M. Burton. Detroit, 1896. 02297. (Pre-1900 Canadiana) – 9 – cn C.I.H.M. [978]
Cadman, H W *see* THE CHRISTIAN UNITY OF CAPITAL AND LABOR
Cadman, James Piper *see* CHRIST IN THE GOSPELS
Cadogan, W *see* A DISSERTATION ON THE GOUT
Cadot, Michel *see* 19TH CENTURY RUSSIA: CONTEMPORARY FRENCH OPINION
LE CADUCEE *see* LES NOUVELLES DE L'ECOLE DES H.E.C
Cadwalader, J *see* CADWALADER'S CASES IN THE DISTRICT COURT OF PENNSYLVANIA, 1858-1879
[Cadwalader, J L] *see* DIGEST...
CADWALADER'S CASES IN THE DISTRICT COURT OF PENNSYLVANIA, 1858-1879 / Cadwalader, J – Philadelphia: Welsh & Co. v1-2. 1907 – 15mf – 9 – $22.50 – LLMC 81-440 – us L.L.M.C. [340]
CADWELL BAPTIST CHURCH. LAURENS COUNTY. CADWELL, GEORGIA : CHURCH RECORDS – Aug 1941-Sept 1962, Oct 1965-1990 – 1 – $40.64 – us Baptist [240]
Cady, Lyman van Law *see* THE PSYCHOLOGY OF RELIGION (CCC5)
Cady, Philander Kinney *see* THE REWARDS OF THE PROFESSION OF THE LAW
CAECILIA : A CATHOLIC REVIEW – Dayton, 1877-1939 – 1 – £380.00 – uk Chadwyck [780]
CAECILIA : EINE ZEITSCHRIFT FUER DIE MUSIKALISCHE WELT – Mainz, 1824-1848. v1-27 – 125mf – P-574/1 – ne IDC [780]
CAECILIA : EINE ZEITSCHRIFT FUER DIE MUSIKALISCHE WELT – v1-27. 1824-48 – 4r – 1 – us Ross [780]
CAECILIA : EINE ZEITSCHRIFT FUER DIE MUSIKALISCHE WELT / ed by Weber, Gottfried & Dehn, Siegfried Wilhelm – Mainz, 1824-48. Hildesheim, 1979 – 143mf – 9 – DM1,200.00 diazo DM1,400.00 silver – gw Olms [073]
CAECILIA. EINE ZEITSCHRIFT FUER DIE MUSIKALISCHE WELT – Paris-Mainz. v. 1-27. 1824-1848 – 1 – us NY Public [780]
CAECILIA: EINE ZEITSCHRIFT FUER DIE MUSIKALISCHE WELT – Mainz. 1824-48. 4 reels – 1 – 75.00 – us L of C Photodup [780]
CAECILIA VON ALBANO : DRAMATISCHES GEDICHT IN FUENF AUFZUEGEN / Mosenthal, Salomon Hermann – Wien: [s. n.], 1849 (U Klopf Senior & A Eurich) – 1r – 1 – us U.W. Library [820]
CAECILIEN-KALENDER – Regensburg, 1876-1885. v1-10 – 21mf – P-575/1 – ne IDC [780]
CAED REPORT / Iowa State University. College of Agriculture. Center for Agricultural and Rural Development – No.1-38.1959-70 – 1,5 – us Spaulding [630]
CAEDMON MANUSCRIPT – c.1000. Bodleian Library. Ms. Junius II – 1. 22.50; ; 14 – uk Microform Academic [810]
CAELII AVGVSTINI CVRIONIS SARRACENICAE HISTORIAE LIBRI TRES, ... / Curio, C A – Francofvrdi, 1596 – 4mf – 9 – H-8387/1 – ne IDC [945]
CAELII CALCAGNINI, FERRARIENSIS.. / Calcagnini, Celio – Basileae, 1544. 6,657,44p. First ed. Ed. by A.M. Brasavola. Includes index.1 reel. 1206 – 1 – us U.W. Library [520]
CAELII SEDULII OPERA / Arevalo, Faustino – Roma: Antonio Fulgonium, 1794 – 1 – sp Bibl Santa Ana [780]
Caeneghem, E P R van *see*
– HEKSERIJ BIJ DE BALUBA VAN KASAI
– STUDIE OVER DE GEWOONTELIJKE STRAFBEPALINGEN TEGEN HET OVERSPEL BIJ DE BALUBA EN BA LULUA VAN KASAI
Caesar, Juan Hugo *see* PALABRAS DE UN GOBERNANTE PERONISTA
Caesar, Julius *see* OPERA/EPITOME LIVII ETC
Caesariensis, Procopii *see*
– ARCANA HISTORIA (CBH 3,3)
– DE AEDIFICIIS DN. IUSTINIANI LIBRI 6 (CBH 3,2)
– HISTORIARUM SUI TEMPORIS LIBRI 8 (CBH 3,1)
Caesarii Heisterbasensis *see* HOMILIAE
Caesarius, S *see* ARELATENSIS EPISCOPUS, REGULA SANCTARUM VIRGINUM ALIAQUE OPUSCULA AD SANCTIMONIALES DIRECTA
CAESARIUS VON ARELATE UND DIE GALLISCHE KIRCHE SEINER ZEIT / Arnold, Carl Franklin – Leipzig: J.C. Hinrichs, 1894 – 2mf – us A.T.L.A. [240]
Caetani, L *see* ANNALI DELL'ISLAM, 1-10
O CAETE : ORGAO POLITICO E NOTICIOSO – Caete, 4 Jul 1948 – 1,5,6 – bl Biblioteca [072]
Cafasso, Arthur *see* DAS BILD IN DER DRAMATISCHEN SPRACHE GRILLPARZERS
CAFFARO – Genoa, Italy. -d. 27 Jan 1918-5 Aug 1919. Imperfect. 4 reels – 1 – uk British Libr Newspaper [072]
CAFFEINE : EFFECTS ON BLOOD PRESSURE, HEART RATE AND SHORT TERM MUSCULAR ENDURANCE IN STATIC EXERCISE OF MUSCLE GROUPS OF VARYING MASS / Bailey, Mark L – 1988 – 147p 2mf – 9 – $8.00 – us Microform Publ [612]
CAFFEINE, CARBOHYDRATE LOADING, AND PHYSICAL PERFORMANCE / O'Connor, MaryLou & McMurray, Robert G – 1992 – 1mf – 9 – $4.00 – us Microform Publ [613]
Cafferata, Juan F *see* LABOR PARLAMENTARIA 1912-1916, 1920-1924, 1924-1928. BUENOS AIRES, 1928
Caffese, Maria E *see* MAYO EN LA BIBLIOGRAFIA. BUENOS AIRES, 1961
Cafiero, Antonio Francisco *see*
– CINCO ANOS DESPUES
– DESDE QUE GRIT E VIVA PERON!
CAGE AND PEN FISH FARMING : CARRYING CAPACITY MODELS AND ENVIRONMENTAL IMPACT – 1984 – 139p – it F.A.O. [639]
Cagigal, Jose *see* LA MUERTE DE LUIS 16
Cagigal, Juan Manuel *see* ESCRITOS LITERARIOS Y CIENTIFICOS
CAGLAYAN – Balikesir: Karesi Matbaasi, 1925-1926 – 9 – $65.00 – us MEDOC [956]
Cagnolo, C *see* THE AKIKUYU, THEIR CUSTOMS, TRADITIONS AND FOLKLORE
Cahen, C *see* LA SYRIE DU NORD A L'EPOQUE DES CROISADES ET LA PRINCIPAUTE FRANQUE D'ANTIOCHE
CAHETE : ORGAO REPUBLICANO NATIVISTA – Maceio, Alagoas. 12 Out-26 Nov 1896 – 1,5,6 – bl Biblioteca [072]
LE CAHIER – Revue mensuelle des lettres et des arts. Paris. 1929-avr 1940 – 1 – fr A.C.R.P.P. [800]
CAHIER DE SPICILEGES – SEM35P310 – 1r – 1 – Can$12.00 – cn Bibl Nat [971]
UN CAHIER D'HISTOIRE LITTERAIRE / Feydel, Gabriel – Paris. Delaunay. 1818 – 9 – fr Hachette [440]
LES CAHIERS ALGERIENS – no. 2. Paris. juil aout 1950 – 1 – fr A.C.R.P.P. [073]
CAHIERS BLEUS – no. 1-119. Paris. aout 1928-mai 1932. Elements repris par: Chantiers cooperatifs voir a ce titre – 1 – fr A.C.R.P.P. [073]
LES CAHIERS COMMUNISTES – no. 1-6. Paris. 9 nov-21 dec 1922. deux no. 6 differents – 1 – fr A.C.R.P.P. [073]
CAHIERS CONGOLAIS D'ANTHROPOLOGIE ET D'HISTOIRE – v1-6. 1976-82. Brazzaville, Congo: s.n. illus. In French, with some summaries in English. Issued by Laboratoire d'Anthropologie, Universite de Brazzaville – 1 – us U.W. Library [301]
LES CAHIERS D'AMANI-Y – Saint-Marc, [Haiti: s.n. [v1 n2-9]. (1953-1954) 1955 – 3 sheets – us Res Libr [972]
LES CAHIERS D'AUJOURD'HUI – no. 1-9. Paris. oct 1912-fevr 1914 – 1 – fr A.C.R.P.P. [073]
LES CAHIERS D'AUJOURD'HUI – no.1-10. Oct 1912-Avr 1914; n.s. nos.1-15. Nov 1920-24. -irr – 1 – us U.W. Library [073]
CAHIERS DE CITE LIBRE – (Cont: Cite Libre) – Montreal, Canada. sep/oct 1966-winter 1971 – 1r – 1 – Can$60.00 – cn Can Microfilming [073]
CAHIERS DE CITE LIBRE *see* CITE LIBRE
LES CAHIERS DE CONTRE-ENSEIGNEMENT PROLETARIEN – Paris. dec 1931-mai 1937 – 1 – fr A.C.R.P.P. [073]
LES CAHIERS DE DROIT – Quebec: Faculte de droit. v1 no 1- 1954-. SEM16P310 – 11r – 5 – Can$374.00 – cn Bibl Nat [073]
CAHIERS DE GEOGRAPHIE DE QUEBEC – (1976- . 5,6,9) – v. 1-. 1956- – 1 – us UMI [910]
CAHIERS DE GEOGRAPHIE DE QUEBEC – Quebec: Les Presses universitaires Laval. v1- 1956-. SEM16P313 – 7r – 5 – Can$181.00 – cn Bibl Nat [910]
LES CAHIERS DE LA DECOLONISATION DU FRANC-CANADA : REVUE / ed by Roy, Raoul – Montreal, oct 1968-summer 1969 – 1r – 1 – Can$25.00 – cn Can Microfilming [073]
CAHIERS DE LA DEMOCRATIE – no. 1-54. Paris. juin 1933-avr 1939. mq no. 13 – 1 – fr A.C.R.P.P. [073]
LES CAHIERS DE LA JEUNESSE – Revue des jeunes de notre temps. no. 1-21. Paris. juil 1937-avr 1939 – 1 – fr A.C.R.P.P. [073]
CAHIERS DE LA NOUVELLE JOURNEE – Paris. 1924-avr 1932 (I-XXI) – 1 – fr A.C.R.P.P. [073]
CAHIERS DE LA QUINZAINE – Paris. 1900-juil 1914, 1925-34 – 1 – fr A.C.R.P.P. [073]
CAHIERS DE LA QUINZAINE – Paris. ser. 1-15. Jan 5 1900-July 7 1914; ser. 16-27, no. 2. Jan 1925-1936. Incomplete – 1 – us NY Public [073]
LES CAHIERS DE LA REPUBLIQUE DES LETTRES, DES SCIENCES ET DES ARTS – no. 1-12, avec un suppl. de mai-juil 1926. Paris. avr 1926-28 – 1 – fr A.C.R.P.P. [073]
CAHIERS DE L'AFRIQUE ET DE L'ASIE – Paris. v 1-3 n.d – 1 – us NY Public [950]
LES CAHIERS DE L'ENFANCE INADAPTEE – Paris. 1952-May 1973 – 5 – fr A.C.R.P.P. [305]
LES CAHIERS DE L'HEXAGONE – no. 1-56 57. Paris. avr 1961-juin 1972 – 5 – fr A.C.R.P.P. [073]
CAHIERS DE L'IEP – Beyrouth-Liban: Institut d'etudes palestiniennes. n10. 1980 – 1r – us Res Libr [956]
CAHIERS DE L'INSTITUT MAURICE THOREZ – no. 1-24. Paris. avr 1966-71 – 5 – fr A.C.R.P.P. [944]
CAHIERS DE NOTES – Manuscrits en Houailou, Nouvelle-Caledonie. 1906-17 – 9 – F30.00 – fr Ethnologie [306]
CAHIERS DE TERRAIN, KIMBERLEY, AUSTRALIE DU NORD-OUEST / Worms, E A – 9 – F300.00 – fr Ethnologie [980]
CAHIERS DES COMITES DE PREVENTION DU BATIMENT ET DES TRAVAUX PUBLICS – Issy-les-Moulineaux. sept oct 1968-73 – 1 – fr A.C.R.P.P. [073]
LES CAHIERS DES DROITS DE L'HOMME – Paris. 1920-fevr 1940 – 1 – fr A.C.R.P.P. [073]
LES CAHIERS DES ETATS GENERAUX – Montreal, Canada. n1. 9 jan 1967-mar 1969 – 1r – 1 – Can$65.00 – cn Can Microfilming [072]
CAHIERS DES QUATRE SAISONS – devenu: Cahiers des saisons. no. 1-49. Paris. aout 1955-67 – 1 – fr A.C.R.P.P. [073]
CAHIERS D'ETUDES AFRICAINES – Paris, 1960. v1-4 – 13mf – A-418/2 – ne IDC [960]
CAHIERS D'ETUDES DE RADIO-TELEVISION – no. 1-27 28. Paris. 1954-sept dec 1960 – 1 – fr A.C.R.P.P. [073]
CAHIERS D'ETUDES REVOLUTIONNAIRES – no. 1-6. Marseille. nov dec 1963-juil 1965 – 1 – fr A.C.R.P.P. [073]
CAHIERS [D'HISTOIRE] DE LA SEIGNEURIE DE CHAMBLY – Chambly. v1 n1. jun 1979-n17. nov 1991 – 1r – 1 – cn Can Microfilming [072]
CAHIERS D'HISTOIRE DE LA SOCIETE D'HISTOIRE DE BELOEIL/MONT ST-HILAIRE – Beloeil, oct 1937-n39 oct 1992 – 1r – 1 – cn Can Microfilming [072]
CAHIERS D'HISTOIRE DE LA SOCIETE D'HISTOIRE DE LONGUEUIL – Longueuil. n1. Printemps 1972-n21. Printemps 1991 – 1r – 1 – cn Can Microfilming [072]
CAHIERS D'HISTOIRE DE LA STE HISTORIQUE DE LA COTE-DU-SUD – La Pocatiere. v1 n1. 1963-n21. 1986f – 1r – 1 – cn Can Microfilming [072]
CAHIERS D'HISTOIRE DES DEUX-MONTAGNES – Saint-Eustache. v1 n1. mar 1978-v12 n1. avr 1992 – 2r – 1 – cn Can Microfilming [072]
CAHIERS D'HISTOIRE DES PAYS D'EN HAUT – Saint-Sauveur. v1 n1. Printemps 1979-n54. jun 1992 – 1r – 1 – cn Can Microfilming [072]
CAHIERS D'HISTOIRE – LA SOCIETE D'HISTOIRE REGIONALE DE QUEBEC – Quebec. n1. 1947-n35. 1983f – 5r – 1 – cn Can Microfilming [072]
LES CAHIERS D'OCCIDENT – I, no. 1-10. Paris. 1926-27; 2e s., no. 1-10. 1928-30. fusionne avec: Latinite. Revue des pays d'Occident et La Reaction pour l'ordre pour former: La Revue du siecles voir a ces titres – 1 – fr A.C.R.P.P. [073]
CAHIERS DU BOLCHEVISME – Paris. nov 1924-aout 1939. A partir de juil 1939, parait sous le titre de: Cahiers du communisme. Pour les suppl. voir Les Dossiers de l'agitateur et Bulletin colonial – 1 – fr A.C.R.P.P. [073]
CAHIERS DU CERCLE PROUDHON – Paris. 1912, 1914 – 1 – fr A.C.R.P.P. [320]
CAHIERS DU COLLEGE DE PATAPHYSIQUE – devenu: College de pataphysique. Dossiers. Paris. 1952-63 – 1 – fr A.C.R.P.P. [073]
CAHIERS DU COMMUNISME – Paris. v.3-25. Dec 31, 1927-Dec 1948. Incomplete – 1 – 69.00 – us L of C Photodup [335]
LES CAHIERS DU CONTADOUR – Paris. puis Saint-Paul. ete 1936-fevr 1939 – 1 – fr A.C.R.P.P. [073]
CAHIERS DU GROUPE FRANCOISE MINKOWSKA – Paris. juil 1958-65 – 1 – fr A.C.R.P.P. [073]
LES CAHIERS DU JAZZ – nos.1-16 17 (all publ). Nov 1959-68. (Jazz Periodicals) – 1 reel – 1 – $135.00 – us UPA [780]
LES CAHIERS DU MILITANT / Parti communiste francais (S F IC) – no. 1, 4, 9-10. Paris. mai 1924-juil 1925 – 1 – fr A.C.R.P.P. [335]
LES CAHIERS DU MOIS – no. 1-25 26. Paris. mai 1924-juin 1927 – 1 – fr A.C.R.P.P. [073]
LES CAHIERS DU PLATEAU – no. 17-18, 20. Passy (Haute-Savoie). 1938-juin 1939 – 1 – fr A.C.R.P.P. [073]
CAHIERS DU SUD – 1924-50 – 1 – 24480.00 – uk Dawson [073]
LES CAHIERS DU SUD – Marseille. 1924-66 – 1 – fr A.C.R.P.P. [073]
LES CAHIERS DU THEATRE – no. 1-10. Paris. mars 1926-avr 1932, sept 1936 – 1 – fr A.C.R.P.P. [790]
CAHIERS ECONOMIQUES ET SOCIAUX DE L'INSTITUT DE RECHERCHES ECONOMIQUES ET SOCIALES – Lovanium, Kinshasa, 1962-1966. v1-4 – 38mf – A-671/1 – ne IDC [330]
CAHIERS FRANCAIS – London, UK. Jul 1944 – 1 – uk British Libr Newspaper [072]
LES CAHIERS FRANCAIS – 1992-1995 – 8 times per yr – 9 – F1,280.00 – sz Infoprint [073]
CAHIERS G.L.M – Paris. mai 1936-mars 1939, 1954-56 – 1 – fr A.C.R.P.P. [073]
CAHIERS HISTORIQUES / ed by Blanchet, L J N – Chambly, Canada. 15 jan 1929 – 1r – 1 – Can$25.00 – cn Can Microfilming [900]
CAHIERS INTERNATIONAUX DE SOCIOLOGIE – v. 4. Paris. 1948. BH-1802 1 – 9 – ne IDC [300]
LES CAHIERS JAUNES – Paris. No.1-2,4. 1932-33 – 1 – fr A.C.R.P.P. [073]
CAHIERS LEON BLOY – La Rochelle. sept oct 1924-mai aout 1939, mars avr 1952 – 5 – fr A.C.R.P.P. [073]
CAHIERS MANUSCRITS DE COMPTES RENDUS DES CONFERENCES PASTORALES, NOUVELLE-CALEDONIE / Leenhardt, Maurice – 9 – F220.00 – fr Ethnologie [306]
LES CAHIERS NATURALISTES – no. 1-36. Paris. 1955-68 – 1 – fr A.C.R.P.P. [073]
CAHIERS PIERRE LOTI – Paris. juin 1950-72 – 5 – fr A.C.R.P.P. [073]
LES CAHIERS RATIONALISTES – No.1, 1931-. Paris: Union Rationaliste. -m. -irr. Indexes 1931-65. Includes index to Courrier Rationaliste. 1v. 1289 – 1 – us U.W. Library [140]
LES CAHIERS ROUGES – no. 3-12. Paris. aout sept 1937-juin juil 1938. mq no. 6 – 1 – fr A.C.R.P.P. [073]
Cahill, Daniel William *see* WORKS. FIRST AMERICAN EDITION OF THE WORKS OF THE REV. D.W. CAHILL, D.D.
Cahill, M *see* A SCOTTISH KNIGHT-ERRANT
Cahm, C *see* KROPOTKIN AND LAW
CAHPER JOURNAL – Gloucester. v53-60. 1987-94 – 9 – Can$20.00y – 0834-1915 – cn Micromedia [073]
CAHUIDE: REVISTA NACIONAL – Lima. 2-22, 1939-59. Incomplete – 1 – 69.00 – us L of C Photodup [972]
LA CAIDA DE PERON, DE JUNIO A SETIEMBRE DE 1955 / Godio, Julio – [Buenos Aires]: Granica, [1st ed 1973] – 1 – CSUXADJ2337-B – us Hoover Inst Photo [320]
Caietanus, Thomas de Vio Cardinalis *see* DE NOMINUM ANALOGIA
CAIFENG – China. Folklore. -bim.1986-. M-D110 – 1 – $23.00r – cc Microforms [072]

CAILLAUX: STATESMAN OF PEACE / Franzius, Enno – Hoover Institution Press, 1976. Manuscript in Microfilm Series 2+5. 268 pp – 1 – $35.00r – us Hoover Inst Photo [920]
Caillemer, E *see* LA NATURALISATION A ATHENES
Cailler-Bois, Ricardo *see*
- ENSAYO SOBRE EL RIO DE LA PLATA Y LA REVOLUCION FRANCESA
- NUESTROS CORSARIOS 1. BROWN Y BOUCHARD EN EL PACIFICO, 1815-1816

Cailleux, E *see* LA QUESTION CHINOISE...
Cailliaud, F *see* VOYAGE A MEROE, AU FLEUVE BLANC AU-DELA DE FAZOQL DANS LE MIDI DU ROYAUME DE SENNAR, A SYOUAH ET DANS CINQ AUTRES OASIS; FAIT DANS LES ANNEES 1819, 1820, 1821 ET 1822
Caillie, R *see* TRAVELS THROUGH CENTRAL AFRICA TO TIMBUCTOO
EL CAIMAN BARBUDO – Havana. nos. 1-95. Jan 1966-1977 – 1 – 35.00r – us Hoover Inst Photo [073]
CAIN / Shaikevich, N M – Warsaw. 1911. BJ-422-82 1 – 9 – ne IDC [305]
CAIN AND ABEL, THE UNINTENTIONAL MURDER / Arrigoni, Enrico – Biblical Fairy Tales, No.2 – 9 – 1.00f – at Libertarian Micro [335]
Caine, Hall *see*
- MY STORY
- RECOLLECTIONS OF DANTE GABRIEL ROSSETTI

Caine, William Sproston *see* A TRIP ROUND THE WORLD IN 1887-8
Caines, George *see* PRACTICAL FORMS OF THE SUPREME COURT, TAKEN FROM TIDD'S APPENDIX OF THE FORMS OF THE COURT OF KING'S BENCH.
Caird, Edward *see*
- LAY SERMONS AND ADDRESSES
- THE SOCIAL PHILOSOPHY AND RELIGION OF COMTE

Caird, John *see*
- ESSAYS FOR SUNDAY READING
- THE FUNDAMENTAL IDEAS OF CHRISTIANITY
- INTRODUCTION TO THE PHILOSOPHY OF RELIGION
- SPINOZA
- UNIVERSITY ADDRESSES
- UNIVERSITY SERMONS

Caird, William Renny *see* CHRISTI WORTE UEBER VOLLENDUNG DER WEGE GOTTES
CAIRNS ARGUS – Australia. 3 Nov 1891-10 Dec 1897 (very imperfect).-w. 6 reels – 1 – uk British Libr Newspaper [072]
Cairns, David Smith *see* CHRISTIANITY IN THE MODERN WORLD
Cairns, John *see*
- CHRIST THE CENTRAL EVIDENCE OF CHRISTIANITY
- CHRIST, THE MORNING STAR
- THE HONGKONG REGISTER
- UNBELIEF IN THE EIGHTEENTH CENTURY

Cairo, Angel *see* PERONISMO
CAIRO BAPTIST CHURCH. MISSOURI : CHURCH RECORDS – 1888-1956 – 1 – 22.95 – us Baptist [240]
CAIRO PRESS REVIEW – Sept-Dec 1962; May 1963-Dec 1982 – 1 – 4485.00 – us L of C Photodup [073]
CAIRO RECORD – Cairo, NE. -w. Apr. 1907-Aug. 1909; Feb. 1920- – 1 – us NE Hist [071]
CAISSA – Revista Argentina de Ajedrez. Buenos Aires. v. 1-14. 1937-1950. Incomplete – 1 – us NY Public [073]
Caisse Ecclesiastique St. Joseph. Quebec *see* REGLES DE LA SOCIETE...ETABLIE DANS L'ARCHDIOCESE DE QUEBEC
Caisse, Joseph Camille *see* L'INSTITUT DES FRERES DES ECOLES CHRETIENNES
CAISSE NATIONALE D'ECONOMIE, FONDEE LE 1ER JANVIER, 1899: ARTHUR GAGNON, SECRETAIRE-TRESORIER / Caisse Nationale d'economie. Montreal – Montreal, La Caisse, 1899. 00378. (Pre-1900 Canadiana) – 9 – cn C.I.H.M. [971]
Caisse Nationale d'economie. Montreal *see* CAISSE NATIONALE D'ECONOMIE, FONDEE LE 1ER JANVIER, 1899: ARTHUR GAGNON, SECRETAIRE-TRESORIER
Caisse Nationale des Monuments Historiques et des Sites. Paris *see*
- ANTIQUITIES
- DECORATIVE ART
- DRAWINGS IN PROVINCIAL AND OTHER MUSEUMS
- DRAWINGS IN THE LOUVRE AND NATIONAL MUSEUMS
- INDEXES
- MANUSCRIPTS
- PAINTINGS IN PROVINCIAL AND OTHER MUSEUMS
- PAINTINGS IN THE LOUVRE
- SCULPTURE

Caisse Nationale des Monuments Historiques et des Sites. Paris. Archives Photographiques *see* ARCHITECTURE AND EARLY PHOTOGRAPHY IN FRANCE
CAITHNESS COURIER – 1 – £42.00r – uk Scot News [072]
CAITHNES-SHIRE, 1837 : BRITISH ISLES CENSUS DIRECTORIES PROJECT, SCOTLAND. VOL 33 – 1mf – 9 – A$9.00 – at Vine [941]
CAITHNESSHIRE, 1852 : BRITISH ISLES CENSUS DIRECTORIES PROJECT, SCOTLAND. VOL 20 – 1mf – 9 – A$9.00 – at Vine [941]
Caius, John *see*
- A BOKE OR COUNSEILL AGAINST THE DISEASE CALLED THE SWEATE
- A BOKE, OR COUNSEILL AGAINST THE DISEASE COMMONLY CALLED THE SWEATE, OR SWEATING SICKNESSE

O CAIXEIRO : ORGAO DEFENSOR DA CLASSE CAIXEIRAL – Pilar, Alagoas. 16 Mar 1892 – 1,5,6 – bl Biblioteca [072]
O CAIXEIRO : PERIODICO NOTICIOSO, COMMERCIAL E LITTERARIO – Maceio, Alagoas. 7 Mar-7 Set 1880 – 1,5,6 – bl Biblioteca [072]
O CAIXEIRO : PUBLICACAO LITTERARIA, SCIENTIFICA E NOTICIOSA – [s.l.]. 1 Mar 1878 – 1,5,6 – bl Biblioteca [072]
O CAIXEIRO NACIONAL – [s.l.]. 24 Ago 1855 – 1,5,6 – bl Biblioteca [072]
CAIZHENG – Finance.1986. F/P 276 – 9 – $4.50f – cc Microforms [073]
Caja Ahorros y Monte de Piedad de Caceres *see*
- MEMORIA Y DATOS ESTADISTICOS CORRESPONDIENTES AL ANO 1954
- REGLAMENTO PROVISIONAL DE PROCEDIMIENTO ELECTORAL

Caja Ahorros y Monte de Piedad de Caceres. *see* ESTATUTOS GENERALES
Caja de Ahorros de Plasencia *see* TRUJILLO EN FIESTAS
CAJA DE AHORROS, PRESTAMOS Y SOCORROS FONTES. MEMORIA, BALANCE Y ESTADISTICA DEL EJERCICIO 1ST DE SU FUNCIONAMIENTO, CERRADO EL 31 DE AGOSTO DE 1909 – Almendralejo: Imp. Juan Bote, 1909 – 1 – sp Bibl Santa Ana [946]
Caja de Ahorros y Monte de Piedad *see*
- GUION DE CONFERENCIAS PRONUNCIADAS EN EL AULA DE CULTURA DE LA CAJA DE AHORROS Y MONTE DE PIEDAD DE PLASENCIA. ABRIL-MAYO 1971
- MEMORIA Y DATOS ESTADISTICOS CORRESPONDIENTES AL EJERCICIO 1958
- MEMORIA Y DATOS ESTADISTICOS CORRESPONDIENTES AL EJERCICIO DE 1957

Caja de Ahorros y Monte de Piedad. Caceres *see*
- ESTATUTOS GENERALES
- MEMORIA CORRESPONDIENTE AL EJERCICIO DE 1961
- MEMORIA CORRESPONDIENTE AL EJERCICIO DE 1962
- MEMORIA CORRESPONDIENTE AL EJERCICIO DE 1963
- MEMORIA CORRESPONDIENTE AL EJERCICIO DE 1964
- MEMORIA DE 1976
- MEMORIA Y DATOS ESTADISTICOS CORRESPONDIENTES AL ANO 1952
- MEMORIA Y DATOS ESTADISTICOS CORRESPONDIENTES AL ANO DE 1955

Caja de Ahorros y Monte de Piedad. Plasencia *see*
- MEMORIA. 1958
- MEMORIA 1972

CAJA EXTREMENA DE PREVISION SOCIAL – Madrid: Imp. de Minuesa, 1930 – 1 – sp Bibl Santa Ana [946]
Caja General Frexnense *see* EJERCICIO SOCIAL DEL ANO 1912. MEMORIA Y BALANCE LEIDOS Y APROBADOS EN JUNTA GENERAL DE SOCIOS...1913
Caja Postal de Ahorros *see* 15TH CERTAMEN NACIONAL DEL AHORRO
CAJA REAL DE FILIPINAS (ANNO 1565-1701) – Sevilla – 1r – 5,6 – sp Cultura [950]
CAJA REAL DE MEJICO (ANNO 1553-1563) – Sevilla – 1r – 5,6 – sp Cultura [972]
CAJA REAL DE NUEVA ESPANA (ANNO 1533-1553) – Sevilla – 1r – 5,6 – sp Cultura [946]
CAJA REAL DE NUEVA ESPANA (ANNO 1540-1549) – Sevilla – 1r – 5,6 – sp Cultura [946]
CAJA REAL DE PANAMA. CUENTAS DE DESCARGAS (ANNO 1550-1576) – Sevilla – 1r – 5,6 – sp Cultura [972]
CAJA REAL DE PUERTO RICO (ANNO 1627-1633) – Sevilla – 1r – 5,6 – sp Cultura [972]
CAJA REAL DE SAN FRANCISCO DE QUITO (ANNO 1549-1590) – Sevilla – 1r – 5,6 – sp Cultura [977]
CAJA REALES DE INDIAS – Sevilla – 17r – 5,6 – sp Cultura [970]
Caja Rural de Ahorros y Prestamos de Almendralejo *see*
- ESTATUTOS Y REGLAMENTOS
- MEMORIA CORRESPONDIENTE AL EJERCICIO DE 1967 APROBADA EN JUNTA GENERAL DE ACCIONISTAS CELEBRADA EL 18-2-1968
- MEMORIA Y BALANCE DEL TERCER EJERCICIO SOCIAL, LEIDA Y APROBADA EN LA JUNTA GENERAL DE SOCIOS...1909

Caja Rural de Ahorros y Prestamos de Fuente de Cantos *see* MEMORIA LEIDA EN LA JUNTA GENERAL DE SOCIOS, CELEBRADA EL DIA 3 DE MARZO DE 1907
Caja Rural de Ahorros y Prestamos de los Santos de Maimona *see* ESTATUTOS
Caja Rural de Ahorros y Prestamos Nuestra Senora de Botoa *see*
- MEMORIA. EJERCICIO DE 1966
- MEMORIA. EJERCICIOS DE 1956-57
- MEMORIA Y EJERCICIO DE 1961

Caja Rural de Almendralejo *see* MEMORIA 1975
CAJAS REALES DE PANAMA Y PORTOBELO (ANNO 1514-1760) – Sevilla – 24r – 5,6 – sp Cultura [972]
Cajetan, T de V *see* OPERA OMNIA QUOTQUOT IN SACRAE SCRIPTURAE EXPOSITIONUM REPERIUNTUR
Cajetanus *see*
- COMM. IN SUMMAM THEOL. TH. AQ. VOL. 1
- DE NOMINUM ANALOGIA – DE CONCEPTU ENTIS
- OPUSCULA OMNIA 1558

Cajetanus, Cardinal, Thomas a Vio *see* COMMENTARII ILLUSTRES...IN QUINQUE MOSAICOS LIBROS
IL (!) CAJO FABRIZIO : OPERA EN 3 ATTI DEL SIG. JOMELLI – Ms, [1772] – 1 – us Sibley [780]
CAJON DE SASTRE / Sanchez Arjona, Vicente – Sevilla: Imprenta Zambrano, 1956 – 1 – sp Bibl Santa Ana [946]
CALAHAN FIRST BAPTIST CHURCH. CALAHAN, FLORIDA : CHURCH RECORDS – 1841-1943 – 1 – 20.97 – us Baptist [240]
Calame-Griaule, G. et al *see* SERRURES DOGON. ANALYSE ETHNO-MORPHOLOGIQUE
Calamy, Edmund *see* FOUR SPEECHES DELIVERED IN GUILD-HALL, 1643
Caland, W *see* BAUDHAYANA S'RAUTA SUTRA
Calandrelli, A *see*
- CUESTIONES DE DERECHO INTERNACIONAL PRIVADO (EL DIVORCIO)
- EL DIVORCIO ANTE EL DERECHO INTERNACIONAL PRIVADO...

CALAS OU LE FANATISME / Lemierre, D'Argy – (French Theatre Series). Paris. Bureau des revolutions de Paris, et au Theatre du Palais-Royal. 1791 – 9 – fr Hachette [820]
Calasibeta, M *see* LA ROSA DE PALERMO, ANTIDOTO DE LA PESTE Y DE TODO MAL CONTAGIOSO
THE CALAVERAS CALIFORNIAN – Angels Camp, CA. 1994- – 1+ r – 1 – $50.00 ($50.00y) – B02014 – us Library Micro [071]
CALAVERAS CHRONICLE – Mokelumne Hill, CA. 1870-1908 – 8r – 1 – $400.00 – C03339 – us Library Micro [071]
CALAVERAS COUNTY, 1893 – 1r – 1 – $50.00 – D009 – us Library Micro [978]
CALAVERAS PROSPECT – San Andreas, CA. Jul 1893-1944 – 17r – 1 – $850.00 – C02757 – us Library Micro [071]
CALAVERAS PROSPECT, WEEKLY CITIZEN AND CHRONICLE – San Andreas, CA. 1945- – 32+ r – 1 – $1,600.00 ($100.00y) – C02758 – us Library Micro [071]
CALAVERAS, SAN JOAQUIN, STANISLAUS AND TUOLUMNE COUNTIES – Calaveras Co, CA. 1856 – 1r – 1 – $50.00 – D010 – us Library Micro [978]
CALAVERAS, SAN JOAQUIN, STANISLAUS AND TUOLUMNE COUNTIES – San Joaquin Co, CA. 1856 – 1r – 1 – $50.00 – D010 – us Library Micro [978]
CALAVERAS, SAN JOAQUIN, STANISLAUS AND TUOLUMNE COUNTIES – Stanislaus Co, CA. 1856 – 1r – 1 – $50.00 – D010 – us Library Micro [978]
CALAVERAS, SAN JOAQUIN, STANISLAUS AND TUOLUMNE COUNTIES – Tuolumne Co, CA. 1856 – 1r – 1 – $50.00 – D010 – us Library Micro [978]
CALAVERAS/LOS GATOS/SARATOGA – 1992 – 1r – 1 – $50.00 – P00012 – us Library Micro [910]
CALAVERAS/TUOLUMNE – 1910-38; 1992- – 31+ r – 1 – $1,550.00 – P00013 – us Library Micro [910]
Calberla, H *see* DIE MACROLEPIDOPTEREN-FAUNA DER ROEMISCHEN CAMPAGNA UND DER ANGRENZENDEN PROVINZEN MITTEL-ITALIENS
Calcagnini, Celio *see* CAELII CALCAGNINI, FERRARIENSIS..
CALCAREOUS SOILS – 1977 – 300p – it F.A.O. [631]
CALCIFIED TISSUE ABSTRACTS – Quarterly – 9 – us C.S.A. [610]
CALCIFIED TISSUE INTERNATIONAL – v. 1-32. 1967-80 – 1,5,9 – us UMI [073]
CALCIUM REQUIREMENTS : REPORT OF AN FAO/WHO EXPERT GROUP; ROME, 1961 – 1968 – 54p – it F.A.O. [640]
Calckman, I I *see* ANTIDOTUM: TEGEN-GIFT VANT GEBRUYCK OF ONGEBRUYCK VANT ORGEL
Calcott, D *see* INTERIM REPORT ON EDUCATION IN A RURAL AREA ...
DU CALCUL INTEGRAL / Condorcet, Marie Jean Antoine Nicolas de – Paris: Imp. Didot, 1765.vii,94p. 2 fiches. (Science Collection) – 9 – 6.00 – fr Bibl Nationale [510]
CALCULATIONES NOUITER EMENDATE ATQUE REUISE. QUAESTIO INSUPER DE REACTIONE IUXTA ARISTOTELIS SENTENTIAM COMMENTATORIS / Swineshead, Richard – Venetijs, 1520 – 1 – us U.W. Library [180]
CALCUTTA CHRISTIAN HERALD – India. -w. 17 July 1844-2 Dec 1845. 1 reel – 1 – uk British Libr Newspaper [072]
CALCUTTA GAZETTE – Calcutta, 1784-1815 – 13r – IF-107/3 – ne IDC [950]
CALCUTTA GAZETTE – India. -w. Jan 1792-March 1800. 5 reels – 1 – uk British Libr Newspaper [072]
THE CALCUTTA GAZETTE – Alipore. 1903-1940; 1957-1966 – 1 – us NY Public [324]
Calcutta Geographical Society *see* GEOGRAPHICAL REVIEW OF INDIA
CALCUTTA GOVERNMENT GAZETTE / Calcutta. India – 1815-32 – 1 – uk Microform Academic [950]
Calcutta. India *see*
- CALCUTTA GOVERNMENT GAZETTE
- MUNICIPAL GAZETTE

CALCUTTA JOURNAL OF NATURAL HISTORY AND MISCELLANY OF THE ARTS AND SCIENCES IN INDIA – Calcutta, 1841-1847. v1-8 – 90mf – I-276/2 – ne IDC [500]
CALCUTTA JOURNAL OF POLITICS AND GENERAL LITERATURE – 1818-23. Lacking: 1822 (4), nr. 194-195; 1823 (1). BI-274 2 – 8 – ne IDC [073]
CALCUTTA LAW JOURNAL – (Missing: 1910-1911, v11-14; 1940-1942, v72-75) – Calcutta, 1905-1948. v1-82 – 1,003mf – I-557/2 – ne IDC [340]
CALCUTTA LITERARY GAZETTE AND JOURNAL OF BELLES LETTRES SCIENCE AND THE ARTS – v. 1-10. Calcutta. 1832-34. Available: 1832, v. 7. BI-524 2 – 8 – ne IDC [800]
CALCUTTA MAGAZINE AND MONTHLY REGISTER – (Missing: 1832. v2) – Calcutta, 1830-1832. v1-3 – 74mf – I-275/2 – ne IDC [950]
CALCUTTA MONTHLY JOURNAL – (Missing: v1-14; 18-19; 28; 43(340); 45(354); 65; 73(456)) – Calcutta, 1798-1830. v1-65; N.S. 1831-1834. v66-79; S.3 1835-1841. v1-7 – 950mf – I-536/2 – ne IDC [950]
CALCUTTA MORNING POST – India. 1812-13 – 1 – uk Microform Academic [072]
CALCUTTA REVIEW – Calcutta, 1913-1920. v1-7 – 73mf – I-108/2 – ne IDC [950]
CALCUTTA REVIEW – (Missing: 1853. v20) – Calcutta, 1844-1912. v1-135 – 1,071mf – I-107/2 – ne IDC [950]
CALCUTTA REVIEW – (Missing: 1943/1944. v87(4-12)) – Calcutta, 1921-1956. v1-141 – 997mf – I-109/2 – ne IDC [950]
CALCUTTA WEEKLY NOTES – (Missing: Various pages in v44; 45; 46; 47) – Calcutta, 1896-1965. v1-69 – 2,127mf – I-537/2 – ne IDC [950]

Caldecott, Alfred *see* THE PHILOSOPHY OF RELIGION IN ENGLAND AND AMERICA
Caldecott, William Shaw *see*
- SOLOMON'S TEMPLE: ITS HISTORY AND ITS STRUCTURE
- THE TABERNACLE

CALDER / Reunion des musees nationaux. Paris – 1965. 51 illus. 1 fiche – 9 – fr Réunion [700]
CALDERON : POEMITA DRAMATICO / Baumgartner, Alexander – Madrid: Libreria de San Jose, 1882 – 1r – 1 – us U.W. Library [820]
Calderon Altamirano de Chaves Hinojosa y Paredes, Luis Francisco *see* OPUSCULOS DE ORO, VIRTUDES MORALES CHRISTIANAS
Calderon, Cesareo *see* APUNTES BIOGRAFICAS DEL M.I. SR. D. FRANCISCO DE PAULA SOTO Y MANCERA, ARCIPRESTE DE LA SANTA Y APOSTOLICA IGLESIA DE SANTIAGO DE COMPOSTELA, NATURAL DE ZAFRA, PROVINCIA DE BADAJOZ
CALDERON DE LA BARCA / Frutos Cortes, Eugenio – Barcelona: Labor S.A., 1949 – sp Bibl Santa Ana [946]
CALDERON DE LA BARCA. AUTOS SACRAMENTALES. ANTOLOGIA / Frutos Cortes, Eugenio – Madrid: Editora Nacional, 1947 – sp Bibl Santa Ana [440]
Calderon de la Barca, Francisco E I de *see* LA VIDA EN MEXICO DURANTE UNA RESIDENCIA DE DOS ANOS EN ESE PAIS(...)
Calderon de la Barca, Pedro *see*
- EL ALCALDE DE ZALAMEA
- ALCALDE DE ZALAMEA, EL
- AURORA EN COPACAVANA, LA

Calderon de Robles, Juan *see* PRIVILEGIA SELECTIORA MILITIAE SANCTI IULIANI..
Calderon S *see* METEORITO DE GUARENA
Calderon, S *see*
- ESTUDIO PETROGRAFICO DEL METEORITO DE GUARENA
- LISTA PRELIMINAR DE LAS PLANTAS DE EL SALVADOR

Calderwood, Henry *see*
- DAVID HUME
- RELATIONS OF SCIENCE AND RELIGION

Caldwell, A B *see* MAKERS OF AMERICAN
Caldwell, Erskine *see* SCRAPBOOKS OF ERSKINE CALDWELL
Caldwell, J A *see* HISTORY OF BELMONT AND JEFFERSON COUNTIES
Caldwell, J R *see* HISTORY OF TAMA COUNTY
Caldwell, James Ernest *see* SONGS OF THE PINES
Caldwell. Kansas *see*
- POLICE DOCKET
- RECORDS

Caldwell, Louis Goldsborough *see* A SUGGESTED METHOD OF COMPLIANCE WITH THE DAVIS AMENDMENT TO THE RADIO LAW
Caldwell, Robert *see* CHI-NYANJA SIMPLIFIED
CALEB STRONG PAPERS, 1657-1818 / Strong, Caleb – Massachusetts Historical Society – 1r – 1 – $85.00 – us UMI [920]
Caledonia, Bill de *see*
- DONDE ESTUVO?
- DONDE ESTUVO? REFUTANDO CON LOS HECHOS UN PANFLETO INSIDIOSO Y ANONIMO

THE CALEDONIA INTERCHANGE – Nass River, B.C: Printed at C.M.S. Mission ... by ... J B McCullagh's Indian Boys, [1899?-19–] – 9 – cn C.I.H.M. [971]
CALEDONIAN – An illustrated family magazine. v. 1-23. 1901-23 – 1 – 109.00 – us L of C Photodup [073]
CALEDONIAN MERCURY – Edinburgh, Scotland, UK.1832. -w. 2 reels – 1 – uk British Libr Newspaper [072]
THE CALEDONIAN RECORD – St Johnsbury, VT. v12 n175. 1 feb 1928 – 1r – 1 – Can$25.00 – cn Can Microfilming [071]
CALEDONIENS, REPERTOIRE BIO-BIBLIOGRAPHIQUE DE LA NOUVELLE-CALEDONIE / O'Reilly, P – 9 – F90.00 – fr Ethnologie [980]
CALEF AND CHUTER LETTER BOOK – 1783-96.From Rhodes House Library, Oxford. BRRAM – 1 – uk Microform Academic [975]
Calegari, Francesco A *see* AMPLA DIMOSTRAZIONE DEGLI ARMONIALI MUSICALE..
Calello, Hugo *see* PODER POLITICO Y POPULISMO
CALENDAR / Montreal Gazette – Montreal, Canada. Comp. by A. R. M. Lower. 1778-1841 – 1 reel – 1 – $68.00 – cn Library Assoc [971]
THE CALENDAR – Kenora, Mar-Oct 1973 – 1r – 1 – cn Preston [971]
CALENDAR: AN ANTHOLOGY OF POETRY – Prairie City, Ill. 1940-1942. 3 v – 1 – us NY Public [810]
CALENDAR OF AFRICAN LETTERS / United Society for the Propagation of the Gospel in Foreign Parts – 1837-1896 – 1 – uk Microform Academic [240]
CALENDAR OF ANCIENT RECORDS OF DUBLIN: IN THE POSSESSION OF THE MUNICIPAL CORPORATION OF THAT CITY / Dublin – By John T. Gilbert; pub. by authority of the Municipal Council. Dublin: J. Dollard, 1889-1919 – 1 – us U.W. Library [941]
CALENDAR OF CORONERS ROLLS OF THE CITY OF LONDON, 1300-1378 / ed by Sharpe, R R – H 1261 2. 1913 – 8 – ne IDC [025]
CALENDAR OF ENTRIES IN THE PAPAL REGISTERS RELATING TO GREAT BRITAIN AND IRELAND. PAPAL LETTERS / Great Britain. Public Record Office – v. 1-11. 1893-1921 – 1 – 85.00 – us L of C Photodup [240]
CALENDAR OF ITEMS MICROFILMED AT THE INDIA OFFICE, LONDON / [Crane, Robert I] – [Ann Arbor: Center for South and Southeast Asian Studies? 196-] – us Res Libr [950]
CALENDAR OF MANUSCRIPTS / New York Public Library.Schomburg Collection of Negro Literature and History – 1r – 1 – us Ross [975]
THE CALENDAR OF ST WILLIBRORD / Wilson, H Austin – 1919 – 4mf – 8 – ne Slangenburg [240]
CALENDAR OF STATE PAPERS, COLONIAL SERIES, 1574-1668 : AMERICA AND THE WEST INDIES – London. v1-2. 1860-1880 – 26mf – 9 – ne IDC [970]
CALENDAR OF STATE PAPERS, DOMESTIC SERIES OF THE REIGN OF CHARLES I, 1625-1649 / Great Britain. Public Record Office – 1858-97 – 1 – 160.00 – us L of C Photodup [941]
A CALENDAR OF THE COURT MINUTES ETC. OF THE EAST INDIA COMPANY 1635-1679 – Oxford, 1907-1938 – 89mf – 1606/2 – ne IDC [950]
A CALENDAR OF THE WARRANTS FOR LAND IN KENTUCKY, GRANTED FOR SERVICE IN THE FRENCH & INDIAN WAR – Abstracted by Philip Fall Taylor, 1967. Excerpted and reprinted from Year Book of the Society of Colonial Wars in the Commonwealth of Kentucky, 1917. Indexed. 1 fiche. F-0858 – 9 – us A.G.L.L. [520]
A CALENDAR OF THE...RECORDS, 1505-1750 – (v1-3 ed by F A Inderwick. v4 ed by R A Roberts) – London: Masters of the Bench, 1896 – 20mf – 9 – $30.00 – LLMC 84-297 – us L.L.M.C. [520]
CALENDAR OF VIRGINIA STATE PAPERS AND OTHER MANUSCRIPTS / Virginia – Richmond. 1875-93 – 1 – 138.00 – us L of C Photodup [978]
CALENDARING PRACTICES OF THE EASTERN DISTRICT OF NORTH CAROLINA / Olson, Susan M – Washington: FJC, 1987 – 1mf – 9 – $1.50 – LLMC 95-354 – us L.L.M.C. [340]
Calendario de Extremadura *see* 1851
CALENDARIO DE EXTREMADURA PARA EL ANO 1863...Y AUMENTADO CON EL CALENDARIO PORTUGUES DE BARDA D'AGUA / Extremadura. Spain (Province.) – 1863 – 9 – 1.50f – sp Bibl Santa Ana [520]
CALENDARIO DEL CAMPEONATO 1972-73 / Federacion Extremena de Futbol – Caceres: Tip. Extremadura, 1972 – 1 – sp Bibl Santa Ana [790]
CALENDARIO ESCOLAR 1968/69 / Seminario Diocesano de San Anton – Badajoz: Graficas Tejado, 1968 – sp Bibl Santa Ana [240]
CALENDARIO ESCOLAR 1969/70 / Seminario Diocesano de San Anton – Badajoz: Graficas Tejado, 1970 – sp Bibl Santa Ana [240]
CALENDARIO, MANUAL, Y GUIA DE FORESTEROS DE LAS ISLAS FILIPINAS, PARA EL ANO DE... – Manila: Impreso en Sto Tomas a cargo de D Candido Lopez, 1839-40 – 1r – 1 – us Res Libr [520]
CALENDARIO PARA 1901 – [s.l.] 1901 – 1,5,6 – bl Biblioteca [072]
CALENDARIO PARA LA PROVINCIA DE EXTREMADURA.. / Extremadura. Spain (Province.) – 1827 – 9 – 1.50f – sp Bibl Santa Ana [520]
CALENDARIO Y PLAN DE ESTUDIOS DEL CURSO ACADEMICO 1972-73. SEMINARIO DIOCESANO / Coria-Caceres – Caceres: Edit. Extremadura, 1972 – 1 – sp Bibl Santa Ana [370]
CALENDARIO Y PLAN DE ESTUDIOS DEL CURSO ACADEMICO 1975-76. SEMINARIO MAYOR DIOCESANO / Diocesis – Caceres: Edit. Extremadura, 1975 – 1 – sp Bibl Santa Ana [370]
CALENDARS OF CHARTERS AND ROLLS IN THE MANUCRIPT COLLECTIONS OF THE BRITISH LIBRARY / British Library – 19r – 1 – £1,320.00 – uk Chadwyck [940]
CALENDARS OF CHARTERS AND ROLLS IN THE MANUSCRIPT COLLECTIONS OF THE BODLEIAN LIBRARY / Bodleian Library – 327mf – 9 – £1,260.00 – uk Chadwyck [090]
CALENDARUL ORTODOX CREDINTA – Detroit, MI. 1966-1971 – 2r – 1 – us I.H.R.C. [073]
CALENDARUL ZIALURUI DESTEPTAREA – Detroit, MI. 1922, 1927, 1928, 1937, 1938, 1946-1958, 1964 – 5r – 1 – us I.H.R.C. [073]
CALENDONIA ROMANA / Stuart, R – H 1135 2. 1845 – 8 – ne IDC [941]
CALENDRIER POUR LES CHANTRES POUR L'ANNEE 1827 – Saint-Philippe: Imp Ecclesiastique, 1826. SEM16P7 – 1r – 5 – Can$9.00 – cn Bibl Nat [240]
CALENDRIER POUR LES CHANTRES POUR L'ANNEE BISSEXTILE 1824 – Saint-Philippe: Joseph Hebert, imprimeur, 1824. SEM16P8 – 1r – 5 – Can$9.00 – cn Bibl Nat [520]
CALENDRIER SAINT SIMONIEN – Paris, Carpentier-Mericourt, 1833, 26 p. Les Saint-Simoniens, 1825-1834. 6898 – 9 – fr Hachette [520]
LES CALENDRIERS TURCS ANCIENS ET MEDIEVAUX / Bazin, Louis – 1973 – 9 – fr Orientalistes [520]
LA CALENTURA MESENTERICA... / Lloret y Marti, F – Madrid, 1730 – 6mf – 9 – sp Cultura [616]
Calepinus, A *see* DICTIONARIUM LATINO LUSITANICUM
Calera de Leon *see*
- FIESTAS DE TENTUDIA, 1969
- FIESTAS DE TENTUDIA, 1970
- TENTUDIA. FIESTAS DE SEPTIEMBRE 1973
- TENTUDIA. REVISTA DE FERIAS Y FIESTAS DE 1975
- TENTUDIA. REVISTA OFICIAL DE FIESTAS, 1972

Calera de Leon, Ayuntamiento *see* TENTUDIA
CALEXICO CHRONICLE – Calexico, CA. 1906- – 71+ r – 1 – $3,550.00 ($50.00y) – R02087 – us Library Micro [071]
Caley, Earle R *see* ANALYSES OF ANCIENT GLASSES
Caley, J *see* MONASTICON ANGLICANUM
CALGARY DAILY HERALD – Canada. -d. April 1911-Dec 1920. 59 1 2 reels – 1 – uk British Libr Newspaper [072]
THE CALGARY DIOCESAN MAGAZINE – [Innisfail, Alta.: s.n., 1899-19–]; (Innisfail [Alta]: Free Lance Print) – 9 – cn C.I.H.M. [240]
CALGARY EYE OPENER – Calgary, Alberta, CN. 1902-22 – 1r – 1 – cn Commonwealth Micro [072]
CALGARY EYE-OPENER – High River and Calgary, Canada. 1902-22 – 1 – $68.00 – cn Library Assoc [971]
CALGARY HERALD – Calgary, Alberta, CN. Sept 1888- – 36r per yr – 1 – Can$53.00r – cn Commonwealth Micro [072]
CALGARY JEWISH TIMES – Calgary, Albert, Canada.1980 – 1 – us A.J.P.C. [072]
CALGARY MAGAZINE – Vancouver. v1-11. 1978-88 – 9 – Can$28.00y – cn Micromedia [073]
CALGARY MIRROR – Alberta, CN. 1983-87 – 20r – 1 – cn Commonwealth Micro [072]
CALGARY NEWS TELEGRAM – Alberta, CN. Mar 1907-Sept 1918 – 45r – 1 – cn Commonwealth Micro [072]
CALGARY OPTIMIST – Calgary. Alberta. Canada. Nov 27, 1909-Feb 12, 1910 – 1 – cn Commonwealth Micro [072]
CALGARY PERIODICALS – Alberta, CN. 1884-94 – 1r – 1 – cn Commonwealth Micro [072]
CALGARY REAL ESTATE AND LIVE STOCK BULLETIN – Calgary [Alta.]: Fitz Gerald & Lucas, [1892?-189- or 19–] – 9 – cn C.I.H.M. [333]
CALGARY REBEL – Calgary. Alberta. Canada. 1937-38 – 1 – cn Commonwealth Micro [072]
CALGARY SUN – (1980-1992.-329r) – Calgary, 1993 – 36r – 1 – cn Preston [971]
CALGARY TRIBUNE – Calgary, Alberta, CN. 1885-1899 – 1r – 1 – cn Commonwealth Micro [072]
CALGARY WEEKLY HERALD – Calgary, Alberta, CN. Aug 1883-Dec 1901 – 4r – 1 – cn Commonwealth Micro [072]
Calhoun, Alfred R *see* A SOLDIER'S STORY
THE CALHOUN CHRONICLE – Grantsville, West Virginia. -w.1911-36 – 1 – us UMI [071]
CALHOUN CITY FIRST BAPTIST CHURCH. CALHOUN CITY, MISSISSIPPI : CHURCH RECORDS – 1904-83. 840p – 1 – 37.80 – us Baptist [240]
Calhoun, Frederick S *see*
- LETTERS RECEIVED BY THE ATTORNEY GENERAL, 1809-1870
- LETTERS RECEIVED BY THE ATTORNEY GENERAL, 1871-1884

Calhoun, John C *see*
- A DISQUISITION ON GOVERNMENT
- LETTERS
- PAPERS

CALHOUN MONITOR – Pittsboro. Miss. 1902-1921 – 1 – us UMI [071]
Calhoun, Robert L *see* THE DILEMMA OF HUMANITARIAN MODERNISM
CALIBAN – Selection d'articles internationaux. no. 1-55. Paris. fevr 1947-51 – 1 – fr A.C.R.P.P. [073]
Calice, F *see* GRUNDLAGEN DER AEGYPTISCH-SEMITISCHEN WORTVERGLEICHUNG
CALICO PRINT – San Bernardino, CA. 1882-1951 – 2r – 1 – $100.00 – R02760 – us Library Micro [071]
CALICO PRINT – Yermo. Calif. 1951-1953 – 1 – us UMI [071]
THE CALIDONIAN – St Johnsbury, VT. v11 n27. 22 jan 1848 – 1r – 1 – Can$25.00 – cn Can Microfilming [071]
CALIENTE EXPRESS – Caliente, NV. 1905 – 1r – 1 – $50.00 – U04429 – us Library Micro [071]
CALIENTE EXPRESS – Lincoln, NV. Mar 1905 – 1r – 1 – $50.00 – U04617 – us Library Micro [071]
THE CALIENTE PROGRESS – Caliente, NV. 1904 – 1r – 1 – $50.00 – U04833 – us Library Micro [071]
CALIFORNIA : SESSION LAWS OF AMERICAN STATES AND TERRITORIES – 1849-1990 – 9 – $4,244.00 set – us Hein [340]
CALIFORNIA : WEST'S ANNOTATED CALIFORNIA CODE – St Paul: West Publ Co, 1954-Feb 1996 update – 9 – $7,525.00 set – us Hein [340]
California *see*
- CODE OF REGULATIONS
- COFFEY'S PROBATE REPORTS
- LABATT'S DISTRICT REPORTS
- MYRICK'S PROBATE DECISIONS
- RAGLAND'S SUPERIOR COURT DECISIONS
- REPORTS AND OPINIONS (A-G)
- REPORTS, POST-NRS
- REPORTS, PRE-NRS
- STATE LABOR REPORTS

THE CALIFORNIA – Eureka, CA. 1898-1909 – 5r – 1 – $250.00 – B02209 – us Library Micro [071]
CALIFORNIA ACADEMY OF SCIENCES VASCULAR PLANT TYPE COLLECTION – (Families can be purchased separately. Index £160.00) – 263mf – 9 – £1090.00 – uk Chadwyck [580]
CALIFORNIA AFL-CIO – Los Angeles, CA. 1981-1992 – 11r – 1 – $550.00 – R03282 – us Library Micro [071]
CALIFORNIA AGGIE – Davis, CA: University Campus Davis, 1922- – 42+ r – 1 – $2,100.00 ($90.00y) – B02163 – us Library Micro [370]
CALIFORNIA AND CALIFORNIANS / Hunt, Rockwell A – Chicago: Lewis Publ. Co., 1932. v1-2, California Reel 1. v3-4, California Reel 2. (The Cox Library Collection) – 5 – us Americana [978]
CALIFORNIA APPELLATE COURT BRIEFS – 3rd series: v1-235. 4th series: v1-10 – 9 – $14,500.00 set 3rd ser. $800.00 4th ser ($80.00v update service) – B50570 3rd ser. B50571 4th ser – us Library Micro [340]

CALIFORNIA APPELLATE REPORTS – (Vols after v40 will be filmed as they fall out of copyright) – 1st series: v1-40. 1905-19 – 66mf (1:42) 180mf (1:24) – 9 – $567.00 – LLMC 84-124 – us L.L.M.C. [340]
CALIFORNIA APPELLATE REPORTS *see*
- COFFEY'S PROBATE REPORTS
- LABATT'S DISTRICT REPORTS
- MYRICK'S PROBATE DECISIONS
- RAGLAND'S SUPERIOR COURT DECISIONS

CALIFORNIA ARCHITECT AND BUILDING NEWS – (Also known as: California Architect and Building Review; Quarterly Architectural Review) – San Francisco, CA. 1879-99 – 5r – 1 – $250.00 – B02792 – us Library Micro [720]
THE CALIFORNIA ARCHITECT AND BUILDING NEWS – 1879-99 – 1 – £210.00 – uk World [978]
CALIFORNIA ARCHITECT AND BUILDING REVIEW *see* CALIFORNIA ARCHITECT AND BUILDING NEWS
CALIFORNIA ART RESEARCH / U.S. Works Progress Administration. San Francisco Office; ed by Hailey, Genevieve – First Series. 1936, '37. Biographies of 100 Northern Calif. artists working 1850-1930's. Updated Bibliogs. New Introd. by Ellen Schwartz. Indexed. 12 fiches – 9 – $57.50 (silver halide); $50.00 (positive vesicular) – us McGilvery [920]
CALIFORNIA BAR JOURNAL – v1. 1994 – 9 – $15.00 – us Hein [340]
California Block Book & Map Co *see* MERY'S BLOCK BOOK OF SAN FRANCISCO
California Botanical Society *see* MADRONA 90
CALIFORNIA BUSINESS – (v.14-. 1979- 5,6,9) – v.1-. 1965- – 1 – us UMI [073]
CALIFORNIA CEMETRY INSCRIPTION SOURCES : PRINT AND MICROFORM / Kot, Elizabeth G & Thomson, Shirley P – 1994 – 9 – $29.95 – 0-9641213-1-X – us Indices [920]
CALIFORNIA CENSUS OF 1852 : COUNTIES OF SIERRA, SOLANO, TRINITY AND TULARE – 1r – 1 – $50.00 – B50004 – us Library Micro [310]
CALIFORNIA CHRISTIAN ADVOCATE – San Franciso CA. Sep 28 1881 – 1 – us U.O. Library [071]
CALIFORNIA CHRONIK – (First German paper in California) – San Francisco, CA. 1866 – 1r – 1 – $50.00 – B02807 – us Library Micro [071]
CALIFORNIA CITY AND COUNTY DIRECTORIES : 1852 – PRESENT – (Individual counties listed separately) – 1 – $50.00r – us Library Micro [978]
CALIFORNIA CITY SUN – Boron Valley. Calif. 1960$69 – 1 – us UMI [071]
CALIFORNIA CODE OF REGULATIONS – (Comprehensive index gives access to both microfiche and looseleaf editions and has retrospective history table of changes to regulations. 1991 Index $350) – Barclays Law Publishers – Ca 300mf – $980.00 current year including updating – us UMI [340]
CALIFORNIA COUNTY AGRICULTURAL COMMISSION REPORTS, 1920-1981 – (Years vary for each county) – CA. – 9 – $300.00 – B50524 – us Library Micro [630]
CALIFORNIA: COUNTY AND REGIONAL HISTORIES – Listed in Blumann, "California Local History" through 1910 – 1 – us Primary [978]
CALIFORNIA CULTIVATOR – Los Angeles, CA. 1892-1947 – 54r – 1 – $2.700.00 – B02369 – us Library Micro [071]
CALIFORNIA CULTIVATOR – San Francisco, CA. 1892-1947 – 54r – 1 – $2,700.00 – B02793 – us Library Micro [071]
California. Dept. of Employment *see* RESEARCH SERIES BULLETINS
California. Dept. of Industrial Relations *see* REPORT
California. Dept. of Insurance *see* REPORT OF THE INSURANCE COMMISSIONER OF CALIFORNIA
California. Dept. of Savings and Loan *see* REPORT: SAVINGS AND LOAN COMMISSIONER OF CALIFORNIA
CALIFORNIA, DISCOVERY OF GOLD IN – 1 – us Ross [976]
California. Division of Industrial Welfare *see* REPORTS: INDUSTRIAL WELFARE COMMISSIONERS
CALIFORNIA EAGLE – Los Angeles, CA. 1943-51 – 15r – 1 – $750.00 – C02370 – us Library Micro [071]
CALIFORNIA ELECTION RETURNS COMPILATION BY DISTRICT OF ALL PRIMARY AND GENERAL ELECTION RETURNS FEDERAL STATE AND COUNTY – 1849-May 1916 – 24r – 1 – $1,200.00 – B50520 – us Library Micro [340]
California. Employment Development Dept *see* OPERATIONS REPORTS
CALIFORNIA EXPRESS LINE – El Cajon, 1989 – 61+ r – 1 – $3,050.00 ($765.00y) – R04023 – us Library Micro [071]
California. Fair Employment Practice Commission *see* REPORTS
CALIFORNIA FARM OBSERVER – Woodland, CA. 1972-78 – 3r – 1 – $150.00 – C03110 – us Library Micro [630]
CALIFORNIA FARMER : CENTRAL EDITION – (See: Los Angeles, San Francisco) – Fresno, CA. 1959-Jun 1991 – 54r – 1 – $2,700.00 – B02256 – us Library Micro [071]
CALIFORNIA FARMER : NORTHERN EDITION – (Cont: Pacific Rural Press. See also Los Angeles, Fresno) – San Francisco, CA. 1949-91 – 59r – 1 – $2,950.00 – B02794 – us Library Micro [071]
CALIFORNIA FARMER : SOUTHERN EDITION – (Cont: Pacific Rural Press. See also San Francisco, Fresno) – Los Angeles, CA. 1949-1991 – 54r – 1 – $2,700.00 – C02371 – us Library Micro [071]
CALIFORNIA FARMER *see* PACIFIC RURAL PRESS
CALIFORNIA FARMER (SOUTHERN EDITION) *see* PACIFIC RURAL PRESS
California. Franchise Tax Board *see* REPORTS
CALIFORNIA FREIE PRESSE – (Cont by: Amerika-Woche, Chicago) – San Francisco, CA. 1972-78 – 1 – gw Mikrofilm [071]
CALIFORNIA GOLD BOOK / Allen, W W & Avery, R V – San Francisco and Chicago: Donahue & Henneberry, 1893. 1 roll – 1 – $20.00 – uk Libr Preservation [978]
California. Governor's Commission on the Los Angeles Riots, 1965 *see* MCCONE COMMISSION REPORT
THE CALIFORNIA GREAT REGISTER OF VOTERS INDEXES, 1900-1944 – (Coll of over 1700v contains records of all 58 California counties. Individual counties also listed separately) – California State Library – 1 – $50.00r (1-20r) $48.00r (21r or more) (Entire coll – inquire for price) – R03720 – us Library Micro [910]
CALIFORNIA HISTORICAL COURIER – San Francisco, CA. Jul 1973-Nov 1979 – 1r – 1 – $50.00 – B02796 – us Library Micro [071]
CALIFORNIA HISTORICAL MATERIALS CONCERNING THE NEGRO BAPTIST – 1899-1964. 194p – 1 – 6.79 – us Baptist [240]
CALIFORNIA HISTORICAL QUARTERLY *see* CALIFORNIA HISTORY
CALIFORNIA HISTORY – (Formerly: California Historical Quarterly. Also available on mf and 16mm) – San Francisco, CA. 1922- – 45+ r – 1 – $2,250.00 ($50.00Y) – B02795 – us Library Micro [978]
CALIFORNIA INDIAN HERALD – 1923-24. (American Indian Periodicals in the Princeton University Library). 2 fiches – 9 – $45.00 – us UPA [305]
CALIFORNIA JEWISH BULLETIN – Los Angeles, CA. 1933-1934 (California Jewish Review); 1924-1929 – 1r – 1 – $50.00 – B02372 – us Library Micro [071]
CALIFORNIA JEWISH LIFE – Los Angeles. Calif. 1950-51 – 1 – us A.J.P.C. [071]
CALIFORNIA JEWISH PRESS – Los Angeles, CA. Jun 1956-Jan 1969 – 4r – 1 – $200.00 – B02373 – us Library Micro [071]
CALIFORNIA JEWISH PRESS – Los Angeles. Calif. 1957-62 – 1 – us A.J.P.C. [071]
CALIFORNIA JEWISH RECORD – San Francisco, CA. Sept 1960-Apr 1971 (broken file) – 2r – 1 – $100.00 – B02797 – us Library Micro [071]
CALIFORNIA JEWISH REVIEW – Los Angeles, CA.1922-29 – 1 – us A.J.P.C. [071]
CALIFORNIA JEWISH REVIEW *see* CALIFORNIA JEWISH BULLETIN
CALIFORNIA JEWISH VOICE – Los Angeles. Calif. 1960 67 – 1 – us A.J.P.C. [071]
CALIFORNIA JOB JOURNAL – Sacramento, CA. 1983-1989 – 6r – 1 – $300.00 – B06052 – us Library Micro [331]
CALIFORNIA JOURNAL – (In German) – San Francisco, CA. 1919-40 – 11r – 1 – $550.00 – C03472 – us Library Micro [073]
CALIFORNIA JOURNAL : THE MONTHLY ANALYSIS OF STATE GOVERNMENT AND POLITICS – Sacramento, CA. 1970- – 20+ r – 1 – $1,000.00 ($50.00y) – B02730 – us Library Micro [320]
CALIFORNIA JOURNAL OF EDUCATIONAL RESEARCH – (1971-75. 5,6) – v. 1-26. 1950-75 – 1 – us UMI [370]
CALIFORNIA JOURNAL OF TEACHER EDUCATION – (1977- . 5,6,9) – 1972- – 1 – us UMI [370]
CALIFORNIA LAW JOURNAL AND LITERARY REVIEW – v1-2. 1862-63 (all publ) – 9 – LLMC 82-910 – us L.L.M.C. [073]
CALIFORNIA LAW REVIEW – (1985- . 5,6,9) – v1- . 1912- – 1 – us UMI [073]
CALIFORNIA LAW REVIEW – v1-8. 1912-1919/29 (all publ) – 45mf – $67.00 – LLMC 90-317 – us L.L.M.C. [073]
CALIFORNIA LAW REVIEW – v1-84. 1912-96 – 1,5,6,9 – $2,205.00 – us Hein [073]
California. Laws, Statutes, etc *see* ADMINISTRATIVE CODE
CALIFORNIA LAWYER – (1983-. 1,5,6,9) – v1-. 1981- – 1 – us UMI [073]
CALIFORNIA LAWYER – (Cont: California State Bar Journal) – v1-15. 1981-95 – 9 – $314.00 set – us Hein [340]
CALIFORNIA LAWYER *see* CALIFORNIA STATE BAR JOURNAL
THE CALIFORNIA LEADER – San Francisco, CA. 1865-1866 – 1r – 1 – $45.00 – C03473 – us Library Micro [071]
CALIFORNIA LEGAL STUDIES JOURNAL – v1. 1995 – 9 – $15.00 – us Hein [340]
CALIFORNIA LEGIONNAIRE – Berkeley, CA. 1940-67 – 5r – 1 – $250.00 – C02053 – us Library Micro [071]
CALIFORNIA LEGIONNAIRE – Berkeley. Calif. 1940-1967 – 1 – us UMI [071]
CALIFORNIA LEGIONNAIRE – San Francisco, CA. 1968-82 – 2r – 1 – $100.00 – C02798 – us Library Micro [071]
CALIFORNIA LEGISLATIVE BILLS – 1963- – over 1600mf ea 2yr session – 9,5 ($950.00/update B50513) – us Library Micro [323]
California. (Lower). Southern territory *see* BOLETIN OFICIAL
CALIFORNIA MAGYARSAG – Los Angeles, CA. 1957- – 14+ r – 1 – $700.00 ($50.00) – C02374 – us Library Micro [071]
CALIFORNIA MAGYARSAG – Los Angeles. Calif. 1957-1965 – 1 – us UMI [071]
CALIFORNIA MANAGEMENT REVIEW – (1970- . 5,6. 1975- . 9) – v1- . 1958- – 1 – us UMI [650]
CALIFORNIA MANAGEMENT REVIEW – 1984-. -q – 1 – us UMI [650]
CALIFORNIA MAPS : BUTTE, GLENN, SUTTER, AND YUBA COUNTIES – 1884-1949. 571 maps. 19 towns. Sanborn Company Fire Insurance Maps – 1 – $80.00r – us Shkurkin [910]
CALIFORNIA MAPS : FRESNO, MADERA, AND MERCED COUNTIES – 1885-1914. 513 maps. 27 towns. Sanborn Company Fire Insurance Maps – 1 – $80.00r – us Shkurkin [910]
CALIFORNIA MAPS : KINGS, TULARE AND KERN COUNTY TOWNS – 1885-1913. 398 maps. 26 towns – 1 – $70.00r – us Shkurkin [910]
CALIFORNIA MAPS : NORTH-COAST TOWNS – 1886-1946. 362 maps. 23 towns – 1 – $67.00r – us Shkurkin [910]
CALIFORNIA MAPS : SAN BERNARDINO AND INYO COUNTIES – 1885-1919. 400 maps. 17 towns. Sanborn Company Fire Insurance Maps – 1 – $80.00r – us Shkurkin [910]
CALIFORNIA MAPS : TOWNS IN FOUR SOUTHERN COUNTIES – 1885-1911. 629 maps. 33 towns. Sanborn Company Fire Insurance Maps – 1 – $80.00r – us Shkurkin [910]
CALIFORNIA MAPS : TOWNS OF 9 NORTHERN COUNTIES – 1885-1950. 547 maps. 40 towns. Sanborn Company Fire Insurance Maps – 1 – $80.00r – us Shkurkin [910]
CALIFORNIA MAPS 1 : ALAMEDA COUNTY; THE EAST BAY – 1884-1908. 700 maps. 19 towns. Sanborn Company Fire Insurance Maps – 1 – $80.00r – us Shkurkin [910]
CALIFORNIA MISSIONARY BAPTIST – 1 May 1940-15 Apr 1973, 15 Jun 1973 – 1 – 54.04 – us Baptist [240]
CALIFORNIA MONTHLY – Berkeley, CA. 1981-1982 – 2r – 1 – $100.00 – R02054 – us Library Micro [073]
CALIFORNIA MOTHER LODE MAPS – 1884-1906. 212 maps. 30 communities. Sanborn Company Fire Insurance Maps – 1 – $40.00r – us Shkurkin [910]
CALIFORNIA NURSE – (1983-. 1,5,6,9) – v65-. 1969- – 1 – us UMI [073]
CALIFORNIA OIL WORLD – Los Angeles, CA. 1909-12; 1915-23 – 8r – 1 – $400.00 – C02375 – us Library Micro [071]
CALIFORNIA, OREGON, WASHINGTON – 1899 – 1r – 1 – $50.00 – P00145 – us Library Micro [910]
CALIFORNIA PERIODICALS ON MICROFILM – 1978. California Periodicals Index. 1978. Collection: CTA NEA Action; Cal-Tax News; California Agriculture; California Business; California Cattleman; California Communities; California Energy Commission News; California Engineer; California English; California Fish and Game; California Geology; California Historian; California Mining Journal; California Nurse; California Prepared; California Reader; California Savings and Loan Journal; California Senior Citizen; California State Employee; California Woman; California Youth Authority. Quarterly; Coastal News; Crime Prevention Review; Energy Commission. Newsletter; FACCC. Bulletin; Forum; Los Angeles Lawyer; Outdoor California; Pacific Coast Archaeological Quarterly; Pacific Oil World; Performing Arts; Santa Barbara Magazine; Senior World; Staff Reporter; Surfing; Trans Actions; Transition; Watermarks Newsletter; Western City; Western Outdoors – 1 – $240.00y; Index $90.00y – us Gabriel Micro [073]
California. Pooled Money Investment Board *see*
- REPORT

California. Public Utilities Commission *see*
- DECISIONS
- REPORTS

CALIFORNIA SENATE AND ASSEMBLY DAILY JOURNALS : LEGISLATURE OF THE STATE OF CALIFORNIA – 1850- – 9 ($225.00/update B50590) – us Library Micro [073]
CALIFORNIA SERIALS COLLECTION : 1800'S-PRESENT – (A collaboration with California State Library and local California libraries to preserve a piece of California's history and provide a source for researchers. Project is entitled "Preserving the Dream". Available as a coll or on a per reel basis) – 1995 – 1 – Apply for prices and complete listing – us Library Micro [978]
CALIFORNIA SOCIAL DEMOCRAT – v1-6. Nos. 1-263 (all publ). 1911-1916 – 1 reel – 1 – $115.00 – us UPA [335]
CALIFORNIA SOCIAL SCIENCE REVIEW – Hanford, CA. 1962-1968 – 1r – 1 – $50.00 – R03236 – us Library Micro [071]
CALIFORNIA SOUTHERN BAPTIST – Nov 1941-1991 – 1 – $1,086.16 – us Baptist [240]
CALIFORNIA SPIRIT AND CORRIDORS – Fullerton, CA: CSU Fullerton, 1979-81 – 2r – 1 – $100.00 – R02261b – us Library Micro [370]
CALIFORNIA SPIRIT OF THE TIMES AND FIREMANS JOURNAL – San Francisco, CA. 1859-1962 – 1r – 1 – $50.00 – C03474 – us Library Micro [071]
CALIFORNIA STAATS ZEITUNG – (Includes 6 issues of the California Democrat) – San Francisco, CA. 1917-18 – 1r – 1 – $50.00 – C02799 – us Library Micro [071]
CALIFORNIA STAATS-ZEITUNG – Los Angeles. 3 May 1917-4 Apr 1918; 27 Feb 1920-8 Jul 1938 (incomplete); 1972- – 1 – gw Mikrofilm [071]
CALIFORNIA STANDARD – San Francisco. v1-3. 1894-96 – 1r – 1 – us Ross [073]
CALIFORNIA STAR – (Cont by: Alta California) – San Francisco, CA. 1847-48 – 1r – 1 – $50.00 – C02800 – us Library Micro [071]
CALIFORNIA STAR – San Francisco. Calif. 1847-48 – 1 – us UMI [071]
CALIFORNIA STAR *see* ALTA CALIFORNIA
THE CALIFORNIA STATE ASSEMBLY FILE ANALYSIS – 1975-94 – 9 – $500.00 set ($50.00/update B50543) – B50542 – us Library Micro [324]
California. State Banking Department. Superintendant of Banks *see* REPORT
California. State Bar Association *see* PROCEEDINGS

CALIFORNIA STATE BAR JOURNAL – (Title varies: v1-17 1926-1942 as State Bar Journal of the State Bar of California. v18-46 1942-1971 as Journal of the State Bar of California. Cont as: California Lawyer) – v1-56. 1926-1981 – 9 – $625.00 set – us Hein [340]
CALIFORNIA STATE BAR JOURNAL *see* CALIFORNIA LAWYER
California. State Board of Equalization *see* REPORTS
California. State Conciliation Service *see* ADJUSTMENT OF LABOR-MANAGEMENT DISPUTES IN CALIFORNIA
California State Council of Cannery Unions, Teamsters *see* AFL CANNERY REPORTER, 1949-1954 : UNITED DAIRY FARMER, 1941, 1944-1945
CALIFORNIA STATE DIRECTORIES AND GAZETTEERS – State of California. 1875-1876; 1880-1881; 1888-1889; 1890; 1893-1894; 1898; 1904-1905 – 12r – 1 – $600.00 – D111 – us Library Micro [978]
California State Govt *see* TEACHERS GUIDE TO THE EDUCATION OF SPANISH SPEAKING CHILDREN
CALIFORNIA STATE NURSES' ASSOCIATION – BULLETIN *see* PACIFIC COAST JOURNAL OF NURSING
CALIFORNIA STATESMAN – Sacramento, CA. 1854-1855 – 1r – 1 – $50.00 – C03422 – us Library Micro [071]
California. Superior Court. San Francisco Probate Department *see* REPORTS OF DECISIONS IN PROBATE
California. Supreme Court *see*
- CALIFORNIA SUPREME COURT REPORTS
- CALIFORNIA UNREPORTED CASES
- LATE POLITICAL DECISIONS.

CALIFORNIA SUPREME COURT BRIEFS – (Update and addendum service. Includes special index) – 3rd series: v1-54. Oct 1969-94. 4th series: v1- – 9 – $4,000.00 set 3rd ser. $95.00v 4th ser – B50535 3rd ser. B50536 4th ser – us Library Micro [340]
CALIFORNIA SUPREME COURT REPORTS / California. Supreme Court – (Pre-NRS: v1-63 1850-83 497mf $745.00. Updates planned) – v1-180. 1850-1919 – 1618mf – 9 – $2,427.00 – LLMC 80-800 – us L.L.M.C. [340]
CALIFORNIA TELEPHONE DIRECTORY COLLECTION *see*
- AIRPORT AREA
- ALAHAMBRA
- ALAMEDA COUNTY
- AMADOR/EL DORADO
- ANTELOPE VALLEY
- AUBURN
- BAKERSFIELD
- BENICIA-VALLEJO
- BEVERLY HILLS
- BEVERLY HILLS/SANTA MONICA
- BURBANK
- BUTTE COUNTY
- CALAVERAS/LOS GATOS/SARATOGA
- CALAVERAS/TUOLUMNE
- CALIFORNIA, OREGON, WASHINGTON
- CAMPBELL/LOS GATOS/SARATOGA
- CAMPBELL/SARATOGA
- CANOGA PARK
- CATALINA
- COLTON
- COLUSA
- CONTRA COSTA COUNTY GREATER
- CORONA/NORCO
- CULVER CITY
- CULVER SITY/MARINA DEL REY
- DOWNEY
- DOWNEY/NORWALK
- EL DORADO/AMADOR
- FAIR OAKS/FOLSOM
- FAIRFIELD/VACAVILLE
- FREMONT/HAYWARD
- FRESNO/CLOVIS
- FRESNO/MADERA
- GLENDALE
- GLENDALE/BURBANK
- GLENN/TEHAMA COUNTIES
- GRASS VALLEY/NEVADA CITY
- HUMBOLDT COUNTY
- HUNTINGTON BEACH
- IMPERIAL COUNTY
- INLAND EMPIRE-NORTH
- INLAND EMPIRE-SPANISH
- KERN COUNTY
- KINGS/TULARE COUNTIES
- LAKE TAHOE AREA
- LAKE/MENDOCINO COUNTIES
- LAKE/MENDOCINO/SONOMA
- LASSEN/PLUMAS COUNTIES
- LODI/GALT
- LONG BEACH
- LOS ALTOS/LOS ALTOS HILLS
- LOS ANGELES: BUSINESS-TO-BUSINESS
- LOS ANGELES: CENTRAL
- LOS ANGELES: EAST
- LOS ANGELES: EXTENDED
- LOS ANGELES: GREATER
- LOS ANGELES: NORTHEASTERN
- LOS ANGELES: NORTHWESTERN
- LOS ANGELES: SOUTH
- LOS ANGELES: SOUTHEASTERN
- LOS ANGELES: SOUTHWESTERN
- LOS ANGELES: SPANISH
- LOS ANGELES: WEST
- MARIN COUNTY
- MENDOCINO/LAKE COUNTIES
- MENDOCINO/LAKE/SONOMA COUNTIES
- MERCED/MARIPOSA
- MID-CITIES
- MODESTO
- MOJAVE DESERT-UPPER
- MONTEREY/SAN BENITO COUNTIES
- NAPA COUNTY
- NAPA VALLEY
- NAPA/SOLANO COUNTIES
- NEVADA BELL
- NORTH HOLLYWOOD
- NORTHERN CALIFORNIA AND BUSINESS
- NORTHWESTERN AREA
- OAKLAND
- OAKLAND/ALAMEDA
- ORANGE COUNTY: BUSINESS-TO-BUSINESS
- ORANGE COUNTY: CENTRAL
- ORANGE COUNTY: CENTRAL AND NORTH
- ORANGE COUNTY: CENTRAL AND SOUTH
- ORANGE COUNTY: COASTAL
- ORANGE COUNTY: INLAND
- ORANGE COUNTY: NORTH
- ORANGE COUNTY: NORTHWEST
- ORANGE COUNTY: ORANGE
- ORANGE COUNTY: SOUTH
- ORANGE COUNTY: SPANISH
- PALO ALTO/REDWOOD CITY
- PASADENA
- PIEDMONT/MONTCLAIR
- PLUMAS/LASSEN COUNTIES
- QUINCY
- REDONDO BEACH
- REDWOOD CITY
- RIVERSIDE
- RIVERSIDE COUNTY
- SACRAMENTO
- SAN BENITO/MONTEREY COUNTIES
- SAN BERNARDINO COUNTY
- SAN DIEGO COUNTY: EAST
- SAN DIEGO COUNTY: INLAND
- SAN DIEGO COUNTY: NORTH
- SAN DIEGO COUNTY: NORTH COAST
- SAN DIEGO COUNTY: SOUTH
- SAN DIEGO COUNTY: SOUTHEAST
- SAN DIEGO COUNTY: SOUTHWEST
- SAN DIEGO COUNTY: SPANISH
- SAN DIEGO COUNTY: SUBURBAN AND GREATER
- SAN FERNANDO
- SAN FERNANDO VALLEY-EAST
- SAN FERNANDO VALLEY-SPANISH
- SAN FERNANDO VALLEY-WEST
- SAN FRANCISCO
- SAN FRANCISCO-CHINESE
- SAN GABRIEL VALLEY
- SAN GABRIEL-SPANISH
- SAN JOSE
- SAN JOSE/SANTA CLARA
- SAN LUIS OBISPO
- SAN MATEO COUNTY
- SAN MATEO COUNTY-CENTRAL
- SAN MATEO COUNTY-NORTH
- SANTA ANA
- SANTA BARBARA
- SANTA CLARA COUNTY
- SANTA CLARITA VALLEY
- SANTA CRUZ COUNTY
- SANTA ROSA
- SHASTA/SISKIYOU/TRINITY
- SHASTA/TEHAMA/TRINITY
- SIMI VALLEY/MOORPARK
- SOLANO/NAPA COUNTIES
- SONOMA COUNTY
- SONOMA COUNTY-NORTH
- SONOMA COUNTY-SOUTH
- SONOMA/LAKE/MENDOCINO COUNTIES
- SOUTH BAY
- SOUTH BAY-LONG BEACH (SPANISH)
- SOUTH BAY-REDONDO
- SOUTHERN AREA (SPANISH)
- STANISLAUS COUNTY
- STOCKTON
- SUNNYVALE/SANTA CLARA COUNTY
- SUTTER/YUBA COUNTIES
- TEHAMA/GLENN COUNTIES
- TRACY
- TRINITY/SHASTA/TEHAMA
- TRI-VALLEY
- TURLOCK
- VALLEJO-BENICIA
- VENTURA-OXNARD
- YOLO COUNTY
- YUBA/SUTTER COUNTIES

California. University. Berkeley. Bancroft Library *see* CATALOG OF PRINTED BOOKS
California. University. Berkeley. East Asiatic Library *see*
- AUTHOR-TITLE CATALOG
- SUBJECT CATALOG

California. University. Los Angeles *see*
- DICTIONARY CATALOG OF THE WILLIAM ANDREWS CLARK MEMORIAL LIBRARY
- UCLA DAILY BRUIN

California. University Los Angeles. Phonetics Laboratory *see* WORKING PAPERS IN PHONETICS
California. University of Southern California *see* SOCIOLOGY AND SOCIAL RESEARCH
California. University of Southern California. Los Angeles *see* CATALOG OF THE HOOSE LIBRARY OF PHILOSOPHY
California. University of Southern California. Los Angeles. Ethel Percy Andrus Gerontology Center *see* AUTHOR-TITLE AND SUBJECT CATALOGS
California. University. San Diego. Scripps Institution of Oceanography *see* AUTHOR/TITLE CATALOG
California. University.Berkeley. Bancroft Library *see* INDEX TO PRINTED MAPS
California. University.San Diego. Scripps Institution of Oceanography *see* SUBJECT CATALOG, SHELF LIST, SHELF LIST OF DOCUMENTS AND REPORTS
CALIFORNIA UNREPORTED CASES / California. Supreme Court – (A Pre-NRS title) – v1-7 (all publ) – 74mf – 9 – $111.00 – LLMC 90-003 – us L.L.M.C. [340]
CALIFORNIA VECKOBLAD – (Library has: v.33,no.4-v.34,no.45,47-v.35,no.52; v.38,no.1-v.39,no.12; Jan. 1942-Mar. 1948) – Los Angeles: California veckoblad, 19??- – 1 – CSUX86-S200 – us Hoover Inst Photo [978]
CALIFORNIA VOICE – Oakland, CA. 1961-72; 1977-78 (incomplete); 1979- – 20+ r – 1 – $1,000.00 ($90.00y) – C02539 – us Library Micro [071]
CALIFORNIA VOICE – San Francisco. Calif. 1961- – 1 – us UMI [071]
CALIFORNIA VOICE *see* VOICE
CALIFORNIA WAREHOUSE BOOK (1885 WITH UPDATES TO 1897) – 192 map plates of warehouses in hundreds of California communities. Fire map of Chico, CA (1885). San Francisco: Dakin Publ. Co. Fire Insurance Maps – 1 – $40.00r – us Shkurkin [910]
CALIFORNIA WESTERN INTERNATIONAL LAW JOURNAL – v1-24. 1970-94 – 1,5,6 – $270.00 – us Hein [073]
CALIFORNIA WESTERN LAW REVIEW – v1-30. 1965-94 – 1,5,6 – $405.00 – us Hein [073]
California. Youth Authority *see* QUARTERLY
CALIFORNIAN – Bakersfield. Calif. 1945-1950 – 1 – us UMI [071]
CALIFORNIAN – Monterey, CA. 1846-48 – 1r – 1 – $45.00 – C02478 – us Library Micro [071]
CALIFORNIAN – Monterey. Calif. -w. 1946-48 – 1 – us UMI [071]
CALIFORNIAN – Salinas. Calif. 1945-47 – 1 – us UMI [071]
CALIFORNIAN – Temecula, CA. 1983 – 74+ r – 1 – $3,700.00 ($340.00y) – RH03546 – us Library Micro [071]
CALIFORNIAN *see* INDEX JOURNAL
THE CALIFORNIAN – Salinas, CA. 1942- – 544+ r – 1 – $27,200.00 ($450.00y) – B02749 – us Library Micro [071]
THE CALIFORNIAN – San Francisco. v. 1-6. 1880-1882 – 1 – us NY Public [978]
CALIFORNIAN AND OVERLAND MONTHLY – San Francisco. v1-6. 1880-82 – 1r – 1 – us Ross [073]
LE CALIFORNIEN – San Francisco, CA. 1974 – 1r – 1 – $50.00 – B02834 – us Library Micro [071]
Calinich, Hermann Julius Robert *see* LUTHER UND DIE AUGSBURGISCHE CONFESSION
CALIPATRIA HERALD – Calipatria, CA. 1920-22 – 1r – 1 – $50.00 – R02088 – us Library Micro [071]
THE CALIPH HAROUN ALRASCHID AND SARACEN CIVILIZATION / Palmer, Edward Henry – New York: G.P. Putnam's Sons, 1881. 228p. fold. geneal. tab – 1 – us U.W. Library [900]
CALISPELL VALLEY TIMES – Cusick. Wash. 1909-1910 – 1 – us UMI [071]
Calker, W van *see* DAS PROBLEM DER MEERESFREIHEIT...
Calkin, John Burgess *see* HISTORY OF BRITISH AMERICA: FOR THE USE OF SCHOOLS
Calkins, Mary Whiton *see* THE METAPHYSICAL SYSTEM OF HOBBES AS CONTAINED IN TWELVE CHAPTERS FROM HIS ELEMENTS OF PHILOSOPHY CONCERNING BODY...AND HUMAN NATURE...AND LEVIATHAN
Calkins, R *see* JEREMIAH THE PROPHET
Calkins, Wolcott *see*
- KEYSTONES OF FAITH
- KEYSTONES OF FAITH, OR, WHAT AND WHY WE BELIEVE

CALL – (Also known as: Call Advertiser) – Norwalk, CA. 1960-72 – 31r – 1 – $1,550.00 – C02533 – us Library Micro [071]
CALL – Cleveland. Ohio. and Post. 1934- – 1 – us UMI [071]
CALL – Kansas City. Mo. -w. 1955-66, 1970- – 1 – us UMI [071]
CALL – Norwalk. Calif. -w. 1960- – 1 – us UMI [071]
CALL – Seattle. Wash. 1885-1886 – 1 – us UMI [071]
CALL – Woonsocket. R.I. 1889- – 1 – us UMI [071]
THE CALL – Chicago, IL. 1974-1982 – 7r – 1 – $350.00 – R04304 – us Library Micro [071]
THE CALL / Communist Party. Great Britain – 1916-1920 – 1 – uk World [072]
THE CALL – London, England. An organ of international socialism. -w. 24 Feb 1916-29 July 1920. 2 reels – 1 – uk British Libr Newspaper [072]
THE CALL – San Francisco, CA. Index for years 1894-1903, AZ – 3r – 1 – $150.00 – C02801 – us Library Micro [071]
THE CALL – Schuylkill, PA., 1981-1983, 1952-1985 – 13 – $25.00r – us I.M.R. [071]
THE CALL – Seattle, WA. -w. 1895-98 – 1 – $48.00 – us Oregon Hist [071]
CALL ADVERTISER *see* CALL
CALL AND POST – 1966-67 – 1r – 1 – us Ross [073]
THE CALL AND POST *see* THE DAILY MORNING CALL
CALL BULLETIN – San Francisco. Calif. 1937-1939; 1941-1959 – 1 – us UMI [071]
CALL BULLETIN *see* THE BULLETIN
A CALL FOR A CONVENTION TO EFFECT A NATIONAL ORGANIZATION FOR THE IMPROVEMENT OF RELIGIOUS AND MORAL EDUCATION THROUGH THE SUNDAY SCHOOL AND OTHER AGENCIES : TO BE HELD IN CHICAGO IN FEBRUARY OR MARCH 1903 – Chicago: under the auspices of the Council of Seventy...., [1902?] – 1mf – 9 – 0-8370-7537-8 – 1986-1537 – us A.T.L.A. [370]
CALL FROM GOD = SHEN CHAO – (In Chinese) – v7 no 6 Sep 1932; v9 no 4 Jul 1934 (incomplete) – 1r – 1 – ATLA S0296P – us A.T.L.A. [073]
CALL LEADER – Elwood. Ind. 1904- – 1 – us UMI [071]
THE CALL OF A CHILD (CCC83) / Chao, Wei-jan – (In Chinese) – 1st ed. Hong Kong: Council on Christian Literature for Overseas Chinese, 1959 – 1r – 1 – 1984-B500 – us A.T.L.A. [820]
THE CALL OF CATHAY : A STUDY IN MISSIONARY WORK AND OPPORTUNITY IN CHINA OLD AND NEW / Cornaby, William Arthur – (Includes index) – London: Wesleyan Methodist Missionary Society, 1910 – 1mf – 9 – 0-8370-6483-X – 1986-0483 – us A.T.L.A. [240]
THE CALL OF KOREA : POLITICAL, SOCIAL, RELIGIOUS / Underwood, Horace Grant – (Includes bibliographies) – New York: Fleming H Revell, c1908 – 1mf – 9 – 0-8370-6433-3 – 1986-0433 – us A.T.L.A. [950]
THE CALL OF THE HARVEST / McKay, Charles L – Convention Press. 1956 – 1 – 5.00 – us Baptist [240]
THE CALL OF THE MINARET / Cragg, Kenneth – New York, 1956 – 7mf – 8 – ne Slangenburg [260]

THE CALL OF THE NEW ERA : ITS OPPORTUNITIES AND RESPONSIBILITIES / Muir, William – (Includes index) – London: Morgan & Scott, 1910 – 1mf – 9 – 0-8370-6223-3 – 1986-0223 – us A.T.L.A. [240]
THE CALL, QUALIFICATIONS AND PREPARATION OF CANDIDATES FOR FOREIGN MISSION SERVICE – New York: Stud. Vol. Mov. for Mis., 1901. 158p.1 fiche – 9 – us A.T.L.A. [240]
Callaghan, Thomas *see* ACTS AND ORDINANCES OF THE GOVERNOR AND COUNCIL OF NEW SOUTH WALES
Callahan *see* BENCH AND BAR OF ILLINOIS – 1920
Callahan, J M *see* THE NEUTRALITY OF...
CALLAWAY COURIER – Callaway, NE. -w. Mar. 1968- – 1 – us NE Hist [071]
Callaway Jr., M *see* STUDIES IN THE SYNTAX OF THE LINDISFARNE GOSPELS
Callbreath, Cook *see* LETTERPRESS COPY BOOKS
Callbreath, Grant *see* LETTERPRESS COPY BOOKS
Callbreath, J C *see* NOTES SUR LES SAUVAGES TAHL-TAN
Calleca Barahona Fernandes, MH *see* L'ELEVAGE INTENSIF DES LARVES ET DES JUVENILES DU BAR (DICENTRAXILIUS LABRAX (L.). DONNEES BIOLOGIQUES, ZOOTECHNIQUES ET PATHOLOGIQUES
CALLED OF GOD / Davidson, Andrew Bruce – New York: Scribner, (1902). 1 fiche – 9 – us A.T.L.A. [240]
Calleja, James *see* INTERNATIONAL EDUCATION AND THE UNIVERSITY
CALLEJERO Y GUIA HISTORICA DE BADAJOZ / Lopez e Sosoaga y Borinaga, Benigno – Badajoz: La Minerva Extremena, 1963 – sp Bibl Santa Ana [946]
Callejo, Carlos *see* EL MONASTERIO DE GUADALUPE
Callejo Serrano, Carlos *see*
- LA ARQUEOLOGIA DE NORBA CESARINA
- CACERES MONUMENTAL
- CATALOGO DE LAS PINTURAS DE LA CUEVA DE MALTRAVIESO
- CEDULAS EPIGRAFICAS DEL CAMPO NORBENSE
- NUEVO REPERTORIO EPIGRAFICO DE LA PROVINCIA DE CACERES
- EL ORIGEN Y EL NOMBRE DE CACERES

Callender, Clarence N *see* SELECTED CASES ON CONTRACTS
CALLENDER I. FAYSSOUX COLLECTION OF WILLIAM WALKER PAPERS, 1856-1860 – (With printed guide) – 4r – 1 – $450.00 – Latin American Library, Tulane University – us Ross [972]
Callender, John *see* AN HISTORICAL DISCOURSE ON THE CIVIL AND RELIGIOUS AFFAIRS OF THE COLONY OF RHODE-ISLAND
CALLER – Corpus Christi. Tex. (morning). 1883- – 1 – us UMI [071]
Callery, J M *see* CORRESPONDANCE DIPLOMATIQUE...
Calles Mariscal, Alfredo *see* GANADO PORCINO EXTREMENO
Calles Mariscal, Juan *see* GANADO PORCINO EXTREMENO
Callet, P M *see* GLOSSAIRE VAUDOIS
Callewaert, C *see* SACRIS ERUDIRI
CALLIE SELF BAPTIST CHURCH. GREENWOOD COUNTY. SOUTH CAROLINA : CHURCH RECORDS – 1942-71 – 1 – 25.20 – us Baptist [240]
Callieres, F de *see*
- DU BON ET DU MAUVAIS USAGE DANS LES MANIERES DE S'EXPRIMER
- DE LA MANIERE DE NEGOCIER AVEC LES SOUVERAINS,...
- DES BONS MOTS ET DES BONS CONTES
- DES MOTS A LA MODE

Callimachus, P *see* DE BELLO TURCIS INFERENDO, ORATIO GRAUISSIMA, ...
THE CALLIOPE – Trois-Rivieres, Quebec: s.n., 1859 – 9 – cn C.I.H.M. [971]
THE CALLIOPEAN – Hamilton, C W [Ont]: P Ruthven, [1847-18–?] – 9 – cn C.I.H.M. [971]
Callisen, Adolph Peter *see* MEDICNISCHES SCHRIFTSTELLER-LEXIKON DER JETZT LEBENDEN AERZTE, WUNDAERZTE UND GEBURTSHELFER, APOTHEKER UND NATURFORSCHER ALLER GEBILDETEN VOELKER (AEL, ABT 3;17)
CALLSIGN INDEX TO NON-GOVERNMENT MASTER FREQUENCY DATA BASE / U.S. National Technical Information Service – Annual. Includes two suppl. issued in May and Oct of each year – 9 – us N.T.I.S. [000]
A CALM REPLY TO THE FALLACIOUS ARGUMENTS AND VIRULENT INVECTIVES CONTAINED IN MR. JOSEPH BENSON'S 'FARTHER DEFENCE OF THE METHODISTS' / Russel, W – Wolverhampton, 1794 – 2mf – 9 – MP-583/1 – ne IDC [240]
A CALM REVIEW OF THE INAUGURAL ADDRESS OF PROF. CHARLES A. BRIGGS / Morris, Edward D – 1891 – 9 – $50.00 – us Presbyterian [240]
Calman, David *see* CALMAN'S CODE TIME-TABLE
CALMAN'S CODE TIME-TABLE / Calman, David – 3rd ed. New York: Strouse, 1891. 143p. LL-622 – 1 – us L of C Photodup [340]
Calmeil, Louis Florentin *see* DE LA FOLIE CONSIDEREE SOUS LE POINT DE VUE PATHOLOGIQUE, PHILOSOPHIQUE, HISTORIQUE ET JUDICIAIRE
Calmet, A *see* DISSERTATIONS SUR LA POESIE ET LA MUSIQUE DES ANCIENS EN GENERAL, ET DES HEBREUX EN PARTICULIER
Calmet, Dom Aug. *see*
- COMMENTAIRE LITTERAL
- COMMENTARIUS LITERALIS, HISTORICO-MORALIS IN REGULAM S.P. BENEDICTI

Calnek, William Arthur *see*
- A BRIEF MEMOIRE OF THE LATE HONORABLE JAMES WILLIAM JOHNSTON, FIRST JUDGE IN EQUITY OF NOVA SCOTIA
- HISTORY OF THE COUNTY OF ANNAPOLIS

Calnin, R J *see* THE EFFECT OF MODERATE EXERCISE ON LIPID PROFILES IN A HEALTHY COLLEGE AGE POPULATION
Caloensis. Leonis Diaconi *see* HISTORIAE LIBRI X ET LIBER DE VELITATIONE BELLICA NICEPHORI AUGUSTI E REC. CAR. BEN. HASII (CSHB 5)
CALOGERA, D.A. *see* ARKHIV VENETSIANSKOGO IZDATELIA A. KALADZHERA V LENINGRADE
Calogeras, Pandia *see* PROBLEMAS DE GOVERNO
CALOMNIES ANTI-PROTESTANTES / Doumergue, Emile – Paris: Bureaux de foi et vie; Lausanne: G. Bridel, 1912 – 1mf – us A.T.L.A. [240]
Calonne-Beaufaict, Adolphe de *see* ETUDES BAKONGO
CALOOSA BELLE – La Belle. Fla. 1972- – 1 – us P.K. Yonge [071]
Caloyanni, M A *see* LA JUSTICE PENALE INTERNATIONALE
CALPHAD : COMPUTER COUPLING OF PHASE DIAGRAMS AND THERMOCHEMISTRY – v1-1977- – 5,6,9 – us UMI [000]
Caltex Pacific Oil Company *see* INDONESIA, LAPORAN SEBUAH PENANAM MODEL ASING
Caltex Pacific Petroleum Company *see* REPORT OF OPERATIONS, UP TO AND INCLUDING DECEMBER, 1954
CALUMET – v1-2. Apr 1831-1835 – 10mf – 9 – $55.00 – us UPA [305]
Calumet Book and Engraving Co *see* ALBUM OF GENEALOGY AND BIOGRAPHY COOK COUNTY
CALVARY BAPTIST CHURCH. AIKEN COUNTY. SOUTH CAROLINA : CHURCH RECORDS – 1962-68, Sept 1975-1983.342p – 1 – 15.39 – us Baptist [240]
CALVARY BAPTIST CHURCH. DALLAS, TEXAS : CHURCH RECORDS – Nov 1914-39 – 1 – 14.58 – us Baptist [240]
CALVARY BAPTIST CHURCH. FLORENCE COUNTY. FLORENCE, SOUTH CAROLINA : CHURCH RECORDS – 1949-72 – 1 – 14.22 – us Baptist [240]
CALVARY BAPTIST CHURCH. HANNIBAL, MISSOURI : CHURCH RECORDS – 1887-1976 – 1 – 112.13 – us Baptist [240]
CALVARY BAPTIST CHURCH. KLAMATH FALLS, OREGON : CHURCH RECORDS – 1947-May 1973 – 1 – 35.37 – us Baptist [240]
CALVARY BAPTIST CHURCH. LANCASTER COUNTY. SOUTH CAROLINA : CHURCH RECORDS – 1924-43, 1951-54. 509p – 1 – 22.91 – us Baptist [240]
CALVARY BAPTIST CHURCH. MCPHERSON, KANSAS : CHURCH RECORDS – 8Nov 1953-Dec 1962 – 1 – 5.00 – us Baptist [240]
CALVARY BAPTIST CHURCH. RENTON, WASHINGTON : CHURCH RECORDS – 2Jun 1950-71 – 1 – 35.28 – us Baptist [240]
CALVARY BAPTIST CHURCH. SHELBY, NORTH CAROLINA : CHURCH RECORDS – 1935-63 – 1 – 52.74 – us Baptist [240]
CALVARY BAPTIST CHURCH. TUSCALOOSA, ALABAMA : CHURCH RECORDS – 1Jan 1911-Oct 1958 – 1 – 48.78 – us Baptist [240]
CALVARY BAPTIST CHURCH. VANCOUVER, WASHINGTON : CHURCH RECORDS – 30 Dec 1948-71 – 1 – 27.14 – us Baptist [240]
CALVARY BAPTIST CHURCH. VILLE PLATTE, LOUISIANA : CHURCH RECORDS – 1846-1947 – 1 – 34.20 – us Baptist [240]
Calve, Adolphe (Azal pseud) *see* SYLVES NOIRES
Calverley, Charles Stuart *see*
- TRANSLATIONS INTO ENGLISH AND LATIN
- VERSES AND TRANSLATION

Calvert, Frances Pery *see* AN IRISH BEAUTY OF THE REGENCY
THE CALVERT PAPERS / ed by Cox, Richard J – (With printed guide) – 27r – 1 – $2,295.00 – S1611 – us Scholarly Res [920]
Calvete de Estrella, Juan Cristobal *see* REBELION DE PIZARRO EN EL PERU
Calvez, J Y *see* DROIT INTERNATIONAL ET SOUVERAINETE EN URSS
CALVIN ALS UNIONSMANN / Reichel, Gerhard – Tuebingen: J.C.B. Mohr, 1909 – 1mf – us A.T.L.A. [320]
CALVIN AND THE REFORMATION : FOUR STUDIES / Doumergue, Emile – New York: Fleming H. Revell, c1909 – 1mf – us A.T.L.A. [240]
CALVIN IN HIS LETTERS / Henderson, Henry F – London: J.M. Dent, 1909 – 1mf – us A.T.L.A. [240]
Calvin, J *see* OPERA OMNIA
Calvin, Jean *see*
- INSTITUTES OF THE CHRISTIAN RELIGION
- TRACTS RELATING TO THE REFORMATION

Calvin, Johannes *see* LA FORME DES PRIERES ET CHANTS ECCLESIASTIQUES
Calvin, John *see* A TREATISE ON RELICS
CALVIN, LE PREDICATEUR DE GENEVE / Doumergue, Emile – Geneve: Atar, [1909?] – 1mf – us A.T.L.A. [240]
CALVIN MEMORIAL ADDRESSES / Reed, R C – Richmond, Va.: Presbyterian Committee of Publication, c1909 – 1mf – us A.T.L.A. [240]
CALVIN, TWISSE AND EDWARDS ON THE UNIVERSAL SALVATION OF THOSE DYING IN INFANCY / Stagg, John Weldon – (Includes bibliographical references) – Richmond, VA: Presbyterian Comm of Publ, c1902 – 1mf – 9 – 0-8370-5518-0 – 1985-3518 – us A.T.L.A. [240]
CALVIN UND BASEL BIS ZUM TODE DES MYCONIUS, 1535-1552 / Wernle, Paul – Basel: F. Reinhardt, 1909 – 1mf – us A.T.L.A. [949]
CALVINIANA RELIGIO, ODER CALVINISTEREY, SO FAELSCHLICH DIE REFORMIRTE RELIGION GENENNET WIRD... / Gedik, S – Leipzig, 1615 – 8mf – ne IDC [240]
CALVINISCHER BETLERSMANTEL DARIN ANGEZEIGET WIRD MIT WAS KLEIDER SIE SICH BEKAPEN DEN SCHALCK VERBERGEN VND ZUDECKEN KOENNEN... / Engel, A – N.p., 1598 – 1mf – 9 – ne IDC [240]
CALVINISM : SIX LECTURES / Kuyper, Abraham – New York: F.H. Revell, [1899?] – 1mf – us A.T.L.A. [240]
CALVINISM AND EVANGELICAL ARMINIANISM : COMPARED AS TO ELECTION, REPROBATION, JUSTIFICATION, AND RELATED DOCTRINES / Girardeau, John Lafayette – (Includes bibliographical references and index) – Columbia, SC: W J Duffie; New York: Baker & Taylor, 1890 – 2mf – 9 – 0-8370-8672-8 – 1986-2672 – us A.T.L.A. [230]
CALVINISM DEFENDED AND ARMINIANISM REFUTED : OR, REMARKS ON A PAMPHLET (LATELY PUBLISH'D) BY PHILALETHES ENTITLED 'A SOLEMN CAUTION AGAINST THE TEN HORNS OF CALVINISM' / Calvinisticus – Leeds, 1780 – 1mf – 9 – MP-538/1 – ne IDC [240]
CALVINISM, PURE AND MIXED : A DEFENCE OF THE WESTMINSTER STANDARDS / Shedd, William Greenough Thayer – New York: Charles Scribner, 1893 – 1mf – 9 – 0-8370-8788-0 – 1986-2788 – us A.T.L.A. [240]
HET CALVINISME = CALVINISM : ZES STONE-LEZINGEN IN OCTOBER 1898 TE PRINCETON (N.-J.) GEHOUDEN / Kuyper, Abraham – (Includes bibliographical references) – Amsterdam: Boekhandel voorheen Hoeveker & Wormser, [ca 1898] – 1mf – 9 – 0-8370-8757-0 – 1986-2757 – us A.T.L.A. [240]
HET CALVINISME EN DE KUNST : REDE BIJ DE OVERDRACHT VAN HET RECTORAAT DER VRIJE UNIVERSITEIT OP 20 OCTOBER 1888 / Kuyper, Abraham – Amsterdam: J.A. Wormser, 1888 – 1mf – us A.T.L.A. [240]
CALVINISTARUM VERA, VIVA ET GENUINA DESCRIPTIO / Hoenegg, M Hoe von – Lipsiae, 1620 – 2mf – ne IDC [240]
Calvinistic Conference on Psychology and Psychiatry *see* PROCEEDINGS
THE CALVINISTIC DOCTRINE OF ELECTION AND REPROBATION NO PART OF ST PAUL'S TEACHINGS : BIBLE-STUDY / Harris, John Andrews – Philadelphia: Porter & Coates, 1890 – 1mf – 9 – 0-8370-5015-4 – 1985-3015 – us A.T.L.A. [220]
Calvinistic Methodist Church in the U.S.A. General Assembly *see* MINUTES
Calvinisticus *see* CALVINISM DEFENDED AND ARMINIANISM REFUTED
CALVINS PRAEDESTINATIONSLEHRE : EIN BEITRAG ZUR WUERDIGUNG DER EIGENART SEINER THEOLOGIE UND RELIGIOSITAET / Scheibe, Max – (Includes bibliographical references) – Halle a. S: Ehrhardt Karras, 1897 – 1mf – 9 – 0-8370-5139-8 – 1985-3139 – us A.T.L.A. [240]
CALVINVS IVDAIZANS, HOC EST: IVDAICAE GLOSSAE ET CORRVPTELE, QVIBVS IOHANNES CALVINVS ILLUSTRISSIMA... / Hunnius, A – VVitebergae, 1593 – 2mf – ne IDC [240]
Calvisius, S *see*
- HARMONIA CANTIONUM ECCLESIASTICARUM.
- MUSICAE ARTIS PRAECEPTA NOVA ET FACILIMA, PER SEPTEM VOCES MUSICALES

Calvo Abeytar, Fernando *see* LIBRO DE ALBAYTERIADE
Calvo, C *see*
- DICTIONNAIRE DE DROIT...
- LE DROIT INTERNATIONAL...
- RECUEIL COMPLET DES TRAITES,...DE TOUS LES ETATS DE L'AMERIQUE LATINE...
- RECUEIL HISTORIQUE COMPLET DES TRAITES...DE TOUS LES ETATS DE L'AMERIQUE LATIN, DEPUIS L'ANNEE 1493 JUSQU'A NOS JOURS

Calvo Flores, Josquin *see*
- POESIAS
- VIENTOS ALEGRES, VIENTOS DESOLADOS

Calvo Serer, Rafael *see* EUROPA EN 1949
Calwer Verlagsverein *see* DER CHRISTLICHE GLAUBE IN ACHT BUECHERN
Calzada, Bernardo Maria de *see*
- EL TRIUNFO DE LA MORAL CRISTIANA
- VIDA DE FEDERICO 2 REY DE PRUSIA

LA CALZADA DE OROPESA, SU SANTO CRISTO Y SUS MONJAS / Ayape, Eugenio – Madrid: Editorial Augustinus, 1976 – sp Bibl Santa Ana [240]
Calzado Pedrilla, Felipe *see*
- DEFENSA DE D. LUIS CALDERON...PRESOS DE CONFESION
- OPINION FORMADA EN EL ASUNTO DE LOS FERROCARRILES DE LA PROVINCIA DE CACERES

Camacho Macias, Aquilino *see* DON FRANCISCO DE NAVARRA, OBISPO DE BADAJOZ (1545-1556). SUS INTERVENEIONES EN TRENTO SOBRE LA OBLIGACION EPISCOPAL DE RESIDIR
Camara Argentina de la Construccion *see* EL PROBLEMA DE LA VIVIENDA
Camara Castro, Tomas Jenaro *see* CONTESTACION A LA HISTORIA DEL CONFLICTO ENTRE LA RELIGION Y LA CIENCIA
Camara, Ezequiel Enrique *see* TABLAS DE REDUCCIONES Y EQUIVALENCIAS DEL ANTIGUO SISTEMA DE PESAS
Camara Oficial de Comercio e Industria Badajoz *see* MEMORIA COMERCIAL Y ESTADISTICA RELATIVA AL ESTADO DE LOS NEGOCIOS EN LA PROVINCIA DE BADAJOZ
Camara Oficial de Comercio e Industria de Badajoz *see*
- DECRETO Y RESOLUCION DE LA DIRECCION GENERAL DE EXPANSION COMERCIAL SOBRE ORGANIZACION DEL REGISTRO GENERAL DE EXPORTADORES Y DE LOS REGISTROS ESPECIALES
- MEMORIA ACERCA DEL MOVIMIENTO DE LOS NEGOCIOS EN LOS ANOS 1962-1963

- MEMORIA ACERCA DEL MOVIMIENTO DE LOS NEGOCIOS EN LOS ANOS 1964-1965
- MEMORIA COMERCIAL Y ESTADISTICA RELATIVA AL ESTADO DE LOS NEGOCIOS EN LA PROVINCIA DE BADAJOZ

Camara Oficial de Comercio e Industria de Caceres *see*
- INFORME DE LOS RESULTADOS DE LA ENCUESTA SOBRE LA SITUACION DEL COMERCIO, INDUSTRIA Y SERVICIOS
- REGLAMENTO DE REGIMEN INTERIOR DE LA...

Camara Oficial de la Propiedad Urbana *see* MEMORIA DE LOS TRABAJOS REALIZADOS DURANTE EL EJERCICIO DE 1931, QUE SE ELEVA AL EXCMO. SR. MINISTRO DE TRABAJO Y PREVISION

Camara Oficial de la Propiedad Urbana de la Provincia de Caceres *see* MEMORIA DE LOS TRABAJOS REALIZADOS DURANTE EL ANO 1940...

Camara Oficial Sindical Agraria *see*
- MEMORIA DE ACTIVIDADES
- MEMORIA DE ACTIVIDADES, 1967
- MEMORIA DE ACTIVIDADES, 1968
- REGLAMENTO DE TRABAJO AGRICOLA PARA LA PROVINCIA DE BADAJOZ

Camara Oficial Sindical Agraria. Caceres *see*
- ORDEN DE 31 DE ENERO DE 1958...LA INCOACION PARA LAS HERMANDADES SINDICALES DE LABRADORES Y GANADEROS...EXACCION POR LA VIA DE APREMIO DE LOS CUPONES IMPAGADOS
- REGLAMENTO PARA EL REGIMEN Y FUNCIONAMIENTO DE LAS SECCIONES SOCIALES DE LAS ENTIDADES SINDICALES MENORES, 12 ABRIL, 1950

Camara Privada de Compensacion Bancaria de Caceres *see*
- MEMORIA 1977
- REGLAMENTO DE LA...

LE CAMARADE – Quebec, Canada. v2 n1. 11 jan 1913-v2 n11. 7 jun 1913 – 1r – 1 – Can$25.00 – cn Can Microfilming [072]

CAMARAGIBE : BI-SEMANARIO POLITICO, LITTERARIO, COMMERCIAL E NOTICIOSO – Passo de Camaragibe, Alagoas. 20 Out-Nov 1880; Out 1881; 22 Fev 1882 – 1,5,6 – bl Biblioteca [072]

THE CAMAS-WASHOUGAL RECORD AND SHOPPERS GUIDE – Camas-Washougal, WA. 1982-1984; 1987 – 12+ r – 1 – $600.00 ($80.00y) – B05407 – us Library Micro [071]

Camau, Emile *see* LES INSTITUTIONS DE BIENFAISANCE, DE CHARITE ET DE PREVOYANCE A MARSEILLE

Cambell, Arthur *see* THE MYSTERY OF MARTHA WARNE

Cambell, Jacques *see* I FIORI DEI TRE COMPAGNI...MILANO, 1967

Cambell, W *see* MATERIALS FOR A HISTORY OF THE REIGN OF HENRY 7 (RS60)

Camberos de Yegros, Fernando *see*
- EL HEROE SERAFICO DE SAN PEDRO DE ALCANTARA
- VERDAD ILUSTRADA CONTRA LAS IMPOSTURAS QUE HA ESCRITO EL R.P. FR. MARCOS DE ALCALA

CAMBERWELL & PECKHAM TIMES – London, UK. Apr 1870-27 Feb 1969. -w. 118 reels – 1 – uk British Libr Newspaper [072]

Cambessedes, J *see* ENUMERATIO PLANTARUM, QUAS IN INSULIS BALEARIBUS COLLEGIT

Cambiagi, G *see* DESCRIZIONE DELL'IMPERIALE GIARDINO DI BOBOLI

LA CAMBIALE... / Contuzzi, F P – Milano, 1898 – 1mf – 1 – ILM-3648/1 – ne IDC [327]

CAMBIALE E ASSEGNO BANCARIO... / Giannini, A – Roma, 1934 – 5mf – 1 – ILM-3764/1 – ne IDC [327]

LA CAMBIALE E IL VAGLIA CAMBIARIO / Angeloni, V – Ed 2. Roma, [1946] – 5mf – 9 – ILM-3969/1 – ne IDC [340]

LA CAMBIALE E IL VAGLIA CAMBIARIO / Angeloni, V – Roma, 1934 – 7mf – 9 – ILM-3970/1 – ne IDC [340]

LA CAMBIALE E IL VAGLIA CAMBIARIO... / Crespolani, R – Modena, 1934 – 3mf – 1 – ILM-3285/1 – ne IDC [327]

Cambiasi, P *see* LA SCALA, 1778-1906; NOTE STORICHE E STATISTICHE

Cambier *see* ESSAI SUR LA LANGUE CONGOLAISE

Cambini, A *see*
- COMMENTARIO...DELLA ORIGINE DE TVRCHI, ET IMPERIO DELLA CASA OTTOMANNA
- LIBRO...DELLA ORIGINE DE TVRCHI ET IMPERIO DELLI OTTOMANNI

Cambini, G *see*
- SIX DUOS A DEUX VIOLONES, OP. 4
- SIX NOUVEAUX QUATUORS, VOL 1
- SIX NOUVEAUX QUATUORS, VOL. 2
- SIX QUATUORS D'AIR CONNUS
- SIX QUATUORS, OP. 10
- SIX SONATAS FOR TWO GERMAN FLUTES AND VIOLONCELLO WITH A THORO'BASS FOR HARPSICHORD OR ORGAN

CAMBIO 16 – Madrid. Nov 22, 1971- – 1 – us L of C Photodup [073]

CAMBIO DIEZ Y SEIS *see* CAMBIO 16

Cambodia *see*
- BULLETIN ADMINISTRATIF
- BULLETIN OFFICIEL
- JOURNAL OFFICIEL DE LA REPUBLIQUE KHMERE
- JOURNAL OFFICIEL DU CAMBODGE
- PLAN D'EQUIPEMENT BIENNAL, 1956-1957

CAMBODIA. HISTORICAL DOCUMENTS AND MANUSCRIPTS *see* HISTORICAL DOCUMENTS AND MANUSCRIPTS

Cambodia. Ministere du Plan *see*
- DEUXIEME PLAN QUINQUENNAL PREAH NORODNOM SURAMARIT 1968-1972
- PREMIER PLAN QUINQUENNAL, (1960-1964)

CAMBODIAN TIPITAKA / Institut Bouddhique, Phnom-Penh – 1931-1969 – 1,142mf – $800.00 – us I.A.S.W.R. [090]

Cambon, J M *see* LA DIPLOMATIE

Los Camborios *see* ESTATUTOS POR LOS QUE SE RIGE LA PENA "LOS CAMBORIOS"

CAMBOURNE-REDRUTH PACKET – England.20 Sept 1955-18 Dec 1956; 1957-59. -w. 2 reels – 1 – uk British Libr Newspaper [072]

CAMBRIA COUNTY PIONEERS / Swank, James M – Philadelphia: Allen, Lane and Scott, Printers, 1910. Pennsylvania Reel 14. (The Cox Library Collection) – 5 – us Americana [978]

CAMBRIA FREEMAN – Ebensburg, PA. -w 1899-1912 – 13 – $25.00r – us I.M.R. [071]

CAMBRIAN – Cambria. Calif. -w. 1931-50 – 1 – us UMI [071]

THE CAMBRIAN – Cambria, CA. 1931-73; 1979; 1981-82 – 21r – 1 – $1,050.00 – B02091 – us Library Micro [071]

CAMBRIAN LAW REVIEW – (v1-15 1970-84 in reel $92.00. v16-26 1985-95 in mf $129.00) – v1-26. 1970-95 – 5,6,9 – $221.00 set – us Hein [340]

CAMBRIDGE 1635-1849 – (Mf 1T-2T: Vital Records 1635-92. Mf 2T-4T,29T: Births 1688-1822. Mf 4T-5T: Marriage Intentions 1800-21. Mf 5T-7T: Marriages 1700-1821. Mf 7T-8T: Deaths 1699-1819. Mf 8T-15T: Marriages & Intentions 1814-45. Mf 13T-17T: Deaths & Burials 1825-64. Mf 14T-15T: Births 1794-1852. Mf 17T-18T: Marriage Intentions 1845-49. Mf 18T-19T: Out-of-Town Marriages 1686-1799. Mf 19T-27T: Vital Records 1843-49. Mf 27T-28T: Births & Deaths 1849. Mf 28T-29T: Marriage Intentions 1772-80) – (mf ed 1995) – 29mf – 9 – 0-87623-223-3 – us Holbrook [920]

THE CAMBRIDGE BIBLE FOR SCHOOLS AND COLLEGES *see* THE BOOK OF EXODUS

CAMBRIDGE CHARACTERISTICS IN THE SEVENTEENTH CENTURY, OR, THE STUDIES OF THE UNIVERSITY AND THEIR INFLUENCE ON THE CHARACTER AND WRITINGS OF THE MOST DISTINGUISHED GRADUATES DURING THAT PERIOD / Mullinger, James Bass – London: Macmillan, 1867 – 1mf – us A.T.L.A. [370]

CAMBRIDGE CHRONICLE – Cambridge, Great Britain. 1770-1934 – 1 – uk Microform Academic [072]

CAMBRIDGE CLARION – Cambridge, NE. (-w. except -sw. 1909-16, 1952-54.) May 1887-Jun. 1892. Incomplete; Oct. 1895-May 1898; Jul. 1898-Feb. 1904; Apr.1904-Oct. 1908. Incomplete; Aug. 1909- – 1 – us NE Hist [071]

CAMBRIDGE DAILY NEWS – Cambridge, England. -d. Jan-Dec 1893. 3 reels – 1 – uk British Libr Newspaper [072]

CAMBRIDGE GENERAL ADVERTISER – Cambridge, England. Cambridge Advertiser – New Cambridge Advertiser. -w. 9 Jan 1839-25 Dec 1850. 6 reels – 1 – uk British Libr Newspaper [072]

Cambridge, George *see* PAPERS

CAMBRIDGE INDEPENDENT PRESS – Cambridge, England. -w. 11 May 1839-Dec 1870. 22 reels – 1 – uk British Libr Newspaper [072]

CAMBRIDGE INTELLIGENCER – Cambridge. England. -w. 27 Jul 1793-18 Apr 1795, 13, 20 Jun, 1 Aug 1795-9 Sep 1797, 6 Jan 1798-17 Aug, 2 Nov-28 Dec 1799, 15 Feb-27 Dec 1800. (2 reels) – 1 – uk British Libr Newspaper [072]

CAMBRIDGE JEFFERSONIAN – (Weekly Democratic newspaper) – Cambridge, OH. may 19, 1870-may 15, 1873 – 2r – 1 – us Western Res [071]

CAMBRIDGE JOURNAL OF EDUCATION – (1975- . 5,6,9) – 1971- – 1 – us UMI [370]

CAMBRIDGE JOURNAL OF EDUCATION – 1988- 23v – 9 – £137.50 – 0305-764X – uk Carfax [370]

Cambridge, Lark A *see* EXPRESSING UNIVERSAL THEMES THROUGH STORYDANCE CHOREOGRAPHY

Cambridge Peace Aims Group *see* CHARTER OF THE RIGHTS AND DUTIES OF MODERN MAN

Cambridge Philological Society *see* PROCEEDINGS OF THE CAMBRIDGE PHILOLOGICAL SOCIETY

Cambridge Philosophical Society *see*
- BIOLOGICAL REVIEWS
- BIOLOGICAL REVIEWS AND BIOLOGICAL PROCEEDINGS
- PROCEEDINGS
- PROCEEDINGS...BIOLOGICAL SCIENCES
- TRANSACTIONS

THE CAMBRIDGE PLATONISTS : BEING SELECTIONS FROM THE WRITINGS OF BENJAMIN WHICHCOTE, JOHN SMITH AND NATHANAEL CULVERWEL / Whichcote, Benjamin – Oxford: Clarendon Press, 1901 – 1mf – us A.T.L.A. [180]

CAMBRIDGE QUARTERLY – 1965-71. v. 1-8. Plus index – 1 – uk Microform Academic [420]

CAMBRIDGE REPORTER – (1993.-18r; 1902-1975.-273r) – Cambridge, 1976-1992 – 210r – 1 – cn Preston [971]

Cambridge University *see* REPORT OF THE COMMISSIONERS APPOINTED TO ENQUIRE INTO THE STATE, DISCIPLINE, STUDIES, AND REVENUES, ETC

Cambridge University. Botany School *see* CATALOGUE OF THE LIBRARY OF CHARLES DARWIN..

Cambridge University. Library *see*
- A CATALOG OF THE MANUSCRIPTS PRESERVED IN THE LIBRARY OF THE UNIVERSITY OF CAMBRIDGE
- UNION CATALOGUE OF SCIENTIFIC LIBRARIES IN THE UNIVERSITY OF CAMBRIDGE: BOOKS PUBLISHED BEFORE 1801

THE CAMBRIDGE UNIVERSITY LIBRARY : STAGE 7 – 1185mf – 9 – H-1930-1933/1 – ne IDC [340]

CAMBRIDGESHIRE, 1805 : BRITISH ISLES CENSUS DIRECTORIES PROJECT, ENGLAND. VOL 169 – 1mf – 9 – A$9.00 – at Vine [941]

CAMBRIDGESHIRE, 1823 : BRITISH ISLES CENSUS DIRECTORIES PROJECT, ENGLAND. VOL 224 – 1mf – 9 – A$9.00 – at Vine [941]

CAMBRIDGESHIRE, 1830 : BRITISH ISLES CENSUS DIRECTORIES PROJECT, ENGLAND. VOL 224 – 1mf – 9 – A$9.00 – at Vine [941]

CAMBRIDGESHIRE, 1839 : BRITISH ISLES CENSUS DIRECTORIES PROJECT, ENGLAND. VOL 19 – 2mf – 9 – A$15.00 – at Vine [941]

CAMBRIDGESHIRE, 1846 : BRITISH ISLES CENSUS DIRECTORIES PROJECT, ENGLAND – at Vine [941]

CAMBRIDGESHIRE, 1851 : BRITISH ISLES CENSUS DIRECTORIES PROJECT, ENGLAND. VOL 2 – 5mf – 9 – A$33.00 – at Vine [941]

CAMBRIDGESHIRE, 1858 : BRITISH ISLES CENSUS DIRECTORIES PROJECT, ENGLAND – at Vine [941]

CAMBRIDGESHIRE, 1864 : BRITISH ISLES CENSUS DIRECTORIES PROJECT, ENGLAND – at Vine [941]

CAMBRIDGESHIRE, 1879 : BRITISH ISLES CENSUS DIRECTORIES PROJECT, ENGLAND. VOL 46 – 3mf – 9 – A$21.00 – at Vine [941]

CAMBRIDGESHIRE, 1883 : BRITISH ISLES CENSUS DIRECTORIES PROJECT, ENGLAND – at Vine [941]

CAMBRIDGESHIRE, 1900 : BRITISH ISLES CENSUS DIRECTORIES PROJECT, ENGLAND. VOL 48 – 6mf – 9 – A$39.00 – at Vine [941]

CAMBRIDGESHIRE, 1912 : BRITISH ISLES CENSUS DIRECTORIES PROJECT, ENGLAND – at Vine [941]

CAMBRIDGESHIRE, 1925 : BRITISH ISLES CENSUS DIRECTORIES PROJECT, ENGLAND – (In prep) – at Vine [941]

Cambronne, P *see* RECHERCHES SUR LA STRUCTURE DE L'IMAGINAIRE DANS LES CONFESSIONS DE SAINT AUGUSTIN

Cambrony, M *see* RECRUTEMENT ET BIOLOGIE DES STADES JUVENILES DE MUGILIDAE (POISSONS-TELEOSTEENS) DANS TROIS MILIEUX LAGUNAIRES DU ROUSSILLON ET DU NARBONNAIS (SALSES-LEUCATE, LAPALME, BOURDIGOU)

Cambry, Jacques *see* DESCRIPTION DU DEPARTEMENT DE L'OISE

CAMDEN JOURNAL AND HAMPSTEAD NEWS – London. -w. 1973-80. (15mqn reels) – 1 – uk British Libr Newspaper [072]

CAMDEN MAIL & NEW JERSEY ADVERTISER – Camden, NJ. 1834-40 – 1 – us Readex [071]

CAMDEN NEWS – Jun 13 1895-Dec 23 1968 – 9 – at Pascoe [072]

CAMDEN REPUBLICAN – United States. 26 Oct 1839-27 May 1843.-w. 1 reel – 1 – uk British Libr Newspaper [071]

Camden, W *see* CHRONOGRAPHICAL DESCRIPTION OF ENGLAND, SCOTLAND, IRELAND AND ISLANDS ADJACENT

Camden, William *see* INSTITUTIO GRAECAE GRAMMATICES COMPENDIARIA

THE CAMEL (CAMELUS DROMEDARIUS) = LE CHAMEAU (CAMELUS DROMEDARIUS). ETUDE BIBLIOGRAPHIQUE : A BIBLIOGRAPHICAL REVIEW / Mukasa-Mugerwa, E – 1981 – 9 – $9.00 – 92-9053-129-0 – et ILRI [590]

Camelot, PT *see* FOI ET GNOSE. INTRODUCTION A L'ETUDE DE LA CONNAISSANCE MYSTIQUE CHEZ CLEMENT D'ALEXANDRIE

CAMELS AND CAMEL MILK – 1982 – 72p – it F.A.O. [636]

CAMEO GLASS, MASTERPIECES FROM 2000 YEARS OF GLASSMAKING / Goldstein, Sidney M & Rakow, Leonard S & Rakow, Juliette K – 1982. 144p. 193 illus., 41 color. 3 fiches. Fiche No.6683 – 9 – $6.25 – us Corning Mus [740]

CAMEOS / Corelli, Marie – British Fiction Archive: Unit 1 – 9 – uk Bell [830]

Camera Club of New York *see* CAMERA NOTES AND PROCEEDINGS

CAMERA CRAFT – San Francisco, CA. 1900-1942 – 17r – 1 – $850.00 – C03475 – us Library Micro [770]

CAMERA CRAFTSMAN – v. 1-26. 1955-80 – 1,5,6,9 – us UMI [770]

CAMERA DI COMMERCIO, INDUSTRIA E AGRICOLTURA – Asmara. Il Bollettino; Notiziario. v2-16. 1946-60 – 2r – 1 – us Ross [380]

CAMERA NOTES – New York: Camera Club. v1-6. 1897-1903 – 2r – 1 – us Res Libr [760]

CAMERA NOTES AND PROCEEDINGS / Camera Club of New York – New York. v1-6.1897-1903 – 1r – 1 – us Ross [770]

Camerarius, J *see*
- CAPITA PIETATIS ET RELIGIONIS CHRISTIANAE...
- DE PHILIPPI MELANCHTHONIS ORTV, TOTIVS VITAE CVRRICVLO ET MORTE,...
- DE REBVS TVRCICIS COMMENTARII DVO ACCVRATISSIMI
- HOMILIAE QVI SVNT SERMONES HABITI DE IIS, QVAE IN CHRISTIANIS ECCLESIIS LEGVNTVR...

Camerarius, R J *see* DISPUTATIO INAUGURALIS MEDICA DE LOLIO TEMULENTO

Camerer, W *see* EDUARD MOERIKE UND KLARA NEUFFER

Camerlynck, Achille *see* COMMENTARIUS IN ACTUS APOSTOLORUM

Cameron, A E et al *see* THE HEATHER BEETLE

Cameron, Charles Innes *see* POEMS AND HYMNS

CAMERON COUNTY ECHO – Emporium, PA. -w 1972-1980. 7 rolls – 13 – $25.00r – us I.M.R. [071]

CAMERON COUNTY PRESS – Emporium, PA. -w 1889-1928 – 13 – $25.00r – us I.M.R. [071]

CAMERON COUNTY PRESS – Emporium. Pa. -w. 1962- – 1 – us UMI [071]

Cameron, Donald *see* MEMOIR OF THE LIFE OF DONALD CAMERON: WITH REMARKS BY HIS SON ARCHIBALD OF VELLORE, VAUGHAN TOWNSHIP, COUNTY OF YORK, ONTARIO
Cameron, DR *see*
- REMARKS UPON THE TRUE LOCATION OF THE INTERNATIONAL BOUNDARY LINE: AT THE MOUTH OF THE RIVER ST CLAIR, WITH REFERENCE TO THE SO-CALLED AMERICAN CANAL
- REPORT ON THE LOCATION OF THE BRITISH-ALASKAN BOUNDARY

Cameron, George Frederick *see*
- AN ENTIRELY NEW AND ORIGINAL MILITARY OPERA IN THREE ACTS, ENTITLED: LEO, THE ROYAL CADET
- LYRICS ON FREEDOM, LOVE AND DEATH

Cameron, George G *see* PERSEPOLIS TREASURY TABLETS
Cameron, J *see*
- CATALOGUE OF PLANTS IN THE BOTANICAL GARDEN...
- OSTEOLOGY OF THE WESTERN AND CENTRAL ESKIMOS

Cameron, J Hillyard *see* A COLLECTION OF LEGAL OPINIONS: COMPRISING UPWARDS OF ONE HUNDRED AND THIRTY LEADING OPINIONS ON CASES SUBMITTED TO THE LATE HON. J. HILLYARD CAMERON
Cameron, James Chalmers *see* MCGILL OBSTETRIC NOTE BOOK
Cameron, Malcolm Graeme *see* PATRIOTIC ADDRESS: DELIVERED AT DUNGANNON, MARCH 15, 1900 AT A CONCERT IN AID FOR THE FUND FOR THE BENEFIT OF THE WIDOWS AND ORPHANS OF THE CANADIAN SOLDIERS KILLED IN THE SOUTH AFRICAN WAR
Cameron, P *see* A MONOGRAPH OF THE BRITISH PHYTOPHAGOUS HYMENOPTERA
Cameron, Robert *see*
- DOCTRINE OF THE AGES
- THE DOCTRINE OF THE AGES BY ROBERT CAMERON
- WATCHWORD AND TRUTH, 1897-1921

Cameron, Saint Robert *see* THE WATCHWORD
Cameron, Simon *see*
- PAPERS
- SIMON CAMERON PAPERS

Cameron, Verney L *see*
- A TRAVERS L'AFRIQUE. VOYAGE DE ZANZIBAR A BANGUELA
- A TRAVERS L'AFRIQUE, VOYAGE DE ZANZIBAR A BENGUELA
- ACROSS AFRICA

Cameron, William *see* A MONTH IN THE UNITED STATES AND CANADA IN THE AUTUMN OF 1873
CAMERON'S DIRECTORY AND RAILWAY AND STEAMSHIP GUIDE TO TORONTO – Toronto?: Cameron, 1892-189- or 19– – 9 – cn C.I.H.M. [380]
CAMERON'S LEGAL OPINIONS / Canada. General – 1v. 1859-76 (all publ) – 3mf – 9 – $4.50 – LLMC 81-006 – us L.L.M.C. [340]
CAMERON'S SUPREME COURT CASES / Canada. Supreme Court – 1v. 1880-1900 (all publ) – 7mf – 9 – $10.50 – LLMC 81-007 – us L.L.M.C. [340]
CAMEROON : NOTE ANNUELLE DE STATISTIQUE 1973-1975 / Cameroon. Direction de la Statistique et de la Comptabilite Nationale – (Coll title: African Official Statistical Serials, 1867-1982) – 9mf – 9 – £75.00 – uk Chadwyck [960]
Cameroon *see*
- ECONOMIE ET PLAN DE DEVELOPPEMENT
- PLAN DE DEVELOPPEMENT
- THIRD FIVE YEAR DEVELOPMENT PLAN 1971-1976
- TROISIEME PLAN QUADRIENNAL DU CAMEROON, 1958-1962

Cameroon. Direction de la Statistique et de la Comptabilite Nationale *see* CAMEROON
Cameroon. Direction du Plan et de la Coop. Technique *see* RAPPORT GENERAL SUR L'EXECUTION DE L'AN 1 DU PLAN QUINQUENNAL
Cameroon. Ministere des Affaires Economiques et du Plan *see* DEUXIEME PLAN QUINQUENNAL DE DEVELOPPEMENT ECONOMIQUE ET SOCIALD-1009/1. 2 V. JUL. 1966-JUNE. 1971
Cameroon. Ministere des Finances et du Plan *see*
- PREMIER PLAN QUINQUENNAL DE DEVELOPPEMENT ECONOMIQUE ET SOCIAL
- RAPPORT GENERAL SUR L'EXECUTION DU PREMIER PLAN QUINQUENNAL (JUSQU AU 30 JUIN 1963)

Cameroon. Ministere du Plan et de l'Amenagement du Territoire *see* TROISIEME PLAN QUINQUENNAL DE DEVELOPPEMENT ECONOMIQUE ET SOCIAL, 1971-1976
Cameroon. Service d'Orientation Scolaire, Universitaire et Professionnelle. Ministere Education Nationale *see* RAPPORT NATIONAL SUR LE DEVELOPPEMENT DE L'EDUCATION AU CAMEROUN (PERIODE 1981-1984)
Cameroon. Societe Generale d'Etudes et de Planification, Paris *see* PLAN DE DEVELOPPEMENT ECONOMIQUE ET SOCIAL-TRAVAUX PREPARATOIRE
CAMEROON TRIBUNE : ENGLISH EDITION – (Scattered issues lacking) – Yaounde, Cameroon. Sept 5 1984-Feb 7 1992 – 13r – 1 – us L of C Photodup [072]
CAMEROONS UNDER UNITED KINGDOM ADMINISTRATION / Great Britain. Colonial Office – 1947-49 – 1 – us Res Libr [960]
CAMEROUN : PLAN DE DEVELOPPEMENT – 1960 – 1r – $49.50 – us African Imprint [330]
CAMEROUN POLITICAL EPHEMERA, 1952-1961 – St Louis, MO: Washington Uni Libraries, 1964 – 1 – us Res Libr [080]
CAMEROUN POLITICAL EPHEMERA, 1954-1963 / Welch, Claude Emerson – Palo Alato, CA: Stanford Uni Photographic Dept, 1965 – 1 – us Res Libr [960]
Camille, M *see* LE VOIX DES BOIS-FRANCS
CAMILLE OU LE SOUTERRAIN / Marsollier et Dalayrac – (French Theatre Series). Paris. Brunet. 1791 – 9 – fr Hachette [820]
CAMILLE PISSARRO. CENTENAIRE DE SA NAISSANCE / Reunion des musees nationaux. Paris – 1930. 9 illus. 1 fiche – 9 – fr Réunion [750]
Camilleri, C *see* CULTURAL ANTHROPOLOGY AND EDUCATION
Camilli, Camillo *see* IMPRESE ILLUSTRI DI DIVERSI
O CAMINHO DA ESCOLA : LUTA POPULAR PELA ESCOLA PUBLICA / Ribero, Vera Masagao – (Texto baseado nos depoimentos de Adriano Diogo...[et al]) – Sao Paulo: Centro Ecumenico de Documentacao e Informacao, 1986 – us Res Libr [972]
Camino Burgos, Luis G *see* LOS BESOS BAJO TIERRA (POEMAS DEL AMOR Y DEL DESAMOS)
EL CAMINO DE LA UNIDAD: UN DISCURSO SOCIALISTA / Lamoneda, Ramon – Madrid? 1937? Fiche W984. (Blodgett Collection of Spanish Civil War Pamphlets) – 9 – us H.U. College Libr [946]
EL CAMINO DE LA VICTORIA: LLAMAMIENTO...A TODOS LOS PUEBLOS DE ESPANA Y A CUANTOS AMAN LA PAZ, EL PROGRESO Y LA LIBERTAD / Communist Party. Spain – Valencia, 193? Fiche W 771. (Blodgett Collection of Spanish Civil War Pamphlets) – 9 – us H.U. College Libr [946]
CAMINO DEL CIELO / Purificacion y Tornavacas, Pedro de – 1818 – 9 – 1.50f – sp Bibl Santa Ana [240]
CAMINO DEL CIELO / Suarez de Figueroa, Diego – 1739. 3v – 9 – 1.50f – sp Bibl Santa Ana [946]
UN CAMINO EN LA SELVA / Barreda, Ernesto Maria – Buenos Aires. 1916 – 1 – us Res Libr [830]
CAMINO ESPIRITUAL / San Pedro de Alcantara, Domingo de – Caceres: Tip. Extremadura, 1962 – 1 – sp Bibl Santa Ana [240]
CAMINOS DE ESPANA : PLASENCIA 2 – Madrid: Compania Espanola de Penicilina, S.A., 1951 – sp Bibl Santa Ana [910]
CAMINOS DE ESPANA : ZAFRA 1 – Madrid: Compania Espanola de Penicilina, S.A., 1952 – sp Bibl Santa Ana [910]
CAMINOS DE ESPANA : ZAFRA 2 – Madrid: Compania Espanola de Penicilina, S.A., 1958 – sp Bibl Santa Ana [910]
CAMINOS DE ESPANA. MERIDA. RUTA 44 – Madrid: Imp. Lonja y Cia, 1960 – 1 – sp Bibl Santa Ana [910]
CAMINOS DE ESPANA: MERIDA-ZAFRA – Madrid: Compania Espanola de Penicilina, 1960 – 1 – sp Bibl Santa Ana [946]
EN LOS CAMINOS DE LA LIBERTAD / Albornoz, Alvaro de – Brooklyn, NY. 1939. Fiche W 706. (Blodgett Collection of Spanish Civil War Pamphlets) – 9 – us H.U. College Libr [946]
CAMINOS DE SERVIDUMBRE / Romero Mendoza, Pedro – Madrid: Imp. G. Hernandez y Galo Saez, 1926 – 1 – sp Bibl Santa Ana [830]
CAMINOS DEL ALMA / Merchan Cantisan, Felisa – Madrid: Tip. Rubio y Castro, S.L. 1975 – 1 – sp Bibl Santa Ana [946]
Camirand, J A *see* BULLETIN SUR LES CHEMINS
Camirand, Wilfrid *see* INTRONISATION DE SA GRANDEUR MGR. ELPHEGE GRAVEL, PREMIER EVEQUE DE NICOLET: SUIVIS SIC DE SON MANDEMENT D'ENTREE ET DE RENSEIGNEMENTS INTERESSANTS SUR LE NOUVEAU DIOCESE
EN CAMISA ROSA. LAS SONATAS DEL OTONO / Trigo, Felipe – Madrid: Renacimiento, 1921 – sp Bibl Santa Ana [810]
Camisado *see* YO, Y MISAN ECDOTAS
THE CAMISARDS : A SEQUEL TO THE HUGUENOTS IN THE SEVENTEENTH CENTURY / Tylor, Charles – London: Simpkin, Marshall, Hamilton, Kent: E. Hicks, 1893 – 2mf – us A.T.L.A. [305]
Camlibel, Faruk Nafiz *see* SUDA HALKALAR
Cammaille Saint-Aubin *see* LE MOINE
Cammann, Henry J *see* THE CHARITIES OF NEW YORK, BROOKLYN, AND STATEN ISLAND
Camocio, G F *see* L'ORDINE DELLE GALERE ET LE INSEGNE LORO, CON LI FANO, NOMI, ET COGNOMI DELLI MAGNIFICI, ET GENEROSI PATRONI DI ESSE, ...
CAMOENS A CALDERON EN EL CENTENARIO DE ESTE / Coronado, Carolina – 1881 – 9 – sp Bibl Santa Ana [440]
Camoes, Luiz de *see* RIMAS VARIAS DE LUIS DE CAMOENS...COMMENTADAS PRO MANUEL DE FARIA Y SOUSA
CAMP ADAIR SENTRY – Camp Adair, OR. -w. 23 Apr 1942-21 Jul 1944. 1 roll – 1 – us U.O. Library [071]
CAMP AND LAMP: RAMBLES IN REALMS OF SPORT, STORY, SONG / Baylis, Samuel Mathewson – Montreal: W. Drysdale, 1897. 03508. (Pre-1900 Canadiana) – 9 – cn C.I.H.M. [790]
CAMP CRIER – 1971-76. (American Indian Periodicals in the Princeton University Library). 33 fiches – 9 – $125.00 – us UPA [305]
LE CAMP DE CHALONS, 1857 / Le Gray, Gustave – 47 plates recording scenes and military maneuvers. 1 reel. (Collections of the Department of Prints and Photographs) – 1 – 50.00 – fr Bibl Nationale [355]
Camp, Edgar W et al *see* ENCYCLOPAEDIA OF EVIDENCE
THE CAMP FIRE – Toronto: F S Spence, [1894-189- or 19–] – 9 – cn C.I.H.M. [971]
Camp, Hugh N *see* THE CHARITIES OF NEW YORK, BROOKLYN, AND STATEN ISLAND
CAMP KETTLE *see* NEW SOUTH (BEAUFORT, SOUTH CAROLINA), MARCH 7, 1895
CAMP MEETING MANUAL / Gorham, Barlow Weed – 1854 – 9 – us A.T.L.A. [240]
Camp, Walter Chauncey *see* HOW TO PLAY FOOTBALL
LE CAMPAGNARD – Napierville, Canada. jul; v1 n6. dec 1975 – 1r – 1 – Can$25.00 – cn Can Microfilming [072]
LA CAMPAGNE : QUOTIDIEN / ed by Nantel, Alphonse – St Jerome, Canada. 25 aut 1886-23 avr 1887 – 1r – 1 – Can$40.00 – cn Can Microfilming [072]
Campagne, Alexandre Auguste de *see* PRINCIPES D'UN BON GOUVERNEMENT OU REFLEXIONS MORALES ET POLITIQUES TENDANTES A PROCURER LE BONHEUR DE L'HOMME ET CELUI DES SOCIETES POLITIQUES
CAMPAGNE DANS LE HAUT SENEGAL ET DANS LE HAUT NIGER, 1885-1886 / Frey, Henri Nicolas – Paris: E Plon, Nourrit, 1888 – 1 – us Res Libr [960]
CAMPAGNE DU DAHOMEY 1892-1894 / Poirier, Jules – Paris, Limoges, Henri-Charles Lavauzelle. 1895 – 9 – 10.00 – fr Orientalistes [960]
UNE CAMPAGNE SUR LES COTES DU JAPON / Roussin, Alfred – Paris, Hachette. 1866 – 9 – 7.50 – fr Orientalistes [950]
Campagnoli, B *see* L'ARTE D'INCENTER A L'IMPROVISTE DES FANTAISIES ET CADENCES POUR LE VIOLON FORMENT UN RECUEIL DE 246 PIECES AMUSANTS ET UTILES EN TOUS MAJEURS ET MINEURS...OEUV 17
CAMPAIGN ACT AMENDMENTS, 1974, 1976 AND 1979 – Washington, 1977, 1983. LLMC 90-370 – 33mf – 9 – $49.50 – us L.L.M.C. [340]
CAMPAIGN CIRCULAR / Nebraska. College of Agriculture. Extension Service – n.7-209. 1939-68 – 1, 5 – us Spaulding [630]
CAMPAIGN FINANCE LAW / Federal Election Commission – 1984, 1986, 1988, 1990, 1992. LLMC 95-027 – 24mf – 9 – $36.00 – us L.L.M.C. [340]
CAMPAIGN FOR WOMEN'S SUFFRAGE 1895-1920 – (N.U.W.S.S. vols.1-29; Manchester Men's League for W.S. 1913-1918; Minute Books; I.W.S.A. Files 1-15; I.W.S.A. Correspondence Files A-Z) – 1 – us Primary [305]
CAMPAIGN HERALD – Portland OR. Apr 11 1868 – 1 – us U.O. Library [071]
CAMPAIGN NOTES – Virginia City, NV. Oct-Nov 1900 – 1r – 1 – $50.00 – U04782 – us Library Micro [071]
THE CAMPAIGN OF TRAFALGAR / Corbett, J Stafford – 1910 – 9 – $20.00 – uk Libr Preservation [941]
CAMPAIGN STAR – Portland OR. Oct 15-24 1887 – 1 – us U.O. Library [071]
CAMPAIGNS AND ELECTIONS – v.1-. 1980- – 1,5,6,9 – us UMI [073]
CAMPAIGNS IN BELGIUM DURING WORLD WAR 2 PAMPHLET COLLECTION – 1940-1970 – 1 – CSUXANM9128-B – us Hoover Inst Photo [355]
CAMPAIGNS IN GERMANY DURING WORDL WAR 2 PAMPHLET COLLECTION – 1943-19?? – 1 – CSUXANM8191-B – us Hoover Inst Photo [355]
CAMPAIGNS IN ITALY DURING WORLD WAR 2 PAMPHLET COLLECTION – 1942-1945 – 1 – CSUXANM9136-B – us Hoover Inst Photo [355]
CAMPAIGNS IN THE NETHERLANDS DURING WORLD WAR 2 PAMPHLET COLLECTION – 1984-1986 – 1 – CSUXANM9146-B – us Hoover Inst Photo [355]
CAMPAIGNS OF THE RUSSIAN REVOLUTION PAMPHLET COLLECTION – 1918-1932 – 1 – CSUXANS8472-B – us Hoover Inst Photo [947]
CAMPAIGNS OF THE WAR OF 1812-15, AGAINST GREAT BRITAIN, SKETCHED AND CRITICISED: WITH BRIEF BIOGRAPHIES OF THE AMERICAN ENGINEERS / Cullum, George Washington – New York: J. Miller, 1879. 03637. (Pre-1900 Canadiana) – 9 – cn C.I.H.M. [971]
CAMPAMENTOS 1971. CACERES / Delegacion Provincial de la Juventud – Caceres: Imp. M. Sergio Dorado, 1971 – 1 – sp Bibl Santa Ana [946]
LOS CAMPAMENTOS DE QUINTO CECILIO METELO PIO / Lumbreras Valiente, Pedro – Caceres: Edit. Extremadura, 1973 – 1 – sp Bibl Santa Ana [946]
LA CAMPANA – Paris. 5 janv-8 juil 1898, 1 avr-5 aout 1900 – 1 – fr A.C.R.P.P. [073]
Campana, C *see* COMPENDIO HISTORICO, DELLE GVERRE VLTIMAMENTE SUCCESSE TRA CHRISTIANI, ET TURCHI, ET TRA TURCHI, ET PERSIANI: ...
CAMPANA DE CAMPAMENTOS 1974 / Delegacion Provincial de la Juventud – Caceres: Imp. M. Sergio Dorado, 1974 – 1 – sp Bibl Santa Ana [350]
CAMPANA DE PORTUGAL...EXTREMADURA / Garcia, Miguel – 1762 – 9 – 1.50f – sp Bibl Santa Ana [946]
CAMPANA DE PORTUGAL...EXTREMADURA / Mascarenas, Geronimo – 1662 – 9 – 1.50f – sp Bibl Santa Ana [910]
CAMPANA DEL BRASIL. ANTECEDENTES COLONIALES. TOMO 1 : (DOCUMENTOS REFERENTES A LA...INDEPENDENCIA...DE... ARGENTINA...SEGUNDA SERIE) / Bayle, Constantino – Buenos Aires, 1931; Madrid: Razon y Fe, 1932 – 1 – sp Bibl Santa Ana [972]
LA CAMPANA PROTESTANTE EN AMERICA / Bayle, Constantino – Madrid: Razon y Fe, 1928 – 9 – sp Bibl Santa Ana [240]
CAMPANA REAUNDADA / Bayle, Constantino – Madrid: Razon y Fe, 1928 – 9 – sp Bibl Santa Ana [999]
Campanario *see* PROGRAMA OFICIAL DE FERIA Y FIESTAS EN HONOR DE LA SANTISIMA VIRGEN DE PIEDRA-ESCRITA
O CAMPANARIO : PERIODICO LITTERARIO E NOTICIOSO – Pilar, Alagoas. 30 Maio 1897 – 1,5,6 – bl Biblioteca [072]
Campanario. Ayuntamiento *see* ORDENANZAS MUNICIPALES

CAMPANAS EN EL RIF Y GEBALA, DEL GENERAL BERENGUER / Bayle, Constantino – Madrid: Razon y Fe, 1923 – 1 – sp Bibl Santa Ana [355]
Campanella, Tommaso *see* THE SONNETS OF MICHAEL ANGELO BUONARROTI AND TOMMASO CAMPANELLA.
THE CAMPANER THAL, AND OTHER WRITINGS / Richter, Johann Paul Friedrich – (From the German) – New York: United States Book Co., n.d. 383p – 1 – us U.W. Library [430]
A CAMPANHA – Campanha, 19 May, 29 Aug 1908 – 1,5,6 – bl Biblioteca [072]
Campano, Jose *see* PERON Y ESPANA
Campanus, J *see* TVRCICORVM TYRANNORVM QVI INDE VSQVE AB OTOMANNO REBUS TURCICIS PRAEFUERUNT, ...
Camparo, Hector, Jose *see* LA REVOLUCION PERONISTA
Campbell, A. et al *see* PSALMS, HYMNS AND SPIRITUAL SONGS
Campbell, A J *see* NESTS AND EGGS OF AUSTRALIAN BIRDS
Campbell, Alexander *see*
- CANADIAN PACIFIC RAILWAY: CONTRACT WITH THE SYNDICATE
- THE MEMORABLE SERMON ON THE LAW
- SPEECHES ON DIVERS OCCASIONS

Campbell, Alfred *see*
- THE CRIME OF PAUL SACRISTAN: A TALE
- THE MYSTERY OF MARTHA WARNE: A TALE OF MONTREAL

Campbell, Archibald *see*
- THE CHURCH OF THE FUTURE
- THE PRESENT CONDITION OF THE CHURCH OF ENGLAND
- THE "ROYAL WILLIAM", THE PIONEER OF STEAM NAVIGATION: A PAPER READ BEFORE THE LITERARY AND HISTORICAL SOCIETY OF QUEBEC, ON THE 31ST DAY OF MARCH, 1891

Campbell, Arthur *see* A RIDE IN MOROCCO, AND OTHER SKETCHES
Campbell, Belle McPherson *see* MADAGASCAR
Campbell, C A *see* THE CATACOMBS OF ROME: A LECTURE
Campbell, Charles *see* CANADA: A METRICAL STORY
CAMPBELL CHRONICALS AND FAMILY SKETCHES / Early, R H – Lynchburg, J. P. Bell and Co., 1927. Virginia Reel 2. (The Cox Library Collection) – 5 – us Americana [978]
CAMPBELL CITIZEN – Campbell, NE. -w. Mar. 1908-Jun. 1914; Aug. 1916-Aug. 1917; Apr. 1919-Dec. 1925; Jan. 1927-Dec. 1939; Jan. 1941-Feb. 1944 – 1 – us NE Hist [071]
Campbell, Clarence Thomas *see* PERSONALITY OF HAHNEMANN
Campbell, Colin *see* VITRUVIUS BRITANNICUS
Campbell, D H *see*
- THE STRUCTURE AND DEVELOPMENT OF MOSSES AND FERNS

Campbell, D S *see* ACTIVE AND PASSIVE ELECTRONIC COMPONENTS
Campbell, Donald *see* MEMORIALS OF JOHN MCLEOD CAMPELL, D.D.
Campbell, Dugald *see* IN THE HEART OF BANTULAND
Campbell, Duncan *see* NOVA SCOTIA IN ITS HISTORICAL, MERCANTILE AND INDUSTRIAL RELATIONS
Campbell Family *see* PAPERS OF CAMPBELL, PRESTON AND FLOYED FAMILIES
Campbell, FBF *see*
- AN INDEX-CATALOGUE OF BIBLIOGRAPHICAL WORKS (CHIEFLY IN THE ENGLISH LANGUAGE) RELATING TO INDIA
- INDEX-CATALOGUE OF INDIAN OFFICIAL PUBLICATIONS IN THE LIBRARY OF THE BRITISH MUSEUM
- INDIA: AN INDEX-CATALOGUE OF BIBLIOGRAPHICAL WORKS

Campbell, Francis *see* INDEX-CATALOGUE OF INDIAN OFFICIAL PUBLICATIONS IN THE LIBRARY, BRITISH MUSEUM
Campbell, Francis Wayland *see* THE WAR OF 1812-13-14 BETWEEN GREAT BRITAIN AND THE UNITED STATES: A LECTURE DELIVERED AT THE MONTREAL MILITARY INSTITUTE AND BEFORE THE NUMISMATIC AND ANTIQUARIAN SOCIETY OF MONTREAL IN FEBRUARY 1899
Campbell, Frank *see* CATALOGUE OF OFFICIAL REPORTS RELATING TO INDIA ISSUED AS ENGLISH PARLIAMENTARY PAPERS (AND IN CONNECTION WITH THE INDIA OFFICE) DURING THE YEAR 1892
Campbell, Gerald Fitzgerald *see* EDWARD AND PAMELA FITZGERALD.
Campbell, H *see* THE LAW OF WAR...
Campbell, H C *see* DEVELOPING PUBLIC LIBRARY SYSTEMS AND SERVICES
Campbell, J *see* TRAVELS IN SOUTH AFRICA
Campbell, J H *see* GEORGIA BAPTISTS: HISTORICAL & BIOGRAPHICAL
Campbell, James B *see* FOR CANADA, TRANSPORTATION THE PROBLEM
Campbell, James Dykes *see* THE POETICAL WORKS OF SAMUEL TAYLOR COLERIDGE
Campbell, James Mann *see*
- THE HEART OF THE GOSPEL: A POPULAR EXPOSITION OF THE ATONEMENT
- PAUL THE MYSTIC
- PAUL, THE MYSTIC: A STUDY IN APOSTOLIC EXPERIENCE
- THE TEACHINGS OF THE BOOKS

Campbell, James Mannann *see* THE INDWELLING CHRIST
Campbell, James R *see* MISSIONS IN HINDUSTAN
Campbell, James Valentine *see* OUTLINES OF THE POLITICAL HISTORY OF MICHIGAN
Campbell, Jessie Buchanan *see* THE PIONEER PASTOR: SOME REMINISCENCES OF THE LIFE AND LABORS OF THE REV. GEO. BUCHANAN, M.D., THE FIRST PRESBYTERIAN MINISTER OF BECKWITH, LANARK COUNTY, UPPER CANADA
Campbell, John *see*
- THE BIRTHPLACE OF ANCIENT RELIGIONS AND CIVILIZATION
- THE COPTIC ELEMENT IN LANGUAGES OF THE INDO-EUROPEAN FAMILY
- THE EARLY HISTORY OF AMERICA MICROFORM: OUTLINE OF A SERIES OF LECTURES DELIVERED UNDER THE AUSPICES OF THE LADIES' EDUCATION ASSOCIATION OF MONTREAL DURING THE SESSION 1881-82
- THE GREAT ELECTION
- THE HORITES
- JOHN ANGELL JAMES
- LIFE OF JOHN, LORD CAMPBELL, LORD HIGH CHANCELLOR OF GREAT BRITAIN; CONSISTING OF A SELECTION FROM HIS AUTOBIOGRAPHY, DIARY, AND LETTERS
- LIVES OF THE LORD CHANCELLORS
- THE LOST TRIBES: A REFUTATION OF THE THEORIES OF MESSRS. WILSON, HINE AND OTHER WRITERS WHO HAVE IDENTIFIED THEM WITH THE ENGLISH NATION: A LECTURE DELIVERED UNDER THE AUSPICES OF THE YOUNG MEN'S SOCIETY OF ERSKINE CHURCH, MONTREAL ON 17TH DECEMBER, 1877
- THE MARTYR OF ERROMANGA, OR, THE PHILOSOPHY OF MISSIONS, ILLUSTRATED FROM THE LABOURS, DEATH, AND CHARACTER OF THE LATE REV. JOHN WILLIAMS
- NEW LIGHT ON THE OLD PRAYER
- ORIGIN OF THE ABORIGINES OF CANADA: A PAPER READ BEFORE THE SOCIETY, 17TH DECEMBER 1880
- THE SHEPHERD KINGS OF EGYPT
- TWO KNAPSACKS: A NOVEL OF CANADIAN SUMMER LIFE

Campbell, John McLeod *see* THOUGHTS ON REVELATION
Campbell, John M'Leod *see* CHRIST THE BREAD OF LIFE
Campbell, John P *see* VINDEX OR THE DOCTRINES OF THE STRICTURES VINDICATED
CAMPBELL, JOHN Q.A., DIARIES MS 3560 – 1861-1905 – 1r – 1 – us Western Res [976]
Campbell, John Roy *see*
- AN ANSWER TO SOME STRICTURES IN BROWN'S SEQUEL TO CAMPBELL'S HISTORY OF YARMOUTH
- A HISTORY OF THE COUNTY OF YARMOUTH, NOVA SCOTIA

CAMPBELL LAW REVIEW – v1-17. 1979-95 – 9 – $207.00 set – us Hein [340]
Campbell, Lewis *see* RELIGION IN GREEK LITERATURE
Campbell, Mary Helen *see* SUNDAYS IN YOHO: TWELVE STORIES FOR CHILDREN AND THEIR FRIENDS
Campbell, ML *see* RATING OF COLLEGE COURSES BY SPRINGFIELD COLLEGE ELEMENTARY PHYSICAL EDUCATION TEACHER PREPARATION PROGRAM GRADUATES
Campbell, N W *see* GEOGRAPHICAL HANDBOOK OF THE COUNTY OF GREY
CAMPBELL NEWS – Campbell,NE. -w. Nov. 1944-Dec. 1973 – 1 – us NE Hist [071]
Campbell, Persia Crawford *see* CHINESE COOLIE EMIGRATION TO COUNTRIES WITHIN THE BRITISH EMPIRE
CAMPBELL PRESS – Campbell, CA. 1895-1948; 1973-85 – 30r – 1 – $1,500.00 – B02092 – us Library Micro [071]
CAMPBELL PRESS – Campbell, NE. -w. Mar. 1892-Nov. 1895. Incomplete; Apr. 1896-May 1898; Dec. 1898-Aug. 1903 – 1 – us NE Hist [071]
Campbell, R *see* A GUIDE TO THE GOLDEN CITY
Campbell, R G *see* NEUTRAL RIGHTS...
Campbell, R J *see* NEW THEOLOGY SERMONS
Campbell, Reginald John *see*
- A FAITH FOR TO-DAY
- THE NEW THEOLOGY
- THE RESTORED INNOCENCE

CAMPBELL RIVER COURIER – British Columbia, CN. 1946-72 – 14r – 1 – cn Commonwealth Micro [072]
Campbell, Robert, 1808-94 *see* THE DISCOVERY AND EXPLORATION OF THE PELLY (YUKON) RIVER
Campbell, Robert, 1835-1921 *see*
- A HISTORY OF THE SCOTCH PRESBYTERIAN CHURCH, ST GABRIEL STREET, MONTREAL
- ON THE UNION OF PRESBYTERIANS IN CANADA: PRIZE ESSAY
- THE PRETENSIONS EXPOSED OF MESSRS. LANG, BURNET & CO. TO BE "THE PRESBYTERIAN CHURCH IN CANADA IN CONNEXION WITH THE CHURCH OF SCOTLAND"

Campbell, Rollo *see*
- THE PILOT
- THE ROYAL STANDARD

Campbell, T L *see* DIONYSIUS THE PS.-AREOPAGITE: THE ECCLESIASTICAL HIERARCHY
Campbell, Thomas *see*
- GERTRUDE OF WYOMING
- THE PLEASURES OF HOPE
- THE POETICAL WORKS OF THOMAS CAMPBELL
- SPECIMENS OF THE BRITISH POETS
- THEODRIC

Campbell, W *see*
- CAMPBELL'S COLLECTION OF THE NEWEST AND MOST FAVORITE COUNTRY DANCES, REELS, STRATHSPEYS, AND COTILLONS FOR THE VIOLIN, HARPSICHORD, PIANOFORTE, OR (?) GERMAN FLUTE. BOOK ONE.
- CAMPBELL'S THIRD COLLECTION OF THE NEWEST AND MOST FAVORITE COUNTRY DANCES AND COTILLONS, FOR THE VIOLIN, HARP, HARPSICHORD, AND GERMAN FLUTE...

Campbell, W Graham *see* THE NEW WORLD, OR, RECENT VISIT TO AMERICA: TOGETHER WITH INTRODUCTORY OBSERVATIONS FOR TOURISTS, AND FOUR APPENDIXES CONTAINING ALL SUITABLE INFORMATION FOR EMIGRANTS, ETC
Campbell, W S *see* THE FLOWERING PLANTS AND FERNS OF NEW SOUTH WALES
Campbell, Wilfred *see*
- BEYOND THE HILL OF DREAMS
- THE DREAD VOYAGE: POEMS
- LAKE LYRICS AND OTHER POEMS
- MORDRED AND HILDEBRAND: A BOOK OF TRAGEDIES

Campbell, William *see* BRITISH INDIA
Campbell, William Cecil *see* PREPARATION FOR CHURCH GROWTH IN THE MIAMI SPRINGS BAPTIST CHURCH, MIAMI SPRINGS, FLORIDA
Campbell, William J *see* CHRONOLOGICAL LIST OF THE PRACTICING MEMBERS OF THE PHILADELPHIA BAR
Campbell, William S *see* FORMS OF CODE PLEADING FOR NEBRASKA, KANSAS AND OKLAHOMA, FULLY ANNOTATED
CAMPBELL/LOS GATOS/SARATOGA – 1993 – 3+ r – 1 – $150.00 – P00014 – us Library Micro [910]
CAMPBELL'S COLLECTION OF THE NEWEST AND MOST FAVORITE COUNTRY DANCES, REELS, STRATHSPEYS, AND COTILLONS FOR THE VIOLIN, HARPSICHORD, PIANOFORTE, OR (?) GERMAN FLUTE. BOOK ONE. / Campbell, W – London: Campbell, 1785 – 1 – us Sibley [780]
CAMPBELL'S THIRD COLLECTION OF THE NEWEST AND MOST FAVORITE COUNTRY DANCES AND COTILLONS, FOR THE VIOLIN, HARP, HARPSICHORD, AND GERMAN FLUTE... / Campbell, W – London: William Campbell, [1786?] – 1 – us Sibley [780]
CAMPBELL/SARATOGA – 1942 – 1r – 1 – $50.00 – P00015 – us Library Micro [910]
CAMPBELLSVILLE BAPTIST CHURCH. KENTUCKY : CHURCH RECORDS – (records beginning with Church of Christ on Pitman's Creek). 1802-28, 1885-1955, 1961-67 – 1 – 174.96 – us Baptist [240]
CAMPBELLTOWN HERALD – Feb 14 1880-Sep 7 1881; Jan 5 1889-Oct 11 1919 – 9 – at Pascoe [072]
CAMPBELLTOWN NEWS – Jan 2 1920-Dec 23 1968 – 9 – at Pascoe [072]
CAMPBELTOWN COURIER – 1 – £42.00r – uk Scot News [072]
Campe, Julius *see* ZWEI BISHER UNVEROEFFENTLICHTE ZEIT-DOKUMENTE DES VERLAGS-ARCHIVES UEBER HEINES "REISEBILDER" UND "BUCH DER LIEDER"
CAMPEAO BRAZILEIRO : PERIODICO MENSAL POLITICO, HISTORICO E LITERARIO – [s.l.]. Set 1830 – 1,5,6 – bl Biblioteca [072]
Campeche. Mexico (State) *see* PERIODICO OFICIAL DEL GOBIERNO CONSTITUCIONAL DEL ESTADO DE CAMPECHE
Campello, Enrico di *see* COUNT CAMPELLO
Campeonato de Pesca 1, 1975 *see* 1ST CAMPEONATO DE PESCA EN LA MODALIDAD DE C. GRUPO IBERDUERO. EMBALSE DE ALCANTARA EN AGUAS DEL RIO TAJO. FINCA LA CARRASCOSA. DIA 21 DE JUNIO DE 1975. REGLAMENTO Y PROGRAMA DE ACTOS
CAMPEONATO DE PESCA 2 1976. ...EN LA MODALIDAD DE CARPIDOS...DIA 19 DE JUNIO 1976. REGLAMENTO Y PROGRAMA DE ACTOS – Caceres: Imp. Rodriguez, 1976 – 1 – sp Bibl Santa Ana [350]
CAMPERDOWN CEMETERY REGISTER – 1854-1984. CCT1 – 1r – 1 – at Corangamite [920]
CAMPERDOWN CHRONICLE – 1875-1879. 1876 Lost. CC1-4 – 4r – 1 – at Corangamite [072]
CAMPERDOWN CHRONICLE – 1921-1994 – 87r – 1 – at Corangamite [072]
CAMPERDOWN TOWN COUNCIL MINUTES – 1953-1982. CTC1-7 – 7mf – 9 – at Corangamite [910]
CAMPERDOWN TOWN COUNCIL REPORTS – 1962-1967. CTCR1 – 1r – 1 – at Corangamite [910]
CAMPERDOWN TOWN COUNCIL SEWERAGE – 1950-1983. CTCSA1 – 1r – 1 – at Corangamite [910]
EL CAMPESINO / Gonzalez, Valentin – Paris: Plon, 1950 – 1 – sp Bibl Santa Ana [946]
LOS CAMPESINOS Y LA REPUBLICA / Uribe, Vicente – Conferencia pronunciada el dia 22 de enero en el Teatro Apolo, de Valencia.Valencia, 1938? Fiches W1239, 1240. (Blodgett Collection of Spanish Civil War Pamphlets) – 9 – us H.U. College Libr [946]
Campet, E *see* LA QUESTION DES NEUTRES...
CAMPFIRES OF THE AFRO-AMERICANS : OR, THE COLORED MAN AS A PATRIOT, SOLDIER, SAILOR AND HERO IN THE CAUSE OF FREE AMERICA... / Guthrie, Jas M – Philadelphia: Afro-American Publ Co, 1899 – us Res Libr [305]
Camphuysen, DR *see* THEOLOGISCHE WERKEN
Campian, Th *see* A BRIEF INTRODUCTION TO THE ART OF DESCANT OR COMPOSING MUSICK IN PARTS
Campililiensis, Christanus *see* OPERA POETICA
Campillo Ruiz, Ana *see* ESTUDIO AGROECOLOGICO
CAMPING IN THE MUSKOKA REGION / Dickson, James – Toronto: C. B. Robinson, 1886. 02660. (Pre-1900 Canadiana) – 9 – cn C.I.H.M. [971]
CAMPING MAGAZINE – (1969- 5,6. 1970- 9) – 1- 1923- – 1 – us UMI [639]
CAMPING MAGAZINE – Riverside, CA. 1973-1975 – 1r – 1 – $50.00 – R03409 – us Library Micro [071]
Campion, Edmund *see* A HISTORIE OF IRELAND
Campion, Lord *see* LA PROCEDURE PARLEMENTAIRE EN EUROPE
Campioni, C *see*
- DUO, 6, A DEUX VIOLONS, OP. 8
- HUIT SONATES A 2 FLUTES TRAVERSIERES ET BASSE, OP. 5
- TRIO-SONATAS, 2 VLNS AND CONT., OP. 3

Campis, Thoma a *see* OPERA THOMAE
Campisi, Paul *see* THE ADJUSTMENT OF ITALIAN-AMERICANS TO THE WAR CRISIS

Campistron, Jean-G de *see* ACIS ET GALATEE, PAROLES DE CAMPISTRON, MUSIQUE DE LULLI

O CAMPO BELLO – Campo Belo, 17 Sep 1893; Jan, Aug-Sep 1895; Jun 1897; Feb-22 Mar 1898 – 1,5,6 – bl Biblioteca [072]

Campo Cardona, Antonio del *see*
- ESTUDIO DEMOGRAFICO COMPARATIVO DE ESPANA Y LA PROVINCIA DE CACERES (DECENIO 1921-1930)
- LA LUCHA ANTIPANEIDICA EN LA PROVINCIA DE CACERES

EL CAMPO DE GIBRALTAR – Algeciras, Spain. -d. 22 Aug 1916-7 March 1919. 3 reels – 1 – uk British Libr Newspaper [072]

Campo, Hugo del *see* SINDICALISMO Y PERONISMO

CAMPO MISIONERO – Buenos Aires: Fundacion Cristiana de Evangelizacion. v34 n7-v49 n588. jan 1978-jun 1993 – 8r – 1 – us Res Libr [240]

CAMPO PROPIO DEL SACERDOTE SECULAR EN LA EVANGELIZACION AMERICANA, EL / Bayle, Constantino – Madrid: Missionalia Hispanica, 1946 – 1 – sp Bibl Santa Ana [240]

Campoamor y Campoosorio, Ramon de *see*
- LO ABSOLUTO
- EL PERSONALISMO. APUNTES PARA UNA FILOSOFIA

Campomanes, Conde de *see* MEMORIAL AJUSTADO AL EXPEDIENTE DE CONCORDIA...MESTA CON LA DIPUTACION PROVINCIAL...EXTREMADURA

Campora, Hector Jose *see*
- DISCURSO PRONUNCIADO
- EL MANDATO DE PERON

Campori, G *see*
- MEMORIA BIOGRAFICHE DEGLI SCULTORI, ARCHITETTI, PITTORI EC. NATIVI DI CARRARA E DI ALTRI LUOGHI DELLA PROVINCIA DI MASSA
- MEMORIE BIOGRAFICHE DEGLI SCULTORI, ARCHITETTI, PITTORI ECC. NATIVI DI CARRARA E DI ALTRI LUOGHI DELLA PROVINCIA DI MASSA.

Campos, Humberto de *see* SOMBRAS QUE SOFREM

Campos, Jorge *see* VIDA Y TRABAJOS DE UN LIBRO VIEJO

Campra, A *see*
- L'AMOUR SALTINBANQUE
- LE BAL
- IDOMENEE
- MOTETS A 1, 2, ET 3 VOIX AVEC BASSE CONTINUE. LIVRE PREMIER-TROISIEME
- LES SERENADES ET LES JOUERS...BALLET

CAMPS IN THE ROCKIES: BEING A NARRATIVE OF LIFE ON THE FRONTIER, AND SPORT IN THE ROCKY MOUNTAINS, WITH AN ACCOUNT OF THE CATTLE RANCHES OF THE WEST / Baillie-Grohman, William Adolph – London: S.Low, Marston, Searle & Rivington, 1882. 03971. (Pre-1900 Canadiana) – 9 – cn C.I.H.M. [910]

Campton, New Hampshire. Campton Baptist Church *see* RECORDS

CAMPUS – Rio de Janeiro: OPUS da Junta de Mocidade da Convencao Batista Brasileira. v1-9 n36. 1977-90 – 1r – us Res Libr [972]

THE CAMPUS – Visalia, CA: College of the Sequoias, 1946-80 – 4r – 1 – $200.00 – B03072 – us Library Micro [370]

CAMPUS CANADA – Toronto. v1-11. 1983-1994 – 9 – Can$20.00y – cn Micromedia [073]

CAMPUS ESTRIEN *see* LE JOURNAL DES ETUDIANTS DE L'UNIVERSITE DE SHERBROOKE

CAMPUS LAW ENFORCEMENT JOURNAL – (v.9-. 1979- 5,6,9) – v.2-. 1972- – 1 – us UMI [360]

CAMROSE CANADIAN – Alberta, CN. 1898- – 2r per yr – 1 – Can$55.00r – cn Commonwealth Micro [072]

Camus, J P *see* (I.P.C. DE BELLEY). REPARTIES SUCCINCTES A L'ABREGE DES CONTROVERSES DE M. CHARLES DRELINCOURT...ENSEMBLES LES ANTITHESES PROTESTANTES...

CAN EQUITY BE ORGANIZED? : EQUITY, DEVELOPMENT ANALYSIS AND PLANNING / Schaffer, Bernhard & Lamb, Geoff – 1981 – 166p – 9 – 92-3-101843-4 – fr UNESCO [320]

CAN THE OLD FAITH LIVE WITH THE NEW? : OR, THE PROBLEM OF EVOLUTION AND REVELATION / Matheson, George – 3rd ed. Edinburgh: William Blackwood, 1889 – 1mf – 9 – 0-8370-4308-5 – 1985-2308 – us A.T.L.A. [210]

CAN WE BELIEVE IN MIRACLES? / Warington, George – London: SPCK, [1871] – 1mf – 9 – 0-8370-5711-6 – 1985-3711 – us A.T.L.A. [210]

CAN WE STILL BE CHRISTIANS? / Eucken, Rudolf – New York: Macmillan, 1914 – 1mf – us A.T.L.A. [240]

Cana, Frank Richardson *see* SOUTH AFRICA

CANAANITE MYTHS AND LEGENDS / Driver, G R – T. and T. Clark, 1956 – 9 – $10.00 – us I.R.C. [390]

(Canada) *see*
- PROFILE
- PUBLICAT

CANADA – Benton, N.B: M R Knight, [1891?-1892] – 9 – cn C.I.H.M. [971]

CANADA – Benton, New Brunswick. 1-12 jan-nov 1891 – 1r – 1 – Can$30.00 – cn Can Microfilming [072]

CANADA : FURTHER PAPERS RELATIVE TO THE AFFAIRS OF CANADA – London: W Clowes and sons..., 1849. SEM105P406 – 1mf – 9 – Can$2.25 – cn Bibl Nat [971]

CANADA – Hampton, N.B: M R Knight, [1892-189- or 19–] – 9 – cn C.I.H.M. [971]

CANADA : PAPERS RELATIVE TO THE AFFAIRS OF CANADA – London: William Clowes and sons..., 1849. SEM105P441 – 1mf – 9 – Can$2.25 – cn Bibl Nat [971]

CANADA : RETURN OF THE NAMES AND QUALITY OR STATION OF THE SEVERAL PERSONS ARRESTED AND PLACED IN CONFINEMENT IN THE PRISONS OF TORONTO, AND C. – House of Commons, 1839. SEM105P388 – 3mf – 9 – Can$6.75 – cn Bibl Nat [971]

CANADA : SESSION LAWS OF CANADA – 1792-94 – 9 – $2,949.00 set – us Hein [340]

Canada *see*
- ACTE POUR POURVOIR PLUS AMPLEMENT A L'INCORPORATIN DE LA VILLE DE ST HYACINTHE, ET POUR ETENDRE SES LIMITES
- ANNUAIRE DU CANADA
- CANADA GAZETTE, PTS 1-3
- CANADA YEARBOOK
- CENSUS OF CANADA
- CORRESPONDENCE BETWEEN THE COLONIAL OFFICE AND THE GOVERNORS OF CANADA, RELATIVE TO THE SEIGNIORIAL AND FEUDAL TENURE..
- CORRESPONDENCE BETWEEN THE FRENCH GOVERNMENT AND THE GOVERNORS AND INTENDANTS OF CANADA, RELATIVE TO THE SEIGNEURIAL TENURE..
- FURTHER PAPERS RELATIVE TO THE AFFAIRS OF CANADA
- GENERAL STATEMENT OF THE ANNUAL REVENUE AND EXPENDITURE OF THE PROVINCE OF CANADA..
- GOVERNMENT PUBLICATIONS CATALOGUE
- PAPERS RELATIVE TO THE AFFAIRS OF CANADA
- PATENT OFFICE RECORD
- PLANS OFFICIELS DES COMTES DE HOCHELAGA AND JACQUES CARTIER, L.-W. SICOTTE
- PRE-CONFEDERATION STATUTES, 1774-1871
- REPONSE A L'ADRESSE DU CONSEIL LEGISLATIF, DEMANDANT COPIE DU TRAITE FAIT A MANITOULIN EN 1836 ENTRE LE GOUVERNEMENT ET CERTAINES TRIBUS SAUVAGES, ETC
- REPONSE A UN ORDRE DE L'ASSEMBLEE LEGISLATIVE...DU 20 FEVRIER. POUR COPIE...DE LA BROCHURE DU PREMIER MINISTRE INTITULEE: ESQUISSE GENERALE DE LA PROVINCE DE QUEBEC
- REPONSE A UN ORDRE DE L'ASSEMBLEE LEGISLATIVE...DU 30 MAI 1888, POUR UNE COPIE DE LA PRISE DE POSSESSION PAR LE SHERIF...DE QUEBEC,...DES BIENS DES JESUITES.
- REPONSE A UNE ADRESSE DE L'ASSEMBLEE LEGISLATIVE DU 22 DU COURANT POUR COPIE DE CERTAINE CORRESPONDANCE RELATIVE AU HAVRE DE MONTREAL
- REPONSE A UNE ADRESSE DE L'ASSEMBLEE LEGISLATIVE POUR COPIE DU RAPPORT D'A.C. BUCHANAN, ECUYER, SUR L'EMIGRATION
- REPONSE A UNE ADRESSE DE L'ASSEMBLEE LEGISLATIVE...DEMANDANT TOUS DOCUMENTS CONCERNANT L'OUVERTURE DU...TERRITOIRE DU NORD-OUE..EN LA POSSESSION DU GOUVERNEMENT DEPUIS LE 1ER JANVIER 1862
- REPONSE A UNE ADRESSE DE L'ASSEMBLEE LEGISLATIVE...DU 2 DU COURANT POUR DES RENSEIGNEMENTS RELATIFS AU CONTRAT...ENTRE LE GOUVERNEMENT ET MM. MCKEAN ET MELARTY, POUR LE SERVICE DES COMMUNICATIONS TRANSATLANTIQUES A VAPEUR
- REPONSE A UNE ADRESSE DE L'ASSEMBLEE LEGISLATIVE...DU 2 JUIN 1881, PRIANT...LE LIEUTENANT-GOUVERNEUR...COPIE DE LA REQUETE EN FAVEUR DE L'ETABLISSEMENT AUX TROIS RIVIERES D'UNE ECOLE NORMALE.
- REPONSE A UNE ADRESSE DE L'ASSEMBLEE LEGISLATIVE...DU 4 JUIN 1888, DEMANDANT UN RAPPORT DE TOUTES DECISIONS DU CONSEIL PRIVE FEDERAL, DESAVOUANT TOUS ACTES...DE CETTE LEGISLATURE DEPUIS 1882.
- REPONSE A UNE ADRESSE DE L'ASSEMBLEE LEGISLATIVE...DU 6 DECEMBRE 1854, DEMANDANT COPIES DE TOUTES LES PLAINTES PORTEES CONTRE M. MAGUIRE, INSPECTEUR ET SURINTENDANT DE POLICE DE QUEBEC
- REPONSE A UNE ADRESSE DE L'ASSEMBLEE LEGISLATIVE...DU 7 MARS 1864, DEMANDANT COPIE DES RAPPORTS DE DIVERSES EXPLORATIONS FAITES DANS LE DISTRICT DU SAGUENAY
- REPONSE A UNE ADRESSE DE L'ASSEMBLEE LEGISLATIVE...DU 22 DU MOIS DERNIER, DEMANDANT COPIE DE LA CORRESPONDANCE...RELATIFS AUX ECOLES DU DISTRICT D'OUTAOUAIS.
- REPONSE A UNE ADRESSE DE L'ASSEMBLEE LEGISLATIVE...DU 22 JUIN DERNIER... COPIE DE LA CORRESPONDANCE...ENTRE LUI ET SON EXCELLENCE LE GOUVERNEUR GENERAL RELATIVEMENT AU RENVOI D'OFFICE DU MINISTRE DE BOUCHERVILLE.
- REPONSE A UNE ADRESSE DE L'ASSEMBLEE LEGISLATIVE...DU 25 FEVRIER 1889, DEMANDANT COPIES...CONCERNANT LA RECLAMATION DE M.W.P. LOCKWOOD, MENTIONEE A L'ARTICLE 254 DU BUDGET POUR 1889-1890
- REPONSE A UNE ADRESSE DE L'ASSEMBLEE LEGISLATIVE...DU 26 DU MOIS DERNIER POUR COPIE DES DOCUMENTS CONCERNANT LA CONSTRUCTION DES PHARES ET DES QUAIS EN BAS DE QUEBEC ET LES SOUMISSIONS ET CONTRAT POUR LES BATEAUX REMORQUEURS.
- REPONSE A UNE ADRESSE DE L'ASSEMBLEE LEGISLATIVE...DU 30 ULTIMO, POUR COPIE...DES RECLAMATIONS DE CERTAINS HABITANTS DE L'ETABLISSEMENT DU RUISSEAU DES SAUVAGES, DANS LES TOWNSHIPS DE L'EST DU BAS-CANADA
- REPONSE A UNE ADRESSE DU CONSEIL LEGISLATIF, DEMANDANT LA CORRESPONDANCE RELATIVE A LA COMPAGNIE DES VAPEURS-OCEANIQUES DE MONTREAL
- REPONSE A UNE ADRESSE POUR RENSEIGNEMENTS CONCERNANT LES ILES MANITOULINES
- REPONSE POUR UN ETAT RELATIF AUX DEMANDES DE LA COMPAGNIE DU GRAND TRONC DE CHEMIN DE FER POUR REMISES DE DEBENTURES PROVINCIALES ET POUR COPIE DE TOUT MEMOIRE DEPUIS LE 1ER JANVIER, 1856
- REPONSE RELATIVE A L'EXPLORATION FAITE PAR M. BLAIKLOCK DU TERRITOIRE ENTRE QUEBEC ET LE LAC SAINT JEAN
- RETURN TO AN ADDRESS FROM THE LEGISLATIVE ASSEMBLY TO HIS EXCELLENCY THE GOVERNOR GENERAL DATED THE 2ND INSTANT, PRAYING... TO THE TRIAL AND CONVICTION OF THE AYLWARDS, EXECUTED AT BELLEVILLE ON THE 8TH DECEMBER 1862
- ROYAL COMMISSION ON BILINGUALISM: RESEARCH STUDIES
- SIR F.B. HEAD: COPY OF A DESPATCH FROM SIR F.B. HEAD, IN ANSWER TO CHARGES PREFERRED AGAINST HIM BY DR. C. DUNCOMBE..
- UPPER CANADA REPORTS

LE CANADA / Champion, Paul – Paris: Societe bibliographique, 1886. 00550. (Pre-1900 Canadiana) – 9 – cn C.I.H.M. [971]

LE CANADA / ed by Gagnon, Jean-Louis – Montreal, 11 oct 1954-7 nov 1954 – 1r – 1 – Can$60.00 – cn Can Microfilming [072]

LE CANADA : GRAND COUNCIL OF THE C.M.B.A. OF CANADA – Montreal. v27 n7. jul 1921 – 1r – 1 – Can$25.00 – cn Can Microfilming [072]

LE CANADA : HEBDO – Montreal, Canada. 9 avr 1903-26 mar 1925 – 10r – 1 – Can$60.00r – cn Can Microfilming [072]

LE CANADA – Montreal, 1951-1953 – 14r – 1 – cn Preston [971]

LE CANADA – Ottawa, Canada. 1865-69 – 4r – 1 – $260.00 – cn Library Assoc [971]

LE CANADA – (Suspended. Resumed as: Le Canada Nouveau 24 mai 1954-10 oct 1954, with Jean-Louis Gagnon as editor) – Montreal, Canada. 4 avr 1903-26 nov 1953 – 124r – 1 – Can$60.00r – cn Can Microfilming [072]

LE CANADA *see* UN PORTRAIT DU CANADA

CANADA 1862: POUR L'INFORMATION DES IMMIGRANTS / Canada. Bureau d'Agriculture et d'Immigration – Quebec: Imprimerie de Leger Brousseau, 1862. SEM105P233 – 1mf – 9 – Can$2.25 – cn Bibl Nat [323]

CANADA: A BRIEF OUTLINE OF HER GEOGRAPHICAL POSITION, PRODUCTIONS, CLIMATE, CAPABILITIES, EDUCATIONAL AND MUNICIPAL INSTITUTIONS, FISHERIES, RAILROADS, ETC / Canada. Ministere de l'Agriculture – 2nd ed. Quebec: Printed by John Lovell, 1860. SEM105P226 – 1mf – 9 – Can$2.25 – cn Bibl Nat [971]

CANADA, A MEMORIAL VOLUME – General reference book on Canada, describing the Dominion at large, and its various provinces and territories, with statistics... Montreal: E. Biggar, 1889. 02302. (Pre-1900 Canadiana) – 9 – cn C.I.H.M. [971]

CANADA: A METRICAL STORY / Campbell, Charles – Toronto: W. Briggs, 1897. 00404. (Pre-1900 Canadiana) – 9 – cn C.I.H.M. [971]

CANADA: A PORTRAIT – (Cont: Canada Handbook) – Ottawa, 1986- – 9 – 1986 Can$22.00 1989-93 Can$20.00y – cn Micromedia [910]

CANADA: A PORTRAIT *see* UN PORTRAIT DU CANADA

CANADA, A SHORT HISTORY OF THE DOMINION OF CANADA / Archer, Andrew – St. John, N.B.: J.& A. McMillan, 1884. 06061. (Pre-1900 Canadiana) – 9 – cn C.I.H.M. [971]

CANADA: AN HISTORICAL MAGAZINE – Toronto. v1-3. 1973-76 – 9 – Can$46.00 – cn Micromedia [073]

CANADA AND HER COMMERCE: FROM THE TIME OF THE FIRST SETTLERS TO THAT OF THE REPRESENTATIVE MEN OF TODAY.. / ed by Hedley, James – Montreal: Sabiston Litho. & Pub. Co., 1894. (Pre-1900 Canadiana) – 9 – cn C.I.H.M. [971]

CANADA AND HER RELATIONS TO THE EMPIRE / Dennison, George Taylor – Toronto: Week Pub., 1895. 02635. (Pre-1900 Canadiana) – 9 – cn C.I.H.M. [971]

CANADA AND HER RESOURCES / Armstrong, Charles Newhouse – London: Metchim, 1885? 02469. (Pre-1900 Canadiana) – 9 – cn C.I.H.M. [971]

CANADA AND ITS CAPITAL: WITH SKETCHES OF POLITICAL AND SOCIAL LIFE AT OTTAWA / Edgar, James David – Toronto: G. Morang, 1898. 02878. (Pre-1900 Canadiana) – 9 – cn C.I.H.M. [971]

CANADA AND NEW BRUNSWICK BOUNDARY: PAPERS RELATIVE TO THE SETTLEMENT OF THE DISPUTED BOUNDARIES BETWEEN THE PROVINCES OF CANADA AND NEW BRUNSWICK – London: Printed by William Clowes and Sons, 1851. SEM105P438 – 2mf – 9 – Can$4.50 – cn Bibl Nat [323]

CANADA, AND OTHER POEMS / Herbin, John Frederic – Windsor: J. Anslow, 1891. 05548. (Pre-1900 Canadiana) – 9 – cn C.I.H.M. [810]

CANADA AND THE UNITED STATES: A STUDY IN COMPARATIVE POLITICS / Bourinot, John George – 1890. 02531. (Pre-1900 Canadiana) – 9 – cn C.I.H.M. [971]

CANADA AND THE UNITED STATES: AN HISTORICAL RETROSPECT / Bourinot, John George – 1891? 02530. (Pre-1900 Canadiana) – 9 – cn C.I.H.M. [971]

CANADA AND THE UNITED STATES: THEIR PAST AND PRESENT RELATIONS – 1891. 00413. (Pre-1900 Canadiana) – 9 – cn C.I.H.M. [971]

CANADA AND THE WORLD – (v41- . 1975- . 5,6,9) – v. 1-. 1935- – 1 – us UMI [971]

CANADA AND THE WORLD – (Vols 1-35 1936/37-1969/70 were titled World Affairs) – Oakville. v1-60. 1936/37-1994/95 – 9 – Can$20.00y – cn Micromedia [971]

CANADA AND THE WORLD *see* WORLD AFFAIRS
CANADA ARTISTIQUE / ed by Filiatrault, Aristide – (Cont by: Canada-Revue) – Montreal, Canada. dec 1889-dec 1890 – 1r – 1 – Can$40.00 – cn Can Microfilming [073]
CANADA ARTISTIQUE *see* CANADA-REVUE
CANADA AS A HOME / Bourinot, John George – London: Truebner, 1882. 03812. (Pre-1900 Canadiana) – 9 – cn C.I.H.M. [971]
CANADA AT THE COLONIAL AND INDIAN EXHIBITION – London: McCorquedale, 1886. 00414. (Pre-1900 Canadiana) – 9 – cn C.I.H.M. [971]
CANADA AT THE UNIVERSAL EXHIBITION OF 1855 / Canada. Parliament. Legislative Assembly. Committee – Toronto: Printed by John Lovell, 1856. SEM105P154 – 5mf – 9 – Can$11.25 – cn Bibl Nat [324]
THE CANADA BANK-NOTE REGISTER – Montreal, Canada. v3 n6. 1 dec 1859 – 1r – 1 – Can$25.00 – cn Can Microfilming [072]
THE CANADA BAPTIST MAGAZINE AND MISSIONARY REGISTER – Montreal: Pub by W Greig ... for the Canadian Baptist Missionary Society, [1837-1841] – 9 – cn C.I.H.M. [240]
Canada. Bas-Canada *see*
- CODE CIVIL..
- CODE CIVIL DU BAS CANADA D'APRES LE ROLE AMENDE DEPOSE DANS LE BUREAU DU GREFFIER DU CONSEIL LEGISLATIF...
- CODE CIVILE DU BAS-CANADA
- CODE CIVILE...D'APRES LE ROLE AMENDE DEPOSE DANS LE BUREAU DU GREFFIER DU CONSEIL LEGISLATIF, TEL QUE PRESCRIT PAR L'ACTE 29 VICT. CHP. 41, 1865

Canada. Bas-Canada. Bureau de l'Education *see*
- RAPPORT DU SURINTENDANT DE L'EDUCATION POUR LE BAS-CANADA, POUR...
- RAPPORT DU SURINTENDANT D'EDUCATION POUR LE BAS-CANADA POUR L'ANNEE 1846
- RAPPORT SUR L'EDUCATION DANS LE BAS CANADA SUIVI DE TABLEAUX STATISTIQUES POUR L'ANNEE SCOLAIRE...1849/1850
- REPORT OF THE SUPERINTENDANT OF EDUCATION FOR LOWER CANADA, FOR THE YEAR 1846
- REPORT OF THE SUPERINTENDENT OF EDUCATION FOR LOWER CANADA FOR.
- REPORT ON EDUCATION IN LOWER CANADA, FOLLOWED BY STATISTICAL TABLES FOR THE SCHOOL YEAR.
- TABLE PREPARED BY THE SUPERINTENDENT OF EDUCATION FOR LOWER CANADA, SHOWING THE COUNTIES WHICH HAVE RECEIVED SUMS OF MONEY FOR THE CONSTRUCTION OF SCHOOL HOUSES
- TABLEAU DU SURINTENDANT D'EDUCATION DU BAS-CANADA, INDIQUANT LES COMTES QUI ONT RECU DES SOMMES D'ARGENT POUR LA CONSTRUCTION DE MAISONS D'ECOLE.

Canada. Bas-Canada. Commissaires nommes pour l'exploration du pays entre les rivieres St. Maurice et Outaouais *see* RAPPORT
Canada. Bas-Canada. Commissaires nommes pour l'exploration...borné par les rivieres Saguenay, Saint-Maurice et Saint-Laurent *see* RAPPORT
Canada. Bas-Canada. Commissaires pour Explorer le Saguenay *see* RAPPORT
Canada. Bas-Canada. Commissaires pour l'Exploration du Pays Situe entre les Rivieres Saint-Maurice et Ottawa *see* RAPPORT DES COMMISSAIRES NOMMES. POUR EXPLORER CETTE PARTIE DE LA PROVINCE QUI SE TROUVE ENTRE LES RIVIERES SAINT-MAURICE ET OTTAWA
Canada. Bas-Canada. Cour du Banc du Roi *see* RULES AND ORDERS OF PRACTICE, FOR THE COURT OF KING'S BENCH, DISTRICT OF MONTREAL
Canada. Bas-Canada. Departement de l'Instruction publique *see* ACTES D'EDUCATION ELEMENTAIRE ET LES CIRCULAIRES Y RELATIVES NOS. 9 ET 12 DU SURINTENDANT DE L'EDUCATION POUR LE BAS-CANADA
Canada. Bas-Canada. Laws, Statutes, etc *see*
- AN ABSTRACT OF THE MOST MATERIAL PARTS OF AN ACT...INTITULED AN ACT FOR MAKING, REPAIRING AND ALTERING THE HIGHWAYS AND BRIDGES WITHIN THIS PROVINCE.
- BILL: AN ACT TO REPEAL CERTAIN ACTS THEREIN MENTIONED, AND TO PROVIDE FOR THE FURTHER ENCOURAGEMENT OF ELEMENTARY EDUCATION IN THIS PROVINCE
- ORDINANCES PASSED BY THE GOVERNOR AND SPECIAL COUNCIL OF LOWER CANADA, IN THE THIRD AND FOURTH YEAR OF THE REIGN OF HER MAJESTY QUEEN VICTORIA
- ORDONNANCE POUR POURVOIR A L'AMELIORATION DES CHEMINS DANS LE VOISINAGE DE LA CITE DE MONTREAL.

Canada. Bas-Canada. Parlement. Chambre d'Assemblee *see*
- BILL INTRODUIT...POUR MIEUX REGLER LA MILICE DE CETTE PROVINCE
- ENQUETE...SUR LES EVENEMENTS DU 21 MAI 1832 A MONTREAL
- PROCEEDING OF THE HOUSE OF ASSEMBLY UPON THE PETITION OF THE ELECTORS OF THE COUNTRY OF BEDFORD
- QUESTIONS SUBMITTED BY A SPECIAL COMMITTEE ON THE HOUSE OF ASSEMBLY OF LOWER CANADA TO THE CURATES OF THE DIOCESE OF QUEBEC
- RAPPORT...NOMME POUR S'ENQUERIR DE L'ETAT ACTUEL DE L'EDUCATION DANS LA PROVINCE DU BAS-CANADA
- RAPPORT...RELATIVE A L'ORGANISATION DE LA MILICE
- RAPPORT...RELATIVEMENT AUX BIENS DU SEMINAIRE DE MONTREAL
- RAPPORTS DU COMITE SPECIAL SUR LES CHEMINS ET AUTRES COMMUNICATIONS INTERIEURES
- REPORTS AND EVIDENCE OF...THE INHABITANTS OF THE COUNTY OF YORK
- STANDING RULES AND REGULATIONS..

Canada. Bas-Canada. Parlement. Chambre d'Assemblee. Bibliotheque *see*
- CATALOGUE DES LIVRES APPARTENANT A LA BIBLIOTHEQUE DE LA CHAMBRE D'ASSEMBLEE
- CATALOGUE OF BOOKS IN THE LIBRARY OF THE HOUSE OF ASSEMBLY
- CATALOGUE OF ENGLISH BOOKS IN THE LIBRARY OF THE HOUSE OF ASSEMBLY

Canada. Bas-Canada. Parlement. Chambre d'Assemblee. Comite choisi sur le Gouvernement civil du Canada *see*
- RAPPORT
- REPORT..

Canada. Bas-Canada. Parlement. Chambre d'Assemblee. Comite special *see*
- RAPPORTS ET TEMOIGNAGES..
- REPORT...ON THE PETITION OF CERTAINS SIC INHABITANTS OF THE DISTRICT OF GASPE

Canada. Bas-Canada. Parlement. Chambre d'assemblee. Comite special nomme pour s'enquerir de l'etat...de l'education dans la province. *see* REPORT
Canada. Bas-Canada. Parlement. Conseil legislatif *see*
- EXTRACT FROM THE JOURNALS OF THE LEGISLATIVE COUNCIL OF THE 2ND OF MARCH 1814
- EXTRACTS FROM THE JOURNALS OF THE LEGISLATIVE COUNCIL OF THE PROVINCE OF LOWER-CANADA FROM THE YEAR 1795-1813 INCLUSIVE..

(Canada). Bass-Canada. Chambre d'Assemblee *see* ACTE POUR FAIRE UNE DIVISION NOUVELLE ET PLUS COMMODE DE LA PROVINCE EN COMTES AFIN D'AVOIR UNE REPRESENTATION (SIC) DANS L'ASSEMBLEE PLUS EGALE..
CANADA BOOKSELLER – 1870-72 – 1 – 25.00 – cn McLaren [971]
THE CANADA BOOKSELLER – (Contd by: The Canada Bookseller Miscellany and Advertiser) – Toronto: Adam, Stevenson, [1870-1871?] – 9 – cn C.I.H.M. [020]
THE CANADA BOOKSELLER – Toronto: Rollo & Adam, [1865?-1869?] – 9 – cn C.I.H.M. [020]
THE CANADA BOOKSELLER *see* THE CANADA BOOKSELLER MISCELLANY AND ADVERTISER
CANADA BOOKSELLER AND STATIONER – (Cont: Books and Notions. Contd by: Bookseller and Stationer) – Toronto: MacLean, 1896-1897 – 9 – cn C.I.H.M. [020]
CANADA BOOKSELLER AND STATIONER *see*
- BOOKS AND NOTIONS
- BOOKSELLER AND STATIONER

THE CANADA BOOKSELLER MISCELLANY AND ADVERTISER – (Cont: The Canada Bookseller) – [Toronto]: Adam, Stevenson, [1872?-18–] – 9 – cn C.I.H.M. [020]
Canada. Bureau Central de la Sante *see*
- RAPPORT DU BUREAU CENTRAL DE LA SANTE, EN REPONSE A L'ADRESSE CI-ANEXEE DE L'ASSEMBLEE LEGISLATIVE, 1854
- REPORT OF THE CENTRAL BOARD OF HEALTH, IN RETURN TO THE ANNEXED ADDRESS OF THE LEGISLATIVE ASSEMBLY, 1854

Canada. Bureau d'Agriculture et de Statistiques *see* MEMOIRE SUR LE CHOLERA
Canada. Bureau d'Agriculture et d'Immigration *see* CANADA 1862: POUR L'INFORMATION DES IMMIGRANTS
Canada. Bureau de l'Instruction Publique pour le Bas-Canada *see*
- EDUCATION, BAS-CANADA
- RAPPORT...POUR S'ENQUIRER DE L'ETAT DE L'EDUCATION ET DU FONCTIONNEMENT DE LA LOI DES ECOLES DANS LE BAS-CANADA

Canada. Bureau d'Enregistrement et de Statistiques *see*
- RECAPITULATION, BY DISTRICTS AND COUNTIES, OF THE RETURNS OF THE ENUMERATION OF THE INHABITANTS OF LOWER CANADA
- RECAPITULATION, PAR DISTRICTS ET COMTES, DES RETOURS DU DENOMBREMENT DES HABITANTS DU BAS-CANADA..

Canada. Bureau des Brevets *see* PATENTS OF CANADA
Canada. Bureau des inspecteurs d'asiles, prisons, etc. *see* RAPPORT PRELIMINAIRE DU BUREAU DES INSEPCTEURS D'ASILES, PRISONS, ETC., 1859
CANADA CANAL COMMUNICATION – s.l., House of Commons, 1831. SEM105P387 – 2mf – 9 – Can$4.50 – cn Bibl Nat [380]
Canada. Chambre d'Agriculture du Bas-Canada *see* COMPTE-RENDU DES TRAVAUX...
Canada. Chief Electoral Officer *see* REPORTS
THE CANADA CHRISTIAN MONTHLY – Chatsworth [Ont]: J Morrison, [1873-1878?] – 9 – cn C.I.H.M. [240]
THE CANADA CITIZEN AND TEMPERANCE HERALD – Toronto: Citizen Pub. Co, [1879?-18– or 19–] – 9 – cn C.I.H.M. [240]
Canada. Colonial Conferences *see* MINUTES AND DOCUMENTS
Canada. Comite special sur l'Immigration *see* RAPPORT DU COMITE SPECIAL NOMME POUR S'ENQUIRER DES CAUSES DE L'EMIGRATION DU CANADA AUX ETATS-UNIS D'AMERIQUE OU AILLEURS
CANADA COMMERCE – (Cont: Foreign Trade. Ceased 1986) – Ottawa, 1973-1986 – 5 – Price varies with yr – cn Micromedia [380]
CANADA COMMERCE *see* FOREIGN TRADE
Canada. Commissaires de l'Amerique Britannique du nord nommes pour s'enquerir du commerce des Antilles, Mexique et Bresil *see* RAPPORT
Canada. Commissaires nommes pour... *see* RAPPORT DES COMMISSAIRES ENQUETEURS DANS L'AFFAIRE DU MEURTRE DE CORRIGAN
Canada. Commissaires nommes pour faire une enquete sur les affaires du departement des postes dans l'Amerique septentrionale britannique *see* RAPPORT DES COMMISSAIRES NOMMES POUR FAIRE UNE ENQUETE SUR LES AFFAIRES DU DEPARTEMENT DES POSTES DANS L'AMERIQUE SEPTENTRIONALE BRITANNIQUE
Canada. Commissaires nommes pour preparer un projet afin de mieux organiser le Departement de l'Adjudant-General de la milice *see* RAPPORT
Canada. Commissaires nommes pour s'enquerir... *see*
- RAPPORT DES COMMISSAIRES NOMMES POUR FAIRE UNE ENQUETE SUR LA CONDUITE DES AUTORITES DE POLICE LORS DE L'EMEUTE DE L'EGLISE CHALMERS, LE 6 JUIN 1853...
- REPORT OF THE COMMISSIONERS APPOINTED TO INQUIRE INTO THE CONDUCT OF THE POLICE AUTHORITIES ON THE OCCASION OF THE RIOT AT CHALMERS CHURCH, ON THE 6TH OF JUNE, 1853...

Canada. Commissaires nommes pour s'enquerir de l'etat des lois et autres circonstances qui se rattachent a la tenure seigneuriale dans le Bas-Canada *see* RAPPORT DES COMMISSAIRES NOMMES POUR S'ENQUERIR DE L'ETAT DES LOIS ET AUTRES CIRCONSTANCES QUI SE RATTACHENT A LA TENURE SEIGNEURIALE DANS LE BAS-CANADA ET APPENDICE
Canada. Commissaires nommes pour s'enquirer de l'origine et des causes de l'incendie qui a consume l'Hospice des Soeurs de la Charite *see* RAPPORT
Canada. Commissaires nommes pour s'enquirer et faire rapport des meilleurs moyens de reorganiser la milice en Canada *see* RAPPORT
Canada. Commission Appointed to Inquire into Matters Connected with the Public Buildings at Ottawa *see*
- REPORT
- REPORT OF THE COMMISSION APPOINTED TO INQUIRE INTO MATTERS CONNECTED WITH THE PUBLIC BUILDINGS AT OTTAWA

Canada. Commission Appointed to Inquire into the Affairs of the Grand Trunk Railway *see* REPORT OF THE COMMISSION APPOINTED TO INQUIRE INTO THE AFFAIRS OF THE GRAND TRUNK RAILWAY
Canada. Commission d'Enquete sur le Transport Scolaire *see* MEMOIRES SOUMIS A LA COMMISSION D'ENQUETE SUR LE TRANSPORT SCOLAIRE
Canada. Commission nommee pour s'enquirer d'une serie d'accidents et retardements sur le Grand Chemin de fer occidental *see* RAPPORTS..
Canada. Commission of Conservation. Committee on Fisheries, Game and Fur-Bearing Animals *see* FUR-FARMING IN CANADA
Canada. Commission of Inquiry into the non-medical use of drugs *see* BRIEFS AND TRANSCRIPTS OF PUBLIC HEARINGS. 1969
Canada. Commission speciale nommee pour s'enquirer des Affaires sauvages en Canada *see* RAPPORT... DES COMMISSAIARES...LE 8 SEPTEMBRE 1856
Canada. Commissioners of State of Law *see* REPORT OF THE COMMISSIONERS APPOINTED TO INQUIRE INTO THE STATE OF THE LAWS AND OTHER CIRCUMSTANCES CONNECTED WITH THE SEIGNIORIAL TENURE IN LOWER CANADA
Canada. Commissioners to Revise the Public General Statutes *see* SPECIAL REPORT.
CANADA COMPANY: LETTER,...SOLICITING APPROPRIATION OF SUM DUE TO THE CROWN TO THE ENCOURAGEMENT OF EMIGRATION TO UPPER CANADA – s.l., House of Commons, 1840. SEM105P390 – 1mf – 9 – Can$2.25 – cn Bibl Nat [336]
Canada, Conde de la *see*
- INSTITUCIONES PRACTICAS DE LOS JUICIOS CIVILES
- OBSERVACIONES PRACTICAS SOBRE LOS RECURSOS DE FUERZA.... 1794

CANADA: COPIES OR EXTRACTS OF DESPATCHES FROM SIR F. B. HEAD, BART., K.C.H. ON THE SUBJECT OF CANADA / Head, Francis Bond – s.l., House of Commons, 1839. SEM105P112 – 6mf – 9 – Can$13.50 – cn Bibl Nat [971]
CANADA CORPORATIONS ACT 1968; CHAP. 53, R.S.C. 1952, AS AMENDED / Canada. Laws, Statutes, etc – 2nd ed. Don Mills, Ont.: CCH Canadian 1968 144p. LL-2373 – 1 – us L of C Photodup [340]
CANADA CORRESPONDENCE / Brown, Thomas Storrow – Montreal: Mitchell & Wilson, 1873? 03728. (Pre-1900 Canadiana) – 9 – cn C.I.H.M. [971]
CANADA: CORRESPONDENCE RELATIVE TO EMIGRATION TO CANADA – London: Printed by W Clowes and sons, 1841. SEM105P232 – 2mf – 9 – Can$4.50 – cn Bibl Nat [324]
CANADA: CORRESPONDENCE RELATIVE TO THE AFFAIRS OF CANADA – London: Printed by William Clowes and Sons, 1840. SEM105P107 – 7mf – 9 – Can$15.75 – cn Bibl Nat [971]
Canada. Departement de la Milice *see*
- THE ANNUAL VOLUNTEER AND SERVICE MILITIA LIST OF CANADA
- LIST OF OFFICERS OF THE SEDENTARY MILITIA OF LOWER CANADA, 1862
- RAPPORT SUR L'ETAT DE LA MILICE DE LA PROVINCE

- RETURN TO AN ADDRESS OF THE LEGISLATIVE ASSEMBLY, OF 1ST SEPTEMBER, 1863

Canada. Departement de l'Instruction Publique pour le Haut-Canada *see*
- COPIES DE CORRESPONDANCES ENTRE LE SURINTENDANT-EN-CHEF DES ECOLES POUR LE HAUT-CANADA ET AUTRES PERSONNES, AU SUJET DES ECOLES SEPAREES
- COPIES OF CORRESPONDENCE BETWEEN MEMBERS OF THE GOVERNMENT AND THE CHIEF SUPERINTENDENT OF SCHOOLS ON THE SUBJECT OF THE SCHOOL LAW FOR UPPER CANADA AND EDUCATION GENERALLY, WITH APPENDICES
- COPIES OF CORRESPONDENCE BETWEEN THE ROMAN CATHOLIC BISHOP OF TORONTO AND THE CHIEF SUPERINTENDENT OF SCHOOLS IN UPPER CANADA
- CORRESPONDENCE BETWEEN THE ROMAN CATHOLIC BISHOP OF TORONTO AND THE CHIEF SUPERINTENDENT OF SCHOOLS ON THE SUBJECT OF SEPARATE COMMON SCHOOLS IN UPPER CANADA
- THE EDUCATIONAL MUSEUM AND SCHOOL OF ART AND DESIGN FOR UPPER CANADA..
- GENERAL INSTRUCTIONS FOR MAKING THE METEOROLOGICAL OBSERVATIONS AT THE SENIOR COUNTY GRAMMAR SCHOOLS IN UPPER CANADA
- LAW OF SEPARATE SCHOOLS IN UPPER CANADA BY THE ROMAN CATHOLIC BISHOPS AND THE CHIEF SUPERINTENDENT OF SCHOOLS

Canada. Departement de l'instruction publique pour le Haut-Canada *see*
- SPECIAL REPORT OF THE MEASURES WHICH HAVE BEEN ADOPTED FOR THE ESTABLISHMENT OF A NORMAL SCHOOL
- SPECIAL REPORT ON THE SEPARATE SCHOOL PROVISIONS OF THE SCHOOL LAW OF UPPER CANADA

Canada. Departement des finances *see*
- DISCOURS PRONONCE PAR L'HONORABLE A.T. GALT,...EN PRESENTANT LE BUDGET
- REPORT OF THE MINISTER OF FINANCE ON THE RECIPROCITY TREATY WITH THE UNITED STATES, ALSO...

Canada. Department of Energy, Mines and Resources *see* GEOS

Canada. Department of External Affairs *see*
- STATEMENTS AND SPEECHES
- TREATIES

Canada. Department of Finance *see*
- ESTIMATES
- PUBLIC ACCOUNTS

Canada. Department of Indian Affairs *see* ANNUAL REPORT

Canada. Department of Indian Affairs and Northern Development *see* CONSERVATION CANADA

Canada. Department of Labour *see*
- LABOUR GAZETTE
- WINNIPEG GENERAL STRIKE CLIPPINGS

Canada. Department of National Health and Welfare *see* MENTAL HEALTH LEGISLATION IN CANADA, 1959

Canada. Department of National Revenue *see* REPORT, CONTAINING STATEMENTS RELATIVE TO CUSTOMS-EXCISE REVENUE AND OTHER SERVICES

THE CANADA DIRECTORY FOR 1857-1858 / Lovell, John – Montreal: 1857. Canada reel 1. (Cox Library Collection) – 5 – us Americana [971]

Canada. Dominion Bureau of Statistics *see* PUBLICATIONS

CANADA DURING THE VICTORIAN ERA: A HISTORICAL REVIEW / Bourinot, John George – Ottawa: J. Durie; Toronto: Copp, Clark, 1897. 00984. (Pre-1900 Canadiana) – 9 – cn C.I.H.M. [971]

IL CANADA E L'EMIGRAZIONE / Bossange, Gustave – Paris: Symonds, 1872? 03711. (Pre-1900 Canadiana) – 9 – cn C.I.H.M. [971]

LE CANADA ECONOMIQUE /LE CAPITALISTE – Paris, France. 14 dec 1902-17 avr 1904 – 1r – 1 – Can$50.00 – cn Can Microfilming [072]

CANADA EDUCATIONAL MONTHLY *see* THE CANADA EDUCATIONAL MONTHLY AND SCHOOL CHRONICLE

THE CANADA EDUCATIONAL MONTHLY – (Cont: The Canada Educational Monthly and School Chronicle. Contd by: The Educational Monthly of Canada) – Toronto: Canada Educational Monthly Pub. Co, 1897-1902 – 9 – cn C.I.H.M. [370]

CANADA EDUCATIONAL MONTHLY AND SCHOOL CHRONICLE *see* THE SCHOOL MAGAZINE

THE CANADA EDUCATIONAL MONTHLY AND SCHOOL CHRONICLE – (Absorbed: School Magazine. Contd by: Canada Educational Monthly) – Toronto: Educational Monthly Pub. Co, 1879?-1897 – 9 – cn C.I.H.M. [370]

THE CANADA EDUCATIONAL MONTHLY AND SCHOOL CHRONICLE *see* THE CANADA EDUCATIONAL MONTHLY

LE CANADA EN 1868 – Microform – Paris: E. Belin, 1868? 04277. (Pre-1900 Canadiana) – 9 – cn C.I.H.M. [971]

LE CANADA ET LES CANADIENS-FRANCAIS PENDANT LA QUERRE FRANCO-PRUSSIENNE / Faucher de Saint-Maurice, Narcisse – Quebec: A. Cote, 1888. 03060. (Pre-1900 Canadiana) – 9 – cn C.I.H.M. [306]

LE CANADA ET LES ZOUAVES PONTIFICAUX:...L'EXPEDITION...A ROME...1868 / Bellefeuille, Edouard Lefebvre de – Montreal: Typ. du Journal Le Nouveau Monde, 1868. 00110. (Pre-1900 Canadiana) – 9 – cn C.I.H.M. [240]

LE CANADA ET L'EXPOSITION UNIVERSELLE DE 1855 / Canada. Parliament. Legislative Assembly. Committee – Toronto: Des presses a vapeur de John Lovell, 1856. SEM105P153 – 6mf – 9 – Can$13.50 – cn Bibl Nat [324]

CANADA ET TERRENEUVE, ETC.: CHRONOLOGIE: DIOCESES, VICARIATS, APOSTOLIQUES, PREFECTURES APOSTOLIQUES, CARDINALS, ARCHEVEQUES, EVEQUES: GOUVERNEURS, LIEUTENANTS-GOURVERNEURS ET ADMINISTRATEURS, DECOUVERTES ET FONDATIONS : MARTYROLOGE: STATISTIQUES ECLESIASTIQUES: 1508 A 1891? / Baillairge, George F – 1891? 04357. (Pre-1900 Canadiana) – 9 – cn C.I.H.M. [971]

Canada. Exchequer Court *see* EXCHEQUER REPORTS OF CANADA

Canada. Exploration Geologique *see*
- DESCRIPTIVE CATALOGUE OF A COLLECTION OF THE ECONOMIC MINERALS OF CANADA, AND OF ITS CRYSTALLINE ROCKS
- MESSAGE DE SON EXCELLENCE, LE GOUVERNEUR GENERAL, AVEC RAPPORTS SUR UNE EXPLORATION GEOLOGIQUE DE LA PROVINCE DE CANADA...
- MESSAGE FROM HIS EXCELLENCY THE GOVERNOR GENERAL, WITH REPORTS ON A GEOLOGICAL SURVEY OF THE PROVINCE OF CANADA..
- PLANS DES DIFFERENTS LACS ET RIVIERES ENTRE LE LAC HURON ET LA RIVIERE DES OUTAOUAIS, POUR ACCOMPAGNER LES RAPPORTS GEOLOGIQUES DU CANADA POUR LES ANNEES 1853, 54, 55, 56
- PLANS OF VARIOUS LAKES AND RIVERS BETWEEN LAKE HURON AND THE RIVER OTTAWA, TO ACCOMPANY THE GEOLOGICAL REPORTS FOR 1853, 54, 55, 56
- RAPPORT DE PROGRES DEPUIS SON COMMENCEMENT JUSQU'A 1863
- REPORT OF PROGRESS FROM ITS COMMENCEMENT TO 1863

CANADA FARMER – (Absorbed: Canadian Agriculturist. Merged with: Globe (Toronto, Ont.). Merged to become: Globe and Canada Farmer) – Toronto: G Brown, 1864-1876 – 9 – cn C.I.H.M. [630]

CANADA FARMER *see* CANADIAN AGRICULTURIST

THE CANADA FARMER – Hamilton [Ont]: J E Force, [1855?-18–] – 9 – cn C.I.H.M. [630]

THE CANADA FARMER – (Merged with: British American Cultivator. Merged to become: The Agriculturalist and Canadian Journal) – Toronto: R Brewer, 1847 – 9 – cn C.I.H.M. [630]

Canada. Federal Royal Commission *see* REPORTS

Canada. Federal-Provincial Conferences *see* REPORTS

CANADA FIRST – Montreal, Canada. 17 dec 1881-v2 n34. 10 oct 1885 – 1r – 1 – Can$35.00 – cn Can Microfilming [072]

Canada. Fisheries Research Board of Canada *see*
- JOURNAL

CANADA FOR CANADIANS: A ROYALIST ROLAND FOR THE ANNEXATIONIST OLIVER / Hague, John – Toronto: Hart, 1889?. 05144. (Pre-1900 Canadiana) – 9 – cn C.I.H.M. [971]

CANADA FRANCAIS – Laval. v1-4. 1888-1891 – 1 – cn Precision [971]

CANADA FRANCAIS – v1-33. Sept 1918-Sept 1946 – 1 – cn Precision [971]

CANADA FROM THE ATLANTIC TO THE PACIFIC AND ARCTIC OCEANS, ARCTIC VOYAGES OF DISCOVERY IN THE NORTH AND PUBLIC WORKS, ETC, ETC / Baillairge, George F – Ottawa?, 1891? 03315. (Pre-1900 Canadiana) – 9 – cn C.I.H.M. [971]

CANADA GAZETTE – (Backfile: 1881-1969 2-3r per y inquire) – Ottawa, 1970- – 9 – inquire – us Ross [072]

CANADA GAZETTE – (Second Series, 1867-92. 27r. $1,755.00) – 1841-69 – 35r – 1 – $2,275.00 – cn Library Assoc [971]

CANADA GAZETTE PART 1 – (v118-121 1984-9) – Hull. v104-117. 1970-83 5 – 5,9 – Price varies with yr – cn Micromedia [340]

CANADA GAZETTE PART 2 – Hull. v83-1949- – 9 – Price varies with yr – cn Micromedia [340]

CANADA GAZETTE, PTS 1-3 / Canada – (Bilingual. Pt 3 included from v115) – Ottawa. v1- 1881- – 1 – Price varies with yr – cn Micromedia [971]

Canada. General *see*
- CAMERON'S LEGAL OPINIONS
- CANADA STATUTES, SESSION LAWS AND REVISIONS
- CANADIAN LAW TIMES
- CANADIAN REPORTS
- CARTWRIGHT'S CASES ON THE BRITISH NORTH AMERICAN ACT
- EASTERN LAW REPORTER
- HUNTER'S TORRENS CASES
- LAPERRIERE'S SPEAKER'S DECISIONS
- WESTERN LAW REPORTER

CANADA GO BRAGH: BEING AN INAUGURAL ADDRESS TO THE YOUNG LIBERAL CLUB, OF SEAFORTH, ONT., ON THE 27TH OCTOBER, 1886 / Cartwright, Richard – Toronto: Hunter, Rose, 1886. 00499. (Pre-1900 Canadiana) – 9 – cn C.I.H.M. [971]

Canada. Gouverneur general *see*
- CHEMIN DE FER DE HALIFAX ET DE QUEBEC ET TRAVAUX PUBLICS
- CORRESPONDENCE RELATING TO THE CIVIL LIST AND MILITARY EXPENDITURE IN CANADA; AND TO THE PROJECTED RAILWAY FROM HALIFAX TO QUEBEC
- FURTHER CORRESPONDENCE RELATIVE TO THE PROJECTED RAILWAY FROM HALIFAX TO QUEBEC
- HALIFAX RAILWAY AND PUBLIC WORKS
- REPONSE A DEUX ADRESSES DE L'HONORABLE ASSEMBLEE LEGISLATIVE A SON EXCELLENCE LE GOUVERNEUR-GENERAL, DATES LE 28 FEVRIER 1856,...
- RETURN TO TWO ADDRESSES OF THE HONORABLE THE LEGISLATIVE ASSEMBLY TO HIS EXCELLENCY THE GOVERNOR GENERAL DATED 28TH FEBRUARY, 1856,...

Canada. Greffier de la Couronne en Chancellerie *see* COMMUNICATION DU GREFFIER DE LA COURONNE EN CHANCELLERIE, TRANSMETTANT LE RAPPORT DU NOMBRE DE VOTES DONNES DURANT LA DERNIERE ELECTION, ETC

CANADA HANDBOOK = LE CANADA – (Cont by Canada: a Portrait 1986) – Ottawa, 1930-1982/83 – 9 – Price varies with yr – cn Micromedia [971]

Canada. Haut-Canada. Chambre d'Assemblee *see*
- PROCEEDINGS HAD IN THE LEGISLATURE OF UPPER CANADA DURING THE YEARS 1831-2 AND 3 ON THE SUBJECT OF THE LANDS
- REPORT FROM THE SELECT COMMITTEE OF THE HOUSE OF ASSEMBLY OF UPPER CANADA, APPOINTED TO REPORT ON THE STATE OF THE PROVINCE
- REPORT OF THE COMMISSIONERS FOR IMPROVEMENT OF THE NAVIGATION OF THE RIVER ST-LAWRENCE

Canada. Haut-Canada. Conseil Legislatif *see* REPORT FROM THE SELECT COMMITTEE OF THE LEGISLATIVE COUNCIL OF UPPER CANADA ON THE STATE OF THE PROVINCE

CANADA HEALTH JOURNAL – (Cont: The Health Journal) – Ottawa: Canada Health Journal, [1890?-189- or 19–] – 9 – cn C.I.H.M. [613]

CANADA HEALTH JOURNAL *see* THE HEALTH JOURNAL

THE CANADA HEALTH JOURNAL – (Cont: Man. Contd by: the Health Journal) – Ottawa: Health Journal, 1886-1888 – 9 – cn C.I.H.M. [613]

CANADA HEALTH JOURNAL (OTTAWA, ONT: 1886) *see* MAN

CANADA, HISTORICAL AND DESCRIPTIVE, FROM SEA TO SEA / Adam, Graeme Mercer – Toronto: W. Bryce, 1888. 00771. (Pre-1900 Canadiana) – 9 – cn C.I.H.M. [910]

CANADA, ILLUSTRATED WEEKLY – (36p re Canadians at War) – Toronto, sep 1918 – 1r – 1 – Can$30.00 – cn Can Microfilming [072]

CANADA IN MEMORIAM, 1812-14: HER DUTY IN THE ERECTION OF MONUMENTS IN MEMORY OF HER DISTINGUISHED SONS AND DAUGHTERS / Curzon, Sarah Anne – A paper read by Mrs. Curzon. Welland Ont.: Telegraph, 1891. 03641. (Pre-1900 Canadiana) – 9 – cn C.I.H.M. [971]

CANADA IN THE SEVENTEENTH CENTURY / Boucher, Pierre – From the French...Trans. by Edward Louis Montizambert. Montreal: G. Desbarats, 1883. 00874. (Pre-1900 Canadiana) – 9 – cn C.I.H.M. [971]

Canada. Indian Dept *see* RECORDS

CANADA: INSTRUCTIONS TO THE EARL OF GOSFORD, AND THE COMMISSIONERS APPOINTED TO INQUIRE INTO THE GRIEVANCES COMPLAINED OF IN LOWER CANADA. – s.l., House of Commons, 1836. SEM105P410 – 1mf – 9 – Can$2.25 – cn Bibl Nat [971]

THE CANADA JOURNAL OF DENTAL SCIENCE – Hamilton [Ont]: W G Beers, C S Chittenden, R Trotter, [1868-1879?] – 9 – cn C.I.H.M. [617]

CANADA LANCET – Montreal, Canada. v1 n7. 15 sep-v1 n10. 15 dec 1863 – 1r – 1 – Can$25.00 – cn Can Microfilming [073]

Canada Land Law Amendment Association *see*
- LAND TRANSFER REFORM: PROCEEDINGS OF A PUBLIC MEETING HELD IN...TORONTO, ON 12TH FEBRUARY, 1890
- PROSPECTUS AND CONSTITUTION.

CANADA LAW JOURNAL / Canada. Ontario – (Cont: v3 of Upper Canada Law Journal, New Series. Also known as: Canada Law Journal, New Series) – v4-58. 1868-1922 (all publ) – 358mf – 9 – $537.00 – LLMC 81-015 – us L.L.M.C. [073]

CANADA LAW JOURNAL – (Title varies: OS: as Upper Canada Law Journal) – Toronto. 68v. 1855-1922. OS: v1-10. 1855-64; NS: 1-58. 1865-1922 – 1 – $480.00 – us Hein [073]

CANADA LAW JOURNAL *see* UPPER CANADA LAW JOURNAL

THE CANADA LAW JOURNAL – (Cont: The Lower Canada Law Journal) – Montreal: J Lovell, 1867-[1868] – 9 – cn C.I.H.M. [340]

THE CANADA LAW JOURNAL – (Cont: The Upper Canada Law Journal and Local Courts Gazette. Merged with: The Canadian Law Times. Merged to Become: The Canadian Bar Review) – Toronto: W C Chewett, 1868-[1922] – 9 – cn C.I.H.M. [340]

THE CANADA LAW JOURNAL *see*
- THE LOWER CANADA LAW JOURNAL
- THE UPPER CANADA LAW JOURNAL AND LOCAL COURTS' GAZETTE

CANADA LAW JOURNAL: A MAGAZINE OF JURISPRUDENCE *see* LOWER CANADA LAW JOURNAL

CANADA LAW JOURNAL, NEW SERIES *see* CANADA LAW JOURNAL

CANADA LAW REPORTS, EXCHEQUER COURT *see* EXCHEQUER REPORTS OF CANADA

Canada. Laws, Statutes, etc *see*
- AN ACT CONCERNING BANKRUPTS, AND THE ADMINISTRATION OF THEIR EFFECTS
- AN ACT FOR LIMITING THE TIME OF SERVICE IN THE ARMY
- AN ACT FOR THE ABOLITION OF FEUDAL RIGHTS AND DUTIES IN LOWER CANADA
- AN ACT RESPECTING THE MILITIA, EXTRACTED FROM CONSOLIDATED STATUTES OF CANADA
- AN ACT RESPECTING THE PRESERVATION OF THE PUBLIC HEALTH
- AN ACT TO AMEND THE ACTS RELATING TO THE GRAND TRUNK RAILWAY COMPANY OF CANADA
- AN ACT TO AUTHORIZE THE GRAND TRUNK RAILWAY COMPANY OF CANADA TO CONSTRUCT A BRIDGE OVER THE RIVER ST CLAIR AT SARNIA
- AN ACT TO GRANT ADDITIONAL AID TO THE GRAND TRUNK RAILWAY COMPANY OF CANADA
- L'ACTE D'AGRICULTURE ET L'ACTE D'AMENDEMENT DES MUNICIPALITES ET CHEMINS DU BAS-CANADA DE 1857

- ACTE D'AMENDEMENT DES MUNICIPALITES ET DES CHEMINS DU BAS-CANADA, DE 1856, AVEC SOMMAIRE ET INDEX
- L'ACTE D'AMENDEMENT SEIGNEURIAL DE 1859
- ACTE DES MUNICIPALITES ET DES CHEMINS DE 1855.
- ACTE DES MUNICIPALITES ET DES CHEMINS DE 1855...LES ACTES DE LA REPRESENTATION PARLEMENTAIRE...ET LES ACTES SEIGNEURIAUX...
- L'ACTE MUNICIPAL DU BAS CANADA DE 1860
- ACTE POUR ABROGER CERTAINES LOIS Y MENTIONNEES POUR MIEUX POURVOIR A LA DEFENSE DE CETTE PROVINCE ET POUR EN REGLER LA MILICE
- ACTE POUR ABROGER CERTAINS ACTES Y MENTIONNES ET ETABLIR DE MEILLEURES DISPOSITIONS RELATIVEMENT A L'ADMISSION DES ARPENTEURS ET A L'ARPENTAGE DES TERRES EN CETTE PROVINCE
- ACTE POUR ABROGER CERTAINS ACTES Y MENTIONNES, ET POUR AMENDER, REFONDRE ET RESUMER EN UN SEUL ACTE.....
- ACTE POUR AMENDER LES LOIS EN FORCE CONCERNANT LA VENTE DES LIQUEURS ENIVRANTES ET L'OCTROI DE LICENCES A CET EFFET.
- ACTE POUR AMENDER LES LOIS RELATIVES A LA MILICE DE CETTE PROVINCE ET LES RENDRE PERMANENTES
- ACTE POUR FAIRE DE PLUS AMPLES DISPOSITIONS POUR L'INCORPORATION DE LA VILLE DES TROIS-RIVIERES
- ACTE POUR L'ABOLITION DES DROITS ET DEVOIRS FEODAUX DANS LE BAS-CANADA
- ACTE POUR POURVOIR A LA DECISION SOMMAIRE DES PETITES CAUSES, DANS LE BAS-CANADA
- ACTE POUR REGLER LA MILICE DE CETTE PROVINCE ET POUR ABROGER LES ACTES MAINTENANT EN FORCE A CETTE FIN
- ACTES CONCERNANT L'EDUCATION ET LES ECOLES DANS LE BAS-CANADA
- ACTES DES MUNICIPALITES DU BAS-CANADA
- ACTES POUR PROMOUVOIR L'EDUCATION DANS LE BAS CANADA
- ACTES RELATIFS AUX POUVOIRS, AUX DEVOIRS ET A LA PROTECTION DES JUGES DE PAIX DANS LE BAS-CANADA AVEC UN INDEX ANALYTIQUE
- ACTES RELATIFS AUX POUVOIRS, AUX DEVOIRS ET A LA PROTECTION DES JUGES DE PAIX DANS LE BAS-CANADA, AVEC UN INDEX ANALYTIQUE COMPLET
- ACTS RELATING TO THE POWERS, DUTIES AND PROTECTION OF THE JUSTICES OF THE PEACE IN LOWER CANADA WITH A FULL SYNOPTICAL INDEX
- AERONAUTICS ACT AND REGULATIONS
- ARCTIC WATERS POLLUTION PREVENTION ACT AND REGULATIONS
- BILL: ACTE POUR REFONDRE LES STATUTS RELATIFS AUX MUNICIPALITES ET AUX CHEMINS DANS LE BAS-CANADA
- BILL: AN ACT TO CONSOLIDATE THE ACTS RESPECTING MUNICIPALITIES AND ROADS IN LOWER CANADA
- BILL: AN ACT TO REGULATE THE INSPECTION AND MEASUREMENT OF TIMBER, MASTS, SPARS,...IN THE PORTS OF QUEBEC AND MONTREAL
- CANADA CORPORATIONS ACT 1968; CHAP. 53, R.S.C. 1952, AS AMENDED
- CANADA SHIPPING ACT AND REGULATIONS
- COLLECTION DE PLUSIEURS DES ACTES ET ORDONNANCES LES PLUS UTILES EN FORCE DANS LE BAS-CANADA, CONCERNANT LA LOI CRIMINELLE ET LES DEVOIRS DES MAGISTRATS
- A COLLECTION OF SOME OF THE MOST USEFUL ACTS AND ORDINANCES IN FORCE IN LOWER CANADA, RELATING TO CRIMINAL LAW AND TO THE DUTIES OF MAGISTRATES
- THE CONSOLIDATED STATUTES FOR LOWER CANADA
- THE CONSOLIDATED STATUTES FOR UPPER CANADA
- THE CONSOLIDATED STATUTES OF CANADA
- CONSOLIDATED STATUTES RESPECTING THE MILITIA
- CUSTOMS, EXCISE AND COMMERCIAL LAWS OF CANADA
- INDEX TO DOMINION STATUTE AMENDMENTS (1907-1921)
- INDEX TO EASTERN PROVINCES AND DOMINION STATUTE AMENDMENTS TO 1926.
- AN INDEX TO THE STATUTES OF CANADA, FROM 3 & 4 VICTORIA TO 12 & 13 VICTORIA, INCLUSIVE, 1840 TO 1850.
- INDEX TO WESTERN PROVINCES AND DOMINION STATUTE AMENDMENTS TO 1926.
- LOIS D'EDUCATION, B. C
- THE LOWER CANADA MUNICIPAL ACT OF 1860
- LOWER CANADA MUNICIPAL AND ROAD ACT OF 1855...THE PARLIAMENTARY REPRESENTATION ACTS...AND THE SEIGNIORIAL ACTS.
- THE LOWER CANADA MUNICIPAL AND ROAD AMENDMENT ACT OF 1856
- THE LOWER CANADA MUNICIPAL AND ROAD AMENDMENT ACT OF 1857
- MOTOR VEHICLE SAFETY ACT, REGULATIONS & TEST METHODS
- MOTOR VEHICLE TIRE SAFETY ACT, REGULATIONS & TEST METHODS
- MUNICIPAL ACT OF LOWER CANADA, 10 AND 11 VICT. 1847.
- NAVIGABLE WATERS PROTECTION ACT AND REGULATIONS
- PILOTAGE ACT AND REGULATIONS
- THE PROVINCIAL LAW OF THE CUSTOMS, AND A COLLECTION OF THOSE PARTS OF THE IMPERIAL ACTS ON THE SAME SUBJECT
- THE PROVINCIAL LAWS OF THE CUSTOMS, AND A COLLECTION OF THOSE PARTS OF THE IMPERIAL ACTS ON THE SAME SUBJECT.
- RAILWAY CLAUSES CONSOLIDATION ACTS AND ACTS RELATING TO THE GRAND TRUNK RAILWAY OF CANADA
- REVISED STATUTES OF CANADA
- SAFE CONTAINERS CONVENTION ACT AND REGULATIONS
- ST. LAWRENCE SEAWAY AUTHORITY ACT, REGULATIONS & ST LAWRENCE SEAWAY AUTHORITY HANDBOOK
- THE SEIGNIORIAL ACTS: VIZ: THE SEIGNIORIAL ACT OF 1854, 16 VICT. CAP. 3
- STATUTES REGULATING JUDICATURE OF LOWER CANADA.
- STATUTES RELATING TO THE DUTIES OF JUSTICES OF THE PEACE IN LOWER CANADA
- STATUTS CONCERNANT LES DEVOIRS DES JUGES DE PAIX DANS LE BAS-CANADA
- LES STATUTS REFONDUS DU CANADA
- LES STATUTS REFONDUS POUR LE BAS-CANADA
- A SYNOPTICAL INDEX OF THE CONSOLIDATED STATUTES OF CANADA AND UPPER CANADA, WITH NOTICES OF THE LATER ACTS WHICH AFFECT THEM; INCLUDING THE SESSION OF 1864
- TRANSPORTATION OF DANGEROUS GOODS ACT AND REGULATIONS

LE CANADA, LE CURE LABELLE ET LA COLONISATION – Paris: L'Oeuvre de Saint Paul, 1885.... 02191. (Pre-1900 Canadiana) – 9 – cn C.I.H.M. [971]

CANADA: LE GUIDE DU COLON FRANCAIS, BELGE, SUISSE, ETC.: BROCHURE PREPAREE ET PUBLIEE / Drapeau, Stanislas – Ottawa: s.n., 1887. 02760. (Pre-1900 Canadiana) – 9 – cn C.I.H.M. [306]

Canada. Legislative Council *see* EXTRACTS FROM THE JOURNALS OF THE LEGISLATIVE COUNCIL OF THE PROVINCE OF LOWER-CANADA FROM THE YEAR 1795 TO 1813 INCLUSIVE,...

Canada. Lois, etc *see* ACTES D'EDUCATION ELEMENTAIRE ET POUR L'ETABLISSEMENT D'ECOLES NORMALES...

CANADA LUMBERMAN – (Other ed. is: Canada Lumberman. Contd by: Canada Lumberman and Woodworker) – Toronto: C H Mortimer, [1895-1905] – 9 – cn C.I.H.M. [630]

CANADA LUMBERMAN *see*
- CANADA LUMBERMAN
- THE CANADA LUMBERMAN

THE CANADA LUMBERMAN – (Cont: The Canada Lumberman and Miller's, Manufacturers' and Miners Gazette. Contd by: The Canada Lumberman and Woodworker. Other edition is: Canada Lumberman) – Peterborough [Ont]: A G Mortimer, [1887-1904] – 9 – cn C.I.H.M. [630]

THE CANADA LUMBERMAN *see* THE CANADA LUMBERMAN AND MILLERS', MANUFACTURER'S AND MINERS GAZETTE

THE CANADA LUMBERMAN AND MILLER'S MANUFACTURERS' AND MINERS GAZETTE *see* THE CANADA LUMBERMAN

THE CANADA LUMBERMAN AND MILLERS', MANUFACTURER'S AND MINERS GAZETTE – (Contd by: The Canada Lumberman) – Toronto: A Begg, [1880-1887] – 9 – cn C.I.H.M. [630]

CANADA LUMBERMAN AND WOODWORKER – Toronto, Canada. -w. Nov 1919-Dec 1921. 7 reels – 1 – uk British Libr Newspaper [073]

CANADA LUMBERMAN AND WOODWORKER *see* CANADA LUMBERMAN

THE CANADA LUMBERMAN AND WOODWORKER *see* THE CANADA LUMBERMAN

CANADA LUTHERAN – (Lacking: v1-3 and some issues. Some original pgs damaged) – v4-24. 1966-85 – 3r – 1 – ATLA S0360 – us A.T.L.A. [073]

Canada. Mackenzie Valley Pipeline Inquiry *see* BRIEFS AND TRANSCRIPTS

CANADA MEDICAL JOURNAL AND MONTHLY RECORD OF MEDICAL AND SURGICAL SCIENCE – Montreal: Printed for the Proprietors by J Lovell, 1852-1853 – 9 – cn C.I.H.M. [610]

CANADA MILITARY GAZETTE – Ottawa: D Kerr, [1857-18–?] – 9 – cn C.I.H.M. [355]

Canada. Ministere de l'Agriculture *see* CANADA: A BRIEF OUTLINE OF HER GEOGRAPHICAL POSITION, PRODUCTIONS, CLIMATE, CAPABILITIES, EDUCATIONAL AND MUNICIPAL INSTITUTIONS, FISHERIES, RAILROADS, ETC

Canada. Ministere de l'Environnement. Service de l'Environnement Atmospherique. Bureau des Previsions du Quebec *see* CARTES: SURFACE

Canada. Ministere des Affaires Culturelles. Archives *see* GREFFES DES NOTAIRES (1637-1668) (20)

Canada. Ministere des Finances *see*
- RAPPORT DU MINISTRE DES FINANCES SUR LE TRAITE DE RECIPROCITE AVEC LES ETATS UNIS.
- SPEECH OF THE HON. A.T. GALT, BRINGING DOWN THE FINANCIAL STATEMENT, AUGUST 29TH, 1865
- SPEECH OF THE HON. A.T. GALT...ON INTRODUCING THE BUDGET OF 1862, TOGETHER WITH STATISTICAL AND FINANCIAL STATEMENTS
- SPEECH OF THE HONORABLE A.T. GALT...IN INTRODUCING THE BUDGET

Canada. Ministere des Postes *see* RETURN TO AN ADDRESS FOR COPIES OF PAPERS CONNECTED WITH THE GRAND TRUNK MAIL SERVICE SINCE 1863

Canada. Ministere des Terres de la Couronne *see*
- ETAT DES SOMMES DEPENSEES A MEME L'OCTROI DE 30,000 VOTE DANS LE BUT D'AIDER A L'ETABLISSEMENT DES TERRES VACANTES DE LA COURONNE DANS LE BAS-CANADA
- INFORMATION FOR IMMIGRANTS, SETTLERS AND PURCHASERS OF PUBLIC LANDS, WITH MAPS..
- RAPPORT SUR L'EXPLORATION DE LA CONTREE SITUEE ENTRE LE LAC SUPERIEUR ET LES ETABLISSEMENTS DE LA RIVIERE ROUGE

Canada. Ministere des Travaux Publics *see*
- DOCUMENTS RELATING TO THE CONSTRUCTION OF THE PARLIAMENTARY AND DEPARTMENTAL BUILDINGS AT OTTAWA
- RAPPORT...QUI CONCERNE LE LAC ST PIERRE
- RETURN OF SUMS PAID BY GOVERNMENT, AND CORRESPONDENCE BETWEEN ENGINEERS AND OTHER OFFICERS. RELATIVE TO CERTAIN RAIL-ROADS

O CANADA, MON PAYS, MES AMOURS / Labelle, Jean Baptiste – Montreal: A J Boucher, c1860. SEM105P908 – 1mf – 9 – Can$2.25 – cn Bibl Nat [971]

CANADA MONTH – Montreal. v1-12. 1961-72 – 5 – Price varies with yr – cn Micromedia [073]

CANADA MONTHLY – London. v4-23. 1908-17 – 5 – Can$100.00 – cn Micromedia [971]

THE CANADA (MONTHLY) GENERAL RAILWAY AND STEAM NAVIGATION GUIDE – Toronto: Pub. for the Proprietor by MacLear, [1856-18–?] – 9 – cn C.I.H.M. [380]

LE CANADA MUSICAL – Montreal, Canada. 5 mai 1917-v8 n8. 20 dec 1930 – 2r – 1 – Can$50.00r – cn Can Microfilming [780]

LE CANADA MUSICAL : REVUE – Montreal, Canada. 1 sep 1866-v7 n12. 1 avr 1881 – 1 – Can$45.00 – cn Can Microfilming [780]

Canada. National Aeronautics Establishment and Division of Mechanical Engineering *see* NATIONAL RESEARCH COUNCIL, CANADA-COLLECTION

Canada. National Energy Board *see* TRANSCRIPTS OF HEARINGS

Canada. New France. Laws, Statutes, etc *see* EDITS, ORDONNANCES ROYAUX, DECLARATIONS ET ARRET DE CONSEIL DU ROI, CONCERNANT LE CANADA.

LE CANADA NOUVEAU *see* LE CANADA

Canada. Ontario *see*
- CANADA LAW JOURNAL
- UPPER CANADA LAW JOURNAL

CANADA PACIFIC RAILWAY: ELEMENTS FOR A PROSPECTUS / Waddington, Alfred – Ottawa, 1870?. 02043. (Pre-1900 Canadiana) – 9 – cn C.I.H.M. [971]

Canada. Parlement Assemblee legislative *see* REPONSE A UNE ADRESSE DE L'ASSEMBLEE LEGISLATIVE DEMANDANT COPIE DE CERTAINS DOCUMENTS SEIGNEURIAUX

Canada. Parlement. Assemblee Legislative *see* DEBATS DANS L'ASSEMBLEE LEGISLATIVE SUR LA TENURE SEIGNEURIALE

Canada. Parlement. Assemblee legislative. Comite pour... *see* REPORT OF THE COMMITTEE APPOINTED BY THE LEGISLATIVE ASSEMBLY TO ENQUIRE INTO THE ADMIRALTY TARIFF OF FEES

Canada. Parlement. Assemblee legislative. Comite special... *see*
- RAPPORT [DU] COMITE SPECIAL AUQUEL A ETE RENVOYE LE BILL, INTITULE, "ACTE POUR AMENDER LA LOI RELATIVE A LA PRATIQUE DE LA MEDECINE, DE LA CHIRURGIE ET DE L'ART OBSTETRIQUE DANS LE BAS-CANADA"...
- RAPPORT DU COMITE SPECIAL DE L'ASSEMBLEE LEGISLATIVE, NOMME POUR S'ENQUERIR DES CAUSES ET DE L'IMPORTANCE DE L'EMIGRATION QUI A LIEU TOUS LES ANS DU BAS-CANADA VERS LES ETATS-UNIS

Canada. Parlement. Assemblee legislative. Comite special auquel... *see* RAPPORT DU COMITE SPECIAL DE L'ASSEMBLEE LEGISLATIVE SUR LA CONVENANCE DE DEFENDRE LE TRAVAIL DU DIMANCHE DANS LES DEPARTEMENTS PUBLICS DE LA PROVINCE

Canada. Parlement. Assemblee legislative. Comite special sur la colonisation *see* REPORT OF THE SPECIAL COMMITTEE ON COLONISATION

Canada. Parlement. Assemblee legislative. Select Committee on the Hudson's Bay Company *see* REPORT FROM THE SELECT COMMITTEE ON THE HUDSON'S BAY COMPANY

Canada. Parlement. Assemblee legislative. Standing Committee on Railroads *see* PROCEEDINGS OF THE STANDING COMMITTEE ON RAILROADS, AND C. IN RELATION TO THE GREAT SOUTHERN RAILWAY

Canada. Parlement. Chambre des Communes. Comite.. *see* RAPPORT SUR LES AVANTAGES ET LA NECESSITE D'ETABLIR UN RESEAU DE TELEGRAPHE SOUS-MARIN DANS LE FLEUVE ET LE GOLFE ST LAURENT

Canada. Parlement. Chambre des Communes. Comite permanent des Privileges et Elections *see* RAPPORT...SUR LA DERNIERE ELECTION POUR LE DISTRICT ELECTORAL DE KAMOURASKA

Canada. Parlement. Chambre des communes. Comite permanent des privileges et elections *see* RAPPORT ET TEMOIGNAGE SUR LA DERNIERE ELECTION POUR LE DISTRICT ELECTORAL DE KAMOURASKA

Canada. Parlement. Conseil legislatif *see* EXTRACT FROM A RETURN DATED THE 2ND OF DECEMBER, 1854, TO ADDRESSES PRESENTED BY THE LEGISLATIVE COUNCIL TO HIS EXCELLENCY THE GOVERNOR GENERAL, ON THE SUBJECT OF THE SEIGNIORIAL TENURE

Canada. Parlement. Conseil legislatif. Select Committee on Immigration *see* REPORT OF THE SELECT COMMITTEE ON IMMIGRATION

Canada. Parliament *see*
- BILLS
- DEBATES

- DEBATS PARLEMENTAIRES SUR LA QUESTION DE LA CONFEDERATION DES PROVINCES A L'AMERIQUE BRITANNIQUE DU NORD
- PARLIAMENTARY DEBATES ON THE SUBJECT OF THE CONFEDERATION OF THE BRITISH NORTH AMERICAN PROVINCES..
- PROCEEDINGS: SESSIONAL PAPERS
- SESSIONAL PAPERS
- UNPRINTED SESSIONAL PAPERS

Canada. Parliament. Commission *see* REPORT...TO INQUIRE INTO THE AFFAIRS OF THE GRAND TRUNK RAILWAY

Canada. Parliament. House of Assembly *see*
- PROCEEDINGS OF THE HOUSE OF ASSEMBLY UPON THE PETITION OF THE ELECTORS OF THE COUNTY OF BEDFORD AGAINST THE LEGALITY OF THE ELECTION FOR THE SAID COUNTY
- REPORT OF THE SPECIAL COMMITTEE OF THE HOUSE OF ASSEMBLY ON THE POST OFFICE DEPARTMENT IN THE PROVINCE OF LOWER CANADA

Canada. Parliament. House of Commons *see*
- COPIES OF CORRESPONDENCE RELATIVE TO THE AFFAIRS OF CANADA
- COPIES OR EXTRACTS OF CORRESPONDENCE RELATIVE TO THE AFFAIRS OF CANADA
- DEBATES
- JOURNALS
- PROCEEDINGS: HANSARD DEBATES
- PROCEEDINGS: JOURNALS
- RETURN OF THE NAMES AND QUALITY OR STATION OF THE SEVERAL PERSONS ARRESTED AND PLACED IN CONFINEMENT IN THE PRISONS OF TORONTO

Canada. Parliament. House of Commons. Committees *see* MINUTES OF PROCEEDINGS AND EVIDENCE

Canada. Parliament. Legislative Assembly *see*
- CHEMIN DE FER DE QUEBEC ET HALIFAX
- DEBATS...SUR LA TENURE SEIGNEURIALE
- DEPECHES DU SECRETAIRE DE SA MAJESTE POUR LES COLONIES ET AUTRES DOCUMENTS RELATIFS A L'UNION FEDERALE DES COLONIES BRITANIQUES DE L'AMERIQUE DU NORD.
- DEPECHES DU SECRETAIRE DE SA MAJESTE POUR LES COLONIES, ET AUTRES DOCUMENTS RELATIFS AU SIEGE DU GOUVERNEMENT.
- GENERAL INDEX TO THE JOURNALS OF THE LEGISLATIVE ASSEMBLY OF CANADA
- PAROCHIAL AND TOWNSHIP SUBDIVISIONS OF LOWER CANADA, IN RETURN TO THE ANNEXED ADDRESS OF THE LEGISLATIVE ASSEMBLY, 1853
- PROCEEDINGS: JOURNALS
- RAPPORT: LE COMITE SPECIAL AUQUEL A ETE RENVOYE LE BILL "POUR REGLER LE PILOTAGE DANS LE PORT DE QUEBEC ET AU DESSOUS".
- REPONSE A UNE ADRESSE DE L'ASSEMBLEE LEGISLATIVE DU 23 ULTIMO, POUR UN ETAT DES AFFAIRES FINANCIAIRES SIC DE LA PROVINCE.
- REPONSE A UNE ADRESSE...DEMANDANT COPIE DE CERTAINS DOCUMENTS SEIGNEURIAUX
- REPONSE A UNE ADRESSE...RELATIVE A L'ADMINISTRATION DES AFFAIRES DE LA SEIGNEURIE DE LAUZON
- REPORT OF THE SPECIAL COMMITTEE TO WHOM WAS REFERRED THE BILL TO REGULATE THE PILOTAGE IS AND BELOW THE PORT OF QUEBEC
- RETURN TO AN ADDRESS FROM...FOR COPIES OF ALL TRANSACTIONS, SALES OR CONTRACTS...CONNECTED WITH THE ALIENATION OF THE ST-MAURICE FORGES.
- RETURN TO AN ADDRESS OF THE LEGISLATIVE ASSEMBLY FOR COPIES OF CERTAIN SEIGNIORIAL DOCUMENTS
- SUBDIVISIONS DU BAS CANADA, EN PAROISSES ET TOWNSHIPS, DEPUIS 1853
- TRENTE-SEPTIEME RAPPORT DU COMITE DES BILLS PRIVES

Canada. Parliament. Legislative Assembly. Committee *see*
- CANADA AT THE UNIVERSAL EXHIBITION OF 1855
- LE CANADA ET L'EXPOSITION UNIVERSELLE DE 1855
- PROCEEDINGS... IN RELATION TO THE GREAT SOUTHERN RAILWAY
- RAPPORT DU COMITE NOMME POUR S'ENQUERIR DU TARIF D'HONORAIRES DE LA COUR D'AMIRAUTE
- RAPPORT DU COMITE NOMME POUR S'ENQUIRER DES TRANSACTIONS DE LA COMPAGNIE DU CHEMIN DE FER DE MONTREAL ET BYTOWN
- RAPPORT DU COMITE SPECIAL AUQUEL A ETE RENVOYE LE RAPPORT ANNUEL DU PRINCIPAL AGENT DE L'EMIGRATION..
- RAPPORT DU COMITE SPECIAL NOMME POUR PRENDRE EN CONSIDERATION LA COLONISATION DES TERRES INCULTES DU BAS-CANADA
- RAPPORT DU COMITE SPECIAL NOMME POUR S'ENQUIRER ET FAIRE RAPPORT SUR L'ETAT, L'ADMINISTRATION ET L'AVENIR DE LA COMMPAGNIE DU CHEMIN DE FER GRAND TRONC
- RAPPORT DU COMITE SPECIAL SUR LA COLONISATION
- RAPPORT SUR LA PETITION DE WM. L. MACKENZIE, ECUYER AGISSANT COMME EXECUTEUR TESTAMENTAIRE DE FEU ROBERT RANDALL, ECUYER DE CHIPPAOUAIS
- RAPPORT SUR LES TERRAINS AURIFERES DU CANADA, ET LES MEILLEURS MOYENS D'EN DEVELOPPER L'EXPLOITATION
- REPORT OF SELECT COMMITTEE ON GEORGIAN BAY AND LAKE ONTARIO SHIP CANAL
- REPORT OF THE SPECIAL COMMITTEE ON COLONIZATION
- REPORT ON THE CANADIAN GOLD FIELDS AND THE BEST MEANS OF THEIR DEVELOPMENT

Canada. Parliament. Legislative Assembly. Library *see*
- CATALOGUE OF BOOKS IN THE LIBRARY OF THE LEGISLATIVE ASSEMBLY OF CANADA
- CATALOGUE OF BOOKS RELATING TO THE HISTORY OF AMERICA, FORMING PART OF THE LIBRARY OF THE LEGISLATIVE ASSEMBLY OF CANADA
- SUPPLEMENTARY CATALOGUE OF BOOKS ADDED TO THE COLLECTION ON THE HISTORY OF AMERICA, DURING THE YEAR 1848

Canada. Parliament. Legislative Assembly. Select Committee *see*
- FIRST AND SECOND REPORTS OF THE SELECT COMMITTEE...APPOINTED TO ENQUIRE INTO THE PUBLIC INCOME AND EXPENDITURE OF THE PROVINCE
- REPORT OF THE SELECT COMMITTEE APPOINTED TO INQUIRE AND REPORT SIC UPON THE PRESENT SYSTEM OF MANAGEMENT OF THE PUBLIC LANDS
- REPORT OF THE SELECT COMMITTEE...APPOINTED TO INQUIRE WHETHER ANY, AND WHAT MEASURERS CAN BE ADOPTED, TO REPRESS THE EVILS OF INTEMPERANCE
- REPORT...ON THE HUDSON'S BAY COMAPNY

Canada. Parliament. Legislative Assembly. Select Committee on the Geological Survey *see* REPORT

Canada. Parliament. Legislative Assembly. Special Committee *see*
- RAPPORT
- RAPPORT DU COMITE SPECIAL DE L'ASSEMBLEE LEGISLATIVE,...POUR REMEDIER AUX MAUX QUI RESULTENT DE L'INTEMPERANCE
- RAPPORT DU COMITE SPECIAL SUR LA LOI POUR PROHIBER LA VENTE DES LIQUEURS FORTES
- TROISIEME RAPPORT ET DELIBERATIONS DU COMITE SPECIAL..

Canada. Parliament. Legislative Assembly. Special Committee.. *see* ANNUAL REVENUE AND EXPENDITURE OF LOWER CANADA FROM ITS CONSTITUTION TO THE PERIOD OF THE UNION

Canada. Parliament. Legislative Council *see*
- EXTRACT FROM A RETURN DATED THE 2ND OF DECEMBER, 1854..
- RULES, ORDERS AND FORMS OF PROCEEDING....
- RULES, ORDERS, AND FORMS OF PROCEEDING OF THE UPPER HOUSE OF THE PARLIAMENT OF CANADA
- STANDING RULES AND REGULATIONS.

Canada. Parliament. Legislative Council. Library *see* ALPHABETICAL CATALOGUE OF THE LIBRARY OF THE HON. THE LEGISLATIVE COUNCIL OF CANADA: AUTHORS AND SUBJECTS

Canada. Parliament. Library *see* CATALOGUE OF BOOKS IN THE LIBRARY OF PARLIAMENT

Canada. Parliament. Senate *see*
- DEBATES
- JOURNALS
- PROCEEDINGS: DEBATES OF THE SENATE
- PROCEEDINGS: JOURNAL

Canada. Parliament. Senate. Committees *see* MINUTES OF PROCEEDINGS AND EVIDENCE

Canada. Parliament. Senate. Special Committee on the Mass Media *see* BRIEFS AND TRANSCRIPTS OF PUBLIC HEARINGS 1970

Canada. Patent Office *see* RECORD

CANADA PENITENTIARY – s.l., s.n., 1842. SEM105P347 – 1mf – 9 – Can$2.25 – cn Bibl Nat [360]

CANADA PERMANENT LOAN AND SAVINGS COMPANY – Inc. A.D. 1855. Toronto?, 1884?. 02022. (Pre-1900 Canadiana) – 9 – cn C.I.H.M. [336]

Canada Permanent Loan and Savings Company *see* RULES...: ALSO THE COMPANY'S ACT OF 1886

CANADA POULTRY JOURNAL – Brooklin, Ont: [H M Thomas & E R Grant], 1875-[18– or 19–] – 9 – cn C.I.H.M. [630]

THE CANADA PRESBYTERIAN – Toronto: Presbyterian Print. & Pub. Co., [1877-189- or 19–] – 9 – cn C.I.H.M. [240]

THE CANADA PRESBYTERIAN *see* BRITISH AMERICAN PRESBYTERIAN

Canada. Privy Council. War Cabinet Committee *see* MINUTES AND DOCUMENTS

Canada Province *see*
- RAPPORT DES COMMISSAIRES NOMMES POUR PREPARER UN PROJET AFIN DE MIEUX ORGANISER LE DEPARTEMENT DE L'ADJUDANT-GENERAL DE LA MILICE ET RECHERCHER...
- RAPPORT DES COMMISSAIRES NOMMES POUR S'ENQUERIR DE L'ORIGINE ET DES CAUSES DE L'INCENDIE QUI A CONSUME L'HOSPICE DES SOEURS DE LA CHARITE, LE TROIS MAI DERNIER, AINSI QUE DES CIRCONSTANCES QUI S'Y RATTACHENT
- RAPPORT DES COMMISSAIRES NOMMES POUR S'ENQUERIR ET FAIRE RAPPORT DES MEILLEURS MOYENS DE REORGANISER LA MILICE EN CANADA, ET POUR RAPPORTER UN PLAN PERFECTIONNE DE POLICE
- REPORT OF THE COMMISSIONERS APPOINTED TO INVESTIGATE AND REPORT UPON THE BEST MEANS OF RE-ORGANIZING THE MILITIA OF CANADA, AND UPON AN IMPROVED SYSTEM OF POLICE

Canada Province. *see* REPORT OF THE COMMISSIONERS APPOINTED TO ENQUIRE INTO THE AFFAIRS AND FINANCIAL CONDITION OF TORONTO UNIVERSITY AND UNIVERSITY COLLEGE, UPPER CANADA

Canada. (Province) *see* STATUTS PROVINCIAUX DU CANADA, PASSES PAR SA TRES-EXCELLENTE MAJESTE, NOTRE SOUVERAINE DAME VICTORIA...VOL 3, 1RE SESS. 3E PARLT

Canada (Province) Acte Pour Amender et Refondre... *see* ACTE POUR AMENDER ET REFONDRE LES DIFFERENTS ACTES CONCERNANT LE NOTARIAT

Canada. Province. Acte Pour Amender l'Acte Municipal du Bas-Canada *see* ACTE POUR AMENDER L'ACTE MUNICIPAL REFONDU DU BAS-CANADA

Canada. Province. Assemblee legislative. Comite pour s'enquirir des causesqui retardent la colonisation des townships de l'Est du Bas-Canada *see* PREMIER ET SECOND RAPPORTS

Canada (Province). Assemblee Legislative. Comite...comptes publics *see* RAPPORT

Canada (Province). Assemblee legislative. Comite...le sujet de la Formation d'un pont de glace sur le Saint-Laurent devant Quebec *see* RAPPORT

Canada (Province). Assemblee legislative. Comite...petitions relatives au travail, le dimanche dans le Departement des postes et sur les canaux *see* RAPPORT

Canada Province. Bureau central de la sante *see* RAPPORT DU BUREAU CENTRAL DE LA SANTE, EN REPONSE A L'ADRESSE CI-ANNEXEE DE L'ASSEMBLEE LEGISLATIVE, 1854

Canada Province. Bureau de l'education (Bas-Canada) *see* REPORT OF THE SUPERINTENDENT OF EDUCATION FOR LOWER CANADA, FOR THE YEAR 1846

Canada Province. Chief Superintendent of Education for Upper Canada *see* EXTRACTS FROM THE CHIEF SUPERINTENDENT'S REPORT ON EDUCATION IN UPPER CANADA FOR THE YEAR 1857

Canada (Province). Commissaire sous l'Acte seigneurial refondu *see*
- CADASTRE ABREGE DE LA SEIGNEURIE DE LEVRARD...
- CADASTRE ABREGE DE LA SEIGNEURIE DE ROCQUETAILLADE,...
- CADASTRE ABREGE DE LA SEIGNEURIE DE ST VALIER...
- CADASTRE ABREGE DU FIEF COTEAU ST LOUIS...
- CADASTRE ABREGE DU FIEF ST JOSEPH OU L'EPINAY,...

Canada (Province). Commissaires Nomme Pour s'Enquerir de l'Etat des Lois et Autres Circonstances... *see* REPORT OF THE COMMISSIONERS APPOINTED TO INQUIRE INTO THE STATE OF THE LAWS AND OTHER CIRCUMSTANCES CONNECTED...

Canada. (Province). Commissaires nommes pour s'enquerir de la Cause de l'incendie qui a detruit l'Hotel du Parlement *see* RAPPORT

Canada. (Province). Commissaires nommes pour s'enquerir de la conduite ..de police lors de l'emeute qui a eu lieu en... Quebec, le 6 juin dernier *see* REPORT

Canada. (Province). Commissaires nommes pour s'enquerir des Circonstances... la mort de feu Robert Corrigan *see* RAPPORT...DANS L'AFFAIRE DU MEURTRE DE CORRIGAN

Canada (Province). Commissaires nommes pour s'enquirer de la conduite des autorites de police.. *see* RAPPORT

Canada. (Province). Commissaires nommes... de reorganiser la Milice en Canada. *see* REPORT

Canada (Province). Commissioners Appointed to Enquire as to the Affairs and Financial Condition of Toronto University and University College, Upper Canada *see* REPORT

Canada (Province). Commissioners Appointed to Inquire into the Cause of the Fire at the Parliament Buildings.. *see* REPORT

Canada. (Province). Laws, Statutes, etc *see*
- APPENDICES DU ONZIEME VOLUME DES JOURNAUX DE L'ASSEMBLEE LEGISLATIVE DE LA PROVINCE DU CANADA, DEPUIS LE 19 AOUT 1852...14 JUIN 1853.
- STATUTS...PASSES DANS LA PREMIERE ANNEE DU REGNE DE SA MAJESTE LE ROI GEORGE 6...DEUXIEME SESSION DE LA VINGTIEME LEGISLATURE.

Canada (Province). Legislative Assembly. Select Committee...State of Education and Working of School Laws in Lower Canada *see* REPORT

Canada. Province. Legislature. Assemblee legislative. Comite... des causes et de l'importance de l'emigration qui a lieu tous les ans du Bas-Canada vers les Etats Unis *see* RAPPORT

Canada (Province) Lois, etc. *see*
- ACTES RELATIFS AUX CHEMINS A BARRIERES ET PONTS DANS ET PRES QUEBEC
- STATUTS DE LA PROVINCE DU CANADA... 1852-1866

Canada (Province). Lois, etc. *see* LES STATUTS PROVINCIAUX DU CANADA...

Canada Province. Parlement *see* REPORT OF THE SELECT COMMITTEE ON THE GEOLOGICAL SURVEY

Canada (Province). Parlement. Assemblee legislative *see*
- RAPPORT DU COMITE CHARGE DE S'ENQUERIR DE LA CAUSE DES DESASTRES EPROUVES PAR LES BATIMENTS ET PAQUEBOTS TRANSPORTANT...
- RAPPORT DU COMITE SPECIAL DE L'ASSEMBLEE LEGISLATIVE NOMME POUR S'ENQUERIR DE L'ETAT DE L'EDUCATION ET DU FONCTIONNEMENT DE LA LOI DES ECOLES DANS LE BAS-CANADA
- RAPPORT DU COMITE SPECIAL SUR LA CULTURE DE LA VIGNE AU CANADA
- RAPPORT DU COMITE SPECIAL SUR L'ETAT DE L'AGRICULTURE DU BAS-CANADA
- REPORT ON TRADE AND COMMERCE

Canada Province. Parlement. Assemblee legislative *see* RAPPORT DU COMITE SPECIAL SUR L'ETAT DE L'AGRICULTURE DU BAS-CANADA

Canada. (Province). Parlement. Assemblee legislative. Comite... Acte pour amender la loi relative a la pratique de la medecine, ...la chirurgie et de l'art obstetrique...dans le Bas-Canada *see* RAPPORT

Canada. (Province). Parlement. Assemblee legislative. Comite charge...des circonstances relatives a la reduction recente des droits sur le pin rouge *see* RAPPORT

Canada. (Province). Parlement. Assemblee legislative. Comite... des desastres eprouves par les batiments et paquebots transportant les passagers du Royaume-Uni et d'ailleurs au Canada *see* RAPPORT
Canada (Province). Parlement. Assemblee Legislative. Comite pour s'enquerir du tarif d'honoraire de la Cour d'Amiraute *see* RAPPORT
Canada. (Province). Parlement. Assemblee legislative. Comite... prendre en consideration l'opportunite d'attirer l'emigration de la France, de la Belgique et de la Suisse en Canada *see* RAPPORT
Canada. (Province). Parlement. Assemblee legislative. Comite... quelle maniere ont ete depenses les Fonds votes en 1855 pour l'achat de grains de semence dans le Bas-Canada et du montant rembourse *see* RAPPORT
Canada. (Province). Parlement. Assemblee legislative. Comite... s'enquerir de la possibilite de cultiver la vigne dans ce pays *see* RAPPORT
Canada (Province). Parlement. Assemblee legislative. Comite special... *see* RAPPORT: LE COMITE SPECIAL AUQUEL A ETE RENVOYEE CETTE PARTIE DU RAPPORT DU PRESIDENT DU BUREAU DES TRAVAUX PUBLICS, QUI CONCERNE LE LAC ST-PIERRE...
Canada. (Province). Parlement. Assemblee legislative. Comite... sur les accusations contre la derniere administration *see* THE SELECT COMMITTEE APPOINTED ON THE 21ST DAY OF SEPTEMBER LAST FOR ..INQUIRING INTO THE ACCUSATIONS MADE AGAINST THE MEMBERS OF THE LATE ADMINISTRATION
Canada. (Province). Parlement. Assemblee legislative. Comite... sur l'etat de l'agriculture du Bas-Canada *see* RAPPORT
Canada. (Province). Parlement. Assemblee legislative. Comite...le bill pour regler le pilotage dans le port de Quebec et au dessous *see* RAPPORT
Canada. (Province). Parlement. Assemblee legislative. Comite...le rapport annuel du principal agent de l'emigration...le rapport supplementaire de l'agent allemand a Quebec *see* REPORT
Canada. (Province). Parlement. Assemblee legislative. Comite...l'etat du Bureau du surintendant des mesureurs de bois *see* RAPPORT
Canada Province. Parlement. Assemblee legislative. Select Committee... *see* REPORT OR THE SELECT COMMITTEE OF THE LEGISLATIVE ASSEMBLY, APPOINTED TO ENQUIRE INTO THE STATE OF EDUCATION AND THE WORKING OF THE SCHOOL LAWS IN LOWER CANADA
Canada. (Province). Parlement. Conseil legislatif. Select Committee on Immigration *see* REPORT
Canada (Province). Parlement...Comite Nomme Pour s'Enquerir des Relations Commerciales Entre le Canada et la Grande-Bretagne... *see* RAPPORT SUR LE COMMERCE
Canada. Public Archives *see* ANNUAL REPORTS
Canada. Public Archives. National Map Collection *see* CATALOGUE OF THE NATIONAL MAP COLLECTION
Canada. Quebec *see*
- DESJARDIN'S SPEAKER'S DECISIONS
- DORION'S DECISIONS ON APPEAL
- JUDGMENT DE CONSEIL SOUVERAIN
- LOWER CANADA JURIST
- LOWER CANADA LAW JOURNAL
- LOWER CANADA REPORTS
- MONTREAL CONDENSED REPORTS
- MONTREAL LAW REPORTS
- PERRAULT'S CONSEIL SUPERIEUR
- PERRAULT'S PREVOSTE DE QUEBEC
- PYKE'S LOWER CANADA REPORTS
- QUEBEC LAW REPORTS
- QUEBEC PRACTICE REPORTS
- QUEBEC REVISED REPORTS
- RAMSAY'S APPEAL CASES
- RAPPORTS JUDICIAIRES DE QUEBEC
- LA REVUE DE JURISPRUDENCE
- REVUE DE LEGISLATION ET DE LA JURISPRUDENCE
- LA REVUE LEGALE
- STUART'S LOWER CANADA COURT KING'S BENCH REPORTS
- STUART'S LOWER CANADA VICE-ADMIRALTY REPORTS

Canada. Quebec Province *see* COOK'S LOWER CANADA ADMIRALTY COURT CASES
Canada. Quebec. (Province) *see* BEAUBIEN
Canada. Royal Commission on Bilingualism and Biculturalism *see* BRIEFS AND TRANSCRIPTS OF PUBLIC HEARINGS
Canada. Royal Commission on Broadcasting *see* BRIEFS AND TRANSCRIPTS OF PUBLIC HEARINGS
Canada. Royal Commission on Dominion-Provincial Relations *see* BRIEFS AND TRANSCRIPTS
Canada. Royal Commission on Energy *see* BRIEFS AND TRANSCRIPTS
Canada. Royal Commission on National Development in the Arts, Letters, and Sciences *see* BRIEFS AND TRANSCRIPTS OF PUBLIC HEARINGS
Canada. Royal Commission on Newspapers *see* TRANSCRIPTS OF PUBLIC HEARINGS
Canada. Royal Commission on Taxation *see* BRIEFS AND TRANSCRIPTS
Canada. Royal Commission on the Economic Union and Development Prospects for Canada *see* BRIEFS AND TRANSCRIPTS
Canada. Royal Commission on the Status of Women *see* BRIEFS AND TRANSCRIPTS OF PUBLIC HEARINGS
Canada. Royal Commissions *see* REPORTS
CANADA SCHOOL JOURNAL *see* THE CANADA SCHOOL JOURNAL AND WEEKLY REVIEW
THE CANADA SCHOOL JOURNAL – (Cont: the Canada School Journal and Weekly Review, Merged with: Educational Weekly. Merged to Become: Educational Journal) – Toronto: Canada School Journal Pub. Co., [1886-1887] – 9 – cn C.I.H.M. [370]
THE CANADA SCHOOL JOURNAL – (Contd by: Canada School Journal and Weekly Review) – Toronto: [A Miller, 1877-1885] – 9 – cn C.I.H.M. [370]
CANADA SCHOOL JOURNAL AND WEEKLY REVIEW *see* THE CANADA SCHOOL JOURNAL
THE CANADA SCHOOL JOURNAL AND WEEKLY REVIEW – (Cont: Canada School Journal) – Toronto: Canada School Journal Pub. Co., [1885-1886?] – 9 – cn C.I.H.M. [370]
THE CANADA SCHOOL JOURNAL AND WEEKLY REVIEW *see* THE CANADA SCHOOL JOURNAL
Canada. Select Committee on Emigration *see*
- REPORT OF THE SELECT COMMITTEE APPOINTED TO ENQUIRE INTO THE CAUSES OF EMIGRATION FROM CANADA TO THE UNITED STATES OF AMERICA OR ELSEWHERE
- REPORT OF THE SELECT COMMITTEE TO WHOM WAS REFERRED THE ANNUAL REPORT OF THE CHIEF EMIGRATION AGENT, AND SUPPLEMENTARY REPORT OF THE GERMAN ASSISTANT AT QUEBEC

CANADA SHIPPING ACT AND REGULATIONS / Canada. Laws, Statutes, etc – (Amendment service. YX76-S9-EM) – Basic set. YX76-S9-1EM – 9 – Can$54.00 – cn Communication [340]
CANADA STAMP AND COIN JOURNAL – (Contd by: The Canada Stamp Journal) – Halifax, N.S: J R Findlay, [1888-1889] – 9 – cn C.I.H.M. [760]
THE CANADA STAMP JOURNAL *see* CANADA STAMP AND COIN JOURNAL
THE CANADA STAMP SHEET – (Merged with: Energy. Merged to become: Canada Stamp Sheet and Energy) – Quebec: W G L Paxman, [1899?-1901?] – 9 – cn C.I.H.M. [760]
CANADA STAMP SHEET AND ENERGY *see*
- THE CANADA STAMP SHEET
- THE PHILATELIC AND ADVOCATE

Canada. Statistics Canada *see* PUBLICATIONS
CANADA STATUTES, SESSION LAWS AND REVISIONS / Canada. General – (Updates planned) – 1st Parliament-32nd Parliament 2nd sess. 1867-1984 – 1420mf – 9 – $2,130.00 – LLMC 90-100 – us L.L.M.C. [340]
LE CANADA STENOGRAPHIQUE – Montreal: M Gabard, [1900-19–] – 9 – cn C.I.H.M. [650]
CANADA SUNDAY SCHOOL ADVOCATE – Toronto: S Rose, [1865?-18– or 19–] – 9 – cn C.I.H.M. [240]
Canada. Supreme Court *see*
- CAMERON'S SUPREME COURT CASES
- RULES AND ORDERS OF PRACTICE OF THE SUPERIOR COURT, LOWER CANADA; RULES AND ORDERS OF PRACTICE OF THE CIRCUIT COURT, LOWER CANADA
- SUPREME COURT REPORTS

Canada. Supreme Court for Lower Canada *see*
- TRANSCRIPT OF RECORD AND PROCEEDINGS IN THE COURTS OF LOWER CANADA APPEALED FROM IN A CAUSE BETWEEN GIDEON ROBERT AND OTHERS
- TRANSCRIPT OF RECORD AND PROCEEDINGS IN THE COURTS OF LOWER CANADA, APPEALED FROM IN A CAUSE BETWEEN ZEPHIR DORION, APPELLANT, AND ALEXANDRE EDOUARD KIERZKOWSKI; RESPONDENT..

CANADA TEMPERANCE ADVOCATE – Montreal, Canada. v1 n3. mai 1837-oct 1843 – 1r – 1 – Can$50.00 – cn Can Microfilming [073]
THE CANADA TEMPERANCE ADVOCATE – [Montreal: s.n, 1835-18–]; (Montreal: R Campbell) – 9 – cn C.I.H.M. [240]
THE CANADA TEMPERANCE MANUAL AND PROHIBITIONIST'S HANDBOOK / Foster, George Eulas – Toronto: Dominion Alliance for the Total Suppression of the Liquor Traffic, 1881. 05592. (Pre-1900 Canadiana) – 9 – cn C.I.H.M. [971]
CANADA. THE PRINTED RECORD. A BIBLIOGRAPHIC REGISTER WITH INDEXES – Cumulated annually. Indexed by author, title, series, subject (French and English headings) and class numbers. Individual Titles available – 17 – cn C.I.H.M. [010]
THE CANADA TIMES : REFORMISTE – Montreal, Canada. v1 n53. 7 mai 1841-v2 n79. 5 aut 1842 – 1r – 1 – Can$25.00 – cn Can Microfilming [072]
CANADA TREATY SERIES – 1928- – 9 – cn Micromedia [971]
CANADA UNDER BRITISH RULE: 1760-1900 / Bourinot, John George – Cambridge: University Press, 1900. 03344. (Pre-1900 Canadiana) – 9 – cn C.I.H.M. [971]
CANADA UNDER THE ADMINISTRATION OF LORD LORNE / Collins, Joseph Edmund – Toronto: Rose, 1884. 00715. (Pre-1900 Canadiana) – 9 – cn C.I.H.M. [971]
Canada. Upper Canada. House of Assembly *see* JOURNALS AND APPENDICES
THE CANADA VISITOR, OR, MONTHLY MAGAZINE – Montreal: Pub. for the Proprietor by W Greig, [1837-18–] – 9 – cn C.I.H.M. [971]
CANADA WEST – (Cont by: Canadian West, v7 1985 begins New Series) – Lnagley. v1-11. 1969-81 – 9 – Can$20.00y – cn Micromedia [073]
CANADA WEST *see* CANADIAN WEST
CANADA YEARBOOK / Canada – (See also: Annuaire du Canada) – Ottawa, 1867- – 9 – Price varies – cn Micromedia [971]
CANADA-ASIA WORKING GROUP – Toronto. 51 docs. 1980-1991 – 28mf – 9 – ne IDC [320]
LE CANADA-FRANCAIS – Longueuil. 29 aut 1972-7/13 fev 1973 – 1r – 1 – Can$45.00 – cn Can Microfilming [072]
LE CANADA-FRANCAIS / ed by Perrier, O & Gagnon, Yves – (31 mai 1918-30 dec 1992 148r) – St-Jean, Canada. 3 aut 1893-17 jul 1914 – 7r – 1 – Can$75.00r – cn Can Microfilming [072]
LE CANADA-FRANCAIS – Quebec: L-J Demers, 1888-1891 – 9 – cn C.I.H.M. [440]
CANADA-NORMANDIE / Association Canada-Normandie. Section de Montreal – Montreal. v1-4. 1970-74. SEM35P15 – 1r – 1 – Can$15.00 – cn Bibl Nat [072]
CANADA-PATRIE : "FILS NATIFS DU CANADA" / ed by Blanchet, L J N – Chambly, Canada. 31 jan-28 fev 1930 – 1r – 1 – Can$25.00 – cn Can Microfilming [072]
CANADA-REVUE – (Cont: Canada Artistique) – Montreal, Canada. v2 n1. jan 1891-aut 1894 – 1r – 1 – Can$40.00 – cn Can Microfilming [073]
CANADA-REVUE *see*
- CANADA ARTISTIQUE
- LE REVEIL

CANADA'S ACTUAL CONDITION / Bender, Prosper – Boston, 1886. 03569. (Pre-1900 Canadiana) – 9 – cn C.I.H.M. [971]
CANADA'S BUSINESS CLIMATE – Toronto, 1968-1994/95 – 9 – Can$20.00y – 0045-4303 – cn Micromedia [338]
CANADA'S FIRST MOVEMENT: WILLIAM ALEXANDER FOSTER SCRAPBOOK – 1 reel – 1 – $68.00 – cn Library Assoc [920]
CANADA'S LATE PREMIER / Aberdeen and Temair, Ishbel Gordon – 1895? 00766. (Pre-1900 Canadiana) – 9 – cn C.I.H.M. [971]
CANADA'S MARINE AND FISHERIES / Bourinot, John George – 1872? 00201. (Pre-1900 Canadiana) – 9 – cn C.I.H.M. [639]
CANADA'S MENTAL HEALTH – (1953-84 Can$460.00. Index 1960-83 Can$20.00) – Ottawa, 1953-84 1; 1985-94 9 – 1,9 – Can$20.00y – cn Micromedia [616]
CANADA'S MENTAL HEALTH – Ottawa, 1953-88 – 9r – 1 – cn Commonwealth Micro [073]
CANADA'S NATIONAL POLICY: MR. C. C. COLBY'S GREAT SPEECH ON TARIFF REVISION, HOUSE OF COMMONS, MARCH, 1878 : TO WHICH IS ADDED AN OPEN LETTER FROM MR. COLBY AND THE AMENDMENT MOVED BY SIR JOHN MACDONALD ON A RE-ADJUSTMENT OF THE DOMINION TARIFF WITH THE DIVISION THEREON / Colby, Charles Carroll – Ottawa?, 1878?. 00698. (Pre-1900 Canadiana) – 9 – cn C.I.H.M. [330]
CANADA-UNITED STATES LAW JOURNAL – (v1-8 1978-84 in reel $82.00. v9-21 1985-95 in mf $158.00) – Case Western Reserve University. v1-21. 1978-95 – 5,6,9 – $235.00 set – us Hein [340]
CANADENSIUM PLANTARUM / Cornut, J P – 7521 2. 1635 – 8 – ne IDC [580]
DER CANADER YID = THE CANADIAN JEW – (In Yiddish) – v2 n15. 14 apr 1911-v2 n26. 30 jun 1911 – 1r – 1 – Can$40.00 – cn Can Microfilming [072]
DER CANADER YID = THE CANADIAN JEW – Winnipeg, CN. v2 no 15,16. 1911 – 1r – 1 – Can$40.00 – cn Can Microfilming [072]
CANADER YIDDISHE WOCHENBLATT = CANADIAN JEWISH WEEKLY – Toronto, CN. v5 no 244, v38 no 419. 1945-1978 – 9r – 1 – Can$65.00r – cn Can Microfilming [072]
CANADIAN – (Cont as: Canadian Magazine 1968-1978) – Toronto, 1965-1967 – 9 – cn Micromedia [073]
CANADIAN – Toronto. v1-27. 1893-1907 – 5 – Can$100.00 – cn Micromedia [073]
CANADIAN – v1-91. Mar 1893-Aug 1939 – 1 – cn Precision [971]
THE CANADIAN – London, Ont: Grand Council of the CMBA of Canada, [1895-19–] – 9 – cn C.I.H.M. [971]
THE CANADIAN – Toronto, 1893-1907 – 9 – Can$100.00y – cn Micromedia [300]
Canadian Academy of Arts *see* CONSTITUTION AND LAWS
CANADIAN ADMINISTRATOR – (v.19-. 1979- 5,6,9) – v.1-. 1961- – 1 – us UMI [073]
THE CANADIAN ADVERTISER – Toronto: Canadian Advertiser Pub. Co., 1893-[189- or 19–] – 9 – cn C.I.H.M. [072]
CANADIAN AERONAUTICS AND SPACE JOURNAL – (v32-40 1986-94 9) – Ottawa. v1-40. 1955-94 – 5 – Price varies – cn Micromedia [629]
CANADIAN AGRICULTURAL JOURNAL *see* LE JOURNAL D'AGRICULTURE CANADIEN
THE CANADIAN AGRICULTURAL JOURNAL – (Contd by: Agricultural Journal and Transactions of the Lower Canada Agricultural Society) – Montreal: Lovell & Gibson, [1844?-1847] – 9 – cn C.I.H.M. [630]
THE CANADIAN AGRICULTURAL JOURNAL *see* AGRICULTURAL JOURNAL AND TRANSACTIONS OF THE LOWER CANADA AGRICULTURAL SOCIETY
CANADIAN AGRICULTURIST – (Cont: Agriculturist and Canadian Journal. Is absorbed by: Canada Farmer) – Toronto: [W McDougall, G Buckland, 1848?]-1863 – 9 – cn C.I.H.M. [630]
CANADIAN AGRICULTURIST *see*
- CANADA FARMER
- LOWER CANADA AGRICULTURIST, MANUFACTURING, COMMERCIAL, AND COLONIZATION INTELLIGENCER

THE CANADIAN ALBUM-MEN OF CANADA; OR, SUCCESS BY EXAMPLE IN RELIGION, PATRIOTISM, BUSINESS, LAW, MEDICINE, EDUCATION AND AGRICULTURE / ed by Cochrane, William – Brantford: Bradley, Garretson and Co., 1891. v1-2. Canada reel 2. (Cox Library Collection) – 5 – us Americana [971]
CANADIAN ALMANAC AND DIRECTORY – (1948-1970 available in positive only. v1-131 1848-1978 Can$2,400) – Cooksville. v1-139. 1848-1986; 1987-1995 – 9 – Can$37.00y – cn Micromedia [971]

CANADIAN AMERICAN REVIEW OF HUNGARIAN STUDIES – (Cont by: Hungarian Studies Review at v11 1984) – Toronto. v1-10. 1974-83 – 9 – Can$20.00y – cn Micromedia [940]
CANADIAN AND INTERNATIONAL EDUCATION – (v15-23 1986-94 9) – Calgary. v1-23. 1972-94 – 5 – Price varies – cn Micromedia [370]
CANADIAN ANNUAL REVIEW OF PUBLIC AFFAIRS – (Publ delayed. 1987 ed publ in 1991. 1901-1986 Can$28.00y) – Downsview. v1-35. 1901-88 – 9 – Can$20.00y – cn Micromedia [073]
CANADIAN ANTIQUARIAN AND NUMISMATIC JOURNAL – (Chronological and alphabetical indexes, 1872-1933 1r Can$25.00) – Montreal, Canada. jul 1872-1933 – 4r – 1 – Can$45.00r – cn Can Microfilming [730]
CANADIAN ANTIQUARIAN AND NUMISMATIC JOURNAL – v1-13 1872-1886; 1889-1894; 1898-1916; 1930-1933 – 1 – cn Precision [730]
CANADIAN ANTIQUER – (Cont by: Canadian Antiquer and Collector v12 1986/87) – Toronto. v1-11. 1975-86 – 1 – Price varies – cn Micromedia [740]
CANADIAN ANTIQUER AND COLLECTOR – (Incorporates: Canadian Collector) – Toronto. v12-15 n10. 1986/87-1989/90 – 1 – Can$60.00y – cn Micromedia [073]
CANADIAN ANTIQUER AND COLLECTOR *see*
– CANADIAN ANTIQUER
– CANADIAN COLLECTOR
CANADIAN APPRAISER – (Cont: Aim at v29 1985) – Winnipeg. v29-39. 1985-95 – 9 – Can$20.00y – cn Micromedia [073]
CANADIAN APPRAISER *see* AIM
CANADIAN AQUACULTURE – (Cont by: Northern Aquaculture v7 1991) – Victoria. v5-6. 1989-90 – 9 – Can$20.00y – cn Micromedia [073]
CANADIAN AQUACULTURE *see* NORTHERN AQUACULTURE
CANADIAN ARCHITECT – (v1-13 1955-68 Can$100.00 5) – Don Mills. v1-40. 1955-95 – 5,9 – Can$28.00y – cn Micromedia [720]
CANADIAN ARCHITECT AND BUILDER – Toronto: C H Mortimer. v1-22. 1888-1908. SEM35P99 – 1r – 1 – Can$60.00 – cn Bibl Nat [720]
CANADIAN ARCHITECT AND BUILDER – v1-21 1888-1908 – 1 – $725.00 – cn McLaren [720]
CANADIAN ART – Toronto. v1-12. 1984-95 – 9 – Can$20.00y – cn Micromedia [700]
Canadian Association of Amateur Oarsmen *see* CONSTITUTION AND BY-LAWS..., AS IN FORCE AUGUST 8TH, 1890: WITH LAWS OF BOAT RACING
THE CANADIAN ATHLETIC NEWS – Montreal, Canada. 7 mai-16 jul 1886 – 1r – 1 – Can$35.00 – cn Can Microfilming [790]
THE CANADIAN ATLANTIC TELEGRAPH – 18?? 05701. (Pre-1900 Canadiana) – 9 – cn C.I.H.M. [971]
CANADIAN AUTHOR AND BOOKMEN – Toronto, Ontario, CN. 1922-75 – 7r – 1 – cn Commonwealth Micro [073]
CANADIAN AUTOMOTIVE TRADE – v1-51,no.8. 1919-69 – 1 – us UMI [073]
CANADIAN AUTOMOTIVE TRADE – (v52-70 1970-88 9. Microform available to v70 1988. v1-51 1918-69 Can$500.00) – Toronto. v1-70. 1918-88 – 5,9 – Can$20.00y – cn Micromedia [380]
CANADIAN AUTOPARTS MARKETING – Toronto, 1986-89 – 9 – Can$20.00y – cn Micromedia [629]
CANADIAN AVIATION – v. 1-36. 1928-63 – 1 – 640.00 – us L of C Photodup [629]
CANADIAN AVIATION – (v1-42 1928-69 5 Can$990.00. Cont by: Aviation and Aerospace at v63 1990) – Toronto. v1-62. 1928-89 – 5,9 – Can$28.00y – cn Micromedia [629]
CANADIAN AVIATION – (v48- . 1975- . 5,6,9) – v. 1-. 1928- – 1 – us UMI [629]
CANADIAN AVIATION *see* AVIATION AND AEROSPACE
CANADIAN AVIATION AND AEROSPACE FOR SALE *see* AVIATION AND AEROSPACE
CANADIAN AVIATION AND AIRCRAFT FOR SALE – (Cont: Aviation and Aerospace at v66 no 5/6 1993) – v67- 1994- – 9 – Can$20.00y – cn Micromedia [629]
CANADIAN BANKER – (Cont: Canadian Banker and ICB Review v90 1983) – Toronto, v90-1983- – 5 – Price varies – cn Micromedia [073]
CANADIAN BANKER – v1-72. 1893-1965 – 1 – cn Precision [332]
CANADIAN BANKER *see* CANADIAN BANKER AND ICB REVIEW
CANADIAN BANKER AND ICB REVIEW – (Cont by: Canadian Banker at v90 1983. 1977-1982 Can$50.00y) – Toronto. v1-89. 1893-1982 – 5 – Can$100.00 – cn Micromedia [073]
CANADIAN BANKER AND ICB REVIEW *see* CANADIAN BANKER
THE CANADIAN BANKING SYSTEM, 1817-1890 / Breckenridge, Roeliff Morton – Toronto, 1894. 03719. (Pre-1900 Canadiana) – 9 – cn C.I.H.M. [971]
THE CANADIAN BANKING SYSTEM: AN EXPOSITION AND A DEFENCE / Canadian Journal of Commerce – By the editors of the Canadian Journal of Commerce. Toronto: E. T. Bromfield, 1869. 02033. (Pre-1900 Canadiana) – 9 – cn C.I.H.M. [971]
CANADIAN BAPTIST – Toronto, 1987-94 – 9 – Can$28.00y – cn Micromedia [240]
CANADIAN BAR ASSOCIATION JOURNAL – (Supersedes: Canadian Bar Journal) – v1-4. 1970-73 – 9 – $20.00 set – us Hein [340]
CANADIAN BAR ASSOCIATION YEARBOOK – (Regular updates planned) – 1896/97; 1915-85 – 108mf – 9 – $486.00 – LLMC 84-431 – us L.L.M.C. [340]
CANADIAN BAR JOURNAL – (Superseded by: Canadian Bar Association Journal) – v1-12. 1958-69 – 9 – $210.00 set – us Hein [340]
CANADIAN BAR JOURNAL *see* CANADIAN BAR ASSOCIATION JOURNAL
CANADIAN BAR REVIEW – (v1-61 1923-94 in reel or mf $804.00. v62-73 1984-94 in mf $237.00) – v1-73. 1923-94 – 5,6,9 – $1,041.00 set – us Hein [340]
THE CANADIAN BAR REVIEW *see*
– THE CANADA LAW JOURNAL
– CANADIAN LAW TIMES
THE CANADIAN BEE JOURNAL – (Contd by: Canadian Horticulturist and Beekeeper) – Beeton, Ont: D A Jones, [1885-1913] – 9 – cn C.I.H.M. [630]
CANADIAN BEVERAGE REVIEW – (Publ suspended at v60 1990) – Ajax. v50-60. 1980-90 – 9 – Can$20.00y – cn Micromedia [640]
THE CANADIAN BIBLIOGRAPHER AND LIBRARY RECORD – Hamilton [Ont: Griffin & Kidner, 1889-1890] – 9 – cn C.I.H.M. [020]
THE CANADIAN BIOGRAPHICAL DICTIONARY AND PORTRAIT GALLERY OF EMINENT AND SELF-MADE MEN – Ontario volume. Toronto, Chicago and New York, 1880. Canada reel 1. (Cox Library Collection) – 5 – us Americana [920]
THE CANADIAN BIOGRAPHICAL DICTIONARY: AND PORTRAIT GALLERY OF EMINENT AND SELF-MADE MEN – Quebec and Maritime provinces volume. Chicago; Toronto: American Biographical Pub. Co., 1881. 00749. (Pre-1900 Canadiana) – 9 – cn C.I.H.M. [920]
CANADIAN BIOGRAPHIES; ARTISTS, AUTHORS AND MUSICIANS – 1948-52 – 1 reel – 1 – $68.00 – cn Library Assoc [920]
CANADIAN BIOTECH NEWS – v1- 1992/93- – 9 – Can$20.00y – cn Micromedia [660]
CANADIAN BOATING – (v1-45 1925-69 Can$770.00 5) – Mississauga. v1-70. 1925-94 – 5,9 – Can$28.00y – cn Micromedia [790]
CANADIAN BOOKMAN – Toronto.v1-22, 1919-Oct/Nov 1939 – 1 – 395.00 – cn McLaren [073]
CANADIAN BOOKMAN; A MONTHLY REVIEW OF CONTEMPORARY LITERATURE DEVOTED TO THE INTERESTS OF THE CANADIAN BOOKBUYERS – 1909-10 – 1 – 45.00 – cn McLaren [073]
CANADIAN BOOKS FOR CHILDREN *see* IN REVIEW
CANADIAN BOOKS IN PRINT : AUTHOR AND TITLE INDEX / ed by Butler, Marian – Toronto: U.T. Press, 1995 – 15mf – $210.00 – 0-8020-4987-7 – cn U.T. Pr [010]
CANADIAN BORN (LADY MERTON, COLONIST) / Ward, Mary Augusta – British Fiction Archive: Unit 2 – 9 – uk Bell [830]
THE CANADIAN BOY – Guelph, Ont: Canadian Boy Pub. Co., [1900?-19–] – 9 – cn C.I.H.M. [971]
CANADIAN BREEDER AND AGRICULTURAL REVIEW – Toronto: [s.n., 1884?-18– or 19–] – 9 – cn C.I.H.M. [630]
CANADIAN BROADCASTER – Toronto, Canada. 8 Jan 1959-1 Oct 1964.-w. 5 reels – 1 – uk British Libr Newspaper [072]
CANADIAN BROADCASTER – Toronto, CN. 1942-79 – 36r – 1 – cn Commonwealth Micro [073]
CANADIAN BUILDING – (5,6,9 v25- 1975-) – v1- 1951- – 1 – us UMI [690]
CANADIAN BUILDING – (v1-24 1951-74 Can$550.00 5) – Toronto. v1-40. 1951-90 – 5,9 – Can$28.00y – cn Micromedia [600]
CANADIAN BUILDING *see* BUILDING
CANADIAN BUSINESS – (1976- . 5,6,9) – v. 1- 1928- – 1 – us UMI [650]
CANADIAN BUSINESS – Toronto. v12-68. 1939-95 – 5,9 – Price varies – cn Micromedia [380]
CANADIAN BUSINESS – v25-40. 1952-1967 – 1 – cn Precision [380]
CANADIAN BUSINESS REVIEW – (v.7-. 1980-. 5,6,9) – v.1-. 1974- – 1 – us UMI [380]
CANADIAN CAMP LIFE / Herring, Frances Elizabeth – London: T.F. Unwin, 1900. 05560. (Pre-1900 Canadiana) – 9 – cn C.I.H.M. [971]
CANADIAN CAMPING ASSOCIATION MAGAZINE – (v1-37 1949-85/86 Can$440.00) – Toronto. v1-39. 1949-1987/88 – 5,9 – Can$20.00y – cn Micromedia [790]
CANADIAN CARTOGRAPHER *see* CARTOGRAPHICA/CANADIAN CARTOGRAPHER
THE CANADIAN CARTOGRAPHER – v5-16. 1968-79 – 1 – us UMI [910]
THE CANADIAN CASKET – Hamilton, U.C. [Ont]: A Crosman, [1831-18–?] – 9 – cn C.I.H.M. [971]
Canadian Catholic Conference. National Commission on Liturgy *see* BULLETIN OF THE NATIONAL COMMISSION ON LITURGY
THE CANADIAN CATTLE AGITATION: MR. GARDNER'S POLICY DENOUNCED: PLAIN SPEAKING BY FARMERS AT PUBLIC MEETING IN TOWN HALL, DUNDEE, ON 1ST AUGUST, 1893 – Dundee Scotland: W. & D. C. Thomson, 1893. 02034. (Pre-1900 Canadiana) – 9 – cn C.I.H.M. [971]
CANADIAN CATTLEMAN – Winnipeg, CN. 1938-87 – 33r – 1 – cn Commonwealth Micro [073]
THE CANADIAN CENTENNIAL GUIDE TO NEW YORK AND PHILADELPHIA BY THIRTY DIFFERENT ROUTES. – (Brockville: Leavitt and Southworth), 1876. 02035. (Pre-1900 Canadiana) – 9 – cn C.I.H.M. [975]
CANADIAN CENTURY – Montreal, Canada. Canadian Century and Canadian Life & Resources. -w. Jan 1910-Nov 1911. 3 1 2 reels – 1 – uk British Libr Newspaper [072]
THE CANADIAN CENTURY – Montreal, Canada. 8 jan 1910-v4 n19. 11 nov 1911 – 2r – 1 – Can$50.00r – cn Can Microfilming [072]
Canadian Ceramic Society *see* JOURNAL
CANADIAN CHAMPION – Milton, 1946-1967 – 10r – 1 – cn Preston [971]
CANADIAN CHAMPION – Milton, Canada. 1862-73 – 3r – 1 – $204.00 – cn Library Assoc [971]
THE CANADIAN CHAMPION – Milton, Ontario, CN. 1870-74; 1949-51; 1984 – 4r – 1 – cn Commonwealth Micro [072]
CANADIAN CHARTERED ACCOUNTANT – v1-78. 1911-1961 – 1 – cn Precision [650]
CANADIAN CHECKERIST – Toronto: W H Darlington, [1888-18–] – 9 – cn C.I.H.M. [971]
THE CANADIAN CHEESE AND BUTTER MAKER – Williamstown, Ont: G F Brown, 1898? – 9 – cn C.I.H.M. [630]
CANADIAN CHEMICAL AND PROCESSING INDUSTRIES – (Cont: Canadian Chemistry and Metallurgy at v23 1939. Cont by: Canadian Chemical Processing at v35 1951) – Unionville. v23-34. 1939-50 – 5 – Can$100.00 – cn Micromedia [073]
CANADIAN CHEMICAL AND PROCESSING INDUSTRIES *see*
– CANADIAN CHEMICAL PROCESSING
– CANADIAN CHEMISTRY AND METALLURGY
CANADIAN CHEMICAL JOURNAL – (Cont by: Canadian Chemistry and Metallurgy at v6 1922) – Unionville. v1-5. 1917-21 – 5 – Can$100.00 – cn Micromedia [660]
CANADIAN CHEMICAL JOURNAL *see* CANADIAN CHEMISTRY AND METALLURGY
CANADIAN CHEMICAL NEWS – (Cont: Chemistry in Canada v36 1984) – Ottawa. v36- 1984- – 9 – Can$28.00y – cn Micromedia [073]
CANADIAN CHEMICAL NEWS *see* CHEMISTRY IN CANADA
CANADIAN CHEMICAL PROCESSING – (Cont: Canadian Chemical and Processing Industries at v35 1951. Cont by: Process Industries Canada at v60 1976) – Unionville, v35-59. 1951-75 – 5 – Can$100.00 – cn Micromedia [660]
CANADIAN CHEMICAL PROCESSING *see*
– CANADIAN CHEMICAL AND PROCESSING INDUSTRIES
– PROCESS INDUSTRIES CANADA
CANADIAN CHEMISTRY AND METALLURGY – (Cont: Canadian Chemical Journal at v6 1922. Cont by: Canadian Chemical and Processing Industries at v23 1939) – Unionville. v6-22. 1922-38 – 5 – Can$100.00 – cn Micromedia [660]
CANADIAN CHEMISTRY AND METALLURGY *see*
– CANADIAN CHEMICAL AND PROCESSING INDUSTRIES
– CANADIAN CHEMICAL JOURNAL
Canadian Christian Conference. First. 1878. Toronto, Ontario *see* THE FIR..CONFERENCE HELD IN SHAFTESBURY HALL, TORONTO, FROM MONDAY OCT. 21ST UNTIL FRIDAY, OCT. 25TH, 1878
THE CANADIAN CHRISTIAN EXAMINER AND PRESBYTERIAN REVIEW – Niagara, U.C. [Ont]: W D Miller, 1837-[1840] – 9 – cn C.I.H.M. [240]
CANADIAN CHRONICLE – Montreal, Canada. 27 sep 1955-v2 n28. 24 jul 1956 – 1r – 1 – Can$25.00 – cn Can Microfilming [072]
CANADIAN CHRONICLE *see* THE NEW ERA, OR, CANADIAN CHRONICLE
THE CANADIAN CHURCH JUVENILE – Toronto: Board of Management of the Domestic and Foreign Missionary Society, [1893?-191-?] – 9 – cn C.I.H.M. [240]
CANADIAN CHURCH MAGAZINE AND MISSION NEWS *see* OUR MISSION NEWS
THE CANADIAN CHURCH MAGAZINE AND MISSION NEWS – (Cont: Our Mission News) – Hamilton, Ont: Domestic and Foreign Missionary Society of the Church of England in Canada, [1887-1898] – 9 – cn C.I.H.M. [240]
THE CANADIAN CHURCH MISSIONARY GLEANER – Toronto: Canadian Church Missionary Society, [1896?-1903?] – 9 – cn C.I.H.M. [240]
THE CANADIAN CHURCH PRESS – Toronto: Lovell and Gibson, 1860 – 9 – cn C.I.H.M. [240]
CANADIAN CHURCHMAN – (Cont by: Anglican Journal/Journal Anglican at v115 1989) – Toronto. v54-114. 1927-88 – 1 – Price varieS – cn Micromedia [240]
CANADIAN CHURCHMAN – Toronto, 1927-1933 – 7r – 1 – cn Preston [971]
CANADIAN CHURCHMAN – Toronto, Canada. 1876-1926 – 36r – 1 – $2,340.00 – cn Library Assoc [971]
CANADIAN CHURCHMAN *see* ANGLICAN JOURNAL/JOURNAL ANGLICAN
CANADIAN COIN NEWS – (v1-8 1962-69 Can$260.00) – St. Catherines. v1-31. 1962-93/94 – 1 – Can$85.00y – cn Micromedia [730]
CANADIAN COLLECTOR – (Cont by: The Canadian Collector and Philatelic Punch (ID 04571)) – Berlin [Kitchener], Ont.: F.I. Weaver, [1898] – 9 – cn C.I.H.M. [760]
CANADIAN COLLECTOR – (Incorporated within: Canadian Antiquer and Collector 1987) – Toronto. v1-22. 1966-87 – 9 – Can$20.00y – cn Micromedia [740]
CANADIAN COLLECTOR *see* CANADIAN ANTIQUER AND COLLECTOR
THE CANADIAN COLLECTOR AND PHILATELIC PUNCH – Berlin [Kitchener], Ont.: E.A. Giller, [1899] – 9 – cn C.I.H.M. [760]
THE CANADIAN COLONIST : MENSUEL / ed by Foley, S – Montreal, Canada. mai 1886 – 1r – 1 – Can$25.00 – cn Can Microfilming [073]
THE CANADIAN COLONIST AND COMMERCIAL ADVERTISER / ed by Jacquies, A – Montreal, Canada. v2 n4. 14 jul 1840-v2 n86. 26 avr 1841 – 1r – 1 – Can$25.00 – cn Can Microfilming [072]
CANADIAN COMMENT – v. 1-7. 1932-38 – 1 – 175.00 – cn McLaren [971]

CANADIAN COMPOSER – (Numbering changes from issues to vols in 1990. Ceased: v4 1993) – Toronto. nos 1-246. 1965-89. v1-4. 1990-93 – 5,9 – Price varies – cn Micromedia [073]

CANADIAN COMPUTER RESELLER – Toronto. v1-7. 1988-94 – 9 – Price varies – cn Micromedia [000]

THE CANADIAN CONSTITUTION; A STUDY OF THE WRITTEN AND UNWRITTEN FEATURES OF OUR SYSTEM OF GOVERNMENT / Lawson, W J – Ottawa, Queen's Printer, 1960. 29 p. LL-2398 – 1 – us L of C Photodup [340]

CANADIAN CONSTITUTIONAL HISTORY AND LAW / Hassard, Albert Richard – Toronto: Carswell, 1900.05207.(Pre-1900 Canadiana) – 9 – cn C.I.H.M. [971]

CANADIAN CONSULTING ENGINEER – Don Mills. v1- 1959- – 5,9 – Price varies – cn Micromedia [073]

CANADIAN CONSUMER – (Cont: Canadian Consumer/Le consommateur canadien 1971) – Nepean. v1-23. 1971-93 – 9 – Price varies – cn Micromedia [073]

CANADIAN CONSUMER *see*
- CANADIAN CONSUMER / LE CONSOMMATEUR CANADIEN
- CONSOMMATEUR CANADIEN

CANADIAN CONSUMER / LE CONSOMMATEUR CANADIEN – (Cont by: Canadian Consumer 1971) – Nepean. v1-8. 1963-70 – 9 – Can$20.00y – cn Micromedia [073]

CANADIAN CONSUMER/LE CONSOMMATEUR CANADIEN *see* CANADIAN CONSUMER

THE CANADIAN CONTINGENT: AN EXTRACT FROM A SPEECH BY THE HON. MINISTER OF RAILWAYS, AT CAMPBELLTON, N. B. ON 21ST NOV., 1899 / Blair, Andrew George – 1899? 00152. (Pre-1900 Canadiana) – 9 – cn C.I.H.M. [971]

CANADIAN CONTRACT RECORD – (Merged with: Canadian Architect and Builder to become: Contract Record) – Toronto: C.H. Mortimer, v1 no 1 (Nov 27 1889)- – 9 – cn C.I.H.M. [690]

CANADIAN CONTROLS AND INSTRUMENTATION – (v14- . 1975- . 5,6,9) – v. 1-. 1962- – 1 – us UMI [600]

THE CANADIAN CO-OPERATOR AND PATRON – Owen Sound [Ont.]: R.J. Doyle, [1882-1900] – 9 – cn C.I.H.M. [971]

CANADIAN COPYRIGHT: THE FOLLOWING EDITORIALS HAVE APPEARED IN THE TORONTO TELEGRAM. – Canadian Copyright Association, 1884. 05702. (Pre-1900 Canadiana) – 9 – cn C.I.H.M. [070]

CANADIAN CORRESPONDENT *see* CORRESPONDENT AND ADVOCATE

THE CANADIAN CORRESPONDENT – York, Toronto. v1 n29. 28 mai 1833-v1 n34. 29 jun 1833 – 1r – 1 – Can$25.00 – cn Can Microfilming [072]

CANADIAN COUNSELLOR/CONSEILLER CANADIEN – (v10- . 5,6,9) – v. 1-. 1967- – 1 – us UMI [150]

CANADIAN COUNTRYMAN – Toronto. Canada. -w. Apr 1913-Dec 1939; 22 Mar 1941-22 Sep 1951. (62mqn reels) – 1 – uk British Libr Newspaper [072]

CANADIAN COURANT AND MONTREAL ADVERTISER – Montreal, Canada. 11 mai 1807-31 dec 1826 – 4r – 1 – Can$35.00r – cn Can Microfilming [072]

CANADIAN COURANT AND MONTREAL ADVERTISER – Montreal, Canada. 1807-34 – 9r – 1 – $585.00 – cn Library Assoc [971]

CANADIAN COURIER – (Lacking: v24) – v1-25. Dec 1906-Oct 1920 – 1 – cn Precision [971]

THE CANADIAN CRAFTSMAN AND MASONIC RECORD – Port Hope, Ont.: J.B. Trayes, 1877- – 9 – cn C.I.H.M. [360]

THE CANADIAN CRAFTSMAN AND MASONIC RECORD *see* THE CRAFTSMAN AND CANADIAN MASONIC RECORD

THE CANADIAN CRICKET FIELD – [Toronto]: A.G. Brown, G.G.S. Lindsey, v1 no 1 (May 10 1882)- – 9 – cn C.I.H.M. [790]

CANADIAN CULTIVATOR AND HOUSEHOLD MAGAZINE – Sherbrooke, Quebec: G.H. Bradford, 1890- – 9 – cn C.I.H.M. [640]

THE CANADIAN DAIRYMAN *see* THE FARMING WORLD

CANADIAN DAIRYMAN AND FARMING WORLD *see*
- FARM AND DAIRY AND RURAL HOME
- THE FARMING WORLD

THE CANADIAN DAIRYMAN AND FARMING WORLD – (Cont by: Farm and Dairy and Rural Home) – Peterboro [Peterborough], Ont.: Dairyman Pub Co and Farming World, [1908] – 9 – cn C.I.H.M. [630]

CANADIAN DATASYSTEMS – (Contains: Software Canada. Cont by: I.T. Magazine at v25 1993) – Toronto. v1-24. 1969-92 – 9 – Price varies – cn Micromedia [510]

CANADIAN DATASYSTEMS – (v8- . 1976- . 5,6,9) – v. 1-. 1969- – 1 – us UMI [510]

CANADIAN DATASYSTEMS *see* SOFTWARE CANADA

THE CANADIAN DAY STAR – Montreal. v1 n-. nov 1861-v3 n-. dec 1864 – 1r – 1 – Can$30.00 – cn Can Microfilming [072]

THE CANADIAN DAY-STAR – [Montreal: s.n., 1861-1864?] – 9 – cn C.I.H.M. [971]

CANADIAN DEFENCE QUARTERLY – Ottawa. v14-16. 1936-1939 – 1 – cn Precision [355]

CANADIAN DEFENCE QUARTERLY – Toronto. v10-23. 1980/81-93/94 – 9 – Can$20.00y – cn Micromedia [073]

Canadian Development Company *see* SAN FRANCISCO, PORTLAND, SEATTLE, TACOMA, VICTORIA, VANCOUVER TO ATLIN LAKE AND DAWSON CITY (VIA SKAGWAY AND LAKE BENNETT): AND ALL INTERMEDIATE POINTS ON THE LEWIS AND YUKON RIVERS

CANADIAN DIMENSION – Winnipeg. v1-29. 1963/64-95 – 9 – Can$20.00y – cn Micromedia [971]

CANADIAN DOCTOR – (v1-35 1935-69 Can$1,650.00) – Richmond Hill. v1-57. 1935-1991 – 5 – Can$60.00y – cn Micromedia [073]

CANADIAN DRIVER/OWNER – v1-12,no.4. 1972/73-1984 – 1 – us UMI [073]

CANADIAN DRIVER/OWNER *see* DRIVER/ OWNER

THE CANADIAN DRY GOODS REVIEW – Toronto: Dry Goods Review Co, v1 no 1 (Jan 1891)- – 9 – cn C.I.H.M. [680]

THE CANADIAN ECCLESIASTICAL GAZETTE – Quebec: G. Stanley, [1850-1853?] – 9 – cn C.I.H.M. [240]

THE CANADIAN ECCLESIASTICAL GAZETTE, OR, MONTHLY CHURCH REGISTER FOR THE DIOCESES OF QUEBEC, TORONTO, AND MONTREAL – Toronto: H. Rowsell, [1854?-1862] – 9 – cn C.I.H.M. [240]

THE CANADIAN ECLECTIC MAGAZINE OF FOREIGN LITERATURE, SCIENCE AND ART – [Toronto: s.n., 1871-1872] – 9 – cn C.I.H.M. [400]

CANADIAN ECONOMIC OBSERVER = L'OBSERVATEUR ECONOMIQUE CANADIEN – (Cont: Canadian Statistical Review and Revue statistique du Canada) – Ottawa, 1988- – 9 – Can$55.00y – cn Micromedia [073]

CANADIAN ECONOMIC OBSERVER *see* REVUE STATISTIQUE DU CANADA

CANADIAN ECONOMICS: BEING PAPERS PREPARED FOR READING BEFORE THE ECONOMICAL SECTION, WITH AN INTRODUCTORY REPORT: MONTREAL MEETING, 1884 / British Association for the Advancement of Science. Canada – Montreal: Dawson Bros., 1885. 03723. (Pre-1900 Canadiana) – 9 – cn C.I.H.M. [330]

THE CANADIAN ECONOMIST – Montreal: Printed for the Committee of the Montreal Free Trade Association, Donoghue and Mantz, [1846-1847] – 9 – cn C.I.H.M. [380]

CANADIAN EDUCATION AND RESEARCH DIGEST – (Cont by: Education Canada) – Toronto. v1-8. 1961-68 – 9 – Can$28.00y – cn Micromedia [370]

CANADIAN EDUCATION AND RESEARCH DIGEST *see* EDUCATION CANADA

Canadian Education Association *see* NEWSLETTER

CANADIAN EDUCATION ASSOCIATION NEWSLETTER – (Missing: n223) – Toronto. n1- 1946- – 5,9 – Price varies – cn Micromedia [370]

THE CANADIAN ELECTRICAL NEWS – Montreal, Canada. 31 mar-15 jun 1884 – 1r – 1 – Can$25.00 – cn Can Microfilming [621]

THE CANADIAN ELECTRICAL NEWS – Montreal: Hart Bros., v1 no 1 (Mar 31 1884)- – 9 – cn C.I.H.M. [621]

CANADIAN ELECTRICAL NEWS AND ENGINEERING JOURNAL – Toronto: C.H. Mortimer, v9 no 1 (Jan 1899)- – 9 – cn C.I.H.M. [621]

CANADIAN ELECTRICAL NEWS AND ENGINEERING JOURNAL *see* CANADIAN ELECTRICAL NEWS AND STEAM ENGINEERING JOURNAL

CANADIAN ELECTRICAL NEWS AND ENGINEERING JOURNAL. (ELECTRICAL NEWS) – Toronto, Canada. Dec 1908-Jun 1922.-w. 20 reels – 1 – uk British Libr Newspaper [073]

CANADIAN ELECTRICAL NEWS AND STEAM ENGINEERING JOURNAL – (Cont by: Canadian Electrical News and Engineering Journal) – Toronto: C.H. Mortimer, v1 no 1 (Jan 1891)-v2 no 12 (Dec 1892); new ser. v3 no 1 (Jan 1893)-new ser. v8 no 12 (Dec 1898) [1891?-1898] – 9 – cn C.I.H.M. [621]

CANADIAN ELECTRONICS – Willowdale. v6-9. 1991-94 – 1 – Can$60.00y – cn Micromedia [621]

CANADIAN ELECTRONICS ENGINEERING – (v1-18 1957-74 Can$440.00 5) – Willowdale. v1-34. 1957-90 – 5,9 – Can$28.00y – cn Micromedia [621]

CANADIAN ELECTRONICS ENGINEERING – (v19- . 1975- . 5,6,9) – v. 1-. 1957- – 1 – us UMI [621]

CANADIAN EMIGRANT AND WESTERN DISTRICT COMMERCIAL AND GENERAL ADVERTISER – Sandwich, Canada. 1831-36 – 1 reel – 1 – $68.00 – cn Library Assoc [971]

THE CANADIAN ENGINEER – Toronto: Canadian Engineer Co, v1 no 1 (May 1893)- – 9 – cn C.I.H.M. [620]

CANADIAN ENGINEER. (CANADIAN ENGINEER WEEKLY) – (CANADIAN ENGINEER WEEKLY). Canada. May 1893-May 1922 (missing 1910-11). -w – 41r – 1 – uk British Libr Newspaper [620]

THE CANADIAN ENGINEERING NEWS – Montreal: W.E. Gower, v1 no 1 (Jan 31 1893)- – 9 – cn C.I.H.M. [620]

CANADIAN ENTOMOLOGIST – London, Toronto, 1869-1920. v1-52 – 321mf – Z-931/2 – ne IDC [590]

CANADIAN ENTOMOLOGIST – v. 1-107. 1868-1975 – 1,5,6 – us Princeton Micro [590]

CANADIAN ENTOMOLOGIST – (v103- . 5,6. v109- . 9) – v. 1-. 1868- – 1 – us UMI [590]

CANADIAN ENTOMOLOGIST – v.1-28. 1868-96 – 1,5,6 – $2267.00 – us Princeton Micro [590]

THE CANADIAN ENTOMOLOGIST – Toronto: Copp, Clark, [1868]- – 9 – cn C.I.H.M. [590]

THE CANADIAN EPWORTH ERA – Toronto: W. Briggs, v1 no 1 (Jan 1899)- – 9 – cn C.I.H.M. [971]

CANADIAN ESTATE TAX AND SUCCESSION DUTIES ACTS; INCLUDING ALL AMENDMENTS TO DECEMBER 1, 1966 / Commerce Clearing House Canadian Limited – 6th ed. Don Mills, Ont. 1966 vii, 215 p. LL-2370 – 1 – us L of C Photodup [340]

CANADIAN ETHNIC STUDIES – (Cont by: Canadian Ethnic Studies/Etude Ethniques au Canada at v11 1979) – Calgary. v1-10. 1969-78 – 9 – Can$20.00y – cn Micromedia [305]

CANADIAN ETHNIC STUDIES = ETUDE ETHNIQUES AU CANADA – (Cont: Canadian Ethnic Studies v11 1979) – Calgary. v11-27. 1979-95 – 9 – Can$28.00y – cn Micromedia [305]

CANADIAN ETHNIC STUDIES *see*
- CANADIAN ETHNIC STUDIES

THE CANADIAN EVANGEL *see* DER EVANGELIUMS-BOTE

THE CANADIAN EVANGELIST – (Cont by: The Disciple of Christ and Canadian Evangelist) – Toronto: Evangelist Pub Co, [1890-1895] – 9 – cn C.I.H.M. [240]

THE CANADIAN EVANGELIST *see*
- THE DISCIPLE OF CHRIST AND CANADIAN EVANGELIST
- THE ONTARIO EVANGELIST

THE CANADIAN EVANGELIST AND DISCIPLE OF CHRIST – Hamilton, Ont.: G. Munro, [1896] – 9 – cn C.I.H.M. [240]

THE CANADIAN EVANGELIST AND DISCIPLE OF CHRIST *see* THE DISCIPLE OF CHRIST AND CANADIAN EVANGELIST

CANADIAN EXHIBITOR – Toronto: Trades Pub Co, [1886-18– or 19–] – 9 – cn C.I.H.M. [650]

THE CANADIAN FAMILY HERALD – Toronto: Printed for D. McDougall by J. Stephens, [1851-18–?] – 9 – cn C.I.H.M. [971]

CANADIAN FARM AND HOME *see*
- THE FARMING WORLD
- THE FARMING WORLD AND CANADIAN FARM AND HOME

CANADIAN FARM ECONOMICS – (Cont: Economic Annalist 1931-65: Current Review of Agricultural Conditions. Publ delay between 1988 and 1991. To publ irregularly from 1991) – Ottawa. v1-23. 1966/67-1991 – 9 – Can$20.00y – cn Micromedia [636]

CANADIAN FARM ECONOMICS *see*
- CURRENT REVIEW OF AGRICULTURAL CONDITIONS
- ECONOMIC ANNALIST

CANADIAN FARMER – Montreal: J. Smith, [1851-18–] – 9 – cn C.I.H.M. [630]

CANADIAN FARMER AND GRANGE RECORD *see* THE RURAL CANADIAN

THE CANADIAN FARMER AND GRANGE RECORD AND ORGAN OF THE ONTARIO BEE-KEEPERS' ASSOCIATION – Welland, Ont.: N.B. Colcock, [1880?-1884] – 9 – cn C.I.H.M. [630]

THE CANADIAN FARMER AND MECHANIC – Kingston [Ont.]: Garfield & Good, 1841 – 9 – cn C.I.H.M. [630]

CANADIAN FARMERS' GAZETTE – Brantford, C.W. [Ont.]: A. Webber, [1861?-18–?] – 9 – cn C.I.H.M. [630]

CANADIAN FICTION MAGAZINE – Toronto. n1-1971- – 9 – Price varies – cn Micromedia [073]

THE CANADIAN FIELD-NATURALIST / Ottawa Field-Naturalists' Club – [Ottawa?: The Club?, 1919] – 9 – cn C.I.H.M. [630]

THE CANADIAN FIELD-NATURALIST *see* THE OTTAWA NATURALIST

CANADIAN FINANCE – Winnipeg, Canada. Jun 1911-Dec 1921.-w. 12 reels – 1 – uk British Libr Newspaper [073]

THE CANADIAN FIRESIDE – Montreal: W. Bennet, v1 no 1 (Feb 1888)- – 9 – cn C.I.H.M. [971]

CANADIAN FISH-EGGS AND LARVAE / Dannevic, A – Z-2 2. 1919 – 8 – ne IDC [590]

CANADIAN FISHERMAN – Sainte Anne de Bellevue, Canada. Sep 1919-Dec 1921; Jan 1933.-w. 2 reels – 1 – uk British Libr Newspaper [073]

THE CANADIAN FLORIST AND COTTAGE GARDENER – Peterborough [Ont.]: F. Mason, v1 no 1 (Jan 1885)- – 9 – cn C.I.H.M. [630]

CANADIAN FOLK SONG AND HANDICRAFT FESTIVAL... FIFTH CONCERT... = FESTIVAL DE LA CHANSON ET DES METIERS DU TERROIR... – [Quebec?]: [s.n.], [cop. 1927]. SEM105P1354 – 1mf – 9 – Can$2.25 – cn Bibl Nat [780]

CANADIAN FOLK SONG AND HANDICRAFT FESTIVAL... FIRST CONCERT... = FESTIVAL DE LA CHANSON ET DES METIERS DU TERROIR... – [Quebec?]: [s.n.], [cop. 1927]. SEM105P1351 – 1mf – 9 – Can$2.25 – cn Bibl Nat [780]

CANADIAN FOLK SONG AND HANDICRAFT FESTIVAL... FOURTH CONCERT... = FESTIVAL DE LA CHANSON ET DES METIERS DU TERROIR... – [Quebec?]: [s.n.], [cop. 1927]. SEM105P1353 – 1mf – 9 – Can$2.25 – cn Bibl Nat [780]

CANADIAN FOLK SONG AND HANDICRAFT FESTIVAL... SECOND CONCERT... = FESTIVAL DE LA CHANSON ET DES METIERS DU TERROIR... – [Quebec?]: [s.n.], cop, 1927. SEM105P1363 – 1mf – 9 – Can$2.25 – cn Bibl Nat [780]

CANADIAN FOLK SONG AND HANDICRAFT FESTIVAL... THIRD CONCERT... = FESTIVAL DE LA CHANSON ET DES METIERS DU TERROIR.... – [Quebec?]: [s.n.], [cop. 1927]. SEM105P1352 – 1mf – 9 – Can$2.25 – cn Bibl Nat [780]

CANADIAN FOOTWEAR JOURNAL – (Previous title: Shoe and Leather Journal) – Ste. Anne de Bellevue. v1- 1888- – 5,9 – Price varies – cn Micromedia [073]

CANADIAN FOOTWEAR JOURNAL *see* THE CANADIAN SHOE AND LEATHER JOURNAL

CANADIAN FOREST INDUSTRIES – (v1-99 1882-1979 Can$2,400.00 5) – Don Mills. v1-110. 1882-1990; 1991-95 – 5,9 – Can$28.00y – cn Micromedia [634]

CANADIAN FORUM – 1920-1950 – 1 – us Princeton Micro [971]

CANADIAN FORUM – (Publ delays between v67 and 68) – Ottawa. v2-74. 1921/22-1995/96 – 9,5 – Price varies – cn Micromedia [073]

CANADIAN FORUM – (v48- . 5,6) – v. 1-. 1920- – 1 – us UMI [073]

CANADIAN FRANCHISE AND ELECTION LAWS: A MANUAL FOR THE USE OF REVISING OFFICERS, MUNICIPAL OFFICERS, CANDIDATES, AGENTS, AND ELECTORS: WITH SUPPLEMENT CONTAINING THE AMENDING ACTS OF 1886 / Ermatinger, Charles Oakes – Toronto: Carswell, 1886. 02920. (Pre-1900 Canadiana) – 9 – cn C.I.H.M. [971]

CANADIAN FREE PRESS – (Ottawa Free Press Aug 1968, Octopus 1 feb 1969-dec 1970) – Ottawa, 25 feb 1967-jul 1968 – 1r – 1 – cn Can Microfilming [072]

CANADIAN FREEMAN – Toronto, Canada. 1825-34 – 1 reel – 1 – $68.00 – cn Library Assoc [971]

CANADIAN FREEMAN – Toronto, Canada. 1862-73 – 5r – 1 – $325.00 – cn Library Assoc [971]

CANADIAN FREEMAN – York, Toronto. v3 n18. 1 nov 1827-v3 n52. 26 jun 1828 – 1r – 1 – Can$30.00 – cn Can Microfilming [072]

THE CANADIAN FREEMAN – Toronto, 16 jul 1858-v12 n3. 5 jul 1869 – 1r – 1 – Can$35.00 – cn Can Microfilming [072]

THE CANADIAN FREEMASON – Montreal: Hill's Book Store, [1860-1861] – 9 – cn C.I.H.M. [360]

THE CANADIAN FREEMASON – Toronto: Aldrich & Co, v1 no 1 (Aug 1874)- – 9 – cn C.I.H.M. [360]

CANADIAN FRIEND – v78-89. 1982-93 (complete) – Inquire – 1 – ATLA S0807 – us A.T.L.A. [073]

CANADIAN FRONTIER – (Ceased: 1978) – New Westminster. v1-4. 1972-75; 1976-78 – 9 – Can$20.00y – cn Micromedia [971]

CANADIAN FRUIT, FLOWER, AND KITCHEN GARDENER:.. / Beadle, Delos White – Toronto: J. Campbell, 1872. 02995. (Pre-1900 Canadiana) – 9 – cn C.I.H.M. [630]

CANADIAN GALLUP POLLS – (1941-60 Can$330.00 5) – Toronto, 1941-1995 – 5,9 – Can$28.00y – cn Micromedia [310]

THE CANADIAN GARLAND – 1832-33 – 1 – 60.00 – cn McLaren [800]

THE CANADIAN GAZETTE = LA GAZETTE CANADIENNE / ed by Brown, James & Brown, Charles – Montreal, Canada. 3 aut 1807-10 mar 1808 – 1r – 1 – Can$35.00 – cn Can Microfilming [072]

Canadian Gazetteer Publishing Co *see* DOMINION OF CANADA AND NEWFOUNDLAND GAZETTEER AND CLASSIFIED BUSINESS DIRECTORY-1922

CANADIAN GEM AND FAMILY VISITOR – 1848-49 – 1 – 35.00 – cn McLaren [073]

THE CANADIAN GENTLEMAN'S JOURNAL AND SPORTING TIMES – Toronto: P. Collins, [187-?-188-?] – 9 – cn C.I.H.M. [790]

CANADIAN GEOGRAPHER – (3yr delay in micropubl) – Montreal. v1- 1950- – 5 – Price varies – cn Micromedia [910]

CANADIAN GEOGRAPHER = GEOGRAPHE CANADIEN – (1983-. 1,5,6,9) – v1-. 1950- – 1 – us UMI [910]

CANADIAN GEOGRAPHICAL JOURNAL – (v78- . 5,6. v90- . 9) – v. 1- 1930- – 1 – us UMI [910]

CANADIAN GEOTECHNICAL JOURNAL – Toronto. v1-32. 1963-95 – 9 – Price varies – cn Micromedia [073]

CANADIAN GEOTECHNICAL JOURNAL – (v14- . 5,6,9) – v. 1- 1963- – 1 – us UMI [550]

CANADIAN GLEANER – Huntingdon, Canada. 1863-1900 – 12r – 1 – $780.00 – cn Library Assoc [971]

CANADIAN GLEANER / THE GLEANER – (Title varies) – Huntingdon, Canada. 18 sep 1863-18 dec 1991 – 47r – 1 – Can$70.00r – cn Can Microfilming [072]

THE CANADIAN GOLD FIELDS AND FARM LANDS – How to get there. Allan Line. Liverpool: Allan Line Offices, 1899. 00036. (Pre-1900 Canadiana) – 9 – cn C.I.H.M. [971]

Canadian Golf Association *see* CONSTITUTION AND BY-LAWS

THE CANADIAN GRANGER – London, Ont.: [s.n.1876-18– or 19–] – 9 – cn C.I.H.M. [630]

THE CANADIAN GRANGER *see* THE GRANGER

THE CANADIAN GREEN BAG – Montreal: J. Lovell, [1895] – 9 – cn C.I.H.M. [332]

CANADIAN GROCER – (1985- 5,6,9) – v1- 1886- – 1 – us UMI [640]

CANADIAN GROCER – (v27-54 1913-1940 5. v55-109 1941-95 9) – Toronto. v1-109. 1886-1995 – 1,5,9 – Price varies – cn Micromedia [640]

CANADIAN HARDWARE AND METAL MERCHANT – (Cont by: Hardware and Metal) – Toronto: J.B. McLean Pub Co, [1889 or 189–1904?] – 9 – cn C.I.H.M. [680]

CANADIAN HARDWARE AND METAL MERCHANT *see* HARDWARE

THE CANADIAN HEBREW = KANEDER ID – Montreal, CN, 1938-1941 – 1r – 1 – Can$30.00 – cn Can Microfilming [072]

CANADIAN HERITAGE – Ottawa, v6-1979/80 – 9 – Can$20.00y – cn Micromedia [971]

CANADIAN HERITAGE *see* HERITAGE CANADA

CANADIAN HIGH NEWS *see* TEEN GENERATION MAGAZINE

CANADIAN HISTORICAL QUARTERLY – [Toronto?]: Hunter, Rose, v1 no 1 (Dec 1899)- – 9 – cn C.I.H.M. [971]

CANADIAN HISTORICAL REVIEW – 1920-1948 – 1,5,6 – us Princeton Micro [971]

CANADIAN HISTORICAL REVIEW – (Annual indexes included in each volume from 1950 to date) – Downsview. v1-76. 1920-95 – 9 – Can$28.00y – cn Micromedia [971]

CANADIAN HISTORICAL REVIEW – (v54- . 5,6. v50- . 9) – v. 1- 1920- – 1 – us UMI [971]

CANADIAN HISTORY – St. John, N.B.: G.U. Hay, 1898-1900 – 9 – cn C.I.H.M. [971]

CANADIAN HISTORY READINGS, VOL. 1: FOR SCHOOLS, LIBRARIES, AND GENERAL READERS: EMBRACING SEVENTY-TWO TOPICS. – Ed. and publ. by George U. Hay, Saint John, N.B.: Barnes, 1900. 05520. (Pre-1900 Canadiana) – 9 – cn C.I.H.M. [971]

CANADIAN HISTORY: THE SIEGE AND BLOCKADE OF QUEBEC BY GENERALS MONTGOMERY AND ARNOLD IN 1775-6 / Anderson, William James – A paper read before the Literary and Historical Society of Quebec, March 6th, 1872. Quebec: Middleton & Dawson, 1872. 00034. (Pre-1900 Canadiana) – 9 – cn C.I.H.M. [971]

CANADIAN HOME ECONOMICS JOURNAL – Ottawa. v25-45. 1975-95 – 9 – Can$20.00y – cn Micromedia [640]

CANADIAN HOME ECONOMICS JOURNAL/ REVUE CANADIENNE D'ECONOMIE FAMILIALE – (v29- 1979- 5,6,9) – 1950- – 1 – us UMI [640]

CANADIAN HOME JOURNAL – Toronto: Home Journal Pub Co, [1895-1958] – 9 – cn C.I.H.M. [640]

CANADIAN HOME RULE HERALD – Parkdale, Ont: G.D. Griffin, no 1 (1890)- – 9 – cn C.I.H.M. [320]

THE CANADIAN HONEY PRODUCER – Brantford, Ont.: E.L. Goold, [1887-1889] – 9 – cn C.I.H.M. [630]

THE CANADIAN HORTICULTURAL MAGAZINE – [Montreal?]: Montreal Horticultural Society, v1 no 1 (Apr 1897)- – 9 – cn C.I.H.M. [630]

THE CANADIAN HORTICULTURIST – St. Catharines [Ont.]: Fruit Growers' Association of Ontario, 1878-[1914] – 9 – cn C.I.H.M. [630]

CANADIAN HORTICULTURIST AND BEEKEEPER *see* THE CANADIAN BEE JOURNAL

CANADIAN HOTEL AND RESTAURANT – (Somes issues in v67 and 68 entitled "Hotel and Restaurant". Ceased 1993) – Toronto. v1-71. 1923-93 – 5,9 – cn Micromedia [640]

CANADIAN HOTEL & RESTAURANT – (1985- 5,6,9) – v43 no 4- 1984- . Continuation of: Canadian Hotel Review & Restaurant – 1 – us UMI [640]

CANADIAN HOTEL REVIEW & RESTAURANT – v1-43 no 3 1922-Mar 1965 – 1 – us UMI [640]

CANADIAN HOUSING – Ottawa. v1-10. 1984-1993/94 – 9 – Can$20.00y – cn Micromedia [360]

CANADIAN HUMAN RIGHTS ADVOCATE – Maniwaki. v1-6. 1985-90 – 9 – Can$20.00y – cn Micromedia [320]

CANADIAN HUMAN RIGHTS FOUNDATION – Montreal. 101 docs. 1980-1990 – 60mf – 9 – ne IDC [320]

THE CANADIAN ICE AGE: BEING NOTES ON THE PLEISTOCENE GEOLOGY OF CANADA, WITH ESPECIAL REFERENCE TO THE LIFE OF THE PERIOD AND ITS CLIMATAL CONDITIONS / Dawson, John William – Montreal: W. Dawson, 1893. 00741. (Pre-1900 Canadiana) – 9 – cn C.I.H.M. [560]

CANADIAN ICOR – Toronto, CN. v3 no 1. 1934-1936 – 1r – 1 – Can$30.00 – cn Can Microfilming [072]

CANADIAN ILLUSTRATED NEWS – Hamilton, C.W. v. 1-3. 1862-64 – 1 – 165.00 – cn McLaren [072]

CANADIAN ILLUSTRATED NEWS – Montreal, Canada. 30 oct 1869-29 dec 1883; dec 1885 – 9r – 1 – Can$65.00r – cn Can Microfilming [073]

CANADIAN ILLUSTRATED SHORTHAND WRITER – (Cont by: Bengough's Cosmopolitan Shorthand Writer) – Toronto: Bengough Bros., [1880-1881] – 9 – cn C.I.H.M. [650]

CANADIAN INDEPENDENCE, ANNEXATION AND BRITISH IMPERIAL FEDERATION / Douglas, James – New York: G. P. Putnam, 1894. 02744. (Pre-1900 Canadiana) – 9 – cn C.I.H.M. [971]

CANADIAN INDEPENDENCE MAGAZINE – v1-2. Oct. 1929-Dec. 1930 – 1 – cn Precision [320]

THE CANADIAN INDEPENDENT – Toronto: MacLear, [1854-1894] – 9 – cn C.I.H.M. [971]

Canadian India Famine Fund *see* SUBSCRIPTIONS TO CANADIAN NATIONAL FUND FOR THE RELIEF OF THE DISTRESS IN INDIA:.

CANADIAN INDIAN – 1890-91 – 1 – 60.00 – cn McLaren [073]

CANADIAN INFORMATION PROCESSING – (Cont: CIPS Review 1990/91: Ceased 1993) – Toronto, 1990/91-1993 – 9 – Can$20.00y – cn Micromedia [000]

CANADIAN INFORMATION PROCESSING *see* CIPS REVIEW

CANADIAN INSECT PEST REVIEW – v1-44. v8 index. April 1923-1966 – 1 – cn Precision [630]

CANADIAN INSOLVENCY LEGISLATION : REPORT OF MEETING OF THE LEAGUE HELD ON WEDNESDAY, DECEMBER 4TH, 1895: INCLUDING A STATEMENT BY THE HON. SIR CHARLES TUPPER / British Empire League. Canada – London: Commerce Print. and Pub. Co., 1895? 00296. (Pre-1900 Canadiana) – 9 – cn C.I.H.M. [971]

THE CANADIAN INSPECTOR – Montreal, Canada. n1. jul 1815 – 1r – 1 – Can$25.00 – cn Can Microfilming [072]

Canadian Institute *see*
- PROCEEDINGS OF THE CANADIAN INSTITUTE
- TRANSACTIONS OF THE CANADIAN INSTITUTE

CANADIAN INSTITUTE FOR HISTORICAL MICROREPRODUCTIONS *see*
- EARLY CANADIANA

Canadian Institute for Ukrainian Studies. University of Alberta *see* THE CANADIAN UKRAINIAN COLLECTION

Canadian Institute of Architects *see* CONSTITUTION AND BY-LAWS

Canadian Institute of Food Science and Technology *see* JOURNAL

CANADIAN INSTITUTE. PROCEEDINGS OF THE CANADIAN INSTITUTE *see* THE CANADIAN JOURNAL OF SCIENCE, LITERATURE, AND HISTORY

CANADIAN INTERIORS – Toronto. v1-31. 1964-94 – 9 – Can$28.00y – cn Micromedia [740]

CANADIAN INTERIORS – (v8- . 1975- . 5,6,9) – v. 1-. 1964- – 1 – us UMI [740]

CANADIAN INVESTMENT REVIEW – Toronto. v1-7. 1988-94 – 9 – Can$20.00y – cn Micromedia [332]

THE CANADIAN JEW = KANADER ID – Montreal, CN. v1 no-, v9 no 34. 1926-1936 – 1r – 1 – Can$30.00 – cn Can Microfilming [072]

CANADIAN JEWELER *see* THE TRADER AND CANADIAN JEWELER

CANADIAN JEWELLER – (v1-90 1879-1969 Can$1,650.00 5. Previous title: Trader and Canadian Jeweller) – Toronto. v1-115. 1879-1994 – 5,9 – Can$28.00y – cn Micromedia [730]

CANADIAN JEWELLER – v81- . 1960- – 1,5,6,9 – us UMI [730]

CANADIAN JEWISH ANNUAL – Montreal, CN, 1928 – 1r – 1 – Can$25.00 – cn Can Microfilming [072]

CANADIAN JEWISH CHRONICLE : REVUE – (In English) – Montreal, 22 mai 1914-nov/dec 1976 – 32r – 1 – Can$65.00r – cn Can Microfilming [073]

CANADIAN JEWISH NEWS : MONTREAL EDITION – Montreal. v- n-. 25 nov 1977-dec 1989 – 10r – 1 – Can$65.00 – cn Can Microfilming [072]

THE CANADIAN JEWISH NEWS – v1- . 1960- – 1 – 197.50y – cn McLaren [270]

CANADIAN JEWISH OUTLOOK – v1-21, 1963-88 – 1 – 385.00 – cn McLaren [270]

CANADIAN JEWISH POST = KENEDER IDISHE POST – (In English and Yiddish) – Montreal, CN. v2 no-. 1939-1951 – 1r – 1 – Can$30.00 – cn Can Microfilming [072]

CANADIAN JEWISH REVIEW : ILLUSTRATED – Montreal. v1 n1. 4 nov 1921-16 dec 1966f – 32r – 1 – Can$65.00 – cn Can Microfilming [072]

THE CANADIAN JEWISH REVIEW – Montreal, 1921-1966 – 35r – 1 – Can$60.00r – cn Can Microfilming [072]

THE CANADIAN JEWISH STAR = DER SHTERN – Montreal, CN. v1 no 1. 1931-1932 – 1r – 1 – Can$30.00 – cn Can Microfilming [072]

CANADIAN JEWISH WEEKLY – (In Jewish) – Canada, 1924-78 – 55r – 1 – cn Commonwealth Micro [072]

THE CANADIAN JEWISH WEEKLY = KENEDER VOKHNBLAT – Montreal, CN, 1926-1927 – 1r – 1 – Can$25.00 – cn Can Microfilming [072]

THE CANADIAN JEWISH WORLD = KENEDER IDISHEVELT – Montreal, CN. v2 no 9. 1932 – 1r – 1 – Can$25.00 – cn Can Microfilming [072]

THE CANADIAN JOURNAL – (Cont by: The Canadian Journal of Industry, Science and Art) – Toronto: Published by H. Scobie, for the Council of the Canadian Institute, 1852-1855 – 9 – cn C.I.H.M. [971]

THE CANADIAN JOURNAL – Toronto: W.R. Haight, v1 no 1 (Oct 14 1882)- – 9 – cn C.I.H.M. [971]

CANADIAN JOURNAL FOR THE STUDY OF ADULT EDUCATION – Toronto. v1-8. 1987-94 – 9 – Can$20.00y – cn Micromedia [370]

CANADIAN JOURNAL OF ADMINISTRATIVE SCIENCES – Montreal. v7-12. 1990-95 – 9 – Can$20.00y – cn Micromedia [350]

CANADIAN JOURNAL OF AGRICULTURAL ECONOMICS – (v25- . 5,6,9) – v. 1-. 1952- – 1 – us UMI [630]

CANADIAN JOURNAL OF AGRICULTURAL SCIENCE – (See also: Canadian Journal of Animal Science; Canadian Journal of Plant Science; and Canadian Journal of Soil Science) – v. 1-36. 1921-56 – 1 – us UMI [630]

CANADIAN JOURNAL OF AGRICULTURAL SCIENCE – v30-36. 1950-56 – 1,5,6 – us Princeton Micro [630]

CANADIAN JOURNAL OF ANIMAL SCIENCE – v37-66. 1957-86 – 1,5,6 – us Princeton Micro [073]

CANADIAN JOURNAL OF ANIMAL SCIENCE – (v56- . 5,6,9) – v. 37- 1957- – 1 – us UMI [636]

CANADIAN JOURNAL OF BEHAVIORAL SCIENCE – Old Chelsea. v1-27. 1969-95 – 9 – Can$28.00y – cn Micromedia [300]

CANADIAN JOURNAL OF BEHAVIORAL SCIENCE/REVUE CANADIENNE DES SCIENCES DU COMPORTEMENT – (v7- . 5,6. v8- . 1976- . 9) – v. 1-. 1969- – 1 – us UMI [150]

CANADIAN JOURNAL OF BIOCHEMISTRY – (Cont: Canadian Journal of Biochemistry and Physiology. Cont by: Canadian Journal of Biochemistry and Cellular Biology at v61 1983) – Ottawa. v42-60. 1964-82 – 9 – Can$55.00y – cn Micromedia [574]

CANADIAN JOURNAL OF BIOCHEMISTRY – v. 42-53. 1964-75 – 1,5,6 – us Princeton Micro [540]

CANADIAN JOURNAL OF BIOCHEMISTRY – (v54- . 5,6. v55- . 9) – v. 42- 1964- – 1 – us UMI [540]

CANADIAN JOURNAL OF BIOCHEMISTRY *see* CANADIAN JOURNAL OF BIOCHEMISTRY AND CELLULAR BIOLOGY

CANADIAN JOURNAL OF BIOCHEMISTRY AND CELLULAR BIOLOGY – (Cont: Canadian Journal of Biochemistry. Cont by: Biochemistry and Cellular Biology at v64 1986) – Ottawa. v61-63. 1983-85 – 9 – Can$55.00y – cn Micromedia [574]

CANADIAN JOURNAL OF BIOCHEMISTRY AND CELLULAR BIOLOGY *see*
- BIOCHEMISTRY AND CELL BIOLOGY
- CANADIAN JOURNAL OF BIOCHEMISTRY

CANADIAN JOURNAL OF BIOCHEMISTRY AND PHYSIOLOGY – (Cont: Canadian Journal of Medical Sciences. Cont by: Canadian Journal of Physiology and Pharmacology at v42 1964) – Ottawa. v32-41. 1954-63 – 9 – Can$55.00y – cn Micromedia [073]

CANADIAN JOURNAL OF BIOCHEMISTRY AND PHYSIOLOGY – Ottawa. v32-41.1954-63. H-206/2 – 8 – ne IDC [073]

CANADIAN JOURNAL OF BIOCHEMISTRY AND PHYSIOLOGY – (See also: Canadian Journal of Physiology and Pharmacology) – v22-41. 1944-63 – 1 – us UMI [540]

CANADIAN JOURNAL OF BIOCHEMISTRY AND PHYSIOLOGY – v. 29-41. 1951-1963 – 1,5,6 – us Princeton Micro [540]

CANADIAN JOURNAL OF BIOCHEMISTRY AND PHYSIOLOGY *see*
- CANADIAN JOURNAL OF BIOCHEMISTRY
- CANADIAN JOURNAL OF MEDICAL SCIENCES
- CANADIAN JOURNAL OF PHYSIOLOGY AND PHARMACOLOGY

CANADIAN JOURNAL OF BOTANY = JOURNAL CANADIEN DE BOTANIQUE – (v 29-38 Can$37.00y.v 53-66 Can$73.00y. v 67 Can$82.00) – Ottawa, v29- 1951- – 9 – Can$64.00y – cn Micromedia [073]

CANADIAN JOURNAL OF BOTANY – v. 29-53. 1951-75 – 1,5,6 – us Princeton Micro [580]

CANADIAN JOURNAL OF BOTANY – (v55- . 5,6,9) – v. 13- 1935- – 1 – us UMI [580]

CANADIAN JOURNAL OF BOTANY *see* CANADIAN JOURNAL OF RESEARCH, SECTION C

CANADIAN JOURNAL OF CHEMICAL ENGINEERING – v29-53. 1951-75 – 1,5,6 – us Princeton Micro [660]

CANADIAN JOURNAL OF CHEMICAL ENGINEERING – (v55- . 5,6,9) – v. 22-. 1944- – 1 – us UMI [540]

CANADIAN JOURNAL OF CHEMICAL ENGINEERING – (v59- 1981-.-9) – Ottawa, v32-58 1954-80 – 5 – Can$37.00y – cn Micromedia [660]

CANADIAN JOURNAL OF CHEMICAL ENGINEERING *see* CANADIAN JOURNAL OF TECHNOLOGY

CANADIAN JOURNAL OF CHEMISTRY – (Cont: Canadian Journal of Research, Section B (Chemical Sciences)) – Ottawa. v29- 1951- – 9 – Price varies – cn Micromedia [540]

CANADIAN JOURNAL OF CHEMISTRY – v. 29-53. 1951-75 – 1,5,6 – us Princeton Micro [540]

CANADIAN JOURNAL OF CHEMISTRY – (v53- . 5,6. v54- . 9) – v. 13- 1935- – 1 – us UMI [073]

CANADIAN JOURNAL OF CHEMISTRY *see* CANADIAN JOURNAL OF RESEARCH, SECTION B

CANADIAN JOURNAL OF CIVIL ENGINEERING – Ottawa, v1- 1974- – 9 – Price varies – cn Micromedia [624]

CANADIAN JOURNAL OF CIVIL ENGINEERING/ REVUE CANADIENNE DE GENIE CIVIL – v1- 1974- – 1,5,6,9 – us UMI [624]

CANADIAN JOURNAL OF COMMERCE – Montreal, Canada. v2 n5. 9 fev 1954-v3 n8. 1 mar 1955 – 1r – 1 – Can$40.00 – cn Can Microfilming [073]

Canadian Journal of Commerce *see* THE CANADIAN BANKING SYSTEM: AN EXPOSITION AND A DEFENCE

CANADIAN JOURNAL OF COMMUNICATION – Waterloo, v1- 1974/75- – 9 – Price varies – cn Micromedia [380]

CANADIAN JOURNAL OF COMPARATIVE MEDICINE = REVUE CANADIENNE DE MEDECINE COMPAREE – (1983-. 1,5,6,9) – v32-. 1968- – 1 – us UMI [073]

CANADIAN JOURNAL OF COMPARATIVE MEDICINE – v1-3. 1937-39 – 1 – us UMI [073]

CANADIAN JOURNAL OF COMPARATIVE MEDICINE AND VETERINARY SCIENCE – v4-32. 1940-68 – 1 – us UMI [073]

CANADIAN JOURNAL OF COUNSELLING – Victoria. v21-28. 1987-94 – 9 – Can$20.00y – cn Micromedia [150]

CANADIAN JOURNAL OF DERMATOLOGY – Baie D'Urfe. v1-6. 1989-94 – 9 – Can$20.00y – cn Micromedia [616]

CANADIAN JOURNAL OF EARTH SCIENCES – v1-14. 1964-77 – 1,5,6 – us Princeton Micro [340]

CANADIAN JOURNAL OF EARTH SCIENCES – (v14- . 5,6,9) – v. 1- 1964- – 1 – us UMI [550]

CANADIAN JOURNAL OF EARTH SCIENCES – (v26 1989 Can$64.00) – Ottawa. v1- 1964- – 9 – Can$55.00y – cn Micromedia [550]

CANADIAN JOURNAL OF ECONOMICS – (Cont: Canadian Journal of Economics and Political Science. Index 1968-77 Can$20.00) – Downsview, v1- 1968- – 9 – Price varies – cn Micromedia [330]

CANADIAN JOURNAL OF ECONOMICS – v1-8. 1968-75. See also: Canadian Journal of Economics and Political Science – 1,5,6 – us Princeton Micro [330]

CANADIAN JOURNAL OF ECONOMICS *see* CANADIAN JOURNAL OF ECONOMICS AND POLITICAL SCIENCE

CANADIAN JOURNAL OF ECONOMICS AND POLITICAL SCIENCE – (Cont by: Canadian Journal of Economics and Canadian Journal of Political Science) – Downsview. v1-33. 1935-67 – 5 – Can$100.00 – cn Micromedia [330]

CANADIAN JOURNAL OF ECONOMICS AND POLITICAL SCIENCE – v. 1-33. 1935-67 – 1,5,6 – us Princeton Micro [330]

CANADIAN JOURNAL OF ECONOMICS AND POLITICAL SCIENCE *see* CANADIAN JOURNAL OF ECONOMICS

CANADIAN JOURNAL OF EDUCATION – Vancouver, v1- 1976- – 9 – Can$28.00y – cn Micromedia [370]

CANADIAN JOURNAL OF EDUCATION. REVUE CANADIENNE DE L'EDUCATION – (1983-. 5,6,9) – v1-. 1976- – 1 – us UMI [073]

CANADIAN JOURNAL OF EXPERIMENTAL PSYCHOLOGY – (Cont: Canadian Journal of Psychology at v47 1993) – v47- 1993- – 9 – Can$28.00y – cn Micromedia [150]

CANADIAN JOURNAL OF EXPERIMENTAL PSYCHOLOGY *see* CANADIAN JOURNAL OF PSYCHOLOGY

CANADIAN JOURNAL OF FABRICS – (Cont by: Canadian Textile Journal) – Montreal: E.B. Biggar, [1883-1906?] – 9 – cn C.I.H.M. [670]

CANADIAN JOURNAL OF FAMILY LAW/REVUE CANADIENNE DE DROIT FAMILIAL – v1- 1978- – 1,5,6,9 – us UMI [340]

CANADIAN JOURNAL OF FOREST RESEARCH – Ottawa, v1- 1971- – 9 – Price varies – cn Micromedia [634]

CANADIAN JOURNAL OF FOREST RESEARCH – (v7- . 1977- . 5,6,9) – v. 1-. 1971- – 1 – us UMI [634]

CANADIAN JOURNAL OF GENETICS AND CYTOLOGY – (Cont: Canadian Journal of Genetics and Cytology. Cont by: Genome at v29 1987) – Ottawa. v25-28. 1983-86 – 9 – Can$28.00y – cn Micromedia [574]

CANADIAN JOURNAL OF GENETICS AND CYTOLOGY = JOURNAL CANADIEN DE GENETIQUE ET DE CYTOLOGIE – (Cont by: Canadian Journal of Genetics and Cytology v25 1983) – Ottawa. v10-24. 1968-82 – 9 – Can$28.00y – cn Micromedia [574]

CANADIAN JOURNAL OF GENETICS AND CYTOLOGY – v1-25. 1959-78 – 1,5,6 – us Princeton Micro [574]

CANADIAN JOURNAL OF GENETICS AND CYTOLOGY *see*
- CANADIAN JOURNAL OF GENETICS AND CYTOLOGY
- GENOME

THE CANADIAN JOURNAL OF HEALTH – Toronto: H. Fox, [1894-189- or 19–] – 9 – cn C.I.H.M. [613]

CANADIAN JOURNAL OF HIGHER EDUCATION – (Previous title: Stoa) – Winnipeg, v1- 1971- – 9 – Can$20.00y – cn Micromedia [370]

CANADIAN JOURNAL OF HIGHER EDUCATION *see* STOA

CANADIAN JOURNAL OF HIGHER EDUCATION/LA REVUE CANADIENNE DE L'ENSEIGNEMENT SUPERIEUR. V.5- 1975- – (v.8- 1979- 5,6,9) – 1 – us UMI [073]

CANADIAN JOURNAL OF HISTORY *see* CANADIAN JOURNAL OF HISTORY AND SOCIAL SCIENCE

CANADIAN JOURNAL OF HISTORY AND SOCIAL SCIENCE – (Continued by History and Social Science Teacher) – Toronto, v5-9 1969/70-1973/74 – 5 – Can$100.00set – cn Micromedia [073]

CANADIAN JOURNAL OF HISTORY AND SOCIAL SCIENCE – (See also: History and Social Science Teacher) – v1-9. 1965-1974 – 1 – us UMI [900]

CANADIAN JOURNAL OF HISTORY AND SOCIAL SCIENCE *see* HISTORY AND SOCIAL SCIENCE TEACHER

CANADIAN JOURNAL OF HOSPITAL PHARMACY – (v.32-. 1979- 5,6,9) – v.22-. 1969- – 1 – us UMI [610]

THE CANADIAN JOURNAL OF INDUSTRY, SCIENCE, AND ART – (Cont by: The Canadian Journal of Science, Literature, and History) – Toronto: Printed for the Canadian Institute by Lovell and Gibson, [1856?-1867] – 9 – cn C.I.H.M. [338]

CANADIAN JOURNAL OF INFORMATION AND LIBRARY SCIENCE – (Cont: Canadian Journal of Information Science at v18 1993) – v18- 1993- – 9 – Can$20.00y – cn Micromedia [020]

CANADIAN JOURNAL OF INFORMATION SCIENCE – (Cont by: Canadian Journal of Information and Library Science at v18 1993) – Downsview. v1-17. 1976-92 – 9 – Can$20.00y – cn Micromedia [020]

CANADIAN JOURNAL OF LAW AND JURISPRUDENCE – (Supersedes: University of Western Ontario Law Review) – University of Western Ontario. v1-8. 1988-1995 – 9 – $176.00 set – us Hein [340]

CANADIAN JOURNAL OF LAW AND JURISPRUDENCE *see* UNIVERSITY OF WESTERN ONTARIO LAW REVIEW

CANADIAN JOURNAL OF LIFE INSURANCE – Elmira. v1- 1978/79- – 9 – Can$20.00y – cn Micromedia [360]

CANADIAN JOURNAL OF MATHEMATICS = JOURNAL CANADIEN DE MATHEMATIQUES – (1983-. 1,5,6,9) – v1-. 1949- – 1 – us UMI [073]

CANADIAN JOURNAL OF MATHEMATICS – v. 1-23. 1949-71 – 1,5,6 – us Princeton Micro [510]

CANADIAN JOURNAL OF MEDICAL SCIENCES – (Cont by: Canadian Journal of Biochemistry and Physiology, 1954-63) – Ottawa. v29-31. 1951-53 – 9 – Can$28.00y – cn Micromedia [610]

CANADIAN JOURNAL OF MEDICAL SCIENCES *see*
- CANADIAN JOURNAL OF BIOCHEMISTRY AND PHYSIOLOGY
- CANADIAN JOURNAL OF RESEARCH, SECTION E

CANADIAN JOURNAL OF MICROBIOLOGY – Ottawa. v1-40. 1954-94 – 9 – Can$37.00y – cn Micromedia [576]

CANADIAN JOURNAL OF MICROBIOLOGY – v. 1-21. 1954-75 – 1,5,6 – us Princeton Micro [576]

CANADIAN JOURNAL OF MICROBIOLOGY – (v23- . 5,6,9) – v. 1- 1954- – 1 – us UMI [073]

CANADIAN JOURNAL OF NATIVE EDUCATION – (v1-17 1973/74-1990 Can$80.00) – v1- 1973- – 9 – Can$20.00y – cn Micromedia [370]

CANADIAN JOURNAL OF NATIVE EDUCATION *see* INDIAN ED

CANADIAN JOURNAL OF NATIVE STUDIES – Brandon. v1-14. 1981-94 – 9 – Can$20.00y – cn Micromedia [306]

CANADIAN JOURNAL OF OB/GYN AND WOMEN'S HEALTH CARE – (Cont: Canadian Journal of Obstetrics and Gynecology at v3 no 3 1991) – Baie Durfe. v3- 1991- – 9 – Can$20.00y – cn Micromedia [618]

CANADIAN JOURNAL OF OB/GYN AND WOMEN'S HEALTH CARE *see* CANADIAN JOURNAL OF OBSTETRICS AND GYNECOLOGY

CANADIAN JOURNAL OF OBSTETRICS AND GYNECOLOGY – (Cont by: Canadian Journal of Ob/Gyn and Women's Healthcare at v3 no 3 1991) – Baie D'Urfe, 1989-90 – 9 – Can$20.00y – cn Micromedia [618]

CANADIAN JOURNAL OF OBSTETRICS AND GYNECOLOGY *see* CANADIAN JOURNAL OF OB/GYN AND WOMEN'S HEALTH CARE

CANADIAN JOURNAL OF OCCUPATIONAL THERAPY – v1-3. Sept 1933-37 – 1 – us UMI [073]

THE CANADIAN JOURNAL OF OCCUPATIONAL THERAPY – (1983-. 5,6,9) – v6-. Oct 1939- – 1 – us UMI [073]

CANADIAN JOURNAL OF OCCUPATIONAL THERAPY AND PHYSIOTHERAPY – v4-6. 1937-Apr 1939 – 1 – us UMI [073]

THE CANADIAN JOURNAL OF ODD-FELLOWSHIP – Stratford [Ont.]: Odd-Fellows' Print and Pub Assoc, [1875?-1876] – 9 – cn C.I.H.M. [360]

CANADIAN JOURNAL OF PAEDIATRICS – (Cont: Canadian Journal of Pediatrics at v1 1994) – v1- 1994- – 9 – Can$20.00y – cn Micromedia [618]

CANADIAN JOURNAL OF PEDIATRICS – (Cont by: Canadian Journal of Paediatrics at v1 1994) – Baie D'Urfe, 1989-93 – 9 – Can$20.00y – cn Micromedia [618]

CANADIAN JOURNAL OF PHARMACEUTICAL SCIENCES *see* THE CANADIAN PHARMACEUTICAL JOURNAL

THE CANADIAN JOURNAL OF PHILATELY – Toronto: H.A. Fowler, [1893] – 9 – cn C.I.H.M. [760]

THE CANADIAN JOURNAL OF PHILATELY *see* THE INTERNATIONAL PHILATELIST

CANADIAN JOURNAL OF PHILOSOPHY – Calgary. v10-24. 1980-94 – 9 – Can$28.00y – cn Micromedia [100]

CANADIAN JOURNAL OF PHOTOGRAPHY – 1870-75 – 1 – 45.00 – cn McLaren [770]

CANADIAN JOURNAL OF PHYSICS = JOURNAL CANADIEN DE PHYSIQUE – (v29-66 Can$55.00y) – Ottawa, v29- 1951- – 9 – Can$46.00y – cn Micromedia [073]

CANADIAN JOURNAL OF PHYSICS – v. 29-53. 1951-75 – 1,5,6 – us Princeton Micro [530]

CANADIAN JOURNAL OF PHYSICS – (v54- . 5,6,9) – v. 13- 1935- – 1 – us UMI [073]

CANADIAN JOURNAL OF PHYSICS *see* CANADIAN JOURNAL OF RESEARCH, SECTION A

CANADIAN JOURNAL OF PHYSIOLOGY AND PHARMACOLOGY = JOURNAL CANADIEN DE PHYSIOLOGIE ET PHARMACOLOGIE – (Cont: Canadian Journal of Biochemistry and Physiology) – Ottawa. v42-72. 1964-94 – 9 – Price varies – cn Micromedia [612]

CANADIAN JOURNAL OF PHYSIOLOGY AND PHARMACOLOGY – v. 42-53. 1964-75 – 1,5,6 – us Princeton Micro [612]

CANADIAN JOURNAL OF PHYSIOLOGY AND PHARMACOLOGY – (v55- . 5,6,9) – v. 42- 1964- – 1 – us UMI [612]

CANADIAN JOURNAL OF PHYSIOLOGY AND PHARMACOLOGY *see* CANADIAN JOURNAL OF BIOCHEMISTRY AND PHYSIOLOGY

CANADIAN JOURNAL OF PLANT SCIENCE – v37-66. 1957-86 – 1,5,6 – us Princeton Micro [580]

CANADIAN JOURNAL OF PLANT SCIENCE – (v56- . 5,6,9) – v. 37- 1957- – 1 – us UMI [580]

CANADIAN JOURNAL OF POLITICAL SCIENCE – (Mf available to v9 1976 only) – Ottawa. v1-9. 1968-76 – 9 – Can$28.00y – cn Micromedia [320]

CANADIAN JOURNAL OF POLTICAL SCIENCE *see* CANADIAN JOURNAL OF ECONOMICS AND POLITICAL SCIENCE

CANADIAN JOURNAL OF PSYCHIATRIC NURSING – (v.20-. 1979- 5,6,9) – v.17-. Jun 1966- – 1 – us UMI [610]

CANADIAN JOURNAL OF PSYCHOLOGY – (Cont by: Canadian Journal of Experimental Psychology at v47 1993. v44-46 1990-92 Can$28.00y) – Old Chelsea. v1-46. 1947-92 – 9 – Can$20.00y – cn Micromedia [150]

CANADIAN JOURNAL OF PSYCHOLOGY *see* CANADIAN JOURNAL OF EXPERIMENTAL PSYCHOLOGY

CANADIAN JOURNAL OF PUBLIC AND COOPERATIVE ECONOMY – Montreal, v1- 1968- – 9 – Can$20.00y – cn Micromedia [330]

CANADIAN JOURNAL OF PUBLIC HEALTH – v. 36-62. 1945-1971 – 1,5,6 – us Princeton Micro [610]

CANADIAN JOURNAL OF REHABILITATION – Edmonton. v1-7. 1987/88-1993/94 – 9 – Can$20.00y – cn Micromedia [360]

CANADIAN JOURNAL OF RELIGIOUS THOUGHT – v1-9. 1924-32 (complete) – Inquire – 1 – ATLA 1993-S512 – us A.T.L.A. [073]

CANADIAN JOURNAL OF REMOTE SENSING – (v3- . 1977- . 5,6,9) – v. 1-. 1975- – 1 – us UMI [621]

CANADIAN JOURNAL OF RESEARCH – (all sections). v. 1-28. 1929-1950 – 1,5,6 – us Princeton Micro [000]

CANADIAN JOURNAL OF RESEARCH / National Research Council of Canada – Ottawa, 1930. V.3 – 10mf – 9 – ne IDC [500]

CANADIAN JOURNAL OF RESEARCH – Ottawa. v1-12. 1929-35 – 9 – Can$28.00y – cn Micromedia [000]

CANADIAN JOURNAL OF RESEARCH – (See also: Canadian Journal of Physics; Canadian Journal of Chemistry; Canadian Journal of Botany; Canadian Journal of Zoology; Canadian Journal of Biochemistry and Physiology; and Canadian Journal of Chemical Engineering) – v1-12. 1929-35 – 1 – us UMI [500]

CANADIAN JOURNAL OF RESEARCH *see* CANADIAN JOURNAL OF CHEMISTRY

CANADIAN JOURNAL OF RESEARCH IN SEMIOTICS – (Cont by RSSI-Researches Semiotiques/Semiotic Inquiry, 1981) – Montreal. v1-7. 1973-79/80 – 9 – Can$20.00y – cn Micromedia [400]
CANADIAN JOURNAL OF RESEARCH IN SEMIOTICS *see* RSSI-RESEARCHES SEMIOTIQUES
CANADIAN JOURNAL OF RESEARCH, SECTION A : PHYSICAL SCIENCES – (Cont by: Canadian Journal of Physics, 1951) – Ottawa. v13-28. 1935-1950 – 9 – Can$20.00y – cn Micromedia [530]
CANADIAN JOURNAL OF RESEARCH SECTION A (PHYSICAL SCIENCE) *see* CANADIAN JOURNAL OF PHYSICS
CANADIAN JOURNAL OF RESEARCH, SECTION B : CHEMICAL SCIENCES – (Cont by: Canadian Journal of Chemistry, 1951) – Ottawa. v13-28. 1935-1950 – 9 – Can$20.00y – cn Micromedia [540]
CANADIAN JOURNAL OF RESEARCH, SECTION C : BOTANICAL SCIENCES – (Cont by: Canadian Journal of Botany, 1951) – Ottawa. v13-28. 1935-1950 – 9 – Can$20.00y – cn Micromedia [580]
CANADIAN JOURNAL OF RESEARCH SECTION C (BOTANICAL SCIENCES) *see* CANADIAN JOURNAL OF BOTANY
CANADIAN JOURNAL OF RESEARCH SECTION C (ZOOLOGICAL SCIENCES) *see* CANADIAN JOURNAL OF ZOOLOGY
CANADIAN JOURNAL OF RESEARCH, SECTION D : ZOOLOGICAL SCIENCES – (Cont by: Canadian Journal of Zoology, 1951) – Ottawa. v13-28. 1935-1950 – 9 – Can$20.00y – cn Micromedia [590]
CANADIAN JOURNAL OF RESEARCH, SECTION E : MEDICAL SCIENCES – (Cont by: Canadian Journal of Medical Sciences, 1951-1953) – Ottawa. v22-28. 1944-1950 – 9 – Can$20.00y – cn Micromedia [610]
CANADIAN JOURNAL OF RESEARCH, SECTION F : TECHNOLOGY – (Cont by: Canadian Journal of Technology, 1951-1956/57) – Ottawa. v22-28. 1944-1950 – 9 – Can$20.00y – cn Micromedia [600]
CANADIAN JOURNAL OF SCHOOL PSYCHOLOGY – Vancouver. v3-10. 1987/88-1994 – Can$20.00y – cn Micromedia [150]
CANADIAN JOURNAL OF SCIENCE, LITERATURE AND HISTORY – v1-3. Aug 1852-Jul 1877. Title varies. Missing Aug 1878-Jan 1879 – 1 – cn Precision [500]
THE CANADIAN JOURNAL OF SCIENCE, LITERATURE AND HISTORY *see* THE CANADIAN JOURNAL OF INDUSTRY, SCIENCE, AND ART
THE CANADIAN JOURNAL OF SCIENCE, LITERATURE, AND HISTORY – (Cont by: Canadian Institute. Proceedings of the Canadian Institute) – Toronto: Canadian Institute, [1868-1878] – 9 – cn C.I.H.M. [500]
CANADIAN JOURNAL OF SOCIOLOGY = CAHIERS CANADIENS DE SOCIOLOGIE – Edmonton. v1-20. 1975-95 – 9 – Can$28.00y – cn Micromedia [301]
CANADIAN JOURNAL OF SOIL SCIENCE – v37-59. 1957-79 – 1,5,6 – 2287.00 – us Princeton Micro [631]
CANADIAN JOURNAL OF SOIL SCIENCE – (v56- . 5,6,9) – v. 37- 1957- – 1 – us UMI [631]
CANADIAN JOURNAL OF SPECIAL EDUCATION – Vancouver. v1-10. 1985-94 – 9 – Can$20.00y – cn Micromedia [370]
CANADIAN JOURNAL OF SPORT SCIENCE – (Microfilming rights to 1990 only) – Champaign, v1-11. 1976-90 – 9 – Can$20.00y – cn Micromedia [790]
CANADIAN JOURNAL OF TECHNOLOGY – (Cont by: Canadian Journal of Chemical Engineering) – Toronto. v29-34. 1951-56/57 – 9 – Can$20.00y – cn Micromedia [660]
CANADIAN JOURNAL OF TECHNOLOGY *see*
– CANADIAN JOURNAL OF CHEMICAL ENGINEERING
– CANADIAN JOURNAL OF RESEARCH, SECTION F
CANADIAN JOURNAL OF UNIVERSITY CONTINUING EDUCATION – Ottawa. v1-20. 1973-94 – 9 – Can$20.00y – cn Micromedia [370]
CANADIAN JOURNAL OF WOMEN AND THE LAW – Ottawa. v1-8. 1985/86-1995 – 9 – Can$28.00y – cn Micromedia [340]
CANADIAN JOURNAL OF ZOOLOGY – Ottawa, v29- 1951- – 9 – Can$73.00y – cn Micromedia [073]
CANADIAN JOURNAL OF ZOOLOGY – v. 29-53. 1951-75 – 1,5,6 – us Princeton Micro [590]
CANADIAN JOURNAL OF ZOOLOGY – (v54- . 5,6,9) – v. 13- 1935- – 1 – us UMI [073]
CANADIAN JOURNAL OF ZOOLOGY *see* CANADIAN JOURNAL OF RESEARCH, SECTION D
THE CANADIAN JOURNALIST = LE JOURNALISTE CANADIEN – Montreal, Canada. 1 aut 1920 – 1r – 1 – Can$25.00 – cn Can Microfilming [072]
CANADIAN LABORATORY – (Incorporates: Canadian Research. Ceased v2 1990) – Willowdale. v1-2. 1989-1990 – 1 – Can$60.00y – cn Micromedia [500]
CANADIAN LABOUR = LE TRAVAILLEUR CANADIEN – (French filmed separately as Travailleur Canadien 1971-1977. Billingual from 1978. Ceased v34 1989) – Ottawa. v1-34. 1956-89 – 5,9 – Price varies – cn Micromedia [073]
CANADIAN LABOUR *see* TRAVAILLEUR CANADIEN
THE CANADIAN LAW OF FIXTURES / Manning, Harold Ernest – Toronto: Canada Law Book Co. 1927. 289-364p. LL-2378 – 1 – us L of C Photodup [340]
THE CANADIAN LAW OF PARTNERSHIP / Henderson, Robert B – Montreal: Snow Law Pub. Co., 1900. 05540. (Pre-1900 Canadiana) – 9 – cn C.I.H.M. [971]
CANADIAN LAW REVIEW – Toronto, CN: Canadian Law Review Co. v1-6. 1901-07 (all publ) – 14mf – 9 – $63.00 – LLMC 84-432 – us L.L.M.C. [073]
CANADIAN LAW REVIEW – Toronto. v1-6. 1901-07 – 1 – $80.00 – us Hein [073]
CANADIAN LAW TIMES / Canada. General – (Includes 2v of digest/index. Cont by: The Canadian Bar Review which is not offered by LLMC) – v1-42. 1881-1922 (all publ) – 467mf – 9 – $700.00 – LLMC 81-016 – us L.L.M.C. [340]
CANADIAN LAW TIMES – Toronto. v1-42. 1881-1922 – 1 – $560.00 – us Hein [073]
CANADIAN LAW TIMES – v1-42. Jan. 1881-Dec. 1922 – 1 – cn Precision [323]
THE CANADIAN LAW TIMES *see* THE CANADA LAW JOURNAL
Canadian Lawn Tennis Association *see* CONSTITUTION AND BY-LAWS
CANADIAN LAWYER – v1-19. 1977-95 – 9 – $177.50 set – us Hein [340]
CANADIAN LEAVES: HISTORY, ART, SCIENCE, LITERATURE, COMMERCE: A SERIES OF NEW PAPERS READ BEFORE THE CANADIAN CLUB OF NEW YORK – Ed. by G. M. Fairchild, illus. by Thomson Willing. New York: N. Thompson, 1887. 00428. (Pre-1900 Canadiana) – 9 – cn C.I.H.M. [971]
Canadian Library Association *see*
– CANADIAN LIBRARY JOURNAL
– CM
CANADIAN LIBRARY JOURNAL / Canadian Library Association – 1944-90 – 16r – 1 – $1,040.00 – cn Library Assoc [971]
CANADIAN LIFE = KENEDER LEBN – Toronto, CN, 1937 – 1r – 1 – Can$25.00 – cn Can Microfilming [072]
CANADIAN LIFE AND SCENERY : WITH HINTS TO INTENDING IMMIGRANTS AND SETTLERS / Argyll, John Douglas Sutherland Campbell, Duke of – London: Religious Tract Society, 1886. 00048. (Pre-1900 Canadiana) – 9 – cn C.I.H.M. [971]
CANADIAN LITERARY JOURNAL *see* THE CANADIAN MAGAZINE
THE CANADIAN LITERARY JOURNAL – (Cont by: The Canadian Magazine) – Toronto: Flint & Van Norman, [1870-1871] – 9 – cn C.I.H.M. [420]
THE CANADIAN LITERARY MAGAZINE – York [Toronto]: G Gurnett, [1883] – 9 – cn C.I.H.M. [400]
THE CANADIAN LITERARY NEWS LETTER AND BOOKSELLERS' ADVERTISER – Montreal: H Ramsey, [1855] – 9 – cn C.I.H.M. [400]
CANADIAN LITERATURE/LITTERATURE CANADIENNE – (v51- . 5,6. v63- . 9) – Summer 1959- – 1 – us UMI [420]
CANADIAN LIVE-STOCK AND FARM JOURNAL *see* FARMING
THE CANADIAN LIVE-STOCK AND FARM JOURNAL – (Cont: Canadian Live-Stock Journal. Contd by: Farming. Has Supplement: The Household Companion) – Hamilton [Ont.]: Stock Journal Co., [1886-1895?] – 9 – cn C.I.H.M. [630]
THE CANADIAN LIVE-STOCK AND FARM JOURNAL *see* CANADIAN LIVE-STOCK JOURNAL
CANADIAN LIVE-STOCK JOURNAL – (Cont: Canadian Stock Raisers' Journal. Contd by: The Canadian Live-Stock and Farm Journal) – Hamilton [Ont]: Stock Journal Co., [1885?-1886] – 9 – cn C.I.H.M. [630]
CANADIAN LIVE-STOCK JOURNAL *see*
– THE CANADIAN LIVE-STOCK AND FARM JOURNAL
– CANADIAN STOCK-RAISERS' JOURNAL
CANADIAN MACHINERY AND MANUFACTURING NEWS *see* CANADIAN MACHINERY AND METALWORKING
CANADIAN MACHINERY AND METAL WORKING – v1-. 1905- – 1,5,6,9 – us UMI [670]
CANADIAN MACHINERY AND METALWORKING – (v66- 1970-.-9) – Toronto, v1-65 1905-69 – 5 – Can$37.00y – cn Micromedia [621]
CANADIAN MACHINERY & MANUFACTURING NEWS – Toronto, Canada. 1909-12; Jan 1919-Mar 1928.-w. 31mqn reels – 1 – uk British Libr Newspaper [073]
CANADIAN MAGAZINE – (Cont by: Canadian Weekend 1979; Today's Magazine 1980-1982) – Toronto, 1968-78 – 9 – Can$55.00 – cn Micromedia [073]
CANADIAN MAGAZINE – York [Toronto]: R Stanton, [1883] – 9 – cn C.I.H.M. [971]
CANADIAN MAGAZINE *see* CANADIAN WEEKEND
THE CANADIAN MAGAZINE – (Cont: Canadian Literary Journal) – Toronto: Irving, Flint, 1871-[1872?] – 9 – cn C.I.H.M. [400]
THE CANADIAN MAGAZINE – Montreal, Canada. jul 1823-jun 1825 – 1r – 1 – Can$40.00 – cn Can Microfilming [073]
THE CANADIAN MAGAZINE *see* THE CANADIAN LITERARY JOURNAL
THE CANADIAN MAGAZINE OF POLITICS, ART, SCIENCE AND LITERATURE – 1904-39 – 25r – 1 – $1,625.00 – cn Library Assoc [971]
CANADIAN MAGAZINE OF SCIENCE AND THE INDUSTRIAL ARTS *see* SCIENTIFIC CANADIAN MECHANICS' MAGAZINE AND PATENT OFFICE RECORD
THE CANADIAN MAGAZINE OF SCIENCE AND THE INDUSTRIAL ARTS, PATENT OFFICE RECORD – (Cont: Scientific Canadian Mechanics' Magazine and Patent Office Record) – Montreal?: s.n., 1883-1891? – 9 – cn C.I.H.M. [600]
CANADIAN MAIL – Montreal, Canada. v5 n1. jan 1948-v14 n1. jan/fev 1957 – 1r – 1 – Can$35.00 – cn Can Microfilming [072]
THE CANADIAN MAIL AND MONTREAL GAZETTE FOR EUROPE *see* THE CANADIAN MAIL AND MONTREAL WEEKLY GAZETTE
THE CANADIAN MAIL AND MONTREAL WEEKLY GAZETTE / ed by Raid, Fenian – (The Canadian Mail and Montreal Gazette for Europe n 264 9 jan 1860. n341 5 jul 1861) – Montreal, Canada. n583. 2 dec 1864-n592. 3 fev 1865 – 1r – 1 – Can$35.00 – cn Can Microfilming [072]
CANADIAN MANAGER – Willowdale. v1-20. 1976-95 – 9 – Can$20.00y – cn Micromedia [650]
A CANADIAN MANUAL ON THE PROCEDURE AT MEETINGS OF MUNICIPAL COUNCILS, SHAREHOLDERS AND DIRECTORS OF COMPANIES, SYNODS, CONVENTIONS, SOCIETIES AND PUBLIC BODIES GENERALLY : WITH AN INTRODUCTORY REVIEW OF THE RULES AND USAGES OF PARLIAMENT THAT GOVERN PUBLIC ASSEMBLIES IN CANADA / Bourinot, John George – Toronto: Carswell Co., 1894. 00224. (Pre-1900 Canadiana) – 9 – cn C.I.H.M. [350]
CANADIAN MANUFACTURER – (Title changed to: The Manufacturer at v4 1989. Ceased v4 no 10 1989. v1-2 1985/86-1987 Can$85.00) – Toronto. v1-4. 1985/86-1989 – 1 – Can$60.00y – cn Micromedia [670]
CANADIAN MANUFACTURER *see* THE CANADIAN MANUFACTURER AND INDUSTRIAL WORLD
THE CANADIAN MANUFACTURER – (Cont: The Canadian Manufacturer and Industrial World) – Toronto: Canadian Manufacturer Pub. Co., [1908-19–] – 9 – cn C.I.H.M. [670]
CANADIAN MANUFACTURER AND INDUSTRIAL WORLD *see* INDUSTRIAL WORLD AND NATIONAL ECONOMIST
THE CANADIAN MANUFACTURER AND INDUSTRIAL WORLD – (Contd by: Canadian Manufacturer. Continues: Industrial World and National Economist) – Toronto: Canadian Manufacturer Co., [1882-1908] – 9 – cn C.I.H.M. [670]
Canadian Manufacturers' Association *see* SOUVENIR, 1893
THE CANADIAN MANUFACUTRER AND INDUSTRIAL WORLD *see* THE CANADIAN MANUFACTURER
CANADIAN MASONIC PIONEER – Montreal: Owler & Stevenson, [1856-1857] – 9 – cn C.I.H.M. [360]
CANADIAN MATRIMONIAL NEWS – Toronto: M. Watson, [1892-189- or 19–] – 9 – cn C.I.H.M. [306]
CANADIAN MECHANIC'S MAGAZINE AND PATENT OFFICE RECORD *see* SCIENTIFIC CANADIAN MECHANICS' MAGAZINE AND PATENT OFFICE RECORD
CANADIAN MECHANICS MAGAZINE AND PATENT OFFICE RECORD – (Cont: The Canadian Patent Office Record and Mechanics' Magazine. Contd by: Scientific Canadian Mechanics' Magazine and Patent Office Record) – Ottawa: Burland-Desbarats Litho. Co., 1876-1878 – 9 – cn C.I.H.M. [600]
CANADIAN MECHANICS' MAGAZINE AND PATENT OFFICE RECORD *see* THE CANADIAN PATENT OFFICE RECORD AND MECHANICS' MAGAZINE
Canadian Medical Association *see* ORIGINE ET ORGANISATION DE L'ASSOCIATION MEDICALE CANADIENNE: AVEC LES MINUTES DES ASSEMBLEES TENUE A QUEBEC, OCTOBRE 1867, ET A MONTREAL, SEPTEMBRE 1868
Canadian Medical Association – Association medicale Canadienne *see* JOURNAL
THE CANADIAN MEN AND WOMEN OF THE TIME: A HANDBOOK OF CANADIAN BIOGRAPHY OF LIVING CHARACTERS / ed by Morgan, Henry J – Toronto: William Briggs, 1912. Canada reel 3. (Cox Library Collection) – 5 – us Americana [920]
CANADIAN MENNONITE REPORTER – v1, no.1-9. 1971 – 1 – us UMI [240]
THE CANADIAN MERCANTILE TEST – Toronto: [s.n., 18—18– or 19–] – 9 – cn C.I.H.M. [380]
CANADIAN MERCHANTS MAGAZINE AND COMMERCIAL REVIEW – Montreal, Canada. v2 n1. oct 1857 – 1r – 1 – Can$25.00 – cn Can Microfilming [073]
CANADIAN MESSENGER – Montreal. v10 n13. 1 jul 1875 – 15r – 1 – Can$25.00 – cn Can Microfilming [072]
THE CANADIAN MESSENGER – (Cont: Messenger of the Sacred Heart. Contd by: The Canadian Messenger of the Sacred Heart) – Montreal: s.n., 1892-1899 – 9 – cn C.I.H.M. [240]
THE CANADIAN MESSENGER *see*
– THE CANADIAN MESSENGER OF THE SACRED HEART
– LE MESSAGER CANADIEN DU SACRE-COEUR DE JESUS
– MESSENGER OF THE SACRED HEART
THE CANADIAN MESSENGER OF THE SACRED HEART – (Cont: The Canadian Messenger) – Montreal: s.n., 1899-1961 – 9 – cn C.I.H.M. [240]
THE CANADIAN MESSENGER OF THE SACRED HEART *see* THE CANADIAN MESSENGER
CANADIAN METALLURGICAL QUARTERLY – v1- 1962- – 5,6,9 – us UMI [660]
THE CANADIAN METHODIST MAGAZINE – (Absorbed: Earnest Christianity. Contd by: The Methodist Magazine) – Toronto: S Rose, 1875-1888 – 9 – cn C.I.H.M. [240]
THE CANADIAN METHODIST MAGAZINE *see* THE METHODIST MAGAZINE
THE CANADIAN METHODIST QUARTERLY – (Contd by: The Canadian Methodist Review) – Toronto: Published Under the Auspices of the Theological Union, [1889-1893] – 9 – cn C.I.H.M. [240]
THE CANADIAN METHODIST QUARTERLY *see* THE CANADIAN METHODIST REVIEW
THE CANADIAN METHODIST REVIEW – (Cont: The Canadian Methodist Quarterly. Is Absorbed by: Methodist Magazine and Review) – Toronto: Published Under the Auspices of the Theological Union, 1894-1895 – 9 – cn C.I.H.M. [240]
THE CANADIAN METHODIST REVIEW *see* THE METHODIST MAGAZINE AND REVIEW

THE CANADIAN MILITARY GAZETTE – Montreal: [s.n., 1878-18–?] – 9 – cn C.I.H.M. [355]
CANADIAN MILITARY GAZETTE. (MILITIA GAZETTE) – v1-10. May 1885-95 – 1 – cn Precision [355]
Canadian Military Institute *see* CONSTITUTION AND BY-LAWS, AS ADOPTED AT A GENERAL MEETING HELD ON MARCH 3RD, 1890
CANADIAN MILITARY REVIEW – (Other Language ed: Partie Francaise de la Revue Militaire Canadienne) – Quebec: [s.n., 1880-1881] – 9 – cn C.I.H.M. [355]
THE CANADIAN MILITARY REVIEW – Ottawa?: s.n., 1877-18– or 19– – cn C.I.H.M. [355]
CANADIAN MILITARY REVIEW, (QUEBEC, QUEBEC) *see* PARTIE FRANCAISE DE LA REVUE MILITAIRE CANADIENNE
THE CANADIAN MILITIA GAZETTE – Montreal, Canada. v7 n24. 16 jul 1892 – 1r – 1 – Can$25.00 – cn Can Microfilming [073]
THE CANADIAN MILITIA: ITS ORGANIZATION AND PRESENT CONDITION / Davis, Robert Henry – By Lieut.-Col. Davis, Commanding 37th Regt. of Militia or Haldimand Rifles Batt. Caledonia, Ont.: W. Sawle, 1873. 02599. (Pre-1900 Canadiana) – 9 – cn C.I.H.M. [971]
THE CANADIAN MILITIA MAN – Toronto: G M Rose, [1899-19–] – 9 – cn C.I.H.M. [355]
THE CANADIAN MILLER AND GRAIN TRADE REVIEW – Toronto: A G Mortimer, [188–1894] – 9 – cn C.I.H.M. [630]
THE CANADIAN MINER – Montreal, Canada. v4 n11. 4 jan 1934; v4 n12. 11 jan 1934 – 1r – 1 – Can$25.00 – cn Can Microfilming [073]
THE CANADIAN MINER – Toronto: Canadian Miner Pub. Co., 1897-[189- or 19–] – 9 – cn C.I.H.M. [622]
CANADIAN MINING AND MECHANICAL REVIEW – (Cont: Canadian Mining Review (1882-1890). Continued by: Canadian Mining Review (1894-1907)) – Ottawa: [Review Pub. Co., 1891-1894] – 9 – cn C.I.H.M. [622]
CANADIAN MINING AND MECHANICAL REVIEW *see* THE CANADIAN MINING REVIEW
CANADIAN MINING AND MECHNICAL REVIEW *see* CANADIAN MINING REVIEW
CANADIAN MINING AND METALLURGICAL BULLETIN – v16-47. 1923-1954 – 1,5,6 – us Princeton Micro [622]
THE CANADIAN MINING GAZETTE – Toronto: [s.n., 1899-19–] – 9 – cn C.I.H.M. [622]
CANADIAN MINING HANDBOOK – Toronto, Ontario, CN. 1931-80 – 40r – 1 – cn Commonwealth Micro [073]
CANADIAN MINING JOURNAL – Toronto and Gardenvale, Canada. Jul 1912-Dec 1938; Jul-Dec 1939; Apr 1941- Sep 1951 (imperfect). -w – 70r – 1 – uk British Libr Newspaper [622]
CANADIAN MINING JOURNAL – (v108-116 1987-95 9) – Don Mills. v1-116. 1883-1995 – 5,9 – Price varies – cn Micromedia [622]
CANADIAN MINING JOURNAL – v31-93. 1910-1972 – 1,5,6 – us Princeton Micro [622]
THE CANADIAN MINING JOURNAL *see* THE CANADIAN MINING REVIEW
CANADIAN MINING OPINION / ed by Isbell, Irving J – Montreal, Canada. 30 jan 1926 – 1r – 1 – Can$25.00 – cn Can Microfilming [072]
CANADIAN MINING REVIEW – Canada. -m. Jan 1889-May 1890; May 1891; Jul, Aug, Dec 1892; Feb 1893-Jun 1902 – 812r – 1 – uk British Libr Newspaper [622]
CANADIAN MINING REVIEW – (Contd by: Canadian Mining and Mechnical Review) – Ottawa: [Review Pub. Co., 1882?-1890] – 9 – cn C.I.H.M. [622]
CANADIAN MINING REVIEW *see*
- CANADIAN MINING AND MECHANICAL REVIEW

THE CANADIAN MINING REVIEW – (Cont: Canadian Mining and Mechanical Review. Continued by: The Canadian Mining Journal) – Ottawa: [Review Pub. Co., 1894-1907] – 9 – cn C.I.H.M. [622]
THE CANADIAN MISCELLANY : OR, THE RELIGIOUS, LITERARY AND STATISTICAL INTELLIGENCER – Montreal, Canada. avr 1828-aut 1838 – 1r – 1 – Can$25.00 – cn Can Microfilming [073]
THE CANADIAN MISSIONARY LINK – (Merged with: Baptist Visitor. Merged to Become: The Link & Visitor) – Toronto: [s.n., 1878-1927]; (Toronto: Dudley & Burns) – 9 – cn C.I.H.M. [240]
CANADIAN MODERN LANGUAGE REVIEW – Willowdale. v36-50. 1979/80-1993/94 – 9 – Can$28.00y – cn Micromedia [400]
CANADIAN MONETARY TIMES AND INSURANCE CHRONICLE *see* THE TRADE REVIEW AND INTERCOLONIAL JOURNAL OF COMMERCE
CANADIAN MONEY SAVER – Bath. v1-13. 1981/82-1993/94 – 9 – Can$20.00y – cn Micromedia [336]
CANADIAN MONTHLY AND NATIONAL REVIEW – v1-13. Jan. 1872-June 1878. Joined Belford's Monthly Magazine to form Rose Belford's Monthly and National Review – 1 – cn Precision [971]
THE CANADIAN MONTHLY AND NATIONAL REVIEW – (Merged with: Belford's Monthly Magazine. Merged to Become: Rose-Belford's Canadian Monthly and National Review) – Toronto: Adam, Stevenson, [1872-1878] – 9 – cn C.I.H.M. [971]
THE CANADIAN MONTHLY AND NATIONAL REVIEW *see* ROSE-BELFORD'S CANADIAN MONTHLY AND NATIONAL REVIEW
THE CANADIAN MONTHLY FREE PRESS – Montreal: Devins & Bolton, [1877-18–?] – 9 – cn C.I.H.M. [070]
CANADIAN MUNICIPAL JOURNAL – Canada. 1905-17.-m. 6 reels – 1 – uk British Libr Newspaper [073]
THE CANADIAN MUNICIPAL JOURNAL – Toronto: A.L. Willson, [1891?-1892] – 9 – cn C.I.H.M. [350]
CANADIAN MUSEUM OF CIVILIZATION : MERCURY SERIES – Ottawa, 1972-1990 – 9 – cn Micromedia [060]
THE CANADIAN MUSIC AND DRAMA – Kingston [Ont.]: Canadian Music and Drama, [1895-189- or 19–] – 9 – cn C.I.H.M. [780]
CANADIAN MUSIC AND TRADES JOURNAL – Toronto: D C Nixon, [1900-1930?] – 9 – cn C.I.H.M. [780]
CANADIAN MUSIC EDUCATOR – v34-36. 1991/92-1993/94 – 9 – Can$20.00y – cn Micromedia [780]
CANADIAN MUSIC FOLIO – Toronto: D J Johnston Canadian Music Folio Co., [18–?-18– or 19–] – 9 – cn C.I.H.M. [780]
CANADIAN MUSIC TRADE – (1990/91 vol numbered 12 in error by publ) – Toronto. v1-15. 1979/80-1993/94 – 9 – Can$20.00y – cn Micromedia [073]
CANADIAN MUSICIAN – Toronto. v1-17. 1979-95 – 9 – Can$28.00y – cn Micromedia [780]
THE CANADIAN MUSICIAN – (Contd by: Musician (Toronto, Ont.)) – Toronto: Whaley, Royce, [1889?-1899?] – 9 – cn C.I.H.M. [780]
THE CANADIAN MUTE – Belleville, Ont.: Institution for the Deaf and Dumb, [1892-19–] – 9 – cn C.I.H.M. [305]
CANADIAN NATION – v1-2. Feb Apr 1928-May Jun 1929 – 1 – cn Precision [971]
THE CANADIAN NATION – Toronto: [s.n., 1890?-189- or 19–] – 9 – cn C.I.H.M. [971]
Canadian National Association *see* CONSTITUTION AND BY-LAWS.
CANADIAN NATIONAL MAGAZINE – v25. 1939-40 – 1 – cn Precision [971]
CANADIAN NATIONALISM AND THE WAR – Montreal: s.n., 1916. SEM105P392 – 1mf – 9 – Can$2.25 – cn Bibl Nat [971]
THE CANADIAN NATIONALITY / Binmore, Charles J – London: Hamilton, Adams & Co., Montreal: Drysdale & Co., 1888. 04364. (Pre-1900 Canadiana) – 9 – cn C.I.H.M. [305]
Canadian Native Friendship Center *see* EDMONTON NATIVE NEWS
THE CANADIAN NATURALIST AND GEOLOGIST – (Contd by: The Canadian Naturalist and Quarterly Journal of Science) – Montreal: B Dawson, [1856-1868] – 9 – cn C.I.H.M. [500]
THE CANADIAN NATURALIST AND GEOLOGIST *see* THE CANADIAN NATURALIST AND QUARTERLY JOURNAL OF SCIENCE
THE CANADIAN NATURALIST AND QUARTERLY JOURNAL OF SCIENCE – (Cont: The Canadian Naturalist and Geologist. Contd by: The Canadian Record of Science) – Montreal: Dawson Bros., 1869-1883 – 9 – cn C.I.H.M. [500]
THE CANADIAN NATURALIST AND QUARTERLY JOURNAL OF SCIENCE *see*
- THE CANADIAN NATURALIST AND GEOLOGIST
- THE CANADIAN RECORD OF SCIENCE

THE CANADIAN NEGRO – v. 1-4. 1953-56 – 1 – 65.00 – cn McLaren [305]
CANADIAN NEWS – London, England. 1856-75 – 9r – 1 – $585.00 – cn Library Assoc [971]
CANADIAN NEWS – London. -w. 11 Jun 1856-16 Mar 1876. (16 reels) – 1 – uk British Libr Newspaper [072]
THE CANADIAN NORTH WEST – Winnipeg: A Begg, [1880?-18– or 19–] – 9 – cn C.I.H.M. [971]
CANADIAN NOTABILITIES VOL.1 / Dent, John Charles – Toronto: J. Magurn, 1880. 03601. (Pre-1900 Canadiana) – 9 – cn C.I.H.M. [971]
CANADIAN NOTABILITIES VOL.2 / Dent, John Charles – Toronto: J. Magurn, 1880. 03602. (Pre-1900 Canadiana) – 9 – cn C.I.H.M. [971]
CANADIAN NUCLEAR TECHNOLOGY – v1-6 1961-67 – 1,5,6 – us Princeton Micro [621]
CANADIAN NUMISMATIC BIBLIOGRAPHY: A REVIEW OF MR. R. W. MCLACHLAN'S 'CANADIAN NUMISMATICS', AND OTHER BOOKS AND PAMPHLETS DESCRIBING CANADIAN COINS AND MEDALS – Montreal: Reprinted from 'The Gazette,' 1886. 02826. (Pre-1900 Canadiana) – 9 – cn C.I.H.M. [730]
CANADIAN NUMISMATIC JOURNAL – Barrie. v1-39. 1956-94 – 9 – Can$28.00y – cn Micromedia [730]
CANADIAN NURSE – v. 47-61. 1951-65 – 1,5,6 – us Princeton Micro [610]
CANADIAN NURSE – (v67- . 5,6. v72- . 9) – 1- 1905- – 1 – us UMI [610]
CANADIAN OPINIONS ON THE BILL INTRODUCED INTO THE DOMINION PARLIAMENT BY DESIRE GIROUARD, ESQ., M.P.; (JACQUES CARTIER), LEGALIZING MARRIAGE WITH THE SISTER OF A DECEASED WIFE, AND WITH THE WIDOW OF A BROTHER – 1880? 02825. (Pre-1900 Canadiana) – 9 – cn C.I.H.M. [971]
THE CANADIAN ORNITHOLOGIST – Toronto: Willing & Williamson, 1973 – 9 – cn C.I.H.M. [590]
THE CANADIAN PACIFIC AND NORTH SHORE RAILWAYS: CORRESPONDENCE RELATING TO THE EFFORTS OF THE CANADIAN PACIFIC RAILWAY CO. TO REACH QUEBEC / Canadian Pacific Railway Company – Montreal?, 1885? 00450. (Pre-1900 Canadiana) – 9 – cn C.I.H.M. [380]
THE CANADIAN PACIFIC RAILWAY: AN INSIGHT INTO ITS MANAGEMENT AND POLICY: FACTS AND FIGURES – Quebec, Saturday Budget, 1889. 02047. (Pre-1900 Canadiana) – 9 – cn C.I.H.M. [380]
Canadian Pacific Railway Company *see*
- ANNOTATED TIME TABLE: WITH INFORMATION AS TO C.P.R. TRANSCONTINENTAL ROUTES
- THE CANADIAN PACIFIC AND NORTH SHORE RAILWAYS: CORRESPONDENCE RELATING TO THE EFFORTS OF THE CANADIAN PACIFIC RAILWAY CO. TO REACH QUEBEC
- CIRCULAR TO THE SHAREHOLDERS.
- CONTRACT BETWEEN THE GOVERNMENT OF THE DOMINION AND THE CANADIAN PACIFIC RAILWAY COMPANY: ALSO, THE CONSOLIDATED RAILWAY ACT (1879), AND THE ACT OF 1881 AMENDING IT
- EXPLORATORY SURVEY: REPORTS, RECOMMENDATIONS AND ORDERS IN COUNCIL IN REFERENCE TO THE LOSS OF LIFE OF OFFICERS AND MEN, IN CONNECTION WITH THE SURVEY IN THE YEAR 1873
- FOLDER A
- LAW BONDS: INDENTURE OF MORTGAGE; THE COMPANY TO THE HON. GEORGE EULAS FOSTER, THE HON. JOHN JOSEPH CALDWELL ABBOTT AND RICHARD BLADWORTH ANGUS, TRUSTEES: 2ND JUNE, 1888
- REPORT OF PROCEEDINGS AT A SPECIAL GENERAL MEETING OF THE SHAREHOLDERS...HELD AT MONTREAL ON THE 3RD AND 6TH DAYS OF MARCH, 1884
- REPORTS AND DOCUMENTS IN REFERENCE TO THE LOCATION OF THE LINE AND A WESTERN TERMINAL HARBOUR
- RULES FOR THE CARE AND USE OF THE COMMINGLER STEAM HEATING SYSTEM AND THE BAKER HEATER
- TIME TABLE: UPPER LAKE EXPRESS STEAMSHIPS OF THE CANADIAN PACIFIC RAILWAY
- A TIME-TABLE, WITH NOTES OF THE WESTBOUND TRANSCONTINENTAL TRAIN: THE GREAT LAKES ROUTE: TORONTO AND CHICAGO LINE
- TO THE SHAREHOLDERS

Canadian Pacific Railway Company. Passenger Department *see* SUMMER TOURS
CANADIAN PACIFIC RAILWAY: CONTRACT WITH THE SYNDICATE / Campbell, Alexander – Speech, 1881? 00396. (Pre-1900 Canadiana) – 9 – cn C.I.H.M. [971]
CANADIAN PACIFIC RAILWAY, OTTAWA, 1ST JULY, 1880 / Fleming, Sandford – Ottawa?: s.n., 1880?. 03127. (Pre-1900 Canadiana) – 9 – cn C.I.H.M. [971]
CANADIAN PACIFIC RAILWAY: REPORTS IN REFERENCE TO LOCATION OF SECOND SECTION WEST OF RED RIVER / Fleming, Sandford – Ottawa?: s.n., 1880. 05454. (Pre-1900 Canadiana) – 9 – cn C.I.H.M. [971]
CANADIAN PACIFIC RESOLUTIONS: THOROUGH SIFTING OF A GREAT SCANDAL: ASTOUNDING DISCREPANCIES IN GOVERNMENT ESTIMATES: CONVINCING ARGUMENT FOR REJECTION OF TERMS / Blake, Edward – Mr. Blake's reply to Sir Charles Tupper's explanation. 1884? 00158. (Pre-1900 Canadiana) – 9 – cn C.I.H.M. [971]
CANADIAN PACIFIC STAFF BULLETIN : FIFTIETH ANNIVERSARY SUPPLEMENT – Montreal. n13. 1 aug 1936 – 1r – 1 – Can$25.00 – cn Can Microfilming [072]
CANADIAN PACKAGING – (v1-22 1948-69 Can$550.00 5) – Toronto. v1-22. 1948-94 – 5,9 – Can$28.00y – cn Micromedia [680]
CANADIAN PACKAGING – (v28- . 1975- . 5,6,9) – v. 1-. 1948- – 1 – us UMI [680]
CANADIAN PAINT AND FINISHING – (v49- . 1975- . 5,6,9) – v. 1-. 1927- – 1 – us UMI [660]
CANADIAN PAPERMAKER – (Cont: Pulp and Paper Journal at v45 n7 1992) – v45-47. 1992-94 – 9 – Can$28.00y – cn Micromedia [670]
CANADIAN PAPERMAKER *see*
- JOURNAL DES PATES ET PAPIERS
- PULP AND PAPER JOURNAL

CANADIAN PARLIAMENTARY GUIDE – Toronto, 1862-1912 – 9 – Can$460.00 – cn Micromedia [971]
THE CANADIAN PATENT OFFICE RECORD – Montreal: G.E. Desbarats, 1873-1960 – 9 – cn C.I.H.M. [340]
THE CANADIAN PATENT OFFICE RECORD AND MECHANICS' MAGAZINE – (Contd by: Canadian Mechanics' Magazine and Patent Office Record) – Montreal: G E Desbarats, [1873-1875] – 9 – cn C.I.H.M. [340]
THE CANADIAN PATENT OFFICE RECORD AND MECHANICS' MAGAZINE *see* CANADIAN MECHANICS MAGAZINE AND PATENT OFFICE RECORD
THE CANADIAN PATRIOT : MONTHLY MAGAZINE – Montreal, Canada. jan 1864-v1 n7. jul 1864 – 1r – 1 – Can$30.00 – cn Can Microfilming [073]
THE CANADIAN PATRIOT – Stanstead, Canada. v1 n7. 2 fev 1838; v1 n9. 16 fev 1838 – 1r – 1 – Can$25.00 – cn Can Microfilming [072]
CANADIAN PEN AND INK SKETCHES / Fraser, John – Montreal?: s.n., 1890 (Montreal: Gazette). 03177. (Pre-1900 Canadiana) – 9 – cn C.I.H.M. [971]
CANADIAN PERIODICAL INDEX – (1987.-1r; 1989.-1r; 1938-1959.-2r) – Toronto, 1966 and 1969 – 1r – 1 – cn Preston [971]
CANADIAN PERIODICAL INDEX – Author and Subject Index. 1938-47, 1948-59 – 2r – 1 – $136.00 – cn Library Assoc [010]
CANADIAN PETROLEUM – (Ceased v25 1984) – Don Mills. v1-25. 1959-84 – 5 – Price varies – cn Micromedia [660]
CANADIAN PHARMACEUTICAL JOURNAL – (v119-127 1986-94 Can$28.00y 9) – Ottawa. v1-127. 1898-1994 – 5,9 – cn Micromedia [615]
THE CANADIAN PHARMACEUTICAL JOURNAL – (Contd in Part by: Canadian Journal of Pharmaceutical Sciences. Contd by: CPJ: Canadian Pharmaceutical Journal) – Toronto: J M Trout, [1868-1984] – 9 – cn C.I.H.M. [615]
THE CANADIAN PHILATELIC AND CURIO ADVERTISER – Montreal: A L Hamilton, [1886?-188-?] – 9 – cn C.I.H.M. [760]
CANADIAN PHILATELIC JOURNAL *see*
- THE CANADIAN PHILATELIST
- THE NIAGARA FALLS PHILATELIST

THE CANADIAN PHILATELIC JOURNAL – (Cont: The Canadian Philatelist (Niagara Falls, Ont.). Is Absorbed by: the Niagara Falls Philatelist) – [St. Catharines, Ont] H E French, [1888-188-?] – 9 – cn C.I.H.M. [760]

THE CANADIAN PHILATELIC JOURNAL – Merritton, Ont: Canadian Pub. Co., [1894] – 9 – cn C.I.H.M. [760]

THE CANADIAN PHILATELIC MAGAZINE – Halifax, N.S: A M Muirhead, [1893-1901?] – 9 – cn C.I.H.M. [760]

THE CANADIAN PHILATELIC REVIEW – (Cont: The Canadian Philatelic Weekly) – Berlin [Kitchener], Ont: F I Weaver, [1899] – 9 – cn C.I.H.M. [760]

THE CANADIAN PHILATELIC REVIEW *see* THE CANADIAN PHILATELIC WEEKLY

THE CANADIAN PHILATELIC WEEKLY – (Cont: The Boys Own Philatelist. Contd by: The Canadian Philatelic Review) – Berlin [Kitchener], Ont: F I Weaver, [1898-1899] – 9 – cn C.I.H.M. [760]

THE CANADIAN PHILATELIC WEEKLY – London [Ont]: L M Staebler, [1894] – 9 – cn C.I.H.M. [760]

THE CANADIAN PHILATELIC WEEKLY – Toronto: Canadian Philatelic Weekly, [1898-189- or 19–] – 9 – cn C.I.H.M. [760]

THE CANADIAN PHILATELIC WEEKLY *see*
– THE BOYS' OWN PHILATELIST
– THE CANADIAN PHILATELIC REVIEW

CANADIAN PHILATELIST – Ottawa. v8-45. 1957-94 – 9 – Can$28.00y – cn Micromedia [760]

CANADIAN PHILATELIST *see* THE CANADIAN PHILATELIST AND NUMISMATIST

THE CANADIAN PHILATELIST – (Contd by: Canadian Philatelic Journal (St. Catherines, Ont.)) – Niagara Falls, Ont: Canadian Philatelic Co., [1888] – 9 – cn C.I.H.M. [760]

THE CANADIAN PHILATELIST – (Contd by: The Canadian Philatelist and Numismatist) – Whitby, Ont: L F Barker, [1884?-1885] – 9 – cn C.I.H.M. [760]

THE CANADIAN PHILATELIST – London, Ont: L M Staebler, [1891-1896] – 9 – cn C.I.H.M. [760]

THE CANADIAN PHILATELIST – Quebec: Birt, Williams & Co., [1872] – 9 – cn C.I.H.M. [760]

THE CANADIAN PHILATELIST – Quebec: International Stamp Co., [1872-1873?] – 9 – cn C.I.H.M. [760]

THE CANADIAN PHILATELIST – Toronto: G A Lowe, [1886] – 9 – cn C.I.H.M. [760]

THE CANADIAN PHILATELIST *see* THE CANADIAN PHILATELIC JOURNAL

THE CANADIAN PHILATELIST AND NUMISMATIST – (Cont: Canadian Philatelist (Whitby, Ont.)) – Whitby, Ont: L F Barker, [1885] – 9 – cn C.I.H.M. [760]

THE CANADIAN PHILATELIST AND NUMISMATIST *see* THE CANADIAN PHILATELIST

THE CANADIAN PHONETIC PIONEER – Oshawa, C W [Ont]: W H Orr, [1858-18–] – 9 – cn C.I.H.M. [400]

CANADIAN PHOTO STANDARD *see* CANADIAN PHOTOGRAPHIC STANDARD

CANADIAN PHOTOGRAPHIC JOURNAL – v1-6 1892-1897 – 1 – $225.00 – cn McLaren [770]

CANADIAN PHOTOGRAPHIC STANDARD – (Cont: Canadian Photo Standard) – Montreal: D H Hogg, [1893?-1899?] – 9 – cn C.I.H.M. [770]

CANADIAN PHOTOGRAPHY – (1975- . 5,6,9) – 1970- – 1 – us UMI [770]

CANADIAN PHRENOLOGICAL AND PSYCHOLOGICAL MAGAZINE – S.l.: s.n., 1891-189- or 19– – 9 – cn C.I.H.M. [130]

CANADIAN PICTORIAL – (Abundantly illustrated) – Montreal, Canada. oct 1906-jul 1914 – 1r – 1 – Can$45.00 – cn Can Microfilming [073]

CANADIAN PICTORIAL – Montreal, Canada. -m. Jan 1908-Nov 1916. 4 reels – 1 – uk British Libr Newspaper [072]

CANADIAN PICTORIAL AND ILLUSTRATED WAR NEWS – 1885 – 1 – 65.00 – cn McLaren [971]

CANADIAN PICTURES : DRAWN WITH PEN AND PENCIL / Argyll, John Douglas Sutherland Campbell, Duke of – London: Religious Tract Society, 1884?. 02222. (Pre-1900 Canadiana) – 9 – cn C.I.H.M. [971]

CANADIAN PLASTICS – v3-28. 1945-70 – 1,5,6 – us Princeton Micro [073]

CANADIAN PLASTICS – (v35-53 1977-95 9) – Don Mills. v1-53. 1943-95 – 5 – Price varies – cn Micromedia [660]

CANADIAN POETS IN MINIATURE / Clio – 1892? 00685. (Pre-1900 Canadiana) – 9 – cn C.I.H.M. [810]

THE CANADIAN POLAR EXPEDITION, OR, WILL CANADA CLAIM HER OWN / Browne, R H C – Canada: s.n, 1901. SEM105P476 – 1mf – 9 – Can$2.25 – cn Bibl Nat [910]

CANADIAN POLITICAL HISTORY: OUTLINES OF A COURSE OF TEN LECTURES... YOUNG MEN'S CHRISTIAN ASSOCIATION...1894 / Ames, Herbert Brown – Montreal: The Association, 1894?. 04012. (Pre-1900 Canadiana) – 9 – cn C.I.H.M. [971]

Canadian Political Science Association *see* PAPERS AND PROCEEDINGS

THE CANADIAN POULTRY CHRONICLE – Toronto: Published for the Proprietors by the Globe Print. Co., [1870-1872?] – 9 – cn C.I.H.M. [630]

CANADIAN POULTRY REVIEW – (Contains: The Pigeon Foncier) – Strathroy, Ont: J Fullerton, 1877-1975 – 9 – cn C.I.H.M. [630]

THE CANADIAN POULTRY REVIEW *see* THE PIGEON FANCIER

CANADIAN POWER FARMER *see* THE CANADIAN THRESHERMAN AND FARMER

THE CANADIAN PRESBYTER – Montreal: J Lovell, 1857-1858 – 9 – cn C.I.H.M. [240]

THE CANADIAN PRESBYTERIAN MAGAZINE – Toronto: [s.n., 1851-1854]; (Toronto: J Cleland) – 9 – cn C.I.H.M. [240]

CANADIAN PRESS NEWSFILE – (Canadian press news articles on mf) – 1983- – 9 – cn Micromedia [072]

CANADIAN PRINTER – (Cont: Canadian Printer and Publisher at v99 no 9 1989) – Toronto. v99-103. 1990-95 – 9 – Price varies – cn Micromedia [680]

CANADIAN PRINTER *see* CANADIAN PRINTER AND PUBLISHER

THE CANADIAN PRINTER – Montreal: C T Palsgrave, [1860?-18–?] – 9 – cn C.I.H.M. [680]

CANADIAN PRINTER AND PUBLISHER – (v1-78 1892-69 Can$1,980.00 5. Cont by: Canadian Printer at v99 no 9 1989) – Toronto. v1-99. 1892-1989 – 5,9 – Can$37.00y – cn Micromedia [070]

CANADIAN PRINTER AND PUBLISHER – (v84- . 1975- . 5,6,9) – v. 1-. 1892- – 1 – us UMI [070]

THE CANADIAN PRISON SUNDAY – Toronto: Prisoners' Aid Association of Canada, [1892-189- or 19–] – 9 – cn C.I.H.M. [360]

Canadian Protesting Committee *see* AN ACCOUNT OF THE CANADIAN PROTEST AGAINST THE INTRODUCTION INTO CANADA OF MUSICAL EXAMINATIONS BY OUTSIDE MUSICAL EXAMINING BODIES

CANADIAN PSYCHOLOGICAL REVIEW *see* CANADIAN PSYCHOLOGY

CANADIAN PSYCHOLOGY – (Previous title: Canadian Psychological Review. v21-30 1980-89 Can$20.00y) – Old Chelsea. v21-36. 1980-95 – 9 – Can$28.00y – cn Micromedia [150]

CANADIAN PUBLIC ADMINISTRATION – (Index 1979-82 Can$20.00) – Toronto. v1-38. 1958-95 – 9 – Can$28.00y – cn Micromedia [350]

CANADIAN PUBLIC LANDS: SPEECH...HOUSE OF COMMONS...MONDAY, 5TH APRIL, 1880 / Plumb, Josiah Burr – 1880?. 02294. (Pre-1900 Canadiana) – 9 – cn C.I.H.M. [971]

CANADIAN PUBLIC POLICY – Burnaby. v1-21. 1975-95 – 9 – Can$28.00y – cn Micromedia [350]

CANADIAN PULP AND PAPER INDUSTRY – (v1-22 1948-69 Can$660.00 5. Mill ed cont by: Pulp and Paper Journal v35 1982. Woodlands ed cont by: Logging and Sawmilling Journal v13 1982) – Toronto. v1-34. 1948-81 – 5,9 – Can$37.00y – cn Micromedia [660]

CANADIAN PULP AND PAPER INDUSTRY – (v28- . 1975- . 5,6,9) – v. 1-34. 1948-81 – 1 – us UMI [670]

CANADIAN PULP AND PAPER INDUSTRY *see*
– LOGGING AND SAWMILLING JOURNAL
– PULP AND PAPER JOURNAL

THE CANADIAN PUNCH – Montreal, Canada. 5 fev 1868-v1 n2. 12 fev 1868 – 1r – 1 – Can$25.00 – cn Can Microfilming [073]

THE CANADIAN QUARTERLY AGRICULTURAL INDUSTRIAL MAGAZINE – Montreal, Canada. mai 1838; v1 n2. aut 1838 – 1r – 1 – Can$25.00 – cn Can Microfilming [073]

THE CANADIAN QUARTERLY REVIEW – Toronto?: s.n., 1856?-18– or 19– – 9 – cn C.I.H.M. [971]

THE CANADIAN QUARTERLY REVIEW AND FAMILY MAGAZINE – Hamilton, Ont?: Pub. for G D Griffin ... by Donnelley & Lawson, [1863-1866] – 9 – cn C.I.H.M. [971]

THE CANADIAN QUEEN – 1890-92 – 1 – $65.00 – cn McLaren [360]

CANADIAN RAILWAY AND STEAMBOAT GUIDE – Montreal: Pub. for the Proprietor by H Rose, [1855?-18– or 19–] – 9 – cn C.I.H.M. [380]

CANADIAN REAL ESTATE = L'IMMOBILIER CANADIENNE – (v1-5 1980-95 Can$115.00. Previous title: CREA Reporter. Mf to 1991 only) – Ottawa. v1-11. 1980-91 – 5 – Can$60.00y – cn Micromedia [333]

CANADIAN RECIPROCITY : WHY SOME CANADIANS WANT RECIPROCITY: WHY ENGLISHMEN WANT IT: WHY WE DON'T WANT IT – Philadelphia: American Iron and Steel Association, 18. 00789. (Pre-1900 Canadiana) – 9 – cn C.I.H.M. [977]

CANADIAN RECORD – Saint John, N.B: J E Hopper, [1881-1887?] – 9 – cn C.I.H.M. [971]

THE CANADIAN RECORD OF SCIENCE – (Cont: The Canadian Naturalist and Quarterly Journal of Science) – Montreal: Natural History Society, [1884?-1916] – 9 – cn C.I.H.M. [500]

THE CANADIAN RECORD OF SCIENCE *see* THE CANADIAN NATURALIST AND QUARTERLY JOURNAL OF SCIENCE

THE CANADIAN REGISTER : QUEBEC EDITION – (Cont: The Beacon, Montreal) – Montreal, Canada. v1 n1. 28 fev 1942-v7 n35. 28 oct 1948 – 4r – 1 – Can$50.00r – cn Can Microfilming [072]

CANADIAN REPORTS : APPEAL CASES / Canada. General – v1-14. 1807-1905; 10v. 1906-13 (all publ) – 140mf – 9 – $210.00 – LLMC 81-008 – us L.L.M.C. [324]

CANADIAN RESEARCH – (Incorporated within Canadian Laboratory, September 1989. 1975-1987 Can$28.00y) – Willowdale, v8- 1975- – 9 – Can$20.00y – cn Micromedia [073]

CANADIAN RESEARCH – (See also: Canadian Research and Development) – v9-. 1976- – 1,5,6,9 – us UMI [600]

CANADIAN RESEARCH *see*
– CANADIAN LABORATORY
– CANADIAN RESEARCH AND DEVELOPMENT

CANADIAN RESEARCH AND DEVELOPMENT – (Cont by: Canadian Research) – Willowdale. v1-8. 1968-75 – 9 – Can$20.00y – cn Micromedia [073]

CANADIAN RESEARCH AND DEVELOPMENT – (v8. 1975. 5,6,9. See also: Canadian Research) – v1-8. 1968-1975 – 1 – us UMI [600]

CANADIAN RESEARCH AND DEVELOPMENT *see* CANADIAN RESEARCH

CANADIAN REVENUES – s.l., s.n., 1831. SEM105P433 – 1mf – 9 – Can$2.25 – cn Bibl Nat [971]

CANADIAN REVIEW – (Ceased v4 1977) – Toronto. v1-4. 1974-77 – 9 – Can$20.00y – cn Micromedia [073]

THE CANADIAN REVIEW AND LITERARY AND HISTORICAL JOURNAL – (Contd by: Canadian Review and Magazine) – Montreal: H H Cunningham, [1824-1825] – 9 – cn C.I.H.M. [400]

THE CANADIAN REVIEW AND LITERARY AND HISTORICAL JOURNAL *see* THE CANADIAN REVIEW AND MAGAZINE

CANADIAN REVIEW AND MAGAZINE *see* THE CANADIAN REVIEW AND LITERARY AND HISTORICAL JOURNAL

THE CANADIAN REVIEW AND MAGAZINE – (Cont: The Canadian Review and Literary and Historical Journal) – Montreal: Printed for the Proprietor at the Office of the Montreal Gazette, [1826] – 9 – cn C.I.H.M. [971]

CANADIAN REVIEW OF MUSIC AND ART – v. 1-6. 1942-1948 – 1 – 135.00 – cn McLaren [780]

CANADIAN REVIEW OF STUDIES IN NATIONALISM – Charlottetown. v16-21. 1989-94 – 9 – Can$20.00y – cn Micromedia [320]

CANADIAN RIGHTS AND LIBERTIES FEDERATION – Ottawa. 35 docs. 1982-1990 – 19mf – 9 – ne IDC [320]

THE CANADIAN ROCKY MOUNTAINS IN TOPOGRAPHIC MAPS (1888-1892) = LES ROCHEUSES CANADIENNES EN CARTES TOPOGRAPHIQUES (1888-1892) / National Archives of Canada – 1994 – 21mf – 15 – $199.00 – us Comics [971]

THE CANADIAN ROSE BUD SONG BOOK: CONTAINING ALL THE POPULAR SONGS OF THE DAY – Toronto: A. Irving, 18–. 00445. (Pre-1900 Canadiana) – 9 – cn C.I.H.M. [780]

THE CANADIAN ROYAL ARCANUM JOURNAL – Toronto: [s.n., 1894-189- or 19–] – 9 – cn C.I.H.M. [971]

CANADIAN RUTHENIAN – Winnipeg, Canada. 1911-30 – 14r – 1 – $910.00 – cn Library Assoc [971]

CANADIAN SCENERY / Willis, N P – England. 2v. 1842 – 1r – 1 – Can$50.00 – cn Can Microfilming [971]

CANADIAN SCHOOL EXECUTIVE – Vancouver. v114. 1981/82-1994/95 – 9 – Can$20.00y – cn Micromedia [370]

THE CANADIAN SCIENCE MONTHLY – (Cont: The Acadian Scientist) – Wolfville, N.S: A J Pineo, [1884-1885] – 9 – cn C.I.H.M. [500]

CANADIAN SECRETARY – (Ceased v15 no4 1990) – Toronto. v15. 1990 – 9 – Can$20.00y – cn Micromedia [650]

CANADIAN SELECT HOMES – (Cont: Select Homes and Food at v21 no 7 1994) – v21- 1994- – 9 – Can$28.00y – cn Micromedia [640]

CANADIAN SELECT HOMES *see* SELECT HOMES AND FOOD

CANADIAN SHAREOWNER – Windsor. v4-7. 1990/91-1993/94 – 9 – Can$20.00y – cn Micromedia [332]

CANADIAN SHIPPING AND MARINE ENGINEERING – (Ceased v60 1989) – Mississauga. v41-60. 1969/70-1989 – 9 – Price varies – cn Micromedia [380]

THE CANADIAN SHOE AND LEATHER JOURNAL – (Contd by: Canadian Footwear Journal) – Toronto: J Acton, 1888-1910 – 9 – cn C.I.H.M. [680]

CANADIAN SLOVAK LEAGUE BRANCH 10 – Ft. William, Ontario, 1933-1943 – 1 reel – 1 – us I.H.R.C. [971]

THE CANADIAN SOCIAL CREDITER – Edmonton, Alberta. 12 oct 1944-v2 n13. 24 jan 1946 – 1r – 1 – Can$45.00 – cn Can Microfilming [072]

CANADIAN SOCIAL STUDIES – (Cont: History and Social Science Teacher at v26 1991/92) – v26- 1993/94- – 9 – Can$20.00y – cn Micromedia [300]

CANADIAN SOCIAL STUDIES *see* HISTORY AND SOCIAL SCIENCE TEACHER

CANADIAN SOCIAL TRENDS – (Only 3 issues publ in 1989-Summer, Autumn, and Winter) – Ottawa, 1986-95 – 9 – Can$20.00y – cn Micromedia [306]

Canadian Society of Authors *see* REPORT ON COPYRIGHT: ADOPTED AT A MEETING...HELD AT THE CANADIAN INSTITUTE, TORONTO, ON MONDAY EVENING, MARCH 13, 1899

CANADIAN SOCIETY OF BIBLICAL STUDIES – v1-49. 1935-89 (complete) – 2r – 1 – ATLA S0780 – us A.T.L.A. [073]

CANADIAN SON OF TEMPERANCE – (Cont: Canadian Son of Temperance and Literary Gem. Contd by: The Canadian Son of Temperance[and] Literary Gem) – Toronto: [s.n., 1852] – 9 – cn C.I.H.M. [971]

CANADIAN SON OF TEMPERANCE *see*
– THE CANADIAN SON OF TEMPERANCE [AND] LITERARY GEM
– CANADIAN SON OF TEMPERANCE AND LITERARY GEM

CANADIAN SON OF TEMPERANCE AND LITERARY GEM – (Contd by: Canadian Son of Temperance) – Toronto: [s.n., 1851] – 9 – cn C.I.H.M. [971]

CANADIAN SON OF TEMPERANCE AND LITERARY GEM *see*
– CANADIAN SON OF TEMPERANCE
– THE SON OF TEMPERANCE AND CANADIAN LITERARY GEM

THE CANADIAN SON OF TEMPERANCE [AND] LITERARY GEM – (Contd by: The Son of Temperance and Canadian Literary Gem. Cont: Canadian Son of Temperance) – Toronto: [s.n., 1853] – 9 – cn C.I.H.M. [971]

THE CANADIAN SON OF TEMPERANCE [AND] LITERARY GEM *see* CANADIAN SON OF TEMPERANCE

THE CANADIAN SPEAKER AND ELOCUTIONARY READER – Ed. and comp. by Edward Hartley Dewart. Toronto: A. Miller, 1868. 02675. (Pre-1900 Canadiana) – 9 – cn C.I.H.M. [410]

CANADIAN SPECIALITY FOODS RETAILER – (Ceased v3 1987) – Port Credit. v1-3. 1985-1987 – 9 – Can$20.00y – cn Micromedia [380]

THE CANADIAN SPECTATOR – Montreal, Canada. v2 n8. 22 fec 1879-v4 n22. 29 mai 1881 – 2r – 1 – Can$35.00r – cn Can Microfilming [072]

THE CANADIAN SPECTATOR / ed by Waller, Jocelyn – Montreal, Canada. 19 Oct 1822-v7 n26. 7 fev 1829 – 1r – 1 – Can$50.00 – cn Can Microfilming [072]

THE CANADIAN SPECTATOR *see* LE SPECTATEUR CANADIEN

CANADIAN SPEECHES – (v3-8 1989/90-1994/95 Can$28.00y) – Woodville, v1-8. 1987/88-1994/95 – 9 – Can$20.00y – cn Micromedia [850]

CANADIAN SPORTSMAN AND LIVESTOCK JOURNAL – Toronto: E K Dodds, [187-?-19–] – 9 – cn C.I.H.M. [790]

THE CANADIAN SPORTSMAN AND NATURALIST – Montreal, Canada. v2 n1. jan 1882-v3 n11/12. dec 1883 – 1r – 1 – Can$25.00 – cn Can Microfilming [790]

CANADIAN STAMP NEWS – (v1-13 1975/76-1988/89 Can$60.00y) – St Catherines. v1-18. 1975/76-1993/94 – 1 – Can$85.00y – cn Micromedia [730]

CANADIAN STATESMAN – Bowmanville, Canada. 1868-1900 – 16r – 1 – $1,040.00 – cn Library Assoc [971]

CANADIAN STATISTICAL REVIEW – (Continued by Canadian Economic Observer, 1988) – Ottawa, v56 1981- – 9 – Can$55.00y – cn Micromedia [310]

CANADIAN STATISTICAL REVIEW = REVUE STATISTIQUE DU CANADA – (Cont by: Canadian Statistical Review and Revue statistique du Canada) – Ottawa. v1-55. 1926-80 – 9 – Price varies – cn Micromedia [310]

CANADIAN STATISTICAL REVIEW *see*
- CANADIAN ECONOMIC OBSERVER
- CANADIAN STATISTICAL REVIEW
- REVUE STATISTIQUE DU CANADA

CANADIAN STOCK RAISERS' JOURNAL *see* CANADIAN LIVE-STOCK JOURNAL

CANADIAN STOCK-RAISERS' JOURNAL – (Contd by: Canadian Live-Stock Journal) – Hamilton, Ont: Stock Journal Co., [1883?-1884?] – 9 – cn C.I.H.M. [630]

CANADIAN STUDIES IN COMPARATIVE POLITICS / Bourinot, John George – Montreal: Dawson Bros., 1890. 00226. (Pre-1900 Canadiana) – 9 – cn C.I.H.M. [971]

THE CANADIAN SUNDAY MAGAZINE – Montreal, Canada. dec 1872-v1 n12. nov 1873 – 1r – 1 – Can$30.00 – cn Can Microfilming [073]

Canadian Synod. (Pres. Ch. in the U.S.A.) *see* MINUTES, 1907-55

Canadian Telebook Agency *see* CTA MICROFICHE

CANADIAN TELECOM – Toronto. v1-8. 1987-94 – 9 – Can$20.00y – cn Micromedia [380]

CANADIAN TEXTILE JOURNAL *see* CANADIAN JOURNAL OF FABRICS

CANADIAN THEATRE REVIEW – (nos1-49 1974-86 Can$28.00y) – Downsview. nos 1-85. 1974-95 – 9 – Can$20.00y – cn Micromedia [790]

CANADIAN THESES / National Library of Canada – (1985/86- . Can$58.50; Can$70.20 (outside Canada)) – 1980/81-1984/85 – 9 – Can$50.50; Can$60.50 (outside Canada) – cn Nat'l Library [370]

THE CANADIAN THRESHERMAN AND FARMER – (Contd by: Canadian Power Farmer) – Winnipeg: E H Heath, 1[1902-1919] – 9 – cn C.I.H.M. [630]

CANADIAN TIMBER TREES: THEIR DISTRIBUTION AND PRESERVATION / Drummond, Andrew Thomas – Montreal?: s.n., 1879 (Montreal: "Witness" Print). 02766. (Pre-1900 Canadiana) – 9 – cn C.I.H.M. [971]

THE CANADIAN TIMES – Montreal, Canada. 23 oct-v1 n7. 4 dec 1909 – 1r – 1 – Can$30.00 – cn Can Microfilming [072]

THE CANADIAN TIMES – Sherbrooke, Canada. 4 jan 1855-v3 n53. 31 dec 1857 – 1r – 1 – Can$50.00 – cn Can Microfilming [072]

THE CANADIAN TIMES AND WEEKLY LITERARY AND POLITICS RECORDER – Montreal. v1 n1. 17 jan 1823-v1 n72. 13 fev 1824 – 1r – 1 – Can$35.00 – cn Can Microfilming [072]

CANADIAN TIT-BITS – [Toronto?: s.n., 1891-189- or 19–] – cn C.I.H.M. [072]

THE CANADIAN TOURIST AND MONTREAL CITY GUIDE – Montreal, Canada. v2 n2. jul 1862 – 1r – 1 – Can$25.00 – cn Can Microfilming [910]

THE CANADIAN TRADE QUESTION / Edgar, James David – Discussed in an open letter from J. D. Edgar to his constituents of the west riding of Ontario sic. Toronto?: s.n., 1893?. 05216. (Pre-1900 Canadiana) – 9 – cn C.I.H.M. [971]

THE CANADIAN TRADE REVIEW – Montreal: H. Harvey, [1885-1906?] – 9 – cn C.I.H.M. [380]

CANADIAN TRANSPORTATION – (Cont: Canadian Transportation and Distribution Management at v92 no 11 1989. Cont by: Canadian Transportation Logistics at v94 no 9 1991) – Don Mills. v93. 1990 – 9 – Can$28.00y – cn Micromedia [380]

CANADIAN TRANSPORTATION *see*
- CANADIAN TRANSPORTATION AND DISTRIBUTION MANAGEMENT
- CANADIAN TRANSPORTATION LOGISTICS

CANADIAN TRANSPORTATION AND DISTRIBUTION MANAGEMENT – (v1-73. 1891-1970 Can$1,650.00 5. Cont by: Canadian Transportation at v92 no 11 1989) – Don Mills. v1-92. 1891-1989 – 5,9 – Can$28.00y – cn Micromedia [380]

CANADIAN TRANSPORTATION LOGISTICS – (Cont: Canadian Transportation at v94 no 9 1991) – v94- 1991- – 9 – Can$28.00y – cn Micromedia [380]

CANADIAN TRANSPORTATION RAILWAY AND MARINE WORLD – Jan. 1906-Dec. 1960. Title and numbering varies – 1 – cn Precision [380]

CANADIAN TRAVEL COURIER – (1975- . 5,6,9) – 1965- – 1 – us UMI [910]

CANADIAN TRAVEL COURIER – (Mf available to v24 1988/89 only) – Toronto. v1-24. 1965/66-1988/89 – 5 – Can$60.00y – cn Micromedia [910]

CANADIAN TRIBUNE – Toronto, 1971-1986 – 1 – Can$485.00 – cn Micromedia [072]

THE CANADIAN TRIBUNE : THE CANADIAN COMMUNIST PAPER – Toronto, Ontario, CN. 1940-89 – 33r – 1 – cn Commonwealth Micro [072]

THE CANADIAN UKRAINIAN COLLECTION / Canadian Institute for Ukrainian Studies. University of Alberta – 1906-70 – 170r – 1 – cn Commonwealth Micro [080]

CANADIAN UNDERWRITER – Don Mills. v56-61. 1989-94 – 9 – Can$28.00y – cn Micromedia [360]

CANADIAN UNION CATALOGUE OF LIBRARY MATERIALS FOR THE PRINT-HANDICAPPED (CANUC:H) / National Library of Canada – 1985- . 80,000 entries. Register, 3 indexes. Updated semi-annually – 9 – cn Nat'l Library [010]

Canadian Union of Fascists *see* THE THUNDERBOLT

CANADIAN UNIONIST – v1-30 Jun 1927 – Mar 1956 – 1 – cn Precision [971]

CANADIAN UNITED PRESBYTERIAN MAGAZINE – Toronto: C. Fletcher, [1854?-1861] – 9 – cn C.I.H.M. [240]

THE CANADIAN UNITED SERVICE MAGAZINE – [Ottawa?]: United Service Club, [1895?-189- or 19–] – 9 – cn C.I.H.M. [360]

CANADIAN VETERINARY JOURNAL – v. 7-18. 1966-1977 – 1,5,6 – us Princeton Micro [636]

Canadian Vocational Association *see* CVA JOURNAL

CANADIAN VOCATIONAL JOURNAL = JOURNAL DE L'ASSOCIATION CANADIENNE DE LA FORMATION PROFESSIONNELLE – (v19-. 1983-. 5,6,9) – v3- Summer 1967- – 1 – us UMI [073]

CANADIAN VOCATIONAL JOURNAL – (v23-29 1987/88-1993/94 9) – Ottawa. v1-29. 1965-93/94 – 5 – Price varies – cn Micromedia [073]

CANADIAN WEEKEND – (Cont: Canadian Magazine 1979. Cont by: Today Magazine 1980) – Toronto, 1979 – 9 – Can$46.00 – cn Micromedia [073]

CANADIAN WEEKEND *see*
- CANADIAN MAGAZINE
- TODAY MAGAZINE

THE CANADIAN WEEKLY STAMP NEWS – Toronto: W.R. Adams, [1896-1897?] – 9 – cn C.I.H.M. [760]

CANADIAN WELFARE – (Ceased v53 1977. v1-51 Can$100.00v. v52-53 Can$50.00v) – Ottawa. v1-53. 1924-77 – 5 – cn Micromedia [360]

CANADIAN WESLEYAN – Hamilton, U.C. [Ont.]: H. Ryan, [183–18–] – 9 – cn C.I.H.M. [240]

CANADIAN WEST – Langley, No.1 1985/86 – 9 – Can$20.00y – cn Micromedia [971]

CANADIAN WEST *see* CANADA WEST

CANADIAN WEST INDIA TRADING ASSOCIATION (LIMITED) – Halifax, N.S.: W. Macnab, 1893. 00455. (Pre-1900 Canadiana) – 9 – cn C.I.H.M. [380]

THE CANADIAN WHEELMAN – London [Ont.: Canadian Wheelmen's Association] v1 no 1 (Sept 1883)- – 9 – cn C.I.H.M. [790]

CANADIAN WHO'S WHO IN MICROFICHE – (1979-88. 131 fiches. 150.00) – 1898-1988. 308 fiches – 9 – 400.00 – cn U.T. Pr [920]

CANADIAN WILD FLOWERS – Montreal: Montreal Star, 1893. 00459. (Pre-1900 Canadiana) – 9 – cn C.I.H.M. [580]

CANADIAN WOMAN STUDIES = LES CAHIERS DE LA FEMME – (v1-10 1978/79-1988 Can$28.00y) – Downsview. v1-15. 1978/79-1994/95 – 9 – Can$20.00y – cn Micromedia [305]

CANADIAN WOODWORKER – Toronto, Canada. 1911-28. -w – 16r – 1 – uk British Libr Newspaper [640]

CANADIAN WORKMEN'S COMPENSATION ACTS AND CASES, CONTAINING COMPARATIVE TABLES AND REFERENCES TO THE ACTS OF BRITISH COLUMBIA, ALBERTA, MANITOBA AND SASKATCHEWAN. / Dale, Edgar Thorniley – Winnipeg, Butterworth, 1915. 162 p. LL-2333 – 1 – us L of C Photodup [340]

CANADIAN WORKSHOP – (v1-14 1977/78-1990/91 Can$28.00y) – Markham. v1-18. 1977/78-1994/95 – 9 – Can$37.00y – cn Micromedia [073]

CANADIAN YACHTING – (v1-14 1976-89 Can$46.00y. Inconsistent vol numbering in 1990) – Mississauga. v1-20. 1976-94 – 9 – Can$28.00y – cn Micromedia [790]

CANADIAN YEARBOOK OF INTERNATIONAL LAW – v1-27. 1963-89 – 1,5,6 – $270.00 – us Hein [340]

CANADIANA – [Montreal?: s.n.], 1889-1890 – 9 – cn C.I.H.M. [971]

CANADIANA / National Library of Canada – Monthly with cumulating indexes – 17 (0225-3216) – cn Nat'l Library [010]

CANADIANA 1867-1900: MONOGRAPHS/ MONOGRAPHIES / National Library of Canada – Base file, semi-annual supplements – 17 – 0-660-50465-0 – cn Nat'l Library [010]

CANADIANA 1973-1980 / National Library of Canada – (Canadiana 1981-85. Canadiana 1986-87) – 17 – 0-660-50860-5 – cn Nat'l Library [010]

CANADIANA AUTHORITIES/CANADIANA VEDETTES D'AUTORITE / National Library of Canada – Quarterly with cumulating biweekly supplements – 17 (0225-1574) – cn Nat'l Library [010]

CANADIANA MULTI-YEAR CUMULATIONS / National Library of Canada – Cumulating annual bibliography – 17 (0225-3216) – cn Nat'l Library [010]

CANADIANA, TRAVEL LITERATURE – 196r – 1 – $12,250.00 – us OmniSys [971]

THE CANADIAN-AMERICAN FISHERIES / Ellison, William Bruce – New York?: s.n., 1886 (New York: Burgoyne). 05236. (Pre-1900 Canadiana) – 9 – cn C.I.H.M. [971]

CANADIAN-AMERICAN LAW JOURNAL – v1-4. 1982-1985 – 9 – $30.00 set – us Hein [340]

CANADIAN-AMERICAN REVIEW OF HUNGARIAN STUDIES *see* HUNGARIAN STUDIES REVIEW

THE CANADIAN-AMERICAN REVIEW OF HUNGARIAN STUDIES – v1-7. 1974-80 – 1 – us UMI [073]

CANADIANS ALL – 1943-46 – 1 – 65.00 – cn McLaren [971]

LE CANADIEN – Chatham, Ontario. v2 n53. mai 19? – 1r – 1 – Can$20.00 – cn Can Microfilming [072]

LE CANADIEN / ed by Frenette, Alf. – (Includes section magazine) – Thetford Mines, Canada. 17 jun 1915-29 dec 1965 – 15r – 1 – Can$65.00r – cn Can Microfilming [072]

LE CANADIEN : HEBDO / ed by Sauve, Arthur – Montreal, Canada. 22 dec 1906-11 dec 1909 – 1r – 1 – Can$45.00 – cn Can Microfilming [072]

LE CANADIEN – Levis. v3 n38. 22 sep 1939 – 1r – 1 – Can$25.00 – cn Can Microfilming [072]

LE CANADIEN : PREMIER JOURNAL ENTIEREMENT DE LANGUE FRANCAISE – (ns: 7 mai 1831-11 fev 1893 43r Can$65.00) – Quebec, Canada. 22 nov 1806-14 mar 1810; 14 jun 1817-2 mar 1825; 17 aut 1825-21 sep 1825 – 3r – 1 – Can$180.00r – cn Can Microfilming [072]

LE CANADIEN – Quebec, 1853-1890 – 11r – 1 – cn Preston [971]

LE CANADIEN – Quebec City, Canada. 1806-25 – 3r – 1 – $204.00 – cn Library Assoc [971]

LE CANADIEN – St Paul, MN. v14 n44. 11 jun 1891; v14 n46. 16 jul 1891 – 1r – 1 – Can$25.00 – cn Can Microfilming [071]

LE CANADIEN – Windsor, Canada. v1 n-. 25 jul 1891 – 1r – 1 – Can$25.00 – cn Can Microfilming [072]

LE CANADIEN DE L'ONTARIO-NORD – Timmins, Ontario. v1 n7. 13 jul 1961 – 1r – 1 – Can$25.00 – cn Can Microfilming [072]

LE CANADIEN DES ETATS-UNIS – New York City, NY. 1 mai 1884-v2 n13. 26 mar 1885 – 1r – 1 – Can$50.00 – cn Can Microfilming [071]

LE CANADIEN D'OTTAWA – Ottawa, Ontario. 28 nov 1924-v2 n10. 29 jan 1926 – 1r – 1 – Can$40.00 – cn Can Microfilming [072]

UN CANADIEN ERRANT / ed by Bilodeau, Ernest – Ottawa, Ontario. v3 n9. 15 jun 1918 – 1r – 1 – Can$25.00 – cn Can Microfilming [072]

LE CANADIEN FRANCAIS – Quebec, Canada. 24 jun 1889-24 jun 1922 – 1r – 1 – Can$35.00 – cn Can Microfilming [072]

LE CANADIEN ILLUSTRE – Montreal, Canada. 5 mai 1881-19 jan 1882 – 1r – 1 – Can$35.00 – cn Can Microfilming [072]

LE CANADIEN INDEPENDENT / ed by Aubin, Napoleon – Quebec, Canada. 21 mai 1849-31 oct 1849 – 1r – 1 – Can$35.00 – cn Can Microfilming [072]

LE CANADIEN LIBERAL : ORGANE DU PARTI LIBERAL PROVINCIAL / ed by Denault, Jean-Marc – Quebec, Canada. 15 dec 1944-23 jul 1948 – 1r – 1 – Can$60.00 – cn Can Microfilming [072]

Canadien-francais *see* LETTRES AU PEUPLE: PREMIER SERIE

LE CANADIEN-FRANCAIS – Edmonton, Alberta. nov 1915-nov 1920 – 1r – 1 – Can$35.00 – cn Can Microfilming [072]

LE CANADIEN-FRANCAIS – New York City, NY. Prosp fev 1930 – 1r – 1 – Can$25.00 – cn Can Microfilming [071]

LA CANADIENNE / ed by Plinguet, Jacques-A – Montreal, Canada. 4 jun-26 oct 1840 – 1r – 1 – Can$30.00 – cn Can Microfilming [072]

LES CANADIENS-FRANCAIS DE LOWELL, MASS – Recensement valeur commerciale, valeur immobiliere, condition religieuse, civile et politique, noms et addresses, suivis de la constitution et des reglements de l'Union Franco-Americaine, Lowell, Mass. A. Bourbonniere, 1896. 00987. (Pre-1900 Canadiana) – 9 – cn C.I.H.M. [978]

CANADIENSUM PLANTARUM / Cornutti – Paris, France. 1v. 1635 – 1r – 1 – cn Can Microfilming [580]

LE CANADO-AMERICAIN / Association Canado-Americaine – Manchester, NH. v10 n38. 6 jul 1910-30 nov 1929 – 1r – 1 – Can$30.00 – cn Can Microfilming [071]

CANAKKALE MUHAREBESI – Istanbul: Askeri Matbaasi, 1927 – $58.00 – us MEDOC [956]

CANAL BOATMAN'S MAGAZINE – Apr 1829-Dec 1832 – 1 – uk Microform Academic [073]

THE CANAL CHRONICLE – Lachine. n1. April 1984-jul 1987f – 1r – 1 – Can$40.00 – cn Can Microfilming [072]

EL CANAL DE PANAMA EN LAS GUERRAS FUTURAS / Olmedo, Alfaro – Guayaquil, 1930; Madrid: Razon y Fe, 1931 – 1 – sp Bibl Santa Ana [380]

LE CANAL DE SUEZ / Voisin-Bey, Francois Philippe – v1-6. Paris 1902-1906 – 1 – us NY Public [627]

Canal, P *see* DICTIONNAIRE FRANCOIS ET ITALIEN

Canal Rosado, Jose *see* VIENTO AMARRADO

Caney. Kansas. Methodist Episcopal Church *see* CANEY, HARRISONVILLE, AND SPRING HILL CHURCH RECORDS
Canfield, George L *see* THE LAW OF THE SEA
Canfield, James Hulme *see* RELIGION AND PUBLIC EDUCATION
Canfield, Leon Hardy *see* THE EARLY PERSECUTIONS OF THE CHRISTIANS
Canfield. Ohio. Presbyterian Church of Christ *see* CHURCH RECORDS, MS 1303
Cange, C du *see*
- ANNALES (CBH 22)
- CHRONICON PASCHALE (CBH 21)
- DE IMPERATORUM CONSTANTINOPOLITANORUM SEU DE INFERIORIS AEVI
- HISTORIA BYZANTINA DUPLICI COMMENTARIO ILLUSTRATA (CBH 25,1)
- HISTORIA BYZANTINA DUPLICI COMMENTARIO ILLUSTRATA (CBH 25,2)
- IMPERATORII GRAMMATICI HISTORIARUM LIBRI SEX SEU DE REBUS GESTIS A JOANNE ET MANNUELE GOMMENSIS IMPP. CP. (CBH 11,1)

Cange, Ch. Dufresne Du *see* GLOSSARIUM MEDIAE ET INFIMAE LATINITATIS. ED. NOVA
CANGE OU LE COMMISSIONNAIRE BIENFAISANT / Villiers et Gouffe – (French Theatre Series). Paris. Plassan. s.d – 9 – fr Hachette [820]
CANH NONG LUAN – Saigon. 24 aout 1929-4 avr 1931 – 1 – fr A.C.R.P.P. [073]
O CANICO : ORGAO IMPARCIAL E NOTICIOSO – Manaos, Amazonas. 16 Maio-13 Jun 1897 – 1,5,6 – bl Biblioteca [072]
Caninius, (A Canini) *see* INSTITUTIONES. LINGUAE SYRIACAE, ASSYRIACAE
Canivet, Charles *see* LES COLONIES PERDUES: OUVRAGE ILLUSTRE DE 65 GRAVURES SUR BOIS
O CANIVETE : ORGAO CRITICO E HUMORISTICO – Manaus, Amazonas. 16 Ago 1914 – 1,5,6 – bl Biblioteca [072]
Canivez, J -M *see* L'ORDRE DE CITEAUX EN BELGIQUE DES ORIGINES (1132) AU 800 SIECLE
Canivez, J-M *see*
- AUCTARIUM D.C. DE VISCH AD BIBLIOTHECAM SCRIPTORUM S.O. CISTERCIENSIS
- STATUTA CAPITULORUM GENERALIUM ORDINIS CISTERCIENSIS

Canizo Gomez, Jose del *see* IDEAS ACTUALES SOBRE LAS PLAGAS DE LANGOSTA
CANKAYA – No 1. – 1 Mayis 1928 – 2mf – 9 – $21.00 – us MEDOC [949]
Cannabich, Christian *see* A PERIODICAL OVERTURE IN EIGHT PARTS...NO. 1
Cannart d'Hamale, Arthur de *see* UN VOYAGE DE NOCES A CHICAGO
Canne, John *see* A NECESSITY OF SEPARATION FROM THE CHURCH OF ENGLAND PROVED BY THE NONCONFORMIST PRINCIPLES....1849
Cannegieter, Tjeerd *see*
- DE GODSDIENST UIT PLICHTBESEF EN DE GELOOFSVOORSTELLING UIT DICHTENDE VERBEELDING GEBOREN?
- DE GODSDIENST UIT...EN DE GELOOFSVOORSTELLING UIT DICHTENDE VERBEELDING GEBOREN?

CANNERY AND FIELD UNION NEWS, 1937 : CIO NEWS CANNERY WORKERS EDITION, 1938-1939 : UCAPAWA NEWS, 1939-1944 : FTA NEWS, 1945-1950 / United Cannery, Agricultural, Packing and Allied Workers of AmericaFood, Tobacco, and Agricultural and Allied Workers Union of America – (Coll title: Labor Union Periodicals, Pt 3) – 1996 – 1r – 1 – $135.00 – 1-55655-610-1 – us UPA [331]
Cannery Workers' Union of the Pacific, Los Angeles County Harbor District *see* FISHERY WORKER
Cannes, Henri *see* L'INFLUENCE DE L'EMIGRATION DES CAMPAGNES SUR LA NATALITE FRANCAISE
Canniff, William *see*
- THE EFFECTS OF ALCOHOL UPON THE HUMAN SYSTEM: AN ESSAY UPON THE CAUSE, NATURE AND TREATMENT OF ALCOHOLISM
- HISTORY OF THE SETTLEMENT OF UPPER CANADA (ONTARIO): WITH SPECIAL REFERENCE TO THE BAY QUINTE

CANNING WORKER'S UNION PAPERS – 6r – 1 – sa Microfile [960]
CANNINGTON GLEANER – (Some missing issues) – Ontario, CN. 1888-1977 – 31r – 1 – cn Commonwealth Micro [072]
CANNOCK ADVERTISER – England. -w. Aug 1893-Dec 1924. (Wanting 1896, 1911). (19 reels) – 1 – uk British Libr Newspaper [072]
CANNOCK CHASE EXAMINER – Hednesford. England. -w. 2 May 1874-5 Oct 1877. (2 reels) – 1 – uk British Libr Newspaper [072]
CANNOCK CHASE NEWS – (Cannock Chase Courier). England. -w. May 1889-Dec 1928. (Wanting 1911). (30 reels) – 1 – uk British Libr Newspaper [072]
Cannon, Clarence *see*
- CANNON'S PRECEDENTS OF THE HOUSE OF REPRESENTATIVES
- CANNON'S PROCEDURE IN THE HOUSE
- CANNON'S PROCEDURE IN THE HOUSE OF REPRESENTATIVES

Cannon, Harry Sharp *see* SUDERMANN'S TREATMENT OF VERSE
CANNON'S PRECEDENTS OF THE HOUSE OF REPRESENTATIVES / Cannon, Clarence – Washington: GPO. 11v. 1935-41 (all publ) – 56mf – 9 – $84.00 – LLMC 105 – us L.L.M.C. [323]
CANNON'S PROCEDURE IN THE HOUSE / Cannon, Clarence – (New ed with notes and addenda by William T. Roy) – Washington: GPO, 1959 – 6mf – 9 – $9.00 – LLMC 84-107 – us L.L.M.C. [323]
CANNON'S PROCEDURE IN THE HOUSE OF REPRESENTATIVES / ed by Cannon, Clarence – 3rd ed. Washington: GPO, 1939 (all publ) – 6mf – 9 – $9.00 – LLMC 84-106 – us L.L.M.C. [323]
Cano, M *see* OPERA
CANOE – (v6- . 1978- . 5,6,9) – v. 1-. 1973- – 1 – us UMI [790]
CANOE AND BOAT BUILDING : A COMPLETE MANUAL FOR AMATEURS: CONTAINING PLAIN AND COMPREHENSIVE DIRECTIONS FOR THE CONSTRUCTION OF CANOES, ROWING AND SAILING BOATS AND HUNTING CRAFT / Stephens, W P – 5th rev enl ed. New York: Forest & Stream Publ Co, 1891 – us Res Libr [790]
A CANOE TRIP THROUGH TEMAGAMING THE PEERLESS IN THE LAND OF HIAWATHA / Armstrong, Louis Olivier – Montreal?: Canadian Pacific Railway, 1900. 03883. (Pre-1900 Canadiana) – 9 – cn C.I.H.M. [790]
CANOGA PARK – 1946-47; 1982-87 – 9r – 1 – $450.00 – P00016 – us Library Micro [910]
THE CANOL PROJECT / U.S. Army. Office of the Chief of Military History. Eastern Defense Command – 1945. 7 v. illus., charts, maps, photos. 1 reel – 1 – 39.00 – us L of C Photodup [977]
Canon, Alexander *see* THE INVISIBLE INFLUENCE
CANON AND TEXT OF THE NEW TESTAMENT / Gregory, Caspar Rene – New York: C. Scribner's Sons, 1907. vii,539p. (International Theological Library) – 1 – us U.W. Library [240]
THE CANON AND TEXT OF THE NEW TESTAMENT (CCC15) / Chang, Pe-Huai – (In Chinese) – Hong Kong: Bible Book and Tract Depot, 1954 – 1r – 1 – 0-8370-1715-7 – 1984-6097 – us A.T.L.A. [220]
CANON LAW : A BASIC COLLECTION – initial ed. Honolulu, 1987 – 1mf – 9 – LLMC 87-000A – us L.L.M.C. [340]
CANON LAW : A BASIC COLLECTION – permanent ed. Kaneohe, 1996 – 1mf – 9 – LLMC 87-000B – us L.L.M.C. [340]
CANON LAW : A BASIC COLLECTION / ed by Reynolds, Thomas H – (Titles are too numerous to list separately. Free catalog available on request. Full cataloguing as a major microform collection available from OCLC) – From the Berkeley Law Library, Uni of California. Additional materials from the law libraries of Yale, Uni of Michigan and other law schools. Complete index – 222 titles 5730mf – 9 – $8,055.00 – us L.L.M.C. [340]
CANON LAW ABSTRACTS – (1984- . 5,6,9) – No.1- . 1958- – 1 – us UMI [073]
CANON LAW ON MICROFILM – 20r – 1 – $1,425.00 – us OmniSys [240]
THE CANON OF THE BIBLE : ITS FORMATION, HISTORY, AND FLUCTUATIONS / Davidson, Samuel – (From the 3rd rev enl ed of this same work publ in 1878) – New York: Peter Eckler, [1899] – 1mf – 9 – 0-8370-2836-1 – 1985-0836 – us A.T.L.A. [220]
Canon Vaughan *see* THE LIFE AND LABOURS OF SAINT THOMAS OF AQUIN
CANONES ET DECRETA: DES HOCHHEILIGEN, OEKUMENISCHEN UND ALLGEMEINEN CONCILS VON TRIENT CANONES UND BESCHLUESSE : NEBST DEN DARAUF BEZUEGLICHEN PAEPSTLICHEN BULLEN UND VERORDNUNGEN UND EINEM VOLLSTAENDIGEN INHALTSVERZEICHNISSE: IN TREUER VERDEUTSCHUNG NEBST EINEM GESCHICHTLICHEN ABRISSE DES CONCILS / Smets, Wilhelm – (In German and Latin) – 5. Aufl. Bielefeld: Velhagen & Klasing, 1858 – 2mf – 9 – 0-8370-8330-3 – 1986-2330 – us A.T.L.A. [240]
CANONICAL AND UNCANONICAL GOSPELS : WITH A TRANSLATION OF THE RECENTLY DISCOVERED FRAGMENT OF THE GOSPEL OF PETER, AND A SELECTION FROM THE SAYINGS OF OUR LORD NOT FOUND IN THE FOUR GOSPELS / Barnes, William Emery – (Appendix contains translation of the gospel of Peter) – London: Longmans, Green, 1893 – 1mf – 9 – 0-8370-2183-9 – 1985-0183 – us A.T.L.A. [220]
CANONICARUM QUAESTIONUM / Gutierrez, Juan – (Liber Secundus. 1729. 1.50f; 9. Liber Tertius. 1730. 1.50f; BSA; 9) – Liber Primus. 1730 – 9 – 1.50f – sp Bibl Santa Ana [240]
CANONICARUM UTRUSQUE FORI LIBER PRIMUS / Gutierrez, Juan – (Liber Secundus. 1608. 1.50f; 9. Liber Tertius. 1617. 1.50f; BSA; 9) – 1587 – 9 – 1.50f – sp Bibl Santa Ana [240]
Canonici, Luciano *see* LA PORZIENCULA NEI PIU ANTICHI DOCUMENTI FRANCESCANI...
CANONICI REGULARIS SCTI VICTORIS PARISIENSIS OPERA OMNIA / Victore, Hugo de St. – Rothomagi, 1648 Tomi 1-2-3 – 87mf – 8 – ne Slangenburg [240]
CANONIS MISSE EXPOSITIO EDIDERUNT : OBERMAN-COURTENAY / Biel, G – Wiesbaden, 1963 – 7mf – 8 – ne Slangenburg [240]
THE CANONS OF ATHANASIUS OF ALEXANDRIA : THE ARABIC AND COPTIC VERSIONS / Athanasius, Patriarch of Alexandria; ed by Riedel, Wilhelm & Crum, W E – London: Williams and Norgate, 1904 – 1mf – us A.T.L.A. [240]
THE CANONS OF INTERNATIONAL LAW / Baty, T – London, n.d. – 6mf – 9 – ILM-990/1 – ne IDC [340]
CANONS OF PROFESSIONAL ETHICS / American Bar Association – Chicago, 1947. 54p. LL-2246 – 1 – us L of C Photodup [340]
THE CANONS OF THE FIRST FOUR GENERAL COUNCILS OF NICAEA, CONSTANTINOPLE, EPHESUS AND CHALCEDON / Bright, William – Oxford: Clarendon Press, 1892 – 1mf – us A.T.L.A. [240]
CANONS OF THE SYNOD...AND OF THE PROVINCIAL SYNOD OF CANADA: WITH A COLLECTION OF STATUTES AFFECTING ECCLESIASTICAL RIGHTS AND FORMS OF GRANTS, REQUESTS AND TRUSTS FOR CHURCH PURPOSES / Church of England. Canada. Diocese of Ontario – Kingston, Ont.: Daily News, 1891. 00639. (Pre-1900 Canadiana) – 9 – cn C.I.H.M. [971]
CANONSBURG HERALD – Canonsburg, PA. -w 1872-1888 – 13 – $25.00r – us I.M.R. [071]
CANONSBURG NOTES WEEKLY – Canonsburg, PA. -w 1902-1904 – 13 – $25.00r – us I.M.R. [071]
EN CANOT DE PAPIER DE QUEBEC AU GOLFE DU MEXIQUE: 2,500 MILLES. / Bishop, Nathaniel Holmes – Traduit par Hephell. Paris: E. Plon, 1879. 00140. (Pre-1900 Canadiana) – 9 – cn C.I.H.M. [910]
Canovas del Castillo, Antonio *see* DISCURSO PRONUNCIADO 8 NOVIEMBRE DE 1888
CANPLAST '76 : PLASTICS CANADA OPPORTUNITY UNLIMITED. PROCEEDINGS / Society of Plastics Industry of Canada – 1976 – 9 – Can$40.00 – 0-88769-001-7 – cn Nash Info [660]
CANPLAST '77 : PROCEEDINGS OF THE SOCIETY OF THE PLASTICS INDUSTRY OF CANADA / Society of Plastics Industry of Canada – 1977 – 9 – Can$50.00 – 0-88769-004-1 – cn Nash Info [660]
CANPLAST '79 : PROCEEDINGS OF THE SOCIETY OF THE PLASTICS INDUSTRY OF CANADA / Society of Plastics Industry of Canada – 1979 – 9 – Can$50.00 – 0-88769-005-X – cn Nash Info [660]
Cansacchi, G *see* L'OCCUPAZIONE DEI MARI COSTIERI
Canseco, Manuel *see*
- CIRCULAR EN LA QUE EL DIRECTOR..
- CIRCULAR RECOMENDANDO LA PUNTUALIDAD DEL AYUNTAMIENTO..

Cantacuzeni, Ioannis *see* HISTORIARUM LIBRI 4 (CBH 17)
Cantarella, Adelina *see* GUIA PARA ANALISIS ANALOGICO DE "LA RAZON DE ME VIDA" DE EVA PERON
CANTARES DE JUVENTUD / Sanchez Arjona, Vicente – Sevilla: Imprenta Alvarez, Tomo 1-9 y 10-29. 1957 – 1 – sp Bibl Santa Ana [780]
CANTARES VIEJOS / Sanchez Arjona, Vicente – Sevilla: Imprenta Carlos Acuna, s.a. – 1 – sp Bibl Santa Ana [780]
CANTATE, LA CONFEDERATION / Achintre, Auguste – Paroles de A. Achintre: musique de J. Bte. Labelle, 1868? 02387. (Pre-1900 Canadiana) – 9 – cn C.I.H.M. [780]
CANTATE: LES CYGNES MALADES – Montreal, 1879. 02571. (Pre-1900 Canadiana) – 9 – cn C.I.H.M. [780]
CANTATE MORALI A VOCE SOLA, OP. 3 / Albergati, C – Bologna: G Monti, 1685 – 1 – us Sibley [780]
CANTATES FRANCOISES A 1 ET 2 VOIX: AVEC SIMPHONIE, ET SANS SIMPHONIE...LIVRE PREMIER / Clerambault, Louis Nicolas – Paris: Ches l'autuer, Sr. Foucault, 1710 – 1 – us Sibley [780]
CANTEMUS DOMINO / Plasencia. Secretariado Catequistico – Plasencia: Imp. La Victoria, 1960 – sp Bibl Santa Ana [946]
Cantera, Eugenio *see* HISTORIA DEL SANTISIMO CRISTO DE LA VICTORIA QUE SE VENERA EN LA VILLA DE SERRADILLA (CACERES)
Cantera y Burgos, Francisco *see* ALVAR GARCIA DE SANTA MARIA.
Canterbury *see* CHRONICLES OF CONVOCATION
Canterbury. Archbishop *see* REGISTERS OF THE ARCHBISHOPS OF CANTERBURY
THE CANTERBURY BENEDICTIONAL / Woolley, R M – 1917 – 4mf – 8 – ne Slangenburg [240]
CANTERBURY: CATALOGUE OF THE ARCHIVES OF THE DEAN AND CHAPTER / Bunce, C R – Ms. 1805-06 – 1 – uk Microform Academic [010]
CANTERBURY CATHEDRAL. ARCHIVES *see*
- CANTERBURY: CATALOGUE OF THE ARCHIVES OF THE DEAN AND CHAPTER
- REGISTER, 1294-1313

CANTERBURY CATHEDRAL LIBRARY CATALOGUE OF PRE-1801 BOOKS – (Binder with guide included) – Marlborough: Adam Matthew Publications, 1996 – 15mf – 9 – $130.00 – uk Matthew [020]
Canterbury. Christ Church Priory *see* LITERAE CANTUARIENSES (RS85)
Canterbury, New Hampshire. Canterbury Free Will Baptist Church *see* RECORDS
Canterbury, New Hampshire. First Free Will Baptist Society *see* RECORDS
CANTERBURY PROVINCIAL ROLL 1868-69 – 2mf – 9 – NZ$9.00 – 0-908797-65-6 – nz BAB [324]
CANTERBURY PROVINCIAL ROLL 1870-71 – 2mf – 9 – NZ$9.00 – 0-908797-66-4 – nz BAB [324]
CANTERBURY PROVINCIAL ROLL 1872-73 – 3mf – 9 – NZ$14.00 – 0-908797-28-1 – nz BAB [324]
CANTERBURY PROVINCIAL ROLL 1873-74 – 4mf – 9 – NZ$18.00 – 0-908797-29-X – nz BAB [324]
CANTERBURY PSALTER – (12th century). Trinity College Library, Cambridge – 14 – uk Microform Academic [780]
THE CANTERBURY TALES / Chaucer, Geoffrey – and Faerie Queene, Edmund Spenser; edited...with current illustrations and explanatory notes by D. Laing Purves. Boston: Lee and Shepard, pref. 1869. viii,624p. With: Report of the Commission on Industrial Education Pennsylvania – 1 – us U.W. Library [810]
THE CANTICLES OF THE CHRISTIAN CHURCH : EASTERN AND WESTERN, IN EARLY AND MEDIEVAL TIMES / Mearns, James – Cambridge: University Press, 1914 – 1mf – us A.T.L.A. [240]
IL CANTICO DEI CANTICI: STUDIO ESEGETICO / Castelli, David – Firenze: G.C. Sansoni, 1892. 1 fiche – 9 – us A.T.L.A. [240]
CANTIGAS DE SANTA MARIA / Alfonso 10 el Sabio, Rey de Castilla – Madrid: Editorial Patrimonio Nacional, 1974 – 1 – sp Bibl Santa Ana [240]

Cantillon de Tramont, P *see* DE LA NATIONALITE DES NAVIRES
CANTILUPE SOCIETY – (Coll title: Publications of the English Record Societies, 1835-1972...) – v1-20. 1906-32 – 74mf – 9 – £545.00 – uk Chadwyck [941]
Cantin, Louise *see* BIBLIOGRAPHIE ANALYTIQUE DE L'OEUVRE DE MADAME MARCELLE LEPAGE-THIBAUDEAU, LICENCIEE EN SCIENCES NATURELLES, LICENCIEE EN PHYCHOLOGIE ET PSYCHOTHERAPIE
CANTIONAL, ODER GESANGBUCH AUGSPURGISCHER CONFESSION. IN WELCHEM DES HERRN D. MARTINI LUTHERI UND ANDERER FROMMEN CHRISTAN... / Schein, J H – [Leipzig]: in Verlegung des Austoris, 1627 – 1 – us Sibley [780]
CANTIONES BOHEMICAE : LEICHE, LIEDER UND RUFE DES 13., 14. UND 15. JAHRHUNDERTS NACH HANDSCHRIFTEN AUS PRAG, JISTEBNICZ, WITTINGAU, HOHENFURT UND TEGERNSEE / ed by Dreves, Guido Maria – (Includes bibliographical references) – Leipzig: Fues, 1886 – 1mf – 9 – 0-8370-7454-1 – 1986-1454 – us A.T.L.A. [220]
CANTIONES ECCLESIASTICAE LATINAE... – Magdeburg: Impressum per M Lotther, 1545 – 1 – us Sibley [780]
LE CANTIQUE DES CANTIQUES / Renan, Ernest – (Includes bibliographical references) – 2e rev corr ed. Paris: Michel Levy, 1861 – 1mf – 9 – 0-8370-9414-3 – 1986-3414 – us A.T.L.A. [220]
LE CANTIQUE DES CANTIQUES / Robert-Tournay-Feuillet – 1963 – 8mf – 8 – ne Slangenburg [220]
CANTO A EXTREMADURA / Quijano Quijano, Adolfo – Cadiz: Libreria Universal de Morillas, s.a. – sp Bibl Santa Ana [780]
CANTO A LA VERA / Verde, Josefina – Plasencia: Sanguino offset y Tip., 1979 – 1 – sp Bibl Santa Ana [780]
EL CANTO DE RELACION EN EL FOLKLORE INFANTIL DE EXTREMADURA / Gil Garcia, Bonifacio – Badajoz, 1963 – 1 – sp Bibl Santa Ana [380]
CANTO DI BALDASSARE DONATO IL PRIMO LIBRO DI MADRIGALI A CINQUE E A SEI VOCI CON TRE DIALOGHI A SETTE NOVAMENTE PER ANTONIO GARDANO / Donato, Baldassare – Venice, 1560. 6v – 1 – 23.00 – us L of C Photodup [780]
IL CANTO FERMO IN PRATTICA.. / Caselli, Domenico A – 1724 – 9 – us Sibley [780]
CANTO FUNEBRE – 1821 – 9 – 1.50f – sp Bibl Santa Ana [810]
Cantoclarus, CaR *see* EXCERPTA DE LEGATIONIBUS (CBH 1,2)
Canton, Dario *see*
- ELECCIONES Y PARTIDOS POLITICOS EN LA ARGENTINA
- LAS INTERVENCIONES MILITARES EN LA ARGENTINA, 1900-66
- EL PARLAMENTO ARGENTINO EN EPOCAS DE CAMBIO
- LA POLITICA DE LOS MILITARES ARGENTINOS
- LA SAGA DEL PERONISMO

CANTON ESTREMENOFEL (SIC), PLASENCIA – 1884-89.No. sueltos – 9 – 1.50f – sp Bibl Santa Ana [072]
EL CANTON EXTREMENO – Plasencia, 1887-1889 – 5 – sp Bibl Santa Ana [073]
CANTON GENERAL PRICE CURRENT – China. -w. 7 Jan 1834-26 Dec 1837. (1 reel) – 1 – uk British Libr Newspaper [072]
CANTON IND. SENTINEL – Canton, PA., 1939-1979 – 13 – $25.00r – us I.M.R. [071]
Canton, Mississippi *see* MISCELLANEOUS EARLY NEWSPAPERS
Canton. Municipal Administration *see* KUANG-CHOU-SHIH SHIH-CHENG KAI-YAO
Canton. Ohio. (Elkton Circuit). Methodist-Episcopal Church *see* CHURCH RECORDS, MS 2822
Canton. Ohio. First Baptist Church *see* RECORDS
Canton. Ohio. First United Church of Christ *see* RECORDS
THE CANTON PRESS – Canton: [s.n.] sep 12 1835-mar 30 1944 – 4r – 1 – us Res Libr [072]
CANTON REGISTER – (Filmed with: Hongkong, Late Canton, Register jun 20-dec 26 1843) – Canton: [James Matheson], nov 8 1827-jun 10 1843 – 4r – 1 – us Res Libr [072]
CANTON SENTINEL – Canton, PA. 1875-1939. 41 rolls – 13 – $25.00r – us I.M.R. [071]
CANTON TIMES – Canton, China. v1-2. 1919-20 – 2r – 1 – us Ross [072]
Canton. University *see*
- KUANG-TA-HSUEH-PAO

CANTON WORLD – Canton, PA. 1909-15. 2 rolls – 13 – $25.00r – us I.M.R. [071]
Cantonese Union Church *see* CANTONESE UNION CHURCH BULLETIN
CANTONESE UNION CHURCH BULLETIN = SHANGHAI KUANG-TUNG CHUNG-HUA CHI-TU-CHIAO-HUI YUEH PAO / Cantonese Union Church – 1917-24 – 2r – 1 – ATLA S0310 – us A.T.L.A. [073]
DER CANTOR / Wolff, Gottfried August Benedikt – [S.l: s.n, 1872?] – 1r – 1 – us U.W. Library [390]
Cantor, Georg *see* OEUVRES TRADUITES EN FRANCAIS, AVEC UNE INTRODUCTION DE P. DUGAC
IL CANTORE ADDOTTRINATO, OVVERO REGOLE DEL CANTO CORALE / Coferati, Matteo – P-218. 1682 – 9 – ne IDC [780]
Cantos Benitez, Pedro de *see* ESCRUTINIO DE MARAVEDISES
CANTOS DEL PUEBLO DE DIOS – Caceres: Tip. El Noticiero, 1975 – 1 – sp Bibl Santa Ana [780]
CANTOS EN NEGRO Y ESPERANZA / Montero Monago, Nemesio E – Madrid: Altamira Tip, 1980 – 1 – sp Bibl Santa Ana [780]
CANTOS LITURGICOS / Colegio San Francisco Javier. Fuente de Cantos (Badajoz) – Zafra: Industrias Tipgraficas Extremenas, 1969 – sp Bibl Santa Ana [780]
CANTOS LITURGICOS / Iglesia – Badajoz: Tip. Manuel Barrena, 1969 – 1 – sp Bibl Santa Ana [240]
CANTOS Y CUENTOS / Sanchez Arjona y Sanchez Arjona, Jose – 1877 – 9 – 1.50f – sp Bibl Santa Ana [810]
Cantraine, F J *see* MALACOLOGIE MEDITERRANEENNE ET LITTORALE
CANTUM ECCLESIASTICUM PRAECIBUS APUD DEUM ANIMAS JUVANDI, CORPOR RAQUE HUMAND... / Magalhaes, F – Antverpine: H Aertssens, 1691 – 1 – us Sibley [780]
Canturbury Cathedral *see* CANTERBURY: CATALOGUE OF THE ARCHIVES OF THE DEAN AND CHAPTER
CANTUS GREGORIANO-MOGUNTINUS, BREVIARIO ROMANO ACCOMODATUS: JUSSU ET AUTORITATE JOANNIS PHILIPPI SACRAE SEDIS MOGUNTINAE ARCHIEPISCOPI – 1666-(1667). 2v – 1 – us Sibley [780]
CANUC:H *see* CANADIAN UNION CATALOGUE OF LIBRARY MATERIALS FOR THE PRINT-HANDICAPPED (CANUC:H)
CANUC:S *see* UNION LIST OF SERIALS IN THE SOCIAL SCIENCES AND HUMANITIES (CANUC:S)
O CANUDO : ORGAM DA ACTUALIDADE – Canudos, Alagoas. 21 Abr 1897 – 1,5,6 – bl Biblioteca [072]
Canuto, V et al *see* FUNDAMENTALS OF COSMIC PHYSICS
CANYON CREEK CURRENT – Canyonville, OR. -w. 21 Mar 1974-24 Dec 1975+. 1 roll – 1 – us U.O. Library [071]
CANYON LAKE COMMUNITY NEWS – Canyon Lake, CA. 1986- – 1r – 1 – $50.00 ($50.00y) – R04010 – us Library Micro [071]
CANYON LAKE MENIFEE VALLEY NEWS – Canyon Lake, CA. 1989- – 1r – 1 – $50.00 ($50.00y) – R04012 – us Library Micro [071]
CANYON LAKE WEEKLY – Canyon Lake, CA. 1990- – 1+ r – 1 – $50.00 ($50.00y) – R04011 – us Library Micro [071]
CANZON A SELIN IMPERATOR DE TURCHI : IN DESPERATION DELLA SUA ARMATA, E GENTE PERSA – [1571] – 1mf – 9 – H-8181/1 – ne IDC [956]
CANZONE NELLA FELICISSIMA VITTORIA CHRISTIANA CONTRA INFIDELI AL SERENISS. D. GIO. D'AVSTRIA / Guarnello, A – Venice, 1571 – 1mf – 9 – H-8313/1 – ne IDC [956]
CANZONE NELLA NATIVITA DI NOSTRO SIGNOR GIESV CHRISTO. NELLA ALLEGREZZA DELLA VITTORIA HAUUTA CONTRA TURCHI / Forzanini, G P – Venetia, 1572 – 1mf – 9 – H-8325/1 – ne IDC [956]
CANZONE NELLA VITTORIA DELL' ARMATA DELLA SANTISSIMA LEGA CONTRA LA TURCHESCA – Venice, 1571 – 1mf – 9 – H-8174/1 – ne IDC [956]
CANZONE SOPRA LA VITTORIA OTTENVTA DALL' ARMATA DE' PRENCIPI CHRISTIANI CONTRA LA TURCHESCA – Venetia, 1571 – 1mf – 9 – H-8175/1 – ne IDC [956]
CANZONE...PER LA FELICISSIMA VITTORIA NAUALE CONTRA TURCHI / Tiepolo, G – Vinegia, 1572 – 1mf – 9 – H-8334/1 – ne IDC [956]
CANZONETTA IN A PER UNA VOCE COL CEMBALO....AUTOGRAPH MS. PHILEMON UND BAUCIS : EIN TAG, DER ALLEN FREUDE BRINGT / Haydn, Joseph – Arranged 1790? – 9 – us Sibley [780]
CANZONETTA IN A-MAJOR PER UNA VOCE COL CEMBALO... / Haydn, Joseph – (Title page in the hand of Aloys Fuchs with an authentication statement by him) – Autograph manuscript, 179? – 1mf – 9 – us Sibley [780]
CANZONETTE A QUATTRO VOCI, COMPOSTE DE DIUVERSI ECCTI MUSICI, CON L'INTAUOLATURA DEL CIMBALO ET DEL LIUTO – Roma: S Verovio, 1591 – 1 – us Sibley [780]
CANZONETTE MUSICALI / Romano, R – 1622-26. Contains: Prima raccolta. 1622; Seconda raccolta. 1622; Terza raccolta. 1622; Nuova raccolta. 1625; Ressiduo alla quarta parte. 1626 – 9 – us Sibley [780]
CANZONETTE SPIRITUALI / Casini, G – Firenze, Pietro Antonio Brigonci, 1703 – 1 – us Sibley [780]
CAO SHUN QIYI SHILIAO HUIBIAN – Collection of materials on the uprising led by Cao Shun. Comp. by Qiao Zhiqiang. 2 fiches. F H84 – 9 – $4.50 – cc Microforms [950]
EL CAOS DE RELIGIONES NUEVAS / Bayle, Constantino – Madrid: Razon y Fe, 1929 – 9 – sp Bibl Santa Ana [240]
Caouette, Jean Baptiste *see* LES VOIX INTIMES
LE CAOUTCHOUC ET LA GUTTA-PERCHA – Paris, France. -m. March 1904-Dec 1909. 4 reels – 1 – uk British Libr Newspaper [410]
CAOUTCHOUS ET LA GUTTA-PERCHA – v. 1-34. 1904-1937 – 1,5,6 – us Princeton Micro [800]
LE CAP AU DIABLE: LEGENDE / Deguise, Charles – Montreal: E. Senecal, 1873. 03789. (Pre-1900 Canadiana) – 9 – cn C.I.H.M. [971]
LE CAP DE BONNE-ESPERANCE AU 17E SIECLE : L'ESCALE MARITIME – JOHAN VAN RIEBEECK – LES COLONS EUROPEENS... – Paris: Hatchette, 1909 – 1 – us Res Libr [960]
CAP JOURNAL – v1- 1991- – 9 – Can$20.00y – cn Micromedia [971]
CAP OF LIBERTY – London, UK. 1819-20. -irr. 13 feet – 1 – uk British Libr Newspaper [072]
CAPA, BASICLICA, MONASTERIUM ET LE CULTE DE ST MARTIN DE TOURS / Bosch, J Van den – Nijmegen, 1959 – 4mf – 8 – ne Slangenburg [240]
Capaccio, Giulio Cesare *see* DELLE IMPRESE
LA CAPACIDAD CAMBIARIA EN EL DERECHO INTERNACIONAL PRIVADO : ESTUDIO COMPARATIVO DE LAS LEGISLACIONES AMERICANAS / Garcia Calderon K, Manuel – Lima: Libreria e Impr. Gil, 1951. 267p. LL-8008 – 1 – us L of C Photodup [340]
LA CAPACITA PATRIMONIALE DELLA DONNA MARITATA... / Baldassarri, A – Roma, 1910 – 1mf – 9 – ILM-3088/1 – ne IDC [340]
CAP-AUX-DIAMANTS : REVUE D'HISTOIRE DU Q'C – Quebec. v1 n1. Printemps 1985-n28. Hiver 1992 – 1r – 1 – cn Can Microfilming [072]
CAPE ARGUS – Cape Town, South Africa. 3 Jan 1857- – 1637 rolls – 1 – sa Microfile [960]
CAPE ARGUS WEEKLY EDITION – Cape Town, South Africa. 1880-1911 – 26r – 1, 16 diazo available – sa SA Libr [960]
CAPE BRETON POST – (1973-1992.-292r) – Sydney, 1993 – 22r – 1 – cn Preston [971]
CAPE BRETON RAILWAY EXTENSION COMPANY OF CANADA – Halifax, N.S., 1890? 02068. (Pre-1900 Canadiana) – 9 – cn C.I.H.M. [380]
CAPE BRETONS' MAGAZINE – (v1-37, 38-46 Can$100.00) – Cape Breton. nos 1-67. 1972-94 – 5 – Can$50.00y – cn Micromedia [971]
THE CAPE CHRONICLE – Cape Town, South Africa.W.F. Mathew, 1860-62. 4 May 1860-14 Nov 1862. 1 reel.Continues: The Cape Weekly Chronicle – 1, 16 diazo available at reduced price – sa SA Libr [072]
THE CAPE CHRONICLE – Cape Town, South Africa.William Foster, 1870-71. 1 Jul 1870-30 Jun 1871. 1 reel – 1, 16 diazo available at reduced price – sa SA Libr [072]
CAPE COAST CASTLE RECORD BOOK, 1777-1803 – [s.l: s.n, 19–?] – 1 – us Res Libr [960]
Cape Colony *see* GOVERNMENT PUBLICATIONS
THE CAPE DAILY TELEGRAPH – Port Elizabeth, South Africa, 4 Jan 1848-30 Sept 1908 – 107r – 1,16 diazo available – sa SA Libr [072]
CAPE FEAR RECORD – Wilmington. N.C. 1829-1832 – 1 – us UMI [071]
CAPE FRONTIER TIMES – Grahamstown, South Africa. 1 Jan 1840-30 Sept 1864. 10 reels. Title varies: The Colonial Times, Jan-May 1840. Absorbed by: The Anglo African – 1, 16 diazo available at reduced price – sa SA Libr [072]
Cape Girardeau. Missouri *see* PROCEEDINGS OF THE BETHEL CHURCH
CAPE GUARDIAN – Cape Town: Stewart Printing Co, feb 19-jun 11 1937 – 1r – 1 – us Res Libr [072]
THE CAPE HORNET – Port Elizabeth, South Africa. 5 Jan-20 Nov 1879. 1 reel – 1, 16 diazo available at reduced price – sa SA Libr [072]
CAPE LAW JOURNAL – v1-17. 1984-1900 – 9 – $214.00 – us Hein [340]
CAPE LAW JOURNAL *see*
- SOUTH AFRICAN LAW JOURNAL

THE CAPE MERCURY – King William's Town, South Africa: 20 Jun 1875-23 Dec 1947 – 123r – 1 (diazo also available at reduced price) – sa SA Libr [072]
CAPE MERCURY AND WEEELY MAGAZINE *see* CAPE TOWN WEEKLY MAGAZINE
THE CAPE MERCURY AND WEEKLY MAGAZINE – Cape Town, South Africa. 14 Jan 1859-28 Oct 1859. 1r Title varies: Cape Town Weekly Magazine, Jan-Mar 1859 – 1 – sa SA Libr [072]
THE CAPE MONITOR – Cape Town, South Africa.18 Oct 1850-20 Dec 1862. 6 reels. Frequency varies – 1, 16 diazo available at reduced price – sa SA Libr [072]
CAPE MONTHLY MAGAZINE – Capetown. v1-9; ns: v1-18; series 2: v1-4. 1857-81 – 5r – 1 – us Ross [960]
THE CAPE MONTHLY MAGAZINE – (v11 jan-jun 1862) – Cape Town: J C Juta. 1857-81 – 1 – us Res Libr [073]
THE CAPE OF GOOD HOPE GOVERNMENT GAZETTE – Cape Town, South Africa: Government Printer 1800-1910 – 155r – 1,16 diazo also available – sa SA Libr [324]
CAPE OF GOOD HOPE IMPARTIAL OBSERVER *see* MEDITATOR
Cape of Good Hope. Laws, Statutes, etc *see* STATUTES...1652-1905
THE CAPE OF GOOD HOPE LITERARY MAGAZINE – (Filmed with: The Cape Monthly Magazine v1 1847. v2 n5-10 feb-dec 1848) – Cape Town: [s.n.], 1847- – 1 – us Res Libr [800]
CAPE OF GOOD HOPE OFFICIAL PUBLICATIONS, 1854-1910 : PARLIAMENTARY REPORTS, 1882-1910 – Cape Town: Government Printer, 1882-1910 – 3,181mf – 9 – sa SA Libr [324]
Cape of Good Hope. Parliament. House *see* INDEX TO THE ANNEXURES AND PRINTED PAPERS OF THE HOUSE OF ASSEMBLY... 1854-1897
CAPE OF GOOD HOPE. PARLIAMENTARY PAPERS, 1854-1910 : SESSIONAL PAPERS AND REPORTS (A, C AND G SERIES) – (Cape Offipubs, section 2) – Cape Town, South Africa: Government Printer, 1854-1910 – 3,181mf – 9 – sa SA Libr [324]
CAPE OF GOOD HOPE. PARLIAMENTARY PAPERS, 1854-1910 : VOTES AND PROCEEDINGS (HOUSE OF ASSEMBLY AND LEGISLATIVE COUNCIL) – (Cape Offipubs, section 3) – Cape Town, South Africa: Government Printer, 1854-1910 – 871mf – 9 – sa SA Libr [324]
CAPE OF GOOD HOPE & PORT NATAL SHIPPING & MERCANTILE GAZETTE – Cape Town, South Africa.5 Jan 1844-30 Dec 1861. 10 reels – 1, 16 diazo available at reduced price – sa SA Libr [072]

CAPE OF GOOD HOPE SHIPPING LIST – Cape Town, South Africa. Cape of Good Hope & Port Natal Shipping & Mercantile Gazette. -w. 7 Jan 1840-28 Dec 1855. Imperfect. – 212r – 1 – £24.00r – uk British Libr Newspaper [380]
Cape of Good Hope. South Africa. Parliament *see*
– PAPERS 1854-1910
– REPORT OF THE SELECT COMMITTEE 1909
Cape of Good Hope. South Africa. Parliament. Legislative Council *see* REPORT OF THE SELECT COMMITTEE 1856-1909
Cape of Good Hope. Surveyor-General's Office *see* REPORT...WITH APPENDICES
CAPE PROVINCE. RECORDS OF THE PROVINCIAL AUDITOR. CAPE TOWN, 1910-19; 1928-50/51 – 5r microfiche – 9 – sa SA Libr [324]
THE CAPE REGISTER – Cape Town, South Africa.25 Apr 1890-4 Dec 1903. 15 reels – 1, 16 diazo available at reduced price – sa SA Libr [072]
CAPE STANDARD – Cape Town: Stewart Printing Co, may 11 1936-nov 25 1947 – 10r – 1 – us Res Libr [072]
CAPE STANDARD *see* SOUTH AFRICAN ADVERTISER AND MAIL
THE CAPE STANDARD – Cape Town, South Africa.1936-47. 13 reels – 1, 16 diazo available at reduced price – sa SA Libr [072]
THE CAPE STANDARD – Cape Town, South Africa.2 Jan 1866-30 Sept 1869. 8 reels. Morgod with: South African Advertiser and Mail – 1, 16 diazo available at reduced price – sa SA Libr [072]
CAPE TIMES – Cape Town: R W Murray & F Y St Leger, jul 1938-jan 1986; mar-may 1986 – 1 – us Res Libr [072]
CAPE TIMES – Cape Town, South Africa. 2 Apr 1984- – 197reels – 1 – sa Microfile [960]
CAPE TIMES – Capetown. Republic of South Africa. 1913-1935 – 1 – us UMI [072]
THE CAPE TIMES – Cape Town, South Africa. 27 Mar 1876-Dec 1913. 1 Jul 1980-Dec 1984. – 268r Jul 1980-Oct 1982; 41r – 1 – sa SA Libr [072]
THE CAPE TIMES WEEKLY EDITION – (Fiche are also available in diazo) – Cape Town, South Africa: Cape Times, 4 Jan 1887-26 Jan 1917 – 39r – 1,16 – sa SA Libr [960]
CAPE TOWN DIOCESAN MAGAZINE – (Some original pgs damaged) – v1-10. Aug 1939-May 1949 – 3r – 1 – ATLA S0689 – us A.T.L.A. [073]
THE CAPE TOWN ENGLISH PRESS INDEX 1871-75 / Coates, Peter Ralph – Cape Town: South African Library – 64mf – 11 – sa SA Libr [010]
THE CAPE TOWN MAIL – Cape Town, South Africa.6 Mar 1841-28 Jun 1853. 8 reels. Absorbed by: The South African Commercial Advertiser – 1, 16 diazo available at reduced price – sa SA Libr [072]
THE CAPE TOWN MIRROR – Cape Town, South Africa.5 Sept 1848-26 Jun 1849. 1 reel – 1, 16 diazo available at reduced price – sa SA Libr [072]
Cape Town. South Africa. Civil Rights League *see* NEWSLETTER
CAPE TOWN WEEKLY MAGAZINE – Cape Town, South Africa – sa SA Libr [072]
CAPE VERDE ISLANDS : ANUARIO ESTATISTICO 1933-1952 / Cape Verde Islands. Seccao de Estatistica – (Coll title: African Official Statistical Serials, 1867-1982) – 28mf – 9 – £235.00 – uk Chadwyck [960]
Cape Verde Islands *see*
– BOLETIM OFICIAL DE CABO VERDE
– BOLETIN OFICIAL, AND SUPPLEMENTS
– PRIMEIRO PLANO DE FOMENTO, 1953-58
– SEGUNDO PLANO DE FOMENTO, 1959-64
– TERCEIRO PLANO DE FOMENTO, 1968-73
Cape Verde Islands. Seccao de Estatistica *see* CAPE VERDE ISLANDS
CAPE VINCENT AND ITS HISTORY / Casler, Nelie H – Watertown: Hungerford-Horton Co., 1906. New York Reel 18. (The Cox Library Collection) – 5 – us Americana [978]
THE CAPE WEEKLY CHRONICLE – Cape Town, South Africa.W.F. Mathew, 1859-60. 4 Feb 1859-27 Jan 1860. 1 reel.Continued by: The Cape Chronicle – 1, 16 diazo available at reduced price – sa SA Libr [072]
Capeau, Charles *see* LA CONVENTION COLLECTIVE DE TRAVAIL (LOI DU 24 JUIN 1936) ET L'ARBITRAGE OBLIGATOIRE
Capecelatro, Alfonso *see* CHRIST, THE CHURCH, AND MAN
Capefigue, J B H R *see* HISTOIRE AUTHENTIQUE...
Capeletti, G *see* THE SCOTCH GHOST, OR, LITTLE FANNY'S LOVE
CAPELLA LIPSIAE / Martinius – 1866 – 1 – uk Microform Academic [590]
Capella y Pons, F *see* MONROISME?...
Capello, de Brito *see* GUIDE POUR L'USAGE DES CARTES DES VENTS ET DES COURANTS DU GOLFE DE GUINEE
Capello, Hermenegildo Carlos de Brito *see* DE BENGUELLA AS TERRAS DO IACCA..
Capers, John G *see* FEDERAL LAWS GOVERNING LICENSED DEALERS
Capes, J M *see* TO ROME AND BACK
Capes, John Moore *see*
– THE CHURCH OF THE APOSTLES
– WHAT CAN BE CERTAINLY KNOWN OF GOD AND OF JESUS OF NAZARETH?
Capes, W W *see* THE ENGLISH CHURCH IN THE FOURTEENTH AND FIFTEENTH CENTURIES
O CAPETA : PERIODICO CRITICO, LITTERARIO E NOTICIOSO – Maceio, Alagoas. 10 Jul 1887 – 1,5,6 – bl Biblioteca [072]
CAPETOWN (SOUTH AFRICA) DIOCESAN RECORDS / United Society for the Propagation of the Gospel. Archives – 19th Century – 1 – uk Microform Academic [025]
Capgrave, John *see*
– CHRONICLE OF ENGLAND (RS1)
– LIBER DE ILLUSTRIBUS HENRICIS (RS7)
CAPISTRANO VALLEY NEWS – South Co, CA. 1993 – 4r – 1 – $200.00 – R04117 – us Library Micro [071]
CAPITA PIETATIS ET RELIGIONIS CHRISTIANAE... / Camerarius, J – Lipsiae, 1551 – 1mf – 9 – ne IDC [240]
LE CAPITAINE CASSE-COU / Boussenard, Louis – Montreal: Montreal Printing and Publishing, 1903. SEM105P527 – 3mf – 9 – Can$6.75 – cn Bibl Nat [830]
A CAPITAL – Lisbon, 2 Sep 1916-7 Aug 1919 – 6r – 1 – uk British Libr Newspaper [072]
A CAPITAL – Manaus, Amazonas. 16 Jul 1917-15 Nov 1918 – 1,5,6 – bl Biblioteca [072]
A CAPITAL – Rio Branco, Acre. 29 Jul 1921-10 Dez 1922 – 1,5,6 – bl Biblioteca [072]
A CAPITAL – [s.l.]. 20 Set 1926-31 Mar 1927 – 1,5,6 – bl Biblioteca [072]
CAPITAL – 1980-1995 – 1r per y – 5,6 – Sfr428.00 – sz Infoprint [336]
CAPITAL – 1993 – 9 – DM144.00y – gw IOS [332]
CAPITAL – Ellensburg. Wash. 1896-1897; 1903-1940 – 1 – us UMI [071]
CAPITAL – Fredericton, Canada. 1880-89 – 8r – 1 – $520.00 – cn Library Assoc [971]
CAPITAL – Guthrie. Okl. 1889-91 – 1 – us UMI [071]
CAPITAL – Sedalia. Mo. 1922-32 – 1 – us UMI [071]
CAPITAL – Topeka. Kan. 1879- – 1 – us UMI [071]
LA CAPITAL – Rosario, Argentina: [s.n.] 1945-aug 1948; oct 1948-mar 1949; may 1949-feb 1950; july-oct, 1950; 1951-jun 1953 – 1 – us Res Libr [072]
LE CAPITAL – Paris. 1922-juin 1940 – 1 – fr A.C.R.P.P. [073]
CAPITAL AND INTEREST / Bastiat, Frederic – 48p – 9 – 1.00f – at Libertarian Micro [335]
CAPITAL AND LABOUR – London, UK. 25 Feb 1874-20 Dec 1882. -w. 9 reels – 1 – uk British Libr Newspaper [072]
CAPITAL AND LABOUR: ARCHIVES OF EMPLOYERS' AND WORKERS' ORGANISATIONS, 1850-1939 – (Part One: Federation of British Industries Minutes, 1916-39) – Series One: Archives of the Confederation of British Industry and Predecessors – 1 – us Primary [331]
CAPITAL AND LABOUR: ARCHIVES OF EMPLOYERS' AND WORKERS' ORGANISATIONS, 1850-1939 – (Part One: Minutes and Reports of the Amalgamated Assoc. of Card and Blowing Room Operatives, 1888-1940. Part Two: Central Committee and General Council Minutes of the Amalgamated Weavers' Association, 1885-1939) – Series Two: Trade Union Archives – 1 – us Primary [331]
CAPITAL BAPTIST – 1959, 1963-91 – 1 – $313.52 – us Baptist [240]
CAPITAL CHRONICLE – Salem, OR. 31 Aug 1867-16 Mar 1868. 1 roll – 1 – us U.O. Library [071]
THE CAPITAL CITY OF CANADA AND ITS SURROUNDINGS: THE MOST PICTURESQUE CAPITAL IN THE WORLD – Ottawa: H. E. Dickson, 1892. 02067. (Pre-1900 Canadiana) – 9 – cn C.I.H.M. [910]
CAPITAL CITY SUN – Lincoln, NE. -w. Nov 1961; Jan 1962-Dec 1972 – 1 – us NE Hist [071]
CAPITAL CITY SUN – Lincoln. Neb. 1962- – 1 – us UMI [071]
CAPITAL DEVELOPMENT PLAN, 1957/61 / Nyasaland – Zomba. 1957 – 9 – ne IDC [338]
CAPITAL EXPENDITURE PROGRAMME, 1955/56-1959/60 / Mauritius – (Sessional Paper No. 6 of 1956). Port Louis. 1956. BD-662 1 – 9 – ne IDC [338]
CAPITAL EXPENDITURE PROGRAMME, 1957-1962 INTERIM REPORT OF THE ECONOMIC PLANNING COMMITTEE / Mauritius – (Sessional Paper no. 10 of 1957). Port Louis. 1957 – 9 – ne IDC [338]
EL CAPITAL EXTERNO EN EL DESARROLLO ECONOMICO DE ARGENTINA : 1880-1964 / Fischer, Peter W – Santiago de Chile: Instituto Latinoamericano de Investigaciones Sociales, 1973 – 1 – CSUXAHZ5237-B – us Hoover Inst Photo [330]
CAPITAL FORMATION AND INCREASE IN NATIONAL INCOME IN SUDAN IN 1955/1959 / Sudan. Dept. of Statistics – J. G. Klove. 1961. DNE-7612 1 – 9 – ne IDC [310]
CAPITAL JOURNAL – Salem. Or. 1956- – 1 – us UMI [071]
CAPITAL JOURNAL – Salem, OR. -d. 1 Mar 1888-10 Jul 1957. 187 rolls – 1 – us U.O. Library [071]
CAPITAL JOURNAL – Salem, OR. -w. 10 Jan 1890-25 Dec 1913. 8 rolls – 1 – us U.O. Library [071]
CAPITAL NEWS – Carson City, NV. Dec 1950 – 1r – 1 – $50.00 – U04440 – us Library Micro [071]
CAPITAL NEWS – Jefferson City. Mo. 1910-1911; 1916- – 1 – us UMI [071]
CAPITAL PRESS – (Set incl. Hollywood Press (Salem)) – Salem, OR. -w. 10 Feb 1928-23 Jun 1978. – 30r – 1 – us U.O. Library [071]
Capital Publishing Co *see* WHO'S WHO IN DENVER AND COLORADO, 1940, 1941 AND 1942
CAPITAL REVIEW – Salem OR. Apr 18 1923 – 1 – us U.O. Library [071]
CAPITAL TIMES – Madison. Wis. 1918- – 1 – us UMI [071]
CAPITAL UNIVERSITY LAW REVIEW – v1-23. 1972-94 – 9 – $378.00 set – us Hein [340]
LA CAPITALE – Denver, CO: La Capitale Publ Co, [dec 29 1917-oct 1923] – us Res Libr [071]
LA CAPITALE – Sacramento, CA: V Panattoni, [dec 8 1917-apr 1944] – 22r – us Res Libr [071]
LOS CAPITALES YANQUIS EN LA ARGENTINA / Sommi, Luis Victor – Buenos Aires: Editorial Monteagudo, 1949. 212p.Illus.Incl. bibliog. 1 reel. 1273 – 1 – us U.W. Library [336]
CAPITALIST WORKER – 8p, sample copy, Journal of the Young Monday Club, London, n.d., Feb 1984 samply copy, 4p – 9 – 1.00f – at Libertarian Micro [335]
LE CAPITALISTE *see* LE CANADA ECONOMIQUE /LE CAPITALISTE
EL CAPITAN DIEGO DE CACERES OVANDO PALADIN EXTREMENO DE LOS REYES CATOLICOS / Munoz de San Pedro, Miguel – Badajoz: Imp. de la Dipt.Prov., 1952 – 1 – sp Bibl Santa Ana [946]
EL CAPITAN DON GONZALO PIZARRO, PADRE DE PIZARRO HERNANDO, JUAN Y GONZALO PIZARRO, CONQUISTADORES DEL PERU / Cuneo-Vidal, Romulo – Madrid: Rev. Arch. Bibliot. y Museos, 1926 – 1 – sp Bibl Santa Ana [920]
EL CAPITAN GENERAL MARQUES DE MONSALUD / Monsalud, Marques de – Madrid: Suc, de Rivadeneyra, 1909 – 1 – sp Bibl Santa Ana [920]
CAPITANES GENERALES. CARTAS FLORIDA Y LUISIANA (ANNO 1764-1823) – Sevilla – 43r – 5,6 – sp Cultura [977]
CAPITANES GENERALES DE LA HABANA – Sevilla – 34r – 5,6 – sp Cultura [972]
LES CAPITAUX ET LA REGION : ETUDE GEOGRAPHIQUE. ESSAI SUR LE COMMERCE ET LA CIRCULATION DES CAPITAUX DANS LA REGION LYONNAISE / Labasse, J – F90.00 – fr Ethnologie [332]
CAPITO UND BUTZER, STRASSBURGS REFORMATOREN : NACH IHREM HANDSCHRIFTLICHEN BRIEFSCHATZE, IHREN GEDRUCKTEN SCHRIFTEN UND ANDEREN GLEICHZEITIGEN QUELLEN / Baum, Johann Wilhelm – Elberfeld: R.L. Friderichs, 1860. (Leben und ausgewaehlte Schriften der Vaeter und Begruender der reformirten Kirche; 3. T.) – 2mf – us A.T.L.A. [240]
CAPITOL HILL BEACON – Oklahoma City. Okl. 1948-56 – 1 – us UMI [071]
CAPITULARIA REGUM FRANCORUM (MGH LEGES. 1: 1.BD) – 1835 – Dfl56.00 – ne Slangenburg [240]
O CAPITULO : JORNAL SATYRICO E LITTERARIO – Feira de Sant'Anna, BA. 28 Set 1877 – 1,5,6 – bl Biblioteca [072]
Capmany Montpalau, Antonio *see*
– FILOSOFIA DE LA ELOCUENCIA
– MEMORIA HISTORICAS DE LA CIUDAD DE BARCELONA. TOMO 3
– MEMORIAS HISTORICAS DE LA CIUDAD DE BARCELONA. TOMO 1
– MEMORIAS HISTORICAS DE LA CIUDAD DE BARCELONA. TOMO 2
– MEMORIAS HISTORICAS DE LA CIUDAD DE BARCELONA. TOMO 4
– TEATRO DE LA ELOCUENCIA ESPANOLA. TOMO 1
– TEATRO DE LA ELOCUENCIA ESPANOLA TOMO 2
– TEATRO DE LA ELOCUENCIA ESPANOLA. TOMO 3
– TEATRO DE LA ELOCUENCIA ESPANOLA. TOMO 4
– TEATRO DE LA ELOCUENCIA ESPANOLA. TOMO 5
Capomazza, Ilario *see* LA LINGUA DEGLI AFAR; VOCABOLARIO ITALIANO-DANKALO E DANKALO-ITALIANO
CAPOT! : OU, LES ADIEUX AU POUVOIR, CHANSON NOUVELLE – Paris [1848?] – us Res Libr [944]
Cappa, Ricardo S J *see*
– ESTUDIOS CRITICOS ACERCA DE LA DOMINACION ESPANOLA EN AMERICA
– HISTORIA DE PERU
Cappel, J *see* CRITICA SACRA
Cappel, L *see* CRITICA SACRA
Capper, Arthur *see* LETTERS AND SPEECHES
Capper, Charles *see* THE PORT AND TRADE OF LONDON, HISTORICAL, STATISTICAL, LOCAL, AND GENERAL
CAPPRICCIOS, TWO, FOR THE PIANO, OP. 47 / Clementi, M – (Ist ed. Signed by Clementi) – London: Clementi et al, 1821 – 1 – us Sibley [780]
CAPRENO – Reno, NV. 1948-49 – 1r – 1 – $50.00 – U04660 – us Library Micro [071]
Capreolus, Johannes *see*
– DEFENSIONES THEOLOGIAE DIVI THOMAE AQUINATIS
– DEFENSIONES THEOLOGIAE DIVI THOMAE AQUINATIS. VOL 1-7
CAPRICE BRILLIANT POUR PIANO ET VIOLON / Saint-Saens, Camille – Autograph manuscirpt, [1859] – 1 – us Sibley [780]
CAPRICE IN A MINOR, ARRANGED BY KREISLER / Wieniawski, H – New York: Carl Fisher, 1913 – 1 – us Sibley [780]
CAPRICE NO. 20, ARRANGED FOR VIOLIN AND PIANO BY KREISLER / Paganini, N & Kreisler, F – (Score and part) – New York: C Fisher, 1913 – 1 – us Sibley [780]
CAPRICORN AFRICA – [London?: s.n. 1953?] – us Res Libr [960]
Capricorn Africa Society *see* HANDBOOK FOR SPEAKERS
THE CAPRICORN CONVENTION : THE WORLD PRESS ON THE CAPRICORN AFRICA SOCIETY'S DECLARATIONS – [London: Neane, 1953] – 1 – us Res Libr [960]
THE CAPRICORN CONVENTION : THE WORLD PRESS ON THE CAPRICORN AFRICA SOCIETY'S DECLARATIONS – [London: Neane, 1953] – us Res Libr [960]
THE CAPRICORNIAN – Rockhampton, Australia. 3 Jan 1885-26 Dec 1929.-d. 105 reels – 1 – uk British Libr Newspaper [072]
CAPS BULLETIN – (Christian Association for Psychological Studies). v.1-. 1975- – 1,5,6,9 – us UMI [073]
CAPSTONE JOURNAL OF EDUCATION – (v4-. 1983-. 5,6,9) – v1-. Jun 1980- – 1 – us UMI [073]
CAPSULAS GELATINOSAS / Gonzalez, Antonio – 1 – sp Bibl Santa Ana [946]

CAPTAIN AMERICA – Issue Nos. 1-5 March 1941-Aug 1941 – 5mf – 15 – $31,95 – us Comics [760]

CAPTAIN AMERICA – Issue Nos. 6-10 Sept 1941-Jan 1942 – 5mf – 15 – $31,95 – us Comics [760]

CAPTAIN AMERICA – Issue Nos. 11-15 Feb 1942-June 1942 – 5mf – 15 – $31,95 – us Comics [760]

CAPTAIN AMERICA – Issue Nos. 16-20 July 1942-Nov 1942 – 5mf – 15 – $31,95 – us Comics [760]

CAPTAIN AMERICA – Issue Nos. 21-25 Dec 1942-Apr 1943 – 5mf – 15 – $31,95 – us Comics [760]

CAPTAIN AMERICA – Issue Nos. 26-30 May 1943-Sept 1943 – 5mf – 15 – $31,95 – us Comics [760]

CAPTAIN AMERICA – Issue Nos. 31-35 Oct 1943-Feb 1944 – 5mf – 15 – $31,95 – us Comics [760]

CAPTAIN AMERICA – Issue Nos. 36-40 March 1944-July 1944 – 5mf – 15 – $31,95 – us Comics [760]

CAPTAIN AMERICA – Issue Nos. 41-45 Aug 1944-March 1945 – 5mf – 15 – $31,95 – us Comics [760]

CAPTAIN AMERICA – Issue Nos. 46-50 Apr 1945-Oct 1945 – 5mf – 15 – $31,95 – us Comics [760]

CAPTAIN BILLY'S WHIZ BANG – December 1920 – August 1936 – 5r – 1 – $150.00 $30.00r – us M.H.S. [073]

CAPTAIN CLAPPERTON'S LAST EXPEDITION TO AFRICA / Lander, Richard – 1830 – 7 – uk Microform Academic [910]

Captain, Gwendolyn *see* SOCIAL, RELIGIOUS, AND LEISURE PURSUITS OF NORTHERN CALIFORNIA'S AFRICAN AMERICAN POPULATION

CAPTAIN LIGHTFOOT : THE LAST OF THE NEW ENGLAND HIGHWAYMEN / G FD – Topsfield, MA: The Wayside Press, 1926 – 2mf – 9 – $3.00 – LLMC 92-125 – us L.L.M.C. [975]

CAPTAIN MARVEL – Issue Nos. 1-5 1941-Dec 1941 – 5mf – 15 – $31.95 – us Comics [760]

CAPTAIN MARVEL – Issue Nos. 6-10 Jan 1942-May 1942 – 5mf – 15 – $31.95 – us Comics [760]

THE CAPTAIN OF THE VULTURE / Braddon, Mary Elizabeth – British Fiction Archive: Unit 5 – 9 – uk Bell [830]

CAPTAINS AND COMRADES IN THE FAITH : SERMONS HISTORICAL AND BIOGRAPHICAL / Davidson, Randall Thomas – London: John Murray, 1911 – 1mf – us A.T.L.A. [240]

THE CAPTIVE CITY OF GOD, OR, THE CHURCHES SEEN IN THE LIGHT OF THE DEMOCRATIC IDEAL / Heath, Richard – London: Headley, 1905 – 1mf – us A.T.L.A. [240]

CAPTIVE INSURANCE COMPANY REPORTS – (v.5-. 1981. 5,6,9) – v.1-. 1977- – 1 – us UMI [336]

THE CAPTIVE MISSIONARY / Stern, Henry A – 1869 – 1 – us A.T.L.A. [240]

CAPTURED BY FRANCO / Ornitz, Lou – N.Y., 1939. Fiche W 1091. (Blodgett Collection of Spanish Civil War Pamphlets) – 9 – us H.U. College Libr [946]

CAPTURED GERMAN DOCUMENTS FILMED AT BERLIN / American Historical Association – 1960 – 986r – 1 – $22,678.00 – T580 – us Nat'l Archives [324]

CAPTURED GERMAN RECORDS FILMED AT BERLIN / University of Nebraska – 49r – 1 – $1,127.00 – T611 – us Nat'l Archives [324]

Capus, Alfred *see* LE PERSONNEL FEMININ DES P.T.T. PENDANT LA GUERRE

CAR AND DRIVER – (1971-. 5,6. 1975-. 9) – 1- 1955- – 1 – us UMI [073]

CAR REVIEW – London, UK. Aug, Nov, Dec 1906.-irr. 13 feet – 1 – uk British Libr Newspaper [072]

CAR TRUST SECURITIES / Rawle, Francis – A paper read at the eighth annual meeting of the American Bar Association at Saratoga Springs, New York, August 20th, 1885. Philadelphia, Dando, 1885. 48 p. LL-1208 – 1 – us L of C Photodup [340]

CARABELAS DE ESPANA...PINZON, JUAN DE LA COSA, DIAZ DE SOLIS JUAN SEBASTIAN ELCANO / Bayle, Constantino & Cabal, Juan – Madrid: Razon y Fe, 1944 – 1 – sp Bibl Santa Ana [946]

AN CARABHAN = KARAVANE: IRISH : PADRAIC O MOGHRAIN D'AISTRIGH O GHEARMAINIS UILHELM HAUFF / Hauff, Wilhelm – [Baile Atha Cliath]: O Fallamhain i Gcomhar le hOifig an tSolathair, 1930 – 1r – 1 – us U.W. Library [830]

LE CARABIN : UNIVERSITE LAVAL – Quebec. v1 n1. 27 sep 1941-v21 n43. 10 avr 1969 – 4r – 1 – Can$50.00 – cn Can Microfilming [072]

Caracas *see* BOLETIN DE LA ACADEMIA NACIONAL DE LA HISTORIA

CARACAS, 1935 / Parra, Caracciolo – Madrid: Razon y Fe, 1935 – 1 – sp Bibl Santa Ana [946]

CARACAS POLITICA, INTELECTUAL Y MUNDANA. CARACAS, 1966 / Parra Marquez, Hector – Madrid: Graf. Calleja, 1968 – 1 – sp Bibl Santa Ana [320]

Caracciolo, Henrietta *see* MEMOIRS OF HENRIETTA CARACCIOLO

Caracciolo, Luis Antonio *see*
– EL IDIOMA DE LA RAZON
– EL IDIOMA DE LA RELIGION
– VERDADEROS INTERESES DE LA PATRIA

Caracosa *see* DIALOGO DI CARACOSA, E CARONTE, IL QUALE GLI NEGA IL PASSO DELLA SUA BARCA

O CARACTER – (Cont as: Cidade de Lavras) – Lavras, 18 Feb-Dec 1894; Jan-Sep, 17 Nov 1895 – 1,5,6 – bl Biblioteca [072]

O CARACTER *see* CIDADE DE LAVRAS

EL CARACTER. DEFINICION, IMPORTANCIA, IDEAL, ORIGENES... / Guibert, J; ed by Bayle, Constantino – Madrid: Razon y Fe, 1928 – 9 – sp Bibl Santa Ana [150]

LE CARACTERE HOSTILE... / Gillet, F – Paris, 1911 – 2mf – 1 – ILM-383/1 – ne IDC [327]

LES CARACTERES DES PASSIONS... / La Chambre, Marin Cureau de – Paris: Chez Jacques d'Allin...5v. 1662. SEM35P159 – 1r – 1 – Can$57.00 – cn Bibl Nat [150]

CARACTERES: PAGES CHOISIES / La Bruyere, Jean de – Preface d'Augustin Filon. London: J.M. Dent; New York: G.P. Putnam, 1907. xviii,214p. With: the modern buddhism and his followers in Orissa N. Vasu – 1 – us U.W. Library [830]

LAS CARACTERISTICAS DE LA REVOLUCION ESPANOLA / Togliatti, Palmiro – Barcelona, 193? Fiche W1229. Blodgett Collection of Spanish Civil War Pamphlets – 9 – us H.U. College Libr [946]

CARACTERIZACION Y PROPIEDADES DE UNA VERMICULITA DE BADAJOZ / Gonzalez, F et al – Madrid: CSIC, 1954. Sep Ana. Edaf. y Fisio. Veg. Tomo 13. no 2. 1954 – 1 – sp Bibl Santa Ana [946]

Caradeuc de la Chalotais, Louis-Rene *see* ESSAI D'EDUCATION NATIONALE

O CARADURA – Maceio, Alagoas. 21 Out 1888; Mar, Ago, 21 Out 1889 – 1,5,6 – bl Biblioteca [072]

THE CARAFAS OF MADDALONI: NAPLES UNDER SPANISH DOMINION / Reumont, Alfred von – Trans. from the German of Alfred von Reumont. London: H.G. Bohn, 1854. xiv,465p. Incl. geneal. tables. 1 reel. 1262 – 1 – us U.W. Library [945]

CARAJA...KOU TROIS ANS CHEZ LES INDIENS DU BRASIL / Falaise, Rayliane de la – Madrid: Razon y Fe, 1940 – sp Bibl Santa Ana [306]

Caramuel, J *see* [P]RAECURSOR LOGICUS...; CUIUS PARTES TRES

Carande, Bernardo Victor *see* MANUEL CONMIGO, ILUSTRACIONES DE ENRIQUE SOPENA SCAPARDINI

CARANGOLA-CADES – Carangola, 4 Feb 1961 – 1,5,6 – bl Biblioteca [072]

Caraoso, Fabrito *see* RACCOLTA DI VARIJ BALLI IN OCCORRENZE DI NOZZE, E FESTINI DA NOBILI CAVALIERI, E DAME DI DIUERSE NATIONI

A CARAPUCA : PERIODICO SATYRICO, NOTICIOSO, JOCO-SERIO – Maceio, Alagoas. 23 Ago 1877 – 1,5,6 – bl Biblioteca [072]

CARAPUCA : ORGAO DE TODAS AS CLASSES – '(s.l.')-Sao Luiz, Brazil. 12 Jun-20 Jul 1884. Incomplete – 1,5,6 – bl Biblioteca [072]

O CARAPUCEIRO : PERIODICO SEMPRE MORAL E SO PER ACCIDENS POLITICO – Recife, 7 Apr 1832-Dec 1833; Feb-Dec 1834; Apr 1837-28 Dec 1842 – 1,5,6 – bl Biblioteca [072]

CARAS Y CARETAS – Buenos Aires. v. 6-42. 26 Dec 1903-7 Oct 1939 – 1 – us NY Public [073]

Caratheodory, E *see* DU DROIT INTERNATIONAL CONCERNANT...D'EAU

CARATTERI DI ALCUNI NUOVI GENERI / Rafinesque-Schmaltz, Constantine S – Palermo. 1810. B-2136 2 – 8 – ne IDC [510]

THE CARAVAN – Brooklyn, NY, 1953-1961 – 4r – 1 – us I.H.R.C. [978]

CARAVANA : ORGAO DOS ALUMNOS DO "ATHENEU ITACOATIARENSE" – Itacoatiara, Amazonas. 1 Fev-3 Abr 1918 – 1,5,6 – bl Biblioteca [072]

CARAVEL – Marjorca. no. 1-5. Summer 1934-Mar 1936 – 1 – us NY Public [073]

CARAVELLE – Cahiers du monde hispanique et luso-bresilien. no. 1-17. Toulouse. 1963-71 – 1 – fr A.C.R.P.P. [073]

Carbajal, C *see* NUESTRO DOMINIO FLUVIAL...

Carballo, Julio *see* TEATRO INFANTIL

CARBOHYDRATE FOODS IN THE INDONESIAN DIET / Mears, Leon A – SE-4713 1. 1962? – 9 – ne IDC [640]

CARBOHYDRATE LETTERS / ed by Sinay, Pierre G – 9,5,1 – us Harwood [540]

CARBOHYDRATE POLYMERS – v1-4. 1981-84 – 1,5,6,13 – sz Elsevier [073]

CARBOHYDRATE RESEARCH – v1-132. 1965-84 – 1,5,6,13 – sz Elsevier [616]

CARBOHYDRATES IN HUMAN NUTRITION – 1980 – 89p – it F.A.O. [640]

CARBON – v1- 1963- – 5,6,9 – us UMI [073]

THE CARBON ADVOCATE – Mauch Chunk, PA. 1890-94. 1 roll – 13 – $25.00r – us I.M.R. [071]

Carbon, Anthime *see* LE SECRET DU PEUPLE DE PARIS

CARBON COUNTY DEMOCRAT – Mauch Chunk, PA., 1847-1873 – 13 – $25.00r – us I.M.R. [071]

CARBON COUNTY DEMOCRAT AND MAUCH – Mauch Chunk, PA., 1848-1849 – 13 – $25.00r – us I.M.R. [071]

CARBON COUNTY GAZETTE – Mauch Chunk, PA., 1844-1847 – 13 – $25.00r – us I.M.R. [071]

CARBON COUNTY GAZETTE AND MAUCH – Mauch Chunk, PA., 1849-1852 – 13 – $25.00r – us I.M.R. [071]

CARBON COUNTY NEWS – Red Lodge. Mont. 1958-1959; 1966- – 1 – us UMI [071]

CARBON COUNTY SENTINEL – Gebo. Mont. 1898-1901 – 1 – us UMI [071]

CARBON COUNTY TRANSIT – Mauch Chunk, PA., 1843-1844 – 13 – $25.00r – us I.M.R. [071]

CARBON COUNTY TRANSIT & GAZETTE – Mauch Chunk, PA. 1843-1846. Also incl. Carbon County Gazette (Mauch Chunk), 1844-47; Carbon Democrat (Mauch Chunk), 1847-48; Carbon County Gazette & Mauch Chunk Courier, 1847-48. 1 roll – 13 – $25.00r – us I.M.R. [071]

Carbon de Flins, Des Oliviers *see* LE REVEIL D'EPIMENIDE A PARIS

THE CARBON DEMOCRAT – Mauch Chunk, PA. 1853-1869. Also incl. Mauch Chunk Gazette, 1856-58. 1 roll – 13 – $25.00r – us I.M.R. [071]

CARBON NEWS – Alberta, CN. 1927-60 – 12r – 1 – cn Commonwealth Micro [072]

CARBON-13 NMR SPECTRAL DATA : A LIVING COM-MICROFICHE COLLECTION OF REFERENCE MATERIAL / Bremser, W et al – 4th ed 1987 – 235mf – DM4,000.00 – 3-527-26198-2 – gw V.C.H. [540]

Carbonero Bravo, D *see* GANADO KARAKUL

Carbonneau, Fred *see* THE GIRL I CAN'T FORGET

Carbonneau, Leopold *see*
– BIBLIOGRAPHIE ANALYTIQUE DE L'OEUVRE DE M. ALBERT RIOUX, AGRONOME...
– BIO-BIBLIOGRAPHIE DE M. ALBERT RIOUX

Carbonneau, Louis *see* FIEVRES D'AFRIQUE

Carbra, Romulo D *see* LA CRONICA OFICIAL DE LAS INDIAS OCCIDENTALES. LA PLATA 1934

Carbutt, E H *see* FIVE MONTHS' FINE WEATHER IN CANADA, WESTERN U. S. AND MEXICO

CARCAJOU WOLVERINE : VILLAGE HURON – (In Cri., English and French) – Loretteville, Canada. 1972-v1 n2. no date – 1r – 1 – Can$25.00 – cn Can Microfilming [072]

Carcano, Miguel Angel *see*
– LA AMISTAD ANGLO-ARGENTINA
– LA PRESIDENCIA DE CARLOS PILLEGINI; POLITICA DE ORDEN, 1890-92

O CARCARA : ORGAO INDEPENDENTE, DE CIRCULACAO MENSAL, DE UM PUNHADO DE ESTUDANTES DA FACULDADE DE DIREITO DO OESTE DE MINAS GERAIS – Divinopolis, Feb-Dec 1967; Jun 1968-Jan 1969 – 1,5,6 – bl Biblioteca [072]

LA CARCEL DE MUJERES DE MADRID / Bayle, Constantino – Burgos: Razon y Fe, 1938 – 1 – sp Bibl Santa Ana [946]

Carco, Francis *see* PRISONS DE FEMMES

CARD CATALOG / Martinique. French West Indies. Archives Departementales – 1 – us UMI [990]

CARD CATALOG / Mystic Seaport Museum. Library – 1986. 150,000 cards. Maritime Research Resources – 9 – $600.00 – us Opus [910]

CARD CATALOG OF GUBERNSKIE, OBLASTNYE AND VOISKOVYE VEDOMOSTI : FROM THE NATIONAL LIBRARY OF RUSSIA, ST PETERSBURG – (87 vedomosti listed, comprising the biggest coll in a single library) – 87mf – 9 – $590.00 – us Ross [020]

CARD CATALOG OF GUBERNSKIE, OBLASTNYE AND VOISKOVYE VEDOMOSTI FROM THE NATIONAL LIBRARY OF RUSSIA, ST PETERSBURG – 87mf – 9 – $590.00 – us Ross [020]

CARD CATALOG OF RUSSIAN BOOKS AND SERIALS – 480mf – 9 – $2,700.00 coll – us Ross [460]

CARD CATALOG OF RUSSIAN PERSONALITIES (B.L. MODZALEVSKII COLLECTION) : FROM THE MANUSCRIPT DEPARTMENT OF THE INSTITUTE OF RUSSIAN LITERATURE OF THE RUSSIAN ACADEMY OF SCIENCE (PUSHKINSKII DOM) / Modzalevskii, B L – (A coll of biographical materials from the 18th to early 20th century, reflecting little-known facts and background material relating to nearly 100,000 influential people in Russian art and society. A large number of cards pertain to less well known people but whose contribution to the development of Russian culture was essential) – 364mf – 9 – $2,200.00 coll – us Ross [920]

CARD CATALOG OF THE BOSTON ATHENAEUM PRINT AND PHOTOGRAPH COLLECTION / Boston Athenaeum Library. Boston – 1989 – ca 100,000 cards on 79mf – 9 – $435.00; Export $470.00 – 0-8161-1749-7 – uk Hall [760]

CARD CATALOG OF THE DEPARTMENT OF THE LITERATURE OF THE NATIONALITIES OF THE FORMER SOVIET UNION / Russian National Library – 2703mf – 9 – $13,500.00 coll – us Ross [020]

CARD CATALOG OF THE FORMER LIBRARY OF THE RUSSKII ZAGRANICHNYI ISTORICHESKII ARKHIV (RZIA) – Prague, 1992 – 267mf – 9 – $1,500.00 – us Ross [020]

CARD CATALOG OF THE G.W. BLUNT WHITE RESEARCH LIBRARY AT MYSTIC SEAPORT MUSEUM – 133mf – 9 – £600.00 – uk Chadwyck [355]

CARD CATALOG OF THE HARVARD UNIVERSITY MUSIC LIBRARY TO 1985 – (Includes guide) – 1986 – 224mf (1:42) – 9 – DM2,700.00 diazo (silver 2,980.00 ISBN 3-598-40150-7) – 3-598-40151-5 – gw Saur [780]

CARD CATALOG OF THE LIBRARY OF THE STATE HERMITAGE MUSEUM, ST PETERSBURG *see* CARD CATALOG OF RUSSIAN BOOKS AND SERIALS

THE CARD CATALOG OF THE MUSIC LIBRARY OF THE ST PETERSBURG STATE CONSERVATORY (RIMSKY-KORSAKOV) – 312mf – 9 – $2,000.00 coll – us Ross [780]

CARD CATALOG OF THE SLAVIC COLLECTION OF THE LIBRARY OF THE ACADEMY OF SCIENCES, ST PETERSBURG, 16TH CENTURY TO 1930 / Russian National Library – 1996 – 434mf – 9 – $2,500.00 – us Ross [460]

CARD CATALOG OF THE SLAVONIC COLLECTION OF THE LIBRARY OF THE NATIONAL MUSEUM OF THE CZECH REPUBLIC – New York: Norman Ross Publ, 1992 – 117mf – 9 – $990.00 – us Ross [943]

CARD CATALOG OF THE SLOVANSKA KNIHOVNA PRAGUE – New York: Norman Ross Publ, 1992 – 368mf – 9 – $5,000.00 – us Ross [943]

CARD CATALOGS OF THE HARVARD LAW SCHOOL LIBRARY 1817-1981 – (Author-Title Catalog. silver $3,000. diazo $2,400. Anglo-American Subject Catalog. silver $810. diazo $670. Foreign and Comparative Law Subject Catalog. silver $895. diazo $740. Catalog of International Law and Relations. silver $790. diazo $655. Jurisdictional Shelflist. silver $945. diazo $785. International Shelflist. silver $345. diazo $285.) – 1984-1985 – 6 pts; 2,422 fiches (1:42) – diazo DM14,800.00 (Silver DM17,600.00 ISBN: 3-598-40114-0) – 3-598-40100-0 – gw Saur [020]

CARD CATALOGS OF THE HARVARD UNIVERSITY FINE ARTS LIBRARY 1895-1981 – (Dictionary Catalog. silver $1,475. diazo $1,280. Catalog of Auction Sales Catalogs. silver $140. diazo $120. Catalog of the Rubel Asiatic Research Collection. silver $140. diazo $120. Shelflist Catalog. silver $320. diazo $280.) – 1984 – 4 pts 516 fiches (1:42) – diazo DM4,980.00 (silver DM5,800.00 ISBN 3-598-40135-3) – 3-598-40130-2 – gw Saur [020]

CARD CATALOGUE / Peace Palace Library. The Hague – (Periodicals Reference Guide $2,820.00; Universal Bibliographical Catalogue $4,925.00; Supplement through 1984 $1,605.00) – 1814 fiches – 9 – $7,475.00 set – us UPA [010]

[CARD CATALOGUE (AUTHORS AND TITLES) OF THE INSTITUTE'S LIBRARY] / South African Institute of Race Relations Library – Johannesburg, Microfile, 1969 – us Res Libr [020]

CARD CATALOGUE FILE / Southern Baptist Theological Seminary. Library – 240,000p – 1 – us Baptist [240]

CARD CATALOGUE OF THE WORKING CLASS MOVEMENT : BOOKS AND PAMPHLETS. 1. AUTHOR. 2. SUBJECT – 50 reels with printed guide – uk World [331]

CARD CATALOGUE TO 75 YEARS OF NEWSREELS / EMI-Pathe Film Library – (With printed index) – 1896-1970 – 5,9 – £2,250.00 – uk World [900]

CARD FILE OF BAPTIST MATERIALS / Southern Baptist Theological Seminary. Library – 6,000p – 1 – us Baptist [240]

CARD INDEX TO 'OLD LOAN' LEDGERS..., 1790-1836 / U.S. Treasury Department. Bureau of the Public Debt – 15 rolls. M521. Printed guide – 5 – us Nat'l Archives [336]

CARD INDEX TO PICTURES COLLECTED BY THE GEORGE WASHINGTON BICENTENNIAL COMMISSION / U.S. Congress – 1roll – 5 – T271 – us Nat'l Archives [324]

CARD MANIFESTS (ALPHABETICAL) OF INDIVIDUALS ENTERING THROUGH THE PORT OF DETROIT, MICHIGAN, 1906-1954 – 117r – 1 – M1478 – us Nat'l Archives [340]

CARD REPORT / Iowa State University. College of Agriculture. Center for Agricultural and Rural Development – No.39-96. 1971-80 – 1,5 – us Spaulding [630]

Cardaire, Michel *see* L'ISLAM ET LE TERROIR AFRICAINE

Cardano, Girolamo *see* DE RERVM VARIETATE LIBRI 17

Cardauns, Hermann *see* AUS LUISE HENSELS JUGENDZEIT

Cardauns, Ludwig *see* ZUR GESCHICHTE DER KIRCHLICHEN UNIONS- UND REFORMBESTREBUNGEN VON 1538 BIS 1542

Cardecera, Valentin *see* RETRATO DE DON PEDRO DE VALDIVIA. INFORME

Carden, Allen D *see*
- HISTORY OF FAYETTE COUNTY
- THE MISSOURI HARMONY
- UNITED STATES HARMONY

CARDENAL ANTONIO CAGGIANO, OBISPO DE ROSARIO. LA FIGURA DE SAN FRANCISCO SOLANO Y SU ACTUACION EN EL LOCUMAN... / Bayle, Constantino – Madrid: Missionalia Hispanica, 1951 – 1 – sp Bibl Santa Ana [240]

EL CARDENAL GOMA, PRIMADO DE ESPANA. MADRID, 1969 / Granados, Anastasio – Madrid: Graf. Calleja, 1970 – 1 – sp Bibl Santa Ana [240]

Cardenal Iracheta, Manuel *see* VIDA DE GONZALO PIZARRO

Cardenas, Daniel *see* EL ESPANOL DE JALISCO. MADRID, 1967

Cardenas, Gonzalo *see* EL PERONISMO

Cardenas, Gonzalo Horacio *see* LAS LUCHAS NACIONALES CONTRA LA DEPENDENCIA

CARDIFF TIMES – Wales. -w. 1858, 1863, 1868. 2 1 2 reels – 1 – uk British Libr Newspaper [072]

Cardillo, Francisco Ramon *see* EL SINDICATO OBRERO EN FUNCION DE PATRIA

Cardim, Fernao *see*
- TRATADOS DA TERRA E GENTE DO BRASIL

Cardinal, Bradley J *see* THE EFFECTIVENESS OF THE STAGES OF CHANGE MODEL AND EXPERIMENTAL EXERCISE PRESCRIPTIONS IN INCREASING FEMALE ADULTS' PHYSICAL ACTIVITY AND EXERCISE BEHAVIOR

CARDINAL ELEMENTS OF THE CHRISTIAN FAITH / Adam, D S – London, New York: Hodder and Stoughton, [1911?] – 1mf – us A.T.L.A. [240]

CARDINAL JOZSEF MINDSZENTY PAMPHLET COLLECTION – 194?-194? – 1 – CSUXANL2839-B – us Hoover Inst Photo [240]

CARDINAL MANNING / Hutton, Arthur Wollaston – London: Methuen, 1892 – 1mf – us A.T.L.A. [240]

LE CARDINAL MANNING ET SON ACTION SOCIALE / Lemire, J – Paris: V. Lecoffe, 1893 – 1mf – us A.T.L.A. [240]

Cardinal, Marita K *see* A SURVEY ANALYSIS OF DANCE WELLNESSRELATED CURRICULA IN AMERICAN HIGHER EDUCATION

CARDINAL NEWMAN / Hutton, Richard Holt – London: Methuen, 1891 – 1 roll – 1 – 1-55879-179-5 – uk Libr Preservation [240]

CARDINAL NEWMAN / Meynell, Wilfrid – London: Burns and Oates, 1907 – 1mf – us A.T.L.A. [240]

CARDINAL NEWMAN : REMINISCENCES OF FIFTY YEARS SINCE / Lockhart, William – London: Burns & Oates; New York: Catholic Publication Society, 1891 – 1mf – us A.T.L.A. [240]

CARDINAL NEWMAN : THE STORY OF HIS LIFE / Jennings, Henry J – Birmingham: Houghton; London: Simpkin, Marshall, 1882 – 1mf – us A.T.L.A. [240]

LE CARDINAL NICOLAS DE CUES (1401-1464) / Vansteenberghe, E – L'Action – La Pensee: Paris, 1920 – 14mf – 8 – ne Slangenburg [100]

CARDINAL VON GEISSEL : AUS SEINEM HANDSCHRIFTLICHEN NACHLASS GESCHILDERT / Pfuelf, Otto – Freiburg i.B., 1895 – 2pts 8mf – 9 – DM198.00 – 3-89349-208-9 – gw Hänsel [240]

CARDINAL WOLSEY / Creighton, Mandell – London; New York: Macmillan, 1888 (Twelve English statesmen) – 1mf – us A.T.L.A. [240]

IL CARDINALE RAFFAELE...DEL VAL...ROMA / Cenci, Pio – Torino, 1933; Madrid: Razon y Fe, 1933 – 1 – sp Bibl Santa Ana [240]

Cardinall, Allan Wolsey *see* THE NATIVES OF THE NORTHERN TERRITORIES OF THE GOLD COAST

Cardinell, A W *see* THE NATIVES OF THE NORTHERN TERRITORIES OF THE GOLD COAST: THEIR CUSTOMS, RELIGION AND FOLKLORE

CARDIO – v1-. 1984- – 1,5,6,9 – us UMI [073]

CARDIOLOGIA – v.1-26. 1937-55 – 1,5,6 – us Princeton Micro [610]

CARDIOLOGY – v60-. 1975- – 1,5,9 – us UMI [073]

CARDIOLOGY CLINICS – v1-. 1983- – 1,5,6,9 – us UMI [616]

CARDIOLOGY IN REVIEW – v1-4. 1993-1996 – 4r – 1,5,6,9 – $65.00r – us Williams [616]

CARDIOPULMONARY MEDICINE – v14-. 1975- – 1,5,6,9 – us UMI [616]

CARDIOPULMONARY RESPONSES TO UNSUPPORTED AND SUPPORTED ARM EXERCISE IN NORMAL SUBJECTS AND PATIENTS WITH OBSTRUCTIVE PULMONARY DISEASE / Lebzelter, Joseph – Temple University, 1996 – 3mf – 9 – $12.00 – PH 1500 – us Microform Publ [612]

CARDIO-RESPIRATORY RESPONSES TO UPRIGHT AND AERO-POSTURE CYCLING / Origenes, M M – 1991 – 1mf – 9 – $4.00 – us Microform Publ [612]

CARDIORESPIRATORY RESPONSES OF CONTROLLED FREQUENCY BREATHING DURING SUBMAXIMAL EXERCISE / Tracy, Michael L – 1980 – 1mf – 9 – $4.00 – us Microform Publ [790]

CARDIORESPIRATORY RESPONSES OF WORLD CLASS WHITEWATER SLALOM PADDLERS / Law, R Craig – 1988 – 88p 1mf – 9 – $4.00 – us Microform Publ [612]

CARDIORESPIRATORY RESPONSES TO CIRCUIT WEIGHT TRAINING AS MEASURED BY A BIOKINETIC SWIM-BENCH TEST AND A TREADMILL RUN TEST / Chiang, J – 1989 – 2mf – 9 – $8.00 – us Microform Publ [612]

CARDIOVASCULAR AND BODY COMPOSITION RESPONSES TO AEROBIC DANCE TRAINING OF VARYING FREQUENCIES AND TOTAL PROGRAM LENGTHS / Ipsen, Lillas F & Roundy, Elmo S – 1990 – 2mf – $8.00 – us Microform Publ [612]

CARDIOVASCULAR AND INTERVENTIONAL RADIOLOGY – A journal of imaging in Diagnosis and Treatment. v.1-4, 1978-81. Continues: cardiovascular radiology. ISSN: 0174-1551 – 1,5,6,9,13 – 67.00v – us UMI [616]

THE CARDIOVASCULAR AND METABOLIC RESPONSES OF MEN WITH CARDIOVASCULAR DISEASE TO AQUA DYNAMIC EXERCISE / Miller, K A – 1990 – 1mf – 9 – $4.00 – us Microform Publ [612]

CARDIOVASCULAR MEDICINE – (1984-. 1,5,6,9) – v1-4. 1976-79 – 1 – us UMI [610]

Cardona Rossell, Mariano *see* ASPECTOS ECONOMICOS DE NUESTRA REVOLUCION

Cardoni, Giuseppe *see* ELUCUBRATIO DE DOGMATICA ROMANI PONTIFICIS INFALLIBILITATE EIUSQUE DEFINIBILITATE

Cardoso, C Lopes *see* CONTRIBUICAO PARA E BIBLIOGRAFIA DAS LINGUAS "BANTU" DE ANGOLA

Cardoso, F *see* UTILIDADES DEL AGUA I DE LA NIEVE, DEL BEVER FRIO I CALIENTE...

Cardoso, Joaquin *see* SANGRE EN LOS TAPEHUANES

Cardot, J *see* MOUSSES

CARDOZA WOMEN'S LAW JOURNAL – Yeshiva University. v1. 1993-94 – 9 – us Hein [340]

CARDOZO ARTS AND ENTERTAINMENT LAW JOURNAL – Yeshiva University. v1-13. 1982-1995 – 9 – $185.00 set – us Hein [340]

Cardozo, Benjamin Nathan *see* AN ADDRESS DELIVERED IN CHANCELLORS HALL, STATE EDUCATION BUILDING, ALBANY, NY

Cardozo, L *see* BIBLIOGRAFIA DE LA LITERATURA INDIGENA VENEZOLANA

Cardozo, Michael H *see* EXCHANGE OF PATENT RIGHTS AND TECHNICAL INFORMATION UNDER MUTUAL AID PROGRAMS

CARDSTON NEWS – Alberta, CN. Sept 1925-Jun 1958 – 14r – 1 – cn Commonwealth Micro [072]

Carducho, Vincencio *see* DIALOGOS DE LA PINTURA

Cardwell, Edward *see*
- DOCUMENTARY ANNALS OF THE REFORMED CHURCH OF ENGLAND
- A HISTORY OF CONFERENCES
- A HISTORY OF CONFERENCES AND OTHER PROCEEDINGS...REVISION OF THE BOOK OF COMMON PRAYER

THE CARE AND CATALOGUING OF MANUSCRIPTS: AS PRACTICED BY THE MINNESOTA HISTORICAL SOCIETY / Nute, Grace Lee – 1936 – 1r – 1 – $5.00 – us M.H.S. [025]

Care, Henry *see* THE TUTOR TO TRUE ENGLISH

THE CARE OF DEPENDENT, NEGLECTED AND WAYWARD CHILDREN / International Congress of Charities, Correction, and Philanthropy. Chicago. 1893. Second Section – Ed. by Anna Garlin Spencer and Charles Wesley Birtwell. 1894 – 9 – us A.T.L.A. [360]

THE CARE OF THE SOUL / Fuller, Andrew – 1805 – 1 – 5.00 – us Baptist [240]

O CARECA – Maceio, Alagoas. 16 Nov 1884 – 1,5,6 – bl Biblioteca [072]

CAREER DEVELOPMENT FOR EXCEPTIONAL INDIVIDUALS – (v.3-. 1980- 5,6,9) – v.1-. 1978- – 1 – us UMI [073]

CAREER DEVELOPMENT QUARTERLY *see* VOCATIONAL GUIDANCE QUARTERLY

CAREER EDUCATION QUARTERLY – v1-4, no.1. 1976-Winter 1979 – 1,5,6,9 – us UMI [370]

Career Guidance Foundation *see*
- COLLEGE CATALOG COLLECTIONS: NATIONAL
- COLLEGE CATALOG COLLECTIONS: REGIONAL
- FINANCIAL AID COLLECTION
- THE INTERNATIONAL COLLECTION
- SPECIAL COLLECTION
- STATE EDUCATION DIRECTORIES
- THE TOP 250

CAREER GUIDE – 1979-Spring, Summer 1981 – 1,5,6,9 – us UMI [073]

CAREER SATISFACTION OF DENTAL HYGIENISTS PERFORMING EXPANDED FUNCTIONS AS COMPARED TO DENTAL HYGIENISTS PERFORMING ONLY TRADITIONAL DUTIES / Sylvis, Robin – 1981 – 1mf – 9 – $4.00 – us Microform Publ [617]

CAREER WORLD ONE – v. 1-. 1977- – 1,5,6,9 – us UMI [370]

CAREER WORLD TWO – (v6- . 1977- . 5,6,9) – v. 1-. 1972- – 1 – us UMI [370]

CAREERS IN SPACE – 1984 – 2mf – 9 – $12.00 – 0-87703-206-8 – us Univelt [331]

CAREERS TODAY – Corona Del Mar, CA. 1969 – 1r – 1 – $50.00 – R02144 – us Library Micro [331]

A CAREFUL AND FREE INQUIRY INTO THE TRUE NATURE AND TENDENCY OF THE RELIGIOUS PRINCIPLES OF THE SOCIETY OF FRIENDS, COMMONLY CALLED QUAKERS / Brownlee, William C – Two parts. 1824 – 1 – us A.T.L.A. [240]

Carell, Paul *see* THE FOXES OF THE DESERT

CARETA – Rio de Janeiro, 6 Jun 1908-Sep 1927; Jan 1928-Dec 1929; Jan-Mar, Jul-Dec 1930; Jan 1931-29 Oct 1960 – 1,5,6 – bl Biblioteca [072]

Carew, Harold D *see* HISTORY OF PASADENA AND THE SAN GABRIEL VALLEY

THE CAREW PAPERS / Lambeth Palace. Library – (The Settlement of Ulster). With printed index – 1 – £650.00 – uk World [025]

CAREW POYNTZ BOOK OF HOURS – 1350. Fitzwilliam Museum, Cambridge – 14 – uk Microform Academic [240]

Carey, George W *see* THE VESSEL, THE DEED AND THE IDEA: ANARCHISM IN PATERSON

Carey, Henry C *see*
- THE CREDIT SYSTEM IN FRANCE, GREAT BRITAIN AND THE UNITED STATES
- FAILURE OF REVENUE TARIFF AND OTHER SUBJECTS

Carey, Henry Charles *see*
- THE BRITISH TREATIES OF 1871 & 1874: LETTERS TO THE PRESIDENT OF THE UNITED STATES
- THE SLAVE TRADE, DOMESTIC AND FOREIGN: WHY IT EXISTS AND HOW IT MAY BE EXTINGUISHED

Carey. Ohio. Memorial United Methodist Church *see* RECORDS

CAREY PROGRESSOR – Carey, Ohio. 1968-71 – 2r – 1 – $32.50r – us Archival [071]

Carey, Robert *see* MEMOIRS...WRITTEN BY HIMSELF. AND FRAGMENTA REGALIA: BEING A HISTORY OF QUEEN ELIZABETH'S FAVOURITES

Carey, T H *see* CHRISTIAN BAPTISM (ILLUSTRATED): ITS PROPER SUBJECTS AND PROPER ACT, WITH A BRIEF HISTORY OF BAPTIST PRINCIPLES AND PRACTICES...

Carey, Thomas Joseph *see*
- LAW AT A GLANCE
- THE LEGAL ADVISOR

CAREY TIMES – Carey, Ohio. 1888-1971 – 38r – 1 – $32.50r – us Archival [071]

Carey, W *see* BIOGRAPHICAL AND LITERARY NOTICES...

Carey, William *see*
- COLLEGE LIBRARY: CATALOGUE OF EARLY INDIAN IMPRINTS, 1714-1850
- FIFTY-TWO LETTERS TO DR. JOHN RYLAND

CAREY'S MANITOBA REPORTS / Manitoba. Canada – 1v. 1875 (all publ) – 2mf – 9 – $3.00 – LLMC 81-024 – us L.L.M.C. [340]

CAREY'S UNITED STATES RECORDER – Philadelphia, Pennsylvania. 1798. Constitutional Diary. 1799-1800 – 1,3 – us Readex [071]

CARGO AIRLIFT *see* AIR CARGO

CARGO EXPRESS – (Incorporates: Transportation Business at v12 no 4 1991. Ceased v15 no 7/8 1994) – Toronto. v12-15. 1991-1993/94 – Can$20.00y – cn Micromedia [380]

CARGO EXPRESS *see* TRANSPORTATION BUSINESS

CARGOS / Comision de Monumentos – Madrid: Ed. Reus, 1922. B.R.A.H. 80. p. 304 – 1 – sp Bibl Santa Ana [946]

CARGOS QUE RESULTAN CONTRA...EL P. DIEGO DE CACERES, GENERAL DE...S. GERONIMO.. / Caceres, Diego de – 1641 – 9 – 1.50f – sp Bibl Santa Ana [240]

CARIB HORIZONS – Montreal, Canada. 3 jun 1967 – 1r – 1 – Can$25.00 – cn Can Microfilming [072]
CARIBBEAN CONFERENCE OF CHURCHES – Barbados. 135 docs. 1980-1991 – 61mf – 9 – ne IDC [240]
CARIBBEAN – GENERAL : AN ABSTRACT OF STATISTICS OF THE LEEWARD ISLANDS, WINDWARD ISLANDS AND BARBADOS / West Indies University. Institute of Social and Economic Research. (Eastern Caribbean) – (Coll title: Latin American and Caribbean Official Statistical Serials, 1821-1982) – 4mf – 9 – £7.00f (set £42.00 5mf) – uk Chadwyck [972]
CARIBBEAN – GENERAL : STATISTICS FOR THE STUDY OF BRITISH CARIBBEAN ECONOMIC HISTORY 1763-1833 / Ragatz, Lowell J – (Coll title: Latin American and Caribbean Official Statistical Serials, 1821-1982) – 1mf – 9 – £7.00f (set £42.00 5mf) – uk Chadwyck [972]
CARIBBEAN HUMAN RIGHTS NETWORK *see* CARIBBEAN RIGTHS
CARIBBEAN JOURNAL OF EDUCATION – (v.7:. 1980- 5,6,9) – v.1-. 1974- – 1 – us UMI [073]
CARIBBEAN JOURNAL OF RELIGIOUS STUDIES – Kingston, Jamaica: United Theological College of the West Indies. v1-12. sep 1975-sep 1991 – 1r – 1 – us Res Libr [240]
CARIBBEAN LABOUR CONGRESS : BULLETINS, REPORTS AND OTHER MATERIAL, 1945-1951 FROM THE RICHARD HARK COLLECTION – 3mf – 9 – uk Microform Academic [320]
CARIBBEAN RIGTHS – Bridgetown. 2 docs. 1990-1991 – 4mf – 9 – ne IDC [320]
EL CARIBE – Ciudad Trujillo, Dominican Republic: Editora del Caribe, 1956-57 – 1 – us Res Libr [072]
EL CARIBE – Dominican Republic. 1948- – 1 – us UMI [072]
THE CARIBOU ESKIMOS / Birket-Smith, K – Material on social life and their cultural position. 2 pts. BN 133 2. 1929 – 8 – ne IDC [305]
CARIBOU NEWS – (v1-11 1981/82-1991 Can$115.00) – v1- 1981/82- – 1 – Can$60.00y – cn Micromedia [071]
CARIBOU SHOOTING IN NEW FOUNDLAND: WITH A HISTORY OF ENGLAND'S OLDEST COLONY FROM 1001 TO 1895 / Davis, Samuel T – s.l.: s.n., 1895 (Lancaster, Pa: New Era Print). 02600. (Pre-1900 Canadiana) – 9 – cn C.I.H.M. [971]
LA CARICATURE 1830-1835 : POLITICAL-SATIRICAL FRENCH WEEKLY MAGAZINE – (Color microfiche edition accompanied by a printed commentary text) – Wildberg: BELSER WISS. DIENST, 1988 – 26mf/1mf – 15,9 – DM1,490.00 color – 3-628-95000-7 – gw Belser Wiss [320]
CARICATURE, CARTOONS, AND HUMOR DURING IN WORLD WAR 2 PAMPHLET COLLECTION – 1940?-1945 – 1 – CSUXANM8121-B – us Hoover Inst Photo [870]
CARICATURE DE LA "CONFERENCE DE LA PAIX" – 233 Images de tous les Pays. Paris, 1908 – 3mf – 1 – ILM-4083/1 – ne IDC [327]
A CARICATURE HISTORY OF CANADIAN POLITICS: EVENTS FROM THE UNION OF 1841.. / Benough, John Wilson – Toronto: Grip Print. and Pub. Co., 1886.07443.(Pre-1900 Canadiana) – 9 – cn C.I.H.M. [971]
CARICATURES, CARTOONS, AND HUMOR IN DENMARK IN RELATION TO WORLD WAR 2 PAMPHLET COLLECTION – 194?-1945 – 1 – CSUXANM8146-B – us Hoover Inst Photo [870]
CARICATURES, CARTOONS, AND HUMOR IN FRANCE DURING WORLD WAR 2 PAMPHLET COLLECTION – 1941?-19?? – 1 – CSUXANM8134-B – us Hoover Inst Photo [870]
CARICATURES, CARTOONS, AND HUMOR IN GERMANY IN RELATION TO WORLD WAR 2 PAMPHLET COLLECTION – 1941?-1959 – 1 – CSUXANM8139-B – us Hoover Inst Photo [870]
CARICATURES, CARTOONS, AND HUMOR IN GREAT BRITAIN DURING WORLD WAR 2 PAMPHLET COLLECTION – 1942-1944 – 1 – CSUXANM8128-B – us Hoover Inst Photo [870]
CARICATURES, CARTOONS, AND HUMOR IN ITALY DURING WORLD WAR 2 PAMPHLET COLLECTION – 1945? – 1 – CSUXANM8150-B – us Hoover Inst Photo [870]
LA CARIDAD CRISTIANA / Fernandez Fernandez, Juan – Badajoz: Tip. Arqueros, 1953 – 1 – sp Bibl Santa Ana [946]
LA CARIDAD EN LOS PRIMEROS SIGLOS DEL CRISTIANISMO / Cicognani, H J – Madrid, 1931; Madrid: Razon y Fe, 1931 – 1 – sp Bibl Santa Ana [240]
LA CARIDAD MISIONAL Y LA EPISTOLA DE SAN PABLO A LOS FILIPENSES. BADAJOZ / Vera, E de & Fernandez y Fernandez, J – Madrid: Razon y Fe, 1947 – 1 – sp Bibl Santa Ana [240]
A CARIDADE – Maceio, Alagoas. 9 Maio 1885 – 1,5,6 – bl Biblioteca [072]
A CARIDADE – Manaos, Amazonas. 17 Dez 1893 – 1,5,6 – bl Biblioteca [072]
A CARIDADE : ORGAO DO GRUPO SPIRITA ANTONIO DE PADUA – Ouro Preto, 1 Apr-19 May 1898 – 1,5,6 – bl Biblioteca [072]
Caridge, Alberto J *see* INFILTRACION JUSTICIALISTA EN AMERICA
CARIES RESEARCH – v9-. 1975- – 1,5,9 – us UMI [073]
Caril, Bonifacio del. *see* PROBLEMAS DE LA REVOLUCION Y LA DEMOCRACIA
LE CARILLON – Hawkesbury, Ontario. 20 nov 1947-31 dec 1991 – 52+ r – 1 – Can$75.00r – cn Can Microfilming [072]
LE CARILLON : HUMORISTIQUE – Quebec, Canada. 24 oct-13 dec 1879 – 1r – 1 – Can$25.00 – cn Can Microfilming [072]
LE CARILLON : JOURNAL DE NOEL – Quebec – 1r – 1 – Can$25.00 – cn Can Microfilming [072]
CARINTHIA PAMPHLET COLLECTION – 1918-1974 – 1 – CSUXANL5564-B – us Hoover Inst Photo [999]
Cario, Louis *see* L'EXOTISME
CARIS : AGRICULTURE RESEARCH IN DEVELOPING COUNTRIES – 1978 – 3v 2656p – it F.A.O. [630]
Caris, H E *see* DES DIVERS MODES DE PAIEMENTS INTERNATIONAUX
Carissimi, G G *see*
- ARS CANTANDI
- ARS CANTANDI: DAS IST: RICHTIGER UND AUSSFUERHLICHER WEG/DIE JUGEND AUS DEM RECHTEN GRUND IN DER SING-KUNST ZU UNTERRICHTEN

CARISTAS DIOCESANAS / Caritas Diocesana de Coria – Caceres: Tip. Extremadura, S.A. 1955 – sp Bibl Santa Ana [240]
Caristia, C *see* IL DIRITTO INTERNAZIONALE E LA SUA CRISI
Caritas *see* UNA CARITAS PARROQUIAL SENCILLA
CARITAS ANGLICANA, OR, AN HISTORICAL INQUIRY INTO THOSE RELIGIOUS AND PHILANTHROPICAL SOCIETIES THAT FLOURISHED IN ENGLAND BETWEEN THE YEARS 1678 AND 1740 / Portus, Garnet V – London: A.R. Mowbray, 1912 – 1mf – us A.T.L.A. [240]
Caritas Diocesana *see*
- CARITAS DIOCESANA DE ACCION CATOLICA. CORIA-CACERES. 1955
- MEMORIA 1957
- MEMORIA-INFORME 1973. RECONCILIACION? SER JUSTO Y FRATERNAL CON TODOS

CARITAS DIOCESANA DE ACCION CATOLICA. CORIA-CACERES. 1955 / Caritas Diocesana – s.l., s.i., s.a. – 1 – sp Bibl Santa Ana [240]
Caritas Diocesana de Coria *see* CARISTAS DIOCESANAS
UNA CARITAS PARROQUIAL SENCILLA / Caritas – Badajoz: Tip. A. Mangas, 1969 – sp Bibl Santa Ana [946]
CARL BERNHARD TRINIUS, 1778-1844 / Komarov Botanical Institute, St. Petersburg – 438mf – 9 – ne IDC [580]
Carl, Erzherzog von Oesterreich *see* AUSGEWAEHLTE SCHRIFTEN
CARL GUSTAV CARUS ALS ERBE UND DEUTER GOETHES / Wilhelmsmeyer, Hans – (Includes bibliographical references) – Berlin: Junker und Duennhaupt, 1936 – 1 – us U.W. Library [430]
CARL M. MARCY, SENATE SERVICE 1950-1973 : CHIEF OF STAFF, SENATE FOREIGN RELATIONS COMMITTEE – 4mf – 9 – $20.00 – us Scholarly Res [320]
CARL PHILIPP EMANUEL BACHS VERSUCH UEBER DIE WAHRE ART DAS CLAVIER ZU SPIELEN / Bach, C P E – Zweyter Theil. Berlin. 1762. BP-142 1 – 9 – ne IDC [780]
CARL VON LINNES BREFVEXLING / Aehrling, E – Stockholm, 1885.(Bibliotheca Sertum Botanicum.Nr.1 Reprint Series). B-8120/1 – 9 – ne IDC [580]
Carlblom, August *see* ZUR LEHRE VON DER CHRISTLICHEN GEWISSHEIT: DREI ABHANDLUNGEN
Carlebach, David *see* BIBLISCHE KOENIGSDRAMEN IN DER FRANZOESISCHEN TRAGOEDIE DES 16. UND 17. JAHRHUNDERTS
Carlebach, S *see* FESTSCHRIFT
CARLETON ENTERPRISE – Carleton, NE. -w.Nov. 1919-May 1941 – 1 – us NE Hist [071]
Carleton, Guy *see* SIR GUY CARLETON PAPERS
Carleton, Hiram *see* GENEALOGICAL AND FAMILY HISTORY OF THE STATE OF VERMONT
Carleton, James G *see* THE PART OF RHEIMS IN THE MAKING OF THE ENGLISH BIBLE
CARLETON LEADER – Carleton, NE. -w. Aug. 1906-Oct. 1914 – 1 – us NE Hist [071]
CARLETON LEADER – Carleton, Nebraska, 1905 weekly – 1 – $35.00r – us NE Hist [071]
CARLETON NEWS – British Columbia, CN. Jan 1938-Dec 1943 – 1r – 1 – cn Commonwealth Micro [072]
CARLETON PLACE CANADIAN – (1978-1992.-15r) – Carleton Place, 1993 – 1r – 1 – cn Preston [971]
Carleton, Will *see*
- DRIFTED IN
- FARM BALLADS

Carletti, Tomaso *see* ATTRAVERSO IL BENADIR
Carli, Gian Rinaldo *see* LETTRES AMERICAINES, DANS LESQUELLES ON EXAMINE L'ORIGINE, L'ETAT CIVIL, POLITIQUE, MILITAIRE ET RELIGIEUX, LES ARTS, L'INDUSTRIE, LES SCIENCES, LES MOEURS, LES USAGES DES ANCIENS HABITANTS DE L'AMERIQUE. POUR SERVIR DE SUITE AUX MEMOIRES DE D. ULLOA
CarlidePlaisance, D de *see* RELATION CURIEUSE ET NOUVELLE D'UN VOYAGE DE CONGO FAIT LES ANNEES 1666 ET 1667
Carlile, John C *see* THE STORY OF THE ENGLISH BAPTISTS
CARLIN EXPRESS – Carlin, NV. 1993 – 2+ r – 1 – $100.00 ($50.00y) – U04835 – us Library Micro [071]
Carling, Jon *see* THE EFFECT OF TRANSVERSE PEDAL SPACING ON CYCLING EFFICIENCY
CARLISLE 1732-1849 – (Mf 1T: Births & Deaths 1741-56. Mf 1T-4T,6T: Marriage Intentions 1780-1849. Mf 1T-4T: Marriages 1780-1843. Mf 4T: Out-of-Town Marriages 1755-98. Mf 4T-6T: Births & Deaths 1732-1843. Mf 6T: Births & Deaths 1843-49; Marriages 1844-49) – (mf ed 1995) – 6mf – 9 – 0-87623-224-1 – us Holbrook [920]
CARLISLE AMERICAN – Carlisle, PA. -w 1856-64. 3 rolls – 13 – $25.00r – us I.M.R. [071]
CARLISLE BAPTIST CHURCH. STEWART COUNTY. TENNESSEE : CHURCH RECORDS – 1913-Aug 1966 – 1 – 9.36 – us Baptist [240]
Carlisle Cathedral. Library *see* ELIZABETHAN PART-SONG BOOKS
CARLISLE GAZETTE – Carlisle, PA. -w 1823-1897; 1897-1900. 4 rolls – 13 – $25.00r – us I.M.R. [071]
THE CARLISLE GAZETTE – Carlisle. Pa. 1785-1817 – 1,3 – us Readex [071]
CARLISLE HERALD – Carlisle, PA. -d 1802-1920 – 58 rolls – 13 – $25.00r – us I.M.R. [071]
CARLISLE HERALD AND EXPOSITER – Carlisle, PA., 1837-1847 – 13 – $25.00r – us I.M.R. [071]
Carlisle, John G *see* FREE TRADE
CARLISLE JOURNAL – Cumbria. 1958-68 – 1 – uk Microform Academic [072]
CARLISLE MIRROR – Carlisle, PA. -w 1875-79. 2 rolls – 13 – $25.00r – us I.M.R. [071]
Carlisle. Presbytery (Pres. Ch. in the U.S.A.) *see* MINUTES
CARLISLE REP. AND FRAMERS MECN. – Carlisle, PA., 1830-1931 – 13 – $25.00r – us I.M.R. [071]
CARLISLE REPUBLICAN – Carlisle, PA. -w 1831-38; 1890-91. 3 rolls – 13 – $25.00r – us I.M.R. [071]
CARLISLE REPUBLICAN *see* SPIRIT OF THE TIMES
CARLISLE VOLUNTEER – Carlisle, PA. -w 1905-13. 6 rolls – 13 – $25.00r – us I.M.R. [071]
CARLISLE WHIG & VARIOUS PAPERS – Carlisle, PA. -w 1822-23. 2 rolls – 13 – $25.00r – us I.M.R. [071]
CARLMONT-ENQUIRER BULLETIN – (Cont: Courier Bulletin. Cont by: San Carlos Enquirer Bulletin) – Belmont, CA. 1982-1985 – 4r – 1 – $200.00 – B03153 – us Library Micro [071]
Carlomagno, J C *see* EL DERECHO FLUVIAL INTERNACIONAL
CARLOS 4 Y MARIA LUISA, DE JUAN PEREZ DE GUZMAN Y GALLO / Godoy, Manuel & Fernandez de Bethencourt, Francisco – Madrid: Fortanet, 1913. B.R.A.H. 62. pp. 460-464 – 1 – sp Bibl Santa Ana [946]
Carlos, Alberto *see* SOCIALISMO NACIONAL
Carlos de Jesus Maria *see* RESUMO DAS REGRAS GERAES MAIS IMPORTANTES
CARLOS DE LAET, O POLMISTA / Chediak, Antonio Jose – Segunda serie. Rio de Janeiro: Z. Valverde, 194- – 1 – us U.W. Library [920]
CARLOW MORNING POST – Ireland. -d. 3 Jan 1828-27 May 1833, 30 Nov 1833-24 Jan 1835. (6 reels) – 1 – uk British Libr Newspaper [072]
CARLOW NATIONALIST, AND LEINSTER TIMES – Ireland. The Nationalist, and Leinster Times. -w. 22 Sept 1883-Dec 1923. 37 reels – 1 – uk British Libr Newspaper [072]
CARLOW SENTINEL – Ireland. -w. 1832-1920. 32 reels – 1 – uk British Libr Newspaper [072]
CARLOW STANDARD – Ireland. -w. 2 Jan-19 Apr 1832. (21 ft) – 1 – uk British Libr Newspaper [072]
Carlowitz, K W von *see* DE FOEDERIBUS FINIUM DISPUTATIO
CARLSBAD CHAMPION *see* CARLSBAD JOURNAL
CARLSBAD JOURNAL – (Also known as: Carlsbad Champion) – Carlsbad, CA. 1926-1928; 1930- – 68+ r – 1 – $3,400.00 ($50.00y) – H03173 – us Library Micro [073]
Carlsberg Laboratory. Copenhagen *see* CARLSBERG RESEARCH COMMUNICATIONS
CARLSBERG RESEARCH COMMUNICATIONS / Carlsberg Laboratory. Copenhagen – v.42-46, 1977-81. ISSN: 0105-1938 – 1,5,6,9,13 – 85.00v – us UMI [500]
Carlson, A J *see* SCIENCE AND THE SUPERNATURAL
Carlson, Frank *see*
- PAPERS
- SELECTED PAPERS

Carlson, PD *see* THE EFFECT OF TACTILE AND WHOLE/PART DRILL ON THE ACQUISITION OF OPPOSITION IN A SUCCESSFUL BASKETBALL LAY-UP
Carlton, Frank T *see* HISTORY AND PROBLEMS OF ORGANIZED LABOR
CARLTON NEWS – Carlton, OR. -w. 31 Oct 1940-28 Feb. 1946. 1 roll – 1 – us U.O. Library [071]
CARLTON SENTINEL – Carlton, OR. -w. 1 Jan 1926-27 Nov 1931. 2 rolls – 1 – us U.O. Library [071]
CARLTON TIMES – 1938 – 1 – at Corangamite [072]
Carlyle, A J *see* THE INFLUENCE OF CHRISTIANITY UPON SOCIAL AND POLITICAL IDEAS
Carlyle, Gavin *see* THE LIGHT OF ALL AGES
Carlyle, John Aitken *see* THE HISTORY OF SCOTISH POETRY
CARLYLE, PERSONALLY AND IN HIS WRITINGS : TWO EDINBURGH LECTURES / Masson, David – London: Macmillan, 1885 – 1 roll – 1 – 1-55879-514-6 – uk Libr Preservation [420]
Carlyle, Rev. G *see* THE COLLECTED WRITINGS OF EDWARD IRVING
Carlyle, S *see* FOR LIBERTY (LIBERTY LUMINANTS)
Carlyle, Thomas *see*
- COLLECTANEA THOMAS CARLYLE, 1821-1855
- CORRESPONDENCE
- THE LIFE OF JOHN STERLING
- ON HEROES, HERO WORSHIP AND THE HEROIC IN HISTORY
- PASSAGES SELECTED FROM THE WRITINGS OF THOMAS CARLYLE
- PAST AND PRESENT
- RESCUED ESSAYS OF THOMAS CARLYLE
- SARTOR RESARTUS
- TALES FROM MUSAEUS, TIECK, RICHTER
- TWO NOTEBOOKS OF THOMAS CARLYLE FROM 23D MARCH, 1822, TO 16TH MAY, 1832

CARLYLES EINFLUSS AUF KINGSLEY IN SOZIALPOLITISCHER UND RELIGIOES-ETHISCHER HINSICHT / Meyer, Maria – Leipzig, 1914 – 2mf – DM62.00 – 3-8267-3074-7 – gw Hänsel [170]

CARLYLES STELLUNG ZU CHRISTENTUM UND REVOLUTION / Schultze-Gaevernitz, G von – Leipzig, 1891 – 9 – DM48.00 – 3-89349-261-5 – gw Hänsel [240]

CARLYLE'S TRANSLATION OF WILHELM MEISTER / Marx, Olga – (Includes bibliographical references) – Baltimore: Waverly Press, 1925 – 1r – 1 – us U.W. Library [430]

Carlysle, G Raht *see* BIG BEND COUNTRY

LA CARMAGNOLE – Au Marais [Paris]: Dondey-Dupre, jun 1-11/15 1848 – us Res Libr [072]

Carman, Albert *see* THE GUIDING EYE, OR, THE HOLY SPIRIT'S GUIDANCE OF THE BELIEVER

Carman, Bliss *see*
- AT MICHAELMAS: A LYRIC
- BALLADS OF LOST HAVEN: A BOOK OF THE SEA
- BY THE AURELIAN WALL: AND OTHER ELEGIES
- THE GIRL IN THE POSTER: FOR A DESIGN BY MISS ETHEL REED
- THE GREEN BOOK OF THE BARDS
- LOW TIDE ON GRAND PRE: A BOOK OF LYRICS
- SAINT KAVIN: A BALLAD
- A SEAMARK: A THRENODY FOR ROBERT LOUIS STEVENSON

CARMARTHEN JOURNAL – Wales: The Journal, 1821-22; 1832-35; 1841-43; 1845-65; 1867-68; 1871; 1876-78; 1880; 1886; 1889; 1893-96; Jun 1910-Dec 1911; 1925; 1950-51; 1976- – 95+ r – 1 – uk British Libr Newspaper [072]

CARMARTHEN WEEKLY REPORTER ETC – (Missing: 1872) – Wales, UK. 2 Sept 1860-1870; 8 Apr 1871-1878; 3 Jan 1879-1895; 189?-1899 – 13 1/2r – 1 – uk British Libr Newspaper [072]

CARMEL : ALLGEMEINE ILLUSTRIERTE JUDENZEITUNG – Pest. v1-2? 1860-1861? Complete? 1 reel. B49. (Leo Baeck Institute. German-Jewish Periodicals, Pt 1) – 1 – $75.00 – us UPA [270]

CARMEL BAPTIST CHURCH. MANSFIELD, GEORGIA : CHURCH RECORDS – 30 Nov 1835-3 Jan 1943 – 1 – 40.68 – us Baptist [240]

CARMEL BAPTIST CHURCH. RUTHER GLEN, VIRGINIA : CHURCH RECORDS – 1799-1819, 1864-72, 1872-89, 1889-1901, 1902-35. WMS records. 1885-1933 – 1 – 43.20 – us Baptist [240]

CARMEL IN IRELAND : A NARRATIVE OF THE IRISH PROVINCE OF TERESIAN, OR, DISCALCED CARMELITES, A.D. 1625-1896: WITH A SUPPLEMENT CHIEFLY FROM LETTERS OF IRISH MISSIONARIES OF THE SEVENTEENTH CENTURY / Rushe, James P – (Includes indexes) – Dublin: Sealy, Bryers and Walker, M H Gill; New York: Benziger, 1903 – 1mf – 9 – 0-8370-7101-1 – 1986-1101 – us A.T.L.A. [240]

LE CARMEL. PARIS, 1929 / Vaussard, M-M – Madrid: Razon y Fe, 1930 – 1 – sp Bibl Santa Ana [944]

CARMEL PINE CONE – Carmel, CA. 1941-59 – 14r – 1 – $700.00 – C02095 – us Library Micro [071]

THE CARMELITE – Carmel. Calif. 1928-1932 – 1 – us UMI [071]

THE CARMELITE REVIEW – (Cont by: The New Carmelite review) – Falls View [Niagara Falls, Ont.]: Carmelite Fathers of North America, 1893-1903 – 9 – cn C.I.H.M. [240]

CARMEN DE BELLO SAXINICO (MGH 7: 17.BD) : ACCEDIT CONQUESTIO HEINRICI 4 IMPERATORIS – 1889 – Dfl6.00 – ne Slangenburg [240]

CARMEN DES GESTIS FREDERICI 1. IMPERATORIS IN LOMBARDIA (MGH 7: 62.BD) – 1965 – Dfl22.00 – ne Slangenburg [240]

CARMEN MAMERANI POETAE LAVREATI. CONTRA TEMPLARIOS PERIPATETICOS AC PROPHANATORES – Bruxellae, M. Hamontanus. 1564. BME-196 1 – 9 – ne IDC [240]

CARMEN PACIS : LE CHANT DE LA PAIX / Famin, N P – Paris, [1799] – 1mf – 1 – ILM-2582/1 – ne IDC [327]

Carmes, Nantes *see* REGISTRE DES FONDATIONS FAITES DANS LA COMMUNAUTE DES RELIGIEUX CARMES DE NANTES, DEPUIS 1318 JUSQU'EN 1767

Carmichael, Amy *see* THINGS AS THEY ARE

CARMICHAEL COURIER – Carmichael, CA. 1952-75 – 12r – 1 – $600.00 – R02096 – us Library Micro [071]

Carmichael, D F *see* A MANUAL OF THE DISTRICT OF VIZAGAPATAM

Carmichael, J Kevin *see* THE EFFECT OF CRANKLENGTH ON OXYGEN CONSUMPTION WHEN CYCLING AT A CONSTANT WORK RATE

Carmichael, James *see*
- CHURCH OF ENGLAND TEACHING
- THE CHURCH SERVICE: A SERIES OF SERMONS IN ST GEORGE'S CHURCH, MONTREAL
- THE CHURCH YEAR: A SERIES OF SERMONS FOR THE SACRED SEASONS
- THE ERRORS OF THE PLYMOUTH BRETHREN: BEING THE SUBSTANCE OF THREE SERMONS PREACHED IN ST GEORGE'S CHURCH, MONTREAL
- HOW TWO DOCUMENTS MAY BE FOUND IN ONE: A MONOGRAPH IN CONNECTION WITH THE HIGHER CRITICISM
- ORGANIC UNION OF CANADIAN CHURCHES: WITH A COMPARISON OF AUTHORIZED STANDARDS
- A PLEA FOR YOUNG MEN OF MONTREAL

CARMICHAEL TIMES – Carmichael, CA. 1981-1994 – 4r – 1 – $200.00 – B02093 – us Library Micro [071]

CARMINA / Albertinus Mussatus – 14th century. Holkham ms. 425. Holkham Hall, Norfolk, England – 1 – uk Microform Academic [025]

CARMINA / Sanchez Arjona, Vicente – Sevilla: Imprenta Alvarez, 1957 – 1 – sp Bibl Santa Ana [810]

CARMINA CANTABRIGIENSIA (MGH 7: 40.BD) – 1926 – Dfl13.00 – ne Slangenburg [240]

CARMINA. LIRIKA (1911-1912) / Shershenevich, V – v. 1. M. 1913. BR-1082 2 – 8 – ne IDC [460]

CARMINA SCRIPTURARUM / Marbach, C – Strasbourg, 1907 – 13mf – 8 – ne Slangenburg [220]

Carmona Alonso, Miguel *see* PRIMERAS JORNADAS DE COMERCIO EXTERIOR. CAMARA OFICIAL DE COMERCIO E INDUSTRIA DE CACERES. PONENTE D. ...

Carmona Guillen, Juan *see* LIBRO DEL MAESTRO. DIOS ES NUESTRO PADRE

Carmona, Juan *see*
- TRACTATUS DE PESTE AC FEBRIBUS CUM PUNCTICULIS VULGO TAVARDILLO
- TRACTATUS DE PESTE...AC FEBRIBUS CUM PUNCTICULIS VULGO TABARDILLO

Carmona, Miguel *see* EXCAVACIONES DE AMERICA

CARNARVON AND DENBIGH HERALD *see* CARNARVON HERALD

CARNARVON HERALD – Caernarvon, Wales. 1831-82 – 40r – 1 – uk British Libr Newspaper [072]

DER CARNAVAL UND DIE SOMNAMBUELE / Immermann, Karl Leberecht – Potsdam: Ruetten & Loening, [1944?] – 1r – 1 – us U.W. Library [830]

Carnazza Amara, G *see* DEL BLOCCO MARITTIMO

Carnazza Amaro, G *see* TRAITE DE DROIT...

Carnazza, C *see* IL CONTRATTO DI TRASPORTO...

Carnegie, Andrew *see* THE GOSPEL OF WEALTH

CARNEGIE CLASSICS OF INTERNATIONAL LAW / Carnegie Endowment for International Law – 8r – 1 – $350.00 – us Trans-Media [340]

Carnegie Endowment for International Law *see* CARNEGIE CLASSICS OF INTERNATIONAL LAW

CARNEGIE ENDOWMENT FOR INTERNATIONAL PEACE : REPORT ON THE TEACHING OF INTERNATIONAL LAW IN THE...UNITED STATES – N.p., 1913 – 1mf – 1 – ILM-3747/1 – ne IDC [327]

Carnegie Institution. Washington *see* MOUNT WILSON SOLAR OBSERVATORY

CARNEGIE QUARTERLY – (v23- . 1975- . 5,6. v24- . 1976- . 9) – 1953- – 1 – us UMI [370]

CARNEGIE ROCHESTER CONFERENCE SERIES ON PUBLIC POLICY – v10-21. 1978-84 – 1,5,6,13 – sz Elsevier [073]

CARNEGIE SCHOLARSHIP MEMOIRS / Iron and Steel Institute. London – v1-27 1909-1938 – 1 – us Princeton Micro [670]

THE CARNEGIE SURVEY OF THE ARCHITECTURE OF THE SOUTH : PHOTOGRAPHS / Johnston, Frances Benjamin – (mf ed 1984) – 132mf – 9 – £500.00 – uk Chadwyck [720]

Carnegie, William Hartley *see* CHURCHMANSHIP AND CHARACTER

Carnel, D *see* QUELQUES RECHERCHES SUR LE DIALECTE FLAMAND EN FRANCE

CARNET D'UN VOYAGEUR AU PAYS DES VEDDAS, CEYLAX / Deschamps, Emile Felix – Paris: Societe d'Editions Scientifiques, 1892 – 1 – us U.W. Library [950]

LE CARNET POSTAL – Neuville, Canada. n10. mai 1945 – 1r – 1 – Can$25.00 – cn Can Microfilming [072]

LES CARNETS D'UN CURIEUX COLLABORATION SPECIALE A "LA PATRIE" / Fauteux, Aegidius – Montreal: Bibliotheque nationale du Quebec, 1971. SEM35P47 – 1r – 1 – Can$15.00 – cn Bibl Nat [971]

CARNETS, NOUVELLE-CALEDONIE, 1905-1919 / Leenhardt, Maurice – 9 – F90.00 – fr Ethnologie [306]

Carnevale, E *see* DIRITTO INTERNAZIONALE E DIRITTO CRIMINALE

Carney, Deborah A *see* THE EFFECTS OF A SIX-MONTH EXERCISE MAINTENANCE PROGRAM ON THE CARDIOVASCULAR FITNESS LEVELS OF PARTICIPANTS

Carney, Thomas *see* LETTERS

Carney, William P *see* NO DEMOCRATIC GOVERNMENT IN SPAIN. RUSSIA'S PART IN SPAIN'S CIVIL WAR. MURDER AND ANTIRELIGION IN SPAIN

Carnochan, Janet *see*
- CENTENNIAL ST ANDREW'S, NIAGARA, 1794-1894
- CENTENNIAL, ST MARK'S CHURCH, NIAGARA
- NIAGARA ONE HUNDRED YEARS AGO: THE ANCIENT CAPITAL AND ITS VICINITY
- TWO FRONTIER CHURCHES: A PAPER READ BEFORE THE CANADIAN INSTITUTE AT NIAGARA, ON THE 2ND DAY OF JULY, 1890?

Carnot, Hippolyte *see* SYSTEME GENERAL DES OPERATIONS MILITAIRES DE LA CAMPAGNE PROCHAINE

Carnot, R *see* L'ETATISME INDUSTRIEL

Caro Baroja, Julio *see* LOS PUEBLOS DE ESPANA. ENSAYO DE ETNOLOGIA

Caro, Elme *see*
- ETUDES MORALES SUR LE TEMPS PRESENT
- NOUVELLES ETUDES MORALES SUR LE TEMPS PRESENT

Caro, Hermann Isaak *see* BEITRAEGE ZUR AELTESTEN EXEGESE DES BUCHES THRENI

Caro, Hugo de S *see* OPERA OMNIA IN UNIVERSUM VETUS ET NOVUM TESTAMENTUM

Caro, Leopold *see*
- AUSWANDERUNG UND AUSWANDERUNGSPOLITIK IN OESTERREICH
- EMIGRACYA I POLITYKA EMIGRACYJNA
- STATYSTYKA
- "WYCHODZTWO POLSKIE"

CARO MIA BEN / Giordani, G – (Score) – London: I Preston, 1785 – 1 – us Sibley [780]

Carocciolo, F *see* I COMMENTARI I DELLE GVERRE FATTO CO' TURCHI DA D. GIOVANNI D'AVSTRIA, ...

CAROLI LINNAEI...GENERA PLANTARUM / Sprengel, K P J – Goettingen, Ed.9 1830-1831. 2v – 16mf – 9 – ne IDC [615]

Carolina *see* FUNDAMENTAL CONSTITUTION

CAROLINA CORONADO / Blanco Garcia, Francisco – Madrid: Saenz de Jubera, 1909 – sp Bibl Santa Ana [440]

CAROLINA CORONADO / Munoz de San Pedro, Miguel – (Notas y papales ineditos) – Madrid, 1953. Sep.Ind. nº 64 Junio, 1953 – 1 – sp Bibl Santa Ana [946]

CAROLINA IN THE OLDEN TIME / Poyas, Elizabeth A – ca.1860. 2 fiches – 9 – us South Carolina Historical [978]

CAROLINA ISRAELITE – Charlotte. N.C. 1944-68 – 1 – us A.J.P.C. [071]

CAROLINA ISRAELITE – Charlotte. v1 n1; v3 n4; v12 n7; v16 n6 – 1r – 1 – us Ross [071]

THE CAROLINA ISRAELITE – Charlotte. v. 1-v. 3, no. 4, v. 12 no. 7-v. 16 no. 6. Feb 1944-May 1946; Mar 1954-Nov Dec 1958. Incomplete – 1 – us NY Public [073]

CAROLINA LAW JOURNAL – Columbia, S.C.: 1v. 1830-31 (all publ) – 2mf – 9 – $9.00 – LLMC 82-911 – us L.L.M.C. [073]

CAROLINA LAW REPOSITORY – Raleigh. v1-2. 1813-1816 – 1,5,6 – $40.00 – us Hein [073]

CAROLINA LAW REPOSITORY – (Title renumbered into official run of the North Carolina Supreme Court Reports as 4 N.C.) – 9 – us L.L.M.C. [073]

CAROLINA NEWS – Chapin. S.C. 1897-1899 – 1 – us UMI [071]

CAROLINA QUARTERLY – (v27- . 1975- . 5,6. v28- . 1976- . 9) – v. 1-. 1948- – 1 – us UMI [073]

Carolina Rifle Club. Charleston, South Carolina *see* MINUTES

CAROLINA SPARTAN – Spartanburg. S.C. 1849-1893 – 1 – us UMI [071]

CAROLINE H. DALL PAPERS, 1811-1917 / Dall, Caroline H – Massachusetts Historical Society – 45r – 1 – $3415.00 – us UMI [920]

CAROLINE PICHLER GEBORNE VON GREINER : DENKWUERDIGKEITEN AUS MEINEM LEBEN / ed by Bluemml, E K – ° (Missing: v1) – Muenchen. 2v. 1914 – 9mf – 9 – ne IDC [943]

CAROLINE PROGRESS – Bowling Green. Va. -w. 1947- – 1 – us UMI [071]

CAROLINE UND DOROTHEA SCHLEGEL IN BRIEFEN / Schelling, Karoline Michaelis – Ed. by Ernst Wieneke. Weimar: G. Kiepenheuer, 1914. 596p – 1 – us U.W. Library [920]

CAROLINE VON WOLZOGENS "AGNES VON LILIEN" (1798) : EIN BEITRAG ZUR GESCHICHTE DES FRAUENROMANS / Brock, Stephan – (Includes bibliographical references) – Berlin: H Blanke, 1914 – 1r – 1 – us U.W. Library [430]

CAROLINE VON WOLZOGENS "AGNES VON LILIEN" (1798) / Brock, Stephan – 1995 – 2mf – 9 – DM62.00 – 3-8267-3112-3 – gw Hänsel [430]

CAROLINIAN FLORIST / Drayton, John – 1798. 2 fiches – 9 – us South Carolina Historical [580]

Carolus, Sebastian *see*
- DISPUTATIO MUSICA
- DISPUTATIO MUSICA PRIMA (-TERTIA).

Caron, Adolphe *see*
- MANIFESTE POLITIQUE ADRESSE AUX ELECTEURS DU COMTE DE DORCHESTER
- MILICE ET DEFENSE DU CANADA: DISCOURS PRONONCE DANS LA CHAMBRE DES COMMUNES LE 10 AVRIL 1883
- SPEECH OF SIR ADOLPHE CARON, M.P. ON THE REMEDIAL BILL, OTTAWA, WEDNESDAY, 4TH MARCH 1896
- SPEECH OF SIR ADOLPHE CARON ON THE EXECUTION OF LOUIS RIEL: OTTAWA, MARCH 17TH AND 18TH, 1886

Caron, Alfred *see* BIO-BIBLIOGRAPHIE DU R.P. FERNAND PORTER, O.F.M.

Caron, Francois *see* A TRUE DESCRIPTION OF THE MIGHTY KINGDOMS OF JAPAN AND SIAM

Caron, Max *see* JESUS, DOCTOR

Caron, Mere *see* DIRECTIONS DIVERSES DONNEES PAR LA REV. MERE CARON, SUP. GEN. DES SOEURS DE LA PROVIDENCE POUR AIDER SES SOEURS A FORMER DE BONNES CUISINIERES

Caron, Napoleon *see*
- DEUX VOYAGES SUR LE SAINT MAURICE
- PETIT VOCABULAIRE A L'USAGE DES CANADIENS-FRANCAIS: CONTENANT LES MOTS DONT IL FAUT REPANDRE L'USAGE ET SIGNALANT LES BARBARISMES QU'IL FAUT EVITER POUR BIEN PARLER NOTRE LANGUE

Caron, R *see* OBJETS ETHNOGRAPHIQUES D'AMAZONIE

Caroso, Fabrito *see*
- IL BALLARINO DI M. FABRITO CAROSO DA SERMONETA, DIUISO IN DU TRATTATI...
- IL BALLARINO. DIVISO IN DUE TRATTATI

Carossa, Hans *see* WIRKUNGEN GOETHES IN DER GEGENWART

THE CARP REVIEW – Carp, Ontario. v2 n1. 24 feb 1905-25 dec 1930 – 9r – 1 – Can$75.00 – cn Can Microfilming [072]

Carpani, Ricardo *see* NACIONALISMO, PERONISMO Y SOCIALISMO NACIONAL

THE CARPATHIAN – [Pittsburgh, PA: Carpathian Pub Co. v1 n1-v3 n7-9. oct 1941-jul-sep 1943] – 1 – us Res Libr [073]

THE CARPATHO-RUSSIAN AMERICAN – Yonkers, NY: Lemko Association of the United States and Canada, 1968-jan 1969 – us Res Libr [305]

THE CARPATHO-RUSSIAN YOUTH – Stanford, CT: [s.n.] v1 n1-v2 n6 jan 20 1938-nov 1940; n1-2 apr,aug 1941 – 1 – us Res Libr [073]
CARPENTER / Dwight, Charles Abbott Schneider – New York: E.B. Treat, 1900. 1 fiche – 9 – us A.T.L.A. [240]
Carpenter, Edward *see*
- CIVILISATION; ITS CAUSE AND CURE, AND OTHER ESSAYS
- NON-GOVERNMENTAL SOCIETY
- PAGAN AND CHRISTIAN CREEDS: THEIR ORIGIN AND MEANING

Carpenter, G H *see* THE LIFE-STORY OF INSECTS
Carpenter, J Estlin *see* THE LIFE AND WORK OF MARY CARPENTER
Carpenter, James C *see* I CROSSED THE PLAINS IN THE '50'S
Carpenter, Joseph Estlin *see*
- THE BIBLE IN THE NINETEENTH CENTURY
- FIRST THREE GOSPELS: THEIR ORIGIN AND RELATIONS
- RELATION OF JESUS TO HIS AGE AND OUR OWN

Carpenter, Mason B *see* MINING CODE
Carpenter & Millberry *see* MENDOCINO AND LAKE COUNTIES
Carpenter, W B *see* INTRODUCTION TO THE STUDY OF FORAMINIFERA
Carpenter, William *see* POLITICAL LETTERS AND PAMPHLETS BY WILLIAM CARPENTER
Carpenter, William B *see* MESMERISM, SPIRITUALISM, AND C.: HISTORICALLY AND SCIENTIFICALLY CONSIDERED
Carpenter, William Boyd *see*
- GREAT CHARTER OF CHRI..STUDIES IN THE SERMON ON THE MOUNT
- A POPULAR HISTORY OF THE CHURCH OF ENGLAND
- SON OF MAN AMONG THE SONS OF MEN
- WISDOM OF JAMES THE JUST
- WITNESS OF THE HEART TO CHRIST
- WITNESS TO THE INFLUENCE OF CHRIST

CARPENTERIA HERALD – Carpenteria, CA. 1911-1954; 1976-1980 – 19r – 1 – $950.00 – H03176 – us Library Micro [071]
CARPENTER'S MONTHLY POLITICAL MAGAZINE – 1-2 2+2 (all publ). 1831-1832 – 6mf – 9 – $65.00 – us UPA [335]
CARPENTER'S MONTHLY POLITICAL MAGAZINE – London. v1-2. 1831-32 – 1r – 1 – us Ross [320]
Carpentier *see* NOUVEAU PLAN D'EDUCATION POUR FORMER DES HOMMES INSTRUITS ET DES CITOYENS UTILES
Carpentier Alting, A S *see* WOORDENBOEK VOOR VRIJMETSELAREN
Carpentier, Denyse *see* BIBLIOGRAPHIE ANALYTIQUE DE LOUIS HEMON
Carpentier, L J M *see* LE GRADUS FRANCAIS OU DICTIONNAIRE DE LA LANGUE POETIQUE
Carpentier, N J *see* DICTIONNAIRE DU BON LANGAGE
CARPENTRY AND BUILDING – New York: David Williams Co, 1879-1909. v3 1881. v14-15 1892-93 – us Res Libr [690]
Carpmael, A *see* PATENT LAWS OF THE WORLD
Carpmael, Charles *see* REPORT OF THE CANADIAN OBSERVATIONS OF THE TRANSIT OF VENUS, 6TH DECEMBER, 1882
Carpmael, E *see* PATENT LAWS OF THE WORLD
Carpue, J C *see* A HISTORY OF THE HIGH OPERATION FOR THE STONE
Carr, Arthur *see* THE GOSPEL ACCORDING TO SAINT MATTHEW
Carr, B *see* THE GENTLEMENS AMUSEMENT
Carr, Benjamin *see*
- DEAD MARCH AND MONODY
- MANUSCRIPT COLLECTION OF PIANOFORTE MUSIC
- MANUSCRIPT COLLECTION OF VOCAL MUSIC
- MASSES, VESPERS, LITANIES, HYMNS, PSALMS, ANTHEMS & MOTETS
- SIX IMITATIONS OF ENGLISH, SCOTCH, IRISH, WELCH, SPANISH & GERMAN AIRS
- THREE DIVERTIMENTOS (FOR THE PIANO)

Carr, H Wildon *see* THE PHILOSOPHY OF CHANGE
Carr, Herbert Wildon *see* LEIBNIZ
Carr, J H *see* THE EFFECT OF ARM MOVEMENT ON THE BIOMECHANICS OF STANDING UP
Carr, Joseph *see* UEBER DAS VERHAELTNIS DER WICLIFITISCHEN...BIBELUEBERSETZUNG
Carr, Ralph *see* AMERICAN PAPERS
Carracedo, San Salvador de *see* REGISTRO DE DOCUMENTOS SIECLE 11-16 (ANNO 1792)
Carrach, I P *see* DE EXEMTIONIBUS TERRITORIORUM GERMANIAE
Carradine, B *see* THE SANCTIFIED LIFE
Carradori, Arcangelo *see* ...DIZIONARIO DELLA LINGUA ITALIANA E NUBIANA
Carral Oviedo, Don Benigno *see* MEMORIAS DE UN LOCO
CARRARA MINER – Carrara, NV. Jul 1929 – 1r – 1 – $50.00 – U04438 – us Library Micro [071]
Carrasco, Adolfo *see* DESCUBRIMIENTO Y CONQUISTA DE CHILE
Carrasco Alvarez, Antonio *see*
- COMENTARIO AL ARTICULO 1361 DEL CODIGO CIVIL
- INCONGRUENCIAS LEGALES DE LAS FALTAS CONTRA LA PROPIEDAD DE CORCHERO Y COMPANIA

Carrasco, Antonio *see* DOCUMENTOS DE 1584 A 1595, RELATIVOS A DON LUIS ZAPATA DE CHAVES, EXISTENTES EN EL ARCHIVO MUNICIPAL DE LLERENA
Carrasco Canales, Jose *see* PASATIEMPOS ARROYANOS
Carrasco, Castulo *see*
- CORRESPONDENCIA CON JUAN ALCAIDE SANCHEZ
- PELICULAS DE AVENTURAS
- POR LOS BLANCOS CAMINOS DEL MARGEN. NOTAS PARA UNA PSICOLOGIA DEL LECTOR

Carrasco Lianes, Virgilio *see*
- DOCUMENTOS Y MONUMENTOS EPIGRAFICOS DEL MUSEO PROVINCIAL DE BADAJOZ
- LOS PUEBLOS TRAS SU HISTORIA. BIENVENIDA

Carrasco Montero, Gregorio *see* NOVENA AL SANTISIMO CRISTO DE LA SALUD. BROZAS
CARRATRACA EN EXTREMADURA – 1842 – 9 – 1.50f – sp Bibl Santa Ana [946]
Carrau, Ludovic *see* LA PHILOSOPHIE RELIGIEUSE EN ANGLETERRE
Carre, H *see* LES INCIDENTS...DE LA GUERRE RUSSO-JAPONAISE...
Carre, I *see* LES PEDAGOGUES DE PORT-ROYAL
Carre, William H *see*
- ART WORK OF BRITISH COLUMBIA, CANADA
- ART WORK ON HAMILTON, CANADA
- ART WORK ON MONTREAL, CANADA
- ART WORK ON OTTAWA, CANADA
- ART WORK – QUEBEC, CANADA

Carred, Henri *see* LA GUERRE
CARREFOUR – Montreal, 8 avr 1979-16 dec 1979f – 1r – 1 – Can$50.00 – cn Can Microfilming [072]
CARREFOUR – Paris. aout 1944-15 Oct 1977; 1978-Nov 1986 – 1 – fr A.C.R.P.P. [073]
CARREFOUR *see* PERSPECTIVES/DIMANCHE-MATIN
CARREFOUR AFRICAIN – Ouagadougou: [s.n, mar 10 1960-may 1967] – 2r – 1 – us Res Libr [072]
CARREFOUR CHRETIEN – Montreal: Les Buissonnets inc. ca 1962-1985. SEM35P84 – 2r – 1 – Can$103.00 – cn Bibl Nat [971]
Carreira, A *see* MANDINGAS DA GUINE PORTUGUESA
Carreno, Alberto Maria *see* UN DESCONOCIDO CEDULARIO DEL SIGLO 16. MEXICO, 1944
Carreno, J.-A. et al *see* LE QUARTIER DE LA PORTE D'AIX A MARSEILLE
Carrera Justiz, F *see* ORIENTACIONES NECESARIAS CUBA Y PANAMA
Carrera Stampa, M *see* MISIONES MEXICANAS EN ARCHIVOS EUROPEOS
Carreras Gargallo, Alberto *see* CRITICA DE LAS BASES TEORICAS DE LA TERAPIA FAMILIAR DE M. SELVINI
Carreras y Gonzalez, M *see*
- DERECHO MERCANTIL DE ESPANA
- ELEMENTOS DEL DERECHO MERCANTIL DE ESPANA...

Carrere, Frederic *see* DE LA SENEGAMBIE FRANCAISE
Carretas, J *see* INDICE DE LOS PAPELES DE LA JUNTA CENTRAL SUPREMA GUBERNATIVA DEL REINO Y...
Carri, Roberto *see* PODER IMPERIALISTA Y LIBERACION NACIONAL
THE CARRIAGE AND IMPLEMENT JOURNAL (OF CANADA) – Toronto: W.H. Miln, v1 no 1 (Mar 1900)- – 9 – cn C.I.H.M. [680]
Carriage and Wagon Workers International Union of North America *see* CARRIAGE AND WAGON WORKERS JOURNAL
Carriage and Wagon Workers' International Union of North AmericaMechanics Educational Society of America *see* CARRIAGE AND WAGON WORKERS JOURNAL, 1899-1908 : OFFICIAL JOURNAL, 1912-1915 : MESA EDUCATOR, 1944-1951
CARRIAGE AND WAGON WORKERS JOURNAL / Carriage and Wagon Workers International Union of North America – v1-8. 1899-1908 – 1r – 1 – us Ross [331]
CARRIAGE AND WAGON WORKERS JOURNAL, 1899-1908 : OFFICIAL JOURNAL, 1912-1915 : MESA EDUCATOR, 1944-1951 / Carriage and Wagon Workers' International Union of North AmericaMechanics Educational Society of America – (Coll title: Labor Union Periodicals, Pt 1) – 1r – 1 – $135.00 – 1-55655-231-9 – us UPA [331]
CARRICK DEMOCRAT ETC – Ireland, 13 Sept 1883 – 6ft – 1 – uk British Libr Newspaper [072]
CARRICK GAZETTE – 1 – £42.00r – uk Scot News [072]
CARRICK HERALD – 1 – £42.00r – uk Scot News [072]
Carrick, John *see* TORYISM IN THE CANADIAN CONFEDERATION
CARRICKFERGUS ADVERTISER – (Missing: 1923, 1925) – Ireland, 4 Apr 1884-9 Jan 1931; 25 Oct 1946-Sep 1982; Dec 1982- – 68r – 1 – uk British Libr Newspaper [072]
CARRICKFERGUS FREEMAN – Ireland, 22 Apr 1865-28 Jul 1866 – 38ft – 1 – uk British Libr Newspaper [072]
Carrick-on-Shannon, Ireland *see*
- LEITRIM JOURNAL
- LEITRIM OBSERVER

Carrier, Augustus Stiles *see* THE HEBREW VERB
Carrier, Joseph C *see* HISTOIRE CHIMIQUE ET PHYSIOLOGIQUE D'UNE BOUCHEE DE PAIN: CONFERENCE FAITE A L'UNION CATHOLIQUE DE MONTREAL, LE 27 AVRIL 1890
Carrier, Nicole *see* ALMANACHS ET ANNUAIRES DE LA VILLE DE QUEBEC DE 1780 A 1900
THE CARRIER, U.S. NAVAL AIR STATION – Alameda, CA. 1948-1979 – 5r – 1 – $250.00 – B06000 – us Library Micro [071]
Carriere, Gaston *see* HISTOIRE DOCUMENTAIRE DE LA CONGREGATION DES MISSIONNAIRES...OTAWA, 1963
LES CARRIERES FEMININES INTELLECTUELLES / Bourdeaux, Jean – Paris: France-edition, 1923 – 3mf – 9 – $8.00 – fr Bibl Nationale [305]
Carrighan, Terentius *see* THE CHANCERY STUDENT'S GUIDE IN THE FORM OF A DIDACTIC POEM.
Carriker, Robert C *see*
- THE ALASKA INDIAN LANGUAGE COLLECTION OF THE OREGON PROVINCE ARCHIVES OF THE SOCIETY OF JESUS
- THE ALASKA MISSION COLLECTION OF THE OREGON PROVINCE ARCHIVES OF THE SOCIETY OF JESUS
- THE PACIFIC NORTHWEST TRIBES INDIAN LANGUAGE COLLECTION OF THE OREGON PROVINCE ARCHIVES OF THE SOCIETY OF JESUS
- THE PACIFIC NORTHWEST TRIBES MISSIONS COLLECTION OF THE OREGON PROVINCE ARCHIVES OF THE SOCIETY OF JESUS, 1853-1960

O CARRIL : JORNAL PARA A DISTRACCAO DOS VIAJANTES – [s.l.]. 1 Dez 1870 – 1,5,6 – bl Biblioteca [072]
Carril, Bonifacio del *see*
- LA CRISIS ARGENTINA
- CRONICA INTERNA DE LA REVOLUCION LIBERTADORA

Carrillo Chumacero, Fernando *see* EPISTOLA DE LAUDIBUS PAETRIAE NOSTRAE
Carrillo de Albornoz, A *see* DIE SPANISCHE INQUISITION UND DIE ALUMBRADOS. BERLIN-BONN, 1934
Carrillo Lopez, Ignacio *see* PENSIL AMERICANO FLORIDO...MARIA DE GUADALUPE DE MEXICO. 1797
Carrillo, Rafael *see* AMBIENTE AXIOLOGICO DE LA TEORIA PURA DEL DERECHO
Carrillo, Santiago *see*
- LA JUVENTUD: FACTOR DE LA VICTORIA
- EN MARCHA HACIA LA VICTORIA
- POR LA REPUBLICA Y LA LEGALIDAD CONSTITUCIONAL: TODOS UNIDOS A LA LUCHA
- UNIDAD Y LUCHA

CARRINGTON AND KIRWAN'S REPORTS : REPORTS OF CASES ARGUED AND RULED AT NISI PRIUS IN THE COURTS OF QUEEN'S BENCH, COMMON PLEAS AND EXCHEQUER, TOGETHER WITH CASES TRIED ON THE CIRCUITS, AND IN THE CENTRAL CRIMINAL COURT, ALSO THE CROWN CASES RESERVED / Carrington, F A & Kirwan, A V – v1-3. 1843-53. London: S Sweet, 1845-52 – 25mf – 9 – $37.50 – LLMC 84-759 – us L.L.M.C. [324]
CARRINGTON AND MARSHMAN'S REPORTS : REPORTS OF CASES ARGUED AND RULED AT NISI PRIUS IN THE COURTS OF QUEEN'S BENCH, COMMON PLEAS AND EXCHEQUER, TOGETHER WITH CASES TRIED ON THE CIRCUITS, AND IN THE CENTRAL CRIMINAL COURT... / Carrington, F A & Marshman, J R – v1-2 in 1bk. 1841-42. London: S Sweet, 1843 (all publ) – 8mf – 9 – $12.00 – LLMC 84-758 – us L.L.M.C. [324]
CARRINGTON AND MARSHMAN'S REPORTS *see* CARRINGTON AND PAYNE'S REPORTS
CARRINGTON AND PAYNE'S REPORTS : REPORTS OF CASES ARGUED AND RULED AT NISI PRIUS IN THE COURTS OF KING'S BENCH AND COMMON PLEAS...AND ON THE OXFORD SUMMER CIRCUIT / Carrington, Frederick A & Payne, J – (With v9 title is described as: Carrington and Marshman's Reports) – v1-9. 1823-41. London: S Sweet, 1825-41 (all publ) – 74mf – 9 – $111.00 – LLMC 84-760 – us L.L.M.C. [324]
Carrington, F A *see*
- CARRINGTON AND KIRWAN'S REPORTS
- CARRINGTON AND MARSHMAN'S REPORTS

Carrington, Frederick A *see* CARRINGTON AND PAYNE'S REPORTS
Carrington, Henry Beebee *see* BATTLES OF THE AMERICAN REVOLUTION, 1775-1781: HISTORICAL AND MILITARY CRITICISM WITH TOPOGRAPHICAL ILLUSTRATION
Carrion, C *see* BIBLIOTECA MANUAL MEDICO-PRACTICA...
Carrion Garcia, Andres *see* AGREGACION TEMPORAL PROCESOS ESTOCASTICOS DISCRETOS DE MEDIAS MOVILES
Carrion Marquez, Jesus *see* DEFENSA DE LA NATURALEZA
Carrion-Nisas *see*
- MONTMORENCY
- PIERRE-LE-GRAND

Carrizo, Juan Alfonso *see* ANTECEDENTES HISPANO-MEDIOEVALES DE LA POESIA TRADICIONAL ARGENTINA
EL CARRO DE LA ALEGRIA, 1967 / Los Santos de Maimona – Madrid: Industrias Graficas M.S.A., 1967 – sp Bibl Santa Ana [946]
CARRO DE LA ALEGRIA EN LAS LOCALIDADES DE HERVAS, JARANDILLA... / Delegacion Provincial de Ministerio de Informacion y Turismo – Febrero, 1970. Caceres: La Minerva, 1969 – 1 – sp Bibl Santa Ana [946]
Carro, P *see* GRAMATICA ILOCANA
Carrol, James *see* THE AMERICAN CRITERION OF THE ENGLISH LANGUAGE
Carroll, Anna E *see* THE ROMISH CHURCH OPPOSED TO THE LIBERTIES..
Carroll, BH *see*
- ECCLESIA THE CHURCH, BIBLE CLASS LECTURES
- THE GENESIS OF AMERICAN ANTI-MISSIONISM

Carroll, Charles *see* THE CHARLES CARROLL PAPERS
Carroll County. Arkansas *see* INVENTORY OF THE COUNTY ARCHIVES OF ARKANSAS: CARROLL
CARROLL COUNTY HISTORICAL QUARTERLY – v2-5, 1957-60. F-0036 to F-0038 – 9 – us A.G.L.L. [978]
Carroll, Edward, Jr *see* LAW PRINTING LAWS.
Carroll, H K *see* THE RELIGIOUS FORCES OF THE UNITED STATES
Carroll, H K et aL *see* WHAT METHODISM OWES TO WOMEN
CARROLL INDEX – Carroll, NE. -w. Nov.1901-Dec. 1911; Jan. 1925-May 1928 – 1 – us NE Hist [071]
Carroll, J M *see* HISTORY OF TEXAS BAPTISTS
Carroll, John *see*
- THE "EXPOSITION" EXPOUNDED, DEFENDED AND SUPPLEMENTED
- "FATHER CORSON", OR, THE OLD STYLE CANADIAN ITINERANT:

- A HUMBLE OVERTURE FOR METHODIST UNIFICATION IN THE DOMINION OF CANADA
- MY BOY LIFE, PRESENTED IN A SUCCESSION OF TRUE STORIES: A BOOK FOR OLD OR YOUNG
- REASONS FOR METHODIST BELIEF AND PRACTICE: RELATIVE TO WATER BAPTISM, EXPRESSED IN PLAIN WORDS AND ARRANGED IN A SUMMARY MANNER
- THE SCHOOL OF THE PROPHETS, OR, FATHER MCROREY'S CLASS, AND SQUIRE FIRSTMAN'S KITCHEN FIRE: A FICTION FOUNDED ON FACTS, A BOOK FOR THE METHODISTS
- THOUGHTS AND CONCLUSIONS OF A MAN OF YEARS: CONCERNING CHURCHES AND CHURCH CONNECTION

Carroll, K K *see* DEVELOPMENT OF A PREDICTIVE EQUATION FOR MAXIMAL OXYGEN CONSUMPTION ON THE STEPTREADMILL

Carroll, Lewis *see*
- THE HUNTING OF THE SNARK
- THE LEWIS CARROLL PICTURE BOOK

Carroll, New Hampshire. Carroll Baptist Church *see* RECORDS

CARROLL NEWS – Vaiden. Miss. 1915-1917 – 1 – us UMI [071]

Carroll, Phidellia Patton *see* SOUL-WINNING

Carroll, T D *see* ACCOUNT OF THE T'U-JUHUN IN THE HISTORY OF THE CHIN DYNASTIE

Carrollton, Mississippi *see* MISCELLANEOUS EARLY NEWSPAPERS

Carrothers, Julia D *see* THE SUNRISE KINGDOM

CARROTTOMAN BAPTIST CHURCH. OTTOMAN, VIRGINIA : CHURCH RECORDS – 1886-1967 – 1 – 29.16 – us Baptist [240]

LE CARROUSEL – Journal de la cour, de la ville et des departements. no. 1-32. Paris. mars 1836-juil 1837 – 1 – fr A.C.R.P.P. [073]

CARRS HILL BAPTIST CHURCH. TRANSYLVANIA COUNTY. NORTH CAROLINA : CHURCH RECORDS – 1882-1927 – 1 – 8.19 – us Baptist [240]

CARRUM BOROUGH GAZETTE – 1922-1929 – 2mf – 9 – at Corangamite [980]

Carruth, Hayden *see* TRACK'S END; BEING THE NARRATIVE OF JUDSON PITCHER'S STRANGE WINTER SPENT THERE AS TOLD BY HIMSELF

Carruthers, Robert *see* THE LIFE OF ALEXANDER POPE, INCLUDING EXTRACTS FROM HIS CORRESPONDENCE

Carruthers, SW *see* THE WESTMINSTER CONFESSION OF FAITH

Carry, John *see*
- AN EXPOSURE OF THE MISCHIEVIOUS PERVERSIONS OF HOLY SCRIPTURE IN THE NATIONAL TEMPERANCE SOCIETY'S PUBLICATIONS: ADDRESSED TO MEN OF SENSE AND CANDOR
- RESTORATIONISM: TWO SERMONS PREACHED IN ST STEPHEN'S CHURCH, TORONTO, ON THE LAST SUNDAY AFTER TRINITY, 1875

CARRYING THE GOSPEL TO ALL THE NON-CHRISTIAN WORLD : WITH SUPPLEMENT, PRESENTATION AND DISCUSSION OF THE REPORT IN THE CONFERENCE ON 15TH JUNE 1910 – (Includes indexes) – Edinburgh: Publ for the World Missionary Conference by Oliphant, Anderson & Ferrier; New York: Fleming H Revell, [1910?] – 2mf – 9 – 0-8370-6472-4 – 1986-0472 – us A.T.L.A. [240]

CARRYOVER STOCKS OF CEREALS, 1975-1980 – 1981 – 41p – it F.A.O. [338]

CARS AND TRUCKS *see* AUTOMOTIVE EXECUTIVE

Carson, Alexander *see* THE KNOWLEDGE OF JESUS, THE MOST EXCELLENT OF THE SCIENCES

CARSON BOYS – Carson City, NV. 1885-1886 – 1r – 1 – $50.00 – U04441 – us Library Micro [071]

CARSON CITY NEWS *see* MORNING NEWS

CARSON DAILY APPEAL – (Also known as: Morning Appeal. Cont by: Nevada Appeal) – Carson City, NV. 1865-1877; 1877-1946 – 142r – 1 – $7,100.00 – N04443 – us Library Micro [071]

CARSON DAILY APPEAL *see* NEVADA APPEAL

CARSON DAILY BEE – Carson City, NV. Oct-Nov 1882, 14 Jul 1883 (scats) – 1r – 1 – $50.00 – U04449 – us Library Micro [071]

CARSON DAILY TIMES – Carson City, NV. 1880-81 – 1r – 1 – $50.00 – 10037 – us Library Micro [071]

CARSON EVENING GAZETTE – Carson City, NV. 21-23 Jul 1914 – 1r – 1 – $50.00 – U04444 – us Library Micro [071]

CARSON FREE LANCE – Carson City, NV. 1885-86 – 2r – 1 – $100.00 – N04447 – us Library Micro [071]

Carson, J *see* AN INQUIRY INTO THE CAUSES OF RESPIRATION ON THE MOTION OF THE BLOOD

CARSON REVIEW – Carson City, NV. 1972-1973 – 2r – 1 – $100.00 – N4447 – us Library Micro [071]

CARSON VALLEY HISTORICAL NEWSLETTER – Minden, NV. 1980-1992 – 1r – 1 – $50.00 – B06064 – us Library Micro [071]

CARSON VALLEY NEWS – Genoa, NV. 1875-76, 1883-89 – 2r – 1 – $90.00 – U04536 – us Library Micro [071]

Carson, W R *see* REUNION ESSAYS

CARSON-CHRONICLE – (Also known as: Morning Chronicle) – Carson City, NV. 1935-52; 1927-48 (incomplete); Feb-Dec 1967; 1969 – 9r – 1 UN04442 – $450.00 – us Library Micro [071]

CARSTAIRS JOURNAL – Alberta, CN. 1907-23 – 5r – 1 – cn Commonwealth Micro [072]

CARSTAIRS NEWS – Alberta. Canada. Au 1924-D 1924, 1926 – 1 – cn Commonwealth Micro [072]

Cart, J *see* PIERRE VIRET, LE REFORMATEUR VAUDOIS

CARTA / Cortes, Hernando – 1865 – 9 – 1.50f – sp Bibl Santa Ana [910]

CARTA A LOS PATRIOTAS Y ANTIFASCISTAS DE LA ARGENTINA / Codovilla, Victorio – Montevideo: Editorial Selecciones, 1944 – 1 – CSUXAGP8750-B – us Hoover Inst Photo [320]

CARTA A MIS CAMARADAS : EL PODER Y LA REVOLUCION / Giudici, Ernesto – [Buenos Aires]: Granica Editor, [1st ed 1973] – 1 – CSUXAGP8743-B – us Hoover Inst Photo [320]

CARTA ABIERTA AL EMINENTISIMO SR. CARDENAL VERDIER, ARZOBISPO DE PARIS – n.p. 1937. Fiche W 779. (Blodgett Collection of Spanish Civil War Pamphlets) – 9 – us H.U. College Libr [946]

CARTA ABIERTA DE UN PERONISTA A UN CONFUNDIDO / Daneri, Alberto – Buenos Aires: Ediciones Macacha Guemes, 1974 – 1 – CSUXADQ6392-B – us Hoover Inst Photo [320]

CARTA AL AUTOR DE LA ORACION APOLOGETICA POR LA ESPENA Y SU MERITO LITERARIO / Conchudo, J – 1787 – 9 – 1.50f – sp Bibl Santa Ana [840]

CARTA AL MARQUES DE SAN SIMON / Godoy, Manuel – Madrid: Fortanet, 1891. B.R.A.H. 18, pp. 470-472 – sp Bibl Santa Ana [946]

CARTA CIRCULAR – (Cont by: Espana Evangelica) – 1967-72; 1978-89 (incomplete) – Inquire – 1 – ATLA S0365 – us A.T.L.A. [240]

CARTA CIRCULAR *see* ESPANA EVANGELICA

CARTA COLECTIVA DE LOS OBISPOS ESPANOLES A LOS DE TODO EL MUNDO CON MOTIVO DE LA GUERRA EN ESPANA – Pamplona, 1937. Fiche W 780. (Blodgett Collection of Spanish Civil War Pamphlets) – 9 – us H.U. College Libr [946]

CARTA DE A...AL PARTIR PARA ROMA / Ramirez Vazquez, Fernando – (1866 ed.1.50f; 9) – 1867 – 9 – 1.50f – sp Bibl Santa Ana [440]

CARTA DE BARTOLO / Ipnocausto, Paulo – 1790 – 9 – 1.50f – sp Bibl Santa Ana [830]

CARTA DE BARTOLO SOBRINO DE DON FERNANDO PEREZ / Forner Segarra, Juan Pablo – 1790 – 9 – $1.50f – sp Bibl Santa Ana [946]

CARTA DE DON...EN QUE DEMUESTRA QUAN INACCESIBLES HAN SIDO LOS ESFUERZOS DE D. BERNARDO ARAYO PARA DEFENDER QUE NO QUE PHTISIS PULMONAR... / Herrero, Antonio Maria – Madrid, 1757 – 1mf – 9 – sp Cultura [616]

CARTA DE FERNANDO EL CATOLICO COMUNICANDO LA TOMA DE GRANADA (ANNO 1492) – Cordoba – 1r – 5,6 – sp Cultura [946]

CARTA DE PARACUELLOS / Perez, Fernando – 1789 – 9 – 1.50f – sp Bibl Santa Ana [946]

CARTA DE PEDRO PONCE DE LEON, OBISPO DE PLASENCIA, A FELIPE 2, SOBRE LAS RELIQUIAS Y LIBRERIAS DE SU OBISPADO Y SUS ACTIVIDADES LITERARIAS / Andres Martinez, Gregorio – Badajoz: Dip. Provincial, 1967 – sp Bibl Santa Ana [240]

CARTA DE PRIVILEGIO DE LOS REYES CATOLICOS A LA CIUDAD DE BADAJOZ, FECHADA EN EL CAMPAMENTO REAL "SOBRE TORO" EL DIA 21 DE JULIO DE 1475 / Guerra Guerra, Arcadio – Badajoz: Dip. Provincial, 1974. Sep. REE – 1 – sp Bibl Santa Ana [240]

CARTA DEL DOCTOR MARIANO SEGUER...A UN ERUDITO Y SABIO... / Seguer, Mariano – SL, SA – 1mf – 9 – sp Cultura [616]

LA CARTA DEL NAVEGAR PITORESCO / Boschini, Marco – O-167. 1660 – 9 – ne IDC [910]

Carta Diocesanas *see* MEMORIA 1959

CARTA EDITORIALE – Riverside, CA. 1963-1969 – 1r – 1 – $50.00 – R03410 – us Library Micro [071]

Carta, F *see* MONUMENTA PALAEOGRAPHICA SACRA ATLANTE PALAEOGRAFICO-ARTISTICO

CARTA MEDITA DE LA DUQUESA DE PLASENCIA DONA LEONOR PIMENTEL. DONANDO A LOS DOMINICOS EL CONVENTO DE SAN VICENTE FERRER DE LA CIUDAD DE PLASENCIA (22 DE AGOSTO Y 10 DE OCTUBRE DE 1484) / Palomo Iglesias Crescensio – Badajoz: Imprenta de la Diputacion Prov., 1975 – sp Bibl Santa Ana [920]

CARTA PASTORA / Ortiz y Gutierrez, Luis Felipe – 1886 – 9 – 1.50f – sp Bibl Santa Ana [240]

CARTA PASTORAL : 1ST ASAMBLEA DIOCESANA DE ACCION DE CATOLICA / Alcazar Alenda, Jose Maria – Badajoz: Tipografia Espanola, 1933 – 1 – sp Bibl Santa Ana [240]

CARTA PASTORAL / Becerra y Valcarzel, Diego – 1694 – 9 – 1.50f – sp Bibl Santa Ana [240]

CARTA PASTORAL / Garcia Gil, Manuel – 1854 – 9 – 1.50f – sp Bibl Santa Ana [830]

CARTA PASTORAL / Torrijos y Gomez, Ramon – 1895 – 9 – 1.50f – sp Bibl Santa Ana [240]

CARTA PASTORAL / Valero y Lossa, Francisco – 1759 – 9 – 1.50f – sp Bibl Santa Ana [240]

CARTA PASTORAL AL INAUGURAR SU PONTIFICADO / Conde y Corral, Bernardo – Plasencia, 1858 – 1 – sp Bibl Santa Ana [240]

CARTA PASTORAL. CONFIRMACION / Garcia Gil, Manuel – 1856 – 9 – 1.50f – sp Bibl Santa Ana [830]

CARTA PASTORAL DE ENTRADA QUE DIRIGE A SUS DIOCESANOS / Casanas, E – Tarragona, 1901 – 1mf – 1 – ILM-4084/1 – ne IDC [327]

CARTA PASTORAL DEL ILMO. SR. OBISPO DE PLASENCIA AL CLERO Y FIELES DE SU DIOCESIS / Casas Souto, Pedro – 1876 – 9 – 1.50f – sp Bibl Santa Ana [240]

CARTA PASTORAL DEL...CON OCASION DEL 4TH CENTENARIO DE LA MUERTE DE HERNANDO CORTES Y DEL HOMENAJE DE ESPANA A NUESTRA SENORA DE GUADALUPE / Alcazar Alenda, Jose Maria – Badajoz: Imp. Provincial, 1947 – 1 – sp Bibl Santa Ana [240]

CARTA PASTORAL QUE EL EXCMO...ADOLFO PEREZ MUNOZ DIRIGE AL CLERO Y FIELES DE SU DIOCESIS / Perez Munoz, Adolfo – Badajoz: Tip.Uceda Hnos, 1915 – 1 – sp Bibl Santa Ana [240]

CARTA PASTORAL QUE...AL...DEAN Y CABILDO / Ramirez Vazquez, Fernando – 1866 – 9 – 1.50f – sp Bibl Santa Ana [240]

CARTA PASTORAL QUE...DIRIGE A SUS DIOCESANOS EN SU PONTIFICADO EN MARZO DE 1864 / Lopez y Zaragoza, Gregorio Mª. – Madrid: Imp. y Lib. de D. Eusebio Aguado, 1864 – 1 – sp Bibl Santa Ana [240]

CARTA PASTORAL QUE...OBISPO DE BADAJOZ DIRIGE AL CLERO Y FIELES DE SU DIOCESIS / Perez Munoz, Adolfo – Badajoz: Tip. Uceda Hermanos, 1920 – 1 – sp Bibl Santa Ana [240]

CARTA PASTORAL...A TODOS LOS PRELADOS Y RELIGIOSOS DE DICHA PROVINCIA... / Molina, Gaspar de – 1 – sp Bibl Santa Ana [240]

CARTA PASTORAL...AL CLERO / Ramirez Vazquez, Fernando – 1867 – 9 – 1.50f – sp Bibl Santa Ana [240]

CARTA PASTORAL...AL CLERO / Ramirez Vazquez, Fernando – 1879 – 9 – 1.50f – sp Bibl Santa Ana [240]

CARTA PASTORAL...QUENTA CURA / Hernandez y Herrero, Joaquin – 1865 – 9 – 1.50f – sp Bibl Santa Ana [240]

CARTA REAL POR LA QUE SE EXIME A SERRADILLA DE LA JURISDICCION DE PLASENCIA (24 DE NOVIEMBRE DE 1557) / Archivo Municipal, Serradilla – Ayuntamiento de Serradilla, Plasencia: Tip. La Victoria, 1956 – sp Bibl Santa Ana [946]

CARTA SIN SOBRE ESCRITO AL SR. OSSORIO Y GALLARDO / Salazar Alonso, Rafael – Madrid: Roca, Impresor, 1929 – 1 – sp Bibl Santa Ana [946]

CARTA SOBRE LA LONJA DE MALLORCA / Jovellanos, Melchor Gaspar de – 1812 – 1mf – 9 – Pta1,000.00 – 84-7848-123-0 – sp Pentalfa [946]

CARTA Y OTROS DOCUMENTOS DE HERNANDO CORTES / Becker, Jeronimo – Madrid: Fortanet, 1916. B.R.A.H. lxix/pp. 313-316 – 1 – sp Bibl Santa Ana [350]

Cartagena, A *see* LIBER DE PESTE, DE SIGNIS FEBRIUM ET DE DIEBUS CRITICIS

Cartapanis, Andre *see* TRANSNATIONAL CORPORATIONS AND ENDOGENOUS DEVELOPMENT

Cartari, V *see*
- IMAGINES DEORUM
- IMAGINI DELLI DEI DE GLI ANTICHI

CARTAS A FLORO. SOBRE PRIMERA ENSENANZA Y EDUCACION / Codina, Luis – 1864 – 9 – 1.50f – sp Bibl Santa Ana [370]

CARTAS A LA NOVIA / Aradillas Agudo, Antonio – Madrid: Ediciones Stadium, 1962 – sp Bibl Santa Ana [946]

CARTAS A LOPEZ PRUDENCIO / Guerra Guerra, Arcadio – Badajoz: Imp. Dip. Provincial, 1966. Sep. REE – sp Bibl Santa Ana [946]

CARTAS BOCA ARRIBA / Sanchez Felipe, Juan A – Caceres: Tip. Editorial Extremadura, s.a. 1954? Anaquel de Forja no 8 – sp Bibl Santa Ana [946]

CARTAS CONFIDENCIALES DE LA REINA MARIA LUISA Y DE DON MANUEL GODOY – Madrid: M. Aguilar – 1 – sp Bibl Santa Ana [946]

CARTAS DE ARTURO GAZUL A FERNANDO VILLALBA / Segura Otano, Enrique – Badajoz: Imp. Dipt. Provincial, 1971 – sp Bibl Santa Ana [910]

CARTAS DE BAROLOME JOSE GALLARDO. NOTICIA / Fita, Fidel – Madrid: Fortanet, 1913. B.R.A.H. 62. p. 182 – 1 – sp Bibl Santa Ana [946]

CARTAS DE D...QUE TRATAN DEL DESCUBRIMIENTO Y CONQUISTA DE CHILE / Valdivia, Pedro de – Sevilla: Est. tip. de M. Carmona, 1929 – 1 – sp Bibl Santa Ana [350]

CARTAS DE GODOY A FERRER DEL RIO / Valgoma y Diaz-Varela, Dalmiro de la – Madrid: Imp. y Edit. Maestre, 1968. B.R.A.H. 163. Cuaderno I. pp. 57-58 – 1 – sp Bibl Santa Ana [946]

CARTAS DE JUAN DE LA ENCINA / Isla, Jose Francisco – 1787 – 1mf – 9 – Pta1,000.00 – 84-7848-245-8 – sp Pentalfa [440]

CARTAS DE LOS PADRES DE LA COMPANIA DE LA MISION DE FILIPINAS / Society of Jesus. Philippine Islands – Letters from missions. Manila. 10v. 1877-95 – 1 – 23.00r – us L of C Photodup [240]

CARTAS DE RELACION DE LA CONQUISTA DE MEJICO / Hernan Cortes – (Tambien Tomo 2, 5th ed) – Madrid: Espasa Calpe, 5th ed. tomo 1. 1942 – 1 – sp Bibl Santa Ana [350]

CARTAS DEL LIBERTADOR. TOMOS 1 A 10 / Lecuna, Vicente – Caracas, 1929-30; Madrid: Razon y Fe, 1931 – 1 – sp Bibl Santa Ana [946]

CARTAS DIOCESANAS. MEMORIA 1957 – S.L., s.i., 1957 – 1 – sp Bibl Santa Ana [240]

CARTAS DO BRASIL / Leclerc, Max – Sao Paulo, 1942 – 4mf – 8 – ne Slangenburg [910]

CARTAS ERUDITAS DE ALGUNOS LITERATOS ESPANOLES / Jordan de Asso, Ignacio – 1775 – 1mf – 9 – Pta1,000.00 – 84-7848-194-X – sp Pentalfa [440]

CARTAS ERUDITAS. TOMO 1 / Feijoo Montenegro, Benito J – 1742 – 2mf – 9 – Pta1,500.00 – 84-7848-004-8 – sp Pentalfa [370]
CARTAS ERUDITAS. TOMO 2 / Feijoo Montenegro, Benito J – 1746 – 2mf – 9 – Pta1,500.00 – 84-7848-005-6 – sp Pentalfa [370]
CARTAS ERUDITAS. TOMO 3 / Feijoo Montenegro, Benito J – 1750 – 2mf – 9 – Pta1,500.00 – 84-7848-006-4 – sp Pentalfa [370]
CARTAS ERUDITAS. TOMO 4 / Feijoo Montenegro, Benito J – 1753 – 2mf – 9 – Pta1,500.00 – 84-7848-007-2 – sp Pentalfa [370]
CARTAS ERUDITAS. TOMO 5 / Feijoo Montenegro, Benito J – 1760 – 2mf – 9 – Pta1,500.00 – 84-7848-008-0 – sp Pentalfa [370]
CARTAS ESCRITAS A LOS MUY NOBLES DOCTORES...SE DIZE QUE EL SAL AZIDOY ALCALI... / Juanini, J – Madrid, 1691 – 2mf – 9 – sp Cultura [610]
CARTAS FAMILIARES DE DON BARTOLOME JOSE GALLARDO / Perez de Guzman, Juan – Madrid: Fortanet, 1920. B.R.A.H. 77. pp. 312-318 – 1 – sp Bibl Santa Ana [946]
CARTAS INEDITAS Y SEMI-INEDITAS DE DONOSO CORTES / Valle, Antonio – Madrid: Razon y Fe, 1936 – 1 – sp Bibl Santa Ana [946]
CARTAS LITERARIAS...SOBRE GREGORIO SILVESTRE / Fernandez Almuzara, E – Madrid: Razon y Fe, 1940 – 1 – sp Bibl Santa Ana [440]
CARTAS MARRUECAS / Cadalso Vazquez, Jose – 1793 – 1mf – 9 – Pta1,000.00 – 84-7848-139-7 – sp Pentalfa [550]
CARTAS MORALES, MILITARES, CIVILES Y LITERARIAS, TOMO 1 / Mayans y Siscar, Gregorio – 1773 – 2mf – 9 – Pta1,500.00 – 84-7848-293-8 – sp Pentalfa [440]
CARTAS MORALES, MILITARES, CIVILES Y LITERARIAS, TOMO 2 / Mayans y Siscar, Gregorio – 1773 – 2mf – 9 – Pta1,500.00 – 84-7848-294-6 – sp Pentalfa [440]
CARTAS MORALES, MILITARES, CIVILES Y LITERARIAS, TOMO 3 / Mayans y Siscar, Gregorio – 1773 – 2mf – 9 – Pta1,500.00 – 84-7848-295-4 – sp Pentalfa [440]
CARTAS MORALES, MILITARES, CIVILES Y LITERARIAS, TOMO 4 / Mayans y Siscar, Gregorio – 1773 – 2mf – 9 – Pta1,500.00 – 84-7848-296-2 – sp Pentalfa [440]
CARTAS MORALES, MILITARES, CIVILES Y LITERARIAS, TOMO 5 / Mayans y Siscar, Gregorio – 1773 – 1mf – 9 – Pta1,000.00 – 84-7848-297-0 – sp Pentalfa [440]
CARTAS PASTORALES. BAHIA, 1928 / Schumacher, Pedro – Madrid: Razon y Fe, 1930 – 1 – sp Bibl Santa Ana [240]
CARTAS PASTORALES Y OTRAS EXHORTACIONES...DOCTOR DON PEDRO CASAS SOUTO...OBISPO DE PLASENCIA / Casas y Gonzalez, Juan Bautista – 1898 – 9 – $1.50f – sp Bibl Santa Ana [240]
CARTAS PEDAGOGICAS / Saiz Otero, Concepcion y Urbano Gonzales Serrano – 1895 – 9 – 1.50f – sp Bibl Santa Ana [370]
CARTAS (SIECLE 16) / Cruz, San Juan de la – Andujar – 1r – 5,6 – sp Cultura [946]
CARTAS SOBRE QUINTOS / Delicado, Juan M – 1827 – 9 – 1.50f – sp Bibl Santa Ana [946]
CARTAS Y DOCUMENTOS DE LAS MISIONES DE LOS P.P. CAPUCHINOS EN VENEZUELA 1781-1788 / Rionegro, Friolan – Vigo, 1931; Madrid: Razon y Fe, 1933 – 1 – sp Bibl Santa Ana [240]
CARTAS Y EXTASIS DE GEMA GALGANI. BARCELONA, 1933 / San Estanislao, German de – Madrid: Razon y Fe, 1934 – 1 – sp Bibl Santa Ana [946]
CARTAS Y MEMORIAL AL REY. MANILA, 23 JUNIO 1584 / Plasencia, Juan de – Archivo Ibero-Americano, 1916 – 1 – sp Bibl Santa Ana [946]
CARTAS Y OTROS DOCUMENTOS NOVISIMAMENTE DESCUBIERTOS EN EL ARCHIVO GENERAL DE INDIAS DE SEVILLA / Cortes, Hernando – Sevilla: Tipografia de F. Diaz y Compania, 1915 – 1 – sp Bibl Santa Ana [946]
CARTAS Y RELACIONES DE HERNANDO CORTES AL EMPERADOR CARLOS V / Cortes, Hernando – 1866 – 9 – 1.50f – sp Bibl Santa Ana [946]
CARTAS...BARTOLO GALLAR.. / Zapatilla, Lupianejo (pseud. de Adolfo de Castro) – 1851 – 9 – 1.50f – sp Bibl Santa Ana [920]
O CARTAZ : FOLHA HUMORISTICA SATIRICA – [s.l.]. 27 Fev 1890 – 1,5,6 – bl Biblioteca [072]
CARTE GENERALE DE LA MONARCHIE FRANCOISE, CONTENANT L'HISTOIRE MILITAIRE, DEPUIS CLOVIS...JUSQU'A...LOUIS 15 / Lemau de la Jaisse, Pierre – SEM35P205 – 1r – 1 – Can$15.00 – cn Bibl Nat [944]
CARTE SCOLAIRE DE L'ENSEIGNEMENT PRIMAIRE, ANNEE SCOLAIRE 1984-1985 / Rwanda. Direction Generale des Etudes et Recherches Pedagogiques – Ed 9. [Kigali, 1986] – 2mf – 9 – DE-646/1 – ne IDC [370]
CARTEGGIO INEDITO D'ARTISTI DEI SECOLI 14, 15, 16... / Gaye, J W – Firenze. 3v. 1839-1840 – 24mf – ne IDC [700]
CARTELAS – Habana. v.1-41, 1919-60 – 1 – 3082.00 – us L of C Photodup [073]
CARTELLA MUSICALE NEL CANTO FIGURATO FERMO, ET CONTRAPUNTO. NOVAMENTE IN QUESTA TERZA IMPRESSIONE RIDOTTA DALL'ANTICA ALLA MODERNA PRATICA / Banchieri, A – 1614 – 9 – us Sibley [780]
Carter *see* HISTORY OF PEMBROKE, NEW HAMPSHIRE 1730-1895
Carter, Alfred George Washington *see* THE OLD COURT HOUSE
Carter, C Sydney *see* THE ENGLISH CHURCH IN THE EIGHTEENTH CENTURY
Carter, Clarence E *see* THE TERRITORIAL PAPERS OF THE UNITED STATES
Carter, E R *see* BIOGRAPHICAL SKETCHES OF OUR PULPIT
Carter, Elizabeth (Simerwell) *see* DIARY
THE CARTER FAMILY PAPERS, 1659-1797, IN THE SABINE HALL COLLECTION / University of Virginia Library – (With printed guide) – 4r – 1 – $340.00 – D3182 – us Scholarly Res [920]
Carter, Howard *see* THE TOMB OF TUT-ANKH-AMEN, 3
Carter, J *see* AMERICAN MUSIC: A VOLUME OF TUNES...FROM THE LIBRARY OF ROBERT CARTER OF VIRGINIA
Carter, J F M *see* LIFE AND WORK OF THE REV. T.T. CARTER
Carter, James Coolidge *see*
- LAW
- THE PROPOSED CODIFICATION OF OUR COMMON LAW

Carter, James Treat *see* THE NATURE OF THE CORPORATION AS A LEGAL ENTITY, WITH ESPECIAL REFERENCE TO THE LAW OF MARYLAND
Carter, Jesse Benedict *see* THE RELIGION OF NUMA, AND OTHER ESSAYS ON THE RELIGION OF ANCIENT ROME
Carter, John *see*
- BOOK OF ANGLICAN CHANT...IN MANUSCRIPT
- JOURNAL AND ACCOUNT BOOK

Carter, Merle *see* DIARIES AND CORRESPONDENCE
Carter, R Kelso *see* THE SUPERNATURAL GIFTS OF THE SPIRIT
Carter, Ruth C *see*
- CATALOGING AND CLASSIFICATION QUARTERLY
- JOURNAL OF INTERNET CATALOGING

Carter, Sydney *see* THE ENGLISH CHURCH IN THE SEVENTEENTH CENTURY
Carter, T T *see* A MEMOIR OF JOHN ARMSTRONG, D.D.
Carter, Thomas H *see* PAPERS
CARTERET PAPERS, FROM THE ARCHIVES OF THE MARQUESS OF BATH / Bath. Archives (Marquess). Longleat – 1 – uk Microform Academic [941]
CARTER-KARIS COLLECTION OF SOUTH AFRICAN POLITICAL MATERIALS – Chicago: Uni of Chicago, Photodup Dept, 1974 (mf ed) – 1 – us Res Libr [960]
CARTER'S FORD BAPTIST CHURCH. COLLETON COUNTY. SOUTH CAROLINA : CHURCH RECORDS – (Membership Rolls 1855-1979. Total, 916p) – 1855-1933, 1945-1979 – 1 reel – 1 – $41.22 – us Baptist [240]
CARTER'S FORD BAPTIST CHURCH. LODGE, SOUTH CAROLINA : CHURCH RECORDS – 1855-1953 – 1 – 28.89 – us Baptist [240]
CARTERSVILLE BAPTIST CHURCH. CARTERSVILLE, GEORGIA : CHURCH RECORDS/WMU BOOK – 1873-94; Manuscript letters from Lottie Moon. 1874 – 1 – $12.51 – us Baptist [240]
CARTES DES PROVINCES ET DES MISSIONS DE LA COMPAGNIE AVANT LA SUPPRESSION (1763-1773) / Pfister, L – N.p., n.d. – 3mf – 9 – HTM-228/1 – ne IDC [240]
CARTES MARINES A L'USAGE DES ARMEES DU ROY DE LA GRANDE BRETAGNE. / Hooghe, Romein de – Amsterdam: Chez Pierre Mortier..., 1693. SEM35P172 – 1r – 1 – Can$15.00 – cn Bibl Nat [910]
CARTES: SURFACE / Canada. Ministere de l'Environnement. Service de l'Environnement Atmospherique. Bureau des Previsions du Quebec – 1972-75. SEM35P139 – 14r – 1 – Can$695.00 – cn Bibl Nat [910]
CARTHAGINIAN – Carthage. Miss. 1881-1920; 1936-1954 – 1 – us UMI [071]
Cartheuser, J F *see* DE GENERICIS QUIBUSDAM PLANTARUM
CARTIER AND HOCHELAGA: MAISONNEUVE AND VILLE-MARIE: TWO HISTORIC POEMS OF MONTREAL / Evans, Walter Norton – Montreal: W. Drysdale & Co., 1895. 02928. (Pre-1900 Canadiana) – 9 – cn C.I.H.M. [810]
CARTIER ET SON TEMPS / DeCelles, Alfred Duclos – 1907. SEM105P513 – 3mf – 9 – Can$6.75 – cn Bibl Nat [920]
CARTIER ET SON TEMPS / DeCelles, Alfred Duclos – 1913. SEM105P514 – 3mf – 9 – Can$6.75 – cn Bibl Nat [920]
CARTIER ET SON TEMPS / DeCelles, Alfred Duclos – 1925. SEM105P532 – 3mf – 9 – Can$6.75 – cn Bibl Nat [920]
Cartier, Georges Etienne *see* DISCOURS... ACCOMPAGNES DE NOTICES PAR JOSEPH TASSE
Cartier, Jacques *see* BRIEF RECIT ET SUCCINCTE NARRATION DE LA NAVIGATION FAICTE ES YLES DE CANADA, HOCHELAGA, SAGUENAY ET AUTRES
CARTIER NEWS – (In English and Yiddish) – Montreal, CN, 1945 – 1r – 1 – Can$25.00 – cn Can Microfilming [072]
CARTILLA AGRARIA EN VERSO PARA USO DE LAS ESCUELAS DE PRIMERA ENSENANZA / Cuadrado Retamosa, Joaquin – 1887 – 9 – 1.50f – sp Bibl Santa Ana [630]
CARTILLA DIVULGADORA. SOBRE EXPLOTACION OVINA EN SU FACETA DE LANA / Direccion General de Ganaderia. Junta Provincial de Fomento Pecuario de Badajoz – Badajoz: Graficas Iberia, 1945 – 1 – sp Bibl Santa Ana [350]
CARTILLA HISTORICO-POLITICA / Moreno, Francisco – 1871 – 9 – 1.50f – sp Bibl Santa Ana [946]
CARTILLA POLITICA DONOSIANA / Becerro de Bengoa, Ricardo – Caceres: Imp. y Enc. Vda. de Garcia Floriano, 1948 – sp Bibl Santa Ana [320]
CARTILLA REDACTADA PARA DAR A CONOCER LOS TRABAJOS QUE SE REALIZAN EN LA GRANJA ESCUELA PRACTICA DE AGRICULTURA DE BADAJOZ. PUBLICADA E EXPENSAS DEL CONSEJO PROVINCIAL DE FOMENTO / Consejo Provincial de Fomento. Badajoz – Badajoz: Tip. y Enc. de Uceda Hermanos, 1913 – sp Bibl Santa Ana [630]
Cartland, Fernando G *see* SOUTHERN HEROES, OR, THE FRIENDS IN WAR TIME
Cartmell, E *see* NEW TRENDS IN CHEMISTRY TEACHING
Cartnell, T K *see* SHENANDOAH VALLEY PIONEERS AND THEIR DECENDANTS
CARTOGRAFIA JESUISTICA DEL RIO DE LA PLATA... / Furlong Cardiff, Guillermo – Madrid: Razon y Fe, 1940 – 1 – sp Bibl Santa Ana [240]
THE CARTOGRAPHER – v1-4. 1964-67 – 1 – us UMI [910]
CARTOGRAPHIC MATERIALS : INDEXES, REGISTERS / U.S. Library of Congress – (1997 current subscription includes registers and fully cumulated indexes) – 1983-96 Registers only – 9 – us Advanced Libr [910]
CARTOGRAPHICA – (1983-. 1,5,6,9) – v17-. 1980- – 1 – us UMI [910]
CARTOGRAPHICA/CANADIAN CARTOGRAPHER – Downsview. v17-31. 1980-94 – 9 – Can$28.00y – cn Micromedia [910]
CARTOGRAPHY AND GEOGRAPHIC INFORMATION SYSTEMS *see* AMERICAN CARTOGRAPHER
Carton, C L *see* NOTICE BIOGRAPHIQUE SUR LE PERE FERDINAND VERBIEST, MISSIONAIRE A LA CHINE
Carton, Michel *see* EDUCATION AND THE WORLD OF WORK
Carton, R *see* LA SYNTHESE DOCTRINALE DE ROGER BACON
THE CARTOON – St. John, N.B: R. & Armstrong, [1878] – 9 – cn C.I.H.M. [740]
CARTOON OF THE CAMPAIGN: DOMINION OF CANADA GENERAL ELECTIONS, 1900 / Bengough, John Wilson – Toronto: Poole,1900. 03572. (Pre-1900 Canadiana) – 9 – cn C.I.H.M. [971]
CARTOONIST AND ILLUSTRATOR / Nast, Thomas – (Examples of his work scrapbook) – New York. v1-8. 1930 – 3r – 1 – us Ross [760]
CARTOONS AND SATIRE : SUBJECT COLLECTIONS – (Individual titles not listed separately) – 9 catalogues on 9mf – 9 – £75.00 – uk Chadwyck [700]
CARTOONS AND SATIRE PERTAINING TO ADOLF HITLER PAMPHLET COLLECTION – 1949-19?? – 1 – CSUXANR9547-B – us Hoover Inst Photo [870]
CARTOONS FOR THE CAUSE, 1886-1896 / Crane, Walter – London: Twentieth Century Press, 1896. "A Souvenir of the International Socialist Workers and Trade Union Congress, 1896." Cartoons reprinted from various journals, with some accompanying verses and a fable – 1 – us U.W. Library [760]
CARTOONS FOR THE LEGAL PROFESSION – Crane Paper Co, n.d. – 1mf – 9 – $1.50 – LLMC 91-081 – us L.L.M.C. [740]
THE CARTOONS OF ST. MARK / Horton, Robert Forman – New York: Fleming H Revell, 1894 – 1mf – 9 – 0-8370-3666-6 – 1985-1666 – us A.T.L.A. [220]
CARTOPHILIC WORLD – v. 11. 1955-56 – 7 – uk Microform Academic [910]
CARTOTHECA PATROLOGIAE GRAECO-LATINAE : ACCURANTE FACULTATE THEOLOGICA TILBURGENSE – 9,244mf – 9 – Bf14,500.00 set – be Brepols [240]
LE CARTULAIRE DE CORMERY. / Cormery. France. Benedictine Abbey – Tours. 1861 – 1 – us Res Libr [090]
CARTULAIRE DE LA CHARTREUSE DU VAL DE STE-ALDEGONDE PRES SAINT-OMER / Pas, J de – Saint-Omer, 1805 – Dfl35.00 – ne Slangenburg [240]
CARTULAIRE DE L'ABBAYE DE BONNEVAL EN ROUERGUE / Verlaguet, P A & Rigal, J L – Rodez, 1938 – 17mf – 8 – Dfl60.00 – ne Slangenburg [240]
CARTULAIRE DE L'ABBAYE DE CAMBRON / Smet, J J de – Bruxelles. 2v. 1869 – v1+2 17mf ea – 8 – Dfl119.00 – ne Slangenburg [240]
CARTULAIRE DE L'ABBAYE DE FLINES / Hautcoeur, E – Lille. 2v. 1873 – v1 11mf; v2 12mf – 8 – Dfl81.00 – ne Slangenburg [240]
CARTULAIRE DE L'ABBAYE DE NOTRE DAME DES VAUX DE GERNAY / Merlet, L & Moutie, A – Paris. 2v. 1857 – v1 15mf; v2 17mf – 8 – Dfl112.00 – ne Slangenburg [240]
CARTULAIRE DE L'ABBAYE DE NOTRE DAME D'OURSCAMP / Peigne-Delacourt, M – Amiens, 1865 – 20mf – 8 – Dfl70.00 – ne Slangenburg [240]
CARTULAIRE DE L'ABBAYE DE SAINT TROND / Piot, Ch. – Brussel. v1. 1870; Brussel. v2. 1874 – v1 22mf; v2 25mf – 8 – Dfl165.00 – ne Slangenburg [240]
CARTULAIRE DE L'ABBAYE DE SILVANES / Verlaguet, P A – Rodez, 1910 – 16mf – 8 – Dfl56.00 – ne Slangenburg [240]
CARTULAIRE DE L'ABBAYE D'ORVAL / Goffinet, Hippolyte – Brussel, 1879 – 27mf – 8 – Dfl95.00 – ne Slangenburg [240]
CARTULAIRE DE L'ABBAYE DU VAL-BENOIT / Cuvelier, J – Brussel, 1906 – 31mf – 8 – Dfl109.00 – ne Slangenburg [240]
CARTULAIRE DE L'ANCIEN CONSULAT D'ESPAGNE A BRUGES / Gilliodts-Van Severen, Louis – Bruges. 1901-02 – 1 – us Res Libr [949]
CARTULAIRE DE L'ORDRE DES HOSPITALIERS DE SAINT-JEAN DE JERUSALEM (1100-1310) / Delaville le Roulx, Joseph M A – Paris: E Leroux. 4v. 1894-1906. SEM35P60 – 4r – 1 – Can$155.00 – cn Bibl Nat [090]

CARTULAIRE DE MARCIGNY-SUR-LOIRE, 1045-1144 / Richard, Jean – Dijon, 1962 – 8mf – 8 – Dfl30.00 – ne Slangenburg [240]

CARTULAIRE DE MARMOUTIER POUR LE PERCHE : [N.-D. DU VIEUX-CHATEAU, COLLEGIALE DE SAINT LEONARD DE BELLEME, ET PRIEURE DE ST.-MARTIN-DU-VIEUX-BELLEME / Barret, M l'Abbe – Mortagne: Impr Georges Meaux, 1894 – 1 – us Res Libr [090]

CARTULAIRE DE NOTRE DAME DE PROUILLE / Guiraud, Jean – Paris. 2v. 1907 – v1 21mf; v2 18mf – 8 – Dfl137.00 – ne Slangenburg [240]

CARTULAIRE DES ABBAYES SAINT-PIERRE DE LA COUTURE ET DE SAINT-PIERRE DE SOLESMES – Le Mans, 1881 – Dfl88.00 – ne Slangenburg [240]

CARTULAIRE DU CHAPITRE DE SAINT-LAUD D'ANGERS. / Angers. France. St. Laud (Church) – Angers. 1903 – 1 – us Res Libr [090]

CARTULAIRE DU PRIEURE DE SAINT MARCEL-LES-CHALON, PUBLIS D'APRES LES MANUSCRITS DE MARCEL CANAT DE CHIZY PAR PAUL CANAT DE CHIZY / St. Marcel-les-Chalon, France. (Benedictine priory) – Chalon-sur-Saone, L. Marceau, 1894 – 1 – us U.W. Library [240]

CARTULAIRE NOIR DE LA CATHEDRALE D'ANGERS. / Angers. France. Cathedrale – Angers. 1908 – 1 – us Res Libr [090]

CARTULARIO DEL ARCHIVO CON DOCUMENTOS DE LOS ANOS 1362-1618 – Albarracin – 1r – 5,6 – sp Cultura [946]

CARTULARIO (SIECLE 13-17) – Albarracin – 1r – 5,6 – sp Cultura [946]

CARTULARIUM MONASTERII DE RAMESEIA (RS79) / Ramsey Abbey; ed by Hart, W H & Lyons, P A – (v1 1884 Dfl32.00. v2 1886 Dfl28.00. v3 1893 Dfl39.00) – ne Slangenburg [240]

Cartwright, Otho Grandford *see* THE MIDDLE WEST SIDE; A HISTORICAL SKETCH

Cartwright, Peter *see*
- AUTOBIOGRAPHY OF PETER CARTWRIGHT
- FIFTY YEARS AS A PRESIDING ELDER

Cartwright, Richard *see*
- BUDGET SPEECH DELIVERED IN THE HOUSE OF COMMONS OF CANADA ON TUESDAY, FEBRUARY 20TH, 1877
- THE BUDGET...SPEECH IN THE HOUSE OF COMMONS, IN REPLY TO THE FINANCE MINISTER'S STATEMENT: DELIVERED TUESDAY, MARCH 5, 1889
- CANADA GO BRAGH: BEING AN INAUGURAL ADDRESS TO THE YOUNG LIBERAL CLUB, OF SEAFORTH, ONT., ON THE 27TH OCTOBER, 1886
- DISCOURS DE SIR RICHARD CARTWRIGHT, PRONONCE A TORONTO LE 24 AOUT 1899: UN EXPOSE MAGISTRAL DE LA SITUATION FINANCIERE DU PAYS
- THE ECONOMIC CONDITION OF CANADA AND HER TRADE POLICY
- LIFE AND LETTERS.
- SIR RICHARD CARTWRIGHT AT MASSEY MUSIC HALL, TORONTO, AUGUST 24TH 1899
- SPEECH AT LONDON, SEPT. 19TH, 1900
- SPEECH OF SIR RICHARD CARTWRIGHT AT INGERSOLL, NOV. 14TH, 1889

Cartwright, Thomas *see* COMMENTARY UPON THE EPISTLE OF PAUL WRITTEN TO THE COLOSSIANS

CARTWRIGHT'S CASES ON THE BRITISH NORTH AMERICAN ACT / Canada. General – v1-5. 1868-96 (all publ) – 41mf – 9 – $61.00 – LLMC 81-009 – us L.L.M.C. [340]

Caruel, T *see* PRODROMO DELLA FLORA TOSCANA

Carufel, L-E *see* LE COLONISATEUR CANADIEN

Carulla, Juan Emiliano *see*
- AL FILO DEL MEDIO SIGLO
- GENIO DE LA ARGENTINA

Carus, Paul *see*
- BUDDHISM AND ITS CHRISTIAN CRITICS
- CROWN OF THORNS: A STORY OF THE TIME OF CHRIST
- GOD: AN ENQUIRY INTO THE NATURE OF MAN'S HIGHEST IDEAL...FROM THE STANDPOINT OF SCIENCE
- GOETHE AND SCHILLER'S XENIONS
- HOMILIES OF SCIENCE
- THE MECHANISTIC PRINCIPLE AND THE NON-MECHANICAL
- NIETZSCHE AND OTHER EXPONENTS OF INDIVIDUALISM
- RELIGION OF SCIENCE
- WHENCE AND WHITHER

Carus, Victor *see* HISTOIRE DE LA ZOOLOGIE DEPUIS L'ANTIQUITE JUSQU'AU XIXE SIECLE

Carus, Victor A *see* DAS ALTARWERK ZU LAUENSTEIN UND DIE ANFAENGE DES BAROCK IN SACHSEN

Carus Wilson, Ashley *see* CLEWS TO HOLY WRIT, OR, THE CHRONOLOGICAL SCRIPTURE CYCLE

Caruso, Christina M *see* PSYCHOLOGICAL AND PHYSIOLOGICAL CHANGES ASSOCIATED WITH A PERIOD OF INCREASED TRAINING

Caruthers, Abraham *see* HISTORY OF A LAWSUIT

Carvajal, Gaspar de *see* DESCUBRIMIENTO DEL RIO AMAZONAS

Carvajal, Micael *see*
- CORTES DE LA MUERTE
- TRAGEDIA JOSEPHINE

Carvajal, Pedro de *see* CONSTITUCIONES SYNODALES DEL OBISPADO DE CORIA

Carvajal y Mendoza, Luisa de *see* POESIAS ESPIRITUALES

CARVER 1733-1900 – (Mf 1-7: Town & Vital Records 1733-1847. Mf 8-12: Vital Records Index 1733-1847. Mf 13-18: Town Records 1814-52. Mf 18-19: Marriage Intentions 1814-52. Mf 19-22: Misc Town Records 1834-56: Mf 23-32: Town Record Copy 1790-1854. Mf 32-34: Intentions Transcript 1791-1852. Mf 34-35: Marriage Transcript 1788-1844. Mf 36-37: Vital Records 1843-57. Mf 38: Vital Records Index 1858-1905. Mf 39-41: Births 1859-1900. Mf 42-43: Marriages 1859-1900. Mf 44-46: Deaths 1895-1905) – (mf ed 1992) – 46mf – 9 – 0-87623-145-8 – us Holbrook [920]

CARVER 1748-1849 – (Mf 1T: Index to Vitals 1748-1844. Mf 1T-4T: Births & Deaths 1748-1844. Mf 1T-2T: Marriages 1788-1844. Mf 2T: Intentions 1791-1814. Mf 4T-5T: Intentions 1814-49. Mf 5T-6T: Births 1843-49. Mf 6T: Marriages & Deaths 1843-49) – (mf ed 1995) – 6mf – 9 – 0-87623-225-X – us Holbrook [920]

Carver, George Washington *see* PAPERS

Carver School of Missions and Social Work (Woman's Missionary Union Training School for Christian Workers). Louisville, Ky *see* CATALOGS AND COLLEGE RECORDS

Carver, T A *see* COMPARISON OF BILATERAL NORMAL TIBIAL ROTATION IN ADULT MALES

Carver, T G *see* INTERNATIONAL MARINE INSURANCE RULES

Carver, W O *see* COLLECTION

Carver, William Owen *see*
- MISSIONS AND MODERN THOUGHT
- MISSIONS IN THE PLAN OF THE AGES

Carwitham, J *see* VARIOUS KINDS OF FLOOR DECORATIONS

Cary, Elisabeth Luther *see*
- THE ROSSETTIS
- WILLIAM MORRIS

Cary, George Lovell *see*
- THE SYNOPTIC GOSPELS
- SYNOPTIC GOSPELS: TOGETHER WITH A CHAPTER ON THE TEXT-CRITICISM OF THE NEW TESTAMENT

Cary, Henry *see* A COLLECTION OF STATUTES AFFECTING NEW SOUTH WALES

Cary, J *see* A DISCOURSE ON TRADE, AND OTHER MATTERS RELATIVE TO IT...

Cary, Orland R *see* CORRESPONDENCE

Cary, Otis *see*
- A HISTORY OF CHRISTIANITY IN JAPAN
- JAPAN AND ITS REGENERATION

Cary, W *see*
- A BOKE OF THE PROPERTIES OF HERBES
- THE HAMMER FOR THE STONE

Carzo, Jose M *see* LA PARTE SUBJETIVA EN EL CONOCIMIENTO INTELECTUAL SEGUN SANTO TOMAS DE AQUINO

CAS – Banska Bystrica, Czechoslovakia. Sept 1944-Feb 1948 – 12r – 1 – us L of C Photodup [072]

CAS BULLETIN – Curriculum Advisory Service. v. 1-7. 1961-1967 – 1 – us UMI [370]

UN CAS DE CONSCIENCE / Diana, Pierre – Paris, 193? Fiche W 1505. (Blodgett Collection of Spanish Civil War Pamphlets) – 9 – us H.U. College Libr [946]

LE CAS DES CATHOLIQUES BASQUES / Hiriartia, J de – Paris, 193? Fiche W945. (Blodgett Collection of Spanish Civil War Pamphlets) – 9 – us H.U. College Libr [946]

CAS QUARTERLY – Curriculum Advisory Service. v. 8-13. 1969-1974 – 1 – us UMI [370]

CAS REGISTRY HANDBOOK-COMMON NAMES – 6,9 – $1,190.00 – us Chemical [540]

CAS REVIEW – Curriculum Advisory Service. v. 14. 1975 – 1 – us UMI [370]

LA CASA DE BERNARDA ALBA / Garcia Lorca, Federico – MS DE 1936 – 2mf – 9 – sp Cultura [820]

Casa de la Cultura. Cine Club de la O.S. de E. y D. *see* NOVIEMBRE 1975. SESIONES CINEMATOGRAFICAS DE ARTE Y ENSAYO

CASA DE LAS AMERICAS – Havana, CU. 1970-1977 – 8r – $400.00 – R04196 – us Library Micro [440]

CASA DE LAS AMERICAS – Havana. nos. 1-99. Jan 1960-Dec 1977 – 1 – 35.00r – us Hoover Inst Photo [073]

LA CASA DE MONTALVO – Ecuador. 1-24, 1931-56. Incomplete – 1 – 23.00 – us L of C Photodup [073]

LA CASA DONDE NACIO SAN FRANCISCO DE ASIS, PATRONATO DEL ESTADO ESPANOL / Barrado, Angel – Madrid, 1944. Sep. Rev. Verda y vida no 7, 1944 – sp Bibl Santa Ana [946]

LA CASA EN QUE MURIO HERNAN CORTES EN CASTILLEJA DE LA CUESTA / Caballero, Fernando – 1844 – 9 – $1.50f – sp Bibl Santa Ana [946]

LA CASA NATALE DI S. FRANCESCO...SECOLO 13. ROMA (1966) / Abate, Giuseppe – Madrid: Graf. Calleja, 1966 – 1 – sp Bibl Santa Ana [946]

CASAL FELIZ – [Rio de Janeiro: s.n., 1985-] n1 – us Res Libr [972]

Casal, G *see*
- HISTORIA NATURAL Y MEDICA DEL PRINCIPADO DE ASTURIAS
- MAL DE LA ROSA

Casal, Horacio Nestor *see* LA REVOLUCION DEL 43

Casal Julian, Gaspar *see* HISTORIA NATURAL Y MEDICA DE ASTURIAS

Casalis, Eugene *see*
- LES BASSOUTOS OU VINGT-TROIS ANNEES DE SEJOUR ET D'OBSERVATIONS AU SUD DE L'AFRIQUE
- ETUDES SUR LA LANGUE SECHUANA

Casanas, E *see* CARTA PASTORAL DE ENTRADA QUE DIRIGE A SUS DIOCESANOS

Casanova di Seingalt, Giacomo G *see* AMOURS ET AVENTURES DE CASANOVA

CASANOVA IN WIEN : KOMOEDIE, DREI AKTE IN VERSEN / Auernheimer, Raoul – Muenchen: Drei Masken Verlag, 1924 – 1r – 1 – us U.W. Library [820]

CASAR BAPTIST CHURCH. CASAR, NORTH CAROLINA : CHURCH RECORDS – 1901-63 – 1 – 17.01 – us Baptist [240]

Casaregi, G L M *see* IL CONSOLATO DEL MARE

Casaretto, G *see* NOVARUM STIRPIUM BRASILIENSIUM DECADES (1-10)

Casas, Bartolome de las *see*
- COLECCION DE LAS OBRAS
- DEL UNICO MODO DE ATRAER A TODOS LOS PUEBLOS A LA VERDADERA RELIGION. ADVERTENCIA...MEXICO, 1942
- DEL UNICO MODO DE ATRAER TODOS LOS PUEBLOS A LA VERDADERA RELIGION

Casas, J B *see* LA QUERRA SEPARATISTA DE CUBA...

Casas Souto, Pedro *see*
- CARTA PASTORAL DEL ILMO. SR. OBISPO DE PLASENCIA AL CLERO Y FIELES DE SU DIOCESIS
- CONSTITUCIONES SINODALES DEL OBISPADO DE PLASENCIA
- PASTORAL DEL VENERABLE OBISPO DE PLASENCIA

Casas y Gonzalez, Juan Bautista *see* CARTAS PASTORALES Y OTRAS EXHORTACIONES...DOCTOR DON PEDRO CASAS SOUTO...OBISPO DE PLASENCIA

Casas y Souto, Pedro *see* PASTORAL

Casatejada. Ayuntamiento *see*
- 136TH FERIA DE SANTIAGO PARA TODA CLASE DE GANADOS 1971
- 142ND FERIA DE SANTIAGO PARA TODA CLASE DE GANADOS
- 144TH FERIA DE SANTIAAGO. JULIO DE 1979
- FERIA DE SANTIAGO DE TODA CLASE DE GANADO. DURANTE...JULIO, 1961
- FERIA DE SANTIAGO DE TODA CLASE DE GANADOS. DURANTE...JULIO, 1962
- FIESTAS DE LA SOLEDAD, 1961
- FIESTAS DE LA SOLEDAD...1960
- GRANDES FIESTAS DE SANTIAGO DE TODA CLASE DE GANADOS Y GENEROS DE COMERCIO...24, 25 Y 26 DE JULIO, 1960
- REVISTA ANUAL DE CULTURA 1980

Casati, Gaetano *see*
- DIX ANNEES EN EQUATORIA
- TEN YEARS IN EQUATORIA AND THE RETURN WITH EMIN PASHA

Casaubon, E A *see*
- LA FEMME ET LA FAMILLE
- LE NOUVEAU CONTRAT SOCIAL

EL CASCABEL – Madrid, Spain. Oct 1863-Apr 1877 – 4r – 1 – uk British Libr Newspaper [072]

CASCABULHO : GAZETA LITTERARIA E CRITICA – Manaos, Amazonas. 1 Abr-27 Ago 1894 – 1,5,6 – bl Biblioteca [072]

Cascales Munoz, Jose *see*
- APUNTES PARA LA HISTORIA DE VILLAFRANCA DE LOS BARROS (BADAJOZ)
- APUNTES Y MATERIALES PARA LA BIOGRAFIA DE DON JOSE DE ESPRONCEDA
- EL AUTENTICO ESPRONCEDA PORNOGRAFICO Y EL APOCRIFO EN GENERAL
- LAS BELLAS ARTES PLASTICAS EN SEVILLA
- LAS BELLAS ARTES PLASTICAS EN SEVILLA...DESDE EL SIGLO 13 HASTA NUESTROS DIAS...
- LA CONFEDERACION DE LAS CLASES. EL PROGRAMA DE UN NUEVO PARTIDO
- LOS CONFLICTOS DEL PROLETARIADO. EL MOVIMIENTO SOCIAL CONTEMPORANEO: POR QUE, CUANDO Y COMO HA NACIDO EL PROBLEMA OBRERO
- DE SEVILLA A BATALHA. EXCURSION...DE SEVILLA A MERIDA Y BADAJOZ..
- DEMOCRACIA COLECTIVISTA. LECCIONES DE SOCIOLOGIA SOBRE UNA NUEVA POLITICA A LA ANTIGUA ESPANOLA...POR...
- ESPRONCEDA SU EPOCA SU VIDA Y SUS OBRAS
- FRANCISCO DE ZURBARAN. SU EPOCA, SU VIDA Y SUS OBRAS
- HISTORIA DE A CUERDA GRANADINA CONTADA POR ALGUNOS DE SUS NUDOS, APUNTES PARA LA MISMA RECOPILADOS POR...
- LOS PRIMEROS FRUTOS DE MI HUERTA. (VERSOS MUY MALOS)
- RASGOS DE NUESTRA EPOPEYA (EPISODIOS Y PERSONAJES)
- SEVILLA INTELECTUAL, SUS ECRITORES Y ARTISTAS CONTEMPORANEOS
- SOLO DIOS ES GRANDE

O CASCAVEL : JORNAL POLITICO E LITTERARIO – [s.l.]. 2 Jul 1852 – 1,5,6 – bl Biblioteca [072]

Cascella, Armando *see* TRASCENDENCIA DE LA TERCERA POSICION

Casco, Marcos *see* PERONISMO DENTRO DEL PERONISMO

CASE AGAINST PROFESSOR BRIGGS / Briggs, Charles Augustus – New York: Scribner's, 1892-93. 2 fiches – 9 – us A.T.L.A. [240]

THE CASE AGAINST THE NAZI WAR CRIMINALS : OPENING STATEMENT FOR THE U.S.A., AND OTHER DOCUMENTS / Jackson, Robert Houghwout – 1st ed. New York: A.A. Knopf, 1946. xiii,216p. plates – 1 – us U.W. Library [340]

Case, Alan J *see* AN EXPLORATION OF THE OPINIONS OF RECREATION AND PARKS/ LEISURE STUDIES FACULTY AND PUBLIC SECTOR PRACTITIONERS CONCERNING THE COMPUTER COMPETENCY SKILLS OF RECREATION AND PARKS/LEISURE STUDIES BACCA-LAUREATE STUDENTS

Case, Alden Buell *see* THIRTY YEARS WITH THE MEXICANS: IN PEACE AND REVOLUTION

CASE AND COMMENT – (Lacking: v2 no 5. v13, v14. Updates planned) – v1-18. 1894-1912 – 74mf – 9 – $111.00 – LLMC 84-434 – us L.L.M.C. [073]

CASE AND CORRESPONDENCE RESPECTING THE PRICES OF BOOKS FOR SCHOOL LIBRARIES AND PRIZES / Ryerson, Adolphus Egerton – Toronto: Hunter, Rose, 1874. 00508. (Pre-1900 Canadiana) – 9 – cn C.I.H.M. [070]

CASE AND OPINION ON THE WILL OF THE REVEREND GEORGE POWELL, DECEASED, EX-PARTE THE PRESIDENT AND GOVERNORS OF THE RADCLIFFE INFIRMARY, OXFORD / Sewell, Richard Clarke – Oxford: Trash, 1840. 20p. LL-2311 – 1 – us L of C Photodup [340]

CASE CURRENTS – (v2- . 1976- . 5,6,9) – v. 1-. 1975-. Council for Advancement and Support of Education – 1 – us UMI [370]

CASE FILE 35-30 / O'Hare, Kate Richards – Washington, DC: National Archives and Records Service [19–] – us Res Libr [324]

CASE FILES / Allen County. Ohio. Common Pleas. Juvenile Div – 1915-1923 – 1r – 1 – $32.50r – us Archival [324]

CASE FILES / Ottawa County. Ohio. Soldiers Relief Commission – 1887-1894 – 1r – 1 – $32.50r – us Archival [324]

CASE FILES / Paulding County. Ohio. Soldiers Relief Commission – 1870-1920 – 1r – 1 – $32.50r – us Archival [324]

CASE FILES / Putnam County. Ohio. Soldiers Relief Commission – 1895-1912 – 1r – 1 – $32.50r – us Archival [324]

CASE FILES – APPLICATIONS AND CORRESPONDENCE / Ottawa County. Ohio. Soldiers Relief Commission – 1889-1894 – 1r – 1 – $32.50r – us Archival [324]

CASE FILES IN SUITS INVOLVING CONSULS AND VICE CONSULS AND THE REPEAL OF PATENTS OF THE U.S. DISTRICT COURT FOR THE SOUTHERN DISTRICT OF NEW YORK / U.S. Circuit and District Courts. New York – 1806-60 – 2r – 1 – M965 – us Nat'l Archives [324]

CASE FILES OF CHINESE IMMIGRANTS, 1895-1920, FROM DISTRICT NO.4 (PHILADELPHIA) OF THE IMMIGRATION AND NATURALIZATION SERVICE / U.S. Immigration and Naturalization Service – RG 85. M1144. 51 rolls – 1 – us Nat'l Archives [975]

CASE FILES OF INVESTIGATIONS BY LEVI C. TURNER AND LAFAYETTE C. BAKER, 1861-66 / U.S. War Department. Adjutant General's Office – 137 rolls. M797. Printed guide – 1 – us Nat'l Archives [324]

CASE FILES – REPORTS / Ottawa County. Ohio. Soldiers Relief Commission – 1887-1895 – 1r – 1 – $32.50r – us Archival [324]

THE CASE FOR THE GOVERNMENT / Langdon-Davies, John – N.Y., 1939. Fiche W986. (Blodgett Collection of Spanish Civil War Pamphlets) – 9 – us H.U. College Libr [946]

THE CASE FOR THE JEWS / Gribetz, L J – New York, 1930 – 2mf – 1 – ILM-2160/1 – ne IDC [327]

THE CASE FOR TOWN PLANNING / Aldridge, Henry R – London, 1915 – 1 – £35.00r – uk Altair [710]

Case, Ira *see* COMMENTS ON THE REVELATION, AND OTHER PROPHECIES

CASE LAW AND INDEX; A COMPLETE SERIES OF CONDENSED REPORTS, FEDERAL, STATE, AND ENGLISH, INCLUDING CANADIAN, AUSTRALIAN, NEW ZEALAND AND HAWAIIAN REPORTS. VOL. I. BANKS AND BANKING – (Index to Vol. I. New York 1903. 207p) – New York: Case Law Co. 1903. 1432p. LL-331 – 1 – us L of C Photodup [340]

CASE MANAGEMENT AND COURT MANAGEMENT IN U.S. DISTRICT COURTS / Flanders, Steven – Washington: FJC, Sept 1977 – 2mf – 9 – $3.00 – LLMC 95-813 – us L.L.M.C. [340]

Case, Nelson *see*
- COPIES OF SPEECHES
- HISTORY OF LABETTE COUNTY

THE CASE OF BENN VS. MAXTON, A CORRESPONDENCE ON CAPITALISM AND SOCIALISM / Benn, Ernest J P – 2fiches (29x) – 9 – 1.00f – at Libertarian Micro [320]

THE CASE OF PETER DU CALVET, ESQ. OF MONTREAL IN THE PROVINCE OF QUEBEC / Du Calvet, Pierre – London: (s.n.), 1784. SEM16P24 – 1r – 5 – Can$9.00 – cn Bibl Nat [910]

THE CASE OF RICHARD MEYNELL / Ward, Mary Augusta – British Fiction Archive: Unit 2 – 9 – uk Bell [830]

THE CASE OF THE BLACK WARRIOR... – Washington, 1854 – 5mf – 1 – ILM-1891/1 – ne IDC [327]

THE CASE OF THE DISSENTING MINISTERS / Mauduit, I – London, 4th ed 1772 – 1mf – 9 – MP-475/1 – ne IDC [240]

THE CASE OF THE MARSHAL BELLISLE... – London, 1745 – 1mf – 1 – ILM-925/1 – ne IDC [327]

THE CASE OF WEST IRIAN (WEST NEW GUINEA) / Indonesia. Kedutaan Besar. Egypt – SE-2018 1. 1954? – 9 – ne IDC [950]

THE CASE OF WEST IRIAN (WEST NEW GUINEA); DISPUTE BETWEEN INDONESIA AND THE NETHERLANDS / Indonesia. Kementerian Luar Negeri – SE-3345 1. 1954 – 9 – ne IDC [950]

THE CASE OF...THE OPPRESSED AFRICANS,... – London, 1784 – 1mf – 1 – ILM-1201/1 – ne IDC [327]

CASE PAPERS / New York. Court of Admiralty – 1784-88. 1 roll. M948 – 1 – us Nat'l Archives [324]

CASE PAPERS OF THE COURT OF ADMIRALTY OF THE STATE OF NEW YORK, 1784-1788 – 1r – 1 – M948 – us Nat'l Archives [340]

CASE PAPERS OF THE U.S. DISTRICT COURT FOR THE EASTERN DISTRICT OF VIRGINIA, 1863-1865, RELATING TO THE CONFISCATION OF PROPERTY – 1r – 1 – M435 – us Nat'l Archives [340]

CASE PAPERS...1863-65, RELATING TO THE CONFISCATION OF PROPERTY / U.S. District Courts. Virginia, Eastern District – 1roll. M435 – 1 – us Nat'l Archives [324]

CASE STUDIES OF ARRANGEMENTS FOR EVALUATION AND UTILIZATION OF POPULATION CENSUS RESULTS : REPORT 1: THE REPUBLIC OF THE SUDAN / United Nations. Dept. of Economic and Social Affairs – 1959 – 9 – BNE-7693 1 – ne IDC [304]

CASE STUDIES ON DESERTIFICATION / ed by Mabbutt, J A & Floret, C – 1981 – 9 – 92-3-101820-5 – fr UNESCO [550]

A CASE STUDY OF SELECTED EFFECTS OF AN ORGANIZED SUMMER RESIDENTIAL CAMP UPON STAFF MEMEBERS / Glick, Jeffrey – 1980 – 4mf – 9 – $16.00 – us Microform Publ [790]

CASE STUDY OF SEVEN COMMERCIAL SEAWEED RESOURCES – 1987 – 320p – it F.A.O. [639]

Case, Walter H *see* LONG BEACH AND VICINITY

CASE WESTERN RESERVE JOURNAL OF INTERNATIONAL LAW – v1-23. 1968-91 – 1,5,6 – $270.00 – us Hein [340]

CASE WESTERN RESERVE JOURNAL OF INTERNATIONAL LAW – v1-27. 1968-95 – 9 – $254.00 set – us Hein [340]

CASE WESTERN RESERVE LAW REVIEW – v1-43. 1949-93 – 1,5,6 – $945.00 – us Hein [073]

CASEBOOK OF METHODS FOR COMPUTING HYDROLOGICAL PARAMETERS FOR WATER PROJECTS : A CONTRIBUTION TO THE INTERNATIONAL HYDROLOGICAL PROGRAMME / ed by Lowing, M J – 1987 – 324p – 9 – 92-3-102472-8 – fr UNESCO [627]

CASEBOOK ON METHODS OF COMPUTATION OF QUANTITATIVE CHANGES IN THE HYDROLOGICAL REGIME OF RIVER BASINS DUE TO HUMAN ACTIVITIES – 1980 – 330p – 9 – 92-3-101798-5 – fr UNESCO [550]

Caselli, Domenico A *see* IL CANTO FERMO IN PRATTICA..

THE CASELOAD EXPERIENCES OF THE DISTRICT COURTS FROM 1972 TO 1983 : A PRELIMINARY ANALYSIS / Meierhoefer, Barbara S & Armen, Eric V – Washington: FJC, 1985 – 1mf – 9 – $1.50 – LLMC 95-836 – us L.L.M.C. [340]

CASEMIRO DE ABREU : ORGAO DO CLUB LITTERARIO CASEMIRO DE ABREU – Maceio, Alagoas. 16 Jul-16 Set 1884 – 1,5,6 – bl Biblioteca [072]

LA CASERNE – puis Organe de defense des matelots. Paris. nov 1924-fevr 1929 – 1 – fr A.C.R.P.P. [073]

CASES / Scotland. Court of Session – (Shaw. 1-16. Dunlop. 1-24. Macpherson. 1-11. Rettie. 1-25. Frazer. 1-8) – 1821-1873. Scottish Council of Law Reporting – 9 – uk Skinner [941]

CASES ADJUDGED IN THE U.S. CIRCUIT COURTS OF APPEAL – (With 2 index vols. Each title page carries the legend "Official Edition") – New York: Banks. v1-63. 1893-99 (al publ) – 612mf – 9 – $918.00 – LLMC 79-422 – us L.L.M.C. [340]

CASES AND MATERIALS ON LEGISLATION / Parkinson, Thomas Ignatius – Rev. 1936. New York, 1936. 2v. in 3. LL-1132 – 1 – us L of C Photodup [340]

CASES AND MATERIALS ON SECURITY TRANSACTIONS / Maloney, John Philip – New York: St. John's Univ. Press, 1947. 748p. LL-300 – 1 – us L of C Photodup [340]

CASES AND MATERIALS ON THE LAW OF SALES / Llewellyn, Karl N – Chicago, Callaghan, 1930. 1081 p. LL-290 – 1 – us L of C Photodup [340]

CASES AND MATERIALS ON THE LAW OF VENDOR AND PURCHASE / Handler, Milton – St. Paul: West, 1933. 238p. LL-173 – 1 – us L of C Photodup [340]

Cases, Cesare *see* STICHWORTE ZUR DEUTSCHEN LITERATUR

CASES IN BUSINESS ADMINISTRATION; PERISTIWA-PERISTIWA PERUSAHAAN / Hawkins, Everett D – SE-4117 1. 1959 – 9 – ne IDC [650]

CASES IN COMMON LAW ACTIONS. / Keigwin, Charles Albert – Rochester, N.Y., The Lawyers Co-Operating Publishing Co., 1928. 302 p. LL-522 – 1 – us L of C Photodup [340]

CASES IN GEORGIA REPORTS THAT HAVE BEEN OVERRULED, DOUBTED, CRITICISED, OR MODIFIED / Downing, Hugh Urquhart – Columbia, Ga. 1922. LL-1306 – 1 – us L of C Photodup [340]

CASES OF THE LAW OF BILLS AND NOTES SELECTED FROM DECISIONS OF ENGLISH AND AMERICAN COURTS / Smith, Howard Leslie – St. Paul: West, 1910. 756p. LL-1117 – 1 – us L of C Photodup [340]

THE CASES OF THE U.S. COURT OF APPEALS FOR THE D.C. CIRCUIT / Beremant, Gordon et al – Washington: FJC, July 1982 – 1mf – 9 – $1.50 – LLMC 95-349 – us L.L.M.C. [340]

CASES ON BAILMENTS AND CARRIERS / Roberts, John Stuart – Chicago: Thompson 1911. 233p. LL-1455 – 1 – us L of C Photodup [340]

CASES ON CERTAIN EQUITABLE DOCTRINES AND REMEDIES / Lloyd, William Henry – Philadelphia, International Printing Co. 1917 418 p. LL-807 – 1 – us L of C Photodup [340]

CASES ON COMMON LAW PLEADING. 2ND ED / Sunderland, Edson Read – Chicago, Callaghan, 1932. 693 p. LL-1564 – 1 – us L of C Photodup [340]

CASES ON CONSTITUTIONAL LAW / Thayer, James Bradley – Cambridge Mass. Sever, 1895. 2 v. LL-1315 – 1 – us L of C Photodup [340]

CASES ON CRIMINAL LAW / Mikell, William Ephraim – (3rd ed. St. Paul: West, 1933. 775p. LL-738) – Philadelphia: International Printing Co., 1903. 983p. LL-509 – 1 – us L of C Photodup [340]

CASES ON DAMAGES SELECTED FROM DECISIONS OF ENGLISH AND AMERICAN COURTS / Mechem, Floyd Russell – St. Paul: West, 1909. 626p. LL-875 – 1 – us L of C Photodup [340]

CASES ON EQUITABLE RELIEF AGAINST DEFAMATION AND INJURIES TO PERSONALITY. SUPPLEMENTARY TO AMES'S CASES IN EQUITY JURISDICTION / Pound, Roscoe – v.1. Cambridge, Mass., 1920. 77p. LL-1205 – 1 – us L of C Photodup [340]

CASES ON EQUITY JURISDICTION; RESTRAINT OF INFRINGEMENT OF INCORPOREAL RIGHTS. PART 1. A COLLECTION OF CASES WITH NOTES / Lewis, William Draper – Philadelphia, International Printing Co., 1904. 200 p. LL-1617 – 1 – us L of C Photodup [340]

CASES ON FEDERAL JURISDICTION AND PROCEDURE. / Medina, Harold Raymond – St. Paul: West, 1926. 674p. LL-1463 – 1 – us L of C Photodup [340]

CASES ON LABOR LAW. / Landis, James McCauley – (1947. Supplement. Brooklyn, 1948. 181 p. LL-1130) – 2nd ed. Chicago, Foundation Press, 1942. v. 1-2. LL-1130 – 1 – us L of C Photodup [340]

CASES ON PERSONAL PROPERTY. / Griffin, Levi Thomas – St. Paul: West, 1895. 202p. LL-259 – 1 – us L of C Photodup [340]

CASES ON PERSONS AND DOMESTIC RELATIONS, SELECTED FROM DECISIONS OF ENGLISH AND AMERICAN COURTS / Kales, Albert Martin – St. Paul, West, 1911. 654 p. LL-1544 – 1 – us L of C Photodup [340]

CASES ON RESTRAINT OF TRADE / Wyman, Bruce – Cambridge, Harvard, 1902-?4. 5 pt. LL-1625 – 1 – us L of C Photodup [340]

CASES ON THE FEDERAL ANTI-TRUST LAWS OF THE UNITED STATES / MacLachlan, James Angell – New York, Ad Press 1930 684 p. LL-237 – 1 – us L of C Photodup [340]

CASES ON THE LAW OF ADMIRALTY / Lord, George de Forest – 2nd ed. St. Paul, West, 1939. 1044p. LL-215 – 1 – us L of C Photodup [340]

CASES ON THE LAW OF ADMIRALTY / Lord, George de Forest – St. Paul, West, 1926. 837p. LL-216 – 1 – us L of C Photodup [340]

CASES ON THE LAW OF AGENCY, INCLUDING THE LAW OF PRINCIPAL AND AGENT AND THE LAW OF MASTER AND SERVANT / Huffcut, Ernest Wilson – 2d ed. Boston: Little, Brown, 1907. 837p. LL-409 – 1 – us L of C Photodup [340]

CASES ON THE LAW OF EVIDENCE. / Hughes, Thomas Welburn – (Chicago: Callaghan, 1921. 922p. LL-1332) – St. Paul: West, 1896. 141p. LL-1285 – 1 – us L of C Photodup [340]

CASES ON THE LAW OF EVIDENCE, SELECTED FROM DECISIONS OF ENGLISH AND AMERICAN COURTS / Hinton, Edward Wilcox – St. Paul: West, 1919. 1098p. LL-1182 – 1 – us L of C Photodup [340]

CASES ON THE LAW OF EXECUTORS AND ADMINISTRATORS / Vosseler, Edward Adolph – Brooklyn, 1948. 208 p. LL-1555 – 1 – us L of C Photodup [340]

CASES ON THE LAW OF INSURANCE...2ND ED / Vance, William Reynolds – St. Paul, West, 1931. 1020 p. LL-1254 – 1 – us L of C Photodup [336]

CASES ON THE LAW OF MUNICIPAL CORPORATIONS / Tooke, Charles Wesley – 1931 ed. New York, Commerce Clearing House, 1931. 896 p. LL-1249 – 1 – us L of C Photodup [340]

CASES ON THE LAW OF PARTNERSHIP / Mechem, Floyd Russell – 2d ed. by Floyd R. Mechem and Frank L. Sage...3d ed. Chicago: Callaghan, 1905. 1104, 209-224p. LL-526 – 1 – us L of C Photodup [340]

CASES ON THE LAW OF PRIVATE CORPORATIONS. / Burnett, Daniel Frederick – Boston, Little, Brown, 1917. 828 p. LL-1272 – 1 – us L of C Photodup [340]

CASES ON THE LAW OF PUBLIC SERVICE / Burdick, Charles Kellog – Boston, Little, Brown, 1916. 544 p. LL-234 – 1 – us L of C Photodup [340]

CASES ON THE LAW OF SUCCESSION TO PROPERTY AFTER THE DEATH OF THE OWNER. / Mechem, Floyd Russell – St. Paul: West, 1895. 184p. LL-93 – 1 – us L of C Photodup [340]

CASES ON THE LAW OF TAXATION: PARTS 1, 2 AND 3...4 AND 5 / Maguire, John MacArthur – New York: Commerce Clearing House. 1931. 950p LL-265 – 1 – us L of C Photodup [340]

CASES ON THE LAW OF WILLS / Schmid, John Henry – Brooklyn, 1924. 365p. LL-1325 – 1 – us L of C Photodup [340]

CASES SUBMITTED TO THE HOUSE OF LORDS ON APPEAL FROM THE COURTS OF ENGLAND, SCOTLAND, AND NORTHERN IRELAND / Great Britain. Parliament. House of Lords – London, etc. On film: cases 1-1027. LL-052 – 1 – us L of C Photodup [340]

LA CASETA DE LA CORDIALIDAD. FERIA DE SAN MIGUEL, 1972. BAILES, ACTOS CULTURALES. CONCURSOS. CENA DE GALA / Zafara 72 – Caceres: Edit. Extremadura, 1972 – 1 – sp Bibl Santa Ana [390]

CASEWORK SOSIAL DI INDONESIA; PEDOMAN KANTONG / Jaspan, Helen – SE-4141 1. 1961 – 9 – ne IDC [360]

Casey, George Elliott *see* MONEY AND PAPER CURRENCY: A STUDY FOR THE TIMES

Casey, Kevin M *see* CONCENTRIC AND ECCENTRIC STRENGTH DIFFERENCES IN THE LEAD AND BACK LEGS OF DIVISION 1 COLLEGE LEVEL FENCERS

Casey, Robert E *see* THE DECLARATION OF INDEPENDENCE

Casey, Thomas Lincoln *see* REVISION OF THE CUCUJIDAE OF AMERICA NORTH OF MEXICO

Casgrain, Eugene *see* LE MOUTON: TRAITE PRATIQUE SUR L'ELEVAGE DES MOUTONS EN CANADA

Casgrain, Henri-Raymond *see*
- A. GERIN-LAJOIE: D'APRES SES MEMOIRES
- A.S. FALARDEAU ET A.E. AUBRY
- BIOGRAPHIES DE A.S. FALARDEAU ET A.E. AUBRY
- CHAMPLAIN: SA VIE ET SON CARACTERE
- DE GASPE ET GARNEAU
- UNE EXCURSION A L'ILE AUX COUDRES
- UNE EXCURSION A L'ILE AUX COUDRES: LEGENDE CANADIENNE
- FRANCIS PARKMAN

- THE FRENCH-WAR PAPERS OF THE MARECHAL DE LEVIS
- HISTOIRE DE L'HOTEL-DIEU DE QUEBEC
- LA JONGLEUSE: LEGENDE CANADIENNE
- LEGENDES CANADIENNES
- LES MIETTES: DISTRACTIONS POETIQUES
- MONTCALM ET LEVIS: LES FRANCAIS AU CANADA
- MONTCALM ET LEVIS: LES HEROS DE QUEBEC
- NOTES RELATIVES AUX INSCRIPTIONS DU MONUMENT DE CHAMPLAIN
- OPUSCULES
- P.A. DE GASPE ET FRANCIS PARKMAN
- UNE PAROISSE CANADIENNE AU XVIIE SIECLE
- UN PELERINAGE AU PAYS D'EVANGELINE
- PHILIPPE AUBERT DE GASPE
- LES PIONNIERS CANADIENS ET LE TABLEAU DE LA RIVIERE-QUELLE: LEGENDES
- LA QUESTION ACADIENNE ET LE RAPPORT SUR LES ARCHIVES DU CANADA POUR 1894
- UNE SECONDE ACADIE
- LES SULPICIENS ET LES PRETRES DES MISSIONS-ETRANGERES EN ACADIE, 1676-1762
- THE WITCH: A CANADIAN LEGEND

Casgrain, Philippe Baby *see*
- MEMORIAL DES FAMILLES CASGRAIN, BABY ET PERRAULT DU CANADA
- LA VIE DE JOSEPH-FRANCOIS PERRAULT: SURNOMME LE PERE DE L'EDUCATION DU PEUPLE CANADIEN

Casgrain, Thomas Chase *see* THE COURTS OF QUEBEC. MR. CASGRAIN'S MEASURE FOR THEIR RE-ORGANIZATION: ITS PROVISION DISCUSSED: THE NEED OF IMPROVEMENT URGENT: HOW THE PROPOSED LAW WILL MEET THE WANTS OF THE CASE

CASH BOOK / Hancock County, Ohio. Cass Township. Township Clerk – 1864-1908 – 1r – 1 – $32.50r – us Archival [324]

CASH BOOK / Ottawa County. Ohio. Carroll Township. Township Treasurer – 1911-1931 – 1r – 1 – $32.50r – us Archival [324]

CASH BOOKS, MILITARY ORDERS / Hancock County. Ohio. Treasurer – 1865 – 1r – 1 – $32.50r – us Archival [324]

Cash, J *see*
- THE BRITISH FRESHWATER RHIZOPODA AND HELIOZA
- THE BRITISH FRESHWATER RHIZOPODA AND HELIOZOA

CASH JOURNAL / Paulding County. Ohio. Crane Township. Township Clerk – 1902-1925 – 1r – 1 – $32.50r – us Archival [324]

CASH JOURNAL AND APPROPRIATIONS / Hancock County. Ohio. Biglick Township. Township Clerk – 1939-1957 – 1r – 1 – $32.50r – us Archival [324]

CASH JOURNALS / Fulton County. Ohio. Treasurer – 1850-1867 – 1r – 1 – $32.50r – us Archival [324]

CASH JOURNALS / Hancock County. Ohio. Biglick Township. Township Clerk – 1928-1988 – 1r – 1 – $32.50r – us Archival [324]

CASHAWAY BAPTIST CHURCH. DARLINGTON DISTRICT. SOUTH CAROLINA : CHURCH RECORDS – 1767-1805 – 1 – 7.20 – us Baptist [240]

CASHBOOK / Aimar, C P – (1841) 1843. 1 fiche – 9 – us South Carolina Historical [978]

CASHBOOK / Wilton, Adam's Run. South Carolina. Christ (Episcopal) Church – 1834-58.Entries re communion plate and mission at Adam's Run. 3 fiches – 9 – us South Carolina Historical [978]

CASHBOOK OF THE DEPT. OF STATE, 1785-95 / U.S. Department of State – 1 roll. T904 – 1 – us Nat'l Archives [975]

Cashel Diocesan Library. County Tipperary. Republic of Ireland *see* CATALOGUE OF THE CASHEL DIOCESAN LIBRARY

CASHEW NUT PROCESSING – 1969 repr 1979 – 86p – it F.A.O. [338]

CASHIE BAPTIST CHURCH. WINDSON ASSOCIATION. BERIE COUNTY. NORTH CAROLINA : CHURCH RECORDS – 1791-1924 – 1 – 44.73 – us Baptist [240]

Casini, G *see* CANZONETTE SPIRITUALI

Casiri, Miguel *see*
- BIBLIOTECA ARABICO-HISPANA. TOMO 1
- BIBLIOTECA ARABICO-HISPANA. TOMO 2

THE CASKET, OR MUSICAL POCKET COMPANION; A COLLECTION OF THE MOST POPULAR SONGS, DUETTS, MARCHES, WALTZES, DANCES &C – Carefully arranged for the flute, violin, Kent bugle, or flageolet. New York: James L. Hewitt 183-. Includes: "Old King Cole" and "Tis the Last Rose of Summer." MUSIC 1988 – 1 – us L of C Photodup [780]

Casler, Nelie H *see* CAPE VINCENT AND ITS HISTORY

CASNP BULLETIN / Indian-Eskimo Association of Canada – 1960-72. (American Indian Periodicals in the Princeton University Library) – 5mf – 9 – $45.00 – us UPA [305]

CASNP BULLETIN – (v1-14 1960-73 Can$550.00. v15-18 1974-78 Can$110.00) – Toronto. v1-18. 1960-78 – 9 – cn Micromedia [073]

EL CASO ARGENTINO : HABLAN SUS PROTAGONISTAS / Dorrego, Alejandro & Azurduy, Victoria – [Mexico]: Prisma, 1st ed 1977 – 1 – CSUXADQ4931-B – us Hoover Inst Photo [972]

UN CASO CURIOSO DE DERECHO Y DE ANATOMIA MINERAL / Bayle, Constantino – Madrid: Razon y Fe, 1925 – 1 – sp Bibl Santa Ana [611]

UN CASO DE EXTIRPACION DE LA LARINGE... DE ESTA OPERACION / Cisneros, Juan – 1890 – 9 – 1.50f – sp Bibl Santa Ana [610]

EL CASO DEL JUDAIZANTE JERONIMO FRAY DIEGO DE MARCHENA / Sicioff, A A – Madrid: Castalia, 1966 – 1 – sp Bibl Santa Ana [946]

EL CASO DEL OBISPO MARCIAL DE MERIDA / Garcia de la Fuente, P Arturo – Badajoz: Tip. y Enc. la Alianza, 1933 – 1 – sp Bibl Santa Ana [946]

CASOS DE LA SEGUNDA TIRANIA / Comision Nacional de Investigaciones – Buenos Aires: Editorial Integracion, 1958- – 1 – CSUXAHZ6280-B – us Hoover Inst Photo [972]

CASP. BARTHOLINI THOM. FIL. DE TIBIIS VETERUM ET EARUM ANTIQUO USU LIBRI TRES / Bartholinus, C – Editio altera, figuris auctior. Amstelaedami. 1679. BP-152 1 – 9 – ne IDC [780]

CASPAR HAUSER : ODER, DIE TRAEGHEIT DES HERZENS: ROMAN / Wassermann, Jakob – 1. bis 4. Aufl. Stuttgart: Deutsche Verlags-Anstalt, 1908, c1905 – 1r – 1 – us U.W. Library [830]

Caspari, C P *see*
- ALTE UND NEUE QUELLEN ZUR GESCHICHTE DES TAUFSYMBOLS UND DER GLAUBENSREGEL

Caspari, Carl P *see* A GRAMMAR OF THE ARABIC LANGUAGE

Caspari, Ch. Ed *see* CHRONOLOGICAL AND GEOGRAPHICAL INTRODUCTION TO THE LIFE OF CHRIST

Caspari, W *see* DIE BEDEUTUNGEN DER WORTSIPPE "KBD" IM HEBRAEISCHEN

Caspari, Wilhelm *see* DIE BEDEUTUNG DER WORTSIPPE KVD IM HEBRAEISCHEN

LE CASQUE A MECHE – [Paris]: Impr de Beaule et Maignand, may 1849 – us Res Libr [944]

Casquete, Antonio *see* EL CRISTO DE LA REJA

Casquete Hernando, Antonio *see* NOTICIAS DE LA VILLA DE SEGURA DE LEON

LA CASQUETTE DU PERE DUCHENE : PAMPHLET SOCIALISTE – [Paris]: Impr Bonaventure et Ducessois, [1848?] – us Res Libr [320]

Casrilho Barreto e Noronha, Augusto Vidal de *see* O DISTRICTO DE LOURENCO MARQUES, NO PRESENTO E NO FUTURO

CASS COUNTY DEMOCRAT – Plattsmouth, NE. -w. Jun 1901-Sep 1902 – 1 – us NE Hist [071]

CASS COUNTY TRIBUNE – Plattsmouth, NE. -w. Oct 1895; Oct-Nov 1896; Jan-Apr 1897 – 1 – us NE Hist [071]

Cassaday, K *see* SHEEP AND GOATS IN HUMID WEST AFRICA

Cassagnac, Granier de *see* DE L'EMANCIPATION DES ESCLAVES, LETTRES A M. DE LAMARTINE

Cassander, G *see* DE BAPTISMO INFANTIVM, TESTIMONIA VETERUM ECCLESIASTICARUM SCRIPTORUM

Cassar, Francisco del *see* RESPUESTA QUE DA EL M.R.P...FR. J. TORRUBIA...SOBRE LA LEGITIMIDAD DEL LIBRO DE ORACION..

CASSAVA PROCESSING / Grace, M R – rev ed 1977 – 155p – it F.A.O. [338]

Cassegrain, Arthur *see* LA GRANDE TRONICIADE OU ITINERAIRE DE QUEBEC A LA RIVIERE-DU-LOUP: POEME BADIN

Cassel, Paulus *see*
- BOOK OF JUDGES
- BOOK OF RUTH
- KRITISCHE SENDSCHREIBEN UEBER DIE PROBEBIBEL

Cassell, B Abayomi *see* DOCUMENTS AND NEWSPAPERS FROM THE COLLECTION OF B. ABAYOMI CASSELL

CASSELL'S GAZETTEER OF GREAT BRITAIN AND IRELAND – London. 6v. 1894-98 – 1 – 46.00 – us L of C Photodup [910]

Cassels, Robert *see*
- A DIGEST OF CASES: DETERMINED BY THE SUPREME COURT OF CANADA FROM THE ORGANIZATION OF THE COURT IN 1875 TO THE 1ST DAY OF MAY, 1893: COMPRISING THE CASES RECORDED IN VOLUMES 1 TO 21.
- LECTURES ON SOME OF THE GREAT MASTERS OF ART: AND ON THE RISE, PROGRESS AND DECAY OF MODERN ART IN EUROPE
- THE PRACTICE OF THE SUPREME COURT OF CANADA

Cassels, Walter Richard *see*
- A REPLY TO DR. LIGHTFOOT'S ESSAYS
- SUPERNATURAL RELIGION: AN INQUIRY INTO THE REALITY OF DIVINE REVELATION

Casser, Paul *see* DIE WESTFAELISCHEN MUSENALMANACHE UND POETISCHEN TASCHENBUECHER

CASSI KWOC – (Keyword out of context index) – 9 – $100.00 – us Chemical [540]

CASSIER MAGAZINE – Cassier. N.Y. 1895-1913 – 1 – us UMI [073]

Cassini, A H G de *see* OPUSCULES PHYTOLOGIQUES

CASSIODORIS SENATORIS VARIAE (MGH 1: 12.BD) / ed by Mommsen, Theodor – (Accedunt 1: Epistolae Theodoricianae Variae. Ed. Th. Mommsen. 2: Acta Synodorum Habitarum Romae A. 498. Ed. Th. Mommsen. 3: Cassiodori Orationum Reliquiae. Ed. L. Traube) – 1894 – Dfl70.00 – ne Slangenburg [240]

Cassirer, Ernst *see* HEINRICH VON KLEIST UND DIE KANTISCHE PHILOSOPHIE

Cassius, S *see* DE JURE ET JUDICE LEGATORUM DIATRIBE...

Cassuto, D *see*
- CONDIZIONE GIURIDICA DELL'ITALIANO NATURALIZZATO STRANIERO...
- LE SENTENZE ESTERE DI DIVORZIO E IL GIUDIZIO DI DELIBAZIONE

THE CAST – New York. v1-212. 1900-54 – 38r – 1 – us Ross [790]

CAST TRESTNI, 1967 / Czechoslovakia. Justicni Statisticka Rocenha – Praha. 1968. BR-8768 1 – 9 – ne IDC [324]

Castagne, J L M *see* CATALOGUE DES PLANTES QUI CROISSENT NATURELLEMENT AUX ENVIRONS DE MARSEILLE AND SUPPLEMENT

Castagno, Antonio *see* TENDENCIAS Y GUPOS POLITICOS EN LA REALIDAD ARGENTINA

Castalleda, Vicente *see* FALLECIMIENTO

Castaneda, P *see* FIRMES

Castaneda, Vicente *see*
- BIBLIOFILIA SENTIMENTAL
- MUERTE DE D. FRANCISCO BARRADO Y FONT
- TRUJILLO. DECLARACION DE MONUMENTO HISTORICO-ARTISTICO DE SU CASTILLO
- VINIEGRA VERA, VIRGILIO. CORRESPONDIENTE DE LA REAL ACAD. DE LA HISTORIA EN SANTA MARTA

LAS CASTAS DEL MEXICO COLONIAL...1924 / Leon, Nicolas; ed by Bayle, Constantino – Madrid: Razon y Fe, 1928 – 9 – sp Bibl Santa Ana [972]

Castejon-Fiallos, M *see* LE TRAITE BRYAN-CHAMORRO...

Castel, B *see* DU PRINCIPE DE LA LIBERTE DES MERS ET DE SES APPLICATIONS...

Castel de Saint Pierre, Charles Irenee *see*
- PROJET DE TRAITE POUR RENDRE LA PAIX PERPETUELLE ENTRE LES SOUVERAINS CHRETIENS, POUR MAINTENIR TOUJOURS LE COMMERCE LIBRE ENTRE LES NATIONS
- PROJET POUR RENDRE LA PAIX PERPETUELLE EN EUROPE

Castel, Joaquin *see*
- ALGUNAS IDEAS SOBRE EL ENGRANDECIMIENTO DE CACERES
- CUESTION DE ACTUALIDAD
- INFLUENCIA DEL MANANTIAL DE MARCO EN EL DESARROLLA MATERIAL DE CACERES
- REPLICA AL FOLLETO DE DON FRANCISCO GALAN CASTILLO TITULADO "AL PUBLICO"

THE CASTEL OF HELTH / Elyot, Thomas – 1541 – 9 – 15.00 – us Scholars' Facs [610]

THE CASTEL OF HELTH / Elyot, Thomas – London, 1541 – 4mf – 9 – ne IDC [840]

Castelao, Fernanda *see* MONOGRAFIA HISTORICO DEL CASTILLO DE JARNDILLA

Castelar, Emilio *see* DONA CAROLINA CORONADO

Casteljau, X de *see* L'ACCES DES FRANCAIS DEVANT LES TRIBUNAUX ALLEMANDS ET LA CAUTION "JUDICATUM SOLVI"

Castella, P *see* NOTES DE SYNTHESE SUR L'ECONOMIE DE LA VILLE DE BOUAKE

Castellan, Antoine L *see* LETTRES SUR LA MOREE, HYDRA ET ZANTE

LA CASTELLANA DE RIBERA DEL FRESNO. LEYENDA. / Antunez Toriblo, Manuel – 1865 – 9 – 1.50f – sp Bibl Santa Ana [830]

Castellani, Charles Jules *see* MARCHAND L'AFRICAIN

Castellano, Conde de *see* UN COMPLOT TERRORISTA EN EL SIGLO 15TH. MADRID, 1927

Castellano, P *see* VITAE ILLUSTRIUM MEDICORUM...

Castellanos, H C *see* NEW ORLEANS AS IT WAS, EPISODES OF LOUISIANA LIFE

Castellanos, Joaquin *see* EL DOCTOR ALEM Y EL RADICALISMO

Castellanos, Juan de *see* OBRAS. TOMO 1

Castelle, Friedrich *see* DICHTUNGEN DER DROSTE

Castelli, David *see* IL CANTICO DEI CANTICI: STUDIO ESEGETICO

CASTELLUS RENOVATUS. HOC EST LEXICON MEDICUM QUONDAM A BART. CASTELLO MESSANENSI (AEL, ABT 3) / Bruno, Jacobus Pancratius – Nuernberg, 1682 (mf ed 1994) – 17mf – 9 – DM380.00 – 3-89131-178-8 – gw Fischer [610]

Castelmola, di *see* DEL PRINCIPIO DI NON INTERVENTO...

Castelnau *see*
- EXPEDICAO AS REGIOES CENTRAIS DA AMERICA DO SUL. T. 1
- EXPEDICAO AS REGIOES CENTRAIS DA AMERICA DO SUL. T. 2

Castelnau, FL de *see* HISTOIRE NATURELLE ET ICONOGRAPHIE DES INSECTES COLEOPTERES

Castelnau, Francis de *see* RENSEIGNEMENTS SUR L'AFRIQUE CENTRALE ET SUR UNE NATION D'HOMMES A QUEUE QUI S'Y TROUVERAIT

Castelnau, K L de *see* ETUDES ENTOMOLOGIQUES, OU DESCRIPTION D'INSECTES NOUVEAUX ET OBSERVATIONS SUR LEUR SYNONYMIE

Castelo, Garcia *see* TROZOS DE LITERATURA DE AUTORES EXTREMENOS

Castelo-Branco, Fernando A *see* ACTIVIDADES DOS MISSIONARIOS...

CASTES AND TRIBES OF SOUTHERN INDIA / Thurston, E & Rangachari, K – 7v. Madras. 1909. BI-593 2 – 8 – ne IDC [306]

Castier, G A *see* THESE POUR LE DOCTORAT

CASTIGATISSIMI ANNALI CON LA LORO COPIOSA TAVOLA DELLA ECCELSE ET ILLUSTRISSIMA REPUBLI. DI GENOA, DA FIDELI ET APPROUATI SCRITTORE, ... / Giustiniani, A – Genoa, 1537 – 11mf – 9 – H-8250/1 – ne IDC [956]

Castile. Laws, Statutes, etc *see* EXTRACTO DE LAS SIETE PARTIDAS: FORMADO PARA FACILITAR LA LECTURA, INTELIGENCIA Y MEMORIA DE SUS DISPOSICIONES

Castilhon, Jean-Louis *see*
- ESSAI SUR LES ERREURS ET LES SUPERSTITIONS
- ZINGHA, REINE D'ANGOLA, HISTOIRE AFRICAINE

CASTILIAN DAYS / Hay, John – Boston: J.R. Osgood and Company, 1871. 414p – 1 – us U.W. Library [910]

CASTILLA AGRICOLA PARA LA ENSENANZA DE LA AGRICULTURA...CACERES / Quintanilla, Guillermo & Arche, Jose Vicente – Badajoz: Ciudad Real y Albacete; Madrid: Imp. de los Hijos de M.G. Hern'andez, 1905 – sp Bibl Santa Ana [630]

Castilla, Juan de *see* LA JUSTICIA REVOLUCIONARIA EN ESPANA

LA CASTILLA Y EL MAS FAMOSO CASTELLANO / Risco, Manuel – 1792 – 1mf – 9 – Pta1,000.00 – 84-7848-109-5 – sp Pentalfa [946]

Castille, Cheryl L *see* THE PERCEIVED IMPORTANCE OF A LEISURE EDUCATION COMPONENT IN OUTPATIENT WEIGHT MANAGEMENT PROGRAMS SERVING ADULT WOMEN
Castillero, E J *see* LA CAUSA INMEDIATA DE LA EMANCIPACION DE PANAMA
Castillo, Catulo *see* UN TEATRO ARGENTINO PARA LA NUEVA ARGENTINA
Castillo de Bovadilla, J *see* POLITICA PARA COREGIDORES Y SENORES DE VASSALOS EN TIEMPOS DE PAZ Y DE GUERRA...
EL CASTILLO DE CASTELLAR : DATOS PARA LA HISTORIA DE ZAFRA / Salazar Fernandez, Antinio – Zafra: Imp. Segedana, 1955 – 1 – sp Bibl Santa Ana [946]
CASTILLO DE GUADAMUZ / Velo Nieto, Gervasio – Madrid, s.i., 1956 – 1 – sp Bibl Santa Ana [946]
CASTILLO DE LA ALTA EXTREMADURA : ELJAS (CON NOTICIAS HISTORICAS DE LA ENCOMIENDA DE SU NOMBRE) / Velo Nieto, Gervasio – Badajoz: Imprenta Diputacion Provincial, 1968 – sp Bibl Santa Ana [946]
EL CASTILLO DE LOARRE (INFORME) / Monsalud, Marques de – Madrid: Est. Tip. Fortanet, 1905. B.R.A.H. 47, 1905, pp. 448-451 – 1 – sp Bibl Santa Ana [946]
EL CASTILLO DE MEDELLIN EN LA RUTA DEL TURISMO / Garcia Sanchez, Francisco – Don Benito, Sanchez Trejo, 1969 – sp Bibl Santa Ana [946]
EL CASTILLO DE PIEDRABUENA / Escobar Prieto, Eugenio – Caceres: Imp. Luciano Jim'enez, 1908 – 1 – sp Bibl Santa Ana [946]
EL CASTILLO DE SANTIBANEZ EL ALTO / Velo Nieto, Gervasio – Madrid: Accasor, 1956 – 1 – sp Bibl Santa Ana [946]
EL CASTILLO E LOS MARQUESES DE LAS NAVAS / Perez Minguez, Fidel – Madrid: Tip. Arch., Bibl. y Mus, 1930. B.R.A.H. 97, pp 745-816, 19 lam – sp Bibl Santa Ana [946]
Castillo, Manuel *see*
- EXTREMADURA. CONFERENCIA DADA EN EL ATENEO ESPANOL DE MEXICO, EL 2 DE MAYO DE 1950
- GRAMATICA CASTELLANA
- PROGRAMA DE LA ASIGNATURA DE CASTELLANO.(PRIMO CURSO)

Castillo, Marciano *see* LA FEDERACION
EL CASTILLO Y PLAZA FUERTE DE ALCANTARA / Velo Nieto, Gervasio – Madrid, 1963. Sep. Boletin Asociacion Espanola de Amigos de los Castillos – sp Bibl Santa Ana [946]
UN CASTILLO Y VARIOS CASTELLANOS... / Perez Minguez, Fidel – Madrid: Razon y Fe, 1927 – 1 – sp Bibl Santa Ana [946]
CASTILLOS DE LA ALTA EXTREMADURA : PENAFIEL, CON BREVES NOTICIAS DE LA ENCOMIENDA DE SU NOMBRE / Velo Nieto, Gervasio – (Aparte Hidalguia Nov.-Dic. 1957, nº 25, pp. 1-22) – Madrid, 1957 – 1 – sp Bibl Santa Ana [946]
CASTILLOS, TORRES Y CASAS FUERTES DE LA PROVINCIA DE CACERES / Hurtado de Mendoza, Publio – Caceres: Imprenta y libreria Catolica de Santos Floriano, 1912 – sp Bibl Santa Ana [946]
Castle, Eduard *see*
- FERDINAND RAIMUNDS SAEMTLICHE WERKE IN DREI TEILEN
- GESPRAECHE MIT GOETHE IN DEN LETZTEN JAHREN SEINES LEBENS
- LENAU UND DIE FAMILIE LOEWENTHAL
- NIKOLAUS LENAU
- NIKOLAUS LENAUS SAEMTLICHE WERKE IN ZWEI BAENDEN

Castle, Egerton *see* SCHOOLS AND MASTERS OF FENCE, FROM THE MIDDLE AGES TO THE EIGHTEENTH CENTURY
Castle, Henry A *see* MINNESOTA: ITS STORY AND BIOGRAPHY
THE CASTLE OF LOVE 1549?, A TRANSLATION BY JOHN BOURCHIER / San Pedro, Diego de – Lord Berners, of Carcel de Amor. 1492 by Diego de San Pedro – 9 – 15.00 – us Scholars' Facs [830]
THE CASTLE OF OTRANTO / Walpole, Horace; ed by Doughty, Oswald – London: The Scholartis Press, 1929. lxxx,111p. 2 pl – 1 – us U.W. Library [830]
CASTLE RICHMOND : A NOVEL / Trollope, Anthony – London: Chapman & Hall, 1860 – 1 roll – 1 – 1-55879-964-8 – uk Libr Preservation [830]
CASTLEACRE MANOR COURT ROLLS – 1300 to 1700 – 1 – uk Microform Academic [941]
CASTLEACRE ROLLS / Holkham Hall. Norfolk. England – Holkham MS. 433 – 1 – uk Microform Academic [941]
CASTLEACRE ROLLS / Holkham Hall. Norfolk. England – Holkham MS. 482 – 1 – uk Microform Academic [941]
CASTLEACRE ROLLS / Holkham Hall. Norfolk, England – Holkham MSS. 431, 432, 433, 436, 437 and 438 – 1 – uk Microform Academic [941]
CASTLEMAINE MAIL – 1917-1983. CM1-96 – 96r – 1 – at Corangamite [072]
THE CASTLES, PALACES AND PRISONS OF MARY OF SCOTLAND / Mackie, Charles – London, 1849. 480p. illus – 1 – us U.W. Library [941]
Caston, Alfred de *see* LA TURQUIE EN 1873
Castonnet des Fosses, Henri *see* L'ABYSSINIE ET LES ITALIENS
Castonnet des Fosses, Henri Louis *see* MADAGASCAR
LE CASTOR / ed by Aubin, Napoleon – Quebec, Canada. 17 nov 1843-28 jun 1845 – 1r – 1 – Can$50.00 – cn Can Microfilming [072]
LE CASTOR : CARICATURES. NUMERO UNIQUE – Montreal, Canada. 25 sep 1883 – 1r – 1 – Can$25.00 – cn Can Microfilming [072]
LE CASTOR : HUMORISTIQUE ILLUSTRE – Montreal, Canada. 14 jun-23 aut 1879 – 1r – 1 – Can$25.00 – cn Can Microfilming [072]
LE CASTOR : IMPRIME A BORD DU "CANADA" – 1-5 sep 1877 – 1r – 1 – Can$25.00 – cn Can Microfilming [072]
LE CASTOR : JOURNAL HUMORISTIQUE DES FAMILLES – Montreal. 19 Mar 1922 – 1r – 1 – Can$25.00 – cn Can Microfilming [640]
LE CASTOR DECHAINE : SATIRIQUE – Montreal, Canada. 5 sep 1967-v1 n11. 21 nov 1967 – 1r – 1 – Can$35.00 – cn Can Microfilming [072]
LE CASTOR NATIONAL – Quebec, Canada. v2 n1. 24 aut 1878 – 1r – 1 – Can$25.00 – cn Can Microfilming [072]
Castori, C *see* IL DIRITTO DI ESTRADIZIONE
LA CASTREIDA / Salas, Francisco Gregorio de – 1838 – 9 – 1.50f – sp Bibl Santa Ana [830]
Castren, M A *see*
- ETHNOLOGISCHE VORLESUNGEN UEBER DIE ALTAISCHEN VOELKER
- GRUNDZUEGE EINER TUNGUSISCHEN SPRACHLEHRE NEBST KURZEM WOERTERVERZEICHNISS
- REISEBERICHTE UND BRIEFE AUS DEN JAHREN 1845-1849
- VERSUCH EINER BURJAETISCHEN SPRACHLEHRE NEBST KURZEM WOERTERVERZEICHNISS
- VERSUCH EINER KOIBALISCHEN UND KARAGASSISCHEN SPRACHLEHRE, NEBST WOERTERVERZEICHNISSEN AUS DEN TATARISCHEN MINDARTEN DES MINNUSINSCHEN KREISES

Castries, H de *see* SOURCES INEDITES DE L'HISTOIRE DU MAROC DE 1530 A 1845
Castro Albarran, A de *see*
- ESTE ES EL CORTEJO...SALAMANCA 1938
- GUERRA SANTA: EL SENTIDO CATOLICO DE LA GUERRA ESPANOLA. BURGOS, 1938
- POLVO DE SUS SANDALIAS

Castro, Alf. A *see* ADVERSUS OMNES HAERESES LIBRI 14
CASTRO ALVES : ORGAO DO CLUB LITTERARIO DESTE NOME – Maceio, Alagoas. 11 Nov 1883; Abr, 27 Jul 1884 – 1,5,6 – bl Biblioteca [072]
CASTRO ALVES, O POETA E O POEMA / Peixoto, A – Sao Paulo, 1942 – 6mf – 8 – ne Slangenburg [440]
Castro, Antonio de *see*
- PETICION ESCRITO DE CONCLUSIONES AL NUNCIO POR EL P. CACERES CON EL P. JUAN DE LA SERENA Y OTROS
- PETICION...AL NUNCIO POR EL P. CACERES..
- POR...FR. DIEGO DE CACERES, GENERAL... DE S. GERONIMO...Y DEMAS DIPUTADOS QUE SE CONFIRMA LA SENTENCIA

Castro Bajo, Julian *see* FLORES Y ESPINAS
Castro, Carlo A *see* GUIA DE CASTELLANIZACION ORAL PARA INDIGENAS TZELTALES
Castro de Torres *see* PANEGIRICO AL CHOCOLATE
Castro, Fidel *see* THE REVOLUTION AND CULTURAL PROBLEMS IN CUBA
Castro, H D de *see* KEUR VAN GRAFSTEENEN OP DE NEDERL.-PORTUG.-ISRAEL. BEGRAAFPLAATS TE OUDERKERK AAN DEN AMSTEL
Castro, I A *see* DE ON-GHEMASKERDE LIEFDE DES HEMELS
Castro, J *see* HISTORIA DE LAS VIRTUDES Y PROPIEDADES DEL TABACO Y DE LOS MODOS DE TOMARSE...
Castro, Jorge *see* PATERNALISMO Y MUNDO NUEVO
Castro, Jose de *see* ELOGIO...ANTONIO MENDES CORREIA
Castro, Justino M *see* VIDA CIVIL Y MILITAR DE DON HERMENEGILDO GALEANA
Castro, Manuel *see*
- BALTASAR CUARTERO Y HUERTA Y ANTONIO VARGAS ZUNIGA Y MONTERO DE ESPINOSA. MARQUES DE SIETE IGLESIAS. INDICE...
- CRISTOBAL DE SAN ANTONIO, OFM...EN NOTAS BIBLIOGRAFIA FRANCISCANA
- FRANCISCO PIZARROSO, OFM, EN NOTASDE BIBLIOGRAFIA FRANCISCANA...
- JERONIMO ZAPATA, NATURAL DE AZUAGA, EN NOTAS DE BIBLIOGRAFIA FRANCISCANA

Castro, Manuel de *see* MERIDION
Castro, P *see* BURGOS. ARCHIVO HISTORICO PROVINCIAL. LOS PROTOCOLOS DEL ARCHIVO HISTORICO PROVINCIAL
Castro, Pedro Andres de *see* ORTOGRAFIA Y REGLAS DE LENGUA TAGALAG, ORDENADA POR...
EL CASTRO ROMANO DE CACERES EL VIEJO. NUEVAS INSCRIPCIONES / Fita, Fidel – Madrid: Fortanet, 1911. B.R.A.H. LIX, pp. 467-482 – sp Bibl Santa Ana [946]
Castro Sampaio, Manuel de *see* ENSAIOS POETICOS
Castro Seoane, Jose *see* EL P. BARTOLOME DE OLMEDO. CAPELLAN DEL EJERCITO DE CORTES
CASTRO VALLEY REPORTER – San Lorenzo, CA. 1931-49; (broken issues) 1950; Jan-Feb 1951; 1955-60; 1967-79 – 13r – 1 – $650.00 – B02899 – us Library Micro [071]
Castro y Castro, Manuel *see* UNION MISIONAL FRANCISCANA. SU NATURALEZA Y ORGANIZACION
Castro y Oyanguren, E *see* BOLETINES DEL EXTERIOR
Castrofuerte, Marques de *see* NOTICIAS (HALLAZGOS POR EL MARQUES DE CASTROFUERTE EN CACERES
Castrovido, Roberto *see* LAS DOS REPUBLICAS: EL 11 DE FEBRERO Y EL 14 DE ABRIL
CASTROVILLE TIMES/NORTH COUNTY NEWS – (Cont by: North County News, Salinas) – Castroville, CA. 1975-77 – 1r – 1 – $50.00 – B02100 – us Library Micro [071]
CASTROVILLE-TIMES – (Cont: Times Journal) – Castroville, CA. 1959-74 – 6r – 1 – $300.00 – B02099 – us Library Micro [071]
Casualty Actuarial Society *see* PROCEEDINGS
Casulli, A *see* LA SOVRANITA DEGLI STATI...
CASUS PAPALES ET EPISCOPALES (I. ZARAGOZA, 1479-1484) – Burgos – 1r – 5,6 – sp Cultura [220]
Caswell, D J *see* THE OUTWARD AND VISIBLE SIGN: A NEW AND ATTRACTIVE METHOD OF TEACHING RELIGIOUS TRUTHS, AND ESPECIALLY APPLIED TO THE TEACHING OF THE CHURCH CATECHISM.
CAT FANCY – 1976- – 9 – us UMI [073]
LE CATACLYSME DE LA RIVIERE STE.-ANNE: RECIT COMPLET DES CATASTROPHES DE SAINT-ALBAN ET DE SAINTE-ANNE LA PERADE – Quebec: Leclerc & Roy, 1894. 02569. (Pre-1900 Canadiana) – 9 – cn C.I.H.M. [971]
CATACOMB – London, South Africa. 1 Jan 1949-31 Dec 1952. 1 reel – 1, 16 diazo available at reduced price – sa SA Libr [072]
LE CATACOMBE ROMANE : SECONDO GLI ULTIMI STUDI E LE PIU RECENTI SCOPERTE: COMPENDIO DELLA ROMA SOTTERANEA CON MOLTE PIANTE PARZIALI DEI CIMITERI E RIPRODUZIONI DI MONUMENTI / Marucchi, Orazio – Roma: Desclee, Lefebvre, 1903 – 2mf – us A.T.L.A. [240]
Catacombes, Messager *see* SUPRACONFESSIONNEL DE L'EGLISE DU SILENCE
THE CATACOMBS OF ROME: A LECTURE / Campbell, C A – Halifax, N. S.: J. Power, 1896. 00402. (Pre-1900 Canadiana) – 9 – cn C.I.H.M. [240]
THE CATACOMBS OF ROME AS ILLUSTRATING THE CHURCH OF THE FIRST THREE CENTURIES / Kip, William Ingraham – New York: Redfield, 1854, c1853 – 1mf – us A.T.L.A. [240]
O CATAGUAZENSE : PERIODICO IMPARCIAL – Cataguazes, 30 Jan-10 Apr 1887 – 1,5,6 – bl Biblioteca [072]
CATAGUAZES : ORGAO OFICIAL DOS PODERES MUNICIPAIS – Cataguazes, 25 Dec 1953; 9 May 1965 – 1,5,6 – bl Biblioteca [072]
Catala, J A *see* CATALOGO DEL "EL COJO ILUSTRADO", 1892-1915
LOS CATALANES EN GRECIA... / Rubio y Lluch, A; ed by Bayle, Constantino – Madrid: Razon y Fe, 1928 – 9 – sp Bibl Santa Ana [946]
Catalano, Luciano R *see* REVOLUCION CONSTRUCTIVA DEL PUEBLO
Catalanus, J *see*
- RITUALE ROMANUM BENEDICTI PAPAE 14, JUSSU EDITUM ET AUCTUM PERPETUIS COMMENTARIIS EXORNATUM. T. 1
- RITUALE ROMANUM BENEDICTI PAPE 14, JUSSU EDITUM ET AUCTUM PERPETUIS COMMENTARIIS EXORNATUM. T. 2

CATALECTA BOTANICA / Roth, A W – 3v. Lipsiae. 1797-1806. B-296 2 – 8 – ne IDC [580]
CATALECTA BOTANICA / Roth, Alberto G – 1797 and 1806 – 7 – uk Microform Academic [580]
CATALINA – 1992- – 3+ r – 1 – $150.00 – P00017 – us Library Micro [910]
CATALINA ISLANDER – Avalon, CA. 1934-56 – 9r – 1 – $450.00 – C02035 – us Library Micro [071]
THE CATALINA ISLANDER – Avalon. Calif. 1943-56 – 1 – us UMI [071]
CATALOG / Amherst College. Amherst, MA – 1822-26, 1829, 1830, 1832, 1835, 1840 41, 1845 46 – 1 – us Res Libr [370]
CATALOG / Georgetown College. Georgetown, Ky – 1845-75 – 1 – 23.52 – us Baptist [240]
CATALOG / Harvard University. Museum of Comparative Zoology. Library – 1968.-153,000 cards 16 reels.-ISBN: 0-8161-1384-X – 1 – $835.00 – uk Hall [025]
CATALOG / Illinois. University at Urbana-Champaign. Communications Library – 1975.-42,700 cards 3 reels.-ISBN: 0-8161-1408-0 – 1 – $365.00 – uk Hall [380]
CATALOG / Interafrican Committee for Hydraulic Studies. Documentation Center. Ouagadougou, Upper Volta – 1978.-22,000 cards 4 reels.-ISBN: 0-8161-1268-1 – $190.00 – uk Hall [910]
CATALOG / Metropolitan Museum of Art. New York – (Fifth Suppl., 1973.-17,900 cards 2 reels. $130.00 ISBN: 0-8161-1319-X; Sixth Suppl., 1975.-18,300 cards 2 reels. $130.00 ISBN: 0-8161-1320-3) – First ed – 1 – uk Hall [700]
CATALOG / Museum of Modern Art. New York – 1976.-199,000 cards 28 reels.-ISBN: 0-8161-1299-1 – 1 – $1310.00 – uk Hall [700]
CATALOG / National Library of Anthropology and History. Mexico City – 1972.-143,000 cards 20 reels.-ISBN: 0-8161-1315-7 – 1 – $960.00 – uk Hall [306]
CATALOG / Regent's Park College. Angus Library – (Annotated v. 1908 – 1 – 36.75 – us Baptist [240]
CATALOG.. / Florida. University. Gainesville. P.K. Yonge Library of Florida History – 1977.-62,700 card. 8 reels.-ISBN: 0-8161-1379-3 – 1 – $435.00 – uk Hall [010]
CATALOG.. / International Museum of Photography at George Eastman House – 1982.-47,293 cards 4 reels. $400.00 ISBN: 0-8161-1445-5; 66mf.- ISBN: 0-8161-1733-0 – 1,9 – 365.00 – uk Hall [760]
CATALOG DER HEBRAEISCHEN BIBELHANDSCHRIFTEN DER KAISERLICHEN OEFFENTLICHEN BIBLIOTHEK IN ST PETERSBURG / Harkavy, A & Strack, H L – St. Petersburg, Leipzig, 1875. xxxiii,297p. BR-10,878/1 – 9 – ne IDC [220]
CATALOG DER LEPIDOPTEREN EUROPA'S UND DER ANGRENZENDEN LAENDER / Staudinger, O & Wocke, M F – Dresden, 1861 – XVI, 192p – 8 – ne IDC [590]

CATALOG DER REICHHALTIGEN SAMMLUNG HEBRAISCHER U. JUEDISCHER BUECHER, HANDSCHRIFTEN, PORTRAITS ETC : NACHGELASSEN VON N.H. VAN BIEMA; BESCHRIEBEN VON S. SEELIGMANN / Biema, N H van – Amsterdam, Joachimsthal, 1904 – 3mf – ne IDC [270]

CATALOG FILE 1843-1989 / Boston Public Library. Research Library – Dictionary catalog of over four million items in the research library – 9 – us Advanced Libr [010]

CATALOG... HEBRAEISCHER UND JUEDISCHER BUECHER, HANDSCHRIFTEN, KUPFERSTICHE, PORTRAITS ETC. NACHGELASSEN VON G. ALMANZI, J. EMDEN, M.J. LEBENSTEIN U.A. / Roest, M – Amsterdam,. 1868 – 5mf – ne IDC [470]

CATALOG OF AFRICAN GOVERNMENT DOCUMENTS / Boston University. Libraries – Third rev. enl. ed., 1976. 14,100 cards. 1 reel. ISBN 0-8161-1422-6 – 1 – $90.00 – uk Hall [960]

CATALOG OF BIOGRAPHIES IN THE LIBRARY OF THE NEW YORK ACADEMY OF MEDICINE / New York Academy of Medicine – 1960. 3400 cards on 1 reel – 1 – $65.00 export $80.00 – 0-8161-1390-4 – uk Hall [610]

CATALOG OF BOOKS – Allahabad, Supt, Govt Press, United Provinces, mar 1923; sep 1924 – us Res Libr [020]

CATALOG OF BOOKS AS REPRESENTED BY LC PRINTED CARDS / U.S. Library of Congress – 1898-1942 cumulation. Quinquennia: 1942-47; 1948-52. National and international – 9 – us Advanced Libr [010]

CATALOG OF BRAZILIAN ACQUISITIONS OF THE LIBRARY OF CONGRESS, 1964-1974 / Jackson, William V – 1977. 15,400 cards on 1 reel – 1 – $100.00 export $120.00 – 0-8161-1373-4 – uk Hall [972]

CATALOG OF BROADSIDES IN THE RARE BOOK DIVISION / U.S. Library of Congress – 1972. 60,800 cards. 4 reels. ISBN 0-8161-1454-4 – 1 – $490.00 – uk Hall [080]

CATALOG OF BROADSIDES OF AMERICAN VERSE IN THE HARRIS COLLECTION OF AMERICAN POETRY AND PLAYS / Brown University. John Hay Library – 1987. 79,000 cards. 5 reels. ISBN 0-8161-1469-2 – 1 – $715.00 – uk Hall [080]

CATALOG OF COPYRIGHT ENTRIES / U.S. Copyright Office – 1958-81 – 3 – us Readex [324]

CATALOG OF COPYRIGHT ENTRIES / U.S. Copyright Office – no. 1-782. 1 11 Jul 1891-28 Jun 1906 – 1 – 388.00 – us L of C Photodup [010]

CATALOG OF COPYRIGHT ENTRIES: BOOKS / U.S. Copyright Office – New series, v. 42. 1945 – 1 – us Princeton Micro [070]

CATALOG OF COPYRIGHT ENTRIES: MUSICAL COMPOSITIONS / U.S. Copyright Office – 1891-1946 – 1 – 1,613.00 – us L of C Photodup [780]

CATALOG OF COPYRIGHT ENTRIES: PERIODICALS / U.S. Copyright Office – Series 3, v. 1-25. 1946-1971 – 1,5,6 – us Princeton Micro [070]

CATALOG OF COPYRIGHTED DRAMAS, 1870-1916 / U.S. Copyright Office – Washington, D.C. G.P.O., 1918. 2 v. 2 reels – 1 – 40.00 – us L of C Photodup [070]

CATALOG OF ETHIOPIAN MANUSCRIPTS – (v.4. Project nos. 1101-1500. 1979. 38.50; 1) – Microfilmed for the Ethiopian Manuscript Microfilm Library, Addis Ababa, and for the Monastic Manuscript Microfilm Library, Collegeville, Minnesota. v.3. Project nos. 701-1100. 1978 – 1 – 27.75 – us UMI [010]

A CATALOG OF FILES AND MICROFILMS OF THE GERMAN FOREIGN MINISTRY ARCHIVES / Kent, George O – 1920-1945. Volume I, 1962, 835 pp. Volume II, 1963, 1330 pp – 1 – 35.00r – us Hoover Inst Photo [943]

A CATALOG OF FILES AND MICROFILMS OF THE GERMAN FOREIGN MINISTRY ARCHIVES, 1867-1920 / Germany. Foreign Office – 1r – 1 – T322 – us Nat'l Archives [324]

CATALOG OF GOVERNMENT PUBLICATIONS IN THE RESEARCH LIBRARIES / New York Public Library. Research Libraries – (Available on microfilm by request) – 1972. 581,000 cards – 1 – $4,340.00 export $5,265.00 – 0-8161-0781-5 – uk Hall [320]

CATALOG OF MANUSCRIPTS OF THE FOLGER SHAKESPEARE LIBRARY / Folger Shakespeare Library. Washington, DC – 1971. 47,500 cards on 3 reels – 1 – $270.00 export $325.00 – 0-8161-1541-9 – uk Hall [420]

CATALOG OF PERIODICAL LITERATURE IN THE SOCIAL AND BEHAVIORAL SCIENCES SECTION, INCLUDING SUPPLEMENT TO MONOGRAPHS, 1973-75 / Indiana University. Institute for Sex Research. Library; ed by Beasley, Ruth – 1976.-73,400 cards – 8r – 1 – $395.00 export $475.00 – 0-8161-1366-1 – uk Hall [300]

CATALOG OF PRINTED BOOKS / California. University. Berkeley. Bancroft Library – (First Suppl., 1969 86,700 cards 6 reels. $725.00 ISBN: 0-8161-1517-6; Second Suppl., 1974.-92,600 cards 6 reels. $790.00 ISBN: 0-8161-1394-7; Third Suppl., 1979.- 69,500 cards 5 reels. $915.00 ISBN: 0-8161-1163-4) – 1964.-364,000 cards 44 reels.-ISBN: 0-8161-1393-9 – 1 – $2180.00 – uk Hall [010]

CATALOG OF PRINTED BOOKS / Folger Shakespeare Library. Washington, DC – (First Suppl., 1976.-43,200 cards 6 reels. $395.00 ISBN: 0-8161-1338-6; Second Suppl., 1981. 25,000 cards 2 reels. $360.00 ISBN: 0-8161-1530-3) – 1970.-387,000 cards 28 reels.-ISBN: 0-8161-1529-X – 1 – $2575.00 – uk Hall [010]

CATALOG OF PRINTED BOOKS OF THE FOLGER SHAKESPEARE LIBRARY : FIRST SUPPLEMENT / Folger Shakespeare Library, Washington, D.C. – 1976. 43,200 cards on 6 reels – 1 – $360.00 export $435.00 – 0-8161-1338-6 – uk Hall [420]

CATALOG OF PRINTED BOOKS OF THE FOLGER SHAKESPEARE LIBRARY : SECOND SUPPLEMENT / Folger Shakespeare Library. Washington, DC – 1981. 25,000 cards on 2 reels – 1 – $325.00 export $390.00 – 0-8161-1530-3 – uk Hall [420]

CATALOG OF PROTESTANT MISSIONARY WORKS IN CHINESE / Harvard University. Harvard-Yenching Library – 1980.-3000 cards 1 reel.-ISBN: 0-8161-1363-7 – 1 – $100.00 – uk Hall [240]

CATALOG OF PUBLICATIONS / U.S. Bureau of the Census – 1790-1987. Includes guide to programs and publications. 57mf – 9 – $90.00 – us Updata [324]

CATALOG OF PUBLICATIONS ISSUED BY THE GOVERNMENT OF THE UNITED PROVINCES AND OBTAINABLE FROM THE BOOK DEPOT, GOVERNMENT PRESS, ALLAHABAD – Allahabad, Supt, Govt Press, United Provinces, jun 1928-sep 1931; jun 1932-sep 1933; jun-sep 1934; jun-sep 1936; jun 1938 – us Res Libr [350]

CATALOG OF SELECTED DOCUMENTS IN PSYCHOLOGY – v1-5. 1971-75 – 1448mf – 9 – $5.00f – us Ross [150]

CATALOG OF THE ARABIC COLLECTION, HARVARD UNIVERSITY / Harvard University. Widener Library – 1983. 87,093 cards on 6 reels – 1 – $1,510.00 export $1,830.00 – 0-8161-1507-9 – uk Hall [470]

CATALOG OF THE AVERY MEMORIAL ARCHITECTURAL LIBRARY. SECOND EDITION, ENGLARGED : FIRST SUPPLEMENT / Columbia University – (Also available on 90mf ISBN 0-8161-1772-1 $440.00 export $530.00) – 1973. 66,400 cards on 4 reels – 1,9 – $440.00 export $530.00 – 0-8161-1432-3 – uk Hall [720]

CATALOG OF THE AVERY MEMORIAL ARCHITECTURAL LIBRARY. SECOND EDITION, ENGLARGED : FOURTH SUPPLEMENT / Columbia University – (Also available on 65mf ISBN 0-8161-1775-6 $340.00 export $410.00) – 1980. 49,600 cards on 6 reels – 1,9 – $340.00 export $410.00 – 0-8161-1381-5 – uk Hall [720]

CATALOG OF THE AVERY MEMORIAL ARCHITECTURAL LIBRARY. SECOND EDITION, ENGLARGED : SECOND SUPPLEMENT / Columbia University – (Also available on 91mf ISBN 0-8161-1773-X $440.00 export $530.00) – 1975. 66,800 cards on 8 reels – 1,9 – $440.00 export $530.00 – 0-8161-1287-8 – uk Hall [720]

CATALOG OF THE AVERY MEMORIAL ARCHITECTURAL LIBRARY. SECOND EDITION, ENGLARGED : THIRD SUPPLEMENT / Columbia University – (Also available on 63mf ISBN 0-8161-1774-8 $440.00 export $400.00) – 1977. 45,600 cards on 6 reels – 1,9 – $330.00 export $400.00 – 0-8161-1350-5 – uk Hall [720]

CATALOG OF THE AVERY MEMORIAL ARCHITECTURAL LIBRARY. SECOND EDITION, ENLARGED / Columbia University – (Also available on 453mf ISBN 0-8161-1736-5 $1,590.00 export $1,970.00) – 1968. 333,000 cards on 19 reels – 1,9 – $1,590.00 export $1,970.00 – 0-8161-1411-0 – uk Hall [720]

CATALOG OF THE CHESS COLLECTION (INCLUDING CHECKERS) / Cleveland. Public Library. John G. White Dept – 1964. 25,000 entries 2 reels. ISBN: 0-8161-1313-0 – 1 – $145.00 – uk Hall [790]

CATALOG OF THE CHINESE COLLECTION / Hoover Institution – (First Suppl., 1972. 28,300 cards. 4 reels. $295.00 ISBN 0-8161-1381-1; Second Suppl., 1977. 33,400 cards. 4 reels. $300.00 ISBN 0-8161-1341-6) – 1 – uk Hall [950]

CATALOG OF THE COMMUNICATIONS LIBRARY / University of Illinois at Urbana-Champaign, Communications Library – 1975. 42,700 cards on 3 reels – 1 – $330.00 export $400.00 – 0-8161-1408-0 – uk Hall [380]

CATALOG OF THE CONSERVATION LIBRARY / Denver Public Library – (First Supplement, 1978. 24,200 cards 2 reels. $220.00 export $265.00. – ISBN 0-8161-1192-8) – 1 – uk Hall [333]

CATALOG OF THE DEFOE COLLECTION IN THE BOSTON PUBLIC LIBRARY / Boston Public Library – (Available on microfilm by request) – 1966. 1900 cards – 1 – $75.00 export $95.00 – 0-8161-0731-9 – uk Hall [420]

A CATALOG OF THE DESCENDANTS OF THOMAS WATKINS / Watkins, Francis N – 1852 – 1 – $50.00 – us Presbyterian [920]

CATALOG OF THE DOCUMENTATION CENTER, INTERAFRICAN COMMITTEE FOR HYDRAULIC STUDIES = CATALOG DU CENTRE DE DOCUMENTATION, COMITE INTERAFRICAIN D'ETUDES HYDRAULIQUES / Interafrican Committee for Hydraulic Studies. Documentation Center. Ouagadougou, Upper Volta – 1977. 22,000 cards on 4 reels – 1 – $170.00 export $205.00 – 0-8161-1268-1 – uk Hall [550]

CATALOG OF THE E. AZALIA HACKLEY MEMORIAL COLLECTION OF NEGRO MUSIC, DANCE, AND DRAMA.. / Detroit Public Library – 1979.-12,000 cards 1 reel.-ISBN: 0-8161-1382-3 – 1 – $110.00 – uk Hall [780]

CATALOG OF THE EDGAR FAHS SMITH MEMORIAL COLLECTION IN THE HISTORY OF CHEMISTRY / University of Pennsylvania. Library – 1960. 11,000 cards. 1 reel. ISBN 0-8161-1429-3 – 1 – $100.00 – uk Hall [540]

CATALOG OF THE HAMPTON L. CARSON COLLECTION ILLUSTRATIVE OF THE GROWTH OF THE COMMON LAW / Free Library of Philadelphia. Hampton L. Carson Collection – (Available on microfilm by request) – 1962. 38,600 cards – 9 – $200.00 export $240.00 – uk Hall [340]

CATALOG OF THE HARVARD UNIVERSITY FINE ARTS LIBRARY / Harvard University. Fogg Art Museum. Library – (First suppl., 1975. 58,500 cards. 3 reels. $400.00 ISBN 0-8161-1442-0) – 1971. 412,000 cards. 15 reels. ISBN 0-8161-1472-2 – 1 – $1925.00 – uk Hall [700]

CATALOG OF THE HOOSE LIBRARY OF PHILOSOPHY / California. University of Southern California. Los Angeles – 1968.-96,100 cards – 6r – 1 – $595.00 export $720.00 – 0-8161-1465-X – uk Hall [100]

CATALOG OF THE JAPANESE COLLECTION / Hoover Institution – (First suppl., 1972. 125,000 cards. 1 reel. $140.00 ISBN 0-8161-1413-7; Second suppl., 1977. 15,300 cards. 1 reel. $155.00 ISBN 0-8161-1414-5) – 1969. 125,000 cards. 7 reels. ISBN 0-8161-1547-8 – 1 – $765.00 – uk Hall [950]

CATALOG OF THE LATIN AMERICAN COLLECTION / Florida. University. Gainesville. Libraries – 1973. 201,000 cards. 26 reels. ISBN 0-8161-1316-5 – 1 – $1480.00 – uk Hall [972]

CATALOG OF THE LATIN AMERICAN COLLECTION / Texas. University at Austin – (First Suppl., 1971. 75,000 cards. 10 reels. $475.00 ISBN 0-8161-1281-9; Second Suppl., 1973. 42,000 cards. 6 reels. $375.00 ISBN 0-8161-1325-4; Third Suppl., 1975. 131,000 cards. 16 reels. $1025.00 ISBN 0-8161-1360-2) – 1969. 479,000 cards. 31 reels. ISBN 0-8161-1511-7 – 1 – $3255.00 – uk Hall [972]

CATALOG OF THE LATIN AMERICAN COLLECTION / Tulane University. New Orleans. Latin American Library – (First Suppl., 1973. 33,900 cards. 4 reels. $275.00 ISBN 0-8161-1276-2; Second Suppl., 1975. 32,900 cards. 4 reels. $275.00 ISBN 0-8161-1312-2; Third Suppl., 1978. 32,100 cards. 2 reels. $300.00 ISBN 0-8161-1516-8) – 1 – uk Hall [972]

CATALOG OF THE LATIN AMERICAN COLLECTION OF THE UNIVERSITY OF TEXAS LIBRARY : FIRST SUPPLEMENT / University of Texas at Austin – 1971. 75,000 cards on 10 reels – 1 – $430.00 export $520.00 – 0-8161-1281-9 – uk Hall [972]

CATALOG OF THE LATIN AMERICAN COLLECTION OF THE UNIVERSITY OF TEXAS LIBRARY : SECOND SUPPLEMENT / University of Texas at Austin – 1973. 42,200 cards on 6 reels – 1 – $340.00 export $410.00 – 0-8161-1325-4 – uk Hall [972]

CATALOG OF THE LATIN AMERICAN COLLECTION OF THE UNIVERSITY OF TEXAS LIBRARY : THIRD SUPPLEMENT / University of Texas at Austin – 1975. 131,000 cards on 16 reels – 1 – $930.00 export $1,125.00 – 0-8161-1360-2 – uk Hall [972]

CATALOG OF THE LATIN AMERICAN COLLECTION, UNIVERSITY OF FLORIDA LIBRARIES / University of Florida at Gainesville – 1973. 201,000 cards on 26 reels – 1 – $1,345.00 export $1,625.00 – 0-8161-1316-5 – uk Hall [972]

CATALOG OF THE LATIN AMERICAN LIBRARY OF THE TULANE UNIVERSITY LIBRARY : FIRST SUPPLEMENT / Tulane University. New Orleans – 1973. 33,900 cards on 4 reels – 1 – $250.00 export $300.00 – 0-8161-1276-2 – uk Hall [972]

CATALOG OF THE LATIN AMERICAN LIBRARY OF THE TULANE UNIVERSITY LIBRARY : SECOND SUPPLEMENT / Tulane University. New Orleans – 1975. 32,900 cards on 4 reels – 1 – $250.00 export $300.00 – 0-8161-1312-2 – uk Hall [972]

CATALOG OF THE LATIN AMERICAN LIBRARY OF THE TULANE UNIVERSITY LIBRARY : THIRD SUPPLEMENT / Tulane University. New Orleans – 1978. 32,100 cards on 2 reels – 1 – $275.00 export $330.00 – 0-8161-1516-8 – uk Hall [972]

CATALOG OF THE LIBRARY / Columbia University. Avery Memorial Architectural Library – (First suppl., 1973.-66,400 cards, 4 reels or 90mf. $485.00 ISBN: 0-8161-1287-8; second suppl., 1975.-66,800 cards, 8 reels or 91 mf. $485.00 ISBN: 0-8161-1350-5; third suppl., 1977.- 45,600 cards, 6 reels or 63mf. $365.00; fourth suppl.,1980.-49,600 cards, 6 reels or 65mf. $375.00 ISBN: 0-8161-1381-5; fifth suppl., 1982.-12,000 cards 4 reels. $565.00 ISBN: 0-8161-0397-6) – 2nd enl. ed., 1968.-333,000 cards 19 reels, ISBN: 0-8161-1411-0; or 453mf.-ISBN: 0-8161-1736-5 – 1,9 – $1750.00 – uk Hall [010]

CATALOG OF THE LIBRARY / International Archives for the Women's Movement. Amsterdam – 1980.-49,300 cards 4 reels.-ISBN: 0-8161-1473-0 – 1 – $400.00 – uk Hall [010]

CATALOG OF THE LIBRARY / Ohio. State University. School of Home Economics – 1977.-42,300 cards – 3r – 1 – $330.00 – 0-8161-1523-0 – uk Hall [640]

CATALOG OF THE LIBRARY / U. S. Geological Survey – (First Suppl., 1972.-178,000 cards 22 reels. $950.00 ISBN: 0-8161-1270-3; Second Suppl., 1975.-59,600 cards 8 reels. $475.00 ISBN: 0-8161-1267-3; Third Suppl., 1976.-95,400 cards 12 reels. $690.00 ISBN: 0-8161-1271-1) – 1964.-416,000 cards – 1 – uk Hall [910]

CATALOG OF THE LIBRARY / U. S. Naval Observatory. Washington, DC – 1976. 86,400 cards. 6 reels. ISBN 0-8161-1515-X – 1 – $655.00 – uk Hall [520]

CATALOG OF THE LIBRARY / University of Chicago. Oriental Institute – 1970. 284,000 cards. 32 reels. ISBN 0-8161-1283-5 – 1 – $1745.00 – uk Hall [950]

CATALOG OF THE LIBRARY / Whitney Museum of American Art. New York. Library – 1979. 28,200 cards. 2 reels. ISBN 0-8161-1428-5 – 1 – $220.00 – uk Hall [700]

CATALOG OF THE LIBRARY / Woods Hole Oceanographic Institution. Marine Biological Laboratory – 1971. 338,000 cards. 23 reels. ISBN 0-8161-1229-0 – 1 – $1215.00 – uk Hall [580]

CATALOG OF THE LIBRARY OF THE INTERNATIONAL ARCHIVES FOR THE WOMEN'S MOVEMENT / International Archives for the Women's Movement. Amsterdam – 1980. 49,300 cards on 4 reels – 1 – $365.00 export $440.00 – 0-8161-1473-0 – uk Hall [320]

CATALOG OF THE LIBRARY OF THE MARINE BIOLOGICAL LABORATORY AND THE WOODS HOLE OCEANOGRAPHIC INSTITUTION / Woods Hole Oceanographic Institution. Marine Biological Laboratory. Woods Hole, Massachusetts – 1971. 338,000 cards on 23 reels – 1 – $1,105.00 export $1,335.00 – 0-8161-1229-0 – uk Hall [574]

CATALOG OF THE LIBRARY OF THE MUSEUM OF MODERN ART / Museum of Modern Art. New York – 1976. 199,000 cards on 28 reels – 1 – $1,190.00 export $1,440.00 – 0-8161-1299-1 – uk Hall [700]

CATALOG OF THE LIBRARY OF THE WHITNEY MUSEUM OF AMERICAN ART / Whitney Museum of American Art. New York – 1979. 28,200 cards on 2 reels – 1 – $198.00 export $240.00 – 0-8161-1428-5 – uk Hall [700]

CATALOG OF THE LIBRARY. SECOND EDITION REVISED AND ENLARGED / University of London. Warburg Institute. Library – (First Suppl., 1971. 16,700 cards. 2 reels. $95.00 ISBN 0-8161-1235-5) – 1967. 118,000 cards. 24 reels. ISBN 0-8161-1385-8 – 1 – $1135.00 – uk Hall [900]

CATALOG OF THE MANUSCRIPT AND ARCHIVAL COLLECTIONS AND INDEX TO THE CORRESPONDENCE OF JOHN TORREY / Phillips, W Louis & Stuckey, Ronald L – (Available on microfilm by request) – 1973. 9900 cards – 9 – $75.00 export $83.00 – uk Hall [015]

A CATALOG OF THE MANUSCRIPTS PRESERVED IN THE LIBRARY OF THE UNIVERSITY OF CAMBRIDGE / Cambridge University. Library – v. 1-5. 1866-67 – 1 – 38.00 – us L of C Photodup [090]

CATALOG OF THE MELVILLE J. HERSKOVITS LIBRARY OF AFRICAN STUDIES, NORTHWESTERN UNIVERSITY LIBRARY, AND AFRICANA IN SELECTED LIBRARIES / Northwestern University – (Available on microfilm by request) – 1972. 119,000 cards – 1 – $825.00 export $995.00 – 0-8161-0921-4 – uk Hall [960]

CATALOG OF THE MODERN GREEK COLLECTION / University of Cincinnati – (Available on microfilm by request) – 1978. 59,900 cards – 1 – $430.00 export $520.00 – 0-8161-0089-6 – uk Hall [014]

CATALOG OF THE NAVAL OBSERVATORY LIBRARY / Naval Observatory. Washington, D.C. – 1976. 86,400 cards on 6 reels – 1 – $595.00 export $720.00 – 0-8161-1515-X – uk Hall [520]

CATALOG OF THE OLD SLAVE MART MUSEUM AND LIBRARY / Old Slave Mart Museum and Library. Charleston, South Carolina – (Available on microfilm by request) – 1978. 22,100 cards – 1 – $145.00 export $175.00 – 0-8161-0073-X – uk Hall [306]

CATALOG OF THE ORIENTAL INSTITUTE LIBRARY / University of Chicago – (Also available on 384 mf. $1,585.00 export $1,915.00. – ISBN 0-8161-1746-2) – 1970. 284,000 cards on 32 reels – 1,9 – $1,585.00 export $1,915.00 – 0-8161-1283-5 – uk Hall [950]

CATALOG OF THE P.K. YONGE LIBRARY OF FLORIDA HISTORY / University of Florida at Gainesville – 1977. 62,000 cards on 8 reels – 1 – $395.00 export $475.00 – 0-8161-1379-3 – uk Hall [978]

A CATALOG OF THE PRINTED BOOKS.. / Middle Temple. London. Library – (Alphabetically arranged, with an index of subjects, by C E A Bedwell) – Glasgow: Maclehose & Co. 3v. 1914 – 26mf – 9 – $39.00 – LLMC 84-307 – us L.L.M.C. [340]

CATALOG OF THE PUBLIC DOCUMENTS OF CONGRESS AND ALL DEPARTMENTS OF THE GOVERNMENT OF THE UNITED STATES / U.S. Superintendent of Documents – v. 1-25. 1893-1940. (all pub.) – 1 – us Princeton Micro [324]

CATALOG OF THE SOPHIA F. PALMER MEMORIAL LIBRARY / American Journal of Nursing. Sophia F. Palmer Memorial Library. New York – (Available on microfilm by request) – 1973. 29,600 cards – 9 – $190.00 export $230.00 – uk Hall [610]

CATALOG OF THE TAMIMENT INSTITUTE LIBRARY / New York University. Tamiment Institute Library – 1981.-63,000 cards 4 reels.-ISBN: 0-8161-1553-2 – 1 – $460.00 – uk Hall [010]

CATALOG OF THE THEATRE AND DRAMA COLLECTIONS : PART 2. THEATRE COLLECTION, BOOKS ON THE THEATRE / New York Public Library. Research Libraries. Theatre and Drama Collections – (First Suppl., 1973. 31,800 cards 3 reels. $310.00 ISBN-0-8161-1477-3) – 1967. 121,000 cards 9 reels – 1 – $790.00 – 0-8161-1476-5 – uk Hall [790]

CATALOG OF THE THEATRE AND DRAMA COLLECTIONS. 1967 : FIRST SUPPLEMENT / New York Public Library. Research Libraries – 1973. 31,800 cards on 3 reels – 1 – $280.00 export $340.00 – 0-8161-1477-3 – uk Hall [790]

CATALOG OF THE UNITED STATES GEOLOGICAL SURVEY LIBRARY / U.S. Department of the Interior. United States Geological Survey. Washington, D.C. – (Available on microfilm by request; First Supplement, 1972. 178,00 cards 22 reels. $865.00 export $1045.00. – ISBN 0-8161-1270-3; Second Supplement, 1975. 59,600 cards 8 reels. $430.00 export $520.00. – ISBN 0-8161-1267-3; Third Supplement, 1976. 95,400 cards 12 reels. $625.00 export $755.00. – ISBN 0-8161-1271-1) – 1964. 416,000 cards – 9 – $2,470.00 export $2,990.00 – uk Hall [550]

CATALOG OF THE WARBURG INSTITUTE LIBRARY : SECOND EDITION. REVISED AND ENLARGED / University of London. Warburg Institute. Library – (First Supplement, 1971. 16,700 cards. 2 reels. $95.00 export $115.00. – ISBN 0-8161-1235-5) – 1967. 118,000 cards on 24 reels – 1 – $1,030.00 export $1,245.00 – 0-8161-1385-8 – uk Hall [700]

CATALOG OF THE WESTERN HISTORY DEPARTMENT / Denver. Public Library – (First Supplement., 1975.-18,000 cards 2 reels. $145.00 ISBN: 0-8161-1395-5) – First Suppl., 1975.-18,000 cards 2 reels – 1 – uk Hall [978]

CATALOG OF THE WESTERN LANGUAGES COLLECTION / Hoover Institution – (First Suppl., 1972.-74,900 cards 10 reels. $805.00 ISBN: O-8161-1280-0; Second Suppl., 1977.-88,000 cards 6 reels. $925.00 ISBN: 0-8161-1431-5) – 1969.-1,087,000 cards 63 reels.-ISBN: 0-8161-1542-7 – 1 – $6850.00 – uk Hall [400]

CATALOG OF THE WESTERN LANGUAGES COLLECTION: SERIALS AND NEWSPAPERS / Hoover Institution – 1969.-46,800 cards 3 reels.-ISBN: 0-8161-1494-3 – 1 – $330.00 – uk Hall [010]

CATALOG OF THE YALE COLLECTION OF WESTERN AMERICANA / Yale University. Library – 1961. 55,500 cards. 4 reels. ISBN 0-8161-1455-2 – 1 – $435.00 – uk Hall [975]

CATALOGING AND CLASSIFICATION QUARTERLY / ed by Carter, Ruth C – v1- 1980- – 1, 9 ($175.00 in US $245.00 outside hardcopy subsc) – us Haworth [020]

LA CATALOGNE / Catalonia. Comissariat de Propaganda – Barcelona. 1963? Fiche W 783. (Blodgett Collection of Spanish Civil War Pamphlets) – 9 – us H.U. College Libr [946]

Catalogne, Gerard de *see* DIALOGUE ENTRE DEUX MONDES

Catalogne, Gideon de *see* RECUEIL DE CE QUI S'EST PASSE EN CANADA AU SUJET DE LA GUERRE: TANT DES ANGLAIS QUE DES IROQUOIS DEPUIS L'ANNEE 1682

CATALOGO / Colegio San Jose – 1938-1939. Villafranca. Badajoz – 1 – sp Bibl Santa Ana [946]

CATALOGO / Museo provincial de Bellas artes – Badajoz: Imp. Provincial, 1974 – sp Bibl Santa Ana [060]

CATALOGO ANNOTADO DOS LIBROS SOBRE O BRASIL...PERTENCENTES A J.C. RODRIGUES..., PARTE 1... / Rodrigues, Jose C – Rio de Janeiro: "Jornal do Commercio", 1907 – 1 – F341,57 – fr Armell [972]

CATALOGO CENTRALIZADO DE LA BIBLIOTECA JUSTICIALISTA / Argentine Republic. Ministerio de Agricultura y Ganaderia. Departamento de Bibliotecas – Buenos Aires, 1955 – 1 – CSUXADJ2510-B – us Hoover Inst Photo [020]

CATALOGO DE DOCUMENTOS RELATIVOS A LAS ISLAS FILIPINAS EXISTENTES EN EL ARCHIVO DE INDIAS DE SEVILLA / Bayle, Constantino – Madrid: Razon y Fe, 1926 – 1 – sp Bibl Santa Ana [950]

CATALOGO DE LA BIBLIOTECA NACIONAL DE ANTROPOLOGIA E HISTORIA = CATALOG OF THE NATIONAL LIBRARY OF ANTHROPOLOGY AND HISTORY / National Library of Anthropology and History. Mexico City – 1972. 143,000 cards on 20 reels – 1 – $875.00 export $1,060.00 – 0-8161-1315-7 – uk Hall [972]

CATALOGO DE LA EXPOSICION DE LIBROS DE GEOGRAFIA E HISTORIA DE VENEZUELA, CARACAS, AGOSTO DE 1946 / Instituto Panamericano de Geografia e Historia – Cuernavaca, Mor., Mexico, 1968 – 4mf – 9 – ne IDC [972]

CATALOGO DE LAS LABRAS HERALDICAS DE LA CIUDAD DE VILLANUEVA DE LA SERENA (BADAJOZ) / Cotta y Marquez de Prado, Fernando de et al – Madrid, s.i. 1958 – 1 – sp Bibl Santa Ana [946]

CATALOGO DE LAS LENGUAS. TOMO 1 / Hervas y Panduro, Lorenzo – 1800 – 1mf – 9 – Pta1,000.00 – 84-7848-112-5 – sp Pentalfa [440]

CATALOGO DE LAS LENGUAS. TOMO 2 / Hervas y Panduro, Lorenzo – 1801 – 2mf – 9 – Pta1,500.00 – 84-7848-113-3 – sp Pentalfa [440]

CATALOGO DE LAS LENGUAS. TOMO 3 / Hervas y Panduro, Lorenzo – 1802 – 1mf – 9 – Pta1,000.00 – 84-7848-114-1 – sp Pentalfa [440]

CATALOGO DE LAS LENGUAS. TOMO 4 / Hervas y Panduro, Lorenzo – 1804 – 1mf – 9 – Pta1,000.00 – 84-7848-115-X – sp Pentalfa [440]

CATALOGO DE LAS LENGUAS. TOMO 5 / Hervas y Panduro, Lorenzo – 1804 – 1mf – 9 – Pta1,000.00 – 84-7848-116-8 – sp Pentalfa [440]

CATALOGO DE LAS LENGUAS. TOMO 6 / Hervas y Panduro, Lorenzo – 1805 – 1mf – 9 – Pta1,000.00 – 84-7848-117-6 – sp Pentalfa [440]

CATALOGO DE LAS OBRAS / Davila y Figueroa, Marino – 1898 – 9 – 1.50f – sp Bibl Santa Ana [946]

CATALOGO DE LAS PINTURAS DE LA CUEVA DE MALTRAVIESO / Callejo Serrano, Carlos – Tirada aparte de la Cronica del 11th Congreso Nacional de Arqueologia – 1 – sp Bibl Santa Ana [930]

CATALOGO DE LOS ALUMNOS DEL COLEGIO DE SAN JOSE. 1904-1905 / Colegio San Jose – (Tambien 1905-1906; 1906-1907; 1908-1909; 1910-1911; 1914-1915; 1915-1916; 1909-1910; 1916-1917; 1917-1918; 1918-1919; 1929-1930; 1933-1934) – Madrid: Imp. Aurial, 1905 – 1 – sp Bibl Santa Ana [240]

CATALOGO DE LOS DOCUMENTOS REFERENTES A LA ANTIGUA PROVINCIA DE MARACAIBO, EXISTENTES EN EL ARCHIVO GENERAL DE INDIAS DE SEVILLA / Nectario Maria, H – Caracas: Univ. Cat. Andres Bello, 1973 – 4mf – 9 – ne IDC [972]

CATALOGO DE LOS DOCUMENTOS RELATIVO A LAS ISLAS FILIPINAS EXISTENTES EN EL ARCHIVO DE INDIAS DE SEVILLA. TOMO 7 / Bayle, Constantino – Barcelona, 1932; Madrid: Razon y Fe, 1932. 2v – 1 – sp Bibl Santa Ana [950]

CATALOGO DE LOS DOCUMENTOS RELATIVOS A LAS ISLAS FILIPINAS... / Torres y Lanzas, Pedro; ed by Bayle, Constantino – Madrid: Razon y Fe, 1928 – 9 – sp Bibl Santa Ana [950]

CATALOGO DE LOS DOCUMENTOS RELATIVOS A LAS ISLAS FILIPINAS... / Torres y Lanzas, Pedro – Madrid: Razon y Fe, 1927 – 1 – sp Bibl Santa Ana [950]

CATALOGO DE LOS DOCUMENTOS RELATIVOS A LAS ISLAS FILIPINAS, EXI EN EL ARCH. D. INDIAS DE SEVILLA – Par Pedro Torres y Lanzas. Barcelona, 1925. 51/2 – 8 – ne IDC [950]

CATALOGO DE LOS DOCUMENTOS RELATIVOS A LAS ISLAS FILIPINAS, EXI EN EL ARCH. D. INDIAS DE SEVILLA : PAR TORRES Y LANZAS, P. HISTORIA GENERAL DE FILIPINAS / ed by Pastells, Pablo – Barcelona. v1 1925 (1493-1572). v2 (1573-1587) – 19mf – 9 – ne IDC [950]

CATALOGO DE LOS DOCUMENTOS RELATIVOS A LAS ISLAS FILIPINAS EXISTENTES EN EL ARCHIVO DE INDIAS DE SEVILLA (1592-1602). BARCELONA, 1928 / Torres Lanzas, Pedro & Pastells, Pablo – Madrid: Razon y Fe, 1930 – 1 – sp Bibl Santa Ana [950]

CATALOGO DE LOS FONDOS AMERICANOS DEL ARCHIVO DE PROTOCOLOS DE SEVILLA... / Bayle, Constantino – Burgos: Razon y Fe, 1939 – 1 – sp Bibl Santa Ana [240]

CATALOGO DE LOS LIBROS...CACERES / DE LS – 1871 – 9 – 1.50f – sp Bibl Santa Ana [010]

CATALOGO DE LOS MANUSCRITOS RELATIVOS A LOS ANTIGUOS JESUITAS DE CHILE QUE SE CUSTODIAN EN LA BIBLIOTECA NACIONAL / Santiago de Chile, Biblioteca Nacional – Santiago: Impr. Ercilla, 1891 – 6mf – 9 – ne IDC [240]

CATALOGO DE LOS MATERIALES CODIGOLOGICOS....DE AUSPACH 1966... / Fernandez Caton, Jose Maria – Madrid: Graf. Calleja, 1966 – 1 – sp Bibl Santa Ana [946]

CATALOGO DE LOS OBISPOS DE CORDOBA. 1ST PARTE / Gomez Bravo, Juan – Cordoba: Simon Ortega y Leon, 1739 – 1 – sp Bibl Santa Ana [240]

CATALOGO DE LOS OBJETOS...EXPOSICION / Diaz Perez, Nicolas – 1883 – 9 – 1.50f – sp Bibl Santa Ana [900]

CATALOGO DE MODELACION IMPRESA 1958 / Minerva Extremena – Badajoz, 1958 – 1 – sp Bibl Santa Ana [020]

CATALOGO DE OBRAS DE DERECHO INTERNACIONAL... / Cuba. Oficina Panamericana – Habana, 1928 – 5mf – 1 – ILM-3867/1 – ne IDC [327]

CATALOGO DE OBRAS QUE EXISTEN EN ESTA BIBLIOTECA EN 30 DE MARZO DE 1952 / Biblioteca Publica Municipal – Trujillo: Imp. Sobrino de Benito Pena, s.a. – 1 – sp Bibl Santa Ana [020]

CATALOGO DE PASAJEROS A INDIAS DURANTE LOS SIGLOS 16, 17 Y 18. VOL 2 (1535-1538) / Bayle, Constantino & Bermudez Plata, Cristobal – Madrid: Razon y Fe, 1944 – 1 – sp Bibl Santa Ana [920]

CATALOGO DE TOMOS VARIOS (B.N. DEPARTAMENTO DE MANUSCRITOS) / Paz, J – Madrid, 1938 – 9 – sp Cultura [020]

CATALOGO DE UNA SERIE MISCELANEA PROCEDENTE DEL CONVENTO DE SAN ANTONIO DEL PRADO Y COLEGIOS JESUITICOS... / Hernandez Andres, J M – Madrid. v2. 1967-1968 – 1 – sp Bibl Santa Ana [240]

CATALOGO DEI MANOSCRITTI EBRAICI DELLA BIBLIOTHECA DELLA COMUNITA ISRAELITICA DI MANTOVA / Mortara, M – Livorno, 1878 – 1mf – ne IDC [270]

CATALOGO DEL ARCHIVO DE LA CASA DEL SOL / Rubio Merino, Pedro – Badajoz: Dip. Provincial, 1979 – 1 – sp Bibl Santa Ana [020]

CATALOGO DEL ARCHIVO DE LA DIPUTACION PROVINCIAL DE TERUEL / Floriano Cumbreno, Antonio C – Madrid: Tip. de Archivos, 1930 – sp Bibl Santa Ana [020]

CATALOGO DEL ARCHIVO DE MUSICA DE LA REAL CAPILLA DE PALACIO / Garcia, Marcellan, Jose – Madrid: Editorial del Patrimonic Nacional, 19– – 1 – us U.W. Library [946]

CATALOGO DEL CONCURSO-EXPOSICION DE FOTOGRAFIAS SOBRE TEMAS CACERENOS / Junta Provincial de Turismo – Caceres, 1957 – sp Bibl Santa Ana [338]

CATALOGO DEL "EL COJO ILUSTRADO", 1892-1915 / Perea Romero, M; ed by Catala, J A – (v1: A-K; v2: L-Z) – Caracas. 2v – 7mf – 9 – ne IDC [972]

CATALOGO DEL MUSAO PROVINCIAL DE ANTIGUEDADES DE BARCELONA / Molins, Antonio Elias de – Barcelona, 1888 – 6mf, xiii/502p – 9 – $15.00 – fr Bibl Nationale [930]

CATALOGO DEL MUSEO DE CIENCIAS NATURALES / Janer, F – 1,279mf – 9 – sp Cultura [500]

CATALOGO DELLA RACCOLTA COLOMBIANA = CATALOG OF THE COLUMBUS COLLECTIONS. BERIO CIVIC LIBRARY / Civica Biblioteca Berio. Genoa – 1963. 3100 cards on 1 reel – 1 – $78.00 export $95.00 – 0-8161-1555-9 – uk Hall [910]

CATALOGO DELLE LINGUE CONOSCIUTE E NOTIZIA DELLA LORO AFFINATA, E DIVERSITA / Hervas y Panduro, Lorenzo – Cesena, 1784 – 3mf – 9 – ne IDC [400]
CATALOGO DELLE LINGUE CONOSCIUTE E NOTIZIA DELLA LORO AFFINITA E DIVERSITA / Hervas Y Panduro, Lorenzo – (Linguistic series). 1784 – 9 – fr Hachette [400]
CATALOGO EXPOSICION DE TROFEOS DE CAZA MAYOR 1970 / Jefatura provincial Servicio Pesca Continental, Caza y Parques Nacionales – Caceres: Tip. Extremadura, 1970 – 1 – sp Bibl Santa Ana [946]
CATALOGO EXPOSICION INTERNATIONAL DE ARTESANIA – Caceres, 4 a 11 Enero, 1953 – sp Bibl Santa Ana [700]
CATALOGO FORMADO POR...DE LOS PRINCIPALES ARTICULOS QUE COMPONEN LA SELECTA LIBRERIA DE D.J. BOEHL DE FABER / Gallardo, Bartolome Jose – Madrid: Ed. Reus, 1922. B.R.A.H. 81. pp. 478-494; y 82, pp. 69-94, 165-190 y 248-267 – 1 – sp Bibl Santa Ana [946]
CATALOGO GENERAL DE LA EXPOSICION BETICO EXTREMENA CELEBRADA EN EL ALCAZAR DE SEVILLA – 1874 – 9 – $1.50f – sp Bibl Santa Ana [900]
CATALOGO GENERAL DE LIBROS IMPRESOS, 1982-1987 – 573mf – 9 – £2,265.00 – uk Chadwyck [020]
CATALOGO GENERAL DE LIBROS IMPRESOS, HASTA 1981 – 4409mf – 9 – £16,155.00 – uk Chadwyck [020]
CATALOGO GENERAL DE PRODUCTOS FITOSANITARIOS – Badajoz: Agrotecnica Extremena, 1970 – sp Bibl Santa Ana [630]
CATALOGO GENERAL DEL ARCHIVO ARQUIDIOCESANO DE CARACAS, 1964 / Suria, J – Madrid: Escuelas Profesionales "Sagrado Corazon de Jesus", 1964 – 1mf – 9 – ne IDC [972]
CATALOGO GENERAL POR ORDEN ALFABETICO DE AUTORES DE LA BIBLIOTECA DE LA RECOLECCION DOMINICANA DE SANTIAGO DE CHILE / Recoleta Dominica, Santiago de Chile, Biblioteca – Santiago: Impr. "La Ilustracion", 1910 – 5mf – 9 – ne IDC [972]
CATALOGO MANUSCRITO DE LA BIBLIOTECA DE LA UNIVERSIDAD CENTRAL DE MADRID / Villaamil y Castro, J – Madrid, 1878 – 762mf – 9 – sp Cultura [020]
CATALOGO MONUMENTAL DE ESPANA : CACERES (1914-1916) / Melida, Jose Ramon – Madrid: Razon y Fe, 1926 – 1 – sp Bibl Santa Ana [946]
CATALOGO MONUMENTAL DE ESPANA. PROVINCIA DE BADAJOZ. TEXTO 2 / Melida, Jose Ramon – Madrid: Imp. de la Ciudad Lineal, 1926 – 1 – sp Bibl Santa Ana [946]
CATALOGO MONUMENTAL DE ESPANA. PROVINCIA DE CACERES. (1914-1916) / Melida, Jose Ramon – Madrid: Nº de Instruccion Publica y Bellas Artes, Texto 2. 1924 – 1 – sp Bibl Santa Ana [946]
CATALOGO MONUMENTAL DE ESPANA. PROVINCIA DE CACERES. TEXTO 1 / Melida, Jose Ramon – Madrid: Imp. de la Ciudad Lineal, 1924 – 1 – sp Bibl Santa Ana [946]
CATALOGO... OBISPOS DE CORDOBA / Gomez Bravo, Juan – 1739 – 9 – $1.50f – sp Bibl Santa Ana [240]
CATALOGO OFICIAL ILUSTRADO DE LA EXPOSICION DE LAS OBRAS DE FRANCISCO DE ZURBARAN / Viniegra, Salvador – Madrid: J. Lacoste, 1905 – 1 – sp Bibl Santa Ana [946]
CATALOGO PARCIAL I DEL ARCHIVO HISTORICO DIOCESANO DE SAN CRISTOBAL DE LAS CASAS, CHIAPAS / Pedrero Nieto, G – San Cristobal de las Casas: Centro de Investigaciones Ecologicas del Sureste, Agosto de 1978 – 2mf – 9 – ne IDC [972]
CATALOGO RAZONADO DE OBRAS ANONIMAS Y SEDONIMAS DE AUTORES DE LA COMPANIA DE JESUS / Uriarte, Jose E – Madrid. 1904-16. 5v – 1 – 46.00 – us L of C Photodup [010]
CATALOGO RAZONADO Y CRITICO...EXTREMADURA / Barrantes Moreno, Vicente – 1865 – 9 – 1.50f – sp Bibl Santa Ana [946]
CATALOGO SISTEMATICO E RAGIONATO DE TESTACEI DELLE DUE SICILIE / Costa, O G – Z-482 2. 1829 – 8 – ne IDC [590]
CATALOGO Y GUIA DE LA RIQUEZA DE EXTREMADURA – (Dibujos) – 1 – sp Bibl Santa Ana [946]
CATALOGO Y GUIA DE LA RIQUEZA DE EXTREMADURA – (Texto) – 1 – sp Bibl Santa Ana [946]
CATALOGO...BIBLIOTECA INSTITUTO...CACERES / Lopez Sanchez, Eulogio – 1871 – 9 – 1.50f – sp Bibl Santa Ana [020]
CATALOGO-GUIA 1950 / Mahizflor. Museo Taurino. Aceuchal – Badajoz: Tip. Arqueros, 1950 – 1 – sp Bibl Santa Ana [020]
CATALOGO...INFORMACIONES GENEALOGICAS DE LOS PRETENDIENTES A CARGOS DE SANTO OFICIO – Valladolid, 1928 – 9 – sp Cultura [920]
CATALOGOMETODICO Y RAZONADO DE LOS COLEOPTEROS OBSERVADOS IN CATALUNA / Cuni y Martorell, M & Martorell y Pena, M – Barcelona, 1876. viii,360p. Z-1158/2 – 8 – ne IDC [590]
CATALOGS / American Baptist Theological Seminary. Nashville, Tennessee – 1980-85 – 1 – $7.70 – us Baptist [240]
CATALOGS / Bluefield College. Virginia – 1922-55 – 1 – $109.06 – us Baptist [240]
CATALOGS / Florida Memorial College – 1910-80 – 1 – $47.80 – us A.B.H.S. [370]
CATALOGS, 1870-1935 / Straight University. New Orleans University – 1 – $90.00 – us Amistad [370]
CATALOGS AND COLLEGE RECORDS / Baylor University College of Medicine. Houston, Texas – 1900-57 – 1 – $127.54 – us Baptist [610]
CATALOGS AND COLLEGE RECORDS / Blue Mountain College. Blue Mountain, Mississippi – 1873-Apr 1955 – 1 – $202.58 – us Baptist [240]
CATALOGS AND COLLEGE RECORDS / Brandon. Vermont. Brandon Seminary – 1832-1866 – 1 – $5.00 – us Baptist [240]
CATALOGS AND COLLEGE RECORDS / Carver School of Missions and Social Work (Woman's Missionary Union Training School for Christian Workers). Louisville, Ky – 1908-55 – 1 – $91.28 – us Baptist [240]
CATALOGS AND COLLEGE RECORDS / Clear Creek Baptist School. Pineville, Kentucky – 1936-82 – 1 – $28.80 – us Baptist [370]
CATALOGS AND COLLEGE RECORDS / Decatur Baptist College. Decatur, Texas – 1899-1906 – 1 – $32.76 – us Baptist [240]
CATALOGS AND COLLEGE RECORDS / Grand Canyon College. Phoenix, Arizona – 1949-55 – 1 – $21.35 – us Baptist [240]
CATALOGS AND COLLEGE RECORDS / Greenville Woman's College. South Carolina – 1857-1937 – 1 – $173.74 – us Baptist [240]
CATALOGS AND COLLEGE RECORDS / Murfreesboro. North Carolina. Chowan College – 1886-1916 – 1 – $89.04 – us Baptist [240]
CATALOGS AND COLLEGE RECORDS / New Orleans Baptist Theological Seminary. (Formerly: Baptist Bible Institute). New Orleans, Louisiana – 1918-54 – 1 – $110.95 – us Baptist [240]
CATALOGS AND COLLEGE RECORDS / Norman College. Norman Park, Georgia – (Lacking 1904-06) – 1903-46 – 1 – $79.94 – us Baptist [240]
CATALOGS AND COLLEGE RECORDS / Roger Williams University. Nashville, Tenn – 1881-93 – 1 – $12.95 – us Baptist [370]
CATALOGS AND COLLEGE RECORDS / Southern Baptist College. Walnut Ridge, Ark – 1942-54 – 1 – $30.73 – us Baptist [240]
CATALOGS AND COLLEGE RECORDS / Southern Baptist Theological Seminary – (Also: History of the establishment and organization of the Southern Baptist Theological Seminary, Greenville, S.C., 1860) – 1859-89 – 1 – $23.80 – us Baptist [240]
CATALOGS AND COLLEGE RECORDS / Stetson University. DeLand, Florida – 1885-1953 – 1 – $466.06 – us Baptist [240]
THE CATALOGS OF THE ART EXHIBITION CATALOG COLLECTION *see* ART EXHIBITION CATALOGS SUBJECT INDEX, 1977-1990
CATALOGS OF THE ASIA LIBRARY / Michigan. University – 1978 – 25r – 1 – $2690.00 – 0-8161-1537-0 – uk Hall [950]
CATALOGS OF THE FAR EASTERN LIBRARY. 1973 : AUTHOR-TITLE CHINESE CATALOG / University of Chicago – 16r – 1 – $1,180.00 – 0-8161-1332-7 – uk Hall [950]
CATALOGS OF THE FAR EASTERN LIBRARY. 1973 : AUTHOR-TITLE JAPANESE CATALOG / University of Chicago – 8r – 1 – $645.00 – 0-8161-1321-1 – uk Hall [950]
CATALOGS OF THE FAR EASTERN LIBRARY. 1973 : CLASSIFIED CATALOG AND SUBJECT INDEX / University of Chicago – 12r – 1 – $995.00 – 0-8161-1365-3 – uk Hall [950]
CATALOGS OF THE FAR EASTERN LIBRARY. 1973 / University of Chicago – 36r – 1 – $2,475.00 set – uk Hall [950]
CATALOGS OF THE SCRIPPS INSTITUTION OF OCEANOGRAPHY LIBRARY : FIRST SUPPLEMENT. 1973. AUTHOR-TITLE CATALOG / University of California at San Diego. Scripps Institution of Oceanography – 6r – 1 – $295.00 – 0-8161-1261-4 – uk Hall [550]
CATALOGS OF THE SCRIPPS INSTITUTION OF OCEANOGRAPHY LIBRARY : SECOND SUPPLEMENT. 1980. SUBJECT CATALOG / University of California at San Diego. Scripps Institution of Oceanography – 1r – 1 – $200.00 – 0-8161-1406-4 – uk Hall [550]
CATALOGS OF VOCAL MUSIC / Ditson, Oliver – Boston. 1879, 1882, 1898, 1900, 1901, 1903-04, 1913, 1915, 1924 – 1 – $23.00 – us L of C Photodup [780]
CATALOGUE / British Film Institute. London – (First suppl., 1903.-25,000 cards 2 reels. $265.00 ISBN: 1-8161-1435-8) – uk Hall [410]
CATALOGUE / Ecole Biblique et Archeologique Francaise. Jerusalem – 1975.-215,000 cards 18 reels.-ISBN: 0-8161-1226-6 – 1 – $1545.00 – uk Hall [240]
CATALOGUE / Hok Hoi Association Library. Hong Kong – 1 – uk Microform Academic [950]
CATALOGUE / Holkham Hall. Norfolk. England – Holkham MS 749, 1773 and ACCOUNTS, ETC – 1 – uk Microform Academic [025]
CATALOGUE / Moravian Archives. Bristol – 1 – uk Microform Academic [240]
CATALOGUE / Moravian Archives. Manchester – 7 – uk Microform Academic [240]
CATALOGUE. / American Law Association – Chicago?. 1893. 3-24 numb. LL-923 – 1 – us L of C Photodup [340]
CATALOGUE : POETRY COLLECTION, LOCKWOOD MEMORIAL LIBRARY – Buffalo: State University of New York, [1972?] – us Res Libr [810]
CATALOGUE 1930-32 / Royal Empire Society – 1 – uk Microform Academic [941]
CATALOGUE AND ERRATA OF THE RECORDS OF HOLY TRINITY (OLD SWEDES) CHURCH / Burr, Horace – Wilmington, Charles L. Story Co., 1919. Delaware Reel 2. (The Cox Library Collection) – 5 – us Americana [978]
CATALOGUE AND INDEX TO THE MISCELLANEOUS MANUSCRIPTS IN THE ARCHIVES OF THE MARQUESS OF BATH / Bath. Archives (Marquess). Longleat – Ms Folio, 1864 – 1 – uk Microform Academic [090]
CATALOGUE CARTE ANTIQUAE ET MISCELLANEAE / Lambeth Palace. Library – 1 – uk Microform Academic [240]
CATALOGUE D'ARTICLES DE PERIODIQUES-ARTS DECORATIFS ET BEAUX ARTS / Bibliotheque Forney. Paris – 1972.-50,700 entries 8 reels.-ISBN: 0-8161-1277-0 – 1 – $360.00 – uk Hall [700]
CATALOGUE DE FONDS ROUSSEL / Bibliotheque Municipale. Mende – 6 fiches. (Rare Books Catalogs) – 9 – 15.00 – fr Bibl Nationale [010]
CATALOGUE DE LA BIBLIOTHEQUE / Teyler. Foundation – Haarlem, 1885-1888 – 21mf – 9 – 8578/1 – ne IDC [020]
CATALOGUE DE LA BIBLIOTHEQUE DE LA LEGISLATURE DE LA PROVINCE DE QUEBEC / Quebec. Bibliotheque de la legislature – Quebec: R Paradis, Imprimeur du roi, 1932-1933. SEM105P1986 – 6mf – 9 – Can$13.50 – cn Bibl Nat [320]
CATALOGUE DE LA BIBLIOTHEQUE DE L'APOSTOLAT DES BONS LIVRES : SUPPLEMENT / Apostolat des bons livres. Bibliotheque – Quebec: Typ. Laflamme and Proulx, 1910. SEM105P1608 – 2mf – 9 – Can$4.50 – cn Bibl Nat [240]
CATALOGUE DE LA BIBLIOTHEQUE DE L'ECOLE BIBLIQUE ET ARCHEOLOGIQUE FRANCAISE = CATALOGUE OF THE LIBRARY OF THE FRENCH BIBLICAL AND ARCHEOLOGICAL SCHOOL / Ecole Biblique et Archeologique Francaise. Jerusalem – 1975. 215,000 cards on 18 reels – 1 – $1,405.00 export $1,700.00 – 0-8161-1226-6 – uk Hall [200]
CATALOGUE DE LA BIBLIOTHEQUE DE L'OEUVRE DES BONS LIVRES, ERIGEE A MONTREAL / Bibliotheque paroissiale de Notre-Dame – Montreal: Imprimerie de Louis Perrault, 1845. SEM105P1577 – 1mf – 9 – Can$2.25 – cn Bibl Nat [020]
CATALOGUE DE LA BIBLIOTHEQUE DU MINISTERE DES AFFAIRES ETRANGERES – Bruxelles, 1877-1899 – 26mf – 9 – ILM-2440/1 – ne IDC [327]
CATALOGUE DE LA COLLECTION DE COLEOPTERES DE M. LE BARON DEJEAN / Dejean, P F M A – Paris, 1821. viii,136p.Z-1178/2 – 8 – ne IDC [590]
CATALOGUE DE L'ANCIEN FONDS DE LA BIBLIOTHEQUE INGUIMBERTINE / Bibliotheque Municipale. Carpentras – 33mf. (Rare Books Catalogs) – 9 – $82.00 – fr Bibl Nationale [010]
CATALOGUE DE L'HERBIER DE SYRIE / Puel, T & Gaillardot, C – Paris. 1854-55. B-1047 2 – 8 – ne IDC [580]
CATALOGUE DE L'HISTOIRE DE L'AFRIQUE / Bibliotheque National. France. Dept des Imprimes – Paris, 1895 – 1 – us Res Libr [960]
CATALOGUE DE L'HISTOIRE DE L'AFRIQUE / Bibliotheque Nationale. Paris. Dept. des Imprimes – Paris. 1895. BA-241 2 – 8 – ne IDC [900]
CATALOGUE DE L'HISTOIRE D'ESPAGNE ET DU PORTUGAL / Bibliotheque Nationale – Paris. 1883. 507, 126p. (Historical Studies Series) – 9 – 33.00 – fr Bibl Nationale [946]
CATALOGUE DE LIVRES RARES ET PRECIEUX...COMPOSANT LA BIBLIOTHEQUE DE M. ALPHONSE-L. PINART ET COMPRENANT...LA BIBLIOTHEQUE...DE M. L'ABBE BRASSEUR DE BOURBOURG – Paris: Vve Labitte, 1883 – 1 – F130.93 – fr Armell [090]
CATALOGUE DE MANUSCRITS ARABES CHRETIENS CONSERVES AU CAIRE / Georg, Graf – Citta del Vaticano, 1934 – 9mf – 8 – ne Slangenburg [240]
CATALOGUE DE MUSEE...DONNE PAR M. ACHILLE JUBINAL...A LA VILLE DE BAGNERES-DE-BIGORRE: 1852-1857 / Musee de Peinture et de Sculpture. Bagneres-de-Bigorre – Dossun, 1864 – 1mf, 77p – 9 – $6.00 – fr Bibl Nationale [700]
CATALOGUE DE RARETES BIBLIOGRAPHIQUES CANADIENNES: COMPRENANT 200 OUVRAGES / Booker, Alfred – Montreal?, 1869. 00852. (Pre-1900 Canadiana) – 9 – cn C.I.H.M. [010]
CATALOGUE DE SERVICE / Bibliotheque Interuniversitaire. Montpellier. Bibliotheque de la Faculte de Medecine – 11 fiches. (Rare Books Catalogs) – 9 – 27.00 – fr Bibl Nationale [010]
CATALOGUE DES ACTES DE PHILIPPE AUGUSTE / Delisle, L – Paris, 1856 – 14mf – ne IDC [944]
CATALOGUE DES BROCHURES REVOLUTIONNAIRES DE LA COLLECTION CHARPENTIER / Bibliotheque Municipale. Arras – 3 fiches. (Rare Books Catalogs) – 9 – 8.00 – fr Bibl Nationale [944]
CATALOGUE DES CATALOGUES DE VENTES D'ART = CATALOG OF THE CATALOGS OF SALES OF ART / Bibliotheque Forney. Paris – 1972 – 1r – 1 – $240.00 – 0-8161-1478-1 – uk Hall [700]
CATALOGUE DES COLEOPTERES CARABIQUES DE LA TRIBU DES CARABIDES / Gehin, J J B – Nancy, 1876 – 72p – 8 – ne IDC [590]
CATALOGUE DES COLEOPTERES CARNASSIERS AQUATIQUES... / Branden, C van den – Bruxelles, 1885. 188p (Ann. Soc. Entom. Belgique, v29) – 8 – ne IDC [590]
CATALOGUE DES COLEOPTERES DE FRANCE / Grenier, A – Paris, 1863. Z/1309/2 – 8 – ne IDC [590]
CATALOGUE DES COLEOPTERES DE LA COLLECTION DE J.B. GEHIN... / Gehin, J J B – Metz, 1851-1852 – 2pts – 8 – ne IDC [590]

CATALOGUE DES COLLECTIONS ORNITHOLOGIQUES / Bouvier, A - Z360. 1874 - 9 - ne IDC [590]
CATALOGUE DES DIATOMEES DE L'ILE CAMPBELL ET DE LA NOUVELLE ZELANDE / Petit, P C M - Paris. 1877. B-6392 2 - 8 - ne IDC [980]
CATALOGUE DES DOCUMENTS MICROFILMES PAR L'EQUIPE CIPEA/CRDI; MISSION DU BURUNDI - 1982 - 9 - $5.00 - 92-9053-203-3 - et ILRI [636]
CATALOGUE DES DOCUMENTS MICROFILMES PAR L'EQUIPE CIPEA/CRDI; MISSION DU CAMEROUN - 1982 - 9 - $5.00 - 92-9053-204-1 - et ILRI [636]
CATALOGUE DES GENTILSHOMMES DE NORMANDIE. / La Roque, Louis de - Paris: E Dentu, 1864. SEM105P85 - 2mf - 9 - Can$4.50 - cn Bibl Nat [360]
CATALOGUE DES HEMIPTERES D'EUROPE ET DU BASSIN DE LA MEDITERRANEE / Puton, A - Paris, 1869. Z-1564/2 - 8 - ne IDC [590]
CATALOGUE DES IMPRESSIONS DUE XVI SIECLE / Bibliotheque Municipale. Rouen - Fichier Jubert. 65mf. (Rare Books Catalogs) - 9 - $161.00 - fr Bibl Nationale [010]
CATALOGUE DES LARVES COLEOPTERES CONNUES JUSQU'A CE JOUR / Chapuis, F & Candeze, E C A - Liege, 1853. 313p. 9 pls. Z-1131/2 - 8 - ne IDC [590]
CATALOGUE DES LEPIDOPTERES D'ALSACE / Peyerimhoff, H De - Colmar, 1880-82.2v. Z-1547/2 - 8 - ne IDC [590]
CATALOGUE DES LEPIDOPTERES QUI COMPOSENT LA COLLECTION DE FEU MR. FRANCK / Franck, J R - Strassburg, 1826. ii,108p. Z/1258/2 - 8 - ne IDC [590]
CATALOGUE DES LIVRES APPARTENANT A LA BIBLIOTHEQUE DE LA CHAMBRE D'ASSEMBLEE / Canada. Bas-Canada. Parlement. Chambre d'Assemblee. Bibliotheque - Quebec: Imprime par Frechette and Cie, 1835. SEM105P132 - 1mf - 9 - Can$2.25 - cn Bibl Nat [324]
CATALOGUE DES LIVRES DE L'IMPRIMERIE ARMENIENNE DE SAINT-LAZARE - Venise, 1894 - 2mf - 9 - ne IDC [460]
CATALOGUE DES LIVRES D'HISTOIRE NATURELLE ET PRINCIPALEMENTS D'ENTOMOLOGIE COMPOSANT LA BIBLIOTHEQUE DE... / Audouin, J V - Paris, 1842 - 3mf - ne IDC [590]
CATALOGUE DES LIVRES ORIENTAUX ET AUTRES COMPOSANT LA BIBLIOTHEQUE DE FEU M. GARCIN DE TASSY : SUIVI DU CATALOGUE DES MANUSCRITS HINDOUSTANIS, PERSANS, ARABES, TURCS 111=DELONCLE, M F - Paris: A Labitte, 1879 - us Res Libr [950]
CATALOGUE DES LIVRES QUI SE DONNENT EN LECTURE - Nantes: [S.l.n.], 1793 - fr Armell [020]
CATALOGUE DES LIVRES RARES ET SINGULIERS DE LA BIBLIOTHEQUE DE M. L'ABBE SEPHER. DONT DA VENTE SE FERA LE LUNDI 6 MARS 1786 / Sepher, Pierre Jacques - Paris: Fournier, 1786 - 1 - us U.W. Library [070]
CATALOGUE DES MANUSCRITS ARABES DE LA BIBLIOTHEQUE NATIONALE / Slane, B William MacGuckin de - Paris: Imprimerie nationale, 1883-1895 - 9mf - 9 - fr Bibl Nationale [470]
CATALOGUE DES MANUSCRITS ARABES DES NOUVELLES ACQUISITIONS (1884-1924) / Blochet, Edgar - Paris: E. Leroux, 1925 - 5mf - 9 - fr Bibl Nationale [470]
CATALOGUE DES MANUSCRITS ET XYLOGRAPHES ORIENTAUX DE LA BIBLIOTHEQUE IMPERIALE PUBLIQUE DE ST PETERSBOURG / Dorn, B A - St. Petersburg, 1852. 719p. BR-10,875/1 - 9 - ne IDC [010]
CATALOGUE DES MANUSCRITS ETHIOPIENS DE LA COLLECTION ANTOINE D'ABBADIE / Chaine, M - Paris, 1921 - 2mf - 9 - ne IDC [090]
CATALOGUE DES MANUSCRITS GRECS DE LA BIBLIOTHEQUE IMPERIALE PUBLIQUE - E. de Muralt, comp. St. Petersburg, 1864. 100p. BR-10,855/1 - 9 - ne IDC [010]
CATALOGUE DES MOLLUSQUES TESTACES DES MERS D'EUROPE / Petit de la Saussaye, S - Z-706 2. 1869 - 8 - ne IDC [590]
CATALOGUE DES OISEAUZ D'EUROPE / Hamonville, J C L T d' - Z-1791 2. 1876 - 8 - ne IDC [590]
CATALOGUE DES PERIODIQUES SLAVES ET RELATIFS AUX ETUDES SLAVES DES BIBLIOTHEQUES DE PARIS / Unbegaun, B O - Paris, 1929 - 5mf - 9 - ne IDC [947]
CATALOGUE DES PLANTES DU JARDIN BOTANIQUE DU GYMNASE DE VOLHYNIE A KRZEMIENIEC / Besser, W S JG von - Krzemieniec, 1811 - 3mf - ne IDC [580]
CATALOGUE DES PLANTES DU JARDIN BOTANIQUE ETABLI A BESANCON... / Morel, J FN - Besancon, [1805] - 2mf - ne IDC [580]
CATALOGUE DES PLANTES INDIGENES DES PYRENEES ET DU BAS LANGUEDOC / Bentham, G - Paris. 1826. B-31 2 - 8 - ne IDC [580]
CATALOGUE DES PLANTES OMISES DANS LA BOTANOGRAPHIE BELGIQUE ET DANS LES FLORES DU NORD DE LA FRANCE / Desmazieres, J B H J - Lille. 1823 - 8 - ne IDC [580]
CATALOGUE DES PLANTES QUI CROISSENT NATURELLEMENT AUX ENVIRONS DE MARSEILLE AND SUPPLEMENT / Castagne, J L M - Aix. 1845-51 - 8 - ne IDC [580]
CATALOGUE DES TABLEAUX... PRECEDE D'UNE NOTICE HISTORIQUE PAR JULES LENGLART. / Musee. Lille - Lille: Lefebvre-Ducrocq, 1893 - 5mf, xxvi/381p - 9 - $12.00 - fr Bibl Nationale [700]
CATALOGUE DU FONDS ANCIEN / Bibliotheque Municipale. Fougeres - 18 fiches. (Rare Books Catalogs) - 9 - 45.00 - fr Bibl Nationale [010]
CATALOGUE DU FONDS ANCIEN E'IMPRIMES / Bibliotheque Municipale. Beauvais - 4mf. (Rare Books Catalogs) - 9 - $10.00 - fr Bibl Nationale [010]
CATALOGUE DU JARDIN DE LA REUNION / Richard, [J M] C - [Saint Denis], 1856 - 2mf - ne IDC [580]
CATALOGUE DU JARDIN DES PLANTES DE A. DE RAZOUMOFFSKY A GORENSKI PRES DE MOSCOU / Fischer, FE L von - M. 1812. B-5565 2 - 8 - ne IDC [580]
CATALOGUE DU JARDIN DES PLANTES DE... A. DE RAZOUMOFFSKY... A GORENSKI PRES DE MOSCOU / Fischer, FE L von - M. 1808 - 3mf - ne IDC [580]
CATALOGUE DU JARDIN DES PLANTES DE... A. DE RAZOUMOFFSKY... A GORENSKI PRES DE MOSCOU / Fischer, FE L von - M. 1812 - 2mf - ne IDC [580]
CATALOGUE GENERAL DES ANTIQUITES EGYPTIENNES DU MUSEE DE CAIRE : FAYENCEGEFAESSE / Bissing, FW von - Wien, 1902 - 3mf - 9 - ne IDC [930]
CATALOGUE GENERAL DES ANTIQUITIES EGYPTIENNES DU MUSEE DE CAIRE : METALLGEFAESSE / Bissing, FW von - Wien, 1901 - 2mf - 9 - ne IDC [930]
CATALOGUE GENERAL DES ANTIQUITIES EGYPTIENNES DU MUSEE DE CAIRE : STEINGEFAESSE / Bissing, FW von - Wien, 1907 - 5mf - 9 - ne IDC [930]
CATALOGUE GENERAL DES ANTIQUITIES EGYPTIENNES DU MUSEE DE CAIRE : TONGEFAESSE / Bissing, FW von - Wien, 1913 - 2mf - 9 - ne IDC [930]
CATALOGUE GENERAL DES MONUMENTS D'ABYDOS DECOUVERTS PENDANT LES FOUILLES DE CETTE VILLE / Mariette, A - Paris, 1880 - 11mf - 9 - ne IDC [720]
CATALOGUE GENERAL DES PERIODIQUES DE LA BIBLIOTHEQUE NATIONALE DES ORIGINES A 1959 - France: Chadwick-Healey, 1987 - F28,000.00 - 2-86976-010-8 - fr Bibl Nationale [073]
CATALOGUE (ILLUSTRATED) / Japan - Of The National treasures of Japan,BY Mombusho. Index. CH-536 2. 1927 - 8 - ne IDC [700]
CATALOGUE ILLUSTRE DE LA COLLECTION LAMARCK / Lamarck, J B A P M de - Geneve, 1910-1918 - 19mf - ne IDC [580]
CATALOGUE ILLUSTRE ET DESCRIPTIF DES VIGNES, BAIES ET ROSES CULTIVEES ET EN VENTE AUX VIGNOBLES BEACONSFIELD (PRES LA POINTE-CLAIRE, P.Q.) / Gallagher & Gauthier - s.l.: s.n., 1880 (Montreal: Cie. d'Imprimerie canadienne). 04354. (Pre-1900 Canadiana) - 9 - cn C.I.H.M. [580]
CATALOGUE LATIN ET FRANCOIS DES PLANTES VIVACES,... / Buchoz, P J - Londres, 1786 - 2mf - ne IDC [580]
CATALOGUE MANUSCRIT DE SA COLLECTION / Feaux, M - 9 - F90.00 - fr Ethnologie [025]
CATALOGUE METHODIQUE DES LEPIDOPTERES D'EUROPE / Duponchel, P A J - Paris, 1844. xxx,523p. Z/1208-2 - 8 - ne IDC [590]
CATALOGUE METHODIQUE ET RAISONNE DES LEPIDOPTERES DES ENVIRONS DE DOUAI / Foucart, A - Douai, Paris, 1876. 127p. (Mem. Soc. Agric. Sci. Arts, Douai). Z/1254/2 - 8 - ne IDC [590]
A CATALOGUE (MIMEO.) / Maritime Baptist Historical Collection, in the Library of Acadia University - (Index) - Kentville, Nova Scotia. 1955 - 1mf - 9 - ne IDC [240]
CATALOGUE OF 17TH CENTURY PORTRAITS IN THE NATIONAL PORTRAIT GALLERY, 1625-1714 - London - 11mf - 9 - us UMI [750]
CATALOGUE OF A COLLECTION OF AMERICAN BIRDS / Sclater, P L - Z 1918 2. 1861-1862 - 8 - ne IDC [590]
CATALOGUE OF A COLLECTION OF BIBLES AND PORTIONS OF THE BIBLE IN VARIOUS LANGUAGES... / Allan, T R - Leipzig, 1883 - 1mf - ne IDC [012]
CATALOGUE OF A COLLECTION OF BIBLES AND PORTIONS OF THE BIBLE IN VARIOUS LANGUAGES AS ALSO OF BIBLIOGRAPHICAL WORKS ON BIBLES AND ESPECIALLY ON THOSE IN THE ABOVE COLLECTION... / Allan, T R - Leipzig, 1883. 56p - 1mf - 9 - ne IDC [025]
CATALOGUE OF ARABIC MANUSCRIPTS FROM GHANA AND ADJACENT TERRITORIES FROM INSTITUTE OF AFRICAN STUDIES : UNIVERSITY OF GHANA, LEGON / Wilks, Ivor & Ferguson, Phyllis - Chicago, IL: Uni of Chicago, Photodup Dept, 1974 - 1 - us Res Libr [010]
CATALOGUE OF ARTICLES SHOWN AT THE PROVINCIAL EXHIBITION, HELD AT MONTREAL AND INAUGURATED BY HIS ROYAL HIGHNESS THE PRINCE OF WALES, AUGUST, 1860 - Montreal: Printed by M Langmoore and Co, 1860 - 1mf - 9 - Can$2.25 - SEM105P365 - cn Bibl Nat [020]
CATALOGUE OF BANTU, KHOISAN AND MALAGASY IN THE STRANGE COLLECTION OF AFRICANA / Johannesburg, Public Library; ed by Smith, A H - Johannesburg, 1942 - 11mf - 9 - ne IDC [470]
CATALOGUE OF BIHAR AND ORISSA GOVERNMENT PUBLICATIONS - Patna, Govt Print, 1929-1936, 1939 - us Res Libr [324]
CATALOGUE OF BOOKS / Burma - Burma. 1868 72-1941. BI-610 2 - 8 - ne IDC [010]
CATALOGUE OF BOOKS / Ceylon - Ceylon. 1902-21. Lacking: 1905 (3)-1906 (1); 1915 (2-4)-1916 (2). BI-609 2 - 8 - ne IDC [010]
CATALOGUE OF BOOKS / India - Ajmer-Merwara. 1886-1919. BI-606 2 - 8 - ne IDC [010]
CATALOGUE OF BOOKS / India - Bangalore. 1885-1921. BI-607 2 - 8 - ne IDC [010]
CATALOGUE OF BOOKS / India - Bengal Library. Appendix to the Calcutta Gazette. Calcutta. 1867-1954. Lacking: 1867-99; 1939 (4); 1941 (1, 4); 1946-49; 1951; 1953-54. BI-600 2 - 8 - ne IDC [010]
CATALOGUE OF BOOKS / India - Central Provinces. 1892-1938. Lacking: 1924-30; 1932 (3); 1937 (1). BI-608 2 - 8 - ne IDC [010]
CATALOGUE OF BOOKS / India - Madras. 1875-1944. Suppl. to the Fort St. George Gazette. Lacking: 1875-1916; 1939 (1-4); 1941 (1-4). BI-602 2 - 8 - ne IDC [010]
CATALOGUE OF BOOKS / India - United Provinces. 1894-1964. Lacking: 1894-1903; 1919-21; 1940 (3); 1946-64. BI-603 2 - 8 - ne IDC [010]
CATALOGUE OF BOOKS AND MANUSCRIPTS IN THE LIBRARY AT FREEMASONS' HALL EDINBURGH - Edinburgh, 1906 - 3mf - ne IDC [360]
A CATALOGUE OF BOOKS AND MANUSCRIPTS PRESENTED TO THE WESLEYAN THEOLOGICAL INSTITUTION, IN THE YEAR MDCCCLIX, BY J. HEALD, ESQ. / Wesleyan Theological Institution - London, 1859 - 4mf - 9 - ne IDC [025]
CATALOGUE OF BOOKS AND MSS IN ENGLISH AND IRISH COLLECTIONS, WITH ALPHABETICAL INDEX / Bernard, Edward - Latin. 1697 - 1 - uk Microform Academic [010]
CATALOGUE OF BOOKS AND PERIODICALS PUBLISHED IN AJMERE-MERWARA... - 1886-1919 - 8mf - I-606/2 - ne IDC [020]
CATALOGUE OF BOOKS BENGAL LIBRARY - (Appendix to the Calcutta Gazette. Missing: 1867-1899; 1939 (4); 1941(1,4); 1946-1949; 1951; 1953-1954) - Calcutta, 1867-1954 - 640mf - I-600/2 - ne IDC [020]
A CATALOGUE OF BOOKS CHIEFLY THEOLOGICAL... / Allan, T R - Leipzig, [1881]. 324p - 4mf - 9 - ne IDC [025]
CATALOGUE OF BOOKS CONSISTING OF ENGLISH LITERATURE AND MISCELLANEA / Church, Elihu Dwight - 7v. 1907 - 3 - us Readex [018]
CATALOGUE OF BOOKS CONTAINED IN THE LOCKHART LIBRARY AND IN THE GENERAL LIBRARY / London Missionary Society; ed by Mabbs, G - London. 3pts. 1899 - 7mf - 9 - ne IDC [240]
CATALOGUE OF BOOKS IN THE LIBRARY OF PARLIAMENT / Canada. Parliament. Library - Quebec: Printed at John Lovell's steam printing establishment, 1852. SEM105P223 - 2mf - 9 - Can$4.50 - cn Bibl Nat [010]
CATALOGUE OF BOOKS IN THE LIBRARY OF THE HOUSE OF ASSEMBLY / Canada. Bas-Canada. Parlement. Chambre d'Assemblee. Bibliotheque - Quebec: Printed by Neilson and Cowan, 1831. SEM105P147 - 1mf - 9 - Can$2.25 - cn Bibl Nat [324]
CATALOGUE OF BOOKS IN THE LIBRARY OF THE LEGISLATIVE ASSEMBLY OF CANADA / Canada. Parliament. Legislative Assembly. Library - Kingston: Desbarats and Cary, 1842. SEM105P144 - 1mf - 9 - Can$2.25 - cn Bibl Nat [324]
CATALOGUE OF BOOKS IN THE PIOT COLLECTION / Victoria and Albert Museum. London - 10mf - ne IDC [700]
CATALOGUE OF BOOKS IN THE PWD SECRETARIAT LIBRARY OF THE GOVERNMENT OF BOMBAY - [3rd corr ed]. Bombay, Govt Central Press, 1st nov 1927 - us Res Libr [020]
CATALOGUE OF BOOKS IN THE SECRETARIAT LIBARY OF THE GOVERNMENT OF BOMBAY 150=BOMBAY, GOVT CENTRAL PRESS, 31ST JUL 1938 - us Res Libr [020]
A CATALOGUE OF BOOKS ON ART AND ARCHITECTURE IN MCGILL UNIVERSITY LIBRARY AND THE GORDON HOME BLACKADER LIBRARY OF ARCHITECTURE / McGill University. Library - 2nd rev. ed. Montreal: McGill University Library, 1926. SEM105P1490 - 3mf - 9 - Can$6.75 - cn Bibl Nat [700]
CATALOGUE OF BOOKS, PRINTED IN THE BOMBAY PRESIDENCY - (Missing: 1867-1893. 1951-1959) - Bombay, 1867-1959 - 448mf - 9 - ne IDC [950]
CATALOGUE OF BOOKS PRINTED IN THE CIVIL AND MILITARY STATION OF BANGALORE DURING THE MONTH OF JULY 1884 UNTILL DECEMBER 1921 - Bangalore, 1885-1921 - 6mf - 9 - ne IDC [355]
CATALOGUE OF BOOKS REGISTERED IN THE CENTRAL PROVINCES AND BERAR DURING 1892 UNTILL 1938 - (Missing: 1924-1930; 1932(3); 1937(1)) - N.p., n.d. - 38mf - 9 - ne IDC [950]
CATALOGUE OF BOOKS REGISTERED IN THE MADRAS PRESIDENCY DURING THE MONTH OF JANUARY 1917 UNTILL DECEMBER 1944 - (Supplement to the Fort St George Gazette. Missing: 1939. 1941) - Madras, 1917-1944 - 240mf - 9 - ne IDC [950]
CATALOGUE OF BOOKS REGISTERED IN THE PROVINCE OF BIHAR AND ORISSA DURING 1912-1941 - (Missing: 1912(1); 1936(1)) - 135mf - I-605/2 - ne IDC [950]
CATALOGUE OF BOOKS, REGISTERED IN THE PUNJAB / India - 1867-1940. Lacking: 1867-1909. BI-604 2 - 8 - ne IDC [010]
CATALOGUE OF BOOKS REGISTERED IN THE PUNJAB...1910-1940 - Lahore, 1910-1940 - 195mf - I-604/2 - ne IDC [950]
CATALOGUE OF BOOKS RELATING TO THE HISTORY OF AMERICA, FORMING PART OF THE LIBRARY OF THE LEGISLATIVE ASSEMBLY OF CANADA / Canada. Parliament. Legislative Assembly. Library - Quebec: William Cowan and Son, 1845. SEM105P218 - 1mf - 9 - Can$2.25 - cn Bibl Nat [971]
A CATALOGUE OF BRITISH HEMIPTERA / Douglas, J W & Scott, J - London, 1876. viii,99p.Z/1199/2 - 8 - ne IDC [590]
CATALOGUE OF CANADIAN PLANTS / Macoun, J M - 7582 2. 7 v. 1883-1902 - 8 - ne IDC [580]

CATALOGUE OF CIVIL AND MECHANICAL ENGINEERING DESIGNS / Smeaton, John - 1741-92 - 7 - uk Microform Academic [621]

CATALOGUE OF CIVIL PUBLICATIONS RELATING TO AGRICULTURE, FORESTRY, CIVIC, COMMERCE, FINANCE, LEGISLATION, INDUSTRY, PUBLIC HEALTH, RAILWAYS, SCIENCE, TRADE, ETC - Delhi: Govt Publ Branch, [1925-mar 1970] - us Res Libr [350]

CATALOGUE OF COMPACT DISCS TO DECEMBER 1993 - 9 - NZ$22.50 - nz Nat'l Libr [020]

CATALOGUE OF DOCUMENTS MICROFICHED BY ILCA/IDRC TEAM : TANZANIA MISSION - 1982. 165 Citations - 9 - $4.50 - 92-9053-158-4 - et ILRI [636]

CATALOGUE OF DRIED SPECIMENS OF INDIAN PLANTS DISTRIBUTED BY DR. R. WRIGHT / Wight, R - 1833-37. B-5810 2 - 8 - ne IDC [580]

CATALOGUE OF EARLY INDIAN IMPRINTS / William Carey College. Library - 1714-1850. 1,296p - 1 - 45.36 - us Baptist [240]

CATALOGUE OF ENGLISH AND FRENCH BOOKS IN THE QUEBEC LIBRARY / Quebec. Library - Quebec: S. Neilson, 1792. SEM16P11 - 1r - 5 - Can$9.00 - cn Bibl Nat [070]

CATALOGUE OF ENGLISH AND FRENCH BOOKS IN THE QUEBEC LIBRARY, AT THE BISHOP'S PALACE, WHERE THE RULES MAY BE SEEN / Quebec. Library - Quebec: Printed at the New Printing Office, 1801. SEM16P12 - 1r - 5 - Can$9.00 - cn Bibl Nat [070]

CATALOGUE OF ENGLISH AND FRENCH BOOKS IN THE QUEBEC LIBRARY, AT THE BISHOP'S PALACE, WHERE THE RULES MAY BE SEEN / Quebec. Library - Quebec: Printed at the New Printing Office, 1808. SEM16P13 - 1r - 5 - Can$9.00 - cn Bibl Nat [070]

CATALOGUE OF ENGLISH BOOKS IN THE LIBRARY OF THE HOUSE OF ASSEMBLY / Canada. Bas-Canada. Parlement. Chambre d'Assemblee. Bibliotheque - s.l., s.n. 1825?. SEM105P146 - 1mf - 9 - Can$2.25 - cn Bibl Nat [324]

CATALOGUE OF EUROPEAN PRINTED BOOKS, INDIA OFFICE LIBRARY / Commonwealth Relations Office. India Office Library. Great Britain - (Available on microfilm by request) - 1964. 110,000 cards - 1 - $920.00 export $1,110.00 - 0-8161-0671-1 - uk Hall [960]

CATALOGUE OF FERNS / Riley, J - (plus synoptical table of C.B. Presl's arrangement of genera). 7252. 1841 - 9 - ne IDC [580]

CATALOGUE OF FRESHWATER FISHES OF AFRICA / Boulenger, G A - 1909-16 - 5 - uk Microform Academic [590]

CATALOGUE OF GOVERNMENT PUBLICATIONS - Madras: Printed by the Director of Stationery and Printing, 1950-1951, jul 1954, jun 1958, jan 1961, jan 1963 - us Res Libr [350]

CATALOGUE OF HEBREW MANUSCRIPTS PRESERVED IN THE USSR / Katsh, A I - NYU Libraries, Occasional Papers, nos. 3 and 4. 2 v. New York. 1957-58. BR-11.167 1 - 9 - ne IDC [010]

A CATALOGUE OF HEMIPTERA IN THE COLLECTION OF...F.W. HOPE / Hope, FW - London, 1837. 46p. Z/1351/2 - 8 - ne IDC [590]

CATALOGUE OF KNOWN SPECIES OF ACARI FROM THE GALAPAGOS ISLANDS. (ECUADOR, PACIFIC OCEAN) / Schatz H - F30.00 - fr Ethnologie [590]

A CATALOGUE OF LUCANOID COLEOPTERA / Parry, F J S - Trans. Entom. Soc. London, v2, London, 1864. 113p, 12pls. Z-1531/2 - 8 - ne IDC [590]

CATALOGUE OF MANUSCRIPTS / Oxford University. Colleges - 1852 - 1 - uk Microform Academic [090]

A CATALOGUE OF MANUSCRIPTS AND RELICS, ENGRAVINGS AND PHOTOGRAPHS, MEDALS, BOOKS AND PAMPHLETS, POTTERY, MEDALLIONS, ETC... / John Rylands University Library. Methodist Archives - London, 1921. - 3mf - 9 - ne IDC [700]

CATALOGUE OF MISCELLANEOUS MSS. AND APPENDICES TO THE COVENTRY, SEYMOUR AND PORTLAND PAPERS / Bath. Archives (Marquess). Longleat - 1 - uk Microform Academic [025]

A CATALOGUE OF NATIVE PUBLICATIONS IN THE BOMBAY PRESIDENCY / Grant, A - 1867 - 1 - uk Microform Academic [950]

CATALOGUE OF NATIVE PUBLICATIONS IN THE BOMBAY PRESIDENCY UP TO 31 DEC 1864 / Bombay. India (Presidency). Educational Department - Ed. 2. Bombay. 1867. BI-330 2 - 8 - ne IDC [010]

CATALOGUE OF NATIVE PUBLICATIONS IN THE BOMBAY PRESIDENCY UP TO 31ST DECEMBER, 1864 / Grant, A - Bombay, 1867. rev. ed. 2. 35, 239 pp. BI-359 2 - 8 - ne IDC [305]

CATALOGUE OF NEARCTIC SPIDERS / Banks, N - Z-2161 2. 1910 - 8 - ne IDC [590]

CATALOGUE OF NORTH AMERICAN MUSCI / Rau, A E & Hervey, A B - 7610 2. 1880 - 8 - ne IDC [580]

CATALOGUE OF NORTH-AMERICAN GENERA OF PLANTS / Torrey, J - 6477. 1831 - 9 - ne IDC [580]

A CATALOGUE OF NOTABLE MIDDLE TEMPLE TEMPLARS / Hutchinson, John - London: Butterworth, 1902 - 4mf - 9 - $6.00 - LLMC 84-296 - us L.L.M.C. [920]

CATALOGUE OF OFFICIAL PUBLICATIONS IN ENGLISH AND KANNADA AVAILABLE FOR SALE AT THE GOVERNMENT CENTRAL BOOK DEPOT, BANGALORE - Bangalore: Printed by the Supt of the Govt Press, 1936-1968 - us Res Libr [324]

CATALOGUE OF OFFICIAL REPORTS RELATING TO INDIA ISSUED AS ENGLISH PARLIAMENTARY PAPERS (AND IN CONNECTION WITH THE INDIA OFFICE) DURING THE YEAR 1892 / Campbell, Frank - London: [Truslove & Bray], 1893 - us Res Libr [324]

CATALOGUE OF ORIENTAL COINS IN THE BRITISH MUSEUM / Lane-Poole, Stanley - (Missing: 1881. v6. (p.lv..., 1-37). Suppl. 1889-1890) - London. 8v. 1875-1883 - 67mf - ne IDC [730]

CATALOGUE OF PARLIAMENTARY PAPERS RELATING TO AFRICA / Jones, H V - (Missing: 1901-1910) - London, 1800-1899, 1901-1910, 1911-1920 - 14mf - 9 - ne IDC [324]

CATALOGUE OF PASTORS OF BAPTIST CHURCHES OF NEW HAMPSHIRE / New Hampshire - 1892-1934. By D. Donovan. Unpublished mss, 1934 - 1 - us A.B.H.S. [240]

CATALOGUE OF PLANTS CULTIVATED IN THE ROYAL BOTANIC GARDENS CALCUTTA... / Anderson, T - Calcutta, 1865 - 2mf - ne IDC [580]

CATALOGUE OF PLANTS, EXOTIC AND INDIGENOUS, IN THE BOTANICAL GARDEN, JAMAICA, 1792 / Dancer, T - St. Jago de la Vega, 1792 - 1mf - ne IDC [580]

A CATALOGUE OF PLANTS, GROWING SPONTANEOUSLY WITHIN 30 MILES OF THE CITY OF NEW YORK / Torrey, J - 5173. 1819 - 9 - ne IDC [580]

CATALOGUE OF PLANTS IN THE BOTANICAL GARDEN... / Cameron, J - Bangalore, 1891 - 6mf - ne IDC [580]

CATALOGUE OF PRE-1650 MANUSCRIPT MAPS HELD BY COUNTY RECORD OFFICES IN ENGLAND AND WALES - 8mf - 9 - uk Microform Academic [910]

CATALOGUE OF PUBLICATIONS - Cuttack, Supt, Orissa Govt Press, 1941, 1943, 1950, 1964, 1967, 1969 - us Res Libr [350]

CATALOGUE OF PUBLICATIONS - Delhi: Ministry of Education, 1956, 1962, 1965 - us Res Libr [350]

CATALOGUE OF PUBLICATIONS - Karachi: Govt Book Depot & Record Office, nov 1939; Suppl: aug 1940, jan 1941, 1942 - us Res Libr [350]

CATALOGUE OF PUBLICATIONS - Patna: Supt, Govt Print, 1939 - us Res Libr [350]

CATALOGUE OF RECORDS, DOCUMENTS, PAPERS, ETC. OF KENTUCKY GOVERNORS, 1792-1926 / Cromwell, Emma Guy - 3 fiches. F-0504 - 9 - us A.G.L.L. [025]

CATALOGUE OF REPRODUCTIONS OF PAINTINGS, 1860-1979 - (English/French/Spanish) - 11th rev ed 1981 - 9 - 92-3-001924-0 - fr UNESCO [750]

CATALOGUE OF SANSKRIT AND PRAKRIT MSS IN THE CENTRAL PROVINCES AND BERAR - Nagpur, 1926 - 10mf - 9 - ne IDC [490]

CATALOGUE OF SANSKRIT MSS EXISTING ON OUDH / ed by Browning, Colin - (1873, pt. 1-2 have not been published. Missing: 1876-1877 pt 6-8. 1893 (for the year 1890) pt 22) - Calcutta. 4v in 22 parts. 1873-1893 - 18mf - 9 - ne IDC [490]

A CATALOGUE OF SANSKRIT MSS IN PRIVATE LIBRARIES OF THE NORTH-WEST-WESTERN PROVINCES - Benares, Allahabad. 10 pts. 1874-1886 - 18mf - 9 - ne IDC [490]

A CATALOGUE OF SANSKRIT MSS IN THE LIBRARY OF HIS HIGHNESS THE MAHARAJA OF BIKANER - Calcutta, 1880 - 8mf - 9 - ne IDC [490]

CATALOGUE OF SCHOOL BOOKS, STATIONERY, ETC / D and J Sadlier and Co - Montreal, 1886. SEM16P268 - 1r - 5 - Can$9.00 - cn Bibl Nat [370]

CATALOGUE OF SCIENTIFIC PAPERS / Royal Society of London - London, Cambridge. v1-6. 1867-1914. S1. v7-8. 1800-1863. S2. v9-11. 1864-1873. S3. 1874-1883. Suppl. v12. 1800-1883. S4. v13-19. 1884-1900 - 606mf - 9 - ne IDC [500]

CATALOGUE OF SEALS IN THE DEPARTMENT OF MANUSCRIPTS IN THE BRITISH MUSEUM / Birch, Walter de Gray - London, 1887-1900. 6 vols - 94mf - 8 - ne IDC [760]

CATALOGUE OF SYRIAC MANUSCRIPTS IN THE BRITISH MUSEUM / ed by Wright, W - London Part 1-3 1870-1872 - 81mf - 8 - ne Slangenburg [470]

CATALOGUE OF THE AFRICAN PLANTS COLLECTED BY F. WELWITSCH IN 1853-1861 / Welwitsch, F M J - 550. 2 V. 1896-1901 - 9 - ne IDC [580]

A CATALOGUE OF THE ANIMALS OF NORTH AMERICA, CONTAINING AN ENUMERATION OF KNOWN QUADRUPEDS, FISH / Forctor, J R - 2043 2. 1771 - 8 - ne IDC [590]

A CATALOGUE OF THE ARABIC BOOKS AND MANUSCRIPTS / Asiatic Society of Bengal - Calcutta. 1899-1904. Compiled by Shamsu-l'Ulama Mirza Ashraf. 'Ali. 2v. 153 p. 1 reel - 1 - us U.W. Library [470]

CATALOGUE OF THE ARABIC MANUSCRIPTS PRESERVED IN THE UNIVERSITY LIBRARY, IBADAN, NIGERIA / Kensdale, W E N - Ibadan, 1955-1958 - us Res Libr [090]

CATALOGUE OF THE ARCHIEPISCOPAL MANUSCRIPTS IN LAMBETH PALACE LIBRARY / Todd, H J - 1 - uk Microform Academic [090]

CATALOGUE OF THE ARMENIAN MSS IN THE BODLEIAN LIBRARY / Baronian, S & Conybeare, FC - Oxford, 1918 - 3mf - 9 - ne IDC [460]

A CATALOGUE OF THE ARMENIAN MSS IN THE BRITISH MUSEUM / Conybeare, Frederick C - London, 1913 - 8mf - 9 - ne IDC [460]

CATALOGUE OF THE BIRDS IN THE BRITISH MUSEUM / Sharpe, R B - 2111 2. 27v. 1874-1898 - 8 - ne IDC [590]

CATALOGUE OF THE BIRDS IN THE MUSEUM ASIATIC SOCIETY / Blyth, E - Calcutta, 1849 - 8mf - ne IDC [590]

A CATALOGUE OF THE BIRDS IN THE MUSEUM OF THE HONORABLE EAST INDIA COMPANY / Horsfield, T & Moore, F - 2v. London. 1854-58. BZ-1806 2 - 8 - ne IDC [590]

A CATALOGUE OF THE BIRDS OF THE SOUTHERN PORTION OF THE BOMBAY PRESIDENCY / Butler, E A - Bombay. 1880. BZ-264 2 - 8 - ne IDC [590]

CATALOGUE OF THE BOOK LIBRARY OF THE BRITISH FILM INSTITUTE : FIRST SUPPLEMENT / British Film Institute. London - 1983. 25,000 cards on 2 reels - 1 - $240.00 export $290.00 - 0-8161-1435-8 - uk Hall [790]

CATALOGUE OF THE BOOKS,... IN THE EDWARD FRY LIBRARY OF INTERNATIONAL LAW / ed by Headicar, B M - London, 1923 - 2mf - 9 - ILM-2870/1 - ne IDC [340]

CATALOGUE OF THE CASHEL DIOCESAN LIBRARY / Cashel Diocesan Library. County Tipperary. Republic of Ireland - (Available on microfilm by request; $100.00 export $120.00) - 1973. 11,000 cards - 1 - uk Hall [290]

CATALOGUE OF THE CENTRAL LIBRARY FOR AGRICULTURAL SCIENCE, BONN *see* KATALOG DER ZENTRALBIBLIOTHEK DER LANDBAUWISSENSCHAFT, BONN

CATALOGUE OF THE CENTRAL MEDICAL LIBRARY, COLOGNE *see* KATALOG DER ZENTRALBIBLIOTHEK DER MEDIZIN, KOELN

CATALOGUE OF THE CHARLES WESLEY PAPERS, V1 / Lloyd, Gareth - (Coll title: The People Called Methodists, Phase 1: Reference Tools) - Manchester, 1994 - 4mf - 9 - MP-601/1 - ne IDC [240]

CATALOGUE OF THE CHARLES WESLEY PAPERS, V2 / Lloyd, Gareth - (Coll title: The People Called Methodists, Phase 1: Reference Tools) - Manchester, 1994 - 3mf - 9 - MP-602/1 - ne IDC [240]

CATALOGUE OF THE CHATEAU RAMEZAY MUSEUM / Chateau de Ramezay - Numismatic & Antiquarian Society of Montreal, 1898. 02123. (Pre-1900 Canadiana) - 9 - cn C.I.H.M. [730]

CATALOGUE OF THE CHEELOO SCHOOL OF THEOLOGY (CCC84) = SHANTUNG TSINAN CHEELOO SHEN HSUEH YUAN CHANG CH'ENG / Cheeloo School of Theology - (In Chinese) - [s.l: s.n, 1931] - 1r - 1 - 1984-B500 - us A.T.L.A. [240]

CATALOGUE OF THE CHINESE LIBRARY OF THE ROYAL ASIATIC SOCIETY / Kidd, S - London, 1838 - 1mf - 9 - ne IDC [950]

CATALOGUE OF THE COLLECTION OF DIURNAL LEPITOPTERA / Kirby, W F - London, 1879. iv,246p. Z-1393/2 - 8 - ne IDC [590]

CATALOGUE OF THE COLONIAL OFFICE LIBRARY / Great Britain. Foreign and Commonwealth Office. Library - (Second Suppl.-1968-71.-1972.-25,500 cards 2 reels. $220.00 export $265.00.-ISBN 0-8161-1434-X) - 1964.-187,000 cards plus sheaf entries 30 reels - 1 - $1,490.00 export $1,800.00 - 0-8161-1354-8 - uk Hall [013]

CATALOGUE OF THE COMPARATIVE EDUCATION LIBRARY / University of London. Institute of Education - (First Suppl., 45,000 cards 3 reels. $365.00 ISBN: 0 8161-1558-3) - 1971.-107,000 cards 6 reels.-ISBN: 0-8161-1236-3 - 1 - $630.00 - uk Hall [370]

CATALOGUE OF THE COPTIC MANUSCRIPTS IN THE BRITISH MUSEUM / Crum, WE - London, 1905 - 60mf - 8 - ne Slangenburg [470]

CATALOGUE OF THE DESCRIBED DIPTERA FROM SOUTH ASIA / Wulp, F. M. van der - The Hague. 1896. BZ-1735 2 - 8 - ne IDC [590]

CATALOGUE OF THE DRAWINGS COLLECTION - 4r - 1 - £175.00 - uk World [740]

CATALOGUE OF THE EDWARD E. AYER ORNITHOLOGICAL LIBRARY / Zimmert, J T - Chicago, 2v. 1924 - 13mf - ne IDC [590]

CATALOGUE OF THE ETHIOPIC MSS IN THE BRITISH MUSEUM / Wright, W - London, 1877 - 8mf - 9 - ne IDC [090]

A CATALOGUE OF THE FERNS INDIGENOUS TO CEYLON / Wall, G - 7275. 1873 - 9 - ne IDC [580]

CATALOGUE OF THE FIRST ANNUAL EXHIBITION OF THE ASSOCIATION OF CANADIAN ETCHERS / Association of Canadian Etchers - Toronto: 1885. 00847. (Pre-1900 Canadiana) - 9 - cn C.I.H.M. [760]

CATALOGUE OF THE FISHES IN THE BRITISH MUSEUM / Guenther, A C LG - London. 8v. 1859-1870 - 80mf - ne IDC [590]

A CATALOGUE OF THE FISHES OF JAPAN / Jordan, D S et al - 2635 2. 1913 - 8 - ne IDC [590]

A CATALOGUE OF THE FLOWERING PLANTS AND FERNS FOUND GROWING WILD IN THE ISLAND OF PENANG / Curtis, C - Singapore, 1894. 101p. (Journ. Straits Branch R. Asiatic Soc., no.25). B-7179/1 - 9 - ne IDC [580]

A CATALOGUE OF THE FLOWERING PLANTS AND FERNS GROWING IN THE NEIGHBOURHOOD OF ABERDEEN / MacGillivray, P H - Aberdeen, etc., 1853. 44 pp. B-7220 1 - 9 - ne IDC [580]

CATALOGUE OF THE FLOWERING PLANTS AND FERNS OF CONNECTICUT / Graves, C B & Eamer, E H - 7545 1. 1910 - 9 - ne IDC [580]

CATALOGUE OF THE FOREIGN AND COMMONWEALTH OFFICE LIBRARY - 1977-1980 - 67mf - 9 - £280.00 - uk Chadwyck [320]

CATALOGUE OF THE FOREIGN OFFICE LIBRARY / Great Britain. Foreign and Commonwealth Office. Library - 1926-68.-1972.-130,000 cards 8 reels.-ISBN: 0-8161-1451-X - 1 - $870.00 - uk Hall [941]

CATALOGUE OF THE FOSSIL PLANTS OF THE GLOSSOPTERIS FLORA IN THE DEPARTMENT OF GEOLOGY... BRITISH MUSEUM NATURAL HISTORY / Arber, E A N - London, 1905 - 7mf - ne IDC [580]

CATALOGUE OF THE FRESH-WATER FISHES OF AFRICA IN THE BRITISH MUSEUM (NATURAL HISTORY) / Boulenger, G A – F360.00 – fr Ethnologie [590]

A CATALOGUE OF THE GENERIC AND SUB-GENERIC TYPES OF THE CLASS AVES, BIRDS / Selby, P J – 2109 2. 1840 – 8 – ne IDC [590]

CATALOGUE OF THE GENNADIUS LIBRARY, AMERICAN SCHOOL OF CLASSICAL STUDIES AT ATHENS / American School of Classical Studies at Athens – 1968. 116,000 cards on 7 reels – 1 – $695.00 export $840.00 – 0-8161-1498-6 – uk Hall [930]

CATALOGUE OF THE GENNADIUS LIBRARY, AMERICAN SCHOOL OF CLASSICAL STUDIES AT ATHENS : FIRST SUPPLEMENT / American School of Classical Studies at Athens – 1973. 17,800 cards on 1 reel – 1 – $125.00 export $150.00 – 0-8161-1499-4 – uk Hall [930]

CATALOGUE OF THE GENNADIUS LIBRARY, AMERICAN SCHOOL OF CLASSICAL STUDIES AT ATHENS : SECOND SUPPLEMENT / American School of Classical Studies at Athens – 1981. 17,500 cards on 1 reel – 1 – $170.00 export $205.00 – 0-8161-1500-1 – uk Hall [930]

CATALOGUE OF THE GEORGIA SOCIETY D.A.R. LIBRARY / Daughters of the American Revolution – In the Georgia Dept. of Archives & History, Rhodes Mem. Hall. 4 fiches. F-1310 – 9 – us A.G.L.L. [920]

CATALOGUE OF THE GREAT EXHIBITION – 1851. With printed index – 1 – £225.00 – uk World [900]

CATALOGUE OF THE GREEK MANUSCRIPTS ON MOUNT ATHOS / Lambros, Spyr P – Cambridge. v1-2. 1895-1900 – 28mf – 8 – ne Slangenburg [450]

CATALOGUE OF THE GREENLEE COLLECTION / Newberry Library. Chicago – (Available on microfilm by request) – 1970. 31,000 cards – 1 – $220.00 export $265.00 – 0-8161-0903-6 – uk Hall [450]

CATALOGUE OF THE HEBREW BOOKS IN THE LIBRARY OF THE BRITISH MUSEUM / Zedner, J – London, 1867 – 10mf – ne IDC [270]

CATALOGUE OF THE HEBREW MANUSCRIPTS IN THE BODLEIAN LIBRARY AND IN THE COLLEGE LIBRARIES OF OXFORD: INCLUDING MSS. IN OTHER LANGUAGES WHICH ARE WRITTEN WITH HEBREW CHARACTERS, OR RELATING TO THE HEBREW LANGUAGE OR LITERATURE, AND A FEW SAMARITAN MSS / Bodleian Library – Compiled by A. Neubauer. Oxford: Clarendon Press, 1886-1906 – 1 – us U.W. Library [090]

CATALOGUE OF THE HEBREW MSS IN THE BODLEIAN LIBRARY / Neubauer, A & Cowley, A E – (Missing: 1886 v1.) – Oxford. 2v. 1886-1906 – 4mf – ne IDC [470]

CATALOGUE OF THE HEMIPTERA (HETEROPTERA), WITH BIOLOGICAL AND ANATOMICAL REFERENCES / Kirkaldy, G W – Berlin, 1909. v1. Z-1401/2 – 8 – ne IDC [590]

CATALOGUE OF THE HUGH BOURNE AND WILLIAM CLOWES PAPERS / Lloyd, Gareth – (Coll title: The People Called Methodists, Phase 1: Reference Tools) – Manchester, 1993 – 1mf – 9 – MP-603/1 – ne IDC [240]

CATALOGUE OF THE IMPERIAL COLLEGE OF TROPICAL AGRICULTURE / University of the West Indies. Imperial College of Tropical Agriculture. Trinidad – 1975. 103,000 cards on 16 reels – 9 – $750.00 export $905.00 – 0-8161-1369-6 – uk Hall [630]

CATALOGUE OF THE INDIAN DECAPOD CRUSTACEA IN THE COLLECTION OF THE INDIAN MUSEUM : FASC. 2. ANOMURA. PT. 1. PAGURIDES / Alcock, A W – Calcutta, 1905 – 9mf – ne IDC [590]

A CATALOGUE OF THE INDIGENOUS AND EXOTIC PLANTS GROWING IN CEYLON / Moon, A – Colombo. 1824. B-7316 1 – 9 – ne IDC [580]

CATALOGUE OF THE LAND AND FRESH-WATER MOLLUSCA OF IRELAND / Thompson, W – Z 835 2. 1840 – 8 – ne IDC [590]

CATALOGUE OF THE LAND AND FRESHWATER SHELLS OF BRITISH INDIA / Theobald, W – Z 295 2.. 1876 – 8 – ne IDC [590]

A CATALOGUE OF THE LEPIDOPTEROUS INSECTS IN THE MUSEUM OF THE HONOURABLE EAST INDIA COMPANY / Horsfield, T & Moore, F – London, 1857-1859 – 11mf – ne IDC [590]

CATALOGUE OF THE LIBRARY / Harvard University. Graduate School of Design. Frances Loeb Library – (First Suppl., 1970.-31,500 cards 4 reels. $265.00 ISBN: 0-8161-1361-0) – 1 – uk Hall [740]

CATALOGUE OF THE LIBRARY / Linnean Society – London, 1925 – 13mf – ne IDC [580]

CATALOGUE OF THE LIBRARY OF CHARLES DARWIN.. / Cambridge University. Botany School – Comp. by H.W. Rutherford with introd. by Francis Darwin.Cambridge: University Press, 1908. xiv,91p – 1 – us U.W. Library [575]

CATALOGUE OF THE LIBRARY OF THE GRADUATE SCHOOL OF DESIGN / Harvard University. Graduate School of Design. Frances Loeb Library – 1970. 31,500 cards on 4 reels – 1 – $240.00 export $290.00 – 0-8161-1361-0 – uk Hall [760]

CATALOGUE OF THE LIBRARY OF THE HISPANIC SOCIETY OF AMERICA / Hispanic Society of America. New York – (First Supplement, 1970. 58,000 cards. 4 reels. $440.00 export $530.00. – ISBN 0-8161-1475-7) – 1962. 211,000 cards on 20 reels – 1 – $990.00 export $1,198.00 – 0-8161-1474-9 – uk Hall [946]

CATALOGUE OF THE LIBRARY OF THE LATE HON. SIR JAMES STUART, BART.,CHIEF JUSTICE OF LOWER CANADA / Stuart, James – Quebec: Lovell and Lamoureux, 1854. SEM105P224 – 2mf – 9 – Can$4.50 – cn Bibl Nat [340]

CATALOGUE OF THE LIBRARY OF THE MUSEUM OF COMPARATIVE ZOOLOGY / Harvard University. Museum of Comparative Zoology – 1968. 153,000 cards on 16 reels – 1 – $760.00 export $920.00 – 0-8161-1384-X – uk Hall [590]

A CATALOGUE OF THE LIBRARY OF THE RIGHT HONOURABLE...EARL OF YARMOUTH, LATELY DECEASED. / Paston, William – London, 1734 – 1 – us U.W. Library [010]

A CATALOGUE OF THE LUCANOID COLEOPTERA IN THE COLLECTION OF...F.W. HOPE / Hope, FW – London, 1845. 31p. Z/1353/2 – 8 – ne IDC [590]

CATALOGUE OF THE MARX MEMORIAL LIBRARY / Marx Memorial Library. London – 1979. 46,600 cards on 3 reels – 1 – $298.00 export $360.00 – 0-8161-1520-6 – uk Hall [335]

CATALOGUE OF THE MINGANA COLLECTION OF MSS – Cambridge. 4v. 1933-1963 – 17mf – 9 – ne IDC [956]

A CATALOGUE OF THE MOTHS OF INDIA / Cotes, E C & Swinhoe, C – Z-265 2. 1887 – 8 – ne IDC [590]

CATALOGUE OF THE NAMES OF THE FIRST PURITAN SETTLERS OF THE COLONY OF CONNECTICUT,...THE TIME OF THEIR ARRIVAL...THEIR STANDING IN SOCIETY... THEIR PLACE OF RESIDENCE. – By R.R. Hinman, 1846. 5 fiches.F-0077 – 9 – us A.G.L.L. [920]

CATALOGUE OF THE NATIONAL MAP COLLECTION / Canada. Public Archives. National Map Collection – 1976.-96,000 cards 16 reels.-ISBN: 0-8161-1401-3 – 1 – $1640.00 – uk Hall [910]

CATALOGUE OF THE PLANTS COLLECTED BY MR. AND MRS. TALBOT IN THE OBAN DISTRICT SOUTH NIGERIA / Rendle, A B et al – London, 1913 – X, 153, (5)p, 17pls – 8 – ne IDC [580]

A CATALOGUE OF THE PLANTS GROWING IN BOMBAY AND ITS VICINITY / Graham, J – Bombay. 1839. B-7314 2 – 8 – ne IDC [580]

A CATALOGUE OF THE PLANTS GROWING WILD IN THE ENVIRONS OF LONDON / Curtis, W – London. 1774. B-5119 2 – 8 – ne IDC [580]

CATALOGUE OF THE PLANTS OF KUMAON AND OF THE ADJACENT PORTIONS OF GARHWAL AND TIBET / Strachey, R – London. 1906. B-317 2 – 8 – ne IDC [580]

A CATALOGUE OF THE PLANTS OF THE PUNJAB AND SINDH / Aitchison, J E T – London. 1869. B-1052 2 – 8 – ne IDC [580]

CATALOGUE OF THE POPULATION COUNCIL LIBRARY / Population Council. New York – 1979. 41,100 cards on 3 reels – 1 – $295.00 export $355.00 – 0-8161-1496-X – uk Hall [304]

CATALOGUE OF THE PUBLICATIONS OF THE GOVERNMENT OF BENGAL AVAILABLE FOR SALE AT THE BENGAL SECRETARIAT BOOK DEPOT – Calcutta, Secretariat. pt 1-2 1926; pt 1 1927; pts 1-2 1936 – us Res Libr [350]

CATALOGUE OF THE RECENT SHELLS IN THE MUSEUM ASIATIC SOCIETY OF BENGAL / Theobald, W – Calcutta. 1860. BZ-293 2 – 8 – ne IDC [590]

CATALOGUE OF THE SANSKRIT MSS IN THE LIBRARY OF THE INDIA OFFICE – London. 7 pts. 1887-1904 – 20mf – 9 – ne IDC [490]

CATALOGUE OF THE SANSKRIT MSS IN THE RAGHUNATHA TEMPLE LIBRARY OF HIS HIGHNESS THE MAHARAJA OF JAMMU AND KASHMIR / ed by Stein, M A – Bombay, 1894 – 6mf – 9 – ne IDC [490]

A CATALOGUE OF THE SHELLS CONTAINED IN THE COLLECTION OF THE LATE EARL OF TANKERVILLE / Sowerby, G B – Z 796 2. 1825 – 8 – ne IDC [590]

CATALOGUE OF THE THOMAS COKE PAPERS / Lloyd, Gareth – (Coll title: The People Called Methodists, Phase 1: Reference Tools) – Manchester, 1991 – 3mf – 9 – MP-604/1 – ne IDC [240]

CATALOGUE OF THE WESLEY FAMILY MANUSCRIPTS, V1 / Lloyd, Gareth – (Coll title: The People Called Methodists, Phase 1: Reference Tools) – Manchester, 1992 – 4mf – 9 – MP-605/1 – ne IDC [240]

CATALOGUE OF THE WESLEY FAMILY PAPERS, V2 / Lloyd, Gareth – (Coll title: The People Called Methodists, Phase 1: Reference Tools) – Manchester, 1992 – 4mf – 9 – MP-606/1 – ne IDC [240]

CATALOGUE OF THE WESLEY FAMILY PAPERS, V3 / Lloyd, Gareth – (Coll title: The People Called Methodists, Phase 1: Reference Tools) – Manchester, 1993 – 4mf – 9 – MP-607/1 – ne IDC [240]

CATALOGUE OF THE WORKS RELATIVE TO THE LAW OF NATIONS AND DIPLOMACY IN THE LIBRARY OF THE DEPARTMENT OF STATE – Washington, 1881 – 1mf – 9 – ILM-2869/1 – ne IDC [327]

CATALOGUE OF TIDE GAUGES IN THE PACIFIC – 1985 – 48p – 9 – 92-3-102326-8 – fr UNESCO [550]

CATALOGUE OF WEST INDIAN BIRDS / Cory, C B – 1892 – 8 – Z-2062 2 – ne IDC [590]

CATALOGUE OF WORKS IN REFUTATION OF METHODISM, FROM ITS ORIGIN IN 1729 TO THE PRESENT TIME,... / Decanver, H C pseud. [i.e. Curtis H Cavender] – Philadelphia, 1846 – 1mf – 9 – ne IDC [240]

CATALOGUE OF WORKS RELATING TO THE LAW OF NATIONS AND DIPLOMACY IN THE LIBRARY OF THE DEPARTMENT OF STATE OF THE UNITED STATES – Washington, 1897 – 2mf – 9 – ILM-2868/1 – ne IDC [327]

CATALOGUE OFFICIEL / Exposition Universelle. Paris, 1878 – Tome 1, Oeuvres d'art, classes 1 a 5. 1878 – 1 – us Res Libr [900]

CATALOGUE OFFICIEL – 2e ed. [Paris]: E Panis, [1855] – us Res Libr [324]

CATALOGUE OFFICIEL : TOME 1. GROUPE 1, OEUVRES D'ART, CLASSES 1 A 5 / Exposition universelle internationale de 1878, a Paris. Commissariat General – 2e ed150=. Paris: Impr national 1878 – us Res Libr [324]

CATALOGUE PRESENTATION DEEDS, AUGMENTATION BOOKS AND PARLIAMENTARY SURVEYS / Lambeth Palace. Library – 1 – uk Microform Academic [240]

CATALOGUE PROVISOIRE DES MANUSCRIPTS MAURITANIENS EN LANGUE ARABE PRESERVES EN MAURITANIE / Hamidoun, Mokhtar ould & Heymowski, Adam – Stockholm, 1965-66 [i.e. 1966?] – us Res Libr [960]

CATALOGUE RAISONNE DE MANUSCRITS ETHIOPIENS / Abbadie, Arnauld d' – Paris, 1859 – 5mf – 9 – ne IDC [090]

CATALOGUE RAISONNE DES LEPIDOPTERES DU BERRY ET DE L'AUVERGNE / Sand, M – Paris, 1879. v,206p. Z-1591/2 – 8 – ne IDC [590]

CATALOGUE RAISONNE DES PLANTES VASCULAIRES DU DAUPHINE / Verlot, J B – Grenoble. 1872. B-7327 2 – 8 – ne IDC [580]

CATALOGUE RAISONNE DES SCULPTURES APPELEES "CHAC MOOL." / Bordeianu-Taladoire, R – 9 – F60.00 – fr Ethnologie [730]

CATALOGUE RAISONNE DES TABLEAUX DU ROY, AVEC UNE ABREGE DE LA VIE DES PEINTRES / Lepicie, B – Paris. 2v. 1752-1754 – 8mf – ne IDC [700]

CATALOGUE SOMMAIRE DES MANUSCRITS SANSCRITS ET PALIS / Cabaton, Antoine – 1870-1908 – 2mf – 9 – fr Bibl Nationale [490]

CATALOGUE SYNONYMIQUE DES HYMENOPTERES DE FRANCE / Dours, J A – Amiens, 1874. 229p. (Mem. Soc. Linn. Nord France, v3, 1873). Z/1200/2 – 8 – ne IDC [590]

CATALOGUE SYSTEMATIQUE DE TOUS LES COLEOPTERES DECRITS DANS LES ANNALES DE LA SOCIETE ENTOMOLOGIQUE DE FRANCE DEPUIS 1832 JUSQU'A 1859 / ed by Strauch, A – Halle, 1861 – IV, 159p – 8 – ne IDC [590]

CATALOGUE SYSTEMATIQUE DES PUBLICATIONS SUR LA RUSSIE (1917-25) SE TROUVANT DANS LA BIBLIOTHEQUE DU BUREAU INTERNATIONAL DU TRAVAIL / International Labour Office. Library – Geneve, 1926-1927. v1-2 – 1 – 35.00r – us Hoover Inst Photo [947]

CATALOGUE SYSTEMATIQUE ET SYNONYMIQUE DES LEPIDOPTERES / Bruand D'uzelle, C T – Besancon. 1844-, 1845-47, -55. 142 (102)p., 1 tab. (Mem. Soc. Emul. Doubs., Besancon, v.1-3). Z-1100 2 – 8 – ne IDC [590]

CATALOGUED MANUSCRIPTS, 1847-19? / Catholic Archdiocese of Papeete – 3r – 1 – PMB1082 – at Pacific Mss [090]

CATALOGUE...FROM 1793 TO 1827 INCLUSIVE / Litchfield Law School – Litchfield, CT: Smith, 1828. 27p. LL-2340 – 1 – us L of C Photodup [340]

CATALOGUES / Contemporary Scientific Archives Centre. Oxford – 1973-80 – 31mf – 9 – us UMI [500]

CATALOGUES / Roger Williams University – 1873-1929 – 1 – $81.69 – us Baptist [020]

CATALOGUES DES MANUSCRITS SYRIAQUES ET SABEENS (MANDAITES) DE LA BIBLIOTHEQUE NATIONALE / Zoterberg, H – 1874 – 15mf – 8 – ne Slangenburg [470]

CATALOGUES HORTI BOTANICI SOCIETATIS PHYSICAE TURICENSIS / Roemer, J J – Turici, 1802 – 2mf – ne IDC [580]

CATALOGUES OF THE BERENSON LIBRARY / Harvard University. Center for Italian Renaissance Studies at Villa I Tat – 1972 – 4r – 1 – $480.00 – uk Hall [945]

CATALOGUES OF THE BIRDS, SHELLS AND SOME OF THE MORE RARE PLANTS OF DORSETSHIRE / Pulteney, R – 1799 – 8 – ne IDC [590]

CATALOGUES OF THE COLLECTION OF PRINTS, DRAWINGS AND PAINTINGS IN THE VICTORIA AND ALBERT MUSEUM / Victoria and Albert Museum. London – (Pt 1: Drawings, oil paintings etc $1,444. Pt 2: Prints and photographs $2,204. Pt 3: Subject and topographical indexes $1,489. Also includes printed contents list) – 878mf 6 comfiche – 9,17 – $4,366.00 set – 1-869934-56-3 – uk Emmett [700]

CATALOGUES OF THE UNITED KINGDOM DEPARTMENT OF THE ENVIRONMENT LIBRARY / United Kingdom Department of the Environment. London – (Available on microfilm by request) – 1977 – 9 – $1,785.00 – uk Hall [360]

CATALOGUES THEMATIQUES / Microeditions Hachette – 9 – F120.00 – fr Ethnologie [070]

CATALOGUING RULES FOR INDONESIAN NAMES, CODE OF – SE-10,792 1 – 9 – ne IDC [020]

CATALOGUS BIBLIOTHECA HISTORICO NATURALIS JOSEPHI BANKS / Dryander, J – Londini. 5v. 1796-1800 – 48mf – ne IDC [500]

CATALOGUS CATALOGORUM : AN ALPHABETICAL REGISTER OF SANSKRIT WORKS AND AUTHORS – Leipzig. 2 pts. 1891-1896 – 12mf – 9 – ne IDC [490]

CATALOGUS CODICUM ASTROLOGORUM GRAECORUM – Bruxellis, 1898-1940. v1-5 – 30mf – H-435/2 – ne IDC [520]

CATALOGUS CODICUM COPTICORUM MANUSCRIPTORUM / Zoega, G – Romae, 1808; Leipzig, 1903 – 39mf – 8 – ne Slangenburg [240]
CATALOGUS CODICUM GRAECORUM SINAITICORUM / Gardthausen, V – Oxonii, 1886 – 6mf – 8 – ne Slangenburg [450]
CATALOGUS CODICUM HAGIOGRAPHICORUM LATINORUM ANTIQUIORUM SAECULA XVI... – Bruxelles, etc. 3v. 1889-1893 – 38mf – 9 – ne IDC [240]
CATALOGUS CODICUM MANUSCRIPT BIBLIOTHECAE BODLEIANAE OXONIENSIS / Dillmann, August – Oxonii, 1848 – 2mf – 9 – ne IDC [090]
CATALOGUS CODICUM MSS. QUI IN COLLEGIIS AULISQUE OXONIENSIBUS HODIE ADSERVANTUR EST / Coxe, H O – 1 – uk Microform Academic [010]
CATALOGUS COLEOPTERORUM / Schenkling & Junk – 1 – uk Microform Academic [590]
CATALOGUS COLEOPTERORUM EUROPAE / Schaum, H R – Berlin, 1859. iv,121p. Z-1601/2 – 8 – ne IDC [590]
CATALOGUS COLEOPTERORUM EUROPAE / Stein, J P E F – Berlin, 1868 – 8 – ne IDC [590]
CATALOGUS COLEOPTERORUM HUCUSQUE DESCRIPTORUM SYNONYMICUS ET SYSTEMATICUS / Gemminger, M & Harold, B de – Monachii, etc. 12v. 1868-1876 – 75mf – ne IDC [590]
CATALOGUS (DE LEGATORUM JURE TRACTATUUM) COMPLETUS AB ANNO 1625 USQUE AD ANNUM 1700 / Grabar', VE – Iur'ev, 1918 – 4mf – ne IDC [340]
CATALOGUS DER TENTOONSTELLING IN HET PORTUGEESCH ISREALIETISCH SEMINARIUM "ETS HAIM" TE AMSTERDAM... / Silva Rosa, J S da & Menasje, A – Amsterdam, 1927 – 1mf – ne IDC [270]
CATALOGUS HERBARII PLANTARUM IN HORTO BOGORIENSI CULTARUM / Boldingh, I – Batavia, 1914 – 3mf – 9 – ne IDC [580]
CATALOGUS HISTORICO-CIRTICUS LIBRORUM RARIORUM / Vogt, J – Hamburg, 1753 – 13mf – 8 – ne Slangenburg [020]
CATALOGUS HORTI ACADEMICI VINDOBONENSIS / Endlicher, S L – Wien. 2v. 1842-1843 – 12mf – ne IDC [580]
CATALOGUS HORTI IMPERIALIS PETROPOLITANI / Fischer, FE L von & Meyer, C A von – Index plantarum. Petropoli. 1824. B-705 2 – 8 – ne IDC [580]
CATALOGUS INSECTARUM / Grey, W – Petropoli, 1866.vi,138p. Z/1310/2 – 8 – ne IDC [590]
CATALOGUS LICHENUM UNIVERSALIS / ed by Zahlbruckner, A – Leipzig. 1921-40. v. 1-10 – 131mf – 8 – ne IDC [580]
CATALOGUS MUNUSCRIPTORUM... 1786 : ANHANG VON UNTERSCHIEDLICHEN CHYMISCHEN,... – N.p., 1786 – 2mf – ne IDC [090]
CATALOGUS MUSCORUM FERE OMNIUM QUOS IN TERRIS AMAZONICIS ET ANDINIS / Spruce, R – Londini. 1867. B-5457 1 – 9 – ne IDC [580]
CATALOGUS OF NAAMLIJST VAN SCHILDERIJEN... / Hoet, G – 's-Gravenhage. 3v. 1752 – 30mf – ne IDC [700]
CATALOGUS PLANTARUM AMERICAE SEPTENTRIONALIS / Muhlenberg, G H E – Lancaster, 1813. 112 pp. B-6088 2 – 8 – ne IDC [580]
CATALOGUS PLANTARUM BY A SOCIETY OF GARDENERS / Miller, P – London, 1730. 90 pp., 21 pls. B-6071 1 – 9 – ne IDC [580]
CATALOGUS PLANTARUM COMMENTARIORUM MATHIOLI IN DIOSCORIDEM / Sternberg, K M von – Prague, 1821. 30 pp. B-443 2 – 8 – ne IDC [580]
CATALOGUS PLANTARUM CUBENSIUM / Grisebach, A – Lipsiae. 1866. B-5943 2 – 8 – ne IDC [580]
CATALOGUS PLANTARUM HORTI ACADEMICI ET AGRI GOTTINGENSIS / Zinn, J G – Gottingae. 1757. B-361 2 – 8 – ne IDC [580]
CATALOGUS PLANTARUM HORTI MONSPELIENSIS... / Candolle, A P de – Monspelii, 1813 – 3mf – ne IDC [580]
CATALOGUS PLANTARUM HORTI REGII PANORMITANI AD ANNUM 1827 / Tineo, V – Panormi, 1827 – 6mf – ne IDC [580]
CATALOGUS PLANTARUM HORTI REGII PARISIENSIS / Desfontaines, R L – Ed. 3. Paris. 1829. Additamentum. Paris. 1832 – 8 – ne IDC [580]
CATALOGUS PLANTARUM HORTI ULENPASSIANI / Gorter, D de – Zutphaniae, [1783] – 4mf – ne IDC [580]
CATALOGUS PLANTARUM IN HELVETIA CIS- ET TRANSALPINA SPONTE NASCENTIUM / Schleicher, J C – Bex. 1800. B-5716 2 – 8 – ne IDC [580]
CATALOGUS PLANTARUM IN HELVETIA CIS- ET TRANSALPINA SPONTE NASCENTIUM / Schleicher, J C – ed. 3. Bex. 1815. B-5718 2 – 8 – ne IDC [580]
CATALOGUS PLANTARUM IN HELVETIA CIS- ET TRANSALPINA SPONTE NASCENTIUM / Schleicher, J C – ed. 4. Camberii. 1821. B-5201 2 – 8 – ne IDC [580]
CATALOGUS PLANTARUM IN HORTO AKSAKOVIANO... / Regel, E A von – [Spb.], 1860 – 2mf – ne IDC [580]
CATALOGUS PLANTARUM IN HORTO BOTANICO BOGORIENSI CULTARUM ALTER / Hasskarl, J K – Bataviae, 1844 – 5mf – 9 – ne IDC [580]
CATALOGUS PLANTARUM IN HORTO BOTANICO GYMNASII VOLHYNIENSIS CREMENECI CULTARUM / Besser, W S JG von – Krzemieniec [Kremenets], 1816 – 5mf – ne IDC [580]
CATALOGUS PLANTARUM LATINE, GRAECE, GERMANICE AND GALLICE / Gessner, C – Tiguri: C. Froschoverus, 1542 – 4mf – ne IDC [580]
CATALOGUS PLANTARUM QUAE IN INSULA JAMAICA SPONTE PROVENIUNT / Sloane, H – Londini, 1696 – 5mf – ne IDC [580]
CATALOGUS PLANTARUM REGII HORTI BOTANICI TAURINENSIS / Birolli, G – Augustae, Taurinorum, 1815 – 2mf – ne IDC [580]
CATALOGUS SYSTEMATICUS COLEOPTERORUM / Voet, J E – La Haye. 2v. [1769-]1806 – 27mf – ne IDC [590]
CATALOGUS SYSTEMATICUS DIPTERORUM EUROPAE / Schiner, J R – Vindobonae, 1864. xii,115p. Z-1609/2 – 8 – ne IDC [590]
CATALOGUS TESTIUM VERITATIS, QUI ANTE NOSTRAM AETATEM RECLAMARUNT PAPAE / Flacius, M – Basileae, 1556 – 12mf – 8 – ne Slangenburg [240]
CATALOGUS TESTIVM VERITATIS, QVI ANTE NOSTRAM AETATEM RECLAMARUNT PAPAE / Flacius Illyricus d.A E, M – Basileae, [1556] – 12mf – 9 – ne IDC [240]
CATALOGUS VAN NEDERLANDSCHE HANDSCHRIFTEN, WELKE BERUSTEN IN DE KEIZERLIJKE BIBLIOTHEEK TE ST PETERSBURG / Bleeck van Rijsewijk, FG B van – Utrecht, 1848 – 1mf – 9 – ne IDC [090]
CATALOGUS VEGETABILIUM MUSEI SUI / Targioni-Tozzetti, G – Florentiae, 1826. 91 pp., 3 pls. B-6474 1 – 9 – ne IDC [580]
CATALOGUS...'S LANDS PLANTENTUIN TE BUITENZORG... / Blume, C L – Batavia, 1823 – 2mf – 9 – ne IDC [580]
Catalonia. Comissariat de Propaganda *see*
– LA CATALOGNE
– EL FASCISMO PRETENDE ENCARCELAR ESPANA
– A PLEA FOR SUPPORT
CATALYSIS REVIEWS – v1-8. 1968-73 – 1 – us UMI [073]
CATALYSIS REVIEWS: SCIENCE AND ENGINEERING – (v26-. 1984-. 5,6,9) – v9-. 1974- – 1 – us UMI [073]
CATALYST – Vancouver. v32-37. 1988/89-1993/94 – 9 – Can$20.00y – cn Micromedia [073]
CATALYST FOR CHANGE – (v4- . 1974- . 5,6. v5- . 1975- . 9) – v. 1-. 1971- – 1 – us UMI [073]
Catamarca. Argentine Republic. (Province) *see* BOLETIN OFICIAL Y JUDICIAL
Cataneo, P *see*
– L'ARCHITETTURA
– I QUATTRO PRIMI LIBRI DI ARCHITETTURA
CATARINE OF SIENA : A BIOGRAPHY / Butler, Josephine E – London: Dyer, 1878 – 1mf – us A.T.L.A. [240]
CATASAUQUA INDEPENDENT – Catasauqua, PA., 1892-1897 – 13 – $25.00r – us I.M.R. [071]
CATASAUQUA VALLEY RECORD – Catasauqua, PA. -w 1889-1892 – 13 – $25.00r – us I.M.R. [071]
LA CATASTROFE DE BARCELONA / Escudero Gonzalez, Jose – Merida: Imp. Juan Rejas Lopez, 1969 – sp Bibl Santa Ana [946]
CATASTROPHE MODEL OF ANXIETY AND PERFORMANCE : APPLICATION TO FIELD HOCKEY / Mills, Brett D & Gray, Marvin – 1992 – 1mf – 9 – $4.00 – us Microform Publ [150]
CATASTROPHIC INJURIES IN JUNIOR HIGH AND HIGH SCHOOL WRESTLING : A FIVE-SEASON STUDY / Laudermilk, Julie I – 1988 – 49p 1mf – 9 – $4.00 – us Microform Publ [617]
CATAWBA BAPTIST CHURCH. YORK COUNTY. SOUTH CAROLINA : CHURCH RECORDS – 1949-72 – 1 – 22.14 – us Baptist [240]
Catawba. Synod (Pres. Ch. in the U.S.A.) *see* MINUTES, 1887-1913
CATCHES AND LANDINGS – it F.A.O. [639]
Cate, S Blaupot ten *see*
– GESCHIEDENIS DER DOOPSGEZINDEN IN FRIESLAND
– GESCHIEDENIS DER DOOPSGEZINDEN IN HOLLAND, ZEELAND, UTRECHT EN GELDERLAND
– GESCHIEDKUNDIG ONDERZOEK NAAR DEN WALDENZISCHEN OORSPRONG VAN DE NEDERLANDSCHE DOOPSGEZINDEN
CATECHESIS DAT IS, ONDERWIJSLICK GESPRECK, TUSSCHEN VADER VNDE SOON / Joris, David – BME-377 1 – 9 – ne IDC [240]
CATECHESIS DAVIDIS CHYTRAEI POSTREMO RECOGNITA / Chytraeus, D – Magdeburgae, 1578 – 3mf – 9 – ne IDC [240]
CATECHETICAL NOTES AND CLASS QUESTIONS, LITERAL AND MYSTICAL / Neale, John Mason – London: Rivingtons, 1869 – 9 – us A.T.L.A. [240]
LE CATECHIME DES COMMENCANTS / Gosselin, David – Ste. Anne de la Pocatiere: F. Proulx, 1886. 03480. (Pre-1900 Canadiana) – 9 – cn C.I.H.M. [240]
CATECHISM (CCC158) = CHIAO YU WEN TA / Ho, Shou-liang & Lin, Chih-szu – (In Chinese) – 1st ed. Kowloon: Chinese Christian Literature Council, 1967 – 1r – 1 – 1984-B500 – us A.T.L.A. [240]
THE CATECHISM FOR THE METHODIST CHURCH MEMBERS (CCC157) = CHI TU CHIAO WEI LI KUNG CHIAO YU WEI TA / Ho, Siew Liong & Ling, James – (In Chinese) – Sarawak: Christian Literature of Sarawak Methodist Church, 1958 – 1r – 1 – 1984-B500 – us A.T.L.A. [240]
CATECHISM OF PRIVATE AND PUBLIC HYGIENE / Desroches, J Israel; ed by Alexander Wright – Translated from the French – 9 – cn C.I.H.M. [971]
THE CATECHISM OF THE ORTHODOX, CATHOLIC, EASTERN CHURCH : EXAMINED AND APPROVED BY THE MOST HOLY GOVERNING SYNOD, AND PUBLISHED FOR THE USE OF SCHOOLS AND OF ALL ORTHODOX CHRISTIANS – San Francisco, CA: Murdock Press, 1901 – 1mf – 9 – 0-8370-7501-7 – 1986-1501 – us A.T.L.A. [240]
A CATECHISM ON CHURCH GOVERNMENT : WITH SPECIAL REFERENCE TO THAT OF THE METHODIST EPISCOPAL CHURCH, SOUTH / McTyeire, Holland N – Nashville, Tenn.: Publishing House of the M.E. Church, South, 1894, c1878 – 1mf – us A.T.L.A. [240]
A CATECHISM ON THE DOCTRINES OF THE PLYMOUTH BRETHERN / Croskery, Thomas – Toronto: "Canada Presbyterian", 1879. 05261. (Pre-1900 Canadiana) – 9 – cn C.I.H.M. [971]
CATECHISME A L'USAGE DES FIDELES DE LA CAMPAGNE DANS LES CIRCONSTANCES ACTUELLES [SUIVI DE] CATECHISME A L'USAGE DES VRAIS FIDELES ET CATHOLIQUES ROMAINS – 1 – F50.00 – fr Armell [240]
CATECHISME ABREGE EN LA LANGUE DE MADAGASCAR / Caulier – 1785 – 9 – $5.00 – fr Orientalistes [240]
LE CATECHISME DE LA PAIX / Constant, Alphonse Louis – Quatrains sur la Bible et la Bible de la Liberte. Extraits. Paris: Chamuel, 1896.238p. 3 fiches. (Political Science Collection) – 9 – 8.00 – fr Bibl Nationale [320]
LE CATECHISME DES ELECTEURS D'APRES L'OUVRAGE DE A. GERIN-LAJOIE – Nouv. ed. Montreal: J.-B Thivierge & fils, editeurs, [1935 ?]. SEM105P1660 – 2mf – 9 – Can$4.50 – cn Bibl Nat [971]
LE CATECHISME DES PROVINCES ECCLESIASTIQUES DE QUEBEC, MONTREAL, OTTAWA / Eglise Catholique. Province de Quebec – Nouv. ed. Quebec: A.O. Pruneau Editeur, [1908?] – 2mf – 9 – Can$4.50 – cn Bibl Nat [240]
CATECHISME D'HYGIENE PRIVEE / Desroches, J Israel – Montreal: W. F. Daniel, 1889. 02667. (Pre-1900 Canadiana) – 9 – cn C.I.H.M. [971]
CATECHISME D'HYGIENE PRIVEE ET PUBLIQUE / Desroches, J Israel – Montreal: Cadieux & Derome, 1897. 02668. (Pre-1900 Canadiana) – 9 – cn C.I.H.M. [971]
CATECHISME DU DIOCESE DE SENS / Languet, Jean Joseph – Quebec: Brown & Gilmore, 1765. SEM105P887 – 2mf – 9 – Can$4.50 – cn Bibl Nat [240]
CATECHISME HISTORIQUE, CONTENANT EN ABREGE L'HISTOIRE SAINTE ET LA DOCTRINE CHRETIENNE / Fleury, Claude – Nouv. ed. Quebec: Nouvelle Imprimerie, 1807. SEM16P39 – 1r – 5 – Can$9.00 – cn Bibl Nat [240]
CATECHISME NATIONAL / Thiery, Avocat – En France, de l'imprimerie des bons citoyens. 1789 – 9 – fr Hachette [321]
CATECHISMI TRES SYSTEMATICE COORDINATI PRO PLENA JUVENTUTIS CHRISTIANAE INSTRUCTIONE / Weninger, Francis Xavier – Cincinnati, OH: Roberti Clarke, 1871 – 1mf – 9 – 0-8370-6714-6 – 1986-0714 – us A.T.L.A. [240]
CATECHISMS – Baptist Catechsim, 1866; Baptist Catechism, a Catechism for little children; Boyce, James P., A brief Catechism of Bible doctrine, 1864; Broadus, John A., A Catechism of Bible teachings, 1892; Dayton, A. C., A catechism for the little children; Graves, A. D., The child's scripture catechism in rhyme, v. 1, 1861; Sunday School primer, 1864; Winkler, Edwin T., Notes and questions for the oral instruction of colored people, 1857 – 1 – 16.10 – us Baptist [240]
CATECHISMS OF THE SECOND REFORMATION : WITH HISTORICAL INTRODUCTION AND BIOGRAPHICAL NOTICES / Mitchell, Alexander F – London: James Nisbet, 1886 – 1mf – us A.T.L.A. [240]
CATECHISMUS, DAS IST: TROSTREICHE VND NUETZLICHE AUSLEGUNG VBER DIE FUENFF HEUBTSTUECK DER CHRISTLICHE LEHRE / Mathesius, Johannes – Leipzig, 1586 – 6mf – ne IDC [240]
CATECHISMUS HISTORICUS MINOR / Bessieux – Creatio. Lex antiqua. Lex nova. Catechisme en langue pongouee. Amiens, Caron et Lambert. 1847 – 9 – 5.00 – fr Orientalistes [240]
DER CATECHISMUS MIT VIEL SCHOENEN SPRUECHEN DER HEILIGEN SCHRIFFT GEGRUENDET... / Huberinus, Caspar – [Magdeburg: Michael Lotther], 1544. [G.F.: 16.3] – 8mf – 9 – HUB-40/1 – ne IDC [240]
DER CATECHISMUS. MIT VIL SCHOENEN SPRUECHEN VN HISTORIEN DER HAILIGE SCHRIFFT GEGRUENDET... / Huberinus, Caspar – [Augsburg: Philipp Ulhart, 1543]. [G.F.: 16.1] – 6mf – 9 – HUB-39/1 – ne IDC [240]
CATECHISMUS ODER KINDERLEHR VON DEN FUERNEMMEN HAEUPTPUNCTEN CHRISTLICHER RELIGION ALS DA SIND:... / Hunnius, A – Franckfort am Mayn, 1596 – 10mf – ne IDC [240]
CATECHISMUS, ODER KURTZE UNTERRICHT CHRISTLICHER LEHRE, WIS DER IN KIRCHEN UND SCHULEN DER CHURFIERST; OCJEM 1/4FATTE GETROEBEM WIRD... – Berlin: Gedruckt bey Christoft Runge, 1657 – 1 – us Sibley [780]
CATECHISMUSPREDIGTEN... / Eber, P – [Nuernberg], 1578 – 4mf – 9 – ne IDC [240]
CATECHISMVS, HOC EST, CHRISTIANAE DOCTRINAE METHODVS. ITEM, OBIECTIONES IN EVNDEM,... / Lossius, L – Vvitebergae, 1560 – 5mf – ne IDC [240]
CATECHISMVS PREDIGSWEISE GESTELT FUER DIE KIRCHE ZU REGENSPURG... / Gallus, N – [Regenspurg], 1554 – 5mf – 9 – ne IDC [240]
CATECHIST – (v10- . 1976- . 5,6,9) – v. 1-. 1967- – 1 – us UMI [240]
O CATECHISTA : FOLHA COMMERCIAL, NOTICIOSA E ANALYTICA – Manaus, Amazonas. 12 Jul 1862; Ago 1863-Jun 1865; Mar, Nov-Dez 1869; Jan-26 Set 1871 – 1,5,6 – bl Biblioteca [072]

LE CATECHUMENE / Borde, Charles – (D'Holbach series). 1768 – 9 – fr Hachette [240]

CATECISMO DE LA DOCTRINA CRISTIANA Y NOCIONES DE URBANIDAD / Llanes Garcia, Enrique – Don Benito: Tip. de Trejo, 1926 – sp Bibl Santa Ana [240]

CATECISMO PATRIOTICO ESPANOL / Gonzalez Menendez-Reigada, Albino – 3rd ed. Salamanca, 1939. Fiche W1043. (Blodgett Collection of Spanish Civil War Pamphlets) – 9 – us H.U. College Libr [946]

CATECISMO POLITICO...MONARQUIA ESPANOLA / D JC – 1820 – 9 – 1.50f – sp Bibl Santa Ana [946]

CATECISMO SOCIAL / Fernandez Santana, Ezequiel – Portada de Orduna: Huelva, Imp Munoz, 1947 – 1 – sp Bibl Santa Ana [240]

CATECISMO SOCIAL / Sanchez Ruiz, Valentin M – Madrid: Apostolado de la Prensa, 2nd ed 1935 – 1 – sp Bibl Santa Ana [240]

CATECISMO SOCIAL... / Sanchez Ruiz, Valentin M – Madrid: Apostolado de la Prensa, 1933 – 1 – sp Bibl Santa Ana [240]

CATECISMO SOCIAL A SEA LA ENCICLICA "RERUM NOVARUM" DEL PAPA LEON 13 PUESTA EN PREGUNTAS Y RESPUETAS PARA SU MEJOR INTELIGENCIA / Crespo, Manuel Maria – Don Benito: Colegio del Corazon de Maria, 1920 – sp Bibl Santa Ana [946]

A CATEDRAL – (Suppl to: Boletim Interdiocesano) – Diamantina, 9 Jun 1935 – 1,5,6 – bl Biblioteca [072]

LA CATEDRAL DE CARACAS Y SUS FUNCIONES DE CULTO / Navarro, Nicolas E – Caracas, 1931; Madrid: Razon y Fe, 1931 – 1 – sp Bibl Santa Ana [240]

CATEGORIES GRAMMATICALES ET DISTRIBUTION : LES LIMITES ENTRE PREPOSITION, CONJONCTION, ADVERBE / Xatard, Veronique – 1mf – 9 – 10092 – fr Atelier National [440]

Catel, Albert *see* CHARTES ET DOCUMENTS DE L'ABBAYE CISTERCIENNE DE PREUILLY

Catel, Charles-Simon *see* (SEMIRAMIS). PREMIERE SUITE D'HARMONIE A HUIT PARTIES...TIREE DE L'OPERA DE SEMIRAMIS.

Catelan, Laurent *see* RARE ET CURIEUX DISCOURS DE LA PLANTE APPELEE MANDRAGORE

Catellani, E *see* IL CANALE DI PANAMA

Catellani, E L *see*
- METODO E FINE...DIRITTO INTERNATIONALE
- LA NAVIGAZIONE FLUVIALE...

CATENAE GRAECORUM PATRUM IN NOVUM TESTAMENTUM / ed by Cramer, J A – London, 1839-1844. 8v – 73mf – 8 – ne Slangenburg [240]

Cates, J M D *see*
- THE COMPANION
- THE SACRED HARP
- THE VOICE OF TRUTH

Catesby, M *see* NATURAL HISTORY OF CAROLINA, FLORIDA AND THE BAHAMA ISLANDS

CATFISH CREEK BAPTIST CHURCH. DILLON COUNTY. LANGLEY, SOUTH CAROLINA : CHURCH RECORDS – 1802-1971 – 1 – 24.12 – us Baptist [240]

Cathala, Pierre Adolphe Juste *see* FACE AUX REALITES, LA DIRECTION DES FINANCES FRANCAISES SOUS L'OCCUPATION

CATHARINE FURZE. BY MARK RUTHERFORD. EDITED BY HIS FRIEND, REUBEN SHAPCOTT / White, William Hale – London: T. Fisher Unwin, 1893 – 1 roll – 1 – 1-55879-972-9 – uk Libr Preservation [920]

CATHARINE MARIA SEDGWICK PAPERS, 1798-1867 / Sedgwick, Catharine Maria – Massachusetts Historical Society – 18r – 1 – $1385.00 – us UMI [920]

CATHARINE OF ARAGON AND THE SOURCES OF THE ENGLISH REFORMATION / Boys, Albert Du; ed by Yonge, Charlotte Mary – London: Hurst and Blackett, 1881 – 2mf – us A.T.L.A. [240]

CATHARRI SUFFOCATIVI EJESQUE CURATIONES HISTORIA / Rotundis, P – Madrid, 1728 – 9 – sp Cultura [615]

CATHAY AND THE WAY THITHER / Yule, H – A collection of medieval notices of China. New ed. revised by H. Cordier. 4 v. Hakluyt Soviety. v. 38. 1915; v. 33. 1913; v. 37. 1914; v. 41. 1916. BU-668 2 – 8 – ne IDC [910]

Cathcart, Wallace Daniel *see* COMMERCIAL LAW QUESTIONS

Cathcart, William *see*
- ANCIENT BRITISH AND IRISH CHURCHES
- THE ANCIENT BRITISH AND IRISH CHURCHES
- THE BAPTISM OF THE AGES AND OF THE NATIONS
- THE BAPTISTS AND THE AMERICAN REVOLUTION
- THE PAPAL SYSTEM

CATHEDRA PETRI / Greenwood, Thomas – 6v. 1856-65 – 1 – us A.T.L.A. [240]

THE CATHEDRAL : ITS NECESSARY PLACE IN THE LIFE AND WORK OF THE CHURCH / Benson, Edward White – London: J. Murray, 1878 – 1mf – us A.T.L.A. [240]

CATHEDRAL CITIZEN – Cathedral, CA. 1981-83 – 6r – 1 – $300.00 – R02101 – us Library Micro [071]

THE CATHEDRAL MONTHLY – [Fredericton, N.B.: Christ Church Cathedral, 1888?-189- or 19–] – 9 – cn C.I.H.M. [240]

CATHEDRALES. SCULPTURES, VITRAUX, OBJETS D'ART, MANUSCRITS DES XIIE ET XIIIE SIECLES / Reunion des musees nationaux. Paris – 1962. 200 illus. 3 fiches – 9 – fr Réunion [700]

THE CATHEDRALS OF ENGLAND AND WALES / Bond, Francis – ("English Cathedrals Illustrated," Ed. 4) H-1234 2. 1912 – 8 – ne IDC [941]

LES CATHEDRALS. PRELUDE POUR ORCHESTRE; VERSION AVEC OU SANS CHOEURS / Pierne, G – Paris: Rouart, Leroille & Co, 1916 – 1 – us Sibley [780]

Cathell, D W *see* BOOK ON THE PHYSICIAN HIMSELF

Catherine 2, Empress of Russia *see*
- BERIGTSCHRIFT VAN...TER VERVAARDOJING VAN EEN ONTWERP VOOR EEN VIEUW RUSSISCH WETBOEK
- ISTRUZIONE EMANATA DA CATERINA SECONDA, IMPERATRICE E LEGISLATRICE DI TUTTA LA RUSSIA...TRADOTTA NUOVAMENTE DAL FRANCESE IN LINGUA TOSCANA

Catherine 2, Tsarina of Russia *see*
- INSTRUCTION DONNEE PAR...IMPERATRICE ET LEGISLATRICE DE TOUTES LES RUSSIES..
- INSTRUCTIONS ADDRESSEES...A LA COMMISSION ETABLIE POUR TRAVAILLER A L'EXECUTION DU PROJET D'UN NOUVEAU CODE DE LOIS
- NAKAZ EIA IMPERATORSKAGO VELICHESTVA EKATERINY VTORIIA..

Catherine of Sienna *see* SAINT CATHERINE OF SIENNA AS SEEN IN HER LETTERS

Catherinot, Nicolas *see* TRAITE DE L'ARCHITECTURE

Catherwood, Mary Hartwell *see*
- THE CHASE OF SAINT-CASTIN: AND OTHER STORIES OF THE FRENCH IN THE NEW WORLD
- HEROES OF THE MIDDLE WEST: THE FRENCH
- MACKINAC AND LAKE STORIES
- OLD KASKASKIA
- THE ROMANCE OF DOLLARD

Cathey, James H et al *see* A LINCOLN LEARNER'S ORIGINAL

CATHOLIC – Indianapolis. Ind. 1910-1915 – 1 – us UMI [071]

THE CATHOLIC – Kingston [Ont.]: Patriot and Farmer's Monitor, 1830- – 9 – cn C.I.H.M. [240]

THE CATHOLIC – Kingston, Ontario. 22 oct 1830-v1 n52. 14 oct 1831 – 1r – 1 – Can$45.00 – cn Can Microfilming [072]

THE CATHOLIC : LETTERS ADDRESSED BY A JURIST TO A YOUNG KINSMAN PROPOSING TO JOIN THE CHURCH OF ROME / Derby, Elias Hasket – (Includes bibliographical references) – Boston: John P Jewett, 1856 – 1mf – 9 – 0-8370-8499-7 – 1986-2499 – us A.T.L.A. [240]

CATHOLIC AND PROTESTANT COUNTRIES COMPARED : IN CIVILIZATION, POPULAR HAPPINESS, GENERAL INTELLIGENCE, AND MORALITY / Young, Alfred – (Includes index) – 9th ed. New York: Catholic Book Exchange, 1898, c1895 – 2mf – 9 – 0-8370-7039-2 – 1986-1039 – us A.T.L.A. [230]

CATHOLIC AND PROTESTANT NATIONS COMPARED IN THEIR THREEFOLD RELATIONS TO WEALTH, KNOWLEDGE, AND MORALITY / Roussel, Napoleon – With an introduction by Baptiste Noel. 2 v. in 1. 1855 – 1 – us A.T.L.A. [240]

CATHOLIC AND PROTESTANT PRIESTS, FREEMASONS AND LIBERALS SHOT BY THE REBELS / Spain. Embajada. Great Britain – London, 1937. Fiche W1171. (Blodgett Collection of Spanish Civil War Pamphlets) – 9 – us H.U. College Libr [946]

Catholic Archdiocese of Papeete *see*
- ADMINISTRATIVE ARCHIVES, 1833-1969
- CATALOGUED MANUSCRIPTS, 1847-19?

CATHOLIC BELIEF : OR, A SHORT AND SIMPLE EXPOSITION OF CATHOLIC DOCTRINE / Di Bruno, Joseph Fa a; ed by Lambert, Louis Aloisius – (Includes index) – Author's American ed. New York: Benziger, c1912 – 1mf – 9 – 0-8370-8337-0 – 1986-2337 – us A.T.L.A. [240]

CATHOLIC BIBLICAL QUARTERLY – 1(1939)-8(1946) – 67mf – 9 – Dfl235.00 – ne Slangenburg [073]

CATHOLIC BIBLICAL QUARTERLY – (v33- . 5,6. v37- . 9) – v. 11- 1949- – 1 – us UMI [240]

THE CATHOLIC BIBLICAL QUARTERLY – Washington, DC. v1-8. 1939-1946 – 67mf – 9 – ne IDC [220]

CATHOLIC CARE OF THE ITALIAN IMMIGRANT IN THE UNITED STATES / Perrotta, Christopher – 1925 – 1r – 1 – us I.H.R.C. [240]

CATHOLIC CHAMPION – v1-13. Dec 1888-1901 (complete) – 3r – 1 – ATLA S0131 – us A.T.L.A. [073]

CATHOLIC CHARISMATIC – v. 1-. 1976- – 1,5,6,9 – us UMI [073]

CATHOLIC CHARITIES REVIEW – v. 1-58. 1917-1974 – 1 – us UMI [360]

CATHOLIC CHURCH AND CHRISTIAN STATE : A SERIES OF ESSAYS ON THE RELATION OF THE CHURCH TO THE CIVIL POWER / Hergenroether, Joseph – London: Burns and Oates, 1876 – 2mf – us A.T.L.A. [240]

CATHOLIC CHURCH AND STATE PAMPHLET COLLECTION – 195?-19?? – 1 – CSUXANK5680-B – us Hoover Inst Photo [240]

THE CATHOLIC CHURCH AND THE RACE QUESTION / Congar, Y M J – 7 – uk Microform Academic [240]

THE CATHOLIC CHURCH FROM WITHIN – (Includes bibliographical references and index) – London; New York: Longmans, Green, 1901 – 1mf – 9 – 0-8370-6939-4 – 1986-0939 – us A.T.L.A. [240]

CATHOLIC CHURCH IN FRANCE PAMPHLET COLLECTION – 1942-1944 – 1 – CSUXAMJ7794-B – us Hoover Inst Photo [240]

CATHOLIC CHURCH IN GERMANY PAMPHLET COLLECTION – 1954-1966 – 1 – CSUXAMK5673-B – us Hoover Inst Photo [240]

THE CATHOLIC CHURCH IN INDONESIA : ARCHIVES OF THE ARCHBISHOPRIC OF BATAVIA/JAKARTA, 1807-1949 – (Inventory available separately for Dfl300.00) – MMF. Subsections available separately – 3302mf – 9 – Dfl22,425.00 – ne MMF Publ [240]

CATHOLIC CHURCH IN LITHUANIA PAMPHLET COLLECTION – 1973-1977 – 1 – CSUXANL2823-B – us Hoover Inst Photo [240]

CATHOLIC CHURCH IN NORTHERN IRELAND PAMPHLET COLLECTION – 197? – 1 – CSUXAMJ7791-B – us Hoover Inst Photo [240]

THE CATHOLIC CHURCH IN THE NIAGARA PENINSULA, 1626-1895 / Harris, William Richard – Toronto: W. Briggs, 1895. 05379. (Pre-1900 Canadiana) – 9 – cn C.I.H.M. [971]

CATHOLIC CHURCH IN THE UKRAINE PAMPHLET COLLECTION – 1981 – 1 – CSUXANR2565-B – us Hoover Inst Photo [240]

CATHOLIC CHURCH IN YUGOSLAVIA PAMPHLET COLLECTION – 19??-1973 – 1 – CSUXANL2791-B – us Hoover Inst Photo [240]

CATHOLIC CHURCH, LITURGY AND RITUAL [MASS 16TH CENT MSS.] – Ms – 1 – us Sibley [780]

THE CATHOLIC CHURCH, THE RENAISSANCE AND PROTESTANTISM : LECTURES GIVEN AT THE CATHOLIC INSTITUTE OF PARIS, JANUARY TO MARCH 1904 / Baudrillart, Alfred – London: Kegan Paul, Truebner, 1908 – 1mf – us A.T.L.A. [240]

CATHOLIC CHURCHMEN IN SCIENCE. FIRST SERIES : SKETCHES OF THE LIVES OF CATHOLIC ECCLESIASTICS WHO WERE AMONG THE GREAT FOUNDERS IN SCIENCE / Walsh, James Joseph – 2nd ed. Philadelphia: American Ecclesiastical Review, 1910 – 1mf – 9 – 0-8370-7034-1 – 1986-1034 – us A.T.L.A. [920]

CATHOLIC CITIZEN – Milwaukee. Wis. -w. 1878-80, 1882-1935 – 1 – us UMI [071]

THE CATHOLIC CITIZEN – Toronto. v4 n4. 19 nov 1857-v5 n28. 8 jul 1858 – 1r – 1 – Can$25.00 – cn Can Microfilming [072]

CATHOLIC COLONIAL MISSIONS / Westminster Cathedral – 1808-27 – 1 – uk Microform Academic [240]

CATHOLIC COMMISSION FOR JUSTICE AND PEACE IN ZIMBABWE – Harare. 23 docs. 1983-1990 – 4mf – 9 – ne IDC [320]

CATHOLIC COMMISSION FOR JUSTICE AND PEACE IN ZIMBABWE – Harare. 24 docs. 1983-1991 – 5mf – 9 – ne IDC [320]

CATHOLIC COURIER – Rochester. N.Y. 1935-1944 – 1 – us UMI [071]

THE CATHOLIC COURIER JOURNAL – Rochester. N.Y. -w. 1945- – 1 – us UMI [071]

CATHOLIC DIGEST – v. 1-10. 1936-1945 – 1 – us Princeton Micro [240]

CATHOLIC DIGEST – (v35- . 5,6. v40- . 9) – 1- 1936- – 1 – us UMI [073]

THE CATHOLIC DOCTRINE OF FAITH AND MORALS, GATHERED FROM SACRED SCRIPTURE; DECREES OF COUNCILS, AND APPROVED CATECHISMS / Byrne, William – (Includes index) – Boston: Cashman, Keating, 1892 – 2mf – 9 – 0-8370-8323-0 – 1986-2323 – us A.T.L.A. [240]

CATHOLIC DOGMA: THE ANTIDOTE OF DOUBT / McLaren, William Edward – New York: James Pott, 1884. 1 fiche – 9 – us A.T.L.A. [240]

CATHOLIC EDUCATIONAL CONDITIONS IN THE UNITED STATES / Macksey, Charles – Columbus, OH: Catholic Educational Association, 1913 – 1mf – 9 – 0-8370-8590-X – 1986-2590 – us A.T.L.A. [240]

CATHOLIC EDUCATIONAL REVIEW – 1-67. 1911-69 – 1 – us UMI [240]

CATHOLIC EDUCATOR – (Formerly: Journal of Religious Instruction.) v. 1-16. 1930-1946 – 1 – us Princeton Micro [240]

CATHOLIC ESSAYS ON THE PROBLEMS OF WAR TODAY: MORALS AND MISSILES – 1fiche (29x) – 9 – 1.00f – at Libertarian Micro [320]

THE CATHOLIC FAITH : OR, DOCTRINES OF THE CHURCH OF ROME CONTRARY TO SCRIPTURE AND THE TEACHING OF THE PRIMITIVE CHURCH / Treat, John Harvey – (In English, Greek and Latin. Includes index) – Nashotah, WI: Bishop Welles Brotherhood, 1888, c1886 – 2mf – 9 – 0-8370-8555-1 – 1986-2555 – us A.T.L.A. [240]

The Catholic Health Association of the United States *see* HEALTH PROGRESS

CATHOLIC HERALD – 1888-1993. Continued annually – 1 – £3,450.00 – uk World [072]

CATHOLIC HERALD – (Includes The Register 1930-38; Superior California Register 1939-Jul 1949) – Sacramento, CA. Mar 1908-44+ r – 1 – $2,200.00 ($50.00y) – B02731 – us Library Micro [240]

CATHOLIC HERALD – Milwaukee. Wis. -w. 1922-35 – 1 – us UMI [071]

CATHOLIC HERALD – v1-3. Jun 1872-Nov 1873 (complete) – 1r – 1 – ATLA S0267A – us A.T.L.A. [073]

THE CATHOLIC HERALD – Philadelphia. Pennsylvania. v. 1-12. 1833-44. Scattered issues wanting – 1 – 65.00 – us L of C Photodup [240]

THE CATHOLIC HERALD AND VISITOR *see* THE UNIVERSE. THE CATHOLIC HERALD AND VISITOR

CATHOLIC HERALD CITIZEN – Milwaukee. Wis. -w. 1936-67 – 1 – us UMI [071]

CATHOLIC HIGH SCHOOL QUARTERLY / National Catholic Education Association – v. 1-27. 1942-69 – 1 – us Princeton Micro [370]

CATHOLIC HISTORICAL RESEARCHES *see* AMERICAN CATHOLIC HISTORICAL RESEARCHES

CATHOLIC HISTORICAL REVIEW – (v56- . 5,6. v62- . 9) – 1- 1915- – 1 – us UMI [240]

CATHOLIC HISTORICAL REVIEW – (Washington)v. 1-27. 1915-1942 – 1,5,6 – us Princeton Micro [240]

CATHOLIC HYMNS / Pustardos, C – (Music in number notation). In part Latin words. SE-4827 1. 1962 – 9 – ne IDC [240]
CATHOLIC INSTITUTE FOR INTERNATIONAL RELATIONS – London. 228 docs. 1980-1991 – 106mf – 9 – ne IDC [320]
CATHOLIC INTERESTS IN THE NINETEENTH CENTURY / Montalembert, Charles Forbes – London: C. Dolman, 1852 – 1mf – us A.T.L.A. [240]
CATHOLIC LAWYER – v1-32. 1955-89 – 1,5,6 – $270.00 – us Hein [073]
CATHOLIC LIBRARY WORLD – (v42- . 5,6. v49- . 9) – 1- 1929- – 1 – us UMI [240]
CATHOLIC LONDON A CENTURY AGO / Ward, Bernard – London: Catholic Truth Society, 1905 – 1mf – us A.T.L.A. [941]
A CATHOLIC LOOKS AT SPAIN / Semprun Gurrea, Jose Maria – London, 1937. Fiche W787. (Blodgett Collection of Spanish Civil War Pamphlets) – 9 – us H.U. College Libr [946]
THE CATHOLIC MAGAZINE – 1931-41 (complete) – 2r – 1 – ATLA S0534 – us A.T.L.A. [073]
CATHOLIC MIND – v1-50. 1903-52 – 1,5,6 – us Princeton Micro [240]
Catholic Mission, Solomon Islands *see* NA TURUPATU NA LOTU KATOLIKA
THE CATHOLIC MONTHLY CALENDAR – Toronto: G.M. Rose, [1898-189- or 19–] – 9 – cn C.I.H.M. [240]
CATHOLIC NEW TIMES – Toronto, De1976-1988 – 95r – 1 – cn Preston [971]
CATHOLIC NEW TIMES – Toronto. v13-19. 1989-95 – 1 – Can$60.00y – cn Micromedia [240]
CATHOLIC OPINION – London, 10 Jul 1869-31 Dec 1870 – 1r – 1 – uk British Libr Newspaper [072]
Catholic Order of Foresters. De Breboeuf Court. Montreal *see* MONTREAL SOUVENIR
CATHOLIC ORTHODOXY AND ANGLO-CATHOLICISM : A WORD ABOUT INTERCOMMUNION BETWEEN THE ENGLISH AND THE ORTHODOX CHURCHES / Overbeck, J J – London: N. Truebner, 1866 – 1mf – us A.T.L.A. [240]
Catholic Poor-School Committee. Great Britain *see* ANNUAL REPORTS: ROMAN CATHOLIC VOLUNTARY SCHOOLS
CATHOLIC PRINCIPLES : AS ILLUSTRATED IN THE DOCTRINE, HISTORY, AND ORGANIZATION OF THE AMERICAN CATHOLIC CHURCH IN THE UNITED STATES COMMONLY CALLED THE PROTESTANT EPISCOPAL CHURCH / Westcott, Frank Nash – Milwaukee: Young Churchman, c1902 – 1mf – 9 – 0-8370-8799-6 – 1986-2799 – us A.T.L.A. [240]
CATHOLIC RECORD – Ontario Prov., Canada. 1874-1947 – 1 – cn Commonwealth Micro [072]
THE CATHOLIC RECORD – London, Ontario. v3 n118. 14 jan 1881-v32 n1665. 17 sep 1910 – 1r – 1 – Can$35.00 – cn Can Microfilming [072]
Catholic Record Society. London *see* PUBLICATIONS
THE CATHOLIC REFORMATION / ed by Blum, Paul Richard – 2,950mf – 9 – ne IDC [240]
THE CATHOLIC REFORMATION *see*
- ABBREGE DES METHODES DE TRAICTER DES CONTROVERSES
- ACCOMPLISSEMENT DES PROPHETIES...
- AD VIRUM NOBILEM DE CULTU CONFUCII PHILOSOPHI ET PROGENITORUM APUD SINAS
- ANALYSIS FIDEI CATHOLICAE, HOC EST RATIO METHODICA EAM IN UNIVERSUM FIDEM...
- L'ANATOMIE DU CALVINISME...
- ANTILUTHERUS..., TRES LIBROS COMPLECTENS
- APOLOGIE POUR LA REFORMATION, POUR LES REFORMATEURS, ET POUR LES REFORMEZ
- APOLOGIE POUR LES CATHOLIQUES CONTRE LES FAUSSETEZ ET LES CALOMNIES D'UN LIVRE INTITULE
- LES ARTIFICES DES HERETIQUES
- AVERTISSEMENT SUR LES DISPUTES ET LE PROCEDE DES MISSIONNAIRES
- BIBLIOTHECA SANCTA
- LE CATHOLIQUE ORTHODOXE OPPOSE AU CATHOLIQUE PAPISTE,...
- CLYPEUS THEOLOGIAE THOMISTICAE CONTRA NOVOS EIUS IMPUGNATORUS
- COMMENTARIA UNA CUM QUAESTIONIBUS, IN UNIVERSAM ARISTOTELIS LOGICAM
- COMMENTARII COLLEGII CONIMBRICENSIS E SOCIETATIS IESU IN UNIVERSAM DIALECTICAM ARISTOTELIS
- COMMENTARII COLLEGII CONIMBRICENSIS SOCIETATIS IESU IN ARISTOTELIS LOGICAM
- COMMENTARII COLLEGII CONIMBRICENSIS SOCIETATIS IESU, IN DUOS LIBROS DE GENERATIONE ET CORRUPTIONE ARISTOTELIS
- COMMENTARII ET ANNOTATIONES IN EPISTOLAM B. PAULI APOSTOLI AD ROMANOS
- COMMENTARII IN LIBROS ARISTOTELIS STAGIRITAE PHILOSOPHORUM PRINCIPIS DE ANIMA...
- COMMENTARII IN LIBROS ARISTOTELIS STAGYRITAE PHILOSOPHORUM PRINCIPIS, DE ANIMA...
- COMMENTARII IN OCTO LIBROS ARISTOTELIS DE PHYSICO AUDITU, SEU AUSCULTATIONE CONTINENTUR
- COMMENTARII IN PRIMA 12 CAPITA...EVANGELII SECUNDAM LUCAM
- COMMENTARIORUM THEOLOGICORUM...
- COMMENTARIUM ET DISPUTATIONUM IN GENESIM, TOMI QUATUOR
- COMMENTARIUM IN QUARTUM SENTENTIARUM
- COMPENDIUM MORALIS THEOLOGIAE
- COMPENDIUM VERITATUM AD FIDEM PERTINENTIUM...
- CONFERENCE AVEC M. CLAUDE...SUR LA MATIERE DE L'EGLISE
- CONFORMITE DE LA CONDUITE DE L'EGLISE DE FRANCE...AVEC CELLE DE L'EGLISE D'AFFRIQUE...
- CONTROVERSIARUM EPITOMES...
- COURS ENTIER DE PHILOSOPHIE, OU SYSTEME GENERAL SELON LES PRINCIPES DE M. DESCARTES
- CURRICULUM PHILOSOPHIAE PERIPATETICAE...
- CURSUS PHILOSOPHICUS...
- CURSUS PHILOSOPHICUS
- CURSUS PHILOSOPHICUS AD USUM STUDENTIUM TOTIUS ORDINIS MINORAM
- CURSUS PHILOSOPHICUS THOMISTICUS, SECUNDUM EXACTAM, VERAM ET GENUINAM ARISTOTELIS...
- CURSUS THEOLOGICI IN PRIMAM SECUNDAM PARTEM D. THOMAE
- DE COMMUNIBUS OMNIUM RERUM NATURALIUM PRINCIPIIS ET AFFECTIONIBUS
- DE LA PRIMAUTE EN L'EGLISE
- DE L'EDIT DE NANTES EXECUTE SELON...
- DE SACRAMENTO EUCHARISTIAE CONTRA OECOLAMPADIUM OPUSCULUM...
- DE THEOLOGIA GENTILI ET PHYSIOLOGIA CHRISTIANA
- DE VENERATIONE SANCTORUM, OPUSCULUM DUOS LIBROS COPLECTENS
- DE VITA ET MORIBUS SACERDOTUM OPUSCULUM...
- DEFENSE DES NOUVEAUX CHRESTIENS ET DES MISSIONARES DE LA CHINE...
- DEFENSE DU CULTE EXTERIEUR DE L'EGLISE
- DEMONSTRATIONS CATHOLIQUES, OU L'ART DE REUNIR LES PRETENDUS REFORMEZ
- DIALOGUES FAMILIERS SUR LES PRINCIPALES OBJECTIONS DES MISSIONNAIRES DE CE TEMPS
- DISPUTATIONES DE CONTROVERSIIS CHRISTIANAE FIDEI, ADVERSUS HUIUS TEMPORIS HAERETICOS...
- DISPUTATIONES DE UNIVERSA PHILOSOPHIA
- DISPUTATIONES META PHYSICAE...
- DISPUTATIONUM DE SANCTO MATRIMONII SACRAMENTUM
- DISPUTATIONUM THEOLOGICARUM... TOMUS PRIMUS
- DISTINCTIONES PHILOSOPHICAE
- LA DOCTRINE CURIEUSE DES BEAUX ESPRITS DE CE TEMPS...
- DU IUGE DES CONTROVERSES
- DU TRES-SAINCT ET TRES-AUGUSTE SACREMENT, ET SACRIFICE DE LA MESSE
- DUNS SCOTUS...PER UNIVERSAM PHILOSOPHIAM,...CONTRA ADVERSANTES DEFENSUS
- ELUCIDATORIUM ECCLESIASTICUM AD OFFICIUM ECCLESIAE PERTINENTIA PLANIUS EXPONENS IN QUATTUOR LIBROS COMPLETENS
- ELUCIDATORIUM ECCLESIASTICUM AD OFFICIUM ECCLESIAE PERTINENTIA PLANIUS EXPONENS IN QUATUOR LIBROS COMPLETENS
- ENCHIRIDION CONTROVERSIARUM PRAECIPUARUM...
- ESCHANTILLON DES PRINCIPAUX PARADOXES DE LA PAPAUTE
- EXPEDITIONUM SPIRITUALIUM SOCIETATIS IESU, LIBRI QUINQUE
- EXPLICATION DE L'EDICT DE NANTES PAR LES AUTRES EDICTS DE PACIFICATION, DECLARATIONS ET ARRESTS DE REGLEMENT
- L'EXPLICATION DE L'EDIT DE NANTES DE M. BERNARD, AVEC DE NOUVELLES OBSERVATIONS...
- EXPOSITION DE LA DOCTRINE DE L'EGLISE CATHOLIQUE SUR LES MATIERES DE CONTROVERSE
- LA FACE DE L'EGLISE PRIMITIVE
- GENEVE PLAGIAIRE, ...
- HISTOIRE CRITIQUE DU VIEUX TESTAMENT
- HISTOIRE DES EDITS DE PACIFICATION ET DES MOYENS QUE LES PRETENDUS REFORMEZ ONT EMPLOYE POUR LES OBTENIR...
- HISTOIRE DU CALVINISME
- HISTOIRE DU CALVINISME, CONTENANT SA NAISSANCE...
- HISTOIRE DU LUTHERANISME
- HISTORIA CONTROVERSIARUM DE RITIBUS SINICIS
- HOMILIAE SEU SERMONES
- L'IDOLATRIE HUGUENOTE FIGUREE AU PATRON DE LA VIEILLE PAYENNE...
- IMPROBATIO QUORUNDAM ARTICULORUM MARTINI LUTHERI...
- IN SACROSANCTUM JOANNIS EVANGELIUM COMMENTARII
- INSTITUTION CATHOLIQUE, OU EST DECLAREE ET CONFIRMEE LA VERITE DE LA FOY
- INSTITUTIONUM DIALECTICARUM...LIBRO OCTO
- INSTITUTIONUM THEOLOGICARUM...
- INTEGER CURSUS PHILOSOPHICUS
- (I.P.C. DE BELLEY). REPARTIES SUCCINCTES A L'ABREGE DES CONTROVERSES DE M. CHARLES DRELINCOURT...ENSEMBLES LES ANTITHESES PROTESTANTES...
- ITINERARIUM PARADISI...
- JOSEPH AMIOT ET LES DERNIERS SURVIVANTS DE LA MISSION FRANCAISE A PEKIN (1780-1795)
- LETTRE INEDITE DU P. PREMARE SUR LE MONOTHEISME DES CHINOIS
- LIBELLUS SODALITATIS
- LOGICA INSTITUTIONIBUS PRAEVIIS QUAESTIONIBUS CONTEXTA
- MANUALE THOMISTARUM SEU BREVIS THEOLOGIAE CURSUS...
- NEUESTE SAMMLUNG JENER SCHRIFTEN, DIE VON EINIGEN JAHREN HER UEBER VERSCHIEDENE WICHTIGSTE GEGENSTAENDE ZUR STEUER DER WAHRHEIT IM DRUCK ERSCHIENEN SIND
- NOTATIONES IN TOTAM SCRIPTURAM SACRAM
- NOUVEAUX MEMOIRES SUR L'ETAT PRESENT DE LA CHINE
- ONUITGE GEVEN BRIEVEN VAN EENIGE PATERS DER SOCIETEIT VAN JESUS, MISSIONARISSEN IN CHINA VAN DE 17 EN 18 EEUW
- OPERA
- OPERA OMNIA
- OPERA OMNIA QUAE SUPERSTES ADHUC EDITIT
- OPERA OMNIA QUOTQUOT IN SACRAE SCRIPTURAE EXPOSITIONUM REPERIUNTUR
- OPERA PIA ET SPIRITUALIA...
- OPUS MORALE IN PRAECEPTA DECALOGI
- LE PANTHEON HUGUENOT DECOUVERT ET RUINE...
- LA PERPETUITE DE LA FOY DE L'EGLISE CATHOLIQUE TOUCHANT L'EUCHARISTIE
- PHILOSOPHIA ACADEMICA...
- PHILOSOPHIA AD MENTEM...DIVI THOMAE AQUINATIS...EXPLICATA
- PHILOSOPHIA IUXTA INCONCUSSA TUTISSIMAQUE DIVI THOMAE DOGMATA...
- PHILOSOPHIA MAGNETICA...
- PHILOSOPHIA METAPHYSICAM PHYSICAMQUE COMPLECTENS QUESTIONIBUS CONTEXTA
- PHILOSOPHIA PERIPATETICA
- PHILOSOPHIA POLLINGANA AD NORMAM BURGUNDICAE
- PHILOSOPHIA SCOTI A PROLIXITATE ET SUBTILITAS EJUS AB OBSCURITATE LIBERA ET VINDICATA...
- PHILOSOPHIAE, AC MATHEMATICAE TOTIUS... INSTITUTIO
- PHILOSOPHIAE AD MENTEM SCOTI CURSUS INTEGER
- PHILOSOPHIEAE MAGNI PATRIS ET ECCLESIAE DOCTORIS AUGUSTINI...PARS ALTERA
- LA PIERRE DE TOUCHE, OU LA VRAYE METHODE POUR DESABUSER LES ESPRITS
- LA POLITIQUE DU CLERGE DE FRANCE
- [P]RAECURSOR LOGICUS...; CUIUS PARTES TRES
- PREJUGEZ LEGITIMES CONTRE LE PAPISME
- PREJUGEZ LEGITIMES CONTRE LES CALVINISTES
- LES PRETENDUS REFORMEZ CONVAINCUS DE SCHISME...
- PROMPTUARIUM CATHOLICUM...
- PROPUGNACULUM ECCLESIAE ADVERSUS LUTERANOS...
- QUADRAGESIMALE...
- LE RABELAIS REFORME PAR LES MINISTRES,...
- RECHEUTE DE GENEVE PLAGIAIRE
- REFLEXIONS SUR LES DIFFERENDS DE LA RELIGION
- REGLE GENERALE DE LA FOY CATHOLIQUE
- LE RENVERSEMENT DE LA MORALE DE JESUS-CHRIST PAR LES ERREURS DES CALVINISTES, TOUCHANT LA JUSTIFICATION
- REPLIQUE A LA RESPONSE DU SERENISSIME ROY DE LA GRANDE BRETAGNE
- REPONSE AU LIVRE DE M. EVEQUE DE CONDOM
- REPONSE AU LIVRE DE MONSIEUR DE CONDOM
- RESPONSE AU LIVRE INTITULE LE MYSTERE D'INIQUITE
- REVEILLE-MATIN A DOUBLE MONTRE
- LA SAINCTE LIBERTE DES ENFANS DE DIEU
- SCHOLASTICA COMMENTARIA IN PRIMAM PARTEM, SUMMAE THEOLOGICAE S. THOMAE AQUINATIS
- SCHOLIAE IN QUATUOR EVANGELIA
- SERMONES DE ADVENTU
- SERMONES DOMINICALES DE TEMPORE...
- SUMMA DE ECCLESIA
- SUMMA PHILOSOPHIAE SCHOLASTICAE ET SCOTISTICAE...
- SUMMA...D. THOMAE AQUINATIS...IN ORDINEM CURSUS PHILOSOPHICI ACCOMMODATA
- TABLE CHRONOGRAPHIQUE DE L'ESTAT DU CHRISTIANISME
- THEOLOGIA DOGMATICO-POLEMICA...
- THEOLOGIA DOGMATICO-SCHOLASTICA...
- THEOLOGIA MORALIS...
- THEOLOGIA MORALIS AD MENTEM DD
- THEOLOGIA MORALIS, LIBER QUINTUS DE SACRAMENTIS, ET SACRIFICIO, NOVAE LEGIS
- THEOLOGIA NATURALIS SIVE ENTIS INCREATI ET CREATI INTRA SUPREMAM ABSTRACTIONEM EX NATURAE LUNINE INVESTIGATIO
- THEOLOGIA POLEMICA...
- THEOLOGIA SCHOLASTICA MORALI-POLEMICA...
- THEOLOGIA TRIPARTITA UNIVERSA...
- THEOLOGIAE SCHOLASTICAE
- TRACTATUS DE INSTITUTIONE SACERDOTUM, QUI SUB EPISCOPIS ANIMARUM CURAM GERUNT
- TRACTATUS THEOLOGICI IN PRIMUM SENTENTIARUM LIBRUM...
- TRAITTE DES HERESIES, CONTENANT LES CAUSES DES HERESIES, LES MOEURS ET ARTIFICES...
- TRAITTE DES IUSTES CAUSES DE LA SEPARATION DES PROTESTANS D'AVEC L'EGLISE ROMAINE
- TRAITTE DU SAINCT SACREMENT DE L'EUCHARISTIE,...
- TRAITTE QUI CONTIENT LA METHODE LA PLUS FACILE...
- LE TRIOMPHE DE LA FOY CATHOLIQUE
- TROIS DISCOURS POUR LA RELIGION CATHOLIQUE
- UNIVERSA PHILOSOPHIA DE MORIBUS

THE CATHOLIC REGISTER – (Cont by: Catholic Register and Canadian Extension) – Toronto: Catholic Register Print & Pub Co, [1893-1908?] – 9 – cn C.I.H.M. [240]
CATHOLIC SCHOOL – London. -irr. Oct 1853, 14 Oct 1854, 14 Mar 1855. (8 ft) – 1 – uk British Libr Newspaper [073]
CATHOLIC SENTINEL – Portland, OR. -w. 5 Feb 1870-19 May 1978+. 48 rolls – 1 – us U.O. Library [071]
THE CATHOLIC SHIELD – Ottawa: [s.n., 1881-1882] – 9 – cn C.I.H.M. [240]
CATHOLIC SOCIALISM / Nitti, Francesco S – London: S. Sonnenschein; New York: Macmillan, 1895 – 2mf – us A.T.L.A. [240]
CATHOLIC SOCIETIES IN FRANCE PAMPHLET COLLECTION – 1961 – 1 – CSUXAMJ7775-B – us Hoover Inst Photo [240]
CATHOLIC STANDARD – (Incomplete) – Georgetown, Guyana. Jan 17 1954-Aug 4 1967; Sept 5 1969-Dec 18 1977; Jan 7 1979-1992 – 15r – 1 – us L of C Photodup [072]

CATHOLIC STANDARD – (Weekly Register and Catholic Standard). London. -w. 20 Oct 1849-Dec 1870. (43 reels) – 1 – uk British Libr Newspaper [072]

THE CATHOLIC STANDARD – (Lacking: v17 1882. v22 1886) – Philadelphia. v1-30. 1866-95 – 16r – 1 – ATLA S0266 – us A.T.L.A. [073]

THE CATHOLIC STANDARD – Washington, DC. v1-44. 1951-94 (complete) – 50r – 1 – ATLA S0185 – us A.T.L.A. [073]

CATHOLIC STANDARD AND TIMES – (Some issues lacking) – Philadelphia, 1895-1992 – Inquire – 1 – us A.T.L.A. [073]

Catholic Theological Society of America *see* PROCEEDINGS OF THE ANNUAL CONVENTION

CATHOLIC THOUGHTS ON THE BIBLE AND THEOLOGY / Myers, Frederic – London: Daldy, Isbister, 1879. 1 fiche – 9 – us A.T.L.A. [240]

THE CATHOLIC TIMES – (Incorporated by: Universe) – v1-3. 3 Dec 1892-23 Nov 1895 (incomplete) – 1r – 1 – ATLA S0267 – us A.T.L.A. [073]

CATHOLIC TRANSCRIPT – Hartford. Conn. -w. 1898- – 1 – us UMI [071]

Catholic Truth Society of Canada *see* CONSTITUTION AND BY-LAWS: ADOPTED JUNE, 1890

Catholic Truth Society of Ottawa *see* ...ITS AIMS AND OBJECTS

CATHOLIC UNIVERSITY LAW REVIEW – (v1-34 1959-65 in reel $400.00. v35-44 1985-95 in mf $256.00) – v1-44. 1950-95 – 5,6,9 – $656.00 set – us Hein [340]

The Catholic University of America Studies in Sacred Theology *see*
- DIONYSIUS THE PS.-AREOPAGITE: THE ECCLESIASTICAL HIERARCHY
- ST. AUGUSTINE, THE DIVINATION OF DEMONS AND CARE FOR THE DEAD

Catholic University of America, Washington D.C. *see* IRISH PAMPHLETS, C. 1700-1850

CATHOLIC VINDICATOR – Milwaukee. Wis. -w. 1871-72, 1874 – 1 – us UMI [071]

CATHOLIC VISITOR – Leavenworth. Kan. 1882-1890 – 1 – us UMI [071]

THE CATHOLIC VISITOR – Quebec: F. Belanger, [1874-1875] – 9 – cn C.I.H.M. [240]

CATHOLIC VOICE – Omaha, NE. -w. Jul 1903 to date – 1 – us NE Hist [071]

THE CATHOLIC VOICE – Oakland, CA. 1963-67; 1986- – 10+ r – 1 – $500.00 ($50.00y) – B02540 – us Library Micro [240]

THE CATHOLIC VOICE – San Francisco, CA. 1963-67 – 6r – 1 – $300.00 – B02803 – us Library Micro [071]

CATHOLIC WEEK – Mobile. Ala. 1935-1967 – 1 – us UMI [071]

THE CATHOLIC WEEKLY REVIEW – (Merged with: Irish Canadian merged to become: Catholic Register) – Toronto: A.C. Macdonell and F.W.G. Fitzgerald [1887-1892] – 9 – cn C.I.H.M. [240]

CATHOLIC WITNESS – Harrisburg, PA., 1966 – 13 – $25.00r – us I.M.R. [071]

CATHOLIC WORKER – 1-27. 1933-1961 – 2r – 9 – $230.00 – us UPA [335]

CATHOLIC WORLD – v. 1-150. 1865-1940 – 1,5,6 – us Princeton Micro [240]

CATHOLICA – 1(1932)-25(1971) – 142mf – 9 – Dfl497.00 – ne Slangenburg [073]

CATHOLICA – Muenster. v1-25. 1932-1971 – 142mf – 9 – ne IDC [240]

CATHOLICISM AND INDEPENDENCE : BEING STUDIES IN SPIRITUAL LIBERTY / Petre, Maude Dominica – London; New York: Longmans, Green, 1907 – 1mf – 9 – 0-8370-8778-3 – 1986-2778 – us A.T.L.A. [240]

CATHOLICISM, ROMAN AND ANGLICAN / Fairbairn, Andrew Martin – New York: Scribner, 1899 – 2mf – us A.T.L.A. [240]

CATHOLICISME EN ANGLETERRE AU 19E SIECLE = THE ENGLISH CATHOLIC REVIVAL IN THE NINETEENTH CENTURY / Thureau-Dangin, Paul; ed by Wilberforce, Wilfred – (In English. Includes bibliographical references and index) – New York: E P Dutton. 2v. [19–] – 4mf – 9 – 0-8370-7030-9 – 1986-1030 – us A.T.L.A. [240]

CATHOLICISME ET CRITIQUE : REFLEXIONS D'UN PROFANE SUR L'AFFAIRE LOISY / Desjardins, Paul – Paris: Libres entretiens, 1905 – 1mf – 9 – 0-8370-8734-1 – 1986-2734 – us A.T.L.A. [240]

CATHOLICISME ET LOYALISME / Moreno, Enrique – Paris, 1937. Fiche W 1062. (Blodgett Collection of Spanish Civil War Pamphlets) – 9 – us H.U. College Libr [946]

CATHOLICISME ET REBELLION / Martin-Chauffier, Louis – Conference prononcee le 30 octobre 1936 dans la Salle des Societes Savantes sous les auspices du Comite Franco-Espagnol. Paris, 1936? Fiche W 1030. (Blodgett Collection of Spanish Civil War Pamphlets) – 9 – us H.U. College Libr [946]

CATHOLICITY AND PANTHEISM: ALL TRUTH OR NO TRUTH / De Concilio, Januarius – New York: D. & J. Sadlier, 1874.1 fiche – 9 – us A.T.L.A. [240]

CATHOLICITY, PROTESTANTISM AND INFIDELITY : AN APPEAL TO CANDID AMERICANS / Weninger, Francis Xavier – (Also issued under title: Protestantism and infidelity) – 13th ed. New York: Sadlier; Cincinnati: John P Walsh, 1869, c1861 – 1mf – 9 – 0-8370-6856-8 – 1986-0856 – us A.T.L.A. [240]

CATHOLICON, OU DICTIONNAIRE UNIVERSEL DE LA LANGUE FRANCOISE, CATHOLICON ODER FRANZOESISCH-DEUTSCHES UNIVERSALWOERTERBUCH DER FRANZOESISCHEN SPRACHE (AEL, ABT 2;12) / Schmidlin, Johann Josef – Hamburg, 1771-1779 (mf ed 1995) – 44mf – 9 – DM690.00 – 3-89131-195-8 – gw Fischer [040]

THE CATHOLICOS OF THE EAST AND HIS PEOPLE : BEING THE IMPRESSIONS OF FIVE YEARS' WORK IN THE "ARCHBISHOP OF CANTERBURY'S ASSYRIAN MISSION" / Maclean, Arthur John & Browne, William Henry – London: S.P.C.K.; New York: E.& J.B. Young, 1892 – 1mf – us A.T.L.A. [240]

CATHOLICS AND THE CIVIL WAR IN SPAIN; A COLLECTION OF STATEMENTS BY WORLD-FAMOUS CATHOLIC LEADERS ON THE EVENTS IN SPAIN – New York, 1936. Fiche W 788. (Blodgett Collection of Spanish Civil War Pamphlets) – 9 – us H.U. College Libr [946]

CATHOLICS AND THE SPANISH STATE / Moreno, Enrique – London, 1937. Fiche W 1063. (Blodgett Collection of Spanish Civil War Pamphlets) – 9 – us H.U. College Libr [946]

THE CATHOLICS OF SCOTLAND: FROM 1593, AND THE EXTINCTION OF THE HIERARCHY IN 1603, TILL THE DEATH OF BISHOP CARRUTHERS IN 1852 / Dawson, Aeneas McDonell – London, Ont.: T. Coffey, 1890. 02602. (Pre-1900 Canadiana) – 9 – cn C.I.H.M. [971]

CATHOLICS REPLY TO OPEN LETTER OF 150 PROTESTANT SIGNATORIES ON SPAIN – New York, 1937? Fiche W 1221. (Blodgett Collection of Spanish Civil War Pamphlets) – 9 – us H.U. College Libr [946]

CATHOLICS SPEAK FOR SPAIN – NY, 1937. Fiche W 789. (Blodgett Collection of Spanish Civil War Pamphlets) – 9 – us H.U. College Libr [946]

CATHOLICUS REFORMATUS; HOC EST, EXPOSITIO ET DECLARATIO / Perkins, William – 1601 – 1 – us A.T.L.A. [240]

LE CATHOLIQUE – I, no. 1-53. Paris. 5 nov 1881-20 mai 1883. mq no. 14, 32, 50; II, no. 1-20 – 1 – fr A.C.R.P.P. [073]

LE CATHOLIQUE ORTHODOXE OPPOSE AU CATHOLIQUE PAPISTE,... / Rivet, A – Ed.3. Saumur, 1616 – 15mf – 9 – CA-148/1 – ne IDC [240]

CATHOLIQUES ET HUGUENOTS A LA COUR DE CHARLES IX – 2eme ed.Paris.1924. 355p. BH-380/2 – 8 – ne IDC [240]

THE CATHOLOGRAPHER, OR UNIVERSAL WRITER – Rockwood, Ont: E, Collom, 1868- – 9 – cn C.I.H.M. [400]

Cathrein, V *see* DIE GRUNDLAGE DES VOELKERRECHTS

Cathrein, Victor *see*
- DIE FRAUENFRAGE
- SOCIALISM
- SOCIALISM EXPOSED AND REFUTED

Catilia *see* ORATIONES

CATILINA ET JUGURTHA AND OFFICIUM B. V. MARIAE / Sallust – Italian.14th and 15th cents. Holkham mss. 336, 42. Holkham Hall, Norfolk, England – 1 – uk Microform Academic [760]

CATILINA ET JUGURTHA, ETC / Sallust – 15th cent. Holkham ms. 539. Holkham Hall, Norfolk, England – 1 – uk Microform Academic [760]

Catinella, Salvatore *see* LA CORTE SUPREMA FEDERALE NEL SISTEMA COSTITUZIONALE DEGLI STATI UNITI D'AMERICA

Catley, Delwyn *see* PSYCHOLOGICAL ANTECEDENTS OF THE FREQUENCY AND INTENSITY OF FLOW IN GOLFERS

Catlow, M E *see* POPULAR BRITISH ENTOMOLOGY

CATO JOURNAL – v.1-. 1981- – 1,5,6,9 – us UMI [073]

CATO VON EISEN / Laube, Heinrich – 2. Aufl. Leipzig: J J Weber, 1892 – 1 – us U.W. Library [820]

CATOCTIN ENTERPRISE – Thurmont. Md. 1940- – 1 – us UMI [071]

EL CATOLICISMO LIBERAL / Tejado, Gabino – 1875 – 9 – 1.50f – sp Bibl Santa Ana [240]

EL CATOLICO FILIPINO – Manila: [s.n.], dec 13-17,20-21,24 1898 – us Res Libr [240]

CATOLICO O KRAUSISTA? / Fernandez Valbuena, Ramiro – 1882 – 9 – 1.50f – sp Bibl Santa Ana [240]

UN CATOLICO VA AL CINE / Perez Lozano, Jose Maria – Barcelona: Editorial Juan Flors, 1956 – 1 – sp Bibl Santa Ana [240]

Caton, James R *see* LEGISLATIVE CHRONICLES OF THE CITY OF ALEXANDRIA

Caton, John Dean *see* A SUMMER IN NORWAY; WITH NOTES ON THE INDUSTRIES, HABITS, CUSTOMS AND PECULIARITIES OF THE PEOPLE.

Cator, Leonce *see* PRECIS ELEMENTAIRE DE DROIT COMMERCIAL.

CATRIONA : A SEQUEL TO "KIDNAPPED", BEING MEMOIRS OF THE FURTHER ADVENTURES OF DAVID BALFOUR AT HOME AND ABROAD / Stevenson, Robert Louis – London: Cassell, 1893 – 1 roll – 1 – 1-55879-562-6 – uk Libr Preservation [830]

Catrufo, G *see*
- FELICE. SI J'ADORAI LISETTE; ARR
- L'INTRIGUE AU CHATEAU

Cats, J *see*
- MAECHDEN-PLICHT OFTE AMPT DER IONCK-VROUWEN
- MAEGDEN-PLICHT OFTE AMPT DER IONGHVROUWEN, IN EERBAER LIEFDE, AANGEWESEN DOOR SINNE-BEELDEN
- MONITA AMORIS VIRGINEI, SIVE OFFICIUM PUELLARUM IN CASTIS AMORIBUS, EMBLEMATE EXPRESSUM
- PROTEUS OFTE MINNE-BEELDEN VERANDERT IN SINNE-BEELDEN
- PROTEUS OFTE MINNE-BEELDEN VERANDERT IN SINNEBEELDEN
- SILENUS ALCIBIADIS, SIVE PROTEUS
- SILENUS ALCIBIADIS SIVE PROTEUS, HUMANAE VITAE IDEAM, EMBLEMATE TRIFARIAM VARIATO, OCULIS SUBJICIENS
- SILENUS ALCIBIADIS, SIVE PROTEUS, VITAE HUMANAE IDEAM, EMBLEMATE TRIFARIÀM VARIATO, OCULIS SUBIJCIENS
- SILENUS ALCIBIADIS SIVE PROTEUS, VOORGHESTELT IN MINN'-EN-ZINNE-BEELDEN...
- SPIEGEL VAN DEN OUDEN EN NIEUWEN TYD. BESTAENDE UYT SPREECK-WOORDEN...
- SPIEGEL VAN DEN OUDEN EN NIEUWEN TYDT, BESTAANDE UYT SPREKWOORDEN...
- SPIEGEL VAN DEN OUDEN ENDE NIEUWEN TIJT
- SPIEGEL VAN DEN OUDEN ENDE NIEUWER TIJDT
- ZINNE-EN MINNE-BEELDEN

Catt, Carrie Clinton Chapman *see* PAPERS

Cattaneo, Atilio E *see* GEOPOLITICA IMPERIALISTA Y LA NUEVA ARGENTINA

Cattaneo, E *see* IL BREVIARIO AMBROSIANO

Cattano, Carlo *see* SCRITTI ECONOMICI

CATTARAUGUS REPUBLICAN – Ellicottville. N.Y. 1844-1854 – 1 – us UMI [071]

CATTARAUGUS REPUBLICAN – Salamanca. N.Y. -w. 1867-1904 – 1 – us UMI [071]

CATTARAUGUS UNION – Salamanca. N.Y. 1910-1914 – 1 – us UMI [071]

Catterall, Carla *see* BEHAVIOURAL STRATEGIES OF A SILVEREYE POPULATION IN RELATION TO FOOD RESOURCES ON A CORAL CAY ISLAND

CATTLE FEEDERS' DAY / South Dakota. State University. Agricultural Experiment Station – nos.1-18. 1962-74 – 1,5,6 – us Spaulding [636]

CATTLE HERD DYNAMICS = DYNAMIQUE DU TROUPEAU DE BOVINS: UN MODELE ENTIER ET STOCHASTIQUE POUR L'EVALUATION DES OPTIONS DE PRODUCTION : AN INTEGER AND STOCHASTIC MODEL FOR EVALUATING PRODUCTION ALTERNATIVES / Konandreas, P A & Anderson, F M – 1982 – vii/95p – 9 – $10.00 – 92-9053-107-X – et ILRI [636]

IL CATTOLICISMO ROSSO: STUDIO SUL PRESENTE MOVIMENTO DE RIFORMA NEL CATTOLICISMO / Prezzolini, Giuseppe – Napoli: R. Ricciardi, 1908. xx,348p – 1 – us U.W. Library [240]

Catullus, Gaius Valerius *see* SELECT POEMS...EDITED, WITH INTRODUCTIONS, NOTES, AND APPENDICES, BY FRANCIS P. SIMPSON

Caturla, Maria Luisa *see*
- BODAS Y OBRAS JUVENILES DE ZURBARAN
- ZURBARAN EN SAN PABLO DE SEVILLA

CATV *see* VUE

"CAT-WAGON TRAILS." / Clugston, W G – 1 – us KS Hist [978]

Caty-Lacroix, Marie-Paule *see* COLLECTION MARIE-PAULE CATY-LACROIX

THE CAUCASIAN HERBARIUM / Komarov Botanical Institute, St. Petersburg – (Includes printed guide) – 279mf – 9 – ne IDC [580]

CAUCE – Badajoz, 1958-1964 – 5 – sp Bibl Santa Ana [073]

LE CAUCHEMAR DES INTRIGANTS POLITIQUES – [Paris]: Typographie Benard et Comp. n1. oct 9 1848 – us Res Libr [320]

Cauchon, Joseph *see*
- DISCOURS SUR LA QUESTION DE LA CONFEDERATION, PRONONCE A LA SEANCE DE L'ASSEMBLEE LEGISLATIVE DU 2 MARS 1865
- JOURNAL DE QUEBEC

Cauchy, E F *see*
- LE DROIT MARITIME...
- DU RESPECT DE LA...

CAUCUS *see* LE JOURNAL DES ETUDIANTS DE L'UNIVERSITE DE SHERBROOKE

Caudeli Peiro, Jesus *see* 25 ANIVERSARIO DE LA SOCIEDAD ESPANOLA DE PSICOLOGIA

EL CAUDILLO Y LOS COMBATIENTES – Bilbao, 1938. Fiche W 807. (Blodgett Collection of Spanish Civil War Pamphlets) – 9 – us H.U. College Libr [946]

Caufeild, Miss. *see* MARTYRS OMITTED BY FOXE

Caughnawaga Ship Canal Company *see* MEMORANDUM FOR CONTRACTORS

Caulier *see* CATECHISME ABREGE EN LA LANGUE DE MADAGASCAR

Caumont, Armand *see* GOETHE ET LA LITTERATURE FRANCAISE

Caus, Salomon de *see*
- LA PERSPECTIVE AVEC LA RAISON DES OMBRES ET MIROIRS
- LES RAISONS DES FORCES MOUVANTES AVEC DIVERSES MACHINES

LA CAUSA INMEDIATA DE LA EMANCIPACION DE PANAMA / Castillero, E J – Panama, 1933 – 3mf – 1 – ILM-2331/1 – ne IDC [327]

CAUSA SAMAMA...SENTENZA...1880 / Corte d'Apello di Lucca – Livorno, 1880 – 2mf – 1 – ILM-3965/1 – ne IDC [327]

CAUSAL ATTRIBUTIONS AND TASK PERSISTENCE OF LEARNED-HELPLESS AND MASTERY-ORIENTED SIXTH GRADERS IN MATH, PHYSICAL EDUCATION, AND READING / Griffith, Joseph B – 1994 – 2mf – $8.00 – us Microform Publ [370]

DIE CAUSALBETRACHTUNG IN DEN GEISTESWISSENSCHAFTEN / Ritschl, Otto – Bonn: A. Marcus u. E. Weber, 1901 – 1mf – us A.T.L.A. [120]

CAUSALITE ET CREATION : LE CONTINU ET LE DISCONTINU DANS L'OEUVRE D'HENRI BERGSON / Anastassopoulou, Itheoni – 2mf – 9 – 10531 – fr Atelier National [110]

CAUSAS CELEBRES : NULIDAD DE MATRIMONIO... – Mexico, 1883 – 1mf – 1 – ILM-3862/1 – ne IDC [327]

LA CAUSE DE L'ECOLE VICTORIA DEVANT LE ST SIEGE: DECRETS DE 1876 ET 1881 ET LEURS APPLICATIONS DANS UN DOCUMENT RENDU PUBLIC: PLAINTES ET DOUTES PROPOSES – Montreal?: Au bureau du proprietaire, 1883. 02567. (Pre-1900 Canadiana) – 9 – cn C.I.H.M. [370]

LA CAUSE DES ESCLAVES NEGRES ET DES HABITANTS DE LA GUINEE, PORTEE AU TRIBUNAL DE LA JUSTICE, DE LA RELIGION, DE LA POLITIQUE; OU HISTOIRE DE LA TRAITE ET DE L'ESCLAVAGE DES NEGRES, PREUVES DE LEUR ILLEGITIMITE, MOYEN DE LES ABOLIR SANS NUIRE AUX COLONIES / Frossart, Benjamin-Sigismond – (Slave Trade and Abolitionism in France Series). 1789 – 9 – fr Hachette [360]
LA CAUSE DES OBLIGATIONS ET PRESTATIONS / Billette, J Emile – Montreal, 1933. 157, 2 p. LL-2325 – 1 – us L of C Photodup [340]
LA CAUSE IMMORALE, ETUDE DE JURISPRUDENCE / Dorat des Monts, Roger – Paris, Librairie Rousseau, 1956. 173 p. LL-4097 – 1 – us L of C Photodup [340]
THE CAUSE OF THE DEGRADATION OF MAN / Adams, Henry – St. John, N.B.: E.J. Armstrong, 1895. 06151. (Pre-1900 Canadiana) – 9 – cn C.I.H.M. [240]
CAUSE OF THE PEOPLE – Isle of Man. 1848 – 1 – uk Microform Academic [073]
CAUSE/EFFECT – (v.3-. 1980 5,6,9) – v.1-. 1978- – 1 – us UMI [073]
LA CAUSERIE – Paris. 1859-avr 1862 – 1 – fr A.C.R.P.P. [073]
UNE CAUSERIE AGRICOLE – St. Hyacinthe Quebec: Courrier, 1872. 02566. (Pre-1900 Canadiana) – 9 – cn C.I.H.M. [630]
CAUSERIE SOCIALE *see* TROIS ETUDES
CAUSERIES CONGOLAISES / Torday, E – Bruxelles: A Dewit, 1925 – 1 – us Res Libr [490]
CAUSERIES: LA LIBERTE VS. LA MODE & AL, ET LA POLITIQUE / Anti-dude – Saint Hyacinthe, Quebec, 1886. 04360. (Pre-1900 Canadiana) – 9 – cn C.I.H.M. [971]
CAUSERIES SCIENTIFIQUES: DECOUVERTES ET INVENTIONS, PROGRES DE LA SCIENCE ET DE L'INDUSTRIE – v. 1-31. 1862-95 – 3 – us Readex [500]
CAUSERIES SUR LE PROTESTANTISME D'AUJOURD'HUI. ENGLISH = PLAIN TALK ABOUT THE PROTESTANTISM OF TO-DAY / Segur, Louis Gaston – (In English. Includes bibliographical references) – Boston: Patrick Donahoe, 1868 – 1mf – 9 – 0-8370-6838-X – 1986-0838 – us A.T.L.A. [240]
CAUSES AND ORIGINS OF WORLD WAR 1 PAMPHLET COLLECITON – 1914-1988 – 5r – 1 – CSUXAML2935-B – us Hoover Inst Photo [355]
DES CAUSES DE DIVORCE... / Cheron, L – Paris, 1934 – 5mf – 1 – ILM-3001/1 – ne IDC [327]
LES CAUSES DE DIVORCE... / Cheron, L – Paris, 1934 – 5mf – 1 – ILM-3000/1 – ne IDC [327]
DES CAUSES DE LA DEPOPULATION ET DES MOYENS D'Y REMEDIER / Jaubert, Pierre – Londres et Paris, Dessain Jr., 1767. xii, 198 p. 4 fiches. (Statistics Series: Demography) – 9 – 10.00 – fr Bibl Nationale [310]
DES CAUSES DE NOS MAUX, DE LEURS PROGRES ET DES MOYENS D'Y REMEDIER / Gin, Pierre L C – Paris, Pichard. 1791 – 9 – fr Hachette [190]
THE CAUSES LEADING TO THE ORGANIZATION OF THE CUMBERLAND PRESBYTERIAN CHURCH / Stephens, John Vant – Nashville: Cumberland Presbyterian Pub. House, 1898 – 1mf – us A.T.L.A. [240]
THE CAUSES OF FOREIGN INVASION IN SPAIN – n.p. 193? Fiche W 790. (Blodgett Collection of Spanish Civil War Pamphlets) – 9 – us H.U. College Libr [946]
THE CAUSES OF THE CORRUPTION OF THE TRADITIONAL TEXT OF THE HOLY GOSPELS / Burgon, John William – London: George Bell, 1896. 1 fiche – 9 – us A.T.L.A. [240]
CAUSES OF THE DECLINE OF INTEREST IN CRITICAL THEOLOGY / Noyes, George Rapall – (The Christian Examiner and Religious Miscellany, v. 43 (4th series, v. 8), Nov. 1874, p. 325-344) – 9 – us A.T.L.A. [240]
CAUSES OF THE INCREASES OF THE CHURCHES / Williams, William R – (A discourse). 1842 – 1 – 5.00 – us Baptist [240]
CAUSES OF WORLD WAR 2 PAMPHLET COLLECTION – 1939-1982 – 1 – CSUXANM6336-B – us Hoover Inst Photo [355]
CAUSES, RESULTS, AND INFLUENCES OF WORLD WAR 2 IN BELGIUM PAMPHLET COLLECTION – 1941-1942? – 1 – CSUXANM6340-B – us Hoover Inst Photo [355]
CAUSES, RESULTS, AND INFLUENCES OF WORLD WAR 2 IN DENMARK PAMPHLET COLLECTION – 1938-1945 – 1 – CSUXANM6346-B – us Hoover Inst Photo [355]
CAUSES, RESULTS, AND INFLUENCES OF WORLD WAR 2 IN ENGLAND PAMPHLET COLLECTION – 1939-1944 – 2r – 1 – CSUXANM6366-B – us Hoover Inst Photo [355]
CAUSES, RESULTS, AND INFLUENCES OF WORLD WAR 2 IN FRANCE PAMPHLET COLLECTION – 1939-1945 – 2r – 1 – CSUXANM6350-B – us Hoover Inst Photo [355]
CAUSES, RESULTS, AND INFLUENCES OF WORLD WAR 2 IN ITALY PAMPHLET COLLECTION – 1940-1943? – 1 – CSUXANM6374-B – us Hoover Inst Photo [355]
CAUSES, RESULTS, AND INFLUENCES OF WORLD WAR 2 IN LUXEMBOURG PAMPHLET COLLECTION – 1980 – 1 – CSUXANM6380-B – us Hoover Inst Photo [355]
CAUSES, RESULTS, AND INFLUENCES OF WORLD WAR 2 IN NORWAY PAMPHLET COLLECTION – 1941-1943 – 1 – CSUXANM6397-B – us Hoover Inst Photo [355]
CAUSES, RESULTS, AND INFLUENCES OF WORLD WAR 2 IN THE NETHERLANDS PAMPHLET COLLECTION – 1939?-1944 – 1 – CSUXANM6386-B – us Hoover Inst Photo [355]
CAUSES, RESULTS, AND INFLUENCES OF WORLD WAR 2 IN THE UNITED STATES PAMPHLET COLLECTION – 1941-1946 – 1 – CSUXANM6412-B – us Hoover Inst Photo [355]
CAUT BULLETIN – (v1-30 1953-83 1) – Ottawa. v1-42. 1953-1995 – 5,1 – Price varies – cn Micromedia [073]
Cauthorn, Henry S *see* A HISTORY OF THE CITY OF VINCENNES
A CAUTION AGAINST RELIGIOUS DELUSION : A SERMON ON THE NEW BIRTH, OCCASIONED BY THE PRETENSIONS OF THE METHODISTS / Stebbing, Henry – London, 1739 – 1mf – 9 – MP-256/1 – ne IDC [240]
CAUTIONS AGAINST METHODISM : OR, UNITY RECOMMENDED, IN A SERMON ON EPHESIANS, CHAP. IV, VER. 3 PREACHED BEFORE THE RELIGIOUS SOCIETIES...EASTER-MONDAY 1759;... / Dodd, W – London, 3rd ed 1769 – 1mf – 9 – MP-383/1 – ne IDC [240]
Cauwenbergh, P Van *see* ETUDES SUR LES MOINES D'EGYPTE
Cauwes, G *see* L'EXTENSION DES PRINCIPES DE LA CONVENTION DE GENEVE AUX GUERRES MARITIMES
Caux de Cappeval, N de *see* APOLOGIE DU GOUT FRANCOIS RELATIVEMENT A L'OPERA. POEME, AVEC UN DISCOURS APOLOGETIQUE, ET DES ADIEUX AUX BOUFFONS
Cavaglieri, A *see*
– LA COSA GIUDICATA E LE QUESTIONI DI STATO...
– IL DIRITTO INTERNAZIONALE COMMERCIALE
– LA DOTTRINA DELLA SUCCESSIONE DI STATO A STATO...
– L'OPINIONE PUBBLICA NELLE...
Cavagnari, V W *see* DELL'EFFICACIA DEL DIRITTO DI PEGNO...
CAVAIGNAC ET LOUIS-NAPOLEON DEVANT LE PAYS – Paris, [1848?] – us Res Libr [944]
Cavaille, Jean Pierre *see* LE MONDE DE DESCARTES
Cavaille-Coll, Aristide *see* DE L'ORGUE ET DE SON ARCHITECTURE
CAVALCADE OF JACKSON COUNTY / Taylor, IT – San Antonio: Naylor Co., 1938. Texas Reel 11. (The Cox Library Collection) – 5 – us Americana [978]
Cavalcanti, A *see* PAN-AMERICAN QUESTIONS
Cavalerie Signale *see* MANUSCRIPT OF MILITARY MARCHES
Cavalieri, Pio Franchi de *see* GLI ATTI DEI SS. MONTANO
Cavallera, F *see* LE SCHISME D'ANTIOCHE (4E-5E SIECLE)
CAVALRY TACTICS, U.S. ARMY, ASSIMILATED TO THE TACTICS OF INFANTRY AND ARTILLERY (NEW YORK, 1874) / U.S. War Department. Adjutant General's Office – T1109 – 1r – 1 – us Nat'l Archives [324]
CAVAN WEEKLY NEWS – Ireland. -w. 1893. 30 ft – 1 – uk British Libr Newspaper [072]
Cavanagh, William Henry *see* THE WORD PROTESTANT IN LITERATURE, HISTORY AND LEGISLATION
Cavanillas y Munoz, Juan Alonso *see* ARTICULOS DE COSTUMBRES
Cavanilles, A J *see*
– COLLECCION DE PAPELES SOBIE CONTROVERSIAS BOTANICAS
– DESCRIPCION DE LAS PLANTAS
– ELENCHUS PLANTARUM HORTI REGII BOTANICI MATRITENSIS
– ICONES ET DESCRIPTIONES PLANTARUM, QUAE AUT SPONTE IN HISPANIA...
– MONADELPHIAE CLASSIS DISSERTATIONES DECEM
Cavarozzi, Marcelo *see*
– CONSOLIDACION DEL SINDICALISMO PERONISTA Y EMERGENCIA DE LA FORMULA POLITICA ARGENTINA DURANTE EL GOBIERNO FRONDIZISTA
– SINDICATOS Y POLITICA EN ARGENTINA
Cavarretta, G *see*
– DIRITTI SUI TERRITORIAL ALTRUI...
– LA PRESCRIZIONE NEL DIRITTO INTERNAZIONALE PRIVATO
– LA RAPPRESENTANZA CONVENZIONALE NEL DIRITTO INTERNAZIONALE CONTEMPORANEO
Cavazzi, Giovanni Antonio *see*
– ISTORIA DESCRIZIONE DE TRE REGNI CONGO, MATAMBA ET ANGOLA
– RELATION HISTORIQUE DE L'ETHIOPIE OCCIDENTALE
Cave, Alfred *see*
– THE BATTLE OF STANDPOINTS
– THE INSPIRATION OF THE OLD TESTAMENT INDUCTIVELY CONSIDERED
Cave, H W *see* THE RUINED CITIES OF CEYLON
CAVE SPRING BAPTIST CHURCH. ROANOKE, VIRGINIA : CHURCH RECORDS – 1899-1935, 1948-59. Bulletins. 1947-57 – 1 – 77.18 – us Baptist [240]
A CAVEAT AGAINST THE METHODISTS, SHEWING HOW UNSAFE IT IS FOR ANY CHRISTIAN TO JOIN HIMSELF TO THEIR SOCIETY OR TO ADHERE TO THEIR TEACHERS / Challenor, R – London, 1760 – 1mf – 9 – MP-401/1 – ne IDC [240]
A CAVEAT AGAINST UNSOUND DOCTRINES, BEING THE SUBSTANCE OF A SERMON PREACHED IN THE PARISH CHURCH OF ST ANN, BLACKFRYARS, ON SUNDAY, APRIL 29, 1770 / Toplady, Augustus Montague – London, 1770 – 1mf – 9 – MP-466/1 – ne IDC [240]
Caven, William *see*
– EQUAL RIGHTS: THE LETTERS OF WILLIAM CAVEN
– A VINDICATION OF DOCTRINAL STANDARDS: WITH SPECIAL REFERENCE TO THE STANDARDS OF THE PRESBYTERIAN CHURCH
Cavendish, Henry *see* DEBATES OF THE HOUSE OF COMMONS IN THE YEAR 1774 ON THE BILL FOR MAKING MORE EFFECTUAL PROVISION FOR THE GOVERNMENT OF THE PROVINCE OF QUEBEC
Cavenne *see* STATISTIQUE DU DEPARTEMENT DE LA MEUSE-INFERIEURE
Caverly, A M *see* HISTORY OF THE TOWN OF PITTSFORD
Caviglia, Hector *see* QUIEN ES EL GENERAL PERON
Cavoleau, Jean A *see* DESCRIPTION ABREGEE DU DEPARTEMENT DE LA VENDEE
Cawdrey, Robert *see*
– A TABLE ALPHABETICALL OF HARD USUAL ENGLISH WORDES
– A TREASURIE OR STOREHOUSE OF SIMILES
Cayet, P V *see* PARADIGMATA DE QVATOR LINGVIS ORIENTALIBVS, PRAECIPVIS ARABICA, ARMENA, SYRA, AETHIOPICA
Cayetano, Luis *see* PROMPTUARIO LLENERENSE GRAMATICO-LATINO
Cayetano Rosado, Moises *see* HE TENIDO SUJETA LA PALABRA ENTRE LOS DIENTES
Cayley, George *see* AERONAUTICAL AND MISCELLANEOUS NOTEBOOKS
Caylus, A C P de *see* PREMIER MEMOIRE SUR GUILLAUME DE MACHAUT; POETE ET MUSICIEN DANS LE XIV SIECLE
CAYMANIAN COMPASS : OR THE DAILY CAYMANIAN COMPASS – George Town, Cayman Islands. Jan-Sept 16 1986; Mar 1987-Aug 1990 – 18r – 1 – us L of C Photodup [072]
Cayol, C *see* A LA CORSE
Cayton. Yorkshire *see* PARISH REGISTERS
CAYUGA CHIEF – Weedsport. N.Y. 1877-1953 – 1 – us UMI [071]
LA CAZA DE LA PERDIZ CON RECLAMO / Gonzales Borreguero, G – Caceres: Tip. de El Noticiero – 1 – sp Bibl Santa Ana [790]
LA CAZA DEL PERDIGON / Vela Hidalgo y Burriel, Angel – Madrid, 1920 – 1 – sp Bibl Santa Ana [630]
Cazeau, R *see* DES ASSOCIATIONS ETRANGERES EN FRANCE
Cazenove, John Gibson *see* HISTORIC ASPECTS OF THE...ARGUMENT CONCERNING THE BEING...OF GOD: FOUR LECTURES
Cazes, Paul de *see*
– LA FRONTIERE NORD DE LA PROVINCE DE QUEBEC
– L'INSTRUCTION PUBLIQUE DANS LA PROVINCE DU QUEBEC
– MANUEL DE L'INSTITUTEUR CATHOLIQUE DE LA PROVINCE DE QUEBEC
– OBSERVATIONS SUR L'ETUDE ARCHEOLOGIQUE DU DR. DIONNE
– PETITES NOTES SUR LE CANADA
Cazet, Cl *see* DU MODE DE FILIATION DES RACINES SEMITIQUES ET DE L'INVERSION
CBA BUILDER / Conservative Baptist Association of America – Oct 1957-Aug 1970 – 1 – 37.03 – us Baptist [240]
CBA RECORD – (Supersedes: Chicago Bar Record) – v1-9. 1987-95 – 9 – $140.00 set – us Hein [340]
CBA RECORD *see* CHICAGO BAR RECORD
CBIA (CONNECTICUT BUSINESS AND INDUSTRY ASSOCIATION) NEWS – v. 55-. 1977- – 1,5,6,9 – us UMI [650]
CBS NEWS – (Parts available; index available) – 9 (1963-88); 1 (1975-88) – $12,995.00 (complete backfile collection, 1963-88) – us UMI [975]
CBS NEWSLETTER – (Caucus of Black Sociologists). 1970-77. Continued as: Black Sociologist – 1 – us UMI [073]
CCA NEWS / Christian Conference of Asia – 1974-85.Continued annually – 1 – uk World [240]
THE CCC AND WILDLIFE – Washington, DC: GPO, 1938 – us Res Libr [630]
CCEA NEWSLETTER / East China Christian Education Association – v2-3. 1948-49 (incomplete) – 1r – 1 – ATLA S0707A – us A.T.L.A. [073]
CCF NEWS FOR BRITISH COLUMBIA AND THE YUKON – v1-25, no. 9. Aug. 1936-Sept. 1961 – 1 – cn Precision [971]
CCF NEWS FOR BRITISH COLUMBIA AND THE YUKON – Vancouver, British Columbia. v. 10, no. 22-v. 25, no. 9. Jan 3 1946-Sept 19 1961. Incomplete – 1 – us NY Public [971]
CCQ : CRITICAL CARE QUARTERLY – (v.3-. 1980- 5,6,9) – v.1-. 1978- – 1 – us UMI [073]
CCSSQ. COMMUNITY COLLEGE SOCIAL SCIENCE QUARTERLY – v. 1-6. 1970-76 – 1 – us UMI [300]
CCTA CSA Joint Secretariat. African Headquarters. London *see* SCIENCE AFRIQUE
CDU-INFORMATIONSDIENST : INFORMATIONSDIENST DES ZONENAUSSCHUSSES DER CDU – (Titelaenderung in: Informationsdienst der CDU Deutschlands 1950-1952. Union im Wahlkampf 1949. Union in Deutschland 1949-1951) – Koeln, 1947-Jan 1950 – 2r – 1 – DM220.00 – gw Mikro Press [072]
CDU-INFORMATIONSDIENST FUER DIE BRITISCHE ZONE – (Cont by: Informationsdienst der CDU/CSU, Frankfurt/Main) – Koeln, West Germany. 1947-51. (incomplete) – 1 – gw Mikrofilm [072]
CE CONTRAT ET MARCHE CONCLU ENTRE SA MAJESTE LA REINE AGISSANT EN CE QUI CONCERNE LA PUISSANCE DU CANADA, ET A CES FINS REPRESENTEE PAR L'HONORABLE SIR CHARLES TUPPER, K.C.M.G., MINISTRE DES CHEMINS DE FER ET CANAUX – 1880? 03413. (Pre-1900 Canadiana) – 9 – cn C.I.H.M. [971]
C.E. Kempe & Co *see* COMMISSION REGISTERS OF THE KEMPE STUDIO
CE QUE JE FERAIS SI J'ETAIS PRETRE – Montreal: D. Bentley, 1880. 04122. (Pre-1900 Canadiana) – 9 – cn C.I.H.M. [240]

CE QUE LES FACTIEUX VEULENT QU'ON OUBLIE – Madrid, 1936. Fiche W 791. (Blodgett Collection of Spanish Civil War Pamphlets) – 9 – us H.U. College Libr [946]
CE QUE PENSENT LES FLEURS: SAYNETE ENFANTINE / Dandurand, Josephine – Montreal: Beauchemin, 1895. 05416. (Pre-1900 Canadiana) – 9 – cn C.I.H.M. [971]
CE QUE TOUT CANADIEN DEVRAIT SAVOIR CONCERNANT LES FILATURES DE LAINE ET LES TRICOTERIES DU CANADA – [Quebec (Province)]: [s.n.], 1925. SEM105P1541 – 1mf – 9 – Can$2.25 – cn Bibl Nat [971]
CE QUI DONNERA BEAUCOUP DE CONNOISSANCE A MR LE LIEUTENANT CRIMINEL POUR LE JUGEMENT DE LA PETITE MERE FRANCOISE SUPERIEURE DES RELIGIEUSES DE LA PLACE ROYALE – 9 – fr Hachette [360]
CE QU'IL FAUT DIRE – Paris. avr 1916-17 – 1 – fr A.C.R.P.P. [073]
CE QU'IL FAUT SAVOIR SUR L'ECONOMIE MAROCAINE / Morocco. Ministere de l'Economie Nationale – 1962. BNE-3075 1 – 9 – ne IDC [338]
CE QU'ON VOIT ET CE QU'ON NE VOIT PAS / Bastiat, Frederic – 5th ed., Paris, 1879. 63p. Bibliography – 9 – 1.00f – at Libertarian Micro [335]
CE SOIR – Paris. 2 mars 1937-25 aout 1939, 22 aout 1944-1 2 mars 1953 – 1 – fr A.C.R.P.P. [073]
Cean Bermudez, Juan A *see*
- DICCIONARIO HISTORICO DE LOS MAS ILLUSTRES PROFESORES DE LAS BELLAS ARTES EN ESPANA

Ceballos, Ernesto S *see* HISTORIA POLITICA DEL MOVIMIENTO OBRERO ARGENTINO (1944-1985)
LA CECA DE LA VILLA IMPERIAL DE POTOSI Y LA MONEDA COLONIAL BUENOS AIRES, 1945 / Burcio, Humberto F – Madrid: Razon y Fe, 1947 – 1 – sp Bibl Santa Ana [972]
CECAF *see*
- REPORT OF THE 4TH SESSION OF THE WORKING PARTY ON FISHERY STATISTICS
- REPORT OF THE 6TH SESSION OF THE SUB-COMMITTEE ON MANAGEMENT OF RESOURCES WITHIN THE LIMITS OF NATIONAL JURISDICTION. LOME, TOGO, 1985
- REPORT OF THE 7TH SESSION OF THE CECAF SUB-COMMITTEE ON MANAGEMENT OF RESOURCES WITHIN THE LIMITS OF NATIONAL JURISDICTION
- REPORT OF THE 8TH SESSION OF THE CECAF SUB-COMMITTEE ON MANAGEMENT OF RESOURCES WITHIN THE LIMITS OF NATIONAL JURISDICTION
- REPORT OF THE 8TH SESSION OF THE WORKING PARTY ON RESOURCES EVALUATION
- REPORT OF THE 9TH SESSION OF THE WORKING PARTY ON RESOURCES EVALUATION
- REPORT OF THE 11TH SESSION OF THE FISHERY COMMITTEE FOR THE EASTERN CENTRAL ATLANTIC
- REPORT OF THE 12TH SESSION OF THE FISHERY COMMITTEE FOR THE EASTERN CENTRAL ALTANTIC

CECC (CENELEC ELECTRONIC COMPONENTS COMMITTEE) – Printed index. Updated every 60 days – 6,9 – us Info Handling [600]
Cecco, John P De *see* JOURNAL OF HOMOSEXUALITY
CECH – Prague, Czechoslovakia. -d. 1 Feb-23 July 1919. Imperfect. 1 reel – 1 – uk British Libr Newspaper [072]
CECHOSLOVACI V RUSHU / STRUCN E VYPRAVUJE OTAKAR VAN EK – Praha: Tiskem knihtisk. Ant. Reise, [1920?] – 1 – CSUX89-B1665 – us Hoover Inst Photo [947]
CECHOSLOVAK *see* CECHOSLOVAK V ANGLII
CECHOSLOVAK V ANGLII – (Cechoslovak. 26 Jul 1940-6 Apr 1945. Cechoslovak v Zahranici. 13 Apr-31 Dec 1945; 24 Apr 1953-29 Nov 1967) – London, UK. 20 Oct 1939-12 Jul 1940 – 1 – uk British Libr Newspaper [072]
CECHOSLOVAK V ZAHRANICI *see* CECHOSLOVAK V ANGLII
Cecil, Algernon *see* SIX OXFORD THINKERS
CECIL CASTLEMAINE'S GAGE / Ouida – British Fiction Archive: Unit 3 – 9 – uk Bell [830]
Cecil, David *see*
- THE STRICKEN DEER
- THE STRICKEN DEER: OR, THE LIFE OF COWPER

Cecil, Joe S *see*
- ADMINISTRATION OF JUSTICE IN A LARGE APPELLATE COURT
- DECIDING CASES WITHOUT ARGUMENT
- THE ROLE OF STAFF ATTORNEYS AND FACE-TO-FACE CONFERENCING IN NON-ARGUMENT DECISIONMAKING
- SUMMARY JUDGEMENT PRACTICE IN THREE DISTRICT COURTS

Cecil, Joe S et al *see* JURY SERVICE IN LENGTHLY CIVIL TRIALS
Cecil. Ohio. Immaculate Conception Church *see* RECORDS
CECIL SHARP AUTOGRAPH NOTEBOOK COLLECTION – (Folk Words 19v; Folk Tunes 23v; Folk Dance 4v; Index 4v. Contains 4977 tunes, only 1118 of which have been published) – 9r – 1 – $630.00 complete collection – us UMI [780]
CECILIA BAPTIST CHURCH (FORMERLY: RUDES CREEK). KENTUCKY : CHURCH RECORDS – 1819-1968 – 1 – 60.21 – us Baptist [240]
CEDAR BLUFF BAPTIST CHURCH. NEBO, MISSOURI : CHURCH RECORDS – (572p) – 1910-Aug 1990 – 1 reel – 1 – $25.74 – us Baptist [240]
CEDAR BLUFFS STANDARD – Cedar Bluffs, NE. -w. Oct. 1895-Jan. 1896; Apr. 1896-Jun. 1899; Aug. 1899-Jul. 1944; Sep. 1944-Aug. 1945. Incomplete; Oct. 1945-Jun. 1967 – 1 – us NE Hist [071]
CEDAR BLUFFS STANDARD – Cedar Bluffs, Saunders County, NE: July 20, 1944-Jan 5, 1961 – us NE Hist [978]
CEDAR COUNTY NEWS – Hartington, NE. -w. Feb 1898-Dec 1901; Feb 1902 to date – 1 – us NE Hist [071]
CEDAR COUNTY WACHTER – Hartington, NE. -w. Jan 1908-Aug 1918 – 1 – us NE Hist [071]
CEDAR COUNTY WATCHER – Hartington. Neb. 1908-1918 – 1 – us UMI [071]
CEDAR GROVE BAPTIST CHURCH. MARYVILLE, TENNESSEE : CHURCH RECORDS – 1890-Apr 1962. Lacking: Feb 1930-Jul 1941 – 1 – 30.69 – us Baptist [240]
CEDAR GROVE BAPTIST CHURCH. SOUTH CAROLINA : CHURCH RECORDS – 1825-1943 – 1 – 34.65 – us Baptist [240]
CEDAR RAPIDS LEADER – Cedar Rapids, NE. -w. May 1935-Apr. 1937 – 1 – us NE Hist [071]
CEDAR RAPIDS LEADER-OUTLOOK – Cedar Rapids, NE. -w. Jul. 1887-Nov. 1892. Incomplete; Oct. 1895-Jan. 1910; May 1910-Sep. 1910; Jun. 1914-Mar. 1943 – 1 – us NE Hist [071]
CEDAR RAPIDS PRESS – Cedar Rapids, NE. -w. Jun. 1949- – 1 – us NE Hist [071]
CEDAR SPRING BAPTIST CHURCH. SPARTANBURG COUNTY. SOUTH CAROLINA : CHURCH RECORDS – 1794-1972 – 1 – 85.14 – us Baptist [240]
Cedarville. Ohio. Reformed Presbyterian Church *see* CENTENNIAL SOUVENIR, 1809-1909
CEDR QUARTERLY – (v.13-. 1980- 5,6,9) – Center on Evaluation, Development and Research. v.7-15. 1974-82 – 1 – us UMI [073]
Cedreni, Georgii *see* COMPENDIUM HISTORIARUM (CBH 8)
Cedrenus, Georgius *see* IOANNIS SCYLITZAE OPE AB IMM. BEKKERO SUPPLETUS ET EMENDATUS (CSHB 34, 35)
CEDRORUM LIBANI HISTORIA / Trew, C J – Norimbergae. 1757. B-5777 2 – 8 – ne IDC [580]
CEDULARIO CUBANO (LOS ORIGENES DE LA COLONIZACION 1. (1493-1512)...TOMO 6 / Chacon y Calvo, Jose Maria – Madrid: Razon y Fe, 1929 – 1 – sp Bibl Santa Ana [946]
CEDULARIO DEL PERU : SIGLOS 16, 17 Y 18 / Porras Barrenechea, Paul – Lima: Dept de Relaciones Culturales del Ministerio de Relciones Exteriores del Peru. v1-2. 1944-48 – 1 – us Res Libr [972]
CEDULAS EPIGRAFICAS DEL CAMPO NORBENSE / Callejo Serrano, Carlos – Salamanca, 1968. Sep. Zephyrus 18th, 1967, pp. 85-120 – 1 – sp Bibl Santa Ana [946]
CEDULE DE CERTAINS ETATS RELATIFS A L'IMPORTATION ET EXPORTATION DE LA PROVINCE DU CANADA – Montreal: Lovell & Gibson, [1846]. SEM105P1734 – 1mf – 9 – Can$2.25 – cn Bibl Nat [380]
CEDULE DES DIVERSES COMPAGNIES INCORPOREES POUR LA CONSTRUCTION DE CHEMINS DE FER EN CANADA,... – [Quebec: Lovell et Lamoureux, 1853 ?]. SEM105P1760 – 1mf – 9 – Can$2.25 – cn Bibl Nat [690]
CEFP JOURNAL / Council of Educational Facility Planners – v1- 1962- 1; v13- 1975- 5,6,9 – us UMI [370]
CEHUI XUEBAO – (1983 $3.50f; 1984- $4.50f) – Acta Geodetica et Cartographica Sinica. In Chinese but English abstracts to the main articles. F p62 – 9 – cc Microforms [073]
CEI – Rio de Janeiro: Centro Ecumenico de Informacao. [n17-149/150]. oct 1966-apr/may 1979 – 1r – us Res Libr [972]
CEI DOCUMENTO – [Rio de Janeiro: Tempo e Presenca. [n58-92]. nov 1974-may 1979 – 1r – us Res Libr [972]
Ceillier, R *see* HISTOIRE GENERALE DES AUTEURS SACRES ET ECCLESIASTIQUES
Cejp, K *see* MONOGRAFIE HYDNACEI REPUBLIKY CESKOSLOVENSKE, FAUNA ET FLORA CECHOSLOVENICA
Celakovsky, L *see* PRODROMUS DER FLORA VON BOEHMEN
Celal, Mehmed *see* ZADE-I SA'IR
Celaleddin *see* DIVAN
Celaya, J de *see* EXPOSITIO IN OCTO LIBROS PHISICORUM ARISTOTELIS...
Celebi, Ibrahim Cevri *see* TARIH-I CEVRI CELEBI
Celebi, Katib *see* FEZKEKE-I TARIH
Celebi, Solakzade Mehmed Hemdemi *see* SOLAKZADE TARIHI
THE CELEBRATED CANON NON NOBIS DOMINE : ADAPTED AS A FUGUE FOR STRING QUARTET OR ORCHESTRA / Diettenhofer, J – London: Skillern, Forster, 178- – 1 – us Sibley [780]
CELEBRATED CRIMES / Dumas, Alexandre – Boston. 3v 1902 – 1r – 1 – us Ross [830]
CELEBRATION DES NOCES D'OR DE M. LE CHANOINE ARCHAMBEAULT A ST HUGUES, 13 JANVIER 1887 – Montreal?: Gebhardt-Berthiaume, 1887. 00751. (Pre-1900 Canadiana) – 9 – cn C.I.H.M. [240]
CELESTE ET FALDONI OU LES AMANTS DE LYON / Hapde, Augustin – (French Theatre Series). Paris. Martinet. 1812 – 9 – fr Hachette [820]
CELESTIAL EMPIRE – Shanghai. China. -w. 4 Jul 1874-26 Dec 1883, 25 Apr 1884-31 Dec 1897, 17 Oct 1908, 5 Jan 1918-28 Mar 1927. (56 reels) – 1 – uk British Libr Newspaper [072]
THE CELESTIAL EMPIRE – Shanghai: Loureiro & Co, jul 4 1874-1897; 1902-sep 1905; 1906-13; 1922-mar 1927 – 66r – 1 – us Res Libr [072]
CELESTIAL LIRIO / Domingo de San Pedro de Alcantara – 1755 – 9 – 1.50f – sp Bibl Santa Ana [810]
CELESTIAL MECHANICS – (v32-. 1984-. 5,6,9) – v1-. Jun 1969- – 1 – us UMI [073]
LE CELIBAT – St-Hyacinthe. v1 n2. aut 1904-oct 1904 – 1r – 1 – Can$25.00 – cn Can Microfilming [072]
CELIBATES / Moore, George – London: Walter Scott, Ltd, 1895 – 1 roll – 1 – 1-55879-604-5 – uk Libr Preservation [890]
Celine, Louis-Ferdinand *see*
- BAGATELLES POUR UN MASSACRE
- MORT A CREDIT; ROMAN

CELINE, OU, UNE AUTRE MAGDELEINE A L'ASILE DU BON PASTEUR DE QUEBEC / Amicus – 1886. 02563. (Pre-1900 Canadiana) – 9 – cn C.I.H.M. [240]
Celine-de-la-Presentation, Soeur *see* BIBLIOGRAPHIE DE L'OEUVRE DE MONSIEUR L'ABBE ANDRE JOBIN, L. TH., PRINCIPAL DE L'ECOLE NORMALE NOTRE-DAME, ST-ROCH, QUEBEC, PROFESSEUR AU COLLEGE UNIVERSITAIRE GARNEAU, QUEBEC...
CELL ADHESION AND COMMUNICATION / ed by Buck, Clayton A & Thiery, Jean-Paul – 9,5,1 – us Harwood [574]
CELL AND TISSUE RESEARCH – v. 20-213. 1933-80 – 1,5,9 – 34,629.00 – us UMI [073]
CELL AND TISSUE RESEARCH *see* ZEITSCHRIFT FUER ZELLFORSCHUNG UND MIKROSKOPISCHE ANATOMIE
CELL CALCIUM – (1982-. 1,5,6,9) – v1-. 1980- – 1 – us UMI [073]
CELL DIFERENTIATION – v1-15. 1972-84 – 1,5,6,13 – sz Elsevier [073]
CELL TRANSPLANTATION – 1,5,69 – us UMI [611]
Cella, Paolo della *see* VOYAGE EN AFRIQUE AU ROYAUME DE BARCAH ET DANS LE CYRENAIQUE A TRAVERS DE DESERT
Cellarius, C *see*
- CVRAE POSTERIORES DE BARBARISMIS ET IDIOTISMIS SERMONIS LATINI
- DISSERTATIONES ACADEMICAE VARII ARGUMENTI IN SUMMAN REDACTAE...
- EXERCITATIO HISTORICA DE ORIGINE LINGVAE ITALICAE EX BARBARORUM INCVRSIONIBUS NATAE

Cellensis, Petrus *see* COMMENTARIA IN RUTH
Cellerier, Jacob Elisee *see*
- BIBLICAL HERMENEUTICS
- MANUEL D'HERMENEUTIQUE BIBLIQUE

Celles, Alfred Duclos de *see*
- LA CRISE DU REGIME PARLEMENTAIRE
- PAPINEAU: EXTRAITS DE SA CORRESPONDANCE INTIME

CELLESCHE ZEITUNG *see*
- ZELLESCHER ANZEIGER

CELLESCHE ZEITUNG UND ANZEIGEN *see*
- ZELLESCHER ANZEIGER

Cellier, Florent de *see* HISTOIRE DES CLASSES OUVRIERES EN FRANCE DEPUIS LA CONQUETE DE LA GAULE JUSQU'A NOS JOURS
Cellini, B *see*
- DUE TRATTATI UNO INTORNO ALLE OTTO PRINCIPALI ARTI DELL' OREFICERIA. L'ALTRO IN MATERIA DELL' ARTE DELLA SCULTURA
- VITA. DA LUI MEDESIMO SCRITTA

Cellini, Benvento *see* THE LIFE OF B. CELLINI
CELLULAR AND MOLECULAR BIOLOGY – (Including Cyto-Enzymology. Formerly Annales D'Histochemie) – v22- 1977- – 5,6,9 – us UMI [574]
CELLULAR AND MOLECULAR NEUROBIOLOGY – (v11-14. 1991-94. $80.00v) – v1-10. 1981-90 – 1,5 – $60.00v – us UMI [574]
CELLULAR BUSINESS – v1-. 1984- – 1,5,6,9 – us UMI [073]
CELLULAR PHYSIOLOGY AND BIOCHEMISTRY – v3-. 1993- – 1,5,9 – us UMI [574]
CELLULAR SIGNALLING – 1,5,69 – us UMI [611]
DIE CELLULARPATHOLOGIE IN IHRER BEGRUENDUNG AUF PHYSIOLOGISCHE UND PATHOLOGISCHE GEWEBELEHRE / Virchow, R LK – Berlin, 1858 – 8mf – 9 – ne IDC [611]
CELLULE / Recueil de Cytologie et d'Histologie Generale – Louvain, 1885-1939/1940. v1-48 – 318mf – 7705c/1 – ne IDC [574]
CELLULE – v. 1-59. 1884-1959 – 1,5,6 – us Princeton Micro [073]
DIE CELLULOID-INDUSTRIE : BEILAGE DER GUMMI-ZEITUNG, BERLIN – Berlin, 22 Mar 1912-24 Jul 1914 – 1 – uk British Libr Newspaper [073]
DIE CELLULOID-INDUSTRIE, BERLIN *see* GUMMI-ZEITUNG
CELT-HELLENISME / Trippault, L – 1581 – 9 – fr I.C.S. [450]
THE CELTIC CHURCH IN BRITAIN AND IRELAND / Zimmer, Heinrich – London: David Nutt, 1902 – 1mf – us A.T.L.A. [240]
THE CELTIC CHURCH IN IRELAND : THE STORY OF IRELAND AND IRISH CHRISTIANITY FROM BEFORE THE TIME OF ST. PATRICK TO THE REFORMATION / Heron, James – London: Service & Paton, 1898 – 1mf – us A.T.L.A. [240]
THE CELTIC CHURCH IN SCOTLAND : BEING AN INTRODUCTION TO THE HISTORY OF THE CHRISTIAN CHURCH IN SCOTLAND DOWN TO THE DEATH OF SAINT MARGARET / Dowden, John – London: S.P.C.K.; New York: E.& J.B. Young, 1894 – 1mf – us A.T.L.A. [240]
THE CELTIC CHURCH OF WALES / Willis Bund, John William – London: D. Nutt, 1897. vii,533p – 1 – us U.W. Library [240]
THE CELTIC REVIVAL IN ENGLISH LITERATURE 1760-1800 / Snyder, Edward Douglas – Cambridge: Harvard University Press, 1923 – 1 roll – 1 – 1-55879-612-6 – uk Libr Preservation [420]
CELTIC STUDIES IN WALES : A SURVEY / International Congress of Celtic Studies. Cardiff, Wales. 2nd, 1963 – Cardiff: University of Wales Press, 1963. xix,182p. illus., map, 7 plates – 1 – us U.W. Library [940]

THE CELTS / Maclear, George Frederick – London: S.P.C.K.; New York: Pott, Young, [1878?] (Conversion of the West) – 1mf – us A.T.L.A. [305]

Celulosas *see* CELULOSAS DE EXTREMADURA

CELULOSAS DE EXTREMADURA / Celulosas – Merida: Sarrio Compania papelera de Leiza, S.A. – 1 – sp Bibl Santa Ana [946]

CEM – (Continues Djem) – Istanbul, nos 34-39. – 12 Birincihanuni 1928-2 Mayis 1929 [12 Dec. 1928-2 May 1929] – 4mf – 9 – $45.00 – us MEDOC [949]

CEM *see* DJEM

CEMENT AND CONCRETE RESEARCH – (Formerly Journal of Cement and Concrete Research) – v1- 1971- – 5,6,9 – us UMI [690]

CEMENT, CONCRETE, AND AGGREGATES – v1- 1979- – 1,5,6,9 – us UMI [690]

CEMENT ERA – v1-15 1903-17. Continued as: Concrete Products – 1 – us UMI [690]

THE CEMETERIES OF ABYDOS (MEES VOL 33) : PART 1, THE MIXED CEMETERY AND UMM EL-GA'AB / Naville, E et al – London, 1914 – 5mf – 8 – Dfl22.00 – ne Slangenburg [930]

THE CEMETERIES OF ABYDOS (MEES VOL 34) : PART 2 / Peet, T E – London, 1914 – 10mf – 8 – Dfl35.00 – ne Slangenburg [930]

THE CEMETERIES OF ABYDOS (MEES VOL 35) : PART 3 / Peet, T E & Loat, W LS – London, 1913 – 5mf – 8 – Dfl22.00 – ne Slangenburg [930]

CEMETERIES OF MENDOCINO COUNTY, CALIFORNIA – By Phyllis Gilley. Item H. Includes index. 37p. SW16-0149 – 5 – us A.G.L.L. [978]

CEMETERY CARDS / St. Mary's Cemetery, Geary County, KS – undated – 1 – us KS Hist [920]

CEMETERY DEED ACCOUNT RECORD / Huron County. Ohio. Plymouth, Village. Cemetery Trustees – 1933-1966 – 1r – 1 – $32.50r – us Archival [324]

CEMETERY DEED MEMORANDUM / Ottawa County. Ohio. Carroll Township. Board of Trustees – 1r – 1 – $32.50r – us Archival [324]

CEMETERY DEED RECORD / Ottawa County. Ohio. Erie Township. Board Of Trustees – 1910-1963 – 1r – 1 – $32.50r – us Archival [324]

CEMETERY DEED RECORD / Wood County. Ohio. Bowling Green, City. Safety/Service Director – 1907-1921 – 1r – 1 – $32.50r – us Archival [324]

CEMETERY DEED RECORDS / Hardin County. Ohio. Kenton. City Safety Service Director – 1883-1892 – 1r – 1 – $32.50r – us Archival [324]

CEMETERY DEED RECORDS / Henry County. Ohio. Recorder – 1872-1976 – 1r – 1 – $32.50r – us Archival [324]

CEMETERY DEED RECORDS / Huron County. Ohio. Plymouth, Village. Cemetery Trustees – 1904-1967 – 1r – 1 – $32.50r – us Archival [324]

CEMETERY DEED RECORDS / Lucas County. Ohio. Toledo, City Board of Public Service – 1840-1977 – 1r – 1 – $32.50r – us Archival [324]

CEMETERY DEED RECORDS / Wood County. Ohio. Freedom Township. Board of Trustees – 1910-1985 – 1r – 1 – $32.50r – us Archival [324]

CEMETERY DEED RECORDS / Wood County. Ohio. Portage Township. Board of Trustees – 1884-1980 – 1r – 1 – $32.50r – us Archival [324]

CEMETERY INSCRIPTIONS / Blytheville. Arkansas – Coll. and comp. by Ophelia Richardson Wade. 1969. Indexed. 7 fiches. F-1307 – 9 – us A.G.L.L. [978]

CEMETERY LOT OWNERS INDEX / Wood County. Ohio. Bowling Green, City. Safety/Service Director – 1r – 1 – $32.50r – us Archival [324]

CEMETERY PLAT MAPS / Hancock County, Ohio. Engineer – 1940-1983 – 1r – 1 – $32.50r – us Archival [324]

CEMETERY PLOT MAPS (VETERANS) / Putnam County. Ohio. Recorder – 1939-1940 – 1r – 1 – $32.50r – us Archival [324]

CEMETERY RECORD / Ottawa County. Ohio. Erie Township. Board of Trustees – 1918-1979 – 1r – 1 – $32.50r – us Archival [324]

CEMETERY RECORD OF THE FRANKLIN WARD, GRAHAM COUNTY, ARIZONA / Graham County. Arizona – Copied by Ethel Woolf. Item J. 7p. SW16-0163 – 5 – us A.G.L.L. [978]

CEMETERY RECORDS / Cherokee County, KS – 1916-1924, Galena, KS, Undertakers' Records – 1 – us KS Hist [920]

CEMETERY RECORDS / Effingham County. Georgia – Item H. 20p. of different cemeteries in this county. SW16-0001 – 5 – us A.G.L.L. [920]

CEMETERY RECORDS / Monroe County. Mich, Bedford Township. Board of Trustees – 1880-1964 – 1r – 1 – $32.50r – us Archival [324]

CEMETERY RECORDS / Ottawa County. Ohio. Carroll Township. Board of Trustees – 1867-1985 – 1r – 1 – $32.50r – us Archival [324]

CEMETERY RECORDS / Van Wert County. Ohio. Pleasant Township. Board of Trustees – 1859-1981 – 8r – 1 – $32.50r – us Archival [324]

CEMETERY RECORDS / Wood County. Ohio. Bloom Township. Board of Trustees – 1909-1988 – 1r – 1 – $32.50r – us Archival [324]

CEMETERY RECORDS / Wood County. Ohio. Freedom Township. Board of Trustees – 1910-1986 – 1r – 1 – $32.50r – us Archival [324]

CEMETERY RECORDS / Wood County. Ohio. Pemberville, Village. Cemetery Association – 1879-1975 – 1r – 1 – $32.50r – us Archival [324]

CEMETERY RECORDS / Wood County. Ohio. Weston. Village Council – 1883-1979 – 2r – 1 – $32.50r – us Archival [324]

CEMETERY RECORDS IN WINDSOR, CT / Ellsworth, Abigal Wolcott – 1929. Item C. SW16-0228 – 5 – us A.G.L.L. [920]

CEMETERY RECORDS OF MARION, CLARK, & TAYLOR COUNTIES. / Kentucky – Copied by members of the East Central States Mission, 1948. F-0688 – 2mf – 9 – us A.G.L.L. [920]

CEMETERY RECORDS OF STANISLAUS COUNTY, CALIFORNIA – Comp. by Downey Historical Society. 1960. Item O. 124p, index included. SW16-0031 – 5 – us A.G.L.L. [978]

CEMETERY TOMBSTONE AND OBITUARY CARDS / Jefferson County, KS – undated – 1 – us KS Hist [920]

CEMETRY DEED RECORDS / Wood County. Ohio. Lake Township. Township Trustees – 1876-1995 – 5r – 1 – $32.50r – us Archival [920]

CEMIYET-I TEDRISIYE-YI ISLAMIYE SALNAMESI – 1332 [1913] – 4mf – 9 – $50.00 – us MEDOC [949]

CENACULO – '(s.l.')-Curitiba, Brazil. Apr 1895-Jun 1897 – 1,5,6 – bl Biblioteca [072]

CEN/CENELEC EUROPEAN STANDARDS SERVICE – (Updated Every 60 Days) – Information Handling Services – 5,9 – us Info Handling [380]

Cenci, Pio *see* IL CARDINALE RAFFAELE...DEL VAL...ROMA

Cenecay, A B de *see* LETTRE DE CLEMENT MAROT A MONSIEUR DE. TOUCHANT CE QUI S'EST PASSE A L'ARRIVEE DE JEAN BAPTISTE DE LULLI, AUX CHAMPS ELISEES

Cenitagoya, Vicente *see* LOS MACHIGUENGAS. LIMA, 1944

CENNI SULLA ORGANOGRAFIA E FISIOLOGIA DELLE ALGHE / Meneghini, G – Padova, 1838. 64 pp. (Nuovi Saggi, Accad. Sci. Padova, v. 4). B-6381 1 – 9 – ne IDC [580]

Cennick, J *see* AN ACCOUNT OF A LATE RIOT AT EXETER

Cennini, C *see*
- TRAITE DE LA PEINTURE
- TRATTATO DELLA PITTURA
- A TREATISE ON PAINTING

CENOVE ZPRAVY / Czechoslovakia. Statni Urad Statisticky – Prague. v. 1-19, 26-28. 1921-39, 1946-48. Incomplete – 1 – us NY Public [310]

CENOVE ZPRAVY / Czechoslovakia. Statni Urad Statisticky – v1-28. 1921-48 – 2r – 1 – us Ross [324]

LE CENSEUR DES JOURNAUX – Paris. nov 1795-sept 1797 – 1 – fr A.C.R.P.P. [073]

LE CENSEUR EUROPEEN – Paris. 1-XII. Fevr 1817-17 avr 1819; 1-172, 15 juin 1819-20 juin 1820 – 1 – fr A.C.R.P.P. [073]

LE CENSEUR HEBDOMADAIRE – Utrecht, Paris. 1760-aout 1761 – 1 – fr A.C.R.P.P. [073]

CENSO DA POPULACAO EM 1940 – Lourenco Marques. v5. 1942 – us Res Libr [310]

CENSO DE LA POBLACION DE ESPANA / Spain. Direction general de estadistica – 1797-1940. Lacks 1860 – 1 – us Res Libr [310]

CENSO DE LA POBLACION DE ESPANA. REGION DE EXTREMADURA. CUADERNO N° 8 / Ministerio de Trabajo – Madrid: Sucesores de Rivadeneyra, S.A. 1941 – 1 – sp Bibl Santa Ana [304]

CENSO DE LAS POBLACIONES DE ESPANA SEGUN LA INSCRIPCION DE 31 DE DICIEMBRE DE 1940 / Direccion General de Estadistica, Ministerio de Trabajo – Madrid: Barranco, 1945 – 1 – sp Bibl Santa Ana [304]

CENSO DE POBLACION DE ESPANA SEGUN EL EMPADRONAMIENTO DE...1887, TOMO 1-3 / Instituto Geografico – Madrid, 1887 – 43mf – 9 – sp Cultura [946]

CENSO DE POBLACION DE ESPANA SEGUN EL RECUENTO DE 21 DE MAYO DE 1857 / Comision de Estadistica – Madrid, 1858 – 16mf – 9 – sp Cultura [946]

CENSO DE POBLACION DE LAS PROVINCIAS Y PARTIDOS DE LA CORONA DE ARAGON EN EL SIGLO 16 / Gonzalez, T – Madrid, 1829 – 7mf – 9 – sp Cultura [946]

CENSO ESCOLAR CORRESPONDIENTE A FINES DE 1883, PRINCIPIOS DE 1884-1885, TOMO 1-3 – Buenos Aires, 1885 – 27mf – 9 – sp Cultura [972]

CENSO ESCOLAR NACIONAL. RESUMENES GENERALES Y PRELIMINARES LEVANTADO A FINES DE 1883, PRINCIPIOS DE 1884 – Buenos Aires, 1884 – 1,093mf – 9 – sp Cultura [972]

CENSO ESPANOL / Floridablanca, Conde de – Madrid, 1787 – 2mf – 9 – sp Cultura [946]

CENSO ESPANOL EXECUTADO POR ORDEN DEL REY EN EL ANO 1787 / Floridablanca, Conde de – Madrid, 1787 – 4mf – 9 – sp Cultura [946]

CENSO GENERAL DE BUENOS AIRES DE 1887, TOMO 1-2 – Buenos Aires, 1889 – 23mf – 9 – sp Cultura [972]

CENSO GENERAL DE LA REPUBLICA DE GUATEMALA EN 1893 – Guatemala, 1894 – 5mf – 9 – sp Cultura [972]

CENSO GENERAL DE LA REPUBLICA DE GUATEMALA LEVANTADO EL ANO 1880 – Guatemala, 1881 – 9mf – 9 – sp Cultura [972]

CENSO GENERAL DE LA REPUBLICA MEXICANA, 1895, 1900, 1910, 1921, 1930 / Mexico. Direccion general de estadistica – 1897-1936 – 1 – 350.00 – us L of C Photodup [310]

CENSO OFICIAL DE LOS SENORES AGENTES COMERCIALES EN 1ST DE JUNIO DE 1961 / Colegio Oficial de Agentes Comerciales – Caceres: Imp. Sanguino, 1961 – 1 – sp Bibl Santa Ana [304]

CENSORED – aguide. 11th ed. 1981. Hard to locate sources of information. 1 fiche (29x) – 9 – 1.00f – at Libertarian Micro [320]

CENSORED / Corbett, B – 13th ed., 1983. 58p – 9 – 1.00f – at Libertarian Micro [321]

DIE CENSORIADE : FUENF BUECHER CENSORENLIEDER / Sehring, Wilhelm – Strassburg: G L Schuler, 1943 – 1r – 1 – us U.W. Library [780]

CENSORIAL – Eureka. Kan. 1875-79 – 1 – us UMI [071]

CENSORSHIP DURING WORLD WAR 1 PAMPHLET COLLECTION – 1916 – 1 – CSUXANL3558-B – us Hoover Inst Photo [350]

CENSORSHIP IN TSARIST RUSSIA / ed by O'Flaherty, Dennis M – 65 titles – 9 – ne IDC [350]

CENSURA SENCILLA DEL PAPEL QUE PUBLICO EN ESTA CORTE EL REVERENDO FRAY BUENAVENTURA ANGELERES CON EL TITULO DE DESENGANO DE LA FILOSOFIA REAL Y DESEMPENO DE LA MEDICINA SANATIVA / Gamez, A – Madrid, S.A. – 1mf – 9 – sp Cultura [610]

CENSURE DE "L'EXAMEN DE LA POSSESSION DES RELIGIEUSES DE LOUVIERS" – 1643 – 9 – fr Hachette [360]

LES CENSURES DES THEOLOGIENS DE PARIS / Estienne, Robert – Geneve: Jules-Guillaume Fick, 1866. 1 fiche – 9 – us A.T.L.A. [240]

CENSUS 86 – 9 – at Statistics [304]

CENSUS, 1885 / Colorado – (Arapahoe County. M158-0001. Archuleta, Bent, Boulder, Chaffee & Clear Creek Counties. M158-0002. Conejos, Costilla, Custer, Delta, Delores, Douglas, Eagle & Elbert Counties. M158-0003. Gilpin, Grand, Gunnison, Hinsdale & Huerfano Counties. M158-0004. Jefferson, Lake & La Plata Counties. M158-0005. Larimer, Las Animas, Mesa, Montrose & Ouray Counties. M158-0006. Park, Pitkin, Pueblo, Rio Grande & Routt Counties. M158-0007. Saguache, San Juan, San Miguel, Summit & Weld Counties. M158-0008) – 1 – us A.G.L.L. [310]

CENSUS COMMISSIONER'S NOTES ON CENSUS ARRANGEMENTS IN INDIVIDUAL PROVINCES AND STATES / India. Census Commissioner – 1st series. 1912? – 1 – us Res Libr [310]

CENSUS DATA FOR SMALL AREAS OF NEW YORK CITY: 1910-60 – 1 – us Primary [310]

CENSUS ETHNOGRAPHY, 1901-1931 / Hodson, T C – Delhi. 1937. BI-477 – 8 – ne IDC [304]

CENSUS: MORTALITY SCHEDULES / District of Columbia – 1880. Includes index. T655-0006 – 1 – us A.G.L.L. [920]

CENSUS OF AGRICULTURE, 1953 / Jordan. Department of Statistics – A joint project with the United States technical cooperation service of Jordan. 1954. BNE-9766 1 – 9 – ne IDC [310]

CENSUS OF CANADA / Canada – (See: Government Document Catalogue) – 1851-1986 – 9 – cn Micromedia [310]

THE CENSUS OF CEYLON – Colombo: Govt Press. v1 pts1-2, v2-3 1946; v4 – 1 – us Res Libr [310]

THE CENSUS OF CEYLON – [s.l., s.n.] v3 1891; v1,3 1901 – 1 – us Res Libr [310]

CENSUS OF CREEK INDIANS TAKEN BY PARSONS AND ABBOTT IN 1832 / U.S. Bureau of Indian Affairs – 1roll. T275 – 1 – us Nat'l Archives [324]

CENSUS OF ENGLAND AND WALES – 1861-1901 – 9 – ie Microforms [310]

CENSUS OF ENGLAND AND WALES, 1871 / Great Britain. Census Office – 1872-73 – 1 – 38.00 – us L of C Photodup [941]

CENSUS OF GLASS WORKING AND GLASS DECORATING SCHOOLS – 1970. 4p. 1 fiche. Fiche no. 966 – 9 – $2.50 – us Corning Mus [740]

CENSUS OF GREAT BRITAIN : ENGLAND, SCOTLAND AND WALES, 1801-1901 – (Individual years available seperately) – 1801-1901. Index, 1801-1851 – 9 – Ir£493.00 set – ie Microforms [310]

CENSUS OF IDIOTS / Wood County. Ohio. County Home – 1903 – 1r – 1 – $32.50r – us Archival [324]

CENSUS OF INDIA *see*
- ADMINISTRATIVE REPORT OF THE CENSUS OF COCHIN
- BALUCHISTAN, 1901 (ADMINISTRATIVE REPORT)
- BARODA STATE, 1901
- BIHAR AND ORISSA
- BURMA
- CENTRAL INDIA
- COCHIN
- DISTRICT CENSUS STATISTICS
- HYDERABAD
- MADRAS
- MYSORE CENSUS
- PUNJAB
- RAJPUTANA
- TRAVANCORE

CENSUS OF INDIA : PRICE LIST OF PUBLICATIONS / India. Ministry of Home Affairs. Office of the Registrar General – New Delhi, 1957 – us Res Libr [310]

CENSUS OF INDIA REPORTS / India – 1872-1951. E-1600-1 through E-1600-9 – 8 – ne IDC [310]

CENSUS OF INDIAN MOSSES / Bruehl, P A – (Records of the Botanical Survey of India, v. 13, pt. 1-2. 1931). B-362 2 – 8 – ne IDC [580]

CENSUS OF INDUSTRIAL PRODUCTION / Egypt. Dept. of Statistics and Census – 7v. 1950-61. (lacking 1951, 1953, 1955, 1957, 1959). BNE-4626 1 – 9 – ne IDC [310]

THE CENSUS OF IOWA / Palmer, F.W., State Printer – (1867. 5. 1869. 5) – Census returns of the different counties of the state of Iowa. 1862. Des Moines, 1863. Iowa Reel 44. The Cox Library Collection – 5 – us Americana [978]

CENSUS OF IOWA FOR 1836-1880 / Hull, John ST – Des Moines: F.M. Mills and George E. Roberts, 1883. Iowa Reel 43. (The Cox Library Collection) – 5 – us Americana [978]

CENSUS OF IRELAND – (Individual years available seperately) – 1813-1911. 444 fiches – 9 – Ir£510.00 set – ie Microforms [941]

CENSUS OF MINING AND MANUFACTURING INDUSTRIES IN JORDAN, 1954 / Jordan. Ministry of Economy – 1955. BNE-9803 1 – 9 – ne IDC [338]

CENSUS OF POPULATION AND HOUSING FORMS, 1911-1991 – 9 – at Statistics [304]

CENSUS OF RUSSIA, 1897 / Russia – Pervaia vseobshchaia perepis' naseleniia Rossisskoi Imperii. 1897. v. 1-89. Spb. 1897-1904. B-3000 2 – 8 – ne IDC [310]

CENSUS OF SAN MATEO AND SANTA CRUZ COUNTIES – San Mateo Co, CA. 1860 – 1r – 1 – $50.00 – B40258 – us Library Micro [978]

CENSUS OF SCOTLAND – 1861-1901 – 9 – ie Microforms [310]

CENSUS OF THE GENERA OF PLANTS HITHERTO KNOWN AS INDIGENOUS TO AUSTRALIA / Mueller, Ferdinand Jakob Heinrich von – Sydney. 1882; Additions. Sydney. 1883; Further additions. Sydney. 1886. B-8042 1 – 9 – ne IDC [580]

CENSUS OF THE ISLAND OF BOMBAY : FEBRUARY 2ND, 1864 / Leith – Bombay. 1864. 26p. Maps. BI-561/2 – 8 – ne IDC [310]

CENSUS OF THE PHILIPPINE ISLANDS. 1918 / Philippines. Census Office – 1-4 v. 1920-21 – 1 – 54.00 – us L of C Photodup [950]

CENSUS OF THE PHILIPPINES, 1939 / Philippines. (Commonwealth). Commission of the Census – 5v. 1940-43 – 1 – $161.00 – us L of C Photodup [310]

CENSUS OF THE TERRITORY OF KANSAS, FEBRUARY 1855 / Kansas.Census – Extracted by W. Heiss and index comp. by R.T. Mayhill. 1967. Indexed. 1 fiche. F-0737 – 9 – us A.G.L.L. [310]

CENSUS OF TRAVANCORE : CODE OF PROCEDURE – Trivandrum. pt1. 1911 – 1 – us Res Libr [310]

CENSUS RECORDS OF HEADS OF FAMILIES AT THE FIRST U.S. CENSUS TAKEN IN 1790 – 12 v – 1 – us UMI [920]

CENSUS REPORT – 9 – ne IDC [304]

CENSUS REPORTS 1926 / Russia – Vsesoiuznaia perepis' naseleniia 1926 goda. M. 1926. Index. BR-160 2 – 8 – ne IDC [310]

CENSUS REPORTS OF INDIA *see* BHAVNAGAR STATE CENSUS

CENSUS ROLL, 1835, OF THE CHEROKEE INDIANS EAST OF THE MISSISSIPPI AND INDEX TO THE ROLL / U.S. Bureau of Indian Affairs – 1roll. T496 – 1 – us Nat'l Archives [324]

CENSUS ROLL OF INDIANS OF CALIFORNIA, SAN JOSE/SANTA CLARA/SANTA CRUZ – State of California. 1890-1891; Act of 1928; Eureka 1936-1938; 1941-1942 – 9r – 1 – $450.00 – B06083 – us Library Micro [978]

CENT ANS DE SEDENTARISATION CHEZ LES MARAZIGUES DU SUD-TUNISIEN / Modrowski, K – 9 – F60.00 – fr Ethnologie [305]

CENT CUEILLETTES : POUR OUVRIERS ET CULTIVATEURS – Montreal, Canada. v1 n1. 4 jan-v1 n5. 1 fev 1883 – 1r – 1 – Can$25.00 – cn Can Microfilming [305]

CENT DEUX POEMES INDONESIENS (1925-1950) / Damais, Louis Charles – SE-4876 1. 1965 – 9 – ne IDC [810]

CENT DIXIEME CONGRES NATIONAL DES SOCIETES SAVANTES *see*
- BIOGRAPHICAL REGISTER OF THE OFFICERS AND GRADUATES OF THE U.S. MILITARY ACADEMY AT WEST POINT, NY FROM ITS ESTABLISHMENT IN 1802, TO 1890
- CITY OF SPOKANE AND SPOKANE COUNTY
- HISTORY OF NATRONA COUNTY 1888-1922
- HISTORY OF WALLA WALLA COUNTY
- UINTA COUNTY – ITS PLACE IN HISTORY
- WYOMING FROM TERRITORIAL DAYS TO THE PRESENT
- WYOMING STATE BUSINESS DIRECTORY 1929

CENT HUITIEME CONGRES NATIONAL DES SOCIETES SAVANTES *see*
- HISTORY OF SNOHOMISH COUNTY
- WILLIAM CHAPIN DEMING OF WYOMING

CENT NEUVIEME CONGRES NATIONAL DES SOCIETES SAVANTES *see* THE HISTORY OF WYOMING

CENT SEPTIEME CONGRES NATIONAL DES SOCIETES SAVANTES *see*
- AN ILLUSTRATED HISTORY OF SKAGIT AND SNOHOMISH COUNTIES
- MEN OF WYOMING 1915
- WHO'S WHO IN WASHINGTON STATE 1927

CENT TRENTE-CINQ ANS APRES, OU, LA RENAISSANCE ACADIENNE: SUIVI DE NOTU LES HISTORIQUES ET ANECDOTIQUES, ET D'UN PETIT DISCOURS PRONONCE PAR L'AUTEUR LE 15 AOUT 1890 A ANNAPOLIS, NOUVELLE-ECOSSE (ANCIENNE ACADIE) / Fontaine, L Urgele – Montreal: Cebhardt-Berthiaume, 1890. 03140. (Pre-1900 Canadiana) – 9 – cn C.I.H.M. [971]

CENTAINS: G. MOREAU, DEGAS, CHERET, WHISTLER, ROPS / Huysmans, Joris Karl – Paris: Tresse et Stock, 1889. 230p. 3 fiches. (Literature Collection) – 9 – $8.00 – fr Bibl Nationale [760]

CENTANERIO DE COLON Y FERIAS / Badajoz – 1892 – 9 – 1.50f – sp Bibl Santa Ana [946]

LE CENTAURE – Paris. 1896-97 – 1 – fr A.C.R.P.P. [073]

CENT-DIX LETTRES GRECQUES / Filelfe, Francois – Publiees par Emile Legrand. 1893 – 9 – fr Orientalistes [450]

CENTENAIRE DE LA FAYETTE, 1757-1834 / Reunion des musees nationaux. Paris – 1934. 3 fiches – 9 – fr Réunion [700]

CENTENAIRE DE MAURICE LEENHARDT, ETHNOLOGUE / Leenhardt, Maurice – Commissaire: Jean Guiart – 9 – F50.00 – fr Ethnologie [920]

CENTENARIO DE DON FRAY JUAN DE ZUMARRAGA, EL 4TH / Bayle, Constantino – Madrid: Missionalia Hispanica, 1948 – 1 – sp Bibl Santa Ana [240]

CENTENARIO DE LA CONGREGACION DE MISIONEROS DE LA PRECIOSA SANGRE. RECUERDOS DE LAS FIESTAS DE SU CELEBRACION EN CACERES, 15 AGOSTO 1815-15 DE AGOSTO 1915... – Caceres: Tip. Jimenez Merino, 1915? – 1 – sp Bibl Santa Ana [240]

CENTENARIO DE LA INDEPENDENCIA ESPANOLA. NOTICIA GENEALOGICA Y BIOGRAFICA Y BIOGRAFICA DEL MARISCAL CAMPO... / Croquer Cabezas, Emilio – Cadiz: Tipografia Comercial, 1912 – 1 – sp Bibl Santa Ana [920]

EL CENTENARIO DE MAGALLANES / Bayle, Constantino – Madrid: Razon y Fe, 1920 – 1 – sp Bibl Santa Ana [946]

CENTENARIO DE UN EPISODIO DE LA GUERRA DE LA INDEPENDENCIA OCURRIDO EL 21 DE AGOSTO DE 1809 / Jerte, Ayuntamiento de – Madrid: Asilo de Huerfanos de S.C. Jesus, 1909 – 1 – sp Bibl Santa Ana [320]

THE CENTENARY OF AMERICAN METHODISM : A SKETCH OF ITS HISTORY, THEOLOGY, PRACTICAL SYSTEM, AND SUCCESS / Stevens, Abel – New York: Carlton & Porter, 1866, c1865 – 1mf – us A.T.L.A. [240]

THE CENTENARY OF METHODISM : BEING A CONDENSED AND CLASSIFIED HISTORY OF THE RISE, EXTENSION AND CONTINUANCE OF THAT SYSTEM... FOUNDED BY THE REV. JOHN WESLEY, A.M., IN THE YEAR 1739 [WITH SPECIAL REFERENCE TO DEVELOPMENTS IN IRELAND] – Dublin, 1839 – 5mf – 9 – ne IDC [240]

CENTENARY OF METHODISM IN EASTERN BRITISH AMERICA – Halifax: S. F. Huestis, 1882?. 02171. (Pre-1900 Canadiana) – 9 – cn C.I.H.M. [240]

THE CENTENARY OF SAINT PETER AND THE GENERAL COUNCIL : A PASTORAL LETTER TO THE CLERGY ETC / Manning, Henry Edward – (Includes bibliographical references) – London: Longmans, Green, 1867 – 1mf – 9 – 0-8370-8727-9 – 1986-2727 – us A.T.L.A. [240]

THE CENTENARY OF THE METHODIST NEW CONNEXION, 1797-1897 / ed by Packer, G – London, [1897]. vii/272p – 3mf – 9 – ne IDC [240]

THE CENTENARY OF WESLEYAN METHODISM : A BRIEF SKETCH OF THE RISE, PROGRESS AND PRESENT STATE OF THE WESLEYAN-METHODIST SOCIETIES THROUGHOUT THE WORLD / Jackson, T – London, 1839. viii/388p – 5mf – 9 – ne IDC [240]

CENTENARY SOUVENIR, 1851-1951 / Fernando, J S A & Jayewardene, Gustavus – [Colombo: Lanka Trading Co, 1951] – 1 – us Res Libr [950]

A CENTENARY STUDY, UPPER CANADA: A PAPER READ BEFORE THE LUNDY'S LANE HISTORICAL SOCIETY / Fessenden, Elisha Joseph – s.l., s.n., 1892?. 03093. (Pre-1900 Canadiana) – 9 – cn C.I.H.M. [971]

THE CENTENARY VOLUME OF THE CHURCH MISSIONARY SOCIETY FOR AFRICA AND THE EAST, 1799-1899 – London: Church Missionary Society, 1902 – 3mf – us A.T.L.A. [240]

THE CENTENNIAL ADVERTISER – Bolton Centre, Knowlton, Canada. 9 mar 1967-23 jun 1971 – 1r – 1 – Can$40.00 – cn Can Microfilming [072]

THE CENTENNIAL ANNIVERSARY OF THE CITY OF HAMILTON 1791-1891 / McClub, D W – Cincinnati, 1892. Ohio Reel 16.(The Cox Library Collection) – 5 – us Americana [978]

THE CENTENNIAL ANNIVERSARY OF THE ELEVATION OF JOHN MARSHALL TO THE OFFICE OF CHIEF JUSTICE OF THE SUPREME COURT OF THE UNITED STATES OF AMERICA. / Marshall, John – Philadelphia: Buchanan, 1901. 68p. LL-485 – 1 – us L of C Photodup [340]

CENTENNIAL BAPTIST CHURCH. NASHVILLE, TENNESSEE : CHURCH RECORDS – Feb 1894-Mar 1982 – 1 – 60.66 – us Baptist [240]

THE CENTENNIAL BIOGRAPHICAL DIRECTORY OF FRANKLIN COUNTY / Kiel, Herman Gottlieb – 1925. Missouri Reel 16.(The Cox Library Collection) – 5 – us Americana [978]

A CENTENNIAL BIOGRAPHICAL HISTORY OF CHAMPAIGN COUNTY – Chicago, 1902. Ohio Reel 18. (The Cox Library Collection) – 5 – us Americana [978]

A CENTENNIAL BIOGRAPHICAL HISTORY OF CRAWFORD COUNTY – Chicago, 1902. Ohio Reel 24. (The Cox Library Collection) – 5 – us Americana [978]

A CENTENNIAL BIOGRAPHICAL HISTORY OF FRANKLIN COUNTY AND THE CITY OF COLUMBUS – Chicago, 1901. Ohio Reel 32. (The Cox Library Collection) – 5 – us Americana [978]

A CENTENNIAL BIOGRAPHICAL HISTORY OF HANCOCK COUNTY – Chicago: 1903. Ohio Reel 37. (The Cox Library Collection) – 5 – us Americana [978]

A CENTENNIAL BIOGRAPHICAL HISTORY OF RICHLAND COUNTY / Baughman, A J – Chicago: Lewis Publ. Co., 1901. Ohio Reel 55. (The Cox Library Collection) – 5 – us Americana [978]

CENTENNIAL BIOGRAPHICAL HISTORY OF SENECA COUNTY – Chicago: 1902. Ohio Reel 58. (The Cox Library Collection) – 5 – us Americana [978]

THE CENTENNIAL CELEBRATION OF THE EVACUATION OF DETROIT BY THE BRITISH, JULY 11, 1796-JULY 11, 1896: REPORT OF THE PROCEEDINGS – With the addresses of H. M. Duffield, J. C. Burrows and Jas. B. Angell. Detroit, 1896. 00752. (Pre-1900 Canadiana) – 9 – cn C.I.H.M. [978]

THE CENTENNIAL CELEBRATION OF THE THEOLOGICAL SEMINARY OF THE PRESBYTERIAN CHURCH IN THE UNITED STATES OF AMERICA, AT PRINCETON, NEW JERSEY : MAY FIFTH, MAY SIXTH, MAY SEVENTH, NINETEEN HUNDRED AND TWELVE – Princeton: At the Theological seminary, 1912 – 2mf – us A.T.L.A. [240]

THE CENTENNIAL CELEBRATION OF TOLARSVILLE BAPTIST CHURCH. ST PAULS, NORTH CAROLINA : CHURCH RECORDS – 1874-1974 – 1 – $5.00 – us Baptist [240]

CENTENNIAL DIRECTORY OF FOND DU LAC COUNTY / M.G. Tousley and Co – Fond Du Lac, 1876. Wisconsin Reel 10. The Cox Library Collection – 5 – us Americana [978]

CENTENNIAL EDITION OF THE APPEAL-DEMOCRAT – Marysville, CA. 1960 – 1 – $50.00 – B06003 – us Library Micro [071]

CENTENNIAL EDITION OF THE BAPTIST DENOMINATION : BEING THE PAST AND PRESENT OF THE BAPTIST CHURCH THROUGHOUT THE WORLD / Haynes, Dudley C – (Includes index) – New York: Sheldon, 1875 – 1mf – 9 – 0-8370-8907-7 – 1986-2907 – us A.T.L.A. [240]

CENTENNIAL HISTORY OF AKRON 1825-1925 / Olin & Allen & Brouse & Braden – Summit County Historical Society, 1925. Ohio Reel 62. (The Cox Library Collection) – 5 – us Americana [978]

CENTENNIAL HISTORY OF ALLEGANY COUNTY / Morton, Oren F – Dayton, J. K. Ruebush Co., 1923. Virginia Reel 2. (The Cox Library Collection) – 5 – us Americana [978]

CENTENNIAL HISTORY OF ALPENA COUNTY / Oliver, David D – Alpena: Argus Printing House, 1903. Michigan Reel 4. (The Cox Library Collection) – 5 – us Americana [978]

CENTENNIAL HISTORY OF AMERICAN METHODISM : INCLUSIVE OF ITS ECCLESIASTICAL ORGANIZATION IN 1784 AND ITS SUBSEQUENT DEVELOPMENT UNDER THE SUPERINTENDENCY OF FRANCIS ASBURY... / Atkinson, John – New York: Phillips & Hunt; Cincinnati: Cranston & Stowe, 1884 – 2mf – us A.T.L.A. [240]

CENTENNIAL HISTORY OF ANDERSON COUNTY / Hohes, Pauline B – San Antonio: Naylor Co., 1936. Texas Reel 10. (The Cox Library Collection) – 5 – us Americana [978]

CENTENNIAL HISTORY OF ARKANSAS / Herdon, Dallas T – (Little Rock: S. J. Clarke Publ. Co., 1922). Vol. 1. Arkansas Reel 1; Vols. 2-3. Arkansas Reel 2. (The Cox Library Collection) – 5 – us Americana [978]

CENTENNIAL HISTORY OF BELMONT COUNTY / McKelvey, A T – Chicago: Biographical Publ. Co., 1903. Ohio Reel 15. (The Cox Library Collection) – 5 – us Americana [978]

CENTENNIAL HISTORY OF BUTLER COUNTY / Bartlow et al – Local biography. Indianapolis: B.F. Bowen and Co., 1905. Ohio Reel 17. (The Cox Library Collection) – 5 – us Americana [978]

THE CENTENNIAL HISTORY OF CHAUTAUQUA COUNTY / Chautauqua History Co – Jamestown, 1904. Vol. 1. New York Reel 10; Vol. 2. New York Reel 11. (The Cox Library Collection) – 5 – us Americana [978]

CENTENNIAL HISTORY OF COLUMBUS AND FRANKLIN COUNTIES / Taylor, William A – Chicago: S.J. Clarke Publ. Co., 1909. 2v. Ohio Reel 33. (The Cox Library Collection) – 5 – us Americana [978]

CENTENNIAL HISTORY OF COSHOCTON COUNTY / Bahmer, William J – Chicago: S.J. Clarke Publ. Co., 1909. 2v. Ohio Reel 23. (The Cox Library Collection) – 5 – us Americana [978]

CENTENNIAL HISTORY OF DAVIDSON COUNTY / Leonard, Jacob C – Raleigh: Edwards and Broughton Co., 1927. North Carolina Reel 1. (The Cox Library Collection) – 5 – us Americana [978]

CENTENNIAL HISTORY OF DECATUR AND MACON COUNTY / Richmond, Mabel E – Decatur: The Decatur Review, 1930. Illinois Reel 41. (The Cox Library Collection) – 5 – us Americana [978]

CENTENNIAL HISTORY OF ERIE COUNTY / Johnson, Crisfield – Buffalo: Matthews and Warren, 1876. New York Reel 14. (The Cox Library Collection) – 5 – us Americana [978]

CENTENNIAL HISTORY OF LANCASTER, OHIO AND LANCASTER PEOPLE / Wiseman, C M – Lancaster: C.M.L. Wiseman, 1898.Ohio Reel 30. (The Cox Library Collection) – 5 – us Americana [978]

CENTENNIAL HISTORY OF MADISON COUNTY / Netterville, J J – 100 years progress, 1823-1923. 2v. Anderson: Historians Assoc., 1925. Indiana Reel 20. (The Cox Library Collection) – 5 – us Americana [978]

CENTENNIAL HISTORY OF MASON COUNTY / Cochrane, Joseph – Springfield: Rokker's Steam Printing House, 1876. Illinois Reel 42. (The Cox Library Collection) – 5 – us Americana [978]

CENTENNIAL HISTORY OF MISSOURI – 1921. Missouri Reel 3. The Cox Library Collection – 5 – us Americana [978]

THE CENTENNIAL HISTORY OF OREGON / Gaston, Joseph – (v2-4. Oregon reel 2) – Chicago: S.J. Clarke Publ. Co., 1912. v1. Oregon reel 1. (Cox Library Collection) – 5 – us Americana [978]

CENTENNIAL HISTORY OF RUSH COUNTY / Gary & Thomas – Indianapolis: Historical Publishing Company, 1921. v1. Indiana Reel 25. (The Cox Library Collection) – 5 – us Americana [978]
CENTENNIAL HISTORY OF SUMMIT COUNTY AND REPRESENTATIVE CITIZENS / Doyle, William B – Chicago: Biographical Publ. Co., 1908. Ohio Reel 61. (The Cox Library Collection) – 5 – us Americana [978]
CENTENNIAL HISTORY OF SUSQUEHANNA COUNTY / Stocher, Rhamanthus M – Philadelphia, R. T. Peck and Company, 1887. Pennsylvania Reel 39. (The Cox Library Collection) – 5 – us Americana [978]
CENTENNIAL HISTORY OF THE CITY OF NEWARK AND LICKING COUNTY / Brister, E M P – Chicago: S. J. Clarke Publ. Co., 1909. Vols. 1-2. Ohio Reel 42. (The Cox Library Collection) – 5 – us Americana [978]
CENTENNIAL HISTORY OF TROY, PIQUA AND MIAMI COUNTY AND REPRESENTATIVE CITIZENS / Harbaugh, Thomas C – Chicago: Richmond-Arnold Publ. Co., 1909. Ohio Reel 49. (The Cox Library Collection) – 5 – us Americana [978]
CENTENNIAL HOMESTEADS, 1977 APPLICATIONS / Ohio Historical Society – 2 reels – 1 – us Ohio Hist [977]
CENTENNIAL HYMN, OP. 27 / Paine, John Knowles – Holograph, 1867 – 1 – us Sibley [780]
THE CENTENNIAL MEDITATION OF COLUMBIA / Buck, Dudley – A cantata for the inaugural ceremonies at Philadelphia, May 10, 1876. Poem by Sidney Lanier, of Georgia. Music by Dudley Buck, of Connecticut. New York: G. Schirmer, 1876. Piano-vocal score. music 902 – 1 – us L of C Photodup [780]
CENTENNIAL OF HOME MISSIONS...114TH GENERAL ASSEMBLY...16-20 MAY 1902 – Philadelphia: Pres. Bd. of Pub. & Sun. Sch. Wk., 1902. 288p. 1 fiche – 9 – us A.T.L.A. [240]
CENTENNIAL OF THE PROVINCE OF UPPER CANADA, 1792-1892: PROCEEDINGS AT THE GATHERING HELD AT NIAGARA-ON-THE-LAKE, JULY 16, 1892 – And also proceedings at the meeting held in front of the new Parliament buildings, Toronto, September 17, 1892. Printed for the Cent. Comm. by Arbuthnot & Adamson, 1893. 02562. (Pre-1900 Canadiana) – 9 – cn C.I.H.M. [971]
THE CENTENNIAL OF THE SETTLEMENT OF UPPER CANADA BY THE UNITED EMPIRE OF LOYALISTS, 1784-1884 – The celebrations at Adolphustown, Toronto, and Niagara; with an appendix containing a copy of the U.E. list, preserved in the Crown Lands Department at Toronto. Toronto: Rose, 1885. 02561. (Pre-1900 Canadiana) – 9 – cn C.I.H.M. [971]
CENTENNIAL PORTRAIT AND BIOGRAPHICAL RECORD OF CITY OF DAYTON AND MONTGOMERY COUNTY / Conover, Frank – Chicago: A. W. Bowen and Co., 1897. Ohio Reel 50. (The Cox Library Collection) – 5 – us Americana [978]
A CENTENNIAL REVIEW OF THE BOWDOINHAM ASSOCIATION OF BAPTIST CHURCHES IN MAINE / Small, Edwin S – 1887 – 1 – 5.00 – us Baptist [240]
CENTENNIAL SOUVENIR, 1809-1909 / Cedarville. Ohio. Reformed Presbyterian Church – 9 – $50.00 – us Presbyterian [240]
CENTENNIAL SOUVENIR OF MARIETTA, OHIO 1788-1888 / E.R. Alderman and Sons – 1887. Ohio Reel 65. The Cox Library Collection – 5 – us Americana [978]
CENTENNIAL ST ANDREW'S, NIAGARA, 1794-1894 / Carnochan, Janet – Toronto: W. Briggs, 1895. 00994. (Pre-1900 Canadiana) – 9 – cn C.I.H.M. [240]
CENTENNIAL, ST MARK'S CHURCH, NIAGARA / Carnochan, Janet – Toronto: J. Bain, 1892. 00461. (Pre-1900 Canadiana) – 9 – cn C.I.H.M. [240]
Centennius, Ralph *see* THE DOMINION IN 1983
Centeno, A *see* HISTORIA DE COSAS DEL ORIENTE PRIMERA Y SEGUNDA PARTE. CONTIENE VNA DESCRIPCION GENERAL DE LOS REYNOS DE ASSIA CON LAS COSAS MAS NOTABLES DELLOS
CENTER BAPTIST CHURCH. MARION, ILLINOIS : CHURCH RECORDS – Feb 1887-Jan 1950. 606p – 1 – 27.27 – us Baptist [240]
Center Creek. Baptist Church, Jefferson County, Mo. *see* RECORDS
CENTER FIRST BAPTIST CHURCH. CENTER, TEXAS : CHURCH RECORDS – Sep 1889-Sep 1941. 998p. Lacks May 1908-Dec 1917 – 1 – 44.91 – us Baptist [240]
Center for Applied Linguistics. Washington, D.C. *see* DICTIONARY CATALOG OF THE LIBRARY OF THE CENTER FOR APPLIED LINGUISTICS
CENTER FOR CUBAN STUDIES NEWSLETTER – NY City, NY. 1974-1976 – 1r – 1 – $50.00 – R04920 – us Library Micro [071]
CENTER FOR DEMOCRATIC RENEWAL – Atlanta. 27 docs. 1986-1992 – 9mf – 9 – ne IDC [320]
CENTER FOR ENERGY AND MINERAL RESOURCES: ALCOHOL-FUEL SYMPOSIUM / Texas A & M University. Agricultural Experiment Station and Agricultural Extension Service – 1980 – 2mf – 9 – us Spaulding [660]
CENTER FOR INTERNATIONAL POLICY – Washington D.C. 69 docs. 1980-1991 – 11mf – 9 – ne IDC [320]
CENTER FOR INTERNATIONAL POLICY, INDOCHINA PROJECT *see* INDOCHINA PROJECT
Center for Self-Sufficiency Staff *see* THE A TO Z SMALL BUSINESS REFERENCE ENCYCLOPEDIA-WORD MAPPING EDITION
CENTER HILL BAPTIST CHURCH. NESHOBA COUNTY. MISSISSIPPI : CHURCH RECORDS – 1866-78 – 1 – 5.00 – us Baptist [240]
CENTER JOURNAL – (1985-. 5,6,9) – v1-4. 1981-85 – 1 – us UMI [073]
CENTER MAGAZINE – (v.4- 1971- 5,6. v.8- 1975- 9) – v.1- 1967- – 1 – us UMI [073]
CENTER NEWS – (V36, No29, (10 Apr. 1975)-v36, No32, (19 May 1975)) – Rochester, N.Y. – 1 – us A.J.P.C. [071]
CENTER NEWS *see* CENTERPIESE
Center of Scientific and Technological Information *see* ARTIFICIAL RAINFALL
CENTER REGISTER – Center, NE. -w. Mar. 1905-Sep. 1906 – 1 – us NE Hist [071]
CENTER TOWNSHIP, RECORDS, MS 566 – (Docket book for various justices of the peace and constables from this township) – 1818-21 – 1r – 1 – us Western Res [978]
CENTER WHITE CREEK BAPTIST CHURCH (LITTLE WHITE CREEK; WHITE CREEK). CAMBRIDGE, NEW YORK : CHURCH RECORDS – 1779-84, 1806-13, 1784-1816, 1827-94 – 1 – 32.94 – us Baptist [240]
CENTERFOLD – Toronto.Aug 1976-Sept 1979. Continued by: Fuse Magazine – 1 – 75.00 – cn McLaren [073]
CENTERLINE PRESS – Van Dyke. Mich. 1926-31 – 1 – us UMI [071]
CENTERPIESE – (Vol. 1, no. 2 (Winter 1983)-v. 1, no. 3 (early spr. 1984); V. 2, no. 5 (Fall 1985)-v. 3, no. 6 (Mar. 1986); v. 5, no. 9 (May 1988)-v. 6, no. 2 (Oct. 1988)) – Palo Alto, California – 1 – us A.J.P.C. [978]
CENTINEL – Easton. Pa. 1821-89; 1897-1917 – 1 – us UMI [071]
CENTINEL OF FREEDOM – Newark. N.J. 1796-1820 – 1,3 – us Readex [071]
CENTINEL OF THE NORTHWESTERN TERRITORY – Cincinnati. Ohio. 1793-96 – 1 – us UMI [071]
CENTINELA – Almendralejo. 1884-86. No. sueltos – 9 – 1.50f – sp Bibl Santa Ana [072]
EL CENTINELA – Mexicali, MX. 1976-1994 – 111 – $5,550.00 – R04215 – us Library Micro [072]
EL CENTINELA – Panama City, Panama. 12 Jul 1857-26 Dec 1858 – 1r – 1 – us L of C Photodup [072]
EL CENTINELA – [Habana]: El Centinela. v12 n1356-1378,1380-1396,1399-1402. mar 9-may 1, may 6-jun 12, jun 19-26 1897; n1405-1411,1413-1417,1419-1422,1425-1450. jul 3-17, jul 22-31, aug 5-14, aug 19-oct 16 1897 – us Res Libr [072]
CENTINELA CONTRA JUDIOS / Torrejoncillo, Francisco de – 1691 – 9 – 1.50f – sp Bibl Santa Ana [270]
EL CENTINELA DE ISRAEL / H G C – 1873 – 9 – 1.50f – sp Bibl Santa Ana [830]
LA CENTINELA DE LA PATRIA – Cadiz, Spain. 21 Jun-22 Aug 1810.-w. 6 ft – 1 – uk British Libr Newspaper [072]
Centner, E *see* DROIT ROMAIN: DU LEGS DE LA DOT ET EN GENERAL DE LA CHOSE DUE...
Cento, Fernando *see* PEGINAS ESCOGIDAS
CENTON EPISTOLARIO DEL BACHILLER FERNAN GOMEZ DE CIBDADREAL. GENERACIONES... / Vera y Figueroa, Juan Antonio – Madrid, 1775 – 4mf – 9 – sp Cultura [946]
CENTRAAL BLAD VOOR ISRAELIETEN IN NEDERLAND – Amsterdam, 1885-1940. v. 1-56. Lacking: 1885, v1; 1894/95, v10; 1899, v14(5 2); 1909, v25(12) – 614mf – 9 – ne IDC [073]
CENTRAAL ECONOMISCH PLAN, 1947. VOL. 1, EERSTE NOTA, GLOBAAL PLAN. (CENTRAL ECONOMIC PLAN, 1947. VOL. 1, FIRST MEMORANDUM, GLOBAL PLAN). 'S-GRAVENHAGE. 1946. BD-1699/1 / Netherlands. Centraal Planbureau – 9 – ne IDC [338]
CENTRAAL ECONOMISCH PLAN, 1949 / Netherlands. Centraal Planbureau – 's-Gravenhage. 1949 – 9 – ne IDC [338]
CENTRAAL ECONOMISCH PLAN, 1950 / Netherlands. Centraal Planbureau – 's-Gravenhage. 1950. BD-320 1 – 9 – ne IDC [338]
CENTRAAL ECONOMISCH PLAN, 1951 / Netherlands. Centraal Planbureau – 's-Gravenhage. 1951 – 9 – ne IDC [338]
CENTRAAL ECONOMISCH PLAN, 1952 / Netherlands. Centraal Planbureau – 's-Gravenhage. 1952. BD-322 1 – 9 – ne IDC [338]
CENTRAAL ECONOMISCH PLAN, 1953 / Netherlands. Centraal Planbureau – 's-Gravenhage. 1953. BD-323 1 – 9 – ne IDC [338]
CENTRAAL ECONOMISCH PLAN, 1954 / Netherlands. Centraal Planbureau – 's-Gravenhage. 1954 – 9 – ne IDC [338]
CENTRAAL ECONOMISCH PLAN, 1955 / Netherlands. Centraal Planbureau – 's-Gravenhage. 1955 – 9 – ne IDC [338]
CENTRAAL ECONOMISCH PLAN, 1956 / Netherlands. Centraal Planbureau – 's-Gravenhage. 1956 – 9 – ne IDC [338]
CENTRAAL ECONOMISCH PLAN, 1957 / Netherlands. Centraal Planbureau – 's-Gravenhage. 1957. BD-327 1 – 9 – ne IDC [338]
CENTRAAL ECONOMISCH PLAN, 1958 / Netherlands. Centraal Planbureau – 's-Gravenhage. 1958 – 9 – ne IDC [338]
CENTRAAL ECONOMISCH PLAN, 1959 / Netherlands. Centraal Planbureau – 's-Gravenhage. 1959. BD-329 1 – 9 – ne IDC [338]
CENTRAAL ECONOMISCH PLAN, 1960 / Netherlands. Centraal Planbureau – 's-Gravenhage. 1960 – 9 – ne IDC [338]
CENTRAAL ECONOMISCH PLAN, 1961 / Netherlands. Centraal Planbureau – 's-Gravenhage. 1961. BD-331 1 – 9 – ne IDC [338]
CENTRAAL ECONOMISCH PLAN, 1962 / Netherlands. Centraal Planbureau – 's-Gravenhage. 1962. BD-765 1 – 9 – ne IDC [338]
CENTRAAL ECONOMISCH PLAN, 1963 / Netherlands. Centraal Planbureau – 's-Gravenhage. 1963 – 9 – ne IDC [338]
CENTRAAL ECONOMISCH PLAN, 1964 / Netherlands. Centraal Planbureau – 's-Gravenhage. 1964. BD-766 1 – 9 – ne IDC [338]
CENTRAAL ECONOMISCH PLAN, 1965 / Netherlands. Centraal Planbureau – 's-Gravenhage. 1965. BD-767 1 – 9 – ne IDC [338]
CENTRAAL ECONOMISCH PLAN, 1966 / Netherlands. Centraal Planbureau – 's-Gravenhage. 1966. BD-768 1 – 9 – ne IDC [338]
CENTRAAL ECONOMISCH PLAN, 1967 / Netherlands. Centraal Planbureau – 's-Gravenhage. 1967 – 9 – ne IDC [338]
CENTRAAL ECONOMISCH PLAN 1973 / Netherlands. Centraal Planbureau – 's-Gravenhage. 1973. BD-1708 1 – 9 – ne IDC [338]
CENTRAAL ECONOMISCH PLAN, 1974 / Netherlands. Centraal Planbureau – 's-Gravenhage. 1974. BD-2012 1 – 9 – ne IDC [338]
CENTRAAL ECONOMISCH PLAN, 1975 / Netherlands. Centraal Planbureau – 's-Gravenhage. 1975. BD-1867 1 – 9 – ne IDC [338]
CENTRAAL PLANBUREAU / Netherlands. Economic plans – (Centraal Economisch Plan 1968. D-916; 2. SF 12.00; 8. Centraal Economisch Plan 1969. D-1132; 1. SF 12.00; IDC; 9. Centraal Economisch Plan 1970. D-1133; 1. 1970. SF 14.00; IDC; 9. Centraal Economisch Plan 1971. D-1134; 1. 1971. SF 14.00; IDC; 9. Centraal Economisch Plan 1972. D-1550; 1. 1972. SF 12.00; IDC; 9) – ne IDC [338]
CENTRAL AFRICA : A RECORD OF THE WORK OF THE UNIVERSITIES' MISSION TO CENTRAL AFRICA – (Some issuses lacking) – v1-82. 1883-1964 – 11r – 1 – ATLA S0224 – us A.T.L.A. [073]
CENTRAL AFRICA / Universities' Mission to Central Africa – (The monthly magazine of the Universities' Mission to Central Africa). 1883-1964 – 1 – uk Microform Academic [240]
CENTRAL AFRICA, JAPAN, AND FIJI: A STORY OF MISSIONARY ENTERPRISE, TRIALS AND TRIUMPHS / Pitman, Emma Raymond – London: Hodder and Stoughton, 1882. 296p. ill – 1 – us U.W. Library [240]
CENTRAL AFRICAN EXAMINER – Salisbury. Rhodesia. Jun 1957-Dec 1965 – 1 – 35.00r – us Hoover Inst Photo [072]
CENTRAL AFRICAN GAME AND ITS SPOOR / Stigand, C H & Lyell, D D – 2430 2. 1906 – 8 – ne IDC [639]
CENTRAL AFRICAN MAIL *see* AFRICAN MAIL
CENTRAL AFRICAN POST – Lusaka, Zambia. -tw. 30 March 1950-3 May 1951; 2 Aug 1951-22 May 1952; 2 Jan 1954-31 Dec 1958. 18 reels – 1 – uk British Libr Newspaper [072]
CENTRAL AFRICAN REPUBLIC : ANNUAIRE STATISTIQUE DE LA REPUBLIQUE CENTRAFRICAINE 1962 / Central African Republic. Direction de la Statistique et de la Conjoncture – (Coll title: African Official Statistical Serials, 1867-1982) – 2mf – 9 – £17.00 – uk Chadwyck [960]
Central African Republic *see*
– ECONOMIE ET PLAN DE DEVELOPPEMENT
– JOURNAL OFFICIEL DE LA REPUBLIQUE CENTRAFRICAINE
– PLAN DE DEVELOPPEMENT ECONOMIQUE ET SOCIAL, 1967-1970
Central African Republic. Direction de la Statistique et de la Conjoncture *see* CENTRAL AFRICAN REPUBLIC
Central African Republic. Haut Commissariat *see* PLAN INTERMEDIAIRE BIENNAL, 1965-66
Central African Republic. Ministere de l'Education Nationale *see* ANNUAIRE DES STATISTIQUES 1986/87-1988/89
Central African Republic. Presidence du Gouvernement. Haut Commissariat au Plan et a l'Assistance Technique *see* PLAN INTERMEDIAIRE 1965-66
CENTRAL AFRICAN TIMES – Blantyre. Malawi. -w. 22 Jul 1899-27 Jun 1908. (10 reels) – 1 – uk British Libr Newspaper [072]
CENTRAL AMERICA AND THE CARIBBEAN, 1930-45 : CONFIDENTIAL U.S. DIPLOMATIC POST RECORDS / U.S. Department of State – (See also indiv. listings) – 1 – $24,255.00 set – us UPA [972]
CENTRAL AND AUTONOMIC NERVOUS SYSTEM ACTIVITY DURING SELF-PACED MOTOR PERFORMANCE: A STUDY OF THE ACTIVATION CONSTRUCT IN MARKSMEN / Hatfield, Bradley D – 1982 – 2mf – 9 – $8.00 – us Microform Publ [790]
CENTRAL AND SOUTHERN CALIFORNIA, ARIZONA AND NEW MEXICO – West Coast. 1882-1883 – 1r – 1 – $50.00 – D128 – us Library Micro [978]
Central Arbitration Council *see* DIEU LE TAM THOI VE CHE DO HOP DONG KINH TE
CENTRAL ASIA AND THE ANGLO-RUSSIAN FRONTIER QUESTION; A SERIES OF POLITICAL PAPERS / Vambery, Armin – Transl. by F.E. Bunnett.London: Smith, Elder & Co., 1874. viii,385p. First publ. in "Unsere Zeit" – 1 – us U.W. Library [950]
CENTRAL ASIAN SERIALS FROM LATE IMPERIAL RUSSIA – (Supplement No1. 50r. Sfr6,750.00) – 200r – 1 – Sfr22,500.00 set Sfr1.00r – sz Infoprint [950]
CENTRAL ASIAN SERIALS, LATE 19TH-EARLY 20TH CENTURY – (1st suppl 50r $3,750. 2nd suppl 50r $3,750. 3rd suppl "Kaspii" 1881-1917 108r $8,000. 4th suppl "Shark Iulduzi" 1931-91 122r $9,000. 5th suppl "Historical Caucasian Newspapers" 32r. 6th suppl 35r $2,600) – 1994 – 200r – 1 – $15,000.00 set $80.00r – us Ross [073]

CENTRAL ASIAN SURVEY – 1982- 12v – 9 – £170.50 – 0263-4937 – uk Carfax [950]
CENTRAL AVENUE BAPTIST CHURCH. MEMPHIS, TENNESSEE : CHURCH RECORDS – 1873-1937 – 1 – 5.00 – us Baptist [240]
CENTRAL AVENUE NEWS – Los Angeles, CA. Nov 1910-May 1911 – 1r – 1 – $50.00 – C02376 – us Library Micro [071]
CENTRAL BANKING IN EGYPT / Abushady, M – 1951. BNE-4602 1 – 9 – ne IDC [332]
CENTRAL BAPTIST – Missouri. Aug 1868-1912. Lacking 1873-76 – 1 – 825.75 – us Baptist [240]
CENTRAL BAPTIST CHURCH. ALCOA, TENNESSEE : CHURCH RECORDS – Sept 1943-Jun 1984 – 1 – 45.63 – us Baptist [240]
CENTRAL BAPTIST CHURCH. GREENVILLE COUNTY. SOUTH CAROLINA : CHURCH RECORDS – 1893-Oct 1982. Includes mission committee minutes, 1974-75. 1713p – 1 – 77.09 – us Baptist [240]
CENTRAL BAPTIST CHURCH. MAYSVILLE, KENTUCKY : CHURCH RECORDS – (Formerly Tabernacle Baptist Church) – Nov 1931-June 1985 – 1 reel – 1 – $82.08 – us Baptist [240]
CENTRAL BAPTIST CHURCH. MORGAN COUNTY. DECATUR, ALABAMA : CHURCH RECORDS – 1892-1956 – 1 – 45.90 – us Baptist [240]
CENTRAL BAPTIST CHURCH. NASHVILLE, TENNESSEE : CHURCH RECORDS – 20 Oct 1858-May 1946 – 1 – 79.29 – us Baptist [240]
CENTRAL BAPTIST CHURCH. PAMPA, TEXAS : CHURCH RECORDS – 1931-60 – 1 – 32.49 – us Baptist [240]
CENTRAL BAPTIST CHURCH. WASHINGTON, D.C. : CHURCH RECORDS – August 1826-February 1835 – 1 reel – 1 – $5.00 – us Baptist [240]
Central Branch Union Pacific Railroad Company *see* REPORT TO SECRETARY OF INTERIOR
Central Canada Chamber of Mines *see* CONSTITUTION
CENTRAL CHINA BAPTIST MISSION MINUTES – Scattered yrs. 1907-48. Also misc. items, scattered years 1889-1940; Executive Committee minutes, scattered years, 1910-42 – 1 – us Baptist [240]
CENTRAL CHRONIK – Omaha, NE. -w. 15 Apr 1897-13 Jan 1898. In German – 1 – us NE Hist [071]
CENTRAL CITY COURIER – Central City, NE. -w. Apr. 1874-Aug. 1874; Dec. 1874-Mar. 1884; Apr. 1885-Mar. 1890; Oct. 1890-Dec. 1891. Incomplete; Mar. 1892-Dec. 1894 – 1 – us NE Hist [071]
CENTRAL CITY NONPAREIL – Central City, NE. -w. Aug. 1882-Jun. 1896. Incomplete; Jul. 1896-Jan. 1953 – 1 – us NE Hist [071]
CENTRAL CITY RECORD – Central City, NE. -w. Aug. 1895-Nov. 1909 – 1 – us NE Hist [071]
CENTRAL CITY REPUBLICAN-NONPAREIL – Central City, NE. -w. Feb. 1896-May 1900. Incomplete; Jun. 1901-Dec. 1901; Nov. 1902- – 1 – us NE Hist [071]
CENTRAL COAST SUN BULLETIN – Morro Bay, CA. 1956-1982 – 31r – 1 – $1,550.00 – C02492 – us Library Micro [071]
CENTRAL COMMITTEE OF INDONESIAN INDEPENDENCE, BRISBANE – (Untitled). SE-4405 1. n1946 – 9 – ne IDC [950]
THE CENTRAL CONCEPTION OF BUDDHISM AND THE MEANING OF THE WORD DHARMA / Shcherbatsky, T – 1923 – 1 – uk Microform Academic [280]
Central Conference of American Rabbis *see*
- VIEWS ON THE SYNOD
- YEARBOOK

Central Conference of American Rabbis. 8th: 1897: Montreal, Quebec *see* SOUVENIR PROGRAMME...FROM JULY 6TH TO JULY 11TH, 1897
CENTRAL COUNTY CLARION *see* COTATI-THE COMMUNITY VOICE
CENTRAL CRIMINAL SESSIONAL PAPERS / Great Britain. Courts – Old Bailey. 1816-1913. 49 reels – 1 – $3,000.00 – us Trans-Media [340]
CENTRAL DEVELOPMENT PROGRAMME 1966-67 / Pakistan. Planning Commission – Jun 1966. BD-1719 1 – 9 – ne IDC [338]
CENTRAL DEVELOPMENT PROGRAMME, 1967-68 / Pakistan. Planning Commission – Karachi. 1967. BD-876 1 – 9 – ne IDC [338]
CENTRAL DEVELOPMENT PROGRAMME 1969-70. (1 JUL 1969 TO 30 JUN 1970) / Pakistan. Planning Commission – Islamabad. 1969 – 9 – ne IDC [338]
CENTRAL DEVELOPMENT PROGRAMME 1970-71 / Pakistan. Planning Commission – (1st Jul 1970 to 30th Jun 1971). Karachi. Jun 1970. BD-1722 1 – 9 – ne IDC [338]
CENTRAL DEVELOPMENT PROGRAMME 1971-72 / Pakistan. Planning Commission – (1st Jul 1971 to 30th Jun 1972). Islamabad. Jun 1971. BD-1724 1 – 9 – ne IDC [338]
CENTRAL ECONOMIC PLAN, 1952 / Netherlands. Centraal Planbureau – The Hague. 1952 – 9 – ne IDC [338]
CENTRAL ECONOMIC PLAN, 1954 / Netherlands. Centraal Planbureau – The Hague. 1954. BD-743 1 – 9 – ne IDC [338]
CENTRAL ECONOMIC PLAN, 1955 / Netherlands. Centraal Planbureau – The Hague. 1955. BD-744 1 – 9 – ne IDC [338]
CENTRAL ECONOMIC PLAN, 1961 / Netherlands. Centraal Planbureau – The Hague. 1961 – 9 – ne IDC [338]
CENTRAL ECONOMIC PLAN, 1964 SUMMARY / Netherlands. Centraal Planbureau – The Hague. 1964 – 9 – ne IDC [338]
CENTRAL ECONOMIC PLAN FOR 1970. SUMMARY / Netherlands. Centraal Planbureau – The Hague. 1970. BD-1706 1 – 9 – ne IDC [338]
THE CENTRAL ESKIMO / Boas, Franz – BN 141 2. 1888 – 8 – ne IDC [305]
CENTRAL ESKIMO AND INDIAN DOT ORNAMENTATION. INDIAN NOTES, V. 2 / Speck, F G – BN 394 2. 1925 – 8 – ne IDC [306]
CENTRAL EUROPEAN MAPS 1832-1870 – 8mf – 9 – A$40.00 – 0-7241-7182-7 – at State Libr Vic [940]
CENTRAL FAITH OF CHRISTIANITY (CCC69) = CHI TU CHIAO TI CHUNG HSIN HSIN YANG / Chao, Tzu-chen – (In Chinese) – 2nd ed. Shanghai: Association Press of China, 1934 – 1r – 1 – 1984-6408 – us A.T.L.A. [240]
CENTRAL FIFE TIMES – 1 – £42.00r – uk Scot News [072]
CENTRAL FIRST BAPTIST CHURCH. CENTRAL, SOUTH CAROLINA : CHURCH RECORDS – 1890-1957 – 1 – 17.28 – us Baptist [240]
CENTRAL GLAMORGAN GAZETTE – Bridgend, Wales, UK. 29 Jun 1866-Mar 1894. -w.15 reels – 1 – uk British Libr Newspaper [072]
Central Government of India *see* LEGISLATIVE SERIES
CENTRAL ILLINOIS WOCHENBLATT – La Salle, IL: H E Hagenbach, 1921-sep 25 1925 – 5r – us Res Libr [072]
CENTRAL INDIA – Lucknow. pt4. 1901 – 1 – us Res Libr [310]
CENTRAL INVERNESS 1851 CENSUS INDEX : ARGYLL AND WEST SCOTLAND CENSUS INDEX, PART 8 / Gibson, Peter & Macinnes, John – 1995 – 2mf – 9 – A$19.95 – 0-646-23636-9 – at Seanachas [920]
Central Java (Province) *see*
- DJAWA TENGAH DALAM ANGKA
- MIMBAR PEMERINTAH DAERAH DJAWA TENGAH

CENTRAL LAW JOURNAL – St Louis. v1-100. 1874-1927 – 1,5,6 – $1,000.00 – us Hein [073]
CENTRAL LAW JOURNAL – v1-100, 1824-1927 + index/digest for v1-54 + index for v1-30 (all publ) – 608mf – 9 – $912.00 – LLMC 82-912 – us L.L.M.C. [073]
CENTRAL LAW JOURNAL *see* THE AMERICAN LAW MAGAZINE
CENTRAL LAW MONTHLY – (Cont by: The Chicago Law Journal) – v1-3. 1880-82 (all publ) – 4mf – 9 – $18.00 – LLMC 84-435 – us L.L.M.C. [073]
CENTRAL LAW MONTHLY *see* CHICAGO LAW JOURNAL
Central Maine Theological Circle *see* RECORDS
CENTRAL METHODIST – Catlettsburg. Ky. 1872-1900 – 1 – us UMI [071]
Central Nacional Sindicalista. Caceres *see* ASAMBLEA ASISTENCIAL DE LA C.N.S. DE CACERES
CENTRAL NEBRASKA REPUBLICAN – Grand Island, NE. -w. Sept 1895-Dec 1899 – 1 – us NE Hist [071]
CENTRAL NEBRASKA REPUBLICAN – Hastings. Neb. 1895-1899 – 1 – us UMI [071]
CENTRAL NEVADAN – Battle Mountain, NV. 1885-1907 – 9r – 1 – $450.00 – U04407 – us Library Micro [071]
CENTRAL NEVADA'S GLORIOUS PAST – Tonopah, NV. v1 1978-v16 1993 – 1r – 1 – $50.00 – U04899 – us Library Micro [071]
Central New York. Synod. (Pres. Ch. in the U.S.A.) *see* MINUTES
CENTRAL NEWS WAVE – Los Angeles, CA. 1980 – 84+ r – 1 – $4,200.00 ($300.00y) – H04049 – us Library Micro [071]
Central Obrera Nacional Sindicalista *see*
- ESTATUTOS

Central Old Settlers Union, Jefferson County, KS *see* RECORDS
CENTRAL OREGON ENTERPRISE – Prineville OR. Dec 4 1919-July 8 1920 – 1 – us U.O. Library [071]
CENTRAL OREGON MIDSTATESMAN – Bend, OR. -w. 21 Oct 1954-8 May 1958 – 1 – us U.O. Library [071]
CENTRAL OREGON PRESS – (Set incl. Bend Daily Press; Bend Press) – Bend, OR. -w. 27 May 1921-21 Nov 1926. – 4r – 1 – us U.O. Library [071]
CENTRAL OREGONIAN – Prineville. Or. -w. 1921-63 – 1 – us UMI [071]
CENTRAL OREGONIAN – Prineville, OR. -w. 1921-63 – 1 – 480.00 – us Oregon Hist [071]
CENTRAL OREGONIAN – Prineville, OR. -w. 2 Jan 1964-8 May 1978+. 13 Rolls – 1 – us U.O. Library [071]
CENTRAL OREGONIAN – Silver Lake OR. Nov 26 1903, Sep 27 1905, Feb 1 1906 – 1 – us U.O. Library [071]
CENTRAL PLAINS RECORD – Kenesaw, NE. -w. Oct 1956-May 1957 – 1 – us NE Hist [071]
CENTRAL POINT AMERICAN – (Set incl Ashland American; Ashland Register) – Central Point, OR. -w. 7 Jan 1926-23 Aug 1956. 29 May 1928-18 Sept 1931 incomplete. – 9r – 1 – us U.O. Library [071]
CENTRAL POINT HERALD – Central Point, OR. -w. 26 Apr 1906-28 Jun 1917. 2 rolls – 1 – us U.O. Library [071]
CENTRAL POINT STAR – Central Point, OR. -w. 5 Apr 1929-5 Sep 1930. 1 roll – 1 – us U.O. Library [071]
CENTRAL POINT STAR – Gold Hill, OR. -w. 26 Apr 1929-5 Sept 1930. 1 roll – 1 – us U.O. Library [071]
CENTRAL POINT TIMES – Central Point, OR. 17 Dec 1964-17 Aug 1967. 1 roll – 1 – us U.O. Library [071]
CENTRAL PRESS – London, UK. 18 Jan-28 Feb 1871; Nov 1873-29 Jun 1874. -d. 5 reels – 1 – uk British Libr Newspaper [072]
Central Provinces. India. Legislative Council *see* PROCEEDINGS OF THE LEGISLATIVE COUNCIL OF THE CHIEF COMMISSIONER OF THE CENTRAL PROVINCES
CENTRAL QUEENSLAND HERALD – Rockhampton, Australia. -w. 2 Jan-31 July 1930. 2 reels – 1 – uk British Libr Newspaper [072]
Central Railway and Engineering Club of Canada *see* OFFICIAL PROCEEDINGS
CENTRAL REGULADORA DE ADQUISICION DE PATATAS : REGLAMENTO DE REGIMEN INTERIOR PARA LA... – Caceres: Tip. El Noticiero, S.A., 1946 – 1 – sp Bibl Santa Ana [060]
THE CENTRAL REPORTER – (Covers NY, NJ, PA, MD, DE and DC) – New York: Lawyers's Co-op. v1-13. 1885-88 (all publ) – 135mf – 9 – $202.00 – LLMC 81-413 – us L.L.M.C. [073]
CENTRAL SCOTLAND A PROGRAMME FOR DEVELOPMENT AND GROWTH / Scotland. Scottish Development Department – Edinburgh. 1963 – 9 – ne IDC [338]
CENTRAL SOMERSET GAZETTE – Glastonbury & Wells, England. 25 Oct 1862-1868; 2-10 Jul 1869; 22 Jan 1870-1981. -w. 128 reels – 1 – uk British Libr Newspaper [072]
CENTRAL STATES NEWS – Belington. West Virginia. 1930-1942 – 1 – us UMI [071]
CENTRAL STATES SPEECH JOURNAL – (1984-. 5,6,9) – v1-. 1949- – 1 – us UMI [410]
CENTRAL STATES SPEECH JOURNAL – Columbus, OH. v1-32. 1949-81 – 7r – 1 – us Ross [400]
Central Statistical Administration of the USSR, Department of Industrial Statistics *see* DINAMIKA PROIZVODITELNOSTI TRUDA I EE VAZHNE ISHIKH FAKTOROV V 1924-25 I 1925-26 G.G.
The Central Study Committee on the History of the Party *see* NOI SAN NHIEN CUU LICH SU DANG
CENTRAL TEACHING OF JESUS CHRI..JOHN XIII TO XVII INCLUSIVE / Bernard, Thomas D – New York: Macmillan, 1892. 1 fiche – 9 – us A.T.L.A. [240]
THE CENTRAL TEACHING OF JESUS CHRIST : A STUDY AND EXPOSITION OF THE FIVE CHAPTERS OF THE GOSPEL ACCORDING TO ST. JOHN, 13 TO 17 INCLUSIVE / Bernard, Thomas Dehany – New York:Macmillan, 1892 – 1mf – 9 – 0-8370-2293-2 – 1985-0293 – us A.T.L.A. [220]
CENTRAL TRADING COMPANY, LTD – (untitled). SE-2930 1. 1958 – 9 – ne IDC [380]
CENTRAL TREASURY RECORDS OF THE CONTINENTAL AND CONFEDERATION GOVERNMENTS – 1775-89. 23 rolls. M1014 – 1 – us Nat'l Archives [324]
CENTRAL TREASURY RECORDS OF THE CONTINENTAL AND CONFEDERATION GOVERNMENTS RELATING TO FOREIGN AFFAIRS / U.S. Treasury Department – 1775-87. 3 rolls. M1004 – 1 – us Nat'l Archives [975]
CENTRAL TREASURY RECORDS OF THE CONTINENTAL AND CONFEDERATION GOVERNMENTS RELATING TO MILILTARY AFFAIRS – 1775-89. 7 rolls. M1015 – 1 – us Nat'l Archives [324]
CENTRAL TRUTHS AND SIDE ISSUES / Balfour, Robert Gordon – Edinburgh: T.&T. Clark, 1895. 1 fiche – 9 – us A.T.L.A. [240]
Central United Presbyterian Church, Topeka, KS *see* RECORDS
CENTRAL VIRGINIAN – Louisa. Va. -w. 1928- – 1 – us UMI [071]
Central Zionist Archives. Jersualem *see*
- INVENTORIES TO OFFICIAL FILES
- INVENTORIES TO PRIVATE ARCHIVES OF D. IDELOVITCH, 1863-1943
- INVENTORIES TO PRIVATE ARCHIVES OF D. YELLIN, 1864-1941
- INVENTORIES TO PRIVATE ARCHIVES OF M. USSISCHKIN, 1863-1941
- INVENTORIES TO PRIVATE ARCHIVES OF THE BENEI MOSHE SOCIETY
- INVENTORIES TO PRIVATE ARCHIVES OF Y. BARZILAI-EISENSTADT, 1856-1918

Central Zionist Archives. Jerusalem *see*
- INVENTORIES TO OFFICIAL FILES
- INVENTORIES TO OFFICIAL FILES: DEPARTMENT OF ORGANIZATION OF THE ZIONIST ORGANIZATION, JERUSALEM, 1935-1948
- INVENTORIES TO OFFICIAL FILES. KEREN HAYESOD (PALESTINE FOUNDATION FUND), CENTRAL EUROPEAN OFFICE
- INVENTORIES TO OFFICIAL FILES: THE CENTRAL ZIONIST OFFICE, BERLIN, 1911-1920
- INVENTORIES TO OFFICIAL FILES: THE CENTRAL ZIONIST OFFICE, VIENNA, 1897-1905
- INVENTORIES TO PRIVATE ARCHIVES OF A. KLEE, 1875-1943
- INVENTORIES TO PRIVATE ARCHIVES OF H. SZOLD, 1860-1945
- INVENTORIES TO PRIVATE ARCHIVES OF L. MOTZKIN, 1867-1933
- INVENTORIES TO PRIVATE ARCHIVES OF S. LEVIN, 1867-1935
- INVENTORIES TO PRIVATE ARCHIVES OF Y. GRUENBAUM, 1879-1970

CENTRALANZEIGER FUER DEN ODENWALD *see* GRAEFLICH ERBACHISCHES WOCHEN-BLATT FUER DEN LANDKREIS ERBACH
CENTRAL-BLATT – v1,no.1-12. Apr 1908-Mar 1909 – 1 – us UMI [073]
CENTRAL-BLATT AND SOCIAL JUSTICE – v2,no.1-32. Apr 1909-Mar 1940 – 1 – us UMI [073]
CENTRALBLATT FUER BAKTERIOLOGIE, PARASITENKUNDE UND INFEKTIONSKRANKHEITEN – (Zweite Abteilung). Jena, 1895-1921. v. 1-52; Index. v. 1-40 – 533mf – 9 – ne IDC [616]
CENTRAL-BLATT FUER DIE DEUTSCHE PAPIER-FABRIKATION – Dresden, Germany. 1876-1902.-m. 15mqn reels – 1 – uk British Libr Newspaper [073]

CENTRALBLATT FUER DIE OESTERR. UNGAR. PAPIERINDUSTRIE – Vienna, Austria. Zentralblatt, etc. -f. Oct 1883-Dec 1909. 26 reels – 1 – uk British Libr Newspaper [072]

CENTRAL-BLATT FUER GLAS-INDUSTRIE UND KERAMIK – Vienna. Internationales Zentralblatt fuer Baukeramik und Glasindustrie. -w. Jan 1897-Dec 1909 – 4r – 1 – uk British Libr Newspaper [660]

CENTRALBLATT FUER MASCHINEN INDUSTRIE UND EISENGIESSEREI – Vienna, Austria. Maschnien und Metallindustrie-Zeitung Oesterreichische Eisenhaendler-Zeitung. -w. 27 Sept 1896-19 Dec 1912. 7 reels – 1 – uk British Libr Newspaper [072]

CENTRALIA ENTERPRISE – Wisconsin Rapids. Wis. and Tribune. 1890-99 – 1 – us UMI [071]

Centralverband der Handlungsgehulfen und Gehulfinnen Deutschlands *see* BERICHT

CENTRAL-VEREIN DEUTSCHER STAATSBUERGER JUEDISCHEN GLAUBENS : BLAETTER FUER DEUTSCHTUM AND JUDENTUM – Berlin. v1-17. 1922-38. Complete. 7 reels. B51. (Leo Baeck Institute. German-Jewish Periodicals, Pt 2) – 1 – $465.00 – us UPA [270]

CENTRAL-VEREINS-DIENST – Berlin, 1924-27 – 1 – Dist. gw Mikrofilm – gw Misc Inst [072]

CENTRAL-VOLKSBLATT FUER DIE KREISE SOEST, ARNSBERG, ISERLOHN, HAMM – Arnsberg, 1856-57 – 1r – 1 – Dist. gw Mikrofilm – gw Misc Inst [943]

CENTR.ASIA LATE IMPERIAL RUSSIA – 1994 – Cumul – 1 – F79,140.00 – sz Infoprint [072]

CENTRE AFRIQUE – (Issues filmed with: Bartlett, Robert E: Collection of African newspapers) – Bukavu: [s.n., dec 27/28 1959. – us Res Libr [072]

Centre Catholique du Cinema de Montreal. Commission des Cine-Clubs *see* SEQUENCES

CENTRE DE DOCUMENTATION PAYSANNE DU PARAGUAY = POPULAR DOCUMENTATION CENTER ON PARAGUAY – Mestre. 60 docs. 1980-1990 – 14mf – 9 – ne IDC [320]

CENTRE DEMOCRAT – Bellefonte, PA. -w 1971-1981 – 13 – $25.00r – us I.M.R. [071]

Centre Documentaire pour L'Oceanie *see* FONDS MANUSCRITS OU EN EDITION RESTREINTE CONCERNANT LA NOUVELLE-CALEDONIE

Centre for East Asian Cultural Studies for Unesco *see* HISTORICAL DOCUMENTS AND MANUSCRIPTS

Centre for Independent Studies:C. I. S *see* EIGHT PAPERS, BOOKS AND STUDIES

CENTRE FOR INVESTIGATIVE JOURNALISM BULLETIN – Ottawa. v1- 1978- – 9 – cn Micromedia [070]

Centre for the History of European Expansion, University of Leiden *see* ITINERARIO

CENTRE FOR THE PRESERVATION OF CONTEMPORARY DOCUMENTATION (TSKHSD) : OPISI SERIES – 3r – 1 – Reel nos 1.12; 1.13; 1.988 – uk Chadwyck [324]

CENTRE FOR THE PRESERVATION OF CONTEMPORARY DOCUMENTATION (TSKHSD), FOND 6 COMMITTEE FOR PARTY CONTROL : OPIS 1: KPK PROTOCOLS 1934-1939 – Dela 1-912 – 159r – 1 – Reel nos 1.15-1.173 – uk Chadwyck [324]

CENTRE FOR THE PRESERVATION OF CONTEMPORARY DOCUMENTATION (TSKHSD), FOND 6 COMMITTEE FOR PARTY CONTROL : OPIS 2: KPK PROTOCOLS, APPEALS TO 18TH VKP(B) CONGRESS 1939-1952 – Dela 1-1938 – 335r – 1 – Reel nos 1.174-1.508 – uk Chadwyck [324]

CENTRE FOR THE PRESERVATION OF CONTEMPORARY DOCUMENTATION (TSKHSD), FOND 6 COMMITTEE FOR PARTY CONTROL : OPIS 3: KPK PROTOCOLS OF MEETINGS AND ADDITIONAL MATERIALS 1952-1956 – Dela 1-956 – 121r – 1 – Reel nos 1.509-1.629 – uk Chadwyck [324]

CENTRE FOR THE PRESERVATION OF CONTEMPORARY DOCUMENTATION (TSKHSD), FOND 6 COMMITTEE FOR PARTY CONTROL : OPIS 4: EXTRAORDINARY 21ST CPSU CONGRESS: PROTOCOLS OF SECRETARIAT MEETINGS 1956-1961 – Dela 1-3217 – 137r – 1 – Reel nos 1.630-1.697; 1.698-1.766 – uk Chadwyck [324]

CENTRE FOR THE PRESERVATION OF CONTEMPORARY DOCUMENTATION (TSKHSD), FOND 6 COMMITTEE FOR PARTY CONTROL : OPIS 5: 22ND CP CONGRESS SECRETARIAT PROTOCOLS OF MEETINGS – Dela 1-1287 – 49r – 1 – Reels nos 1.767-1.815 – uk Chadwyck [324]

CENTRE FOR THE PRESERVATION OF CONTEMPORARY DOCUMENTATION (TSKHSD), FOND 6 COMMITTEE FOR PARTY CONTROL : OPIS 6: REPORTS, REFERENCES, VERBATIM ACCOUNTS, PROTOCOLS 1935-1966 – Dela 1-1836 – 172r – 1 – Reel nos 1.816-1.987 – uk Chadwyck [324]

CENTRE FOR THE PRESERVATION OF CONTEMPORARY DOCUMENTATION (TSKHSD), FOND 89 : THE COMMUNIST PARTY ON TRIAL – Opisi 1-76 – 24r – 1 – Reel nos 1.989-1.1012 – uk Chadwyck [947]

Centre Franco-Chinois d'Etudes Sinologiques de Pekin *see* HAN-HSUEEH

CENTRE INTERNATIONAL DE FORMATION EUROPEENNE PAMPHLET COLLECTION – 1977? – 1 – CSUXANP2006-B – us Hoover Inst Photo [940]

CENTRE INTERNATIONAL DES DROITS DE LA PERSONNE ET DU DEVELOPPEMENT DEMOCRATIQUE = INTERNATIONAL CENTRE FOR HUMAN RIGHTS AND DEMOCRATIC DEVELOPMENT – Montreal. 12 docs. 1990-1991 – 4mf – 9 – ne IDC [320]

CENTRE ISLAND NEWS – Hicksville. N.Y. 1963- – 1 – us UMI [071]

CENTRE POINT – Salisbury (Zimbabwe): Centre Party, nov 1970-feb 1973 – 1r – us Res Libr [960]

CENTRE POLYTECHNICIEN D'ETUDES ECONOMIQUES – Paris. 1933-aout 1939. Les no. 1-6 ont paru sous le titre de: X Crise – 1 – fr A.C.R.P.P. [330]

CENTRE PROTESTANT D'ETUDES : BULLETIN / Centre Protestant d'Etudes – Geneva, Switzerland. 1967-90 – 4r – 1 – ATLA S0391 – us A.T.L.A. [240]

Centre Protestant d'Etudes *see* CENTRE PROTESTANT D'ETUDES

CENTRE PROTESTANT D'ETUDES ET DE DOCUMENTATION : BULLETIN / Centre Protestant d'Etudes et de Documentation – Paris, France. nos 38-356. 1959-90 (incomplete) – 12r – 1 – ATLA S0415 – us A.T.L.A. [240]

Centre Protestant d'Etudes et de Documentation *see* CENTRE PROTESTANT D'ETUDES ET DE DOCUMENTATION

Centre Syndical d'Action Contre la Guerre *see* FEUILLE BIMENSUELLE D'INFORMATIONS SYNDICALES

CENTRE TIMES – State College (Bellefonte). Pa. 1961- – 1 – us UMI [071]

LES CENTRES DE PRODUCTIVITE DE BOUNDA ET DE SAMINIRKO / Ancey, G – (Africa series). 1967 – 9 – fr Hachette [380]

CENTRIPETAL/HAKOL – Palo Alto, CA. 1980-81 – 1 – us A.J.P.C. [071]

O CENTRO : ORGAO DO CENTRO ESTUDANTAL "PLACIDO SERRANO" – [s.l.] Jun 1944 – 1,5,6 – bl Biblioteca [072]

CENTRO DE DEFESA DOS DIREITOS HUMANOS, ASSESSORIA E EDUCACAO POPULAR = CENTER FOR THE DEFENSE OF HUMAN RIGHTS, LEGAL CONSULTATION AND POPULAR EDUCATION – Paraiba. 56 docs. 1980-1991 – 35mf – 9 – ne IDC [320]

CENTRO DE DOCUMENTACION DE HONDURAS = HONDURAS DOCUMENTATION CENTER – Tegucigalpa. 174 docs. 1981-1991 – 40mf – 9 – ne IDC [320]

CENTRO DE DOCUMENTACION E INFORMACION-BOLIVIA = DOCUMENTATION AND INFORMATION CENTER-BOLIVIA – La Paz. 200 docs. 1983-1991 – 68mf – 9 – ne IDC [320]

Centro de Documentacion Justicialista *see* LA DOCTRINA NACIONAL JUSTICIALISTA

Centro de Educacion Especial *see* JORNADAS DE EDUCACION ESPECIAL. 1970

CENTRO DE ESTUDIOS LEGALES Y SOCIALES (CELS) = CENTER FOR LEGAL AND SOCIAL STUDIES – Buenos Aires. 113 docs. 1980-1991 – 44mf – 9 – ne IDC [340]

CENTRO DE ESTUDOS E ACAO SOCIAL (CEAS) = STUDY AND SOCIAL ACTION CENTER – Salvador de Bahia. 67 docs. 1980-1990 – 62mf – 9 – ne IDC [350]

Centro de Iniciativas Turisticas *see*
– PLASENCIA EN FERIAS 1977
– PLASENCIA. NAVIDAD-76

Centro de Iniciativas Turisticas de Plasencia *see* VALLE DEL JERTE

CENTRO DE INVESTIGACION Y EDUCACION POPULAR (CINEP) = CENTER FOR RESEARCH AND POPULAR EDUCATION – Bogota. 159 docs. 1980-1991 – 167mf – 9 – ne IDC [370]

CENTRO DE MINAS – Curvello, 26 Nov-Dec 1909; Jan-Sep, Nov-Dec 1910; Jan-Feb, Aug, Oct 1911; Jan-Mar, Nov-Dec 1912; Jan-Mar 1913; Feb-Mar, Aug, Nov-Dec 1915; Jan-Jun 1916; Jan-Mar 1917; Jan-Feb, Oct 1918; Feb 1920; Mar, May-Aug 1921; Jan, Mar 1923; Aug 1924; Mar, Nov 1925; Dec 1926; May-Dec 1932; Jan-Apr, Dec 1933; Oct-11 Nov 1956 – 1,5,6 – bl Biblioteca [072]

Centro Ecumenico de Documentacao e Informacao. Rio de Janeiro *see* ACONTECEU

CENTRUM NATURAE CONCENTRATUM: OR THE SALT OF NATURE REGENERATED / Alipili – London, 1696 – 1 – us U.W. Library [615]

CENTURIA EUPHORBIARUM / Boissier, E P – Lipsiae. 1860. B-426 2 – 8 – ne IDC [580]

CENTURIA PLANTARUM RARIORUM ROSSIAE MERIDIONALIS.... / Bieberstein, Friedrich August Marschall von – Charkoviae-Petropoli, 1810-1843 – 13mf – 9 – ne IDC [580]

CENTURIA SIMILITUDINUN. 100 GLEICHNUSSEN IN WELCHEN DURCH VORSTELLUNG LEIBLICHER FIGUREN. LEHREN FURGEBILDET WERDEN: VORNEHMLICH AUSS H. SCHRIFT / Sudermann, Daniel – O 866. 1624 – 9 – ne IDC [760]

CENTURIE D'INSECTS, CONTENANT PLUSEIURS GENRES NOUVEAUX DECRITS DANS SA COLLECTION / Kirby, W F – Paris, 1834. iv,92p. 4 pls. Z-1389/2 – 8 – ne IDC [590]

LES CENTURIES DE MAGDEBOURG, OU, LA RENAISSANCE DE L'HISTORIOGRAPHIE ECCLESIASTIQUE AU SEIZIEME SIECLE / Jundt, Auguste – Paris: Fischbacher, 1883 – 1mf – us A.T.L.A. [900]

CENTURY – A Popular Quarterly. (All published. v. 1-22 published as Scribner's Monthly; v. 23-110 published as Century Illustrated Magazine.) v. 1-120. 1870-1930 – 1,5,6 – us Princeton Micro [073]

THE CENTURY – Las Vegas, NV. 15 Nov 1963 – 1r – 1 – $50.00 – U04598 – us Library Micro [071]

CENTURY, A POPULAR QUARTERLY – 1-71. 1870-1906 – 1 – us UMI [073]

THE CENTURY BIBLE *see* HEBREWS

CENTURY HISTORY OF THE SANTA MONICA BAY CITIES / Ingersoll, Luther A – Los Angeles, 1908. California Reel 19. (The Cox Library Collection) – 5 – us Americana [978]

A CENTURY IN THE PACIFIC : SCIENTIFIC, SOCIOLOGICAL, HISTORICAL, MISSIONARY, GENERAL / Colwell, James – London: C.H. Kelly, 1914 – 2mf – us A.T.L.A. [240]

CENTURY MINUTES OF THE PHILADELPHIA BAPTIST ASSOCIATION – 1707-1807 – 1 – $16.94 – us Baptist [240]

A CENTURY OF ACHIEVEMENT / Coyne, James Henry – Hamilton: W. Lancefield, (1899?). 04184. (Pre-1900 Canadiana) – 9 – cn C.I.H.M. [971]

A CENTURY OF AMERICAN DIPLOMACY : BEING A BRIEF REVIEW OF THE FOREIGN RELATIONS OF THE UNITED STATES, 1776-1876 / Foster, John W – Boston, New York: Houghton, Mifflin & Co: 1901 – 6mf – 9 – $9.00 – LLMC 92-188 – us L.L.M.C. [327]

A CENTURY OF BIRDS FROM THE HIMALAYA MOUNTAINS / Gould, J – London. 1832. BZ-269 2 – 8 – ne IDC [590]

A CENTURY OF FAITH / White, Charles L – 1932 – 1 – 11.48 – us Baptist [240]

A CENTURY OF FERNS / Hooker, W J – London. 1854. B-5966 2 – 8 – ne IDC [580]

A CENTURY OF JEWISH MISS[I]ONS / Thompson, Albert Edward – Chicago: Fleming H Revell, c1902 – 1mf – 9 – 0-8370-6624-7 – 1986-0624 – us A.T.L.A. [230]

A CENTURY OF MUNICIPAL HISTORY, 1792-1892. PART 1, 1792-1841 / Cruikshank, Ernest Alexander – Compiled from the municipal records of the County of Welland. Welland, Ont.: Published by authority of the County Counc., 1892?. 03633. (Pre-1900 Canadiana) – 9 – cn C.I.H.M. [971]

A CENTURY OF MUNICIPAL HISTORY: PART 2, 1841-1893 / Cruikshank, Ernest Alexander – Compiled from the municipal records of the County of Welland. Welland, Ont.: Published by the authority of the County Council, 1893?. 03634. (Pre-1900 Canadiana) – 9 – cn C.I.H.M. [971]

A CENTURY OF PROTESTANT MISSIONS IN CHINA *see* THE CHINA MISSION YEARBOOK

A CENTURY OF PROTESTANT MISSIONS IN CHINA (1807-1907) : BEING THE CENTENARY CONFERENCE HISTORICAL VOLUME / ed by MacGillivray, D – Shanghai: Printed at the American Presbyterian Mission Press, 1907 – 2mf – us A.T.L.A. [240]

A CENTURY OF ROUNDELS / Swinburne, Algernon Charles – London: Chatto & Windus, 1883 – 1 roll – 1 – 1-55879-835-8 – uk Libr Preservation [810]

A CENTURY OF SCIENCE AND OTHER ESSAYS / Fiske, John – Boston and New York: Houghton Mifflin and Co., 1900 (c1899). vii,c477p – 1 – us U.W. Library [500]

CENTURY OF WARREN COUNTY, GEORGIA, WILLS: 1790-1890 – Names of Testators listed alphabetically. 2 fiches. F-0735 – 9 – us A.G.L.L. [920]

CENT-VINGT JOURS DE SERVICE ACTIF / Daoust, C Roger – Montreal: E Senecal et fils...1886. SEM105P76 – 3mf – 9 – Can$6.75 – cn Bibl Nat [971]

CEPAL REVIEW / United Nations – (Nos. 1-7. E.34 S.36; Nos. 8-23. E/CEPAL/. E.62 S.64; Nos. 24-39. LC/G. E.58 S.62; No. 38 is not yet available in Spanish; No. 39 is not available in English) – 9 – us U.N. Pubs [330]

CEPAL REVIEW. 1983-86 / United Nations – 103 fiches – 9 – 195.00; 1.90f – uk UNIMICRO [330]

Cepeda, Joaquin *see* FAMOSSISIMOS ROMANCES

CEPHALALGIA – v1-. 1981- – 1,5,6,9 – us UMI [073]

CEPHALOPODS : HANDLING, PROCESSING AND PRODUCTS – 1984 – 115p – it F.A.O. [639]

CEPY – Chicago, IL: Cepy Publ Co. v19 n44-v23 n31. nov 1917-jul 1921 – us Res Libr [071]

CEPY I NOWY SWIAT – Chicago, IL; New York: [s.n.]: [v23 n32-v26 n12]. aug 1921-apr 1 1923 – us Res Libr [071]

CERAMIC ABSTRACTS / American Ceramic Society – v. 1-34. 1922-1955 – 1 – us Princeton Micro [740]

CERAMIC ABSTRACTS – v. 54- 1975- – 1,5,6,9 – us UMI [740]

CERAMIC ABSTRACTS *see*
– AMERICAN CERAMIC SOCIETY BULLETIN
– JOURNAL OF THE AMERICAN CERAMIC SOCIETY

CERAMIC INDUSTRY – (v.112- 1979- 5,6,9) – v.1-. 1923- – 1 – us UMI [073]

CERAMICS : ARCHITECTURE, APPLIED ARTS, STUDIO ARTS – (Individual titles not listed separately) – 68 catalogues on 86mf – 9 – £632.00 – uk Chadwyck [730]

CERAMICS – (Over 6,500 reproductions of Enlish and Continental item, glass and Art Nouveau) – 110mf – 9 – $610.00 – 0-907006-32-9 – uk Mindata [740]

CERAMICS – v1-25 1949-74 – 1 – us UMI [660]

CERAMICS AND GLASS (TIAM, PT 8) – (With printed catalogue ISBN: 0-914146-76-9 £30) – 35mf – 15 – £600.00 – uk Chadwyck [730]

CERAMICS COLLECTION / Victoria and Albert Museum. London – 237mf – 9 – $1,275.00 – 0-907006-15-9 – uk Mindata [740]

CERAMICS INDUSTRIES JOURNAL – (v93- 1984- 5,6,9) – Aug 1974- – 1 – us UMI [660]

CERAMICS MONTHLY – (v16- . 1968- . 5,6. v18- . 1970- . 9) – 1- 1953- – 1 – us UMI [740]

CERAMIQUE ANCIENNE EN PROCHE-ORIENT, ISRAEL ET LIBAN, VI-IIIE MILLENAIRE / Balfet, H – Etude technique – 9 – F60.00 – fr Ethnologie [740]

Cerani, Antonio Maria *see* TRANSLATIO SYRA PESCITTO VETERIS TESTAMENTI

Cercle Catholique de Quebec *see* CONSTITUTION...: AVEC LETTRES DE S. G. MGR. L'ARCHEVEQUE DE QUEBEC

Cercle Catholique de Quebec. Comite de Construction *see* CIRCULAIRE.

CERCLE ET CARRE – no. 1-3. Paris. mars-juin 1930 – 1 – fr A.C.R.P.P. [073]

CERCLE LINGUISTIQUE DE PRAGUE – Travaux, 1929-1939. v1-8 – 38mf – 2271/2 – ne IDC [460]

Cercle Linguistique de Prague *see* TRAVAUX

CERCLE SOCIAL – Paris. Imprimerie du Cercle Social. 1790 – 9 – fr Hachette [321]

Cercle Ville-Marie. Montreal, Canada *see* HISTORIQUE DU CERCLE ET RAPPORT GENERAL DU SECRETAIRE POUR L'ANNEE 1886-87

LES CERCLES AGRICOLES DANS LA PROVINCE DE QUEBEC / Dionne, Narcisse Eutrope – s.l.: s.n., 1881 (Quebec: Brousseau). 02711. (Pre-1900 Canadiana) – 9 – cn C.I.H.M. [971]

EL CERCO DE ZAMORA / Martinez Abeytia, Mateo – 1833 – 9 – 1.50f – sp Bibl Santa Ana [830]

Cerda Rico, Francisco *see*
- CRONICA DE ALFONSO EL ONCENO
- MEMORIAS DEL REY ALONSO EL NOBLE

Cerdan, F *see*
- DISCURSOS PHYSICO-MEDICO, POLITICO-MORAL QUE TRATAN SER TODA CALENTURA HECTICA CONTAGIOSA
- DISERTACION PHYSICO-MEDICA DE LAS VIRTUDES MEDICINALES, USO Y ABUSO DE LAS AGUAS TERMALES DE LA VILLA DE ARCHENA
- NATURALEZA TRIUNFANTE Y CRISOL DE MESENTERICAS...
- TUTA...MEDICATIO PRO LIENTERICIS...

EL CERDO DE TIPO IBERICO EN LA PROVINCIA DE BADAJOZ / Juana Sardon, Amalio de la – Cordoba: Imprenta Moderna, 1954 – sp Bibl Santa Ana [946]

Cere, Paul *see* LES POPULATIONS DANGEREUSES ET LES MISERES SOCIALES

Cereada, F *see* DON JUAN DE CARVAJAL. UN ESPANOL AL SERVICIO DE LA SANTA SEDE. MADRID, 1947

CEREAL AND GRAIN-LEGUME SEED PROCESSING : TECHNICAL GUIDELINES – 1981 – 156p – it F.A.O. [660]

CEREAL BREEDING PROCEDURES / Harrington, J B – 3rd printing 1978 – 122p – it F.A.O. [631]

CEREAL CHEMISTRY – St. Paul. v1-37 1924-60 – 1,5,6 – us Princeton Micro [660]

CEREAL CHEMISTRY – (v47- . 5,6. v48- . 9) – 1- 1924- – 1 – us UMI [540]

CEREAL CHEMISTRY *see* JOURNAL OF THE AMERICAN ASSOCIATION OF CEREAL CHEMISTS

CEREAL NITROGEN FIXATION : PROCEEDINGS OF THE WORKING GROUP MEETING, 9-12 OCT 1984 – 1986 – 128p – $5.00 – ii ICRISAT [630]

CEREAL POLICIES REVIEW 1990-91 – 1991 – 47p – it F.A.O. [630]

CEREAL POLICIES REVIEW 1991-92 – 1992 – 59p – it F.A.O. [630]

CEREAL SEED TECHNOLOGY : A MANUAL OF CEREAL SEED PRODUCTION, QUALITY CONTROL AND DISTRIBUTION / ed by Feistritzer, W P – 3rd printing 1988 – 238p – it F.A.O. [338]

CEREALS : SELECTED ASPECTS OF PRODUCTION, TRADE AND PRICE POLICIES – 1983 – 137p – it F.A.O. [660]

CEREBRI ANATOME: CUI ACCESSIT NERVORUM DESCRIPTIO ET USUS / Willis, Thomas – M 284. 1664 – 9 – ne IDC [611]

CEREBROVASCULAR DISEASES – v3-. 1993- – 1,5,9 – us UMI [616]

Cereceda, F *see*
- GONZALEZ, JULIO. ALFONSO 9TH. MADRID, 1944
- LOS ORIGENES DE EUROPA. TRADUCCION DE FRANCISCO ELIAS DE TEJADA. MADRID, 1945

Cereijo, Ramon Antonio *see*
- DISCURSO PRONUNCIADO POR EL PRESIDENTE DEL CONSEJO ECONOMICO NACIONAL EN LA LIGA POR LOS DERECHOS DEL TRABAJADOR, BUENOS AIRES, AGOSTO 5, 1949
- HACIA UN MAYOR Y MEJOR CONOCIMIENTO DE LA VERDADERA SITUACION ECONOMICA ARGENTINA
- EL PLAN ECONOMICO DE 1952 Y LA CONSOLIDACION DE LA PROSPERIDAD NACIONAL

CEREMONIA DEL...SANTA MARIA DE TUDIA / Grima y Villa-Senor, Gabriel de – 1705 – 9 – 1.50f – sp Bibl Santa Ana [240]

CEREMONIAL DEL ALTAR...SAN GABRIEL / Santano de Membrio, Juan – 1710 – 9 – 1.50f – sp Bibl Santa Ana [240]

LE CEREMONIAL OFFICIEL OU LES HONNEURS... – Ed 2. Paris, 1868 – 4mf – 1 – ILM-652/1 – ne IDC [327]

CEREMONIES AND PROCESSIONS OF THE CATHEDRAL CHURCH OF SALISBURY / ed by Wordsworth, Charles – H 1253 2. 1901 – 8 – ne IDC [240]

CEREMONIES USITEES AU JAPON POUR LES MARIAGES ET LES FUNERAILLES – Traducteur by Isaac Titsingh. Traduit du japonais. Paris, Nepveu. 1819 – 9 – 10.00 – fr Orientalistes [390]

CEREMORIAS EN EL COLEGIO MILITAR DE NUESTRA SRA. STA. MARIA DE TUDIA DEL ORDEN DE SANTIAGO DE LA UNIVERSIDAD DE SALAMANCA / Grima y Villa-Senor Gabriel de – Salamanca, 1705 – 1 – sp Bibl Santa Ana [350]

Cerenville, B de *see* LE SYSTEME CONTINENTAL ET LA SUISSE...

CERES COURIER – Ceres, CA. 1921-56 – 19r – 1 – $950.00 – C02104 – us Library Micro [071]

CERESCO COURIER – Ceresco, NE. -w. Jul. 1892-Oct. 1894. Incomplete; Nov. 1895-Dec. 1910; Jan. 1912-Oct. 1912; Jan. 1914-Jun. 1925 – 1 – us NE Hist [071]

CERESCO NEWS – Ceresco, NE. -w. Jul. 1925-Jun. 1956 – 1 – us NE Hist [071]

Ceresole, Norberto *see*
- ARGENTINA
- EJERCITO Y POLITICA NACIONALISTA
- PERONISMO

Ceresole, Norberto et al *see* PERONISMO

Ceresoles, Mauricio *see*
- ANALISIS DE LA CONTESTACION DEL DIPUTADO DE PROVINCIA DON ANTONIO CONCHA Y DEL LIBELO INFORMATIVO...D. JOAQUIN RODRIGUEZ LEAL...
- ANALISIS DE LA CONTESTACION DEL DIPUTADO...D. JOAQUIN RODRIGUEZ LEAL.
- DEMONSTRACION Y VINDICACION DE LAS INJUSTICIAS...POR ACUSACION DEL DELATOR DON JOAQUIN RODRIGUEZ LEAL
- RESULTADO DE LA VISTA DEL ARTICULO...EN LA CAUSA QUE SIGUE A DON MAURICIO CERESOLES

Cereti, C *see* LE OBLIGAZIONI...

Cerezo Moreno, Antonio *see* UNA MANANA GRIS

Cerfbeer, Auguste-Edouard *see* DES SOCIETES DE BIENFAISANCE MUTUELLE

Cerfvol, de *see* MEMOIRE SUR LA POPULATION: DANS LEQUEL ON INDIQUE LE MOYEN DE LA RETABLIR ET DE SE PROCURER UN CORPS MILITAIRE

Ceria, E *see* DON BOSCOCON DIOS

CERKOVNAJA NAUKA – Church adviser.1, 1903 – 1 – us Res Libr [240]

CERKOVNYJ VISTNIK – Church messenger. 1946-1970, 1973-1974 – 1 – us Res Libr [240]

Cernadas Lamadrid, Juan Carlos *see* LOPEZ REGA

Cerny, Karl H *see* NATO IN QUEST OF COHESION

Cerone, Pedro *see*
- EL MELOPEO Y MAESTRO. TRACTADO DE MUSICA THEORICA Y PRACTICA: EN QUE SE PONE POR EXTENSO
- EL MELOPEO Y MAESTRO. TRACTADO DE MUSICA THEORICA Y PRATICA

Cerralbo, Marques de *see* UNA CRONICA DE LOS MOCTEZUMA, MADRID...1954

Cerreto, Scipione *see* DELLA PRATTICA MUSICA VOCALE ET INSTRUMENTALE.

Cerro Fernandez, Patricio *see* EN DEFENSA DE LA LIBERTAD

Cerro Sanchezherrera, Eduardo *see* APORTACION AL ESTUDIO DEL FUERO DE BAYLIO

Cerro y Contreras, Felix *see* NOCIONES DE ARITMETICA Y SU METRICO DECIMAL... ELEMENTALES DE NINOS... SEXOS

CERTAIN GAMBLING GAMES OF THE KLAMATH INDIANS / Dorsey, G A – N 193. 1901 – 9 – ne IDC [306]

CERTAIN PHYSIOLOGICAL ESSAYS / Boyle, R – M-307. 1661 – 9 – ne IDC [612]

CERTAINE WORKES OF CHIRURGERIE / Gale, T – M 350. 4 pts. 1563 – 9 – ne IDC [617]

CERTAMEN PHARMACEUTICO-GALENICO IN QUO TRES CONTINENTUR DISSERTATIONES... / Arnau, J – Valencia, 1727 – 2mf – 9 – sp Cultura [615]

CERTAMEN POETICO...POR LA REAL ACADEMIA...X DE SU INSTALACION.. – 1872 – 9 – 1.50f – sp Bibl Santa Ana [810]

CERTEZZA DEL DIRITTO INTERNAZIONALE... / Esperson, P – N.p., 1882 – 1mf – 1 – ILM-2476/1 – ne IDC [327]

LE CERTIFICAT D'HERITIER DANS LES DEPARTEMENTS DU BAS-RHIN, DU HAUT-RHIN ET DE LA MOSELLE D'APRES LA LOI D'INTRODUCTION DU DROIT FRANCAIS DU 1ER JUIN 1924 / Krug, Camille – Paris, Recueil Sirey, 1939. 175 p. LL-4109 – 1 – us L of C Photodup [340]

CERTIFICATES OF ADMISSION / Sandusky County. Ohio. County Home – 1917-1929 – 1r – 1 – $32.50r – us Archival [324]

CERTIFICATES OF BIRTHS / Putnam County, Ohio. General Health District – 1908-1996 – 1r – 5 – $32.50r – us Archival [324]

CERTIFICATES OF ELECTION / Hancock County. Ohio. Biglick Township. Township Clerk – 1893-1895 gaps in holdings – 1r – 1 – $32.50r – us Archival [324]

CERTIFICATES OF HEAD TAX PAID BY ALIENS ARRIVING AT SEATTLE FROM FOREIGN CONTIGUOUS TERRITORY, 1917-1924 – 10r – 1 – M1365 – us Nat'l Archives [340]

CERTIFICATES OF RATIFICATION OF THE CONSTITUTION AND THE BILL OF RIGHTS, INCLUDING RELATED CORRESPONDENCE AND REJECTIONS OF PROPOSED AMENDMENTS, 1787-92 / U. S. Constitutional Convention – 1roll – 1 – M338 – us Nat'l Archives [324]

CERTIFICATES OF REGISTRY, ENROLLMENT, AND LICENSE ISSUED AT EDGARTOWN, MASSACHUSETTS, 1815-1913 / U.S. Bureau of Marine Inspection and Navigation – M130 – 9r – 1 – us Nat'l Archives [380]

CERTIFICATES OF STILLBIRTHS / Putnam County, Ohio. General Health District – 1928-1961 – 1r – 5 – $32.50r – us Archival [324]

CERTIFIED ACCOUNTANT – 1905-to date – 1,9 – uk Microform Academic [073]

CERTIFIED PUBLIC ACCOUNTANT – v1-30. 1922-50 – 1 – us UMI [650]

CERTIFYING QUESTIONS OF STATE LAW : EXPERIENCE OF FEDERAL JUDGES / Seron, Carroll – Washington: FJC, Jan 1983 – 1mf – 9 – $1.50 – LLMC 95-833 – us L.L.M.C. [340]

DE LA CERTITUDE CHRETIENNE: ESSAI SUR LA THEOLOGIE DE FRANK / Bois, Henri – Paris: Fischbacher, 1887. 1 fiche – 9 – us A.T.L.A. [240]

LA CERTITUDE DES PREUVES DU MAHOMETISME / Cloots, Jean-Baptiste – (D'Holbach series). 1780 – 9 – fr Hachette [260]

CERULEAN BAPTIST CHURCH. CERULEAN, KENTUCKY : CHURCH RECORDS – 1887-1979. Scattered Minutes: 1904-07; 1928-38. Lacking Minutes: Sept 1948-Aug 1973 – 1 – 38.34 – us Baptist [240]

Cerulli, Enrico *see*
- LA COSTITUZIONE ETIOPICA
- IL LIBRO ETIOPICO DEL MIRACOLO DI MARIA E LE SUE FONTI NELLE LETTERATURE DEL MEDIO EVO LATINO
- STUDI ETIOPICI...

Cerutti, D B *see* RAPPORT SUR LA LETTRE DE CHANGE INTERNATIONALE

Cervantes Bermudez de Cana, Tomas *see* COMPENDIO DE LAS INSTITUCIONES DE DERECHO CANONIGO SEGUN EL METODO DE DOMINGO CAVALLARIO

CERVANTES EN EL ATENEO DE BADAJOZ / Ateneo – Badajoz: Tip. Correo de la Manana, 1918 – 1 – sp Bibl Santa Ana [946]

Cervantes Saavedra, Miguel de *see* LA GALATEA: EDICION PUBLICADA POR RODOLFO SCHEVILL Y ADOLFO BONILLA

Cervarius Tubero, L *see* DE TURCARUM ORIGINE, MORIBUS, ET REBUS GESTIS COMMENTARIUS

Cervati, Raphael C *see*
- ANNUAIRE ORIENTAL DU COMMERCE DE L'INDUSTRIE, DE L'ADMINISTRATION ET DE LA MAGISTRATURE 9ME ANNEE 1889-1890
- ANNUAIRE-ALMANACH DU COMMERCE DE L'INDUSTRIE, DE L'ADMINISTRATION ET DE LA MAGISTRATURE 4ME ANNEE 1883

Cervenka, Zdenek *see* BIBLIOGRAPHY ON THE NIGERIAN CIVIL WAR

Cervi, Emilio *see* COMPARACIONES HISTORICAS

Cervinka, Jaroslav *see* CESTOU NA SEHO ODBOJE

Cervo, F *see* STORIA DEL CODICE DI ALLEANZA DELLE NAZIONI...

Cesalpino, Andrea *see* DE METALLICIS LIBRI TRES ANDREA CAESALPINO ARETINO

CESAR CORTES / Alcala, Manuel – Mexico; Editorial Jus, 1950 – sp Bibl Santa Ana [920]

Cesare, R de *see* THE LAST DAYS OF PAPAL ROME, 1850-1870

CESETTE, HISTOIRE D'UNE PAYSANNE / Pouvillon, Emile – Paris. 1881. (La Condition Ouvriere. Part Two.) – 9 – 7.50 – fr Bibl Nationale [360]

CESIEX EN CIFRAS / Consejo Economico Sindical – Badajoz: CESIEX, 1970 – sp Bibl Santa Ana [946]

CESKA PRISLOVI / Flajshans, V – Sbirka prislovi, prupovedi a porekadel lidu ceskeho v cechach, na morave a v Slezsku. Praha. 1911-13. B-1478 2 – 8 – ne IDC [943]

CESKE A MORAVSKOSLEZSKE ZEMEDELSKE NOVINY *see* ZMEDELESKE NOVINY

CESKE SLOVO – (Filmed with: A-Zet Pondelnik jul 1938-nov 1939) – Prague. jul 1938-jun 5 1940 – 13r – 1 – us Res Libr [072]

CESKE SLOVO – (Scattered issues) – Prague, Czechoslovakia. May 1923-1933; May 1940-Mar 1942 – 2r – 1 – us L of C Photodup [072]

CESKO-AMERICKY VENKOV – Omaha, NE. May 1910-15 Sep 1917. Bohemian-American Country Life magazine. -m – 1 – us NE Hist [073]

CESKO-SLOVANSKY OBZOR – Omaha, NE. -w. 30 Apr 1908-17 Nov 1910 – 1 – us NE Hist [071]

CESKOSLOVENSKA REPUBLIKA – Prague, Czechoslovakia. 7 Jul 1921; 1926-Sept 1932 – 15r – 1 – us L of C Photodup [072]

CESKOSLOVENSKY HORNIK – Prague, Czechoslovakia. Aug 1955-1958 – 1r – 1 – us L of C Photodup [072]

CESKOSLOVENSKY SPORT – (1985-. 5,6,9) – Prague, Czechoslovakia. 1953-63; 1965-Jun 1975.23 reels – 1 – us UMI [240]

CESKY BIOGRAFICKY ARCHIV A SLOVENSKY BIOGRAFICKY ARCHIV = CZECH AND SLOVAKIAN BIOGRAPHICAL ARCHIVE / ed by Kramme, Ulrike & Muena, Zelmira Urra – (Collection of entries from ca 250 biographical reference works from the 9th century through ca 1988) – (mf ed 1993-98) – ca 550mf (1:24) in 12 installments – 9 – diazo DM19,800.00 set DM1,980.00 per installment (silver DM21,600.00 set DM2,160.00 per installment) – 3-598-33430-3 – silver ISBN: 3-598-33431-1 – gw Saur [920]

CESKY BOJ – London, UK. 1 May 1948-8 Jan 1951; 28 Sept 1957-12 Dec 1958; Aug 1959 – 1 – uk British Libr Newspaper [072]

CESKY BRATR – 1924-91 (complete) – Inquire – 1 – ATLA S0620 – us A.T.L.A. [073]

CESKY DENIK – (1995 1r $75.00. Backfile 6r per y $510y. As of Jan 1995: Cesky Tydenik) – 1999- – 1r per y – 1 – $80.00 standing order – us Ross [072]

CESKY DENIK – Plzen, Czechoslovakia. -d. 9 Feb-22 July 1919. Imperfect. 1 reel – 1 – uk British Libr Newspaper [072]

CESKY TYDENIK *see* CESKY DENIK

CESKY ZAPAS – Prague, Czechoslovakia. -w. 19 Oct 1933-24 Aug 1939. 2 reels – 1 – uk British Libr Newspaper [072]

Cespedes, A *see* LIBRO DE INSTRUMENTOS NUEVOS DE GEOMETRIA

LA CESSAZIONE DEL MANDATO INTERNAZIONALE / Borsa, G – Milano, 1934 – 2mf – 9 – ILM-2133/1 – ne IDC [327]

CESSNA AIRCRAFT – Ontario, CA. Roll A-D – 4r – 1 – $200.00 – R04074 – us Library Micro [071]

C'EST LE DIABLE OU LA BOHEMIENNE / Cuvelier de Trie et Mittie – (French Theatre Series). Paris. Barba, an VI. 1797 – 9 – fr Hachette [820]

CESTA MIRU – Liberec, Czechoslovakia. 1953-Mar 1960 – 4r – 1 – us L of C Photodup [072]

CESTOU NA SEHO ODBOJE : PRISP EVEK K HISTORII V YVOJE FORMACI CESKOSLOVENSK EHO VOJSKA NA RUSI V ROCE 1914-1918 / Cervinka, Jaroslav – VPraze: [f. Z d ask y], 1920 – 1 – CSUX89-B2685 – us Hoover Inst Photo [943]

LA CETRA SONARA. SONATE A TRE...OP. 1 / Franchi, G – Amsterdam: E Roger. 4pts. 171- – 1 – us Sibley [780]

CETTE SEMAINE : SUPPLEMENT – Montreal, Canada.v2 n52. 23 mar 1939 – 1r – 1 – Can$25.00 – cn Can Microfilming [072]
Ceuerio de Vera, J *see* VIAIE DE LA TIERRA SANTA, Y DESCRIPCION DE IERUSALEN, Y DEL SANTO MONTE LIBANO, CON SON RELACION DE COSAS MARAUILLOSAS, ...
Ceulemans, Mieke *see* MASS MEDIA
Cevat Pasa, Ahmet *see*
- TARIH-I ASKERI-YI OSMANI
- TARIH-I OSMANI

Cevdet, Ahmet *see* MECELLE-I AHKAMN ADLIYE
Cevdet, Mehmed *see* DUENYAYA IKINCI GELIS YAHUT ISTANBUL'DA NELER OLMUS
Ceylon *see*
- CATALOGUE OF BOOKS
- THE CEYLON GOVERNMENT GAZETTE
- HERBARIUM

CEYLON ALMANAC AND ANNUAL REGISTER *see* CEYLON ALMANAC AND COMPENDIUM OF USEFUL INFORMATION
CEYLON ALMANAC AND COMPENDIUM OF USEFUL INFORMATION – (Cont as: Ceylon Calendar and Compendium of Useful Information, Colombo 1840-1843. Cont as: Ceylon Almanac and Compendium of Useful Information, Colombo 1844-1850. Cont as: Ceylon Almanac and Annual Register, Colombo 1851-1862. Missing: 1814-1832. 1852. 1854-1862) – Colombo, 1814-1839 – 132mf – 9 – ne IDC [950]
CEYLON ALMANAC AND COMPENDIUM OF USEFUL INFORMATION – (Continued as Ceylon Almanac and Compendium of useful information. Colombo, 1840-43; as Ceylon Almanac and Compendium of useful information. Colombo, 1844-50; as Ceylon Almanac and Annual Register. Colombo, 1851-62) – Colombo. 1814-39. Lacking: 1814-32; 1852; 1854-62 – 132mf – ne IDC [950]
CEYLON ALMANAC AND COMPENDIUM OF USEFUL INFORMATION *see* CEYLON ALMANAC AND COMPENDIUM OF USEFUL INFORMATION
CEYLON, AN ACCOUNT OF THE ISLAND PHYSICAL, HISTORICAL, AND TOPOGRAPHICAL WITH NOTICES OF ITS NATURAL HISTORY, ANTIQUITIES AND PRODUCTIONS / Tennent, J E – 2v. London. 1859. BZ-291 2 – 8 – ne IDC [910]
CEYLON ANTIQUARY AND LITERARY REGISTER – v. 1-10, no. 2. Jul 1915-Oct 1924 – 1 – us NY Public [490]
Ceylon. Archaeological Survey *see*
- ANNUAL REPORT
- MEMOIRS OF THE ARCHAEOLOGICAL SOCIETY OF INDIA

CEYLON BLUE BOOK – Colombo. 1821-1938. Available: 1938. BI-799 2 – 8 – ne IDC [950]
CEYLON CALENDAR AND COMPENDIUM OF USEFUL INFORMATION *see* CEYLON ALMANAC AND COMPENDIUM OF USEFUL INFORMATION
CEYLON DAILY NEWS – Colombo, Ceylon: Assoc Newspapers of Ceylon, 1956-66 (mf ed 1981) – 1 – us Res Libr [072]
CEYLON DAILY NEWS – Colombo, Sri Lanka. -d. Jan 1919-Dec 1921. 12 reels – 1 – uk British Libr Newspaper [072]
Ceylon. Department of National Planning *see*
- THE DEVELOPMENT PROGRAMME, 1964-1965
- THE SHORT-TERM IMPLEMENTATION PROGRAMME

THE CEYLON GOVERNMENT GAZETTE / Ceylon – 1902-45 – 1 – us NY Public [950]
Ceylon. Legislative Council *see* CEYLON SESSIONAL PAPERS, 1860-JULY 1931
Ceylon. Ministry of Land, Irrigation and Power *see*
- PLAN OF DEVELOPMENT, 1966-1970 IMPLEMENTATION PROGRAMME AND TARGETS FOR 1967-68
- PLAN OF DEVELOPMENT OF MINISTRY OF LAND, IRRIGATION AND POWER, 1966-1970

Ceylon. Ministry of Planning and Economic Affairs *see*
- AGRICULTURAL DEVELOPMENT PROPOSALS, 1966-1970
- THE DEVELOPMENT PROGRAMME, 1966-67
- ECONOMIC DEVELOPMENT 1966-68 REVIEW AND TRENDS
- HIGHER EDUCATION, ENROLMENT AND OUTPUT 1968-1977

Ceylon. Ministry of Planning and Employment *see* FIVE-YEAR PLAN
Ceylon. Planning Council *see* THE TEN-YEAR PLAN
Ceylon. Planning Secretariat *see* SIX-YEAR PROGRAMME OF INVESTMENT, 1954/55 TO 1959/60
CEYLON SESSIONAL PAPERS, 1860-JULY 1931 / Ceylon. Legislative Council – Papers relating to agriculture, etc – 1 – us Res Libr [950]
Ceylon. Supreme Court *see* DECISIONS...ON APPEAL FROM COURTS OF REQUESTS. PT. 1
CEZA KANUNU – Ibnuerrefik Ahmet Nuri. Istanbul: Orhaniye Matbaasi, 1924 – $35.00 – us MEDOC [956]
CEZANNE / Reunion des musees nationaux. Paris – 1936. 40 illus. 3mf – 9 – fr Réunion [700]
C.F. Cooper and Co *see* HISTORY OF THE RED RIVER VALLEY PAST AND PRESENT
C.F. GELLERTS BRIEFSTILREFORM : TRADITION, ENTWICKLUNG UND WIRKUNGSGESCHICHTE DER GELLERTSCHEN EPISTOLARTHEORIE / Arto-Haumacher, Rafael – 1995 – 2mf – 9 – DM80.00 – 3-8267-2126-8 – gw Hänsel [430]
C.F. MEYERS "ANGELA BORGIA" / Weishaar, Friedrich – (Includes bibliographical references) – Marburg a.L.: N G Elwert, 1928 – 1 – us U.W. Library [430]
CF TC *see*
- SYNDICALISME
- LE SYNDICALISME CHRETIEN

CFO – v1-. 1985- – 1,5,6,9 – us UMI [380]
CGA (COMPRESSED GAS ASSOCIATION) – Standards. Printed index. Updated every 60 days – 6,9 – us Info Handling [622]
CGA MAGAZINE – (v1-15 1967-1980/81 Can$20.00y) – Vancouver. v1-29. 1967-95 – 9 – Can$28.00y – cn Micromedia [073]
CGSB (CANADIAN GENERAL STANDARDS BOARD) – Printed index. Updated every 60 days – 6,9 – us Info Handling [380]
C.H. SPURGEON : A BIOGRAPHY BY W.Y. FULLERTON / Fullerton, William Young – London: W. Williams and Norgate, 1920. xv,385p.plates, ports, facsim – 1 – us U.W. Library [240]
C.H. SPURGEON'S AUTOBIOGRAPHY... / Spurgeon, Charles Haddon – London: Passmore and Alabaster, 1897-1900 – 2 rolls – 1 – 1-55879-229-5 – uk Libr Preservation [920]
Chaadaev, Pla *see* SOCHINENIIA I PIS'MA
Chaadaeva, O N *see*
- ARMII A NAKANUNE FEVRALSKO I REVOLIUTSII
- KORNILOVSHCHINA
- POMESHCHIKI I IKH ORGANIZATSII V 1917 G.

CHABAD LUBAVITCH PRESS – Montreal, Quebec. 1979-1985 – 1 – us A.J.P.C. [072]
CHABAD TIMES – Portland, Oregon, Mar. 1986; Oct. 1986; Dec. 1986; Apr. 1987 – us A.J.P.C. [071]
THE CHABAD TIMES – Cincinnati, OH. 1978-83 – 1 – us A.J.P.C. [071]
Chabanon, M P S de *see* UEBER DIE MUSIK UND DEREN WIRKUNGEN, MIT ANMERKUNGEN. HERAUSGEGEBEN VON JOHANN HILLER
Chabanon, Michel Paul de *see* EPITRE SUR LA MANIE DES JARDINS ANGLAIS
Chabat, Pierre *see*
- BATIMENTS DE CHEMINS DE FER: EMBARCADERES, PLANS DE GARES, STATIONS, ABRIS
- LA BRIQUE ET LA TERRE CUITE.
- LES TOMBEAUX MODERNES, CHAPELLES, CROIX, MAUSOLEES, PIERRES TOMBALES, SARCOPHAGES, STELES.

Chaboillez, Augustin *see* QUESTIONS SUR LE GOUVERNEMENT ECCLESIASTIQUE DU DISTRICT DE MONTREAL
Chabot, J B *see* SYNODICON ORIENTALE OU RECUEIL DES SYNODES NESTORIENS
THE CHACE. SELECTED FROM THE...POEMS OF WILLIAM SAMMERVILLE... / Flackton, W – London: Walsh, 1738 – 2mf – 9 – us Sibley [780]
DER CHACHAM KOHELET ALS PHILOSOPH UND POLITIKER : EIN KOMMENTAR ZUM BIBLISCHEN BUCHE KOHELET, ZUGLEICH EIN STUDIE ZU RELIGIOESEN UND POLITISCHEN ENTWICKLUNG DES VOLKES ISRAEL IM ZEITALTER HERODES DES GROSSEN / Gerson, Adolf – (Includes index) – Frankfurt a. M.: J Kauffmann, 1905 – 1mf – 9 – 0-8370-3257-1 – 1985-1257 – us A.T.L.A. [220]
Chacon, L A *see* APUNTACIONES PARA EL ESTUDIO DE LIMITES DEL ECUADOR CON EL PERU
Chacon Miriam E *see* THE RELATIONSHIP OF TRUNK AND HIP MUSCLE STRENGTH TO LOW BACK PAIN
Chacon Villareso, Carmen *see* COLECCION DE POESIAS
Chacon y Calvo, Jose Maria *see* CEDULARIO CUBANO (LOS ORIGENES DE LA COLONIZACION 1. (1493-1512)...TOMO 6
Chacon Zamora, Fernando *see* LA PEDAGOGIA JURIDICA NORTEAMERICANA
CHAD : ANNUAIRE STATISTIQUE 1966-1975 / Chad. Sous Direction de la Statistique et des Etudes Economiques – (1971, 1973 not publ. 1967, 1968 not available. Coll title: African Official Statistical Serials, 1867-1982) – 9mf – 9 – £75.00 – uk Chadwyck [960]
Chad *see*
- DEVELOPMENT POTENTIAL AND CONSTRAINTS
- ECONOMIE ET PLAN DE DEVELOPPEMENT
- JOURNAL OFFICIEL DU TCHAD

CHAD BROWNE MEMORIAL – 1638-1888. 280p – 1 – us Baptist [240]
Chad. Haut Commissariat Charge du Plan et des Aides Exterieures *see* PROJET POUR UN PLAN DE DEVELOPPEMENT ECONOMIQUE DECENNIE 1971-1980
Chad. Ministere du Plan et de la Cooperation *see* PREMIER PLAN QUINQUENNAL DE DEVLOPPEMENT ECONOMIQUE ET SOCIAL, 1966-1970
Chad. Ministere du Plan et des Aides Exterieures *see* PLAN DE DEVELOPPEMENT ECONOMICQUE ET SOCIAL POUR LA DECENNIE 1971-1980
Chad. Sous Direction de la Statistique et des Etudes Economiques *see* CHAD
Chadbourne, Paul Ansel *see* LECTURES ON NATURAL THEOLOGY, OR, NATURE AND THE BIBLE FROM THE SAME AUTHOR
Chadds Ford, Pennsylvania. Brandywine Baptist Church *see* RECORDS
Chadman, Charles Erehart *see*
- CONSTITUTIONAL LAW.
- ILLUSTRATIVE CASES ON PERSONAL RIGHTS AND THE DOMESTIC RELATIONS INCLUDING TEACHER AND PUPIL
- NEGOTIABLE INSTRUMENTS AND PRINCIPAL AND SURETY.
- PRINCIPLES OF THE LAW OF PRIVATE AND PUBLIC CORPORATIONS.
- PRINCIPLES OF THE LAW OF REAL PROPERTY AND THE LAW OF PLEADING AND PRACTICE AT COMMON LAW
- A TREATISE ON CRIMINAL LAW AND CRIMINAL PROCEDURE.
- WILLS; OR, THE LAW OF SUCCESSION AFTER DEATH.

CHADRON ADVOCATE – Chadron, NE. -w. Dec. 1887-Jan. 1892 – 1 – us NE Hist [071]
CHADRON CHRONICLE – Chadron, NE. -w. Sep. 1919-Nov. 1943 – 1 – us NE Hist [071]
CHADRON CITIZEN – Chadron, NE. -w. Aug.1885-Aug. 1891; Nov. 1891; Feb. 1892-May 1894; Jul. 1894-Dec.1894; Jun. 1895 – 1 – us NE Hist [071]
CHADRON RECORD – Chadron, NE. (-sw. except -w. 1885-1944, 1951-1958.) Nov. 1885-Sep. 1891. Incomplete; Apr. 1892-Sep. 1894; Oct. 1895- – 1 – us NE Hist [071]
CHADRON RECORDER – Chadron, NE. -w. Oct. 1892-Feb. 1896. Incomplete; Apr. 1896-Dec. 1896; Mar. 1897-Aug. 1897 – 1 – us NE Hist [071]
CHADRON TIMES – Chadron, NE. -w. May 1898-Mar. 1900. Incomplete; Aug. 1902-Jul. 1905 – 1 – us NE Hist [071]
Chadwick, Edward H *see* CHADWICK'S HISTORY OF SHELBY COUNTY
Chadwick, George Alexander *see*
- BOOK OF EXODUS
- CHRIST BEARING WITNESS TO HIMSELF
- THE GOSPEL ACCORDING TO ST MARK

Chadwick, George Whitefield *see* JUDITH, LYRIC DRAMA
Chadwick, H M *see*
- THE HEROIC AGE
- ORIGIN OF THE ENGLISH NATION

Chadwick, John White *see*
- THE FAITH OF REASON
- FAITH OF REASON: A SERIES OF DISCOURSES ON THE LEADING TOPICS OF RELIGION
- WILLIAM ELLERY CHANNING

Chadwick, Nora (Kershaw) *see* POETRY AND LETTERS IN EARLY CHRISTIAN GAUL
Chadwick, O *see* JOHN CASSIAN
Chadwick, William Edward *see*
- THE CHURCH, THE STATE, AND THE POOR
- PASTORAL TEACHING OF PAUL: HIS MINISTERIAL IDEALS
- SOCIAL RELATIONSHIPS IN THE LIGHT OF CHRISTIANITY

Chadwick, William Sydney *see* MOTHER AFRICA HITS BACK
CHADWICK'S HISTORY OF SHELBY COUNTY / Chadwick, Edward H – Indianapolis: B.F. Bowen and Co., 1909. Indiana Reel 27. (The Cox Library Collection) – 5 – us Americana [978]
Chaev, N S *see* RUSSKAIA PALEOGRAFIIA
Chafe, William H *see*
- SOUTHERN WOMEN AND THEIR FAMILIES IN THE 19TH CENTURY: PAPERS AND DIARIES
- WOMAN'S SUFFRAGE

Chafee, Zechariah Jr. *see* THE ZECHARIAH CHAFEE, JR. PAPERS
Chafer, Lewis Sperry *see*
- THE KINGDOM IN HISTORY AND PROPHECY
- TRUE EVANGELISM

Chaffault, Silvestre-F du *see* DISCOURS OU ORAISON FUNEBRE PRONONCE(...)AU SERVICE SOLENNEL DU MARQUIS DE LA ROCHE-JACQUELIN(...)
Chafik, H *see* STATUT JURIDIQUE INTERNATIONAL DE L'EGYPTE
Chagnon, Joseph Antoine *see* ETUDE SUR LA LOI CRIMINELLE DU CANADA EN RAPPORT AVEC LES LOIS PENALES DE LA PROVINCE DE QUEBEC
Chagnon, W *see* LA PAIX
CHAGRIN FALLS TOWNSHIP MINUTES – Chagrin Falls, Cuyahoga, OH. 1845-1991 – 4r – 1 – us Western Res [978]
CHAGRIN FALLS VILLAGE CEMETERY DEEDS – Chagrin Falls, Cuyahoga, OH. 1881-1989 – 3r – 1 – us Western Res [978]
CHAGRIN FALLS VILLAGE MINUTES : MINUTES OF THE COUNCIL OF THE VILLAGE OF CHAGRIN FALLS – Cuyahoga, OH. 1844-1992 – 11r – 1 – us Western Res [978]
THE CHAHAR MAQALA / Nizami, 'Aruzi' – (Four Discourses). 1899 – 1 – uk Microform Academic [280]
THE CHAHAR MAQALA OF NIDHAMI-I-ARUNDI-I-SAMARQANDI / Browne, E G – 1 – uk Microform Academic [800]
CHAI LIGHTS – (Feb. 1984; Nov. 1984-Mar. 1985; May 1985; Sept. 1985-Oct. 1985; Dec. 1985; Apr. 1986-May 1986; Sept. 1986-Feb. 1987) – Shreveport, Louisiana – 1 – us A.J.P.C. [073]
Chaianov, A V *see*
- BIUDZHETNYE ISSLEDOVANIIA
- KAK ORGANIZOVAT' KREST'IANSKOE KHOZIAISTVO V NECHERNOZEMNOI POLOSE
- KAPITALY KREST'IANSKOGO KHOZIAISTVA I EGO KREDITOVANIE PRI AGRARNOI REFORME
- KRATKII KURS KOOPERATSII
- MATERIALY PO VOPROSAM ORGANIZATSII PRODOVOL'STVENNOGO DELA
- METODY KOLICHESTVENNOGO UCHETA EFFEKTA ZEMLEUSTROISTVA
- OCHERKI PO TEORII TRUDOVOGO KHOZIAISTVA
- OPTIMAL'NYE ZARMERY SEL'SKO-KHOZIAISTVENNYKH PREDPRIIATII
- OPYT ANKETNOGO ISSLEDOVANIIA DENEZHNYKH ELEMENTOV KRESTIANSKOGO KHOZIAISTVA MOSKOVSKOI GUBERNII
- ORGANIZATSIIA KREST'IANSKOGO KHOZIAISTVA
- ORGANIZATSIIA SEVERNOGO KREST'IANSKOGO KHOZIAISTVA
- OSNOVNYE IDEI I METODY RABOTY OBSHCHESTVENNOI AGRONOMIII
- OSNOVNYE USLOVIIA USPEKHA KOOPERATIVNOGO SBYTA PRODUKTOV SEL'SKOGO KHOZIAISTVA
- PAMIATKA L'NOVODA-KOOPERATORA
- PRODOVOL'STVENNYI VOPROS
- RUSSKOE L'NOVODSTVO, L'NIANOI RYNOK I L'NIANAIA KOOPERATSIIA
- SOIUZNOE STROITEL'STVO KOOPERATIVOV

Chaigniez *see* LE JUGEMENT DE SALOMON
CHAIKA I SOLOMEIA / Voloshin, M – Stikhotvoreniia. Kiev. 1909. BR-892 2 – 8 – ne IDC [460]
Chaikin, Vadim Afanasevich *see* KISTORII ROSSI ISKO I REVOLIUTSII
Chaille-Long *see* L'AFRIQUE CENTRALE, EXPEDITIONS AU LAC VICTORIA-NYANZA ET AU MAKRAKA NIAM NIAM, A L'OUEST DU NIL BLANC

Chailley-Bert, Joseph *see* LES COMPAGNIES DE COLONISATION SOUS L'ANCIEN REGIME

THE CHAIN OF LIFE IN GEOLOGICAL TIME: A SKETCH OF THE ORIGIN AND SUCCESSION OF ANIMALS AND PLANTS / Dawson, John William – London: Religious Tract Society, 1880?. 02373. (Pre-1900 Canadiana) – 9 – cn C.I.H.M. [560]

CHAIN STORE AGE – (1975-. 1,5,6,9) – Drug store ed. v1-50. 1925-74 – 1 – us UMI [073]

Chaine, Leon *see* MENUS PROPOS D'UN CATHOLIQUE LIBERAL

Chaine, M *see* CATALOGUE DES MANUSCRITS ETHIOPIENS DE LA COLLECTION ANTOINE D'ABBADIE

CHAINING AUSTRALIA, CHURCH BUREAUCRACIES AND POLITICAL ECONOMY / ed by Brennan, Geoffrey & Williams, John K – Contributions by Geoffrey Brennan, Paul A. McGavin, John K. Williams, Hugh Henry, Greg Sheridan, Lauchlan Chipman. 1984, 143p. Indexed – 9 – 1.00f – at Libertarian Micro [335]

LA CHAIRE FRANCAISE AU 12 SIECLE : D'APRES LES MANUSCRITS / Bourgain, L – Paris: Societe generale de librairie catholique, 1879 – 1mf – us A.T.L.A. [240]

CHAIRMAN'S CORRESPONDENCE (INDEXED) / New Zealand. Methodist Church. Methodist Overseas Mission. Solomon Islands Mission – 1952-61 – 7r – 1 – PMB1111 – at Pacific Mss [240]

Chairul Basri *see* GEO-POLITIK INDONESIA; POLITIK BOEMI INDONESIA

CHAITANYA AND HIS AGE / Sen, Dinesh Chandra, rai banadur – (Calcutta): University of Calcutta, 1922. 425p – 1 – us U.W. Library [920]

Chaix, Barthelemy *see* PREOCCUPATIONS STATISTIQUES, GEOGRAPHIQUES, PITTORESQUES ET SYNOPTIQUES DU DEPARTEMENT DES HAUTES-ALPES

Chajes, H P *see* MA'AMARIM LE-ZIKHRON R. ZEVI PEREZ CHAJES

Chajes, Hirsch Perez *see* MARKUS-STUDIEN

CHAKKHYGYS-TAASU. SIBIRSKII SKAZ / Remizov, A – Berlin. 1922. BR-816 2 – 8 – ne IDC [460]

Chakravarty, Apurba Kumar *see* ORIGIN AND DEVELOPMENT OF INDIAN CALENDRICAL SCIENCE

CHAKRAVIJAYA / Corps Kehakiman Angkatan Darat – (Irregular. Available: 1962(1); 1963(4); 1966(1)) – Djakarta, 1962-1966 – 3mf – 9 – SE-1378/1 – ne IDC [340]

EN CHALAND SOUS LES TROPIQUES / Neufville, Gilbert de – Paris: B Grasset, 1926 – 1 – us Res Libr [960]

CHALARISESACARYA – English and Sanskrit. Madhva logic. Ed. and trans. by Susil Kumar Maitra. Calcutta: Calcutta University, 1936. xxvi,166p – 1 – us U.W. Library [280]

Chalasinski, Jozef *see*
- "EMIGRACJA JAKO ZJAWISKO SPOLECZNE"
- PARAFJA I SKOLA PARAFJALNA WSROD EMIGRACJI POLSKI W AMERYCE
- SWIASEK I PARAFJA A SWIADOMOSC NARODOWA EMIGRANTA

THE CHALCEDONIAN DECREE, OR, HISTORICAL CHRISTIANITY, MISREPRESENTED BY MODERN THEOLOGY, CONFIRMED BY MODERN SCIENCE, AND UNTOUCHED BY MODERN CRITICISM / Fulton, John – New York: T. Whittaker, 1892. (Charlotte Wood Slocum lectures) – 1mf – us A.T.L.A. [240]

DAS CHALCIDIUS KOMMENTAR ZU PLATOS TIMAEUS : BGPHMA 3/6 / Switalski, B W – Muenster, 1902 – 3mf – 9 – ne Slangenburg [240]

Chalcocondylae, Laonici *see*
- ATHENIENSIS HISTORIARUM LIBRI 10 (CSHB 45)
- HISTORIARUM LIBRI DECEM DE REBUS TURCICIS (CBH 16)

Chalcocondylas, Laonici *see* L'HISTOIRE DE LA DECADENCE DE L'EMPIRE GREC, ET ESTABLISSEMENT DE CELVY DES TURCS; ...

CHALDAEISCHEN WOERTERBUCH UEBER DIE TARGUMIM UND EINEN GROSSEN THEIL DES RABBINISCHEN SCHRIFTTHUMS / Levy, J – 2v. Leipzig. 1867-68. BJ-412 14 1 – 9 – ne IDC [270]

CHALDAEISCHES WOERTERBUCH UEBER DIE TARGUMIM / Levy, J – ed. 3. Leipzig. 1881. BJ-32-50 1 – 28mf – 9 – ne IDC [270]

CHALDAEISCHES WOERTERBUCH UEBER DIE TARGUMIM UND EINEN GROSSEN THEIL DES RABBINISCHEN SCHRIFTTHUMS / Levy, J – Leipzig. 2v. 1867-1868 – 19mf – ne IDC [470]

CHALDAEISCHES WOETERBUCH UEBER DIE TARGUM UND EINEN GROSSEN THEIL DES RABBINISCHEN SCHRIFTTHUMS / Levy, J – (1. Band Aleph-Lamed, Leipzig 1867 12mf; 2. Band Mem-Tav., Leipzig 1868 16mf) – 8 – ne Slangenburg [270]

Chaleard, J L *see* STRUCTURE AGRAIRE ET ECONOMIE DE PLANTATION CHEZ LES ABE, DEPARTEMENT D'AGBOVILLE, COTE D'IVOIRE

CHALET DES BRISES : CINQUIEME REUNION DE BONZES – QUI SE PRENNENT AU SERIEUX / Morin, Victor – Montreal, 1919. SEM105P781 – 1mf – 9 – Can$2.25 – cn Bibl Nat [820]

CHALEUR ET INDUSTRIE : REVUE MENSUELLE DES INDUSTRIES DE FEU – v 1-37 1920-61 – 1,5,6 – us Princeton Micro [621]

Chalil, H Munawar *see* KELENGKAPAN TARICH NABI MUHAMMAD

Challen, G A *see* LES MINES CANADIENNES

CHALLEN TYPESCRIPTS / Challen, W H – vols. 1-87. 16th, 17th and 18th centuries – 1 – uk Microform Academic [920]

Challen, W H *see* CHALLEN TYPESCRIPTS

Challener, Richard *see* THE CORRESPONDENCE SERIES AND SPEECHES SERIES OF THE PERSONAL PAPERS OF JOHN FOSTER DULLES (1888-1959)

CHALLENGE – (1982-. 1,5,6,9) – v2-. 1954- – 1 – us UMI [330]

CHALLENGE – Boston. v. 1-2. Mar 1 1934-Spring Fall 1937 – 1 – us NY Public [073]

CHALLENGE – Clarksdale. Miss. 1905 – 1 – us UMI [071]

CHALLENGE – Gainesville, FL.Fall 1980-Spring 1981 – 1 – us A.J.P.C. [071]

CHALLENGE – Kingstown. St. Vincent. -f. 3 Jan 1959-15 Dec 1960, 6 Jan 1962-15 Jan 1964. (1 reel) – 1 – uk British Libr Newspaper [072]

THE CHALLENGE – Montreal, CN, 1938 – 1r – 1 – Can$25.00 – cn Can Microfilming [072]

CHALLENGE; A LIBERTARIAN WEEKLY – 1-2 2+18 (all publ). 1938-1939 – 1 reel – 1 – $65.00 – us UPA [335]

CHALLENGE IN EDUCATIONAL ADMINISTRATION – (v1-15 Can$20.00y) – Edmonton. v27-31. 1990-94 – 9 – Can$28.00y – cn Micromedia [370]

CHALLENGE IN EDUCATIONAL ADMINISTRATION – (v13- . 1974- . 5,6. v14- . 1975- . 9) – v. 1-. 1961- – 1 – us UMI [370]

CHALLENGE MAGAZINE – v1-2. 1952-54 – 1 – us UMI [330]

THE CHALLENGE OF CHRISTIANITY TO A WORLD AT WAR / Griffith-Jones, Ebenezer – London: Duckworth, 1915 – 1mf – us A.T.L.A. [240]

CHALLENGE OF CONSERVATIVE BAPTIST HOME MISSIONS – Apr 1954-Nov 1972 – 1 – 27.02 – us Baptist [240]

THE CHALLENGE OF FACTS AND OTHER ESSAYS / Sumner, William Graham – 1914. 462p. 1 fiche (29x) – 9 – 1.00f – at Libertarian Micro [320]

THE CHALLENGE OF GERMAN LITERATURE / ed by Daemmrich & Haenicke, Diether H – (Includes bibliographical references) – Detroit: Wayne State University Press, 1971 – 1 – us U.W. Library [430]

THE CHALLENGE OF THE CITY / Strong, Josiah – New York: Eaton & Mains; Cincinnati: Jennings & Graham, c1907 – 1mf – us A.T.L.A. [240]

THE CHALLENGE OF YOUTH *see* CHALLENGE OF YOUTH (YOUNG PEOPLE'S SOCIALIST LEAGUE OF AMERICA)

CHALLENGE OF YOUTH (YOUNG PEOPLE'S SOCIALIST LEAGUE OF AMERICA) – (Library has: v.3, no. 8-9, 11; v.4, no. 1, 3-5; v.5, no. 1; new series. v.1, no. 1-v.4, no. 6; new series. v.1, no. 2-5; v. 2, no. 2, 4-5; Nov. 1935-May 1941) – [Chicago, Ill.: Young People's Socialist League, 1935-1937]. 2v – 1 – CSUX86-S124 – us Hoover Inst Photo [335]

CHALLENGE PRESENTED TO CULTURES BY SCIENCE AND TECHNOLOGY / Ladriere, Jean – 1977 – 165p – 9 – 92-3-101418-8 – fr UNESCO [303]

THE CHALLENGE TO CHRISTIAN MISSIONS : MISSIONARY QUESTIONS AND THE MODERN MIND / Welsh, Robert Ethol – (Includes bibliographical references) – New York: Young People's Missionary Movement, 1908 – 1mf – 9 – 0-8370-6459-7 – 1986-0459 – us A.T.L.A. [230]

CHALLENGE TO OUR CULTURAL HERITAGE : WHY PRESERVE THE PAST? / ed by Isar, Yudhishthir Raj – 1986 – 252p – 9 – 92-3-102370-5 – fr UNESCO [900]

CHALLENGE (YOUNG PEOPLE'S SOCIALIST LEAGUE OF AMERICA) : Y.P.S.L. – (Library has: v.2, no. 5; v.3, no. 2; Aug. 1934, May 1935) – Chicago, Ill.: [Young People's Socialist League of America, 1933-1935]. 3v – 1 – CSUX86-S125 – us Hoover Inst Photo [335]

CHALLENGE! YPSL / Young People's Socialist League – 1-4 2+3 (all publ). 1943-1946 – 5mf – 9 – $40.00 – us UPA [335]

CHALLENGE/DESAFIO – v.1-. 1964- – 1 – us UMI [073]

CHALLENGER – Portland. Or. 1952-1954 – 1 – us UMI [071]

CHALLENGER COMMISSION P.C. NUMBERED DOCUMENTS, 1986 – 73r – 5 – M1496 – us Nat'l Archives [324]

CHALLENGES TO PRESS FREEDOM IN INDIA, 1947 TO 1963 / Irani, Behram S – Madison, 1965 – us Res Libr [360]

Challenor, R *see* A CAVEAT AGAINST THE METHODISTS, SHEWING HOW UNSAFE IT IS FOR ANY CHRISTIAN TO JOIN HIMSELF TO THEIR SOCIETY OR TO ADHERE TO THEIR TEACHERS

Chalmel, J L *see*
- BIBLIOTHEQUE HISTORIQUE DE TOURAINE...
- NOTICES BIOGRAPHIQUES

Chalmers, Alexander *see* THE BRITISH ESSAYISTS

CHALMERS CHURCH WATCHMAN – [Montreal?]: Young Peoples' Society of Christian Endeavor, [1890?-189- or 19–] – 9 – cn C.I.H.M. [240]

Chalmers, G *see* A COLLECTION OF TREATIES BETWEEN GREAT BRITAIN AND OTHER POWERS

Chalmers, James *see* ADVENTURES IN NEW GUINEA

Chalmers, John Aitken *see* TIYO SOGA

Chalmers, Thomas *see*
- ON THE POWER, WISDOM, AND GOODNESS OF GOD AS MANIFESTED IN THE ADAPTATION OF EXTERNAL NATURE TO THE MORAL AND INTELLECTUAL CONSTITUTION OF MAN
- A SELECTION FROM THE CORRESPONDENCE.

Chalons, V C *see* REGLES DE LA POESIE FRANCOISE

Chalout, Pierre *see* VIVRE

CHALUTZ – Gainesville, FL.Fall 1973; Apr 1974 – 1 – us A.J.P.C. [071]

LE CHAMBARD SOCIALISTE – no. 1-78. Paris. 16 dec 1893-8 juin 1895. mq no. 73 – 1 – fr A.C.R.P.P. [073]

Chambaron, D *see* VIE ET TECHNIQUES DE CHASSE DES INDIENS DE MISTASSINI

CHAMBER MUSIC OF THE LOW COUNTRIES : 1570-1820 – 318mf – 9 – MS-r – ne IDC [780]

CHAMBER MUSIC. SELECTIONS : CONTAINS: NO. 1 OF 3 SONATAS FOR THE PIANOFORTE WITH AN ACCOMP. FOR A VIOLIN, OP. 4. ALSO CONTAINS: 2 SONATES, OP. 33.... / Steibelt, Daniel – Philadelphia: E Blake – 1 – us Sibley [780]

Chamber of Commerce. Constantinople *see* JOURNAL

Chamber of Commerce of Japan *see* HONPO SHOGYO KAIGISHO SHIRYO

Chamberlain, Alexander Francis *see*
- THE ESKIMO RACE AND LANGUAGE
- THE LANGUAGE OF THE MISSISSAGA INDIANS OF SKUGOG: A CONTRIBUTION TO THE LINGUISTICS OF THE ALGONKIAN TRIBES OF CANADA

Chamberlain, Basil Hall *see* THINGS JAPANESE; BEING NOTES ON VARIOUS SUBJECTS CONNECTED WITH JAPAN FOR THE USE OF TRAVELLERS AND OTHERS

Chamberlain, Daniel Henry *see* ADDRESS OF HON. DANIEL H. CHAMBERLAIN TO THE GRADUATING CLASS AT THE COMMENCEMENT EXERCISES OF COLUMBIA COLLEGE LAW SCHOOL.

Chamberlain, Franc *see* CONTEMPORARY THEATRE REVIEW

Chamberlain, Houston Stewart *see* DAS DRAMA RICHARD WAGNER'S

Chamberlain, Isabel Fraser *see* ABDUL BAHA ON DIVINE PHILOSOPHY

Chamberlain, J P *see*
- THE DANUBE
- THE REGIME OF...DANUBE AND RHINE

Chamberlain, Jacob *see*
- THE COBRA'S DEN: STORIES OF MISSIONARY WORK AMONG THE TELUGAS OF INDIA
- IN THE TIGER JUNGLE:...MISSIONARY WORK AMONG THE TELUGUS OF INDIA
- THE KINGDOM IN INDIA

Chamberlain, L T *see* UN CHAPITRE DE DESHONNEUR NATIONAL

Chamberlain, Montague *see* SOME CANADIAN BIRDS: A BRIEF ACCOUNT OF SOME OF THE COMMON BIRDS OF EASTERN CANADA: FIRST SERIES – BIRDS OF FIELD AND GROVE

Chamberlain, Walter *see* THE COLONIES, AND THEIR CONNECTION WITH THE MOTHER COUNTRY: WITH A STATISTICAL LIST OF THE BRITISH EMPIRE IN 1886 APPENDED

Chambers, E T D *see* LES PECHERIES DE LA PROVINCE DE QUEBEC

Chambers, Edward Thomas Davies *see*
- THE ANGLER'S GUIDE TO EASTERN CANADA: SHOWING WHERE, WHEN AND HOW TO FISH FOR SALMON, BASS, OUANANICHE AND TROUT
- THE GUIDE TO QUEBEC
- THE OUANANICHE AND ITS CANADIAN ENVIRONMENT
- THE PORT OF QUEBEC: ITS FACILITIES AND PROSPECTS: THE PAST, PRESENT AND FUTURE OF QUEBEC'S SHIPPING TRADE

Chambers, Ephraim *see*
- CYCLOPAEDIA
- CYCLOPAEDIA (AEL, ABT.1;2)

Chambers, Ernest J *see* THE ORIGIN AND SERVICES OF THE PRINCE OF WALES REGIMENT: INCLUDING A BRIEF HISTORY OF THE MILITIA OF FRENCH CANADA AND OF THE CANADIAN MILITIA..

Chambers, George Frederick *see*
- A DIGEST OF THE LAW RELATING TO DISTRICT COUNCILS.
- A DIGEST OF THE LAW RELATING TO PUBLIC HEALTH AND LOCAL GOVERNMENT.

Chambers, John David *see* DIVINE WORSHIP IN ENGLAND IN THE THIRTEENTH AND FOURTEENTH CENTURIES CONTRASTED WITH AND ADAPTED TO THAT IN THE NINETEENTH

Chambers, Robert *see*
- A BIOGRAPHICAL DICTIONARY OF EMINENT SCOTSMEN
- CYCLOPAEDIA OF ENGLISH LITERATURE
- ILLUSTRATIONS OF THE AUTHOR OF WAVERLEY
- VESTIGES OF THE NATURAL HISTORY OF CREATION

Chambers, Robert William *see* THE MASK: AND OTHER STORIES

Chambers, Sue *see* COLLECTIVE ARTISTIC DIRECTION

CHAMBERS SUN – Chambers, NE. -w. Jul. 1892; Oct 1895-Dec. 1895; Feb. 1896-Jan. 1901; Apr. 1901-Feb.1902; Mar. 1908-Dec. 1943; May 1946-Sep. 1948 – 1 – us NE Hist [071]

Chambers, Talbot Wilson *see*
- THE BOOK OF ZECHARIAH
- COMPANION TO THE REVISED OLD TESTAMENT
- THE NOON PRAYER MEETING OF THE NORTH DUTCH CHURCH : FULTON STREET, NEW YORK
- PSALTER: A WITNESS TO THE DIVINE ORIGIN OF THE BIBLE

Chambers, V *see* A DISSERTATION ON ORIENTAL GARDENING

Chambers, W *see* PLANS, ELEVATIONS, SECTIONS, AND PERSPECTIVE VIEWS OF THE GARDENS AND BUILDINGS AT KEW IN SURREY

CHAMBERSBURG DEMOCRATIC-REPUBLICAN *see* SPIRIT OF THE TIMES

CHAMBERSBURG VALLEY SPIRIT – Chambersburg, PA., 1849-1912 – 13 – $25.00r – us I.M.R. [071]

Chamborant, CG de *see* DU PAUPERISME, CE QU'IL ETAIT DANS L'ANTIQUITE ET CE QU'IL EST DE NOS. JOURS

La Chambre d'Agriculture du Bas-Canada. Montreal *see* L'AGRICULTEUR

CHAMBRE D'ASSEMBLEE, VENDREDI LE 2 FEVRIER 1827. RESOLU, QU'IL SOIT NOMME UN COMITE DE SEPT MEMBRES POUR S'ENQUERIR S'IL SEROIT NECESSAIRE D'OUVRIR QUELQUES ET QUELS CHEMINS... – [Quebec]: [Chambre d'Assemblee], [1827] – 1mf – 9 – Can$2.25 – cn Bibl Nat [340]

CHAMBRE D'ASSEMBLEE, VENDREDI, LE 2 FEVRIER 1827. RESOLU, QU'IL SOIT NOMME UN COMITE DE SET MEMBRES POUR... = HOUSE OF ASSEMBLY, FRIDAY, 2ND FEBRUARY 1827 – [Quebec]: [Chambre d'assemblee], [1827]. SEM105P1140 – 1mf – 9 – Can$2.25 – cn Bibl Nat [380]

Chambre de Commerce de Paris *see*
- AVIS EXPRIMES SUR LES PRINCIPALES QUESTIONS SOUMISES A SON EXAMEN PENDANT LES ANNEES 1870 A 1872: ABROGATION DE LA LOI DU 25 MAI 1864 SUR LES COALITIONS
- ENQUETE SUR LES CONDITIONS DE TRAVAIL EN FRANCE PENDANT L'ANNEE 1872
- STATISTIQUE DE L'INDUSTRIE A PARIS, RESULTANT DE L'ENQUETE FAITE PAR LA CHAMBRE DE COMMERCE POUR LES ANNEES 1847-1848. RESULTATS GENERAUX

Chambre de Commerce d'Edmunston *see* LE REPUBLICAIN

CHAMBRE DES PAIRS DE FRANCE. SESSION DE 1821 / Broglie, Leonce Victor – Developpement d'Une Proposition Faite A La Chambre. Relative A L'Execution Des Lois Prohibitives De La Traite Des Noirs. (Slave Trade and Abolitionism in France Series). Seance du jeudi 28 Mars 1822 – 9 – fr Hachette [305]

Chambres Syndicales de la Ville de Paris *see* MONITEUR DE L'ENTREPRISE ET DE L'INDUSTRIE

Chambrun, Charles Adolphe de Pineton *see* LE POUVOIR EXECUTIF AUX ETATS-UNIS, ETUDE DE DROIT CONSTITUTIONNEL

LE CHAMEAU : HUMORISTIQUE / ed by Arcand, Adrien – Montreal, Canada. 14 mar 1930-10 jun 1932 – 1r – 1 – Can$40.00 – cn Can Microfilming [072]

Chamier, Jacques Daniel *see* FABULOUS MONSTER

Chaminade, C *see* VALSE CARNAVALESQUE POUR DEUX PIANOS A 4 MAINS, OP. 73

Chaminaud, Ricardo *see* 17 DE OCTUBRE

Chamisso, Adelbert von *see*
- GEDICHTE
- GESAMMELTE WERKE
- EL HOMBRE QUE PERDIO SU SOMBRA
- WERKE

Chamisso, LA von *see* UEBERSICHT DER NUTZBARSTEN UND SCHAEDLICHSTEN GEWAECHSE,...

Chamizo, Luis *see*
- OBRAS COMPLETAS
- SEMANA SANTA EN GUARENA Y ORACION A LA VIRGEN
- SEMANA SANTA EN GUARENA Y ORACION DE LA VIRGEN

Chamorro Garrido, G *see* LA NACIONALIDAD ANTE EL DERECHO INTERNACIONAL PRIVADO Y EL DERECHO SUD AMERICANO

Chamorro Martinez, Manuel *see* VALOR MILITAR DE LA "ZONA DE DEFENSA DEL NOROESTE PENINSULAR"

Chamorro, Pedro Joaquin *see*
- ENTRE DOS FILOS. MANAGUA, 1927
- EL ULTIMO FILIBUSTERO. NOVELA HISTORICA. MANAGUA, 1933

Champ, B R *see* REPORT OF THE F.A.O. GLOBAL SURVEY OF PESTICIDE SUSCEPTIBILITY OF STORED GRAIN PESTS

CHAMP FLEURY AUQUEL EST CONTENU L'ART ET SCIENCE DE LA DEUE ET VRAYE PROPORTION DES LETTRES ATTIQUES / Tory, G – 1529 – 9 – fr I.C.S. [760]

Champagne, Andre *see* BIO-BIBLIOGRAPHIE ANALYTIQUE DE F. FITZ OSBORNE, GEOLOGUE, TITULAIRE DE LA CHAIRE DE PETROLOGIE A L'UNIVERSITE LAVAL

Champagne, Louis *see* ROMAN D'AMOUR

Champagne, Philias *see* LA GUERRE D'EUROPE

CHAMPAIGN COUNTY DIRECTORY 1870-1871 / Lothrop, J S – Rand, McNally and Co., 1871. Illinois Reel 14. (The Cox Library Collection) – 5 – us Americana [978]

Champaign County. Ohio. Nettle Creek Baptist Church *see* CHURCH RECORDS, MS 646

Champcommunal, J *see*
- ETUDE SUR LA DONATION ET LE TESTAMENT...
- ETUDE SUR LA LETTRE DE CHANGE...
- ETUDE SUR LA SUCCESSION AB INTESTAT...

CHAMPIGNONS DU TONKIN / Patouillard, N T – 1985 – 7mf – 9 – £235.00 – 0-930466-95-0 – uk Chadwyck [580]

CHAMPION – Atchison. Kan. -w. 1869-1909 – 1 – us UMI [071]

CHAMPION – (Champion and Weekly Herald. Nov 1836-Apr 1840) – London, UK. Sept 1836-Apr 1940. -w – 3r – 1 – uk British Libr Newspaper [072]

CHAMPION / Young Communist League – Official Organ – 1 – 145.00 – cn McLaren [971]

THE CHAMPION – 1739-41 – 1 – uk Microform Academic [073]

CHAMPION AND WEEKLY HERALD *see* CHAMPION

Champion, L G *see* OUTLOOK FOR CHRISTIANITY

CHAMPION LABOR MONTHLY – 1-3 2+10 (all publ). 1936-1938 – 1 reel – 1 – $115.00 – us UPA [331]

THE CHAMPION OF VIRTUE : A GOTHIC STORY / Reeve, Clara – [London?]: Printed for the Author, by W. Keymer, Colchester, 1777 – 1 roll – 1 – 1-55879-299-6 – uk Libr Preservation [830]

Champion, P *see* LA VIE DU PERE J. RIGOLEUC

Champion. P *see* LA VIE ET LA DOCTRINE SPIRITUELLE DU PERE LOUIS LALLEMANT

Champion, Paul *see* LE CANADA

Champion, Pierre *see* HISTOIRE POETIQUE DU QUINZIEME SIECLE..

Champion, Thomas Edward *see*
- THE ANGLICAN CHURCH IN CANADA
- HISTORY OF THE 10TH ROYALS AND OF THE ROYAL GRENADIERS, FROM THE FORMATION OF THE REGIMENT UNTIL 1896
- THE METHODIST CHURCHES OF TORONTO: A HISTORY OF THE METHODIST DENOMINATION AND ITS CHURCHES IN YORK AND TORONTO, WITH BIOGRAPHICAL SKETCHES OF MANY OF THE CLERGY AND LAITY

CHAMPIONS OF CHRISTIANITY / Farmer, Silas – New York: Eaton & Mains, 1897. 1 fiche – 9 – us A.T.L.A. [240]

CHAMPLAIN / Dawson, Samuel Edward – Montreal: s.n., 1890. 03775. (Pre-1900 Canadiana) – 9 – cn C.I.H.M. [971]

CHAMPLAIN ET SON OEUVRE: UNE PAGE D'HISTOIRE – Quebec: A. Talbot, 1898. 02873. (Pre-1900 Canadiana) – 9 – cn C.I.H.M. [910]

CHAMPLAIN: SA VIE ET SON CARACTERE / Casgrain, Henri-Raymond – Quebec: L. J. Demers, 1898. 00644. (Pre-1900 Canadiana) – 9 – cn C.I.H.M. [920]

Champlain, Samuel de *see*
- OEUVRES
- LES VOYAGES DE LA NOUVELLE-FRANCE OCCIDENTALE, DICTE CANADA, FAITS PAR LE SR DE CHAMPLAIN,....
- LES VOYAGES DE LA NOUVELLE-FRANCE OCCIDENTALE, DICTE CANADA, FAITS PAR LE SR DE CHAMPLAIN, XAINCTONGEOIS,...
- LES VOYAGES DU SIEUR DE CHAMPLAIN XAINTONGEOIS, CAPITAINE ORDINAIRE POUR LE ROY EN LA MARINE, DIVISEZ EN DEUX LIVRES

CHAMPLAIN SOCIETY PUBLICATIONS : TORONTO, 1907-58 – 209mf – 9 – $755.00 – us UPA [971]

CHAMPLAIN'S AMERICAN EXPERIENCES IN 1613 / Harvey, Arthur – 1886?. 03987. (Pre-1900 Canadiana) – 9 – cn C.I.H.M. [910]

CHAMPLAIN'S TOMB / Harper, John Murdoch – 18–?. 05367. (Pre-1900 Canadiana) – 9 – cn C.I.H.M. [910]

CHAMPOEG PIONEER – Champoeg, OR. -m Mar 1956-Jan 1960. 1 roll – 1 – us U.O. Library [071]

CHAMS *see* EL-CHAMS

Chan, Shui *see* STORY OF ISRAEL (CCC6)

Chancellor, E Beresford *see* THE HISTORY OF THE SQUARES OF LONDON, TOPOGRAPHICAL & HISTORICAL

CHANCEN UND PERSPEKTIVEN EINER DEMOKRATISIERUNG DES RUNDFUNKSYSTEMS IN BRASILIEN : UNTERSUCHUNG ANHAND EINER EXPERTENBEFRAGUNG / Knoebelspies, Karin – 1992 – 202p – 9 – DM98.00 – 3-89349-580-0 – gw Hänsel [380]

THE CHANCERY JURISDICTION AND PRACTICE, ACCORDING TO STATUTES AND DECISIONS IN THE STATE OF ILLINOIS, FROM THE EARLIEST PERIOD TO 1873 / Hill, Edward Judson – Chicago: Myers, 1873. 758p. LL-780 – 1 – us L of C Photodup [340]

CHANCERY RECORD / Fulton County. Ohio. Common Pleas. Civil Division – 1850-1854 – 1r – 1 – $32.50r – us Archival [324]

CHANCERY RECORD NO. 5 / Erie County. Ohio. Common Pleas. Civil Division – 1853-1857 – 1r – 1 – $32.50r – us Archival [324]

CHANCERY RECORDS / Crawford County. Ohio. Common Pleas. Civil Division – 1831-1852 – 1r – 1 – $32.50r – us Archival [324]

CHANCERY RECORDS / Henry County. Ohio. District Court – 1852-1853 – 1r – 1 – $32.50r – us Archival [324]

CHANCERY RECORDS / Huron County. Ohio. Common Pleas. Civil Division – 1822-1901 – 6r – 1 – $32.50r – us Archival [324]

CHANCERY RECORDS / Huron County. Ohio. District Court – 1852-1861 – 1r – 1 – $32.50r – us Archival [324]

CHANCERY RECORDS / Huron County. Ohio. Supreme Court – 1835-1851 – 3r – 1 – $32.50r – us Archival [324]

CHANCERY RECORDS / Van Wert County. Ohio. Common Pleas. Civil Division – 1839-1855 – 1r – 1 – $32.50r – us Archival [324]

CHANCERY RECORDS / Van Wert County. Ohio. Supreme Court – 1848-1855 – 1r – 1 – $32.50r – us Archival [324]

CHANCERY RECORDS / Wyandot County. Ohio. Common Pleas. Civil Division – 1846-1855 – 2r – 1 – $32.50r – us Archival [324]

CHANCERY RECORDS / Wyandot County. Ohio. Supreme Court – 1850-1854 – 1r – 1 – $32.50r – us Archival [324]

THE CHANCERY STUDENT'S GUIDE IN THE FORM OF A DIDACTIC POEM. / Carrighan, Terentius – London: Wildy, 1850. 64p. LL-1672 – 1 – us L of C Photodup [340]

LES CHANCES ECONOMIQUES DE LA COMMUNAUTE FRANCO-AFRICAINE / Moussa, P – F50.00 – fr Ethnologie [338]

LA CHANDELLE DEMOCRATIQUE ET SOCIALE – [Paris]: Madame de Lacombe 1849. – us Res Libr [320]

Chandieu *see* ANT. SAD. OPERA THEOLOGICA 1614

Chandler, Amos Henry *see* LYRICS, SONGS AND SONNETS

Chandler, Arthur *see* SPIRIT OF MAN: AN ESSAY IN CHRISTIAN PHILOSOPHY

Chandler, Henry William *see*
- THE PHILOSOPHY OF MIND
- PHILOSOPHY OF MIND: AN INAUGURAL LECTURE

Chandler, Peleg W *see*
- OBSERVATIONS ON THE AUTHENTICITY OF THE GOSPELS
- THESAURUS THOMAS A KEMPIS

Chandler, William Eaton *see* ADDRESS BEFORE THE GRAFTON AND COOS BAR ASSOCIATION

Chandler, Zachariah *see* PAPERS

CHANDLER'S REPORTS / Wisconsin. Supreme Court – (For purposes of Pre-NRS coverage, all of Chandler's cases are included in pinney) – v1-4. 1849-1852 (all publ) – 13mf – 9 – $19.50 – LLMC 91-303 – us L.L.M.C. [340]

Chandonnet, Gemma *see* BIBLIOGRAPHIE DE L'OEUVRE DE LOUIS-PHILIPPE AUDET, D. PED.

Chandonnet, Thomas Aime *see*
- L'ABBE JOSEPH AUBRY
- NOTRE-DAME-DES-CANADIENS ET LES CANADIENS AUX ETATS-UNIS

CHANDOS / Ouida – British Fiction Archive: Unit 3 – 9 – uk Bell [830]

Chandra Bhanja Deo, Maharaja *see* THEISM: THE NATION'S NEED: AN ADDRESS

Chandra, Lokesh *see* MONGOLIAN KANJUR

Chandra, Satish et al *see* CURRICULA AND SYLLABI IN HYDROLOGY

Chaney, George Leonard *see* WOMAN'S MINISTRY, AS EXEMPLIFIED IN SOUTHERN SCHOOLS

Chaney, George Leonhard *see* BELIEF

Chang, Chih-Chieng *see* THE ART OF PREACHING (CCC8)

Chang, Chin-Shih *see* RELIGIOUS THOUGHT MOVEMENTS IN CHINA DURING THE LAST DECADE (CCC9)

CHANG CHI-TZU CHIU LU – Collected works of Chang Chien. 25v. Shanghai. 1935. 2 reels – 1 – 48.00 – us Chinese Res [072]

Chang, Chun-i *see* THE BUDDHIZATION OF CHRISTIANITY (CCC10)

Chang, Chun-Yen *see* A SIMULATION APPROACH TO CROWDING IN OUTDOOR RECREATION

Chang, F L *see* THE CHRISTIAN RURAL MOVEMENT (CCC252)

Chang, I-Ching *see*
- A CRITICAL REVIEW OF CHU CHIH SIN'S "WHAT THING IS JESUS" (CCC11)
- DISCUSSING CHRISTIANITY WITH CHAN AND TSEN (CCC12)

Chang, Li-sheng chu *see* THE RELIGIOUS FAITH OF DISTINGUISHED PEOPLE OF THE WORLD (CCC13)

Chang, Nae-Ch'i *see* THE NEXT WORLD WAR AND CHINA (CCC14)

Chang, Pe-Huai *see* THE CANON AND TEXT OF THE NEW TESTAMENT (CCC15)

Chang, Pei-ying *see* RURAL WORSHIP SERVICES (CCC110)

Chang, Shao-ching *see* OLD TESTAMENT CHARACTERS (CCC256)

Chang, Shih-Chang *see* CHRISTIANITY AND THE SOCIALIST MOVEMENT (CCC16)

Chang, T T *see* SINO-PORTUGUESE TRADE FROM 1514 TO 1644

Chang, Tao-hsing *see* RUSSIA, CHINA AND THE CHINESE EASTERN RAILWAY

Chang, Tzu-ping *see* THE CHILDREN OF GOD (CCC17)

Chang, Wan-Ju *see* THE GREAT GULF (CCC18)

Chang-chi-chih *see* BIOGRAPHY

CHANGCHUN DIZHI XUEYUAN XUEBAO – Journal of Changchun College of Geology. In Chinese but English abstracts to the main articles. F p199 – 9 – $4.50f – cc Microforms [073]

CHANGE – (v3-14. 5,6. v7-14. 9) – 1-14. 1969-82 – 1 – us UMI [370]

THE CHANGE IN OXYGEN CONSUMPTION OVER TIME IN DOWNHILL VERSUS LEVEL GRADE RUNNING / Pein, Wayne E – 1989 – 60p 1mf – 9 – $4.00 – us Microform Publ [617]

CHANGE: LE CHANGE DES MONNAIES ETRANGERES – Current Banknotes. Quarterly, cumulative – 15 – FF210.00 per year (y) – fr CHANGE [332]

THE CHANGED CROSS AND OTHER RELIGIOUS POEMS – New ed. London: S. Low, Marston, Searle, & Rivington, 1877. 228p. Includes indexes – 1 – us U.W. Library [810]

A CHANGED EXCHANGE BROKER (CCC213) = IH KO SHANG HSI SHANG JEN TI KAI P'IEN / Li, Kuan-shen – (In Chinese) – 6th rev ed. Shanghai: Christian Literature Society, 1939 – 1r – 1 – 1984-B500 – us A.T.L.A. [240]

LE CHANGEMENT DE NATIONALITE DES SOCIETES COMMERCIALES / Demassieux, G – Lille, 1928 – 4mf – 1 – ILM-3207/1 – ne IDC [327]

CHANGES IN BLOOD RESISTIVITY OVER A SUB-MAXIMAL EXERCISE BOUT / De la Cruz Napoli, Jose – Indiana University, 1994 – 1mf – 9 – $4.00 – PH1457 – us Microform Publ [612]

CHANGES IN CLINICAL STUDENTS' PERCEPTIONS OF DEVELOPMENTAL PHYSICAL EDUCATION AND EFFECTIVE TEACHING / Hammel, Patricia A – University of Wisconsin-La Crosse – 1mf – 9 – $4.00 – PE3595 – us Microform Publ [370]

CHANGES IN COGNITIVE APPRAISALS AND METABOLIC INDICES OF PHYSICAL EXERTION DURING AT TWO-HOUR RUN / Acevedo, E O – 1989 – 2mf – 9 – $8.00 – us Microform Publ [613]

CHANGES IN SHIFTING CULTIVATION IN AFRICA – 1984 – 67p – it F.A.O. [631]

CHANGES IN SHIFTING CULTIVATION IN AFRICA : SEVEN CASE STUDIES – 1985 – 192p – it F.A.O. [631]

CHANGES IN SPINAL EXCITABILITY PRECEDING A VOLUNTARY MOVEMENT IN YOUNG AND OLD ADULTS / Burke, J – 1991 – 6mf – 9 – $24.00 – us Microform Publ [613]

CHANGES IN THE DOCUMENTS OF BRITISH INDIA CAUSED BY THE GOVERNMENT OF INDIA ACT 1935 / Cabeen, Violet Abbott – [n.p. 1939] – us Res Libr [950]

CHANGES MADE BY THE 1951 LEGISLATURE IN KANSAS LIBRARY LAWS / Drury, James Westbrook – Lawrence, Bureau of Government Research, University of Kansas 1952. LL-241 – 1 – us L of C Photodup [340]
CH'ANG-HUA HSIEN-CHIH – 1897, 11, 1. BCH-641 2 – 8 – ne IDC [950]
CHANGING ATTITUDES TOWARD PHYSICALLY DISABLED PERSONS USING A VIDEOTAPE SPORT INTERVENTION / Bett, A – 1991 – 2mf – 9 – $8.00 – us Microform Publ [360]
CHANGING PATTERNS AND TRENDS IN FEED UTILIZATION – 1983 – 65p – it F.A.O. [636]
THE CHANGING ROLE OF THE TEACHER AND ITS INFLUENCE ON PREPARATION FOR THE PROFESSION AND ON IN-SERVICE TRAINING IN THAILAND / Thailand. Ministry of Education – Bangkok, 1975 – 1mf – 9 – DE-286/1 – ne IDC [370]
CHANGING RUSSIA / Graham, Stephen – London, New York: John Lane, 1913 – 1mf – us A.T.L.A. [947]
CHANGING TIMES – (v20- 1966- 5,6 v24- 1970- 9) – 1- 1947- – 1 – us UMI [380]
CHANGING VIEW-POINT IN RELIGIOUS THOUGHT AND OTHER SHORT STUDIES / Colestock, Henry Thomas – New York: E.B. Treat, 1901. 1 fiche – 9 – us A.T.L.A. [240]
CHANGING WOMEN – Portland OR. Oct 15 1971-May 31 1973 – 1 – us U.O. Library [071]
CHANGJIANG RIBAO = CHANGJIANG DAILY – China. 1983- . M/D82 – 1 – $55.00r – cc Microforms [072]
CH'ANG-LO HSIEN-CHIH – 1763. 10, 1. Lacking: prefaces. BCH-558 2 – 8 – ne IDC [950]
CHANG-P'ING HSIEN-CHIH – 1830, 10, 1. BCH-582 2 – 8 – ne IDC [950]
CHANGYAN BAO – The Verax. Jul-Oct 1898. 7 fiches. F C26 – 9 – $36.00 – cc Microforms [073]
CHANH DAO – Saigon, South Vietnam. 1965-67 – 1 – us UMI [072]
Chanlaire, Pierre G *see* DESCRIPTION TOPOGRAPHIQUE ET STATISTIQUE
CHANNEL ISLANDS, 1911 : BRITISH ISLES CENSUS DIRECTORIES PROJECT, ENGLAND. VOL 206 – 5mf – 9 – A$33.00 – at Vine [941]
THE CHANNEL TO QUEBEC AND HARBOUR IMPROVEMENTS – Montreal? 187?. 02149. (Pre-1900 Canadiana) – 9 – cn C.I.H.M. [971]
Channell, Leonard Stewart *see* HISTORY OF COMPTON COUNTY: AND SKETCHES OF THE EASTERN TOWNSHIPS, DISTRICT OF ST FRANCIS, AND SHERBROOKE COUNTY
Channing, William E *see*
- UNITARIAN CHRISTIANITY
- WILLIAM ELLERY CHANNING PAPERS, 1791-1892
- WORKS

THE CHANNINGS / Wood, Ellen – British Fiction Archive: Unit 1 – 9 – uk Bell [830]
CHANOINE JEAN BERGERON, 1868-1956 : BIO-BIBLIOGRAPHIE ANALYTIQUE / Bergeron, Juliana – 1958. SEM105P4 – 2mf – 9 – cn Bibl Nat [240]
LES CHANOINES REGULIERS DE SAINT AUGUSTIN. APERCU HISTORIQUE / Ette, A van – Cholet, 1953 – 5mf – 8 – Dfl22.00 – ne Slangenburg [240]
LA CHANSON CANADIENNE : ORIGINES, EVOLUTION, EPANOUISSEMENT / Morin, Victor – Toronto, 1928. SEM105P771 – 1mf – 9 – Can$2.25 – cn Bibl Nat [780]
LE CHANSONNIER CANADIEN DU MICHIGAN – Mich., 1886. 00559. (Pre-1900 Canadiana) – 9 – cn C.I.H.M. [971]
LE CHANSONNIER DES FAMILLES : LYRE CANADIENNE – 3e ed. Montreal: J.B. Rolland & Fils, Editeurs, [1883?] SEM105P1339 – 3mf – 9 – Can$6.75 – cn Bibl Nat [780]
LES CHANSONS DE COLIN MUSET / Muset, Colin; ed by Bedier, Joseph – Paris: H. Champion, 1912. xiii,44p – 1 – us U.W. Library [810]
CHANSONS DU DODECANESE / Baud-Bovy, Samuel – 2v. 1935-38. Modern Greek Dodecanese folk songs – 1 – us I.U. Libraries [390]
CHANSONS ET CHANSONNIERS / Avenel, Henri – Paris: C. Marpon et E. Flammarion, 1889.431p. 9 fiches. (Literature Collection) – 9 – 22.00 – fr Bibl Nationale [780]
CHANSONS ET DANSES DE LA GASCOGNE – 1945 – 1 – us I.U. Libraries [390]
CHANSONS ET MONOLOGUES: PAROLES ET MUSIQUE / Bruant, Aristide – Paris: H. Geffroy, (1896-97). 3v. 1200p. ill.Includes music – 1 – us U.W. Library [780]
CHANSONS ET RONDES ENFANTINES DES PROVINCES DE LA FRANCE / Weckerlin, Jean Baptiste – 1889 – 1 – us I.U. Libraries [390]
CHANSONS POPULAIRES DE LA FRANCE – 1891 – 1 – us I.U. Libraries [390]
CHANSONS POPULAIRES DU CANADA / Gagnon, Ernest – Quebec: Bureaux du "Foyer canadien", 1865. SEM16P140 – 1r – 5 – Can$9.00 – cn Bibl Nat [780]
CHANT ET BAISER / Godard, B – (Inscribed to Arthur Hartmann by composer) – Ms – 5 – us Sibley [780]
CHANT ET MUSIQUE DANS LE CULTE CHRETIEN / Gelineau, J – Paris, 1962 – 4mf – 8 – Dfl19.00 – ne Slangenburg [240]
LE CHANT LITURGIQUE COLLECTIF A L'EPOQUE PATRISTIQUE / Malherbe, G – Bruxelles, 1923 – 1mf – 8 – Dfl6.00 – ne Slangenburg [240]
LE CHANT POPULAIRE DANS NOS EGLISES: DOUZE CANTIQUES NOUVEAUX: EMBELISSONS NOS CIMITIERES / Gingras, Apollinaire – Quebec?: N. Hardy, 1885.04104.(Pre-1900 Canadiana) – 9 – cn C.I.H.M. [240]
CHANTA LEKSIKON / Wright, Allen – A Choctaw in English definition. 1880 – 1 – 11.27 – us Baptist [490]
CHANTE LA VIE... : RECUEIL DE CHANSONS D'HIER ET D'AUJOURD'HUI AVEC ACCORDS DE GUITARE – [Saint-Mathieu-du-Parc: Collection Chante la vie, 1988?]. SEM105P1776 – 5mf – 9 – Can$11.25 – cn Bibl Nat [780]
CHANTECLER – Paris. 1er mai 1926-1er aout 1931 – 1 – fr A.C.R.P.P. [073]
CHANTECLERC – Quebec, Canada. 22 dec 1917-v1 n9. 23 fev 1918 – 1r – 1 – Can$25.00 – cn Can Microfilming [072]
Chanter, C *see* FERNY COMBES. A RAMBLE AFTER FERNS IN THE GLENS AND VALLEYS OF DEVONSHIRE
CHANTIERS COOPERATIFS – Paris. juin 1932-mai 1934. Suite de: Cahiers bleus. devenu: Le Nouvel age voir a ces titres – 1 – fr A.C.R.P.P. [073]
Chan-toon *see* THE NATURE AND VALUE OF JURISPRUDENCE
Chantre, B *see* A TRAVERS L'ARMENIE RUSSE...
CHANTRES ET CHANT DES PSAUMES A GENEVE – 16e siecle. [n.p. 19–] – us Res Libr [780]
CHANTS DE BEAUTE ET DE VIE RECUEILLIS CHEZ LES PEULS NOMADES DU NORD CAMEROUN / Labatut, Roger – 1975 – 9 – fr Orientalistes [306]
LES CHANTS DE LA MESSE AUX 8TH ET 9TH SIECLE / Froger, L – Paris, 1950 – 1mf – 8 – Dfl6.00 – ne Slangenburg [240]
CHANTS DE LA VEILLEE – Montreal: Typographie de Duvernay freres, 1855. SEM105P1356 – 2mf – 9 – Can$4.50 – cn Bibl Nat [780]
CHANTS ET CHANSONS EN PAYS AKYE : VALEUR EXPRESSIVE, VALEUR DIDACTIQUE / Aye, Agnes – 1985 – us Res Libr [780]
CHANTS, POEMES SAINT-SIMONIENS – Les Saint-Simoniens, 1825-1834. 6974 – 9 – fr Hachette [335]
CHANTS POPULAIRES D'AUVERGNE – 1910 – 1 – us I.U. Libraries [390]
CHANTS SACRES : 60 MOTETS AVEC ACCOMPT. D'ORGUE OU PIANO POUR MESSES, SALUTS, MARIAGE, OFFICES DIVERS / Gounod, C – (Sibley has only v1 (solos and duets) and v2 (trios and quatre voix EGALES) – Paris: Le Beau, [187-?] – 1 – us Sibley [780]
Chao, Hsia-yun *see* LIFE'S EXPERIENCES (CCC64)
Chao, Tsung-fu *see* OLD TESTAMENT HISTORY (CCC65)
Chao, Tzu-ch'en *see*
- CHI TU CHIAO CHE HSUEH (CCC66)
- CHRISTIAN ETHICS (CCC70)
- CHRISTIAN FELLOWSHIP HYMNS (CCC80)
- FOUR TALKS ON THEOLOGY (CCC78)
- HSUEH JEN (CCC74)
- HYMNS FOR THE PEOPLE (CCC75)
- I AM CAPTURED (CCC81)
- AN INTERPRETATION OF CHRISTIANITY (CCC68)
- JESUS AND MY CHARACTER (CCC71)
- LIFE OF JESUS (CCC82)
- THE LIFE OF ST. PAUL (CCC79)
- THE MEANING OF THE CHURCH (CCC67)
- MY EXPERIENCE IN PRISON (CCC73)
- THE RECONSTRUCTION OF CHRISTIAN CHURCH IN CHINA (CCC72)
- THE THEOLOGY OF KARL BARTH (CCC76)

Chao, Tzu-chen *see*
- CENTRAL FAITH OF CHRISTIANITY (CCC69)
- A CRITICAL STUDY OF THE FIRST FOUR CHAPTERS OF RETHINKING MISSIONS (CCC77)

Chao, Wei-jan *see* THE CALL OF A CHILD (CCC83)
CHAO-CH'ING FU-CHIH – 1760, 28. BCH-622 2 – 8 – ne IDC [950]
CHAO-CHOU CHIH – 1838, 6. BCH-672 2 – 8 – ne IDC [950]
CHAOS – 1,5,6,9 – us A.I.P. [530]
CHAOS – 1962-1964 – 1r – 1 – at Corangamite [980]
LE CHAOS ESPAGNOL, EVITERNONS-NOUS LA CONTAGION? / Bardoux, Jacques – Paris, 1937. Fiche W 745. (Blodgett Collection of Spanish Civil War Pamphlets) – 9 – us H.U. College Libr [946]
CHAOS IN SPAIN / Bardoux, Jacques – London, 1937. Fiche W 746. (Blodgett Collection of Spanish Civil War Pamphlets) – 9 – us H.U. College Libr [946]
CHAOS, SOLITONS AND FRACTALS – 1,5,69 – us UMI [510]
CH'AO-YANG HSIEN-CHIH – 1884, 22, 1. BCH-615 2 – 8 – ne IDC [950]
Chapado Garcia, Eusebio Maria *see* HISTORIA GENERAL DEL DERECHO ESPANOL
CHAPAEV / Furmanov, Dmitrii – Izd. Trete. Moskva: Gos. izd-vo, 1925 – 1 – CSUX89-B6548 – us Hoover Inst Photo [999]
CHAPAEV / Furmanov, Dmitrii – Moskva: Gos. izd-vo, 1923 – 1 – CSUX89-B6387 – us Hoover Inst Photo [999]
Chapais, Jean Charles *see*
- ARBOR DAY: A FEW ADVICES TO FARMERS ON THE PLANTING OF FOREST AND ORNAMENTAL TREES
- LE JOUR DE LA FETE DES ARBRES: QUELQUES CONSEILS AUX CULTIVATEURS SUR LA PLANTATION DES ARBRES FORESTIERS ET D'ORNEMENT
- LA VIGNE: SA CULTURE ET SA TAILLE

Chapais, Thomas *see*
- LES CONGREGATIONS ENSEIGNANTES ET LE BREVET DE CAPACITE
- LE COURRIER DU CANADA
- DISCOURS ET CONFERENCES
- DISCOURS SUR LA LOI DE L'INSTRUCTION PUBLIQUE: PRONONCE...DEVANT LE CONSEIL LEGISLATIF, LE 10 JANVIER 1898
- DISCOURS SUR LA LOI DE L'INSTRUCTION PUBLIQUE: PRONONCE...DEVANT LE CONSEIL LEGISLATIF, LES 2 ET 3 MARS 1899
- LE SERMENT DU ROI ET LES CATHOLIQUES

CHAPARRAL (COLLEGE OF THE DESERT) – Palm Desert, CA. 1962-79 – 3r – 1 – $150.00 – R02591 – us Library Micro [071]
CHAP-BOOK : SEMI-MONTHLY. A MISCELLANY AND REVIEW OF BELLES LETTRES – Chicago. v1-9. 1894-98 – 1r – 1 – us Ross [073]
CHAPBOOK – London. n1-40. 1919-25 – 1r – 1 – us Ross [073]
THE CHAP-BOOK – Chicago. v. 1-9. May 15 1894-July 1 1898 – 1 – us NY Public [800]
Chapdelaine, Cecile *see* BIBLIOGRAPHIE ANALYTIQUE DE LA DELINQUANCE JUVENILE OU DE L'INADAPTATION FAMILIALE ET SOCIALE DES MAL-AIMES...
Chapek, Constance L *see* THE EFFECTS OF A TEN-WEEK STEP AEROBIC TRAINING PROGRAM ON AEROBIC CAPACITY OF COLLEGE-AGED FEMALES
Chapelain, Jean *see* LETTRES DE JEAN CHAPELAIN, DE L'ACADEMIE FRANCAISE
LE CHAPELET DE L'AMOUR DE DIEU: AVEC DEUX AUTRES EXERCISES PORTANT INDULGENCES – (Quebec: L. Brousseau, 1870). 04121. (Pre-1900 Canadiana) – 9 – cn C.I.H.M. [240]
Chapelle, Howard Irving *see* THE BARK CANOES AND SKIN BOATS OF NORTH AMERICA
Chapelle, P *see*
- L'HEUREUZ DEPIT
- SIX DUETTE POUR DEUX VIOLONS...OP. 3
- SIX DUETTI POUR DEUX VIOLONS...OP. 6

CHAPERON : GENEALOGIE / Chaperon, Henri – Brest: Roger, 1876 – fr Armell [920]
Chaperon, Elisee *see* BIBLIOGRAPHIE DE MONSIEUR L'ABBE J.W. LAVERDIERE, GEOLOGUE-PRETRE
Chaperon, Henri *see* CHAPERON
Chapin, Anna Alice *see*
- THE STORY OF THE RHINEGOLD

Chapin, Gardner B *see* TALES OF THE ST LAWRENCE
Chapin, Howard M *see*
- LIST OF ROGER WILLIAMS' WRITINGS
- TRADING POST OF ROGER WILLIAMS WITH THOSE OF JOHN WILCOX AND RICHARD SMITH

UN CHAPITRE DE DESHONNEUR NATIONAL / Chamberlain, L T – 1912 – 1mf – 1 – ILM-2361/1 – ne IDC [327]
CHAPLAIN SMITH AND THE BAPTISTS / Guild, Reuben A – or Life, journals, letters, and addresses of the Rev. Hezekiah Smith, D.D. 1737-1805 – 1 – 15.01 – us Baptist [240]
CHAPLAINCY – v1-. 1978- – 1,5,6,9 – us UMI [240]
THE CHAPLAINS AND CLERGY OF THE REVOLUTION / Headley, JT – New York: Scribner, 1864, c1861 – 1mf – us A.T.L.A. [240]
Chapleau, Joseph Adolphe *see*
- LE BANQUET DONNE A SIR JOHN A. MACDONALD A QUEBEC, LE 15 OCTOBRE 1879/DISCOURS.
- THE CONSTITUTION AND GOVERNMENT OF CANADA: FROM AN OFFICIAL DOCUMENT, DECEMBER 1893
- CONSTITUTION ET GOUVERNEMENT DU CANADA: EXTRAIT D'UNE PUBLICATION OFFICIELLE, DECEMBRE 1893
- DISCOURS PROGRAMME...AU COMITE CENTRAL DU PARTI CONSERVATEUR A MONTREAL, 10 FEVRIER 1891
- DISCOURS...: PRONONCE A LA GRANDE ASSEMBLEE TENUE A LEVIS, DIMANCHE, 10 MARS
- DISCOURS PRONONCE...AU BANQUET DES OUVRIERS A OTTAWA, LE 18 OCTOBRE 1888
- DISCOURS...: SUBVENTIONS AUX CHEMINS DE FER: RECLAMATIONS DE LA PROVINCE DE QUEBEC (COMPTE RENDU OFFICIEL), CHAMBRE DES COMMUNES, 12 AVRIL 1884
- DISCOURSE DE L'HON. J.A. CHAPLEAU A L'OCCASION DE LA MOTION CENSURANT LE MINISTERE POUR AVOIR PERMIS L'EXECUTION DE LOUIS RIEL
- DISCOURS...EN PROPOSANT LA VENTE DU CHEMIN DE FER QUEBEC, MONTREAL, OTTAWA ET OCCIDENTAL A L'ASSEMBLEE LEGISLATIVE, SEANCES DES 27 ET 28 MARS 1882
- DISCOURS...PRONONCE A L'ASSEMBLEE DE SAINT-LAURENT, COMTE DE JACQUES-CARTIER, LE 6 SEPTEMBRE 1883
- DISCOURS...PRONONCE A STE.THERESE, LE 3 NOVEMBRE 1881
- DISCOURS...SUR L'EXECUTION DE LOUIS RIEL: CHAMBRE DES COMMUNES, 24 MARS 1886
- DU DROIT INTERNATIONALE: DISCOURS PRONONCE A L'UNIVERSITE LAVAL, A MONTREAL, LE 22 JUIN 1886
- L'HON. J. A. CHAPLEAU, RETOUR D'EUROPE: DEMONSTRATION ENTHOUSIASTE: ADDRESSE DE BIENVENUE: DISCOURS EN REPONSE: AVANT TOUT SOYONS CANADIENS: NOTRE POSITION, NOS DEVOIRS, MONTREAL 24 AVRIL 1889
- HON. J. A. CHAPLEAU: WELCOMED AT MONTREAL ON HIS RETURN FROM EUROPE, 24TH APRIL, 1889, HIS ADDRESS IN REPLY: THE POLITICAL POSITION AND RESPONSIBILITIES OF CANADIANS
- LEON 13, HOMME D'ETAT
- LEON 13, HOMME D'ETAT: DISCOURS PRONONCE...LE 11 JANVIER, 1888
- THE POSITION OF THE PROVINCE OF QUEBEC IN THE DOMINION OF CANADA: DELIVERED IN THE HOUSE OF COMMONS ON THE RESOLUTIONS PROVIDING FOR SUBSIDIES TO LOCAL RAILWAY, 12TH APRIL, 1884
- THE QUEBEC COUP D'ETAT: ELOQUENT SPEECH
- THE RIEL QUESTION
- SPEECH OF HON. J. A. CHAPLEAU TO BLAME THE GOVERNMENT FOR HAVING ALLOWED THE EXECUTION OF LOUIS RIEL
- SPEECH...DELIVERED AT ST LAURENT, COUNTY OF JACQUES CARTIER, ON THE 6TH SEPTEMBER, 1883

- SPEECH...ON CANADIAN PACIFIC RAILWAY RESOLUTIONS, HOUSE OF COMMONS, 16TH JUNE 1885

CHAPLEAU SENTINEL – Chapleau, Ontario, CN. 1981-82 – 2r – 1 – cn Commonwealth Micro [072]

Chaplin, J *see*
- LIFE OF CHARLES SUMNER
- LIFE OF HENRY DUNSTER

Chaplin, Thomas B *see* PLANTATION JOURNAL

Chapman *see*
- ANNALS OF NEWBERRY COUNTY
- TRAVELS IN THE INTERIOR OF SOUTH AFRICA

Chapman, Arthur Thomas *see* AN INTRODUCTION TO THE PENTATEUCH

Chapman, Berlin B *see*
- "HOW THE CHEROKEE ACQUIRED AND DISPOSED OF THE OUTLET [OKLAHOMA]"
- OKLAHOMA TERRITORY AND THE NATIONAL ARCHIVES

Chapman, Charles *see*
- HOW TO REASON: A LECTURE DELIVERED BEFORE THE YOUNG MEN'S ASSOCIATION OF ZION CHURCH, AND PUBLLISHED AT THEIR REQUEST, 2ND NOVEMBER, 1871
- THE PECULIARITIES OF DIVINE REVELATION IN ITS EARLIEST STAGE, OR, GENESIS FROM A MODERN POINT OF VIEW
- PRE-ORGANIC EVOLUTION AND THE BIBLICAL IDEA OF GOD

CHAPMAN, CHARLES C. AND CO *see*
- HISTORY OF ELKHART COUNTY
- HISTORY OF FULTON COUNTY
- HISTORY OF KENT COUNTY
- HISTORY OF KNOX COUNTY
- HISTORY OF LAPORTE COUNTY
- HISTORY OF PIKE COUNTY
- HISTORY OF SAGINAW COUNTY
- HISTORY OF ST. JOSEPH COUNTY
- HISTORY OF WASHTENAW COUNTY

Chapman, Clowry *see* TRADE-MARKS

Chapman, David W *see* FROM DATA TO ACTION

Chapman, Edward John *see*
- EAST AND WEST: A SUMMER'S IDLENESS
- A MEMORY
- THE MINERAL INDICATOR: A PRACTICAL GUIDE TO THE DETERMINATION OF GENERALLY-OCCURRING MINERALS
- AN OUTLINE OF THE GEOLOGY OF CANADA: BASED ON A SUBDIVISION OF THE PROVINCES INTO NATURAL AREAS
- THE PILGRIMAGE TO KEVLAAR: A PARAPHRASE FROM HEINE
- PRACTICAL INSTRUCTIONS FOR THE DETERMINATION BY FURNACE ASSAY OF GOLD AND SILVER IN ROCKS AND ORES
- PROFESSOR CHAPMAN'S REPORT ON COLLINS COAL AREA, CAPE BRETON
- REPORT OF THE IVES MINE: BOULTON TOWNSHIP, P.Q
- REPORT ON THE GALWAY MINING LOCATION, COUNTY OF PETERBOROUGH, ONTARIO
- REPORT ON THE PROPERTY OF THE ST ONGE GOLD MINING COMPANY

Chapman, Edward Mortimer *see* THE DYNAMIC OF CHRISTIANITY

Chapman, Harlan P *see* LETTERS, MS P.P.

Chapman, James *see* JESUS CHRIST AND THE PRESENT AGE

Chapman, John *see*
- BISHOP GORE AND THE CATHOLIC CLAIMS
- NOTES ON THE EARLY HISTORY OF THE VULGATE GOSPELS

Chapman, John A *see* HISTORY OF EDGEFIELD COUNTY

Chapman, John Wilbur *see*
- PRESENT-DAY EVANGELISM
- RECORDS, 1880-1918
- S.H. HADLEY OF WATER STREET

Chapman, Mary Weems *see* MOTHER COBB, OR, SIXTY YEARS' WALK WITH GOD

Chapman, PT *see* A HISTORY OF JOHNSON COUNTY, ILLINOIS

Chapman, Samuel M *see* PAPERS

Chapman, Tom *see* COMPARATIVE HYDROLOGY

Chapman, William *see*
- A PROPOS DE LA GUERRE HISPANO-AMERICAINE
- DEUX COPAINS: REPLIQUE A MM. FRECHETTE ET SAUVALLE
- LES FEUILLES D'ERABLE
- GOLD MINES OF BEAUCE
- MINES D'OR DE LA BEAUCE
- LES QUEBECQUOISES

CHAPMAN'S GAZETTEER OF THE PROVINCE OF AUCKLAND – (Details of places, many of which no longer exist) – Auckland, c1867 – 1mf – 9 – NZ$3.00 – 0-908797-12-5 – NZNB 1037 – nz BAB [980]

Chappele, S *see* EIGHT ANTHEMS ON [SELECTED] PSALMS

Chappell, E *see* NARRATIVE OF A VOYAGE TO HUDSON BAY IN H.M.S. ROSAMOND

Chappell, Louis Watson *see* JOHN HENRY

CHAPPELL REGISTER – Chappell, NE. -w. Mar. 1888; Jun. 1892; Oct. 1895-Feb.1901; Apr. 1901-Apr. 1925; Jun. 1925- – 1 – us NE Hist [071]

Chappell, William *see* THE PREACHER, OR THE ART AND METHOD OF PREACHING

Chaprusha *see* GEROI NE- REVOLIUTSII

A CHAPTER OF CANADIAN HISTORY – 1876? 02957. (Pre-1900 Canadiana) – 9 – cn C.I.H.M. [971]

A CHAPTER OF MISSION HISTORY IN MODERN JAPAN : BEING A SKETCH FOR THE PERIOD SINCE 1869 AND A REPORT FOR THE YEARS SINCE 1893... / Pettee, James Horace – [s.l: s.n, 1895?] – 1mf – 9 – 0-8370-6302-7 – 1985-0302 – us A.T.L.A. [240]

CHAPTERS FROM SOME MEMOIRS / Ritchie, Anne Thackeray – London, New York: Macmillan, 1894 – 1 roll – 1 – 1-55879-507-3 – uk Libr Preservation [420]

CHAPTERS FROM THE HISTORY OF THE FREE CHURCH OF SCOTLAND / Walker, Norman Lockhart – Edinburgh: Oliphant, Anderson and Ferrier [1895?] – 1mf – us A.T.L.A. [240]

CHAPTERS FROM THE RELIGIOUS HISTORY OF SPAIN CONNECTED WITH THE INQUISITION / Lea, Henry Charles – Philadelphia: Lea Bros., 1890 – 2mf – us A.T.L.A. [240]

CHAPTERS IN THE EARLY HISTORY OF THE CHURCH OF WELLS, A.D. 1136-1333, FROM DOCUMENTS IN POSSESSION OF THE DEAN AND CHAPTER OF WELLS / Church, Charles Marcus – London: E. Stock, 1894. xiii,450p. illus. pl.plans – 1 – us U.W. Library [941]

CHAPTERS OF EARLY ENGLISH CHURCH HISTORY / Bright, William – Oxford: Clarendon Press, 1897 – 2mf – us A.T.L.A. [240]

CHAPTERS ON INTERNATIONAL LAW... / Charteris, A H – 1940 – 2mf – 1 – ILM-2105/1 – ne IDC [327]

CHAPTERS ON JEWISH LITERATURE / Abrahams, Israel – (Includes index and bibliographies) – Philadelphia: The Jewish Publication Society of America, 1899 – 1mf – 9 – 0-8370-2032-8 – 1985-0032 – us A.T.L.A. [470]

CHAPTERS ON TREES. A POPULAR ACCOUNT OF THEIR NATURE AND USES / Gregg, Mary Kirby & Kirby, Elizabeth – London, Paris, New York: Cassell, Petter & Galpin, 1873. 320p. illus – 1 – us U.W. Library [634]

Chapuis, F *see* CATALOGUE DES LARVES COLEOPTERES CONNUES JUSQU'A CE JOUR

Chapurskii, V P *see* GRAZHDANSKOE PROTSESSUAL'NOE ZAKONODATEL'STVO SSSR; SOIUZNYKH RESPUBLIK

Chapurskii, VP *see* GRAZHDANSKOE PROTSESSUAL'NOE ZAKONODATEL'STVO SSSR; SOIUZNYKH RESPUBLIK

Chapus, G S *see* HISTOIRE DES ROIS

Chapus, G-S *see* HISTOIRE DES POPULATIONS DE MADAGASCAR

Chaput, Marcel *see*
- LE REPUBLICAIN
- LA SANTE

Chaput-Rolland, Solange et al *see* POINTS DE VUE

Chaqueri, Cosroe *see*
- ASNAD-I TARIKHI-I JUBNISH-I KARGARI, SUSIYAL-DIMUKRASI VA KUMUNISTI-I IRAN
- ASNAD-I TARIKHI-I JUNBISH-I KARGARI, SUSIYAL-DIMUKRASI VA KUMUNISTI IRAN
- ASNAD-I TARIKHI-I JUNBISH-I KARGARI, SUSIYAL-DIMUKRASI VA KUMUNISTI-I IRAN

THE CHARACEAE OF AMERICA. / Allen, T F – New York, 1888. B-6336 2 – 8 – ne IDC [580]

THE CHARACTER AND CALL OF THE CHURCH OF ENGLAND : A CHARGE DELIVERED AT HIS SECOND VISITATION OF THE DIOCESE OF CNATERBURY IN FEBRUARY, 1912 / Davidson, Randall Thomas – London; New York: Macmillan, 1912 – 1mf – us A.T.L.A. [240]

CHARACTER AND COMPOSITION OF THE TURKISH PRESS, (1939-1944) – [Washington, DC]: Office of Strategic Services, Research and Analysis Branch, 1945 – us Res Libr [070]

THE CHARACTER, CLAIMS AND PRACTICAL WORKINGS OF FREEMASONRY / Finney, Charles G – Cincinnati: Western Tract and Book Society, c1869 – 1mf – us A.T.L.A. [900]

CHARACTER OF GOD / Todd, John – Northampton: Bridgman and Childs, 1867, c1856 – 1mf – 9 – 0-8370-5660-8 – 1985-3660 – us A.T.L.A. [210]

CHARACTER OF JESUS / Jefferson, Charles Edward – New York: Thomas Y. Crowell, 1908. 1 fiche – 9 – us A.T.L.A. [240]

THE CHARACTER OF JESUS : FORBIDDING HIS POSSIBLE CLASSIFICATION WITH MEN / Bushnell, Horace – (Includes bibliographical references) – New York:Charles Scribner, 1905, c1886 – 1mf – 9 – 0-8370-3063-3 – 1985-1063 – us A.T.L.A. [240]

THE CHARACTER OF JESUS (CCC175) : A SHORT COURSE OF BIBLE STUDIES DESIGNED FOR STUDENT ENQUIRERS / Hsieh, Hung-lai – (In Chinese) – 4th ed. Shanghai: Association Press of China, 1920 – 1r – 1 – 1984-B500 – us A.T.L.A. [240]

THE CHARACTER OF JESUS: FORBIDDING HIS POSSIBLE CLASSIFICATION WITH MEN / Bushnell, Horace – New York: Charles Scribner, 1905. 1 fiche – 9 – us A.T.L.A. [240]

CHARACTER STUDIES / Oates, James F – New York: International Comm. YMCAs, 1903. 1 fiche – 9 – us A.T.L.A. [240]

CHARACTER STUDIES : SOME OF THE LORD'S "MIGHTY MEN": A COURSE OF SUNDAY NIGHT LECTURES GIVEN IN THE FIRST BAPTIST CHURCH, KANSAS CITY, MO., DURING THE WINTER OF 1893-94 / Vassar, T E – Kansas City, Mo.: Pearl Ptg. Co., 1894 – 1mf – us A.T.L.A. [240]

CHARACTER STUDIES IN GENESIS / Blodgett, May N – Chicago: American Com. Y.W.C.A., 1900. 1 fiche – 9 – us A.T.L.A. [220]

CHARACTERES GENERUM PLANTARUM / Forster, J R & Forster, J G A – Londini. 1776. B-1273 2 – 8 – ne IDC [580]

CHARACTERISATION OF KENANA CATTLE AT UM BANEIN, SUDAN / Saeed, A M et al – 1987 – 9 – $8.00 – 92-9053-119-3 – et ILRI [636]

CHARACTERISTIC DIFFERENCES OF THE FOUR GOSPELS / Jukes, Andrew John – London: James Nisbet, 1867. 1 fiche – 9 – us A.T.L.A. [240]

THE CHARACTERISTIC DIFFERENCES OF THE FOUR GOSPELS : CONSIDERED AS REVEALING VARIOUS RELATIONS OF THE LORD JESUS CHRIST / Jukes, Andrew John – 4th ed. London: James Nisbet, 1867 – 1mf – 9 – 0-8370-3816-2 – 1985-1816 – us A.T.L.A. [220]

CHARACTERISTICS COMMON TO LAWYERS / O'Connor, Johnson – Hoboken, N.J.: Human Engineering Laboratories, Steven Institute of Technology, 1934. LL-2254 – 1 – us L of C Photodup [340]

CHARACTERISTICS FROM THE WRITINGS OF ARCHBISHOP ULLATHORNE / Ullathorne, William Bernard – (Includes index) – London: Burns & Oates; New York: Catholic Publ Society Co, 1889 – 1mf – 9 – 0-8370-7514-9 – 1986-1514 – us A.T.L.A. [240]

CHARACTERISTICS OF CHRISTIANITY / Leathes, Stanley – 1884 – 9 – us A.T.L.A. [240]

CHARACTERISTICS OF MEN, MANNERS, OPINIONS, TIMES, ETC / Shaftesbury, Anthony Ashley Cooper – Introd. and notes by John M. Robertson. London: G. Richards, 1900. 2v – 1 – us U.W. Library [840]

CHARACTERISTICS OF THE GOSPEL MIRACLES / Westcott, Brooke Foss – 1859 – 1 – us A.T.L.A. [240]

CHARACTERISTICS OF THOUGHT PROCESSES AND KNOWLEDGE STRUCTURES OF NOVICE TENNIS PLAYERS / Oguchi-Chen, Fumiko & Sinclair, Gary D – 1990 – 2mf – 9 – $8.00 – us Microform Publ [150]

CHARACTERS OF MODERN TIMES (CCC283) : FOR MIDDLE SCHOOLS AND GENERAL READING / Shining Light Staff – (In Chinese) – Hong Kong: Bible Book and Tract Depot, 1952 – 1r – 1 – 1984-6622 – us A.T.L.A. [240]

THE CHARACTERS OF THE OLD TESTAMENT : IN A SERIES OF SERMONS / Williams, Isaac – London:Rivingtons, 1887 – 1mf – 9 – 0-8370-5856-2 – 1985-3856 – us A.T.L.A. [220]

CHARAKTERBILD JESU = A SKETCH OF THE CHARACTER OF JESUS. A BIBLICAL ESSAY / Schenkel, Daniel – (In English. Includes bibliographical references) – London:Longmans, Green, 1869 – 1mf – 9 – 0-8370-5086-3 – 1985-3086 – us A.T.L.A. [240]

CHARAKTERBILDER KATHOLISCHER REFORMATOREN DES 16. JAHRHUNDERTS : IGNATIUS VON LOYOLA, TERESA DE JESUS, FILIPPO NERI, CARLO BORROMEO / Pastor, Ludwig, Freiherr von – Freiburg, 1924 – 1mf – 9 – DM48.00 – 3-89349-733-1 – gw Hänsel [240]

CHARAKTERISIERUNG VON UNMODIFIZIERTEN UND OLIGOMERMODIFIZIERTEN ANORGANISCHEN METALLOXIDOBERFLAECHEN DURCH ELEKTROKINETISCHE MESSMETHODEN / Simon, Frank – 1994 – 2mf – DM80.00 – 3-89349-884-2 – gw Hänsel [540]

CHARAKTERISTIK DER BIBEL / Niemeyer, August Hermann – HP 17 6198-6202 2. ed 5a. v. 1-5. 1830 – 8 – ne IDC [240]

CHARAKTERISTIKEN UND KRITIKEN VON JOSEPH GOERRES / Goerres, Joseph; ed by Schultz, Franz – Koeln, 1902 – 9 – DM48.00 – 3-89349-265-8 – gw Hänsel [430]

CHARAKTERISTIKEN UND KRITIKEN VON JOSEPH GOERRES AUS DEN JAHREN 1804 UND 1805 / Goerres, Joseph; ed by Schultz, Franz – Koeln, 1900 – 9 – DM48.00 – 3-89349-264-X – gw Hänsel [430]

Charavay *see* SYSTEME GENERAL DES OPERATIONS MILITAIRES DE LA CAMPAGNE PROCHAINE

Charbonneau, Jeannine *see* BIBLIOGRAPHIE DE LA PEINTURE AU CANADA

Charcot, Jean Martin *see*
- LECONS DU MARDI A LA SALPETRIERE. V. V.1887-1889
- LECONS SUR LES MALADIES DU SYSTEME NERVEUX

CHARD AND ILLMINSTER NEWS ETC – Chard, England. Jul 1875-1962; 1983- – 98+ r – 1 – uk British Libr Newspaper [072]

Chardin, Jean *see* JOURNAL DU VOYAGE DU CHEVALIER CHARDIN EN PERSE ET AUX INDES ORIENTALES, PAR LA MER NOIRE ET PAR LA COLCHIDE. PREMIERE PARTIE QUI CONTIENT LE VOYAGE DE PARIS A ISPAHAN

CHARDON DEMOCRAT : WEEKLY FREE SOIL NEWSPAPER – Chardon, OH. 22 Oct 1850-23 Mar 1852 – 1r – 1 – us Western Res [071]

Chardon. Ohio. Regular Baptist Church *see* CHURCH RECORDS, MS 542

CHARDON SPECTATOR AND GEAUGA GAZETTE : WEEKLY NATIONAL REPUBLICAN, LATER WHIG NEWSPAPER – Chardon, OH. 27 July 1833-27 Nov 1835 – 1r – 1 – us Western Res [071]

Chardonnet, J *see* LES GRANDS TYPES DE COMPLEXES INDUSTRIELS

Charest, Pauline *see* BIO-BIBLIOGRAPHIE ANALYTIQUE DE MONSIEUR GERALD GODIN

Charette, Pierre Ph *see* NOCES D'OR DE LA SAINT-JEAN-BAPTISTE: COMPTE-RENDU OFFICIEL DES FETES DE 1884 A MONTREAL

LA CHARGE – Paris. janv-sept 1870, juil 1888-89 – 1 – fr A.C.R.P.P. [073]

A CHARGE DELIVER'D TO THE REVEREND THE CLERGY IN SEVERAL PARTS OF THE DIOCESE OF LICHFIELD AND COVENTRY...IN 1741 / Smalbroke, R – London, 1744 – 1mf – 9 – MP-312/1 – ne IDC [240]

A CHARGE DELIVERED TO THE CLERGY AT THE VISITATION HELD IN THE CATHEDRAL CHURCH OF ST LUKE, AT HALIFAX, ON THE 6TH DAY OF JULY, 1870 / Anglican Church of Canada. Diocese of Nova Scotia. Bishop – By Hibbert, Lord Bishop of Nova Scotia. Halifax, N.S. 1890. 00992. (Pre-1900 Canadiana) – 9 – cn C.I.H.M. [240]

A CHARGE DELIVERED TO THE GRAND JURY FOR THE COUNTY OF ESSEX...HELD AT IPSWICH. MAY TERM, 1832 / Massachusetts. Supreme Judicial Court – Boston: Steam Power Press Office, 1832. 16p. LL-976 – 1 – us L of C Photodup [340]

A CHARGE TO THE GRAND JURY IN THE DISTRICT COURT OF THE UNITED STATES FOR THE DISTRICT OF NEW JERSEY, APRIL 21, 1863 / U.S. District Court. New Jersey – Trenton, State Gazette and Republican Print, 1863. 24 p. LL-422 – 1 – us L of C Photodup [340]

CHARIS – Leipzig, feb-dec 1803. 1805 – 1r – 1 – gw Mikrofilm [640]

CHARISMA – (1982-. 1,5,6,9) – v1-. 1975- – 1 – us UMI [073]

CHARISMA MAXIMUM : UNTERSUCHUNG ZU CASSIANS VOLLKOMMENHEITSLEHRE / Kemmer, A – Loewen, 1938 – 3mf – 8 – ne Slangenburg [240]

LA CHARITE – [Montreal?]: L'Association, no 1 (15 Nov 1898)- – 9 – cn C.I.H.M. [360]

LA CHARITE – Joliette: Imp. de l'Etoile, 1891. SEM105P44 – 1mf – 9 – Can$2.25 – cn Bibl Nat [360]

LA CHARITE – Levis, Canada. 1 mai 1900-v2 n12. 1 avr 1903 – 1r – 1 – Can$25.00 – cn Can Microfilming [072]

LA CHARITE – Montreal, Canada. 8 oct-29 oct 1897 – 1r – 1 – Can$30.00 – cn Can Microfilming [072]

LA CHARITE DANS SES RAPPORTS AVEC L'ETAT MORAL ET LE BIEN-ETRE DES CLASSES INFERIEURES DE LA SOCIETE / Duchatel, MT – (Condition of 19th C. French working class series). 1829 – 9 – fr Hachette [305]

CHARITIES AND THE COMMONS *see* SURVEY

THE CHARITIES OF NEW YORK, BROOKLYN, AND STATEN ISLAND / Cammann, Henry J & Camp, Hugh N – New York: Hurd and Houghton, 1868 – 2mf – us A.T.L.A. [360]

CHARITIES REVIEW – 1-10 (all publ). 1891-1901 – 58mf – 9 – $205.00 – us UPA [360]

THE CHARITY OF THE PRIMITIVE CHURCHES / Chastel, Etienne Louis – G.A. Matile, trans. Philadelphia: J.B. Lippincott and Co., 1857. xx, 356p – 1 – us U.W. Library [240]

THE CHARITY OF THE PRIMITIVE CHURCHES : HISTORICAL STUDIES UPON THE INFLUENCE OF CHRISTIAN CHARITY DURING THE FIRST CENTURIES OF OUR ERA, WITH SOME CONSIDERATIONS TOUCHING ITS BEARINGS UPON MODERN SOCIETY / Chastel, Stephen – Philadelphia: J.B. Lippincott, 1857 – 1mf – us A.T.L.A. [240]

THE CHARITY THAT COVERS A MULTITUDE OF SINS: A SERMON PREACHED ON SUNDAY, FEBRUARY 23RD, 1879,..., IN THE CHURCH OF ST ALBAN, THE MARTYR, OTTAWA / Bedford-Jones, T – 1879. 03306. (Pre-1900 Canadiana) – 9 – cn C.I.H.M. [240]

LE CHARIVARI / ed by Bechery, Louis – Montreal, Canada. 3 fev 1887 – 1r – 1 – Can$25.00 – cn Can Microfilming [072]

LE CHARIVARI – Montreal, 23 mar 1918; 16 aut 1919 – 1r – 1 – Can$30.00 – cn Can Microfilming [073]

LE CHARIVARI – Montreal, Canada. 9 avr-v1 n8. 16 sep 1878 – 1r – 1 – Can$25.00 – cn Can Microfilming [072]

LE CHARIVARI – Montreal, Canada. v6 n1. 14 fev 1891; v6 n4. 3 mar 1891 – 1r – 1 – Can$25.00 – cn Can Microfilming [072]

LE CHARIVARI – Paris. 1832-1905; 1907-juin 1908; 1909-1920; 19 juin 1926-27 fevr 1937 juil 1866-67; 25 sept 1870-1902 – 1 – fr A.C.R.P.P. [073]

LE CHARIVARI – Paris, France. v8 n165. 14 jun 1839 – 1r – 1 – Can$25.00 – cn Can Microfilming [072]

LE CHARIVARI CANADIEN : GRAVURES – Montreal, Canada. 10 mai-3 Oct 1844 – 1r – 1 – Can$35.00 – cn Can Microfilming [073]

LE CHARIVARI CANADIEN – Quebec, Canada. 5 jun-13 nov 1868 – 1r – 1 – Can$35.00 – cn Can Microfilming [072]

Charland, Paul Victor *see*
- LE CULTE DE SAINTE ANNE EN AMERIQUE OU SAINTE-ANNE DE BEAU ET SA FILIATION DANS LE NOUVEAU MONDE
- QUESTIONS D'HISTOIRE LITTERAIRE MISES EN RAPPORT AVEC LE PROGRAMME DE L'UNIVERSITE LAVAL

Charland, T -M *see* ARTES PRAEDICANDI

Charlas, A *see* TRACTATUS DE LIBERTATIBUS ECCLESIAE GALLICANAE

Charlebois, CH-T *see* LE TAON

CHARLEMAGNE / Cutts, Edward L – London: S.P.C.K.; New York: E.& J.B. Young, 1882. (The Home library) – 1mf – us A.T.L.A. [940]

Charlemagne, Armand *see*
- L'AGIOTEUR
- LE SOUPER DES JACOBINS

CHARLEMONT 1719-1849 – (Mf 1T-3t: Family Records 1719-1863. Mf 2T: Marriages 1795-1823. Mf 3T-4T: Intentions 1814-185?. Mf 4T: Marriages 1822-44. Mf 4T-5T: Births 1843-49. Mf 5T: Marriages; Deaths 1843-49) – (mf ed 1995) – 5mf – 9 – 0-87623-226-8 – us Holbrook [920]

CHARLEMONT 1765-1899 – (Mf 1-10: Town & Vital Records 1765-1826. Mf 11-12: Births & Deaths 1803-43. Mf 13-14: Marriage Intentions 1814-67. Mf 15-16: Militia Soldiers 1840-1904. Mf 17: B,M,D 1843-54. Mf 18-22: B,M,D 1855-99. Mf 23-34: Marriage Intentions 1917-68) – (mf ed 1987) – 24mf – 9 – 0-87623-047-8 – us Holbrook [920]

Charleroi, Pennsylvania *see* MISCELLANEOUS NEWSPAPERS

CHARLES 5...VIE POLITIQUE / Pichot, Amedee – 1854 – 9 – $1.50f – sp Bibl Santa Ana [320]

CHARLES 9 OU L'ECOLE DES ROIS / Chenier, Marie-Joseph – (French Theatre Series. Paris. Bossange et Nantes, Louis. 1790 – 9 – fr Hachette [820]

CHARLES ABRAMS : PAPERS AND FILES / Abrams, Charles – 53r – 1 – $3930.00 – us UMI [360]

Charles, Archduke of Austria *see* PRINCIPES DE LA STRATEGIE DEVELOPPES PAR LES RELATIONS DE LA CAMPAGNE DE 1796 EN ALLEMAGNE

THE CHARLES BRADLAUGH PAMPHLETS – Selections from his outstanding collection. c.1850-85. With printed index – 5 – £180.00 – uk World [941]

THE CHARLES CARROLL PAPERS / Carroll, Charles; ed by Hanley, Thomas O'Brien – (With printed guide) – 1972 – 3r – 1 – $255.00 – S1612 – us Scholarly Res [920]

CHARLES DARWIN / Allen, Grant – London: Longmans, Green, 1885. 05014. (Pre-1900 Canadiana) – 9 – cn C.I.H.M. [575]

CHARLES DARWIN : HIS LIFE AND WORK / Holder, Charles Frederick – New York: Putnam's, 1891 – 1 roll – 1 – 1-55879-377-1 – uk Libr Preservation [570]

CHARLES DE GAULLE INSTITUTE PAMPHLET COLLECTION – 1974 – 1 – CSUXAMJ3123-B – us Hoover Inst Photo [320]

CHARLES DE GAULLE PAMPHLET COLLECTION – 1940-1974 – 1 – CSUXANQ5611-B – us Hoover Inst Photo [320]

CHARLES DICKENS : HIS LIFE, WRITINGS, AND PERSONALITY / Kitton, Frederic George – London, Edinburgh: T.C. & E.C. Jack, 1902 – 1 roll – 1 – 1-55879-358-5 – uk Libr Preservation [420]

CHARLES DICKENS: A SKETCH OF HIS LIFE AND WORKS / Perkins, Frederic Beecher – New York: G.P. Putnam & Sons, 1870. 264p – 1 – us U.W. Library [420]

CHARLES DICKENS BY PEN AND PENCIL : INCLUDING ANECDOTES AND REMINISCENCES COLLECTED FROM HIS FRIENDS AND CONTEMPORARIES / Kitton, Frederic George – London: F.T. Sabin, J.F. Dexter, 1890-92 – 1 roll – 1 – 1-55879-252-X – uk Libr Preservation [420]

CHARLES DICKENS RESEARCH COLLECTION / ed by Storey, Graham – (Pt 1: The J.F. Dexter Collection at the British Library. Pt 2: Selections from the Suzannet Collection. Printed guide available £50.00) – 102r – 1 – £6,990.00 – uk Chadwyck [420]

CHARLES DICKENS, THE APOSTLE OF THE PEOPLE / Pugh, Edwin William – London: New Age Press, 1908. vi,316p – 1 – us U.W. Library [920]

Charles, Elizabeth Rundle *see*
- EARLY CHRISTIAN MISSIONS OF IRELAND, SCOTLAND AND ENGLAND
- ECCE ANCILLA DOMINI: MARY...STUDIES IN THE CHRISTIAN IDEAL OF WOMANHOOD
- THREE MARTYRS OF THE NINETEENTH CENTURY

CHARLES ET CAROLINE OU LES ABUS DE L'ANCIEN REGIME / Pigault-Lebrun – (French Theatre Series). Paris. Carilleau et fils. 1790 – 9 – fr Hachette [820]

CHARLES FENDERICH : LITHOGRAPHER OF AMERICAN STATESMEN / U.S. Library of Congress; ed by Miller, Lillian B – 1978 – 3mf – 9 – $30.00f – 0-226-69243-4 – us Chicago [760]

CHARLES KINGSLEY : HIS LETTERS AND MEMORIES OF HIS LIFE / Kingsley, Charles – London: Henry S. King, 1877 – 2 rolls – 1 – 1-55879-216-3 – uk Libr Preservation [420]

CHARLES LAMB : HIS FRIENDS, HIS HAUNTS, AND HIS BOOKS / Fitzgerald, Percy Hetherington – London: Richard Bentley, 1866 – 1 roll – 1 – 1-55879-287-2 – uk Libr Preservation [420]

CHARLES LAMB AND THE LLOYDS / ed by Lucas, Edward Verrall – London: Smith, Elder, 1898 – 1 roll – 1 – 1-55879-657-6 – uk Libr Preservation [420]

CHARLES LAMB AND THE LLOYDS / Lucas, Edward Verrall – London: Smith, Elder, 1898 – 1 roll – 1 – 1-55879-658-4 – uk Libr Preservation [420]

CHARLES LE BRUN, PREMIER DIRECTEUR DE LA MANUFACTURE ROYALE DES GOBELINS / Reunion des musees nationaux. Paris – 1962. 29 illus. 1mf – 9 – fr Réunion [700]

CHARLES NOBLE GREGORY / McClain, Emlin – n.p., 1911 4 p. LL-473 – 1 – us L of C Photodup [340]

Charles, P *see* LA PROMOTION DES TRAVAILLEURS NATIONAUX A L'INTERIEUR DES ENTERPRISES INDUSTRIELLES DES PAYS EN VOIE DE DEVELOPPEMENT

Charles, R H *see*
- APOCRYPHA AND PSEUDEPIGRAPHA OF THE OLD TESTAMENT
- THE BOOK OF JUBILEES OR THE LITTLE GENESIS
- A CRITICAL AND EXIGETICAL COMMENTARY ON THE BOOK OF DANIEL
- A CRITICAL HISTORY OF THE DOCTRINE OF A FUTURE LIFE IN ISRAEL, IN JUDAISM AND IN CHRISTIANITY
- THE ETHIOPIC VERSION OF THE BBOK OF ENOCH
- THE ETHIOPIC VERSION OF THE HEBREW BOOK OF JUBILEES

CHARLES READE, D.C.L., DRAMATIST, NOVELIST, JOURNALIST : A MEMOIR COMPILED CHIEFLY FROM HIS LITERARY REMAINS / Reade, Charles L & Reade, Compton – New York: Harper & Brothers, 1887 – 1 roll – 1 – 1-55879-955-9 – uk Libr Preservation [420]

CHARLES S. PEIRCE MICROFICHE COLLECTION / ed by Ketner, Kenneth Laine – (Microfiche Supplement to the ... Collection. 12 fiches. $15.00) – Published writings. 149mf – 9 – $85.00 – us Philosophy [190]

CHARLES SEALSFIELD : ETHNIC ELEMENTS AND NATIONAL PROBLEMS IN HIS WORKS / Uhlendorf, Bernhard A – (INcludes bibliographical references) – 1 – us U.W. Library [400]

CHARLES SEALSFIELD (CARL POSTL) : DER DICHTER BEIDER HEMISPHAEREN : SEIN LEBEN UND SEINE WERKE / Faust, Albert Bernhardt – Weimar: E Felber, 1897 – 1 – us U.W. Library [400]

CHARLES SEALSFIELD (CARL POSTL) / Soffe, Emil – (Includes bibliographical references) – Bruenn: L u A Brecher, [1922?] – 1r – 1 – us U.W. Library [400]

THE CHARLES SIMMS PAPERS – 3r – 1 – $105.00 – Dist. us Scholarly Res – us L of C Photodup [977]

CHARLES STEWART PARNELL; HIS LOVE STORY AND POLITICAL LIFE / Parnell, Katherine Wood – New York: George H. Doran Co., c1914. 2v. illus – 1 – us U.W. Library [320]

CHARLES SUMMER / Storey, Moorfield – Boston & NY: Houghton, Mifflin & Co, 1900 – 6mf – 9 – $9.00 – LLMC 96-033 – us L.L.M.C. [975]

CHARLES THOMSON PAPERS / Thomson, Charles – 1729-1824 – 1 – $27.00 – us L of C Photodup [920]

CHARLES WHITTLESEY PAPERS *see* WHITTLESEY, CHARLES, PAPERS, MS 3196

CHARLES WRIGHT IN CUBA, 1856-1867 / Howard, Richard A – 4mf. – 9 – £95.00 including book – uk Chadwyck [574]

CHARLES WRIGHT ON THE BOUNDARY, 1849-1852 : OR PLANTAE WRIGHTIANAE REVISITED / Shaw, Elizabeth A – 3mf – 9 – £95.00 including book – uk Chadwyck [574]

CHARLES-E. HARPE, PRESIDENT DE LA SOCIETE DES POETES CANADIENS-FRANCAIS, MEMBRE DE LA SOCIETE DES ECRIVAINS CANADIENS, 1909-1952 : BIO-BIBLIOGRAPHIE ANALYTIQUE / Lord, Marie-Paule – 1961. SEM105P4 – 3mf – 9 – cn Bibl Nat [440]

Charleston Association. South Carolina *see* A SUMMARY OF CHURCH-DISCIPLINE

THE CHARLESTON ASSOCIATION TO THE BAPTIST ASSOCIATION OF SOUTH CAROLINA CALLING FOR THE ORGANIZATION OF THE STATE BAPTIST CONVENTION OF SOUTH CAROLINA : ADDRESS – Signed by Richard Furman, John M. Roberts, and Joseph B. Cook, Nov 1820 – 1 – $5.00 – us Baptist [240]

CHARLESTON BAPTIST CHURCH. CHARLESTON COUNTY. SOUTH CAROLINA : CHURCH RECORDS – (Includes Financial Rpts., Deacon Minutes, History 1923-1987) – 1958-1971 – 4r – 1 – $170.10 – us Baptist [240]

Charleston County Democratic Executive Committee *see* MINUTES

Charleston County. South Carolina. St. Andrew's Episcopal Church *see* TRANSCRIPT RECORDS

CHARLESTON DAILY REPUBLICAN – Charleston, SC: [s.n.], feb 19-jul 12 1872 – 3r – 1 – us Res Libr [071]

CHARLESTON FIRST BAPTIST CHURCH. CHARLESTON, ARKANSAS : CHURCH RECORDS – 1894-14 Oct 1934; 1937-56 – 1 – 35.64 – us Baptist [240]

CHARLESTON FIRST BAPTIST CHURCH. CHARLESTON, SOUTH CAROLINA : CHURCH RECORDS – 1821-75 – 1 – 43.79 – us Baptist [240]

CHARLESTON FIRST BAPTIST CHURCH. CHARLESTON, TENNESSEE : CHURCH RECORDS – 1901-68 – 1 – 53.73 – us Baptist [240]

Charleston Heights (now North Charleston). South Carolina. St. Peter's by-the-Sea (Episcopal) Church *see* REGISTERS

Charleston Library Society. Charleston, South Carolina *see*
- BILLS
- LIBRARY SOCIETY COLLECTION
- MISC. MANUSCRIPTS
- PARTIAL MANUSCRIPT CATALOG
- RECORDS

Charleston Siege *see* JOURNAL

Charleston. South Carolina *see*
- MISCELLANEOUS EARLY NEWSPAPERS
- YEARBOOKS

Charleston. South Carolina. Bethel United Methodist Church *see* RECORDS, 1845-1980, AND MINUTES, 1845-1916

Charleston. South Carolina. Calvary Protestant Episcopal Church *see* RECORDS

Charleston. South Carolina. Cumberland St. Methodist Episcopal Church *see* LIST OF SUBSCRIBERS FOR REBUILDING OF CHURCH, 1837

Charleston. South Carolina. First (Scots) Presbyterian Church *see* TOMBSTONE INSCRIPTIONS

Charleston. South Carolina. Grace (Episcopal) Church *see* RECORDS

Charleston. South Carolina. Holy Communion (Episcopal) Church *see* REGISTER

Charleston. South Carolina. Mariner's Church *see* REGISTERS

Charleston. South Carolina. St. James United Methodist Church *see* MISCELLANEOUS CHURCH RECORDS

Charleston. South Carolina. St. Luke's (Episcopal) Church *see* VESTRY MINUTES

Charleston. South Carolina. St. Mark's Protestant Episcopal Church *see* RECORDS

Charleston. South Carolina. St. Michael's Episcopal Church *see* RECORDS

Charleston. South Carolina. St. Paul's Stono (Episcopal) Church *see* RECORDS

Charleston. South Carolina. St. Peter's and Christ (Episcopal) Churches *see* RECORDS

Charleston. South Carolina. St. Philip's (Episcopal) Church *see* RECORDS

Charleston. South Carolina. St. Stephen's (Episcopal) Church *see* RECORDS

Charleston. South Carolina. Trinity Methodist Church *see* REGISTER

Charleston. South Carolina. Unitarian Church *see* TOMBSTONE INSCRIPTIONS

CHARLESTOWN 1692-1874 – (Mf 1-40: B,M,D 1629-1866. Mf 41-80: Births 1843-73. Mf 81-130: Marriage Intentions 1725-1873. Mf 131-171: Marriages 1843-74. Mf 172-249: Deaths 1843-74. Mf 250-258: Church Records 1632-1789, 1817-1889) – (mf ed 1985) – 258mf – 9 – 0-931248-79-5 – us Holbrook [920]

CHARLESTOWN MAIL – Charlestown, South Africa. 1909-10 – 1 – sa State Libr [072]
Charlesworth, J H *see* JOHN AND QUMRAN
Charlesworth, M P *see* TRADE ROUTES AND COMMERCE OF THE ROMAN EMPIRE
Charlevoix, Francois Xavier de *see*
- HISTOIRE DE L'ETABLISSEMENT, DES PROGRES ET DE LA DECADENCE DU CHRISTIANISME DANS L'EMPIRE DU JAPON
- HISTOIRE ET DESCRIPTION GENERALE DE LA NOUVELLE FRANC
- HISTOIRE ET DESCRIPTION GENERALE DE LA NOUVELLE FRANCE
- A VOYAGE TO NORTH-AMERICA, UNDERTAKEN BY COMMAND OF THE PRESENT KING OF FRANCE, CONTAINING THE GEOGRAPHICAL DESCRIPTION AND NATURAL HISTORY OF CANADA AND LOUISIANA....

CHARLIE-HEBDO – Paris. 23 nov 1970-81 – 1 – fr A.C.R.P.P. [073]
LA CHARLOIADE, OU, LE MENTEUR DEMASQUE: POEME HEROI-COMIQUE / Benoit, Samuel – Quebec, 1872. 02315. (Pre-1900 Canadiana) – 9 – cn C.I.H.M. [810]
Charlotin, Marie-Joseph *see* BIBLIOGRAPHIE ANALYTIQUE DU REVEREND PERE PHILIPPE DESCHAMPS, C.S.V., PROVESSEUR AGREGE A LA FACULTE DE PEDAGOGIE ET D'ORIENTATION DE L'UNIVERSITE LAVAL
CHARLOTTE BIRCH-PFEIFFER ALS DRAMATIKERIN : EIN BEITRAG ZUR THEATERGESCHICHTE DES 19. JAHRHUNDERTS / Hes, Else – (Includes bibliographical references) – Stuttgart: J B Metzler, 1914 – 1 – us U.W. Library [430]
CHARLOTTE BRONTE : A MONOGRAPH / Reid, Thomas Wemyss – New York: Scribner, Armstrong & Co., 1877 – 1 roll – 1 – 1-55879-742-4 – uk Libr Preservation [420]
CHARLOTTE HERALD – Punta Gorda. Fl. -w. 1962-63. Herald. 1902, 1904, 1908, 1913 16 Apr 1914, 1915-16, 1918-20, 1922, 1928, 1930-31, 1936, 1938, 1942, Oct 1946-61. Herald News. -w. 1964-73 – 1 – us P.K. Yonge [071]
CHARLOTTE MARY YONGE : AN APPRECIATION / Romanes, Ethel – London: A.R. Mowbray, 1908 – 1mf – us A.T.L.A. [240]
THE CHARLOTTE NEWS – Charlotte, NC: Wade H Harris, 1901 – 4r – 1 – us Res Libr [071]
CHARLOTTE VON SCHILLER UND IHRE FREUNDE : AUSWAHL AUS IHRER KORRESPONDENZ / Schiller, Charlotte; ed by Geiger, Ludwig – (Includes bibliographical references) – Berlin. H Bondy, [1908] – 1r – 1 – us U.W. Library [920]
CHARLOTTE VON STEIN, GOETHE'S FREUNDIN : EIN LEBENSBILD, MIT BENUTZUNG DER FAMILIENPAPIERE ENTWORFEN / Duentzer, Heinrich – Stuttgart: J G Cotta, 1874 – 1r – 1 – us U.W. Library [920]
CHARLOTTE VON STEIN UND CORONA SCHROETER : EINE VERTHEIDIGUNG / Duentzer, Heinrich – Stuttgart: J G Cotta, 1876 – 1r – 1 – us U.W. Library [430]
CHARLOTTE'S INHERITANCE: A NOVEL / Braddon, Mary Elizabeth – British Fiction Archive: Unit 5 – 9 – uk Bell [830]
CHARLOTTETOWN HERALD – Canada, May 1894-Dec 1921 – 9r – 1 – uk British Libr Newspaper [072]
CHARLTON 1742-1890 – (Mf 1-4: Births, Deaths, Int. 1742-1801. Mf 5-9: B,M,D 1773-1826. Mf 10-15: Marriage Intentions 1800-1909. Mf 16-19: Births, Deaths 1826-45. Mf 20-22: B,M,D 1844-72. Mf 23: Births 1871-90. Mf 24-26: Index to Births 1844-90. Mf 27-28: Marriages 1862-90. Mf 29-31: Index to Marriages 1844-90. Mf 32: Deaths 1870-90. Mf 33-35: Index to Deaths 1844-90) – (mf ed 1986) – 35mf – 9 – 0-87623-005-2 – us Holbrook [920]
Charlton, John *see*
- EQUAL RIGHTS: MR. CHARLTON'S OPEN LETTER TO REV. PRINCIPAL CAVEN, D.D., DATED MAY 9TH, 1890
- SABBATH OBSERVANCE: SPEECH OF JOHN CHARLTON, M.P. ON BILL TO PROVIDE FOR BETTER OBSERVANCE OF THE LORD'S DAY, HOUSE OF COMMONS, 26TH FEBRUARY, 1885
- SPEECH OF JOHN CHARLTON, M.P. ON UNRESTRICTED RECIPROCITY WITH THE UNITED STATES: DELIVERED IN THE CANADIAN HOUSE OF COMMONS, THURSDAY, MARCH 7TH, 1889
- SPEECH OF JOHN CHARLTON, M.P. ON UNRESTRICTED RECIPROCITY WITH THE UNITED STATES: DELIVERED IN THE HOUSE OF COMMONS, FRIDAY, MARCH 16TH, 1888
- SPEECH...ON JESUITS' ESTATES ACT: DELIVERED IN THE HOUSE OF COMMONS, OTTAWA ON THURSDAY, MARCH 28TH, 1889
- SPEECH...ON THE BUDGET: DELIVERED IN THE HOUSE OF COMMONS, OTTAWA, FRIDAY, MARCH 28TH, 1890

Charlton, Lionel Evelyn Oswald *see* THE MILITARY SITUATION IN SPAIN AFTER TERUEL
CHARLTON TRIBUNE – 1926-1942. CHT1-7 – 7r – 1 – at Corangamite [072]
Charlton, William Henry *see* FOUR MONTHS IN NORTH AMERICA
CHARLZ DARVIN I EGO UCHENIE / Timiriazev, Kliment Arkad'evich – Moskva: Tipo-Litogr. D.A. Bonch-Bruevicha, 1894.414p – 1 – us U.W. Library [575]
THE CHARM OF SUNDAY SCHOOLS / Bliss, P P – 1871. New York – 1 – us Baptist [240]
Charmetant, Felix *see* LES ORPHELINS ARABES D'ALGER: LEUR PASSE, LEUR PRESENT, LEUR AVENIR: OEUVRE DE LEUR ADOPTION
Charmont, J *see* DE LA VACCINE ET DE SES HEREUX RESULTATS: DEMONTRES PAR DES VISITES FAITES AU DOMICILE DES INDIVIDUS DECEDES A PARIS...EN 1825
Charndler, S *see* AN ANSWER TO THE REV. MR. JOHN WESLEY'S LETTER TO WILLIAM, LORD BISHOP OF GLOUCESTER, CONCERNING THE CHARGES ALLEDGED AGAINST HIM AND HIS DOCTRINE IN A BOOK LATELY PUBLISHED ENTITLED 'THE DOCTRINE OF GRACE;...
Charnet, J *see* NOTIONS DE DROIT MARITIME INTERNATIONAL
Charney, J P *see* STRATEGY AND ART OF WAR FROM FEUDAL TIMES TO THE WORLD WARS
Charnock, Joan Thomson *see* RUSSIA: THE OLD AND THE NEW
Charnock, John *see* AN HISTORY OF MARINE ARCHITECTURE OF ALL NATIONS
Charnoluskaia, E M *see* BIBLIOGRAFICHESKII UKAZATEL' KNIG I STATEI PO NARODNOMU OBRAZOVANIIU ZA 1894 GOD
Charnoluskii, V *see* SHKOL'NOE ZAKONODATEL'STVO V RSFSR
Charns, Alexander *see* U.S. SUPREME COURT AND FEDERAL JUDGES SUBJECT FILES
Charpantier, Jean *see* RECOGNITION OF STUDIES AND COMPETENCE
Charpentier, Fr *see*
- DE L'EXCELLENCE DE LA LANGUE FRANCOISE
- DEFFENSE DE LA LANGUE FRANCOISE

Charpentier, J *see* DIE ETHNOGRAPHISCHE STELLUNG DER TOCHARER
Charpentier, John *see* GOETHE
Charpentier, T von *see*
- HORAE ENTOMOLOGICAE
- ORTHOPTERA DESCRIPTA ET DEPICTA

CHART ANALYSIS OF THE AUTOMOBILE LIABILITY SECURITY LAWS OF THE UNITED STATES AND CANADA. / Association of Casualty and Surety Companies. Law Department – New York, 1947. 10 p. LL-1065 – 1 – us L of C Photodup [340]
CHART OF ELOCUTIONARY DRILL / Browning, Thomas Blair – Toronto: Copp, Clark, 1888. 00285. (Pre-1900 Canadiana) – 9 – cn C.I.H.M. [420]
CHART OF THE ASSESSMENT LIFE ASSOCIATIONS AND FRIENDLY SOCIETIES TRANSACTING BUSINESS IN CANADA. – Toronto: Bulletin Pub. Co. 1898. 00325. (Pre-1900 Canadiana) – 9 – cn C.I.H.M. [310]
LA CHARTE COLONIALE. / Congo. Belgian – Bruxelles, Weissenbruch, 1910-19. 3 v. On film – v. 1 and v. 2 only. LL-12002 – 1 – us L of C Photodup [340]
LA CHARTE DE 1830 – Paris. Journal du soir. oct 1836-juil 1838 – 1 – fr A.C.R.P.P. [072]
CHARTE ET REGLEMENTS DE LA CITE. / Saint Hyacinthe Quebec – St Hyacinthe: Courrier de St. Hyacinthe, 1895. SEM105P866 – 5mf – 9 – Can$11.25 – cn Bibl Nat [971]
THE CHARTER – 1839-40. Journal of Chartist movement-platform for the views of the working class. 4 reels – 1 – uk World [330]
THE CHARTER – London, 27 Jan 1839-15 Mar 1840 – 4r – 1 – uk British Libr Newspaper [072]
CHARTER NOMMENSEN-UNIVERSITY, INSTITUTION OF THE BATAK PROTESTANT CONGREGATION, SUMATRA, INDONESIA / Pematang Siantar, Indonesia. Universitas H.K.B.P. Nommensen – In English and Indonesian. SE-10,955 1. 1966 – 9 – ne IDC [240]
THE CHARTER OF THE CHURCH : SIX LECTURES ON THE SPIRITUAL PRINCIPLE OF NONCONFORMITY / Forsyth, Peter Taylor – London: Alexander & Shepheard, 1896 – 1mf – us A.T.L.A. [240]
CHARTER OF THE RIGHTS AND DUTIES OF MODERN MAN / Cambridge Peace Aims Group – Five welfare rights, with a list of duties – 9 – 1.00f – at Libertarian Micro [335]
CHARTER OF THE RIGHTS OF THE CHILD / Australian Teachers Federation – 1969. 12 collectivists claims – 9 – 1.00f – at Libertarian Micro [335]
CHARTERED ACCOUNTANT IN AUSTRALIA *see* ACCOUNTANT IN AUSTRALIA
Chartered Institute of Patent Agents *see* CIPA
THE CHARTERED INSTITUTE OF PATENT AGENTS TRANSACTIONS – London. v1-50. 1882-1932 – 9 – LLMC 84-341 – us L.L.M.C. [073]
Chartered Institution of Building Services *see* JOURNAL
CHARTERED LAND SURVEYOR/CHARTERED MINERALS SURVEYOR – v1-4 no 4. 1979-Summer 1983 – 1,5,6,9 – us UMI [520]
CHARTERED MECHANICAL ENGINEER – (1976-. 5,6,9) – v. 1-. 1954- – 1 – us UMI [621]
CHARTERED QUANTITY SURVEYOR – v1-1979- – 1,5,6,9 – us UMI [690]
Charteris, A H *see* CHAPTERS ON INTERNATIONAL LAW...
Charteris, Archibald Hamilton *see*
- HISTORICAL NOTE: WOMAN'S WORK IN THE CHURCH
- THE NEW ENCYCLOPAEDIA BRITANNICA ON THEOLOGY
- NEW TESTAMENT SCRIPTURES: THEIR CLAIMS, HISTORY, AND AUTHORITY

CHARTERS AND DOCUMENTS ILLUSTRATING THE HISTORY OF THE CATHEDRAL, CITY AND DIOCESE OF SALISBURY, IN THE TWELFTH AND THIRTEENTH CENTURIES (RS97) : SELECTED FROM THE CAPITULAR AND DIOCESAN REGISTERS BY W RICH-JONES / Salisbury (Diocese); ed by Macray, W D – 1891 – Dfl30.00 – ne Slangenburg [240]
CHARTERS EN BESCHEIDEN OVER DE BETREKKING DER OVERIJSSELSCHE STEDEN BIJZONDER VAN KAMPEN OP HET NOORDEN VAN EUROPA GEDURENDE DE 13E EEUW – Deventer, 1861 – Dfl9.00 – ne Slangenburg [240]
CHARTERS OF AMERICAN LIFE INSURANCE COMPANIES. / Spectator Company. New York – New York, 1906. 408 p. LL-1416 – 1 – us L of C Photodup [340]
CHARTES DE L'ABBAYE DE SAINT-HUBERT EN ARDENNE / Kurth, G – Tome Premier. Bruxelles, 1903 – Dfl126.00 – ne Slangenburg [240]
LES CHARTES DE L'ORDRE DE CHALAIS (1101-1400) / Romain, J Ch. – Tome 1 (1101-1200). 1923 – Dfl13.00 – ne Slangenburg [240]
LES CHARTES DE L'ORDRE DE CHALAIS (1101-1400) / Romain, J Ch. – Tome 2 (1201-1300) – Dfl19.00 – ne Slangenburg [240]
LES CHARTES DE L'ORDRE DE CHALAIS (1101-1400) / Romain, J Ch. – Tome 3 (1301-1400). 1923 – Dfl13.00 – ne Slangenburg [240]
CHARTES ET DOCUMENTS DE L'ABBAYE CISTERCIENNE DE PREUILLY / Catel, Albert & Lecomte, Maurice – Montereau, 1927 – 11mf – 8 – Dfl39.00 – ne Slangenburg [240]
CHARTES INEDITES DE L'ABBAYE D'ORVAL / Deleseluse, A – Brussel, 1896 – 4mf – 8 – Dfl19.00 – ne Slangenburg [240]
CHARTIER ANCIEN DE MONTMORIGNY / Huchet, Albert – Bourges, 1936 – 17mf – 8 – Dfl60.00 – ne Slangenburg [240]
Chartier, Jean Baptiste *see* LA COLONISATION DANS LES CANTON DE L'EST
Chartiers. Presbytery (Assoc. Pres. Ch. of No. Am.) *see* MINUTES, 1805-1815
THE CHARTIST – London, 2 Feb-7 Jul 1839 – 15ft – 1 – uk British Libr Newspaper [072]
CHARTIST CIRCULAR – 1-2 (all publ). 1839-1842 – 7mf – 9 – $65.00 – us UPA [335]
CHARTIST CIRCULAR – Glasgow, Scotland. 28 Sept 1839-18 Sept 1841 – 38ft – 1 – uk British Libr Newspaper [072]
CHARTIST CIRCULAR – nos. 1-146. 1839-42 – 1 – uk Microform Academic [072]
THE CHARTIST MOVEMENT IN SCOTLAND / Wilson, A – 1 – uk Microform Academic [941]
Charton, Charles *see* POPULATION: RECENCEMENT ET MOUVEMENTS DE LA POPULATION DES VOSGES
Charton, E Th *see* MEMOIRE D'UN PREDICATEUR SAINT-SIMONIEN
CHARTS AND GRAPHS SHOWING THE CONDITIONS OF AFRO-AMERICANS IN 1900 – Drawings – 1 – 18.00 – us L of C Photodup [977]
CHARTS OF SOUTH CAROLINA BAPTIST CHURCHES BY ASSOCIATIONS / South Carolina – 1 – 5.00 – us Baptist [240]
CHARTULARIES OF ST MARY'S ABBEY, DUBLIN (RS80) : AND THE REGISTER OF ITS HOUSE AT DUNBRODY; AND ANNALS OF IRELAND / Dublin, St Mary's Abbey; ed by Gilbert, G T – (v1 1884 Dfl39.00. v2 1886 Dfl42.00) – ne Slangenburg [240]
CHARTULARIUM UNIVERSITATIS PARISIENSIS / Denifle, Heinrich – Paris. v1-4. 1889-1897 – 121mf – 8 – Dfl424.00 – ne Slangenburg [240]
CHAS – Chernovtsy, U.S.S.R. -d. 10 Jan 1931-31 Dec 1939. Very imperfect. 9 reels – 1 – uk British Libr Newspaper [947]
CHAS – Fuerth. Germany. -w. 19 Dec 1946-7 Jan 1947, 27 Apr 1947-1 Jul 1949. (1 reel) – 1 – uk British Libr Newspaper [072]
CHAS DOSUGA – Zhurnal igr, zabav i uveselitel'nago chteniia dlia russkago iunochestva. Ezhemesiachnoe periodicheskoe izdanie. Spb. 1858-62. BR-2278 2 – 8 – ne IDC [073]
CHAS E. GOAD COMPANY *see* PLANS D'ASSURANCES DE VILLES DU QUEBEC
CHAS. G. MILLER SCRAPBOOKS *see* MILLER, CHAS. G., SCRAPBOOKS, NO. 112
DIE CHASANIM WELT – (Yiddish monthly) – Warsaw, PL. v3 no16. Feb 1935 – 1r – 1 – cn Can Microfilming [072]
Chase, Chief Justice *see* CHASE'S REPORTS OF CASES IN THE FOURTH CIRCUIT, 1865-1869
CHASE COUNTY COURANT – Cottonwood Falls. Kan. 1874-1900 – 1 – us UMI [071]
CHASE COUNTY ENTERPRISE – Imperial, NE. -w. Oct 1895-Dec 1897, scattered issues missing; Aug 1898-Mar 1899 – 1 – us NE Hist [071]
CHASE COUNTY TRIBUNE – Imperial, NE. -w. Jul 1897-Dec 1898; Mar 1899-Jan 1901; Apr 1901-Dec 1907 – 1 – us NE Hist [071]
CHASE ECONOMIC OBSERVER – v1-. 1981- – 1,5,6,9 – us UMI [330]
Chase, Eliza Brown *see* OVER THE BORDER: ACADIA, THE HOME OF "EVANGELINE"
Chase, Franklin N *see* SYRACUSE AND ITS ENVIRONS
Chase, Frederic Henry *see*
- CREDIBILITY OF THE BOOK OF THE ACTS OF THE APOSTLES
- THE LORD'S PRAYER IN THE EARLY CHURCH
- OLD SYRIAC ELEMENT IN THE TEXT OF CODEX BEZAE
- SUPERNATURAL ELEMENT IN OUR LORD'S EARTHLY LIFE
- THE SYRO-LATIN TEXT OF THE GOSPELS

Chase, Frederick *see*
- CORRESPONDENCE OF FREDERICK CHASE, 1861-1874
- CORRESPONDENCE OF FREDERICK CHASE IN THE YEARS 1861-1874

Chase, George *see*
- JOHNSON'S READY LEGAL ADVISER.
- LEADING CASES UPON THE LAW OF TORTS

Chase, Lisa A *see*
- BLOOD LACTATE RESPONSES FOR THREE COMPETITIVE SWIMMING STROKES
- PERCEIVED BODY IMAGE

THE CHASE OF SAINT-CASTIN: AND OTHER STORIES OF THE FRENCH IN THE NEW WORLD / Catherwood, Mary Hartwell – Boston: Houghton, Mifflin, 1894. 00507. (Pre-1900 Canadiana) – 9 – cn C.I.H.M. [830]
Chase, Philander *see* BISHOP CHASE'S REMINISCENCES

Chase, Salmon Portland *see*
- PAPERS
- SALMON P. CHASE PAPERS

CHASE'S REPORTS OF CASES IN THE FOURTH CIRCUIT, 1865-1869 / Chase, Chief Justice – New York: Diossy. 1v. 1876 (all publ) – 7mf – 9 – $10.50 – LLMC 81-441 – us L.L.M.C. [340]

Chaset, Alan J *see* DISQUALIFICATION OF FEDERAL JUDGES BY PEREMPTORY CHALLENGE

CHASIAT, RATJUN DAN MASAKAN KETELA POHON / Darjanto – SE-4095 1. 1959 – 9 – ne IDC [950]

Chasopis Istorii i Kul'turi. (Naukove Tovaristvo imeni Shevchenka) *see* STARA UKRAINA

CHASOVOI – ("La Sentinelle".) Illiustrirovannyi,voennyi zhurnal-pamiatka. v. 1-285. Asniere-Brussels-Paris. 1929-41, 1947-49. BR-2276 2 – 8 – ne IDC [073]

CHASOVOI – Paris, Brussels. Jan. 1929-May 10, 1941; May 1947-Mar. 1954 – 1 – 35.00r – us Hoover Inst Photo [073]

LA CHASSE A L'HERITAGE / Cote, Stanislas (1846-1920) – Montreal: Imp. et litho. Gebhardt-Berthiaume, 1884. SEM105P30 – 1mf – 9 – Can$2.25 – cn Bibl Nat [830]

LA CHASSE AU FILET DANS LA REGION DU POOL : ETUDE DE CONTES, LEGENDES, PROVERBES DES BALA:DI, BASU:DI, BAKO:NGO. (RECHERCHE ETHNOLINGUISTIQUE) / Seguin, M – 9 – F120.00 – fr Ethnologie [306]

LA CHASSE ET LA PECHE DANS LEURS RAPPORTS AVEC LES CROYANCES RELIGIEUSES PARMI LES POPULATIONS DU LOBI / Labouret, Henri – Goree: [s.n.], 1918 – fr Armell [240]

LA CHASSE GALERIE AND OTHER CANADIAN STORIES / Beaugrand, Honore – Montreal, 1900. 03523. (Pre-1900 Canadiana) – 9 – cn C.I.H.M. [830]

Chasseboeuf, Comte de Volney *see* DISCOURS SUR L'ETUDE PHILOSOPHIQUE DES LANGUES

LE CHASSEUR : IMPRIME A BORD DU "CANADA" – 8 sep 1877 – 1r – 1 – Can$25.00 – cn Can Microfilming [072]

LE CHASSEUR CANADIEN – Montreal: "L'Etendard", 1885. 03018. (Pre-1900 Canadiana) – 9 – cn C.I.H.M. [971]

CHASSEURS CANADIENS / Boussenard, Louis – Paris: E. Flammarion. 1892?. 00221. (Pre-1900 Canadiana) – 9 – cn C.I.H.M. [971]

LES CHASSEURS DE FOURRURES / Bailleul, Louis – Paris: T. Lefevre et E. Guerin, 18–?. 02487. (Pre-1900 Canadiana) – 9 – cn C.I.H.M. [636]

Chassiron, Ch. de *see* NOTES SUR LE JAPON

Chastain, J G *see* PERSONAL DIARY AND SCRAPBOOK

Chastein *see*
- L'APOTHEOSE DU DICTIONNAIRE DE L'ACADEMIE
- L'ENTERREMENT DU DICTIONNAIRE DE L'ACADEMIE

Chastel, Etienne Louis *see*
- THE CHARITY OF THE PRIMITIVE CHURCHES
- CHRISTIANITY IN THE NINETEENTH CENTURY
- ETUDES HISTORIQUES SUR L'INFLUENCE DE LA CHARITE DURANT LES PREMIERS SIECLES CHRETIENS
- MELANGES HISTORIQUES ET RELIGIEUX

Chastel, Stephen *see* THE CHARITY OF THE PRIMITIVE CHURCHES

Chastelein, C P *see* DE FIDE INTER HOSTES,...

Chastellux, Louis Emmanuel de *see* LE TERRITOIRE DU DEPARTEMENT DE LA MOSELLE: HISTOIRE ET STATISTIQUE

Chastenet, L *see* LA VIE DE MGR. ALAIN DE SOLMINIHAC, EVEQUE... DE CAORS

CHASTNY I KAPITAL V TORGOVLE SSSR : KAPITALY, DOKHODY, RASKHODY I REZULTATY TORGOVO I DEIATELNOSTI CHASTNYKH TORGOVYKH PREDPRIIATII SSSR, KAPITALONAKOPLENIE VLADELTSEV CHASTNYKH PREDPRIIATII / POD RED. I S PREDISL. SH. M. DVOLA IT SKOGO – Moskva: Izd-vo Narkomtorga SSSR i RSFSR, 1928 – 1 – CSUX90-B8401 – us Hoover Inst Photo [330]

CHASTUSHKI UGNETENNAGO NARODA – Shankhai: Izd-vo Raboche-kresti ansko-kazachi a oppozitsii a, 1927 – 1 – CSUX88-B5358 – us Hoover Inst Photo [390]

CHASY. ROMAN / Remizov, A – Spb. 1908. BR-818 2 – 8 – ne IDC [460]

LE CHAT BOTTE / ed by Francq, G & Nicolas, Louis – Montreal, Canada. 22 jan 1922 – 1r – 1 – Can$25.00 – cn Can Microfilming [072]

LE CHAT BOTTE : JOURNAL HUMORISTIQUE HEBDOMADAIRE – Montreal: G Francq et Ls Nicolas. v1- 1922-. SEM16P343 – 1r – 5 – Can$9.00 – cn Bibl Nat [073]

LE CHAT NOIR – Paris. 1882-95 – 1 – fr A.C.R.P.P. [073]

Chatard, Francis Silas *see* CHRISTIAN TRUTHS

LE CHATEAU DE MONTENERO / Dalayrac, N – (Score) – Paris: L'Auteur, 1798 – 1 – us Sibley [780]

CHATEAU DE NANTES, DOCUMENTS – 11 pieces – 1 – F258.07 – fr Armell [910]

Chateau de Ramezay *see* CATALOGUE OF THE CHATEAU RAMEZAY MUSEUM

Chateaubriand *see* CONGRES DE VERONE

Chateaubriand, F A de *see* BUONAPARTE UND DIE BOURBONS

Chateaubriand, Francois-Rene de *see*
- DE LA VENDEE
- THE GENIUS OF CHRISTIANITY, OR, THE SPIRIT AND BEAUTY OF THE CHRISTIAN RELIGION

CHATEAUGUAY: QUI EST "TEMOIN OCULAIRE" ET SA DESCRIPTION DE LA BATAILLE EST-ELLE CORRECTE? / Baby, Georges – Montreal: Pelletier, 1900. 03744. (Pre-1900 Canadiana) – 9 – cn C.I.H.M. [971]

CHATEAUGUAY TIMES – Ormstown, Canada. v1 n14. 21 jan 1892-v1 n33. 2 jun 1892 – 1r – 1 – Can$30.00 – cn Can Microfilming [072]

CHATEAUGUAY VALLEY HISTORICAL SOCIETY ANNUAL JOURNAL – Huntingdon. v1 n1. 1968-n25. 1992 – 1r – 1 – cn Can Microfilming [073]

Chateau-Lyon, PL d'Aquin de *see* LA HENRIADE

Chateauneuf, Francois de Castagneres, Abbe de *see*
- DIALOGUE SUR LA MUSIQUE DES ANCIENS
- DIALOGUE SUR LA MUSIQUE DES ANCIENS: A MONSIEUR DE
- DIALOQUE SUR LA MUSIQUE DES ANCIENS: A MONSIEUR DE ***

THE CHATEAUX OF THE LOIRE / Monmarche, M – H-567 2. 7th ed. 1924 – 8 – ne IDC [944]

Chatelain, A *see* AUCTARIUM CHARTULARII UNIVERSITATIS PARISIENSIS

Chatelain, H *see* FOLK TALES OF ANGOLA

CHATELAINE MAGAZINE (ENGLISH) – Toronto, 1928-95 – 1,9 – Can$91.00y – cn Micromedia [073]

CHATELAINE MAGAZINE (FRENCH) – Toronto, 1960-95 – 1,9 – Can$91.00y – cn Micromedia [073]

Chatelet-Lomont, Gabrielle Emilie du *see* DISSERTATION SUR LA NATURE ET PROPAGATION DE FEU

Chatenay, C *see* LES SUCCESSIONS EN DROIT FRANCO-SUISSE

Chatfield. Ohio. Evangelical Lutheran Church. Nazareth Congregation *see* RECORDS

Chatfield. Ohio. Evangelical Lutheran Church. Peace Congregation *see* RECORDS

Chatham *see* TO THE RIGHT HONOURABLE CHARLES POULETT THOMSON, GOVERNOR GENERAL OF HER MAJESTY'S PROVINCES IN NORTH AMERICA

CHATHAM 1693-1900 – (Mf 1-7: B,M,D 1693-1789. Mf 8-11: Vital Records 1704-47. Mf 12-15: Meetings & Marriages 1698-1748. Mf 16-21: Vital Records 1749-87. Mf 22-26: Vital Records & Meetings 1727-1856. Mf 27-33: Vital & Town Records 1814-46. Mf 34-43: Vital Records 1804-68. Mf 44-48: Marriage Intentions & Records 1854-74. Mf 49-51: Marriages 1855-1900. Mf 52-53: Deaths 1869-1900; Births 1891-1900. Mf 54-55: Index to Deaths 1845-1928. Mf 56-57: Index to Births 1846-1944. Mf 57-58: Index to Marriage Intentions 1846-1944. Mf 58-60: Index to Marriages 1846-1944) – (mf ed 1987) – 60mf – 9 – 0-87623-002-8 – us Holbrook [920]

THE CHATHAM COURIER – Chatham, New York. Apr 4 1883-Mar 17 1897 – 1 – us NY Public [071]

THE CHATHAM COURIER – Chatham, New York. v22-35. 1883-97 – 5r – 1 – us Ross [071]

CHATHAM DAILY NEWS – (1975-1992.-223r; 1993.-16r; 1914Ap-Ju1914.-1r) – Chatham, 1925-1974 – 449r – 1 – cn Preston [971]

CHATHAM HOUSE SERIES – Royal Institute of International Affairs – 9 – Inquire – us Hein [327]

CHATHAM JOURNAL – Chatham, Canada. 1841-44 – 1 reel – 1 – $68.00 – cn Library Assoc [971]

CHATHAM NEWSPAPERS – Chatham, Canada. Pt. 1. 1844-55. Includes Canadian Freeman, Chatham Chronicle, Chatham Gleaner, Kent Advertiser, Western Sentinel – 2r – 1 – $136.00 – cn Library Assoc [971]

CHATHAM NEWSPAPERS – Chatham, Canada. Pt. 2. 1853-75. Includes Chatham Growler, Chatham Planet, Western Argus, Western Planet, Western Union – 9r – 1 – $585.00 – cn Library Assoc [971]

CHATHAM OBSERVER – Chatham, England. Chatham & Rochester Observer – Chatham, Rochester & Brompton Observer – Chatham, Rochester & Gillingham Observer – New Observer – Kent Messenger & Observer – Kent Messenger & Chatham Observer. -w. 14 May 1870-2 Aug 1968. Lacking Jan 1896. 105 reels – 1 – uk British Libr Newspaper [072]

Chatillon, Auguste de *see* LES POESIES

Chatillon, Jean *see* COLLECTION DE MUSIQUE CANADIENNE

Chatillonais, R.C.P.Vignet-Zunz, J.Lancelot, F. *see* LES LOISIRS DES JEUNES A CHATILLON-SUR-SEINE; REGARDS SUR LA DANSE POPULAIRE EN CHATILLONAIS

LE CHATIMENT – (Filmed as pt of: Commune de Paris newspapers; newspapers on these reels are filmed chronologically, not alphabetically.) – Ed. de Paris. [Paris: s.n. mar 25 1871 – us Res Libr [072]

CHATTANOOGA DAILY GAZETTE – (Union newspaper) – Chattanooga, TN. mar 5, 1864-sept 2, 1865 – 1r – 1 – us Western Res [071]

CHATTANOOGA DAILY REBEL – (Confederate newspaper) – Chattanooga, TN. aug 9, 1862-july 29, 1863 – 1r – 1 – us Western Res [071]

CHATTANOOGA FIRST BAPTIST CHURCH. CHATTANOOGA, TENNESSEE : CHURCH RECORDS – 1852-1967 – 1 – 71.51 – us Baptist [240]

CHATTANOOGA TIMES – Chattanooga. Tenn. 1873- – 1 – us UMI [071]

Chattard, G P *see* NUOVA DESCRIZIONE DEL VATICANO O SIA DELLA SACROSANTA BASILICA DI S. PIETRO

CHATTEL MORTGAGE / Bahlke, William A – Detroit, Richmond & Backus, 1897. 9 p. LL-2235 – 1 – us L of C Photodup [340]

CHATTEL MORTGAGE INDEX / Monroe County. Mich, Bedford Township. Township Treasurer – 1893-1931 – 1r – 1 – $32.50r – us Archival [324]

CHATTEL MORTGAGE RECORDS / Hancock County. Ohio. Biglick Township. Township Clerk – 1877-1902 – 1r – 1 – $32.50r – us Archival [324]

CHATTEL MORTGAGES / Hancock County. Ohio. Marion Township. Board of Trustees – 1878-1906 – 1r – 1 – $32.50r – us Archival [324]

CHATTEL MORTGAGES AND CONDITIONAL SALES IN THE STATE OF NEW YORK / Smith, Dix W – 3d ed. Albany: Bender, 1900. 272p. LL-1330 – 1 – us L of C Photodup [340]

CHATTEL MORTGAGES AND INDICES / Ottawa County. Ohio. Carroll Township. Township Clerk – 1878-1906 – 2r – 1 – $32.50r – us Archival [324]

Chatterjee, Ashok Kumar *see* THE YOGACARA IDEALISM

Chatterji, M M *see* THE "BHAGAVAD GITA"

Chatterton, Eyre *see* THE STORY OF FIFTY YEARS' MISSION WORK IN CHHOTA NAGPUR

Chatterton, Henrietta Georgiana Marcia *see* MEMORIALS, PERSONAL AND HISTORICAL OF ADMIRAL LORD GAMBIER. WITH ORIGINAL LETTERS FROM WILLIAM PITT FIRST LORD CHATHAM, LORD NELSON, LORD CASTLEREAGH, LORD MULGRAVE, HENRY FOX FIRST LORD HOLLAND, THE RIGHT HON. GEORGE CANNING

Chatterton, Mason Daniel *see* PROBATE LAW

CHATTULISTIWA – Amsterdam. 1947-1960. Incomplete. SE-748 1 – 9 – ne IDC [073]

Chaubard, LA *see*
- EXPEDITION SCIENTIFIQUE DE MOREE
- NOUVELLE FLORE DU PELOPONNESE ET DES CYCLADES

Chaucer, Geoffrey *see*
- THE CANTERBURY TALES
- CHAUCER'S LEGENDE OF GOODE WOMEN

CHAUCER'S LEGENDE OF GOODE WOMEN / Chaucer, Geoffrey – Ed., with introd. and notes, glossarial and critical, by Hiram Corson....Philadelphia: F. Leypoldt; New York: F.W. Christern. 1864. xxxviii, 145p – 1 – us U.W. Library [810]

CHAUCHAMAYO. ESTUDIO DE UNA REGION DE LA SELVA DEL PERU. DEPARTAMENTO...TOMO 1. LIMA, 1969 / Ortiz, Dionisio – Madrid: Graf. Calleja, 1970 – 1 – sp Bibl Santa Ana [972]

Chaudhuri, Bhawani Prasad *see* LEFTIST LEADERS OF INDIA

Chaudoin, E *see* TROIS MOIS DE CAPTIVITE AU DAHOMEY

Chaudoin, William *see* DIARY

Chaughi, Rene *see* LA FEMME ESCLAVE

Chauliac, A *see* HISTOIRE DE L'ABBEYE SAINTE-CROIX DE BORDEAUX

Chaulie, Dionisio *see* COSAS DE MADRID: APUNTES SOCIALES DE LA VILLA Y CORTE

Chaumeix, Abraham J de *see* NOUVEAU PLAN D'ETUDES: ESSAI SUR LA MANIERE DE REMPLIR LES PLACES DANS LES COLLEGES QUE LES JESUITES OCCUPOIENT CI-DEVANT

Chaumeton, F P *see* FLORE MEDICALE

Chaumette, E J M *see* LES ENFANTS CELEBRES

Chaumont, de *see* RELATION DE L'AMBASSADE...SIAM,...

CHAUNCEY W. MEAD PAPERS, MS 3602 / Mead, Chauncey W – 1862-65 – 1r – 1 – us Western Res [920]

Chaundler, Thomas *see* WORKS

CHAUTAUQUA ASSEMBLY HERALD – Ottawa. Kan. 1887-1913 – 1 – us UMI [071]

CHAUTAUQUA COUNTY AND ITS PEOPLE / Downs & Hedley – New York, American Historical Society, 1921. Vols. 1-3. New York Reel 11. (The Cox Library Collection) – 5 – us Americana [978]

Chautauqua History Co *see* THE CENTENNIAL HISTORY OF CHAUTAUQUA COUNTY

THE CHAUTAUQUA MOVEMENT / Vincent, John H – Boston: Chautauqua Press, 1886, c1885 – 1mf – us A.T.L.A. [240]

CHAUTAUQUAN – Merged into Independent. v. 31-72. 1900-1914. All pub – 1,5,6 – us Princeton Micro [240]

CHAUTAUQUAN DAILY – Chautauqua. N.Y. 1906-1967 – 1 – us UMI [071]

Chauveau, Pierre J O *see*
- L'ABBE JEAN HOLMES ET SES CONFERENCES DE NOTRE-DAME: ETUDE LITTERAIRE ET BIOGRAPHIQUE
- DISCOURS PRONONCE LORS DE L'INAUGURATION DU MONUMENT CARTIER-BREBEUF LE 24 JUIN 1889; DONNACORNA: POESIE
- FRANCOIS-XAVIER GARNEAU: SA VIE ET SES OEUVRES
- L'INSTRUCTION PUBLIQUE AU CANADA: PRECIS HISTORIQUE ET STATISTIQUE
- NOCES D'OR DE PIE IX: DISCOURS PRONONCE A CETTE OCCASION A LA SEANCE LITTERAIRE ET MUSICALE DONNEE A L'UNIVERSITE LAVAL, EN L'HONNEUR DU CINQUANTIEME ANNIVERSAIRE DU SACERDOCE DE SA SAINTETE, LE 10 AVRIL 1869
- SOUVENIRS ET LEGENDES: CONFERENCE FAITE A L'INSTITUT CANADIEN DE QUEBEC

Chauvet *see* DU NIGER, DU FLEUVE DE TIMBOUCTOU, DE SON EMBOUCHURE ET DE LA COMMUNICATION DES GRANDS FLEUVES D'AFRIQUE

Chauvin, Etienne *see* NOUVEAU JOURNAL DES SCAVANS, DRESSE A BERLIN

Chauvin, J F *see* RECHERCHES SUR L'ORGANISATION, LA FRUCTIFICATION ET LA CLASSIFICATION DE PLUSIEURS GENRES D'ALGUES

Chauvincourt, Beauvois de *see* DISCOURS DE LA LYCANTHROPIE OU DE LA TRANSFORMATION DES HOMMES EN LOUPS

Chavannes, E *see*
- DIX INSCRIPTIONS CHINOISES DE L'ASIE CENTRALE D'APRES LES ESTAMPAGES DE M. C.E. BONIN
- EPITAPHES DE DEUX PRINCESSES TURQUES DE L'EPOQUE DES TANG
- L'ITINERAIRE D' OU-K'ONG (751-790)
- LES MEMOIRS HISTORIQUES DE SE-MA TS'IEN
- MONOGRAPHIE DES ANTIRRHINEES
- LE NESTORIANISME ET L'INSCRIPTION DE KARA-BALGASSOUN

- NOTES ADDITIONELLES SUR LES TON-KINE (TURCS) OCCIDENTAUX
- LES PAYS D'OCCIDENT D'APRES LE HEOU CHOU
- UN TRAITE MANICHEEN RETROUVE EN CHINE
- VOYAGEURS CHINOIS CHEZ LES KHITAN ET LES JOUTCHEN

Chavard *see*
- ENCORE UN MOT SUR LA RELIGION SAINT-SIMONIENNE
- LA RELIGION SAINT-SIMONIENNE ET SES PRETRES

Chavasse, A *see* SACRAMENTARIUM GELASIANUM

Chaveau, M E *see* LE DROIT DES GENS...

Chaventre, A *see*
- ESQUISSE D'UNE ETUDE GENEALOGIQUE DES SARA KABA M'BANGA DU VILLAGE DE MIAMANE, REPUBLIQUE CENTRE-AFRICAINE
- ETUDE ANTHROPOLOGIQUE DE L'ILE DE SILBA
- ETUDE DU CONTEXTE SOCIAL ET HISTORIQUE DE LA REVOLTE DES IWELLEMMEDDAN DE 1916
- RAPPORT SUR LA MISSION MEDICO-SCIENTIFIQUE FRANCO-MALIENNE

Chavero, Alfredo *see* SAHAGUN

Chaves, Bernabe de *see* APUNTAMIENTO LEGAL DE LA O. SANTIAGO

Chaves, Manuel *see* DON BERNARDO MARQUEZ DE LA VEGA

Chaves Masa, Pedro *see* LLANTOS FUNEBRES A LA SENTIDA, LAMENTABLE,...DONA MA REINA DE PORTUGAL

Chaves y Manso, Rafael *see*
- DE LA LEGISLACION ROMANA EN LAS RELACIONES CON LA DE LOS PUEBLOS EUROPEOS
- DISCURSO

Chavez, A Ezequiel *see* EL PRIMERO DE LOS EDUCADORES DE LA NUEVA ESPANA, FR. PEDRO DE GANTE. MEJICO, 1934

Chavez, Fermin *see* PERON Y EL PERONISMO EN LA HISTORIA CONTEMPORANEA

Chayanov, A V *see* METHODS OF NON-MILITARY ACCOUNTING IN ECONOMIC UNDERTAKINGS

CHAYENU = OUR LIFE : ORGAN FOR JEWISH RELIGIOUS LABOUR – (In English and Hebrew) – London, GB. v6 no8 Aug 1943-v8 no10-11 Oct/Nov 1945 – 1r – 1 – $25.00 – cn Can Microfilming [072]

L'CHAYIM – (Continued by: L'chayim quarterly) – (La Jolla, Calif.) v1, no. 1 (Apr. 1974)-v9, no. 2 (winter 1982) ; v1 (fall 1983) – us A.J.P.C. [270]

CHAZANAH; SUARA SANTRI DAN SISWA PROGESIP / Dept. Penerangan IPNU wil. Djk. Raya – (Monthly. Missing: 1955(1-2)) – Djakarta, 1955(1-3) – 1mf – 9 – SE-1379/1 – ne IDC [950]

Chazaud *see* DICTIONNAIRE DES NOMS DE LIEUX HABITES DU DEPARTEMENT DE L'ALLIER

Chda, Kok Hong *see* PRICE PARITY TABLES FOR THE NETHERLANDS EAST INDIES

Cheadle. England *see* CHEADLE PARISH REGISTERS, 1574-1682/CANNOCK PARISH REGISTERS, 1660-1812/CAVERSWALL PARISH REGISTERS, 1559-1812

CHEADLE PARISH REGISTERS, 1574-1682/CANNOCK PARISH REGISTERS, 1660-1812/CAVERSWALL PARISH REGISTERS, 1559-1812 / Cheadle. England – 1 – uk Microform Academic [920]

Cheatham, Tina R *see* THE ATHLETIC ORGANIZATIONAL STRUCTURE AND ADMINISTRATIVE VIEWS OF UNIVERSITY AND ATHLETIC GOVERNING PERSONNEL IN THE SOUTHWEST CONFERENCE

Cheavens, J S *see* SOBRE INTERPRETACION

Chebotarevskaia, A *see* O SOLOGUBE: KRITIKA, STAT'I ZAMETKI

Chebsey. England *see* CHEBSEY PARISH REGISTERS, 1660-1713/COLWICH PARISH REGISTERS, 1574-1682

CHEBSEY PARISH REGISTERS, 1660-1713/COLWICH PARISH REGISTERS, 1574-1682 / Chebsey. England – 1 – uk Microform Academic [920]

CHEBUCTO AND OTHER POEMS / Bell, John Allison – Halifax: J. Bowes, 1890.05832.(Pre-1900 Canadiana) – 9 – cn C.I.H.M. [810]

Chebyshev-Dmitriev, A P *see* RUSSKOE UGOLOVNOE SUDOPROIZVODSTVO PO SUDEBNYM USTAVAM 20 NOIABRIA 1864 G

Checa, Pedro *see* TAREAS DE ORGANIZACION Y TRABAJO PRACTICO DEL PARTIDO

CHE-CHIANG HSIANG-SHIH LU – List of successful candidates in the imperial examination in Chekiang province: 1835, 1851, 1855, 1870, 1879, 1882, 1885, 1889, 1893. 1 reel – 1 – 29.00 – us Chinese Res [950]

CHE-CHIANG HSUEH-PAO – Chekiang Journal. v. 1-2 (1). Hangchow. 1947-48. BCH-207 2 – 8 – ne IDC [073]

CHE-CHIANG JIH-PAO – Hangchow, Chekiang. May 9, 1949-. Reel 1: Mar-May 10, 1961; Reel 2: Jan-Jul 1962; Reel 3: Aug-Dec. 1962. 3 reels – 1 – 52.50 – us Chinese Res [072]

CHE-CHIANG SHENG-LI T'U-SHU-KUAN KUAN-K'AN. JOURNAL / Chekiang Provincial Library – v. 1-6. Hanchow. 1932-37. Lacking: v. 3 (1-2, 4-6) 1934; v. 4 (3-5) 1935; v. 5-6, 1936 37. BCH-208 1 – 9 – ne IDC [073]

Chechulin, N D *see*
- OCHERKI PO ISTORII RUSSKIKH FINANSOV V TSARSTVORANIE EKATERINY 2
- VNESHNIAIA POLITIKA ROSSII V NACHALE TSARSTVOVANIIA E KATERINY II 1762-1774
- VNESIAIA POLITIKA ROSSII V NACHALE TSARSTVOVANIIA EKATERINY 2

CHECK LIST OF THE SHELLS OF NORTH AMERICA / Prime, T – Z 730 2. 1862 – 8 – ne IDC [580]

A CHECK TO UNCHARITABLENESS : OR, AN ANSWER TO A BOOK ENTITLED 'THE SKELETON; OR, THE ARMINIAN ANATOMIZED AND THE CARNAL PREACHER DISSECTED' BY W.H. IN THREE PARTS:... / King, T – London; 1791 – 2mf – 9 – MP-571/1 – ne IDC [240]

CHECKLIST OF DOCUMENTS, 1946-75 / United Nations – 1,3 – us Readex [900]

CHECKLIST OF HISTORICAL RECORDS SURVEY PUBLICATIONS, APRIL 1943 / U.S. Federal Works Agency – 1roll. T1028 – 1 – us Nat'l Archives [324]

CHECKLIST OF INNS OF COURT HOLDINGS / Louisiana State University. Paul M. Herbert Law Center. Library – (Covers add titles not offered for copyright reasons) – 1984 – 1mf – 9 – $1.50 – LLMC 84-305 – us L.L.M.C. [020]

A CHECKLIST OF SERIALS FOR AFRICAN STUDIES / Duignan, Peter & Glazier, Kenneth M – Based on the libraries of the Hoover Institute and Stanford University. 1963. 104p – 1 – 35.00r – us Hoover Inst Photo [960]

CHECKLIST OF THE COLEOPTERA OF AMERICA, NORTH OF MEXICO / Crotch, G R – Salem, 1873. 136p. Z-1155/2 – 8 – ne IDC [590]

CHECKLIST OF THE FISHES OF THE EASTERN TROPICAL ATLANTIC (CLOFETA) = CLOFETA ATLANTIC / ed by Quero, J C et al – (In English and French) – 1991 – 9 – 92-3-002622-0 – Copublished by JNICT-Portugal – fr UNESCO [590]

CHECKLIST OF THE FISHES OF THE NORTH-EASTERN ATLANTIC AND OF THE MEDITERRANEAN (CLOFNAM) / ed by Hureau, J C & Monod, T – (Text in English and French) – 2nd ed 1979 – 2v (xxii/683p; 394p) – 9 – 92-3-001762-0 – fr UNESCO [590]

CHECKLIST OF UNITED STATES PUBLIC DOCUMENTS / U. S. – (v2 was never publ) – 3rd ed. 1v. 1789-1909. Washington: GPO, 1909 (all publ) – 18mf – 9 – $27.00 – LLMC 81-403 – us L.L.M.C. [324]

CHECKLIST OF U.S. PUBLIC DOCUMENTS. SHELFLIST CARD CATALOG OF THE U.S.G.P.O / U.S. Government Printing Office – 1789-1976 – 1,5,6 – us Princeton Micro [324]

CHEDDAR VALLEY TIMES – England, 29 May-24 Dec 1914 – 23ft – 1 – uk British Libr Newspaper [072]

Chedeville, E P *see* CONCERTS CHAMPETRES POUR LES MUSETTES, VIELES... OP. 3

Chediak, Antonio Jose *see* CARLOS DE LAET, O POLMISTA

Cheeloo School of Theology *see* CATALOGUE OF THE CHEELOO SCHOOL OF THEOLOGY (CCC84)

CHEER FOR LIFE'S PILGRIMAGE / Meyer, Frederick Brotherton – New York: Fleming H Revell, c1897 – 1mf – 9 – 0-8370-7172-0 – 1986-1172 – us A.T.L.A. [240]

CHEERFUL AYRES OR BALLADS, FIRST COMPOSED FOR ONE SINGLE VOICE AND SINCE SET FOR THREE VOICES / Wilson, J – Oxford: William Hall, for Richard Davies, 1660 – 11mf – 9 – us Sibley [780]

Cheeseman, Lewis *see*
- DIFFERENCES BETWEEN OLD AND NEW SCHOOL PRESBYTERIANS
- ISHMAEL AND THE CHURCH

Cheetham, S *see*
- A HISTORY OF THE CHRISTIAN CHURCH DURING THE FIRST SIX CENTURIES
- A HISTORY OF THE CHRISTIAN CHURCH SINCE THE REFORMATION
- THE MYSTERIES, PAGAN AND CHRISTIAN

Cheetham, William *see* LIGHTS AND SHADOWS OF CLERICAL LIFE

Cheever, George B *see* GOD AGAINST SLAVERY

Cheever, George Barrell *see*
- FAITH, DOUBT, AND EVIDENCE: GOD'S VOUCHERS FOR HIS WRITTEN WORD
- GOD'S HAND IN AMERICA
- THE GUILT OF SLAVERY AND THE CRIME OF SLAVEHOLDING

LES CHEFFERIES DE MARE : LES DOCUMENTS / Dubois, M J – 9 – F200.00 – fr Ethnologie [306]

CHEFS D'OEUVRE DE L'AMERIQUE PRECOLOMBIENNE / Institut d'Ethnologie. Museum National d'Histoire Naturelle. Paris – Commissaire: Henri Lehmann avec Georgette Soustelle – 9 – F120.00 – fr Ethnologie [306]

CHEFS D'OEUVRES CLASSIQUES DE L'OPERA FRANCAIS – 38v – 1 – 207.00 – us L of C Photodup [780]

CHEFS-D'OEUVRE DE LA PEINTURE FRANCAISE DANS LES MUSEES DE LENINGRAD ET DE MOSCOU / Reunion des musees nationaux. Paris – 1965. 102 illus. 3 fiches – 9 – fr Réunion [700]

CHEFS-D'OEUVRE DE L'ART PALEOLITHIQUE / Reunion des musees nationaux. Paris – 1969. 7 illus. 1 fiche – 9 – fr Réunion [700]

CHEFS-D'OEUVRE DES COLLECTIONS PRIVEES FRANCAISES RETROUVEES EN ALLEMAGNE PAR LA COMMISSION DE RECUPERATION ARTISTIQUE ET LES SERVICES ALLIES / Reunion des musees nationaux. Paris – 1946. 2 illus. 2 fiches – 9 – fr Réunion [700]

Cheglokov, P N *see* OB ORGANAKH SUDEBNOI VLASTI V ROSSII OT OSNOVANIIA GOSUDARSTVA DO VSTUPLENIIA NO PRESTOL' ALEKSEIA MIKHAILOVICHA

Chehpeliades, M G *see* DE LA CONDITION...

CHE-HSUEH P'ING-LUN – Philosophical Review. v1-11 (2). Peiping. 1927-46. Available: v1-3(4), v4, v5, v6(2-3), v 7, v8, v9(2). BCH-209 2 – 8 – ne IDC [100]

CHE-HSUEH YEN-CHIU – Study of Philosophy. Peking, 1955-66. BCH-931/2 – 8 – ne IDC [100]

Cheikho, L *see* SALIH IBN YAHYA. HISTOIRE DE BEYROUTH...

CHEIROS LANGUAGE OF THE HAND : A COMPLETE PRACTICAL WORK ON THE SCIENCES OF CHEIROGNOMY AND CHEIROMANCY, CONTAINING THE SYSTEM, RULES, AND EXPERIENCE OF CHEIRO (COMTE DE HAMONG) – 7th ed. New York: F Tennyson Neely, c1897 – us Res Libr [130]

CHE-KA : MATERIALY PO DEIATELNOSTI CHREZVYCHAINYKH KOMISSII / Chernov, Viktor Mikhailovich et al – Berlin: Izd. T Sentr. bi uro Partii sotsialistov-revoliutsionerov, 1922 – 1 – CSUX89-B1790 – us Hoover Inst Photo [947]

CHEKA : LICHNYIA VOSPOMINAIAOB ODESSKO I CHREZVYCHAIKIE S PORTRETAMI ZHERTV CH. K. / Alinin, K – Odessa: Sklad izd. Tip. "Tekhnik", 1919 – 1 – CSUX88-B5808 – us Hoover Inst Photo [947]

CHEKHOSLOVAKI V ROSSII, 1914-1920 / Dragomiretskii, VS – Parizh: Izd. avtora, 1928 – 1 – CSUX88-B6788 – us Hoover Inst Photo [947]

CHEKHO-SLOVAKI V SAMARI E – Moskva: Vseros. t sentr. ispolnitelnago kom-ta sovietov r., s., k. i k. deputatov, Voen. otdi el, 1918 – 1 – CSUX88-B7633 – us Hoover Inst Photo [947]

CHEKHOSLOVAT SKOE VO ISKO V ROSSII / Golecek, V – Irkutsk: Izd. Informatsionno-prosvi etitelnago otdi ela Chekhoslovat skago voen. ministerstva, 1919 – 1 – CSUX89-B5215 – us Hoover Inst Photo [947]

Chekhov, A P *see* RUKOPISI, PIS'MA, BIOGRAFICHESKIE DOKUMENTY, VOSPOMINANIIA, TEATRAL'NYE POSTANOVKI, RISUNKI, FOTOGRAFII..

Chekhovskoi, V I A *see* ENTALPIIA, TEPLOEMKOST, TEPLOTA I ENTROPIIA PLAVLENIIA NEKOTORYKH TUGOPLAVKIKH METALLOV

Chekiang Provincial Library *see* CHE-CHIANG SHENG-LI T'U-SHU-KUAN KUAN-K'AN. JOURNAL

A CHEKOSLOVAKIAN WRITER TELLS OF THE WAVE OF TERROR SWEEPING OVER CADIZ – Washington, DC. 193? Fiche W 717. (Blodgett Collection of Spanish Civil War Pamphlets) – 9 – us H.U. College Libr [946]

Chekunov, A V *see* GEOPHYSICAL JOURNAL

Cheles. Ayuntamiento *see* PROGRAMA DE FERIAS Y FIESTAS EN HONOR DEL SANTISIMO CRISTO DE LA PAZ. SEPTIEMBRE 1976

Cheliapov, N I *see* VOPROSY SOVETSKOGO STROITEL'STVA: SBORNIK STATEI

Chellig, Nadia *see* POUVOIRS ET SOCIETE AGRA-PASTORALE DANS LES HAUTES PLAINES STEPPIQUES DE L'ALGERIE

CHELMER SZTYME = VOICE – (In Yiddish) – Chelm, PL. v4 no47(no191) Nov 1928-v4 no49(no193) Dec 1928 – 1r – 1 – $25.00 – cn Can Microfilming [072]

CHELMSFORD 1645-1849 – (Mf 1T-4T: Vital Records 1645-1738. Mf 5T-7T: Births & Deaths 1719-75. Mf 7T: Marriages & Intentions 1714-39. Mf 8T-9T: Marriage Intentions 1745-77. Mf 9T: Births 1704-07, 1774-75. Mf 10T-12T: Births & Deaths 1767-1826. Mf 12T-16T,18T-21T: Intentions 1777-1849. Mf 13T-15T: Marriages 1780-1823. Mf 16T-17T: Births 1799-1844. Mf 9T,17T-18T: Marriages 1741-93, 1836-43. Mf 17T-18T: Out-of-Town Marriages 1661-1799. Mf 21T: Marriages 1822-36; Deaths 1781-1844. Mf 22T-23T: Vital Records 1843-49) – (mf ed 1995) – 23mf – 9 – 0-87623-228-4 – us Holbrook [920]

CHELMSFORD 1653-1900 – (Mf 1-8: Town & Vital 1653-1777. Mf 9-24: Town & Land 1653-1785. Mf 12-32: Vital Records 1653-1826. Mf 33-39: Intentions 1825-1903. Mf 35: Marriages 1822-36. Mf 40-53: Vitals 1653-1843. Mf 47-62: Church Records 1656-1901. Mf 63-88: Town Records 1680-1767. Mf 89-153: Town & Tax 1762-1823. Mf 154-214: Town Record 1789-1904. Mf 214-220: Deeds 1837-52. Mf 221-224: School 1819-69. Mf 225-229: Military 1861-75. Mf 230-234: Paupers 1817-1917. Mf 235-239: Voters 1877-1902. Mf 240: Births 1799-1844. Mf 241-242: Dog License 1863-72. Mf 243-249: Vitals 1834-70. Mf 250-253: Marriages 1854-87. Mf 254-255: Births 1871-99. Mf 255-256: Marriages 1887-1900. Mf 253,256-257: Deaths 1852-1900. Mf 258-266: Birth Index 1843-1900. Mf 267-273: Marriage Index 1844-1900. Mf 274-278: Death Index 1843-1900) – (mf ed 1997) – 278mf – 9 – 0-87623-388-4 – us Holbrook [920]

CHELMSFORD AND SOUTH WOODHAM WEEKLY NEWS *see* CHELMSFORD WEEKLY NEWS

CHELMSFORD WEEKLY NEWS – England, 1978- – 43+ r – 1 – uk British Libr Newspaper [072]

CHELOVECHESKAIA ZHIZN' – Zhurnal. v. 1. 1905. BR-3396 2 – 8 – ne IDC [073]

CHELOVEK / Ivanov, V – Paris. 1939. BR-733 2 – 8 – ne IDC [460]

CHELOVEK – Izd. Akademii nauk SSSR. v. 1-4. L. 1928. BR-2277 2 – 8 – ne IDC [073]

CHELOVEK I PRIRODA (PETROGRAD, R.S.F.S.R. – (Includes c.1: v.1 1920) – Petersburg: Gos. izd-vo, 1920- – 1 – CSUXAKZ6939-S – us Hoover Inst Photo [947]

CHELSEA 1655-1849 – (Mf 1T-3T: Births & Deaths 1718-1842. Mf 3T-4T: Births 1842-49. Mf 4T.5T: Marriage Intentions 1843-50. Mf 5T-7T: Marriages 1841-49. Mf 6T-7T: Deaths 1840-49. Mf 7T: Births & Deaths 1820-49; Out-of-Town Marriages 1655-1798. Mf 7T-9T: Marriage Intentions 1739-1843; Marriages 1738-1844) – (mf ed 1995) – 9mf – 9 – 0-87623-229-2 – us Holbrook [920]

A CHELSEA HOUSEHOLDER / Lawless, Emily – British Fiction Archive: Unit 4 – 9 – uk Bell [830]

CHELSEA JOURNAL – (Ceased v6 no 3 1980) – Saskatoon. v1-6. 1975-80 – 9 – Can$20.00y – cn Micromedia [073]

CHELSEA NEWS – London: Westminster and Chelsea News West London Press, 1865-72; 1875-1975 – 99r – 1 – uk British Libr Newspaper [072]

CHELSEA PICK AND SHOVEL – London, England. Jan-Dec 1900 – 10ft – 1 – uk British Libr Newspaper [072]
CHELSEA TIMES – London, 24 Feb 1872; 4 Jan 1873-11 Dec 1875 – 2r – 1 – uk British Libr Newspaper [072]
Cheltsov-Bebutov, M A *see*
– SOTSIALISTICHESKOE PRAVOSOZNANIE I UGOLOVNOE PRAVO REVOLIUTSII
– SOVETSKII UGOLOVNYI PROTSESS
CHELYS, MINURITIONUM ARTIFICIO EXORNATA...THE DIVISION-VIOL.. / Simpson, Christopher – Editio secunda. 1667 – 2 – us Sibley [780]
O CHEM SHEPCHET DEREVNIA / Bezerov, Rodion Mikhailovich – Moskva: Moskovski i rabochi i, 1925 – 1 – CSUX88-B5100 – us Hoover Inst Photo [947]
CHEMAWA AMERICAN – 1926-35; 1970-76. (American Indian Periodicals in the Princeton University Library). 16 fiches – 9 – $75.00 – us UPA [305]
CHEMEHUEVI NEWSLETTER – 1968-73. (American Indian Periodicals in the Princeton University Library). 6 fiches – 9 – $45.00 – us UPA [305]
CHEMICA SCRIPTA – v1-4. 1971-73. See also: Archiv fuer Kemi – 1,5,6 – us Princeton Micro [540]
CHEMICAL ABSTRACTS / American Chemical Society – Easton, 1907-18. v. 1-12 – 600mf – 8 – ne IDC [073]
CHEMICAL ABSTRACTS : COLLECTIVE INDEXES – (1st-6th 1907-61. 7th 1962-66. 8th 1967-71. 9th 1972-76. 10th 1977-81. 11th 1982-86. 12th 1987-91. 13th 1992-96) – 1907-86. 11 indexes – 6,9 – us Chemical [540]
CHEMICAL AGE – (1979-. 9) – v. 108- 1974- (Formerly: Chemical Age International) – 1,5,6 – us UMI [540]
CHEMICAL AGE – v. 1-101. 1919-70 – 1,5,6 – us Princeton Micro [540]
CHEMICAL AGE INTERNATIONAL – (1965-74. 5,6) – v. 1-108. 1919-74 – 1 – us UMI [540]
CHEMICAL AND ENGINEERING NEWS – v1-1923- – 1,5,6,9 – us A.C.S. [540]
CHEMICAL AND PETROLEUM ENGINEERING – v1-30. 1965-94 – 1,5 – $80.00v – us UMI [660]
CHEMICAL AND PHARMACEUTICAL BULLETIN – (Formerly: Pharmaceutical Bulletin). v. 1-21. 1953-1973 – 1,5,6 – us Princeton Micro [540]
CHEMICAL, BIOMEDICAL, AND ENVIRONMENTAL INSTRUMENTATION – v9-12. 1979-83 – 1 – us UMI [073]
CHEMICAL BUSINESS – v1-. 1984- – 1,5,6,9 – us UMI [073]
CHEMICAL ENGINEER – (1976-. 5,6,9) – 1956- – 1 – us UMI [660]
CHEMICAL ENGINEERING – v.1- 1902- – 1,5,6,9 – us UMI [540]
CHEMICAL ENGINEERING – v1-62. 1902-55 – 1,5,6 – us Princeton Micro [660]
CHEMICAL ENGINEERING AND MINING REVIEW – Melbourne, Australia. Apr-Nov 1918; Jan 1920-Dec 1921 (missing Sep 1918; Apr 1920).-m. 2 reels – 1 – uk British Libr Newspaper [073]
CHEMICAL ENGINEERING CATALOG: CEC – 1984- – 1,5,6,9 – us UMI [660]
CHEMICAL ENGINEERING COMMUNICATIONS / ed by Gill, W N et al – 1,5,9 – us Gordon [540]
CHEMICAL ENGINEERING JOURNAL – v1-29. 1970-84 – 1,5,6,13 – sz Elsevier [073]
CHEMICAL ENGINEERING PROGRESS – v1-51. 1908-55 – 1,5,6 – us Princeton Micro [660]
CHEMICAL ENGINEERING SCIENCE – v1-1951- – 5,6,9 – us UMI [073]
THE CHEMICAL GAZETTE: OR, JOURNAL OF PRACTICAL CHEMISTRY, IN ALL ITS APPLICATIONS TO PHARMACY, ARTS, AND MANUFACTURES – London, 1842-1859 – 3 – us Readex [540]
CHEMICAL GEOLOGY – v1-46. 1966-84 – 1,5,6,13 – sz Elsevier [550]
CHEMICAL HEALTH AND SAFETY – v1. 1994- – 1,5,6,9 – ACS Division of Chemical Health and Safety – us A.C.S. [540]
THE CHEMICAL HISTORY OF THE SIX DAYS OF CREATION / Phin, John – New York: American News, 1870. 1 fiche.8370-4735-8 – 9 – us A.T.L.A. [240]
CHEMICAL INDUSTRY COMMITTEE / UN Economic Commission for Europe (ECE) – 1968-89 – E/F.112 E.573 F.441 R.384 – 9 – us U.N. Pubs [340]
CHEMICAL INDUSTRY PRODUCT NEWS – v15, no.5-v22, no.6. Oct 1977-Dec 1983 – 1,5,6,9 – us UMI [073]
CHEMICAL INSTRUMENTATION – v1-8. 1968-77 – 1 – us UMI [073]
CHEMICAL MARKETING REPORT – New York, NY. 1963-78 – 38r – 1 – $1,900.00 – R04905 – us Library Micro [071]
CHEMICAL MARKETING REPORTER – (v. 215-. 1979-. 5,6,9) – v. 10- 1876- – 1 – us UMI [540]
THE CHEMICAL NEWS AND JOURNAL OF PHYSICAL SCIENCE – [London: Griffin, Bohn & Co, 1861-1921]. v14-15 1867 – 1r – 1 – us Res Libr [500]
CHEMICAL PATENTS INDEX – (Plastics. 1966-91. Pharmaceuticals. 1963-91. Agricultural Chemistry. 1965-84. Food and Fermentation and Detergents. 1970-91. General Chemistry. 1970-91. Textiles and Paper. 1970-91. Coating and Adhesives and Photography. 1970-91. Petroleum. 1970-91. Glass and Ceramics and Cement. 1970-91. Metallurgy. 1970-91) – 1963-91. Annual. Basic abstracts on microfilm. English lang. abstracts for new patents and applications from 16 major patent issuing authorities covering all chemically oriented technologies. Available by subject and year – 5,6 – uk Derwent [660]
CHEMICAL PATENTS INDEX – (Plastics. 1966-91. Pharmaceuticals. 1963-91. Agricultural chemistry. 1965-84. Food and Fermentation and Detergents. 1970-91. General Chemistry. 1970-91. Textiles and Paper. 1970-91. Coating and Adhesives and Photography. 1970-91. Petroleum. 1970-91. Glass and Ceramics and Cement. 1970-91. Metallurgy. 1970-91) – 1963-91. Annual. Complete specifications on microfilm. Complete patent specifications by subject for all chemically oriented technologies from 15 major patent issuing authorities. Available by subject and year – 5,6 – uk Derwent [660]
CHEMICAL PHYSICS – v1-90. 1973-84 – 1,5,6,13 – sz Elsevier [073]
CHEMICAL PHYSICS LETTERS – v1-112. 1967-84 – 1,5,6,13 – sz Elsevier [073]
CHEMICAL PHYSICS REPORTS / ed by Gol'danskii, V I – 1,5,9 – us Gordon [540]
CHEMICAL PROBLEMS ASSOCIATED WITH THE CONTROL OF PESTS IN STORED GROUNDNIUTS IN WEST AFRICA / Babatunde Somade, H M – London, [1953] – us Res Libr [630]
CHEMICAL PRODUCT NEWS: CPN – v23-. Feb 1984- – 1,5,6,9 – us UMI [073]
CHEMICAL RESEARCH IN TOXICOLOGY – v1-1988- – 1,5,6,9 – us A.C.S. [615]
CHEMICAL REVIEWS – Baltimore. 1924-57. v.1-57. Lacking: 1924-28, v.1-5; 1950, v.47 (1, p.1-175), (3-4, p.306-End). B-7683 1 – 9 – ne IDC [073]
CHEMICAL REVIEWS – Baltimore. v36-45. 1945-49. 279/2 – 8 – ne IDC [073]
CHEMICAL REVIEWS – (Missing: 1924-1928. v1-5) – Baltimore, 1924-1941. v1-29 – 157mf – 7683c/1 – ne IDC [660]
CHEMICAL REVIEWS – v1- 1924- – 1,5,6,9 – us A.C.S. [540]
Chemical Society *see*
– JOURNAL
– PROCEEDINGS
– REVIEWS
Chemical Society. Analytical Division *see* PROCEEDINGS
Chemical Society. Japan *see* BULLETIN
Chemical Society. London *see*
– ANNUAL REPORTS OF THE PROGRESS OF CHEMISTRY
– ANNUAL REPORTS ON THE PROGRESS OF CHEMISTRY
– JOURNAL
– JOURNAL, DALTON TRANSACTIONS
– JOURNAL, FARADAY TRANSACTIONS 2
– JOURNAL, PERKIN TRANSACTIONS 1
– JOURNAL, PERKIN TRANSACTIONS 2
– JOURNAL, SECTION A: INORGANIC, PHYSICAL, AND THEORETICAL CHEMISTRY
– JOURNAL, SECTION B: PHYSICAL ORGANIC CHEMISTRY
– JOURNAL, SECTION C: ORGANIC CHEMISTRY
– JOURNAL, SECTION D: CHEMICAL COMMUNICATIONS
– MEMOIRS AND PROCEEDINGS OF THE CHEMICAL SOCIETY OF LONDON FOR 1841-48
– PROCEEDINGS
– QUARTERLY REVIEWS
CHEMICAL SOCIETY REVIEWS – Royal Society of Chemistry, Great Britain. 1972-84. Available to current subscribers to the equivalent printed editions – 1 – us UMI [073]
CHEMICAL WEEK – v.1- 1926- – 1,5,6,9 – us UMI [073]
CHEMICO-BIOLOGICAL INTERACTIONS – v1-52. 1969-84 – 1,5,6,13 – sz Elsevier [073]
CHEMIE-INGENIEUR-TECHNIK (CIT) : VERFAHRENSTECHNIK, TECHNISCHE CHEMIE, APPARATEWESEN, BIOTECHNOLOGIE – v1-68. 1928-96 – 1,5,6,13 – us V.C.H. [540]
CHEMIKER ZEITUNG – v. 1-68. 1877-1944 – 1,5,6 – us Princeton Micro [540]
CHEMIKER-ZEITUNG – Koethen, Germany. 1880-1909.-w. 56 reels – 1 – uk British Libr Newspaper [073]
CHEMIN DE FER DE HALIFAX ET DE QUEBEC ET TRAVAUX PUBLICS / Canada. Gouverneur general – Montreal: Imprime par Lovell et Gilbson sic, 1849. SEM105P121 – 1mf – 9 – Can$2.25 – cn Bibl Nat [380]
Chemin de fer de Quebec et du Saguenay *see* REPORT OF THE CHIEF ENGINEER..
CHEMIN DE FER DE QUEBEC ET HALIFAX / Canada. Parliament. Legislative Assembly – Quebec: Imprime par John Lovell, 1852. SEM105P128 – 2mf – 9 – Can$4.50 – cn Bibl Nat [380]
LE CHEMIN DE FER DES CANTONS DU NORD – Quebec, 1884. 02985. (Pre-1900 Canadiana) – 9 – cn C.I.H.M. [380]
Chemin de Fer du Grand Tronc *see*
– PROCEEDINGS OF THE...MEETING OF THE SHAREHOLDERS OF THE GRAND TRUNK RAILWAY COMPANY OF CANADA...1854
– REPONSE COMPLEMENTAIRE A UNE ADRESSE DE L'ASSEMBLEE LEGISLATIVE DU 21 DU MOIS DERNIER,...
– REPONSE PARTIELLE..
– STATEMENTS, REPORTS AND ACCOUNTS OF THE GRAND TRUNK RAILWAY COMPANY OF CANADA
LE CHEMIN DE FER DU LAC SAINT-JEAN / Buies, Arthur – Quebec: Leger Brousseau, 1895. SEM105P24 – 2mf – 9 – Can$4.50 – cn Bibl Nat [971]
LE CHEMIN DE FER DU LAC ST-JEAN – Quebec, 1882? 00597. (Pre-1900 Canadiana) – 9 – cn C.I.H.M. [380]
LE CHEMIN DE FRANCE: GILBRALTER / Verne, Jules – Paris: J. Hetzel, 1887. 324p. 4 fiches. (Literature Collection) – 9 – 10.00 – fr Bibl Nationale [830]
LE CHEMIN DES LARMES, OU, UN AMOUR DECU – Anon. Montreal: C. Beauchemin, 1896. 00598. (Pre-1900 Canadiana) – 9 – cn C.I.H.M. [830]
LE CHEMINOT ALGERIEN / Union d'Algerie – Alger. 1930-38 – 1 – fr A.C.R.P.P. [073]
LE CHEMINOT DE L'ETAT / Union des syndicats confederes des Chemins de Fer de l'Etat francais – Paris. mai 1917-avr 1920, mai 1928, 1931-juin juil 1939 – 1 – fr A.C.R.P.P. [331]
CHEMINS DE FER DANS LA PROVINCE DE QUEBEC: DISCOURS PRONONCE A L'ASSEMBLEE LEGISLATIVE LE 29E JOUR DE DECEMBRE 1896, SUR LES RESOLUTIONS TOUCHANT LES SUBSIDES AUX CHEMINS DE FER / Flynn, Edmund James – par l'Honorable E. J. Flynn, premier ministre et commissaire des travaux publics. Quebec: s.n.. 1897 (Quebec: Impr. generale). 03113. (Pre-1900 Canadiana) – 9 – cn C.I.H.M. [971]
LES CHEMINS DE FER DU CAMEROUN / Regie Nationale de Chemins de Fer du Cameroun – 1967-74. – 1r – 1 – $24.75 – us African Imprint [380]
CHEMISCHE BERICHTE : INORGANIC AND ORGANO-METALLIC CHEMISTRY – v1-129. 1868-1996 – 1,5,6,13 – us V.C.H. [540]
CHEMISCHE GASPHASENABSCHEIDUNG VON VANADIUMOXIDEN / Wormer, Oliver Gerd – 1993 – 2mf – 9 – DM98.00 – 3-89349-644-0 – gw Hänsel [540]
CHEMISCHE ZEITSCHRIFT – Germany. Leipzig. -f. Oct 1901-Dec 1908. 4 1 2 reels – 1 – uk British Libr Newspaper [073]
CHEMISCHES JOURNAL FUER DIE FREUNDE DER NATURLEHRE, ARZNEYGELEHRTHEIT, HAUSHALTUNGSKUNST UND MANUFACTUREN – Lemgo, 1778-81 – 3 – us Readex [540]
THE CHEMIST – London. 1840 – 3 – us Readex [540]
CHEMIST AND DRUGGIST – (1975-81. 5,6,9) – 1859-1981 – 1 – us UMI [615]
CHEMISTRY – A EUROPEAN JOURNAL *see* – ANGEWANDTE CHEMIE
CHEMISTRY AND CHEMICAL INDUSTRY – (1975- 5,6,9) – 1948- – 1 – us UMI [540]
CHEMISTRY AND ECOLOGY / ed by Howells, G – 9,5,1 – us Gordon [540]
CHEMISTRY AND INDUSTRY – 1941-82 – 1,5,6 – us Princeton Micro [073]
CHEMISTRY AND PHYSICS OF LIPIDS – v1-36. 1966-84 – 1,5,6,13 – sz Elsevier [073]
CHEMISTRY AND TECHNOLOGY OF FUELS AND OILS – v1-30. 1965-94 – 1,5 – $80.00v – us UMI [660]
CHEMISTRY AND THEOLOGY IN MID-VICTORIAN LONDON : THE DIARY OF HERBERT MCLEOD, 1860-70 / ed by James, Frank A J L – 1987. 23 fiches. Printed booklet – 9 – £135.00 – uk Mansell Publ [540]
CHEMISTRY AS APPLIED TO THE FINE ARTS / Bachoffner, George Henry – London: J. Carpenter, 1837. xvi,172p. Includes index – 1 – us U.W. Library [540]
CHEMISTRY IN BRITAIN – Royal Society of Chemistry, Great Britain. 1965-84 (1965-69 35mm only). Available to current subscribers to the equivalent printed editions – 1 – us UMI [073]
CHEMISTRY IN CANADA – (v26-35 1974-83 Can$28.00y 9. Cont by: Canadian Chemical News at v36 1984) – Ottawa. v1-35. 1949/52-1983 – 5,9 – Price varies – cn Micromedia [540]
CHEMISTRY IN CANADA *see* CANADIAN CHEMICAL NEWS
CHEMISTRY IN ECOLOGY – 1982 – 1,5,9 – us Gordon [540]
CHEMISTRY LETTERS – (1975- 5,6,9) – 1972- – 1 – us UMI [073]
THE CHEMISTRY OF COMMON LIFE / Johnston, James Finlay Weir – New ed., rev. and updated by Arthur Herbert Church. Edinburgh: W. Blackwood, 1879. xxvi,592p. illus. Includes index – 1 – us U.W. Library [390]
CHEMISTRY OF HETEROCYCLIC COMPOUNDS – 1-30. 1965-94 – 1,5 – $120.00v – us UMI [540]
CHEMISTRY OF MATERIALS – v1- 1989- – 1,5,6,9 – us A.C.S. [073]
CHEMISTRY OF NATURAL COMPOUNDS – v1-29. 1965-93 – 1,5 – $80.00v – us UMI [540]
CHEMISTRY REVIEWS / ed by Vol'pin, M E & Phillips, D – 9,5,1 – us Harwood [540]
Chemnitius, M *see* THESES DE JURE BELLI
Chemnitz, J H *see* SYSTEMATISCHES CONCHYLIEN-CABINET
Chemnitz, Martin *see*
– APOLOGIA ODER VERANTWORTUNG DESS CHRISTLICHEN CONCORDIEN BUCHS...
– DE DVABVS NATVRIS IN CHRISTO..
– DE DVABVS NATVRIS IN CHRISTO. DE HYPOSTATICA EARVM VNIONE...
– DE INCARNATIONE FILII DEI ITEM DE OFFICIO ET MAIESTATE CHRISTI TRACTUS
– DIE FUERNEMSTEN HEUPSTUECK DER CHRISTLICHEN LEHRE
– HISTORI DESS SACRAMENTSTREITS...
– HISTORIA DER PASSION VNSERS LIEBEN HERRN VND HEILANDS JESU
– LOCI THEOLOGICI...
– POSTILLA ODER AUSSLEGUNG DER EUANGELIEN...
– REPETITIO SANAE DOCTRINAE DE VERA PRAESENTIA...
CHEMORECEPTION ABSTRACTS – Quarterly – 9 – us C.S.A. [540]
CHEMOSPHERE – v1- 1972- – 5,6,9 – us UMI [500]
CHEMOTHERAPY – v. 11-18. 1966-1973 – 1,5,6 – us Princeton Micro [615]
CHEMOTHERAPY – v21-. 1975- – 1,5,9 – us UMI [073]
CHEMTECH – v1- 1971- – 1,5,6,9 – us A.C.S. [073]
CHEMTRONICS *see* ADVANCED MATERIALS FOR OPTICS AND ELECTRONICS
CHEMU UCHAT NAS PRAVITELSTVOI TRETIA GOSUDARSTVENNAIA DUMA : PISMO DEPUTATA PERVOI GOSUDARSTVENNOI DUMY NA RODINU – [Parizh?: s.n.], 1910 – 1 – CSUX89-B1755 – us Hoover Inst Photo [947]
CHEMUNG COUNTY / Towner, A – 1892. New York Reel 12. (The Cox Library Collection) – 5 – us Americana [978]
Chemung. Presbytery (Pres. Ch. in the U.S.A.) *see* MINUTES, 1836-1894
Ch'en, Ch'ang-feng *see* LONG MARCH DISAMPING KETUA MAU TJE-TUNG

CH'EN CH'ENG COLLECTION / Cheng, Chen – Documents collected by General Ch'en Ch'eng, former Vice President of China. 1931-37 – 1 – 35.00r – us Hoover Inst Photo [950]
Ch'en, Chien-hsun *see* THE BIBLICAL VIEW OF MARRIAGE (CCC88)
Ch'en, Chin-yung *see*
- ADDRESSES AND SERMONS FOR PREACHERS (CCC92)
- HINTS ON PREACHING (CCC91)

Ch'en, Chi-yun *see*
- THE GOSPEL FOR ALL (CCC87)
- THE PREPARATION FOR THE GOSPEL (CCC86)
- WHAT IS THE CHRISTIAN CHURCH? (CCC85)

Ch'en, Chu *see* THE HONOURABLE GUEST (CCC89)
Chen, J A *see* SELECTED PHYSIOLOGICAL VARIABLES AND DISTANCE RUNNING PERFORMANCE AMONG NON-ELITE, HETEROGENEOUS GROUPS OF MALE AND FEMALE RUNNERS
Chen, Kan *see* IVHS JOURNAL
Chen, Kwan *see* PERSONAL INVESTMENT IN EXERCISE AND SPORT
Ch'en, Li-t'ing *see* ESSENTIALS OF YMCA (CCC93)
Ch'en, Lu-wei *see* GUIDE TO INDONESIA
Chen, Moon S *see* PRESSURE SORE PREVENTION SELF-EFFICACY AND OUTCOME EXPECTATIONS IN THE SPINAL CORD-INJURED
Chen, Su Lan *see* THE OPIUM PROBLEM IN BRITISH MALAYA
Ch'en Ta *see* CHUNG-KUO LAO-KUNG WEN-T'I
Chen, Ta-san *see* SCRIPTURE CATECHISM (CCC266)
Ch'en, W Y *see* WHAT RELIGION DOES FOR PERSONALITY (CCC94)
Chen, Xinhua *see*
- DIE BEDEUTUNG DER WIRTSCHAFTLICHEN KOOPERATION FUER DIE WIRTSCHAFTSENTWICKLUNG CHINAS AM BEISPIEL JOINT VENTURES
- DIE CHINESISCHE WIRTSCHAFTSREFORM UND INFLATIONSPROBLEMATIK SEIT 1979

CHENANGO AMERICAN – Greene. N.Y. 1856-1969 – 1 – us UMI [071]
CHENANGO TELEGRAPH – Norwich. N.Y. 1835-1840; 1846-1868; 1872-1904 – 1 – us UMI [071]
CHENANGO WEEKLY ADVERTISER – Norwich. New York; 1811-12. Broome County Patriot. Binghamton. New York. 1811-13; Political Olio. Binghamton, N.Y. 1813-14; Madison County Herald. Peterboro. New York. 1813-18. Sold as one unit – 3 – us Readex [071]
Chenevert, C A *see* LE COURRIER DE SOREL
Cheneviere, A *see* LEXIQUE DE LA LANGUE DE BONAVENTURE DES PERIERS
Cheney Cowles Memorial Museum of the Eastern Washington State Historical Society *see* CORNHUSK BAGS OF THE PLATEAU INDIANS
CHENEY HERALD – Cheney. Kan. 1891-94 – 1 – us UMI [071]
CHEN-FU-KUNG-PAO = OFFICIAL GAZETTE. REPUBLIC OF CHINA FROM 1912-1919 – (In Chinese. Lacks: 1915/1,3,7. 1916/1-3,6. 1918/11) – May 1912-Oct 1919 – 50r – 1 – Y414,000 – ja Yushodo [950]
Cheng, Andrew C Y *see* THE LIFE OF THE EARLY CHURCH (CCC95)
Cheng, Chen *see* CH'EN CH'ENG COLLECTION
Ch'eng, Chih-i *see* A GUIDE TO THE STUDY OF THE NEW TESTAMENT (CCC96)
Cheng, F T *see* THE RULES OF PRIVATE INTERNATIONAL LAW...
Cheng, Hsueeh-chia *see* WHITHER INDONESIA? PKI AND CCP
Ch'eng, I-chen *see* CHINESE CHRISTIAN MONOGRAPH (CCC97)
Cheng, P *see* INTERNATIONAL LAW TIMES OF PEACE
CHENG XIANG JIANSHE – Urban and Rural Construction. 1984-85. F/P 299 – 9 – $4.50f – cc Microforms [624]
CHENG-CHIANG FU-CHIH 5-16 – 1719. BCH-671 2 – 8 – ne IDC [950]
CHENG-CHIH HSUEH-HSI – Political Studies. Peking. 1955-59. Lacking: v. 1 (4-8) 1955; v. 1 (1-26) v. 2, v. 3, v. 4, v. 9, 1956. BCH-892 2 – 8 – ne IDC [320]
CHENGDU KEJI DAXUE XUEBAO – Journal of Chengdu University of Science and Technology. In Chinese but English abstracts to the main articles. F p179 – 9 – 4.00f – cc Microforms [073]
CHENG-FA-YEN-CHIU – (Political and legal studies). Peking. 1954-64. Lacking: 1954; 1955; v. 2-4, v. 6, 1957; v. 1-6, 1958; v. 4-6, 1960; v. 4, 1961. BCH-893 2 – 8 – ne IDC [320]
CHENG-FU KUNG-TSO PAO-KAO HUI-PIEN, 1950 / China. People's Republic – Report of the People's Republic of China. Peking. 1951. BCH-836 2 – 8 – ne IDC [324]
CH'ENG-KUNG HSIEN-CHIH – 1725, 4. BCH-664 2 – 8 – ne IDC [950]
CHENIER: EPISODE DE L'INSURRECTION CANADIENNE DE 1837 / Frechette, Louis-Honore – Montreal: s.n., 1885 (Montreal: La Presse) 03227. (Pre-1900 Canadiana) – 9 – cn C.I.H.M. [971]
Chenier, LS de *see* RECHERCHES HISTORIQUES SUR LES MAURES ET HISTOIRE DE L'EMPIRE DE MAROC PAR M. DE CHENIER, CHARGE DES AFFAIRES DU ROI AUPRES DE L'EMPEREUR DU MAROC
Chenier, Marie-Joseph *see*
- CHARLES 9 OU L'ECOLE DES ROIS
- FENELON OU LES RELIGIEUSES DE CAMBRAI
- TIMOLEON

Chenier, Mehul *see* TIMOLEON
Chen-kuo-fu *see* THE WHOLE SET OF BOOKS BY MR. CHEN-KUO-FU
CHEN-NAN CHOU-CHIH – 1892, 11. BCH-676 2 – 8 – ne IDC [950]
Chenone, E *see* L'HERESIE A LA CHARITE-SUR-LOIRE ET LES DEBUTS DE L'INQUISITION MONASTIQUE DANS LA FRANCE DU NORD AU 13E SIECLE
CHENOPODEARUM MONOGRAPHICA ENUMERATIO / Moquin-Tandon, C H B A – Paris, 1840. 182 pp. B-667 2 – 8 – ne IDC [580]
Chenowith, Edith *see* SCRAPBOOKS
Chen-pu-lei *see* THE INITIAL MANUSCRIPT OF THE WAR HISTORY OF THE NATIONAL REVOLUTIONARY ARMY
LA CHEQUE ET LA LOI DU LIEU DE PAIEMENT / Egnell, H – Paris, 1935 – 2mf – 1 – ILM-3511/1 – ne IDC [327]
CHERAW BAPTIST CHURCH. SOUTH CAROLINA : CHURCH RECORDS – 1822-1934 – 1 – 43.83 – us Baptist [240]
Cherbuliez, A E *see*
- ETUDES SUR LES CAUSES DE LA MISERE TANT MORALE QUE PHYSIQUE ET SUR LES MOYENS D'Y PORTER REMEDE
- RICHESSE OU PAUVRETE. EXPOSITION DES CAUSES ET DES EFFETS DE LA DISTRIBUTION ACTUELLE DES RICHESSES SOCIALES

Cherbury, Edward *see* LORD HERBERT OF -.
LE CHERCHEUR – [Quebec: s.n.], 1888-1889 – 9 – cn C.I.H.M. [440]
Chereau, O *see* JARGON OU LANGAGE DE L'ARGOT REFORME
Cherel-Mora, C *see* VARIATION GEOGRAPHIQUE ET TAXONOMIE DES PLACOSTYLUS (GASTEROPODES PULMONES STYLOMMATOPHORES) EN NOUVELLE-CALEDONIE
Cheremin, G S *see* RANNII MAIAKOVSKII
Cherepnin, LV *see*
- RUSSKAIA PALEOGRAFIIA
- RUSSKIE FEODAL'NYE ARKHIVY XIV-XV VEKOV

Cherepovet ski i gubernski i sovet narodnogo khozi a istva *see* DOKLAD PREDSEDATELIA CHEREPOVETSKOGO GUB. SOV. NARODN. KHOZIAISTVA TOV. VASINOVA K V-MU OCHEREDNOMU GUBERNSKOMU SEZDU SOVETOV
CHEREPOVETSKII KOOPERATOR – (Missing: 1922 n1-12) – Cherepovets, 1922-23 n14 – 22mf – 9 – COR-704/1 – ne IDC [334]
Cherevanin, N *see* SOVREMENNOE POLOZHENIE I VOZMOZHNOE BUDUSHCHEE
CHEREZ GORNILO IMPERIALISTSKOI VOINY : K CHETYREKHLIETII U MIROVOI BOINI: SBORNIK STATEI – Moskva: "Kommunist", 1918 – 1 – CSUX89-B6828 – us Hoover Inst Photo [947]
CHEREZ KOOPERATSIIU K ELEKTRIFIKATSII : KAK KOOPERATSIIA-STARUIU LADU NA NOVYI LAD PEREDELALA / Erokhin, N V – M., L., 1928 – 1mf – 9 – COR-474/1 – ne IDC [334]
DE CHERIBONSCHE OPSTAND VAN 1806 / Broek, J A van den – 's-Gravenhage, 1891. (Overdruk "De Tijdspiegel"). 's-Gravenhage, 1891 – 1mf – 9 – ne IDC [950]
Cherler, J H *see* HISTORIA PLANTARUM UNIVERSALIS
Chermenskii, E D *see* BURZHUAZIIA I TSARIZM V PERVOI RUSSKOI REVOLIUTSII
Chermenskii, V D *see* STACHKA
CHERNAI A GODINA : DVUKHNEDELNY I ZHURNAL SARATOVSKO I GUBERNSKO I KOMISSII POMOSHCHI GOLODAI USHCHIM – Saratov: Komissii a, 1922 – 1 – CSUX89-S858 – us Hoover Inst Photo [947]
CHERNAIA GODINA : SBORNIK O GOLODE V TSARITSYNSKOI GUBERNII I OBZOR DEIATELNOSTI GUBKOMPOMGOLA ZA 1921-22 GOD / Perfilov, B – T Saritsynn-V.: Izd. T S.G.K.P.G., 1922 – 1 – CSUX88-B5399 – us Hoover Inst Photo [947]
CHERNAIA KNIGA : SBORNIK STATEI I MATERIALOV OB INTERVENTSII ANTANTY NA UKRAINE V 1918-1919 GG. / POD REDAKTSIEI ISPREDISLOVIEM A.G. SHLIKHTERA – Ekaterinoslav: Gos. izd-vo Ukrainy, 1925 – 1 – CSUX88-B5415 – us Hoover Inst Photo [947]
CHERNAIA NEMOCH' / Pogodin, M P – Povest. M. 1829. BR-8301 2 – 8 – ne IDC [947]
CHERNAIA SOTNIA – [s.l.]: Izd. L. Gorbunovo i i Kn. S. Shakhovskogo, 1905 (Moskva: Tipolit. t-vo I.N. Kushnerev) – 1 – CSUX88-B752 – us Hoover Inst Photo [947]
Cherneeva, L I et al *see* ENTALPIIA PLAVLENIIA SOLEVYKH EVTEKTIK
Chernenkov, BN *see* EVOLIUTSIIA OSNOVNYKH ELEMENTOV SELSKOGO KHOZIA ISTVA ODESSKOI GUBERNII
Chernenkov, N N *see* OCHERK ISTORII ZEMELNYKH OTNOSHENII V ODESSKOI GUBERNII
Chernetsov, V N *see* NIZHNEE PRIOB'E V I TYSIACHELETII NASHEI ERY
Chernev, Irving *see* CHESSBOARD MAGIC
Chernevskii, P O *see* UKAZATEL' MATERIALOV DLIA ISTORII TORGOVLI, PROMYSHLENNOSTI I FINANSOV Y PREDELAKH ROSSIISKOI IMPERII
CHERNIGOVSKAIA GUB – Sel'skokhoziaistvennyi obzor Chernigovskoi gub. za 1913 god. BRZ-198 2 – 8 – ne IDC [630]
CHERNIGOVSKAIA GUB – Zemskii sbornik Chernikovskoi gub. na 1869-1915 g. Lacking: 1870, v. 7, 10; 1872, v. 5-12; 1873; 1874; 1875, v. 11-12; 1876, v. 5-8; 1877, v. 1-4; 1881, v. 11-12; 1882; 1883; 1884; 1885, v. 1-8, 11-12; 1886, v. 1-2; 1887, v. 3-6; 1888, v. 11-12; 1900, v. 5; 1904-15. BRZ-197 2 – 8 – ne IDC [073]
CHERNIGOVSKII LISTOK – 1861-62. BR-11,329 2 – 8 – ne IDC [630]
CHERNOE PO BELOMU / Gippius, Z N – Piataia kniga razskazov. Spb. 1908. BR-711 2 – 8 – ne IDC [460]
Chernogolovkin, N V *see* FORMY KOLONIAL'NOI ZAVISIMOSTI
CHERNOMORSKI FRONT – Burgas, Bulgaria. -d. 1 Jan 1951-31 Dec 1955. 10 reels – 1 – uk British Libr Newspaper [949]
CHERNOMORSKI FRONT – Burgas, Bulgaria. Jun 1951-1982; 1985-1992 – 39r – 1 – us L of C Photodup [072]
CHERNOMORSKII FLOT V EPOKHU PERVOI REVOLIUTSII : SBORNIK ZHURNALA "KATORGA I SSYLKA." – Moskva: Izd-vo Vses. ob-va polit. katorzhan i ssylno-poselent sev, 1927 – 1 – CSUX88-B592 – us Hoover Inst Photo [947]
Chernov, Viktor Mikhailovich *see*
- CHUZHIMI PUTIAMI
- THE GREAT RUSSIAN REVOLUTION
- INTERNATSIONAL I VO INA
- INTERNATSIONAL I VOINA
- NASHIM OBVINITELI AM
- PROLETARIAT, TRUDOVOE KRESTI ANSTVO I REVOLIUTSII A

Chernov, Viktor Mikhailovich et al *see* CHE-KA
Chernova-Kolbasina, Olga E *see* VOSPOMINANII A O SOVI ETSKIKH TI URMAKH
Chernykh, P Ia *see* IAZYK ULOZHENIIA 1649 GODA
Chernyshevskii, Nikolai Gavrilovich *see*
- OPIS' DOKUMENTAL'NYKH MATERIALOV FONDA LICHNOGO PROISKHOZHDENIIA NO.1
- POLNOE SOBRANIE SOCHINENII V PIATNADTSATI TOMAKH

O CHERNYSHEVSKOM – Bibliografiia 1854-1910. Spb. 1911. BR-5886 2 – 8 – ne IDC [947]
CHEROETENOE – Amsterdam. Available: 1938. v14(2-7); 1939. v15(1-4) – 3mf – J-261-21/1 – ne IDC [073]
CHEROKEE ALMANAC – 1838-60 – 1r – 1 – us Ross [073]
CHEROKEE BIBLE – 1860 – 1 – 14.91 – us Baptist [240]
Cherokee County, KS *see* CEMETERY RECORDS
CHEROKEE HYMN BOOK – 1 – $5.00 – us Baptist [780]
CHEROKEE HYMN BOOK – n.d – 1 – $5.00 – us Baptist [780]
CHEROKEE ONE FEATHER / Eastern Board of Cherokee Indians – 1966-82.(American Indian Periodicals in the Princeton University Library). 98 fiches – 9 – $395.00 – us UPA [305]
CHEROKEE PHOENIX – New Echota, Feb 1828-May 1834 – 3r – 1 – uk British Libr Newspaper [071]
Cheron, A *see* LA FEMME MARIEE ANGLAISE EN ANGLETERRE ET EN FRANCE
Cheron, L *see*
- DES CAUSES DE DIVORCE...
- LES CAUSES DE DIVORCE...

Cherrier, A Benjamin *see* HISTORY OF THE QUEBEC DIRECTORY SINCE ITS FIRST ISSUE IN 1844 UP TO THE PRESENT DAY
Cherrier, Andre R *see* PROCES DE JOSEPH N. CARDINAL ET AUTRES, AUQUEL ON A JOINT LA REQUETE ARGUMENTATIVE EN FAVEUR DES PRISONNIERS ET PLUSIEURS AUTRES DOCUMENTS PRECIEUX,...
Cherrier, Come Seraphin *see* L'HONORABLE F.-A. QUESNEL
Cherriman, John Bradford *see* LOAN TABLES
Cherrington, Ernest H *see*
- PAPERS

Cherrington, Kristy Y *see* RELATIONSHIP BETWEEN THE MARITAL SATISFACTION OF THE WIFE AND THE VIEWING OF TELEVISED SPORTS BY THE HUSBAND
CHERRY COUNTY NEWS – Valentine, NE. -w. Dec 1892; Oct 1895-Dec 1895; Mar 1896-Jan 1957 – 1 – us NE Hist [071]
DES CHERTES EN FRANCE ET DE LEUR INFLUENCE SUR LE MOUVEMENT DE LA POPULATION / Legoyt, Alfred – Reprod. d'un extrait du Journal de la Societe Statistique de Paris, 1860. p93-114. 1 fiche. (Statistics Series: Demography) – 9 – 6.00 – fr Bibl Nationale [310]
CHERTOVA KUKLA / Gippius, Z N – Zhizneopisanie v 33-kh glavakh. M. 1911. BR-712 2 – 8 – ne IDC [460]
Cherubini *see*
- LES DEUX JOURNEES
- ELISA OU LE VOYAGE AU MONT BERNARD

Cherubini, N *see* SACRI CONCENTUS BINIS, TERNIS, QUATERISQUE VOCIBUS
Cherubini, S *see* NUBIE
Cherubins, Marie des *see* BIBLIOGRAPHIE ANALYTIQUE DE L'OEUVRE DE MONSIEUR L'ABBE JEAN-BAPTISTE GAUVIN, L.PH., D.TH., PRINCIPAL DE L'ECOLE NORMALE DE MONT-JOLI
Cheruel, A *see* DICTIONNAIRE DES INSTITUTIONS DE LA FRANCE
CHERVENO ZNAME – Vidin, Bulgaria. Aug 1950-1970 – 14r – 1 – us L of C Photodup [072]
Chervet, Eugenie-Caroline Saffray *see* LA FILLEUL DE L'EVOQUE
Chervet, G *see* DROIT ROMAIN
Chervin, Arthur *see*
- ANTHROPOLOGIE BOLIVIENNE
- COMMUNICATIONS SUR LA NATALITE EN FRANCE
- HISTOIRE STATISTIQUE DE LA POPULATION FRANCAISE

CHERVONOE KAZACHESTVO : SBORNIK MATERIALOV PO ISTORII CHERVONOGO KAZACHESTVA / RISUNKI I OBLOZHKA KHUDOZH. A. MARTYNOVA – Kharkov: Izd-va "Put prosveshchenii a" i "Molodo i rabochi i", [1923 or 1924] – 1 – CSUX88-B5855 – us Hoover Inst Photo [947]
CHESAPEAKE SCIENCE – v. 12-18. 1971-77 – 1,5,6 – us Princeton Micro [580]
Cheselden, W *see*
- OSTEOGRAPHIA
- A TREATISE ON THE HIGH OPERATION FOR THE STONE

CHESHAM EXAMINER *see* BUCKS EXAMINER
CHESHIRE, 1822 : BRITISH ISLES CENSUS DIRECTORIES PROJECT, ENGLAND – (In prep) – at Vine [941]
CHESHIRE, 1830 : BRITISH ISLES CENSUS DIRECTORIES PROJECT, ENGLAND – at Vine [941]
CHESHIRE, 1834 : BRITISH ISLES CENSUS DIRECTORIES PROJECT, ENGLAND – (In prep) – at Vine [941]
CHESHIRE, 1848 : BRITISH ISLES CENSUS DIRECTORIES PROEJCT, ENGLAND. VOL 190 – 1mf – 9 – A$9.00 – at Vine [941]

CHESHIRE, 1850 : BRITISH ISLES CENSUS DIRECTORIES PROJECT, ENGLAND. VOL 70 – 4mf – 9 – A$27.00 – at Vine [941]
CHESHIRE, 1855 : BRITISH ISLES CENSUS DIRECTORIES PROJECT, ENGLAND – at Vine [941]
CHESHIRE, 1874 : BRITISH ISLES CENSUS DIRECTORIES PROJECT, ENGLAND. VOL 160 – 8mf – 9 – A$51.00 – at Vine [941]
CHESHIRE, 1928 : BRITISH ISLES CENSUS DIRECTORIES PROJECT, ENGLAND – (In prep) – at Vine [941]
CHESHIRE 1793-1892 – (Mf 1: Vital Records 1764-1812. Mf 2: Vital Records 1802-37. Mf 3: Marriages & Intent 1837-64. Mf 4: Births & Deaths 1782-1835. Mf 4: Military Pension 1815. Mf 5: Vital Records 1845-59. Mf 6: Deaths 1860-68. Mf 7: Births 1868-83. Mf 8: Births 1883-92. Mf 9: Marriages 1860-83. Mf 10: Marriages 1884-92. Mf 11: Deaths 1860-78. Mf 12: Deaths 1878-92) – (mf ed 1983) – 12mf – 9 – 0-931248-53-1 – us Holbrook [920]
CHESHIRE (CHESTER, STOCKPORT AND MACCLESFIELD), 1805 : BRITISH ISLES CENSUS DIRECTORIES PROJECT, ENGLAND. VOL 172 – 1mf – 9 – A$9.00 – at Vine [941]
CHESHIRE (FAR NORTH EAST), 1832 : BRITISH ISLES CENSUS DIRECTORIES PROJECT, ENGLAND. VOL 193 – 1mf – 9 – A$9.00 – at Vine [941]
CHESHIRE FIRST BAPTIST CHURCH (FORMERLY NEW PROVIDENCE). CHESHIRE, MASSACHUSETTS : CHURCH RECORDS – 1769-1848 (the entire life of the church); Werden Church. Manuscript Copy. 1769-1841 – 1 – 30.33 – us Baptist [240]
Cheshire, Joseph Blount *see* THE CHURCH IN THE CONFEDERATE STATES
CHESHIRE (NORTH EAST), 1825 : BRITISH ISLES CENSUS DIRECTORIES PROJECT, ENGLAND. VOL 147 – 1mf – 9 – A$9.00 – at Vine [941]
CHESHIRE (PART), 1816 : BRITISH ISLES CENSUS DIRECTORIES PROJECT, ENGLAND – (In prep) – at Vine [941]
CHESHIRE (PART), 1841 : BRITISH ISLES CENSUS DIRECTORIES PROJECT, ENGLAND – at Vine [941]
CHESHKO-RUSSKOE EDINENIE – nr. 1. 1915. BR-2317 2 – 8 – ne IDC [947]
CHESHUNT AND WALTHAM CROSS MERCURY *see* LEA VALLEY MERCURY
CHESHUNT AND WALTHAM WEEKLY TELEGRAPH – Cheshunt, Waltham, England. 1876-77; 1879; 1884-85; 1888-90; 1893-94; 1900; 1970- – 63+ r – 1 – uk British Libr Newspaper [072]
Chesneau, Augustin *see* ORPHEUS EUCHARISTICUS
Chesneau du Marsais, C *see*
- LOGIQUE ET PRINCIPES DE GRAMMAIRE (NOUVELLE EDITION PLUS TRAITE D'INVERSION)
- VERITABLES PRINCIPES DE LA GRAMMAIRE

Chesneau, Ernest *see* LES NATIONS RIVALES DANS L'ART.
CHESNEE FIRST BAPTIST CHURCH. CHESNEE, SOUTH CAROLINA : CHURCH RECORDS – 1910-21 – 1 – 29.52 – us Baptist [240]
Chesnut, James et al *see* PAPERS
Chesnutt, Charles W *see*
- PAPERS, MS 3370
- A SELECTION OF WORKS

CHESSBOARD MAGIC / Chernev, Irving – A collection of 160 brilliant chess endings, comp. and annot. by Irving Chernev. New York: N.Y. Chess Review, 1943.xi,162p. illus – 1 – us U.W. Library [790]
Chesson, Frederick William *see*
- THE ATLANTIC CABLES: A REVIEW OF RECENT TELEGRAPHIC LEGISLATION IN CANADA
- MR. CHESSON ON MANITOBA

CHESTER 1762-1849 – (Mf 1T-2T: marriages & Intentions 1770-91. Mf 1T-5T: Births & Deaths 1762-1858. Mf 5T-8T: Marriages & Intentions 1791-1848. Mf 8T-10T: Births & Deaths 1802-58. Mf 10T: Marriages 1831-49. Mf 11T: Births, Marriages 1843-49; Deaths 1846-49) – (mf ed 1995) – 11mf – 9 – 0-87623-230-6 – us Holbrook [920]
CHESTER 1793-1892 – (Mf 1-7: Town & Vital Records 1766-87. Mf 8-11: Births, Marriages, Intentions, Deaths 1829-64. Mf 12: Index to Births: 1842-57. Mf 13: Index to Marriages 1844-57. Mf 14: Index to Deaths 1846-56. Mf 15: B,M,D 1844-57. Mf 16-17: Index to Births 1857-1970. Mf 18-22: B,M,D 1857-93. Mf 23: Index to Deaths 1893-1900. Mf 24-26: Deaths 1893-1940) – (mf ed 1988) – 26mf – 9 – 0-87623-058-3 – us Holbrook [920]
CHESTER CHRONICLE – (1775-92 imperfect. Lacking: 1880) – England, 22 May 1775-9 Nov 1792; 1830-82 – 40r – 1 – uk British Libr Newspaper [072]
CHESTER CHRONICLE (CITY ED) – 1986-90; Jul-Dec 1991; 1992-96 – 93 1/2r – 1 – uk British Libr Newspaper [072]
CHESTER COUNTY DEMOCRAT – West Chester, PA. -w 1889-1898 – 13 – $25.00r – us I.M.R. [071]
Chester County, PA *see* CHESTER COUNTY, PENNSYLVANIA, ESTATE PAPERS, 1700-1820
CHESTER COUNTY, PENNSYLVANIA, ESTATE PAPERS, 1700-1820 / Chester County, PA – (Dorothy Lapp Collection, Chester County Estate Papers 1700-1810 55r $4,675.00 S1821.P1. Chester County Orphans Court, Minors' Estate Papers 1700-1820 11r $935.00 S1821.P2. Chester County Orphans Court, Decedents' Papers 1700-1810 19r $1,615.00 S1821.P3) – 1978 – 1 – us Scholarly Res [978]
CHESTER COUNTY VILLAGE RECORD – West Chester, PA. -w 1889-1895 – 13 – $25.00r – us I.M.R. [071]
CHESTER FIRST BAPTIST CHURCH. CHESTER, SOUTH CAROLINA : CHURCH RECORDS – 1873-1926, 1939-57, 1960-61, 1963-72. Deacons' Minutes. 1921-47 – 1 – $36.59 – us Baptist [240]
CHESTER HERALD – Chester, NE. -w. Aug. 1889-Dec. 1902. Incomplete; Feb. 1903-Sep. 1906;Nov. 1906-Mar. 1911; Nov. 1923-Jan. 1924; Jan. 1925-Feb. 1943; Dec. 1945- – 1 – us NE Hist [071]
Chester, Joseph Lemuel *see* JOHN ROGERS: THE COMPILER OF THE FIRST AUTHORISED ENGLISH BIBLE; THE PIONEER OF THE ENGLISH REFORMATION; AND ITS FIRST MARTYR...A GENEAOLOGICAL ACCOUNT OF HIS FAMILY.
Chester, New Hampshire. Chester Baptist Church *see* RECORDS
Chester. Ohio. Free Will Baptist Church *see* CHURCH RECORDS, MS 669
Chester, Pennsylvania. Crozer Theological Seminary *see* TRUSTEES' MINUTES
Chester. Presbytery (Pres. Ch. in the U.S.A.) *see* MINUTES, 1870-1926
Chester, Samuel Hall *see* LIGHTS AND SHADOWS OF MISSION WORK IN THE FAR EAST
CHESTERFIELD 1762-1892 – (Mf 1-5: Birth Index Cards 1762-1963. Mf 6-8: Death Index Cards 1762-1962. Mf 9-11: Marriage Index Cards 1762-1962. Mf 12-15: Marriage Intention Index Cards 1762-1962. Mf 16: Town Records 1762-1783: B,M,I,D, Vol 1. Mf 17-18: Town Records 1782-97: B,M,I,D, Vol 2. Mf 19-21: B,M,D 1802-45. Mf 22-25: Marriage Intentions 1803-1909 Bk 2. Mf 26-28: B,M,D 1844-75. Mf 29-30: B,M,D 1858-92) – (mf ed 1983) – 30mf – 9 – 0-931248-26-4 – us Holbrook [920]
Chesterfield, Massachusetts. Chesterfield Baptist Church *see* RECORDS
CHESTER-LE-STREET AND DISTRICT ADVERTISER – England. 30 Oct 1891-20 May 1892.-w. men reel – 1 – uk British Libr Newspaper [072]
CHESTER-LE-STREET CHRONICLE – England. Jan 1913-Dec 1940.-w. 16men reels – 1 – uk British Libr Newspaper [072]
CHESTER-LE-STREET OBSERVER – England. 22 March 1894-9 May 1895.-w. 1 reel – 1 – uk British Libr Newspaper [072]
CHESTER-LE-STREET TIMES – Chester-le-Street, England. -w. 26 Nov 1870-3 Sept 1887. 5 1 2 reels – 1 – uk British Libr Newspaper [072]
Chesterton, GK *see*
- LA SUPERSTICION DEL DIVORCIO
- VARIED TYPES

CHESTNUT HILL BAPTIST CHURCH. SALUDA COUNTY. SOUTH CAROLINA : CHURCH RECORDS – 1832-91 – 1 – 7.56 – us Baptist [240]
CHESTNUT RIDGE BAPTIST CHURCH. LAURENS COUNTY. SOUTH CAROLINA : CHURCH RECORDS – 1816-90, 1920-55, 1959, 1964, 1971-74 – 1 – 38.16 – us Baptist [240]
CHESTNUTHILLER WOCHENSCHRIFT – Chestnut Hill. Pa. 1790-1794 – 1,3 – us Readex [071]
CHESTNY I SLON L'HONNETE EL EPHANT – (Includes c.1: 1945:Mar.3-Dec.8) – Paris, 1945 – 1 – CSUXANR1690-S – us Hoover Inst Photo [944]
CHETHAM SOCIETY : REMAINS HISTORICAL AND LITERARY CONNECTED WITH THE PALATINE COUNTIES OF LANCASTER AND CHESTER – (Coll title: Publications of the English Record Societies, 1835-1972...) – New series. v1-110. 1883-1947 – 311mf – 9 – £1,630.00 – uk Chadwyck [941]
CHETHAM SOCIETY : REMAINS HISTORICAL AND LITERARY CONNECTED WITH THE PALATINE COUNTIES OF LANCASTER AND CHESTER – (Coll title: Publications of the English Record Societies, 1835-72.... Includes indexes) – Old series. v1-114. 1844-93 – 349mf – 9 – £1,830.00 – uk Chadwyck [941]
CHETHAM SOCIETY : REMAINS HISTORICAL AND LITERARY CONNECTED WITH THE PALATINE COUNTIES OF LANCASTER AND CHESTER – (Coll title: Publications of the English Record Society, 1835-1972...) – 3rd series. v1-18. 1949-70 – 51mf – 9 – £375.00 – uk Chadwyck [941]
Chetham Society *see* REMAINS HISTORICAL AND LITERARY CONNECTED WITH THE PALATINE COUNTIES OF LANCASTER AND CHESTER
CHETKI. STIKHI / Akhmatova, A – Berlin. 1921. BR-1092 2 – 8 – ne IDC [460]
CHETKI. STIKHI / Akhmatova, A – ed. 2. Petrograd. 1915. BR-1091 2 – 8 – ne IDC [460]
CHETKI. STIKHI / Akhmatova, A – ed. 8. Petrograd. 1922. BR-1093 2 – 8 – ne IDC [460]
CHETKI. STIKHI / Akhmatova, A – Spb. 1914. BR-1090 2 – 8 – ne IDC [460]
CHETMER SZTYME = CHELM VOICE – Chelm, PL. no12 Jun 1925-v4 no49(no193) 1928 – 1r – 1 – $25.00 – cn Can Microfilming [072]
Chetopa. Kansas *see* ORDINANCES
Chetty, N G *see* A MANUAL OF THE KURNOOL DISTRICT IN THE PRESIDENCY OF MADRAS
CHETVERTAIA GODOVSHCHINA NARKOMPRODA : SBORNIK STATEI INFORMATSIONNO-IZDATELSKOGO OTDELA NARKOMPRODA, POSVI ASHCHENNY I 4-I GODOVSHCHINE PRODOVOLSTVENNO I RABOTY SOVESTKOI VLASTI – Moskva: Gos. izd-vo, 1921 – 1 – CSUX90-B9408 – us Hoover Inst Photo [947]
CHETYRE GODA BORBY ZA SOTSIALIZM : MATERIALY K OTCHETU SVERDLOVSKOGO OBLASTNOGO ISPOLNITELNOGO KOMITETA I SEZDU SOVETOV SVERDLOVSKOI OBLASTI – Sverdlovsk: Oblispolkom, 1934 – 1 – CSUX91-B3949 – us Hoover Inst Photo [947]
Chetyrkina, VI *see* V POMOSHCH' UCHITELIU - STROITELIU DEREVENSKOI KOOPERATSII
CHETYRNADTSATYI GOD / Gorodetskii, S – Stikhotvoreniia. Petrograd. 1915. BR-1119 2 – 8 – ne IDC [460]
Chevalier, Auguste *see*
- L'AFRIQUE CENTRALE FRANCAISE, RECIT DU VOYAGE DE LA MISSION, APPENDICE PAR PELLEGRIN, ET AL
- EXPLORATION BOTANIQUE DE L'AFRIQUE OCCIDENTALE FRANCAISE

LE CHEVALIER D'INDUSTRIE / Duval, Alexandre – (French Theatre Series). Paris. L. Vente. 1820 – 9 – fr Hachette [820]
Chevalier, Henri Emile *see* L'ILE DE SABLE
Chevalier, J-Guy *see* LE JOURNAL DE L'ILE JESUS
Chevalier, Jules *see* VISITE PASTORALE DU DIOCESE DE DIE PAR CHARLES-JACQUES DE LEBERON
Chevalier, Michel *see*
- A LYON MENILMONTANT, LE 23 NOVEMBRE 1832
- DOCTRINE DE SAINT-SIMON: LA MARSEILLAISE
- QUESTIONS DES TRAVAILLEURS: L'AMELIORATION DU SORT DES OUVRIERS. LES SALAIRES, L'ORGANISATION DU TRAVAIL

Chevalier, Ulysse *see*
- POESIE LITURGIQUE DES EGLISES DE FRANCE AUX 17 ET 18E SIECLES, OU, RECUEL D'HYMNES ET DE PROSES
- POESIE LITURGIQUE DU MOYEN AGE
- REPERTOIRE DES SOURCES HISTORIQUES DU MOYEN-AGE
- REPERTOIRE DES SOURCES HISTORIQUES DU MOYEN-AGE...
- REPERTORIUM HYMNOLOGICUM

Chevallard, P *see* SAINT AGOBARD, ARCHEVEQUE DE LYON
Chevalley, E *see* ESSAI SUR LE DROIT DES GENS NAPOLEONIEN...
Chevalley, L *see* LA DECLARATION DU DROIT...
Chevallie, J A *see* REPORT OF THE COMMITTEE...THE PETITION OF AMELIE; EUGENIE DE BEAUMARCHAIS...
Chevallier, Emile *see* LES SALAIRES AU XIXE SIECLE
Chevassu, J *see*
- BEOUMI. ETUDE ECONOMIQUE D'UN CENTRE SEMI URBAIN
- ESSAI DE DEFINITION DE QUELQUES INDICATEURS DE STRUCTURE ET DE FONCTIONNEMENT DE L'ECONOMIE DES CENTRES SEMI-URBAINS
- ETUDE DE QUELQUES CENTRES SEMI-URBAINS
- RAPPORT PRELIMINAIRE D'ETUDE DES CENTRES SEMI-URBAINS
- RECENSEMENT DEMOGRAPHIQUE DE SAN PEDRO
- LES ZONES RURALES ET LES CENTRES SECONDAIRES DE LA REGION DE BOUAKE

CHEVES' CASES IN EQUITY / South Carolina. Supreme Court – (A Pre-NRS title) – 1v. 1839-1840 (all publ) – 3mf – 9 – $4.50 – LLMC 94-033 – us L.L.M.C. [340]
Cheves, Langdon, 1st *see* LANGDON CHEVES PAPERS
CHEVES' LAW REPORTS / South Carolina. Supreme Court – (A Pre-NRS title) – 1v. 1839-1840 (all publ) – 4mf – 9 – $6.00 – LLMC 94-021 – us L.L.M.C. [340]
Chevillard, Jacques *see* HISTOIRE GENEALOGIQUE DE LA MAISON DE BEAUVAU ET DE SES ALLIANCES
Chevillard, Valbert *see* PAYSAGES CANADIENS
Chevin *see* DICTIONNAIRE LATIN-FRANCAIS DES NOMS PROPRES DE LIEUX
Chevrette, John M *see* THE EFFECT OF ORAL SMOKELESS TOBACCO ON THE CARDIOVASCULAR AND METABOLIC RESPONSES IN HUMANS DURING REST AND EXERCISE
Chevreul, Eugene *see*
- CONSIDERATIONS GENERALES SUR L'ANALYSE ORGANIQUE ET SUR SES APPLICATIONS
- DE LA LOI DU CONTRASTE SIMULTANE DES COULEURS...
- RECHERCHES CHIMIQUES SUR LES CORPS GRAS D'ORIGINE ANIMALE
- RECHERCHES CHIMIQUES SUR PLUSIEURS CORPS GRAS ET PARTICULIEREMENT SUR LEURS COMBINAISONS AVEC LES ALCALIS

Chevreul, M E *see* THE LAWS OF CONTRAST OF COLOUR
Chevrier, Rodolphe *see* TENDRES CHOSES: POESIES CANADIENNES
Chevrolat, LA A *see* COLEOPTERES DU MEXIQUE
CHEWAUCAN POST – Paisley OR. Oct 17 1901-Jan 1 1903 – 1 – us U.O. Library [071]
CHEWAUCAN PRESS – Paisley OR. Nov 23 1911, Jan 4 1912, Mar 19 1914, Jan 11 1916, Jan 25 1917 – 1 – us U.O. Library [071]
CHEWAUCAN RIPPLE – Paisley OR. Mar 24 1923, Sep 29 1923-Apr 7 1924, Jan 26 May 4 1926 – 1 – us U.O. Library [071]
CHEYENNE COUNTY CITIZEN – Gurley, NE. -w. Feb-Oct 1925 – 1 – us NE Hist [071]
CHEYENNE COUNTY RECORD – Sidney, NE. -w. Aug 1934-Aug 1936 – 1 – us NE Hist [071]
Cheyenne Indians *see* COLLECTION
Cheyne, G *see*
- THE ENGLISH MALADY
- OBSERVATIONS CONCERNING THE NATURE AND DUE METHOD OF TREATING THE GOUT

Cheyne, J *see* ESSAY ON HYDROCEPHALUS ACUTUS
Cheyne, Thomas Kelly *see*
- AIDS TO THE DEVOUT STUDY OF CRITICISM
- BIBLE PROBLEMS AND THE NEW MATERIAL FOR THEIR SOLUTION
- BOOK OF ISAIAH CHRONOLOGICALLY ARRANGED
- THE BOOK OF PSALMS
- CHRISTIAN USE OF THE PSALMS
- FOUNDERS OF OLD TESTAMENT CRITICISM
- HALLOWING OF CRITICISM: NINE SERMONS ON ELIJAH
- HOSEA
- INTRODUCTION TO THE BOOK OF ISAIAH
- JEREMIAH, HIS LIFE AND TIMES
- JEWISH RELIGIOUS LIFE AFTER THE EXILE
- JOB AND SOLOMON, OR, THE WISDOM OF THE OLD TESTAMENT

- ORIGIN AND RELIGIOUS CONTENT OF THE PSALTER
- THE PROPHECIES OF ISAIAH: A NEW TRANSLATION WITH COMMENTARY
- TRADITIONS AND BELIEFS OF ANCIENT ISRAEL

CHEZ LE BEY DE TUNIS / Ague de Lassus, Lucien – Versailles: L. Bernard, 1881. 62p. ill. 1 fiche. (Literature Collection) – 9 – 6.00 – fr Bibl Nationale [910]

CHEZ LES FANG AU QUINZE ANNEES DE SEJOUR AU CONGO FRANCAIS / Trilles, H – Lille: Soc St Augustan, Desclee, de Brouwer, [1912] – 1 – us Res Libr [960]

CHEZ LES SAUVAGES BAHNARS : JOURNAL DE VOYAGE... / Guerlach, le pere M – (Chez les sauvages de la Cochinchine orientale: Bahnar, Reungao, Sedang. – Lyon:[s.n.], 1894. Theogonie, genies ou lang superieurs: moeurs et superstitions des sauvages Bahnars. -[Lyon?: s.n.], 1887) – Lyon: [s.n.], 1884 – 1 – F151.81 – fr Armell [305]

CHEZ M. SULLY-PRUDHOMME : HELENE VACARESCO / Xau, Fernand-Arthur-Pierre – [S.l.n.d.] – fr Armell [920]

CHEZ-NOUS / ed by Cote, Chanoine V – Rimovski, Canada. nov 1920-v3 n7. mai/jun 1923 – 1r – Can$30.00 – cn Can Microfilming [072]

CHEZ-NOUS : DANS L'EST – Montreal, Canada. v1 n5. sep 1939-v2 n7. 6 oct 1941 – 1r – 1 – Can$25.00 – cn Can Microfilming [073]

CHI TU CHIAO CHE HSUEH (CCC66) / Chao, Tzu-ch'en – (In Chinese) – [s.l: s.n, 1925] – 1r – 1 – 1984-B500 – us A.T.L.A. [240]

CHI TU CHIAO YU SHIH CHIEH HO P'ING (CCC223) / ed by Liu, Liang-mou – (In Chinese) – [s.l: s.n, 1951] – 1r – 1 – 1984-B500 – us A.T.L.A. [240]

CHI TU HUA CHING CHI KUAN HSI CH'UAN KUO TA HUI PAO KAO (CCC253) / National Christian Council of China – (In Chinese) – [s.l: s.n, 1927] – 1r – 1 – 1984-6592 – us A.T.L.A. [240]

CHI TU T'U SHENGHUO TI P'EI YANG (CCC218) / Liang, Hsiao-ch'u – (In Chinese) – [s.l: s.n, 1963] – 1r – 1 – 1984-B500 – us A.T.L.A. [240]

CHIA CHIH-FANG. CHIN-TAI CHUNG-KUO CHING-CHI SHE-HUI – Modern Chinese Economic Society. 1950. BCH-849 2 – 8 – ne IDC [330]

CHIAH LUAN – South Vietnam. 1964- – 1 – us UMI [072]

Chiang, J *see* CARDIORESPIRATORY RESPONSES TO CIRCUIT WEIGHT TRAINING AS MEASURED BY A BIOKINETIC SWIM-BENCH TEST AND A TREADMILL RUN TEST

CHIANG-AN HSIEN-CHIH – 1829, 2. BCH-777 2 – 8 – ne IDC [950]

CHIANG-HSI HSIANG-SHIH LU – List of successful candidates in the imperial examination in Kiangsi province: 1873, 1875, 1876, 1879, 1885, 1888, 1889, 1891, 1893, 1894, 1897, 1900, 1901. 1 reel – 1 – 21.00 – us Chinese Res [950]

CHIANG-HSI MIN-CHENG KUNG-PAO / Kiangsi. China. (Province) – Gazette of Civil Affairs... 16 Jan 1928-1 Jul 1930. Incomplete. 5 reels – 1 – 120.00 – us Chinese Res [950]

CHIANG-HSI SHENG-CHENG FU KUNG-PAO / Kiangsi. China. (Province) – Kiangsi Provincial government Gazette. 1st series. Oct 1927-Dec 1928. 45 issues. 2nd series. Jan 1929-Apr 1931. 87 issues. 3rd series. May 1931-Dec 1931. 32 issues. 4th series. Jan 1932-Sep 1934. 99 issues. 5th series. Oct 1934-Dec 1948. 1680 issues – 7r – 1 – $185.00 – us Chinese Res [950]

CHIANG-NAN HSIANG-SHIH LU – List of successful candidates in the imperial examination in Kiangsu province: 1879, 1885, 1888, 1893, 1901, 1903. 1 reel – 1 – 28.00 – us Chinese Res [950]

CHIANG-NING HSEUH-WU TSA-CHIH – Nanking Educational Magazine. v. 1-10. Nanking. 1907. BCH-783 2 – 8 – ne IDC [073]

CHIANG-SU. (KIANGSU) – No.1-35, 37-40, 42, 45. 1 Sept 1928-11 Dec 1929. Propaganda of the Chinese Revolution. 2 reels – 1 – 60.00 – us Chinese Res [950]

CHIANG-SU SHENG-LI KUO-HSUEH T'U-SHU-KUAN NIEN-K'AN / Kiang Su. Provincial Sinological Library – Annual. v. 1-9. Nanking. 1928-36. Lacking: v. 1-2, 1928-29, v. 8, 1935. BCH-214 2 – 8 – ne IDC [073]

CHIAO HUI TI CHENG T'UNG (CCC98) – (In Chinese) – [s.l: s.n, 1955] – 1r – 1 – 1984-B500 – us A.T.L.A. [240]

CHIAO T'UNG KUNG PAO / China. Ministry of Communications – Official Gazette. Nanking. 1929-37. Lacking: (1-20, 74, 76) 1929; (113, 132, 144) 1930; (160-633, 635-640, 642-649, 651-653, 655-665, 670-674, 676-677, 679-682, 686-688) 1930 35; (691-895) 1935 37. BCH-1060 1 – 9 – ne IDC [380]

CHIAO T'UNG KUNG PAO / China. Ministry of Communications – Official Gazette. Nanking, Chunking. 1938-48. Lacking: v. 1-5 (1) 1938 42; v. 6 (1, 10-12) 1943; v. 7 (2, 3, 6, 12) 1944; v. 8 (2, 9-12) 1945; v. 11 (21-?) 1948. BCH-1061 1 – 9 – ne IDC [380]

CHIAO T'UNG KUNG PAO / China. Ministry of Communications – Official Gazette. Peking. 1917-28. Lacking: (1-1686) 1917-27; (1745-1801) 1927 28; (1940-1943) 1928. BCH-1059 1 – 9 – ne IDC [380]

CHIAO T'UNG PU T'UNG CHI NIEN PAO / China. Ministry of Communications – Statistical yearbook. Nanking. 1928-44. BCH-1062 1 – 9 – ne IDC [380]

CHIAO T'UNG YUEH K'AN / China. Ministry of Communications – Monthly bulletin. Peking. 1917-19. Lacking: (11, 13) 1917; (15-19, 21, 24) 1918; (27, 28, 32) 1919. BCH-1063 1 – 9 – ne IDC [380]

CHIAO YU KUNG PAO / China. Ministry of Education – Gazette. Peking. v.3, n.5-v.12, n.2. May 1916-Mar 1925, Very incomplete. 14 reels – 1 – 262.00 – us Chinese Res [324]

CHIAO YU PU KUNG PAO / China. Ministry of Education – Gazette. Nanking, Chungking. 1929-48. v.1-v.20, n.6. Lacking: v.2, n.25, 28-31,34,36,37; v.9, n.17-40; v.10,n.9-12; v.11-17. 18 reels – 1 – 336.50 – us Chinese Res [324]

CHIAO-T'UNG TSA-CHIH – Journal of Communications. v. 1-5. Nanking. 1932-37. Lacking: v. 5 (7-12) 1937. BCH-215 1 – 9 – ne IDC [073]

CH'IAO-WU PAO – Bulletin of Overseas Chinese Affairs. Peking. 1957-66. Lacking: 1957-60; v. 3, 1961; v. 11, 12, 1966. BCH-908 2 – 8 – ne IDC [950]

CHIAO-YU HSUEH-PAO – Journal of Education. v. 1-9. Peking. 1939-42. BCH-784 2 – 8 – ne IDC [073]

CHIAO-YU TSA-CHIH – Chinese Educational Review. v. 1-33. Shanghai, Changsha and Hongkong. 1909-48. monthly. Available: v. 8 (10)-v. 25, 1916-33. Lacking: v. 24 (5-12) 1932. BCH-2172 – 8 – ne IDC [370]

Chiapas. Mexico (State) *see* PERIODICO OFICIAL DEL GOBIERNO CONSTITUCIONAL DEL ESTADO DE CHIAPAS

Chiara, V *see*
- NOTES SUR QUELQUES CATEGORIES RELIGIEUSES DES INDIENS WAURA DU HAUT-XINGU, BRESIL
- LES POUPEES DES INDIENS KARAJA

Chiaretti, Giuseppe *see* ARCHIVO LEONESSANO. DOCUMENTI RIGUARDANTI LA VITA E IL CULTO DI SAN GIUSEPPE DE LEONESSA. ROMA 1965

CHIA-TING FU-CHIH – 1803, 48. BCH-752 2 – 8 – ne IDC [950]

Chiavelloni, Vincenzo *see* DISCORSI DELLA MUSICA..

CHIA-YIN TSA-CHIH – (The Tiger. v. 1-10. Shanghai. 1914-15; v. 1-45. Tientsin. 1925-27. BCH-213 2 – 8 – ne IDC [073]

CHIBA NIPPO – January 1957-December 1994 – 366r – 1 – Y3,732,000 – ja Japan Micro [950]

CHIBATA – Sao Paulo, Feb-Mar 1932 – 1,5,6 – bl Biblioteca [072]

CHIC / ed by Oligny, Odette – Montreal. v1 n4. 28 fev 1954-28 nov 1954 – 1r – 1 – Can$35.00 – cn Can Microfilming [072]

O CHIC : ORGAM CRITICO, LITERARIO, HUMORISTICO, HEBDOMADARIO E NOTICIOSO – Manaos, Amazonas. 6 Fev 1915 – 1,5,6 – bl Biblioteca [072]

Chicago and Canada Southern Railway Company *see*
- PROSPECTUS, AND OTHER DOCUMENTS
- THIS INDENTURE...BETWEEN THE CHICAGO AND CANADA SOUTHERN RAILWAY COMPANY...AND ANDREW T. HALL...AND KENYON COX 111 TRUSTEES

CHICAGO AND THE BAPTISTS / Stackhouse, Perry J – 1782-1933 – 1 – 9.87 – us Baptist [240]

CHICAGO ANTIQUITIES / Hurlbut, Henry H – Chicago: Fergus Printing Co., 1881. Illinois Reel 17. (The Cox Library Collection) – 5 – us Americana [978]

Chicago. Art Institute. Ryerson Library *see* INDEX TO ART PERIODICALS

Chicago Bar Association. Board of Managers *see* REPORT...CONCERNING AN INQUIRY CONDUCTED BY IT IN REFERENCE TO THE ACTIVITIES OF JUDGES IN PARTISAN POLITICS

CHICAGO BAR RECORD – (Cont as: CBA Record) – v1-67. 1910-1986 – 9 – $725.00 set – us Hein [340]

CHICAGO BAR RECORD *see* CBA RECORD

THE CHICAGO BEE – Chicago: Bee Publ Co, jan 1943-aug 17 1947 – 9r – us Res Libr [071]

Chicago. Board of Trade *see*
- ANNUAL REPORT
- ANNUAL REPORT OF THE TRADE AND COMMERCE OF CHICAGO

CHICAGO BUSINESS REVIEW – v. 1-. 1978- – 1 – us UMI [380]

CHICAGO CITY COUNCIL PROCEEDINGS FILES, 1833-1871 : INVENTORY AND INDEX 1987 – 93mf – 9 – $35.00 – us IL Archives [324]

CHICAGO DAILY JOURNAL – Chicago, IL: R L Wilson, jun 1847-dec 1849 – 1 – us Res Libr [071]

CHICAGO DAILY SOCIALIST / Chicago Socialist Party – Chicago, 1906-12 – 1 – us NY Public [335]

CHICAGO DAILY TIMES – 1929-47 – 1 – us UMI [071]

CHICAGO DAILY TRIBUNE – Chicago: Tribune Co, 1872-1963. jul 1873-75; may-dec 1881; jun-nov 1892; may 16-31 1923; oct 16-31 1933 – us Res Libr [071]

Chicago. Educational Commission *see* REPORT...OF THE COMMISSION...APPOINTED BY THE MAYOR, HON. CARTER H. HARRISON, JAN 19TH, 1898

CHICAGO FIELD – v1-15 (all publ). Feb 1874-Jun 1881 – 5r – 1 – $525.00 – us UPA [970]

THE CHICAGO HERALD – Chicago: [s.n.], jan-jun 1891; sep-oct 1891; may-jun 1893 – us Res Libr [071]

CHICAGO HISTORY – (NSv7- . 1978- . 5,6,9) – NSv1- . 1970- – 1 – us UMI [970]

THE CHICAGO JUVENILE COURT / Jeter, Helen Rankin – Washington, Govt. Print. Off., 1922. 119 p. LL-1294 – 1 – us L of C Photodup [340]

CHICAGO KENT LAW REVIEW – (v1-60 1923-84 in reel $578.00. v61-70 1985-95 in mf $230.00) – v1-70. 1923-95 – 5,6,9 – $808.00 set – us Hein [340]

CHICAGO LAW JOURNAL / ed by Barber, G L – E B Meyers Co. v1-2 n1. 1876-78 (all publ) – 8mf – $12.00 – LLMC 91-095 – us L.L.M.C. [073]

CHICAGO LAW JOURNAL – v1-2. 1876-77 – 1 – $40.00 – us Hein [073]

CHICAGO LAW JOURNAL / ed by Wachob, I S – (Cont: The Central Law Monthly. In 1896, absorbed by: The Chicago Law Journal Weekly) – Chicago Law Book Co. os: v4-10 1883-89. ns: v1-7 1890-96 (all publ) – 94mf – 9 – $141.00 – LLMC 82-913 – us L.L.M.C. [073]

CHICAGO LAW JOURNAL *see*
- CENTRAL LAW MONTHLY
- CHICAGO LAW JOURNAL WEEKLY

THE CHICAGO LAW JOURNAL – Chicago. v1, n.9-v9,n.12, 1880-88. Title varies. Incomplete. LL-048 – 1 – us L of C Photodup [340]

CHICAGO LAW JOURNAL WEEKLY – (Absorbs: Chicago Law Journal in 1896. The set is complete as provided by LLMC, but its vol numeration is very confused, with some vol numbers, 7-16 & 20, not being used at all. v6 ends in 1901 and the next vol, v17, starts in 1902) – v1-24. 1896-1907 (all publ) – 378mf – $328.00 – LLMC 91-096 – us L.L.M.C. [073]

CHICAGO LAW JOURNAL WEEKLY *see* CHICAGO LAW JOURNAL

CHICAGO LAW TIMES – v1-3. 1886-89 – 1 – $40.00 – us Hein [073]

THE CHICAGO LAW TIMES – (Lacking: v2) – v1-3. 1886-89 (all publ) – 3mf – 9 – $13.50 – LLMC 84-436 – us L.L.M.C. [073]

CHICAGO LAWYER – 1979- – 9 – us UMI [340]

CHICAGO LEGAL NEWS – v1-57. 1868-1925 – 1 – $840.00 – us Hein [073]

CHICAGO LITERARY TIMES – 1 – us U.W. Library [073]

Chicago Medical Society *see* OFFICIAL PROCEEDINGS

CHICAGO MUSICAL REVIEW – v1-9. Sept 1866-May 1867 – 1 – 195.00 – us Opus [073]

CHICAGO MUSICAL TIMES – Chicago, 1881-1926 – 1 – £165.00 – uk Chadwyck [780]

THE CHICAGO PACKER – Kansas City, MO: The Packer. [v17 n4-v46 n39]. jan 9 1915-sep 7 1946 – 32r – 1 – us Res Libr [071]

THE CHICAGO REPUBLICAN – Chicago: A W Mack, 1865- [1869-70] – us Res Libr [071]

CHICAGO REVIEW – (v22- . 5,6. v27- . 9) – v. 1- 1946- – 1 – us UMI [073]

CHICAGO SENTINEL – Chicago. Ill. 1911-23 – 1 – us A.J.P.C. [071]

CHICAGO SOCIALIST – Chicago. Daily. Oct 25 1906-Dec 4 1912. Incomplete – 1 – us NY Public [071]

Chicago Socialist Party *see* CHICAGO DAILY SOCIALIST

CHICAGO SUN – Chicago. Ill. 1941-48 – 1 – us UMI [071]

CHICAGO SUN TIMES – Chicago. 1948- With index – 1 – us UMI [071]

CHICAGO THEOLOGICAL SEMINARY : REGISTER – v1-80. Mar 1908-1990 (complete) – 12r – 1 – ATLA S0258 – us A.T.L.A. [073]

THE CHICAGO TIMES – Chicago: Wilbur F Storey, [jul 22 1862; ,ar 22 1863; sep 22 1863-jun 10 1864; apr-sep 1869; apr-dec 1870] – us Res Libr [071]

CHICAGO TRIBUNE – Chicago, IL. 1849-72 – 1 – us UMI [071]

CHICAGO TRIBUNE INDEX – Chicago. 1972- – 1 – us UMI [071]

THE CHICAGO WORLD – Chicago. Ill. Sept. 2, 9, 30; Oct. 7, 1950; Dec. 29, 1951 – 1 – us NY Public [071]

CHICAGOER ARBEITER-ZEITUNG – Chicago, IL: Socialistic Publ Soc, feb 13,18,28, mar 16,25, apr 11, may 25, nov 12 1885; may 19, jun 22,24,26,28, jul 1, oct 2-dec 1886; 1887-jun 1894; jul 1897-1900; may 1910-apr 1920 – 1 – us Res Libr [071]

CHICAGOER DEUTSCHE ZEITUNG : WOCHEN-AUSGABE – Chicago: Chicago-German Gazette Publ Co, dec 20 1924; jan 10 1925; aug 1925-may 22 1926 – 1r – 1 – us Res Libr [071]

CHICAGOER FRAUEN-ZEITUNG – Chicago: [German-American Publ Co, [dec 10 1893-jun 2 1901] – us Res Libr [071]

CHICAGOER FREIE PRESSE – Chicago: Richard Michaelis, [1891-1901] – 49r – 1 – us Res Libr [071]

CHICAGO'S AMERICAN – Chicago. Ill. 1950- – 1 – us UMI [071]

EL CHICANO – Colton, CA. 1968- – 39+ r – 1 – $1,950.00 ($90.00y) – R04017 – us Library Micro [071]

EL CHICANO – San Bernardino, CA. 1968- – 33+ r – 1 – $1,650.00 ($135.00y) – R02764 – us Library Micro [071]

CHICANO HISTORY NEWSPAPER CLIPPING FILE : UNION CITY, ALAMEDA COUNTY LIBRARY BRANCH CLIPPINGS FROM REGIONAL AND LEADING PAPERS ON ARTICLES OF IMPORT TO THE CHICANO COMMUNITY IN THE SAN FRANCISCO BAY AREA – June 1968-Jan 1976 – 46mf – 9 – $400.00 – B63007 – us Library Micro [071]

CHICANO LAW REVIEW – Los Angeles, CA. 1972-1975 – 1r – 1 – $50.00 – R03284 – us Library Micro [071]

CHICANO SCRAPBOOK : CLIPPINGS FROM CALIFORNIA NEWSPAPERS OF HAPPENINGS IN SANTA CLARA VALLEY – (Also available on mf $100.00) – San Jose, CA: Mexican-American Services Agency, 1968-73 – 1 B63020 – $50.00 – us Library Micro [305]

CHICANO STUDIES LIBRARY SERIAL COLLECTION : COMPLETE COLLECTION, SECTIONS 1-12 – (Sect 1 + 2: 5r $375.00 B62001. Sect 3: 3r $225.00 B62002. Sect 4 39r $2,145 B62003. Sect 5: 89r $4,895 B62004. Sect 6: 64r $3,520 B62005. Sect 7: 75r $4,125 B62006. Sect 8: 16r $880 B62007. Sect 9: 32r $1,760 B62008. Sect 10: 27r $1,485 B62009. Sect 11: 32r $1,815 B62010. Sect 12: 44r $2,385 B62011) – 426r – 1 – $21,485.00 set – B62000 – us Library Micro [305]

CHICANO THEATER – San Juan Bautista, Mar 1973-Spr 1974 – 1r – 1 – $50.00 – R03506 – us Library Micro [071]

Chichagov, N *see* ZHIZN' GENERAL-FEL'DMARSHALA GR

CHI-CH'ENG CH'U-P'U – (Collection of Chinese Music). v. 1-32. 1925. BCH-815 2 – 8 – ne IDC [780]

Chicherin, Boris N *see*
- FEELOSOFIA PRAVA
- OBLASTNYE UCHREZHDENIIA ROSSII V 17 V
- OPYTY PO ISTORII RUSSKAGO PRAVA

CHICHESTER COURIER – England. -w. 21 Oct-16 Nov 1868, 6-20 Jan 1869. (14 ft) – 1 – uk British Libr Newspaper [072]
CHICHESTER EXPRESS AND WEST SUSSEX JOURNAL – England. -w. 6 Jan 1863-30 Dec 1902. (13 reels) – 1 – uk British Libr Newspaper [072]
CHICHESTER JOURNAL – (Southern Star). England. -w. 28 Nov 1860-27 Apr 1864. (2 reels) – 1 – uk British Libr Newspaper [072]
Chichester, New Hampshire. Chichester Baptist Church and Society *see* RECORDS
Chick, Susan A *see* GENDER CLASSIFICATIONS OF FEMALE ATHLETES AND NONATHLETES AT WOMEN'S AND COEDUCATIONAL COLLEGES
CHICO AND OROVILLE CITY DIRECTORIES – Butte Co, CA. 1904-1905; 1913-1914; 1921-1928; 1937-1938; 1948-1950 – 9r – 1 – $450.00 – D006 – us Library Micro [910]
CHICO ENTERPRISE RECORD – (Also known as: Chico Record) – Chico, CA. 1907- – 439+ r – 1 BC02017 – $21,950.00 ($800.00y) – us Library Micro [071]
CHICO NEWS AND REVIEW – Chico, CA. 1994- – 1+ r – 1 – $50.00 ($50.00y) – B06016 – us Library Micro [071]
CHICO RECORD *see* CHICO ENTERPRISE RECORD
CHICOPEE 1848-1890 – (Mf 1-7: Births 1848-79 Vol A 1-192. Mf 8-11: Births 1880-90 Vol B 193-283. Mf 12-16: Index to Births 1848-91. Mf 17-27: Marriage Intentions 1848-61 Vol 1. Mf 28-38: Marriage Intentions 1861-81 Vol 2. Mf 39-48: Marriage Intentions 1881-93. Mf 49-53: Index to Marriage Intention 1848-90. Mf 54-60: Marriages 1848-62 Vol A. Mf 61-66: Marriages 1862-82 Vol B. Mf 67-70: Marriages 1883-90 Vol 3. Mf 71-75: Index to Marriages 1848-90. Mf 76-82: Deaths 1848-82 Vol A. Mf 83-84: Deaths 1883-90 Vol B. Mf 85-88: Index to Deaths 1848-90) – (mf ed 1984) – 88mf – 9 – 0-931248-66-3 – us Holbrook [920]
CHICOREL INDEX SERIES – 334mf – 9 – $1075.00 – us UMI [010]
LE CHICOT – Quebec, Canada. n3. 1858 (s.d.) – 1r – 1 – Can$25.00 – cn Can Microfilming [072]
CHICOT: COMEDIE EN UN ACTE / Braseau, Alphonse Victor – Montreal: C. Beauchemin, 18??. 00248. (Pre-1900 Canadiana) – 9 – cn C.I.H.M. [820]
O CHICOTE : ORGAM CRITICO E NOTICIOSO – Manaos, Amazonas. 6 Jul-Dez 1913; Jan-Set, 7 Nov 1915 – 1,5,6 – bl Biblioteca [072]
O CHICOTE : SEMANARIO VESPERTINO, CRITICO E NOTICIOSO – Itacoatiara, Amazonas. 15 Nov-13 Dez 1914 – 1,5,6 – bl Biblioteca [072]
Chiddingstone Castle, Kent. Denys Bower Collection *see* STUART PAPERS
CHIEF – Perry. Iowa. 1957- – 1 – us UMI [071]
CHIEF – Red Cloud. Neb. 1873-1923 – 1 – us UMI [071]
THE CHIEF ACTORS IN THE PURITAN REVOLUTION / Bayne, Peter – London: James Clarke, 1879 – 2mf – us A.T.L.A. [941]
THE CHIEF END OF REVELATION / Bruce, Alexander Balmain – London: Hodder & Stoughton, 1890 – 1mf – 9 – 0-8370-2482-X – 1985-0482 – us A.T.L.A. [220]
CHIEF JOSEPH HERALD – Joseph, OR. -w. 3 Jan 1952-26 Feb 1959. 3 rolls – 1 – us U.O. Library [071]
CHIEF JUSTICE MARSHALL'S DECISIONS *see* BROCKENBROUGH'S REPORTS OF CASES IN THE FOURTH CIRCUIT, 1802-1833
THE CHIEF PERIODS OF EUROPEAN HISTORY : SIX LECTURES READ IN THE UNIVERSITY OF OXFORD IN TRINITY TERM, 1885: WITH AN ESSAY ON GREEK CITIES UNDER ROMAN RULE / Freeman, Edward A – London; New York: Macmillan, 1886 – 1mf – us A.T.L.A. [940]
Chief Secretary's Office *see* VOLUMES OF ENROLLED LETTERS OF NATURALIZATION, 1863-1903
Chief Secretary's Office, Queensland *see*
– AGREEMENT FOR TRANSPORT OF QUEENSLAND CONTINGENT TO SOUTH AFRICA, 1899-1899
– ARMY ORDERS; SOUTH AFRICA 1901-1902
– COPIES OF CORRESPONDENCE BETWEEN AUSTRALIAN PREMIERS CONCERNING RATES OF PAY, 1900-1900
– LIST OF MEN ABSENT FROM REGIMENT, QUEENSLAND DEFENCE FORCE, CHRONOLOGICAL SERIES, 1901-1902
– LIST OF NAMES OF THOSE TO WHOM INSURANCE HAS BEEN PAID IN RESPECT OF THE DEATH OF MEMBERS OF THE FIRST FOUR QUEENSLAND CONTINGENTS, QUEENSLAND DEFENCE FORCE, 1900-1902
– MEDAL ROLLS AND CLASPS OF THE QUEENSLAND DEFENSE FORCE, 1902-1903
– MEDICAL HISTORY SHEETS OF MEMBERS OF THE 6TH QUEENSLAND CONTINGENT RETURNING BY TSS "DEVON" 1902-1902
– MEDICAL RECORDS OF THE QUEENSLAND DEFENCE FORCE, LEXICOGRAPHICAL SERIES, 1900-1901
– NOMINAL ROLLS OF THE QUEENSLAND DEFENCE FORCE FOR SERVICE IN SOUTH AFRICA, 1900-1903
– PAY LISTS FOR "H" COMPANY, 4TH CONTINGENT, QUEENSLAND DEFENCE FORCE, CHRONOLOGICAL SERIES, 1900-1901
– PAY SHEETS OF THE 5TH AND 6TH CONTINGENTS FROM THE QUEENSLAND DEFENCE FORCE WHO SERVED IN THE BOER WAR, CHRONOLOGICAL SERIES, 1901-1902
– PAYLISTS AND PAY INSTRUCTION ROLLS FOR THE QUEENSLAND DEFENCE FORCE MEMBERS WHO SERVED IN THE BOER WAR, 1901-1902
– REGISTER OF MEDICAL EXAMINATIONS FOR THE 1ST CONTINGENT, QUEENSLAND DEFENCE FORCE, 1899-1899
– REGISTERED OF RETURNED SOLDIERS OF THE QUEENSLAND DEFENCE FORCE WHO SERVED IN THE BOER WAR, 1901-1903
– RETURNS OF MEMBERS OF THE QUEENSLAND DEFENCE FORCE WHO HAVE BEEN KILLED OR DIED IN SOUTH AFRICA, 1899-1902
– RETURNS OF QUEENSLAND CONTINGENTS WHICH HAVE PROCEEDED TO SOUTH AFRICA, 1899-1902
– ROLL OF THE 4TH QUEENSLAND IMPERIAL BUSHMEN FROM NEWCASTLE TO STORMBERG, 1901-1901
– SERVICE ROLLS OF CONTINGENTS OF THE QUEENSLAND DEFENCE FORCE WHO SERVED IN THE BOER WAR, 1899-1901
– VOLUMES OF SUPPLEMENTS TO THE QUEENSLAND GOVERNMENT GAZETTE RELATING TO CONTINGENTS FOR SOUTH AFRICA, 1900-1903
CHIEFLY AMONG WOMEN – From: Catholic World (1875) – 9 – us A.T.L.A. [073]
CHIEFS OF STATE AND CABINET MEMBERS OF FOREIGN GOVERNMENTS / U.S. Central Intelligence Agency – 1966-86 – 352mf – 9 – $550.00 – us Updata [920]
CHIEFS OF STATE AND CABINET MEMBERS OF FOREIGN GOVERNMENTS / U.S. Central Intelligence Agency – Aug 1962-Dec 1975 – 1 $262.00 $18.00y 8 $58.00y – us L of C Photodup [324]
CHIEFTAIN – La Crosse. Kan. 1881; 1882-1885 – 1 – us UMI [071]
CHIEFTAIN – Pueblo. Col. 1947- – 1 – us UMI [071]
CHIEFTAIN – Tecumseh. Neb. 1873-1961 – 1 – us UMI [071]
THE CHIEFTAINS OF CEYLON / Sanden, J C van – Colombo: Plate, 1936 – 1 – us Res Libr [950]
THE CHIEFTAINS OF CHAMPLAIN: A STORY OF ADVENTURE IN THE NEW WORLD – New York: Hickey, 1883. 00607. (Pre-1900 Canadiana) – 9 – cn C.I.H.M. [920]
CHIEH-FANG JIH-PAO – Yenan. China. 1941-47 – 1 – 216.00 – us Chinese Res [072]
CHIEN CHU HSUEH PAO – Incomplete. CH-897 2. 1955-1966 – 8 – ne IDC [073]
LE CHIEN D'OR – Quebec, Canada. v2 n12. mai-jun 1927; v3 n10/11. mar/avr 1928 – 1r – 1 – Can$25.00 – cn Can Microfilming [072]
CHIEN KUOKUO CHI LIEN HO PAO – Saigon. South Vietnam. 1969 – 1 – us UMI [072]
Chien, Timothy Yu-wan *see*
– THE NEW POINT OF VIEW (CCC99)
– RELIGION AND LIFE (CCC101)
– RELIGION AND SCIENCE (CCC102)
Chien, Yu-wan *see*
– PIONEERS OF THE PROTESTANT CHURCH IN CHINA (CCC100)
– STORY OF THE JEWISH REVOLT (CCC103)
CHIENGMAI KHONMUANG – Chiengmai, Thailand. 1953-54; 1975-76 – 3r – 1 – us L of C Photodup [072]
CH'IEN-T'U (THE FUTURE) – Shanghai, Feb 1933-Feb 1939. Scattered issues missing. 7 reels – 1 – 195.00 – us Chinese Res [073]
CHIEN-YANG HSIEN-CHIH – 1929. 12. BCH-575 2 – 8 – ne IDC [950]
CH'IEN-YEH YUEH-PAO – "Native Banker's Monthly". 20 v. Shanghai. 1921-49. Lacking: v. 14 (3) 1934; v. 15-v. 19 (1-9) 1935-48; v. 19 (11-12)-v. 20 (1-4) 1948-49. BCH-218 1 – 9 – ne IDC [073]
Chiera, E *see*
– JOINT EXPEDITION WITH THE IRAQ MUSEUM AT NUZI
– SUMERIAN RELIGIOUS TEXTS
Chiesa, Carlos *see* IGLESIA Y JUSTICIALISMO
LA CHIESA GALDEA NEL SECOLO DELL' UNIONE / Beltrami, G – 1392 2. 1933 – 8 – ne IDC [240]
LA CHIESA NUOVA IN AISSI... / Terzi, Arduino – Madrid: Arch. Ibero Americano, 1964 – 1 – sp Bibl Santa Ana [240]
Chiesi, Gustavo *see* LA COLONIZZAZIONE EUROPEA NELL'EST AFRICA
Chiflet, L *see* ESSAY D'UNE PARFAITE GRAMMAIRE DE LA LANGUE FRANCOISE
Chigi, Zondadari, 1 *see* RIFLESSIONI FATTE DE EUCHERO PASTORE ARCADE SOPRA ALLA MAGGIOR FACILITA CHE TROVASI NELL' APPRENDERE IL CANTO
CHIH LOUK KOUOH YUH TCHI – Geographie historique traduite du chinois par A. Des Michels. 1892 – 9 – fr Orientalistes [950]
CHIH-CHIANG HSUEH-PAO (HANGCHOW JOURNAL) – Hangchow, China.1932-35. BCH-219/1 – 9 – ne IDC [950]
CHIH-LI MIEN-CHOU CHIH – 1871, 55. BCH-779 2 – 8 – ne IDC [950]
CHIH-SHENG HSIANG-SHIH LU – List of successful candidates in the imperial examination in Chih-li province: 1831, 1834, 1843, 1851, 1904, 1907. 2 reels – 1 – 62.00 – us Chinese Res [950]
Chihuahua. Mexico. (State) *see*
– PERIODICO OFICIAL
– PERIODICO OFICIAL DEL GOBIERNO DEL ESTADO
Chilcote, Ronald *see* PORTUGUESE AFRICA
THE CHILD / Dupanloup, Felix – Boston: P Donahoe, 1875 – 1r – 1 – us U.W. Library [920]
CHILD ABUSE AND NEGLECT – v1- 1977- – 5,6,9 – us UMI [360]
CHILD AND ADOLESCENT SOCIAL WORK JOURNAL: C & A – v1-. 1984- – 1,5,6,9 – us UMI [073]
CHILD AND FAMILY BEHAVIOR THERAPY / ed by Franks, Cyril M – v1- 1989- – 1,9 ($325.00 in US $455.00 outside hardcopy subsc) – us Haworth [306]
CHILD AND PLAY : THEORETICAL APPROACHES AND TEACHING APPLICATIONS – 1980 – 68p – 9 – 92-3-101658-X – fr UNESCO [306]
CHILD AND YOUTH SERVICES / ed by Beker, Jerome – v1- 1977- – 1,9 ($200.00 in US $280.00 outside hardcopy subsc) – us Haworth [305]
CHILD ART : RHODA KELLOGG COLLECTION – $755.00 – us UPA [700]
CHILD CARE QUARTERLY – (v3- 5,6 v7- 9) – v1- 1971- – 1 – us UMI [640]
Child, David Lee *see* THE CULTURE OF THE BEST
CHILD DAY CARE PLANNING PROJECT – 1983-1990 – 9r – 1 – us Western Res [360]
CHILD DEVELOPMENT – (v42- v48- 1977-) – v37- 1966- – 1,5,6,9 – us UMI [370]
CHILD EDUCATION SPECIAL – n. 1-. 1978- – 1 – us UMI [370]
Child, George Chaplin *see* BENEDICITE, OR, THE SONG OF THE THREE CHILDREN
Child, Gilbert W *see* CHURCH AND STATE UNDER THE TUDORS
Child, Hamilton *see*
– GAZETTEER AND BUSINESS DIRECTORY OF CHEMUNG AND SCHUYLER COUNTIES 1868-69
– GAZETTEER AND BUSINESS DIRECTORY OF FRANKLIN AND GRAND ISLE COUNTIES
– GAZETTEER AND BUSINESS DIRECTORY OF LAMOILLE AND ORLEANS COUNTIES
– GAZETTEER AND BUSINESS DIRECTORY OF NIAGARA COUNTY 1869
– GAZETTEER AND BUSINESS DIRECTORY OF ORANGE COUNTY
– GAZETTEER AND BUSINESS DIRECTORY OF RENSSELAER COUNTY, NEW YORK 1870/71
– GAZETTEER AND BUSINESS DIRECTORY OF RUTLAND COUNTY
– GAZETTEER AND BUSINESS DIRECTORY OF WINDHAM COUNTY
– GAZETTEER OF CHESHIRE COUNTY 1736-1885
– GAZETTEER OF GRAFTON COUNTY 1709-1886
– GAZETTEER OF WASHINGTON COUNTY
Child, Hamiltoniler and publisher *see* GAZETTEER AND BUSINESS DIRECTORY OF NIAGARA COUNTY 1869
Child, James E *see* CHILD'S HISTORY OF WASECA COUNTY
CHILD LABOR AND STREET TRADES PERMITS ISSUED IN WISCONSIN / Wisconsin. Division of Labor Standards – 1915-68. 14 fiches. (Harvard Law School Library Collection.) – 9 – 1.50f – us H.U. Law [331]
CHILD LABOR BULLETIN *see* AMERICAN CHILD
CHILD LANGUAGE SURVEY: TRANSCRIPTS – (Nuffield Foundation) – 9 – uk Microform Academic [370]
Child, Lydia Maria *see* A SELECTION OF WORKS
CHILD PSYCHIATRY AND HUMAN DEVELOPMENT – (v4- 5,6,9) – v1- 1970- – 1 – us UMI [616]
Child, Theodore *see* THE PRAISE OF PARIS
CHILD WELFARE – Sept 1985- – 1 – us UMI [073]
CHILD WELFARE – (v50- 5,6) – v1- 1922- – 1 – us UMI [360]
CHILD WELFARE *see* PTA MAGAZINE
CHILD WELFARE INFORMATION SERVICE, BULLETIN *see* WASHINGTON BULLETIN
CHILD WELFARE MAGAZINE *see* PTA MAGAZINE
Child, William H *see* HISTORY OF THE TOWN OF CORNISH
CHILD WORKERS IN NEPAL – Kathmandu. 12 docs. 1989-1991 – 7mf – 9 – ne IDC [331]
CHILDBIRTH AND CEREMONIES IN A WONOSOBO VILLAGE – SE 1168 1. 1956 – 9 – ne IDC [306]
Childers, Hugh Culling Eardley *see* PRINCE EDWARD ISLAND: HOW IT WAS BOUGHT BACK FROM THE LANDLORDS
Childers, Spencer *see* A MARINER OF ENGLAND: AN ACCOUNT OF THE CAREER OF WILLIAM RICHARDSON... 1780-1819, AS TOLD BY HIMSELF
CHILDHOOD EDUCATION – v1-17 1925-1941 – 1 – us Princeton Micro [370]
CHILDHOOD EDUCATION – (v44- . 5,6. v52- . 9) – v. 1-. 1924- – 1 – us UMI [370]
CHILDHOOD OF JESUS / Gannett, William C – London: Sunday School Assoc., 1885. 1 fiche – 9 – us A.T.L.A. [240]
THE CHILDHOOD OF JESUS / Gannett, William Channing – English ed. London: Sunday School Association, 1885 – 1mf – 9 – 0-8370-3228-8 – 1985-1228 – us A.T.L.A. [240]
CHILDREN – (Cont by: Children Today) – Washington. v1-18. 1954-71 – 2r – 1 – us Ross [305]
CHILDREN – v1-9 1954-62 – 1,5,6 – $28.00 – us Princeton Micro [305]
CHILDREN ADVENT HERALD – v. 1. 1846-1847 – 1 – us UMI [240]
CHILDREN AND THEIR PRIMARY SCHOOLS / Great Britain. Central Advisory Committee for England – Reports of the Central Advisory Council for England. (Plowden Report). 1967 – 9 – uk Microform Academic [324]
CHILDREN AND WORLD WAR 1 PAMPHLET COLLECTION – 1915-1919 – 2r – 1 – CSUXANL3610-B – us Hoover Inst Photo [305]
CHILDREN AND YOUTH SERVICES REVIEW – v1- 1979- – 5,6,9 – us UMI [360]
CHILDREN IN CONCENTRATION CAMPS / Medical Bureau and North American Committee to Aid Spanish Democracy – N.Y., 1939? Fiche W 1035. (Blodgett Collection of Spanish Civil War Pamphlets) – 9 – us H.U. College Libr [946]
CHILDREN IN COURT / Puner, Helen Walker – 1st ed. New York: Public Affairs Committee, 1954. 28p – 1 – us L of C Photodup [340]
CHILDREN IN EXILE – The story of ile de Re. NY. n.d. Fiche W 796. (Blodgett Collection of Spanish Civil War Pamphlets) – 9 – us H.U. College Libr [946]
Children, J G *see* AN ABSTRACT OF THE CHARACTERS OF OCHSENHEIMER'S GENERA OF THE LEPIDOPTERA OF EUROPE

CHILDREN OF CENTRAL AFRICA / Wareham, J M – London: Longmans, Green, [1957] – us Res Libr [305]
CHILDREN OF GOD AND UNION WITH CHRIST / Schieffelin, Samuel Bradhurst – NY: Board of Publication of the Reformed Church in America, 1896 – 1mf – 9 – 0-8370-5418-4 – 1985-3418 – us A.T.L.A. [240]
THE CHILDREN OF GOD (CCC17) = SHANG TI TI ERH NU MEN / Chang, Tzu-ping – (In Chinese) – Shanghai: Kuang ming shu chu, 1931 – 1r – 1 – 0-8370-1717-3 – 1984-6089 – us A.T.L.A. [240]
THE CHILDREN OF MADAGASCAR / Standing, Herbert F – [London]: Religious Tract Society, 1887 – 1mf – 9 – 0-8370-6413-9 – 1986-0413 – us A.T.L.A. [960]
THE CHILDREN OF WISDOM AND OTHER SERMONS PREACHED IN CANADIAN PULPITS / De Soyres, John – Toronto: W. Briggs, 1897. 02665. (Pre-1900 Canadiana) – 9 – cn C.I.H.M. [971]
CHILDREN TODAY – v1- 1972- – 1,5,6,9 – us UMI [305]
CHILDREN TODAY *see* CHILDREN
CHILDREN WITH SPECIFIC READING DIFFICULTIES / Great Britain. Advisory Committee on Handicapped Children – Report of the Advisory Committee on Handicapped Children. 1972 – 9 – uk Microform Academic [324]
CHILDREN'S AND WORLD WAR 2 PAMPHLET COLLECTION – 1941-1946 – 1 – CSUXANN2519-B – us Hoover Inst Photo [305]
THE CHILDREN'S BIBLE (CCC141) : SCRIPTURE SELECTIONS / ed by Happy Childhood Staff – (In Chinese) – Hong Kong: Bible Book and Tract Depot, 1952 – 1r – 1 – 1984-B500 – us A.T.L.A. [220]
CHILDREN'S BOOKS *see* EARLY AMERICAN CHILDREN'S BOOKS IN MICROFICHE
CHILDREN'S LEGAL RIGHTS JOURNAL – v1-15. 1979-95 – 9 – $181.00 set – us Hein [340]
CHILDREN'S LITERATURE IN EDUCATION – (v7- . 5,6,9) – v. 1-. 1970- – 1 – us UMI [370]
THE CHILDREN'S MISSIONARY AND SABBATH SCHOOL RECORD – Montreal: J.C. Becket, 1844-[1845?] – 9 – cn C.I.H.M. [240]
THE CHILDREN'S RECORD – (Cont by: King's Own) – New Glasgow, N.S.: E. Scott, [1886?-1899] – 9 – cn C.I.H.M. [240]
CHILDREN'S THEATRE CONFERENCE NEWSLETTER – v.8-15. 1958-66. Continued by: Children's Theatre Review – 1 – us UMI [790]
CHILDREN'S THEATRE NEWSLETTER – v.1-8. 1954-58. Continued by: Children's Theatre Conference Newsletter – 1 – us UMI [790]
CHILDREN'S THEATRE REVIEW – (v.28- 1979- 5,6,9) – v.16- 1967- – 1 – us UMI [790]
CHILDREN'S TREASURY OF BIBLE STORIES : PART 2: NEW TESTAMENT / Gaskoin, Herman (Mrs); ed by Maclear, George Frederick – London: Macmillan, 1879 – 1mf – 9 – 0-8370-7382-0 – 1986-1382 – us A.T.L.A. [220]
THE CHILD'S BIBLE EXPOSITOR, OR, LESSONS AND RECORDS OF THE SUNDAY SCHOOL – Toronto: H.Rowsell, [1840?-18–] – 9 – cn C.I.H.M. [220]
THE CHILDS DELIGHT / Lye, Thomas – 1671. 183p. (English Linguistics Series 1500-1800) – 9 – us UMI [420]
CHILD'S FIRST LEARNING ENVIRONMENT : SELECTED READINGS IN HOME ECONOMICS – 1980 – 9 – 92-3-101751-9 – fr UNESCO [150]
CHILD'S GEM – 1900-29 – 1 – 217.84 – us Baptist [240]
CHILD'S HISTORY OF WASECA COUNTY / Child, James E – From the first settlement to 1904. 1905. Minnesota Reel 16. (The Cox Library Collection) – 5 – us Americana [978]
CHILD'S INDEX – v. 1, no. 1-V. 3, no. 4. Sep 1862-Apr 1865 – 1 – 5.63 – us Baptist [240]
Childs, Nancy M *see* JOURNAL OF NUTRACEUTICALS, FUNCTIONAL AND MEDICAL FOODS
CHILD'S PAPER – New York, NY. -w. Jan 1852-Nov 1880. 2 reels – 1 – uk British Libr Newspaper [071]
CHILD'S RIGHT TO EDUCATION / ed by Mialaret, Gaston – 1979 – 258p – 9 – 92-3-101737-3 – fr UNESCO [370]

CHILE : ANUARIO ESTADISTICO 1848/58-1937 / Chile. Servicio Nacional de Estadistica y Censos – (Some missing vols and pts. Coll title: Latin American and Caribbean Official Statistical Serials, 1821-1982) – 512mf – 9 – £4.00f (set £3,630.00 691mf) – uk Chadwyck [972]
Chile *see*
- DIARIO OFICIAL
- DIARIO OFICIAL DE LA REPUBLICA DE CHILE
- GACETA DE LOS TRIBUNALES

Chile. Centro de Investigacion y Desarrollo de la Educacion *see* INDICE DE RESUMENES ANALITICOS SOBRE EDUCACION EN AMERICA LATINA Y EL CARIBE
Chile. Corporacion de Fomento de la Produccion *see*
- PLAN DE DESARROLLO AGRICOLA Y DE TRANSPORTE 1954-1961
- PROGRAMA NACIONAL DE DESARROLLO ECONOMICO, 1961-1970

Chile. Direccion General de Correos y Telegrafos *see* BOLETIN OFICIAL
CHILE HOY – Santiago, CL. 1972-1973 – 3r – $150.00 – R04189 – us Library Micro [072]
Chile. Inspeccion Jeneral de Tierras i Colonizacion *see* MEMORIA
Chile. Inter-American Economic and Social Council *see* EVALUACION DEL PROGRAMA NAC. DE DES. EC. Y SOCIAL DE CHILE
Chile. Ministerio de Hacienda *see* BOLETIN
Chile. Ministerio de Justica *see* MEMORIA
Chile. Ministerio de Relaciones Exteriores *see* MEMORIA
CHILE MISSIONS: OUR BAPTIST WORK IN CHILE – By Mary P. Moore and "Reminiscenses of Baptist Missions in Chile" by W. E. Davidson. (Unpubl. mss.). 168p – 1 – 5.88 – us Baptist [240]
Chile. Oficina Central de Estadistica *see* ESTADISTICA COMERCIAL DE LA REPUBLICA DE CHILE
Chile. Oficina de Planificacion Nacional *see*
- PLAN ANUAL 1971
- PLAN DE DESARROLLO DE LA 4 REGION VALPAIRASO-ACONCAGUA, 1971-1976
- PLAN DE LA ECONOMIA NACIONAL 1971-1976
- PLAN DE RECONSTRUCCION 1971-1973, DE LA PROVINCIAS DE COQUIMBO, ACONCAGUA, SANTIAGO, VALPARASIO Y O'HIGGINS, AFECTADAS POR EL SISMO DEL 8 DE JULIO DE 1971
- PLAN NACIONAL DE EDUCACION
- POLITICA DE DESARROLLO NAC DIRECTIVAS NAC. Y REG
- RESUMEN DEL PLAN ANUAL 1971
- RESUMEN DEL PLAN ANUAL 1972
- RESUMEN DEL PLAN DE LA ECONOMICA NACIONAL 1971-1976
- SINTESIS DE LA ESTRATEGIA PARA EL DESARROLLO DE LA REGION DE MAGALLANES

Chile. Servicio Nacional de Estadistica y Censos *see* CHILE
CHILGOOPIE THE GLAD : A STORY OF KOREA AND HER CHILDREN / Perry, Jean – London: S W Partridge, [1906] – 1mf – 9 – 0-8370-6594-1 – 1986-0594 – us A.T.L.A. [240]
Chili, New York. Chili Baptist Church *see* RECORDS
CHI-LIN JIH PAO – Ch'ang-ch'un, China. 1958-1960 – 6r – 1 – us L of C Photodup [072]
CHI-LIN JIH-PAO – Kirin, Kirin. Oct 10, 1945-. Reel 1: Jan, Apr-Jun 1962; Reel 2: Jul-Dec 1962. 2 reels – 1 – 35.00 – us Chinese Res [072]
Chilipaine, F A *see* ESSAI DE RECHERCHE EN LINGUISTIQUE CONTRASTIVE: LE SYSTEME VERBAL CHICHEWA-FRANCAIS
Chillicothe. Ohio. First New Jerusalem Society *see* CHURCH RECORDS, MS 399
CHILLIWACK PROGRESS – Chilliwack, British Columbia, CN. Apr 1891- – 4r per yr – 1 – Can$55.00r – cn Commonwealth Micro [072]
CHILMARK 1673-1849 – (Mf 1T-2T: Vital Records 1673-1881. Mf 2T-3T: Marriages & Intentions 1699-1849. Mf 3T: Family Records 1752-1859. Mf 4T: Births 1810-49; Marriages, Deaths 1844-49; Births & Deaths 1718-1806) – (mf ed 1995) – 4mf – 9 – 0-87623-231-4 – us Holbrook [920]

CHILMARK 1674-1900 – (Mf 1-6: Town & Vitals 1688-1871. Mf 7-13: Town Records 1801-67. Mf 8-13: Marriges 1824-38. Mf 13: Out-of-Town Marriages. Mf 14: Vitals. Mf 14-16: Marriages 1838-90; Intentions 1838-1905. Mf 17: Marriages 1674-1837. Mf 17-18: Births 1690-1807. Mf 18: Intentions 1800-38; Deaths 1691-1829+. Mf 19-20: West Family 1606-1944. Mf 21: Baptisms 1852-1908; Marriages 1819-1905. Mf 21-23: Churchgoers 1810-1921. Mf 24-27: Church Records 1837-88. Mf 28-30: Treasurer 1820-55. Mf 31: Valuation List 1862. Mf 32-33: Valuation List 1891. Mf 34: Voters 1892-1915. Mf 35-36: Birth Index 1844-1975. Mf 37-38: Marriage Index 1844-1975. Mf 39-40: Death Index 1845-1975. Mf 41,43: Births 1810-1900. Mf 41-43: Marriages 1844-1905. Mf 42-43: Deaths 1845-1910) – (mf ed 1994) – 43mf – 9 – 0-87623-193-8 – us Holbrook [920]
CHILOQUIN REVIEW – Chiloquin, OR. 1925-26 – 1 – 17.00 – us Oregon Hist [071]
CHILOQUIN REVIEW – Chiloquin, OR. -w. 4 Sept. 1925-25 Dec 1947. 3 rolls – 1 – us U.O. Library [071]
Chilton, Robert S *see* POEMS
CHILTON'S AUTOMOTIVE INDUSTRIES – v.154-. 1976- – 1,5,6,9 – us UMI [073]
CHILTON'S CCJ – (v121-139, no.8. Mar 1971-Aug 1982. 5,6. v125-139, no.8. Mar 1973-Aug 1982. 9) – v1-139, no.8. Mar 1911-Aug 1982 – 1 – us UMI [073]
CHILTON'S CCJ – v141, no.4-. Apr 1984- – 1,5,6,9 – us UMI [073]
CHILTON'S COMMERCIAL CARRIER JOURNAL – v139, no.9-v141, no.3. Sept 1982-Mar 1984 – 1,5,6,9 – us UMI [073]
CHILTON'S DISTRIBUTION WORLD WIDE – (v69- . 5,6. v75- . 9) – v. 8- 1909- – 1 – us UMI [380]
CHILTON'S DISTRIBUTOR NEWS – v3-. 1986- – 1,5,6,9 – us UMI [380]
CHILTON'S FOOD ENGINEERING INTERNATIONAL – (v3- 1978- 5,6,9) – v3- 1978- – 1 – us UMI [660]
CHILTON'S HARDWARE AGE *see*
- HARDWARE AGE
- HARDWARE AGE HOME IMPROVEMENT MARKETPLACE

CHILTON'S IMPO – v43, no.5-. May 1982- – 1,5,6,9 – us UMI [330]
CHILTON'S IMPO DISTRIBUTOR NEWS: INDUSTRIAL MAINTENANCE AND PLANT OPERATION – v1-2. 1984-85 – 1 – us UMI [380]
CHILTON'S INDUSTRIAL SAFETY AND HYGIENE NEWS – v16-. 1982- – 1,5,6,9 – us UMI [073]
CHILTON'S IRON AGE – Manufacturing management. v227-. 1984- – 1,5,6,9 – us UMI [330]
CHILTON'S REVIEW OF OPTOMETRY – v. 114-. 1977- – 1,5,6,9 – us UMI [617]
Chimba, Barnabas *see* A HISTORY OF THE BAUSHI
CHIMERE – no. 1-6, 8-9, 19. Montpellier. aout 1891-avr 1893 – 1 – fr A.C.R.P.P. [073]
THE CHIMES : A GOBLIN STORY OF SOME BELLS THAT RANG ON OLD YEAR OUT AND A NEW YEAR IN / Dickens, Charles – London: Chapman and Hall, 1845 – 1 roll – 1 – 1-55879-289-9 – uk Libr Preservation [830]
LA CHIMICA INDUSTRIALE. (L'INDUSTRIA CHIMICA) – Turin, Italy. Oct 1899-dec 1904.-f. 3 reels – 1 – uk British Libr Newspaper [073]
LA CHIMIE AGRICOLE MISE A LA PORTEE DE TOUT LE MONDE : OUVRAGE TRES SIMPLIFIE A L'USAGE DES AGRICULTEURS CANADIENS ET PARTICULIEREMENT DES ECOLES ELEMENTAIRES / Aubin, Napoleon – Quebec: de l'imprimerie de J B Frechette, pere, 1847. SEM16P264 – 1r – 5 – Can$9.00 – cn Bibl Nat [370]
CHIMIE ET INDUSTRIE – v. 1-106. 1968-1973 – 1,5,6 – us Princeton Micro [540]
CHIN JIH HSIN WEN – Peking. China. 1962- – 1 – us UMI [072]
CHIN YEN KUNG PAO / China. National Committee for Opium Suppression – Gazette. Nanking, Jan 1930, n.12. Also: CHIN YEN WEI YUAN HUI KUNG PAO. Gazette, Nanking. 1931. n.1-12. 2 reels – 1 – 35.20 – us Chinese Res [360]
Chin, Yo-Lin *see* LUN TAO (CCC104)
Chin, Yung *see*
- PI HSUEH CHIEN
- SIN TIAUW HIAP LU, ATAU SI RADJAWALI SAKTI DAN PASANGAN PENDEKAR

CHINA : AZOLLA PROPAGATION AND SMALL-SCALE BIOGAS TECHNOLOGY – 1979 – 93p – it F.A.O. [630]
CHINA : DEVELOPMENT OF OLIVE PRODUCTION. REPORT OF A STUDY TOUR IN THE PEOPLE'S REPUBLIC OF CHINA, 1979 – 1980 – 163p – it F.A.O. [634]
CHINA : DOCUMENTS ON CONTEMPORARY CHINA – (Inventory contents; Bibliography, Reference and Leadership Information; Enactments of Party and Government; Provincial and Municipal Data; Research and Analysis Reports; Red Guard Translations with index; Inquire regarding indexes) – 1949-75 + index – 525mf – 9 – $5.00f – us Ross [950]
CHINA : ITS STATE AND PROSPECTS,... / Medhurst, W H – London, 1838 – 7mf – 9 – ne IDC [320]
CHINA : LAWS, STATUTES ETC. NATURALIZATION LAW – Peking, 1925 – 1mf – 1 – ILM-3869/1 – ne IDC [327]
CHINA : MULTIPLE CROPPING AND RELATED CROP PRODUCTION TECHNOLOGY – 1980 – 66p – it F.A.O. [631]
CHINA : RECENT CHINESE ECONOMIC REFORMS, STUDIES OF TWO INDUSTRIAL ENTERPRISES / Byrd, W et al – Washington, 1984 – 3mf – 9 – DE-140/1 – ne IDC [370]
CHINA : RECYCLING OF ORGANIC WASTES IN AGRICULTURE – 1981 – 122p – it F.A.O. [631]
China *see*
- CHUNG-KUO CHAN-SHIH CHING-CHI FA-KUI HUI-PIEN
- HISTORICAL DATA OF THE NATIONAL ASSEMBLY FROM 1938-1947
- TAIRIKU NENKAU
- WAI CHIAO KUNG PAO
- YANG TZU CHIANG SHUI TAO CHI K'AN

CHINA, 1911-41 : REPORTS / U.S. Military Intelligence; ed by Kesaris, Paul – 1982. Series: US Military Intelligence Reports. 15 reels with printed guide – 1 – $1,515.00 – us UPA [355]
CHINA, 1946-76 / U.S. Central Intelligence Agency – 1982. Series: CIA Research Reports – 1 – $580.00 – 0-89093-424-X – us UPA [950]
CHINA (1949-1979), DOCUMENTS ON CONTEMPORARY / ed by Lowey, George – 9 – $5.00f – us Ross [950]
CHINA, 1970-80 : SPECIAL STUDIES / ed by Kesaris, Paul – 1981 – 8r – 1 – $880.00 – 0-89093-386-3 – us UPA [320]
CHINA, AGRICULTURE IN TRANSITION : REPORT OF AN F.A.O. MISSION ON AGRICULTURAL PLANNING AND POLICY, 1980 – 1981 – 53p – it F.A.O. [338]
CHINA, AN OUTLINE OF ITS GOVERNMENT, LAWS AND POLICY / Auber, P – London, 1834 – 8mf – 9 – CH-817/2 – ne IDC [950]
CHINA AND FRANCE, OR TWO TREATISES – London, 1676 – 3mf – 9 – ne IDC [327]
CHINA AND INDIA : 1941-49 / U.S. Office of Strategic Services – (1950-61, Suppl. 1979. Series, Pt 9. $480.00 ISBN 0-89093-249-2) – 1977. Series: OSS State Department Intelligence and Research Reports, Pt 3 – 1 – $580.00 – 0-89093-119-4 – us UPA [950]
CHINA AND METHODISM / Bashford, James Whitford – (Includes bibliography) – Cincinnati: Jennings and Graham; New York: Eaton and Mains, c1906 – 1mf – 9 – 0-8370-7201-8 – 1986-1201 – us A.T.L.A. [240]
CHINA AND PROTESTANT MISSIONS : A COLLECTION OF THEIR EARLIEST MISSIONARY WORKS IN CHINESE – (Includes an illustrated catalogue by Mr. John Yung-Hsiang Lai. A detailed free catalogue available) – 1,750mf – 9 – ne IDC [240]
CHINA AND THE CHINESE : A GENERAL DESCRIPTION OF THE COUNTRY AND ITS INHABITANTS, ITS CIVILIZATION AND FORM OF GOVERNMENT, ITS RELIGIOUS AND SOCIAL INSTITUTIONS, ITS INTERCOURSE WITH OTHER NATIONS, AND ITS PRESENT CONDITION AND PROSPECTS / Nevius, John L – Philadelphia: Presbyterian Board of Publication, c1882 – 2mf – us A.T.L.A. [950]
CHINA AND THE CHINESE / Nevius, John L – 1869 – 1 – $50.00 – us Presbyterian [950]
CHINA AND THE CHINESE : THEIR RELIGION, CHARACTER, CUSTOMS, AND MANUFACTURES;... / Sirr, H C – London. 2v. 1849 – 10mf – 9 – ne IDC [950]

China Association *see* ANNUAL REPORTS
China. Bank of China *see* CHUNG-HANG YUEH-K'AN
CHINA BEING A MILITARY REPORT. AN ACCOUNT OF CHINA CIVIL, NAVAL, AND MILITARY ADMINISTRATION / Bell, M S – 2v. Calcutta, Simla. 1888. BCH-818 2 – 8 – ne IDC [950]
CHINA: BEING "THE TIMES" SPECIAL CORRESPONDENCE FROM CHINA IN THE YEARS 1857-1858 / Cooke, G W – London. 1858. BCH-820 2 – 8 – ne IDC [072]
CHINA BOOKMAN = CHEW BUNG CHI – (Lacking: v21-23) – v1-28. 1918-51 – 3r – 1 – ATLA S0299 – us A.T.L.A. [073]
THE CHINA BUSINESS REVIEW – (1983-. 5,6) – 1974- – 1,9 – us UMI [950]
CHINA CENTENARY MISSIONARY CONFERENCE – 1907 – 1 – us A.T.L.A. [240]
China. Central Bank *see* CHUNG YANG YIN HANG YUEH PAO
CHINA CHRISTIAN ADVOCATE / Methodist Church. China Central Conference – v1-29, no. 10 11 (?) (all publ ?). Feb 1914-Oct Nov 1941 (?) – 4r – 1 – $485.00 – us UPA [240]
CHINA CHRISTIAN EDUCATION QUARTERLY = CHUNG-HUA CHI-TU-CHIAO CHIAO-YU CHI-K'AN – v1-12. 1925-36 (complete) – 2r – 1 – ATLA S0303 – us A.T.L.A. [073]
CHINA CHRISTIAN EDUCATIONAL ASSOCIATION. COUNCIL OF HIGHER EDUCATION *see* CHRISTIAN HIGHER EDUCATION IN CHINA
China Christian Educational Association. Shanghai *see* THE EDUCATIONAL REVIEW
CHINA CHRISTIAN YEARBOOK *see* THE CHINA MISSION YEARBOOK
THE CHINA COLLEGES – v1-20. 1934-53 (complete) – 1r – 1 – ATLA S0701A – us A.T.L.A. [073]
China. Commission of Mongolian and Tibetan Affairs *see*
- MENG TSANG WEI YUAN HUI KUNG PAO
- MENG TSANG YUEH PAO

China. Commission on Rural Reconstruction of the Executive Yuan *see* NUNG TS'UN FU HSING WEI YUAN HUI HUI PAO
CHINA CONTINUATION COMMITTEE *see* THE ART OF USING THE CHINA MISSIONARY SURVEY
CHINA CRITIC – v24-34. 1939-46 – 1r – 1 – us Ross [072]
CHINA DAILY – 1982-1995 – 1 – F742.00 – sz Infoprint [072]
CHINA DAILY – China. 1 Jun 1981-. In English. M E1. Semi-annual delivery – 1 – $45.00 – cc Microforms [072]
CHINA DAILY – (In English) – 1982- – 2r per y – 1 – inquire – us Ross [072]
CHINA DAILY NEWS – New York. July 8 1940-Dec 1947 – 1 – us NY Public [071]
CHINA DAILY NEWS – New York. N.Y. 1962- – 1 – us UMI [071]
CHINA DAILY NEWS – Taipei, Taiwan. 1973-83. 44 reels – 1 – 2200.00 – ch Transmission [072]
CHINA DIENST – Shanghai. 1932-33. KCHF-6-3 – 1 – ne IDC [072]
CHINA DIGEST – v1, no.1-v7, no.9. 31 Dec 1946-1 Feb 1950. Fortnightly published by Communist Party of Hong Kong. China, combined with People's China in 1950. F E10 – 9 – $4.50f – cc Microforms [073]
China. Director of Military Medical Service *see* CHUN I KUNG PAO
CHINA. ERGEBNISSE EIGENER REISEN UND DARAUF GEGRUENDETEN STUDIEN / Richthofen, F P W von – 2542 2. 5 v. 1877-1912 – 9 – ne IDC [950]
CHINA FOR CHRIST – v145-219. 1934-41 (incomplete) – 1r – 1 – ATLA S0699 – us A.T.L.A. [073]
CHINA. FORESTRY SUPPORT FOR AGRICULTURE : REPORT OF AN F.A.O./ U.N.D.P. STUDY TOUR TO THE PEOPLE'S REPUBLIC OF CHINA, 1977 – 1978 – 115p – it F.A.O. [634]
THE CHINA FUNDAMENTALIST – Oct Dec 1929-2nd qtr 1940 (incomplete) – 1r – 1 – ATLA S0500 – us A.T.L.A. [073]
CHINA, GRAIN STORAGE STRUCTURES : REPORT ON AN F.A.O./U.N.D.P. WORKSHOP STUDY TOUR IN THE PEOPLE'S REPUBLIC OF CHINA, 1979 – 1982 – 122p – it F.A.O. [631]
China. Inspectorate General of Customs *see* RETURNS OF TRADE AT THE TREATY PORTS
CHINA. INTEGRATED WOOD PROCESSING INDUSTRIES : REPORT OF AN F.A.O./ U.N.D.P. STUDY TOUR TO THE PEOPLE'S REPUBLIC OF CHINA, 1978 – 1979 – 79p – it F.A.O. [670]
CHINA JOURNAL OF SCIENCE AND ARTS – Shanghai, 1923-40. v1-33 – 446mf – 8 – ne IDC [073]
China. Judicial Yuan *see* SSU FA YUAN KUNG PAO
China. Kwangtung Provincial Government *see* KWANG-TUNG CHING-WU CHUANG-K'UANG
CHINA LAW REPORTER (ABA) – v1-7. 1980-1993 – 9 – $90.00 set – us Hein [340]
China. Laws, Statutes, etc *see*
- MANUEL DU CODE CHINOIS
- NUNG TSUN CHING CHI CHIN JUNG FA KUEI HUIPIEN

CHINA LIAISON OFFICE OF THE BOARD OF GLOBAL MINISTRIES, UNITED METHODIST CHURCH – Kowloon. 43 docs. 1980-1991 – 10mf – 9 – ne IDC [320]
CHINA MAIL – Hong Kong. -w. 1856-58, 1863-64; 1866-73. (25mqn reels) – 1 – uk British Libr Newspaper [072]
THE CHINA MAIL – Hong Kong: Andrew Shortrede, 1861-65; 1874-1961 – 1 – us Res Libr [072]
THE CHINA MEDICAL JOURNAL / China Medical Missionary Association – v1-35, no. 6. Mar 1887-Nov 1921 – 6r – 1 – $710.00 – us UPA [950]
China Medical Missionary Association *see* THE CHINA MEDICAL JOURNAL
THE CHINA METHODIST FORUM – v1-4. 1902-07 (complete) – 1r – 1 – ATLA S0707B – us A.T.L.A. [073]
China. Ministry of Communications *see*
- CHIAO T'UNG KUNG PAO
- CHIAO T'UNG PU T'UNG CHI NIEN PAO
- CHIAO T'UNG YUEH K'AN

China. Ministry of Education *see*
- CHIAO YU KUNG PAO
- CHIAO YU PU KUNG PAO
- TA HSUEH YUAN KUNG PAO

China. Ministry of Finance. Director of Salt Administration *see*
- YE WU YUEH PAO
- YEN WU HUI K'AN
- YEN WU YUEH PAO

China. Ministry of Foreign Affairs *see*
- WAI CHIAO KUNG PAO
- WAI CHIAO PU KUNG PAO

China. Ministry of Industries *see*
- SHIH YEH PU YUEH K'AN. MONTHLY BULLETIN
- WU CHIA T'UNG CHI YUEH K'AN

China. Ministry of Public Health *see*
- WEI SHENG KUNG PAO

China. Ministry of Railways *see*
- T'IEH TAO KUNG PAO
- T'IEH TAO PAN YUEH K'AN

THE CHINA MISSION : EMBRACING A HISTORY OF THE VARIOUS MISSIONS OF ALL DENOMINATIONS AMONG THE CHINESE: WITH BIOGRAPHICAL SKETCHES OF DECEASED MISSIONARIES / Dean, William – New York: Sheldon, 1859 – 1mf – 9 – 0-8370-6487-2 – 1986-0487 – us A.T.L.A. [240]
THE CHINA MISSION ADVOCATE – 1v., nos. 1-12 (all publ). Jan-Dec 1939 – 1 reel – 1 – $60.00 – us UPA [240]
CHINA MISSION HANDBOOK *see* THE CHINA MISSION YEARBOOK
THE CHINA MISSION YEARBOOK / Christian Literature Society for China – Shanghai. v1-21 (all publ). 1910-1938/39. Includes: The China Mission Handbook. Shanghai. 1896; and A Century of Protestant Missions in China. Shanghai. 1907 – 6r – 1 – $720.00 – us UPA [240]
CHINA MONTHLY REVIEW – Shanghai. Sept 1950-Dec 1952 – 1 – 46.00 – us L of C Photodup [950]
China. National Committee for Opium Suppression *see* CHIN YEN KUNG PAO
China. National Financial Conference *see* PROCEEDINGS
THE CHINA NEWS – Taipei, Taiwan. 1973-83. 44 reels – 1 – 2200.00 – ch Transmission [072]
CHINA NEWSLETTER – v3-9. 1948-55 (incomplete) – 1r – 1 – ATLA S0701B – us A.T.L.A. [073]
CHINA NOTES – v1-23. Sept 1962-1985 (complete) – 1r – 1 – ATLA S0794 – us A.T.L.A. [073]
CHINA OCEAN ENGINEERING – 1,5,69 – us UMI [620]
CHINA, OR, ILLUSTRATION OF THE SYMBOLS, PHILOSOPHY,... EDUCATION, AND LITERATURE OF THE CHINESE / Kidd, S – London, 1841 – 5mf – 9 – ne IDC [950]
China. Parliament. Lower House *see*
- TSUNG I YUAN KUNG PAO
- TSUNG I YUAN KUNG PAO FU LU, TI I TZU HUI I SU CHI LU

China. Parliament. Upper House *see* TS'AN I YUAN KUNG PAO
China. People's Republic *see*
- CHENG-FU KUNG-TSO PAO-KAO HUI-PIEN, 1950
- CHUNG HUA JEN MIN KUNG HO KUA FA CHAN MIN CHING CHI TI YI KO WU NIEN CHI HUA 1953-1957
- CHUNG-HUA JEN-MIN KUNG-HO-KUO FA-KUEI HUI-PIEN
- FIRST FIVE-YEAR PLAN FOR DEVELOPMENT OF THE NATIONAL ECONOMY IN 1953-1957
- MIN-TSU T'UAN-CHIEH
- LE PREMIER PLAN QUINQUENNAL POUR LE DEVELOPPEMENT DE L'ECONOMIE NATIONALE. (1953-1957)
- PROPOSALS OF THE 8TH NATIONAL CONGRESS OF THE COMMUNIST PARTY OF CHINA FOR THE 2ND FIVE-YEAR PLAN (1958-62)
- PROPUESTAS DEL 8 CONGRESO NACIONAL DEL PARTIDO COMMUNISTA DE CHINA PARA EL 2 PLAN QUINQUENAL (1958-1962)
- RAPPORT SUR LE 1ER PLAN QUINQUENNAL DE CHINE (1953-57)
- REPORT ON THE FIRST FIVE-YEAR PLAN OF CHINA IN 1953-57

China. People's Republic. Economic Stabilization Board *see* HIGHLIGHTS OF THE SECOND FOUR-YEAR PLAN FOR THE ECONOMIC DEVELOPMENT IN TAIWAN
China. People's Republic of China *see* CHUAN KUO CHIN JUNG CHI KOU I LAN
China. People's Republic. Statistical Bureau *see*
- REPORT ON FULFILLMENT OF THE CHINESE NATIONAL ECONOMIC PLAN...IN 1955
- REPORT ON NATIONAL ECONOMIC DEVELOPMENT AND FULFILLMENT OF THE STATE PLAN IN 1954

CHINA PICTORIAL – Peking. 1951-67. Lacking: 1951; 1952 (Jan-Feb). – 457mf – 8 – ne IDC [073]
CHINA, POST-HARVEST GRAIN TECHNOLOGY : REPORT OF A STUDY GROUP IN THE PEOPLE'S REPUBLIC OF CHINA, 1977 – 1982 – 70p – it F.A.O. [631]
THE CHINA PRESS – Shanghai. Jun 1946-11 May 1949. Incomplete issues. 7 reels – 1 – 174.00 – us Chinese Res [950]
China. Provisional Government of the Republic of China *see* SSU FA KUNG PAO
China. Provisional Legislative Assembly *see* TS'AN I YUAN I SHIH LU
CHINA QUARTERLY – London. 1960-67. Nos.1-32. Lacking: 1967 (30). BCH-150/2 – 8 – ne IDC [073]
CHINA RECONSTRUCTS – 1973- – 9 – us UMI [073]
CHINA RECONSTRUCTS – China. 1977-81. -m. Illus. Pub. by China Welfare Institute. Available in English, French, Spanish, Arabic, German or Chinese. Annual delivery. M E3 – 1 – $50.00r ($4.50f) – cc Microforms [072]
CHINA RECONSTRUCTS – Peking. 1952-72. v. 1-21 – 405mf – 8 – ne IDC [950]
China. Republic *see* HIGHLIGHTS OF THE FIFTH FOUR-YEAR ECONOMIC DEVELOPMENT PLAN OF THE REPUBLIC OF CHINA
China. Republic. Council for Economic Planning *see* SIXTH FOUR-YEAR PLAN FOR ECONOMIC DEVELOPMENT OF TAIWAN 1973-1976
China. Republic. Council for International Economic Cooperation and Development *see*
- ANNUAL PLAN FOR THE THIRD YEAR (1971) UNDER THE FIFTH FOUR-YEAR ECONOMIC DEVELOPMENT
- FIFTH FOUR-YEAR ECONOMIC DEVELOPMENT PLAN, 1969-1972
- FOURTH ANNUAL PLAN, 1972
- FOURTH FOUR-YEAR PLAN FOR ECONOMIC DEVELOPMENT OF THE PROVINCE OF TAIWAN, 1965-1968
- LONGRANGE (1971-80) ECONOMIC DEVELOPMENT PLAN FOR TAIWAN AREA.
- THE REPUBLIC OF CHINA'S TARGETS AND BASIC POLICIES IN THE SIXTH FOUR-YEAR PLAN FOR ECONOMIC DEVELOPMENT OF TAIWAN, 1973-76
- SIXTH FOUR-YEAR PLAN FOR ECONOMIC DEVELOPMENT OF TAIWAN

China. Republic. Government Information Office. Executive Yuan *see* MANUSCRIPT OF THE INFORMATION DATA
China. Republic. Ministry of Economic Affairs. Industrial Planning and Coordination Group *see*
- THE INDUSTRIAL AND MINING PROGRAM UNDER TAIWAN'S THIRD FOUR-YEAR PLAN
- THIRD FOUR-YEAR DEVELOPMENT PLAN OF TAIWAN 1961-1964

China. Republic. Ministry of Economic Affairs.Agricultural Planning and Coordination Committee *see* THE AGRICULTURAL PROGRAM UNDER TAIWANS THIRD 4-YEAR PLAN
China. Republic. Ministry of Education *see* EDUCATIONAL PLANNING PRELIMINARY DRAFT OF THE LONG-RANGE EDUCATIONAL PLAN, 1964-1982
China. Republic of China *see* TAIWAN SOTOKUFU TOKEISHO
CHINA REVIEW : OR NOTES AND QUERIES ON THE FAR EAST – Hong Kong, 1872-1901. v. 1-25 Lacking: 1896/97, v22(4); 1897/98, v23(1-3) – 1899/1900, v24(1) – 181mf – 8 – ne IDC [073]
CHINA, RURAL PROCESSING TECHNOLOGY – 1979 – 63p – it F.A.O. [600]
China. Second National Financial Conference *see* PROCEEDINGS
CHINA, SERICULTURE – 1980 – 133p – it F.A.O. [636]
China Series Committee *see* CHRONOLOGICAL BIOGRAPHY OF MR. TAI-CHI-TAO
CHINA, THE AGRICULTURAL TRAINING SYSTEM : REPORT OF AN F.A.O./U.N.D.P. STUDY TOUR TO THE PEOPLE'S REPUBLIC OF CHINA – 1980 – 141p – it F.A.O. [630]
China. Third National Financial Conference *see* PROCEEDINGS
CHINA THROUGH WESTERN EYES : MANUSCRIPT RECORDS OF TRADERS, TRAVELLERS, MISSIONARIES AND DIPLOMATS, 1792-1942 – (Pt 1: Sources from the William R. Perkins Library, Duke University 15r. Pt 2: Sources from the William R. Perkins Library, Duke University 15r. A single guide accompanies Pts 1 + 2) – Marlborough: Adam Matthew Publications, 1996 – 2pts 30r – 1 – $1850.00 – uk Matthew [950]
CHINA TODAY – 1977-1986 – 1 – F742.00 – sz Infoprint [072]
CHINA TODAY – 1987-1995 – 9 – F742.00 – sz Infoprint [072]
CHINA TODAY / American Friends of the Chinese People – (Series 1: nos. 1-8 (all publ). 1934. Series 2: v1-8 (all publ). 1934-42) – 23mf – 9 – $130.00 – us UPA [950]
CHINA TODAY – (In English) – 1977- – 9 – inquire – us Ross [072]
CHINA WEEKLY HERALD – China. -w. 28 Jan-27 Feb 1932. 3 ft – 1 – uk British Libr Newspaper [072]
CHINA WEEKLY REVIEW – China. 1917-1953 – 1 – us UMI [072]
CHINA WEEKLY REVIEW – Shanghai. Jan 4, 1930-Aug 5, 1950 – 1 – 414.00 – us L of C Photodup [950]
THE CHINA WEEKLY REVIEW / ed by Powell, John William – 1917-1947 – 50r – 1 – $3,000.00 – us Universal [320]
THE CHINA WEEKLY REVIEW – Shanghai, China, 1917-47 – 50r – 1 – inquire – us Ross [072]
CHINA YEAR BOOK / ed by Montague Bell, H T & Woodhead, H G W – London, New York. 1912-39. Lacking: 1915 (1-38, 40-53); 1917/18 (82-95); 1920 (117-234); 1927 (255-386); 1932 (397-419). BCH-981 2 – 339mf – 8 – ne IDC [950]
CHINA-DIENST – Halbmonatsschrift fuer die foerderung der deutsch-chinesischen Beziehungen. Shanghai, China. Oct 1932-33 – 1r – 1 – gw Mikrofilm [072]
THE CHINAMAN AS WE SEE HIM : AND FIFTY YEARS OF WORK FOR HIM / Condit, Ira M – Chicago: F.H. Revell, c1900 – 1mf – us A.T.L.A. [240]
CHINA'S CHALLENGE IN MANCHURIA : ANTI-JAPANESE ACTIVITIES IN MANCHURIA PRIOR TO THE MUKDEN INCIDENT / Ito, Takeo – Darien?: South Manchuria Railway Company, 1932. 117p – 1 – us U.W. Library [950]

CHINA'S DIAMONDS IN THE ROUGH (CCC123) / Fan, I – (In Chinese) – Shanghai: Association Press of China, 1921 – 1r – 1 – 1984-B500 – us A.T.L.A. [950]
CHINA'S LEGISLATION GAZETTE *see* FAZHI RIBAO
CHINA'S MILLIONS – 1875-1952 – 1 – us UMI [240]
CHINA'S MILLIONS – London, 1875-92. v.1-17; N.S., 1893-99. v.1-7 – 118mf – ne IDC [073]
CHINA'S NEW LITERATURE AND ART : ESSAYS AND ADDRESSES / Yang, Chou – Peking: Foreign Language Press, 1954 – us Res Libr [950]
CHINA'S PROBLEMS AND THEIR SOLUTION / Wang, Chao-Ming – Shanghai: United Press, 1934. xxii,199p. China Today series, 2 – 1 – us U.W. Library [950]
Chinchilla, Anastasio *see* ANALES...MEDICINA...Y BIOGRAFICO
Chinchon, Condesa de *see* ESPOSOCION(SIC) QUE DIRIGE A LAS CORTES CONSTINTUYENTES EN DEFENSA DE SU PADRE DON MANUEL GODOY...
LA CHINE, MOEURS, USAGES, COSTUMES... / Malpiere, DB de – Paris. 2v. 1825-1827 – 8mf – 9 – ne IDC [950]
LA CHINE, OU DESCRIPTION GENERALE... / Davis, J F – Paris. 2v. 1837 – 10mf – 9 – ne IDC [950]
CHINE OU DESCRIPTION HISTORIQUE, GEOGRAPHIQUE ET LITTERAIRE DE CE VASTE EMPIRE, D'APRES DES DOCUMENTS CHINOIS / Pauthier, PG – Paris, 1837 – 7mf – 9 – ne IDC [950]
THE CHINESE : A GENERAL DESCRIPTION OF THE EMPIRE OF CHINA AND ITS INHABITANTS / Davis, J F – London. 2v. 1836 – 11mf – 9 – ne IDC [950]
CHINESE AND ENGLISH DICTIONARY : CONTAINING ALL THE WORDS IN THE CHINESE IMPERIAL DICTIONARY, ARRANGED ACCORDING TO THE RADICALS / Medhurst, W H – Batavia. 2v. 1842-1843 – 18mf – ne IDC [480]
THE CHINESE AS THEY ARE : THEIR MORAL, SOCIAL, AND LITERARY CHARACTER; A NEW ANALYSIS OF THE LANGUAGE;... / Lay, GT – London, 1841 – 4mf – 9 – ne IDC [950]
CHINESE ASTRONOMY *see* CHINESE ASTRONOMY AND ASTROPHYSICS
CHINESE ASTRONOMY AND ASTROPHYSICS – (English Translation of Acta Astronomica Sinica. Continues: Chinese Astronomy) – v1-1977- – 5,6,9 – us UMI [520]
A CHINESE BOY'S PERSONAL PROBLEM (CCC210) / Rounds, H J – (In Chinese) – Shanghai: Publication Dept., National Committee, YMCAs of China, 1923 – 1r – 1 – 1984-B500 – us A.T.L.A. [920]
CHINESE CANADIAN DAILY – Toronto, 1984-1988 – 28r – 1 – cn Preston [971]
CHINESE CHEMICAL LETTERS – 1,5,69 – us UMI [540]
CHINESE CHRISTIAN ADVOCATE = HSING HUA – 1904-27 (complete) – 3r – 1 – ATLA S0307 – us A.T.L.A. [073]
CHINESE CHRISTIAN COLLECTION : SERIALS IN CHINESE – (Individual titles also listed separately) – 44 serial titles 307 monographs – 55r – 1 – ATLA S0296 (A-S)-0321 – us A.T.L.A. [073]
CHINESE CHRISTIAN COLLECTION *see*
– THE ABC CATECHISM (CCC265)
– ABIDING FAITH FOR A NATION IN CRISIS (CCC340)
– ABIDING KNOWLEDGE OF CHRISTIAN TRUTH (CCC202)
– ACADEMIC MONTHLY
– ADDRESSES AND SERMONS FOR PREACHERS (CCC92)
– THE ADVENTURES OF MISS KANG (CCC327)
– AIDS TO THE STUDY OF ACTS (CCC236)
– THE ARMOUR OF LIGHT (CCC276)
– THE ART OF PREACHING (CCC8)
– ASSOCIATION PROGRESS
– AUTOBIOGRAPHY OF HOLLINGTON K. TONG (CCC302)
– A BALLAD OF FOUR RELIGIONS (CCC222)
– BASIC ELEMENTS OF THE CHRISTIAN FAITH (CCC321)
– BIBLE AND FILIAL PIETY (CCC194)
– BIBLE (CCC289)
– THE BIBLICAL VIEW OF MARRIAGE (CCC88)
– BOOK OF COMMON WORSHIP (CCC120)
– A BRIEF HISTORY OF THE FIRST 25 YEARS' HISTORY OF THE YMCA'S IN CHINA (CCC237)
– THE BUDDHIZATION OF CHRISTIANITY (CCC10)
– CALL FROM GOD
– THE CALL OF A CHILD (CCC83)
– THE CANON AND TEXT OF THE NEW TESTAMENT (CCC15)
– CANTONESE UNION CHURCH BULLETIN
– CATALOGUE OF THE CHEELOO SCHOOL OF THEOLOGY (CCC84)
– CATECHISM (CCC158)
– THE CATECHISM FOR THE METHODIST CHURCH MEMBERS (CCC157)
– CENTRAL FAITH OF CHRISTIANITY (CCC69)
– A CHANGED EXCHANGE BROKER (CCC213)
– THE CHARACTER OF JESUS (CCC175)
– CHARACTERS OF MODERN TIMES (CCC283)
– CHI TU CHIAO CHE HSUEH (CCC66)
– CHI TU CHIAO YU SHIH CHIEH HO P'ING (CCC223)
– CHI TU HUA CHING CHI KUAN HSI CH'UAN KUO TA HUI PAO KAO (CCC253)
– CHI TU T'U SHENGHUO TI P'EI YANG (CCC218)
– CHIAO HUI TI CHENG T'UNG (CCC98)
– THE CHILDREN OF GOD (CCC17)
– THE CHILDREN'S BIBLE (CCC141)
– CHINA BOOKMAN
– CHINA CHRISTIAN EDUCATION QUARTERLY
– CHINA'S DIAMONDS IN THE ROUGH (CCC123)
– A CHINESE BOY'S PERSONAL PROBLEM (CCC210)
– CHINESE CHRISTIAN ADVOCATE
– CHINESE CHRISTIAN MONOGRAPH (CCC97)
– CHINESE CHRISTIAN MONOGRAPH (CCC134)
– CHINESE CHRISTIAN MONOGRAPH (CCC180)
– CHINESE CHRISTIAN MONOGRAPH (CCC187)
– CHINESE CHRISTIAN MONOGRAPH (CCC203)
– CHINESE CHRISTIAN MONOGRAPH (CCC247)
– CHINESE CHRISTIAN MONOGRAPH (CCC281)
– CHINESE CHRISTIAN MONOGRAPH (CCC310)
– CHINESE CHRISTIAN MONOGRAPH (CCC316)
– CHINESE CHRISTIAN MONOGRAPH, VOLS 3-5 (CCC140)
– CHINESE CHURCHMAN
– CHINESE CLASSICAL STORIES (CCC308)
– CHINESE MUSLIM
– THE CHINESE NATION THROUGH THE EYES OF JESUS (CCC196)
– CHIN-LING SCHOOL OF THEOLOGY
– CHIN-LING THEOLOGICAL MAGAZINE
– CHI-TU-CHIAO YU CHUNG-KUO (CCC168)
– THE CHRISTIAN AWAKENING OF FAITH (CCC195)
– CHRISTIAN BIOGRAPHIES (CCC270)
– CHRISTIAN CHURCH IN CHINA (CCC334)
– CHRISTIAN EDUCATION AND THE NATIONAL CONSCIOUSNESS IN CHINA (CCC320)
– CHRISTIAN ETHICS (CCC70)
– CHRISTIAN FAITH AND LIFE (CCC150)
– THE CHRISTIAN FAMILY (CCC225)
– THE CHRISTIAN FAMILY IN CHANGING EAST ASIA (CCC246)
– CHRISTIAN FARMER
– CHRISTIAN FELLOWSHIP HYMNS (CCC80)
– CHRISTIAN HOME EDUCATION (CCC2)
– CHRISTIAN HOPE
– THE CHRISTIAN HOPE (CCC330)
– CHRISTIAN INTERPRETATION OF HISTORY (CCC217)
– CHRISTIAN LIFE WEEKLY
– CHRISTIAN MARRIAGE (CCC117)
– CHRISTIAN MORALITY AND TRADITIONAL CHINESE ETHICS (CCC329)
– CHRISTIAN OCCUPATION OF CHINA
– THE CHRISTIAN RURAL MOVEMENT (CCC252)
– CHRISTIAN SALVATION OF CHINA (CCC189)
– CHRISTIAN SERIES
– A CHRISTIAN STUDY OF BUDDHISM (CCC305)
– CHRISTIAN WORK IN RURAL CHINA (CCC350)
– CHRISTIAN YOUTH AT THE FRONT (CCC224)
– CHRISTIANITY AND CHINA (CCC106)
– CHRISTIANITY AND CHINESE CULTURE (CCC192)
– CHRISTIANITY AND CHINESE CULTURE (CCC331)
– CHRISTIANITY AND COMMUNISM (CCC4)
– CHRISTIANITY AND FILIAL PIETY (CCC151)
– CHRISTIANITY AND LITERATURE (CCC114)
– CHRISTIANITY AND MARX-LENINISM (CCC205)
– CHRISTIANITY AND MODERN THOUGHT (CCC166)
– CHRISTIANITY AND NEW CHINA (CCC229)
– CHRISTIANITY AND SCIENCE (CCC173)
– CHRISTIANITY AND THE NEW CHINA (CCC333)
– CHRISTIANITY AND THE NEW PHYSICS (CCC299)
– CHRISTIANITY AND THE RURAL RECONSTRUCTION MOVEMENT IN CHINA (CCC351)
– CHRISTIANITY AND THE SOCIALIST MOVEMENT (CCC16)
– CHRISTIANITY IN THE LIGHT OF TODAY (CCC200)
– CHRISTIANITY IN THE T'ANG DYNASTY (CCC208)
– CHRISTIANS AND THE NATIONAL SALVATION MOVEMENT (CCC278)
– CHRISTIANS AND WARTIME SERVICE (CCC311)
– CHRIST'S SERMON ON THE MOUNT AND ORIENTALISM (CCC112)
– CHU JIH YUAN LIU (CCC272)
– CHUANGTZE (CCC118)
– CHUNG-HUA CHI-TU-CHIAO TS'ING-NIEN-HUI CH'UAN KUO HSIEH-HUI CHIAO-HUI TSU (CCC119)
– CHUNG-KUO HSIANG TS'UN CHIAO WEN TI HSIN CHIEN SHE (CCC108)
– CHUNG-KUO HUI CHIAO SHIH CHIEN (CCC239)
– CHUNG-KUO LI SHIH TI SHANG TI KUAN (CCC306)
– CHUNG-KUO T'IEN CHU CHIAO CH'UAN CHIAO SHIH (CCC121)
– CHUNG-KUO TSUNG CHIAO SZU SHIH TA KANG (CCC309)
– CHURCH HISTORY (CCC145)
– CHURCH MEMBER (CCC 116)
– COLLECTION OF THE TEACHINGS OF FAMOUS CHINESE (CCC300)
– THE COMMON GROUND OF CONFUCIANISM, TAOISM AND CHINESE BUDDHISM (CCC169)
– COMMONISM (CCC105)
– CONCERNING THE TRUE RELIGION (CCC131)
– CONFERENCE NEWSLETTER
– CONSCIENCE (CCC137)
– CONSOLATIONS OF THE TRUE RELIGION (CCC132)
– CONVERSION
– COUNTRYSIDE CHURCHES
– COVENANT PEOPLE OF GOD (CCC324)
– A CRITICAL REVIEW OF CHU CHIH SIN'S "WHAT THING IS JESUS" (CCC11)
– A CRITICAL STUDY OF THE FIRST FOUR CHAPTERS OF RETHINKING MISSIONS (CCC77)
– CUP OF BLESSING (CCC152)
– THE DEVELOPMENT OF CHRISTIANITY IN TAIWAN (CCC301)
– A DIALOGUE ON CHRISTIANITY FOR MY CHINESE FRIENDS (CCC1)
– THE DISCOVERY OF CHINA'S EARLIEST STORY OF JESUS CHRIST (CCC214)
– DISCUSSING CHRISTIANITY WITH CHAN AND TSEN (CCC12)
– DOCTRINE OF SALVATION IN THE CHINESE LANGUAGE (CCC136)
– DOES GOD CARE FOR ME? (CCC191)
– EDUCATION OF LIFE (CCC153)
– ELEMENTS OF RELIGIOUS PEDAGOGY (CCC260)
– ESSENTIALS OF YMCA (CCC93)
– ETHICAL TEACHINGS FOR THE YOUNG (CCC111)
– EVANSTON SPEAKS (CCC90)
– EVENING DRUM (CCC144)
– EXAMPLE (CCC287)
– AN EXPERIMENTAL RURAL CHURCH (CCC109)
– EXPERIMENTS IN PERSONAL RELIGION (CCC297)
– EXPLANATIONS AND ILLUSTRATIONS OF THE SACRED EDICT, VOL 1 (CCC122)
– EXPOSITORY LIFE OF CHRIST (CCC146)
– A FAITH FOR A NEW AGE (CCC170)
– FAITH IN PRACTICE (CCC155)
– FAR ABOVE RUBIES (CCC257)
– FINDINGS ON FIVE YEAR MOVEMENT (CCC254)
– FOUNDATION CHARACTERS, BK 1 (CCC128)
– FOUR TALKS ON THEOLOGY (CCC78)
– FRIENDS (CCC288)
– FROM BUDDHISM TO CHRISTIANITY (CCC207)
– GOD (CCC163)
– THE GOOD NEWS (CCC323)
– GOOD SAMARITAN
– GOOD YEARS
– THE GOSPEL FOR ALL (CCC87)
– GOSPEL NEWS REPORT
– THE GREAT GULF (CCC18)
– GREAT HYMNS AND HYMN WRITERS (CCC317)
– GUARDIAN OF TRUTH
– A GUIDE TO THE STUDY OF THE NEW TESTAMENT (CCC96)
– A GUIDE TO THE STUDY OF THE OLD TESTAMENT (CCC216)
– HANDBOOK ON PASTORAL THEOLOGY (CCC244)
– HAPPY CHRISTMAS STORIES (CCC142)
– HAPPY STORIES (CCC143)
– HARMONY OF THE GOSPELS (CCC234)
– HEAVENLY WIND
– HINTS ON PREACHING (CCC91)
– HISTORICAL STUDY OF THE ACTS AND THE EPISTLES (CCC235)
– A HISTORY OF CHRISTIAN THOUGHT (CCC261)
– HISTORY OF CHRISTIANITY IN CHINA (CCC307)
– HISTORY OF THE EASTERN CHURCH (CCC262)
– A HISTORY OF THE FOOCHOW YMCA (CCC348)
– HOMILETICS (CCC243)
– THE HONOURABLE GUEST (CCC89)
– HOW TO COMMEND CHRISTIANITY TO THE CHINESE (CCC165)
– HSIANG KANG CHI TU CHIAO HUI SHIH (CCC228)
– HSIAO CHING TONG KAO (CCC295)
– HSIU YANG WEI TI (CCC342)
– HSUEH JEN (CCC74)
– HYMNS FOR THE PEOPLE (CCC75)
– I AM CAPTURED (CCC81)
– INDIGENIZATION OF THE YMCA IN CHINA (CCC349)
– INDIVIDUAL EVANGELISM (CCC241)
– INDUSTRY REFORM
– AN INTERPRETATION OF CHRISTIANITY (CCC68)
– AN INTRODUCTION TO CHURCH HISTORY (CCC271)
– AN INTRODUCTION TO THE CREEDS (CCC221)
– INTRODUCTORY CATECHISM, VOL 2 (CCC344)
– JESUS AND MY CHARACTER (CCC71)
– JESUS (CCC291)
– JESUS (CCC325)
– THE JESUS I KNOW (CCC313)
– THE JESUS I KNOW (CCC335)
– JESUS THROUGH THE EYES OF THE CHINESE NATION (CCC193)
– K'ANG CHAN SHIH KO CHI, VOL 5 (CCC126)
– THE KEY TO LIFE (CCC154)
– THE LIFE AND TEACHINGS OF JESUS (CCC318)
– LIFE AND WORK OF THE MINISTER (CCC280)
– THE LIFE OF H.L. ZIA (CCC176)
– LIFE OF JESUS (CCC82)
– LIFE OF LEUNG FAAT (CCC212)
– LIFE OF LI SHU-CH'ING (CCC215)
– THE LIFE OF ST. PAUL (CCC79)
– THE LIFE OF THE EARLY CHURCH (CCC95)
– LIFE'S EXPERIENCES (CCC64)
– LIGHT AND DARKNESS (CCC336)
– THE LIGHT OF THE OCEAN
– LIGHTHOUSE
– LITURGIES OF CHRISTIAN CHURCHES (CCC248)
– LIVES OF PROMINENT CHINESE PASTORS (CCC174)
– LORD, TEACH US TO PRAY (CCC242)
– THE LORD'S PRAYER AND ORIENTALISM (CCC113)
– LOVE, MARRIAGE AND HOME (CCC238)
– LOVE OTHERS AS YOURSELF (CCC286)
– LUN TAO (CCC104)
– MARCHING IN HARMONY
– THE MEANING OF THE CHURCH (CCC67)
– MEDITATIONS ON THE LORD'S PRAYER (CCC162)
– METZE (CCC249)
– THE MINISTRY (CCC284)
– MISSIONARY REVIEW
– MODEL PERSONAL WORK (CCC319)
– MODERN BUDDHISM
– MOTZE AND JESUS (CCC332)
– MY EXPERIENCE IN PRISON (CCC73)
– MY EXPERIENCE IN RURAL WORK (CCC190)
– MY LIFE DECISIONS (CCC269)
– MY PHILOSOPHY OF RELIGION (CCC347)
– NATIONAL CULTURE AND THE DEVELOPMENT OF THE INDIVIDUAL (CCC232)
– NATIVE RELIGIONS AND CHRISTIANITY (CCC204)
– A NEW HISTORY OF SOCIALISM (CCC277)
– NEW PARENTS (CCC227)
– THE NEW POINT OF VIEW (CCC99)
– THE NEW TESTAMENT (CCC312)
– NEW TESTAMENT CHARACTERS (CCC181)
– THE NEW TESTAMENT IN CHINESE (CCC130)
– NEWS
– NEWSPAPERS OF THE TAIWANESE CHURCH
– THE NEXT WORLD WAR AND CHINA (CCC14)

- NINETY YEARS' HISTORY OF THE PRESBYTERIAN CHURCH IN NORTH FORMOSA (CCC188)
- NO MAN HATH SEEN GOD (CCC338)
- NORTHERN CHINESE FARMERS UNION NEWSLETTER
- NOT "THEIR" JESUS (CCC345)
- NOTES ON THE NESTORIAN INSCRIPTION OF SI-AN (CCC129)
- THE OLD TESTAMENT AND THE CHINESE CLASSICAL BOOKS (CCC285)
- OLD TESTAMENT CHARACTERS (CCC256)
- OLD TESTAMENT HISTORY (CCC65)
- ON ANTI-RELIGION (CCC124)
- THE ORIGIN AND CAUSE OF THE ANTI-CHRISTIAN MOVEMENT BY CHINESE OFFICIALS AND GENTRY, 1860-1874 (CCC233)
- OUT OF THE DEPTHS (CCC292)
- OUTLOOK
- PEACE ON EARTH (CCC220)
- P'EI LING YEN CHING HUI (CCC259)
- PEOPLE'S STORIES (CCC178)
- PERFECT MAN'S MODEL (CCC135)
- PHILOSOPHY OF RELIGION (CCC171)
- PHILOSOPHY OF THEISM (CCC352)
- THE PIONEER (CCC245)
- PIONEERS OF THE CHUNG HUA SHEN KUNG HUI (CCC263)
- PIONEERS OF THE PROTESTANT CHURCH IN CHINA (CCC100)
- THE PLOUGHMAN'S SONG (CCC264)
- PRAYERS FOR THE DAILY TASK (CCC226)
- A PREACHER'S BOOK OF RELIGIOUS EDUCATION (CCC182)
- PREACHER'S MAGAZINE
- THE PREPARATION FOR THE GOSPEL (CCC86)
- PRINCIPLES IN CHILD TRAINING (CCC3)
- PRINCIPLES OF THE YOUNG MEN'S CHRISTIAN ASSOCIATION (CCC167)
- PROCEEDINGS (CCC337)
- PROGRESS
- THE PSYCHOLOGY OF RELIGION (CCC5)
- PUBLIC NEWSPAPER
- A READER ON THE APOSTLES' CREED (CCC274)
- A READER ON THE LORD'S PRAYER (CCC273)
- A READER ON THE TEN COMMANDMENTS (CCC275)
- REASONS FOR CHRISTIAN FAITH (CCC172)
- THE RECONSTRUCTION OF CHRISTIAN CHURCH IN CHINA (CCC72)
- RELIGION AND LIFE (CCC101)
- RELIGION AND SCIENCE (CCC102)
- RELIGIOUS EDUCATION
- THE RELIGIOUS FAITH OF DISTINGUISHED PEOPLE OF THE WORLD (CCC13)
- RELIGIOUS THOUGHT MOVEMENTS IN CHINA DURING THE LAST DECADE (CCC9)
- THE ROAD TO MATURE MANHOOD (CCC209)
- ROBERT MORRISON
- ROBERT MORRISON, 1782-1934 (CCC250)
- RURAL WORSHIP SERVICES (CCC110)
- SCRIPTURE CATECHISM (CCC266)
- SELECTED CHRISTIAN ESSAYS (CCC230)
- SERMONS FOR CHURCH WORKERS (CCC115)
- SERMONS FOR THE YEAR (CCC303)
- SERVE ONE ANOTHER (CCC290)
- A SHORT LIFE OF D L MOODY (CCC184)
- A SHORT LIFE OF SPURGEON (CCC185)
- SHORT SHORT STEPS (CCC267)
- SHORT STEPS TO GREAT TRUTHS (CCC268)
- SHORT STORIES FOR YOUNG PEOPLE, VOL 1 (CCC328)
- A SHORT STUDY OF EDUCATION IN THE CHRISTIAN HOME
- A SHORT STUDY OF RELIGIONS (CCC183)
- SHORT TERM READERS FOR ILLITERATE CHURCH MEMBERS (CCC186)
- SIMPLE SUGGESTION ON CLUBS AND OTHER WORK WITH BOYS (CCC138)
- SIN AND SALVATION (CCC160)
- THE SOCIAL GOSPEL (CCC341)
- THE SPIRIT OF CHRISTIANITY (CCC231)
- STORY OF ISRAEL (CCC6)
- THE STORY OF MY BECOMING A CHRISTIAN (CCC346)
- STORY OF THE JEWISH REVOLT (CCC103)
- THE SUCCESS AND FAILURE OF THE CHURCH (CCC282)
- THE SUMMONS TO A LARGER EVANGELISM (CCC255)
- SYSTEMATIC THEOLOGY (CCC147)
- TALES FOR CHILDREN, BK 1 (CCC326)
- TALKS ON CHRISTIAN FAITH (CCC339)
- TALKS TO YOUNG CHRISTIANS (CCC315)
- TAO CHIAO SHIH, VOL 1 (CCC197)
- TAO TE CHING (CCC211)
- TEN TALKS ON THE APOSTLES' CREED (CCC322)
- THEOLOGICAL QUARTERLY; NANKING SEMINARY REVIEW
- THE THEOLOGY OF KARL BARTH (CCC76)
- THINGS NEW AND OLD (CCC125)
- THREE-SELF MOVEMENT (CCC304)
- TIEN FENG CHOU KAN TZU LIAO SHIH (CCC293)
- TIEN FENG CHOU KAN TZU LIAO SHIH (CCC294)
- TO THE YOUTH (CCC201)
- TRACTATUS DE DEO UNO ET TRINO (CCC198)
- THE TRIBULATIONS OF THE CHURCH IN CHINA, A.D. 1900 (CCC240)
- TRUE LIGHT REVIEW
- TSUI YING CHUNG HSUEH SHU PAN SHE (CCC298)
- TUNG-WEN NEWSPAPER
- TWELVE TALKS ON CHRISTIANITY (CCC156)
- TWENTIETH ANNIVERSARY PUBLICATION OF THE UNION GIRLS' SCHOOL, HANGCHOW (CCC139)
- UNDERSTANDING THE BIBLE (CCC159)
- VICTORIOUS LIVING (CCC177)
- VICTORY OF LOVE (CCC148)
- WEI LIAO HSIEN CH'IH CHIU KUO KEI AI KUO P'ENG YU TI (CCC127)
- WHAT IS CHRISTIANITY (CCC279)
- WHAT IS THE CHRISTIAN CHURCH? (CCC85)
- WHAT IS THE CHRISTIAN FAITH? (CCC206)
- WHAT RELIGION DOES FOR PERSONALITY (CCC94)
- WHAT SORT OF THING IS JESUS? (CCC107)
- WHISPER
- WHISPER MONTHLY
- WHY FEAR EVOLUTION? (CCC161)
- WHY I BECAME A CHRISTIAN (CCC164)
- WHY I FOLLOW JESUS (CCC296)
- WHY WE ARE CHRISTIANS (CCC219)
- THE WORDS OF MY MOUTH (CCC314)
- WORLD OF JESUS (CCC133)
- YEH SU TI YEN CHIN (CCC258)
- YOUNG CHRISTIAN WOMEN
- YOUNG SUN
- YOUTH AND VOCATION (CCC149)
- THE YOUTHS' BOOK-READING MOVEMENT (CCC199)

CHINESE CHRISTIAN MONOGRAPH (CCC97) / Ch'eng, I-chen – (In Chinese) – [s.l: s.n, 1950] – 1r – 1 – 1984-B500 – us A.T.L.A. [240]

CHINESE CHRISTIAN MONOGRAPH (CCC134) / Gutzlaff, Karl Friedrich August – (In Chinese) – [s.l: s.n, 1837] – 1r – 1 – 1984-B500 – us A.T.L.A. [240]

CHINESE CHRISTIAN MONOGRAPH (CCC180) / ed by Hsieh, Sung-kao – (In Chinese) – [s.l: s.n, 1927] – 1r – 1 – 1984-B500 – us A.T.L.A. [240]

CHINESE CHRISTIAN MONOGRAPH (CCC187) / Hsiu, Yao-ch'un – (In Chinese) – [s.l: s.n, 1899] – 1r – 1 – 1984-B500 – us A.T.L.A. [240]

CHINESE CHRISTIAN MONOGRAPH (CCC203) / Hughes, E R – (In Chinese) – [s.l: s.n, 19–?] – 1r – 1 – 1984-B500 – us A.T.L.A. [240]

CHINESE CHRISTIAN MONOGRAPH (CCC247) / Mao-tun – (In Chinese) – [s.l: s.n, 1935] – 1r – 1 – 1984-6586 – us A.T.L.A. [240]

CHINESE CHRISTIAN MONOGRAPH (CCC281) / Shih ch'uan, San szu lang – (In Chinese) – [s.l: s.n, 1929] – 1r – 1 – 1984-6620 – us A.T.L.A. [240]

CHINESE CHRISTIAN MONOGRAPH (CCC310) / Wang, Chung-min – (In Chinese) – [s.l: s.n, 1927] – 1r – 1 – 1984-6649 – us A.T.L.A. [240]

CHINESE CHRISTIAN MONOGRAPH (CCC316) / Wang, Ming-tao – (In Chinese) – [s.l: s.n, 1950] – 1r – 1 – 1984-6655 – us A.T.L.A. [240]

CHINESE CHRISTIAN MONOGRAPH, VOLS 3-5 (CCC140) / ed by Happy Childhood Staff – (In Chinese) – [s.l. s.n. 5v. 1926] – 1r – 1 – 1984-B500 – us A.T.L.A. [240]

CHINESE CHURCHMAN = SHENG KUNG HUI PAO – 1929-51 (complete) – 1r – 1 – ATLA S0312 – us A.T.L.A. [073]

CHINESE CLASSICAL STORIES (CCC308) / Wang, Chih-hsin – (In Chinese) – 1st rev HK ed. Hong Kong: Council on Christian Literature for Overseas Chinese. 2v. 1956 – 1r – 1 – 1984-6647 – us A.T.L.A. [480]

CHINESE COMMUNISM 1 – 50 unique monographs and 11 periodicals covering the period 1927-1964. (Write for breakdown of titles and prices) – 1 – $35.00r – us Hoover Inst Photo [335]

CHINESE COMMUNISM 2 – 52 monographs covering five categories: (1) Chinese Communism (2) Wang Chao-ming, head of Nanking Government under Japanese occupation (3) Wartime Chinese publications (4) Biographies (5) Books on secret societies. (Write for specifics.) – 1 – $35.00r – us Hoover Inst Photo [335]

CHINESE COMMUNISM 3 – 74 monographs covering four categories: (1) The border area of Shensi, Kansu, Ninghsia (2) History of the Chinese Communist Party (3) Chinese Communist Military tactics (4) Economic Policies of Communist China. (Write for specifics.) – 1 – $35.00r – us Hoover Inst Photo [335]

CHINESE COMMUNIST BIOGRAPHICAL INFORMATION / U.S. Consulate General. Hong Kong – Biographic cards of Leaders in Communist China. Text in English. Includes Master Index 16 mm. 1951-1967 – 1 – 35.00r – us Hoover Inst Photo [335]

CHINESE COMMUNIST PERIODICALS AND NEWSPAPERS / Hoover Institution – Inventory list of 997 titles of Chinese Communist periodicals and newspapers published in 1949-1969. (9698.3 4685) – 1 – 35.00r – us Hoover Inst Photo [335]

CHINESE COMMUNIST PROPAGANDA ACTIVITIES RE INDONESIA; RESEARCH BACKGROUNDER / Chung-kuo kung ch'an tang – SE-4875 1.. 1960? – 9 – ne IDC [335]

CHINESE COOLIE EMIGRATION TO COUNTRIES WITHIN THE BRITISH EMPIRE / Campbell, Persia Crawford – Reel 4001. 1923 – 1 – ja CEACS [941]

CHINESE COURIER *see* CHINESE COURIER AND CANTON GAZETTE

CHINESE COURIER AND CANTON GAZETTE – (Filmed with: Chinese Courier jul 28 1831-apr 5 1832) – Canton: [Markwick & Lane], 1831-32 – 1r – 1 – us Res Libr [072]

CHINESE CULTURE / Hwa Kang et al – 1957-1966. v1-7 – 97mf – 8 – ne IDC [073]

CHINESE CULTURE SERIES – 1967- – 38r – 1 – $2,700.00 – us OmniSys [306]

CHINESE ECONOMIC JOURNAL AND BULLETIN – Peking, 1927-37 – 12r – 1 – $960.00 – us Ross [950]

CHINESE ECONOMIC JOURNAL AND BULLETIN – Peking, January 1927-June 1937 – 12r – 1 – $720.00 – us Universal [330]

CHINESE EDUCATION – (1982-. 1,5,6,9) – v1-. 1968- – 1 – us UMI [073]

CHINESE EMPIRE – 34p – 9 – 92-3-102594-5 – Co-published with Childrens Press, Chicago, who have exclusive sales rights in the USA and Canada – fr UNESCO [950]

THE CHINESE EMPIRE : A GENERAL AND MISSIONARY SURVEY: WITH PORTRAITS AND ILLUSTRATIONS / ed by Broomhall, Marshall – (Includes indexes) – New York: Fleming H Revell; Philadelphia: China Inland Mission, [ca 1907] – 2mf – 9 – 0-8370-6806-1 – 1986-0806 – us A.T.L.A. [950]

CHINESE EXPRESS *see* K'UAI PAO

THE CHINESE IN BRITISH GUIANA / Clementi, Cecil – [Georgetown? British Guiana]: Argosy, 1915 – 1 – CSUXANM8073-B – us Hoover Inst Photo [950]

CHINESE IN THE MOTHER LODE / Minke, Pauline – 1r – 1 – $50.00 – C63001 – us Library Micro [305]

CHINESE JOURNAL – (mei-chou jih pao) (Chinese Language). New York. N.Y. 1962-67 – 1 – us UMI [480]

CHINESE JOURNAL OF ACOUSTICS – 1982- – 1,5,9 – us Gordon [073]

CHINESE JOURNAL OF LASERS B – Bimonthly – 9,6 – $396.00 in US $414.00 outside – us Optical Soc [621]

CHINESE KUNGFU STORIES IN INDONESIAN : A BIBLIOGRAPHY SELECTED FROM THE IDC COLLECTION / Tan, Siew Eng – 1982 – A$10.00 – 0-86758-097-6 – at BISA [830]

CHINESE LABOUR IN TRANSVAAL MINES – 1 – uk Microform Academic [305]

CHINESE LAW : JOURNALS AND SERIALS – (CHENG-FA YEN-CHIU (Political and Legal Research): Peking, 1954-1963 (some incomplete years) 3r L9300129. CHUNG-YANG JEN-MIN CHENG-FU FA-LING HUI-PIEN (Compendium of Laws and Decrees of the Central People's Government): Peiping, 1949-54 2r L9300130. CHUNG-HUA JEN-MIN KUNG-HO-KUO CH'UEAN-KUO JEN-MIN TAI-PIAO TA-HUI CH'ANG-WU WEI-YUEAN-HUI KUNG-PAO (Official Gazette of Standing Committee of the National People's Congress of the People's Republic of China): Peking, 1959-1963 3r L9300131. CHUNG-HUA JEN-MIN KUNG-HO-KUO KUO-WU-YUEAN KUNG-PAO (Official Gazette of the State Council of the People's Republic of China): Peking, 1957, 1958 and Index, 1959 and Index (some incomplete years) 3r L9300132. CHUNG-HUA JEN-MIN KUNG-HO-KUO FA-KUEI HUI-PIEN (Compendium of Laws and Regulations of the People's Republic of China): Jul-Dec 1956, 1959-Jun 1960, Jul-Dec 1961, Jan-Dec 1963 3r L9300133, FA HSUEEH (Jurisprudence): Shanghai, 1956-1958 1r L9300134. In Chinese) – 15r – 1 – $525.00 in US $40.00r outside – L9300129-L9300134 – Dist. us Scholarly Res – us L of C Photodup [340]

CHINESE LAW AND GOVERNMENT – (v1-17 1968-85 in reel $300.00. v18-28 1985-95 in mf $626.00) – v1-28. 1968-95 – 5,6,9 – $926.00 set – us Hein [340]

CHINESE LITERATURE – 1977-1995 – 9 – F742.00 – sz Infoprint [072]

CHINESE LITERATURE – 1977-81. Monthly in English, quarterly in French. Quarterly delivery. F E5 – 9 – $4.50f – cc Microforms [480]

CHINESE LITERATURE – Peking: Cultural Press, 1951-54 – 1 – us Res Libr [480]

CHINESE LITERATURE, 1951-1969 – Monthly. Foreign Languages Press. Peking. 1951-69. – 496mf – 8 – ne IDC [480]

CHINESE LITERATURE. ESSAYS, ARTICLES, REVIEWS – v. 1-. 1979- – 1,5,6,9 – us UMI [480]

CHINESE MATHEMATICS – v1-9. 1962-67 – 1 – us UMI [073]

CHINESE MEDICAL JOURNAL – 1,5,69 – us UMI [610]

CHINESE MEDICAL JOURNAL – 1979-81. -m. In English. Publ. by Chinese Medical Assoc. Annual delivery. F E7 – 9 – $4.50f – cc Microforms [073]

CHINESE MEDICAL MISSION / Gutzlaff, KF A – (Missing: Title page) – Bath, n.d. – 1mf – 9 – ne IDC [610]

CHINESE MILITARY STUDIES AND MATERIALS IN ENGLISH TRANSLATION – (Collection can only be purchased as a set. In English) – 10r – 1 – $350.00 in US $40.00r outside – L9300070-9 – Dist. us Scholarly Res – us L of C Photodup [355]

THE CHINESE MISCELLANY;... / ed by Medhurst, W H – Shanghai, 1845-1850. 4v – 10mf – HT-573/1 – ne IDC [480]

CHINESE MOSLEMS – In Chinese. No.25, 10 Jan 1960.1 reel – 1 – us A.T.L.A. [073]

Chinese Museum Association *see* CHUNG-KUO PO-WU-KUAN HSIEH-HUI HUI-PAO

CHINESE MUSLIM = HUNG KUO MU SUU LIN – (In Chinese) – no25. 10 Jan 1960 (incomplete) – 1r – 1 – ATLA S0296G – us A.T.L.A. [073]

THE CHINESE NATION THROUGH THE EYES OF JESUS (CCC196) = YEH SU YEN LI TI CHUNG-HUA MIN TSU : A STUDY OF CHINESE CONCEPTIONS OF LIFE AS COMPARED WITH CHRISTIAN CONCEPTIONS AND A FORECAST OF THE ULTIMATE WAY FOR CHINA / Hsu, Sung-shih – (In Chinese) – Shanghai: Publication Dept., National Committee, YMCAs of China, 1934 – 1r – 1984-B500 – us A.T.L.A. [230]

CHINESE NATIONALIST – (Lacks 8 issues) – New York. v43 n279-341. 1 jan-31 mar 1958 – 1r – 1 – us Ross [073]

CHINESE NATIONALIST DAILY – New York. Jan 21 1927-Mar 1958 – 1 – us NY Public [071]

CHINESE NEWSPAPERS, 1 – (Ch'ang Chiang Jih Pao, Hankow: Nov 1949-59 15r L9400090. Che-Chiang Jih Pao, Hangchow: Dec 1949-Oct 1954, 1955-Nov 1959 12r L9400091. Chieh Fang Jih Pao, Shanghai: May 1949-Jul 1955, Feb 1956-Dec 1959, May 1960-Nov 1962 16r L9300092. Chiang Hsi Jih Pao, Nanchang: Nov 1950-Dec 1960 9r L9300093. Chin Jih Hsin Wen, Peking: Sep 1959-1961 4r L9300094. Ch'ing-Tao Jih Pao, Tsingtoo: Apr 1950-Aug 1959 9r L9300095. Ch'un Chung Jih Pao, Shansi: Mar 1950-Oct 1954 9r L9300096. Ch'ung Ch'ing Jih Pao, Chungking: Sep 1952-59 3r L9300097. Chung Kuo Hsin Wen, Canton: Sep 1954-56, 1957-90 96r L9300098. Chung kuo shih pao, Taipei: 1970-88 85r L9300099. Chung Pao, Nanking: Apr 1940-Jun 1945 10r L9300100. Ho-Nan Jih Pao, Kaifeng: Nov 12 1950-Apr 1962 9r L9300101. Ho-Pei

Jih Pao, Pao-ting: Aug 1950-Jan 1958, Oct-Nov 1959 11r L9300102. Hsin Chiang Jih Pao, Urmuchi: 1943-Sep 1945, 1948-60 9r L9300103. Hsin-Chien Jih Pao, Kewichow: Jul 1951-Nov 1956 5r L9300104. Hsin Hua Jih Pao: Chungking: 1942-46, Oct 1950-54 14r L9300105. Nanking, Sep 1949-Aug 1961 11r L9300106. Hsin Min Pao, Peking: Feb 1941-Apr 1944 5r L9300107. Hsin Shen Pao, Shanghai: Oct 1937-May 1945 20r L9300108. Hsin Wen Pao, Shanghai: Aug-Dec 1928, Jul 1944-May 1946, May 1947-Dec 1959 23r L9300109;) – 471r including section 2 – 1 – $40.00r – Dist. us Scholarly Res – us L of C Photodup [072]

CHINESE NEWSPAPERS, 2 – (Kan Su- Jih Pao Lanchow. July 1951-60. 10r. L9300110; Kuang Chou Jih Pao, Canton. 1952-54; 1956-60. 4r. L9300111; Kuang Hsi Jih Pao, Nanning. Dec 1942-43; Dec 1951-Nov 1954. 9r. L9300112; Lao-Tung Pao, Shanghai. July 1949-May 1958. 5r. L9300113; Li Pao, Hengyang. July 1940-42; Apr-Oct 1943. 5r. L9300114; Lu Ta Jih Pao, Liaoning. Apr 1956-Oct 1958. 4r. L9300115; Nang-Fang Jih Pao, Canton, Feb 1950-64. 20r. L9300116; Shan-Hsi Jih Pao, Taiyuan. 1950-59. 13r L9300117; Shih Chia Chuang Jih Pao, Hopeh. Aug 1950-Nov 1957. 4r L9300118; Ssu-Ch'uan Jih Pao, Chengtu. 1952-3; 1955-59. 4r. L9300119; Su Nan Jih Pao, Wusih. Dec 1949-52. 5r. L9300120; Tung Pei Jih Pao, Mukden. Mar 1949-Dec 1950; Aug 1951-July 1954. 7r. L9300121; Yun-Nan Jih Pao, Kunming. 1950; 1952-55; 1957; Sept 1958-Oct 1960. 6r. L9300122; Comes in Chinese) – 471r including section 1 – 1 – $16,485.00 set including section 1 $30.00r – Dist. us Scholarly Res – us L of C Photodup [072]

CHINESE PACIFIC WEEKLY – San Francisco. Calif. 1948-59 – 1 – us UMI [071]

THE CHINESE PACIFIC WEEKLY – San Francisco, CA. 1947-59 – 10r – 1 – $500.00 – C02804 – us Library Micro [071]

CHINESE PEASANT CULTS / Day, Clarence B – 1940 – 1 – 12.32 – us Baptist [290]

CHINESE PEASANT CULTS / Day, Clarence B – Shanghai. 1940. BCH-858 2 – 8 – ne IDC [290]

CHINESE PEOPLE'S MOVEMENT, SPRING 1989 / International Institute of Social History. Amsterdam – (The microfiches and the inventory are supplied in a plastic binder with dust cover) – 34mf – CPM-1/1 – ne IDC [320]

CHINESE PRESS – San Francisco, CA. 1948-52 – 2r – 1 – $100.00 – C02805 – us Library Micro [071]

CHINESE PRESS – San Francisco. Calif. -w. 1948-51 – 1 – us UMI [071]

CHINESE PRESS REVIEW / U. S. Consulate. Peiping-Tientsin – Peiping-Tientsin: US Consulate, 1946-Jul 1948 – 3r – 1 – us L of C Photodup [073]

CHINESE PRESS REVIEW / U.S. Consulate General.Canton, China – Chungking, China: US Consulate General, 1945-Oct 21 1946 – 3r – 1 – us L of C Photodup [073]

THE CHINESE PRESS REVIEW / U.S. Consulate General.Chungking, China – Mukden, China: US Consulate General, Jun 6 1947-Jul 26 1948 – 2r – 1 – us L of C Photodup [073]

CHINESE PRESS SUMMARIES AND RELATED PUBLICATIONS, 1944-1950 – (US Consulate General (& US Information Service), Canton, China, Chinese Press Review, 1946-48 L9300045 3r. US Consulate General (& US Office of War Information), Chungking, China, Chinese Press Review, 1945-46 L9300046 3r. US Information Service, Chungking, China, Domei News, 1944-45 L9300047 1r. US Consulate General, Kunming, China, Chinese Press Review, 1945-48 L9300048 2r. US Consulate General, Mukden, China, Chinese Press Review, 1947-48 L9300049 2r. US Embassy, Nanking, China, Chinese Magazine Review, 1948-49 L9300050 1r. US Embassy, Nanking, China, Chinese Press Review, 1946-48 L9300051 3r. US Consulate General (& US Information Service), Peiping, China, Chinese Press Review, 1946-48 L9300052 3r. US Consulate General, Peiping, China, Translations Radio Broadcasts of Communist Hsin Hua Station, North Shensi, 1947-49 L9300053 1r. US Consulate General (& US Information Service), Shanghai, China, Chinese Press Review, 1945-50 L9300054 10r. US Information Service, Shanghai, China, For Your Informations: Yenan Broadcasts, 1946-47 L9300055 1r. US Consulate General (& US Information Service), Tientsin, China, Tientsin Chinese Review, 1945-48 L9300056 2r. US Consulate General, Hong Kong, China, Summary of New China News Agency Chinese News Dispatches, Jun- Oct 1950 L9300057 1r. In English) – 33r – 1 – $1,155.00 in US $40.00r outside – L9300045-L9300057 – Dist. us Scholarly Res – us L of C Photodup [320]

THE CHINESE PUBLIC OPINION = YING-WEN PEI-CHING JIH-PAO – (Filmed with: Pekinger deutsche Zeitung) – Peking: Chinese Public Opinion, may 5 1908-apr 1909 – us Res Libr [072]

CHINESE RECORDER – China. 1868-1940 – 1 – us UMI [072]

CHINESE RECORDER – v. 1-67. 1868-1936 – 1 – us Princeton Micro [950]

CHINESE RECORDER *see* MISSIONARY RECORDER

THE CHINESE RECORDER, 1867-1941 – (The Chinese Recorder Index: A Guide to the Christian Missions in Asia 1867-1941, 1986 2v $15000 ISBN:0-8420-2250-3) – 1986 – 18r – 1 – $1,530.00 – us Scholarly Res [950]

CHINESE REPOSITORY – Canton, 1832-51. 20v – 142mf – 1 – ne IDC [073]

CHINESE REPOSITORY – v1-20. May 1832-Dec 1851 (complete) – 5r – 1 – ATLA S0014 – us A.T.L.A. [073]

CHINESE SCIENCE ABSTRACTS SERIES A – 1,5,69 – us UMI [500]

CHINESE SCIENCE ABSTRACTS SERIES A AND B – 1,5,69 – us UMI [500]

CHINESE SCIENCE ABSTRACTS SERIES B – 1,5,69 – us UMI [500]

CHINESE SOCIAL AND POLITICAL REVIEW – Peking. 1916-41. v.l-24. Lacking: 1916-24, v1(2)-8. – 202mf – 8 – ne IDC [300]

THE CHINESE SOCIAL AND POLITICAL SCIENCE REVIEW – Peking, April 1916-March 1941. v1, No1-v24, No 4 – 13r – 1 – $780.00 – us Universal [320]

A CHINESE ST FRANCIS, OR, THE LIFE OF BROTHER MAO / Brown, C Campbell – London; New York: Hodder and Stoughton, [1911?] – 1mf – us A.T.L.A. [240]

THE CHINESE STUDENT MOVEMENT 1927-1937 / Israel, John – A bibliographical essay based on the resources of the Hoover Institution. 1959. 22p – 1 – $35.00r – us Hoover Inst Photo [950]

CHINESE THEOLOGICAL MAGAZINE – In Chinese. No.6,7. Feb, Aug 1957. Incomplete. 1 reel – 1 – us A.T.L.A. [073]

CHINESE TIMES – (In Chinese) – British Columbia, CN. 1914-1970 – 148r – 1 – cn Commonwealth Micro [072]

CHINESE TIMES – San Francisco, CA. 1960- – 151+ r – 1 – $7,550.00 ($270.00y) – C02806 – us Library Micro [071]

CHINESE TIMES – San Francisco. Calif. 1960- – 1 – us UMI [071]

CHINESE TIMES – Tientsin. China. -w. Nov 1886-Mar 1891. (4 reels) – 1 – uk British Libr Newspaper [072]

THE CHINESE TIMES – Tientsin: Printed & publ for the proprietors by Tientsing Printing Co, nov 6 1886-mar 28 1891 – 4r – 1 – us Res Libr [072]

THE CHINESE TRAVELLER : CONTAINING A GEOGRAPHICAL, COMMERCIAL, AND POLITICAL HISTORY OF CHINA – London. 2v. 1775 – 7mf – 9 – ne IDC [950]

CHINESE VOICE – (In Chinese) – British Columbia, CN. 1954-70 – 37r – 1 – cn Commonwealth Micro [072]

CHINESISCHE FELDZUEGE DURCH DIE MONGOLEI IM FRUEHEN 15. JAHRHUNDERT / Franke, W – (Sinologica III. 1953, p 81-88) – 8 – ne IDC [950]

DER CHINESISCHE RITENSTREIT / Huonder, Anton – Aachen, (um 1903) – 1mf – 9 – DM38.00 – 3-89349-320-4 – gw Hänsel [950]

CHINESISCHE SOLDATEN BESTIMMTEN DIE GRENZEN DES MILITAERISCHEN GEHORSAMS / Beckerath, Ulrich von – Military Jiu Jitsu or, How Chinese Soldiers Determined the Limits of Military Obedience – 9 – 1.00f – at Libertarian Micro [335]

EINE CHINESISCHE TEMPELINSCHRIFT AUS INDIKUSAHRI BEI TURFAN / Franke, O – (APAW. Anhang. 1907). Turkistan. BU-803 2 – 8 – ne IDC [410]

CHINESISCHE URKUNDEN ZUR GESCHICHTE ASIENS / ed by Groot, J J M de – Vol 1, Die Hunnen der vorchristlichen Zeit (1921); Vol 2, Die westlande Chinas in de vorchristlichen Zeit (1926); Ed. by O. Franke. Berlin, Leipzig – 8 – ne IDC [900]

DIE CHINESISCHE WIRTSCHAFTSREFORM UND INFLATIONSPROBLEMATIK SEIT 1979 / Chen, Xinhua – 1995 – 4mf – 9 – DM112.00 – 3-8267-2188-8 – gw Hänsel [330]

CHING FENG – (1985-. 5,6,9) – English ed. v8-. 1964- – 1 – us UMI [073]

Ching, R C *see*
- A REVISION OF THE CHINESE AND SIKKIM HIMALAYAN DRYOPTERIS
- A REVISION OF THE CHINESE AND SIKKIM-HIMALAYAN DRYOPTERIS

CHING-CHI PAN-YUEH K'AN – Peking and Shanghai, China. Nov 1927-Nov 1928. Semi-monthly economic journal – 1 – 44.00 – us Chinese Res [073]

CHING-CHI T'UNG-CHI YUEH-CHIH = THE CHINESE ECONOMIC AND STATISTICAL REVIEW – Shanghai. v1-8(1-12). 1934-41.Lacking: 1935,v2(10); 1936,v3(9); 1941,v8(10-12). BCH-222/1 – 9 – ne IDC [310]

CHING-CHI YEN-CHIU – (Economic Studies). Peking. 1955-66. Lacking: v. 6-12, 1955; v. 7-12, 1956; v. 7-12, 1957; v. 7-12, 1960; v. 1-12, 1961; v. 1, v. 7-12, 1964; v. 6-12, 1966. BCH-943 2 – 8 – ne IDC [330]

CH'ING-HO = THE BLUE CRANE – Art magazine. Shanghai.v1-5(14), 1932-37. Lacking: 1933,v1(13); 1937,v5(9-13).BCH-1046/1 – 9 – ne IDC [073]

CH'ING-HUA HSUEH-PAO – Peking. 1-15, no.1, 1924-Oct 1948, n.s.1, no.1-2, 1956-57 – 1 – 138.00 – us L of C Photodup [950]

CHINGLEPUT DISTRICT MANUAL / Crole, C S – Madras. 1879. BI-150-15 2 – 8 – ne IDC [950]

CH'ING-NIEN CHIEH – (Youth Magazine). Shanghai. 1931-48. Lacking: v. 2 (2?)-v. 5 (5) 1932-34; v. 10 (2-?)1936-45; v. 2 (3-5) 1946-v. 3 1947. BCH-956 2 – 8 – ne IDC [073]

CHING-SHIH PAO – Current Affairs. v1-3 (1). Peking. 1922. BCH-785 2 – 8 – ne IDC [950]

Chiniquy, Charles *see*
- DR. CHINIQUY TO SENATOR TASSE AND MGR. LYNCH: ARCHBISHOP OF TORONTO
- L'EGLISE DE ROME
- LE PRETRE, LA FEMME ET LE CONFESSIONNAL
- THE PRIEST, THE WOMAN, AND THE CONFESSIONAL

CHINKI, HISTOIRE COCHINCHINOISE QUI PEUT SERVIR A D'AUTRES PAYS / Coyer, Gabriel-Francois – (Utopias in the Enlightenment series). 1768 – 9 – fr Hachette [830]

CHIN-LING SCHOOL OF THEOLOGY = CHIN-LING SHEN HSUEH YUAN HUA HSI T'EH K'AN – no 1 Aug 1945 (complete) – 1r – 1 – ATLA S0296B – us A.T.L.A. [073]

CHIN-LING THEOLOGICAL MAGAZINE – (In Chinese) – nos6-7. Feb-Aug 1957 (incomplete) – 1r – 1 – ATLA S0296A – us A.T.L.A. [073]

CHINO CHAMPION – (Also known as: Chino Hills News) – Chino, CA. Nov 1887- – 93+ r – 1 – $4,650.00 ($150.00y) – R02108 – us Library Micro [071]

CHINO HILLS NEWS *see* CHINO CHAMPION

CHINOOK ADVANCE – Alberta, CN. 1915-45 – 6r – 1 – cn Commonwealth Micro [072]

CHINOOK OBSERVER – Long Beach, WA. 1900-19043; 1906-09; 1989- – 8+ r – 1 – $400.00 ($90.00y) – B05401 – us Library Micro [071]

CHINOOK TEXTS / Boas, Franz – Washington: GPO, 1894. 00155. (Pre-1900 Canadiana) – 9 – cn C.I.H.M. [490]

CHIN-SHAN SHIH-PAO = CHINESE TIMES – San Francisco: Chinese Times Publ Co, [oct 4 1928-jun 1929; jun 1930-aug 1931] – us Res Libr [071]

CHIN-SHEN LU – List of Chinese gentry. Government posts (Ching Dynasty) and lists of those who filled them. 1757-1917. Many years missing – 1 – 2360.00 – us Chinese Res [950]

CHINTAO KINKO NI OKERU NOSON JITTAI CHOSA HOKOKU / South Manchurian Railway. North China Office – Peking. 1939. Rural conditions and agriculture of Tsingtao and vicinity. (J 612.221 M137s) – 1 – 35.00r – us Hoover Inst Photo [630]

CHI-NYANJA SIMPLIFIED / Caldwell, Robert – 2nd ed. London: Zambesi Industrial Mission, [1897] – 1 – us Res Libr [490]

Chiovenda, E *see*
- LE COLLEZIONI BOTANICHE DELLA MISSIONE STEFANINI-PAOLI NELLA SOMALIA ITALIANA
- FLORA SOMALA

Chipman, D *see* D. CHIPMAN'S REPORTS

Chipman, Lauchlan *see*
- LIBERTY, EQUALITY AND UNHAPPINESS
- LIBERTY, JUSTICE AND THE MARKET
- TO EACH HIS OWN

Chipman, N *see* N. CHIPMAN'S REPORTS

Chippewa and Munsee Indians *see* JOURNAL OF PROCEEDINGS OF COUNCIL

Chippewa Lake. Ohio. First Presbyterian Church of Lafayette *see* CHURCH RECORD, MS 1217

CHIPS – London, Ont.: London Collegiate Institute, Dec 1890- – 9 – cn C.I.H.M. [370]

CHIPS / New Hampshire. Cooperative Extension Service – 1938-46 – 1,5,6 – us Spaulding [630]

CHIPS FROM MANY BLOCKS / Burritt, Elihu – Toronto: Rose-Belford, 1878. 00353. (Pre-1900 Canadiana) – 9 – cn C.I.H.M. [971]

EL CHIQUITIN CHARLATAN – Villafranca de los Barros, 1896. 1 numero – 5 – sp Bibl Santa Ana [073]

CHIRAGH – Shumarah-'i 1-5 (Pa'iz 1360-Mihr 1363 [Fall 1981-Sep 1984]) – 18mf – 9 – $75.00 – us MEDOC [950]

Chirikov, Evgeni i Nikolaevich *see* KRASNYI PAIATS

CHIROLOGIA / Bulwer, J – M 319. 1644 – 9 – ne IDC [610]

CHIRON ACHILLIS, SIVE NAVARCHUS HUMANAE VITAE / Bonomi, Giovanni Francesco – O-164. 1661 – 9 – ne IDC [450]

CHIRONOMIA / Bulwer, J – M-320 2. 1644 – 8 – ne IDC [610]

CHIROPRACTIC SPORTS MEDICINE – v1-10. 1987-1996 – 1,5,6,9 – $65.00r – us Williams [617]

CHIROPRACTIC TECHNIQUE – v1-8. 1989-1996 – 1,5,6,9 – $65.00r – us Williams [615]

DER CHIRURG – v. 17 18-51. 1946 47-80 – 1,5,9 – 3990.00 – us UMI [617]

CHIRURGIA PLASTICA – v. 1-5. 1971-80 – 1,5,9 – 383.00 – us UMI [617]

CHIRURGICAL OBSERVATIONS RELATIVE TO THE CATARACT, THE POLYPUS OF THE NOSE, THE CANCER OF THE SCROTUM,... / Pott, P – London, 1775 – 4mf – 9 – ne IDC [615]

CHIRURGIE D'ARMEE / Ravaton, H – M 235. 1768 – 9 – ne IDC [617]

CHIRURGISCHE BEHANDLUNGSERGEBNISSE GUTARTIGER SCHILDDRUESENERKRANKUNGEN / Sengupta, Rahul – 1995 – 1mf – 9 – DM60.00 – 3-8267-2220-5 – gw Hänsel [617]

CHIRURGISKE FOERSOEK OCH ANMAERKNINGAR VID OEGONSJUKDOMAR / Ribe, CF – Kongl. Swenska Wetenskaps Academiens Handlingar, 1745 – 1mf – 9 – ne IDC [617]

CHIS: CONSUMER HEALTH INFORMATION SERVICE – (1983 ed. $465; 1985 ed. $245; 1987 ed. $245; 1989 ed $315) – 1983- – 9 – us UMI [613]

Chisholm, Alexander *see*
- THE BIBLE IN THE LIGHT OF NATURE, OF MAN, AND OF GOD
- BIBLE IN THE LIGHT OF NATURE, OF MAN, AND OF GOD

Chisholm, Murdoch *see* THE EARLY CHRISTIAN CHURCH AS FORESHADOWED IN OLD TESTAMENT PROPHECY

CHISLA – Paris. v. 1-10. 1930-1934 – 1 – us NY Public [073]

CHISLEHURST AND DISTRICT TIMES – 1911; 1950-51; 1984-89; 7-28 Jun 1990-1993; Jan-Jun, 7 Jul-25 Aug 1994; 1995-96 – 60 1/2r – 1 – uk British Libr Newspaper [072]

CHISLENNOST SELSKOGO NASELENIIA V SAMARSKOI GUBERNII / Samarskoe gubernskoe statisticheskoe biuro – Samara: [Biuro], 1920 – 1 – CSUX91-B1380 – us Hoover Inst Photo [947]

CHISLENNOST SKOTA V SSSR : STATISTICHESKII SBORNIK / T Sentralnoe statisticheskoe upravlenie pri Sovete Ministrov SSSR – Moskva: Gos. statisticheskoe izd-vo, 1957 – 1 – CSUX90-B9197 – us Hoover Inst Photo [947]

CHISLENNYE METODY MEKHANIKI SPLOSHNOI SREDY / Akademiia nauk SSSR, Sibirskoe otdelenie & Otdelenie mekhaniki i protsessov upravleniia Novosibirsk: VTS SO AN SSSR 1970-1986. v1 n1-5 (1970) & v2 (1971) & v3 n1,4-5 1972) – us Res Libr [947]
Chislov, PI *see* ISTORIIA RUSSKAGO PRAVA OT IZDANIIA SOBORNAGO ULOZHENIIA TSARIA ALEKSEIA MIKHAILOVICHA DO IZDANIIA SVODA ZAKONOV
CHISPAZOS (AQUI-DULCES DE TIEMPOS PASADOS) / Sanchez Arjona, Vicente – Sevilla: Imprenta Carlos Acuna, Tomo 1-3. 1942, 1943, 1945 – 1 – sp Bibl Santa Ana [810]
Chistiakov, P S *see* RIECHI OKTIABRISTA 1905-1907 GG.
CHISTILISHCHE. STIKHI, KNIGA VTORAIA / Adamovich, G – Spb. 1922. BR-1107 2 – 8 – ne IDC [460]
Chistovich, I A *see* FEOFAN PROKOPOVICH I EGO VREMIA
CH'I-TA CHI-K'AN – Cheeloo University Journal. 1932-37. v1-8. BCH-212- – 8 – ne IDC [073]
CHITATEL' – Moskva. 1896-97, 1901. Lacking: 1896 (1-50); 1897 (25); 1901 (4-50). BR-1576 2 – 8 – ne IDC [073]
CHITATEL I KNIGA : SBORNIK NAUCHNYKH TRUDOV / Nauchnyi sovet po istorii mirovoi kultury Akademii nauk SSSR, Gosudarstvennaia ordena Lenina biblioteka SSSR imeni V I Lenina [redaktsionnaia 111=Markushevich, A I et al – Moskva: Gos. bib-ka SSSR im. V I Lenina 1978 – us Res Libr [947]
Chittenden, Newton H *see* SETTLERS, MINERS AND TOURISTS GUIDE FROM OCEAN TO OCEAN BY THE C. P. R., THE GREAT TRANS-CONTINENTAL SHORT LINE THROUGH A REGION OF UNSURPASSED ATTRACTION FOR SETTLER, MINER AND TOURIST
Chitty, J *see* A PRACTICAL TREATISE ON THE LAW OF NATIONS...
Chitty, Joseph *see*
- A PRACTICAL TREATISE ON THE CRIMINAL LAW
- A TREATISE ON PLEADING, AND PARTIES TO ACTIONS.
- A TREATISE ON PLEADING, AND PARTIES TO ACTIONS, WITH SECOND AND THIRD VOLUMES, CONTAINING PRECEDENTS OF PLEADINGS, AND AN APPENDIX OF FORMS
- A TREATISE ON THE LAW OF BILLS OF EXCHANGE, CHECKS ON BANKERS, PROMISSORY NOTES, BANKERS' CASH NOTES, AND BANKNOTES
- A TREATISE ON THE LAWS OF COMMERCE AND MANUFACTURES, AND THE CONTRACTS RELATING THERETO, WITH AN APPENDIX OF TREATIES, STATUTES, AND PRECEDENTS

CHITTY'S LAW JOURNAL – v1-29. 1950-81 – 1,5,6 – $270.00 – us Hein [073]
CHI-TU-CHIAO YU CHUNG-KUO (CCC168) / Hsieh, Fu-ya – (In Chinese) – [s.l: s.n, 1965] – 1r – 1 – 1984-B500 – us A.T.L.A. [240]
CH'IUNG-CHOU FU-CHIH – 1774, 10. BCH-635 2 – 8 – ne IDC [950]
CH'I-YUEH – (July: A Literary Magazine). 1957. BCH-974 2 – 8 – ne IDC [480]
Chizhevskii, D *see* O POEZII FUTURIZMA
Chizhikov, OL *see* PROIZVODSTVENNAIA KOOPERATSIIA I ELEKTRIFIKATSIIA SEL'SKOGO KHOZIAISTVA
Chizmadzhev *see* BIOLOGICAL MEMBRANES
Chkhikvadze, V M *see*
- SOVETSKOE VOENNO-UGOLOVNOE PRAVO

Chladni, E FF *see* ENTDECKUNGEN UEBER DIE THEORIE DES KLANGES VON ERNST FLORENS FRIEDRICH CHLADNI
Chlebowska, Krystyna *see*
- KNOWING AND DOING
- LITERACY FOR RURAL WOMEN IN THE THIRD WORLD

CHLENI 1-I GOSUDARSTVENNOI DUMY : BIOGRAFII, KHARAKTERISTIKI, POLITICHESKIE VZGLIADY, OBSHCHESTVENNAIA DEIATEL'NOST', VYBORY I PROCHEE – M., 1906. 79p – 2mf – 9 – ne IDC [320]
CHLOPSKA DROGA – Warsaw, Poland. 1981-92 – 12r – 1 – us L of C Photodup [072]
CHLORIDE BELT – Candelaria, NV. 1890-92 – 1r – 1 – $50.00 – U04434 – us Library Micro [071]
CHLORIS AETNENSIS, ETC / Rafinesque-Schmaltz, Constantine S – Palermo. 1813. B-5648 1 – 9 – ne IDC [580]
CHLORIS ANDINA. ESSAI D'UNE FLORE DE LA REGION ALPINE DES CORDILLERES DE L'AMERIQUE DU SUD / Weddell, H A – 2v. Paris. 1855-1857-61. B-1357 2 – 8 – ne IDC [580]
CHLOROFORM EXPOSURE AND DOSE DETERMINATION ASSOCIATED WITH COMPETITIVE SWIMMERS DURING A TWO-HOUR SWIM PRACTICE / Berkoff, David C – University of Montana, 1995 – 1mf – 9 – PE 3629 – us Microform Publ [617]
Chlumecky, P von *see* DIE REGESTEN ODER DIE CHRONOLOGISCHEN VERZEICHNISSE DER URKUNDEN IN DEN ARCHIVEN ZU IGLAU, TREBITSCH...
Cho, Ho S *see* FACTORS RELATED TO FASTING BEHAVIOR AMONG AMERICAN ADULTS
Cho, Kwang M et al *see* ATTITUDES OF KOREAN NATIONAL ATHLETES AND COACHES TOWARD ATHLETICS PARTICIPATION
Choate, J H *see* THE TWO HAGUE CONFERENCES
Chobham, Thomas de *see*
- SERMONES
- SUMMA DE ARTE PRAEDICANDI

Choboy, Jon A *see* INFLUENCE OF MENTAL IMAGERY ON TENNIS SERVICE ACCURACY OF INTERMEDIATE LEVEL TENNIS PLAYERS
CHOC : SOCIETE ST-JEAN BAPTISTE – Saint Jerome, Canada. jun 1965 – 1r – 1 – Can$25.00 – cn Can Microfilming [072]
LE CHOC DES IDEES : EN COLLABORATION. LE JOURNAL CHOC POUR L'INDEPENDANCE SOCIALISTE DU QUEBEC – (Cont by: Le Journal Choc nov 1972-11 jan 1980) – Montreal, 21 avr 1969-jun 1972 – 2r – 1 – Can$50.00r – cn Can Microfilming [072]
CHOCTAW BAPTIST HYMNAL – Orig. and trans. hymns – 1 – 5.00 – us Baptist [240]
CHOCTAW PLAINDEALER – Ackerman. Miss. 1915- – 1 – us UMI [071]
Chodat, R *see* MONOGRAPHIA POLYGALACEARUM
Choderlos de Laclos, P AF *see* DE L'EDUCATION DES FEMMES
Chodowski, S *see* KRITIK DES MIDRASCH SCHIR-HASCHIRIM, NACH DER MUENCHENER HANDSCHRIFT NO. 50 ORIENTAL
Chodzko, L *see*
- LE CONGRES DE VIENNE ET LES TRAITES DE 1815
- RECUEIL DES TRAITES, CONVENTIONS ET ACTES DIPLOMATIQUES CONCERNANT LA POLOGNE, 1762-1862 PAR LE COMTE D'ANGEBERG

CHOH LIN : THE CHINESE BOY WHO BECAME A PREACHER / Davis, John A – Philadelphia: Presbyterian Board of Publ and Sabbath-School Work, 1901, c1884 – 1mf – 9 – 0-8370-7209-3 – 1986-1209 – us A.T.L.A. [920]
CHOHATSU BUKKEN ICHIRANHYO = REQUISTIONED MATERIALS LIST IN THE MEIJI ERA / Special Staff Office of the Japanese Army; ed by Hora, Tomio – 1875-1911 – 24r – 1 – Y220,000 – ja Yushodo [950]
Choi, Monica W *see* CHOOSING WHETHER OR NOT TO USE HORMONE REPLACEMENT THERAPY DURING THE MENOPAUSAL TRANSITION
CHOICE – (v9- . 5,6. v12- . 9) – v. 1- 1964- – 1 – us UMI [020]
CHOICE AND EXPERIMENTED RECEIPTS IN PHYSICK AND CHIRURGERY / Digby, K – London, 1668 – 6mf – 9 – ne IDC [617]
CHOICE SELECTIONS IN PROSE AND POETRY – From favorite authors. Quebec: J. Walsh, 1891. 00630. (Pre-1900 Canadiana) – 9 – cn C.I.H.M. [830]
THE CHOIR – 1869-1963 – 1 – uk Manchester Libr [780]
THE CHOIR JOURNAL – Boston, 1901-08 – 1 – £115.00 – uk Chadwyck [780]
CHOISEUL ET LA FRANCE D'OUTRE-MER APRES LE TRAITE DE PARIS: ETUDE SUR LA POLITIQUE COLONIALE AU XVIIIE SIECLE, AVEC UN APPENDICE SUR LES ORIGINES DE LA QUESTION DE TERRE-NEUVE / Daubigny, Eugene – Paris: Hachette, 1892. 02508. (Pre-1900 Canadiana) – 9 – cn C.I.H.M. [971]
Choiseul-Stainville, Etienne F *see* MEMOIRE HISTORIQUE SUR LA NEGOCIATION DE LA FRANCE ET DE L'ANGLETERRE, DEPUIS LE 26 MARS 1761 JUSQU'AU 20 SEPTEMBRE DE LA MEME ANNEE, AVEC LES PIECES JUSTIFICATIVES
Choisy, Eugene *see*
- L'ETAT CHRETIEN CALVINISTE A GENEVE
- LA THEOCRATIE A GENEVE AU TEMPS DE CALVIN

Choisy, J D *see*
- CONVOLVULACEAE ORIENTALES
- PRODROMUS D'UNE MONOGRAPHIE DE LA FAMILLE DES HYPERICINEES

CHOIX DE CHANSONS – 3e ed., 14e mille. Montreal: [les freres des ecoles chretiennes], 1916. SEM105P1679 – 3mf – 9 – Can$6.75 – cn Bibl Nat [780]
CHOIX DE CHANSONS – 5e ed., 23e mille. Montreal: les freres des escoles chretiennes, 1936. SEM105P1680 – 3mf – 9 – Can$6.75 – cn Bibl Nat [780]
CHOIX DE CHANSONS ET POESIES WALLONNES – Pays de Liege. 1844 – 1 – us I.U. Libraries [440]
CHOIX DE PLANTES DU COROLLAIRE DES INSTITUTS DE TOURNEFORT / Desfontaines, R L – Paris. 1808. B-681 2 – 8 – ne IDC [580]
CHOIX DE RAPPORTS ET INSTRUCTIONS PUB. SOUS LES AUSPICES DU MINISTERE DE L'INSTRUCTION PUBLIQUE ET DES BEAUX-ARTS / Archives des Missions scientifiques et litteraires – v1-8, 1850-57. 2nd series, v1-7, 1864-72. 3rd series, v1-15, 1873-90. 30v. plates, maps, plans, facsims., tables – 1 – us U.W. Library [073]
CHOIX D'EDIFICES PUBLICS PROJETES ET CONSTRUITS EN FRANCE DEPUIS LE COMMENCEMENT DU XIXE SIECLE / Gourlier, Charles – Paris. L. Colas, 1825-50. 3v. in fol., ill. (Architecture Series) – 9 – fr Hachette [720]
CHOIX DES VACHES LAITIERES D'APRES LE SYSTEME GUENON / Couture, Joseph Alphonse – Quebec: L. Brousseau, 1884. 05271. (Pre-1900 Canadiana) – 9 – cn C.I.H.M. [971]
LE CHOIX, LE MONDE, L'EXISTENCE / Wahl, J A et al – Paris, 1948 – 4mf – 8 – ne Slangenburg [110]
LE CHOIX, LE MONDE, L'EXISTENCE / Wahl, J A et al – Paris, 1948 – 4mf – 8 – ne Slangenburg [120]
Chokier, I A *see* TRACTATUS DE LEGATO
Choksey, Rustom Dinshaw *see* A HISTORY OF BRITISH DIPLOMACY AT THE COURT OF THE PESHWAS, 1786-1818
LE CHOLERA : SON HISTORIQUE, SON ORIGINE, SA NATURE, LES CAUSES QUI LE PRODUISENT, AINSI QUE CELLES DES AUTRES MALADIES EPIDEMIQUES OU CONTAGIEUSES PRODUITES PAR LES MICROBES... / Crevier, Joseph Alexandre – Montreal: Imprimerie generale..., 1885. SEM105P48 – 1mf – 9 – Can$2.25 – cn Bibl Nat [616]
LE CHOLERA A TOULOUSE / Armieux, Louis Leon Cyrille – Toulouse, Douladoure, 1866. 31 p. 1 fiche. (Statistics: Medical Studies Series) – 9 – 6.00 – fr Bibl Nationale [310]
LE CHOLERA ELECTORAL : DE PROFUNDIS PROUDHONIEN – Paris [1848?] – us Res Libr [944]
CHOLERA EPIDEMICS IN EAST AFRICA. : AN ACCOUNT OF THE SEVERAL DIFFUSIONS OF THE DISEASE IN THAT COUNTRY FROM 1821 TILL 1872 / Christie, James – London: Macmillan, 1876 – 1 – us Res Libr [610]
LE CHOLERA (HISTOIRE D'UNE EPIDEMIE, FINISTERE 1885-1886) / Monod, Henri Charles – Melum, Impr. administrative, 1892. 656 p. 8 fiches. (Statistics Series: Medical Studies) – 9 – 20.00 – fr Bibl Nationale [310]
Cholet, C *see* L'ABORDAGE INTERNATIONAL...
Cholmondeley, Mary *see*
- THE DANVERS JEWELS
- A DEVOTEE
- DIANA TEMPEST
- THE LOWEST RUNG
- MOTH AND RUST
- NOT WITHSTANDING
- PRISONERS
- RED POTTAGE
- THE ROMANCE OF LIFE
- SIR CHARLES DANVERS
- UNDER ONE ROOF

Cholvat, John *see* VALUES EDUCATION
CHOMEDEY DE MAISONNEUVE: DRAME CHRETIEN EN TROIS ACTES: SAMUEL DE CHAMPLAIN, PAGES ORATOIRES: TROIS AUREOLES / Corbeil, Sylvio – Montreal: Cadieux et Derome, 1899. 00233. (Pre-1900 Canadiana) – 9 – cn C.I.H.M. [820]
Chon, K S (Kaye) *see* JOURNAL OF TRAVEL AND TOURISM MARKETING
Chong Pyong-Hi *see* DANSES MASQUEES ET JEUX DE MARIONNETTES EN COREE
CHONGQING DAXUE XUEBAO – (1980 $3.50f; 1981 $4.50f) – Journal of Chongqing University. In Chinese but English abstracts to the main articles. F p177 – 9 – cc Microforms [073]
CHONGQING RIBAO – China. Chongqing Daily. 1985-. M D86 – 1 – $55.00r – cc Microforms [072]
CHONGQING TANPAN ZILIAO – Materials on the Chongqing Negotiations.Comp. by Sichuan Renmin Chubanshe. 1980. 3 fiches. F/H 141 – 9 – $13.50 – cc Microforms [950]
Choniatae, Nicetae *see* HISTORIA (CSHB 23)
CHOOSING WHETHER OR NOT TO USE HORMONE REPLACEMENT THERAPY DURING THE MENOPAUSAL TRANSITION : A QUALITATIVE STUDY / Choi, Monica W & Ruzek, Sheryl – 1993 – 3mf – 9 – $12.00 – us Microform Publ [613]
Chopin, Jules *see* SOIUZNICHESKAIA INTERVENTSIIA NA DALNEM VOSTOKE I V SIBIRI
Chopra, Ram Nath *see* INDIGENOUS DRUGS INQUIRY
Choque, Pierre *see*
- COMMEMORACION ET ADVERTISSEMENT DE LA MORT DE TRES CRESTIENNE ET TRES HAULTE...DAME MADAME ANNE...DUCHESSE DE BRETAIGNE...
- RECIT DES FUNERAILLES D'ANNE DE BRETAGNE...AVEC UNE INTROD. ET DES NOTES PAR L. MERLET ET MAX. DE GOMBERT

Choquet, A *see* STATISTIQUES VITALES DES CATHOLIQUES DE MONTREAL POUR L'ANNEE 1874
Choquette, Ernest *see*
- CLAUDE PAYSAN
- LES RIBAUD: UNE IDYLLE DE 37

Choquette, Ph-Aug *see* LA SENTINELLE
CHORAL ADVOCATE AND SINGING CLASS JOURNAL – v1-24. Jun 1850-Apr 1873 – 1 – 550.00 – us Opus [073]
THE CHORAL ADVOCATE AND SINGING CLASS JOURNAL – New York City. v1-24. 1850-73 – 11r – 1 – £600.00 – uk Chadwyck [780]
DER CHORAL BEI JOHANN SEBASTIAN BACH / Meyer, Juergen – 1995 – 1mf – 9 – DM60.00 – 3-8267-2224-8 – gw Hänsel [780]
CHORAL BOOK OF THE EPHRATA CLOISTER – Manuscript, ca.1745. MUSIC 1154, Reel 1 – 1 – us L of C Photodup [780]
CHORAL HARMONIE. ENTHALTEND KIRCHEN-MELODIEN / Gerhart, Isaac – 1822. with Pennsylvanische Sammlung von Kirchen-Musik. 1840 – 1 – $50.00 – us Presbyterian [780]
CHORALBUCH, 4 STIMMIGES. / Bach, Johann Sebastian – 238 Choralmelodien mit beziffertem Bass; Handschrift...mitte des 18. Jahrhunderts. MS – 9 – us Sibley [780]
CHORAL-SYSTEM / Vogler, Georg Joseph – Offenbach a M: J. Andre ca. 1800 – 1 – us U.W. Library [780]
CHOREOGRAPHY AND DANCE : AN INTERNATIONAL JOURNAL / ed by Cohan, Robert P – 9,5,1 – us Harwood [790]
THE CHOREOGRAPHY AND PERFORMANCE OF A JAPANESE FOLK TALE / Ito, Sayuri – Brigham Young University, 1993 – 1mf – 9 – $4.00 – PE3602 – us Microform Publ [790]
DIE CHORFUGE IN HAENDELS WERKEN / Wieber, Georg-Friedrich – Frankfurt a.M., 1958 – 3mf – DM76.00 – 3-89349-847-8 – gw Hänsel [780]
Choriolanus, Ambrosius *see* CHRONICA O.E.S.A
CHORLEY GUARDIAN – Lancashire – 1 – uk Microform Academic [072]
Chorley, Henry Fothergill *see* THIRTY YEARS' MUSICAL RECOLLECTIONS
CHORLEY STANDARD & DISTRICT ADVERTISER – England.Sept 1864-1869; 1885-86. -w. 3 1/2 reels – 1 – uk British Libr Newspaper [072]
CHOROGRAFIA / Barrientos, Gaspar – 1561 – 9 – 1.50f – sp Bibl Santa Ana [946]
CHORT ZA RULEM : ZAMI ETKI O BOLSHEVIZMIE / Gorielov, M – Berlin: Tip. E.A. Gutnova, 1920 – 1 – CSUX89-B6609 – us Hoover Inst Photo [947]
CHORTOV LOG I POLUNOSHCHNOE SOLNTSE. RAZSKAZY I POEMY / Remizov, A – Spb. 1908. BR-819 2 – 8 – ne IDC [460]

CHOSEN DOKURITSU UNDO NI KANSURU MONJO – Korean nationalistic activities in Korea and other countries. 300 p. 1921. (J 316.821 C54) – 1 – 35.00r – us Hoover Inst Photo [950]

THE CHOSEN FRIEND – Toronto: Chosen Friend Print and Pub Co, v1 no 1 (Jan 15 1892)- – 9 – cn C.I.H.M. [971]

CHOSEN SOTOKUFU / Korea. (Government-General of Chosen, 1910-45) – Official Gazette. Seoul. On film: v1-5521; 1910-45 (incomplete). LL-02008 – 1 – us L of C Photodup [340]

CHOSES D'AUTREFOIS : FEUILLES EPARSES / Gagnon, Ernest – Quebec: Typ. Dussault & Proulx, 1905. SEM105P1610 – 4mf – 9 – Can$9.00 – cn Bibl Nat [971]

CHOSES DU PAYS : MELANGES, LITTERATURE, HISTOIRE – Montreal: Bibliotheque de l'Action Francaise, [1921?]. SEM105P1290 – 2mf – 9 – Can$4.50 – cn Bibl Nat [440]

Chossat, Ed de *see* REPERTOIRE SUMERIEN (ACCADIEN)

Chossat, R P M *see* LA GUERRE ET LA PAIX

CHOSUN ILBO – 1920-1995 – 6 times per yr – 1 – F989.00 – sz Infoprint [072]

CHOSUN ILBO – (Yrly reel count varies) – 1920- – 1 – inquire – us Ross [072]

Chotard, Jean-Bapt. L *see* ENSEMBLE DE PIECES MANUSCRITES CONCERNANT

CHOTEAU COUNTY INDEPENDENT – Fort Benton. Mont. 1912-1914 – 1 – us UMI [071]

Chotib, A *see* BANK DALAM ISLAM

CHOTSCHO / Le Coq, A von – Facsimile Wiedergaben. der wichtigeren Funde der Ersten Koenigl. Preuss. Expedition nach Turfan. Berlin. 1913. BU-624 2 – 8 – ne IDC [550]

Chotzner, J *see* HEBREW SATIRE

Chou, Keng-sheng *see* OUTLINE OF INTERNATIONAL LAW

Chou, Pai-ch'in *see* COMMONISM (CCC105)

Chou, Shu-jen *see* PILIHAN TJERPEN; TERDJEMAHAN SHANNU

CHOUBAN YIWU SHIMO (XIANFENG CHAO) – Preparations and Arrangements for Foreign Affairs During the Reign of Xianfeng. Comp. by Zhonghua Shuju. 2 reels. M H200 – 5 – $80.00 – cc Microforms [950]

Chouinard, Honore Julien Jean Baptiste *see* PAUL DE CHOMEDEY, SIEUR DE MAISONNEUVE, FONDATEUR DE MONTREAL: ETUDE HISTORIQUE ET BIOGRAPHIQUE

Choulant, J L *see*
- GESCHICHTE UND BIBLIOGRAPHIE DER ANATOMISCHEN ABBILDUNG
- HANDBUCH DER BUECHERKUNDE FUER DIE AELTERE MEDICIN ZUR KENNTNISS DER GRIECHISCHEN,...

Chouman, Joumana *see* LES RELATIONS PUBLIQUES AU LIBAN, ENTRE LE SECTEUR PUBLIC ET PRIVE, DE 1982 A 1988

Chouraqui, A *see* LES JUIFS D'AFRIQUE DU NORD ENTRE L'ORIENT ET L'OCCIDENT

Chow, B C *see* COMPARISONS OF DOMAIN SCORE AND RELIABILITY ESTIMATES USING TRIALS-TOCRITERION, SEQUENTIAL PROBABILITY RATIO, AND PRE-SET TRIAL LENGTH TESTS

Chow, Sergio et al *see* DIE TAETIGKEIT DES KINDES IN DER SPIELTHERAPIE

Chow, Yi-Fu *see* CHRISTIANITY AND CHINA (CCC106)

CHOWAN BAPTIST CHURCH. CHOWAN ASSOCIATION. NORTH CAROLINA : CHURCH RECORDS – 1884-90 – 1 – 6.48 – us Baptist [240]

CHOWCHILLA CITY DIRECTORY – Madera Co, CA. 1926-1927 – 1r – 1 – $50.00 – D056 – us Library Micro [978]

CHOWCHILLA NEWS – Chowchilla, CA. 1913-81; 1987- – 29+ r – 1 RC02110 – $1,450.00 ($50.00y) – us Library Micro [071]

CHOWCHILLA TODAY – Chowchilla, CA. Apr-Dec 1980; 1985-86 – 4r – 1 – $200.00 – B02111 – us Library Micro [071]

Choy, Valerie E *see* THE EFFECT OF EXOGENOUS RECOMBINANT PORCINE SOMATOTROPIN ON PIG COMMON CALCANEAN TENDON BIOCHEMISTRY

CHOZER CHEWRATH-'OLIM – Amsterdam, 1933-1937 – 8mf – J-261-22/1 – ne IDC [073]

CHR. JAC. BOSTROEMS FOERELAESNINGAR I RELIGIONSFILOSOFI / Bostroem, Christopher Jacob; ed by Ribbing, Sigurd – Stockholm: Norstedt, 1885 – 1mf – us A.T.L.A. [240]

CHRANITEL = GUARDIAN – [Johnstown, PA: St Mary's Greek Catholic Congregation. v1 n1-v1 n9/10. jul 1920-mar/apr 1921 – 1 – us Res Libr [073]

LA CHRECHE D'YOUVILLE ET L'ADOPTION DES ENFANTS – [Montreal: s.n.], 1933. SEM105P1641 – 1mf – 9 – Can$2.25 – cn Bibl Nat [360]

Chrehan, J *see* EARLY CHRISTIAN BAPTISM AND THE CREED

CHRESTOMATHIA AETHIOPICA EDITA ET GLOSSARIO EXPLANATA / Dillmann, August – (Includes an Ethiopic-Latin glossary) – Lipsiae [Leipzig]: T O Weigel, 1866 – 1mf – 9 – 0-8370-2915-5 – 1985-0915 – us A.T.L.A. [470]

CHRESTOMATHIA AETHIPICA EDITA ET GLOSSARIO EXPLANATA / Dillmann, August – Lipsiae, 1866 – 4mf – ne IDC [470]

CHRESTOMATHIA SYRIACA : QUAM GLOSSARIO ET TABULIS GRAMMATICIS – (Texts and glossary in Syriac; discussion in Latin) – Halis Saxonum: Sumptibus Orphanotrophei, 1868 – 1mf – 9 – 0-8370-8614-0 – 1986-2614 – us A.T.L.A. [470]

CHRESTOMATHIA TARGUMICO-CHALDAICA : ADDITO LEXICO / Kaerle, Joseph – Viennae: Typis Caes Reg Aulae et Imperii Typographiae, 1852 – 1mf – 9 – 0-8370-7550-5 – 1986-1550 – us A.T.L.A. [470]

CHRESTOMATHIE MANDCHOU, OU RECUEIL DE TEXTES MANDCHOU / Klaproth, Julius von – Paris. 1828. BU-488 2 – 8 – ne IDC [490]

CHRESTOMATHIE PERSANE / Schefer, C – 1883, 1885 – 9 – fr Orientalistes [470]

Chretien, A *see* ETUDE SUR LA LETTRE DE CHANGE

LES CHRETIENS DANS L'EMPIRE ROMAIN : DE LA FIN DES ANTONINS AU MILIEU DU 3E SIECLE (180-249) / Aube, Benjamin – Paris: Didier, 1881 – 2mf – us A.T.L.A. [240]

LES CHRETIENS ET L'EMPIRE ROMAIN A L'EPOQUE DU NOUVEAU TESTAMENT / Goguel, Maurice – Paris: Fischbacher, 1908 – 1mf – us A.T.L.A. [240]

LA CHRETIENTE AFRICAINE DE DAKAR : PARTIE DESCRIPTIVE ET STATISTIQUE / Martin, V – Dakar, Fraternite Saint-Dominique 1964 – us Res Libr [960]

LA CHRETIENTE ROMAINE, 1198-1274 (10) – Paris, 1950 – Dfl46.00 – ne Slangenburg [240]

LES CHRETIENTES CELTIQUES / Gougaud, Louis – Paris: Lecoffre, 1911 – 2mf – us A.T.L.A. [240]

CHREZVYCHA INY I VSEROSSI ISKI I SOI EZD RABOTNIKOV VODNAGO TRANSPORTA (1918: LENINGRAD, RSFSR) *see* TRUDY CHREZVYCHAINAGO VSEROSSIISKAGO SOIEZDA RABTONIKOV VODNAGO TRANSPORTA RESPUBLIKI: 14-27 FEVRALI A 1918 G

CHREZVYCHAINAIA SLEDSTRENNAIA – 7v. (Fall of the Tsarist Regime). 1924-27 – 3 – us Readex [947]

CHRISCHONA BLAETTCHEN – (Filmed with: Chrischona Gruesse) – 1934-60 (complete) – 1r – 1 – ATLA S0718A – us A.T.L.A. [073]

CHRISCHONA BLAETTCHEN *see* CHRISCHONA GRUESSE

CHRISCHONA GRUESSE – (Filmed with: Chrischona Blaettchen) – 1961-72 (complete) – 1r – 1 – ATLA S0718B – us A.T.L.A. [073]

CHRISCHONA GRUESSE *see* CHRISCHONA BLAETTCHEN

Chriscoe, Stephen B *see* THE VALIDITY OF THE TECUMSEH SELF-ADMINISTERED OCCUPATIONAL ACTIVITY QUESTIONNAIRE

CHRIST, A HOME MISSIONARY / Williams, William R – (A discourse). 1836 – 1 – 5.00 – us Baptist [240]

CHRIST AND CHRISTENDOM : THE BOYLE LECTURES FOR THE YEAR 1866 / Plumptre, Edward Hayes – London: Alexander Strahan, 1867 – 1mf – 9 – 0-8370-5480-X – 1985-3480 – us A.T.L.A. [240]

CHRIST AND CHRISTIANITY / Schaff, Philip – 1885 – 1 – us A.T.L.A. [240]

CHRIST AND CRITICISM...THE RELATION OF CHRISTIAN FAITH TO BIBLICAL CRITICISM / Mead, Charles Marsh – New York: A.D.F. Randolph, (1892). 1 fiche – 9 – us A.T.L.A. [240]

CHRIST AND HIS RELIGION / Reid, John – 1880 – 9 – us A.T.L.A. [240]

CHRIST AND HIS SEED: CENTRAL TO ALL THINGS...IN PAUL'S EPISTLE TO THE EPHESIANS / Pulsford, John – London: Hamilton, Adams, 1872. 1 fiche – 9 – us A.T.L.A. [240]

CHRIST AND HUMANITY : WITH A REVIEW, HISTORICAL AND CRITICAL, OF THE DOCTRINE OF CHRIST'S PERSON / Goodwin, Henry Martyn – (Includes bibliographical references) – New York: Harper, 1875 – 1mf – 9 – 0-8370-4910-5 – 1985-2910 – us A.T.L.A. [240]

CHRIST AND MODERN THOUGHT: WITH A...LECTURE, ON...MEETING MODERN UNBELIEF – Various authors.Boston: Roberts, 1881.1 fiche – 9 – us A.T.L.A. [240]

CHRIST AND MODERN UNBELIEF / McKim, Randolph Harrison – (Includes bibliographical references) – New York: Thomas Whittaker, 1893 – 1mf – 9 – 0-8370-4359-X – 1985-2359 – us A.T.L.A. [230]

CHRIST AND OTHER MASTERS : AN HISTORICAL INQUIRY INTO SOME OF THE CHIEF PARALLELISMS AND CONTRASTS BETWEEN CHRISTIANITY AND THE RELIGIOUS SYSTEMS OF THE ANCIENT WORLD / Hardwick, Charles – London: Macmillan, 1874 – 2mf – us A.T.L.A. [240]

CHRIST AND THE BIBLE: FOUR LECTURES / Leathes, Stanley – London: S.W. Partridge, 1885. 1 fiche – 9 – us A.T.L.A. [240]

CHRIST AND THE CHERUBIM, OR, THE ARK OF THE COVENANT A TYPE OF CHRIST / Otts, John Martin Philip – Richmond: Presb. Comm. of Pub., 1896. 1 fiche. 8370-4650-5 – 9 – us A.T.L.A. [240]

CHRIST AND THE DRAMAS OF DOUBT : STUDIES IN THE PROBLEM OF EVIL / Flewelling, Ralph Tyler – New York: Eaton & Mains, c1913 – 1mf – us A.T.L.A. [210]

CHRIST AND THE EASTERN SOUL / Hall, Charles Cuthbert – Chicago: University of Chicago Press, 1909. 1 fiche – 9 – us A.T.L.A. [240]

CHRIST AND THE ETERNAL ORDER / Buckham, John Wright – (Includes bibliographical references) – Boston:Pilgrim Press, 1906 – 1mf – 9 – 0-8370-3034-X – 1985-1034 – us A.T.L.A. [240]

CHRIST AND THE JEWISH LAW / Mackintosh, Robert – London: Hodder & Stoughton, 1886. 1 fiche – 9 – us A.T.L.A. [240]

CHRIST BEARING WITNESS TO HIMSELF / Chadwick, George Alexander – New York: A.D.F. Randolph, (1879?). 1 fiche – 9 – us A.T.L.A. [240]

CHRIST CHURCH ALLANSFORD – 1879-1976. Marr., Bapt. etc. CCRA1-2 – 2mf – 9 – at Corangamite [920]

CHRIST CHURCH ANNUAL REPORTS – 1950-1986. CCAR1 – 1r – 1 – at Corangamite [910]

CHRIST CHURCH BAPTISMS – 1850-1986. CCRB1 – 1r – 1 – at Corangamite [920]

CHRIST CHURCH BAPTISMS – 1986-1993 – 1mf – 9 – at Corangamite [920]

Christ Church Cathedral. Montreal, Quebec *see* CHRIST CHURCH, MONTREAL AS PARISH CHURCH AND CATHEDRAL

CHRIST CHURCH CENTRAL COUNCIL MINS – 1960-1986. CCC1 – 1r – 1 – at Corangamite [910]

CHRIST CHURCH CONFIRMATIONS – 1891-1986. CCRC1 – 1r – 1 – at Corangamite [920]

CHRIST CHURCH DEATHS REGISTER – 1909-1986. CCRD1 – 1r – 1 – at Corangamite [920]

CHRIST CHURCH DEATHS REGISTER – 1987-1993 – 4mf – 9 – at Corangamite [920]

CHRIST CHURCH LETTER BOOKS – 1862-1899. CCRL1 – 1r – 1 – at Corangamite [920]

CHRIST CHURCH MARRIAGES – 1853-1986. CCRM1-4 – 4r – 1 – at Corangamite [920]

CHRIST CHURCH MARRIAGES – 1987-1993 – 3mf – 9 – at Corangamite [920]

CHRIST CHURCH MISC. MINUTES – 1901-1960. CCRD1 – 1r – 1 – at Corangamite [910]

CHRIST CHURCH, MONTREAL AS PARISH CHURCH AND CATHEDRAL : A REPORT TO THE RECTOR OF THE PARISH...CONTAINING OPINIONS OF CANADIAN COUNSEL AND EVIDENCE OF THE CHIEF CATHEDRAL AUTHORITIES IN ENGLAND, RELATIVE TO ECCLESIASTICAL LAW AND USAGE IN ENGLAND AND CANADA / Christ Church Cathedral. Montreal, Quebec – By the select vestry of the church. Montreal: Lovell, 1875. 00634. (Pre-1900 Canadiana) – 9 – cn C.I.H.M. [971]

CHRIST CHURCH: OTHER CHURCH SERVICES – 1886-1964. CCRSO1 – 1r – 1 – at Corangamite [910]

CHRIST CHURCH "PARISH RECORD" – 1909-1986. CCPR1-3 – 3r – 1 – at Corangamite [920]

CHRIST CHURCH SERVICES – 1874-1984. CCRS1-2 – 2r – 1 – at Corangamite [910]

CHRIST CHURCH VESTRY MINUTES – 1853-1986. CCR1-4 – 4r – 1 – at Corangamite [920]

CHRIST ENOUGH / Smith, Hannah Whitall – 1895 – 9 – us A.T.L.A. [240]

CHRIST FOR INDIA : BEING A PRESENTATION OF THE CHRISTIAN MESSAGE TO THE RELIGIOUS THOUGHT OF INDIA / Lucas, Bernard – London: Macmillan, 1910 – 2mf – 9 – 0-8370-6583-6 – 1986-0583 – us A.T.L.A. [230]

THE CHRIST FROM WITHOUT AND WITHIN : A STUDY OF THE GOSPEL BY ST JOHN / Clark, Henry William – New York: Fleming H Revell, 1907 – 1mf – 9 – 0-8370-2666-0 – 1985-0666 – us A.T.L.A. [220]

Christ, Grace H *see* JOURNAL OF PSYCHOSOCIAL ONCOLOGY

Christ, H *see*
- DIE FARNKRAEUTER DER ERDE
- DIE GEOGRAPHIE DER FARNE

CHRIST HIMSELF / McKenzie, Alexander – Boston: D. Lothrop, 1891. 1 fiche – 9 – us A.T.L.A. [240]

CHRIST IN ISAIAH : EXPOSITIONS OF ISAIAH 40-55 / Meyer, Frederick Brotherton – New York:Fleming H. Revell, c1895 – 1mf – 9 – 0-8370-4405-7 – 1985-2405 – us A.T.L.A. [220]

CHRIST IN LITERATURE: BEING A TREASURY OF CHOICE READINGS, IN PROSE AND VERSE / Eggleston, Edward – New York: J.B. Ford, 1875. 1 fiche – 9 – us A.T.L.A. [240]

CHRIST IN SONG : HYMNS OF IMMANUEL / ed by Schaff, Philip – New York: Anson D.F. Randolph, c1895 – 8mf – us A.T.L.A. [780]

CHRIST IN THE CHRISTIAN YEAR AND IN THE LIFE OF MAN / Huntington, Frederic Dan – 1881 – 9 – us A.T.L.A. [240]

CHRIST IN THE GOSPELS : OR, THE LIFE OF OUR LORD IN THE WORDS OF THE EVANGELISTS, AMERICAN REVISION, A.D. 1881 WITH SELFINTERPRETING SCRIPTURE, MAPS OF JESUS' TRAVELS, AND A DICTIONARY OF PROPER NAMES / Cadman, James Piper – (Includes index) – 6th ed. Chicago: American Publ Society of Hebrew, 1886 – 1mf – 9 – 0-8370-9132-2 – 1986-3132 – us A.T.L.A. [240]

CHRIST IN THE TABERNACLE: WITH SOME REMARKS ON THE OFFERINGS / White, Frank H – London: S.W. Partridge, 1883. 1 fiche. 8370-5821-X – 9 – us A.T.L.A. [240]

CHRIST IN THEOLOGY / Bushnell, Horace – 1851 – 1 – $50.00 – us Presbyterian [240]

Christ, J L *see* NATURGESCHICHTE. KLASSIFICATION UND NOMENCLATUR DER INSEKTEN VOM BIENEN

CHRIST LEGENDS / Lagerlof, Selma – New York: Henry Holt, 1908. 1 fiche – 9 – us A.T.L.A. [240]

CHRIST LORE : BEING THE LEGENDS, TRADITIONS, MYTHS, SYMBOLS, CUSTOMS, AND SUPERSTITIONS OF THE CHRISTIAN CHURCH / Hackwood, Frederick William – London: Elliot Stock, 1902 – 1mf – 9 – 0-8370-3444-2 – 1985-1444 – us A.T.L.A. [230]

CHRIST MYSTICAL : OR, THE BLESSED UNION OF CHRIST AND HIS MEMBERS / Hall, Joseph – London: Hodder & Stoughton, 1908 – 1mf – 9 – 0-8370-4745-5 – 1985-2745 – us A.T.L.A. [240]

THE CHRIST MYTH : A STUDY / Evans, Elizabeth Edison – New York:Truth Seeker Co., c1900 – 1mf – 9 – 0-8370-3078-1 – 1985-1078 – us A.T.L.A. [240]

CHRIST MYTH: A STUDY / Evans, Elizabeth Edison – New York: Truth Seeker Co., 1900. 1 fiche – 9 – us A.T.L.A. [240]

THE CHRIST OF HISTORY : AN ARGUMENT GROUNDED IN THE FACTS OF HIS LIFE ON EARTH / Young, John – New York: Robert Carter, 1857 – 1mf – 9 – 0-8370-5737-X – 1985-3737 – us A.T.L.A. [240]

THE CHRIST OF THE GOSPELS AND THE CHRIST OF MODERN CRITICISM : LECTURES ON M. RENAN'S "VIE DE JESUS" / Tulloch, John – Cincinnati: Poe & Hitchcock, 1865 – 1mf – 9 – 0-8370-5585-7 – 1985-3585 – us A.T.L.A. [240]

THE CHRIST OF THE GOSPELS AND THE CHRIST OF MODERN CRITICISM...M. RENAN'S VIE DE JESUS / Tulloch, John – Cincinnati: Poe & Hitchcock, 1865. 1 fiche – 9 – us A.T.L.A. [240]

THE CHRIST OF TO-DAY / Gordon, George Angier – (Includes bibliographical references) – Boston: Houghton, Mifflin, 1895 – 1mf – 9 – 0-8370-4843-5 – 1985-2843 – us A.T.L.A. [240]

CHRIST ON PARNASSUS : LECTURES ON ART, ETHIC, AND THEOLOGY / Forsyth, Peter Taylor – New York: Hodder and Stoughton, [1911?] – 1mf – us A.T.L.A. [240]

CHRIST ON THE THRONE OF POWER AND ANTICHRIST / Brown, Fortune Charles – Rochester: Union & Advertiser, 1885. 1 fiche – 9 – us A.T.L.A. [240]

CHRIST OR FRANCE? AN ANSWER TO THE COLLECTIVE LETTER WHICH THE SPANISH EPISCOPATE ISSUED TO THE BISHOPS OF THE WORLD – London, 1937. Fiche W 797. (Blodgett Collection of Spanish Civil War Pamphlets) – 9 – us H.U. College Libr [946]

Christ, Paul *see* DIE LEHRE VOM GEBET NACH DEM NEUEN TESTAMENT

LE CHRIST REPUBLICAIN – Paris: Bonaventure et Ducessois, jun 8-22/25 1848 – us Res Libr [944]

LE CHRIST REPUBLICAIN-DEMOCRATE-SOCIALISTE – Paris: Beaule et Maignand, jan-mar 1849 – us Res Libr [944]

CHRIST SEUL – 1962-93 (complete) – 9r – 1 – ATLA S0422 – us A.T.L.A. [240]

THE CHRIST THAT IS TO BE / Dougall, Lily – (Includes bibliographical references) – New York: Macmillan, 1907 – 1mf – 9 – 0-8370-3634-8 – 1985-1634 – us A.T.L.A. [240]

CHRIST THD VITALIZING PRINCIPLE OF CHRISTIAN THEOLOGY: AN ADDRESS / Brown, William Adams – New York: Wm. C. Martin, 1898. 1 fiche – 9 – us A.T.L.A. [240]

CHRIST THE BREAD OF LIFE : AN ATTEMPT TO GIVE A PROFITABLE DIRECTION TO THE PRESENT OCCUPATION OF THOUGHT WITH ROMANISM / Campbell, John M'Leod – London: Macmillan, 1869 – 1mf – us A.T.L.A. [240]

CHRIST THE CENTRAL EVIDENCE OF CHRISTIANITY / Cairns, John – New York:American Tract Society, [188-?] – 1mf – 9 – 0-8370-2567-2 – 1985-0567 – us A.T.L.A. [230]

CHRIST, THE CHURCH, AND MAN : AN ESSAY ON NEW METHODS IN ECCLESIASTICAL STUDIES AND WORKSHOP: WITH SOME REMARKS ON A NEW APOLOGIA FOR CHRISTIANITY IN RELATION TO THE SOCIAL QUESTION / Capecelatro, Alfonso – London: Burns & Oates; St Louis, MO: B Herder, 1909 – 1mf – 9 – 0-8370-6970-X – 1986-0970 – us A.T.L.A. [240]

CHRIST THE LORD: THE REVEALER OF GOD...WITH A REPLY TO BISHOP COLENSO ...JEHOVAH / Tyler, Thomas – London: Hamilton, Adams, 1863. 1 fiche – 9 – us A.T.L.A. [240]

CHRIST, THE MORNING STAR : AND OTHER SERMONS / Cairns, John – London: Hodder and Stoughton, 1892 – 1mf – us A.T.L.A. [240]

CHRIST THE ORATOR : OR, NEVER MAN SPAKE LIKE THIS MAN: ECCE ORATOR / Hyde, Thomas Alexander – Boston: Arena, 1893 – 1mf – 9 – 0-8370-3713-1 – 1985-1713 – us A.T.L.A. [240]

DER CHRIST UND DIE SUENDE BEI PAULUS / Wernle, Paul – (Includes bibliographical references) – Freiburg i.B.: J C B Mohr (Paul Siebeck), 1897 – 1mf – 9 – 0-8370-9345-7 – 1986-3345 – us A.T.L.A. [220]

CHRIST UND WELT – Stuttgart, 6 Jun 1948-26 Mar 1971 – 24r – DM1800.00 – gw Mikro Press [240]

CHRIST UND WELT – Stuttgart. Jan.-Dec. 1955 (complete) – 1 – 35.00r – us Hoover Inst Photo [240]

CHRIST UND WELT *see*
- DEUTSCHE ZEITUNG / CHRIST UND WELT
- DEUTSCHE ZEITUNG/CHRIST UND WELT
- RHEINISCHER MERKUR / CHRIST UND WELT

CHRIST UND WELT/RHEINISCHER MERKUR – Koblenz. 1979- – 22125.00y; CPC; 9 – gw Alpha Com [072]

CHRIST VERSUS CHRISTIANITY : THE CHRISTIAN CHURCH CROSS-EXAMINED BY A MODERN LAWYER / Hale, William Pillsbury – Boston: American Elzevir, 1892 – 1mf – 9 – 0-8370-3450-7 – 1985-1450 – us A.T.L.A. [240]

Christ, W *see* ANTHOLOGIA GRAECA CARMINUM CHRISTIANORUM

CHRISTABEL / Coleridge, Samuel Taylor – London: H. Frowde, 1907 – 1 roll – 1 – 1-55879-737-8 – uk Libr Preservation [810]

Christaller, Johann Gottlieb *see*
- A COLLECTION OF THREE THOUSAND AND SIX HUNDRED TSHI PROVERBS IN USE AMONG THE NEGROES OF THE GOLD COAST SPEAKING THE ASANTE AND FANTE LANGUAGE
- TWI MANUSCRIPTS, 1855-1907

Christaller, Th. *see* HANDBUCH DER DUALA-SPRACHE

O CHRISTAO BRASILEIRO : PERIODICO MENSAL DESTINADO PARA O ESTADO DE ALAGOAS – Maceio, Alagoas. 1 Ago 1901 – 1,5,6 – bl Biblioteca [072]

CHRISTCHURCH STAR-SUN – New Zealand. Christchurch Star. -d. 21 March 1941-16 Dec 1944; 7-25 May, 20 July 1945-10 Sept 1960; 7, 11 March, 30 Nov, 1, 30 Dec 1961; 3 Jan-19 Feb, 14 Sept 1962; 3 April 1963-Oct 1971. 292 reels – 1 – uk British Libr Newspaper [072]

CHRISTELIICKEN WAERSEGGHER, DE PRINCIPALE STUCKEN VAN T'CHRISTEN GELOOF EN LEVEN INT CORT BEGRIJPENDE / David, J – Antwerpen, 1603 – 7mf – 9 – ne IDC [700]

EEN CHRISTELIJCKE ENDE LIEFLIJCKE VERMANINGE AEN ALLEN OUERHEYDEN, GHELEERDEN. GHEMENEN VOLCKE, SECTEN, ENDE BRUYDT CHRISTI, DIE VAN DIE HETTE DER SONNEN NIET WEYNICH OP ALLE PLAETSEN VERBRANT WORT / Simons, Menno – BME-281 1 – 9 – ne IDC [240]

EEN CHRISTELIJCKE SENTBRIEF, GESCHREUEN WTER GEUANCKENISSE / Joriaensz, Thijs – 1579. BME-203 1 – 9 – ne IDC [240]

EEN CHRISTELIJCKE SENTBRIEF, GESCHREUEN WTER GEUANCKNISSE...WAARACHTER NOG EEN SENTBRIEF EN EEN LIEDEKEN / Joriaensz, Thijs – 1577. BME-202 1 – 9 – ne IDC [240]

EEN CHRISTELIJCKE SENTBRIEF, VAN DE SENDINGHE, INLEYDINGHE ENDE COEMSTE JESU CHRISTI IN DESER WERELT / Joriaensz, Thijs – Amstelredam, W. J. Buys. 1586. BME-204 1 – 9 – ne IDC [240]

CHRISTELIJCKE VERANTWOORDINGHE, ENDE BILLIJCKE NEDERLEGGINGE DES VALSCHEN ONGHEGRONDEDEN OORDEELS, LASTERENS ENDE SCHELDENS / Blesdijk, Nicolaas M van – Wtgegaen int Jaer 1546. 1607. BME-385 1 – 9 – ne IDC [240]

CHRISTELIJCKE WAERSCHOUWINGHE. DATMENT NIEMANT OM SIJN GHELOOF EN BEHOORT TE BELEYDIGHEN NOCH TE VERVOLGEN, VEELE MIN TE DOODEN / Joris, David – 1554. BME-370 1 – 9 – ne IDC [240]

CHRISTELIJKE GEREFORMEERDE KERKEN : JAARBOEK – 1968-92 (complete) – Inquire – 1 – ATLA S0506 – us A.T.L.A. [240]

CHRISTELYKE AANDACHTEN OF VLAMMENDE ZIEL-ZUCHTEN, EENER GODVREESENDE ZIELE, MET EEN GODDELIJK ANTWOORD DAAR OP PASSENDE : SAMEN-GESTELT EN GERYMT DOOR GERRIT HESMAN, DOKKUMER / Hesman, Gerrit – (Frontispiece missing) – 1st ed. Deventer, 1728 – 2mf – 9 – O-3080/1 – ne IDC [760]

CHRISTELYKE BEDENKINGEN EN VOORBEELDLYKE ZEEDELESSEN AFGELEID UIT 'S WERELDS EERSTE TOESTAND : DES MENSCHEN LEEVEN, AMPTEN, STAATEN, KONSTEN EN NEIGINGEN DES GEMOEDS / Graauwhart, Hendrik – Amsterdam, 1756 – 4mf – 9 – O-3072/1 – ne IDC [760]

CHRISTELYKE STAETS-VORST IN HONDERT SIN-SPREUKEN... / Saavedra, Faxardo D de – Amsterdam, 1662 – 11mf – 9 – ne IDC [700]

Christen, Ada *see* UNSERE NACHBARN

CHRISTENDOM : THE CHRISTIAN CHURCHES CONSTITUTIONAL, FORMS AND WAYS / Molland, E – London, 1959 – 9mf – 8 – ne Slangenburg [240]

CHRISTENDOM : A JOURNAL OF CHRISTIAN SOCIOLOGY – v1-16. 1931-50 (complete) – 3r – 1 – ATLA S0006 – us A.T.L.A. [073]

CHRISTENDOM'S DIVISIONS : BEING A PHILOSOPHICAL SKETCH OF THE DIVISIONS OF THE CHRISTIAN FAMILY IN EAST AND WEST: TO BE FOLLOWED BY A HISTORY OF THE DIFFERENT RE-UNIONS WHICH HAVE BEEN PROJECTED IN BOTH UP TO THE PRESENT TIME / Ffoulkes, Edmund S – Pt 1. London: Longman, Green, Longman, Roberts & Green, 1865. (Christendom's divisions) – 1mf – us A.T.L.A. [240]

DIE CHRISTENKATASTROPHE UNTER NERO : NACH IHREN QUELLEN, INSBESONDERE NACH TAC. ANN. XV, 44 / Klette, E Theodore – Tuebingen: J.C.B. Mohr, 1907 – 1mf – us A.T.L.A. [930]

CHRISTENLEHRE – 1948-92 (complete) – Inquire – 1 – ATLA S0657 – us A.T.L.A. [073]

EINE CHRISTENLICHE ANTWORDT DENEN / Greyffenberger, H – 1524. BME-23 1 – 9 – ne IDC [240]

CHRISTENLICHE VNDTERWEISUNG AN DIE WIDERTAUFFER VON DEM TAUFF DER JUNGEN KINDLEIN. VND VON DER GAISTLICHEN VNND WELTLICHEN OBERKAIT, AN DIE WIDERTAUFFER / Fabri von Hailbrunn, J – Ingolstatt, A. u. S. Weissenhorn gebrued. 1550. BME-133 1 – 9 – ne IDC [240]

Christensen, C F A *see*
- INDEX FILICUM
- INDEX OF FLORA AEGYPTIACO-ARABICA AND HERBARIUM FORSKALII
- A MONOGRAPH OF THE GENUS DRYOPTERIS
- REGISTER TIL FLORA AEGYPTIACO-ARABICA OG HERBARIUM. FORSKALII
- UEBER EINIGE FARNE IN O.P. SWARTZ' HERBARIUM

Christensen, Kimberly M *see* EFFECTS OF AN INTERVAL TRAINING DANCE CLASS ON SELECT CARDIOVASCULAR VARIABLES

Christensen, Mogens et al *see* DIE GRATULANTEN KOMMEN

DAS CHRISTENTHUM UND DIE EINSPRUECHE SEINER GEGNER : EINE APOLOGETIK FUER JEDEN GEBILDETEN / Vosen, Christian Hermann – 4. Aufl. Freiburg i.B.; St Louis, MO: Herder, 1881 – 2mf – 9 – 0-8370-6954-8 – 1986-0954 – us A.T.L.A. [230]

CHRISTENTHUM UND SOCIALISMUS / Hohoff, Kaplan – Leipzig, 1878 – 1 – DM30.00 – gw Mikro Press [240]

DAS CHRISTENTUM : FUENF EINZELDARSTELLUNGEN / Cornill, Carl Heinrich et al – Leipzig:Quelle & Meyer, 1908 – 1mf – 9 – 0-8370-2656-3 – 1985-0656 – us A.T.L.A. [240]

DAS CHRISTENTUM / Hammerstein, Ludwig von – (Includes index) – Trier: Paulus-Druckerei, 1893 – 1mf – 9 – 0-8370-7064-3 – 1986-1064 – us A.T.L.A. [230]

DAS CHRISTENTUM IN DEN ERSTEN DREI JAHRHUNDERTEN / Achelis, Hans – Leipzig: Quelle & Meyer, 1912 – 2mf – us A.T.L.A. [240]

DAS CHRISTENTUM UND DIE CHRISTLICHE KIRCHE DER DREI ERSTEN JAHRHUNDERTE / Baur, Ferdinand Christian – Tuebingen: Fues, 1853 – 5mf – us A.T.L.A. [240]

CHRISTENTUM UND DIE GESCHICHTE / Harnack, Adolf von – London: Adam & Charles Black, 1896 – 1mf – 9 – 0-8370-3478-7 – 1985-1478 – us A.T.L.A. [240]

DAS CHRISTENTUM UND DIE MONISTISCHE RELIGION / Werner, Max – (Includes bibliographical references) – Berlin: Karl Curtius, 1908, c1905 – 1mf – 9 – 0-8370-5791-4 – 1985-3791 – us A.T.L.A. [240]

DAS CHRISTENTUM UND DIE PHILOSOPHIE : EIN VORTRAG / Kaftan, Julius – Leipzig: J C Hinrichs, 1895 – 1mf – 9 – 0-8370-3828-6 – 1985-1828 – us A.T.L.A. [240]

CHRISTENTUM UND KIRCHENTUM / Knortz, Karl – Leipzig: Teichmann, 1909. 1 fiche – 9 – us A.T.L.A. [240]

CHRISTENTUM UND KULTUR : EIN ORIENTIERENDER VORTRAG / Haack, Ernst – Schwerin i. M.: Fr Bahn, 1897 – 1mf – 9 – 0-8370-3438-8 – 1985-1438 – us A.T.L.A. [306]

DIE CHRISTENVERFOLGUNGEN IM ROEMISCHEN REICHE / Cohn, Max Conrat – Leipzig: J.C. Hinrichs, 1897 – 1mf – us A.T.L.A. [240]

CHRISTI WORTE UEBER VOLLENDUNG DER WEGE GOTTES : MIT SEINER KIRCHE, DEM VOLKE ISRAEL UND DER GANZEN MENSCHHEIT UND SCHOEPFUNG / Caird, William Renny & Lutz, Johann Georg – Augsburg:Richard Preyss, 1879 – 1mf – 9 – 0-8370-2565-6 – 1985-0565 – us A.T.L.A. [240]

LA CHRISTIADE OU LE PARADIS RECONQUIS: POUR SERVIR DE SUITE AU "PARADIS PERDU" DE MILTON / La Baume-Desdossat, Jacques Francois de – Paris: M. Lambert, 1752.46p. 1 fiche.(Literature Collection) – 9 – $6.00 – fr Bibl Nationale [810]

CHRISTIAN – Cambridge, England. v1-11. 1973-86 (complete) – 3r – 1 – ATLA S0749 – us A.T.L.A. [073]

THE CHRISTIAN – Kansas City. v5-10, 1929-34. 2 reels – 1 – us A.T.L.A. [073]

THE CHRISTIAN – Saint John, N.B.: W.W. Eaton, 1839-1848 – 9 – cn C.I.H.M. [240]

THE CHRISTIAN : A WEEKLY RECORD OF CHRISTIAN LIFE – (Lacking: 1890-93. 1908-12) – London, 1882-1925 – 34r – 1 – ATLA S0445 – us A.T.L.A. [073]

Christian A Herter *see* THE PAPERS OF JOHN FOSTER DULLES AND OF CHRISTIAN A. HERTER, 1953-61

CHRISTIAN ACHIEVEMENT IN AMERICA / Beardsley, Frank Grenville – Chicago, Ill.: Winona, c1907 – 1mf – us A.T.L.A. [240]

CHRISTIAN ADVENTURES IN SOUTH AFRICA / Taylor, William MacKergo – London: Jackson, Walford, and Hodder; New York: Carlton & Porter, [1867?] – 2mf – 9 – 0-8370-6529-1 – 1986-0529 – us A.T.L.A. [240]

CHRISTIAN ADVENTURES IN SOUTH AFRICA / Taylor, William MacKergo – New York: Nelson & Phillips, 1877. 557p. illus. Introd. by William B. Boyce – 1 – us U.W. Library [240]

CHRISTIAN ADVOCATE – (Lacking: v100.106) – Pittsburgh. v1-99 no 5; v107 no 6-24. 1834-1932 (incomplete) – 59r – 1 – ATLA S0071 – us A.T.L.A. [073]

CHRISTIAN ADVOCATE – (Lacking: v13 no 9. v26-28 1862-68) – Nashville. v11-75. 1846-1914 – 49r – 1 – ATLA S0023 – us A.T.L.A. [073]

CHRISTIAN ADVOCATE – London. -w. Jan 7 1830-Sep 2 1839. 4 reels – 1 – uk British Libr Newspaper [072]

CHRISTIAN ADVOCATE – New York. v1-131. 1826-1956 (complete) – 148r – 1 – ATLA S0012 – us A.T.L.A. [073]

CHRISTIAN ADVOCATE – (Some pgs lacking) – Northwestern ed. v1-188. 1853-1940 – 99r – 1 – ATLA S0133 – us A.T.L.A. [073]

CHRISTIAN ADVOCATE – (Title varies. Some vols missing) – Central ed. v1-143. 1866-1968 – 76r – 1 – ATLA S0180 – us A.T.L.A. [073]

CHRISTIAN ADVOCATE – (v57- . 5,6,9) – Western ed. v. 1- 1921- – 1 – us UMI [240]

CHRISTIAN AGE – 1849-56 (complete) – 2r – 1 – ATLA R0125 – us A.T.L.A. [073]

CHRISTIAN ALLIANCE AND FOREIGN MISSIONARY WEEKLY *see* ALLIANCE WITNESS

CHRISTIAN ALTERNATIVE MOVEMENT OF AUSTRALIA – With: The Integrity Policies, 1983. 3p – 9 – $1.00f – at Libertarian Micro [360]

CHRISTIAN AND CHURCH (A SERMON) / Clarke, W Newton – 1882 – 1 – 5.00 – us Baptist [240]

CHRISTIAN AND MISSIONARY ALLIANCE *see* ALLIANCE WITNESS

Christian and Missionary Alliance *see* PRAYER MANUAL FOR THE INDONESIAN MISSION

CHRISTIAN AND MOHAMMEDAN : A PLEA FOR BRIDGING THE CHASM / Herrick, George F – New York: F.H. Revell, c1912 – 1mf – us A.T.L.A. [230]

THE CHRISTIAN AND THE STATE / Brennan, Geoffrey – Comments by J.K. Williams and W.R. Stent. 1983, 35p – 9 – 1.00f – at Libertarian Micro [335]

CHRISTIAN APOLOGETICS : A SERIES OF ADDRESSES / Henslow, George et al; ed by Seton, Walter Warren – New York: E P Dutton, 1903 – 1mf – 9 – 0-8370-5232-7 – 1985-3232 – us A.T.L.A. [230]

CHRISTIAN ARCHAEOLOGY / Bennett, Charles W – New York: Hunt & Eaton; Cincinnati: Cranston & Jennings, c1888. (Library of biblical and theological literature; v4) – 2mf – us A.T.L.A. [240]

CHRISTIAN ASPECTS OF PEACE PAMPHLET COLLECTION – 1983 – 1 – CSUXAMJ7765-B – us Hoover Inst Photo [240]
Christian Association for Psychological Studies *see* PROCEEDINGS OF THE ANNUAL CONVENTION
CHRISTIAN ATTITUDES ON JEWS AND JUDAISM – (v46- . 1976- . 5,6,9) – v. 1-. 1968- – 1 – us UMI [240]
THE CHRISTIAN AWAKENING OF FAITH (CCC195) = SHENG TAO CH'I HSIN LUN / Hsu, Sung-shih – (In Chinese) – Shanghai: Christian Literature Society, 1940 – 1r – 1 – 1984-B500 – us A.T.L.A. [240]
CHRISTIAN BANNER – Philadelphia. New England Missionary and Educational Baptist Convention/South Jersey Association/National Baptist Convention of America. 1900-01, 1915-19 – 1 – 38.00 – us A.B.H.S. [073]
THE CHRISTIAN BANNER – (Cont by: The Banner of the Faith) – Cobourg [Ont.]: D. Oliphant, [1852?-1858] – 9 – cn C.I.H.M. [240]
THE CHRISTIAN BANNER *see* THE WITNESS OF TRUTH
CHRISTIAN BAPTISM: A LECTURE IN REPLY TO A SERMON BY REV. D. M. WILSON / Annand, Edward – Halifax, 1870. 04110. (Pre-1900 Canadiana) – 9 – cn C.I.H.M. [240]
CHRISTIAN BAPTISM (ILLUSTRATED): ITS PROPER SUBJECTS AND PROPER ACT, WITH A BRIEF HISTORY OF BAPTIST PRINCIPLES AND PRACTICES... : ALSO A BIOGRAPHICAL SKETCH OF THE LIFE AND LABORS OF REV. CHARLES HADDON SPURGEON, PASTOR OF THE METROPOLITAN TABERNACLE, LONDON, ENGLAND / Carey, T H – Essex, Ont.: Free Press Book Rooms, 1891. 00478. (Pre-1900 Canadiana) – 9 – cn C.I.H.M. [240]
CHRISTIAN BEACON – Collingswood, NJ. v15-28. 1950-64 (complete) – 5r – 1 – ATLA S0089 – us A.T.L.A. [073]
CHRISTIAN BELIEF AND LIFE / Peabody, Andrew Preston – Boston: Roberts, 1876, c1875 – 1mf – 9 – 0-8370-5255-6 – 1985-3255 – us A.T.L.A. [240]
CHRISTIAN BELIEF INTERPRETED BY CHRISTIAN EXPERIENCE / Hall, Charles Cuthbert – Chicago: University of Chicago Press, 1905. 1 fiche – 9 – us A.T.L.A. [240]
CHRISTIAN BELIEFS RECONSIDERED IN THE LIGHT OF MODERN THOUGHT / Henslow, George – (Includes bibliographical references) – London: Frederic Norgate, 1884 – 1mf – 9 – 0-8370-3562-7 – 1985-1562 – us A.T.L.A. [240]
CHRISTIAN BERARD / Reunion des musees nationaux. Paris – 1950. 16 illus. 1 fiche – 9 – fr Réunion [750]
CHRISTIAN BIOGRAPHIES (CCC270) / Richard, Timothy, Mrs – (In Chinese) – Shanghai: Society for the Diffusion of Christian and General Knowledge among the Chinese. 10v. 1900-1901 – 1r – 1 – 1984-6609 – us A.T.L.A. [920]
CHRISTIAN BROADCAST BULLETIN – v1-5. 1937-40 (incomplete) – 1r – 1 – ATLA S0707C – us A.T.L.A. [073]
CHRISTIAN BROTHERHOODS / Leete, Frederick Deland – Cincinnati: Jennings and Graham; New York: Eaton and Mains, c1912 – 1mf – us A.T.L.A. [240]
Christian Brothers *see*
- ARITHMETIQUE: COURS ELEMENTAIRE: LIVRE DE L'ELEVE
- HISTOIRE DU CANADA: COURS ELEMENTAIRE

THE CHRISTIAN CALLING / Davies, John Llewelyn – London: Macmillan, 1875 – 1mf – us A.T.L.A. [240]
CHRISTIAN CENTURY – (v. 85-. 1968- 5,6. v. 87-. 1970- 9) – v. 17- 1900- – 1 – us UMI [240]
THE CHRISTIAN CHALLENGE – v1-31. 1962-92 (complete) – Inquire – 1 – ATLA S0865 – us A.T.L.A. [073]
CHRISTIAN CHARITY IN THE ANCIENT CHURCH / Uhlhorn, Gerhard – 1883 – 1 – us A.T.L.A. [240]
CHRISTIAN CHARITY IN THE ANCIENT CHURCH / Uhlhorn, Gerhard – Trans. from the German with author's sanction. New York: Scribners, 1883. vi,424p – 1 – us U.W. Library [240]
CHRISTIAN CHRONICLE – 1846-63 (complete) – 3r – 1 – ATLA R0108 – us A.T.L.A. [073]
CHRISTIAN CHURCH IN CHINA (CCC334) = KUAN YU CHUNG-KUO CHI-TU-CHIAO SAN-TZU AI-KUO YUN- TUNG TI PAO-KAO : REPORT OF THE THREE-SELF PATRIOTIC MOVEMENT AT NATIONAL CHRISTIAN CONFERENCE, 1956 / Wu, Yao-tsung – (In Chinese) – [s.l: s.n, 1956?] – 1r – 1 – 1984-6673 – us A.T.L.A. [240]
THE CHRISTIAN CHURCH IN THESE ISLANDS BEFORE THE COMING OF AUGUSTINE / Browne, G F – London: S.P.C.K.; New York: E. & J.B. Young, 1899 – 1mf – us A.T.L.A. [240]
CHRISTIAN CIVILISATION : WITH SPECIAL REFERENCE TO INDIA / Cunningham, William – London: Macmillan, 1880 – 1mf – us A.T.L.A. [900]
CHRISTIAN CONCEPTION AND EXPERIENCE / Gill, William Icrin – New York: Authors' Publ Co, 1877 – 1mf – 9 – 0-8370-3286-5 – 1985-1286 – us A.T.L.A. [240]
THE CHRISTIAN CONCEPTION OF HOLINESS / Askwith, Edward Harrison – London, New York: Macmillan, 1900 – 1mf – 9 – 0-8370-2515-X – 1985-0515 – us A.T.L.A. [230]
Christian Conference. 1888. Montreal, Quebec *see* VITAL QUESTIONS: THE DISCUSSIONS OF THE GENERAL CHRISTIAN CONFERENCE...OCTOBER 22ND TO 25TH
Christian Conference of Asia *see* CCA NEWS
THE CHRISTIAN CONQUEST OF ASIA : STUDIES AND PERSONAL OBSERVATIONS OF ORIENTAL RELIGIONS: BEING THE MORSE LECTURES OF 1898 / Barrows, John Henry – New York: Scribner, 1899 – 1mf – us A.T.L.A. [240]
THE CHRISTIAN CONQUEST OF INDIA / Thoburn, James Mills – (Includes index) – 1st ed. New York: Young People's Missionary Movement, c1906 – 1mf – 9 – 0-8370-6420-1 – 1986-0420 – us A.T.L.A. [240]
THE CHRISTIAN CONSERVATOR *see* THE UNITED BRETHREN
CHRISTIAN CONTRIBUTOR – 1846-50 (complete) – 1r – 1 – ATLA R0102 – us A.T.L.A. [073]
CHRISTIAN COUNCIL QUARTERLY – (Lacking: nos 24,44,45. Cont by: Kairos) – nos 23-88. 1949-68 – 1r – 1 – ATLA S0704B – us A.T.L.A. [073]
THE CHRISTIAN CREED / Leathes, Stanley – 1878 – 9 – us A.T.L.A. [240]
CHRISTIAN DEMOCRATIC REVIEW – 1954-61 (complete) – 1r – 1 – ATLA S0547 – us A.T.L.A. [073]
CHRISTIAN DIETRICH GRABBE / Gottschall, Rudolf von – (Includes index) – Leipzig: P Reclam, [1901] – 1r – 1 – us U.W. Library [430]
CHRISTIAN DIETRICH GRABBE IN DER NACHSCHILLERISCHEN ENTWICKELUNG / Gieben, Joseph – (Includes bibliographical references) – [Luedinghausen]: Selbstverlag, [19–?] – 1 – us U.W. Library [430]
CHRISTIAN DOCTRINE / Greene, William Brenton – Philadelphia: Westminster Press, 1906, c1905 – 1mf – 9 – 0-8370-4803-6 – 1985-2803 – us A.T.L.A. [240]
CHRISTIAN DOCTRINE: A SERIES OF DISCOURSES / Dale, Robert William – New York: A.C. Armstrong, 1895. 1 fiche – 9 – us A.T.L.A. [240]
CHRISTIAN DOCTRINE AND MORALS VIEWED IN THEIR CONNEXION : BEING THE TWENTY-FOURTH FERNLEY LECTURE / Findlay, George G – London: C.H. Kelly, 1894 – 1mf – us A.T.L.A. [240]
THE CHRISTIAN DOCTRINE OF GOD / Clarke, William Newton – New York: C. Scribner, 1910, c1909 – 2mf – us A.T.L.A. [240]
CHRISTIAN DOCTRINES AND MODERN THOUGHT : THE BOYLE LECTURES FOR 1891 / Bonney, Thomas G – London, New York: Longmans, Green, 1892 – 1mf – us A.T.L.A. [240]
CHRISTIAN EDUCATION / O'Connell, Cornelius Joseph – New York: Benziger, 1906 – 1mf – 9 – 0-8370-6925-4 – 1986-0925 – us A.T.L.A. [370]
CHRISTIAN EDUCATION: A SERMON PREACHED IN CHRIST CHURCH CATHEDRAL, SUNDAY, JANUARY 22, 1871 / Baldwin, Maurice Scollard – Montreal: J. Lovell, 1871. 00839. (Pre-1900 Canadiana) – 9 – cn C.I.H.M. [240]
CHRISTIAN EDUCATION AND THE NATIONAL CONSCIOUSNESS IN CHINA (CCC320) = TSUNG CHIAO CHIAO YU YU KUO HUN / Webster, James B – (In Chinese) – Shanghai: Christian Literature Society, 1926 – 1r – 1 – 1984-6659 – us A.T.L.A. [240]
CHRISTIAN EDUCATION IN AMERICA : A LECTURE / Keane, John J – Washington: Church News Pub Co, 1892 – 1mf – 9 – 0-8370-7551-3 – 1986-1551 – us A.T.L.A. [240]
CHRISTIAN EDUCATION JOURNAL – (1985-. 5,6,9) – v3-. 1983- – 1 – us UMI [240]
CHRISTIAN EGYPT : PAST, PRESENT, AND FUTURE / Fowler, Montague – (Includes bibliographical references and index) – London: Church Newspaper Co, 1901 – 1mf – 9 – 0-8370-7632-3 – 1986-1632 – us A.T.L.A. [240]
CHRISTIAN EPOCH-MAKERS : THE STORY OF THE GREAT MISSIONARY ERAS IN THE HISTORY OF CHRISTIANITY / Vedder, Henry Clay – (Includes bibliographies and index) – Philadelphia: Griffith & Rowland, 1908 – 1mf – 9 – 0-8370-6438-4 – 1986-0438 – us A.T.L.A. [240]
CHRISTIAN ETHICS : EIGHT LECTURES / Strong, Thomas Banks – (Includes bibliographical references and index) – London; New York: Longmans, Green, 1896 – 1mf – 9 – 0-8370-6417-1 – 1986-0417 – us A.T.L.A. [170]
CHRISTIAN ETHICS AND MODERN THOUGHT / D'Arcy, Charles Frederick – London, New York: Longmans, Green, 1912 – 1mf – us A.T.L.A. [170]
CHRISTIAN ETHICS AND SOCIAL PROGRESS / Harper, J Wilson – London: J. Nisbet, 1912 – 1mf – us A.T.L.A. [170]
CHRISTIAN ETHICS AND WISE SAYINGS – (Includes index) – London: James Nisbet, 1883 – 1mf – 9 – 0-8370-6078-8 – 1986-0078 – us A.T.L.A. [080]
CHRISTIAN ETHICS (CCC70) = CHI TU CHIAO TI LUN LI / Chao, Tzu-ch'en – (In Chinese) – Shanghai: Association Press of China, 1948 – 1r – 1 – 1984-B500 – us A.T.L.A. [240]
THE CHRISTIAN EVANGEL – Chicago, IL. v1-23. 1910-33 (complete) – 4r – 1 – ATLA 1993-S012 – us A.T.L.A. [073]
THE CHRISTIAN EVANGEL – Scottdale, PA. v24-45. 1936-57 (complete) – 3r – 1 – ATLA 1993-S013 – us A.T.L.A. [073]
Christian Evidence Society *see* POPULAR OBJECTIONS TO REVEALED TRUTH
CHRISTIAN EVIDENCES / Robinson, Ezekiel Gilman – New York: Silver, Burdett, 1895.1 fiche. 8370-4935-0 – 9 – us A.T.L.A. [240]
CHRISTIAN EVOLUTIONISM AND ITS INFLUENCE ON RELIGIOUS THOUGHT / Martin, Daniel Strobel – New York: Wilbur B. Ketcham, 1887. 1 fiche. 8370-4294-1 – 9 – us A.T.L.A. [240]
CHRISTIAN EXAMINER – Lexington. Kentucky. v. 1. 1830 – 1 – 16.87 – us Baptist [240]
CHRISTIAN EXAMINER – London. Jan 1841-June 1848. -m. 1mqn reels – 1 – uk British Libr Newspaper [072]
CHRISTIAN EXERTION / Peck, George – 1845 – 9 – us A.T.L.A. [240]
THE CHRISTIAN EXPONENT – v1-5. 1924-28 (complete) – Inquire – 1 – ATLA 1993-S010 – us A.T.L.A. [073]
CHRISTIAN EXPRESS – Lovedale, South Africa – sa SA Libr [072]
CHRISTIAN EXPRESS *see* SOUTH AFRICAN OUTLOOK
CHRISTIAN FAITH : FIVE SERMONS / Smith, William Saumarez – London: Macmillan, 1869 – 1mf – 9 – 0-8370-5166-5 – 1985-3166 – us A.T.L.A. [240]
CHRISTIAN FAITH : ITS NATURE, OBJECT, CAUSES, AND EFFECTS / Godwin, John Henry – London: Jackson, Walford, & Hodder, 1862 – 1mf – 9 – 0-8370-4918-0 – 1985-2918 – us A.T.L.A. [240]
THE CHRISTIAN FAITH / Curtis, Alfred – New York: Eaton & Mains; Cincinnati: Jennings & Graham, c1905 – 2mf – us A.T.L.A. [240]
CHRISTIAN FAITH AND LIFE – v37-45. 1931-39 (complete) – Inquire – 1 – ATLA 1993-S518 – us A.T.L.A. [073]
CHRISTIAN FAITH AND LIFE (CCC150) / Ho, Shih-ming – (In Chinese) – 1st ed. Hong Kong: Council on Christian Literature for Overseas Chinese, 1956 – 1r – 1 – 1984-B500 – us A.T.L.A. [240]
THE CHRISTIAN FAITH AND THE OLD TESTAMENT / Thomas, John Martin – New York: Thomas Y. Crowell, 1908. 1 fiche – 9 – us A.T.L.A. [240]
CHRISTIAN FAITH IN AN AGE OF SCIENCE / Rice, William North – New York: Hodder & Stoughton, 1903. 1 fiche. 8370-4892-3 – 9 – us A.T.L.A. [240]
Christian Faith Society *see* PAPERS
THE CHRISTIAN FAMILY (CCC225) / Liu, Mary – (In Chinese) – 1st ed. Hong Kong: Council on Christian Literature for Overseas Chinese, 1955 – 1r – 1 – 1984-B500 – us A.T.L.A. [240]
THE CHRISTIAN FAMILY IN CHANGING EAST ASIA (CCC246) / ed by Manikam, Rajah B & Highbaugh, Irma – (In Chinese) – 1st ed. Hong Kong: Council on Christian Literature for Overseas Chinese, 1956 – 1r – 1 – 1984-6585 – us A.T.L.A. [640]
CHRISTIAN FARMER = T'IEN CHIA – v1-18. 1934-52 (complete) – 2r – 1 – ATLA S0316 – us A.T.L.A. [073]
CHRISTIAN FELIX WEISSE UND SEINE BEZIEHUNGEN ZUR DEUTSCHEN LITERATUR DES ACHTZEHNTEN JAHRHUNDERTS / Minor, Jacob – (Includes bibliographical references) – Innsbruck: Wagner, 1880 – 1r – 1 – us U.W. Library [430]
CHRISTIAN FELLOWSHIP HYMNS (CCC80) : PREPARED IN THE NAME OF THE YENTA CHRISTIAN FELLOWSHIP / ed by Chao, Tzu-ch'en – (In Chinese) – Peiping: School of Religion, Yenching University, 1931 – 1r – 1 – 1984-B500 – us A.T.L.A. [240]
Christian Foodship Committee *see* CHRISTIANS AND SPAIN
CHRISTIAN FREE PRESS – (Library has: no. 2-13, 15, 17, 19-27, 29 (Oct. 1936-June 1939)) – Glendale, Calif.: Militant Christian Patriots, 193u – 1 – CSUX89-S91 – us Hoover Inst Photo [240]
CHRISTIAN FREEMAN – 1867-70 (complete) – 2r – 1 – ATLA R0110 – us A.T.L.A. [073]
CHRISTIAN FRIEDRICH HUNOLD (MENANTES) : (1681-1721): SEIN LEBEN UND SEINE WERKE: EINE MONOGRAPHIE / Vogel, Hermann – (Includes bibliographical references) – Leipzig: E Graefe, [1898] – 1r – 1 – us U.W. Library [920]
CHRISTIAN FRIEDRICH SCHERENBERG UND DAS LITERARISCHE BERLIN VON 1840 BIS 1860 / Fontane, Theodor – Berlin: W Hertz, 1885 – 1r – 1 – us U.W. Library [430]
THE CHRISTIAN FRONT – v1-4. 1936-39 (complete) – Inquire – 1 – ATLA 1994-S500 – us A.T.L.A. [073]
THE CHRISTIAN FUNDAMENTALIST – v1-6. 1927-32 (complete) – Inquire – 1 – ATLA 1993-S513 – us A.T.L.A. [073]
THE CHRISTIAN GEM – Halifax, N.S.: W. Cunnabell & J. Belcher, no 1 (Sept 1845)- – 9 – cn C.I.H.M. [240]
THE CHRISTIAN GLEANER – [Halifax, N.S.?: s.n., 1833-1838?] – 9 – cn C.I.H.M. [240]
THE CHRISTIAN GRAPHIC – 1932-35 (incomplete) – 1r – 1 – ATLA S0717A – us A.T.L.A. [073]
CHRISTIAN GUARDIAN – Toronto, 1830-1863 – 7r – 1 – cn Preston [971]
THE CHRISTIAN HELPER – Toronto: Dudley & Burns, v1 no 1 (May 15 1877)- – 9 – cn C.I.H.M. [240]
CHRISTIAN HERALD – Middlebury, Vt. 1816; Christian Messenger, 1816-19; Columbian Patriot, 1813-15; yNational Standard, 1815-20. Sold as one unit – 3 – us Readex [071]
CHRISTIAN HERALD – Monmouth, OR. 4 Sept 1908-28 Dec 1917. – 1r – 1 – us U.O. Library [071]
CHRISTIAN HEROISM: ILLUSTRATED IN THE LIFE AND CHARACTER OF ST PAUL / Lipscomb, Andrew Adgate – Macon: J.W. Burke, 1880.1 fiche – 9 – us A.T.L.A. [240]
CHRISTIAN HIGHER EDUCATION IN CHINA / Cressy, Earl H – A study for the year 1925-26 – us A.T.L.A. [370]
CHRISTIAN HISTORY IN ITS THREE GREAT PERIODS / Allen, Joseph Henry – Boston: Roberts Bros., 1884-1890, c1882-1883 – 3mf – us A.T.L.A. [240]
CHRISTIAN HOFMANN VON HOFMANNSWALDAU : EIN BEITRAG ZUR LITERATURGESCHICHTE DES SIEBZEHNTEN JAHRHUNDERTS / Ettlinger, Josef – (Includes bibliographical references) – Halle a.d.S.: M Niemeyer, 1891 – 1r – 1 – us U.W. Library [430]

CHRISTIAN HOFMANN VON HOFMANNSWALDAUS GRABSCHRIFTEN / Friebe, Karl – Greifswald: F W Kunike, 1893 – 1r – 1 – us U.W. Library [430]

CHRISTIAN HOME EDUCATION (CCC2) = CHI TU CHIAO HUA TI CHIAO TING CHIAO YU / Barbour, Dorothy Dickinson – (In Chinese) – 5th ed Shanghai: Christian Literature Society, 1933 – 1r – 1 – 0-8370-1702-5 – 1984-6083 – us A.T.L.A. [240]

CHRISTIAN HOPE = HSI WANG YUEH K'AN – (Lacking: v1-5) – v6 no 1-v9 no 3. 1924-32 – 1r – 1 – ATLA S0604 – us A.T.L.A. [073]

THE CHRISTIAN HOPE : A STUDY IN THE DOCTRINE OF IMMORTALITY / Brown, William Adams – London: Duckworth, 1912 – 1mf – us A.T.L.A. [240]

THE CHRISTIAN HOPE (CCC330) / Wu, Lei-ch'uan – (In Chinese) – Shanghai: Association Press of China, 1940 – 1r – 1 – 1984-6669 – us A.T.L.A. [240]

CHRISTIAN HORIZONS – v1-9. 1938-46 (complete) – 1r – 1 – ATLA 1994-S516 – us A.T.L.A. [073]

THE CHRISTIAN IN THE WORLD / Faunce, Daniel Webster – 1875 – 9 – us A.T.L.A. [240]

CHRISTIAN INDEX – Georgia. 1822-1991 – 1 – $5,168.32 – us Baptist [240]

THE CHRISTIAN INDEX – (v75 not publ) – v69-78. 1938-46 (complete) – 9r – 1 – ATLA S0883 – us A.T.L.A. [073]

THE CHRISTIAN INDIAN – Wheaton, IL. 1978-Oct 1980. (American Indian Periodicals from the State Historical Society of Wisconsin). 1 reel – 1 – $50.00 – us UPA [073]

CHRISTIAN INQUIRER *see* THE INQUIRER

THE CHRISTIAN INQUIRER – New York City, NY. v1 n27. 17 apr 1847 and 4 Devotional Tracts – 1r – 1 – Can$30.00 – cn Can Microfilming [071]

CHRISTIAN INSTINCTS AND MODERN DOUBT : ESSAYS AND ADDRESSES IN AID OF A REASONABLE, SATISFYING, AND CONSOLATORY RELIGION / Craufurd, Alexander Henry – New York:T. Whittaker, 1897 – 1mf – 9 – 0-8370-2770-5 – 1985-0770 – us A.T.L.A. [230]

CHRISTIAN INSTITUTIONS / Allen, Alexander V G – New York: Scribner, 1897. (The International theological library) – 2mf – us A.T.L.A. [240]

THE CHRISTIAN INSTRUCTED IN THE NATURE AND USE OF INDULGENCES = CHRETIEN ECLAIRE SUR LA NATURE ET L'USAGE DES INDULGENCES / Maurel, F Antoine – (In English. Includes index) – 6th rev enl ed. Dublin: M H Gill, 1901 – 1mf – 9 – 0-8370-7410-X – 1986-1410 – us A.T.L.A. [240]

THE CHRISTIAN INSTRUCTOR AND MISSIONARY REGISTER OF THE PRESBYTERIAN CHURCH OF NOVA SCOTIA – (Cont by: The Home and Foreign Record of the Presbyterian Church of the Lower Provinces of British North America) – [Halifax, N.S.?: s.n., 1856?-1860] – 9 – cn C.I.H.M. [240]

THE CHRISTIAN INSTRUCTOR AND MISSIONARY REGISTER OF THE PRESBYTERIAN CHURCH OF NOVA SCOTIA *see* MISSIONARY REGISTER OF THE PRESBYTERIAN CHURCH OF NOVA-SCOTIA

CHRISTIAN INTELLIGENCER – New York. v1-105 no 18. 7 Aug 1830-15 Sep 1934 (complete) – 51r – 1 – ATLA S0067 – us A.T.L.A. [073]

CHRISTIAN INTERPRETATION OF HISTORY (CCC217) = CHI TU CHIAO TI LI SHIH KUAN / Liang, Hsiao-ch'u – (In Chinese) – 1st ed. Hong Kong: Chinese Christian Literature Council, 1968 – 1r – 1 – 1984-B500 – us A.T.L.A. [240]

Christian, John *see*
- BEHAR PROVERBS
- THE OXFORD UNION MURALS

Christian, John T *see* HISTORY OF BAPTISTS OF LOUISIANA

Christian, Juan T *see* INMERSION; EL ACTO DEL BAUTISMO CRISTIANO

CHRISTIAN LAYMAN – 1942-52 (complete) – 1r – 1 – ATLA S0721 – us A.T.L.A. [073]

CHRISTIAN LEGAL SOCIETY QUARTERLY – v1-2,no.1. 1980-81 – 1 – us UMI [073]

CHRISTIAN LIBERTY AND ITS ENEMIES: A BOOK FOR YOUTH / Foote, LeRoy – s.l.: s.n., 1868 (Montreal: J. Lovell). 03143. (Pre-1900 Canadiana) – 9 – cn C.I.H.M. [971]

CHRISTIAN LIBRARIAN – (v.23-. 1979- 5,6,9) – v.1-. 1957- – 1 – us UMI [240]

THE CHRISTIAN LIFE: A STUDY / Bowne, Borden Parker – Cincinnati: Jennings & Pye, 1899. 1 fiche – 9 – us A.T.L.A. [240]

CHRISTIAN LIFE AND CHARACTER OF THE CIVIL INSTITUTIONS OF THE UNITED STATES : DEVELOPED IN THE OFFICIAL AND HISTORICAL ANNALS OF THE REPUBLIC / Morris, BF – Philadelphia: George W. Childs; Cincinnati: Rickey & Carroll, 1864 – 2mf – us A.T.L.A. [240]

CHRISTIAN LIFE BULLETIN – 1955-58. Reel also includes Light, 1948-79. 406p – 1 – 14.21 – us Baptist [240]

Christian Life Commission. Advisory Council of Southern Baptist Work with Negroes *see* MINUTES, REPORTS AND CORRESPONDENCE

CHRISTIAN LIFE WEEKLY = CHI-TU-CHIAO SHENG-HO CHOU-K'AN – (In Chinese) – v1 nos17-34. 7 May 1955-10 Sep 1955 (incomplete) – 1r – 1 – ATLA S0296C – us A.T.L.A. [073]

CHRISTIAN LITERATURE SOCIETY FOR CHINA : ANNUAL REPORTS / Christian Literature Society for China – (Lacking: v54-58 1941-45) – v1-60. 1887-1947 – 2r – 1 – ATLA S0111 – us A.T.L.A. [240]

Christian Literature Society for China *see*
- THE CHINA MISSION YEARBOOK
- CHRISTIAN LITERATURE SOCIETY FOR CHINA

CHRISTIAN LIVING / Meyer, Frederick Brotherton – New York: Fleming H Revell, c1892 – 1mf – 9 – 0-8370-7173-9 – 1986-1173 – us A.T.L.A. [240]

THE CHRISTIAN LYRE / Leavitt, Joshua – Collections of hymns and tunes. Boston. 1832 – 1 – 18.83 – us Baptist [240]

CHRISTIAN MARRIAGE (CCC117) = CH'UAN KUO CHI-TU-CHIAO HUA CHIA T'ING WEI YUAN HUI : CHRISTIANIZING THE HOME WEEK PAMPHLET: PROGRAMS AND MATERIALS OF THE WEEK, OCT. 24-31, 1948 / ed by Christianizing the Home Committee of the National Christian Council of China – (In Chinese) – Shanghai: Christian Literature Society, 1948 – 1r – 1 – 1984-B500 – us A.T.L.A. [240]

CHRISTIAN MARTYRDOM IN RUSSIA: PERSECUTION OF THE SPIRIT-WRESTLER (OR DOUKHOBORTSI) IN THE CAUCASUS – Ed. by Vladimir Tchertkoff; containing a concluding chapter and letter by Leo Tolstoy. London: Brotherhood Pub. Co., 1897. 00600. (Pre-1900 Canadiana) – 9 – cn C.I.H.M. [240]

CHRISTIAN MEDICAL SOCIETY JOURNAL – (1985-. 5,6,9) – v1-. 1970- – 1 – us UMI [610]

CHRISTIAN MEDICAL SOCIETY JOURNAL – v1-21. 1949-69 – 1 – us UMI [610]

CHRISTIAN MEMORIALS OF THE WAR, OR, SCENES AND INCIDENTS ILLUSTRATIVE OF RELIGIOUS FAITH AND PRINCIPLE, PATRIOTISM AND BRAVERY IN OUR ARMY : WITH HISTORICAL NOTES / Hackett, Horatio Balch – Boston: Gould and Lincoln, 1864 – 1mf – us A.T.L.A. [240]

A CHRISTIAN MERCHANT, A MEMOIR OF JAMES C. CRANE / Burrows, J L – 1858 – 1 – 5.00 – us Baptist [240]

CHRISTIAN MESSENGER – Monmouth, OR. 8 Oct 1870-20 Jan 1875; 30 Jan 1976-17 May 1977 – 1 – us U.O. Library [071]

THE CHRISTIAN MESSENGER – London, 1884-1889. v19-24 – 31mf – H-2740/1 – ne IDC [240]

THE CHRISTIAN MINISTRY : ITS ORIGIN, CONSTITUTION, NATURE, AND WORK: A CONTRIBUTION TO PASTORAL THEOLOGY / Lefroy, William – London: Hodder and Stoughton, 1890 – 2mf – us A.T.L.A. [240]

THE CHRISTIAN MINISTRY / Lightfoot, Joseph B – 1879 – 1 – us A.T.L.A. [240]

THE CHRISTIAN MINISTRY AND MODERN THOUGHT: HIGHER CRITICISM / Armstrong, William Dunwoodie – Toronto: W. Briggs, 1896? 02467. (Pre-1900 Canadiana) – 9 – cn C.I.H.M. [240]

THE CHRISTIAN MINISTRY AND THE SOCIAL ORDER : LECTURES DELIVERED IN THE COURSE IN PASTORAL FUNCTIONS AT YALE DIVINITY SCHOOL, 1908-1909 / ed by Macfarland, Charles S – New Haven, Conn.: Yale University Press; London: Henry Frowde, 1909 – 1mf – us A.T.L.A. [240]

THE CHRISTIAN MINISTRY AT THE CLOSE OF THE NINETEENTH CENTURY / Littlejohn, AN – New York: T. Whittaker, 1884 – 1mf – us A.T.L.A. [240]

THE CHRISTIAN MINISTRY IN RELATION TO POLITICS AND PUBLIC QUESTIONS / Armstrong, William Dunwoodie – A Sermon preached before the Synod of Montreal and Ottawa, April 16th, 1889, in St. Andrew's Church, Quebec. Ottawa: J. Hope, 1889. 00823. (Pre-1900 Canadiana) – 9 – cn C.I.H.M. [240]

THE CHRISTIAN MIRACLES AND THE CONCLUSIONS OF SCIENCE / Thomson, William Duncan – Edinburgh: T.& T. Clark, 1888.1 fiche – 9 – us A.T.L.A. [240]

THE CHRISTIAN MIRROR – (Lacking: 24 Jul 1866. Title varies) – v1-78. 13 Jul 1822-6 May 6 1899 – 29r – 1 – ATLA S0257 – us A.T.L.A. [073]

THE CHRISTIAN MIRROR – Montreal, Canada. 2 aut-v1 n52. 12 sep 1844 – 1r – 1 – Can$35.00 – cn Can Microfilming [240]

THE CHRISTIAN MISSION MAGAZINE – 1870-78 – 1 – uk Microform Academic [073]

CHRISTIAN MISSIONS / Seelye, Julius Hawley – (Includes bibliographical references) – New York: Dodd, Mead, c1875 – 1mf – 9 – 0-8370-6514-3 – 1986-0514 – us A.T.L.A. [240]

CHRISTIAN MISSIONS : THEIR AGENTS, AND THEIR RESULTS / Marshall, T W M – London: Longman, Green, Longman, Roberts, & Green, 1863 – 3mf – us A.T.L.A. [240]

CHRISTIAN MISSIONS AND FOREIGN RELATIONS IN CHINA,AN HISTORICAL STUDY / Drury, Clifford Merril – 1932 – 1 – us A.T.L.A. [240]

CHRISTIAN MISSIONS AND SOCIAL PROGRESS: A SOCIOLOGICAL STUDY / Dennis, James Shepard – New York: Fleming H. Revell, 1899. 3v. 6 fiches – 9 – us A.T.L.A. [240]

CHRISTIAN MISSIONS IN BURMA / Purser, W C B – Westminster: Societey for the Propagation of the Gospel in Foreign Parts, 1911 – 1mf – us A.T.L.A. [240]

CHRISTIAN MISSIONS IN THE TELUGU COUNTRY / Hibbert-Ware, G – Westminster: Society for the Propagation of the Gospel in Foreign Parts, 1912 – 1mf – us A.T.L.A. [240]

CHRISTIAN MONASTICISM : FROM THE FOURTH TO THE NINTH CENTURIES OF THE CHRISTIAN ERA / Smith, Gregory – London: A.D. Innes, 1892 – 1mf – us A.T.L.A. [240]

CHRISTIAN MONASTICISM IN EGYPT TO THE CLOSE OF THE FOURTH CENTURY / Mackean, W H – London, 1920 – 3mf – 8 – Dfl13.00 – ne Slangenburg [240]

CHRISTIAN MONITOR – v1-45. 1909-53 (complete) – 15r – 1 – ATLA 1991-S001 – us A.T.L.A. [073]

CHRISTIAN MONITOR AND WEEKLY REGISTER – Providence, Rhode Island. May 22-Nov 13 1824 – 1r – 1 – us L of C Photodup [071]

CHRISTIAN MONTHLY – v1-47. 1944-91 (complete) – Inquire – 1 – ATLA S0435 – us A.T.L.A. [073]

CHRISTIAN MONTHLY HISTORY – 1743-46 – 1 – $50.00 – us Presbyterian [240]

CHRISTIAN MORALITY AND TRADITIONAL CHINESE ETHICS (CCC329) = CHI-TU-CHIAO TAO-TE-KUAN YU CHUNG-KUO LUN-LI / Wong, Hwa Chieh – (In Chinese) – 1st ed. Hong Kong: Council on Christian Literature for Overseas Chinese, 1962 – 1r – 1 – 1984-6668 – us A.T.L.A. [230]

CHRISTIAN MORGENSTERNS DICHTUNGEN VON "ICH UND DU" / Klemm, Guenther – (Includes bibliographical references) – Bonn a. Rh.: L Roehrscheid, 1933 – 1r – 1 – us U.W. Library [430]

CHRISTIAN MOURNING: A SERMON, OCCASIONED BY THE DEATH OF MRS. ISABELLA GRAHAM, AND PREACHED ON THE EVENING OF SABBATH, THE 14TH AUG. 1814 / Mason, John Mitchell – 1814 – 9 – us A.T.L.A. [920]

CHRISTIAN NEWS – Glasgow, Scotland. -w. 1859-1870. Lacking 1868. 11 reels – 1 – uk British Libr Newspaper [072]

CHRISTIAN NEWS FROM ISRAEL / Israel. Ministry of Religious Affairs. Christian Affairs Department – 24 v. 1949-74. Lacking: v. 24, 1974. BJ-81-7 1 – 9 – ne IDC [240]

CHRISTIAN NEWS FROM ISRAEL / Israel. Ministry of Religious Affairs. Christian Affairs Department – Jerusalem, 1949-. Quarterly – 9 – 120.00; 4.00y – is I.T.T.I. [240]

CHRISTIAN OBSERVER – Catlettsburg. Ky. 1867-71 – 1 – us UMI [071]

CHRISTIAN OBSERVER – (Cont by: Toronto Christian Observer) – Toronto: A.T. McCord and J. Pyper, [1851?-1852] – 9 – cn C.I.H.M. [240]

CHRISTIAN OBSERVER – Louisville. v. 83-97. 1895-1909 – 1 – us NY Public [073]

CHRISTIAN OBSERVER *see* THE TORONTO CHRISTIAN OBSERVER

CHRISTIAN OCCUPATION OF CHINA = CHUNG HUA KUEI CHU : A TRANSLATION – nos 36-216. Nov 1923-May 1941 (incomplete) – 1r – 1 – us A.T.L.A. [073]

THE CHRISTIAN OPPORTUNITY : BEING SERMONS AND SPEECHES / Davidson, Randall Thomas – New York: Macmillan; London: Macmillan, 1904 – 1mf – us A.T.L.A. [240]

CHRISTIAN ORACLE – (Some issues lacking) – v1-16. 1884; 1886-99 – 8r – 1 – ATLA S0015 – us A.T.L.A. [073]

CHRISTIAN ORGANIZER – Lynchburg, VA. Virginia Baptist State Convention. 1899, 1902-03 – 1 – 16.40 – us A.B.H.S. [073]

CHRISTIAN ORIGINS / Pfleiderer, Otto – New York: B.W. Huebsch, 1906. 1 fiche – 9 – us A.T.L.A. [240]

THE CHRISTIAN OUTLOOK: AN ADDRESS / Spencer, William Gabriel – Hartford: Case, Lockwood, 1878. 1 fiche – 9 – us A.T.L.A. [240]

CHRISTIAN PATIENCE : THE STRENGTH AND DISCIPLINE OF THE SOUL: A COURSE OF LECTURES / Ullathorne, William Bernard – (Includes bibliographical references) – 4th ed. London: Burns and Oates; New York: Catholic Publication Society, 1890 – 1mf – 9 – 0-8370-7110-0 – 1986-1110 – us A.T.L.A. [240]

CHRISTIAN PATRIOT – Belfast. Ireland. -w. 13 Apr 1838-13 Mar 1840. (1 reel) – 1 – uk British Libr Newspaper [072]

THE CHRISTIAN PATRIOT – (Lacking: v8 no 5 p3-6) – v1-27 no 7. 1945-Jul 1971 – 2r – 1 – ATLA S0197 – us A.T.L.A. [073]

CHRISTIAN PEACE CONFERENCE – 1962-90 (complete) – 3r – 1 – ATLA S0586 – us A.T.L.A. [073]

CHRISTIAN PEACE CONFERENCE – (1985-. 5,6,9) – 1962- – 1 – us UMI [240]

Christian Peace Conference *see* CPC (CHRISTIAN PEACE CONFERENCE) INFORMATION

CHRISTIAN PHILOSOPHY / Frothingham, Ephraim L & Frothingham, Arthur L – Baltimore: A.L. Frothingham, 1888-1890 – 1mf – us A.T.L.A. [240]

THE CHRISTIAN PLATONISTS OF ALEXANDRIA : BEING THE BAMPTON LECTURES OF THE YEAR 1886 / Bigg, Charles – Oxford: Clarendon Press, 1913 – 1mf – us A.T.L.A. [240]

THE CHRISTIAN POINT OF VIEW : THREE ADDRESSES / Knox, George William et al – New York:Charles Scribner, 1902 – 1mf – 9 – 0-8370-3326-8 – 1985-1326 – us A.T.L.A. [240]

THE CHRISTIAN POLICY OF LIFE / Brown, James Baldwin – London: E. Stock, 1870 – 1mf – us A.T.L.A. [240]

CHRISTIAN PROGRESS IN CHINA : GLEANINGS FROM THE WRITINGS AND SPEECHES OF MANY WORKERS / Foster, Arnold – (Includes bibliographical references) – London: Religious Tract Society, 1889 – 1mf – 9 – 0-8370-6044-3 – 1986-0044 – us A.T.L.A. [240]

THE CHRISTIAN PROPHETS AND THE PROPHETIC APOCALYPSE / Selwyn, Edward Carus – (Includes bibliographical references, indexes) – London; New York:Macmillan, 1900 – 1mf – 9 – 0-8370-5229-7 – 1985-3229 – us A.T.L.A. [220]

THE CHRISTIAN PSALMIST / Leonard, SW – Louisville. 1850 – 1 – 16.34 – us Baptist [240]

CHRISTIAN RECONSTRUCTION IN THE SOUTH / Douglass, Harlan Paul – 1909 – 1r – 1 – us Ross [977]

CHRISTIAN RECONSTRUCTION IN THE SOUTH / Douglass, Harlan Paul – (Includes bibliographical references and index) – Boston: Pilgrim Press, c1909 – 1mf – 9 – 0-8370-6488-0 – 1986-0488 – us A.T.L.A. [240]

CHRISTIAN RECORD – (Lacking some issues) – Bloomington, IN. Jul 1843-Oct 1884 – 12r – 1 – ATLA S0145 – us A.T.L.A. [073]

THE CHRISTIAN RECORD – Pictou, N.S.: Stiles and Fraser, 1843- – 9 – cn C.I.H.M. [240]

CHRISTIAN RECORDER – v16-19. 1967-69 (complete) – 1r – 1 – ATLA S0726A – us A.T.L.A. [073]

THE CHRISTIAN RECORDER – [Toronto: s.n.], 1819-[1821] – 9 – cn C.I.H.M. [240]

CHRISTIAN REFORMER AND SIGNS OF THE TIMES – v. 1-2. 1855-1856 – 1 – us UMI [240]

THE CHRISTIAN REGISTER – Montreal, Canada. 1 jan-15 dec 1823 – 1r – 1 – Can$30.00 – cn Can Microfilming [072]

THE CHRISTIAN RELIGION / Fisher, George Park – (Includes bibliographical references) – New York: Chautauqua Press, 1886 – 1mf – 9 – 0-8370-4977-6 – 1985-2977 – us A.T.L.A. [240]

THE CHRISTIAN REPORTER – Toronto: Bengough, Moore, [1880?-18– or 19–] – 9 – cn C.I.H.M. [240]

THE CHRISTIAN REVELATION / Bowne, Borden Parker – 2nd ed. Cincinnati: Curts & Jennings, 1898 – 1mf – 9 – 0-8370-2428-5 – 1985-0428 – us A.T.L.A. [240]

CHRISTIAN REVIEW – Philadelphia. Afro-American Baptist. 1949-51 – 1 – 38.50 – us A.B.H.S. [073]

CHRISTIAN REVIEW – v. 1-28. 1836-1863 – 1,5,6 – us Princeton Micro [240]

THE CHRISTIAN REVIEW – v1-10. 1932-41 (complete) – 3r – 1 – ATLA 1993-S515 – us A.T.L.A. [073]

THE CHRISTIAN RURAL MOVEMENT (CCC252) / Chang, F L – (In Chinese) – Shanghai: Christian Literature Society, 1930 – 1r – 1 – 1984-6591 – us A.T.L.A. [240]

CHRISTIAN SALVATION OF CHINA (CCC189) = CHI TU CHIAO CHIU KUO CHU I K'AN HSING CHIH SAN / Hsu, Ch'ien – (In Chinese) – [s.l: s.n, 1920] – 1r – 1 – 1984-B500 – us A.T.L.A. [240]

CHRISTIAN SCIENCE : THE FAITH AND ITS FOUNDER / Powell, Lyman P – New York: Putnam, 1907 – 1mf – us A.T.L.A. [240]

CHRISTIAN SCIENCE BEFORE THE BAR OF REASON / Lambert, Louis Aloisius; ed by Quinlan, Aloysius Stanislaus – New York: Christian Press Association Publ, 1908 – 1mf – 9 – 0-8370-6991-2 – 1986-0991 – us A.T.L.A. [210]

CHRISTIAN SCIENCE MONITOR – Boston. Mass. 1908-1918; 1922- – 1 – us UMI [071]

CHRISTIAN SCIENCE MONITOR INDEX – Boston. Massachusetts. 1950- – 1 – us UMI [071]

CHRISTIAN SCIENCE SO-CALLED : AN EXPOSITION AND AN ESTIMATE / Sheldon, Henry Clay – New York: Abingdon, c1913 – 1mf – us A.T.L.A. [240]

CHRISTIAN SECRETARY – 1822-95 (complete) – 8r – 1 – ATLA R0130 – us A.T.L.A. [073]

THE CHRISTIAN SENTINEL AND ANGLO-CANADIAN CHURCHMAN'S MAGAZINE – Montreal, Canada. v1 n5. sep/oct 1827-apr 1829 – 1r – 1 – Can$25.00 – cn Can Microfilming [240]

THE CHRISTIAN SENTINEL, VOLS 1-19 (1883-1901) – (Incomplete) – Pittsburgh, PA – 1r – 1 – $50.00 – us Presbyterian [240]

CHRISTIAN SERIES = CHI-TU-CHIAO TS'UNG K'AN – no 4 1943 (incomplete) – 1r – 1 – ATLA S0296D – us A.T.L.A. [073]

CHRISTIAN SERVICE AND THE MODERN WORLD / Macfarland, Charles S – New York: F.H. Revell, c1915 – 1mf – us A.T.L.A. [240]

CHRISTIAN SINGERS OF GERMANY / Winkworth, Catherine – [London]: Macmillan, [1869?] – 1mf – us A.T.L.A. [780]

CHRISTIAN SOCIAL ACTION – v4-7. 1939-42 (complete) – Inquire – 1 – ATLA 1994-S501 – us A.T.L.A. [073]

CHRISTIAN SOCIAL ASSOCIATION : INFORMATION BULLETIN – 1965-79; 1985-89 – Inquire – 1 – ATLA S0356 – us A.T.L.A. [073]

CHRISTIAN SOCIAL UNION – (Cont: Church Social Union) – Apr 1895-Apr 1908 (complete) – 2r – 1 – ATLA S0583 – us A.T.L.A. [073]

CHRISTIAN SOCIALIST – Chicago. v. 2-18. 1905-1921. Incomplete – 1 – us NY Public [240]

CHRISTIAN SOCIALIST – London. v. 1 no. 1-v. 9 no. 103. June 1883-Dec 1891. Incomplete – 1 – us NY Public [240]

CHRISTIAN SOCIALIST – London. v1-9. 1883-91 – 1r – 1 – us Ross [335]

THE CHRISTIAN SOCIALIST – (Lacking some issues) – v1-125. 1960-87 – 1r – 1 – ATLA S0848 – us A.T.L.A. [073]

CHRISTIAN SOCIOLOGY / Stuckenberg, John Henry Wilburn – New York: I.K. Funk, 1880 – 1mf – us A.T.L.A. [300]

THE CHRISTIAN STANDARD – v1-27, 1866-95. 27 reels – 1 – us A.T.L.A. [073]

THE CHRISTIAN STATE OF LIFE = CHRISTLICHE SITTEN-LEHRE UEBER DIE EVANGELISCHEN WAHRHEITEN : OR, SERMONS ON THE PRINCIPAL DUTIES OF CHRISTIANS IN GENERAL, AND OF DIFFERENT STATES IN PARTICULAR / Hunolt, Franz – (In English. Includes indexes of sermons and subjects) – 2nd ed. New York: Benziger, 1886 – 4mf – 9 – 0-8370-7295-6 – 1986-1295 – us A.T.L.A. [240]

CHRISTIAN STATESMAN – (1985-. 5,6,9) – v1-. 1867- – 1 – us UMI [240]

THE CHRISTIAN STATESMAN – (Lacking: v63-66) – v57-132. 1923-89 – 6r – 1 – us A.T.L.A. [073]

THE CHRISTIAN STATESMAN – (v1-31, 1867-1897) – 12r – 1 – $600.00 – us Presbyterian [240]

THE CHRISTIAN STATESMAN, 1867-1897 – 12r – 1 – $1,020.00 – D3331 – Co-publ with the Presbyterian Historical Society, Dept of History, Presbyterian Church (U.S.A.) 1995 – us Scholarly Res [302]

CHRISTIAN STEWARDSHIP, MORRISTOWN, TENN / Cox, E K – 1887 – 1 – 5.00 – us Baptist [240]

A CHRISTIAN STUDY OF BUDDHISM (CCC305) = CHI TU TU CHIH FO HSUEH YEN CHIU / Wang, Chih-hsin – (In Chinese) – 3rd ed. Shanghai: Christian Literature Society, 1941 – 1r – 1 – 1984-6644 – us A.T.L.A. [230]

CHRISTIAN THEISM : ITS CLAIMS AND SANCTIONS / Purinton, Daniel Boardman – (Includes bibliographies & index) – New York: G P Putnam, 1889 – 1mf – 9 – 0-8370-4812-5 – 1985-2812 – us A.T.L.A. [240]

CHRISTIAN THEISM:...THE EVIDENCE...AND THE OBJECTIONS URGED AGAINST IT / Row, Charles Adolphus – New York: Thomas Whittaker, 1890. 1 fiche. 8370-4984-9 – 9 – us A.T.L.A. [240]

CHRISTIAN THEOLOGY : A CONCISE AND PRACTICAL VIEW OF THE CARDINAL DOCTRINES AND INSTITUTIONS OF CHRISTIANITY / Weaver, Jonathan – (Includes index) – Memorial ed. Dayton, Ohio: United Brethren Publ House, 1900 – 1mf – 9 – 0-8370-5665-9 – 1985-3665 – us A.T.L.A. [240]

CHRISTIAN THEOLOGY / Robinson, Ezekiel Gilman – (Includes bibliographical references and index) – Rochester, NY: E R Andrews, c1894 – 1mf – 9 – 0-8370-6353-1 – 1986-0353 – us A.T.L.A. [240]

CHRISTIAN THEOLOGY AND SOCIAL PROGRESS / Bussell, FW – London: Methuen, 1907 – 1mf – us A.T.L.A. [240]

CHRISTIAN THOUGHT TO THE REFORMATION / Workman, Herbert Brook – New York: Scribner, 1911 – 1mf – us A.T.L.A. [240]

CHRISTIAN TIMES AND WITNESS – Illinois. 1853-67 – 1 – 87.69 – us Baptist [240]

CHRISTIAN TRUTH AND MODERN OPINION : SEVEN SERMONS PREACHED IN NEW YORK BY CLERGYMEN OF THE PROTESTANT EPISCOPAL CHURCH – 4th ed. New York: Thomas Whittaker, 1885, c1884 – 1mf – 9 – 0-8370-3488-4 – 1985-1488 – us A.T.L.A. [210]

CHRISTIAN TRUTH VIEWED IN RELATION TO PLYMOUTHISM / Mearns, Peter – Edinburgh: William Oliphant, 1874 – 1mf – us A.T.L.A. [240]

CHRISTIAN TRUTHS : LECTURES / Chatard, Francis Silas – (Includes appendix) – New York: Catholic Publ Society, 1881 – 1mf – 9 – 0-8370-7050-3 – 1986-1050 – us A.T.L.A. [230]

CHRISTIAN TYPES OF HEROISM : A STUDY OF THE HEROIC SPIRIT UNDER CHRISTIANITY / Adams, John Coleman – Boston: Universalist Pub. House, 1891, c1890 – 1mf – us A.T.L.A. [240]

CHRISTIAN UND DIE KATALOGE : EINE ERZAEHLUNG FUER BUECHERFREUNDE / Hoinkes, Carl – Berlin: Verlag Die Heimbuecherei, 1942 – 1r – 1 – us U.W. Library [830]

CHRISTIAN UNION : A HISTORICAL STUDY / Garrison, J H – St. Louis, Mo.: Christian Pub. Co., c1906 – 1mf – us A.T.L.A. [240]

CHRISTIAN UNION AND THE PROTESTANT EPISCOPAL CHURCH IN ITS RELATIONS TO CHURCH UNITIY / Lewis, William H – New York: Published for the author by F.D. Harriman, 1858 – 1mf – us A.T.L.A. [240]

CHRISTIAN UNION PAMPHLET COLLECTION – 1946 – 1 – CSUXAMJ7772-B – us Hoover Inst Photo [240]

CHRISTIAN UNION QUARTERLY : INTERDENOMINATIONAL AND INTERNATIONAL – v1-24. Jul 1911-Apr 1935 (complete) – 4r – 1 – ATLA S0024 – us A.T.L.A. [073]

CHRISTIAN UNITY AND THE HISTORIC EPISCOPATE / Forrester, Henry – New York: T. Whittaker, 1889 – 1mf – us A.T.L.A. [240]

CHRISTIAN UNITY AT WORK : THE FEDERAL COUNCIL OF THE CHURCHES OF CHRIST IN AMERICA, IN QUADRENNIAL SESSION AT CHICAGO, ILLINOIS, 1912 / ed by Macfarland, Charles S – New York: The Council, c1913 – 1mf – us A.T.L.A. [240]

THE CHRISTIAN UNITY OF CAPITAL AND LABOR / Cadman, H W – Philadelphia: American Sunday-School Union, c1888. (Green fund book; no. 6) – 1mf – us A.T.L.A. [240]

CHRISTIAN USE OF THE PSALMS / Cheyne, Thomas Kelly – New York: E.P. Dutton, 1900. 1 fiche – 9 – us A.T.L.A. [240]

THE CHRISTIAN VIEW OF THE WORLD : NATHANIEL WILLIAM TAYLOR LECTURES FOR 1910-1911, DELIVERED BEFORE THE DIVINITY SCHOOL OF YALE UNIVERSITY / Blewett, George John – New Haven: Yale University Press, 1912 – 1mf – us A.T.L.A. [240]

CHRISTIAN VISITOR : FAMILY NEWSPAPER – St-John, New Brunswick. v1 n8. 12 jan 1848-v2 n5. 20 dec 1848 – 1r – 1 – Can$45.00 – cn Can Microfilming [072]

CHRISTIAN WAHNSCHAFFE / Wassermann, Jakob – Berlin: S Fischer. 2v. 1928 – 1 – us U.W. Library [830]

THE CHRISTIAN WATCHMAN – 1866-68 (complete) – 1r – 1 – ATLA R0137 – us A.T.L.A. [073]

CHRISTIAN WEEKLY – In Chinese. v1:17-34, 7 May-10 Sept 1955. Incomplete. 1 reel – 1 – us A.T.L.A. [073]

CHRISTIAN WEISE : EIN SAECHSISCHER GYMNASIALREKTOR AUS DER REFORMZEIT DES 17. JAHRHUNDERTS / Kaemmel, Otto – (A commissioned Festschrift. Includes bibliographical references) – Leipzig: B G Teubner, 1897 – 1r – 1 – us U.W. Library [943]

CHRISTIAN WEISE UND MOLIERE : EINE STUDIE ZUR ENTWICKLUNGSGESCHICHTE DES DEUTSCHEN LUSTSPIELS / Levinstein, Kurt – 1995 – 1mf – 9 – DM48.00 – 3-8267-3136-0 – gw Hänsel [410]

CHRISTIAN WEISE UND MOLIERE : EINE STUDIE ZUR ENTWICKLUNGSGESCHICHTE DES DEUTSCHEN LUSTSPIELS / Levinstein, Kurt – (Includes bibliographical references) – Berlin: G Schade (O Francke), [1899?] – 1 – us U.W. Library [430]

CHRISTIAN WEISE'S BAUERN-KOMOEDIE VON TOBIAS UND DER SCHWALBE : AUFGEFUEHRT IM JAHRE 1682 / Weise, Christian – Berlin: U Hofmann, 1882 – 1r – 1 – us U.W. Library [820]

CHRISTIAN WEISES HISTORISCHE DRAMEN UND IHRE QUELLEN / Hess, Adolf – (Includes bibliographical references) – Rostock: Adler's Erben, 1893 – 1 – us U.W. Library [430]

CHRISTIAN WEISES ROMANE UND IHRE NACHWIRKUNG / Becker, Rudolf – 1910 – 1r – 1 – us U.W. Library [430]

CHRISTIAN WITNESS – (Lacking: 1939. Title varies) – v1-158. Jul 1870-Apr 1959 – 46r – 1 – ATLA S0225 – us A.T.L.A. [073]

CHRISTIAN WOMANHOOD / Hack, Mary Pryor – 1883 – 9 – us A.T.L.A. [240]

CHRISTIAN WORK IN RURAL CHINA (CCC350) : A SYMPOSIUM OF PRACTICAL EXPERIENCES / ed by Yu, Mu-jen – (In Chinese) – Shanghai: Christian Literature Society. 2v. 1949-1950 – 1r – 1 – 1984-6689 – us A.T.L.A. [240]

CHRISTIAN WORKER – Wichita. Kan. 1915-1934 – 1 – us UMI [071]

THE CHRISTIAN WORKER – (Cont by: The Ontario Evangelist) – Meaford, Ont.: H.R. Sherman, [1881-1886] – 9 – cn C.I.H.M. [240]

THE CHRISTIAN WORKER *see* THE ONTARIO EVANGELIST

CHRISTIAN WORLD : NEWS OF THE WEEK – (Lacking some pgs. Some original pgs damaged) – 1894-1961 – 58r – 1 – ATLA S0204 – us A.T.L.A. [073]

CHRISTIAN WORLD – v1-6. 1843-48 (complete) – 2r – 1 – ATLA S0159 – us A.T.L.A. [073]

CHRISTIAN WORSHIP : ITS PRINCIPLES AND FORMS / Richard, J W & Painter, F V N – Philadelphia: Lutheran Publication Society, c1908 – 1mf – us A.T.L.A. [240]

THE CHRISTIAN WRITERS OF THE INNER EMIGRATION / Klieneberger, H R – (Includes bibliographical references and index) – The Hague; Paris: Mouton, c1968 – 1r – 1 – us U.W. Library [430]

THE CHRISTIAN YEAR : ITS PURPOSE AND ITS HISTORY / Gwynne, Walker – New York: Longmans, Green, c1915 – 1mf – us A.T.L.A. [240]

THE CHRISTIAN YEAR : THOUGHTS IN VERSE FOR THE SUNDAYS AND HOLYDAYS THROUGHOUT THE YEAR / Keble, John – Oxford: Printed by W. Baxter, for J. Parker; London: C. and J. Rivington, 1827 – 1 roll – 1 – 1-55879-428-X – uk Libr Preservation [240]

CHRISTIAN YOUTH AT THE FRONT (CCC224) = CH'IEN HSIEN TI CHI TU T'U CH'ING NIEN / Liu, Liang-mou – (In Chinese) – Shanghai: Association Press of China, 1940 – 1r – 1 – 1984-B500 – us A.T.L.A. [950]

LA CHRISTIANA VITTORIA MARITIMA / Bolognetti, F – Bologna, 1572 – 2mf – 9 – H-8323/1 – ne IDC [355]

CHRISTIANAE VERITATIS TELUM, SEU FIDEI CATAPULTA IN PLEROSQUE PSEUDOPROPHETAS, PRAESERTIM IN BERN / Iohannes Daventriae – Coloniae. 1533. BME-359 1 – 9 – ne IDC [240]

CHRISTIAN-ERLANGISCHER ZEITUNGS-EXTRACT – (Title changes: Auszug der neuesten Weltgeschichte, 1742-45, Real-Zeitung, 1 763; Erlanger Real-Zeitung, 1804; Erlanger Zeitung, Dec 1821) – Erlangen, Germany. 1741-1798, 1813-1829 – 42r – 1 – gw Mikrofilm [072]

DIE CHRISTIANISIERUNG DER FUERSTENTUEMER REUSS / Priegel, F – (Koenigsbrueck, um 1905) – 1mf – 9 – DM38.00 – 3-89349-342-5 – gw Hänsel [240]

LE CHRISTIANISME AU VINGTIEME SIECLE – 1966-92 (complete) – Inquire – 1 – ATLA S0678 – us A.T.L.A. [073]

LE CHRISTIANISME DANS L'EMPIRE PERSE : SOUS LA DYNASTIE SASSANIDE (224-632) / Labourt, J – Paris: V. Lecoffre, 1904 – 1mf – us A.T.L.A. [240]

LE CHRISTIANISME DANS L'EMPIRE PERSE SOUS LA DYNASTIE SASSANIDE (224-632) / Labourt, J – Paris, 1904 – Dfl28.00 – ne Slangenburg [240]

LE CHRISTIANISME DE LUTHER / Kuhn, Felix – Paris: Fischbacher, 1900 – 1mf – us A.T.L.A. [240]

LE CHRISTIANISME DEVOILE / Holbach, Paul-Thiry d' – (D'Holbach series). 1756 – 9 – fr Hachette [240]

LE CHRISTIANISME EN CHINE ET EN ASIE CENTRALE SOUS LES MONGOLS / Cordier, Henri – (T'oung Pao). Leide. 1917. BU-710 2 – 8 – ne IDC [240]

LE CHRISTIANISME MODERNE : ETUDE SUR LESSING / Fontanes, Ernest – Paris: G Balliere; New York: Bailliere brothers, 1867 – 1r – 1 – us U.W. Library [240]

CHRISTIANISME SOCIAL – (Suspended: Jul 1914-Oct 1918) – v1 nos 1-69; ns: 1887-1961 – 24r – 1 – ATLA S0049 – us A.T.L.A. [073]

O CHRISTIANISMO : SEMANARIO RELIGIOSO – '(s.l.')-Sao Luis, Brazil. 1 May 1854-Apr 1855 – 1,5,6 – bl Biblioteca [072]

CHRISTIANITY : ITS NATURE AND ITS TRUTH / Peake, Arthur S – London: Duckworth, 1908 – 1mf – 9 – 0-8370-5226-2 – 1985-3226 – us A.T.L.A. [240]

CHRISTIANITY ACCORDING TO CHRIST: A SERIES OF PAPERS / Gibson, John Monro – New York: Robert Carter, 1888. 1 fiche – 9 – us A.T.L.A. [240]

CHRISTIANITY AGREEABLE TO REASON IN ITS EVIDENCE,...ATONEMENT, AND... SACRAMENT / Mortlock, Edmund – Cambridge: Macmillan, 1862. 1 fiche. 8370-4497-9 – 9 – us A.T.L.A. [240]

CHRISTIANITY AND AGNOSTICISM : A CONTROVERSY / Wace, Henry et al – (Includes bibliographical references) – New York: D Appleton, 1889 – 1mf – 9 – 0-8370-2658-X – 1985-0658 – us A.T.L.A. [210]

CHRISTIANITY AND AGNOSTICISM: A CONTROVERSY: CONSISTING OF PAPERS BY HENRY WACE...(ET AL) – New York: Humboldt Pub. Co., (1889). 162p. (Humboldt Library of Popular Science; no.114) – 1 – us U.W. Library [240]

CHRISTIANITY AND AGNOSTICISM: REVIEWS OF SOME RECENT ATTACKS ON THE CHRISTIAN FAITH / Wace, Henry – London: S.P.C.K., 1905. 1 fiche – 9 – us A.T.L.A. [240]

CHRISTIANITY AND BUDDHISM : A COMPARISON AND A CONTRAST: BEING THE DONNELLAN LECTURES FOR THE YEAR 1889-90 / Berry, T Sterling – London: S.P.C.K.; New York: E. & J.B. Young, [1891?] – 1mf – us A.T.L.A. [230]

CHRISTIANITY AND CHINA (CCC106) = CHI-TU-CHIAO YU CHUNG-KUO / Chow, Yi-Fu – (In Chinese) – 1st ed. Hong Kong: Council on Christian Literature for Overseas Chinese, 1965 – 1r – 1 – 1984-B500 – us A.T.L.A. [240]

CHRISTIANITY AND CHINESE CULTURE (CCC192) = CHI-TU-CHIAO YU CHUNG-KUO WEN-HUA / Hsu, Sung-shih – (In Chinese) – Hong Kong: Baptist Press, 1965 – 1r – 1 – 1984-B500 – us A.T.L.A. [230]

CHRISTIANITY AND CHINESE CULTURE (CCC331) = CHI TU CHIAO YU CHUNG-KUO WEI HUA / Wu, Lei-ch'uan – (In Chinese) – Shanghai: Association Press of China, 1936 – 1r – 1984-6670 – us A.T.L.A. [230]

CHRISTIANITY AND COMMUNISM (CCC4) / Bates, Miner Searle – (In Chinese) – Hong Kong: Association Press of China, 1939 – 1r – 1 – 0-8370-1704-1 – 1984-6095 – us A.T.L.A. [240]

CHRISTIANITY AND CRISIS – (v30- . 5,6. v36- . 9) – 1- 1941- – 1 – us UMI [240]

CHRISTIANITY AND ECONOMIC SCIENCE / Cunningham, William – London: John Murray, 1914 – 1mf – us A.T.L.A. [240]

CHRISTIANITY AND EMANCIPATION, OR, THE TEACHINGS AND THE INFLUENCE OF THE BIBLE AGAINST SLAVERY / Thompson, Joseph Parrish – New York: A.D.F. Randolph, 1863 – 1mf – us A.T.L.A. [240]

CHRISTIANITY AND ETHICS : A HANDBOOK OF CHRISTIAN ETHICS / Alexander, Archibald – New York: Scribner, 1914 – 1mf – us A.T.L.A. [240]

CHRISTIANITY AND EUROPE PAMPHLET COLLECTION – 1982 – 1 – CSUXAMJ4564-B – us Hoover Inst Photo [240]

CHRISTIANITY AND EVOLUTION : MODERN PROBLEMS OF THE FAITH / Matheson, George et al – London: James Nisbet, 1887 – 1mf – 9 – 0-8370-2659-8 – 1985-0659 – us A.T.L.A. [210]

CHRISTIANITY AND FILIAL PIETY (CCC151) = TS'UNG CHI TU CHIAO KAN CHUNG-KUO HSIAO TAO / Ho, Shih-ming – (In Chinese) – 1st ed. Hong Kong: Council on Christian Literature for Overseas Chinese, 1963 – 1r – 1 – 1984-B500 – us A.T.L.A. [240]

CHRISTIANITY AND GREEK PHILOSOPHY, OR, THE RELATION BETWEEN SPONTANEOUS AND REFLECTIVE THOUGHT IN GREECE AND THE POSITIVE TEACHING OF CHRIST AND HIS APOSTLES / Cocker, BF – New York: Harper, 1870 – 2mf – us A.T.L.A. [240]

CHRISTIANITY AND HISTORY / Figgis, John Neville – London: James Finch, 1905 – 1mf – us A.T.L.A. [240]

CHRISTIANITY AND HISTORY / Harnack, Adolf von – London: Adam & Charles Black, 1896. 1 fiche – 9 – us A.T.L.A. [240]

CHRISTIANITY AND IDEALISM / Watson, John – New York: Macmillan, 1897. 1 fiche – 9 – us A.T.L.A. [240]

CHRISTIANITY AND ISLAM IN SPAIN, A.D. 756-1031 / Haines, C R – London: K. Paul, Trench, 1889 – 1mf – us A.T.L.A. [230]

CHRISTIANITY AND LITERATURE (CCC114) / Chu, Wei-chih – (In Chinese) – Shanghai: Association Press of China, 1948 – 1r – 1 – 1984-B500 – us A.T.L.A. [230]

CHRISTIANITY AND MARX-LENINISM (CCC205) = CHI TU CHIAO YU MA LIEH CHU I / Kiang, Wen-han – (In Chinese) – [s.l: s.n, 1950] – 1r – 1 – 1984-B500 – us A.T.L.A. [230]

CHRISTIANITY AND MODERN CULTURE: AN ESSAY IN PHILOSOPHY OF RELIGION / Shaw, Charles Gray – Cincinnati: Jennings & Graham, 1906. 1 fiche – 9 – us A.T.L.A. [240]

CHRISTIANITY AND MODERN THOUGHT (CCC166) = CHI TU CHIAO YU HSIEN TAI SZU HSIANG / Hsieh, Fu-ya – (In Chinese) – Shanghai: Association Press of China, 1941 – 1r – 1 – 1984-B500 – us A.T.L.A. [230]

CHRISTIANITY AND NEW CHINA (CCC229) / Lo, Yun-yen – (In Chinese) – 2nd ed. Shanghai: Publ Dept of the M E Church, 1923 – 1r – 1 – 1984-B500 – us A.T.L.A. [240]

CHRISTIANITY AND POLITICS / Cunningham, William – Boston: Houghton Mifflin, 1915 – 1mf – us A.T.L.A. [240]

CHRISTIANITY AND POSITIVISM : A SERIES OF LECTURES TO THE TIMES ON NATURAL THEOLOGY AND APOLOGETICS / McCosh, James – (Includes bibliographical references) – New York: Robert Carter, 1871 – 1mf – 9 – 0-8370-2418-8 – 0418 – us A.T.L.A. [210]

CHRISTIANITY AND SCIENCE: A SERIES OF LECTURES / Peabody, Andrew Preston – New York: Robert Carter, 1875. 1 fiche.8370-4681-5 – 9 – us A.T.L.A. [240]

CHRISTIANITY AND SCIENCE (CCC173) / Hsieh, Hung-lai – (In Chinese) – 2nd ed. Shanghai: Association Press of China, 1921 – 1r – 1 – 1984-B500 – us A.T.L.A. [210]

CHRISTIANITY AND SOCIAL PROBLEMS / Abbott, Lyman – Boston: Houghton, Mifflin, 1896 – 1mf – us A.T.L.A. [240]

CHRISTIANITY AND SOCIAL QUESTIONS / Cunningham, William – London: Duckworth, 1910. (Studies in theology) – 1mf – us A.T.L.A. [240]

CHRISTIANITY AND SOCIETY – v1-21. 1935-56 (complete) – 2r – 1 – ATLA S0007 – us A.T.L.A. [073]

CHRISTIANITY, AND SOME OF ITS EVIDENCES: AN ADDRESS / Mowat, Oliver – Toronto: Williamson, 1890. 1 fiche. 8370-4514-2 – 9 – us A.T.L.A. [240]

CHRISTIANITY AND SPAIN / Negrin, Juan – N.Y., 1938. Fiche W 1070. (Blodgett Collection of Spanish Civil War Pamphlets) – 9 – us H.U. College Libr [946]

CHRISTIANITY AND THE AMERICAN COMMONWEALTH, OR, THE INFLUENCE OF CHRISTIANITY IN MAKING THIS NATION / Galloway, Charles B – Nashville, Tenn.: Publishing House, Methodist Episcopal Church, South, 1898 – 1mf – us A.T.L.A. [240]

CHRISTIANITY AND THE LABOR MOVEMENT / Balch, William Monroe – Boston: Sherman, French, 1912 – 1mf – us A.T.L.A. [240]

CHRISTIANITY AND THE NATIONS / Speer, Robert Elliott – New York: Fleming H Revell, c1910 – 1mf – 9 – 0-8370-6390-6 – 1986-0390 – us A.T.L.A. [240]

CHRISTIANITY AND THE NEW CHINA (CCC333) = CHI TU CHIAO YU HSIN CHUNG-KUO : A SYMPOSIUM / ed by Wu, Yao-tsung – (In Chinese) – Shanghai: Association Press of China, 1940 – 1r – 1 – 1984-6672 – us A.T.L.A. [240]

CHRISTIANITY AND THE NEW IDEALISM : A STUDY IN THE RELIGIOUS PHILOSOPHY OF TO-DAY / Eucken, Rudolf – London, New York: Harper, 1909 – 1mf – us A.T.L.A. [240]

CHRISTIANITY AND THE NEW PHYSICS (CCC299) / Tu, Yu-ching – (In Chinese) – Shanghai: Association Press of China, 1939 – 1r – 1 – 1984-6638 – us A.T.L.A. [210]

CHRISTIANITY AND THE PROGESS OF MAN : AS ILLUSTRATED BY MODERN MISSIONS / Mackenzie, William Douglas – (Includes bibliographical references) – Chicago: Fleming H Revell, 1897 – 1mf – 9 – 0-8370-6147-4 – 1986-0147 – us A.T.L.A. [240]

CHRISTIANITY AND THE RELIGIONS / Lloyd, Arthur Selden – New York: E.P. Dutton, 1909. 1 fiche – 9 – us A.T.L.A. [240]

CHRISTIANITY AND THE ROMAN GOVERNMENT: A STUDY IN IMPERIAL ADMINISTRATION / Hardy, Ernest George – London: Longmans, Green, 1894. 15, 208p – 1 – us U.W. Library [240]

CHRISTIANITY AND THE RURAL RECONSTRUCTION MOVEMENT IN CHINA (CCC351) / Yu, Mu-jen – (In Chinese) – 3rd ed. Shanghai: Christian Literature Society, 1948 – 1r – 1 – 1984-6690 – us A.T.L.A. [240]

CHRISTIANITY AND THE SOCIALIST MOVEMENT (CCC16) = CHI TU CHIAO YU SHE HUI CHU I YUN TUNG / Chang, Shih-Chang – (In Chinese) – Hong Kong: Association Press of China, 1939 – 1r – 1 – 0-8370-1716-5 – 1984-6088 – us A.T.L.A. [230]

CHRISTIANITY AND THE SUPERNATURAL / D'Arcy, Charles Frederick – London: Longmans, Green, 1909. 1 fiche – 9 – us A.T.L.A. [240]

CHRISTIANITY AT THE CROSS-ROADS / Tyrrell, George – London; New York: Longmans, Green, 1910 – 1mf – 9 – 0-8370-8873-9 – 1986-2873 – us A.T.L.A. [240]

CHRISTIANITY IN CELTIC LANDS / Gougaud, L – London, 1932 – Dfl32.00 – ne Slangenburg [240]

CHRISTIANITY IN EARLY BRITAIN / Williams, Hugh – Oxford: Clarendon Press, 1912 – 2mf – us A.T.L.A. [240]

CHRISTIANITY IN ITS RELATION TO THE STATE AND THE CHURCH: TWO SERMONS PREACHED IN ST ANDREW'S CHURCH, OTTAWA, ON APRIL 7TH AND APRIL 14TH 1889 / Herridge, William Thomas – Ottawa: A. Woodburn, 1889. 05557. (Pre-1900 Canadiana) – 9 – cn C.I.H.M. [971]

CHRISTIANITY IN MODERN JAPAN / Clement, Ernest Wilson – (Includes appendix and index) – Philadelphia: American Baptist Publ Soc, 1905 – 1mf – 9 – 0-8370-6096-6 – 1986-0096 – us A.T.L.A. [240]

CHRISTIANITY IN RELATION TO SCIENCE AND MORALS / MacColl, Malcolm – New York: James Pott, 1890. 1 fiche – 9 – us A.T.L.A. [240]

CHRISTIANITY IN THE APOSTOLIC AGE / Purves, George Tybout – New York: Charles Scribner, 1900. 1 fiche. 8370-4813-3 – 9 – us A.T.L.A. [240]

CHRISTIANITY IN THE LIGHT OF TODAY (CCC200) / ed by Woo, Y K – (In Chinese) – 3rd ed. Shanghai: Publication Dept., National Committee, YMCAs of China, 1926 – 1r – 1 – 1984-B500 – us A.T.L.A. [240]

CHRISTIANITY IN THE MODERN WORLD / Cairns, David Smith – New York:A.C. Armstrong ; London:Hodder and Stoughton, [1906?] – 1mf – 9 – 0-8370-3122-2 – 1985-1122 – us A.T.L.A. [240]

CHRISTIANITY IN THE NINETEENTH CENTURY : A RELIGIOUS AND PHILOSOPHICAL SURVEY OF THE IMMEDIATE PAST, ACCORDING TO THE SPIRIT OF JESUS / Chastel, Etienne Louis – London: Williams and Norgate, 1874 – 1mf – us A.T.L.A. [240]

CHRISTIANITY IN THE T'ANG DYNASTY (CCC208) = TANG-CH'AO CHI-TU-CHIAO CHIH YEN-CHIU / Kung, Tien-min – (In Chinese) – 1st ed. Hong Kong: Council on Christian Literature for Overseas Chinese, 1960 – 1r – 1 – 1984-B500 – us A.T.L.A. [240]

CHRISTIANITY JUDGED BY ITS FRUITS / Croslegh, Charles – (Includes bibliographical references) – London: SPCK, 1884 – 1mf – 9 – 0-8370-2783-7 – 1985-0783 – us A.T.L.A. [230]

THE CHRISTIANITY OF JESUS CHRIST / Pearse, Mark Guy – 18– – 9 – us A.T.L.A. [240]

THE CHRISTIANITY OF ST PAUL / Alexander, Sidney Arthur – London, NY: Longmans, Green, 1899 – 1mf – 9 – 0-8370-2063-8 – 1985-0063 – us A.T.L.A. [220]

CHRISTIANITY OLD AND NEW : LECTURES / Bacon, Benjamin Wisner – New Haven: Yale University Press, 1914 – 1mf – us A.T.L.A. [240]

CHRISTIANITY REVIVED IN THE EAST, OR, A NARRATIVE OF THE WORK OF GOD AMONG THE ARMENIANS OF TURKEY / Dwight, H GO – New York: Baker and Scribner, 1850 – 1mf – us A.T.L.A. [240]

CHRISTIANITY, THE RELIGION OF NATURE / Peabody, Andrew Preston – Boston: Gould and Lincoln, 1864.1 fiche. 8370-4682-3 – 9 – us A.T.L.A. [240]

CHRISTIANITY, THE WORLD-RELIGION : LECTURES DELIVERED IN INDIA BY JOHN HENRY BARROWS / Barrows, John Henry – (Includes appendix) – 1st ed. Madras: Christian Lit Society for India, 1897 – 1mf – 9 – 0-8370-2189-8 – 1985-0189 – us A.T.L.A. [230]

CHRISTIANITY TODAY : A PRESBYTERIAN JOURNAL – (Lacking some issues) – v1-11. May 1930-May 1949 – 5r – 1 – ATLA S0189 – us A.T.L.A. [073]

CHRISTIANITY TODAY – (v15- . 5,6,9) – v1- . 1956- – 1 – us UMI [240]

CHRISTIANITY VINDICATED BY ITS ENEMIES / Dorchester, Daniel – New York: Hunt & Eaton, c1896 – 1mf – 9 – 0-8370-2951-1 – 1985-0951 – us A.T.L.A. [230]

CHRISTIANITY'S STORM CENTRE : A STUDY OF THE MODERN CITY / Stelzele, Charles – New York: F.H. Revell, c1907 – 1mf – us A.T.L.A. [240]

CHRISTIANIZATION OF ANCIENT RUSSIA : A MILLENNIUM (988-1988) – 1992 – 9 – 92-3-102642-9 – fr UNESCO [240]

CHRISTIANIZED RATIONALISM AND THE HIGHER CRITICISM : A REPLY TO PROFESSOR HARNACK'S "WHAT IS CHRISTIANITY" / Anderson, Robert – Chicago: Winona Publishing Company, 1903 – 1mf – 9 – 0-8370-2093-X – 1985-0093 – us A.T.L.A. [210]

Christianizing the Home Committee of the National Christian Council of China *see* CHRISTIAN MARRIAGE (CCC117)

IL CHRISTIANO – (Title varies: The New Aurora) – 1913-17 (complete) – 1r – 1 – ATLA RS0144 – us A.T.L.A. [073]

CHRISTIANS AND SPAIN / Christian Foodship Committee – Watford, 1937? Fiche W 799. (Blodgett Collection of Spanish Civil War Pamphlets) – 9 – us H.U. College Libr [946]

CHRISTIANS AND THE NATIONAL SALVATION MOVEMENT (CCC278) / Shen, T'i-lan – (In Chinese) – Shanghai: Association Press of China, 1938 – 1r – 1 – 1984-6617 – us A.T.L.A. [240]

CHRISTIANS AND WARTIME SERVICE (CCC311) = CHI TU T'U YU CHAN SHIH FU WU / Wang, Hsiang-hsien; ed by Ying, Yuan-t'ao – (In Chinese) – Shanghai: Association Press of China, 1940 – 1r – 1 – 1984-6650 – us A.T.L.A. [950]

THE CHRISTIAN'S COMPANION / Whitefield, George – or Sermons on several subjects. 1738 – 1 – 11.06 – us Baptist [240]

THE CHRISTIANS OF ST THOMAS AND THEIR LITURGIES : COMPRISING THE ANAPHORAE OF ST. JAMES, ST. PETER, THE TWELVE APOSTLES, MAR DIONYSIUS, MAR XYSTUS, AND MAR EVANNIS, TOGETHER WITH THE ORDO COMMUNIS / Howard, George Broadley – Oxford: J. Henry and J. Parker, 1864 – 1mf – us A.T.L.A. [240]

THE CHRISTIAN'S PRESENT FOR ALL SEASONS, CONTAINING DEVOTIONAL THOUGHTS OF EMINENT DIVINES FROM JOSEPH HALL TO WILLIAM JAY / Harsha, David A – With an introductory essay on devotion by W. B. Sprague. c1866 – 9 – us A.T.L.A. [240]

THE CHRISTIAN'S RELATION TO EVOLUTION : A QUESTION OF GAIN OR LOSS / Johnson, Franklin – (Includes bibliographical references) – Chicago: Fleming H Revell, 1904 – 1mf – 9 – 0-8370-3787-5 – 1985-1787 – us A.T.L.A. [210]

CHRISTIAN'S SACRIFICE AND SERVICE OF PRAISE / Candlish, Robert Smith – Edinburgh: A. & C. Black, 1867. 1 fiche – 9 – us A.T.L.A. [240]

THE CHRISTIAN'S SECRET OF A HAPPY LIFE / Smith, Hannah Whitall – 1888 – 9 – us A.T.L.A. [240]

CHRISTIANS UNDER THE CRESCENT IN ASIA / Cutts, Edwards L – London: S.P.C.K.; New York: Pott, Young, [1877?] – 1mf – us A.T.L.A. [240]

Christiansen, Carl *see* INDEX FILICUM

Christiansen, Monty L *see* AN EXPLORATION OF THE OPINIONS OF RECREATION AND PARKS/LEISURE STUDIES FACULTY AND PUBLIC SECTOR PRACTITIONERS CONCERNING THE COMPUTER COMPETENCY SKILLS OF RECREATION AND PARKS/ LEISURE STUDIES BACCA-LAUREATE STUDENTS

CHRISTIANSTADS WECKOBLAD – Kristianstad, Sweden. 1810-40 – 4r – 1 – sw Kungliga [072]

Christianus *see* A LETTER TO THE REVEREND MR. JOHN WESTLY, OCCASION'D BY HIS SERMON AGAINST PREDESTINATION;...

Christie, James *see* CHOLERA EPIDEMICS IN EAST AFRICA.

CHRISTIE JOHNSTONE / Reade, Charles L – British Fiction Archive: Unit 2 – 9 – uk Bell [830]

Christie, Robert *see*
- THE DIGNITY OF LABOR: LECTURE TO THE YOUNG
- THE QUEBEC TELEGRAPH

CHRISTIE'S IMPRESSIONIST AND MODERN ART – (Extension of Christie's Pictorial Archive. 9,400 captioned photographs of items sold by Christie's, with full details of price realized and date of sale. Arranged in alphabetical order by artist, in four sub-sections: British and Foreign, Paintings and Sculpture. Printed Index of Artists. Binder) – 1950-83 – 158mf – 9 – $890.00 – 0-907006-57-4 – uk Mindata [700]

Christie's. London *see* CHRISTIE'S PICTORIAL SALES REVIEW

Christie's. New York *see* CHRISTIE'S PICTORIAL ARCHIVE NEW YORK

CHRISTIE'S PICTORIAL ARCHIVE : DECORATIVE AND APPLIED ART – (Available in 5 binders. Individual titles also listed separately) – 710mf – 9 – $3.580.00 coll – 0-907006-47-7 – uk Mindata [700]

CHRISTIE'S PICTORIAL ARCHIVE : PAINTING AND GRAPHIC ART – (Available in 4 binders. Individual titles also listed separately) – 498mf – 9 – $2,500.00 coll – 0-907006-17-5 – uk Mindata [700]

CHRISTIE'S PICTORIAL ARCHIVE : PAINTING AND GRAPHIC ART – DECORATIVE AND APPLIED ART – (Complete set consists of 9 sections. May be purchased separately. Individual titles also listed) – 1900-79 – 1208mf – 9 – $5,900.00 set – 0-907006-52-3 – uk Mindata [700]

CHRISTIE'S PICTORIAL ARCHIVE: DECORATIVE AND APPLIED ART *see*
- CERAMICS
- GENERAL DECORATIVE AND APPLIED ART
- ORIENTAL WORKS OF ART
- SILVER

Christie's Pictorial Archive. London *see* BRITISH SCHOOL

CHRISTIE'S PICTORIAL ARCHIVE NEW YORK / Christie's. New York – (Over 35,000 captioned photographs of items sold by New York Christie's with full catalogue details, prices realized and date of sale. In alphabetical order, by artist. 6 sections with binder for each) – 599mf – 9 – $3,400.00 set – 0-907006-92-2 – uk Mindata [700]

CHRISTIE'S PICTORIAL ARCHIVE NEW YORK *see*
- 19TH CENTURY PAINTINGS
- AMERICAN DECORATIVE ART
- AMERICAN PAINTINGS
- CONTEMPORARY PAINTINGS, DRAWINGS AND SCULPTURE
- IMPRESSIONIST AND MODERN PAINTINGS, DRAWINGS AND SCULPTURE
- OLD MASTER PAINTINGS AND DRAWINGS

CHRISTIE'S PICTORIAL ARCHIVE: PAINTING AND GRAPHIC ART *see*
- BRITISH SCHOOL
- DUTCH AND FLEMISH SCHOOL
- FURNITURE
- ITALIAN SCHOOL
- OTHER SCHOOLS AND GRAPHIC ART

CHRISTIE'S PICTORIAL SALES REVIEW / Christie's. London – (Comprehensive cumulative update of Christie's Pictorial Archive. Full catalogue details, prices realized, date of sale. Arranged in alphabetical order by artist. Over 40,000 illus. In 4 sections, with binder for each) – 341mf – 9 – $2,000.00 set – 0-907006-18-3 – uk Mindata [700]

CHRISTIE'S PICTORIAL SALES REVIEW *see*
- ENGLISH AND VICTORIAN PICTURES, DRAWINGS AND WATERCOLOURS
- IMPRESSIONIST, MODERN AND CONTEMPORARY PAINTINGS, DRAWINGS AND SCULPTURE AND MODERN PRINTS
- OLD MASTER AND CONTINENTAL DRAWINGS, WATERCOLOURS AND PRINTS
- OLD MASTER, CONTINENTAL AND 19TH CENTURY PICTURES

Christina de Wonderbare *see* GEDENKBOEK 1150-1940

CHRISTINA ROSSETTI : A BIOGRAPHICAL AND CRITICAL STUDY / Bell, Mackenzie – London: Thomas Burleigh, Fourth ed 1898 – 1 roll – 1 – 1-55879-537-5 – uk Libr Preservation [750]

Christinat, J -L *see* PARENTE RITUELLE ET SOCIETE A CHIA, PEROU

Christine-Marie, Soeur *see* BIBLIOGRAPHIE ANALYTIQUE DE L'OEUVRE DU DOCTEUR PIERRE JOBIN...

CHRISTKATHOLISCHES KIRCHENBLATT – v89-114. 1966-91 (incomplete) – Inquire – 1 – ATLA S0359 – us A.T.L.A. [073]

EIN CHRISTL. ERMANUNG ZU WARER HOFFNUNG IN GOTT / Schmid, C – Zuerich, Chr. Froschouer. 1527. BME-91 1 – 9 – ne IDC [240]

DAS CHRISTLICH KINDERLIED : D. MARTINI LUTHERI. ICH SECH STIMMEN. / Walther, J – Wittenberg, 1565 – 1 – us Sibley [780]

EYN CHRISTLICH VNTERRICHT EYNES GOTTSELIGEN LEBENS... / Bugenhagen, J – [Altenburg, 1526] – 1mf – 9 – ne IDC [240]

DIE CHRISTLICH-ARABISCHE LITTERATUR BIS ZUR FRAENKISCHEN ZEIT... / Graf, G – Freiburg. v7(1). 1905 – 1mf – 9 – ne IDC [240]

DER CHRISTLICHE ALTAR / Braun, J – Muenchen. v1-2. 1924 – 50mf – 8 – Dfl175.00 – ne Slangenburg [240]

DAS CHRISTLICHE ALTERTHUM : ODER, DIE KATHOLISCHE KIRCHE IN IHREM KAMPFE MIT DEN VERFOLGUNGEN UND IRRLEHREN: EIN VOLLSTAENDIGES LEBEN DER HEILIGEN DES CHRISTLICHEN ALTERTHUMS IM ANSCHLUSS AN DIE KIRCHENGESCHICHTE / Bayerle, Bernard Gustav – (Includes index of saints) – New York: S Zickel [distributor], 1862 – 2mf – 9 – 0-8370-6883-5 – 1986-0883 – us A.T.L.A. [240]

DIE CHRISTLICHE APOLOGETIK IM NEUNZEHNTEN JAHRHUNDERT : LEBENSBILDER UND CHARAKTERISTIKEN DEUTSCHER EVANGELISCHER GLAUBENSZEUGEN AUS DER JUENGSTEN VERGANGENHEIT / Zoeckler, Otto – (Includes bibliographical references) – Guetersloh: C Bertelsmann, 1904 – 1mf – 9 – 0-8370-8879-8 – 1986-2879 – us A.T.L.A. [230]

DER CHRISTLICHE BOTSCHAFTER – (Lacking some pgs. Some original pgs damaged) – nos 1-111. 1836-1946 – 81r – 1 – ATLA S0106 – us A.T.L.A. [073]

DAS CHRISTLICHE DES PLATONISMUS, ODER, SOKRATES UND CHRISTUS : EINE RELIGIONSPHILOSPHISCHE UNTERSUCHUNG / Baur, Ferdinand Christian – Tuebingen: L.F. Fues, 1837 – 1mf – us A.T.L.A. [240]

CHRISTLICHE DOGMATIK / Biedermann, Alois Emanuel – Berlin: G. Reimer, 1884-1885 – 3mf – us A.T.L.A. [240]

DIE CHRISTLICHE ERFAHRUNG...LUTHERS KATECHISMUS ARTIKEL 3: SECHS VORLESUNGEN / Scholz, Hermann – Berlin: Julius Springer. 1902. 1 fiche – 9 – us A.T.L.A. [240]

DIE CHRISTLICHE FAMILIE : IM KAMPFE GEGEN FEINDLICHE MAECHTE: VORTRAEGE UEBER CHRISTLICHE EHE UND ERZIEHUNG / Hug, Gall Joseph – 2., vielfach verm Aufl. Freiburg (Schweiz): Universitaetsbuchhandlung (B Veith), 1896 – 1mf – 9 – 0-8370-6985-8 – 1986-0985 – us A.T.L.A. [240]

DER CHRISTLICHE FREIHEITSBEGRIFF / Ziegelmeier, Otto W – 1994 – 1mf – 9 – DM60.00 – 3-89349-909-1 – gw Hänsel [240]

DER CHRISTLICHE GLAUBE : NACH DEM BEKENNTNISS DER LUTHERISCHEN KIRCHE: VORTRAEGE / Langbein, Bernhard Adolf – Leipzig: Justus Naumann, 1873 – 1mf – 9 – 0-8370-4390-5 – 1985-2390 – us A.T.L.A. [240]

DER CHRISTLICHE GLAUBE FUER DIE MENSCHEN DER GEGENWART: ZWOELF VORTRAEGE / Kuelpe, Ernst – Wismar i.M.: Hans Bartholdi, 1907. 1 fiche – 9 – us A.T.L.A. [240]

DER CHRISTLICHE GLAUBE IN ACHT BUECHERN / Hackenschmidt, Karl; ed by Calwer Verlagsverein – (Includes index) – Calw: Vereinsbuchh., 1901 – 1mf – 9 – 0-8370-4760-9 – 1985-2760 – us A.T.L.A. [240]

DAS CHRISTLICHE GLAUBENSBEKENNTNIS : PROTESTANTISMUS GEGEN ORTHODOXISMUS / Richter, F – Berlin: Franz Lobeck, 1868 – 1mf – 9 – 0-8370-8707-4 – 1986-2707 – us A.T.L.A. [240]

DIE CHRISTLICHE GLAUBENSLEHRE / Luthardt, Christoph Ernst – 1906 – 9 – us A.T.L.A. [240]

CHRISTLICHE GLAUBENSLEHRE IN LEITSAETZEN : FUER EINE AKADEMISCHE VORLESUNG / Reischle, Max – 2. Aufl. Halle a.S: Max Niemeyer, 1902 – 1mf – 9 – 0-8370-5150-9 – 1985-3150 – us A.T.L.A. [240]

DER CHRISTLICHE GOTTESBEGRIFF : BEITRAG ZUR SPECULATIVEN THEOLOGIE / Rocholl, Rudolf – (Includes authors index) – Goettingen: Vandenhoeck & Ruprecht, 1900 – 1mf – 9 – 0-8370-5275-0 – 1985-3275 – us A.T.L.A. [210]

DER CHRISTLICHE GOTTESGLAUBE : IN SEINEM VERHAELTNIS ZUR HEUTIGEN PHILOSOPHIE UND NATURWISSENSCHAFT / Wobbermin, Georg – 2. umgearb Aufl. Berlin: Alexander Duncker, 1907 – 1mf – 9 – 0-8370-6469-4 – 1986-0469 – us A.T.L.A. [240]

DER CHRISTLICHE GOTTESGLAUBE: SEINE VORGESCHICHTE UN URGESCHICHTE / Holtzmann, Oskar – Giessen: Alfred Toepelmann, 1905. 1 fiche – 9 – us A.T.L.A. [240]

DIE CHRISTLICHE HEILSGEWISSHEIT : EINE SYSTEMATISCHE DARSTELLUNG DES MITTELPUNKTS EVANGELISCHEN HEILSVERSTAENDNISSES / Clasen, L – Halle a. S: Eugen Strien, 1897 – 1mf – 9 – 0-8370-3458-2 – 1985-1458 – us A.T.L.A. [240]

DIE CHRISTLICHE HEILSLEHRE / Buttmann, Philipp Karl – Leipzig: Zangenberg & Himly, 1872. 1 fiche – 9 – us A.T.L.A. [240]

DER CHRISTLICHE JUGEND-FREUND – v1-74. 1878-1951 (gaps) – Inquire – 1 – ATLA 1994-S025 – us A.T.L.A. [073]

CHRISTLICHE KINDER-ZEITUNG – Duesseldorf, Germany. 1833-36 – 1 – gw Mikrofilm [072]

DIE CHRISTLICHE KINDER-ZEITUNG – Augsburg, 1841 n1-12 – 1 – Dist. gw Mikrofilm – gw Misc Inst [370]

DIE CHRISTLICHE KIRCHE DES MITTELALTERS IN DEN HAUPTMOMENTEN IHRER ENTWICKLUNG / Baur, Ferdinand Christian – Leipzig: Fues, 1869. (Geschichte der christlichen Kirche / von Ferdinand Christian Baur; 3. Bd.) – 2mf – us A.T.L.A. [240]

DIE CHRISTLICHE LEHRE : NACH DEM GEGENWAERTIGEN STANDE DER THEOLOGISCHEN WISSENSCHAFT UND IHRE VERMITTLUNG AN DIE GEMEINDE / Dorner, Isaak August – Berlin: Schwetschke, 1904 – 1mf – 9 – 0-8370-2952-X – 1985-0952 – us A.T.L.A. [240]

DIE CHRISTLICHE LEHRE AUF HEILSGESCHICHTLICHEM GRUNDE / Buchholtz, Ludwig – Hoerter: Otto Buchholtz, 1879. 1 fiche – 9 – us A.T.L.A. [240]

DIE CHRISTLICHE LEHRE VON DER SUENDE: EINE UNTERSUCHUNG ZUR SYSTEMATISCHEN THEOLOGIE / Clemen, Carl – Goettingen: Vandenhoeck & Rup., 1897. 1 fiche – 9 – us A.T.L.A. [240]

DIE CHRISTLICHE LEHRE VON DER VERSOEHNUNG : IN IHRER GESCHICHTLICHEN ENTWICKLUNG VON DER AELTESTEN ZEIT BIS AUF DIE NEUESTE / Baur, Ferdinand Christian – Tuebingen: C.F. Osiander, 1838 – 2mf – us A.T.L.A. [240]

DIE CHRISTLICHE LIEBESTHAETIGKEIT / Uhlhorn, Gerhard – Stuttgart: D. Gundert, 1895 – 2mf – us A.T.L.A. [240]

CHRISTLICHE PREDIGT AUS DEM 48. CAPITTEL ESAIAE VON DEN GROSSEN WOLTHATEN GOTTES... / Hoffmann, David – Helmstadt, 1589 – 1mf – ne IDC [240]

EINE CHRISTLICHE PREDIGT VBER DER LEICHE DES...HERRN M : MATTHIAE FLACIJ JLLYRICI...GESTELLET... / Flacius Illyricus d.A E, M – N.p., 1575 – 3mf – 9 – ne IDC [240]

EIN CHRISTLICHE PREDIGT, VON CHRISTLICHER EINIGKEIT DER THEOLOGEN AUGSPUERGISCHER CONFESSION,... / Andreae d.A E, J – Wolffenbuettel, 1570 – 1mf – 9 – ne IDC [240]

CHRISTLICHE PREDIGT VON DER VOCAL UND INSTRUMENTALISCHEN MUSIC... / Anwander, G – Tuebingen: G Gruppenbach, 1606 – 1 – us Sibley [780]

CHRISTLICHE PREDIGTEN. VBER EN CXXIX. PSALM DAUIDS. DARINNE ANGEZEIGET WIRD WIE DIE CALUINISCHE SCHWERMER DER KIRCH ZU WITTEMBERG VNND IM GANTZEN CHURKREISS SEYEN MIT JHREM HEILLOSEN PFLUG... / Huber, S – Wittemberg, 1594 – 1mf – ne IDC [240]

DER CHRISTLICHE RELIGIONS-UNTERRICHT : AUF GRUNDLAGE DER HEILIGEN SCHRIFT UND NACH PAEDAGOGISCHEN GRUNDSAETZEN IN DER OBERKLASSE DER VOLKSSCHULE: EIN HANDBUCH FUER LEHRER / Kehr, C – (Includes bibliographical references) – 3. Aufl. Gotha: C F Thienemann. 2v. 1875 – 2mf – 9 – 0-8370-8583-7 – 1986-2583 – us A.T.L.A. [240]

CHRISTLICHE UND JUEDISCHE OSTERTAFELN / Schwartz, Eduard – (AGWG.PG Bd 8 (1904-1905)) – Berlin, 1905 – 6mf – 8 – Dfl25.00 – ne Slangenburg [240]

AIN CHRISTLICHE VNDERRICHTUNG / Landtsperger, J – 1527. BME-64 1 – 9 – ne IDC [240]

CHRISTLICHE VNDERRICHTUNG *see* AIN CHRISTLICHE VNDERRICHTUNG

DAS CHRISTLICHE VOLKS-BLATT – v1-10. 1856-66 (gaps) – 1r – 1 – ATLA 1994-S024 – us A.T.L.A. [073]

CHRISTLICHE VOLKSZEITUNG – Esseg (Osijek), Jugoslawien. 6 Jan-28 Jul 1938; 4 Mar-19 Dez 1940 – 2r – 1 – gw Mikrofilm [949]

CHRISTLICHE VOLKSZEITUNG – Osijek, Yugoslavia. Sept 1925-Aug 1935; Jun-Dec 1937; Aug-Dec 1938; 1941 – 5r – 1 – us L of C Photodup [949]

DIE CHRISTLICHE WAHRHEITSGEWISSHEIT : IHR LETZTER GRUND UND IHRE ENTSTEHUNG / Ihmels, Ludwig – (Includes bibliographical references) – Leipzig: A Deichert, 1901 – 1mf – 9 – 0-8370-3719-0 – 1985-1719 – us A.T.L.A. [230]

CHRISTLICHE...AUSSLEGUNG IN DAS ERSTE CAPITEL DES EUANGELISTEN S. JOHANNIS... / Mathesius, Johannes – Leipzig, 1589 – 4mf – ne IDC [240]

DIE CHRISTLICHEN GRUNDWAHRHEITEN : ODER, DIE ALLGEMEINEN PRINCIPIEN DER CHRISTLICHEN DOGMATIK / Goltz, Hermann von der – Gotha: F A Perthes, 1873 – 1mf – 9 – 0-8370-3259-8 – 1985-1259 – us A.T.L.A. [240]

DIE CHRISTLICHEN LITERATUREN DES ORIENTS / Baumstark, Anton – Leipzig: G.J. Goeschen, 1911. (Sammlung Goeschen) – 1mf – us A.T.L.A. [240]

CHRISTLICHER BUNDES-BOTE – (In German) – Berne, IN. 1882-1930 – 21r – 1 – $1,785.00 – D3365 – us Scholarly Res [071]

CHRISTLICHER BUNDES-BOTE – v1-66. 1882-1947 (complete) – 21r – 1 – ATLA 1993-S022 – us A.T.L.A. [073]

CHRISTLICHER FAMILIEN-KALENDER – 1884-85 (complete) – 1r – 1 – ATLA 1993-S023 – us A.T.L.A. [073]

CHRISTLICHER, NUETZLICHER, U. NOHTWENDIGER TRACTAT UND BERICHT VON DER KINDER TAUFF, WIDER DEN IRRTHUMB U. FALSCHE LEHRE DER SCHWERMER. EINER VORREDEN NIC. SELNECCERI VOM EXORCISMO / Alberus, E – Notopyrgi ad Menium. 1591. BME-215 1 – 9 – ne IDC [240]

AIN CHRISTLICHER SEDNPRIEFF AN FRAUW ANNA... / Bugenhagen, J – [Augsburg, 1525] – 1mf – 9 – ne IDC [240]

CHRISTLICHER TEXTILARBEITER – (Since 1906: Textilarbeiter-Zeitung) – Krefeld, Germany. 28 Sept 1901-8 Jul 1933 – 7r – 1 – gw Mikrofilm [072]

CHRISTLICHER TEXTIL-ARBEITER/ TEXTILARBEITER-ZEITUNG – Krefeld, 28 Sept 1901-8 Jul 1933 – 7r – 1 – DM780.00 – gw Mikro Press [331]

CHRISTLICHER UNDERRICHT UND WARHAFFTIGE ERWEISZUNG...DAS JHESUS CHRISTUS...DURCH D. PERSONL. VEREINIGUNG D. GOTTL. U. VLEUESCHL. NATUREN...IN ALLE GOETTLICHE HERRLICHKEYT...GESETZT SEYE / Marbach, J – Straszburg, 1567 – 13mf – ne IDC [240]

CHRISTLICHER VND WARHAFFTIGER UNDERRICHT VON DEN WORTEN DER EINSATZUNG DES HEYLIGEN ABENDTMALS JHESU CHRISTI... / Marbach, J – Straszburg, 1566 – 7mf – ne IDC [240]

CHRISTLICHES BEDENCKEN DES MINISTERIJ DER KIRCHEN ZU BRUNSCHWIG. AUFF D. MAIORS REPITITION VND ENDTLICHE ERKLERUNG. GELANGEND DEN STREIT, OB GUTE WERCKE ZUR SELIGKEIT NOETIG SIND, ALSO, DAS ES VNMUEGLICH SEY, OHNE GUTE WERCKE SELIG ZUWERDEN / Major, G – N.p., 1568 – 1mf – ne IDC [240]

CHRISTLICHES GESANGBUCH; CHRISTIAN SONG BOOK OR COLLECTION OF PSALMS AND HYMNS – 1 – 23.10 – us Baptist [240]

CHRISTLICHES VOLK HEIDELBERG *see* DER BOTE AUS KURPFALZ

CHRISTLICHES VOLKS-BLATT KARLSRUHE *see* DER BOTE AUS KURPFALZ

CHRISTLICH-PALAESTINISCHE FRAGMENTE AUS DER OMAJJADEN-MOSCHEE ZU DAMASKUS / Schulthess, Friedrich – Berlin, 1905 – 3mf – 8 – Dfl13.00 – ne Slangenburg [240]

Christlieb, Marie L *see* A STRUGGLE FOR A SOUL AND OTHER STORIES OF LIFE AND WORK IN SOUTH INDIA

Christlieb, Theodor *see*
- AERZTLICHE MISSIONEN
- THE BEST METHODS OF COUNTERACTING MODERN INFIDELITY
- PROTESTANT FOREIGN MISSIONS: THEIR PRESENT STATE
- THEODOR CHRISTLIEB, D.D.: OF BONN

CHRISTLIJCKE SENDTBRIEUEN, INHOLDENDE SEER VEELE VNDE VERSCHEYDENE SCHOONE GODTLIJCKE VERMANINGHEN VNDE ONDERRICHTINGHEN / Joris, David – Brieven van 5146-56. BME-382 1 – 9 – ne IDC [240]

CHRISTMAS.. / Dawson, William Francis – London: E. Stock, 1902 – 1 – us U.W. Library [390]

THE CHRISTMAS BELLS AND NEW YEAR'S CALL – (Suppl of: Morning Chronicle) – Quebec, Canada. 1884; 1885; 1886 – 1r – 1 – Can$35.00 – cn Can Microfilming [072]

CHRISTMAS BOX – 1828-29 – 6mf – 9 – £50.00 – uk Chadwyck [800]

THE CHRISTMAS CHIMES AND NEW YEAR'S CALL – (Suppl of: Quebec Morning Chronicle) – Quebec, Canada. 1887; 1888; 1889 – 1r – 1 – Can$35.00 – cn Can Microfilming [072]

CHRISTMAS EVANS : THE PREACHER OF WILD WALES : HIS COUNTRY, HIS TIMES AND HIS CONTEMPORARIES / Hood, Edwin Paxton – London: Hodder and Stoughton, 1881 – 1mf – us A.T.L.A. [240]

THE CHRISTMAS HIRELINGS / Braddon, Mary Elizabeth – British Fiction Archive: Unit 5 – 9 – uk Bell [830]

CHRISTMAS IN RITUAL AND TRADITION, CHRISTIAN AND PAGAN / Miles, Clement A – London: T. Fisher Unwin, 1912 – 1mf – us A.T.L.A. [306]

CHRISTMAS VALLEY GAZETTE – Christmas Valley, OR. -m. Mar 1962-May 1965. 1 roll – 1 – us U.O. Library [071]

CHRISTMAS-EVE AND EASTER-DAY : A POEM / Browning, Robert – London: Chapman and Hall, 1850 – 1 roll – 1 – 1-55879-931-1 – uk Libr Preservation [810]

Christoffel, Karl *see* REBE UND WEIN IN GOETHES WELTBILD

DIE CHRISTOLOGIE DER APOKALYPSE DES JOHANNES (T.U.U. 5-85) / Holtz, T – Berlin, 1962 – 5mf – 9 – ne Slangenburg [240]

CHRISTOLOGIE DES ALTEN TESTAMENTES / Boehl, Eduard – Wien: Wilhelm Braumueller, 1882.1 fiche – 9 – us A.T.L.A. [240]

DIE CHRISTOLOGIE DES H. IGNATIUS VON ANTIOCHIEN / Rackl, M – Freiburg Brsg., 1914 – 8mf – 9 – ne Slangenburg [240]

DIE CHRISTOLOGIE DES NEUEN TESTAMENTS : EIN BIBLISCH-THEOLOGISCHER VERSUCH / Beyschlag, Willibald – Berlin: Ludwig Rauh, 1866 – 1mf – 9 – 0-8370-2328-9 – 1985-0328 – us A.T.L.A. [220]

DIE CHRISTOLOGIE SEIT SCHLEIERMACHER : IHRE GESCHICHTE UND IHRE BEGRUENDUNG / Faut, S – Tuebingen: J C B Mohr (Paul Siebeck), 1907 – 1mf – 9 – 0-8370-4595-9 – 1985-2595 – us A.T.L.A. [240]

CHRISTOLOGIE TRADITIONNELLE ET LA FOI PROTESTANTE *see* COLLECTED WORKS

THE CHRISTOLOGY OF PAUL'S OPPONENTS IN SECOND CORINTHIANS AND ITS RELATIONSHIP TO THEIR CONCEPT OF APOSTLESHIP / Howell, David B – 1982 – 1 – 5.04 – us Baptist [240]

CHRISTOPH COLUMBUS, DER DON QUICHOTE DES OZEANS : EIN PORTRAET / Wassermann, Jakob – (Includes bibliographical references) – 11. bis 20. Auflage. Berlin: S Fischer, 1929 – 1r – 1 – us U.W. Library [946]

CHRISTOPH ERNST FRHR. V. HOUWALD ALS DRAMATIKER / Schmidtborn, Otto – (Includes bibliographical references) – Marburg a.L.: N G Elwert, 1909 – 1 – us U.W. Library [430]

CHRISTOPH MARLOW : TRAUERSPIEL IN VIER AKTEN / Wildenbruch, Ernst von – 2. Aufl. Berlin: G Grote, 1902 – 1 – us U.W. Library [820]

CHRISTOPH MARTIN WIELAND'S LEBEN UND WIRKEN IN SCHWABEN UND IN DER SCHWEIZ / Ofterdinger, Ludwig Felix – Heilbronn: Gebr. Henninger, 1877 – 1r – 1 – us U.W. Library [430]

CHRISTOPH PANKRATIUS MIESERICH UNTER DEN SELIGEN / Wellems, Hugo – Berlin: Nordland Verlag, [1943] – 1r – 1 – us U.W. Library [943]

CHRISTOPH PANZER : ROMAN / Reichelt, Johannes – Dresden: Wodni & Lindecke, [194-?] – 1r – 1 – us U.W. Library [830]

CHRISTOPH PECHLIN : EINE INTERNATIONALE LEBENSGESCHICHTE / Raabe, Wilhelm Karl – Leipzig: E J Guenther, 1873 – 1r – 1 – us U.W. Library [830]

CHRISTOPHE COLOMB / Lemercier – (French Theatre Series). Paris. L. Collin. 1809 – 9 – fr Hachette [820]

CHRISTOPHER AND GAY: A PARTISAN'S VIEW OF THE GREENWICH VILLAGE HOMOSEXUAL SCENE / Hamilton, Wallace – New York: Saturday Review Press, 1973. 236p – 1 – us U.W. Library [360]

CHRISTOPHER COLUMBUS COLLECTION OF THE LIBRARY OF CONGRESS / ed by Larson, Everette E – (Part 1: Works in English. 631mf. $3,475.00. ISBN 1-55655-391-9; Part 2: Non-English Works. 740mf. $3,025.00. ISBN 1-55655-392-7. With printed guides) – 9 – $6,175.00 set – us UPA [975]

CHRISTOPHER COWAN PAPERS, MS 1328 / Cowan, Christopher – (Letters, agreements relating to lands in Virginia Military District of Ohio) – 1784, 1787, 1798, 1815-26 – 1r – 1 – us Western Res [920]

Christopher, H *see* GEOTHERMAL ENERGY

Christopher, Luella S *see* PALAU'S EVOLVING RELATIONSHIP WITH THE U.S.

Christophers, Samuel W *see* THE EPWORTH SINGERS AND OTHER POETS OF METHODISM

Christophersen, Pedro F *see* LOS PARTIDOS POLITICOS Y EL SUFRAGIO EN UNA DEMOCRACIA ORGANICA

CHRISTOPHORI CLAVII BAMBERGENSIS E SOCIETATE IES OPERUM MATHEMATICORUM TOMUS PRIMUS-QUINTUS / Clavius, Christoph – Moguntiae: sumptibus A Hierat. 5v. 1611-12. SEM35P61 – 1r – 1 – Can$18.00 – cn Bibl Nat [510]

CHRISTOPHORI CLAVII...IN SPHAERAM IOANNIS DE SACRO BOSCO COMMENTARIUS / Clavius, Christoph – Venetiis: apud Bernardum Basam, 1596. 483,(1)p.ill – 1 – us U.W. Library [520]

CHRISTOPHORI MORALIS HYSPANIENSIS MISSARUM LIBER PRIMUS (-SECUNDUS) / Morales, C de – 1546 (-51) – 1 – us Sibley [780]

CHRISTOWELL / Blackmore, Richard Doddridge – British Fiction Archive: Unit 3 – 9 – uk Bell [830]

CHRISTROSEN IM MARIENGARTEN : ODER, DIE GEHEIMNISSE DES HEILIGEN ROSENKRANZES / Hattler, Franz – 3., verm Aufl. Innsbruck: Fel Rauch, 1894 – 1mf – 9 – 0-8370-8347-8 – 1986-2347 – us A.T.L.A. [240]

CHRIST'S COMPANY AND OTHER POEMS / Dixon, Richard Watson – London: Smith, Elder, 1861 – 1 roll – 1 – 1-55879-984-2 – uk Libr Preservation [810]

CHRIST'S CURE FOR CARE / Pearse, Mark Guy – 190- – 9 – us A.T.L.A. [240]

CHRIST'S ESTIMATE OF HIMSELF / Beardslee, Clark S – Hartford: Hartford Seminary Press, 1899.1 fiche – 9 – us A.T.L.A. [240]

Christ's Hospital, Topeka, KS *see* PATIENT REGISTERS

CHRIST'S KINGDOM ON EARTH : OR, THE CHURCH AND HER DIVINE CONSTITUTION, ORGANIZATION, AND FRAMEWORK: EXPLAINED FOR THE PEOPLE / Meagher, James Luke – (Includes index) – New York: Russell, 1892 – 2mf – 9 – 0-8370-6920-3 – 1986-0920 – us A.T.L.A. [240]

CHRIST'S KINGDOM UPON EARTH : A SERIES OF DISCOURSES / Flint, Robert – Edinburgh: W. Blackwood, 1865 – 1mf – us A.T.L.A. [240]

CHRIST'S OBJECT LESSONS / White, Ellen Gould Harmon – Oakland: Pacific Press, 1900. 1 fiche. 8370-5820-1 – 9 – us A.T.L.A. [240]

CHRIST'S SERMON ON THE MOUNT AND ORIENTALISM (CCC112) = PA FUH CHEN CHING / Chu, T'ui-yu – (In Chinese) – Shanghai: Christian Literature Society, 1931 – 1r – 1 – 1984-B500 – us A.T.L.A. [230]

CHRISTUS : DAS EVANGELIUM UND SEINE WELTGESCHICHTLICHE BEDEUTUNG / Schell, Herman – (Includes index) – Mainz: Kirchheim, 1906 – 1mf – 9 – 0-8370-5081-2 – 1985-3081 – us A.T.L.A. [240]

CHRISTUS – no. 1-76. Paris. 1954-72. tb: 1954-63 – 5 – fr A.C.R.P.P. [073]

CHRISTUS COMPROBATOR: THE TESTIMONY OF CHRIST TO THE OLD TESTAMENT: SEVEN ADDRESSES / Ellicott, Charles J – London: S.P.C.K., 1892. 1 fiche – 9 – us A.T.L.A. [240]

CHRISTUS CONSUMMATOR: SOME ASPECTS OF THE WORK AND PERSON OF CHRIST IN RELATION TO MODERN THOUGHT / Westcott, Brooke Foss – 1886 – 9 – us A.T.L.A. [240]

CHRISTUS CONSUMMATOR:...CHRIST IN RELATION TO MODERN THOUGHT / Westcott, Brooke Foss – London: Macmillan, 1887.1 fiche – 9 – us A.T.L.A. [240]

CHRISTUS, DER ZWEITE ADAM = SECOND ADAM : DAS SUEHNOPFER FUER DEN ANGEHORSAM DES ERSTEN ADAM UND FUER DIE SUENDEN SEINER NACHKOMMEN: ZWANZIG CONFERENZEN / Coret, Jacques – (In German. Includes bibliographical references) – Regensburg: Georg Joseph Manz, 1870 – 2mf – 9 – 0-8370-6894-0 – 1986-0894 – us A.T.L.A. [240]

DER CHRISTUS DES GLAUBENS UN DER JESUS DER GESCHICHTE / Strauss, David Friedrich – Berlin: Franz Duncker, 1865. 1 fiche – 9 – us A.T.L.A. [240]

CHRISTUS FUER UNS : PASSIONSPREDIGTEN / Rueling, Joseph – Leipzig: Friedrich Jansa, 1906 – 1mf – 9 – 0-8370-9738-X – 1986-3738 – us A.T.L.A. [240]

CHRISTUS LIBERATOR : AN OUTLINE STUDY OF AFRICA / Parsons, Ellen C – (Includes index) – New York: Macmillan, 1905 – 1mf – 9 – 0-8370-6295-0 – 1985-0295 – us A.T.L.A. [240]

CHRISTUS MAGISTER / Pearson, Alfred – 1892 – 9 – us A.T.L.A. [240]

CHRISTUS REDEMPTOR : AN OUTLINE STUDY OF THE ISLAND WORLD OF THE PACIFIC / Montgomery, Helen Barrett – New York: Macmillan, 1909 – 1mf – us A.T.L.A. [240]

DAS CHRISTUSBILD DER APOSTEL UND DER NACHAPOSTOLISCHEN ZEIT / Schenkel, Daniel – Leipzig: F A Brockhaus, 1879 – 1mf – 9 – 0-8370-5143-6 – 1985-3143 – us A.T.L.A. [220]

DAS CHRISTUSBILD DES URCHRISTLICHEN GLAUBENS IN RELIGIONSGESCHICHTLICHER BELEUCHTUNG = THE EARLY CHRISTIAN CONCEPTION OF CHRIST : ITS SIGNIFICANCE AND VALUE IN THE HISTORY OF RELIGION / Pfleiderer, Otto – (In English) – 1mf – 9 – 0-8370-5449-4 – 1985-3449 – us A.T.L.A. [240]

DAS CHRISTUSBILD DES URCHRISTLICHEN GLAUBENS IN RELIGIONSGESCHICHTLICHER BELEUCHTUNG : VORTRAG / Pfleiderer, Otto – (Includes bibliographical references) – Berlin: Georg Reimer, 1903 – 1mf – 9 – 0-8370-5153-3 – 1985-3153 – us A.T.L.A. [240]

CHRISTUSBILDER : UNTERSUCHUNGEN ZUR CHRISTLICHEN LEGENDE (T.U.U. 2-18) / Dobschuetz, E V – Leipzig, 1899 – 15mf – 9 – ne Slangenburg [240]

CHRISTUSFORMMIGKEIT IN IHRER HISTORISCHEN ENTFALTUNG / Richstaetter, C – Koeln, 1949 – 9mf – 8 – ne Slangenburg [290]

CHRISTUSFROMMIGKEIT IN IHRER HISTORISCHEN ENTFALTUNG / Richstaetter, C – Koeln, 1949 – 9mf – 8 – ne Slangenburg [240]

DAS CHRISTUS-PROBLEM : GRUNDLINIEN ZU EINER SOZIAL-THEOLOGIE / Kalthoff, Albert – 2. Aufl. Leipzig: Eugen Diederichs, 1903 – 1mf – 9 – 0-8370-3838-3 – 1985-1838 – us A.T.L.A. [240]

CHROMATISCHE FANTASIE UND FUGE / Bach, Johann Sebastian – Leipsic: Bureau de musique/Vienne, Hoffmeister et Kuehnel, 1802 – 1 – us Sibley [780]

CHROMATOGRAPHIA – v14- 1981- – 5,6,9 – us UMI [540]

CHROMATOGRAPHIC REVIEWS – v1-15. 1959-71 – 1,5,6,13 – sz Elsevier [073]

CHROME DUST – Nye. Mont. 1954-1960 – 1 – us UMI [071]

CHROMOSOMA – v. 1-80. 1939-80 – 1,5,9 – 15,720.00 – us UMI [073]

CHRONA1MY PRZYRODE OJCZYSTA – Cracow. v. 1-7. 1945-1951. Incomplete – 1 – us NY Public [073]

Chroni, Stiliani *see* INCENTIVE MOTIVATION, COMPETITIVE ORIENTATION AND GENDER IN COLLEGIATE ALPINE SKIERS

CHRONIA MONASTEREII S ALBANI *see*
- ANNALES MONASTERII S. ALBANI (CHRONIA..5)
- CHRONICA ET ANNALES 1259-1296, 1307-1324, 1392-1406 (CHRONIA..3)
- CHRONICA ET ANNALES 1259-1307 (CHRONIA..2)
- GESTA ABBATUM MONASTERII S. ALBANI (CHRONIA..4)
- HISTORIA ANGLICANA (CHRONIA..1)
- REGISTRA QUORUNDAM ABBATUM MONASTERII S. ALBANI QUI SAEC. 15 FLORUERE (JOH. WETHAMSTEDE, WILL. ALBON, ETC.) (CHRONIA..6)
- YPODIGMA NEUSTRIE (CHRONIA..7)

CHRONIA MONASTEREII S ALBANI (RS28) / St Albans Abbey; ed by Riley, H T – (Individual vols listed separately) – ne Slangenburg [240]

CHRONIC EFFECTS OF EXERCISE / Steinhaus, Arthur H – 1933 – 2mf – 9 – $6.00 – us Microform Publ [790]

CHRONICA / Paiaranus, Baptista – 1556. Holkham ms. 466. Holkham Hall, Norfolk, England – 1 – uk Microform Academic [760]

CHRONICA AEVI SUEVICI (MGH 5: 20.BD) : SUPPLEMENTA TOMORUM 1-12 – 1868 – Dfl77.00 – ne Slangenburg [240]

CHRONICA AEVI SUEVICI (MGH 5: 23.BD) – 1874 – Dfl95.00 – ne Slangenburg [240]

CHRONICA AUSTRIAE (MGH 6: 13.BD) / Ebendorfer, Thomas; ed by Lhotsky, A – 1967 – Dfl49.00 – ne Slangenburg [240]

CHRONICA DE 25 ANOS / Badajoz. Espana en Paz – Madrid: Publicaciones Espanolas, 1964 – 1 – sp Bibl Santa Ana [946]

CHRONICA DE A SANTA PROVINCIA DE SAN JOSEPH... / Santa Rosa o Alcala, Marcos de – Madrid: Imp. y Lib. de Manuel Fernandez, s.a. – sp Bibl Santa Ana [240]

CHRONICA DE VEINTICINCO ANOS / Caceres. Espana en Paz – Madrid: Publicaciones Espanolas, 1964 – 1 – sp Bibl Santa Ana [946]

CHRONICA DEL ESFORCADO PRINCIPE Y CAPITAN IORGE CASTRIOTO REY DE EPIRO, O ALBANIA / George, C – Lisboa, 1588 – 7mf – 9 – H-8370/1 – ne IDC [956]

CHRONICA DEL MUY ESCLARECIDO PRINCIPE, Y REY DON ALFONSO.. / Alfonso 10th, King of Castille and Leon, 1221-1284 – Valladolid: (s.n.), 1554. 77 leaves – 1 – us U.W. Library [946]

LA CHRONICA DEL PERU. NUEVAMENTE ESCRITA POR / Cieza de Leon, Pedro de – 1554. Libros en Microficha no. 12 – 1mf – 9 – Pta1,000.00 – 84-85422-37-6 – sp Pentalfa [972]

CHRONICA DO SERENISSIMO SENHOR REI D. MANOEL... / Goes, D de – Lisboa, 1749 – 11mf – ne IDC [946]

CHRONICA ET ANNALES 1259-1296, 1307-1324, 1392-1406 (CHRONIA..3) / Johannis de Trokelowe & Henrici de Blaneforde – 1866 – Dfl35.00 – ne Slangenburg [240]

CHRONICA ET ANNALES 1259-1307 (CHRONIA..2) / William Rishanger – 1865 – Dfl39.00 – ne Slangenburg [240]

CHRONICA ET ANNALES AEVI SALICI (MGH 5: 6.BD) – 1844 – Dfl77.00 – ne Slangenburg [240]

CHRONICA ET ANNALES AEVI SALICI (MGH 5: 9.BD) – 1851 – Dfl84.00 – ne Slangenburg [240]

CHRONICA ET GESTA AEVI SALICI (MGH 5: 7.BD) – 1846 – Dfl84.00 – ne Slangenburg [240]

CHRONICA ET GESTA AEVI SALICI (MGH 5: 8.BD) – 1848 – Dfl63.00 – ne Slangenburg [240]

CHRONICA HEINRICI SURDI DE SELBACH (MGH 6: 1.BD) / ed by Bresslau, H – 1922 – Dfl22.00 – ne Slangenburg [240]

CHRONICA HISPANA SAECULI 12 – 1991 – 4mf – 9 – Bf1,250.00 – 2-503-63712-4 – be Brepols [240]

CHRONICA HISPANA SAECULI 12 PARS 2 CHRONICA NAIERENSIS – 1995 – 4mf – 9 – Bf1,600.00 – 2-503-63714-0 – be Brepols [450]

CHRONICA MAGISTRI ROGERI DE HOUEDENE (RS51) / Roger Of Hoveden; ed by Stubbs, W – (v1 1868 Dfl28.00. v2 1869 Dfl30.00. v3 1871 Dfl30.00. v4 1870 Dfl35.00) – ne Slangenburg [941]

CHRONICA MAIORA / Paris, Matthew – (Illustrations only. 22.50; 14) – vols. 1 and 2. (Corpus Christi College, Cambridge, Mss 16 and 26). 13th century – 1 – uk Microform Academic [760]

CHRONICA MAJORA (RS57) / Matthaei Parisiensis; ed by Luard, H R – (v1: The Creation-1066 1872 Dfl39.00. v2: 1067-1216 1874 Dfl46.00. v3: 1216-1239 1876 Dfl 42.00. v4: 1240-1247 1878 Dfl42.00. v5: 1248-1259 1880 Dfl46.00. v6: Additamenta 1882 Dfl35.00. v7: Index, Glossary 1884 Dfl39.00) – ne Slangenburg [240]

CHRONICA MARANHENSE – '(s.l.')-Sao Luiz, Brazil. 1 Jan 1838-24 Mar 1841 – 1,5,6 – bl Biblioteca [072]

CHRONICA MATHIAE DE NUWENBURG (MGH 6: 4.BD) / ed by Hofmeister, A – 1924-1940 – Dfl46.00 – ne Slangenburg [240]

CHRONICA MINORA SAEC. 4, 5, 6, 7 (MGH 1: 11.BD) / ed by Mommsen, Theodor – v2. 1894 – Dfl46.00 – ne Slangenburg [240]

CHRONICA MINORA SAEC. 4, 5, 6, 7 (MGH 1: 13.BD) / ed by Mommsen, Theodor – v3. 1898 – Dfl67.00 – ne Slangenburg [240]

CHRONICA MINORA SAEC. 4, 5, 6,7 (MGH 1: 9.BD) / ed by Mommsen, Theodor – v1. 1892 – Dfl70.00 – ne Slangenburg [240]

CHRONICA MONASTERII DE MELSA, A FUNDATIONE USQUE AD ANNUM 1396 (RS43) : ACCEDIT CONTINUATIO AD ANNUM 1406 A MONACHO QUODAM IPSIUS DOMUS / Thomas de Burton; ed by Bond, E A – (v1 1866 Dfl35.00. v2 1867 Dfl30.00. v3 1868 Dfl35.00) – ne Slangenburg [240]

CHRONICA O.E.S.A / Choriolanus, Ambrosius – Romae. 53 2. 1481 – 8 – ne IDC [945]

CHRONICA ORDINIS CARTHUSIENSIS AB ANNO 1084 AD ANNUM 1510 / Bohic, Cl. O Carth. – Tornaci-Parkmonasterii. v1-4. 1911-1954 – Dfl490.00 – ne Slangenburg [240]

CHRONICA REGIA COLONIENSIS (ANNALES MAXIMI COLONIENSES) CUM CONTINUATIONIBUS IN MONASTERIO S. PANTALEONIS SCRIPTIS ALIISQUE HISTORIAE COLONIENSIS MONUMENTIS (MGH 7: 18.BD) – 1880 – Dfl32.00 – ne Slangenburg [240]

CHRONICA RELIGIOSA : PERIODICO CONSAGRADO AOS INTERESSES DA RELIGIAO – [s.l.]. 22 Jun 1873; 21 Fev 1875 – 1,5,6 – bl Biblioteca [072]

CHRONICA (RS13) / Johannes de Oxenedes; ed by Ellis, H – 1859 – Dfl32.00 – ne Slangenburg [240]

CHRONICA. ZEITBUCH VNND GESCHICHTBIBELL VON ANBEGYN BISZ IN DISS GEGENWERTIG M.D.XXXVI. JAR VERLENGT / Franck von Woerd, S – Ulm, J. Varnier. 1536. BME-79 – 9 – ne IDC [240]

CHRONICAE BAVARICAE SAEC. 14 (MGH 7: 19.BD) – 1918 – Dfl22.00 – ne Slangenburg [240]

CHRONICA...SAN GABRIEL DE FRANCISCO DESCALZOS / San Francisco Membrio, Andres – 1753 – 9 – $1.50f – sp Bibl Santa Ana [240]

CHRONICA...SAN MIGUEL / Santa Criz, Fr. Jose – 1671 – 9 – 1.50f – sp Bibl Santa Ana [240]

CHRONICLE – Abilene. Kan. 1870-1924; 1927-1933 – 1 – us UMI [071]

CHRONICLE – Allentown. Pa. and News. 1939- – 1 – us UMI [071]

CHRONICLE / The American Baptist Historical Society, Chester, Pa – 1938-57 – 1 – $149.31 – us Baptist [240]

CHRONICLE – Augusta. Ga. 1950- – 1 – us UMI [071]

CHRONICLE – Bluffton. Ind. -w. 1878-1918 – 1 – us UMI [071]

CHRONICLE – Boston. Mass. 1932-39 – 1 – us UMI [071]

CHRONICLE – Bulawayo, Rhodesia. 1 Jun 1950- – 323r – 1 – sa Microfile [960]

CHRONICLE – California City. Calif. 1964-1966 – 1 – us UMI [071]

CHRONICLE – Camden. S.C. 1891-1950 – 1 – us UMI [071]

CHRONICLE – Carson City, NV. 1935-52; 1927-48 (incomplete) – 7r – 1 – $350.00 – U04448 – us Library Micro [071]

CHRONICLE – Centralia. Wash. 1908- – 1 – us UMI [071]

CHRONICLE – Centralia. Wash. -w. 1889-90, 1902, 1907-08, 1910-12 – 1 – us UMI [071]

CHRONICLE – Chadron. Neb. 1920-1943 – 1 – us UMI [071]

CHRONICLE – Crewe. Va. 1935-45; 1950- – 1 – us UMI [071]

CHRONICLE – Davenport, NE. -w. Jun. 1898-Jun. 1899 – 1 – us NE Hist [071]

CHRONICLE – Dominica. British West Indies. 1821-22; 1825-27; 1909-62 – 1 – us UMI [072]

CHRONICLE – Elyria. Ohio. 1901-08; 1914-19 – 1 – us UMI [071]

CHRONICLE – Fayette. Miss. 1893-1903; 1936-1949 – 1 – us UMI [071]

CHRONICLE – Fillmore. Neb. 1896-1957 – 1 – us UMI [071]

CHRONICLE – Franklin. Ohio. 1967- – 1 – us UMI [071]

CHRONICLE – Goldfield, NV. 1907-09 – 4r – 1 – $200.00 – U04549 – us Library Micro [071]

CHRONICLE – Hampton. Iowa. -w. 1951- – 1 – us UMI [071]

CHRONICLE – Jacksonville. Fl. -w. 1949-71 – 1 – us P.K. Yonge [071]

CHRONICLE / Joseph Ben Joshua – 1835-6, Royal Asiatic Society – 1 – uk Microform Academic [950]

CHRONICLE – Katoomba, Aug 15-Oct 10 1929 – 9 – at Pascoe [072]

CHRONICLE – Lamoni. Iowa. -w. 1951- – 1 – us UMI [071]

CHRONICLE – Laurel. Miss. 1902-1912 – 1 – us UMI [071]

CHRONICLE – Logansport. Ind. -w. 1904-12 – 1 – us UMI [071]

CHRONICLE : LONDON MISSIONARY SOCIETY / London Missionary Society – 1892-1966 (complete?) – 13r – 1 – ATLA T0005 – us A.T.L.A. [073]

CHRONICLE – Ludington. Mich. 1901-1915 – 1 – us UMI [071]

CHRONICLE – Marion. Ind. 1887-1968 – 1 – us UMI [071]

CHRONICLE – Marion. Ind. -w, sw. 1867-1908 – 1 – us UMI [071]

CHRONICLE – Marshall. Mich. 1932- – 1 – us UMI [071]

CHRONICLE – Muskegon. Mich. 1880- – 1 – us UMI [071]

CHRONICLE – Muskegon. Mich. -w. 1869-1900 – 1 – us UMI [071]

CHRONICLE – Odebolt. Iowa. -w. 1951- – 1 – us UMI [071]

CHRONICLE – Olympia. Wash. 1918 – 1 – us UMI [071]

CHRONICLE – Omak. Wash. 1927-1958 – 1 – us UMI [071]

CHRONICLE – Pawtucket. R.I. 1826-1838 – 1 – us UMI [071]

CHRONICLE – Portsmouth. N.H. 1854-1898; 1908 – 1 – us UMI [071]

CHRONICLE – Providence. R.I. 1939-51 – 1 – us UMI [071]

CHRONICLE – Providence. R.I. 1952-57.-w – 1 – us UMI [071]

CHRONICLE – San Francisco, CA. 1866; 1889 – 1mf – 1 – $25.00 – B02807 – us Library Micro [071]

CHRONICLE – Santa Paula. Calif. 1955-1958 – 1 – us UMI [071]

CHRONICLE – Spokane. Wash. 1886- – 1 – us UMI [071]

CHRONICLE – Spokane. Wash. -w. 1881-83, 1896- – 1 – us UMI [071]

CHRONICLE – The Dalles. Or. 1948-1952 – 1 – us UMI [071]

CHRONICLE – The Dalles. Or. -sw. 1904-06 – 1 – us UMI [071]

CHRONICLE – The Dalles. Or. -w. 1900-52 – 1 – us UMI [071]

CHRONICLE – Uhrichsville. Ohio. 1958- – 1 – us UMI [071]

CHRONICLE / UNESCO (United Nations Educational, Scientific and Cultural Organization) – v1- 1955- 1; v21- 5,6,9 – us UMI [073]

CHRONICLE – Virginia City. Nev. 1962- – 1 – us UMI [071]

CHRONICLE – Warren. Ohio. 1883-1904 – 1 – us UMI [071]

CHRONICLE – Willimantic. Conn. -w. 1880-94 – 1 – us UMI [071]

CHRONICLE – Wilmington. N.C. -w. 1840-51 – 1 – us UMI [071]

THE CHRONICLE – Arlington. Va. 1941-51 – 1 – us UMI [071]

THE CHRONICLE – (Cont: The Insurance and Finance Chronicle) – Montreal: R. Wilson-Smith, [1898-19–] – 9 – cn C.I.H.M. [360]

THE CHRONICLE – Journal of the American Baptist Historical Society, Chester, P. 1938-57. 4,266p – 1 – 149.31 – us Baptist [240]

THE CHRONICLE – Livingston, CA. 1928-57 (scats); 1958- – 20+ r – 1 – $1,000.00 ($50.00y) – B02359 – us Library Micro [071]

THE CHRONICLE – NY City, NY. 1974-1980 – 6r – 1 – $300.00 – R04921 – us Library Micro [071]

THE CHRONICLE – Pascagoula. Miss. 1911-1920; 1962- – 1 – us UMI [071]

THE CHRONICLE – Sherwood, Ohio. 1909-68 – 15r – 1 – $32.50r – us Archival [071]

THE CHRONICLE *see*
- COLERAINE CHRONICLE
- INSURANCE AND FINANCE CHRONICLE
- THE LAKESHORE NEWS

THE CHRONICLE – Lilongwe: Lilongwe Publ, dec 7-31 1993-jan 11-may 16, jun 2/6-20/21 1994 – 1r – us Res Libr [072]

CHRONICLE ADVERTISER – Centralia. Wash. 1935-1937 – 1 – us UMI [071]

CHRONICLE AND ECHO – (Also known as: Northampton Chronicle and Echo) – 1950-51; 1986-Jun 30 1997 – 206 1/4r – 1 – uk British Libr Newspaper [072]

THE CHRONICLE AND MUNSTER ADVERTISER – Waterford. Ireland. -w. 30 Mar 1844-5 May 1849. (6 reels) – 1 – uk British Libr Newspaper [072]

CHRONICLE AND SENTINEL-MIST – (Set incl. Sentinel-Mist Chronicle (St. Helens)) – St. Helens, OR 2 Jan 1972+ – 10r – 1 – us U.O. Library [071]

CHRONICLE (CHRONICLES..4) / Robert of Torigni – 1890 – Dfl32.00 – ne Slangenburg [941]

CHRONICLE HERALD – Hoopeston. Ill. 1927- – 1 – us UMI [071]

CHRONICLE OF CURRENT EVENTS – (Nos. 1-16 only published on microfiche) – London, 1968-1983. Nos 1-63 – 62mf – H-2615/1 – ne IDC [320]

THE CHRONICLE OF DINO COMPAGNI / Compagni, Dino – Trans. by Else C.M. Benecke and A.G. Ferrers Howell. London: Dent, 1906. vii,284p. illus – 1 – us U.W. Library [945]

CHRONICLE OF ENGLAND (RS1) / Capgrave, John; ed by Hingeston, C – 1958 – Dfl32.00 – ne Slangenburg [941]

CHRONICLE OF HIGHER EDUCATION – Hightstown, NJ. 1966-1982 – 20r – 1 – $1,000.00 – R04976 – us Library Micro [370]

CHRONICLE OF HIGHER EDUCATION – (v.17-. 1978-. 5,6,9) – 1- 1966- – 1 – us UMI [370]

CHRONICLE OF PIERRE DE LANGTOFT (RS47) : IN FRENCH VERSE FROM THE EARLIEST PERIOD TO THE DEATH OF EDWARD 1 / Peter Of Langtoft; ed by Wright, T – v1 1866 v2 1868 – Dfl32.00v – ne Slangenburg [941]

A CHRONICLE OF ST JOHN'S CEMETARY ON THE HUMBER / Denison, George Taylor – Toronto: Printed for the use of the members of the Denison family, 1868. 03767. (Pre-1900 Canadiana) – 9 – cn C.I.H.M. [971]

A CHRONICLE OF THE AUGSBURG CONFESSION – A QUESTION OF LATINITY / Krauth, Charles Porterfield & Jacobs, Henry Eyster – (Includes bibliographical references) – Philadelphia: J Fred'k Smith, 1879 – 1mf – 9 – 0-8370-8755-4 – 1986-2755 – us A.T.L.A. [240]

CHRONICLE OF THE DIOCESE OF FREDERICTON / Church of England. Diocese of Fredericton – St. John [N.B.]: Diocesan Church Society of New Brunswick, v1 no 1 (Jan 1886)- – 9 – cn C.I.H.M. [240]

THE CHRONICLE OF THE DISCOVERY AND CONQUEST OF GUINEA / Azurara de Gomes Eannes – 2v. London. 1896. A-272. BA-272 2 – 8 – ne IDC [960]

THE CHRONICLE OF THE LONDON MISSIONARY SOCIETY *see* MISSIONARY CHRONICLE

THE CHRONICLE OF THE REIGNS OF HENRY 2 AND RICHARD 1, 1169-1192 (RS49) = GESTA REGIS HENRICI SECUNDI BENEDICTI ABBATIS : KNOWN COMMONLY UNDER THE NAME OF BENEDICT OF PETERBOROUGH / ed by Stubbs, W – (v1 1867 Dfl30.00. v2 1867 Dfl35.00) – ne Slangenburg [941]

CHRONICLE OF THE WORLD HEALTH ORGANIZATION *see* WHO CHRONICLE

CHRONICLE REVIEW – Montreal, Quebec, Canada. 1968-76 – 1 – us A.J.P.C. [072]

CHRONICLE (S-M) – Metropolis, NV. 1911-13 – 1r – 1 – $50.00 – U04626 – us Library Micro [071]

CHRONICLE STAR – Pascagoula. Miss. 1921-1926 – 1 – us UMI [071]

CHRONICLE STAR – Pascagoula. Miss. and Moss Point Advertiser. 1909-19, 1924-26, 1953- – 1 – us UMI [071]

CHRONICLE TELEGRAM – Elyria. Ohio. 1919- – 1 – us UMI [071]

CHRONICLE TELEGRAPH – Pittsburgh. Pa. and predecessors. 1842-1927 – 1 – us UMI [071]

CHRONICLE UNION – Bridgeport. Calif. -w. 1947- – 1 – us UMI [071]

CHRONICLE-GUIDE – (1978-1992.-34r) – Arnprior, 1993 – 2r – 1 – cn Preston [971]

CHRONICLE-HERALD – Macon. Mo. 1957- – 1 – us UMI [071]

THE CHRONICLE-HERALD – Halifax, Nova Scotia, CN. 1880- – 24r per yr – 1 – Can$53.00r – cn Commonwealth Micro [072]

CHRONICLE-JOURNAL – (1972-1992.-267r) – Thunder Bay, 1993 – 24r – 1 – cn Preston [971]

CHRONICLES : INTRODUCTION, REVISED VERSION WITH NOTES, INDEX AND MAP / ed by Harvey-Jellie, Wallace Raymond – (Includes an index) – New York: Henry Frowde, 1906 – 1mf – 9 – 0-8370-3515-5 – 1985-1515 – us A.T.L.A. [220]

CHRONICLES / Jerahmeel – 1899 – 1 – uk Microform Academic [240]

CHRONICLES AND DOCUMENTS OF MEDIEVAL ENGLAND, C1150-C1500 – The most important volumes from the Manuscript Holdings of Cambridge University Library – 1 – us Primary [941]

CHRONICLES AND MEMORIALS OF THE REIGN OF RICHARD 1 (RS38) / ed by Stubbs, W – (v1: Itinerarium Peregrinorum Et Gesta Regis Ricardi (1187-1199) Auctore Ut Videtur Can.S. Trinitatis Londoniensis 1864 Dfl42.00. v2: Epistolae Cantuarienses, 1187-1199 1865 Dfl49.00) – ne Slangenburg [941]

CHRONICLES AND THE MOSAIC LEGISLATION / Terry, Milton Spenser – (Includes bibliographical references) – New York: Funk & Wagnalls, 1888, c1887 – 1mf – 9 – 0-8370-5788-4 – 1985-3788 – us A.T.L.A. [220]

CHRONICLES OF AN OLD INN : OR, A FEW WORDS ON GRAY'S INN / Harvey, Annie J – London: Chapman & Hall, 1887 – 3mf – 9 – $4.50 – LLMC 84-292 – us L.L.M.C. [941]

CHRONICLES OF CONVOCATION / Canterbury – 1847-1918. From Lambeth Palace Library – 1 – uk Microform Academic [240]

CHRONICLES OF THE CRUSADES: CONTEMPORARY NARRATIVES OF THE CRUSADE OF RICHARD COEUR DE LION – By Richard of Devizes and Geoffrey de Vinsauf, and of the Crusade of St. Louis, by Lord John de Joinville. London: G. Bell, 1903. 562p – 1 – us U.W. Library [900]

CHRONICLES OF THE REIGNS OF EDWARD 1 AND EDWARD 2 (RS76) / ed by Stubbs, W – v1 1882 v2 1883 – Dfl32.00v – ne Slangenburg [941]

CHRONICLES OF THE REIGNS OF STEPHEN, HENRY 2 AND RICHARD 1 *see*
- CHRONICLE (CHRONICLES..4)
- HISTORIA RERUM ANGLICARUM, BK 5 (CHRONICLES..2)

– HISTORIA RERUM ANGLICARUM, BKS 1-4 (CHRONICLES..1)
CHRONICLES OF THE REIGNS OF STEPHEN, HENRY 2 AND RICHARD 1 (RS82) / ed by Howlett, R – (Individual vols listed separately) – 4v – ne Slangenburg [941]
CHRONICLES OF WESLEYAN METHODISM, FIRST DEPARTMENT : A DIGEST OF ALL ITS LAWS AND REGULATIONS, WITH A COMPREHENSIVE STATEMENT OF ITS PRINCIPAL DOCTRINES / Warren, S – London, 1827 – 5mf – 9 – ne IDC [240]
CHRONICLES OF WESLEYAN METHODISM, SECOND DEPARTMENT / Stephens, J – (Coll title: The People Called Methodists, Phase 1: Reference Tools) – London, 1827 – 3mf – 9 – MP-233/1 – ne IDC [240]
CHRONICLE-TELEGRAPH – Quebec. Canada. 1971- – 1 – us UMI [072]
THE CHRONICLE-TELEGRAPH – (Cont: The Quebec-Chronicle-Telegraph 1764) – Quebec, 2 jul 1925- – 1 – cn Can Microfilming [072]
THE CHRONICLE-TELEGRAPH – Quebec: Chronicle-Telegraph Pub Co. v1-9. 1925-34. SEM35P239 – 26r – 9 – Can$1,559.00 – cn Bibl Nat [072]
CHRONICLE-TRIBUNE – Marion. Ind. 1968- – 1 – us UMI [071]
CHRONICON / Tyrensis, Willelmus – 1986 – 24mf – 9 – Bf2,350.00 – 2-503-60632-6 – be Brepols [240]
CHRONICON ABBATIAE DE EVESHAM AD ANNUM 1418 (RS29) / ed by Macray, W D – 1863 – Dfl30.00 – ne Slangenburg [240]
CHRONICON ABBATIAE RAMESIENSIS (RS83) / Ramsey Abbey; ed by Macray, W D – 1886 – Dfl35.00 – ne Slangenburg [240]
CHRONICON ANGLIAE (RS64) : AB ANNO DOMINI 1328 USQUE AD ANNUM 1388 / ed by Thompson, E M – 1874 – Dfl35.00 – ne Slangenburg [941]
CHRONICON ANGLICANUM (RS66) : DE EXPUGNATIONE TERRAE SANCTAE LIBELLUS / Radulphi de Coggenshall; ed by Stevenson – (THOMAS AGNELLUS: De Morte Et Sepultura Henrici Regis Angliae Juniores; Gesta Fulconis Filii Warini ; Excerpta Ex Otiis Imperialibus Gervasii Tileburiensis) – 1875 – Dfl32.00 – ne Slangenburg [240]
CHRONICON BENEDICTOBURANUM OPERA ET STUDIO CAR. MEICHELBECK – Benedictoburani. v1-2. 1753 – Dfl130.00 – ne Slangenburg [240]
CHRONICON CARTUSIENSE / Diestensis, D Petri Dorlandi & Prioris, Cartusiae – Col. Agrippinae, 1608 – 6mf – 8 – Dfl28.00 – ne Slangenburg [240]
CHRONICON (CBH 30,2) : VERSIO LATINA / Phranzae, Georgii – Venetiis, 1733 – Dfl25.00 – ne Slangenburg [930]
CHRONICON CISTERCIENSIS / Miraeus, A – Colonia Agrippina, 1604 – 6mf – 8 – Dfl25.00 – ne Slangenburg [240]
CHRONICON EPHRATENSE : A HISTORY OF THE COMMUNITY OF SEVENTH DAY BAPTISTS AT EPHRATA, LANCASTER COUNTY, PENN'A / Lamech & Agrippa – Lancaster, Pa.: S.H. Zahm, 1889 – 1mf – us A.T.L.A. [240]
CHRONICON GOTWICENSE SEU ANNALES LIBERI ET EXEMPTI MONASTERII GOTWICENSIS O.S.B. – Tegernsensis. v1-2. 1753 – Dfl165.00 – ne Slangenburg [240]
CHRONICON HENRICI KNIGHTON, VEL CNITTHON, MONACHI LEYCESTRENSIS (RS92) / Henry Knighton; ed by Lumby, J R – (v1 1899 Dfl32.00. v2 1895 Dfl30.00) – ne Slangenburg [240]
CHRONICON HISPANIAE (SIECLE 15) / Rada, Rodrigo Jimenez de – Copenhague – 1r – 5,6 – sp Cultura [946]
CHRONICON MOGUNTINUM (MGH 7: 20.BD) – 1885 – Dfl13.00 – ne Slangenburg [240]
CHRONICON MONASTERII ALDENBURGENSIS / ed by Malou, J B – Brugis, 1840 – Dfl22.00 – ne Slangenburg [240]
CHRONICON MONASTERII DE ABINGTON (RS2) / Abington Abbey; ed by Stevenson, J – (v1 1858 Dfl35.00. v2 1858 Dfl46.00) – ne Slangenburg [240]
CHRONICON MONASTERII EVERSHAMENSIS CONSRIPTUM PER GERARDUM DE MEESTERE WINNOCI-BERGENSEN – Brugis, 1852 – Dfl19.00 – ne Slangenburg [240]
CHRONICON NOVALICIENSE (MGH 7: 21.BD) – 1846 – Dfl13.00 – ne Slangenburg [240]
CHRONICON ORIENTALE : LATINITATE DONATUM A ABR. ECCHELLENSI 20 – Parisiis, 1685 – Dfl42.00 – ne Slangenburg [930]
CHRONICON PASCHALE AD EXEMPLAR VATICANUM (CSHB 16, 17) / ed by Dindorfius, L – Bonnae. v1-2. 1832 – Dfl81.00 – ne Slangenburg [240]
CHRONICON PASCHALE (CBH 21) / ed by Cange, C du – Parisiis, 1688 – Dfl105.00 – ne Slangenburg [240]
CHRONICON SAMARITANUM : ARABICE CONSCRIPTUM, CUI TITULUS EST LIBER JOSUAE / ed by Juynboll, T G J – Lugduni Batavorum, 1848 – 14mf – 8 – ne Slangenburg [200]
CHRONICON SCOTORUM (RS46) : A CHRONICLE OF IRISH AFFAIRS FROM THE EARLIEST TIMES TO 1135 AND A SUPPLEMENT CONTAINING THE EVENTS FROM 1141-1150 / ed by Hennessy, W M – 1866 – Dfl30.00 – ne Slangenburg [941]
CHRONICON VORMELENSE – Brugis, 1847 – Dfl19.00 – ne Slangenburg [240]
CHRONICON WARNESTONIENSIS : ORDINIS CANONICORUM REGULARIUM S. AUGUSTINI – Brugis, 1852 – Dfl9.00 – ne Slangenburg [240]
CHRONICON WINDESHEMENSE UND LIBER DE REFORMATIONE MONASTICA DES AUGUSTINERPROPSTES JOH. BUSCH / ed by Grube, K – Halle, 1887 – Dfl53.00 – ne Slangenburg [240]
CHRONICORUM TURCICORUM / Lonicerus, P – Francofvrti ad Moenvm. 2v. 1584 – 8mf – 9 – H-8365/1 – ne IDC [956]
CHRONICORVM TVRCICORVM, ... / Lonicerus, P – Francoforti ad Moenvm. 3v. 1578 – 20mf – 9 – H-8417/1 – ne IDC [956]
CHRONICVM ... CONTINENS HISTORIAM RERVM MEMORABILIVM, A NINO ASSYRIORVME REGE AD TEMPORA FRIDERICI 2... / Burchardus, U – Argentorati, [1540] – 9mf – 9 – H-8249/1 – ne IDC [956]
CHRONIK DER UKRAINISCHEN SHEVCHENKO-GESELLSCHAFT DER WISSENSCHAFTEN – Lemberg, 1900-1914. v1-59 – 42mf – R-1708/2 – ne IDC [500]
DIE CHRONIK DES HIPPOLYTOS IM MATRITENSIS GRAECUS 121 / Bauer, Adolf – Leipzig: J.C. Hinrichs, 1905. (Texte und Untersuchungen zur Geschichte der altchristlichen Literatur; der ganzen Reihe 29. Bd., Heft 1. n.F., 14. Bd., 1. Heft) – 1mf – us A.T.L.A. [240]
DIE CHRONIK DES HIPPOLYTOS IN MATRITENSIS GRAECUS 121 (T.U.U. 2-29/1) / Bauer, Adolf – Leipzig, 1905 – 5mf – 9 – ne Slangenburg [240]
CHRONIQUE / Tabari – 1836. Trans. by L. Dubeux. Royal Asiatic Society – 1 – uk Microform Academic [950]
CHRONIQUE / Tabari – Translation by H. Zotenberg, Royal Asiatic Society. 1867-74 – 1 – uk Microform Academic [950]
CHRONIQUE *see* ANGLO FRENCH STAGE CHRONICLE (FRENCH EDITION)
LA CHRONIQUE ARTISTIQUE ET LITTERAIRE – Paris. 1857 – 1 – fr A.C.R.P.P. [073]
CHRONIQUE DE CHYPRE PAR LEONCE MACHERAS – Texte grec traduit par E. Miler et C. Sathas. 1882 – 9 – fr Orientalistes [949]
CHRONIQUE DE JERSEY – St. Helier, England. -w. Jan 1814-Dec 1815; Jan 1820-Dec 1821; Jan 1825-Dec 1828; Jan 1830-Dec 1840; April 1849-Dec 1850. 4 1 2 reels – 1 – uk British Libr Newspaper [072]
CHRONIQUE DE LA DYNASTIE ALAOUIE DU MAROC / [Esslaoui, Ahmed Ennasiri] – Paris: E Leroux 1906-1907 – us Res Libr [960]
LA CHRONIQUE DE LA VALLEE DU SAINT-MAURICE – Trois Rivieres, Canada. v1 n13. 6 avr 1929-v1, 28. 20 jul 1929; v11 n48. 6 jan 1940-26 dec 1942; 26 mai 1948; v28 n39. 21 dec 1955 – 2r – 1 – Can$60.00r – cn Can Microfilming [072]
CHRONIQUE DE LONDRES – London, UK. 25 Mar 1899-12 Jul 1924 – 1 – uk British Libr Newspaper [072]
LA CHRONIQUE DE MAGOG – Magog, Canada. 4 jun 1937-28 oct 1964 – 14r – 1 – Can$60.00r – cn Can Microfilming [072]
CHRONIQUE DE MOLDAVIE / Urechi, Gregoire – Texte roumain traduit par Em. Picot. 18– – 9 – fr Orientalistes [943]
CHRONIQUE DE PARIS – Paris. aout. 1789-aout 1793 – 1 – fr A.C.R.P.P. [073]
LA CHRONIQUE DE TRES HAULT ET TRES EXCELLANT PRINCE DE BON MEMOIRE ARTHUR, DEUXZIESME DE CE NOM... / Gruel, Guillaume 15th cont – 1 – F79.70 – fr Armell [920]
CHRONIQUE DITE DE NESTOR – Texte slavon traduit par L. Leger. 1884 – 9 – fr Orientalistes [460]
LA CHRONIQUE DU MOIS OU LES CAHIERS PATRIOTIQUES – Paris. Imprimerie du Cercle Social, nov 1791-jui 1793 – 9 – fr Hachette [321]
CHRONIQUE DU MOIS, OU LES CAHIERS PATRIOTIQUES DE E. CLAVIERE, C. CONDORCET, L. MERCIER, ETC – puis Ou les Cahiers patriotiques des amis de la verite. Paris. nov 1791-juil 1793 – 1 – fr A.C.R.P.P. [073]
CHRONIQUE DU MONASTERE D'OUDENBOURG DE L'ORDRE DE S. BENOIT / ed by Putte, F van de – Gand, 1843 – Dfl28.00 – ne Slangenburg [240]
CHRONIQUE D'UN ANONYME DE BETHUNE, HISTOIRE DES DUCS DE NORMANDIE ET DES ROIS D'ANGLETERRE JUSQU'EN 1220 / Mace de Gastines, Edith – 2mf – 9 – 10339 – fr Atelier National [440]
CHRONIQUE EUROPEENE – London, UK. 20 Jan-8 Jun 1872 – 1 – uk British Libr Newspaper [072]
LA CHRONIQUE GUYANAISE – no. 1-8. Cayenne. oct 1884-janv 1885 – 1 – fr A.C.R.P.P. [073]
LA CHRONIQUE ILLUSTREE – Paris. 14 aout 1868-72 – 1 – fr A.C.R.P.P. [073]
LA CHRONIQUE MUSICALE – Paris: [s.n.] v1 n1-v11 n66. jul 1873-jun 15 1876 – 4r – us Res Libr [780]
LA CHRONIQUE OUVRIERE – Chicoutimi, Canada. 19 dec 1924; n50. 19 jun 1926 – 1r – 1 – Can$25.00 – cn Can Microfilming [072]
CHRONIQUE PARISIENNE ET DEPARTEMENTALE – Paris: Impr de Poussielgue, aug 13 1848 – 1r – us Res Libr [944]
CHRONIQUE RELIGIEUSE – Paris. 1819-21 (I-VI) – 1 – fr A.C.R.P.P. [073]
CHRONIQUES / Fabre, Hector – Quebec: Imp de l'Evenement, 1877. SEM105P21 – 3mf – 9 – Can$6.75 – cn Bibl Nat [920]
CHRONIQUES / Fabre, Hector – Quebec?: s.n., 1877 (Quebec: L'Evenement). 02937. (Pre-1900 Canadiana) – 9 – cn C.I.H.M. [971]
CHRONIQUES DE FOUTA SENEGALAIS DE SIRE-ABBAS-SOH / Delafosse, Maurice – Paris: E Leroux, 1913 – 1 – us Res Libr [960]
CHRONIQUES DE LA MAURITANIE SENEGALAISE / Hamet, Ismael – (Text in Arabic) – Nacer edd. Paris: E Leroux, 1911 – 1 – us Res Libr [960]
CHRONIQUES DE LUNDI DE FRANCOISE / Francoise – s.l.: s.n., 1896?. 03171. (Pre-1900 Canadiana) – 9 – cn C.I.H.M. [971]
LES CHRONIQUES DE OUALATA ET DE NEMA (SOUDAN FRANCAIS) – Paris: P Geuthner, 1927 – 1 – us Res Libr [960]
CHRONIQUES DES COMTES DE FLANDRES – 15th century. Holkham MS 659 – 1 £25.00 14 £35.00 – uk Microform Academic [949]
CHRONIQUES DES COMTES DE HAINAULT / Guise, Jacques de – 15th cent. Holkham ms. 658. Holkham Hall, Norfolk, England – 1 – uk Microform Academic [760]
O CHRONISTA – (Cont as: O Brazil) – Rio de Janeiro, 23 May-Dec 1836; Feb 1837-2 Apr 1839 – 1,5,6 – bl Biblioteca [072]
CHRONOBIOLOGICA – (v4- . 1977- . 5,6,9) – v. 1-. 1974- – 1 – us UMI [574]
CHRONOBIOLOGY INTERNATIONAL *see* ANNUAL REVIEW OF CHRONOPHARMACOLOGY
DER CHRONOGRAPH AUS DEM ZEHNTEN JAHRE ANTONINS / Schlatter, Adolf von – Leipzig: J.C. Hinrichs, 1894. (Texte und Untersuchungen zur Geschichte der altchristlichen Literatur; 12. Bd., Heft 1) – 1mf – us A.T.L.A. [240]
DER CHRONOGRAPH AUS DEM ZEHNTEN JAHRE ANTONINS (T.U.U. 1-12/1A) / Schlatter, Adolf von – Leipzig, 1894 – 2mf – 9 – ne Slangenburg [240]
CHRONOGRAPHIA : LEONIS GRAMMATICI: VITAE RECENTIORUM IMPERATORRUM (CBH 6) / Theophanis; ed by Goar, J – Parisiis, 1655 – Dfl112.00 – ne Slangenburg [930]
CHRONOGRAPHIA : NICEPHORI PATRIARCHAE: BREVIARIUM CHRONOGRAPHICUM (CBH 5) / Syncellus, Georgius; ed by Goar, J – Parisiis, 1652 – Dfl102.00 – ne Slangenburg [930]
CHRONOGRAPHIA / Theophanis; ed by Boor, C de – Lipsiae. v1-2. 1883-85 – 23mf – 8 – Dfl81.00 – ne Slangenburg [240]
CHRONOGRAPHIA (CSHB 15) : ACCEDUNT CHILMEADI HODIIQUE ANNOTATIONES ET RIC. BENTLEI EPISTOLA AD IO. MILLIUM / Malalae, Joannis Antiocheni; ed by Dindorfius, L – Bonnae, 1831 – Dfl53.00 – ne Slangenburg [240]
CHRONOGRAPHIA (CSHB 39, 40) / Theophanis; ed by Classeni, IO – (v2 cont. Anastasii Bibliothecarii: Historiam Ecclesiasticam ex rec. Imm. Bekkeri Dfl46.00) – Bonnae. v1-2. 1839-1840 – Dfl53.00 – ne Slangenburg [240]
CHRONOGRAPHIA (CSHB 44) : ACCEDIT EUSTHATII DE CAPTA THESSALONICA LIBER / Grammatic, Leonis; ed by Bekkeri, Imm – Bonnae, 1842 – Dfl35.00 – ne Slangenburg [930]
CHRONOGRAPHIAE LIBRI QUATUOR / Genebrardus, Gilb. – Parisiis, 1585 – 43mf – 8 – ne Slangenburg [220]
CHRONOGRAPHICAL DESCRIPTION OF ENGLAND, SCOTLAND, IRELAND AND ISLANDS ADJACENT / Camden, W – 1806 – 1 – uk Microform Academic [910]
CHRONOLOGIA SACRA / Usser, J – Editionum acc. 1087 2. 1722 – 8 – ne IDC [240]
CHRONOLOGICAL AND GEOGRAPHICAL INTRODUCTION TO THE LIFE OF CHRIST / Caspari, Ch. Ed – Edinburgh: T. & T. Clark, 1876. 1 fiche – 9 – us A.T.L.A. [240]
CHRONOLOGICAL BIBLIOGRAPHY OF ENGLISH LANGUAGE FICTION IN THE LIBRARY OF CONGRESS THROUGH 1950 / Wright, R Glenn – (Available on microfilm by request; $870.00 export $1045.00. – ISBN 0-8161-1116-2) – 1974. 131,000 entries – 9 – uk Hall [018]
CHRONOLOGICAL BIOGRAPHY OF MR. TAI-CHI-TAO / China Series Committee – 1880-1949. (Tai-chi-tao hsien-sheng pien-nien chuan-chi). 1958. 284p. 1 reel – 1 – $14.50 – ch Transmission [920]
A CHRONOLOGICAL CATALOGUE OF ALL THE TRAVELLING PREACHERS NOW IN THE METHODIST CONNEXION... : TO WHICH IS PREFIXED AN ADDRESS TO THE PREACHERS BY THOMAS COKE / Pawson, J – Liverpool, 1795 – 1mf – 9 – ne IDC [240]
CHRONOLOGICAL COLLECTION OF CARTOONS RELATING TO MR. GAYNOR PUBLISHED IN THE NEW YORK NEWSPAPERS / Gaynor, William J A – 1910-17 – 1r – 1 – us Ross [977]
CHRONOLOGICAL FILES, 1884-1913 / Alaska. Governor's Office – 44 rolls. T1200 – 1 – us Nat'l Archives [978]
CHRONOLOGICAL HISTORY OF THE DISCOVERY AND SETTLEMENT OF GUIANA, 1493-1668 / Rodway, James – 1888 – 1 – us UMI [972]
A CHRONOLOGICAL HISTORY OF THE PEOPLE CALLED METHODISTS, CONTAINING AN ACCOUNT OF THEIR RISE AND PROGRESS, FROM THE YEAR 1729 TO THE YEAR 1799;... / Myles, W – Liverpool, [1799]. [2], iv/223p – 3mf – 9 – ne IDC [240]
A CHRONOLOGICAL HISTORY OF THE PEOPLE CALLED METHODISTS, OF THE CONNEXION OF THE LATE REV. JOHN WESLEY : FROM THEIR RISE, IN THE YEAR 1729, TO THEIR LAST CONFERENCE, IN 1812 / Myles, W – 4th ed London, 1813. xi/487p – 6mf – 9 – ne IDC [240]
CHRONOLOGICAL HISTORY OF THE WEST INDIES / Southey, Thomas – 3v. 1827 – 1r – 1 – us Ross [972]
CHRONOLOGICAL INDEX AND SUMMARY OF COMMUNICATIONS, 1941-45 / General Headquarters, Southwest Pacific Area – 12 reels with printed guide – 1 – $1,170.00 – 0-89093-738-9 – us UPA [950]
CHRONOLOGICAL LIST OF MEMBERS / Lawrence. Kansas. First Christian Church – 1884-1980 – 1 – us KS Hist [920]
A CHRONOLOGICAL LIST OF THE ITINERANT PREACHERS IN THE CONNEXION OF THE LATE REV. JOHN WESLEY, DECEASED, ARRANGED IN ALPHABETICAL ORDER / Atmore, C – Manchester, 1801 – 1mf – 9 – ne IDC [240]

CHRONOLOGICAL LIST OF THE PRACTICING MEMBERS OF THE PHILADELPHIA BAR / Campbell, William J – 2nd ed. Philadelphia: Gallagher, 1890. 48p. With an appendix containing the bar of Camden, N.J. LL-1361 – 1 – us L of C Photodup [340]

CHRONOLOGIE DE L'HISTOIRE DES ETATS UNIS D'AMERIQUE / Begin, Louis Nazaire – Quebec: A. Cote, 1895. 03547. (Pre-1900 Canadiana) – 9 – cn C.I.H.M. [975]

CHRONOLOGIE DE L'HISTOIRE DES ETATS-UNIS D'AMERIQUE / Gagnon, Charles-Octave – Quebec: A. Cote, 1895. 03269. (Pre-1900 Canadiana) – 9 – cn C.I.H.M. [971]

CHRONOLOGIE DE L'HISTOIRE DU CANADA / Begin, Louis Nazaire – Quebec: C. Darveau, 1886. (Pre-1900 Canadiana) – 9 – cn C.I.H.M. [971]

DIE CHRONOLOGIE DER BIBEL : IM EINKLANGE MIT DER ZEITRECHNUNG DER EGYPTER UND ASSYRIER / Raska, Johann – (Includes bibliographical references) – Wien: Wilhelm Braumueller, 1878 – 1mf – 9 – 0-8370-4842-7 – 1985-2842 – us A.T.L.A. [220]

DIE CHRONOLOGIE DER BUECHER DER KOENIGE UND PARALIPOMENON : IM EINKLANG MIT DER CHRONOLOGIE DER AEGYPTER, ASSYRER, BABYLONIER, PHOENIZIER, MEDER... / Alker, Emmerich – (Includes chronological tables. Includes appendix) – Leobschuetz: George Schnurpfeil, 1889 – 1mf – 9 – 0-8370-2075-1 – 1985-0075 – us A.T.L.A. [220]

DIE CHRONOLOGIE DER GENESIS (1. MOSES) IM EINKLANG MIT DER PROFANEN / E A – Regensburg: Georg Joseph Manz, 1881 – 1mf – 9 – 1985-0000 – us A.T.L.A. [240]

DIE CHRONOLOGIE DER GESCHICHTE ISRAELS, AEGYPTENS, BABYLONIENS UND ASSYRIENS VON 2000-700 V. CHR. / Niebuhr, Carl – (Includes bibliographical references) – Leipzig: Eduard Pfeiffer, 1896 – 1mf – 9 – 0-8370-4006X – 1985-2006 – us A.T.L.A. [220]

DIE CHRONOLOGIE DER HEBRAEISCHEN KOENIGE: EINE GESCHICHTLICHE UNTERSUCHUNG / Kamphausen, Adolf – Bonn: Max Cohen, 1883. 1 fiche – 9 – us A.T.L.A. [220]

CHRONOLOGIE DER ROEMISCHEN BISCHOEFE : BIS ZUR MITTE DES VIERTEN JAHRHUNDERTS / Lipsius, Richard Adelbert – (Includes bibliographical references) – Kiel: Schwer, 1869 – 1mf – 9 – 0-8370-8838-0 – 1986-2838 – us A.T.L.A. [240]

DIE CHRONOLOGIE DES JOSEPHUS / Destinon, Justus Von – (In English. Includes bibliographical references) – Kiel: Schmidt & Klaunig, 1880 – 1mf – 9 – 0-8370-2895-7 – 1985-0895 – us A.T.L.A. [270]

CHRONOLOGIE DES LEBENS JESU VON HERMANN SEVIN / Sevin, Hermann – (Includes bibliographical references) – 2. umgearb. Aufl. Tuebingen:H Laupp, 1874 – 1mf – 9 – 0-8370-5234-3 – 1985-3234 – us A.T.L.A. [240]

LA CHRONOLOGIE DU CANZONIERE DE PETRARQUE / Cochin, Henry – Paris: E. Bouillon, 1898. x,160p – 1 – us U.W. Library [440]

CHRONOLOGIES OF WORLD WAR 1 PAMPHLET COLLECTION – 1915-1941 – 2r – 1 – CSUXAML7847-B – us Hoover Inst Photo [355]

CHRONOLOGISCHE TAFEL VOOR DE GESCHIEDENIS DER ISRAELIETEN IN NEDERLAND / Visscher, L G – Utrecht. 1850. BJ-262-69 1 – 9 – ne IDC [949]

DIE CHRONOLOGISCHEN FRAGEN IN DEN BUECHERN ESRA-NEHEMIA / Fischer, Joseph – Freiburg i.B.: Herder, 1903. 1 fiche – 9 – us A.T.L.A. [240]

CHRONOLOGISCHES VERZEICHNIS DER OESTERREICHISCHEN STAATSVERTRAEGE / Bittner, L – Wien. 4v. 1903-1917 – 21mf – 9 – ne IDC [943]

CHRONOLOGY OF AMERICAN CASE LAW COVERING ALL REPORTED CASES, STATE AND FEDERAL, FROM THE EARLIEST PERIOD TO 1897 / Phelps, W W – St. Paul: West, 1897. 506p. LL-1433 – 1 – us L of C Photodup [340]

THE CHRONOLOGY OF ANCIENT NATIONS / Biruni – 1879. Royal Asiatic Society – 1 – uk Microform Academic [900]

THE CHRONOLOGY OF BIBLE HISTORY, AND HOW TO REMEMBER IT / Munger, C – New York: Nelson & Phillips, 1876. 1 fiche – 9 – us A.T.L.A. [240]

THE CHRONOLOGY OF EFFECTS OF CAFFEINE DURING PROLONGED CYCLE ERGOMETRY / Dennis, D – 1991 – 1mf – 9 – $4.00 – us Microform Publ [612]

CHRONOLOGY OF EVENTS PERTAINING TO U.S. INVOLVEMENT IN THE WAR IN VIETNAM AND SOUTHEAST ASIA / U.S. Military Assistance Command. Vietnam – 1v. 1972 – 1 – 18.00 – us L of C Photodup [950]

A CHRONOLOGY OF IMPORTANT MILITARY EVENTS IN REPUBLICAN CHINA, 1924-1950, PART 1, 1924-1928 / U.S. Office of the Chief of Military History – 1971 – 1 – 18.00 – us L of C Photodup [950]

A CHRONOLOGY OF THE BAPTISTS IN NIGERIA, WEST AFRICA, AND RELATED SUBJECTS, 1782-1968 / Roberson, Cecil F – 1978. Rev. ed – 1 – 15.30 – us Baptist [240]

THE CHRONOLOGY OF THE BIBLE / Sharpe, Samuel – London: J Russell Smith, 1868 – 1mf – 9 – 0-8370-5243-2 – 1985-3243 – us A.T.L.A. [220]

CHRONOLOGY OF THE BIBLE CONNECTED WITH CONTEMPORANEOUS EVENTS / de Bunsen, Ernest – London: Longmans, Green, 1874. 1 fiche – 9 – us A.T.L.A. [220]

THE CHRONOLOGY OF THE BIBLE, CONNECTED WITH CONTEMPORANEOUS EVENTS IN THE HISTORY OF BABYLONIANS, ASSYRIANS, AND EGYPTIANS / de Bunsen, Ernest – Preface by A.H. Sayce. London: Longmans, Green and Co., 1874. xiv, 138p – 1 – us U.W. Library [520]

CHRONOLOGY OF WORLD WAR 2 PAMPHLET COLLECTION – 1939-1942 – 1 – CSUXANM6454-B – us Hoover Inst Photo [355]

LA CHRONOPHOTOGRAPHIE / Marey, Etienne J – Paris: Gauthier-Villars, 1899. SEM16P236 – 1r – 5 – Can$9.00 – cn Bibl Nat [770]

CHRONOS ATHENON – Athens, Greece. -d. 9 March 1885-27 Jan 1887. Imperfect. 4 reels – 1 – uk British Libr Newspaper [949]

CHRONOSCOPE – Larned. Kansas. 1878-1930 – 1 – us UMI [071]

Chroust, A *see* HISTORIA DE EXPEDITIONE FRIDERICI IMPERATORIS ET QUIDAM ALII RERUM GESTARUM FONTES EIUSDEM EXPEDITIONIS (MGH 6: 5.BD)

CHRUT UND UCHRUT IM SEELEGAERTLI / Abbondio-Kuenzle, Christine – 1. Ufl. Fryburg: Schwyzerluet-Verlag (G. Schmidt), 1952 – 1r – 1 – us U.W. Library [430]

A CHRYSALIDA : PERIODICO DEDICADO AO BELLO SEXO – [s.l.]. 1879 – 1,5,6 – bl Biblioteca [072]

LA CHRYSALIDE – Port-au-Prince, Haiti: [s.n.], 1re annee n1-n5. 22 avril 1911-22 dec 1911 – 2 sheets – us Res Libr [972]

Chrysander, Friedrich et al *see* VIERTELJAHRSSCHRIFT FUER MUSIKWISSENSCHAFT

LA CHRYSOLITE OU LE SECRET DES ROMANS / Mareschal, Andre – Paris: Toussaint du Bray, 1627 – 1 – F469,66 – fr Armell [440]

Chrysologus, Petrus *see* COLLECTIO SERMONUM

CHRYSOST O. PRAEM. VITA S. NORBERTI / Van Der Sterre, Ioann. – Antverpiae, 1556 – Dfl32.00 – ne Slangenburg [240]

CHRYSOSTOM – Granville, New York. v1-4 n3 oct 1935-mar 1938 – 1 – us Res Libr [073]

CHRYSOSTOM – v1-8. 1960-89 (complete) – 2r – 1 – ATLA S0425 – us A.T.L.A. [073]

CHRYSOSTOM – (v4- . 1974- . 5,6,9) – 1960- – 1 – us UMI [240]

Chrystal, James *see*
- AUTHORITATIVE CHRISTIANITY
- A HISTORY OF THE MODES OF CHRISTIAN BAPTISM

Chrytraeus, D *see* ORATIO DE STATV ECCLESIARVM HOC TEMPORE IN GRAECIA, ASIA, AFRICA, VNGARIA, ...

CHTENIE V BESEDE LIUBITELEI RUSSKAGO SLOVA – v. 1-19. Spb. 1811-15. B-1699 2 – 8 – ne IDC [073]

CHTENIIA IMPERATORSKOI AKADEMII NAUK V S. PETERBURGE ZA 1829 I 1830 GODA – Otdelenie nauk istoricheskikh, filologicheskikh i politicheskikh. v. 1. Spb. 1831. B-1700 2 – 8 – ne IDC [940]

CHTENIIA V ISTORICHESKOM OBSHCHESTVE NESTORA LETOPISTSA – Kiev, 1873-1914.24v. Contains texts of Readings given before the Historical Society of Nestor the Chronicler. B-1217/2 – 8 – ne IDC [947]

CHTENIIA V MOSKOVSKOM OBSHCHESTVIE LIUBITELEI DUKHOVNAGO PROSVIESHCHENIIA – (Includes indexes 1863-80. 1880-94. 1910-12) – nos3,10. 1868; 1874; nos1-4,7,10. 1894 (complete) – 2r – 1 – ATLA S0193B – us A.T.L.A. [073]

CHTENIIA V OBSHCHESTVE LIUBITELEI DUKHOVNAGO PROSVESHCHENIIA – Zhurnal.Moscow, 1910-17. Lacking: 1914 (1-2); 1917 (4-12). BR-1579/2 – 8 – ne IDC [073]

CHTENIIA V TSERKOVNO-ARKHEOLOGICHESKOM OBSHCHESTVE – Kiev, 1883-1915/1916. v1-13. Lacking: 1914 (12). BR-1578/2 – 8 – ne IDC [947]

CHTO CHITAT' NARODNU? – Kriticheskii ukazatel'knig dlia narodnago i detskago chteniia 1 Ed. 2, 2. Spb. 1888-89. BR-5868 2 – 8 – ne IDC [947]

CHTO CHITAT' PO ISTORII KOMMUNISTICHESKOI PARTII SOVETS-KOGO SOIUZA / Gubareva, MN & Filipoov, N G – Ukazatel'literatury. 1. (1883-1918 gg). M. 1955. BR-5711 2 – 8 – ne IDC [947]

CHTO CHITAT' PO PROMYSLOVOI KOOPERATSII / Merkulov, A V – Moscow, 1930 – 2mf – 9 – COR-538/1 – ne IDC [334]

CHTO CHITAT' PO RUSSKOI LITERATURE 19 VEKA? / Malinin, D I – Opyt literaturno-kriticheskago ukazatelia k proizvedeniiam russkoi literatury 19 veka. Ed. 2. M. 1911. BR-7139 2 – 8 – ne IDC [460]

CHTO DALA OKTIABRSKAIA REVOLIUTSIIA : CHTO MY SDELALI ZA GOD I CHEGO MY ESHCHE NE SDELALI? – Moskva: Izd-vo Vseros. t sentr. ispolnitelnogo kom-ta sovetov r., s., k. i k. deputatov, 1919 – 1 – CSUX88-B9829 – us Hoover Inst Photo [947]

CHTO DIELALA I CHTO SDIELALA TRETIA GOSUDARSTVENNAIA DUMA – S.-Peterburg: Tip. T-va "Ekateringofskoe pechatnoe di elo", 1912 – 1 – CSUX88-B9203 – us Hoover Inst Photo [947]

CHTO DIELAT?: NABOLIEVSHIE VOPROSY NASHEGO DVIZHENIIA / Lenin, Vladimir Ilyich – Stuttgart: Verlag von J.H.W. Dietz, 1902. 144p – 1 – us U.W. Library [335]

CHTO DIELAT V UCHREDITELNOM SOBRANII / Breshko-Breshkovskaia, Ekaterina Konstantinovna – Moskva: "Zemli a i vli a", 1917 – 1 – CSUX88-B2063 – us Hoover Inst Photo [947]

CHTO GOVORI AT TSIFRY O GOLODE? : PAMIATKA AGITATORA / Glavpolitprosvet (RSFSR) – Moskva: Tip. Glavpolitprosveta, 1922- – 1 – CSUX89-B1310 – us Hoover Inst Photo [947]

CHTO MOZHET DAT' KOOPERATSIIA RABOCHIM / Kheisin, ML – Ed 2. Ekaterinburg, 1916 – 1mf – 9 – COR-136/1 – ne IDC [334]

CHTO NUZHNO ZNAT KAZHDOMU KRESTI ANINU? / SOSTAVLENO REDAKTSII AMI GAZET : "PRAVDA", "BEDNOTA" I "KOMMUNAR" – Moskva: Izd-vo Vserossi iskogo t sentralnogo ispolnitelnogo komiteta, 1919 – 1 – CSUX91-B2433 – us Hoover Inst Photo [947]

CHTO OZNACHAET ZAKON O SVOBODE SOVESTII OTDELENII TSERKVI OT GOSUDARSTVA? / Burov, I Akov – Moskva: Gos. izd-vo, 1921 – 1 – CSUX91-B1593 – us Hoover Inst Photo [947]

CHTO PROIZOSHLO V ROSSII? / Bobrovnikov, Nikolai – Petrograd: "Osvobozhdennai a Rossii a", 1917 – 1 – CSUX88-B9663 – us Hoover Inst Photo [947]

CHTO PROIZOSHLO VO VLADIVOSTOKIE 10/23 I 11/24 IANVARI A – [S.l.]: Izd. Sotsialistov revoliutsionerov, [1906] – 1 – CSUX88-B7362 – us Hoover Inst Photo [947]

CHTO SDELALO ZEMSTVO I CHTO ONO DALAET? / Abramov, A – St Petersburg, 1889 – 8 – BR-10,542 2 – ne IDC [947]

CHTO TAKOE DEMOKRATICHESKAIA RESPUBLIKA? : POIASNENIE DLIA GRAZHDAN ROSSII – Petrograd: Tip. gazety "Petrogradski i listok", [1917] – 1 – CSUX88-B2897 – us Hoover Inst Photo [947]

CHTO TAKOE FUTURIZM? / Malakhov, S – K postanovke voprosa. Oktiabr'. v. 2. M. 1927. BR-3567 2 – 8 – ne IDC [700]

CHTO TAKOE OBSHCHESTVO POTREBITELEI, KAK EGO OSNOVAT'I VESTI / Ozerov, I Kh. – (Enlarged ed) – Ed 3. M., 1909 – 2mf – 9 – COR-84/1 – ne IDC [334]

CHTO TAKOE PROIZVODITEL'NO-TRUDOVAIA ARTEL' I KAK EE ORGANIZOVAT' / Golikov, Pla. – Pg., 1920 – 1mf – 9 – COR-419/1 – ne IDC [334]

CHTO TAKOE PROMYSLOVAIA ARTEL' I KAK EE USTROIT' / Simakov, V – (Revised and enlarged edition) – Ed.4. M., 1929 – 2mf – 9 – COR-445/1 – ne IDC [334]

CHTO TAKOE SAMODERZHAVIE I POCHEMU ONO PALO / Azvitskii, Valeriilolivich – Moskva: Izd. D. A. Makovskogo, 1917 – 1 – CSUX88-B5874 – us Hoover Inst Photo [947]

CHTO TAKOE SOTSIALNOE STRAKHOVANIE, DLIA CHEGO ONO NUZHNO I KAK EGO PROVODIT V ZHIZN / Gelfer, A – Moskva: [Narodny i komissariat truda], 1918 – 1 – CSUX91-B2138 – us Hoover Inst Photo [947]

CHTO TAKOE SOVETY NARODNOGO KHOZIAISTVA I DLIA CHEGO ONI SOZDANY? / Sovet narodnogo khozi a istva Severnogo ra iona – 2-e ispr. i dop. izd. Petrograd: [Sovet], 1919 – 1 – CSUX91-B1354 – us Hoover Inst Photo [947]

CHTO TAKOE TSENTROSOIUZ? / Merkulov, A V – M., 1919 – 1mf – 9 – COR-335/1 – ne IDC [334]

CHTO-ZHE DOLZHNY MY SDIELAT? / Bielogorskii, N – Nitstsa: N. Bielogorskii, 1930 – 1 – CSUX89-B6496 – us Hoover Inst Photo [947]

Chu, Chih-hsin *see* WHAT SORT OF THING IS JESUS? (CCC107)

Chu, Ching-i *see*
- CHUNG-KUO HSIANG TS'UN CHIAO WEN TI HSIN CHIEN SHE (CCC108)
- AN EXPERIMENTAL RURAL CHURCH (CCC109)
- RURAL WORSHIP SERVICES (CCC110)

Chu, Hsi *see* ETHICAL TEACHINGS FOR THE YOUNG (CCC111)

Chu, Hsieh *see* FRIENDLY RELATIONS AND CULTURAL EXCHANGE BETWEEN THE CHINESE AND INDONESIAN PEOPLES

CHU JIH YUAN LIU (CCC272) / Schramm, George & Li, Jui-fang – (In Chinese) – [s.l: s.n, 1920] – 1r – 1 – 1984-6611 – us A.T.L.A. [240]

Chu, T'ui-yu *see* CHRIST'S SERMON ON THE MOUNT AND ORIENTALISM (CCC112)

Chu, Wei-chih *see* CHRISTIANITY AND LITERATURE (CCC114)

Chu, Wei-yu *see* SERMONS FOR CHURCH WORKERS (CCC115)

CHUAN KUO CHIN JUNG CHI KOU I LAN / China. People's Republic of China – Directory of financial organizations in China. Shanghai, 1947. Rev. ed. 1 reel – 1 – 8.80 – us Chinese Res [324]

CH'UAN KUO TSUNG SHU-MU – (Cumulative national bibliography). Peking, 1958, 1960, 1962-65, 1970, 1972-77. 7 reels – 1 – 150.00 – us Chinese Res [920]

Chuan, S Peter *see* CHURCH MEMBER (CCC 116)

CHUANBO SHIJIE – China. Ship World, Technical Paper. -w. 1979-. M-D101 – 1 – $28.00r – cc Microforms [623]

CH'UANG-TSAO CHOU-K'AN – Creation Weekly.Shanghai, 1923-24. v1-2 (1-52). BCH-227/1 – 9 – ne IDC [073]

CH'UANG-TSAO JIH HUI-K'AN – Collection of Creation Daily. Shanghai. 1933. BCH-786 2 – 8 – ne IDC [072]

CHUANGTZE (CCC118) – (In Chinese) – [s.l: s.n, 1938] – 1r – 1 – 1984-B500 – us A.T.L.A. [240]

CHUANGZAO JIKAN – La Kreo. Mar 1922-Nov 1924. 1 reel. M C38 – 1 – $45.00 – cc Microforms [073]

CHUANGZAO ZHOUBAO – The Creative Weekly. May 1923-May 1924. 1 reel. M C39 – 1 – $40.00 – cc Microforms [073]

CHUANGZUO – Creation. -m. Jul-Sept 1935. 7 fiches. F C51 – 9 – $31.50 – cc Microforms [073]

CHUAN-HU-SHAAN BAILIANJIAO QIYI ZILIAO JILU – Materials on Uprisings of the White Lotus Society in Sichuan, Hubei and Shaanxi Provinces. Comp. by Jiang Weimin. 3 fiches. F H78 – 9 – $18.00 – cc Microforms [950]

CH'UAN-KUO CHU-YAO PAO-K'AN TZU-LIAO SO-YIN – Index to Chinese major periodicals and newspapers. Peking. 1955-59. Lacking: 1955-57; v. 12, 1958; v. 1-2, 1959. BCH-909 2 – 8 – ne IDC [072]

CH'UAN-KUO HSIANG HUI SHIH T'I-MING LU – National lists of successful candidates in the imperial examinations. Scattered years from 1673-1909. 12 reels – 1 – 380.00 – us Chinese Res [950]

CHUANKUO TSUNG SHUMO – China National Cumulative Bibliography. 1949-65, 1970, 1972-78. Suspended 1966-69, 1971. 15 reels. M R1 – 1 – 600.00 – cc Microforms [020]

CH'UAN-PIEN CHI-K'AN – (Szechuan Frontier Quarterly). Chungking. 1935-36. v.1-2(1-6). BCH-226 1 – 9 – ne IDC [073]

CHUANSHAAN GEMING GENJUDI LISHI WENXIAN XUANBIAN, 1-2. SELECTED DOCUMENTS ON THE SICHUAN AND SHAANXI REVOLUTIONARY BASES, 6-2 / ed by Chubanshe, Sichuan Renmin – 1978-80. M/H135. 1r – 5 – $40.00 – cc Microforms [025]

Chubanshe, Sichuan Renmin *see* CHUANSHAAN GEMING GENJUDI LISHI WENXIAN XUANBIAN, 1-2. SELECTED DOCUMENTS ON THE SICHUAN AND SHAANXI REVOLUTIONARY BASES, 6-2

Chubin, Daryl *see* INTERDISCIPLINARY ANALYSIS AND RESEARCH

Chubinskii, M P *see* ZAKON I DIEISTVITELNOST V SOVIETSKOI ROSSII

Chucarro, E M *see* DERECHO MARITIMO...

Chudakov, Gerasim *see* PROLETARSKAIA REVOLIUTSIIA I BURZHUAZNAIA KULTURA

Chudnov, MN *see* POD CHERNYM ZNAMENEM

Chudnovtsev, M *see*
- POLITCHESKAYA ROL' TSERKOVNIKOV I SEKTANTOV V SSSR
- TSERKOVNIKI I SEKTANTI V BOR'BE PROTIV KUL'TURNOI REVOLYUTSEE

Chudnovtsev, M I *see* 1905 NA I AKHROME

CHUDOVSKAIA PSALTYR' / Pogorelov, V – Pamiatniki staroslavianskago iazyka, V. III(1-). Spb. 1910 – 8 – BR-8054 – ne IDC [947]

CHUG. KREIS DER BUECHERFREUNDE – (Title change: Heute und Morgen, Nov 1944; Heute und Morgen/Antifaschistische Revue, Apr 1943-Jun 1945) – Tel Aviv, Haifa, Jerusalem, Israel. – 1r – 1 – gw Mikrofilm [800]

Chugaev, A P *see* MALOZNACHITEL'NOE PRESTUPLENIE I TOVARISHCHESKII SUD

CHUGOKU NENKAN – China yearbook. In Japanese. Shanghai, 1934-37, 1939. 3 reels – 1 – 49.50 – us Chinese Res [950]

CH'U-HSIUNG FU-CHIH – 1716, 10, 1. BCH-675 2 – 8 – ne IDC [950]

CHU-HSUEH YUEH-K'AN = DRAMA MONTHLY – Peiping, 1932-33, v1-2 (12). BCH-248/1 – 9 – ne IDC [820]

Chukovskii, K *see*
- AKHMATOVA I MAIAKOVSKII
- EGO-FUTURISTY I KUBO-FUTURISTY AND OBRAZTSY FUTURISTICHESKIKH PROIZVEDENII
- FUTURISTY
- IZ VOSPOMINANII
- KNIGA OB ALEKSANDRE BLOKE
- LIUDI I KNIGI
- OT CHEKHOVA DO NASHIKH DNEI IZD
- REPIN, GOR'KII, MAIAKOVSKII, BRIUSOV
- SOVREMENNIKI

Chukovskii, N *see* VSTRECHI S MANDEL'SHTAMOM

CHULA VISTA STAR NEWS – Chula Vista, CA. 1930-1937; 1970- – 99+ r – 1 – $4,950.00 ($165.00y) – H03182 – us Library Micro [071]

Chulkov, G I *see*
- GODY STRANSTVII
- K ISTORII "BALAGANCHIKA"
- POKRYVALO IZIDY
- SBORNIK STATEI 1912-1922
- VCHERA I SEGODNIA

CHULKOV I LEVSHIN / Shklovskii, V – L. 1933. BR-7872 2 – 8 – ne IDC [460]

Chulkov, M D *see* SOCHINENIIA

Chumacero y Carrillo, Juan *see* MEMORIAL... ANO DE 1633

Chumalo, F S *see* LESNOE ZAKONODATEL'STVO UKRAINY

CHUN I KUNG PAO / China. Director of Military Medical Service – Official gazette. Nanking. 1929-35. Lacking: (25, 26) 1931; (33, 38) 1932; 1933-35. BCH-1069 1 – 9 – ne IDC [610]

CH'UN-CHUNG JIH-PAO – Sian, China. Ch'un-chung Daily. Starting 16 Oct 1954, title changed to Shensi Daily. May 1952-Oct 1954. 6 reels – 1 – 126.00 – us Chinese Res [072]

CHUNG FA HAN-HSUEEH YEN-CHIU-SO T'U-SHU-KUAN KUAN-K'AN – Scripta Sinica. v. 1-2. Peiping. 1945-46. BCH-228 – 8 – ne IDC [480]

Chung, H *see* KOREAN TREATIES

CHUNG HSI JIH PAO = CHUNG SAI YAT PO – San Francisco [CA: Chung Sai Yat Po Publ Co], jul 1947-1950 – us Res Libr [071]

CHUNG HUA JEN MIN KUNG HO KUA FA CHAN MIN CHING CHI TI YI KO WU NIEN CHI HUA 1953-1957 / China. People's Republic – D-1267 1. 1955 – 9 – ne IDC [324]

CHUNG HUA JEN MIN KUNG HO KUO CH'UAN KUO JEN MIN TAI PIAO TA HUI CH'ANG WU WEI YUAN HUI KUNG PAO – Peking. 1958-66. Lacking: v. 1-34, 1958; v. 42-64, 1959-61. BCH-900 2 – 8 – ne IDC [073]

Chung Hua Tsung Hui *see* MEMORANDUM OUTLINING ACTS OF VIOLENCE AND INHUMANITY PREPETRATED BY INDONESIAN BANDS ON INNOCENT CHINESE BEFORE AND AFTER THE DUTCH POLICE ACTION WAS ENFORCED ON JULY 21, 1947

CHUNG HUA T'U SHU KUAN HSIEH HUI HAI PAO – v1-14. 1925-40 – 1r – 1 – us Ross [020]

Chung, Kuang-hsing *see* HUA CH'IAO TSAI YIN-NI. (OVERSEAS CHINESE IN INDONESIA)

CHUNG NUNG CHING-CHI T'UNG-CHI – (Economic and Statistical review). Chungking, Nanking, China. 31 Jul 1941-31 Dec 1947. v.1, no.2-v.7, no.2. 3 reels – 1 – 62.50 – us Chinese Res [330]

CHUNG NUNG YUEH KAN – Farmers' Bank Monthly. Chungking, Shanghai. May 1940-Oct 1948. v.1, n.5-v.9, no.10. Incomplete. 6 reels – 1 – 112.50 – us Chinese Res [332]

Chung, Pak K *see* SELF-ESTEEM AND HEALTH RELATED PHYSICAL FITNESS OF MALE COLLEGE STUDENTS IN HONG KONG

CHUNG TE HSUEH-CHIH – Aus Deutschen Geistesleben. v. 2-6. Peiping. 1939-44. BCH-246 2 – 8 – ne IDC [073]

CHUNG WAI CHING-CHI CHOU-K'AN – Peking, China. Chinese weekly economic bulletin. March 1923-Oct 1927. Incomplete – 1 – 108.00 – us Chinese Res [330]

CHUNG YANG YIN HANG YUEH PAO / China. Central Bank – (n.s. v1-4. n.3. Lacking: v2, n.8. 5 reels. $93.50) – Shanghai. -m. v1-6, n.6. Aug 1932-Jun 1937. Lacking: v1, n.1-3. 14 reels – 1 – $237.00 – us Chinese Res [332]

CH'UNG-CH'ING HSIEN-CHIH – 1926, 12. BCH-706 2 – 8 – ne IDC [950]

CH'UNG-CHING JIH-PAO – Chungking, China. Chungking Daily. Sept 1952-Jun 1953; Oct 1954-Dec 1960. 14 reels – 1 – 380.00 – us Chinese Res [072]

CHUNG-FA CHAN-CHENG – Documents on Franco-Chinese War. 7 v. 1955. BCH-949 2 – 8 – ne IDC [944]

CHUNG-FA-TA-HSUEH YUEH-K'AN = REVUE DE L'UNIVERSITE FRANCO-CHINOISE – Peiping, 1931-37. v1-11 (1). BCH-229/1 – 9 – ne IDC [073]

CHUNG-HANG YUEH-K'AN / China. Bank of China – Monthly Review. 17 v. Shanghai. 1930-38. BHC-230 1 – 9 – ne IDC [073]

CHUNG-HO YUEH-K'AN – Harmony Monthly. v. 1-6. Peiping. 1940-46. BCH-231 2 – 8 – ne IDC [073]

CHUNG-HO YUEH-K'AN – Peking. (The Neutral Monthly). Jan. 1940-Apr. 1945. (9200 5272) – 1 – 35.00r – us Hoover Inst Photo [073]

CHUNG-HSI CHIAO-HUI PAO *see* MISSIONARY REVIEW

Chung-Hsing [pseud] *see* THE ANTI-COMMUNIST RECORDS OF THE DJAKARTA WARUNG BOND AND OF THE HONG GIE SOEN COOPERATIVE SOCIETY OF DJAKARTA

CHUNG-HUA CHIAO-YU-CHIEH – Chung-hua Educational Review. -m. Shanghai, 1913-37. v1-24, nsv1-4. BCH-232/1. Lacks many issues – 9 – ne IDC [073]

CHUNG-HUA CHI-TU-CHIAO TS'ING-NIEN-HUI CH'UAN KUO HSIEH-HUI CHIAO-HUI TSU (CCC119) : JEN SHIH YU HSING TUNG – (In Chinese) – [s.l: s.n, 1936] – 1r – 1 – 1984-B500 – us A.T.L.A. [240]

CHUNG-HUA CHI-TU-CHIAO-HUI NIEN CHIEN = CHINA CHURCH YEARBOOK – v1-13. 1914-36 (complete) – 4r – 1 – ATLA S0269 – us A.T.L.A. [240]

CHUNG-HUA FA-HSUEH TSA-CHIH – (Chinese Law Journal).-m. Nanking. 1930-33. v.1-4(6). Lacking: 1933, v.4(7,8). BCH-233 1 – 9 – ne IDC [073]

CHUNG-HUA JEN-MIN KUNG-HO-KUO FA-KUEI HUI-PIEN / China. People's Republic – v. 1-13. 1956-64. Lacking: v. 10-12, 1960-63. BCH-853 2 – 8 – ne IDC [324]

CHUNG-HUA T'U-SHU-KUAN HSIEH-HUI HUI-PAO. BULLETIN / Library Association. China – v. 1-21. Peiping. 1924-48. Lacking: v. 1, v. 2 (1) 1924; v. 14 (6) 1940; v. 15, v. 18 (1-4) 1940 44; v. 21 (1-2) 1947 48; v. 21 (5-6) 1948. BCH-236 1 – 9 – ne IDC [073]

CHUNG-JIH CHAN-CHEN – (Documents on Sino-Japanese War, 1894-95). 7 v. 1957. BCH-950 2 – 8 – ne IDC [950]

CHUNGKING DAN YENAN / Stein, Guenther – (Translation of The challenge of Red China). SE 5266 1. 1949 – 9 – ne IDC [950]

CHUNG-KUNG-YEH T'UNG-HSUN – Heavy Industry Bulletin. 1954-56. Lacking (1-36) 1954. BCH-948 2 – 8 – ne IDC [330]

CHUNG-KUO CHAN-SHIH CHING-CHI FA-KUI HUI-PIEN / China – (Collection of Laws and Regulations Governing China's Wartime Economy). Shanghai, 1940. 1 reel – 1 – 14.00 – us Chinese Res [950]

CHUNG-KUO CHIEN-SHE – China Construction. Nanking, 1930-34, v1-9. -m. Lacks some issues. BCH-238/1 – 9 – ne IDC [073]

CHUNG-KUO CHING-CHI KAI-TSAO / Ma Yin-Ch'u – (The Economic Reform of China). Shanghai. 1935. 1 reel – 1 – 11.00 – us Chinese Res [330]

CHUNG-KUO CHING-CHI NIEN-CHIEN – (Chinese economic yearbook. 2 v. 1934. BCH-982 2 – 8 – ne IDC [330]

CHUNG-KUO CHING-CHI (THE CHINESE ECONOMY) – Nanking, Apr 1933-Apr 1937. Scattered issues missing. 7 reels – 1 – 195.00 – us Chinese Res [339]

CHUNG-KUO CH'ING-NIEN – China Youth. Peking. 1948-66. Lacking: (5-32) 1948-49; (36-37, 47, 53) 1950; (13, 23-24) 1952. BCH-903 2 – 8 – ne IDC [360]

CHUNG-KUO CHIN-TAI SHIH TS'AN-K'AO T'U-P'IEN CHI – Illustrations on Modern Chinese History, 1840-1916. Peking. 1958. BCH-953 2 – 8 – ne IDC [950]

CHUNG-KUO HSIANG TS'UN CHIAO WEN TI HSIN CHIEN SHE (CCC108) / Chu, Ching-i – (In Chinese) – [s.l: s.n, 1927] – 1r – 1 – 1984-B500 – us A.T.L.A. [240]

CHUNG-KUO HSIN-SHU YUEH-PAO – (Chinese new publications monthly). 3 v. Shanghai. 1930-33. Lacking: v. 1 (5-7, 10, 11) 1931; v. 2 (11, 12) 1932; v. 3 (4-12) 1933. BCH-241 1 – 9 – ne IDC [073]

CHUNG-KUO HSUEH-PAO – China Journal. v. 1-9. Peking. 1912-13; n.s. v. 1-5. 1916. monthly. BCH-240 2 – 8 – ne IDC [073]

CHUNG-KUO HUI CHIAO SHIH CHIEN (CCC239) / Ma, I-yu – (In Chinese) – [s.l: s.n, 1941] – 1r – 1 – 1984-6578 – us A.T.L.A. [240]

Chung-kuo kung ch'an tang *see* CHINESE COMMUNIST PROPAGANDA ACTIVITIES RE INDONESIA; RESEARCH BACKGROUNDER

CHUNG-KUO KUNG-JEN – Chinese Workers. Peking. 1955. Lacking: v. 1-13, 15-17, 1956; v. 21-24, 1959. BCH-905 2 – 8 – ne IDC [330]

CHUNG-KUO KUNG-LUN = CHINA FORUM – Peking, 1939-45.v1-12 (1-4). Lacking: 1942, v7(1-4); v8(2,6-?)-1943, v9(1,2) 5,6?)-1943, v10(1-4); 1944, v11(1,2,4), 1944, v12(1,3). BCH-1048/1 – 9 – ne IDC [073]

CHUNG-KUO LAO-KUNG WEN-T'I / Ch'en Ta – (Labor Problems in China). Shanghai, 1929. 1 reel – 1 – 12.00 – us Chinese Res [950]

CHUNG-KUO LAO-TUNG FA LING HUI-PIEN / Ku Ping-Yuan – (A Collection of Chinese Labor Laws and Decrees). Shanghai, 1937. 1 reel – 1 – $11.00 – us Chinese Res [950]

CHUNG-KUO LI SHIH TI SHANG TI KUAN (CCC306) / Wang, Chih-hsin – (In Chinese) – [s.l: s.n, 1926] – 1r – 1 – 1984-6645 – us A.T.L.A. [240]

CHUNG-KUO NUNG-TS'UN (CHINESE VILLAGES) – Shanghai, Oct 1934-May 1943. Scattered issues missing. 4 reels – 1 – 108.00 – us Chinese Res [073]

CHUNG-KUO PAN-K O T'U-LU – Collections of selected pages from old and rare editions. 8 v. 1960. BCH-947 2 – 8 – ne IDC [800]

CHUNG-KUO PO-WU-KUAN HSIEH-HUI HUI-PAO / Chinese Museum Association – Bulletin. v1-2(5) 1935-37. Bi-monthly. Lacking: v2(5) 1937. BCH-242 2 – 8 – ne IDC [060]

CHUNG-KUO T'IEN CHU CHIAO CH'UAN CHIAO SHIH (CCC121) / D'Elia, Paschal – (In Chinese) – [s.l: s.n, 1934] – 1r – 1 – 1984-B500 – us A.T.L.A. [240]

CHUNG-KUO TSO-CHIA – (Chinese writers). 1947-48. BCH-957 2 – 8 – ne IDC [890]

CHUNG-KUO TSUNG CHIAO SZU SHIH TA KANG (CCC309) / Wang, Chih-hsin – (In Chinese) – [s.l: s.n, 1933] – 1r – 1 – 1984-6648 – us A.T.L.A. [240]

CHUNG-KUO WEI HSIN PAO = CHINESE REFORM NEWS – New York City: Chinese Reform News Publ Co, [aug 22 1917-1928] – 7r – us Res Libr [071]

CHUNG-KUO YING-TSAO-HSUEH-SHE HUI-K'AN = BULLETIN OF THE SOCIETY FOR RESEARCH IN CHINESE ARCHITEKTURE – Peiping, Szechuan, 1930-45. -q.7v. BCH-244/1 – 9 – ne IDC [073]

CHUNG-NUNG YUEH-K'AN – (The Farmer's Bank Monthly). Chungking Shanghai. v.1, no.5-v.9, no.10. Incomplete. 6 reels – 1 – 112.50 – us Chinese Res [332]

CHUNG-QANG JIH-PAO, 1928-1990 – (In Chinese) – 198r – 1 – $30.00r in U.S. $6,930.00r outside U.S. (L94A0001-L94A0016) – us L of C Photodup [320]

CHUNG-SHAN WEN-HUA CHIAO-YU-KUAN CHI-K'AM / Sun Yat-San Institute for Advancement of Culture and Education – "Quarterly Review. 4 v. Nanking. 1934-37. BCH-245 1 – 9 – ne IDC [000]

CHUNG-YANG JIH-PAO : CHANGSHA (HUNAN) EDITION – Apr-Nov 1938 – 1r – 1 – L94A0001 – Dist. us Scholarly Res – us L of C Photodup [320]

CHUNG-YANG JIH-PAO : CHENGTU (SZECHWAN) EDITION – Apr 1943-Jun 1946 – 4r – 1 – L94A0002 – Dist. us Scholarly Res – us L of C Photodup [320]

CHUNG-YANG JIH-PAO : CHIKIANG (HUNAN) EDITION – Aug-Dec 1943 – 1r – 1 – L94A0003 – Dist. us Scholarly Res – us L of C Photodup [320]

CHUNG-YANG JIH-PAO : CHUNGKING (SZECHWAN) EDITION – Sept 1938-Dec 1941; Apr 1942-Jul 1948 – 8r – 1 – L94A0004 – Dist. us Scholarly Res – us L of C Photodup [320]

CHUNG-YANG JIH-PAO : KUNMING (JUNAN) EDITION – May 1943-Aug 1945 – 1r – 1 – L94A0005 – Dist. us Scholarly Res – us L of C Photodup [320]

CHUNG-YANG JIH-PAO : KWEIYANG (KWEICHOW) EDITION – Apr 1943-48 – 1r – 1 – L94A0006 – Dist. us Scholarly Res – us L of C Photodup [320]

CHUNG-YANG JIH-PAO : NANKING (KIANGSU) EDITION – Nov 1932-Dec 1937; Mar 1945-Apr 1949 – 22r – 1 – L94A0007 – Dist. us Scholarly Res – us L of C Photodup [320]

CHUNG-YANG JIH-PAO : NANKING (KIANGSU) EDITION – (Wang Ching-wei regime). Mar-Jul 1945 – 1r – 1 – L94A0008 – Dist. us Scholarly Res – us L of C Photodup [320]

CHUNG-YANG JIH-PAO : PAI-SE (KWANGSI) EDITION – Jan-Jul 1945 – 1r – 1 – L94A0009 – Dist. us Scholarly Res – us L of C Photodup [320]

CHUNG-YANG JIH-PAO : SHANGHAI EDITION – Feb-Sept 1928; Aug-Dec 1945; 1946; 1947; 1948; 1949 – 12r – 1 – L94A0010 – Dist. us Scholarly Res – us L of C Photodup [320]

CHUNG-YANG JIH-PAO : SHAOYANG (HUNAN) EDITION – Aug 1942-Sept 1945 – 2r – 1 – L94A0011 – Dist. us Scholarly Res – us L of C Photodup [320]

CHUNG-YANG JIH-PAO : SHENYANG (LIAONING) EDITION – Jul 1948 – 1r – 1 – L94A0012 – Dist. us Scholarly Res – us L of C Photodup [320]

CHUNG-YANG JIH-PAO : TAIPEI (TAIWAN) EDITION – Oct-Dec 1950; 1951-1990; 1950-1959: 20r; 1960-1969: 30r; 1970-1979: 35r; 1980-1989: 49r; 1990: 6r – 140r – 1 – L94A0013 – Dist. us Scholarly Res – us L of C Photodup [320]

CHUNG-YANG JIH-PAO : T'UN-HSI (ANHWEI) EDITION – Jul 1944-Jun 1945 – 1r – 1 – L94A0014 – Dist. us Scholarly Res – us L of C Photodup [320]

CHUNG-YANG JIH-PAO : WU-CHOU (KWANGSI) EDITION – Oct 1943-Jul 1944 – 1r – 1 – L94A0015 – Dist. us Scholarly Res – us L of C Photodup [320]

CHUNG-YANG JIH-PAO : YUNG-AN (FUKIEN) EDITION – Jul 1943-Jun 1944 – 1r – 1 – L94A0016 – Dist. us Scholarly Res – us L of C Photodup [320]
CHUNG-YANG JIH-PAO, 1928-1990 = CENTRAL DAILY NEWS – (In Chinese. Individual titles also listed) – 198r – 1 – $6,930.00 in US $40.00r outside – L94A00001-L94A00016 – Dist. us Scholarly Res – us L of C Photodup [072]
CHUNG-YANG LU-CHUN CHUN-KUAN HSUEH-HSIAO – Nanking. 1936. (8924 5573) – 1 – 35.00r – us Hoover Inst Photo [950]
CHUNG-YANG YIN-HANG YUEH-PAO – Shanghai, Chungking, 1932-41. v1-10, n.s.1946-49, v1-4.Lacking: 1932-41, v1-10. BCH-247/1 – 9 – ne IDC [073]
CHUO BIJUTSU : 1915-1936 – 1st period v1-15/no 6(1915-1929). 2nd period no 1-40(1933-1936) – 36r – 1 – Y480,000 – ja Yushodo [700]
Chuprov, A I *see* RECHI I STAT'I
THE CHURCH – Feb 1941-Nov 1950 (incomplete) – 1r – 1 – ATLA S0707D – us A.T.L.A. [073]
THE CHURCH / Luthardt, Christoph Ernst – 1867 – 9 – us A.T.L.A. [240]
THE CHURCH – Toronto. v5 n27. 8 jan 1842 – 1r – 1 – Can$25.00 – cn Can Microfilming [072]
CHURCH ADMINISTRATION – 1927-31. N.S. Oct 1959-61 – 1 – 81.97 – us Baptist [240]
CHURCH ADVOCATE – Findlay, Ohio. 1846- – 77r – 1 – $32.50r – us Archival [071]
CHURCH AND CREED / Newton, Richard Heber – New York: G P Putnam, 1891 – 1mf – 9 – 0-8370-3916-9 – 1985-1916 – us A.T.L.A. [240]
THE CHURCH AND HER CHILDREN / Hulbert, Henry Woodward – New York: F.H. Revell, c1912 – 1mf – us A.T.L.A. [240]
CHURCH AND HOME – Saint John, N.B.: [s.n., 1896-189-?] – 9 – cn C.I.H.M. [240]
THE CHURCH AND LABOR / Stelzele, Charles – Boston: Houghton Mifflin, 1910 – 1mf – us A.T.L.A. [240]
CHURCH AND LIFE – (Cont: Kirche og Folk) – v28-41. 1979-92 (complete) – Inquire – 1 – ATLA S0743 – us A.T.L.A. [073]
CHURCH AND MANOR : A STUDY IN ENGLISH ECONOMIC HISTORY / Addy, Sidney Oldall – London: George Allen, 1913 – 2mf – us A.T.L.A. [330]
THE CHURCH AND MODERN LIFE / Gladden, Washington – Boston: Houghton, Mifflin, 1908 – 1mf – us A.T.L.A. [240]
THE CHURCH AND MODERN MEN / Palmer, William Scott – London: Longmans, Green, 1907. 1 fiche – 9 – us A.T.L.A. [240]
THE CHURCH AND MODERN SOCIETY : LECTURES AND ADDRESSES / Ireland, John – (Includes Indexes) – Chicago: D H McBride. 2v. 1897-1905 – 2mf – 9 – 0-8370-6668-9 – 1986-0668 – us A.T.L.A. [240]
CHURCH AND RACE PROBLEMS PAMPHLET COLLECTION – 19?? – 1 – CSUXAMJ4555-B – us Hoover Inst Photo [305]
CHURCH AND REFORM IN SCOTLAND; A HISTORY FROM 1797 TO 1843 / Mathieson, William Law – Glasgow: James Maclehose, 1916. 412p – 1 – us U.W. Library [941]
THE CHURCH AND RELIGIOUS UNITY / Kelly, Herbert – London; New York: Longmans, Green, 1913 – 1mf – us A.T.L.A. [240]
CHURCH AND SOCIETY – (Lacking: v1-4 p5-6. Title varies) – Philadelphia. v1-81. Sep 1908-Aug 1991 – 19r – 1 – ATLA S0147 – us A.T.L.A. [073]
CHURCH AND STATE : A HISTORICAL HANDBOOK / Innes, Alexander Taylor – Edinburgh: T.& T. Clark; New York: Scribner and Welford, [1890?] (Handbooks for Bible classes and private students) – 1mf – us A.T.L.A. [240]
CHURCH AND STATE : THEIR RELATIONS HISTORICALLY DEVELOPED / Geffcken, Heinrich; ed by Taylor, Edward Fairfax – London: Longmans, Green, 1877 – 3mf – us A.T.L.A. [240]
CHURCH AND STATE IN ARMENIA PAMPHLET COLLECTION – 19?? – 1 – CSUXANL2247-B – us Hoover Inst Photo [320]
CHURCH AND STATE IN BELGIUM PAMPHLET COLLECTION – 197? – 1 – CSUXAMJ4575-B – us Hoover Inst Photo [320]
CHURCH AND STATE IN CZECHOSLOVAKIA PAMPHLET COLLECTION – 1922-1931? – 1 – CSUXANL5039-B – us Hoover Inst Photo [320]
CHURCH AND STATE IN EARLY MARYLAND / Petrie, George – Baltimore: Johns Hopkins Press, 1892 (Johns Hopkins University studies in historical and political science; 10th ser., 4) – 1mf – us A.T.L.A. [320]
CHURCH AND STATE IN EAST GERMANY PAMPHLET COLLECTION – 1979-1983 – 1 – CSUXAMJ5673-B – us Hoover Inst Photo [320]
CHURCH AND STATE IN ESTONIA PAMPHLET COLLECTION – 1979?-1982 – 1 – CSUXANL2237-B – us Hoover Inst Photo [320]
CHURCH AND STATE IN FRANCE, 1300-1907 / Galton, Arthur – London: Edward Arnold, 1907 – 1mf – us A.T.L.A. [944]
CHURCH AND STATE IN GERMANY PAMPHLET COLLECTION – 1939-1974 – 1 – CSUXAMJ5663-B – us Hoover Inst Photo [320]
CHURCH AND STATE IN ITALY PAMPHLET COLLECTION – 1958 – 1 – CSUXAMK5677-B – us Hoover Inst Photo [320]
CHURCH AND STATE IN LATVIA PAMPHLET COLLECTION – 1978 – 1 – CSUXANL1866-B – us Hoover Inst Photo [320]
CHURCH AND STATE IN NEW ENGLAND / Lauer, Paul E – Baltimore: Johns Hopkins Press, 1892 (Johns Hopkins University studies in historical and political science; 10th ser., 2-3) – 1mf – us A.T.L.A. [320]
CHURCH AND STATE IN NORTH CAROLINA / Weeks, Stephen Beauregard – Baltimore: Johns Hopkins Press, 1893 (Johns Hopkins University studies in historical and political science; 11th ser., 5-6) – 1mf – us A.T.L.A. [320]
CHURCH AND STATE IN POLAND PAMPHLET COLLECTION – 1916-1940? – 1 – CSUXANL6574-B – us Hoover Inst Photo [320]
CHURCH AND STATE IN SCOTLAND : A NARRATIVE OF THE STRUGGLE FOR INDEPENDENCE FROM 1560 TO 1843: THE THIRD SERIES OF CHALMERS LECTURES / Brown, Thomas – Edinburgh: MacNiven & Wallace, 1892. (The Chalmers lectures) – 1mf – us A.T.L.A. [240]
CHURCH AND STATE IN THE SOVIET UNION PAMPHLET COLLECTION – 1923-1974 – 1 – CSUXANR0999-B – us Hoover Inst Photo [320]
CHURCH AND STATE IN THE UNITED STATES / Schaff, Philip – 1889 – 1 – $50.00 – us Presbyterian [240]
CHURCH AND STATE IN THE UNITED STATES : WITH AN APPENDIX ON THE GERMAN POPULATION / Thompson, Joseph Parrish – Boston: J.R. Osgood, 1873 – 1mf – us A.T.L.A. [240]
CHURCH AND STATE IN YUGOSLAVIA PAMPHLET COLLECTION – 1953 – 1 – CSUXANL2227-B – us Hoover Inst Photo [320]
THE CHURCH AND STATE RESPONSIBLE TO CHRIST / Irving, Edward – 1829 – 1 – $50.00 – us Presbyterian [240]
CHURCH AND STATE TWO HUNDRED YEARS AGO : A HISTORY OF ECCLESIASTICAL AFFAIRS IN ENGLAND FROM 1660 T0 1663 / Stoughton, John – London: Jackson, Walford, and Hodder, 1862 – 2mf – us A.T.L.A. [240]
CHURCH AND STATE UNDER THE TUDORS / Child, Gilbert W – London; New York: Longmans, Green, 1890 – 2mf – us A.T.L.A. [941]
THE CHURCH AND THE AGE : AN EXPOSITION OF THE CATHOLIC CHURCH IN VIEW OF THE NEEDS AND ASPIRATIONS OF THE PRESENT AGE / Hecker, Isaac Thomas – (Includes bibliographical references) – New York: Catholic Book Exchange, 1896, c1887 – 1mf – 9 – 0-8370-8348-6 – 1986-2348 – us A.T.L.A. [240]
THE CHURCH AND THE BARBARIANS : BEING AN OUTLINE OF THE HISTORY OF THE CHURCH FROM A.D. 461 TO A.D. 1003 / Hutton, William Holden – 1mf 1500 London: Rivingtons, 1906. (The Church universal; v3) – us A.T.L.A. [240]
CHURCH AND THE BIBLE: AN EXPLANATION AND VINDICATION / Bolmer, William Brevoort – New York: E. & J.B. Young, 1896.1 fiche – 9 – us A.T.L.A. [240]
THE CHURCH AND THE CHURCHES, OR, THE PAPACY AND THE TEMPORAL POWER : AN HISTORICAL AND POLITICAL REVIEW / Doellinger, Ignaz von – London: Hurst and Blackett, 1862 – 2mf – us A.T.L.A. [240]
THE CHURCH AND THE CIVIL LAW / Howell, Charles Boynton – Detroit, 1886. 58p. LL-712 – 1 – us L of C Photodup [340]
THE CHURCH AND THE COMMONWEALTH: DISCUSSIONS AND ORATIONS ON QUESTIONS OF THE DAY: PRACTICAL, BIOGRAPHICAL, EDUCATIONAL AND DOCTRINAL, WRITTEN DURING A TWENTY YEARS MINISTRY / Cochrane, William – Brantford, Ont.: Bradley, Garretson & Co., 1887. 00690. (Pre-1900 Canadiana) – 9 – cn C.I.H.M. [240]
THE CHURCH AND THE EASTERN EMPIRE / Tozer, Henry Fanshawe – New York: A.D.F. Randolph, [1888?] – 1mf – us A.T.L.A. [240]
THE CHURCH AND THE FUTURE = L'EGLISE ET L'AVENIR / Bourdon, Hilaire – Abridged and rearranged. [S.l.: s.n.], 1903 (Edinburgh: Turnbull and Spears) – 1mf – 9 – 0-8370-9446-1 – 1986-3446 – us A.T.L.A. [240]
THE CHURCH AND THE HOUR / Scudder, Vida Dutton – 1917 – 9 – us A.T.L.A. [240]
THE CHURCH AND THE KINGDOM / Gladden, Washington – New York: Fleming H Revell, c1894 – 1mf – 9 – 0-8370-9782-7 – 1986-3782 – us A.T.L.A. [240]
THE CHURCH AND THE LABOR CONFLICT / Womer, Parley Paul – New York: Macmillan, 1913 – 1mf – us A.T.L.A. [240]
THE CHURCH AND THE LABOR MOVEMENT / Stelzele, Charles – Philadelphia: American Baptist Publication Society, 1910 – 1mf – us A.T.L.A. [331]
THE CHURCH AND THE NATION : CHARGES AND ADDRESSES / Creighton, Mandell; ed by Creighton, Louise – London; New York: Longmans, Green, 1901 – 1mf – us A.T.L.A. [240]
THE CHURCH AND THE PEOPLE'S PLAY / Atkinson, Henry A – Boston: Pilgrim Press, c1915 – 1mf – us A.T.L.A. [240]
THE CHURCH AND THE PURITANS, 1570-1660 / Wakeman, Henry Offley – New York: A.D.F. Randolph, [1894?] – 1mf – us A.T.L.A. [240]
THE CHURCH AND THE REBELLION : A CONSIDERATION OF THE REBELLION AGAINST THE GOVERNMENT OF THE UNITED STATES AND THE AGENCY OF THE CHURCH, NORTH AND SOUTH, IN RELATION THERETO / Stanton, R L – New York: Derby & Miller, 1864 – 2mf – us A.T.L.A. [240]
THE CHURCH AND THE SOCIAL PROBLEM : A STUDY IN APPLIED CHRISTIANITY / Plantz, Samuel – Cincinnati: Jennings and Graham; New York: Eaton and Mains, c1906 – 1mf – 9 – 0-8370-9728-2 – 1986-3728 – us A.T.L.A. [240]
CHURCH ARMY GAZETTE – 1852-1914 – 1 – uk Microform Academic [240]
THE CHURCH – AS IT WAS, AS IT IS, AS IT OUGHT TO BE : A DISCOURSE / Clarke, James Freeman – Boston: Greene, 1848 – 1mf – us A.T.L.A. [240]
THE CHURCH AT HOME AND ABROAD – Philadelphia, PA. v1-24. 1887-1898 – 6r – 1 – $300.00 – us Presbyterian [240]
THE CHURCH AT THE CENTER / Wilson, Warren H – New York: Missionary Education Movement of the United States and Canada, 1914 – 1mf – us A.T.L.A. [240]
CHURCH AUTHORITY AND POWER IN MEDIEVAL AND EARLY MODERN ENGLAND – (Part 2: Bishops of Lincoln, 1209-1663. Part 3: Bishops of Coventry & Lichfield, 1295-1632; Carlisle, 1292-1656; Chester, 1541-1652; Durham, 1283-1672. Part 4: Bishops of Salisbury, 1297-1689. Part 5: Bishops of London, 1304-1660. Part 6: Christ Church Cathedral, Prior Canterbury, 1284-1661. Part 7: Bishops of Ely, 1337-1619; Oxford, 1592-1663; Wales, 1389-1705. Part 8: Bishops of Chichester, 1396-1675; Gloucester, 1541-1681; and Rochester, 1319-1683.) – Series One: The Episcopal Registers, 1209-1629. Part 1: Registers of the Archbishops of York, 1215-1650 – 1 – us Primary [240]
THE CHURCH BELL – Round Hill, N.B.: [s.n., 1899?-19–] – 9 – cn C.I.H.M. [240]
CHURCH BELLS OF ENGLAND / Walters, H B – H 1248 2. 1912 – 8 – ne IDC [780]
CHURCH BOOK / Evangelical and Reformed Church, Hoisington, KS – 1912-1946 – 1 – us KS Hist [240]
CHURCH BOOK – Greenbottom Church of Jesus Christ (Cabell Co), West Virginia, Jan 1836-Dec 1858 – $20.00 – us A.B.H.S. [240]
CHURCH BOOK / Trinity Lutheran Church, Lehigh, KS – 1900-1953 – 1 – us KS Hist [240]
CHURCH BUILDING : A STUDY OF THE PRINCIPLES OF ARCHITECTURE IN THEIR RELATION TO THE CHURCH / Cram, Ralph Adams – Boston: Small, Maynard, 1901 – 1mf – us A.T.L.A. [720]
CHURCH CALENDAR, CLERGY LIST, AND GENERAL ALMANACK FOR THE DIOCESE OF WORCESTER / Worcester (Hereford and Worcester) – Birmingham, 1862 – 1 – us U.W. Library [240]
THE CHURCH CATECHISM : ITS HISTORY AND CONTENTS: A MANUAL FOR TEACHERS AND STUDENTS / Allen, A J C – London, New York: Longmans, Green, 1892 – 1mf – us A.T.L.A. [240]
THE CHURCH CEVENANT IDEA : ITS ORIGIN AND ITS DEVELOPMENT / Burrage, Champlin – Philadelphia: American Baptist Publication Society, 1904 – 1mf – us A.T.L.A. [240]
Church, Charles A *see*
- HISTORY OF ROCKFORD AND WINNEBAGO COUNTY
- PAST AND PRESENT OF ROCKFORD CITY AND WINNEBAGO COUNTY

Church, Charles Marcus *see* CHAPTERS IN THE EARLY HISTORY OF THE CHURCH OF WELLS, A.D. 1136-1333, FROM DOCUMENTS IN POSSESSION OF THE DEAN AND CHAPTER OF WELLS
CHURCH CHIMES – Toronto: [s.n., 1874-18– or 19–] – 9 – cn C.I.H.M. [240]
CHURCH CHRONICLE – (Some original pgs damaged) – v28-32. 1931-35 – 1r – 1 – ATLA S0740 – us A.T.L.A. [073]
THE CHURCH CHRONICLE – Toronto: H. Rowsell, v1 no 1 (Apr 1863)- – 9 – cn C.I.H.M. [240]
CHURCH CHRONICLE FOR THE DIOCESE OF MONTREAL – Montreal: J. Lovell, 1860-1862 – 9 – cn C.I.H.M. [240]
THE CHURCH COVENANT IDEA / Burrage, Champlin – 1904 – 1 – 8.19 – us Baptist [240]
CHURCH DEFENSE : REPORT OF A CONFERENCE ON THE PRESENT DANGERS OF THE CHURCH / Marshall, Thomas William – New York: Catholic Publ Society, 1873 – 1mf – 9 – 0-8370-6756-1 – 1986-0756 – us A.T.L.A. [230]
CHURCH DISCIPLINE / Dover Baptist Association. Virginia – Summary. 1824. 30p – 1 – 5.00 – us Baptist [240]
CHURCH DISCIPLINE : AN ETHICAL STUDY OF THE CHURCH OF ROME / McCabe, Joseph – London: Duckworth, 1903 – 1mf – us A.T.L.A. [240]
CHURCH ECLECTIC – v1-41. 1873-1908 (complete) – 19r – 1 – ATLA S0882 – us A.T.L.A. [073]
Church, Elihu Dwight *see* CATALOGUE OF BOOKS CONSISTING OF ENGLISH LITERATURE AND MISCELLANEA
THE CHURCH EVANGELIST – Toronto: Church of England Pub Co, [1895-189-] – 9 – cn C.I.H.M. [240]
CHURCH FEDERATION : INTER-CHURCH CONFERENCE ON FEDERATION, NEW YORK, NOVEMBER 15-21, 1905 / ed by Sanford, Elias B – New York: Fleming H. Revell, c1906 – 2mf – us A.T.L.A. [240]
CHURCH FINANCES / Stevens, L C – or God's law. 1849 – 1 – 5.00 – us Baptist [240]
THE CHURCH GUARDIAN – (Montreal: v6 n33 26 nov 1884 4r Can$40.00) – Halifax, Moncton, Canada. v2 n12. 3 jul 1879-v5 n51. 9 avr 1884 – 1r – 1 – Can$25.00 – cn Can Microfilming [240]
THE CHURCH GUARDIAN : REVUE – St-Jean, Halifax, Canada. 3 dec 1879-25 nov 1891; Montreal, 1 dec 1891- 29 mai 1895 – 5r – 1 – Can$50.00r – cn Can Microfilming [073]
THE CHURCH HERALD – Toronto: Church Print and Pub Co, [1869-1875] – 9 – cn C.I.H.M. [240]
CHURCH HERALD AND HOLINESS BANNER – v55-57. 1934-36 (incomplete) – 2r – 1 – ATLA S0691 – us A.T.L.A. [073]
CHURCH HISTORY – v1-17. 1932-48 (complete) – 3r – 1 – ATLA S0064 – us A.T.L.A. [073]
CHURCH HISTORY – (v39- . 5,6. v45- . 9) – 1- 1932- – 1 – us UMI [240]
CHURCH HISTORY ASSOCIATION OF INDIA : BULLETIN – nos7-10. 1965-67 (incomplete) – 1r – 1 – ATLA S0714A – us A.T.L.A. [073]

CHURCH HISTORY ASSOCIATION OF INDIA BULLETIN – No.7-10, 1965-67. Incomplete; filmed with other titles.1 reel – 1 – us A.T.L.A. [073]

CHURCH HISTORY (CCC145) = CHIAO HUI LI SHIH / Hayes, W M – (In Chinese) – 6th ed. Shanghai: Christian Literature Society. 2v. 1931 – 1r – 1 – 1984-B500 – us A.T.L.A. [240]

CHURCH HISTORY IN BRIEF / Moffat, James C – Philadelphia: Presbyterian Board of Publication, c1885 – 2mf – us A.T.L.A. [240]

CHURCH HISTORY IN QUEEN VICTORIA'S REIGN / Fowler, Montague – London: S.P.C.K.; New York: E.& J.B. Young, 1896 – 1mf – us A.T.L.A. [240]

THE CHURCH HISTORY OF SCOTLAND : FROM THE COMMENCEMENT OF THE CHRISTIAN ERA TO THE PRESENT TIME / Cunningham, John – Edingburgh: J Thin, 1882 – 3mf – us A.T.L.A. [240]

THE CHURCH HISTORY OF THE FIRST THREE CENTURIES / Baur, Ferdinand Christian; ed by Menzies, Allan – Theological translation fund library; (v.16, 20) – 2mf – us A.T.L.A. [240]

THE CHURCH IN ENGLAND : FROM WILLIAM 3 TO VICTORIA / Hore, A H – Oxford: Parker, 1886 – 3mf – us A.T.L.A. [240]

THE CHURCH IN FRANCE / Smith, Richard Travers – London: Wells Gardner, Darton, 1894 – 2mf – us A.T.L.A. [240]

THE CHURCH IN GERMANY / Baring-Gould, Sabine – London: Wells Gardner, Darton, 1891. (The National churches) – 1mf – us A.T.L.A. [240]

THE CHURCH IN ITALY / Pennington, Arthur Robert – London: Wells Gardner, Darton, [1893?] – 2mf – us A.T.L.A. [240]

CHURCH IN RELATION TO SCEPTICS: A CONVERSATIONAL GUIDE TO EVIDENTIAL WORK / Harrison, Alexander James – London: Longmans, Green, 1892. 1 fiche – 9 – us A.T.L.A. [240]

THE CHURCH IN ROMAN GAUL / Smith, Richard Travers – London: S.P.C.K.; New York: E. & J.B. Young, [1882?] – 2mf – us A.T.L.A. [240]

THE CHURCH IN SCOTLAND : A HISTORY OF ITS ANTECEDENTS, ITS CONFLICTS, AND ITS ADVOCATES, FROM THE EARLIEST RECORDED TIMES TO THE FIRST ASSEMBLY OF THE REFORMED CHURCH / Moffat, James C – Philadelphia: Presbyterian Board of Publication, c1882 – 2mf – us A.T.L.A. [240]

THE CHURCH IN SCOTLAND / Luckock, Herbert Mortimer – London: Wells Gardner, Darton, [1893?] – 1mf – us A.T.L.A. [240]

THE CHURCH IN SPAIN / Bayle, Constantino & Allison Peers, E – Burgos: Razon y Fe, 1939 – 1 – sp Bibl Santa Ana [240]

THE CHURCH IN THE CATACOMBS : A DESCRIPTION OF THE PRIMITIVE CHURCH OF ROME ILLUSTRATED BY ITS SEPULCHRAL REMAINS / Maitland, Charles – London: Longman, Brown, Green, and Longmans, 1847 – 1mf – us A.T.L.A. [240]

THE CHURCH IN THE CITY / Leete, Frederick Deland – New York: Abingdon, c1915. (Constructive church series) – 1mf – us A.T.L.A. [240]

THE CHURCH IN THE CONFEDERATE STATES : A HISTORY OF THE PROTESTANT EPISCOPAL CHURCH IN THE CONFEDERATE STATES / Cheshire, Joseph Blount – New York: Longmans, Green, 1912, c1911 – 1mf – us A.T.L.A. [240]

THE CHURCH IN THE COUNTRY TOWN / Bemies, Charles O – Philadelphia: Published for the Social Service Commission of the Northern Baptist Convention [by] American Baptist Publ. Society, 1912 – 1mf – us A.T.L.A. [240]

THE CHURCH IN THE HIGHLANDS, OR, THE PROGRESS OF EVANGELICAL RELIGION IN GAELIC SCOTLAND, 563-1843 / Mackay, John – London; New York: Hodder and Stoughton, [1914?] (Chalmers lectures) – 1mf – us A.T.L.A. [240]

THE CHURCH IN THE MIRROR OF HISTORY : STUDIES ON THE PROGRESS OF CHRISTIANITY / Sell, Karl – New York: Scribner & Welford, [1890?] – 1mf – us A.T.L.A. [240]

THE CHURCH IN THE MISSION FIELD : WITH SUPPLEMENT, PRESENTATION AND DISCUSSION OF THE REPORT IN THE CONFERENCE ON 16TH JUNE 1910 – (Includes indexes) – Edinburgh: Publ for the World Missionary Conference by Oliphant, Anderson & Ferrier; New York: Fleming H Revell, [1910?] – 1mf – 9 – 0-8370-6473-2 – 1986-0473 – us A.T.L.A. [240]

THE CHURCH IN THE NETHERLANDS / Ditchfield, P H – London: Wells Gardner, Darton, 1893. (The National churches) – 1mf – us A.T.L.A. [240]

THE CHURCH IN THE SMALLER CITIES / Patterson, FW – Philadelphia: Published for the Social Service Commission of the Northern Baptist Convention [by] American Baptist Publ. Society, 1911 – 1mf – us A.T.L.A. [240]

THE CHURCH IN THE SOUTH AMERICAN REPUBLICS 2ND EDIC. WESTMENSTER, 1943 / Ryan, D D Edwin – Madrid: Missionalia Hispanica, 1946 – 1 – sp Bibl Santa Ana [240]

CHURCH IN THE WORLD – 1942-66 (complete) – 1r – 1 – ATLA S0698 – us A.T.L.A. [073]

THE CHURCH IN VICTORIA DURING THE EPISCOPATE OF THE RIGHT REVEREND CHARLES PERRY : FIRST BISHOP OF MELBOURNE, PRELATE OF THE ORDER OF ST. MICHAEL AND ST. GEORGE / Goodman, George – Melbourne: Melville, Mullen and Slade; London: Seeley, 1892 – 2mf – us A.T.L.A. [240]

CHURCH INTELLIGENCER – Raleigh, NC. 1860-67 (complete) – 1r – 1 – ATLA BS0051 – us A.T.L.A. [073]

THE CHURCH JOURNAL AND GOSPEL MESSENGER – (Title varies) – v1-26. 1853-79. 5 Feb 1853-14 Feb 1878; 7 Apr 1878-11 Jan 1879 – 13r – 1 – ATLA S0128 – us A.T.L.A. [073]

Church, L. Ruggles *see* REPORT OF ARGUMENT SUBMITTED TO THE HONORABLE THE EXECUTIVE COUNCIL FOR THE PROVINCE OF QUEBEC: ON PRESENTATION OF A MEMORIAL RESPECTING THE VESTED RIGHTS OF LIMIT HOLDERS IN THEIR LIMITS, MARCH 16TH, 1880

CHURCH LIBRARY – 1960-61 – 1 – 9.59 – us Baptist [240]

CHURCH LIFE AND THOUGHT IN NORTH AFRICA A.D. 200 / Donaldson, Stuart Alexander – (Includes indexes) – Cambridge: University Press, 1909 – 1mf – 9 – 0-8370-7623-4 – 1986-1623 – us A.T.L.A. [240]

CHURCH LIFE IN COLONIAL MARYLAND / Gambrall, Theodore C – Baltimore: G. Lycett, 1885 – 1mf – us A.T.L.A. [240]

CHURCH LIFE IN THE BLUE GRASS, 1783-1933 – By Ward Russell.4 fiches. F-0160 – 9 – us A.G.L.L. [240]

THE CHURCH MAGAZINE – Montreal: J.D. Borthwick, [v1] no 1 (Jan 1868)- – 9 – cn C.I.H.M. [240]

THE CHURCH MAGAZINE – St. John, N.B.: W.M. Wright, v1 no 1 (May 1865)- – 9 – cn C.I.H.M. [240]

CHURCH MANAGEMENT *see*
– THE RECORD OF CHRISTIAN WORK

CHURCH MEMBER (CCC 116) = CHIAO-YU / Chuan, S Peter – (In Chinese) – Shanghai: Mission Book Co., 1922 – 1r – 1 – 1984-B500 – us A.T.L.A. [240]

CHURCH MEMBERSHIP, OR, THE CONDITIONS OF NEW TESTAMENT AND METHODIST CHURCH MEMBERSHIP EXAMINED AND COMPARED / Bond, S – Toronto: W. Briggs; Montreal: C. Coates; Halifax: S. Huestis, 1882. 07201. (Pre-1900 Canadiana) – 9 – cn C.I.H.M. [240]

THE CHURCH MESSENGER – (Title varies) – v1-21 no 9. Oct 1875-Sep 1896 (complete) – 2r – 1 – ATLA S0097 – us A.T.L.A. [073]

THE CHURCH MESSENGER = TSERKOVNYI VIESTNIK – Pemberton, NJ: [American Carpatho-Russian Orthodox Greek Catholic Diocese in USA. nov 10 1946; aug 15 1947-1975 – us Res Libr [071]

THE CHURCH MESSENGER FOR THE DIOCESE OF QU'APELLE – Qu'Apelle Station [Sask.]: S. John's College, [188- or 189–189- or 19–] – 9 – cn C.I.H.M. [240]

THE CHURCH MESSENGER FOR THE DIOCESE OF QU'APPELLE *see* OUR MESSENGER

CHURCH MINUTES / Cullom Association. North Carolina. Warrenton Baptist Church – 1849-68 – 1 – $14.67 – us Baptist [240]

THE CHURCH MISCELLANY – [Kingston, Ont.?: First Congregational Church, Kingston?, 18–?] – 9 – cn C.I.H.M. [240]

THE CHURCH MISSIONARY ATLAS : CONTAINING AN ACCOUNT OF THE VARIOUS COUNTRIES IN WHICH THE CHURCH MISSIONARY / Society Labours, And Of Its Missionary Operations – London: Church Missionary Society, 1896 – 1mf – us A.T.L.A. [240]

CHURCH MISSIONARY REVIEW – (Lacking some pgs. Several title changes) – v1-78. 1849-1927 – 27r – 1 – ATLA S0213 – us A.T.L.A. [073]

Church Missionary Society *see*
– INTELLIGENCER
– PROCEEDINGS FOR AFRICA AND THE EAST
– UGANDA MISSION
– WEST INDIES MISSION RECORDS

Church Missionary Society. London *see* [RECORDS, 1803?-1914]

Church Missionary Society. South India Mission. Madras *see*
– CORRESPONDENCE, 1830-1865
– RECORDS, 1834-1860

Church Missionary Society. West Africa and Nigeria and Yoruba Missions *see* ARCHIVES

THE CHURCH MONTHLY AND THE HALDIMAND DEANERY MAGAZINE – (Cont by: The Haldimand Deanery Magazine) – [Dunnville, Ont.?: s.n., 1900] – 9 – cn C.I.H.M. [240]

THE CHURCH MONTHLY AND THE HALDIMAND DEANERY MAGAZINE *see*
– THE HALDIMAND DEANERY MAGAZINE

CHURCH MUSIC, A MANUSCRIPT OF AN ESSAY-SERMON 14 MAR 1875 / Smith, W S D – 1 – 5.00 – us Baptist [240]

CHURCH MUSIC IN THEORY AND PRACTICE IN SELECTED BAPTIST CHURCHES, AN EXPLORATORY STUDY / Benson, David P – 1961 – 1 – 5.00 – us Baptist [240]

CHURCH MUSICIAN – v. 1. 1950-61 – 1 – 64.96 – us Baptist [240]

CHURCH NURSERY GUIDE – 1957-61 – 1 – 31.71 – us Baptist [240]

CHURCH OBSERVER – Montreal: P. Wilson, [1868?-18– or 19–] – 9 – cn C.I.H.M. [240]

THE CHURCH OBSERVER – Montreal, Canada. v2 n1. 14 jan-29 dec 1869; v4 n45. 22 nov 1871 – 1r – 1 – Can$65.00 – cn Can Microfilming [240]

THE CHURCH OBSERVER – Springhill, N.S.: [s.n., 1896?-189- or 19–] – 9 – cn C.I.H.M. [240]

THE CHURCH OF ARMENIA : HER HISTORY, DOCTRINE, RULE, DISCIPLINE, LITURGY, LITERATURE, AND EXISTING CONDITION / Ormanian, Malachia – London: A.R. Mowbray, [1912?] – 1mf – us A.T.L.A. [240]

THE CHURCH OF CHRIST / Phillips, Thomas Wharton – (Includes index) – New York: Funk & Wagnalls, 1907, c1906 – 1mf – 9 – 0-8370-6077-X – 1986-0077 – us A.T.L.A. [240]

CHURCH OF CHRIST ADVOCATE – Circleville. Ohio. 1908-26 – 1 – us UMI [240]

THE CHURCH OF CHRIST IN JAPAN : A COURSE OF LECTURES / Imbrie, William – Philadelphia: Westminster Press, c1906 – 1mf – 9 – 0-8370-6578-X – 1986-0578 – us A.T.L.A. [240]

THE CHURCH OF CHRIST THE SAME FOREVER / McErlane, Daniel – (Includes index) – St Louis, MO: B Herder, 1900 – 1mf – 9 – 0-8370-6684-0 – 1986-0684 – us A.T.L.A. [240]

THE CHURCH OF CYPRUS / Duckworth, H T F – London: S.P.C.K.; New York: E.& J.B. Young, 1900 – 1mf – us A.T.L.A. [240]

Church of England *see*
– BOOK OF COMMON PRAYER
– GROVE BOOKLET ON MINISTRY AND WORSHIP
– RECORDS OF THE CHURCH OF ENGLAND DURING THE COMMONWEALTH PERIOD (1643-61)

THE CHURCH OF ENGLAND / Watson, Edward William – London: Williams and Norgate; New York: H. Holt, 1914 – 1mf – us A.T.L.A. [240]

THE CHURCH OF ENGLAND AND EPISCOPACY / Mason, Arthur James – Cambridge: University Press; New York: Putnam [distributor], 1914 – 2mf – us A.T.L.A. [240]

Church of England. Canada. Diocese of Ontario *see* CANONS OF THE SYNOD...AND OF THE PROVINCIAL SYNOD OF CANADA: WITH A COLLECTION OF STATUTES AFFECTING ECCLESIASTICAL RIGHTS AND FORMS OF GRANTS, REQUESTS AND TRUSTS FOR CHURCH PURPOSES

Church of England. Diocese of Fredericton *see* CHRONICLE OF THE DIOCESE OF FREDERICTON

THE CHURCH OF ENGLAND IN NOVA SCOTIA AND THE TORY CLERGY OF THE REVOLUTION / Eaton, Arthur Wentworth – New York: T. Whittaker, 1891 – 1mf – us A.T.L.A. [240]

THE CHURCH OF ENGLAND: ITS CONTINUOUS ORGANIC LIFE, AND ITS CATHOLIC RESTORATION: A LECTURE DELIVERED BEFORE THE CHURCH OF ENGLAND INSTITUTE, HALIFAX, AND SUBSEQUENTLY IN MONTREAL AND SHERBROOKE, PROVINCE OF QUEBEC, AND IN WINDSOR, NOVA SCOTIA / Brock, Isaac – Halifax: Morton, 1891. 00858. (Pre-1900 Canadiana) – 9 – cn C.I.H.M. [240]

Church of England. Liturgy and Ritual. Missal *see* MISSALE AD USUM INSIGNIS ECCLESIE SARISBURIENSIS

CHURCH OF ENGLAND TEACHING / Carmichael, James – Montreal: W. Drysdale, 1890. 00494. (Pre-1900 Canadiana) – 9 – cn C.I.H.M. [240]

THE CHURCH OF ENGLAND VINDICATED FROM THE CHARGE OF ARMINIANISM AND THE CASE OF ARMINIAN SUBSCRIPTION PARTICULARLY CONSIDERED,... / Toplady, Augustus Montague – London, 1769 – 2mf – 9 – MP-459/1 – ne IDC [240]

CHURCH OF GOD : YEARBOOK / Church of God – Anderson, IN. 1902-90 (complete) – 9r – 1 – ATLA S0198 – us A.T.L.A. [240]

Church of God *see* CHURCH OF GOD

THE CHURCH OF GOD AND THE BISHOPS = KIRCHE GOTTES UND DIE BISCHOEFE : AN ESSAY SUGGESTED BY THE CONVOCATION OF THE VATICAN COUNCIL / Liaeno, Heinrich St A von – (In English) – London: Rivingtons; New York: Pott and Amery, 1870 – 1mf – 9 – 0-8370-8444-X – 1986-2444 – us A.T.L.A. [240]

THE CHURCH OF OLD ENGLAND – Montreal: J.P. McMillin, 1866-[1867?] – 9 – cn C.I.H.M. [240]

THE CHURCH OF SANCTA SOPHIA CONSTANTINOPLE : A STUDY OF BYZANTINE BUILDING / Lethaby, W R & Swainson, H – London, 1894 – Dfl30.00 – ne Slangenburg [720]

CHURCH OF SCIENTOLOGY, CREED – Making 14 human rights points – 9 – 1.00f – at Libertarian Micro [290]

THE CHURCH OF SCOTLAND : HER DIVISIONS AND HER RE-UNIONS / McCrie, CG – Edinburgh: Macniven & Wallace, 1901 – 1mf – us A.T.L.A. [240]

Church of Scotland. General Assembly *see* RECORDS OF THE KIRK OF SCOTLAND

Church of Scotland. General Assembly. Committee for the Propagation of the Gospel in Foreign Parts *see* EDUCATIONAL MISSIONS IN INDIA

THE CHURCH OF SCOTLAND IN THE THIRTEENTH CENTURY : THE LIFE AND TIMES OF DAVID DE BERHAM OF ST. ANDREWS, BISHOP A.D. 1239 TO 1253: WITH LIST OF CHURCHES DEDICATED BY HIM, AND DATES / Lockhart, William – Edinburgh: W. Blackwood, 1892 – 1mf – us A.T.L.A. [240]

Church of Seventh Day Adventists (Columbus Grove, Ohio) *see* RECORDS

THE CHURCH OF THE APOSTLES : AN HISTORICAL INQUIRY / Capes, John Moore – London: Kegan Paul, Trench, 1886 – 1mf – 9 – 0-8370-6569-0 – 1986-0569 – us A.T.L.A. [240]

THE CHURCH OF THE APOSTLES / Kip, William Ingraham – New York: D. Appleton, 1877 – 1mf – us A.T.L.A. [240]

THE CHURCH OF THE APOSTLES / Ragg, Lonsdale – New York: Macmillan, 1909. 1 fiche – 9 – us A.T.L.A. [240]

CHURCH OF THE BRETHREN : DIRECTORY – 1973-81 (complete) – 2r – 1 – ATLA S0886 – us A.T.L.A. [030]

CHURCH OF THE BRETHREN : STATISTICS – 1973-80 (complete) – 1r – 1 – ATLA S0891 – us A.T.L.A. [240]

CHURCH OF THE BRETHREN : YEARBOOK (1918) – 1918-72 (complete) – 4r – 1 – ATLA S0901 – us A.T.L.A. [030]

CHURCH OF THE BRETHREN : YEARBOOK (1982) – 1982-1989 (complete) – 2r – 1 – ATLA S0902 – us A.T.L.A. [030]
CHURCH OF THE EPIPHANY PARISH MAGAZINE – Parkdale [Ont.: s.n., 189-?-19–] – 9 – cn C.I.H.M. [240]
THE CHURCH OF THE FUTURE : ITS CATHOLICITY, ITS CONFLICT WITH THE ATHEIST, ITS CONFLICT WITH THE DEIST, ITS CONFLICT WITH THE RATIONALIST, ITS DOGMATIC TEACHING ... / Campbell, Archibald – New York: Macmillan, 1881 – 1mf – us A.T.L.A. [240]
THE CHURCH OF THE MOTHER OF GOD, A CENTENNIAL CHRONICLE. / Kentucky – By Sis Mary Carmelite Brungs. 1941. 2 fiches. F-0408 – 9 – us A.G.L.L. [240]
THE CHURCH OF THE OPEN COUNTRY : A STUDY OF THE CHURCH FOR THE WORKING FARMER / Wilson, Warren H – New York: Literature Dept., Presbyterian Home Missions, c1911 – 1mf – us A.T.L.A. [240]
CHURCH OF THE REDEEMER PARISH MAGAZINE – Toronto: [s.n., 1891?-18– or 19–] – 9 – cn C.I.H.M. [240]
THE CHURCH OF THE SIXTH CENTURY : SIX CHAPTERS IN ECCLESIASTICAL HISTORY / Hutton, William Holden – London, New York: Longmans, Green, 1897 – 1mf – us A.T.L.A. [240]
THE CHURCH OF THE SUB-APOSTOLIC AGE : ITS LIFE, WORSHIP, AND ORGANIZATION, IN THE LIGHT OF "THE TEACHING OF THE TWELVE APOSTLES" / Heron, James – London: Hodder and Stoughton, 1888 – 1mf – us A.T.L.A. [240]
CHURCH ORGANIZATION AND METHODS – 1917 – 1 – 5.00 – us Baptist [240]
THE CHURCH, PAST AND PRESENT : A REVIEW OF ITS HISTORY / Gwatkin, Henry Melvill – London: J. Nisbet, 1900 – 1mf – us A.T.L.A. [240]
CHURCH PASTORALS / Adams, Nehemiah – Hymns and tunes for public and social worship. w index. Boston. 1864 – 9 – us A.T.L.A. [240]
Church, Pharcellus *see*
– RELIGIOUS DISSENSIONS
– SEED-TRUTHS
THE CHURCH PRESS – v1-5. Jul 1884-17 Apr 1888 (complete) – 3r – 1 – ATLA S0494 – us A.T.L.A. [073]
CHURCH PROBLEMS : A VIEW OF MODERN ANGLICANISM / ed by Henson, H Hensley – London: J. Murray, 1900 – 2mf – us A.T.L.A. [240]
CHURCH QUARTERLY – v.1-4. 1968-71 – 1 – us UMI [240]
CHURCH QUARTERLY REVIEW – 1955 – 1 – uk Microform Academic [073]
Church, R W *see*
– ESSAYS AND REVIEWS
– OCCASIONAL PAPERS
– ON SOME INFLUENCES OF CHRISTIANITY UPON NATIONAL CHARACTER
– THE OXFORD MOVEMENT
THE CHURCH RECORD – (Cont by: The Church Record for Diocese of New Westminster) – New Westminster, B.C.: H. Morey, [1897-1897 or 1898] – 9 – cn C.I.H.M. [240]
THE CHURCH RECORD FOR DIOCESE OF NEW WESTMINSTER – New Westminster [B.C.]: H. Morey, [1897 or 1898-189- or 19–] – 9 – cn C.I.H.M. [240]
CHURCH RECORD, MS 1217 / Chippewa Lake. Ohio. First Presbyterian Church of Lafayette – 1853-83 – 1r – 1 – us Western Res [240]
CHURCH RECORDS / Attica. Ohio. First Baptist Church of Attica – 1841-1944 – 1r – 1 – $32.50r – us Archival [240]
CHURCH RECORDS / Findlay.Ohio. St. Paul's United Methodist Church – 1870-1945 – 1r – 1 – $32.50r – us Archival [240]
CHURCH RECORDS / First Presbyterian Church, Topeka, KS – 1962-1984, Records of the church and the Synod of Kansas – 1 – us KS Hist [240]
CHURCH RECORDS / Galion. Ohio. Peace Evangelical Lutheran Church – 1846-1924 – 1r – 1 – $32.50r – us Archival [240]
CHURCH RECORDS / Garfield Heights. Ohio. St. John Evangelical Lutheran Church – 1854-1953 – 1r – 1 – us Western Res [240]
CHURCH RECORDS / Grand River. Ohio. Grand River Baptist Association – 1817-42, 1853-71 – 1r – 1 – us Western Res [240]
CHURCH RECORDS / Hardin County. Ohio. St. Paul's Evangelical Lutheran Church – 1842-1925 – 1r – 1 – $32.50r – us Archival [240]
CHURCH RECORDS / Mungen. Ohio. Church of Christ – 1883-1925 – 1r – 1 – $32.50r – us Archival [240]
CHURCH RECORDS / St. Paul's Church, Geary County, KS – 1870-1915 – 1 – us KS Hist [240]
CHURCH RECORDS / United Emmanuel Lutheran Church (ALC), Milberger, KS – 1883-1973, Records of the church and its predecessors – 1 – us KS Hist [240]
CHURCH RECORDS / U.S. Works Projects Administration. South Carolina Historical Records Survey – 1930s. 244 fiches. (Courtesy of the South Caroliniana Library, University of South Carolina) – 9 – us South Carolina Historical [240]
CHURCH RECORDS, 1836-1839, MS 444 / Presbyteries of Lorain and Elyria, Ohio – The Presbytery of Elyria, 1842-63 – 1r – 1 – us Western Res [240]
CHURCH RECORDS, MS 40 / Randolph. Ohio. First Congregational Church – 1846-99 – 1r – 1 – us Western Res [240]
CHURCH RECORDS, MS 241 / Cleveland. Ohio. Presbytery. The Women's Foreign Mission Society – 1872-1914 – 1r – 1 – us Western Res [240]
CHURCH RECORDS, MS 384 / Muskingham. Ohio. Presbytery – 1861-87 – 1r – 1 – us Western Res [240]
CHURCH RECORDS, MS 399 / Chillicothe. Ohio. First New Jerusalem Society – 1838-79 – 1r – 1 – us Western Res [240]
CHURCH RECORDS, MS 415 / Cleveland. Ohio. Woodland Ave. Methodist-Episcopal Church – 1874-86 – 1r – 1 – us Western Res [240]
CHURCH RECORDS, MS 418 / Elyria. Ohio. Presbytery – 1864-66 – 1r – 1 – us Western Res [240]
CHURCH RECORDS, MS 421 / Franklin. Ohio. First Congregational Church – 1819-98 – 1r – 1 – us Western Res [240]
CHURCH RECORDS, MS 477 / West Union. Ohio. Mt. Leigh Presbyterian Church – 1838-51 – 1r – 1 – us Western Res [240]
CHURCH RECORDS, MS 482 / Western Reserve. Ohio. Presbytery – 1858-70 – 1r – 1 – us Western Res [240]
CHURCH RECORDS, MS 500 / Grand River. Ohio. Presbytery of Grand River – 1814-18; 1829-70 – 1r – 1 – us Western Res [240]
CHURCH RECORDS, MS 501 / Portage. Ohio. Presbytery – 1818-43 – 1r – 1 – us Western Res [240]
CHURCH RECORDS, MS 542 / Chardon. Ohio. Regular Baptist Church – 1831-1905 – 1r – 1 – us Western Res [240]
CHURCH RECORDS, MS 642 / Jefferson. Ohio. First Baptist Church – 1811-1921 – 1r – 1 – us Western Res [240]
CHURCH RECORDS, MS 646 / Champaign County. Ohio. Nettle Creek Baptist Church – 1822-84 – 1r – 1 – us Western Res [240]
CHURCH RECORDS, MS 647 / Cleveland. Ohio. First Regular Baptist Church – 1820-92; 1901-16 – 1r – 1 – us Western Res [240]
CHURCH RECORDS, MS 654 / Mentor Willoughby. Ohio. Baptist Church. (Ohio Plains Conference) – 1836-48 – 1r – 1 – us Western Res [240]
CHURCH RECORDS, MS 668 / Dover. Ohio. Baptist Church – 1836-56 – 1r – 1 – us Western Res [240]
CHURCH RECORDS, MS 669 / Chester. Ohio. Free Will Baptist Church – 1863-1904 – 1r – 1 – us Western Res [240]
CHURCH RECORDS, MS 670 / Bethel Township. Ohio. Honey Creek Baptist Church – 1811-44 – 1r – 1 – us Western Res [240]
CHURCH RECORDS, MS 788 / Elyria. Ohio. First Baptist Church, Women's Home Mission Society – 1887-1900 – 1r – 1 – us Western Res [240]
CHURCH RECORDS, MS 1204 / Montville. Connecticut. Baptist Church – 1749-79; 1779-1801; 1807-27 – 1r – 1 – us Western Res [240]
CHURCH RECORDS, MS 1303 / Canfield. Ohio. Presbyterian Church of Christ – 1804-60 – 1r – 1 – us Western Res [240]
CHURCH RECORDS, MS 1468 / Parma. Ohio. First Congregational Church – 1835-74 – 1r – 1 – us Western Res [240]
CHURCH RECORDS, MS 1509 / New Hope. Ohio. Second Creek New Hope Baptist Church – 1836-81 – 1r – 1 – us Western Res [240]
CHURCH RECORDS, MS 1512 / Warren County. Ohio. Providence Baptist Church – 1820-46 – 1r – 1 – us Western Res [240]
CHURCH RECORDS, MS 1528 / East Cleveland. Ohio. First Presbyterian Church – 1807-1911 – 1r – 1 – us Western Res [240]
CHURCH RECORDS, MS 1559 / Upper Sandusky. Ohio. First Universalist Church – 1870-1912 – 1r – 1 – us Western Res [240]
CHURCH RECORDS, MS 1585 / Jefferson. Ohio. Bethel Union Baptist Church – 1829-87 – 1r – 1 – us Western Res [240]
CHURCH RECORDS, MS 1797 / Bradford. New Hampshire. Christian Church – 1829-45 – 1r – 1 – us Western Res [240]
CHURCH RECORDS, MS 2041 / Bellevue,. Ohio. Methodist Episcopal Church – 1852-86 – 1r – 1 – us Western Res [240]
CHURCH RECORDS, MS 2087 / Garrettsville. Ohio. Baptist Church – 1808-60 – 1r – 1 – us Western Res [240]
CHURCH RECORDS, MS 2125 / Farmington. Ohio. United Presbyterian and Congregational Church – 1817-66 – 1r – 1 – us Western Res [240]
CHURCH RECORDS, MS 2335 / Cleveland. Ohio. Third Baptist Church – 1852-67; 1880-1900 – 1r – 1 – us Western Res [240]
CHURCH RECORDS, MS 2822 / Canton. Ohio. (Elkton Circuit). Methodist-Episcopal Church – 1864-1940 – 1r – 1 – us Western Res [240]
CHURCH RECORDS, MS 2843 / Garrettsville. Ohio. Church of Christ – 1889-1902 – 1r – 1 – us Western Res [240]
CHURCH RECORDS, MS 3066 / Cleveland. Ohio. St. John's Episcopal Church – 1835-71 – 1r – 1 – us Western Res [240]
CHURCH RECORDS, MS 3168 / Brecksville. Ohio. Brecksville Congregational Church – 1816-1947 – 1r – 1 – us Western Res [240]
CHURCH RECORDS, MS 3190 / Streetsboro. Ohio. Congregational Church – 1833-81 – 1r – 1 – us Western Res [240]
CHURCH RECORDS, MS 3324 / Cleveland. Ohio. Bethany Presbyterian Church – 1889-1917 – 1r – 1 – us Western Res [240]
CHURCH RECREATION – 1960-61 – 1 – 9.45 – us Baptist [240]
CHURCH REFORM IN SPAIN AND PORTUGAL : A SHORT HISTORY OF THE REFORMED EPISCOPAL CHURCHES OF SPAIN AND PORTUGAL, FROM 1868 TO THE PRESENT TIME / Noeyes, H E – London: Cassell, 1897 – 1mf – us A.T.L.A. [240]
CHURCH REGISTER / Ogallah. Kansas. Swedish Evangelical Lutheran Church – 1900-45 – 1 – us KS Hist [978]
CHURCH REGISTER / St. Mark's Episcopal Church, Medicine Lodge, KS – 1890-1981, The canonical church register (ledger) (1890-1981), 1904-1981 – 1 – us KS Hist [240]
THE CHURCH REVIEW – Lunenburg, N.S.: G. Haslam, [1891?-1893?] – 9 – cn C.I.H.M. [240]
THE CHURCH REVIEW – v1-30. 1940-72 (complete) – 1r – 1 – ATLA S0677 – us A.T.L.A. [073]
THE CHURCH REVIVAL : THOUGHTS THEREON AND REMINISCENCES / Baring-Gould, Sabine – London: Methuen, 1914 – 2mf – us A.T.L.A. [240]
THE CHURCH SERVICE: A SERIES OF SERMONS IN ST GEORGE'S CHURCH, MONTREAL / Carmichael, James – Montreal: Gazette, 1872. 00496. (Pre-1900 Canadiana) – 9 – cn C.I.H.M. [240]
CHURCH SERVICES AND SERVICE-BOOKS BEFORE THE REFORMATION / Swete, Henry Barclay – London: S.P.C.K.; New York: E. & J.B. Young, 1896 – 1mf – us A.T.L.A. [240]
CHURCH SLAVONIC AND RUSSIAN HAGIOGRAPHIES / ed by Danilenko, Boris – 57 titles – 9 – ne IDC [220]
CHURCH SOCIAL UNION *see* CHRISTIAN SOCIAL UNION
THE CHURCH STANDARD – Toronto: [s.n., 1868?-18–] – 9 – cn C.I.H.M. [240]
CHURCH, STATE AND POLITICS IN SIXTEENTH AND SEVENTEENTH CENTURY ENGLAND – (Part 1: 1648-99. Part 2: 1570-1647. Part 3: 1600-1700. Part 4: 1550-1700) – Selected volumes from the Tanner Manuscripts in the Bodleian Library, Oxford – 1 – us Primary [321]
CHURCH STRUGGLE *see* DER KIRCHENKAMPF
CHURCH & SYNAGOGUE LIBRARIES – (1985-. 5,6,9) – v1-. 1968- – 1 – us UMI [020]
Church T *see* SOME FARTHER REMARKS ON THE REV. MR. JOHN WESLEY'S LAST JOURNAL, TOGETHER WITH A FEW CONSIDERATIONS ON HIS 'FARTHER APPEAL',...
Church, T *see*
– REMARKS ON THE REVEREND MR. JOHN WESLEY'S LAST JOURNAL, WHEREIN HE GIVES AN ACCOUNT OF THE TENETS AND PROCEEDINGS OF THE MORAVIANS,...
– A SERIOUS AND EXPOSTULATORY LETTER TO THE REV. MR. GEORGE WHITEFIELD ON OCCASION OF HIS LATE LETTER TO THE BISHOP OF LONDON AND OTHER BISHOPS,...
THE CHURCH THAT FOUND HERSELF : THE STORY OF OUR CENTENARY COMMEMORATION, 1907-1911 / Thompson, J D – London, 1912. 96p – 2mf – 9 – ne IDC [240]
THE CHURCH, THE PEOPLE, AND THE AGE / Scott, Robert & Gilmore, George William – New York: Runk & Wagnalls, 1914 – 2mf – us A.T.L.A. [240]
THE CHURCH, THE STATE, AND THE POOR : A SERIES OF HISTORICAL SKETCHES / Chadwick, William Edward – London: R. Scott, 1914 – 1mf – us A.T.L.A. [303]
CHURCH TIMES – (Lacking some issues. Some original pgs damaged) – v1-157. 1863-1974 – 112r – 1 – ATLA S0072 – us A.T.L.A. [073]
CHURCH TIMES – London. -w. 1863-92. (21 reels) – 1 – uk British Libr Newspaper [072]
CHURCH TIMES : A WEEKLY JOURNAL OF RELIGIOUS NEWS – New York, Utica, NY. v1-6. 1940-46 (complete) – 2r – 1 – ATLA P0003 – us A.T.L.A. [073]
THE CHURCH TIMES – Halifax, N.S.: W. Gossip, [1848-1858] – 9 – cn C.I.H.M. [240]
THE CHURCH UNDER QUEEN ELIZABETH : AN HISTORICAL SKETCH / Lee, Frederick George – London: W.H. Allen, 1892 – 1mf – us A.T.L.A. [240]
THE CHURCH UNIVERSAL : A SERIES OF DISCOURSES ON THE TRUE COMPREHENSION OF THE CHURCH, AS EXHIBITED MAINLY IN THE HOLY SCRIPTURES AND SUBORDINATELY IN THE STANDARDS OF THE PROTESTANT EPISCOPAL CHURCH / Stone, John S – New York: Houel & Macoy, Printers, 1846 – 1mf – us A.T.L.A. [240]
Church, W S *see* CHURCH'S DIGEST OF CASES IN VOLS 25-48 OF THE AMERICAN STATE REPORTS
CHURCH WATCHMAN – Springfield/Ashtabula, OH. Ohio Free Communion Baptist Association (Free Will Baptist General Conference). 1892-93, 1895, 1897-98. Incomplete – 1 – 15.50 – us A.B.H.S. [073]
CHURCH WORK – Dorchester, N.B.: J.D.H. Browne, [1876?-19–?] – 9 – cn C.I.H.M. [240]
THE CHURCH YEAR: A SERIES OF SERMONS FOR THE SACRED SEASONS / Carmichael, James – Montreal: W. Foster Brown, 1893. 00498. (Pre-1900 Canadiana) – 9 – cn C.I.H.M. [240]
THE CHURCH YEAR AND KALENDAR / Dowden, John – Cambridge: University Press; New York: Putnam [distributor], 1910. (The Cambridge handbooks of liturgical study) – 1mf – us A.T.L.A. [240]
THE CHURCHES AND EDUCATED MEN : A STUDY OF THE RELATION OF THE CHURCH TO MAKERS AND LEADERS OF PUBLIC OPINION / Hardy, Edwin Noah – Boston: Pilgrim Press, c1904 – 1mf – us A.T.L.A. [240]
THE CHURCHES AND MONASTERIES OF EGYPT AND SOME NEIGHBOURING COUNTRIES, ATTRIBUTED TO ABU SALIH, THE ARMENIAN / ed by Evetts, B T A & Butler, A J – Anecdota Oxoniensia, Semitic Series: Oxford. v1-P7. 1895 – Dfl63.00 – ne Slangenburg [720]
THE CHURCHES AND SECTS OF THE UNITED STATES : CONTAINING A BRIEF ACCOUNT OF THE ORIGIN, HISTORY, DOCTRINES, CHURCH GOVERNMENT, MODE OF WORSHIP, USAGES, AND STATISTICS OF EACH RELIGIOUS DENOMINATION, SO FAR AS KNOWN / Gorrie, P Douglass – New York: L. Colby, 1850 – 1mf – us A.T.L.A. [200]

THE CHURCHES AND THE WAGE EARNERS : A STUDY OF THE CAUSE AND CURE OF THEIR SEPARATION / Thompson, C Bertrand – New York: Scribner, 1909 – 1mf – us A.T.L.A. [240]
CHURCHES AT BOSRA AND SAMARIA-SEBASTE / Crowfoot, J W – BSA, 1937 – 9 – $10.00 – us I.R.C. [240]
CHURCHES AT JERASH / Crowfoot, J W – BSA, 1931 – 9 – $10.00 – us I.R.C. [240]
THE CHURCHES IN BRITAIN BEFORE A.D. 1000 / Plummer, Alfred – London: R. Scott, 1911-1912 – 2mf – us A.T.L.A. [240]
CHURCHES IN THE MODERN STATE / Figgis, John Neville – London; New York: Longmans, Green, 1914 – 1mf – us A.T.L.A. [200]
CHURCHES OF CHRIST : A HISTORICAL, BIOGRAPHICAL, AND PICTORIAL HISTORY OF CHURCHES OF CHRIST IN THE UNITED STATES, AUSTRALASIA, ENGLAND AND CANADA / ed by Brown, John T – Louisville, Ky.: J.P. Morton, 1904 – 2mf – us A.T.L.A. [240]
CHURCHES OF CHRISTENDOM: LECTURES, CRITICAL AND HISTORICAL / Bray, Alfred James – Montreal: Milton League, 1877. 00252. (Pre-1900 Canadiana) – 9 – cn C.I.H.M. [240]
THE CHURCHES OUTSIDE THE CHURCH / Coleman, George W – Philadelphia: Published for the Social Service Commission of the Northern Baptist Convention [by] American Baptist Publ. Society, 1910 – 1mf – us A.T.L.A. [240]
THE CHURCHES SEPARATED FROM ROME / Duchesne, Louis – London: Kegan Paul, Trench, Truebner, 1907. (The International Catholic library; v9) – 1mf – us A.T.L.A. [240]
THE CHURCH-IDEA : AN ESSAY TOWARDS UNITY / Huntington, William Reed – New York: E.P. Dutton, 1870 – 1mf – us A.T.L.A. [240]
CHURCHILL COUNTY COURIER – Fallon. Nev. 1961- – 1 – us UMI [071]
CHURCHILL COUNTY COURIER – Fallon, NV. 1961-62 – 1r – 1 – $50.00 – U04522 – us Library Micro [071]
CHURCHILL COUNTY EAGLE – (Also known as: Fallon Eagle) – Fallon, NV. 1906-49 (incomplete) – 17r – 1 – $850.00 – U04523 – us Library Micro [071]
CHURCHILL COUNTY STANDARD *see* CHURCHILL STANDARD
CHURCHILL DRIVE BAPTIST CHURCH. SHELBY, NORTH CAROLINA : CHURCH RECORDS – 1950-63 – 1 – 8.37 – us Baptist [240]
Churchill, J *see* A COLLECTION OF VOYAGES AND TRAVELS..
Churchill, John Awsham *see* A COLLECTION OF VOYAGES AND TRAVELS..
CHURCHILL NEWS – White Plains, NV. 1888 – 1r – 1 – $50.00 – U04810 – us Library Micro [071]
CHURCHILL STANDARD – (Also known as: Churchill County Standard) – Fallon, NV. 1904-50 – 18r – 1 – $900.00 – U04524 – us Library Micro [071]
Churchill, Winston S *see*
- THE PEOPLES' RIGHTS
- SCRAPBOOKS OF WINSTON CHURCHILL
- THE SCRAPBOOKS OF WINSTON CHURCHILL, AMERICAN NOVELIST AND POLITICIAN

THE CHURCH-KINGDOM : LECTURES ON CONGREGATIONALISM / Ross, A Hastings – Boston: Congregational Sunday-school and Publ. Society, c1887 – 1mf – us A.T.L.A. [240]
CHURCHMAN – London, England. v62-64. 1948-50 (complete) – Inquire – 1 – ATLA 1993-S507 – us A.T.L.A. [073]
Churchman *see* FAILURE OF THE CHURCHES
THE CHURCHMAN – New York. Jan 1893-Dec 1909; Jul 1910-Jun 1911; Jul-Dec 1914.-w. 37 reels – 1 – uk British Libr Newspaper [073]
THE CHURCHMAN – St Petersburg, FL. v1-180. 1831-1966 (complete) – 146r – 1 – ATLA S0129 – us A.T.L.A. [073]
Churchman, Philip H *see* BYRON AND ESPRONCEDA
THE CHURCHMAN'S FRIEND – Windsor, C.W. [Ont.: s.n., 1855-1857?] – 9 – cn C.I.H.M. [240]
THE CHURCHMAN'S MAGAZINE AND MONTHLY REVIEW – Hamilton, Ont: T and R White, 1869-[1871?] – 9 – cn C.I.H.M. [240]
THE CHURCHMAN'S REASONS FOR HIS FAITH AND PRACTICE / Richardson, Nathaniel Smith – (Includes bibliographical references) – 2nd ed. New York: Pott & Amery, 1863 – 1mf – 9 – 0-8370-8612-4 – 1986-2612 – us A.T.L.A. [240]
CHURCHMANSHIP AND CHARACTER : THREE YEARS' TEACHING IN BIRMINGHAM CATHEDRAL / Carnegie, William Hartley – (Includes index) – New York: E P Dutton, 1909 – 1mf – 9 – 0-8370-3189-3 – 1985-1189 – us A.T.L.A. [240]
THE CHURCHMANSHIP OF JOHN WESLEY AND THE RELATIONS OF WESLEYAN METHODISM TO THE CHURCH OF ENGLAND / Rigg, James H – London: Wesleyan-Methodist Book-Room, [1886?] – 1mf – us A.T.L.A. [240]
THE CHURCHMEMBER'S GUIDE AND COMPLETE CHURCH MANUAL / Essig, Montgomery F – Nashville, Tenn.: Southwestern Co., c1907 – 1mf – us A.T.L.A. [240]
CHURCH-MEMBERS' HANDBOOK OF THEOLOGY / Robertson, Norvell – 1874. 328p – 1 – 11.48 – us Baptist [240]
THE CHURCH'S BEST STATE, OR, CONSTANT REVIVALS OF RELIGION / Harkey, Simeon W – Baltimore: Publication Rooms, 1843 – 1mf – us A.T.L.A. [240]
THE CHURCH'S CERTAIN FAITH GRAY / Gray, George Zabriskie – Boston: Houghton, Mifflin; Cambridge: Riverside Press, 1890 – 1mf – 9 – 0-8370-4805-2 – 1985-2805 – us A.T.L.A. [240]
THE CHURCH'S CREED, OR THE CROWN'S CREED? : A LETTER TO THE MOST REV. ARCHBISHOP MANNING, ETC / ed by Foulkes, Edmund Salisbury – (Includes bibliographical references) – New York: Pott & Amery, 1869 – 1mf – 9 – 0-8370-8422-9 – 1986-2422 – us A.T.L.A. [240]
CHURCH'S DIGEST OF CASES IN VOLS 25-48 OF THE AMERICAN STATE REPORTS / Church, W S – San Francisco: Bancroft-Whitney, 1896 (all publ) – 14mf – 9 – $21.00 – LLMC 78-038H – us L.L.M.C. [340]
CHURCH'S MUSICAL VISITOR – Cincinnati. v1-26. 1871-97 – 1r – 1 – £60.00 – uk Chadwyck [780]
CHURCH'S MUSICAL VISITOR – v1-26. Oct 1871-1897 – 1 – 310.00 – us Opus [073]
CHURCH'S MUSICAL VISITOR, 1878-1883 – With which is incorporated Root's Song Messenger. 1862 – 1 – 45.50 – us Baptist [240]
THE CHURCH'S ONE FOUNDATION : CHRIST AND RECENT CRITICISM / Nicoll, William Robertson – (Includes bibliographical references) – New York: A.C. Armstrong, 1902 – 1mf – 9 – 0-8370-6234-9 – 1986-0234 – us A.T.L.A. [240]
CHURCH'S QUARREL EXPOUSED – 1715. and A vindication of the government of the New England churches. 1717 – 1 – 5.00 – us Baptist [240]
THE CHURCH'S TASK UNDER THE ROMAN EMPIRE : FOUR LECTURES, WITH PREFACE, NOTES, AND AN EXCURSUS / Bigg, Charles – Oxford: Clarendon Press, 1905 – 1mf – us A.T.L.A. [240]
THE CHURCH'S WORK IN OUR LARGE TOWNS / Huntington, George – Oxford: J. Parker, 1871 – 1mf – us A.T.L.A. [240]
CHURCHWARDENS' ACCOUNTS : FROM THE FOURTEENTH CENTURY TO THE CLOSE OF THE SEVENTEENTH CENTURY / Cox, John Charles – London: Methuen, 1913. (The Antiquary's books) – 1mf – us A.T.L.A. [240]
CHURCHWARDENS' ACCOUNTS OF ST. MARY THE GREAT / ed by Foster, J E – 1504-1635 – 1r – 1 – us Ross [240]
Churman, Philip H *see* BLANCA DE BORBON
Churton, Edward *see* MEMOIR OF JOSHUA WATSON
O CHUTE – Rio Branco, Acre. 14 Maio-4 Jun 1973 – 1,5,6 – bl Biblioteca [072]
LA CHUTE DE L'EMPIRE DE RABAH / Gentil, Emile – Paris: Hatchette, 1902 – 1 – us Res Libr [960]
LES CHUTES DE SHAWINIGAN – Shawinigan, Canada. v1 n43. 26 oct 1938-24 dec 1968 – 8r – 1 – Can$55.00r – cn Can Microfilming [072]
CHUTE'S WESTERN HERALD – (The Western Herald). Tralee. Ireland. -w. 27 Aug 1812, 2 Jan 1828-4 May 1835. (7 reels) – 1 – uk British Libr Newspaper [072]
CHUTZPAH – Chicago, IL. 1972-79 – 1 – us A.J.P.C. [071]
CHUUK – TRUK DISTRICT CHARTER, 1977 : AS APPROVED BY THE SEVENTH CONGRESS OF MICRONESIA / Federated States of Micronesia – 1st spec sess. Saipan: the Congress, 29 Aug 1977 – 2mf – 9 – $3.00 – LLMC 82-100H Title 2 – us L.L.M.C. [324]
CHUUNICHI SHIMBUN – September 1942-December 1994 – 798r – 1 – Y7,210,400 – ja Japan Micro [950]
Chuvinskii, P P *see* TRUDY ETNOGRAFICHESKO-STATISTICHESKOI EKSPEDITSII V ZAPODNO-RUSSKII KRAI, SNARIAZHENNOI IMP. RUSSKIM GEOGRAFICHESKIM OBSHCHESTVOM. LUGO-ZAPADNYI OTDEL
Chuzhak, N K *see* DIALEKTIKE ISKUSSTVA
CHUZHIMI PUTIAMI : SBORNIK STATE / Chernov, Viktor Mikhailovich & Gardenin, U – Geneve: "Zhizn", 1916 – 1 – CSUX89-B7307 – us Hoover Inst Photo [947]
CHUZHOE NEBO / Gumilev, Nikolai Sepanovich – Tret'ia kniga stikhov. S predisloviem G. Ivanova. Berlin. 1936. BR-1136 2 – 8 – ne IDC [460]
CHUZHOE NEBO / Gumilev, Nikolai Sepanovich – Tret'ia kniga stikhov. Spb. 1912. BR-1135 2 – 8 – ne IDC [460]
Chwalewik, E *see* ZBIORY POLSKIE, ARCHIWA, BIBLIOTEKI, GABINETY, GALERJE, MUZEA I INNE ZBIORY PAMIATEK PRZESZLOSCI W OJCZYZNIE I NA OBCZYZNIE
CHWARELWR CYMREIG *see* Y CHWARELWR CYMREIG
CHWILA : MORNING EDITION – (In Polish) – Lwow, PL. no6348 21 Nov 1936-no7302 23 Jul 1939 – 1r – 1 – $35.00 – cn Can Microfilming [072]
CHWILA : PM EDITION – (In Polish) – Lwow, PL. no677 10 Nov 1936-no1100 24 Jul 1939 – 1r – 1 – $35.00 – cn Can Microfilming [072]
Chwolson, D A *see* SYRISCH-NESTORIANISCHE GRABINSCHRIFTEN AUS SEMIRJETSCHIE
CHYMICUS RATIONALIS: OR, THE FUNDAMENTAL GROUNDS OF THE CHYMICAL ART RATIONALLY STATED AND DEMONSTRATED / Y-Worth, William – London, 1692 – 1 – us U.W. Library [540]
CHYMIE HUDRAULIQUE, POUR EXTRAIRE LES SELS ESSENTIELS DES VEGETAUX ET DES MINERAUX, PAR LE MOYEN DE L'EAU PURE / La Garaye, Claude Toussaint Marot – Nouvelle edition, revue corrigee et augmentee de notes par M. Parmentier. Paris, 1775 – 1 – us U.W. Library [540]
CHYMISCHE UNTERSUCHUNGEN WELCH FURNEHMLICH VON.. / Pott, Johann Heinrich – Berlin, 1757 – 1 – us U.W. Library [540]
CHYMISCHER SCHRIFTEN. ERSTER -ZWEYTER THEIL. NEUE VERBESSERTE AUFLAGE / Marggraf, Andreas Siegismund – Berlin, 1768 – 1 – us U.W. Library [540]
DER CHYMSICHE WARSAGER, ODER EINE IN ZWANZIG WOCHEN-BLAETTERN HERAUSGEGEBENE UNTERWEISUNG.. – Hamburg, 1748 – 1 – us U.W. Library [540]
CHYN-NU I GUNNY / Inostrantsev, K – Zhivaia starina X. 1900. BU-633 2 – 8 – ne IDC [950]
Chytraeus, D *see*
- CATECHESIS DAVIDIS CHYTRAEI POSTREMO RECOGNITA
- COMMENTARIVS IN MATTHAEVM EVANGELISTAM,...
- EXPLICATIO MALACHIAE PROPHETAE,...
- HISTORIA AVGVSTANAE CONFESSIONIS,...
- IN DEVTERONOMIVM MOSIS ENARRATIO...
- IN EXODVM ENARRATIO,...
- IN GENESIN ENARRATIO,...
- IN HISTORIAM IUDICUM POPULI ISRAEL... COMMENTARIUS
- IN LEVITICVM,...COMPLECTEN...
- IN NVMEROS...ENARRATIO
- IN PSALMVM 118TH...PRAELECTIONES,...
- ORATIO DE STATV ECCLESIARVM HOC TEMPORE IN GRAECIA, ASIA, BOHEMIA, ...
- TERTIUS LIBER MOYSIS, QVI INSCRIBITVR LEVITICVS. ADDITA ENARRATIONE

CIA RESEARCH REPORTS / U.S. Central Intelligence Agency – (See indiv. titles: Africa; China; Europe; Japan, Korea, and the Security of Asia; Latin America; The Middle East; The Soviet Union; Vietnam and Southeast Asia) – $4,085.00 set – us UPA [324]
Ciacono, A *see* HISTORIA UTRIUSQUE BELLI DACICI A TRAIANO CAESARE GESTI...QUAE IN COLUMNA EIUSDEM ROMAE VISUNTUR
Ciadoncha, Marques de *see*
- ALONSO FERNANDEZ DE BARRANTES. SU TESTAMENTO (1390) APUNTES GENEALOGICOS DE SU CASA
- MARINOS EXTREMNOS

Ciakciak, E *see* DIZIONARIO ARMENO-ITALIANO
Ciamarra, Guglielmo *see* LA GIUSTIZIA NELLA SOMALIA, GUGLIELMO CIAMARRA. RACCOLTA DI GIURISPRUDENZA COLONIALE.
Ciano, Galeazzo, Count *see* PAPERS...(LISBON PAPERS) RECEIVED FROM THE DEPT. OF STATE (U.S.A.)
CIAS / Buenos Aires. Centro de Investigacion y Accion Social – Buenos Aires: El Centro. v10 n105 july 1961. v11 n113, 119 may, nov 1962. v12 n128 oct 1963. v13 n136, n138 aug, oct 1964. v18 n181/182 apr/may 1969 – us Res Libr [350]
CIAU ATHLETES' USE AND INTENTIONS TO USE PERFORMANCE ENHANCING DRUGS : A STUDY UTILIZING THE THEORY OF PLANNED BEHAVIOUR / Allemeier, Meredith Frances – University of British Columbia, 1996 – 3mf – 9 – $12.00 – PSY 1878 – us Microform Publ [150]
Cibat, A *see*
- ELEMENTOS DE MATEMATICAS O...INTRODUCCION A LA FISICA EXPERIMENTAL
- MEMORIA SOBRE LA CALENTURA AMARILLA...QUE INVADIO A CADIZ Y SEVILLA
- MEMORIA SOBRE LA NATURALEZA DEL CONTAGIO DE LA FIEBRE AMARILLA...
- MEMORIAS FISICAS SOBRE EL INFLUJO DELGES INDIOGENO EN LA ANESTITUCION DEL NOMBRE SOBRE EL OPIGENO... DEL AIRE ATMOSFERICO
- POR QUE MOTIVOS O CAUSAS LAS TERCIANAS SE HAN HECHO TAN COMUNES Y GRAVES...

Cibot, P M *see*
- ARMOISE
- NOTICE DU CONG-FOU DES BONZES TAO-SEE

Cicero, Marcus Tullius *see*
- DE AMICITIA, ETC
- DE INVENTIONE RHETORICA
- EPISTOLA AD QUINTUM FRATREM, ETC
- MARCUS TULLIUS CICERO
- PRINCIPIA LATINE LOQUENDI
- RECUEIL D'OEUVRES RELIEES ET MICROFILMEES ENSEMBLE, ENRICHIES DE NOMBREUSES NOTES MANUSCRITES
- RHETORICA AD HERENNIUM, ETC

CICERON ORATEUR: ANALYSE ET CRITIQUE DES DISCOURS DE CICERON / Cucheval, Victor – Paris: E. Belin, 1901. 2v. Bibliog. references – 1 – us U.W. Library [450]
DER CICERONE : HALBMONATSSCHRIFT FUER DIE INTERESSEN DES KUNSTFORSCHERS UND SAMMLERS – Leipzig, 1909-1930. v1-22 – 305mf – O-498/1 – ne IDC [700]
EL CICERONE / Pascual Ayago, Julian – Guia Kilometrica de la provincia de Badajoz, Ano 1946. Badajoz, Graficas Iberia – 1 – sp Bibl Santa Ana [946]
EL CICERONE / Pascual, Julian – Puerta de Palma: Guia-Callejero de Badajoz. Badajoz, Imp. Clasica – 1 – sp Bibl Santa Ana [946]
EL CICERONE DEL PUEBLO / Gutierrez Macias, Valeriano – Badajoz: Dip. Provincial, 1969. Sep. REE – 1 – sp Bibl Santa Ana [946]
CICERONIS AMOR: TULLIES LOVE / Greene, Robert – 1589. A quip for an upstart courtier. 1592 – 9 – 10.00 – us Scholars' Facs [840]
CICLO : COLOQUIOS EMPRESARIALES / Delegacion Provincial de Sindicatos – Caceres: Imp. T. Rodriguez, 1972 – 1 – sp Bibl Santa Ana [946]
EL CICLO DEL CERDO EN ESPANA. INVESTIGACIONES SOBRE LAS FLUCTUACIONES DE LA PRODUCCION Y DE LOS PRECIOS DESDE 1939 A 1956 POR...Y..., BAJO LA DIRECCION DE GASPAR GONZALEZ / Wienberg, Dieter & Sobrino, Francisco – Madrid: Consejo S.I.C. y Diput. Prov. de Badajoz, 1958 – 1 – sp Bibl Santa Ana [946]
EL CICLON – Badajoz, 1921. 1 numero – 5 – sp Bibl Santa Ana [073]
Cicognani, H J *see* LA CARIDAD EN LOS PRIMEROS SIGLOS DEL CRISTIANISMO
Cicognara, L *see* STORIA DELLA SCULTURA

CICSB NEWSLETTER / Coalition of Indian-Controlled School Boards – 1973-76. (American Indian Periodicals in the Princeton University Library) – 5mf – 9 – $45.00 – us UPA [370]

DER CID : NACH SPANISCHEN ROMANZEN BESUNGEN DURCH JOHANN GOTTFRIED VON HERDER: MIT EINER EINLEITUNG UEBER HERDER UND SEINE BEDEUTUNG FUER DIE DEUTSCHE LITERATUR – Leipzig: F A Brockhaus, 1868 – 1 – us U.W. Library [830]

Cid Lopez, Rosa Maria *see* EL CULTO AL EMPERADOR EN NUMIDIA. DE AUGUSTO A DIOCLECIANO

A CIDADE – (Cont of: A Cidade de Vicosa) – Vicosa, 15 Oct-Dec 1961; Jan, Mar-Nov 1962; Jan-Apr 1963; Aug, Nov 1964; May, Jul-Aug, Nov 1967; Mar-21 Jul 1968 – 1,5,6 – bl Biblioteca [072]

A CIDADE – Ouro Preto, 15 Oct 1901-Dec 1902; 20 Oct 1904 – 1,5,6 – bl Biblioteca [072]

CIDADE – Maceio, Alagoas. 20 Abr 1898; Out 1899; Jan-15 Fev 1900 – 1,5,6 – bl Biblioteca [072]

CIDADE DA EMPREZA : ORGAM OFFICIAL DA PREFEITURA DO ALTO ACRE – Empreza, Acre. 15 Jul-22 Out 1910 – 1,5,6 – bl Biblioteca [072]

CIDADE DA FEIRA – Feira de Sant' Anna, BA. 18 Nov 1888 – 1,5,6 – bl Biblioteca [072]

CIDADE DE BARBACENA : ORGAM DOS INTERESSES DO MUNICIPIO E DO POVO – Barbacena, 23 Jan 1898-Dec 1906; 6 Mar 1949 – 1,5,6 – bl Biblioteca [072]

CIDADE DE COARI : ORGAO DE PROPAGANDA DO MUNICIPIO – Coari, Amazonas. 26 Fev. 1941 – 1,5,6 – bl Biblioteca [072]

CIDADE DE ITABIRA : ORGAO DOS INTERESSES DO MUNICIPIO E SEUS LIMITROPHES – Itabira de Matto Dentro, 28 Jun 1896; 2 Jul 1897 – 1,5,6 – bl Biblioteca [072]

CIDADE DE LABREA – Labrea, Amazonas. 25 Maio-Jun, Set-20 Dez 1917 – 1,5,6 – bl Biblioteca [072]

CIDADE DE LAVRAS – (Cont of: O Caracter) – Lavras, 24 Nov-Dec 1895; Jan-Jun, Aug-Sept, Nov-Dec 1896; 17 Jan 1897 – 1,5,6 – bl Biblioteca [072]

CIDADE DE LAVRAS *see* O CARACTER

CIDADE DE MACEIO : JORNAL CRITICO E HUMORISTICO – Maceio, Alagoas. 19 Ago 1888 – 1,5,6 – bl Biblioteca [072]

CIDADE DE MANACAPURU : ORGAM INDEPENDENTE – Manacapuru, Amazonas. 17 Set 1933 – 1,5,6 – bl Biblioteca [072]

A CIDADE DE PALMA : HEBOMADARIO ALHEIO A POLITICA – Cidade de Palma, 4 Jul 1897 – 1,5,6 – bl Biblioteca [072]

CIDADE DE PATOS – Patos de Minas, Brazil. Nov 1917 – 1 – bl Biblioteca [072]

CIDADE DE POUSO ALEGRE – Pouso Alegre, 30 Apr 1906 – 1,5,6 – bl Biblioteca [072]

CIDADE DE PRADOS – Prados, 13 Apr 1902 – 1,5,6 – bl Biblioteca [072]

CIDADE DE S. MIGUEL – S. Miguel, Alagoas. 23 Mar, 4 Maio 1890 – 1,5,6 – bl Biblioteca [072]

A CIDADE DE SANTOS – Santos, Brazil. 1898-99 – 1 – bl Biblioteca [072]

CIDADE DE UBA : ORGAO DEDICADO AOS INTERESSES DO MUNICIPIO DE UBA – Cidade de Uba, 27 Dec 1953; 6 May 1973 – 1,5,6 – bl Biblioteca [072]

CIDADE DE UBERABA – Uberaba, 8, 29 Sep 1895 – 1,5,6 – bl Biblioteca [072]

A CIDADE DE VICOSA – (Cont as: A Cidade) – Vicosa, 12 Jul 1897; Jul-Dec 1933; Jun-Dec 1935; Apr-May, Aug, Sep, Nov 1936; 30 Sep 1961 – 1,5,6 – bl Biblioteca [072]

A CIDADE DE VICOSA *see* A CIDADE

CIDADE DO BOMFIM : ORGAM DOS INTERESSES DO POVO – Bomfim, 4 Dec 1898; Feb-Mar 1899; Jul 1908; May-Dec 1935; Jan, 17-31 May 1936 – 1,5,6 – bl Biblioteca [072]

A CIDADE DO PARA : FOLHA POPULAR – Cidade do Para, 20-27 May, Aug-Sept, Nov-Dec 1894; Jan-May, Jul-8 Sept 1895 – 1,5,6 – bl Biblioteca [072]

CIDADE DO PATROCINIO : ORGAO DEDICADO AOS INTERESSES DO POVO – Patrocinio, 13 May, Jul, Sep, Nov-Dec 1911; Jul, Oct, Dec 1912; Jan, May-Dec 193; Jan-Sep 1914; Sep, Dec 1915; Sep, Dec 1916; Jul 1917; Jan, May-Jun, Oct 1918; Apr, Jun 1929; 3 Apr 1932 – 1,5,6 – bl Biblioteca [072]

CIDADE DO PILAR – Pilar, Alagoas. 1 Maio-13 Jun 1889 – 1,5,6 – bl Biblioteca [072]

CIDADE DO PRATA – Cidade do Prata, 4 Jun-Jul, Nov 1911; Jul 1913; Dec 1915; Mar 1916; Aug-Sep 1917; Nov 1919 – 1,5,6 – bl Biblioteca [072]

CIDADE DO PYRANGA – Piranga, Brazil. Jul 1918; Jul 1923; Jul 1932 – 1 – bl Biblioteca [072]

CIDADE DO SACRAMENTO : ORGAO BI-SEMANARIO DOS INTERESSES MUNICIPAES – Sacramento, 21 Feb 1903 – 1,5,6 – bl Biblioteca [072]

CIDADE DO SALVADOR – Salvador, BA. 1 Jul 1897-25 Maio 1899 – 1,5,6 – bl Biblioteca [072]

Cidoncha, Marques de *see* DONA MENCIA DE LOS NIDOS

CIE COMPULSORY EDUCATION – Topical bibliography. 3p – 9 – 1.00f – at Libertarian Micro [370]

CIE REPORT – March 1971, no.1. 3p – 9 – 1.00f – at Libertarian Micro [335]

CIEL – Zilina, Czechoslovakia. Nov 1955-Mar 1960 – 2r – 1 – us L of C Photodup [072]

LE CIEL BLEU – Brussels, 1945 – 1r – 1 – £60.00 – uk Chadwyck [750]

LE CIEL, SEJOUR DES ELUS / Ghyvelde, Frederic de – Montreal, 1912. SEM105P536 – 5mf – 9 – Can$13.50 – cn Bibl Nat [240]

CIEN LETRILLAS / Sanchez Arjona, Vicente – Sevilla: Graficas Sevillanas, 1951 – 1 – sp Bibl Santa Ana [810]

LAS CIEN MEJORES POESIAS (LIRICAS) DE LA LENGUA CASTELLANA / Menendez y Pelayo, Marcelino; ed by Artigas, Miguel – Madrid, rev ed 1932 – 1 – sp Bibl Santa Ana [810]

CIEN RAZONES (AUNQUE SEA TARDE) / Galan, Leocadio – Caceres: Tip. El Noticiero, 1977 – 1 – sp Bibl Santa Ana [946]

LA CIENAGA / Reyes Huertas, Antonio – Madrid: Edic. Hispano-Americanas, s.a. – 1 – sp Bibl Santa Ana [946]

LA CIENAGA / Reyes Huertas, Antonio – Madrid: Ediciones Hispano Americanas, 1921 – 1 – sp Bibl Santa Ana [946]

LA CIENCIA DE LAS MUGERES / Sanchez Arjona y Sanchez Arjona, Jose – 1874 – 9 – 1.50f – sp Bibl Santa Ana [810]

LA CIENCIA, LA NATURALEZA Y EL MILAGRO / Caba, Pedro – Madrid: Diana, Artes Graficas, 1965. Sep. Rev. Filosofia, vol XXIV, no 92-93, Enero-Junio 1965 – sp Bibl Santa Ana [240]

CIENCIA PARA TODOS – (Suppl to: A Manha) – Rio de Janeiro, 28 Mar 1948-31 Dec 1950. – 1,5,6 – bl Biblioteca [072]

CIENCIA POLITICA – 1-9, 1941-44. Incomplete – 1 – 23.00 – us L of C Photodup [320]

CIENCIA Y FE / San Miguel FCP. Facultades de Filosofia y Teologia – Buenos Aires ; Montivideo: Editorial Verbum. v1-20. 1944-1964 – 7r – us Res Libr [972]

Cienfuegos Linares, Julio *see* PREGON DE LA FIESTAS PATRONALES DE L'ERENA, 11 DE AGOS TO DE 1968

CIENTO CINCUENTA ANOS DE PERIODISMO EN CACERES Y SALAMANCA / Colegio Universitario de Caceres – Caceres: Imprenta Diputacion Provincial, 1973 – sp Bibl Santa Ana [946]

Cieza de Leon, Pedro de *see*
- LA CHRONICA DEL PERU. NUEVAMENTE ESCRITA POR
- LA CRONICA DEL PERU
- GUERRAS CIVILES DEL PERU

Cieza Leon, Pedro de *see*
- SEGUNDA PARTE DE LA CRONICA...INCAS YUPANQUIS..
- TERCERO LIBRO DE LAS GUERRAS CIVILES...DE QUITO

CIFA *see*
- REPORT OF THE 1ST SESSION OF THE WORKING PARTY ON POLLUTION AND FISHERIES. ACCRA, GHANA, 1986
- REPORT OF THE 2ND SESSION OF THE WORKING PARTY ON POLLUTION AND FISHERIES
- REPORT OF THE 3RD SESSION OF THE SUB-COMMITTEE FOR LAKE TANGANYIKA. LUSAKA, 1985
- REPORT OF THE 3RD SESSION OF THE SUB-COMMITTEE FOR THE PROTECTION AND DEVELOPMENT OF THE FISHERIES IN THE SAHELIAN ZONE. ACCRA, 1986
- REPORT OF THE 3RD SESSION OF THE WORKING PARTY ON POLLUTION AND FISHERIES
- REPORT OF THE 4TH SESSION OF THE SUB-COMMITTEE FOR THE DEVELOPMENT AND MANAGEMENT OF THE FISHERIES OF LAKE VICTORIA. KISUMU, KENYA, APRIL 1987
- REPORT OF THE 4TH SESSION OF THE SUB-COMMITTEE FOR THE PROTECTION AND DEVELOPMENT OF THE FISHERIES IN THE SAHELIAN ZONE
- REPORT OF THE 5TH SESSION OF THE SUB-COMMITTEE FOR THE DEVELOPMENT AND MANAGEMENT OF THE FISHERIES OF LAKE VICTORIA
- REPORT OF THE 6TH SESSION OF THE SUB-COMMITTEE FOR THE DEVELOPMENT AND MANAGEMENT OF THE FISHERIES OF LAKE VICTORIA
- REPORT OF THE 8TH SESSION OF THE COMMITTEE FOR INLAND FISHERIES OF AFRICA

Ciganek, David S *see* A STUDY OF MULTI-DIMENSIONAL EVALUATION PROCESSES IN THE PROFESSIONAL PREPARATION OF ATHLETIC TRAINERS

Cigar Makers' International Union of America *see* CIGAR WORKERS OFFICIAL JOURNAL

Cigar Makers Progressive Union of America *see* PROGRESS

CIGAR WORKERS OFFICIAL JOURNAL : 1876-1972 / Cigar Makers' International Union of America – (Coll title: Labor Union Periodicals, Pt 3) – 1996 – 15r – 1 – $2,025.00 – 1-55655-624-1 – us UPA [331]

A CIGARRA – Rio de Janeiro, 9 May 1895-16 Jan 1896 – 1,5,6 – bl Biblioteca [072]

A CIGARRA – '(s.l.')-Sao Luiz, Brazil. 12 Oct 1829-17 Apr 1830 – 1,5,6 – bl Biblioteca [072]

Cilleros. Ayuntamiento *see*
- FERIAS Y FIESTAS 1971
- TRADICIONALES FIESTAS EN HONOR DE LA SANTISIMA VIRGEN DE NAVELONGA
- TRADICIONALES FIESTAS EN HONOR DE LA SANTISIMA VIRGEN DE NAVELONGA, 1978

CILLIER ZEITUNG – Celje, Yugoslavia. 1921; 1923-Feb 1928 – 5r – 1 – us L of C Photodup [072]

CILLIER ZEITUNG – (Cont by: Deutsche Zeitung) – Cilli (Celje), Jugoslawien. 1922 – 1r – 1 – gw Mikrofilm [949]

Cilliers, Andries Charl *see* THE STATE AND THE UNIVERSITIES (1910-1943)

CIM BULLETIN – 1984- – 1,5,6,9 – us UMI [660]

CIM TECHNOLOGY: CASA, SME'S MAGAZINE OF COMPUTERS IN DESIGN AND MANUFACTURING – v3, no.4-. Winter 1984- – 1,5,6,9 – us UMI [073]

Cima, A *see* IL SECONDRO LIBRO DELLI CONCERTI A DUE, TRE, & QUATTRO VOCI... OPERA SECONDA

CIMAISE – Revue de l'art actuel. no. 1-50. Paris. nov 1953-60 – 1 – fr A.C.R.P.P. [073]

Cimarosa, D *see*
- L'ARTEMISIA L'ANNO 1801 A VENEZIA
- GLI ORAZI E CURIAZI
- RECUEIL D'AIRS. 3 DUETTI AVEC ACCOMPAGNEMENT DE COR HAUBOIS, VIOLON ET VIOLE
- LE STAVEGANZE DI AMORE
- VI DIRO SENTITE BENE

Cimbali, E *see*
- DELLA NECESSITA DI UN NUOVO DIRITTO INFORMAZIONALE...
- IL DIRITTO INTERNAZIONALE IN ITALIA...
- DIRITTO INTERNAZIONALE OPPRESSORE E GUERRESCO...
- IL MATRIMONIO DELLO STRANIERO
- IL MATRIMONIO DINANZI AGLI AGENTI DIPLOMATICI
- TRIONFI E COMPITI DEL NUOVO DIRITTO INTERNAZIONALE...

LA CIMBARRA / Martinez de Carnero y Diaz, Rafael – 1846 – 9 – 1.50f – sp Bibl Santa Ana [830]

CIMBRI, EMBLEMATA. CHRISTIANO 4. DICATA / Westhovius, W W W – O 802 1. 1640 – 9 – ne IDC [740]

CIMBRISHAMNSBLADET – Simrishamn, Sweden. 1857-1944 – 1 – sw Kungliga [072]

Cimon, Constance *see* BIBLIOGRAPHIE ANALYTIQUE DES ECRITS CANADIENS SUR L'OEUVRE ET LA PERSONNALITE DE CORNELIUS KRIEGHOFF

CIN – Brno, Czechoslovakia. Aug 1945-Oct 1946 – 2r – 1 – us L of C Photodup [072]

CINA, LATVIA – (Missing: 1916) – Riga, 1904-45 – 8r – 1 – $680.00 – us Ross [072]

Cinagli, Ang. *see* LE MONETE DEI PAPI DESCRITTE IN TAVOLLE SINOTTICHE

THE CINCHONA SPECIES OF NEW GRANADA / Markham, C R – London, 1867. 139 pp., 5 pls. B-5140 2 – 8 – ne IDC [580]

CINCINNATI COMMERCIAL – Cincinnati, Ohio. Daily. Apr 12 1861-Dec 30 1865. Incomplete – 1 – us NY Public [071]

CINCINNATI COMMERCIAL – Cincinnati. v22-26. 1861-65 – 7r – 1 – us Ross [071]

CINCINNATI DAILY COMMERCIAL – Cincinnati, OH: M D Potter & Co, [nov 13 1854-may 25 1861] – 1 – us Res Libr [071]

CINCINNATI DAILY GAZETTE – Cincinnati, 1828-81 – 89r – 1 – us Ross [071]

CINCINNATI DEMOCRAT – Cincinnati, dec 8 1845 – 1r – us Res Libr [071]

CINCINNATI ENQUIRER – Covington. Ky. (Ky. Edition). 1901- – 1 – us UMI [071]

CINCINNATI GAZETTE – Cincinnati, Ohio. Daily. June 26 1828-Dec 31 1881. Incomplete – 1 – us NY Public [071]

CINCINNATI JEWISH WORLD – Cincinnati, OH. 4 Apr 1952 – 1 – us A.J.P.C. [071]

CINCINNATI JOURNAL – (Some original pgs damaged) – v1-11. 1828-39 – 3r – 1 – ATLA S0161 – us A.T.L.A. [073]

CINCINNATI NORTH JOURNAL – Hamilton. Ohio. -w. 1973- – 1 – us UMI [071]

Cincinnati, Ohio *see* DAY STAR

THE CINCINNATI POST – Cincinnati. Ohio. 1882- – 1 – us UMI [071]

Cincinnati. Presbytery (Presbyterian Church in the USA) *see* MINUTES, 1822-1911

CINCINNATI REPUBLIKANER = CINCINNATI REPUBLICAN – Cincinnati, OH: Carl Hiller & Wm Ed Becht, [jan 4 1858-mar 23 1861] – 1r – 1 – us Res Libr [071]

THE CINCINNATI STAR – Cincinnati, Ohio. Weekly. Mar 14 1872-June 23 1880. Incomplete – 1 – us NY Public [071]

CINCINNATI SUPERIOR COURT DECISIONS / Ohio. Superior Court – 1v. 1903-07 (all publ) – 6mf – 9 – $9.00 – LLMC 84-181 – us L.L.M.C. [340]

CINCINNATI SUPERIOR COURT DECISIONS / Ohio. Superior Court – v1-2. 1854-1855 (all publ) – 8mf – 9 – $12.00 – LLMC 91-036 – us L.L.M.C. [340]

CINCINNATI SUPERIOR COURT DECISIONS / Ohio. Superior Court – v1-2. 1870-1873 (all publ) – 14mf – 9 – $21.00 – LLMC 91-035 – us L.L.M.C. [340]

CINCINNATI TIMES – Cincinnati, Ohio. Weekly. July 15 1880-Dec 27 1888 – 1 – us NY Public [071]

CINCINNATI TIMES STAR – Covington. Ky. (Ky. Edition). 1902-58 – 1 – us UMI [071]

CINCINNATI WEEKLY HERALD *see* CINCINNATI WEEKLY HERALD AND PHILANTHROPIST

CINCINNATI WEEKLY HERALD – (Filmed with: Philanthropist (New Richmond, OH), and: Cincinnati Weekly Herald and Philanthropist) – Cincinnati: Sperry & Brewster, dec 16 1846-feb 7 1847 – 1r – us Res Libr [071]

CINCINNATI WEEKLY HERALD AND PHILANTHROPIST – (Filmed with: Philanthropist (New Richmond, Ohio) and Cincinnati Weekly Herald oct 18 1843-dec 9 1846) – Cincinnati, OH: Gamaliel Bailey, Jr., 1843-46 – 1r – 1 – us Res Libr [071]

CINCINNATI WEEKLY STAR – Cincinnati. v1-17. 1872-80 – 3r – 1 – us Ross [071]

CINCINNATI WEEKLY TIMES – Cincinnati, 1880-88 – 3r – 1 – us Ross [071]

CINCINNATIER ZEITUNG – Cincinnati, OH: Cincinnatier Zeitung Pub Co, jul 1887-oct 20 1901 – 59r – 1 – us Res Libr [071]

CINCINNATI-KURIER – (Cont by: Amerika-Woche, Chicago) – Omaha. 1972-76 – 1 – gw Mikrofilm [071]

CINCO ANOS DESPUES : [DE LA ECONOMIA SOCIAL-JUSTICIALISTA AL REGIMEN LIBERAL-CAPITALISTA] / Cafiero, Antonio Francisco – Buenos Aires, [1961] – 1 – CSUXAHZ2324-B – us Hoover Inst Photo [330]

CINCO DE JANEIRO : ORGAO DO PARTIDO LIBERAL DO AMAZONAS – Manaos, Amazonas. 29 Maio 1879 – 1,5,6 – bl Biblioteca [072]

CINCO D'OUTUBRO – Manaos, Amazonas. 5 Out 1911 – 1,5,6 – bl Biblioteca [072]

CINCO LIBROS DE ARQUITECTURA / Serlio, Sebastian – SL, 1563 – 8mf – 9 – sp Cultura [720]

CINCPACFLT INTERIM EVALUATION REPORTS, 1950-1953 – Korean conflict. 1978 – 6r – 1 – $510.00 – S1653 – us Scholarly Res [950]

CINDERELLA FROM THE PAMPAS : MARIA EVA DUARTE DE PERON, ARGENTINE FIRST LADY, 1919-1952 / Akridge, Sharon A Hollenbeck – Ann Arbor, Mich.: University Microfilms International, 1983 – 1 – CSUXAJB7762-B – us Hoover Inst Photo [320]

CINEASTE – (v8- . 1977- . 5,6,9) – v. 1-. 1967- – 1 – us UMI [790]

CINEGRAM MAGAZINE – v. 1. 1976 – 1,5,6,9 – us UMI [770]

CINE-LIBERTE – no. 1-5. Paris. mai-nov 1936. Collection privee – 1 – fr A.C.R.P.P. [790]

CINEMA – 17 no. Paris. oct 1952-janv 1955 – 1 – fr A.C.R.P.P. [790]

CINEMA *see* "LITTLE MAGAZINES" SERIES 1889-1972

CINEMA CANADA – Montreal, Quebec, CN. 1972-Nov 1989 – 9r – 1 – cn Commonwealth Micro [073]

LE CINEMA CANADIEN : VALSE CHANTEE / Dandurand, J L – Montreal, 1921. SEM105P927 – 1mf – 9 – Can$2.25 – cn Bibl Nat [790]

CINEMA DURING WORLD WAR 2 PAMPHLET COLLECTION – 1942-19?? – 1 – CSUXANM6429-B – us Hoover Inst Photo [790]

CINEMA EDITIONS ON MICROFICHE: BIRTH OF A NATION – 9 – us Primary [790]

LE CINEMA ET L'ECHO DU CINEMA REUNIS – Paris. mars 1912-mars 1914, mai 1916-mai 1923 – 1 – fr A.C.R.P.P. [790]

CINEMA JOURNAL – (1983-. 1,5,6,9) – v6-. 1966- – 1 – us UMI [790]

CINEMA PRESSBOOKS, 1920-1940 / British Film Institute – (Includes printed list of titles in alphabetical order with the date, studio, director and main stars with 4 indexes) – 1,864mf – 9 – £2,865.00 – British Film Institute – uk Chadwyck [790]

CINEMA PRESSBOOKS FROM THE ORIGINAL STUDIO COLLECTIONS – (Part Two: Pressbooks for United Artists, 1919-49; Warner Bros., 1922-49; and Monogram Pictures, 1937-46, Section B) – Part One: Pressbooks for United Artists, 1919-49; Warner Bros., 1922-49; Monogram Pictures, 1937-46, Section A – 1 – us Primary [790]

CINEMA QUARTERLY *see* "LITTLE MAGAZINES" SERIES 1889-1972

CINEMA RISING *see* "LITTLE MAGAZINES" SERIES 1889-1972

CINEMA STUDIES *see* "LITTLE MAGAZINES" SERIES 1889-1972

CINEMA TV TO-DAY – 1 – uk World [790]

CINEMATOGRAPHIC INSTITUTIONS / International Film and Television Council – 1973 – 98p – 9 – 92-3-101076-X – fr UNESCO [380]

A CINEMATOGRAPHICAL ANALYSIS AND FORCE MEASURE OF THREE STYLES OF THE KARATE BACK PUNCH AND SIDE KICK / Powell, Steven W – 1989 – 215p 3mf – 9 – $12.00 – us Microform Publ [790]

LA CINEMATOGRAPHIE / Bull, Lucien – Paris: A. Colin, 1928. viii,180p. illus., diagrs. (Collection Armand Colin, no.94. Section de physique) – 1 – us U.W. Library [770]

LA CINEMATOGRAPHIE FRANCAISE – Paris. nov 1918-29 nov 1928 – 1 – fr A.C.R.P.P. [790]

CINEMONDE – Montreal, Canada. v2 n1. 2 oct 1943-v5 n13. 12 jul 1947 – 1r – 1 – Can$50.00 – cn Can Microfilming [770]

CINE-REPORTER : SEMANARIO CENEMATOGRAFICO – Sao Paulo, 2 Jan, Jun-Dec 1946; Jan 1947-Oct 1961; Aug, Sep 1962; Feb, May-Dec 1964; Feb, Jun 1965; Jan 1966 – 1,5,6 – bl Biblioteca [072]

CINGIRAKLI TATAR – Nos 1-29. – 24 Mart-6 Temmuz 1289 – 3mf – 9 – $31.50 – us MEDOC [949]

Cinnami, Joannis *see*
– EPITOME RERUM AB IOANNE ET ALEXIO COMNENIS GESTARUM (CSHB 26)
– IMPERATORII GRAMMATICI HISTORIARUM LIBRI SEX SEU DE REBUS GESTIS A JOANNE ET MANNUELE GOMMENSIS IMPP. CP. (CBH 11,1)

CINQ ANNEES AU CONGO,1879-1884 / Stanley, Henry Morton – Voyages, explorations, fondation de l'etat libre du Congo. Paris, Dreyfous. 1885 – 9 – 20.00 – fr Orientalistes [960]

CINQ ANNEES D'ADMINISTRATION REFORMISTE – La ruine a l'interieur quand la fortune est a la porte: Choisissiez 1878? 03189. (Pre-1900 Canadiana) – 9 – cn C.I.H.M. [971]

CINQ ANS DE SEJOUR AU SOUDAN FRANCAIS / Bechet, Eugene – Paris: E Plon, 1889 – 9 – us Res Libr [910]

CINQ ANS D'EXECUTION DU PLAN DE MODERNISATION ET D'EQUIPEMENT DE L'UNION FRANCAISE REALISATIONS 1947-1951 ET PROGRAMME 1952 / France. Commissariat general du plan de modernisation et d'equipement – (Five years of implementation of the modernization and equipment plan of the French Union; achievements 1947-1951 and program 1952). Paris. 1952. BD-1653 1 – 9 – ne IDC [338]

LES CINQ CENTS MILLIONS DE LA BEGUM / Verne, Jules – and Les Revoltes de la Bounty. Paris: J. Hetzel, s.d. 312p. 4 fiches. (Literature Collection) – 9 – 10.00 – fr Bibl Nationale [830]

CINQ HISTOIRES ADMIRABLES / Blendecq, D Charles – Paris. 1582 – 9 – fr Hachette [360]

CINQ LIVRES DE L'IMPOSTURE ET TROMPERIE DES DIABLES, DES ENCHANTEMENTS ET SORCELLERIES / Wier, Johann – Paris. 1569 – 9 – fr Hachette [360]

LES CINQ ORDRES D'ARCHITECTURE. / Scamozzi, Vincenzo – Paris, Coignard, 1685. 14, 143p., ill. (Architecture Series) – 9 – fr Hachette [720]

CINQ TRAITES D'ALCHIMIE DES PLUS GRANDS PHILOSOPHES. – Paris, 1890 (Science Collection) – viii/134p 2mf – 9 – $6.00 – fr Bibl Nationale [180]

LE CINQ TROIS UN SIX : ECOLE DE JOURNALISME / ed by Gagnon, J-L & Germain, Nicole – Montreal, Canada. jun 1964-v2 n4. jun 1966 – 1r – 1 – Can$25.00 – cn Can Microfilming [370]

Cinq-Mars, F *see* L'AURORE DES CANADAS

CINQ-MARS: OR, A CONSPIRACY UNDER LOUIS 13 / Vigny, Alfred de – Transl. by William Hazlitt. Boston: Little, Brown and Co., 1889. 2v – 1 – us U.W. Library [944]

CINQUANTENAIRE DE LA BANQUE D'EPARGNE.. / Banque d'epargne de la cite et du district de Montreal – Montreal?, 1896?. 04080. (Pre-1900 Canadiana) – 9 – cn C.I.H.M. [332]

CINQUANTENAIRE DES OBLATS DE MARIE IMMACULEE EN CANADA – Fetes jubilaires les 7, 8 et 9 decembre, 1891. Montreal: Beauchemin, 1891? 03189. (Pre-1900 Canadiana) – 9 – cn C.I.H.M. [240]

CINQUANTENAIRE DES OBLATS DE MARIE IMMACULEE EN CANADA: FETES JUBILAIRES LES 7, 8 ET 9 DECEMBRE 1891 / Guillet, Didace – Montreal: C.O. Beauchemin, 1891?. 05131. (Pre-1900 Canadiana) – 9 – cn C.I.H.M. [240]

CINQUANTENAIRE DU COLLEGE DE L'ASSOMPTION – Fetes jubilaires celebrees les 12, 13 et 14 juin 1883. Montreal: Beauchemin, 1893. 03041. (Pre-1900 Canadiana) – 9 – cn C.I.H.M. [370]

CINQUANTIEME ANNIVERSAIRE DU REV. M. GAGNON, CURE DE BERTHIER – 1868? 00653. (Pre-1900 Canadiana) – 9 – cn C.I.H.M. [920]

CINQUE PORTS *see* THE WHITE AND BLACK BOOKS OF THE CINQUE PORTS

CINQUE PORTS CHRONICLE AND EAST SUSSEX OBSERVER – (Cinque Ports Chronicle and Southern Advertiser. 1840-41) – England. 8 Sept 1838-29 Dec 1841. -w – 3r – 1 – uk British Libr Newspaper [072]

CINQUE PORTS CHRONICLE AND SOUTHERN ADVERTISER *see* CINQUE PORTS CHRONICLE AND EAST SUSSEX OBSERVER

CINQUIEME CONFERENCE ECONOMIQUE NATIONALE / Toure, Ahmed Sekou – Conakry: Imprimerie nationale "Patrice Lumumba" 1976 – 9 – us Res Libr [330]

CINQUIEME PLAN / Martinique. French West Indies. Commission locale du plan – D-1122 1. 1966-1970 – 9 – ne IDC [338]

CINQUIEME PLAN, 1966-1970 RAPPORT GENERAL DE LA COMMISSION DE L'EQUIPEMENT CULTUREL ET DU PATRIMOINE ARTISTIQUE / France. Commissariat General du Plan – Paris 1966 – 9 – ne IDC [330]

CINQUIEME PLAN, 1966-1970 RAPPORT GENERAL DE LA COMMISSION DES BUREAUX ET ORGANISMES D'ETUDES TECHNIQUES / France. Commissariat General du Plan – Paris. 1966 – 9 – ne IDC [650]

CINQUIEME PLAN, 1966-1970 RAPPORT GENERAL DE LA COMMISSION DES PRESTATIONS SOCIALES / France. Commissariat General du Plan – Paris. 1966. BD-610 1 – 9 – ne IDC [360]

CINQUIEME PLAN DE DEVELOPPEMENT ECONOMIQUE ET SOCIAL 1966-1970 / French Overseas Departments. Departement de la Martinique – D-1058 1. 1965 – 9 – ne IDC [338]

CINTA – Communist Party of India, (Marxist) Kerala State Committee. v10. 1973-74. Incomplete. -w. In Malayalam – 1 – us U.W. Library [073]

EL CINTURON DE AFRODITA / Hurtado de Mendoza, Publio – Caceres: Luciano Jimenez Merino, Impresor, 1922 – 1 – sp Bibl Santa Ana [946]

THE CIO FILES OF JOHN L. LEWIS, PART 1 : CORRESPONDENCE WITH CIO UNIONS, 1929-1962 – 9 – $2,750.00 – 1-55655-048-0 – us UPA [331]

THE CIO FILES OF JOHN L. LEWIS, PART 2 : CIO GENERAL FILES, 1929-1955 – 9 – $2,200.00 – 1-55655-049-9 – us UPA [331]

CIO INDUSTRIAL WORKER – Portland OR. July 11 18 Aug 8 29 1941, Feb 21 Mar 7 21 Apr 4 18 1941, May 2 16 30 June 13 27 1941 + – 1 – us U.O. Library [071]

CIO NEWS : ALUMINIUM WORKERS EDITION, 1938-1943 : ALUMINIUM WORKERS NEWS DIGEST, 1943-1944 / Aluminium Workers of America, CIO – (Coll title: Labor Union Periodicals, Pt 1) – 2r – 1 – $270.00 – 1-55655-232-7 – us UPA [331]

CIO NEWS : DIE CASTERS EDITION, 1938-1942 / National Association of Die Casting Workers, CIO – (Coll title: Labor Union Periodicals, Pt 1) – 1r – 1 – $135.00 – 1-55655-233-5 – us UPA [331]

CIO NEWS : MINE, MILL AND SMELTER WORKERS INTERNATIONAL EDITION, 1938-1942 / International Union of Mine, Mill and Smelter Workers – (Coll title: Labor Union Periodicals, Pt 1) – 1r – 1 – $135.00 – 1-55655-234-3 – us UPA [331]

CIO NEWS : PACKINGHOUSE WORKERS EDITION, 1938-1942 / United Packinghouse Workers of America – (Coll title: Labor Union Periodicals, Pt 3) – 1996 – 2r – 1 – $270.00 – 1-55655-622-5 – us UPA [331]

CIO NEWS : UNITED FARM EQUIPMENT AND METAL WORKERS EDITION, 1938-1943 / United Farm Equipment and Metal Workers of America – (Coll title: Labor Union Periodicals, Pt 1) – 1r – 1 – $135.00 – 1-55655-235-1 – us UPA [331]

CIO NEWS – Washington, DC. 1937-1955 – 5r – 1 – $250.00 – R05506 – us Library Micro [071]

CIO NEWS CANNERY WORKERS EDITION *see* CANNERY AND FIELD UNION NEWS, 1937 : CIO NEWS CANNERY WORKERS EDITION, 1938-1939 : UCAPAWA NEWS, 1939-1944 : FTA NEWS, 1945-1950

CIO WORLD AFFAIRS BULLETIN – Washington, DC. 1951-1952 – 1r – 1 – $50.00 – R05507 – us Library Micro [073]

Ciolfi, E *see* LE SUCCESSIONI NEL DIRITTO INTERNAZIONALE...

Cioriceanu, G *see* LES MANDATS INTERNATIONAUX

CIPA / Chartered Institute of Patent Agents – (v4- . 1974- . 5,6. v5- . 1975- . 9) – v. 1-. 1971- – 1 – us UMI [340]

CIPEA *see*
– EVALUATION DES PRODUCTIVITES DES RACES BOVINES MAURE ET PEUL A LA STATION DU SAHEL, NIONO, MALI
– POTENTIEL D'IMPACT
– RECUEIL STATISTIQUE SUR LA PRODUCTION ANIMALE EN AFRIQUE

THE CIPHER IN THE PLAYS, AND ON THE TOMBSTONE / Donnelly, Ignatius – Minneapolis: The Verulam Publ. Co., 1899. 5,(9),372p. With: Shaksper Not Shakespeare by W.H. Edwards. 1 reel. 1295 – 1 – us U.W. Library [420]

O CIPO – Rio Branco, Acre. Mar 1984 – 1,5,6 – bl Biblioteca [072]

Cipolletti, Emilio Domingo *see* ANTE LOS OJOS DE AMERICA

CIPS REVIEW – (Cont by Canadian Information Processing) – Toronto. v1-13. 1976/77-1989/90 – 9 – Can$20.00y – cn Micromedia [073]

CIPS REVIEW *see* CANADIAN INFORMATION PROCESSING

Ciquard, Francois *see* PORTRAIT D'UN MISSIONNAIRE APOSTOLIQUE

CIRCE: THREE ACTS IN THE LIFE OF AN ARTIST / Braddon, Mary Elizabeth – By Babington White. British Fiction Archive: Unit 5 – 9 – uk Bell [830]

THE CIRCLE OF CHRISTIAN DOCTRINE : A HANDBOOK OF FAITH FRAMED OUT OF A LAYMAN'S EXPERIENCE / Kinloch, William Penney – 2nd ed. Edinburgh:Edmonston & Douglas, 1861 – 1mf – 9 – 0-8370-4470-7 – 1985-2470 – us A.T.L.A. [230]

THE CIRCLE OF THEOLOGY : AN INTRODUCTION TO THEOLOGICAL STUDY / Clarke, William Newton – (Includes bibliographical references) – Cambridge: University Press, 1897 – 1mf – 9 – 0-8370-2673-3 – 1985-0673 – us A.T.L.A. [200]

THE CIRCLES OF GOMER, OR AN ESSAY TOWARDS AN INVESTIGATION AND INTRODUCTION TO THE ENGLISH, AS AN UNIVERSAL LANGUAGE / Jones, Rowland – 1771. 258p. (English Linguistics Series 1500-1800) – 9 – us UMI [420]

EL CIRCO ROMANO DE MERIDA. MEMORIA DE LAS EXCAVACIONES PRACTICADAS DE 1920 A 1925 / Melida, Jose Ramon – Madrid: Rev. Arch. Bibl, 1925 – 1 – sp Bibl Santa Ana [946]

CIRCOLO MATEMATICO DI PALERMO – 1-62, no.3, 1884 87-1938 39; ser. 2, v.1-. 1952. Irregular. 3 no. a year. 6 indexes – 1 – us U.W. Library [073]

CIRCUIT REPORTS, 1835-1898, AND THE SWANSTON COLLECTION ON THE RA AND BA MILITARY CAMPAIGNS, 1873 / Fiji. Methodist Church – 5r – 1 – PMB1093 – at Pacific Mss [355]

THE CIRCUIT RIDER : A TALE OF THE HEROIC AGE / Eggleston, Edward – New York: J.B. Ford, 1874 – 1mf – us A.T.L.A. [240]

CIRCUIT SUPERIOR COURT : THE NAME INDEX AND ABSTRACT / Virginia. Fairfax County – 1831-1859 – 9 – $375.00 – us Bloch [340]

CIRCUIT WEST – Claremont, CA. 1975-1976 – 1r – 1 – $50.00 – R03183 – us Library Micro [071]

CIRCUITS AND MINISTERS, 1924-1980 / Leary, William – 1983 – 8mf – 9 – ne IDC [240]

CIRCULAIRE. / Cercle Catholique de Quebec. Comite de Construction – 1878? 00753. (Pre-1900 Canadiana) – 9 – cn C.I.H.M. [240]

CIRCULAIRE DER ALGEMEENE VEREENIGING VAN RUBBER PLANTERS TER OOSTKUST VAN SUMATRA – Medan, 1910-1940. Nos. 1-1465 – 22mf – 9 – ne IDC [670]

CIRCULAR / Alabama. Agricultural Experiment Station – v. 1-180. 1906-70 – 1,5,6 – us Spaulding [630]

CIRCULAR / Auburn University. Agricultural Experiment Station – No.181-263. 1970-82 – 1, 5 – us Spaulding [630]

CIRCULAR / Auburn University. Cooperative Extension Service – (PH-S). 1963-69 – 1,5,6 – us Spaulding [630]

CIRCULAR / Auburn University. Extension Service – n.s. v. 1-5. 1949-50 – 1,5,6 – us Spaulding [630]

CIRCULAR / Auburn University. Extension Service – v. 1-636. 1916-63 – 1,5,6 – us Spaulding [630]

CIRCULAR / Clemson University. Agricultural Experiment Station – No.161-191. 1970-82. 1 reel – 1,5 – us Spaulding [630]

CIRCULAR / Colorado. Agricultural Extension Service. Fort Collins Cooperative Extension Service – nos.1-207. 1925-59 – 1,5,6 – us Spaulding [630]

CIRCULAR / Connecticut. Agricultural Experiment Station. New Haven – v. 1-231. 1905-69 – 1,5,6 – us Spaulding [630]

CIRCULAR / Florida. Agricultural Experiment Station – S-1-S-202. 1949-69 – 1,5,6 – us Spaulding [630]
CIRCULAR / Florida. Agricultural Extension Service – v. 1-342. 1917-69 – 1,5,6 – us Spaulding [630]
CIRCULAR / Georgia. Agricultural Experiment Station. Athens – n.s. v. 1-51. 1954-66 – 1,5,6 – us Spaulding [630]
CIRCULAR / Georgia. Agricultural Experiment Station. Athens – v. 1-6. 1952-54 – 1,5,6 – us Spaulding [630]
CIRCULAR / Georgia. Coastal Plain Experiment Station. Tifton – v. 1-23. 1921-53 – 1,5,6 – us Spaulding [630]
CIRCULAR / Georgia. Experiment Station. Experiment – v. 61-170. 1907-53 – 1,5,6 – us Spaulding [630]
CIRCULAR / Georgia. University. Agricultural Extension Service – n.1-610. 1913-69 – 1,5 – us Spaulding [630]
CIRCULAR / Illinois. Cooperative Extension Service in Agriculture and Home Economics – Nos 1-1011 1897-1969 – 1,5 – us Spaulding [630]
CIRCULAR / Iowa State University. Agricultural Experiment Station – No.1-148. 1912-33 – 1,5 – us Spaulding [630]
CIRCULAR / Kansas. State University. Agricultural Experiment Station – nos.1-411. 1909-77 – 1,5,6 – us Spaulding [630]
CIRCULAR / Kentucky. Agricultural Experiment Station – v. 1-71. 1885-1952 – 1,5,6 – us Spaulding [630]
CIRCULAR / Kentucky. Agricultural Extension Service – v. 1-631. 1912-72 – 1,5,6 – us Spaulding [630]
CIRCULAR / Louisiana State University. Agricultural Experiment Station – No.92-116. 1970-83. 1 reel – 1,5 – us Spaulding [630]
CIRCULAR / Massachusetts. Agricultural Experiment Station – v. 1-74. 1907-27 – apply; AGR; 1,5,6 – us Spaulding [630]
CIRCULAR / Minnesota. Agricultural Extension Service. Agricultural Extension Division – nos.1-59. 1919-38 – 1,5,6 – us Spaulding [630]
CIRCULAR / Mississippi. Agricultural Experiment Station. State College – v. 1-213. 1900-58 – 1,5,6 – us Spaulding [630]
CIRCULAR / Montana. Agricultural Experiment Station – nos.1-251. 1908-71 – 1,5,6 – us Spaulding [630]
CIRCULAR / Nebraska. Agricultural Experiment Station. Lincoln – n.1-104. 1917-61 – 1,5 – us Spaulding [630]
CIRCULAR / North Carolina. Agricultural Experiment Station. Raleigh – n.1-35. Jul 1913-May 1917 – 1,5 – us Spaulding [630]
CIRCULAR / North Dakota. Agricultural Experiment Station. Fargo – nos.1-73. 1914-46 – 1,5,6 – us Spaulding [630]
CIRCULAR / Oklahoma State University. Cooperative Extension Service – E812-E828. 1970-82. 1 reel – 1,5 – us Spaulding [630]
CIRCULAR / Purdue University. Agricultural Experiment Station – No.1-419. 1906-55 – 1,5 – us Spaulding [630]
CIRCULAR / Rhode Island. Agricultural Extension Service – v. 1-159. 1928-68 – 1,5,6 – us Spaulding [630]
CIRCULAR / South Carolina. Agricultural Experiment Station. Clemson – n.1-160. Oct 1910-May 1969 – 1,5 – us Spaulding [630]
CIRCULAR / South Dakota. Agricultural Extension Service. State College of Agriculture and Mechanic Arts – nos.1-693. 1917-73 – 1,5,6 – us Spaulding [630]
CIRCULAR / South Dakota. State University. Agricultural Experiment Station – nos.1-213. 1920-75 – 1,5,6 – us Spaulding [630]
CIRCULAR / Stephen F. Austin University. Texas Forest Service – 1970-82.No.75-107 (revisions of pre-1970 circulars); No.202-260. 1 reel – 1,5 – us Spaulding [630]
CIRCULAR / Tennessee. University. Agricultural Experiment Station – n.1-111. Feb. 1926-Jan 1955 – 1,5 – us Spaulding [630]
CIRCULAR / University of Florida. Agricultural Experiment Station – No.S203-S294. 1970-82. 1 reel – 1, 5 – us Spaulding [630]
CIRCULAR / University of Florida. Cooperative Extension Service – No.343-542 and revisions. 1970-82 – 1, 5 – us Spaulding [630]
CIRCULAR / University of Georgia. Agricultural Extension Service – No.610-739. 1970-82. 12 fiches – 9 – us Spaulding [630]
CIRCULAR / Vermont. Agricultural Extension Service – v. 1-140. 1914-69 – 1,5,6 – us Spaulding [630]
CIRCULAR / Virginia. Agricultural Experiment Station. Blacksburg – 1908-09.n.1-8 – 1,5 – us Spaulding [630]
CIRCULAR / Virginia. Polytechnic Institute. Extension Division – n.1-1065. May 1915-Feb 1968 – 1,5 – us Spaulding [630]
CIRCULAR / Virginia. Truck Experiment Station. Norfolk – v. 1-2. 1909 – 1,5,6 – us Spaulding [630]
CIRCULAR / Washington. Agricultural Experiment Station – nos.1-573. 1943-74 – 1,5,6 – us Spaulding [630]
CIRCULAR / American Academy of Language and Belles Lettres – (Ceased publ) – New York. v1-3. oct 1820-jan 1822* – 1 – D5208 – us UMI [800]
CIRCULAR 4-H / Wisconsin. Agricultural Extension Service – n.1-121, 1926-63 – 1,5 – us Spaulding [630]
CIRCULAR 996 / Great Britain. Consultative Committee on Examinations in Secondary Schools – 1917 – 9 – uk Microform Academic [324]
CIRCULAR A / Auburn University. Extension Service – No.3-53.1970-78. 1 reel – 1, 5 – us Spaulding [630]
CIRCULAR ADDRESS / The Mississippi Society for Baptist Missions – 1817 – 1 – $5.00 – us Baptist [240]
CIRCULAR ADDRESS ON BOTANY AND ZOOLOGY / Rafinesque-Schmaltz, Constantine S – Philadelphia. 1816. B-8102 1 – 9 – ne IDC [580]
CIRCULAR (A-EX) / Auburn University. Extension Service – 1963-69 – 1,5,6 – us Spaulding [630]
CIRCULAR AND REVISIONS / Wisconsin. Agricultural Experiment Station – Jul 1909-Nov 1914.n.1-54. Revisions through 1924 – 1,5 – us Spaulding [630]
CIRCULAR AND REVISIONS / Wisconsin. Agricultural Extension Service – 1915-71. no.55-694 – 1,5 – us Spaulding [630]
CIRCULAR ANR / Auburn University. Extension Service – No.1-343. 1978-82 – 1, 5 – us Spaulding [630]
CIRCULAR CRD / Auburn University. Cooperative Extension Service – No.1-20.1978-82. 1 reel – 1, 5 – us Spaulding [630]
CIRCULAR DE LA AGRUPACION SOCIALISTA DE VALENCIA / Academia...Valencia. Academia Socialista Preparatoria para el Ingreso en las Escuelas Populares de Guerra – Valencia, 1937. Fiche W 801. (Blodgett Collection of Spanish Civil War Pamphlets) – 9 – us H.U. College Libr [946]
CIRCULAR E / Auburn University. Service – No.E2-E38. 1970-82. 1 reel – 1, 5 – us Spaulding [630]
CIRCULAR EN LA QUE EL DIRECTOR.. / Canseco, Manuel – 1824 – 9 – 1.50f – sp Bibl Santa Ana [946]
CIRCULAR EX / Auburn University. Extension Service – No.1-8. 1978-82. 1 reel – 1, 5 – us Spaulding [630]
CIRCULAR HE / Auburn University. Cooperative Extension Service – No.146-503 and Revisions No.4-144 – 1, 5 – us Spaulding [630]
CIRCULAR HE / Auburn University. Extension Service – v. 1-145. 1963-69 – 1,5,6 – us Spaulding [630]
CIRCULAR LETTER / Association of Research Libraries. Foreign Newspaper Microfilm Project – v1-16 1955-63 – 1 – us Res Libr [020]
CIRCULAR LETTER / Cone, Spencer H – 1824 – 1 – 5.00 – us Baptist [240]
CIRCULAR LETTER / South Dakota. Agricultural Extension Service. State College of Agriculture and Mechanic Arts – nos.1-160. 1925-38 – 1,5,6 – us Spaulding [630]
A CIRCULAR LETTER SUGGESTING A PETITION TO PARLIAMENT FOR THE PROTECTION OF THE TEMPORALITIES FUND / Barclay, John – Toronto: J. Barclay, 1882. 02973. (Pre-1900 Canadiana) – 9 – cn C.I.H.M. [971]
CIRCULAR LETTERS OF MINISTERS AND MESSENGERS / Northamptonshire Baptist Association, England – (ms.). 1765-1820 – 1 – 34.44 – us Baptist [240]
CIRCULAR LETTERS OF THE SECRETARY OF THE TREASURY (T SERIES), 1789-1878 / U.S. Treasury Department – 5 rolls. M735. Printed guide – 1 – us Nat'l Archives [336]
CIRCULAR M / Auburn University. Cooperative Extension Service – No.3, 13, 18 (revisions only). 1970-82.1 reel – 1, 5 – us Spaulding [630]
CIRCULAR M / Auburn University. Extension Service – v. 1-20. 1963-68 – 1,5,6 – us Spaulding [630]
CIRCULAR N° 11 DE ORGANIZACION ENCUADRAMIENTO DE PROFESIONES POR SINDICATOS Y SECCIONES / Servicio Nacional de Sindicatos – Caceres: Garcia Floriano, 1938 – 1 – sp Bibl Santa Ana [946]
CIRCULAR OF INFORMATION / Tennessee. University. Agricultural Experiment Station – n.1-88. 1932-Apr 1951 – 1,5 – us Spaulding [630]
CIRCULAR OF THE ANTI-PERSECUTION UNION – London. 1845 – 1 – uk Microform Academic [073]
CIRCULAR P / Auburn University. Cooperative Extension Service – v. 1-84. 1963-69 – 1,5,6 – us Spaulding [630]
CIRCULAR P / Auburn University. Extension Service – No.2-123. 1970-79. 1 reel – 1, 5 – us Spaulding [630]
CIRCULAR R / Auburn University. Extension Service – No.1-73.1970-82. 1 reel – 1, 5 – us Spaulding [630]
CIRCULAR RECOMENDANDO LA PUNTUALIDAD DEL AYUNTAMIENTO.. / Canseco, Manuel – 1828 – 9 – 1.50f – sp Bibl Santa Ana [946]
CIRCULAR SAW MANUAL : FAO/SIDA SAWMILL MANUALS – 1983 – 75p – it F.A.O. [621]
CIRCULAR SR / Auburn University. Extension Service – No.1000-9004. 1978-82. 1 reel – 1, 5 – us Spaulding [630]
CIRCULAR TO BANKERS – 1827-60 – 1 – uk Microform Academic [336]
CIRCULAR TO THE SHAREHOLDERS. / Canadian Pacific Railway Company – Montreal?, 1883?. 02044. (Pre-1900 Canadiana) – 9 – cn C.I.H.M. [336]
CIRCULARS / Clemson University. Agricultural Extension Division – n.1-513. 1918-Jun 1961 – 1,5 – us Spaulding [630]
CIRCULARS / Clemson University. Agricultural Extension Division – No.514-633 – 1,5 – us Spaulding [630]
CIRCULARS / Montana. Agricultural Extension Service – nos.1-294. 1929-67 – 1,5,6 – us Spaulding [630]
CIRCULARS / U.S. Department of Agriculture – No.1-982. 1927-56. 425 fiches – 9 – 760.00 – us Updata [630]
CIRCULARS / U.S. National Marine Fisheries Service (NOAA) – Nos. 1-451. 1941-84. 536 fiches – 9 – 1200.00 – us Updata [324]
CIRCULARS / University of Missouri. Agricultural Experiment Station – No.1-360. 1895-1951 – 1,5 – us Spaulding [630]
CIRCULARS 113-46 AND 168-48 / Great Britain. Consultative Committee on Examinations in Secondary Schools – 1946 and 1948 – 9 – uk Microform Academic [324]
CIRCULARS AND REGULATIONS.. / U.S. Department of the Interior. General Land Office – With reference tables and index.Comp. by C.G. Fisher. 1696p. Washington: GPO, 1930.85-303 – 9 – 12.00 – us L.L.M.C. [324]
CIRCULATION – (v. 33-. 1966- 5,6. v. 41-. 1970- 9) – 1- 1950- – 1 – us UMI [610]
CIRCULATION – v1-12. 1950-55 – 1,5,6 – us Princeton Micro [610]
LA CIRCULATION DANS LE SUD CAMEROUN / Billard, Pierre – Lyons, Impr des beaux-arts 1961 – us Res Libr [960]
LA CIRCULATION DU SANG. DES MOUVEMENTS DU COEUR CHEZ L'HOMME ET CHEZ LES ANIMAUX, DEUX REPONSES A RIOLAN / Harvey, William – Paris, Masson, 1879, iii-287 p. 10 fig. Histoire des Sciences XVIIe-XIXe Siecles. 7946 – 9 – fr Hachette [590]
THE CIRCULATION OF THE BLOOD / Arcieri, Giovanni P – Also, Andrea Cesalpino of Arezzo. Dr. John P. Arcieri. New York: S.F. Vanni, 1945. 193p. ill. Bibliography and indexes. With: In pursuit of Happiness-L.N. Tolstoy. 1 reel. 1282 – 1 – us U.W. Library [612]
CIRCULATION RESEARCH – New York. v1-45. 1953-79 – 1,5,6 – us Princeton Micro [610]
CIRCULATION RESEARCH – (v. 18-. 1966- 5,6. v. 26-. 1970- 9) – v. 1-. 1953- – 1 – us UMI [610]
Circulo de Artesanos *see*
– MEMORIA, ANO 1937
– MEMORIA, ANO 1958
Circulo de Artesanos. *see* MEMORIA, ANO 1938
CIRCUS – (v10- . 1975- . 5,6,9) – v. 1-. 1966- – 1 – us UMI [790]
CIRCUS RAVES – v. 1-2. 1974-75 – 1 – us UMI [790]
CIRENAICA SCONOSCIUTA – [Firenze] Sansoni, [1952] – 9 – us Res Libr [960]
Ciria, Alberto *see*
– ENGLISH PARTIES AND POWER IN MODERN ARGENTINA (1930-1946)
– PERON Y EL JUSTICIALISMO
– PERONISMO
CIRIACO PEREZ BUSTAMANTE, LA FUNDACION DE UN IMPERIO... / Bayle, Constantino – Madrid: Razon y Fe, 1941 – 1 – sp Bibl Santa Ana [946]
Cirigliano, Gustavo F J *see* UNIVERSIDAD Y PUEBLO
Cirillo, D *see* ENTOMOLOGIAE NEAPOLITANAE SPECIMEN PRIMUM
Cirni, AF *see*
– SVCCESSI DELL' ARMATA DELLA M^TA C^CA DESTINATA ALL' IMPRESA DI TRIPOLI DI BARBERIA, DELLA PRESA DELLE GERBE, E PROGRESSI DELL' ARMATA TURCHESCA, ...
– SVCCESSI DELLA ARMATA DELLA MAESTA' CATOLICA DESTINATA ALL' IMPRESA DI TRIPOLI DI BARBERIA, DELLA PRESA DELLE GERBE, E PROGRESSI DELL' ARMATA TURCHESCA, ...
CIRP : ANNALS OF THE INTERNATIONAL INSTITUTION FOR PRODUCTION ENGINEERING RESEARCH – Berne; Stuttgart: Technische Rundschau, v23. 1974 – 1r – us Res Libr [620]
CIRP ANNALS ... MANUFACTURING TECHNOLOGY – Berne: Technische Rundschau. v24 1975; v29 1980 – 2r – us Res Libr [670]
LE CIRQUE EN FRANCE DE LA BELLE EPOQUE A LA FIN DE LA DEUXIEME GUERRE MONDIALE / Vesque, M & Vesque, J – (Pt. 2. F220.00; 9) – Pt. 1 – 9 – F220.00 – fr Ethnologie [790]
Cirri, G B *see* SEI TRIJ PER VIOLINO, VIOLA, E VIOLONCELLO CONCERTANTI, OP. 18
Ciruelo, P *see*
– CURSO DE GEOMETRIA Y MATEMATICAS
– CURSUS QUATTOR MATHEMATICORUM ARTIUM LIBERALIUM
CIRUGIA, OSTEOLOGIA, MIOLOGIA Y VASOS, OPERACIONES, MEDICAMENTOS, SUPURACION... – SL, SA – 10mf – 9 – sp Cultura [617]
CIS – 3 leaflets. 4p – 9 – 1.00f – at Libertarian Micro [335]
CIS CONGRESSIONAL BILLS, RESOLUTIONS AND LAWS ON MICROFICHE : RETROSPECTIVE COLLECTION / U.S. Congress – 73rd Congress (1933-34)-104th Congress (1995-96) – 9 – Apply for prices – us CIS [324]
CIS CONGRESSIONAL MEMBER ORGANIZATIONS AND CAUCUSES : GUIDE TO PUBLICATIONS AND POLICY MATERIALS / U.S. Congress – 1991- – ca 325mf per yr – 9 – Apply for price – us CIS [324]
CIS POLICY FORUMS 1 – The Economics of Bureaucracy and Statutory Authorities. By Gordon Tullock, A.S. Watson, Peter L. Swan et al. 1983. 104p – 9 – 1.00f – at Libertarian Micro [335]
CIS POLICY FORUMS 2 – The Entrepreneur in Society. Contributors: Barry Maley, Malcolm Fisher, Michael G. Porter et al. 1983. 82p – 9 – 1.00f – at Libertarian Micro [335]
CIS POLICY FORUMS 3 – Changes in the Air: Issues in Domestic Aviation Policy. With: Christopher Findlay, Michael Kirby, Frank Gallagher et al. 1984. 112p – 9 – 1.00f – at Libertarian Micro [380]
CIS POLICY FORUMS 4 – Policies and Prescriptions: Current Directions in Health Policy.By Cotton M. Lindsay, Michael A. Walker, John Logan et al. 1986.211p – 9 – 1.00f – at Libertarian Micro [616]
CIS POLICY FORUMS 5 – Takeovers and Corporate Controls: Towards a New Regulatory Environment. Proceedings, 9 Jun 1986 (Auckland) and 13 Jun 1986 (Sydney). 1987. 246p – 9 – 1.00f – at Libertarian Micro [335]
CIS PRESIDENTIAL EXECUTIVE ORDERS AND PROCLAMATIONS ON MICROFICHE – (Index and mf set $34,800.00. Index Pts 1 + 2 $8,675.00) – 2pts. 1789-1983 – 9117mf – 9 – $29,990.00 set – us CIS [324]

CIS UNPUBLISHED U.S. CONGRESSIONAL COMMITTEE HEARINGS *see*
- CIS UNPUBLISHED U.S. HOUSE OF REPRESENTATIVES COMMITTEE HEARINGS ON MICROFICHE
- CIS UNPUBLISHED US SENATE COMMITTEE HEARINGS ON MICROFICHE

CIS UNPUBLISHED U.S. HOUSE OF REPRESENTATIVES COMMITTEE HEARINGS ON MICROFICHE : RETROSPECTIVE INDEX COVERAGE AND MICROFICHE COLLECTION / U.S. Congress. House of Representatives – (1833-1936 1691mf $6,925 Index $820. 1937-46 2491mf $10,200 Index $1,345. 1947-54 5211mf $19,900 Index $1,495. 1955-58 2975mf $13,355 Index $845. 1959-64 ca 3500mf $14,995 Index $995) – Pts 1-5. 1833-1964 – 9 – us CIS [324]

CIS UNPUBLISHED US SENATE COMMITTEE HEARINGS ON MICROFICHE : RETROSPECTIVE INDEX COVERAGE AND MICROFICHE COLLECTION / U.S. Congress. Senate – (1823-1964 9072mf $29,815 Index $2,585. 1965-68 853mf $3,945 Index $425. 1969-72 ca 725mf $3,355 Index $345) – Pts 1-3. 1823-1972 – 9925+ mf – 9 – us CIS [324]

CIS U.S. CONGRESSIONAL COMMITTEE HEARINGS ON MICROFICHE LIBRARY CATALOG RECORDS / U.S. Congress – (Print index accompanies 8pt coll. Available individually or as a complete coll (except pts1-3, sold only as a combined coll). Pts 1-3: 1833-1934 23rd-74th Congress. Pt 4: 1935-94 74th-78th Congress. Pt 5: 1945-52 79th-82nd Congress. Pt 6: 1953-58 83rd-85th Congress. Pt 7: 1959-64 86th-88th Congress. Pt 8: 1965-69 89th-91st Congress, 1st Session.) – Pts 1-8. 1833-1969 – 84,067mf – 9 – Apply for prices – us CIS [324]

CIS U.S. CONGRESSIONAL COMMITTEE PRINTS ON MICROFICHE : RETROSPECTIVE INDEX COVERAGE AND MICROFICHE COLLECTION / U.S. Congress – (Pt 1: 1911-1969 $22,585. Pt 2: 1917-1969 $5,095. Pt 3: 1830-1969 $29,475. Combined coll: Pts 1-3 1830-1969 $51,440. Complete index set $2,170.00) – Pts 1-3. 1830-1969 – 17,743mf – 9 – us CIS [324]

CIS U.S. CONGRESSIONAL JOURNALS ON MICROFICHE : RETROSPECTIVE COLLECTION / U.S. Congress – 1789-1978 – 4177mf – 9 – $8,380.00 – us CIS [073]

CIS U.S. EXECUTIVE BRANCH DOCUMENTS, 1789-1909 ON MICROFICHE – (Provides precise access to documents from federal executive agencies in existence during the time covered by the US govt's "Checklist of United States Public Documents, 1789-1909". Printed index) – 1995 – Pts 1-6 + suppl – 9 – Apply for prices – us CIS [324]

CIS U.S. EXECUTIVE BRANCH DOCUMENTS, 1910-1932 – (7pt-series to be publ over 7-yr period between 1996-2002) – Pts 1-7. 1996- – ca 8500mf – 9 – Apply for price – us CIS [324]

CIS U.S. SENATE EXECUTIVE DOCUMENTS AND REPORTS ON MICROFICHE : RETROSPECTIVE INDEX COVERAGE AND MICROFICE COLLECTION / U.S. Senate – (Index available $820.00. Access to facts behind treaties and nominations) – 1817-1969 – 1153mf + index – 9 – $6,125.00 – us CIS [324]

CIS U.S. SERIAL SET ON MICROFICHE / U.S. Congress – (Provides access to pre-1970 congressional reports and documents. Group 1: American State Papers and the 15th-34th Congresses (1789-1857). Groups 2-12: 35th-91st Congresses (1857-1969). Group 13: Index by Reported Bill Numbers (1819-1969). Group 14: Index and Carto-Bibliography of Maps (1789- 1897, 1897-1925 and 1925-1969)) – Pts 1-14. 1789-1969 – 116,000mf – 9 – Apply for individual prices, $241,100.00 set – us CIS [324]

CIS/INDEX AND CIS/MICROFICHE LIBRARY – (Microfiche and index coll include: Complete, Hearings, Limited Edition, and Serial Set) – 1970-1997 – 9 – Apply for prices – us CIS [020]

CISNE DE APOLO, DE LAS EXCELENCIAS, Y DIGNIDAD Y TODO QUE AL ARTE POETICA Y VERSIFICATORIA PERTENECE : LOS METODOS Y ESTYLOS QUE EN SUS OBRAS DEUE SEGUIR EL POETA – Medina del Campo: Godinez de Millis, 1602 – 9 – us Res Libr [810]

Cisneros, D *see* SITIO, NATURALEZA Y PROPIEDADES DE LA CIUDAD DE MEJICO, AGUAS Y VIENTOS. A QUE ESTA SUJETA Y SI TIEMPOS DEL ANO. NECESIDAD DE SU CONO CIMIENTO PARA EL EXERCICIO DE LA MEDICINA...

Cisneros, Juan *see*
- UN CASO DE EXTIRPACION DE LA LARINGE...DE ESTA OPERACION
- CONGRESO INTERNACIONAL DE MEDICINA VERIFICADO EN BERLIN DEL 4 AL 9 DE AGOSTO DE 1890
- CONTRIBUCION AL ESTUDIO DEL COLERA
- PAPILOMA COMEO DE LA LARINGE, LARINGOTOMIA CURACION

Cisse, S Y *see* L'EDUCATION EN AFRIQUE A LA LUMIERE DE LA CONFERENCE DE HARARE (1982)

Cissell, William B *see* DENTAL HEALTH ATTITUDES AND KNOWLEDGE LEVELS OF RURAL AND SUBURBAN TEXAS

CISTERCIAN STUDIES – (1981-. 1,5,6,9) – v1-. 1966- – 1 – us UMI [073]

CISTERCIENSER-CHRONIK – 1(1889)-38(1926) – 387mf – 9 – Dfl1,335.00 – ne Slangenburg [073]

CISTERCIENSER-CHRONIK – Bregenz. v1-38. 1889-1926 – 387mf – 9 – ne IDC [240]

CISTERCII REFLORESCENTIS / Morotius, C – Augustae Taurinorum, 1690 – 13mf – 8 – Dfl46.00 – ne Slangenburg [240]

DER CISTERZIENSER : EINE ERZAEHLUNG AUS DER ZEIT DES MARKGRAFEN OTTO 1. VON BRANDENBURG / Schmidt, Ferdinand – Duesseldorf: Felix Bagel, [18–?] – 1r – 1 – us U.W. Library [830]

CIST'S WEEKLY ADVERTISER – (Bound with: Western General Advertiser) – Cincinnati: Charles Cist, mar 22 1847-apr 29 1853 – us Res Libr [071]

CISTULA ENTOMOLOGICA – London, 1869-1885. v1-3 – 27mf – Z-932/2 – ne IDC [590]

CITADEL SQUARE BAPTIST CHURCH. CHARLESTON COUNTY. SOUTH CAROLINA : CHURCH RECORDS – 1868-Apr 1969 – 1 – 142.52 – us Baptist [240]

CITADEL SQUARE BAPTIST CHURCH. CHARLESTON COUNTY. SOUTH CAROLINA : CHURCH RECORDS – April 17, 1955-1969; Ladies Benevolent Society, 1867-1904; Burial Records and List of Members. 1828-1830; Register of Names of Colored Members. 1826 – 1 – 33.60 – us Baptist [240]

LA CITADELLE – Quebec, Canada. 9 mai 1857-dec 1859 – 1r – 1 – Can$25.00 – cn Can Microfilming [072]

CITANIAS EXTREMENAS / Monsalud, Marques de – Caceres: Tip. Enc. y Lib. de Jimenez, 1901. Rev. Extremadura, 1901 – 1 – sp Bibl Santa Ana [946]

CITATION AND EXAMINATION OF WILLIAM SHAKESPEARE, EUSEBY TREEN, JOSEPH CARNABY, AND SILAS GOUGH, CLERK. / Landor, Walter Savage – New York: Dodd, Mead, 1891?. xviii,229p – 1 – us U.W. Library [420]

CITATIONS OF THE STATUTES OF ALBERTA AND SASKATCHEWAN (1886-1912) / Miall, Edward – (Supplement. (1912-17). Toronto, 1917. 105p. LL-2330) – 2nd.ed. Toronto: Carswell, 1912 – 1 – us L of C Photodup [340]

CITE – London, UK. 26 Jul 1880-9 Jun 1882 – 1 – uk British Libr Newspaper [072]

LA CITE *see* LE JOURNAL DU VIEUX-MONTREAL

CITE LIBRE – 1950-1955 and 1965 – 1 – cn Precision [971]

CITE LIBRE / ed by Hebert, J et al – (Cont by: Cahiers de Cite Libre) – Montreal, Canada. jun 1950-aut 1966 – 2r – 1 – Can$60.00r – cn Can Microfilming [073]

CITE LIBRE *see* CAHIERS DE CITE LIBRE

CITEAUX IN DE NEDERLANDEN – 1(1950)-25(1974) – 161mf – 9 – Dfl172.00 – ne Slangenburg [073]

CITES NOUVELLES – Pointe-Claire, Canada. 7 mar 1974 – 1r – 1 – Can$25.00 – cn Can Microfilming [072]

LA CITHARE ZHENG / Rault, L – 9 – F160.00 – fr Ethnologie [306]

CITHERA MELICA, VEL OPUS MUSICUM PLANE NOVUM... VOCIBUS 12, 10 AND 8 / Duling, Anton – Magdaeburgi, typis J. Joachimi Boelij, sumptibus Johannis Neumanni, 1620 – 1 – us Sibley [780]

THE CITIES AND BISHOPRICS OF PHRYGIA, VOL 1 PTS 1 AND 2 : PART 1: THE LYCOS VALLEY AND SOUTH-WESTERN PHRYGIA; PART 2: WEST AND WEST-CENTRAL PHRYGIA / Ramsay, William Mitchell – Oxford, 1895 + 1897 – 15mf – 8 – Dfl53.00 – ne Slangenburg [240]

CITIES OF BELGIUM / Allen, Grant – London: G. Richards, 1897. 05015. (Pre-1900 Canadiana) – 9 – cn C.I.H.M. [910]

CITIES OF PAUL : BEACONS OF THE PAST REKINDLED FOR THE PRESENT / Wright, William Burnet – Boston: Houghton, Mifflin, 1905 – 1mf – 9 – 0-8370-7438-X – 1986-1438 – us A.T.L.A. [930]

CITIES OF SOUTHERN ITALY & SICILY / Hare, Augustus John Cuthbert – New York: G. Routledge & Sons, 188-. viii,535p.ill – 1 – us U.W. Library [910]

CITIES OF THE EASTERN ROMAN PROVINCES / Jones, A H M – 1937 – 9 – $21.00 – us I.R.C. [930]

CITIZEN – Anacortes. Wash. -w. 1914-15, 1916-27 – 1 – us UMI [071]

CITIZEN – Ansley, NE. -w. May 1901-Sep. 1902 – 1 – us NE Hist [071]

CITIZEN – Asheville. N.C. 1873- – 1 – us UMI [071]

CITIZEN – Battle Creek. Mich. 1882-1884 – 1 – us UMI [071]

CITIZEN – Beaver Dam. Wis. 1954- – 1 – us UMI [071]

CITIZEN – Birmingham. Ala. 1914-1918 – 1 – us UMI [071]

CITIZEN – Cairo. Ill. -w. 1885-1900 – 1 – us UMI [071]

CITIZEN – Columbus. Ohio. 1899-1939; 1947-1959 – 1 – us UMI [071]

CITIZEN – Ellwood City. Pa. 1894-1920 – 1 – us UMI [071]

CITIZEN – Fallon. Nev. 1963- – 1 – us UMI [071]

CITIZEN – Fallon, NV. 1964-1967 – 3r – 1 – $150.00 – N04521 – us Library Micro [071]

CITIZEN – Greeley. Neb. 1895-1911 – 1 – us UMI [071]

CITIZEN – Holdrege. Neb. 1892-1968; 1970- – 1 – us UMI [071]

CITIZEN – Hot Springs. Mont. 1948-1959; 1966-1967- – 1 – us UMI [071]

CITIZEN – Hudson. Ohio. 1914-1916 – 1 – us UMI [071]

CITIZEN – Iowa City. Iowa. 1894-1919 – 1 – us UMI [071]

CITIZEN – Irving. Tex. 1955-1960 – 1 – us UMI [071]

CITIZEN – Jackson. Mich. -d. 1865-1904 – 1 – us UMI [071]

CITIZEN – Jackson. Mich. -w, sw. 1849-1903 – 1 – us UMI [071]

CITIZEN – Key West. Fl. 1933-43, 1945$82 – 1 – us P.K. Yonge [071]

CITIZEN – Lakewood. N.J. -w. 1966- – 1 – us UMI [071]

CITIZEN – Lima. Ohio. 1957-1964 – 1 – us UMI [071]

CITIZEN – Linton. Ind. 1921-1928; 1935- – 1 – us UMI [071]

CITIZEN – London, UK. 1913-Jun 1922. -w.4 reels – 1 – uk British Libr Newspaper [072]

CITIZEN – Los Angeles. Calif. -w. 1943-48 – 1 – us UMI [071]

CITIZEN – Milford. Conn. -w. 1952-55 – 1 – us UMI [071]

CITIZEN – North Vancouver, British Columbia, CN. Apr 1958-Dec 1973 – 22r – 1 – cn Commonwealth Micro [072]

CITIZEN – Point Pleasant, West Virginia. 1934-39 – 1 – us UMI [071]

CITIZEN – Urbana. Ohio. 1923- – 1 – us UMI [071]

CITIZEN – Urbana. Ohio. and Gazette. 1845-50, 1853, 1863-91 – 1 – us UMI [071]

CITIZEN – (Weekly Republican newspaper publ in a Cleveland suburb later annexed to the city; issues are intermixed on the film with those of the Nottingham Citizen and the Collinwood Citizen) – Collinwood, OH. feb 1, 1901-sept 15, 1905 – 2r – 1 – us Western Res [071]

CITIZEN *see* KIMBERLEY CITIZEN

THE CITIZEN – Reno, NV. 1965-66 – 1r – 1 – $50.00 – U04661 – us Library Micro [071]

CITIZEN ADVERTISER – Auburn. N.Y. 1963- – 1 – us UMI [071]

CITIZEN AIRMAN *see* AIR RESERVIST

CITIZEN ALERT – Reno, NV. 1982-1993 – 1r – 1 – $50.00 – U04879 – us Library Micro [071]

THE CITIZEN AND EVENING CHRONICLE – Halifax, Nova Scotia. v11 n284. 4 dec 1886 – 1r – 1 – Can$25.00 – cn Can Microfilming [072]

THE CITIZEN. (CHICAGO CITIZEN) – Chicago. 4 Jan 1890-25 Dec 1897.-w. 8 reels – 1 – uk British Libr Newspaper [071]

CITIZEN DEMOCRAT – Poplar Bluff. Mo. -w. 1933-42, 1947-50, 1952- – 1 – us UMI [071]

CITIZEN GARDEN CITY RECORD AND ADVERTISING JOURNAL – (Also known as: The Gazette (Letchworth and Baldock); Letchworth and Baldock Citizen; Letchworth and Baldock Citizen Gazette) – Sep 22-Nov 24, Dec 1 1906; 1908-10; Jan 14-Dec 29 1911; 1912-Jun 1925; Jul 3-Dec 25 1925; 1926-Dec 25 1931; 1932-38; Jan 6-Jun 30 1939; Jul 7-Dec 29 1939; 1940-Aug 1978; Sep 21 1978-89; Jul 1990-92; Jan 8-Jun 25 1993; Jul 1993-Sep 1994; Oct 7-Dec 23 1994; 1995-Jun 1996; Jul 5-Dec 1996 – 153 1/2r – 1 – uk British Libr Newspaper [072]

THE CITIZEN OF ENGLAND, HIS RIGHTS AND DUTIES / Armitage-Smith, G – London/ Edinburgh, 1895 – 2mf – 9 – $3.00 – LLMC 92-163 – us L.L.M.C. [320]

CITIZEN PATRIOT – Jackson. Mich. and pred. 1912- – 1 – us UMI [071]

CITIZEN TIMES – Honesdale. Pa. 1956-1966 – 1 – us UMI [071]

CITIZEN-JOURNAL – Columbus. Ohio. 1960- – 1 – us UMI [071]

Citizens Alliance of Minneapolis *see* RECORDS

THE CITIZEN'S CLAW – May 1984, sample issue. 8p. A Freedom Movement Newspaper. ed. by S.A. Freeman, Citizens for Constitutional Law – 9 – 1.00f – at Libertarian Micro [335]

CITIZEN'S COUNCIL – Jackson. Miss. -m. 1955-61 – 1 – us UMI [071]

CITIZENS VOICE – Kohima, India. May 1969-1975 – 5r – 1 – us L of C Photodup [072]

CITIZENSHIP AND SALVATION, OR, GREEK AND JEW : A STUDY IN THE PHILOSOPHY OF HISTORY / Lloyd, Alfred Henry – Boston: Little, Brown, 1897 – 1mf – 9 – 0-8370-4296-8 – 1985-2296 – us A.T.L.A. [100]

CITIZENSHIP EDUCATION PROJECT / Columbia University. Teachers College – SE-4919 1. c.1955 – 9 – ne IDC [370]

CITIZENSHIP OF THE UNITED STATES / Dyne, F van – New York, 1904 – 5mf – 1 – ILM-3165/1 – ne IDC [327]

LE CITOYEN – (Cont: L'Asbestos) – Asbestos, Canada. 4 avr 1950-30 dec 1986 – 31r – 1 – Can$65.00r – cn Can Microfilming [072]

LE CITOYEN / ed by Larose, P – Quebec, Canada. 21 jan 1897-v1 n89. 17 mai 1897 – 1r – 1 – Can$30.00 – cn Can Microfilming [072]

LE CITOYEN – Montreal, Canada. 10 sep-18 oct 1844 – 1r – 1 – Can$25.00 – cn Can Microfilming [072]

LE CITOYEN – Northampton, MA. 11 avr 1908 – 1r – 1 – Can$25.00 – cn Can Microfilming [071]

LE CITOYEN – Paris. Journal quotidien politique, industriel et commercial. no. 1-54. 4 mars-29 avr 1870 – 1 – fr A.C.R.P.P. [072]

LE CITOYEN – Paris. no. 1-602. 1er oct 1881-27, mai 1883. mq no. 8-12, 83 – 1 – fr A.C.R.P.P. [072]

LE CITOYEN *see* L'ASBESTOS

LE CITOYEN DU NORD – Montreal, Canada. v1 n2. 6 dec 1929 – 1r – 1 – Can$25.00 – cn Can Microfilming [072]

LE CITOYEN FRANCO-AMERICAIN – Springfield, MA. v6 n12. 10 mar 1892-v7 n43. 30 dec 1893 – 1r – 1 – Can$45.00 – cn Can Microfilming [071]

LA CITOYENNE – Paris. no. 1-165. 13 fevr 1881-90. mq no. 78 – 1 – fr A.C.R.P.P. [072]

Citrine, Walter McLennan *see* I SEARCH FOR TRUTH IN RUSSIA

CITRUS COUNTY CHRONICLE – Inverness. Fl. -w. 1940-1941. 1945- – 1 – us P.K. Yonge [071]

CITRUS GROWER – Orlando, Fl. 1-4. 1938-1942 – 1 – us P.K. Yonge [634]

CITRUS JUICES : TRENDS AND PROSPECTS IN WORLD PRODUCTION AND INTERNATIONAL TRADE – 1989 – 56p – it F.A.O. [338]

IL CITTADINO – New York. Weekly, Italian Jan 14 1915-Aug 28 1919. Incomplete. Not collated – 1 – us NY Public [071]
CITTAVISUDDHIPRAKARANA: SANSKRIT AND TIBETAN TEXTS / ed by Prabhubhai Bhikhabhai Patel – 1 – us U.W. Library [280]
CITY ADVANCE – Elizabeth. N.C. 1905- – 1 – us UMI [071]
THE CITY ADVERTISER AND MONTHLY VISITOR – Montreal: Wilsons and Nolan, [1852-185-?] – 9 – cn C.I.H.M. [971]
CITY ADVOCATE – Lyons. Iowa. 1856-1861; 1866-1873 – 1 – us UMI [071]
CITY AND COUNTRY HOME – (v12 1993 Can$28.00y) – Toronto. v1- 1982/83- – 9 – Can$37.00y – cn Micromedia [640]
CITY AND COUNTY CORK GENERAL ADVERTISER *see* SCRAGGS GENERAL ADVERTISER
CITY AND COUNTY OF SAN DIEGO / Leberthon & Taylor – San Diego, 1888.California Reel 25. (The Cox Library Collection) – 5 – us Americana [978]
THE CITY AND DIOCESE OF LONDON, ONTARIO, CANADA: AN HISTORICAL SKETCH COMPILED IN COMMEMORATION OF THE OPENING OF ST PETER'S CATHEDRAL, LONDON, JUNE 28TH, 1885 / Coffey, John F – London, Ont.: T. Coffey, 1885. 03205. (Pre-1900 Canadiana) – 9 – cn C.I.H.M. [971]
CITY AND STATE – Jan 1985- – 1,5,6,9 – us UMI [073]
"THE CITY BELOW THE HILL": A SOCIOLOGICAL STUDY OF A PORTION OF THE CITY OF MONTREAL, CANADA / Ames, Herbert Brown – Montreal, 1897. 02168. (Pre-1900 Canadiana) – 9 – cn C.I.H.M. [300]
CITY CENTRES OF EARLY CHRISTIANITY / Aytoun, Robert Alexander – London; New York: Hodder and Stoughton, 1915 – 1mf – us A.T.L.A. [720]
CITY CHAMBERLAIN ACCOUNT BOOKS, 1446-1600 / York. England – 1 – uk Microform Academic [941]
CITY CHAMBERLAIN ROLLS, 1396-1600 / York. England – 1 – uk Microform Academic [941]
THE CITY CHURCH AND ITS SOCIAL MISSION : A SERIES OF STUDIES IN THE SOCIAL EXTENSION OF THE CITY CHURCH / Trawick, A M – New York: Association Press, 1913 – 1mf – us A.T.L.A. [240]
CITY CLUB OF CLEVELAND SPEECHES, MS 3517 – Cleveland, Cuyahoga, OH. 6 Nov 1917-25 May 197? – 1 – us Western Res [978]
CITY DIRECTORIES / Columbus. Ohio – 1843-62. There are 2 35mm rolls in this set. Related Guide Book not available – 1 – us Ohio Hist [975]
CITY DIRECTORIES OF THE UNITED STATES – (Segment 1: through 1860. Segment 2: 1861-1881. Segment 3: 1882-1901. Segment 4: 1902-35. Segment 5: 1936-60) – 1,9 – us Primary [978]
CITY DIRECTORIES OF THE UNITED STATES: ALABAMA – 1860-1935 – 1,9 – us Primary [978]
CITY DIRECTORIES OF THE UNITED STATES: ARIZONA – 1902-1935 – 1 – us Primary [978]
CITY DIRECTORIES OF THE UNITED STATES: ARKANSAS – 1861-1935 – 1 – us Primary [978]
CITY DIRECTORIES OF THE UNITED STATES: CALIFORNIA – 1860-1935 – 1,9 – us Primary [978]
CITY DIRECTORIES OF THE UNITED STATES: COLORADO – 1860-1935 – 1,9 – us Primary [978]
CITY DIRECTORIES OF THE UNITED STATES: CONNECTICUT – 1849-1935 – 1,9 – us Primary [978]
CITY DIRECTORIES OF THE UNITED STATES: DELAWARE – 1860-1901 – 1,9 – us Primary [978]
CITY DIRECTORIES OF THE UNITED STATES: DISTRICT OF COLUMBIA – 1822-1935 – 1,9 – us Primary [978]
CITY DIRECTORIES OF THE UNITED STATES: FLORIDA – 1902-35 – 1 – us Primary [978]
CITY DIRECTORIES OF THE UNITED STATES: GEORGIA – 1850-1935 – 1,9 – us Primary [978]
CITY DIRECTORIES OF THE UNITED STATES: HAWAII – 1902-1935 – 1 – us Primary [978]
CITY DIRECTORIES OF THE UNITED STATES: IDAHO – 1902-1935 – 1 – us Primary [978]
CITY DIRECTORIES OF THE UNITED STATES: ILLINOIS – 1847-1935 – 1,9 – us Primary [978]
CITY DIRECTORIES OF THE UNITED STATES: INDIANA – 1858-1935 – 1,9 – us Primary [978]
CITY DIRECTORIES OF THE UNITED STATES: IOWA – 1846-1901 – 1,9 – us Primary [978]
CITY DIRECTORIES OF THE UNITED STATES: KANSAS – 1860-81 – 1,9 – us Primary [978]
CITY DIRECTORIES OF THE UNITED STATES: KENTUCKY – 1859-1901 – 1,9 – us Primary [978]
CITY DIRECTORIES OF THE UNITED STATES: LOUISIANA – 1860-1935 – 1,9 – us Primary [978]
CITY DIRECTORIES OF THE UNITED STATES: MAINE – 1849-1935 – 1,9 – us Primary [978]
CITY DIRECTORIES OF THE UNITED STATES: MARYLAND – 1860-1935 – 1,9 – us Primary [978]
CITY DIRECTORIES OF THE UNITED STATES: MASSACHUSETTS – 1835-1935 – 1,9 – us Primary [978]
CITY DIRECTORIES OF THE UNITED STATES: MICHIGAN – 1838-1935 – 1,9 – us Primary [978]
CITY DIRECTORIES OF THE UNITED STATES: MINNESOTA – 1860-1935 – 1,9 – us Primary [978]
CITY DIRECTORIES OF THE UNITED STATES: MISSISSIPPI – 1860 – 9 – us Primary [978]
CITY DIRECTORIES OF THE UNITED STATES: MISSOURI – 1860-1935 – 9,1 – us Primary [978]
CITY DIRECTORIES OF THE UNITED STATES: MONTANA – 1861-1935 – 1,9 – us Primary [978]
CITY DIRECTORIES OF THE UNITED STATES: NEBRASKA – 1861-1935 – 1 – us Primary [978]
CITY DIRECTORIES OF THE UNITED STATES: NEVADA – 1861-1881 – 1 – us Primary [978]
CITY DIRECTORIES OF THE UNITED STATES: NEW ENGLAND – 1849-1860 – 9 – us Primary [978]
CITY DIRECTORIES OF THE UNITED STATES: NEW HAMPSHIRE – 1849-1935 – 1,9 – us Primary [978]
CITY DIRECTORIES OF THE UNITED STATES: NEW JERSEY – 1850-1935 – 1,9 – us Primary [978]
CITY DIRECTORIES OF THE UNITED STATES: NEW MEXICO – 1902-1935 – 1 – us Primary [978]
CITY DIRECTORIES OF THE UNITED STATES: NEW YORK (STATE) – 1842-1935 – 1,9 – us Primary [978]
CITY DIRECTORIES OF THE UNITED STATES: NORTH CAROLINA – 1902-1935 – 1 – us Primary [978]
CITY DIRECTORIES OF THE UNITED STATES: NORTH DAKOTA – 1902-1935 – 1 – us Primary [978]
CITY DIRECTORIES OF THE UNITED STATES: OHIO – 1860-1935 – 1,9 – us Primary [978]
CITY DIRECTORIES OF THE UNITED STATES: OKLAHOMA – 1902-1935 – 1 – us Primary [978]
CITY DIRECTORIES OF THE UNITED STATES: OREGON – 1861-1935 – 1 – us Primary [978]
CITY DIRECTORIES OF THE UNITED STATES: PENNSYLVANIA – 1860-1935 – 1,9 – us Primary [978]
CITY DIRECTORIES OF THE UNITED STATES: RHODE ISLAND – 1849-1935 – 1,9 – us Primary [978]
CITY DIRECTORIES OF THE UNITED STATES: SOUTH CAROLINA – 1860-1935 – 1,9 – us Primary [978]
CITY DIRECTORIES OF THE UNITED STATES: SOUTH DAKOTA – 1902-35 – 1 – us Primary [978]
CITY DIRECTORIES OF THE UNITED STATES: TENNESSEE – 1860-1935 – 1,9 – us Primary [978]
CITY DIRECTORIES OF THE UNITED STATES: TEXAS – 1860-1935 – 1,9 – us Primary [978]
CITY DIRECTORIES OF THE UNITED STATES: UTAH – 1861-1935 – 1 – us Primary [978]
CITY DIRECTORIES OF THE UNITED STATES: VERMONT – 1849-1935 – 1,9 – us Primary [978]
CITY DIRECTORIES OF THE UNITED STATES: VIRGINIA – 1852-1935 – 1,9 – us Primary [978]
CITY DIRECTORIES OF THE UNITED STATES: WASHINGTON (STATE) – 1861-1935 – 1 – us Primary [978]
CITY DIRECTORIES OF THE UNITED STATES: WEST VIRGINIA – 1860 – 9 – us Primary [978]
CITY DIRECTORIES OF THE UNITED STATES: WISCONSIN – 1857-1935 – 1,9 – us Primary [978]
CITY DIRECTORIES OF THE UNITED STATES: WYOMING – 1902-35 – 1 – us Primary [978]
CITY DIRECTORY / Barberton. Ohio – 1928. 1 reel – 1 – us Ohio Hist [978]
CITY DIRECTORY – Ottawa, 1861-1960 – 38r – 1 – cn Preston [971]
CITY ENTERPRISE – McComb. Miss. 1889-1915; 1917; 1919-1922 – 1 – us UMI [071]
THE CITY ENTERPRISE – Hamilton [Ont]: R Theophilus, [1864] – 9 – cn C.I.H.M. [971]
CITY GAZETTE – Charleston. South Carolina. Jan 3-Dec 31 1789 – 1 – us NY Public [071]
CITY GAZETTE AND DAILY ADVERTISER – Charleston, 1789 – 1r – 1 – us Ross [071]
CITY JOURNAL – Canyon City, OR. -w. 1 Jan 1869, 28 June 1869. 1 roll – 1 – us U.O. Library [071]
THE CITY LIFE – Montreal: The City Life Pub. Co., [1879?-187- or 188-] – 9 – cn C.I.H.M. [971]
THE CITY LIFE – Montreal. v1 n1. 9 apr 1879 – 1r – 1 – Can$25.00 – cn Can Microfilming [072]
CITY LIGHTS – (Lacking August 1935 issue v1, no 10) – Toronto, v1-2, no 2, Nov 1934-Dec 1935 – 1 reel – 1 – Can$85.00 – cn McLaren [790]
CITY MAGAZINE – Winnipeg. v1- 1974- – 9 – Can$20.00y – cn Micromedia [073]
THE CITY MAGAZINE – Montreal: Printed for the Proprietors by J W Harrison [1847-18–?] – 9 – cn C.I.H.M. [910]
CITY NEWS – Holland. Mich. 1872- – 1 – us UMI [071]
CITY NEWS – Los Angeles, CA. 1972-1975 – 1r – 1 – $50.00 – H03285 – us Library Micro [071]
THE CITY OF AKHENATEN (MEES VOL 38) : PART 1: EXCAVATIONS OF 1921 AND 1922 AT EL-'AMARNEH / Peet, T E & Woolley, C L – London, 1921 – 14mf – 8 – Dfl49.00 – ne Slangenburg [930]
THE CITY OF BENIN / Egharevba, Jacob U – [Benin City: s.n, 1952?] – 1 – us Res Libr [960]
CITY OF BRISTOL, NEWPORT AND WELCH TOWNS DIRECTORY / Edward Hunt & Co. Bristol, England – London, 1848. 1v – 1 – us U.W. Library [941]
CITY OF CHELSEA GAZETTE – 1929 – 1 – at Corangamite [980]
CITY OF CHELSEA NEWS – 1929-1930 – 1mf – 9 – at Corangamite [980]
CITY OF DECATUR AND MACON COUNTY / Nelson, William E – Chicago: Pioneer Publ. Co., 1910. Vols. 1-2. Illinois Reel 41. (The Cox Library Collection) – 5 – us Americana [978]
THE CITY OF DETROIT, MICHIGAN 1701-1922 / Burton, Clarence Monroe – Chicago: S. J. Clarke Publ. Co., 1922. Vol. 1. Michigan Reel 23; Vols. 2-4. Michigan Reel 24. (The Cox Library Collection) – 5 – us Americana [978]
THE CITY OF DREADFUL NIGHT : AND OTHER POEMS / Thomson, James – London: Reeves and Turner, 1880 – 1 roll – 1 – 1-55879-558-8 – uk Libr Preservation [810]
City of Edinburgh Charity Organisation Society *see* REPORT ON THE PHYSICAL CONDITION OF FOURTEEN HUNDRED SCHOOL CHILDREN IN THE CITY, TOGETHER WITH SOME ACCOUNT OF THEIR HOMES AND SURROUNDINGS
THE CITY OF GRAND RAPIDS AND KENT COUNTY / A.W. Bowen and Co – Biographical sketches. Chicago, 1900. Michigan Reel 15. The Cox Library Collection – 5 – us Americana [978]
CITY OF HOPE NATIONAL MEDICAL CENTER PILOT – (Missing: Spr.-Sum. 1962, Spr. 1963, 1964-1969, Wint. 1969/70, Spr. 1970, Fall 1973, Wint. 1973/4, Fall 1974-Fall 1975, Wint. 1979-1980, Sum. 1980, Spr.-Sum. 1981, Fall 1982-Sum. 1984, Spr.-Sum. 1985) – (Los Angeles, CA) Winter 1962-Winter 1985 – us A.J.P.C. [073]
CITY OF HOPE REPORTER – Los Angeles, CA.Jan-Feb 1959; Jan 1960 – 1 – us A.J.P.C. [071]
CITY OF LONDON, ONTARIO, CANADA: THE PIONEER PERIOD AND THE LONDON OF TODAY / Bremner, Archie – London, Ont.: London Print. and Lithographing, 1897. 00260. (Pre-1900 Canadiana) – 9 – cn C.I.H.M. [971]
City of London Polytechnic *see* FAWCETT LIBRARY ON WOMEN'S STUDIES
CITY OF OTTAWA: CAPITAL OF THE DOMINION OF CANADA – Ottawa: Ottawa Free Press, 1899. 03044. (Pre-1900 Canadiana) – 9 – cn C.I.H.M. [971]
CITY OF SAN DIEGO AND SAN DIEGO COUNTY / McGrew, Clarence A – Chicago: American Historical Society, 1922. 2v.California Reel 26. (The Cox Library Collection) – 5 – us Americana [978]
CITY OF SAN FRANCISCO : FINANCIAL RECORDS – San Francisco, 1849-50 – 1r – 1 – $50.00 – B40304 – us Library Micro [978]
CITY OF SPOKANE AND SPOKANE COUNTY / Durham, N W – Spokane: S.J. Clarke Publ. Co., 1912. v1-3. Washington reel 6.(Cox Library Collection) – 5 – us Americana [978]
THE CITY OF THREE RIVERS AS A SEA-PORT: AND HER NET-WORK OF RAIL-ROADS / Balcer, Georges – 1880. 02483. (Pre-1900 Canadiana) – 9 – cn C.I.H.M. [910]
CITY OF VICTORIA AND SUBURBAN DIRECTORY : COMPRISING AN IMPROVED STREET AND AVENUE GUIDE, AND A CLASSIFIED BUSINESS DIRECTORY – Victoria, B.C.: Henderson Publishing Co, 1905 – 1r – 1 – cn U.B.C. Preserve [910]
CITY OF VICTORIA AND SUBURBAN DIRECTORY FOR 1908 : COMPRISING STREET DIRECTORY OF THE CITY, AN ALPHABETICALLY ARRANGED LIST OF BUSINESS FIRMS AND COMPANIES, PROFESSIONAL MEN AND PRIVATE CITIZENS AND A CLASSIFIED BUSINESS DIRECTORY – Victoria, B.C.: Henderson Publishing Co, 1908 – 1r – 1 – cn U.B.C. Preserve [910]
CITY OF WASHINGTON GAZETTE – Washington, DC. 1817-20 – 1,3 – us Readex [071]
CITY OF WATSONVILLE DIRECTORIES – Santa Cruz Co, CA. 1873; 1912-13; 1922; 1925-28; 1936-40 – 10r – 1 – $500.00 – D096 – us Library Micro [978]
THE CITY ON THE HILL – Santa Cruz, CA: UC Santa Cruz Press, Sept 1966-Jun 1986 – 10r – 1 – $500.00 – B02950 – us Library Micro [370]
CITY PLAT MAPS / Lucas County. Ohio. Toledo, City Planning Commission – 1979 – 2r – 1 – $32.50r – us Archival [324]
CITY POEMS / Smith, Alexander – Cambridge: Macmillan and Co., 1857 – 1 roll – 1 – 1-55879-337-2 – uk Libr Preservation [810]
CITY PRESS – London, UK. 8 Jul 1857-31 May 1976. -w. 140 reels – 1 – uk British Libr Newspaper [072]
CITY PRESS – Otay, CA. 1888-1900 – 1r – 1 – $50.00 – C02581 – us Library Micro [071]
CITY SMOKE SIGNALS – 1968-79. (American Indian Periodicals in the Princeton University Library). 8 fiches – 9 – $45.00 – us UPA [305]
CITY STAR – Blantyre, [Malawi]: G E Publ, apr 16/23 1993 – 1r – us Res Libr [072]
CITY TAX ROLL – San Jose, CA. 1853 – 1r – 1 – $50.00 – B50005 – us Library Micro [978]
CITY TIMES – Akron. Ohio. 1869-92 – 1 – us UMI [071]
CITY TIMES – Auburn. R.I. 1895-1927 – 1 – us UMI [071]
CITY TIMES – Zanesville. Ohio. 1855-1860 – 1 – us UMI [071]
CITY WEEKLY – (See also: Nation's Cities Weekly) – v1. 1978 – 1 – us UMI [073]
THE CITY-STATE OF THE GREEKS AND ROMANS : A SURVEY INTRODUCTORY TO THE STUDY OF ANCIENT HISTORY / Fowler, William Warde – London; New York: Macmillan, 1893 – 1mf – us A.T.L.A. [930]

LA CIUDAD DE DIOS, REVISTA QUINCENAL RELIGIOSA, CIENTIFICA Y LITERARIA DEDICADA AL GRAN PADRE SAN AGUSTIN – v. 1-153. Jun 1881-Aug 1936. v. 6, no. 1; v. 9, no. 3; v. 18; v. 117 wanting – 1 – 897.00 – us L of C Photodup [073]

CIUDADANIA Y NACIONALIZACION / Gomez, C F – Buenos Aires, 1913 – 2mf – 1 – ILM-3570/1 – ne IDC [327]

CIUDADANIA Y NATURALIZACION / Arbo, H – Buenos Aires, 1926 – 2mf – 9 – ILM-3170/1 – ne IDC [340]

CIVIC – v24-30, 1972-78.Continued by: Civic Public Work – 1 – us UMI [073]

CIVIC ADMINISTRATION – v1-23, Apr 1949-1971. Continued by: Civic – 1 – us UMI [073]

CIVIC AFFAIRS – (1963-79 Can$73.00. Ceased 1983) – Toronto, 1963-83 – 9 – Can$20.00y – cn Micromedia [350]

CIVIC CENTER NEWS – Los Angeles, CA. 1978-1981 – 2r – 1 – $100.00 – R04055 – us Library Micro [071]

CIVIC PUBLIC WORKS – (v.31- Jan 1979-5,6,9) – v.30- May 1978- – 1 – us UMI [073]

THE CIVIC REPORTER AND OAKLAND REVIEW – Oakland, CA. 1916 – 1r – 1 – $50.00 – B05043 – us Library Micro [071]

CIVIC TRAINING IN SOVIET RUSSIA / Harper, Samuel Northrup – Chicago: The University of Chicago Press, 1929. xvii,401p. (Studies in the Making of Citizens) – 1 – us U.W. Library [947]

Civica Biblioteca Berio. Genoa *see* CATALOGO DELLA RACCOLTA COLOMBIANA

CIVIC/PUBLIC WORKS – (v21-47 1969-47 9) – Toronto. v1-47. 1948-95 – 5,9 – Price varies – cn Micromedia [350]

CIVIL AERONAUTICS ADMINISTRATION ANNUAL REPORTS / U.S. Civil Aeronautics Board – (Cont by: Civil Aeronautics Board Annual Reports) – 1940-42 (all publ) – 3mf – 9 – $4.50 – LLMC 81-202 – us L.L.M.C. [324]

CIVIL AERONAUTICS ADMINISTRATION ANNUAL REPORTS *see* CIVIL AERONAUTICS AUTHORITY ANNUAL REPORTS

CIVIL AERONAUTICS AUTHORITY ANNUAL REPORTS / U.S. Civil Aeronautics Board – (Cont by: Civil Aeronautics Administration Annual Reports) – 1939-40 (all publ) – 2mf – 9 – $3.00 – LLMC 81-203 – us L.L.M.C. [324]

CIVIL AERONAUTICS AUTHORITY'S AIR COMMERCE BULLETIN *see* CIVIL AERONAUTICS JOURNAL

CIVIL AERONAUTICS BOARD ANNUAL REPORTS / U.S. Civil Aeronautics Board – (Lacking: 1979-80) – 1941-83 (all publ) – 67mf – 9 – $100.00 – LLMC 81-204 – us L.L.M.C. [324]

CIVIL AERONAUTICS BOARD ANNUAL REPORTS *see* CIVIL AERONAUTICS ADMINISTRATION ANNUAL REPORTS

CIVIL AERONAUTICS BOARD REPORTS – v1-75 – 838mf – 9 – $1,257.00 – LLMC 78-204 – us L.L.M.C. [380]

CIVIL AERONAUTICS BOARD REPORTS *see*
- CIVIL AERONAUTICS ADMINISTRATION ANNUAL REPORTS
- CIVIL AERONAUTICS AUTHORITY ANNUAL REPORTS
- CIVIL AERONAUTICS BOARD ANNUAL REPORTS

CIVIL AERONAUTICS JOURNAL – (Cont: Civil Aeronautics Authority's Air Commerce Bulletin) – v1-13 no 7 – 31mf – 9 – $46.50 – LLMC 81-201 – us L.L.M.C. [380]

CIVIL AFFAIRS AND MILITARY GOVERNMENT IN THE MEDITERRANEAN THEATER / U.S. Army. Office of Military History – v. 1. 1948? – 5 – 28.00 – us L of C Photodup [945]

CIVIL AND CRIMINAL CODES OF PRACTICE OF KENTUCKY; REV. AND COR. TO JULY 1, 1908 / Kentucky. Laws, Statutes, etc – Pocket ed. Lexington: Hughes 1908. 481p. LL-936 – 1 – us L of C Photodup [340]

CIVIL AND CRIMINAL DOCKETS / Paulding County, Ohio. Crane Township. Justice of the Peace – 1869-1955 – 4r – 1 – us Archival [324]

CIVIL AND CRIMINAL DOCKETS / Paulding County. Ohio. Crane Township. Justice of the Peace – 1869-1955 – 4r – 1 – $32.50r – us Archival [324]

CIVIL AND MECHANICAL ENGINEERING DESIGNS / Smeaton, John – 1 – uk Microform Academic [621]

CIVIL AND MILITARY GAZETTE – Lahore, Pakistan. May 1876-Dec 1931. 629 reels – 1 – uk British Libr Newspaper [072]

THE CIVIL AND NATURAL HISTORY OF JAMAICA / Browne, P – Ed. 2. London. 1789. B-2600 2 – 8 – ne IDC [910]

THE CIVIL AND NATURAL HISTORY OF JAMAICA / Browne, P – London. 1756. B-1272 2 – 8 – ne IDC [910]

THE CIVIL AND PENAL CODES OF THE TERRITORY OF GUAM, 1953 / Bohn, John A – Agana: Office of the Sec of the Gov of Guam, 1953 – 10mf – 9 – $15.00 – LLMC 82-100B Title 3 – us L.L.M.C. [324]

THE CIVIL CODE / Field, David Dudley – New York, 1886. 10p. LL-676 – 1 – us L of C Photodup [340]

THE CIVIL CODE IN FORCE IN CUBA, PORTO RICO, AND THE PHILIPPINES, 1899 – Washington: GPO, 1899 – 4mf – 9 – $6.00 – LLMC 92-305 – us L.L.M.C. [324]

THE CIVIL CODE OF GUAM, 1933 : APPROVED BY THE NAVAL GOVERNMENT OF GUAM MAY 1 1933, EFFECTIVE FEBRUARY 1 1934 IN 4 DIVISIONS / Robinson, Stephen B – Govt House, 28 Dec 1933 – 8mf – 9 – $12.00 – LLMC 82-100B Title 1 – us L.L.M.C. [324]

THE CIVIL CODE OF GUAM, 1947 : IN 4 DIVISIONS / Guam. (Commonwealth). Laws, Statutes, etc – Washington: GPO, 1947 – 4mf – 9 – $6.00 – LLMC 82-100B Title 9 – us L.L.M.C. [324]

THE CIVIL CODE OF LOUISIANA AS A DEMOCRATIC INSTITUTION / Fenner, Charles Erasmus – New Orleans? n.d. 19p. LL-656 – 1 – us L of C Photodup [340]

THE CIVIL CODE OF THE REPUBLIC OF PANAMA AND AMENDATORY LAWS CONTINUED IN FORCE IN THE CANAL ZONE, ISTHMUS OF PANAMA, BY EXECUTIVE ORDER OF MAY 9 1904 / Panama Canal Zone – (Also contains decree no 4 Nov 4 1903 of the Junta of the Provisional Government of the Republic, and a historical introduction to the development of the Panamanian Civil Law) – Washington: Isthmanian Canal Commission, 1905 – 8mf – 9 – $12.00 – LLMC 82-100D Title 1 – us L.L.M.C. [340]

THE CIVIL CODE OF THE TERRITORY OF GUAM, 1970 / Bohn, John A – (With 1974 suppl) – Agana: n.p. 2v. 1970 – 13mf – 9 – $19.50 – LLMC 82-100B Title 4 – us L.L.M.C. [324]

CIVIL DEFENSE DURING WORLD WAR 2 PAMPHLET COLLECTION – 1933-1944 – 1 – CSUXANN2525-B – us Hoover Inst Photo [355]

CIVIL DISTURBANCE, CHARTISM AND RIOTS IN NINETEENTH CENTURY ENGLAND / Great Britain. Home Office – (Part 2: Disturbance Papers, 1847-76) – (PRO Class H045). Part 1: Disturbance Papers, 1841-44 – 1 – us Primary [941]

CIVIL DISTURBANCES / Mullik, B N – (Filmed with: Dutt, Surendra Nath. The life of Benoyendra Nath Sen) – Delhi: Manager of Publ, 1966 – us Res Libr [303]

CIVIL DOCKET / Erie County. Ohio. Kelley's Island Twp Justice of the Peace – 1876-1907 – 1r – 1 – $32.50r – us Archival [324]

CIVIL DOCKET / Wood County. Ohio. Freedom Township. Justice of the Peace – 1847-1851 – 1r – 1 – $32.50r – us Archival [324]

CIVIL DOCKETS / Fulton County. Ohio. Swan Creek Township. Justice of the Peace – 1889-1931 – 2r – 1 – $32.50r – us Archival [324]

CIVIL DOCKETS / Ottawa County. Ohio. Carroll Township. Justice of the Peace – 1839-1937 – 2r – 1 – $32.50r – us Archival [324]

CIVIL DOCKETS / Seneca County. Ohio. Liberty Township. Justice of the Peace – 1842-1879 – 1r – 1 – $32.50r – us Archival [324]

CIVIL DOCKETS / Wyandot County. Ohio. Probate Court – 1892-1926 – 2r – 1 – $32.50r – us Archival [324]

CIVIL DOCKETS (INDEXED) / Ottawa County. Ohio. Carroll Township. Justice of the Peace – 1862-1876 – 1r – 1 – $32.50r – us Archival [324]

CIVIL ENGINEER IN SOUTH AFRICA – (5,6,9 v17- 1975-) – v1- 1959- – 1 – us UMI [624]

CIVIL ENGINEERING – (5,6 v35- ; 9 v43-) – v1- 1930- – 1 – us UMI [624]

CIVIL ENGINEERING – (5,6,9 v72-) – v69-1974- . Continues: Civil Engineering and Public Works Review – 1 – us UMI [624]

CIVIL ENGINEERING AND PUBLIC WORKS REVIEW – 1945-59 – 1 – uk Microform Academic [624]

CIVIL ENGINEERING AND PUBLIC WORKS REVIEW – (Continued as: Civil Engineering) – v1-68 1906-73 – 1 – us UMI [624]

CIVIL ENGINEERING DATA SERVICE (CED) – (Updated Every 60 Days) – Information Handling Services – 5 – us Info Handling [624]

CIVIL ENGINEERING SYSTEMS / ed by Brown, C B & Jowitt, P W – 9,5,1 – us Gordon [624]

CIVIL GOVERNMENT IN THE UNITED STATES : CONSIDERED WITH SOME REFERENCE TO ITS ORIGINS / Fiske, John – Boston/New York/Chicago: Houghton, Mifflin, 1890 – 5mf – 9 – $7.50 – LLMC 95-079 – us L.L.M.C. [323]

CIVIL LAW 1 : FRANCE: A BASIC COLLECTION / ed by Combe, David A & Reynolds, Thomas H – (Individual titles of coll not listed. Free catalog available on request. Full cataloguing as a major microform collection available from OCLC) – Source materials from Berkeley and Tulane libraries and others. Complete index – 165 titles 8451mf – 9 – $12,676.00 – LLMC 82-300 – us L.L.M.C. [340]

CIVIL LAW 1 : FRANCE: A BASIC COLLECTION – initial ed. Honolulu, 1988 – 1mf – 9 – LLMC 86-000A – us L.L.M.C. [340]

CIVIL LAW 1 : FRANCE: A BASIC COLLECTION – permanent ed. Kaneohe, 1996 – 1mf – 9 – LLMC 86-000B – us L.L.M.C. [340]

CIVIL LAW 2 : ITALY, SPAIN, PORTUGAL AND THE LOW COUNTRIES: A BASIC COLLECTION – initial ed. Honolulu, 1991 – 1mf – 9 – LLMC 86-001A – us L.L.M.C. [340]

CIVIL LAW 2 : ITALY, SPAIN, PORTUGAL AND THE LOW COUNTRIES: A BASIC COLLECTION – permanent ed. Kaneohe, 1996 – 1mf – 9 – LLMC 86-001B – us L.L.M.C. [340]

CIVIL LAW 2 : ITALY, SPAIN, PORTUGAL AND THE LOW COUNTRIES: A BASIC COLLECTION / ed by Reynolds, Thomas H – (Titles in coll not listed individually. Free catalog available on request. Full cataloguing as a major microform collection available from OCLC) – Civil Law and Codification in Spain and Its Empire, Italy, Portugal and the Low Countries. From the foreign law collections of the Uni of California at Berkeley – 95 titles 3294mf – 9 – $4,941.00 – LLMC 82-300B – us L.L.M.C. [340]

CIVIL LAW 3 / ed by Reynolds, Thomas H – (Will be publ Feb 1998. Total fiche count and final price not yet known. Full catalog will be available on request. Full OCLC cataloguing will also be available) – Civil law development in Germany, Austria and Switzerland. From the collections of the U.C. Berkeley Law Library – 9 – LLMC 82-300C – us L.L.M.C. [340]

Civil law sub-group of the Legal Studies group of the National Scientific Committee *see* HOI VA DAP VE HOP-DONG KINH TE

CIVIL LIBERTIES – London, UK: The National Council for Civil Liberties. v1 1937-1970 (all publ) – 21mf – 9 – $31.50 – LLMC 84-437 – us L.L.M.C. [073]

CIVIL LIBERTIES – New York, NY. 1980-81 nos 331-340 – 3r – 1 – $150.00 – R04906 – us Library Micro [071]

CIVIL LIBERTIES AND POLICE – Berlin. 38 docs. 1980-1991 – 45mf – 9 – ne IDC [320]

CIVIL LIST AND CONSTITUTIONAL HISTORY OF THE COLONY AND STATE OF NEW YORK / Hutchins, Stephen C – Albany: Weed, Parsons and Co., 1882. New York Reel 1. (The Cox Library Collection) – 5 – us Americana [978]

CIVIL LIST AND FORMS OF GOVERNMENT OF THE COLONY AND STATE OF NEW YORK – 1879. New York Reel 1. (The Cox Library Collection) – 5 – us Americana [978]

CIVIL REGULATIONS WITH THE FORCE AND EFFECT OF LAW IN GUAM, 1947 / Guam. (Commonwealth) – Washington: GPO, 1947 – 2mf – 9 – $3.00 – LLMC 82-100B Title 10 – us L.L.M.C. [324]

CIVIL RIGHTS – Cape Town, Civil Rights League. [4-15] 1957-1968; v16 n5 jun 1969; v17 n8 sep 1970 – us Res Libr [320]

CIVIL RIGHTS DIGEST / U.S. Commission on Civil Rights – (v1-11 titled: Civil Rights Digest. After v11: New Perspectives: Civil Rights Quarterly) – v1-18 no 1. 1968-86 – 56mf – 9 – $84.00 – LLMC 81-206 – us L.L.M.C. [340]

CIVIL RIGHTS DIGEST *see*
- CIVIL RIGHTS DIGEST
- NEW PERSPECTIVES

CIVIL RIGHTS DURING THE JOHNSON ADMINISTRATION – (Part 2. Equal Employment Opportunity Commission Administrative History. Printed guide. ISBN: 0-89093-691-9. $330.00; Part 3. Oral Histories. Printed guide. ISBN: 0-89093-692-7. $330.00) – 1963-69. Part 1. White House Central Files and Aides Files. Printed guide. ISBN: 0-89093-690-0 – 1 – $1,655.00 – us UPA [360]

CIVIL RIGHTS DURING THE JOHNSON ADMINISTRATION – Part 4. Papers of the White House Conference on Civil Rights. 20 reels with printed guide – 1 – $2,200.00 – us UPA [360]

CIVIL RIGHTS DURING THE JOHNSON ADMINISTRATION – Part 5. Records of the National Advisory Commission on Civil Disorders (Kerner Commission). 28 reels with printed guide – 1 – $3,080.00 – 0-89093-903-9 – us UPA [360]

CIVIL RIGHTS DURING THE KENNEDY ADMINISTRATION – (Part 1: The White House Central Files and Staff Files and the President's Office Files. 19 reels. ISBN 0-89093-900-4. $2,090.00; Part 2: The Papers of Burke Marshall, Assistant Attorney General for Civil Rights. 28 reels. ISBN 0-89093-364-2. $3,080.00) – 1 – $4,910.00 set – us UPA [360]

CIVIL RIGHTS DURING THE NIXON ADMINISTRATION, 1969-1974, PART 1 : THE WHITE HOUSE CENTRAL FILES – 9 – $5,225.00 – 1-55655-133-9 – us UPA [320]

CIVIL RIGHTS ISSUES OF EURO-ETHNIC AMERICANS IN THE U.S. : OPPORTUNITIES AND CHALLENGES / U.S. Commission on Civil Rights – Washington: GPO, 1980. LLMC 94-332 – 7mf – 9 – $10.50 – us L.L.M.C. [320]

CIVIL RIGHTS LEAGUE – Cape Town. 76 docs. 1980-1991 – 12mf – 9 – ne IDC [320]

Civil Rights League. Cape Town *see* ANNUAL REPORT

CIVIL RIGHTS MOVEMENT OF SRI LANKA – Colombo. 136 docs. 1980-1991 – 17mf – 9 – ne IDC [320]

CIVIL SERVICE EXAMINATIONS / India – v. 60. P.P. 1894. Paper C 7378. BI-517 2 – 8 – ne IDC [324]

CIVIL SERVICE JOURNAL – Perth, Australia. -m. May 1914-Dec 1921. 2 reels – 1 – uk British Libr Newspaper [073]

CIVIL SERVICE NEWS; THE PUBLIC EMPLOYES' WEEKLY – v. 6, no. 10-v. 11, no. 36. 8 Jan 1914-23 Oct 1919. (Wanting scattered numbers) – 1 – 38.00 – us L of C Photodup [350]

THE CIVIL SERVICE REVIEW – Ottawa: Paynter, [1893-189- or 19–] – 9 – cn C.I.H.M. [350]

CIVIL WAR ARMY NURSES' SCRAPBOOK / North, Mary – 1925 – 1 – 18.00 – us L of C Photodup [976]

CIVIL WAR BAND BOOKS / U.S. Army. Brigade, 1st Division, 3rd Band – 1st Brigade Band of Brodhead, Wisconsin (3rd Division, 15th Army Corps). 1864-65. 12 mss – 1 – us U.W. Library [780]

CIVIL WAR BATTLES AND CAMPAIGNS – (Individual titles listed and may be acquired separately) – 3pts ca 2,051mf – 9 – ca $12,180.00 coll – us UPA [976]

CIVIL WAR BATTLES AND CAMPAIGNS, PART 1 : EASTERN THEATER: OFFICIAL HISTORIES AND PERSONAL NARRATIVES – (With printed guide) – 1995 – 801mf – 9 – $5,005.00 – 1-55655-589-X – us UPA [976]

CIVIL WAR BATTLES AND CAMPAIGNS, PART 2 : WESTERN THEATER: OFFICIAL HISTORIES AND PERSONAL NARRATIVES – (With printed guide) – 1996 – ca 500mf – 9 – ca $3,125.00 – 1-55655-590-3 – us UPA [976]

CIVIL WAR BATTLES AND CAMPAIGNS, PART 3 : GENERAL REFERENCES AND COLLECTED WORKS – (With printed guide) – 1996 – ca 750mf – ca $4,690.00 – 1-55655-591-1 – us UPA [976]

CIVIL WAR BOUNTIES / Wood County. Ohio. Auditor – 1864-1865 – 1r – 1 – $32.50r – us Archival [324]

CIVIL WAR BOUNTIES AND PAPERS / Williams County. Ohio. Auditor – 1859-1892 – 10r – 1 – $32.50r – us Archival [324]

CIVIL WAR BOUNTY RECORD / Ottawa County. Ohio. Auditor – 1864 – 1r – 1 – $32.50r – us Archival [324]

CIVIL WAR BOUNTY RECORD / Van Wert County. Ohio. Pleasant Township. Township Clerk – 1863-1877 – 1r – 1 – $32.50r – us Archival [324]

CIVIL WAR CORRESPONDENCE / Alexander, Isaac & Alexander, Rebecca – 1854-1890 – 1r – 1 – $32.50r – us Archival [976]

CIVIL WAR CORRESPONDENCE, DIARIES, AND JOURNALS – Massachusetts Historical Society – 29r – 1 – us UMI [976]

CIVIL WAR CORRESPONDENCE, DIARIES, AND JOURNALS AT THE MASSACHUSETTS HISTORICAL SOCIETY – (30,000p of material by 29 soldiers of Massachusetts military units) – Massachusetts Historical Society – 29r – 1 – $2150.00 – us UMI [976]

CIVIL WAR DIARY / Beck, Aaron N – 1861-64 – 1 – us KS Hist [920]

CIVIL WAR DIRECT TAX ASSESSMENT LISTS: TENNESSEE / Confederate States of America – 6rolls. – 1 – T227 – us Nat'l Archives [324]

CIVIL WAR DRAWINGS BY EDWIN FORBES / U.S. Library of Congress. Prints and Photographs Division – 322 pencil drawings and 15 oil paintings. 1 reel. P&P11950 – 1 – $23.00r – us L of C Photodup [976]

CIVIL WAR HISTORY – (v17- . 5,6. v21- . 9) – v. 1- 1955- – 1 – us UMI [976]

CIVIL WAR IN CHINA, 1945-1950 / U.S. Office of the Chief of Military History – v. 1-2 – 1 – 29.00 – us L of C Photodup [950]

THE CIVIL WAR IN SPAIN / Morrow, Felix – N.Y., 1936. Fiche W 1064. (Blodgett Collection of Spanish Civil War Pamphlets) – 9 – us H.U. College Libr [946]

CIVIL WAR LETTERS / Flanders, George E – 1861-64 – 1 – us KS Hist [976]

CIVIL WAR LETTERS / Fleischer, George W – 1861-65 – 1 – us KS Hist [976]

CIVIL WAR LETTERS / Searles Family (Rachel Stanton Papers) – 1856-1905 – 1r – 1 – $32.50r – us Archival [976]

CIVIL WAR LETTERS / Wakefield, Amor William – 20 May 1861-5 Aug 1864 – 1 – us KS Hist [978]

CIVIL WAR LETTERS / Weddell Family – 1862-1864 – 1r – 1 – $32.50r – us Archival [920]

CIVIL WAR RAILROAD ALBUM / U.S. Library of Congress. Prints and Photographs Division – Produced by U.S. Military Railroad Department in 1862-63. 82 Photoprints. 1 reel. P&P9209 – 1 – 23.00r – us L of C Photodup [080]

CIVIL WAR TIMES ILLUSTRATED – v.1-. Apr 1962- – 1,5,6,9 – us UMI [073]

CIVIL WAR UNIT HISTORIES: REGIMENTAL HISTORIES AND PERSONAL NARRATIVES : PART 2: THE UNION – NEW ENGLAND – (Connecticut 246mf $2,035.00. Maine 248mf $2,050.00. Massachusetts 807mf $6,670.00. New Hampshire 251mf $2,075.00. Rhode Island 218mf $1,800.00. Vermont 129mf $1,065.00. Printed guide ISBN 1-55655-259-9 $175.00 (not included with indiv. States)) – 1,899mf – 9 – $11,775 – 1-55655-258-0 – us UPA [976]

CIVIL WAR UNIT HISTORIES: REGIMENTAL HISTORIES AND PERSONAL NARRATIVES : PART 3: THE UNION – MID-ATLANTIC – (Delaware 11mf $90.00. District of Columbia 12mf $100.00. New Jersey 162mf $1,340.00. New York 1630mf $13,475.00. Pennsylvania 762mf $6,300.00. West Virginia 54mf $445.00. Printed guide ISBN 1-55655-387-0 $175.00 (not included with indiv. states)) – 2,631mf – 9 – $16,310.00 – 1-55655-386-2 – us UPA [976]

CIVIL WAR UNIT HISTORIES: REGIMENTAL HISTORIES AND PERSONAL NARRATIVES : PART 4: THE UNION – MIDWEST AND WEST – (Illinois 553mf $4,570.00. Indiana 372mf $3,075.00. Iowa 397mf $3,190.00. Kansas 62mf $530.00. Michigan 323mf $2,670.00. Minnesota 89mf $735.00. Ohio 670mf $5,540.00. Wisconsin 338mf $2,795.00. West 89mf $735.00. Printed guide ISBN 1-55655-441-9 $175.00 (not included with indiv. states)) – 2,893mf – 9 – $17,935.00 – 1-55655-440-0 – us UPA [976]

CIVIL WAR UNIT HISTORIES: REGIMENTAL HISTORIES AND PERSONAL NARRATIVES : PART 5: THE UNION – HIGHER AND INDEPENDENT COMMANDS AND NAVAL FORCES – (Printed guide only ISBN 1-55655-451-6 $175.00) – 1995 – 971mf – 9 – $5,995.00 – 1-55655-450-8 – us UPA [976]

CIVIL WAR UNIT HISTORIES; REGIMENTAL HISTORIES AND PERSONAL NARRATIVES : PART 1: THE CONFEDERATE STATES OF AMERICA AND BORDER STATES – (Alabama 84mf $695.00. Arkansas 13mf $105.00. Florida 16mf $130.00. Georgia 150mf $1,240.00. Kentucky 155mf $1,280.00. Louisiana 94mf $775.00. Maryland 83mf $685.00. Mississippi 55mf $455.00. Missouri 113mf $1,100.00. North Carolina 142mf $1,175.00. South Carolina 123mf $1,015.00. Tennessee 126mf. $1,040.00. Texas 92mf $760.00. Virginia 333mf $2,755.00. Higher and Independent Commands and Naval Forces 338mf $2,795.00. Printed guide only (not included with indiv. states) ISBN 1-55655-257-2 $175.00) – 1,937mf – 9 – $12,010.00 – 1-55655-216-5 – us UPA [976]

CIVILIAN ADMINISTRATION IN THE OCCUPIED WEST BANK – 1982 – sz I.C.J. [320]

THE CIVILIAN CONSERVATION CORPS : WHAT IT IS AND WHAT IT DOES – Washington, DC: Civilian Conservation Corps, Office of the Director 1939 – us Res Libr [060]

THE CIVILIAN CONSERVATION CORPS AND COLORED YOUTH / Brown, Edgar G – Washington, DC: Office of the Director, 1939 – us Res Libr [060]

CIVILIAN CONSERVATION CORPS BIBLIOGRAPHY : A LIST OF REFERENCES ON THE UNITED STATES CIVILIAN CONSERVATION CORPS 102=CIVILIAN CONSERVATION CORPS. OFFICE OF THE DIRECTOR – Washington, DC: [GPO], 1939 – us Res Libr [060]

CIVILIAN CONSERVATION CORPS CAMP PAPERS – Chicago, IL: Filmed by Mid-Atlantic Preservation Service for The Center for Research Libraries, 1989-1991 – 306r 7694mf – 1,9 – us Res Libr [060]

CIVILIAN CONSERVATION CORPS EDUCATIONAL ACTIVITIES – [Spokane, Washington?: s.n.] 1937 – us Res Libr [060]

CIVILIAN RELIEF DURING WORLD WAR 1 PAMPHLET COLLECTION – 1915-1920 – 1 – CSUXANL3616-B – us Hoover Inst Photo [355]

CIVILIAN WORK TOWARDS THE WAR EFFORT DURING WORLD WAR 1 PAMPHLET COLLECTION – 1914-1918 – 1 – CSUXANM5014-B – us Hoover Inst Photo [355]

DER CIVILINGENIEUR – Freiberg: Verlag von J G Engelhardt, 1854-1896 – us Res Libr [624]

CIVILISACAO – '(s.l.')-Sao Luiz, Brazil. 18-25 Jun 1881; Jan-May, Jul-Dec 1887; Jul 1888; Jan 1889-4 Oct 1890 – 1,5,6 – bl Biblioteca [072]

LE CIVILISATEUR – ou Les Hommes illustres. Par M. de Lamartine. Paris. oct 1852-54 – 1 – fr A.C.R.P.P. [073]

CIVILISATION AT THE CROSS ROADS : FOUR LECTURES / DELIVERED BEFORE HARVARD UNIVERSITY IN THE YEAR 1911 ON THE WILLIAM BELDEN NOBLE FOUNDATION / Figgis, John Neville – London; New York: Longmans, Green, 1913, c1912 – 1mf – us A.T.L.A. [240]

LA CIVILISATION DU TCHAD...: SUIVI D'UNE ETUDE SUR LES BRONZES SAO, PAR RAYMOND LANTIER / Lebeuf, Jean Paul – Paris: Payot, 1950. 198p. illus. maps – 1 – us U.W. Library [306]

CIVILISATION; ITS CAUSE AND CURE, AND OTHER ESSAYS / Carpenter, Edward – 2nd ed. London: S. Sonnenschein, 1891. 156p – 1 – us U.W. Library [000]

LES CIVILISATIONS DE L'INDE / Le Bon, G – Paris. 1887. BI-1134 1 – 9 – ne IDC [930]

LA CIVILITE DES PETITES FILLES / Juranville, Clarisse – Paris: Larousse, 1900. 107p. (Les Femmes Collection) – 2mf – 9 – $6.00 – fr Bibl Nationale [390]

CIVILIZACAO : REVISTA TRIMESTRAL DE CULTURA E EDUCACAO – Campo Grande, 30 Jun, 30 Set 1934 – 1,5,6 – bl Biblioteca [073]

LA CIVILIZACION CRISTIANA DEL CHOCO (1554-1810) / Tommasini, Gabriel – Buenos Aires, 1937; Madrid: Razon y Fe, 1941.- 2v – 1 – sp Bibl Santa Ana [306]

CIVILIZATION AND CULTURE IN ROMANIA PAMPHLET COLLECTION – 1913-1943 – 1 – CSUXANL8096-B – us Hoover Inst Photo [306]

CIVILIZATION AND CULTURE IN RUSSIA AND THE SOVIET UNION PAMPHLET COLLECTION – 1918-1972 – 1 – CSUXANR4709-B – us Hoover Inst Photo [306]

CIVILIZATION AND CULTURE IN RUSSIA PAMPHLET COLLECTION – 1854-1945 – 1 – CSUXANR3770-B – us Hoover Inst Photo [306]

CIVILIZATION AND CULTURE IN THE SOVIET UNION PAMPHLET COLLECTION – 1929-1960 – 1 – CSUXANR3796-B – us Hoover Inst Photo [306]

CIVILIZATION AND CULTURE IN YUGOSLAVIA PAMPHLET COLLECTION – 1919-1930 – 1 – CSUXANQ5279-B – us Hoover Inst Photo [306]

CIVILIZATION IN THE UNITED STATES : FIRST AND LAST IMPRESSIONS OF AMERICA / Arnold, Matthew – Boston: Cupples and Hurd, 1888 – 1 roll – 1 – 1-55879-519-7 – uk Libr Preservation [975]

THE CIVILIZATION OF CHRISTENDOM : AND OTHER STUDIES / Bosanquet, Bernard – London: S. Sonnenschein; New York: Macmillan, 1893 – 1mf – us A.T.L.A. [240]

DIE CIVILPROCESS-ORDNUNG NACH MOSAISCH-RABBINISCHEM RECHTE / Bloch, Moses – Budapest: Universitaets-Buchdruckerei, 1882 – 1mf – 9 – 0-8370-5982-8 – 1985-3982 – us A.T.L.A. [270]

Civilus *see* EINE FREIDIGE VERMANUNG, ZU KLAREM VND OEFFENTLICHEM BEKENTNIS JHESU CHRISTI, SEHR NUETZLICH ZU LESEN

Civinini, Guelfo *see* RECORDI DI CAROVANA

CIVITATES ORBIS TERRARVM / Braun, G & Hohenberg, F – Cologne, 1575-1618 – 44mf – 9 – H-8199/1 – ne IDC [900]

Cizos, Duplessis De. (La Citoyenne Villeneuve) *see* LE VERITABLE AMI DES LOIS OU LES REPUBLICAINS A L'EPREUVE

CJ INTERNATIONAL – 1985- – 1,5,6,9 – us UMI [340]

THE CL PSALMS OF DAVID, IN SCOTTISH METER.. – 1615 – 1 – $50.00 – us Presbyterian [240]

C.L.A. *see* CM

Claassen, Johannes *see* DAS LICHT UND DIE FARBEN

CLACKAMAS COUNTY BANNER – Lake Oswego OR. Mar 15 1918 – 1 – us U.O. Library [071]

CLACKAMAS COUNTY BANNER – Oregon City OR. Mar 22 1918-July 3 1919 – 1 – us U.O. Library [071]

CLACKAMAS COUNTY INDEPENDENT – Canby, OR. -w. 5 Feb 1898-12 May 1899. 1 roll – 1 – us U.O. Library [071]

CLACKAMAS COUNTY RECORD – Oregon City, OR. -sw. 5 Jan 1903-30 Jul 1903, 29 Oct 1918. – 1r – 1 – us U.O. Library [071]

CLACKAMAS COUNTY REVIEW – Milwaukie OR. June 30 1983-Sep 4 1986 – 1 – us U.O. Library [071]

CLACKAMAS DEMOCRAT – Oregon City OR. Apr 8 1880 – 1 – us U.O. Library [071]

CLACKMANNANSHIRE, 1837 : BRITISH ISLES CENSUS DIRECTORIES PROJECT, SCOTLAND. VOL 34 – 1mf – 9 – A$9.00 – at Vine [941]

CLACKMANNANSHIRE ADVERTISER – Alloa. Scotland. -w. 1844-59. (3 reels) – 1 – uk British Libr Newspaper [072]

Cladel, Leon *see* REVANCHE

EEN CLAER ONDERWYSINGHE WT DES HEEREN WOORT VAN DIE GHEESTELICKE VERRYSENISSE, ENDE NIEUWE GEBOORTE / Simons, Menno – BME-280 1 – 9 – ne IDC [240]

EEN CLAERE ENDE SCHRIFTELICKE ONDERRICHTINGHE VANDEN EEDT. WAER TOEGHEDAEN IS EEN CLEIN ANHANCKSEL, DEN SELUEN HANGAEL ANGAENDE / Meeuszlin, W & Musculus, W – Door Marten Mikroen. 1555. BME-126 1 – 9 – ne IDC [240]

Claes Ganglofs *see* EEN GRONDICH BEWIJS WT DE GODLIJCKE SCHRIFTUERE VERTOONT, DAT GODS GEMEYNTE, DE GHELOOUIGEN OP AERDEN

Claeys, Hector *see* LEVEN VAN SINTE GODELIEVE

Clagett, Charles *see* A REVIEW RELATIVE TO THE COURT OF APPEALS OF MARYLAND

Clagett, Helen Lord *see* A GUIDE TO THE LAW AND LEGAL LITERATURE OF ARGENTINA, 1917-1946

AN CLAIDHEAMH SOLAIS – Dublin, Ireland.18 Mar 1899-5 Jan 1918 – 1 – ie Microforms [072]

CLAIMS BETWEEN SHIPPERS AND CARRIERS: A DIGEST OF THE AMERICAN DECISIONS / Merriam, Ralph – Chicago: La Salle Extension University, 1916. 1815p. LL-773 – 1 – us L of C Photodup [340]

THE CLAIMS OF CHRISTIANITY / Lilly, William Samuel – New York: D. Appleton, 1894. 1 fiche – 9 – 12.50f – us A.T.L.A. [240]

THE CLAIMS OF THE OLD TESTAMENT: LECTURES / Leathes, Stanley – New York: Charles Scribner, 1897. 1 fiche – 9 – us A.T.L.A. [240]

Clairaut, Alexis-Claude *see*
- RECHERCHES SUR LES COURBES A DOUBLE COURBURE
- THEORIE DE LA FIGURE DE LA TERRE, TIREE DES PRINCIPES DE L'HYDROSTATIQUE

LE CLAIRON – Chicoutimi, Canada. 11 mai 1916-v1 n3. 20 mai 1916 – 1r – 1 – Can$30.00 – cn Can Microfilming [072]

LE CLAIRON – (Includes: Le Clairon Maskoutain 21 mai 1954-31 aut 1961. Le Clairon de St-Hyacinthe 7 sep 1961-24 mar 1971. Le Nouveau Clairon 14 avr 1971-18 dec 1992) – St Hyacinthe, Canada. 5 jan 1912-7 mal 1954 – 59r – 1 – Can$70.00r – cn Can Microfilming [072]

LE CLAIRON / ed by Langlois, G E et al – Montreal, Canada. 7 dec 1889-22 mar 1890 – 1r – 1 – Can$25.00 – cn Can Microfilming [072]

LE CLAIRON – Paris. no. 1-1153. Red. en chef J. Cornely. 7 mars 1881-, 1er mai 1884. mq no. 730. 4 mars 1889-91, janv-24 juin 1893, 22 mars-5 juin 1902 – 1 – fr A.C.R.P.P. [072]

LE CLAIRON – Quebec. v1 n13. 20 fev 1897 – 1r – 1 – Can$25.00 – cn Can Microfilming [072]

LE CLAIRON – Trois-Rivieres, Canada. 10 jan-11 jul 1884 – 1r – 1 – Can$35.00 – cn Can Microfilming [072]

LE CLAIRON – Windsor, Ontario. 25 sep 1913-v1 n5. 23 oct 1913 – 1r – 1 – Can$30.00 – cn Can Microfilming [072]

LE CLAIRON – Port-au-Prince: P Errie. 1re annee. n2-n30. 28 juin 1902-17 dec 1902 – 2 sheets – us Res Libr [072]

LE CLAIRON DE ST-HYACINTHE *see* LE CLAIRON

LE CLAIRON MASKOUTAIN *see* LE CLAIRON

Clair-Tisdall, W St. *see* MANUAL OF THE LEADING MUHAMMADAN OBJECTIONS TO CHRISTIANITY

CLAMOR AFRICANO : LOURENCO MARQUES: "O BRADO AFRICANO", [DEC 10 1932-FEB 25 1933] – reel 5 – us Res Libr [960]

CLAMOR AFRICANO – Quelimane: Tip. Progresso, apr 21-27, aug 30 1892; aug 30 1893 – us Res Libr [960]

Clancy, James J *see* IRELAND: AS SHE IS, AS SHE HAS BEEN, AND AS SHE OUGHT TO BE

CLANGORES TUBAE ADVERSVS THEODORVM BEZAM. VT PRIUSQUAM IN ALTERUM EXSPIRAT SECVLVM, HVC RESPICIAT UND PERPENDAT,... / Huber, S – Vrsellis, 1598 – 1mf – ne IDC [240]

Clanin, Douglas E *see* THE PAPERS OF WILLIAM HENRY HARRISON 1800-1815

THE CLANS OF THE BAGANDA / Kagwa, Apolo – (Filmed with: Rowe, J A: Selected articles on the Bataka controversy ... Bukalasa 1922-1923. Gray, J M: Mutesa of Buganda 1934. Katate, A G: Abagabe B'Ankole, Kampala 1955) – Mengo, Uganda 1949 – us Res Libr [307]

CLAO JOURNAL – v9-. 1983- – 1,5,6,9 – us UMI [616]

Claparede, A R *see* DIE VOELKERRECHTLICHE REPATRIATIONSPFLICHT...

CLAPHAM OBSERVER – London. 1 May 1869-17 Jun 1871; 7, 21, 28 Sep 1872; 31 May 1873-Dec 1965.-w. 113 reels – 1 – uk British Libr Newspaper [072]

Clapham, S *see* HOW FAR METHODISM CONDUCES TO THE INTERESTS OF CHRISTIANITY AND THE WELFARE OF SOCIETY,...

Clapin, Sylvia *see*
- DICTIONNAIRE CANADIEN-FRANCAIS
- DICTIONNAIRE CANADIEN-FRANCAIS OU LEXIQUE-GLOSSAIRE DES MOTS, EXPRESSIONS ET LOCUTIONS NE SE TROUVANT PAS DAN LES DICTIONNAIRES COURANTS ET DONT L'USAGES APPARTIENT SURTOUT AUX CANADIENS-FRANCAIS
- LA FRANCE TRANSATLANTIQUE: LE CANADA
- HISTOIRE DES ETATS UNIS DEPUIS LES PREMIERS ETABLISSEMENTS JUSQU'A NOS JOURS

Clapperton *see* VOYAGES ET DECOUVERTES DANS LE NORD ET LES PARTIES CENTRALES DE L'AFRIQUE

Clapperton, Hugh *see*
- JOURNAL OF A SECOND EXPEDITION INTO THE INTERIOR OF AFRICA, FROM THE BIGHT OF BENIN TO SOCCATOO
- JOURNAL OF A SECOND EXPEDITION TO AFRICA
- NARRATIVE OF TRAVELS AND DISCOVERIES IN NORTHERN AND CENTRAL AFRICA IN THE YEARS 1822, 1823 AND 1824
- SECOND VOYAGE DANS L'INTERIEUR DE L'AFRIQUE, DEPUIS DE GOLFE DE BENIN JUSQUA SACKATOU. PENDANT LES ANNEES 1825, 1826, ET 1827
- TRAVELS AND DISCOVERIES IN AFRICA

Clapperton, John Alexander *see*
- FIRST STEPS IN NEW TESTAMENT GREEK
- PITFALLS IN BIBLE ENGLISH

Claproths, J C *see* GRUNDRISS DES RECHTS DER NATUR

Clapton, Edward *see* PRECIOUS STONES OF THE BIBLE...A TREATISE ON THE BREASTPLATE OF THE HIGH PRIEST

LA CLAQUE – Montreal, no 1 1970-. SEM35P161 – 1r – 1 – Can$15.00 – cn Bibl Nat [073]

THE CLARA BARTON PAPERS – 123r – 1 – $4,305.00 – Dist. us Scholarly Res – us L of C Photodup [360]

CLARA HOPGOOD. EDITED BY HIS FRIEND, REUBEN SHAPCOTT / White, William Hale – London: T.F. Unwin, 1896 – 1 roll – 1 – 1-55879-706-8 – uk Libr Preservation [920]

CLARA VAUGHAN / Blackmore, Richard Doddridge – British Fiction Archive: Unit 3 – 9 – uk Bell [830]

CLARE ADVERTISER – Kilrush, Ireland. 17 Jul 1869-29 Nov 1873; 1875-76; 1878-82; 1887. -w. 15 1/2 reels – 1 – uk British Libr Newspaper [072]

Clare College. Cambridge *see* HORAE

CLARE INDEPENDENT ETC – (Independent 1885-) – Ennis, Ireland. 1877-81; 1885 – 4r – 1 – uk British Libr Newspaper [072]

Clare, John *see*
- MANUSCRIPTS AND PAPERS FROM THE COLLECTION IN NORTHAMPTON CENTRAL LIBRARY
- MANUSCRIPTS FROM THE COLLECTION IN PETERBOROUGH MUSEUM
- THE SHEPHERD'S CALENDAR

Clare, William *see* A COMPLEAT SYSTEM OF GRAMMAR ENGLISH AND LATIN

CLAREMONT COURIER – Claremont, CA. Sept 1912-Mar 1913; 1969- – 53+ r – 1 CR02112 – $2,650.00 – us Library Micro [071]

Claremont, New Hampshire. Claremont Baptist Church and Society *see* RECORDS

CLARENCE AND RICHMOND EXAMINER – Grafton, Australia. 10 Sep 1892-31 Dec 1901; 8 Mar 1902.-d. 15 reels – 1 – uk British Libr Newspaper [072]

CLARENCE AND RICHMOND EXAMINER – Grafton, Jul 26-Nov 29 1859; Jan 7 1873-Dec 29 1885; Jan 7-Dec 29 1908 – 9 – at Pascoe [072]

CLARENCE CAMERON WHITE PAPERS : FROM THE HOLDINGS OF THE SCHOMBURG CENTER FOR RESEARCH IN BLACK CULTURE, MANUSCRIPTS, ARCHIVES AND RARE BOOKS DIVISION: THE NEW YORK PUBLIC LIBRARY, ASTOR, LENOX AND TILDEN FOUNDATIONS – (Guide which covers all coll under "Literature and the Arts" sold separately for $20.00 D3305.G6) – 1995 – 10r – 1 – $850.00 – D3305P20 – Dist. us Scholarly Res – us L of C Photodup [780]

CLARENCE DARROW'S TWO GREAT TRIALS : REPORTS OF THE SCOPES AND THE DR. SWEET NEGRO TRIAL / Halderman-Julius, M – Girard, Kansas: H-J Company, 1927 – 1mf – 9 – $1.50 – LLMC 91-059 – us L.L.M.C. [340]

Clarence, Frere *see* BIBLIOGRAPHIE ANALYTIQUE DE OEUVRES DE M. JEAN-MARIE LAURENCE, DIRECTEUR LINGUISTIQUE ET CHEF DES SERVICES D'ANNONCEURS DES RESEAUX FRANCAIS DE RADIO-CANADA

CLARENCE JORDAN: A PROPHET IN BLUE JEANS / Barnette, Henlee H – 1982. Lecture delivered at Southern Baptist Theological Seminary, Louisville, KY – 1 – $5.00 – us Baptist [240]

CLARENDON PAPERS 1853-1870 : THE AMERICAN PAPERS OF THE 4TH EARL OF CLARENDON – 15r – 1 – uk Microform Academic [975]

THE CLARENDON PAPERS, 1867-1870 / Villiers, George William Frederick – State Papers Foreign Collection 361. Orig. publ. by Michael Glazier Inc – 1r – 1 – $85.00 – D3264 – us Scholarly Res [941]

CLARENDON SECOND BAPTIST CHURCH. CLARENDON, VERMONT : CHURCH RECORDS – 1798-1832 – 1 – 5.58 – us Baptist [240]

CLARESHOLM ADVERTISER – Alberta, CN. 1914-16 – 1r – 1 – cn Commonwealth Micro [072]

CLARESHOLM LOCAL PRESS – Alberta, CN. 1926-95 – 32r – 1 – cn Commonwealth Micro [072]

CLARESHOLM REVIEW – Alberta, CN. 1907-16 – 3r – 1 – cn Commonwealth Micro [072]

Clareson, Thomas D *see* EARLY SCIENCE FICTION NOVELS

Claretie, Jules *see* RECITS DE GUERRE

LA CLARIDAD – [Habana: s.n. v1 n5,6,?,? (nov 1,8, [no date], 29 1890); v2 n12-22,?,?-? (mar 21-may 22, may 30, jun 20-27 1891) – 3mf – us Res Libr [072]

Claridge, R *see*
- AN ANSWER TO RICHARD ALLEN'S ESSAY

O CLARIM – Cuiaba, 25 Apr, Jul-Aug, 11 Oct 1894 – 1,5,6 – bl Biblioteca [072]

O CLARIM : PERIODICO LITTERARIO, CRITICO E JOCO-SERIO – Maceio, Alagoas. 9 Jun 1894; Jul-30 Ago 1896 – 1,5,6 – bl Biblioteca [072]

CLARINES DE FERIA – Merida, 1964, 1965 y 1969 – 5 – sp Bibl Santa Ana [073]

CLARION – Medford OR. June 16 1922-Oct 3 1924 – 1 – us U.O. Library [071]

CLARION – Princeton. Ind. and Pred. 1846-1930; 1964- – 1 – us UMI [071]

CLARION – Sandusky. Ohio. -w. 1822-34, 1843-49 – 1 – us UMI [071]

CLARION – v1-2. no. 2 (all publ). 1932-1934 – 1 reel – 1 – $65.00 – us UPA [335]

CLARION *see* GUARDIAN

THE CLARION – Belize. British Honduras. (Daily Clarion). -d. 19 Nov 1897-31 May 1940; 1 Feb-30 Nov 1943, 1 Oct 1951-6 Nov 1954, 2 Jan 1957-20 Oct 1961. (90 reels) – 1 – uk British Libr Newspaper [072]

THE CLARION / Communist Party of Canada – 1940-41 – 1 – 45.00 – cn McLaren [335]

THE CLARION – Manchester and London. England. -w. 12 Dec 1891-22 Apr 1927. (31mqn reels) – 1 – uk British Libr Newspaper [072]

THE CLARION *see* COTATI-THE COMMUNITY VOICE

THE CLARION – Cape Town [South Africa]: Stewart Printing Co Ltd, may 29-aug 14 1952 – us Res Libr [072]

CLARION DEFENDER – Portland OR. Dec 16 1965-Oct 15 1970 – 1 – us U.O. Library [071]

CLARION DEFENDER – (Set incl. Northwest Clarion (Portland); Northwest Defender (Portland)) – Portland, OR. 7 Dec 1965-15 Oct 1970. 1 roll. – 1 – us U.O. Library [071]

THE CLARION DEMOCRAT – Clarion, PA. -w 1868-69; 1884-1941; 1945-46. 22 rolls – 13 – $25.00r – us I.M.R. [071]

CLARION LEADER – Princeton. Ind. -w. 1897-1901 – 1 – us UMI [071]

CLARION LEDGER – Jackson. Miss. 1865-1868; 1875-1878; 1890-1902; 1922- – 1 – us UMI [071]

CLARION LEDGER – Jackson. Miss. -sw. 1870-72 – 1 – us UMI [071]

CLARION LEDGER – Jackson. Miss. -w. 1890-1911 – 1 – us UMI [071]

CLARION NEWS – Clarion, PA., 1972-1975 – 13 – $25.00r – us I.M.R. [071]

CLARION NEWS – Princeton. Ind. 1902-1939- – 1 – us UMI [071]

THE CLARION REPUBLICAN – Clarion, PA., 1899-1958 – 13 – $25.00r – us I.M.R. [071]

CLARION REPUBLICAN/GAZETTE – Clarion, PA. -w 1884-1899. 5 rolls – 13 – $25.00r – us I.M.R. [071]

CLARITY / Young Communist League – 1-4 2+1 (all publ). 1940-1943 – 10mf – 9 – $65.00 – us UPA [335]

Clark *see* HISTORY OF HARRISON COUTNY

CLARK AND FINNELLY'S REPORTS : REPORTS OF CASES HEARD AND DECIDED IN THE HOUSE OF LORDS ON APPEALS AND WRITS OF ERROR / Clark, Charles & Finnelly, W – v1-12. 1831-46. London: J & W T Clark, 1835-47 (all publ) – 112mf – 9 – $168.00 – LLMC 95-248 – us L.L.M.C. [324]

CLARK AND SCULLY'S ONTARIO DRAINAGE CASES / Ontario. Canada – v1-2. 1898-1903 (all publ) – 13mf – 9 – $19.50 – LLMC 81-059 – us L.L.M.C. [340]

Clark, Charles *see*
- CLARK AND FINNELLY'S REPORTS
- HOUSE OF LORDS CASES (CLARK AND FINNELLY)

Clark, Christopher Saint George *see* OF TORONTO THE GOOD; A SOCIAL STUDY

Clark, Colin *see*
- PROPERTY AND ECONOMIC PROGRESS; SCHOOLS CAN PAY DIVIDENDS
- PUTTING THE POPULATION EXPLOSION IN PERSPECTIVE

CLARK COUNTY CLIPPER – Ashland. Kan. 1884-1930 – 1 – us UMI [071]

Clark, Daniel *see*
- AN ANIMATED MOLECULE AND ITS NEAREST RELATIVE: AN ESSAY READ BEFORE THE AMERICAN ASSOCIATION OF MEDICAL SUPERINTENDENTS OF ASYLUMS FOR THE INSANE, AT WASHINGTON, D.C., ON THE 10TH OF MAY, 1878
- MENTAL DISEASES: A SYNOPSIS OF TWELVE LECTURES DELIVERED AT THE HOSPITAL FOR THE INSANE, TORONTO, TO THE GRADUATING MEDICAL CLASSES
- PEN PHOTOGRAPHS OF CELEBRATED MEN AND NOTED PLACES, GHOSTS AND THEIR RELATIONS: TALES, SKETCHES, ESSAYS, ETC., ETC

Clark, Dawn *see* AN INTERPRETIVE INQUIRY OF THE PROFESSIONAL LIFE HISTORIES OF SELECTED WOMEN DANCE/PHYSICAL EDUCATORS

Clark, DL *see* SINGLE TAX, FREE TRADE & LAND VALUES TAXATION: HENRY GEORGE IN THE SYDNEY SINGLE TAX LEAGUE

Clark, Dougan *see*
- THE HOLY GHOST DISPENSATION
- INSTRUCTIONS TO CHRISTIAN CONVERTS
- THE THEOLOGY OF HOLINESS

Clark, E C *see* HISTORY OF ROMAN PRIVATE LAW

Clark, Edson Lyman *see* FUNDAMENTAL QUESTIONS

Clark, Francis Barnard *see* CLARK'S FORM BOOK, CONTAINING LEGAL AND BUSINESS FORMS USEFUL TO THE PRIVATE CITIZEN, AS WELL AS TO JUDGES, ATTORNEYS.

Clark, Francis Edward *see*
- THE GOSPEL IN LATIN LANDS
- OUR JOURNEY AROUND THE WORLD: AN ILLUSTRATED RECORD OF A YEAR'S TRAVEL OF FORTY THOUSAND MILES THROUGH INDIA, CHINA, JAPAN, AUSTRALIA, NEW ZEALAND, EGYPT, PALESTINE, GREECE, TURKEY, ITALY, FRANCE, SPAIN, ETC

Clark, Gabriel Penn *see* BUSINESS RECORDS

Clark, Gavin Brown *see* THE TRANSVAAL AND BECHUANALAND

Clark, Gilbert J *see* LIFE SKETCHES OF EMINENT LAWYERS

Clark, Grenville *see* PAPERS OF GRENVILLE CLARK

Clark, Hannah Belle *see* THE PUBLIC SCHOOLS OF CHICAGO: A SOCIOLOGICAL STUDY

Clark, Henry Martyn *see* ROBERT CLARK OF THE PUNJAB

Clark, Henry W *see*
- HISTORY OF ENGLISH NONCONFORMITY FROM WICLIF TO THE CLOSE OF THE NINETEENTH CENTURY
- LAWS OF THE INNER KINGDOM
- LIBERAL ORTHODOXY

Clark, Henry William *see* THE CHRIST FROM WITHOUT AND WITHIN

Clark, Horace F et al *see* CLARK'S MINERAL LAW

Clark, Hugh *see* AN INTRODUCTION TO HERALDRY: WITH NEARLY ONE THOUSAND ILLUSTRATIONS, INCLUDING THE ARMS OF ABOUT FIVE HUNDRED DIFFERENT FAMILIES

Clark, J *see* MONTANUS REDIVIVUS

Clark, J Reuben Jr *see* EMERGENCY LEGISLATION OF THE U.S. 1775-1918

Clark, J W *see* FASCICULUS IOANNI WILLIS CLARK DICATUS

Clark, Janet M *see* WOMEN AND POLITICS

Clark, Jeremiah Simpson *see* RAND AND THE MICMACS

Clark, JK *see* TWO CURRICULAR SETTINGS OF A HIV EDUCATION UNIT RELATED TO SECONDARY SCHOOL STUDENTS' HIV KNOWLEDGE AND ATTITUDE

Clark, John King *see* SYSTEMATIC MORAL EDUCATION: WITH DAILY LESSONS IN ETHICS

Clark, John Murray *see* THE FUNCTIONS OF A GREAT UNIVERSITY: INAUGURAL ADDRESS DELIVERED ON NOVEMBER 16TH, 1894

Clark, Joseph B *see*
- BLUE SKY
- LEAVENING THE NATION ; THE STORY OF AMERICAN (PROTESTANT) HOME MISSIONS

Clark, Katherine A *see*
- GLEANINGS FROM MY PORTFOLIO: ORIGINAL POEMS
- LYRICAL ECHOES

CLARK KINSEY LOGGING PHOTOGRAPHS / Kinsey, Clark – (More than 5000 views of logging and milling operations, crews, equipment, towns, and landscapes dated 1914-45. A 147p-printed inventory and description included) – 95mf – 9 – $100.00 set – us U.W. Libraries [634]

Clark, Lucien *see* RELIGION FOR THE TIMES

Clark, M B Sterling *see* SCRIPTURE HISTORY OF OUR BLESSED LORD AND SAVIOUR

Clark, Marona M (Still) *see* AUTOBIOGRAPHICAL NOTES

Clark, Mary *see* BIOGRAPHICAL SKETCHES OF THE FATHERS OF NEW ENGLAND

Clark, Mary Alice *see* OUR RECENT VISIT TO TRINIDAD: AND THE OPENING OF THE PRESBYTERIAN COLLEGE IN SAN FERNANDO

Clark, Robert *see* THE MISSIONS OF THE CHURCH MISSIONARY SOCIETY AND THE CHURCH OF ENGLAND ZENANA MISSIONARY SOCIETY IN THE PUNJAB AND SINDH

Clark, Rufus W *see*
- A REVIEW OF THE REV. MOSES STUART'S PAMPHLET ON SLAVERY ENTITLED CONSCIENCE AND THE CONSTITUTION
- ROMANISM IN AMERICA
- THE WORK OF GOD IN GREAT BRITAIN

Clark, S H *see* PRACTICAL PUBLIC SPEAKING

Clark, Salter S *see* THE GOVERNMENT CLASS BOOK

Clark, Sidney J W *see* THE ART OF USING THE CHINA MISSIONARY SURVEY

Clark, Tara J *see* THE RELATIONSHIP BETWEEN PHYSICAL SELF-PERCEPTIONS AND FUNCTIONAL MUSCULAR STRENGTH IN YOUNG ADULT FEMALES

Clark, Thomas March *see* PRIMARY TRUTHS OF RELIGION

Clark, WA *see* CONTRIBUTIONS TO THE HISTORICAL SOCIETY OF MONTANA

Clark, Walter A *see* UNDER THE STARS AND BARS: MEMORIES OF FOUR YEARS SERVICE WITH THE OGLETHORPES, OF AUGUSTA, GEORGIA

Clark, Walter H *see* HISTORY OF PLATTE PRESBYTERY

Clark, William *see*
- THE ANGLICAN REFORMATION
- PASCAL AND THE PORT ROYALISTS
- WITNESSES TO CHRIST

Clark, William George *see* ESSAYS BY THE LATE GEORGE BRIMLEY

Clark, William Lawrence *see* A TREATISE ON THE LAW OF CRIMES

Clarke, A *see* OUT-LETTERS 1785-1832

Clarke, A M *see* THE LIFE OF ST. FRANCIS BORGIA OF THE SOCIETY OF JESUS

CLARKE AND HALL'S CASES IN CONTESTED ELECTIONS IN CONGRESS, 1789-1834 / Clarke, M St. Clair & Hall, David A – Washington: Gales & Seaton. 1v. 1834 (all publ) – 9 – LLMC 95-122 – us L.L.M.C. [340]

Clarke, Andrew *see* OCEAN ROUTE TO AUSTRALASIA THROUGH ATLANTIC AND PACIFIC

Clarke, B *see* FOREST FIRE CONTROL

Clarke, Bella *see* A PRAYER FOR GUIDANCE

Clarke, C B *see*
- COMMELYNACEAE ET CYRTANDRACEAE BENGALENSES
- A LIST OF THE FLOWERING PLANTS, FERNS AND MOSSES OF ANDOVER
- A REVIEW OF THE FERNS OF NORTHERN INDIA

Clarke, Charles Cowden *see* SHAKESPEARE-CHARACTERS

Clarke, Charles Cowley *see* HANDBOOK OF THE DIVINE LITURGY

CLARKE COUNTY TRIBUNE – Quitman. Miss. 1937-1950 – 1 – us UMI [071]

Clarke, E D *see* TRAVELS IN VARIOUS COUNTRIES OF EUROPE, ASIA AND AFRICA

Clarke, George Sydenham *see* THE NAVY AND THE NATION; OR, NAVAL WARFARE AND IMPERIAL DEFENCE

Clarke, Henry Harrison *see*
- BIOGRAPHIES OF FELLOWS, AMERICAN ACADEMY OF PHYSICAL EDUCATION
- "MUSCULAR STRENGTH AND ENDURANCE IN MAN" 1966
- OREGON CABLE-TENSION STRENGTH TEST BATTERIES FOR BOYS AND GIRLS FROM FOURTH GRADE THROUGH COLLEGE
- REFLECTIONS

Clarke, Henry Lowther *see* STUDIES IN THE ENGLISH REFORMATION

Clarke, Hyde *see* SERPENT AND SIVA WORSHIP AND MYTHOLOGY, IN CENTRAL AMERICA, AFRICA, AND ASIA

Clarke, J I *see* AMERICAN LEADING CASES

Clarke, James Freeman *see*
- THE CHURCH – AS IT WAS, AS IT IS, AS IT OUGHT TO BE
- EVENTS AND EPOCHS IN RELIGIOUS HISTORY
- EVENTS AND EPOCHS IN RELIGIOUS HISTORY; BEING THE SUBSTANCE OF A COURSE OF TWELVE LECTURES...LOWELL INSTITUTE, BOSTON, IN 1880
- FALSE WITNESSES ANSWERED
- THE FOURTH GOSPEL
- THE INTRODUCTION TO THE GOSPEL OF JOHN
- MEMORIAL AND BIOGRAPHICAL SKETCHES
- NINETEENTH CENTURY QUESTIONS
- SERMON ON CHANNING
- THE TRANSFIGURATION OF LIFE

Clarke, James Stanier *see* THE LIFE AND SERVICES OF HORATIO VISCOUNT NELSON

Clarke, John *see*
- DUX GRAMMATICUS TYRONEM SCHOLASTICUM
- AN INTRODUCTION TO THE MAKING OF LATIN
- SPECIMENS OF DIALECTS

Clarke, John B *see* SKETCHES OF SUCCESSFUL NEW HAMPSHIRE MEN

Clarke, John Caldwell Calhoun *see* THE ORIGIN AND VARIETIES OF THE SEMITIC ALPHABET

Clarke, M St. Clair *see* CLARKE AND HALL'S CASES IN CONTESTED ELECTIONS IN CONGRESS, 1789-1834

Clarke, Peter Dooyentate *see* ORIGIN AND TRADITIONAL HISTORY OF THE WYANDOTTS: AND SKETCHES OF OTHER INDIAN TRIBES OF NORTH AMERICA, TRUE TRADITIONAL STORIES OF TECUMSEH AND HIS LEAGUE, IN THE YEARS OF 1811 AND 1812

Clarke, R Floyd *see* THE SCIENCE OF LAW AND LAWMAKING

Clarke, Robin *see* MORE THAN ENOUGH

Clarke, Samuel Robinson *see*
- THE CONSTABLES' MANUAL: BEING A SUMMARY OF THE LAW RELATING TO THE RIGHTS, POWERS, AND DUTIES OF CONSTABLES
- THE LAW OF LIS PENDENS AND IN PART OF MECHANICS' LIENS.
- A NEW LIGHT ON ANNEXATION: A POLITICAL BROCHURE
- A TREATISE OF THE LAW OF LANDLORD AND TENANT APPLICABLE TO THE DOMINION OF CANADA
- A TREATISE ON CRIMINAL LAW AS APPLICABLE TO THE DOMINION OF CANADA
- A TREATISE ON THE LAW OF INSURANCE
- A TREATISE ON THE LAW RELATING TO BILLS, NOTES, CHEQUES AND IOU'S

Clarke, W C *see* THE INFLUENCE OF A GODLY LIFE: A SERMON PREACHED ON THE OCCASION OF THE DEATH OF THE LATE REV. A. WALLACE, A.B., HUNTINGDON, QUEBEC

Clarke, W K Lowther *see* LITURGY AND WORSHIP

Clarke, W Newton *see* CHRISTIAN AND CHURCH (A SERMON)

Clarke, Walter E *see* WEST VIRGINIA TODAY

Clarke, William F *see* A BIRD'S-EYE VIEW OF BEE-KEEPING

Clarke, William Fletcher *see* IN MEMORIAM: A DISCOURSE OCCASIONED BY THE DEATH OF THE LATE A. W. LILLIE, ESQ., AND DELIVERED IN THE CONGREGATIONAL CHURCH, GUELPH, ON SABBATH EVENING, OCTOBER 18TH, 1868

Clarke, William Newton *see*
- THE CHRISTIAN DOCTRINE OF GOD
- THE CIRCLE OF THEOLOGY
- OUTLINE OF CHRISTIAN THEOLOGY
- A STUDY OF CHRISTIAN MISSIONS
- THE USE OF SCRIPTURES IN THEOLOGY
- USE OF THE SCRIPTURES IN THEOLOGY
- WHAT SHALL WE THINK OF CHRISTIANITY?

Clarke, Wm. H *see* TRAVELS AND EXPLORATIONS OF

CLARKE'S CHANCERY APPEALS REPORTS / New York. (State) – (A Pre-NRS title) – 1v. 1839-41 (all publ) – 5mf – 9 – $7.50 – LLMC 80-200 – us L.L.M.C. [340]

CLARKS ENTERPRISE – Clarks, NE. -w. Nov. 1892; Oct. 1896-Sep. 1918; Jan. 1919-Apr. 1949 – 1 – us NE Hist [071]

CLARK'S FORM BOOK, CONTAINING LEGAL AND BUSINESS FORMS USEFUL TO THE PRIVATE CITIZEN, AS WELL AS TO JUDGES, ATTORNEYS. / Clark, Francis Barnard – Montgomery, Ala.: Hold & Crawford, 1882. 460p. LL-12 – 1 – us L of C Photodup [340]

CLARK'S MINERAL LAW : DIGEST OF DECISIONS OF THE COURTS AND LAND DEPARTMENT UNDER THE PUBLIC MINERAL LAWS / Clark, Horace F et al – Chicago: Callaghan. 1v. 1897 (all publ) – 9 – LLMC 95-134 – us L.L.M.C. [340]

CLARKS NEWS – Clarks, NE. -w. Sep. 1950-Jan. 1957; Mar. 1957-Dec. 1964 – 1 – us NE Hist [071]

CLARKSBURG 1798-1915 – (Mf 1-5: Town Records 1798-1846. Mf 6: Births 1846-1900. Mf 8: Marriages 1847-1916; Deaths 1846-72. Mf 9: Deaths 1873-1915) – (mf ed 1988) – 9mf – 9 – 0-87623-072-9 – us Holbrook [920]

Clarkson, T *see*
- AN ESSAY ON THE SLAVERY...
- THOUGHTS...IMPROVING THE CONDITION OF THE SLAVES...

Clarkson, Thomas *see* LETTERS ON THE SLAVE-TRADE AND THE STATE OF THE NATIVES IN THOSE PARTS OF AFRICA WHICH ARE CONTIGUOUS TO FORT ST LOUIS AND GOREE.

Claros, Jose Ma de *see* DISCURSOS DE...SOBRE CUESTIONES DE CARACTER POLITICO...LEGISLATURA DE 1864-65

CLARTE – Montreal, Canada. 14 jan 1935-4 oct 1939 – 1 – cn Can Microfilming [072]

CLARTE – no. 1-35, no. special de dec 1938. Paris. aout 1936-aout 1939. mq no. 3-5; no. 18, 20, 29 – 1 – fr A.C.R.P.P. [073]

CLARTE – Paris, 1921-28 – 1r – 1 – us Ross [335]

CLARTE – Paris. 25 oct 1919-dec 1927 janv 1928 – 1 – fr A.C.R.P.P. [072]

CLARTE, REVISTA DE SCIENCIAS SOCIAES – Rio de Janeiro, BL. 1921-1922 – 1r – $50.00 – R04169 – us Library Micro [072]

Clary, J M *see* EATING DISORDERS AMONG ATHLETES

CLASE OBRERA Y PERONISMO / Durruty, Celia – Cordoba [Argentina]: Ediciones Pasado y Presente, [1969] – 1 – CSUXADH7729-B – us Hoover Inst Photo [320]

Clasen, L *see* DIE CHRISTLICHE HEILSGEWISSHEIT

Clasey, Jody Lee *see* THE RELATIONSHIP BETWEEN FINGER FLEXION FORCE PRODUCTION AND SELECTED HAND, FOREARM AND BODY PHYSIQUE MEASUREMENTS

CLASS BULLETINS / Minnesota. University. Agricultural Experiment Station. St. Paul – nos.1-15. 1898-1904 – 1,5,6 – us Spaulding [630]

CLASS. (Cooperative Library Agency for Systems and Services) *see* CULP. (CALIFORNIA UNION LIST OF PERIODICALS)

THE CLASS LEADER: HIS WORK AND HOW TO DO IT, WITH ILLUSTRATIONS OF PRINCIPLES, DEEDS, METHODS AND RESULTS / Atkinson, John – Halifax: A. Nicolson, 1875. 02453. (Pre-1900 Canadiana) – 9 – cn C.I.H.M. [370]

CLASS REGISTER / Sandusky County. Ohio. Fremont Township. Board of Education – 1849-1852 – 1r – 1 – $32.50r – us Archival [324]

CLASS REGISTER, FELLERS SCHOOL / Hancock County, Ohio. Eagle Township. Board of Education – 1896-1903 – 1r – 1 – $32.50r – us Archival [324]

CLASS REGISTERS / Putnam County. Ohio. Board of Education – 1861-1864 – 1r – 1 – $32.50r – us Archival [324]

CLASS REGISTERS / Wood County. Ohio. Lake Township. Board of Education – 1883-1888 – 1r – 1 – $32.50r – us Archival [324]

CLASS STRUGGLE / Communist League of Struggle – 1-7 2+9 (all publ). 1931-1937 – 17mf – 9 – $85.00 – us UPA [335]

CLASS STRUGGLE : DEVOTED TO INTERNATIONAL SOCIALISM – 1-3 no. 4 (all publ). 1917-1919 – 18mf – 9 – $85.00 – us UPA [335]

CLASS STRUGGLE – New York. v. 1-3. May 1917-Nov 1919 – 1 – us NY Public [335]

A CLASS-BOOK OF BIBLICAL HISTORY AND GEOGRAPHY / Osborn, Henry Stafford – New York: American Tract Society, 1890. 1 fiche – 9 – us A.T.L.A. [240]

A CLASSE OPERARIA – Rio de Janeiro, BL. 1962-1964 – 1r – $50.00 – R04164 – us Library Micro [320]

CLASSED SUBJECT CATALOG OF THE ENGINEERING SOCIETIES LIBRARY AND INDEX TO THE CLASSED SUBJECT CATALOG / Engineering Societies. New York – 1982. 335,000 cards on 22 reels – 1 – $2,550.00 export $3.085.00 – 0-8161-1333-5 – uk Hall [620]

Classen, Walther *see* SUCHEN WIR EINEN NEUEN GOTT?

Classeni, IO *see* CHRONOGRAPHIA (CSHB 39, 40)

CLASSES CONCHYLIORUM / Bergen, C A von – Z-397 2. 1760 – 8 – ne IDC [590]

DES CLASSES DANGEREUSES DE LA SOCIETE DANS LES GRANDES VILLES ET DES MOYENS DE LES RENDRE MEILLEURES / Fregier, H A – (Condition of 19th C. French working class series). 1840 – 9 – fr Hachette [305]

LES CLASSES LABORIEUSES, LEUR CONDITION ACTUELLE, LEUR AVENIR PAR LA REORGANISATION DU TRAVAIL / Compagnon, A – (Condition of 19th C. French working class series). 1858 – 9 – fr Hachette [305]

LES CLASSES OUVRIERES EN FRANCE DEPUIS 1789 / Du Cellier, Florent – (Condition of 19th C. French working class series). 1857 – 9 – fr Hachette [360]

DES CLASSES OUVRIERES EN FRANCE PENDANT L'ANNEE 1848 / Blanqui, Adolphe – (Condition of 19th C. French working class series). 1849 – 9 – fr Hachette [305]

CLASSES PLANTARUM / Linnaeus, Carl – Lugduni Batavorum. 1738. B-160 2 – 8 – ne IDC [580]

CLASSIC LITERATURE ON INVERTEBRATE PALAEONTOLOGY / ed by Hallam, A – (A: Palaeozoic Corals, 17 titles, ed. Scrutton, Colin T., $140; B: Crinoid Literature, 14 titles, ed. Lane, N.G., $70; C: Trilobite Works, 29 titles, ed. Hughs, C.P., et al., $125; D: Mesozoic Bivalves, 81 titles, ed. Morris, N.J., $305; E: Graptolite Literature, 24 titles, ed. Rickards, R.B. and Palmer, D.C., $115; F: Mesozoic Brachiopods, 6 titles, ed. Owen, Ellis, $110; G: Mesozoic Ammonites, 9 titles, ed. Howarth, M.K., $205. Includes printed guide: Classical Literature on Invertebrate Palaeontology: an Introduction and Detailed Catalogue, by A. Hallam (Former title: The Palaeontological Microfiche Library.)) – 313mf – 9 – $1070.00 – us UMI [560]

THE CLASSIC TEST OF AUTHORSHIP, AUTHENTICITY AND AUTHORITY / Samson, George Whitefield – New York: F. Scott, 1893. 1 fiche – 9 – us A.T.L.A. [240]

THE CLASSICAL AGE OF GERMAN LITERATURE, 1748-1805 / Willoughby, Leonard Ashley – (Includes bibliographical references and index) – London: Oxford University Press, H Milford, 1926 – 1 – us U.W. Library [430]

THE CLASSICAL AGE OF GERMAN LITERATURE, 1748-1805 / Willoughby, Leonard Ashley – (Includes bibliographical references and index) – London: Oxford University Press, H Milford, 1926 – 1 – us U.W. Library [430]

CLASSICAL AND QUANTUM GRAVITY – v1- . 1984- – 1,5,6,9 – £662.00 – uk I.O.P. [520]

CLASSICAL ANTIQUITY – (1985- . 5,6,9) – v1- . 1982- – 1 – us UMI [073]

Classical Association *see* PROCEEDINGS

A CLASSICAL DICTIONARY OF INDIA, ILLUSTRATIVE OF THE MYTHOLOGY, PHILOSOPHY, LITERATURE, ANTIQUITIES, ARTS, MANNERS, CUSTOMS, ETC. OF THE HINDUS / Garrett, John – (Supplement, 1873. 160p. 1) – Madras: Higginbotham and Co., 1871 – 1 – us U.W. Library [950]

A CLASSICAL DICTIONARY OF THE VULGAR TONGUE / Grose, Francis – 1785. 217p. (English Linguistics Series 1500-1800) – 9 – us UMI [420]

THE CLASSICAL HERITAGE OF THE MIDDLE AGES / Taylor, Henry Osborn – New York: Macmillan, 1911 – 1mf – us A.T.L.A. [900]

CLASSICAL JOURNAL – v. 1-36. 1905-1940 – 1 – us Princeton Micro [450]

CLASSICAL JOURNAL – (v64- . 5,6. v72- . 9) – 1- 1905- – 1 – us UMI [930]

THE CLASSICAL MORALISTS...SOCRATES TO MARTINEAU / Rand, Benjamin – Boston: Houghton, Mifflin, 1909 – xix/797p 2mf – 9 – us A.T.L.A. [170]

CLASSICAL PHILOLOGY – Chicago, 1923-40. v.18-35 – 111mf – 8 – ne IDC [073]

CLASSICAL PHILOLOGY – v1-35. 1906-40 – 1,5,6 – us Princeton Micro [450]

CLASSICAL PHILOLOGY – (v64- . 5,6. v73- . 9) – v. 1- 1906- – 1 – us UMI [450]

CLASSICAL QUARTERLY – (v. 1-13. /34.50v; 9. v. 14-19. 247.50v; WDS; 9) – n.s. v. 1-19. London. 1951-69 – 9 – 24100.00 – uk Dawson [930]

CLASSICAL QUARTERLY – (v. 1-8. 246.00v; 9. v. 9-33. 244.50v; WDS; 9. v. 34-44. 243.00v; WDS; 9) – orig. s. v. 1-44. London. 1907-50 – 9 – 24190.00 – uk Dawson [930]

CLASSICAL QUARTERLY – (v21- . 5,6. v25- . 9) – v. 1- 1907- – 1 – us UMI [450]

CLASSICAL REVIEW – (Old Series). v. 1-57. 1887-1943 – 1 – us Princeton Micro [450]

CLASSICAL REVIEW – (v21- . 5,6. v25- . 9) – Oxford. v. 1- 1887- – 1 – us UMI [450]

CLASSICAL REVISION OF THE GREEK NEW TESTAMENT : TESTED AND APPLIED ON UNIFORM PRINCIPLES WITH SUGGESTED ALTERATIONS OF THE ENGLISH VERSION / Nicolson, W Millar – (Includes an appendix and index) – London: Williams and Norgate, 1878 – 1mf – 9 – 0-8370-4590-8 – 1985-2590 – us A.T.L.A. [450]

CLASSICAL TRANSLATIONS / Hartley, H A S – St. John, N.B.: J. & A. McMillan, 1889. 02430. (Pre-1900 Canadiana) – 9 – cn C.I.H.M. [450]

CLASSICAL WORLD – (v64- . 5,6. v71- . 9) – v. 1- 1907- – 1 – us UMI [450]

CLASSICS IN SOUTH-EAST ASIAN STUDIES – (Individual titles available. Also listed separately) – 225mf – 9 – ne IDC [950]

CLASSICS OF INTERNATIONAL LAW. CARNEGIE INSTITUTION. MICRO-MINI-PRINTS EDITION... / ed by Scott, James Brown – (22 titles in 40 books) – Washington: Carnegie Institution, 1911- – 9 – $575.00 set – 0-89941-203-3 – us Hein [340]

CLASSIFICATION AND DEFINITIONS OF FOREST PRODUCTS – 1982 – 256p – it F.A.O. [338]

A CLASSIFICATION AND DESCRIPTION OF SOME NEWLY DISCOVERED FERNS, COLLECTED IN THE NORTHERN ISLAND OF NEW ZEALAND IN 1841-42 / Colenso, W – (Tasman Journ. Nat. Sc. Launceston). 1845 – 9 – ne IDC [580]

CLASSIFICATION DEFINITIONS (PATENTS) *see* UNITED STATES PATENT CLASSIFICATION DEFINITIONS

CLASSIFICATION DES DIALECTES ARMENIENS / Adjarian, H – Paris, 1909 – 2mf – ne IDC [460]

CLASSIFICATION OF BIRDS / Seebohm, H – Z 1924 2. Suppl. 1895. 1890 – 8 – ne IDC [590]

CLASSIFICATION OF ILLINOIS HIGHWAYS / Illinois County Records – 1951. Adams-Woodford Co – 1 – us A.G.L.L. [910]

CLASSIFICATION OUTLINE WITH TOPICAL INDEX FOR DECISIONS OF THE N.L.R.B. AND RELATED COURT DECISIONS / U.S. National Labor Relations Board – Washington: GPO, 1988 – 12mf – 9 – $18.00 – LLMC 95-033 – us L.L.M.C. [340]

CLASSIFIED CATALOG AND SUBJECT INDEX / University of Chicago. Far Eastern Library – 1973. 86,400 cards. 12 reels. ISBN 0-8161-1365-3 – 1 – $910.00 – uk Hall [950]
CLASSIFIED CATALOG OF THE ECUMENICAL MOVEMENT / World Council of Churches. Geneva – (First Suppl., 1981. 1 reel. $115.00 ISBN 0-8161-1556-7) – 1972. 20,300 entries. 2 reels. ISBN 0-8161-1262-2 – 1 – $205.00 – uk Hall [240]
CLASSIFIED CATALOGUE (DEWEY DECIMAL SYSTEM) / Jewish National and University Library, Jerusalem – (Includes index) – 1647mf – 9 – J-10-21/1 – ne IDC [020]
CLASSIFIED CATALOGUE OF PRINTED TRACTS AND BOOKS IN SINHALESE / Murdoch, John & Nicholson, J – Madras. 1868. BI-352 2 – 1mf – 8 – ne IDC [010]
CLASSIFIED CATALOGUE OF TAMIL PRINTED BOOKS, WITH INTRODUCTORY NOTICES / Murdoch, John – Madras, 1865 – 7mf – 9 – ne IDC [490]
CLASSIFIED CATALOGUE OF THE LIBRARY OF THE DIRECTOR GENERAL OF ARCHAEOLOGY 1908-1915 – (Supplement 1-3) – Calcutta, 1911-1916 – 3mf – 9 – ne IDC [930]
CLASSIFIED INDEX OF RATE CASES, YEARS 1925, 1926, 1927 / American Telephone and Telegraph Co – New York 1928 75 p. LL-1066 – 1 – us L of C Photodup [340]
CLASSIFIED INDEX, REGIONAL DIRECTORS' DECISIONS IN REPRESENTATION PROCEEDINGS / U.S. National Labor Relations Board – 1977-89 (all publ) – 13mf – 9 – $19.50 – LLMC 95-034 – us L.L.M.C. [340]
A CLASSIFIED LIST OF CAMBRO-SILURIAN AND POST-TERTIARY FOSSILS, FROM OTTAWA AND VICINITY / Ami, Henry Marc – Ottawa: Citizen, 1884. 02371. (Pre-1900 Canadiana) – 9 – cn C.I.H.M. [560]
CLASSIFIED SUBJECT CATALOG / Engineering Societies. New York – (Tenth Suppl., 1973-74) – 1reel 8600 cards – 1 – $70.00 – 0-8161-1269-X – uk Hall [620]
LE CLASSIQUE ET LE ROMANTIQUE: DIALOGUE / Baour-Lormian, Pierre Marie Francois Louis – Paris: U. Canel, 1825. 45p. 1 fiche. (Literature Collection) – 9 – 6.00 – fr Bibl Nationale [810]
CLASSIS CRUCIFORMIUM EMENDATA / Crantz, H J N von – Lipsiae. 1769 – 8 – ne IDC [580]
CLASSROOM COMPUTER NEWS – v1-. 1980- – 1,5,6,9 – us UMI [073]
CLATONIA LEADER – Clatonia, NE. -w. Dec. 1935-Jun. 1938; Aug. 1944 – 1 – us NE Hist [071]
CLATONIA OBSERVER – Clatonia, NE. -w. Jun. 1907-Apr. 1909 – 1 – us NE Hist [071]
CLATSKANIE CHIEF – Clatskanie, OR. -w. 4 Sept 1891-29 Dec 1917+. 22 rolls – 1 – us U.O. Library [071]
THE CLAUDE A. BARNETT PAPERS, PART 1 : ASSOCIATED NEGRO PRESS NEWS RELEASES, 1928-64 / The Associated Negro Press – (Series A: 1928-44. 29r. $3,200.00 ISBN: 0-89093-698-6; Series B: 1945-55. 29r. $3,200.00 ISBN: 0-89093-699-4; Series C: 1956-64. 25r. $2,750.00 ISBN: 0-89093-697-8. With printed guides) – 1 – $8,685.00 set – us UPA [380]
THE CLAUDE A. BARNETT PAPERS, PART 2 : ASSOCIATED NEGRO PRESS ORGANIZATIONAL FILES, 1920-66 / The Associated Negro Press – (With printed guide) – 24r – 1 – $2,645.00 – 0-89093-739-7 – us UPA [380]
THE CLAUDE A. BARNETT PAPERS, PART 3 : SUBJECT FILES ON BLACK AMERICANS, 1918-67 / The Associated Negro Press – (Series A: Agriculture, 1923-66. 11r. ISBN 0-89093-759-1 $1,210.00; Series B: Colleges and Universities, 1918-66. 16r. ISBN 0-89093-760-5 $1,760.00; Series C: Economic Conditions, 1918-66. 13r. ISBN 0-89093-761-3 $1,430.00; Series D: Entertainers, Artists and Authors, 1928-65. 7r. ISBN 0-89093-762-1 $770.00; Series E: Medicine, 1927-65. 7r. ISBN 0-89093-763-X $770.00; Series F: The Military, 1925-65. 3r. ISBN 0-89093-764-8 $330.00; Series G: Philanthropic and Social Organizations, 1925-66. 5r. ISBN 0-89093-765-6 $550.00; Series H: Politics and Law, 1920-66. 9r. ISBN 0-89093-766-4 $990.00; Series I: Race Relations, 1923-65. 8r. ISBN 0-89093-767-2 $885.00; Series J: Religion, 1924-66. 9r. ISBN 0-89093-768-0 $990.00; Series K: Claude A. Barnett Papers, Personal and Financial, 1920-67. 3r. ISBN 0-89093-769-9 $330.00. All with printed guides) – 1 – $9,515.00 set – us UPA [380]
CLAUDE MONET. EXPOSITION RETROSPECTIVE / Reunion des musees nationaux. Paris – 1931. 1 fiche – 9 – fr Réunion [700]
CLAUDE PAYSAN / Choquette, Ernest – Illus. par Leduc. Montreal: Bishop, 1899. 00631. (Pre-1900 Canadiana) – 9 – cn C.I.H.M. [920]
O CLAUDIENSE : ORGAM POPULAR, DEDICADO AOS INTERESSES DA LAVOURA, COMMERCIO E INDUSTRIA – Claudio, 21 Nov 1897; Feb-May, Jul 1898 – 1,5,6 – bl Biblioteca [072]
CLAUDII CLAUDIANI CARMINA (MGH 1: 10.BD) / ed by Birt, Th – 1892 – Dfl77.00 – ne Slangenburg [240]
Claudin, Fernando *see* LA JUVENTUD ESPANOLA CONTINUA SU LUCHA
Claudius Matthias *see* DER WANDSBECKER BOTHE
Claudius, Matthias *see*
– DER WANDSBECKER BOTE
– WERKE
Claudon, F *see* ABBAYES ET PRIEURES DE L'ANCIENNE FRANCE
THE CLAUSE COMPROMISSOIRE, ITS VALIDITY IN QUEBEC / Johnson, Walter Seely – Montreal, Johnson, 1945. 166 p. LL-2319 – 1 – us L of C Photodup [340]
Clausen, Ernst Alexander *see* DER HEILIGEN KIND
[Clausen, H F C] *see* RECUEIL DE TOUS LES TRAITES,...
Clausen, Julius *see* JENS BAGGESEN
Clausewitz, C von *see* ON WAR
Clausewitz, Carl von *see* HINTERLASSENE WERKE UEBER KREIG UND KRIEGFUEHRUNG
Clausewitz, Karl von *see* PRINCIPLES OF WAR
Clauss, Gertrud *see* DIE FRAU IN DER DICHTUNG CONRAD FERDINAND MEYERS
Clauss, Walter *see* DEUTSCHE LITERATUR
Claussen, Martin P *see* THE STATE-WAR-NAVY COORDINATING COMMITTEE (SWNCC) AND STATE-ARMY-NAVY-AIR FORCE COORDINATING COMMITTEE (SANACC) CASE FILES, 1944-49
Claussen, Sophus *see* BYEN: JUNKER FRIKLOVER: NUTIDSROMAN
CLAVE HISTORIAL / Florez Setien, Enrique – 1743 – 2mf – 9 – Pta1,500.00 – 84-7848-045-5 – sp Pentalfa [240]
LE CLAVECIN BIEN TEMPERE: OU PRELUDES ET FUGUES DANS TOUS LES TONS ET DEMINTONS DU MODE MAJEUR ET MINEUR / Bach, Johann Sebastian – Vienne: Hoffmeister & Comp; Leipsic: Bureau de Musique, 18– – 1 – us Sibley [780]
Clavego, P *see* EL TRABAJO DE LOS COMISARIOS POLITICOS
Clavel, Charles *see* LES MARQUISIENS
THE CLAVERINGS / Trollope, Anthony – London: Smith, Elder, 1867 – 1 roll – 1 – 1-55879-965-6 – uk Libr Preservation [830]
CLAVICULA SALOMONIS = THE KEY OF SOLOMON THE KING / Clavicula Salomonis – (In English. Includes bibliographical references) – London: Kegan Paul, Trench, Truebner, 1909 – 1mf – 9 – 0-8370-4179-1 – 1985-2179 – us A.T.L.A. [920]
Clavicula Salomonis *see* CLAVICULA SALOMONIS
Clavier, Irene *see* SAMARITANA
Claviere, Etienne *see* DE LA CONJURATION CONTRE LES FINANCES ET DES MESURES A PRENDRE POUR EN ARRETER LES EFFETS
CLAVIERUEBUNG BESTEHEND IN EINER ARIA MIT VERSCHIEDENEN VERAENDERUNGEN VORS CLAVICIMBAL MIT 2 MANUALEN. DENEN LIEBHABERN ZUR GEMUETHSERGETZUNG VERFERTIGT VON... / Bach, Johann Sebastian – Nuernberg: im Verlagung Balthasar Schmids, [1742] – 1 – us Sibley [780]
CLAVIERUEBUNGEN / Kirnberger, Johann P – 1761-63.Erste (-Dritte) Sammlung – 9 – us Sibley [780]
Clavijo y Clavijo, Salvador *see* LA TRAYECTORIA HOSPITALARIA DE LA ARMADA ESPANOLA. MADRID, 1944
CLAVIS AGROSTOGRAPHIAE ANTIQUIORIS : UEBERSICHT DES ZUSTANDES DER AGROSTOGRAPHIE BIS AUF LINNE.... / Trinius, Carl Bernhard – Coburg, 1822 – 8mf – 9 – ne IDC [580]
CLAVIS MEDICINAE DUPLEX, EXTERIOR AND INTERIOR / Linnaeus, Carl – 161. 1766 – 9 – ne IDC [610]
CLAVIS NOVI HYMENOPTERORUM SYSTEMATIS / Dahlbom, A G – Lund. 1835. v, 40p. 1pl. Z-1166 2 – 8 – ne IDC [590]
CLAVIS RIVINIANA, SCHLUESSEL ZU DEN KUPFERWERKEN DES A. Q. RIVINUS / Huth, E – Frankfurt a. D. 1891. B-5680 2 – 8 – ne IDC [580]
CLAVIS SYNOPTICA HYMENOMYCETUM EUROPAEORUM / Cooke, M C & Quelet, L – London, etc. 1878. B-6257 2 – 8 – ne IDC [580]
Clavius, Christoph *see*
– CHRISTOPHORI CLAVII BAMBERGENSIS E SOCIETATE IES OPERUM MATHEMATICORUM TOMUS PRIMUS-QUINTUS
– CHRISTOPHORI CLAVII...IN SPHAERAM IOANNIS DE SACRO BOSCO COMMENTARIUS
Clay, A T *see* BABYLONIAN RECORDS IN THE LIBRARY OF J. PIERPONT MORGAN
CLAY AND OWEN COUNTIES / Blanchard, Richard – Historical and biographical sketches. Chicago: F. A. Battey and Co., 1884. Indiana Reel 8. (The Cox Library Collection) – 5 – us Americana [978]
CLAY COUNTY CRESCENT – Green Cove Springs. Fl. -w. 1946- – 1 – us P.K. Yonge [071]
CLAY COUNTY FREE PRESS – Clay. West Virginia. -w. 1934-66 – 1 – us UMI [071]
CLAY COUNTY LEADER – Clay Center, NE. -w. Sep. 1963-Dec. 1976 – 1 – us NE Hist [071]
CLAY COUNTY NEWS – Sutton, NE. -w. May 1942 to date – 1 – us NE Hist [071]
CLAY COUNTY REPUBLICAN – Clay Center, NE. -w. Mar. 1895-Apr. 1895; Oct. 1895-Aug. 1921 – 1 – us NE Hist [071]
CLAY COUNTY SUN – Clay Center, NE. -w. May 1887; Dec. 1892; Jul. 1895-Oct. 1910;Dec. 1917- – 1 – us NE Hist [071]
CLAY CROSS CHRONICLE – Clay Cross, England. -w. 11 May 1900-Dec 1910. 10 reels – 1 – uk British Libr Newspaper [072]
Clay, Henrietta *see* BITS OF FAMILY HISTORY
Clay, Henry *see*
– 1832 SPEECH IN DEFENCE OF THE AMERICAN SYSTEM
– PAPERS
Clay, Rotha Mary *see*
– THE HERMITS AND ANCHORITIES OF ENGLAND
– THE MEDIAEVAL HOSPITALS OF ENGLAND
Claybaugh, Joseph *see* HISTORY OF CLINTON COUNTY
Clayden, Arthur *see* THE REVOLT OF THE FIELD: A SKETCH OF THE RISE AND PROGRESS OF THE MOVEMENT AMONG THE AGRICULTURAL LABOURERS, KNOWN AS THE "NATIONAL AGRICULTURAL LABOURERS' UNION"
Clayden, Peter William *see* THE EARLY LIFE OF SAMUEL ROGERS
CLAYPOOLE'S AMERICAN DAILY ADVERTISER – Philadelphia, Penna. 1796-1800 – 3 – us Readex [071]
CLAYS AND CLAY MINERALS – v16-25. 1968-77 – 5,6,9 – us UMI [550]
CLAYTON COMMERCIAL – Plainfield. Ind. -w. 1934-35, 1937-40, 1944-45, 1948-52 – 1 – us UMI [071]
Clayton, F H *see* SCENES AND INCIDENTS IN IRISH LIFE
Clayton, Henry R *see* ANGLO-CANADIAN COPYRIGHTS
Clayton, J M *see* SPEECH...1853
Clayton, Joseph *see* ST. HUGH OF LINCOLN, A BIOGRAPHY..
Clayton, W Woodford *see*
– HISTORY OF DAVIDSON COUNTY
– HISTORY OF ONONDAGA COUNTY
– HISTORY OF UNION AND MIDDLESEX COUNTIES
CLAYTON'S WEEKLY – Seattle. Wash. 1917-1920 – 1 – us UMI [071]
CLAYWORKER – Sept 1973-Jul 1974 – 1 – us UMI [073]
CLE – no. 1-2. Paris. janv-fevr 1939 – 1 – fr A.C.R.P.P. [073]
LA CLE D'OR : REVUE MENSUELLE ILLUSTREE DE L'ANNONCE – Quebec, Canada. mar 1926-fev 1928 – 1r – 1 – Can$30.00 – cn Can Microfilming [072]
CLE JOURNAL AND REGISTER (ALI-ABA) – v1-41. 1965-95 – 9 – $684.00 set – us Hein [340]
CLEAN AIR – (1976- . 5,6,9) – 1967- – 1 – us UMI [574]
CLEAR CREEK BAPTIST CHURCH. ADAMS COUNTY. MISSISSIPPI : CHURCH RECORDS – 1835-1873 – 1 – 5.13 – us Baptist [240]
Clear Creek Baptist School. Pineville, Kentucky *see* CATALOGS AND COLLEGE RECORDS
CLEAR CUT : THE DEFORESTATION OF AMERICA / Wood, Nancy – 1r – 5,9 – $50.00 – B70008 – us Library Micro [574]
CLEAR HILLS STANDARD – Jun 20 1914 – 9 – at Pascoe [072]
CLEARING HOUSE – (v. 43-56. 1968-83. 5,6. v. 44-56. 1969-83. 9) – 1-56. 1920-83 – 1 – us UMI [370]
CLEARINGHOUSE REVIEW – (v.13-. 1979- 5,6,9) – v.1-. 1967- – 1 – us UMI [073]
CLEARLAKE COURIER – Lakeport, CA. 1870-1871 – 1 – 1 – $50.00 – C03608 – us Library Micro [071]
CLEARLAKE OBSERVER-AMERICAN – Clearlake Highlands, CA. 1976- – 31+ r – 1 – $1,550.00 ($140.00y) – B02114 – us Library Micro [071]
CLEARLAKE PRESS – Lakeport, CA. 1894-1914 – 10r – 1 – $500.00 – BC03263 – us Library Micro [071]
CLEARMONT BAPTIST CHURCH. OCONEE COUNTY. WESTMINSTER, SOUTH CAROLINA : CHURCH RECORDS – 1890-1909, 1922-53 – 1 – 9.45 – us Baptist [240]
CLEARWATER HEADLIGHT – Clearwater, NE. -w. Sep. 1886-Jun. 1887 – 1 – us NE Hist [071]
CLEARWATER MESSAGE – Clearwater, NE. -w. Ju. 1887-Sep. 1888; May 1890-Mar. 1895. Incomplete; Oct. 1895-Oct. 1896 – 1 – us NE Hist [071]
CLEARWATER RECORD-EWING NEWS – Clearwater, NE. -w. Apr. 1897-Aug. 1904; Jul. 1905; Aug. 1908- – 1 – us NE Hist [071]
Cleary, James Vincent *see* CORRESPONDENCE BETWEEN ARCHBISHOP CLEARY, OF KINGSTON, AND W. R. MEREDITH, LEADER OF THE ONTARIO OPPOSITION; ALSO, THE ARCHBISHOP'S REMARKS AT TWEED, AND HIS CIRCULAR ON SEPARATE SCHOOLS, ADDRESSED TO HIS CLERGY
Cleary, Jon *see* THE LONG PURSUIT
Cleary, Michelle A *see* THE TIME COURSE OF THE REPEATED BOUT EFFECT OF ECCENTRIC EXERCISE ON DELAYED ONSET MUSCLE SORENESS
Cleary, N P *see* GO THE RIGHTS WAY, DO THE RIGHTS THING, A POLICY STATEMENT
Cleary, Reuben *see* MANUSCRIPT OF HIS CHRONICOS LAGEANAS
CLEAVELAND GAZETTE AND COMMERCIAL REGISTER – (Weekly newspaper, the first publ in Cleveland) – Cleveland, OH. Jul 31 1818-Mar 7 1820 – 1r – 1 – us Western Res [071]
CLEAVELAND HERALD – (Weekly Whig newspaper, the second newspaper published in Cleveland) – Cleveland, OH. oct 19, 1819-april 12, 1832 – 4r – 1 – us Western Res [071]
CLECKHEATON ADVERTISER – Yorkshire. 1871-85 – 1 – uk Microform Academic [072]
Clee. Shropshire *see* REGISTERS
CLEF – v1, nos. 1-7 (all publ). Mar-Sep 1946. (Jazz Periodicals) – 1 reel – 1 – $60.00 – us UPA [780]
LA CLEF DU CABINET DES PRINCES DE L'EUROPE / Jordan, Claude – or Recueil historique et politique sur les matieres du tems. Luxembourg. juil 1704-06 (I-V) – 1 – fr A.C.R.P.P. [073]
LA CLEF DU CABINET DES PRINCES DE L'EUROPE,... – N.p., 1707 – 2mf – 1 – ILM-2809/1 – ne IDC [327]
LA CLEF DU CABINET DES SOUVERAINS – Paris. 1797-sept 1805 (I-XXXII) – 1 – fr A.C.R.P.P. [073]
CLEF SYNOPTIQUE, OU, ABREGEE DU TABLEAU STEREOMETRIQUE BAILLAIRGE / Baillairge, Charles – Quebec: C. Darveau, 1874. 02497. (Pre-1900 Canadiana) – 9 – cn C.I.H.M. [624]
Cleghorn, H F C *see* THE FORESTS AND GARDENS OF SOUTH INDIA

Cleghorn, Robert *see* A SHORT HISTORY OF BAPTIST MISSIONARY WORK IN BRITISH HONDURAS, 1822-1939

Cleinow, G *see* RUSSLAND UND ASIEN

Cleirac, Estienne *see*
- US ET COUSTUMES DE LA MER
- LES US ET COUTUMES DE LA MER

Cleland, James *see* THE INSTITUTION OF A YOUNG NOBLE MAN

Cleland, John *see* THE WAY TO THINGS BY WORDS

Cleland, William *see* HISTORY OF THE PRESBYTERIAN CHURCH IN IRELAND; FOR READERS ON THIS SIDE OF THE ATLANTIC

Clelland, Thomas *see* MARRIAGE REGISTER AND ACCOUNT BOOK

LES CLEMATITES A GRANDES FLEURS / Lavallee, P A M – Paris. 1884. B-6008 2 – 8 – ne IDC [580]

Clemen, August *see*
- DER GEBRAUCH DES ALTEN TESTAMENTS IN DEN NEUTESTAMENTLICHEN SCHRIFTEN
- DIE WUNDERBERICHTE UEBER ELIA UND ELISA IN DEN BUECHERN DER KOENIGE

Clemen, Carl *see*
- DIE APOSTELGESCHICHTE IM LICHTE DER NEUEREN TEXTQUELLEN
- DIE CHRISTLICHE LEHRE VON DER SUENDE: EINE UNTERSUCHUNG ZUR SYSTEMATISCHEN THEOLOGIE
- DER EINFLUSS DER MYSTERIENRELIGIONEN AUF DAS AELTESTE CHRISTENTUM
- DIE EINHEITLICHKEIT DER PAULINISCHEN BRIEFE
- DIE ENTWICKLUNG DER CHRISTLICHEN RELIGION: INNERHALB DES NEUEN TESTAMENTS
- DIE RELIGIONEN DER ERDE: IHR WESEN UND IHRE GESCHICHTE, MIT BEITRAEGEN VON FRANZ RABINGER...ET AL
- DIE RELIGIONSPHILOSOPHISCHE BEDEUTUNG DES STOISCH-CHRISTLICHEN EUDAEMONISMUS IN JUSTINS APOLOGIE
- DER URSPRUNG DES HEILIGEN ABENDMAHLS

CLEMENS ALEXANDRINUS UND DIE SEPTUAGINTA / Staehlin, Otto – Nuernberg: J.L. Stich, 1901. 1 fiche – 9 – us A.T.L.A. [240]

CLEMENS BRENTANOS FRUEHLYRIK : CHRONOLOGIE UND ENTWICKLUNG / Jaeger, Hans – (Includes bibliographical references) – Frankfurt am Main: M Diesterweg, 1926 – 1 – us U.W. Library [430]

CLEMENS BRENTANOS WELTLICHE LYRIK / Schubert, Kurt – (Includes bibliographical references) – Breslau: F Hirt, 1910 – 1 – us U.W. Library [430]

Clemens, Samuel Langhorne *see* CONTRIBUTIONS TO THE GALAXY 1868-1871

Clement *see* GUILLAUME LE CONQUERANT, DUC DE NORMANDIE

Clement 1st, Pope *see* BRUCHSTUECKE DES ERSTEN CLEMENSBRIEFES

Clement, Alex *see* AUX JEUNES GENS QUI VEULENT REUSSIR

Clement, Ambroise *see* RECHERCHES SUR LES CAUSES DE L'INDIGENCE

Clement, Charles-F *see* ESSAI SUR L'ACCOMPAGNEMENT DU CLAVECIN

CLEMENT D'ALEXANDRIE : ETUDE SUR LES RAPPORTS DU CHRISTIANISME ET DE LA PHILOSOPHIE GRECQUE AU IIE SIECLE / Faye, Eugene de – Paris: Ernest Leroux, 1906. (Bibliotheque de l'Ecole des hautes etudes. Sciences religieuses; t. 12) – 1mf – us A.T.L.A. [240]

CLEMENT D'ALEXANDRIE / Freppel, Monseigneur – Paris: Retaux-Bray, [1873?] (Cours d'eloquence sacree / fait a la Sorbonne pendant l'annee 1864-1965) – 1mf – us A.T.L.A. [240]

Clement de Ris, Louis Torterat *see* NOTICE DU MUSEE HISTORIQUE DE VERSAILLES

Clement, Ernest Wilson *see* CHRISTIANITY IN MODERN JAPAN

Clement, F E *see* PRIMITIVE CONCEPTS OF DISEASE

Clement, Francis *see* THE PETIE SCHOLE WITH AN ENGLISH ORTHOGRAPHIE

Clement, G *see* LES OEUVRES RUPESTRES DU MASSIF DE SUMIDOURO, REGION DE LAGOA SANTA, MINAS GERAIS, BRESIL

Clement, J M B *see* ANECDOTES DRAMATIQUES

Clement, James Wilkenson Legare, Jr. *see* PAPERS OF JAMES WILKENSON LEGARE CLEMENT, JR.

CLEMENT OF ALEXANDRIA, A STUDY IN CHRISTIAN LIBERALISM / Tollinton, Richard Bartram – London: Williams and Norgate, 1914. 2v – 1 – us U.W. Library [240]

CLEMENT OF ALEXANDRIA, QUIS DIVES SALVETUR : WITH AN INTRODUCTION ON THE MSS OF CLEMENT'S WORKS / ed by Barnard, P M – 1897 – 2mf – 9 – ne Slangenburg [240]

Clement, P *see*
- LETTRES, INSTRUCTIONS ET MEMOIRES DE COLBERT PUBLIES...
- VIENNE SUR LE RHONE

Clement, William Henry Pope *see*
- THE HISTORY OF THE DOMINION OF CANADA
- THE LAW OF THE CANADIAN CONSTITUTION

Clementi, Cecil *see* THE CHINESE IN BRITISH GUIANA

Clementi, G *see* SERTULUM ORIENTALE SEU RECENSIO PLANTARUM IN OLYMPO BITHYNICO

Clementi, M *see*
- CAPPRICCIOS, TWO, FOR THE PIANO, OP. 47
- INTRODUCTION O THE ART OF PLAYING THE PIANOFORTE
- SONATA PER CLAVICEMBALO O PIANOFORTE CON UN VIOLINE O FLAUTO E VIOLONCELLO, OP. (33)/T. 6
- SONATAS, PIANO, OP. 2, C MAJOR
- SONATE PER CLAVICEMBALO OPIANOFORTE, CON VIOLINE O FLAUTO
- SONATES, 3 POUR LE CLAVECIN OU PIANOFORTE AVEC FLUTE ET BASSE
- SONATES, TROIS. HEFT 1 OF REPERTOIRE DES CLAVECINISTES

Clementi, Muzio *see* SAMMLUNG BERUEHMTER SONATEN, REVIDIRT UND MIT FINGERSATZ VERSEHEN VON LOUIS KOEHLER UND F.A. ROITZSCH

Clements, J B *see* HISTORY OF IRWIN COUNTY

Clements, Rex S *see* SERMONS

Clements, W G *see* ON A COLLECTION OF SIERRA LEONE LEPIDOPTERA

Clements, W H *see* THE GLAMOUR AND TRAGEDY OF THE ZULU WAR

Clemmer, Myrtle M *see* UNITED PRESBYTERIAN HISTORICAL DIRECTORY

CLEMSON NATURE STUDY LEAFLET / Clemson University. College of Agriculture – n.1-23 – 1,5 – us Spaulding [630]

Clemson University. Agricultural Experiment Station *see*
- AE AGRICULTURAL ECONOMICS AND RURAL SOCIOLOGY REPORT
- AGRICULTURAL CHEMICAL SERVICES SERIES
- AGRICULTURAL ENGINEERING RESEARCH SERIES
- AGRICULTURAL WEATHER RESEARCH SERIES
- AGRONOMY AND SOILS RESEARCH SERIES
- ANIMAL SCIENCE RESEARCH SERIES
- ANNUAL REPORT
- ANNUAL REPORT OF ECONOMIC POISONS ANALYSES
- BULLETIN
- CIRCULAR
- CLIMATIC RESEARCH SERIES
- DAIRY RESEARCH SERIES
- DEPARTMENT OF HORTICULTURE RESEARCH SERIES
- DEPARTMENT OF SEED CERTIFICATION RESEARCH SERIES
- LEAFLETS
- POULTRY RESEARCH SERIES
- RESEARCH SUMMARIES
- TECHNICAL BULLETIN

Clemson University. Agricultural Extension Division *see*
- AGRICULTURAL CHEMICALS HANDBOOK
- AGRICULTURAL ENGINEERING HANDBOOK
- BULLETINS
- CIRCULARS
- COTTON LEAFLET
- DAIRY SCIENCE EXTENSION LEAFLET
- EXTENSION BULLETIN
- FORESTRY NOTES
- HORTICULTURE LEAFLET
- LIVESTOCK LEAFLET
- MISCELLANEOUS EXTENSION PUBLICATION
- MISCELLANEOUS PUBLICATIONS
- REPORTS

Clemson University. College of Agriculture *see* CLEMSON NATURE STUDY LEAFLET

Clemson University. Department of Agricultural Economics and Rural Sociology *see* RESEARCH REPORT

Clemson University. Department of Forestry *see*
- FOREST RESEARCH SERIES
- FORESTRY BULLETIN
- FORESTRY PUBLICATIONS
- TECHNICAL PAPER

Clemson University. Department of Horticulture *see* MISCELLANEOUS PUBLICATION

Clemson University. South Carolina Agricultural Experiment Station *see* PUBLICATION: AN INDEX

Clendenen, Clarence C *see* AMERICANS IN BLACK AFRICA UP TO 1865

CLEOPHAS LACHANCE: SON CRIME, SON PROCES, SON EXECUTION – Levis Quebec: A. Routhier, 1881. 03014. (Pre-1900 Canadiana) – 9 – cn C.I.H.M. [360]

Clephane, Walter Collins *see* THE ORGANIZATION AND MANAGEMENT OF BUSINESS CORPORATIONS

Cler, Jean Joseph Gustave *see* REMINISCENCES OF AN OFFICER OF ZOUAVES

Clerambault, Louis Nicolas *see* CANTATES FRANCOISES A 1 ET 2 VOIX: AVEC SIMPHONIE, ET SANS SIMPHONIE...LIVRE PREMIER

Clerambault, Louis Nicolas et al *see* NEUF CANTATES

Clerc, Jean le *see*
- OPERA OMNIA
- LE SPECTACLE DE LA VIE HUMAINE

Clerc, Michel *see* CONTRIBUTION A L'ETUDE DES RELATIONS VITAMINIQUES A ET C

Clercq, A J H de *see* RECUEIL DES TRAITES DE LA FRANCE, 1763-1906

Clercq, E F J de *see* RECUEIL DES TRAITES DE LA FRANCE, 1763-1906

Clercq, Louis de *see* VOYAGE EN ORIENT

Clercq, V C De *see* OSSIUS OF CORDOVA

THE CLERC'S BOOK OF 1549 / Wickham Legg, J – 1901 – 4mf – 8 – Dfl19.00 – ne Slangenburg [240]

Clerfeyt, Joseph Maximilian Louis *see* L'AFFAIRE CLERFEYT.

LE CLERGE CANADIEN: SA MISSION, SON OEUVRE / David, Laurent Olivier – Montreal: s.n., 1896. 02510. (Pre-1900 Canadiana) – 9 – cn C.I.H.M. [971]

THE CLERGY AND THE CREEDS : A SERMON / Gore, Charles – London: Rivingtons, 1887 – 1mf – us A.T.L.A. [240]

THE CLERGY IN AMERICAN LIFE AND LETTERS / Addison, Daniel Dulany – New York: Macmillan, 1900. (National studies in American letters) – 1mf – us A.T.L.A. [240]

CLERGYMEN OF THE CHURCH OF ENGLAND / Trollope, Anthony – London: Chapman and Hall, 1866 – 1 roll – 1 – 1-55879-890-0 – uk Libr Preservation [240]

CLERICAL POLITICS IN THE METHODIST EPISCOPAL CHURCH / Townsend, Luther Tracy – Boston: McDonald, Gill, c1892 – 1mf – us A.T.L.A. [240]

LE CLERICALISME AU CANADA – (Fasc 1: Cures et bedeaux. Fasc 2: Saintes comedies) – Montreal, 1896. SEM16P282 – 1r – 5 – Can$9.00 – cn Bibl Nat [240]

Clerici, J *see* OPERA OMNIA

LOS CLERIGOS Y LA EXTIRPACION DE LA IDOLATRIA ENTRE LOS NEOFITOS AMERICANOS / Bayle, Constantino – Madrid: Missionalia Hispanica, 1946 – 1 – sp Bibl Santa Ana [240]

Clerk, E *see* THE TRUE WITNESS

Clerk, John *see* AN ESSAY ON NAVAL TACTICS, SYSTEMATICAL AND HISTORICAL

Clerke, Francis *see* PRAXIS FRANCISCI CLERKE, TAM JUS DICENTIBUS QUAM ALIIS OMNIBUS QUI IN FORO ECCLESIASTICO VERSANTUR APPRIME UTILIS

THE CLERK'S ASSISTANT, CONTAINING A LARGE VARIETY OF LEGAL FORMS AND INSTRUMENTS. / McCall, Henry Strong – (5th ed. New York, Banks, 1898. 1136p. LL-930. 1. 6th ed. New York, Banks, 1902. 1216p. LL-1412. 1) – 4th ed. Albany, Gould, 1884. 618 p. LL-874 – 1 – us L of C Photodup [340]

CLERK'S RECORD / Shawnee County. Kansas. School District 26 – 1927-43 – 1 – us KS Hist [978]

CLERMONT CO, OHIO, RECORDS, MSS 1086 – (Scattered census records, tax accounts, treasurers' reports, loose papers of the Sheriff, Justices of Peace, and Court of Common Pleas, vital statistics, and poll books) – Clermont, OH. 1801-63 – 1r – 1 – us Western Res [350]

Clermont County. Ohio *see* MISCELLANEOUS RECORDS, MS 1086

CLERMONT SUN : WEEKLY DEMOCRATIC NEWSPAPER – Batavia, OH. 22 Feb 1854-26 Dec 1860 – 1r – 1 – us Western Res [071]

EL CLERO SECULAR Y LA EVANGELIZACION DE AMERICA / Bayle, Constantino – Madrid: CSIC Instituto Santo Toribio de Mogroviejo, 1950. Bib. Missionalia Hispanica. vol. 6 – 1 – sp Bibl Santa Ana [240]

EL CLERO VASCO, FIEL AL GOBIERNO DE LA REPUBLICA, SE DIRIGE AL SUMO PONTIFICE / Vitoria. Spain (Diocese) – Madrid, 1937. Fiche W804. (Blodgett Collection of Spanish Civil War Pamphlets) – 9 – us H.U. College Libr [946]

EL CLERO Y LOS CATOLICOS VASCO-SEPARATISTAS Y EL MOVIMIENTO NACIONAL – Madrid: Imp. y Enc. de los sobrinos de la Sucesoera de M. Minuesa, 1940 – sp Bibl Santa Ana [240]

Clery, Jean Baptiste Cant Hanet *see* JOURNAL DE CE QUI S'EST PASSE A LA TOUR DU TEMPLE, PENDANT LA CAPTIVITE DE LOUIS XVI, ROI DE FRANCE

Clessin, S *see* DEUTSCHE EXCURSIONS-MOLLUSKEN FAUNA

Cleve, Karl *see*
- GOETHES VERHAELTNIS ZU HANS SACHS
- NICOLAIS FEYNER KLEYNER ALMANACH

CLEVELAND ADVOCATE : WEEKLY AFRICAN-AMERICAN REPUBLICAN NEWSPAPER – Cleveland, OH. May 1915-Dec 1920 – 1 – us Western Res [071]

Cleveland, Akron and Columbus Railway *see* OBSERVATION CAR

CLEVELAND ANZEIGER – Cleveland, OH. July 30-Aug 1 1872 – 1r – 1 – us Western Res [071]

CLEVELAND ANZEIGER : DAILY GERMAN LANGUAGE NEWSPAPER – Cleveland, OH. Oct 2 1876-Sept 18 1891 – 27r – 1 – us Western Res [071]

CLEVELAND ANZEIGER : SUNDAY EDITION – Cleveland, OH. Sept 29 1878-Sept 13 1891 – 7r – 1 – us Western Res [071]

CLEVELAND ANZEIGER : WEEKLY EDITION – Cleveland, OH. Jan 3 1878-Sept 16 1891 – 5r – 1 – us Western Res [071]

CLEVELAND ANZEIGER AND DEUTSCHE PRESSE – Cleveland, OH. Sept 19 1891-Sept 30 1893 – 3r – 1 – us Western Res [071]

CLEVELAND ANZEIGER AND DEUTSCHE PRESSE : SUNDAY EDITION GERMAN LANGUAGE NEWSPAPER – Cleveland, OH. Sept 20 1891-Oct 1 1893 – 3r – 1 – us Western Res [071]

CLEVELAND ANZEIGER AND DEUTSCHE PRESSE : WEEKLY EDITION – Cleveland, OH, Sept 23 1891-Sept 27 1893 – 1r – 1 – us Western Res [071]

CLEVELAND BAR ASSOCIATION JOURNAL *see* CLEVELAND BAR JOURNAL

CLEVELAND BAR JOURNAL – (Cont: Cleveland Bar Association Journal. Lacking: v1 no 5,11. v2 no 2. v5 nos 1-4. v32 no 9. v47 no 8. Updates planned) – v1-55. 1927-84 – 197mf – 9 – $295.00 – LLMC 84-438 – us L.L.M.C. [073]

CLEVELAND BAR JOURNAL – (Title varies: v1-40 1927-68 as Journal of the Cleveland Bar Association. Suspended March 1933-Sept 1936) – v1-66. 1927-95 – 9 – $682.00 set – us Hein [340]

Cleveland, Charles Dexter *see* LYRA SACRA AMERICANA, OR, GEMS FROM AMERICAN SACRED POETRY

Cleveland, Clyde C *see* INDONESIAN ADVENTURE FOR CHRIST

CLEVELAND CORRESPONDENT : WEEKLY GERMAN LANGUAGE NEWSPAPER – Cleveland, OH. 14 Sep 1908-4 Mar 1911 – 2r – 1 – us Western Res [071]

CLEVELAND DAILY EXPRESS : DAILY KNOW NOTHING/AMERICAN PARTY NEWSPAER – Cleveland, OH. 21 June-30 Dec 1854 – 1r – 1 – us Western Res [071]

CLEVELAND DAILY HERALD : DAILY WHIG NEWSPAPER – Cleveland, OH. 21 July 1856-22 June 1857 – 2r – 1 – us Western Res [071]

CLEVELAND DAILY HERALD : DAILY WHIG NEWSPAPER – Cleveland, OH. 6 Aug 1839-20 Sept 1843 – 6r – 1 – us Western Res [071]

CLEVELAND DAILY HERALD – (Evening ed of this daily Republican newspaper) – Cleveland, OH. Jun 1-Dec 31 1874 – 2r – 1 – us Western Res [071]

CLEVELAND DAILY HERALD – (Morning ed of this daily Republican newspaper) – Cleveland, OH. Jan 2-Nov 30 1871 – 3r – 1 – us Western Res [071]
CLEVELAND DAILY HERALD – (Morning ed of this daily Republican newspaper) – Cleveland, OH. Jul 1-Dec 2 1874 – 1r – 1 – us Western Res [071]
CLEVELAND FEDERATIONIST : WEEKLY LABOR PAPER, PUBLISHED BY THE CLEVELAND BRANCH, AMERICAN FEDERATION OF LABOR – Cleveland, OH. 1910-33 – 8r – 1 – us Western Res [071]
CLEVELAND GAZETTE : DAILY WHIG NEWSPAPER – Cleveland, OH. 1 June 1836-21 Mar 1837 – 1r – 1 – us Western Res [071]
CLEVELAND GERMANIA – (Daily German language, Republican newspaper) – Cleveland, OH. Jan 2-Jun 30 1889 – 2r – 1 – us Western Res [071]
Cleveland, Grover *see* PAPERS
CLEVELAND HERALD – Cleveland, OH. 1869-74 – 1 – us Western Res [071]
CLEVELAND HERALD : DAILY WHIG NEWSPAPER – Cleveland, OH. 21 Sept 1843-9 Apr 1853 – 17r – 1 – us Western Res [071]
CLEVELAND HERALD : MORNING EDITION – (Daily Republican newspaper) – Cleveland, OH. june 5, 1880-june 30, 1884 – 6r – 1 – us Western Res [071]
CLEVELAND HERALD – (Weekly Whig, later Republican newspaper) – Cleveland, OH. sept 27, 1843-dec 30, 1865 – 5r – 1 – us Western Res [071]
CLEVELAND HERALD AND GAZETTE – (Weekly Whig newspaper) – Cleveland, OH. mar 25, 1837-sept 20, 1843 – 2r – 1 – us Western Res [071]
CLEVELAND JEWISH MISCELLANY, MS 3669 / Nebel, Abraham Lincoln – (Correspondence, clippings, notes and legal documents relating to Jewish American genealogy and Jewish community in Cleveland, Ohio) – 1831-1971 – 1 – us Western Res [920]
THE CLEVELAND JEWISH NEWS – Cleveland. Ohio. 1964-67 – 1 – us A.J.P.C. [071]
CLEVELAND JOURNAL : WEEKLY AFRICAN-AMERICAN REPUBLICAN NEWSPAPER – Cleveland, OH. Mar 1903-Apr 1910 – 2r – 1 – us Western Res [073]
CLEVELAND JOURNAL AND SOUTH DURHAM ADVERTISER – Cleveland, South Durham, England. 13 Feb-23 Oct 1873. 45 ft – 1 – uk British Libr Newspaper [072]
CLEVELAND LAW RECORD – v1. 1855-56 (all publ) – 1mf – 9 – $1.50 – LLMC 84-441 – us L.L.M.C. [340]
CLEVELAND LAW REPORTER – v1-2. 1878-79 (all publ) – 9mf – 9 – $13.50 – LLMC 84-439 – us L.L.M.C. [340]
CLEVELAND LAW SCHOOL JOURNAL – v1. 1916 (all publ) – 1mf – 9 – $1.50 – LLMC 84-440 – us L.L.M.C. [073]
CLEVELAND MARSHAL LAW REVIEW *see* CLEVELAND STATE LAW REVIEW
CLEVELAND METHODIST MESSENGER – Cleveland, England. -m. Oct 1874-Jan 1875. 5 ft – 1 – uk British Libr Newspaper [072]
CLEVELAND MORNING DAILY HERALD – (Morning ed of this daily Republican newspaper) – Cleveland, OH. Dec 2 1871-May 30 1874 – 5r – 1 – us Western Res [071]
CLEVELAND MORNING EXPRESS : DAILY KNOW NOTHING/AMERICAN PARTY NEWSPAPER – Cleveland, OH. 22 Jan-30 June 1855 – 1r – 1 – us Western Res [071]
CLEVELAND NEWS – England. 7-28 Jun 1873; 6 Aug 1875-29 Oct 1887.-w. 12 reels – 1 – uk British Libr Newspaper [072]
CLEVELAND OBSERVER – (Weekly Presbyterian newspaper; originally published in Hudson, OH, as the Ohio Observer, the title returned to Hudson in 1840) – Cleveland, OH. sept 28, 1837-apr 1, 1840 – 1r – 1 – us Western Res [071]
Cleveland. Ohio. Bethany Presbyterian Church *see* CHURCH RECORDS, MS 3324
Cleveland. Ohio. Fifth Circuit Court *see* TAPPAN'S COMMON PLEAS REPORTS
Cleveland. Ohio. First Regular Baptist Church *see* CHURCH RECORDS, MS 647
Cleveland. Ohio. Presbytery. The Women's Foreign Mission Society *see* CHURCH RECORDS, MS 241
Cleveland. Ohio. St. John's Episcopal Church *see* CHURCH RECORDS, MS 3066
CLEVELAND, OHIO, TAXES, MS V.F. O – (Appraisement of Cleveland giving proprietors, owners or occupiers names) – 1802 – 1r – 1 – us Western Res [978]
CLEVELAND, OHIO, TAXES, MS V.F. O / Ayres, Ebenezer – (Return of list of inhabitants of the district of Cleveland) – 1802 – 1r – 1 – us Western Res [978]
CLEVELAND, OHIO, TAXES, MS V.F. O / Gilbert, Stephen & Spafford, Amos – (Lists all properties liable to be appraised for raising county levies in the town of Cleveland in County Trumbull) – 1801 – 1r – 1 – us Western Res [350]
CLEVELAND, OHIO, TAXES, MS V.F.O. – (List of all the polls and taxable property found in Cleveland town) – 1801 – 1r – 1 – us Western Res [978]
Cleveland. Ohio. Third Baptist Church *see* CHURCH RECORDS, MS 2335
Cleveland. Ohio. Woodland Ave. Methodist-Episcopal Church *see* CHURCH RECORDS, MS 415
CLEVELAND POST : DAILY GERMAN LANGUAGE NEWSPAPER – Cleveland, OH. Oct 1879-Jan 1880 – 1r – 1 – us Western Res [071]
Cleveland. Presbytery (Pres. Ch. in the U.S.A.) *see* MINUTES, 1830-1883
Cleveland, President *see*
– AMERICAN RIGHTS IN SAMOA
– SAMOAN AFFAIRS
CLEVELAND PRESS – Cleveland, Ohio. 1878- – 1 – us UMI [071]
Cleveland. Public Library. John G. White Dept *see* CATALOG OF THE CHESS COLLECTION (INCLUDING CHECKERS)
CLEVELAND SHOPPING NEWS – (Biweekly advertising newspaper) – Cleveland, Cuyahoga, OH. 15 Oct 1921-27 Jun 19? – 9r – 1 – us Western Res [071]
CLEVELAND SHOPPING NEWS – (Bi-weekly advertising newspaper) – Cleveland, Cuyhoga, OH. 26 Dec 1945-1 Jul 195? – 23r – 1 – us Western Res [071]
Cleveland, Stafford C *see* HISTORY OF AND DIRECTORY OF YATES COUNTY
CLEVELAND STANDARD – Cleveland, England. -w. 1 Feb, 21 Aug 1908-1 May 1953. 28 1 2 reels – 1 – uk British Libr Newspaper [072]
CLEVELAND STATE LAW REVIEW – (v1-33 1972-85 in reel $208.00. v34-42 1985-94 in mf $192.00. Title varies: v1-18 1952-69 as Cleveland-Marshall Law Review) – v1-42. 1952-94 – 5,6,9 – $400.00 set – us Hein [340]
CLEVELAND UND SEIN DEUTSCHTHUM – (A German language history and biographical dictionary of Cleveland) – [Cleveland], Cuyahoga, OH. 1907 – 1r – 1 – us Western Res [920]
CLEVELAND UNION LEADER : WEEKLY LABOR NEWSPAPER, PUBLISHED BY THE CLEVELAND CONGRESS OF INDUSTRIAL O RGANIZATIONS – Cleveland, OH. 1937-39 – 1r – 1 – us Western Res [331]
CLEVELAND WEEKLY GAZETTE – (Weekly Whig newspaper) – Cleveland, OH. Jun 1 1836-21 Mar 1837 – 1r – 1 – us Western Res [071]
CLEVELAND WEEKLY HERALD – (Weekly Republican newspaper) – Cleveland, OH. mar 28, 1868-dec 30, 1876 – 4r – 1 – us Western Res [071]
CLEVELAND WHIG – (Weekly Whig newspaper) – Cleveland, OH. aug 20, 1834-dec 28, 1836 – 1r – 1 – us Western Res [071]
CLEVELAND WORKHOUSE RECORDS, MS 3681 – 1855-1950 – 24r – 1 – us Western Res [978]
CLEVELAND WORLD – Cleveland, OH. Apr 1 1890-Jun 30 1905 – 64r – 1 – us Western Res [071]
CLEVELANDER HEROLD : WEEKLY, LATER DAILY, GERMAN LANGUAGE, FRATERNAL NEWSPAPER – Cleveland, OH. 2 Mar 1901-24 Aug 1908 – 13r – 1 – us Western Res [071]
CLEVELANDSKA AMERIKA – Cleveland, OH, 1909, 1914 – 2mf or 1 reel – 9,1 – us I.H.R.C. [975]
CLEVELANDSKA AMERIKA – Cleveland, Oh. 1918 – 1 – us Res Libr [071]
Clevenger, Shobal Vail *see* MEDICAL JURISPRUDENCE OF INSANITY; OR, FORENSIC PSYCHIATRY
Clevenger, William May *see* THE COURTS OF NEW JERSEY; THEIR ORIGIN, COMPOSITION AND JURISDICTION
CLEWISTON NEWS – Clewiston. Fl. 1928- – 1 – us P.K. Yonge [071]
CLEWS TO HOLY WRIT, OR, THE CHRONOLOGICAL SCRIPTURE CYCLE / Carus Wilson, Ashley – New York: American Tract Society, (1893). 1 fiche – 9 – us A.T.L.A. [240]
Cleymaet, G *see* EEN NIEUW GELUID OVER DEN VOLKENBOND
DE CLEYN WERELT / Moerman, J – O 827. 1608 – 9 – ne IDC [949]
Cleyre, Voltairine de *see* SELECTED WORKS
Clichtouei, J *see*
– DE BELLO ET PACE OPUSCULUM...
– DE BELLO ET PACE OPUSCULUM, CHRISTIANOS PRINCIPES AD SEDANOS BELLORUM TUMULTUS ET PACEM COMPONENDAM EXHORTANS...
Clichtove, J *see*
– ANTILUTHERUS..., TRES LIBROS COMPLECTENS
– COMPENDIUM VERITATUM AD FIDEM PERTINENTIUM...
– DE SACRAMENTO EUCHARISTIAE CONTRA OECOLAMPADIUM OPUSCULUM...
– DE VENERATIONE SANCTORUM, OPUSCULUM DUOS LIBROS COPLECTENS
– DE VITA ET MORIBUS SACERDOTUM OPUSCULUM...
– ELUCIDATORIUM ECCLESIASTICUM AD OFFICIUM ECCLESIAE PERTINENTIA PLANIUS EXPONENS IN QUATTUOR LIBROS COMPLETENS
– ELUCIDATORIUM ECCLESIASTICUM AD OFFICIUM ECCLESIAE PERTINENTIA PLANIUS EXPONENS IN QUATUOR LIBROS COMPLETENS
– HOMILIAE SEU SERMONES
– IMPROBATIO QUORUNDAM ARTICULORUM MARTINI LUTHERI...
– PROPUGNACULUM ECCLESIAE ADVERSUS LUTERANOS...
Click, Barry Clinton *see* TOWARD A THEOLOGY OF MARRIAGE AND FAMILY MINISTRY: A PRACTICUM DEVELOPMENT IN A PASTORAL COUNSELING CENTER. 1982
THE CLIENT PRINCES OF THE ROMAN EMPIRE UNDER THE REPUBLIC / Sands, P C – Cambridge: University Press, 1908 – 1mf – us A.T.L.A. [240]
CLIFFORD HENDERSON PAPERS *see* HENDERSON, CLIFFORD, PAPERS, MS 4309
Clifford, John *see*
– THE ENGLISH BAPTISTS
– THE INSPIRATION AND AUTHORITY OF THE BIBLE
– TYPICAL CHRISTIAN LEADERS
– THE ULTIMATE PROBLEMS OF CHRISTIANITY
Clifford, John Henry *see* JOHN H. CLIFFORD, ESQ., ATTORNEY-GENERAL, &C
Clifford, N *see* CLIFFORD'S REPORTS OF CASES IN THE FIRST CIRCUIT, 1858-1878
Clifford, W H *see* CLIFFORD'S REPORTS OF CASES IN THE FIRST CIRCUIT, 1858-1878
Clifford, William Kingdon *see* LECTURES AND ESSAYS BY WILLIAM KINGDON CLIFFORD
CLIFFORD'S REPORTS OF CASES IN THE FIRST CIRCUIT, 1858-1878 / Clifford, N & Clifford, W H – Boston: Little-Brown. v1-4. 1869-80 (all publ) – 32mf – 9 – $48.00 – LLMC 81-442 – us L.L.M.C. [340]
CLIFTON AND REDLAND FREE PRESS – Bristol, England. 9 May 1890-15 Jan 1931. -w. -irr. 14 reels – 1 – uk British Libr Newspaper [072]
CLIFTON HILL GAZETTE – 1888 – 1r – 1 – at Corangamite [072]
CLIFTON HILL GAZETTE *see* TIMES
CLIFTON HILL LEADER – 1888-1889 – 1 – at Corangamite [072]
CLIFTON HILL TIMES – 1937-1938 – 1 – at Corangamite [072]
Clifton Park, New York. Clifton Park Baptist Church *see* RECORDS
Clifton, Robert T *see* GENDER DIFFERENCES IN THE RELATIONSHIPS AMONG SELF-CONFIDENCE, GENDER-APPROPRIATENESS, AND VALUE
CLIFTON SOCIETY – Bristol, England. Nov 1890-Mar 1916. Missing: 1893, 1898. -w. 23 1/4 reels – 1 – uk British Libr Newspaper [072]
CLIFTONVILLE AND HOVE MERCURY – Cliftonville, Hove, England. -w. 13 Sept 1878-16 Jan 1880. 43 ft – 1 – uk British Libr Newspaper [072]
CLIMA, PAISAJE Y NATURALEZA EN LA OBRA DE GABRIEL Y GALAN / Lopez Bustos, Carlos – Badajoz: Dip. Provincial, 1970. Sep. REE – 1 – sp Bibl Santa Ana [440]
Climacus, John *see* THE LADDER OF DIVINE ASCENT
CLIMATIC CHANGE – (v6- 1984- 5,6,9) – v1-Mar 1977- – 1 – us UMI [550]
CLIMATIC RESEARCH SERIES / Clemson University. Agricultural Experiment Station – Nos 7-15 1970-73 (ceased) – 1r – 1,5 – us Spaulding [550]
CLIMATIC RESEARCH SERIES / South Carolina. Agricultural Experiment Station. Clemson – Nos 1-6 1967-69 – 1,5 – us Spaulding [550]
CLIMATOLOGICAL OBSERVATIONS / Minnesota. College of Agriculture. Cloquet Forest Research Center – 1956-69 – 1,5,6 – us Spaulding [550]
CLIMATOLOGICAL RECORDS OF THE WEATHER BUREAU, 1819-92 / U.S. Weather Bureau – T907 – 564r – 1 – us Nat'l Archives [550]
CLIMATOLOGIE, PEDOLOGIE ET ECOLOGIE FORESTIERES AU CANADA, 1937-1956 : BIBLIOGRAPHIE / Deslandes, Germain – 1958. SEM105P4 – 2mf – 9 – cn Bibl Nat [550]
Climo, V C *see* PRECIS OF INFORMATION CONCERNING THE COLONY OF THE GOLD COAST AND ASHANTI
Climstein, M *see* MYOCARDIAL STRUCTURE AND FUNCTION DIFFERENCES BETWEEN STEROID USING AND NON-STEROID USING ELITE POWERLIFTERS AND ENDURANCE ATHLETES
CLINCH VALLEY NEWS – Tazewell. Va. -w. 1955- – 1 – us UMI [071]
Clinchy, Russell J *see* WHAT DOES FREEDOM MEAN TO YOU?
CLINICA CHIMICA ACTA – v1-144. 1956-84 – 1,5,6,13 – sz Elsevier [073]
CLINICAL AND EXPERIMENTAL DIALYSIS AND APHERESIS – v5-7. 1981-83 – 1 – us UMI [616]
CLINICAL AND EXPERIMENTAL HYPERTENSION – v1-3. 1978-81 – 1 – us UMI [616]
CLINICAL AND EXPERIMENTAL HYPERTENSION: PART A: THEORY AND PRACTICE – (v6-. 1984-. 5,6,9) – v4-. 1982- – 1 – us UMI [616]
CLINICAL AND EXPERIMENTAL HYPERTENSION: PART B: HYPERTENSION IN PREGNANCY – (v3-. 1984-. 5,6,9) – v1-. 1982- – 1 – us UMI [616]
CLINICAL AND EXPERIMENTAL IMMUNOLOGY – v1-30. 1966-77 – 1,5,6 – us Princeton Micro [073]
CLINICAL AND GENETIC INVESTIGATIONS INTO TUBEROUS SCLEROSIS AND RECKLINGHAUSEN'S NEUROFIBROMATOSIS : CONTRIBUTION TO ELUCIDATION OF INTERRELATIONSHIP AND EUGENICS OF THE SYNDROMES / Borberg, Allan – (Transl fr the Danish by Elisabeth Aagesen) – Copenhagen: Munksgaard 1951 – us Res Libr [616]
CLINICAL AND INVESTIGATIVE MEDICINE = MEDECINE CLINIQUE ET EXPERIMENTALE – v1- . 1978- – 1,5,6,9 – us UMI [073]
CLINICAL AND INVESTIGATIVE MEDICINE – v. 1-. 1978- – 5,6,9 – us UMI [610]
CLINICAL BIOCHEMISTRY – 1,5,69 – us UMI [540]
CLINICAL BIOFEEDBACK AND HEALTH *see* AMERICAN JOURNAL OF CLINICAL BIOFEEDBACK
CLINICAL BULLETIN / Memorial Sloan-Kettering Cancer Center – (v.9. 1979- 5,6,9) – v.1-. 1971- – 1 – us UMI [073]
CLINICAL BULLETIN OF MYOFASCIAL THERAPY : THE PRACTICAL JOURNAL FOR THE SOFT-TISSUE PRACTITIONER / ed by Lowe, John C – v2 n1. 1997- – 1,9 – $105.00 in US $147.00 outside hardcopy subsc – us Haworth [615]
CLINICAL CHEMISTRY – v. 1-25. 1955-79 – 1,5,6 – us Princeton Micro [540]
CLINICAL CHEMISTRY – (v.25-. 1979- 5,6,9) – v.1-. 1955- – 1 – us UMI [540]
CLINICAL CHEMISTRY AND ENZYMOLOGY COMMUNICATIONS / ed by Federici, G – 9,5,1 – us Harwood [574]
CLINICAL CHEMISTRY NEWS – (v.5-. 1979- 5,6,9) – v.1-. 1975- – 1 – us UMI [540]
CLINICAL ELECTROENCEPHALOGRAPHY – (v6-, 1975- . 9) – v. 1-. 1970- – 1 – us UMI [616]

CLINICAL, FUNCTIONAL, AND RADIOGRAPHIC ASSESSMENT OF THE CONVENTIONAL AND MODIFIED BOYD-ANDERSON SURGICAL PROCEDURES FOR REPAIR OF DISTAL BICEPS TENDON RUPTURES : A 3-YEAR FOLLOW-UP STUDY / D'Arco, Patrick H – Temple University, 1996 – 2mf – 9 – $8.00 – PE 3635 – us Microform Publ [617]
CLINICAL GERONTOLOGIST / ed by Brink, T L – v1- 1982- – 1, 9 ($300.00 in US $420.00 outside hardcopy subsc) – us Haworth [618]
CLINICAL HEMORHEOLOGY – v1- 1981- – 5,6,9 – us UMI [610]
CLINICAL IMMUNOLOGY REVIEWS – (v3-. 1984-. 5,6,9) – v1-. 1981- – 1 – us UMI [073]
CLINICAL INSTRUCTION IN ATHLETIC TRAINING / Gardner, Gregory A – University of Southern Mississippi, 1995 – 2mf – 9 – $8.00 – PE3590 – us Microform Publ [617]
CLINICAL KINESIOLOGY *see* AMERICAN CORRECTIVE THERAPY JOURNAL
CLINICAL LECTURES ON AMBLYOPIA AND AMAUROSIS, AND THE EXTRACTION OF CATARACT / Graefe, A von – Boston, 1866 – 2mf – 9 – ne IDC [617]
Clinical Ligand Assay Society *see* JOURNAL OF CLINICAL IMMUNOASSAY
CLINICAL NUCLEAR MEDICINE – v. 1-. 1976- – 1,5,6,9 – us UMI [616]
CLINICAL NURSE SPECIALIST : THE JOURNAL FOR ADVANCED NURSING PRACTICE – v1-10. 1987-1996 – 1,5,6,9 – $65.00r – us Williams [610]
CLINICAL NUTRITION / European Society of Parenteral and Enteral Nutrition – v1-. 1982- – 1,5,6,9 – us UMI [613]
CLINICAL PHARMACOLOGY AND THERAPEUTICS – (v. 6-. 1965- 5,6. v. 11-. 1970- 9) – 1- 1960- – 1 – us UMI [615]
CLINICAL PHARMACY *see* AMERICAN JOURNAL OF HOSPITAL PHARMACY
CLINICAL PSYCHIATRY NEWS – (v.9-. 1981-. 5,6,9) – v.1-. 1973- – 1 – us UMI [610]
CLINICAL PSYCHOLOGY REVIEW – v1- 1981- – 5,6,9 – us UMI [150]
CLINICAL RESEARCH PRACTICES AND DRUG REGULATORY AFFAIRS – v1-. 1983- – 1,5,6,9 – us UMI [073]
CLINICAL SCIENCE – London, New York. v22-31. 1962-66. M-17/2 – 8 – ne IDC [073]
CLINICAL SCIENCE AND MOLECULAR MEDICINE – v. 9-41. 1950-1971 – 1,5,6 – us Princeton Micro [610]
CLINICAL SOCIAL WORK JOURNAL – v1-. 1973- – 1,5,6; v3-. 9 – us UMI [360]
THE CLINICAL SUPERVISOR : A JOURNAL OF SUPERVISION IN PSYCHOTHERAPY AND MENTAL HEALTH / ed by Munson, Carlton – v1- 1983- – 1, 9 ($275.00 in US $385.00 outside hardcopy subsc) – us Haworth [610]
CLINICAL TOXICOLOGY – (v.18-. 1981-. 5,6,9) – v.1-. 1968- – 1 – us UMI [615]
CLINICAL VISION SCIENCES – v1- 1985- – 5,6,9 – us UMI [616]
CLINICAL VISION SCIENCES *see* VISION RESEARCH
CLINICS IN ANAESTHESIOLOGY – 1983- – 1,5,6,9 – us UMI [617]
CLINICS IN CHEST MEDICINE – v.1-. 1980- – 1,5,6,9 – us UMI [616]
CLINICS IN DERMATOLOGY – v1-. 1983- – 1,5,6,9 – us UMI [616]
CLINICS IN ENDOCRINOLOGY AND METABOLISM – (1980- 5,6,9) – 1972- – 1 – us UMI [616]
CLINICS IN GASTROENTEROLOGY – (1980- 5,6,9) – 1972- – 1 – us UMI [616]
CLINICS IN GERIATRIC MEDICINE – v1-. 1985- – 1,5,6,9 – us UMI [618]
CLINICS IN HAEMATOLOGY – (1980- 5,6,9) – 1972- – 1 – us UMI [616]
CLINICS IN IMMUNOLOGY AND ALLERGY – 1981- – 1,5,6,9 – us UMI [616]
CLINICS IN LABORATORY MEDICINE – v1-. 1981- – 1,5,6,9 – us UMI [073]
CLINICS IN OBSTETRICS AND GYNECOLOGY – (v.7- 1980- 5,6,9) – v.1-. 1974- – 1 – us UMI [618]
CLINICS IN ONCOLOGY – v1-. 1982- – 1,5,6,9 – us UMI [616]
CLINICS IN PERINATOLOGY – (v4- . 5,6,9) – v. 1-. 1974- – 1 – us UMI [618]
CLINICS IN PLASTIC SURGERY – v. 1-. 1974- – 1,5,6,9 – us UMI [617]
CLINICS IN PODIATRY – v1-. 1984- – 1,5,6,9 – us UMI [617]
CLINICS IN RHEUMATIC DISEASES – (v6- , 1980- . 5,6,9) – v.1-. 1975- – 1 – us UMI [616]
CLINICS IN SPORTS MEDICINE – v1-. 1982- – 1,5,6,9 – us UMI [617]
Clint, Harold Cuthbert *see* COLONEL WILLIAM WOOD, SOLDIER, HISTORIAN, ARCHIVIST
CLINTON 1850-1900 – (Mf 1-5: Births 1850-81. Mf 6-10: Births 1882-98. Mf 11-15: Marriages 1850-83. Mf 16-20: Marriages 1884-1900. Mf 21-25: Deaths 1850-92. Mf 26-30: Death 1893-1903. Mf 31-39: Birth Index 1850-1990. Mf 40-47: Marriage Index 1850-1990. Mf 48-54: Death Index 1850-1990) – (mf ed 1991) – 54mf – 9 – 0-87623-138-5 – us Holbrook [920]
CLINTON COUNTY ADVERTISER – Lyons. Iowa. 1874-1876; 1878-1881 – 1 – us UMI [071]
CLINTON COUNTY DEMOCRAT – Wilmington. Ohio. 1888-1918; 1921; 1925-1926; 1929-1950 – 1 – us UMI [071]
THE CLINTON DEMOCRAT – Lock Haven, PA. -w 1889-1912; 1918-1923 – 13 – $25.00r – us I.M.R. [071]
CLINTON FIRST BAPTIST CHURCH. CLINTON, SOUTH CAROLINA : CHURCH RECORDS – 1881-1966 – 1 – 27.45 – us Baptist [240]
Clinton, Henry Lauren *see* EXTRAORDINARY CASES
Clinton, Mississippi *see* MISCELLANEOUS EARLY NEWSPAPERS
CLINTON NEW ERA – Ontario, CN. Apr 1894-95 – 13r – 1 – cn Commonwealth Micro [072]
CLINTON REPUBLICAN – Wilmington. Ohio. 1846-1881; 1892 – 1 – us UMI [071]
THE CLINTON REPUBLICAN – Lock Haven, PA. -w 1889-1912 – 13 – $25.00r – us I.M.R. [071]
CLINTON STREET QUARTERLY – Portland OR. Spring 1979 + – 1 – us U.O. Library [071]
CLINTON/HURON NEWS – Ontario, CN. 1874-1911 – 29r – 1 – cn Commonwealth Micro [072]
Clio *see* CANADIAN POETS IN MINIATURE
Clionian Debating Society. Charleston, South Carolina *see* MINUTES
CLIPPER – 1-2 2+9 (all publ). 1940-1941 – 5mf – 9 – $35.00 – us UPA [073]
CLIPPER – Argonia. Kan. 1884-1915 – 1 – us UMI [071]
CLIPPER – New York. v1-72. 1853-1924 – 49r – 1 – us Ross [071]
CLIPPER – Shelton. Neb. 1895-1964 – 1 – us UMI [071]
THE CLIPPER – New York. v. 1-72 no. 3. May 7 1853-July 12 1924. Lack: Jan 1855-Apr 19 1856 and few scattered issues – 1 – us NY Public [073]
(CLIPPINGS AND HANDBILLS BY OR ABOUT ISABELO DE LOS REYES FROM HIS PERSONAL NOTEBOOK...UNIVERSITY OF THE PHILIPPINES LIBRARY....) / Reyes y Florentino, Isabelo de los – 1 reel. With marginal notations in his hand – 1 – us U.W. Library [025]
CLIPPINGS SCRAPBOOKS / Northern Pacific Railway Company – 1866-1904. 10 rolls including filmed inventory – 1 – $300.00; $30.00r – us M.H.S. [380]
CLITHEROE ADVERTISER – Lancashire – 1 – uk Microform Academic [072]
Clive, Caroline *see*
- PAUL FERROLL, A TALE
- WHY PAUL FERROLL KILLED HIS WIFE
THE CLOAK ROOM AND WEEKLY LETTER / Lambertson, William Purnell – 1930-1950, Lambertson communicated with his constituents through a weekly newspaper column called "The Cloak Room" or "The Crossroads" (used between sessions) and a weekly letter to certain supporters. The microfilm consists of typed drafts but not the acutal newspaper columns – 1 – us KS Hist [978]
LA CLOCHE – 19 dec 1869-17 dec 1870, 6 fevr 1871-21 dec 1872. devenu: L' Etat. 22 dec 1872-13 mai 1873. Paris – 1 – fr A.C.R.P.P. [073]
LA CLOCHE – Journal litteraire, artistique, satirique et humoristique. no. 1-52. Paris. avr 1892-nov 1894. mq no. 21, 27, 40-43, 50 – 1 – fr A.C.R.P.P. [073]
LA CLOCHE – Tamatave. oct 1880-juil 1892. remplace par: The Bee. d'oct a dec 1880 – 1 – fr A.C.R.P.P. [073]
LA CLOCHE – (Issues at MF-7496 and Neg. MF-1751 filmed as part of: Commune de Paris newspapers; newspapers on these reels are filmed chronologically, not alphabetically.) – Paris: Imp. Dubuisson et Ce, mar 26-apr 9, apr 11-16, 18-19 1871-1872] – us Res Libr [072]
LA CLOCHE DU DIMANCHE / ed by Vekeman, G – Montreal, Woonsocket, Canada. 14 oct 1897-29 dec 1900 – 1r – 1 – Can$30.00 – cn Can Microfilming [072]
LA CLOCHE FELEE – Saigon. dec 1923-mai 1926 – 1 – fr A.C.R.P.P. [073]
LE CLOCHER – [Paris]: A Desrez, apr 8 1849- – us Res Libr [072]
LES CLOCHES DE PLURS = DIE GLOCKEN VON PLURS / Pasque, Ernst – Geneve: H Robert, 1901 – 1r – 1 – us U.W. Library [830]
Clockmakers Company *see* RECORDS
Clodd, Edward *see*
- GRANT ALLEN: A MEMOIR, WITH A BIBLIOGRAPHY
- JESUS OF NAZARETH
Cloete, Henry *see* THE HISTORY OF THE GREAT BOER TREK AND THE ORIGINS OF SOUTH AFRICAN REPUBLICS
THE CLOISTER AND THE HEARTH / Reade, Charles L – British Fiction Archive: Unit 2 – 9 – uk Bell [830]
CLOISTER LIFE IN THE DAYS OF COEUR DE LION / Spence, H Donald M – London: Isbister; Philadelphia: J.B. Lippincott, 1892 – 1mf – us A.T.L.A. [240]
Cloninger, Karl W *see* OFF SEASON RESIDENT CAMP UTILIZATION IN THE CONTIGNOUS UNITED STATES
CLONMEL ADVERTISER – Ireland. -w. 2 Jan 1828-7 Apr 1838. (10 reels) – 1 – uk British Libr Newspaper [072]
CLONMEL ADVERTISER AND LITERARY JOURNAL – Ireland. -w. 8 Jul-16 Sep 1843. (10 ft) – 1 – uk British Libr Newspaper [072]
CLONMEL CHRONICLE ETC – Ireland.21 Jul 1848-96. -w. 48 reels – 1 – uk British Libr Newspaper [072]
Cloots, Jean-Baptiste *see* LA CERTITUDE DES PREUVES DU MAHOMETISME
Cloran, Henry Joseph *see* REPORT ON THE JURY SYSTEM
CLORIANYDD *see* Y CLORIANYDD
THE CLOSE OF THE TENTH CENTURY OF THE CHRISTIAN ERA / Dixon, Richard Watson – Oxford: T. & G. Shrimpton, 1858 – 1mf – us A.T.L.A. [900]
Close, Percy L *see* A PRISONER OF THE GERMANS IN SOUTHWEST AFRICA
CLOSE UP – London. v. 1-10. July 1927-Dec 1933 – 1 – us NY Public [073]
CLOSELY HELD BUSINESS IDEAS – (v.3-. 1979- 5,6,9) – v.1-. 1976- – 1 – us UMI [073]
CLOSE-UP – v1-10. 1927-33 – 2r – 1 – us Ross [770]
CLOSE-UP – (v6- . 1975- . 5,6,9) – v. 1-. 1970- – 1 – us UMI [073]
CLOSE-UP ON THE LAND = CROS PLAN DU TERRITOIRE : THE COUNTY MAPS OF CANADA / National Archives of Canada – (New Brunswick/Westmoreland, 1862. 4mf; Nova Scotia / Digby, 1864. 4mf; Nova Scotia / Guysborough, 1864. 4mf; Nova Scotia / Inverness, 1864. 4mf; Nova Scotia / Yarmouth, 1864. 4mf; Prince Edward Island, 1863. 4mf; Quebec, 1863. 6mf. $57.00; Quebec, 1864. 4mf; Ontario / Lanark, 1863. 4mf; Ontario / Leeds & Grenville, 1861-62. 4mf; Ontario / Lincoln & Welland, 1862. 4mf; Ontario / Ontario, 1860. 4mf; Ontario / Perth, 1888. 4mf; Ontario / Stormont, Dundas, 1862. 6mf. $57.00; Ontario / York, 1860. 4mf) – 1994 – 64mf – 15 – $577.00 set $38.00 ea subset – us Comics [971]
CLOSING CEREMONY: GENERAL PROGRAMME / Games of the New Emerging Forces. 1st, Djakarta, 1963 – In Indonesian, French and English. SE-3886 1. 1963 – 9 – ne IDC [790]
Closs, August *see* MEDUSA'S MIRROR
CLOTHILDA : THE MOST CELEBRATED AIRS AND DUETS IN THE OPERA...(ARR. FOR 2 FLUTES) / Conti, F – (Parts) – London: Walsh & Hare, 170- – 1 – us Sibley [780]
THE CLOUD OF UNKNOWING AND THE BOOK OF PRIVY COUNSELLING / ed by Hodgson, Phyllis – 9mf – 8 – ne Slangenburg [290]
THE CLOUDS OF THE BIBLE / Wallace, Alexander – Glasgow: John S. Marr, 1878. 1 fiche – 9 – us A.T.L.A. [240]
CLOUDS ON THE HORIZON : AN ESSAY ON THE VARIOUS FORMS OF BELIEF, WHICH STAND IN THE WAY OF THE ACCEPTANCE OF REAL CHRISTIAN FAITH BY THE EDUCATED NATIVES OF ASIA, AFRICA, AMERICA, AND OCEANIA / Cust, Robert Needham – Hertford: S. Austin, 1904 – 1mf – us A.T.L.A. [240]
Cloudsey-Thompson, J L *see* BIOLOGY OF DESERTS
CLOUGH, ARTHUR H. AMBARVALIA : POEMS / Burbidge, Thomas – London: Chapman and Hall, 1849 – 1 roll – 1 – 1-55879-430-1 – uk Libr Preservation [810]
Clough, Arthur Hugh *see*
- POEMS
Clough, Emma *see* WHILE SEWING SANDALS, OR, TALES OF A TELUGU PARIAH TRIBE
Clough, John Everett *see*
- FROM DARKNESS TO LIGHT: THE STORY OF A TELUGU CONVERT
- SOCIAL CHRISTIANITY IN THE ORIENT
Cloughly, Alfred *see* MECHANICS' LIEN LAW OF THE STATE OF NEW JERSEY AND BUILDERS' GUIDE.
Clouston, T S *see* FEMALE EDUCATION FROM A MEDICAL POINT OF VIEW
Clouston, Thomas Smith *see* UNSOUNDNESS OF MIND
THE CLOVEN FOOT / Braddon, Mary Elizabeth – British Fiction Archive: Unit 5 – 9 – uk Bell [830]
CLOVER CREEK BAPTIST CHURCH. MEDON, TENNESSEE : CHURCH RECORDS – Sep 1848-99, 1937-67 – 1 – 49.32 – us Baptist [240]
CLOVERDALE COURIER – Cloverdale, OR. -w. 6 Aug 1909-29 Aug 1918. 1 roll – 1 – us U.O. Library [071]
CLOVERDALE REVEILLE – (Detailed index available) – Cloverdale, CA. 1880-96 (broken series); 1897-1907; 1908-24 (broken series); 1925-26; 1928- – 50+ r – 1 – $2,500.00 ($50.00y) – B02115 – us Library Micro [071]
CLOVERDALE SENTINEL – Cloverdale, CA. 1965-66 – 1r – 1 – $50.00 – B02116 – us Library Micro [071]
CLOVIS INDEPENDENT – Clovis, CA. 1933-66; 1967-76 – 27r – 1 BC02117 – $1,350.00 – us Library Micro [071]
CLOVIS, POEME HEROI-COMIQUE AVEC DES REMARQUES HISTORIQUES ET CRITIQUES / Lejeune – Paris: Fournier, 1763. 3v. 13 fiches. (Literature Collection) – 9 – 32.00 – fr Bibl Nationale [810]
CLOVIS. TOME 2 / Kurth, G – Bruxelles, 3e ed 1923 – 7mf – 8 – ne Slangenburg [240]
CLOVIS TRIBUNE – Clovis, CA. 1915-25 – 6r – 1 – $300.00 – B02119 – us Library Micro [071]
Clowes, W *see* NOTEBOOKS, 1836-1838
Clowes, William *see*
- A PROFITABLE AND NECESSARIE BOOKE OF OBSERVATIONS
- PROFITABLE AND NECESSARIE BOOKE OF OBSERVATIONS
- A PROOVED PRACTISE FOR ALL YOUNG CHIRURGIANS, CONCERNING BURNINGS WITH GUNPOWDER, AND WOUNDES MADE WITH GUNSHOT
Clowes, William Laird *see* THE ROYAL NAVY: A HISTORY FROM THE EARLIEST TIMES TO THE PRESENT
Clozel, Francois Joseph *see* DIZ ANS A LA COTE D'IVOIRE
CLU FORUM REPORT – (1979-81. 5,6,9) – (American Society of Chartered Life Undewriters.) 1967-81 – 1 – us UMI [073]
CLU JOURNAL – (v26-37, no.4. 1972-Oct 1983. 5,6. v29-37, no.4. 1975-Oct 1983. 9) – v1-37, no.4. 1946-Oct 1983 – 1 – us UMI [073]
Club Alfaya *see* ESTATUTOS
CLUB CURITYBANO : INSTRUCCAO E RECCREIO – '(s.l.')-Curitiba, Brazil. 16 Jan 1890-Apr 1893; Mar 1894-Dec 1900; 19 Dec 1903; Jun 1912-Oct 1913 – 1,5,6 – bl Biblioteca [072]
Club de Chasse et de Peche du Chenal-du-Moine *see* STATUTS ET REGLEMENTS DE LA COMPAGNIE
Club de Chasse et de Peche 'Les Laurentides' *see* CONSTITUTION ET REGLEMENTS...ET LISTE DES ACTIONNAIRES
Club de Raquettes Frontenac *see* CONSTITUTION ET REGLEMENTS
Club de Raquettes 'Le Canadien' *see* REGLEMENT ET CONSTITUTION...FONDE LE 20 NOVEMBRE 1878

Club de Tenis Cabeza-Rubia *see* REGLAMENTO DE REGIMEN INTERIOR
Club Deportivo Cacereno *see* REGLAMENTO DELA SOCIEDAD...
Club der Filmindustrie *see* GESCHAEFTSBERICHT
Club Liberal de la Partie Est de Montreal *see* CONSTITUTION...FONDE LE 20 NOVEMBRE 1898
CLUB LIFE – London. -w. Jan 1899-Dec 1902. (4 reels) – 1 – uk British Libr Newspaper [073]
CLUB LITTERARIO – Cuyaba, Brazil. 2 Apr 1882 – 1 – bl Biblioteca [410]
Club Nautico Lago Gabriel y Galan. Plasencia *see* 11TH CAMPEONATO DE ESPANA DE LA CLASE DE...Y COPA NACIONAL JUVENIL 1974: INSTRUCCIONES DE REGATA
Club Polideportivo de Tiro Puerto de los Castanos (Caceres) *see* TIRADAS EXTRAORDINARIAS PUNTUABLES PARA EL PRIMER CAMPEONATO RUTA DE LA PLATA. 1971
CLUB SERIES / North Carolina. State University. Raleigh. Agricultural Extension Service – n.1-158. 1936-Feb 19? – 1,5 – us Spaulding [630]
Club Taurino Emeritense *see* MEMORIA DE ACTIVIDADES 1975-76
THE CLUB WOMAN – v1-12 no 2 (all publ) 1897-1904 – 1r – 1 – $125.00 – us UPA [305]
CLUE : A GUIDE THROUGH GREEK TO HEBREW SCRIPTURE / Abbott, Edwin Abbott – (Includes bibliographical references) – London: Adam and Charles Black; New York: Macmillan [distributor], 1900 – 1mf – 9 – 0-8370-9680-4 – 1986-3680 – us A.T.L.A. [220]
Clugston, W G *see* "CAT-WAGON TRAILS."
CLUNES BOROUGH RATES – 1864-1935 – 5r – 1 – at Corangamite [910]
Clunet, E *see* UN ETRANGER PEUT-IL PRATIQUER UNE SAISIE-ARRET EN FRANCE SUR UN FRANCAIS?
Cluniacensis abbas, Petrus *see* DE MIRACULIS LIBRI DUO
DAS CLUNIAZENSISCHE TOTENGEDAECHTNISWESEN (910-954) / Jorden, W – Muenster Westf., 1930 – 3mf – 8 – Dfl13.00 – ne Slangenburg [240]
Clusius, C *see*
- RARIORUM ALIQUOT STIRPIUM PER HISPANIAS OBSERVATARUM HISTORIA
- RARIORUM PLANTARUM HISTORIA

THE CLUSTER OF SPIRITUAL SONGS, DIVINE HYMNS AND SACRED POEMS / Mercer, Jesse – 3rd ed. Philadelphia. 1823 – 1 – 19.04 – us Baptist [240]
Clyde *see* HISTORY OF MITCHELL AND WORTH COUNTIES
CLYDE BILL OF ENTRY & SHIPPING LIST – Glasgow, Scotland. -tw. 7 July 1874-Dec 1914. 44 reels – 1 – uk British Libr Newspaper [072]
CLYDE ENTERPRISE – Clyde, Ohio. 1878- – 2r – 1 – $32.50r – us Archival [071]
CLYDE ENTERPRISE AND SENTINEL – Clyde, Ohio. 1880-81 – 53r – 1 – $32.50r – us Archival [071]
Clyde Mitchell, J *see* THE KALELA DANCE: ASPECTS OF SOCIAL RELATIONSHIPS AMONG URBAN AFRICANS IN NORTHERN RHODESIA
Clyde. Ohio. Clyde Baptist Church *see* RECORDS
Clyde, P H *see* JAPAN'S PACIFIC MANDATE
CLYDEBANK & REFREW PRESS – Scotland, UK. 15 Aug 1891-1913.-w. 11 reels – 1 – uk British Libr Newspaper [072]
Clymer, Joseph Floyd *see* INDIANAPOLIS 500-MILE RACE HISTORY
CLYPEUS THEOLOGIAE THOMISTICAE CONTRA NOVOS EIUS IMPUGNATORUS / Gonet, J B – Parisiis. 5v. 1669 – 57mf – 9 – CA-51/1 – ne IDC [240]
CM : A REVIEWING JOURNAL OF CANADIAN MATERIALS FOR YOUNG PEOPLE 1981-90 / Canadian Library Association – Ottawa, Ontario – 5r – 1 – $325.00 – cn Library Assoc [370]
CMA MAGAZINE – Hamilton. v63-69. 1989/90-1995/96 – 9 – Can$28.00y – cn Micromedia [650]
CMAJ: CANADIAN MEDICAL ASSOCIATION JOURNAL – (CMAJ publishes 2 vols each calendar year) – Ottawa. v122-153. 1980-95 – 9 – Price varies – cn Micromedia [610]
CMBA – Montreal, Canada. v1 n10. fev 1891; v4 n6. dec 1892 – 1r – 1 – Can$25.00 – cn Can Microfilming [073]
THE C.M.B.A. HERALD – Kingston [Ont.]: The Association, [1891] – 9 – cn C.I.H.M. [240]
CMBA JOURNAL AND CATHOLIC SOCIETY NEWS – Montreal: Catholic Societies Pub. Co., [1891-189- or 19–] – 9 – cn C.I.H.M. [240]
CMS OUTLOOK – (New Zealand Section Supplement) – 1934-53 (complete) – 1r – 1 – ATLA S0716A – us A.T.L.A. [073]
CNA BULLETIN – California Nurses Association. v57-65. 1961-69 – 1 – us UMI [073]
CNRS : FUNDAMENTAL PHYSICS AND ASTROPHYSICS – 1,5,9 – us Gordon [530]
CNRS : NEW PHYSICAL, MECHANICAL AND CHEMICAL PROPERTIES OF VERY HIGH PURITY IRON – 1,5,9 – 0-677-30730-6 – us Gordon [530]
C.N.S. Vicesecretaria Provincial de O. Sindicales de E.D. *see* 3RD EXPOSICION FILATELICA CACERNA
CNT (BARCELONA, SPAIN) – (Library has: v.1, no.111-v.2, no.181; Oct. 1938-Jan. 1939; many issues missing) – Barcelona: [La Confederacion, 19??- – 1 – CSUX88-S369 – us Hoover Inst Photo [946]
CNT (MADRID, SPAIN) – (Library has: v.6, no.578-V.7, no. 1138; March 1937-Feb. 1939; innumrable issues missing and/or mutilated) – Madrid: [La Confederacion, 19??- – 1 – CSUX88-S448 – us Hoover Inst Photo [946]
CNUTONIS REGIS GESTA SIVE ENCOMIUM EMMAE REGINAE AUCTORE MONACHO S. BERTINI (MGH 7: 22.BD) – 1865 – Dfl6.00 – ne Slangenburg [240]
CO DA A ROSYJSKA REWOLUCJA ROBOTNIKOM MIAST I WSI – Warszawa: Wydawn. Komitetu Warszawskiego Komunistycznej Partji Robotniczej Polski, 1919 – 1 – CSUX88-B7303 – us Hoover Inst Photo [947]
CO DALI BOLSZEWICY LUDOWI W ROSJI? / Gryzynski, Waclaw – Wyd. 2. Warszawa: "Plac owka", 1918 – 1 – CSUX88-B8416 – us Hoover Inst Photo [947]
C.O. Owen and Co *see* PORTRAIT AND BIOGRAPHICAL RECORD OF RALLS, MARION AND PIKE COUNTIES
CO – PARTNERSHIP AND PROFIT – SHARING / William, Aneurin – 1913. 1 fiche (29x) – 9 – 1.00f – at Libertarian Micro [320]
COACHELLA VALLEY SUBMARINE – Coachella, CA. 1917-42 – 13r – 1 – $650.00 – R02121 – us Library Micro [071]
COACHELLA VALLEY SUN NEWS – Coachella, CA. 1911-89 – 43r – 1 – $2,150.00 – R02123 – us Library Micro [071]
COACHING REVIEW – (Ceased v10 no 2 1987) – Gloucester. v1-10. 1978-87 – 9 – Can$20.00y – cn Micromedia [790]
COACHING: WOMEN'S ATHLETICS – v3- . 1976- . Continues: Woman Coach – 1,5,6,9 – us UMI [790]
Coade, George *see* A BRIEF ACCOUNT OF THE LATE PERSECUTION AND BARBAROUS USAGE OF THE METHODISTS AT EXETER,...
THE COAHOMIAN – Friar's Point. Miss. 1865-1866 – 1 – us UMI [071]
Coahuila. Mexico *see* PERIODICO OFICIAL-GOBIERNO CONSTITUCIONAL DEL ESTADO INDEPENDIENTE, LIBRE Y SOBERANO DE COAHUILA DE ZARAGOZA
Coahuila. Mexico. (State) *see* PERIODICO OFICIAL
COAL AGE – 1- 1911- 1; v72- 5,6; v80- 9 – us UMI [622]
COAL CITY CHRONICLE – New Castle, PA. -sw 1860 – 13 – $25.00r – us I.M.R. [071]
COAL CITY ITEM – New Castle, PA. -w 1856-1858 – 13 – $25.00r – us I.M.R. [071]
COAL COMMITTEE / UN Economic Commission for Europe (ECE) – 1947-89 – E/F.325 E.1333 F.1156 R.796 – 9 – us U.N. Pubs [340]
THE COAL FIELDS AND COAL TRADE OF THE ISLAND OF CAPE BRETON / Brown, Richard FGS – London: S. Low, Marston, Low and Searle, 1871. 02176. (Pre-1900 Canadiana) – 9 – cn C.I.H.M. [622]
COAL GASIFICATION AND LIQUEFACTION COLLECTION – No 1- . All NTIS and U.S. Bureau of Mines documents from 1910 to 1975 with paper copy index by title, subject, author and report numbers. Collection no 1 – 1195mf – 9 – $1700.00 – us Updata [324]
THE COAL MINES OF NOVA SCOTIA: THE GOVERNMENT'S SCHEME OF EXTENDING THE COAL TRADE / Fielding, William Stevens – Speech of W.S. Fielding. Halifax, N.S.: Nova Scotia Printing Co., 1893. 03101. (Pre-1900 Canadiana) – 9 – cn C.I.H.M. [971]
COAL MINING – v21 no 4-. Apr 1984- – 1,5,6,9 – us UMI [622]
COAL MINING AND PROCESSING – v1-21 no3. Oct 1964-Mar 1984 – 1,5,6,9 – us UMI [622]
COAL PREPARATION : A MULTINATIONAL JOURNAL / ed by Laskowski, J S – 9,5,1 – us Gordon [622]
COAL TRADE BULLETIN : A JOURNAL DEVOTED TO THE COAL INDUSTRY – v6-39. Dec 1901-Nov 1918 – 1 – $336.00 – us L of C Photodup [380]
COAL UTILIZATION : AN INTERNATIONAL FORUM ON NEW TECHNOLOGIES – 1983 – 9 – 92-3-102081-1 – fr UNESCO [622]
COAL VALLEY NEWS – Madison. West Virginia. -w. 1943-67 – 1 – us UMI [071]
COALFIELD PROGRESS – Norton. Va. -w. 1935- – 1 – us UMI [071]
COALFIELD TIMES – Dhanbad, India. 1962-9 Apr 1980; Apr 1967-1970; 1972-1980 – 18r – 1 – us L of C Photodup [072]
A COALICAO – Sao Luiz, 6 Feb 1862-11 Mar 1866 – 1,5,6 – bl Biblioteca [072]
LA COALICIOB – Badajoz, 1895 y 1895-1900 – 5 – sp Bibl Santa Ana [073]
LA COALICION – Badajoz, 1902-1904, 1906-1908 y 1911 – 5 – sp Bibl Santa Ana [073]
COALINGA CITY DIRECTORIES – Fresno Co, CA. 1910-1914 – 4r – 1 – $200.00 – D022 – us Library Micro [910]
COALINGA RECORD – Coalinga, CA. 1983-1985 – 3r – 1 – $150.00 – B03186 – us Library Micro [071]
COALITION AFFIRMING FREEDOM IN EDUCATION (CAFE) – 6p-pamphlet – 9 – 1.00f – at Libertarian Micro [370]
Coalition for Alternatives in Jewish Education *see* NEWS
Coalition of Indian-Controlled School Boards *see* CICSB NEWSLETTER
COALVILLE TIMES – Sep 29, 1893-95; 1897-1996 – 153 1/2r – 1 – uk British Libr Newspaper [072]
Coan, Charles F *see* A HISTORY OF NEW MEXICO
Coan, Lydia Bingham *see* TITUS COAN
Coan, Titus *see* LIFE IN HAWAII
LES COAPTATIONS SEXUELLES DES ONISCOIDEA / Legrand, J J – 5366 2. 1946 – 8 – ne IDC [590]
O COARYENSE : ORGAO IMPARCIAL E SEMANAL – Coary, Amazonas. 13-20 Jun 1895 – 1,5,6 – bl Biblioteca [072]
COAST BURGH'S REPORTER – Anstruther, Scotland, UK. 8 Oct 1896-22 Dec 1898. -w. 1 reel – 1 – uk British Libr Newspaper [072]
COAST COUNTY DIRECTORY – West Coast. 1884-1885 – 1r – 1 – $50.00 – D131 – us Library Micro [978]
COAST DEFENDER *see* THE REPUBLICAN
COAST DISPATCH – Encinitas. Calif. -w. 1943-58 – 1 – us UMI [071]
Coast Federal Savings *see* FREE ENTERPRISE, MYTHS AND TRUTHS
COAST GUARD – Taft OR. Aug 13 1931 (one issue) – 1 – us U.O. Library [071]
THE COAST INDIANS OF SOUTHERN ALASKA AND NORTHERN BRITISH COLUMBIA / Niblack, A P – BN 327 2. 1888 – 8 – ne IDC [910]
COAST MAIL – Marshfield OR. Dec 15 1887-Nov 26 1896, Dec 8 1900-Nov 22 1902 – 1 – us U.O. Library [071]
COAST VALLEY JOURNAL – Greenleaf, OR. -w. 30 Nov 1972-20 Jun 1974. 1 roll – 1 – us U.O. Library [071]
COASTAL AQUACULTURE : DEVELOPMENT PERSPECTIVES IN AFRICA AND CASE STUDIES FROM OTHER REGIONS – 1982 – 246p – it F.A.O. [639]
COASTAL ENGINEERING – v1-8 1976-84 – 1,5,6,13 – sz Elsevier [624]
COASTAL MANAGEMENT – (Title varies: v1-14 1973-86 as Coastal Zone Management Journal) – v1-23. 1973-95 – 9 – $822.00 set – us Hein [333]
COASTAL STATE REQUIREMENTS FOR FOREIGN FISHING – 1985 – 302p – it F.A.O. [340]
COASTAL TELEGRAPH – 1979-1986. CTE1-8 – 8r – 1 – at Corangamite [072]
COASTAL ZONE MANAGEMENT JOURNAL – v1- 1973- 1; v3- 5,6,9 – us UMI [550]
COASTAL ZONE MANAGEMENT JOURNAL *see* COASTAL MANAGEMENT
COASTAL ZONE SPACE : PRELUDE TO CONFLICT? / Goldberg, Edward D – 1994 – 138p – 9 – 92-3-102953-3 – fr UNESCO [360]
COASTLINE DISPATCH – San Clemente, CA. 1980 – 14+ r – 1 – $700.00 – H04060 – us Library Micro [071]
COASTSIDE CHRONICLE – Pacifica, CA. 1959-71 – 13r – 1 – $650.00 – B02582 – us Library Micro [071]
COASTSIDE TRIBUNE – Pacifica, CA. 1954-59 – 5r – 1 – $250.00 – B02583 – us Library Micro [071]
COATBRIDGE EXPRESS – Scotland. 14 Oct 1885-27 Jun 1951.-w. 23 reels – 1 – uk British Libr Newspaper [072]
COATBRIDGE READER – Scotland, UK. 1905-28 Dec 1957.-w. 26 reels – 1 – uk British Libr Newspaper [072]
Coates, E *see* JOURNAL OF THE SIEGE OF QUEBEC, 1759
Coates, James *see* PHOTOGRAPHING THE INVISIBLE
Coates, Joseph F *see*
- ISSUES MANAGEMENT: HOW YOU CAN PLAN, ORGANIZE AND MANAGE FOR THE FUTURE
- WHAT FUTURISTS BELIEVE

Coates, Peter Ralph *see* THE CAPE TOWN ENGLISH PRESS INDEX 1871-75
COATESVILLE WEEKLY TIMES – Coatesville, PA. -w 1889-1923 – 13 – $25.00r – us I.M.R. [071]
COATHAM PARISH CHURCHYARD MONUMENTAL INSCRIPTIONS / Redcar. Yorkshire – 1 – uk Microform Academic [941]
THE COATICOOK OBSERVER – Coaticook, Canada. v21 n9. 18 apr 1890-17 apr 1891; 7 jan 1927-27 dec 1928; 8 dec 1939-5 jan 1961 – 2r – 1 – Can$130.00r – cn Can Microfilming [072]
Coats, W *see* THE GEOGRAPHY OF HUDSON'S BAY
Cobb, David *see* DAVID COBB PAPERS, 1708-1833
Cobb, Irvin S *see* OLD JUDGE PRIEST
Cobb, Ivo Geikie *see* THE GLANDS OF DESTINY (A STUDY OF THE PERSONALITY)
Cobb, Joe *see* THE FALLACY OF CENTRAL BANKING
Cobb, L E *see* THE INFLUENCE OF GOAL SETTING ON EXERCISE ADHERENCE OF APPARENTLY HEALTHY ADULTS
Cobb, Louise S *see* A STUDY OF THE FUNCTIONS OF PHYSICAL EDUCATION IN HIGHER EDUCATION
Cobb, Sanford H *see*
- THE RISE OF RELIGIOUS LIBERTY IN AMERICA

Cobb, William Frederick *see*
- BOOK OF PSALMS: WITH INTRODUCTION AND NOTES
- MYSTICISM AND THE CREED
- ORIGINES JUDAICAE
- THEOLOGY OLD AND NEW

Cobb, William Henry *see* A CRITICISM OF SYSTEMS OF HEBREW METRE
Cobbe, Frances Power *see* DARWINISM IN MORALS
Cobbet, W *see* LETTERS TO THE RIGHT HONOURABLE LORD HAWKESBURY AND THE RIGHT HONOURABLE HENRI ADDINGTON...
Cobbett, William *see*
- ADVICE TO YOUNG MAN
- ENGLISH STATE TRIALS, 1163-1858
- A GRAMMAR OF THE ENGLISH LANGUAGE
- A GRAMMAR OF THE ENGLISH LANGUAGE, IN A SERIES OF LETTERS
- A HISTORY OF THE PROTESTANT REFORMATION IN ENGLAND AND IRELAND
- PARLIAMENTARY HISTORY OF ENGLAND FROM THE NORMAN CONQUEST IN 1066 TO 1803
- RURAL RIDES IN THE COUNTIES OF SURREY, KENT, SUSSEX, HAMPSHIRE, WILTSHIRE...

COBBETT'S COMPLETE COLLECTION OF STATE TRIALS – Cases included: Sir Thomas Moore, Anne Boleyn, Mary Queen of Scots, Lady Jane Grey, William Land, Thomas Cranmer, Lord George Gordon, and the Cato Street Conspirators – 288 fiches – 9 – $870.00 – us UPA [340]
COBBETT'S EVENING POST – London, UK. 1820. -d. 1 1/2 reels – 1 – uk British Libr Newspaper [072]

COBBETT'S POLITICAL REGISTER – 1-89 (all publ). 1802-1835 – 501mf – 9 – $1,690.00 – us UPA [941]
COBBETT'S STATE TRIALS / HOWELL'S STATE TRIALS / Great Britain. England – (Cobbett's complete collection of State Trials and Proceedings for High Treason and other crimes and misdemenors. From the earliest to the present time. 5th ed by Thomas B. Howell. First 10v of ed known as "Cobbett's State Trials" and the remainder as "Howell's State Trials") – London: Bagshaw/Longman. v1-33 + index. 1809-28 (all publ) – 268mf – 9 – $402.00 – LLMC 84-762 – us L.L.M.C. [324]
COBDEN CEMETERY RECORDS – 1863-1993 – 5mf – 9 – at Corangamite [920]
Cobden Club *see* TARIFF MAKERS, THEIR AIMS AND METHODS
COBDEN FIRST BAPTIST CHURCH. COBDEN, ILLINOIS : CHURCH RECORDS – 1876-1973 – 1 – 96.03 – us Baptist [240]
COBDEN PAPERS / British Library – (Inquire to publisher for details) – 1 – uk World [941]
Cobden, Richard *see*
- FREE TRADE
- RICHARD COBDEN PAPERS
- RUSSIA BY A MANCHESTER MANUFACTURER
- SPEECHES ON FREE TRADE

COBDEN TIMES – 1941-1993 – 27r – 1 – at Corangamite [072]
Cobern, Camden M *see* THE NEW ARCHAEOLOGICAL DISCOVERIES
COBERNADORES Y CAPITANES GENERALES DE VENEZUELA / Sucre, Luis Alberto – Caracas, 1928; Madrid: Razon y Fe, 1932 – 1 – sp Bibl Santa Ana [350]
COBETT'S MAGAZINE SHILLING MAGAZINE – London, UK. 1833-34. -w. 1 reel – 1 – uk British Libr Newspaper [072]
Cobham, Claude Delaval *see*
- EXCERPTA CYPRIA
- THE PATRIARCHS OF CONSTANTINOPLE

Cobham, H W *see* THE EFFECTS OF CARDIAC REHABILITATION ON CORONARY HEART DISEASE RISK FACTORS IN POST MYOCARDIAL INFARCTION PATIENTS
Coblans, H et al *see* SCIENCE AND TECHNOLOGY POLICIES INFORMATION EXCHANGE SYSTEM (SPINES)
Coblenz, Felix *see* UEBER DAS BETENDE ICH IN DEN PSALMEN
COBLENZER TAGEBLATT – Koblenz, Germany. Apr 1848-1849 – 2r – 1 – gw Mikrofilm [072]
COBLENZER VOLKSZEITUNG – (Cont by: Koblenzer Volkszeitung, jul 1 1926) – Koblenz, jul 3-sep 30 1916. oct 1-dec 31 1924 – 2r – 1 – gw Mikrofilm [943]
COBLENZER ZEITUNG – Koblenz, jul 2-dec 31 1870. jan 2-jul 31 1900 – 3r – 1 – gw Mikrofilm [943]
Cobo Sampedro, Ramon *see* SERMON...A MARIA SANTISMA...EL BENEFICIO DE LA LLUVIA
Cobos de Belchite, Baron de *see* MARQUESADO DE AGUILAFUENTE, EL
Cobos de Villalobos, Amantina *see* ROMANCES CABALLERESCOS
COBOURG DAILY STAR – (1993.-4r; 1948-1976.-37r) – Cobourg, 1978-1992 – 64r – 1 – cn Preston [971]
COBOURG WORLD – Cobourg, Ju1899-1908De – 2r – 1 – cn Preston [971]
COBRAM COURIER – 1921-1956. CCO1-14 – 14r – 1 – at Corangamite [072]
COBRAM COURIER – Jan 12 1956-Dec 23 1965 – 9 – at Pascoe [072]
THE COBRA'S DEN: STORIES OF MISSIONARY WORK AMONG THE TELUGAS OF INDIA / Chamberlain, Jacob – New York: Fleming H. Revell, 1900. 270p. 1 fiche – 9 – us A.T.L.A. [240]
COBRO COERCITIVO... / Drago, L M – Buenos Aires, 1906 – 2mf – 1 – ILM-509/1 – ne IDC [327]
COBURGER TAGEBLATT – Coburg, Germany. 19 Jan 1918- 20 Apr 1939 – 42r – 1 – gw Mikrofilm [072]
COCAINE AND EXCERCISE : TEMPORAL CHANGES IN THE PLASMA CONCENTRATIONS OF CATECHOLAMINES, LACTATE, GLUCOSE, AND COCAINE / Han, Dong H – 1994 – 2mf – $8.00 – us Microform Publ [612]
COCAINE AND EXERCISE : ALTERATION IN CARBOHYDRATE METABOLISM IN ADRENODEMEDULLATED RATS / Ojuka, Edward O – 1994 – 2mf – $8.00 – us Microform Publ [619]
LA COCARDE – Paris, 13 Mar 1888-31 Dec 1897 – 28r – 1 – uk British Libr Newspaper [072]
LA COCARDE – Paris. 17 janv 1888, 13 mars 1888-15 oct 1897, 3 mai 1898-13 sept 1906, 12 oct 1907-25, 1928-mars 1932. contient egalement: La Cocarde du lundi. 8, 14 oct 1907, 13 mai 1908, 9 juin, 2 oct 1913 et 1 no. de mai juin 1906 de La Cocarde – 1 – fr A.C.R.P.P. [073]
Coccejus, J *see* OPERA OMNIA THEOLOGICA
THE COCCIDAE OF CEYLON / Green, E E – Z-174 2. 1896-1922 – 8 – ne IDC [580]
COCCINELLE : JOURNAL DES JEUNES / ed by Vendiere, Louise – Montreal, 30 mai 1971-28 oct 1973 – 1r – 1 – Can$25.00 – cn Can Microfilming [072]
Coccius, M A *see* LE HISTORIE VINITIANE DI MARCO ANTONIO SABELLICO, ...
Coche, A G *see*
- SOIL AND FRESHWATER FISH CULTURE
- WATER FOR FRESHWATER FISH CULTURE

Cochelet, Charles *see* NAUFRAGE DU BRICK FRANCAIS "LA SOPHIE" PERDU LE 30 MAI 1819, SUR LA COTE OCCIDENTALE D'AFRIQUE
Cochenhausen, Friedrich von *see* GEDANKEN
Cocheril, Maurice *see* ETUDES SUR LE MONACHISME EN ESPAGNE...PARIS, 1966
Cocheris, J *see* SITUATION INTERNATIONALE DE L'EGYPTE ET DU SOUDAN
COCHIN : ADMINISTRATIVE VOLUME – Ernakulam: Printed at the Cochin Govt Press, 1911-21 – 9 – us Res Libr [310]
Cochin, Augustin *see*
- LA CONDITION DES OUVRIERS FRANCAIS D'APRES LES DERNIERS TRAVAUX
- PARIS, SA POPULATION, SON INDUSTRIE

Cochin, Henry *see* LA CHRONOLOGIE DU CANZONIERE DE PETRARQUE
LA COCHINCHINE RELIGIEUSE / Louvet, Louis Eugene – 2v. 1885 – 1 – us A.T.L.A. [240]
Cochlaeus, J *see* HISTORIAE HUSITARUM
Cochleus, J *see* VON NEWEN SCHWERMEREYEN SECHS CAPITEL. DER SEELEN SELIGKEIT BETREFFENDE
LE COCHON – Montreal, Canada. 24 jun-18 jul 1878 – 1r – 1 – Can$25.00 – cn Can Microfilming [072]
Cochon de Lapparent, Charles *see* DESCRIPTION GENERALE DU DEPARTEMENT DE LA VIENNE
Cochran, John *see*
- THE REVELATION OF JOHN ITS OWN INTERPRETER IN VIRTUE OF THE DOUBLE VERSION IN WHICH IT IS DELIVERED
- REVELATION OF JOHN ITS OWN INTERPRETER IN...THE DOUBLE VERSION

Cochran, John H *see* DALLAS COUNTY
Cochran, William Cox *see* THE STUDENTS' LAW LEXICON.
Cochrane, Henry Park *see* AMONG THE BURMANS
Cochrane, Hugh *see* 'IDEAL' AND OTHER POEMS
Cochrane, Joseph *see* CENTENNIAL HISTORY OF MASON COUNTY
COCHRANE NORTHERN POST – Canada, Feb 1914-Dec 1919 – 2r – 1 – uk British Libr Newspaper [072]
Cochrane, William *see*
- THE CANADIAN ALBUM-MEN OF CANADA; OR, SUCCESS BY EXAMPLE IN RELIGION, PATRIOTISM, BUSINESS, LAW, MEDICINE, EDUCATION AND AGRICULTURE
- THE CHURCH AND THE COMMONWEALTH: DISCUSSIONS AND ORATIONS ON QUESTIONS OF THE DAY: PRACTICAL, BIOGRAPHICAL, EDUCATIONAL AND DOCTRINAL, WRITTEN DURING A TWENTY YEARS MINISTRY
- FUTURE PUNISHMENT, OR, DOES DEATH END PROBATION: MATERIALISM, IMMORTALITY OF THE SOUL, CONDITIONAL IMMORTALITY OR ANNIHILATIONISM.
- MEMOIRS AND REMAINS OF THE REVEREND WALTER INGLIS, AFRICAN MISSIONARY AND CANADIAN PASTOR

Cock, Alfons de *see* KINDERSPEL UND KINDERLUST IN ZUID-NEDERLAND
Cock, C *see* SPECIMEN JURIDICUM INAUGURALE DE JURE POSTLIMINII
Cock, H *see* ORATIO DE JURIS PUBLICI UNIVERSALIS STUDIO,...
Cock, V *see* CONCEPCIONES MODERNAS SOBRE LA TEORIA...CIVILES, COMERCIALES Y FINANCIERAS
THE COCKATOO AND NORTH QUEENSLAND FIGARO – Townsville, Australia. 1-15 Sept 1883 – 4ft – 1 – uk British Libr Newspaper [072]
Cockayne, T O *see* LEECHDOMS, WORTCUNNING AND STARCRAFT OF EARLY ENGLAND (RS35)
Cockburn, George Ralph Richardson *see* SPEECH...ON UNRESTRICTED RECIPROCITY DELIVERED IN THE HOUSE OF COMMONS, OTTAWA, ON TUESDAY, MARCH 19TH, 1889
Cockburn, James *see* THE BOUNDARY QUESTION
Cockburn, W *see* AN ACCOUNT OF DISTEMPERS INCIDENT TO SEAFARING PEOPLE
Cocke, Alonzo Rice *see* STUDIES IN EPHESIANS
Cocker, Benjamin *see* THEISTIC CONCEPTION OF THE WORLD: AN ESSAY IN OPPOSITION TO CERTAIN TENDENCIES
Cocker, Benjamin Franklin *see* THE THEISTIC CONCEPTION OF THE WORLD
Cocker, BF *see*
- CHRISTIANITY AND GREEK PHILOSOPHY, OR, THE RELATION BETWEEN SPONTANEOUS AND REFLECTIVE THOUGHT IN GREECE AND THE POSITIVE TEACHING OF CHRIST AND HIS APOSTLES
- LECTURES ON THE TRUTH OF THE CHRISTIAN RELIGION

Cocker, Edward *see* COCKERS ACCOMPLISH'D SCHOOL-MASTER
Cockeram, Henry *see* THE ENGLISH DICTIONARIE
Cockerell, Sydney Carlyle *see* THE WORK OF W. DE BRAILES, AN ENGLISH ILLUMINATOR OF THE 13TH CENTURY
COCKERS ACCOMPLISH'D SCHOOL-MASTER / Cocker, Edward – 1696. 125p. (English Linguistics Series 1500-1800) – 9 – us UMI [420]
Cockin, Hereward Kirby *see* GENTLEMAN DICK OF THE GREYS: AND OTHER POEMS
Cockin, William *see* THE ART OF DELIVERING WRITTEN LANGUAGE
Cockrell, Ewing *see* HISTORY OF JOHNSON COUNTY
Cockrill, W R *see*
- BUFFALOES OF CHINA
- HUSBANDRY AND HEALTH OF THE DOMESTIC BUFFALO

Cockshott, H M *see* THE STATUTES OF NEW SOUTH WALES OF RACTICAL UTILITY PASSED PRIOR TO 1894 AND STILL IN FORCE
Cockton, Peter *see* HOUSE OF COMMONS PARLIAMENTARY PAPERS, 1801-1900
Coclico, A P *see* COMPENDIUM MUSICES. DE REGULA CONTRAPUNCTI. DE COMPOSITIONE
COCOA PEST AND DISEASE MANAGEMENT IN SOUTHEAST ASIA AND AUSTRALASIA – 1992 – 227p – it F.A.O. [360]
COCOA TRIBUNE – Cocoa. Fl. 1930-1967 – 1 – us P.K. Yonge [071]
COCONUT PALM PRODUCTS : THEIR PROCESSING IN DEVELOPING COUNTRIES / Grimwood, BE – 1975 – 261p – it F.A.O. [670]
COCONUT, TREE OF LIFE – 1984 – 456p – it F.A.O. [580]
COCONUT WOOD : PROCEEDINGS AND USE – 1985 – 60p – it F.A.O. [670]
COCUK DUENYASI – Istanbul: Ikdam Matbaasi, Kader Matbaasi, Ayyildiz Matbaasi, ahmediye Matbaasi, 1913-1919; Mesuel Mueduerue: Tevfik Nureddin, Muallim Ahmed Halid, Nos 12, 41, 83-91, 93-94. – 30 Mayis 1329 [1913]-9 Kanunisani 1919 – 4mf – 9 – $90.00 – us MEDOC [949]
COD Cattle Ranch *see* RECORD BOOK
CODA – (nos 212-253 1987/88-1993/94 Can$20.00 9) – Toronto. nos 1-253. 1958/59-1993/94 – 5,9 – Price varies – cn Micromedia [073]
CODA: POETS AND WRITERS NEWSLETTER – (v. 6-. 1978$ 9) – v. 1-. 1973- – 1,5,6 – us UMI [420]
CODE : U.S. LAWS, STATUTES, ETC / U. S. – Official ed. 1925-94 ed v25 – 9 – $5,450.00 set – us Hein [324]
LE CODE BOLCHEVIK DU MARIAGE / Prouvost, Leon – Conflans-Ste-Honorine: L'Idee libre, 1921. 4p. (Les Femmes Collection) – 1mf – 9 – $6.00 – fr Bibl Nationale [340]
CODE CIVIL.. / Canada. Bas-Canada – Quebec: Imp. Stewart Derbishire and Georges Desbarats, 1863. SEM105P380 – 19mf – 9 – Can$42.75 – cn Bibl Nat [340]
CODE CIVIL DE L'EMPIRE DU JAPON / Japan – (Livres 1, 2 et 3). Dispositions generales Droits reels Droit de creance. Traducteurs by I. Motono et M. Tomii. Traduction du japonais. Paris, Librairie de la societe du recueil general des lois et des arrets. 1898 – 9 – 5.00 – fr Orientalistes [340]
CODE CIVIL DU BAS CANADA – Quebec: Imp. Georges E Desbarats, 1865. SEM105P426 – 16mf – 9 – Can$36.00 – cn Bibl Nat [340]
CODE CIVIL DU BAS CANADA. / Quebec. (Province). Laws, Statutes, etc – (Table analytique du Code civil du Bas-Canada... Ottawa, 1867. 98p. LL-2387. Analytical index to the Civil code of Lower-Canada. Ottawa, 1867. 100p. LL-2387) – Ottawa: Cameron, 1866. 4, 747p. LL-2387 – 1 – us L of C Photodup [340]
CODE CIVIL DU BAS CANADA D'APRES LE ROLE AMENDE DEPOSE DANS LE BUREAU DU GREFFIER DU CONSEIL LEGISLATIF... = CIVIL CODE OF LOWER CANADA FROM THE AMENDED ROLL DEPOSITED IN THE OFFICE OF THE CLERK OF THE LEGISLATIVE COUNCIL.. / Canada. Bas-Canada – Ottawa: Printed by Malcom Cameron, 1866. SEM105P430 – 8mf – 9 – Can$18.00 – cn Bibl Nat [340]
CODE CIVILE DU BAS-CANADA / Canada. Bas-Canada – Quebec: Stewart Derbishire et Georges Desbarats..., 1863. SEM105P380 – 19mf – 9 – Can$42.75 – cn Bibl Nat [971]
CODE CIVILE...D'APRES LE ROLE AMENDE DEPOSE DANS LE BUREAU DU GREFFIER DU CONSEIL LEGISLATIF, TEL QUE PRESCRIT PAR L'ACTE 29 VICT. CHP. 41, 1865 / Canada. Bas-Canada – Ottawa: Malcom Cameron..., 1866. SEM105P430 – 8mf – 9 – Can$18.00 – cn Bibl Nat [971]
CODE CONSTITUTIONEL DE LA BELGIQUE, OU COMMENTAIRE SUR LA CONSTITUTION, LA LOI ELECTORALE, LA LOI COMMUNALE ET LA LOI PROVINCIALE / Bivort, Jean Baptiste – Nouv. ed. rev. Bruxelles, Decq, 1859-62 4 pt. in 1 v. LL-4017 – 1 – us L of C Photodup [340]
CODE CRIMINEL DE L'EMPEREUR CHARLES, VULGAIREMENT APPELLE LA CAROLINE : CONTENANT LES LOIX QUI SONT SUIVIES DANS LES JURISDICTIONS CRIMINELLES DE L'EMPIRE; ET A L'UFAGE DES CONSEILS DE GUERRE DES TROUPES SUISSES – A Maestricht: Chez Jean-Edme Dufour & Phil Poux, 1779 – 4mf – 9 – $6.00 – LLMC 89-018 – us L.L.M.C. [340]
CODE CRIMINEL, OU COMMENTAIRE SUR L'ORDONNANCE DE 1670 / Serpillon, Francois – Nouv. ed. Lyon: chez les Freres Perisse. 2v. 1788. SEM35P80 – 1r – 1 – Can$51.00 – cn Bibl Nat [360]
CODE DE LA PATRIE ET DE L'HUMANITE / Baumier – Ouvrage periodique par M. Baumier. Paris, Imp. de Cellot. no. 1 (30-7-1789) no. 2 (7-8-1789) – 9 – fr Hachette [321]
LE CODE DE L'AIR; ... / Bonnefoy, G – Paris, 1909 – 3mf – 9 – ILM-1107/1 – ne IDC [327]
CODE DE MUSIQUE PRATIQUE / Rameau, Jean-Phillippe – 1760 – 9 – us Sibley [780]
CODE DES CURES, MARGUILLIERS ET PAROISSIENS: ACCOMPAGNE DE NOTES HISTORIQUES ET CRITIQUES / Beaudry, Joseph Ubald – Montreal: La Minerve, 1870. 03034. (Pre-1900 Canadiana) – 9 – cn C.I.H.M. [240]
CODE DES ETRANGERS... / Gand, M – Paris, 1853 – 6mf – 1 – ILM-849/1 – ne IDC [327]
CODE DES PRISES ET DU COMMERCE DE TERRE ET DE MER / Dufriche-Foulaines, F N – Paris, 1804 – 7mf – 1 – ILM-642/1 – ne IDC [327]
CODE DIPLOMATIQUE... / Garden, G – Paris, n.d. – 3mf – 1 – ILM-172/1 – ne IDC [327]
LE CODE DU TRAVAIL MALGACHE : SON APPLICATION PRATIQUE / Goyat, Michel & Mouric, Rene – (Filmed with Garlick, Peter: African traders in Kumasi, Legon 1959; and Nypan, Astrid: Market trade, Legon 1960) – Tananarive [1962] – 1 – us Res Libr [960]
CODE FISCAL SYRIEN: CODE PERMANENT / Syria – (Recueil des lois syriennes et de la legislation financiere). 1953. BNE-9736 1 – 9 – ne IDC [332]

CODE INTERNATIONAL DE L'ABORDAGE, DE L'ASSISTANCE... / Autran, F C – Ed 2. Paris, 1902 – 7mf – 9 – ILM-3918/1 – ne IDC [340]

CODE INTERNATIONAL DE L'ABORDAGE MARITIME... / Autran, F C – Paris, 1890 – 3mf – 9 – ILM-3917/1 – ne IDC [340]

Code, Joseph Bernard *see* THE SPANISH WAR AND LYING PROPAGANDA

CODE MILITAIRE / Suzor, L T – Quebec: G and G E Desbarats, 1864. SEM105P317 – 3mf – 9 – Can$6.75 – cn Bibl Nat [355]

CODE MILITAIRE OU COMPILATION DES ORDONNANCES DES ROIS DE FRANCE, CONCERNANT LES GENS DE GUERRE / Briquet, Pierre de – Paris: Chez Durand..., 1761. SEM16P344 – 1r – 5 – Can$45.00 – cn Bibl Nat [355]

CODE MUNICIPAL DE LA PROVINCE DE QUEBEC ANNOTE 1898-1902 / Quebec Province – Montreal: C Theoret, editeur librairie generale de droit et de jurisprudence, 1902. SEM105P1865 – 7mf – 9 – Can$15.75 – cn Bibl Nat [340]

CODE MUNICIPAL DE LA PROVINCE DE QUEBEC, ANNOTE; COMPRENANT TOUS LES AMENDEMENTS JUSQU'AU 1 JANVIER 1888. / Quebec. (Province). Laws, Statutes, etc – 1er. ed. Quebec: Filteau, 1888. 494p. LL-1654 – 1 – us L of C Photodup [340]

CODE MUNICIPAL DE LA PROVINCE DE QUEBEC ANNOTE MIS AU COURANT DE LA LEGISLATION ET DE LA JURISPRUDENCE / Quebec Province; ed by Theoret, C – 2e ed. Montreal, 1905. SEM105P1864 – 8mf – 9 – Can$18.00 – cn Bibl Nat [340]

CODE MUNICIPAL DE LA PROVINCE DE QUEBEC MIS AU COURANT DE LA LEGISLATION ET DE LA JURISPRUDENCE / Quebec Province – Montreal: A. Periard, libraire-editeur, librairie generale de droit et de jurisprudence, 1887. SEM105P1863 – 5mf – 9 – Can$11.25 – cn Bibl Nat [340]

CODE NATIONAL, OU MANUEL FRANCAIS A L'USAGE DES 3 ORDRES, ET PRINCIPALEMENT DES DEPUTES AUX PROCHAINS ETATS GENERAUX / Saige, Joseph – En France. 1789 – 9 – fr Hachette [321]

CODE OF AMERICAN SAMOA, 1946 EDITION / American Samoa – Office of the Governor, n.d. – 4mf – 9 – $6.00 – LLMC 82-100C Title 1 – us L.L.M.C. [324]

CODE OF AMERICAN SAMOAN, 1973 EDITION / American Samoa – (With 1979 pocket pts) – Equity Publ Co. 2v. 1973 – 22mf – 9 – $33.00 – LLMC 82-100C Title 3 – us L.L.M.C. [324]

CODE OF CENSUS PROCEDURE / Punjab. India. Superintendent of Census Operations – 1911, pt. 1 – 1 – us Res Libr [310]

THE CODE OF CIVIL PROCEDURE AND PROBATE CODE OF GUAM, 1953 / Bohn, John A – (Includes 1964 suppl) – Agana: Off of the Sec of the Gov of Guam, 5 Nov 1953 – 10mf – 9 – $15.00 – LLMC 82-100B Title 7 – us L.L.M.C. [324]

THE CODE OF CIVIL PROCEDURE AND PROBATE CODE OF GUAM, 1970 / Bohn, John A – (With 1972 and 1974 suppls) – 2v – 12mf – 9 – $18.99 – LLMC 82-100B Title 13 – us L.L.M.C. [324]

THE CODE OF CIVIL PROCEDURE OF GUAM, 1947 / Guam. (Commonwealth). Laws, Statutes, etc – Washington: GPO. 4pts. 1947 – 3mf – 9 – $4.50 – LLMC 82-100B Title 11 – us L.L.M.C. [324]

THE CODE OF CIVIL PROCEDURE OF THE CANAL ZONE : ENACTED BY EXECUTIVE ORDER OF PRESIDENT THEODORE ROOSEVELT – 1 May 1907. Washington: GPO, 1907 – 3mf – 9 – $4.50 – LLMC 82-100D Title 17 – us L.L.M.C. [340]

CODE OF COMMERCE IN FORCE IN CUBA, PORTO RICO, AND THE PHILIPPINES, 1897 : INCLUDING THE COMMERCIAL REGISTRY REGULATIONS, EXCHANGE REGULATIONS,AND OTHER PROVISIONS OF A SIMILAR CHARACTER, THE CODE OF 1885 AS AMENDED BY THE LAW OF JUNE 10, 1897 – Washington: GPO, 1899 – 4mf – 9 – $6.00 – LLMC 92-306 – us L.L.M.C. [340]

CODE OF CRIMINAL PROCEDURE: PRELIMINARY DRAFT / American Law Institute – Philadelphia The Institute, 1927. 88 p. LL-2341 – 1 – us L of C Photodup [340]

THE CODE OF EVIDENCE... / New York. (State). Commissioners to Report a Code of Evidence – Albany? 1889. LL-326 – 1 – us L of C Photodup [340]

CODE OF FEDERAL REGULATIONS – (1975-94 $750.00y. 1938-74 price varies. 1995 $775.00) – Backfile 1938-1995 – 9 – $25,500.00 set (1996 subsc $795.00 set) – 0-89941-200-9 – us Hein [324]

CODE OF FEDERAL REGULATIONS / U. S. National Archives and Records Administration, Office of the Federal Register – 1994 – 9 – $264.00y in US; $330.00y outside – S-N 869-029-00000-9. Sub-list ID-CFRM4 – us Gov't Printing [324]

CODE OF FEDERAL REGULATIONS / U.S. National Archives and Records Service – (Containing codification of documents of general applicability and future effect as of Jan 1 1970, with ancillaries: title 25 Indians 1970) – 9 – $5.00f – us Ross [340]

CODE OF FEDERAL REGULATIONS: 1939-1982 / U. S. Laws, Statutes, etc – 577 reels. Includes printed guide – 1 – us Trans-Media [324]

CODE OF FEDERAL REGULATIONS ON MICROFICHE / U. S. – (Printed index available separately) – 1938- – ca 36,000mf – 9 – Apply for price – us CIS [340]

CODE OF LAW, PRACTICE AND FORMS FOR JUSTICES' AND OTHER INFERIOR COURTS IN THE WESTERN STATES / Hillyer, Curtis – San Francisco: Bender-Moss Co., 1912. 2v. LL-1251 – 1 – us L of C Photodup [340]

CODE OF MASSACHUSETTS REGULATIONS – Boston: Office of the Massachusetts Secretary of State, 1992 revision with 1996 service – 9 – $670.00 set – us Hein [324]

THE CODE OF NOMENCLATURE AND CHECK-LIST OF NORTH AMERICAN BIRDS. / American Ornithologists' Union. Committee on Classification and Nomenclature – New York: The Union, 1886. c1895. 00042. (Pre-1900 Canadiana) – 9 – cn C.I.H.M. [590]

A CODE OF REFORM AND PRISON DISCIPLINE. / Livingston, Edward – New York, National Prison Association of the United States 1872 140 p. LL-4077 – 1 – us L of C Photodup [340]

CODE OF REGULATIONS / California – 9 – us UMI [324]

CODE OF REGULATIONS OF THE TTPI / Trust Territory of the Pacific Islands. (U.S.) – Saipan: TTPI Gov, n.d. – 4mf – 9 – $6.00 – LLMC 82-100F Title 5 – us L.L.M.C. [324]

CODE OF THE TRUST TERRITORY OF THE PACIFIC, 1952 – (With an appendix of Executive Orders) – Honolulu: Office of the High Commissioner, 22 Dec 1952 – 5mf – 9 – $7.50 – LLMC 82-100F Title 20 – us L.L.M.C. [324]

CODE OF THE TRUST TERRITORY OF THE PACIFIC, 1959 REVISION – Agana, Guam: Office of the High Commissioner, 31 Dec 1959 – 5mf – 9 – $7.50 – LLMC 82-100F Title 21 – us L.L.M.C. [324]

CODE OF THE TRUST TERRITORY OF THE PACIFIC, 1966 REV – Saipan: Off of the High Commissioner, oct 10 1966 – 6mf – 9 – $9.00 – LLMC 82-100F Title 22 – us L.L.M.C. [323]

CODE OF THE TRUST TERRITORY OF THE PACIFIC, 1970 REV / ed by Steincipher, John – (Includes 1973 & 1975 suppl) – Seattle: Book Publ Co. 2v. 1970 – 21mf – 9 – $31.50 – LLMC 82-100F Title 23 – us L.L.M.C. [323]

CODE OF THE TRUST TERRITORY OF THE PACIFIC, 1980 – Charlottesville: Michie. 2v. 1980 – 14mf – 9 – $21.00 – LLMC 82-100F Title 24 – us L.L.M.C. [323]

CODE PENAL / Congo. Free State. Laws, Statutes, etc – Bruxelles, Hayez, 1888. 21 p. LL-12004 – 1 – us L of C Photodup [340]

CODE PENAL / Guinea. French. Laws, Statutes, etc – Conakry, Imprimerie Lumumba, 1966. 122 p. LL-12035 – 1 – us L of C Photodup [340]

LE CODE PENAL – Montreal, Canada. n.d.; 1909; v3 n25. mar 1912 – 1r – 1 – Can$25.00 – cn Can Microfilming [340]

CODE PENAL DU ROYAUME DE SIAM PROMULGUE LE LER JUIN 1908, ENTRE EN VIGEUR LE 22 SEPTEMBRE 1908 / Thailand. Laws, Statutes, etc – Paris, Imprimerie Nationale, 1909. 110 p. LL-10015 – 1 – us L of C Photodup [340]

CODE PENAL INTERNATIONAL EN 1314 ARTICLES / Cosentini, F – Paris, 1937 – 4mf – 1 – ILM-2082/1 – ne IDC [327]

CODE PENAL PROMULGUE PAR LE DECRET NO. 36 – Traduction du japonais. Tokyo, Imprimerie Imperiale. 1881 – 9 – 5.00 – fr Orientalistes [340]

CODE POUR L'ANALYSE DES REPRESENTATIONS FIGURES SUR LES VASES MOCHICAS / Hocquenghem, Anne Marie – 9 – F100.00 – fr Ethnologie [740]

CODE REMEDIES AND REMEDIAL RIGHTS BY THE CIVIL ACTION ACCORDING TO THE REFORMED AMERICAN PROCEDURE. / Pomeroy, John Norton – 4th ed. Boston: Little, Brown, 1904. 983p. LL-1399 – 1 – us L of C Photodup [340]

CODEBOOKS / U.S. Department of State – 1867-76. 1 roll. T1171 – 1 – us Nat'l Archives [975]

Codera, Francisco *see*
- LOS BENIVERMAN EN MERIDA Y BADAJOZ
- INSCRIPCION ARABE EN TRUJILLO
- NUEVA LAPIDA ROMANA DE MONTANCHEZ, CAPITAL DE PARTIDO EN LA PROVINCIA DE CACERES

LES CODES CAMBODGIENS / Leclere, Adhemard – Paris (I-II). 1898 – 1 – fr A.C.R.P.P. [950]

CODES CONGOLAIS ET LOIS USUELLES EN VIGUEUR AU CONGO, COLLATIONNES D'APRES LES TEXTES OFFICIELS ET ANNOTES / Congo. Free State. Laws, Statutes, etc – Bruxelles, Larcier, 1900. 604 p. LL-12005 – 1 – us L of C Photodup [340]

LES CODES DU CONGO, SUIVIS DES DECRETS, ORDONNANCES ET ARRETES COMPLEMENTAIRES. / Congo. Free State. Laws, Statutes, etc – 2. ed. Bruxelles, Larcier, 1892. 360 p. LL-12001 – 1 – us L of C Photodup [340]

CODES OF CENSUS PROCEDURES FOR THE HYDERABAD ASSIGNED DISTRICTS / Hyderabad. India. (State). Superintendent of Census Operations – 1901. pt. 1 – 1 – us Res Libr [310]

THE CODES OF HAMMURABI AND MOSES, WITH COPIOUS COMMENTS, INDEX, AND BIBLE REFERENCES / Hammurabi, King of Babylonia – Cincinnati: Jennings and Graham, 1905. 126p LL-2294 – 1 – us L of C Photodup [340]

CODES OF PRACTICE AND MANUAL OF PROCEDURES FOR CONSIDERATION OF INTRODUCTIONS AND TRANSFERS OF MARINE AND FRESHWATER ORGANISMS – 1988 – 60p – it F.A.O. [639]

CODEX 1 OF THE GOSPELS AND ITS ALLIES / Lake, Kirsopp – 1902 – 5mf – 9 – ne Slangenburg [220]

CODEX ALIMENTARIUS : VOL 1 – GENERAL REQUIREMENTS – 1992 – 347p – it F.A.O. [060]

Codex Alimentarius Commission *see* PROCEDURAL MANUAL OF THE CODEX ALIMENTARIUS COMMISSION

DER CODEX ARABICUS MONACENSIS AUMER 238: EINE SPANISCH-ARABISCHE EVANGELIENHANDSCHRIFT / Roemer, Karl – Leipzig: W. Drugulin, 1905. 1 fiche – 9 – us A.T.L.A. [240]

CODEX BORBONICUS – A sacred almanac of the Aztecs ed. by George C. Vaillant. New York, 1940 – 1 – us U.W. Library [520]

DER CODEX D IN DER APOSTELGESCHICHTE (T.U.U. 2-17/1) / Weiss, Bernhard – Leipzig, 1897 – 2mf – 9 – ne Slangenburg [240]

CODEX DIPLOMATICUS AEVI SAXONICI / Kemble, J M – H-1144 2. 6 v. 1839-1848 – 8 – ne IDC [025]

CODEX DIPLOMATICUS BRANDENBURGENSIS : SAMMLUNG DER URKUNDEN, CHRONIKEN UND SONSTIGEN QUELLEN FUER DIE GESCHICHTE DER MARK BRANDENBURG UND IHRER REGESTEN / ed by Riedel, Adolf Friedrich – Berlin. 41v. 1838-69 – 237mf – 9 – subsc: DM1,300 diazo DM1,500.00 silver – gw Olms [943]

CODEX DIPLOMATICUS RHENO-MOSELLANUS – Koblenz.v1-3. 1822-25. 25 fiches – 9 – DM250.00 – gw Mikro Press [073]

CODEX DIPLOMATICUS SILESIAE / ed by Verein fuer Geschichte und Altertum Schlesien – Breslau. 36v. 1857-1933 – 120mf – 9 – subsc: DM700.00 diazo DM800.00 silver – gw Olms [943]

CODEX DUNENSIS / ed by Lettenhove, J Kervijn de – Brussel, 1875 – 20mf – 8 – Dfl70.00 – ne Slangenburg [240]

CODEX FULDENSIS : NOVUM TESTAMENTUM LATINE INTERPRETE HIERONYMO / ed by Ranke, Ernst – Marburgi: Sum[p]tibus N G Elwerti Bibliopolae Academici, 1868 – 2mf – 9 – 0-8370-9499-2 – 1986-3499 – us A.T.L.A. [220]

CODEX LITURGICUS ECCLESIAE UNIVERSA / Daniel, H A – (Tome 1, Eccl. Romano-Catholicae.-8mf; Tome 2, Eccl. Lutheranae.-11mf; Tome 3, Eccl. Reformatae Atque Anglicanae.-11mf; Tome 4, Eccl. Orientalis.-13mf) – Lipsiae, 1847, 1848, 1851, 1853 – 8 – ne Slangenburg [240]

CODEX LITURGICUS ECCLESIAE UNIVERSAE / Assemanus, J A – Roma. v1-13. 1749-66 – 106mf – 8 – Dfl371.00 – ne Slangenburg [240]

Codex Mariano Jimenez *see* CODICE MARIANO JIMENEZ. NOMINA DE TRIBUTOS DE LOS PUEBLOS OTLAZPAN Y TEPEXIC..., 1549

CODEX MARIANUS GLAGOLITICUS. QUATTUOR EVANGELIORUM VERSIONIS PALAEOSLOVENICAE / ed by Iagich, V – Berolini, St. Petersburg, 1883. In Latin and Russian. B/770/2 – 8 – ne IDC [240]

CODEX MENDOZA / Galarza, J – (Lecture nahuatl. 7 fiches. F180.00; 9) – 1ere page: 2 recto. Methode d'analyse. 3 fiches – 9 – F100.00 – fr Ethnologie [306]

CODEX NAPOLEON [CODE NAPOLEON], UEBERSETZT NACH DER NEUEN OFFIZIELLEN AUSGABE VON EINER GESELLSCHAFT RECHTSGELEHRTER UND DURCH NOTEN ERLAEUTERT VON L. SPIELMANN – 1995 – 8mf – 9 – DM148.00 – 3-8267-3155-7 – gw Hänsel [944]

CODEX PURPUREUS PETROPOLITANUS (CODEX N OF THE GOSPELS) / ed by Cronin, H S – 1899 – 3mf – 9 – ne Slangenburg [220]

Codex Ramirez *see* RELACION DEL ORIGEN DE LOS INDIOS QUE HABITAN ESTA NUEVA ESPANA...

CODEX REGULARUM : AMPLIFICATUS A M. BROCKIE / Holstenius, L – Aug. Vindelicorum. v1-6. 1759 – Dfl539.00 – ne Slangenburg [240]

CODEX REGULARUM ET CONSTITUTIONUM CLERICALIUM / Miraeus, A – Antverpiae, 1638 – Dfl22.00 – ne Slangenburg [240]

CODEX SAECULI XI, CONTINENS TRATATUS VARIOS AD HISTORIAM MUSICAE MEDIIAEVI PERTINENTES / Rochester Codex – c. 1070-1103 – 9 – us Sibley [780]

THE CODEX SANGALLENSIS : A STUDY IN THE TEXT OF THE OLD LATIN GOSPELS / Harris, James Rendel – London: C J Clay, 1891 – 1mf – 9 – 1986-3243 – us A.T.L.A. [220]

CODEX SCHLIERBACH 1, 31.(12 SAEC.) : KALENDARIUM ANTIPHONALE MISSAE, SACRAMENTARIUM, LECTIONARIUM MONASTERII S. AGAPITI CREMIFANI (KREMSMUENSTER) – 14mf – 8 – Dfl49.00 – ne Slangenburg [240]

CODEX VERCELLENSIS – Der Vercelli-Codex CXVII, nebst Abdruck einiger altenglischer Homilien der Handschrift, von Max Foa5rster. Halle, a. S., M. Niemeyer, 1913. 163 p. "Sonderabdruck aus 'Studien zur englischen Philologie' Heft L." Film Mas 8139 – 1 – us H.U. Library [090]

Codey, H A *see* AN APOSTLE OF THE NORTH

THE CODIACEAE OF THE SIBOGA EXPEDITION / Gepp, A & Gepp, E S – Including a monograph of Flabellarieae and Uloteae. (Siboga-Expedite, Mon. 62, Livr. 56). Leyden. 1911. B-5517 2 – 8 – ne IDC [580]

CODICE FRANCISCANO S. 16. INFORME DE LA PROVINCIA DEL SANTO EVANGELIO AL VISITADOR LC. JUAN DE OVANDO – 1869 – 9 – $1.50f – sp Bibl Santa Ana [240]

CODICE MARIANO JIMENEZ. NOMINA DE TRIBUTOS DE LOS PUEBLOS OTLAZPAN Y TEPEXIC..., 1549 / Codex Mariano Jimenez – Mexico: Instit. de antropologia e historia, 1967 – 1 – F50.00 – fr Armell [305]

CODICE MENDIETA / Mendieta, Geronimo – (Tomo II.1892. 1.50f; 9) – Tomo I. 1892 – 9 – 1.50f – sp Bibl Santa Ana [890]

CODICE SIETE PARTIDAS DE ALFONSO X / Lopez de Tovar, Gregorio – (Tomo II.1887. 1.50f; 9) – 1877. Tomo I, primera partida – 9 – 1.50f – sp Bibl Santa Ana [946]

CODICES MAYAS... / Villacorte, J Antonio & Villacorta, Carlos A – Guatemala, 1933; Madrid: Razon y Fe, 1934 – 1 – sp Bibl Santa Ana [340]

CODICES MEJICANOS DE FR. BERNARDINO DE SAHAGUN / Ramirez, J F – Madrid: Fortanet, 1885. B.R.A.H. vi/pp. 85-124 – 1 – sp Bibl Santa Ana [240]

CODICILLUS – (v.21-. 1980-. 5,6,9) – v.1-. 1960- – 1 – us UMI [340]

CODICUM MANUSCRIPTORUM ECCLESIAE CATHEDRALIS DUNELMENSIS CATALOGUS CLASSICUS / Durham Cathedral Library – Compiled by Raine and Rud, Thomas – 1 – uk Microform Academic [010]

LA CODIFICATION DU DROIT INTERNATIONAL / Alvarez, Arturo – Paris, 1912 – 4mf – 9 – ILM-1004/1 – ne IDC [340]

LA CODIFICATION DU DROIT INTERNATIONAL / Alvarez, Arturo – Paris, 1931 – 1mf – 9 – ILM-1584/1 – ne IDC [340]

LA CODIFICATION DU DROIT INTERNATIONAL... / Constantinoff, J – Paris, 1929 – 3mf – 1 – ILM-1582/1 – ne IDC [327]

CODIFICATION OF AMERICAN INTERNATIONAL LAW – Washington, DC, 1925 – 2mf – 1 – ILM-1720/1 – ne IDC [327]

CODIFICATION OF THE REGULATIONS AND ORDERS FOR THE GOVERNMENT OF AMERICAN SAMOA : 1921, 1931 AND 1937 EDITIONS / American Samoa. Executive Branch – 1921-37 – 13mf – 9 – $19.50 – LLMC 82-100C Title 9 – us L.L.M.C. [324]

CODIGO CIVIL DE LA REPUBLICA DOMINICANA. / Dominican Republic. Laws, Statutes, etc – Edicion autorizada. Santo Domingo, Casanova N., 1930. 279 p. LL-8006 – 1 – us L of C Photodup [340]

CODIGO CIVIL DE LA REPUBLICA ORIENTAL DEL URUGUAY / Uruguay.Laws, Statutes, etc – Montevideo: Impr. de la Nacion, 1893 – 1 – us U.W. Library [972]

CODIGO CIVIL PAN-AMERICANO / Cosentini, F – Habana, [1929] – 2mf – 1 – ILM-1581/1 – ne IDC [327]

CODIGO DE LA CIRCULACION / Espana. Leyes, decretos, etc – Caceres: Imprenta Moderna, 1959 – 1 – sp Bibl Santa Ana [340]

CODIGO DE LAS SIETE PARTIDAS DEL REY D. ALFONSO EL SABIO GLOSADAS POR EL LIC. GREGORIO LOPEZ DE TOVAR / Alfonso 10 el Sabio, Rey de Castilla – Partida 1st. Madrid: Imp. de la Nueva Prensa, 1877 – 1 – sp Bibl Santa Ana [340]

CODIGO DE PROCEDIMIENTOS ADMINISTRATIVOS / Honduras. Laws, Statutes, etc – Tegucigalpa: Nacional, 1930. 22p. LL-8031 – 1 – us L of C Photodup [340]

CODIGO PENAL BOLIVIANO / Bolivia. Laws, Statutes, etc – La Paz, Gamarra, 1902. 267 p. LL-8003 – 1 – us L of C Photodup [340]

CODIGO PENAL DE 1879 : PARA LAS ISLAS DE CUBA Y PUERTO RICO, Y LEY PROVISIONAL PARA LA APLICACION DE SUS DISPOSICIONES, CONCORDADO CON LAS LEGISLACIONES ROMANA, PATRIA Y EXTRANJERAS... / Orozco y Arascot, Andres de – Habana: Imprenta de G Montiel, 1879 – 2mf – 9 – $3.00 – LLMC 92-314 – us L.L.M.C. [340]

CODIGO PENAL PARA LAS ISLAS DE CUBA Y PUERTO RICO / ed by Ochotorena, Manuel D – (With catalogue) – 2nd ed. Madrid: Centro Editorial de Gongora, 1891 – 7mf – 9 – $10.50 – LLMC 92-302 – us L.L.M.C. [340]

LOS CODIGOS ESPANOLES / Lopez de Tovar, Gregorio – Tomo V. 1872 – 9 – 1.50f – sp Bibl Santa Ana [946]

Codina, Luis *see* CARTAS A FLORO. SOBRE PRIMERA ENSENANZA Y EDUCACION

CODING AND DEVELOPMENT OF MOVEMENT RECALL IN LABORATORY AND FIELD SETTINGS / Quek, Jin-Jong – University of Queensland, 1990 – 6mf – 9 – $24.00 – PSY 1899 – us Microform Publ [150]

CODINI CUROPALATAE (CSHB 37) : DE OFFICIALIBUS PALATII CONSTANTINOPOLITANI ET DE OFFICIIS MAGNAE ECCLESIAE LIBER / ed by Bekkeri, Imm – Bonnae, 1839 – Dfl30.00 – ne Slangenburg [240]

Codini, Georgii *see*
- DE OFFICIIS MAGNAE ECCLESIAE ET AULAE CONSTANTINOPO- LITANAE (CBH 18)
- EXCERPTA DE ANTIQUITATIBUS CONSTANTINOPOLITANI (CSHB 46)

Codini, Georgii et al *see* EXCERPTA DE ANTIQUITATIBUS CONSTANTINOPOLITANIS (CBH 12,2)

CODKA MACALLINKA = TEACHER'S VOICE – Mogadishu, Somalia, feb, may, dec 1973; jun 1975; jul 1976; apr 1978; feb, jun, sep 1989; feb 1990 – 1r – us Res Libr [370]

Codman, John *see* TEN MONTHS IN BRAZIL: WITH INCIDENTS OF VOYAGES AND TRAVELS, DESCRIPTIONS OF SCENERY AND CHARACTER, NOTICES OF COMMERCE.

Codo, B C *see* LA PRESSE DAHOMEENNE FACE AUX ASPIRATIONS DES "EVOLUES"

Codovilla, Victorio *see*
- BATIR AL NAZI-PERONISMO PARA ABRIR UNA ERA DE LIBERTAD Y PROGRESO
- CARTA A LOS PATRIOTAS Y ANTIFASCISTAS DE LA ARGENTINA
- DONDE DESEMBOCARA LA SITUACION POLITICA ARGENTINA?
- EL SIGNIFICADO DEL "GIRO A LA IZQUIERDA" DEL PERONISMO
- SOBRE EL PERONISMO Y LA SITUACION POLITICA ARGENTINA

Codrington, Edward *see* MEMOIR OF THE LIFE OF ADMIRAL SIR EDWARD CODRINGTON, WITH SELECTIONS FROM HIS PUBLIC AND PRIVATE CORRESPONDENCE

CODY COW BOY – Cody, NE. -w. Dec. 1900-Nov. 1912; Jan. 1913-Jun. 1927 – 1 – us NE Hist [071]

CODY ROUND-UP – Cody, NE. -w. May 1936; Oct. 1936; Jul. 1937-Sep. 1937; Nov. 1937-Oct. 1943 – 1 – us NE Hist [071]

Cody, SM *see* THE EFFECTS OF THE STRENGTH SHOE ON VERTICAL JUMP PERFORMANCE IN MALE COLLEGIATE BASKETBALL PLAYERS

Coe, Harrie B *see* MAINE

Coe, Joseph *see* THE TRUE AMERICAN

Coedes, G *see*
- THE EMPIRE OF THE SOUTH SEAS
- TEXTES D'AUTEURS GRECS ET LATINS RELATIFS A L'EXTREME ORIENT, DEPUIS LE IVE SIECLE AVANT J.C. JUSQU'AU XIVE SIECLE

COEDUCACION / Aradillas Agudo, Antonio – Madrid: Ediciones Studium, 1970 – sp Bibl Santa Ana [370]

Coeffeteau, N *see* RESPONSE AU LIVRE INTITULE LE MYSTERE D'INIQUITE

COELESTIS URBS IERUSALEM : APHORISMEN: NEBST EINER BEILAGE / Laemmer, Hugo – (Includes bibliographical references) – Freiburg i.B.: Herder, 1866 – 1mf – 9 – 0-8370-7300-6 – 1986-1300 – us A.T.L.A. [780]

COELINA OU L'ENFANT DU MYSTERE / Pixerecourt – (French Theatre Series). Paris. Au Theatre et au Palais du Tribunal, an XI. 1803 – 9 – fr Hachette [820]

Coello, Francisco *see*
- BOLETIN DE LA REAL ACADEMIA DE LA HISTORIA. INFORMES
- VIAS ROMANAS ENTRE TOLEDO Y MERIDA. INFORMES

COELUM EMPYREUM, NON VANIS ET FICTIS CONSTELLATIONUM MONSTRIS BELLUATUM, SED DIVUM DOMUS DOMINI JESU CHRISTI, EJUSQUE ILLIBATAE VIRGINIS MATRIS MARIAE, SANCTORUM APOSTOLORUM, MARTYRUM..... / Engelgrave, H – Koeln, Amsterdam, 1669 – 17mf – 9 – ne IDC [700]

Coenen, H W *see* DAS KUESTENMEER IM FRIEDEN

COENS EERHERSTEL / Gerretson, Frederik Carel – Amsterdam: P.N. van Kampen, 1944. 110p – 1 – us U.W. Library [950]

Coerper, F *see* JEREMIA

LE COEUR – Illustre paraissant tous les mois. Esoterisme, litterature, sciences, arts. Red. en chef Jules Bois. no. 1-10. Paris. avr 1893-juin 1895. mq no. 8 – 1 – fr A.C.R.P.P. [073]

Coeurderoy, Ernest *see* HURRAH OU LA REVOLUTION PAR LES COSAQUES

COEVOLUTION QUARTERLY – (v.25-. 1980-5,6,9) – v.1-. 1974- – 1 – us UMI [073]

COEXISTENCE – v1-31. 1964-94 – 9 – $595.00 set – us Hein [333]

Coferati, Matteo *see*
- IL CANTORE ADDOTTRINATO, OVVERO REGOLE DEL CANTO CORALE
- MANUALE DEGLI INVITATORI CO'SUOI SALMI..

Coffey, Achilles *see* HISTORY OF THE REGULAR BAPTISTS

Coffey, John F *see* THE CITY AND DIOCESE OF LONDON, ONTARIO, CANADA: AN HISTORICAL SKETCH COMPILED IN COMMEMORATION OF THE OPENING OF ST PETER'S CATHEDRAL, LONDON, JUNE 28TH, 1885

COFFEY'S PROBATE REPORTS / California – v1-6. 1883-1908 (all publ) – 41mf – 9 – $61.00 – LLMC 91-037 – us L.L.M.C. [340]

Coffin, Charles Carleton *see* THE SEAT OF EMPIRE

Coffin, Fulton Johnson *see* THE THIRD COMMANDMENT

Coffin, Thomas Aston *see* PLANTATION RECORDS

Coffin, Victor *see*
- DIE ORGANISATION DES HOEBEREN UNTERRICHTS IM KANADISCHEN BUND
- THE PROVINCE OF QUEBEC AND THE EARLY AMERICAN REVOLUTION: A STUDY IN ENGLISH-AMERICAN COLONIAL HISTORY

Coffin-Roney *see* GUILLAUME LE CONQUERANT, DUC DE NORMANDIE

COFI *see*
- REPORT OF THE 2ND SESSION OF THE SUB-COMMITTEE ON FISH TRADE
- REPORT OF THE 3RD SESSION OF THE SUB-COMMITTEE ON FISH TRADE
- REPORT OF THE 18TH SESSION OF THE COMMITTEE ON FISHERIES

LA COFRADIA CACERENA DE NUESTRA SENORA DE LA PAZ / Munoz de San Pedro, Miguel – Badajoz: Diput.Prov. Badajoz, 1949 – 1 – sp Bibl Santa Ana [946]

Cofradia de la Santisima Virgen del Pilar de Casas de Don Antonio *see* ESTATUTOS PARA EL REGIMEN Y ADMINISTRACION DE LA...

Cofradia de los Ramos, Cristo de la Buena Muerte y Virgen de la Esperanza *see* ESTATUTOS DE LA COFRADIA DE LOS RAMOS, CRISTO DE LA BUENA MUERTE Y VIRGEN DE LA ESPERANZA

Cofradia de Ntra. Sra. de la Montana, Real. Caceres *see*
- MEMORIA Y CUENTA GENERAL 1947-48
- MEMORIA Y CUENTA GENERAL...ANO 1942
- MEMORIA Y CUENTA GENERAL...ANO 1949

Cofradia de Nuestra Senora De la Santisima Virgen de la Montana *see* ORDENANZAS PARA SU REGIMEN Y ADMINISTRACION. ESTATUTOS A ACTUALIZAR

Cofradia de Nuestra Senora de la Soledad y del Santo Entierro *see* ESTATUTOS DE LA REAL...DE CACERES

Cofradia de San Cristobal *see*
- FIESTAS DE SAN CRISTOBAL 1974
- FIESTAS DE SAN CRISTOBAL 1976

Cofradia Santisimo Sacramento *see* ESTATUTOS DE LA...EN LA IGLESIA PARROQUIAL DE ALMENDRALEJO

LAS COFRADIAS RELIGIOSAS DEL VALLE DEL RIO MIERA SIGLOS 17 Y 18 / Mantecon Movellan, T Antonio – 2mf – 9 – Pta1,500.00 – 84-85422-72-4 – sp Pentalfa [200]

Cofrancesco, Lisa *see* HOSTILITY AND CORONARY RISK FACTORS AMONG NATIVE AMERICANS AND CAUCASIANS

Coggin, Frederick Ernest *see* MAN'S ESTATE

COGGINS MEMORIAL BAPTIST CHURCH'S INVOLVEMENT IN A MEANINGFUL WORLD HUNGER MINISTRY / Bunce, Dearl Linwood I – 1982 – 1 – 5.84 – us Baptist [240]

Coggiola, Osvaldo *see* HISTORIA DEL TROTSKISMO ARGENTINO, 1929-1960

Coghlan, T A *see*
- COLONIAL MICROFICHE

COGITATA PHYSICOMATHEMATICA, IN QUIBUS TAM NATURAE QUAM ARTIS EFFECTUS ADMIRANDI CERTISSIMIS DEMONSTRATIONIBUS EXPLICANTUR / Mersenne, Marin – Avec une introduction de A. Beaulieu, Paris, A. Bertier, 1644, pieces liminaires et 606 p. Historie des Sciences XVIIe-XIXe Siecles. 7964 – 9 – fr Hachette [510]

COGITO – 1987- 7v – 9 – £114.50 – 0950-8864 – uk Carfax [073]

LA COGNEE : ORGANE DU FRONT DE LIBERATION DU QUEBEC – Quebec, no 1-no 66. oct 1963-15 avril 1967. SEM35P164 – 1r – 1 – Can$18.00 – cn Bibl Nat [971]

COGNITION – v1-18 1972-84 – 1,5,6,13 – sz Elsevier [150]

COGNITIVE THERAPY AND RESEARCH – v1-18. 1977-94 – 1,5 – $80.00v – us UMI [150]

Cogolludo, Francisco de *see* HISTORIA DE LAS VIDAS Y MILAGROS DE NUESTRO BEATO P. FR. PEDRO DE ALCANTARA

Cohan, Robert P *see* CHOREOGRAPHY AND DANCE

COHASSET 1717-1900 – (Mf 1-2: Births & Deaths 1732-1864. Mf 2: Marriages 1798-1835. Mf 3-4: Vital & Town Records 1739-1864. Mf 5-10: Town Meetings 1717-1813. Mf 11-18: Town Records 1814-50. Mf 19-21: Vital Records 1844-66. Mf 22-24: Marriage Certificates 1848-76. Mf 25-26: Index to Births 1844-1900. Mf 27-28: Index to Marriages 1844-1900. Mf 29-30: Index to Deaths 1844-1900. Mf 31-32: Births 1844-66; Marriages 1844-53. Mf 32-34: Deaths 1844-1900. Mf 35-36: Births 1867-1900. Mf 36-38: Marriages 1862-19004) – (mf ed 1992) – 38mf – 9 – 0-87623-120-2 – us Holbrook [920]

COHASSET 1737-1849 – (Mf 1T-2T: Births & Deaths 1737-1843. Mf 2T: Marriages 1798-1849. Mf 2T-4T: Births & Deaths 1769-1881. Mf 4T: Marriages 1837-1844. Mf 4T,6T: Marriages & Intentions 1846-49. Mf 4T-5T: Hingham Marriages 1747-91. Mf 5T: Out-of-Town Marriages 1770-96; Births, Deaths 1844-49. Mf 6T: Deaths 1844-49) – (mf ed 1995) – 6mf – 9 – 0-87623-232-2 – us Holbrook [920]

Cohen, A *see*
- DECLARATION OF LONDON
- LE TALMUD

Cohen, Avigdor *see* PATTERNS OF SOME GEOLOGICAL CHARACTERISTICS FROM OIL FIELDS IN THE GULF OF SUEZ

Cohen, David *see* TAKING DRUDGERY OUT OF SCHOOL-TOWARDS AN UNINHIBITED FUTURE

Cohen, E G W *see* AN AIR OF MOZART, WITH VARIATIONS FOR A VIOLIN AND VIOLONCELLO

Cohen, Gustave *see* UN GRAND ROMANCIER D'AMOUR ET D'AVENTURE AU 13E SIECLE. CHRETIEN DE TROYES.

Cohen, H *see* JUDAICA, FESTSCHRIFT

Cohen, H Robert et al *see* REPERTOIRE INTERNATIONAL DE LA PRESSE MUSICALE (RIPM)

Cohen, Joseph *see*
- THE DEICIDES
- LES DEICIDES

Cohen, Joseph J *see* THE RIGHT TO SELF-DETERMINATION

Cohen, Margalit *see* ASPECTS PSYCHOLOGIQUES DE L'ACCULTURATION DES JUIFS MAROCAINS

Cohen, Morris L *see* THE YALE LAW LIBRARY BLACKSTONE COLLECTION

COHEN'S LEGAL AND COMMERCIAL GUIDE – West Coast, 1881 – 1r – 1 – $50.00 – B06078 – us Library Micro [340]

COHESION OF COACTING AND INTERACTING FEMALE INTERCOLLEGIATE ATHLETES / Matheson, H E – 1991 – 2mf – 9 – $8.00 – us Microform Publ [150]

Cohn, G *see*
- BEITRAEGE ZUR LEHRE VOM EINHEITLICHEN WECHSELRECHT
- QUID INTERSIT INTER CONFOEDERATIONEM CIVITATUM...

Cohn, Max Conrat *see* DIE CHRISTENVERFOLGUNGEN IM ROEMISCHEN REICHE

Cohn, Michael A *see* SOME QUESTIONS AND AN APPEAL

Cohn, Tobias *see* DER TALMUD: EIN VORTRAG

Cohnitz, E *see* DIE INTERNATIONALEN RECHTSBEZIEHUNGEN...

Cohn-Reiss, E *see* MI-ZIKHRONOT ISH YERUSHALAYIM

Cohrs, Ferdinand *see* PHILIPP MELANCHTHON, DEUTSCHLANDS LEHRER

Cohu, J R *see* THROUGH EVOLUTION TO THE LIVING GOD

COHUNA NEW TIMES – 1913. CNT1 – 1r – 1 – at Corangamite [072]

Coignet, Clarisse Gauthier *see* FRANCIS THE FIRST AND HIS TIMES

Coillard, Francois *see* ON THE THRESHOLD OF CENTRAL AFRICA

COILLARD OF THE ZAMBESI : THE LIVES OF FRANCOIS AND CHRISTINA COILLARD, OF THE PARIS MISSIONARY SOCIETY, IN SOUTH AND CENTRAL AFRICA, 1858-1904 / MacKintosh, Catherine Winkworth – London: T.F. Unwin, 1907 – 2mf – us A.T.L.A. [240]
COILLARD OF THE ZAMBESI / MacKintosh, Catherine Winkworth – London. 1907. BA-400 2 – 8 – ne IDC [900]
THE COIMBATORE DISTRICT MANUAL / Nicholson, F A – I-150-8 2. 1898 – 8 – ne IDC [950]
COIN AND STAMP – Toronto: Greenslade Bros., [1882] – 9 – cn C.I.H.M. [730]
LE COIN DU FEU – Basse-Ville [Quebec]: Frechette, 1840-1841 – 9 – cn C.I.H.M. [730]
LE COIN DU FEU – Montreal: s.n., 1829 – 9 – cn C.I.H.M. [730]
LE COIN DU FEU : REVUE FEMININE – Montreal: [s.n.] v1-4. 1893-96. SEM16P342 – 5 – Can$26.00 – cn Bibl Nat [073]
COIN PRICES – v2-69 1968-79 – 1,5,6 – us Princeton Micro [730]
COINS – v20-25 1973-78 – 1,5,6 – us Princeton Micro [730]
COINS OF BIBLE DAYS / Banks, Florence Aiken – 1959 – 9 – $10.00 – us I.R.C. [730]
COINTELPRO : THE COUNTERINTELLIGENCE PROGRAM OF THE FBI / U.S. Federal Bureau of Investigation – 1978 – 30r – 1 – $2,550.00 – S1753 – us Scholarly Res [360]
O COIO : HEBDOMADARIO ILLUSTRADO E HUMORISTICO – Rio de Janeiro, 1 Apr-Jun 1901; Jan-13 Mar 1902 – 1,5,6 – bl Biblioteca [072]
O COIO – Santa Rita do Sapucai, Brazil. Sept 1911 – 1 – bl Biblioteca [072]
Coit, Thomas Winthrop *see* LECTURES ON THE EARLY HISTORY OF CHRISTIANITY IN ENGLAND
Coke, Edward *see*
- AXIOMATA EX COMMENTARIIS EJUS
- LEGAL AND STATE MEMORANDA
- LEGAL POLITICAL AND PERSONAL PAPERS
- MINUTES OF MEETINGS OF HIS EXECUTORS

Coke Family *see* CORRESPONDENCE
Coke, Henry John *see* THE DOMAIN OF BELIEF
Coke, T *see* ACCOUNT BOOKS OF HIS EXPENSES ABROAD
Coke, Thomas *see* A HISTORY OF THE WEST INDIES...
Coke, Thomas William *see* LETTERS TO T. W. COKE, FROM DR. SAMUEL PARR, ETC
Coke, Zachary *see* THE ART OF LOGICK: OR THE ENTIRE BODY OF LOGICK IN ENGLISH
Coker, Daniel *see* JOURNAL...
COL. H. C. HART'S NEW AND IMPROVED INSTRUCTOR FOR THE DRUM / Hart, H C – New York: the Author, 1862. MUSIC 3081 – 1 – us L of C Photodup [780]
COL. ROBERT G. INGERSOLL, AS HE IS: A COMPLETE REFUTATION OF HIS CLERICAL ENEMIES' MALICIOUS SLANDERS.. / Macdonald, Eugene Montague – 3rd ed. with additions. New York: Truth Seeker Co., (189-). 196,(4)p – 1 – us U.W. Library [240]
LA COLABORACION DE LA CAJA EXTREMENA DE PREVISION SOCIAL EN EL FOMENTO DE LAS CONSTRUCCIONES ESCOLARES / Leal Ramos, Leon – Caceres: Imprenta Moderna, 1929 – sp Bibl Santa Ana [946]
COLAC CITY COUNCIL MINUTES – (1989-91 2r 5) – 1938-1993. CCC1-25. 1990- 16mm – 30r – 1,5 – at Corangamite [910]
COLAC FIRE BRIGADE MINUTES – 1887-1980. CFB1-3 – 3r – 1 – at Corangamite [910]
COLAC HERALD – 1921-1994 – 168r – 1 – at Corangamite [072]
COLAC LIBRARIANS REPORTS – 1950-1967. CMRL1 – 1r – 1 – at Corangamite [910]
COLAC SHIRE RATE BOOKS – 1865-1955. COC1-21 – 21r – 1 – at Corangamite [910]
Colani, Timothee *see* JESUS CHRIST ET LES CROYANCES MESSIANIQUES DE SON TEMPS
Colardeau, Charles Pierre *see* LES HOMMES DE PROMETHEE
COLAS ET COLINETTE OU LE BAILLI DUPE / Quesnel, Joseph – Quebec: John Neilson, 1808. SEM105P889 – 1mf – 9 – Can$2.25 – cn Bibl Nat [830]
Colasse, Pascal *see* ACHILLE ET POLIXENE
Colbert de Croissy, Charles *see* ETAT DE POITOU SOUS LOUIS XIV
COLBERT ET LE CANADA / Desmazures, Adam Charles Gustave – Paris?: s.n., 1879 (Paris: V. E. Bolin). 02690. (Pre-1900 Canadiana) – 9 – cn C.I.H.M. [971]
COLBERT ET LE CANADA – Saint-Cloud France: E. Belin, 1889. 00697. (Pre-1900 Canadiana) – 9 – cn C.I.H.M. [971]
THE COLBERTINE BREVIARY / Gambier-Parry, T R – 2v. 1912-1913 – 10mf – 8 – ne Slangenburg [240]
Colby, Charles Carroll *see*
- CANADA'S NATIONAL POLICY: MR. C. C. COLBY'S GREAT SPEECH ON TARIFF REVISION, HOUSE OF COMMONS, MARCH, 1878
- PARLIAMENTARY GOVERNMENT IN CANADA: A LECTURE READ BEFORE THE LAW SCHOOL OF BISHOP'S COLLEGE, SHERBROOKE
- SPEECH...ON JESUITS' ESTATES ACT: DELIVERED IN THE HOUSE OF COMMONS, OTTAWA, ON TUESDAY, MARCH 26TH, 1889

Colby, John H *see* THE STATUTE RAILROAD LAWS OF THE STATE OF NEW YORK.
Colby. Kansas. Public Library. Board of Directors *see* PIONEER MEMORIAL LIBRARY RECORDS
Colchen *see* MEMOIRE STATISTIQUE DU DEPARTEMENT DE LA MOSELLE
COLCHESTER BAPTIST CHURCH. COLCHESTER, CONNECTICUT : CHURCH RECORDS – 1780-1939. (Scott Hill). 2v. 276p – 1 – 12.42 – us Baptist [240]
COLD REGIONS SCIENCE AND TECHNOLOGY – v1-9. 1979-84 – 1,5,6,13 – sz Elsevier [500]
Colden, C *see* THE HISTORY OF THE FIVE INDIAN NATIONS OF CANADA
Coldstream, John Phillips *see* THE DEVELOPMENT OF THE TEACHING OF LAW IN THE UNIVERSITY OF EDINBURGH
COLDWATER BAPTIST CHURCH. COLLIERVILLE, TENNESSEE : CHURCH RECORDS – 1867-1979. 1276p – 1 – 51.04 – us Baptist [240]
Coldwater. Kansas. Police Court *see* DOCKET
Cole, C A *see* MEMORIALS OF HENRY THE FIFTH (RS11)
Cole, C W *see* REPORT ON LAND TENURE
COLE COUNTY DEMOCRAT – Jefferson City. Mo. 1884-1895; 1904-1909 – 1 – us UMI [071]
Cole, Cyrenus *see* A HISTORY OF THE PEOPLE OF IOWA
Cole, David *see* THE TEACHING OF OUR LORD
Cole, E L *see* AN APPLICATION OF ITEM RESPONSE THEORY TO THE REST OF GROSS MOTOR DEVELOPMENT
Cole Family *see* PAPERS
Cole, H H *see*
- AGRA AND GWALIOR
- BUILDINGS IN THE PUNJAB
- DELHI
- GOLDEN TEMPLE AT AMRITSAR, PUNJAB
- GRAECO-BUDDHIST SCULPTURES FROM YUSUFZAI
- GREAT BUDDHIST TOPE AT SANCHI
- GREAT TEMPLE TO SIVA AND HIS CONSORT AT MADURA
- MEYWAR, RAJPUTANA
- TEMPLES AT TRICHINOPOLY
- TOMB OF JAHANGIR AT SHAHDARA NEAR LAHORE

Cole, H OF LA HOGUE *see* DOCUMENTS ILLUSTRATIVE OF ENGLISH HISTORY IN THE 13TH AND 14TH CENTURIES
Cole, H W *see* ON THE DOMICIL OF ENGLISHMEN IN FRANCE
Cole, Henry *see* THE JOURNAL OF DESIGN AND MANUFACTURES
Cole, Isaac *see* DIARY
Cole, J S *see* A CONFIRMATION TRACT: TOUCHING A FEW PRACTICAL AND VITAL QUESTIONS, IN THAT CONNECTION NOT USUALLY TREATED
Cole, Jim *see* THE SERIALS LIBRARIAN
Cole, John Y *see* THE LIBRARY OF CONGRESS
Cole, Kelly J *see*
- THE EFFECT OF ALTERING SPEED OF BACKWARD MOVEMENT OF THE TRUNK ON ANTICIPATORY POSTURAL ADJUSTMENTS
- THE EFFECTS OF IMAGINARY MAXIMAL MUSCLE CONTRACTION TRAINING ON THE VOLUNTARY NEURAL DIRVE TO MUSCLE

Cole, S D *see*
- THE HAGUE RULES 1921 EXPLAINED
- THE HAGUE RULES EXPLAINED...

Cole, T *see* THE RECOGNITION POLICY OF THE UNITED STATES SINCE 1901
Cole, William *see* LIFE IN THE NIGER
COLECAO ESPECIAL-JORNAIS OPERARIOS, 1 / Biblioteca Nacional. Rio de Janeiro – (Acao popular 1-16 May 1951. O bond 2 Nov 1881; Nov-Dec 1882. A bomba 1 Sept-28 Dec 1894. O baluarte May-Jun 1910 (2a epoca). Vante 7 Aug-10 Oct 1908. Vante 7 Aug-2 Oct 1904. O artista Jun 1905. O artista 7 Mar-24 May 1883. O artista 27 Nov 1870-12 Mar 1871. O archote 17 May-2 Jun 1908. Brazil Operario 1 May 1903-1 May 1904. O caixeiro 5 Mar-23 Apr 1899. O clamor May-Dec 1951; Jun 1953-Sept 1954. A classe operaria Mar 1951-Jun 1952. O componedor May-Nov 1909. Correiro operario 1 Aug-1 Sept 1910. O corsario 26 Nov 1903; 9 Mar 1904. O debate July-Oct 1917. O despertar 2 Nov 1898-Jan 1899. O Domingo 10 Jun 1888. O echo do Mar Jun-Dec 1909. Echo Popular 6 Mar-7 Nov 1890. O Estrangeiro Oct-Nov 1894. O Figaro 17 Sept-3 Oct 1909. O Futuro Popular 31 Oct-5 Nov 1901. Gazeta dos Operarios 8-21 Dec 1875. Gazeta maritima 12 Nov-20 Dec 1903. Gazeta operaria Sept 1902-Feb 1903; Sept-Dec 1906. A gazeta Portuaria Mar 1949. Gazeta Sindical 24 Mar 1948-Mar 1949; Aug-Dec 1951. O Graphico 1 Jan 1916-16 Nov 1919. O Grito do Povo 16 Apr 1879. A Guerra Social Jun-Nov 1911) – Rio de Janeiro, 70 titles (all publ) – 5r – 1 – bl Biblioteca [020]
COLECAO ESPECIAL-JORNAIS OPERARIOS, 2 / Biblioteca Nacional. Rio de Janeiro – (O Independente. 11 Mar 1909. O Internacional. 20 Apr-1 May 1911.. O Jacobino. 19 Sept 1894-29 Jun 1897. Jornal dos Tipografos. 10 Jan-12 Mar 1858. Liberdade. Aug-Oct 1909. O Libertario. 9 Oct 1904. O Libertarista. 24 Dec 1899-9 Feb 1900. Lumen. 16 Jun-1 Jul 1904. O Mensageiro. Aug-Sept 1899. A Nacao. Dec 1903-Feb 1904. O Niilista. 30 Mar-6 Apr 1883. L'Operai italiano. 5 Dec 1897-2 Apr 1898. O Operario. 6 Dec 1908-3 Feb 1909. O Operario. 14 May 1910. O Panificador. 1 Jan-11 Feb 1900. O Protesto. 24 Dec 1899. Reaccao. 4 Jun 1902. Revolucao. 7 Apr-12 May 1881. Revolucao. 12-24 Sept 1882. Rio de Janeiro. 20 Oct-10 Nov 1910. Roma. 20 Sept-10 Nov 1888.. A Semana. 30 Jul, 3 Sept 1911. Semana Operaria. 20 May, 3 Jun 1907. O Trabalho. 11 Oct-1 Nov 1868. Trabalho e Direito. 10 Oct-Dec 1891. A Tribuna do povo. 18 Mar, 18 Apr 1909. Tribuna Operaria. 15 Oct-1 Nov 1900. A Uniao. 15 Oct, 15 Nov, 15 Dec 1911. Uniao Caixeral. 1 May, 1 Jul 1903. A uniao do povo. 2 Oct 1877. A uniao operaria. 1 May 1904. A voz do chauffer. 13 Sept 1924-28 Dec 1926. A voz do Povo. 6-9 Jan 1890. A voz do Povo. Oct-Dec 1911. Voz do Povo. 6 Feb-6 Dec 1920. A voz do Trabalhador. Aug 1908-Dec 1909. Voz Operaria. Jan-Dec 1955) – 5 reels total. continued from above – bl Biblioteca [072]
LA COLECCION CANONICA HISPANA 1. ESTUDIO POR...MADRID, 1966 / Martinez Diez, Gonzalo – Madrid: Graf. Calleja, 1966 – 1 – sp Bibl Santa Ana [946]
COLECCION COMPLETA DE LEYES NACIONALES SANCIONADAS POR EL HONORABLE CONGRESO / Argentine Republic. Laws, Statutes, etc – 1852-1934 – 1 – 115.00 – us L of C Photodup [324]
COLECCION DE CARTAS PASTORALES Y EDICTOS. TOMO 1 / Bertran, Felipe – 1783 – 2mf – 9 – Pta1,500.00 – 84-7848-174-5 – sp Pentalfa [240]
COLECCION DE CARTAS PASTORALES Y EDICTOS. TOMO 2 / Bertran, Felipe – 1783 – 1mf – 9 – Pta1,000.00 – 84-7848-175-3 – sp Pentalfa [240]
COLECCION DE "CUADROS SINOPTICOS" DE LOS PUEBLOS, HACIENDAD Y RANCHOS DEL ESTADO LIBRE Y SOBERANO DE OAXACA: ANEXO NUMERO 50 A LA MEMORIA ADMINISTRATIVA PRESENTADA AL H. CONGRESO DEL MISMO EL 17 DE SETIEMBRE DE 1883 / Martinez Gracida, Manuel – Oaxaca: Impr. del Estado, a cargo de I. Candiani, 1883 – 1 – us U.W. Library [972]
COLECCION DE CUENTOS / Febres Cordero, Julio – Caracas, 2nd ed 1930; Madrid: Razon y Fe, 1931 – 1 – sp Bibl Santa Ana [390]
COLECCION DE DECRETOS DEL REY FERNANDO 7TH – Madrid, 1814-1833 – 178mf – 9 – sp Cultura [340]
COLECCION DE DECRETOS Y ORDENES EXPEDIDAS POR LAS CORTES GENERALES YEXTRAORDINARIAS – 1810-1814; 1820-1823 – 63mf – 9 – sp Cultura [340]
COLECCION DE DIARIOS Y RELACIONES PARA LA HISTORIA DE LOS VIAJES Y DESCUBRIMIENTOS. VOL. 1...VOL 2...MADRID, 1943 / Bayle, Constantino – Madrid: Razon y Fe, 1946 – 1 – sp Bibl Santa Ana [946]
COLECCION DE DISCURSOS Y POESIAS LEIDOS EN EL ACTO DE LA INAUGURACION DEL MONUMENTO QUE SE HA DE ERIGIR EN BADAJOZ A LA MEMORIA DE D. JOSE MORENO NIETO – Fregenal: Imprenta El Eco, 1883 – 1 – sp Bibl Santa Ana [810]
COLECCION DE DISERTACIONES / Huerta Vega, Fco. M and Alii – s.a. – 2mf – 9 – Pta1,500.00 – 84-7848-222-9 – sp Pentalfa [370]
COLECCION DE DOCUMENTOS DE SIGLOS 15 A 20 AND SOSA : INDICE DE LOS DOCUMENTOS RELATIVOS A LA CONQUISTA Y COLONIZACION DEL ISTMO DE PANAMA, 1513-1700 – Panama: Biblioteca Nacional de Panama, 1513-1700 – 1r – 1 – inquire – us Ross [972]
COLECCION DE DOCUMENTOS HISTORICOS – v1-. 1915-. Separately paged section of: Boletin de la Real Academia Gallega, ano 10, num. 94 (Jun 1915)- – 1 – us U.W. Library [900]
COLECCION DE DOCUMENTOS INEDITOS PARA LA HISTORIA DE CHILE / Medina, Jose Toribio – Santiago de Chile. v. 1-30. 1888-1902. (Wanting v. 19) – 1 – 122.00 – us L of C Photodup [972]
COLECCION DE DOCUMENTOS INEDITOS PARA LA HISTORIA DE ESPANA / Spain – v. 44-112. 1864-95 – 1 – 317.00 – us L of C Photodup [946]
COLECCION DE DOCUMENTOS INEDITOS PARA LA HISTORIA DE IBEROAMERICA / Montoto, Santiago; ed by Bayle, Constantino – Madrid: Razon y Fe, 1928 – 9 – sp Bibl Santa Ana [972]
COLECCION DE DOCUMENTOS INEDITOS, RELATIVOS AL DESCUBRIMIENTO, CONQUISTA Y ORGANIZACION DE LAS ANTIGUAS POSESIONES ESPANOLAS DE AMERICA Y OCEANIA / America – v. 1-42. 1864-84 – 1 – 181.00 – us L of C Photodup [946]
COLECCION DE DOCUMENTOS RELATIVOS AL ADELANTADO CAPITAN DON SEBASTIAN DE BELALCAZAR 1535-1560 / Bayle, Constantino – Quito, 1936; Burgos: Razon y Fe, 1938 – 1 – sp Bibl Santa Ana [946]
COLECCION DE EPIGRAMES / Salas, Francisco Gregorio de – (1827. 1.50f; 9) – 1816 – 9 – 1.50f – sp Bibl Santa Ana [880]
COLECCION DE ESCRITORES CASTELLANOS / Lopez de Ayala, Adelardo – 1885 – 9 – 1.50f – sp Bibl Santa Ana [800]
COLECCION DE HISTORIADORES DE CHILE / Olivares, Miguel de, y otro – 1864 – 9 – 1.50f – sp Bibl Santa Ana [972]
COLECCION DE HISTORIADORES DE CHILE...: HISTORIA DE GONGORA MARMOLEJO – 1536-1575. 1862 – 9 – 1.50f – sp Bibl Santa Ana [972]
COLECCION DE HISTORIADORES DE CHILE Y DOCUMENTOS RELATIVOS A LA HISTORIA NACIONAL / Marino de Lovera, Pedro – Santiago de Chile: Imprenta del Ferrocarril, 1865 – 1 – sp Bibl Santa Ana [972]
COLECCION DE INSCRIPCIONES Y ANTIGUEDADES DE EXTREMADURA / D F de Viu – Caceres: Imp. Concha y Cia, 1846 – 1 – sp Bibl Santa Ana [946]
LA COLECCION DE LAPIDAS DE D. CLAUDIO CONSTANZO / Jimenez Navarro, Ernesto – Badajoz, 1949 – 1 – sp Bibl Santa Ana [946]
COLECCION DE LAS MEMORIAS O RELACIONES QUE ESCRIBIERON LOS VIRREYES DEL PERU ACERCA DEL ESTADO EN QUE DEJABAN LAS COSAS GENERALES DEL REINO. TOMO 2 / Altolaguirre, Angel de – Madrid, 1931 – 1 – sp Bibl Santa Ana [972]
COLECCION DE LAS OBRAS / Casas, Bartolome de las; ed by Llorente, J A – Paris. Tomes 1-2. 1822 – 18mf – 8 – ne Slangenburg [240]
COLECCION DE LEYES...CIRCULARES...DE LA MESTA DESDE EL ANO 1729 AL DE 1827 / Brieva, Matias – Madrid: Imp. de Repulles, 1828 – 1 – sp Bibl Santa Ana [946]
COLECCION DE LEYES...RAMO DE LA MESTA / Brieva, Matias – 1828 – 9 – 1.50f – sp Bibl Santa Ana [946]

COLECCION DE LIBROS CUBANOS – (A collection of Cuban literary and historical works under the general editorship of Fernando Ortiz) – 42v. 1927-39 – 187mf – 9 – $5.00f – us Ross [440]
COLECCION DE LIBROS Y DOCUMENTOS REFERENTES A LA HISTORIA DE AMERICA / America – Madrid. v. 1-21. 1904-29 – 1 – 118.00 – us L of C Photodup [972]
COLECCION DE LOS DISCURSOS MAS NOTABLES...CONGRESO DE LOS DIPUTADOS... EN LA LEGISLATURA 1818-19 – 1849 – 9 – 1.50f – sp Bibl Santa Ana [323]
COLECCION DE LOS EPIGRAMAS Y OTRAS POESIAS CRITICAS, SATIRICAS Y JOCOSAS / Salas, Francisco Gregorio de – Madrid: Repulles, 1827 – 1 – sp Bibl Santa Ana [800]
COLECCION DE LOS MAS PRECIOSOS ADELANTAMIENTOS DE LA MEDICINA... / Ellerker, R – Malaga, S.A. – 11mf – 9 – sp Cultura [610]
COLECCION DE OBRAS. TOMO 1 / Iriarte, Tomas – 1787 – 1mf – 9 – Pta1,000.00 – 84-7848-235-0 – sp Pentalfa [440]
COLECCION DE OBRAS. TOMO 2 / Iriarte, Tomas – 1787 – 1mf – 9 – Pta1,000.00 – 84-7848-236-9 – sp Pentalfa [440]
COLECCION DE OBRAS. TOMO 3 / Iriarte, Tomas – 1787 – 1mf – 9 – Pta1,000.00 – 84-7848-237-7 – sp Pentalfa [440]
COLECCION DE OBRAS. TOMO 4 / Iriarte, Tomas – 1787 – 1mf – 9 – Pta1,000.00 – 84-7848-238-5 – sp Pentalfa [440]
COLECCION DE OBRAS. TOMO 5 / Iriarte, Tomas – 1787 – 1mf – 9 – Pta1,000.00 – 84-7848-239-3 – sp Pentalfa [440]
COLECCION DE OBRAS. TOMO 6 / Iriarte, Tomas – 1787 – 1mf – 9 – Pta1,000.00 – 84-7848-240-7 – sp Pentalfa [440]
COLECCION DE OBRAS Y DOCUMENTOS RELATIVOS A LA HISTORIA ANTIGUA Y MODERNA DE LAS PROVINCIAS DEL RIO DE LA PLATA / Angelis, Pedro de – 5v. 1910 – 1 – 40.00 – us L of C Photodup [972]
COLECCION DE POESIAS / Chacon Villareso, Carmen – Madrid: Hijos de Rens. Impresores, 1914 – 1 – sp Bibl Santa Ana [810]
COLECCION DE POESIAS / Malendez Valdes, Juan – 1798 – 9 – 1.50f – sp Bibl Santa Ana [810]
COLECCION DE POESIAS LATINAS Y CASTELLANAS / Santa Lucia y Amaya, Jose – 1883 – 9 – 1.50f – sp Bibl Santa Ana [450]
COLECCION DE SILOGISMOS (POR VIA INDUCTIVA) (PROMANUSCRIPTO) / Colegio de San Antonio – Caceres: Imp. La Minerva, 1963 – 1 – sp Bibl Santa Ana [946]
COLECCION DE SILOGISMOS (POR VIA INDUCTIVA) T. 2. EL UNIVERSAL "IN RE"... / Colegio de San Antonio – Caceres: Imp. La Minerva, 1963 – 1 – sp Bibl Santa Ana [946]
COLECCION DE TODAS LAS LEYES / Spain. Laws, Statutes, etc – 1792 – 9 – 1.50f – sp Bibl Santa Ana [324]
COLECCION DE TRATADOS CELEBRADOS POR LA REPUBLICA ARGENTINIA... – Buenos Aires, 1863 – 5mf – 1 – ILM-2532/1 – ne IDC [327]
COLECCION DE TRATADOS, CONVENCIONES...DE LA REPUBLICA ORIENTAL DEL URUGUAY (1830-1930) – Montevideo. 5v. 1923-1928 – 36mf – 1 – ILM-2939/1 – ne IDC [327]
COLECCION DE TRATADOS DE PAZ. TOMO 1 / Abreu Bertodano, Jose Antonio – 1740 – 5mf – 9 – Pta3,000.00 – 84-7848-210-5 – sp Pentalfa [340]
COLECCION DE TRATADOS DE PAZ. TOMO 2 / Abreu Bertodano, Jose Antonio – 1740 – 5mf – 9 – Pta3,000.00 – 84-7848-211-3 – sp Pentalfa [340]
COLECCION DE TRATADOS DE PAZ. TOMO 3 / Abreu Bertodano, Jose Antonio – 1744 – 5mf – 9 – Pta3,000.00 – 84-7848-212-1 – sp Pentalfa [340]
COLECCION DE TRATADOS DE PAZ. TOMO 4 / Abreu Bertodano, Jose Antonio – 1745 – 5mf – 9 – Pta3,000.00 – 84-7848-213-X – sp Pentalfa [340]
COLECCION DE TRATADOS DE PAZ. TOMO 5 / Abreu Bertodano, Jose Antonio – 1746 – 5mf – 9 – Pta3,000.00 – 84-7848-214-8 – sp Pentalfa [340]
COLECCION DE TRATADOS DE PAZ. TOMO 6 / Abreu Bertodano, Jose Antonio – 1750 – 5mf – 9 – Pta3,000.00 – 84-7848-215-6 – sp Pentalfa [340]
COLECCION DE TRATADOS DE PAZ. TOMO 7 / Abreu Bertodano, Jose Antonio – 1750 – 5mf – 9 – Pta3,000.00 – 84-7848-216-4 – sp Pentalfa [340]
COLECCION DE TRATADOS DE PAZ. TOMO 8 / Abreu Bertodano, Jose Antonio – 1751 – 4mf – 9 – Pta2,500.00 – 84-7848-217-2 – sp Pentalfa [340]
COLECCION DE TRATADOS DE PAZ. TOMO 9 / Abreu Bertodano, Jose Antonio – 1751 – 6mf – 9 – Pta3,500.00 – 84-7848-218-0 – sp Pentalfa [340]
COLECCION DE TRATADOS DE PAZ. TOMO 10 / Abreu Bertodano, Jose Antonio – 1751 – 5mf – 9 – Pta3,000.00 – 84-7848-219-9 – sp Pentalfa [340]
COLECCION DE TRATADOS DE PAZ. TOMO 11 / Abreu Bertodano, Jose Antonio – 1752 – 4mf – 9 – Pta2,500.00 – 84-7848-220-2 – sp Pentalfa [340]
COLECCION DE TRATADOS DE PAZ. TOMO 12 / Abreu Bertodano, Jose Antonio – 1752 – 6mf – 9 – Pta3,500.00 – 84-7848-221-0 – sp Pentalfa [340]
COLECCION DE...DEL PERU / Odriozola, Manuel de – 1863 – 9 – 1.50f – sp Bibl Santa Ana [800]
COLECCION DIPLOMATICA DE SAN ANDRES DE FAULO (958-1270). ZARAGOZA, 1964 / Canellas, Angel – Madrid: Graf. Calleja, 1966 – 1 – sp Bibl Santa Ana [320]
COLECCION DOCUMENTOS...CHILE / Medina, Jose Toribio – (Tomo 9. 1896. 1.50f; 9. Tomo 10.1896. 1.50f; BSA; 9. Tomo 11.1897. 1.50f; BSA; 9. Tomo 13.1897. 1.50f; BSA; 9. Tomo 15.1898. 1.50f; BSA; 9. Tomo 17.1899. 1.50f; BSA; 9. Tomo 18.1899. 1.50f; BSA; 9. Tomo 20.1899. 1.50f; BSA; 9) – Tomo 8. 1896 – 9 – 1.50f – sp Bibl Santa Ana [972]
COLECCION GENERAL DE DOCUMENTOS RELATIVOS A LAS ISLAS FILIPINAS / Bayle, Constantino – Madrid: Razon y Fe, 1924.-v5 – 1 – sp Bibl Santa Ana [950]
COLECCION HISTORIADORES DE CHILE-DOCUMENTO / Marino de Lovera, Pedro – 1865 – 9 – 1.50f – sp Bibl Santa Ana [972]
COLECCION LEGISLATIVA DE ESPANA, CONTINUACION DE LA COLECCION DE DECRETOS – 1869-1874 – 275mf – 9 – sp Cultura [340]
COLECCION LEGISLATIVA DE ESPANA, CONTINUACION DE LA COLECCION DE DECRETOS – 1874-1885 – 388mf – 9 – sp Cultura [340]
COLECCION LEGISLATIVA DE ESPANA. TOMOS 19 A 100 – Madrid, 1833-1808 – 9 – sp Cultura [340]
COLECCION LEGISLATIVA DE INSTRUCCION PUBLICA...1888-1935 – Madrid, 1889-1940 – 293mf – 9 – sp Cultura [340]
COLECCION LEGISLATIVA DE PRIMERA ENSENANZA / Pimentel y Donaire, Miguel – Badajoz: Tip La Economica. Rodriguez y Cia, 1894 – 1 – sp Bibl Santa Ana [350]
COLECCION LEGISLATIVA...ENSENANZA / Pimentel y Donaire, Miguel – 1894 – 9 – 1.50f – sp Bibl Santa Ana [340]
COLECCION NUMISMATICA ANTIGUA DEL MUSEO MUNICIPAL BB.AA. DE SANTANDER / Marcos-Garcia, Miguel Angel – 1mf – 9 – Pta1,000.00 – 84-85422-78-3 – sp Pentalfa [730]
COLECCION OBRAS PREMIADAS. OBRAS DE ELOCUENCIA / Academia Espanola – 1799 – 1mf – 9 – Pta1,000.00 – 84-7848-127-3 – sp Pentalfa [440]
COLECCION OBRAS PREMIADAS. OBRAS DE POESIA / Academia Espanola – 1799 – 1mf – 9 – Pta1,000.00 – 84-7848-128-1 – sp Pentalfa [440]
COLECCION OFICIAL DE LEYES, DECRETOS, ORDENES, RESOLUCIONES. / Bolivia. Laws, Statutes, etc – Paz de Ayacucho. v1-16; 1825-54; 2nd series, v1-6; 1857-63. LL-065 – 1 – 92.00 – us L of C Photodup [340]
COLECCION POESIAS CASTELLANAS ANTERIORES AL SIGLO 15. TOMO 1 / Sanchez, Tomas Antonio – 1779 – 2mf – 9 – Pta1,500.00 – 84-7848-344-6 – sp Pentalfa [810]
COLECCION POESIAS CASTELLANAS ANTERIORES AL SIGLO 15. TOMO 2 / Sanchez, Tomas Antonio – 1780 – 2mf – 9 – Pta1,500.00 – 84-7848-345-4 – sp Pentalfa [810]
COLECCION POESIAS CASTELLANAS ANTERIORES AL SIGLO 15. TOMO 3 / Sanchez, Tomas Antonio – 1782 – 2mf – 9 – Pta1,500.00 – 84-7848-346-2 – sp Pentalfa [810]
COLECCION POESIAS CASTELLANAS ANTERIORES AL SIGLO 15. TOMO 4 / Sanchez, Tomas Antonio – 1790 – 1mf – 9 – Pta1,000.00 – 84-7848-347-0 – sp Pentalfa [810]
COLECCION...ANTIGUEDADES DE ESTREMADURA (SIC) / Viu, Jose de – 1846 – 9 – 1.50f – sp Bibl Santa Ana [930]
COLECCION...CHILE Y DOCUMENTOS.. / Ovalle, Alonso de – v12. 1888 – 9 – 1.50f – sp Bibl Santa Ana [972]
COLECCION...LA DIPLOMACIA / Donoso Cortes, Juan Francisco – 1848 – 9 – 1.50f – sp Bibl Santa Ana [946]
COLECCION...MEJORES POETAS ESPANOLES / Blanco, Indalecio – 1883 – 9 – 1.50f – sp Bibl Santa Ana [810]
COLECCION...PROYECTO DE LEY / Donoso Cortes, Juan Francisco – 1848 – 9 – 1.50f – sp Bibl Santa Ana [946]
Colegio de Abogados de Badajoz *see* LISTA DE ABOGADOS DEL ILUSTRE COLEGIO DE BADAJOZ. ANO DE 1930
Colegio de Abogados de Caceres *see* LISTA DE LOS ABOGADOS DEL ILUSTRE COLEGIO DE CADERES EN ESTE ANO DE 1873
EL COLEGIO DE LA CONSTANCIA. ROBO DE CUATRO RUILLONES / Plasencia, Juan de – Plasencia: Tip. E. Pinto Sanchez, 1900 – sp Bibl Santa Ana [946]
Colegio de la Inmaculada Concepcion *see*
- JMJ REGLAMENTO PARA EL COLEGIO DE SENORITAS...SAGRADA FAMILIA... PLASENCIA
- REGLAMENTO PARA EL COLEGIO DE SENORITAS DIRIGIDO POR LAS HERMANAS DE LA SAGRADA FAMILIA BAJO EL TITULO DE LA INMACULADA CONCEPCION ESTABLECIDO EN PLASENCIA

Colegio de San Antonio *see*
- COLECCION DE SILOGISMOS (POR VIA INDUCTIVA) (PROMANUSCRIPTO)
- COLECCION DE SILOGISMOS (POR VIA INDUCTIVA) T. 2. EL UNIVERSAL "IN RE"...
- MESA REVUELTA. REDACCIONES DE NO 6 Y PREN. T. 4-B. DIA DE LA ASUNCION 1961

Colegio de San Antonio. Caceres *see*
- MESA REVUELTA. REDACCIONES DE 6° Y PREU COGIDAS AL VUELO. 2 DE MAYO DE 1957 (PROMANUSCRIPTO). T.I.
- MESA REVUELTA. REDACCIONES DE 6TH Y PREU. DIA DE SAN PEDRO DE ALCANTARA DE 1961 (PRO-MANUSCRITO)

Colegio de San Jose de Villafranca (Badajoz) *see*
- MEMORIA DEL ANO ESCOLAR 1936-37
- MEMORIA DEL ANO ESCOLAR 1938-39
- MEMORIA DEL ANO ESCOLAR DE 1927 A 1928
- MEMORIA DEL ANO ESCOLAR DE 1928 A 1929
- MEMORIA DEL ANO ESCOLAR DE 1929 A 1930
- MEMORIA DEL ANO ESCOLAR DE 1931-1932

Colegio de San Jose de Villafranca de los Barros (Badajoz) *see* MEMORIA DEL A.ESC.37-38
COLEGIO DE SAN JOSE DE VILLAFRANCA. DISTRIBUCION DE PREMIOS 1922-1923 – Villafranca: Imp Rodriguez, 1923 – 1 – sp Bibl Santa Ana [946]
COLEGIO DE SAN JOSE DE VILLAFRANCA. DISTRIBUCION DE PREMIOS. ANO 1921-1922 – Villafranca: Imp Rodriguez, (1922) – 1 – sp Bibl Santa Ana [946]
COLEGIO DE SAN JOSE. DISTRIBUCION DE PREMIOS. CURSO 1920-1921 – Zafra: Morera, 1921 – 1 – sp Bibl Santa Ana [946]
Colegio de San Jose. Estremoz (Portugal) *see*
- MEMORIA DEL ANO ESCOLAR 1932-1933
- MEMORIA DEL ANO ESCOLAR 1933-34
- MEMORIA DEL ANO ESCOLAR 1934-35
- MEMORIA DEL ANO ESCOLAR 1935-36

COLEGIO DE SAN JOSE. MEMORIA DEL CURSO ACADEMICO 1917-18 – Villafranca de los Barros, Madrid: Blass y Cia., 1918 – 1 – sp Bibl Santa Ana [946]
Colegio de San Jose. Villafranca de los Barros (Badajoz) *see* LAUDATE PUERI. ORACIONES Y CANTOS
Colegio de Santa Cecilia de Caceres *see*
- DIRIGIDO POR HERMANAS CARMELITAS DE LA CARIDAD LEGALMENTE RECONOCIDO PARA ENSENANZA MEDIA
- REGLAMENTO DEL...PARA LA EDUCACION DE SENORITAS DIRIGIDO POR LAS RELIGIOSAS CARMELITAS DE LA CARIDAD

Colegio Extremeno de Arbitros de Futbol *see* REGLAMENTO DE FUTBOL
Colegio Maristas San Calixto *see*
- PROYECTO EDUCATIVO 1977-78
- PROYECTO EDUCATIVO CURO 1980-1981
- PROYECTO EDUCATIVO. CURSO 1976-77

Colegio Mayor del Conde Duque *see* APROBACION Y CONFIRMACION QUE DIO EL...AL PARECER Y ADICION QUE HIZO. FRAY JUAN DE LOS REYES...
Colegio Oficial de Abogados de Badajoz *see*
- LISTA OFICIAL DE LOS SENORES ABOGADOS Y PROCURADORES Y GUIA JUDICIAL DE LA PROVINCIA. ANO 1958
- LISTA OFICIAL DE LOS SRES. ABOGADOS Y PROCURADORES Y GUIA JUDICIAL DE LA PROVINCIA. ANO DE 1965

Colegio Oficial de Agentes Comerciales *see*
- CENSO OFICIAL DE LOS SENORES AGENTES COMERCIALES EN 1ST DE JUNIO DE 1961
- MEMORIA DE LOS TRABAJOS REALIZADOS DURANTE EL ANO 1959...
- MEMORIA DE LOS TRABAJOS REALIZADOS DURANTE EL ANO 1960 LEIDA Y APROBADA EN SESION DEL 25 DE MARZO DE 1961

Colegio Oficial de Ayudantes Tecnicos Sanitarios *see* TARIFA DE HONORARIOS MINIMOS APROBADA POR JUNTA DE GOBIERNO: SESION ORDINARIA DEL 12-2-80
Colegio Oficial de Farmaceuticos. Caceres *see*
- ANALES. 1959
- LISTA DE FARMACEUTICOS COLEGIADOS ANO 1943
- LISTA DE FARMACEUTICOS COLEGIADOS, ANO 1945

Colegio Oficial de Medicos de la Provincia de Badajoz *see* LISTA DE SRES. MEDICOS COLEGIADOS 1969
Colegio Oficial de Medicos de la Provincia de Caceres *see*
- LA ESCUELA DE MEDICINA DE GUADALUPE
- LISTA DE SENORES COLEGIADOS POR PARTIDOS JUDICIALES Y POR ORDEN DE INCORPORACION A ESTE COLEGIO PROVINCIAL

COLEGIO OFICIAL DE PERITOS AGRICOLAS DE BADAJOZ. ARANCELES 1960 – Badajoz: Graficas Jimenez, 1960 – sp Bibl Santa Ana [630]
COLEGIO OFICIAL DE SECRETARIOS, INTERVENTORES Y DEPORTIVOS DE ADMINISTRACION LOCAL DE LA PROVINCIA DE CACERES. MEMORIA QUE FORMULA EL SECRETARIO...DEL EJERCICIO 1941... / Rubio, Julio – Caceres: Tip. El Noticiero – sp Bibl Santa Ana [350]
COLEGIO OFICIAL VETERINARIO DE BADAJOZ. CIRCULAR NO 144 – Badajoz: La Minerva Extremena, 1945 – sp Bibl Santa Ana [946]
Colegio Provincial de Abogados *see*
- LISTA OFICIAL DE LOS SENORES ABOGADOS Y PROCURADORES Y GUIA JUDICIAL
- LISTA OFICIAL DE LOS SENORES ABOGADOS Y PROCURADORES Y GUIA JUDICIAL. ANO 1967

Colegio Provincial de Abogados de Badajoz *see*
- BASES ORIENTADORAS PARA LA FIJACION DE HONORARIOS APROBADOS POR LA JUNTA GENERAL DE ESTE ILUSTRE COLEGIO, EL 31 DE MARZO DE 1961
- LISTA OFICIAL DE LOS SENORES ABOGADOS Y PROCURADORES Y GUIA JUDICIAL DE LA PROVINCIA. ANO DE 1953
- LISTA OFICIAL DE LOS SENORES ABOGADOS Y PROCURADORES Y GUIA JUDICIAL DE LA PROVINCIA. ANO DE 1957
- LISTA OFICIAL DE LOS SRES. ABOGADOS Y PROCURADORES Y GUIA JUDICIAL DE LA PROVINCIA. ANO DE 1959
- LISTA OFICIAL DE LOS SRES. ABOGADOS Y PROCURADORES Y GUIA JUDICIAL DE LA PROVINCIA. ANO DE 1960
- LISTA OFICIAL DE LOS SRES. ABOGADOS Y PROCURADORES Y GUIA JUDICIAL DE LA PROVINCIA. ANO DE 1961
- LISTA OFICIAL DE LOS SRES. ABOGADOS Y PROCURADORES Y GUIA JUDICIAL DE LA PROVINCIA. ANO DE 1962
- LISTA OFICIAL DE LOS SRES. COLEGIADOS, DE LOS SRES. PROCURADORES Y GUIA JUDICIAL DE LA PROVINCIA. ANO DE 1968

- LISTA OFICIAL DE LOS SRES. COLEGIADOS, DE LOS SRES. PROCURADORES Y GUIA JUDICIAL DE LA PROVINCIA. ANO DE 1971
Colegio Provincial de Abogados de Caceres *see*
- LISTA OFICIAL DE LOS SENORES ABOGADOS DEL ILUSTRE COLEGIO PROVINCIAL DE CACERES Y GUIA JUDICIAL DE LOS TRIBUNALES DE DICHA CIUDAD PARA EL ANO 1956
- LISTA OFICIAL DE LOS SENORES ABOGADOS DEL ILUSTRE COLEGIO PROVINCIAL DE CACERES Y GUIA JUDICIAL DE LOS TRIBUNALES DE DICHA CIUDAD PARA EL ANO 1959
- LISTA OFICIAL DE LOS SENORES ABOGADOS DEL ILUSTRE COLEGIO PROVINCIAL DE CACERES Y GUIA JUDICIAL DE LOS TRIBUNALES DE DICHA CIUDAD PARA EL ANO 1960
- LISTA OFICIAL DE LOS SENORES COLEGIADOS Y GUIA JUDICIAL DE LOS TRIBUNALES DE LA CIUDAD. ANO 1961
- NORMAS DE HONORARIOS MINIMOS

Colegio Provincial de Procuradores de Badajoz *see* ESTATUTOS DEL...Y EL GENERAL DE PROCURADORES DE LOS TRIBUNALES DE ESPANA
COLEGIO PROVINCIAL DE VETERNARIOS DE BADAJOZ. CIRCULAR NO 1 – Badajoz: Imp. Barrena, 1944 – sp Bibl Santa Ana [946]
COLEGIO, REVISTA DE CULTURA E ARTE – Sao Paulo, BL. 1948-1949 – 1r – $50.00 – R04184 – us Library Micro [073]
Colegio San Antonio *see* ENSAYOS DE ETICE. DUNS ESCOTO EN EXTREMADURA. 2
Colegio San Francisco Javier. Fuente de Cantos (Badajoz) *see* CANTOS LITURGICOS
Colegio San Jose *see*
- CATALOGO
- CATALOGO DE LOS ALUMNOS DEL COLEGIO DE SAN JOSE. 1904-1905
- CONGREGACIONES MARIANAS DEL...BAJO LA ADVOCACION DE LA INMACULADA CONCEPCION, SAN LUIS GORZAGA Y SAN ESTANISLAO DE KOSTKA (1900-1901)

Colegio San Jose de Azuaga *see* PROCULTURA. TRABAJOS DE EXTENSION PEDAGOGICA
Colegio Santiago y Santa Margarita. Sociedad Cooperativa *see* IDEARIO DE LA COLEGIO DE EGB Y FORMACION PROFESIONAL
Colegio Universitario de Caceres *see* CIENTO CINCUENTA ANOS DE PERIODISMO EN CACERES Y SALAMANCA
Coleman, Arthur Philemon *see*
- GLACIAL AND INTER-GLACIAL DEPOSITS NEAR TORONTO
- THE IROQUOIS BEACH
- NORTHEASTERN PART OF LABRADOR AND NEW QUEBEC

Coleman, Christopher Bush *see* CONSTANTINE THE GREAT AND CHRISTIANITY
Coleman, Eli *see* JOURNAL OF PSYCHOLOGY AND HUMAN SEXUALITY
Coleman, George W *see* THE CHURCHES OUTSIDE THE CHURCH
Coleman, J Winston *see* COLLECTED MINOR WRITINGS OF J. WINSTON COLEMAN, JR
Coleman, James M *see* COLEMAN'S GENERAL INDEX TO PRINTED PEDIGREES; WHICH ARE TO BE FOUND IN ALL THE PRINCIPAL COUNTY AND LOCAL HISTORIES, AND IN...GENEALOGIES.
Coleman, John Noble *see* ECCLESIASTES: A NEW TRANSLATION WITH NOTES
Coleman, Julius Archer *see*
- THE MECHANIC'S LIEN LAW OF THE STATE OF ILLINOIS
- A TREATISE ON THE MECHANIC'S LIEN LAW OF THE STATE OF ILLINOIS, AS IN FORCE MARCH 1, 1894, SO FAR AS THE SAME RELATES TO REAL ESTATE

Coleman, Lyman *see* GENEALOGY OF THE LYMAN FAMILY
Coleman, Robert H *see* PUBLICATIONS OF MUSIC
COLEMAN'S GENERAL INDEX TO PRINTED PEDIGREES; WHICH ARE TO BE FOUND IN ALL THE PRINCIPAL COUNTY AND LOCAL HISTORIES, AND IN...GENEALOGIES. / Coleman, James M – With an appendix. London: J. Coleman, 1866. vii,155p – 1 – us U.W. Library [920]
COLEMOKEE BAPTIST CHURCH. EARLY COUNTY. GEORGIA : CHURCH RECORDS – 1889-1908 – 1 – 12.00 – us Baptist [240]
Colenbrander, G J *see* OBSERVATIONES...DE PACTIS
Colenso, John William *see*
- THE PENTATEUCH AND THE BOOK OF JOSHUA CRITICALLY EXAMINED
- ST. PAUL'S EPISTLE TO THE ROMANS

Colenso, W *see* A CLASSIFICATION AND DESCRIPTION OF SOME NEWLY DISCOVERED FERNS, COLLECTED IN THE NORTHERN ISLAND OF NEW ZEALAND IN 1841-42
COLEOPTERA MICROPTERA BRUNSVICENSIA / Gravenhorst, J L C – Brunsvigae, 1802. lxvi,106p. Z/1301/2 – 8 – ne IDC [590]
COLEOPTERA NEERLANDICA / Everts, E J G – 's-Gravenhage, 1898-1903. 2v. Suppl., 's-Gravenhage, 1903, 138p. 6pls. Z/1223/2 – 8 – ne IDC [590]
THE COLEOPTERA OF INDIANA / Blatchley, W S – 1910 – 7 – uk Microform Academic [590]
THE COLEOPTERA OF THE BRITISH ISLANDS / Fowler – v. 1-5. 1887-91 – 1 – uk Microform Academic [590]
THE COLEOPTERA OF THE BRITISH ISLANDS / Fowler, W W – London, 1886/87-1891/92.5v. Suppl., London, 1913. Z/1257/2 – 8 – ne IDC [590]
COLEOPTERA UND LEPIDOPTERA: EIN SYSTEMATISDIES VERZEICHNISS / Dahl, G – Wien. 1823. vi, 105p. Z-1164 2 – 8 – ne IDC [590]
COLEOPTEREN-STUDIEN / Daniel, K & Daniel, J – Muenchen, 1891-98. Pt.1-2. Z-1176/2 – 8 – ne IDC [590]
LES COLEOPTERES D'EUROPE: FRANCE ET REGIONS VOISINES / Houlbert, C – Paris, 1921. V1. Z/1357/2 – 8 – ne IDC [590]
COLEOPTERES DU MEXIQUE / Chevrolat, LA A – Strasbourg, 1834 (1833-35). Z-1135/2 – 8 – ne IDC [590]
THE COLEOPTERIST'S MANUAL. CONTAINING LAMELLICORN INSECTS BY LINNEUS AND FABRICIUS / Hope, FW – Z-1352 2. 3 v. 1837-1840 – 8 – ne IDC [590]
COLEOPTERORUM CATALOGUS / ed by Schenkling, S – Berlin, 1910-1924 – v1-31 – 8 – ne IDC [590]
COLEPHOUS DE MANUSCRITO / Bounere, Benedictius du – Madrid: Graf. Calleja, 1967 – 1 – sp Bibl Santa Ana [946]
Coler, Bird S *see* DEUX ET DEUX FONT QUATRE
Coler, J *see*
- BERICHT VON DEM EXORCISMO BEY DER TAUFFE...
- HISTORIA DISPVTATIONIS SEV POTIVS COLLOQVII INTER IACOBVM COLERVM ET MATHIAM FLACIVM ILLYRICVM DE PECCATO ORIGINIS,...

Coler, William Nichols *see* A PRACTICAL TREATISE ON THE LAW OF MUNICIPAL BONDS.
EL COLERA / Oliveres, Luis – 1884 – 9 – 1.50f – sp Bibl Santa Ana [610]
EL COLERA MORBO EN BADAJOZ EN 1883 / Guerra Camacho, Mercedes – Badajoz: Dip. Provincial, 1970. Sep. REE – 1 – sp Bibl Santa Ana [946]
COLERAINE CHRONICLE – (Missing: Jan-Jun 1930) – Ireland, 13 Apr 1844- – 212+ r – 1 – uk British Libr Newspaper [072]
COLERAINE CONSTITUTION – Ireland, 21 Apr 1877- – 170+ r – 1 – uk British Libr Newspaper [072]
LA COLERE ET LE DESESPOIR D'UN VIEUX REPUBLICAIN – [Paris]: Bonaventure et Ducessoi. n1-2. 1848 – reel 1, item 27 – us Res Libr [944]
COLERIDGE BLADE – Coleridge, NE. -w. Jun. 1892; Apr. 1896-Aug. 1896; Dec. 1896-Aug. 1909; Oct. 1909-Dec. 1918; Jun. 1927-Feb. 1933; Aug. 1933; Jan. 1935; Aug. 1935- – 1 – us NE Hist [071]
Coleridge, Derwent *see* THE DRAMATIC WORKS OF SAMUEL TAYLOR COLERIDGE
Coleridge, Ernest Hartley *see* ANIMA POET
Coleridge, John *see* A CRITICAL LATIN GRAMMAR
Coleridge, Samuel Taylor *see*
- ANIMA POET
- CHRISTABEL
- THE DRAMATIC WORKS OF SAMUEL TAYLOR COLERIDGE
- ESSAYS ON HIS OWN TIMES
- HINTS TOWARDS THE FORMATION OF A MORE COMPREHENSIVE THEORY OF LIFE
- LECTURES AND NOTES ON SHAKESPEARE AND OTHER ENGLISH POETS
- MISCELLANIES, AESTHETIC AND LITERARY
- OSORIO
- POEMS
- THE POETICAL WORKS OF SAMUEL TAYLOR COLERIDGE
- SEVEN LECTURES ON SHAKESPEARE AND MILTON
- SIBYLLINE LEAVES
- SPECIMENS OF THE TABLE TALK OF THE LATE SAMUEL TAYLOR COLERIDGE
- THE STATESMAN'S MANUAL; OR, THE BIBLE, THE BEST GUIDE TO POLITICAL SKILL AND FORESIGHT...

Coleridge, Sara Coleridge *see* PHANTASMION
Coles, Elisha *see*
- THE COMPLEAT ENGLISH SCHOOLMASTER
- AN ENGLISH DICTIONARY: EXPLAINING THE DIFFICULT TERMS.
- SYNCRISIS, OR, THE MOST NATURAL AND EASY METHOD OF LEARNING LATIN

COLE'S LACROSSE CHAMPIONSHIP DIARY AND ATHLETIC GUIDE – Montreal: H. Cole, 1886. 00702. (Pre-1900 Canadiana) – 9 – cn C.I.H.M. [790]
Coles, William *see* THE ART OF SIMPLING
THE COLESBERG ADVERTISER – Colesberg, South Africa.1 Jan 1861-25 Dec 1900. 22 reels. 1899 incomplete – 1, 16 diazo available at reduced price – sa SA Libr [072]
THE COLESBERG HERALD – Colesberg, South Africa.15 May 1869-16 Jun 1876. 3 reels. Suspended: Sept 1873-Jun 1875 – 1, 16 diazo available at reduced price – sa SA Libr [072]
Colestock, Henry Thomas *see* CHANGING VIEW-POINT IN RELIGIOUS THOUGHT AND OTHER SHORT STUDIES
Colet, John *see*
- AEDITIO
- IOANNIS COLETI ENARRATIO IN PRIMAM EPISTOLAM S. PAULI AD CORINTHIOS
- A SHORTE INTRODUCTION OF GRAMMAR

Coleti, NiC *see* ITALIA SACRA SIVE DE EPISCOPIS ITALIAE
Colette, A *see* HISTOIRE DU BREVIAIRE DE ROUEN
COLFAX CO. PRESS – Clarkson. Neb. and pred. 1909-62 – 1 – us UMI [071]
COLFAX COUNTY CALL – Schuyler, NE. -w. Jul 1933-May 1955 – 1 – us NE Hist [071]
COLFAX COUNTY PRESS – Clarkson, NE. -w. Sep. 1909; Dec. 1909-Dec. 1913; Feb. 1914; Jun. 1916- – 1 – us NE Hist [071]
COLFAX RECORD – Colfax, CA. 1944-58 – 9r – 1 – $450.00 – C02124 – us Library Micro [071]
Colfax, Schuyler *see* PAPERS
COLFAX SENTINEL – Colfax, CA. 1893-1907 – 8r – 1 – $400.00 – B02125 – us Library Micro [071]
Colfer, George W *see* MANUAL FOR THE USE OF ROAD & RURAL INSPECTORS & POUND-KEEPERS: CONTAINING ALSO A MONTHLY CALENDAR OF DUTIES COMPILED FROM THE LATEST EDITION OF THE MUNICIPAL CODE (1888) WITH DECISIONS OF THE TRIBUNALS QUOTED
Colgan, John C *see* THE POEMS OF JOHN C. COLGAN
COLGATE BAPTIST CHURCH. BALTIMORE, MARYLAND : CHURCH RECORDS – 1945-69 – 1 – 15.71 – us Baptist [240]
Colgate, Robert *see* THE IMMIGRANT
COLGATE ROCHESTER DIVINITY SCHOOL : BEXLEY HALL BULLETIN – v41-42 no4. 1968-70 (gaps) – Inquire – 1 – ATLA 1994-S526 – us A.T.L.A. [073]
COLGATE ROCHESTER DIVINITY SCHOOL BULLETIN – v1-40. 1928-68 (complete) – Inquire – 1 – ATLA 1994-S525 – us A.T.L.A. [073]
O COLIBRI : ORGAO DEDICADO AO BELLO SEXO – Manaos, Amazonas. 24 Fev 1888 – 1,5,6 – bl Biblioteca [072]
Coligny, Gaspard de *see* DISCOURS SUR LA GUERRE DES FLANDRES
COLIGNY – GUSTAV ADOLF – WALLENSTEIN : DREI ZEITGENOESSISCHE LATEINISCHE DRAMEN VON RHODIUS, NARSSIUS, VERNULAEUS / ed by Bolte, Johannes – (Latin texts with introduction in German. Includes bibliographical references) – Leipzig: K W Hiersemann, 1933 – 1 – us U.W. Library [820]
Colima. Mexico. (State) *see*
- EL ESTADO DE COLIMA
- PERIODICO OFICIAL

Colin *see* OBSERVATIONS SUR LA SITUATION DU DEPARTEMENT DE LA DROME
Colin, Auguste *see* AUX MARSEILLAIS, UN COMPAGNON DE LA FEMME PARTANT POUR L'ORIENT
Colin, Frederic Louis de Gonzague *see*
- DISCOURS SUR L'OUVRIER PRONONCE PAR LE REVEREND M. COLIN DEVANT L'INSTITUT DES ARTISANS CANADIENS LE 2 AVRIL 1869
- ORAISONS FUNEBRES DE MGR. BOURGET: PRONONCEES DANS L'EGLISE NOTRE-DAME LE 12 JUIN 1885
- ORAISONS FUNEBRES DE MONSEIGNEUR IGNACE BOURGET, SECOND EVEQUE DE MONTREAL, ARCHEVEQUE DE MARIANOPOLIS, PRONONCEE DANS L'EGLISE DE NOTRE-DAME DE MONTREAL, LE 12 JUIN 1885
- REPLY TO TWO LETTERS ADDRESSED BY MR. VANKOUGHNET TO THE SUPERIOR OF THE SEMINARY OF ST SULPICE: DATED RESPECTIVELY, SEPTEMBER 12TH, 1884, AND JANUARY 13TH, 1885
- REPONSE A DEUX LETTRES ADRESSEES PAR M. VANKOUGHNET AU SUPERIEUR DU SEMINAIRE DE ST SUPLICE EN DATE DU 12 SEPTEMBRE 1884 ET DU 13 JANVIER 1885

COLIN LEGUM'S PRESS CUTTINGS VOLUMES, 1936-1987 : MATERIAL FROM THE PERSONAL LIBRARY OF COLIN LEGUM / Legum, Colin – Printed introd. and index. Press Cuttings Volumes, 1936-1987 – 10r – 1 – £400.00 – uk Altair [960]
COLIN LEGUM'S THIRD WORLD REPORTS, 1982-1989 : MATERIAL FROM THE PERSONAL LIBRARY OF COLIN LEGUM / Legum, Colin – (Printed introd and index. To be updated on regular basis) – 9 – £180.00 – uk Altair [960]
COLIN LEGUM'S THIRD WORLD REPORTS, 1992-1995 – 53mf – 9 – uk Microform Academic [300]
COLIN LEGUM'S WRITINGS FROM 1940'S TO 1980'S : MATERIAL FROM THE PERSONAL LIBRARY OF COLIN LEGUM / Legum, Colin – Printed introd. and index – 40mf – 9 – £280.00 – uk Altair [960]
COLINIST – Quebec, 1856 – 1r – 1 – cn Preston [971]
Colizzi, J AK *see* THE FIRST LESSONS FOR THE HARPSICHORD OR SPINNET
Coll, Blanche D *see* MINUTES OF TRUSTEES OF THE POOR
Colla, L A *see* HERBARIUM PEDEMONTANUM, AUGUSTAE TAURINORUM, 1833-1837
COLLABORATIONISTS IN BELGIUM DURING WORLD WAR 2 PAMPHLET COLLECTION – 1944-1946 – 1 – CSUXANN2530-B – us Hoover Inst Photo [355]
COLLABORATIVE ADULT LEARNING PRINCIPLES IN BACCALAUREATE COMMUNITY HEALTH EDUCATION CURRICULA / Lucas, Martha M – 1987 – 114p 2mf – 9 – $8.00 – us Microform Publ [360]
Collado, Fr. Diego *see*
- ARS GRAMATICA JAPONICAE LINGUAE
- DICTIONARUM SIVE THESAURI LINGUAE JAPONICAE

Collado, L *see*
- EX HIPPOCRATIS ET GALENI MONUMENTIS ISAGOGE...
- PLATICA MANUAL DE ARTILLERIA

Colladon, LT F *see* HISTOIRE NATURELLE ET MEDICALE DES CASSES,...
EL COLLAR DE LESCOT / Hurtado, Antonio – 1868 – 9 – 1.50f – sp Bibl Santa Ana [830]
COLLARENEBRI EXPRESS – Mar 4 1965-Jul 13 1967 – 9 – at Pascoe [072]
COLLARENEBRI GAZETTE – Aug 28 1935-Nov 1 1961 – 9 – at Pascoe [072]
COLLATERAL CONSANGUINITY – Philadelphia 1860. 11 p. LL-14 – 1 – us L of C Photodup [340]
THE COLLATERAL GUIDE – Pittsburgh. Pa. 1908-1935 – 1 – us UMI [071]
COLLATIO CODICIS LEWISIANI RESCRIPTI EVANGELIORUM SACRORUM SYRIACORUM CUM CODICE CURETONIANO / Bonus, Alb. – Oxford, 1896 – Dfl19.00 – ne Slangenburg [220]
COLLATION DU DIPLOME DE DOCTEUR EN LETTRES A M. L'ABBE VERREAU, PRINCIPAL DE L'ECOLE NORMALE JACQUES CARTIER – Montreal: E. Senecal, 1882. 04157. (Pre-1900 Canadiana) – 9 – cn C.I.H.M. [370]
Colle, F M *see* DISSERTAZIONE SOPRA IL QUESITO DIMONSTRARE CHE COSA FOSSE E QUANTA PARTE AVESSE LA MUSICA NELL' EDUCAZIONE DE 'GRECI
Colle, R P *see* LES BALUBA (CONGO BELGE)

COLLECCION DE DOCUMENTOS PARA LA HISTORIA DE LA OPOSICION POLITICA AL ESTADO AUTORITARIO EN CHILE (1973-1981) / Fernandez Jilberto, Alex E – 14mf – 9 – ne IDC [320]

COLLECCION DE LOS TRATADOS... / Ministerio de Relaciones Exteriores – Lima, 1890-1911. 14v – 129mf – Dfl 783 – ILM-3836/1 – ne IDC [972]

COLLECCION DE PAPELES SOBIE CONTROVERSIAS BOTANICAS : CON ALGUNAS NOTAS DEL MISMO A LOS ESCRITOS DE SUS ANTAGONISTAS / Cavanilles, A J – Madrid, 1796 – 6mf – 9 – ne IDC [580]

COLLECTANEA AD OMNEM REM BOTANICAM SPECTANTIA / Roemer, J J – Turici. 1809. B-291 2 – 8 – ne IDC [580]

COLLECTANEA AUSTRIACA AD BOTANICAM, CHEMIAM ET HISTORIAM NATURALEM SPECTANTIA / Jacquin, N J von – 5v. Vindobonae. 1786-96. B-1577 2 – 8 – ne IDC [580]

COLLECTANEA BOTANICA / Lindley, J – London. 1821-25. B-816 2 – 8 – ne IDC [580]

COLLECTANEA CHEMICA; BEING CERTAIN SELECT TREATISES ON ALCHEMY AND HERMETIC MEDICINE – By Eirenaeus Philalethes (pseud.), Dr. Francis Antony, George Starkey, Sir George Ripley, and anon. unknown. London: J. Elliott & Co., 1893.160p – 1 – us U.W. Library [540]

COLLECTANEA COMMISSIONIS SYNODALIS : DIGEST OF THE SYNODAL COMMISSION OF THE CATHOLIC CHURCH IN CHINA – 1928-47. 229 fiches – 9 – $1,440.00 – us UPA [240]

COLLECTANEA DE REBUS HIBERNICIS / ed by Vallancey, Charles – 2d ed. Dublin: L. White etc. 1786 – 1 – us U.W. Library [941]

COLLECTANEA MONUMENTORUM VETERUM ECCLESIAE GRAECAE ET LATINAE / ed by Zacagnio, A – Romae, 1698 – Dfl81.00 – ne Slangenburg [240]

COLLECTANEA THOMAS CARLYLE, 1821-1855 / Carlyle, Thomas; ed by Jones, Samuel Arthur – Canton, Pa.: The Kirgate Press, 1903 – 1 roll – 1 – 1-55879-838-2 – uk Libr Preservation [800]

COLLECTANEUM MISCELLANEUM / Scottus, Sedulius – 1990 – 8mf – 9 – Bf2,175.00 – 2-503-63472-9 – be Brepols [240]

COLLECTE POUR PAYER LA DETTE DE L'EGLISE ST JEAN-BAPTISTE DE QUEBEC – Quebec?: Paroisse de St. Jean-Baptiste de Quebec, 1900-1909 – 9 – cn C.I.H.M. [971]

COLLECTED ADDRESSES AND WRITINGS / Tucker, William Jewett; ed by Leavens, Robert French – 1893-1909 – 2r – 1 – $30.00 – us Dartmouth [920]

THE COLLECTED CORRESPONDENCE OF LYDIA MARIA CHILD, 1817-1880 / ed by Holland, Patricia & Meltzer, Milton – (With printed guide) – 1980 (mf ed) – 97mf – 9 – $5.00f – us Ross [920]

COLLECTED DIPLOMATIC DOCUMENTS RELATING TO THE OUTBREAK OF THE EUROPEAN WAR / Great Britain. Foreign Office – London: H.M. Stationery Office, 1915. xix,561p. Includes index – 1 – us U.W. Library [941]

COLLECTED ESSAYS OF RUDOLF EUCKEN : PROFESSOR OF PHILOSOPHY IN THE UNIVERSITY OF JENA, NOBEL PRIZEMAN, 1908 / ed by Booth, Meyrick – London: T.F. Unwin, 1914 – 1mf – us A.T.L.A. [100]

COLLECTED JOURNALS / American Society of Civil Engineers – v109- 1983- – 1,5,6,9 – us UMI [624]

COLLECTED LEGAL PAPERS / Holmes, Oliver Wendell, Jr – New York: Harcourt, Brace and Howe, 1920. 316p. LL-347 – 1 – us L of C Photodup [340]

COLLECTED MINOR WRITINGS OF J. WINSTON COLEMAN, JR / Coleman, J Winston – 2r – 1 – $150.00 – us OmniSys [920]

COLLECTED PAMPHLETS / Lenin, N – 1917-24 – 1 – 19.00 – us L of C Photodup [943]

COLLECTED PAPERS / Maitland, Frederick William – H-1251 2. 3 v. 1911 – 9 – ne IDC [025]

COLLECTED PAPERS, MS 3031 / Lincoln, Abraham – 1841-70 – 1r – 1 – us Western Res [920]

THE COLLECTED PAPERS OF CHARLES WILLSON PEALE AND HIS FAMILY / ed by Miller, Lillian B – (With guidebook) – 1980 – 449mf – 9 – $5.00f – us Ross [975]

COLLECTED PAPERS. ZOOLOGY : A COLLECTION OF 15 ARTICLES PUBLISHED IN VARIOUS JOURNALS / Rafinesque-Schmaltz, Constantine S – 9 – ne IDC [590]

COLLECTED PAPERS-BOTANY / Rafinesque-Schmaltz, Constantine S – A collection of 42 articles published in various journals. B-8119 1 – 9 – ne IDC [580]

THE COLLECTED POEMS OF WILLIAM WATSON / Watson, William – London, New York: John Lane, 2nd ed 1899 – 1 roll – 1 – 1-55879-541-3 – uk Libr Preservation [810]

COLLECTED RECORDS / Afro-American Clubwoman's Project – undated – 1 – us KS Hist [305]

COLLECTED RECORDS OF THE WOMAN'S PEACE PARTY, 1914-20 / Swarthmore College Peace Collection Staff. Woman's Peace Party – (With printed guide) – 23r – 1 – $1,955.00 – D3052 – us Scholarly Res [305]

COLLECTED SPEECHES DELIVERED WHILE AMBASSADOR OF REP. OF INDONESIA TO COURT OF ST JAMES / Subandrio – SE 1229 1. 1950-1954 – 9 – ne IDC [025]

COLLECTED WORKS / Lobstein, Paul – A corpus of the monographic publications of Paul Lobstein (1850-1922) – 1 – us A.T.L.A. [240]

COLLECTED WORKS / Melanchthon, Philip – In Latin and German on Theology and Pedagogy. Includes: Loci Communes Rerum Theologicarum – 231 fiches – 9 – $685.00 – us UPA [180]

COLLECTED WORKS OF LYSANDER SPOONER / Spooner, Lysander; ed by John Zube & Watner, Carl – (Private Mails. No Treason. Revolution. Natural Law. Letter to Bayard and Letter to Cleveland. Trial by Jury.. Intellectual Property. Unconstitutionality of Slavery, etc. Credit, Currency and Banking; Poverty and a New System of Paper. Currency and Our Mechanical Industry; Considerations for Bankers. A New Banking System & Our Financiers...; Gold and Silver; Universal Wealth. Vices are Not Crimes.. Second Letter to Bayard; Various Comments; Index. Towards a Proprietary Theory of Justice by Carl Watner. 1971) – 7vols. Indexed, with some comments. 1834-86. Compiled and 24 fiches (24x). Among the titles are: – 9 – 1.00f – at Libertarian Micro [320]

THE COLLECTED WORKS OF WILLIAM MORRIS. WITH INTRODUCTIONS BY HIS DAUGHTER MAY MORRIS / Morris, William – London, New York [etc.]: Longmans, Green and Company, 1910-15 – 12 rolls – 1 – 1-55879-795-5 – uk Libr Preservation [830]

COLLECTED WORKS ON SOCIALIST LEGAL SYSTEMS / ed by Butler, W E – (Harold J. Berman 124mf Dfl753.00. William E. Butler 22mf Dfl141.00. John N. Hazard 43mf Dfl267.00. Rudolf Schlesinger 94mf Dfl573.00. Marc M. Wolff 8mf Dfl57.00. Every part comes with a printed bibliography.) – 291mf – 9 – ne IDC [340]

THE COLLECTED WRITINGS OF EDWARD IRVING / Irving, Edward; ed by Carlyle, Rev. G – Alexander & Straham & Co., 1864. 5v – 9 – $96.00 – us I.R.C. [920]

LE COLLECTIF *see* LE JOURNAL DES ETUDIANTS DE L'UNIVERSITE DE SHERBROOKE

COLLECTING DATA ON LIVESTOCK – 1992 – 113p – it F.A.O. [636]

COLLECTING STATISTICS ON AGRICULTURAL POPULATION AND EMPLOYMENT – 1978 – 179p – it F.A.O. [304]

COLLECTIO CANONUM ECCLESIAE HISPANAE... – Matriti, 1808 – 14mf – 8 – ne Slangenburg [240]

COLLECTIO NOVA PATRUM ET SCRIPTORUM GRAECORUM : STUDIO ET OPERA / de Montfaucon, D Bern – (Tomus 1 34mf; Tomus 2 32mf) – Parisiis, 1707 – 9 – Dfl231.00 – ne Slangenburg [250]

COLLECTIO PLANTARUM / Wendland, J C – 3v. Hannover. 1808-19. B-5803 2 – 8 – ne IDC [580]

COLLECTIO SCRIPTORUM RERUM HISTORICO-MONASTICO-ECCLESIASTICARUM VARIORUM RELIGIOSORUM ORDINUM / Kuen, M – Ulmae. Tom 1-6. 1755-1768 – 75mf – 9 – Dfl263.00 – ne Slangenburg [220]

COLLECTIO SERMONUM / Chrysologus, Petrus – 1982 – 15mf – 9 – Bf1,500.00 – 2-503-60242-8 – be Brepols [240]

COLLECTIO SERMONUM (CCSL 24-24A-24B) / Petrus Chrysologus – 1982 – 10mf – 9 – Bf975.00 – 2-503-70242-2 – be Brepols [240]

COLLECTION / Adair, Samuel Lyle and Florella (Brown) Family – undated, Correspondence between S.L. and Florella Adair and with other members of their family. The Adairs were missionaries at Osawatomie, KS, and were involved with the territorial conflict in eastern Kansas. The Adairs were relatives of John Brown – 1 – us KS Hist [920]

COLLECTION / Bailey, Lawrence D – 1855-1881, A one volume scrapbook of newspaper clippings, correspondence, and personal manuscripts. Much of the material relates to the monetary question of the 1870's – 1 – us KS Hist [920]

COLLECTION / Carver, W O – Handwritten notes by John A. Broadus and E. C. Dargan while students at Southern Baptist Theological Seminary. 1522p – 1 – 53.27 – us Baptist [240]

COLLECTION / Cheyenne Indians – undated, Material relating to the Cheyenne Indians in Kansas – 1 – us KS Hist [305]

COLLECTION / Cooley, Anna M – 1891-1950 – 1 – us KS Hist [920]

COLLECTION / Courtenay, William Ashmead – 1781-1906. 148 fiches – 9 – us South Carolina Historical [025]

COLLECTION / Cranfield College of Aeronautics. England – 1946-77.Reports, notes, reviews. 480 fiches – 9 – 600.00 – us Updata [629]

COLLECTION / Crigler, Sara Gossett – 1956. 4 fiches – 9 – us South Carolina Historical [025]

COLLECTION / Crottet, Alexandre – 1578-1787. 127 fiches – 9 – us South Carolina Historical [240]

COLLECTION / Custer, Elizabeth B – undated, Letters and related papers of Mrs. Custer; mostly about her experiences and her husband – 1 – us KS Hist [920]

COLLECTION / Force, Peter – Series 8 and 9 – 1 – us L of C Photodup [920]

COLLECTION / Fumimaro, Konoe, Prince – 1 – 35.00r – us Hoover Inst Photo [920]

COLLECTION / Institute of Aerospace Studies. University of Toronto. Canada – (Notes 1954-86 $1000.00. Reports 1948-86 $600.00. Reviews 1950-86 $180.00) – 1948-86 – 881mf – 9 – $1500.00 – us Updata [629]

COLLECTION / Jackson, Sheldon – Alaska selected documents – 1 – $50.00 – us Presbyterian [978]

COLLECTION / Massicotte, Edouard-Zotique – (Contains papers and clippings, dated ca 1886-1947.) – Montreal: Bibliotheque Nationale du Quebec, 1979. SEM35P162 – 2r – 1 – Can$99.00 – cn Bibl Nat [920]

COLLECTION / Monday, Henry A – 1822-1932 – 1 – 897.00 – us L of C Photodup [972]

COLLECTION / Morgan, Dale L – undated, Correspondence as an advisor to the Kansas State Historical Society on various historical research projects – 1 – us KS Hist [978]

COLLECTION / Nelson, Erik Alfred – 1 – 42.21 – us Baptist [240]

COLLECTION / Newton, Louis Devotie – Correspondence, pamphlets, addresses and manuscripts. Papers prepared while he was President of the Southern Baptist Convention. Also materials relating to naming and dedication of Louis D. Newton Hall, Mercer University. 388p – 1 – 13.58 – us Baptist [240]

COLLECTION / Purysburg Colony-Bourquin Family – 18th and 20th cents. 11 fiches. (Courtesy of Eugenia M. Howard, comp. and coll., 1980) – 9 – us South Carolina Historical [025]

COLLECTION / Roche, William Lundy – 1873-1976, Papers of a prominent Washington, KS, family containing much local history – 1 – us KS Hist [920]

COLLECTION / Spilman, B W – 1871-1950. 2558p – 1 – 89.53 – us Baptist [240]

COLLECTION / U.S. National Aeronautics and Space Administration – (Report Memorandum, 1958-59. 1000.00; 9. Special Publications, 1961-63. 340.00; UPD; 9. Technical Memorandum, 1959-63. 3000.00; UPD; 9. Technical Notes, 1958-63. 6000.00; UPD; 9. Technical Reports, 1958-63. 540.00; UPD; 9. Technical Translations, 1958-63.900.00; UPD; 9) – 1958-63.4458 fiches – 9 – 11,340.00 – us Updata [324]

COLLECTION / Wallace, David Duncan – 1879-80, 1942. 1 fiche – 9 – us South Carolina Historical [025]

COLLECTION / Woodson, Carter Godwin – 1804-1936 – 1 – 202.00 – us L of C Photodup [920]

COLLECTION, 1985 / U.S. Bureau of Mines – (Information Circulars $90.00; Minerals Yearbooks $50.00; Open File Reports $550.00; Reports of Investigations $110.00; all other publications $70.00) – Part 5 – 456mf – 9 – $750.00 – us Updata [622]

COLLECTION, 1986 UPDATE / U.S. Bureau of Mines – (Information Circulars $130; Reports of Investigations $120; Mineral Yearbooks $50; Open File Reports $550; all other publications $60) – 1986 – 391mf – 9 – $700.00 – us Updata [622]

COLLECTION, 1987 UPDATE / U.S. Bureau of Mines – (Bulletins. 30.00; 9. Reports of Investigations. 150.00; UPD; 9. Information Circulars. 150.00; UPD; 9. Mineral Yearbooks. 50.00; UPD; 9. Open File Reports. 280.00; UPD; 9. All other publications. 90.00; UPD; 9) – 1987 – 360mf – 9 – 650.00 – us Updata [324]

COLLECTION, 1988 UPDATE / U.S. Bureau of Mines – (Bulletins. 10.00; 9. Reports of Investigations. 175.00; UPD; 9. Information Circulars. 150.00; UPD; 9. Mineral Yearbooks. 50.00; UPD; 9. Open File Reports. 450.00; UPD; 9. All other publications. 15.00; UPD; 9) – 1988 – 390mf – 9 – 750.00 – us Updata [324]

COLLECTION, 1989 UPDATE / U.S. Bureau of Mines – (Reports of Investigations. $150.00; Information Circulars. $60.00; Mineral Yearbooks. $50.00; Openfile Reports. $280.00; All Other Publications. $15.00) – 1989 – 229mf – 9 – $500.00 – us Updata [324]

COLLECTION, 1990 UPDATE / U.S. Bureau of Mines – (Reports of Investigations. $100.00; UPD; 9. Information Circulars. $80.00; UPD; 9. Mineral Yearbooks. $50.00; UPD; 9. Open File Reports. $400.00; UPD; 9. All Other Publications. $70.00; UPD; 9) – 1990 – 291mf – 9 – $600.00 – us Updata [622]

COLLECTION, 1991 UPDATE / U.S. Bureau of Mines – (Reports of Investigations. $150.00; UPD; 9. Information Circulars. $90.00; UPD; 9. Mineral Yearbooks. $60.00; UPD; 9. Open File Reports. $400.00; UPD; 9. All Other Publications. $70.00; UPD; 9.) – 1991 – 314mf – 9 – $650.00 – us Updata [622]

COLLECTION, 1910-69 / U.S. Bureau of Mines – (Bulletins $1925; Information Circulars $1800; Mineral Yearbooks and Mineral Resources $1400; Reports of Investigations $3100; Technical Papers $1430; all other publications, including complete Index, Miners' Circulars, Co-op Publications, Handbooks, Annual Reports, Open File Reports, Technical Progress Reports, Special Publications, Miscellaneous and Economic Papers $1200.00) – Part 1 – 7440mf – 9 – $9900.00 – us Updata [622]

COLLECTION, 1910-87 / U.S. Bureau of Mines – Complete. Five parts – 17,516mf – 9 – $22,000.00 – us Updata [622]

COLLECTION, 1925-52 / Norris, J Frank – 46,360p – 1 – 1622.60 – us Baptist [240]

COLLECTION, 1970-75 / U.S. Bureau of Mines – (Bulletins $65; Information Circulars $600; Mineral Yearbooks $230; Open File Reports $1000; Reports of Investigations $1000; Technical Progress Reports, Special Publications, Translations and Miscellaneous $600) – Part 2 – 2589mf – 9 – $3100.00 – us Updata [622]

COLLECTION, 1976-80 / U.S. Bureau of Mines – (Bulletins $30; Information Circulars $310; Mineral Yearbooks $300; Mineral Commodity Profiles $90; Open File Reports $3000; Reports of Investigations $640; all other publications $450) – Part 3 – 2988mf – 9 – $4000.00 – us Updata [622]

COLLECTION, 1981-84 / U.S. Bureau of Mines – (Bulletins $50; Reports of Investigations $700; Information Circulars $300.00; Mineral Yearbooks $200.00; Open File Reports $3500.00; all other publications $230.00) – Part 4 – 2891mf – 9 – $4500.00 – us Updata [622]

COLLECTION ACADEMIQUE – Academic collection: composed of dissertations, acts or journals. t.1-t.13. 1755-79 – 3 – us Readex [500]

COLLECTION COMPLETE DES OEUVRES DE GRETRY PUBLIEE PAR LE GOUVERNEMENT BELGE / Gretry, Andre E M – Leipzig and Bruxelles. 42 v – 1 – 168.00 – us L of C Photodup [780]

COLLECTION DE (10) MEMOIRES / Candolle, A P de – Paris. 1828-30. 1. Melastomacees. 2. Crassulacees. 3. 4. Onagraires, Paronychiees. 5. Ombelliferes. 6. Loranthacees. 7. Valerianees. 8. Cactees. 9. Composees. (struct.). 10. (statist.). Paris. 1828-38. B-438 2 – 8 – ne IDC [580]

COLLECTION DE DOCUMENTS CONCERNANT MADAGASCAR ET LES PAYS VOISIONS – Tananarive, Academie malgache. v4. 1953-58 – us Res Libr [960]

COLLECTION DE DOCUMENTS IMPR. OU MANUS. CONCERNANT DIVERS PERSONNAGES DE L'EPOQUE REVOLUTIONNAIRE = COLLECTION OF PRINTED OR HANDWRITTEN DOCUMENTS ABOUT PEOPLE OF THE REVOLUTIONARY ERA / Dugast-Matifeux, Charles – v1. 18-19th cent – 36r – 1 – F18,780.55 – fr Armell [920]

COLLECTION DE DOCUMENTS IMPR. OU MANUS. CONCERNANT L'HISTOIRE DE SEDAN ET DES ARDENNES = COLLECTION OF PRINT. OR HANDWR. DOCUMENTS ABOUT THE STORY OF SEDAN AND THE ARDENNES DEPARTMENT / Gourjault – 17th-19th c. – fr Armell [944]

COLLECTION DE DOCUMENTS INEDITS SUR L'HISTOIRE ECONOMIQUE DE LA REVOLUTION FRANCAISE – Paris, 1906-52 – 1,129mf – 8 – ne IDC [330]

COLLECTION DE DOCUMENTS MANUS. OU IMPR. CONCERNANT L'HISTOIRE DE LAVAL ET DU BAS-MAINE = COLLECTION OF HANDWRITTEN OR PRINTED DOCUMENTS ABOUT THE STORY OF LAVAL AND THE BAS-MAINE / Lefizelier, Jules – 19th cent – 14r – 1 – F4,788.60 – fr Armell [944]

COLLECTION DE DOCUMENTS RELATIFS A L'HISTOIRE DE PARIS PENDANT LA REVOLUTION FRANCAISE – Paris, 1883-1923 – 706mf – 690B/2 – ne IDC [944]

LA COLLECTION DE FRANCOIS 1ER / Reunion des Musees Nationaux. Paris – 1972 – 9 – fr Réunion [700]

COLLECTION DE MANUSCRITS RELATIFS A LA NOUVELLE-FRANCE – Quebec, Canada. 4v. 1883-85 – 2r – 1 – Can$50.00r – cn Can Microfilming [971]

COLLECTION DE MONOGRAPHIES ETHNOGRAPHIQUES PUBLIEES PAR CYRILLE VAN OVERBERGH / Overbergh, Cyrille van – Bruxelles: de Wit: Institut internat. de bibliographie – 1 – fr Armell [305]

COLLECTION DE MUSIQUE CANADIENNE / Chatillon, Jean – Montreal: Bibliotheque nationale du Quebec, 1971. SEM35P112 – 3r – 1 – Can$152.00 – cn Bibl Nat [780]

COLLECTION DE PLUSIEURS DES ACTES ET ORDONNANCES LES PLUS UTILES EN FORCE DANS LE BAS-CANADA, CONCERNANT LA LOI CRIMINELLE ET LES DEVOIRS DES MAGISTRATS / Canada. Laws, Statutes, etc – Quebec: Imprime par Stewart Derbishire & George Desbarats, 1854. SEM105P190 – 2mf – 9 – Can$4.50 – cn Bibl Nat [324]

COLLECTION DELOYNES : DOCUMENTS ON THE FINE ARTS, 1675-1808 – (A panorama of art criticism in the Old Regime, the Revolution and the Empire. Over 2000 pamphlets, manuscripts, salon and exhibition catalogs) – 9 – 1100.00 – fr Bibl Nationale [700]

COLLECTION DES BONS ROMANS – Montreal: Lamarre, [1887] – 9 – cn C.I.H.M. [440]

COLLECTION DES MEILLEURS DISSERTATIONS, NOTICES ET TRAITES RELATIFS A L'HISTOIRE DE FRANCE / Leber, [J M]C – Paris. 20v. 1838 – 115mf – 9 – ne IDC [440]

COLLECTION DES MONOGRAPHIES ETHNOGRAPHIQUES / Overbergh, Cyr. van – Bruxelles: Albert de Wit. v1-11. 1907-13 – 1 – us Res Libr [305]

COLLECTION DES OUVRAGES ANCIENS CONCERNANT MADAGASCAR / Grandidier, Alfred et al – Paris: Comite de Madagascar. 5v. 1903-20 – 1 – us Res Libr [080]

COLLECTION: DIARIES, 1832-85; NOTEBOOKS, MANUSCRIPTS AND CORRESPONDENCE WITH CONTEMPORARIES / Crane, William Carey – 40,629p – 1 – 1422.01 – us Baptist [240]

COLLECTION D'OBJETS DES INDIENS OTOMI ET D'ETHNIES APPARENTEES / Soustelle, J & Soustelle, G – 9 – F100.00 – fr Ethnologie [306]

COLLECTION, FIVE NOTEBOOKS. / Dawson, J M – 594p – 1 – 20.79 – us Baptist [240]

A COLLECTION IN THE MAKING : WORKS FROM THE PHILLIPS COLLECTION / Phillips Collection; ed by Grogan, Kevin – 1v. 1976 – 15 – $54.00f – 0-226-69538-7 – us Chicago [760]

COLLECTION INDEX / U.S. Bureau of Mines – 1910-84 – 36mf – 9 – $70.00 – us Updata [622]

THE COLLECTION LAWS, SPECIAL, EXEMPTION, PROPERTY, BANKING, AND INTEREST LAWS, OF ILLINOIS, INDIANA, MICHIGAN, IOWA, WISCONSIN AND MINNESOTA. / Hoyt, James T – Chicago: Cooke, 1859. 406p. LL-734 – 1 – us L of C Photodup [340]

COLLECTION MANAGEMENT / ed by Lee, Sul H – v1- 1976- – 1, 9 ($125.00 in US $175.00 outside hardcopy subsc) – us Haworth [020]

COLLECTION, MANUSCRIPTS AND BOOKS / Howell, Robert Boyte C – 1820. 6190p – 1 – 216.65 – us Baptist [240]

COLLECTION MARIE-PAULE CATY-LACROIX / Caty-Lacroix, Marie-Paule – Montreal: Bibliotheque nationale du Quebec, 1987. SEM105P559 – 2mf – 9 – Can$4.50 – cn Bibl Nat [780]

A COLLECTION OF 16TH CENTURY MANUSCRIPTS, MANY OF WHICH HAVE NEVER APPEARED IN PRINT / Joris, David – BME-401 1 – 9 – ne IDC [240]

THE COLLECTION OF 17TH AND 18TH CENTURY MANUSCRIPTS / Winchester College. Warden and Fellows' Library – With printed index – 1,14 – £795.00 – uk World [025]

COLLECTION OF 18TH AND 19TH-CENTURY SONGS AND PIANO PIECES – (32 songs, mostly by unidentified composers) – Ms in several hands – 1 – us Sibley [780]

COLLECTION OF 42 HOLOGRAPH MANUSCRIPTS / Mason, William – Music-3069 – 1 – us L of C Photodup [780]

A COLLECTION OF 500,000 ALGAL ILLUSTRATIONS, WITH INDEX AND FOREWORD BY DR. J.W.G. LUND / Fritsch, F E – (A printed cumulative alphabetical genus index of 77 pages, made by Dr. Pertii Eloranta is available free of charge to purchasers of the complete collection) – 2,759mf – 9 – 5211, 5211A-E/2,1 – ne IDC [580]

COLLECTION OF AFRICAN NEWSPAPER ISSUES MAINLY IN AFRICA, 1959 TO MAY 1962 – [s.l, s.n, 19–?] – 1 – us Res Libr [072]

COLLECTION OF AFRICAN TRAVELS / Ogilvy, J – London. 1670. BA-126 2 – 8 – ne IDC [960]

[COLLECTION OF AFRICANA] / St Clair Drake – Chicago, IL: Uni of Chicago Photodup Dept, [19–?] – 43r – 1 – us Res Libr [080]

COLLECTION OF AIRS FOR ONE AND TWO FLUTES, OR OTHER TREBLE INSTRUMENTS / Ewell, D Jesse – Manuscript, "presented to W. L. Wharton...by D. Jesse Ewell, March 23, 1826." MUSIC 3054 – 1 – us L of C Photodup [780]

COLLECTION OF AKAN (TWI-FANTE) MATERIALS / Warren, Denise M – 1 – us Res Libr [960]

THE COLLECTION OF ALGAE ILLUSTRATIONS / Fritsch, FE – (Supplement 1. Zug. 1972. B-5211A; 2 SF980.00; 8. Supplement 2. Zug. 1978. B-5211B; 1 SF970.00; IDC; 9. Collection Price. SF3357.00; IDC; 8 and 9) – With index and forward by Dr. J. W. G. Lund. Zug. 1964. B-5211 2 – 8 – ne IDC [580]

A COLLECTION OF ANCIENT TUNES, STEP SHUFFLING AND QUICK. FROM VARIOUS AUTHERS [!] AND CHURCHES OF BELIEVERS, BOTH FAR AND NEAR, AND HEREIN TRANSCRIBED FOR THE PURPOSE OF RETAINING THEM / Haskins, O – Manuscript, begun 1852 – 1 – us Sibley [780]

COLLECTION OF ARCHIVES OF C.E.P. (CENTRE D'ETUDES POLITIQUES) AND I.R.E.S. (INSTITUTE DE RECHERCHES ECONOMIQUES ET SOCIALES) / Congo – Kinshasa. Provinces. BA-565/2 – 8 – ne IDC [960]

COLLECTION OF AUTOGRAPH FIRST EDITIONS / Decker, P – Includes works of Schumann, Loewe, Marschner, Hensel, Reinthaler, and others – 9 – us Sibley [780]

COLLECTION OF BOOKLETS AND PAMPHLETS OBTAINED IN 1965-66 IN THE LOWER CONGO / Janson, John M – (Items are primarily official publs of several religious organizations) – [n.p.], 1959-65 – 1r – 1 – us Res Libr [960]

COLLECTION OF CARTOONS / Keppler, J A – Scrapbooks. v1-8. 1933 – 2r – 1 – us Ross [740]

A COLLECTION OF CHRONICLES AND ANCIENT HISTORIES OF GREAT BRITAIN (RS40) : NOW CALLED ENGLAND / Jehan De Wavrin; ed by Hardy, W & Hardy, E L C P – (v1 1864 Dfl35.00. v2 1887 Dfl32.00. v3 1891 Dfl28.00) – ne Slangenburg [941]

COLLECTION OF CORRESPONDENCE..., 1881-83 / Bismarck, Herbert von – 1roll. T972. Finding Aid: T176 roll 33. (Captured German rcords Filmed at Alexandria, VA.) – 1 – us Nat'l Archives [920]

A COLLECTION OF CURIOUS TRAVELS AND VOYAGES / Ray, J – 7731 1. 2 v. Ed. 2. 1738 – 9 – ne IDC [910]

A COLLECTION OF CURIOUS TRAVELS AND VOYAGES / Ray, J – v. 2: Observations made in many parts of Greece, Asia minor, Egypt. B-7095 2. 1693 – 8 – ne IDC [910]

COLLECTION OF CZECHOSLOVAK CHEMICAL COMMUNICATIONS – v. 1-40. 1929-75 – 1,5,6 – us Princeton Micro [540]

COLLECTION OF DATA, 1784-1840 / Lane, Tidence – 166p – 1 – 5.81 – us Baptist [240]

COLLECTION OF DRAWINGS WITH NOTES OF ORCHIDACEAE OF MEXICO / O Estlund, KE M – Cuernavaca – 68mf – 9 – 8300/1 – ne IDC [580]

COLLECTION OF EARLY AMERICAN MUSIC PUBLISHED AND MANUSCRIPT, VARIOUS PUBLISHERS / Custis, Eleanor – Contains 42 compositions, including a manuscript copy of "Adams and Liberty". music 1974 – 1 – us L of C Photodup [780]

A COLLECTION OF EMBLEMS, ANCIENT AND MODERNE / Wither, F – O 825. 1635 – 9 – ne IDC [740]

COLLECTION OF ENGLISH VOCAL MUSIC : TWELVE GLEES FOR THREE OR FOUR VOICES / Corfe, Joseph – (Binder's collection) – 1 – us Sibley [780]

A COLLECTION OF ENGLISH WORDS NOT GENERALLY USED / Ray, John – 1691. 245p. (English Linguistics Series 1500-1800) – 9 – us UMI [420]

[COLLECTION OF EPHEMERA RELATED TO THE AFRICAN NATIONAL CONGRESS AND DR. S.M. MOLEMA / Molema, S M – (Presumably collected by Dr S M Molema. Contains minutes and programs of the Congress, photos, newspaper clippings, correspondence, etc) – Johannesburg: Microfile, [19–] – 1r – 1 – us Res Libr [960]

A COLLECTION OF FACTS AND OBSERVATIONS MADE RELATIVE TO THE STATE OF MORALS AND RELIGION IN HOLLAND IN 1814 / Romeyn, John B – 1 – $50.00 – us Presbyterian [949]

A COLLECTION OF FAVORITE SONGS ARRANGED FOR THE VOICE AND PIANO FORTE / Reinagle, Alexander – Philadelphia: Printed for A. Reinagle 1789?. music 1456 – 1 – us L of C Photodup [780]

THE COLLECTION OF FINNISH LITERATURE 1810-1944 – (Collection increases annually with 5,500 mf) – Helsinki – ca 80,000mf – 9 – fi H.U. Libr [490]

A COLLECTION OF GAELIC PROVERBS AND FAMILIAR PHRASES – 1882 – 1 – us I.U. Libraries [390]

COLLECTION OF GOVERNMENT DOCUMENTS, MAINLY ECONOMIC AND STATISTICAL 150=OUAGADOUGOU 1960-[67?] – 3r – us Res Libr [324]

COLLECTION OF HAUSA MANUSCRIPTS IN ARABIC SCRIPT – Chicago, Uni of Chicago, Photodup Dept, [19–?] – 20r – us Res Libr [470]

COLLECTION OF HISTORIES OF GAUL AND FRANCE – 1 – $1,055.00 – us UPA [944]

COLLECTION OF HUNGARIAN POLITICAL AND MILITARY RECORDS, 1909-45 – 21r – 1 – $483.00 – T973 – us Nat'l Archives [324]

COLLECTION OF ITALIAN MILITARY RECORDS, 1935-43 – 506r – 1 – $11,638.00 – T821 – us Nat'l Archives [324]

A COLLECTION OF LEGAL OPINIONS: COMPRISING UPWARDS OF ONE HUNDRED AND THIRTY LEADING OPINIONS ON CASES SUBMITTED TO THE LATE HON. J. HILLYARD CAMERON / Cameron, J Hillyard – Comp. by W. A. Orr. Toronto: R. Carswell, 1878. 00390. (Pre-1900 Canadiana) – 9 – cn C.I.H.M. [340]

A COLLECTION OF LESSONS AND SONGS ADAPTED TO THE CELESTINA / Walker, A – London: Napiers, 1775 – 1 – us Sibley [780]

A COLLECTION OF LETTERS OF THACKERAY 1847-1855... / Thackeray, William Makepeace – London: Smith, Elder & Co., 1887 – 1 roll – 1 – 1-55879-614-2 – uk Libr Preservation [860]

THE COLLECTION OF MEDIAEVAL AND RENAISSANCE MANUSCRIPTS / Trinity College. Dublin – (Section 1: The Roman Inquisition £1,500.00. Section 2: Secular Studies (music, law, heraldry, genealogy, general) £2,500.00. Section 3: Waldensian and Icelandic Manuscripts £530.00 Section 4: Literature £950.00) – With printed index. The complete manuscript holdings organized by subject areas – 1,14 – uk World [090]

COLLECTION OF NEGRO SPIRITUALS / Work, John – 1874 – 1 – 23.17 – us Baptist [240]

[COLLECTION OF PAMPHLETS ON THE CHURCHES AND MISSIONS IN THE FORMER FEDERATION OF RHODESIA AND NYASALAND] – Chicago, IL: Uni of Chicago Photodup Dept, 1967 (mf ed) – 1r – 1 – us Res Libr [080]

COLLECTION OF PAMPHLETS RELATING TO THE METHODIST CHURCH IN FIJI, 1878-1970 / Gribble, Cecil F – Suva, Fiji – 1r – 1 – PMB Doc408 – at Pacific Mss [240]

A COLLECTION OF PAPERS LATELY PRINTED IN THE 'DAILY ADVERTISER' – [London, 1740] – 1mf – 9 – MP-280/1 – ne IDC [240]

COLLECTION OF PHILIPPINE LITERATURE IN THE BIKOL LANGUAGE – 1895?-1913? – 1 – us I.U. Libraries [800]

COLLECTION OF PHILIPPINE LITERATURE IN THE BISAYA LANGUAGE – 1894?-1913? – 1 – us I.U. Libraries [800]

COLLECTION OF PHILIPPINE LITERATURE IN THE PAMPANGA LANGUAGE – 1902?-05? – 1 – us I.U. Libraries [800]

COLLECTION OF PHILIPPINE LITERATURE IN THE TAGALOG LANGUAGE – 1904?-23?. 28 pieces – 1 – us I.U. Libraries [800]

COLLECTION OF PIANO AND VOCAL MUSIC – (Most composers are not identified but are identifiable from the titles...Hook, Reinagle, Shuster, Shield et al) – Ms, ca 1800 – 1 – us Sibley [780]

COLLECTION OF PIONEER STORIES / Monroe, Lilla Day – undated, Copyright protected. No copies without permission – 1 – us KS Hist [920]

A COLLECTION OF POETRY OF THE SOAK COTTAGE / Li-wei-yuan – (Ou-lu shih-chi). 1935. 458 poems. 1 reel – 1 – $12.50 – ch Transmission [810]

A COLLECTION OF PRIVATE ACTS OF PRACTICAL UTILITY IN FORCE IN NEW SOUTH WALES : EMBRACING THE LOCAL PRIVATE LEGISLATION FROM THE YEAR 1832 TO THE YEAR 1885 / Tarleton, W W – Sydney: Thomas Richards, 1886 – 14mf – 9 – $21.00 – LLMC 96-005 – us L.L.M.C. [323]

COLLECTION OF PROGRAMS / Daly's Fifth Avenue Theatre. New York – (Ada Rehan Collection). New York. 1879-1899 – 1 – us NY Public [790]

A COLLECTION OF PUBLISHED MUSIC INCLUDING 17 PIANO PIECES AND 3 VOCAL SELECTIONS / Bethune, Thomas Greene – Music-3087 – 1 – us L of C Photodup [780]

COLLECTION OF RARE BOOKS ON ACCOUNTING AND RELATED SUBJECTS, 15TH-19TH CENTURIES / Institute of Chartered Accountants – (Group A: English. Includes early North American. 1. Group B: Italian. 1. Group C: Dutch. 1. Group D: French. 1. Group E: German. 1. Group F: Spanish and Portuguese. 1. Group G: Japanese. 1. Group H: Special Subjects.

1) – With printed index – 1 – £1695.00 – uk World [380]

COLLECTION OF REPORTS OF MEETINGS HELD IN FAVOUR OF MR. JAMES PEIRIS' NOMINATION AS REPRESENTATIVE OF THE LOW COUNTRY SINHALESE IN THE LEGISLATIVE COUNCIL – [Colombo]: Printed at the "Ceylon Examiner" Press, [1895?] – 1r – 1 – us Res Libr [950]

A COLLECTION OF RIGHT MERRIE GARLANDS FOR NORTH COUNTRY ANGLERS – 1864 – 1 – us I.U. Libraries [810]

A COLLECTION OF ROSES FROM NATURE / Lawrance, M – London. 1799. B-7495 1 – 9 – ne IDC [580]

A COLLECTION OF SOME OF THE MOST USEFUL ACTS AND ORDINANCES IN FORCE IN LOWER CANADA, RELATING TO CRIMINAL LAW AND TO THE DUTIES OF MAGISTRATES / Canada. Laws, Statutes, etc – Quebec: Printed by Stewart Derbishire and George Desbarats, 1854. SEM105P191 – 2mf – 9 – Can$4.50 – cn Bibl Nat [324]

COLLECTION OF SONGS AND PIANO MUSIC IN MANUSCRIPT – (7 vols of miscellaneous songs and piano music) – Bethlehem, PA: 181- – 1 – us Sibley [780]

COLLECTION OF SOUTHERN RHODESIA ARCHIVES, MANUSCRIPTS AND DOCUMENTS / Haddon, Eileen – 1950s and 1960s – 1 – us Res Libr [960]

COLLECTION OF SPANISH DEVOTIONAL LITERATURE – 1882?-1907 – 1 – us I.U. Libraries [390]

COLLECTION OF SPIRITUALS (JOHN W. WORK, FISK UNIVERSITY) – 1 – 23.17 – us Baptist [240]

COLLECTION OF STATE DOCUMENTS / Harvard University. Law School Library – (All 32 banking titles. 6359mf. $1.50f. All 18 insurance titles. 12,655mf. $1.50f. All 60 labor titles. 3115mf. $1.50f. All 4 public utilities titles. 10,294mf. $1.50f. All 40 taxation titles. 2846mf. $1.50f. All 15 California titles. 2685mf. $1.50f. All 14 Connecticut titles. 3357mf. $1.50f. All 14 Illinois titles. 2154mf. $1.50f. All 11 Indiana titles. 642mf. $1.50f. All 9 Maryland titles. 1119mf. $1.50f. All 28 Massachusetts titles. 4271mf. $1.50f. All 13 Michigan titles. 1693mf. $1.50f. All 17 New Jersey titles. 1674mf. $1.50f. All 26 New York titles. 8273mf. $1.50f. All 13 Ohio titles. 2261mf. $1.50f. All 10 Pennsylvania titles. 2805mf. $1.50f. All 7 Virginia titles. 1386mf. $1.50f. All 22 Wisconsin titles. 2949mf. $1.50f) – Banking, insurance, labor, public utilities and taxation. 199 serial titles from 13 states: California, Connecticut, Illinois, Indiana, Maryland, Massachusetts, Michigan, New Jersey, New York, Ohio, Pennsylvania, Virginia and Wisconsin. 35,269mf. See individual states for further information – 9 – ca $44,087.00 – us H.U. Law [336]

A COLLECTION OF STATUTES AFFECTING NEW SOUTH WALES : CONTAINING ALL THE STATUTES OF PRACTICAL UTILITY TO THE PRESENT TIME / ed by Cary, Henry – Sydney/Melbourne: Sands & Kenny. v1-2. 1841 – 24mf – 9 – $36.00 – LLMC 96-003 – us L.L.M.C. [323]

COLLECTION OF SYRIAN LAWS AND FINANCIAL TEXTS / Syria. Ministry of Finance – 1949. BNE-9717 1 – 9 – ne IDC [336]

A COLLECTION OF TELUGU LITERATURE – India: s.n., n.d. 1v – 1 – us U.W. Library [800]

A COLLECTION OF THE CHARGES, OPINIONS AND SENTENCES OF GENERAL COURTS-MARTIAL : AS PUBLISHED BY AUTHORITY, FROM THE YEAR 1795 TO THE PRESENT TIME / James, Charles – (Intended to serve as an appendix Tytler's "Essay on Military Law...", and forming a book of cases and references, with a copious index) – 10mf – 9 – $15.00 – LLMC 88-119 – us L.L.M.C. [340]

THE COLLECTION OF THE HONOURABLE LOUIS ARTHUR GRIMES – 6r – 1 – $297.00 – us African Imprint [340]

COLLECTION OF THE NATIONAL CONFERENCE OF INDUSTRY AND COMMERCE IN CHINA – Nan King, 1931. Chinese text. 1 reel – 1 – 17.00 – us Chinese Res [950]

COLLECTION OF THE OFFICIAL ACCOUNTS IN DETAIL OF ALL THE BATTLES FOUGHT BY SEA AND LAND, BETWEEN THE NAVY AND ARMY OF THE UNITED STATES, AND THE NAVY AND THE ARMY OF GREAT BRITAIN DURING THE YEARS 1812-15 / Fay, H A – 1817 – 9 – $20.00 – uk Libr Preservation [941]

A COLLECTION OF THE STATE PAPERS... DANISH AND RUSSIAN WARS;... – London, 1808 – 1mf – 1 – ILM-1214/1 – ne IDC [327]

A COLLECTION OF THE STATUTES OF PRACTICAL UTILITY, COLONIAL AND IMPERIAL, IN FORCE IN NEW SOUTH WALES : EMBRACING THE LOCAL LEGISLATION FROM THE YEAR 1824 TO 1879 / Oliver, Alexander – Sydney: Thomas Richards. v1-2 + app. 1879 – 28mf – 9 – $42.00 – LLMC 96-004 – us L.L.M.C. [323]

COLLECTION OF THE TEACHINGS OF FAMOUS CHINESE (CCC300) / ed by Tung, Ching-an – (In Chinese) – [s.l: s.n, 19–?] – 1r – 1 – 1984-6639 – us A.T.L.A. [180]

A COLLECTION OF THREE THOUSAND AND SIX HUNDRED TSHI PROVERBS IN USE AMONG THE NEGROES OF THE GOLD COAST SPEAKING THE ASANTE AND FANTE LANGUAGE / Christaller, Johann Gottlieb – Basel: Basel German Evangelical Missionary Society, 1879 – 1 – us Res Libr [390]

A COLLECTION OF TRACTATEN / Joris, David – 1537-55. BME-400 1 – 9 – ne IDC [240]

A COLLECTION OF TREATIES BETWEEN GREAT BRITAIN AND OTHER POWERS / Chalmers, G – London, 1790 – 13mf – 1 – ILM-618/1 – ne IDC [327]

A COLLECTION OF TREATIES, ENGAGEMENTS AND SANADS / ed by Aitchison, C U. – Calcutta, 1923-1933. v1-14. Ed.5 – 113mf – 9 – Dfl 687 – I-327/1 – ne IDC [950]

A COLLECTION OF TREATIES, ENGAGEMENTS AND SUNNUDS, RELATING TO INDIA AND NEIGHBOURING COUNTRIES / ed by Aitchison, C U. – (Index. Missing: 1864. v3) – Calcutta, 1862-1866. v1-6 – 35mf – 9 – Dfl 219 – ILM-2929/1 – ne IDC [950]

A COLLECTION OF TRIALS ON MICROFICHE / ed by Csaky, Susan D – (Based on the trial materials collected by John Davison Lawson, editor of American State Trials. Includes introd., list of items included, index by subject and names of persons involved in hard cover) – 2290mf – 9 – $6,165.00 – us Hein [340]

COLLECTION OF TUNES, DANCES AND MARCHES, CA. 1780-1834 / Duport, Pierre Landrin – Composer's manuscript. Includes several dance tunes by A. Reinagle. MUSIC 136, Item 3 and MUSIC 1029 – 1 – us L of C Photodup [780]

COLLECTION OF UNPUBLISHED INVENTORIES TO ARCHIVES ON ASIA AND OCEANIA / Jaquet, FG P – 230mf – 9 – ne IDC [950]

COLLECTION OF UPPER VOLTA POLITICAL AND OTHER EPHEMERA / Martens, George F – 1 – us Res Libr [080]

A COLLECTION OF VOYAGES AND TRAVELS.. / Churchill, John Awsham & Churchill, J – London, 1704. 4v. Lacking v3. KHT-672-1 – 9 – ne IDC [910]

A COLLECTION OF WILLS / Grutze, Albert Lewis – Portland, Ore., Title and Trust Co. 1927 99 p. LL-334 – 1 – us L of C Photodup [340]

COLLECTION OF WORKS : CONTAINS: THE CHILDREN IN THE WOOD/GRAY'S ELEGY/ LAVINIA/MARIA'S EVENING SERVICE TO THE VIRGIN/POPE'S ELEGY/POPE'S EBISA TO ABELARD/POPE'S MESSIAH/PRIOR'S GARLAND/TE DEUM ETC. / Billington, T – London, 1780 – 1 – us Sibley [780]

COLLECTION ON THE EXCLUSION OF DR. CALVIN AND CAROLINE CUTTER / Nashua, New Hampshire. First Baptist Church – c1838 – 1 – us A.B.H.S. [240]

COLLECTION PAUL SAURIOL : CHRONIQUE INTERNATIONALE, EDITORIAUX, BLOC NOTES – Montreal, Canada. 15 mai 1925-28 aut 1971 – 6r – 1 – Can$50.00r – cn Can Microfilming [072]

COLLECTION "QUESTION LIBANAISE" – [Beirut?: s.n.] 1975-76 – 1r – us Res Libr [956]

COLLECTION WITH MAPS / U.S. Central Intelligence Agency – 1972-86. Maps regrid as entity with one-inch overlap on each frame – 2160mf – 9 – $3800.00 – us Updata [977]

COLLECTION(MEXICAN AND PERUVIAN DOCUMENTS) / Harkness, Edward S – 1 – 186.00 – us L of C Photodup [972]

LE COLLECTIONNEUR – Montreal, Canada. mai; jun 1886 – 1r – 1 – Can$25.00 – cn Can Microfilming [073]

LE COLLECTIONNEUR – Stoneham, Canada. 20 mai 1961-v2 n4. avr 1963 – 1r – 1 – Can$30.00 – cn Can Microfilming [073]

COLLECTIONS / Dekalb Historical Society – v1, 1952. Biog. and hist. sketches. Indexed. 3 fiches. F-0682 – 9 – us A.G.L.L. [920]

COLLECTIONS / Georgia Historical Society – (v1, 1840. Biog. & hist. sketches. 5 fiches. F-0744. v2, 1842. 5 fiches. F-0745. v3, 1873. 7 fiches. F-0746. v4, 1878. 6 fiches. F-0747. v5, 1901. Indexed.6 fiches. F-0748. v6, 1904. The Letters of Hon. James Habersham, 1756-75. 4 fiches. F-0749. v7, 1909. Letters of Montiano. Siege of St. Agustine. 5 fiches. F-0750. v8, 1913. Letters of Joseph Clay (1776-93), List of ships & vessels entered at the port of Savannah for May 1765, 1766 & 1767. 4 fiches. F-1292) – 9 – us A.G.L.L. [978]

COLLECTIONS / Jewish Theological Seminary of America – (Hebrew Incunabula. Benaim Collection. Liturgy Collection. Biblical Manuscripts. Steinschneider Collection. Rare Books Collection. Philological Manuscripts. Polemical Manuscripts. Poetry and Belles Lettres Collection. Kabbalah and Mysticism Collection. Philosophy Manuscripts. History of Science. Maimonides' Mishneh Torah. Adler Special Manuscript Collection) – 14 collections. 383 reels – 1 – us UMI [270]

COLLECTIONS / Minnesota Historical Society – 1872-1920. 9 rolls. Printed guide 2210.00, available separately – 1 – $270.00; $30.00r – us M.H.S. [025]

COLLECTIONS / Missouri Historical Society – v.2-6. 1900-1931. Continued as Glimpses of the Past – 1 – us UMI [073]

COLLECTIONS / South Carolina Historical Society – 1857-97. 5v – 34mf – 9 – us South Carolina Historical [978]

COLLECTIONS DE DECRETS DE L'ASSEMBLEE NATIONALE(...)ENREGISTRES AU GREFFE DU DEPARTEMENT DE LA LOIRE-INFERIEURE / Assemblee Nationale – Nantes: Malassis, 1791 – fr Armell [324]

COLLECTIONS FOR A HISTORY OF STAFFORDSHIRE / Staffordshire Record Society – 1880-97. v.1-18; N.S., 1898-1909; S.3, 1910-1939. Lacking: 1937 – 442mf – 9 – ne IDC [941]

COLLECTIONS FROM THE BODLEIAN LIBRARY *see*
- CLASSIC LITERATURE ON INVERTEBRATE PALAEONTOLOGY
- SEVENTEENTH- AND EIGHTEENTH-CENTURY BOOK PROSPECTUSES

COLLECTIONS FROM THE JEWISH THEOLOGICAL SEMINARY OF AMERICA – (Adler Special Manuscript Collection $995; Benaim Collection $685; Biblical Manuscripts $4335; Hebrew Incunabula 109 titles $1150; History of Science 200 MS, ca 400 titles $995; Kabbalah and Mysticism 700 MS $3740; Liturgy Collection $3820; Maimonides' Mishneh Torah 71 MS $595; Philological Manuscripts 150 MS $1035; Philosophy Manuscripts ca 300 MS $1255; Poetry and Belles Lettres 378 MS $1435; Polemical Manuscripts $290; Rare Books ca 100 items $695; Steinschneider Collection $1155. Cataloging available) – 383r – 1 – $22,180.00 complete collection – us UMI [270]

COLLECTIONS FROM THE ROYAL SOCIETY / Royal Society – (See also indiv. titles: Book Catalogue of the Library; Council Minutes; The Early Letters and Classified Papers; Journal Books of Scientific Meetings; Letters and Papers of Robert Boyle; Letters and Papers of Sir John Herschel; Misc. Manuscripts) – $10,575.00 set – us UPA [500]

COLLECTIONS ICONOGRAPHIQUES ET HISTORIQUES DES CHENILLES...D'EUROPE / Boisduval, J B A D de et al – Paris, 1832-43. 128 pls. Z-1084/2 – 8 – ne IDC [590]

COLLECTIONS OF THE ALCUIN CLUB – London, 1899-1901. v1-4 – 16mf – H-762/2 – ne IDC [941]

COLLECTIONS OF THE CONNECTICUT HISTORICAL SOCIETY – v11, 1907. The Law Papers, 1741-50, v1 & 2. Indexes for each. V132-0001 – 1 – us A.G.L.L. [920]

COLLECTIONS OF THE ILLINOIS STATE HISTORICAL LIBRARY – v2 by Clarence Walworth Alvord. 1907. V148-0006 – 1 – us A.G.L.L. [920]

LES COLLECTIONS POLYNESIENNES DU MUSEE DU PALAIS DES BEAUX-ARTS, LILLE / Lavondes, A – 9 – F80.00 – fr Ethnologie [306]

COLLECTION(SPANISH-AMERICAN DOCUMENTS) / Kraus, Hans P – 1500-1819 – 1 – 87.00 – us L of C Photodup [972]

COLLECTIVE ARTISTIC DIRECTION : THE DYNAMICS OF A MODERN DANCE COMPANY / Chambers, Sue – Texas Woman's University, 1994 – 1mf – 9 – PE 3634 – us Microform Publ [790]

COLLECTIVE BARGAINING SETTLEMENTS IN NEW YORK STATE / New York. Dept. of Labor. Division of Research and Statistics – 1948-79. 174 fiches. (Harvard Law School Library Collection.) – 9 – 1.50f – us H.U. Law [331]

THE COLLECTIVE CATALOGUE OF HEBREW MANUSCRIPTS / The Jewish National and University Library. Jerusalem – (Includes user's guide) – From the Institute of Microfilmed Hebrew Manuscripts and the Dept of Manuscripts – 812mf + update on 50 COM – 9 – £4,250.00 – uk Chadwyck [090]

COLLECTIVE PHENOMENA – 1973-. – 1,5,9 – us Gordon [530]

LA COLLECTIVISATION DE L'AGRICULTURE : U.R.S.S., CHINE, DEMOCRATIES POPULAIRES / Bouvier, Ch. – F50.00 – fr Ethnologie [630]

COLLECTIVISM, A STUDY OF THE LEADING SOCIAL QUESTIONS OF THE DAY / Beaulieu, Paul Leroy – Abr.and trans. by Sir Arthur Clay, 1908.343p. Indexed – 9 – 1,00f – at Libertarian Micro [335]

THE COLLECTOR – (Selections from 'The Queen') – London, 1902-07 – 1r – 1 – uk British Libr Newspaper [072]

THE COLLECTOR AND ART CRITIC – 1899-1907 – 17mf – 9 – £95.00 – uk Chadwyck [700]

COLLECTOR EDITIONS – v10-. 1982- – 1,5,6,9 – us UMI [073]

COLLECTOR EDITIONS QUARTERLY – v5-1977- – 1,5,6,9 – us UMI [090]

COLLECTOR EDITIONS QUARTERLY *see* ACQUIRE

COLLECTOR INVESTOR – v.1-3. 1980-82 – 1,5,6,9 – us UMI [336]

Collector of Customs, Adelaide *see*
- REGISTER OF BRITISH SHIPS

Collector of Customs, Brisbane *see*
- REGISTER OF BRITISH SHIPS

Collector of Customs, Darwin *see* REGISTER OF BRITISH SHIPS

Collector of Customs, Hobart *see*
- REGISTER OF BRITISH SHIPS

Collector of Customs, Melbourne *see*
- REGISTER OF BRITISH SHIPS

Collector of Customs, Sydney *see*
- ALPHABETICAL INDEX TO REGISTER OF BRITISH SHIPS, 1948-
- REGISTER OF BRITISH SHIPS
- REGISTER OF TRANSACTION RELATING TO SHIPS REGISTERED UNDER THE 8TH AND 9TH VICTORIA, CAP. 89, 1855-1862

Collector of Customs, Western Australia *see*
- REGISTER OF BRITISH SHIPS

Collectors Club Library. New York *see* PHILATELY

THE COLLECTOR'S MAGAZINE = LE COLLECTIONEUR – Quebec. v1 n1. oct 1933-sep 1934 – 1r – 1 – Can$30.00 – cn Can Microfilming [072]

COLLECTORS MART – 1986- – 1,5,6,9 – us UMI [740]

COLLECTORS' SHOWCASE – (v3-. 1983-. 5,6,9) – v1-. 1981- – 1 – us UMI [073]

Colledge, T R *see* THE MEDICAL MISSIONARY SOCIETY IN CHINA

Colledge, T R et al *see* SUGGESTIONS FOR THE FORMATION OF A MEDICAL MISSIONARY SOCIETY, OFFERED TO THE CONSIDERATION OF ALL CHRISTIAN NATIONS, MORE ESPECIALLY TO THE KINDRED NATIONS OF ENGLAND AND THE UNITED STATES OF AMERICA

COLLEGE ADDRESSES AND SERMONS / Lindsay, Thomas M – Glasgow: J. Maclehose, 1915 – 1mf – us A.T.L.A. [240]

COLLEGE AND CAREER – 1956-70 – 1 – 42.52 – us Baptist [240]

COLLEGE AND RESEARCH LIBRARIES NEWS – v.41-. 1980- – 1,5,6,9 – us UMI [370]

COLLEGE AND UNDERGRADUATE LIBRARIES / ed by Bahr, Alice Harrison – v3 n1. 1996- – 1,9 – $60.00 in US $84.00 outside hardcopy subsc – us Haworth [370]

COLLEGE AND UNIVERSITY – 1- 1910- 1; v44- 5,6; v22- 9 – us UMI [370]

COLLEGE AND UNIVERSITY BULLETIN *see* AAHE BULLETIN
LE COLLEGE ANGLAIS DE DOUAI : SON HISTOIRE HEROIQUE (REVUE DE LITTERATURE COMPAREE 10, 1930) / Fabre, F – Dfl6.00 – ne Slangenburg [370]
College Art Association *see* BULLETIN
COLLEGE CATALOG COLLECTIONS: NATIONAL / Career Guidance Foundation – More than 2900 accredited postsecondary schools represented by approx. 3600 catalogs. Annual subscription includes supplements and indexes and most recent catalogs – 1314mf – 9 – $698.00 – us Career [370]
COLLEGE CATALOG COLLECTIONS: REGIONAL / Career Guidance Foundation – (Eastern, 350mf; Western, 256mf; North Central, 354mf; Southern, 355mf) – More than 700 regional schools and 900 or more catalogs – 9 – $298.00 each region – us Career [370]
COLLEGE COMPOSITION AND COMMUNICATION – 1- 1950- 1; 1971- 5,6; 1976- 4 x 6 in9 – us UMI [370]
COLLEGE CRAMPTON : KOMOEDIE IN 5 AKTEN / Hauptmann, Gerhart – 3. Aufl. Berlin: S Fischer, 1896 – 1r – 1 – us U.W. Library [820]
THE COLLEGE DAYS OF CALVIN / Blackburn, W M – Philadelphia: Presbyterian Board of Publication, c1865 – 1mf – us A.T.L.A. [240]
COLLEGE DE CHAMBLY: FONDE EN 1836 PAR MONSIEUR P. M. MIGAULT – Montreal: E. Senecal, 1882. 02040. (Pre-1900 Canadiana) – 9 – cn C.I.H.M. [370]
College des Medecins et Chirurgiens de la Province de Quebec. Bureau Medical *see* BULLETIN DU BUREAU MEDICAL DU COLLEGE DES MEDECINS ET CHIRURGIENS DE LA PROVINCE DE QUEBEC
COLLEGE ENGLISH – v.1- 1939- – 1,5,6,9 – us UMI [420]
COLLEGE LIBRARY: CATALOGUE OF EARLY INDIAN IMPRINTS, 1714-1850 / Carey, William – 1,296p – 1 – us Baptist [240]
COLLEGE LITERATURE – v1- 1974- 1,5,6; v3- 1976- 9 – us UMI [410]
COLLEGE MANAGEMENT – 1-9 1966-74 1; v6-9 5,6,9 – us UMI [650]
COLLEGE MANAGEMENT – Palm Desert, CA. 1966-1967 – 2r – 1 – $100.00 – R03379 – us Library Micro [370]
COLLEGE MUSIC SYMPOSIUM – (1985- . 5,6,9) – v1- . 1961- – 1 – us UMI [073]
THE COLLEGE OF APOSTLES: A STUDY OF THE TWELVE / Vance, James Isaac – New York: Fleming H. Revell, 1896. 1 fiche – 9 – us A.T.L.A. [240]
A COLLEGE OF COLLEGES / ed by Shanks, T J – Chicago: Fleming H Revell, c1887 – 1mf – 9 – 0-8370-6614-X – 1986-0614 – us A.T.L.A. [240]
College of Ottawa *see*
– APERCU DU PLAN D'ETUDES ET DE LA METHODE D'ENSEIGNEMENT SUIVIS AU COLLEGE D'OTTAWA
– PROSPECTUS OF COURSE OF STUDIES
COLLEGE OF THE DESERT – Palm Desert, CA. 1958-1985 – 4r – 1 – $200.00 – R02592 – us Library Micro [370]
College Physical Education Association Committee on Terminology *see* GLOSSARY OF PHYSICAL EDUCATION TERMS, PART 1
College Sainte-Marie. Montreal. Archives *see* DICTIONNAIRES ALGONQUINS, HURONS, ETC
COLLEGE STATION FIRST BAPTIST CHURCH. COLLEGE STATION, TEXAS : CHURCH RECORDS – 1920-63. 1688p – 1 – 67.52 – us Baptist [240]
COLLEGE STORE JOURNAL – 1934- 1; 1975- 5,6,9 – us UMI [370]
COLLEGE STUDENT AFFAIRS JOURNAL – v4-. 1982- – 1,5,6,9 – us UMI [073]
COLLEGE STUDENT PERSONNEL ABSTRACTS – v9-19. Fall 1973-Summer 1984 – 1,5,6,9 – us UMI [073]
COLLEGE TIMES – [Toronto?]: Upper Canada Literary Society, [1871?-19–] – 9 – cn C.I.H.M. [370]
COLLEGE TIMES *see* THE SPARTAN DAILY
COLLEGE TOPICS – Toronto: [s.n, 1897-1902?]; (Toronto: [C B Robinson]) – 9 – cn C.I.H.M. [370]
COLLEGE TOPICS – Toronto.v1-5, 2 Nov 1897-14 Jan 1902 – 1 – 85.00 – cn McLaren [073]
COLLEGE VIEW HERALD – College View, NE. -w. Nov. 1910-Mar. 1912. Incomplete; Apr. 1912-Dec. 1922; Feb. 1923-Sep. 1925. Incomplete – 1 – us NE Hist [071]
COLLEGE WOMEN, ALCOHOL CONSUMPTION, AND NEGATIVE SEXUAL OUTCOMES / Good, DL – 1992 – 2mf – 9 – $8.00 – us Microform Publ [613]
COLLEGE WOMEN ATHLETES' KNOWLEDGE AND PERCEPTIONS OF TITLE 9 / Jacob, Michael P – Iowa State University, 1993 – 2mf – 9 – $8.00 – PE3603 – us Microform Publ [790]
THE COLLEGES AND THEOLOGICAL INSTITUTIONS OF AMERICA : A LECTURE DELIVERED BY DESIRE OF THE PRINCIPAL AND PROFESSORS AT THE OPENING OF THE NEW COLLEGE, EDINBURGH, 2D NOVEMBER 1870 / Blaikie, William Garden – Edinburgh: A. Elliot, 1870 – 1mf – us A.T.L.A. [370]
O COLLEGIAL : ORGAO DO GREMIO-LITTERO-CIVICO OLAVO BILAC – Manoas, Amazonas. 31 Mar-Set 1914; 16 Jul 1916 – 1,5,6 – bl Biblioteca [072]
O COLLEGIAL : PERIODICO LITTERARIO, RELIGIOSO E RECREATIVO – Maceio, Alagoas. 3 Ago 1869 – 1,5,6 – bl Biblioteca [072]
COLLEGIAN – Ashland, Ohio, 1922-1993 – 11r – 1 – $32.50r – us Archival [978]
COLLEGIAN – Toledo, Ohio. 1984-1994 – 12r – 1 – $32.50r – us Archival [071]
THE COLLEGIAN – (Also known as: The Daily Collegian) – Fresno, CA. CSU Fresno: 1922 – 41+ r – 1 – $2,050.00 ($90.00y) – B03715 – us Library Micro [370]
COLLEGIATE CHURCH : YEARBOOK OF THE REFORMED PROTESTANT DUTCH CHURCH OF THE CITY OF NEW YORK – New York, NY. 1950-78 (complete) – 3r – 1 – ATLA S0387 – us A.T.L.A. [240]
COLLEGIATE COACHES' KNOWLEDGE OF EATING DISORDERS / Turk, Joanne C – University of North Carolina at Chapel Hill, 1995 – 2mf – 9 – $8.00 – HE559 – us Microform Publ [616]
COLLEGIATE MICROCOMPUTER – v1-. 1983- – 1,5,6,9 – us UMI [073]
COLLEGIATE SOCCER PLAYERS' PERCEPTIONS OF SPORT PSYCHOLOGY, SPORT PSYCHOLOGISTS AND SPORT PSYCHOLOGICAL SERVICES / Francis, Nicholas C & Gould, Daniel – 1991 – 2mf – 9 – $8.00 – us Microform Publ [150]
LE COLLEGIEN – St-Hyacinthe, Canada. 31 oct 1873-v3 n20. 23 jun 1876 – 1r – 1 – Can$25.00 – cn Can Microfilming [072]
COLLEGIT OTTO KERN / Orphicorum Fragmenta – Berolini, 1963 – 7mf – 8 – ne Slangenburg [100]
COLLEGIUM – Villafranca de los Barros: Colegio de San Jose, 1939. 1 numero – 5 – sp Bibl Santa Ana [073]
Colletet, G *see* L'ART POETIQUE
Colleton County. South Carolina. St. Bartholomew's (Episcopal) Parish *see* RECORDS
Collett, H *see* FLORA SIMLENSIS
Colletta, N J *see* THE USE OF INDIGENOUS CULTURE AS A MEDIUM FOR DEVELOPMENT
Collette, Charles Hastings *see* THE NOVELTIES OF ROMANISM
LE COLLEZIONI BOTANICHE DELLA MISSIONE STEFANINI-PAOLI NELLA SOMALIA ITALIANA / Chiovenda, E – Appendice: Le raccolte di Mangano, Scassellati, Mazzocchie Provenzale in Somalia. (Pubblic. R. Inst. Studi Super. Firenze). Firenze. 1916. B-6125 2 – 8 – ne IDC [580]
COLLIER COUNTY DAILY NEWS – Naples. Fl. 1966- – 1 – us UMI [071]
COLLIER COUNTY NEWS – Naples. Fl. -w, sw. 1946-69 – 1 – us P.K. Yonge [071]
LE COLLIER DE COQUILLAGES / Ouane, Ibrahima Mamadou – [Andrezieux, France, Impr moderne 1958] – us Res Libr [944]
Collier, J *see* MUSICAL TRAVELS THROUGH ENGLAND
Collier, J Payne *see* MALCOLM LOWRY'S SHAKESPEARE
Collier, John *see* JOHN COLLIER PAPERS, 1922-1968
COLLIER ON BANKRUPTCY – 1st-14th ed. 1898-1982 – 9 – $750.00 set – us Hein [332]
Collier, Robert Laird *see* MEDITATIONS ON THE ESSENCE OF CHRISTIANITY
Collier, William Miller *see* THE LAW AND PRACTICE IN BANKRUPTCY UNDER THE NATIONAL BANKRUPTCY ACT OF 1898
COLLIER'S, THE NATIONAL WEEKLY – v. 8-139. 1891-1957 – 1 – us UMI [073]
COLLIERY WORKMAN'S TIMES – Manchester, 2 Dec 1893-13 Jan 1894 – 7ft – 1 – uk British Libr Newspaper [072]
Colligan, J Hay *see*
– THE ARIAN MOVEMENT IN ENGLAND
– EIGHTEENTH CENTURY NONCONFORMITY
Collin de Plancy, J A S *see* DICTIONNAIRE INFERNAL; REPERTOIRE UNIVERSEL DES ETRES, DES PERSONNAGES, DES LIVRES, DES FAITS ET DES CHOSES QUI TIENNENT AUX ESPRITS.
Collin d'Harleville, Jean Francois *see*
– LES MOEURS DU JOUR OU L'ECOLE DES JEUNES FEMMES
– LE VIEUX CELIBATAIRE
Collin, Henry P *see* A 20TH CENTURY HISTORY AND BIOGRAPHICAL RECORD OF BRANCH COUNTY
Collin, P C *see* ESSAI SUR LA MEMOIRE COLLECTIVE DES HABITANTS DES MONTS DU LYONNAIS
Collinet, Paul *see* RECHERCHES STATISTIQUES SUR LA POPULATION DES ARDENNES AVANT LE 19EME SIECLE
Collinge, WE *see* A MANUAL OF INJURIOUS INSECTS
Collingwood, Cuthbert *see* A SELECTION FROM THE PUBLIC AND PRIVATE CORRESPONDENCE OF VICE-ADMIRAL LORD COLLINGWOOD: INTERSPERSED WITH MEMOIRS OF HIS LIFE
Collingwood, Stuart Dodgson *see* THE LEWIS CARROLL PICTURE BOOK
Collingwood, WG *see*
– THE ART TEACHING OF JOHN RUSKIN
– RUSKIN RELICS
Collini, Alexandre *see* MON SEJOUR AUPRES DE VOLTAIRE ET LETTRES INEDITES QUE M'ECRIVIT CET HOMME CELEBRE JUSQU'A LA DERNIERE ANNEE DE SA VIE
COLLINS – An appendix concerning the ordinance of singing. London. 1680 – 1 – $5.00 – us Baptist [240]
Collins *see* HISTORY OF KENTUCKY
Collins, A Jefferies *see* MANUALE AD USUM PER CELEBRIS ECCL. SARISBURIENSIS
Collins, Almer M *see* THE CONTRADICTIONS OF ORTHODOXY, OR, "WHAT SHALL I DO TO BE SAVED?"
Collins, Anthony *see*
– ESSAI SUR LA NATURE ET LA DESTINATION DE L'AME
– EXAMEN DES PROPHETIES QUI SERVENT DE FONDEMENT A LA RELIGION CHRETIENNE. AVEC UN ESSAI DE CRITIQUE SUR LES PROPHETES ET LES PROPHETIES EN GENERAL
Collins, Cornelius Francis *see* THE MUNICIPAL COURT PRACTICE ACT, ANNOTATED.
Collins, Fred K *see* AN ABSTRACT OF THE STATUTORY LAW OF CORPORATIONS AS RESPECTS THEIR FORMATION, OFFICERS, MEETINGS, LIABILITY OF MEMBERS, ETC
Collins, G N *see*
– THE MANGO IN PORTO RICO
– NOTES ON ALGAE
Collins, George *see*
– AN EXPLANATION OF THE ELEVENTH CHAPTER OF THE BOOK OF DANIEL
– AN EXPLANATION OF THE VISIONS OF THE FOUR BEASTS. DANIEL 7
Collins, H B *see*
– ARCHEOLOGY OF ST LAWRENCE ISLAND, ALASKA
– ESKIMO ARCHAEOLOGY AND ITS BEARING ON THE PROBLEM OF MAN'S ANTIQUITY IN AMERICA
– OUTLINE OF ESKIMO PREHISTORY
Collins, Hugh *see* A VAST PUBLIC UTILITY: THE STATE IN AUSTRALIANS' EXPERIENCE AND EXPECTATIONS
Collins, John H *see* PROPAGANDA, ETHICS AND PSYCHOLOGICAL ASSUMPTIONS IN CAESAR'S WRITINGS
Collins, Joseph Edmund *see*
– ANNETTE, THE METIS SPY: A HEROINE OF THE N. W. REBELLION
– CANADA UNDER THE ADMINISTRATION OF LORD LORNE
– LIFE AND TIMES OF THE RIGHT HONOURABLE SIR JOHN A. MACDONALD, K.C.B., D.C.L., ETC., PREMIER OF THE DOMINION OF CANADA
Collins, Lewis *see* HISTORY OF KENTUCKY, V2: BY THE LATE LEWIS COLLINS
Collins, Perry McDonough *see* A VOYAGE DOWN THE AMOOR: WITH A LAND JOURNEY THROUGH SIBERIA, AND INCIDENTAL NOTICES OF MANCHOORIA, KAMSCHATKA, AND JAPAN
Collins, Richard *see*
– THE PHILOSOPHY OF JESUS CHRIST AS UNFOLDED IN THE PHYSICAL ASPECT OF HIS MIRACLES
– PHILOSOPHY OF JESUS CHRIST AS UNFOLDED IN...HIS MIRACLES
Collins, S *see* A SYSTEME OF ANATOMY
Collins, Sherry L *see* IMPRESSIONISM IN THE ARTS AND ITS INFLUENCE ON SELECTED DANCE WORKS
Collins, W H *see* PAST AND PRESENT OF THE CITY OF QUNINCY AND ADAMS COUNTY
Collins, William A *see* THE DIVORCE QUESTION
Collins, William Edward *see*
– THE BEGINNINGS OF ENGLISH CHRISTIANITY
– LECTURES ON ARCHBISHOP LAUD
– THE STUDY OF ECCLESIASTICAL HISTORY
– TYPICAL ENGLISH CHURCHMEN FROM PARKER TO MAURICE
Collins, Winfield Hazlitt *see* THE DOMESTIC SLAVE TRADE OF THE SOUTHERN STATES
Collinson, Richard *see*
– ACCOUNT OF THE PROCEEDINGS OF H.M.S. ENTERPRISE FROM BEHRING STRAIT TO CAMBRIDGE BAY
– JOURNAL OF H. M. S. ENTERPRISE: ON THE EXPEDITION IN SEARCH OF SIR JOHN FRANKLIN'S SHIPS BY BEHRING STRAIT 1850-55
– JOURNAL OF H.M.S. ENTERPRISE, 1850-55
– JOURNAL OF H.M.S. ENTERPRISE, ON THE EXPEDITION IN SEARCH OF SIR JOHN FRANKLIN'S SHIPS BY BEHRING STRAIT, 1850-55
COLLINWOOD CITIZEN : WEEKLY REPUBLICAN NEWSPAPER – Cleveland, OH. Sept 22 1905-Jun 27 1918 – 6r – 1 – us Western Res [071]
Collis, Dirmid R F *see* ARCTIC LANGUAGES
Collis, Maurice *see* CORTES AND MONTEZUME
COLLIS P. HUNTINGTON PAPERS – 1856-1901 – 115r – 1 – us UMI [920]
COLLIS P. HUNTINGTON PAPERS, 1856-1901 / Huntington, Collis P – 115r – 1 – $7250.00 – us UMI [920]
Collis, Septima Maria *see* A WOMAN'S TRIP TO ALASKA: BEING AN ACCOUNT OF A VOYAGE THROUGH THE INLAND SEAS OF THE SITKAN ARCHIPELAGO IN 1890
Collison, William *see* THE APOSTLE OF FREE LABOUR, THE LIFE OF WILLIAM COLLISON, FOUNDER AND GENERAL SECRETARY OF THE NATIONAL FREE LABOUR ASSOCIATION
Collocott, E E V *see* 'KING TAUFA'
COLLOID AND POLYMER SCIENCE – v1-138. 1906-54 – 1,5,6 – us Princeton Micro [660]
COLLOID JOURNAL – v14-55. 1952-93 – 1,5 – $80.00v – us UMI [540]
COLLOIDS AND SURFACE – v1-9. 1980-84 – 1,5,6,13 – sz Elsevier [073]
Collomb, G *see* L'ALLIANCE ET LA PARENTE A VILLAREMBERT
COLLOQUE KINO-QUEBEC. (7E: 1983: GASPE, QUEBEC) – Quebec: Ministere du loisir, de la chasse et de la peche, 1983. SEM105P435 – 3mf – 9 – Can$6.75 – cn Bibl Nat [790]
LES COLLOQUES SCOLAIRES DU XVIE SIECLE / Massebieau, L – 1878 – 9 – fr I.C.S. [370]
COLLOQUIAL ARABIC; SHUWA DIALECT OF BORNU, NIGERIA, AND OF THE REGION OF THE CHAD / Lethem, Gordan James et al – (Grammar & vocabulary, with some proverbs & songs) – London: Publ for the Govt of Nigeria by the Crown Agents for the Colonies, 1920 – 1 – us Res Libr [470]
COLLOQUIUM – (Cont: New Zealand Theological Review) – v1-8. 1964-86 (complete) – 3r – 1 – ATLA S0843 – us A.T.L.A. [073]
COLLOQUIUM DE PECCATO ORIGINIS. INTER D. IACOBUM ANDREAE, ET. M. MATTHIAM FLACCIVM ILLYRICUM... / Andreae d.A E, J – Tvbingae, 1574 – 2mf – 9 – ne IDC [240]
COLLOQUIUM ON MEDICAL PLANTS, ORGANIZED BY THE BOTANICAL SOCIETY OF FRANCE / Paris, R. and G. Dilleman – 1590 2. 1961 – 8 – ne IDC [580]
COLLOQUIUM ON REGULATORY DESIGN IN THEORY AND PRACTICE : 1982-83 AND 1984-85, IN 3 VOLS / Administrative Conference of the U.S. (ACUS) – Acus: np. nd. (all publ) – 3mf – 9 – $4.50 – LLMC 94-342 – us L.L.M.C. [340]

Collyer, James N *see* AN HISTORICAL RECORD OF THE LIGHT HORSE VOLUNTEERS OF LONDON AND WESTMINSTER
Collyer, John *see*
- THE GENERAL PRINCIPLES OF GRAMMAR
- A PRACTICAL TREATISE ON THE LAW OF PARTNERSHIP; WITH AN APPENDIX OF FORMS

Colm, Gerhard *see* BEITRAG ZUR GESCHICHTE UND SOZIOLOGIE DES RUHRAUFSTANDES VOM MARZ-APRIL 1920
Colman, Benjamin *see* PAPERS OF BENJAMIN COLMAN, 1641-1763
Colman, George *see* INKLE AND YARICO: AN OPERA, IN THREE ACTS..
COLMAN-SCHWARZENBERG FAMILY SCRAPBOOK – (Manuscripts, documents, photographs, artifacts, and memorabilia chronicaling the Colman and Schwarzenberg families, early Jewish settlers in Cleveland ca. 1840, and their careers) – 1840-1972 – 1r – 1 – us Western Res [920]
Colmeiro, D M *see* APUNTES PARA LA FLORA DE LAS DOS CASTILLAS
Colmenero, J *see* REPROBACION DEL...ABUSO DE LOS POLVOS DEL QUARANGO...
Colmenero Ledesma, A *see* CURIOSO TRATADO DE LA NATURALEZA Y CALIDAD...DEL CHOCOLATE...
Colmer, Joseph Grose *see*
- ACROSS THE CANADIAN PRAIRIES: A TWO MONTHS' HOLIDAY IN THE DOMINION
- THE DOMINION OF CANADA: AS IT WILL APPEAR TO THE MEMBERS OF THE BRITISH ASSOCIATION FOR THE ADVANCEMENT OF SCIENCE IN 1884: A PAPER READ BEFORE THE SOCIETY OF ARTS, TUESDAY, JANUARY 29, 1884
- RECENT AND PROSPECTIVE DEVELOPMENT IN CANADA: BEING A PAPER READ BEFORE THE FELLOWS OF THE ROYAL COLONIAL INSTITUTE, JANUARY 12, 1886

COLNE TIMES – Lancashire – 1 – uk Microform Academic [072]
Colnett, James *see* A VOYAGE TO THE SOUTH ATLANTIC AND ROUND CAPE HORN INTO THE PACIFIC OCEAN, FOR THE PURPOSE OF EXTENDING THE SPERMACETI WHALE FISHERIES
Cologne. Museum fuer Ostasiatische Kunst *see* VEROEFFENTLICHUNGEN
COLOGNE POST : UPPER SILESIAN EDITION – Oppeln, Germany. 17 June-6 Aug 1921 – 15ft – 1 – uk British Libr Newspaper [072]
THE COLOGNE POST – Eine Tageszeitung veroeffentlicht von der Armee am Rhein. Koeln, Germany. 31 Mar 1919-13 Feb 1920 – 1r – 1 – gw Mikrofilm [072]
THE COLOGNE POST : EINE TAGESZEITUNG VEROEFFENTLICHT VON DER ARMEE AM RHEIN – Koeln, 1919-1920 – 1r – 1 – DM80.00 – gw Mikro Press [072]
Cologne. Regierungsbezirk *see* AMTSBLATT DER REGIERUNG ZU COELN
Colom, Eduardo *see* 17 [I.E DIECISIETE] DE OCTUBRE
Colomb, Philip Howard *see*
- MEMOIRS OF ADMIRAL THE RIGHT HON. SIR ASTLEY COOPER, K.G.C.B
- NAVAL WARFARE

Colombia *see*
- THE DESTINATION AND EARLY CAREER PERFORMANCE OF SECONDARY SCHOOL GRADUATES IN COLOMBIA
- DIARIO OFICIAL
- EVALUACION DEL PROGRAMA GENERAL DE DESARROLLO ECONOMICO Y SOCIAL DE COLOMBIA

COLOMBIA DE NORTE A SUR. 2 VOL. MADRID, 1943 / Perez de Barrados, Jose – Madrid: Razon y Fe, 1946 – 1 – sp Bibl Santa Ana [946]
Colombia. Departamento Administrativo de Planeacion.. *see*
- PLAN CUATRIENAL DE INVERSIONES PUBLICAS NACIONALES, 1961-1964
- PLAN GENERAL DE DESARROLLO ECONOMICO Y SOCIAL

Colombia. Departamento Administrativo Nacional de Estadistica *see* ANUARIO GENERAL DE ESTADISTICA
Colombia. Departamento Nacional de Planeacion *see*
- EL PLAN DE DESAROLLO COLOMBIANO EN MARCHA
- PLAN DE DESARROLLO
- PLAN DE DESARROLLO ECONOMICO Y SOCIAL 1970-73
- PLANES Y PROGRAMAS DE DESARROLLO 1969-72

Colombia. Direccion Nacional de Planeacion.. *see*
- PLAN DE BOYACA, INVERCIONES 1954-1958
- PLAN DE SANTANDER, INVERSIONES 1954-1958

Colombia. Inter-American Economic and Social Council *see* EVALUATION OF THE GENERAL ECONOMIC AND SOCIAL DEVELOPMENT PROGRAM OF COLOMBIA
Colombia. Laws, Statutes, etc *see*
- HISTORIA DE LAS LEYES
- LEYES Y DECRETOS

Colombia. Ministerio de la Economia Nacional *see* EL PLAN DE FOMENTO DE LA ECONOMIA NACIONAL
Colombia. Senado *see* ANALES
LA COLOMBIADE OU LA FOI PORTEE AU NOUVEAU MONDE / DuBoccage, Anne Marie – Paris: Desaint et Saillant, et Durand, 1756. viii, 184p. (Literature Collection) – 3mf – 9 – 8.00 – fr Bibl Nationale [810]
LA COLOMBIE – Vancouver, BC. v1 n4. 27 fev 1946-v1 n6. 27 mar 1946 – 1r – 1 – Can$25.00 – cn Can Microfilming [072]
COLOMBO : SEMANARIO REPUBLICANO – Campanha, 1 Jan 1873-Dec 1874; Jan 1878-Jun 1885 – 1,5,6 – bl Biblioteca [072]
Colombo Plan Conference of National Information Officers *see* SPEECHES
Colomer, B M *see* IDYLLS ET CAPRICES
LE COLON – (Cont by: L'Etoile du Lac) – Roberval, Canada. 1 mar 1917-19 sep 1946 – 6r – 1 – Can$70.00r – cn Can Microfilming [072]
LE COLON – Saint-Sauveur, Quebec, Canada. 23 jun 1884 – 1r – 1 – Can$25.00 – cn Can Microfilming [072]
LE COLON *see* L'ETOILE DU LAC
LE COLON DU LAC SAINT-JEAN – Roberval, Canada. 15 mar 1900-v3 n13. 2 oct 1902 – 1r – 1 – Can$40.00 – cn Can Microfilming [072]
COLON EN BARCELONA. SEVILLA, 1944 / Rumeu de Armas, Antonio – Madrid: Razon y Fe, 1947 – 1 – sp Bibl Santa Ana [946]
COLON ESTREMENA / Fita, Fidel & Fernandez D, Cesareo – Madrid: Tip. de Fortanet, 1903 – 1 – sp Bibl Santa Ana [946]
COLON EXTREMENO? DE VICENTE PAREDES / Fita, Fidel & Fernandez D, Cesareo – Madrid: Fortanet, 1903. B.R.A.H. 42, 1903, pp. 237-238 – sp Bibl Santa Ana [946]
Colon, Hernando *see* HISTORIA DEL ALMIRANTE DON CRISTOBAL COLON. TOMO 1
COLON ITALIANO? COLON ESPANOL? / Bayle, Constantino – Madrid: Razon y Fe, 1923 – 1 – sp Bibl Santa Ana [440]
COLON STARLET – Colon, Panama. 1904; 1905-08; misc dates – 3r – 1 – us L of C Photodup [072]
COLON TELEGRAM – Colon, Panama. 1902-11 (incomplete) – 4r – 1 – us L of C Photodup [072]
LE COLONEL C. M. DE SALABERRY / David, Laurent Olivier – Montreal: s.n., 1872 (Montreal: G. Desbarats). 02512. (Pre-1900 Canadiana) – 9 – cn C.I.H.M. [971]
COLONEL WILLIAM WOOD, SOLDIER, HISTORIAN, ARCHIVIST : AN ANALYTICAL BIBLIOGRAPHY OF THE WRITINGS OF COLONEL WILLIAM WOOD / Clint, Harold Cuthbert – 1951. SEM105P4 – 1mf – 9 – cn Bibl Nat [355]
A COLONIA – S Tome: C Lopes Alpoim, sep 29 1923-apr 10 1924; apr 24-oct 5 1924 – us Res Libr [072]
LA COLONIA ERITREA DALLE SUR ORIGINI FINO AL IO. MARZO 1899... – Parma: L Battei 1899 – us Res Libr [960]
A COLONIA PARAENSE – Manaos, Amazonas. Mar 1896 – 1,5,6 – bl Biblioteca [072]
LA COLONIA SVIZZERA – San Francisco, CA: Swiss Pub Co, [dec 7 1917-1933] – 32r – us Res Libr [071]
EL COLONIAJE Y SUS DETRACTORES. EL PASO, 1927 / Planchet, Regis; ed by Bayle, Constantino – Madrid: Razon y Fe, 1928 – 9 – sp Bibl Santa Ana [972]
COLONIAL ADVOCATE – Hobart, 1828 – 1r – 1 – A$31.00 silver A$27.00 vesicular – at Pascoe [072]
COLONIAL ADVOCATE *see* ADVOCATE
THE COLONIAL AND STATE JUDICIARY OF DELAWARE / Grubb, I C – Wilmington, The Historical Society of Delaware, 1897. Delaware Reel 1. (The Cox Library Collection) – 5 – us Americana [978]
THE COLONIAL AND STATE POLITICAL HISTORY OF HERTFORD COUNTY / Winborne, Benjamin B – Raleigh: Edwards and Broughton, 1906. North Carolina Reel 2. (The Cox Library Collection) – 5 – us Americana [978]
THE COLONIAL CHURCH IN VIRGINIA / Goodwin, Edward Lewis – Milwaukee. 1927 – 1 – us Res Libr [975]
THE COLONIAL CHURCHMAN – Lunenburg, N.S: E A Moody, [1835?-1841?] – 9 – cn C.I.H.M. [240]
THE COLONIAL ERA / Fisher, George Park – New York: Scribner, 1892 (The American history series) – 1mf – us A.T.L.A. [975]
COLONIAL FAMILIES OF THE SOUTHERN STATES OF AMERICA – By Stella P. Hardy, 1911. Item H. History and geneal. of families who settled in the colonies prior to the revolution. 643p, indexed. SW16-0019 – 5 – us A.G.L.L. [978]
COLONIAL FAMILIES OF THE UNITED STATES OF AMERICA – Ed. by George Norbury Mackenzie 1966 followed by Nelson Osgood Rhoades. Orig. publ., 1907-20. 7v. SW16-0080, V300-0039, V300-0040 – 1 – apply; and 5 – us A.G.L.L. [978]
COLONIAL FARMER – Fredericton, Canada. 1863-73 – 3r – 1 – $204.00 – cn Library Assoc [971]
THE COLONIAL FARMER – [Halifax, N.S?]: R Nugent, [1841-1843?] – 9 – cn C.I.H.M. [630]
COLONIAL GAZETTE – London. -w. Dec 1838-Jan 1847. (8 reels) – 1 – uk British Libr Newspaper [072]
COLONIAL HEIGHTS BAPTIST CHURCH. FAIRFIELD COUNTY. COLUMBIA, SOUTH CAROLINA : CHURCH RECORDS – 1971-76 – 1 – 30.24 – us Baptist [240]
COLONIAL HERALD – Charlottetown, Canada. 1840-44 – 2r – 1 – $136.00 – cn Library Assoc [971]
COLONIAL HISTORY OF THE STATE OF NEW YORK / New York. (State) – 1856-1887 – 1 – us UMI [978]
COLONIAL HOMES – v.5-. 1979- – 1,5,6,9 – us UMI [720]
COLONIAL LAW JOURNAL : REPORTS OF CASES ARGUED AND DETERMINED IN THE SUPREME COURT OF NEW ZEALAND, AND ON APPEAL TO THE COURT OF APPEAL OF NEW ZEALAND – (Covers selected cases from 1865-75 and includes some articles, a 14-pg biography of Wilson Gray, and other editorial matter. Missing title-pg) – n.p. 1v. n.d. – 2mf – 9 – $3.00 – LLMC 96-016 – us L.L.M.C. [340]
COLONIAL LAWYER – (Superseded by: William and Mary Bill of Rights Journal) – College of William and Mary. v1-20. 1967-91 – 9 – $102.00 set – us Hein [340]
COLONIAL LAWYER *see* WILLIAM AND MARY BILL OF RIGHTS JOURNAL
COLONIAL MICROFICHE / ed by Australian Bureau of Statistics – (New South Wales (558mf) A$2,200.00. Queensland (400mf) A$1,600.00. South Australia (380mf) A$1,500.00. Tasmania (387mf) A$1,500.00. Victoria (866mf) A$3,450.00. Western Australia (416mf) A$1,650.00. A Statistical Account of the Seven Colonies of Australasia (57mf) A$300.00) – 3035mf – 9 – A$11,000.00 full set – at Statistics [980]
COLONIAL MICROFICHE : AUSTRALIA/NEW ZEALAND, STATISTICAL ACCOUNT OF THE SEVEN COLONIES OF AUSTRALASIA / Coghlan, T A – 57mf – A$300.00 set – at Statistics [980]
COLONIAL MICROFICHE : NEW SOUTH WALES, A STATISTICAL, HISTORICAL AND POLITICAL DESCRIPTION OF THE COLONY / Wentworth, W C – 5mf – 9 – at Statistics [980]
COLONIAL MICROFICHE : NEW SOUTH WALES, ANALYTICAL VIEW OF THE CENSUS – 1841, 1846 – 3mf – 9 – at Statistics [980]
COLONIAL MICROFICHE : NEW SOUTH WALES, CENSUS – 1833, 1836, 1841, 1846, 1851 – Abstract Only 1856, 1861, 1871, 1881, 1891, 1901 – 54mf – 9 – at Statistics [980]
COLONIAL MICROFICHE : NEW SOUTH WALES, CENSUS INDUSTRIAL RETURNS – 1891 – 2mf – 9 – at Statistics [980]
COLONIAL MICROFICHE : NEW SOUTH WALES, CENSUS LIFE ASSURANCE – 1901 – 2mf – 9 – at Statistics [980]
COLONIAL MICROFICHE : NEW SOUTH WALES, HANDBOOK TO THE STATISTICAL REGISTER – 1885-1886. Continued by Handbook of Statistics 1887-1888 – 16mf – 9 – at Statistics [980]
COLONIAL MICROFICHE : NEW SOUTH WALES, REGISTRATION. ANNUAL REPORT FROM REGISTRAR GENERAL – 1856-1866. Continued by Vital Statistics. Annual Report from the Registrar General on Vital Statistics 1867-1885... – 67mf – 9 – at Statistics [980]
COLONIAL MICROFICHE : NEW SOUTH WALES, STATISTICAL RETURNS – 1822/1842-1836/1845. Continued by Statistics 1837/1846-1848/1857. Continued by Statistical Register 1849/1858-1900 – 273mf – 9 – at Statistics [980]
COLONIAL MICROFICHE : NEW SOUTH WALES, STATISTICAL SURVEY OF NEW SOUTH WALES / Coghlan, T A – 4mf – 9 – at Statistics [980]
COLONIAL MICROFICHE : NEW SOUTH WALES, WEALTH AND PROGRESS (OFFICIAL YEARBOOK 1-13) – No 1, 1886/1887 – No 13, 1900/1901 – 132mf – 9 – at Statistics [980]
COLONIAL MICROFICHE : QUEENSLAND, BLUE BOOK – 1869-1900 – 80mf – 9 – at Statistics [980]
COLONIAL MICROFICHE : QUEENSLAND, CENSUS – 1861, 1864, 1868, 1871, 1876, 1881, 1886, 1891, 1901 – 54mf – 9 – at Statistics [980]
COLONIAL MICROFICHE : QUEENSLAND, QUEENSLAND PAST AND PRESENT – No 1 (1896) – No 2 (1897) – 9 – at Statistics [980]
COLONIAL MICROFICHE : QUEENSLAND, REGISTRATION OF BIRTHS, MARRIAGES AND DEATHS – No 1 (1860)... – 65mf – 9 – at Statistics [980]
COLONIAL MICROFICHE : QUEENSLAND, REPORT OF THE REGISTRAR GENERAL ON RETURNS ON AGRICULTURE AND LIVE STOCK – 1883-1896... – 18mf – 9 – at Statistics [980]
COLONIAL MICROFICHE : QUEENSLAND, STATISTICAL REGISTER – 1859-1868... – 174mf – 9 – at Statistics [980]
COLONIAL MICROFICHE : SOUTH AUSTRALIA, AGRICULTURAL AND LIVE STOCK STATISTICS – 1860/61-1876 – 16mf – 9 – at Statistics [980]
COLONIAL MICROFICHE : SOUTH AUSTRALIA, ANNUAL REPORT OF THE REGISTRAR GENERAL OF BIRTHS, DEATHS, AND MARRIAGES – 1862-1900 – 39mf – 9 – at Statistics [980]
COLONIAL MICROFICHE : SOUTH AUSTRALIA, BLUE BOOK – 1838-1865 – 101mf – 9 – at Statistics [980]
COLONIAL MICROFICHE : SOUTH AUSTRALIA, CENSUS – 1844, 1846, 1851, 1855 – Abstract Only 1860, 1861, 1866, 1871, 1876, 1881, 1891, 1901 – 52mf – 9 – at Statistics [980]
COLONIAL MICROFICHE : SOUTH AUSTRALIA, STATISTICAL RETURNS – 1841-1858 (Incomplete) Continued by Statistical Register 1859-1900 – 170mf – 9 – at Statistics [980]
COLONIAL MICROFICHE : SOUTH AUSTRALIA, STATISTICAL SKETCH – 1876 – 2mf – 9 – at Statistics [980]
COLONIAL MICROFICHE : TASMANIA, BLUE BOOK – 1822-1855 (Incomplete) – 123mf – 9 – at Statistics [980]
COLONIAL MICROFICHE : TASMANIA, CENSUS – 1842, 1848, 1851, 1857, 1861, 1870 – Abstract Only 1881, 1891, 1901 – 22mf – at Statistics [980]
COLONIAL MICROFICHE : TASMANIA, HANDBOOK – 1891-1893 – 5mf – 9 – at Statistics [980]
COLONIAL MICROFICHE : TASMANIA, OFFICIAL HANDBOOK – 1883, 1887 – 4mf – 9 – at Statistics [980]
COLONIAL MICROFICHE : TASMANIA, OFFICIAL RECORD (TASMANIA) – 1890-1892 – 24mf – 9 – at Statistics [980]
COLONIAL MICROFICHE : TASMANIA, STATISTICAL RETURNS (VAN DIEMEN'S LAND) – 1824/1839 – 2mf – 9 – at Statistics [980]
COLONIAL MICROFICHE : TASMANIA, STATISTICAL SUMMARY (TASMANIA) – 1816/1865 – 1mf – 9 – at Statistics [980]
COLONIAL MICROFICHE : TASMANIA, STATISTICAL TABLES (VAN DIEMEN'S LAND) – 1804/1823 – 1mf – 9 – at Statistics [980]

COLONIAL MICROFICHE : TASMANIA, STATISTICS – 1838/1841-1865 (Incomplete) Continued by Statistics of the Colony 1866-1900 – 205mf – 9 – at Statistics [980]
COLONIAL MICROFICHE : VICTORIA, ABSTRACT OF THE STATISTICS – 1893/98-1900 – 3mf – 9 – at Statistics [980]
COLONIAL MICROFICHE : VICTORIA, AGRICULTURAL AND LIVE STOCK STATISTICS – 1857-1867 – 21mf – 9 – at Statistics [980]
COLONIAL MICROFICHE : VICTORIA, ANNUAL REPORT OF THE REGISTRAR GENERAL ON BIRTHS, DEATHS AND MARRIAGES – 1854-1858 – 5mf – 9 – at Statistics [980]
COLONIAL MICROFICHE : VICTORIA, BLUE BOOK – 1851-1855... – 48mf – 9 – at Statistics [980]
COLONIAL MICROFICHE : VICTORIA, CENSUS – 1854, 1857, 1861, 1871, 1881, 1891, 1901 – 100mf – 9 – at Statistics [980]
COLONIAL MICROFICHE : VICTORIA, CRIMINAL STATISTICS – 1858-1867 – 13mf – 9 – at Statistics [980]
COLONIAL MICROFICHE : VICTORIA, GOLD FIELD STATISTICS – 1860-1863. Continued by Mineral Statistics 1864-1883 – 29mf – 9 – at Statistics [980]
COLONIAL MICROFICHE : VICTORIA, HANDBOOK TO THE COLONY – 1885 – 2mf – 9 – at Statistics [980]
COLONIAL MICROFICHE : VICTORIA, NOSOLOGICAL INDEX – 1863 – 1mf – 9 – at Statistics [980]
COLONIAL MICROFICHE : VICTORIA, PORT PHILLIP DISTRICT STATISTICS MISCELLANEOUS – 1836-1867/59 – 53mf – 9 – at Statistics [980]
COLONIAL MICROFICHE : VICTORIA, REPORT OF THE REGISTRAR GENERAL ON THE PROGRESS AND STATISTICS OF VICTORIA FROM 1851 TO 1858 – 1mf – 9 – at Statistics [980]
COLONIAL MICROFICHE : VICTORIA, STATISTICAL NOTES ON THE PROGRESS OF VICTORIA – 1st 1835/1860. Continued by Progress of Victoria: A Statistical Essay 2nd 1867, 3rd 1873 – 7mf – at Statistics [980]
COLONIAL MICROFICHE : VICTORIA, STATISTICAL REGISTER...FROM THE FOUNDATION OF THE COLONY WITH AN ASTRONOMICAL CALENDER FOR 1855 – 7mf – 9 – at Statistics [980]
COLONIAL MICROFICHE : VICTORIA, STATISTICS OF THE FRIENDLY SOCIETIES – 1873 – 2mf – 9 – at Statistics [980]
COLONIAL MICROFICHE : VICTORIA, YEARBOOK – No 1 (1873) – No 22 (1895/98) – 185mf – 9 – at Statistics [980]
COLONIAL MICROFICHE : VICTORIA,PORT PHILLIP DISTRICT STATISTICS – 1850... – 389mf – 9 – at Statistics [980]
COLONIAL MICROFICHE : WESTERN AUSTRALIA, BLUE BOOK – 1837-1895 – 250mf – 9 – at Statistics [980]
COLONIAL MICROFICHE : WESTERN AUSTRALIA, CENSUS – 1848, 1854, 1859, 1861, 1870, 1881, 1891, 1901 – 36mf – 9 – at Statistics [980]
COLONIAL MICROFICHE : WESTERN AUSTRALIA, MISCELLANEOUS STATISTICAL RETURNS FOR BUSSELTON – 1841/1850 – 1mf – 9 – at Statistics [980]
COLONIAL MICROFICHE : WESTERN AUSTRALIA, MONTHLY STATISTICAL ABSTRACT JUNE-DEC. 1900 – 2mf – 9 – at Statistics [980]
COLONIAL MICROFICHE : WESTERN AUSTRALIA, PAPERS RELATIVE TO THE COLONY – 1837 – 1mf – 9 – at Statistics [980]
COLONIAL MICROFICHE : WESTERN AUSTRALIA, REPORT OF THE REGISTRAR GENERAL ON THE VITAL STATISTICS (ANNUAL) – 1889-1896 – 8mf – 9 – at Statistics [980]
COLONIAL MICROFICHE : WESTERN AUSTRALIA, REPORT OF THE REGISTRAR GENERAL ON THE VITAL STATISTICS (QUARTERLY RETURNS) – 1888 (Dec Only)-1901 – 14mf – 9 – at Statistics [980]
COLONIAL MICROFICHE : WESTERN AUSTRALIA, STATISTICAL REGISTER OF THE COLONY – 1896-1900 – 54mf – 9 – at Statistics [980]
COLONIAL MICROFICHE : WESTERN AUSTRALIA, YEARBOOK – 1886-1900/1901 – 50mf – 9 – at Statistics [980]
COLONIAL NAMES – Genealogical records of births, deaths & marriages from family bible, 1581-1917. Item B. SW16-0225 – 5 – us A.G.L.L. [920]
COLONIAL NUMBERED SERIES / Great Britain. Foreign and Commonwealth Office – (Individual sections available) – London. n1-269, 271-320, 323-352. 1924-60 – 755mf – 9 – $5.00f – us Ross [941]
COLONIAL OFFICE RECORDS ON EARLY AMERICAN HISTORY AND INDIAN AFFAIRS / Great Britain. Colonial Office – (Part One: Westward Expansion, 1700-1783. 1982. $1,150.00; Part Two: The Board of Trade, 1689-1775. 1982. $575.00; Part Three: The French and Indian War, 1754-1763. 1982. $770.00; Part Four: Royal Instructions and Commissions to Colonial Officials, 1702-1771. 1983. $1,150.00; Part Five: The American Revolution, 1792-1784. 1983. $1,450.00) – 1982 – 1 – us UPA [975]
COLONIAL PARLIAMENTARY BULLETIN – London, African Press Agency. v1 n3-v3 n6 mar/apr 1946-sep 1948 – us Res Libr [320]
COLONIAL PATRIOT – Pictou, Canada. 1827-34 – 2r – 1 – $136.00 – cn Library Assoc [971]
COLONIAL PHRENOLOGICAL JOURNAL AND REPOSITORY OF SCIENCE, LITERATURE, AND GENERAL INTELLIGENCE – Pictou, N.S: A B Parker, [1860] – 9 – cn C.I.H.M. [130]
THE COLONIAL PROTESTANT AND JOURNAL OF LITERATURE AND SCIENCE – Montreal: Printed and Published by R Campbell, 1848-[1849] – 9 – cn C.I.H.M. [240]
COLONIAL PURPOSES IN WEST IRIAN; AN EXPOSE OF DUTCH INTENTIONS / Indonesia. Departemen Luar Negeri – SE-5996 1. 1962 – 9 – ne IDC [321]
THE COLONIAL RECORDS OF THE STATE OF GEORGIA / Georgia – v1-22 and Suppls. Comp. by Allen D. Candler. F-0110- – 9 – us A.G.L.L. [978]
COLONIAL RESEARCH PUBLICATIONS / Great Britain. Foreign and Commonwealth Office – (Individual sections available) – London. n1-13,15,17-25. 1948-61 – 41mf – 9 – $5.00f – us Ross [941]
THE COLONIAL REVIEW – Saint John, N.B: J & A McMillan, [1862-186-?] – 9 – cn C.I.H.M. [971]
COLONIAL SECRETARY'S PAPERS, 1788-1825 / The Archives Authority of New South Wales – (Set includes index, leaflet and guide) – 1989 – 72r 312mf – 9,1 – A$3,500.00 reels A$1,500.00 mf A$500.00 index – 0-7240-8038-4 – at N.S.W. Archives [980]
COLONIAL SESSION LAWS – 9 – $5,250.00 set – us Hein [340]
COLONIAL STANDARD – Pictou, Canada. 1862-73 – 4r – 1 – $260.00 – cn Library Assoc [971]
THE COLONIAL STANDARD – (Continued as: The Colonial Standard and Jamaica Despatch. Kingston, 1850(July)-1853(June); 1864(June)-1879(July); 1879(Nov.)-1895(June)) – Kingston, 1850(Jan.-June) – 45r – EF-7/3 – ne IDC [990]
Colonial Williamsburg Foundation *see* EARLY AMERICAN HISTORY RESEARCH REPORTS FROM THE COLONIAL WILLIAMSBURG FOUNDATION LIBRARY
COLONIAL WILLIAMSBURG RESEARCH COLLECTIONS IN MICROFORM : A GUIDE – 9 – $710.00 – 1-55655-284-X – us UPA [975]
COLONIAL-HISPANIC LEGAL DOCUMENTS (18TH-19TH CENTURIES) / U.S. Library of Congress. Law Library – 820 items on 13 reels. Jurisdictions: Colombia, Mexico, Peru, Portugal, Puerto Rico – 1 – 23.00r – us L of C Photodup [340]
UNE COLONIE DE COMMERCE... / Bacquart, A – Paris, 1907 – 3mf – 9 – ILM-331/1 – ne IDC [340]
LE COLONIE STRANIERE... / Fedozzi, P – Bologna, 1895 – 1mf – 1 – ILM-3353/1 – ne IDC [327]
LES COLONIES – St. Pierre. Martinique. French West Indies. Omissions. 1881-1902 – 1 – us UMI [072]
THE COLONIES – London. The Colonies and India. 17 Jan 1872-20 May 1898.-f. 40mqn reels – 1 – uk British Libr Newspaper [072]
THE COLONIES, 1492-1950 / Thwaites, Reuben Gold – 4th ed. New York: Longmans, Green, 1893 c1890. xviii,301p. maps – 1 – us U.W. Library [975]
LES COLONIES AGRICOLES – Port-au-Prince: [s.n. v1 n1-4 june-dec 1938; v2-v3 n5/1 aug 1939-apr/jun 1940 – 2 sheets – us Res Libr [630]
THE COLONIES AND INDIA IN LONDON: READ BEFORE THE LITERARY AND SCIENTIFIC SOCIETY OF OTTAWA, 5TH APRIL, 1887 / Cross, Thomas – Ottawa?: s.n., 188? (Ottawa: Woodburn). 02134. (Pre-1900 Canadiana) – 9 – cn C.I.H.M. [971]
THE COLONIES, AND THEIR CONNECTION WITH THE MOTHER COUNTRY: WITH A STATISTICAL LIST OF THE BRITISH EMPIRE IN 1886 APPENDED / Chamberlain, Walter – An address to the members of the above institute, on Tuesday, February 1st, 1887. Birmingham: J. Allday, 1887? 00546. (Pre-1900 Canadiana) – 9 – cn C.I.H.M. [971]
COLONIES DES VALLEES DE LA ROUGE, DE LA KIAMIKA ET DE LA LIEVRE – Quebec, 1898? SEM105P959 – 1mf – 9 – Can$2.25 – cn Bibl Nat [910]
LES COLONIES EUROPEENNES DU MARKLAND ET DE L'ESCORILAND (DOMINATION CANADIENNE) AU XIVE SIECLE ET LES VESTIGES QUI EN SUBSISTERENT JUSQU'AUX XVIE ET XVIIE SIECLES / Beauvois, Eugene – Nancy, France: G. Crepin-Leblond, 1877. 04362. (Pre-1900 Canadiana) – 9 – cn C.I.H.M. [971]
DES COLONIES FRANCAISES. ABOLITION IMMEDIATE DE L'ESCLAVAGE / Schoelcher, Victor – Pagnerre. 1842 – 9 – 15.00 – fr Orientalistes [305]
DES COLONIES FRANCAISES. ABOLITION IMMEDIATE DE L'ESCLAVAGE / Schoelcher, Victor – (Slave Trade and Abolitionism in France series). 1842 – 9 – fr Hachette [305]
LES COLONIES PERDUES: OUVRAGE ILLUSTRE DE 65 GRAVURES SUR BOIS / Canivet, Charles – Paris: Jouvet, 1884. 00464. (Pre-1900 Canadiana) – 9 – cn C.I.H.M. [971]
LE COLONISATEUR – Montreal, Canada. 2 jan 1862-27 jun 1863 – 1r – 1 – Can$35.00 – cn Can Microfilming [072]
LE COLONISATEUR CANADIEN / ed by Carufel, L-E – Montreal, Canada. 1 dec 1885-22 dec 1898 – 1r – 1 – Can$45.00 – cn Can Microfilming [072]
LA COLONISATION – Sherbrooke. n1 1886-n27 15 dec 1889 – 1r – 1 – Can$50.00 – cn Can Microfilming [072]
LA COLONISATION BIEN FAITE PAR LES OUVRIERS ET LES TRAVAILLEURS / Ancien Colon – 1897. 00719. (Pre-1900 Canadiana) – 9 – cn C.I.H.M. [971]
LA COLONISATION DANS LES CANTON DE L'EST / Chartier, Jean Baptiste – St. Hyacinthe, Quebec: Courrier de St. Hyacinthe, 1871. 02980. (Pre-1900 Canadiana) – 9 – cn C.I.H.M. [971]
LA COLONISATION FRANCAISE SOUS L'ANCIEN REGIME / Saintoyant, J F – 2v. Paris. 1929. BA-349 2 – 8 – ne IDC [900]
LA COLONISATION FRANCAISE SOUS L'ANCIEN REGIME / Saintoyant, J F – A 349. 2 v. 1929 – 9 – ne IDC [360]
LE COLONISE – (Filmed with Les continents and 11 other titles) – Paris: Isaac Becon, nov 15-dec 20 1936 – us Res Libr [944]
COLONIST – Dominica. 1848-1866 – 1 – us UMI [072]
COLONIST – Sydney, 1835-40 – 3r – 1 – A$93.00 silver A$81.00 vesicular – at Pascoe [072]
THE COLONIST – (Cont: Manitoba Colonist) – Winnipeg: The Colonist, [1890-1898] – 9 – cn C.I.H.M. [971]
THE COLONIST – Georgetown, Guyana. 11 Dec 1863-9 Feb 1884.-d. 38 reels – 1 – uk British Libr Newspaper [072]
THE COLONIST – Maryborough, Australia. 3 Jan 1885-15 Jul 1916; 7 Apr 1917-30 Mar 1940.-w. 106mqn reels – 1 – uk British Libr Newspaper [072]
THE COLONIST – Stevenson, CA. 1911-1912 – 1r – 1 – $50.00 – B06058 – us Library Micro [071]
THE COLONIST – Sydney, Australia. -w. 1836-37. 1 reel – 1 – uk British Libr Newspaper [072]
THE COLONIST – Winnipeg, Canada. -m. June 1892-Nov 1897. 2 reels – 1 – uk British Libr Newspaper [072]
COLONIZACION Y PARCELACIONES / Merchan Merchan, Felipe & Lopez Santamaria, Francisco – Badajoz: Graficas Iberia, 1950 – 1 – sp Bibl Santa Ana [946]
COLONIZATION AND ENVIRONMENT : LAND SETTLEMENT PROJECTS IN CENTRAL AMERICA / Jones, Jeffrey R – 9 – $12.00 – ja U.N. Univ [307]
COLONIZATION AND MISSIONS : A HISTORICAL EXAMINATION OF THE STATE OF SOCIETY IN WESTERN AFRICA, AS FORMED BY PAGANISM AND MUHAMMEDANISM, SLAVERY, THE SLAVE TRADE AND PIRACY / Tracy, Joseph – Boston: T.R. Marvin, 1844 – 1mf – us A.T.L.A. [960]
COLONIZATION AND REVOLUTION, 1775 – (Regional History) – 1 – us Ross [975]
COLONIZATION HERALD – Series 1, no.63 (Oct. 21, 1837). Philadelphia, Pennsylvania Colonization Society sometimes published as: Colonization Herald and General Register. With Liberia Christian Advocate, and New York Colonization Journal – 1 – us U.W. Library [073]
THE COLONIZER – Toronto: Temperance Colonization Society, [1881?-18– or 19–] – 9 – cn C.I.H.M. [971]
THE COLONIZER; AN IMPERIAL MEDIUM OF COLONIZATION, EMIGRATION, EXPLORATION, AND TRAVEL – v. 1-37, no. 1-439. Jan 1896-Jul 1932 – 1 – 169.00 – us L of C Photodup [073]
LA COLONIZZAZIONE DELLA CIRENAICA NELL'ANTICHITA E NEL PRESENTE – Bengasi: Stabilimento tipografico Fratelli Pavone, 1934 – 1 – us Res Libr [960]
LA COLONIZZAZIONE EUROPEA NELL'EST AFRICA : ITALIA, INGHILTERRA, GERMANIA / Chiesi, Gustavo – Torino: Unione tipografico-editrice torinese 1909 – us Res Libr [960]
Colonna, F *see*
– DISCOURS DU SONGE DE POLIPHILE
– LA SAMBUCA LINCEO, OVERO DELL'INSTROMENTO MUSICO PERFETTO LIB 3, DI FABIO COLONNA LINCEO NE'QUALIOLTRE LA DESCRITTIONE
LA COLONNA ITALIANA IN SPAGNA – Paris, 1936? Fiche W 806. (Blodgett Collection of Spanish Civil War Pamphlets) – 9 – us H.U. College Libr [946]
Colonna, M A *see* I TRION FI FESTE, ET LIVREE FATTE DALLI SIGNORI CONSERVATORI, ET POPOLO ROMANO, ET DA TUTTE LE ARTI DI ROMA, ...
LES COLONS DU SALTUS BURUNITAKUS MOMMSEN / Esmein, Adhemar – Paris. 1880. 20p. (Historical Studies Series) – 9 – 3.00 – fr Bibl Nationale [900]
THE COLONY AND PROVINCIAL REPORTER – (Colonial and Provincial Reporter West Africa Mail and Trade Gazette). Freetown. Sierra Leone. -w. 25 May 1911-Dec 1932. (Imperfect). (19 reels) – 1 – uk British Libr Newspaper [072]
THE COLONY NEWS – Stevenson, CA. 1911-1912 – 1r – 1 – $50.00 – B06059 – us Library Micro [071]
THE COLONY OF BRITISH HONDURAS, ITS RESOURCES AND PROSPECTS. / Morris, Daniel – London. 1883 – 1 – us Res Libr [972]
THE COLONY OF NATAL : AN ACCOUNT OF THE CHARACTERISTICS AND CAPABILITIES OF THIS BRITISH DEPENDENCY – (Publ under the authority of the Govt Immigration Board for the guidance and info of emigrants) – London: Jarold, [1860] – 1 – us Res Libr [960]
COLOPHONS DE MANUSCRITS... / Bonaeret, Benedictius de – Madrid: Graf. Calleja, 1966 – 1 – sp Bibl Santa Ana [240]
COLOQUES FAMILIERS / Meurier, G – 1568 – 9 – fr I.C.S. [440]
COLOQUIO : PUBLICACION PERIODICA DEL CONGRESO JUDIO LATINOAMERICANO, RAMA DEL CONGRESO JUDIO MUNDIAL – Buenos Aires: Congreso Judio Latinoamericano. n1-24. 1979-92 – 2r – us Res Libr [972]
COLOR : A TIP-TOP WORLD MAGAZINE – v1-11. 1944-57 – 5r – 1 – us Ross [073]
COLOR COMPUTER MAGAZINE – 1984 – 1 – us UMI [000]
COLOR LINE; A MONTHLY ROUND-UP OF THE FACTS OF NEGRO AMERICAN PROGRESS AND OF THE GROWTH OF AMERICAN DEMOCRACY – v1-2 2+6 (all publ). 1946-1947 – 1mf – 9 – $55.00 – us UPA [975]
COLOR RESEARCH AND APPLICATION – v1-1976 1; v2- 1976- 5,6,9 – us UMI [600]
COLOR RESEARCH AND APPLICATION – v1-11. 1976-86 – 1,5,6 – us Princeton Micro [073]

COLOR VISION IN BEES : SIMILARITY MEASURES AND METRIC SCALES OF THE PERCEPTUAL SPACE / Backhaus, Werner – 1993 – 2mf – 9 – DM98.00 – 3-89349-650-5 – gw Hänsel [574]
COLOR VISION IN HONEYBEES AND OTHER INSECTS / Backhaus, Werner – 1993 – 3mf – 9 – DM98.00 – 3-89349-648-3 – gw Hänsel [574]
COLORADO : COLORADO REVISED STATUTES – Bradford-Robinson, 1973-Feb 1996 update – 9 – $791.50 set – us Hein [340]
COLORADO : SESSION LAWS OF AMERICAN STATES AND TERRITORIES – 1859-1995 – 9 – $1,424.00 set – us Hein [340]
Colorado *see*
- CENSUS, 1885
- COLORADO LAW REPORTER
- COLORADO NISI PRIUS DECISIONS
- REPORTS AND OPINIONS (A-G)
- REPORTS, PRE-NRS
- STATE LABOR REPORTS

COLORADO A AND M NEWS / Colorado. State University. Agricultural and Mechanical College. Fort Collins – nos.1-10. 1946-56 – 1,5,6 – us Spaulding [630]
COLORADO ADDENDUM TO GREEN'S PLEADING AND PRACTICE / Green, Thomas Andre – St. Louis: Gilbert, 1880. 123p. LL-601 – 1 – us L of C Photodup [340]
Colorado. Agricultural Experiment Station *see*
- COLORADO FARM AND HOME RESEARCH
- COLORADO FARM BULLETIN

Colorado. Agricultural Experiment Station. Fort Collins *see*
- ANNUAL REPORT
- BULLETIN
- GENERAL SERIES
- PRESS BULLETIN
- PROGRESS REPORT
- RESEARCH BULLETIN
- SCIENTIFIC JOURNAL SERIES
- SPECIAL RIVER BULLETIN
- TECHNICAL BULLETIN

Colorado. Agricultural Experiment Station. Fort Collins. *see* B NOTES
Colorado. Agricultural Extension Service *see* COLORADO EXTENSION RECORD
Colorado. Agricultural Extension Service. Fort Collins Cooperative Extension Service *see*
- BULLETIN
- BULLETIN, D SERIES
- CIRCULAR

COLORADO AND ITS PEOPLE: PERSONAL AND FAMILY HISTORY – New York, 1948. Colorado reel 3. (Cox Library Collection) – 5 – us Americana [978]
COLORADO APPELLATE REPORTS / Colorado. Court of Appeals – (No Pre-NRS vols. Updates planned) – v1-27. 1891-1917 – 59mf (1:42) 21mf (1:24) – 9 – $297.00 – LLMC 84-126 – us L.L.M.C. [340]
COLORADO APPELLATE REPORTS *see*
- COLORADO LAW REPORTER
- COLORADO NISI PRIUS DECISIONS

COLORADO ATTORNEY GENERAL REPORTS AND OPINIONS – (6 1887-1966 $105.00. 9 1967-1995 $567.00) – 1887-1995 – 6,9 – $672.00set – us Hein [340]
COLORADO BAPTIST BULLETIN – Denver. Colorado and Wyoming Baptist Bulletin/ Colorado Baptist. Colorado Baptist State Convention, Wyoming Baptist Convention. 1904, 1911-12, 1915, 1917, 1929-30, 1931-72. Incomplete. Single reels available – 1 – $120.10 – us A.B.H.S. [240]
COLORADO BAR ASSOCIATION ANNUAL REPORTS – (Cont by: Colorado Looseleaf Service, 1941-46) – v1-43. 1884-1940 (all publ) – 50mf – 9 – $225.00 – LLMC 84-442 – us L.L.M.C. [340]
COLORADO CEMETERY INSCRIPTIONS / McQueary, Lela O – Z10-0001 – 5 – us A.G.L.L. [920]
Colorado. College of Agriculture *see* AGRICOLA ARIDUS
Colorado. Committee on Child Welfare Legislation *see* FIRST AND SECOND REPORTS OF GOVERNOR SHOUP'S COMMITTEE ON CHILD WELFARE LEGISLATION FOR COLORADO
Colorado. Court of Appeals *see* COLORADO APPELLATE REPORTS
Colorado. Dept of Natural Resources. Div of Game, Fish and Parks *see* 1970 COLORADO COMPREHENSIVE OUTDOOR RECREATION PLAN
Colorado Division of Parks and Outdoor recreation *see* INTERIM COLORADO COMPREHENSIVE OUTDOOR RECREATION PLAN, 1974
COLORADO EXTENSION RECORD / Colorado. Agricultural Extension Service – v.4-15. 1934-44 – 1,5,6 – us Spaulding [630]
COLORADO FARM AND HOME RESEARCH / Colorado. Agricultural Experiment Station – v1-19 1950-69 – 1,5,6 – us Spaulding [630]
COLORADO FARM BULLETIN / Colorado. Agricultural Experiment Station – nos.1-8. 1939-46 – 1,5,6 – us Spaulding [630]
COLORADO GENEALOGIST – v1-21, 1941-1960. F-0946 to F-0964 – 9 – us A.G.L.L. [073]
Colorado Genealogist *see* INDEX
COLORADO HEROLD – Denver, CO: Harburg & Co, sep 2 1917-jun 27 1918 – 4r – us Res Libr [071]
COLORADO JOURNAL OF INTERNATIONAL ENVIRONMENTAL LAW AND POLICY – v1-6. 1990-95 – 9 – $75.00 set – us Hein [333]
COLORADO LAW REPORTER / Colorado – v1-24. 1880-1884 (all publ) – 31mf – 9 – $46.50 – LLMC 91-026 – us L.L.M.C. [340]
COLORADO LAW REPORTER – Denver. v1-4. 1880-84 – 1 – $40.00 – us Hein [073]
COLORADO LAW REPORTER – v1-4. 1880-84 (all publ) – 9 – LLMC 82-914 – us L.L.M.C. [073]
Colorado. Laws, Statutes, etc *see* THE JUVENILE COURT LAWS OF THE STATE OF COLORADO
COLORADO LAWYER – v1-24. 1971-95 – 9 – $1,258.00 set – us Hein [340]
COLORADO LAWYER – (v.8-. 1979- 5,6,9) – v.1-. 1972- – 1 – us UMI [073]
COLORADO LOOSELEAF SERVICE *see* COLORADO BAR ASSOCIATION ANNUAL REPORTS
COLORADO MAGAZINE – (1976-80. 1,5,6,9) – v52-57. 1975-80 – 1 – us UMI [073]
COLORADO NISI PRIUS DECISIONS / Colorado – 1v. 1900-1902 (all publ) – 6mf – 9 – $9.00 – LLMC 91-027 – us L.L.M.C. [340]
COLORADO RANCHER AND FARMER – Denver. Col. 1948- – 1 – us UMI [071]
Colorado School of Mines *see* SUBJECT CATALOG OF THE ARTHUR LAKES LIBRARY OF THE COLORADO SCHOOL OF MINES
Colorado. State Bar Association *see* PROCEEDINGS 1882-1940
Colorado. State University. Agricultural and Mechanical College. Fort Collins *see* COLORADO A AND M NEWS
THE COLORADO STATESMAN – Denver. Colo. aug. 16, 1940; Oct. 30, 1948 – 1 – us NY Public [071]
Colorado. Supreme Court *see* COLORADO SUPREME COURT REPORTS
COLORADO SUPREME COURT REPORTS / Colorado. Supreme Court – (Pre-NRS: v1-6 1864-83 15mf $67.00. Updates planned) – v1-66. 1864-1919 – 152mf – 9 – $799.00 – LLMC 84-125 – us L.L.M.C. [340]
Colorado. Synod (Cum. Pres. Ch.) *see* MINUTES, 1854-1887
Colorado, Vicente *see* FUNDAMENTOS DE SOCIOLOGIA
THE COLORADOAN – Fort Collins. Colo. 1972- – 1 – us UMI [071]
COLORADO-ROCKY MOUNTAIN WEST – v14-16, no.5. Sept 1978-Mar-Apr 1980 – 1,5,6,9 – us UMI [550]
COLORADSKE NOVICE – Pueblo, CO, 1905 – 1mf or 1 reel – 9,1 – us I.H.R.C. [975]
COLORADSKE SOLNCE – Denver, CO, 1908 – 1mf or 1 reel – 9,1 – us I.H.R.C. [975]
COLORED AMERICAN – New York, 1840-41 – 1r – 1 – us Ross [071]
THE COLORED AMERICAN – New York. Mar 14 1840-Mar 13 1841 – 1 – us NY Public [071]
THE COLORED AMERICAN FROM SLAVERY TO HONORABLE CITIZENSHIP / Gibson, John W & Crogman, William Henry – (Special features: National Negro Business League and introduction by Prof Booker T Washington. Club Movement among Negro Women by Fannie Barrier Williams) – 1902 – 1r – 1 – us Ross [976]
COLORED AMERICAN MAGAZINE – 1-17 2+5 (all publ). 1900-1909 – 89mf – 9 – $325.00 – us UPA [305]
COLORED AMERICAN MAGAZINE – v1-17. 1900-09 – 2r – 1 – us Ross [073]
THE COLORED AMERICAN MAGAZINE – v. 1-17. May 1900-Nov 1909 – 1 – 74.00 – us L of C Photodup [073]
COLORED BAPTISTS FAMILY TREE: A COMPENDIUM OF ORGANIZED NEGRO BAPTISTS CHURCH HISTORY / Moses, W H – Nashville, TN: The Sunday School Publishing Board of the National Baptist Convention, U.S.A., Inc., c1925 – 1r – 1 – $5.00 – us Baptist [240]
THE COLORED CITIZEN – Bakersfield, CA. Apr-Oct 1914 – 1r – 1 – $50.00 – C02041 – us Library Micro [071]
THE COLORED INVENTOR : A RECORD OF FIFTY YEARS / Baker, Henry Edwin – New York, 1913 – 1r – 1 – us Ross [975]
THE COLORED LADY EVANGELIST: BEING THE LIFE, LABORS AND EXPERIENCES OF MRS. HARRIET A. BAKER / Acornley, John Holmes – 1892 – 9 – us A.T.L.A. [240]
THE COLORED LUTHERAN *see* MISSIONARY LUTHERAN
THE COLORED MAN IN THE METHODIST EPISCOPAL CHURCH / Hagood, L M – Cincinnati: Cranston & Stowe; New York: Hunt & Eaton, 1890 – 1mf – us A.T.L.A. [240]
THE COLORED PATRIOTS OF THE AMERICAN REVOLUTION / Nell, William C – (Filmed with: [Baird, H C] Washington, u. Jackson uber die Neger als Soldaten) – New York: Arno Press 1968 – us Res Libr [975]
LA COLORINA. BADAJOZ, ARQUEROS, 1928 / Reyes Huertas, Antonio; ed by Zurbitu, D – Madrid: Razon y Fe, 1929 – 9 – sp Bibl Santa Ana [946]
Colosi, Christopher B *see*
- LA MEDIACION
- MEDIATION

Colosi, Thomas R *see*
- LA MEDIACION
- MEDIATION

Colossa, N A *see* ...SEV TVRCARVM EXPEDITIO IN SICULUM FRETUM
COLOSSIAN STUDIES: LESSONS IN FAITH AND HOLINESS / Moule, Handley Carr Glynn – New York: A.C. Armstrong, 1898. 1 fiche – 9 – us A.T.L.A. [240]
COLOURED ENGRAVINGS OF HEATHS / Andrews, H C – London: 1794- 1802-05 -1830. B-5369 2 – 8 – ne IDC [760]
COLOURED ENGRAVINGS TO EDWARD YOUNG'S "NIGHT THOUGHTS" FROM SIR JOHN SOANE'S MUSEUM, LONDON / Blake, William – 14 – uk Microform Academic [760]
THE COLOURS OF FLOWERS: AS ILLUSTRATED IN BRITISH FLORA / Allen, Grant – London: Macmillan, 1882. 05018. (Pre-1900 Canadiana) – 9 – cn C.I.H.M. [580]
THE COLOUR-SENSE: ITS ORIGIN AND DEVELOPMENT: AN ESSAY IN COMPARATIVE PSYCHOLOGY / Allen, Grant – London: Truebner, 1879. 05017. (Pre-1900 Canadiana) – 9 – cn C.I.H.M. [150]
Colpitts, W W *see* BAPTISM: HOW AND FOR WHOM?
LE COLPORTEUR PARISIEN – [Paris]: H Vrayet de Surcy, jul 2 1848 – us Res Libr [072]
Colquhoun, P *see*
- A TREATISE ON THE POLICE OF THE METROPOLIS
- A TREATISE ON THE WEALTH, POWER AND RESOURCES OF THE BRITISH EMPIRE...

COLRAIN 1740-1849 – (Mf 1T: Baptisms 1828-38; Church Marriages 1829-35; Church Deaths 1829-62. Mf 1T-2T: Births 1792-1849. Mf 2T: Marriages 1844-49. Mf 2T-3T: Births & Deaths 1740-1822. Mf 3T: Marriages 1789-92. Mf 3T-4T: Deaths 1843-49. Mf 4T,7T: Marriages 1842-49. Mf 4T: Marriage Intentions 1773-88; Out-of-Town Marriges 1747-95. Mf 4T-7T: Marriages & Intentions 1804-49) – (mf ed 1995) – 7mf – 9 – 0-87623-233-0 – us Holbrook [920]
COLRAIN 1741-1895 – (Mf 1-6: Town & Vital Records 1741-96. Mf 7-15: Town & Vital Records 1803-39. Mf 16-17: Marriages & Publishments 1803-25. Mf 18-20: Marriage Intentions 1828-1908. Mf 21-22: B,M,D 1843-53. Mf 23-25: Index to Births 1854-1986. Mf 26-28: Index to Marriages: 1854-1986. Mf 29-30: Index to Deaths 1854-1986. Mf 31-32: Births 1854-95 Bk 3. Mf 33-34: Marriages 1854-95. Mf 35-36: Deaths 1854-95) – (mf ed 1987) – 36mf – 9 – 0-87623-052-4 – us Holbrook [920]
Colsmann, J *see* PRODROMUS DESCRIPTIONIS GRATIOLAE
Colson, E *see* PLATEAU TONGA OF NORTHERN RHODESIA: STUDIES
Colson, Leon Clement *see* TRANSPORTS & TARIFS; REGIME ADMINISTRATIF DES VOIES DE COMMUNICATION, CONDITIONS TECHNIQUES ET COMMERCIALES DES TRANSPORTS.
Colsoni, Francesco *see* THE NEW TRISMAGISTER, OR THE NEW TEACHER OF THREE LANGUAGES
Colston, J G *see* RES JUDICATA IN THE CIVIL AND CRIMINAL LAW OF QUEBEC
COLTON – 1909-34 – 25r – 1 – $1,250.00 – P00018 – us Library Micro [910]
Colton, California *see* MISCELLANEOUS NEWSPAPERS
Colton, Calvin *see*
- THE GENIUS AND MISSION OF THE PROTESTANT EPISCOPAL CHURCH IN THE UNITED STATES
- HISTORY AND CHARACTER OF AMERICAN REVIVALS OF RELIGION

COLTON COURIER – Colton, CA. 1971- – 23+ r – 1 – $1,150.00 ($50.00y) – R02127 – us Library Micro [071]
COLTON PAGE (THE SUN) – Colton, CA. 1971-1973 – 2r – 1 – $100.00 – R03188 – us Library Micro [071]
COLTON SEMITROPIC – Colton, CA. 1877-1878 – 1r – 1 – $50.00 – R04016 – us Library Micro [071]
Colucci, M *see* PRINCIPLE DI DIRITTO CONSUETUDINARIO DELLA SOMALIA, ITALIANA MERIODINALE
THE COLUMBIA – Columbia Falls. Mont. 1891-1896; 1908-1924 – 1 – us UMI [071]
COLUMBIA AND THE UNITED STATES / Thomson, N – London, [1915] – 3mf – 9 – ILM-2357/1 – ne IDC [327]
COLUMBIA BEACON – Warrenton, OR. -w. 24 Jul 1954-27 Oct 1955. 1 roll – 1 – us U.O. Library [071]
COLUMBIA BUSINESS LAW REVIEW – 1986-95 – 9 – $152.00 set – us Hein [340]
THE COLUMBIA COLLEGE MSS OF MEGHILLA (BABYLONIAN TALMUD) : WITH AN AUTOTYPE FACSIMILE / Margolis, Max Leopold – New York: s.n., 1892 (A Ginsberg) – 1mf – 9 – 0-8370-4277-1 – 1985-2277 – us A.T.L.A. [270]
COLUMBIA COUNTY HERALD – Scappoose, OR. 26 Sept 1974-21 Sept 1978. – 2r – 1 – us U.O. Library [071]
COLUMBIA COUNTY NEWS – St. Helens, OR. -w. 27 Apr 1900-3 Jan 1902. 1 roll – 1 – us U.O. Library [071]
Columbia County.Georgia *see* EARLY COURT RECORDS
COLUMBIA EMPIRE – Umatilla OR. Dec 10 1948-Mar 25 1949 – 1 – us U.O. Library [071]
COLUMBIA FIRST BAPTIST CHURCH. COLUMBIA, SOUTH CAROLINA : CHURCH RECORDS – 1809-40, 1870-1949, 1984-1988 – 1 – $528.57 – us Baptist [240]
COLUMBIA HERALD – Houlton OR. June 12 1914 – 1 – us U.O. Library [071]
COLUMBIA HISTORICAL REVIEW – 1895-1948 – 1,5,6 – us Princeton Micro [073]
COLUMBIA HUMAN RIGHTS LAW REVIEW – v1- 1968- 1; v8- 1976- 5,6,9 – us UMI [340]
COLUMBIA HUMAN RIGHTS LAW REVIEW – (v1-16 1967-85 on reel or mf $200.00. v17-26 1985-95 on mf $219.00. Title varies: v1-3, 1967-71 as Columbia Survey of Human Rights Law) – v1-26. 1967-95 – 5,6,9 – $419.00 set – us Hein [340]
COLUMBIA INDEPENDENT – Columbia, PA. -w 1891-1912 – 13 – $25.00r – us I.M.R. [071]
COLUMBIA JOURNAL OF ENVIRONMENTAL LAW – (v1-9 1974-84 on reel or mf $110.00. v10-20 1985-95 on mf $255.00) – v1-20. 1974-95 – 5,6 – $365.00 set – us Hein [340]
COLUMBIA JOURNAL OF LAW AND SOCIAL PROBLEMS – (v1-18 1965-85 on reel or mf $240.00. v19-28 1985-95 on mf $245.00) – v1-28. 1965-95 – 5,6,9 – $485.00 set – us Hein [360]
COLUMBIA JOURNAL OF TRANSNATIONAL LAW – (v1-23 1961-85 on reel or mf $285.00. v24-33 1985-95 on mf $261.00. Title varies: v1-2 1961, 1963-63 as Columbia Society of International Law Bulletin. v2 1963 as International Law Bulletin) – v1-33. 1961-95 – 5,6,9 – $546.00 set – us Hein [340]
COLUMBIA JOURNAL OF WORLD BUSINESS – v6- 1971- 1; v2- 5,6; v10- 9 – us UMI [380]

COLUMBIA JOURNALISM REVIEW – (v10-1971- 5,6, v14- 1975- 9) – v1- 1962- – 1 – us UMI [073]
COLUMBIA JURIST – New York. v1-3. 1885-87 – 1 – $40.00 – us Hein [073]
THE COLUMBIA JURIST – v1-3. 1885-87 (all publ) – 4mf – 9 – $18.00 – LLMC 82-915 – us L.L.M.C. [073]
COLUMBIA LAW REVIEW – (Lacking: p179-80 v13. Updates planned) – v1-20. 1901-20 – 160mf – 9 – $240.00 – LLMC 84-443 – us L.L.M.C. [073]
COLUMBIA LAW REVIEW – v1-96. 1901-96 – 1,5,6,9 – $3,015.00 – us Hein [073]
COLUMBIA LAW TIMES – (Lacking: v3,4,6) – v1-6. 1887-93 (all publ) – 9 – LLMC 82-916 – us L.L.M.C. [073]
COLUMBIA LAW TIMES – New York. v1-6. 1887-93 – 1 – $40.00 – us Hein [073]
COLUMBIA PRESS – Astoria, OR. -m. 2 Sept 1949-20 Apr 1951. 1 roll – 1 – us U.O. Library [071]
COLUMBIA PRESS – (Cont as: Warrenton, Columbia Press) – Astoria, OR. 6 Apr 1961-15 Jun 1978 – 9r – 1 – us U.O. Library [071]
COLUMBIA PRESS – Umatilla OR. July 20 1867-Aug 29 1868 + – 1 – us U.O. Library [071]
COLUMBIA PRESS – Warrenton OR. June 22 1978 + – 1 – us U.O. Library [071]
COLUMBIA REGISTER – Houlton, OR. -w. 29 Apr 1904-1 Jun 1906. 1 roll – 1 – us U.O. Library [071]
COLUMBIA RIVER PILOT – Rainier OR. Aug 28-Sep 25 1930, Apr 13 1931 – 1 – us U.O. Library [071]
COLUMBIA RIVER SUN – Cathlamet. Wash. 1906-1938 – 1 – us UMI [071]
COLUMBIA SECOND BAPTIST CHURCH. COLUMBIA, SOUTH CAROLINA : CHURCH RECORDS – 1890-1915 – 1 – 7.16 – us Baptist [240]
COLUMBIA SOCIETY OF INTERNATIONAL LAW BULLETIN *see* COLUMBIA JOURNAL OF TRANSNATIONAL LAW
COLUMBIA SPY – Columbia, PA. -w 1889-1912 – 13 – $25.00r – us I.M.R. [071]
COLUMBIA SURVEY OF HUMAN RIGHTS LAW *see* COLUMBIA HUMAN RIGHTS LAW REVIEW
Columbia University *see*
- CATALOG OF THE AVERY MEMORIAL ARCHITECTURAL LIBRARY. SECOND EDITION, ENGLARGED
- CATALOG OF THE AVERY MEMORIAL ARCHITECTURAL LIBRARY. SECOND EDITION, ENLARGED
- COLUMBIANA
- LECTURES ON SCIENCE, PHILOSOPHY AND ART, 1907-8
- REPORTS OF THE BUREAU OF APPLIED SOCIAL RESEARCH
- THE SPINOZA BIBLIOGRAPHY

Columbia University. Ancient Near Eastern Society *see* JOURNAL..
Columbia University. Avery Memorial Architectural Library *see*
- ARCHITECTURAL TRADE CATALOGS
- AVERY INDEX TO ARCHITECTURAL PERIODICALS, SECOND EDITION
- AVERY OBITUARY INDEX OF ARCHITECTS
- CATALOG OF THE LIBRARY

Columbia University. East Asian Library *see* INDEX TO LEARNED CHINESE PERIODICALS
Columbia University. Law Library *see*
- DICTIONARY CATALOG
- DICTIONARY CATALOG OF THE COLUMBIA UNIVERSITY LAW LIBRARY

Columbia University Libraries *see* EARLY NONCONFORMITY, 1566-1800
Columbia University. Psychology Library *see* AUTHOR INDEX TO PSYCHOLOGICAL INDEX, 1894 TO 1935, AND PSYCHOLOGICAL ABSTRACTS, 1927 TO 1958
Columbia University. Teachers College *see* CITIZENSHIP EDUCATION PROJECT
Columbia University. Teachers College Library *see*
- DICTIONARY CATALOG
- DICTIONARY CATALOG OF THE TEACHERS COLLEGE LIBRARY

COLUMBIAN – New Westminster, British Columbia, CN. Sept 1899-Nov 1983 – 425r – 1 – cn Commonwealth Micro [072]
COLUMBIAN – St. Helens, OR. -w. 10 Mar 1882-4 Feb 1886; 27 Aug 1880; 13 June 1923 – 1r – 1 – us U.O. Library [071]
COLUMBIAN – Vancouver. Wash. 1908-1909; 1912-1913; 1921- – 1 – us UMI [071]
COLUMBIAN – Vancouver. Wash. -w. 1890-1921 – 1 – us UMI [071]
COLUMBIAN CENTINEL – Boston. Mass. 1790-1820. The Massachusetts Centinel. 1784-1790. Sold as one unit – 1,3 – us Readex [071]
Columbian College *see* CORRESPONDENCE
COLUMBIAN COLLEGE CORRESPONDENCE – Baptist records in Library of Congress, 1822-1936. 144p – 1 – us Baptist [240]
COLUMBIAN GAZETTE – Ithaca, NY. 1813-15 – 1r – 1 – us Western Res [071]
THE COLUMBIAN HARMONIST, OR SONGSTER'S REPOSITORY: BEING A SELECTION OF THE MOST APPROVED SENTIMENTAL, PATRIOTIC, AND OTHER SONGS – New York: Smith & Forman, 1814. Text only. MUSIC 519 – 1 – us L of C Photodup [780]
COLUMBIAN HERALD – Charleston. S.C. 1784-1790 – 1 – us UMI [071]
COLUMBIAN METHODIST RECORDER – (Contd by: Methodist Recorder) – Victoria, B.C: Province Pub. Co., [1899] – 9 – cn C.I.H.M. [240]
COLUMBIAN METHODIST RECORDER *see* METHODIST RECORDER
COLUMBIAN PROGRESS – Columbia. Miss. 1936-1966; 1968 – 1 – us UMI [071]
THE COLUMBIAN STAR – 1823-28 (complete) – 1r – 1 – ATLA R0123 – us A.T.L.A. [240]
COLUMBIANA / Columbia University – New York. N.Y. 1877- – 1 – us UMI [370]
COLUMBIANA AMERICAN AND NEW-LISBON FREE PRESS – (Weekly National Republican newspaper) – New Lisbon, OH. Feb9.Mar 1 1828 – 1r – 1 – us Western Res [071]
COLUMBIANA BAPTIST CHURCH. COLUMBIANA, ALABAMA : CHURCH RECORDS – 1909-52 – 1 – 17.52 – us Baptist [240]
COLUMBIANA COUNTY RECORDS, MS 1134 – (General records of county including court cases, Ohio laws, township voting abstracts, justices of the peace...) – 1803-54 – 2r – 1 – us Western Res [978]
COLUMBIA-VLA ART AND THE LAW *see* COLUMBIA-VLA JOURNAL OF LAW AND THE ARTS
COLUMBIA-VLA JOURNAL OF LAW AND THE ARTS – (v1-9 1974-85 on reel $104.00. v10-19 1985-95 on mf $259.99. Title varies: v1-6 1974-81 as Art and the Law. v7-9 1982-85 as Columbia-VLA Art and the Law) – v1-19. 1974-95 – 5,6,9 – $363.00 set – us Hein [340]
Columbus, Christopher *see* SELECT LETTERS AND OTHER ORIGINAL DOCUMENTS RELATING TO THE NEW WORLD
COLUMBUS CITIZEN JOURNAL – Columbus, Ohio. 1959- – 1 – us UMI [071]
COLUMBUS, DON QUIXOTE OF THE SEAS / Wassermann, Jakob – (Includes index) – Boston: Little, Brown, and Company, 1930 – 1r – 1 – us U.W. Library [946]
COLUMBUS EVENING DISPATCH – Columbus, Ohio. 1871- – 1 – us UMI [071]
Columbus Grove. Ohio. First Presbyterian Church *see* RECORDS
COLUMBUS, ITS HISTORY, RESOURCES AND PROGRESS / Studer, Jacob H – 1873. Ohio Reel 31. (The Cox Library Collection) – 5 – us Americana [978]
COLUMBUS JOURNAL – Columbus, NE. (-w. except -d. 1904-08.) May 1870-Jul. 1917 – 1 – us NE Hist [071]
Columbus, Mississippi *see* MISCELLANEOUS EARLY NEWSPAPERS
COLUMBUS MONTHLY – (v10-. 1984-. 5,6,9) – v1-. 1975- – 1 – us UMI [073]
COLUMBUS NEWS – Columbus, NE. -w. Nov. 1933-Aug. 1961 – 1 – us NE Hist [071]
Columbus. Ohio *see* CITY DIRECTORIES
COLUMBUS RECORD – Portland, OR. 1954-57. Incomplete – 1 – 17.00 – us Oregon Hist [071]
COLUMBUS RECORD MONTHLY – Portland, OR. 13 Apr 1935-Jan 1964. 1 roll – 1 – us U.O. Library [071]
COLUMBUS REPUBLICAN – Columbus, NE. -w. May 1875-Jan. 1877 – 1 – us NE Hist [071]
COLUMBUS THEOLOGICAL MAGAZINE – v1-30. Feb 1881-1910 (complete) – 6r – 1 – ATLA S0259 – us A.T.L.A. [073]
COLUMBUS TIMES – Columbus, NE. -w. May 1896-Jan. 1904 – 1 – us NE Hist [071]
COLUMBUS TRIBUNE – Columbus, NE. -w. Oct. 1906-May 1911 – 1 – us NE Hist [071]
COLUMIA BASIN HERALD – Moses Lake. Wash. -d, w, sw. 1941- – 1 – us UMI [071]
COLUMNA ANTONINIANA MARCI AURELII ANTONINI AUGUSTI. CUM NOTIS EXCERPTIS EX DECLARATIONIBUS J. P. BELLORII / Bartolo, P S – O-1083 1. 1672 – 9 – ne IDC [930]
LA COLUMNA VERTEBRAL : SINDICATOS Y PERONISMO / Abos, Alvaro – Buenos Aires: Editorial Legasa, 1983 – 1 – CSUXADH7647-B – us Hoover Inst Photo [612]
COLUMNAS VOLANTES – (Filmed with other miscellaneous titles from Duke University) – Lipa: Club Democratico Independista, jun 18-jul 2 1899 – us Res Libr [072]
COLUSA – 1913-50 – 18r – 1 – $900.00 – P00019 – us Library Micro [910]
COLUSA COUNTY – Calaveras Co, CA. 1878 – 1r – 1 – $50.00 – D011 – us Library Micro [978]
COLUSA COUNTY / Rogers, Justus H – Orland, 1891. California Reel 11. (The Cox Library Collection) – 5 – us Americana [978]
COLUSA COUNTY SUN HERALD – Colusa, CA. 1934- – 107+ r – 1 – $4,815.00 ($105.00y) – C02131 – us Library Micro [071]
COLUSA SUN – Colusa, CA. 1911 – 1r – 1 – $50.00 – C01228 – us Library Micro [071]
Colwell, Gregory B *see* INTERRELATIONSHIPS AMONG STRESS, SOCIAL SUPPORT, HEALTH BEHAVIORS AND SELF-ASSESSED HEALTH STATUS
Colwell, James *see* A CENTURY IN THE PACIFIC
Colwell, Stephen *see*
- NEW THEMES FOR THE PROTESTANT CLERGY : CREEDS WITHOUT CHARITY, THEOLOGY WITHOUT HUMANITY, AND PROTESTANTISM WITHOUT CHRISTIANITY
- THE POSITION OF CHRISTIANITY IN THE UNITED STATES

Colyn, H A *see* LA DECISION...CONCERNANT LES ILES D'ALAND
Colzel, M *see* BIBLIOGRAPHIE DES OUVRAGES RELATIFS A LA SENEGAMBIE ET AU SOUDAN OCCIDENTAL
COM CATALOG TO NOAA REPORTS / U.S. National Oceanic and Atmospheric Administration – Indexed by contract, personal author, subject, corporate author, title and access number. Cumulated Dec. 1978. 72mf – 9 – $80.00 – us Updata [324]
COM (MICROFICHE) CATALOGUE – 1990 – 287mf – 9 – Can$385.00 – 0-665-90295-6 – cn C.I.H.M. [010]
LES COMALIS / Ferrand, Gabriel – Paris: E Leroux, 1903 – 1 – us Res Libr [960]
Comanche County. Kansas. Union Church Ediface Society *see* HISTORY
COMARCA DE CALDAS – Caldas, 27 Apr-May, Jul-28 Sep 1894 – 1,5,6 – bl Biblioteca [072]
COMARCAS NATURALES DE LA ALTA EXTREMADURA. LA JARA CACERENA / Gutierrez Macias, Valeriano – Badajoz: Dip. Provincial, 1975. Sep. REE – 1 – sp Bibl Santa Ana [946]
Comas Roca, Jose M *see* LA RUTA DE LO DESCONOCIDO...
Comba, E *see* HISTOIRE DES VAUDOIS
Comba, Emilio *see*
- ENRICO ARNAUD
- HISTORY OF THE WALDENSES OF ITALY
- I NOSTRI PROTESTANTI
- LEZIONI DI STORIA DELLA CHIESA
- WALDO AND THE WALDENSIANS BEFORE THE REFORMATION

Combalusier, Francois de P *see* MEMOIRE DE L'UNIVERSITE SUR LES MOYENS DE POURVOIR A L'INSTRUCTION DE LA JEUNESSE, ET DE LA PERFECTIONNER
COMBAT – Dir. J. de Fabregues et Th. Maulnier. Paris. mens. 1936-juin 1939 – 1 – fr A.C.R.P.P. [073]
COMBAT – Paris. Le journal de Paris. Quot. aout 1944-30 aout 1974 – 1 – fr A.C.R.P.P. [072]
LE COMBAT – Chicago, IL. v3 n28. 27 jun 1891 – 1r – 1 – Can$25.00 – cn Can Microfilming [071]
LE COMBAT : COMMUNISTE – (Becomes and filmed with: L'Alternative 27 oct 1988-nov 1990) – Montreal, Canada. 23 nov 1946-mar 1949; ns: n100. 30 mar 1951-1 aut 1957; v1 n3. jul 1958-13 oct 1988 – 5r – 1 – Can$65.00r – cn Can Microfilming [072]
LE COMBAT – Dir. E. Le Blond. Cayenne. aout 1897-sept 1898 – 1 – fr A.C.R.P.P. [073]
LE COMBAT – Dir. Felix Pyat. no. 1-131. Paris. 6 sept 1870-23 janv 1871 – 1 – fr A.C.R.P.P. [073]
LE COMBAT – Federation socialiste de l'Allier. Montlucon. oct 1903-aout 1911 – 1 – fr A.C.R.P.P. [073]
LE COMBAT – French Guiana. 1897-99 with omissions – 1 – us UMI [072]
LE COMBAT / ed by Lavergne, Armand et al – Quebec, Canada. 23 fev-7 dec 1929 – 1r – 1 – Can$35.00 – cn Can Microfilming [072]
LE COMBAT – Montreal, Canada. 18 nov 1916-v1 n15. 10 mar 1917 – 1r – 1 – Can$30.00 – cn Can Microfilming [072]
LE COMBAT / ed by Morrissette, J-F – Montreal, Canada. 1 fev 1896; v2 n1. 25 mar 1897 – 1r – 1 – Can$25.00 – cn Can Microfilming [072]
LE COMBAT – Paris. Aug. 21, 1944-Aug. 20, 1948. Missing: 2 issues – 1 – 35.00r – us Hoover Inst Photo [072]
LE COMBAT – Paris. Organe republicain quotidien. 20 janv-25 26 juin 1893 – 1 – fr A.C.R.P.P. [944]
LE COMBAT – Sherbrooke, Canada. v1 n9. 8 aut 1935 – 1r – 1 – Can$25.00 – cn Can Microfilming [072]
COMBAT CONSTITUTIONNEL: 1868-1886 / Weiss, Jean Jacques – Paris: G. Charpentier et E. Fasquelle, 1893. 334p. 4 fiches. (Political Science Collection) – 9 – 10.00 – fr Bibl Nationale [323]
COMBAT ESTIMATES : EUROPE AND THE WESTERN HEMISPHERE, 1920-43 / U.S. Military Intelligence – (Europe: 4r $415.00 ISBN 0-89093-665-X; The Western Hemisphere: 2r $210.00 ISBN 0-89093-658-7) – Reports. With printed guides – 1 – us UPA [355]
COMBAT LE JOURNAL DE PARIS – Paris: Combat, 1951-57. 1953-55; 1956-62 – us Res Libr [073]
LE COMBAT MARXISTE – no. 1-30. Paris. oct 1933-avr 1936. mq no. 12-14 – 1 – fr A.C.R.P.P. [073]
LE COMBAT NATIONAL : ORGANE DU PARTI DE L'UNITE NATIONALE DU CANADA – Montreal, Canada. jul 1938-aut 1939 – 1r – 1 – Can$50.00 – cn Can Microfilming [073]
LE COMBAT NATIONAL *see* LE FACISTE CANADIEN
LE COMBAT SOCIAL – Dir. Pappalardo. no. 1-5. Alger. mars-juin 1927 – 1 – fr A.C.R.P.P. [073]
COMBAT SOCIALISTE – Dir. alain Rannou. no. 1-41. Paris. 15 nov 1971-nov 1980 – 1 – fr A.C.R.P.P. [073]
COMBAT SOCIALISTE – Montreal: O.C.S., 1980-81. SEM35P201 – 1r – 1 – Can$15.00 – cn Bibl Nat [335]
COMBAT SOCIALISTE : POUR LA REPUBLIQUE DES TRAVAILLEURS DU QUEBEC – Montreal: (Groupe marxiste revolutionnaire), 1975-77. SEM35P199 – 1r – 1 – Can$18.00 – cn Bibl Nat [335]
LE COMBAT SYNDICALISTE – Confederation generale du travail syndicaliste revolutionnaire. no. 140-200. Limoges. 1936-19 mars 1937 – 1 – fr A.C.R.P.P. [073]
COMBATE – [s.l.]. 2 Maio 1891 – 1,5,6 – bl Biblioteca [072]
O COMBATE – Caratinga, 16 Dec 1894-17 Mar 1895 – 1,5,6 – bl Biblioteca [072]
O COMBATE : JORNAL DE PROPAGANDA ANTI-CLERICAL – Curitiba, 6 Jan-5 May 1907 – 1,5,6 – bl Biblioteca [072]
O COMBATE – Manaos, Amazonas. 26 Set 1912 – 1,5,6 – bl Biblioteca [072]
O COMBATE : ORGAO INDEPENDENTE – Manaus, Amazonas. 23 Set 1946 – 1,5,6 – bl Biblioteca [072]
O COMBATE : ORGAO LITTERARIO E NOTICIOSO – Manaos, Amazonas. 25 Jul 1915 – 1,5,6 – bl Biblioteca [072]
O COMBATE – [s.l.]. 7 Jun 1927-Jan 1928 – 1,5,6 – bl Biblioteca [072]
O COMBATE – S Tome: Joas Carragoso, mar 21-apr 25 1925 – us Res Libr [072]
LES COMBATS DE COQS DANS LE NORD DE LA FRANCE / Petitjean-Roget, V – 9 – F30.00 – fr Ethnologie [390]
LE COMBATTANT EUROPEEN – Paris. juin 1943-juil 1944 – 1 – fr A.C.R.P.P. [073]
LES COMBATTANTS FRANCAIS DE LA GUERRE AMERICAINE (1778-1783) – (Avec un index d'environ 46,000 noms) – Washington, DC. 1905 – 1r – 1 – Can$60.00 – cn Can Microfilming [975]
Combe, David A *see* CIVIL LAW 1

Combe, E *see* HISTOIRE DU CULTE DE SIN EN BABYLONIE ET EN ASSYRIE
Combe, W *see*
- FANATICAL CONVERSION
- PERFECTION
- THE SAINTS
- A SKETCH OF THE TIMES
- VOLTAIRE'S GHOST TO THE APOSTLE OF THE SINLESS FOUNDERY

Combe, William *see*
- DOCTOR SYNTAX, HIS THREE TOURS IN SEARCH OF THE PICTURESQUE, OF CONSOLATION, OF A WIFE
- THE LOVE-FEAST
- SKETCHES FOR TABERNACLE-FRAMES
- THE TEMPLE OF IMPOSTURE

Combefis, FR *see* SCRIPTORES POST THEOPHANEM (CBH 7)
Combes, EdmondTamisier, M. *see* VOYAGE EN ABYSSINIE, DANS LE PAYS DES GALLA, DE CHOA ET D'IFAT
Combes, Ernest *see* PROFILS ET TYPES DE LA LITTERATURE ALLEMANDE
Combes, F *see* HISTOIRE GENERALE DE LA DIPLOMATIE EUROPEENNE
Combes, Paul *see* EXPLORATION DE L'ILE D'ANTICOSTI.
Combes, Pierre de *see* RECUEIL TIRE DES PROCEDURES CIVILES FAITES EN L'OFFICIALITE DE PARIS, ET AUTRES OFFICIALITEZ DU ROYAUME.
COMBINATION LAWS: SELECT COMMITTEE / Great Britain. Laws, Statutes, etc – 1825 – 1 – uk Microform Academic [324]
COMBINED HISTORY OF SCHUYLER COUNTY AND BROWN COUNTY – Biographical sketches. Philadelphia, 1882. Illinois. The Cox Library Collection – 54r – 5 – us Americana [978]
COMBINED HISTORY OF SHELBY AND MOULTRIE COUNTIES / Brink, McDonough and Co – Biographical sketches. Philadelphia, 1881. Illinois Reel 55. The Cox Library Collection – 5 – us Americana [978]
COMBUSTION – v1- 1929- 1; v42- 5,6; v47- 9 – us UMI [660]
COMBUSTION – Battleboro. Engineering & Finance. -m. Sep 1924-Jul 1931 – 5r – 1 – uk British Libr Newspaper [621]
COMBUSTION AND FLAME – v1-58. 1963-84 – 1,5,6,13 – sz Elsevier [073]
COMBUSTION, EXPLOSION AND SHOCK WAVES – v1-30. 1965-94 – 1,5 – $80.00v – us UMI [530]
COMBUSTION SCIENCE AND TECHNOLOGY / ed by Glassman, I et al – 1969- – 1,5,9 – us Gordon [660]
COME HOME : AN APPEAL ON BEHALF OF REUNION / Langtry, John – Toronto: Church of England Pub. Co., 1900 – 1mf – us A.T.L.A. [240]
COME, LET US CELEBRATE : MEETING GOD IN CHRISTIAN AND NON-CHRISTIAN FEASTS / ed by Puthiadam, I – Bangalore: Asian Trading Corp, 1976 – us Res Libr [230]
COME OUT FIGHTING – v1-21, 1975-77. Hollywood, CA: Lavender and Red Union, 1975 – 1 – us U.W. Library [073]
COME TO JOGJAKARTA / Indonesia. Jogjakarta – SE-4748 1 – 9 – ne IDC [910]
LA COMEDIA DE LA VIDA / Hurtado, Antonio – 1871 – 9 – $1.50f – sp Bibl Santa Ana [870]
LA COMEDIA IN COMEDIA : THE FAVORITE SONGS IN THE OPERA / Lattila, G – (Orchestral Score) – London: I Walsh, 1748? – 1 – us Sibley [780]
LA COMEDIA NUEVA / Fernandez de Moratin, Leandro – 1802 – 1mf – 9 – Pta1,000.00 – 84-7848-187-7 – sp Pentalfa [830]
COMEDIA PRODIGA / Miranda, Luis de – 1868 – 9 – 1.50f – sp Bibl Santa Ana [820]
COMEDIA SIN TITULO. MS. / Garcia Lorca, Federico – MS. DE 1935. Fragmento – 1mf – 9 – sp Cultura [820]
COMEDIA TROFEA / Torres Naharro, Bartolome – Reimp. prefaciada por Fidelino de Figueiredo. Sao Paulo. Oficina Jose Magalhaes, 1943 – 1 – sp Bibl Santa Ana [946]
COMEDIAE 18 / Plautus – 15th cent. Holkham ms. 298. Holkham Hall, Norfolk, England – 1 – uk Microform Academic [760]
LA COMEDIANTA. MS. / Garcia Lorca, Federico – MS DE 1923 – 2mf – 9 – sp Cultura [820]
COMEDIAS NUEVAS ESCOGIDAS DE LOS MEJORES INGENIOS DE ESPANA – Madrid, 1652-1704 – 447mf – 9 – sp Cultura [820]
LES COMEDIES DU PACIFIQUE – Montreal?, 1884?. 03404. (Pre-1900 Canadiana) – 9 – cn C.I.H.M. [971]
THE COMEDIES OF ARISTOPHANES / Aristophanes – Ed., transl., and explained by Benjamin Bickley Rogers. London: G. Bell & Sons, 1902-16. Greek and English on opposite pages – 1 – us U.W. Library [450]
THE COMEDY OF CATHERINE THE GREAT / Gribble, Francis Henry – London: E. Nash, 1912. xix,367p. Front., ports – 1 – us U.W. Library [920]
COMENDADORES...ALCANTARA / Manera de Rezar – 1663 – 9 – $1.50f – sp Bibl Santa Ana [946]
Comenius, Johann Amos *see*
- THE ORBIS PICTUS OF JOHN AMOS COMENIUS
- ORBIS SENSUALIUM PICTUS
- PORTA LINGUARUM TRILINGUIS
- A REFORMATION OF SCHOOLES

COMENTAIRE...POEME...IBN ABDOUN / Ibn-Badroun – 1846 – 9 – 1.50f – sp Bibl Santa Ana [440]
COMENTARII IN QUATOR EVANGELISTAS / Maldonado, Juan – (Tomo I. 1862. 1.50f; 9. Tomo II-IV. 1841. 1.50f; BSA; 9. Tomo II.1874. 1.50f; BSA; 9. 1601. 1.50f; BSA; 9. 1611. 1.50f; BSA; 9) – Tomo I. 1840 – 9 – 1.50f – sp Bibl Santa Ana [240]
COMENTARII..3 LIBRUM...DUNS SCOTI / Ovando, Juan de – 1597 – 9 – $1.50f – sp Bibl Santa Ana [240]
COMENTARIO AL ARTICULO 1361 DEL CODIGO CIVIL / Carrasco Alvarez, Antonio – 1898 – 9 – 1.50f – sp Bibl Santa Ana [340]
COMENTARIO IN PROFETAS MIMOS / Arias Montano, Benito – Amberes: Plantino, 1571 – 1 – sp Bibl Santa Ana [946]
COMENTARIOS A LA VIDA DE PEDRO DE VALDIVIA : ESCRITA POR A. MIGUEL-ROMERO Y GIL DE ZUNIGA / Mena, Vicente – Madrid: Impresos Madrid, 1929 – 1 – sp Bibl Santa Ana [920]
COMENTARIOS DE DON GARCIA DE SILVA Y FIGUEROA DE LA EMBAJADA QUE DE PARTE DEL REY DE ESPANA DON FELIPE 3RD HIZO AL REY XA ABAS DE PERSIA / Asin Palacios, Miguel – de Serrano Sanz. Madrid: Tip. de la Rev. de Archivos. Bibliotecas y Museos, 1928 – 1 – sp Bibl Santa Ana [946]
COMENTO – London, UK. 8 Jul 1922; 10 May, 10 Sept-26 Nov 1924 – 1 – uk British Libr Newspaper [072]
COMENTO – London, UK. Monthly Bulletin of the Italian Antifascist Federation. Nov 1943 – 1 – uk British Libr Newspaper [072]
COMENTO DE LOS MAJORETES, 1500 / Meseguer Fernandez, Juan – Madrid: Graf. Calleja, 1500 – 1 – sp Bibl Santa Ana [946]
COMENTOS CRITICOS SOBRE LA FUNDACION DE CARTAGENA DE INDIAS. BOGOTA / Otero D'Acosta, Enrique – Madrid: Razon y Fe, 1935 – 1 – sp Bibl Santa Ana [950]
Comer, G *see* A GEOGRAPHICAL DESCRIPTION OF SOUTHAMPTON ISLAND AND NOTES ON THE ESKIMO
Comer, John *see* DIARY
EL COMERCIO – Lima: Jose Ayarza, 1938- – 1 – us Res Libr [072]
EL COMERCIO – Quito, Ecuador: Carlos Mantilla, jan 4 1940- – 1 – us Res Libr [072]
EL COMERCIO – Quito, Ecuador. Jan 1948-Dec 1955 – 44r – 1 – us L of C Photodup [072]
COMERCIO ANGLO-LATINO – London, UK. Apr-Aug 1912 – 1 – uk British Libr Newspaper [072]
COMERCIO ARGENTINO-BRITANICO – (Comercio britanico. Dec 1942/Feb 1943-Jul 1948. Ingenieria Britanico. Aug 1948-Mar/Apr 1958) – London, UK. Mar/May 1940-Sept/Nov 1942 – 1 – uk British Libr Newspaper [072]
COMERCIO BRITANICO *see* COMERCIO ARGENTINO-BRITANICO
COMERCIO EXTERIOR / Honduras. Direccion General de Estadistica y Censos – 1957-65 – 1 – 46.00 – us L of C Photodup [380]
COMERCIO HISPANO-BRITANICO – London, UK. Aug 1939-Oct/Dec 1945 – 1 – uk British Libr Newspaper [072]
COMERCIO HISPANO-BRITANICO – London, UK. Jan/Mar 1921-Apr/Jun 1936; Jan/Mar 1948 – 1 – uk British Libr Newspaper [072]
EL COMERCIO Y LA BANCA / Martinez Perez, Eloy – 1892 – 9 – 1.50f – sp Bibl Santa Ana [380]
Comes de Blumegen, F H *see* TENTAMEN EX IURISPRUDENTIA NATURALI
Comes, R et al *see* CONDENSED MATTER NEWS
COMES THE DAWN / Read, Leonard E – 1976. 168p. Together with: "Censored", 10th ed. of a directory by Bayliss Corbett. 1980. 45p. 1 fiche (24x) – 9 – 1.00f – at Libertarian Micro [320]
COMET – Hamilton, OH. Nov 1865 – 1r – 1 – us Western Res [073]
COMET – v1, nos. 1-5 (all publ). 1940-41 – 1 reel – 1 – $50.00 – us UPA [830]
THE COMET – Dublin. Ireland. -w. 1 May 1831-1 Dec 1833. (1 reel) – 1 – uk British Libr Newspaper [072]
THE COMET – Lagos, Nigeria. Daily Comet. -d. 16 May 1944-1 Dec 1945; 23 April-2 Nov 1946. Imperfect. 2 reels – 1 – uk British Libr Newspaper [072]
THE COMET – Lagos, Nigeria. -w. 22 July 1933-13 May 1944. 6 reels – 1 – uk British Libr Newspaper [072]
THE COMET – Ottawa: Thoburn, [1894-189-?] – 9 – cn C.I.H.M. [971]
THE COMET – Quebec, Canada. v1 n4. 17 nov 1866 – 1r – 1 – Can$25.00 – cn Can Microfilming [072]
THE COMET – Quebec: [s.n., 1866-1868?] – 9 – cn C.I.H.M. [971]
THE COMET, A WEEKLY NEWS-MAGAZINE OF WEST AFRICA – Lagos, Nigeria. June 12, 1937-May 26, 1943 – 1 – us NY Public [073]
THE COMET AND LOCAL ADVERTISER – Johannesburg, South Africa. 22 May 1897-31 Jul 1897 – 1r – 1, 16 diazo available – sa SA Libr [960]
COMETA / Hermoso, Eugenio – Madrid: Chulilla y Angel, 1932 – 1 – sp Bibl Santa Ana [946]
COMETA – Villa de Traipu, Alagoas. 10 Fev 1886 – 1,5,6 – bl Biblioteca [072]
O COMETA – Manaos, Amazonas. 26 Maio-1 Set 1912 – 1,5,6 – bl Biblioteca [072]
LA COMETE: CONTE EN L'AIR / Bricaire de la Dixmarie, Nicolas – Reprod. d'une edition s.l., s.d. 42p. 1 fiche. (Literature Collection) – 9 – 6.00 – fr Bibl Nationale [830]
COMETH UP AS A FLOWER : AN AUTOBIOGRAPHY / Broughton, Rhoda – London: Richard Bentley, 1883 – 1 roll – 1 – 1-55879-548-0 – uk Libr Preservation [920]
COMETH UP AS A FLOWER: AN AUTOBIOGRAPHY / Broughton, Rhoda – British Fiction Archive: Unit 4 – 9 – uk Bell [830]
Comettant, O *see* HISTOIRE DE CENT MILLE PIANOS ET D'UNE SALLE DE CONCERT...
A COMFORTABLE AYDE FOR SCHOLERS / Rowland, David – 1568. 173p. (English Linguistics Series 1500-1800) – 9 – us UMI [420]
Comhaire, J *see* URBAN CONDITIONS IN AFRICA
THE COMIC BLACKSTONE : (PARODIES ON THE COMMENTARIES) – ca 22mf – 9 – LLMC 82-800 Titles 185-197 – us L.L.M.C. [340]
COMIC OFFERING – 1831-35 – 21mf – 9 – £180.00 – uk Chadwyck [800]
COMIC WORLD – New York, NY. 1876 – 1r – 1 – us Western Res [073]
COMIENCA EL LIBRO PRIMERO DELA D'CLARACIO DE INSTRUMETOS, DIRIGIDO AL ELEMENTISSIMO Y MUY PODEROSE DON JOAN TERCERO DESTE NOMBRE / Bermudo, J – P 640. 1549 – 9 – ne IDC [780]
COMINCIAMENTO E PROGRESSO DELL' ARTE DELL' INTAGLIARE IN RAME, COLLE VITE DI MOLTI DE' PIU ECCELLENTI MAESTRI DELLA STESSA PROFESSIONE / Baldinucci, Filippo – Firenze. 1686. BO-137 1 – 9 – ne IDC [760]
THE COMING ARISTOCRACY / Read, Leonard E – 1969. 194p. Together with: Vision, 1978, 160p. 1 fiche (24x) – 9 – 1.00f – at Libertarian Micro [320]
THE COMING INDUSTRIAL STRUGGLE / Maitland, William – 1894. 1 fiche (29x) – 9 – 1.00f – at Libertarian Micro [320]
THE COMING NATION – (Sold with: The Progressive Woman) – ns: v1 n1-8. 1913-14 (all publ) – 1 – $90.00 – us UPA [305]
COMING NEW ERA – Wahoo, NE. -w. Aug 1890-May 1906 – 1 – us NE Hist [071]
THE COMING OF LOVE: RHONA BOSWELL'S STORY : AND OTHER POEMS / Watts-Dunton, Theodore – London, New York: John Lane, 1899 – 1 roll – 1 – 1-55879-763-7 – uk Libr Preservation [810]
THE COMING OF MESSIAH IN GLORY AND MAJESTY / Irving, Edward – Preliminary discourse. Also includes Irving's Ordination Charge and an introductory essay to Bishop Harnes' Commentary on the Psalms. Bosworth & Harrison, 1859 – 9 – $10.00 – us I.R.C. [240]
THE COMING OF PEACE : A FAMILY CATASTROPHE / Hauptmann, Gerhart – Chicago: C H Sergel, 1900 – 1r – 1 – us U.W. Library [830]
THE COMING OF THE FRIARS AND OTHER HISTORIC ESSAYS / Jessopp, Augustus – London: T.F. Unwin; New York: Putnam, 1913 – 1mf – us A.T.L.A. [240]
COMING OF THE LOYALISTS / Haight, Canniff – Toronto: Haight, 1899. 05146. (Pre-1900 Canadiana) – 9 – cn C.I.H.M. [971]
COMINTERN ARCHIVE : INSTALLMENT 1 – (Congress 1-4 1919-1922 now available) – 1995 – 1,792mf – 9 (Dfl16,130.00 standing order) – ne IDC [947]
THE COMINTERN: HISTORICAL HIGHLIGHTS / ed by Drachkovitch, M M – Essays, recollections, documents. New York 1966 – 1 – 35.00r – us Hoover Inst Photo [335]
COMISARIA DEL PLAN DE DESARROLLO ECONOMICO Y SOCIAL / Canary Islands. Spain – D-1203 f.83-92). 1968 – 9 – ne IDC [338]
Comisetti, L *see* MANDATS ET SOUVERAINETE
COMISION ANDINA DE JURISTAS (CAJ) = ANDEAN COMMISSION OF JURISTS – Lima. 123 docs. 1980-1991 – 109mf – 9 – ne IDC [340]
COMISION CATEQUISTICA DE ZARAGOZA. RELIGION Y CULTURA, UN GRAFICO Y EJEMPLOS ZARAGOZA, 1940 / Marquez, Gabino – Madrid: Razon y Fe, 1945 – 1 – sp Bibl Santa Ana [240]
COMISION CHILENA DE DERECHOS HUMANOS = CHILEAN HUMAN RIGHTS COMMISSION – Santiago. 236 docs. 1980-1991 – 147mf – 9 – ne IDC [320]
COMISION DE CANARIAS. 3 PLAN DE DESARROLLO ECONOMICO Y SOCIAL. CANARIAS / Canary Islands. Comisaria del Plan de Desarrollo Economico y Social – (3rd Economic and Social Development Plan. Canary Islands). Madrid. 1972. BD-1628 1 – 9 – ne IDC [338]
UNA COMISION DE CARLOS 5TH AL...P. FRANCISCO DE LOS ANGELES QUINONES (DESPUES OBISPO DE CORIA) / Gracia Villacampa, Carlos – Archivo Ibero-Americano, 1916 – 1 – sp Bibl Santa Ana [240]
Comision de Estadistica *see*
- CENSO DE POBLACION DE ESPANA SEGUN EL RECUENTO DE 21 DE MAYO DE 1857
- NOMENCLATOR DE LOS PUEBLOS DE ESPANA

Comision de Monumentos *see*
- ACTA DE 22 DE OCTUBRE DE 1918
- ACTA DE LA SESION DE 1 DE OCTUBRE DE 1920
- ACTA DE LA SESION DE 22 DE MARZO DE 1920
- ACTA DE LA SESION DEL 14 DE MARZO DE 1920
- CARGOS

COMISION DE MONUMENTOS, ANTIGUEDADES ROMANAS / Alcuescar – 1900 – 9 – $1.50f – sp Bibl Santa Ana [930]
Comision de Monumentos de Caceres *see* ANTIGUEDADES ROMANAS DE ALCUESCAR
Comision de Semana Santa *see*
- SEMANA SANTA CACERENA 1960
- SEMANA SANTA. CACERES 1974

Comision Diocesana de Apostolada Rural *see* LA FAMILIA RURAL HACIA LA CONQUISTA DE UN MEJOR NIVEL DE CULTURA. ENCUESTA CAMPANA EXPERIMENTAL 1963-1964
COMISION ESPECIAL DE AGUAS. DICTAMEN... / Caceres – Caceres: Imp. Moderna, 1936 – sp Bibl Santa Ana [946]
COMISION ESPECIAL DE AGUAS. DICTAMEN... 6.11.1934 / Caceres – Caceres: Imprenta Moderna, 1935 – sp Bibl Santa Ana [628]

Comision Nacional de Investigaciones *see* CASOS DE LA SEGUNDA TIRANIA
COMISION NO 2 : TRANSFORMACIO EN REGADIO / Consejo Economico Sindical Provincial – Badajoz: Imprenta Inca, 1965 – sp Bibl Santa Ana [330]
COMISION NO 4: INDUSTRIAS BASICAS DEL HIERRO / Consejo Economico Sindical Provincial – Badajoz: Imp. Inca, 1965 – sp Bibl Santa Ana [338]
COMISION NO 5: PRODUCTOS QUIMICOS / Consejo Economico Sindical Provincial – Badajoz: Imp. Inca, 1965 – sp Bibl Santa Ana [338]
COMISION NO 6: INDUSTRIAS RELACIONADAS – CON LA ALIMENTACION / Consejo Economico Sindical Provincial – Badajoz: Imprenta Inca, 1965 – sp Bibl Santa Ana [338]
COMISION NO 8: TRANSPORTES. COMUNICACIONES Y SERVICIOS DE INFORMACION / Consejo Economico Sindical Provincial – Badajoz: Imp. Inca, 1965 – sp Bibl Santa Ana [380]
COMISION NO 9: TURISMO / Consejo Economico Sindical Provincial – Badajoz: Imp. Inca, 1965 – sp Bibl Santa Ana [338]
COMISION NO 13: FINANCIACION / Consejo Economico Sindical Provincial – Badajoz: Imprenta Inca, 1965 – sp Bibl Santa Ana [332]
COMISION NO 14: TRABAJO / Consejo Economico Sindical Provincial – Badajoz: Imp. Inca, 1965 – sp Bibl Santa Ana [331]
COMISION NO 15: FACTORES HUMANOS Y SOCIALES. PRODUCTIVIDAD / Consejo Economico Sindical Provincial – Badajoz: Imprenta Inca, 1965 – sp Bibl Santa Ana [338]
COMISION ORGANIZADORA DE FESTEJOS. MEMORIA DE 1920 / Fomento de Caceres – Caceres: Tip. de Santos Floriano Gonzalez, y 1921-22, 1924 – sp Bibl Santa Ana [946]
COMISION PERMANENTE DE DERECHOS HUMANOS DE NICARAGUA (CPDH) = PERMANENT COMMISSION FOR HUMAN RIGHTS IN NICARAGUA – Managua. 153 docs. 1980-1990 – 28mf – 9 – ne IDC [320]
Comision Provincial de Monumentos *see*
- CONSTITUCION EN 1925. NOTICIA DE VICENTE CASTANEDA
- CONSTITUCION EN 1928, NOTICIA DE VICEN TE CASTANEDA

COMISION PROVINCIAL DE MONUMENTOS HISTORICOS Y ARTISTICOS DE BADAJOZ / Solar, Antonio del – Madrid: Fortanet, 1918. B.R.A.H 73, pp.383-384 – sp Bibl Santa Ana [946]
Comision Provincial de subsidio el Combatiente *see* DECRETO DE 25 DE ABRIL DE 1938 Y REGLAMENTO DEL MIS MO MES, REORGANIZANDO EL SERVICIO DEL SUBSIDIO AL COMBATIENTE
Comision Semana Santa. Caceres *see*
- SEMANA SANTA CACERENA, 1958
- SEMANA SANTA CACERENA, 1959
- SEMANA SANTA CACERENA 1961
- SEMANA SANTA CACERENA 1976
- SEMANA SANTA CACERENA 1978
- SEMANA SANTA. CACERES, 1963
- SEMANA SANTA CACERES 1977
- SEMANA SANTA DE PLASENCIA. MARZO 1959

COMISON ECUMENICA DE DERECHOS HUMANOS (CEDHU) = ECUMENICAL COMMISSION FOR HUMAN RIGHTS – Quito. 75 docs. 1980-1991 – 25mf – 9 – ne IDC [320]
Comite Central des Artistes *see* LA VOIX DES ARTISTES
Comite Contra el Racismo y el Antisemitismo de la Argentina *see* 2ND CONGRESO (1. ORDINARIO) DEL COMITE CONTRA EL RACISMO Y ANTISEMITISMO DE LA ARGENTINA
Comite d'Action Antifasciste et de Vigilance *see* VIGILANCE
LE COMITE DE BIENFAISANCE / Kahn, Leon – Paris. 1886. (La Condition Ouvriere. Part Two.) – 9 – 10.00 – fr Bibl Nationale [360]
Comite de Collaborateurs *see* HISTORIQUE DU SAGUENAY: SOUVENIR DE L'EXCURSION DE LA PRESSE D'ONTARIO ET DE QUEBEC A CHICOUTIMI, AU GRAND-BRULE ET A ST ALPHONSE, LE 9 AOUT 1883
Un Comite de Collaborateurs *see* HISTORIQUE DU SAGUENAY
Comite de la Troisieme Internationale *see* BULLETIN COMMUNISTE
Comite de l'Afrique francaise *see* BULLETIN
Comite de l'Asie francaise *see*
- L'ASIE FRANCAISE
- ASIE FRANCAISE

Comite de Recrutement Canadien-Francais. Montreal *see* ALBUM DE LA GRANDE GUERRE
Comite de Vigilance des Intellectuels Antifascistes *see* LA PRESSE DE FRANCO
Comite der Chicago Schiller Gedenkfeier, Mai 1905 *see* ZUR WUERDIGUNG SCHILLER'S IN AMERIKA
Comite des Monuments Francais *see* AMI DES MONUMENTS ET DES ARTS PARISIENS ET FRANCAIS
Comite d'Etudes Berberes de Rabat *see* LES ARCHIVES BERBERES
Comite d'Etudes Historiques et Scientifiques de l'Afrique Occidentale Francaise *see* BULLETIN
Comite du Monument de Maisonneuve. Montreal, Quebec *see* MONUMENT MAISONNEUVE: SOUVENIR DE LA CEREMONIE D'INAUGURATION, LE LER JUILLET 1895
Comite Executif nomme pour venir en aide aux victimes de l'incendie du 9 mai 1886 en la cite de Hull *see* RAPPORT
Comite Franco-Espagnole *see* DURANGO, VILLE MARTYRE; CE QUE FURENT LES BOMBARDEMENTS DE LA VILLE DE DURANGO PAR LES AVIONS ALLEMANDS
COMITE LATINOAMERICANO PARA LA DEFENSA DE LOS DERECHOS DE LA MUJER = LATIN AMERICAN COMMITTEE FOR THE DEFENSE OF WOMEN'S RIGHTS – Lima. 4 docs. 1988-1991 – 5mf – 9 – ne IDC [320]
Comite Maritime International *see* CONFERENCE DE BRUXELLES, JUIN 1897
Comite Regional de l'Oranie du Parti Communiste *see* L'ENCHAINE
Comite Special du Katanga. Congres Scientifique du Cinquantenaire, Elisabethville, 1950 *see* COMPTES-RENDUS
COMITE SUISSE CONTRE LA TORTURE = SWISS COMMITTEE AGAINST TORTURE : SCHWEIZERISCHES KOMITEE GEGEN DIE FOLTER – Geneva. 46 docs. 1980-1990 – 18mf – 9 – ne IDC [320]
Comite Tecnico de Ayuda a los Espanoles en Mexico *see*
- CULTURAL CREATIONS.
- SPANISH PROFESSORS AND ARTISTS IN THE EMIGRATION

Comite...pour venir en aide aux victimes de l'incendie du 5 juin 1888 en la cite de Hull *see* RAPPORT
Comley *see* THE FUTURE GREAT STATE – CINCINNATI AND CLEVELAND
Comly, James M *see*
- THE JAMES M. COMLY PAPERS
- PAPERS

COMM. IN SUMMAM THEOL. TH. AQ. VOL. 1 / Cajetanus – 1892 – 27mf – 8 – ne Slangenburg [290]
COMMAND MAGAZINE – v. 1-. 1978 – 1,5,6,9 – us UMI [324]
THE COMMAND OF THE SEA / Wilkinson, Henry Spenser – 3rd ed. 1894 – 9 – uk Libr Preservation [941]
COMMAND PO MCCLELLAN FIELD – Sacramento. Calif. -w. 1943-46 – 1 – us UMI [071]
COMMAND POLICY – v.2- 1979- – 1,5,6,9 – us UMI [073]
COMMAND POST (MCCLELLAN FIELD) – Sacramento, CA. 1943-46 – 2r – 1 – $100.00 – C03423 – us Library Micro [071]
LE COMMANDANT MARCHAND ET SES COMPAGNONS D'ARMES A TRAVERS L'AFRIQUE : HISTOIRE COMPLETE ET ANECDOTIQUE DE LA MISSION – Paris: E Geffroy, [1892] – 1 – us Res Libr [960]
COMMANDER IN CHIEF, U.S. FLEET, BATTLE EXPERIENCES, DEC. 1941-AUG. 1945 / U.S. Navy – (With printed guide) – 1989 – 2r – 5 – $170.00 – S3178 – us Scholarly Res [355]
COMME IL VOUS PLAIRA – Mensuel d'art et de litterature. no. 1-2. Bruxelles. oct-nov 1897 – 1 – fr A.C.R.P.P. [800]
Commelin, C *see* FLORA MALABARICA
Commelin, J *see* HORTI MEDICI AMSTELODAMENSIS RARIORUM TAM ORIENTALIS, QUAM OCCIDENTALIS INDIAE
COMMELINACEAE INDICAE,... / Hasskarl, J K – Vindobonae, 1870 – 2mf – 9 – ne IDC [580]
COMMELYNACEAE ET CYRTANDRACEAE BENGALENSES / Clarke, C B – Calcutta. 1874 – 9 – ne IDC [580]
COMMEMORACION ET ADVERTISSEMENT DE LA MORT DE TRES CRESTIENNE ET TRES HAULTE...DAME MADAME ANNE...DUCHESSE DE BRETAIGNE... / Choquo, Pierre – 16th cent – 1 – F50.00 – fr Armell [944]
COMMEMORATIVE BIOGRAPHICAL AND HISTORICAL RECORD OF KANE COUNTY / Beers, Leggett and Co – Chicago, 1888. (Illinois Reel 31). (The Cox Library Collection) – 5 – us Americana [978]
COMMEMORATIVE BIOGRAPHICAL CYCLOPEDIA OF DAUPHIN COUNTY / J.M. Runk and Co – Chambersburg, 1896. Pennsylvania Reel 18. The Cox Library Collection – 5 – us Americana [978]
COMMEMORATIVE BIOGRAPHICAL ENCYCLOPEDIA OF THE COUNTIES OF HUNTINGTON, MUFFLIN, JUNIATA AND PERRY / J.M. Runk and Co – Chambersburg, 1897. v1-2. Pennsylvania Reel 4. The Cox Library Collection – 5 – us Americana [978]
COMMEMORATIVE BIOGRAPHICAL RECORD OF CENTRE, CLINTON, UNION AND SNYDER COUNTIES / J.H. Beers and Co – Chicago, 1898. Pennsylvania Reel 2. The Cox Library Collection – 5 – us Americana [978]
COMMEMORATIVE BIOGRAPHICAL RECORD OF DUTCHESS COUNTY / J.H. Beers and Co – Chicago, 1897. New York Reel 13. The Cox Library Collection – 5 – us Americana [978]
COMMEMORATIVE BIOGRAPHICAL RECORD OF HARTFORD COUNTY, CONNECTICUT / J.H. Beers and Co – Chicago, 1901. Connecticut Reel 4. The Cox Library Collection – 5 – us Americana [978]
COMMEMORATIVE BIOGRAPHICAL RECORD OF NORTHEASTERN PENNSYLVANIA / J.H. Beers and Co – Chicago, 1900. Pennsylvania Reel 1. The Cox Library Collection – 5 – us Americana [978]
COMMEMORATIVE BIOGRAPHICAL RECORD OF ROCK, GREEN, GRANT, IOWA AND LAFAYETTE COUNTIES / J.H. Beers and Co – Chicago: 1901. Wisconsin Reel 18. The Cox Library Collection – 5 – us Americana [978]
COMMEMORATIVE BIOGRAPHICAL RECORD OF THE COUNTIES OF SANDUSKY AND OTTAWA / J.H. Beers and Co – Chicago, 1896. Ohio Reel 56. The Cox Library Collection – 5 – us Americana [978]
COMMEMORATIVE BIOGRAPHICAL RECORD OF THE UPPER LAKE REGION / J.H. Beers and Co – Biographical sketches. Chicago, 1905. Wisconsin Reel 4. The Cox Library Collection – 5 – us Americana [978]
COMMEMORATIVE BIOGRAPHICAL RECORD OF THE UPPER WISCONSIN / J.H. Beers and Co – Chicago, 1895. Wisconsin Reel 4. The Cox Library Collection – 5 – us Americana [978]
COMMEMORATIVE BIOGRAPHICAL RECORD OF THE WEST SHORE OF GREEN BAY / J.H. Beers and Co – Brown, Oconto, Marinette and Florence Counties. Chicago, 1896. Wisconsin Reel 6. The Cox Library Collection – 5 – us Americana [978]
COMMEMORATIVE BIOGRAPHICAL RECORD OF WASHINGTON COUNTY / J.H. Beers and Co – Chicago, 1893. Pennsylvania Reel 41. The Cox Library Collection – 5 – us Americana [978]
COMMEMORATIVE BIOGRAPHICAL RECORD OF WAYNE AND HOLMES COUNTIES / J.H. Beers and Co – Chicago, 1889. Ohio Reel 66. The Cox Library Collection – 5 – us Americana [978]
COMMEMORATIVE BIOGRAPHICAL RECORDS OF THE COUNTIES OF HURON AND LORAIN / J.H. Beers and Co – Biographical sketches. Chicago, 1894. Ohio Reel 39. The Cox Library Collection – 5 – us Americana [978]
COMMEMORATIVE BIOGRAPHICAL RECORDS OF ULSTER COUNTY / J.H. Beers and Co – Chicago, 1896. New York Reel 36. The Cox Library Collection – 5 – us Americana [978]
COMMEMORATIVE HISTORICAL AND BIOGRAPHICAL RECORD OF WOOD COUNTY / J.H. Beers and Co – Chicago, 1897. Ohio Reel 68. The Cox Library Collection – 5 – us Americana [978]
THE COMMEMORATIVE SERVICES OF THE FIRST BAPTIST CHURCH OF BOSTON, MASSACHUSETTS (250TH ANNIVERSARY) / Wells, Edwin P – 1915 – 1 – 9.17 – us Baptist [240]
COMMENT – London. 1963-93. Continued annually – 1 – uk World [073]
COMMENT – (Issues for mar 3 1981-jun 21 1982 filmed with: Current affairs (South African Broadcasting Corporation), may 31 1978-mar 2 1981) – Johannesburg: Broadcasting Centre, [1981- – us Res Libr [070]
COMM/ENT: A JOURNAL OF COMMUNICATIONS AND ENTERTAINMENT *see* HASTINGS COMMUNICATIONS AND ENTERTAINMENT LAW JOURNAL (COMM/ENT)
COMM/ENT: HASTINGS JOURNAL OF COMMUNICATIONS AND ENTERTAINMENT LAW *see* HASTINGS COMMUNICATIONS AND ENTERTAINMENT LAW JOURNAL (COMM/ENT)
COMMENT IL FAUT PLEURER NOS CHERS D'EFUNTS / Francois de Sales – s.l.: s.n., 1882 (Quebec: A. Cote). 04331. (Pre-1900 Canadiana) – 9 – cn C.I.H.M. [971]
COMMENT LA FRANCE EST DEVENUE REPUBLICAINE / Gouault, J – Les elections generales et partielles a l'Assemblee Nationale. 5 fiches – 9 – F70.00 – fr Ethnologie [320]
A COMMENT ON RUTH / Fuller, Thomas – Edinburgh: James Nichol, 1865. 1 fiche – 9 – us A.T.L.A. [240]
A COMMENT ON THE SO-CALLED PROBLEM OF INFLATION IN LIBYA / United Nations. Dept. of Economic and Social Affairs – Commentary no. 2, 14 Aug 1964. Farley, R. (Senior Economist and United Nations TAB (OPEX) Expert). BNE-603 1 – 9 – ne IDC [324]
A COMMENT OR PARAPHRASE ON THE EXTRACT FROM THE MINUTES OF THE REV. MR. WESLEY, AND C., EXTRACTED FROM 'THE GOSPEL MAGAZINE' – London, 1771 – 1mf – 9 – MP-468/1 – ne IDC [240]
COMMENT SONT PRESENTES LES PREDETERMINANTS DU SUBSTANTIF DANS LES OUVRAGES DES GRAMMAIRIENS DU 17E ET 18E SIECLE / Poupardin, C – F100.00 – fr Ethnologie [440]
COMMENTAAR OP DE BRIEVEN VAN PAULUS AAN DE THESSALONIKERS, EFEZIERS, KOLOSSERS IN AAN FILEMON / Baljon, Johannes Marinus Simon – Utrecht: J van Boekhoven, 1907 – 1mf – 9 – 0-8370-2168-5 – 1985-0168 – us A.T.L.A. [220]
LE COMMENTAIRE D'ORIGENE SUR ROM. 3, 5-V, 7 D'APRES LES EXTRAITS DU PAPYRUS NO 88748 DU MUSEE DU CAIRE / Origenes; ed by Scherer, Jean – Le Caire, 1957 – 10mf – 9 – ne Slangenburg [240]
COMMENTAIRE HISTORIQUE SUR LE POEME D'IBN-ABDOEN / Ibn-Badroun; ed by Dozy, R – Leyde, 1846 – Dfl30.00 – ne Slangenburg [470]
COMMENTAIRE LITTERAL : HISTORIQUE ET MORAL SUR LA REGLE DE SAINT BENOIT / Calmet, Dom Aug. – Paris. v1-2. 1734 – Dfl137.00 – ne Slangenburg [240]
COMMENTAIRE SUR LA REGLE DE S. BENOIT / Mege, Joseph – Paris, 1687 – 22mf – 8 – Dfl77.00 – ne Slangenburg [240]
COMMENTAIRE SUR LE THEATRE DE VOLTAIRE / La Harpe, Jean Francois de – Paris: Maradan, 1814 – 9 – fr Hachette [410]
COMMENTAIRES SUR LE TRAITE "DE LA GUERRE" DE CLAUZEWITZ / La Barre DuParq, Edouard – Paris. J. Correard. 1853. 340p. (Strategy of War Series) – 9 – fr Hachette [355]
COMMENTAR UEBER DAS BUCH IOB ERSTER TEIL, UEBERSETZUNG UND SPRACHLICHE ANALYSE / Winterfeld, Ernst von – Anklam: Hermann Wolter, 1898. 1 fiche – 9 – us A.T.L.A. [240]
COMMENTAR UEBER DAS BUCH JUDITH UND UEBER BEL UND DRACHE / Scholz, Anton – (Includes appendixes) – Wuerzburg: Leo Woerl, 1896 – 1mf – 9 – 0-8370-5140-1 – 1985-3140 – us A.T.L.A. [220]
COMMENTAR UEBER DEN BRIEF AN DIE HEBRAEER / Keil, Carl Friedrich – Leipzig: Doerffling und Franke, 1885 – 1mf – 9 – 0-8370-3865-0 – 1985-1865 – us A.T.L.A. [220]
COMMENTAR UEBER DEN BRIEF PAULI AN DIE GALATER : MIT BESONDERER RUECKSICHT AUF DIE LEHRE UND GESCHICHTE DES APOSTELS / Wieseler, Karl – (Includes indexes) – Goettingen: Dieterich, 1859 – 2mf – 9 – 0-8370-9671-5 – 1986-3671 – us A.T.L.A. [220]

COMMENTAR UEBER DIE APOSTELGESCHICHTE DES LUKAS / Nosgen, CF – Leipzig, 1882 – 9mf – 8 – ne Slangenburg [220]

COMMENTAR UEBER DIE BRIEFE DES PETRUS UND JUDAS / Keil, Carl Friedrich – (Includes bibliographical references) – Leipzig: Doerffling & Franke, 1883 – 1mf – 9 – 0-8370-3866-9 – 1985-1866 – us A.T.L.A. [220]

COMMENTAR ZU DER WEISSAGUNG DES PROPHETEN OBADJA / Johannes, Adolf – Wuerzburg: Thein, 1885 – 1mf – 9 – 0-8370-3784-0 – 1985-1784 – us A.T.L.A. [220]

COMMENTAR ZUM BUCHE DES PROPHETEN HOSEAS / Scholz, Anton – Wuerzburg, Leo Woerl, 1882 – 1mf – 9 – 0-8370-5141-X – 1985-3141 – us A.T.L.A. [220]

COMMENTAR ZUM BUCHE DES PROPHETEN JOEL / Scholz, Anton – Wuerzburg:Leo Woerl, 1885 – 1mf – 9 – 0-8370-5142-8 – 1985-3142 – us A.T.L.A. [220]

COMMENTARI IN PROPHETAS. JEREMIAN EZECHIELEM / Maldonado, Juan – Turnoni: Horatij Candon, 1611 – 1 – sp Bibl Santa Ana [240]

COMMENTARIA IN CONCORDIAM ET HISTORIAM EVANGELICAM / Barradas, S – Antverpiae. Tomi 1-4. 1622 – 94mf – 8 – ne Slangenburg [220]

COMMENTARIA IN DECRETALES (SIECLE 14) – Barcelona – 4r – 5,6 – sp Cultura [240]

COMMENTARIA IN DUODECIM PROPHETAS / Arias Montano, Benito – 1583 – 9 – 1.50f – sp Bibl Santa Ana [240]

COMMENTARIA IN HOSSEAN PROPHETAM / Guadelupe, Andres – 1581 – 9 – 1.50f – sp Bibl Santa Ana [240]

COMMENTARIA IN ISIAE PROPHETAE / Arias Montano, Benito – 1599 – 9 – 1.50f – sp Bibl Santa Ana [240]

COMMENTARIA IN RUTH – 1990 – 9mf – 9 – Bf1,950.00 – 2-503-63812-0 – be Brepols [240]

COMMENTARIA IN RUTH : TRACTATUS DE TABERNACULO / Cellensis, Petrus – 1983 – 8mf – 9 – Bf975.00 – 2-503-60542-7 – be Brepols [220]

COMMENTARIA IN RUTH : TRACTATUS DE TABERNACULO (CCCM 54) / Petrus Cellensis – 1987 – 6mf – 9 – Bf975.00 – 2-503-73542-8 – be Brepols [240]

COMMENTARIA IN SCRIPTURAM SACRAM = THE GREAT COMMENTARY OF CORNELIUS A LAPIDE / Lapide, Cornelius a – 3rd ed. London: John Hodges. 6v. 1891-96 – 9mf – 9 – 0-8370-6992-0 – 1986-0992 – us A.T.L.A. [220]

COMMENTARIA (LIBRI 13) / Sylvius, Aeneas – 18th Century. Holkham Ms 482 – 1 – uk Microform Academic [760]

COMMENTARIA QUAEDAM IN CANTICA CANTICORUM / Alfonso de Orozco, Beato – 1581 – 9 – 1.50f – sp Bibl Santa Ana [780]

COMMENTARIA UNA CUM QUAESTIONIBUS, IN UNIVERSAM ARISTOTELIS LOGICAM / Toletus, Franciscus – Coloniae Agrippinae, 1583 – 5mf – 9 – CA-39/1 – ne IDC [100]

COMMENTARIES ON AMERICAN LAW / Kent, James – (12th ed. Boston, Little, Brown, 1873. 4 v. LL-1665. New and thoroughly rev. ed. Philadelphia, Blackstone, 1889. 4 v. LL-775.. New and thoroughly revised ed., by William M. Lacy. New York, Banks, 1891-92. 4 v. LL-852. 12th ed. Ed. by O. W. Holmes, Jr. 14th ed. Ed. by John M. Gould. Boston, Little, Brown, 1896. 4 v. LL-903) – 4th ed. New York, 1840. 4 v. LL-861 – 1 – us L of C Photodup [340]

COMMENTARIES ON COLONIAL AND FOREIGN LAWS GENERALLY AND IN THEIR CONFLICT WITH EACH OTHER AND WITH THE LAW OF ENGLAND / Burge, W – New ed. London. 5v. 1907 – 45mf – 1 – ILM-446/1 – ne IDC [327]

COMMENTARIES ON EQUITY JURISPRUDENCE, AS ADMINISTERED IN ENGLAND AND AMERICA. 11TH ED / Story, Joseph – (12th Ed. Boston, Little, Brown, 1877. 2v. LL-1068. 1) – Boston, Little, Brown, 1873. 2 v. LL-1011 – 1 – us L of C Photodup [340]

COMMENTARIES ON EQUITY PLEADINGS, AND THE INCIDENTS THEREOF, ACCORDING TO THE PRACTICE OF THE COURTS OF EQUITY, OF ENGLAND AND AMERICA. 6TH ED / Story, Joseph – (8th ed. Boston, Little, Brown, 1870. 816 p. LL-532. 1. 10th ed. Boston, Little, Brown, 1892. 823 p. LL-1640 1) – Boston, Little, Brown, 1857. 871 p. LL-1114 – 1 – us L of C Photodup [340]

COMMENTARIES ON THE CONFLICT OF LAWS, FOREIGN AND DOMESTIC, IN REGARD TO CONTRACTS, RIGHTS, AND REMEDIES, AND ESPECIALLY IN REGARD TO MARRIAGES, DIVORCE, WILLS, SUCCESSIONS, AND JUDGMENTS. 8TH ED / Story, Joseph – Boston Little, Brown, 1883. 901 p. LL-1013 – 1 – us L of C Photodup [340]

COMMENTARIES ON THE CONSTITUTION OF THE UNITED STATES / Story, Joseph – 4th ed. Boston: Little, Brown and Co. 2v. 1873 – 17mf – 9 – $25.50 – LLMC 90-367 – us L.L.M.C. [323]

COMMENTARIES ON THE HISTORY AND CURE OF DISEASE / Heberden, William – 2nd ed. London, 1803. M-443/1 – 9 – ne IDC [610]

COMMENTARIES ON THE HISTORY, CONSTITUTION, AND CHARTERED FRANCHISES OF THE CITY OF LONDON / Norton, George – 3rd ed., rev. London: Longmans, Green, 1869. xxviii,421p – 1 – us U.W. Library [941]

COMMENTARIES ON THE JURISDICTION OF COURTS / Brown, Timothy – Chicago, Callaghan, 1891. 624 p. LL-1465 – 1 – us L of C Photodup [340]

COMMENTARIES ON THE LAW OF AGENCY AS A BRANCH OF COMMERCIAL AND MARITIME JURISPRUDENCE...4TH ED / Story, Joseph – (7th ed., Boston, Little, Brown, 1869. 674 p. LL-1156. 1. 8th ed., Boston, Little, Brown, 1874. 706 p. LL-1143. 1) – Boston, Little and Brown, 1851. 719 p. LL-1151 – 1 – us L of C Photodup [340]

COMMENTARIES ON THE LAW OF BAILMENTS, WITH ILLUSTRATIONS FROM THE CIVIL AND FOREIGN LAW. 8TH ED / Story, Joseph – Boston, Little, Brown, 1870. 653 p. LL-1413 – 1 – us L of C Photodup [340]

COMMENTARIES ON THE LAW OF MUNICIPAL CORPORATIONS / Dillon, John Forrest – 4th ed. Boston, Little, Brown, 1890. 2 v. LL-803 – 1 – us L of C Photodup [340]

COMMENTARIES ON THE LAW OF NEGLIGENCE IN ALL RELATIONS. / Thompson, Seymour Dwight – (A supplement. Being Volume VII of the series. Indianapolis, 1907. 1148 p. A supplement. Being volume VIII of the series. Indianapolis, 1914. 1192 p) – Indianapolis, Bowen-Merrill, 1901-05. 6 v. LL-1250 – 1 – us L of C Photodup [340]

COMMENTARIES ON THE LAW OF RECEIVERS. / Beach, Charles Fisk – New York, Strouse, 1888. 796 p. LL-899 – 1 – us L of C Photodup [340]

COMMENTARIES ON THE LAWS OF ENGLAND : (AMERICAN EDITIONS OF THE COMMENTARIES) – 814mf – 9 – LLMC 82-800 Titles 80-146 – us L.L.M.C. [340]

COMMENTARIES ON THE LAWS OF ENGLAND / Blackstone, William – (This ed was missing from the Yale Law Library Blackstone Collection) – 8th ed. Oxford: Clarendon Press. v1-4. 1778 – 16mf – 9 – $24.00 – LLMC 90-463 – us L.L.M.C. [340]

COMMENTARIES ON THE LAWS OF ENGLAND : (ENGLISH AND IRISH EDITIONS OF THE COMMENTARIES) – 1st-23rd ed + new ed – ca 774mf – 9 – LLMC 82-800 Titles 1-45 – us L.L.M.C. [340]

COMMENTARIES ON THE LAWS OF ENGLAND : (FOREIGN EDITIONS, ABRIDGEMENTS AND EXTRACTS): FRENCH – 62mf – 9 – LLMC 82-800 Titles 179-182 – us L.L.M.C. [340]

COMMENTARIES ON THE LAWS OF ENGLAND : (FOREIGN EDITIONS, ABRIDGEMENTS AND EXTRACTS): GERMAN – 10mf – 9 – LLMC 82-800 Title 183 – us L.L.M.C. [340]

COMMENTARIES ON THE LAWS OF ENGLAND : (FOREIGN EDITIONS, ABRIDGEMENTS AND EXTRACTS): ITALIAN – 6mf – 9 – LLMC 82-800 Title 184 – us L.L.M.C. [340]

COMMENTARIES ON THE LAWS OF ENGLAND : (WORKS FOUNDED ON BLACKSTONE'S COMMENTARIES) – 395mf – 9 – LLMC 82-800 Titles 198-216 – us L.L.M.C. [340]

COMMENTARIES ON THE LAWS OF ENGLAND; IN FOUR BOOKS / Blackstone, William – 4th ed. Chicago, Callaghan, 1899. 2 v. LL-840 – 1 – us L of C Photodup [340]

COMMENTARIES ON THE LAWS OF MOSES / Michaelis, Johann David – Trans. from German by Alexander Smith. London: Rivington, 1814.4v – 1 – us U.W. Library [240]

COMMENTARIES ON THE MODERN LAW OF MUNICIPAL CORPORATIONS...BEING A REV., RE-WRITTEN AND ENL. ED. OF BEACH ON PUBLIC CORPORATIONS. / Smith, John Wilson – Indianapolis: Bowen-Merrill, 1903. 2v. LL-1304 – 1 – us L of C Photodup [340]

COMMENTARIES ON THE THE LAW OF MARRIAGE AND DIVORCE. / Bishop, Joel Prentiss – 6th ed. Boston, Little, Brown, 1881. 2 v. LL-902 – 1 – us L of C Photodup [340]

COMMENTARIES ON THE WRITTEN LAWS AND THEIR INTERPRETATION / Bishop, Joel Prentiss – Boston, Little, Brown, 1882. 354 p. LL-378 – 1 – us L of C Photodup [340]

COMMENTARIES UPON TOPICS DEMANDING THEM – Halifax, N.S: W S Hall, [1878-18–?] – 9 – cn C.I.H.M. [971]

COMMENTARII / Akademie der Wissenschaften. Goettingen – (Commentationes v1-2 Goettingen 1758-68. Commentationes v1-16 Goettingen 1778-1808. Commentationes recentiores v1-8 Goettingen 1808-37) – v1-4. Goettingen. 1751-54. BH-644-2 – 8 – ne IDC [500]

COMMENTARII / Akademie der Wissenschaften. Goettingen – v1-4. 1752-(1755) – 3 – us Readex [500]

COMMENTARII ACADEMIAE SCIENTIARUM IMPERIALIS PETROPOLITANAE / Leningrad – Petropoli, 1726-46. v.1-14 – 159mf – 8 – ne IDC [500]

COMMENTARII COLLEGII CONIMBRICENSIS E SOCIETATIS IESU IN UNIVERSAM DIALECTICAM ARISTOTELIS / Conimbricenses – Lugduni. 2v. 1605 – 14mf – 9 – CA-11/1 – ne IDC [100]

COMMENTARII COLLEGII CONIMBRICENSIS SOCIETATIS IESU IN ARISTOTELIS LOGICAM / Conimbricenses – Venetiis. 2v. 1607 – 7mf – 9 – CA-180/1 – ne IDC [100]

COMMENTARII COLLEGII CONIMBRICENSIS SOCIETATIS IESU, IN DUOS LIBROS DE GENERATIONE ET CORRUPTIONE ARISTOTELIS / Conimbricenses – Lugduni, 1606 – 6mf – 9 – CA-12/1 – ne IDC [100]

COMMENTARII DE REBUS BYZANTINIS (CBH 3,4) / Bryennii, Nicephori Caesaris; ed by Possinus, P, – Parisiis, 1661 – Dfl270.00 – ne Slangenburg [930]

COMMENTARII DE RELIGIONE REVELATA EJUSQUE FONTIBUS AC DE ECCLESIA CHRISTI / MacGuinness, Joannes – (Includes bibliographical references) – Parisiis: Des Irlandais; Turonibus: Bousrez, 1900 – 1mf – 9 – 0-8370-6915-7 – 1986-0915 – us A.T.L.A. [240]

COMMENTARII ET ANNOTATIONES IN EPISTOLAM B. PAULI APOSTOLI AD ROMANOS / Toledo, Francisco de – Romae, 1602 – 10mf – 9 – CA-71/1 – ne IDC [240]

COMMENTARII HIERONYMI COMITIS ALEXANDRINI DE ACERRIMO, AC OMNIUM DIFFICILLIMO TURCARUM BELLO, IN INSULAM MELITAM GESTO, ANNO MDLXV / Conti, N – Venetiis, 1566 – 2mf – 9 – H-8304/1 – ne IDC [956]

COMMENTARII ILLUSTRES...IN QUINQUE MOSAICOS LIBROS / Cajetanus, Cardinal, Thomas a Vio – Parisiis, 1539 – 24mf – 8 – ne Slangenburg [240]

COMMENTARII IN EPISTOLAM PAULI AD ROMANOS *see* IONNIS CALVIN COMMENTARII IN EPISTOLAM PAULI AD ROMANOS

COMMENTARII IN EVANGELICAM HISTORIAM, ET IN ACTA APOSTOLORUM... / ed by Salmeron, A – Coloniae Agrippinae. 16v. 1602-1604 – 154mf – 9 – CA-63/1 – ne IDC [240]

COMMENTARII IN LIBROS ARISTOTELIS STAGIRITAE PHILOSOPHORUM PRINCIPIS DE ANIMA... / Rubio, A – [Alcala], 1611 – 7mf – 9 – CA-36/1 – ne IDC [100]

COMMENTARII IN LIBROS ARISTOTELIS STAGYRITAE PHILOSOPHORUM PRINCIPIS, DE ANIMA... / Rubio, A – Lugduni, 1620 – 9mf – 9 – CA-37/1 – ne IDC [100]

COMMENTARII IN OCTO LIBROS ARISTOTELIS DE PHYSICO AUDITU, SEU AUSCULTATIONE CONTINENTUR / Rubio, A – (Missing: Title page) – Lugduni, 1620 – 9mf – 9 – CA-35/1 – ne IDC [100]

COMMENTARII IN OMNES PAULI EPI ET EPI CATHOLICAS : DE TESTAMENTO...DEI – DE UTRAQUE IN CHRISTO NATURA / Bullinger, H – Tiguri, 1539 – 41mf – 8 – ne Slangenburg [220]

COMMENTARII IN OMNES PAULI EPISTOLAS, IN EPISTOLAM AD HEBRAEOS ET IN EPISTOLAS CANONICAS / Bullingeri, Heinrichi – Tiguri, 1603 – 30mf – 8 – ne Slangenburg [220]

COMMENTARII IN PRIMA 12 CAPITA...EVANGELII SECUNDAM LUCAM / Toledo, Francisco de – Romae, 1600 – 15mf – 9 – CA-70/1 – ne IDC [240]

COMMENTARII IN QUATTUOR EVANGELISTAS / Maldonatus, Ioan. – Mussiponti. v1-2. 1596-97 – 49mf – 8 – ne Slangenburg [220]

COMMENTARII IN SACROSANCTUM IESU CHRISTI D.N. EVANGELIUM SECUNDUM LUCAM / Toletus, Franciscus – Parisiis, 1600 – 37mf – 8 – ne Slangenburg [220]

COMMENTARII JURIS CIVILIS. / Acevedo, Alfonso de – 1737. v. I-VI – 9 – 1.50f – sp Bibl Santa Ana [340]

COMMENTARII LINGUAE GRAECA / Bude, G – Parisiis, 1548 – 20mf – 9 – ne IDC [450]

COMMENTARII SOCIETATIS REGIAE SCIENTIARUM GOTTINGENSIS : COMMENTARII – (Commentationes. Goettingen, 1758-1768. v1-2; Commentationes, Goettingen, 1778-1808. v1-16; Commentationes...recentiores. Goettingen, 1808-1837. v1-8) – Goettingen, 1751-1754. v1-4 – 407mf – H-644/2 – ne IDC [500]

COMMENTARIO DE LE COSE DE TVRCHI, DI PAVLO IOVIO, VESCOVO DI NOCERA, A CARLO QVINTO IMPERADORE AVGVSTO / Giovio, P – [Venice], 1538 – 1mf – 9 – H-8252/1 – ne IDC [956]

COMMENTARIO DE LE COSE DE TVRCHI, DI PAVLO IOVIO, VESCOVO DI NOCERE, A CARLO QVINTO IMPERADORE AVGVSTO / Giovio, P – Venetia, 1540 – 1mf – 9 – H-8263/1 – ne IDC [956]

COMMENTARIO DE LE COSE DE TVRCHI, ET DEL S. GEORGIO SCANDERBEG, PRINCIPE DI EPYRRO / Giovio, P – [Venice], 1539 – 2mf – 9 – H-8257/1 – ne IDC [956]

COMMENTARIO DE LE COSE DE TVRCHI, ET DEL S. GEORGIO SCANDERBEG, PRINCIPE DI EPYRRO / Giovio, P – (Venice], 1541 – 2mf – 9 – H-8268/1 – ne IDC [956]

COMMENTARIO...DELLA ORIGINE DE TVRCHI, ET IMPERIO DELLA CASA OTTOMANNA / Cambini, A – N.p., 1538 – 2mf – 9 – H-8251/1 – ne IDC [956]

COMMENTARIO...DELLA ORIGINE DE TVRCHI, ET IMPERIO DELLA CASA OTTOMANNA / Cambini, A – [Venice], 1540 – 2mf – 9 – H-8261/1 – ne IDC [956]

COMMENTARIORUM CONTINUATIO AD LEGES REGIAS. / Acevedo, Alfonso de – 1600 – 9 – 1.50f – sp Bibl Santa Ana [340]

COMMENTARIORUM DE PLANTIS AFRICAE AUSTRALIORIS / Meyer, E H F – Lipsiae, 1835-1837. 326 pp. B-207 2 – 8 – ne IDC [580]

COMMENTARIORUM ET DISPUTATIONUM IN GENESIM / Peperius, Ben. – Moguntiae. v1-4. 1612 – 46mf – 8 – ne Slangenburg [220]

COMMENTARIORUM IURIS CIVILIS / Acevedo, Alfonso de – 1591 – 9 – 1.50f – sp Bibl Santa Ana [340]

COMMENTARIORUM IURIS CIVILIS / Acevedo, Alfonso de – 1612. v. I-VI – 9 – 1.50f – sp Bibl Santa Ana [340]

COMMENTARIORUM IURIS CIVILIS, TOMUS QUINTUS / Acevedo, Alfonso de – 1596 – 9 – 1.50f – sp Bibl Santa Ana [340]

COMMENTARIORUM IURIS CIVILIS, TOMUS SECUNDUS / Acevedo, Alfonso de – 1595 – 9 – 1.50f – sp Bibl Santa Ana [340]

COMMENTARIORUM IURIS CIVILIS, TOMUS SEXTUS / Acevedo, Alfonso de – 1598 – 9 – 1.50f – sp Bibl Santa Ana [340]

COMMENTARIORUM LIBRI 10 IN...EVANGELIUM SECUNDUM IOANNEM / Bullinger, H – Tiguri, 1543 – 20mf – 8 – ne Slangenburg [240]

COMMENTARIORUM LIBRI 12 IN...EVANGELIUM SECUNDUM MATTHAEUM / Bullinger, H – Tiguri, 1542 – 25mf – 8 – ne Slangenburg [240]

COMMENTARIORUM THEOLOGICORUM... / Gregorius de Valencia – Lugduni. 4v. 1603-09 – 60mf – 9 – CA-76/1 – ne IDC [240]

COMMENTARIORUM THEOLOGICORUM TOMI QUATUOR / Valentia, Greg. De – Inglostadii, 1592-1597 – 178mf – 8 – ne Slangenburg [240]

COMMENTARIOS INEDITOS A LA TERCERA PARTE DE SANTO TOMAE, T1-2 / Banes, Dom – Matriti, 1951-1953 – 17mf – 8 – ne Slangenburg [240]

COMMENTARIUM ET DISPUTATIONUM IN GENESIM, TOMI QUATUOR / Pererius, B – Coloniae Agrippinae. 4v. 1601 – 39mf – 9 – CA-29/1 – ne IDC [100]

COMMENTARIUM IN QUARTUM SENTENTIARUM / Soto, D de – [Salamanca]. 2v. 1581 – 32mf – 9 – CA-73/1 – ne IDC [240]

COMMENTARIUM JURIS CIVILIS...SALMANTICAL, DIDACUSCUSIO, 1591 / Acevedo, Alfonso de – 1 – sp Bibl Santa Ana [340]

COMMENTARIUS CAPTAE VRBIS, DVCTORECAROLO BORBONIO, AD EXQUISITUM MODUM CONFECTUS / Giovio, P – Parisiis, 1539 – 1mf – 9 – H-8258/1 – ne IDC [956]

COMMENTARIUS CRITICUS IN N.T. QUO LOCA GRAVIORA ET DIFFICILIORA LECTIONIS DUBIAE ACCURATE RECENSENTUR ET EXPLICANTUR / Reiche, Johann Georg – 3v. 1853-62 – 1 – us A.T.L.A. [240]

COMMENTARIUS DE SACRIS ECCLESIAE ORDINATIONIBUS / Morin, J – Parisiis, 1686 – 37mf – 8 – Dfl130.00 – ne Slangenburg [240]

COMMENTARIUS D.IAC.CHRI SCHAEFFERI FUNGORUM BAVARIAE INDIGENORUM ICONES PICTAS / Persoon, C H – Erlangae. 1800. B-6297 2 – 8 – ne IDC [580]

COMMENTARIUS IN ACTUS APOSTOLORUM / Camerlynck, Achille – (Includes indexes) – Editio 6. Brugis: Car Beyaert, 1910 – 2mf – 9 – 0-8370-7131-3 – 1986-1131 – us A.T.L.A. [220]

COMMENTARIUS IN APOCALYPSIN / Primasius – 1985 – 7mf – 9 – Bf1,550.00 – 2-503-60922-8 – be Brepols [210]

COMMENTARIUS IN EPISTOLAM B. PAULI APOSTOLI AD HEBRAEOS / Paenek, Joannes – (Includes bibliographical references) – Oeniponte [Innsbruck]: Libraria Academica Wagneriana, 1882 – 1mf – 9 – 0-8370-4662-9 – 1985-2662 – us A.T.L.A. [220]

COMMENTARIUS IN VATICINIUM MICHAE / Roorda, Taco – (Includes index) – Lugduni Batavorum [Leiden]: P Engels; Lipsiae [Leipzig]: T O Weigel, 1869 – 1mf – 9 – 0-8370-4962-8 – 1985-2962 – us A.T.L.A. [220]

COMMENTARIUS ISAACIDIS QUATENUS AD TEXTUM TALMUDIS...POSSIT TRACTATU ERUBHIN / Margolis, Max Leopold – New York, 1891. 1 fiche – 9 – us A.T.L.A. [270]

COMMENTARIUS LITERALIS, HISTORICO-MORALIS IN REGULAM S.P. BENEDICTI / Calmet, Dom Aug. – Lincii. 2v. 1750 – 8 – Dfl63.00 – ne Slangenburg [240]

COMMENTARIUS PORRETANUS IN PRIMAM EPISTOLAM AD CORINTHIOS 1945 STUDI E TESTI 117 / Landgraf, Arthur M – 7mf – 8 – ne Slangenburg [220]

COMMENTARIUS SUPER GENESIN, IN QUO TEXTUS DECLARATUR, QUAESTIONES DUBIAE SOLVUNTUR, OBSERVATIONES ERUUNTUR,... / Gerhard, J – Jenae, 1637 – 10mf – ne IDC [240]

COMMENTARIVS DE REGIBVS PERSICIS, SEV FAMILIA ARTAXERXIS MAGVSAEI / Reineck, R – Helmaestadii, 1588 – 1mf – 9 – H-8373/1 – ne IDC [956]

COMMENTARIVS IN MATTHAEVM EVANGELISTAM,... / Chytraeus, D – [Strassburg], 1556 – 5mf – 9 – ne IDC [240]

COMMENTARY – (v. 47-. 1969- 5,6. v. 49-. 1970- 9) – v. 1- 1945- – 1 – us UMI [000]

A COMMENTARY, CRITICAL, EXEGETICAL, AND DOCTRINAL, ON ST. PAUL'S EPISTLE TO THE GALATIANS : WITH A REVISED TRANSLATION / Gwynne, George John – (Includes appendixes) – Dublin: University Press, 1863 – 1mf – 9 – 0-8370-3437-X – 1985-1437 – us A.T.L.A. [220]

A COMMENTARY, GRAMMATICAL AND EXEGETICAL, ON THE BOOK OF JOB, VOL 1 : WITH A TRANSLATION / Davidson, Andrew Bruce – (No more publ) – [London]:Williams and Norgate, 1862 – 1mf – 9 – 0-8370-2833-7 – 1985-0833 – us A.T.L.A. [220]

A COMMENTARY ON ECCLESIASTES / Stuart, Moses; ed by Robbins, Rensselaer David Chanceford – Boston: Draper and Halliday, 1880, c1862 – 1mf – 9 – 0-8370-9422-4 – 1986-3422 – us A.T.L.A. [220]

COMMENTARY ON EZRA AND NEHEMIAH / Saadiah, Rabbi; ed by Mathews, H J – Oxford v1-pt 1. 1882 – 3mf – 8 – ne Slangenburg [220]

COMMENTARY ON MECHANIC'S LIEN LAW FOR THE STATE OF NEW YORK; CHAPTER XLIX OF THE GENERAL LAWS. / Heydecker, Edward Le Moyne – Albany, NY: Bender, 1897. 251p. LL-790 – 1 – us L of C Photodup [340]

A COMMENTARY ON ST PAUL'S EPISTLE TO THE GALATIANS / Beet, Joseph Agar – (Includes index) – 3rd ed. New York: Thomas Whittaker, 1891 – 1mf – 9 – 0-8370-6014-1 – 1986-0014 – us A.T.L.A. [220]

A COMMENTARY ON ST PAUL'S EPISTLE TO THE ROMANS / Beet, Joseph Agar – (Includes indexes of biblical and extra-biblical citations, and of subjects) – 2nd ed. London: Hodder & Stoughton, 1881 – 1mf – 9 – 0-8370-2246-0 – 1985-0246 – us A.T.L.A. [220]

A COMMENTARY ON ST PAUL'S EPISTLES TO THE EPHESIANS, PHILIPPIANS, COLOSSIANS, AND TO PHILEMON / Beet, Joseph Agar – (Includes dissertations on Paul's thought and letters) – NY: Thomas Whittaker, 1891 – 1mf – 9 – 0-8370-2247-9 – 1985-0247 – us A.T.L.A. [220]

A COMMENTARY ON THE ACTS OF THE APOSTLES / Hackett, Horatio Balch; ed by Hovey, Alvah – (Includes indexes) – rev enL Philadelphia: American Baptist Publication Society, c1882 – 1mf – 9 – 0-8370-3442-6 – 1985-1442 – us A.T.L.A. [220]

A COMMENTARY ON THE ACTS OF THE APOSTLES *see* PUBLICATIONS

COMMENTARY ON THE ACTS OF THE APOSTLES / Summers, Thomas Osmond – Nashville: M.E. Church, So., 1882. 1 fiche – 9 – us A.T.L.A. [240]

A COMMENTARY ON THE BOOK OF DANIEL / Japheth ben Eli; ed by Margoliouth, D S – (Text in Arabic & Hebrew with transl in English) – Oxford: Clarendon Press, 1889 – 1mf – 9 – 0-8370-3770-0 – 1985-1770 – us A.T.L.A. [220]

A COMMENTARY ON THE BOOK OF ECCLESIASTES / Young, Loyal – Philadelphia: Presb. Bd. of Pub., 1865. 1 fiche – 9 – us A.T.L.A. [240]

COMMENTARY ON THE BOOK OF JOB / Ewald, Heinrich – London: Williams & Norgate, 1882. 1 fiche – 9 – us A.T.L.A. [240]

A COMMENTARY ON THE BOOK OF LEVITICUS / Bonar, A A – 9 – $18.00 – us I.R.C. [220]

A COMMENTARY ON THE BOOK OF PROVERBS / Stuart, Moses – Andover: Warren F Draper, 1870, c1852 – 1mf – 9 – 0-8370-9423-2 – 1986-3423 – us A.T.L.A. [220]

A COMMENTARY ON THE BOOKS OF AMOS, HOSEA, AND MICAH / Smith, John Merlin Powis – (Includes bibliographies and index) – New York:Macmillan, 1914 – 1mf – 9 – 0-8370-4630-0 – 1985-2630 – us A.T.L.A. [220]

COMMENTARY ON THE BOOKS OF KINGS / Keil, Karl Friedrich – Translated by James Murphy; supplemented by Commentary on the books of Chronicles, by Ernst Berteau, translated by James Martin. 2 v. 1857 – 1 – us A.T.L.A. [220]

A COMMENTARY ON THE CONFESSION OF FAITH / Hodge, Archibald Alexander – 1869 – 9 – us A.T.L.A. [240]

COMMENTARY ON THE DE CONSOLATIONE PHILOSOPHIAE BY BOETHIUS / Trivet, Nicholas – 1 – uk Microform Academic [180]

COMMENTARY ON THE EPISTLE OF PAUL TO THE GALATIANS / Bacon, Benjamin Wisner – New York: Macmillan, 1909. 1 fiche – 9 – us A.T.L.A. [240]

A COMMENTARY ON THE EPISTLE TO THE ROMANS / Foster, Robert Verrell – Nashville, TN:Cumberland Presbyterian Pub. House, 1891 – 1mf – 9 – 0-8370-3169-9 – 1985-1169 – us A.T.L.A. [220]

A COMMENTARY ON THE EPISTLE TO THE ROMANS / Stuart, Moses; ed by Robbins, Rensselaer David Chanceford – (Includes bibliographical references) – 4th ed. Andover: Warren F Draper, 1868, c1859 – 2mf – 9 – 0-8370-9831-9 – 1986-3831 – us A.T.L.A. [220]

COMMENTARY ON THE EPISTLE TO THE ROMANS : EMBRACING THE LATEST RESULTS OF CRITICISM / Brown, David – Glasgow: William Collins, 1860 – 1mf – 9 – 0-8370-2475-7 – 1985-0475 – us A.T.L.A. [220]

COMMENTARY ON THE EPISTLE TO THE ROMANS / Foster, Robert V – Nashville: Cumberland Presb. Bd., 1891. 1 fiche – 9 – us A.T.L.A. [240]

COMMENTARY ON THE EPISTLES OF ST PAUL TO THE CORINTHIANS / Stanley, Arthur Penrhyn – 5th ed. 1882 – 9 – us A.T.L.A. [240]

COMMENTARY ON THE EPISTLES TO THE SEVEN CHURCHES IN ASIA : REVELATION 2, 3 / Trench, Richard Chenevix – (Includes also Revelation 1, 4-20) – New York:Charles Scribner, 1872 – 1mf – 9 – 0-8370-5569-5 – 1985-3569 – us A.T.L.A. [220]

COMMENTARY ON THE EPISTLES TO THE THESSALONIANS / Stevens, William Arnold – Philadelphia: Am. Bapt. Pub. Soc., 1890.1 fiche – 9 – us A.T.L.A. [240]

COMMENTARY ON THE EPISTLES TO...ASIA: REVELATION 2, 3 / Trench, Richard Chenevix – New York: Charles Scribner, 1872. 1 fiche – 9 – us A.T.L.A. [240]

COMMENTARY ON THE GOSPEL ACCORDING TO LUKE / Rice, Edwin Wilbur – Philadelphia: Union Press, 1898.1 fiche – 9 – us A.T.L.A. [240]

COMMENTARY ON THE GOSPEL ACCORDING TO MATTHEW / Rice, Edwin Wilbur – Philadelphia: Am. Sun. Sch. Un., 1909. 1 fiche – 9 – us A.T.L.A. [240]

COMMENTARY ON THE GOSPEL ACCORDING TO ST. JOHN / Cyrillus, Patriarch of Alexandria – 1 – us A.T.L.A. [240]

A COMMENTARY ON THE GREEK TEXT OF THE EPISTLE OF PAUL TO THE COLOSSIANS / Eadie, John; ed by Young, W – (Includes indexes) – 2nd ed. Edinburgh: T & T Clark, 1884 – 1mf – 9 – 0-8370-3015-3 – 1985-1015 – us A.T.L.A. [220]

A COMMENTARY ON THE GREEK TEXT OF THE EPISTLE OF PAUL TO THE PHILIPPIANS / Eadie, John – (Includes indexes of subjects and Greek terms) – London: Richard Griffin, 1859 – 1mf – 9 – 0-8370-3016-1 – 1985-1016 – us A.T.L.A. [220]

A COMMENTARY ON THE GREEK TEXT OF THE EPISTLES OF PAUL TO THE THESSALONIANS / Eadie, John; ed by Young, William – London: Macmillan, 1877 – 1mf – 9 – 0-8370-3017-X – 1985-1017 – us A.T.L.A. [220]

COMMENTARY ON THE HERBARIUM AMBOINENSE / Hamilton, F – Memoirs of the Wernerian Natural History Society, v5, 1824. p. 307-383 – 2mf – 9 – ne IDC [580]

A COMMENTARY ON THE HORTUS MALABARICUS / Hamilton, F – (Transactions of the Linnean Society). London. 1821-26. B-8308 1 – 9 – ne IDC [580]

A COMMENTARY ON THE LAW OF AGENCY AND AGENTS / Wharton, Francis A – Philadelphia, Kay, 1876. 620 p. LL-1532 – 1 – us L of C Photodup [340]

A COMMENTARY ON THE LAW OF EVIDENCE IN CIVIL ISSUES / Wharton, Francis A – Philadelphia, Kay, 1877. 2 v. LL-1478 – 1 – us L of C Photodup [340]

A COMMENTARY ON THE MINING LEGISLATION OF CONGRESS WITH A PRELIMINARY REVIEW OF THE REPEALED SECTIONS OF THE MINING ACT OF 1866...2ND ED / Weeks, Edward P – San Francisco, Whitney, 1880. 580 p. LL-1645 – 1 – us L of C Photodup [340]

A COMMENTARY ON THE NEW TESTAMENT. VOLUME 2, LUKE-THE ACTS = NEUE TESTAMENT. 1. HAELFTE / Weiss, Bernhard – New York: Funk & Wagnalls, 1906 – 2mf – 9 – 0-8370-9664-2 – 1986-3664 – us A.T.L.A. [220]

A COMMENTARY ON THE NEW TESTAMENT. VOLUME 3, ROMANS-COLOSSIANS = NEUE TESTAMENT. 2. HAELFTE / Weiss, Bernhard – New York: Funk & Wagnalls, 1906 – 2mf – 9 – 0-8370-9665-0 – 1986-3665 – us A.T.L.A. [220]

A COMMENTARY ON THE NEW TESTAMENT. VOLUME 4, THESSALONIANS-REVELATION = NEUE TESTAMENT. 2. HAELFTE / Weiss, Bernhard – New York: Funk & Wagnalls, 1906 – 2mf – 9 – 0-8370-9666-9 – 1986-3666 – us A.T.L.A. [220]

A COMMENTARY ON THE SECOND EPISTLE OF THE APOSTLE PETER / Demarest, John Terhune – New York: Sheldon, 1862 – 1mf – 9 – 0-8370-2884-1 – 1985-0884 – us A.T.L.A. [220]

COMMENTARY ON THE SOBIESKY BOOK OF HOURS IN WINDSOR CASTLE LIBRARY / Ameisenowa, Z – 1 – uk Microform Academic [760]

COMMENTARY ON THE SONG OF SONGS AND ECCLESIASTES / Delitzsch, Franz – Trans. from German by M. G. Easton. 1877 – 1 – us A.T.L.A. [240]

COMMENTARY ON WATER DEVELOPMENT IN THE JORDAN VALLEY REGION / The Arab Palestine Office – Beirut, Lebanon: The Arab Palestine Office 1954 – us Res Libr [333]

A COMMENTARY OR EXPOSITION UPON THE PROPHECY OF HABAKKUK / Marbury, Edward – Edinburgh: James Nichol, 1865. 1 fiche – 9 – us A.T.L.A. [240]

COMMENTARY UPON THE EPISTLE OF PAUL WRITTEN TO THE COLOSSIANS / Cartwright, Thomas – Edinburgh: James Nichol, 1864. 1 fiche – 9 – us A.T.L.A. [240]

COMMENTARY UPON THE GOSPEL OF ST MATTHEW / Valdes, Juan de – 1882 – 1 – us A.T.L.A. [240]

A COMMENTARY UPON THE PROPHECY OF MALACHI / Stock, Richard – (Includes indexes) – Edinburgh: James Nichol, 1865 – 1mf – 9 – 0-8370-5422-2 – 1985-3422 – us A.T.L.A. [220]

COMMENTATIO BOTANICA DE CONIFEREIS ET CYCADEIS / Richard, L C M – Stuttgardiae. 1826. B-5019 2 – 8 – ne IDC [580]

COMMENTATIO DE FUNGIS CLAVAEFORMIBUS / Persoon, C H – Lipsiae. 1797. B-6294 2 – 8 – ne IDC [580]

COMMENTATIO DE JURE PEREGRINANTIUM : ED NOVISSIMA / Engelbrecht, I W – Helmstadii, 1751 – 1mf – 1 – ILM-1223/1 – ne IDC [327]

COMMENTATIO DE VARIO LICHENUM USU / Hoffmann, G F – Lyon. 1787. B-922 2 – 8 – ne IDC [580]

COMMENTATIO SEU DECLARATIO ADILLUD GENESEOS / Correas, Gonzalo – 1622 – 9 – 1.50f – sp Bibl Santa Ana [400]

COMMENTATIONES BOTANICAE / Dumortier, B C J – Tournay. 1822, 1823 – 8 – ne IDC [580]

COMMENTATIONES DE LEGUMINOSARUM GENERIBUS / Bentham, G – Vindobonae. 1837. B-850 2 – 8 – ne IDC [580]

COMMENTATIONES MATHEMATICAE UNIVERSITATIS CAROLINAE – (v1-4. Dfl35.00v; v5-7. Dfl90.00v; v8-23. Dfl160.00v) – Prague. v1-23. 1960-82 – 5,9 – Dfl2,970.00 – ne Swets [510]

COMMENTATOR OF THE COMMUNITY COUNCIL – Jacksonville, FL. 28 Oct, 8 Dec 1960; 10 Mar, 6 May, 25 May 1961; 12 Jan, 16 Apr 1962; 28 Oct 1964.Ceased publication. In English – 1 – us A.J.P.C. [071]

COMMENTING AND COMMENTARIES: LECTURES / Spurgeon, Charles Haddon – New York: Sheldon, 1876.1 fiche – 9 – us A.T.L.A. [240]

COMMENTO EN DEFENSA DEL LIBRO 4... NEBRIJA / Lopez, Diego – Salamanca: Casa de Autoria. Ramirez Vda., 1610 – 1 – sp Bibl Santa Ana [440]

COMMENTS OF THE FEDERAL MILITARY GOVERNMENT ON THE REPORT OF THE TRIBUNAL OF INQUIRY INTO THE AFFAIRS OF WAAC (NIGERIA) LIMITED : OTHERWISE KNOWN AS NIGERIA AIRWAYS, FOR THE PERIOD 1ST MARCH 1961 TO 31ST DECEMBER 1965 – Lagos, Federal Ministry of Information, Printing Division 1968 – us Res Libr [380]

COMMENTS OF THE LAGOS STATE GOVERNMENT ON THE REPORT OF THE TRIBUNAL OF INQUIRY INTO THE AFFAIRS OF THE LAGOS EXECUTIVE DEVELOPMENT BOARD FOR THE PERIOD 1ST OCTOBER 1960 TO 31ST DECEMBER 1965 – Lagos, Information Division, Lagos State Government 1968 – us Res Libr [350]

COMMENTS ON AGRICULTURAL AND FOOD CHEMISTRY : A JOURNAL OF CRITICAL DISCUSSION OF THE CURRENT LITERATURE AND FUTURE TRENDS / ed by Feeney, Robert E – 1,5,9 – us Gordon [660]
COMMENTS ON ASTROPHYSICS – 1969- – 1,5,9 – us Gordon [530]
COMMENTS ON ATOMIC AND MOLECULAR PHYSICS – 1,5,9 – us Gordon [530]
COMMENTS ON CONDENSED MATTER PHYSICS / ed by Mills, D L et al – 9,5,1 – us Gordon [530]
COMMENTS ON DOXIADIS REPORT "HOUSING IN LIBYA" / Libya. Advisor on Housing and Town Planning – Advisor on Housing and Town Planning, to H.E. Abdul Mawla Longhi, Minister of Labour and Social Affairs. 27 Jul 1964. BNE-1103 1 – 9 – ne IDC [360]
COMMENTS ON EARTH SCIENCES: GEOPHYSICS – 1970- – 1,5,9 – us Gordon [530]
COMMENTS ON GEOCHEMISTRY AND COSMOCHEMISTRY – 1,5,9 – us Gordon [073]
COMMENTS ON INORGANIC CHEMISTRY – 1,5,9 – us Gordon [540]
COMMENTS ON INORGANIC CHEMISTRY : A JOURNAL OF CRITICAL DISCUSSION OF THE CURRENT LITERATURE / ed by Basolo, Fred & Marzilli, L G – 9,5,1 – us Gordon [540]
COMMENTS ON MOLECULAR AND CELLULAR BIOPHYSICS / ed by Jameson, D – 1,5,9 – us Gordon [530]
COMMENTS ON NUCLEAR AND PARTICLE PHYSICS – v1- 1968- – 1,5,9 – us Gordon [530]
COMMENTS ON PLASMA PHYSICS AND CONTROLLED FUSION – 1972- – 1,5,9 – us Gordon [621]
COMMENTS ON SOLID STATE PHYSICS – 1968- – 1,5,9 – us Gordon [530]
COMMENTS ON TECTONOPHYSICS AND PHYSICS OF THE INTERIOR – 1,5,9 – us Gordon [073]
COMMENTS ON THE DECISION TO ESTABLISH A PERMANENT CONSULTATIVE COMMITTEE TO PROMOTE ECONOMIC COORDINATION AMONG THE MAGHRIB COUNTRIES AND TO SET UP A CENTRE FOR INDUSTRIAL STUDIES IN TRIPOLI / Libya. Industrial Planning Section – From Industrial Planning section. To Dr. Rawle Farley, Senior Economist. Paper nr. 6. 6th Feb 1965. BNE-1205 – 9 – ne IDC [330]
COMMENTS ON THE HAGUE RULES, 1921... – N.p., n.d. – 1mf – 1 – ILM-3890/1 – ne IDC [327]
COMMENTS ON THE POLSERVICE REPORT ON SUGAR BEET PLANT / Libya. Industrial Planning Section – nr. 7. S. Bofarull, Industrial Planning Officer. BNE-1206 1 – 9 – ne IDC [660]
COMMENTS ON THE PROPOSED WAR WITH FRANCE, ON THE STATE OF PARTIES, AND ON THE NEW ACT RESPECTING ALIENS – London, 1793 – 2mf – 1 – ILM-2829/1 – ne IDC [327]
COMMENTS ON THE REVELATION, AND OTHER PROPHECIES / Case, Ira – Providence, 1871. 1 fiche – 9 – us A.T.L.A. [240]
COMMENTS ON THEORETICAL BIOLOGY : A JOURNAL OF CRITICAL DISCUSSION OF THE CURRENT LITERATURE / ed by Blum, J Joseph et al – 9,5,1 – us Gordon [574]
COMMENTS ON TOXICOLOGY : A JOURNAL OF CRITICAL DISCUSSION OF THE CURRENT LITERATURE / ed by Hayes, A Wallace – 9,5,1 – us Gordon [615]
LE COMMERCANT – (The Negotiator: 1 page sur 4) – St-Cesaire, Canada. v1 n2. 9 dec 1876-6 avr 1878 – 1r – 1 – Can$30.00 – cn Can Microfilming [072]
COMMERCE – Montreal: Chambre de commerce, 1899-1991. SEM105P1 – 762mf – 9 – Can$1,714.50 (1992 12mf Can$27.00y) – cn Bibl Nat [073]
COMMERCE / Sydney Chamber of Commerce – Official Journal. Sydney. v. 29-46 no. 1. Jan 1940-Feb 1957 – 1 – us NY Public [073]
LE COMMERCE – Journal commercial, politique, scientifique et litteraire. Dir. P. Douvet. no. 1-17. Paris. 6 juin-26 sept 1869 – 1 – fr A.C.R.P.P. [073]
LE COMMERCE – Port-au-Prince: J J Andain, [6e annee n8-n42]. (12 fevr. 1876-31 mars 1877) – 2 sheets – us Res Libr [072]
COMMERCE AMERICA – v. 1-. 1976- – 1,5,6,9 – us UMI [380]
Commerce Clearing House *see* BUSINESS LAW CASE METHOD.
Commerce Clearing House Canadian Limited *see*
– CANADIAN ESTATE TAX AND SUCCESSION DUTIES ACTS; INCLUDING ALL AMENDMENTS TO DECEMBER 1, 1966
– EXPENSES UNDER CANADIAN INCOME TAX ACT
LE COMMERCE DE MONTREAL ET DE QUEBEC ET LEURS INDUSTRIES EN 1889 – Montreal: J. Kane, 1889. 00723. (Pre-1900 Canadiana) – 9 – cn C.I.H.M. [971]
DU COMMERCE DES COLONIES: SES PRINCIPES ET SES LOIS – Reprod. d'un edition 1785. 63p. 1 fiche. (Economics Collection) – 9 – 6.00 – fr Bibl Nationale [380]
COMMERCE ET TRAITE DES NOIRS AUX COTES OCCIDENTALES D'AFRIQUE / Bouet-Willaumez, E – (Slave Trade and Abolitionism in France Series). Ier janvier 1848 – 9 – fr Hachette [380]
COMMERCE EXTERIEUR DE L'ALGERIE / Algeria. Direction Generale du Plan et des Etudes Economiques – Tablaux statistiques. 1965. BNE-8631 1 – 9 – ne IDC [380]
LE COMMERCE EXTERIEUR DE L'ALGERIE / Algeria. Direction Nationale des Douanes – 4v. in 3. 1959-64. (lacking 1962). BNE-8639 1 – 9 – ne IDC [380]
LE COMMERCE EXTERIEUR DU MAROC / Beaud, M – Rabat. 1960. BNE-3014 1 – 9 – ne IDC [380]
COMMERCE FIRST BAPTIST CHURCH. COMMERCE, GEORGIA : CHURCH RECORDS – 1874-1989. 2030p – 1 – 91.35 – us Baptist [978]
COMMERCE TODAY – v1-6 1970-75 1,5,6; v6-9 – us UMI [380]
COMMERCE TODAY – Washington, DC. v1-6. 1970-75 – 142mf – 9 – $5.00f – us Ross [380]
COMMERCIAL – Caldwell. Kan. 1880-1883 – 1 – us UMI [071]
COMMERCIAL – Columbus. Miss. 1902-1918 – 1 – us UMI [071]
COMMERCIAL – Danville. Ill. 1878-99 – 1 – us UMI [071]
COMMERCIAL – Danville. Ill. -w. 1866-90, 1899 – 1 – us UMI [071]
COMMERCIAL – Pittsburgh. Pa. 1864-1877 – 1 – us UMI [071]
COMMERCIAL – Toledo. Ohio. 1863-1899 – 1 – us UMI [071]
COMMERCIAL – Wilmington. N.C. -tw. 1846-58 – 1 – us UMI [071]
COMMERCIAL – Ypsilanti. Mich. -w. 1864-98 – 1 – us UMI [071]
COMMERCIAL – Bangor, ME. may 4-aug 4 1956 – 3r – us Res Libr [072]
O COMMERCIAL : ORGAO INDEPENDENTE, PROPAGANDISTA, LITTERARIO E NOTICIOSO – Manaos, Amazonas. 3 Maio-18 Dez 1916 – 1,5,6 – bl Biblioteca [072]
O COMMERCIAL – [s.l.]. 11 Fev, Maio 1882; Jul 1885; Fev 1886; 31 Jul 1888 – 1,5,6 – bl Biblioteca [072]
THE COMMERCIAL – (Contd by: Commercial and Retail Merchants Review) – Winnipeg: Steen & Boyce, [1882?-1922] – 9 – cn C.I.H.M. [380]
THE COMMERCIAL – Meyersdale, PA., 1894-1897 – 13 – $25.00r – us I.M.R. [071]
THE COMMERCIAL – Winnipeg, Canada. -w. 1886-1907. 41 reels – 1 – uk British Libr Newspaper [072]
COMMERCIAL ACCOUNTANT/ACCOUNTANTS REVIEW – 1947-77 – 1 – uk Microform Academic [073]
COMMERCIAL ADVERTISER – Canton. N.Y. 1952-58 – 1 – us UMI [071]
COMMERCIAL ADVERTISER – Huron. Ohio. 1837-42 – 1 – us UMI [071]
COMMERCIAL ADVERTISER – New York. 1797-1820 – 3 – us Readex [071]
COMMERCIAL ADVERTISER – New York. Oct 2 1797-Jan 31 1904. Incomplete – 1 – us NY Public [071]
COMMERCIAL ADVERTISER – Red Cloud. Neb. 1908-1968 – 1 – us UMI [071]
COMMERCIAL ADVERTISER – Waterford. Ireland. -w. 15 Jan-4 Mar 1848. (6 ft) – 1 – uk British Libr Newspaper [072]
THE COMMERCIAL ADVERTISER – (Filmed together with: The Morning Courier) – Montreal, Canada. v23 n3. 29 jun 1858; v26 n196. 16 aut 1869 – 3r – 1 – Can$45.00r – cn Can Microfilming [072]
THE COMMERCIAL ADVERTISER *see* THE MORNING COURIER
COMMERCIAL ADVISORY FOUNDATION IN INDONESIA : AGRICULTURE SECTION – (Irregular. Missing: 1972(34)) – Djakarta, 1970-1972 – 21mf – 9 – SE-1383/1 – ne IDC [630]
COMMERCIAL ADVISORY FOUNDATION IN INDONESIA : BANKING SECTOR – (In English. Irregular) – Djakarta. nos 1-5. 1970-1972 – 3mf – 9 – SE-1384/1 – ne IDC [332]
COMMERCIAL ADVISORY FOUNDATION IN INDONESIA : CAPITAL INVESTMENT SECTOR – (Irregular. Missing: 1970-1971(1-40,42,43,58,83)) – Djakarta. nos 1-84. 1970-1972 – 11mf – 9 – SE-1385/1 – ne IDC [332]
COMMERCIAL ADVISORY FOUNDATION IN INDONESIA : CIRCULAR 1. COST OF LIVING INDEX FOR FOREIGN FAMILY – (In English. Monthly. Missing: 1967-1969) – Djakarta, 1967-1971 – 1mf – 9 – SE-1380/1 – ne IDC [339]
COMMERCIAL ADVISORY FOUNDATION IN INDONESIA : ECONOMIC SECTION – (In English. Irregular) – Djakarta, 1969(1-7) – 2mf – 9 – SE-1388/1 – ne IDC [330]
COMMERCIAL ADVISORY FOUNDATION IN INDONESIA : ECONOMIC SECTION – (Irregular. Some vols missing) – Djakarta. nos 1-2059. [1960]-1963 – 25mf – 9 – SE-1387/1 – ne IDC [330]
COMMERCIAL ADVISORY FOUNDATION IN INDONESIA : ECONOMIC SECTION – (Missing: 1964(10-12); 1964/65(16)) – Djakarta, 1964-1969 – 45mf – 9 – SE-278/1 – ne IDC [330]
COMMERCIAL ADVISORY FOUNDATION IN INDONESIA : FINANCE SECTOR – (Irregular. Missing: 1972(39,50)) – Djakarta. nos 1-51. 1970-1972 – 22mf – 9 – SE-1389/1 – ne IDC [332]
COMMERCIAL ADVISORY FOUNDATION IN INDONESIA : GENERAL SECTION – (Irregular. Some vols missing) – Djakarta, 1965-1972 – 27mf – 9 – SE-1381/1 – ne IDC [380]
COMMERCIAL ADVISORY FOUNDATION IN INDONESIA : INDUSTRIES SECTOR – (Irregular) – Djakarta, 1970-1972 – 5mf – 9 – SE-1390/1 – ne IDC [338]
COMMERCIAL ADVISORY FOUNDATION IN INDONESIA : LABOUR AND SOCIAL SECTION – (Irregular. Missing: nos 1-278[196?]-65; no 306 1966) – Djakarta. nos 1-316. [196?]-1966 – 3mf – 9 – SE-1391/1 – ne IDC [331]
COMMERCIAL ADVISORY FOUNDATION IN INDONESIA : LEGAL SECTION – (Some vols missing) – Djakarta, 195?-1969 – 119mf – SE-643/1 – ne IDC [340]
COMMERCIAL ADVISORY FOUNDATION IN INDONESIA – (Missing: 1962(April); 1964(June-July); 1965(June-July, Oct.)) – Djakarta, 1962-1966 – 40mf – SE-678/1 – ne IDC [380]
COMMERCIAL ADVISORY FOUNDATION IN INDONESIA : SECTOR OF MINING – (Irregular. Missing: 1972(49)) – Djakarta. nos 1-54. 1970-1972 – 14mf – 9 – SE-1392/1 – ne IDC [622]
COMMERCIAL ADVISORY FOUNDATION IN INDONESIA – (Some vols missing) – Djakarta, 1953-1973. v1-21(43) – 961mf – SE-680/1 – ne IDC [380]
COMMERCIAL ADVISORY FOUNDATION IN INDONESIA : STATISTICS AND PRICE SURVEY SECTION – (Irregular) – Djakarta, 1965(1-11) – 2mf – 9 – SE-1393/1 – ne IDC [338]
COMMERCIAL ADVISORY FOUNDATION IN INDONESIA : STATISTICS AND PRICE SURVEY SECTION – (Irregular. Missing: 1966(2-13)) – Djakarta, 1965-1967 – 7mf – 9 – SE-1394/1 – ne IDC [338]
COMMERCIAL ADVISORY FOUNDATION IN INDONESIA : SUMMARIES LAWS/ REGULATIONS AND OTHER INFORMATION MATERIALS – (Monthly. Missing: 1970(9)-1971(1,5,6)) – Djakarta, 1970-1971 – 7mf – 9 – SE-1382/1 – ne IDC [340]
COMMERCIAL ADVISORY FOUNDATION IN INDONESIA : TRADE SECTOR – (Irregular. Missing: 1970(1-10); 1971(24,26)) – Djakarta. nos1-39. 1970-1971 – 11mf – 9 – SE-1396/1 – ne IDC [380]
COMMERCIAL AGE – Olympia. Wash. -w. 1868-70 – 1 – us UMI [071]
COMMERCIAL AND FINANCIAL CHRONICLE – New York. Nov 1875-Dec 1876; Jan 1897-Dec 1908.-w. 63 reels – 1 – uk British Libr Newspaper [071]
COMMERCIAL AND FINANCIAL CHRONICLE – New York. v1-19. 1865-74 – 7r – 1 – us Ross [380]
COMMERCIAL AND FINANCIAL CHRONICLE – Riverside, CA. 1975-80 – 23r – 1 – $1,150.00 – R02715 – us Library Micro [071]
COMMERCIAL AND FINANCIAL CHRONICLE – v. 1- 1865- – 1 – us UMI [380]
THE COMMERCIAL AND FINANCIAL CHRONICLE – New York. v. 1-19 no. 496. July 1865-Dec 1874 – 1 – us NY Public [071]
COMMERCIAL AND NOTARIAL PRECEDENTS. / Montefiore, Joshua – 2d Amer. ed. from the last London ed. Philadelphia: Carey & Lea, 1822. 480p. LL-867 – 1 – us L of C Photodup [340]
COMMERCIAL AND RETAIL MERCHANTS REVIEW *see* THE COMMERCIAL
COMMERCIAL APPEAL – Danville. Va. -w. 1947- – 1 – us UMI [071]
COMMERCIAL APPEAL – Knoxville. Tenn. 1965- – 1 – us UMI [071]
COMMERCIAL APPEAL – Memphis. Tenn. 1894- – 1 – us UMI [071]
COMMERCIAL BULLETIN – Marshfield OR. Nov 1890 – 1 – us U.O. Library [071]
COMMERCIAL BULLETIN – New Orleans. La. 1836-1871 – 1 – us UMI [071]
COMMERCIAL CHRONICLE AND DAILY MARYLANDER – Baltimore, Maryland. Apr 14 1829-Dec 27 1833 – 1r – 1 – us L of C Photodup [071]
COMMERCIAL COURIER/COURRIER COMMERCIAL / ed by Drapeau, Stanislas – Quebec, Canada. v1 n8. 13 mar 1845 – 1r – 1 – Can$25.00 – cn Can Microfilming [072]
COMMERCIAL DAILY LIST – London. 2 March 1838-26 March 1870.-d. 39mqn reels – 1 – uk British Libr Newspaper [072]
COMMERCIAL DIRECTORY OF MANILA – [Manila: s.n.], 1901 – 1 – us Res Libr [380]
COMMERCIAL EGG CLINIC COMPENDIUM / Texas A & M University. Department of Poultry Science – No.10-27. 1965-71. 11 fiches – 9 – us Spaulding [636]
COMMERCIAL FERTILIZER AND PLANT FOOD INDUSTRY *see* AG CHEM AND COMMERCIAL FERTILIZER
COMMERCIAL GAZETTE – Montreal, Canada. v13 n31. 19 aut 1897; v13 n32. 24 aut 1897 – 1r – 1 – Can$25.00 – cn Can Microfilming [380]
COMMERCIAL HERALD AND MARKET REVIEW – San Francisco, CA. 1868-1875 – 2r – 1 – $90.00 – C03665 – us Library Micro [071]
THE COMMERCIAL INDEPENDENCE OF CANADA: AN ADDRESS DELIVERED 26TH JANUARY, 1883 TO THE REFORM ASSOCIATIONS OF CENTRE TORONTO, ON "THE RIGHT OF CANADA TO MAKE HER OWN COMMERCIAL TREATIES" / Edgar, James David – Toronto: Published by a Committee of the Associations, 1883?. 02879. (Pre-1900 Canadiana) – 9 – cn C.I.H.M. [971]
COMMERCIAL INDUSTRIES OF CANADA – Historical and commercial sketches of Quebec, Point Levi, Three Rivers, Richmond, Sherbrooke, St. Johns and environs: its prominent places and people, representative merchants and manufacturers; its improvements, progress and enterprise. Toronto: M. Bixby, 1888. 03406. (Pre-1900 Canadiana) – 9 – cn C.I.H.M. [971]
COMMERCIAL JOURNAL – Pittsburgh. Pa. 1846-1852 – 1 – us UMI [071]
COMMERCIAL LAW / Gano, Darwin Curtis – (commercial law. New York: American Book Co. 1913. 399p. LL-205) – New York: American Book Co. 1904. 399p. LL-247 – 1 – us L of C Photodup [340]
COMMERCIAL LAW / Lyon, Newell – New York, 1901-04. 148l. LL-1238 – 1 – us L of C Photodup [340]
COMMERCIAL LAW JOURNAL – (Title varies: v6-27 no 7 1902-1922 as Bulletin of Commercial Law League of America. v27 no 8 1922-23 as Commercial Law Legal Bulletin. v28-35 1923-30 as Commercial Law League Journal) – v6-99. 1902-94 – 9 – $1,373.00 set – us Hein [340]
COMMERCIAL LAW LEAGUE JOURNAL *see* COMMERCIAL LAW JOURNAL
COMMERCIAL LAW LEGAL BULLETIN *see* COMMERCIAL LAW JOURNAL

COMMERCIAL LAW QUESTIONS / Cathcart, Wallace Daniel – San Francisco: Pacioli, 1946. 74p. LL-210 – 1 – us L of C Photodup [340]

THE COMMERCIAL LAWS OF THE STATES: A SUMMARY OF THE LAWS RELATING TO ARREST ASSIGNMENTS ATTACHMENT...&C / Homans, Isaac Smith – New York: Bankers', 1870. 328p. LL-900 – 1 – us L of C Photodup [340]

THE COMMERCIAL LIST – Quebec, Canada. v3 n1. 14 mai 1818-29 nov 1819; v10 n1. 21 mai 1825-v11 n28. 27 nov 1826; v17 n1. 22 mai 1832-v17 n31. 15 mar 1833; 22 mai 1836-6 nov 1837 – 1r – 1 – Can$40.00 – cn Can Microfilming [072]

COMMERCIAL MASTER FILE-RESTRICTED / U.S. National Technical Information Service – Commercial operator and restricted operator licensees in operator name sequence. Cross-reference by serial number included. Covers last 7 years – 9 – us N.T.I.S. [000]

COMMERCIAL MESSENGER AND BRITISH CANADIAN LITERARY GAZETTE / ed by Gibson, John – Montreal, Canada. v1 n11. 9 avr 1840-v3 n119. 14 dec 1842 – 1r – 1 – Can$35.00 – cn Can Microfilming [072]

THE COMMERCIAL MONTHLY – Montreal, Canada. v2 n3. avr 1910 – 1r – 1 – Can$25.00 – cn Can Microfilming [073]

COMMERCIAL MOTOR – v111-142. 1960-75 – 1,5,6 – us Princeton Micro [073]

COMMERCIAL NEWS – Danville. Ill. 1904- – 1 – us UMI [071]

COMMERCIAL NEWS – Sacramento, CA. 1924-54 – 8r – 1 – $400.00 – C03424 – us Library Micro [071]

COMMERCIAL NEWS – Sacramento. Calif. 1942-54 – 1 – us UMI [071]

COMMERCIAL NEWS – San Francisco. Calif. 1947- – 1 – us UMI [071]

COMMERCIAL OPERATIONS IN SPACE – (Suppl to vol 51, Science and Technology) – 1981 – 1mf – 9 – $10.00 – 0-87703-165-7 – us Univelt [338]

COMMERCIAL PRECEDENTS : SELECTED FROM THE COLUMN OF REPLIES AND DECISIONS OF THE NEW YORK JOURNAL OF COMMERCE, ALSO SELECTED DECISIONS FROM OTHER SOURCES / Putzel, Charles & Baehr, H A – Hartford, CO: American Publ Co, 1897 – 8mf – 9 – $12.00 – LLMC 92-122 – us L.L.M.C. [340]

COMMERCIAL PRICE CURRENT – Canton. China. -w. 12 Sep 1835-3 Sep 1836. (16 ft) – 1 – uk British Libr Newspaper [072]

COMMERCIAL REFRIGERATION AND AIR CONDITIONING see AIRCONDITIONING AND REFRIGERATION BUSINESS

COMMERCIAL REVIEW – Portland. Ind. 1952-58; 1963- – 1 – us UMI [071]

THE COMMERCIAL REVIEW – Montreal, Canada. ns: v7 n7. fev 1880 – 1r – 1 – Can$25.00 – cn Can Microfilming [072]

COMMERCIAL SHIPPING AND GENERAL ADVERTISER FOR WEST CORNWALL – Penryn, England. 8 Jun 1867-27 Sep 1912.-w. 10 reels – 1 – uk British Libr Newspaper [072]

COMMERCIAL SKETCH OF MONTREAL AND ITS SUPERIORITY AS A WHOLESALE MARKET – Montreal: Chisholm & Dodd, 1868. 03408. (Pre-1900 Canadiana) – 9 – cn C.I.H.M. [971]

COMMERCIAL SPACE – v1- . 1985- – 1,5,6,9 – us UMI [073]

THE COMMERCIAL TRIBUNE – Cincinnati, Ohio. Jan 1 1928-Dec 3 1930. Incomplete – 1 – us NY Public [071]

COMMERCIAL UNION: A STUDY – By a Quebec liberal. 1886?. 00724. (Pre-1900 Canadiana) – 9 – cn C.I.H.M. [971]

COMMERCIAL UNION BETWEEN CANADA AND THE UNITED STATES: AN ADDRESS DELIVERED BEFORE THE CANADIAN CLUB OF NEW YORK / Butterworth, Benjamin – 1887? 02058. (Pre-1900 Canadiana) – 9 – cn C.I.H.M. [975]

COMMERCIAL UNION BETWEEN THE UNITED STATES AND CANADA: TWO LETTERS FROM EDWARD ATKINSON, ESQ., OF BOSTON, IN RESPONSE TO RESOLUTIONS OF THE NEW YORK CHAMBER OF COMMERCE / Atkinson, Edward – New York: E. Wiman, 1887? 02209. (Pre-1900 Canadiana) – 9 – cn C.I.H.M. [380]

COMMERCIAL UTILIZATION OF SPACE – (Suppl to vol 23, Advances) – 1968 – 24mf – 9 – $35.00 – 0-87703-216-5 – us Univelt [380]

COMMERCIAL-DISPATCH – Columbus. Miss. 1919-1923; 1937-1962; 1973- – 1 – us UMI [071]

COMMERCIAL-MAIL – Columbia City. Ind. 1927-28 – 1 – us UMI [071]

COMMERCIAL-MAIL – Columbia City. Ind. -w. 1879-1919 – 1 – us UMI [071]

O COMMERCIARIO : ORGAO DA ASSOCIACAO DOS EMPREGADOS NO COMMERCIO AMAZONAS – Manaos, Amazonas. 1 Ago 1933 – 1,5,6 – bl Biblioteca [072]

O COMMERCIO : ORGAO DOS INTERESSES DA INDUSTRIA, LAVOURA E COMMERCIO – Senna Madureira, Acre. 22-29 Jun 1913 – 1 – bl Biblioteca [380]

O COMMERCIO – Patos de Minas, Brazil. Nov-Dec 1910; 1911; Jan 1912; Mar-Dec 1913; 1914 – 1 – bl Biblioteca [072]

O COMMERCIO : PERIODICO COMMERCIAL, LITTERARIO E NOTICIOSO – Patrocinio, 7 Jan-23 Sep 1934 – 1,5,6 – bl Biblioteca [072]

O COMMERCIO – Pirapora, 1 Jun 1932; Mar-Dec 1933; Jan-15 Apr 1934 – 1,5,6 – bl Biblioteca [072]

O COMMERCIO – [s.l.]. 3 Nov 1842; Jan-Dez 1843; 22 Fev 1847 – 1,5,6 – bl Biblioteca [072]

COMMERCIO DE ALAGOAS : ORGAO DEDICADO AOS INTERESSES DO COMMERCIO, DA INDUSTRIA E DA LAVOURA – Maceio, Alagoas. 2-4 Jun 1898 – 1,5,6 – bl Biblioteca [072]

O COMMERCIO DE LOURENCO MARQUES – Lourenco Maraques: Baptista de Carvalho & Irmao, sep 3-17 1892 – us Res Libr [380]

COMMERCIO DO ACRE – Xapury, Acre. 11 Jun 1915-29 Dez 1918 – 1,5,6 – bl Biblioteca [072]

COMMERCIO DO AMAZONAS – Manaos, Amazonas. 1-27 Jul, Dez 1870; Abr 1872; Jan, Maio-Jun 1874; Jun-Jul 1875; Dez 1876; Dez 1877; Jan 1878; Maio 1879; Maio-Out 1880; Ago, Dez 1881; Mar 1884; Out 1891; Ago 1897; Maio 1898-Dez 1899; Abr-Jun, Out-Dez 1900; Ago 1903; 29 Mar 1912 – 1,5,6 – bl Biblioteca [072]

COMMERCIO DO MADEIRA : ORGAO ESPECIAL DO COMMERCIO – Villa de Manicore, Amazonas. 11 Maio 1884 – 1,5,6 – bl Biblioteca [072]

O COMMERCIO DO PORTO – Oporto, Portugal. -d. 1 Aug 1916-9 Aug 1919. Imperfect. 6 reels – 1 – uk British Libr Newspaper [072]

LE COMMIS DE BANQUE / ed by Ferriere, Philippe La – Quebec. v1 n1. jul 1938-v1 n3. jan 1939f – 1r – 1 – Can$35.00 – cn Can Microfilming [072]

Commissaires du Havre de Montreal see REGLEMENTS...PASSES LE 26 JANVIER 1875, SANCTIONNES LE 10 AVRIL 1875

COMMISSION / UN Economic Commission for Europe (ECE) – 1947-89 – E/F.100 E.2359 F.2439 R.2079 – 9 – us U.N. Pubs [340]

COMMISSION see PERIODICALS

LA COMMISSION CENTRALE POUR LA NAVIGATION DU RHIN / Eysinga, W J M van – Leyde, 1935 – 2mf – 1 – ILM-1868/1 – ne IDC [327]

Commission de colonisation de la province de Quebec see
- RAPPORT DE LA COMMISSION DE COLONISATION DE LA PROVINCE DE QUEBEC
- REPORT OF THE COLONIZATION COMMISSION OT THE PROVINCE OF QUEBEC

COMMISSION D'ENQUETE SUR LA SITUATION DES OUVRIERS ET DES INDUSTRIES D'ART / France. Ministere De l'Instruction Publique Et Des Beaux-Arts – (Condition of 19th C. French working class series). 1884 – 9 – fr Hachette [305]

Commission des assurances sociales de Quebec see RAPPORTS/COMMISSION DES ASSURANCES SOCIALES DE QUEBEC

Commission du Chemin de Fer de Quebec, Montreal, Ottawa et Occidental see RAPPORT

COMMISSION FOR JUSTICE AND PEACE – Dhaka-1000. 46 docs. 1982-1991 – 8mf – 9 – ne IDC [320]

COMMISSION INSTITUTEE PAR DECISION ROYALE DU 26 MAI 1840 POUR L'EXAMEN DES QUESTIONS RELATIVES A L'ESCLAVAGE ET A LA CONSTITUTION POLITIQUE DES COLONIES / France. Ministere de la Marine et des Colonies – (Slave Trade and Abolitionism in France Series). 1840-43 – 9 – fr Hachette [305]

Commission Internationale pour l'Aide aux Refugies Espanols see LISTES DE SOUSCRIPTION

COMMISSION MINUTES, COMMITTEE MINUTES AND PROPOSALS, JANUARY 1966-JUNE 1966 / Florida. Constitution Revision Commission – Tallahassee 1966. LL-2248 – 1 – us L of C Photodup [340]

COMMISSION OF ENQUIRY INTO THE 1986 UNREST AND ALLEGED MISMANAGEMENT IN KWANDEBELE – Hamden, CT: Micrographic Systems of Connecticut 1992 – us Res Libr [350]

Commission of the European Communities see
- THE HISTORICAL RECORDS OF THE HIGH AUTHORITY OF THE EUROPEAN COAL AND STEEL COMMUNITY, PART 1
- THE HISTORICAL RECORDS OF THE HIGH AUTHORITY OF THE EUROPEAN COAL AND STEEL COMMUNITY, PART 2

COMMISSION ON HUMAN RIGHTS : 1ST-30TH SESSIONS / UN Commission on Human Rights – 1947-75 – E/F.7 E.1666 F.1641 – 9 – us U.N. Pubs [340]

Commission on Interracial Cooperation see SOUTHERN FRONTIER

COMMISSION ON INTERRACIAL COOPERATION, 1919-1944 – (Price together with Southern Regional Council Papers, 1944-1968 plus Association of Southern Women for the Prevention of Lynching, 1930-1942 $18,985) – 55r – 1 – $4045.00 – us UMI [360]

COMMISSION ON NARCOTIC DRUGS : 1ST 30TH SESSIONS AND 8TH SPECIAL SESSIONS / UN Commission on Narcotic Drugs – E/F.11 E.683 F.691 R.226 S.375 – 9 – E/CN.7/ – us U.N. Pubs [340]

COMMISSION REGISTERS OF THE KEMPE STUDIO : STAINED GLASS DESIGNS 1893-1933 / C.E. Kempe & Co – (With printed index) – 25mf – 9 – $144.00 – 1-869934-14-8 – uk Emmett [730]

COMMISSION REPORTS (SLIM) / U.S. National Institute of Justice NCJRS – Full-text reports of 5 major national commissions. 51 documents – 9 – $55.00 – us N.C.J.R.S. [360]

COMMISSIONER OF INDIAN AFFAIRS ANNUAL REPORTS / U.S. Department of the Interior – (Lacking: 1899 pt 2. 1901 pt2. 1902 pt2. 1961-62. 1964) – 1837-1968 (all publ) – 504mf – 9 – $756.00 – LLMC 88-002 – us L.L.M.C. [340]

COMMISSIONERS JOUR.-CO HOME / Defiance County, Ohio. Board of County Commissioners – 1910-1927 – 1r – 1 – $32.50r – us Archival [324]

COMMISSIONERS' JOURNAL / Seneca County. Ohio. Board of County Commissioners – 1824-1939 – 1r – 1 – $32.50r – us Archival [324]

COMMISSIONERS' JOURNALS / Defiance County, Ohio. Board of County Commissioners – 1845-1971 – 14r – 1 – $32.50r – us Archival [324]

COMMISSIONERS' JOURNALS / Erie County. Ohio. Board of County Commissioners – 1838-1975 – 23r – 1 – $32.50r – us Archival [324]

COMMISSIONERS' JOURNALS / Fulton County. Ohio. Board of County Commissioners – 1863-1938 – 10r – 1 – $32.50r – us Archival [324]

COMMISSIONERS' JOURNALS / Hardin County. Ohio. Board of County Commissioners – 1853-1961 – 19r – 1 – $32.50r – us Archival [324]

COMMISSIONERS' JOURNALS / Henry County. Ohio. Board of County Commissioners – 1847-1987 – 34r – 1 – $32.50r – us Archival [324]

COMMISSIONERS' JOURNALS / Ottawa County. Ohio. Board of County Commissioners – 1840-1971 – 14r – 1 – $32.50r – us Archival [324]

COMMISSIONERS' JOURNALS / Putnam County. Ohio. Board of County Commissioners – 1852-1958 – 17r – 1 – $32.50r – us Archival [324]

COMMISSIONERS' JOURNALS / Sandusky County. Ohio. Board of County Commissioners – 1820-1959 – 27r – 1 – $32.50r – us Archival [324]

COMMISSIONERS' JOURNALS / Van Wert County. Ohio. Board of County Commissioners – 1835-1973 – 18r – 1 – $32.50r – us Archival [324]

COMMISSIONERS' JOURNALS / Williams County. Ohio. Board of County Commissioners – 1859-1970 – 14r – 1 – $32.50r – us Archival [324]

COMMISSIONERS' JOURNALS / Wood County. Ohio. Board of County Commissioners – 1836-1941 – 25r – 1 – $32.50r – us Archival [324]

COMMISSIONERS' JOURNALS / Wyandot County. Ohio. Board of County Commissioners – 1845-1980 – 20r – 1 – $32.50r – us Archival [324]

COMMISSIONER'S SIC JOURNAL / Leavenworth County. Kansas. Board of Commissioners – 1855-62 – 1 – us KS Hist [978]

LES COMMISSIONS ... / Bokanowski, M – Paris, 1908 – 2mf – 9 – ILM-431/1 – ne IDC [327]

Committee for Anglophone Social Action see SPEC (NEW CARLISLE, QUEBEC)

COMMITTEE FOR DEFENCE OF DEMOCRATIC RIGHTS IN TURKEY (CDDRT) = TRKIYE DEMOKRATIK HAKLARI SAVUNMA KOMITESI – London. 88 docs. 1980-1990 – 22mf – 9 – ne IDC [320]

Committee for Inland Fisheries of Africa see REPORT OF THE 3RD SESSION OF THE SUB-COMMITTEE FOR THE DEVELOPMENT AND MANAGEMENT OF THE FISHERIES OF LAKE VICTORIA, JINJA, UGANDA, 1984

Committee for Non-violent Revolution see ALTERNATIVE

COMMITTEE FOR THE DEVELOPMENT AND MANAGEMENT OF FISHERY RESOURCES OF THE GULFS : REPORT OF THE 6TH SESSION. ROME, OCTOBER 1986 / IOFC – 1987 – 81p – it F.A.O. [639]

COMMITTEE HEARINGS AND PRINTS / U.S. Congress – (84th Congress. 1956. Second Session. 85th Congress. 1957-58. Complete. 86th Congress. 1959-60. Complete. 87th Congress. 1961-62. Complete. 88th Congress. 1963-64. Complete. 89th Congress. 1965-66. Complete. 90th Congress. 1967-68. Complete. 91st Congress. 1969-70. Complete. 92nd Congress. 1971-72. Complete. 93rd Congress. 1973-74. Complete. 94th Congress. 1975-76. Complete.. 95th Congress. 1977-78. Complete. 96th Congress. 1979-80. Complete. 97th Congress. 1981-82. In prep) – 3 – us Readex [324]

COMMITTEE HEARINGS, PRINTS, REPORTS / U.S. Congress – 82nd-86th Congress. 1952-60 – 1 – us UMI [324]

COMMITTEE IN SOLIDARITY WITH THE PEOPLE OF EL SALVADOR (CISPES) – Washington DC. 139 docs. 1980-1991 – 42mf – 9 – ne IDC [320]

COMMITTEE IN SUPPORT OF SOLIDARITY – New York. 107 docs. 1981-1991 – 38mf – 9 – ne IDC [320]

Committee of Enquiry into Breaches of International Law Relating to Intervention in Spain see REPORT AND FINDINGS.

COMMITTEE OF FIFTEEN RECORDS, 1900-1901 : FROM THE HOLDINGS OF THE RARE BOOKS AND MANUSCRIPTS DIVISION – (With Guide) – Center for the Humanities, the New York Public Library; Astor, Lenox, Tilden Foundations, 1997 – ca 24r – 1 – ca $2,040.00 – S3358 – us Scholarly Res [300]

Committee of the Sturbridge Association see HISTORY OF THE BAPTIST CHURCHES COMPOSING THE STURBRIDGE ASSOCIATION FROM THEIR ORIGIN TO 1843

Committee of University Industrial Relations Librarians see
- EXCHANGE BIBLIOGRAPHIES. NUMERICAL LIST
- EXCHANGE BIBLIOGRAPHIES. SUBJECT INDEX

Committee of Writers see HISTORICAL SKETCH OF SAGUENAY

Committee on Data for Science and Technology of the International Council of Scientific Unions see INVENTORY OF DATA SOURCES IN SCIENCE AND TECHNOLOGY

COMMITTEE ON DISARMAMENT, 1962-1984 : MEETINGS AND DOCUMENTS – (With printed guide) – 30r – 1 – $2,890.00 – 0-89093-517-3 – us UPA [327]

COMMITTEE ON ELIMINATION OF RACIAL DISCRIMINATION : 1ST-36TH SESSIONS / UN Commission on Human Rights – 1969-89 – E.350 F.355 R.150 S.234 – 9 – us U.N. Pubs [340]

Committee on EthicsEthics Commission of the American Association of Law Libraries *see* PAPERS ON THE AALL CODE OF ETHICS

Committee on Fisheries *see* REPORT OF THE 1ST SESSION OF THE SUB-COMMITTEE ON FISH TRADE. ROME, 1986

COMMITTEE ON SOUTH AFRICAN WAR RESISTANCE (COSAWR) – London. 67 docs. 1980-1990 – 19mf – 9 – ne IDC [320]

Committee on Space Research *see* COSPAR INFORMATION BULLETIN

COMMITTEE ON THE ADMINISTRATION OF JUSTICE – Belfast. 92 docs. 1984-1991 – 29mf – 9 – ne IDC [340]

COMMITTEE ON THE PEACEFUL USES OF OUTER SPACE : LEGAL SUB-COMMITTEE / UN – (General Series: 1962-80 A/ AC.105/C./1-14 mf: E.13 F.13; Information Series: 1968-87 A/AC.105/C.2/INF.1-19 mf: E/F/S.17; Summary Records: 1962-87 A/ AC.105/C.2/SR.1-479 mf: E.98 F.90 S.92) – 9 – us U.N. Pubs [340]

COMMITTEE ON THE PEACEFUL USES OF OUTER SPACE : MAIN COMMISSION / UN – (Agenda: 1961-1962 A/AC.105/Agenda mf: E.3 F.3; General Series: 1962-1987 A/ AC.105/1-432 mf: E.525 F.480; Information Series: 1962-1984 A/AC.105/INF.1-394 mf: E.51 F.47; Verbatim Records: 1962-1988 A/AC.105/PV.1-319 mf: E.246 F.236; 1987 is not yet available in French) – 9 – us U.N. Pubs [340]

COMMITTEE ON THE PEACEFUL USES OF OUTER SPACE : SCIENTIFIC AND TECHNICAL SUB-COMMITTEE / UN – (Information Series: 1972-89 A/ AC.105/C.1/INF.1-14 mf: E/F/S.16; Summary Records: 1962-79 A/AC.105/C.1/SR.1-222 mf E.47 F.49; A/AC.105/C.1/INF.5 and 6 of 1976 and 1977 are not available) – 9 – us U.N. Pubs [340]

COMMITTEE REPORTS N1-67 : AND OUTLINE OF CONSTITUTION AND ARTICLES 1-16 – (Various pagination) – Saipan, n.p, 1975 – 12mf – 9 – $18.00 – LLMC 82-100F, Title 91 – us L.L.M.C. [323]

COMMITTEE REPORTS OF THE EUROPEAN PARLIAMENT : (IRREGULAR) / European Parliament – (Available in 9 languages. Interinstitutional catalogue in paper version available free of charge) – 9 – ECU590.00 subsc – AY-CO-96-000-EN-A – lu EEC [340]

COMMITTEE REPORTS, SURVEYS AND OTHER MISCELLANEOUS PUBLICATIONS / Atomic Industrial Forum – 17v 1953-56 – 3 – us Readex [330]

Committee to Frame a World Constitution *see* DOCUMENT

COMMITTEE TO PROTECT JOURNALISTS – New York. 90 docs. 1980-1991 – 23mf – 9 – ne IDC [320]

Committee to Restore the Constitution *see*
– BULLETIN

THE COMMITTEES OF THE CONTINENTAL CONGRESS, CHOSEN TO HEAR AND DETERMINE APPEALS FROM COURTS OF ADMIRALTY / Davis, John Chandler Bancroft – New York, Banks, 1888. 24 p. LL-438 – 1 – us L of C Photodup [976]

COMMLAW CONSPECTUS : JOURNAL OF COMMUNICATION LAW AND POLICY – Catholic University: v1-2. 1993-1994 – 9 – $20.00set – us Hein [380]

COMMODITY EXCHANGES / Baer, Julius Bernard & Woodruff, George P – New York and London: Harper & Bros., 1929. xii,319p. illus. plates – 1 – us U.W. Library [380]

COMMODITY TRADE IMPLICATIONS OF THE EUROPEAN ECONOMIC ENLARGEMENT – 1983 – 44p – it F.A.O. [380]

COMMODORE PERRY IN JAPAN – 1 – us Ross [976]

COMMODORE WORLD – Spanish ed. 1984- – 1,5,6,9 – us UMI [510]

COMMOEDIAE, ETC / Terentius – 15th cent. Holkham mss. 300, 339. Holkham Hall, Norfolk, England – 1 – uk Microform Academic [760]

Common, A *see* HOW TO REPAIR VIOLINS AND OTHER MUSICAL INSTRUMENTS...

COMMON BENCH REPORTS, NEW SERIES : CASES ARGUED AND DETERMINED IN THE COURT OF COMMON PLEAS, THE EXCHEQUER CHAMBER AND IN THE COURTS OF ERROR / Great Britain. England. Court of Common Pleas – (Includes index to series bound into v20) – v1-20. 1856-65. London: W G Benning & Co/Wm W Gearing, 1857-66 (all publ) – 197mf – 9 – $295.00 – LLMC 95-270 – us L.L.M.C. [324]

COMMON BENCH REPORTS, OLD SERIES : CASES ARGUED AND DETERMINED IN THE COURT OF COMMON PLEAS AND IN THE EXCHEQUER CHAMBER / Great Britain. England. Court of Common Pleas – v1-18 + index. 1845-56. London: Wm Benning & Co, 1846-56; 1858 (all publ) – 195mf – 9 – $292.00 – LLMC 95-269 – us L.L.M.C. [324]

THE COMMON BOND – Powell River. B.C. Canada. Jul-Oct 1946 – 1 – cn Commonwealth Micro [072]

COMMON CARP – it F.A.O. [580]

COMMON CARRIER LAND MOBILE BASE STATION CUMULATIVE STAFF STUDY LISTING / U.S. National Technical Information Service – Weekly – 9 – us N.T.I.S. [000]

COMMON CARRIER LAND MOBILE BASE STATIONS DATA BASE (SUPPLIERS) / U.S. National Technical Information Service – Monthly.Lists all telephone companies in the Common Carrier Land Mobil Base Station System that provide service to individual consumers–in call sign sequence – 9 – us N.T.I.S. [000]

COMMON CARRIER MICROWAVE CONSTRUCTION PERMIT FILE / U.S. National Technical Information Service – Every two months. Permit data such as licensee name, address, transmitter, receiver, path link and antenna information. Data is in State, county latitude and longitude sequence – 9 – us N.T.I.S. [000]

COMMON CARRIER MICROWAVE PENDING APPLICATION DUMP / U.S. National Technical Information Service – Every two months – 9 – us N.T.I.S. [621]

COMMON CAUSE – v6,no.4-v9,no.3.Oct 1980-Jun 1983 – 1 – us UMI [073]

COMMON CAUSE MAGAZINE – (1985- . 5,6,9) – v9,no.4- . Jul 1983- – 1 – us UMI [073]

COMMON GOOD – London, UK. 1880-81. -irr. 21 feet – 1 – uk British Libr Newspaper [072]

THE COMMON GROUND OF CONFUCIANISM, TAOISM AND CHINESE BUDDHISM (CCC169) = CHUNG-KUO SAN-CHIAO TI KUNG TUNG PEN CHIH / Hsieh, Fu-ya – (In Chinese) – Hong Kong: Christian Study Centre on Chinese Religion and Culture, 1966 – 1r – 1 – 1984-B500 – us A.T.L.A. [280]

THE COMMON LAW; ITS ORIGIN, SOURCES, NATURE AND DEVELOPMENT, AND WHAT THE STATE OF NEW YORK HAS DONE TO IMPROVE UPON IT / Daly, Charles Patrick – New York, Banks, 1894. 71 p. LL-539 – 1 – us L of C Photodup [340]

THE COMMON LAW JURISDICTION AND PRACTICE, ACCORDING TO STATUTES AND DECISIONS IN THE STATE OF ILLINOIS, FROM THE EARLIEST PERIOD TO 1872 / Hill, Edward Judson – Chicago: Myers, 1872. 2v. LL-779 – 1 – us L of C Photodup [340]

COMMON LAW PRACTICE IN CIVIL ACTIONS / Cox, Walter Smith – Washington, D.C., Morrison, 1877. 362 p. LL-521 – 1 – us L of C Photodup [340]

COMMON LAW PRACTICE IN CIVIL ACTIONS / Cox, Walter Smith – Washington, D.C., Morrison, 1880. 362 p. LL-530 – 1 – us L of C Photodup [340]

COMMON MARKET BROADSHEET – 1961-63.(Britain and Europe Since 1945) – 9 – us Primary [330]

COMMON MARKET LAW REVIEW – v1-32. 1963-95 – 9 – $2,091.00 set – us Hein [340]

COMMON SCHOOL LIBRARY FUNDS / Allen County. Ohio. Auditor – 1855-1860 – 1r – 1 – $32.50r – us Archival [324]

COMMON SCHOOL RECORD BOOK / Erie County. Ohio. Milan Township. Board of Education – 1838-1890 – 1r – 1 – $32.50r – us Archival [324]

COMMON SENSE – 1-15 2+1 (all publ). 1932-1946 – 63mf – 9 – $360.00 – us UPA [335]

COMMON SENSE – Johannesburg: Soc of Jews & Christians. v1-12. jul 1939-51 – 1 – us Res Libr [073]

COMMON SENSE – (Library has v.3,no.84-87,90-v.6,no.161,163-v.13,no.313; Sept. 1948-Dec.1958) – Union, N.J.: Common Sense, 19??- – 1 – CSUX86-S185 – us Hoover Inst Photo [978]

COMMON SENSE – London. -w. 1 Aug 1824-5 Feb 1826; 7 Oct 1916-Dec 1919. 3 reels – 1 – uk British Libr Newspaper [072]

COMMON SENSE – (Nos. 36-42, Sept 1984-May 1986. Ed., Viv Forbes. 72p) – Brisbane. Nos.16-35, Jan-Apr 1984. Ed., Viv Forbes – 9 – 1.00f – at Libertarian Micro [335]

COMMON SENSE VERSUS JUDICIAL LEGISLATION. / Sargent, John Osborne – New York: Putnam, 1871. 34p. LL-580 – 1 – us L of C Photodup [340]

COMMON TRADITION OF THE SYNOPTIC GOSPELS / Abbott, Edwin Abbott & Rushbrooke, WG – London: Macmillan, 1884.1 fiche – 9 – us A.T.L.A. [240]

COMMON WEEDS OF EAST AFRICA – 1987 – 184p – it F.A.O. [631]

A COMMON WRITING / Lodowyck, Francis – 1647. 45p. (English Linguistics Series 1500-1800) – 9 – us UMI [420]

COMMONEFACTIO HISTORICA DE STATV EIVS TEMPORIS,...CUI INSERTA EST BREUITER CONFESSIO...DE DOCTRINA IUSTIFICATIONIS AND BONORUM OPERUM,.. / Major, G – VVitebergae, 1567 – 1mf – ne IDC [240]

COMMONER – Colfax. Wash. -w. 1888-99, 1901-32 – 1 – us UMI [071]

THE COMMONER – Lincoln, NE. v1-23. 1901-23 – 9r – 1 – us Ross [320]

THE COMMONER – Lincoln. Neb. 1901-1923 – 1 – us UMI [071]

THE COMMONER – William J. Bryan, Editor. Lincoln, Nebraska. v. 1-23 no. 4. Jan 23 1901-Apr 1923 – 1 – us NY Public [073]

COMMONISM (CCC105) : THE TENTH CHAPTER OF CHRISTIANITY AND COMMUNISM / Chou, Pai-ch'in – (In Chinese) – 1st ed. Hong Kong: Too Hung Printing Co, 1953 – 1r – 1 – 1984-B500 – us A.T.L.A. [230]

COMMONPLACE BOOK / Darwin, Erasmus – 1 – uk Microform Academic [920]

COMMONPLACE BOOK / Lowndes, William Thomas – 1803. 1 fiche – 9 – us South Carolina Historical [025]

COMMONS *see* SURVEY

Commons, John R *see* RACES AND IMMIGRANTS IN AMERICA

A COMMONSENSE DIGEST OF AMERICAN NEGLIGENCE CASES – (Covers mainly American Negligence Cases but recommended that it be used also for American Negligence Reports) – Chicago: Callaghan. 1v. 1914 (all publ) – 13mf – 9 – $19.50 – LLMC 84-699C – us L.L.M.C. [340]

A COMMONSENSE INDEX TO THE NOTES OF AMERICAN NEGLIGENCE CASES – Chicago: Callaghan. 1v. 1914 (all publ) – 2mf – 9 – $3.00 – LLMC 84-699D – us L.L.M.C. [340]

COMMONWEAL – 1885-94 – 1 – uk Microform Academic [073]

COMMONWEAL – (v. 88-. 1968- 5,6. v. 90-. 1969- 9) – v. 1-. 1924- – 1 – us UMI [240]

COMMONWEAL – v1-34. 1921-41 – 1 – 22279.00 – us Princeton Micro [073]

THE COMMONWEAL : ORGAN OF THE SOCIALIST LEAGUE / Socialist League – (Series 1: v1-7. 1-328 (all publ). 1885-1892. Series 2: v1-2 (all and last publ). 1893-94) – 2r – 1 – $140.00 – us UPA [335]

THE COMMONWEAL / Socialist League – London. -w. Feb. 1885-Sep. 1892; May 1893-May 1894. 2 reels – 1 – uk British Libr Newspaper [073]

COMMONWEALTH – A Monthly Magazine and Library of Sociology. v. 1-9. 1893-1902 – 1 – 85.00 – us L of C Photodup [335]

COMMONWEALTH – Grand Rapids. Mich. -w, m. 1919-32 – 1 – us UMI [071]

COMMONWEALTH – Greenwood. Miss. 1905-1910; 1919-1920; 1946-1964; 1966- – 1 – us UMI [071]

COMMONWEALTH – Harrisburg, OR. -w. 19 Feb 1915-1 Dec 1916. – 2r – 1 – us U.O. Library [071]

COMMONWEALTH – London, UK. 1880. -irr. 1 foot – 1 – uk British Libr Newspaper [072]

THE COMMONWEALTH – Deeth, NV. 1910-14 – 2r – 1 – $100.00 – U04486 – us Library Micro [071]

THE COMMONWEALTH – Freetown. Sierra Leone. -f. 4 Aug-1 Sep 1888. (4 ft) – 1 – uk British Libr Newspaper [072]

THE COMMONWEALTH – Gary. Ind. 1930-32 – 1 – us UMI [071]

THE COMMONWEALTH : INDEPENDENT – Montreal, Canada. 3 mar 1883 – 1r – 1 – Can$25.00 – cn Can Microfilming [072]

COMMONWEALTH ADVOCATE – Manila. v. 1 no. 10-v. 7 no. 9. Nov 1935-Oct 1941 – 1 – us NY Public [073]

COMMONWEALTH ENGINEER – Melbourne, Australia. -m. Mar 1920-Dec 1921. Lacking Dec 1920 – 2r – 1 – uk British Libr Newspaper [620]

COMMONWEALTH ENGLAND / Brown, John – London: National Council of Evangelical Free Churches, 1904. (Eras of nonconformity; 6) – 1mf – us A.T.L.A. [240]

COMMONWEALTH HOME – Sydney, Australia. -w. 14 Aug 1925-1 Nov 1927. 2 reels – 1 – uk British Libr Newspaper [072]

Commonwealth Institute *see* THE ARTS OF THE HAUSA

COMMONWEALTH LAW REVIEW – Australia. v1-6. 1903-09 (all publ) – 6mf – 9 – $27.00 – LLMC 84-444 – us L.L.M.C. [073]

COMMONWEALTH LEGISLATION CATALOGUE ON MICROFICHE – (Updated regularly) – 9 – at AusInfo [340]

COMMONWEALTH OF AUSTRALIA GAZETTE – Melbourne, 1950-70 – 33r – 1 – us Ross [980]

COMMONWEALTH OF AUSTRALIA GAZETTE – Canberra. General ed: jul 1977-apr 28 1987 (24r); Public Service ed: jul 1977-dec 20 1984 (20r) – us Res Libr [980]

COMMONWEALTH OF AUSTRALIA GAZETTE – Canberra, etc, 1950-jun 1973 – 59r – us Res Libr [980]

COMMONWEALTH OF MASSACHUSETTS PUBLICATIONS – July 1975- – 5,6 – us Primary [324]

COMMONWEALTH OF NATIONS PAMPHLET COLLECTION – 1917-1974 – 1 – CSUXANP2015-B – us Hoover Inst Photo [320]

COMMONWEALTH POLITICAL EPHEMERA: BAHAMAS AND THE CARIBBEAN : PAMPHLETS ETC. ISSUED BY POLITICAL PARTIES, TRADE UNIONS AND PRESSURE GROUPS / Institute of Commonwealth Studies. University of London – (Available separately by country – fiche details and prices supplied) – ca 328mf – 9 – ca £1,700.00 – uk Altair [320]

Commonwealth Relations Office. India Office Library. Great Britain *see*
– CATALOGUE OF EUROPEAN PRINTED BOOKS, INDIA OFFICE LIBRARY
– INDEX OF POST-1937 EUROPEAN MANUSCRIPT ACCESSIONS. INDIA OFFICE LIBRARY

COMMONWEALTH REPORTER – Fond Du Lac. Wis. 1965- – 1 – us UMI [071]

COMMONWEALTH SPY – Carlisle, PA., 1823 – 13 – $25.00r – us I.M.R. [071]

THE COMMONWEALTHS AND THE KINGDOM : A STUDY OF THE MISSIONARY WORK OF STATE CONVENTIONS / Padelford, Frank W – Philadelphia: Griffith & Rowland, 1913 – 1mf – us A.T.L.A. [240]

COMMUNALE *see* HEIDELBERGER RUNDSCHAU

COMMUNATE DES CHRETIENS – 1960-85 (complete) – 3r – 1 – ATLA S0737 – us A.T.L.A. [073]

LA COMMUNAUTE – Senate. Debats. 1959-1960 – 1 – us NY Public [073]

COMMUNAUTE DES CHRETIENS – 1960-85.3 reels – 1 – us A.T.L.A. [073]

UNE COMMUNAUTE D'ORIGINE YEMENITE EN ISRAEL / Landau, L – 9 – F30.00 – fr Ethnologie [306]

COMMUNAUTE LOCALE ET ORGANISATION COMMUNAUTAIRE AUX ETATS-UNIS / Medard, J F – 6 fiches – 9 – F90.00 – fr Ethnologie [320]

COMMUNAUTE OU SECESSION? / Ehrhard, Jean – Paris, Calmann-Levy [1959] – us Res Libr [944]

COMMUNAUTE VILLAGEOISE ET HABITAT RURAL A GOZO / Henriet, MO – 9 – F90.00 – fr Ethnologie [305]

LES COMMUNAUTES DES CORDONNIERS, BASANIERS ET SAVETIERS DE TROYES / Morin, Louis – Troyes. 1895. (La Condition Ouvriere. Part Two.) – 9 – 2.50 – fr Bibl Nationale [360]

COMMUNAUTES SYRIAQUES EN IRAN ET IRAK DES ORIGINES A 1552 / Fiey, J M – London, 1979 – 7mf – 8 – Dfl28.00 – ne Slangenburg [956]

Communay, Arnaud *see* LES GRANDS NEGOCIANTS BORDELAIS AU XVIIIE SIECLE

COMMUNE – puis Revue litteraire. pour la defense de la culture. Paris. juil 1933-sept 1939 – 1 – fr A.C.R.P.P. [800]

LA COMMUNE – Geneve. Almanach socialiste pour l'annee 1877, par Elisee Reclus – 1 – fr A.C.R.P.P. [073]
LA COMMUNE – no. 1-6. Paris. avr-sept 1874 – 1 – fr A.C.R.P.P. [073]
LA COMMUNE – Paris. Journal quotidien, politique et socialiste. Dir. politique Felix Pyat. no. spec. du 17 aout, no. 1-45. 21 sept-4 nov 1880 – 1 – fr A.C.R.P.P. [072]
LA COMMUNE / Parti Communiste Internationaliste Bolchevik-Leniniste pour la Construction de la IVe Internationale – Paris. dec 1935-38 – 1 – fr A.C.R.P.P. [335]
LA COMMUNE – (Filmed as pt of: Commune de Paris newspapers; newspapers on these reels are filmed chronologically, not alphabetically.) – Paris: Impr Dubuisson et Ce, mar 26-31, apr 1-8,10-16,20-30, may 1,3-4,6-15 ,17-19 1871 – us Res Libr [072]
LA COMMUNE DE PARIS – no. 1-86 Paris. 9 mars-7 juin 1848; no. 1-2. fevr-mars 1849 – 1 – fr A.C.R.P.P. [073]
LA COMMUNE DEVOILEE PAR UN AMI DES TRAVAILLEURS – (Filmed as pt of: Commune de Paris newspapers; newspapers on these reels are filmed chronologically, not alphabetically) – Paris: [Auguste Petit, 1871] – us Res Libr [072]
LA COMMUNE ET LA MILICE DE NANTES / Mellinet, Camille – Nantes: C. Mellinet, 1840. 12v – fr Armell [355]
COMMUNE ET SOCIETE RURALE EN ALGERIE: ADMINISTRATION LOCALE ET PARTICIPATION AU DEVELOPPEMENT DANS L'AURES / Descloitres, R & Cornet, R – Aix-en-Provence. 1968. BNE-8629 1 – 9 – ne IDC [350]
THE COMMUNE OF LONDON / Round, J H – H 1154 2. 1899 – 8 – ne IDC [941]
COMMUNE SIGILLI SECRET (ANNO 1412-1416) / Fernando 1 – Barcelona – 1r – 5,6 – sp Cultura [946]
COMMUNICATION AND BROADCAST ENGINEERING – New York. v.1-4. 1934-37 – 1,5,6 – 2229.00 – us Princeton Micro [621]
COMMUNICATION AND RURAL DEVELOPMENT / Diaz Bordenave, Juan E – 2nd ed 1979 – 109p – 9 – 92-3-101370-X – fr UNESCO [380]
COMMUNICATION DU GREFFIER DE LA COURONNE EN CHANCELLERIE, TRANSMETTANT LE RAPPORT DU NOMBRE DE VOTES DONNES DURANT LA DERNIERE ELECTION, ETC / Canada. Greffier de la Couronne en Chancellerie – Toronto: Imprime par John Lovell, 1858. SEM105P169 – 1mf – 9 – Can$2.25 – cn Bibl Nat [380]
COMMUNICATION EDUCATION – (See also: Speech Teacher) – v25- 1976- 1; v25- 5,6,9 – us UMI [370]
COMMUNICATION ET LANGAGE – Paris. mars 1969-75; 1985-1993 – 1 – fr A.C.R.P.P. [073]
COMMUNICATION IN THE COMMUNITY : AN INTERNATIONAL STUDY ON THE ROLE OF THE MASS MEDIA IN SEVEN COMMUNITIES – 1982 – 85p – 9 – 92-3-101679-2 – fr UNESCO [302]
COMMUNICATION MONOGRAPHS – (See also: Speech Monographs) – v43- 1976 – 1,5,6 – us UMI [621]
COMMUNICATION PLANNING FOR DEVELOPMENT : AN OPERATIONAL FRAMEWORK / Hancock, A – 1980 – 198p – 9 – 92-3-101786-1 – fr UNESCO [380]
COMMUNICATION PLANNING REVISITED / Hancock, Alan – 9 – 92-3-102754-9 – fr UNESCO [380]
COMMUNICATION POLICIES IN COSTA RICA / Fonseca, Jaime M – 1977 – 89p – 9 – 92-3-101348-3 – fr UNESCO [380]
COMMUNICATION POLICIES IN THE REPUBLIC OF KOREA – 1978 – 50p – 9 – 92-3-101582-6 – fr UNESCO [380]
COMMUNICATION RESEARCH – (v.7-. 1980-5,6,9) – v.1-. 1974- – 1 – us UMI [073]
COMMUNICATION REVIEW / ed by Horwitz, R – 1974- – 1,5,9 – us Gordon [380]
COMMUNICATION STRATEGIES FOR HEIGHTENING AWARENESS OF WATER / ed by Sadler, B S – 1987 – x/25p – 9 – 92-3-102469-8 – fr UNESCO [360]
COMMUNICATION TECHNOLOGY AND DEVELOPMENT / Mowlana, Hamid & Wilson, Laurie J – 1988 – 9 – 92-3-102519-8 – fr UNESCO [380]
COMMUNICATIONS / Kamerlingh Onnes Laboratorium. Leiden – v. 1-29, nos. 1-325. 1895-1961 – 1,5,6 – us Princeton Micro [500]
COMMUNICATIONS – v1-. 1984- – 1,5,6,9 – us UMI [380]
COMMUNICATIONS – v17-29. 1937-49 – 1,5,6 – us Princeton Micro [073]
COMMUNICATIONS, 1862-1990 – (Guide only $310.00) – 474mf – 9 – $2,820.00 – 1-55655-475-3 – us UPA [380]
COMMUNICATIONS AND THE LAW – (v1-6 1979-84 on reel $130. v7-17 1985-95 on mf $296.00) – v1-17. 1979-95 – 5,6,9 – $426.00 set – us Hein [340]
COMMUNICATIONS BETWEEN THE COLONIAL OFFICE AND THE GOVERNORS OF UPPER AND LOWER CANADA, ON THE SUBJECT OF THE CIVIL GOVERNMENT OF CANADA,... / Grande-Bretagne. Colonial Office – [S.l.]: [s.n.], [1830]. SEM105P103 – 1mf – 9 – Can$2.25 – cn Bibl Nat [323]
LES COMMUNICATIONS DE MERCATOR / Ellice, Edward – Montreal: C B Pasteur et H Meziere, 1817. SEM16P37 – 1r – 5 – Can$9.00 – cn Bibl Nat [971]
LES COMMUNICATIONS DES INDIGENES DU KASAI AVEC LES AMES DES MORTS / Tiarko Fourche, J A & Morlighem, H – Bruxelles: G van Campenhout, 1939 – 1 – us Res Libr [290]
COMMUNICATIONS DURING WORLD WAR 1 PAMPHLET COLLECTION – 1917 – 1 – CSUXANM2798-B – us Hoover Inst Photo [380]
COMMUNICATIONS DURING WORLD WAR 2 PAMPHLET COLLECTION – 1941-194? – 1 – CSUXANN2535-B – us Hoover Inst Photo [380]
COMMUNICATIONS EVALUATION REPORT / Illinois. College of Agriculture. Extension Service in Agriculture and Home Economics – Nos 1-7 1963-65 – 1,5 – us Spaulding [630]
COMMUNICATIONS IN ALGEBRA – (v12-. 1984-. 5,6,9) – v1-. 1974- – 1 – us UMI [073]
COMMUNICATIONS IN MATHEMATICAL PHYSICS – v. 1-77. 1965-80 – 1,5,9 – 11,781.00 – us UMI [073]
COMMUNICATIONS IN PARTIAL DIFFERENTIAL EQUATIONS – (v9-. 1984-. 5,6,9) – v1-. 1976- – 1 – us UMI [073]
COMMUNICATIONS IN PSYCHOPHARMACOLOGY – v.1- 1977- – 5,6,9 – us UMI [150]
COMMUNICATIONS IN SOIL SCIENCE AND PLANT ANALYSIS – (1984-. 5,6,9) – v1-. 1970- – 1 – us UMI [631]
COMMUNICATIONS IN STATISTICS – v1-4. 1973-75 – 1 – us UMI [073]
COMMUNICATIONS IN STATISTICS: ECONOMETRIC REVIEWS – v1-2. 1982-83 – 1 – us UMI [073]
COMMUNICATIONS IN STATISTICS: SEQUENTIAL ANALYSIS – v1-2. 1982-84 – 1 – us UMI [073]
COMMUNICATIONS IN STATISTICS: SIMULATION AND COMPUTATION – (v13-. 1984-. 5,6,9) – v5-. 1976- – 1 – us UMI [073]
COMMUNICATIONS IN STATISTICS: THEORY AND METHODS – (v13-. 1984-. 5,6,9) – v5-. 1976- – 1 – us UMI [073]
COMMUNICATIONS NEWS – v21-. 1984- – 1,5,6,9 – us UMI [380]
COMMUNICATIONS OF THE ACM – (v.21-. 1978- 5,6,9) – v.2-. 1959- – 1 – us UMI [073]
COMMUNICATIONS OF THE ASSOCIATION FOR COMPUTING MACHINERY – v.1-2. 1958-59. Continued as: yCommunications of the ACM – 1 – us UMI [073]
COMMUNICATIONS OF THE INTERNATIONAL ASSOCIATION OF MARINE UNDERWRITERS... / Brueders, P – Berlin. v1 only – 2mf – 1 – ILM-3883/1 – ne IDC [327]
COMMUNICATIONS ON PURE AND APPLIED MATHEMATICS – v. 1-. 1948- – 1,5,6,9 – us UMI [510]
COMMUNICATIONS ON PURE AND APPLIED MATHEMATICS – v1-39. 1948-86 – 1,5,6 – us Princeton Micro [073]
COMMUNICATIONS SUR LA NATALITE EN FRANCE / Chervin, Arthur – Reprod. d'un extrait du Bulletin ste. anthrop. de Paris, 1888, p540-578. 1 fiche. (Statistics Series: Medical Studies) – 9 – 6.00 – fr Bibl Nationale [310]
COMMUNICATIONS SYSTEMS EQUIPMENT DESIGN – v1-. 1984- – 1,5,6,9 – us UMI [621]
COMMUNICATIONS WITH FRANCE AND SPAIN, RELATING TO THE SPANISH AMERICAN PROVINCES – London, [1824] – 1mf – 1 – ILM-2823/1 – ne IDC [327]
Communications Workers of America *see* CWA NEWS
COMMUNICATIONS WORLD – 1986- – 1 – us UMI [510]
COMMUNICATOR – v1- 1970- 1; v10- 1978- 5,6,9 – us UMI [370]
COMMUNICATOR – Cincinnati, Ohio. Aug 1976-Aug 1984 – 1 – us A.J.P.C. [071]
COMMUNIO – Santiago, Chile: Communio. v1-7 n25. jun/jul 1982-1991 – 2r – us Res Libr [072]
COMMUNIO, AMERICAN EDITION – (v.7-. 1980-5,6,9) – v.1-. 1974- – 1 – us UMI [073]
COMMUNION – (Includes: Cone, Spencer H. The Terms of Communion at the Lord's Table. n.d. Haldane, James Alex. The Foundation of the Observance of the Lord's Day and of the Lord's Supper. 1807) – 11 miscellaneous pamphlets – 1 – $13.30 – us Baptist [240]
THE COMMUNION OF LIFE / Fry, Joan Mary – London: Publ for the Woodbrooke Extension Committee by Headley, 1910 – 1mf – 9 – 0-8370-8901-8 – 1986-2901 – us A.T.L.A. [240]
COMMUNION SERMON MANUSCRIPTS / Tennent, William – 1r – 1 – $50.00 – us Presbyterian [240]
COMMUNIQUE / Gouvernement revolutionnaire de l'Angola en exil – [Alger]: Gouvernement. n45 feb 4 1965; n51-52 mar 26-29 1965; n54 apr 15 1965; jul 12 1972 – us Res Libr [320]
COMMUNIQUE / Partido Africano da Independencia da Guine e Cabo Verde – Conakry: O Partido, jun 9 1961-sep 25 1972 – us Res Libr [320]
COMMUNIQUE: CANADIAN STUDIES – v. 1-3. 1974-77 – 1 – 65.00 – cn McLaren [971]
COMMUNIQUE DE LA CHAMBRE DE COMMERCE FRANCAISE DE LONDRES – (Bulletin de la Chambre de Commerce francaise de Grande-Bretagne. Oct 1943-Sept 1956. Bulletin de la Chambre de Commerce francaise de Londres. March/Apr-Jun 1916; 1917-Jun 1924; 1930-Mar 1934. Deux Cotes du Detroit. Apr 1934-Sept 1943. Revue du Commerce franco-britannique. Oct 1956-1973) – London, UK. Jun 1913-Jan/Feb 1916 – 1 – uk British Libr Newspaper [072]
COMMUNIQUES OF MILITARY OPERATIONS – dec 11 1967-may 2 1969 – us Res Libr [355]
COMMUNIQUES OF MILITARY OPERATIONS – [mid-sep 1968-mid-dec 1969] – us Res Libr [355]
COMMUNISM AND THE IMPORTATION OF ADVANCED TECHNOLOGY: THE CASE OF POLAND / Andreski, Stanislav – 1986, LA Economic Notes, No.5, 2p – 9 – 1.00f – at Libertarian Micro [335]
COMMUNISM CAN BE DEFEATED WITHOUT A THIRD WORLD WAR / Butler, Eric D – 2fiches (29x) – 9 – 1.00f – at Libertarian Micro [320]
COMMUNISM IN SPAIN, 1931-36 / Godden, Gertrude M – New York, 1937. Fiche W918. (Blodgett Collection of Spanish Civil War Pamphlets) – 9 – us H.U. College Libr [946]
LE COMMUNISME / Baillairge, Charles – 1895? 00047. (Pre-1900 Canadiana) – 9 – cn C.I.H.M. [335]
LE COMMUNISME EN FRANCE / Bon, F. et al – 9 – F90.00 – fr Ethnologie [335]
COMMUNIST / Communist Party of America – (Series 1: nos. 1-7 (all publ). 1919. Series 2: v1-3 (all publ). 1919-21) – 1 reel – 1 – $115.00 – us UPA [335]
THE COMMUNIST – Great Britain. (Newspaper). 1920-23 – 1 – uk World [072]
THE COMMUNIST – Great Britain. (Theoretical journal). 1927-1928 – 1 – uk World [073]
COMMUNIST ACTIVITY IN THE ENTERTAINMENT INDUSTRY : FBI SURVEILLANCE FILES ON HOLLYWOOD, 1942-1958 / ed by Leab, Daniel – (Printed guide) – 14r – 1 – $1,540.00 – 1-55655-414-1 – us UPA [324]
COMMUNIST ATTACK IN GREAT BRITAIN, LONDON 1938 / Bayle, Constantino & Godden, G M – Burgos: Razon y Fe, 1938 – 1 – sp Bibl Santa Ana [335]
COMMUNIST ECONOMIES AND ECONOMIC TRANSFORMATION – 1989- 5v – 9 – £170.50 – 0954-0113 – uk Carfax [330]
COMMUNIST INFILTRATION OF THE SOUTHERN CHRISTIAN LEADERSHIP CONFERENCE : FBI INVESTIGATION FILE, 1958-1980 / U.S. Federal Bureau of Investigation – 1984 – 9r – 1 – $765.00 – S1754 – us Scholarly Res [360]
COMMUNIST INTERNATIONAL / Communist International. Library – Hamburg. no.1-40 – 1 – us NY Public [335]
COMMUNIST INTERNATIONAL – Earl Browder, Editor. New York. no. 1-12. Jan-Dec 1940 – 1 – us NY Public [073]
COMMUNIST INTERNATIONAL – (English Edition). London etc. v. 6-12. May 1929-Aug 1935. Incomplete – 1 – us NY Public [073]
COMMUNIST INTERNATIONAL – Leningrad. London. New York. Apr. 1919-Dec. 1940. Missing 1921-22 – 1 – 35.00r – us Hoover Inst Photo [073]
COMMUNIST INTERNATIONAL – New York. n1-12. 1940 – 1r – 1 – us Ross [335]
COMMUNIST INTERNATIONAL – New York. v. 11 no. 2-v. 16 no 12. Jan 15 1934-Dec 1939 – 1 – us NY Public [073]
COMMUNIST INTERNATIONAL – ns: v6-16. 1929-39 – 5r – 1 – us Ross [335]
COMMUNIST INTERNATIONAL – (Series 1: nos. 1-30 (all publ). 1919-1924. Series 2: v1-17 (all publ), 1924-40) – 9r – 1 – $1,040.00 – us UPA [335]
COMMUNIST INTERNATIONAL – (Special American Edition). New York. v. 9 no. 8-12. May 15-July 1 1932 – 1 – us NY Public [073]
Communist International *see*
- PAMPHLETS
- UNITY FOR SPAIN; CORRESPONDENCE BETWEEN THE COMMUNIST INTERNATIONAL AND THE LABOR AND SOCIALIST INTERNATIONAL, JUN-JULY, 1937

Communist International. Comite Executif *see* L'INTERNATIONALE SYNDICALE ROUGE
Communist International. Congress. 3. (1921) *see* BULLETIN DES 3. KONGRESSES DER KOMMUNISTISCHEN INTERNATIONALE
Communist International. Congress. 4. (1922) *see* BULLETIN DES 4. KONGRESSES DER KOMMUNISTISCHEN INTERNATIONALE
Communist International. Congress (4th: 1922: Petrograd and Moscow, R.S.F.S.R.) *see* 4TH KONGRESS KOMINTERNA
Communist International. Congress. 5. (1924) *see* PIATYI VSEMIRNYI KONGRESS KOMMUNISTI-CHESKOGO INTERNATSIONALA
Communist International. Executive Committee *see*
- BULLETIN OF THE EXECUTIVE COMMITTEE OF THE COMMUNIST INTERNATIONAL
- I APONII A NA RUSSKOM DALNEM VOSTOKE

Communist International. Library *see* COMMUNIST INTERNATIONAL
COMMUNIST INTERNATIONAL PERIODICALS FROM THE FELTRINELLI ARCHIVES – (See indiv. listings: Bulletin Communiste; Bulletin des Kongresses der Kommunistischen Internationale; Bulletin of the Executive Committee of the Communist International; Contre le Courant; La Correspondance Internationole; Die Internationale; L'Internationale Communiste; Internationale Presse- Korrespondenz; Kommunismus; Rundschau ueber Politik, Wirtschaft und Arbeiterbewegung) – 9 – $3,770.00 set – us UPA [320]
Communist Labor Party *see* REVOLUTIONARY AGE
Communist League of America *see*
- MILITANT
- YOUNG SPARTACUS

Communist League of Struggle *see* CLASS STRUGGLE
THE COMMUNIST NETWORK / Hinkel, John Vincent – N.Y., 1939. Fiche W944. (Blodgett Collection of Spanish Civil War Pamphlets) – 9 – us H.U. College Libr [946]
COMMUNIST OPERATIONS IN SPAIN / Godden, Gertrude M – London, 1937. Fiche W919. (Blodgett Collection of Spanish Civil War Pamphlets) – 9 – us H.U. College Libr [946]
COMMUNIST PAMPHLETS, 1907-1982 – (With free printed list of titles) – Labadie Collection, University of Michigan – 1,429mf – 9 – £5,670.00 – uk Chadwyck [320]

Communist Party Congress. 1917. (Sixth) *see* VSESOIUZNAIA KOMMUNISTICHESKAIA PARTIIA
Communist Party. France *see*
- L'ARALDO. ORGANO IN LINGUA ITALIANA DEL PARTITO COMUNISTA FRANCESE (S.F.I.C.)
- BULLETIN COLONIAL
- FRANCE-NOUVELLE
- L'HUMANITE
- L'HUMANITE-DIMANCHE
- LA TERRE
- LA VOIX DES TRAVAILLEURS
- LA VOIX DU PEUPLE

Communist Party. France. 6-15 Congres National *see* COMPTES RENDUS ET RAPPORTS
Communist Party. Germany *see*
- BERICHT UEBER DEN PARTEITAG
- BERICHT UEBER DIE VERHANDLUNGEN
- PAMPHLETS

Communist Party. Great Britain *see*
- THE CALL
- COMPLETE ARCHIVES, 1916-92
- THE LINK
- MARXIST QUARTERLY. 1954-57
- WORKERS' LIFE
- THE WORKERS' WEEKLY
- WORKER'S WEEKLY

Communist Party. Indonesia *see*
- ABC POLITIK. KAWTOKAKE MITURUT PESENAN C.D.B.-P.K.I. DJAWA TENGAH
- AC POLITIK
- KONSTITUSI PARTAI KOMUNIS INDONESIA (P K I)
- PATRIOTISME DANS INTERNATIONALISME
- REVOLUSI SOSIALIS, 7 NOV 1917
- SERBA-SERBI DOKUMEN PARTAI 1961

Communist Party. Indonesia. Comite Central *see*
- EIGHTH PLENUM OF THE CENTRAL COMMITTEE OF THE COMMUNIST PARTY OF INDONESIA; POLITICAL REPORT AND RESOLUTION
- EVER FORWARD TO STORM IMPERIALISM AND FEUDALISM BY D.N. AIDIT. DOCUMENTS OF THE SECOND PLENUM, END DECEMBER, 1960
- PESAN TAHUN BARU POLITBURO CC PKI
- SIXTH PLENUM OF THE CENTRAL COMMITTEE OF THE COMMUNIST PARTY OF INDONESIA, MARCH 31-APRIL 3, 1958: DOCUMENTS
- STRENGTHEN NATIONAL UNITY AND COMMUNIST UNITY: DOCUMENTS OF THE THIRD PLENUM OF THE CENTRAL COMMITTEE OF THE COMMUNIST PARTY OF INDONESIA, END DECEMBER 1961

Communist Party. Indonesia. Kongres Nasional *see*
- MATERIALS OF THE SIXTH NATIONAL CONGRESS OF THE COMMUNIST PARTY OF INDONESIA
- SIXTH, DJAKARTA, 1959. (TENTANG PROGRAM PKI)

Communist Party of America *see* COMMUNIST
Communist Party of Canada *see* THE CLARION
COMMUNIST PARTY OF INDONESIA – 661mf – 9 – ne IDC [320]
Communist Party. South Africa *see* UMSEBENZI
Communist Party. Spain *see* EL CAMINO DE LA VICTORIA: LLAMAMIENTO...A TODOS LOS PUEBLOS DE ESPANA Y A CUANTOS AMAN LA PAZ, EL PROGRESO Y LA LIBERTAD
Communist Party. U.S.A *see*
- PARTY ORGANIZER
- REVOLUTIONARY AGE

Communist Party. U.S.A. International Labor Defense *see* EQUAL JUSTICE
Communist Party. U.S.A. National Committee *see* NATIONAL ISSUES
Communist Party.U.S.A *see* WESTERN WORKER
THE COMMUNIST PLOT IN SPAIN / Azcarate y Florez, Pablo de – n.p. 1938? Fiche W 743. (Blodgett Collection of Spanish Civil War Pamphlets) – 9 – us H.U. College Libr [946]
COMMUNIST REVIEW – Great Britain. 1921-1927 – 1 – uk World [073]
COMMUNIST REVIEW – Great Britain. 1929-1935 – 1 – uk World [073]
COMMUNIST REVIEW – Great Britain. 1946-1953 – 1 – uk World [073]
COMMUNIST VIETNAMESE PUBLICATIONS – 1 – 59.00 – us L of C Photodup [950]
LE COMMUNISTE – no. 1. Paris. mars 1849 – 1 – fr A.C.R.P.P. [073]
LE COMMUNISTE – no. 1-13 14. Paris. nov 1931-sept 1933. mq no. 2-3, 5. n.s., no. 1-2 – 1 – fr A.C.R.P.P. [073]
LE COMMUNISTE / Parti Communiste et des Soviets – Paris. oct-dec 1919, juil-aout 1920 – 1 – fr A.C.R.P.P. [335]
THE COMMUNISTIC SOCIETIES OF THE UNITED STATES : FROM PERSONAL VISIT AND OBSERVATION / Nordhoff, Charles – New York: Harper, 1875, c1874 – 2mf – us A.T.L.A. [335]
DIE "COMMUNITARIANS" / Beierwaltes, Andreas – 1995 – 1mf – 9 – DM60.00 – 3-8267-2137-3 – gw Hänsel [320]
COMMUNITY – v1- 1941- 1; v34- 6; v35- 1975- 9 – us UMI [300]
COMMUNITY ACTION – 1972-80.(The Underground and Alternative Press in England) – 9 – us Primary [073]
COMMUNITY AND JUNIOR COLLEGE JOURNAL – (v. 39-. 1968- 5,6. v. 40-. 1969- 9) – v. 1- 1930- – 1 – us UMI [370]
COMMUNITY AND JUNIOR COLLEGE LIBRARIES / ed by Todaro, Julie Beth – v1- 1982- – 1, 9 ($60.00 in US $84.00 outside hardcopy subsc) – us Haworth [020]
COMMUNITY CARE-SOCIAL WORK IN ACTION – v. 1-. 1974- – 1,5,6,9 – us UMI [360]
COMMUNITY CIVICS / Hughes, R O – Boston etc: Allyn & Bacon, 1917 – 6mf – 9 – $9.00 – LLMC 96-062 – us L.L.M.C. [360]
COMMUNITY COLLEGE FRONTIERS – v. 1-9. 1972-81, 1; v. 4-9, 5,6,9 – us UMI [370]
COMMUNITY COLLEGE JOURNALIST – v. 3-. 1974- – 1,5,6,9 – us UMI [070]
COMMUNITY COLLEGE REVIEW – v. 1-. 1973- , 1; v. 3- 1975- 5,6,9 – us UMI [370]
COMMUNITY COLLEGE SOCIAL SCIENCE JOURNAL – v. 1- 1977- – 1,5,6,9 – us UMI [300]
COMMUNITY COMMUNICATIONS : THE ROLE OF COMMUNITY MEDIA IN DEVELOPMENT / Berrigan, Frances J – 1981 – 50p – 9 – 92-3-101771-3 – fr UNESCO [380]
COMMUNITY CONGRESS : MINUTES – (In Yiddish) – Kaunas, LT. (-) 14 Feb 1922 – 1r – 1 – $30.00 – cn Can Microfilming [072]
COMMUNITY DENTISTRY AND ORAL EPIDEMIOLOGY – Copenhagen. v1-14. 1973-86 – 5,9 – Dfl1,470.00; Dfl105.00v – ne Swets [614]
COMMUNITY DEVELOPMENT : COMPARATIVE CASE STUDIES IN INDIA, REPUBLIC OF KOREA, MEXICO AND UNITED REPUBLIC OF TANZANIA / ed by Dore, Ronald & Mars, Zoe – 1981 – 446p – 9 – 92-3-101877-9 – fr UNESCO [307]
COMMUNITY EDUCATION IN INDONESIA / Indonesia. Ministry of Education – Tartib Prawirodihardjo and T. Krishnamurthy. 1960. SE-5122-1 – 9 – ne IDC [370]
COMMUNITY FISHERY CENTRES : GUIDELINES FOR ESTABLISHMENT AND OPERATION – 1985 – 105p – it F.A.O. [636]
COMMUNITY LEVEL STATISTICS – 1983 – 91p – it F.A.O. [310]
COMMUNITY MENTAL HEALTH JOURNAL – v1- 1965- 1; v10- 5,6; v11- 9 – us UMI [360]
COMMUNITY MIRROR – Maumee, Ohio. 1981-88 – 7r – 1 – $32.50r – us Archival [071]
COMMUNITY NEWS – Flint. Mich. 1945-1947 – 1 – us UMI [071]
COMMUNITY NEWS – Marcus. Wash. 1922-1923 – 1 – us UMI [071]
COMMUNITY NEWS REPORTER / Jewish Telegraphic Agency – New York. N.Y. 1962-67 – 1 – us A.J.P.C. [073]
COMMUNITY ONTARIO – (Cont: Housing Ontario. Ceased v26 1982) – Toronto. v25-26. 1981-82 – 5 – Can$50.00y – cn Micromedia [307]
COMMUNITY ONTARIO *see* HOUSING ONTARIO
COMMUNITY PRESS – Maquoketa. Iowa. -w. 1951- – 1 – us UMI [071]
COMMUNITY PRESS – Portland, OR. 2 Jan 1974-27 Feb 1980. – 10r – 1 – us U.O. Library [071]
COMMUNITY PROPERTY JOURNAL – (1985- . 5,6,9) – v1- . 1974- – 1 – us UMI [073]
COMMUNITY PUBLICATIONS – Chicago. Ill. -w. 1969- – 1 – us UMI [071]
COMMUNITY REPORTER – Mount Airy. Md. 1930-1949; 1958- – 1 – us UMI [071]
COMMUNITY RESOURCE DEVELOPMENT NEWSLETTER / Tennessee. University. Agricultural Extension Service – n.1-71. Jul 1951-69 – 1,5 – us Spaulding [307]
COMMUNITY REVIEW – 1985- – 1 – us UMI [073]
COMMUNITY REVIEW – (v.3-. 1979- 5,6,9) – v.1-. 1977- – 1 – us UMI [073]
COMMUNITY SCHOOLS – 1971-74 – 9 – 68.50 – cn McLaren [370]
COMMUNITY SERVICES CALENDAR/ALAMEDA HOUSING NEWS – Alameda, CA. 1948-1955 – 1r – 1 – $50.00 – B06001 – us Library Micro [071]
COMMUNITY SERVICES CATALYST – (v14-. 1984-. 5,6,9) – v1-. Winter 1971- – 1 – us UMI [073]
COMMUNITY SURVEY FOR RURAL AREAS OF THE SPECIAL DISTRICT, JOGJAKARTA / Indonesia. National Malaria Eradication Service – SE-5554 1. 1960 – 9 – ne IDC [610]
COMMUNITY UNIT CABLE FULL RECORD / U.S. National Technical Information Service – Every two years – 9 – us N.T.I.S. [000]
COMMUNITY/JUNIOR COLLEGE RESEARCH QUARTERLY – v. 1-. 1976- – 1,5,6,9 – us UMI [370]
COMMUNITY/JUNIOR COLLEGE RESEARCH QUARTERLY – v. 1-. 1976- – 1,5,6,9 – us UMI [370]
Comnena, Anna *see* ALEXIADIS LIBRI 15 (CSHB 49)
COMO CUMPL I EL MANDATO DE PERON *see* EL MANDATO DE PERON
COMO EL FASCISMO DEFIENDE A LOS TRABAJADORES, PARA QUE EL PUEBLO SEPA – Bilbao, 1939. Fiche W 812. (Blodgett Collection of Spanish Civil War Pamphlets) – 9 – us H.U. College Libr [946]
COMO ENSENAR A LOS HIJOS A VIVIR CON ALEGRIA / Aradillas Agudo, Antonio – Madrid: Alameda, 1968 – sp Bibl Santa Ana [946]
COMO ES LA VIDA / Fernandez Abelehira, Maria Isabel – Sevilla: Ed. Catolica Espanola, S.A., s.a. – sp Bibl Santa Ana [240]
COMO NACE UN MONASTERIO Y MUERE UN CESAR / Jimenz Vasco, Felipe – Jaraiz de la Vera: Imp. Romero, 1969 – 1 – sp Bibl Santa Ana [240]
COMO NACE Y SE DESARROLLA UNA COOPERATIVA / Repetto, Nicolas – Buenos Aires: A.M. Gimenez, 3rd ed 1944 – 1 – CSUXADH5684-B – us Hoover Inst Photo [334]
COMO NOS VEN LOS DE FUERA : ANECDOTARIO DE COSAS EXTREMENAS / Vera Camacho, Juan Pedro – Caceres: Diputacion Provincial de Caceres, 1953 – 1 – sp Bibl Santa Ana [946]
COMO PIENSA EL PARTIDO SINDICALISTA EN ESTE MOMENTO HISTORICO DE LA VIDA ESPANOLA; TRES MANIFESTOS DEL COMITE NACIONAL, CON NUEVE REPRODUCCIONES DE LOS CARTELES DE PROPAGANDA ANTIFASCISTA / Partido Sindicalista. Spain – Valencia? 1937? Fiche W1099. (Blodgett Collection of Spanish Civil War Pamphlets) – 9 – us H.U. College Libr [946]
COMO SE ALHAJABAN CASAS E IGLESIAS EN MAYNAS / Bayle, Constantino – Madrid: Missionalia Hispanica, 1948 – 1 – sp Bibl Santa Ana [240]
COMO SE EDUCA UN NINO EN LA ARGENTINA / Argentina. Direccion General de Relaciones Culturales y Difusion – [Buenos Aires?, 1950?] – 1 – CSUXAGN1686-B – us Hoover Inst Photo [972]
COMO SE ENFRENTO AL FASCISMO EN TODA ESPANA – Buenos Aires, 1938. Fiche W 813. (Blodgett Collection of Spanish Civil War Pamphlets) – 9 – us H.U. College Libr [946]
COMO SE INICIO EL GLORIOSO MOVIMIENTO NACIONAL EN VALLADOLID Y LA GESTA HEROICA DEL ALTO DEL LEON / Raymundo, Francisco J – Valladolid, 1936. Fiche W1129. (Blodgett Collection of Spanish Civil War Pamphlets) – 9 – us H.U. College Libr [946]
COMOEDIA – Paris. 1er oct 1907-6 aout 1914, 1er oct 1919-1er janv 1937, 21 juin 1941-5 aout 1944 – 1 – fr A.C.R.P.P. [073]
Comolli, A *see* DE COLEOPTERIS NOVIS AC RARIORIBUS MINUSUE COGNITIS PROVINCIAE NOVOCOMI
Comolli, Louis Antoine *see* LES PONTS DE L'AMERIQUE DU NORD: ETUDE, CALCUL, DESCRIPTION DE CES PONTS: COMPARAISON DES SYSTEMES AMERICAIN ET EUROPEEN
COMOX DISTRICT FREE PRESS – Comox, British Columbia, CN. 1931-73 – 37r – 1 – cn Commonwealth Micro [072]
COMPACT – v1- 1966- 1; v12- 1978- 5,6,9 – us UMI [370]
COMPACT OF FREE ASSOCIATION : REDRAFT 1983 – (Unpag) – Koror: Off of the President of Palau, oct 1983 – 2mf – 9 – $3.00 – LLMC 82-100G, Title 26 – us L.L.M.C. [323]
THE COMPACT OF FREE ASSOCIATION : HISTORY AND MATERIALS / Schwalbenberg, Henry M – (Covers all Micronesian jurisdictions) – Henry M. Schwalbenberg, 29 Jan 1983 – 2mf – 9 – $3.00 – LLMC 82-100F Title 13 – us L.L.M.C. [324]
COMPACT OF FREE ASSOCIATION ACT OF 1985 (FSM AND MARSHALL ISLANDS) : PUBLIC LAW 99-239, JAN 14, 1986 / U.S. Congress – (Unpag) – Washington: GPO, 1986 – 1mf – 9 – $1.50 – LLMC 82-100F, Title 106 – us L.L.M.C. [323]
COMPACT OF FREE ASSOCIATION AND RELATED AGREEMENTS BETWEEN THE FEDERATED STATES OF MICRONESIA AND THE UNITED STATES, 1 OCTOBER 1982 / Federated States of Micronesia – Kolonia, Ponape: Plebiscite Commission, 1982 – 3mf – 9 – $4.50 – LLMC 82-100H Title 7 – us L.L.M.C. [324]
COMPACT OF FREE ASSOCIATION AND SUBSIDIARY AGREEMENTS – (Various pagination) – Koror: Off of the President, mar 1981 – 8mf – 9 – $12.00 – LLMC 82-100G, Title 21 – us L.L.M.C. [323]
COMPACT OF FREE ASSOCIATION BETWEEN THE UNITED STATES AND THE GOVERNMENTS OF PALAU, THE MARSHALL ISLANDS AND THE FEDERATED STATES OF MICRONESIA / Micronesia. (U.S.) – (Mimeo of initialed copies, with add agreement between the US and the FSM regarding aspects of marine sovereignty and jurisdiction) – 31 Oct 1980; 11 Nov 1980 – 2mf – 9 – $3.00 – LLMC 82-100F Title 10 – us L.L.M.C. [324]
COMPACT OF FREE ASSOCIATION BETWEEN THE U.S. AND PALAU : HEARINGS AND MARKUP BEFORE THE HOUSE COMM ON FOREIGN AFFAIRS AND ITS SUBCOMM ON ASIAN AND PACIFIC AFFAIRS, 99TH CONG, 2ND SESS, MAY-JUN 1986 / U.S. Congress – Washington: GPO, 1986 – 3mf – 9 – $4.50 – LLMC 82-100G, Title 9 – us L.L.M.C. [327]
THE COMPACT OF FREE ASSOCIATION, FOREIGN POLITICAL PROVISIONS : A SECTION BY SECTION LEGAL ANALYSIS / Zafren, Daniel H – Washington: The Library of Congress Congressional Research Service, jul 19, 1984 – 1mf – 9 – $1.50 – LLMC 82-100F, Title 63 – us L.L.M.C. [323]
COMPACT OF FREE ASSOCIATION WITH PALAU : (AS SIGNED ON MAY 23, 1984) / U.S. Congress. Hse.Comm on Interior and Insular Affairs – Washington: GPO, 1985 – 1mf – 9 – $1.50 – LLMC 82-100G, Title 27 – us L.L.M.C. [327]
COMPACT OF FREE ASSOCIATION WITH PALAU : HEARING BEFORE THE SENATE COMM ON ENERGY AND NATURAL RESOURCES, 99TH CONG, 2ND SESS, MAY 9, 1986 / U.S. Congress – Washington: GPO, 1986 – 3mf – 9 – $4.50 – LLMC 82-100G, Title 30 – us L.L.M.C. [327]
Compagni, Dino *see* THE CHRONICLE OF DINO COMPAGNI
COMPAGNIE D'ASSURANCE MUTUELLE CONTRE LE FEU DES COMTES DE RIMOUSKI, TEMISCOUATA ET KAMOURASKA – (Quebec: C. Darveau), 1876. 03412. (Pre-1900 Canadiana) – 9 – cn C.I.H.M. [336]
Compagnie de colonisation et de credit des cantons de l'est *see* NOTICE SUR SON BUT ET SON ORGANISATION
Compagnie du chemin a lisses de colonisation du nord de Montreal *see*
- RAPPORT DE L'EXPLORATION A LA BAIE GEORGIENNE
- RAPPORT SUR LA SECTION D'HOCHELAGA ET ST JEROME

Compagnie du Grand Tronc *see*
- REPONSE COMPLEMENTAIRE A UNE ADDRESSE DE L'ASSEMBLEE LEGISLATIVE.
- STATEMENTS, REPORTS AND ACCOUNTS..

La compagnie du haras national *see* VENTE ET AFFERMAGE DE CHEVAUX PERCHERONS, ARABES, ET CAROSSIERS NORMANDS: CATALOGUE POUR 1889-1890

LES COMPAGNIES DE COLONISATION SOUS L'ANCIEN REGIME / Chailley-Bert, Joseph – Paris: A. Colin, 1898. 02875. (Pre-1900 Canadiana) – 9 – cn C.I.H.M. [971]

Compagnon, A *see* LES CLASSES LABORIEUSES, LEUR CONDITION ACTUELLE, LEUR AVENIR PAR LA REORGANISATION DU TRAVAIL

LE COMPAGNON DES VACANCES: PRESENTE A LA JEUNESSE CHRETIENNE – Montreal: Libr. St. Joseph, 1887. 05411. (Pre-1900 Canadiana) – 9 – cn C.I.H.M. [790]

EL COMPANERO – v1-4, n.d.; 1962, no.1-5. 374p – 1 – 13.09 – us Baptist [240]

UN COMPANERO DE HERNANDO CORTES, JUAN CANO DE SAAVEDRA, VERNO DE MOCTEZUMA (CACERES, ?1501? SEVILLA, 2 DE SEPTIEMBRE DE 1572) / Lopez de Meneses, Amada – Badajoz: Dip. Provincial, 1965. Sep. REE – sp Bibl Santa Ana [946]

COMPANIA FUNDIDORA DE FIERRO Y ACERO DE MONTERREY, S.A. ... / ed by Bayle, Constantino – Madrid: Razon y Fe, 1926 – 1 – sp Bibl Santa Ana [946]

THE COMPANIES ORDINANCE OF HONGKONG, BEING NO. 1 OF 1865. / Hong Kong. Laws, Statutes, etc – Hongkong: Kelly & Walsh, 1907. 121p. LL-10005 – 1 – us L of C Photodup [340]

THE COMPANION / Cates, J M D – Second ed. contains 239 hymns published in 1846 – 1 – $8.82 – us Baptist [240]

COMPANION AND TEACHER – London, Ont: Companion Pub. Co., [1875?-18– or 19–] – 9 – cn C.I.H.M. [971]

A COMPANION TO LATIN STUDIES / ed by Sandys, John Lewis – Cambridge: University Press, 1910 – 3mf – 9 – us A.T.L.A. [450]

COMPANION TO THE BIBLE / Barrows, Elijah Porter – (Includes appendixes. Includes indexes of subjects and texts cited) – New York: American Tract Society, c1867 – 2mf – 9 – 0-8370-2188-X – 1985-0188 – us A.T.L.A. [220]

COMPANION TO THE BOTANICAL MAGAZINE / Hooker, W J – London. 1835-36. 2v – 16mf – 8 – ne IDC [580]

COMPANION TO THE BOTANICAL MAGAZINE – London, 1835-36 – 1,3 – us Readex [580]

COMPANION TO THE GREEK TESTAMENT / Barrett, A C – Cambridge: Deighton, Bell, 1890.1 fiche – 9 – us A.T.L.A. [240]

COMPANION TO THE MINUTES OF CONFERENCE : BEING AN ALPHABETICAL ARRANGEMENT OF THE MINISTERS... / Gunstone, W D – Dewsbury, 1896 – 1mf – 9 – ne IDC [240]

COMPANION TO THE MINUTES OF CONFERENCE : BEING AN ALPHABETICAL ARRANGEMENT OF THE MINISTERS OF THE METHODIST NEW CONNEXION,... / Gunstone, W D – Hull, 1888 – 1mf – 9 – ne IDC [240]

COMPANION TO THE REVISED OLD TESTAMENT / Chambers, Talbot Wilson – (Includes index) – New York: Funk & Wagnalls, 1885 – 1mf – 9 – 0-8370-2624-5 – 1985-0624 – us A.T.L.A. [220]

COMPANION TO THE REVISED VERSION OF THE NEW TESTAMENT / Roberts, Alexander – New York: Cassell, Petter, 1881. 1 fiche. 8370-4915-6 – 9 – us A.T.L.A. [240]

THE COMPANIONS OF ST PAUL / Howson, John Saul – London: Strahan, 1871 – 1mf – 9 – 0-8370-3680-1 – 1985-1680 – us A.T.L.A. [920]

THE COMPANIONS OF THE LORD: CHAPTERS ON THE LIVES OF THE APOSTLES / Reed, Charles Edward Baines – London: Religious Tract Society, 1883.1 fiche – 9 – us A.T.L.A. [240]

The Company of the Haras National *see* IMPORTERS AND BREEDERS OF FRENCH COACH, PERCHERON AND ARABIAN HORSES: CATALOGUE FOR 1889-90

Companys, Lluis *see* DISCURSO PRONUNCIADO POR LUIS COMPANYS EL DIA 27 DE DICIEMBRE DE 1936 EN EL PALACIO DE BELLAS ARTES DE BARCELONA, CON MOTIVO DEL 3 ANIVERSARIO DEL FALLICIMIENTO DE FRANCISCO MACIA

COMPARACIONES HISTORICAS / Cervi, Emilio – Madrid: Razon y Fe, 1940 – sp Bibl Santa Ana [240]

LA COMPARAISON DE LA LANGUE ET DE LA POESIE FRANCOISE AVEC LA GRECQUE ET LA LATINE / Desmarets de Saint-Sorlin, J – 1670 – 9 – fr I.C.S. [450]

COMPARATA DELLE R. UNIVERSITA DI TORINO / Musei di Zoologia ed Anatomia – Torino, 1893-1894. V.8-9 – 12mf – 9 – ne IDC [590]

Comparata delle R. Universita di Torino *see* MUSEI DI ZOOLOGIA ED ANATOMIA

COMPARATIVE ADVANTAGE OF AGRICULTURAL PRODUCTION SYSTEMS AND ITS POLICY IMPLICATIONS IN PAKISTAN – 1987 – 138p – it F.A.O. [338]

A COMPARATIVE ANALYSIS OF EQUIVALENT SUBMAXIMAL TREADMIL AND BICYCLE ERGOMETER EXERCISE / Black, John G – 1980 – 1mf – 9 – $4.00 – us Microform Publ [790]

COMPARATIVE ANALYSIS OF FACTORS INFLUENCING PARTICIPATION IN AN EMPLOYEE HEALTH PROMOTION PROGRAM, INCLUDING CHARACTERIZATIONS OF PARTICIPANTS AND NONPARTICIPANTS / Teschner, Pamela J S & Donatelle, Rebecca J – 1992 – 2mf – 9 – $8.00 – us Microform Publ [613]

A COMPARATIVE ANALYSIS OF THE LEADERSHIP STYLES OF HEAD FOOTBALL COACHES FROM TADITIONALLY BLACK AND WHITE UNIVERSITIES AND COLLEGES / Thomas, Johnny D & Waigandt, Alex – 1992 – 3mf – 9 – $12.00 – us Microform Publ [150]

COMPARATIVE AND GENERAL PHARMOCOLOGY *see* GENERAL PHARMACOLOGY

COMPARATIVE AND INTERNATIONAL LAW JOURNAL OF SOUTHERN AFRICA – (v1-17 1968-84 on reel $185.00. v18-28 1985-95 on mf $277.00) – v1-28. 1968-95 – 5,6,9 – $462.00 set – us Hein [340]

THE COMPARATIVE ARCHEOLOGY OF EARLY MESOPOTAMIA / Perkins, Ann L – 1948 – 9 – $10.00 – us I.R.C. [930]

COMPARATIVE BIOCHEMISTRY AND PHYSIOLOGY : PARTS A, B AND C – (Back issues of journal available from UMI) – v104-106. 33 issues/y. 1993 – 9 – £2,724.00 set – uk Elsevier Sci [540]

COMPARATIVE BIOCHEMISTRY AND PHYSIOLOGY – (v38- 1971- available separately; Part A: Comparative Physiology; Part B: Comparative Biochemistry; Part C: Comparative Pharmacology & Toxicology) – v1-37. 1961-70 – 5,6,9 – us UMI [540]

COMPARATIVE BIOCHEMISTRY AND PHYSIOLOGY, PART A: COMPARATIVE PHYSIOLOGY – v38- 1971- – 5,6,9 – us UMI [540]

COMPARATIVE BIOCHEMISTRY AND PHYSIOLOGY. PART A: COMPARATIVE PHYSIOLOGY – (Back issues of journal available from UMI) – v104-106. 12 issues/y. 1993 – 9 – £1,051.00y – uk Elsevier Sci [540]

COMPARATIVE BIOCHEMISTRY AND PHYSIOLOGY, PART B: COMPARATIVE BIOCHEMISTRY – v38- 1971- – 5,6,9 – us UMI [540]

COMPARATIVE BIOCHEMISTRY AND PHYSIOLOGY. PART B: COMPARATIVE BIOCHEMISTRY – (Back issues of journal available from UMI) – v104-106. 12 issues/y. 1993 – 9 – £1,072.00y – uk Elsevier Sci [540]

COMPARATIVE BIOCHEMISTRY AND PHYSIOLOGY, PART C: COMPARATIVE PHARMACOLOGY – v50- 1975- – 5,6,9 – us UMI [540]

COMPARATIVE BIOCHEMISTRY AND PHYSIOLOGY. PART C: COMPARATIVE PHARMACOLOGY – (Back issues of journal available from UMI) – v104-106. 9 issues/y. 1993 – 9 – £783.00y – uk Elsevier Sci [615]

COMPARATIVE DRAMA – v1- 1967- 1; v9- 1975- 5,6,9 – us UMI [790]

COMPARATIVE ECOLOGY AND BEHAVIOUR OF SWAMP HARRIERS AND SPOTTED HARRIERS AND OTHER RAPTORS IN AUSTRALIA AND NEW ZEALAND / Baker-Gabb, David – (PhD Thesis) – 1982 – 9 – A$15.00 – at R.A.O.U. [590]

COMPARATIVE EDUCATION – 1965- 29v – 9 – £225.50 – 0305-0068 – uk Carfax [370]

COMPARATIVE EDUCATION REVIEW – v1- 1957- 1; v15- 5,6; v20- 9 – us UMI [370]

THE COMPARATIVE EFFECTIVENESS OF STATIC STRETCHING AND PROPRIOCEPTIVE NEUROMUSCULAR FACILITATION STRETCHING TECHNIQUES IN INCREASING HIP FLEXION RANGE OF MOTION / Sundquist, Robert D – Oregon State University, 1996 – 1mf – 9 – PH 1511 – us Microform Publ [612]

A COMPARATIVE EVALUATION OF STENOGRAPHIC AND AUDIOTAPE METHODS FOR U.S. DISTRICT COURT REPORTING / Greenwood, Michael et al – Washington: FJC, July 1983 – 3mf – 9 – $4.50 – LLMC 95-353 – us L.L.M.C. [340]

A COMPARATIVE GRAMMAR OF THE HEBREW LANGUAGE : FOR THE USE OF CLASSICAL AND PHILOLOGICAL STUDENTS / Donaldson, John William – London: John W Parker, 1853 – 1mf – 9 – 0-8370-9227-2 – 1986-3227 – us A.T.L.A. [470]

A COMPARATIVE GRAMMAR OF THE HITTITE LANGUAGE / Sturtevant, Edgar H – 1933 – 9 – $12.00 – us I.R.C. [470]

A COMPARATIVE HISTORY OF METROLOGY / Griffin, H J – 1984. 5 fiches – 9 – £35.00 – uk Mansell Publ [380]

COMPARATIVE HYDROLOGY : AN ECOLOGICAL APPROACH TO LAND AND WATER RESOURCES / ed by Falkenmark, Malin & Chapman, Tom – 1989 – 479p – 9 – 92-3-102571-6 – fr UNESCO [333]

COMPARATIVE IMMUNOLOGY MICRO-BIOLOGY AND INFECTIOUS DISEASES – v1- 1978- – 5,6,9 – us UMI [576]

COMPARATIVE LABOR LAW *see* COMPARATIVE LABOR LAW JOURNAL

COMPARATIVE LABOR LAW JOURNAL – (Title varies: v1-7 1976-1986 as Comparative Labor Law) – University of Pennsylvania. v1-16. 1976-1995 – 9 – $274.00 set – us Hein [340]

COMPARATIVE LAW YEARBOOK *see* COMPARATIVE LAW YEARBOOK OF INTERNATIONAL BUSINESS

COMPARATIVE LAW YEARBOOK OF INTERNATIONAL BUSINESS – (Title varies: v1-11 1977-87 as Comparative Law Yearbook) – v1-17. 1977-95 – 9 – $506.00 set – us Hein [340]

COMPARATIVE LITERATURE – (v.1-7. 1949-55; v.20- 1968- 5,6. v.1-7. 1949-55; v.27- 1975- 9) – v.1- 1949- – 1 – us UMI [410]

COMPARATIVE MEDICINE EAST AND WEST – (See also: American Journal of Chinese Medicine) – v5-. 1977- – 1,5,6,9 – us UMI [610]

COMPARATIVE MEDICINE EAST AND WEST *see* – AMERICAN JOURNAL OF CHINESE MEDICINE

COMPARATIVE MORPHOLOGY AND BIOLOGY OF THE FUNGI, MYCETOZOA AND BACTERIA / Bary, H A de – English trans. by H. E. F. Garnsey. Rev. by I. B. Balfour. Oxford. 1887. B-7401 1 – 9 – ne IDC [580]

COMPARATIVE PRINT OF THE TEXTS OF THE IMMIGRATION AND NATURALIZATION ACT AND THE IMMIGRATION AND NATURALIZATION LAWS EXISTING PRIOR TO THE ENACTMENT OF P.L. 414, JUNE 27, 1952, 66 STAT. 163 / U.S. Dept of Immigration. Senate Committee on the Judiciary – Washington: GPO, 1952 (all publ) – 3mf – 9 – $4.50 – LLMC 81-500 – us L.L.M.C. [340]

COMPARATIVE PSYCHOLOGY; OR, THE GROWTH AND GRADES OF INTELLIGENCE / Bascom, John – New York: G.P. Putnam's Sons, 1878. 297p – 1 – us U.W. Library [150]

COMPARATIVE STATISTICS OF EDUCATION 1953/54-1960/61 / United Arab Republic. Southern Region. Ministry of Education. Department of Statistics – Cairo, 1961 – 2mf – 9 – DE-705/1 – ne IDC [370]

COMPARATIVE STRATEGY – v. 1-. 1978- – 1,5,6,9 – us UMI [320]

COMPARATIVE STUDIES IN SOCIETY AND HISTORY – (1981-. 1,5,6,9) – v1-. 1958- – 1 – us UMI [073]

A COMPARATIVE STUDY OF AMERICAN AND DUTCH ACCOUNTANCY AND THEIR IMPACT ON THE PROFESSION IN INDONESIA / Suhadji Hadibroto – SE 4381 1. 1962? – 9 – ne IDC [650]

A COMPARATIVE STUDY OF EXPERIENTIAL LEARNING UTILIZING INDOOR-CENTERED TRAINING AND OUTDOOR-CENTERED TRAINING / Moorefield, David L – Texas Woman's University, 1994 – 1mf – 9 – PSY 1895 – us Microform Publ [150]

COMPARATIVE STUDY OF FOOD CONSUMPTION DATA FROM FOOD BALANCE SHEETS AND HOUSEHOLD SURVEYS – 1983 – 36p – it F.A.O. [310]

A COMPARATIVE STUDY OF LEISURE LIFESTYLES : THREE DEVELOPMENTALLY DISABLED AND THREE NON-DISABLED OLDER ADULTS / Kerr, S R – 1991 – 2mf – 9 – $8.00 – us Microform Publ [301]

COMPARATIVE STUDY OF SOME METHODS OF CENSUSING BIRDS / Hermes, Neil – (BSc Thesis) – 1977 – microfiche – A$15.00 – at R.A.O.U. [590]

A COMPARATIVE STUDY OF THE LITERATURES OF EGYPT, PALESTINE AND MESOPOTAMIA / Peet, T E – 1929 – 9 – $10.00 – us I.R.C. [470]

A COMPARATIVE STUDY OF THE SOCIAL BACKGROUND OF ADULT EDUCATION PROBLEMS IN AFRICA AND INDIA / Banerji, Santi Kumar – London: [s.n.], 1950 – 1 – us Res Libr [370]

A COMPARATIVE STUDY OF THE SOCIAL BACKGROUND OF ADULT EDUCATION PROBLEMS IN AFRICA AND INDIA / Banerji, Santi Kumar – London: [s.n.] 1950 – us Res Libr [370]

A COMPARATIVE STUDY ON THE EFFECTIVENESS OF PREVENTIVE KNEE BRACES / Szczodrowski, Daniel F – 1988 – 91p 1mf – 9 – $4.00 – us Microform Publ [617]

COMPARATIVE STUDY ON THE NATIONAL SCIENCE AND TECHNOLOGY POLICY-MAKING BODIES IN THE COUNTRIES OF EASTERN AND SOUTHERN AFRICA – (English/French) – 1987 – 186p – 9 – 92-3-002470-8 – fr UNESCO [350]

COMPARATIVE STUDY ON THE NATIONAL SCIENCE AND TECHNOLOGY POLICY-MAKING BODIES IN THE COUNTRIES OF WEST AFRICA – 1986 – 104p – 9 – 92-3-102280-6 – fr UNESCO [350]

COMPARATIVE STUDY ON THREE COUNTRIES WITH REGARD TO THEIR ECONOMIC STRUCTURE AND LONG TERM DEVELOPMENT. A STUDY IN THE BEHAVIOR OF FAMILY CONSUMPTION EXPENDITURE ON HOUSEHOLD DURABLE EQUIPMENT / Tjan, Thay-an – SE 5464 1. 1962? – 9 – ne IDC [338]

COMPARATIVE THEOLOGY / MacCulloch, John Arnott – London: Methuen, 1902. 1 fiche – 9 – us A.T.L.A. [230]

COMPARATIVE URBAN RESEARCH – v1- 1972- 1; 1976- 5,6,9 – us UMI [300]

COMPARATIVE URBAN RESEARCH – 1985- – 1 – us UMI [073]

A COMPARATIVE VIEW OF THE GOSPELS / Platt, Isaac L – New York: Thomas Holman, 1860. 1 fiche – 9 – us A.T.L.A. [240]

A COMPARATIVE VOCABULARY OF THE WESTERN ESKIMO DIALECTS / Jenness, D – BN 272 2. 1928 – 8 – ne IDC [490]

A COMPARATIVE VOCABULARY OF THE WESTERN ESKIMO DIALECTS / Jenness, D – Ottawa, 1928 – 3mf – ne IDC [490]

COMPARE – New York, NY. 1976-? – us I.H.R.C. [073]

COMPARE: A JOURNAL OF COMPARATIVE EDUCATION – 1971- 23v – 9 – £216.00 – 0305-7925 – uk Carfax [370]

COMPARING TORT LIABILITY KNOWLEDGE OF FUTURE TEACHER COACHES AND CURRENT PRACTICING TEACHER COACHES / Kautz, Robert E & Adams, Samuel Houston – 1993 – 2mf – $8.00 – us Microform Publ [340]

A COMPARISON AMONG THE TRACK AND GRAB STARTS IN SWIMMING AND A STAND-UP RESPONSE TASK / Stone, Randall A – 1988 – 68p 1mf – 9 – $4.00 – us Microform Publ [612]

COMPARISON AND FIT OF THE TWO AND SIX BAND K.P. MODELS FOR THE BAND EDGE STRUCTURE OF PB, SN, TE 1-X X / Israel. Prime Minister's Office – By Y. Weissman. Oct 1975. 21 p. Diagr – 9 – 2.00 – is I.T.T.I. [530]

THE COMPARISON BETWEEN AN AQUATIC RUNNING PROGRAM VERSUS A HARD SURFACE RUNNING PROGRAM ON AEROBIC CAPACITY AND BODY COMPOSITION / Hartman, H – 1988 – 1mf – 9 – $4.00 – us Microform Publ [612]

A COMPARISON BETWEEN ANTHROPOMETRIC REGRESSION EQUATIONS AND HYDROSTATIC WEIGHING FOR PREDICTING PERCENT BODY FAT OF ADULT MALES WITH DOWN SYNDROME / Ovalle, S E –

1992 – 2mf – 9 – $8.00 – us Microform Publ [790]

A COMPARISON BETWEEN STAIRCLIMBING AND GRADED WALKING IN PERIPHERAL VASCULAR OCCLUSIVE DISEASE / Vaughan, N R – 1991 – 2mf – 9 – $8.00 – us Microform Publ [612]

A COMPARISON BETWEEN THE NUMBER OF EUROPEAN AMERICANS, AFRICAN AMERICANS, AND OTHER MINORITY RACES WHO ENTER PHASE 1 AND PHASE 2 CARDIAC REHABILITATION PROGRAMS / Shields, Lionell – University of Wisconsin-La Crosse, 1995 – 1mf – 9 – HE 571 – us Microform Publ [613]

THE COMPARISON OF ACTIVE PLANTARFLEXOR MUSCLE STIFFNESS BETWEEN YOUNG AND ELDERLY HUMAN FEMALES / Blanpied, Peter R & Smidt, Gary L – 1989 – 3mf – 9 – $12.00 – us Microform Publ [617]

COMPARISON OF ACUTE HEART RATE AND BLOOD PRESSURE RESPONSES AMONG ISOMETRIC, ISOTONIC, AND ISOKINETIC EXERCISE / Hui, Sai C & Mahar, Matthew T – 1992 – 2mf – $8.00 – us Microform Publ [612]

THE COMPARISON OF AEROBIC FITNESS LEVELS IN REPECT TO VISUAL-PERCEPTUAL PERFORMANCE AT REST AND DURING EXERCISE / Pate, John G & Pleasants, Frank – 1993 – 1mf – $4.00 – us Microform Publ [150]

COMPARISON OF ANDROGYNY LEVELS IN TEAM AND INDIVIDUAL SPORT FEMALE ATHLETES / Thibodeau, Laura – 1990 – 67p 1mf – 9 – $4.00 – us Microform Publ [150]

A COMPARISON OF ANTERIOR TIBIAL-FEMORAL LAXITY IN FEMALE INTERCOLLEGIATE GYMNASTS TO A NORMAL POPULATION / Brannan, Tori L – 1994 – 1mf – $4.00 – us Microform Publ [617]

A COMPARISON OF ATHLETIC ANKLE TAPING TECHNIQUES WITH RESPECT TO ANKLE INVERSION / Plummer, P E – 1991 – 1mf – 9 – $4.00 – us Microform Publ [790]

COMPARISON OF BALANCE AND MAXIMAL OXYGEN CONSUMPTION AMONG HEARING, CONGENITAL NON-HEARING AND ACQUIRED NON-HEARING FEMALE INTERCOLLEGIATE ATHLETES / Ellis, Marjorie K – 1991 – 1mf – $4.00 – us Microform Publ [612]

COMPARISON OF BEHAVIOR MODIFICATION TECHNIQUES USED IN PHYSICAL EDUCATION WITH INSTITUTIONALIZED PROFOUNDLY MENTALLY RETARDED STUDENTS AT DIFFERENT AGES / Culver, April D – 1989 – 120p 2mf – 9 – $8.00 – us Microform Publ [150]

COMPARISON OF BILATERAL NORMAL TIBIAL ROTATION IN ADULT MALES / Carver, T A – 1990 – 1mf – 9 – $4.00 – us Microform Publ [613]

COMPARISON OF BODY COMPOSITION BETWEEN GERMAN AND AMERICAN ADULTS WITH MENTAL RETARDATION / Frey, Bernd – 1994 – 1mf – $4.00 – us Microform Publ [612]

A COMPARISON OF BODY COMPOSITION CHANGES IN MODERATELY OBESE AND EXTREMELY OBESE WOMEN WHO EXPERIENCE THE SAME CALORIC DEFICIT / Stowe, Stephen R & Fisher, A Garth – 1991 – 1mf – $4.00 – us Microform Publ [617]

A COMPARISON OF BODY DENSITY AND PERCENT BODY FAT USING FUNCTIONAL RESIDUAL CAPACITY AND RESIDUAL VOLUME AND DEVELOPMENT OF IMMERSED FUNCTIONAL RESIDUAL CAPACITY AND RESIDUAL VOLUME PREDICTION FORMULAS / Koenig, Joseph M & Floyd, William – 1990 – 1mf – $4.00 – us Microform Publ [612]

A COMPARISON OF BONE MINERAL DENSITY BETWEEN ACTIVE AND NONACTIVE MEN WITH SPINAL CORD INJURIES / Eddins, William C, Jr – Oregon State University, 1995 – 2mf – 9 – $8.00 – PH 1491 – us Microform Publ [612]

A COMPARISON OF CARDIORESPIRATORY FITNESS OF TRAINED AND UNTRAINED MIDDLE-AGED WOMEN / Upton, S Jill – 1981 – 2mf – 9 – $8.00 – us Microform Publ [790]

A COMPARISON OF COACHES' AND ATHLETIC ADMINISTRATORS' PERCEPTIONS ON THE DESIRABILITY OF HOSTING NON-REVENUE, POSTSEASON ATHLETIC EVENTS / Smith, Linda J – 1994 – 1mf – $4.00 – us Microform Publ [790]

A COMPARISON OF DIRECT INSTRUCTION AND COMPUTER-ASSISTED INSTRUCTION ON LEARNING A MOTOR SKILL BY FOURTH GRADE STUDENTS / Ross, James R & Robertson, James B – 1992 – 2mf – $8.00 – us Microform Publ [150]

A COMPARISON OF DIVISION IA FOOTBALL PLAYERS' GRADES IN SEASON AND OUT OF SEASON / Hickey, Kathleen P – 1994 – 1mf – $4.00 – us Microform Publ [370]

COMPARISON OF FACTORS AFFECTING THE CAREER PATHS OF MALE AND FEMALE DIRECTORS OF INTERCOLLEGIATE ATHLETICS / Sweany, Lisa – Ball State University, 1996 – 1mf – 9 – PE 3674 – us Microform Publ [790]

A COMPARISON OF GRIP STRENGTH IN YOUNG ATHLETES AND NON-ATHLETES / Garcia, R – 1991 – 1mf – 9 – $4.00 – us Microform Publ [790]

A COMPARISON OF HEMODYNAMIC RESPONSES TO ARM AND LEG EXERCISE OF THE SAME INTENSITIES / Holmes, Richard J – 1983 – 9 – $4.00 – us Microform Publ [790]

A COMPARISON OF HYDROSTATIC WEIGHING AND DISPLACEMENT PLETHYSMOGRAPHY FOR DETERMINING BODY DENSITY OF YOUNG ELITE FEMALE GYMNASTS / Graham, Bruce J & Klug, Gary A – 1993 – 1mf – 9 – $4.00 – us Microform Publ [617]

COMPARISON OF HYDROSTATIC WEIGHING TO BIOELECTRICAL IMPEDANCE ANALYSIS IN WOMEN GREATER THAN THIRTY PERCENT BODY FAT / Bauer, Shari R & Porcari, John P – 1991 – 1mf – $4.00 – us Microform Publ [617]

A COMPARISON OF INTERMITTENT EXERCISE AND RELAXATION VERSUS STEADY STATE EXERCISE ON FITNESS LEVELS AND ATTITUDES IN SEVENTH GRADE GIRLS / Jordan, Mary C – 1993 – 1mf – $4.00 – us Microform Publ [612]

A COMPARISON OF ISOMETRIC STRENGTH TEST RESULTS BETWEEN LOW BACK INJURED PATIENTS AND NORMALS / Kendrick, R J – 1991 – 1mf – 9 – $4.00 – us Microform Publ [612]

A COMPARISON OF MALADAPTIVE BEHAVIORS OF ATHLETES AND NON-ATHLETES / Weiss, Steven M – Springfield College – 2mf – 9 – $8.00 – PSY1871 – us Microform Publ [150]

A COMPARISON OF MANUAL AND MACHINE ASSISTED PROPRIOCEPTIVE NEUROMUSCULAR FACILITATION FLEXIBILITY TECHNIQUES / Burke, Darren – Dalhousie University, 1995 – 2mf – 9 – $8.00 – PH1453 – us Microform Publ [612]

A COMPARISON OF OCCUPATIONAL STRESS AND RELATED VARIABLES AMONG SALESPERSONS, CLERICAL STAFF, SERVICE TECHNICIANS, AND MANAGERS OF THE MID-OHIO DISTRICT OF THE XEROX CORPORATION / Gardner, J K – 1991 – 3mf – 9 – $12.00 – us Microform Publ [150]

A COMPARISON OF OFFENSIVE EFFICIENCY BETWEEN THREE TYPES OF BASKETBALL OFFENSE / Papachatzis, Thanasis – 1994 – 3mf – $12.00 – us Microform Publ [301]

A COMPARISON OF ORTHOSTATIC TOLERANCE AND FLUID LOADING IN TRAINED AND NON-TRAINED SUBJECTS DURING SIMULATED WEIGHTLESSNESS / Mauro, B A – 1992 – 2mf – 9 – $8.00 – us Microform Publ [612]

A COMPARISON OF PERCEPTIONS OF THE IMPORTANCE BETWEEN PHYSICAL EDUCATION GRADUATE TEACHING ASSISTANTS AND GRADUATE PROGRAM COORDINATORS ON SELECTION OF GRADUATE TEACHING ASSISTANTS AND THEIR TEACHING PERFORMANCE CRITERIA / Wei, Bing & Cooper, Walter E – 1992 – 2mf – 9 – $8.00 – us Microform Publ [370]

A COMPARISON OF PHYSIOLOGIC RESPONSES TO FORWARD AND RETROGRADE SIMULATED STAIR STEPPING ON THE STAIRMASTER / Ryan, Patrick T – 1993 – 1mf – $4.00 – us Microform Publ [612]

A COMPARISON OF RATING OF PERCEIVED EXERTION IN TREADMILL VS TRACK WALKING AND RUNNING / Schroeder, Lisa M & Butts, Nancy Kay – 1991 – 1mf – $4.00 – us Microform Publ [150]

COMPARISON OF RESTING METABOLIC RATE AND EXCESS POST-EXERCISE OXYGEN CONSUMPTION IN NORMAL AND LOW CALORIE DIETING FEMALES / Hilbert, Carey A – Oregon State University, 1995 – 2mf – 9 – $8.00 – PH 1496 – us Microform Publ [612]

THE COMPARISON OF RESTING METABOLIC RATE IN TRAINED VS. UNTRAINED FEMALES / Allen, D M – 1991 – 1mf – 9 – $4.00 – us Microform Publ [613]

COMPARISON OF RISK FACTORS FOR CORONARY HEART DISEASE IN SEDENTARY AND PHYSICALLY ACTIVE COLLEGE STUDENTS / Jensen, Marian & Heiner, Steven W – 1992 – 2mf – $8.00 – us Microform Publ [613]

A COMPARISON OF SELECTED CORONARY HEART DISEASE RISK FACTORS IN WEIGHT TRAINED MALES / Lambert, Christopher M & Floyd, William – 1991 – 1mf – $4.00 – us Microform Publ [612]

A COMPARISON OF SELECTED NEUROMUSCULAR AND KINEMATIC VARIABLES BEFORE AND AFTER LEARNING AN AIMING TASK / Steciak, David M & Brush, Florence C – 1992 – 1mf – 9 – $4.00 – us Microform Publ [150]

A COMPARISON OF SIX PERSONALITY FACTORS BETWEEN PROFESSIONAL, COLLEGE, AND HIGH SCHOOL BASKETBALL PLAYERS / Bowe, William G Jr – State University of New York College at Brockport, 1994 – 1mf – 9 – $4.00 – PSY1839 – us Microform Publ [150]

A COMPARISON OF SKELETAL MUSCLE RESPONSIVENESS TO EXERCISE IN MALE AND FEMALE SPRAGUE-DAWLEY RATS TREATED WITH AN ANABOLIC STEROID / Brown, Gordon D et al – 1992 – 2mf – 9 – $8.00 – us Microform Publ [613]

COMPARISON OF SKINFOLD MEASUREMENTS UNDER NORMALLY HYDRATED AND DEHYDRATED CONDITIONS IN FEMALES AGES TO 54 / Botenhagen, Kim A & Alejandro-De Leon, Daniel – 1992 – 1mf – 9 – $4.00 – us Microform Publ [617]

COMPARISON OF SPORT ACHIEVEMENT ORIENTATION BETWEEN WHEELCHAIR BASKETBALL ATHLETES AND ABLE-BODY BASKETBALL ATHLETES / Skordilis, Emmanouil K – Springfield College, 1995 – 2mf – 9 – $8.00 – PSY1864 – us Microform Publ [150]

A COMPARISON OF STANDING POSTURE BETWEEN FEMALE JUNIOR HIGH SCHOOL STUDENTS IN HONG KONG WITH AND WITHOUT BALLET TRAINING / Lee, B W – 1991 – 2mf – 9 – $8.00 – us Microform Publ [790]

COMPARISON OF TAGALOG AND ILOKO : DISSERTATION FOR THE OBTENTION OF THE DOCTOR'S DEGREE IN THE FACULTY OF PHILOSOPHY OF THE UNIVERSITY OF HAMBURG / Lopez, Cecilio – 1928 – us Res Libr [490]

A COMPARISON OF TAGALOG AND MALAY LEXICOGRAPHIES (ON PHONETIC-SEMANTIC BASIS) / Lopez, Cecilio – Manila: Bureau of Print, 1939 – us Res Libr [490]

A COMPARISON OF THE AMERICAN RED CROSS AND YOUNG MEN'S CHRISTIAN ASSOCIATION TEACHING METHODS FOR BEGINNING SWIMMING / Roan, Sarah A – 1987 – 117p 2mf – 9 – $8.00 – us Microform Publ [370]

COMPARISON OF THE ASSOCIATION OF CERVICAL SPINAL CANAL STENOSIS AND INTERVERTEBRAL FORAMING CANAL STENOSIS AND TRANSIENT UPPER EXTREMITY PARASTHESIAS / Aliquo, David – Temple University, 1996 – 1mf – 9 – PE 3626 – us Microform Publ [617]

A COMPARISON OF THE EFFECTIVENESS OF INTERACTIVE VIDEO IN TEACHING THE ABILITY TO ANALYZE TWO MOTOR SKILLS IN SWIMMING / Mathias, KE – 1990 – 2mf – 9 – $8.00 – us Microform Publ [790]

A COMPARISON OF THE EFFECTS OF A WRESTLING PRACTICE AND A WEIGHTLIFTING WORKOUT ON THE BODY FAT PERCENT OF WRESTLERS / Bergerson, Mark – 1994 – 1mf – $4.00 – us Microform Publ [612]

COMPARISON OF THE EXAMINATION QUESTIONS ON CHEMISTRY AND PHYSICS: GIVEN BY DR. MCLELLAN, EXAMINER OF PUBLIC SCHOOL TEACHERS WITH THE QUESTIONS GIVEN TO NORMAL SCHOOL STUDENTS BY MR. KIRKLAND A FEW WEEKS BEFORE THE TIME OF EXAMINATION, IN 1874 – 1874? 00734. (Pre-1900 Canadiana) – 9 – cn C.I.H.M. [370]

COMPARISON OF THE LACTATE AND VENTILATORY THRESHOLDS DURING PROLONGED WORK / Loat, Christopher E R & Rhodes, E C – 1991 – 1mf – 9 – $4.00 – us Microform Publ [613]

A COMPARISON OF THE LEADERSHIP BEHAVIOR OF WINNING AND LOSING HIGH SCHOOL BASKETBALL COACHES / Lam, Tak C – Springfield College, 1995 – 2mf – 9 – $8.00 – PSY1849 – us Microform Publ [150]

COMPARISON OF THE LOCATABILITY OF VOCALISATIONS OF BELL MINERS AND NOISY MINERS IN RELATION TO DIFFERENCES IN HABITAT / Date, Elizabeth – (BSc Hons Thesis) – 1982 – microfiche – A$15.00 – at R.A.O.U. [590]

COMPARISON OF THE MID-AMERIACN CONFERENCE ATHLETIC DEPARTMENT REGARDING COMPLIANCE WITH TITLE 9 / Fiscus, Douglas L – Ball State University, 1996 – 1mf – 9 – PE 3639 – us Microform Publ [790]

COMPARISON OF THE NUMBER OF CLASSIFICATION TRIALS FOR VARIOUS CRITERION-REFERENCED TESTING METHODS / McManis, BG – 1991 – 2mf – 9 – $8.00 – us Microform Publ [613]

A COMPARISON OF THE POLITICAL ATTITUDES OF FEMALE AND MALE ATHLETES / Martindell-Jensen, Jane – 1980 – 1mf – 9 – $4.00 – us Microform Publ [790]

A COMPARISON OF THE RATIO OF SHOULDER CONCENTRIC INTERNAL ROTATION TO ECCENTRIC EXTERNAL ROTATION OF MALE SWIMMERS VS. NONSWIMMERS / Werner-Ferrel, Sally D – 1989 – 40p 1mf – 9 – $4.00 – us Microform Publ [612]

A COMPARISON OF THE SPORTSMANSHIP ATTITUDES AND/OR MORAL REASONING OF INTERSCHOLASTIC COACHES / Gillentine, John A – University of Southern Mississippi, 1995 – 1mf – 9 – $4.00 – PSY1845 – us Microform Publ [150]

A COMPARISON OF THE TENSILE STRENGTH OF THE UMBILICAL CORD OF BABIES OF SMOKING AND NON-SMOKING MOTHERS / England, Joyce & McGuire, Don – 1988 – 2mf – 9 – $8.00 – us Microform Publ [613]

A COMPARISON OF THREE HYDROSTATIC WEIGHING TECHNIQUES : WITHOUT HEAD SUBMERSION, TOTAL LUNG CAPACITY, AND RESIDUAL VOLUME / Wa, K M – 1991 – 2mf – 9 – $8.00 – us Microform Publ [790]

A COMPARISON OF THREE WARM-UP PROTOCOLS ON POWER OUTPUT IN THE WINGATE ANAEROBIC TEST / Thomas, R S – 1990 – 1mf – 9 – $4.00 – us Microform Publ [613]

COMPARISON OF TOTAL PERIPHERAL RESISTANCE AND BLOOD VELOCITY AS OBTAINED FROM DOPPLER ULTRASOUND WAVEFORMS DURING REST, EXERCISE AND RECOVERY / Socha, M L – 1991 – 1mf – 9 – $4.00 – us Microform Publ [612]

COMPARISON OF TWO INSTRUMENTS FOR NEEDS ASSESSMENT AND EVALUATION OF AN EMPLOYEE HEALTH PROMOTION PROGRAM / Hoffman, Marilyn A – 1989 – 78p 1mf – 9 – $4.00 – us Microform Publ [613]

A COMPARISON OF TWO INTERMITTENT EXTERNAL COMPRESSION DEVICES ON PITTING ANKLE EDEMA / Lemley, T R – 1991 – 1mf – 9 – $4.00 – us Microform Publ [790]

COMPARISON OF TWO METHODS OF TRAINING SPECIAL OLYMPICS VOLUNTEERS TO TEACH AND COACH BOWLING / Albright, Cindy W – 1989 – 191p 2mf – 9 – $8.00 – us Microform Publ [370]

A COMPARISON OF VALUED OUTCOMES OF YOUTH SPORT PROGRAMS : PARTICIPANTS, PARENTS, COACHES, AND ADMINISTRATORS / Millard, Linda – 1990 – 2mf – 9 – $8.00 – us Microform Publ [150]

A COMPARISON OF VERTICAL JUMP HEIGHT MEASUREMENTS ON THE VERTEC AND BIOTRAN USING THREE JUMPING TECHNIQUES / McCollum, Jennifer D – University of North Carolina at Chapel Hill, 1995 – 1mf – 9 – $4.00 – PE3611 – us Microform Publ [612]
A COMPARISON OF VILLAGE AND STAGED VERSIONS OF SELECTED HUNGARIAN DANCE STYLES / Geslison, Jeannette E K – Brigham Young University, 1995 – 2mf – 9 – $8.00 – PE 3645 – us Microform Publ [790]
COMPARISON OF WAIST TO HIP RATIO MEASUREMENTS IN RELATION TO CARDIOVASCULAR RISK FACTORS IN HEALTHY MENOPAUSAL WOMEN / Hurtubise, Cheryl L – University of Carolina at Greensboro, 1995 – 1mf – 9 – $4.00 – HE555 – us Microform Publ [616]
COMPARISONS OF DOMAIN SCORE AND RELIABILITY ESTIMATES USING TRIALS-TOCRITERION, SEQUENTIAL PROBABILITY RATIO, AND PRE-SET TRIAL LENGTH TESTS / Chow, B C – 1991 – 2mf – 9 – $8.00 – us Microform Publ [370]
COMPASS – Houston, TX. 1967-69 – 1r – 1 – $50.00 – R05002 – us Library Micro [071]
THE COMPASS – Quebec, Canada. 27 jan 1877 – 1r – 1 – Can$25.00 – cn Can Microfilming [072]
Compayre, Gabriel *see*
- ABELARD AND THE ORIGIN AND EARLY HISTORY OF UNIVERSITIES
- L'EDUCATION
- ELEMENTS D'INSTRUCTION MORALE ET CIVIQUE
- HERBERT SPENCER AND SCIENTIFIC EDUCATION
- HISTOIRE CRITIQUE DES DOCTRINES DE L'EDUCATION EN FRANCE DEPUIS LE SEIZIEME SIECLE
- HISTOIRE CRITIQUE DES DOCTRINES DE L'EDUCATION EN FRANCE DEPUIS LE XVIE SIECLE
- PESTALOZZI AND ELEMENTARY EDUCATION

COMPENDARIA IN GRAECAM VIA / Gonzalez, Castro – Tip. Regia, 1792 – sp Bibl Santa Ana [946]
COMPENDIA OF AWARDS / Connecticut. Compensation Commissioners – v.1-12, 1914-48. 102 fiches. (Harvard Law School Library Collection.) – 9 – 1.50f – us H.U. Law [336]
COMPENDIARIA EXPOSITIO DOCTRINAE DE ESSENTIA ORIG: PECCATI / Flacius Illyricus d.A E, M – Vrsellis, 1572 – 1mf – 9 – ne IDC [240]
COMPENDIARIA PRAECIPVARVM RERVM TVRCICARVM / Risebergius, L – Helmaestadii, 1596 – 4mf – 9 – H-8390/1 – ne IDC [956]
COMPENDIO DE ARITMETICA / Munoz de Rivera, Juan – 1868 – 9 – 1.50f – sp Bibl Santa Ana [510]
COMPENDIO DE ARITMETICA.. / Botello del Castillo, Carlos – 1878 – 9 – 1.50f – sp Bibl Santa Ana [510]
COMPENDIO DE ELEMENTOS DE MATEMATICAS / Morales Fernandez, Francisco – 1884 – 9 – 1.50f – sp Bibl Santa Ana [510]
COMPENDIO DE FILOSOFIA ESCOLASTICA. TOMO 1 : LOGICA Y PSICOLOGIA / Marquez, Gabino – Jerez: Tipolitografia de Salido Hermanos, 2nd ed 1917 – 1 – sp Bibl Santa Ana [170]
COMPENDIO DE FILOSOFIA ESCOLASTICA. TOMO 2. FILOSOFIA MORAL / Marquez, Gabino – Jerez: Tipolitografia de Salido Hermanos, 3rd ed 1921 – 1 – sp Bibl Santa Ana [170]
COMPENDIO DE GEOMETRIA Y TRIGONOMETRIA.. / Botello del Castillo, Carlos – 1879 – 9 – 1.50f – sp Bibl Santa Ana [510]
COMPENDIO DE GRAMATICA CASTELLANA / Diez Olivares, J Ma – 1874 – 9 – 1.50f – sp Bibl Santa Ana [440]
COMPENDIO DE HISTORIA DE ESPANA. TOMO 1 / Duchesne – 1786 – 1mf – 9 – Pta1,000.00 – 84-7848-243-1 – sp Pentalfa [946]
COMPENDIO DE HISTORIA DE ESPANA. TOMO 2 / Duchesne – 1787 – 2mf – 9 – Pta1,500.00 – 84-7848-244-X – sp Pentalfa [946]
COMPENDIO DE LA SALUD HUMANA, ZARAGOZA, 1494 / Kethan, J – 9 – sp Cultura [610]
COMPENDIO DE LAS INSTITUCIONES DE DERECHO CANONIGO SEGUN EL METODO DE DOMINGO CAVALLARIO / Cervantes Bermudez de Cana, Tomas – 1870 – 9 – 1.50f – sp Bibl Santa Ana [340]
COMPENDIO DE LOS COMENTARIOS EXTENDIDOS POR EL MAESTRO ANTONIO GOMEZ A LAS OCHENTA Y TRES LEYES DE TORO... / Nolasco de Llano, Pedro – Madrid: Imp. y Lib. de D. Manuel Martin, 1777 – 1 – sp Bibl Santa Ana [946]
COMPENDIO DE LOS COMENTARIOS...ANTONIO GOMEZ...TORO / Nolasco de Llano, Pedro – 1785 – 9 – 1.50f – sp Bibl Santa Ana [636]
COMPENDIO DE TEOLOGIA CRISTIANA / Pendleton, J M – 1910. 292p – 1 – 10.22 – us Baptist [240]
COMPENDIO DE UN CURSO DE HISTORIA UNIVERSAL PARA USO DE LOS ALUMNOS DE SEGUNDA ENSENANZA – 1875 – 9 – 1.50f – sp Bibl Santa Ana [370]
COMPENDIO ... DEL DERECCHO DE GENTES NATURAL, ... / Bolanos y Noboa, P – Madrid, 1808 – 1mf – 9 – ILM-2559/1 – ne IDC [327]
COMPENDIO DEL'HISTORIA ROMANA.. / Leto, Giulio Pomponio – Venice: Aperesso Gabriel di Ferrarii, 1549. 127 leaves. Trans. by Francesco Baldelli – 1 – us U.W. Library [930]
COMPENDIO DELLA FLORA ITALIANA / Arcangeli, G – Torino. 1882. B-5584 2 – 8 – ne IDC [580]
IL COMPENDIO DELLA MUSICA NEL QUALE BREVEMENTE SI TRATTA DELL'ARTE DEL CONTRAPUNTO / Tigrini, O – 1588 – 9 – us Sibley [780]
COMPENDIO HISTORIA ECLESIASTICA / Pedrajas y Nunez-Moreno, Eloy – 1889 – 9 – 1.50f – sp Bibl Santa Ana [240]
COMPENDIO HISTORICO, DELLE GVERRE VLTIMAMENTE SUCCESSE TRA CHRISTIANI, ET TURCHI, ET TRA TURCHI, ET PERSIANI: ... / Campana, C – Vinegia, 1597 – 2mf – 9 – H-8391/1 – ne IDC [956]
COMPENDIO HISTORICO DI FERRARA / Guarini, M A – O 1052. 1621.n – 9 – ne IDC [945]
COMPENDIO HISTORICOS DE LAS VIDAS DE LOS SANTOS...DEL ORDEN DE PREDICADORES / Amado, Manuel – 1829 – 9 – 1.50f – sp Bibl Santa Ana [920]
COMPENDIO INSTRUCTIVO SOBRE EL MEJOR METODO DE CURAR LAS TERCIANAS Y QUARTANAS... / Puig, S – Madrid, 1786 – 3mf – 9 – sp Cultura [615]
COMPENDIO QUIRURGICO... / Robledo, D – Barcelona, 1702 – 8mf – 9 – sp Cultura [617]
COMPENDIO...ANTIGUEDAD...NTR. SRA. GUADALUPE / Vicente Yanez, Juan – 1889 – 9 – 1.50f – sp Bibl Santa Ana [240]
COMPENDIO...ANTONIO GOMEZ...TORO / Llano, Pedro N – 1785 – 9 – 1.50f – sp Bibl Santa Ana [790]
COMPENDIO...CRISTIANA / Rodrigo de la Cerda, Jose – (1888 ed.1.50f; 9) – 1891 – 9 – 1.50f – sp Bibl Santa Ana [240]
COMPENDIO...DE FORTIFICACION... / Rojas, C – Madrid, 1613 – 3mf – 9 – sp Cultura [355]
COMPENDIOLO DI MOLTI DUBBI, SEGRETI ET SENTENZE INTORNO AL CANTO FERMO, ET FIGURATO / Aron, Pietro – CA.1545 – 9 – us Sibley [780]
COMPENDIO...NTRA. SRA. GUADALUPE / Yanez, Juan Vicente – 1899 – 9 – 1.50f – sp Bibl Santa Ana [240]
COMPENDIOSA ANATOMIAE DELINEATIO / Geminus, T – 1545. M 351 – 9 – ne IDC [611]
COMPENDIOSA ANATOMIAE DELINEATIO / Geminus, T – 1553. M 352 – 9 – ne IDC [611]
COMPENDIOSO...TRATADO DE LA ORACION / Pedro de Alcantara, Saint – 1731 – 9 – 1.50f – sp Bibl Santa Ana [410]
A COMPENDIOUS HISTORY OF AMERICAN METHODISM : ABRIDGED FROM TEH AUTHOR'S HISTORY OF THE METHODIST EPISCOPAL CHURCH / Stevens, Abel – New York: Carlton & Porter, 1868, c1867 – 2mf – us A.T.L.A. [240]
A COMPENDIOUS LAW DICTIONARY : CONTAINING BOTH AN EXPLANATION OF THE TERMS AND THE LAW ITSELF; INTENDED FOR THE USE OF THE COUNTRY GENTLEMAN, THE MERCHANT, AND THE PROFESSIONAL MAN / Potts, Thomas – new rev corr enl ed. London: B & R Crosby, 1813 – 8mf – 9 – $12.00 – LLMC 95-424 – us L.L.M.C. [340]
A COMPENDIOUS REGYMENT OR A DYETARY / Boorde, A – London, 1567 – 2mf – 9 – ne IDC [360]
A COMPENDIOUS REGYMENT OR A DYETARY / Boorde, A – M-305. 1567 – 9 – ne IDC [615]
COMPENDIOUS SYRIAC GRAMMAR / Noeldeke, Theodor – 9 – $12.00 – us I.R.C. [470]
A COMPENDIOUS WAY OF TEACHING ANCIENT AND MODERN LANGUAGES / LeFevre, Tannegui – 1723. 196p. (English Linguistics Series 1500-1800) – 9 – us UMI [400]
COMPENDIUM. / American Bar Association. Committee on Unauthorized Practice of the Law – Chicago. 1942. 122, 14 p. LL-1097 – 1 – us L of C Photodup [340]
COMPENDIUM ALCHEMIAE; CUM DICTIONARIO EIUSDEN ARTIS ATQUE DE METALLORUM TINCTURA PRAEPARATIO NEQ / Joannes, de Garlandia – Basle, 1560 – 1 – us U.W. Library [540]
A COMPENDIUM AND DIGEST OF THE LAWS OF MASSACHUSETTS / White, William Charles – Boston, Munroe Francis and Parker, 1809-11. 4 v. in 2. LL-465 – 1 – us L of C Photodup [340]
COMPENDIUM DER KIRCHENGESCHICHTE / Groene, V – Regensburg: G.J. Manz; 1869 – 2mf – us A.T.L.A. [240]
COMPENDIUM FLORAE ATLANTICAE / Cosson, E SC – 2v. Paris. 1881-87 – 8 – ne IDC [580]
COMPENDIUM FLORAE PHILADELPHICAE / Barton, W P C – 2v. Philadelphia. 1818. B-5833 2 – 8 – ne IDC [580]
COMPENDIUM GERMANICO-LATINUM MUSICES PRACTICAE...MUSICA DEUTSCH UND LATEINISCH.. / Machold, Johann – 1596 – 9 – us Sibley [780]
COMPENDIUM HARMONICUM / Sorge, G A – 1760 – 9 – us Sibley [780]
COMPENDIUM HISTORIAE LITERARIAE NOVISSIMAE, 1. 1746- 24. 1769; ERLANGISCHE GELEHRTE ANMERKUNGEN UND NACHRICHTEN, 25. 1770-42. 1787; ANNALEN DER GESAMMTEN LITTERATUR, 1788-1789; ERLANGISCHE GELEHRTE ZEITUNG, 1790-1798 – 1746-1798 (mf ed 1993) – 247mf – 9 – DM4,900.00 – 3-89131-102-8 – gw Fischer [430]
COMPENDIUM HISTORIARUM (CBH 8) : EX VERSIONE GUILLELMI XYLANDRI / Cedreni, Georgii – Parisiis, 1647 – Dfl161.00 – ne Slangenburg [930]
COMPENDIUM JURIS NATURAE / Ditterich, F G – Argents, 1780 – 3mf – 1 – ILM-806/1 – ne IDC [327]
COMPENDIUM MORALIS THEOLOGIAE / Laymann, P – Lugduni, 1631 – 8mf – 9 – CA-67/1 – ne IDC [240]
COMPENDIUM MUSICAE LATINO-GERMANICUM / Gumpelzhaimer, Adam – Nunc editione hac sexta. 1616 – 9 – us Sibley [780]
COMPENDIUM MUSICAE LATINO-GERMANICUM / Gumpelzhaimer, Adam – P 691. 1616 – 9 – ne IDC [780]
COMPENDIUM MUSICAE LATINO-GERMANICUM....NUNC EDITIONE HAC DECIMA.. / Gumpelzhaimer, Adam – 1646 – 9 – us Sibley [780]
COMPENDIUM MUSICAE LATINO-GERMANICUM....NUNC EDITIONE HAC NONA.. / Gumpelzhaimer, Adam – 1632 – 7,9 – us Sibley [780]
COMPENDIUM MUSICAE SIGNATORIAE ET MODULATORIAE VOCALIS / Printz, Wolfgang C – 1714 – 9 – us Sibley [780]
COMPENDIUM MUSICES CONFECTUM AD FACILIOREM INSTRUCTIONEM CANTUMCHORALEM DISCENTIUM – 1513 – 9 – us Sibley [780]
COMPENDIUM MUSICES. DE REGULA CONTRAPUNCTI. DE COMPOSITIONE / Coclico, A P – 1552 – 9 – us Sibley [780]
A COMPENDIUM OF ALL THE INSTRUCTIONS AND INDICTMENTS WHICH ARE APPROVED AND CRITICISED IN THE MISSOURI SUPREME AND APPELLATE COURT REPORTS / West, James Columbus – Ozark, Mo., 1899. 275 11 p. LL-570 – 1 – us L of C Photodup [340]
A COMPENDIUM OF AMERICAN CRIMINAL LAW / Desty, Robert – San Francisco, Whitney, 1882. 713 p. LL-550 – 1 – us L of C Photodup [340]
A COMPENDIUM OF COMMERCIAL LAW / Townsend, Calvin – New York/Chicago: Ivison, Blakeman, Taylor & Co, 1877 – 7mf – 9 – $10.50 – LLMC 92-138 – us L.L.M.C. [340]
COMPENDIUM OF DOMINION LAWS OF CANADA, 1867-1883, IN FORCE ON THE FIRST DAY OF JANUARY, 1884, INDICATING AMENDMENTS, REPEALS, & C., WITH INDEX / Fremont, Joseph – Montreal: A. Periard, 1884. 03254. (Pre-1900 Canadiana) – 9 – cn C.I.H.M. [971]
A COMPENDIUM OF EDENBURG AND EDENBURG PEOPLE / Keatley, Hettie A – Chicago: Clarion Jacksonian Print., 1887. Pennsylvania Reel 16. (The Cox Library Collection) – 5 – us Americana [978]
COMPENDIUM OF EVIDENCE / Straker, David Augustus – Detroit, Mich., Richmond & Backus, 1899. 255 p. LL-1189 – 1 – us L of C Photodup [340]
COMPENDIUM OF FOOD ADDITIVE SPECIFICATIONS : ADDENDUM 1 – 1992 – 148p – it F.A.O. [660]
A COMPENDIUM OF FREEMASONRY IN ILLINOIS / Warvelle, George William – Chicago: Lewis Publ. Co., 1897. Vols. 1-2. Illinois Reel 9. (The Cox Library Collection) – 5 – us Americana [978]
COMPENDIUM OF HISTORY AND BIOGAPHY OF HILLSDALE COUNTY / Reynolds, Elon G – Chicago: A. W. Bowen and Co. Michigan Reel 11. (The Cox Library Collection) – 5 – us Americana [978]
COMPENDIUM OF HISTORY AND BIOGRAPHY OF CASS COUNTY / Henry Taylor and Co – Chicago, 1906. Iowa Reel 9. The Cox Library Collection – 5 – us Americana [978]
COMPENDIUM OF HISTORY AND BIOGRAPHY OF KALAMAZOO COUNTY / Fisher & Little – Chicago: A. W. Bowen and Co. Michigan Reel 14. (The Cox Library Collection) – 5 – us Americana [978]
COMPENDIUM OF HISTORY AND BIOGRAPHY OF LINN COUNTY / Henry Taylor and Co – Chicago, 1912. Missouri Reel 24. The Cox Library Collection – 5 – us Americana [978]
COMPENDIUM OF HISTORY AND BIOGRAPHY OF NORTH DAKOTA / Ogle, George A – Chicago, 1900. North Dakota Reel 2. (The Cox Library Collection) – 5 – us Americana [978]
COMPENDIUM OF HISTORY AND BIOGRAPHY OF THE CITY OF DETROIT AND WAYNE COUNTY / Henry Taylor and Co – Chicago, 1909. Michigan Reel 23. The Cox Library Collection – 5 – us Americana [978]
COMPENDIUM OF HISTORY REMINISCENCE AND BIOGRAPHY OF LYON COUNTY / G.A. Ogle and Co – Chicago, 1904. Iowa Reel 27. The Cox Library Collection – 5 – us Americana [978]
COMPENDIUM OF HISTORY, REMINISCENCE AND BIOGRAPHY OF NEBRASKA / Alden Publishing Co – Chicago, 1912. Nebraska Reel 2.(The Cox Library Collection) – 5 – us Americana [978]
COMPENDIUM OF HISTORY, REMINISCENCE AND BIOGRAPHY OF WESTERN NEBRASKA / Alden Publishing Co – Chicago, 1909. Nebraska Reel 3.(The Cox Library Collection) – 5 – us Americana [978]
COMPENDIUM OF HOUSING STATISTICS *see* COMPENDIUM OF HUMAN SETTLEMENT STATISTICS
COMPENDIUM OF HUMAN SETTLEMENT STATISTICS / UN – E.29 – 9 – ST/STAT/ Ser.N/1, ST/EAS/STAT/Ser.N/2-4 – us U.N. Pubs [340]
A COMPENDIUM OF OFFICIAL DOCUMENTS RELATIVE TO NATIVE AFFAIRS IN THE SOUTH ISLAND / Mackay, Alexander – (With a new Chronology and Index compiled by Rohi Williams and Josie Laing in the Canterbury Museum) – Originally published 1872-3 in 2 vols. 1991 – 14mf – 9 – NZ$49.95 – nz Nat'l Libr [324]
COMPENDIUM OF PAPERS ON BROADENING THE TAX BASE / U.S. Congress. House Committee on Ways and MeansTax Revision Study – Washington: GPO. 3v. 1959 – 26mf – 9 – $43.50 – LLMC 82-701 – us L.L.M.C. [336]
A COMPENDIUM OF PRACTICAL MUSICK IN FIVE PARTS.. / Simpson, Christopher – 1667 – 9 – us Sibley [780]

A COMPENDIUM OF PRACTICAL MUSICK IN FIVE PARTS. TOGETHER WITH LESSONS FOR VIOLS / Simpson, Christopher – The 3rd ed. 1678 – 9 – us Sibley [780]

COMPENDIUM OF PULP AND PAPER TRAINING AND RESEARCH INSTITUTIONS – 1992 – 71p – it F.A.O. [680]

COMPENDIUM OF SOCIAL STATISTICS / UN – E.66 – 9 – ST/STAT/Ser.K/1-3; ST/ESA/STAT/Ser.K/4,5,7 – us U.N. Pubs [340]

COMPENDIUM OF THE ART OF ALWAYS REJOICING / Sarasa, Alphonso Antonio de – Boston: Henry A Young, [1872?] – 1mf – 9 – 0-8370-5404-4 – 1985-3404 – us A.T.L.A. [240]

A COMPENDIUM OF THE COMMON LAW IN FORCE IN KENTUCKY / Humphreys, Charles – Lexington: Hunt, 1822. 594p. LL-868 – 1 – us L of C Photodup [340]

COMPENDIUM OF THE HISTORY OF CANADA AND OF THE BRITISH NORTH AMERICAN PROVINCES / Brothers of the Christian Schools – Montreal, 1873. 00308. (Pre-1900 Canadiana) – 9 – cn C.I.H.M. [971]

A COMPENDIUM OF THE HISTORY OF THE CATHOLIC CHURCH : FROM THE COMMENCEMENT OF THE CHRISTIAN ERA TO THE ECUMENICAL COUNCIL OF THE VATICAN – (Includes chronological table and index) – 22nd rev enl ed. Baltimore: John Murphy, 1882, c1870 – 2mf – 9 – 0-8370-6924-6 – 1986-0924 – us A.T.L.A. [240]

A COMPENDIUM OF THE LAW AND PRACTICE OF INJUNCTIONS, AND OF INTERLOCUTORY ORDERS IN THE NATURE OF INJUNCTIONS / Henley, Robert Henley Eden – 3d ed. New York: Banks, Gould, 1852. 2v. LL-740 – 1 – us L of C Photodup [340]

A COMPENDIUM OF THE LAW OF MARINE INSURANCE / Annesley, Alexander – Middletown, Conn. Alsop 1808. 258 p. LL-102 – 1 – us L of C Photodup [340]

COMPENDIUM OF THE LAW ON PRISONERS' RIGHTS / Sensenich, Ila Jeanne – (Plus suppl Feb 2 1981) – Washington: FJC, Apr 1979 – 7mf – 9 – $11.50 – LLMC 95-391 – us L.L.M.C. [340]

A COMPENDIUM OF THE LAWS AND DECISIONS RELATING TO MOBS, RIOTS, INVASION, CIVIL COMMOTION, INSURRECTION, &C., AS AFFECTING FIRE INSURANCE COMPANIES IN THE UNITED STATES / Ecclesine, Joseph B – New York, Grierson & Ecclesine, 1863. 112 p. LL-584 – 1 – us L of C Photodup [340]

A COMPENDIUM OF THE LAWS AND REGULATIONS OF WESLEYAN METHODISM, WITH NOTES AND AN APPENDIX / Grindrod, E – London, 1842 – 6mf – 9 – ne IDC [240]

A COMPENDIUM OF THE ORNITHOLOGY OF GREAT BRITAIN, WITH REFERENCE TO ANATOMY AND PHYSIOLOGY OF BIRDS / Atkinson, J C – 2067 2. 1820 – 8 – ne IDC [590]

A COMPENDIUM OF THE RATIONAL SECRETES OF THE WORTHY KNIGHT AND MOST EXCELLENT DOCTOR OF PHYSICS – L. PHIERANAM / Fioravanti, L – London, 1582 – 5mf – ne IDC [610]

COMPENDIUM OF THE SPEECHES PRESENTED BY EDUCATORS, OLYMPIC CHAMPIONS, ADMINISTRATORS, AND AVERY BRUNDAGE AT THE INTERNATIONAL OLYMPIC ACADEMY 1961-1985 – (Series: United States Olympic Academy, 10 Selections 2) – Colorado Springs, 1986 – 3mf – 9 – $12.00 – us Microform Publ [790]

COMPENDIUM ON CONTINUING EDUCATION FOR THE PRACTICING VETERINARIAN – (1982-. 1,5,6,9) – v1-. 1979- – 1 – us UMI [073]

COMPENDIUM ON CONTINUING EDUCATION FOR THE SMALL ANIMAL PRACTITIONER – v1-. 1979- – 1 – us UMI [073]

A COMPENDIUM: OR INTRODUCTION TO PRACTICAL MUSIC / Simpson, Christopher – The eighth ed. 1732 – 9 – us Sibley [780]

A COMPENDIUM OR INTRODUCTION TO PRACTICAL MUSIC, IN FIVE PARTS / Simpson, Christopher – The ninth ed. 1775 – 9 – us Sibley [780]

COMPENDIUM THEOLOGIE, METHODI QVAESTIONIBVS TRACTATVM / Heerbrand, J – Tvbingae, 1575 – 7mf – ne IDC [240]

COMPENDIUM VERITATUM AD FIDEM PERTINENTIUM... / Clichtove, J – Parisiis, 1529 – 4mf – 9 – CA-83/1 – ne IDC [240]

COMPENDIUMS OF GENERAL HISTORY, THE HISTORY OF CANADA, AND OTHER BRITISH NORTH AMERICAN PROVINCES / Brothers of the Christian Schools – Quebec: C. Darveau, 1875. 00977. (Pre-1900 Canadiana) – 9 – cn C.I.H.M. [971]

THE COMPENSATOR / Ohio. Bureau of Unemployment Compensation – v.1, n.1-v.13, n.4, 1938-49. 15 fiches. (Harvard Law School Library Collectio.) – 9 – 1.50f – us H.U. Law [336]

COMPERE, E. L. MATERIALS, 1855-94 – 12,757p – 1 – 446.49 – us Baptist [025]

COMPETENCIES FOR ADAPTED PHYSICAL EDUCATORS IN THAILAND / Suphawibul, M – 1992 – 2mf – 9 – $8.00 – us Microform Publ [790]

A COMPETENCY ANALYSIS OF NCAA ATHLETIC ADMINISTRATORS / Nielsen, FE – 1990 – 2mf – 9 – $8.00 – us Microform Publ [790]

THE COMPETENCY OF WITNESSES IN CIVIL CAUSES IN PENNSYLVANIA. / Miller, Nicholas Dubois – Philadelphia: Welsh, 1881. 181p. LL-730 – 1 – us L of C Photodup [340]

LA COMPETENZA DEI TRIBUNALI STRANIERI... / Breschi, B – Macerata, [1925] – 1mf – 1 – ILM-2095/1 – ne IDC [327]

COMPETITION, EXERCISE, PROVOCATION, AND VERBAL COMMENTS: INFLUENCES ON ATTRIBUTIONS AND AGGRESSION? / Miller, David L – 1981 – 1mf – 9 – $4.00 – us Microform Publ [616]

COMPETITION PROGRAMMES DESIGNED TO PROMOTE GRAIN PRODUCTION / Israel. Ministry of Agriculture. Center for Cooperation with Developing Countries – By M. Rehovot Bar-Daroma. Dec 1974. 18 p. In cooperation with the Ministry for Foreign Affairs, International Cooperation Division – 9 – 2.00 – is I.T.T.I. [338]

COMPETITIVE ORIENTATION OF BASKETBALL STARTERS AND NONSTARTERS ACROSS DIFFERENT PLAYING LEVELS / Schoen, Christopher H – 1993 – 2mf – $8.00 – us Microform Publ [150]

Competitive Ratification Office *see* THE COMPETITIVE RATIFICATION ROUTE TOWARD A STRENGHENED UN

THE COMPETITIVE RATIFICATION ROUTE TOWARD A STRENGHENED UN / Competitive Ratification Office – 2p – 9 – $1.00f – at Libertarian Micro [320]

COMPETITOR – 1-3 2+4 (all publ). 1920-1921 – 11mf – 9 – $80.00 – us UPA [305]

COMPFLASH – (1979- 5,6,9) – 1977- – 1 – us UMI [073]

Compiegne *see* L'AFRIQUE EQUATORIALE

COMPIEGNE PAMPHLET COLLECTION – 1915 – 1 – CSUXANQ7787-B – us Hoover Inst Photo [944]

COMPILACION DE ARTICULOS REFERENTES A LAS ORDENES... / Inchaurre Aldape, Diego – Madrid: Archivo Ibero Americano, 1963 – 1 – sp Bibl Santa Ana [240]

O COMPILADOR : DA ASSEMLEIA LEGISLATIVA PROVINCIAL DE MINAS GERAIS – Ouro Preto, 29 May-Aug 1843; Feb-Jun 1844; Feb-Jun 1845; Feb-May 1846; Feb-Jul 1847; 1863 – 1,5,6 – bl Biblioteca [072]

COMPILADOR CONSTITUCIONAL, POLITICO E LITERARIO BRASILIENSE – Rio de Janeiro, 5 Jan-26 Apr 1822 – 1,5,6 – bl Biblioteca [072]

COMPILATION ET RECUEIL DES LOIS STATUTAIRES TOUCHANT L'ENREGISTREMENT DES DROITS REEL ET DES PRIVILEGES ET HYPOTHEQUES. / Auger, Joseph Cyrille – Montreal? 1899. 02450. (Pre-1900 Canadiana) – 9 – cn C.I.H.M. [340]

COMPILATION OF CERTAIN DEPT. CIRCULARS...CITIZENSHIP, REGISTRATION OF AMERICAN CITIZENS, ISSUANCE OF PASSPORTS,... – Washington, 1919 – 1mf – 1 – ILM-3829/1 – ne IDC [327]

COMPILATION OF COURT MARTIAL ORDERS, 1916-1937 / U.S. Naval Department – Washington: GPO. 2v + cum index. 1940 – 11mf – 9 – $16.50 – LLMC 84-213 – us L.L.M.C. [340]

COMPILATION OF LAWS WITH 1937 INSERTS; DIGEST OF STATE, FEDERAL AND CANADIAN LAWS, RELATING TO FOODS, DRUGS, PHARMACY. / Standard Remedies Publishing Company, Inc – Washington, D.C., Proprietary 1937? 1 v. LL-1044 – 1 – us L of C Photodup [340]

A COMPILATION OF MASSACHUSETTS LAW RELATING TO PRIVACY AND PERSONAL DATA / Massachusetts. Laws, Statutes, etc – 2nd ed. Boston. Governor's Special Commission on Privacy and Personal Data, 1974. LL-2343 – 1 – us L of C Photodup [340]

COMPILATION OF REPORTS OF THE FOREIGN RELATIONS COMMITTEE; 1789-1901 / U.S. Senate Committee on Foreign Relations – Washington: GPO. 1st session. 1st Congress-56th Congress. 8v. 1902 – 80mf – 9 – $120.00 – LLMC 81-106 – us L.L.M.C. [323]

COMPILATION OF TENNESSEE CENSUS REPORTS, 1820 / U.S. Bureau of The Census – 1r – 1 – T911 – us Nat'l Archives [324]

A COMPILATION OF THE LAWS AND AMENDMENTS THERETO RELATING TO BUILDING SOCIETIES, LOAN COMPANIES, JOINT STOCK COMPANIES, AND INTEREST ON MORTGAGES AND OTHER ACTS PERTAINING TO MONETARY INSTITUTIONS : AS PASSED BY THE DOMINION PARLIAMENT AND THE SEVERAL PROVINCIAL LEGISLATURES: TO WHICH IS APPENDED A COMPLETE REFERENCE TABLE TO PRIVATE ACTS AND AMENDMENTS / Garland, Nicholas Surrey – Ottawa: A. S. Woodburn, 1882. 03293. (Pre-1900 Canadiana) – 9 – cn C.I.H.M. [971]

COMPILATION OF THE LAWS OF THE UNITED STATES APPLICABLE TO THE DUTIES OF THE GOVERNOR, ATTORNEY, JUDGE, CLERK, MARSHAL, AND COMMISSIONERS OF THE DISTRICT OF ALASKA / U. S. Laws, Statutes, etc – Washington, Govt. Print. Off., 1884. 60 p LL-916 – 1 – us L of C Photodup [340]

COMPILATION OF THE ORGANIC PROVISIONS OF THE ADMINISTRATION OF JUSTICE IN FORCE IN THE SPANISH COLONIAL PROVINCES : AND APPENDICES RELATING THERETO – (A description of the organization of the courts in Puerto Rico, Cuba & the Philippines) – 1891. Washington: GPO, 1899 (mf ed) – 2mf – 9 – $3.00 – LLMC 92-304 – us L.L.M.C. [340]

A COMPILATION OF THE STATUTES PASSED SINCE CONFEDERATION RELATING TO BANKS AND BANKING: GOVERNMENT AND OTHER SAVINGS BANKS, PROMISSORY NOTES AND BILLS OF EXCHANGE, AND INTEREST AND USURY IN NEW BRUNSWICK AND NOVA SCOTIA / Davidson, Charles Peers – s.l.: s.n., 1876 (Montreal: The "Gazette"). 02589. (Pre-1900 Canadiana) – 9 – cn C.I.H.M. [971]

THE COMPILED AND REVISED LAWS OF THE TERRITORY OF IDAHO. / Idaho. (Territory). Laws, Statutes, etc – Boise: Kelly, 1875. 877,22p. LL-2350 – 1 – us L of C Photodup [340]

COMPILED MILITARY SERVICE RECORD, COMPANY F, 15TH KANSAS CAVALRY, RELATING TO ORREN A. CURTIS / U.S. Army. Adjutant General's Office – 1 – us KS Hist [324]

COMPILED MILITARY SERVICE RECORDS OF MICHIGAN AND ILLINOIS VOLUNTEERS WHO SERVED DURING THE WINNEBAGO INDIAN DISTURBANCES OF 1827 – 3r – 1 – M1505 – us Nat'l Archives [355]

COMPILED RECORDS SHOWING SERVICE OF MILITARY UNITS IN CONFEDERATE ORGANIZATIONS / U.S. War Department. Confederate Records – 74 rolls. M861 – 1 – us Nat'l Archives [324]

COMPILED RECORDS SHOWING SERVICE OF MILITARY UNITS IN VOLUNTEER UNION ORGANIZATIONS / U.S. War Department. Adjutant General's Office – 225 rolls. M594. Printed guide – 1 – us Nat'l Archives [324]

COMPILED SERVICE RECORDS OF AMERICAN NAVAL PERSONNEL AND MEMBERS OF THE DEPARTMENTS OF THE QUARTERMASTER GENERAL AND THE COMMISSARY GENERAL OF MILITARY STORES WHO SERVED DURING THE REVOLUTIONARY WAR / U.S. War Department. Collection of Revolutionary War Records – 4rolls. M880 – 1 – us Nat'l Archives [324]

COMPILED SERVICE RECORDS OF CONFEDERATE GENERALS AND STAFF OFFICERS, AND NONREGIMENTAL ENLISTED MEN / U.S. War Department. Confederate Records – 275 rolls. M331. Printed guide – 5 – us Nat'l Archives [324]

COMPILED SERVICE RECORDS OF CONFEDERATE SOLDIERS WHO SERVED IN ORGANIZATIONS FROM THE STATE OF: / U.S. War Department. Confederate Records – (Alabama. 508 rolls. M311. Printed guide. Arizona Territory. 1 roll. M318. Printed guide. Arkansas. 256 rolls. M317. Printed guide. Florida. 104 rolls. M251. Printed guide. Georgia. 607 rolls. M266. Printed guide. Kentucky. 136 rolls. M319. Printed guide. Louisiana. 414 rolls. M320. Printed guide. Maryland. 22 rolls. M321. Printed guide. Mississippi. 427 rolls. M269. Printed guide. Missouri. 193 rolls. M322. Printed guide. North Carolina. 580 rolls. M270. Printed guide. South Carolina. 392 rolls. M267. Printed guide. Tennessee. 359 rolls. M268. Printed guide. Texas. 445 rolls. M323. Printed guide. Virginia. 1,075 rolls. M324. Printed guide) – 5 – us Nat'l Archives [324]

COMPILED SERVICE RECORDS OF CONFEDERATE SOLDIERS WHO SERVED IN ORGANIZATIONS RAISED DIRECTLY BY THE CONFEDERATE GOVERNMENT / U.S. War Department. Confederate Records – 123 rolls. M258. Printed guide – 5 – us Nat'l Archives [324]

COMPILED SERVICE RECORDS OF FORMER CONFEDERATE SOLDIERS WHO SERVED IN THE 1ST THROUGH 6TH U.S. VOLUNTEER INFANTRY REGIMENTS / U.S. War Department. Confederate Records – 1864-66. M1017 – 65r – 1 – us Nat'l Archives [324]

COMPILED SERVICE RECORDS OF SOLDIERS WHO SERVED IN THE AMERICAN ARMY DURING THE REVOLUTIONARY WAR / U. S. War Department Adjutant General's Office – 1096 rolls. M881 – 1 – us Nat'l Archives [324]

COMPILED SERVICE RECORDS OF VOLUNTEER SOLDIERS WHO SERVED DURING THE MEXICAN WAR IN MORMON ORGANIZATIONS / U.S. War Department. Adjutant General's Office – 3rolls. M351. Printed guide – 5 – us Nat'l Archives [324]

COMPILED SERVICE RECORDS OF VOLUNTEER SOLDIERS WHO SERVED DURING THE MEXICAN WAR IN ORGANIZATIONS FROM THE STATE OF: / U.S. War Department. Adjutant General's Office – (Tennessee. 15 rolls. M638. Printed guide. Texas. 19 rolls. M278. Printed guide) – 5 – us Nat'l Archives [324]

COMPILED SERVICE RECORDS OF VOLUNTEER SOLDIERS WHO SERVED DURING THE MEXICAN WAR IN ORGANIZATIONS FROM THE STATE OF MISSISSIPPI / U.S. War Department. Adjutant General's Office – 9rolls. M863 – 1 – us Nat'l Archives [324]

COMPILED SERVICE RECORDS OF VOLUNTEER SOLDIERS WHO SERVED DURING THE MEXICAN WAR IN ORGANIZATIONS FROM THE STATE OF PENNSYLVANIA / U. S. War Department. Adjutant General's Office – M1028 – 13r – 1 – us Nat'l Archives [920]

COMPILED SERVICE RECORDS OF VOLUNTEER SOLDIERS WHO SERVED DURING THE WAR OF 1812 IN ORGANIZATIONS FROM THE TERRITORY OF MISSISSIPPI / U.S. War Department. Adjutant General's Office – 22 rolls. M678. Printed guide – 5 – us Nat'l Archives [324]

COMPILED SERVICE RECORDS OF VOLUNTEER SOLDIERS WHO SERVED FROM 1784 TO 1811 / U.S. War Department. Adjutant General's Office – M905 – 32r – 1 – us Nat'l Archives [920]

COMPILED SERVICE RECORDS OF VOLUNTEER SOLDIERS WHO SERVED IN ORGANIZATIONS FROM THE STATE OF FLORIDA DURING THE FLORIDA INDIAN WARS / U.S. War Department. Adjutant General's Office – 1835-58. 63 rolls. M1086 – 1 – us Nat'l Archives [324]

COMPILED SERVICE RECORDS OF VOLUNTEER SOLDIERS WHO SERVED IN THE FLORIDA INFANTRY DURING THE WAR WITH SPAIN / U.S. War Department. Adjutant General's Office – 13 rolls. M1087 – 1 – us Nat'l Archives [324]

COMPILED SERVICE RECORDS OF VOLUNTEER UNION SOLDIERS WHO SERVED DURING THE CIVIL WAR IN ORGANIZATIONS FROM THE STATE OF: / U.S. War Department. Adjutant General's Office – (Alabama. 10 rolls. M276. Printed guide. Arkansas. 60 rolls. M399. Printed guide. Florida. 11 rolls. M400. Printed guide. Georgia. 1 roll. M403. Printed guide. Kentucky. 515 rolls. M397. Printed guide. Louisiana. 50 rolls. M396. Printed guide. Maryland. 238 rolls. M384. Printed guide. Mississippi. 4 rolls. M404. Printed guide. Missouri. 854 rolls. M405. Printed guide. New Mexico Territory. 46 rolls. M427. Printed guide. North Carolina. 25 rolls. M401. Printed guide. Tennessee. 220 rolls. M395. Printed guide. Texas. 13 rolls. M402. Printed guide. Utah Territory. 1 roll. M692. Printed guide. Virginia. 7 rolls. M398. Printed guide.. West Virginia. 261 rolls. M508. Printed guide) – 5 – us Nat'l Archives [324]

COMPILED STATUTES : FROM THE KINGDOM (1827) TO 1993 / Hawaii Legislature – (Add vols after 1993 planned) – 1827-1993 – 761mf – 9 – $1,141.00 – LLMC 77-103 – us L.L.M.C. [340]

COMPILER – Gettysburg. Pa. 1857-1953 – 1 – us UMI [071]

COMPILER – Wheeling. West Virginia. 1829-30 – 1 – us UMI [071]

THE COMPLAINT OF NATURE / Lille, Alain de – (Translated from the Latin by D.M. Moffat) – New York, 1908 – 2mf – 8 – ne Slangenburg [110]

THE COMPLAINT OF PEACE / Erasmus, Desiderius – 1559 – 9 – 10.00 – us Scholars' Facs [323]

A COMPLEAT ACCOUNT OF THE PORTUGUEZE LANGUAGE / J, A – 1701. 444p. (English Linguistics Series 1500-1800) – 9 – us UMI [440]

THE COMPLEAT AMBASSADOR / Digges, D – London, 1655 – 8mf – 1 – ILM-507/1 – ne IDC [327]

A COMPLEAT ANSWER TO MR. WESLEY'S OBSERVATIONS UPON DR. PRICE'S ESSAY ON CIVIL LIBERTY, WHEREIN THE FATALISM AND INFIDELITY OR MR. WESLEY'S PRINCIPLES ARE CONFUTED,... / Murray, James – Newcastle, [1776] – 1mf – 9 – MP-515/1 – ne IDC [240]

THE COMPLEAT ENGLISH SCHOOLMASTER / Coles, Elisha – 1674. 128p. (English Linguistics Series 1500-1800) – 9 – us UMI [420]

THE COMPLEAT FRENCH-MASTER, FOR LADIES AND GENTLEMEN / Boyer, Abel – 1694. 401p. (English Linguistics Series 1500-1800) – 9 – us UMI [440]

A COMPLEAT HISTORY OF THE PIRATICAL STATES OF BARBARY : VIZ ALGIERS, TUNIS, TRIPOLI AND MOROCCO: CONTAINING THE ORIGINS, REVOLUTIONS, AND PRESENT STATE OF THESE KINGDOMS, THEIR FORCES, REVENUES, POLICY, AND COMMERCE – London: R Griffiths, 1750 – 1 – us Res Libr [960]

COMPLEAT INSTRUCTIONS FOR THE VIOLIN / Geminiani, Francesco – CA.1790 – 9 – us Sibley [780]

THE COMPLEAT LINGUIST / Henley, John – 1719-26. 864p. (English Linguistics Series 1500-1800) – 9 – us UMI [400]

A COMPLEAT SYSTEM OF GRAMMAR ENGLISH AND LATIN / Clare, William – 1690. 165p. (English Linguistics Series 1500-1800) – 9 – us UMI [420]

COMPLEMENT D'ORDONNANCES ET JUGEMENTS : GOUVERNEURS ET INTENDANTS – (Avec une table alphabetique des matieres pour les trois volumes) – Quebec, Canada. 3v. 1856 – 1r – 1 – Can$50.00 – cn Can Microfilming [971]

COMPLEMENT DU DICTIONNAIRE DE L'ACADEMIE FRANCAISE / Barre, L – 1842 – 9 – fr I.C.S. [000]

COMPLETE AAS MICROFICHE SERIES COLLECTION : PAPERS / American Astronautical Society; ed by Jacobs, H – (Vols available separately) – v1-73. 1968-96 – 868mf – 9 – $915.00 – ISSN: 0065-7417 – us Univelt [629]

A COMPLETE AND POPULAR DIGEST OF THE POLITY OF METHODISM, EACH SUBJECT ALPHABETICALLY ARRANGED / Skewes, J H – London, 1869 – 3mf – 9 – ne IDC [240]

COMPLETE ARCHIVE PROGRAM / Human Relations Area Files – 1958. 38 installments – 9 – 2050.00 per installment – us H.R.A.F. [300]

COMPLETE ARCHIVES, 1916-92 / Communist Party. Great Britain – (Series 1: Journals, 1921-88; Series 2: Newspapers, 1916-29; Series 3: Theoretical Journals, 1921-88; Series 4: Pamphlets, 1920-88. With printed index) – 1 – £6,995.00 – uk World [941]

THE COMPLETE CATHOLIC DIRECTORY, ALMANACK AND REGISTRY... / Battersby, W J – Dublin, 1840-1845 – us Res Libr [030]

A COMPLETE CATHOLIC REGISTRY, DIRECTORY AND ALMANACK... / Battersby, W J – Dublin, Printed by W Powell [etc], 1836; 1838-39 – us Res Libr [030]

COMPLETE COLLECTION / U.S. National Advisory Committee on Aeronautics – (Reports. 2000.00; 9. Research Memoranda.7000.00; UPD; 9. Technical Memoranda. 2000.00; UPD; 9. Technical Notes. 6000.00; UPD; 9. Wartime Reports. 2000.00; UPD; 9) – 1915-58.13,941 fiches – 9 – 15,000.00 – us Updata [324]

THE COMPLETE COMMENTARY OF OECUMENIUS ON THE APOCALYPSE / Hoskier, H C – 1928 – 9 – $10.00 – us I.R.C. [240]

THE COMPLETE CONSPIRACY TRIAL BOOK / Hayden, Samuel Augustus – 1907. 356p – 1 – 12.46 – us Baptist [240]

A COMPLETE DICTIONARY OF MUSIC : CONTAINING A FULL AND CLEAR EXPLANATION... / Hoyle, J – London, 1791 – 1mf – ne IDC [780]

COMPLETE DIRECTORY OF HENRY COUNTY / M.J. Minch Co – Portland, 1909. Indiana Reel 15. The Cox Library Collection – 5 – us Americana [978]

THE COMPLETE FIFER'S MUSEUM : A COLLECTION OF MARCHES OF ALL KINDS NOW IN USE IN THE MILITARY LINE. ALSO A NUMBER OF OCCASIONAL TUNES FOR THE ACTUAL SERVICE AND THE MILITIA / Hulbert, J Jr – (P23-24 lacking) – Northhampton, MA: Simeon Butler, [1807] – 1 – us Sibley [780]

COMPLETE FORMS OF PROCEEDINGS IN CIVIL AND CRIMINAL CASES BEFORE JUSTICES OF THE PEACE, IN THE STATE OF OHIO / Palm, Jefferson – Warren, Ohio: Ritezel, 1855. 55p. LL-1392 – 1 – us L of C Photodup [340]

THE COMPLETE HANOVERIAN STATE PAPERS DOMESTIC, 1714-1782 / Great Britain. Home Office – (Part 2: George I, 1722-27. Part 3: George II, 1727-36. Part 4: George II, 1737-45. Part 5: George II, 1746-50. Part 6: George II, 1751-60. Part 7: George III, 1760-82) – Part 1: George I, 1714-22 – 1 – us Primary [941]

A COMPLETE HARMONY OF DANIEL AND THE APOCALYPSE / Litch, Josiah – Philadelphia: Claxton, Remsen, 1873. 1 fiche – 9 – us A.T.L.A. [240]

A COMPLETE HERMENEUTICAL MANUAL ON THE BOOK OF ECCLESIASTES / Strong, James – New York: Hunt & Eaton, 1893. 1 fiche – 9 – us A.T.L.A. [240]

COMPLETE HISTORY OF FAIRFIELD COUNTY / Scott, Harvey – Columbus: Siebert and Lilley, 1877. Ohio Reel 29. (The Cox Library Collection) – 5 – us Americana [978]

A COMPLETE HISTORY OF ILLINOIS FROM 1673 TO 1873: EMBRACING THE PHYSICAL FEATURES OF THE COUNTRY, ITS EARLY EXPLORATIONS, ABORIGINAL INHABITANTS.. / Davidson, Alexander – By Alexander Davidson and Bernard Stuve. Springfield Ill.: Illinois Journal, 1874. 02521. (Pre-1900 Canadiana) – 9 – cn C.I.H.M. [971]

COMPLETE HISTORY OF THE PRESENT WAR, FROM ITS COMMENCEMENT IN 1756, TO THE END OF THE CAMPAIGN, 1760 – London: Printed for W Owen and others, 1761. SEM16P16 – 1r – 5 – Can$12.00 – cn Bibl Nat [971]

COMPLETE INDEX TO THE EXPOSITOR'S BIBLE: TOPICAL AND TEXTUAL / Ayres, Samuel Gardiner – New York: A.C. Armstrong, 1905. 1 fiche – 9 – us A.T.L.A. [240]

A COMPLETE INDEX TO THE NAMES OF PERSONS, PLACES & SUBJECTS MENTIONED IN LITTELL'S LAWS OF KENTUCKY – By W.T. Smith, 1931. 4 fiches. F-0503 – 9 – us A.G.L.L. [340]

A COMPLETE INVESTIGATION OF MR. EDEN'S TREATY,... – London, 1787 – 2mf – 1 – ILM-779/1 – ne IDC [327]

THE COMPLETE LAW QUIZZER...THE OHIO SUPREME COURT EXAMINATION QUESTIONS FOR ADMISSION TO THE BAR / Kinkead, Edgar Benton – 5th ed. Cincinnati, Anderson, 1915. 1025z-10 (i.e. 1731) p. LL-1426 – 1 – us L of C Photodup [340]

COMPLETE LECTURES OF COL. R.G. INGERSOLL / Ingersoll, Robert Green – Chicago: J Regan, [191-?] – 1mf – 9 – 0-8370-6266-7 – 1986-0266 – us A.T.L.A. [080]

A COMPLETE LEGAL ADVERTISING FORM BOOK. / Monaghan, James Patrick – Cincinnati?: Legal Advertising, 1907. 335p. LL-848 – 1 – us L of C Photodup [340]

COMPLETE LIST OF PUBLICATIONS / Iowa State University. Agricultural Experiment Station – 1919. 1 reel – 1,5 – us Spaulding [630]

THE COMPLETE L.R.A. DIGEST – (Covers both series) – New York: Lawyers' Co-op. 10v. 1921-24 (all publ) – 150mf – 9 – $225.00 – LLMC 78-046C – us L.L.M.C. [340]

THE COMPLETE MAIN DICTIONARY CATALOG OF THE LIBRARY OF CONGRESS IN A SINGLE ALPHABETICAL SEQUENCE *see* MAIN CATALOG OF THE LIBRARY OF CONGRESS 1898-1980

THE COMPLETE MAN – v2. 1875 (complete) – 1r – 1 – ATLA 1993-S020 – us A.T.L.A. [073]

THE COMPLETE MARTINDALE-HUBBELL, 1868-1980 *see* LAWYERS' DIRECTORIES, 1868-1980

THE COMPLETE MARTINDALE-HUBBELL'S LAW DIRECTORY, 1868-1980 – (Directories providing a unique, comprehensive and continuous record of the American Bar for the past 114 years) – 11,980mf – 9 – $11,900.00 – LLMC 92-001 – us L.L.M.C. [340]

COMPLETE MICROFICHE CATALOGUE OF BOOKS HELD BY THE BRITISH ARCHITECTURAL LIBRARY / Royal Institute of British Architects – (Pt 1: Author/Title Catalogue. Pt 2: Subject Catalogues) – 1996 – 2pts 1132mf – 9 – £3,500.00 set – uk World [720]

THE COMPLETE NAVIGATOR : OR, AN EASY AND FAMILIAR GUIDE TO THE THEORY AND PRACTICE OF NAVIGATION / Mackay, Andrew – 2nd ed., improved. 1810 – 9 – $20.00 – uk Libr Preservation [623]

COMPLETE PARADIGMS OF THE SAMARITAN VERBS : REGULAR AND IRREGULAR / Young, Robert – Edinburgh: Robert Young, [18–?] – 1mf – 9 – 0-8370-7116-X – 1986-1116 – us A.T.L.A. [470]

THE COMPLETE PHOTOGRAPHIC WORK OF JACOB A. RIIS / Salt Lake Art Center. Salt Lake, Utah; ed by Doherty, Robert J – Macmillan Publishing Co, Inc., 1981 – 8mf – 9 – $70.00 export $80.00 – 0-8161-1732-2 – uk Hall [770]

THE COMPLETE POEMS.. / Dickinson, Emily – With introd. by her niece, Martha Dickinson Bianchi. Boston: Little, Brown, 1925. 330p. Illus – 1 – us U.W. Library [810]

THE COMPLETE POETICAL WORKS... / Darley, George – London: George Routledge & Sons, limited; New York: E.P. Dutton & Co., [1908] – 1 roll – 1 – 1-55879-739-4 – uk Libr Preservation [810]

THE COMPLETE POETICAL WORKS OF DANTE GABRIEL ROSSETTI / Rossetti, Dante Gabriel – Ed. by William M. Rossetti. Author's ed. Boston: Roberts Brothers, 1894 – 1 – us U.W. Library [810]

A COMPLETE POPULAR ENCYCLOPEDIA OF VIRGINIA LAW AND FORMS AND BUSINESS GUIDE OR HOW-BOOK FOR THE BUSINESSMAN AND CITIZEN. / Hurst, Samuel Need – Pulaski, Va.: Hurst, 1922. 2148p. LL-963 – 1 – us L of C Photodup [340]

A COMPLETE PRECEPTOR FOR THE CLARIONET, CONTAINING THE MOST APPROVED INSTRUCTIONS RELATIVE TO THAT INSTRUMENT – New York: W. Dubois 1818. Includes: "General Washingtons March," "Rule Britannia," and "Yankee Doodle." MUSIC 778, Item 4 – 1 – us L of C Photodup [780]

COMPLETE RECORD / Van Wert County. Ohio. Supreme Court – 1843-1875 – 1r – 1 – $32.50r – us Archival [324]

COMPLETE RECORDS / Allen County. Ohio. Circuit Court – 1885-1912 – 4r – 1 – $32.50r – us Archival [324]

COMPLETE RECORDS / Allen County. Ohio. Common Pleas. Civil Division – 1853-1898 – 30r – 1 – $32.50r – us Archival [324]

COMPLETE RECORDS / Allen County. Ohio. Common Pleas. Criminal Div – 1833-1952 – 9r – 1 – $32.50r – us Archival [324]

COMPLETE RECORDS / Fulton County. Ohio. Common Pleas. Civil Division – 1850-1865 – 4r – 1 – $32.50r – us Archival [324]

COMPLETE RECORDS / Fulton County. Ohio. Probate Court – 1864-1930 – 9r – 1 – $32.50r – us Archival [324]

COMPLETE RECORDS / Henry County. Ohio. Common Pleas. Civil Division – 1847-1872 – 3r – 1 – $32.50r – us Archival [324]

COMPLETE RECORDS / Henry County. Ohio. District Court – 1852-1884 – 1r – 1 – $32.50r – us Archival [324]

COMPLETE RECORDS / Henry County. Ohio. Supreme Court – 1847-1858 – 1r – 1 – $32.50r – us Archival [324]

COMPLETE RECORDS / Huron County. Ohio. Common Pleas. Civil Division – 1815-1854 – 8r – 1 – $32.50r – us Archival [324]

COMPLETE RECORDS / Huron County. Ohio. Supreme Court – 1819-1835 – 1r – 1 – $32.50r – us Archival [324]

COMPLETE RECORDS / Van Wert County. Ohio. Common Pleas. Civil Division – 1839-1893 – 23r – 1 – $32.50r – us Archival [324]

COMPLETE RECORDS / Van Wert County. Ohio. Common Pleas. Criminal Div – 1838-1852 – 1r – 1 – $32.50r – us Archival [324]

COMPLETE RECORDS / Van Wert County. Ohio. District Court – 1879-1883 – 1r – 1 – $32.50r – us Archival [324]

COMPLETE RECORDS / Wood County. Ohio. Common Pleas. Civil Division – 1825-1875 – 12r – 1 – $32.50r – us Archival [324]

COMPLETE RECORDS / Wyandot County. Ohio. Common Pleas. Civil Division – 1845-1907 – 28r – 1 – $32.50r – us Archival [324]

COMPLETE RECORDS / Wyandot County. Ohio. District Court – 1869-1878 – 1r – 1 – $32.50r – us Archival [324]

COMPLETE RECORDS / Wyandot County. Ohio. Probate Court – 1887-1914 – 5r – 1 – $32.50r – us Archival [324]

COMPLETE RECORDS / Wyandot County. Ohio. Supreme Court – 1850-1868 – 1r – 1 – $32.50r – us Archival [324]

COMPLETE RECORDS, DIVORCE / Van Wert County. Ohio. Common Pleas. Domestic – 1902-1925 – 3r – 1 – $32.50r – us Archival [324]

COMPLETE RECORDS, LAW RECORDS / Wyandot County. Ohio. Common Pleas. Civil Division – 1845-1854 – 2r – 1 – $32.50r – us Archival [324]

COMPLETE RECORDS OF THE MISSION OF GENERAL GEORGE C. MARSHALL TO CHINA, DEC 1945-JAN 1947 / Marshall, George C – (With printed guide) – 1987 – 50r – 1 – $4,250.00 – S3048 – us Scholarly Res [950]

THE COMPLETE SKI GUIDE. / ed by Elkins, Frank – New York: Doubleday, 1940. xvii,286p. illus., maps, tables, plates – 1 – us U.W. Library [790]

THE COMPLETE STATE PAPERS DOMESTIC, SERIES 1 / Great Britain. Public Record Office – (Pt 2: Elizabeth I, 1569-75. v49-106. Pt 3: Elizabeth I, 1576-85. v107-185. Pt 4: Elizabeth I, 1586-92. v186-243. Pt 5: Elizabeth I, 1593-1603. v244-288. Pt 6: James I, 1603-08. v1-40. Pt 7: James I, 1608-17. v41-94. Pt 8: James I, 1618-23. v95-157. Pt 9: James I, 1624-25. v158-216. Pt 10: Addenda, Edward VI to James I, 1547-1625. v1-43) – Pt 1 Edward VI, 1547-1553 Mary I, 1553-58 Elizabeth I, 1558-68 – 1 – us Primary [941]

THE COMPLETE STATE PAPERS DOMESTIC, SERIES 2 / Great Britain. Public Record Office – (Pt 12: Charles I, 1628-30. v90-181. Pt 13: Charles I, 1631-33. v182-257. Pt 14: Charles I, 1634-35. v258-310. Pt 15: Charles I, 1636-37. v311-377. Pt 16: Charles I, 1638-39. v378-440. Pt 17: Charles I, 1640-42. v441-496. Pt 18: Charles I, 1643-48. v497-542. Pt 19: Interregnum, 1649-52. v1-31. Pt 20: Interregnum, 1653. v32-64. Pt 21: Interregnum, 1654. v65-93. Pt 22: Interregnum, 1655-56. v94-131A. Pt 23: Interregnum, 1656-57. v132-178. Pt 24: Interregnum, 1658-60. v179-225. Pt 25: Charles II, 1660. v1-53. Pt 26: 1662-65. v54-114. Pt 27: 1665-66. v115-180. Pt 28: 1666-68. v181-237. Pt 29: 1668-70. Pt 30: 1671-72. Pt 31: 1672-74. Pt 32: 1675-78. Pt 33: 1678-83. Pt 34: Charles II, 1685-88 James II, 1685-88 William III and Mary, 1689-1702. Pt 35: William III and Mary, 1689-1702. King William's Chest,

1670-1702) – Pt 11: Charles I, 1625-1627. v1-89 – 1 – us Primary [941]

THE COMPLETE STATE PAPERS DOMESTIC, SERIES 3 / Great Britain. Public Record Office – (Pt 36: 1509-28 (SP1, v1-49); Pt 37: 1528-35 (SP1, v50-100); Pt 38: 1536-39 (SP1, v101-150); Pt 39: 1539-45 (SP1, v151-200); Pt 40: 1545-46 (SP1, v201-246); Pt 41: Private papers and stamp signatures (SP2, SP3, SP4)) – The Reign of Henry VIII, 1509-47 – 1 – us Primary [941]

THE COMPLETE STATE PAPERS REGENCIES / Great Britain. Public Record Office – (Part 1: SP43, v1-27. Hanover 1716-40. Part 2: SP43, v28-56. Hanover 1741-55.) – PRO Class SP43. State Papers Regencies – 1 – us Primary [941]

A COMPLETE SYSTEM OF HARMONY / Heck, J C – c1780 – 9 – us Sibley [780]

COMPLETE TEXT OF THE ADDRESS DELIVERED BY THE SPANISH AMBASSADOR...NOVEMBER 5, 1936 / Rios, Fernando de los – n.p., n.d. Fiche W1140. (Blodgett Collection of Spanish Civil War Pamphlets) – 9 – us H.U. College Libr [946]

THE COMPLETE TEXT OF THE PAHLAVI DINKARD UNDER THE SUPERVISION OF D.M. MADAN – Bombay, 1911 – 6mf – NE-20148/1 – ne IDC [490]

COMPLETE WORKS OF ALBERT EINSTEIN / Einstein, Albert – (Scientific and general) – 3 – us Readex [500]

THE COMPLETE WORKS OF FLAVIUS JOSEPHUS / Josephus, Flavius – 1859. By W. Whiston – 1 – uk Microform Academic [270]

COMPLETE WORKS OF GENEVIEVE TAGGARD / Taggard, Genevieve – 3r – 1 – $245.00 – us UMI [810]

THE COMPLETE WORKS OF GENEVIEVE TAGGARD / Taggard, Genevieve – 3r – 1 – $70.00 set – us Dartmouth [800]

THE COMPLETE WORKS OF THE REV. ANDREW FULLER, WITH A MEMOIR OF HIS LIFE BY ANDREW GUNTON FULLER / Fuller, Andrew – London: G. & J. Dyer, 1846. xciii,1012p – 1 – us U.W. Library [920]

THE COMPLETE WRITINGS OF C.S. RAFINESQUE ON RECENT AND FOSSIL CONCHOLOGY / Rafinesque-Schmaltz, Constantine S; ed by Binney, W G & Tryon, G W – New York, 1864 – 2mf – ne IDC [590]

COMPLETED RESEARCH IN HEALTH, PHYSICAL EDUCATION, AND RECREATION – v1- 1959- 1; v19- 1977- 5,6,9 – us UMI [610]

COMPLEX VARIABLES / ed by Gilbert, R P & Habetna, K – 1982- – 1,5,9 – us Gordon [073]

COMPLIMENTARY BANQUET TO SIR CHARLES TUPPER: AT THE HALIFAX HOTEL, THURSDAY, JUNE 14TH, 1883 – Halifax, 1883?. 00735. (Pre-1900 Canadiana) – 9 – cn C.I.H.M. [920]

A COMPLIMENTARY EPISTLE TO JAMES BRUCE, ESQ, THE ABYSSINIAN TRAVELLER / Pindar, Peter [pseud] – London: H D Symonds, 1792 – 1 – us Res Libr [910]

COMPLIMENTS OF COMPANY 670, CIVILIAN CONSERVATION CORPS, CAMP BITELY F-22, BITELY, MICHIGAN, APRIL 4TH 1937 – [Bitely, MI: s.n.] 1937 – us Res Libr [060]

UN COMPLOT TERRORISTA EN EL SIGLO 15TH. MADRID, 1927 / Castellano, Conde de; ed by Bayle, Constantino – Madrid: Razon y Fe, 1928 – 9 – sp Bibl Santa Ana [946]

COMPORTAMIENTO Y CRISIS DE LA CLASE EMPRESARIA / Cuneo, Dardo – Buenos Aires: Pleamar, 2nd ed 1967 – 1 – CSUXADQ3341-B – us Hoover Inst Photo [360]

COMPOSER – v1-12 1969-81 1; v6-12 6; v7-12 1975-81 9 – us UMI [780]

COMPOSICION DEL 4 PLENO DEL CONSEJO ECONOMICO SINDICAL / Organizacion Sindical – Badajoz: Imprenta Inca, 1963 – sp Bibl Santa Ana [330]

COMPOSICIONES...DONA ISABEL 2 / Martinez Abeytia, Mateo – 1852 – 9 – $1.50f – sp Bibl Santa Ana [810]

COMPOSITAE / Hoffmann, O – Engler, A. and K. Prantl. Die natuerlichen Pflanzenfamilien. v. 4, pt. 5. Leipzig. 1897. B-235 2 – 8 – ne IDC [580]

COMPOSITE SCIENCE AND TECHNOLOGY – v1-21. 1968-84 – 1,5,6,13 – sz Elsevier [073]

COMPOSITES – (1982-. 1,5,6,9) – v1-. 1969- – 1 – us UMI [073]

COMPOSITES ENGINEERING – 1,5,69 – us UMI [620]

COMPOSITES SCIENCE AND ENGINEERING – v1- 1980- – 5,6,9 – us UMI [620]

LE COMPOSITEUR *see* LE COMPOSTEUR

COMPOSITION – Pattee, University Park, PA, 1990 – 41p 3 cards – 9 – us Lawrence Pub [720]

THE COMPOSITION AND HISTORICAL VALUE OF EZRA-NEHEMIAH / Torrey, Charles Cutler – Giessen: J. Ricker, 1896. 1 fiche – 9 – us A.T.L.A. [240]

DIE COMPOSITION DES BUCHES DANIEL / Meinhold, Johannes – (Includes bibliographical references) – Greifswald: Julius Abel, 1884 – 1mf – 9 – 0-8370-4378-6 – 1985-2378 – us A.T.L.A. [220]

DIE COMPOSITION DES BUCHES HIOB: EIN LITTERAR-KRITIKISCHER VERSUCH / Laue, Ludwig – Halle a.S.: J. Krause, 1896. 1 fiche – 9 – us A.T.L.A. [240]

DIE COMPOSITION DES HEXATEUCHS UND DER HISTORISCHEN BUECHER DES ALTEN TESTAMENTS / Wellhausen, Julius – (Includes bibliographical references) – Berlin: Georg Reimer, 1899 – 1mf – 9 – 0-8370-5769-8 – 1985-3769 – us A.T.L.A. [220]

DIE COMPOSITION DES MATTHAEUS-EVANGELIUMS VON PAUL SCHANZ / Schanz, Paul – (Includes bibliographical references) – Tuebingen:Ludwig Friedrich Fues, 1877 – 1mf – 9 – 0-8370-5075-8 – 1985-3075 – us A.T.L.A. [220]

LA COMPOSITION DU LIVRE D'HABACUC / Nicolardot, Firmin – (Includes index of authors) – Paris: Librairie Fischbacher, 1908 – 1mf – 9 – 0-8370-4587-8 – 1985-2587 – us A.T.L.A. [220]

COMPOSITION IN BANKRUPTCY / Bump, Orlando Franklin – St. Louis, Jones, 1877. 48 p. LL-583 – 1 – us L of C Photodup [340]

COMPOSITION OF THE BOOK OF GENESIS: WITH ENGLISH TEXT AND ANALYSIS / Fripp, Edgar Innes – London: David Nutt, 1892. 1 fiche – 9 – us A.T.L.A. [240]

THE COMPOSITION OF THE FOUR GOSPELS : A CRITICAL INQUIRY / Wright, Arthur – (Includes indexes) – London; New York: Macmillan, 1890 – 1mf – 9 – 0-8370-6548-8 – 1986-0548 – us A.T.L.A. [220]

LE COMPOSTEUR – (Cont by and filmed with: Le Compositeur 27 mar 1925-v2 n8 4 jun 1926) – Montreal, Canada. 21 fev 1925-14 mar 1925 – 1r – 1 – Can$30.00 – cn Can Microfilming [072]

THE COMPREHENSIVE CHURCH,OR, CHRISTIAN UNITY AND ECCLESIASTICAL UNION / Vail, Thomas H – Hartford: Huntington, 1841 – 1mf – us A.T.L.A. [240]

COMPREHENSIVE FIVE YEAR PLAN FOR ECONOMIC AND SOCIAL DEVELOPMENT, 1960-1965 / United Arab Republic. National Planning Committee – D 1229 1. 1960 – 9 – ne IDC [338]

COMPREHENSIVE HISTORY OF TEXAS / Wooten, Dudley G – Dallas: Wm. G. Scarff, 1898. v1, Texas Reel 1. v2, Texas Reel 2. (The Cox Library Collection) – 5 – us Americana [978]

COMPREHENSIVE INDEX TO ARCHITECTURAL PERIODICALS / British Architectural Library – 1956-72. Printed List – 5 – £690.00 – uk World [720]

THE COMPREHENSIVE MICROFORM EDITION OF HIS PAPERS, 1730-1816 / Mazzei, Philip; ed by Marchione, Margherita – (With printed guidebook) – 9r – 1 – us Ross [920]

COMPREHENSIVE PLAN FOR THE GLOBAL INVESTIGATION OF POLLUTION IN THE MARINE ENVIRONMENT AND BASELINE STUDY GUIDELINES – 1976 – 42p – 9 – 92-3-101430-7 – fr UNESCO [360]

COMPREHENSIVE REPORT ON KALI BRANTAS OVERALL PROJECT / Indonesia. Kementerian Pekerdjaan Umum dan Tenaga – SE-5370 1. 1961 – 9 – ne IDC [624]

COMPRENDIO HISTORIAL DE CORIA PARA USO DEL COLEGIO DE NINAS DEL SAGRADO CORAZON DE DICHA CIUDAD ESCRITO POR... / Prebendado de la Catedral, un sudonimo de Eugenio Escobar Prieto – Madrid: Imp. Viudad e hija de Gomez Fuentenebro, 1897 – 1 – sp Bibl Santa Ana [946]

COMPRENDRE : SERIE BLANCHE – Paris. [n1-48]. may 3 1956-dec 15 1963 – us Res Libr [944]

COMPRENDRE : SERIE BLEUE – Paris. n2-28,30-37. may 16 1956-jan 1 1964 – us Res Libr [944]

COMPRENDRE : SERIE JAUNE – Paris. n1-22,24-25,27-31,33. may 16 1956-feb 1 1964 – us Res Libr [944]

COMPRESSED AIR – 1- 1896- 1; v76- 5,6; v82- 9; – us UMI [621]

COMPRESSED AIR AND HYDRAULICS – 1935-60 – 1 – uk Microform Academic [073]

LE COMPROMIS AUSTROHONGROIS DE 1867 ETUDE SUR LE DUALISME / Eisenmann, L – Paris. 1904. BR-4910 2 – 8 – ne IDC [940]

COMPROMISO Y RESPONSABILIDAD. CAMPAMENTO NACIONAL "FRANCISCO FRANCO". CAVALEDA (SORIA) 74 / Delegacion Nacional de la Juventud – Caceres: Imp. M. Sergio Dorado, 1974 – 1 – sp Bibl Santa Ana [350]

COMPTABILITE DES AFFAIRES A ENZEL ET LEURS CONSEQUENCES JURIDIQUES POUR LES COMMERCANTS / Bonan, Jules – Tunis, Imprimerie commerciale (L. Rombi) 1913. 30 p. LL-12023 – 1 – us L of C Photodup [340]

COMPTE DE LA NATION / Morocco. Division du Plan et des Statistiques – 1958-68. BNE-3046 1 – 9 – ne IDC [310]

COMPTE RENDU : 4 CONGRES DU HAVRE / Congres du Havre – Manuscrit de 51 feuillets au Musee social. 5643 – 9 – fr Hachette [335]

COMPTE RENDU / Congres du Parti Ouvrier Socialiste Francais (Ve), 30 oct-6 nov 1881, Reims. Parti Ouvrier Socialiste Francais – Paris. 1882. 125 p. 5644 – 9 – fr Hachette [335]

COMPTE RENDU / Congres du Parti Ouvrier Socialiste Francais (VIe), 25-31 sept 1882, Saint-Etienne. Parti Ouvrier Socialiste Revolutionnaire Francais – (COMPTE RENDU DE LA SEANCE DE NUIT DU 25 SEPTEMBRE. QUESTION DE DISCIPLINE. Paris. 1882. 39 p. 5647. 2.50; 9) – Paris. 1882. 214 p. et carte repliee. 5646 – 9 – fr Hachette [335]

COMPTE RENDU / Congres du Parti Ouvrier Socialiste Revolutionnaire, Allemanistes. Conference Nationale de 1895, 29 et 30 septembre, Paris – Imp. J. Allemane, Paris. 1896. 86p 5669 – 9 – fr Hachette [335]

COMPTE RENDU / Congres du Parti Ouvrier Socialiste Revolutionnaire, Allemanistes. Congres National (10e), 21 au 29 juin 1891, Paris – Imp. J. Allemane, Paris. 1892. 112p 5659 – 9 – fr Hachette [335]

COMPTE RENDU / Congres du Parti Ouvrier Socialiste Revolutionnaire, Allemanistes. Congres National (11e). 2-9 octobre 1892, St. Quentin – Imp. J. Allemane. Paris. 1893. 71p 5661 – 9 – fr Hachette [335]

COMPTE RENDU / Congres du Parti Ouvrier Socialiste Revolutionnaire, Allemanistes. Congres National (12e). 14-22 juillet, 1894, Dijon – Imp. Carre, Dijon. 1895. 48p 5664 bis – 9 – fr Hachette [335]

COMPTE RENDU / Congres du Parti Ouvrier Socialiste Revolutionnaire, Allemanistes. Congres National (14e), septembre 1896, Paris – Imp. J. Allemane, Paris. 1897. 158p 5673 – 9 – fr Hachette [335]

COMPTE RENDU / Congres du Parti Ouvrier Socialiste Revolutionnaire, Allemanistes. Congres National (15e), 26 septembre au 3 octobre 1897, Paris – Imp. J. Allemane, Paris. 1898. 108p 5675 – 9 – fr Hachette [335]

COMPTE RENDU / Congres du Parti Ouvrier Socialiste Revolutionnaire, Allemanistes. Federation des Travailleurs Socialistes de France. Congres Regional de l'Union Federative du Centre (10e), 1-5 oct, 1890 et 12-17 mars 1891, Paris – Imp. J. Allemane. Paris. 1891. 96p 5658 – 9 – fr Hachette [335]

COMPTE RENDU / Congres du Parti Socialiste Francais, Jauressistes. Congres socialiste de Saint Etienne, 4 au 7 janvier 1904 – Dans la Revue Socialiste, v39, p317-364.5828 – 9 – fr Hachette [335]

COMPTE RENDU / Congres National de la Federation des Travailleurs Socialistes de France (10e), 9 au 15 octobre, 1890, Chatellerault. Parti Ouvrier Socialiste Revolutionnaire ("Possibilistes") – Imp. A. Masson, Poitiers. 1891. 104p 5655 – 9 – fr Hachette [335]

COMPTE RENDU / Congres National de la Federation des Travailleurs Socialistes de France (7e), 30 sept au 7 oct 1883, Paris – Publie par le Comite National aux bureaux du Proletaire. Paris. 1883. 35p 5649 – 9 – fr Hachette [335]

COMPTE RENDU / Congres National de la Federation des Travailleurs Socialistes de France (8e), 12 au 19 octobre 1884, Rennes – Publie par le Comite National aux Bureaux du Proletaire. Paris. 1885. 40p 5652 – 9 – fr Hachette [335]

COMPTE RENDU / Congres National de la Federation des Travailleurs Socialistes de France (9e), 2 au 8 octobre 1887, Charleville. Parti Ouvrier Socialiste Revolutionnaire ("Possibilistes") – Congres regional de l'Union federative du Centre Congres. Imp. F. Harry. Paris. 1888. 5653 – 9 – fr Hachette [335]

COMPTE RENDU / Congres National du Parti Ouvrier Francais, Guesdiste (13e), 8 au 10 septembre 1895, Romilly – Dans "Le Socialiste," organe central du Parti ouvrier, no du 15 septembre 1895; dans "Le Socialiste Troyen," nos. du 14 et du 21 septembre 1895. Un dossier de 40 fevillets, diverses coupures de presse. 5666 8 – 9 – fr Hachette [335]

COMPTE RENDU / Congres National du Parti Ouvrier Francais, Guesdiste (17e), aout 1899, Epernay – Dans "Le Socialiste," organe central du P.O.F., no. 56, 20 aout 1899. 5681 – 9 – fr Hachette [335]

COMPTE RENDU / Congres National du Parti Ouvrier Francais, Guesdiste (18e), octobre 1900, Ivry-sur-Seine – Dans "Le Socialiste," no. 108, 7 octobre 1900. 10p – 9 – fr Hachette [335]

COMPTE RENDU / Congres National du Parti Ouvrier Francais, Guesdiste (20e), 21 au 24 septembre 1902, Issoudun – Dans "Le Socialiste" du 28 septembre 1902 – 9 – fr Hachette [335]

COMPTE RENDU / Congres National du Parti Socialiste (S.F.I.O.). 2 Congres National, 29 octobre au 1 novembre 1905, Chalon s Saone – Dans LE SOCIALISTE, no. 27, 4 novembre 1905. 8p 5690 – 9 – fr Hachette [335]

COMPTE RENDU / Congres Socialiste Ouvrier de Marseille, 1879, Marseille – Lu en assemblee le 15 fev 1880 par I. Dauthier. l'Auteur, Paris, 1880. 104 p. 5642 – 9 – fr Hachette [335]

COMPTE RENDU / Federation des Travailleurs Socialistes de France. Parti Ouvrier Socialiste Revolutionnaire. IXe Congres Regional de l'Union Federative du Centre. Paris du 17 au 26 juin 1888 – Paris, impr. F. Harry. 1888. 175 p. 5654 – 9 – fr Hachette [335]

COMPTE RENDU / Parti Ouvrier Socialiste Revolutionnaire. 14e Congres Regional de l'Union Federative du Centre. Paris, fevrier 1896 – Paris, imp. Jean Allemane. 1896. 36p 5670 – 9 – fr Hachette [335]

COMPTE RENDU / Parti Ouvrier Socialiste Revolutionnaire. 15e Congres Regional, Paris, avril-mai 1899 – Paris, imp. J. Allemane. 1899. 178p 5680 – 9 – fr Hachette [335]

COMPTE RENDU / Parti Ouvrier Socialiste Revolutionnaire. 9e Congres Regional de l'Union Federative du Centre. Paris du 21 aout au 11 septembre 1892 – Paris, imp. J. Allemane. 1892. 92p 5662 – 9 – fr Hachette [335]

COMPTE RENDU.. / International Conference on Unemployment. First. Paris. 1910 – Paris, 18-21 sept 1910. 3v in 1. fold. map, tables. Almost entirely in French; Rapports in French, English or German with a summary in the other two languages – 1 – us U.W. Library [330]

COMPTE RENDU ANALYTIQUE / Congres National du Parti socialiste (S.F.I.O.). 1 et 2 Congres Nationaux, avril 1905, Paris, octobre 1905, Chalon s Saone – Paris, au siege du Conseil National, s.d. 127p 5951 – 9 – fr Hachette [335]

COMPTE RENDU ANALYTIQUE / Congres National du Parti Socialiste (S.F.I.O.). 3 Congres National,1 au 4 novembre, Limoges – Paris, au siege du Conseil National, s.d. 288p 5691 – 9 – fr Hachette [335]

COMPTE RENDU ANALYTIQUE / Congres National du Parti Socialiste (S.F.I.O.). 8 Congres National 2e session, 1 au 2 novembre 1911, Paris – Paris, s.d. 104p 5697 bis – 9 – fr Hachette [335]

COMPTE RENDU ANALYTIQUE. CHAMBRE DES REPRESENTANTS DU CONGO. LE LEGISLATION – Leopoldville, 1960-63. v.1-9 – 97mf – 9 – ne IDC [330]

COMPTE RENDU ANALYTIQUE DU SENAT DU CONGO. 1E LEGISLATION, 1960-63. COMPTES RENDUS OFFICIELS, 2E LEGISLATION, 1965-66 / Congo. Senat – 97mf – 9 – ne IDC [960]

COMPTE RENDU ANALYTIQUE PUBLIE PAR LE SECRETARIAT DU BUREAU SOCIALISTE INTERNATIONAL / International Socialist Congress. 7th. 1907 – Bruxelles. Impr. Veuve D. Brismee. 1908 – 1 – $35.00r – us Hoover Inst Photo [335]

COMPTE RENDU AU ROI SUR L'EMPLOI DES FONDS ALLOUES DEPUIS 1839 POUR L'ENSEIGNEMENT RELIGIEUX ET ELEMENTAIRE DES NOIRS ET DE L'EXECUTION DES LOIS DES 18 ET 19 JUILLET 1845 RELATIVES AU REGIME DES ESCLAVES... – (Slave Trade and Abolitionism in France Series).1846 – 9 – fr Hachette [305]

COMPTE RENDU COMPLET / Congres National du Parti Socialiste de France, Guesdistes (1e), 26 au 28 september 1902, Commentry. (U.S.R.) – Imp. ouvriere M. Dhoossche, Lille. 1902. 88p 5825 – 9 – fr Hachette [335]

COMPTE RENDU COMPLET / Congres National du Parti Socialiste de France, Guesdistes (2e), 27 au 29 septembre, 1903, Reims. (U.S.R.) – Imp. ouvriere du Centre, Bourges. 1903. 66p 5826 – 9 – fr Hachette [335]

COMPTE RENDU DE LA DISTRIBUTION DES PRIX ET DE LA PRESENTATION D'UNE MEDAILLE D'HONNEUR OFFERTE PAR S.E. LE GOUVERNEUR GENERAL ET LA PRINCESSE LOUISE AUX ELEVES. / Academie de St. Augustin – Quebec. s.n.. 1880. 04004. (Pre-1900 Canadiana) – 9 – cn C.I.H.M. [971]

COMPTE RENDU DES DEBATS / Confederation Generale du Travail. Congres – III-XI, XIII-XV, XVII-XXXVIII Congres. 1897-1975 – 1 – fr A.C.R.P.P. [331]

COMPTE RENDU DES SEANCES / Congres International des Traditions Populaires – 1891 – 1 – us I.U. Libraries [390]

COMPTE RENDU DES TRAVAUX DE LA QUATRIEME SESSION TENUE A GENEVE DU 24 AU 29 AOUT 1896 : SOUS LE HAUT PATRONAGE DU CONSEIL FEDERAL SUISSE ET DU GOUVERNEMENT DE LA REPUBLIQUE ET CANTON DE GENEVE – Geneve: Georg & Co, 1897 – us Res Libr [949]

COMPTE RENDU DU DINER DES CITOYENS DE ST HYACINTHE A LA COMPAGNIE MCMARTIN-HAMEL, LE 12 JANVIER 1875 – 1875. 00736. (Pre-1900 Canadiana) – 9 – cn C.I.H.M. [971]

COMPTE RENDU DU GRAND CONCERT DONNE AU BENEFICE DES ZOUAVES PONTIFICAUX A LEVIS, LE 22 FEVRIER 1868 – Suivi du discours de M. Chapleau sous le patronage de l'Hon. orateur de l'Assemblee legislative. Levis: J. N. Doucet, 1868. 04162. (Pre-1900 Canadiana) – 9 – cn C.I.H.M. [971]

COMPTE RENDU ET RESOLUTIONS / Congres National du Parti Ouvrier Francais, Guesdiste (14e), 21 au 25 juillet 1896, Lille – Un dossier de 25 feuillets, articles de presse, au Musee social. 5671 – 9 – fr Hachette [335]

COMPTE RENDU STENOGRAPHIQUE / Congres general des organisations socialistes francaises, 3rd & 26 au 28 mai 1901, Lyon – Societe nouvelle de librarie, Paris. 1901. 581 p. 5685 – 9 – fr Hachette [335]

COMPTE RENDU STENOGRAPHIQUE / Congres National du Parti Socialiste (S.F.I.O.). 10 Congres National, 23 au 25 mars 1913, Brest – Paris, au siege du Conseil national, s.d. 360p 5699 – 9 – fr Hachette [335]

COMPTE RENDU STENOGRAPHIQUE / Congres National du Parti Socialiste (S.F.I.O.). 11 Congres National, 25 au 28 janvier 1914, Amiens – Paris, au siege du Conseil national, s.d. 442p 5948 – 9 – fr Hachette [335]

COMPTE RENDU STENOGRAPHIQUE / Congres National du Parti Socialiste (S.F.I.O.). 4 Congres National, 11 au 14 aout 1907, Nancy – Paris, au siege du Conseil National, s.d. 610p 5692 – 9 – fr Hachette [335]

COMPTE RENDU STENOGRAPHIQUE / Congres National du Parti Socialiste (S.F.I.O.). 5 Congres National, 15 au 18 octobre 1908, Toulouse – Paris, au siege du Conseil national, s.d. 504p 5694 – 9 – fr Hachette [335]

COMPTE RENDU STENOGRAPHIQUE / Congres National du Parti Socialiste (S.F.I.O.). 6e – (Rapport au Ministere de l'Interieure apres le congres de Saint Etienne. MANUSCRITAUX Archives nationales. 5953) – Paris, au siege du Conseil national, s.d. 607p 5695 – 9 – 2.50 – fr Hachette [335]

COMPTE RENDU STENOGRAPHIQUE / Congres National du Parti Socialiste (S.F.I.O.). 7e Congres National, 15 au 16 juillet 1910, Paris, 2e session – Paris, s.d. 209p 5696 bis – 9 – fr Hachette [335]

COMPTE RENDU STENOGRAPHIQUE / Congres National du Parti Socialiste (S.F.I.O.). 7e Congres National, 6 au 8 fevrier, 1910, Nimes – Paris, au siege du Conseil national. s.d. 520p 5696 – 9 – fr Hachette [335]

COMPTE RENDU STENOGRAPHIQUE / Congres National du Parti Socialiste (S.F.I.O.). 8e Congres National, 16 au 19 avril 1911, Saint Quentin – Paris, au siege du Conseil national, s.d. 480p 5697 – 9 – fr Hachette [335]

COMPTE RENDU STENOGRAPHIQUE / Congres National du Parti Socialiste (S.F.I.O.). 9 Congres National, 18 au 21 fevrier 1912, Lyon – Paris, au siege du Conseil national, s.d. 618p 5698 – 9 – fr Hachette [335]

COMPTE RENDU STENOGRAPHIQUE / Parti Socialiste Francais. Comite General. Discussion sur l'unification et l'organisation du Parti – Novembre 1900-Fevrier 1901. Paris. Societe nouvelle de librarie, 1901. 318 p. 5798 – 9 – fr Hachette [335]

COMPTE RENDU STENOGRAPHIQUE OFFICIEL / Congres du Parti Socialiste Francais, Jauressistes. Congres General (4e), 2 au 4 mars 1902, Tous – Societe de nouvelle librarie, Paris. 1902. 460p 5688 – 9 – fr Hachette [335]

COMPTE RENDU STENOGRAPHIQUE OFFICIEL / Congres General des Organisations Socialistes Francaises (1e), 3 au 8 decembre 1899, Paris – Societe nouvelle de librarie, Paris. 1900. 510p 5682 – 9 – fr Hachette [335]

COMPTE RENDU STENOGRAPHIQUE OFICIEL / Congres General des Organisations Socialistes Francaises (2e), 28 au 30 septembre 1900, Paris – Societe nouvelle de librarie, Paris. 1901. 581p 5684 – 9 – fr Hachette [335]

COMPTE-RENDU / Congres National des Droits Civils et du Suffrage des Femmes – Paris. 1908 – 1 – us Res Libr [323]

[COMPTE-RENDU] – Toulouse: Impr regionale, 1950 – 1r – 1 – us Res Libr [616]

COMPTE-RENDU AU ROI DE L'EXECUTION DES LOIS DES 18 ET 19 JUILLET 1845 SUR LE REGIME DES ESCLAVES, LA CREATION D'ETABLISSEMENTS AGRICOLES PAR LE TRAVAIL LIBRE, ETC / France. Ministere de la Marine et des Colonies – (Slave Trade and Abolitionism in France Series). Mar 1847 – 9 – fr Hachette [324]

COMPTE-RENDU DE LA CONFERENCE ... – (Filmed with three conference reports of the Union africaine et malgache: Compte-rendu ... de la Conference de Bangui ... Cotonou [1962?].–Compte-rendu ... de la Conference de Libreville ... Cotonou [1962?].-Compte–rendu... de la Conference de Ouagadougou ... Cotonou [1963?]) – Tananarive, 6-12 sep 1961 [Tananarive, Impr. nationale 1962] – us Res Libr [960]

COMPTE-RENDU DE LA CONFERENCE DE BANGUI, 25-27 MARS 1962 – (Filmed with Conference des chefs d'etat et de gouvernement africains et malgaches, Tananarive 1961 [Tananarive 1962]) – Cotonou: [s.n. 1962?] – us Res Libr [960]

COMPTE-RENDU DE LA NEUVIEME SESSION DU CONGRES PREHISTORIQUE DE FRANCE... / Congres Prehistorique de France – Paris: Soc. prehist. francaise, 1914 – 1 – F473.45 – fr Armell [301]

COMPTE-RENDU DE LA SEIZIEME CONVENTION...: TENUE A RUTLAND, VT., LE 22 ET 23 JUIN 1886 / Convention Nationale des Canadiens-francais des Etats-Unis – s.l.: s.n., 1886 (Plattsburgh, N.Y.: Ateliers typ. du National). 00066. (Pre-1900 Canadiana) – 9 – cn C.I.H.M. [971]

COMPTE-RENDU DES TRAVAUX / Depince, M Ch – Paris: Comite d'organization du Congres, 1909 – 1 – us Res Libr [960]

COMPTE-RENDU DES TRAVAUX... : ANNEE 1859 / Canada. Chambre d'Agriculture du Bas-Canada – Montreal: de Montigny et Compagnie, s.d. SEM105P155 – 5mf – 9 – Can$11.25 – cn Bibl Nat [331]

COMPTE-RENDU DES TRAVAUX DE LA CONFERENCE DE LIBREVILLE 10-13 SEP 1962 / ed by Le Secretariat general de l'UAM – (Filmed with Conference des chefs d'etat et de gouvernement africains et malgaches, Tananarive 1961 [Tananarive 1962]) – Cotonou [1962?] – us Res Libr [960]

COMPTE-RENDU DES TRAVAUX DE LA CONFERENCE DE OUAGADOUGOU 10-14 MARS 1963 / ed by Le Secretariat general de l'UAM – (Filmed with Conference de chefs d'etat et de gouvernement africains et malgaches, Tananarive 1961 [Tananarive 1962]) – Cotonou [1963?] – us Res Libr [960]

[COMPTE-RENDU] INSTITUEE / Maginot, M A – Paris: E Larose, 1917 – 1 – us Res Libr [944]

COMPTE-RENDU OFFICIEL DE LA 17E CONVENTION...: TENUE A NASHUA, N.H.: LES LES SIC 26 ET 27 JUIN 1888 / Convention Nationale des Canadiens-francais des Etats-Unis – s.l.: s.n., 1890 (Lewiston, Me.: Messager). 04405. (Pre-1900 Canadiana) – 9 – cn C.I.H.M. [971]

COMPTE-RENDU STENOGRAPHIQUE DE LA PREMIERE REUNION. / Confederation Generale du Travail. Paris – Villeneuve-St. George. 1919. (La Condition Ouvriere. Part Two.) – 9 – 5.00 – fr Bibl Nationale [360]

LES COMPTES ECONOMIQUES DE L'ALGERIE ET DU SAHARA POUR LES ANNEES 1957 ET 1958 / Algeria. Service de la Statistique Generale – 1960. BNE-8666 1 – 9 – ne IDC [310]

COMPTES RENDUS / Academie des Sciences d'Outre-Mer – Paris. 1941-67 – 1 – fr A.C.R.P.P. [500]

COMPTES RENDUS / Academie des Sciences. Russie – (Serie B: Section historico-philologique. 1924-31. 1. nouvelle serie: 1933-43. 1) – Petrograd-Leningrad. Serie A: Section physico-mathematique et sciences naturelles. 1922-33 – 1 – fr A.C.R.P.P. [500]

COMPTES RENDUS / Parti Republicain Radical et Radical-Socialiste. Congres du Parti – 1933-38 – 1 – fr A.C.R.P.P. [335]

COMPTES RENDUS / Societe de Biologie. Paris – v66-168 1909-74 – 1,5,6 – us Princeton Micro [574]

COMPTES RENDUS DES SEANCES DE L'ACADEMIE DES SCIENCES – (Index 1835-1895, v1-121) – Paris, 1835-1916. v1-163 – 4,896mf – 470/2 – ne IDC [500]

COMPTES RENDUS ET RAPPORTS / Communist Party. France. 6-15 Congres National – 1929-59 – 1 – fr A.C.R.P.P. [335]

COMPTES RENDUS ET RAPPORTS DES 30-44 CONGRES / Parti Socialiste. Section Francaise de l'Internationale Ouvriere – 1933-52 – 1 – fr A.C.R.P.P. [335]

COMPTES RENDUS HEBDOMADAIRES DES SEANCES / Academie des Sciences. Paris – v1-261. 1835-1965 – 1,5,6 – us Princeton Micro [500]

COMPTES RENDUS HEBDOMADAIRES DES SEANCES / Academie des Sciences. Paris – v1-283. 1830-1976 – 5,6 – us UMI [500]

COMPTES RENDUS-SERIE A: SCIENCES MATHEMATIQUES / Academie des Sciences. Paris – v. 264-283. 1967-1976 – 5,6 – us UMI [510]

COMPTES RENDUS-SERIE A: SCIENCES MATHEMATIQUES / Academie des Sciences. Paris – v262-291. 1966-80 – 1,5,6 – us Princeton Micro [510]

COMPTES RENDUS-SERIE B: SCIENCES PHYSIQUES / Academie des Sciences. Paris – v. 264-283. 1967-1976 – 5,6 – us UMI [530]

COMPTES RENDUS-SERIE B: SCIENCES PHYSIQUES / Academie des Sciences. Paris – v262-291. 1966-80 – 1,5,6 – us Princeton Micro [530]

COMPTES RENDUS-SERIE C: SCIENCES CHIMIQUES / Academie des Sciences. Paris – v. 264-283. 1967-1976 – 5,6 – us UMI [540]

COMPTES RENDUS-SERIE C: SCIENCES CHIMIQUES / Academie des Sciences. Paris – v262-291. 1966-80 – 1,5,6 – us Princeton Micro [540]

COMPTES RENDUS-SERIE D: SCIENCES NATURELLES / Academie des Sciences. Paris – v. 264-283. 1967-1976 – 5,6 – us UMI [574]

COMPTES RENDUS-SERIE D: SCIENCES NATURELLES / Academie des Sciences. Paris – v262-291. 1966-80 – 1,5,6 – us Princeton Micro [574]

COMPTES-RENDU ANALYTIQUES DU CONGO – 1961-65 – 259mf – 9 – ne IDC [330]

COMPTES-RENDUS / Comite Special du Katanga. Congres Scientifique du Cinquantenaire, Elisabethville, 1950 – Incomplete. A 402. 7v – 9 – ne IDC [500]

COMPTES-RENDUS DE L'ACADEMIE DES SCIENCES DE RUSSIE / Akademiia Nauk. BSSR – (Continued as DOKLADY AKADEMII NAUK SSSR. S.B.M., 1926-31) – S.B.M., 1924-25 – 38mf – 9 – ne IDC [500]

COMPTES-RENDUS DES CONFERENCES. / Association des Instituteurs de la Circonscription de l'Ecole Normale Jacques-Cartier – Montreal: E. Senecal, 1873. 04099. (Pre-1900 Canadiana) – 9 – cn C.I.H.M. [370]

COMPTES-RENDUS DES SEANCES DE L'ACADEMIE DES INSCRIPTIONS ET BELLES-LETTRES – Paris, 1857-1864. v1-8; N.S., 1865-1871. v1-7; S.3, 1872. v1; S.4, 1873-1920. v1-48 – 450mf – O-1203/1 – ne IDC [440]

LE COMPTOIR FRANCAIS DE JUDA (OUIDAH) AU 18E SIECLE – Paris: E Larose, 1942 – 1 – us Res Libr [336]

Compton, Boyd *see* INDONESIA'S NATIONAL LANGUAGE

COMPTON COUNTY CHRONICLE – Cookshire, Canada. 25 fev 1891; v2 n2. 2 mar 1892-v2 n53. 27 fev 1893 – 1r – 1 – Can$40.00 – cn Can Microfilming [072]

Compton-Rickett, Joseph *see* ORIGINS AND FAITH: AN ESSAY OF RECONCILIATION

COMPTROLLER GENERAL ANNUAL REPORTS – (Missing: 1938-39; 1942; 1986-89. Updates planned) – 1937-91 – 141mf – 9 – $211.00 – LLMC 90-375 – us L.L.M.C. [336]

COMPTROLLER GENERAL DECISIONS / U.S. General Accounting Office – (With index/ digest for 1921-81. Updates planned) – v1-71. 1921-84 – 897mf – 9 – $1,346.00 – LLMC 79-412 + 79-412 – us L.L.M.C. [324]

COMPTROLLER GENERAL DECISIONS *see* COMPTROLLER GENERAL ANNUAL REPORTS

COMPTROLLER OF THE TREASURY DECISIONS : 1894-1921 / U.S. Treasury Department. Comptroller – (Cont by: Decisions of the Comptroller General of the US LLMC 79-412) – v1-27 (all publ) – 283mf – 9 – $424.00 – LLMC 78-212 – us L.L.M.C. [336]

COMPTROLLER OF THE TREASURY DECISIONS *see* FIRST COMPTROLLER, DEPARTMENT OF THE TREASURY, DECISIONS

COMPTROLLER OF THE TREASURY DECISIONS, 1894-1921 *see* INDEX TO THE PUBLISHED DECISIONS OF THE U.S. ACCOUNTING OFFICERS

COMPTROLLER OF THE TREASURY DICISIONS, 1894-1921 *see* DIGEST OF THE DICISIONS OF THE COMPTROLLER OF THE TREASURY

COMPULSORY EDUCATION IN NEW ZEALAND – 2nd ed rev 1975 – 113p – 9 – 92-3-100971-0 – fr UNESCO [370]

COMPULSORY LICENSING OF PATENTS: A LEGISLATIVE HISTORY / U.S. Library of Congress. Legislative Reference Service – Washington, Govt. Print. Off., 1958. 70 p. LL-2310 – 1 – us L of C Photodup [340]

COMPULSORY STANDARDS FOR THE EXPORT OF EDIBLE PEANUTS / Libya. Administration of Tripolitania – Export Standard nr.2. Oct 1954. BNE-1020 1 – 9 – ne IDC [380]

COMPUTATIONAL MATHEMATICS AND MATHEMATICAL PHYSICS – (Formerly U.S.S.R. Computational Mathematics and Mathematical Physics) – v1- 1962- – 5,6,9 – us UMI [510]

COMPUTATIONAL MATHEMATICS AND MODELING – v1-5. 1990-94 – 1,5 – $65.00 – us UMI [000]

COMPUTE – 1979- – 1,5,6,9 – us UMI [510]

COMPUTER – (1985-. 5,6,9) – Sweden. 1983- – 1 – us UMI [000]
COMPUTER ACCESSORIES AND PERIPHERALS: CAP – 1984 – 1,5,6,9 – us UMI [000]
COMPUTER AIDED DESIGN REPORT – 1984- – 1,5,6,9 – us UMI [620]
COMPUTER AND COMMUNICATIONS BUYER – 1985-. -m – 1 – us UMI [073]
COMPUTER AND COMMUNICATIONS TECHNOLOGY DOCUMENTS – 1982. Updated every 6 months – 5,9 – uk Tech [000]
COMPUTER AND CONTROL ABSTRACTS : ABSTRACTS JOURNALS 1898-1995 – (With author-subject indexes) – v1-26. 1966-91 – 1,5,6,9 – uk INSPEC [620]
COMPUTER AND CONTROL ABSTRACTS – (Cont: Control Abstracts 1966-68) – 1969-95 – 1,5,6,9 – uk INSPEC [620]
COMPUTER AND CONTROL ABSTRACTS : CUMULATIVE INDEXES 1898-1992 – (Includes author-subject indexes) – 1966-1992 – 1,5,6,9 – uk INSPEC [620]
COMPUTER AND CONTROL ABSTRACTS – (v. 1. $46.00v v. 2-4. $412.00v. v. 5-6. $430.00v) – (Formerly: Control Abstracts). London. v. 1-6. 1966-71 – 9 – $24100.00 – uk Dawson [000]
COMPUTER AND ELECTRONICS MARKETING *see* ADWEEK'S COMPUTER AND ELECTRONICS MARKETING
COMPUTER BULLETIN – (v. 1-8. $243.00v. v. 9-16. $246.00v) – orig. s. London. 1957-71 – 9 – $2470.00 – uk Dawson [000]
COMPUTER BULLETIN – v1-16. 1957-72 – 1 – us UMI [073]
COMPUTER BULLETIN. SERIES 2 – (1982-. 1,5,6,9) – 1974- – 1 – us UMI [073]
COMPUTER BUSINESS: DAS MAGAZIN FUER HANDEL, OEM, SOFTWARE- UND SYSTEMHAEUSER – 1984- – 1,5,6,9 – us UMI [000]
COMPUTER BUSINESS NEWS – v. 1-5. 1978-82 – 1,5,6,9 – us UMI [000]
COMPUTER COMMUNICATIONS – (1982-. 1,5,6,9) – v1-. 1978- – 1 – us UMI [073]
COMPUTER CRIME DIGEST – v1-. 1982- – 1,5,6,9 – us UMI [360]
COMPUTER CRIME DIGEST *see* WASHINGTON CRIME NEWS SERVICES' CORPORATE SECURITY DIGEST
COMPUTER DATA – (1986-. 1,5,6) – 1983- – 9 – us UMI [000]
COMPUTER DEALER NEWS – (Mf available to 1993 only) – Willowdale. v7-9. 1991-93 – 1 – Can$115.00y – cn Micromedia [000]
COMPUTER GRAPHICS – v1-3. 1978-Feb 1980 – 1 – us UMI [073]
COMPUTER GRAPHICS DIRECTORY – 1985- – 1 – us UMI [073]
COMPUTER GRAPHICS TODAY – v1-. 1984- – 1,5,6,9 – us UMI [000]
COMPUTER GRAPHICS WORLD – (v7-. 1984-. 5,6,9) – v3-. May 1980- – 1 – us UMI [073]
COMPUTER JOURNAL – (1982-. 1,5,6,9) – v1-. 1958- – 1 – us UMI [073]
COMPUTER JOURNAL – v. 1-18. London. 1958-75 – 9 – $24130.00; $7.50v – uk Dawson [000]
COMPUTER LANGUAGE – (1986- . 5,6,9) – v1- . 1984- – 1 – us UMI [073]
COMPUTER LANGUAGES – v1- 1976- – 5,6,9 – us UMI [073]
COMPUTER LAW AND TAX REPORT – v1-22. 1974-96 – 9 – us Hein [340]
COMPUTER LAWYER – v1-12. 1984-1995 – 9 – $300.00 – us Hein [340]
COMPUTER LAWYER *see* INTERNATIONAL COMPUTER LAWYER
COMPUTER MARKETING NEWSLETTER – (1985-. 1,5,6) – v7-. 1983- – 9 – us UMI [000]
COMPUTER METHODS IN APPLIED MECHANICS AND ENGINEERING – v1-47 1972-84 – 1,5,6,13 – sz Elsevier [621]
COMPUTER MUSIC JOURNAL – v. 1-. 1977- – 1,5,6,9 – us UMI [780]
COMPUTER NETWORKS – v1-8. 1976-84 – 1,5,6,13 – sz Elsevier [073]
COMPUTER NEWS – 1983- – 1 – us UMI [000]
COMPUTER OUTPUT MICROFILM (COM) HARDWARE AND SOFTWARE: THE STATE OF THE ART / American Library Association – RLMS Micro-File Series, v. 5. 1977 – 9 – 8.00 – us L of C Photodup [770]
COMPUTER PERFORMANCE – (1982-. 1,5,6,9) – v1-. 1980- – 1 – us UMI [073]
COMPUTER PHYSICS COMMUNICATIONS – v1-36 1969-84 – 1,5,6,13 – sz Elsevier [530]
COMPUTER PROGRAM FOR IRRIGATION PLANNING AND MANAGEMENT / CROPWAT – 1992 – 134p – it F.A.O. [631]
COMPUTER PROGRAMS FOR FISH STOCK ASSESSMENT : ANACO: SOFTWARE FOR THE ANALYSIS OF CATCH DATA BY AGE GROUP ON IBM-PC AND COMPATIBLES – 1989 – 81p – it F.A.O. [639]
COMPUTER PROGRAMS FOR FISH STOCK ASSESSMENT : APPLICATIONS FOR THE HP 41 CV CALCULATOR – 1986 – 232p – it F.A.O. [000]
COMPUTER PROGRAMS FOR FISH STOCK ASSESSMENT : LENGTH-BASED FISH STOCK ASSESSMENT FOR APPLE 2 COMPUTERS – 1987 – 226p – it F.A.O. [639]
COMPUTER PROGRAMS IN BIOMEDICINE – v1-19. 1970-84 – 1,5,6,13 – sz Elsevier [073]
COMPUTER PROGRAMS IN BIOMEDICINE – v.1-3. 1970-73 – 1,5,6 – 2235.00 – us Princeton Micro [610]
COMPUTER SYSTEMS SCIENCE AND ENGINEERING – v1-. 1985- – 1,5,6,9 – us UMI [621]
COMPUTER TECHNOLOGY REVIEW – v1-. 1981- – 9 – us UMI [621]
COMPUTER UPDATE – 1984- – 1,5,6,9 – us UMI [000]
COMPUTER USE IN SOCIAL SERVICES NETWORK (NEWSLETTER) – 1984- – 1,5,6,9 – us UMI [360]
COMPUTER VISION DIRECTORY – 1985- – 1 – us UMI [073]
COMPUTER WEEKLY – 1966- – 1 – us UMI [000]
COMPUTER WORLD – (v13- 1979- 5,6,9) – v1- 1967- – 1 – us UMI [073]
COMPUTER-AIDED DESIGN – (1982-. 1,5,6,9) – v1-. 1968- – 1 – us UMI [073]
COMPUTER-AIDED ENGINEERING – v1-. 1982- – 1,5,6,9 – us UMI [073]
COMPUTER-AIDED RECORDING AND MATHEMATICAL ANALYSIS OF TEAM PERFORMANCE IN VOLLEYBALL / Eom, Han J & Schutz, Robert W – 1989 – 2mf – 9 – $8.00 – us Microform Publ [790]
COMPUTER-AIDED TRANSCRIPTION : A SURVEY OF FEDERAL COURT-REPORTERS' PERCEPTIONS / Greenwood, J Michael – Washington: FJC, 1981 – 1mf – 9 – $1.50 – LLMC 95-306 – us L.L.M.C. [340]
COMPUTER-ENHANCED SPECTROSCOPY – 1983- – 1,5,6,9 – us UMI [073]
COMPUTER-INTEGRATED MANUFACTURING SYSTEMS *see* ADVANCED MANUFACTURING ENGINEERING (AME)
COMPUTERISED INDEX OF AUSTRALIAN ABORIGINAL SONGS, CAPE YORK AREA / Moyle, Alice & Koch, Grace – (Index details name of collector, place, and year of recording, language groups of performers, vocal and instrumental components, and references to spoken song works, published song works and musical notations) – 1981 – 6mf – 9 – A$6.95 – at Aboriginal [780]
COMPUTERIZED MEDICAL IMAGING AND GRAPHICS – 1,5,69 – us UMI [000]
COMPUTERIZED TOMOGRAPHY – v.1- 1977- – 5,6,9 – us UMI [616]
COMPUTER-PROCESSED TABULATIONS OF DATA FROM SEAMEN'S PROTECTIVE CERTIFICATE APPLICATIONS TO THE COLLECTOR OF CUSTOMS FOR THE PORT OF PHILADELPHIA / U.S. Bureau of the Customs – 1812-15. 1 roll. M972 – 1 – us Nat'l Archives [324]
COMPUTERS AND AUTOMATION – v.1-18. 1951-69 – 1 – us UMI [000]
COMPUTERS AND CHEMICAL ENGINEERING – v1- 1977- – 5,6,9 – us UMI [000]
COMPUTERS AND CHEMISTRY – v1- 1977- – 5,6,9 – us UMI [000]
COMPUTERS AND EDUCATION – v1- 1977- – 5,6,9 – us UMI [370]
COMPUTERS AND ELECTRICAL ENGINEERING – v1- 1973- – 5,6,9 – us UMI [000]
COMPUTERS AND ELECTRONICS – n.s.v20-. 1982- – 1,5,6,9 – us UMI [621]
COMPUTERS AND FLUIDS – v1- 1973- – 5,6,9 – us UMI [000]
COMPUTERS AND GEOSCIENCES – v1- 1975- – 5,6,9 – us UMI [550]
COMPUTERS AND GRAPHICS – v1- 1975- – 5,6,9 – us UMI [073]
COMPUTERS AND HUMANITIES – v.1-12. 1966-78 – 5,6,9 – us UMI [000]
COMPUTERS AND INDUSTRIAL ENGINEERING – v1- 1977- – 5,6,9 – us UMI [000]
COMPUTERS AND MATHEMATICS WITH APPLICATIONS – v1- 1975- – 5,6,9 – us UMI [073]
COMPUTERS AND OPERATIONS RESEARCH – v1- 1974- – 5,6,9 – us UMI [073]
COMPUTERS AND STRUCTURES – v1- 1971- – 5,6,9 – us UMI [000]
COMPUTERS AND THE HISTORY OF ART : AN INTERNATIONAL JOURNAL PUBLISHED IN ASSOCIATION WITH CHART / ed by Vaughan, William – 9,5,1 – us Harwood [700]
COMPUTERS AND THE HUMANITIES – (1985-. 5,6,9) – v1-. 1966- – 1 – us UMI [000]
COMPUTERS AND THE HUMANITIES – v13-16. 1979-82 – 1,5,6 – sz Elsevier [073]
COMPUTERS AND THE SOCIAL SCIENCES – v1-. 1985- – 1,5,6,9 – us UMI [300]
COMPUTERS AND TRANSLATIONS – v1-. 1986- – 1,5,6,9 – us UMI [400]
COMPUTERS, ENVIRONMENT AND URBAN SYSTEMS – (Formerly: Urban Systems) – v1- 1975- – 5,6,9 – us UMI [304]
COMPUTERS IN ACCOUNTING *see* ACCOUNTING TECHNOLOGY
COMPUTERS IN BIOLOGY AND MEDICINE – v1- 1971- – 5,6,9 – us UMI [000]
COMPUTERS IN HEALTHCARE – v3-. 1982- – 1,5,6,9 – us UMI [073]
COMPUTERS IN HEALTHCARE *see* HEALTH MANAGEMENT TECHNOLOGY
COMPUTERS IN HOSPITALS – v.1-3. 1980-82 – 1,5,6,9 – us UMI [000]
COMPUTERS IN HUMAN BEHAVIOR – v1- 1986- – 5,6,9 – us UMI [073]
COMPUTERS IN HUMAN SERVICES / ed by Schoech, Dick – v1- 1985- – 1, 9 ($200.00 in US $280.00 outside hardcopy subsc) – us Haworth [000]
COMPUTERS IN INDUSTRY – v1-5. 1980-84 – 1,5,6,13 – sz Elsevier [073]
COMPUTERS IN MECHANICAL ENGINEERING: CIME – v1-. 1982- – 1,5,6,9 – us UMI [073]
COMPUTERS IN NURSING – v1-. 1983- – 1,5,6,9 – us UMI [073]
COMPUTERS IN PHYSICS / American Institute of Physics – v1- 1987- – 1,5,6 – us A.I.P. [530]
COMPUTERS IN THE SCHOOLS / ed by Johnson, D LaMont – v1- 1984- – 1, 9 ($200.00 in US $280.00 outside hardcopy subsc) – us Haworth [000]
COMPUTERWELT – v1- . 1986- – 1 – us UMI [073]
COMPUTERWOCHE – (1985-. 5,6,9) – v1-. 1974- – 1 – us UMI [510]
COMPUTERWORLD – 1983 – 1 – us UMI [073]
COMPUTERWORLD – (1985-. 5,6,9) – Australia. 1978- – 1 – us UMI [510]
COMPUTERWORLD – (1985-. 5,6,9) – Danmark.v1-. 1981- – 1 – us UMI [510]
COMPUTERWORLD – (1985-. 5,6,9) – Espana. v1-. 1981- – 1 – us UMI [510]
COMPUTERWORLD – (1985-. 5,6,9) – Japan. 1982- – 1 – us UMI [510]
COMPUTERWORLD – (1985-. 5,6,9) – Norge. 1983- – 1 – us UMI [510]
COMPUTERWORLD – Boston, MA. 1970-1980 – 24r – 1 – $1,200.00 – R04376 – us Library Micro [000]
COMPUTERWORLD – Hong Kong, China, Korea, Taiwan.1984- – 1,5,6,9 – us UMI [510]
COMPUTERWORLD – Mexico. v1-. 1980- – 1 – us UMI [510]
COMPUTERWORLD – Nederland. v1-. 1984- – 1 – us UMI [510]
COMPUTERWORLD – Schweiz.1985- – 1 – us UMI [510]
COMPUTERWORLD – Southeast Asia. v1-. 1984- – 1,5,6,9 – us UMI [510]
COMPUTERWORLD – Venezuela. v1-. 1985- – 1,5,6,9 – us UMI [510]
COMPUTE'S GAZETTE – v1-. 1983- – 1,5,6,9 – us UMI [073]
COMPUTING: ARCHIV FUER INFORMATIK UND NUMERIK – v.1-27, 1966-81. ISSN: 0010-485X – 1,5,6,9,13 – $130.00v – us UMI [000]
COMPUTING CANADA – (v1-13 1974-87 Can$550.00) – Willowdale. v1-21. 1974-95 – 1 – Can$115.00y – cn Micromedia [000]
COMPUTING NOW – (v1-7 1989/90 Can$37.00y) – North York. v1-12. 1983/84-1994/95 – 9 – Can$28.00y – cn Micromedia [000]
COMPUTING REVIEWS – (v.19-. 1978; 5,6,9) – v.1-. 1960- – 1 – us UMI [073]
COMPUTING SURVEYS – v.1-2. 1969-70. Continued as: A C M Computing Surveys – 1 – us UMI [073]
COMPUTING SURVEYS *see* ACM COMPUTING SURVEYS
COMPUTING SYSTEMS IN ENGINEERING – 1,5,69 – us UMI [000]
COMPUTING TEACHER – (1985-. 1,5,6) – v11-. 1983- – 9 – us UMI [370]
COMRADE – 1-4 2+4 (all publ). 1901-1905 – 12mf – 9 – $75.00 – us UPA [335]
COMRADE – Delhi. 1911-14.v.1-8. Lacking: 1911-12, v. 1-4. – 89mf – 8 – ne IDC [073]
THE COMRADE – Delhi. India. 1913-14 – 1 – uk Microform Academic [072]
THE COMRADE – New York. -m. Oct 1901-Dec 1904. (1 reel) – 1 – uk British Libr Newspaper [071]
COMRADE BILL / Cope, Robert K – [Cape Town: Stewart Printing, 1944?] – 1 – us Res Libr [960]
COMRADES OF THE ROAD, N.D / Andrews, Matthew T – 1 – 5.00 – us Baptist [240]
COMSTOCK CHRONICLE – Virginia City, NV. 1993 – 2+ r – 1 – $100.00 ($50.00y) – U04900 – us Library Micro [071]
Comstock, J H *see* THE SPIDER BOOK
COMSTOCK NEWS – Comstock, NE. -w. Aug. 1909-Dec. 1917; Jan. 1920- – 1 – us NE Hist [071]
Comtat, Paulin *see* NOTRE FRONTIERE
Comte, Auguste *see* DISCOURS D'OUVERTURE DU COURS DE PHILOSOPHIE POSITIVE
LE COMTE DE FRONTENAC / Lorin, Henri – Paris: Armand Colin, 1895. SEM105P31 – 6mf – 9 – Can$13.50 – cn Bibl Nat [971]
Comte, Florent le *see* CABINET DES SINGULARITES D'ARCHITECTURE, PEINTURE, SCULPTURE, ET GRAVEURE
Comte, Gustave *see* LA SEMAINE
LES COMTES DE RIMOUSKI, DE MATANE ET DE TEMISCOUATA: EXPLORATION SPECIALE / Buies, Arthur – Quebec: Imprime par Belleau, 1890. 00342. (Pre-1900 Canadiana) – 9 – cn C.I.H.M. [971]
COMTE'S PHILOSOPHY OF THE SCIENCES : BEING AN EXPOSITION OF THE PRINCIPLES OF THE COURS DE PHILOSOPHIE POSITIVE OF AUGUSTE COMTE / Lewes, George Henry – London: H.G. Bohn, 1853 – 1 roll – 1 – 1-55879-760-2 – uk Libr Preservation [190]
COMUNAS ARGENTINAS – (Includes c.1: v.1.no.1 1948:July) – 1 – CSUXADN3435-S – us Hoover Inst Photo [972]
LA COMUNE – Philadelphia, PA, 1911-1915 – 1r – 1 – us I.H.R.C. [978]
COMUNICACION SOBRE LA ESCULTURA DE JUAN MARTINEZ MONTANES, "SAN JERONIMO PENITENTE" EXISTENTE EN EL CONVENTO DE CLARISAS DE LLERENA / Lepe de la Camara, Jose Maria – Badajoz: Dip. Provincial, 1970. Sep. REE – 1 – sp Bibl Santa Ana [240]
Comunicaciones *see* LINEAS DE AUTOBUSES
COMUNICACOES DO ISER – Rio de Janeiro: Comunicacoes do ISER. v1 n1-9 n39. may 1982-1990 – 2r – us Res Libr [972]
COMUNIDAD DE LABRADORES. ORDENANZAS DE LA COMUNIDAD DE LABRADORES DE VILLAFRANCA DE LOS BARROS / Villafranca de los Barros – Villafranca de los Barros: Impresor Bolanos, 1937 – 1 – sp Bibl Santa Ana [946]
Comunidad de Regantes de Badajoz. Canal Montijo *see* ORDENANZAS Y REGLAMENTOS
Comunidad de regantes de Badajoz por el Canal de Lobon *see* ORDENANZAS Y REGLAMENTOS PARA EL SINDICATO Y JURADO E RIEGO
Comunidad de regantes de la margen derecha del rio Salor *see* ORDENANZAS Y REGLAMENTOS DE LA...
Comunidad de regantes de Merida *see* ORDENANZAS Y REGLAMENTOS
Comunidad de Regantes de Montijo *see* ORDENANZAS Y REGLAMENTOS
COMUNIDAD DE REGANTES DE MONTIJO. CANAL DE MONTIJO (BADAJOZ). ORDENANZAS Y REGLAMENTOS – Badajoz: Imp. Barrena, 1964 – sp Bibl Santa Ana [340]

COMUNIDAD DE REGANTES. ORDENANZAS / Navasfrias (Salamanca) – Caceres: Edit. Extremadura, 1970 – 1 – sp Bibl Santa Ana [060]
LA COMUNION ENTRE LOS INDIOS AMERICANOS / Bayle, Constantino – Madrid: Missionalia Hispanica, 1944 – 1 – sp Bibl Santa Ana [240]
LAS COMUNIONES EN LA ESPANA ROJA / Bayle, Constantino – Burgos: Razon y Fe, 1939 – 1 – sp Bibl Santa Ana [240]
EL COMUNISMO EN ESPANA. CINCO ANOS EN EL PARTIDO : SU ORGANIZACION Y SUS MISTERIOS / Bayle, Constantino & Karl, Mauricio – Madrid, 2nd ed 1931; Madrid: Razon y Fe, 1932 – 1 – sp Bibl Santa Ana [320]
COMUNISMO O JUSTICIALISMO / Badanelli, Pedro – Santa Fe, Argentina: Universidad Nacional del Litoral, 2nd ed 1951 – 1 – CSUXAJA7213-B – us Hoover Inst Photo [320]
COMUNISMO O JUSTICIALISMO : CON UNA CARTA DE PERON AL AUTOR PEDRO BADANELLI / Badanelli, Pedro – [Buenos Aires?: M. Guemes], 3rd ed 1971 – 1 – CSUXAJA7227-B – us Hoover Inst Photo [320]
O COMUNITARIO – Nanuque, Brazil. Oct-Dec 1968; May 1969 – 1 – bl Biblioteca [072]
Comyn, T de *see* STATE OF THE PHILIPPINE ISLANDS
Comyns, John *see* A DIGEST OF THE LAWS OF ENGLAND
CON LA VOZ DEL CORAZON / Quintero Carrasco, J – Fregenal: Imprenta Angel Verde, 1962 – sp Bibl Santa Ana [810]
CON LO QUE TENGO A BORDO (MECANOGRAFIADO) / Belloso Rodriguez, Pedro – 1975 – 1 – sp Bibl Santa Ana [810]
CON PERON EN EL EXILIO : LO QUE NADIE SABIA! / Barrios, Americo – [Buenos Aires: Editorial Treinta Dias, 1964] – 1 – CSUXADP4743-B – us Hoover Inst Photo [320]
LOS CON RAZON OLVIDADOS / Sanchez Arjona, Vicente – Sevilla: Imprenta Zamb, Tomo 1. 1955 – 1 – sp Bibl Santa Ana [810]
CON SAFOS – Los Angeles, CA. 1968-69 – 1r – 1 BR02377 – $50.00 – us Library Micro [071]
CON SAFOS – Riverside, CA. 1968-1969 – 1r – 1 – $50.00 – R03411 – us Library Micro [071]
Conac, G *see* LA FONCTION PUBLIQUE AUX ETATS-UNIS
Conan, Laure *see*
- ELISABETH SETON
- L'OUBLIE
- SILHOUETTES CANADIENNES

Conant, C A *see* TH INTERNATIONAL LAW OF BILLS AND CHECKS
Conant, H C *see* POPULAR HISTORY OF THE TRANSLATION OF THE HOLY SCRIPTURES INTO THE ENGLISH TONGUE
Conant, Thomas *see* UPPER CANADA SKETCHES
Conant, William C *see* NARRATIVES OF REMARKABLE CONVERSIONS AND REVIVAL INCIDENTS
Conard, Howard L *see* HISTORY OF MILWAUKEE COUNTY AND CITY
Concatti, Rolando *see*
- FIN DE LA ECONOMIA PERONISTA?
- NUESTRA OPCION POR EL PERONISMO

A CONCEICAO : FOLHA INDEPENDENTE DEDICADA AOS INTERESSES DO MUNICIPIO – Cidade da Conceicao, 21 Oct 1921; Jan-Mar, May-Sep, Nov-Dec 1934; Jan, Mar-Apr, Jul-Sep, Nov-Dec 1935; Jan-Feb, Apr, Sep-Dec 1936; Feb-May, Jul-Nov 1937; 30 Aug 1938 – 1,5,6 – bl Biblioteca [072]
CONCEICAO DO SERRO : ORGAM OFICIAL DO MUNICIPIO – Cidade da Conceicao, 20 Mar 1904-12 Feb 1905 – 1,5,6 – bl Biblioteca [072]
CONCENTRACION NACIONAL DE LA FALANGES FEMENINAS EN HONOR DEL CAUDILLO Y DEL EJERCITO ESPANOL / Falange Espanola Tradicionalista y de las Juntas Ofensivas Nacional-Sindicalistas. Seccion Femenina – Medina del Campo, 1939. Fiche W816. (Blodgett Collection of Spanish Civil War Pamphlets) – 9 – us H.U. College Libr [946]
CONCENTRATION CAMPS IN POLAND DURING WORLD WAR 2 PAMPHLET COLLECTION – 1944-1955 – 1 – CSUXANQ3153-B – us Hoover Inst Photo [360]
CONCENTRIC AND ECCENTRIC STRENGTH DIFFERENCES IN THE LEAD AND BACK LEGS OF DIVISION 1 COLLEGE LEVEL FENCERS / Casey, Kevin M – 1994 – 1mf – $4.00 – us Microform Publ [612]
CONCEPCIONES MODERNAS SOBRE LA TEORIA...CIVILES, COMERCIALES Y FINANCIERAS / Cock, V – Bogota, n.d. – 1mf – 1 – ILM-3713/1 – ne IDC [327]
CONCEPT OF INTERNATIONAL ORGANIZATION / ed by Abi-Saab, Georges – 1981 – 245p – 9 – 92-3-101742-X – fr UNESCO [060]
THE CONCEPT OF MISSION IN THE ROMAN CATHOLIC CHURCH IN LIGHT OF VATICAN 2 / Lindell, CG – 1967 – 1 – us A.T.L.A. [240]
CONCEPT OF SARASVATI (IN VEDIC LITERATURE) / Airi, Raghunath – 1st ed. Rohtak: Rohtak Co-operative Print & Pub Society, [New Delhi]: exclusively distributed by Munshiram Manoharlal Publ, c1977 – us Res Libr [490]
THE CONCEPT OF THE OBJECTIVE AND LIBERTARIANISM / Alcott, Blake – 1971. 8p – 9 – 1.00f – at Libertarian Micro [320]
CONCEPTION AND DEVELOPMENT OF POETRY IN ZULU / Vilakazi, B W – [Johannesburg] 1937 – us Res Libr [490]
LA CONCEPTION DU MARIAGE D'APRES LES JURISTES ROMAINES / Volterra, Edoardo – Padova, 'La Garangola,' 1940. 66 p. LL-4204 – 1 – us L of C Photodup [340]
THE CONCEPTION OF GOD : A PHILOSOPHICAL DISCUSSION CONCERNING THE NATURE OF THE DIVINE IDEA AS A DEMONSTRABLE REALITY / Royce, Josiah et al – New York: Macmillan, 1897 – 1mf – 9 – 0-8370-4991-1 – 1985-2991 – us A.T.L.A. [210]
THE CONCEPTION OF IMMORTALITY / Royce, Josiah – Boston, New York: Houghton Mifflin, 1900. (The Ingersoll Lecture, 1899) – 1 – us U.W. Library [210]
CONCEPTO DEL FEDERALISMO EN LA GUERRA Y EN LA REVOLUCION; CONFERENCIA PRONUNCIADA EN EL CINE COLISEUM DE BARCELONA, EL DIA 7 DE FEBRERO DE 1937 / Lopez, Juan – Barcelona, 1937? Fiche W1006. (Blodgett Collection of Spanish Civil War Pamphlets) – 9 – us H.U. College Libr [946]
CONCERNED CITIZENS OF PALAU : A PETITION TO THE HON ADRIAN P WINKEL, HIGH COMMISSIONER OF THE TRUST TERRITORY OF THE PACIFIC – Feb 19, 1978 – 1mf – 9 – $1.50 – LLMC 82-100G, Title 15 – us L.L.M.C. [323]
CONCERNING A VOW / Broughton, Rhoda – British Fiction Archive: Unit 4 – 9 – uk Bell [830]
CONCERNING THE TRUE RELIGION (CCC131) / Gutzlaff, Karl Friedrich August – (In Chinese) – [s.l: s.n, 1837] – 1r – 1 – 1984-B500 – us A.T.L.A. [240]
CONCERNING THEM THAT ARE ASLEEP / Gorham, Barlow Weed – 1885 – 9 – us A.T.L.A. [240]
CONCERT FUR DAS PIANOFORTE / Raff, J – Leipzig: C F W Siegel, [1873] – 1 – us Sibley [780]
CONCERT FUR VIOLINE; MIT BEGLEITUNG DES ORCHESTERS, OP. 77 / Brahms, Johannes – (Score) – Berlin: N Simrock, 1879 – 1 – us Sibley [780]
LE CONCERT INTERROMPU. OPERA COMIQUE EN UN ACTE / Berton, H – Paris: Freres Gaveaux, 1802 – 1 – us Sibley [780]
CONCERT POUR LE VIOLONCELL : EDITION POUR VIOLONCELLE ET PIANO / Ritter, P – (Manuscript) – London?, 1904? – 1 – us Sibley [780]
CONCERT POUR LE VIOLONCELL : EDITION POUR VIOLONCELLE ET PIANO / Ritter, P – (Manuscript) – London?, 1904? – 1 – us Sibley [780]
CONCERT-GOER – v1-220. Mar 1897-Jan 1903 – 1 – 775.00 – us Opus [073]
CONCERTI GROSSI [NOS. 1-6] CON DUE VIOLINE, VIOLA E VIOLONCELLE DO CONCERTINO OBBLIGATI, E DUE ALTRI VIOLINI E BASSO DI CONCERTO GROSSE... / Geminiani, Francesco – Amsterdam: M C LeCene. 7pts. 1735? – 1 – us Sibley [780]
CONCERTI GROSSI [NOS. 7-12] CON DUE VIOLINI, VIOLA E VIOLONCELLO DI CONCERTINO OBBLIGATI, E DUE ALTRI VIOLINI E BASSE DI CONCERTO GROSSO...OP. 2 / Geminiani, Francesco – (7 pts) – London: Walsh, 174- – 1 – us Sibley [780]
CONCERTI MUSICALI A DUE, TRE, W QUATTRO VOCI, CON UNA MESSA A QUATTRO CONCERTATA, ET INTROITI, PANGE LINGUA A QUATTRO DA CAPELLA : OPERA TERZA DEL SIG. GIO. BATTISTA BERIA... / Beria, G B – (Parts) – Milano: C Camagno, 1650 – 1 – us Sibley [780]
CONCERTO, [7E] POUR LA FLUTE. [OP. 22?] / Hoffmeister, Franz A – (Parts) – Paris: Sieber, 180-? – 1 – us Sibley [780]
A CONCERTO FOR THE GRAND OR SMALL PIANOFORTE WITH ACCOMPANIMENT...AIR OF THE "PLOUGH BOY", OP. 15 / Dussek, J L – London: Broderip & Wilkinson, No 13, Haymarket, [179-?] – 1mf – 9 – us Sibley [780]
A CONCERTO FOR THE VIOLINCELLO. WITH ACCOMPANIMENT FOR 2VLNS/TENOR/BASS/2FL/2HNS / Paxton, S – (8pts) – London: Goulding, 179- – 1 – us Sibley [780]
CONCERTO (NO 1) FOR PIANOFORTE, OP. 1 / Griffin, G – London: Printed for the author by Clementi & Co, 26 Cheapside, [between 1801 and 1830] – 1 – us Sibley [780]
CONCERTO NO. 1, OP. 23 / Tschaikovsky, PI – (From binder's collection made up by owner) – Hamburg: Rahter, [18–] – 1 – us Sibley [780]
CONCERTO NO. 2 IN B MINOR FOR VIOLIN AND ORCHESTRA, OP. 36 / Nachez, T – (Violino principale part) – Manuscript, 1908 – 1 – us Sibley [780]
CONCERTO [NO. 9]...OP. 50 / Dussek, J L – Leipsic: Breitkopf & Hartel, 184- – 1 – us Sibley [780]
CONCERTO PER IL ORGANO O CEMBALO / Hook, James – 1799. Composer's holograph score for organ and orchestra. MUSIC 1873, Item 3 – 1 – us L of C Photodup [780]
CONCERTO, PIANO, OP. 14, F MAJOR / Dussek, J L – (Parts) – Naderman, ca 1796 – 1 – us Sibley [780]
CONCERTO POUR CLAVECIN OU FORTEPIANO, OP. 17 / Dussek, J L – (Fortepiano part only) – London: Lavenu & Mitchell, 179- – 1 – us Sibley [780]
CONCERTO QUATRIEME POUR PIANO / Viotti, Giovanni B – Ms, 177- – 1 – us Sibley [780]
CONCERTO, THIRD GRAND IN C / Dussek, J L – London: Breoderip & Wilkinson, 1795 – 1 – us Sibley [780]
CONCERTS CHAMPETRES POUR LES MUSETTES, VIELES... OP. 3 / Chedeville, E P – (Musette ou vielle part only) – Paris: Gland, 1740 – 1 – us Sibley [780]
LA CONCESSON EN DROIT INTERNATIONAL / Develle, P – Paris, 1936 – 3mf – 1 – ILM-3020/1 – ne IDC [327]
Concha, Antonio *see* CONTESTACION AL MANIFIESTO PUBLICADO...MAURICIO CERESOLES...PASADAS ELECIONES..
Concha Castaneda, Juan de la *see* DISCURSOS LEIDOS...CIENCIAS MORALES Y POLITICAS
Concha, J V *see* LAS NEGOCIACIONES DIPLOMATICAS DEL CANAL DE PANAMA
CONCHOLOGIA ICONICA = ILLUSTRATIONS OF THE SHELLS OF MOLLUSCOUS ANIMALS / ed by Reeve, L A – London, 1843-1878. 20v – 349mf – 2168/2 – ne IDC [590]
CONCHOLOGIA INDICA / Hanley, S & Theobald, W – London. 1876. Includes: On the dates of Hanley and Theobald's Conchologia Indica. (Journal and Proceedings of the Asiatic Society of Bengal. n.s. 1926, 1927). v. 22. BZ-566 2 – 8 – ne IDC [590]
CONCHOLOGIA SYSTEMATICA, OR / Reeve, LA – Complete System of Conchology. 2167 2. 2 v. 1841-1842 – 8 – ne IDC [590]
A CONCHOLOGICAL DICTIONARY OF THE BRITISH ISLANDS / Turton, W – London, 1819 – 6mf – ne IDC [590]
THE CONCHOLOGICAL ILLUSTRATIONS / Sowerby, G B – Z 797 2. 1832-1844 – 8 – ne IDC [590]
THE CONCHOLOGICAL MAGAZINE – Kyoto, 1907-1909. v1-3 – 41mf – Z-895/2 – ne IDC [590]
A CONCHOLOGICAL MANUAL / Sowerby, G B – Z 798 2. 1839 – 8 – ne IDC [590]
THE CONCHOLOGICAL MISCELLANY / Hanley, S – Z-563 2. 1854-1858 – 8 – ne IDC [590]
CONCHOLOGISCHE MITTHEILUNGEN *see* NOVITATES CONCHOLOGICAE
CONCHOLOGIST – (Continued as: Journal of Malacology. London, 1894-1902. v3-9) – London, 1891-1893. v1-2 – 27mf – 5623/2 – ne IDC [590]
CONCHOLOGY / Perry, G – The Natural History of Shells. Z-705 2. 1811 – 8 – ne IDC [590]
Conchudo, J *see* CARTA AL AUTOR DE LA ORACION APOLOGETICA POR LA ESPENA Y SU MERITO LITERARIO
CONCHYLIOLOGIE FRANCAISE. LES COQUILLES DES EAUX DOUCES ET SAUMATRES DE FRANCE / Locard, A – Z-625 2. 1893 – 8 – ne IDC [590]
CONCHYLIOLOGIE FRANCAISE. LES COQUILLES TERRESTRES DE FRANCE / Locard, A – Z-626 2. 1894 – 8 – ne IDC [590]
CONCIENCIA OBRERA Y FRACASO PERONISTA / Ghioldi, Americo – Buenos Aires: Parlamento Libre, 1951 – 1 – CSUXADJ3447-B – us Hoover Inst Photo [320]
LE CONCIL DE TURIN / Babut, E C – Paris, 1904 – 6mf – 8 – Dfl25.00 – ne Slangenburg [240]
CONCIL UND JESUITSIMUS : BRENNENDE FRAGEN ZUR ORIENTIERUNG FUER DAS DEUTSCHE VOLK – Stuttgart: Vogler & Beinhauer, 1870 – 1mf – 9 – 0-8370-8549-7 – 1986-2549 – us A.T.L.A. [240]
LE CONCILE DE TURIN : ESSAI SUR L'HISTOIRE DES EGLISES PROVENCALES AU VE SIECLE ET SUR LES ORIGINES DE LA MONARCHIE ECCLESIASTIQUE ROMAINE (417-450) / Babut, E C – Paris: A. Picard, 1904 – 1mf – us A.T.L.A. [240]
LE CONCILE DU VATICAN : SON HISTOIRE ET SES CONSEQUENCES POLITIQUES ET RELIGIEUSES / Pressense, Edmond de – Paris: Sandoz et Fischbacher, 1872 – 2mf – 9 – 0-8370-8933-6 – 1986-2933 – us A.T.L.A. [240]
CONCILIA AEVI KAROLINI (MGH LEGES 2C: 2.BD) – 1906-1908 – Dfl95.00 – ne Slangenburg [240]
CONCILIA AEVI MERIVINGICI (MGH LEGES 2C: 1.BD) – 1893 – Dfl30.00 – ne Slangenburg [240]
CONCILIA ANTIQUA GALLIAE : OPERA ET STUDIO / Sirmondi, J – Lutetiae Parisiorum Tomi 1-3 1629 – 91mf – 9 – Dfl319.00 – ne Slangenburg [941]
CONCILIA GALLIAE NARBONENSIS / Baluzius, Stephanus – Parisiis, 1668 – ne Slangenburg [240]
CONCILIA MAGNAE BRITANNIAE ET HIBERNIAE A SYNODO VEROLAMIENSI A.D. 446 AD LONDINENSEM A.D. 1717 A DAVIDE WILKINS COLLECTA – Londini. v1-4. 1737 – Dfl501.00 – ne Slangenburg [240]
CONCILIA OMNIA, TUM GENERALIA, TUM PROVINCIALIA ATQUE PARTICULARIA / Surius, L et al – Coloniae Agrippinae. Tomi 1-4. 1567 – 101mf – 8 – Dfl354.00 – ne Slangenburg [240]
CONCILIA PROVINCIAE TURONENSIS / Travers, Nicolas – (T. 4: annees/years 1400-1499; T. 5: annees/years 1501-1713) – 18th cent – 1 – F691.68 – fr Armell [944]
CONCILIABULO DE BASILEA / Caceres, Diego de – S.l., s.i., s.a. Hacia 1641 – 1 – sp Bibl Santa Ana [946]
A CONCILIACAO – '(s.l.')-Sao Luiz, Brazil. 27 Sep-29 Nov 1856 – 1,5,6 – bl Biblioteca [072]
O CONCILIADOR – Ouro Preto, 2 Jan-19 Dec 1851 – 1,5,6 – bl Biblioteca [072]
O CONCILIADOR – Rio de Janeiro, Brazil. 5 Abr 1828 – 1 – bl Biblioteca [072]
O CONCILIADOR DO MARANHAO – '(s.l.')-Sao Luis, Brazil. 15 Apr-May, Nov-Dec 1821. Jan 1822-Jul 1823 – 1,5,6 – bl Biblioteca [072]
O CONCILIADOR DO REINO UNIDO – Rio de Janeiro, 1 Mar-28 Apr 1821 – 1,5,6 – bl Biblioteca [072]
LE CONCILIATEUR : NOUVELLES DU JOUR – Paris: Bureau du journal. v1 n18-39. jul 7-28 1848 – us Res Libr [073]
CONCILIATION COURTS REVIEW *see* FAMILY AND CONCILIATION COURTS REVIEW
CONCILIATIONES LOCORUM SCRIPTURAE, QUI SPECIE TENVS INTER SE PUGNARE UIDENTUR, CENTURIAE DUAE.. / Althamer, A – Noribergae, 1561 – 1 – us U.W. Library [240]
CONCILIATIONIS ECCLESIAE ARMENAE CUM ROMANA EX IPSIS ARMENORUM PATRUM ET DOCTORUM TESTIMONIIS IN DUAS PARTES / Galanus, Clemens – Historialem et controversialem divisae.... 2 pts. in 3 v. 1658-90 – 1 – us A.T.L.A. [240]

IL CONCILIO 2 DI LEONE... / Franchi, Antonino – Madrid: Graf. Calleja, 1966 – 1 – sp Bibl Santa Ana [946]

EL CONCILIO 3 EMERITENSE / Garcia de la Fuente, P Arturo – Badajoz, 1932 – 1 – sp Bibl Santa Ana [946]

Concilio, Januarius de *see* THE KNOWLEDGE OF MARY

CONCILIO Y VIDA CRISTIANA / Aradillas Agudo, Antonio – Madrid: Sociedad de Educacion. Atenas, 1966 – sp Bibl Santa Ana [240]

CONCILIUM BASILEENSE SCRIPTORES – Tom. 1-4. Vindobonae, 1857; Basileae, 1935 – Dfl445.00 – ne Slangenburg [240]

CONCIO AD CLERUM: A SERMON DELIVERED IN THE CHAPEL OF YALE COLLEGE, 10 SEP 1828 / Taylor, Nathaniel – 1842 – 9 – us A.T.L.A. [240]

CONCIONERO DE JUAN PERON Y EVA PERON / ed by Dario Alessandro, Julio – [Buenos Aires]: Grupo Editor de Buenos Aires, [1966] – 1 – CSUXADP3860-B – us Hoover Inst Photo [320]

CONCISE ACCOUNT OF THE LATE REV. NOAH DAVIS / Davis, Noah – 38p – 1 – 5.00 – us Baptist [240]

A CONCISE ACCOUNT OF THE RELIGIOUS SOCIETY OF FRIENDS, COMMONLY CALLED QUAKERS : EMBRACING A SKETCH OF THEIR CHRISTIAN DOCTRINES AND PRACTICES / Evans, Thomas – Philadelphia: For sale at Friends' Book Store, 1872 – 1mf – 9 – 0-8370-8896-8 – 1986-2896 – us A.T.L.A. [240]

A CONCISE AND PRACTICAL TREATISE OF THE LAW OF VENDORS AND PURCHASERS OF ESTATES / Sugden, Edward Burtneshaw – 14th ed.; 8th American ed., by J.C. Perkins. Philadelphia: Kay, 1873. 2v – 1 – us L of C Photodup [340]

A CONCISE HISTORY OF KEHUKEE BAPTIST ASSOCIATION, N.C / Biggs, Joseph et al – PTS. 1 and 2. 1803, 1834 – 1 – 10.64 – us Baptist [240]

A CONCISE HISTORY OF THE INTRODUCTION OF PROTESTANTISM INTO MISSISSIPPI AND THE SOUTHWEST / Jones, John G – 1772-1817 – 1 – 10.29 – us Baptist [240]

A CONCISE HISTORY OF THE KETOCTON BAPTIST ASSOCIATION / Fristoe, William – 1808 – 1 – 5.81 – us Baptist [240]

CONCISE LIVES OF FAMOUS IYASES OF BENIN / Egharevba, Jacob U – 2nd ed. [Lagos: s.n., 1947] – 1 – us Res Libr [920]

A CONCISE STATEMENT OF THE LAW OF PARTNERSHIP / Brown, B F – Indianapolis, 1871. 32 p. LL-1456 – 1 – us L of C Photodup [340]

A CONCISE SUMMARY OF THE LAW OF LIBEL AS IT AFFECTS THE PRESS / Henderson, William Graham – Rutherford, NJ: Chemical Bank Note Co., 1915. 120p. LL-242 – 1 – us L of C Photodup [340]

A CONCISE TREATISE ON THE PRINCIPLES OF EQUITY PLEADING / Heard, Franklin Fiske – Boston: Boston Book Co., 1889. 217p. LL-535 – 1 – us L of C Photodup [340]

A CONCISE TREATISE ON THE PRINCIPLES OF EQUITY PLEADING. / Heard, Franklin Fiske – Boston: Soule and Bugbee, 1882. 217p. LL-1300 – 1 – us L of C Photodup [340]

EL CONCISO – Ano 1810 (Diciembre)-1814 (Mayo) – 132mf – 9 – sp Cultura [946]

EL CONCISO – Cadiz, Spain. 1 Apr-27 Jun 1811.-w. 32 ft – 1 – uk British Libr Newspaper [072]

THE CONCLAVE OF PHYSICIANS / Harvey, G – M 366. 1683 – 9 – ne IDC [610]

CONCLAVE THESAURI MAGNAE ARTIS MUSICAE.. / Vogt, Mauritius – 1719 – 2 – us Sibley [780]

CONCLUSIONS / Berliner, Emile – New York:Kaufman, 1902 – 1mf – 9 – 0-8370-2292-4 – 1985-0292 – us A.T.L.A. [360]

CONCLUSIONS DE MONSIEUR LE PROCUREUR GENERAL DE ROY AU PARLEMENT D'AIX DU 11 SEP 1731 AU SUJET DU PROCES D'ENTRE LE PERE GIRARD, JESUITE, CATHERINE CADIERE; LE PERE CADIERE DOMINICAIN, LE PRETRE CADIERE ET LE PERE NICOLAS CARME DECHAUSSE – S. 1. 1731 – 9 – fr Hachette [360]

CONCLUSIONS OF THE GOVERNMENT ... ON THE REPORT AND RECOMMENDATIONS OF THE TECHNICAL COMMITTEE FOR THE ASSESSMENT OF THE VIABILITY OF THE EXISTING PRIMARY SCHOOLS ... / Nigeria. Cross River State – Calabar, 1985 – 1mf – 9 – DE-457/1 – ne IDC [370]

CONCLUSIONS OF THE GOVERNMENT ... ON THE REPORT OF THE ADMINISTRATIVE INQUIRY INTO ALLEGATIONS OF MISMANAGEMENT IN THE SCHOOL OF BASIC STUDIES, AKAMKPA / Nigeria. Cross River State – Calabar, 1985 – 1mf – 9 – DE-458/1 – ne IDC [370]

CONCORD = BAPTIST ASSOCIATIONS. TENNESSEE – 1866, 1900, 1957-79 – 1 – 58.32 – us Baptist [240]

CONCORD – Salisbury. Apr. June 1954-Dec. 1957 – 1 – 35.00r – us Hoover Inst Photo [073]

CONCORD BAPTIST CHURCH. ANDERSON COUNTY. SOUTH CAROLINA : CHURCH RECORDS – 1963-72 – 1 – 6.17 – us Baptist [240]

CONCORD BAPTIST CHURCH. BRENTWOOD, TENNESSEE : CHURCH RECORDS – 1804-1901 – 1r – 1 – $16.47 – us Baptist [240]

CONCORD BAPTIST CHURCH. CHATTANOOGA, TENNESSEE : CHURCH RECORDS – 1848-72 – 1 – 5.00 – us Baptist [240]

CONCORD BAPTIST CHURCH. MADISON, FLORIDA : CHURCH RECORDS – 1841-68 – 1 – 6.84 – us Baptist [240]

CONCORD BAPTIST CHURCH. ROSE HILL ASSOCIATION. DUPLIN COUNTY. NORTH CAROLINA : CHURCH RECORDS – 1813-80 – 1 – 17.46 – us Baptist [240]

CONCORD BAPTIST CHURCH. ST LOUIS, MISSOURI : CHURCH RECORDS – 1955-60 – 1 – 18.63 – us Baptist [240]

CONCORD GAZETTE – Concord. New Hampshire. 1806-1819 – 1,3 – us Readex [071]

CONCORD HERALD – Concord. N.H. 1790-94 – 1,3 – us Readex [071]

CONCORD LECTURES ON PHILOSOPHY : COMPRISING OUTLINES OF ALL THE LECTURES AT THE CONCORD SUMMER SCHOOL OF PHILOSOPHY IN 1882, WITH AN HISTORICAL SKETCH / Harris, William Torrey; ed by Bridgman, Raymond L – Cambridge, Mass.: Moses King, c1883 – 1mf – 9 – us A.T.L.A. [100]

Concord, New Hampshire. Concord Baptist Church *see* RECORDS

A CONCORDANCE AND WORD-LISTS TO DYLAN THOMAS' UNDER MILK WOOD / ed by Farringdon, Michael G – (Keyed to New Directions ed (US) and to Everyman pb of J M Dent (UK). Printed preface, introd and 5 appendices) – 1982 – 3mf – 11 – $41.00 – uk Ariel [420]

A CONCORDANCE AND WORD-LISTS TO HENRY FIELDING'S JOSEPH ANDREWS / Farringdon, Michael G – (Keyed to Wesleyan ed. Printed preface, introd and 6 appendices) – 1984 – 17mf – 11 – $72.00 – uk Ariel [420]

A CONCORDANCE AND WORD-LISTS TO HENRY FIELDING'S SHAMELA / ed by Farringdon, Michael G – (Keyed to the Augustan Reprint Society's facsimile of the 2nd ed (1741). Printed preface, introd and 3 appendices) – 1982 – 4mf – 11 – $46.00 – uk Ariel [420]

CONCORDANCE LATINE DES PSEUDEPIGRAPHES D'ANCIEN TESTAMENT : CONCORDANCE. CORPUS DES TEXTES. INDICES – SERIES A-B: FORMAE ET LEMMATA / Denis, A-M – 1993 – 5mf – 9 – Bf9,950.00 – 2-503-50343-8 – be Brepols [220]

A CONCORDANCE OF PARALLELS / Crutwell, Clement – 1790 – 1 – us A.T.L.A. [240]

A CONCORDANCE TO GREGORY OF NYSSA / Fabricus, Cajus & Ridings, Daniel – 1989 – 31mf – 9 – sw G.U. [450]

CONCORDANCE TO THE DIGEST JURISTS – 84mf – 9 – us UMI [340]

A CONCORDANCE TO THE OLNEY HYMNS OF JOHN NEWTON AND WILLIAM COWPER / Newton, John & Cowper, William; ed by Kirkham, E Bruce – (348 hymns and 3 poems of the 1779 ed with concordance to the 61,978 words in the text) – Muncie, IN: Heather Press, 1983 – 6mf – 9 – $19.95 – 0-912459-01-8 – us Heather [780]

A CONCORDANCE TO THE PLYMOUTH COLLECTION OF HYMNS AND TUNES / Beecher, Henry Ward; ed by Kirkham, E Bruce – (1431 hymns of the 1855 ed. Preface, six indexes and concordance to the 144,768 significant words) – Muncie, IN: Heather Press, 1984 – 16mf – 9 – $39.95 – 0-912459-02-6 – us Heather [780]

CONCORDANCE TO THE POEMS OF DYLAN THOMAS – (Based on 1978 ed of Daniel Jones edition of Dylan Thomas: the Poems) – 5mf – 9 – $65.00 – us UMI [420]

CONCORDANCE TO THE SEPTUAGINT AND THE OTHER GREEK VERSIONS OF THE OLD TESTAMENT : VOLS 1-3 / Hatch, E & Redpath, H A – Oxford, 1897 – 102mf – 8 – ne Slangenburg [220]

CONCORDANCES TO THE MAJOR WRITINGS OF WILLIAM HAZLITT – (Characters of Shakespear's Plays: $95.00. Round Table: $95.00. Table Talk: $95.00. Includes printed guides. Also available on CD-ROM and 3 1/4-inch disks in Adobe Acrobat format) – Each concordance reproduces ca 1,000 printed pages. Mf bound within guides. – 9 – us UMI [420]

CONCORDANCES TO THE NOVELS OF VIRGINIA WOOLF / Woolf, Virginia; ed by Haule, James M & Smith, Philip H O – (Based on Harcourt Brace Jovanovich editions. Between the Acts 6mf $70; Jacob's Room 6mf $70; Mrs. Dalloway 7mf $70; Night and Day 14mf $70; Orlando 8mf $70; To the Lighthouse 7mf $70; The Voyage Out 12mf $70; The Waves 14mf $70; The Years 11mf $70) – 85mf – 9 – $630.00 complete collection – us UMI [420]

CONCORDANCES TO THE WORKS OF WILLIAM FAULKNER / Faulkner, William; ed by Faulkner Concordance Advisory Board – (Absalom, Absalom! 12mf $85; A Fable 5mf $95; As I Lay Dying 5mf $50; Go Down, Moses 10mf $75; Intruder in the Dust 7mf $60; Light in August 12mf $85; Pylon 8mf $65; Requiem for a Nun 6mf $55; The Sound and the Fury 10mf $75; The Wild Palms 9mf $70) – us UMI [420]

CONCORDANCIE, DAT IS : DE GHELIJCKLUYDENDE PLAETSEN, DER HEYLIGER SCHRIFT, BY EEN VERGADERT / Hantboecxken, ofte – 1576 – 6mf – 9 – ne IDC [240]

CONCORDANTIAE AUGUSTINIANAE / Lenfant, Davidis – (Tomus Primus. Lutetiae Parisiorum 1656 42mf; Tomus Alter. Lutetiae Parisiorum 1665 41mf) – 8 – ne Slangenburg [240]

CONCORDANTIAE AUGUSTINIANAE. LABORE DAVIDIS LENFANT O.P. – Tomus Primus. Lutetiae Parisiorum 1656 42mf; Tomus Alter. Lutetiae Parisiorum 1665 41mf – 8 – ne Slangenburg [240]

CONCORDANTIAE BIBLIORUM VTRIUSQUE TESTAMENTI,... / Estienne, Robert – [Genevae], 1555 – 19mf – 9 – ne IDC [220]

CONCORDANTIAE IURIS CANONICI CUM LEGIBUS PARTITARUM... / Jimenez, Sebastian – Madrid: Juan de la Cuesta, 1611. 2nd parte – 1 – sp Bibl Santa Ana [946]

CONCORDANTIAE PARTICULORUM EBRAEOCHALDAICARUM VETERIS TESTAMENTI / Noldius, C – Ed. 2, with indices and other additions. Jena. 1734. BJ-412-16 1 – 9 – ne IDC [470]

CONCORDANTIAE VETERIS TESTAMENTI GRAECAE, EBRAEIS, VOCIBUS RESPONDENTES / Kircher, Konrad – 2v. 1607 – 1 – us A.T.L.A. [240]

CONCORDANTIE ENDE AENWYSINGHE DER VERNAEMSTER SPROKEN ALLER BYBELSCHER BOECKEN... / Sattler, M – N.p., n.d. – 2mf – 9 – ne IDC [240]

EEN CONCORDANTIE OFT REGISTER DER GANSCHER BIBEL... / Adam, Pastor – 1559 – 4mf – 9 – ne IDC [220]

CONCORDANTZ VND ZEIGER DER NAMHAFFTIGEN SPRUECH ALLER BIBLISCHEN BUECHER ALTS VND NEWS TESTAMENTS – N.p.[1540] – 4mf – 9 – ne IDC [220]

CONCORDANZ DER DEUTSCHEN NATIONAL-LITERATUR / ed by Berlepsch, H A – Leipzig: A Lehmann. 8v. 1859 – 1 – us U.W. Library [430]

LE CONCORDAT DE 1801. SES ORIGINES SON HISTOIRE / Mathieu, F D – H-552 2. 1904 – 8 – ne IDC [940]

LA CONCORDE – Journal historique, politique et litteraire. Haiti. mai 1821-juil 1822 – 1 – fr A.C.R.P.P. [073]

LA CONCORDE – L'Orignal, Ontario. 5 oct 1899 – 1r – 1 – Can$25.00 – cn Can Microfilming [072]

LA CONCORDE – Ottawa, Ontario. v1 n45. 25 mai 1912 – 1r – 1 – Can$25.00 – cn Can Microfilming [072]

LA CONCORDE – Trois-Rivieres, Canada. 2 mai 1879-2 mai 1884 – 3r – 1 – Can$60.00r – cn Can Microfilming [072]

CONCORDIA – Berlin, Leipzig, Bremen. 1849-50 – 1 – Dist. gw Mikrofilm – gw Misc Inst [943]

CONCORDIA – Neuendettelsau. v1-76. 1914-91 (complete) – 7r – 1 – ATLA S0394 – us A.T.L.A. [073]

CONCORDIA – Paris. v. 3, 5-21. Aug Sept 1897, Dec 1898-July 1914 – 1 – us NY Public [073]

CONCORDIA : ZEITSCHRIFT FUER ARBEITERFRAGE – Berlin, Leipzig, 1849-50; 1871-76 – 5r – 1 – gw Mikrofilm [072]

THE CONCORDIA – Chicago. v1-2. 1866-67 – 1r – 1 – £60.00 – uk Chadwyck [780]

CONCORDIA BAPTIST CHURCH. HAVANA, FLORIDA : CHURCH RECORDS – 1858-1917 – 1 – 14.94 – us Baptist [240]

Concordia Historical Institute. St. Louis *see* QUARTERLY

CONCORDIA INTELLIGENCER – Vidalia. La. 1843-44; 1850-52 – 1 – us UMI [071]

CONCORDIA JOURNAL – 1975-93 (complete) – 5r – 1 – ATLA S0623 – us A.T.L.A. [073]

Concordia Luthern Church, Hoisington, KS *see* RECORDS

CONCORDIA, ODER, DIE BEKENNTNISSCHRIFTEN DER EVANGELISCH-LUTHERISCHEN KIRCHE – (Includes indexes) – 11. Aufl. Basel: P Kober, 1898 – 2mf – 9 – 0-8370-8859-3 – 1986-2859 – us A.T.L.A. [240]

CONCORDIA THEOLOGICAL QUARTERLY – (v.44-. 1980- 5,6,9) – v.41-. 1977- – 1 – us UMI [073]

CONCORDIANTAE...GLOSSEMATIBUSQUE GREGORII LOPEZ / Jimenez, Sebastian – 1611 – 9 – 1.50f – sp Bibl Santa Ana [440]

CONCOURS D'ELOQUENCE SUR L'AGRICULTURE – Eloge de l'agriculture; ce qu'est l'art agricole au Canada: des moyens de l'y faire progresser. Hubert LaRue et trois autres. Quebec: A. Cote, 1879. 05246. (Pre-1900 Canadiana) – 9 – cn C.I.H.M. [630]

LES CONCOURS PUBLICS D'ARCHITECTURE – Paris, 1895-1914. 4 reels – 1 – $330.00 – us UPA [720]

CONCRETE CONSTRUCTION *see* ABERDEEN'S CONCRETE CONSTRUCTION

CONCRETE PRODUCTS – v16- 1918-. Continues: Cement Era – 1,5,6,9 – us UMI [690]

CONCURRENCE – 1969 (complete) – Inquire – 1 – ATLA S0884 – us A.T.L.A. [073]

CONCURRENCE AND DISSENT; SOME RECENT SUPREME COURT CASES / Prenner, Manuel – New York: Merrill, 1933. 243p. LL-1037 – 1 – us L of C Photodup [340]

DIE CONCURRENZ FUER ENTWUERFE ZUM NEUEN REICHSTAGSGEBAEUDE / Eggert, Hermann – O-242. 1882 – 9 – ne IDC [720]

Concurso hipico internacional (No oficial) *see* PROGRAMA GENERAL DEL CONCURSO HIPICO INTERNACIONAL

CONCURSO LITERARIO DE TRUJILLO ORGANIZADO POR LA COMISION DE FIESTAS PARA SOLUCIONAR LA INAUGURACION DEL MONUMENTO A PIZARRO, LEVAN TADO...VDA. DE D. CARLOS RUMSEY / Trujillo – Trujillo: Tip. de Sobrino de Benito Pena, 1928 – sp Bibl Santa Ana [946]

CONCURSO REGIONAL DE GANADOS QUE ORGANIZA LA JUNTA PROVINCIAL DE BADAJOZ EN REPRESENTACION DE LA ASOCIACION GENERAL DE GANADEROS DEL REINO QUE SE CELEBRARA EN DON BENITO...EN 1925 – Don Benito: Tip. de Trejo, 1925 – sp Bibl Santa Ana [946]

CONDADO DE LA GOMERA / Regulo Perez, Juan & Siete Iglesias, Marques de – Madrid, 1955 – 1 – sp Bibl Santa Ana [946]

Condamin, Albert *see* LE LIVRE D'ISAIE: TRADUCTION CRITIQUE AVEC NOTES ET COMMENTAIRES

Conde Berron, Felix see LIBRO PRIMERO. METODO SIMULTANEO DE LECTURA Y DIBUJO
Conde de Canilieros see BROZAS. LA ENCOMIENDA MAYOR
EL CONDE DE CANILLEROS / Valgoma y Diaz-Varela, Dalmiro de la – Madrid: Imp. y Editorial Maestre, 1972. B.R.A.H. 169. Cuaderno II. pp. 453-454 – 1 – sp Bibl Santa Ana [946]
CONDE DE CASTRALLA / Lopez de Ayala, Adelardo – 1856 – 9 – 1.50f – sp Bibl Santa Ana [820]
O CONDE DE LINHARES / Funchal, Agostinho de Sousa Coutinho – Lisboa, Typ: Bayard, 1908 – 1 – us U.W. Library [946]
EL CONDE DE MONTECRISTO / Dumas, Alexandre – 1867. Vicente Barrantes, trans – 9 – 1.50f – sp Bibl Santa Ana [830]
Conde, Louis 1 de Bourbon see
- PROTESTATION DE MOSEIGNEUR LE PRINCE DE CONDE
- REQUESTE PRESENTEE AU ROY PAR, MONSIEUR LE PRINCE DE CONDE: AC COMPAGNE D'UN GRAND NOMBRE DE SEIGNEURS GENTILS-HOMMES, & AUTRES QUI FONT PROFESSION DE LA RELIGION REFORMEE EN CE ROYAUME

Conde, Louis 1st Prince of Bourbon see DISCOURS VERITABLE DES PROPOS TENUS PAR MONSIEUR LE PRINCE DE CONDE, AUEC LES SEIGNEURS DEPUTEZ PAR LE ROY: CONTENANT LES CAUSES GUI ONT CONTRAINT LEDICT SEIGNEUR PRINCE & AUTRES DE SA COPAGNIE A PRENDRE LES ARMS
Conde, Prudencio see ETICA GENERAL
Conde y Corral, Bernardo see CARTA PASTORAL AL INAUGURAR SU PONTIFICADO
CONDENSATION OF PROGRESS AND POVERTY BY HENRY GEORGE / Busey, J L – 9 – 1.00f – at Libertarian Micro [335]
A CONDENSED INDEX TO THE MINOR LIENS FILED IN THE OFFICE OF THE CLERK OF KINGS COUNTY, NY. / Sparrow, George – New York, Lawyers' Real Estate Agency, 1897. 254 1 p. LL-1350 – 1 – us L of C Photodup [340]
CONDENSED MATTER NEWS / ed by Comes, R et al – 9,5,1 – us Gordon [530]
Conder, C R see THE LATIN KINGDOM OF JERUSALEM, 1099 TO 1291 A.D.
Conder, Francis R see HANDBOOK TO THE BIBLE...DERIVED FROM ANCIENT MONUMENTS AND MODERN EXPLORATION
CONDICION OBRERA Y DESPILFARRO OLIG ARQUICO / Balmaceda, Rodolfo – Buenos Aires, Argentina: Ediciones del Mar Dulce, 1982 – 1 – CSUXADH4084-B – us Hoover Inst Photo [947]
CONDICION SOCIAL DE LA MUJER EN ESPANA, LA. SU ESTADO ACTUAL : SU POSIBLE DESARROLLO / Nelken, Margarita – Barcelona: Editorial Minerva, S.A. – 1 – sp Bibl Santa Ana [946]
LAS CONDICIONES DE LA VICTORIA : MANUAL DE POLITICA ARGENTINA / Frigerio, Rogelio – Montevideo: A. Monteverde, [4th ed prologo 1963] – 1 – CSUXAJA7149-B – us Hoover Inst Photo [320]
CONDICIONES Y METODOS PARA LA RECONSTITUCION DEL FRENTE DEL 23 DE FEBRERO / Frigerio, Rogelio – [Buenos Aires, 1960] – 1 – CSUXADJ8388-B – us Hoover Inst Photo [972]
Condict, Alice Byram see OLD GLORY AND THE GOSPEL IN THE PHILIPPINES
Condillac, E B de see
- COURS D'ETUDE POUR L'INSTRUCTION DU PRINCE DE PARME
- PRINCIPES GENERAUX DE GRAMMAIRE POUR TOUTES LES LANGUES
- PRINCIPES GENERAUX DE GRAMMAIRE. POUR TOUTES LES LANGUES. PARIS, (AN 6)

Condis, Pierre see TRAITE DES CENSURES EN FRANCAIS: D'APRES LE DROIT NOUVEAU ETABLI PAR LA BULLE "APOSTOLICAE SEDIS."
Condit, Blackford see SHORT TITLES OF FAMILIAR BIBLE TEXTS, MISTRANSLATED, MISINTERPRETED, AND MISQUOTED
Condit, Ira M see THE CHINAMAN AS WE SEE HIM
Condit, Uzal W see HISTORY OF EASTON
LA CONDITION DES JUIFS DE NICE AUX 17E ET 18E SIECLES / Decourcelle, J – (Les Presses Universitaires de France). Paris. 1923. BJ-22-173 1 – 9 – ne IDC [944]
LA CONDITION DES OUVRIERS FRANCAIS D'APRES LES DERNIERS TRAVAUX / Cochin, Augustin – (Condition of 19th C. French working class series). 1862 – 9 – fr Hachette [360]
LA CONDITION DES PERSONNES DANS LA CITE DU VATICAN / Fragonard, J H – Paris, 1930 – 3mf – 1 – ILM-3212/1 – ne IDC [327]
CONDITION HUMAINE – Dakar. fevr 1948-aout 1956 – 1 – fr A.C.R.P.P. [073]
LA CONDITION INTERNATIONALE DE L'EGYPTE / Edhem, I – Montauban, 1904 – 2mf – 1 – ILM-1946/1 – ne IDC [327]
LA CONDITION JURIDIQUE DE LA FEMME MARIEE... / Guillot, L – Poitiers, 1912 – 4mf – 1 – ILM-3406/1 – ne IDC [327]
LA CONDITION JURIDIQUE DES MINORITES ETHNIQUES... / Budisteano, R – Paris, 1927 – 1mf – 1 – ILM-1565/1 – ne IDC [327]
CONDITION OF AMERICAN SEAMEN AT THE PORT OF HAVANA... – N.p., n.d. – 1mf – 1 – ILM-2864/1 – ne IDC [327]
THE CONDITION OF THE ENGLISH WORKING CLASS – Papers of Rev. Henry Solly, 1813-1903. British Library of Political and Economic Science – 1 – us Primary [320]
CONDITION OF THE FRENCH WORKING CLASS IN THE 19TH CENTURY / ed by Perrot, Michelle – v.1. 133 titles. In French. Printed Index – 9 – fr Hachette [360]
LA CONDITION OUVRIERE / Bibliotheque Nationale – Part Two. (Condition of the French working class). Rare works from 16th through 19th centuries on health, working conditions, occupational studies, government regulations. In French. 139 titles on 483 fiches. Individual titles available – 9 – 1195.00 – fr Bibl Nationale [360]
CONDITION OUVRIERE EN FRANCE AU 19E SIECLE – (Series). Rare books and official government publications, with descriptive and statistical studies of health, working conditions, poverty, etc. In French. Titles also available individually – 9 – fr Hachette [360]
CONDITIONAL AND FUTURE INTERESTS AND ILLEGAL CONDITIONS AND RESTRAINTS IN ILLINOIS / Kales, Albert Martin – Chicago,Callaghan, 1905. 453 p. LL-599 – 1 – us L of C Photodup [340]
CONDITIONAL REFLEX see PAVLOVIAN JOURNAL OF BIOLOGICAL SCIENCE
CONDITIONS AND POLITICS IN OCCUPIED WESTERN EUROPE, 1940-1945, PART 1 – 1940. Belgium, France, Norway, Sweden, Spain – 1 – us Primary [025]
CONDITIONS AND POLITICS IN OCCUPIED WESTERN EUROPE, 1940-1945, PART 2 – 1941. Belgium, Co-ordination Files; Denmark, France, General Files; Italy, Netherlands, Norway, Spain, Sweden, Vatican – 1 – us Primary [025]
CONDITIONS AND POLITICS IN OCCUPIED WESTERN EUROPE, 1940-1945, PART 3 – 1942, Belgium, Co-ordination Files, Denmark, France, General Files, Italy, Netherlands, Norway, Portugal, Spain, Sweden, Switzerland, Vatican – 1 – us Primary [025]
CONDITIONS AND POLITICS IN OCCUPIED WESTERN EUROPE, 1940-1945, PART 4 – 1943, Belgium. Co-ordination files, Denmark, France, General Files, Italy, Netherlands, Norway, Portugal, Spain, Sweden, Switzerland, Vatican – 1 – us Primary [025]
CONDITIONS AND POLITICS IN OCCUPIED WESTERN EUROPE, 1940-1945, PART 5/A – 1944. Belgium and Luxembourg, Denmark, Economic and Reconstruction Files, France, and General Files – 1 – us Primary [025]
CONDITIONS AND POLITICS IN OCCUPIED WESTERN EUROPE, 1940-1945, PART 5/B – 1944. Italy, Netherlands, Norway, Portugal, Spain, Sweden, Switzerland and the Vatican – 1 – us Primary [025]
CONDITIONS AND POLITICS IN OCCUPIED WESTERN EUROPE, 1940-45, PART 6/A – 1945. Belgium, Denmark, European General Files, France – 1 – us Primary [025]
CONDITIONS AND POLITICS IN OCCUPIED WESTERN EUROPE, 1940-45, PART 6/B / Great Britain. Public Record Office – 1945. Italy, Netherlands, Norway, Portugal, Spain, Sweden, Switzerland, Vatican – 1 – us Primary [025]
CONDITIONS DE DEVELOPPEMENT D'UN NOUVEAU TYPE DE TOURISME. IMPLICATIONS POUR LE DEVELOPPEMENT, EXEMPLE DE L'AVEYRON / Berthou, M P – Paris. 1976 – 175p – 9 – F60.00 – fr Ethnologie [300]
LES CONDITIONS DE L'SENSEIGNEMENT RELIGIEUX DANS LES EGLISES NATIONALES DE LA SUISSE ROMANDE : RAPPORT / Dumont, Emile – Lausanne: Georges Bridel, 1898 – 1mf – 9 – 0-8370-7626-9 – 1986-1626 – us A.T.L.A. [370]
LES CONDITIONS DE TRAVAIL CHEZ LES OUVRIERS EN INSTRUMENTS DE PRECISION DE PARIS / Delesalle, Paul – (Condition of 19th century French working class series). 1899 – 9 – fr Hachette [360]
LES CONDITIONS DU RETOUR AU CATHOLICISME : ENQUAETE PHILOSOPHIQUE ET RELIGIEUSE / Rifaux, Marcel – 3e ed. Paris: Librairie Plon, 1907 – 1mf – 9 – 0-8370-8856-9 – 1986-2856 – us A.T.L.A. [240]
CONDITIONS FAVOURABLE TO FASTER GROWTH (1961-1966) / Great Britain. National Economic Development Council – London. 1963 – 9 – ne IDC [338]
CONDITIONS FOR THE SALE OF PRODUCE AND ARBITRATION RULES / Organisasi Exporteur Hasilbumi Indonesia – English and Indonesian on opposite pages. SE-11,212 1. 2nd ed 1959- – 9 – ne IDC [331]
THE CONDITIONS OF OUR LORD'S LIFE ON EARTH : BEING FIVE LECTURES DELIVERED ON THE BISHOP PADDOCK FOUNDATION, IN THE GENERAL SEMINARY AT NEW YORK, 1896 / Mason, Arthur James – (Includes bibliographical references) – New York: Longmans, Green, 1896 – 1mf – 9 – 0-8370-4148-1 – 1985-2148 – us A.T.L.A. [240]
Condivi, Ascanio see DAS LEBEN DES MICHELANGELO BUONARROTI
CONDIZIONE GIURIDICA DELLA VEDOVA... / Diena, G – Torino, 1891 – 4mf – 1 – ILM-3564/1 – ne IDC [327]
CONDIZIONE GIURIDICA DELL'ITALIANO NATURALIZZATO STRANIERO... / Cassuto, D – Livorna, 1901 – 1mf – 1 – ILM-3176/1 – ne IDC [327]
CONDOMINIUM DES NOUVELLES-HEBRIDES : JOURNAL OFFICIEL – 1947-69 – 2r – 1 – us Ross [324]
CONDON GLOBE – Condon, OR. -w. 1 Apr 1892-27 Dec 1918. 5 rolls – 1 – us U.O. Library [071]
CONDON GLOBE TIMES – Condon, OR. -w. 4 Apr 1919-26 Sept 1975. – 18r – 1 – us U.O. Library [071]
CONDON TIMES – Condon, OR. -w. 14 Jul 1900-29 Mar 1919. 4 rolls – 1 – us U.O. Library [071]
CONDOR – Santiago de Chile, Chile. 1972- – 1 – gw Mikrofilm [072]
CONDOR – (v.81-. 1979- 5,6,9) – v.2-. 1900- – 1 – us UMI [073]
O CONDOR : PERIODICO LITTERARIO E NOTICIOSO – Maceio, Alagoas. 1-22 Mar 1903 – 1,5,6 – bl Biblioteca [072]
Condor, Tacuara (MNRT) see EL RETORNO DE PERON
Condorcet, Marie Jean Antoine Nicolas de see
- ADRESSE DE L'ASSEMBLEE AUX FRANCAIS, DUE 10 AOUT 1792
- UN AMI DE VOLTAIRE A M. D'EPREMESNIL AU SUJET D'UN PLAIDOYER, OU L'ON OUTRAGE GRATUITEMENT LE MEMOIRE DE M. VOLTAIRE
- DU CALCUL INTEGRAL
- DE LA REPUBLIQUE, OU UN ROI EST-IL NECESSAIRE A LA CONSERVATION DE LA LIBERTE?
- DES CONVENTIONS NATIONALES
- DISCOURS SUR LES CONVENTIONS NATIONALES PRONONCE A L'ASSEMBLEE DES AMIS DE LA CONSTITUTION SEANTE AUX JACOBINS LE 7 AOUT 1791
- DU PROBLEME DES TROIS CORPS
- ELEMENS DU CALCUL DES PROBABILITES ET SON APPLICATION AUX JEUX DE HASARD, A LA LOTERIE ET AUX JUGEMENS DES HOMMES
- ESSAIS D'ANALYSE
- LETTRE AUX BAILLIAGES DE FRANCE
- MOYENS D'APPRENDRE A COMPTER SUREMENT ET AVEC FACILITE
- OPINION DE M. CONDORCET SUR LE RAPPORT DES COMITES MILITAIRE, DIPLOMATIQUE ET DE L'ORDINAIRE DES FINANCES, REUNIS
- PIECES EXTRAITES DU RECUEIL PERIODIQUE INTITULE LE REPUBLICAIN
- REFLEXIONS DE M. LE MARQUIS DE CONDORCET SUR L'USUFRUIT DES BENEFICIERS
- REFLEXIONS D'UN CITOYEN CATHOLIQUE SUR LES LOIX DE FRANCE RELATIVES AUX PROTESTANTS
- REFLEXIONS D'UN CITOYEN SUR LA REVOLUTION DE 1788
- REFLEXIONS SUR LES AFFAIRES PUBLIQUES
- REGLEMENTS DE LA SOCIETE DES AMIS DES NOIRS

THE CONDUCT AND DOCTRINE OF THE REVEREND MR. WHITEFIELD VINDICATED FROM THE ASPERSIONS AND MALICIOUS INVECTIVES OF HIS ENEMIES;... – London, 1739 – 1mf – 9 – MP-270/1 – ne IDC [240]
THE CONDUCT OF PUBLIC WORSHIP / Greenhough, JG – London: Baptist Union Publication Dept., [1901?] – 1mf – us A.T.L.A. [240]
CONDUCT OF THE UNDERSTANDING / Locke, John – 288p – 1 – us U.W. Library [150]
CONDUCT OF THE VOIR DIRE EXAMINATION : PRACTICES AND OPINIONS OF FEDERAL DISTRICT JUDGES / Bermant, Gordon – Washington: FJC, Sept 1977 – 1mf – 9 – $1.50 – LLMC 95-812 – us L.L.M.C. [340]
CONDUCTING SMALL-SCALE NUTRITION SURVEYS : A FIELD MANUAL – 1990 – 186p – it F.A.O. [640]
CO-NE BSTAN-'GYUR – A.D. 1753-1773 repr 1928 – 2,226mf – $1,100.00 – us I.A.S.W.R. [090]
Cone, Orello see
- THE GOSPEL AND ITS EARLIEST INTERPRETATIONS
- GOSPEL-CRITICISM AND HISTORICAL CHRISTIANITY

Cone, Spencer H see CIRCULAR LETTER
CONEROSS BAPTIST CHURCH. OCONEE COUNTY. SOUTH CAROLINA : CHURCH RECORDS – West Union included. 1833-91, 1907-20, 1934-45 – 1 – 29.34 – us Baptist [240]
CONERTINO PER IL CEMBALO / Benda, G – Lipsia: Schwickert, [1779] – 1 – us Sibley [780]
Conestaggio, G F di see DELL'UNIONE...
CONEXION DE YUSTE CON LOS PUNTOS HISTORICOS DE LA PROVINCIA DE CACERES / Pablos Abril, Juan – (Plasencia): Imprenta La Victoria S.A., 1976? – sp Bibl Santa Ana [946]
CONFABULACION CONTRA LA ARGENTINA / Filippo, Virgilio – Buenos Aires: Editorial Lista Blanca, 1944 – 1 – CSUXADQ0040-B – us Hoover Inst Photo [320]
Confalonieri, Orestes D see PERON CONTRA PERON
A CONFEDERACAO : ORGAM DO PARTIDO REPUBLICANO COLLEGIAL – Manaos, Amazonas. Jan 1972 – 1,5,6 – bl Biblioteca [072]
CONFEDERACAO DO TRABALHO : ORGAM DAS CLASSES LABORIOSAS – Manaos, Amazonas. 14 Nov-25 Dez 1909 – 1,5,6 – bl Biblioteca [072]
LA CONFEDERACION DE LAS CLASES. EL PROGRAMA DE UN NUEVO PARTIDO / Cascales Munoz, Jose – 1894 – 9 – 1.50f – sp Bibl Santa Ana [360]
Confederacion de Trabajadores de America Latina see CTAL WHITE AND BLUE BOOK
Confederacion Nacional de Trabajo. Spain see
- LA OBRA DE LOS TRABAJADORES UNIDOS
- LOS SUCESOS DE BARCELONA: RELACION DOCUMENTAL DE LAS TRAGICAS JORNADAS DE LA SEMANA DE MAYO DE 1937
- LOS SUCESOS DE MAYO EN BARACELONA. RELATO AUTENTICO
- LA VERDAD SOBRE LA TRAGEDIA DE CASAS VIEJAS, POR EL COMITE NACIONALE.

LA CONFEDERACION PERU-BOLIVIANA / Cornejo Bouroncle, J – Gusco, 1935 – 2mf – 1 – ILM-2575/1 – ne IDC [327]
CONFEDERATE BAPTIST – South Carolina. 1862-65 – 1 – 19.53 – us Baptist [240]
THE CONFEDERATE BAPTIST – v1-3. 1862-65 (complete) – 1r – 1 – ATLA R0127 – us A.T.L.A. [240]
CONFEDERATE COURT RECORDS, EASTERN DISTRICT OF NORTH CAROLINA, 1861-1864 – 1r – 1 – M1430 – us Nat'l Archives [340]

CONFEDERATE IMPRINTS – A microfilm collection of the items listed in Marjorie Lyle Crandall's Confederate Imprints: A Check list. Boston. 1955. and Richard B. Harwell's More Confederate Imprints. Richmond. 1957 – 1 – us Primary [976]

CONFEDERATE MILITARY MANUSCRIPTS : SERIES A: HOLDINGS OF THE VIRGINIA HISTORICAL SOCIETY / ed by Glatthaar, Joseph T – (With printed guide) – 1996 – ca 40r – 1 – ca $5,000.00 – 1-55655-632-2 – us UPA [976]

CONFEDERATE PAPERS OF THE U.S. DISTRICT COURT FOR THE EASTERN DISTRICT OF NORTH CAROLINA, 1861-1865 – 1r – 1 – M436 – us Nat'l Archives [340]

CONFEDERATE PAPERS RELATING TO CITIZENS OR BUSINESS FIRMS / U.S. War Department. Confederate Records – M346 – 1158r – 5 – us Nat'l Archives [324]

CONFEDERATE PAPERS...1861-65 / U.S. District Courts. North Carolina, Eastern District – 1roll. M436 – 1 – us Nat'l Archives [324]

THE CONFEDERATE RECORDS OF THE STATE OF GEORGIA / Georgia – v1-5. Comp. by Allen D. Candler. Indexed. F-0105/F-0109 – 9 – us A.G.L.L. [978]

CONFEDERATE STATES ARMY CASUALTIES: LISTS AND NARRATIVE REPORTS, 1861-65 / U.S. War Department. Confederate Records – 7rolls. M836 – 1 – us Nat'l Archives [324]

Confederate States of America *see*
- CIVIL WAR DIRECT TAX ASSESSMENT LISTS: TENNESSEE
- GENERAL ORDERS AND CIRCULARS OF THE CONFEDERATE WAR DEPARTMENT
- LETTERS AND TELEGRAMS SENT BY THE CONFEDERATE QUARTERMASTER GENERAL
- PRESIDENTIAL MESSAGES AND PAPERS OF THE CONFEDERACY
- RECORDS

Confederate States of America. Army *see*
- MILITARY RECORDS
- RECORDS

Confederate States of America. Secretary of the Treasury *see*
- LETTERS RECEIVED BY THE CONFEDERATE SECRETARY..., 1861-65
- LETTERS SENT BY THE CONFEDERATE SECRETARY..., 1861, 1864-65

Confederate States of America. War Department *see* RECORDS OF THE COTTON BUREAU OF THE TRANS-MISSISSIPPI DEPARTMENT

CONFEDERATE VETERAN – v. 1-40. 1893-1932 – 1 – 370.00 – us L of C Photodup [976]

CONFEDERATED UMATILLA JOURNAL – Pendleton OR. Dec 1 1975-May 25 1982 – 1 – us U.O. Library [071]

Confederation Generale du Travail *see*
- L'ATELIER POUR LE PLAN
- LE PEUPLE

Confederation Generale du Travail. Congres *see* COMPTE RENDU DES DEBATS

Confederation Generale du Travail. Paris *see* COMPTE-RENDU STENOGRAPHIQUE DE LA PREMIERE REUNION.

Confederation Generale du Travail Unitaire *see* LA VIE SYNDICALE

CONFEDERAZIONE FASCISTA DEI LAVORATORI DELL'INDUSTRIA : LA REPARTITION DES MATIERES PREMIERES ET DES MANDATS INTERN – Roma, 1936 – 1mf – 1 – ILM-3925/1 – ne IDC [327]

CONFERENCE : MINUTES... 1ST-31ST ANNUAL CONFERENCE / Primitive Methodist Connexion – (Coll title: The People Called Methodists, Phase 3: Primary Sources, 1801-1850) – Nottingham, Burslem, etc. 1819-1850 – 16mf – 9 – H-2737/1 – ne IDC [240]

CONFERENCE AFRICAINE SUR LA TSE-TSE ET LA TRYPANOMIASE (1948 BRAZZAVILLE) *see* [COMPTE-RENDU]

LA CONFERENCE AFRICAINE-FRANCAISE, BRAZZAVILLE, 1944 – Alger: Commissariat aux colonies, 1944 – 1 – us Res Libr [960]

CONFERENCE AVEC M. CLAUDE...SUR LA MATIERE DE L'EGLISE / Bossuet, Jacques B – Paris, 1682 – 6mf – 9 – CA-116/1 – ne IDC [240]

A CONFERENCE BETWEEN A MYSTIC, AN HUTCHINSONIAN, A CALVINIST, A METHODIST, A MEMBER OF THE CHURCH OF ENGLAND... / Dodd, W – London, 1761 – 2mf – 9 – MP-412/1 – ne IDC [240]

CONFERENCE BOARD RECORD – v1-13. 1964-Sept 1976 – 1 – us UMI [073]

CONFERENCE BOARD RECORD *see* ACROSS THE BOARD

CONFERENCE BULLETINS / National Conference of Social Welfare – (1975-5,6,9) – 1873- – 1 – us UMI [360]

CONFERENCE COLONIALE (1917 PARIS) *see* [COMPTE-RENDU] INSTITUEE

CONFERENCE DE BRUXELLES, JUIN 1897 / Comite Maritime International – Anvers, 1897-1938 – 123mf – 1 – ILM-3956/1 – ne IDC [327]

CONFERENCE DE LA HAYE, 1910 : ACTES – N.p., n.d. – 7mf – 1 – ILM-3958/1 – ne IDC [327]

CONFERENCE DE LA HAYE 1912 : DOCUMENTS, 1-2 – N.p., n.d. – 7mf – 1 – ILM-3957/1 – ne IDC [327]

CONFERENCE DEUXIEME POUR L'UNIFICATION DU DROIT EN MATIERE DE LETTRE DE CHANGE, DE BILLET A ORDRE ET DE CHEQUE : RAPPORT... – La Haye, n.d. – 2mf – 1 – ILM-3978/1 – ne IDC [327]

CONFERENCE DU DR. GRIGNON: LE FONCTIONNEMENT DES SOCIETES D'AGRICULTURE PAR LES CERCLES AGRICOLES / Grignon, Wilfrid – 1891?. 04308. (Pre-1900 Canadiana) – 9 – cn C.I.H.M. [630]

CONFERENCE ET LETTRES DE P. SAVORGNAN DE BRAZZA SUR SES TROIS EXPLORATIONS DANS L'OUEST AFRICAIN DE 1875 A 1886 / Ney, Napoleon – Paris: M Dreyfous, 1887 – 1 – us Res Libr [960]

CONFERENCE IN THE INTEREST OF PHYSICAL TRAINING, BOSTON, 1889 / ed by Barrows, Isabel C – 1899 – 3mf – 9 – $9.00 – us Microform Publ [790]

CONFERENCE INTERNATIONALE DE DROIT MARITIME (BRUSSELS, 1909) : REPORT ON THE AMERICAN DELEGATES... – N.p., n.d. – 1mf – 1 – ILM-3955/1 – ne IDC [327]

CONFERENCE INTERNATIONALE DE DROIT MARITIME (BRUXELLES, 1905) : PROCES-VERBAUX DE SEANCES...1905 – Bruxelles, 1906 – 5mf – 1 – ILM-3946-1 – ne IDC [327]

CONFERENCE INTERNATIONALE DE DROIT MARITIME (BRUXELLES, 1909) : PROCES-VERBAUX DES SEANCES...1909 – Bruxelles, 1909 – 5mf – 1 – ILM-3944/1 – ne IDC [327]

CONFERENCE INTERNATIONALE DE DROIT MARITIME (BRUXELLES, 1910) : PROCES-VERBAUX DES SEANCES...1910 – Bruxelles, 1910 – 5mf – 1 – ILM-3945/1 – ne IDC [327]

CONFERENCE INTERNATIONALE DE DROIT MARITIME (BRUXELLES, 1922) : DOCUMENTS ET PROCES-VERBAUX...1922 – Bruxelles, 1922 – 5mf – 1 – ILM-3949/1 – ne IDC [327]

CONFERENCE INTERNATIONALE DE DROIT MARITIME (BRUXELLES, 1923) : PROCES-VERBAUX DES SEANCES...1923 – Ledeberg, 1924 – 3mf – 1 – ILM-3960/1 – ne IDC [327]

CONFERENCE INTERNATIONALE DE DROIT MARITIME (BRUXELLES, 1923) : TEXTES ADOPTES – Ledeberg, 1924 – 1mf – 1 – ILM-3961/1 – ne IDC [327]

CONFERENCE INTERNATIONALE DE DROIT MARITIME (BRUXELLES, 1926) : [DOCUMENTS] – Bruxelles, 1927 – 2mf – 1 – ILM-3959/1 – ne IDC [327]

CONFERENCE INTERNATIONALE DU DROIT MARITIME (BRUXELLES, 1922) : UNIFICATION...REGLES EN MATIERE DE CONNAISSEMENTS – Bruxelles, 1923 – 2mf – 1 – ILM-3977/1 – ne IDC [327]

CONFERENCE. MINUTES... / Wesleyan Methodist Church – (Missing: 1812; 1815; 1819; 1836; 1840; 1844) – London, Bristol, 1791-1850 – 87mf – 9 – MP-345/1 – ne IDC [240]

CONFERENCE. MINUTES ... 1819-1850 / Bible Christians – (Coll title: The People Called Methodists, Phase 3: Primary Sources, 1801-1850) – Devon, Launceston, etc., 1825-1850 – 9mf – 9 – MP-349/1 – ne IDC [240]

CONFERENCE NEWSLETTER = HUI HSUN – v3-4. 1949-50; v5 Jan 1951 (incomplete) – 1r – 1 – ATLA S0296M – us A.T.L.A. [073]

Conference of Bar Association Delegates. Committee on Cooperation of the Press and the Bar *see* REPORT

CONFERENCE OF BRITISH MISSIONARY SOCIETIES ARCHIVES / School of Oriental and African Studies – (Includes printed guide) – 1912-1954 – 6,272mf – 9 – ne IDC [240]

CONFERENCE OF EUROPEAN POSTAL AND TELECOMMUNICATIONS ADMINISTRATIONS (CEPT) AND EUROPEAN TELECOMMUNICATIONS STANDARDS INSTITUTE (ETSI), NETS STANDARDS – (Updated Every 120 Days) – Information Handling Services – 5 – us Info Handling [621]

CONFERENCE OF EUROPEAN STATISTICIANS COMMITTEE / UN Economic Commission for Europe (ECE) – 1954-89 – E/F.50 E.1067 F.906 R.692 – 9 – us U.N. Pubs [340]

Conference of Missionary Societies in Great Britain and Ireland *see*
- BIBLIOGRAPHY OF AFRICAN CHRISTIAN LITERATURE

CONFERENCE OF THE EIGHTEEN-NATION COMMITTEE ON DISARMAMENT / UN – 1962-78 – E.570 F.615 R.623 S.606 – 9 – ENDC/ and CCD/ – us U.N. Pubs [340]

CONFERENCE OF THE HEADS OF STATE OF GOVERNMENTS OF NON-ALIGNED COUNTRIES IN BELGRADE (1961) PAMPHLET COLLECTION – 1961 – 1 – CSUXANL4378-B – us Hoover Inst Photo [320]

Conference on Christian Missions *see* CONFERENCE ON MISSIONS HELD IN 1860 AT LIVERPOOL

Conference on Co-operative Communities *see* MINUTES

CONFERENCE ON DISARMAMENT, 1985-1989 : MEETINGS AND DOCUMENTS – (With printed guide) – 20r – $2,200.00 – 1-55655-224-6 – us UPA [327]

Conference on Foreign Missions...London, 1886 *see* PROCEEDINGS...MILDMAY PARK, LONDON, OCTOBER 5TH TO 7TH 1886

CONFERENCE ON INTERNATIONAL RELATIONS : PROCEEDINGS...HELD AT CORNELL UNIVERSITY...JUNE 15-30, 1915 – Boston, 1916 – 5mf – 1 – ILM-3843/1 – ne IDC [327]

CONFERENCE ON MISSIONS HELD IN 1860 AT LIVERPOOL / Conference on Christian Missions – London: James Nisbet, 1860. xi,428p. 1 fiche – 9 – us A.T.L.A. [240]

CONFERENCE ON TAX PLANNING FOR 501(C)(3) ORGANIZATIONS (NEW YORK UNIVERSITY) : PROCEEDINGS – v1-22. 1953-94 – 1,5,6 – $180.00 – us Hein [340]

CONFERENCE ON THE ACQUISITION OF MATERIAL FROM AFRICA / Bloomfield, V – University of Birmingham, 25th April 1969. Published for the Standing Conference on Library Materials on Afriza. Zug. 1969. BA-731 1 – 9 – ne IDC [960]

CONFERENCE ON THE DISCONTINUANCE OF NUCLEAR WEAPON TESTS / UN – 1958-62 – E.134 R.144 – 9 – GEN/DNT/ PV.1-353 – us U.N. Pubs [340]

CONFERENCE ON THE LAW OF THE SEA / United Nations – 20v in 9bks. 1958-79 – 9 – $285.00 set – us Hein [340]

CONFERENCE PAPER COMPRISING A ROYAL STATEMENT BEFORE PARLIAMENT ON GOVERNMENT POLICY / Libya. Ministry of Information and Culture – Nat. Planning. Khitab al-Arsh. Tripoli. Nov 17 1968. Gazafi, W. BNE-521 1 – 9 – ne IDC [323]

CONFERENCE PROCEEDINGS / National Conference on Law and Poverty. Washington, DC. 1965 – Washington: GPO, 1966 200p. LL-2281 – 1 – us L of C Photodup [340]

CONFERENCE PROCEEDINGS / Virginia. Polytechnic Institute. Extension Division – 18 fiches – 9 – us Spaulding [630]

CONFERENCE PROCEEDINGS / West African Institute of Social and Economic Research. Ibadan – v1-5. 1952-56 – 1 – us Res Libr [960]

CONFERENCE PROCEEDINGS / American Marketing Association – Chicago. 1954-1970; v33-55 1971-1989; v1-8 1990- 1; v38-55 1976-1989; v1-8 1990- 5; v38-55 1976-1989; v1-8 1990- 9 – 1,5,9 – D5966 – us UMI [650]

CONFERENCE PROCEEDINGS / Nigerian Institute of Social and Economic Research – Ibadan, 6th-8th. 1958-1962 – us Res Libr [330]

CONFERENCE SERIES – v.1 1969 – 1,5,6,9 – us UMI [330]

CONFERENCE SUR L'HYGIENE GENERALE / Archambault, Joseph Louis – Montreal: W. Daniel, 1887. 04108. (Pre-1900 Canadiana) – 9 – cn C.I.H.M. [610]

CONFERENCES : LA PRESSE CANADIENNE-FRANCAISE ET LES AMELIORATIONS DE QUEBEC, 20 SEPTEMBRE 1875 / Buies, Arthur – Quebec: C Darveau, 1875. SEM105P25 – 2mf – 9 – Can$4.50 – cn Bibl Nat [971]

CONFERENCES APOLOGETIQUES = LECTURES IN DEFENCE OF THE CHRISTIAN FAITH / Godet, Frederic Louis – (In English) – 4th ed. Edinburgh: T & T Clark, [ca 1895] – 1mf – 9 – 0-8370-3321-7 – 1985-1321 – us A.T.L.A. [230]

CONFERENCES ECONOMIQUES NATIONALES – 2. ed. [Conakry]: Imprimerie National "Patrice Lumumba" 1973 – us Res Libr [330]

CONFERENCES ET DISCOURS / Bourassa, Gustave – Montreal: C. Beauchemin, 1899. 00200. (Pre-1900 Canadiana) – 9 – cn C.I.H.M. [971]

CONFERENCES ET LETTRES SUR L'OUEST AFRICAIN / Savorgnan de Brazza, Pierre Paul Francois Camille – Paris, Maurice Dreyfous. 1887 – 9 – 12.50 – fr Orientalistes [960]

CONFERENCES FAICTES A TURIN...1663,... 1664 – Turin, 1664 – 3mf – 1 – ILM-893/1 – ne IDC [327]

Conferences pour la negociation d'une convention regulant les relations commerciales entre la France et le Canada *see* PREMIERE CONFERENCE, 15 MARS 1882

CONFERENCIA : SEMANA AGRICOLA DE BADAJOZ / Fernandez Santana, Ezequiel – Badajoz: Imp. de Vicente Rguez., 1912 – 1 – sp Bibl Santa Ana [630]

CONFERENCIA BELIGERANTE / Bonifacino, Victor – Buenos Aires: [s.n.], 1951 – 1 – CSUXADN0112-B – us Hoover Inst Photo [355]

Conferencia das Organizacoes Nacionalistas das Colonias Portuguesas (CONCP) *see* BOLETIM DE INFORMACAO

LA CONFERENCIA DE LAUSANA SOBRE FE Y DISCIPLINA / ed by Bayle, Constantino – Madrid: Razon y Fe, 1927 – 1 – sp Bibl Santa Ana [210]

CONFERENCIA DE MINISTROS DE HACIENDA (7TH: 1953: BUENOS AIRES) *see* SEPTIMA CONFERENCIA DE MINISTROS DE HACIENDA

LA CONFERENCIA INTERNACIONAL DE DERECHO MARITIMO DE BRUSELAS – 1922 / Benitoy Endara, L – Madrid, 1924 – 1mf – 9 – ILM-3755/1 – ne IDC [327]

LA CONFERENCIA NACIONAL DE JUVENTUDES / Serrano Poncela, Segundo – Guia de divulgacion y de trabajo. Valencia, 1937. Fiche W1159. (Blodgett Collection of Spanish Civil War Pamphlets) – 9 – us H.U. College Libr [946]

CONFERENCIA RECITAL SOBRE EL ROMANCERO GITANO. MANUSCRITO / Garcia Lorca, Federico – 1mf – 9 – sp Cultura [850]

CONFERENCIA SOBRE EL SEGURO DE MATERNIDAD DEDICADA ESPECIALMENTE A PATRONOS AGRICOLAS / Leal Ramos, Leon – Madrid: Imp. y Enc. de los sobrinos de la sucesora de M. Minussa de los Rios, 2nd ed 1932 – sp Bibl Santa Ana [946]

Conferencias de Ministros de Hacienda, Secretar ia Permanente *see* SEPTIMA CONFERENCIA DE MINISTROS DE HACIENDA

CONFERENCIAS MILITARES / Leon Gutierrez, Florencio – 1894 – 9 – 1.50f – sp Bibl Santa Ana [355]

CONFERENCIAS PRONUNCIADAS EN LA LIGA CONTRA LA BLASFEMIA DE OLIVA DE JEREZ / Serrano Serrano, Ildefonso – Segura de Leon: Imp. de Ntra. Sra. de Gracia, 1924 – sp Bibl Santa Ana [240]

CONFERENCIAS SOBRE LA PLUROTONIA / Huertas y Barrero, Francisco – 1885 – 9 – 1.50f – sp Bibl Santa Ana [946]

CONFERENCIAS TEOSOFICAS EN AMERICA DEL SUR / Roso de Luna, Mario – Madrid: Gregorio Pueyo, editor, S.A. – 1 – sp Bibl Santa Ana [240]

CONFERENCIAS TEOSOFICAS EN AMERICA DEL SUR / Roso de Luna, Mario – Madrid: Libreria de Pueyo, Tomo 2, 1911 – 1 – sp Bibl Santa Ana [290]

CONFERENTIE? PERMOESJAWARATAN MALINO, 15-24 JULY 1946 / Indonesia. Malino Conference, 1946 – (In Dutch and Indonesian) – Resoluties En Dan Moties – 9 – SE-11,203 1 – ne IDC [950]

CONFESSIO / Imbroeck, Thomas van – Een schoone Bekentenisse eens vromen ende Godtureesende Christen. Item een Boecxken van de Verrijssenisse des Lichaems, met een schoon Leideken int eynde. 1579. BME-170 1 – 9 – ne IDC [240]

CONFESSIO ET APOLOGIA PASTORUM... / Amsdorff, N von – Magdeburg, 1550 – 1mf – 9 – ne IDC [240]

LA CONFESSION / Normand, Victor – Paris: F. Rieder, 1926. 172p. (Christianisme) – 1 – us U.W. Library [240]

THE CONFESSION AND PRAYER OF ASENATH, DAUGHTER OF PENTEPHRES, THE PRIEST,(TRANS.) BY E. W. BROOKS – 1918 – 1 – us A.T.L.A. [240]

LA CONFESSION AUX LAIQUES DANS L'EGLISE LATINE DEPUIS LE VILLE / Teetaert, Amedee – Wetteren: J de Meester et fils; Paris: J Gabalda, [etc., etc.], 1926 – 1 – us U.W. Library [240]

THE CONFESSION OF A CAPITALIST / Benn, Ernest J P – 1925. 2 fiches (29x) – 9 – 1.00f – at Libertarian Micro [320]

A CONFESSION OF FAITH – Charleston, South Carolina. 1774. 153p – 1 – 5.35 – us Baptist [240]

CONFESSION OF FAITH ADOPTED BY THE BAPTIST ASSOCIATION MET AT PHILADELPHIA, A, 25 SEP 1742 / Baptist Association – 1 – 5.00 – us Baptist [240]

CONFESSION SOCIALE, COMMENTAIRE CRITIQUE TANT DE LA DECLARATION FAITE AU PEUPLE – Paris, 1848 – us Res Libr [300]

CONFESSION VND BEKENTNIS JOHANNS AGRICOLE EISSLEBENS VOM GESETZE GOTTES / Johannes Agricola aus Eisleben – Berlin, 1541 – 1mf – ne IDC [240]

CONFESSIONAL REVISION; BEING A COLLECTION OF 395 ARTICLES... ON THE SUBJECT OF REVISING THE WESTMINSTER CONFESSION OF THE FAITH.. – 1890 – 1 – us A.T.L.A. [240]

DIE CONFESSIONELLE ENTWICKLUNG DER ALTPROTESTANTISCHEN KIRCHE DEUTSCHLANDS : DIE ALTPROTESTANTISCHE UNION UND DIE GEGENWAERTIGE CONFESSIONELLE LAGE UND AUFGABE DES DEUTSCHEN PROTESTANTISMUS / Heppe, Heinrich – Marburg: N.G. Elwert, 1854 – 2mf – us A.T.L.A. [240]

CONFESSIONES / Augustinus, St – 1983 – 8mf – 9 – Bf975.00 – 2-503-60272-X – be Brepols [240]

LES CONFESSIONS DE THEOROIGNE DE MERICOURT / Ravelsberg, Ferdinand Strobl von – Paris, 1892. 195p. (Les Femmes Collection) – 3mf – 9 – $8.00 – fr Bibl Nationale [360]

CONFESSIONS D'UNE ROUE DE LA REGENCE / Duclos, Charles Pinot & Bretonne, Nicolas Edme Retif de la – Paris: E. Dentu, 1889. 296p. 4 fiches.(Literature Collection) – 9 – 10.00 – fr Bibl Nationale [830]

CONFESSIONS OF A MEDIUM, WITH FIVE ILLUSTRATIONS – London: Griffith & Farran; New York: E.P. Dutton & Co., (1882). xvi,232p incl. front., illus – 1 – us U.W. Library [150]

CONFESSIONS OF A THUG / Taylor, Philip Meadows – British Fiction Archive: Unit 5 – 9 – uk Bell [830]

CONFESSIONS OF AN ENGLISH OPIUM-EATER / De Quincey, Thomas – London: Printed for Taylor and Hessey, 1822 – 1 roll – 1 – 1-55879-309-7 – uk Libr Preservation [920]

CONFESSIONS OF FAITH : AND OTHER PUBLIC DOCUMENTS, ILLUSTRATIVE OF THE HISTORY OF THE BAPTIST CHURCHES OF ENGLAND IN THE 17TH CENTURY / ed by Underhill, Edward B – (382p) – Hanserd Knolleys Society – 1 reel – 1 – $15.28 – us Baptist [240]

CONFESSIONS OF FAITH AND FORMULAS OF SUBSCRIPTION : IN THE REFORMED CHURCHES OF GREAT BRITAIN AND IRELAND ESPECIALLY IN THE CHURCH OF SCOTLAND / Cooper, James – (Includes bibliographical references) – Glasgow: James Maclehose, 1907 – 1mf – 9 – 0-8370-8804-6 – 1986-2804 – us A.T.L.A. [240]

CONFESSIONS OF FAITH AND OTHER PUBLIC DOCUMENTS ILLUSTRATIVE OF THE HISTORY OF THE BAPTIST CHURCHES OF ENGLAND IN THE 17TH CENTURY *see* PUBLICATIONS

THE CONFESSIONS OF HARRY LORREQUER / Lever, Charles James – Dublin: W. Curry; London: William S. Orr and Co., 1839 – 1 roll – 1 – 1-55879-253-8 – uk Libr Preservation [830]

THE CONFESSIONS OF ST AUGUSTINE, BISHOP OF HIPPO / Augustine, Saint, Bishop of Hippo – (Includes bibliographical references & index) – Edinburgh: T & T Clark; New York: Scribner & Welford [distr], 1882 – 2mf – 9 – 0-8370-6084-2 – 1986-0084 – us A.T.L.A. [920]

THE CONFESSIONS OF THE CHURCH OF SCOTLAND: THEIR EVOLUTION IN HISTORY : THE SEVENTH SERIES OF THE CHALMERS LECTURES / M'Crie, Charles Greig – Edinburgh: Macniven & Wallace, 1907 – 1mf – us A.T.L.A. [240]

Confessore, R J *see* QUANTIFICATION FACTORS DESCRIBING PHYSICAL ACTIVITY INVOLVEMENT AND THEIR RELATIONSSHIP TO CURRENT CRITERION REFERENCE STANDARDS FOR AEROBIC CAPACITY IN CHILDREN AND YOUTH

LE CONFIDENT DE CHARLEVOIX/DE LA RIVE-NORD – La Malbaie, Canada. 25 aut 1960-17 mar 1981 – 9r – 1 – Can$65.00r – cn Can Microfilming [072]

CONFIDENTIAL AND UNOFFICIAL LETTERS SENT BY THE SECRETARY..., 1814-47 / U.S. War Department. Office of the Secretary – 2rolls. M7 – 1 – us Nat'l Archives [324]

CONFIDENTIAL BRITISH FOREIGN OFFICE POLITICAL CORRESPONDENCE : SERIES 1: CHINA, 1906-1911 – (Pt 1: 1906-08 105r $14,740.00 ISBN 1-55655-519-9. Pt 2: 1909-11 106r $15,595.00 ISBN 1-55655-559-8. Pt 3: 1912-14 99r $14,035.00 ISBN 1-55655-647-0) – 4pt series ca 441r – 1 – $56,135.00 coll – us UPA [950]

CONFIDENTIAL BRITISH FOREIGN OFFICE POLITICAL CORRESPONDENCE : SERIES 1: GERMANY, 1906-1925 – (Pt 1: 1906-19 105r $14,885.00 ISBN 1-55655-530-X. Pt 2: 1920-21 ca 146r ca $20,695.00 ISBN 1-55655-630-6. Pt 3: 1922-25 ca 150r. Pt 4: 1924-25 ca 94r. All include printed guides) – 4pt series ca 495r – 1 – $63,155 coll – us UPA [943]

CONFIDENTIAL BRITISH FOREIGN OFFICE POLITICAL CORRESPONDENCE FILES : PALESTINE, 1947-1948 – (With printed guide $345.00 ISBN 1-55655-641-1) – 46r – 1 – $6,845.00 – 1-55655-494-X – us UPA [956]

CONFIDENTIAL BRITISH FOREIGN OFFICE POLITICAL CORRESPONDENCE FILES : PALESTINE AND TRANSJORDAN, 1940-1946 – (With printed guide $260.00 ISBN 1-55655-594-6) – 35r – 1 – $5,210.00 – 1-55655-493-1 – us UPA [956]

...CONFIDENTIAL PROSPECTUS / Anticosti Company – 187? 02196. (Pre-1900 Canadiana) – 9 – cn C.I.H.M. [380]

CONFIDENTIAL PUBLICATIONS AND HOME POLITICAL FILES / India. National Archives – Reports, etc. on Indian publications, ca. 1900-45 – 1 – us Res Libr [950]

CONFIDENTIAL PUBLICATIONS AND HOME POLITICAL FILES / India. National Archives – Two major series and two publications. ca. 1920-45 – 1 – us Res Libr [950]

CONFIDENTIAL REPORT ON THE NEGRO MARKET – v1-3. 1960-63 – 1 – us UMI [073]

CONFIDENTIAL REPORT ON THE NORTHERN RHODESIA POLICE : PARTS 3, 4 AND 9 / Dowbiggin, Herbert – (Filmed with: Report on the Northern Rhodesia Police, pts 1-2, 5-9 & summary by Herbert Dowbiggin) – [s.l: s.n.], 1937 (Lusaka Govt Printer) – 1 – us Res Libr [960]

CONFIDENTIAL U.S. STATE DEPARTMENT CENTRAL FILES : JORDAN – Internal and Foreign Affairs, 1955-59. 10 reels. – 1 – $1,185.00 – 1-55655-263-7 – us UPA [327]

CONFIDENTIAL U.S. STATE DEPARTMENT CENTRAL FILES: ARGENTINA : FOREIGN AFFAIRS, 1945-1949 / U.S. Department of State – (With printed guide) – 5r – 1 – $625.00 – us UPA [972]

CONFIDENTIAL U.S. STATE DEPARTMENT CENTRAL FILES: GERMANY : INTERNAL AND FOREIGN AFFAIRS, 1930-1959 / U.S. Department of State – (See also individual listings. All pts with printed guides) – 436r – 1 – $44,645.00 coll – us UPA [320]

CONFIDENTIAL U.S. STATE DEPARTMENT CENTRAL FILES: GERMANY *see* – FEDERAL REPUBLIC OF GERMANY – FEDERAL REPUBLIC OF GERMANY: INTERNAL AFFAIRS, 1950-1954 – GERMANY

CONFIDENTIAL...CENTRAL FILES : ARAB CONFEDERATION AND OTHER ISSUES, 1950-59 / U.S. Department of State – $3,220.00 – us UPA [956]

CONFIDENTIAL...CENTRAL FILES : BRITISH AFRICA / U.S. Department of State – (1945-49. 14r ISBN: 1-55655-405-2. $1,665.00; 1950-54. 29r ISBN: 1-55655-406-0. $3,455.00; 1955-59. 39r ISBN: 1-55655-407-9. $4,645.00) – Internal and Foreign Affairs, 1945-59 – 1 – $9,280.00 set – us UPA [960]

CONFIDENTIAL...CENTRAL FILES : CHINA / U.S. Department of State – (Internal Affairs, 1930-39. $9,215.00; 1940-44. 51r $3,575.00; 1945-49. 75r $5,095.00; 1950-54. 47r $4,125.00; 1955-59, Pt 1: Political, Governmental and National Defense Affairs. $2,890.00; Pt 2: Social, Economic and Industrial Affairs. $1,585.00; Foreign Affairs, 1950-54. $550.00; 1955-59. $965.00; U.S.-China Relations, 1940-49. $620.00) – Internal and Foreign Affairs, 1930-59. With printed guides – 1 – $22,895.00 set – us UPA [950]

CONFIDENTIAL...CENTRAL FILES : CUBA / U.S. Department of State – (1945-49: 29r $3,455.00; 1950-54: 39r $4,640.00; 1955-59: 25r $2,975.00) – Internal Affairs and Foreign Affairs, 1945-59. With printed guides – 1 – $10,515.00 set – us UPA [324]

CONFIDENTIAL...CENTRAL FILES : EGYPT / U.S. Department of State – (1945-49. 19 reels. ISBN: 0-89093-648-X. $2,270.00; 1950-54. 38 reels. ISBN: 0-89093-649-8. $4,525.00; Foreign Affairs, 1955-59. 7 reels. ISBN: 1-55655-145-2. $835.00; Internal Affairs, 1955-59. 30 reels. ISBN: 1-55655-144-4. $3,575.00) – Internal and Foreign Affairs, 1945-59 – 1 – $10,640.00 – us UPA [327]

CONFIDENTIAL...CENTRAL FILES : THE FAR EAST / U.S. Department of State – (1945-49: 21r $2,505.00 ISBN 1-55655-314-5; 1950-54. 26r $3,100.00 ISBN 1-55655-315-3; 1955-59: 30r $3,570.00 ISBN 1-55655-316-1) – Internal and Foreign Affairs, 1945-59. With printed guides – 1 – $8,710.00 set – us UPA [950]

CONFIDENTIAL...CENTRAL FILES : FORMOSA / U.S. Department of State – (Internal, 1945-49. 3r $350.00; Internal and Foreign, 1950-54. 17r $2,015.00) – Internal and Foreign Affairs, 1945-54. With printed guides – 1 – $2,130.00 set – us UPA [324]

CONFIDENTIAL...CENTRAL FILES : FRANCE / U.S. Department of State – (Internal, 1945-49. Pt 1: Political, Governmental and National Defense Affairs. 22r. $2,625.00 ISBN 0-89093-919-5; Pt 2: Social, Economic and Industrial Affairs. 46r. $5,485.00 ISBN 0-89093-920-9; Foreign, 1945-49. $480.00 ISBN 0-89093-921-7; Internal, 1950-54. Pt 1: $2,975.00 ISBN 0-89093-956-X; Foreign, 1950-54. $600.00 ISBN 0-89093-955-1) – Internal and Foreign Affairs, 1945-54 – 1 – $11,560.00 set – us UPA [324]

CONFIDENTIAL...CENTRAL FILES : GREAT BRITAIN / U.S. Department of State – (1930-39: $3,145.00; 1940-44: $1,070.00; 1945-49: $1,195.00) – Foreign Affairs, 1930-49. With printed guides – 1 – us UPA [324]

CONFIDENTIAL...CENTRAL FILES : GREAT BRITAIN / U.S. Department of State – (1930-39, Pt 1: Political, Governmental and National Defense Affairs. $4,410.00; Pt 2: Social, Economic and Industrial Affairs. 42r $5,005.00; 1940-44, Pt 1. 31r $3,705.00; Pt 2. 63r $7,515.00; 1945-49, Pt 1. 26r $3,105.00) – Internal Affairs, 1930-49. With printed guides – us UPA [941]

CONFIDENTIAL...CENTRAL FILES : GREAT BRITAIN / U.S. Department of State – (See also indiv. listings) – Internal and Foreign Affairs, 1930-49. With printed guides – 1 – $24,745.00 set – us UPA [324]

CONFIDENTIAL...CENTRAL FILES : HONDURAS / U.S. Department of State – (1945-49. 10r $1,315.00; 1950-54. 11r $1,315.00; 1955-59. 10r $1,185.00) – Internal Affairs and Foreign Affairs, 1945-59. With printed guides – 1 – $3,625.00 set – us UPA [972]

CONFIDENTIAL...CENTRAL FILES : INDIA / U.S. Department of State – (Internal Affairs: 1945-49, Pt 1: Political, Governmental and National Defense Affairs. 23r $2,740.00; Pt 2: Social, Economic and Industrial Affairs. 20r $2,390.00; 1950-54. $11,925.00; Foreign Affairs: 1945-49. 2r $235.00; 1950-54. $475.00) – Internal Affairs and Foreign Affairs, 1945-59. With printed guides – 1 – $16,875.00 set – us UPA [950]

CONFIDENTIAL...CENTRAL FILES : INDOCHINA / U.S. Department of State – (Internal Affairs: 1945-49. 10r $1,185.00; 1950-54. 44r $5,240.00; Internal and Foreign Affairs, 1955-59. $6,435.00) – Internal and Foreign Affairs, 1945-59. With printed guides – 1 – $12,215.00 set – us UPA [950]

CONFIDENTIAL...CENTRAL FILES : IRAN / U.S. Department of State – (1945-49. 18 reels. ISBN: 0-89093-676-5. $2,155.00; 1950-54. 44 reels. ISBN: 0-89093-677-3. $5,240.00; 1955-59. $3,220.00) – Internal and Foreign Affairs, 1945-59 – 1 – $10,070.00 set – us UPA [327]

CONFIDENTIAL...CENTRAL FILES : IRAQ / U.S. Department of State – (1945-49. 10 reels. ISBN: 0-89093-904-7. $1,185.00; 1950-54. 18 reels. ISBN: 0-89093-905-5. $2,155.00; 1955-59. $2,155.00) – Internal and Foreign Affairs, 1945-59 – 1 – $5,210.00 set – us UPA [327]

CONFIDENTIAL...CENTRAL FILES : ITALY / U.S. Department of State – (1940-44: 6r $720.00 ISBN 0-89093-923-3; 1945-49: $1,070.00 ISBN 0-89093-483-5; 1950-54: $595.00 ISBN 1-55655-040-5) – Foreign Affairs, 1940-54. With printed guides – 1 – us UPA [324]

CONFIDENTIAL...CENTRAL FILES : ITALY / U.S. Department of State – (1940-45: 44r $5,240.00 ISBN 0-89093-922-5; 1945-49, Pt 1: Political, Governmental and National Defense Affairs. $3,455.00 ISBN 0-89093-485-1; Pt 2: Social, Economic and Industrial Affairs. $4,055.00 ISBN 0-89093-489-4; 1950-54, Pt 1: $2,015.00 ISBN 1-55655-038-3; Pt 2: $4,170.00 ISBN 1-55655-039-1) – Internal Affairs, 1940-54. With printed guides – 1 – us UPA [324]

CONFIDENTIAL...CENTRAL FILES : ITALY / U.S. Department of State – (See also indiv. listings) – Internal Affairs and Foreign Affairs, 1940-54 – 1 – $20,255.00 set – us UPA [324]

CONFIDENTIAL...CENTRAL FILES : LEBANON / U.S. Department of State – (1945-49. 5r ISBN 0-89093-908-X. $595.00; 1950-54. 13r ISBN 0-89093-909-8. $1,550.00; 1955-59. 16r ISBN 1-55655-262-9. $1,900.00) – Internal and Foreign Affairs, 1945-59 – 1 – $3,850.00 – us UPA [327]

CONFIDENTIAL...CENTRAL FILES : MEXICO / U.S. Department of State – (1940-44, Pt 1: Political, Governmental and National Defense Affairs. 43r $5,120.00; Pt 2: Social, Economic and Industrial Affairs. 67r $7,975.00; 1945-49, Pt 1. $2,015.00; Pt 2. $4,170.00; 1950-54. 43r $5,120.00; 1955-59. 25r $2,975.00) – Internal Affairs, 1940-59. With printed guides – us UPA [324]

CONFIDENTIAL...CENTRAL FILES : MEXICO / U.S. Department of State – (1950-54. 18r $1,900.00; 1955-59. 11r $1,315.00) – Foreign Affairs, 1950-59. With printed guides – 1 – us UPA [324]

CONFIDENTIAL...CENTRAL FILES : MEXICO / U.S. Department of State – (See also indiv. listings) – Internal Affairs and Foreign Affairs, 1940-59 – 1 – $29,075.00 set – us UPA [324]

CONFIDENTIAL...CENTRAL FILES : NICARAGUA / U.S. Department of State – (1945-49. 12r $1,430.00; 1950-54. 11r $1,315.00; 1955-59. 9r $1,070.00) – Internal and Foreign Affairs, 1945-59. With printed guides – 1 – $3,625.00 set – us UPA [324]

CONFIDENTIAL...CENTRAL FILES : PALESTINE / U.S. Department of State – United Nations Activities, 1945-49. With printed guide – 14r – 1 – $1,665.00 – us UPA [956]

CONFIDENTIAL...CENTRAL FILES : PALESTINE – ISRAEL / U.S. Department of State – (1945-49. 29r ISBN: 0-89093-646-3. $3,455.00; Foreign Affairs, 1950-54. 6r ISBN: 0-89093-715-X. $720.00; Internal Affairs, 1950-54. 21r ISBN: 0-89093-714-1. $2,505.00; Foreign Affairs, 1955-59. 17r ISBN: 1-55655-260-2. $2,025.00; Internal Affairs, 1955-59. 18r ISBN: 1-55655-261-0. $2,270.00) – Internal and Foreign Affairs, 1945-59 – 1 – $12,000.00 set – us UPA [327]

CONFIDENTIAL...CENTRAL FILES : PANAMA / U.S. Department of State – (1930-39, Internal Affairs. $2,860.00; Foreign Affairs.

$1,305.00; 1940-44. $3,100.00; 1945-49. $2,740.00) – Internal and Foreign Affairs, 1930-49. With printed guides – 1 – $9,505.00 set – us UPA [972]

CONFIDENTIAL...CENTRAL FILES : THE PERSIAN GULF STATES AND YEMEN / U.S. Department of State – Internal and Foreign Affairs, 1950-59 – 15r – 1 – $1,665.00 – 1-55655-381-1 – us UPA [956]

CONFIDENTIAL...CENTRAL FILES : THE PHILIPPINE REPUBLIC / U.S. Department of State – (1945-49. 35r $4,170.00; 1950-54. 37r $4,405.00; 1955-59. $2,860.00) – Internal and Foreign Affairs, 1945-59. With printed guides – 1 – $10,860.00 set – us UPA [324]

CONFIDENTIAL...CENTRAL FILES : POLAND / U.S. Department of State – (1945-49. 29r $1,920.00; 1950-54. 17r $1,180.00) – Internal Affairs and Foreign Affairs, 1945-54. With printed guides – 1 – $2,945.00 set – us UPA [947]

CONFIDENTIAL...CENTRAL FILES : EL SALVADOR / U.S. Department of State – (1945-49: 7r $835.00; 1950-54: 13r $1,550.00; 1955-59: 7r $835.00) – Internal Affairs and Foreign Affairs, 1955-59. With printed guides – 1 – $3,055.00 set – us UPA [324]

CONFIDENTIAL...CENTRAL FILES : SAUDI ARABIA / U.S. Department of State – (1945-49. 12r ISBN 0-89093-716-8. $1,430.00; 1950-54. 10r ISBN 0-89093-717-6. $1,185.00; 1955-59. 11r ISBN 1-55655-264-5. $1,315.00) – Internal and Foreign Affairs, 1945-59. With printed guides – 1 – $3,735.00 set – us UPA [327]

CONFIDENTIAL...CENTRAL FILES : SOUTH AFRICA / U.S. Department of State – (1945-49. 14r $1,665.00; 1950-54. 23r $2,740.00; 1955-59. $1,665.00) – Internal and Foreign Affairs, 1945-59. With printed guides – 1 – $5,770.00 set – us UPA [324]

CONFIDENTIAL...CENTRAL FILES : THE SOVIET UNION / U.S. Department of State – (1945-49. 10r $1,185.00; 1950-54. 12r $1,430.00; 1955-59. $1,785.00) – Foreign Affairs, 1945-59. With printed guides – 1 – us UPA [947]

CONFIDENTIAL...CENTRAL FILES : THE SOVIET UNION / U.S. Department of State – (1945-49. 39r $4,640.00; 1950-54. 38r $4,525.00; 1955-59. $5,475.00) – Internal Affairs, 1945-59. With printed guides – 1 – us UPA [947]

CONFIDENTIAL...CENTRAL FILES : THE SOVIET UNION / U.S. Department of State – (See also indiv. listings) – Internal Affairs and Foreign Affairs, 1945-59 – 1 – $18,090.00 set – us UPA [947]

CONFIDENTIAL...CENTRAL FILES : SPAIN / U.S. Department of State – (Internal Affairs 1930-39, Pt 1: Political, Governmental and National Defense Affairs. 66r $7,860.00 ISBN 0-89093-886-5; Pt 2: Social, Economic and Industrial Affairs. $2,625.00 ISBN 0-89093-887-3; Foreign Affairs 1930-39. $350.00 ISBN 0-89093-888-1) – Internal Affairs and Foreign Affairs, 1930-39. With printed guides – 1 – $10,290.00 set – us UPA [946]

CONFIDENTIAL...CENTRAL FILES : SYRIA / U.S. Department of State – (1945-49. 9 reels. ISBN: 0-89093-906-3. $1,070.00; 1950-54. 12 reels. ISBN: 0-89093-907-1. $1,430.00) – Internal and Foreign Affairs, 1945-54 – 1 – $2,380.00 set – us UPA [327]

CONFIDENTIAL...CENTRAL FILES / U.S. Department of State – Argentina: Internal Affairs and Foreign Affairs, 1950-54. 29 reels with printed guide – 1 – $3,455.00 – us UPA [972]

CONFIDENTIAL...CENTRAL FILES / U.S. Department of State – Argentina: Internal Affairs and Foreign Affairs, 1955-59. 29 reels with printed guide – 1 – $3,335.00 – us UPA [972]

CONFIDENTIAL...CENTRAL FILES / U.S. Department of State – Japan: Internal Affairs, 1945-49. 42 reels with printed guide – 1 – $3,850.00 – 0-89093-731-1 – us UPA [324]

CONFIDENTIAL...CENTRAL FILES / U.S. Department of State – Japan: Internal Affairs, 1950-54. 62 reels with printed guide – 1 – $5,365.00 – 0-89093-732-X – us UPA [324]

CONFIDENTIAL...CENTRAL FILES / U.S. Department of State – (Part 1. 26 reels with printed guide. $2,680.00; 1) – Great Britain: Internal Affairs, 1945-49 – us UPA [941]

CONFIDENTIAL...CENTRAL FILES / U.S. Department of State – (Part 1. Political, Governmental, and National Defense Affairs. 28 reels with printed guide. $3,335.00; Part 2. Social, Economic, and Industrial Affairs. 19 reels with printed guide. $2,270.00) – Argentina: Internal Affairs and Foreign Affairs, 1945-49 – us UPA [972]

CONFIDENTIAL...CENTRAL FILES / U.S. Department of State – South Africa: Internal and Foreign Affairs, 1950-54. 23 reels with printed guide – 1 – $2,485.00 – us UPA [324]

CONFIDENTIAL...SPECIAL FILES : KOREA, 1950-57 / U.S. Department of State – 1 – $1,210.00 – us UPA [950]

CONFIDENTIAL...SPECIAL FILES : NORTHEAST ASIA, 1943-56 / U.S. Department of State – 1 – $2,650.00 – us UPA [950]

CONFIDENTIAL...SPECIAL FILES : SOUTHEAST ASIA, 1944-58 / U.S. Department of State – 1 – $4,065.00 – us UPA [950]

CONFINADO EN LAS HURDES (UNA VICTIMA DE LA INQUISICION REPUBLICANA) / Albinana, Jose Maria – Madrid: Imp. El Financiero, 1933 – 1 – sp Bibl Santa Ana [946]

A CONFIRMATION TRACT: TOUCHING A FEW PRACTICAL AND VITAL QUESTIONS, IN THAT CONNECTION NOT USUALLY TREATED / Cole, J S – Toronto: Rowsell & Hutchison, 1879. 00703. (Pre-1900 Canadiana) – 9 – cn C.I.H.M. [240]

A CONFIRMATORY FACTOR ANALYSIS OF THE CAROLINA SPORT CONFIDENCE INVENTORY / Mink, Randi S – University of North Carolina at Chapel Hill, 1995 – 2mf – 9 – $8.00 – PSY1855 – us Microform Publ [150]

CONFITEBOR A 5 VOIX AVEC DES INSTRUMENTS / Pergolesi, G B – (Full score, for soprano solo, SSATB, str, bc) – Pub: Rome, Gli Amici della Muscia da camera, 1942, Ms, 178- – 1 – us Sibley [780]

CONFITEMINI DOMINO [1705] AND CONFITEMINI [1699]. MOTETS A GRAND CHOEUR / Lalande, M R – (Manuscript score) – 1st Work: Paris: Philidor, 1705; 2nd work: Paris: Bovin, 1729 – 1 – us Sibley [780]

CONFLICT – v1- 1978- – 1,5,6,9 – us UMI [320]

THE CONFLICT / Braddon, Mary Elizabeth – British Fiction Archive: Unit 5 – 9 – uk Bell [830]

CONFLICT AND CONSENSUS IN BRITISH INDUSTRIAL RELATIONS / Great Britain. Public Record Office – (Pt 1: Government Industrial Relations Policy, 1921-46; Reconstruction Policy, 1917-18; National Industrial Conference , Wages and Hours Policies; Relationships with the T.U.C. and related subjects (from Lab 2, Lab 10, Lab 31, PRO 30; 69, T1 and T162). 2200.00; 1. NT.-0020 Pt 2: The General Strike, 1926; Industrial Disputes, 1921-46; Trade Disputes Record Books, 1916-46 (from Lab 2, Lab 10, Lab 27, Lab 34). 2500.00; RP; 1. Pt 2: The General Strike, 1926; Industrial Disputes, 1921-46; Trade Disputes Record Books, 1916-46 (from Lab 2, Lab 10, Lab 27, Lab 34). 2500.00; HP; 1. Pt 3: Conciliation Officers' Weekly Reports, 1940-46 (from Lab 10). 1300.00; HP; 1. Pt 3: Conciliation Officers' Weekly Reports, 1940-46 (from Lab 10). 1300.00; RP; 1) – 1916-48. Complete files selected from PRO classes Lab 2, Lab 10, Lab 27, Lab 31, Lab 34, PRO 30 69, T1 and T162 – us Primary [941]

THE CONFLICT BETWEEN DESPOTISM AND LIBERTY, OR THE RIGHT OF TRIAL BY JURY ABOLISHED IN CIVIL SUITS, AND SUSTAINED BY THE COURTS OF THE STATE OF NEW YORK. – Rochester, Curtis, Butts, 1860. 15 p. LL-15 – 1 – us L of C Photodup [340]

THE CONFLICT BETWEEN PAGANISM AND CHRISTIANITY IN THE FOURTH CENTURY / Momigliano, A – Oxford, 1963 – Dfl22.00 – ne Slangenburg [230]

CONFLICT IN SPAIN 1920-1937 / Gooden, G M – London, 1938; Burgos: Razon y Fe, 1938 – 1 – sp Bibl Santa Ana [946]

THE CONFLICT IN SPAIN; COMMUNISTIC MISSTATEMENTS REFUTED / Merry del Val, Alfonso – London, 1938. Fiche W 1046. (Blodgett Collection of Spanish Civil War Pamphlets) – 9 – us H.U. College Libr [946]

THE CONFLICT OF AGES: OR, THE GREAT DEBATE ON THE MORAL RELATIONS OF GOD AND MAN / Beecher, Edward – 7th ed. Boston: Phillips, Sampson, 1855. c1853. xii, 552p – 1 – us U.W. Library [240]

THE CONFLICT OF DUTIES AND OTHER ESSAYS / Gardner, Alice – London: T. Fisher Unwin, 1903 – 1mf – us A.T.L.A. [240]

THE CONFLICT OF LAWS IN CASES OF DIVORCE / Fraser, P – Edinburgh, 1860 – 1mf – 1 – ILM-3101/1 – ne IDC [327]

CONFLICT OF RACES IN SOUTH AFRICA / Aiyar, P S – Durban: African Chronicle Print Works, [1946?] – 1 – us Res Libr [960]

EL CONFLICTO DE ESPANA ANTE EL MUNDO CRISTIANO REPUBLICA, MONARQUIA, FASCISMO Y JUSTICIA DE UNA CAUSA / Thompson, Emmanuel – San Jose, Costa Rica, 1937. Fiche W1225. (Blodgett Collection of Spanish Civil War Pamphlets) – 9 – us H.U. College Libr [946]

CONFLICTO INTERNATIONAL, (ECUADOR Y PERU) / Coral, L – Guayaquil, 1894 – 4mf – 1 – ILM-1989/1 – ne IDC [327]

LOS CONFLICTOS DEL PROLETARIADO. EL MOVIMIENTO SOCIAL CONTEMPORANEO: POR QUE, CUANDO Y COMO HA NACIDO EL PROBLEMA OBRERO / Cascales Munoz, Jose – Madrid: Imp. Alrededor del mundo, 1912 – 1 – sp Bibl Santa Ana [946]

LOS CONFLICTOS INTERNACIONALES Y EL PANAMERICANISMO / [Bustamente, D S] – Bolivia, 1917 – 1mf – 1 – ILM-4082/1 – ne IDC [327]

THE CONFLICTS OF THE AGE (EVOLUTION, AGNOSTICISM, MORALITY) – New York: Scribner, 1881. 1 fiche – 9 – us A.T.L.A. [240]

DES CONFLITS DE LOIS EN MATIERE D'AVARIES... / Darmon, R – Paris, 1908 – 2mf – 1 – ILM-3203/1 – ne IDC [327]

LES CONFLITS DE LOIS EN MATIERE DE CONTRATS / Batiffol, H – Paris, 1938 – 6mf – 9 – ILM-3022/1 – ne IDC [340]

DES CONFLITS DE LOIS...DU TESTAMENT SOUS-SEING PRIVE / Dubrujeaud, A – Paris, 1908 – 3mf – 9 – ILM-3408/1 – ne IDC [327]

CONFLUENCES – Lyon, Paris. juil 1941-47 – 1 – fr A.C.R.P.P. [073]

LA CONFLUENCIA – v. 1- 1976- – 1,5,6,9 – us UMI [000]

THE CONFORMATION OF THE MATERIAL BY THE SPIRITUAL : TO IMPERFECTION BY THE SPIRIT OF ERROR, TO PERFECTION AND BEAUTY BY THE SPIRIT OF TRUTH: CHRISTIAN IDEALISM / Thomas, W Cave – London: Strangeways and Walden, 1862 – 1mf – 9 – 0-8370-7432-0 – 1986-1432 – us A.T.L.A. [210]

CONFORMITE DE LA CONDUITE DE L'EGLISE DE FRANCE...AVEC CELLE DE L'EGLISE D'AFFRIQUE... / Dubois-Goibaud, P – Paris, 1685 – 4mf – 9 – CA-127/1 – ne IDC [240]

CONFORMITE DU LANGAGE FRANCOIS AVEC LE GREC / Estienne, Henri – 1853 – 9 – fr I.C.S. [450]

CONFRATERNIDAD CHILENO-ARGENTINA – [Buenos Aires?: Servicio Internacional Publicaciones Argentinas], 1953 – 1 – CSUXAHZ3518-B – us Hoover Inst Photo [972]

CONFRATERNIDAD LATINOAMERICANA – [Buenos Aires?: Servicio Internacional Publicaciones Argentinas], 1953 – 1 – CSUXADJ2540-B – us Hoover Inst Photo [972]

CONFRATERNIDAD PARAGUAYO ARGENTINA : VISITA REALIZADA POR EL PRESIDENTE DE LA REPUBLICA ARGENTINA, TENIENTE GENERAL JUAN DOMINGO PERON, A LA HERMANA REPUBLICA DEL PARAGUAY, LOS DIAS 6 Y 7 DE JUNIO DE 1974 / Argentina. Secretaria de Prensa – Buenos Aires: Presidencia de la Nacion, Secretaria de Prensa y Difusion, Republica Argentina, 1974 – 1 – CSUXAJB7738-B – us Hoover Inst Photo [320]

LA CONFRERERIE ET SES ECOLES / Nepluyeff, Nicolas de – Paris. 1900. (La Condition Ouvriere. Part Two.) – 9 – 7.50 – fr Bibl Nationale [360]

CONFRERIE DE SAINT JOSEPH DU SUFFRAGE – 2e ed., rev. et augm. 18??. 04238. (Pre-1900 Canadiana) – 9 – cn C.I.H.M. [240]

LA CONFRERIE MUSULMANE DE SIDI MOHAMMED BEN 'ALI ES SENOUSI ET SON DOMAINE GEOGRAOHIQUE EN L'ANNEE 1300 DE L'HEGIRE : 1883 DE NOTRE ERE / Duveyrier, Henri – Paris: Societe de geographie, 1886 – 1 – us Res Libr [260]

CONFRONTATION; A MANIFESTATION OF THE INDONESIAN PROBLEM / Muhammad Ghazali bin Shafie – SE-10,367 1. 1964 – 9 – ne IDC [360]

CONFRONTI – (Cont: Nuovi Tempi) – v16-20. 1989-93 (complete) – 3r – 1 – ATLA S0635 – us A.T.L.A. [073]

CONFRONTI *see* NUOVI TEMPI

CONFUCIANISM AND ITS RIVALS : LECTURES DELIVERED IN THE UNIVERSITY HALL OF DR. WILLIAMS' LIBRARY, LONDON, OCTOBER-DECEMBER 1914 / Giles, Herbert Allen – London: Williams and Norgate, 1915 – 1mf – us A.T.L.A. [290]

CONFUCIUS AND THE CHINESE CLASSICS: OR, READINGS IN CHINESE LITERATURE / Loomis, Augustus Ward – Ed.and comp. by Rev. A.W. Loomis. San Francisco, New York: A. Roman & Company, 1867.xiii,(16)-432p – 1 – us U.W. Library [480]

A CONFUTATION OF THE DUTCH ARMINIAN TENET OF UNIVERSAL REDEMPTION / Brabourn, Theoph – 1651 – 1 – us A.T.L.A. [240]

CONFVSION DE LA SECTE DE MVHAMED / Andres, J – Paris, 1573 – 3mf – 9 – H-8343/1 – ne IDC [956]

CONFVTATIO BREVIS LIBRI, SUB ALIENO NOMINE EDITI, DE CONTROVERSIA INTER THEOLOGOS VVITTEBERGENSES,... / Huber, S – N.p., 1595 – 1mf – ne IDC [240]

CONG BAO / Indochina. French – Bulletin officiel en langue indigene. Bac-ky Bao ho, Quoc ngu Cong bao, Saigon. 1936-40 – 1 – fr A.C.R.P.P. [073]

CONG BAO = OFFICIAL GAZETTE – Jan-Sept 15 1975 – 5mf – 9 SEL-107/1 – ne IDC [340]

CONG BAO VIET-NAM / Vietnam – Journal officiel. juin 1948-50 – 1 – fr A.C.R.P.P. [073]

CONG DON'S CAVALRY COMPENDIUM – West Coast. 1864 – 1r – 1 – $50.00 – D121 – us Library Micro [978]

Cong of Micronesia. Joint Committee on Future Status *see* PROCEEDINGS OF THE 6TH ROUND OF FUTURE POLITICAL STATUS NEGOTIATIONS

Congar, Y M J *see* THE CATHOLIC CHURCH AND THE RACE QUESTION

CONGAREE BAPTIST CHURCH. RICHLAND COUNTY. SOUTH CAROLINA : CHURCH RECORDS – 1849-1953 – 1 – 47.84 – us Baptist [240]

CONG-BAO – no. 3-16. Hanoi. 18 juil-2 aout 1930 – 1 – fr A.C.R.P.P. [073]

CONG-BAO VIET-NAM CONG-HOA : AN-BAN QUOC-HOI – Saigon, 1959-68 – 7r – 1 – us Ross [950]

CONG-BAO VIET-NAM CONG-HOA : AN-BAN QUOC-HOI – Saigon (Thu'o'ng-Nghi-Vien). n1-17. 1969 – 1r – 1 – us Ross [950]

CONG-BAO VIET-NAM CONG-HOA : JOURNAL OFFICIEL DE LA REPUBLIQUE DU VIET NAM – Saigon, 1955-70 – 44r – 1 – us Ross [324]

CONG-BAO VIET-NAM CONG-HOA / Vietnam – An-ban Quoc-hoi; (Ha-Ngi-Vien). Saigon. May 26-July 22, 1968, Jan.-Aug. 29, 1969 – 1 – us NY Public [950]

CONG-BAO VIET-NAM CONG-HOA / Vietnam – Oct 1955-April 1975 – 1 – 2392.00 – us L of C Photodup [950]

Congdon, Frederick Tennyson *see* A DIGEST OF THE NOVA SCOTIA COMMON LAW, EQUITY, VICE-ADMIRALTY AND ELECTION REPORTS: WITH NOTES OF MANY UNREPORTED CASES AND OF CASES APPEALED TO THE PRIVY COUNCIL AND SUPREME COURT OF CANADA FROM NOVA SCOTIA

Conger, Arthur Bloomfield *see* RELIGION FOR THE TIME: SIX CONFERENCES ON NATURAL RELIGION

Conger, John L *see* HISTORY OF THE ILLINOIS RIVER VALLEY

CONG-GIAO DONG-THIN – Saigon. 16 sept 1927-nov 1937 – 1 – fr A.C.R.P.P. [073]

Conginsby, F C *see* SOME INTERNATIONAL ELEMENTS IN MATRIMONIAL CAUSES

CONGLETON CHRONICLE – Oct 14 1893-97; Jan 22-Jun 4 1898; Jun 11 1898-1911; 1950; 1967; 1986-87; Jan 8 1988-Jun 1991; Jul 5-Dec 27 1991; 1992; Jan 8-Jun 25 1993; Jul 1993-96 – 51r – 1 – uk British Libr Newspaper [072]

CONG-LUAN BAO – Xuat ban thu'o'ng ngay. Saigon. 15 mars 1917-18-oct 1939 – 1 – fr A.C.R.P.P. [073]
CONGO – Leopoldville, 1959(Nov. 21)-1960(Sept. 13) – 1 reel – 6 – AF-108/3 – ne IDC [960]
CONGO – (Issues filmed as pt of: R E Bartlett collection of African newspapers) – Leopoldville: [P Kanza, aug 27-sep 2 1960] – us Res Libr [072]
CONGO – Leopoldville: [P Kanza, apr 13-20, jun 1,15, jul 13-20 1957; nov 21-dec 26 1959; jan 2-jul 2, aug 3-sep 13 1960 – us Res Libr [072]
Congo *see*
- BULLETIN PROVINCIAL DU KATANGA ORIENTAL
- COLLECTION OF ARCHIVES OF C.E.P. (CENTRE D'ETUDES POLITIQUES) AND I.R.E.S. (INSTITUTE DE RECHERCHES ECONOMIQUES ET SOCIALES)
- ETUDES CONGOLAISES
- INFORMATIONS OFFICIELLES DE LA REPUBLIQUE DU CONGO
- MONITEUR CONGOLAIS
- MONITEUR KATANGAIS
- NEWSPAPER CLIPPINGS, COLLECTION OF THE C.E.P. AT THE I.R.E.S
- NOUVELLES DU CONGO
- LE PROGRAMME TRIENNAL DE DEVELOPPEMENT 1975-1977
- RAPPORT D'ACTIVITE SUR L'OPERATION CIVILE DES NATIONS UNIES (ORGANISATION ET TRAVAUX)
- RAPPORT DE LA COMMISSION DE CONCILIATION DES NATIONS UNIES POUR LE CONGO
- REPORT OF COMMISSION OF INVESTIGATION INTO THE CONDITIONS AND CIRCUMSTANCES RESULTING IN THE TRAGIC DEATH OF MR. DAG HAMMARSKJOLD.
- LA REPUBLIQUE DU CONGO DEVANT L'OPINION MONDIALE

LE CONGO / Pigafetta, Philippe – La veridique description du royaume africain. Bruxelles, Gay. 1883 – 9 – 7.50 – fr Orientalistes [960]
THE CONGO; A REPORT OF THE COMMISSION OF ENQUIRY..; A COMPLETE AND ACCURATE TRANSLATION / Congo Free State. Commission to Investigate the State Territories – New York and London: G.P. Putnam's Sons, 1906. iii,171p. On cover: Questions of the Day – 1 – us U.W. Library [324]
CONGO AFRIQUE – Leopoldville, 1966-1968. 3v – 20mf – A-693/1 – ne IDC [960]
Congo. Ambassade. Bruxelles *see* BULLETIN HEBDOMADAIRE D'INFORMATION
THE CONGO AND THE FOUNDING OF ITS FREE STATE : A STORY OF WORK AND EXPLORATION / Stanley, Henry Morton – London: S. Low, Marston, Searle, & Rivington, 1885 – 3mf – us A.T.L.A. [960]
LE CONGO BELGE ILLUSTRE : OU, L'ETAT INDEPENDENT DU CONGO (AFRIQUE CENTRALE) SOUS LA SOUVERAINETE DE S M LEOPOLD 2... / Alexis M G – 2. augm. ed. Liege: H Dessain, 1888 – 1 – us Res Libr [960]
Congo. Belgian *see*
- BULLETIN ADMINISTRATIF
- BULLETIN OFFICIEL
- LA CHARTE COLONIALE.
- LE PLAN DECENNAL APRES 6 ANS D'EXISTENCE

Congo. (Belgian). Conseil *see* SESSION GENERALE DU 23 FEVRIER AU 2 MARS 1959: ANNEXE 2: AVANT-PROJECT, DEUXIEME PLAN DECENNAL, NOTES DOCUMENTAIRES (1960-1969)
Congo. (Brazzaville) *see*
- ECONOMIE ET PLAN DE DEVELOPPEMENT, 3EME ED
- JOURNAL OFFICIEL
- PLAN INTERIMAIRE DE DEVELOPPEMENT ECONOMIQUE ET SOCIAL

Congo. Chambre des Deputes. Kinshasa/ Kalina *see* TRAVAUX PARLEMENTAIRES
Congo. Congo Presse *see*
- BULLETIN QUOTIDIEN

CONGO ET AFRIQUE NOIRE : BULLETIN HEBDOMADAIRE INTERAFRICAIN "BELGA N1, 323, 25-96 – aug 30/sep 6 1958-jun 21/30 1960 – us Res Libr [960]
THE CONGO FOR CHRIST : THE STORY OF THE CONGO MISSION / Myers, John Brown – (Includes index) – New York: Fleming H Revell, [1895?] – 1mf – 9 – 0-8370-6229-2 – 1986-0229 – us A.T.L.A. [240]
CONGO (FORMERLY FRENCH CONGO) : ANNUAIRE STATISTIQUE 1958-1963, 1969 / Congo (formerly French Congo). Service National de la Statistique, des Etudes Demographiques et Economiques – (Coll title: African Official Statistical Serials, 1867-1982) – 7mf – 9 – £60.00 – uk Chadwyck [960]
Congo (formerly French Congo). Service National de la Statistique, des Etudes Demographiques et Economiques *see* CONGO (FORMERLY FRENCH CONGO)
LE CONGO FRANCAIS DU GABON A BRAZZAVILLE / Guiral, Leon – Paris: Plon, Nourrit, 1889 – 1 – us Res Libr [960]
Congo Free State. Commission to Investigate the State Territories *see* THE CONGO; A REPORT OF THE COMMISSION OF ENQUIRY..; A COMPLETE AND ACCURATE TRANSLATION
Congo. Free State. Laws, Statutes, etc *see*
- CODE PENAL
- CODES CONGOLAIS ET LOIS USUELLES EN VIGUEUR AU CONGO, COLLATIONNES D'APRES LES TEXTES OFFICIELS ET ANNOTES
- LES CODES DU CONGO, SUIVIS DES DECRETS, ORDONNANCES ET ARRETES COMPLEMENTAIRES.

Congo. (French) *see* JOURNAL OFFICIEL DES POSSESSIONS DU CONGO FRANCAIS
LE CONGO ILLUSTRE – Voyages et travaux des Belges dans l'Etat independant du Congo. Brussels. 1892-Dec. 1895 – 1 – 35.00r – us Hoover Inst Photo [960]
CONGO INDEPENDANT – Stanleyville: Philppe Elebe, mar 19 1960 – us Res Libr [072]
THE CONGO INDEPENDENT STATE : A REPORT ON A VOYAGE OF INQUIRY / Mountmorres, William Geoffrey Bouchard de Montmorency – London: Williams & Norgate, 1906 – 1 – us Res Libr [960]
Congo. Institut de Recherches Economiques et Sociales *see* NOTES ET DOCUMENTS
Congo. (Kinshasa). Ministere du Plan et du Developpement Industriel *see* PLAN QUINQUENNAL DE DEVELOPPEMENT ECONOMIQUE ET SOCIAL. PRINCIPES GENERAUX 1965-1969
Congo. Kwango *see* DOCUMENTATION OF THE COLLECTION I.R.E.S
Congo. Leopoldville. Ministere du Plan.. *see* PLAN DE DEVELOPPEMENT ECONOMIQUE ET SOCIAL PROBLEME, VOTES A SUIVRE, ORGANISATION
Congo. Middle *see* PROJET DE TROISIEME PLAN QUADRIENNAL, SECTION TERRITORIALE
Congo. Ministere des Affaires Sociales *see* BULLETIN.
CONGO MISSION NEWS – 1945-52 – 1r – 1 – us Ross [240]
CONGO MISSION NEWS : ORGAN OF THE GENERAL CONFERENCE OF THE PROTESTANT MISSIONARIES IN CONGO – (Some vols missing) – Leopoldville, 1912-1960. Nos 1-190 – 61mf – H-2009/1 – ne IDC [240]
Congo. Nations Unies *see* PROGRAMMES DE COOPERATION TECHNIQUE.
CONGO NEWS LETTER – 1919-52 (complete) – 2r – 1 – ATLA S0497 – us A.T.L.A. [073]
Congo. Operations civiles des Nations Unies au Congo *see* ONUC-BULLETIN MENSUEL DE STATISTIQUE
Congo (People's Republic). Ministere du Plan ... Ministere du Travail. Ministere de l'Education Nationale *see* PLAN QUINQUENNAL 1982-1986
CONGO POLITICAL EPHEMERA – Chicago, IL: [microfilmed for Coop Africana Microfilm Project by] Uni of Chicago Photodup Dept, 1965 (mf ed) – 4r – 1 – us Res Libr [080]
Congo. Press Services Office of Public Information, United Nations, NY *see* ONUC-CHRONOLOGIES
CONGO PRESSE : BULLETIN QUOTIDIEN – Leopoldville, 1962. Nos 1-112 – 25mf – A-673/1 – ne IDC [960]
CONGO PRESSE – Kinshasa, Kalina, 1966(Sept. 10)-1967 – 72mf – A-674/1 – ne IDC [960]
Congo. Republic *see* JOURNAL OFFICIEL DE LA REPUBLIQUE DU CONGO
CONGO REVUE – Leopoldville, 1963(Aug. 9)-1964(June 29) – 1 reel – 6 – AF-124-3 – ne IDC [960]
Congo. Senat *see*
- ANNALES, 1960-63
- COMPTE RENDU ANALYTIQUE DU SENAT DU CONGO. 1E LEGISLATION, 1960-63. COMPTES RENDUS OFFICIELS, 2E LEGISLATION, 1965-66

CONGOLESE NEWSPAPERS. DURING THE PERIOD 1958-1967 – 6r – 6 – AF-106/3 – ne IDC [072]
CONGOLESE NEWSPAPERS. DURING THE PERIOD 1962-1966 – 151mf – A-598 – A-615/2 – ne IDC [072]
CONGOPRESSE – Leopoldville: Secretariat general du Congo belge, Section information. n4-9,11-18,21-95. nov 1947-jan 1948; feb 15-jun 1 1948; jul 15 1948-sep 1951 – 2r – us Res Libr [072]
A CONGRATULATORY ADDRESS TO THE REV. JOHN CROSSE, VICAR OF BRADFORD, ON THE PROSPECT OF HIS RECOVERY FROM A DANGEROUS DISEASE TO A STATE OF SPIRITUAL HEALTH AND SALVATION... – London, 1791 – 3mf – 9 – MP-569/1 – ne IDC [240]
A CONGRATULATORY LETTER TO THE REVD. DR. TRAPP, OCCASIONED BY HIS FOUR SERMONS AGAINST ENTHUSIASM,... / Finch, R – London, 1739 – 2mf – 9 – MP-252/1 – ne IDC [240]
Congregacion de la Inmaculada San Luis y San Estanislao *see* MEMORIA 1948-49
CONGREGACIONES MARIANAS DEL...BAJO LA ADVOCACION DE LA INMACULADA CONCEPCION, SAN LUIS GORZAGA Y SAN ESTANISLAO DE KOSTKA (1900-1901) / Colegio San Jose – Madrid: Imp. Aurial, 1901 – 1 – sp Bibl Santa Ana [240]
THE CONGREGATION – Philadelphia, PA. v1-16. 1972-87 (complete) – 1r – 1 – ATLA S0340 – us A.T.L.A. [073]
Congregation de la Sainte-Vierge de Ville-Marie. Montreal, Quebec *see* MANUEL DE PIETE A L'USAGE DES CONGREGANISTES.
Congregation de Notre-Dame *see*
- CONSTITUTIONS DES SOEURS.
- PETIT QUESTIONNAIRE POUR FACILITER L'ETUDE DE L'ARBRE HISTORIQUE DU CANADA

Congregation des Sacres-Coeurs et de l'Adoration *see* ANNALES DES SACRES-COEURS
CONGREGATION LUBAVITCH TIMES – South Brookline, Mass., Winter 1990/91-Spring 1991 – us A.J.P.C. [240]
Congregation Sons of Israel and David *see* ORGAN OF CONGREGATION SONS OF ISRAEL AND DAVID
CONGREGATIONAL CHRISTIAN HISTORICAL SOCIETY : NEWS – v5-10. 1973-78 (incomplete) – 1r – 1 – ATLA S0403 – us A.T.L.A. [240]
CONGREGATIONAL CONVENTION OF VERMONT : MINUTES – 1899-1907 (complete) – 1r – 1 – ATLA S0607 – us A.T.L.A. [240]
Congregational Historical Society *see* TRANSACTIONS
CONGREGATIONAL HOME MISSIONARY SOCIETY : REPORTS – nos 1-110. 1827-1936 (complete) – 11r – 1 – ATLA S0184 – us A.T.L.A. [240]
Congregational Ministers and Churches of Vermont *see* GENERAL CONVENTION OF CONGREGATIONAL MINISTERS AND CHURCHES OF VERMONT
CONGREGATIONAL NEWS – Portland OR. June 13 1880 – 1 – us U.O. Library [071]
THE CONGREGATIONAL QUARTERLY – v1-28. 1932-50 (complete) – Inquire – 1 – ATLA 1993-S505 – us A.T.L.A. [073]
CONGREGATIONAL UNION OF SCOTLAND : MANUAL – 1978-82 (complete) – Inquire – 1 – ATLA S0922 – us A.T.L.A. [073]
CONGREGATIONAL UNION OF SCOTLAND : YEAR BOOK (1962) – 1962/1963-77 (complete) – Inquire – 1 – ATLA S0921 – us A.T.L.A. [030]
CONGREGATIONAL UNION OF SCOTLAND : YEAR BOOK (1984) – 1984-93 (complete) – Inquire – 1 – ATLA S0923 – us A.T.L.A. [030]
CONGREGATIONALIST – (Cont: The Free Churches) – v1-152. 1957-92 (complete) – Inquire – 1 – ATLA S0839 – us A.T.L.A. [073]
THE CONGREGATIONALIST – Cape Town, SA. v34-68. 1934-68 (complete) – 1r – 1 – ATLA S0541 – us A.T.L.A. [240]
CONGREGATIONALIST, GOOD REASONS FOR NOT BEING A CONGREGATIONALIST... *see* MISCELLANEOUS PAMPHLETS
CONGREGATIONALISTS IN AMERICA : A POPULAR HISTORY OF THEIR ORIGIN, BELIEF, POLITY, GROWTH AND WORK / Dunning, Albert E – New York: J.A. Hill, c1894 – 2mf – us A.T.L.A. [240]
LES CONGREGATIONS ENSEIGNANTES ET LE BREVET DE CAPACITE / Chapais, Thomas – Quebec: L. Brousseau, 1893. 02868. (Pre-1900 Canadiana) – 9 – cn C.I.H.M. [971]
LE CONGRES – Quebec: C. Darveau, 1875. 00334. (Pre-1900 Canadiana) – 9 – cn C.I.H.M. [971]
CONGRES ARCHEOLOGIQUE DE FRANCE, 114E SESSION 1956, LA ROCHELLE – Orleans, 1956 – 7mf – 8 – ne Slangenburg [930]
Congres Catholique Canadien francais. Ier: 1880. Quebec, Quebec *see* ACTES ET DELIBERATIONS...LES 25, 26 ET 27 JUIN 1880: ANNUAIRE NO. 3 DU CERCLE CATHOLIQUE DE QUEBEC, 1879-80
CONGRES DE DROIT INTERNATIONAL D'ANVERS / Duguit, L – Paris, 1886 – 1mf – 1 – ILM-3282/1 – ne IDC [327]
LE CONGRES DE LA BAIE SAINT PAUL / Auclair, Joseph – Quebec: Darveau, 1882. 02451. (Pre-1900 Canadiana) – 9 – cn C.I.H.M. [971]
Congres de la Colonisation. 1898: Montreal, Quebec *see* RAPPORT...LES 22, 23 ET 24 NOVEMBRE 1898
CONGRES DE VERONE : GUERRE D'ESPAGNE / Chateaubriand – Paris. 2v. 1838 – 12mf – 1 – ILM-2572/1 – ne IDC [327]
LE CONGRES DE VIENNE ET LES TRAITES DE 1815 / Chodzko, L – Paris. 2v. 1863 – 24mf – 9 – Dfl 153 – HQ-9/1 – ne IDC [943]
CONGRES DES CERCLES AGRICOLES SAINT ISIDORE, LABOREUR (LER: 1887: TROIS-RIVIERES, QUEBEC) – Premier Congres... tenu a Trois-Rivieres, les 20, 21 et 22 janvier 1887. Montreal: E. Senecal, 1887. 00754. (Pre-1900 Canadiana) – 9 – cn C.I.H.M. [331]
CONGRES DES INSPECTEURS D'ECOLES (1895: ST HYACINTHE, QUEBEC) – Congres...: tenu a St. Hyacinthe le 21 el le 22 aout 1895. s.l.: s.n., 1895?. 04244. (Pre-1900 Canadiana) – 9 – cn C.I.H.M. [971]
Congres des missionnaires agricoles. 1895: Oka *see* RAPPORT DE LA REUNION DES MISSIONNAIRES AGRICOLES TENUE A OKA LES 9, 10, 11 ET 12 JUILLET, 1895
LE CONGRES DES RELIGIONS A CHICAGO EN 1893 / Bonet-Maury, Gaston – Paris: Hachette, 1895 – 1mf – us A.T.L.A. [240]
Congres du Havre *see* COMPTE RENDU
Congres du Parti Ouvrier Socialiste Francais, 5th30 oct-6 nov 1881, Reims. Parti Ouvrier Socialiste Francais *see* COMPTE RENDU
Congres du Parti Ouvrier Socialiste Francais, 6th25-31 sept 1882, Saint-Etienne. Parti Ouvrier Socialiste Revolutionnaire Francais *see* COMPTE RENDU
Congres du Parti Ouvrier Socialiste Francais (Ve), 30 oct-6 nov 1881, Reims. Parti Ouvrier Socialiste Francais *see* COMPTE RENDU
Congres du Parti Ouvrier Socialiste Francais (Vle), 25-31 sept 1882, Saint-Etienne. Parti Ouvrier Socialiste Revolutionnaire Francais *see* COMPTE RENDU
Congres du Parti Ouvrier Socialiste Revolutionnaire, Allemanistes. Conference Nationale de 1895, 29 et 30 septembre, Paris *see* COMPTE RENDU
Congres du Parti Ouvrier Socialiste Revolutionnaire, Allemanistes. Congres National (10e), 21 au 29 juin 1891, Paris *see* COMPTE RENDU
Congres du Parti Ouvrier Socialiste Revolutionnaire, Allemanistes. Congres National (11e). 2-9 octobre 1892, St. Quentin *see* COMPTE RENDU
Congres du Parti Ouvrier Socialiste Revolutionnaire, Allemanistes. Congres National (12e). 14-22 juillet, 1894, Dijon *see* COMPTE RENDU
Congres du Parti Ouvrier Socialiste Revolutionnaire, Allemanistes. Congres National (14e), septembre 1896, Paris *see*
- COMPTE RENDU
- UN DOSSIER

Congres du Parti Ouvrier Socialiste Revolutionnaire, Allemanistes. Congres National (15e), 26 septembre au 3 octobre 1897, Paris *see* COMPTE RENDU

Congres du Parti Ouvrier Socialiste Revolutionnaire, Allemanistes. Federation des Travailleurs Socialistes de France. Congres Regional de l'Union Federative du Centre (10e), 1-5 oct, 1890 et 12-17 mars 1891, Paris *see* COMPTE RENDU

Congres du Parti Socialiste Francais, Jauressistes. Congres General (4e), 2 au 4 mars 1902, Tous *see* COMPTE RENDU STENOGRAPHIQUE OFFICIEL

Congres du Parti Socialiste Francais, Jauressistes. Congres National (8e), 1908, Marseille *see* RAPPORT DU MINISTERE DE L'INTERIEUR

Congres du Parti Socialiste Francais, Jauressistes. Congres socialiste de Bordeaux, 12 au 14 avril 1903 *see* DIX DISCOURS DE G. HERVE SARRAUTE MILLERAND JEAN JAURES BAUDOT RENAUDEL DE PRESSENSE PREFACE DE ROUANET

Congres du Parti Socialiste Francais, Jauressistes. Congres socialiste de Saint Etienne, 4 au 7 janvier 1904 *see* COMPTE RENDU

Congres General des Organisations Socialistes Francaises (1e), 3 au 8 decembre 1899, Paris *see* COMPTE RENDU STENOGRAPHIQUE OFFICIEL

Congres General des Organisations Socialistes Francaises (2e), 28 au 30 septembre 1900, Paris *see* COMPTE RENDU STENOGRAPHIQUE OFICIEL

Congres general des organisations socialistes francaises, 3rd *see* COMPTE RENDU STENOGRAPHIQUE

CONGRES INTERNACIONAL DES SOCIETES PAR ACTIONS...PARIS...1889 : COMPTE-RENDU STENOGRAPHIQUE – Paris, 1890 – 4mf – 1 – ILM-3916/1 – ne IDC [327]

CONGRES INTERNATIONAL DE DROIT COMMERCIAL : NOTES ET OBSERVATIONS... – Napoli, 1888 – 1mf – 1 – ILM-3901/1 – ne IDC [327]

CONGRES INTERNATIONAL DE DROIT COMMERCIAL : PROGRAMME DES TRAVAUX DE LE DEUXIEME SESSION... – Bruxelles, 1888 – 1mf – 1 – ILM-3906/1 – ne IDC [327]

LE CONGRES INTERNATIONAL DE DROIT COMMERCIAL A ANVERS. L'UNIFICATION DE LA LEGISLATION EN MATIERE DE LETTRES DE CHANGE / Nobele, Edouard de – Gand: Annoot-Braeckman, 1886. 48p. LL-4079 – 1 – us L of C Photodup [340]

CONGRES INTERNATIONAL DE DROIT COMMERCIAL (ANVERS, 1885) / Constant, C – Paris, 1886 – 1mf – 1 – ILM-3905/1 – ne IDC [327]

CONGRES INTERNATIONAL DE DROIT COMMERCIAL (ANVERS, 1885) : DROIT MARITIME... – Bruxelles, 1885 – 1mf – 1 – ILM-3903/1 – ne IDC [327]

CONGRES INTERNATIONAL DE DROIT COMMERCIAL (ANVERS, 1885) : DROIT MARITIME-LETTRE DE CHANGE – Bruxelles, Paris, 1886 – 5mf – 1 – ILM-3907/1 – ne IDC [327]

CONGRES INTERNATIONAL DE DROIT COMMERCIAL (ANVERS, 1885) : RESUME DES TRAVAUX ET RESOLUTIONS... – Berlin, 1885 – 1mf – 1 – ILM-3904/1 – ne IDC [327]

CONGRES INTERNATIONAL DE DROIT COMMERCIAL (BRUXELLES, 1888) : ACTES... – Bruxelles, Paris, 1889 – 6mf – 1 – ILM-3902/1 – ne IDC [327]

LE CONGRES INTERNATIONAL DE DROIT MARITIME DE G-NES (SEMPTEMBRE 1892) / Desjardins, A – Paris, 1893 – 1mf – 1 – ILM-3769/1 – ne IDC [327]

Congres International de folklore *see* TRAVAUX DU 1ER CONGRES..

CONGRES INTERNATIONAL DES ORIENTALISTES – (Missing: 1877-1880. v3-4; 1890. v8(1); 1901. v12(2); 1905-1908. v14) – 1875-1938. v1-19 – 163mf – I-1252/1 – ne IDC [950]

Congres International des Orientalistes *see* SERIE D'ETUDES SUR LE JAPON

Congres international des raquetteurs (1938: Montreal, Quebec) *see* CONGRES INTERNATIONAL DES RAQUETTEURS, MONTREAL 26, 27, 28, 29, 30 JANV. 1938

CONGRES INTERNATIONAL DES RAQUETTEURS, MONTREAL 26, 27, 28, 29, 30 JANV. 1938 = INTERNATIONAL CONVENTION OF SNOWSHOERS / Congres international des raquetteurs (1938: Montreal, Quebec) – [Quebec (Province): s.n., 1938 ?]. SEM105P1695 – 1mf – 9 – Can$2.25 – cn Bibl Nat [971]

CONGRES INTERNATIONAL DES SOCIETES DES AMIS DE LA PAIX,... : LES 26, 27, 28 ET 30 SEBTEMBRE ET LE OCTOBRE 1878 – Paris, 1880 – 2mf – 1 – ILM-4089/1 – ne IDC [327]

Congres International des Traditions Populaires *see* COMPTE RENDU DES SEANCES

Congres International d'Ethnologie Europeenne. (Premier) *see* ACTES

Congres International d'Hygiene et de Demographie *see* LES NAISSANCES ILLEGITIMES EN FRANCE ET DANS QUELQUES PAYS DE L'EUROPE

CONGRES INTERNATIONAL...DES FEMMES, TENU...SEPTEMBRE 1900... – Paris, 1901 – 5mf – 1 – ILM-1196/1 – ne IDC [327]

CONGRES, MAXEVILLE-NANCY, FRANCE, 1907 / Parti republicain radical et radical socialiste – Septieme Congres, Comite Executif. (La Condition Ouvriere. Part Two.) – 9 – 10.00 – fr Bibl Nationale [360]

CONGRES NATIONAL, 2ND, ALGIERS, 1965, ENSEMBLE DES TEXTES ADOPTES / Algeria. Union General des Travaillleurs Algeriens – 1965. RNE-8744 1 – 9 – ne IDC [330]

CONGRES NATIONAL, 19E-38E / Parti socialiste. Section francaise de l'internationale ouvriere – Paris. 1921-46. (La Condition Ouvriere. Part Two.) – 9 – 120.00 – fr Bibl Nationale [360]

Congres National de la Federation des Travailleurs Socialistes de France (7e), 30 sept au 7 oct 1883, Paris *see* COMPTE RENDU

Congres National de la Federation des Travailleurs Socialistes de France (8e), 12 au 19 octobre 1884, Rennes *see* COMPTE RENDU

Congres National de la Federation des Travailleurs Socialistes de France (9e), 2 au 8 octobre 1887, Charleville. Parti Ouvrier Socialiste Revolutionnaire ("Possibilistes") *see* COMPTE RENDU

Congres National de la Federation des Travailleurs Socialistes de France (10e), 9 au 15 octobre, 1890, Chatellerault. Parti Ouvrier Socialiste Revolutionnaire ("Possibilistes") *see* COMPTE RENDU

Congres National des Chambres Syndicales et Groupes Corporatifs *see* LA GREVE GENERALE

Congres National des Droits Civils et du Suffrage des Femmes *see* COMPTE-RENDU

Congres National du Parti Ouvrier Francais, Guesdiste (6e), 26 sept au 1 oct 1882, Roanne *see* SEANCES

Congres National du Parti Ouvrier Francais, Guesdiste (7e), 29 mars au 7 avril 1884, Roubaix *see* SEANCES

Congres National du Parti Ouvrier Francais, Guesdiste (8e), 11 et 12 oct 1890, Lille *see* SEANCES

Congres National du Parti Ouvrier Francais, Guesdiste (9e), 26 au 28 nov 1891, Lyon *see* SEANCES

Congres National du Parti Ouvrier Francais, Guesdiste (10e), 24 au 28 septembre 1892, Marseille *see* SEANCES

Congres National du Parti Ouvrier Francais, Guesdiste (11e), 7-8 octobre, 1893, Paris *see* SEANCES

Congres National du Parti Ouvrier Francais, Guesdiste (12e), 14 au 16 septembre 1894, Nantes *see* SEANCES

Congres National du Parti Ouvrier Francais, Guesdiste (13e), 8 au 10 septembre 1895, Romilly *see* COMPTE RENDU

Congres National du Parti Ouvrier Francais, Guesdiste (14e), 21 au 25 juillet 1896, Lille *see* COMPTE RENDU ET RESOLUTIONS

Congres National du Parti Ouvrier Francais, Guesdiste (15e), 10 au 13 juillet 1897, Paris *see* SEANCES

Congres National du Parti Ouvrier Francais, Guesdiste (16e), 17 au 20 septembre 1898, Montlucon *see* SEANCES

Congres National du Parti Ouvrier Francais, Guesdiste (17e), aout 1899, Epernay *see* COMPTE RENDU

Congres National du Parti Ouvrier Francais, Guesdiste (18e), octobre 1900, Ivry-sur-Seine *see* COMPTE RENDU

Congres National du Parti Ouvrier Francais, Guesdiste (19e), 15 au 18 septembre 1901, Roubaix *see* SEANCES

Congres National du Parti Ouvrier Francais, Guesdiste (20e), 21 au 24 septembre 1902, Issoudun *see* COMPTE RENDU

Congres National du Parti Socialiste de France, Guesdistes (1e), 26 au 28 september 1902, Commentry. (U.S.R.) *see* COMPTE RENDU COMPLET

Congres National du Parti Socialiste de France, Guesdistes (2e), 27 au 29 septembre, 1903, Reims. (U.S.R.) *see* COMPTE RENDU COMPLET

Congres National du Parti socialiste (S.F.I.O.). 1 et 2 Congres Nationaux, avril 1905, Paris, octobre 1905, Chalon s Saone *see* COMPTE RENDU ANALYTIQUE

Congres National du Parti Socialiste (S.F.I.O.). 2 Congres National, 29 octobre au 1 novembre 1905, Chalon s Saone *see* COMPTE RENDU

Congres National du Parti Socialiste (S.F.I.O.). 3 Congres National,1 au 4 novembre, Limoges *see* COMPTE RENDU ANALYTIQUE

Congres National du Parti Socialiste (S.F.I.O.). 4 Congres National, 11 au 14 aout 1907, Nancy *see* COMPTE RENDU STENOGRAPHIQUE

Congres National du Parti Socialiste (S.F.I.O.). 5 Congres National, 15 au 18 octobre 1908, Toulouse *see* COMPTE RENDU STENOGRAPHIQUE

Congres National du Parti Socialiste (S.F.I.O.). 6e *see* COMPTE RENDU STENOGRAPHIQUE

Congres National du Parti Socialiste (S.F.I.O.). 7e Congres National, 6 au 8 fevrier, 1910, Nimes *see* COMPTE RENDU STENOGRAPHIQUE

Congres National du Parti Socialiste (S.F.I.O.). 7e Congres National, 15 au 16 juillet 1910, Paris, 2e session *see* COMPTE RENDU STENOGRAPHIQUE

Congres National du Parti Socialiste (S.F.I.O.). 8 Congres National 2e session, 1 au 2 novembre 1911, Paris *see* COMPTE RENDU ANALYTIQUE

Congres National du Parti Socialiste (S.F.I.O.). 8e Congres National, 16 au 19 avril 1911, Saint Quentin *see* COMPTE RENDU STENOGRAPHIQUE

Congres National du Parti Socialiste (S.F.I.O.). 9 Congres National, 18 au 21 fevrier 1912, Lyon *see* COMPTE RENDU STENOGRAPHIQUE

Congres National du Parti Socialiste (S.F.I.O.). 10 Congres National, 23 au 25 mars 1913, Brest *see* COMPTE RENDU STENOGRAPHIQUE

Congres National du Parti Socialiste (S.F.I.O.). 11 Congres National, 25 au 28 janvier 1914, Amiens *see* COMPTE RENDU STENOGRAPHIQUE

Congres National du Parti Socialiste (S.F.I.O.). Federation de la Seine *see* DOCUMENTS CONCERNANT LE CONGRES NATIONAL DE NANCY 4E ET LE CONGRES INTERNATIONAL DE STUTTGARD (AOUT 1907)

Congres Ouvrier de France (1e), 2-10 oct 1876, Paris *see* SEANCES

Congres Ouvrier de France (2), 28 jan-8 fev 1878, Lyon *see* SEANCES

Congres Ouvrier de France (3rd: 1879: Marseille) *see* SEANCES DU CONGRES OUVRIER SOCIALISTE DE FRANCE.20-31 OCTOBRE 1879

Congres Ouvrier Socialiste de France (3e), 20-31 oct 1879, Marseille *see* SEANCES

LES CONGRES OUVRIERS EN FRANCE DE 1876 A 1897 / Seilhac, Leon de – Paris. 1899. ix-364 p. 5678 – 9 – fr Hachette [335]

Congres Panafricain de Prehistoire, 1976 *see* ACTES DU CONGRES PANAFRICAIN DE PREHISTOIRE...

CONGRES PERIODIQUE INTERNATIONAL A OPHTHALMOLOGIE. COMPTE-RENDU – (Text in several languages: Missing: V.8) – Paris, etc., 1857-1937. V.1-15(7) – 265mf – 9 – ne IDC [617]

LE CONGRES: POEMES / Auclair, Joseph – Quebec: C. Darveau, 1875. 04091. (Pre-1900 Canadiana) – 9 – cn C.I.H.M. [810]

Congres Prehistorique de France *see* COMPTE-RENDU DE LA NEUVIEME SESSION DU CONGRES PREHISTORIQUE DE FRANCE...

Congres Socialiste Ouvrier de Marseille, 1879, Marseille *see* COMPTE RENDU

Les Congres Socialistes moderes. Congres National Ouvrier Socialiste (5e) *see* SEANCES

Les Congres Socialistes Moderes. Congres Socialiste National Ouvrier de Bordeaux (6e) *see* SEANCES

CONGRESA NACIONAL DE PERIODISTAS (ARGENTINA) *see* DIEZ ANOS DE ORGANIZACION SINDICAL

CONGRESO DE ESPIRITUALIDAD FRANCISCANA / Barrado Manzano, Arcangel – Madrid: Archivo Ibero Americano, 1963 – 1 – sp Bibl Santa Ana [240]

EL CONGRESO DE GUINEA / Vinajeras, Antonio – (Filmed with: Fournier, G: La raza negra es la mas antigua de las razas humanas) – Matanzas, Ferro-Carril 1879 – us Res Libr [972]

CONGRESO DE HISTORIA Y GEOGRAFIA HISPANO-AMERICANAS EN COMMEMORACION DEL DESCUBRIMIENTO DEL MAR PACIFICO POR VASCO NUNEZ DE BALBOA / Nunez de Balboa, Vasco – Madrid: Est. Tip. Fortanet, 1914. B.R.A.H. Tomo 64, 1914, pp. 556 – 1 – sp Bibl Santa Ana [946]

Congreso de la Nacion *see* HOMENAJE POSTUMO AL EXCELENTISIMO SENOR PRESIDENTE DE LA NACION TENIENTE GENERAL DON JUAN D. PERON

CONGRESO EUCARISTICO DE DUBLIN / Bayle, Constantino – Madrid: Razon y Fe, 1932 – 1 – sp Bibl Santa Ana [240]

CONGRESO INTERNACIONAL DE BRUSELAS (1888) : INFORMES... / Mille y Suarez, E & Villalon, R Aunony – Madrid, 1889 – 2mf – 1 – ILM-3974/1 – ne IDC [327]

Congreso Internacional de Folklore *see* TRABAJO DE BASE

CONGRESO INTERNACIONAL DE MEDICINA VERIFICADO EN BERLIN DEL 4 AL 9 DE AGOSTO DE 1890 / Cisneros, Juan – Madrid: Revista Clinica de los Hospitales, 1890 – 1 – sp Bibl Santa Ana [610]

EL CONGRESO MARIANO DE SEVILLA / Bayle, Constantino – Madrid: Razon y Fe, 1929 – 1 – sp Bibl Santa Ana [946]

CONGRESO NACIONAL DE PRODUCTIVIDAD Y BIENESTAR SOCIAL : ANTECEDENTES, TEMARIO, CONCLUSIONES – Buenos Aires, 1955 – 1 – CSUXADN3472-B – us Hoover Inst Photo [338]

CONGRESO NACIONAL DE PRODUCTIVIDAD Y BIENESTAR SOCIAL (1955: BUENOS AIRES) *see* CONGRESO NACIONAL DE PRODUCTIVIDAD Y BIENESTAR SOCIAL

CONGRESO SOCIAL Y ECONOMICO HISPANO-AMERICANO REUNIDO EN MADRID EL ANO 1900 – Madrid. 2v. 1903 – 17mf – 1 – ILM-4090/1 – ne IDC [327]

EL CONGRESO Y EXPOSICION. MISIONALES DE BARCELONA / Bayle, Constantino – Madrid: Razon y Fe, 1929 – 1 – sp Bibl Santa Ana [240]

CONGRESS AND THE COURTS : A LEGISLATIVE HISTORY 1787-1984 / ed by Reams, Bernard D Jr & Haworth, Charles B – (v1-6 1781-1978 index and suppl 1 in 30 books (Series 1) $600.00 set. v1-22 1978-84 (Series 2) $395.00 set) – Series 1 and 2 pt 1 (complete) – 9 – $995.00 set – 0-89941-812-0 – us Hein [350]

CONGRESS AND THE COURTS : A LEGISLATIVE HISTORY 1985-1992. SERIES 2 PT 2 / ed by Reams, Bernard D Jr – v23-46. 1985-1992 – 9 – $1,850.00set – 0-89941-868-6 – us Hein [340]

CONGRESS BEACON – Chicago, IL. 2 Jan 1942, 2 Mar-6 Apr 1945-15 Jun 1945. Many missing – 1 – us A.J.P.C. [071]

CONGRESS BI-WEEKLY – v.26-. 1959- – 1 – us UMI [323]

CONGRESS BULLETIN – 1935- – 1 – us UMI [323]

CONGRESS BULLETIN : CANADIAN JEWISH CONGRESS – Montreal, jan 1943-feb 1976 – 2r – 1 – cn Can Microfilming [072]

CONGRESS MONTHLY – New York, NY. 1977-90 – 8r – 1 – $400.00 – R04150 – us Library Micro [071]

CONGRESS MONTHLY – (v.47-. 1980-. 5,6,9) – v.42-. 1975- – 1 – us UMI [323]

Congress of Democrats *see* CORRESPONDENCE, MINUTES, CIRCULARS, CLIPPINGS, ETC

Congress of Industrial Organizations *see*
- AFL-CIO AMERICAN FEDERATIONIST
- AFL-CIO PUBLICATIONS

Congress of Industrial Organizations. Committee on Latin American Affairs *see* THE ARGENTINE REGIME

Congress of Micronesia *see*
- HOUSE JOURNALS 1966-79
- JOURNAL OF THE GENERAL ASSEMBLY
- LAWS AND RESOLUTIONS
- POLITICAL STATUS DIGEST
- SENATE JOURNALS 1966-79

Congress of Racial Equality *see*
- CORE: ADDENDUM
- PAPERS, PART 1
- PAPERS, PART 2: SOUTHERN REGIONAL OFFICE, 1959-66
- PAPERS, PART 3: SEDFRE SERIES A, ADMINISTRATIVE FILES, 1960-76
- PAPERS, PART 3: SEDFRE SERIES B, LEADERSHIP DEVELOPMENT FILES, 1960-76
- PAPERS, PART 3: SEDFRE SERIES C, LEGAL DEPARTMENT FILES, 1960-76

Congress of the Toilers of the Far East. 1. Moscow and Leningrad. 1922 *see*
- DER ERSTE KONGRESS DER KOMMUNISTISCHEN UND REVOLUTIONAEREN ORGANISATIONEN DES FERNEN OSTENS
- PERVYI S'EZD REVOLIUTSIONNYKH ORGANIZATSII DAL'NEGO VOSTOKA

CONGRESS PAPERS / Australian and New Zealand Association for the Advancement of Science – v42- 1970- – 9 – ISSN 0312-8059 – at U.N.S.W. Library [500]

CONGRESS WEEKLY – 1941- – 1 – us UMI [323]

CONGRESSES DURING WORLD WAR 2 PAMPHLET COLLECTION – 1941-1944 – 1 – CSUXANM5486-B – us Hoover Inst Photo [355]

CONGRESSIONAL BILLS AND RESOLUTIONS, 1ST-72D AND 92D CONGRESSES – 595r – 1 – $20,825.00 – Dist. us Scholarly Res – us L of C Photodup [323]

CONGRESSIONAL BI-WEEKLY – NY City, NY. 1971-1984 – 8r – 1 – $400.00 – R04908 – us Library Micro [071]

CONGRESSIONAL BUDGET OFFICE PUBLICATIONS – (Includes chronological and title index) – 1975-96 update 1 – 9 – $2,215.00 set – In Japan: Far Eastern Book-Sellers – us Hein [324]

CONGRESSIONAL DEBATES, 1824-37 / U.S. Congress – 18th, 2nd Sess. to 25th Congress. Gales and Seaton, Publishers.29 books, all published. Followed by Congressional Globe. 80-034 – 9 – 144.00 – us L.L.M.C. [323]

CONGRESSIONAL DIGEST, VOL 1 – 1921-22. Sheppard-Towner maternity bill; public Welfare Dept. bill; Beer bill; Dept. of Educ. bill; Dog bill; Congressional reapportionment; Fed. empl. reclassif.; Peyote bill; Anti-lynching; Cooperative marketing; New naturalization bill; Fordney-McCumber tariff bill; Soldier bonus controversy; Ship subsidy controversy; Political parties and issues-1922; St. Lawrence Seaway – 1,5,9 – us Congressional Digest [324]

CONGRESSIONAL DIGEST, VOL 2 – 1922-23. Muscle shoals development; U. S. budget system; Cancellation of inter-allied war debt; Rural credits legislation; Child labor amendment; Constitution and the maternity act; Federal civil service; World Court proposal; Curbing Supreme Court powers; Immigration problem; Federal taxation – 1,5,9 – us Congressional Digest [324]

CONGRESSIONAL DIGEST, VOL 3 – 1923-24. Congress and the railroads; Organization of the new Congress; Problems before the 68th Congress; Foreign service reorganization; Sterling-Reed education bill; Woman's "equal rights" amendment; Immediate Philippine independence; McNary-Haugen agricultural bill; Peace proposals and the 68th Congress; Political parties and issues-1924; Developing our inland waterways – 1,5,9 – us Congressional Digest [324]

CONGRESSIONAL DIGEST, VOL 4 – 1924-25. Enforcement of prohibition; Dawes plan for reparations payments; Repeal of income tax publicity law; Naval armaments limitation; Postal pay and rate issue; Review of the 68th Congress; Federal Dept. of Aeronautics; Congress and cooperative marketing; Congress and the coal problem; Repeal of the federal estate tax – 1,5,9 – us Congressional Digest [324]

CONGRESSIONAL DIGEST, VOL 5 – 1926. Govt. aid to U. S. shipping; U. S. and the World Court; McFadden banking bill; Adoption of the metric system; A Federal Department of Education; Congress and prohibition enforcement; Changing inauguration day; Direct primary system; Cloture in the U. S. Senate; Settlement of U. S. war claims – 1,5,9 – us Congressional Digest [324]

CONGRESSIONAL DIGEST, VOL 6 – 1927. St. Lawrence Seaway; Boulder Dam project; Problem of railroad consolidations; U. S.-Nicaragua controversy; America and the Chinese conflict; A uniform marriage and divorce law; Question of capital punishment; Problems of copyright revision; Issues involved in seating a senator; Capital of the United States – 1,5,9 – us Congressional Digest [324]

CONGRESSIONAL DIGEST, VOL 7 – (1928). New Congress and tax question; Congress and flood control; Question of outlawing war; Third-term controversy; Immigration problems; Merchant Marine Act; 1928 Presidential election; Problem of radio reallocation; Uncle Sam and the movies; Effect of a "pocket veto" – 1,5,9 – us Congressional Digest [324]

CONGRESSIONAL DIGEST, VOL 8 – 1929. Question of more U. S. cruisers; Congressional reapportionment; New administration begins; Question of a thirteen-month year; 1929 farm relief problem; Making a tariff law; German reparations; Limitation of naval armaments; Modification of the jury system; Congress and the lobby problem – 1,5,9 – us Congressional Digest [324]

CONGRESSIONAL DIGEST, VOL 9 – 1930. Freedom of seas; Censorship of foreign books; 71st Congress and prohibition; Communications problem; Federal operation of Muscle Shoals; London naval treaty; Congress and chain stores; 1930 Congressional elections; Equal nationality rights for women: Outlook for 2nd session, 71st Congress – 1,5,9 – us Congressional Digest [324]

CONGRESSIONAL DIGEST, VOL 10 – 1931. Congress and the employment problem; New maternity and infancy bill; Motor bus controversy; Federal birth control legislation; Philippine independence; Congress and the oil problem; Compulsory unemployment insurance; America's war debt policy; Congress and the silver question; Congress and the banking situation – 1,5,9 – us Congressional Digest [324]

CONGRESSIONAL DIGEST, VOL 11 – 1932. Foreign debts; Tribute to George Washington; Tariff, politics, and the 72nd Congress; Congress considers economic planning; New tax bill; Bankruptcy problem; National campaign of 1932; Five-day work week; Veterans legislation; Investigation of "short" selling – 1,5,9 – us Congressional Digest [324]

CONGRESSIONAL DIGEST, VOL 12 – 1933. Congress and the beer problem; Domestic allotment plan; Congress and currency expansion; Congress faces the banking problem; America and tariff reciprocity; Suspension of anti-trust laws; U.S. vs. British radio control systems; U.S. recognition of the U.S.S.R.; Increasing power of the President; Supreme Court and the N.I.R.A – 1,5,9 – us Congressional Digest [324]

CONGRESSIONAL DIGEST, VOL 13 – 1934. Gold policy and commodity prices; U.S. public school crisis; New food and drug bill; National defense problem; Federal Securities Act of 1933; Congress and the New Deal; Federal monies for public schools; Federal ownership of power utilities; Investigation of munitions industries; Crop control experiment – 1,5,9 – us Congressional Digest [324]

CONGRESSIONAL DIGEST, VOL 14 – 1935. Congress and the New Deal; Compulsory unemployment insurance; Old-age pensions; Congress and the labor problem; Abolition of utility holding cos.; Lynching as a federal crime; Socialized medicine; Federal sedition legislation; Alien deportation controversy; Congress and Supreme Court powers – 1,5,9 – us Congressional Digest [324]

CONGRESSIONAL DIGEST, VOL 15 – 1936. American neutrality; Federal aid to shipping; Substitute for AAA; New Deal's housing activities; New administration tax proposal; Proposed state control of relief; National campaign of 1936; Federal ownership of electric utilities; Minimum wage law controversy; Federal all-risk crop insurance – 1,5,9 – us Congressional Digest [324]

CONGRESSIONAL DIGEST, VOL 16 – 1937. Digest teaching plan; New congress; Aid to farm tenants; Roosevelt Supreme Court plan; Proposed nationalization of munitions; Congress and the sit-down strikes; Congress and the budget; Unicameral legislative system; Roosevelt's reorganization plan; Civil Service reform; Labor and compulsory arbitration – 1,5,9 – us Congressional Digest [324]

CONGRESSIONAL DIGEST, VOL 17 – 1938. Question of regional planning; War referendum proposal; Roosevelt's national defense program; Proposed Japanese boycott; Question of presidential tenure; Pump-priming and recovery; Alliance with Great Britain; Proposed federal sales tax; Roosevelt "Purge"; Monopoly in American radio – 1,5,9 – us Congressional Digest [324]

CONGRESSIONAL DIGEST, VOL 18 – 1939. Profit sharing and increased employment; Moves to control relief; Extension of U.S. defense frontier; 150th anniversary of U.S. Congress; Expansion of social security program; Labor Relations act; Federal ownership of the railroads; Amendment of neutrality law; Investigation of un-American activities; Reciprocal tariff-making powers – 1,5,9 – us Congressional Digest [324]

CONGRESSIONAL DIGEST, VOL 19 – 1940. Extending New Deal borrowing power; Joint committee to balance the budget; Curbing powers of the NLRB; Hatch Act and state officials; Court review of U.S. rulings; War widows and orphans pensions; Increasing federal powers; Prohibition of presidential third term; Conscription of American industry; Financial aid to Latin America – 1,5,9 – us Congressional Digest [324]

CONGRESSIONAL DIGEST, VOL 20 – 1941. Military defense of the Americas; Union of American Republics; Abolition of electoral college; National defense labor-control laws; St. Lawrence Seaway; Federal union of world democracies; Perm. compulsory military training; Federal price controls and inflation; Federal regulation of labor unions; Congress and state poll tax laws – 1,5,9 – us Congressional Digest [324]

CONGRESSIONAL DIGEST, VOL 21 – 1942. Question of a separate air force; Help to small business; Abolition of tax-exempt securities; Fed. unemployment compensation; Abolition of 40-hour week; Abolition of the CCC and NYA; Administration and inflation; Post-war world organization; Poll tax legislation; War manpower problem – 1,5,9 – us Congressional Digest [324]

CONGRESSIONAL DIGEST, VOL 22 – 1943. Problems of the new Congress; The Ruml pay-as-you-go tax plan; Balancing civilian and armed forces; Equal rights for women amendment; Reciprocal trade act extension; Outlawing labor racketeering; Reconstitution of League of Nations; Treaty-making authority of Senate; The New Deal food subsidy program; Proposed federal retail sales tax – 1,5,9 – us Congressional Digest [324]

CONGRESSIONAL DIGEST, VOL 23 – 1944. Absentee soldier voting; Federal aid to public schools; Post-war education of veterans; Civilian conscription for war; Presidential fourth term; Federal vs. states rights in voting; Reduction of voting age to 18; Federal control of insurance; Limitation of federal taxing powers; Demobilization of war workers – 1,5,9 – us Congressional Digest [324]

CONGRESSIONAL DIGEST, VOL 24 – 1945. Comp. peacetime military training; Little Steel formula; Montgomery Ward seizure; Constitutional treaty process; Bretton Woods proposals; Employment discrimination; Reorganizing congressional procedures; Murray "full employment" bill; Proposed increase in minimum wage; A single armed forces department – 1,5,9 – us Congressional Digest [324]

CONGRESSIONAL DIGEST, VOL 25 – 1946. Truman's labor fact-finding boards; Federal funds for public schools; Presidental Succession Act; Control of employment services; Atomic energy control; Prospectus for the 1946 elections; Compulsory prepaid medical care; St. Lawrence Seaway; Administration housing policy; Woman's equal rights amendment – 1,5,9 – us Congressional Digest [324]

CONGRESSIONAL DIGEST, VOL 26 – 1947. Powers of the U. S. President; Outlawing the closed shop; Curbing "unfair" labor practices; Budget, debt, and taxes; Knutson income tax reduction bill; Progress of new Republican Congress; Arbitration of labor disputes; Universal military training; Hawaii and Alaska statehood; Universal "split-income" tax law – 1,5,9 – us Congressional Digest [324]

CONGRESSIONAL DIGEST, VOL 27 – 1948. Admission of displaced persons; Voice of America; Marshall Plan controversy; Electoral College revision; Reciprocal trade program extension; Long-range housing problem; Federal world government; Tideland oil dispute; International Trade Organization; National Science Foundation – 1,5,9 – us Congressional Digest [324]

CONGRESSIONAL DIGEST, VOL 28 – 1949. National aviation policy; Administration's legislative program; Federal compulsory health insurance; Repeal of Taft-Hartley Act; Oleomargarine tax fight; North Atlantic Treaty; Presidential election reform; Curbing communism in the U.S.; Federal aid to education; Extension of Social Security – 1,5,9 – us Congressional Digest [324]

CONGRESSIONAL DIGEST, VOL 29 – 1950. New valley power authorities; Federal civil rights program; Brannan Plan; D. P. program; Big unions and anti-trust laws; Point 4 program; Aid to Great Britain; Welfare state; A non-communist world org.; Question of new states for the U.S.; U.N. genocide treaty – 1,5,9 – us Congressional Digest [324]

CONGRESSIONAL DIGEST, VOL 30 – 1951. 81st Congress and outlook for 82nd; Congress and U.S. foreign relations; Great federal budget; Reciprocal trade program; Government propaganda; Basic principles of American govt.; Civilian conscription in wartime; Federal tax revision; Foreign economic aid; Military factors in U.S. foreign policy – 1,5,9 – us Congressional Digest [324]

CONGRESSIONAL DIGEST, VOL 31 – 1952. Point 4 and world politics; U.S. conflict with the U.N.; U.S. primary system; Great federal payroll; Congressional investigation; St. Lawrence Seaway; U.S. and world federation; 1952 national election; Curbing the treaty power; Home rule for District of Columbia – 1,5,9 – us Congressional Digest [324]

CONGRESSIONAL DIGEST, VOL 32 – 1953. Curbing federal power to tax; Limiting debate in the Senate; U.S.-Spanish relations; Abolition of the RFC; Federal lobbying act; "Stand-by" controls bill; Changing the electoral system; Raising the federal debt limit; Revision of the Taft-Hartley Act; Public lands problem – 1,5,9 – us Congressional Digest [324]

CONGRESSIONAL DIGEST, VOL 33 – 1954. U.S. foreign trade policy; Social Security revision; Lowering the voting age to 18; "Flexible" farm price supports; Internal security measures; Hawaii and Alaska statehood; Foreign economic policy; 1954 Biennial election; Federal funds for public schools; Congress studies juvenile delinquency – 1,5,9 – us Congressional Digest [324]

CONGRESSIONAL DIGEST, VOL 34 – 1955. "Dixon-Yates" controversy; Organization of 84th congress; Federal health reinsurance plan; New national military reserve plan; Ten-year highway program; Federal control of gas producers; Federal subsidies to higher education; Bricker treaty power amendment; U.N. charter review conference; President's partnership power policy – 1,5,9 – us Congressional Digest [324]

CONGRESSIONAL DIGEST, VOL 35 – 1956. U.S. immigration policy; "Right to work" laws; Farm aid proposals; Electoral revision; Organization for Trade Cooperation; Postal rate increase; Federal farm policy; 1956 federal elections; U.S. foreign aid; Federal small business policy – 1,5,9 – us Congressional Digest [324]

CONGRESSIONAL DIGEST, VOL 36 – 1957. Atomic energy policy; Senate cloture rule 22; Mid-East doctrine; Civil rights legislation; Federal budget reduction; Minimum wage legislation; U.S. foreign aid policy; Right-to-work legislation; Federal aid for school construction; Foreign jurisdiction over U.S. forces – 1,5,9 – us Congressional Digest [324]

CONGRESSIONAL DIGEST, VOL 37 – 1958. Provision for presidential disability; Congress and the job ahead; 1958 farm aid proposals; Renewal of reciprocal trade act; Curbing the Supreme Court; Tax cut

proposals; Challenge of today's public schools; Nuclear disarmament; Labor reform legislation; Senate cloture rule 22 – 1,5,9 – us Congressional Digest [324]

CONGRESSIONAL DIGEST, VOL 38 – 1959. Hawaii statehood; Federal aid for depressed areas; Extending federal housing aid; Future financing of REA programs; FY 1960 foreign aid program; Federal aid to public education; Curbing labor union abuses; 86th Congress and the Supreme Court; Raising rate ceiling on U.S. bonds; Unemployment insurance changes – 1,5,9 – us Congressional Digest [324]

CONGRESSIONAL DIGEST, VOL 39 – 1960. New civil rights legislation; Federal minimum wage law; Adding medical aid to OASI program; NDEA loyalty provisions; Congress and the wheat problem; Curtailing U.S. mutual security aid; Strengthening the U. N.; Guide to the 1960 federal elections; U.S. policy and the Caribbean situation; Proposed youth conservation corps – 1,5,9 – us Congressional Digest [324]

CONGRESSIONAL DIGEST, VOL 40 – 1961. U. S. and World Court jurisdiction; Economic aid for Latin America; Kennedy program and the new Congress; Aid to depressed areas; Congress and the railroad situation; New Frontier's housing program; Federal aid to education; Labor unions and anti-trust laws; Dept. of Urban Affairs and Housing; A wilderness area system – 1,5,9 – us Congressional Digest [324]

CONGRESSIONAL DIGEST, VOL 41 – 1962. New medicare plan for the aged; Administered prices in drug industry; Proposed U. N. bond issue; Administration's new farm proposals; Literacy test and poll tax; FY 1963 foreign aid proposals; Foreign Trade Expansion Act; Non-Communist econ. community; U. S. and the situation in Cuba, Record of the 87th Congress – 1,5,9 – us Congressional Digest [324]

CONGRESSIONAL DIGEST, VOL 42 – 1963. Federal aid for urban mass transit; Aid to higher education; Alliance for Progress; Administration's proposed tax revision; Proposed 1964 budget; The FY 1964 foreign aid proposals; Proposed medicare for the aged; Omnibus higher education bill; Civil rights and "public accommodations"; Youth employment legislation – 1,5,9 – us Congressional Digest [324]

CONGRESSIONAL DIGEST, VOL 43 – 1964. A domestic "peace corps"; Communist bloc trade; Civil rights and FEPC; Federal urban renewal; Presidential succession and inability; Federal food stamp program; Disarmament and intl. arms control; Fed. public works and unemployment; Supreme Court and "school prayer"; "Appalachia" program – 1,5,9 – us Congressional Digest [324]

CONGRESSIONAL DIGEST, VOL 44 – 1965. State legislative apportionment; U.S. space program; Administration "medicare" program; U.S. and situation in Vietnam; Amendment of U.S. immigration laws; Fiscal 1966 foreign aid program; Labor-management relations policy; Crime and law enforcement in U.S.; U.S. Latin American policy; Proposed U.S. Soviet consular treaty – 1,5,9 – us Congressional Digest [324]

CONGRESSIONAL DIGEST, VOL 45 – 1966. Administration rent subsidy program; Federal minimum wage revision; Federal anti-poverty program; Review of U.S. Vietnam policy; Proposals for a longer House term; "Truth in packaging" legislation; Controversy over U.S. foreign aid; U. S. foreign policy commitments; "Open housing" controversy; Proposed "gun control" legislation – 1,5,9 – us Congressional Digest [324]

CONGRESSIONAL DIGEST, VOL 46 – 1967. Unemployment compensation revision; "Demonstration cities" program; U.S. policy toward Rhodesia; Controversy over the FY68 budget; Proposed selective service changes; Expansion of east-west trade; Congress and national crime problem; Federally-guaranteed minimum income; Changing the electoral system; Question of "pay television" – 1,5,9 – us Congressional Digest [324]

CONGRESSIONAL DIGEST, VOL 47 – 1968. Federal Job Corps; Community Action Program; Consumer protection proposals; Federal anti-riot legislation; Congress and U.S. travel deficit; Public welfare revision; Revision of the military draft; Congress foreign policy role; Anti-ballistic missile defense; Congress and airport development – 1,5,9 – us Congressional Digest [324]

CONGRESSIONAL DIGEST, VOL 48 – 1969. Nuclear nonproliferation treaty; School desegregation guidelines; Federal postal corporation; Controversy over bail reform; Tax status of foundations; Radio-TV cigarette advertising; U.S. foreign military commitments; Federal revenue sharing; Extension of Voting Rights Act; Federal role in urban mass transit – 1,5,9 – us Congressional Digest [324]

CONGRESSIONAL DIGEST, VOL 49 – 1970. Changing the U.S. electoral system; Casualty insurance regulation; The "Philadelphia Plan"; Federal school racial policy; 18-year voting age; Public welfare revision; The federal anti-pollution role; Standby wage and price controls; Broadening U.S. import controls; Debate over the supersonic transport – 1,5,9 – us Congressional Digest [324]

CONGRESSIONAL DIGEST, VOL 50 – 1971. Women's "Equal Rights Amendment"; Federal consumer protection agency; Federally-subsidized jobs proposals; the Nixon revenue-sharing plan; An all-volunteer U.S. armed force; "No-fault" automobile insurance; Revising the U.S. jury system; Federal information-gathering on private individuals; Strengthening equal employment opportunity laws; Adoption of metric system – 1,5,9 – us Congressional Digest [324]

CONGRESSIONAL DIGEST, VOL 51 – 1972. Federal voter registration by mail; National health insurance proposals; A six-year presidential term; Minimum wage law expansion; Federal day-care proposals; Future U.S. space program; Financing elementary and secondary education; Presidential election issues; Panama Canal treaty revision; Federal spending ceiling controversy – 1,5,9 – us Congressional Digest [324]

CONGRESSIONAL DIGEST, VOL 52 – 1973. Capital punishment controversy; U.S. Rhodesia policy; Future of foreign aid program; Presidential impoundment of funds; Newsmen's "shield" legislation; Reconstruction Aid for North Vietnam; Federal role in public assistance; Federal Petroleum policy; Expansion of U.S.-Soviet trade; Federal-State Land-Use policy – 1,5,9 – us Congressional Digest [324]

CONGRESSIONAL DIGEST, VOL 53 – 1974. A "School Prayer" Amendment; Federal Campaign Financing Reform; Automobile Emission Controls; "School Busing" Controversy; Federal Regulation of Surface Mining; National Health Insurance Program; Revising the U.S. Electoral System; Controversy Over the Amnesty Question; a U.S. Consumer Protection Agency; U.S. Food Export Policy – 1,5,9 – us Congressional Digest [324]

CONGRESSIONAL DIGEST, VOL 54 – 1975. The Problem of Illegal Aliens; Controversy Over Sugar Controls; U.S. Financial Role in the United Nations; U.S. Military Aid to Turkey; The Food Stamp Controversy; Extension of Federal Voting Rights Act; Allocation of Scarce World Resources; Congress & U.S.-Soviet Detente; Safeguarding Classified Information; Controversy over Handgun Controls – 1,5,9 – us Congressional Digest [324]

CONGRESSIONAL DIGEST, VOL 55 – 1976. Basic Principles of American Government; Public Employee Strikes; Mandatory Budget Balancing; Panama Canal Treaty Revision; Breakup of Major Oil Companies; Humphrey-Hawkins Full Employment Bill; Mandatory Sentencing & Crime Control; 1976 Election Campaign Issues: Postal Service Reorganization; B-1 Bomber Controversy – 1,5,9 – us Congressional Digest [324]

CONGRESSIONAL DIGEST, VOL 56 – 1977. U.S. Southern Africa Policy; Nuclear Energy Safety; Congressional Campaign Financing; Executive Reorganization Powers; Minimum Wage Revision; Women's Equal Rights Amendment; National Health Insurance; Amnesty for Illegal Aliens; Mandatory Retirement Age – 1,5,9 – us Congressional Digest [324]

CONGRESSIONAL DIGEST, VOL 57 – 1978. Labor Reform Act; U.S. Cuban Policy; Beverage Container Problem; U.S. Foreign Arms Sales; Welfare Reform; Airline Deregulation; U.S. Energy Policy; Congress Congress seats for D.C.; New U.S. Dept of Education; Alaska Lands Controversy – 1,5,9 – us Congressional Digest [324]

CONGRESSIONAL DIGEST, VOL 58 – 1979. Student Aid Policy; Marihuana Use Policy; Direct Presidential Election; "Real Wage Insurance"; Balanced Budget Amendments; Treaty Termination; SALT Treaty; Trucking Regulation; National Defense Spending; House Campaign Financing – 1,5,9 – us Congressional Digest [324]

CONGRESSIONAL DIGEST, VOL 59 – 1980. Welfare Reform Amendments; The Consumer and Antitrust Law; "Sunset" Legislation; Draft Registration; Limitations on Covert Intelligence; Federal Revenue Sharing; Occupational Safety and Health Act; 1980 Election Campaign Issues; MX Missile Controversy; Congress & "School Prayer" – 1,5,9 – us Congressional Digest [324]

CONGRESSIONAL DIGEST, VOL 60 – 1981. Food Stamp Program; School Busing; "Fair Housing" Proposals; CETA Program; Federal Legal Aid Program; Reagan Tax-Reduction Program; Social Security Financing; Illegal Aliens; International Lending Agencies; Extension of Voting Rights Act – 1,5,9 – us Congressional Digest [324]

CONGRESSIONAL DIGEST, VOL 61 – 1982. Clean Air Act; Freedom of Information Act; Urban Enterprise Zones; Curtailing Federal Student Aid; Curbing Federal Courts; A Gold-Based U.S. Currency; Nuclear Freeze Proposal; Mandatory Balanced Federal Budget; Abolition of Mandatory Retirement; Wilderness Protection Act – 1,5,9 – us Congressional Digest [324]

CONGRESSIONAL DIGEST, VOL 62 – 1983. Law of the Sea Treaty; Auto "Domestic Content"; Caribbean Basin Initiative; Social Security Reform; American Conservation Corps; Export Controls over U.S. Technology; Immigration Reform; Central American Policy; War Powers Act; Legislative Veto – 1,5,9 – us Congressional Digest [324]

CONGRESSIONAL DIGEST, VOL 63 – 1984. Tuition Tax Credit; Federal Budget Deficit; Space Weapons Policy; Broadcast Deregulation; School Prayer Controversy; Federal Criminal Sentencing; NATO Cost Sharing Controversy; 1984 Election Campaign Issues; U.S. Policy towards Nicaragua; The Genocide Treaty – 1,5,9 – us Congressional Digest [324]

CONGRESSIONAL DIGEST, VOL 64 – 1985. Civil Rights Legislation; Acid Rain Controversy; Star Wars Controversy; Subminimum Wage for Youth; Enterprise Zones; The MX Missile; Federal Subsidy of AMTRAK; Policy toward South Africa; Presidential Line-Item Veto; The Clean Water Act – 1,5,9 – us Congressional Digest [324]

CONGRESSIONAL DIGEST, VOL 65 – 1986. Farm Credit System; The Tax Reform Controversy; Immigration Legislation; Policy toward Angola; Gun Control Controversy; Environmental Superfund; Foreign Trade Legislation; SALT II Agreements; Omnibus Drug Legislation; National 55 MPH Speed Limit – 1,5,9 – us Congressional Digest [324]

CONGRESSIONAL DIGEST, VOL 66 – 1987. Product Liability; Limiting PACs; Bilingual Education; Catastrophic Health Insurance; Drug Testing; U.S. Foreign Trade Policy; Minimum Wage; Broadcasting Fairness Doctrine; ABM Treaty; War Powers Act; Persian Gulf – 1,5,9 – us Congressional Digest [324]

CONGRESSIONAL DIGEST, VOL 67 – 1988. Fed. Emp. Polit. Act. Legislation; Welfare Reform; Contra Aid; Missiles Treaty; Med. Leave Policy; Fair Housing Act; Election Camp. Financing; 1988 Elections; Child Care Leg.; Intelligence Oversight Act – 1,5,9 – us Congressional Digest [324]

CONGRESSIONAL DIGEST, VOL 68 – (Text. and Apparel Trade Act; Clean Air Act; Corporate Merger Leg.; Occ. Health Controversy; Minimum Wage Leg.; Savings and Loan Leg.; Flag Desecration; Immigration Reform; Balanced Budget Amend.; Disabilities Act) – 1989 – 1,5,9 – us Congressional Digest [324]

CONGRESSIONAL DIGEST, VOL 69 – (Capital Gains; Child Care; Clean Air; Voter Reg.; National Service; Line Item Veto; Civil Rights; Campaign Finance Reform; 1990 Omnibus Crime Bill; Budget Reconciliation Act) – 1990 – 1,5,9 – us Congressional Digest [324]

CONGRESSIONAL DIGEST, VOL 70 – (Funding of the Arts; Cable TV Reregulation; Persian Gulf Policy; Family and Medical Leave; Energy Policy; Brady Handgun Act; Title X Pregnancy Counseling; U.S.-China Act; Striker Replacement; Choice in Schools) – 1991 – 1,5,9 – us Congressional Digest [324]

CONGRESSIONAL DIGEST, VOL 71 – (Banking Reform; U.S.-Mexico Free Trade Agreement; Campaign Finance; Omnibus Crime Control; Defense Spending and Budget; Capping Fed. Entitlement Programs; Aid to the Former Soviet Union; Election Issues; Product Liability; Economic Competitiveness) – 1992 – 1,5,9 – us Congressional Digest [324]

CONGRESSIONAL DIGEST, VOL 72 – (Family and Medical Leave; Line Item Veto & Rescission Authority; Voter Reg.; Space Station Funding; 1994 Budget; Replacement of Striking Workers; Fed. Employees' Political Activities; Nat. and Comm. Service; N.A. Free Trade Agreement; Violence on TV) – 1993 – 1,5,9 – us Congressional Digest [324]

CONGRESSIONAL DIGEST, VOL 73 – (Education Reform; Proposed Dept. of the Environment; Mining and Public Lands; Campaign Finance; Second-Hand Tobacco Smoke; Crime Control; U.S. Policy toward Haiti; Health Care; Gen. Agreement on Tariffs and Trade) – 1994 – 1,5,9 – us Congressional Digest [324]

THE CONGRESSIONAL DIRECTORY, 1909-1993/94 / U.S. Congress – (Updates planned) – Washington: GPO. 60th Congress 2nd session-103rd Congress – 1099mf – 9 – $1,649.00 – LLMC 81-109 – us L.L.M.C. [323]

CONGRESSIONAL GLOBE / U.S. Congress – 1833-1873 – 1 – us Princeton Micro [324]

CONGRESSIONAL GLOBE / U.S. Congress – v. 23-42. 1833-73 – 1 – us UMI [324]

CONGRESSIONAL GLOBE, 1833-73 / U.S. Congress – 23rd to 42nd Congress. 109 books, all published. Followed by Congressional Record. 80-035 – 9 – 796.00 – us L.L.M.C. [323]

CONGRESSIONAL INVESTIGATING COMMITTEES / Dimock, Marshall Edward – Baltimore, Johns Hopkins Press, 1929. 182 p. LL-1609 – 1 – us L of C Photodup [340]

THE CONGRESSIONAL MANUAL : COMPILED FROM THE CONGRESSIONAL RECORD AND OTHER PUBLIC DOCUMENTS – N.Y./Chicago: International Survey Co, 1901 – 3mf – 9 – $4.50 – LLMC 92-132 – us L.L.M.C. [324]

CONGRESSIONAL QUARTERLY / U.S. Congress – 1945-1961 – 3 – us Readex [323]

CONGRESSIONAL QUARTERLY WEEKLY REPORTS / U.S. Congress – (v. 24- 1966-5,6. v. 28- 1970- 9) – v. 1- 1945- – 1 – us UMI [324]

CONGRESSIONAL RECORD – Law Library Microfilm Corporation, 1873-1975 – 9 – $26,388.00 set – us Hein [340]

CONGRESSIONAL RECORD / Philippines. Congress. House of Representatives – 1945-61 – 1 – 690.00 – us L of C Photodup [950]

CONGRESSIONAL RECORD / Philippines. Congress. Senate – 1945-61 – 1 – 227.00 – us L of C Photodup [950]

CONGRESSIONAL RECORD / U.S. Congress – 1873-1985. 43rd to 99th Congress. 131v in approx. 1630 books. v1-128.pt13. 85-200 – 9 – 14,776.00 – us L.L.M.C. [323]

CONGRESSIONAL RECORD / U.S. Congress – Daily periodical with biweekly indexes when Congress is in session. Subscriptions for six-month or one-year period only – 9 – $118.00y in US; $147.50 outside – S-N 752-029-00000-8. Sub-list ID-CRM – us Gov't Printing [324]

CONGRESSIONAL RECORD / U.S. Congress – (Updated as released by GPO) – Backfile 1976-95 – 9 – $8,400.00 set $450.00y (1995 subsc $695.00) – 0-89941-201-7 – us Hein [324]

CONGRESSIONAL RECORD / U.S. Congress – v1-125. 1873-1980. With appendices and indexes – 1,5 – us Princeton Micro [324]

CONGRESSIONAL RECORD: DAILY DIGEST / U.S. Congress – v. 93-115. 1947-1969 – 1,5,6 – us Princeton Micro [323]

CONGRESSIONAL RECORD (DAILY ED.) / U.S. Congress – 1957-80 – 3 – us Readex [324]

CONGRESSIONAL RECORD ON MICROFICHE : RETROSPECTIVE COLLECTION / U.S. Congress – (Provides a complete transcript of debates and other floor proceedings of the US Congress. Available as a complete coll or by individual congress) – 43rd-100th congresses. v1-134. 1873-1988 – 9 – $31,680.00 coll – us CIS [324]
CONGRESSIONAL RECORD. V. 1- 1873- / U.S. Congress – (v. 122- 1976- 5,6,9) – 1 – us UMI [073]
THE CONGRESSIONAL RECORDS 1789-1990 – (The Annals of Congress 1789-1824 343mf $515.00; The Congressional Debates 1824-1837 216mf $324.00; The Congressional Globe 1833-1873 1,190mf $1,785.00; The Congressional Record 1873-1990 7,415mf $34,073.00) – 4 titles – 9,164mf – 9 – $31,200.00 set – us L.L.M.C. [323]
CONGRESSIONAL VOTING RECORDS – 1961-74 – 5 – 68.00 – us UMI [977]
Congreve, W *see*
- LOVE FOR LOVE
- THE MOURNING BRIDE

Congreve, William *see*
- THE DOUBLE-DEALER
- WILLIAM CONGREVE

Conil Paz, Alberto A *see* POLITICA EXTERIOR ARGENTINA, 1930-1962
Conil-Lacoste, Michel *see* STORY OF A GRAND DESIGN
Conimbricenses *see*
- COMMENTARII COLLEGII CONIMBRICENSIS E SOCIETATIS IESU IN UNIVERSAM DIALECTICAM ARISTOTELIS
- COMMENTARII COLLEGII CONIMBRICENSIS SOCIETATIS IESU IN ARISTOTELIS LOGICAM
- COMMENTARII COLLEGII CONIMBRICENSIS SOCIETATIS IESU, IN DUOS LIBROS DE GENERATIONE ET CORRUPTIONE ARISTOTELIS

LES CONIURATIONS FAITES A UN DEMON POSSEDANT LE CORPS D'UNE GRANDE DAME – Paris. 1619 – 9 – fr Hachette [360]
CONJUGAISONS, REGLES ET INSTRUCTIONS POUR CEUX QUI DESIRENT APPRENDRE FRANCOIS, ITALIEN, ESPAGNOL ET FLAMENS / Meurier, G – 1558 – 9 – fr I.C.S. [440]
CONJUNTO – Havana, CU. 1964-1977 – 5r – $250.00 – R04197 – us Library Micro [790]
A CONJURACAO : ORGAM REPUBLICANO – Campanha, 22 May 1888 – 1,5,6 – bl Biblioteca [072]
CONJURATION WIMAN-LAURIER CONTRE LE CANADA: LE CANADA POUR LES ETATS-UNIS, COMPLOT DEMASQUE / Wiman, Erasus – Montreal, 1891. 05245. (Pre-1900 Canadiana) – 9 – cn C.I.H.M. [971]
Conklin, Charles H *see* A TREATISE ON THE POWERS AND DUTIES OF JUSTICES OF THE PEACE IN CIVIL, CRIMINAL AND SPECIAL CASES IN THE STATE OF IOWA.
Conklin, E C *see* THE ORGANIZATION AND CELL LINEAGE OF THE ASCIDIAN EGG
Conkling, Alfred *see*
- THE POWERS OF THE EXECUTIVE DEPARTMENT OF THE GOVERNMENT OF THE UNITED STATES, AND THE POLITICAL INSTITUTIONS AND CONSTITUTIONAL LAW OF THE UNITED STATES
- A TREATISE ON THE ORGANIZATION AND JURISDICTION OF THE SUPREME, CIRCUIT AND DISTRICT COURTS OF THE UNITED STATES.
- A TREATISE ON THE ORGANIZATION, JURISDICTION AND PRACTICE OF THE COURTS OF THE UNITED STATES
- THE YOUNG CITIZEN'S MANUAL; BEING A DIGEST OF THE LAWS OF THE STATE OF NEW YORK AND OF THE UNITED STATES, RELATING TO CRIMES AND THEIR PUNISHMENTS.

Conkling, Roscoe *see* PAPERS
Conkwright, S J *see* HISTORY OF THE CHURCHES OF BOONE'S CREEK BAPTIST ASSOCIATION OF KENTUCKY, 1780-1923
CONLATIO CRITICA CODICIS SINAITICI CUM TEXTU ELZEVIRIANO : VATICANI QUOQUE CODICIS RATIONE HABITA / Tischendorf, Constantin von – Lipsiae: Hermann Mendelssohn, 1869 – 1mf – 9 – 0-8370-5536-9 – 1985-3536 – us A.T.L.A. [230]
Conlon, P M *see* VOLTAIRE'S LITERARY CAREER FROM 1728 TO 1750
CONNACHT SENTINEL – Galway, Ireland.-d. 1927-86. 125 reels – 1 – PS27.50r – ie European Micro [072]
CONNACHT TRIBUNE – 1909-1980 – ca 160r – 1 – ie Microforms [941]
CONNACHT TRIBUNE – Galway, Ireland.-d. 1909-86. 184 reels – 1 – PS27.50r – ie European Micro [072]
LA CONNAISSANCE – Paris. 1920-nov 1922 – 1 – fr A.C.R.P.P. [073]
CONNAISSANCE DES ARTS – 1952- 1; 1974-5,6; 1975- 9; – us UMI [700]
CONNAISSEMENTS ET REGLES DE LA HAYE / Bladel, G van – Bruxelles, 1929 – 3mf – 9 – ILM-3424/1 – ne IDC [327]
CONNAUGHT CHAMPION – Galway. Ireland. -w. 1904-11. (6 reels) – 1 – uk British Libr Newspaper [072]
CONNAUGHT JOURNAL – Galway. Ireland. -w. Jan 1823-Dec 1836, Feb-Dec 1840. (13 reels) – 1 – uk British Libr Newspaper [072]
CONNAUGHT PATRIOT – Tuam, Ireland. 27 Aug 1859-27 Mar 1869.-w. 4 reels – 1 – uk British Libr Newspaper [072]
CONNAUGHT PEOPLE AND BALLINASLOE INDEPENDENT – Ireland. 19 Apr 1884-25 Sep 1886.-w. 1 reel – 1 – uk British Libr Newspaper [072]
CONNEAUTVILLE COURIER – Conneautville, PA. -w 1876-1955 – 13 – $25.00r – us I.M.R. [071]
CONNECTICUT : SESSION LAWS OF AMERICAN STATES AND TERRITORIES – 1776-1995 – 9 – $2,015.00 set – us Hein [340]
CONNECTICUT – v.34-45. 1970-81 – 1,5,6,9 – us UMI [330]
Connecticut *see*
- THE NEW JOINT STOCK ACT OF CONNECTICUT, PASSED JANUARY SESSION, 1880.
- REPORTS AND OPINIONS (A-G)
- REPORTS, POST-NRS
- REPORTS, PRE-NRS
- STATE LABOR REPORTS
- STATE OF CONNECTICUT REGISTER AND MANUAL, 1910

CONNECTICUT 1670 CENSUS – (Census lists names of all household heads residing in Connecticut between 1667-73. Over 2,400 names indexed alphabetically by surname and by town. For each individual there is a date, place of residence, biographical notation & reference to source document. First-time publ of names fr obscure listings discovered in town records of Guildford, Killingworth, Milford, New London, Norwich, Saybrook and Stamford) – (mf ed 1977) – 1mf – 9 – 0-931248-04-3 – us Holbrook [920]
CONNECTICUT, A GUIDE TO ITS ROADS, LORE & PEOPLE – 1938. Federal Writers' Project, WPA. Indexed. 9 fiches. F-0303 – 9 – us A.G.L.L. [920]
Connecticut Academy of Arts and Sciences *see* TRANSACTIONS
Connecticut. Agricultural Experiment Station. New Haven *see*
- ANNUAL REPORT AND BULLETIN
- CIRCULAR
- FRONTIERS OF PLANT SCIENCE
- REPORTS AND BULLETINS
- UNNUMBERED GENERAL PUBLICATIONS

Connecticut. Agricultural Experiment Station. Storrs *see*
- ANNUAL REPORT AND BULLETIN
- INFORMATION SERIES
- MISCELLANEOUS PUBLICATION
- MONOGRAPHS
- PROGRESS REPORT
- RESEARCH REPORT
- SPECIAL BULLETIN
- UNNUMBERED PUBLICATIONS

CONNECTICUT ATTORNEY GENERAL REPORTS AND OPINIONS – (6 1899-1968 $175.00. 9 1967-1968, 1983-1989 $107.50) – 1899-1989 – 6,9 – $282.50set – us Hein [340]
CONNECTICUT BAPTIST – Rockville/Hartford, CT. Conn. Baptist State Convention/Conn. Convention of American Baptist Churches. 1922-70. Incomplete. Single reels available – 1 – 128.20 – us A.B.H.S. [073]
CONNECTICUT BAPTIST MATERIALS: MISCELLANEOUS BOOKLETS, SERMONS AND ADDRESSES – 1632p – 1 – 65.28 – us Baptist [240]
CONNECTICUT BAR JOURNAL – v1-37. 1927-63 – 173mf – 9 – $259.00 – LLMC 84-445 – us L.L.M.C. [073]
CONNECTICUT BAR JOURNAL – v1-69. 1927-95 – 9 – $886.00 set – us Hein [340]
Connecticut. Board of Compensation Commissioners *see* REPORTS
Connecticut. Bureau of Labor Statistics *see* REPORTS
CONNECTICUT C P A QUARTERLY – v.45-. 1981- – 1,5,6,9 – us UMI [650]
CONNECTICUT CATHOLIC – Hartford. Conn. -w. 1876-97 – 1 – us UMI [071]
Connecticut. College of Agriculture *see* MILESTONES
Connecticut. Compensation Commissioners *see* COMPENDIA OF AWARDS
Connecticut. Comptroller *see* REPORT IN RELATION TO THE CRIMINAL BUSINESS OF THE COURTS..
CONNECTICUT COURANT – Hartford. Conn. 1764-1820 – 1,3 – us Readex [071]
CONNECTICUT COURANT – Hartford, CT. 1734 – 1r – 1 – us Ross [071]
Connecticut. Dept. of Factory Inspection *see* REPORTS
Connecticut. Dept. of Labor and Factory Inspection *see* REPORTS
Connecticut. Dept. of Revenue Services *see* INFORMATION RELATIVE TO THE ASSESSMENT AND COLLECTION OF TAXES
Connecticut. Employment Security Division *see*
- BULLETIN: CONNECTICUT LABOR DEPARTMENT
- REPORTS OF THE ADMINISTRATOR OF THE UNEMPLOYMENT COMPENSATION LAW

CONNECTICUT EVANGELICAL MAGAZINE *see* MISSIONARY SOCIETY OF CONNECTICUT PAPERS, 1759-1948
CONNECTICUT EVANGELICAL MAGAZINE AND RELIGIOUS INTELLIGENCER *see* MISSIONARY SOCIETY OF CONNECTICUT PAPERS, 1759-1948
CONNECTICUT GENERAL STATUTES ANNOTATED – St Paul: West Pub Co, 1958-Feb 1996 update – 9 – $1,380.00 set – us Hein [340]
Connecticut. Insurance Dept *see* REPORTS OF THE INSURANCE COMMISSIONER
CONNECTICUT JOURNAL – New Haven. Ct. 1767-1820 – 3 – us Readex [071]
CONNECTICUT JOURNAL OF INTERNATIONAL LAW – v1-11. 1985-1996 – 9 – $174.00set – us Hein [340]
CONNECTICUT JOURNAL OF INTERNATIONAL LAW – v1-11. 1985-1996 – 9 – $174.00set – us Hein [340]
CONNECTICUT LAW JOURNAL – v1-19. 1935-55 – 120mf – 9 – $180.00 – LLMC 84-446 – us L.L.M.C. [073]
CONNECTICUT LAW, PUBLIC UTILITIES AND CARRIERS / Connecticut. Laws, Statutes, etc – Hartford, Public Utilities Commission, 1944. 264 p. LL-1567 – 1 – us L of C Photodup [340]
Connecticut. Laws, Statutes, etc *see*
- CONNECTICUT LAW, PUBLIC UTILITIES AND CARRIERS
- INDEX TO GENERAL STATUTES OF CONNECTICUT, AND PUBLIC ACTS, FROM 1875 TO 1882
- THE JOINT STOCK ACT OF CONNECTICUT, FROM THE REVISED STATUTES.

CONNECTICUT LAWYER – v1-5 – 9 – us Hein [340]
CONNECTICUT MAGAZINE – Hartford, CT. v1-12. 1895-1908 – 5r – 1 – us Ross [978]
CONNECTICUT MIRROR – Hartford, CT. 1809-32. Run extended from 1820 – 1,3 – us Readex [071]
Connecticut. Office of Bank Commissioner *see*
- REPORTS
- REPORTS OF BANK COMMISSIONER RELATIVE TO LICENSED CREDIT UNIONS

CONNECTICUT PROBATE LAW JOURNAL – University of Bridgeport. v1-9. 1985-95 – 9 – $90.00set – us Hein [340]
Connecticut. Public Utilities Commission *see* REPORTS
Connecticut. Railroad Commissioners *see* REPORTS
CONNECTICUT SOCIETY. SECOND REPORT...AUXILLIARY TO THE BAPTIST BOARD OF FOREIGN MISSIONS...1816 *see* MISCELLANEOUS PAMPHLETS
CONNECTICUT STAATS-ZEITUNG – Holyoke, MA: [s.n.], [mar 1918-jun 1942] – us Res Libr [071]
Connecticut. State Bar Association *see* PROCEEDINGS
Connecticut. State Board of Mediation and Arbitration *see* REPORTS
Connecticut. State Water Commission *see* STATE WATER RESOURCES REPORTS
Connecticut. Supreme Court *see*
- CONNECTICUT SUPREME COURT REPORTS
- DAY'S REPORTS
- KIRBY'S REPORTS
- ROOT'S REPORTS

CONNECTICUT SUPREME COURT REPORTS / Connecticut. Supreme Court – (Pre-NRS: v1-52 1814-85 356mf $534.00. Updates planned) – v1-94. 1814-1920 – 704mf – 9 – $1,056.00 – LLMC 80-801 – us L.L.M.C. [340]
CONNECTICUT SUPREME COURT REPORTS *see*
- DAY'S REPORTS
- KIRBY'S REPORTS
- ROOT'S REPORTS

CONNECTION SCIENCE: A JOURNAL OF NEURAL COMPUTING, ARTIFICIAL INTELLIGENCE, AND COGNITIVE RESEARCH – 1989- 5v – 9 – £205.00 – 0954-0091 – uk Carfax [510]
CONNECTIONS JOURNAL – (Ceased v5 1980) – Edmonton. v5-6. 1989-90 – 9 – Can$20.00y – cn Micromedia [073]
THE CONNECTIONS OF THE GESTE DES LOHERAINS WITH OTHER FRENCH EPICS AND MEDIAEVAL GENRES / Bowman, Russell Keith – 1940 – 1 – us I.U. Libraries [390]
CONNECTIVE TISSUE RESEARCH / ed by Vies, A et al – 1972- – 1,5,9 – us Gordon [610]
Connelley, William Elsey *see*
- HISTORY OF KANSAS
- HISTORY OF KENTUCKY
- PAPERS
- STANDARD HISTORY OF KANSAS AND KANSANS

Conner, J E *see* THE DEVELOPMENT OF BELLIGERENT OCCUPATION
Conner, James *see* THE HISTORY OF A SUIT AT LAW, ACCORDING TO THE PRACTICE OF THIS STATE
Conner, Jeremiah Frederick *see* EMPLOYERS' LIABILITY, WORKMEN'S COMPENSATION AND LIABILITY INSURANCE.
Conners, Jo *see* WHO'S WHO IN ARIZONA
CONNEXIONS – Toronto. 32 docs. 1980-1991 – 23mf – 9 – ne IDC [970]
THE CONNOISSEUR – 1886-89 – 10mf – 9 – £58.00 – uk Chadwyck [700]
THE CONNOISSEUR – 1901-79 – 1 – uk Microform Academic [073]
Connolly, Declan A *see* THE EFFECTS OF AN APPLICATION OF SUNSCREEN ON SELECTED PHYSIOLOGICAL VARIABLES DURING EXERCISE IN THE HEAT
CONNOLLY MEMORIAL BAPTIST CHURCH. DELBARTON, WEST VIRGINIA : CHURCH RECORDS – 1940-81 – 1 – 27.14 – us Baptist [240]
Connolly, R H *see*
- THE EXPLANATIO SYMBOLI AD INITIANDOS
- THE LITURGICAL HOMILIES OF NARSAI
- THE SO-CALLED EGYPTIAN CHURCH ORDER AND DERIVED DOCUMENTS

CONNOQUENESSING VALLEY NEWS – Zelienople. Pa. 1901-1932 – 1 – us UMI [071]
Connors, Lyndsay *see* DON'T CONFUSE THOSE YEARS AT SCHOOL WITH EDUCATION
CONOCIMIENTO, CURACION Y PRESERVACION DE LA PESTE / Frailas, A – Jaen, 1606 – 10mf – 9 – sp Cultura [614]
Conover *see* HISTORY OF ONTARIO COUNTY
Conover, Charlotte R *see* THE STORY OF DAYTON
Conover, Frank *see* CENTENNIAL PORTRAIT AND BIOGRAPHICAL RECORD OF CITY OF DAYTON AND MONTGOMERY COUNTY
CONOVER-MAST INDUSTRIAL PURCHASING DIRECTORY – 1971 – 1 – us UMI [380]
CONOVER-MAST PURCHASING DIRECTORY – 1940-70; 1973-74 – 1 – us UMI [380]
CONOVER-MAST U.S. INDUSTRIAL PURCHASING DIRECTORY – 1972 – 1 – us UMI [380]
CONQUERING ANXIETY IN GRADE SCHOOL AGED SWIMMERS THROUGH THE USE OF IMAGINATIVE PLAY / Gup, Marc L & Jensen, Barbara E – 1992 – 2mf – $8.00 – us Microform Publ [150]
THE CONQUERING CROSS (THE CHURCH) / Haweis, Hugh Reginald – 1887 – 9 – us A.T.L.A. [240]
THE CONQUEROR – Lahore, Shradhe Mohan for the Deva Dharma Mission. v1 n10. feb/mar 1892 – us Res Libr [072]
THE CONQUEST IN CENTRAL ASIA / Gibb, H A R – London. 1923. BU-608 2 – 8 – ne IDC [950]

THE CONQUEST OF DEATH / Kinney, Abbot – New York, 1893. ix,259p. illus – 1 – us U.W. Library [306]
THE CONQUEST OF FLORIDA...HERNANDO DE SOTO / Irving, Theodore – 1877 – 9 – 1.50f – sp Bibl Santa Ana [975]
THE CONQUEST OF QUEBEC : AN EPIC POEM IN EIGHT BOOKS / Murphy, Henry – Dublin: W Porter, 1790. SEM16P72 – 1r – 5 – Can$9.00 – cn Bibl Nat [810]
THE CONQUEST OF RED SPAIN / Fuller, John Frederick Charles – London, 1937. Fiche W 901. (Blodgett Collection of Spanish Civil War Pamphlets) – 9 – us H.U. College Libr [946]
THE CONQUEST OF THE CROSS IN CHINA / Speicher, Jacob – (Includes index) – New York: Fleming H Revell, c1907 – 1mf – 9 – 0-8370-6525-9 – 1986-0525 – us A.T.L.A. [240]
THE CONQUEST OF THE SIOUX / Gilman, Samuel C – new rev ed. Indianapolis: Carlon & Hollenbeck, 1897 – 1mf – 9 – 0-8370-7143-7 – 1986-1143 – us A.T.L.A. [240]
THE CONQUEST OF THE WEAST INDIA / Gomara, Francisco Lopez de – 1578 – 9 – 25.00 – us Scholars' Facs [972]
LES CONQUESTES ET LES TROPHEES DES NORMANDS-FRANCOIS AUX ROYAUMES DE NAPLES ET DE SICILE, AUX DUCHEZ DE CALABRE, D'ANTIOCHE, DE GALILEE. / Du Moulin, Gabriel – Rouen: Chez David du Petit Val...et Jean et David Berthelin, 1658. SEM105P384 – 6mf – 9 – Can$13.50 – cn Bibl Nat [940]
CONQUESTS OF THE CROSS : A RECORD OF MISSIONARY WORK THROUGHOUT THE WORLD / ed by Hodder, Edwin – London, New York: Cassell, 1890 – 5mf – us A.T.L.A. [240]
LA CONQUETE DE LA TERRE PROMISE / Berault-Bercastel, Antoine Henri de – Paris: Delalain, 1766. 282p. 3 fiches.(Literature Collection) – 9 – 8.00 – fr Bibl Nationale [890]
CONQUETE DE L'ANDALOUSIE / Lapene, Edouard – 1823 – 9 – 1.50f – sp Bibl Santa Ana [946]
CONQUETE DU FOUTAH-DJALON / Sanderval, Aime Olivier – Ed. by Augustin Challamel. Paris. 1899 – 9 – 10.00 – fr Orientalistes [960]
LA CONQUETE PACIFIQUE DU MAROC ET DU TAFILALET / Cruchet, Rene – Paris: Berger-Levrault, 1934 – 1 – us Res Libr [960]
LA CONQUETE SPIRITUELLE...DU MEXIQUE... NOUVELLE ESPAGNE 1523-1524 A 1572 / Ricard, Robert – Paris, 1933; Madrid: Razon y Fe, 1934 – 1 – sp Bibl Santa Ana [240]
A CONQUISTA : FOLHA ENCYCLOPEDICA – CONSAGRADA A EVOLUCAO INTELECTUAL DA MOCIDADE – Penedo, Alagoas. 10-24 Maio 1902 – 1,5,6 – bl Biblioteca [072]
A CONQUISTA : JORNAL POLITICO E LITERARIO – Manaos, Amazonas. 2 Out 1920 – 1,5,6 – bl Biblioteca [072]
CONQUISTA DE LAS ISLAS MALUCAS AL REY FELIPE 3 / Leonardo y Argensola, B J – Madrid, 1609 – 5mf – 9 – ne IDC [950]
CONQUISTA DE MEJICO / Lopez de Gomara, Francisco – (Tomo II.1888. 1.50f; 9) – Tomo I. 1887 – 9 – 1.50f – sp Bibl Santa Ana [972]
LA CONQUISTA DE MEJICO / Diaz del Castillo, Bernal – Madrid: Atlas, 1943 – 1 – sp Bibl Santa Ana [972]
LA CONQUISTA DE MEJICO / Gomez de Arteche, Jose – 1892 – 9 – 1.50f – sp Bibl Santa Ana [972]
LA CONQUISTA DEL ESTADO POR LA REVOLUCION NACIONAL / Faleroni, Alberto Daniel – [Buenos Aires: Ediciones "Montoneras", 1947] – 1 – CSUXAGP8767-B – us Hoover Inst Photo [320]
CONQUISTA ESPIRITUAL DO ORIENTE...INTRODUCAO E NOTAS DE F. FELIX LOPES, 3 PARTE. LISBOA, 1967 / Trindade, Paula da – Madrid: Graf. Calleja, 1968 – 1 – sp Bibl Santa Ana [240]
CONQUISTA Y COLONIZACION DE MEJICO / Garcia Icazbalceta, Joaquin – Madrid: Tip. Fortanet, 1894 – 1 – sp Bibl Santa Ana [972]
LAS CONQUISTAS DE CACERES POR FERNANDO 2 Y ALFONSO 9 DE LEON Y SU FUERO LATINO ANOTADO / Orti Belmonte, Miguel Angel – Badajoz: Imp. de la Diputacion Provincial, 1947. Sep. de la Rev. de Estudios Extremenos – sp Bibl Santa Ana [946]
Conrad, Arcturus Zodiac *see* BOSTON'S AWAKENING
Conrad, Christine *see* BERECHTIGUNG UND PRAKTISCHE ANWENDUNG DES VERBOTS DER WERBUNG MIT SONDERANGEBOTEN BEI MENGENMAESSIG BESCHRAENKTER ABGABE
CONRAD FERDINAND MEYER / Holzamer, Wilhelm – Berlin: Schuster & Loeffler, [1904?] – 1r – 1 – us U.W. Library [430]
CONRAD FERDINAND MEYER : LEBEN UND WERKE / Nussberger, Max – (Includes bibliographical references & index) – Frauenfeld: Huber, 1919 – 1r – 1 – us U.W. Library [920]
CONRAD FERDINAND MEYER : SAGGIO PSICOLOGICO ESTETICO / Pensa, Mario – (Includes bibliographical references) – Bologna: R Patron, c1963 – 1r – 1 – us U.W. Library [920]
CONRAD FERDINAND MEYER : SEIN RELIGIOESES UND SITTLICHES VERMAECHTNIS / Fischer, Richard – Stuttgart: Calwer Verlag, 1949 – 1r – 1 – us U.W. Library [170]
CONRAD FERDINAND MEYER UND JULIUS RODENBERG = CORRESPONDENCE. SELECTIONS : EIN BRIEFWECHSEL / Meyer, Conrad Ferdinand; ed by Langmesser, August – (Includes bibliographical references) – Berlin: Paetel, 1918 – 1r – 1 – us U.W. Library [920]
CONRAD GESSNER / Barre, Radet, Desfontaines et Bourgueil; ed by Wellisch, Hans H – (French Theatre Series). Paris. Brunet, an VIII. 1800 – 383mf – 9 – Dfl2,991.00. – fr Hachette [820]
CONRAD GESSNER : EIN BEYTRAG ZUR GESCHICHTE DES WISSENSCHAFTLICHEN STREBENS UND DER GLAUVENSVERBESSERUNG IM 16. JAHRHUNDERT / Hanhart, J – Winterthur, 1824 – 4mf – 9 – ne IDC [500]
CONRAD GESSNER / ed by Wellisch, Hans H – (Includes bio-bibliography) – 77 titles – 9 – ne IDC [500]
Conrad, Howard L *see*
- ENCYCLOPEDIA OF THE HISTORY OF MISSOURI
- ENCYCLOPEDIA OF THE HISTORY OF ST LOUIS

Conrad, Joseph *see*
- THE NIGGER OF THE "NARCISSUS"
- AN OUTCAST OF THE ISLANDS
- A PERSONAL RECORD
- TALES OF UNREST
- TYPHOON AND OTHER STORIES
- YOUTH: A NARRATIVE

Conrad, Sven *see* GRAB- UND WEIHDENKMAELER AUS DEN TERRITORIEN VON AUGUSTA TRAIANA UND KABYLE VOM 1. BIS 3. JAHRHUNDERT N. CHR
Conrad, T A *see* NEW FRESH WATER SHELLS OF THE UNITED STATES
Conrad, V *see* GERLANDS BEITRAEGE ZUR GEOHYSIK
Conradi, LR *see* HISTORY OF THE SABBATH AND FIRST DAY OF THE WEEK
Conradus de Brunopoli *see* SPECULUM BEATAE MARIAE VIRGINIS FR. CONRADI A SAXONIA
Conrady, Ludwig *see* DIE QUELLE DER KANONISCHEN KINDHEITSGESCHICHTE JESUS'
Conrath, Annemarie *see* ADALBERT STIFTERS "WITIKO"
Conroy, Ellen *see* THE SYMBOLISM OF COLOUR
Conroy, Theresa R *see* PLYOMETRIC TRAINING AND ITS EFFECTS ON SPEED, STRENGTH, AND POWER OF INTERCOLLEGIATE ATHLETES
LA CONSACRAZIONE EUCHARISTICA NELLA CHIESA COPTA / Giamberandini, G – Cairo, 1957 – 3mf – 8 – Dfl13.00 – ne Slangenburg [240]
LA CONSAGRACION DE LA REPUBLICA DEL ECUADOR AL SAGRADO CORAZON DE JESUS. QUITO, 1935 / Heredia, Jose Felix – Madrid: Razon y Fe, 1936 – 1 – sp Bibl Santa Ana [972]
THE CONSCIENCE / Maurice, Frederick Denison – Lectures on casuistry, delivered in the University of Cambridge. 1868 – 1 – us A.T.L.A. [170]
CONSCIENCE AND LAW : OR, PRINCIPLES OF HUMAN CONDUCT / Humphrey, William – London: Thomas Baker, [1896] – 1mf – 9 – 0-8370-6127-X – 1986-0127 – us A.T.L.A. [170]
CONSCIENCE (CCC137) / Gutzlaff, Karl Friedrich August – (In Chinese) – [s.l: s.n, 1835] – 1r – 1 – 1984-B500 – us A.T.L.A. [240]
CONSCIENCE ET LIBERTE – nos 1-82 v31-42. 1974-91 (complete) – 6r – 1 – ATLA S0355 – us A.T.L.A. [240]
CONSCIENCE GUYANAIS – French Guiana. 1959-1962 – 1 – us UMI [072]
THE CONSCIENCE OF THE KING / Spence, James Carmichael – 1899. 3 fiches (29x) – 9 – $1.00f – at Libertarian Micro [320]
CONSCIENCE ON THE BATTLEFIELD / Read, Leonard E – 1fiche (29x) – 9 – 1.00f – at Libertarian Micro [320]
CONSCIENCE: WITH PRELUDES ON CURRENT EVENTS / Cook, Joseph – Boston: Houghton, Osgood, 1879. ix,279p. 1 fiche – 9 – us A.T.L.A. [240]
CONSCIENCIA Y OGANIZACION EN EL MUNDO SINDICAL / Marischi, Vicente – [Buenos Aires]: Calicanto, 1968 – 1 – CSUXADH7662-B – us Hoover Inst Photo [320]
CONSCIENTIA – 1924-27 (complete) – 1r – 1 – ATLA R0135 – us A.T.L.A. [073]
CONSCIENTIOUS OBJECTOR – 1-8 2+6 (all publ). 1939-46 – 1 reel – 1 – $115.00 – us UPA [335]
CONSCRIPTION NEWS – (Offered as part of LLMC's Military Law Collection) – nos 1-262. 1944-59 (all publ) – 16mf – 9 – $24.00 – us L.L.M.C. [073]
LE CONSCRIT – Organe antimilitariste revolutionnaire. no. 1-6. Paris. 1900-05. mq no. 4-5 – 1 – fr A.C.R.P.P. [073]
LE CONSCRIT – Paris. 1924-39 – 1 – fr A.C.R.P.P. [073]
LE CONSCRIT OU LE RETOUR DE CRIMEE / Doin, Ernest – Montreal: Librairie Beauchemin, 1902. SEM105P461 – 1mf – 9 – Can$2.25 – cn Bibl Nat [350]
A CONSECRATED LIFE : A SKETCH OF THE LIFE AND LABORS OF REV. RANSOM DUNN, D.D., 1818-1900 / Gates, Helen Dunn – Boston, Mass.: Morning Star, 1901 – 1mf – us A.T.L.A. [240]
CONSECRATED WOMANHOOD: A SERMON PREACHED IN FIRST CONGREGATIONAL CHURCH, PORTLAND, OREGON / Marvin, Frederic R – 1903 – 9 – us A.T.L.A. [240]
CONSECRATED WOMEN / Hack, Mary Pryor – 1882 – 9 – us A.T.L.A. [240]
A CONSECUTIVE HISTORY OF THE RISE, PROGRESS AND PRESENT STATE OF WESLEYAN METHODISM IN IRELAND / Smith, W – Dublin, 1830. iv/320p – 4mf – 9 – ne IDC [240]
Conseil Colonial de Bourbon *see* AVIS DU CONSEIL COLONIAL DE BOURBON SURDIVERSES PROPOSITIONS CONCERNANT L'ESCLAVAGE
LE CONSEIL DE TROIS EVESQUES SUR LA DETERMINATION DU CONCILE GENERAL DE TRENTE / Vergerio, Pietro Paolo – 1564 ed. n.p. (Religion series) – 9 – 3.00 – fr Bibl Nationale [240]
CONSEIL DES ARTS *see* ETUDES LITTERAIRES
CONSEIL ECONOMIQUE ET SOCIAL – Disponible Depuis 1958 – F90.00y – fr Journal Officiel [944]
CONSEIL ECONOMIQUE ET SOCIAL / France – (1958-1980 F2,300.00) – 1981- – 9 – F90.00y – fr Journal Officiel [330]
Conseil General du Commerce. Session de 1845-1846 *see* RAPPORT PRESENTE PAR M. SCHNEIDER, D'AUTUN, AU NOM DE LA COMMISSION CHARGEE D'EXAMINER LA LOI DU 22 MARS 1841, SUR LE TRAVAIL DES ENFANTS DANS LES MANUFACTURES
Conseil International Provisoire des Syndicats Ouvriers *see* MOUVEMENT OUVRIER INTERNATIONAL
LE CONSEILLER DE L'OUEST – (8 missing numbers) – Angers (Maine-et-Loire), Oct. 1853 – Feb. 1855 – 1r – fr Armell [944]
LE CONSEILLER DES BELLES – Montreal, Canada. v1 n3. 1 dec 1901; 1 jan 1902; 1 fev 1902 – 1r – 1 – Can$25.00 – cn Can Microfilming [072]
LE CONSEILLER DU PEUPLE – Journal mensuel publie par A. de Lamartine. Paris. avr 1849-nov 1851 – 1 – fr A.C.R.P.P. [073]
CONSEILS AUX MAUVAIS POETES : POEME / Taki, Mir – Paris: Dondey-Dupre 1826 – us Res Libr [810]
LES CONSEILS DU PERE JEAN : OU DU CHIFFONIER DE PARIS, A SES AMIS DES FAUBOURGS – [Paris]: Bureau central, [1848?] – us Res Libr [944]
CONSEJO DE CASTILLA : SALA DE ALCALDES DE CASA Y CORTE... / Archivo Historico Nacional – Madrid: Razon y Fe, 1926 – 1 – sp Bibl Santa Ana [946]
Consejo de Hacienda *see* DEFENSAS OMITIDAS EN EL MEMORIAL AJUSTADO HECHO POR EL RELATOR EN LA CAUSA DE DON JUAN DE OVANDO...
Consejo Diocesano de los hombres de Accion Catolica *see*
- PLAN DE FORMACION-ACCION (REUNIONES DE EQUIPO). PRIMER CICLO-GUIONES
- REVISION DE VIDA

Consejo Economico Sincial *see* 4TH ASAMBLEA PLENARIA DEL CONSEJO ECONOMICO SINDICAL. PONENCIAS Y CONCLUSIONES
CONSEJO ECONOMICO SINDICAL – Badajoz: Graficas Iberia, 1948 – sp Bibl Santa Ana [330]
Consejo Economico Sindical *see*
- 4 PLENO
- CESIEX EN CIFRAS
- NORMAS DE CONSTITUCION Y FUNCIONAMIENTO DE LOS CONSEJOS ECONOMICOS SINDICALES COMARCALES E INTERCOMARCALES O DE ZONA

CONSEJO ECONOMICO SINDICAL INTERPROVINCIAL DE EXTREMADURA Y HUELVA. EVOLUCION SOCIO-ECONOMICA – Badajoz: Graf. N. Jimenez, 1970 – sp Bibl Santa Ana [330]
Consejo Economico Sindical Provincial *see*
- 4. COMISION NO 1 A: AGRICULTURA
- 4. COMISION NO 1 B: REPOBLACION FORESTAL
- 4. COMISION NO 1: GANADERIA
- 4. COMISION NO 7: ENSENANZA Y FORMACION PROFESIONAL
- 11TH COMISION. SANIDAD Y ASISTENCIA SOCIAL
- COMISION NO 2
- COMISION NO 4: INDUSTRIAS BASICAS DEL HIERRO
- COMISION NO 5: PRODUCTOS QUIMICOS
- COMISION NO 6: INDUSTRIAS RELACIONADAS – CON LA ALIMENTACION
- COMISION NO 8: TRANSPORTES. COMUNICACIONES Y SERVICIOS DE INFORMACION
- COMISION NO 9: TURISMO
- COMISION NO 13: FINANCIACION
- COMISION NO 14: TRABAJO
- COMISION NO 15: FACTORES HUMANOS Y SOCIALES. PRODUCTIVIDAD

Consejo Episcopal Latinoamericano, Secretariado General *see* DOCUMENTACION CELAM
CONSEJO GENERAL. LA CUESTION DE ANDORRA... / Andorra – Barcelona, 1894 – 1mf – 9 – ILM-3935/1 – ne IDC [340]
CONSEJO PROVINCIAL DE AGRICULTURA, INDUSTRIA Y ENERGIA DE CACERES / Caceres. Spain – 1884 – 9 – 1.50f – sp Bibl Santa Ana [946]
Consejo Provincial de Fomento. Badajoz *see* CARTILLA REDACTADA PARA DAR A CONOCER LOS TRABAJOS QUE SE REALIZAN EN LA GRANJA ESCUELA PRACTICA DE AGRICULTURA DE BADAJOZ. PUBLICADA E EXPENSAS DEL CONSEJO PROVINCIAL DE FOMENTO
EL CONSEJO REAL Y SUPREMO DE LAS INDIAS; SU HISTORIA, ORGANIZACION Y LABOR ADMINISTRATIVA HASTA LA TERMINACION DE LA CASA DE AUSTRIA / Schaefer, Ernst – Sevilla: Imp. M. Carmona, 1935-47. 2v. Plates, plan, facsim – 1 – us U.W. Library [970]
CONSEJO REGIONAL INDIGENA DEL CAUCA (CRIC) = INDIGENOUS REGIONAL COUNCIL OF CAUCA – Bogota. 91 docs. 1980-1991 – 35mf – 9 – ne IDC [320]
Consejo Superior de Investigaciones Cientificas *see* MEMORIA, ANO 1967, 1968
CONSEJOS AUN JOVEN / Moreno Torrado, Luis – Villafranca de los Barros: Imp. Ventura Rodriguez, 1909 – 1 – sp Bibl Santa Ana [946]
CONSENSUS – v1-11. 1975-85 (complete) – 2r – 1 – ATLA S0447 – us A.T.L.A. [073]
CONSENSUS AND PEACE / M'Bow, Amadou-Mahtar; ed by Selassie, Besear Kifle – 1980 – 231p – 9 – 92-3-101851-5 – fr UNESCO [320]
Consentius, Ernst *see*
- "FREYGEISTER, NATURALISTEN, ATHEISTEN"
- GEDICHTE IN ZWEI TEILEN

THE CONSEQUENCES OF MANDATORY MINIMUM PRISON TERMS : A SUMMARY OF RECENT FINDINGS / Vincent, Barbara S & Hofer, Paul J – Washington: FJC, 1994 – 1mf – 9 – $1.50 – LLMC 95-831 – us L.L.M.C. [340]

CONSER MICROFICHE / National Library of Canada – Base file, annual supplements – 17 (0707-3747) – cn Nat'l Library [020]

O CONSERVADOR : FOLHA POLITICA E INDUSTRIAL – '(s.l.')-Sao Luis, Brazil. 13 Dec 1858-Dec 1859. Jan-Feb,Apr, Jun-Dec 1860. Jan-Aug 1861. Jan-Oct, 6 Dec 1862 – 1,5,6 – bl Biblioteca [072]

O CONSERVADOR : JORNAL POLITICO E COMMERCIAL – Itacoatiara, Amazonas. 27 Out 1912-Abr 1917; 25 Set 1921 – 1,5,6 – bl Biblioteca [072]

O CONSERVADOR : JORNAL POLITICO LITTERARIO E NOTICIOSO – Aracaju, 24 Dec 1881; Jan, Apr 1882; Jan, 17 Mar 1883 – 1,5,6 – bl Biblioteca [072]

O CONSERVADOR – Maceio, Alagoas. 22 Out 1870 – 1,5,6 – bl Biblioteca [072]

O CONSERVADOR – Oliveira, 22 Dec 1929 – 1,5,6 – bl Biblioteca [072]

O CONSERVADOR : PERIODICO POLITICO, NOTICIOSO, COMERCIAL E LITTERARIO – Penedo, Alagoas. 31 Out 1880 – 1,5,6 – bl Biblioteca [072]

O CONSERVADOR – [s.l.]. 9 Abr 1884 – 1,5,6 – bl Biblioteca [072]

O CONSERVADOR DE MINAS – Ouro Preto, 13 Feb-31 Mar 1870 – 1,5,6 – bl Biblioteca [072]

O CONSERVADOR PENEDENSE – Penedo, Alagoas. 21 Abr, Jun 1876; Jan 1877; 15 Mar 1878 – 1,5,6 – bl Biblioteca [072]

LE CONSERVATEUR – ou Collection de morceaux rares et d'ouvrages anciens et modernes. Paris. 1756-58, janv-nov 1760 – 1 – fr A.C.R.P.P. [073]

LE CONSERVATEUR – Paris. oct 1818-mars 1820 (I-VI) – 1 – fr A.C.R.P.P. [073]

LE CONSERVATEUR LITTERAIRE – Par Abel et Victor Hugo. no. 1-30. Paris. dec 1819-mars 1821 (I-III) – 1 – fr A.C.R.P.P. [073]

LE CONSERVATEUR LITTERAIRE / Societe des textes francais modernes – Paris, 1819-1821 – 23mf – H-1391/2 – ne IDC [440]

LES CONSERVATEURS ET LA POLITIQUE NATIONALE DE 1878 A 1882 – St. Hyacinthe Quebec: Des Presses a moteur hydraulique du Courrier, 1882. 00307. (Pre-1900 Canadiana) – 9 – cn C.I.H.M. [971]

CONSERVATION – Ottawa: Commission of Conservation, [1912-1921] – 9 – cn C.I.H.M. [333]

CONSERVATION *see* AMERICAN FORESTS

CONSERVATION BIOLOGY – v1- . 1987- – 1,5,6,9 – us UMI [574]

CONSERVATION CANADA / Canada. Department of Indian Affairs and Northern Development – (Ceased v5 1980) – Ottawa. v1-5. 1974-1980 – 9 – Can$20.00y – cn Micromedia [333]

CONSERVATION CENTENNIAL SYMPOSIUM: THE QUEST FOR QUALITY IN WISCONSIN / Wisconsin. College of Agriculture. Conservation Education Programs – Jul 1967 – 1,5 – us Spaulding [639]

CONSERVATION OF CULTURAL PROPERTY : WITH SPECIAL REFERENCE TO TROPICAL CONDITIONS – 3rd ed 1976 – 341p – 9 – 92-3-101318-1 – fr UNESCO [306]

CONSERVATION OF GENETIC RESOURCES IN TROPICAL FOREST MANAGEMENT : PRINCIPLES AND CONCEPTS – 1992 – 120p – it F.A.O. [634]

CONSERVATION OF NATIONAL IDEALS / Wells, D B [et al] – New York: F.H. Revell, c1911 – 1mf – us A.T.L.A. [240]

THE CONSERVATION OF WILD LIFE AND NATURAL HABITATS IN CENTRAL AND EAST AFRICA / Huxley, J – Paris. 1961. BA-386 2 – 8 – ne IDC [960]

CONSERVATION SCIENCE AND SOCIETY – 1985 – 2v (xii/638p) – 9 – 92-3-102254-7 – fr UNESCO [306]

CONSERVATION STANDARDS FOR WORKS OF ART IN TRANSIT AND ON EXHIBITION / Stolow, Nathan – 1979 – 129p – 9 – 92-3-101628-8 – fr UNESCO [060]

CONSERVATIONIST – v1- 1946- 1; v27- 5,6; v30- 9; – us UMI [333]

THE CONSERVATIVE – Carrollton. Miss. 1908- – 1 – us UMI [071]

THE CONSERVATIVE – Nebraska City, Otoe County, Nebraska. 14 Jul 1898-29 May 1902 – 1 – us NE Hist [071]

CONSERVATIVE ACTION AND VICTORY FUND – 2p leaflet – 9 – 1.00f – at Libertarian Micro [320]

CONSERVATIVE AND UNIONIST WOMEN'S FRANCHISE REVIEW – London, 1909-1916 – 14mf – W-16/1 – ne IDC [305]

Conservative Baptist Association of America *see* CBA BUILDER

The Conservative Baptist Foreign Mission Society *see* NEWS AND VIEWS

CONSERVATIVE BAPTIST FOREIGN MISSION SOCIETY : ANNUAL REPORT – 1959-65; 1971-83 (complete) – 1r – 1 – ATLA S0450 – us A.T.L.A. [240]

CONSERVATIVE BAPTISTS – Sep 1960-Nov 1965 – 1 – 13.09 – us Baptist [240]

CONSERVATIVE JUDAISM – (v.34-. 1980- 5,6,9) – v.1-. 1945- – 1 – us UMI [270]

Conservative Party. Great Britain *see*
- ANNUAL REPORTS
- ARCHIVES OF THE BRITISH CONSERVATIVE PARTY

THE CONSERVATIVE REFORMATION AND ITS THEOLOGY : AS REPRESENTED IN THE AUGSBURG CONFESSION, AND IN THE HISTORY AND LITERATURE OF THE EVANGELICAL LUTHERAN CHURCH / Krauth, Charles Porterfield – (Includes bibliographical references and index) – Philadelphia: J B Lippincott, 1871 – 2mf – 9 – 0-8370-8686-8 – 1986-2686 – us A.T.L.A. [240]

THE CONSERVATIVE REVIEW – v. 1-5. 1899-1901 – 1 – 19.00 – us L of C Photodup [073]

THE CONSERVATIVE SPEAKERS' CLUB – Australia. 2p leaflet – 9 – 1.00f – at Libertarian Micro [320]

CONSERVATIVER VOLKSFREUND – Bielefeld, jan 4 1862-aug 22 1874 (incomplete) – 1 – Inquire at Mikrofilmarchiv for details – gw Misc Inst [943]

Conservatoire et jardin botanique de Geneve *see* ICONES HEPATICARUM

THE CONSERVATOR – Philadelphia. v. 1-9. Mar 1890-Feb 1899 – 1 – us NY Public [073]

THE CONSERVATOR – Philadelphia. v1-30. 1890-1919 – 3r – 1 – us Ross [800]

Conservatorio di Musica Luigi Cherubini. Florence *see* ANNUARIO

Conseso Provincial de Fomento *see* FOLLETO DE LAS CONFERENCIAS DADAS DURANTE LA SEMANA AGRICOLA DE BADAJOZ DEL 12-18 NOV. 1912

CONSIDERACIONES ACERCA DE LA SEGUNDA PARADOJA DE EL BROCENSE / Gonzalez de la Calle, Pedro Urbano – Caceres: Tip. Extremadura – sp Bibl Santa Ana [946]

CONSIDERACIONES DEMOGRAFICAS SOBRE EL CENSO DE BUENOS AIRES / Instituto Geografico – Buenos Aires, 1883 – 1mf – 9 – sp Cultura [972]

CONSIDERACIONES SOBRE DIVERSAS CATEGORIAS DE FUERZAS... / Nieto y Serrano, M – Madrid, 1886 – 9 – sp Cultura [610]

CONSIDERACIONES SOBRE LA DIPLOMACIA / Donoso Cortes, Juan Francisco – Madrid: Tip. R. Rodriguez de Rivera, Tomo 1. 1848 – 1 – sp Bibl Santa Ana [320]

CONSIDERACIONES SOBRE LA ESPANA Y SUS COLONIAS,... / Flinter, G D – Madrid, 1834 – 1mf – 1 – ILM-2851/1 – ne IDC [327]

CONSIDERACIONES SOBRE LO QUE SIGNIFICA...CRISTIANO / Hernandez Cardenal, Garcia – 1570 – 9 – 1.50f – sp Bibl Santa Ana [240]

CONSIDERACIONES SOBRE LOS DOLORES DE LA SANTISIMA VIRGEN MARIA. PRIMER DOLOR / Tena Fernandez, Juan – Trujillo: Tip. sobrino de B. Pena, 1928 – 1 – sp Bibl Santa Ana [240]

CONSIDERACIONES...FERROCARRILES... CACERES / Godinez de la Paz, Carlos – 9 – 1.50f – sp Bibl Santa Ana [380]

CONSIDERATIEN OVER DE TOESTAND IN MAKASAR, 1699, 1708 – 10-11mf – 9 – ne IDC [950]

CONSIDERATIONS GENERALES APPLICABLES A L'ARCHITECTURE EOLIENNE... / Bazelaire de Rupierre, OP de – [S.l]: Ministere de la France d'Outre mer, 1948 – 1 – F50.00 – fr Armell [720]

CONSIDERATIONS GENERALES SUR LA CLASSE DES INSECTES / Dumeril, A M C – Paris, 1823. xii,272p. 60 pl. Z/1205/2 – 8 – ne IDC [590]

CONSIDERATIONS GENERALES SUR LA CODIFICATION DU DROIT INTERNATIONAL AMERICAIN / Alvarez, Arturo – Rio de Janeiro, 1927 – 1mf – 9 – ILM-1715/1 – ne IDC [340]

CONSIDERATIONS GENERALES SUR L'ANALYSE ORGANIQUE ET SUR SES APPLICATIONS / Chevreul, Eugene – Paris: Levraut, 1824 – 1 – F143.27 – fr Armell [540]

CONSIDERATIONS ON A SEPARATION OF THE METHODISTS FROM THE ESTABLISHED CHURCH, ADDRESSED TO SUCH OF THEM AS ARE FRIENDLY TO THAT MEASURE, AND PARTICULARLY TO THOSE IN THE CITY OF BRISTOL / Knox, Alexander – Bristol, 1794 – 1mf – 9 – MP-588/1 – ne IDC [240]

CONSIDERATIONS ON THE DEFINITIVE TREATY, SIGNED AT AIX LA CHAPELLE,...1748 – London, 1748 – 1mf – 1 – ILM-2741/1 – ne IDC [327]

CONSIDERATIONS ON THE FORMATION OF THE HERMITAGE COLLECTION OF RUSSIAN MANUSCRIPTS / Afferica, J – (Forschungen zur osteuropaeischen Geschichte. 1976). BR-9899 1 – 9 – ne IDC [090]

CONSIDERATIONS ON THE LATE DISTURBANCES / Consistent Whig – London, 1780 – 1mf – 9 – MP-540/1 – ne IDC [240]

CONSIDERATIONS ON THE PENTATEUCH / Taylor, Isaac – London: Jackson, Walford, 1863. 1 fiche – 9 – us A.T.L.A. [240]

CONSIDERATIONS ON THE PRUSSIAN TREATY,... – London, 1789 – 1mf – 1 – ILM-795/1 – ne IDC [327]

CONSIDERATIONS ON THE QUESTION...WHETHER THE PROCEEDINGS OF COMMANDERS IN CHIEF OF FLEETS AND ARMIES...ARE SUBJECT TO THE REVIEW OF THE CIVIL COURTS OF LAW... / Pultenay, William – London: J Stockdale, 1786 – 1mf – 9 – $1.50 – LLMC 89-019 – us L.L.M.C. [340]

CONSIDERATIONS PERTINENT TO A PROPOSED NEW STATISTICAL SERVICE FOR THE GOVERNMENT OF SPECIAL DISTRICT OF JOGJAKARTA / Indonesia. Jogjakarta – Newton B. Knox. 1960. SE-5561-1 – 9 – ne IDC [310]

CONSIDERATIONS PRESENTEES AUX VRAIS AMIS DU REPOS ET DU BONHEUR DE LA FRANCE, A L'OCCASION DES NOUVEAUX MOUVEMENTS DE QUELQUES SOI-DISANT AMIS DES NOIRS / Moreau de Saint Mery, ML E – (Slave Trade and Abolitionism in France series). 1791 – 9 – fr Hachette [360]

CONSIDERATIONS SUR LA NEUTRALITE MARITIME,... – Paris, 1801 – 1mf – 1 – ILM-875/1 – ne IDC [327]

CONSIDERATIONS SUR LA POLITIQUE EXTERIEURE ET INTERIEURE DE LA FRANCE DEPUIS LA REVOLUTION DE 1830 / Laurent, M – Paris, Everat. 1831. 63 p. Les Saint-Simoniens, 1825-1834. 6852 – 9 – fr Hachette [335]

CONSIDERATIONS SUR L'ART DE LA GUERRE / Rogniat, Joseph – Paris. Magimel. Anselin et Pochard. 1817. xi, 608p. (Strategy of War Series) – 9 – fr Hachette [355]

CONSIDERATIONS SUR LE CHOLERA D'ARLES. / Meissonnier, Casimir – Avignon, Rastoul, 1835. 1 fiche. (Statistics Series: Medical Studies) – 9 – 6.00 – fr Bibl Nationale [310]

CONSIDERATIONS SUR LES APPARENCES DE LA PAIX,... – N.p., n.d. – 1mf – 1 – ILM-1056/1 – ne IDC [327]

CONSIDERATIONS SUR LES CORPS ORGANISES / Bonnet, Charles – Amsterdam, MM. Rey, 1761, 2 v., 274 p., 328 p. Histoire des Sciences XVIIe-XIXe Siecles. 7934 4 bis – 9 – fr Hachette [580]

CONSIDERATIONS SUR LES DIATOMEES / Brebisson, L A de – Falaise. 1838. B-6347 1 – 9 – ne IDC [580]

CONSIDERATIONS SUR LES DIVERSES METHODES A SUIVRE DANS L'OBSERVATION DES PEUPLES SAUVAGES / Gerando, Joseph-M de – 1 – F50.00 – fr Armell [301]

CONSIDERATIONS SUR LES EFFETS QU'ONT PRODUIT EN CANADA / Viger, Denis Benjamin – Montreal: J Brown, 1809. SEM16P91 – 1r – 5 – Can$9.00 – cn Bibl Nat [971]

CONSIDERATIONS SUR LES FINANCES DE FRANCE ET DES ETATS-UNIS / Pereire, Emile – Paris, Revue encyclopedique, 1832, 35 p. Les Saint-Simoniens, 1825-1834. 6886 – 9 – fr Hachette [336]

CONSIDERATIONS SUR LES LEPIDOPTERES ENVOYES DU GUATEMALA A M. DE L'ORZA / Boisduval, J B A D de – Rennes, 1870. 100p. Z-1080/2 – 8 – ne IDC [590]

CONSIDERATIONS SUR LES LOIS CIVILES DU MARIAGE / Girouard, Desire – (Montreal: Nouveau Monde), 1868.03437.(Pre-1900 Canadiana) – 9 – cn C.I.H.M. [971]

CONSIDERAZIONI CRITICHE SU ALCUNE TEORIE DEL DIRITTO INTERNAZIONALE... / Diena, G – Torino, 1908 – 1mf – 1 – ILM-3567/1 – ne IDC [327]

Considine, William J *see* THE EFFECT OF TWO TYPES OF PLYOMETRIC TRAINING IN IMPROVING VERTICAL JUMP ABILITY IN FEMALE COLLEGE SOCCER PLAYERS

CONSILIA / Gutierrez, Juan – 1595 – 9 – 1.50f – sp Bibl Santa Ana [240]

CONSILIA...PERFECTA...PER JOHANNEM DE ACEVEDO / Acevedo, Alfonso de – 1737 – 9 – $1.50f – sp Bibl Santa Ana [340]

CONSILIORUM SIVE RESPONSORUM / Gutierrez, Juan – (vl. 1618. 1.50f; 9. vl. 1730. 1.50f; BSA; 9) – vl. 1611 – 9 – 1.50f – sp Bibl Santa Ana [240]

CONSILIUM QUORUNDAM EPISCOPORUM BONONIAE CONGREGATORUM / Vergerio, Pietro Paolo – London. (Religion series) – 9 – 3.00 – fr Bibl Nationale [240]

Consistent Whig *see* CONSIDERATIONS ON THE LATE DISTURBANCES

A CONSOLATION FOR OUR GRAMMAR SCHOOLES / Brinsley, John – 1622 – 9 – 10.00 – us Scholars' Facs [370]

CONSOLATIONS A CEUX QUI PLEURENT OU TRESOR DES MALADES – Montreal: E. Senecal, 1872. 00424. (Pre-1900 Canadiana) – 9 – cn C.I.H.M. [971]

THE CONSOLATIONS OF THE CROSS : ADDRESSES ON THE SEVEN WORDS OF THE DYING LORD / Brent, Charles H – New York: Longmans, Green, 1904 – 1mf – us A.T.L.A. [240]

CONSOLATIONS OF THE TRUE RELIGION (CCC132) / Gutzlaff, Karl Friedrich August – (In Chinese) – [s.l: s.n, 1837] – 1r – 1 – 1984-B500 – us A.T.L.A. [240]

IL CONSOLATO DEL MARE / Casaregi, G L M – Torino, 1911 – 5mf – 1 – ILM-2293/1 – ne IDC [327]

IL CONSOLATO DEL MARE... – Leyden, 1704 – 8mf – 1 – ILM-863/1 – ne IDC [327]

Consoli, Maximiliano *see*
- LOS DERECHOS DEL TRABAJADOR
- POR QUE SOY PERONISTA

CONSOLIDACION DEL SINDICALISMO PERONISTA Y EMERGENCIA DE LA FORMULA POLITICA ARGENTINA DURANTE EL GOBIERNO FRONDIZISTA / Cavarozzi, Marcelo – Buenos Aires, Argentina: Centro de Estudios de Estado y Sociedad, 1979 – 1 – CSUXADH7656-B – us Hoover Inst Photo [320]

CONSOLIDATED EDITION AS AT THE 31ST DEC 1955 OF THE PENAL CODE AND THE CRIMINAL PROCEDURE CODE – (Prepared by the Attorney General under section 44 of the Interpretation and General Clauses ordinance n2 of 1953) – Zomba, Govt print, [1956] – us Res Libr [340]

CONSOLIDATED INDEX TO COMPILED SERVICE RECORDS OF CONFEDERATE SOLDIERS / U.S. War Department. Confederate Records – M253. Printed guide – 535r – 5 – us Nat'l Archives [324]

THE CONSOLIDATED STATUTES FOR LOWER CANADA / Canada. Laws, Statutes, etc – Quebec: Printed by Stewart Derbishire and George Desbarats, 1861. SEM105P139 – 13mf – 9 – Can$29.25 – cn Bibl Nat [324]

THE CONSOLIDATED STATUTES FOR UPPER CANADA / Canada. Laws, Statutes, etc – Toronto: Printed by Stewart Derbishire and George Desbarats, 1859. SEM105P138 – 13mf – 9 – Can$29.25 – cn Bibl Nat [324]

THE CONSOLIDATED STATUTES OF CANADA / Canada. Laws, Statutes, etc – Toronto: Printed by Stewart Derbishire and George Desbarats, 1859. SEM105P126 – 15mf – 9 – Can$33.75 – cn Bibl Nat [340]

CONSOLIDATED STATUTES RESPECTING THE MILITIA / Canada. Laws, Statutes, etc – Toronto: Printed by Stewart Derbishire & George Desbarats, 1859. SEM105P179 – 1mf – 9 – Can$2.25 – cn Bibl Nat [324]

CONSOLIDATED TRANSLATION SURVEYS / U.S. Central Intelligence Agency – 1964-71 – 238mf – 9 – $300.00 – us Updata [977]

THE CONSOLIDATION DEVELOPMENT PLAN (1957/58-1958/59) / Ghana. Ministry of Finance – D-1305 1. 2 v. 1957-1958 – 9 – ne IDC [336]

THE CONSOLIDATION OF THE CHURCH IN CANADA: A PLEA FOR A GENERAL SYNOD WITH LEGISLATIVE POWERS, FROM THE NORTH-WEST:.. / Anson, Adelbert – Toronto: J. P. Clougher, 1892?. 05872. (Pre-1900 Canadiana) – 9 – cn C.I.H.M. [240]

CONSOMMATEUR CANADIEN – (Cont: Canadian Consumer = Le Consommateur canadien, 1971. v1-20 Can$28.00y) – Nepean. v1-22 n4. 1971-92 – 9 – Can$20.00y – cn Micromedia [073]

CONSOMMATION – Annales du C.R.E.D.O.C. Paris. 1958-72 – 1 – fr A.C.R.P.P. [073]

LA CONSOMMATION ET LES DEPENSES DES MENAGES AU MAROC / Morocco. Secretariat d'Etat au Plan – 4v. Avril 1970-Avril 1971. BNE-3125 1 – 9 – ne IDC [310]

LA CONSOMMATION ET LES DEPENSES DES MENAGES MAROCAINS MUSULMANS: RESULTATS DE L'ENQUETE 1959-1960 / Morocco. Service Central des Statistiques – 1961. BNE-3096 1 – 9 – ne IDC [310]

LES CONSOMMATIONS DE PARIS / Husson, Armand – (Condition of 19th C. French working class series). 1856 – 9 – fr Hachette [360]

CONSONANT GRADATION IN ESKIMO / Ulving, T – BN 462 2. 1953 – 8 – ne IDC [490]

CONSONANZEN UND DISSONANZEN : GESAMTE SCHRIFTEN AUS ALTERER UND NEURER ZEIT / Lobe, J C – Leipzig: Baumgartner, 1869 – 1 – us Sibley [780]

CONSPECTUM AVIUM PICINARUM / Sundevall, C J – Stockholmiae. 1866. Z-1940 2 – 8 – ne IDC [590]

CONSPECTUS CRITICUS DIATOMACEARUM / Agardh, C A – Lundae, (1830-32). 66p. IB-2 – 8 – ne IDC [580]

CONSPECTUS FLORA GRAECAE / Halacsy, Eyon – v. 1-3, Suppl. v. 1. Lipsiae. 1900-08. B-2255 2 – 8 – ne IDC [580]

CONSPECTUS FLORAE EUROPAEAE / Nyman, CF – Orebro. 1878-82-1890. B-5574 2 – 8 – ne IDC [580]

CONSPECTUS FUNGORUM / Krombholz, J V von – Prag. 1821. B-5094 2 – 8 – ne IDC [580]

CONSPECTUS FUNGORUM IN LUSATIAE SUPERIORIS AGRO NISKIENSI CRESCENTIUM / Albertini, J B von & DeSchweinitz, LD – Lipsiae. 1805. B-5284 2 – 8 – ne IDC [580]

CONSPECTUS HEPATICARUM ARCHIPELAGI INDICI / Schiffner, V – Batavia, 1898 – 5mf – 9 – 12,472/1 – ne IDC [580]

CONSPECTUS LITTERATURAE BOTANICAE IN SUECIA / Wikstroem, J E – Holmiae. 1831. B-5202 2 – 8 – ne IDC [580]

CONSPECTUS REGNI VEGETABILIS / Reichenbach, Heinrich G L – Lipsiae. 1828. B-5664 1 – 9 – ne IDC [580]

CONSPECTUS SYNOPTICUS STICTEORUM / Nylander, W – (Bull. Soc. Linn. Normandie. S. 2, v. 2). Caen. 1868. B-5389 2 – 8 – ne IDC [580]

CONSPECTUS SYSTEMATICUS CHARACEARUM EUROPAEARUM / Braun, A C H – Berlin. 1867. B-6345 1 – 9 – ne IDC [580]

LA CONSPIRACION DE LA OLIGARQUIA / Guillen, Abraham – Buenos Aires: Editorial Guitem, 1956 – 1 – CSUXADJ9209-B – us Hoover Inst Photo [320]

LA CONSPIRACION DEL '43; EL GOU : UNA EXPERIENCIA MILITARISTA EN LA ARGENTINA / Diaz Araujo, Enrique – Buenos Aires: Ediciones La Bastilla; distribuidor exclusivo: Editorial Astrea de R. Depalma, [1971] – 1 – CSUXADJ2565-B – us Hoover Inst Photo [355]

CONSPIRACY AND REVISIONIST LITERATURE / Albionic Consulting and Research – 9 – 1.00f – at Libertarian Micro [320]

CONSPIRACY TRIALS IN AMERICA, 1919-1953 – (1919: Abrams vs US $75. 1922: People vs Ferguson $75. 1922: People vs Lloyd $225. 1922: People vs Ruthenberg $75. 1925: Gitlow vs NY. $75. 1927: Whitnes vs California $75. 1930: People vs Mintz $75. 1931: People vs Horiuchi $525. 1931: State vs Boloff $75. 1939: Kessler vs Strecker $75. 1941: Gorin vs US $75. 1943: Schneiderman vs US $75. 1943: Dunne vs US $75. 1945: Bridges vs Wixon $300. 1946: US vs Redin $150. 1948: Marzani vs US $150. 1949: US vs Alger Hiss $525. 1950: Brownell vs Communist Party $975. 1951: Coplon vs US $600. 1951: Dennis vs US $600. 1951: US vs Fujimoto $675. 1952: US vs Rosenberg $375. 1953: Orloff vs Willoughby $75) – 1 – $85.00 – D3258 – us Scholarly Res [340]

CONSPIRATION DE RUSSIE; RAPPORT DE LA COMMISSION D'ENQUETE DE SAINT-PETERSBOURG A S.M. L'EMPEREUR NICOLAS 1ER SUR LES SOCIETES SECRETES DECOUVERTES EN RUSSIE ET PREVENUES DE CONSPIRATION CONTRE L'ETAT, LEUR ORIGINE – (Russia – 19th C. series). 1826 – 9 – fr Hachette [947]

LA CONSPIRATION DES POUDRES – [Paris]: Impr Populaire de J Dupont, jun 4-8 1848 – us Res Libr [944]

CONSTABLE AND OLD SUFFOLK ARTISTS / Ipswich. Fine Arts Club – 1887 – 9 – $4.90 – uk Chadwyck [750]

CONSTABLES' ACCOUNTS / East Ardsley. Yorkshire – 1653-92. Ms – 1 – uk Microform Academic [941]

CONSTABLE'S ACCOUNTS, 1629-1866 / Sowerby – 1 – uk Microform Academic [941]

THE CONSTABLE'S GUIDE AND FORM BOOK / Marsh, Howard Franklin – Wellsboro, 167p. LL-675 – 1 – us L of C Photodup [340]

THE CONSTABLES' MANUAL: BEING A SUMMARY OF THE LAW RELATING TO THE RIGHTS, POWERS, AND DUTIES OF CONSTABLES / Clarke, Samuel Robinson – Toronto: Hart & Rawlinson, 1878. 00670. (Pre-1900 Canadiana) – 9 – cn C.I.H.M. [971]

THE CONSTABLES' MANUAL: BEING A SUMMARY OF THE LAW RELATING TO THE RIGHTS, POWERS, AND DUTIES OF CONSTABLES / Clarke, Samuel Robinson – Toronto: Ure, 1881. 120p. LL-2293 – 1 – us L of C Photodup [340]

Constandse, AK *see* RURAL SOCIOLOGY IN ACTION

Constans, Augustin *see* RAPPORT GENERAL A M. LE MINISTRE DE L'INTERIEUR SUR LE SERVICE DES ALIENES EN 1874 PAR LES INSPECTEURS GENERAUX DU SERVICE

Constans, S *see* FETES CHRETIENNES: HISTORIQUE, CONSIDERATIONS ET TRAITS EDIFIANTS: LRE SERIE

THE CONSTANT / Borsodi, Ralph – 2p – 9 – 1.00f – at Libertarian Micro [335]

Constant, A *see* LISTE ANNOTEE DES LEPIDOPTERES ENVOYES A LA SOCIETE D'HISTOIRE NATURELLE D'AUTUN

Constant, Alphonse Louis *see*
- LE CATECHISME DE LA PAIX
- DOGME ET RITUAL DE LA HAUTE MAGIE
- LA MERE DE DIEU: EPOPEE RELIGIEUSE ET HUMANITAIRE
- LE TESTAMENT DE LA LIBERTE
- LES TROIS HARMONIES, CHANSONS ET POESIES

Constant, Benjamin *see* DISCOURS A LA CHAMBRE SUR LA TRAITE DES NOIRS, DES 27 JUIN 1821, 4 AVRIL ET 31 JUILLET 1822

Constant, C *see*
- CONGRES INTERNATIONAL DE DROIT COMMERCIAL (ANVERS, 1885)
- DE L'EXECUTION DES JUGEMENTS ETRANGERS...
- DE L'EXECUTION DES JUGEMENTS ETRANGERS DANS LES DIVERS PAYS

Constant, Claire *see* INVENTAIRE GENERAL DES PEINTURES DU MUSEE DU CHATEAU DE VERSAILLES

Constant, G *see*
- RAPPORT SUR UNE MISSION SCIENTIFIQUE AUX ARCHIVES D'AUTRICHE ET D'ESPAGNE
- THE REFORMATION IN ENGLAND 1: THE ENGLISH SCHISM HENRY 8TH (1509-1547). LONDON, 1934
- THE REFORMATION IN ENGLAND. THE ENGLISH SCHIM. HENRY 7TH 1509-1547. LONDON, 1934

Constant Rebeque, C T J de *see* ...DE NEUTRALITATE TEMPORE BELLI

Constantin, R *see* NOMENCLATOR INSIGNIUM SCRIPTORUM,...

CONSTANTIN TISCHENDORF IN SEINER FUENFUNDZWANZIGJAEHRIGEN SCHRIFTSTELLERISCHEN WIRKSAMKEIT : LITERAR-HISTORISCHE SKIZZE / Volbeding, Joh. Ernst – Leipzig: C. Fr. Fleischer, 1862 – 1mf – us A.T.L.A. [430]

CONSTANTINE THE GREAT : THE REORGANISATION OF THE EMPIRE AND THE TRIUMPH OF THE CHURCH / Firth, John B – New York: G.P. Putnam, 1905. (Heroes of the nations) – 1mf – us A.T.L.A. [240]

CONSTANTINE THE GREAT : THE UNION OF THE STATE AND THE CHURCH / Cutts, Edward L – London: S.P.C.K.; New York: Pott, Young, 1881 – 1mf – us A.T.L.A. [320]

CONSTANTINE THE GREAT AND CHRISTIANITY : THREE PHASES : THE HISTORICAL, THE LEGENDARY, AND THE SPURIOUS / Coleman, Christopher Bush – New York: Columbia University Press; London: P.S. King, 1914. (Studies in history, economics and public law; v60, no.1: whole no. 146) – 1mf – us A.T.L.A. [240]

Constantineau, Philippe *see* PARMENIDES UND HEGEL UEBER DAS SEIN

DIE CONSTANTINISCHE SCHENKUNG / Friedrich, Johann – Noerdlingen: Beck, 1889 – 1mf – us A.T.L.A. [240]

Constantino, I *see* LA PERSONALITA GIURIDICA INTERNAZIONALE

Constantinoff, J *see* LA CODIFICATION DU DROIT INTERNATIONAL...

CONSTANTINOPLE, A SKETCH OF ITS HISTORY FROM ITS FOUNDATION TO ITS CONQUEST BY THE TURKS IN 1453 / Brodribb, William Jackson – London: Seeley, Jackson, and Halliday, 1879. xv,270p – 1 – us U.W. Library [940]

CONSTANTINUS PORPHYROGENITUS IMPERATOR, VOL 1-3 (CSHB 9-11) – (v1 + 2: De Cerimoniis Aulae Byzantinae Libri Duo, Graece Et Latine, E Recensione Io. Iac. Reiskii, Cum Eiusdem Commentariis Integris v1 Bonnae 1829 Dfl53.00. v2 Bonnae 1830 Dfl56.00. v3: De Thematibus Et De Administrando Imperio. Accedit Hieroclis Synecdemus Cum Bandurii Et Wesselingii Commentariis. Rec. Imm. Bekkerus Bonnae 1840 Dfl35.00) – ne Slangenburg [240]

Constantius *see* THE PATRIARCHATE OF ANTIOCH

Constantius, Constantin *see* GJENTAGELSEN

Constanza, M *see* SAGGIO CRITICO DI DIRITTO INTERNAZIONALE "CICLO D'EVOLUZIONE"

THE CONSTELLATION (NO. 4 OF MR. FRANCIS'S BALLROOM ASSISTANT) / Reinagle, Alexander – n.p., n.d.. MUSIC 3082, Item 10 – 1 – us L of C Photodup [780]

CONSTITUCION : LA CONSTITUCION ARGENTINA, ANOTADA CON LA JURISPRUDENCIA DE LA CORTE SUPREMA DE JUSTICIA – Buenos Aires: Editorial Guillermo Kraft ltda., [1945] – 1 – CSUXADQ5221-B – us Hoover Inst Photo [340]

CONSTITUCION (1949) : LA CONSTITUCION NACIONAL DE 1949: [TEXTO ORIGINAL COMPLETO] – (Edicion, Orlande F. Calgaro) – Buenos Aires: R. Alonso, [1974] – 1 – CSUXAH76023-B – us Hoover Inst Photo [340]

CONSTITUCION DE COMISION NACIONAL DE COOPERACION ECONOMICA, UNA ETAPA MAS EN LA EJECUCION DE LA DOCTRINA PERONISTA EN EL ORDEN ECONOMICO – Buenos Aires. 1950 – 1 – us Res Libr [339]

CONSTITUCION DE LA COMISION NACIONAL DE COOPERACION ECONOMICA : UNA ETAPAMAS EN LA EJECUCION DE LA DOCTRINA PERONISTA EN EL ORDEN ECONOMICO – Buenos Aires, 1950 – 1 – CSUXAJA7175-B – us Hoover Inst Photo [330]

CONSTITUCION DE LA CORPORACION MUNICIPAL EL 6 DE FEBRERO DE 1949 / Caceres – Caceres: Tip El Noticiero, 1949 – sp Bibl Santa Ana [628]

CONSTITUCION DE LA CORPORACION MUNICIPAL EL 31 DE JULIO DE 1948 / Caceres – Caceres: Tip. El Noticiero, 1948 – sp Bibl Santa Ana [338]

CONSTITUCION DE LOS ESTADOS-UNIDOS / U. S. Constitution – Mayaguez, Tip. Comercial, 1898. 52 p. LL-1678 – 1 – us L of C Photodup [340]

CONSTITUCION EN 1925. NOTICIA DE VICENTE CASTANEDA / Comision Provincial de Monumentos – Madrid: Tip. Rev. Arch. y Museos, 1927. Boletin R.A. Historia, 1927 – 1 – sp Bibl Santa Ana [324]

CONSTITUCION EN 1928, NOTICIA DE VICEN TE CASTANEDA / Comision Provincial de Monumentos – Madrid: Tip. R.B. Arch. y Museos, 1928 – 1 – sp Bibl Santa Ana [324]

LA CONSTITUCION "JUSTICIALISTA" DE 1949 / Gonzalez Arzac, Alberto Ricardo – Mexico: Editorial El Alba, 1973 – 1 – CSUXAGP9745-B – us Hoover Inst Photo [340]

LA CONSTITUCION JUSTICIALISTA DE SANTA FE : NOTAS A LAS REFORMAS CONSTITUCIONALES DE 1949 DE LA PROVINCIA DE SANTA FE; FUENTES Y CONCORDANCIAS / Berraz Montyn, Carlos – Santa Fe, 1950 – 1 – CSUXADP5150-B – us Hoover Inst Photo [340]

LA CONSTITUCION NACIONAL (LIBERTAD, IGUALDAD Y FRATERNIDAD) Y LOS DERECHOS DEL TRABAJADOR (RAZON DE LEGITIMO AMPARO) : MENTALIDAD JURIDICA REVOLUCIONARIA, SOLIDARIDAD, JUSTICIA SOCIAL, DIGNIDAD HUMANA / Antoni, Norberto Olegario – [Tucuman, Casanova & Cossio, 1948] – 1 – CSUXAHZ3279-B – us Hoover Inst Photo [331]

CONSTITUCION POLITICA...DEL PRINCIPADO DE ANDORRA / Dios Trias, D J de – Barcelona, 1890 – 1mf – 1 – ILM-2535/1 – ne IDC [327]

CONSTITUCIONAL : JORNAL POLITICO, LITTERARIO E NOTICIOSO – Ouro Preto, 18 Aug 1866-23 Nov 1868 – 1,5,6 – bl Biblioteca [072]

O CONSTITUCIONAL : FOLHA POLITICA, LITTERARIA E COMMERCIAL – [s.l.]-Sao Luis, Brazil. 28 Oct 1851-Jan 1854. Jan 1863-31 Dec 1864 – 1,5,6 – bl Biblioteca [072]

O CONSTITUCIONAL – Maceio, Alagoas. 25 Mar-22 Nov 1851 – 1,5,6 – bl Biblioteca [072]

O CONSTITUCIONAL : ORGAO DO PARTIDO CONSERVADOR – Maceio, Alagoas. 14 Ago 1873 – 1,5,6 – bl Biblioteca [072]

O CONSTITUCIONAL – Ouro Preto, 25 Apr-7 Aug 1878 – 1,5,6 – bl Biblioteca [072]

O CONSTITUCIONAL : PERIODICO POLITICO, LITTERARIO E NOTICIOSO – [s.l.]. 25 Jul 1872 – 1,5,6 – bl Biblioteca [072]

O CONSTITUCIONAL – Rio de Janeiro, 1822 – 1,5,6 – bl Biblioteca [072]

O CONSTITUCIONAL – [s.l.]-BA, Brazil. 10 abr-21 ago 1822 – 1,5,6 – bl Biblioteca [072]

CONSTITUCIONES / Escuelas de Maria Santisima – 1832 – 9 – 1.50f – sp Bibl Santa Ana [370]

CONSTITUCIONES DE CATALUNA (IMPRESAS EN PERGAMINO, SIECLE 15) – Barcelona – 1r – 5,6 – sp Cultura [340]

CONSTITUCIONES DE LA CONGREGACION Y ESCUELA DE CRISTO – 1788 – 9 – 1.50f – sp Bibl Santa Ana [240]

CONSTITUCIONES DE LA PROVINCIA DE SAN GABRIEL (1580) / Barrado Manzano, Arcangel – Madrid: Graf. Calleja, 1967 – 1 – sp Bibl Santa Ana [340]

CONSTITUCIONES ECLESIASTICAS (SIECLE 14) – Zamora – 1r – 5,6 – sp Cultura [240]

CONSTITUCIONES SINODALES DEL OBISPADO DE PLASENCIA / Casas Souto, Pedro – 1892 – 9 – 1.50f – sp Bibl Santa Ana [240]

CONSTITUCIONES SYNODALES / Roys y Mendoza, Francisco – 1673 – 9 – 1.50f – sp Bibl Santa Ana [240]

CONSTITUCIONES SYNODALES DEL OBISPADO DE CORIA / Carvajal, Pedro de – 1608 – 9 – 1.50f – sp Bibl Santa Ana [240]

CONSTITUCIONES SYNODALES...GRANADA / Guerrero, Pedro – 1573 – 9 – 1.50f – sp Bibl Santa Ana [240]

CONSTITUCIONES Y EXERCICIOS DE LA VENERABLE MADRE SOR MARIA DE LA ANTIGUA...IGLESIA PARROQUIAL SANTA MARIA LA REAL – Ecija: Benito Daza. S. XVIII – 1 – sp Bibl Santa Ana [240]

CONSTITUCIONES Y REGLA DE LA MINIMA CONGREGACION DE LOS HERMANOS ENFERMEROS / Obregon, B – Madrid, 1634 – 9 – sp Cultura [610]

CONSTITUIDO...2 DE FEBRERO DE 1958 / Caceres – Caceres: Imprenta Moderna, s.a. – sp Bibl Santa Ana [946]

A CONSTITUINTE : ORGAM LIBERAL – Sao Paulo, 7 Sep 1879-17 Jul 1880 – 1,5,6 – bl Biblioteca [072]

LA "CONSTITUTIO ANTONINIANA" ED I "DEDITICII" / Bozzoni, R – Napoli, 1933 – 1mf – 1 – ILM-3172/1 – ne IDC [327]

CONSTITUTION / Central Canada Chamber of Mines – Winnipeg: Stovel, 1899. 02560. (Pre-1900 Canadiana) – 9 – cn C.I.H.M. [380]
CONSTITUTION – Chillicothe. Mo. 1889-1927 – 1 – us UMI [071]
CONSTITUTION – Chillicothe. Mo. -w. 1901-21, 1950- – 1 – us UMI [071]
CONSTITUTION / Jewish Agency for Palestine – London. 1949. BJ-28-34 1 – 9 – ne IDC [956]
CONSTITUTION – Keokuk. Iowa. 1862-75; 1876-1916 – 1 – us UMI [071]
CONSTITUTION – Robinson. Ill. -w. 1865-77, 1888-94, 1908-17 – 1 – us UMI [071]
CONSTITUTION – Toronto, Canada. 1836-37 – 1 reel – 1 – $68.00 – cn Library Assoc [971]
CONSTITUTION – (Weekly Republican newspaper) – Erie, PA. july 16, 1856-oct 20, 1858 – 1r – 1 – us Western Res [071]
CONSTITUTION / World Zionist Organization – Jerusalem. 1939. BJ-28-51 1 – 9 – ne IDC [956]
THE CONSTITUTION – London. -w. 3 Apr 1831-22 Jan 1832. (1 reel) – 1 – uk British Libr Newspaper [072]
THE CONSTITUTION – or Anti-union Evening Post. Dublin. Ireland. -sw. 17 Dec 1799-7 Jan 1800, 11, 14, 21 Jan, 8, 15, 18 Feb, 22 Mar, 7 Jun 1800. (16 ft) – 1 – uk British Libr Newspaper [072]
THE CONSTITUTION – Quebec, Canada. v1 n3. 7 mar-v1 n7. 12 mar 1878 – 1r – 1 – Can$25.00 – cn Can Microfilming [072]
THE CONSTITUTION – Quebec: [s.n, 1878] – 9 – cn C.I.H.M. [971]
THE CONSTITUTION – Woodbury, NJ. 1834-1945 – 1,3 – us Readex [071]
CONSTITUTION, 1786-1956 / Presbyterian Church in the U.S.A. General Assembly – 1 – $800.00 – us Presbyterian [240]
CONSTITUTION, 1958-1983 / United Presbyterian Church in the U.S.A – 1 – $200.00 – us Presbyterian [240]
CONSTITUTION AND ADDRESS TO THE CHRISTIAN PUBLIC / Southern Aid Society – 1854. Annual report. v1-7. 1854-60 – 1 – $50.00 – us Presbyterian [240]
CONSTITUTION AND BY-LAWS / Aurora Snow Shoe Club – Quebec: C. Darveau, 1879. 04089. (Pre-1900 Canadiana) – 9 – cn C.I.H.M. [060]
CONSTITUTION AND BY-LAWS / British Columbia Agricultural and Horticultural Society – Victoria, B.C., 1872. 00863. (Pre-1900 Canadiana) – 9 – cn C.I.H.M. [060]
CONSTITUTION AND BY-LAWS / Canadian Golf Association – Ottawa: Faynter & Abbott, 1895. 02037. (Pre-1900 Canadiana) – 9 – cn C.I.H.M. [060]
CONSTITUTION AND BY-LAWS / Canadian Institute of Architects – Toronto: The Institute, 18?? 02040. (Pre-1900 Canadiana) – 9 – cn C.I.H.M. [720]
CONSTITUTION AND BY-LAWS / Canadian Lawn Tennis Association – Toronto: Mail Job Print., 1890. 02051. (Pre-1900 Canadiana) – 9 – cn C.I.H.M. [060]
CONSTITUTION AND BY-LAWS. / Canadian National Association – Toronto: Hunter, Rose, 1884. 02144. (Pre-1900 Canadiana) – 9 – cn C.I.H.M. [971]
CONSTITUTION AND BY-LAWS: ADOPTED JUNE, 1890 / Catholic Truth Society of Canada – Toronto: Catholic Review, 1890. 02568. (Pre-1900 Canadiana) – 9 – cn C.I.H.M. [060]
CONSTITUTION AND BY-LAWS, AS ADOPTED AT A GENERAL MEETING HELD ON MARCH 3RD, 1890 / Canadian Military Institute – Toronto: Mail Job Print., 1890? 02050. (Pre-1900 Canadiana) – 9 – cn C.I.H.M. [971]
CONSTITUTION AND BY-LAWS..., AS IN FORCE AUGUST 8TH, 1890: WITH LAWS OF BOAT RACING / Canadian Association of Amateur Oarsmen – 1890? 00422. (Pre-1900 Canadiana) – 9 – cn C.I.H.M. [060]
CONSTITUTION AND BY-LAWS OF THE FEDERATED ASSOCIATION OF LETTER CARRIERS OF THE DOMINION OF CANADA, ADOPTED SEPTEMBER 28 AND 29, 1892 / Federated Association of Letter Carriers of the Dominion of Canada – Toronto: W. Johnston, 1892. 05474. (Pre-1900 Canadiana) – 9 – cn C.I.H.M. [060]
CONSTITUTION AND BY-LAWS...1891 / Liberal Conservative Association of the Eastern Townships – Montreal: Mitchell & Wilson, 1894. 05212. (Pre-1900 Canadiana) – 9 – cn C.I.H.M. [060]
THE CONSTITUTION AND GOVERNMENT OF CANADA: FROM AN OFFICIAL DOCUMENT, DECEMBER 1893 / Chapleau, Joseph Adolphe – (Montreal: E. Senecal), 1894. 00565. (Pre-1900 Canadiana) – 9 – cn C.I.H.M. [971]
CONSTITUTION AND LAWS / Canadian Academy of Arts – Ottawa? 1879. 02824. (Pre-1900 Canadiana) – 9 – cn C.I.H.M. [060]
CONSTITUTION AND LAWS / Order of Canadian Home Circles – 1885. 00438. (Pre-1900 Canadiana) – 9 – cn C.I.H.M. [060]
CONSTITUTION AND LAWS OF THE KNIGHTS OF THE KU KLUX KLAN (INCORPORATED) – Atlanta, GA: The Klan, c1921 – us Res Libr [360]
CONSTITUTION AND PLAYING RULES / National League and American Association of Professional Baseball Clubs – 1876-1900 – 1r – 1 – us Ross [790]
CONSTITUTION AND PLAYING RULES / National League and American Association of Professional Baseball Clubs – New York etc. 1876-1890; 1895-1900 – 1 – us NY Public [790]
CONSTITUTION AND RULES OF THE FISH AND GAME CLUB...IN CONNECTION WITH THE FISH AND GAME PROTECTION CLUB OF THE PROVINCE OF QUEBEC: ADOPTED MAY 12TH, 1882. / Fish and Game Club. Montreal. – Montreal?: s.n., 1882 (Montreal: Becket). 04275. (Pre-1900 Canadiana) – 9 – cn C.I.H.M. [060]
THE CONSTITUTION AND WHAT IT MEANS TODAY / Corwin, Edward A – Princeton, London: Princeton UP, Oxford UP, 1920 – 2mf – 9 – $3.00 – LLMC 95-093 – us L.L.M.C. [323]
CONSTITUTION...: AVEC LETTRES DE S. G. MGR. L'ARCHEVEQUE DE QUEBEC / Cercle Catholique de Quebec – Quebec: L. Brousseau, 1878. 00650. (Pre-1900 Canadiana) – 9 – cn C.I.H.M. [240]
LA CONSTITUTION COMME JE LA VOUDRAIS, AVEC DES DEBATS IMAGINAIRES – [Paris]: Impr centrale de Napoleon Chaix, oct 1848 – us Res Libr [944]
CONSTITUTION DE L'INDUSTRIE ET ORGANISATION PACIFIQUE DU COMMERCE ET DU TRAVAIL OU TENTATIVE D'UN FABRICANT DE LYON / Derrion, M – Lyon, Durval, 1834, 56 p. Les Saint-Simoniens, 1825-1834. 6896 – 9 – fr Hachette [338]
CONSTITUTION DEMOCRAT – Keokuk. Iowa. -sw. 1902-03, 1905-07, 1910-12 – 1 – us UMI [071]
CONSTITUTION DEMOCRAT – Keokuk. Iowa. -w. 1889-1902 – 1 – us UMI [071]
CONSTITUTION DES SOCIETES ANONYMES EN FRANCE, DANS L'EMPIRE ALLEMAND ET EN GRANDE-BRETAGNE / Ostrorog, Leon – Paris: Larose & Forcel, 1893. 178p. LL-4080 – 1 – us L of C Photodup [340]
CONSTITUTION ESTABLISHING SELF-GOVERNMENT IN THE ISLANDS OF CUBA AND PORTO RICO : PROMULGATED BY ROYAL DECREE OF NOVEMBER 25, 1897 – Washington: GPO, 1899 – 1mf – 9 – $1.50 – LLMC 92-303 – us L.L.M.C. [324]
DE LA CONSTITUTION ET DU GOUVERNEMENT QUI POURRAIENT CONVENIR A LA REPUBLIQUE FRANCAISE / Kersaint, Armand G S – Paris. Imp. du Cercle Social. 1792 – 9 – fr Hachette [321]
CONSTITUTION ET GOUVERNEMENT DU CANADA: EXTRAIT D'UNE PUBLICATION OFFICIELLE, DECEMBRE 1893 / Chapleau, Joseph Adolphe – Montreal: E. Senecal, 1894. 00566. (Pre-1900 Canadiana) – 9 – cn C.I.H.M. [971]
CONSTITUTION ET REGLEMENTS / Association Saint Antoine de Montreal – Montreal: Senecal et Daniel, 1857. SEM105P524 – 1mf – 9 – Can$2.25 – cn Bibl Nat [360]
CONSTITUTION ET REGLEMENTS / Club de Raquettes Frontenac – (Ottawa: A. Bureau), 1883. 03200. (Pre-1900 Canadiana) – 9 – cn C.I.H.M. [060]
CONSTITUTION ET REGLEMENTS....AMENDES... 31 MAI 1878 / Association des Instituteurs de la Circonscription de l'Ecole Normale Jacques Cartier – (Montreal: Impr. de la Minerve), 1880. 02458. (Pre-1900 Canadiana) – 9 – cn C.I.H.M. [370]
CONSTITUTION ET REGLEMENTS...ET LISTE DES ACTIONNAIRES / Club de Chasse et de Peche 'Les Laurentides' – (Quebec: I. Turcot), 1890. 04149. (Pre-1900 Canadiana) – 9 – cn C.I.H.M. [060]
THE CONSTITUTION IN THE YEAR 2000 : CHOICES AHEAD IN CONSTITUTIONAL INTERPRETATION, 11 OCT 1988 – n.p., n.d. – 3mf – 9 – $4.50 – LLMC 94-367 – us L.L.M.C. [340]
CONSTITUTION MANGAREVIENNE DU 13 DECEMBRE, 1869. CODES MANGAREVIENS DU 18 JANVIER, 1870 – 9 – F40.00 – fr Ethnologie [306]
CONSTITUTION MEDICALE ET MORTALITE DE LA VILLE DE METZ PENDANT L'ANNEE 1851: RAPPORT STATISTIQUE / Saunois, Victor – Metz, Verronnais, 1852. 77 p., depl. 2 fiches. (Statistics Series: Medical Studies) – 9 – 6.00 – fr Bibl Nationale [310]
CONSTITUTION OF AMERICAN SAMOA, 1960 / Samoa – (Effective Oct 17 1960. Contained in Committe Print no 1, US Hse. Comm. on Interior and Insular Affairs, 87th Congress 1st session) – Washington: GPO, 1961 – 1mf – 9 – $1.50 – LLMC 82-100C Title 20 – us L.L.M.C. [324]
CONSTITUTION OF CANADA THE BRITISH NORTH AMERICA ACT, 1867; ITS INTERPRETATION. / Doutre, Joseph – Montreal, Lovell, 1880. 414 p. LL-2376 – 1 – us L of C Photodup [340]
CONSTITUTION OF CANADA: THE BRITISH NORTH AMERICA ACT, 1867: ITS INTERPRETATION, GATHERED FROM THE DECISIONS OF COURTS, THE DICTA OF JUDGES, AND THE OPINIONS OF STATESMEN AND OTHERS : TO WHICH IS ADDED THE QUEBEC RESOLUTIONS OF 1864: AND THE CONSTITUTION OF THE UNITED STATES / Doutre, Joseph – Montreal: J. Lovell, 1880. 02751. (Pre-1900 Canadiana) – 9 – cn C.I.H.M. [971]
THE CONSTITUTION OF MCGILL UNIVERSITY: BEING THE ANNUAL UNIVERSITY LECTURE IN THE SESSION OF 1888-89 / Dawson, John William – Montreal?: s.n., 1888 (Montreal: Gazette Printing Co.). 02137. (Pre-1900 Canadiana) – 9 – cn C.I.H.M. [971]
THE CONSTITUTION OF NGONDE / Wilson, G – 7 – uk Microform Academic [960]
THE CONSTITUTION OF NORTHERN NIGERIA LAW, 1953 / Nigeria. Northern Region – Kanduna: Gov't. Printer 1963 35p. LL-12039 – 1 – us L of C Photodup [340]
CONSTITUTION OF THE AMERICAN FEDERATION OF LABOR AND CONGRESS OF INDUSTRIAL ORGANIZATIONS : AS AMENDED BY THE 13TH CONSTITUTIONAL CONVENTION OF THE AFL-CIO, NOV 15-20 1979 – n.p., n.d. (AFL-CIO publ no 1) – 1mf – 9 – $1.50 – LLMC 96-045 – us L.L.M.C. [323]
CONSTITUTION OF THE COMMONWEALTH OF THE NORTHERN MARIANA ISLANDS, 1976 / Government of the Northern Mariana Islands – (Contains also President Carter's "certification" and proclamation dated Oct 24 1977) – n.d. – 1mf – 9 – $1.50 – LLMC 82-100J Title 1 – us L.L.M.C. [324]
CONSTITUTION OF THE FEDERATED STATES OF MICRONESIA – (Multi-lingual ed) – Micronesian Constitutional Convention, 1975 – 6mf – 9 – $9.00 – LLMC 82-100F Title 103 – us L.L.M.C. [323]
THE CONSTITUTION OF THE FEDERATION OF RHODESIA AND NYASALAND... ST 109=INCORPORATING RELEVANT PAPERS AND INDICES – Salisbury, Government Printer 1959 – us Res Libr [323]
CONSTITUTION OF THE INDONESIAN REPUBLIC / Indonesia. Constitution – SE-11,900 1. 1945? – 9 – ne IDC [323]
CONSTITUTION OF THE KINGDOM OF LIBYA, AS MODIFIED BY LAW NR. 1 OF 1963 / Libya – Benghazi. 1964. BNE-524 1 – 9 – ne IDC [324]
THE CONSTITUTION OF THE LATER ROMAN EMPIRE : CREIGHTON MEMORIAL LECTURE / Bury, J B – Cambridge: University Press; New York: Putnam [distributor], 1910 – 1mf – us A.T.L.A. [930]
CONSTITUTION OF THE MARSHALL ISLANDS, 1979 / Marshall Islands – Micronitor News and Printing Co, May 1983 – 1mf – 9 – $1.50 – LLMC 82-100I Title 5 – us L.L.M.C. [324]
CONSTITUTION OF THE MARSHALL ISLANDS, DECEMBER 1 1978 / Republic of the Marshall Islands – Majuro: Constitutional Convention, 4 Jan 1979 – 2mf – 9 – $3.00 – LLMC 82-100I Title 1 – us L.L.M.C. [324]
THE CONSTITUTION OF THE REPUBLIC OF PALAU, 1979 / Palau Constitutional Convention, Koror – (Palauan and English versions. Various pagination) – Koror: Palau Constitutional Convention, 1979 – 1mf – 9 – $1.50 – LLMC 82-100G, Title19 – us L.L.M.C. [323]
THE CONSTITUTION OF THE REPUBLIC OF PALAU, 1979 / Palau. (The Republic of Belau) – (Mimeo copy of the original signed version from the Palau Constitution Convention, Jan 28-Apr 2 1979) – Koror, Palau. 1979 – 1mf – 9 – $1.50 – LLMC 82-100G Title 1 – us L.L.M.C. [324]
CONSTITUTION OF THE STATE OF LOUISIANA – 1975 – 9 – 1.00f – at Libertarian Micro [323]
CONSTITUTION OF THE STATE OF YAP, 1982 / Federated States of Micronesia – n.p, n.d. – 1mf – 9 – $1.50 – LLMC 82-100H Title 14 – us L.L.M.C. [324]
THE CONSTITUTION OF THE UNITED STATES : A CRITICAL DISCUSSION OF ITS GENESIS, DEVELOPMENT AND INTERPRETATION / Tucker, John Randolph; ed by Tucker, Henry ST George – Chicago: Callaghan. 2v. 1899 – 12mf – 9 – $18.00 – LLMC 95-066 – us L.L.M.C. [323]
THE CONSTITUTION OF THE UNITED STATES / Hickey, W – 7th ed. Philadelphia: T K & F G Collins, 1854 – 6mf – 9 – $9.00 – LLMC 91-084 – us L.L.M.C. [323]
THE CONSTITUTION OF THE UNITED STATES / Tucker, John Randolph – Chicago, Callaghan, 1899. 2 v. LL-1603 – 1 – us L of C Photodup [340]
THE CONSTITUTION OF THE UNITED STATES AT THE END OF THE FIRST CENTURY / Boutwell, George S – Boston: D C Heath, 1896 – 5mf – 9 – $7.50 – LLMC 95-096 – us L.L.M.C. [323]
THE CONSTITUTION OF THE UNITED STATES DEFINED AND CAREFULLY ANNOTATED / Paschal, George Washington – (3d ed. Washington, D.C.: Morrison, 1882. 644p LL-1155) – 2nd ed. Washington, D.C.: Morrison, 1876. 644p LL-1039 – 1 – us L of C Photodup [340]
THE CONSTITUTION OF THE UNITED STATES WITH NOTES OF THE DECISIONS OF THE SUPREME COURT THEREON. / Bryant, Edwin Eustace – Madison, Wis., Democrat, 1901. 418 p. LL-503 – 1 – us L of C Photodup [340]
LA CONSTITUTION POLITIQUE ET SOCIALE – (Filmed as pt of: Commune de Paris newspapers; newspapers on these reels are filmed chronologically, not alphabetically. Le constitutionnel Port-au-Prince: Libr. Bouchereau & Cie., (2 sheets) [1ere annee n1-2e annee n37/38/39] (29 avril 1876-23 mars 1878)) – Paris: Impr Ch Schiller, may 18, 20 1871 – us Res Libr [072]
CONSTITUTION, STATUTES, RULES AND ORDER OF BUSINESS, RULES OF PROCEDURE OF GRAND FORUM, INCORPORATION OF THE ORDER, AND FORM OF COMPLAINT OF THE BENEVOLENT AND PROTECTIVE ORDER OF ELKS OF THE UNITED STATES OF AMERICAN – Ed 1970-71. Chicago, 1970 – 2mf – 9 – $3.00 – LLMC 92-243 – us L.L.M.C. [360]
DIE CONSTITUTION UNIGENITUS : IHRE VERANLASSUNG UND IHRE FOLGEN: EIN BEITRAG ZUR GESCHICHTE DES JANSENISMUS / Schill, Andreas – (Includes bibliographical references) – Freiburg in Breisgau; St Louis, MO: Herder, 1876 – 1mf – 9 – 0-8370-8711-2 – 1986-2711 – us A.T.L.A. [240]
CONSTITUTIONAL AND GOVERNMENTAL RIGHTS OF THE MORMONS, AS DEFINED BY CONGRESS AND THE SUPREME COURT OF THE UNITED STATES. – Salt Lake City, Parry, 1890. 116 p. LL-162 – 1 – us L of C Photodup [340]
CONSTITUTIONAL AND PARLIAMENTARY HISTORY OF THE METHODIST EPISCOPAL CHURCH / Buckley, James Monroe – New York: Methodist Book Concern, c1912 – 1mf – us A.T.L.A. [240]

A CONSTITUTIONAL ANSWER TO THE REV. MR. JOHN WESLEY'S 'CALM ADDRESS TO THE AMERICAN COLONIES' – London, 1775 – 1mf – 9 – MP-503/1 – ne IDC [240]

THE CONSTITUTIONAL AUTHORITY OF BISHOPS IN THE CATHOLIC CHURCH : ILLUSTRATED BY THE HISTORY AND CANON LAW OF THE UNDIVIDED CHURCH, FROM THE APOSTOLIC AGE TO THE COUNCIL OF CHALCEDON, A.D. 451 / Wirgman, A Theodore – London, New York: Longmans, Green, 1899 – 1mf – us A.T.L.A. [240]

CONSTITUTIONAL COMMENTARY – University of Minnesota. v1-12. 1984-95 – 9 – $149.00 set – us Hein [320]

Constitutional Convention, Koror *see* DRAFT CONSTITUTIONS. ALTERNATIVES 1 AND 2

CONSTITUTIONAL DECISIONS OF JOHN MARSHALL / Cotton, Joseph Jr – New York, London: Putnam's Sons. 2v. 1905 – 11mf – 9 – $16.50 – LLMC 84-248 – us L.L.M.C. [340]

CONSTITUTIONAL DEVELOPMENT OF PALAU : FACT SHEET – Washington: The State Department?, jul 1980 – 1mf – 9 – $1.50 – LLMC 82-100G, Title 20 – us L.L.M.C. [323]

THE CONSTITUTIONAL DOCUMENTS OF THE PURITAN REVOLUTION, 1625-1660 / ed by Gardiner, Samuel R – Oxford: Clarendon Press, 1906 – 2mf – us A.T.L.A. [240]

CONSTITUTIONAL GOVERNMENT IN THE UNITED STATES / Wilson, Woodrow – New York: Columbia UP, 1908 – 3mf – 9 – $4.50 – LLMC 95-069 – us L.L.M.C. [323]

CONSTITUTIONAL GOVERNMENT TODAY IN SOVIET RUSSIA / Lefevre, Robert – 1962. 1 fiche (24x) – 9 – 1.00f – at Libertarian Micro [320]

THE CONSTITUTIONAL GUARANTEES OF THE RIGHT OF PROPERTY AS AFFECTED BY RECENT DECISIONS. / Hoadly, George – New York: Evening Post Job Printing Office, 1889. 53p. LL-427 – 1 – us L of C Photodup [340]

THE CONSTITUTIONAL HISTORY AND CONSTITUTION OF THE CHURCH OF ENGLAND / Makower, Felix – London: Swan Sonnenschein; New York: Macmillan, 1895 – 2mf – us A.T.L.A. [240]

THE CONSTITUTIONAL HISTORY OF ENGLAND IN ITS ORIGIN AND DEVELOPMENT / Stubbs, W – v I-III. Oxford, 1874-1878 – Dfl123.00 – ne Slangenburg [323]

CONSTITUTIONAL HISTORY OF THE AMERICAN PEOPLE / Thorpe, Francis F – New York, London: Harper. 2v. 1898 – 23mf – 9 – $34.50 – LLMC 84-255 – us L.L.M.C. [323]

A CONSTITUTIONAL HISTORY OF THE HOUSE OF LORDS / Pike, L O – H 1213 2. 1894 – 8 – ne IDC [941]

THE CONSTITUTIONAL HISTORY OF THE PRESBYTERIAN CHURCH IN THE UNITED STATES OF AMERICA / Hodge, Charles – Philadelphia: W.S. Martien, 1839-1840 – 2mf – us A.T.L.A. [240]

CONSTITUTIONAL HISTORY OF THE UNITED STATES : AS SEEN IN THE DEVELOPMENT OF AMERICAN LAW. A COURSE OF LECTURES BEFORE THE POLITICAL SCIENCE ASSOCIATION OF THE UNIVERSITY OF MICHIGAN / Cooley, Thomas M et al – New York, London: G P Putnam's Sons, 1890 – 4mf – 9 – $6.00 – LLMC 95-075 – us L.L.M.C. [323]

CONSTITUTIONAL HISTORY OF THE UNITED STATES : FROM THEIR DECLARATION OF INDEPENDENCE TO THE CLOSE OF THEIR CIVIL WAR / Curtis, George Ticknor – New York: Harper & Bros. 2v. 1897 – 18mf – 9 – $27.00 – LLMC 95-061 – us L.L.M.C. [323]

CONSTITUTIONAL HISTORY OF THE UNITED STATES / Holst, Herman E von – (Includes index and list of authorities) – Chicago: Callaghan. v1-7. 1889-92 – 45mf – 9 – $67.50 – LLMC 84-251 – us L.L.M.C. [323]

CONSTITUTIONAL HISTORY OF THE UNITED STATES, 1765-1895 / Thorpe, Francis Newton – New York: Harper. 3v. 1901 – 23mf – 9 – $34.50 – LLMC 82-714 – us L.L.M.C. [323]

CONSTITUTIONAL HISTORY OF THE UNITED STATES AS SEEN IN THE DEVELOPMENT OF AMERICAN LAW. / Michigan. University. Political Science Association – New York: Putnam's, 1889. 296p. LL-192 – 1 – us L of C Photodup [340]

CONSTITUTIONAL LAW. / Chadman, Charles Erehart – Chicago: American School of Law, 1906. 316p. LL-1322 – 1 – us L of C Photodup [340]

CONSTITUTIONAL LAW; FROM THE ARTICLE ON THIS SUBJECT IN THE ENCYCLOPEDIA OF UNITED STATES SUPREME COURT REPORTS. / Richey, Homer – Charlottesville, Va.: Michie, 1928. 4v. LL-1033 – 1 – us L of C Photodup [340]

THE CONSTITUTIONAL LAW OF THE UNITED STATES / Willoughby, Westel Woodbury – New York, Baker, Voorhis, 1910. 2 v. LL-1543 – 1 – us L of C Photodup [340]

CONSTITUTIONAL LAW QUESTIONS NOW PENDING IN THE METHODIST EPISCOPAL CHURCH / Warren, William Fairfield – 1894 – 9 – us A.T.L.A. [240]

CONSTITUTIONAL POWER AND WORLD AFFAIRS / Sutherland, George – New York: Columbia UP, 1919 – 3mf – 9 – $4.50 – LLMC 95-082 – us L.L.M.C. [323]

CONSTITUTIONAL REVIEW – v1-13. 1917-29 – 1,5,6 – us Princeton Micro [073]

CONSTITUTIONAL RIGHTS OF MILITARY PERSONNEL : SUMMARY-REPORT OF HEARINGS BY THE SUBCOMMITTEE ON CONSTITUTIONAL RIGHTS OF THE COMMITTEE ON THE JUDICIARY – Senate. 88th Congress, 1st session. Washington: GPO, 1963 – 1mf – 9 – $1.50 – LLMC 96-087 – us L.L.M.C. [340]

CONSTITUTIONAL RIGHTS OF MILITARY PERSONNEL : SUMMARY-REPORT OF HEARINGS BY THE SUBCOMMITTEE ON CONSTITUTIONAL RIGHTS OF THE COMMITTEE ON THE JUDICIARY – US Senate Pursuant to Senate Resolution 58. 88th Congress, 1st session. Washington: GPO, 1963 – 1mf – 9 – $1.50 – LLMC 96-080 – us L.L.M.C. [340]

CONSTITUTIONAL RIGHTS PROJECT – Surulere, Lagos. 3 docs. 1989-1991 – 3mf – 9 – ne IDC [320]

CONSTITUTIONAL ROUTES TO SMALLER GOVERNMENT / Brennan, Geoffrey – 1986. 22p – 9 – 1.00f – at Libertarian Micro [335]

CONSTITUTIONAL TELEGRAPH – Boston. Mass. 1799-1802 – 3 – us Readex [071]

CONSTITUTIONALIST – Exeter. N.H. 1810-1814 – 3 – us Readex [071]

THE CONSTITUTIONALITY OF THE LAWYERS TEST OATH; ARGUMENT OF W. D. PORTER, IN THE DISTRICT COURT OF THE UNITED STATES / Porter, William Dennison – Charleston: Walker, 1866. 26p. LL-2357 – 1 – us L of C Photodup [340]

DAS CONSTITUTIONELLE TEUTSCHLAND – Darmstadt, 1831 – 1mf – 1 – ILM-2729/1 – ne IDC [327]

CONSTITUTIONELLE ZEITUNG – Berlin, 1849-jun 30 1852 – 3r – 1 – Dist. gw Mikrofilm – gw Mikrofilm [072]

CONSTITUTIONELLES BLATT AUS BOEHMEN – Prag (Praha), Austria-Hungary. Apr 1848-49 – 3r – 1 – gw Mikrofilm [072]

CONSTITUTIONES CANONICORUM REGULARIUM ORDINIS S.P. AUGUSTINI EP. CONGREGATIONIS WINDESEMENSIS – Lovanii, 1639 – 7mf – 8 – Dfl28.00 – ne Slangenburg [240]

CONSTITUTIONES ET ACTA GENERALIUM / Jimenez Samaniego, Jose – 1704 – 9 – 1.50f – sp Bibl Santa Ana [340]

CONSTITUTIONES ET ACTA REGUM GERMANICORUM (MGH LEGES. 1: 2.BD. PARS 1A) : TOMI PRIMI SUPLLEMENTA – (Pars 2a: Capitularia Spuria. Canones Ecclesiastici. Bullae Pontificum) – 1837 – Dfl74.00 – ne Slangenburg [240]

CONSTITUTIONES O.E.S.A. (VENETIIS), 1508 – Republication of the 1290 Constitutions. BH-54 2 – 8 – ne IDC [323]

CONSTITUTION...FONDE LE 20 NOVEMBRE 1898 / Club Liberal de la Partie Est de Montreal – (Montreal: La Patrie), 1898? 04151. (Pre-1900 Canadiana) – 9 – cn C.I.H.M. [060]

CONSTITUTION...MONTREAL, INSTITUTED A.D. 1875: ALSO BY-LAWS, AS REVISED AT ANNUAL MEETING, DECEMBER 23RD, 1880 / Dominion Commercial Travellers' Association – s.l.: s.n., 1881 (Montreal: D. Bentley). 04297. (Pre-1900 Canadiana) – 9 – cn C.I.H.M. [060]

LE CONSTITUTIONNEL – A paru sous le titre: Journal du commerce de juil. 1817 a mai 1819. Paris. oct 1815-21 juil 1914, 1907-juil 1914 lac – 1 – fr A.C.R.P.P. [073]

LE CONSTITUTIONNEL / ed by Duvernay, Ludger – Trois-Rivieres, Canada. v1 n5. 8 avr 1823-v2 n26. 14 sep 1824 – 1r – 1 – Can$30.00 – cn Can Microfilming [072]

LE CONSTITUTIONNEL : QUOTIDIEN – (Hebdo: 28 dec 1871-26 mai 1881 2r Can$45.00. Semi-quotidien: v16 n1 5 jan 1883-30 avr 1883 1r Can$40.00) – Trois-Rivieres, Canada. Edition bi-hebdomadaire: 4 jun 1868-25 jul 1884 – 8mf – 1 – Can$45.00 – cn Can Microfilming [072]

CONSTITUTIONS AND LAWS OF THE AMERICAN INDIANS – (Based on A Bibliography of the Constitutions and Laws of the American Indian by Lester Hargarett) – 7r – 1 – us Ross [970]

CONSTITUTIONS DES SOEURS. / Congregation de Notre-Dame – Montreal, 1889. 04243. (Pre-1900 Canadiana) – 9 – cn C.I.H.M. [240]

LES CONSTITUTIONS DU CANADA / DeCelles, Alfred Duclos – 1918. SEM105P517 – 1mf – 9 – Can$2.25 – cn Bibl Nat [971]

CONSTITUTIONS OF INDONESIAN TRADE-UNIONS / Indonesian Trade-unions – In Indonesian. SE-11,598 1. 2 v. 1966 – 9 – ne IDC [331]

THE CONSTITUTIONS OF THE SEVERAL STATES OF THE UNION AND UNITED STATES IN THE YEAR 1859 – New York, Barnes 1879? 602, 17 p. LL-1131 – 1 – us L of C Photodup [340]

CONSTITUTION-TRIBUNE – Chillicothe. Mo. 1928- – 1 – us UMI [071]

DAS CONSTITUTUM CONSTANTINI (KONSTANTINISCHE SCHENKUNG) TEXT (MGH LEGES 4: 10.BD) – 1968 – Dfl13.00 – ne Slangenburg [240]

CONSTITVTIONES REGVM REGNI VTRIVSQVE SICILIAE MANDANTE FRIDERICO 2 IMPERATORE PER PETRVM DE VINEA. / Naples. (Kingdom). Laws, Statutes, etc – Neapoli, ex Roma Typographia, 1786. 459p. LL-4015 – 1 – us L of C Photodup [340]

CONSTRAINED BY JESUS' LOVE / Berg, J van den – Kampen, 1956 – 5mf – 8 – ne Slangenburg [240]

CONSTRAINED BY JESUS' LOVE / Van den Berg – 1956 – 1 – us A.T.L.A. [240]

CONSTRUCCION NACIONAL : JULIO-DICIEMBRE 1974 / ed by Presidencia de la Nacion, Secretaria de Prensa y Difusion – Buenos Aires: The Presidencia, [1974] – 1 – CSUXADQ7966-B – us Hoover Inst Photo [320]

CONSTRUCCION Y EXPLICACION DE LAS REGLAS DE LOS GENEROS Y PRETERITOS, CONFORME AL ARTE DE ANTONIO, MUY UTIL Y PROVECHOSA PARA LOS QUE COMIENZAN A ESTUDIAR / Lopez, Diego – Sevilla: Imprenta Castellana y Latina de los Herederos de Tomas Lopez de Haro, s.a. – sp Bibl Santa Ana [946]

THE CONSTRUCT VALIDITY OF A SCALE TO MEASURE TEACHER ENTHUSIASM IN SECONDARY PHYSICAL EDUCATION / Fischer, Joseph C & Brockmeyer, Gretchen A – 1992 – 3mf – $12.00 – us Microform Publ [790]

LE CONSTRUCTEUR D'USINES A GAZ – Paris, France. -m. July 1894-Dec 1905. 1 2 reel – 1 – uk British Libr Newspaper [073]

CONSTRUCTION : A JOURNAL FOR THE ARCHITECTURAL, ENGINEERING AND CONTRACTING INTERESTS OF CANADA – v1-27 1907-34 – 1 – $865.00 – cn McLaren [690]

CONSTRUCTION – Port-au-Prince, Haiti: Imp Construction, [1ere annee n10-2eme annee n253]. 1951-1953 – 11 sheets – us Res Libr [072]

CONSTRUCTION AND CIVIL ENGINEERING INDEX – 1v. 1983. 5 sections. Updated quarterly – 9 – uk Tech [624]

CONSTRUCTION AND HOUSING / Libya – Report of the Annual Survey: large construction. 1969, 1970. BNE-311 1 – 9 – ne IDC [690]

THE CONSTRUCTION AND INITIAL VALIDATION OF THE PHYSIQUE ANXIETY SCALE / Lutter, Candice D – 1993 – 2mf – $8.00 – us Microform Publ [150]

CONSTRUCTION AND OPERATION OF MEDIUM-SIZED ABATTOIRS IN DEVELOPING COUNTRIES – 1992 – 222p – it F.A.O. [660]

CONSTRUCTION AND OPERATION OF SMALL SOLID-WALL BINS – 1987 – 73p – it F.A.O. [631]

CONSTRUCTION CONTRACTING – (See also: Construction Methods and Equipment) – v60-1978- – 1,5,6,9 – us UMI [690]

LA CONSTRUCTION DE L'OPINION PUBLIQUE DANS LE SONDAGE DE LA QUESTION AU DISCOURS DE REFORMULATION / Zappella, Jeannine – 2mf – 9 – 10345 – fr Atelier National [380]

LA CONSTRUCTION DES NAVIRES A QUEBEC ET SES ENVIRONS / Rosa, Narcisse – Ouvrage inedit. Quebec: Imprimerie Leger Brousseau, 1897. SEM16P275 – 1r – 5 – Can$9.00 – cn Bibl Nat [623]

CONSTRUCTION MANAGEMENT AND ECONOMICS – v1-. 1983- – 1,5,6,9 – us UMI [650]

CONSTRUCTION METHODS AND EQUIPMENT – v1-60 1919-78 1; v52-60 5,6; v57-60 9 – us UMI [690]

THE CONSTRUCTION NEWS – Chicago, IL: Construction News Co. v5-20 may 1897-dec 1905; v31 jan-june 1911; v35 jan-jun 1913 – 17r – 1 – us Res Libr [690]

CONSTRUCTION OF CRIBS FOR DRYING AND STORAGE OF MAIZE – 1987 – 82p – it F.A.O. [631]

CONSTRUCTION OF THE GREAT VICTORIA BRIDGE IN CANADA / Hodges, James – London: John Weale, 1860. SEM35P301 – 1r – 1 – Can$15.00 – cn Bibl Nat [624]

CONSTRUCTION REPAIRS AND MAINTENANCE – v1-. 1985- – 1,5,6,9 – us UMI [620]

CONSTRUCTIVE EDUCATION FOR ADOLESCENTS / Wall, W D – 1977 – xi/333p – 9 – 92-3-101421-8 – fr UNESCO [370]

CONSTRUCTIVE EDUCATION FOR SPECIAL GROUPS : HANDICAPPED AND DEVIANT CHILDREN / Wall, W D – 1979 – 144p – 9 – 92-3-101588-5 – fr UNESCO [370]

CONSTRUCTIVE STUDIES IN JOHN / Gregory, Daniel Seeley – New York: Bible League of North America, 1908.1 fiche – 9 – us A.T.L.A. [240]

O CONSTRUCTOR CIVIL : ORGAM DA "ASSOCIACAO DE CLASSE DAS QUATRO ARTES DE CONSTRUCCAO CIVIL" – Manaos, Amazonas. 5 Jan 1920 – 1,5,6 – bl Biblioteca [072]

CONSUELO / Lopez de Ayala, Adelardo – 1878 – 9 – 1.50f – sp Bibl Santa Ana [820]

CONSUETUDINES MONASTICAE / Albers, B – Stuttgardiae et Vindobonae. 5v. 1900-1912 – 30mf – 8 – Dfl105.00 – ne Slangenburg [240]

CONSUETUDINES SANCTI VICTORIS PARISIENSIS : ZUTPHEN STED. ARCHIEF MS.15 – Dfl13.00 – ne Slangenburg [240]

CONSUETUDINES SCI VICTORIS PARISIENSIS / Zutphen – Sted. Archief, 15e.s. – 3mf – 8 – Dfl13.00 – ne Slangenburg [240]

EL CONSOLIDADO DE BUENOS AIRES Y SUS PROYECCIONES EN LA HISTORIA DEL RIO DE LA PLATA. BUENOS AIRES, 1962 / Barrado Manzano, Arcangel – Madrid: Graf. Calleja, 1969 – 1 – sp Bibl Santa Ana [972]

CONSULAR INSTRUCTIONS OF THE DEPARTMENT OF STATE, 1801-1834 / U. S. Department of State – 7r – 1 – M78 – us Nat'l Archives [327]

CONSULAR INSTRUCTIONS...1801-34 / U.S. Department of State – M78 – 7r – 1 – us Nat'l Archives [976]

CONSULTA CANONICA, ECLESIASTICA, REGULAR Y CEREMONIAL POR LOS CONVENTOS... / Zambrano, Juan – Sevilla: s.i., s.a. – 9 – sp Bibl Santa Ana [240]

CONSULTA...SOBRE ASUNTO P. CACERES Y RESPUESTA DE ANDRES BARBOSA / Davila, Andres – S.l., s.i., 1641 – 1 – sp Bibl Santa Ana [946]

CONSULTATION – (v3-. 1984-. 5,6,9) – v1-. Fall 1981- – 1 – us UMI [073]

CONSULTATION AMONG THE AMERICAN REPUBLICS WITH RESPECT TO THE ARGENTINE SITUATION / U.S. Department of State – Washington: U.S. Govt. print. off., 1946 – 1 – CSUXADJ8382-B – us Hoover Inst Photo [327]

CONSULTATION DE M. DUPIN, AVOCAT A LA COUR ROYALE DE PARIS, POUR LE SEMINAIRE DE MONTREAL, EN CANADA / Dupin, Andre Marie Jean Jacques – Paris: Everat, 1826. SEM105P921 – 1mf – 9 – Can$2.25 – cn Bibl Nat [971]

CONSULTATION DES TROIS EVEQUES SUR LES MOYENS DE SOUTENIR L'EGLISE ROMAINE PRESENTEE AU PAPE JULES 3 EN 1553 / Besson, Paul – Rouillac. 1884. 11p (Religion series) – 9 – $3.00 – fr Bibl Nationale [240]

CONSULTATION ON CHURCH UNION – Fourth meeting. Lexington, Apr. 1965. Reports, papers, etc – 1 – us A.T.L.A. [240]
CONSULTATION ON IRRIGATION IN AFRICA – 1987 – 210p – it F.A.O. [631]
A CONSULTATIVE DOCUMENT ON THE REORGANISATION OF SECONDARY EDUCATION IN NORTHERN IRELAND / Great Britain. Department of Education – 1976 – 9 – uk Microform Academic [324]
CONSULTA...UNIVERSIDAD DE SALAMANCA... CENSURAS IMPUESTAS...P. CACERES / Toledo, Jose de – 1641 – 9 – 1.50f – sp Bibl Santa Ana [946]
CONSULTING ENGINEER – (5,6 1971-; 9 1975-) – v1- 1952- – 1 – us UMI [620]
CONSUMER AND MARKETING RESERVES: HEARINGS...MARCH 21 AND 22, 1974 / U.S. Congress. Senate. Committee on Agriculture and Forestry. Subcommittee on Agricultural Production, Marketing and Stabilization of Prices – Washington, Govt. Print. Off., 1974. 222 p. LL-2256 – 1 – us L of C Photodup [340]
CONSUMER BULLETIN – (1967-73. 5,6,9) – v1-56 1931-73. Continued by: Consumers' Research Magazine – 1 – us UMI [380]
CONSUMER EGG SURVEY / Wisconsin. College of Agriculture. Dept. of Poultry Husbandry – 1959 – 1,5 – us Spaulding [636]
CONSUMER ELECTRONICS – 1986- – 1,5,6,9 – us UMI [621]
CONSUMER FINANCES IN THE REGION OF JOGJAKARTA; PRELIMINARY REPORT ON RESEARCH CONDUCTED IN AUGUST, 1959 / Hawkins, Everett D – SE-2258 1. 1960 – 9 – ne IDC [336]
CONSUMER HEALTH PERSPECTIVES – v5-9, no.5. Apr 1978-Sept 1983 – 1,5,6,9 – us UMI [073]
CONSUMER INFORMATION: HEARINGS...FEBRUARY 27, MARCH 13, AND APRIL 15, 1975 / U.S. Congress. House. Committee on Banking, Currency and Housing Subcommittee on Consumer Affairs – Washington, Govt. Print. Off., 1975. 156 p. LL-2393 – 1 – us L of C Photodup [340]
CONSUMER NEW AND REVIEWS *see* NEWSLETTER
CONSUMER PRODUCT FLAMMABILITY – v1-2 1974-75 – 1,5,6 – us UMI [360]
CONSUMER PRODUCT SAFETY COMMISSION ANNUAL REPORTS – 1980-83 (each year in 2 pts) – 14mf – 9 – $21.00 – LLMC 95-022 – us L.L.M.C. [340]
CONSUMER REPORTS – (v. 32-. 1967- 5,6. v. 35-. 1970- 9) – 1- 1936- – 1 – us UMI [336]
CONSUMER'S COMMERCIAL CYCLONE – Yutan, NE. -w. Mar 1905-Mar 1910 – 1 – us NE Hist [071]
Consumer's League of Ohio *see* RECORDS, MS 3546
CONSUMERS' NEWS – Nos 1-60 1942-47 – 5 – $45.00 – cn McLaren [640]
CONSUMERS' RESEARCH MAGAZINE – v56- 1973-. Continues: Consumer Bulletin – 1,5,6,9 – us UMI [380]
CONSUMERS UNION NEWS DIGEST – v1- 1976- – 1,5,6,9 – us UMI [334]
CONTACT – Cape Town, South Africa. 8 Feb 1958-1967 – 1r – 1, 16 diazo available – sa SA Libr [960]
CONTACT – Capetown. Republic of South Africa. 1959-1962 – 1 – us UMI [072]
CONTACT – (Ceased v10 1954) – Toronto. nos 1-10. 1952-54 – 5 – Can$100.00 – cn Micromedia [073]
CONTACT – Granby, Canada. v9 n9. 15 mai 1935-v19 n11. 1 jun 1945 – 1r – 1 – Can$25.00 – cn Can Microfilming [072]
CONTACT : REVUE CANADIENNE DESTINEE AUX PROFESSEURS DE FRANCAIS – (Ceased v12 no 1 1993) – Burnaby. v8-12. 1989-93 – 9 – Can$20.00y – cn Micromedia [440]
CONTACT – Scotland, 1960-88 (complete) – 4r – 1 – ATLA S0560 – us A.T.L.A. [073]
CONTACT – Sherbrooke, Canada. nov 1972 – 1r – 1 – Can$25.00 – cn Can Microfilming [072]
CONTACT – Cape Town, Selemela Publications. [v1-10 n1. feb 8 1958-jan 1967] – us Res Libr [072]
CONTACT AND INTRAOCULAR LENS MEDICAL JOURNAL – (1982. 1,5,6,9) – v1-8. 1975-82 – 1 – us UMI [617]
CONTACT DERMATITIS – Copenhagen. v1-15. 1975-86 – 5,9 – Dfl1,575.00; Dfl105.00v – ne Swets [610]
CONTACT ET ADAPTATION : ETHNOHISTOIRE DE L'ADOPTION DE L'ELEVAGE ET DES CHANGEMENTS SOCIO-ECONOMIQUES CHEZ LES INDIENS GUAJIROS, COLOMBIE / Picon, F R – 9 – F120.00 – fr Ethnologie [972]
CONTACT MINER – Contact, NV. 1915 – 1r – 1 – $50.00 – U03704 – us Library Micro [622]
THE CONTACT NEWS – Contact, NV. 1909 – 1r – 1 – $50.00 – U04837 – us Library Micro [071]
CONTACTO LIPOCRATICO Y ENTRADA DE NUEVOS CONCEPTOS EN EL SABER MEDICO DE DOS EPOCAS MUY LIGADAS : FRACASTORO-LUIS DE TORO-SYDENHAM / Sayans Castanos, Marcelo – Plasencia: Graf. Sandoval, 1973 – 1 – sp Bibl Santa Ana [610]
CONTACTS : REVUE FRANCAISE DE L'ORTHODOXIE – 12(1960)-29(1977) – 114mf – 9 – Dfl399.00 – ne Slangenburg [073]
CONTACTS – Revue francaise de l'orthodoxie. Dr. J. Balzon. no. 1-10. Paris. avr 1949-janv 1950; n.s., no. 1-80. 1955-72 – 1 – fr A.C.R.P.P. [073]
CONTACTS ET ANTAGONISMES CULTURELS EN PAYS KIKUYU (KENYA) / Jamin, J – 9 – F60.00 – fr Ethnologie [960]
CONTADURIA. MEMORIA DEL ANO 1910 / Caceres – Tip. El noticiero – 1 – sp Bibl Santa Ana [946]
LA CONTAGION SACREE OU HISTOIRE NATURELLE DE LA SUPERSTITION / Holbach, Paul-Thiry d' – (D'Holbach series). 1768 – 9 – fr Hachette [210]
CONTAGIOUS BOVINE PLEUROPNEUMONIA – 1971 – 120p – it F.A.O. [636]
CONTAGIOUS DISEASES OF CATTLE: PRIZE ESSAY / Duncan, J T – Ottawa: s.n., 1880 (Ottawa: Maclean, Roger). 02798. (Pre-1900 Canadiana) – 9 – cn C.I.H.M. [971]
CONTAINERISATION INTERNATIONAL – 1967-1; 1977- 5,6,9 – us UMI [380]
CONTAINING THE ART OF SINGING / Ornithoparcus, Andrea – P 734. 1609 – 9 – ne IDC [780]
CONTAINS NEWS ITEMS AND THE POLITICAL PROGRAMME OF THE INDONESIAN SOCIALIST PARTY / Indonesia. Union of Democratic Control – SE-6435 1. 1946 – 9 – ne IDC [335]
Contant, Alexis *see* VIVE LAURIER
Contant de la Molette, P du *see* TRAITE SUR LA POESIE ET LA MUSIQUE DES HEBREUX
Contant d'Orville, Andre Guillaume *see*
- HISTOIRE DE L'OPERA BOUFFON. POUR SERVIR A L'HISTOIRE DES THEATRES DE PARIS
- HISTOIRE DES DIFFERENS PEUPLES DU MONDE.
- HISTOIRE DES DIFFERENTS PEUPLE DU MONDE, CONTENANT LES CEREMONIES RELIGIEUSES ET CIVILES, L'ORIGINE DES RELIGIONS, LEURS SECTES ET SUPERSTITIONS ET LES MOEURS ET USAGES DE CHAQUE NATION

Contarini, G P *see* HISTORIAE DE BELLO NVPER VENETIS A SELIMO 2. TVRCARVM IMPERATORE ILLATO, LIBER VNVS, EX ITALICO SERMONE IN LATINUM CONUERSUS, ...
Contarsy, Steven A *see* PHYSIOLOGICAL COMPARISON OF HIGH PERFORMANCE SWIMMERS AND RUNNERS
CONTEMPLATIVE REVIEW – (1985- . 5,6,9) – v1-19,no.2. 1968-Summer 1986 – 1 – us UMI [073]
LES CONTEMPORAINS – Revue hebdomadaire illustree. Paris. oct 1892-1914 – 1 – fr A.C.R.P.P. [073]
CONTEMPORANEO – Maceio, Alagoas. 5 Mar, 7 Maio 1894 – 1,5,6 – bl Biblioteca [072]
O CONTEMPORANEO – Porto Alegre, Brazil. Jan-feb, Apr-Dec 1886; Jan-Mar 1888 – 1 – bl Biblioteca [072]
O CONTEMPORANEO – Sabara, 29 Jun-Aug, Oct-Dec 1890; Jan, Apr-Dec 1891; Jan, Mar-Apr, Oct-Dec 1892; Jan 1893-Dec 1894; Jan-Feb, Apr-Jun 1895; Jun, Sep-Oct 1896; Oct-Dec 1897; Jan, Mar-May, Jul, Nov 1898; Apr 1899; May-Jul, Sep-Dec 1902 – 1,5,6 – bl Biblioteca [072]
CONTEMPORANUL – Bucuresti, 1976-79 – 4r – 1 – DM300.00 – gw Mikro Press [949]
CONTEMPORARIES / Higginson, Thomas Wentworth – Boston: Houghton, Mifflin, 1900, c1899 – 1mf – us A.T.L.A. [240]
CONTEMPORARY CHINA – v.1-3. 1977-79 – 1 – us UMI [073]
CONTEMPORARY CRISES – v1-8. 1977-84 – 1,5,6,13 – sz Elsevier [073]
CONTEMPORARY EDUCATION – v1- 1929- 1; v41-50 5,6; v47- 9 – us UMI [370]
CONTEMPORARY ESTIMATES OF HIS LIFE AND CHARACTER / Gladstone, William Ewart – v. 1-19. 1898. W ind – 1 – 81.00 – us L of C Photodup [920]
CONTEMPORARY GLASS : A WORLD SURVEY FROM THE CORNING MUSEUM OF GLASS / Frantz, Susanne K – Corning, NY: Corning Museum of Glass, 1989 – 6mf – 9 – $10.00 – 0-81091-038-1 – us Corning Mus [740]
CONTEMPORARY JEWRY – v. 3-. 1976- – 1,5,6,9 – us UMI [270]
CONTEMPORARY KEYBOARD – v1- 1975- 1; v2- 1976- 5,6,9 – us UMI [780]
CONTEMPORARY LITERATURE – Formerly: Wisconsin Studies in Contemporary Literature – 1- 1960- 1; v12- 5,6; v16- 9 – us UMI [370]
CONTEMPORARY LITERATURE IN TRANSLATION – Mission City. nos 1-32. 1968-78/79 – 9 – Can$20.00y – cn Micromedia [400]
CONTEMPORARY MANCHURIA : A BI-MONTHLY MAGAZINE – South Manchuria Railway Company, April 1937-January 1941 – 2r – 1 – $125.00 – us Universal [380]
CONTEMPORARY MUSIC REVIEW / ed by Osborne, Nigel – 9,5,1 – us Harwood [780]
CONTEMPORARY NEWSPAPERS OF THE NORTH AMERICAN INDIAN – 1924-74.49 newspapers.Printed table of contents – 1 – us UMI [071]
CONTEMPORARY OPINIONS ON CURRENT TOPICS – Translated from Japanese Magazines, Books, and Government Bulletins, Pamphlets, and Reports from Various Sources. nos. 117-378. 1936-41. 95 scattered issues wanting – 1 – 41.00 – us L of C Photodup [950]
CONTEMPORARY PAINTINGS, DRAWINGS AND SCULPTURE – (Extensive coverage of post war and living artists. 3,600 reproductions) – 61mf – 9 – $400.00 – 0-907006-87-6 – uk Mindata [700]
CONTEMPORARY PHYSICS – v. 1-16. 1959-75 – 1,5,6 – us Princeton Micro [530]
CONTEMPORARY PHYSICS – v.1-16. 1959-75 – 9 – 24200.00; 2413.00v – uk Dawson [530]
CONTEMPORARY POLICY ISSUES – v1-. 1982- – 1,5,6,9 – us UMI [073]
CONTEMPORARY PORTRAITS : THIERS, STRAUSS COMPARED WITH VOLTAIRE, ARNAUD DE L'ARIEGE, DUPANLOUP, ADOLPHE MONOD, VINET, VERNY, ROBERTSON / Pressense, Edmond de – New York: A.D.F. Randolph, 1880 – 1mf – us A.T.L.A. [920]
CONTEMPORARY PROGRESSIVE INDONESIAN POETRY / Suradi, Bintang – SE 3651 1. 1962 – 9 – ne IDC [810]
CONTEMPORARY PSYCHOANALYSIS – (v20-. 1984-. 5,6,9) – v1-. Fall 1964- – 1 – us UMI [616]
CONTEMPORARY PSYCHOLOGY – (v. 10-. 1965- 5,6. v. 15-. 1970- 9) – v. 1- 1956- – 1 – us UMI [150]
CONTEMPORARY PYSCHOLOGY – v. 1-24. 1956-79 – 1,5,6 – us Princeton Micro [150]
CONTEMPORARY REVIEW – v183- 1953- 1; v218- 5,6; v228- 9 – us UMI [073]
CONTEMPORARY REVIEW – London. v. 1-198. 1866-1960 – 1 – us Princeton Micro [073]
CONTEMPORARY SCIENTIFIC ARCHIVES CENTER CATALOGUES – 31mf – 9 – $110.00 – us UMI [500]
Contemporary Scientific Archives Centre. Oxford *see* CATALOGUES
CONTEMPORARY SOCIALISM / Rae, John – 2nd ed., rev. and enl. New York: C. Scribner, 1891. 508p – 1 – us U.W. Library [335]
CONTEMPORARY SOCIALISM / Rae, John – New York: C. Scribner's Sons, 1910. xii,555p – 1 – us U.W. Library [335]
CONTEMPORARY SOCIOLOGY – v1- 1972- 1; v5- 5,6,9 – us UMI [300]
THE CONTEMPORARY SOUTH AFRICAN SHORT STORY IN ENGLISH WITH SPECIAL REFERENCES TO THE WORK OF NADINE GORDIMER, DORIS LESSING, ALAN PATON, JACK COPE, UYS KRIGE AND DAN JACOBSON / Millar, Clive – Cape Town 1962 – us Res Libr [420]
CONTEMPORARY SOUTH ASIA – 1992- 2v – 9 – £113.50 – 0958-4935 – uk Carfax [910]
CONTEMPORARY THEATRE REVIEW : AN INTERNATIONAL JOURNAL / ed by Chamberlain, Franc – 9,5,1 – us Harwood [790]
CONTEMPORARY VERSE 2 – Winnipeg. v1-16. 1975-1993/94 – 9 – Can$20.00y – cn Micromedia [400]
CONTEMPORARY WOMEN ARTISTS / Women's Art Library – (Accompanied by full catalogue details and artists' statements) – 1992 – 17 colour mf – 15 – $532.00 – 1-869934-48-2 – uk Emmett [700]
CONTENANT LA 1,2,3,4 (RGFS 20-23) : LIVRAISON DES MONUMENTS DES REGNES DE SAINT LOUIS, DE PHILIPPE LE HARDI, DE PHILIPPE LE BEL, DE LOUIS 10, DE PHILIPPE 5 ET DE CHARLES 4, DEPUIS L'AN 1226-1328 – l'Academie Des Inscriptions: 1893-1894 – Dfl368.00 – ne Slangenburg [240]
CONTENT : FOR CANADIAN JOURNALISTS – (Cont: Content) – Toronto, 1984- – 9 – cn Micromedia [070]
CONTENT – (Incorporated in: Media v1 1994) – Mountain, 1970-1992 – 9 – Can$20.00y – cn Micromedia [073]
CONTENT *see* CONTENT
THE CONTENT OF BROADCASTING IN NIGERIA / Ekwelie, Sylvanus Ajani – Madison, 1968 – us Res Libr [070]
CONTENTA. RICOLDI ORDINIS PRAEDICATORUM CONTRA SECTAM MA-HUMETICAM... / Riccoldo, Montecroce de – Parisiis, 1509 – 2mf – 9 – H-8222/1 – ne IDC [956]
CONTENTIO VERITATIS : ESSAYS IN CONSTRUCTIVE THEOLOGY / Rashdall, Hastings et al – London:John Murray, 1902 – 1mf – 9 – 0-8370-2728-4 – 1985-0728 – us A.T.L.A. [240]
THE CONTENTS AND ORIGIN OF THE ACTS OF THE APOSTLES, CRITICALLY INVESTIGATED / Zeller, Eduard – To which is prefixed, Dr. F. Overbeck's Introduction to the Acts, from De Wette's handbook. 2 v. 1875-76 – 1 – us A.T.L.A. [240]
CONTENTS OF 1913 CORNERSTONE / Nashville. Tennessee. Grace Baptist Church – 1 – 5.00 – us Baptist [240]
CONTENTS OF EDUCATION : A WORLDWIDE VIEW OF THEIR DEVELOPMENT FROM THE PRESENT TO THE YEAR 2000 / Rassekh, Shapour & Vaideanu, G – 1987 – 297p – 9 – 92-3-102421-3 – fr UNESCO [370]
CONTES AFRICAINS : LIVRE DE LECTURES AFRICAINES / Beaumont, Pierre de – [Abidjan]: Editions Africaines 1964 – us Res Libr [960]
LES CONTES D'AMADOU-KOUMBA / Diop, Birago – Paris: Fasquelle, [1947] – 1 – us Res Libr [490]
CONTES DE LA MONTAGNE LIBANAISE / Gay-Para, P – Procedes stylistiques et signification – 9 – F200.00 – fr Ethnologie [306]
LES CONTES DE M. MERCIER – s.l.: s.n., 1883?. 03431. (Pre-1900 Canadiana) – 9 – cn C.I.H.M. [810]
LES CONTES DE PERRAULT ET LES RECITS PARALLELES / Saintyves, Pierre – 1923 – 1 – us I.U. Libraries [390]
CONTES DES FEES / Aulnoy, Marie-Catherine d' – English fairy tales. 1855 – 1 – us I.U. Libraries [390]
LES CONTES D'OGRES (IBISIZIMWE) : CONTRIBUTION A L'ANALYSE DES TEXTES NARRATIFS DE LITTERATURE ORALE AU BURUNDI / Nizigiyimana, D – 9 – F150.00 – fr Ethnologie [490]
CONTES DU LARHALLE, SUIVIS D'UN RECUEIL DE PROVERBES ET DE DEVISES DU PAYS MOSSI / Tiendrebeogo, Yamba – Ouagadougou: Tiendrebeogo, 1963 [cover 1964] – us Res Libr [960]
CONTES ET LEGENDES DE L'INDE ANCIENNE / Foucaux, Marie Filon – Paris: E. Leroux, 1878. x,152p.2 fiches. (Literature Collection) – 9 – 6.00 – fr Bibl Nationale [390]
CONTES ET ROMANS DE L'EGYPTE CHRETIENNE / Amelineau, E – Paris: E. Leroux, 1888. 2v. lxxxvii, 189; ix,263p 6 fiches. (Literature Collection) – 9 – 15.00 – fr Bibl Nationale [240]
CONTES LIGURES, TRADITIONS DE LA RIVIERE: RECUEILLIS ENTRE MENTON ET GENES / Andrews, James Bruyn – Paris: E. Leroux, 1892. iv,355p. 4 fiches. (Literature Collection) – 9 – 10.00 – fr Bibl Nationale [830]
CONTES PERSANS – 1910 – 1 – us I.U. Libraries [830]

CONTES POPULAIRES / Roussey, Charles – 1894 – 1 – us I.U. Libraries [390]

CONTES POPULAIRES D'AFRIQUE / Basset, Rene – Ed. by E. Guimolto – 9 – 12.50 – fr Orientalistes [390]

CONTES POPULAIRES DES PROVENCAUX DE L'ANTIQUITE ET DU MOYEN-AGE / Berenger-Feraud, Laurent Jean Baptiste – Paris: E. Leroux, 1887. vii,261p. 3 fiches. (Literature Collection) – 9 – 8.00 – fr Bibl Nationale [390]

CONTES POPULAIRES DES SAKALAVA ET DES TSIMIHETY DE LA REGION D'ANALALAVA / Dandouau, Andre – Algiers: J Carbonel, 1922 – 1 – us Res Libr [390]

CONTES POUR ENFANTS CANADIENS / Marjolaine – Montreal: Librairie d'Action canadienne-francaise, limitee, 1931. SEM105P1316 – 2mf – 9 – Can$4.50 – cn Bibl Nat [971]

CONTESTACION A LA HISTORIA DEL CONFLICTO ENTRE LA RELIGION Y LA CIENCIA / Camara Castro, Tomas Jenaro – 1880. Libros en Microficha no 21 – 2mf – 9 – Pta1,500.00 – 84-85422-64-3 – sp Pentalfa [240]

CONTESTACION AL INFORME...JOAQUIN MUNOZ BUENO...LINEA FERREA...CACERES / Tamarit de Plaza – 1867 – 9 – 1.50f – sp Bibl Santa Ana [946]

CONTESTACION AL MANIFIESTO PUBLICADO...MAURICIO CERESOLES...PASADAS ELECIONES.. / Concha, Antonio – 1839 – 9 – 1.50f – sp Bibl Santa Ana [946]

CONTESTACION DE ROCAFUERTE AL ARTICULO...EN LA CONCORDIA 5 DE FEBRERO DE 1844 / Rocafuerte, Vicente – 1 – us Res Libr [972]

CONTESTACION DE TEORIA AL PROGRAMA DE MUSICA DE MAGISTERIO SEGUNDO – Caceres: Imprenta Moderna, 1960 – 1 – sp Bibl Santa Ana [780]

CONTESTACION QUE DA LA SENORA DONA AGUSTINA ORELLANA – Caceres, 1849. Imp. de D.A. Concha y Cia – 1 – sp Bibl Santa Ana [946]

CONTESTACIONES AL DERECHO HIPOTECARIO / Munoz Casillas, Juan & Munoz Casillas, Joaquin – Caceres: Tip.El Noticiero, Tomo 1. 1921 – 1 – sp Bibl Santa Ana [946]

CONTESTACIONES OFICIALES DE DOCTRINA DEL MOVIMENTO, PARA OPOSICIONES EN LAS QUE SE EXIGE TITULO ELEMENTAL / Falange Espanola Tradicionalista y de las Juntas Ofensivas Nacional-Sindicalistas – Madrid, 1945. Fiche W 818. (Blodgett Collection of Spanish Civil War Pamphlets) – 9 – us H.U. College Libr [946]

CONTESTACION...EXTREMADURA POR EL AVISO / Hore, Rafael – 1811 – 9 – 1.50f – sp Bibl Santa Ana [946]

CONTESTACION...PLEITO...FALSEDAD Y NULIDAD / Quintanilla, Condessa de – 1849 – 9 – 1.50f – sp Bibl Santa Ana [340]

CONTESTACION...VECINO DE BURGUILLOS... VENTA DE ARBOLADA / Martinez de Santa Maria, Juan – 1863 – 9 – 1.50f – sp Bibl Santa Ana [830]

CONTEXT – Venice, CA. Spring 1982-Winter 1985 – 1 – us A.J.P.C. [071]

CONTEXT; A COMMENTARY ON THE INTERACTION OF RELIGION AND CULTURE – (1985- . 5,6,9) – v1- . 1969- – 1 – us UMI [073]

Conti, F *see* CLOTHILDA

Conti, Giovanni *see* LA GIUSTIZIA FRA INTRIGHI E TRADIMENTI

Conti, Luigi de *see*
- MERCURY'S CADUCEAN ROD: OR, THE GREAT AND WONDERFUL OFFICE OF THE UNIVERSAL MERCURY, OR GOD'S VICEGERENT, DISPLAYED..
- TRIFERTES SAGANI, OR, IMMORTAL DISSOLVENT: BEING A BRIEF BUT CANDID DISCOURCE OF THE MATTER AND MANNER OF PREPARING THE LIQUOR ALKAHEST OF HELMONT, THE GREAT HILECH OF PAROCELSUS..

Conti, N *see* COMMENTARII HIERONYMI COMITIS ALEXANDRINI DE ACERRIMO, AC OMNIUM DIFFICILLIMO TURCARUM BELLO, IN INSULAM MELITAM GESTO, ANNO MDLXV

Conti Rossini, Carlo *see* LA LANGUE DES KEMANT EN ABYSSINIE

CONTIENT CE QUI S'EST PASSE DANS LES GAULES (RGFS 2,3) : ET CE QUE LES FRANCOIS ONT FAIT SOUS LES ROIS DE LA PREMIERE RACE – (Tom. 2 Dfl84.00. Tom. 3 Dfl81.00) – 1869 – ne Slangenburg [240]

CONTIENT CE QUI S'EST PASSE DEPUIS LE COMMENCEMENT DU REGNE DE LOUIS LE BEGUE, FILS DE CHARLES LE CHAUVE, JUSQU'A LA FIN DU REGNE DE LOUIS 5, DERNIERE ROI DE LA SECONDE RACE, C'EST-A-DIRE DEPUIS L'AN 877-987 (RGFS 8) – 1871 – Dfl84.00 – ne Slangenburg [240]

CONTIENT CE QUI S'EST PASSE SOUS LES REGNES DE PEPIN ET DE CHARLEMAGNE (RGFS 5) : C'EST A DIRE DEPUIS L'AN 752-814, AVEC LES LOIS, ETC. DE CES DEUX ROIS – 1869 – Dfl84.00 – ne Slangenburg [240]

CONTIENT LA SUITE DES MONUMENTS DES TROIS REGNES DE PHILIPPE 1, DE LOUIS 6 ET DE LOUIS VII DEPUIS L'AN 1060-1180 (RGFS 13) – 1869 – Dfl88.00 – ne Slangenburg [240]

CONTIENT LA SUITE DES MONUMENTS DES TROIS REGNES...DEPUIS L'AN 1060-1180 (RGFS 14-16) – M. J.-J. Brial: 1877-1878 – Dfl263.00 – ne Slangenburg [240]

CONTIENT LE 1,2,3 (RGFS 17-19) : LIVRAISON DES MONUMENTS DES REGNES DE PHILIPPE-AUGUSTE ET DE LOUIS 8, DEPUIS L'AN 1180-1226 – 1818-1833 – Dfl249.00 – ne Slangenburg [240]

CONTIENT LES ENQUETES ADMINISTRATIVES DU REGNE DE SAINT LOUIS ET LA CHRONIQUE DE L'ANONYME DE BETHUNE (RGFS 24) – 1904 – Dfl119.00 – ne Slangenburg [240]

CONTIENT LES GESTES DE LOUIS LE DEBONNAIRE, D'ABORD ROI D'AQUITAINE, ET ENSUITE EMPEREUR, DEPUIS L'AN 781-840, AVEC LES LOIS, ETC. DE CE PRINCE, ETC (RGFS 6) – 1870 – Dfl77.00 – ne Slangenburg [240]

CONTIENT LES LETTRES HISTORIQUES (RGFS 4) : LES LOIX QUI CONCERNENT LES GAULES ET LA FRANCE SOUS LES ROIS DE LA PREMIERE RACE – 1869 – Dfl74.00 – ne Slangenburg [240]

CONTIENT PRINCIPALEMENT CE QUI S'EST PASSE SOUS LE REGNE DE HENRI1, FILS DE ROBERT LE PIEUX, C.A.D. DEPUIS L'AN 1031-1060 (RGFS 11) – 1876 – Dfl102.00 – ne Slangenburg [240]

CONTIENT SURTOUT CE QUI S'EST PASSE DEPUIS LE COMMENCEMENT DU REGNE DE HUGUES CAPET JUSQU'A CELUI DU ROI HENRI 1, FILS DE ROBERT LE PIEUX (RGFS 10) – 1874 – Dfl84.00 – ne Slangenburg [240]

CONTIENT TOUT CE QUI A ETE FAIT PAR LES GAULOIS, ET QUI S'EST PASSE DANS LES GAULOIS AVANT L'ARRIVE DES FRANCOIS (RGFS 1) : ET PLUSIEURS AUTRES CHOSES QUI REGARDENT LES FRANCOIS DEPUIS LEUR ORIGINE JUSQU'A CLOVIS – 1869 – Dfl95.00 – ne Slangenburg [240]

CONTIENT UNE PARTIE DE CE QUI S'EST PASSE SOUS LES TROIS REGNES DE PHILIPPE 1, DE LOUIS 6 DIT LE GROS, ET DE LOUIS 6 SURNOMME LE JEUNE, DEPUIS L'AN 1060-1180 (RGFS 12) – 1877 – Dfl95.00 – ne Slangenburg [240]

THE CONTINENT – A weekly magazine. 1882-84. 6v – 9 – us Primary [800]

THE CONTINENT – (Lacking some issues. Title varies. Cont: The Interior) – v1-57. Mar 1870-Apr 1926 – 90r – 1 – ATLA S0160 – us A.T.L.A. [073]

CONTINENTAL AND ISLAND LIFE, A REVIEW OF WALLACE: WITH REFERENCE TO THE BEARING OF GEOLOGICAL FACTS AND THEORIES OF EVOLUTION ON THE DISTRIBUTION OF LIFE / Dawson, John William – s.l.: s.n., 1881?. 02104. (Pre-1900 Canadiana) – 9 – cn C.I.H.M. [560]

CONTINENTAL DRIFT EMPHASIZING THE HISTORY OF THE SOUTH ATLANTIC AREA / ed by Wilson, J T – 1972 – ca 1000p – 1,5,6,9 – $10.00 – us A.G.U. [550]

CONTINENTAL JOURNAL – Boston. Mass. 1776-1787 – 1,3 – us Readex [071]

CONTINENTAL NEWS-REVIEW – Continental, Ohio. 1919- – 20r – 1 – $32.50r – us Archival [071]

CONTINENTAL NOTES FOR PRIVATE CIRCULATION / Bagg, Stanley Clark – Montreal: S. Bagg, 1870. 02377. (Pre-1900 Canadiana) – 9 – cn C.I.H.M. [971]

THE CONTINENTAL REFORMATION IN GERMANY, FRANCE AND SWITZERLAND : FROM THE BIRTH OF LUTHER TO THE DEATH OF CALVIN / Plummer, Alfred – London: R. Scott, 1912 – 1mf – us A.T.L.A. [940]

CONTINENTAL SHELF RESEARCH – v1- 1982- – 5,6,9 – us UMI [550]

THE CONTINENTAL TEUTONS / Merivale, Charles – London: S.P.C.K.; New York: Pott, Young, [1878?] – 1mf – us A.T.L.A. [240]

CONTINENTAL TIMES – Berlin, 18 Sep 1914-14 Jul 1919 (imperfect) – 2r – 1 – uk British Libr Newspaper [072]

THE CONTINENTAL TIMES – Toronto.1948-82. In Japanese and English – 1 – 1925.00 – cn McLaren [072]

CONTINENTAL UNION: A SHORT STUDY OF ITS ECONOMIC SIDE: BY CONSTITUTIONAL MEANS INVOLVING THE CONSENT OF THE MOTHER COUNTRY, TO BRING ABOUT THE UNION, ON FAIR AND HONORABLE TERMS, OF CANADA AND THE UNITED STATES / Continental Union Association of Ontario – Issued by the Continental..., May, 1893. Toronto: Continental Union, 1893. 00013. (Pre-1900 Canadiana) – 9 – cn C.I.H.M. [971]

Continental Union Association of Ontario *see* CONTINENTAL UNION: A SHORT STUDY OF ITS ECONOMIC SIDE: BY CONSTITUTIONAL MEANS INVOLVING THE CONSENT OF THE MOTHER COUNTRY, TO BRING ABOUT THE UNION, ON FAIR AND HONORABLE TERMS, OF CANADA AND THE UNITED STATES

LES CONTINENTS – (Filmed with 12 other titles) – Paris: M Boivent, may 15, jun 15, jul 15, sep 1-dec 15 1924 – us Res Libr [072]

CONTINGENT ACCOUNTS OF THE SHERIFF OF THE DISTRICT OF MONTREAL, FROM THE 11TH APRIL TO THE 10TH OCTOBER 1833 – [Quebec]: the Standing Committee on Public Accounts, [1834 ?]. SEM105P1393 – 3mf – 9 – Can$6.75 – cn Bibl Nat [971]

CONTINGENT PAY LEDGERS FOR NEW SOUTH WALES FORCES WHO SERVED IN THE BOER WAR, 1899-1908 – 3r – 1 – CRS B5200 – at Archives [920]

CONTINUACION DE LAS NUEVAS POESIAS DE... / Salas, Francisco Gregorio de – Madrid: Andres Ramirez, 1776 – 1 – sp Bibl Santa Ana [946]

CONTINUACION DEL JUICIO CRITICO DEL ANO DE 1788 / Salas, Francisco Gregorio de – Madrid: Joseph Otero, 2ª ed 1788 – 1 – sp Bibl Santa Ana [946]

CONTINUACION...POESIAS / Salas, Francisco Gregorio de – 9 – 1.50f – sp Bibl Santa Ana [810]

CONTINUATIO CHRONICARUM (RS93) / Adam Murimuth; ed by Thompson, E M – (Continuation of: Robertus De Avesbury "De Gestis Mirabilibus Regis Edwardii Tertii") – 1889 – Dfl35.00 – ne Slangenburg [240]

CONTINUATION AF HANS EGEDES RELATIONER FRA GRONLAND; SAMT NIELS EGEDES BESKRIVELSE OVER GRONLAND; RE-ED. VED H. OSTERMANN / Egede, P & Egede, N – MoG. v. 120. Kobenhavn. 1939. BN-197 2 – 8 – ne IDC [430]

THE CONTINUATION COMMITTEE CONFERENCES IN ASIA, 1912-1913 : A BRIEF ACCOUNT OF THE CONFERENCES TOGETHER WITH THEIR FINDINGS AND LISTS OF MEMBERS / World Missionary Conference (1910 : Edinburgh, Scotland) Continuation Committee – New York: Chairman of the Continuation Committee, 1913 – 2mf – us A.T.L.A. [240]

CONTINUATION DE L'ENTRETIEN DE SCIPION ET SEVERE SUR LA LETTRE D'UN AMI DE L'AUTHEUR DES REFLEXIONS – Rouen. 1699 – 9 – fr Hachette [360]

CONTINUATION OF THE INDEX TO 1826 AND THE COLON FIRE DISASTER, 1885 – Panama: Biblioteca Nacional de Panama, 1885 – 1r – 1 – inquire – us Ross [972]

CONTINUED PROFESSIONAL LEARNING AND THE EXPERIENCED ELEMENTARY SCHOOL PHYSICAL EDUCATION SPECIALIST / Pissanos, B W – 1989 – 4mf – 9 – $16.00 – us Microform Publ [790]

CONTINUING EDUCATION FOR THE FAMILY PHYSICIAN – v. 1-. 1973- – 1,5,6,9 – us UMI [610]

CONTINUITY OF SCRIPTURE / Wood, William Page – London: S.P.C.K., (1869). 1 fiche – 9 – us A.T.L.A. [240]

THE CONTINUITY OF SCRIPTURE : AS DECLARED BY THE TESTIMONY OF OUR LORD AND OF THE EVANGELISTS AND APOSTLES / Wood, William Page – rev ed. London:Society for Promoting Christian Knowledge, [ca. 1869] – 1mf – 9 – 0-8370-3522-8 – 1985-1522 – us A.T.L.A. [220]

CONTINUOUS CREATION: AN APPLICATION OF THE EVOLUTIONARY PHILOSOPHY / Adams, Myron Winslow – Boston: Houghton, Mifflin, 1889.1 fiche – 9 – us A.T.L.A. [240]

CONTRA ADVERSARIUM LEGIS ET PROPHETARUM – CONTRA PRISCILLIANISTAS ET ORIGENISTAS; OROSIUS – DE ERRORE PRISCILLIANISTARUM ET ORIGENISTARUM / Augustinus, St – 1985 – 4mf – 9 – Bf975.00 – be Brepols [240]

CONTRA ALCHORANUM ET SECTAM MACHOMENTICAM LIBRI QUINQUE / Leuwis, D de, de Rickel – Coloniae, 1533 – 7mf – 9 – H-8242/1 – ne IDC [956]

CONTRA ANABAPTISTAS UNICI BAPTISMATIS ASSERTIO / Corbachius, I – Coloniae, M. Nouesianus. 1535. BME-192 1 – 9 – ne IDC [240]

CONTRA COSTA COUNTY 1, CALIFORNIA – 1884-1906. 122 maps. 12 towns. Sanborn Company Fire Insurance Maps – 1 – $32.00r – us Shkurkin [910]

CONTRA COSTA COUNTY 2, CALIFORNIA – 1907-43. 540 maps. 25 towns. Sanborn Company Fire Incurance Maps – 1 – $68.00r – us Shkurkin [910]

CONTRA COSTA COUNTY, 1871-1872 – 1r – 1 – $50.00 – D012 – us Library Micro [978]

CONTRA COSTA COUNTY GREATER – (East 1992- 3+ r $150.00. West 1992- 3+ r $150.00. North 1992- 4+ r $200.00. South 1992- 4+ r $200.00. North and South 1994- 2+ r $100.00) – 1906-38 – 32r – 1 – $1,600.00 – P00020 – us Library Micro [910]

CONTRA COSTA COURIER *see* COURIER JOURNAL

CONTRA COSTA GAZETTE – Martinez, CA. 1860-1975 – 190r – 1 BC02420 – $9,500.00 – us Library Micro [071]

CONTRA COSTA INDEPENDENT – (Cont: North East Bay Independent and Gazette) – Richmond, CA. Mar-Jul 1982; Oct 1982-1984 – 27r – 1 – $1,350.00 – B02690 – us Library Micro [071]

CONTRA COSTA INDEPENDENT – Livermore, CA. 1978-80 – 3r – 1 – $150.00 – B02348 – us Library Micro [071]

CONTRA COSTA INDEPENDENT *see* NORTH EAST BAY INDEPENDENT AND GAZETTE

CONTRA COSTA STANDARD – Martinez, CA. 1901-11; 1930-56 – 17r – 1 – $850.00 – C02421 – us Library Micro [071]

CONTRA COSTA STANDARD – Martinez. Calif. -w. 1945-56 – 1 – us UMI [071]

CONTRA COSTA SUN – (Cont: Lafayette Sun and Midweek Sun) – Lafayette, CA. Jul 1980- – 21+ r – 1 – $1,050.00 ($90.00y) – B02328 – us Library Micro [071]

CONTRA COSTA SUN *see*
- THE MIDWEEK SUN
- SUN

CONTRA COSTA TIMES – Walnut Creek, CA. 1952- – 547+ r – 1 – $27,350.00 ($1,100.00y) – B03082 – us Library Micro [071]

CONTRA COSTA TIMES – Walnut Creek. Calif. 1972- – 1 – us UMI [071]

THE CONTRA COSTAN – El Cerrito, CA. 1917-1924 – 1r – 1 – $50.00 – B03592 – us Library Micro [071]

CONTRA FELICEM / Aquileiensis, Paulinus – 1990 – 4mf – 9 – Bf1,175.00 – 2-503-63952-6 – be Brepols [240]

CONTRA KOMINTERN – Berlin, apr 1937-aug 1939 – 1 – Dist. gw Mikrofilm – gw Misc Inst [072]

CONTRA LOS TRAJES Y ADORNOS PROFANOS / Belluga Moncada, Luis – 1722 – 3mf – 9 – Pta2,000.00 – 84-7848-029-3 – sp Pentalfa [946]

CONTRA RUFINUM / Hieronymus – 1982 – 4mf – 9 – Bf750.00 – 2-503-60792-6 – be Brepols [240]

CONTRACT BETWEEN THE GOVERNMENT OF THE DOMINION AND THE CANADIAN PACIFIC RAILWAY COMPANY: ALSO, THE CONSOLIDATED RAILWAY ACT (1879), AND THE ACT OF 1881 AMENDING IT / Canadian Pacific Railway Company – Ottawa?: Maclean, Roger, 1882. 02046.

(Pre-1900 Canadiana) – 9 – cn C.I.H.M. [380]

CONTRACTING BUSINESS *see* AIRCONDITIONING AND REFRIGERATION BUSINESS

CONTRACTORS GUIDE – 1984- – 1,5,6,9 – us UMI [600]

CONTRACTS AND COMBINATIONS IN RESTRAINT OF TRADE / Kales, Albert Martin – Chicago, Callaghan, 1918. 169 p. LL-1623 – 1 – us L of C Photodup [340]

THE CONTRADICTIONS OF ORTHODOXY, OR, "WHAT SHALL I DO TO BE SAVED?" : AS ANSWERED BY SEVERAL REPRESENTATIVE CLERGYMEN OF CHICAGO / Collins, Almer M – Chicago, Ill.: Central Book Concern, 1880 – 1mf – us A.T.L.A. [240]

CONTRAST – London. 1961-66 – 1 – uk World [073]

THE CONTRAST, OR, THE EVANGELICAL AND TRACTARIAN SYSTEMS COMPARED IN THEIR STRUCTURE AND TENDENCIES / Stone, John S – New York: Protestant Episcopal Society for the Promotion of Evangelical Knowledge, 1853 – 1mf – us A.T.L.A. [240]

CONTRAST; SERVING THE BLACK COMMUNITY – v1- . 1969- – 1 – 60.00y – cn McLaren [971]

LE CONTRAT D'APPRENTISSAGE EXPLIQUE AUX MAITRES ET AUX APPRENTIS, SELON LES LOIS, REGLEMENTS ET USAGES ET LA JURISPRUDENCE DES CONSEILS DE PRUD'HOMMES / Mollot – (Condition of 19th C. French working class series). 1847 – 9 – fr Hachette [340]

CONTRATOS Y CUASICONTRATOS MINEROS EN LAS LEGISLACIONES SUDAMERICANAS / Alvarez Madariaga, Luz – Santiago de Chile, Talleres graficos "Simiente" 1944. 67 p. LL-8001 – 1 – $23.00r – us L of C Photodup [340]

IL CONTRATTO DI TRASPORTO... / Carnazza, C – Catania, 1898 – 2mf – 1 – ILM3246/1 – ne IDC [327]

CONTRE LA GUERRE – Journal bi-mensuel. Dir. Charles Rappoport. no. 1-4. Paris. 23 nov 1912-5 mars 1913 – 1 – fr A.C.R.P.P. [073]

CONTRE LE COURANT / Organe de l'opposition Communiste – Paris. v1,no1-5-v2,no38. Nov 1927-Oct 1929. Organ of the Communist Opposition. 7 fiches – 9 – $45.00 – us UPA [944]

CONTRE LE COURANT – Organe de l'opposition communiste. no. 1-38. Paris. nov 1927-oct 1929 – 1 – fr A.C.R.P.P. [073]

CONTRE LES ETRANGERS: ETUDE POUR LA PROTECTION DES OUVRIERS FRANCAIS / Barres, Maurice – Paris. 1893. (La Condition Ouvriere. Part Two.) – 9 – 6.00 – fr Bibl Nationale [360]

LE CONTRE-POISON – ou Preservatif contre les motions insidieuses, cabales, erreurs, mensonges, calomnies et faux principes repandus dans les feuilles de la semaine. Par Dusaulchoy, Estienne, et autres. no. 1-36. Paris. janv-avr 1791 – 1 – fr A.C.R.P.P. [073]

Contreras, Eduardo et al *see* CROSS-CULTURAL BROADCASTING

Contreras Labarca, Carlos *see* HACIA DONDE VA CHILE

CONTRIBUCION A LA HISTORIA DE LA COLONIA DEL SACRAMENTO. LA EPOPEYA DE MANUEL LOBO... / Arazola Gil, Luis Enrique – Madrid, 1931; Madrid: Razon y Fe, 1932 – 1 – sp Bibl Santa Ana [946]

CONTRIBUCION A UNA ANTOLOGIA DE LA REALIDAD HISTORICA / Frutos Cortes, Eugenio – Madrid, 1943. Rev. Filosofia (Tomo II. Num. 4) del Instituto Luis Vives – sp Bibl Santa Ana [100]

CONTRIBUCION AL ESTUDIO DE LA COMPOSICION ACOMATICA DE LOS VINOS Y DERIVADOS VINICOS DE TIERRA DE BARROS / Maynar Marino, Juan – Badajoz: Universidad de Extremadura, 1981 – 1 – sp Bibl Santa Ana [370]

CONTRIBUCION AL ESTUDIO DE LA FAUNA ENTOMOLOGICA DE PATAGONIA / Berg, C – Buenos Aires, 1877. 30p. Z-1057/2 – 8 – ne IDC [590]

CONTRIBUCION AL ESTUDIO DE LA OSTEOSINTESIS EN CARACAS / Parra Leon, Jose Antonio – Caracas, 1930; Madrid: Razon y Fe, 1931 – 1 – sp Bibl Santa Ana [610]

CONTRIBUCION AL ESTUDIO DE LAS ORACIONES FINALES Y CAUSALES EN FRANCES / Corcuera Manso, Fidel – 2mf – 9 – Pta1,500.00 – 84-85422-48-1 – sp Pentalfa [140]

CONTRIBUCION AL ESTUDIO DE LOS PASTOS EXTREMENOS / Moreno Marquez, Victor – Madrid: Graficas Agma, 1952 – 1 – sp Bibl Santa Ana [946]

CONTRIBUCION AL ESTUDIO DE LOS VINAGRE DE VINO DE "TIERRA DE BARROS" Y ESTUDIO DE ALGUNOS COMPONENTES VOLATILES DE LOS MISMOS / Olivares del Valle, Francisco Javier – Badajoz: Universidad de Extremadura, Facultad de Ciencias. Departamento de Quimica-fisica, 1975 – 1 – sp Bibl Santa Ana [550]

CONTRIBUCION AL ESTUDIO DE NUESTRA TOPONIMIA / Deletang, Luis F – Buenos Aires, 1931; Madrid: Razon y Fe, 1933 – 1 – sp Bibl Santa Ana [972]

CONTRIBUCION AL ESTUDIO DEL COLERA / Cisneros, Juan – 1886 – 9 – 1.50f – sp Bibl Santa Ana [610]

CONTRIBUCION AL PROCESO DE CONCIENTIZACION EN AMERICA LATINA – Montevideo, Uruguay: Junta Latino Americana de Iglesia y Sociedad, 1968 – us Res Libr [972]

CONTRIBUCIONES. IMPUESTOS, ARANCELES Y GRAVAMENES / Bardaji y Buitrago, A – Madrid: Mag, 1954 – 1 – sp Bibl Santa Ana [946]

CONTRIBUICAO PARA E BIBLIOGRAFIA DAS LINGUAS "BANTU" DE ANGOLA / Almeida Santos, J & Cardoso, C Lopes – Lisboa, 1966 – 1mf – 9 – ne IDC [960]

CONTRIBUTION A LA CONNAISSANCE DE LA BIOLOGIE DU LOUP, DICENTRARCHUS LABRAX (L) : POISSON SERRANIDAE / Barnabe, G – Montpellier, 1976 – 426p – 9 – F130.00 – fr Ethnologie [590]

CONTRIBUTION A LA CONNAISSANCE DES PEUPLEMENTS BENTHIQUES DU GOLFE NORMANNO-BRETON / Retiere, C – 9 – F120.00 – fr Ethnologie [574]

CONTRIBUTION A LA FLORE BRYOLOGIQUE DE L'ANNAM / Potier de la Varde, R – (Revue Generale de Botanique). v. 27. 1917. B-6191 2 – 8 – ne IDC [580]

CONTRIBUTION A LA FLORE BRYOLOGIQUE DU TONKIN / Bescherelle, E – 3 articles, published in 1887, 1892, 1894. B-745 2 – 8 – ne IDC [580]

CONTRIBUTION A LA TYPOLOGIE DES EPINGLES DE L'AGE DU BRONZE / Audouze, F – 9 – F130.00 – fr Ethnologie [306]

CONTRIBUTION A L'ETUDE BIOLOGIQUE DU LEPTOPORUS LIGNOSUS / Boisson, Claude – (Africa series) – 9 – fr Hachette [580]

CONTRIBUTION A L'ETUDE BIOLOGIQUE ET ECOLOGIQUE DE CYCLOTHONE BRAUERI JESPERSEN ET TANING, 1926 (GONOSTOMATIDAE), EN MER LIGURE / Palma, S – 9 – F60.00 – fr Ethnologie [590]

CONTRIBUTION A L'ETUDE DE LA BIOLOGIE ET DE LA DYNAMIQUE DES POPULATIONS DE BRACHYDEUTERUS AURITUS VAL. 1831 (TELEOSTEEN, POMADASIIDAE) AU LARGE DE LA COTE D'IVOIRE / Barro, M – 9 – F50.00 – fr Ethnologie [590]

CONTRIBUTION A L'ETUDE DE LA NUTRITION ET DE SES ASPECTS ENERGETIQUES CHEZ DES FORMES JUVENILES DE DELTENTOSTEUS QUADRIMACULATUS (VALENCIENNES) (PISCES: GOBIIDAE) / Villiers, L – 9 – F60.00 – fr Ethnologie [590]

CONTRIBUTION A L'ETUDE DE LA SOCIETE DE FAIT... / Baudouin, L – Paris, 1931 – 2mf – 9 – ILM-3414/1 – ne IDC [340]

CONTRIBUTION A L'ETUDE DE LA SOCIOLOGIE ET DE L'HISTOIRE DU MOUVEMENT NATIONAL KURDE / Viennot, Jean-Pierre – 1975 – 9 – fr Orientalistes [300]

CONTRIBUTION A L'ETUDE DE L'HISTOIRE DE L'ANCIEN ROYAUME DE PORTO-NOVA / Akindele, Adolphe & Aguessy, C – Dakar: IFAN, 1953 – 1 – us Res Libr [960]

UNE CONTRIBUTION A L'ETUDE DES PARTIS POLITIQUES NIGERIENS: LE TEMOIGNAGE DE ADAMOU MAYAKI / Talba, Aly – Centre d'Etude d'Afrique noire (Institut d'Etudes politiques de Bordeaux). 1984 – 1 – us U.W. Library [960]

CONTRIBUTION A L'ETUDE DES RELATIONS VITAMINIQUES A ET C / Clerc, Michel – (Africa series). 1968 – 9 – fr Hachette [615]

CONTRIBUTION A L'ETUDE DU DROIT COUTUMIER BERBERE MAROCAIN : ETUDE SUR LES COUTUMES DES TRIBUS ZAYANES / Aspinion, Robert – Casablanca: A Moynier, 1937 – 1 – us Res Libr [960]

CONTRIBUTION A L'ETUDE DU PALEOLITHIQUE ANCIEN ET MOYEN DES CAUSSES / Jaubert, J – 9 – F160.00 – fr Ethnologie [560]

CONTRIBUTION A L'ETUDE DYNAMIQUE DE PEUPLEMENTS MARINS DE SUBSTRATS MEUBLES: LES PEUPLEMENTS MACROBENTHIQUES CIRCALITTORAUX SOUMIS A L'ENVASEMENT DANS LA REGION PROVENCALE / Salen-Picard, C – 9 – F70.00 – fr Ethnologie [574]

CONTRIBUTION A L'ETUDE DYNAMIQUE ET FONCTIONNELLE DES PEUPLEMENTS DE SABLES FINS DU GOLFE NORMANO-BRETON / Rivain, V – 9 – F40.00 – fr Ethnologie [590]

CONTRIBUTION A L'ETUDE ETHNOLOGIQUE DE LA TERMINOLOGIE DE LA PARENTE AU "PAYS" DE LOVISTEA, ROUMANIE / Marcu-Pandrea, A – 10 fiches – 9 – F150.00 – fr Ethnologie [306]

CONTRIBUTION A L'ETUDE PHYTOGEOGRAPHIQUE DE LA FORET DU GABON / Nicolas, P – 9 – F120.00 – fr Ethnologie [910]

CONTRIBUTION A L'HISTOIRE DES CLASSES RURALES EN FRANCE AU 19E SIECLE: LA COTE D'OR / Martin, Germain – Dijon. 1909. (La Condition Ouvriere. Part Two.) – 9 – 17.00 – fr Bibl Nationale [360]

CONTRIBUTION A L'HISTOIRE DU COMMERCE BULGARE (DOCUMENTS OFFICIELS ET RAPPORTS CONSULAIRES) / Michoff, N V – 4v. Sofia. 1941-53. BR-3937 2 – 8 – ne IDC [949]

CONTRIBUTION A L'INVENTAIRE DES RESSOURCES DU TIBESTI / Massip, J M – 9 – F100.00 – fr Ethnologie [306]

CONTRIBUTION OF BOTH PUBLIC AND PRIVATE SECTORS TO THE ECONOMIC INDICATORS FOR 1970 AT 1963 CONSTANT PRICES / Syria. Central Bureau of Statistics – Damascus. 1972 – 9 – ne IDC [310]

THE CONTRIBUTION OF FORCE AND VELOCITY IN THE DEVELOPMENT OF PEAK POWER OUTPUT / McLario, David J – 1981 – 1mf – 9 – $4.00 – us Microform Publ [790]

THE CONTRIBUTION OF SUMATRA AND KALIMANTAN TIMBER TO THE INDONESIAN ECONOMY / Anwar, Chairul – SE-6445 1. 1957 – 9 – ne IDC [338]

CONTRIBUTION POTENTIELLE DES LEGUMINEUSES FOURRAGERES AUX SYSTEMES AGRAIRES DE L'AFRIQUE AU SUD DU SAHARA : ACTES DU SEMINAIRE TENU AU CIPEA, ADDIS-ABEBA (ETHIOPIE) DU 16 AU 19 SEPTEMBRE 1985 / Haque, I et al – 1987 – 9 – 92-9053-199-1 – et ILRI [631]

CONTRIBUTION SEMIOTIQUE A L'ETUDE DU CONTE AFRICAIN : APPLICATIONS PRATIQUES ET THEORISATION A PARTIR DE QUELQUES CONTES DE BIRAGO DIOP – Saer Dione, 1983 – us Res Libr [960]

CONTRIBUTION TO A BIBLIOGRAPHY OF INDIAN ART AND AESTHETICS / Mitra, H – Santiniketan, 1951 – 5mf – 9 – ne IDC [700]

CONTRIBUTION TO KNOWLEDGE OF THE MARINE ALGAE OF NORWAY. PTS.1-2 / Foslie, M – (Tromso Museums Aarshefter, v13 and 14. Tromso. 1890-1891) – 8 – ne IDC [580]

A CONTRIBUTION TO THE CAUSE OF CHRISTIAN UNITY, OR, THE THOUGHTS OF AN INDIAN MISSIONARY ON THE CONTROVERSIES OF THE DAY / O'Neill, Simeon Wilberforce – London: J.T. Hayes, [1879?] – 1mf – us A.T.L.A. [240]

A CONTRIBUTION TO THE FLORA OF AUSTRALIA / Woolls, W – 5176. 1867 – 9 – ne IDC [580]

A CONTRIBUTION TO THE FRESHWATER ALGAE OF THE NORTH OF IRELAND / West, W – 6421. 1902 – 9 – ne IDC [580]

THE CONTRIBUTION TO THE NATIONAL INCOME OF INDONESIA, 1957 AND 1958, BY THE AGRICULTURE SECTOR / Indonesia. National Income Committee – SE-6289 1. 1960 – 9 – ne IDC [338]

CONTRIBUTIONES AD ALGOLOGIAM ET FUNGOLOGIAM / Reinsch, P F – Lipsiae. 1875. B-6403 2 – 8 – ne IDC [580]

CONTRIBUTIONS A L'ETUDE DE LA VEGETATION DU SENEGAL / Trochain, Jean-Louis – Paris: Larose, 1940 – 1 – us Res Libr [580]

CONTRIBUTIONS A L'ETUDE DU DETERMINISME FONCTIONNEL DE L'INDUSTRIE DANS L'EDUCATION DE L'INDIGENE CONGOLAIS / Mottoulle, Leopold – [Bruxelles: G van Campenhout, 1934] – 1 – us Res Libr [960]

CONTRIBUTIONS CHIEFLY TO THE EARLY HISTORY OF THE LATE CARDINAL NEWMAN : WITH COMMENTS / Newman, Francis William – London: K. Paul, Trench, Truebner, 1891 – 1mf – us A.T.L.A. [240]

CONTRIBUTIONS FROM THE PHYSICAL LABORATORIES / Harvard University – v. 1-22. 1903-1933. Series 2, v. 1-5. 1933-1938 – 1,5,6 – us Princeton Micro [370]

CONTRIBUTIONS FROM THE U.S. NATIONAL HERBARIUM / U.S. Department of Agriculture. Division of Botany – Washington, 1890/1895-1967. v1-38 – 637mf – 6503/2 – ne IDC [580]

CONTRIBUTIONS OF MYCOLOGIA BRITANNICA / Cooke, M C – The Myxomycetes of Great Britain. London. 1877 – 8 – ne IDC [580]

CONTRIBUTIONS OF THE VISUAL AND SOMATOSENSORY PERCEPTUAL SYSTEMS TO THE DEVELOPMENT OF POSTURAL CONTROL IN INFANTS / Sveistrup, Heidi – 1993 – 2mf – $8.00 – us Microform Publ [150]

CONTRIBUTIONS TO AN INSECT FAUNA OF THE AMAZON VALLEY / Bates, Henry Walter – London, 1861-66.-255p – 5mf – 8 – ne IDC [590]

CONTRIBUTIONS TO BIBLICAL AND PATRISTIC LITERATURE / ed by Robinson, J A – London. v1-10. 1891-1952 – 123mf – 9 – ne Slangenburg [240]

CONTRIBUTIONS TO BOTANY / Miers – 1851-1871 – 5 – uk Microform Academic [580]

CONTRIBUTIONS TO BOTANY / Miers, J – London, 1851-1871. 3 vols. B-5142 2 – 8 – ne IDC [580]

CONTRIBUTIONS TO CHIPEWYAN ETHNOLOGY / Birket-Smith, K – BN 134 2. 1930 – 8 – ne IDC [970]

CONTRIBUTIONS TO EMBRYOLOGY – v. 1-4. 1915-1916 – 1,5,6 – us Princeton Micro [611]

CONTRIBUTIONS TO MINERALOGY AND PETROLOGY – v. 1-75. 1947-80 – 1,5,9 – 14,513.00 – us UMI [550]

CONTRIBUTIONS TO NORTH AMERICAN BOTANY / Gray, A – (Proc. Amer. Acad. Arts and Sciences, v. 1-23. 1846-88). B-5937 2 – 8 – ne IDC [580]

CONTRIBUTIONS TO THE ANTHROPOLOGY OF THE CENTRAL AND SMITH SOUND ESKIMO / Hrdlicka, A – BN 260 2. 1910 – 8 – ne IDC [301]

CONTRIBUTIONS TO THE BOTANY OF INDIA / Wight, R – London. 1834. B-5811 2 – 8 – ne IDC [580]

CONTRIBUTIONS TO THE ETHNOLOGY AND ANTHROPOGEOGRAPHY OF THE POLAR ESKIMOS / Steensby, H P – BN 400 2. 1910 – 8 – ne IDC [306]

CONTRIBUTIONS TO THE ETHNOLOGY OF THE HAIDA / Swanton, J R – BN 409 2. 1905-09 – 8 – ne IDC [306]

CONTRIBUTIONS TO THE GALAXY 1868-1871 / Clemens, Samuel Langhorne – 9 – $10.00 – us Scholars' Facs [830]

CONTRIBUTIONS TO THE HISTORICAL SOCIETY OF MONTANA / Clark, WA – Helena: Independent Publ. Co., Rocky Mountain Publ. Co., 1876. Montana reel 4. (Cox Library Collection) – 5 – us Americana [978]

CONTRIBUTIONS TO THE HISTORICAL SOCIETY OF MONTANA – Helena, 1896-1940. v2-10. Montana reel 4. (Cox Library Collection) – 5 – us Americana [978]

CONTRIBUTIONS TO THE HISTORY OF STATISTICS / Westergaard, Harald – 1932 – 1 – uk Microform Academic [310]

CONTRIBUTIONS TO THE KNOWLEDGE OF SOUTH AFRICAN MARINE MOLLUSCA / Barnard, K H – Pt. 1: Gastropoda, Prosobranchiata, Toxoglossa. 2841 2. 1958 – 8 – ne IDC [590]

CONTRIBUTIONS TO THE NATURAL HISTORY OF THE UNITED STATES OF AMERICA / Agassiz, Louis – Boston, 1857-1862. 4v – 54mf – 8 – ne IDC [574]

CONTRIBUTIONS TO THE PHYTOGRAPHY OF AUSTRALIA / Mueller, Ferdinand Jakob Heinrich von – 1887. B-8044 1 – 9 – ne IDC [580]

CONTRIBUTIONS TO THE STUDY OF THE INDONESIAN IDENTITY / Tobing, Ph. O L – SE 3761 1. 1962 – 9 – ne IDC [300]

CONTRIBUTIONS TOWARDS A GLOSSARY OF THE ASSYRIAN LANGUAGE / Talbot, William Henry Fox – (In English and Akkadian. Includes bibliographical references) – [S.l.: s.n., 18–?] – 1mf – 9 – 0-8370-8622-1 – 1986-2622 – us A.T.L.A. [470]

CONTRIBUTIONS TOWARDS A MONOGRAPH OF THE LABOULBENIACEAE / Thaxter, R – Boston. 1895-1930. B-5382 2 – 8 – ne IDC [580]

CONTRIBUTO ALLA STORIA DELLA RIFORMA DEL MESSALE PROMULGATO DA SAN PIO 5TH NEL 1570 / Frutaz, A P – 1960 – 1mf – 8 – Dfl6.00 – ne Slangenburg [240]

CONTRIBUTORY NEGLIGENCE. A COMPARATIVE STUDY OF THE LAW OF TORTS (U.S.A., ENGLAND AND DENMARK) / Kragh, Karsten – Nykobing, Forfatteren, 1965. 5, 89 p. LL-2323 – 1 – us L of C Photodup [340]

CONTRIBUZIONO ALLA BIOLOGIA VEGETALE / Borzi, A – Palermo, 1894-1909. v1-4 – 8 – ne IDC [580]

CONTROL ABSTRACTS *see*
– COMPUTER AND CONTROL ABSTRACTS

Control Council for Germany *see* THE STATUTORY CRIMINAL LAW OF GERMANY

CONTROL DE NATALIDAD. INFORME PARA EXPERTOS, LLOS DOCUMENTOS DE ROMA / Javierre, Jose Maria et al – Madrid: Editorial Alameda, 1967 – 1 – sp Bibl Santa Ana [946]

CONTROL ENGINEERING – (v. 12-. 1965- 5,6. v. 17-. 1970- 9) – v. 1- 1954- – 1 – us UMI [510]

CONTROL ENGINEERING PRACTICE – v1- 1993- – 5,6,9 – us UMI [620]

CONTROL OF EUTROPHICATION OF LAKES AND RESERVOIRS / ed by Ryding, S-O & Rast, W – 1989 – xxii/314p – 9 – 92-3-102550-3 – Co-published with Parthenon Publishing – fr UNESCO [333]

THE CONTROL OF MOVEMENTS WHICH VARY IN ACCURACY AND COMPLEXITY / Lajoie, Jennifer M – University of British Columbia, 1996 – 2mf – 9 – $8.00 – PSY 1892 – us Microform Publ [150]

CONTROL SERIES BULLETIN / Massachusetts. Agricultural Experiment Station – v. 1-216. 1914-69 – 1,5,6 – us Spaulding [630]

LE CONTROLE DES CHANGES DANS LES OPERATIONS DU COMMERCE EXTERIEUR / Morocco. Banque Marocaine du Commerce Exterieur – 1961. BNE-3007 1 – 9 – ne IDC [380]

CONTROLES MORPHOGENETIQUES DU DEVELOPPEMENT ET DE LA REGENERATION DES NAGEOIRES PAIRES DES TELEOSTEENS / Geraudie, J – 9 – F90.00 – fr Ethnologie [590]

CONTROLLED BREEDING AND LARVAL REARING OF SELECTED MEDITERRANEAN MARINE SPECIES – 1980 – 177p – it F.A.O. [639]

CONTROLLED CLINICAL TRIALS – v1-5. 1980-84 – 1,5,6,13 – sz Elsevier [073]

IL CONTRO-PELO – Barre, VT, 1911-1912 – 7mf or 1r – 1,9 – us I.H.R.C. [978]

CONTROVERSIA TRA LA GRECIA E LA ROMANIA / Fiore, P – Roma, 1894 – 3mf – 1 – ILM-3667/1 – ne IDC [327]

CONTROVERSIAE INTER THEOLOGOS VVITTENBERGENSES DE REGENERATIONE ET ELECTIONE DILVCIDA EXPLICATIO D.D. EGIDII HVNNII, POLYCARPI LEYSERI, SALOMONIS GESNERI,... / Gesner, S – (Title page missing) – [Francoforti ad Moenvm, 1594] – 1mf – ne IDC [240]

CONTROVERSIARUM EPITOMES... / Gordon, J – Coloniae Agrippinae. 3v. 1620 – 10mf – 9 – CA-52/1 – ne IDC [240]

CONTROVERSIE OF SINGING BROUGHT TO AN END / Marlow, Isaac – London. 1696 – 1 – 5.00 – us Baptist [240]

CONTROVERSY BETWEEN REV. MESSRS. HUGHES AND BRECKENRIDGE : ON THE SUBJECT "IS THE PROTESTANT RELIGION THE RELIGION OF CHRIST?" / Hughes, John – 6th ed. Philadelphia: Eugene Cummiskey, 1885 – 2mf – 9 – 0-8370-7546-7 – 1986-1546 – us A.T.L.A. [230]

THE CONTROVERSY OVER A NEW CANAL TREATY BETWEEN THE U.S. AND PANAMA : A SELECTIVE, ANNOTATED BIBLIOGRAPHY OF U.S., PANAMANIAN, COLUMBIAN, FRENCH AND INTERNATIONAL ORGANIZATION TITLES / Bray, Wayne D – Washington: Library of Congress, 1976 – 1mf – 9 – $1.50 – LLMC 82-100D Title 15 – us L.L.M.C. [340]

A CONTROVERSY WITH THE PEOPLE CALLED METHODISTS CONCERNING THE TRUE NATURE OF THE CHRISTIAN RELIGION,... / Free, J – London, 1760 – 1mf – 9 – MP-386/1 – ne IDC [240]

Contuzzi, F P *see*
– LA CAMBIALE...
– IL DIRITTO EREDITARIO INTERNAZIONALE...
– LA NEUTRALIZZAZIONE DEL CANALE DI SUEZ...

Convencion Nacional Constituyente *see* ARGENTINE REPUBLIC

CONVENCION SOBRE DERECHO INTERNACIONAL PROVADO Y OTROS DOCUMENTOS – Bogota, 1931 – 2mf – 1 – ILM-4026/1 – ne IDC [327]

CONVENCION Y REGLAMENTOS... / Guatemala. Secretaria de relaciones exteriores – Guatemala, 1913 – 1mf – 1 – ILM-3834/1 – ne IDC [327]

CONVENCIONES PARA LA UNIFICACION DE DETERMINADAS REGLAS EN MATERIA DE ABORDAJE... – Mexico, 1929 – 1mf – 1 – ILM-3849/1 – ne IDC [327]

CONVENIO COLECTIVO SINDICAL DE SIDERMETALURGIA (N° 188 DE 18.8.76) / Sindicato Provincial del Metal – Caceres: Tip. El Noticiero, 1976 – 1 – sp Bibl Santa Ana [946]

CONVENIO COLECTIVO SINDICAL DE SIDEROMETALURGICA. NUMERO 159 DE 13-7-74 / Sindicato Provincial del Metal – Caceres: Rdit. Extremadura, 1974 – 1 – sp Bibl Santa Ana [946]

CONVENIO COLECTIVO SINDICAL DE TRABAJO AGRICOLA, APROBADO Y SUSCRITO POR LOS REPRESENTANTES...DE CORIA / Delegacon Provincial de Sindicatos – Caceres: Imprenta Moderna, 1961 – 1 – sp Bibl Santa Ana [630]

CONVENIO COLECTIVO SINDICAL DE TRABAJO AGRICOLA, APROBADO Y SUSCRITO POR LOS REPRESENTANTES...DE VILLAMIEL (CACERES) / Delegacion Provincial de Sindicatos – Caceres: Imp. Moderna, 1963 – 1 – sp Bibl Santa Ana [630]

CONVENIO COLECTIVO SINDICAL DE TRABAJO AGRICOLA DE ALCANTARA (CACERES) Y SUS AGREGADOS DE ESTORNINOS Y PIEDRAS ALBAS / Delegacion Provincial de Sindicatos – Caceres: Imp. Moderna, 1962 – 1 – sp Bibl Santa Ana [630]

CONVENIO COLECTIVO SINDICAL DE TRABAJO AGRICOLA...DE CASAS DE MILLAN CACERES / Delegacion Provincial de Sindicatos – Caceres: Imprenta Moderna, 1962 – 1 – sp Bibl Santa Ana [630]

CONVENIO COLECTIVO SINDICAL DE TRABAJO AGRICOLA...DE GUADALUPE / Delegacion Provincial de Sindicatos – (Caceres): Imprenta Moderna, 1962 – 1 – sp Bibl Santa Ana [630]

CONVENIO COLECTIVO SINDICAL DE TRABAJO, DE AMBITO PROVINCIAL PARA EL COMERCIO DE LA ALIMENTACION (MAYOR Y MENOR) APROBADO POR EL ILMO. SR. DELEGADO PROV. DE TRABAJO / Sindicato Prov. de la Alimentacion y Productos Coloniales, Badajoz – Badajoz: Imp. Inca, 1969 – sp Bibl Santa Ana [331]

CONVENIO COLECTIVO SINDICAL DE TRABAJO...DE LA EMPRESA TEXTIL LANERA SOBRINO DE BENITO MATAS EN HERVAS (CACERES) / Delegacion Provincial de Sindicatos – Caceres: Imp. Moderna, 1962 – 1 – sp Bibl Santa Ana [331]

CONVENIO COLECTIVO SINDICAL PROVINCIAL PARA LAS INDUSTRIAS DEL ACEITE Y SUS DERIVADOS DE BADAJOZ / Delegacion Prov. de la Org.Sindical – Badajoz: Tipografia Clasica, 1961 – sp Bibl Santa Ana [338]

CONVENIO DE ARBITRAJE COMERCIAL – Washington, 1917 – 1mf – 1 – ILM-3746/1 – ne IDC [327]

CONVENTION BAPTIST PRESS RELEASE MATERIALS – SBC, 1954-60. 2818p – 1 – us Baptist [240]

LA CONVENTION COLLECTIVE DE TRAVAIL (LOI DU 24 JUIN 1936) ET L'ARBITRAGE OBLIGATOIRE / Capeau, Charles – Nice? 1937. 81p. LL-4091 – 1 – us L of C Photodup [340]

CONVENTION DE LA BAIE JAMES ET DU NORD QUEBECOIS. AGREEMENT BETWEEN THE GOVERNMENT OF QUEBEC AND THE SOCIETE D'ENERGIE DE LA BAIE JAMES AND.. – Montreal: Conseil executif: Negociations indiens Inuit de la Baie James, 1974. SEM105P448 – 11mf – 9 – Can$24.75 – cn Bibl Nat [971]

CONVENTION DE LA BAIE JAMES ET DU NORD QUEBECOIS. CONVENTION ENTRE LE GOUVERNEMENT DU QUEBEC ET LA SOCIETE DE LA BAIE JAMES.. – Montreal: Conseil executif: Negociations indiens Inuit de la Baie James, 1974. SEM105P447 – 11mf – 9 – Can$24.75 – cn Bibl Nat [971]

CONVENTION DE LA BAIE JAMES ET DU NORD QUEBECOIS. CONVENTION ENTRE LE GOUVERNEMENT DU QUEBEC ET LA SOCIETE DE LA BAIE JAMES – Quebec: Editeur officiel du Quebec, ca 1976. SEM105P445 – 6mf – 9 – Can$13.50 – cn Bibl Nat [971]

CONVENTION DE LA BAIE JAMES ET DU NORD QUEBECOIS....LES CONVENTIONS COMPLEMENTAIRES NOS. 1,2,3,4,5 ET 6 – Quebec: Editeur officiel, ca 1980. SEMP105449 – 8mf – 9 – Can$18.00 – cn Bibl Nat [971]

LA CONVENTION DE RECIPROCITE LAURIER, 1911 – [Quebec (Province)]: [s.n.], [1911?] – 2mf – 9 – Can$4.50 – cn Bibl Nat [971]

CONVENTION DES MEDECINS DU DISTRICT DE QUEBEC: DISCOURS PRONONCE AU BANQUET DU 25 JUIN 1900, LE JOUR DE LA SAINT JEAN BAPTISTE, A L'HOTEL CHATEAU FRONTENAC / Brouchu, Delphis – Quebec: du Patronage, 1900? 02975. (Pre-1900 Canadiana) – 9 – cn C.I.H.M. [610]

CONVENTION DU 15 SEPTEMBRE ET L'ENCYCLIQUE DU 8 DECEMBRE = REMARKS ON THE ENCYCLICAL OF THE 8TH OF DECEMBER, A.D. 1864 / Dupanloup, Felix – (In English) – 2nd ed. London:Burns, Lambert, & Oates, 1865 – 1mf – 9 – 0-8370-3651-8 – 1985-1651 – us A.T.L.A. [240]

Convention Evangelica Bautista. Argentine Baptist convention *see* MINUTES

CONVENTION FOR PROMOTING SAFETY OF LIFE AT SEA : HEARING BEFORE A SUBCTTEE...FOREIGN RELATIONS U.S. SENATE – Washington, 1932 – 1mf – 1 – ILM-3950/1 – ne IDC [327]

LA CONVENTION FRANCO-BADOISE...1846... / Desbois, R – Paris, 1920 – 3mf – 1 – ILM-2090/1 – ne IDC [327]

CONVENTION JOURNAL – Saipan, n.p, 1975 – 42mf – 9 – $63.00 – LLMC 82-100F, Title 93 – us L.L.M.C. [323]

Convention Nationale des Canadiens-francais des Etats-Unis *see*
– COMPTE-RENDU DE LA SEIZIEME CONVENTION...: TENUE A RUTLAND, VT., LE 22 ET 23 JUIN 1886
– COMPTE-RENDU OFFICIEL DE LA 17E CONVENTION...: TENUE A NASHUA, N.H.: LES LES SIC 26 ET 27 JUIN 1888

Convention of Bible Societies of New Jersey, 1880 *see* THE WYCLIFFE SEMI-MILLENNIAL BIBLE CELEBRATION

Convention of the American Street Railway Association *see* SOUVENIR AND OFFICIAL PROGRAMME: FOURTEENTH ANNUAL CONVENTION...HELD IN MONTREAL, 15TH, 16TH, 17TH + 18TH OF OCTOBER, 1895

Convention of the Canada Temperance Union *see* WHAT DOES IT COST?: STATISTICAL REPORT, &C, PRESENTED TO THE CONVENTION..., HELD IN TORONTO, SEPTEMBER 7TH, 8TH, AND 9TH, 1869

Convention of the Canadian Association of Stationary Engineers *see* SOUVENIR NUMBER OF THE FOURTH ANNUAL CONVENTION... 1893

CONVENTION PAPERS / International Reading Association – 1956-68 – 1 – us UMI [370]

THE CONVENTION SYSTEM OF TEACHER TRAINING / Burroughs, P E – 1914 – 1 – 5.00 – us Baptist [240]

A CONVENTION THE ONLY MEANS OF SAVING US FROM RUIN... / Gerrald, J – Ed 3. London, 1794 – 2mf – 1 – ILM-2591/1 – ne IDC [327]

THE CONVENTION VINDICATED FROM THE MISREPRESENTATIONS OF THE ENEMIES OF OUR PEACE – London, 1739 – 1mf – 1 – ILM-2767/1 – ne IDC [327]

LE CONVENTIONI INTERNAZIONALI DI DIRITTO MARITTIMO / Giannini, A – Milano, 1930 – 6mf – 1 – ILM-1649/1 – ne IDC [327]

CONVENTIONS AND AGREEMENTS: TREATY SERIES / Israel. State Records – Jerusalem. 1949- – 9 – $200.00; $8.00y – is I.T.T.I. [956]

DES CONVENTIONS CONSULAIRES... / Ditte, M – Paris, 1903 – 4mf – 1 – ILM-3409/1 – ne IDC [327]

CONVENTIONS MADE BETWEEN THE GOVERNMENT OF THE SYRIAN REPUBLIC AND THE IRAQ PETROLEUM COMPANY LTD, THE 11TH / Syria. Ministry of Finance – Nov 1955, approved by Law nr. 128 dated with the 1931 convention. 1956? (in French). BNE-9716 1 – 9 – 2.00 – ne IDC [336]

EL CONVENTO DE SANTA MARIA DE JESUS... / Marti Mayor, Jose – Madrid: Archivo Ibero Americano, 1963 – 1 – sp Bibl Santa Ana [240]

EL CONVENTO DE TEPOTZOTLAN...1924 / Eliodoro Valle, Rafael; ed by Bayle, Constantino – Madrid: Razon y Fe, 1928 – 9 – sp Bibl Santa Ana [946]

EL CONVENTO DOMINICANO DE NUESTRA SRA. DEL ROSARIO EN SANTA FE Y SU UNIVERSIDAD / Mesanza, Andres – Burgos: Razon y Fe, 1939 – 1 – sp Bibl Santa Ana [240]

CONVENTOS DE MONJAS EN LA NUEVA ESPANA. MEXICO, 1946 / Mauriel, Josefina – Madrid: Razon y Fe, 1947 – 1 – sp Bibl Santa Ana [946]

LA CONVENZIONE INTERNAZIONALE E LA LEGGE UNIFORME CAMBIARIA... / Francesco, P – Napoli, 1914 – 5mf – 1 – ILM-3651/1 – ne IDC [327]

CONVERGENCE – (v20-27 1987-94 Can$20.00y 9. Index v1-25 1968-92 Can$20.00y 9) – Toronto. v1-27. 1968-94 – 5 – Price varies – cn Micromedia [073]

CONVERGENCE DES SYSTEMES ET COEXISTENCE PACIFIQUE : LA POSITION SOVIETIQUE / Portier, J – F100.00 – fr Ethnologie [320]

CONVERGENCIA – Rio de Janeiro: CRB. v6 n55-v8 n79 mar 1973-mar 1975; v8 n82-v10 n99 jun 1975-jan/feb 1977; v10 n102 may 1977; v10 n104-v26 n258 jul/aug 1977-dec 1992 – 7r – us Res Libr [072]

CONVERSACIONES CON GOETHE EN LOS ULTIMOS ANOS DE SU VIDA / Eckermann, Johann Peter – Madrid: Calpe, 1920 – 1r – 1 – us U.W. Library [920]

CONVERSACIONES CON OSCAR ALENDE / Corbiere, Emilio J – Buenos Aires: Colihue; Hachette, c1978 – 1 – CSUXAJA7783-B – us Hoover Inst Photo [972]

CONVERSACIONES CON ROGELIO FRIGERIO SOBRE LA CRISIS POLITICA ARGENTINA / Diaz, Fanor – Buenos Aires: Colihue/Hachette, 1st ed 1977 – 1 – CSUXAJA7306-B – us Hoover Inst Photo [320]

CONVERSACIONES FAMILIARES ENTRE EL CENSOR / Forner Segarra, Juan Pablo – 1787 – 9 – 1.50f – sp Bibl Santa Ana [840]

CONVERSACIONES FAMILIARES ENTRE EL CENSOR, EL APOLOGISTA / Liberio, Silvio – 1787 – 9 – 1.50f – sp Bibl Santa Ana [946]

A CONVERSATION BETWEEN RICHARD HILL, ESQ., THE REV. MR. MADAN AND FATHER WALSH,...HELD...JULY 13, 1771,... / Hill, Richard – London, 1771 – 1mf – 9 – MP-470/1 – ne IDC [240]

CONVERSATIONS NOUVELLES SUR DIVERS SUJETS, DEDIEES AU ROY / Scudery, Madeleine de – La Haye: Abraham Arondeus. 2v. 1685. SEM16P81 – 1r – 5 – Can$9.00 – cn Bibl Nat [840]

CONVERSATIONS OF JESUS CHRIST WITH REPRESENTATIVE MEN / Adams, William – New York: American Tract Society, c1868 – 1mf – 9 – 0-8370-2045-X – 1985-0045 – us A.T.L.A. [240]

CONVERSATIONS OF LORD BYRON WITH THE COUNTESS OF BLESSINGTON / Blessington, Marguerite – London: Published for Henry Colburn by R. Bentley, 1834 – 1 roll – 1 – 1-55879-731-9 – uk Libr Preservation [840]

CONVERSATIONS ON LIBERALISM AND THE CHURCH / Brownson, Orestes Augustus – New York: D & J Sadlier, 1870, c1869 – 1mf – 9 – 0-8370-7369-3 – 1986-1369 – us A.T.L.A. [240]

CONVERSATIONS WITH CHRIST : A BIOGRAPHICAL STUDY / Lucas, Bernard – London, New York: Macmillan, 1905 – 1mf – 9 – 0-8370-2729-2 – 1985-0729 – us A.T.L.A. [240]
DAS CONVERSATIONSBLATT – Berlin, 1836-39 – 1r – 1 – Dist. gw Mikrofilm – gw Misc Inst [072]
CONVERSATIONS-LEXIKON (AEL, ABT 1; 35.10) – Neue Folge. Leipzig. 2 Bde. 1822-26 (mf ed 1997) – 23mf – 9 – DM420.00 – 3-89131-260-1 – gw Fischer [943]
CONVERSATIONS-LEXIKON (AEL, ABT 1; 35.21) – 12. Aufl. Leipzig. 15 Bde. 1875-79 (mf ed 1997) – 82mf – 9 – DM1,390.00 – 3-89131-270-9 – gw Fischer [943]
CONVERSATIONSLEXIKON MIT VORZUEGLICHER RUECKSICHT AUF DIE GEGENWAERTIGEN ZEITEN (AEL, ABT 1; 35.1) : LOEBEL-AUSGABE – Leipzig. 6 Theile. 1796-1808 (mf ed 1997) – 18mf – 9 – DM390.00 – 3-89131-251-2 – gw Fischer [943]
CONVERSATIONS-LEXIKON ODER ENCYCLOPAEDISCHES HANDWOERTERBUCH FUER GEBILDETE STAENDE (AEL, ABT 1; 35.5) – 3. Aufl. Leipzig. 10 Bde. 1814-19 (mf ed 1997) – 57mf – 9 – DM1,050.00 – 3-89131-255-5 – gw Fischer [943]
CONVERSATIONS-LEXIKON ODER ENZYCLOPAEDISCHES HANDWOERTERBUCH FUER GEBILDETE STAENDE (AEL, ABT 1; 35.6) – 4. Aufl. Leipzig. 10 Bde. 1817-19 (mf ed 1997) – 59mf – 9 – DM1,100.00 – 3-89131-256-3 – gw Fischer [943]
CONVERSATIONS-LEXIKON ODER HANDWOERTERBUCH FUER DIE GEBILDETEN STAENDE UEBER DIE IN DER GESELLSCHAFTLICHEN UNTERHALTUNG UND BEI DER LECTUERE VORKOMMENDEN GEGENSTAENDE, NAMEN UND BEGRIFFE... (AEL, ABT 1; 35.4) – 2. Aufl. Leipzig. 10 Bde. 1812-19 (mf ed 1997) – 55mf – 9 – DM990.00 – 3-89131-254-7 – gw Fischer [943]
CONVERSATIONS-LEXIKON ODER KURZGEFASSTES HANDWOERTERBUCH FUER DIE IN DER GESELLSCHAFTLICHEN UNTERHALTUNG AUS DEN WISSENSCHAFTEN UND KUENSTEN VORKOMMENDEN GEGENSTAENDE... (AEL, ABT 1; 35.2) – 1. Auflage. Amsterdam. 6 Bde. 1809 (mf ed 1997) – 18mf – 9 – DM390.00 – 3-89131-252-0 – gw Fischer [943]
CONVERSATIONS-LEXIKON ODER KURZGEFASSTES HANDWOERTERBUCH FUER DIE IN DER GESELLSCHAFTLICHEN UNTERHALTUNG AUS DEN WISSENSCHAFTEN UND KUENSTEN VORKOMMENDEN GEGENSTAENDE... (AEL, ABT 1; 35.3) : NACHTRAEGE – Amsterdam. 2 Bde. 1809; Leipzig, 1811 (mf ed 1997) – 8mf – 9 – DM170.00 – 3-89131-253-9 – gw Fischer [943]
CONVERSAZIONI DELLA DOMENICA – Milan, Italy. -w. 3 Jan 1886-28 Dec 1890. 2 reels – 1 – uk British Libr Newspaper [072]
Converse, John Melvin *see*
– DIARY
– SCRAPBOOK
CONVERSION – (In Chinese) – 19 Aug 1924-25 Feb 1925 (incomplete) – 1r – 1 – ATLA S0296E – us A.T.L.A. [073]
LA CONVERSION – Journal hebdomadaire paraissant le mardi. Dir. J. Tregoli. Paris. 29 nov 1881-25 dec 1882 – 1 – fr A.C.R.P.P. [073]
THE CONVERSION OF CHILDREN : CAN IT BE EFFECTED? HOW YOUNG? WILL THEY REMAIN STEADFAST?... / Hammond, Edward Payson – Chicago: Fleming H Revell, [1877?] – 1mf – 9 – 0-8370-6065-6 – 1986-0065 – us A.T.L.A. [240]
THE CONVERSION OF INDIA : FROM PANTAENUS TO THE PRESENT TIME, A.D. 193-1893 / Smith, George Adam – (Includes bibliographical references and index) – New York: Young People's Missionary Movement, [1894] – 1mf – 9 – 0-8370-6518-6 – 1986-0518 – us A.T.L.A. [240]
THE CONVERSION OF ST PAUL : THREE DISCOURSES / Geer, George Jarvis – New York: Samuel R Wells, 1871 – 1mf – 9 – 0-8370-3241-5 – 1985-1241 – us A.T.L.A. [240]
CONVERSION OF ST PAUL: THREE DISCOURSES / Geer, George Jarvis – New York: Samuel R. Wells, 1871.1 fiche – 9 – us A.T.L.A. [240]
THE CONVERSION OF THE MAORIS / MacDougall, Donald – Philadelphia, PA: Presbyterian Board of Publication and Sabbath-Schoolwork, 1899 – 1mf – 9 – 0-8370-6584-4 – 1986-0584 – us A.T.L.A. [240]
THE CONVERSION OF THE NORTHERN NATIONS : THE BOYLE LECTURES FOR THE YEAR 1865 / Merivale, Charles – London: Longmans, Green, 1866 – 1mf – us A.T.L.A. [240]
THE CONVERSION OF THE ROMAN EMPIRE : THE VOYLE LECTURES FOR THE YEAR 1864 / Merivale, Charles – London: Longman, Green, Longman, Roberts, & Green, 1864 – 1mf – us A.T.L.A. [240]
THE CONVERSION POLICY OF THE JESUIT IN INDIA. BOMBAY, 1933 / Heras, H – Madrid: Razon y Fe, 1934 – 1 – sp Bibl Santa Ana [240]
CONVERTER – 1938-44. Superseded by: American paper converter – 1 – us UMI [600]
CONVERTER – (v. 13-. 1976-. 5,6,9) – v. 1-1964- – 1 – us UMI [600]
CONVERTER *see* PAPER CONVERTERS AND ENVELOPE INDUSTRY
CONVERTING PRODUCT NEWS *see* PAPER AND CONVERTING PRODUCT NEWS
THE CONVEYANCER'S AND NOTARY'S MANUAL...IN THE STATE OF MINNESOTA / Booth, Walter Sherman – 1st ed. Minneapolis, Booth, 1892. 135 p. LL-665 – 1 – us L of C Photodup [340]
THE CONVEYANCER'S AND NOTARY'S MANUAL...IN THE STATE OF SOUTH DAKOTA / Booth, Walter Sherman – 1st ed. Minneapolis, Booth, 1892. 135 p. LL-1677 – 1 – us L of C Photodup [340]
A CONVICCAO – Feira de Sant' Anna, BA. 12 Jan 1884 – 1,5,6 – bl Biblioteca [072]
CONVICTING THE INNOCENT; ERRORS OF CRIMINAL JUSTICE / Borchard, Edwin Montefiore – New Haven, Yale, 1932. 421 p. LL-398 – 1 – us L of C Photodup [340]
CONVICTS.. / Kansas. State Penitentiary – 1864-84 – 1 – us KS Hist [360]
IL CONVIVIO: THE BANQUET OF DANTE ALIGHIERI / Dante, Alighieri – Trans. by Elizabeth Price Sayer.London, New York: G. Routledge and Sons, 1887. 286p – 1 – us U.W. Library [810]
Convocation of Charleston. South Carolina *see* RECORDS
Convocatoria Peronista *see* BASES PARA UNA PROPUESTA PROGRAMATICA JUSTICIALISTA
CONVOCATORIA Y REGLAMENTO DE LA 1ST ASAMBLEA PROVINCIAL DE CULTURA POPULAR / Badajoz, Delegacion Provincial de Informacion y Turismo – Badajoz: Direccion General de Cultura del Ministerio de Informacion y Turismo, 1970 – sp Bibl Santa Ana [338]
CONVOLVULACEAE ORIENTALES / Choisy, J D – 3pts. Geneve. 1834. B-5882 2 – 8 – ne IDC [580]
Convoy Research Club (Convoy, Ohio) *see* RECORDS
CONWAY 1749-1892 – (Mf 1-3: Births & Deaths 1750-1849. Mf 4-7: Town & Vital Records 1752-91. Mf 8-12: Town & Vital Records 1770-1806. Mf 13-20: Town & Vital Records 1806-36. Mf 21-28: Town & Vital records 1829-51. Mf 29-33: Index: B,M,D 1843-1986. Mf 34-35: B,M,D 1843-58. Mf 36-38: Births 1859-92. Mf 38-40: Marriages 1856-92. Mf 40-43: Deaths 1855-92) – (mf ed 1989) – 43mf – 9 – 0-87623-100-8 – us Holbrook [920]
CONWAY 1750-1849 – (Mf 1T: Out-of-Town Marriages 1784-90; Births & Deaths 1752-81. Mf 1T-2T: Marriage Intentions 1769-91. Mf 1T-5T: Births 1750-1849. Mf 4T,6T,8T: Deaths 1768-1845. Mf 4T-7T: Marriage Intentions 1791-1849. Mf 5T-6T: Births & Deaths 1758-1801. Mf 6T-9T: Marriages 1791-1801, 1828-48. Mf 7T-8T: Births 1787-1808. Mf 9T-10T: Vital Records 1843-49) – (mf ed 1995) – 10mf – 9 – 0-87623-234-9 – us Holbrook [920]
Conway, Bertrand Louis *see* THE QUESTION-BOX ANSWERS
CONWAY FIRST BAPTIST CHURCH. CONWAY, SOUTH CAROLINA : CHURCH RECORDS – (Deacon Minutes and Financial Reports, 1973-1981) – 1899-1981 – 1 – us Baptist [240]
Conway, James Joseph *see* THE FUNDAMENTAL PRINCIPLES OF CHRISTIAN ETHICS
Conway, Jim *see* MARX AND JESUS
Conway Library *see* THE COURTAULD INSTITUTE OF ART, THE UNIVERSITY OF LONDON
THE CONWAY LIBRARY : 5 YEAR UPDATE 1987-1992 / Courtauld Institute of Art – (With printed contents list) – 860mf – 9 – $7,600.00 – 1-869934-52-0 – uk Emmett [720]
THE CONWAY LIBRARY : PHOTOGRAPHIC RESEARCH LIBRARY FOR ART HISTORY / Courtauld Institute of Art – (800,000 photographs in 6pts. Pt 1: Architecture: France and Italy $6,712. Pt 2: Architecture: Rest of the world $6,608. Pt 3: Architecture: Architectural drawings $1,477. Pt 4: Sculpture: 15th-20th C. $5,028. Pt 5: Medieval Arts $4,906. Pt 6: Illuminated Mss $3,888. With printed contents lists) – 1987 – 7047mf – 9 – $22,796.00 set – 1-869934-00-8 – uk Emmett [720]
Conwell, Effie (Wood) *see* REMINISCENCES
Conwell, Russell H *see* HISTORY OF THE GREAT FIRE IN SAINT JOHN, JUNE 20 AND 21, 1877
Conwray, G R G *see* POSTRERA VOLUNTAD Y TESTAMENTO DE HERNANDO CORTES MARQUES DEL VALLE
Conybeare, FC *see* CATALOGUE OF THE ARMENIAN MSS IN THE BODLEIAN LIBRARY
Conybeare, Frederick C *see*
– A CATALOGUE OF THE ARMENIAN MSS IN THE BRITISH MUSEUM
– MYTH, MAGIC AND MORALS: A STUDY OF CHRISTIAN ORIGINS
– RITUALE ARMENORUM
– ROMAN CATHOLICISM AS A FACTOR IN EUROPEAN POLITICS
Cook, Albert S *see* A DEFENSE OF POETRY
Cook, Albert Stanburrough *see*
– THE AUTHORIZED VERSION OF THE BIBLE AND ITS INFLUENCE
– EXTRACTS FROM THE ANGLO-SAXON LAWS
Cook, Ben T *see* AN INVESTIGATION OF NORTH CAROLINA HIGH SCHOOL FOOTBALL COACHES
Cook, Charles Augustus *see*
– STEWARDSHIP AND MISSIONS
– SYSTEMATIC GIVING: THE CHURCH'S SAFEGUARD AGAINST NINETEENTH CENTURY EVILS
Cook, Charles Henry *see* THE CURIOSITIES OF ALE AND BEER: AN ENTERTAINING HISTORY
COOK CHRONICLE – Cook, NE. -w. Dec. 1947-Jun. 1949 – 1 – us NE Hist [071]
Cook, Elizur *see* STATE OF CONNECTICUT REGISTER AND MANUAL, 1884
Cook, Eveline Bosworth *see* RECOLLECTIONS, MS 3143
Cook, Forrest *see* EQUITY
Cook, Frederic Charles *see*
– REVISED VERSION OF THE FIRST THREE GOSPELS
– THE REVISED VERSION OF THE FIRST THREE GOSPELS
Cook, Frederick *see* MANUAL FOR THE USE OF THE LEGISLATURE OF THE STATE OF NEW YORK
Cook, George Cram *see* GREEK COINS; POEMS...WITH MEMORABILIA BY FLOYD DELL, EDNA KENTON AND SUSAN GLASPELL
Cook, Herman Henry *see* LISEZ LA CONDAMNATION DU REGIME LAURIER-TANE
COOK ISLANDS ANNUAL REPORTS – (Lacking: 1896/97/98, 1903, 1918, 1920, 1921 and 1929) – Wellington: Dept of Island Territories, 1894-1945 (incomplete) – 1r – PMB Doc403 – at Pacific Mss [350]
Cook Islands Collector of Customs *see* RECORDS OF ARRIVALS AND DEPARTURES, 1920-93
Cook Islands Library and Museum Society *see*
– MISCELLANEOUS MANUSCRIPTS, 1847-1977
– MISCELLANEOUS MANUSCRIPTS, 1891-1973
– MISCELLANEOUS MANUSCRIPTS, 1903-1939
– MISCELLANEOUS MANUSCRIPTS, 1933-1970
Cook, James *see*
– COOK'S LOGS OF HIS VOYAGES ROUND THE WORLD IN H.M.S. ENDEAVOUR 1768-71
– JOURNAL OF HIS VOYAGE ROUND THE WORLD IN H.M.S. "RESOLUTION"
– LOG AND JOURNAL OF HIS JOURNEY ROUND THE WORLD IN THE BARK "ENDEAVOUR"
– MANUSCRIPT JOURNAL OF COOK'S SECOND VOYAGE, 1772-75
– A VOYAGE TO THE PACIFIC OCEAN
Cook, Joel *see*
– AMERICA PICTURESQUE AND DESCRIPTIVE VOL. 1
– AMERICA PICTURESQUE AND DESCRIPTIVE. VOL. 2
– AMERICA PICTURESQUE AND DESCRIPTIVE. VOL. 3
Cook, John *see* SERMONS PREACHED IN ST ANDREW'S CHURCH, QUEBEC
Cook, John C *see* HOW TO END INFLATION
Cook, John W *see* EDUCATIONAL HISTORY OF ILLINOIS
Cook, Joseph *see*
– CONSCIENCE: WITH PRELUDES ON CURRENT EVENTS
– CURRENT RELIGIOUS PERILS: WITH...ADDRESSES ON LEADING REFORMS
– HEREDITY, WITH PRELUDES ON CURRENT EVENTS
– LABOR, WITH PRELUDES ON CURRENT EVENTS
– OCCIDENT, WITH PRELUDES ON CURRENT EVENTS
– ORTHODOXY, WITH PRELUDES ON CURRENT EVENTS
– TRANSCENDENTALISM, WITH PRELUDES ON CURRENT EVENTS
Cook, Joseph Simpson *see* THE OLD TESTAMENT ITS OWN DEFENCE: BEING A REPLY TO "THE OLD TESTAMENT VINDICATED"
Cook, Stanley Arthur *see* CRITICAL NOTES ON OLD TESTAMENT HISTORY
Cook, Yvonne H *see* THE RELATIVE EFFECTS OF A LIVE AND VIDEOTAPED INSTRUCTOR O RATINGS OF PERCEIVED EXERTION AND SUBJECTIVE FEELINGS OF STUDENTS IN AN AEROBIC EXERCISE CLASS
Cooke, Edmund Vance *see* UNCIVILIZED: A POEM ON TITLE DEEDS
Cooke, G A *see* A TEXT BOOK OF NORTH-SEMITIC INSCRIPTIONS
Cooke, G W *see* CHINA: BEING "THE TIMES" SPECIAL CORRESPONDENCE FROM CHINA IN THE YEARS 1857-1858
Cooke, George Albert *see*
– THE BOOK OF JOSHUA
– THE BOOK OF JUDGES
– THE BOOK OF RUTH
Cooke, George Alexander *see* TOPOGRAPHICAL LIBRARY OF GREAT BRITAIN. THE BRITISH TRAVELLERS' GUIDE; OR, POCKET COUNTY DIRECTORY
Cooke, George Willis *see* A GUIDE-BOOK TO THE POETIC AND DRAMATIC WORKS OF ROBERT BROWNING
Cooke, Harriette J *see* MILDMAY
Cooke, John H *see* JOHANN GERHARD ONCKEN, HIS LIFE AND WORK
Cooke, John Hunt *see* PREACHER'S PILGRIMAGE: A STUDY OF THE BOOK OF ECCLESIASTES
Cooke, John T *see* RELIGIOUS LEGISLATION: SHALL GOD OR CIVIL RULERS GOVERN THE CONSCIENCE?
Cooke, John William *see*
– APUNTES PARA LA MILITANCIA
– JOHN WILLIAM COOKE
– LA LUCHA POR LA LIBERACION NACIONAL
– PERONISMO E INTEGRACION
– EL PERONISMO Y EL GOLPE DE ESTADO
– PERONISMO Y PETROLEO
– EL RETORNO
– LA REVOLUCION Y EL PERONISMO
Cooke, Joseph Parsons *see* CREDENTIALS OF SCIENCE: THE WARRANT OF FAITH
Cooke, Josiah Parsons *see* RELIGION AND CHEMISTRY: A RE-STATEMENT OF AN OLD ARGUMENT
Cooke, M A *see* MICROGRAPHIA SUE ICONES FUNGERUM
Cooke, M C *see*
– BRITISH DESMIDS
– BRITISH EDIBLE FUNGI: HOW TO DISTINGUISH AND HOW TO COOK THEM
– BRITISH FRESH-WATER ALGAE
– CLAVIS SYNOPTICA HYMENOMYCETUM EUROPAEORUM
– CONTRIBUTIONS OF MYCOLOGIA BRITANNICA
– A FERN BOOK FOR EVERYBODY
– HANDBOOK OF BRITISH FUNGI, WITH DESCRIPTION OF ALL THE SPECIES
– ILLUSTRATIONS OF BRITISH FUNGI (HYMENOMYCETES) TO SERVE AS AN ATLAS TO THE "HANDBOOK OF BRITISH FUNGI"
– MYCOGRAPHIA, SEU LCONES FUNGORUM
– RUST, SMUT, MILDEW, AND MOULD

Cooke, Maud C *see* SOCIAL ETIQUETTE, OR, MANNERS AND CUSTOMS OF POLITE SOCIETY: CONTAINING RULES OF ETIQUETTE FOR ALL OCCASIONS..
Cooke, Richard Joseph *see* THE INCARNATION AND RECENT CRITICISM
Cooke, Sarah A Bass *see* THE HANDMAIDEN OF THE LORD, OR, WAYSIDE SKETCHES
Cooke, W *see* IN-LETTERS, 1836-1848, RELATING TO THE METHODIST NEW CONNEXION IN IRELAND
Cooke, Willis *see* UNITARIANISM IN AMERICA
COOKERY FOR THE MILLION : WITH USEFUL HINTS TO HOUSEWIVES – Montreal: W. Drysdale, 1877. 04164. (Pre-1900 Canadiana) – 9 – cn C.I.H.M. [640]
COOKEVILLE FIRST BAPTIST CHURCH. COOKEVILLE, TENNESSEE : CHURCH RECORDS – 1873-1956 – 1 – 58.59 – us Baptist [240]
Cookinham, Henry J *see* HISTORY OF ONEIDA COUNTY 1700 TO PRESENT
COOK'S AUSTRALASIAN TRAVELLER'S GAZETTE (THE AUSTRALASIAN TRAVELLER'S GAZETTE) – Melbourne, Australia. -m. 1911-15; 1918-21. 1 1 2 reels – 1 – uk British Libr Newspaper [073]
COOK'S LOGS OF HIS VOYAGES ROUND THE WORLD IN H.M.S. ENDEAVOUR 1768-71 / Cook, James – From the National Maritime Museum. Mss JOD and JOD 56. And R. Pickersgill's Narrative account of the voyage of H.M.S. Resolution. 1772-73 – 1 – uk Microform Academic [910]
COOK'S LOWER CANADA ADMIRALTY COURT CASES / Canada. Quebec Province – (Contains decisions by the Hon. George O Smart) – 1v. 1873-84 (all publ) – 5mf – 9 – $7.50 – LLMC 81-071 – us L.L.M.C. [340]
Cool, Amanda *see* DIARY
Cool, J *see* DIARY
Cool, M F J *see* STRUKTUURVERANDERINGEN IN NEDERLANDSCH-INDIE IN DE LAATSTE 25 JAAR
A COOL REPLY TO A 'CALM ADDRESS' LATELY PUBLISHED BY MR. JOHN WESLEY – London, 2nd ed 1775 – 1mf – 9 – MP-504/1 – ne IDC [240]
Cool, W *see* WITH THE DUTCH IN THE EAST
Cooledge, Charles Edwin *see* THE RELIGIOUS LIFE OF GOETHE AS ILLUSTRATED IN THE TRAGEDY OF FAUST
Cooley, Anna M *see* COLLECTION
Cooley, Roger William *see* BRIEFS ON THE LAW OF INSURANCE
Cooley, Thomas M *see* A TREATISE ON THE CONSTITUTIONAL LIMITATIONS
Cooley, Thomas M et al *see* CONSTITUTIONAL HISTORY OF THE UNITED STATES
Cooley, Thomas McIntyre *see*
- THE ELEMENTS OF TORTS
- THE GENERAL PRINCIPLES OF CONSTITUTIONAL LAW IN THE UNITED STATES
- THE LAW OF TAXATION
- LIABILITY OF PUBLIC OFFICERS TO PRIVATE ACTIONS FOR NEGLECT OF OFFICIAL DUTY
- A TREATISE ON THE CONSTITUTIONAL LIMITATIONS
- A TREATISE ON THE LAW OF TAXATION, INCLUDING THE LAW OF LOCAL ASSESSMENTS
- A TREATISE ON THE LAW OF TORTS, OR THE WRONGS WHICH ARISE INDEPENDENT OF CONTRACT

COOLGARDIE MINER – Australia. Sep 1902-Oct 1910 (1910 imperfect). -w – 17r – 1 – uk British Libr Newspaper [622]
COOLGARDIE PIONEER – Australia. 22 Apr 1899-30 Mar 1901.-w. 4mqn reels – 1 – uk British Libr Newspaper [072]
Coolidge, Calvin *see* PAPERS
Coolidge, Orville W *see* A 20TH CENTURY HISTORY OF BERRIEN COUNTY
Coomaraswamy, Ananda Kentish *see* THE INDIAN CRAFTSMAN
COOMBE LODGE REPORT – v1- 1967- 1; v10-5,6,9 – us UMI [370]
Coombs, Margaret *see* THE ENDLESS HUNT FOR A HAPPY SCHOOL
COON TAIL COURRIER – Beebe, Canada. 1 jul 1967 – 1r – 1 – Can$20.00 – cn Can Microfilming [072]
COONAMBLE INDEPENDENT – Jan 7 1898-Dec 31 1909 – 9 – at Pascoe [072]
CO-OP MAGAZINE – v.7-. 1980- – 1,5,6,9 – us UMI [334]
CO-OP: THE HARBINGER OF ECONOMIC DEMOCRACY – (See also: Journal of the New Harbinger; New Harbinger: A Journal of the Cooperative Movement) – v6. 1979. Continued as: Co-op Magazine – 1,5,6,9 – us UMI [334]
Cooper, A P *see* THE ANATOMY AND SURGICAL TREATMENT OF INGUINAL AND CONGENITAL HERNIA
Cooper, Charles Henry *see* MEMOIR OF MARGARET, COUNTESS OF RICHMOND AND DERBY
Cooper, Charles William *see*
- DIGEST OF REPORTS OF CASES DECIDED IN THE COURT OF CHANCERY, IN THE COURT OF ERROR & APPEAL, ON APPEAL FROM THE COURT OF CHANCERY, AND IN CHANCERY CHAMBERS.
- THE MECHANICS' LIEN LAW OF ILLINOIS, AS AMENDED BY ACT OF 1887.

Cooper, Christopher *see*
- THE ENGLISH TEACHER
- GRAMMATICA LINGUAE ANGLICANAE

Cooper, Elizabeth *see* MY LADY OF THE CHINESE COURTYARD
Cooper, James *see*
- CONFESSIONS OF FAITH AND FORMULAS OF SUBSCRIPTION
- JOURNAL OF GERIATRIC DRUG THERAPY

Cooper, James Fenimore *see*
- EARLY CRITICAL ESSAYS 1820-1822
- TALES FOR FIFTEEN

Cooper, John *see*
- MISCELLANIES IN VERSE AND PROSE
- SCIENCE OF SPIRITUAL LIFE

Cooper, M M *see* HISTORY OF JERSEYVILLE 1822-1901
Cooper, Morris *see* THE LAW AND PRACTICE OF REFEREES AND REFERENCES UNDER THE CODE OF CIVIL PROCEDURE AND STATUTES OF THE STATE OF NEW YORK
Cooper, Reginald Davey *see* HUNTING AND HUNTED IN THE BELGIAN CONGO
COOPER RIVER BAPTIST CHURCH. CHARLESTON COUNTY. SOUTH CAROLINA : CHURCH RECORDS – 1955-72 – 1 – 17.01 – us Baptist [240]
Cooper, Thomas *see*
- BRIDGE OF HISTORY OVER THE GULF OF TIME
- GOD, THE SOUL, AND A FUTURE STATE: A TWOFOLD POPULAR TREATISE
- THESAURUS LINGUAE ROMANAE ET BRITAINICAE
- VERITY AND VALUE OF THE MIRACLES OF CHRIST

Cooper, Trevor K *see* PERIPHERAL CHEMORESPONSIVENESS AND EXERCISE INDUCED ARTERIAL HYPOXEMIA IN HIGHLY TRAINED ENDURANCE ATHLETES
Cooper Union Museum for the Arts of Decoration. New York *see* ITALIAN DRAWINGS FOR JEWELRY 1700-1875
Cooper, Walter E *see* A COMPARISON OF PERCEPTIONS OF THE IMPORTANCE BETWEEN PHYSICAL EDUCATION GRADUATE TEACHING ASSISTANTS AND GRADUATE PROGRAM COORDINATORS ON SELECTION OF GRADUATE TEACHING ASSISTANTS AND THEIR TEACHING PERFORMANCE CRITERIA
Cooper, William Frierson *see* REMOVAL OF CAUSES FROM STATE TO FEDERAL COURTS
Cooper, William H *see* PROBLEMS OF THE FUTURE STATE: A SERIES OF SERMONS DELIVERED IN EMMANUEL REFORMED EPISCOPAL CHURCH OTTAWA, ONTARIO
Cooper, William M *see* FLAGELLATION AND THE FLAGELLANTS
Cooper, William Ricketts *see* EGYPT AND THE PENTATEUCH: AN ADDRESS
COOPERACION DE ROMAN GOMEZ VILLAFRANCA A LA BIBLIOGRAFIADE ARIAS MONTANO. N° 1 : LA BIBLIA REGIA / Gomez Villafranca, Ramon – Badajoz: Imp. Provincial, 1928. Rev. Centro de Estudios Extremenos Tomo 2, no 1-2 – 1 – sp Bibl Santa Ana [946]
LE COOPERATEUR / ed by Barbeau, Victor – Montreal, Canada. 21 nov 1940-v4 n4. 19 dec 1943 – 1r – 1 – cn Can Microfilming [072]
COOPERATION – Journal francais paraissant a Alger. Dir. J. Kamenka. Alger. mars 1963-65 – 1 – fr A.C.R.P.P. [073]
COOPERATION AND CONFLICT – (1981-. 1,5,6,9) – v1-. 1965- – 1 – us UMI [073]
CO-OPERATION AND THE PROMOTION OF UNITY : WITH SUPPLEMENT, PRESENTATION AND DISCUSSION OF THE REPORT IN THE CONFERENCE ON 21ST JUNE 1910 – (Includes indexes) – Edinburgh: Publ for the World Missionary Conference by Oliphant, Anderson & Ferrier; New York: Fleming H Revell, [1910?] – 1mf – 9 – 0-8370-6474-0 – 1986-0474 – us A.T.L.A. [240]
LA COOPERATION AUDIOVISUELLE FRANCO-ALGERIENNE DE 1975 A NOS JOURS / Rabia, Ali – 2mf – 9 – 10271 – fr Atelier National [790]
COOPERATION BETWEEN JEWS AND ARABS – I. Letter of Col. F. H. Kisch to the Chairman, XVII Zionist Congress, 1931. II. Report of the Joint Bureau for Arab relations. London. 1931. BJ-28-134 1 – 9 – ne IDC [956]
COOPERATION CANADA – (Ceased no 26 1977) – Ottawa. nos 1-26. 1972-77 – 5 – Can$100.00 – cn Micromedia [073]
COOPERATION ET INTERVENTION, LA POLITIQUE MILITAIRE DE LA FRANCE EN AFRIQUE NOIRE FRANCOPHONE ET A MADAGASCAR / Guillemin, J – 9 – F90.00 – fr Ethnologie [306]
COOPERATIVA DE PEQUENOS CAMPESINOS DE CASTUERA – Castuera: Tip. Republica, 1937 – sp Bibl Santa Ana [946]
Cooperativa de Suministros y Consumo de Nuestra Senora de Guadalupe de Caceres *see* ESTATUTOS DE LA...
Cooperativa de viviendas de proteccion oficial *see* SAN FRANCISCO DE ASIS
Cooperativa de Viviendas "San Antonio" *see* ESTATUTOS Y REGLAMENTO DE LA...
Cooperativa del Campo *see* ESTATUTOS...
Cooperativa del campo "Arrago" *see* ESTATUTOS DE LA COOPERATIVA DEL CAMPO "ARRAGO"
Cooperativa del campo Nuestra Senora de Botoa y de la Caja Rural de Badajoz *see*
- MEMORIA, 1970
- MEMORIA 1970 Y CINCUENTA ANIVERSARIO DE SU PRECURSORA LA CAJA RURAL DE AHORROS Y PRESTAMOS DEL SINDICATO CATOLICO AGRARIO
- MEMORIA 1972

Cooperativa del Campo Union de Cultivadores de tabaco de Jaraiz de la Vera *see* ESTATUTOS DE LA...
Cooperativa Farmaceutica Extremena "Cofex" *see* ESTATUTOS DE LA...
Cooperativa Industrial Cacerena *see* ESTATUTOS POR LOS QUE HA DE REGIRSELA...
Cooperativa Local de Consumo *see* ESTATUTOS DE LA...DENOMINADA DE SANTIAGO Y SANTA MARGARITA
Cooperativa Local del Campo y Ganaderos "San Isidro". Miajadas *see* ESTATUTOS
Cooperativa se Casas Baratas *see* ESTATUTOS DE LA COOPERATIVA DE CASAS BARATAS NUESTRA SENORA DE LA ASUNCION DE CACERES
Cooperativa y Caja Rural Comarcal del Campo Nuestra Senora de Piedraescrita. Espinaso *see* MEMORIA Y BALANCES 1975
THE COOPERATIVE BUILDER – Superior, Wisconsin. 1928-17 Dec 1932, 6 Jan 1977-20 Sept 1982.3 reels – 1 – us I.H.R.C. [071]
THE COOPERATIVE CALIFORNIA – Fresno, CA. 1912-1923 – 1r – 1 – $50.00 – B07452 – us Library Micro [370]
THE CO-OPERATIVE COLONIST – Fallon, NV. 1916-18 – 1r – 1 – $50.00 – U04525 – us Library Micro [071]
THE COOPERATIVE COMMONWEALTH IN ITS OUTLINES. AN EXPOSITION OF MODERN SOCIALISM / Gronlund, Laurence – Boston: Lee and Shepard; New York: C.T. Dillingham, 1884. 278p – 1 – us U.W. Library [335]
Co-operative Congress *see* REPORTS
CO-OPERATIVE INFORMATION / International Labour Organisation – 1924-92. Continued annually – 1 – uk World [331]
CO-OPERATIVE INFORMATION / International Labour Organisation – 1928-68 – 17 – Sfr275.00 – 92-2-106573-1 – sz I.L.O. [334]
THE CO-OPERATIVE MOVEMENT AS AN INSTITUTION FOR TEACHING AUTO-ACTIVITY AND A HIGH ECONOMIC CHARACTER / Hatta, Mohammad – (Speech delivered on Aug. 8, 1955). SE-2630 1 – 9 – ne IDC [370]
THE CO-OPERATIVE MOVEMENT IN INDONESIA / Hatta, Mohammad – (Speech delivered at IInd Co-operatives Day, 12th July, 1952). SE-2123 1 – 9 – ne IDC [360]
THE COOPERATIVE MOVEMENT IN RUSSIA / ed by Pries, Anne – (This mf coll lists highly theoretical works by outstanding authors, educational literature, notebooks of the members and leaders of the movement, periodicals, bibliographies and economical works. Titles also listed individually) – 675 titles – 9 – ne IDC [334]
THE COOPERATIVE MOVEMENT IN RUSSIA *see*
- ALTAISKII KRESTIANIN
- ARTEL'NOE DELO
- ARTEL'NYI MIR
- BELORUSSKII KOOPERATOR
- BIBLIOGRAFICHESKII DESIATIGODNIK PO KOOPERATSII
- BIBLIOGRAFICHESKII UKAZATEL' KNIG I STATEI, OTNOSIASHCHIKHSIA DO OBSHCHESTV, OSNOVANNYKH NA NACHALAKH VZAIMNOSTI, ARTELEI, POLOZHENIIA RABOCHEGO SOSLOVIIA I MELKOI KUSTARNOI PROMYSHLENNOSTI V ROSSII
- BIBLIOGRAFICHESKII UKAZATEL' KOOPERATIVNOI LITERATURY ZA 1927 G
- BIUDZHET KREST'IANSKOGO KHOZIAISTVA
- BIULLETEN' GUBSOIUZA
- BIULLETEN' KOOPERATIVNOI SEKTSII KOMINTERNA
- BIULLETEN' NIZHEGORODSKOGO GUBERNSKOGO KOOPERATIVNOGO SOVETA
- BIULLETEN' PROMKOOPERATSII
- BIULLETEN' VSEROSSIISKOGO KOOPERATIVNOGO BANKA
- CHEREPOVETSKII KOOPERATOR
- CHTO CHITAT' PO PROMYSLOVOI KOOPERATSII
- DAL'NEVOSTOCHNAIA KOOPERATSIIA
- DEISTVUIUSHCHEE KOOPERATIVNOE ZAKONODATEL'STVO
- DEREVENSKAIA KOOPERATSIIA
- DONSKOI PRODOVOL'STVENNIK I KOOPERATOR
- DUMY KOOPERATORA
- EKONOMICHESKII ZHURNAL
- ENISEISKII KOOPERATOR
- EZHEGODNIK PROIZVODSTVENNOI KOOPERATSII 1925 G
- GOLOS KOOPERATORA
- GOLOS KOOPERATSII
- GOLOS SIMBIRSKOI KOOPERATSII
- GOROD I DEREVNIA
- IAKUTSKAIA KOOPERATSIIA
- IRKUTSKII KOOPERATOR
- IUZHNYI KOOPERATOR
- IUZNYI POTREBITEL'
- IZDANIIA TSENTROSOIUZA ZA 25 LET (1898-1923)
- IZVESTIIA CHELIABINSKOGO OBSHCHESTVA POTREBITELEI RABOCHIKH I SLUZHASHCHIKH
- IZVESTIIA MOSKOVSKOGO NARODNOGO BANKA
- IZVESTIIA OMGUBSOIUZA
- IZVESTIIA PERMSKOGO GORODSKOGO OBSHCHESTVA POTREBITELEI
- IZVESTIIA PSKOVSKOGO GUBSOIUZA
- IZVESTIIA TVERSKOGO GUBSOIUZA
- IZVESTIIA VOLOGDSKOGO OBSHCHESTVA SEL'SKOGO KHOZIAISTVA
- IZVESTIJA SAMARSKOGO OBSHCHESTVA POTREBITELEI "SAMOPOMOSHCH"
- KAK KREST'IANINU OBZAVESTIS' MASHINOI
- KALUZHSKII KOOPERATOR
- KATALOG IZDANII PO KUSTARNOI PROMYSHLENNOSTI I PROMYSLOVOI KOOPERATSII
- KLASSY I KOOPERATSIIA V DEREVNE SSSR
- KOOPERATIVNAIA MYSL'
- KOOPERATIVNAIA SIBIR'
- KOOPERATIVNAIA VIATKA
- KOOPERATIVNAIA ZHIZN'
- KOOPERATIVNAIA ZHIZN' KARELII
- KOOPERATIVNOE DELO
- KOOPERATIVNOE SLOVO
- KOOPERATIVNOE STROITEL'STVO
- KOOPERATIVNOE ZHILISHCHE
- KOOPERATIVNYI BIULLETEN'
- KOOPERATIVNYI BIULLETEN' SUMRAISOIUZA
- KOOPERATIVNYI BYT
- KOOPERATIVNYI KREDIT
- KOOPERATIVNYI KREDIT V SEVERO-ZAPADNOM KRAE
- KOOPERATIVNYI LISTOK
- KOOPERATIVNYI MIR
- KOOPERATIVNYI MOLOT
- KOOPERATIVNYI PUT'

- KOOPERATIVNYI URAL
- [/KOOPERATIVNYI/] VESTNIK NIZHEGORODSKOI SOIUZA UCHREZHDENII MELKOGO KREDITA
- KOOPERATOR
- KOOPERATSIIA
- KOOPERATSIIA I ZHIZN'
- KOOPERATSIIA SEVERA
- KOOPERATSIIA V SOVETSKOI DEEREVNE
- KOSTROMSKOI KOOPERATOR
- KUBANSKII KOOPERATOR
- KURSKII KOOPERATOR
- KUSTAR'-KOOPERATOR
- LESNAIA KOOPERATSIIA
- MATERIALY PO KOOPERATSII NOVGORODSKOI GUBERNII
- OBSHCHESTVA, TOVARISHCHESTVA, TRESTY, ARTELI, KOOPERATIVY I DRUGIE OB"EDINENIIA
- OCHERKI DEREVENSKOI KOOPERATSII
- REKOMENDATE L'NYI SPISOK KNIG DLIA KOMPLEKTOVANIIA I POPOLNENIIA BIBLIOTEK SEL'SKOKHOZIAISTVENNOI, KUST.-PROM. KOOPERATSII I OBSHCHESTV SEL.-KHOZ. KREDITA
- SEL'SKOKHOZIAISTVENNAIA KOOPERATSIIA I GOSPROMYSHLENNOST'
- SISTEMATICHESKII SPISOK KOOPERATIVNOI LITERATURY, BYVSHEI NA VYSTAVKE PRI KURSAKH PO ORGANIZATSII MESTNYKH KOOPERATIVNYKH KURSOV S 27 MARTA PO 5 APRELIA 1915 GODA
- SISTEMATICHESKII UKAZATEL' RUSSKOI LITERATURY PO KOOPERATSII 1856-1924 GG
- SVODNYI BALANS PO KRYMSKOI MESTNOI TRESTIROVANNOI GOSPROMYSHLENNOSTI,...I KOOPERATSII ZA 1924-1925 OPERATSIONNYI GOD
- TRUDY INSTRUKTORSKOGO SOVESHCHANIIA PO SCHETOVODSTVU SEL'SKOKHOZIAISTVENNYKH KOOPERATIVOV
- UKAZATEL' KNIG DLIA CHTENIIA PO VOPROSAM KOOPERATSII
- UKAZATEL' KNIG I STATEI O KOOPERATSII I MELKOM NARODNOM KREDITE
- UKAZATEL' KNIG PO SEL'SKOMU KHOZIAISTVU ZA 1923-25 GG
- V POMOSHCH' SEL'SKOMU KOOPERATORU
- VTOROE SOBRANIE UPOLNOMOCHENNYKH VSEROSSIISKOGO SOIUZA SEL'SKOKHOZIAISTVENNOI KOOPERATSII 22-27 FEVRALIA 1924 GODA

COOPERATIVE NEWS – Portland OR. May 1895 – 1 – us U.O. Library [071]

Cooperative Women's Guild *see* MINUTES, CORRESPONDENCE, REPORTS, ETC

LES COOPERATIVES ET L'ALGERIE / Algeria. Chambre de Commerce et d'Industrie d'Alger – 1969. BNE-8702 1 – 9 – ne IDC [334]

CO-OPERATOR – Auburn. Wash. 1923-1924 – 1 – us UMI [071]

CO-OPERATOR – v1-12. 1898-1906 – 2r – 1 – us Ross [073]

THE CO-OPERATOR – (Library has: v.1, no. 22, 25, 27; v.2, no. 37 (April, July, Sept. 1962; Oct./Nov. 1963) – Accra, Ghana: The Cooperator, 1960 – 1 – CSUX86-S96 – us Hoover Inst Photo [960]

IL CO-OPERATORE – Pueblo, CO, 1918-1919 – 1r – 1 – us I.H.R.C. [978]

LA COOPERAZIONE – Barre, VT, 1911 – 3r – 1 – us I.H.R.C. [978]

COOPER'S CHANCERY REPORTS / Tennessee. Supreme Court – v1-3. 1872-1878 (all publ) – 25mf – 9 – $37.50 – LLMC 91-040 – us L.L.M.C. [340]

COOPER'S CLARKSBURG REGISTER – Clarksburg. West Virginia. 1851-58 – 1 – us UMI [071]

COOPER'S JOURNAL : OR UNFETTERED THINKER AND PLAIN SPEAKER FOR TRUTH, FREEDOM AND PROGRESS – 1-30 (all publ). 1850 – 5mf – 9 – $65.00 – us UPA [335]

Cooray, L J M *see* LIBERAL DEMOCRACY: PROBLEMS AND CHALLENGES

COORDINATING GROUP FOR RELIGION IN SOCIETY (CGRS) – Bangkok. 32 docs. 1980-1989 – 15mf – 9 – ne IDC [320]

COORDINATING SECRETARIAT FOR PLANTATION AREAS – Kandy. 47 docs. 1980-1991 – 11mf – 9 – ne IDC [320]

COORDINATION CHEMISTRY REVIEWS – v1-59. 1966-84 – 1,5,6,13 – sz Elsevier [073]

LA COORDINATION EN FRANCAIS MODERNE : THEORIE A L'EPREUVE D'UN CORPUS / Ruppli, M – 1988 – F190.00 – fr Ethnologie [440]

COORDINATOR *see* FAMILY COORDINATOR

Coornhert, D V *see*
- IVSTIFICATIE DES MAGISTRAETS TOT LEYDEN IN HOLLANDT, TEGHENS DE CALUMNIEN, TER SAKEN VANDE DIFFERENTEN
- RECHT GHEBRUYCK ENDE MISBRUYCK, VAN TIJDLICKE HAVE
- RECHT GHEBRUYCK ENDE MISBRUYCK VAN TYDLICKE HAVE
- VANDE BEIAERDEN DOOPE: CORTE ENDE GETROUWE WAERSCHOUWINGHE
- ZEDEKUNST, DAT IS WELLEVENSKUNSTE, UITG. B. BECKER

COOS BAY HARBOR – North Bend, OR. -w. 14 Jan 1905-28 Dec 1950. 18 rolls – 1 – us U.O. Library [071]

COOS BAY NEWS – Marshfield OR. Mar 17 1875, Aug 12 19 26 1902, Jan 13 1903, Oct 4 1904 + – 1 – us U.O. Library [071]

COOS BAY NEWS – Marshfield, OR. -w. 1893-1917 – 1 – 113.00 – us Oregon Hist [071]

COOS BAY NEWS – Marshfield. Or. -w. 1900-01, 1907-17 – 1 – us UMI [071]

COOS BAY NEWS – Marshfield, OR. -w. 5 Dec 1877-26 Dec 1899. – 1r – 1 – us U.O. Library [071]

COOSAWHATCHIE BAPTIST CHURCH. JASPER COUNTY. SOUTH CAROLINA : CHURCH RECORDS – 1941-73 – 1 – $17.78 – us Baptist [240]

COOTAMUNDRA HERALD – Jan 1 1898-Dec 30 1910 – 9 – at Pascoe [072]

Coote, Edmund *see* THE ENGLISH SCHOOLMASTER

LE COPAIN – St-Henri a Montreal, Canada. avr 1963-v1 n3. jul 1963 – 1r – 1 – Can$25.00 – cn Can Microfilming [072]

Copart, J *see* UNE RUE DE TOMBEAUX A SAQQARAH

Copas, J V *see* DIARY

Cope, Edward Drinker *see* THEOLOGY OF EVOLUTION: A LECTURE

Cope, Elmer Fern *see*
- ELMER FERN COPE PAPERS
- THE ELMER FERN COPE PAPERS

Cope, Henry Frederick *see* THE EVOLUTION OF THE SUNDAY SCHOOL

Cope, Robert K *see* COMRADE BILL

COPEIA – (1980- 5,6,9) – 1913- – 1 – us UMI [073]

Copeland, E B *see*
- HYMENOPHYLLUM
- TRICHOMANES

Copeland, Edward Brent *see* THE DEVELOPMENT OF LONG-RANGE GOALS FOR THE FIRST BAPTIST CHURCH OF FAIRFIELD, OHIO

Copeland Island. Co. Down. Ireland *see* DONAGHADEE CEMETERY, MONUMENTAL INSCRIPTIONS

Copeland, R P *see* SPORT SPONSORSHIP IN CANADA

COPERNICUS ATAU RAHASIA-RAHASIA LANGIT, BERSAMA RIWAJAT GIORDANO BRUNO, GALILEI, KEPLER DAN NEWTON – SE-2002 1. 1948? – 22mf – 9 – ne IDC [520]

COPESCAL *see*
- REPORT OF THE 2ND SESSION OF THE WORKING PARTY ON AQUACULTURE. GUAYAQUIL, ECUADOR, SEPTEMBER 1986
- REPORT OF THE 2ND SESSION OF THE WORKING PARTY ON FISHERIES TECHNOLOGY. SAN SALVADOR, 1985
- REPORT OF THE 5TH SESSION OF THE COMMISSION FOR INLAND FISHERIES OF LATIN AMERICA

COPIA CERTIFICADA DEL PRIVILEGIO REAL DE LA VILLA DE ACEHUCHE. ANO 1573 – 1 – sp Bibl Santa Ana [946]

COPIA DE LA PROTESTA...CONGRESO... ELECCION DE CORIA / Gutierrez Utrera, Benigno – 1886 – 9 – 1.50f – sp Bibl Santa Ana [946]

COPIA DE LA RELACION...VIAGE...CADIZ A CARTAGENA DE INDIAS / Soto y Marne, Francisco de – 1753 – 9 – 1.50f – sp Bibl Santa Ana [946]

COPIA POETICA DEL CUADRO DE LA ANUNCIACION... / Salas, Francisco Gregorio de – Madrid, 1781 – 1 – sp Bibl Santa Ana [810]

COPIA...ANUNCIACION...ANTONIO R. MENGS / Salas, Francisco Grogorio de – 1781 – 9 – 1.50f – sp Bibl Santa Ana [810]

COPIAH CO. NEWS – Hazelhurst. Miss. 1942-1951 – 1 – us UMI [071]

COPIE D'AVTRES NOVVELLES DE ROME: ... – Paris, 1561 – 1mf – 9 – H-8158/1 – ne IDC [910]

COPIE DE LA CORRESPONDENCE ECHANGEE ENTRE L'EVEQUE CATHOLIQUE ROMAIN DE TORONTO DE LE SURINTENDANT-EN-CHEF DES ECOLES, AU SUJET DES ECOLES SEPAREES DANS LE HAUT-CANADA. – Quebec: Imp. John Lovell, 1852. SEM105P367 – 1mf – 9 – Can$2.25 – cn Bibl Nat [370]

COPIE DE LA LETTRE ENUOIEE PAR SELIM EMPEREUR DES TURQZ, AU SEIGNEUR DOMP IOUAN D'AUSTRIE, CAPITAINE GENERAL DE LA LIGUE SAINCTE – Paris, 1572 – 1mf – 9 – H-8190/1 – ne IDC [956]

COPIE DE LA PETITION ADRESSEE AU GOUVERNEUR EN CONSEIL PAR LES HONORABLES MESSIEURS CHAPLEAU, CHURCH ET ANGERS DEMANDANT LA DESTITUTION DE SON HONNEUR LUC LETELLIER, LIEUTENANT-GOUVERNEUR DE LA PROVINCE DE QUEBEC – Ottawa: Maclean, Roger, 1879. SEM105P833 – 2mf – 9 – Can$4.50 – cn Bibl Nat [971]

COPIE DES LETTRES DE SON EX[CE] **ENVOIEES A MONSEIGNEUR LE BARON DE BILLY GOUVERNEUR DE LILLE, DOUAY ET ORCHIES, TOUCHANT LA GRANDE HEUREUSE ET MEMORABLE VICTOIRE DE L'ARMEE DE SA MAJESTE IMPERIALLE CONTRE LES TURCS ET HONGRES** – Dovay, 1594 – 1mf – 9 – H-8210/1 – ne IDC [956]

COPIE DU PRONONCE DE L'ARREST DE LA COUR DU PARLEMENT DE PROVENCE AU SUJET DE L'AFFAIRE DU PERE JEAN-BAPTISTE GIRARD, JESUITE; ET DE CATHERINE CADIERE – S. 1. 1731 – 9 – fr Hachette [360]

COPIES DE CORRESPONDANCES ENTRE LE SURINTENDANT-EN-CHEF DES ECOLES POUR LE HAUT-CANADA ET AUTRES PERSONNES, AU SUJET DES ECOLES SEPAREES / Canada. Departement de l'Instruction Publique pour le Haut-Canada – Toronto: Lovell et Gibson, 1855. SEM105P338 – 3mf – 9 – Can$6.75 – cn Bibl Nat [370]

COPIES DE PIECES SUR LA PEROUSE, APPARTENANT A M. DE LAJARIETTE / La Perouse, Jean-Francois de G de – 19th cent – 1 – F50.00 – fr Armell [944]

COPIES OF ADDRESS OF THE HOUSE OF ASSEMBLY TO THE GOVERNOR-GENERAL RESPECTING THE CIVIL LIST; OF REPORT OF SEIGNIORIAL TENURES; AND C. – [London, England: s.n., 1844]. SEM105P1737 – 1mf – 9 – Can$2.25 – cn Bibl Nat [333]

COPIES OF ALL ORDINANCES, ...PASSED BY THE SPECIAL COUNCIL AND GOVERNOR OF LOWER CANADA, SINCE THE 24TH DAY OF NOVEMBER 1838 – London: s.n., 1839. SEM105P1372 – 1mf – 9 – Can$2.25 – cn Bibl Nat [324]

COPIES OF CORRESPONDENCE BETWEEN AUSTRALIAN PREMIERS CONCERNING RATES OF PAY, 1900-1900 / Chief Secretary's Office, Queensland – 1 reel – 1 – CRS B5160 – at Archives [920]

COPIES OF CORRESPONDENCE BETWEEN MEMBERS OF THE GOVERNMENT AND THE CHIEF SUPERINTENDENT OF SCHOOLS ON THE SUBJECT OF THE SCHOOL LAW FOR UPPER CANADA AND EDUCATION GENERALLY, WITH APPENDICES / Canada. Departement de l'Instruction Publique pour le Haut-Canada – Toronto: Printed by Lovell and Gibson, 1850. SEM105P339 – 1mf – 9 – Can$2.25 – cn Bibl Nat [370]

COPIES OF CORRESPONDENCE BETWEEN THE ROMAN CATHOLIC BISHOP OF TORONTO AND THE CHIEF SUPERINTENDENT OF SCHOOLS IN UPPER CANADA / Canada. Departement de l'Instruction Publique pour le Haut-Canada – Quebec: Printed by John Lovell, 1852. SEM105P331 – 1mf – 9 – Can$2.25 – cn Bibl Nat [370]

COPIES OF CORRESPONDENCE RELATIVE TO THE AFFAIRS OF CANADA / Canada. Parliament. House of Commons – House of Commons: s.l., 1839. SEM105P402 – 1mf – 9 – Can$2.25 – cn Bibl Nat [324]

COPIES OF LETTERS AND TELEGRAMS RECEIVED AND SENT BY GOVERNOR ZEBULON B. VANCE OF NORTH CAROLINA, 1862-65 / U.S. War Department. Confederate Records – 1roll. T731 – 1 – us Nat'l Archives [324]

COPIES OF LETTERS SENT BY THE OUTFACTORS OF THE ROYAL AFRICAN COMPANY OF ST ENGLAND TO THE CHIEF AGENTS AT CAPE COAST CASTLE FROM JANUARY 1681-1699 – [Cape Coast Castle, 1699] – us Res Libr [960]

COPIES OF LISTS OF PASSENGERS ARRIVING AT MISCELLANEOUS PORTS ON THE ATLANTIC AND GULF COASTS AND AT PORTS ON THE GREAT LAKES, 1820-73 / U.S. Bureau of the Customs – 16 rolls. M575 – 1 – us Nat'l Archives [324]

COPIES OF SPEECHES / Case, Nelson – 1867-1920 – 1 – us KS Hist [978]

COPIES OF WAR DEPT. CORRESPONDENCE AND REPORTS, 1791-96 / U.S. War Department. Office of the Secretary – 1roll. T982 – 1 – us Nat'l Archives [324]

COPIES OR EXTRACTS OF CORRESPONDENCE RELATIVE, TO THE AFFAIRS OF BRITISH NORTH AMERICA – [London, England]: [s.n.], [1839]. SEM105P111 – 5mf – 9 – Can$11.25 – cn Bibl Nat [971]

COPIES OR EXTRACTS OF CORRESPONDENCE RELATIVE TO THE AFFAIRS OF CANADA / Canada. Parliament. House of Commons – House of Commons: s.l., 1839. SEM105P403 – 1mf – 9 – Can$2.25 – cn Bibl Nat [324]

COPIES OR EXTRACTS OF CORRESPONDENCE RELATIVE TO THE AFFAIRS OF CANADA – House of Commons: s.l., 1839. SEM105P403 – 1mf – 9 – Can$2.25 – cn Bibl Nat [971]

COPIES OR EXTRACTS OF CORRESPONDENCE RELATIVE TO THE AFFAIRS OF CANADA – s.l., s.n., 1839. SEM105P404 – 1mf – 9 – Can$2.25 – cn Bibl Nat [971]

COPILACION...ORDEN...SANTIAGO DEL ESPADA / Tapia, Gregorio de – 1605 – 9 – 1.50f – sp Bibl Santa Ana [946]

COPING WITH CRISIS : AUSTERITY, ADJUSTMENT AND HUMAN RESOURCES / ed by Samoff, Joel – 1995 – 284p – 9 – 92-3-102973-8 – Co-publ with Cassell/ UNESCO Publishing – fr UNESCO [300]

Copinger, WA *see* ON THE ENGLISH TRANSLATIONS OF THE "IMITATIO CHRISTI"

Copinger, Walter Arthur *see* THE MANORS OF SUFFOLK; NOTES ON THEIR HISTORY AND DEVOLUTION, WITH SOME ILLUSTRATIONS OF THE OLD MANOR HOUSES

Copland, James *see* A DICTIONARY OF PRACTICAL MEDICINE (AEL, ABT 3;14)

Copland, John A *see* A METEOR KING

COPLAS DEL BAILE DEL PANDERO / Gutierrez Macias, Valeriano – (Sep. Rev. Dialectologia y Tradiciones Populares. Tomo 17, 1961. Cuaderno No 3, pp. 401-415) – Madrid: C. Bermejo Impresor, 1961 – 1 – sp Bibl Santa Ana [946]

Copp, Henry N *see* U.S. MINERAL LANDS

Copp, Henry Norris *see*
- AMERICAN MINING CODE
- "COPP'S MINING DECISIONS"
- MINING DECISIONS OF THE SECRETARY OF THE INTERIOR AND THE COMMISSIONER OF THE GENERAL LAND OFFICE
- PUBLIC LAND LAWS OF THE UNITED STATES, 1869-1882
- PUBLIC LAND LAWS OF THE UNITED STATES, 1882-1890
- PUBLIC LAWS PASSED BY CONGRESS FROM APRIL 1, 1882 TO JANUARY 1, 1890.
- UNITED STATES MINERAL LANDS.

Coppell, William George *see* MISCELLANEOUS PAPERS CONCERNING EDUCATION IN THE COOK ISLANDS, 1922-66

Coppens, Charles *see*
- A BRIEF TEXT-BOOK OF MORAL PHILOSOPHY
- MORAL PRINCIPLES AND MEDICAL PRACTICE
- THE MYSTIC TREASURES OF THE HOLY MASS

Coppens, J *see* L'IMPOSITION DES MAINS ET LES RITES CONNEXES DANS LE NOUVEAU TESTAMENT ET DANS L'EGLISE ANCIENNE

Coppenstein, Ioan *see*
- EX BELLARMINO EPITOME CONTROVERSIARUM OMNIUM HUIUS AEVI LUTHERO-CALVINISTICARUM
- HOMILIAE

COPPER ORE – McGill, NV. Jul-Dec 1910 – 1r – 1 – $50.00 – U04635 – us Library Micro [071]

COPPER-GOLD ERA – Rouyn, Canada. v1 n4. 9-16 oct 1926 – 1r – 1 – Can$25.00 – cn Can Microfilming [072]

COPP'S LAND OWNER – (Lacking: v8 p45-46. v9 p181-82. Index vol v18 p40. Suppl to: The Western Landowner which is not offered by LLMC) – v1-18 + index; 1874-92 (all publ) – 68mf – 9 – $102.00 – LLMC 84-448 – us L.L.M.C. [073]

"COPP'S MINING DECISIONS" / Copp, Henry Norris – Decisions of the Commissioner of the General Land Office and the Secretary of the Interior Under the U.S. Mining Statutes. 1 vol. Bancroft & Co., S.F., 1874. 84-113 – 9 – $8.00 – us L.L.M.C. [340]

COPROGENE, OU, PROCEDE DE BOMMER POUR FABRIQUER TOUTES SORTES D'ENGRAIS SURTOUT LES ENGRAIS VEGETAL ET MINERAL – Methode pratique Americaine. Traduit de l'anglais par Arthur Thiboutot. s.l.: Chs. Cote, 1881. 05398. (Pre-1900 Canadiana) – 9 – cn C.I.H.M. [971]

COPTIC AOPCRYPHAL GOSPELS / Robinson, F – 1986 – 6mf – 9 – ne Slangenburg [220]

THE COPTIC ELEMENT IN LANGUAGES OF THE INDO-EUROPEAN FAMILY / Campbell, John – Toronto: Copp, Clark, 1872. 00369. (Pre-1900 Canadiana) – 9 – cn C.I.H.M. [400]

COPTIC MANUSCRIPTS : A CHECK LIST OF COPTIC MANUSCRIPTS IN THE PIERPONT MORGAN LIBRARY – New York, 1919 – 4mf – 8 – ne Slangenburg [240]

THE COPTIC MORNING SERVICE FOR THE LORD'S DAY / John, Marquis of Butet – London, 1908 – 4mf – 8 – Dfl19.00 – ne Slangenburg [240]

Coptius, F *see* AD CAESAREM ORATIO PRO CHRISTIANA REPV...

COPTS AND MOSLEMS UNDER BRITISH CONTROL : A COLLECTION OF FACTS AND A RESUME OF AUTHORITATIVE OPINIONS ON THE COPTIC QUESTION / Mikhail, Kyriakos – London: Smith, Elder, 1911 – 1mf – us A.T.L.A. [230]

LA COPULATA DE LEYES DE INDIAS Y LAS ORDENANZAS OVANDINAS / Pena Camara, Jose de la – Madrid: Revista de Indias, 1941 – 1 – sp Bibl Santa Ana [950]

COPY : ESSAYS FROM AN EDITOR'S DRAWER ON RELIGION, LITERATURE, AND LIFE / Thompson, Hugh Miller – Hartford, CT: M H Mallory, 1872 – 1mf – 9 – 0-8370-5586-5 – 1985-3586 – us A.T.L.A. [240]

COPY OF A COMMUNICATION AND OTHER PAPERS...FROM THE HONORABLE DENIS BENJAMIN VIGER / Viger, Denis Benjamin – s.l., s.n., 1831. SEM105P398 – 2mf – 9 – Can$4.50 – cn Bibl Nat [971]

COPY OF A DESPATCH, AND ITS ENCLOSURES, ADDRESSED TO EARL AMHERST BY THE EARL OF ABERDEEN, ON THE 2ND APRIL 1835 / Gordon, George Hamilton – [London, England: s.n., 1838]. SEM105P1392 – 1mf – 9 – Can$2.25 – cn Bibl Nat [971]

COPY OF A DESPATCH FROM LORD GODERICH TO LORD AYLMER / Goderich, Frederick John Robinson, Viscount – [London: s.n., 1841]. SEM105P1379 – 1mf – 9 – Can$2.25 – cn Bibl Nat [324]

COPY OF A DESPATCH FROM THE GOVERNOR-GENERAL OF BRITISH NORTH AMERICA, TRANSMITTING A RETURN FROM THE PRINCIPAL OF THE SEMINARY OF MONTREAL... – [London, England: s.n., 1841 ?]. SEM105P1157 – 1mf – 9 – Can$2.25 – cn Bibl Nat [240]

COPY OF A MEMORIAL FROM JAMES STUART,...TO THE RIGHT HONORABLE LORD VISCOUNT GODERICH,. / Stuart, James – s.l., s.n., s.d. SEM105P116 – 5mf – 9 – Can$11.25 – cn Bibl Nat [971]

COPY OF A MEMORIAL FROM JAMES STUART...TO THE RIGHT HONORABLE LORD VISCOUNT GODERICH.. – s.l., s.n., 1831?. SEM105P412 – 1mf – 9 – Can$2.25 – cn Bibl Nat [920]

COPY OF CORRESPONDENCE RELATING TO THE ESTABLISHMENT OF THE EARL OF DURHAM, AS GOVERNOR GENERAL OF BRITISH NORTH AMERICA AND HER MAJESTY'S HIGH COMMISSIONER – [London, England: s.n., 1838]. SEM105P1389 – 1mf – 9 – Can$2.25 – cn Bibl Nat [971]

COPY OF MEMORIAL AND PETITION FROM INHABITANTS OF THE RED RIVER SETTLEMENT,... / Hudson's Bay Company – [s.l.]: The House of Commons, 1849. SEM105P124 – 2mf – 9 – Can$4.50 – cn Bibl Nat [971]

COPY OF THE CHARTER OF THE CORPORATION OF SAINT NICOLET IN LOWER CANADA, WITH INSTRUCTIONS OF LORD BATHURST ON THE SUBJECT / Bas-Canada – [S.l.: s.n., 1841?]. SEM105P1384 – 1mf – 9 – Can$2.25 – cn Bibl Nat [370]

COPY OF THE FOURTH REPORT OF THE STANDING COMMITTEE OF THE GRIEVANCES... / Bas-Canada. Parlement. Chambre d'Assemblee. Comite Permanent des Griefs – [London]: [s.n.], [1836] – 1mf – 9 – Can$2.25 – cn Bibl Nat [971]

COPYBOOK / Palmer, Thomas – 1803. 3 fiches – 9 – us South Carolina Historical [025]

COPYBOOKS OF GEORGE WASHINGTON'S CORRESPONDENCE WITH SECRETARIES OF STATE, 1789-96 / U.S. Department of State – 1 roll. M570. Printed guide – 1 – us Nat'l Archives [975]

Copyright Association of Canada *see* INTERVIEWING THE CABINET: THE COPYRIGHT ASSOCIATION LAY THEIR CASE BEFORE THE GOVERNMENT: ABLE SPEECH BY THE PRESIDENT OF THE ASSOCIATION

COPYRIGHT BULLETIN – v1- 1967- 1; v11-5,6,9 – us UMI [340]

THE COPYRIGHT CONFERENCE – 1905, 1906. 1 reel – 1 – $50.00 – us Trans-Media [340]

COPYRIGHT IN CONGRESS, 1789-1904 : A BIBLIOGRAPHY AND CHRONOLOGICAL RECORD OF ALL PROCEEDINGS IN CONGRESS / Solberg, Thorvald – Washington: GPO, 1905 – 5mf – 9 – $7.50 – LLMC 82-312 – us L.L.M.C. [340]

COPYRIGHT, ITS HISTORY AND ITS LAW / Bowker, Richard Rogers – (Contains a chronological table of laws and cases, English and American) – New York: Houghton-Mifflin, 1912 – 3mf – 9 – $13.50 – LLMC 82-309 – us L.L.M.C. [340]

COPYRIGHT LAW : PROVISIONS OF THE U.S. COPYRIGHT LAW WITH SUMMARY OF PARALLEL PROVISIONS OF THE LAWS OF FOREIGN COUNTRIES / U. S. Laws, Statutes, etc – Washington: GPO, 1905 – 1mf – 9 – $1.50 – LLMC 82-307 – us L.L.M.C. [324]

COPYRIGHT LAW REVISION : LEGISLATIVE HISTORY: 89TH CONGRESS 2ND SESSION / U.S. Congress. House Committee of the Whole – Washington: GPO. rept no 2237 for HR4347. 1966 – 3mf – 9 – $4.50 – LLMC 82-505 – us L.L.M.C. [340]

COPYRIGHT LAW REVISION / U.S. Copyright Office – Washington: GPO. 6v. 1961-65 (all publ) – 25mf – 9 – $37.50 – LLMC 82-302 – us L.L.M.C. [340]

COPYRIGHT LAW REVISIONS : STUDIES / U.S. Copyright Office – (Prepared for the Senate Subcomm. on Patents, Trademarks and Copyright) – Washington: GPO. 86th Congress nos 1-35. 1960-72 – 23mf – 9 – $34.50 – LLMC 82-303/304 – us L.L.M.C. [324]

COPYRIGHT LAWS AND TREATIES OF THE WORLD – 3v and 25 supplements – 9 – 92-3-102650-X – fr UNESCO [340]

COPYRIGHT LAWS AND TREATIES OF THE WORLD : SUPPLEMENT NO. 26, 1989-1990 – 1993 – 9 – 92-3-102776-X – fr UNESCO [340]

COPYRIGHT OFFICE ANNUAL REPORTS / U.S. Copyright Office – (Some issues lacking) – Washington: GPO, 1912; 1928-39; 1941-71; 1977; 1979; 1982-84 – 9 – LLMC 82-311 – us L.L.M.C. [340]

COPYRIGHT OFFICE DECISIONS – (Add vols planned) – US Copyright Office, Library of Congress, 1783-1985 – 365mf – 9 – $547.00 – LLMC 78-064 – us L.L.M.C. [340]

COPYRIGHT OFFICE DECISIONS *see* COPYRIGHT OFFICE ANNUAL REPORTS

THE COPYRIGHT QUESTION – s.l.: s.n., 189?. 00231. (Pre-1900 Canadiana) – 9 – cn C.I.H.M. [971]

Copyright Society of the U.S.A. *see* JOURNAL OF THE COPYRIGHT SOCIETY OF THE U.S.A.

LE COQ – Montreal. Canada. n23. 12 mar-n25. 26 mar 1892 – 1r – 1 – Can$25.00 – cn Can Microfilming [072]

LE COQ – Quebec, Canada. 10-31 aut 1878 – 1r – 1 – Can$25.00 – cn Can Microfilming [072]

Coquelin, Ch *see* DU CREDIT ET DES BANQUES

Coquerel, Athanase *see*
- THE FINE ARTS IN ITALY IN THEIR RELIGIOUS ASPECT
- LES FORCATS POUR LA FOI

Coqueugniot, G *see* DE LA CONCLUSION DES TRAITES INTERNATIONAUX D'APRES LE DROIT PUBLIC ROMAIN

Coquilhat, Camille *see*
- SUR LE HAUT-CONGO

COQUILLE TRIBUNE – (Set incl. Coos County Courier (Coquille); Oregon Coos District Courier (Coquille)) – Coquille, OR. -w. 7 July 1934-28 Mar 1947. – 4r – 1 – us U.O. Library [071]

COQUILLE VALLEY SENTINEL – Coquille, OR. -w. 14 Nov 1913-29 Dec 1916 (Gap from 1 Jan 1917 through 31 Dec 1952) – 17r – 1 – us U.O. Library [071]

COQUILLE VALLEY SENTINEL – Coquille, OR. -w. 1917-77 – 1 – $672.00 – us Oregon Hist [071]

LES COQUILLES MARINES DES COTES DE FRANCE. DESCRIPTION DES FAMILLES, GENRES ET ESPECES / Locard, A – Z-624 2. 1892 – 8 – ne IDC [590]

COR – Havana, CU. 1967-1969 – 1r – $50.00 – R04198 – us Library Micro [072]

COR ARDENS / Ivanov, V – Plamennoe serdtse. Kniga pervaia. Kniga vtoraia. M. 1911-12. BR-734 2 – 8 – ne IDC [460]

O CORACAO DOS CRITICOS – [s.l.]. 16 Mar 1890 – 1,5,6 – bl Biblioteca [072]

THE CORACLE – 1953-88 (complete) – 3r – 1 – ATLA S0630 – us A.T.L.A. [073]

THE CORAL ISLAND : A TALE OF THE PACIFIC OCEAN / Ballantyne, Robert Michael – London: T. Nelson, 1858 – 1 roll – 1 – 1-55879-546-4 – uk Libr Preservation [830]

Coral, L *see* CONFLICTO INTERNATIONAL, (ECUADOR Y PERU)

CORAL REEFS – 1993 – 36p – 9 – 92-3-102601-1 – fr UNESCO [910]

CORAL TRIBUNE – Key West. Fl. -w. 1954-1963 Sept – 1 – us P.K. Yonge [071]

CORALS FROM THE GULF OF CALIFORNIA AND THE NORTH PACIFIC COAST OF AMERICA / Durham, John Wyatt – New York; 1947 – 1 – us U.W. Library [590]

LE CORAN : TRADUCTION SELON UN ESSAI DE RECLASSEMENT DES SOURATES / Blachere, R – Paris, 1947. v1, 2, 3 – 21mf – 8 – ne Slangenburg [260]

Corancez, Olivier de *see* DE JEAN-JACQUES ROUSSEAU

Corbachius, I *see* CONTRA ANABAPTISTAS UNICI BAPTISMATIS ASSERTIO

Corbeil, F *see* LE VRAI LOUP-GAROU

Corbeil, Sylvio *see* CHOMEDEY DE MAISONNEUVE: DRAME CHRETIEN EN TROIS ACTES: SAMUEL DE CHAMPLAIN, PAGES ORATOIRES: TROIS AUREOLES

Corbeil, Wilfrid *see* L'ESTUDIANT

Corbett, B *see* CENSORED

Corbett, Boston *see* PAPERS OF BOSTON CORBETT

Corbett, Charles H *see* OLD TESTAMENT STORY

Corbett, F *see* LA GUITARRE ROYALLE

Corbett, J Stafford *see*
- THE CAMPAIGN OF TRAFALGAR
- SOME PRINCIPLES OF MARITIME STRATEGY

Corbett, John Maxwell *see* AZTEC RUINS NATIONAL MONUMENT, NEW MEXICO

CORBETTS HERALD – Providence. R.I. 1884-1886; 1891-1918 – 1 – us UMI [071]

Corbiere, Emilio J *see*
- CONVERSACIONES CON OSCAR ALENDE
- EL MITO ALFONSINISTA

THE CORBIN COLLECTION, 1 / Corbin, Walter E & Corbin, Lottie S – (MASSACHUSETTS: Hampshire County: Reel 1: Amherst; Reel 2: Amherst; Reel 3: Belchertown; Reel 4: Belchertown; Reel 5: Chesterfield; Reel 6: Easthampton; Reel 7: Enfield, Florence, Goshen, Granby; Reel 8: Hadley; Reel 9: Hatfield; Reel 9A: Hatfield; Reel 10: Huntington, Middlefield; Reel 11: Northampton; Reel 12: Northampton; Reel 13: Northampton; Reel 13A: Northampton; Reel 14: Northampton; Reel 15: Northampton; Reel 16: Northampton; Reel 17: Norwich, Pelham, Prescott, South Hadley; Reel 18: Southampton; Reel 19: Southampton; Reel 20: Ware; Reel 21: Washington; Reel 22: Williamsburg; Reel 23: Williamsburg; Hampden County: Reel 24: Brimfield;) – 1650-1850 – 60r – 1 – $1,800.00 $30.00r – us New England [920]

THE CORBIN COLLECTION, 2 : COLLECTION DIVIDED INTO TWO PARTS FOR EDITORIAL PURPOSES – (Reel 25: Brimfield; Reel 26: Chicopee, Hampden, Holland, Holyoke, Ludlow; Reel 27: Monson; Reel 28: Monson; Reel 29: Monson; Reel 30: Montgomery, Russell, Springfield; Reel 31: Wales; Reel 32: Wales; Reel 33: Westfield, West Springfield, Wilbraham; Franklin County: Reel 34: Ashfield, Bernardston, Charlemont, Colrain, Hawley; Reel 35: Leverett, Leyden, New Salem, Northfield; Reel 36: Shutesbury, South Deerfield, Sunderland; Reel 36A: Warwick, Wendell, Whately; Berkshire County: Reel 37: Cheshire, Great Barrington, Hancock, Lanesborough, Monterey; Reel 38: New Marlborough, Otis, Peru; Reel 39: Pittsfield; Reel 40: Sandisfield, Savoy, Williamstown; Worcester County, Middlesex County, and Suffolk County: Reel 41: Paxton. Dunstable, Groton, Pepperell, Shirley, Watertown. Charlestown, Dorchester; Plymouth County, Norfolk County, and Bristol County: Reel 42: Hingham, Marshfield, Middleborough. Dedham. Dighton; Connecticut, Rhode Island, and New Hampshire: Reel 43: Gilead (in Hebron), Norwalk, Stafford, Stamford, West Stafford, Willington, Connecticut. South Kingston, Rhode Island. Gosport, New Hampshire; GENEALOGIES: Reel 44: Alexander-Daniels; Reel 45: Dickinson-Fisk; Reel 46: Granger-Holton; Reel 47: King; Reel 47A: Kirkland-Page; Reel 48: Parker-Utley; Reel 49: Wahl-Woodruff; Reel 50: Achilles-Hyde; Reel 51: Ingersoll-Wylly; SOURCE NOTES – Massachusetts, Connecticut, and Phillimore Index: Reel 52: Cape Cod, Hampshire County, Massachusetts State. Bible Records: Allen-Wright. Connecticut State. Phillimore Index; GENERAL: Reel 53: Notes on sources in New England records. General Catalog; Reel 53A: Notes on sources in New England records. General Catalog; Reel 54: General Catalog; Reel 55: General Catalog) – 1650-1850 – 60r – 1 – $1,800.00 set $30.00r – us New England [920]

Corbin, David Timothy *see* THE LAW OF PERSONAL INJURIES IN THE STATE OF ILLINOIS, AND THE REMEDIES AND DEFENSES OF LITIGANTS

Corbin, Le P *see* MEMOIRE SUR LES PRINCIPAUX OBJETS DE L'EDUCATION PUBLIQUE

Corbin, Lottie S *see* THE CORBIN COLLECTION, 1

Corbin, Walter E *see* THE CORBIN COLLECTION, 1

Corbin, William Horace *see*
- THE ACT CONCERNING CORPORATIONS IN THE STATE OF NEW JERSEY, APPROVED APRIL 7, 1875
- AN ACT CONCERNING CORPORATIONS (REVISION OF 1896), TAKING EFFECT JULY 4, 1896, IN THE STATE OF NEW JERSEY.

Corbon, Anthime *see* DE L'ENSEIGNEMENT PROFESSIONNEL

Corbu, A C *see* ESSAI SUR LA NOTION DE REGLE DE DROIT...

LE CORBUSIER. OEUVRES PLASTIQUES / Reunion des musees nationaux. Paris – 1953. 8 illus. 1 fiche – 9 – fr Réunion [730]

Corcho Asenjo, Leopoldo *see* QUIENES SON LOS TESTIGOS DE JEHOVA

Corchon Garcia, Justo *see* INSCRIPCIONES CACERENAS INEDITAS

Corcoran, A *see* SAINT ASELLUS: TRANSLATION DE SES RELIQUES DAN LA CHAPELIE DU COLLEGE JOLIETTE, LE 3 NOVEMBRE 1892: SERMON PRONONCE A CETTE OCCASION

CORCORAN JOURNAL – Corcoran, CA. 1971- – 19+ r – 1 – $950.00 ($50.00y) – B02137 – us Library Micro [071]

Corcuera Manso, Fidel *see* CONTRIBUCION AL ESTUDIO DE LAS ORACIONES FINALES Y CAUSALES EN FRANCES

Cord, Steven *see* RIGHTS COME NOT FROM NATURE BUT FROM REASON

Cord, William H *see* A TREATISE ON THE LEGAL AND EQUITABLE RIGHTS OF MARRIED WOMEN

Corda, A C *see*
- ICONES FUNGORUM HUCUSQUE COGNITORUM

Cordain, Loren *see* INFLUENCE OF BODY FAT MASS ON EXCESS POST-EXERCISE OXYGEN CONSUMPTION

Cordeiro da Matta, J D *see*
- ENSAIO DE DICCIONARIO KIMBUNDU-PORTUGUEZ.
- JISABU, JIHENG'ELE, IFIKA NI JINONGONONGO, JOSONEKE MU LIMOUNDU NI PUTU, KUA MON'ANGOLA JAKIM RIA MATTA

Cordell, Victor V *see* JOURNAL OF TRANSNATIONAL MANAGEMENT DEVELOPMENT

Cordemoy, G de *see* DISCOURS PHISIQUE DE LA PAROLE

Cordemoy, J L de *see* NOUVEAU TRAITE DE TOUTE L'ARCHITECTURE.
CORDER BAPTIST CHURCH. CORDER, MISSOURI : CHURCH RECORDS – 1871-1901 – 1 – 7.11 – us Baptist [240]
Cordero, Juan Luis *see*
- HOJAS DE ARBOL CAIDAS
- MI PATRIA Y MI DAMA
- MI TORRE DE BABEL
- LA MUSA DEL PECADO
- LA MUSA INGENUA...LA MUSA DEL CONSUELO...LA MUSA CIVICA
- REGIONALISMO
- LA ROMERIA DE LA LUZ
- VIDA Y ENSUENO

Cordero Marina, Pedro *see* DON JUAN DE AUSTRIA
LOS CORDEROS DE LA PASCUA Y NINGUNA TRUJILLANA ES GUAPA / Ramos Sanguino, Joaquin – Trujillo: Tip. Sobrino de B. Pena, 1919 – 1 – sp Bibl Santa Ana [946]
Cordes, Marie-Dominique *see* L'EXTENSION ET L'UTILISATION DES TERRAINS CONQUIS SUR LA MER AU JAPON
Cordeu, Mora *see* PERONISMO, LA MAYORIA PERDIDA
Cordier, F S *see* BESCHREIBUNG UND ABBILDUNG DES ESSBAREN UND GIFTIGEN SCHWAEMME, WELCHE IN DEUTSCHLAND UND FRANKREICH WACHSEN
Cordier, Henri *see*
- BIBLIOTHECA SINICA
- LE CHRISTIANISME EN CHINE ET EN ASIE CENTRALE SOUS LES MONGOLS
- DICTIONNAIRE BIBLIOGRAPHIQUE DES OUVRAGES RELATIFS A LA PENINSULE INDOCHINOISE

Cordner, John *see*
- IS PROTESTANTISM A FAILURE?: THE QUESTION CONSIDERED IN FIVE LECTURES: ALSO A DISCOURSE ON CHRISTIAN MONOTHEISM
- TWENTY-FIVE SERMONS: A MEMORIAL OF TWENTY-FIVE YEARS' MINISTRY

Cordoba, Tomas *see* LA ARGENTINA, PERON Y DESPUES
CORDOBESAS / Fernandez de Molina Menitez Donoso, Antonio – 1894 – 9 – 1.50f – sp Bibl Santa Ana [946]
Cordonnier, R *see* FEMMES AFRICAINES ET COMMERCE
Cordovani, P M *see* ELEMENTA IURIS NATURALIS INTERNATIONALIS
Cordovez Moure, J M *see* REMINISCENCIAS
Cordus, V *see*
- ANNOTATIONES IN PEDACII DIOSCORIDIS ANAZARBEI DE MATERIA MEDICA...
- ANNOTATIONES IN PEDACII DIOSCORIDIS ANAZARBEIDE DE MEDICA MATERIA

CORE = COLLECTED ORIGINAL RESOURCES IN EDUCATION – 1977- 17v – 9 – £313.00y – 0308-6909 – uk Carfax [370]
CORE: ADDENDUM / Congress of Racial Equality – 1944-68 – 25r – 1 – us UMI [360]
COREFICHE : ANTHOLOGIES LISTED IN GRANGER'S INDEX TO POETRY – (Phase 2: 298 additional vols from Granger's and other select indexes 354mf. Phase 3: 281 new vols 330mf. Both $2,245.00) – Phase 1: 150,000 poems in 781 vols (747 anthologies) from the first 8 eds. of Granger's.... Covers 1904-73. Master index-author, title, first line, with subject classification, for Phases 1,2 and 3 – 950mf – 9 – $5,000.00 – us Roth [810]
COREFICHE : BOOKS LISTED IN THE SHORT STORY INDEX – (Phase 2: 125v 150mf $1,000.00. Phase 3: 125v 155mf $1,000.00. Phase 4: 125v 136mf $1,000.00. Phase 5: 125v 130mf $1,000.00. Phase 6: 125v 130mf $1,000.00. Phase 7 65v 100mf $800.00) – Phase 1: 314v indexed in the 1st cumulative ed of the Short Story Index (1900-49). Roth's Index to Short Stories author/title index with genre classification – 345mf – 9 – $2,500.00 – us Roth [830]
COREFICHE : CORE POETRY COLLECTION – (Part 1: 90 books on 106mf. ISBN 0-8486-7049-3. $800.00; Part 2: 101 vols on 135mf. ISBN 0-8486-7048-5. $800.00) – us Roth [420]
COREFICHE : FULL-TEXT OF BOOKS LISTED IN THE ESSAY AND GENERAL LITERATURE INDEX – (Phase 2: 290v listed in 1st 7 eds of EGLI (1900-69) 334mf in storage trays $2,500.00. Phase 3: 260v indexed in 1st 7 permanent cumulative eds of the EGLI (1900-69) 341mf $2,250.00. Phase 4: 224v indexed in the 1st 7 permanent cumulative eds of the EGLI (1900-69) 248mf $2,000.00. Phase 5: 300v 335mf $2,500.00. Phase 6: 300v 334mf $2,500.00. Phase 7: 300v 361mf $2,500.00. Phase 8: 300v 379mf $2,500.00. Phase 9: 300v 329mf $2,500.00. Phase 10: 300v 379mf $2,500.00. Phase 11: 300v 379mf $2,500.00. Phase 12: 100v 200mf $1,750.00. Essay Index by author/title/subject) – Phase 1: 136 complete vols listed in 1st ed of EGLI (1900-33) – 280mf – 9 – $1,568.00 – us Roth [840]
COREFICHE : GREAT AMERICAN AND ENGLISH ESSAYS – 2,376 essays by 1,239 authors on 147mf – $500.00 – 0-8486-4141-8 – us Roth [420]
COREFICHE : LITERARY CRITICISM – A BASIC COLLECTION – 102 vols. 115 fiches. Roth's Index to Literary Criticism-author/title/subject index – 9 – $700.00 – us Roth [840]
COREFICHE : WORLD'S BEST DRAMA – Nine hundred plays by 275 dramatists in 50,000p. 160 fiches. Roth's Index to World's Best Drama by author/title/character/genre/topic/nationality – 9 – $1,000.00 – 0-8486-9000-1 – us Roth [790]
THE COREGENCY OF RAMSES 2 / Seele, Keith – 9 – $10.00 – us I.R.C. [930]
Corelli, Arcangelo *see*
- CORELLI'S 12 SOLOS...OP. 5
- CORELLI'S CELEBRATED TWELVE CONCERTOS...
- OEUVRES DE CORELLY EN TRIO [TRIO SONATAS OP. 1 – 4]
- PARTE PRIMA (-SECONDA) SONATE A VIOLINO O CEMBALO...OP. 5
- SARABANDE AND ALLEGRO
- SIX SOLOS FOR A FLUTE AND A BASS... BEING THE SECOND PART OF HIS FIFTH OPERA.
- SONATE A VIOLINO E VIOLINE O CEMBALO.
- SONATES, 12...TIRES DE TOUS SES OUVRAGES AND TRANSPORTES POUR LA FLUTE, DONT IL EN A 6 A 2 FL. AND A BASSE CONTINUE...
- [TRIO SONATAS, OP. 1 AND 2, SELECTIONS]
- TRIO SONATAS, VIOLINS AND CONTINUO, OP. 1-4

Corelli, Marie *see*
- ARDATH
- BARABBAS
- BOY
- CAMEOS
- THE DEVIL'S MOTOR
- FREE OPINIONS
- GOD'S GOOD MAN
- HOLY ORDERS
- INNOCENT
- JANE
- THE LIFE EVERLASTING
- LOVE AND THE PHILOSOPHER
- THE LOVE OF LONG AGO
- THE MASTER-CHRISTIAN
- THE MIGHTY ATOM
- THE MURDER OF DELICIA
- A ROMANCE OF TWO WORLDS
- THE SECRET POWER
- THE SILVER DOMINO
- THE SORROWS OF SATAN
- THE SOUL OF LILITH
- THE STRANGE VISITATION
- TEMPORAL POWER
- THELMA
- THE TREASURE OF HEAVEN
- VENDETTA
- WORMWOOD
- THE YOUNG DIANA
- ZISKA

CORELLI'S 12 SOLOS...OP. 5 / Corelli, Arcangelo – (Piano part only) – London: D'Almaine & Co, 1834; 1858 – us Sibley [780]
CORELLI'S CELEBRATED TWELVE CONCERTOS... : ADAPTED FOR THE ORGAN, HARPSICHORD, OR PIANO, BY THOMAS BILLINGTON...OPERA 9 / Corelli, Arcangelo – London: Printed for Mr Billington, [ca 1790] – 1 – us Sibley [780]
Coret, Jacques *see* CHRISTUS, DER ZWEITE ADAM
Corey, Henry Bascom *see* THE AMERICAN AGRICULTURIST LAW BOOK, A COMPENDIUM OF EVERY DAY LAW, FOR FARMERS, MECHANICS, BUSINESS MEN, MANUFACTURERS, ETC..
Corey, M D *see* MISSISQUOI RECORD
Corfe, Joseph *see* COLLECTION OF ENGLISH VOCAL MUSIC
Coria. Ayuntamiento *see*
- CULTOS EN HONOR DE LA SANTISIMA VIRGEN DE ARGEME. PATRONA DE LA CIUDAD DE CORIA Y CONSAGRACION DE SU NUEVO SANTUARIO
- FERIAS DE SAN JUAN. JUNIO 1956

CORIA (CACERES) / Junta Provincial de Turismo – (Fotos Gudiol) – Vitoria: Tip. Fournier, s.a. – 1 – sp Bibl Santa Ana [338]
CORIA COMPOSTELANA Y TEMPLARIA / Fita, Fidel – Madrid: Tip. Fortanet, 1912. B.R.A.H. 61. pp. 346-351 – 1 – sp Bibl Santa Ana [946]
Coria, Joaquin de *see* NUEVA GRAMATICA TAGALOG.TEORICO-PRACTICA
CORIA Y EL MANTEL DELA SAGRADA CENA (LA CIUDAD, SU CATEDRAL, SU RELICARIO Y SU GRAN RELIQUIA) / Munoz de San Pedro, Miguel – Madrid: Caja Ahorros y Monte de Piedad de Caceres, 1964 – 1 – sp Bibl Santa Ana [946]
CORIA Y SUS FIESTAS 1963 – Coria: Imp. Fernandez, 1963 – 1 – sp Bibl Santa Ana [390]
Coria-Caceres *see* CALENDARIO Y PLAN DE ESTUDIOS DEL CURSO ACADEMICO 1972-73. SEMINARIO DIOCESANO
Coria-Caceres. Caritas Diocesana *see* MEMORIA, ANO 1959
CORIA-CACERES. DIOCESIS. ORGANIZACION CURSO 1968-69 – Caceres: Edit. Extremadura, 1968 – 1 – sp Bibl Santa Ana [240]
CORINTH BAPTIST CHURCH. COLLETON, SOUTH CAROLINA : CHURCH RECORDS – 1869-1919, 1922-72 – 1 – 17.78 – us Baptist [240]
CORINTH BAPTIST CHURCH. MCQUADY, KENTUCKY : CHURCH RECORDS – 1892-1969 – 1 – 26.37 – us Baptist [240]
CORINTH BAPTIST CHURCH. STEWART COUNTY. MODEL, TENNESSEE : CHURCH RECORDS – 1915-64 – 1 – 12.33 – us Baptist [240]
CORINTHIAN HORSE SPORT – (v25 1992 Can$37.00y) – Aurora. v2327. 1990-94 – 9 – Can$28.00y – cn Micromedia [790]
CORINTHIANS : INTRODUCTION, AUTHORIZED VERSION, REVISED VERSION, WITH NOTES, INDEX, AND MAP / Massie, John – (Includes index) – New York: Henry Frowde, [1902?] – 1mf – 9 – 0-8370-4307-7 – 1985-2307 – us A.T.L.A. [220]
CORINTO A TRAVES DE LA HISTORIA (1514-1933). CORINTO (NICARAGUA) / D'Arbelles, Salvador – Madrid: Razon y Fe, 1934 – 1 – sp Bibl Santa Ana [946]
CORIPPI AFRICANI GRAMMATICI LIBRI QUI SUPERSUNT (MGH1: 3.BD. 2.TEIL) / ed by Partsch, J – 1879 – Dfl28.00 – ne Slangenburg [240]
Corippus *see* CORPUS SCRIPTORUM HISTORIAE BYZANTINAE (CSHB 28)
O CORISCO : PERIODICO CRITICO E PITORESCO – [s.l.]. 3 Dez 1867 – 1,5,6 – bl Biblioteca [072]
CORK AND SOUTH OF IRELAND GENERAL ADVERTISER – Ireland. -w. 24 May 1851-2 April 1853. 1 reel – 1 – uk British Libr Newspaper [072]
CORK (CORK), 1805 : BRITISH ISLES CENSUS DIRECTORIES PROJECT, IRELAND. VOL 12 – 1mf – 9 – A$9.00 – at Vine [941]
CORK DAILY ADVERTISER – Ireland. -d. 1 Oct 1836-21 Jan 1837. (1 reel) – 1 – uk British Libr Newspaper [072]
CORK EVENING HERALD – Ireland. -d. 9 Sep 1833-7 Oct 1836. (4 reels) – 1 – uk British Libr Newspaper [072]
CORK EVENING POST – Cork, Ireland. 1757-1806. 4 reels – 1 – ie Microforms [072]
CORK EXAMINER – Ireland. Jan-Aug 1923; Jul-Dec 1926; Jan-Sep 1928.-d. 10 reels – 1 – uk British Libr Newspaper [072]
THE CORK EXAMINER – (1845-1980 is available for Ir£9,000.00) – Cork, Ireland. 1841- – 1 – ie Microforms [072]
CORK MERCANTILE CHRONICLE – Cork, Ireland. 1801-18 – 1 – ie Microforms [072]
CORK MERCANTILE CHRONICLE – Ireland. -tw. 2 Jan 1832-11 Nov 1835. (4 reels) – 1 – uk British Libr Newspaper [072]
THE CORK OAK FORESTS AND THE EVOLUTION OF THE CORK INDUSTRY IN SOUTHERN SPAIN AND PORTUGAL / Parsons, James J – 1 – sp Bibl Santa Ana [338]
CORK SENTINEL – Ireland. -m. 19 Jan-3 Sep 1831. (8 ft) – 1 – uk British Libr Newspaper [072]
CORK SPORTSMAN – Ireland. -w. 30 May 1908-19 Oct 1911. (1 reel) – 1 – uk British Libr Newspaper [072]
CORK STANDARD – Ireland.10 Oct 1836-1837. -d.2 1/2 reels – 1 – uk British Libr Newspaper [072]
CORK SUN – Ireland. 18 Apr 1903-30 Sep 1905.-w. 3mqn reels – 1 – uk British Libr Newspaper [072]
CORK WEEKLY CHRONICLE – Ireland. -w. 24 April-20 Nov 1909. 1 2 reel – 1 – uk British Libr Newspaper [072]
CORK WEEKLY HERALD *see* WEEKLY HERALD
CORK WEEKLY TIMES – Ireland. -w. 4 Oct 1833-26 Sep 1834. (35 ft) – 1 – uk British Libr Newspaper [072]
CORKMAN – Kerry, Ireland. -d. 1904-86 – 1 – PS27.50r – ie European Micro [072]
Cormery. France. Benedictine Abbey *see* LE CARTULAIRE DE CORMERY.
Cormiguano de Brenta, Arthur *see* MISSION DIPLOMATIQUE DE LAURENT DE BRINDES... PADOUE, 1964
Corminboeuf, C *see* LE JEU DE L'IDENTITE ET DE LA DIFFERENCE. LE CAS D'ESSE ZOGBEDJI, MINI-DIASPORA ADANGME DANS LE SUD-EST DU TOGO
THE CORN PROJECT IN INDONESIA / International Cooperation Administration – Robert Isaac Jackson. 1957. SE-4806-1 – 9 – ne IDC [630]
CORN VARIETIES FOR ALABAMA / Alabama. Agricultural Experiment Station – 1948-63 – 1,5,6 – us Spaulding [630]
Cornaby, William Arthur *see* THE CALL OF CATHAY
Cornaeus, M *see* CURRICULUM PHILOSOPHIAE PERIPATETICAE...
Cornede-Miramont, A C *see* LES SAINTS-SIMONIENS, COMEDIE BURLESQUE EN TROIS ACTES ET EN PROSE
LA CORNEILLE DU NORD – St-Lin, Canada. 28 dec 1877 – 1r – 1 – Can$25.00 – cn Can Microfilming [072]
Corneille, Th *see* LE DICTIONNAIRE DES ARTS ET DES SCIENCES
LA CORNEJA SIN PLUMAS / Ipnocausto, Paulo – 1795 – 9 – 1.50f – sp Bibl Santa Ana [830]
Cornejo Bouroncle, J *see* LA CONFEDERACION PERU-BOLIVIANA
Cornejo, J *see* DISCURSO PARTICULAR Y PRESERVATIVO DE LA GOTA, EN QUE SE DESCUBRE SU NATURALEZA Y SE PONE SU PROPIA CURA
Cornejo M, P *see* LA DEFENSA PERUANA
Cornejo, P *see* EL ECUADOR Y EL PERU...
CORNELIE OU LA PUPILLE DE VOLTAIRE / Princeteau, T – Comedie en un acte et en vers (nouvelle proie de la censure theatrale). Lyon. J.-M. Barret. 1825. XII – 9 – fr Hachette [820]
Cornelison, Isaac A *see*
- THE NATURAL HISTORY OF RELIGIOUS FEELING : A QUESTION OF MIRACLES IN THE SOUL
- THE RELATION OF RELIGION TO CIVIL GOVERNMENT IN THE UNITED STATES OF AMERICA

Cornelius, A E *see* SOURCES OF STRESS IN ATHLETES
Cornelius, Asher Lynn *see* THE LAW OF SEARCH AND SEIZURE.
Cornelius, C A *see*
- HISTORISCHE ARBEITEN VORNEHMLICH ZUR REFORMATIONSZEIT
- NAGRA BIDRAG TILL UPSALA THEOLOGISKA FAKULTETS HISTORIA

CORNELIUS FREUNDT : EIN BEITRAG ZUR GESCHICHTE DER EVANGELISCHEN KIRCHENMUSIK INSBESONDERE DER SAECHSISCHEN KANTOREIEN IN DER 2. HAELFTE DES 16. JAHRHUNDERTS / Goehler, Georg – Leipzig, 1896 – 1mf – 9 – DM48.00 – 3-89349-332-8 – gw Hänsel [780]
Cornelius, Peter *see* GEDICHTE
CORNELL DAILY SUN – Ithaca. N.Y. 1880- – 1 – us UMI [071]
CORNELL HOTEL AND RESTAURANT ADMINISTRATION QUARTERLY – (v21-1980- 5,6,9) – v1- 1960- – 1 – us UMI [640]
CORNELL INTERNATIONAL LAW JOURNAL – v1-25. 1968-92 – 1,5,6 – $315.00 – us Hein [073]
Cornell, John A *see* THE PIONEERS OF BEVERLY, SERIES OF SKETCHES
CORNELL LAW FORUM – (v.6-. 1979- 5,6,9) – v.1-. 1974- – 1 – us UMI [073]
CORNELL LAW QUARTERLY – (Add vols as copyright expires) – v1-5. 1915/16-1919/20 (all publ) – 21mf – $31.50 – LLMC 90-319 – us L.L.M.C. [073]
CORNELL LAW REVIEW – v1-80. 1915-95 – 1,5,6,9 – $1,620.00 – us Hein [073]

CORNELL UNIVERSITY LIBRARIES : SOUTHEAST ASIA CATALOG / Cornell University. Libraries – 1976. 111,000 cards on 13 reels – 1 – $620.00 export $750.00 – 0-8161-1329-7 – uk Hall [010]

Cornell University. Libraries *see*
- CORNELL UNIVERSITY LIBRARIES
- SOUTHEAST ASIA CATALOG

Cornell University. New York State School of Industrial and Labor Relations. Martin P. Catherwood Library *see*
- LIBRARY CATALOG OF THE NEW YORK STATE SCHOOL OF INDUSTRIAL AND LABOR RELATIONS

Corner, C *see*
- EPISTOLA D. PAVLI AD GALATAS...CVM COMMENTARIO...
- IN EPISTOLAM D. PAVLI AD ROMANOS SCRIPTAM COMMENTARIVS...

CORNERSTONE BAPTIST CHURCH. LINCOLN COUNTY. MISSOURI (EXTINCT) : CHURCH RECORDS – 1872-1910. 214p – 1 – 9.63 – us Baptist [240]

THE CORNER-STONE, OR, A FAMILIAR ILLUSTRATION OF THE PRINCIPLES OF CHRISTIAN TRUTH / Abbott, Jacob – Boton: W. Peirce; New York: J.P. Haven, 1834. 360p – 1 – us U.W. Library [240]

CORNER-STONES OF FAITH, OR THE ORIGIN AND CHARACTERISTICS OF THE CHRISTIAN DENOMINATIONS OF THE UNITED STATES / Small, Charles H – New York: E.B. Treat, 1898 – 2mf – us A.T.L.A. [240]

Cornet, Charles Joseph Alexandre *see* AU TCHAD

Cornet, R *see* COMMUNE ET SOCIETE RURALE EN ALGERIE: ADMINISTRATION LOCALE ET PARTICIPATION AU DEVELOPPEMENT DANS L'AURES

O CORNETA : ORGAO REPUBLICANO – Manaos, Amazonas. 12 Jan-15 Mar 1888 – 1,5,6 – bl Biblioteca [072]

CORNHILL MAGAZINE – v1-1082 1860-1975 1; v1067-1082 1971-75 5,6 – us UMI [073]

CORNHILL MAGAZINE – v. 1-175. 1860-1967 – 1,5,6 – us Princeton Micro [940]

CORNHUSK BAGS OF THE PLATEAU INDIANS / Cheney Cowles Memorial Museum of the Eastern Washington State Historical Society – (28p accompanying text) – 1976 – 4 color mf – 15 – $36.00f – 0-226-68987-5 – us Chicago [060]

CORNHUSKER COUNTRYMAN / Nebraska. College of Agriculture – n.1-25. 1921-52 – 1,5 – us Spaulding [630]

Corni, Guido *see* SOMALIA ITALIANA

Cornick, Delroy L *see* AUDITING IN THE ELECTRONIC ENVIRONMENT: THEORY, PRACTICE AND LITERATURE

Cornill, Carl Heinrich *see*
- DAS BUCH JEREMIA
- EINLEITUNG IN DIE KANONISCHEN BUECHER DES ALTEN TESTAMENTS
- INTRODUCTION TO THE CANONICAL BOOKS OF THE OLD TESTAMENT
- DIE METRISCHEN STUECKE DES BUCHES JEREMIA

Cornill, Carl Heinrich et al *see* DAS CHRISTENTUM

CORNING DEMOCRAT – Ithaca. N.Y. 1857-1896 – 1 – us UMI [071]

THE CORNING FLOOD: MUSEUM UNDER WATER / ed by Martin, John H – 1977. 72p. 120 illus. 2 fiches. Fiche no. 6662 – 9 – $5.00 – us Corning Mus [700]

Corning, Iowa. Corning Baptist Church *see* RECORDS

Corning Museum of Glass *see*
- THE CUT AND ENGRAVED GLASS OF CORNING, 1868-1940
- GLASS FROM THE CORNING MUSEUM OF GLASS
- THE HISTORY AND ART OF GLASS
- THE HISTORY AND ART OF GLASS: INDEX OF PERIODICAL LITERATURE
- HISTORY OF GLASS
- NEW GLASS REVIEW 9
- NEW GLASS REVIEW 10
- NEW GLASS REVIEW 11
- NEW GLASS REVIEW 12
- NEW GLASS REVIEW 13
- NEW GLASS REVIEW 14
- RARE BOOKS FROM THE CORNING MUSEUM OF GLASS
- THE STORY OF GLASS DECORATION
- TRADE CATALOGUES

CORNING OBSERVER – Corning, CA. 1888- – 100+ r – 1 – $5,000.00 ($90.00y) – B02141 – us Library Micro [071]

CORNISH BAPTIST CHURCH. CORNISH FLAT, NEW HAMPSHIRE : CHURCH RECORDS – 1791-1802. 12p – 1 – 5.00 – us Baptist [240]

CORNISH ECHO *see* FALMOUTH AND PENRYN WEEKLY TIMES

Cornish, Francis Warre *see* THE ENGLISH CHURCH IN THE NINETEENTH CENTURY

Cornish, George H *see* HAND-BOOK OF CANADIAN METHODISM

CORNISH GUARDIAN – Bodmin, England. 1901-71.-w. 84 reels – 1 – uk British Libr Newspaper [072]

Cornish, Louisa S *see* PRINCE OF THE KINGS OF THE EARTH

Cornish, New Hampshire. Cornish Baptist Church *see* RECORDS

CORNISH TIMES AND GENERAL ADVERTISER – Liskeard, England. 21 Feb 1859 sic; 2 May 1857-7 May 1859. -w. 1 reel – 1 – uk British Libr Newspaper [072]

THE CORNISHMAN – Penzance, England. Jul 1878-Dec 1900.-w. 20mqn reels – 1 – uk British Libr Newspaper [072]

Cornu, Charles *see* DER VERGLEICH BEI GOETHE UNTER BESONDERER BERUECKSICHTIGUNG DER VERGLEICHENDEN LITERATURKRITIK

Cornu, Paul *see* GREVES DE FLOTTEURS SUR L'YONNE AUX 18E ET 19E SIECLES

Cornulier, Louis de *see* REPONSE SOMMAIRE POUR LES HERITIERS DE LOUIS DE CORNULIER...AU MEMOIRE PUBLIE AU NOM DE M. MUSSEAU...

Cornut, J P *see* CANADENSIUM PLANTARUM

CORNUTI THEOLOGIAE GRAECAE COMPENDIUM : RECENSUIT ET EMENDABAT CAROLUS LANG – Lipsiae: In aedibus B.G. Teubneri, 1881 – 1mf – us A.T.L.A. [240]

Cornutti *see* CANADIENSUM PLANTARUM

CORNWALL, 1823 : BRITISH ISLES CENSUS DIRECTORIES PROJECT, ENGLAND. VOL 223 – 1mf – 9 – A$9.00 – at Vine [941]

CORNWALL, 1830 : BRITISH ISLES CENSUS DIRECTORIES PROJECT, ENGLAND. VOL 51 – 1mf – 9 – A$9.00 – at Vine [941]

CORNWALL, 1844 : BRITISH ISLES CENSUS DIRECTORIES PROJECT, ENGLAND. VOL 118 – 3mf – 9 – A$21.00 – at Vine [941]

CORNWALL, 1852 : BRITISH ISLES CENSUS DIRECTORIES PROJECT, ENGLAND. VOL 152 – 3mf – 9 – A$21.00 – at Vine [941]

CORNWALL, 1889 : BRITISH ISLES CENSUS DIRECTORIES PROJECT, ENGLAND – at Vine [941]

CORNWALL, 1902 : BRITISH ISLES CENSUS DIRECTORIES PROJECT, ENGLAND – at Vine [941]

CORNWALL, 1910 : BRITISH ISLES CENSUS DIRECTORIES PROJECT, ENGLAND. VOL 228 – 7mf – 9 – A$45.00 – at Vine [941]

CORNWALL, 1923 : BRITISH ISLES CENSUS DIRECTORIES PROJECT, ENGLAND. VOL 265 – 7mf – 9 – A$45.00 – at Vine [941]

THE CORNWALL CANAL: ITS LOCATION AND CONSTRUCTION, BREAKS AND PRESENT CONDITION / Bergin, Darby – House of Commons, Ottawa, 18–. 02308. (Pre-1900 Canadiana) – 9 – cn C.I.H.M. [627]

CORNWALL CHRONICLE – Launceston, Australia. Jan 1850-Aug 1880 (missing 1853, 1857).-w. 15mqn reels – 1 – uk British Libr Newspaper [072]

CORNWALL CHRONICLE – West Indies. 1776-94 – 1 – uk Microform Academic [072]

CORNWALL (EAST), 1901 : BRITISH ISLES CENSUS DIRECTORIES PROJECT, ENGLAND – at Vine [941]

CORNWALL (FALMOUTH, TRURO AND PENRYN), 1805 : BRITISH ISLES CENSUS DIRECTORIES PROJECT, ENGLAND. VOL 179 – 1mf – 9 – A$9.00 – at Vine [941]

CORNWALL PARISH REGISTERS. MARRIAGES / ed by Phillimore, William Phillimore Watts & Taylor, Thomas – London, issued to subscribers, 1900- – 1 – us U.W. Library [920]

Cornwallis, William *see* DISCOURSES UPON SENECA THE TRAGEDIAN

Cornwell, William Caryl *see* THE CURRENCY AND THE BANKING LAW OF THE DOMINION OF CANADA: CONSIDERED WITH REFERENCE TO CURRENCY REFORM IN THE UNITED STATES

COROLLARIUM AD PHILOSOPHIAM BOTANICAM / Necker, N J de – Neowedae ad Rhenum, 1790. 29, 2 pp., 63 pls. B-6092 1 – 9 – ne IDC [580]

COROLLARIUM INSTITUTIONUM REI HERBARIAE IN QUO PLANTAE 1356 IN ORIENTALIBUS REGIONIBUS OBSERVATAE / Tournefort, Joseph Pitton de – Paris. 1703; Impr. cum editione tertia. Lugdunum. 1719. B-5439 2 – 8 – ne IDC [580]

Corona Baratech, Carlos E *see* HERNANDO CORTES

CORONA DE LA INMACULADA / Corredor Garcia, Antonio – Caceres: Tip. El Noticiero, SL, 1954 – 1 – sp Bibl Santa Ana [946]

CORONA DELLE NOBILI, ET VIRTUOSE DONNE / Vecellio, C – O 1130 1. 1592 – 9 – ne IDC [440]

CORONA DI SACRAE CANZONI O LAUDE DI PIV... – Pirenze, Da C Bindi, per il Parlierei, 1710 – 1 – us Sibley [780]

CORONA FUNEBRE, A LA MEMORIA DE LA VIRTUOSA SENORA MARIA CRISTINA ROJAS DE HERDOCIA / Bayle, Constantino – Madrid: Razon y Fe, 1926 – 1 – sp Bibl Santa Ana [920]

CORONA PER LA VITTORIA DEL SERENISS. DON GIO. D'AVSTRIA / Gualtieri, F – Venetia, 1572 – 1mf – 9 – H-8329/1 – ne IDC [956]

CORONA POETICA / Asociacion Santa Eulalia. Spain – 1875 – 9 – 1.50f – sp Bibl Santa Ana [810]

CORONA POETICA DE SANTA EULALIA, NATURAL Y PATRONA DE LA CIUDAD DE MERIDA – 1875 – 9 – 1.50f – sp Bibl Santa Ana [240]

CORONA QUERNEA : FESTGABE FUER KARL STRECKER (MGH SCHRIFTEN... 6.BD) – 1941 – Dfl42.00 – ne Slangenburg [240]

CORONACA BAPTIST CHURCH. GREENWOOD COUNTY. SOUTH CAROLINA : CHURCH RECORDS – 1943-72. Historical statistics. 1881-1942 – 1 – 10.31 – us Baptist [240]

CORONACION CANONIGA DE LA SANTISIMA VIRGEN DE LA VICTORIA – Trujillo: Tip. Sobrino de B. Pena, 1953 – sp Bibl Santa Ana [240]

CORONACION DE LA VIRGEN DE CHIGUINGUIRA / Mesanza, Andres – Madrid: Razon y Fe, 1935 – 1 – sp Bibl Santa Ana [240]

LA CORONACION DE LA VIRGEN DE GUADALUPE / Bayle, Constantino – Madrid: Razon y Fe, 1928 – 9 – sp Bibl Santa Ana [972]

CORONACION DE NUESTRA SENORA DE CONSOLACION DEL CASTILLO DE MONTANCHEZ – Caceres: Tip. El Noticiero, s.a., (1950) ? – 1 – sp Bibl Santa Ana [240]

Coronado, Carolina *see*
- ANANLES DE TAJO LISBOA
- CAMOENS A CALDERON EN EL CENTENARIO DE ESTE
- INTRODUCCION A LA POESIA DE LA SENORITA ARMINO
- NOVELAS. JARILLA
- PAQUITA ADORACION. NOVELAS ORIGINALES
- POESIAS
- POESIAS COMPLETAS
- RUEDA DE LA DESGRACIA. MANUSCRITO DE UN CONDE
- LA SIEGA

CORONADO EVENING MERCURY – Coronado, CA. May 1887-Jul 1896 (incomplete) – 4r – 1 – $200.00 – C02145 – us Library Micro [071]

CORONADO JOURNAL COMPASS – Coronado, CA. Sept 1948-Dec 1952 – 2r – 1 – $100.00 – C02146 – us Library Micro [073]

Coronado, Nicolas *see* CRITICA NEGATIVA

CORONA/NORCO – 1930-33; 1992- – 6+ r – 1 – $300.00 – P00021 – us Library Micro [910]

CORONARY HEART DISEASE RISK FACTORS IN CHILDREN AGES 9 TO 11 YEARS / Brewer, Julia R & Wilson, Philip K – 1991 – 1mf – $4.00 – us Microform Publ [616]

Coronas, Juan Enrique *see* EL SEGUNDO PLAN QUINQUENAL Y EL PODER JUDICIAL

CORONATION BOOK OF CHARLES 5 OF FRANCE / Dewick, E S – 1899 – 4mf – 8 – Dfl19.00 – ne Slangenburg [390]

Coronel, Ambrosio *see* MEMORIAL AJUSTADO DE LOS ACTOS ACREEDORES...IGLESIA COLEGIAL Y HOSPITAL DE ZAFRA

EL CORONEL DE CABALLERIA DON ANTONIO DEL SOLAR E IBANEZ / Solar y Taboada, Antonio – Badajoz: Florencio Ger Castro, 1916 – 1 – sp Bibl Santa Ana [350]

Coronel de Palma, Luis *see* TRES PROBLEMAS Y EL FUTURO ECONOMICO DE ESPANA

CORONERS GUIDE AND THE CORONERS ACT, R. S. O. 1927, CHAPTER 123, AS AMENDED BY 1931, CHAPTER 31. / Magone, Clifford Richard – 1st ed. Toronto: Bowman, 1936? 111p. LL-2317 – 1 – us L of C Photodup [340]

CORONER'S INQUESTS / Defiance County, Ohio. Common Pleas. Criminal Div. – 1847-1941 – 5r – 1 – $32.50r – us Archival [324]

CORONER'S INQUESTS / Williams. County, Ohio. Common Pleas. Criminal Div. – 1898-1920 – 1r – 1 – $32.50r – us Archival [324]

CORONERS' INQUESTS / Fulton County. Ohio. Common Pleas. Criminal Div – 1888-1948 – 1r – 1 – $32.50r – us Archival [324]

CORONERS' INQUESTS / Seneca County. Ohio. Common Pleas. Criminal Division – 1883-1950 – 6r – 1 – $32.50r – us Archival [324]

CORONERS' INQUESTS / Van Wert County, Ohio. Common Pleas. Criminal Div. – 1861 – 1r – 1 – $32.50r – us Archival [324]

CORONERS' INQUESTS / Van Wert County. Ohio. Common Pleas. Criminal Div – 1880-1938 – 1r – 1 – $32.50r – us Archival [324]

CORONERS' INQUESTS / Wood County. Ohio. Common Pleas. Criminal Div. – 1888-1902 – 2r – 1 – $32.50r – us Archival [324]

CORONER'S SOCIETY OF ENGLAND AND WALES REPORTS – 2 bound vols. 1890-1903 (all publ) – 36mf – 9 – $54.00 – LLMC 84-449 – us L.L.M.C. [340]

CORONET – 1-50. 1936-1961 – 1 – us UMI [073]

CORPO CLIP : LE BULLETIN DES BIBLIOTHECAIRES PROFESSIONNELS DU QUEBEC – Montreal, 1988-. SEM105P1120 – 5mf – 9 – Can$2.25f – cn Bibl Nat [073]

CORPORATE ACCOUNTING – v1-. 1983- – 1,5,6,9 – us UMI [650]

CORPORATE ADVANTAGES WITHOUT INCORPORATION. / Warren, Edward Henry – New York, Baker, Voorhis, 1929. 1012 p. LL-1642 – 1 – us L of C Photodup [340]

CORPORATE COUNSEL'S ANNUAL – 1966-85 – 1,5,6 – $675.00 – us Hein [340]

CORPORATE DESIGN – (1984-. 5,6,9) – v1-3. 1982-84 – 1 – us UMI [338]

CORPORATE DESIGN AND REALTY – v3-. 1984- – 1,5,6,9 – us UMI [330]

CORPORATE PRACTICE REVIEW – v1-4. 1928-32 (all publ) – 12mf – 9 – $54.00 – LLMC 84-450 – us L.L.M.C. [073]

CORPORATE REORGANIZATION. 1-312, AUG. 11, 1938-JULY 12, 1972 / U.S. Securities and Exchange Commission – 9 – us UMI [332]

CORPORATE REORGANIZATION RELEASES / U.S. Securities and Exchange Commission – nos 1-312. 17 Aug 1938-12 Jul 1972 (all publ) – 35mf – 9 – $52.00 – LLMC 84-360 – us L.L.M.C. [340]

CORPORATION ACT BOOKS OF THE CITY OF WELLS, 1377-1835 – 6r – 1 – uk Microform Academic [941]

CORPORATION ASSESSMENT LISTS, 1909-15 / U.S. Internal Revenue Service – 82 rolls. M667. Printed guide – 1 – us Nat'l Archives [324]

Corporation des Arpenteurs-Geometres de la Province de Quebec *see* STATUTS ET REGLEMENTS DU BUREAU DE DIRECTION DE LA CORPORATION...PREPARES PAR UN COMITE DU BUREAU DE DIRECTION, APPROUVES ET SANCTIONNES A UNE ASSEMBLEE GENERALE TENUE LE 9 AVRIL 1890

Corporation des Bibliothecaires Professionnels du QuebecCorporation of Professional Librarians of Quebec *see* ARGUS

THE CORPORATION DIGEST *see* THE INDIANA LAW MAGAZINE

CORPORATION, FINANCE AND BUSINESS LAW SECTION JOURNAL *see* MICHIGAN BUSINESS LAW JOURNAL

CORPORATION HOUSE BOOKS, 1490-1603 / York. England – 1 – uk Microform Academic [941]

THE CORPORATION JOURNAL – (Lacking: v1) – v1-11. 1913-35 (all publ) – 45mf – 9 – $67.50 – LLMC 84-451 – us L.L.M.C. [073]

CORPORATION LAW REVIEW – v. 1-. 1978- – 1,5,6,9 – us UMI [338]

THE CORPORATION LAWS OF 1883; BEING A SUPPLEMENT TO THE GENERAL CORPORATION LAWS OF PENNSYLVANIA / Freedley, Angelo Tillinghast – Philadelphia, 1883. 30p. LL-75 – 1 – us L of C Photodup [340]
THE CORPORATION LAWS OF NEW JERSEY / New Jersey Corporation Guarantee and Trust Company. Camden, NJ – (Ibid. Camden, NJ., 1896. 119p. LL-228) – Camden, 1896 16p. LL-973 – 1 – us L of C Photodup [340]
CORPORATION LETTER BOOKS / Aldeburgh. Suffolk – 1625-63 – 1 – uk Microform Academic [941]
Corporation of London Record Office, London *see* THE WHITECHAPEL MURDERS PAPERS. LETTERS RELATING TO JACK THE RIPPER
CORPORATION RECORDS / Henry County. Ohio. Recorder – 1876-1903 – 1r – 1 – $32.50r – us Archival [324]
THE CORPORATION REPORTER *see* THE INDIANA LAW MAGAZINE
CORPORATIONS ET METIERS DE CLAMECY A LA FIN DU 18E SIECLE / Destray, Paul – Moulins. 1914. (La Condition Ouvriere. Part Two.) – 9 – 2.50 – fr Bibl Nationale [360]
CORPORATIONS IN PENNSYLVANIA / Murphy, Walter – Philadelphia: Welsh, 1891. 2v. LL-663 – 1 – us L of C Photodup [340]
LE CORPS ANDROGYNE. L'HABITAT AU BURUNDI / Stanford, A – 9 – F60.00 – fr Ethnologie [306]
Corps Bukit Barisan *see* BERKALA BERITA
Corps Kehakiman Angkatan Darat *see* CHAKRAVIJAYA
CORPUS ANTIPHONALIUM OFFICII / ed by Hesbert, R J – Roma. v1-2. 1963 – 43mf – 8 – Dfl151.00 – ne Slangenburg [240]
CORPUS APOLOGETARUM CHRISTIANORUM SAECULI SECUNDI / ed by Otto, J C T – Ienae v1-9 1847-1872 – 62mf – 8 – ne Slangenburg [240]
CORPUS BYZANTINAE HISTORIAE *see*
- ANNAE COMMENAE PORPHYROGENITAE CAESARISSAE ALEXIAS SIVE DE REBUS AB ALEXIO IMPERATORE VEL EJUS TEMPORE GESTIS (CBH 10)
- ANNALES A MUNDI EXORDIO USQUE AD OBITUM ALEXII COMMENI IMPER. (CBH 9)
- ANNALES (CBH 22)
- ARCANA HISTORIA (CBH 3,3)
- BREVIARIUM HISTORICUM (CBH 2,2)
- BREVIARIUM HISTORICUM (CBH 12,1)
- BYZANTINA HISTORIA (CBH 23)
- CHRONICON (CBH 30,2)
- CHRONICON ORIENTALE
- CHRONICON PASCHALE (CBH 21)
- CHRONOGRAPHIA
- COMMENTARII DE REBUS BYZANTINIS (CBH 3,4)
- COMPENDIUM HISTORIARUM (CBH 8)
- DE AEDIFICIIS DN. IUSTINIANI LIBRI 6 (CBH 3,2)
- DE HISTORIAE BYZANTINAE SCRIPTORIBUS EMITTENDIS PROTREPTICON
- DE IMPERIO ET REBUS GESTIS IUSTINIANI (CBH 4)
- DE OFFICIIS MAGNAE ECCLESIAE ET AULAE CONSTANTINOPO- LITANAE (CBH 18)
- DE REBUS CONSTANTINOPOLITANIS LIBRI 4 (CBH30,1)
- DESCRIPTIO MAGNAE ECCLESIAE SEU SANCTAE SOPHIAE (CBH 11,2)
- ECLOGAE HISTORICORUM DE REBUS BYZANTINIS (CBH 1,3)
- EXCERPTA DE ANTIQUITATIBUS CONSTANTINOPOLITANIS (CBH 12,2)
- EXCERPTA DE LEGATIONIBUS (CBH 1,2)
- HISTOIRE DE L'EMPIRE DE CONSTANTINOPLE SOUS LES EMPEREURS FRANCOIS (CBH 26)
- HISTORIA
- HISTORIA BYZANTINA (CBH 15)
- HISTORIA BYZANTINA DUPLICI COMMENTARIO ILLUSTRATA (CBH 25,1)
- HISTORIA BYZANTINA DUPLICI COMMENTARIO ILLUSTRATA (CBH 25,2)
- HISTORIA (CBH 13)
- HISTORIA CHRONICA
- HISTORIA CHRONICA (CBH 30,3)
- HISTORIA DE VITIS ROMANORUM PONTIFICUM (CBH 19,2)
- HISTORIA ECCLESIASTICA SIVE CHRONOGRAPHIA TRIPERTITA (CBH 19,1)
- HISTORIA RERUM A MICHAELE PALAEOLOGO (CBH 28,1)
- HISTORIA RERUM AB ANDRONICO SENIORE (CBH 28,2)
- HISTORIA SCRIPTORESQUE ALII AD RES BYZANTINAS PERTINENTES (CBH 39)
- HISTORIARUM LIBRI 4 (CBH 17)
- HISTORIARUM LIBRI 8 (CBH 2,1)
- HISTORIARUM LIBRI DECEM DE REBUS TURCICIS (CBH 16)
- HISTORIARUM SUI TEMPORIS LIBRI 8 (CBH 3,1)
- IMPERATORII GRAMMATICI HISTORIARUM LIBRI SEX SEU DE REBUS GESTIS A JOANNE ET MANNUELE GOMMENSIS IMPP. CP. (CBH 11,1)
- IMPERIUM ORIENTALE SIVE ANTIQUITATES CONSTANTINOPOLITANI (CBH 24,1)
- IMPERIUM ORIENTALE SIVE ANTIQUITATES CONSTANTINOPOLITANI (CBH 24,2)
- LIBRI DUO DE CEREMONIIS AULAE BYZANTINAE (CBH 33)
- NOTITIA DIGNITATUM IMPERII ROMANI (CBH 27)
- NOVA APPENDIX
- SCRIPTORES POST THEOPHANEM (CBH 7)
- SYMMICTA SIVE OPUSCULA GRAECA ET LATINA (CBH 30,5)
- TRACTATUS DE PATRIARCHIS CONSTANTINOPOLITANIS (CBH 32)

CORPUS BYZANTINAE HISTORIAE (CBH) – (Individual vols also listed separately) – Parisiis. Tom. 1-27. 1648-1711 – 734mf – Dfl2,569.00 coll – ne Slangenburg [930]
Corpus Christi College, Cambridge *see* THE ANGLO-SAXON AND MEDIAEVAL MANUSCRIPT COLLECTION
CORPUS D'ARCHIVES HISTORIQUES DE L'ETHNIE GURO / Deluz, A – (Tome 1. F280.00. Tome 2. F150.00. Tome 3. F100.00) – Republique de Cote d'Ivoire – 9 – fr Ethnologie [960]
EL CORPUS DE LOS NEOFITOS AMERICANOS / Bayle, Constantino – Madrid: Razon y Fe, 1944 – 1 – sp Bibl Santa Ana [972]
CORPUS DE TEXTES DE BELEP / Dubois, M J – 9 – F90.00 – fr Ethnologie [490]
CORPUS DE TEXTES DE L'ILE DES PINS / Dubois, M J – 9 – F60.00 – fr Ethnologie [306]
CORPUS DOCUMENTORUM INQUISITIONIS HAERETICAE / ed by Fredericq, P – Gent. v1-5. 1889-1902 – Dfl249.00 – ne Slangenburg [240]
CORPUS GLOSSARIORUM LATINORUM / ed by Loewe, G – Lipsiae. v1-7. 1889-1901 – 85mf – ne IDC [450]
CORPUS IGNATIANUM: A COMPLETE COLLECTION OF THE IGNATIAN EPISTLES TRANSL. AND ANNOTATED BY WILLIAM CURETON / Ignatius, Saint – 1849 – 1 – us A.T.L.A. [240]
CORPUS INSCRIPTIONUM BHAVNAGARI – A selection of Arabic and Persian inscriptions. Bombay. 1889. BI-788 2 – 8 – ne IDC [410]
CORPUS INSCRIPTIONUM LATINARUM – Berolini, 1893-1933. v.1-15 – 907mf – 9 – ne IDC [410]
CORPUS INSCRIPTIONUM LATINARUM / Huebner, Emilio – (Supplemento, 2v 1892 $1.50f) – 2v 1869 – 9 – $1.50f – sp Bibl Santa Ana [410]
CORPUS IURIS CANONICI 1-2 / Friedberg, A – Leipzig, 1879 – 63mf – 8 – ne Slangenburg [240]
CORPUS JURIS – (With annotation vols) – v1-72. 1921-1955 – 9 – $2,395.00 set – 0-89941-709-4 – us Hein [340]
CORPUS OF RUSSIAN ORTHODOX PERIODICALS – (Individual titles also listed separately) – 5 serial titles – 12r – 1 – ATLA S0193 – us A.T.L.A. [073]
CORPUS OF RUSSIAN ORTHODOX PERIODICALS *see*
- AFONSKIE LISTKI
- CHTENIIA V MOSKOVSKOM OBSHCHESTVIE LIUBITELEI DUKHOVNAGO PROSVIESHCHENIIA
- DUKH KHRISTIANINA
- DUKHOVNAIA BESIEDA
- PRAVOSLAVNYI SOBESIEDNIK

Corpus pacificationum *see* SYSTEMATISCHE ZUSAMMENSTELLUNG DER TEXTE DER FRIEDENSVERTRAEGE 1792-1913
CORPUS REFORMATORUM / ed by Bretschneider, C G – (Missing: 1936. v93) – Halis, Saxonum, 1834-1938. v1-100 – 1,450mf – 1176c/2 – ne IDC [240]
CORPUS SCRIPTORUM ECCLESIASTICORUM LATINORUM – (Individual titles in this series not listed. Please apply to publisher.) – Wien v1-68 1866 ss – 696mf – 98 – Dfl2,400.00 – ne Slangenburg [220]
CORPUS SCRIPTORUM ECCLESIASTICORUM LATINORUM – v1-68 – 686mf – 8 – ne Slangenburg [220]
CORPUS SCRIPTORUM ECCLESIASTICORUM LATINORUM . – Vindobonae, 1867-1917. v.1-66(1) – 711mf – 8 – ne IDC [240]
CORPUS SCRIPTORUM HISTORIAE BYZANTINAE *see*
- ALEXIADIS LIBRI 15 (CSHB 49)
- ANNAE COMMENAE ALEXIADIS LIBRI 15 (CSHB 38)
- ANNALES (CSHB 27)
- ANNALES (CSHB 42, 43)
- ATHENIENSIS HISTORIARUM LIBRI 10 (CSHB 45)
- BREVIARIUM HISTORIAE METRICUM (CSHB 29)
- BYZANTINA HISTORIA (CSHB 6-8)
- CHRONICON PASCHALE AD EXEMPLAR VATICANUM (CSHB 16, 17)
- CHRONOGRAPHIA (CSHB 15)
- CHRONOGRAPHIA (CSHB 39, 40)
- CHRONOGRAPHIA (CSHB 44)
- CODINI CUROPALATAE (CSHB 37)
- CONSTANTINUS PORPHYROGENITUS IMPERATOR, VOL 1-3 (CSHB 9-11)
- CORPUS SCRIPTORUM HISTORIAE BYZANTINAE (CSHB 12, 13)
- CORPUS SCRIPTORUM HISTORIAE BYZANTINAE (CSHB 28)
- CORPUS SCRIPTORUM HISTORIAE BYZANTINAE (CSHB 30)
- CORPUS SCRIPTORUM HISTORIAE BYZANTINAE (CSHB 31)
- CORPUS SCRIPTORUM HISTORIAE BYZANTINAE (CSHB 33)
- CORPUS SCRIPTORUM HISTORIAE BYZANTINAE (CSHB 36)
- CORPUS SCRIPTORUM HISTORIAE BYZANTINAE (CSHB 41)
- CORPUS SCRIPTORUM HISTORIAE BYZANTINAE (CSHB 18-20
- DE MICHAEL ET ANDROICO PALAEOLOGIS LIBRI 13 (CSHB 24, 25)
- DESCRIPTIO TEMPLI SANCTAE SOPHIAE (CSHB 32)
- EPITOMAE HISTORIARUM LIBRI 18 (CSHB 50)
- EPITOME RERUM AB IOANNE ET ALEXIO COMNENIS GESTARUM (CSHB 26)
- EXCERPTA DE ANTIQUITATIBUS CONSTANTINOPOLITANI (CSHB 46)
- HISTORIA BYZANTINA (CSHB 21)
- HISTORIA (CSHB 23)
- HISTORIA (CSHB 48)
- HISTORIA POLITICA ET PATRIARCHICA (CSHB 47)
- HISTORIAE LIBRI X ET LIBER DE VELITATIONE BELLICA NICEPHORI AUGUSTI E REC. CAR. BEN. HASII (CSHB 5)
- HISTORIARUM LIBRI 5 (CSHB 1)
- HISTORIARUM LIBRI 8 (CSHB 22)
- HISTORIARUM QUAE SUPERSUNT (CSHB 14)
- IOANNIS CANTACUZENI EXIMPERATORIS HISTORIARUM LIBRI 4 (CSHB 2-4)
- IOANNIS SCYLITZAE OPE AB IMM. BEKKERO SUPPLETUS ET EMENDATUS (CSHB 34, 35)

CORPUS SCRIPTORUM HISTORIAE BYZANTINAE (CSHB) : EDITIO EMENDATIOR ET COPIOSIOR CONSILIO B. G. NIEBUHRII C.F. INSTITUTA, AUCTORITATE ACADEMIAE LITTERARUM REGIAE BORUSSICANAE CONTINUATA – (Individual vols also listed separately) – Bonnae. v 1-50. 1828-1897 – Dfl2,037.00 coll – ne Slangenburg [240]
CORPUS SCRIPTORUM HISTORIAE BYZANTINAE (CSHB 12, 13) / Syncellus, Georgius & Nicephorus Cp; ed by Dindorfii, GuiL – (v2 Bonnae 1829 Dfl39.00) – Bonnae. v1. 1829 – Dfl49.00 – ne Slangenburg [240]
CORPUS SCRIPTORUM HISTORIAE BYZANTINAE (CSHB 28) / Merobaudes & Corippus; ed by Bekkerus, Imm – Bonnae, 1836 – Dfl35.00 – ne Slangenburg [240]
CORPUS SCRIPTORUM HISTORIAE BYZANTINAE (CSHB 30) / Zosimus; ed by Bekkeri, Imm – Bonnae, 1837 – Dfl32.00 – ne Slangenburg [240]
CORPUS SCRIPTORUM HISTORIAE BYZANTINAE (CSHB 31) / Lydus, Ioannes; ed by Bekkeri, Imm – 1837 – Dfl32.00 – ne Slangenburg [240]
CORPUS SCRIPTORUM HISTORIAE BYZANTINAE (CSHB 33) / Theophanes Continuatus et al; ed by Bekkeri, Imm – Bonnae, 1838 – Dfl56.00 – ne Slangenburg [930]
CORPUS SCRIPTORUM HISTORIAE BYZANTINAE (CSHB 36) / Phrantzes, Georgius et al; ed by Bekkeri, Imm – Bonnae, 1838 – Dfl39.00 – ne Slangenburg [930]
CORPUS SCRIPTORUM HISTORIAE BYZANTINAE (CSHB 41) / Ephraemius; ed by Bekkeri, Imm – Bonnae, 1840 – Dfl30.00 – ne Slangenburg [930]
CORPUS SCRIPTORUM HISTORIAE BYZANTINAE (CSHB 18-20 / Procopius; ed by Dindorfii, GuiL – Bonnae. v1-2. 1833-1838 – Dfl112.00 – ne Slangenburg [240]
CORPUS TANNAITICUM : ABT. 3 HALACHISCHE MIDRASCHIM. TEIL 3 SIPHRE ZU DEUTERONOMIUM / ed by Finkelstein, L – Breslau, 1935 – 12mf – 8 – ne Slangenburg [200]
Corral Acedo, Francisco et al *see* 1ST CONGRESO SINDICAL AGRARIO DE EXTREMADURA 2. PONENCIA REGINEN DE PRECIOS Y MERCADOS EN LA AGRICULTURA
Corral, Juan del *see* NOBLEZA DE CATALUNA
Corrales Lazaro, Juan Luis *see* MEMORIA DE LAS OBRAS DE RESTAURACION Y AMPLIACION DE LA IGLESIA PARROQUIAL DE NUESTRA SENORA DE LOS ANGELES DE FUENTES DE LEON. ANOS 1940-1943
Corrales Vicente, Manuel *see* LOS PROBLEMAS DE LA FABRICACION DEL QUESO
Corraliza, Jose V *see*
- HERNANDO CORTES
- IDEAL DE LOS CONQUISTADORES
- EL PUENTE DE ALCANTARA

Correa y Zafrilla, P *see* LA FEDERACION
Correal y Frente de Andrade, Narciso *see* EL VENERABLE BARRANTES
Correard, A.Savigny, H. *see* NAUFRAGE DE LA FREGATE "LA MEDUSE"
Correas, Gonzalo *see*
- COMMENTATIO SEU DECLARATIO ADILLUD GENESEOS
- ORTOGRAFIA KASTELLANA...EL MANUAL EPIKTETO
- TRILINGUE DE TRES ARTS DE LAS TRES LENGUAS
- TRILINGUE DE TRES...CASTELLANA, LATINA Y GRIEGA

CORRECCION DEL LENGUAJE... / Obando, Luis de – Madrid: Razon y Fe, 1940 – 1 – sp Bibl Santa Ana [946]
CORRECCIONES AL TRILLO INVENTADO POR DON JUAN ALVAREZ GUERRA, EXECUTADAS POR DON JUAN FRANCISCO GUTIERREZ / Alvarez Guerra, Juan – 1817 – 9 – $1.50f – sp Bibl Santa Ana [621]
CORRECTED IMPRESSIONS : ESSAYS ON VICTORIAN WRITERS / Saintsbury, George – London: W. Heinemann, 1895 – 1 roll – 1 – 1-55879-578-2 – uk Libr Preservation [840]
CORRECTIF A LA REVOLUTION / Marechal, Pierre-Sylvain – Paris. Chez les Directeurs du Cercle Social. 1793 – 9 – fr Hachette [321]
CORRECTIONS DIGEST – v1-6 1970- 1; v7- 9 – us UMI [360]
CORRECTIONS MAGAZINE – (v.5-. 1979- 5,6,9) – v.1-. 1974- – 1 – us UMI [073]
CORRECTIONS PERSPECTIVE – v. 1-. 1975- – 1,5,6,9 – us UMI [073]
CORRECTIONS RAISONNEES DES FAUTES DE LANGAGE ET DE PRONONCIATION / Reynier, J B – 1829.M – 9 – fr I.C.S. [440]
CORRECTIONS TODAY – v1-48. 1939-1986 + index 1-12 – 13r – 1 – us Ross [360]
CORRECTIONS TODAY – v.41-. 1979- – apply; photo copies of articles – us UMI [360]
CORRECTIONS TODAY *see* AMERICAN JOURNAL OF CORRECTION
CORRECTIVE AND SOCIAL PSYCHIATRY AND JOURNAL OF APPLIED BEHAVIOR – v.19. 1973 – 1 – us UMI [610]
CORRECTIVE AND SOCIAL PSYCHIATRY AND JOURNAL OF BEHAVIOR TECHNOLOGY METHODS AND THERAPY – (v.27-. 1981-. 5,6,9) – v.20-. 1974- – 1 – us UMI [610]
CORRECTIVE CHURCH DISCIPLINE / Mell, Patrick H – Reprint from ed. of 1860 – 1 – 5.00 – us Baptist [240]
CORRECTIVE PSYCHIATRY AND JOURNAL OF SOCIAL THERAPY – v.8-19 – 1 – us UMI [610]
CORRECTOR – New York, NY. 1804; Remembrancer. 1804-1805; Weekly Inspector. 1806-1807; New York Spy. 1806. Sold as one unit – 3 – us Readex [071]
Corredor, Antonio *see*
- EN EL ALCAZAR DE LA REINA. ANTOLOGIA POETICA GUADALUPENSE. CACERES, 1967
- DEVOCIONES ANTONIANAS

- DIALOGO CON UN TURISTA. REPORTAJE GRAFICO-HISTORICO SOBRE SAN PEDRO DE ALCANTARA. MADRID, 1969
- LEYENDAS MARIANAS RECOPILADAS...

Corredor Garcia, Antonio *see*
- ANECDOTAS MISIONALES...
- AQUI LA CODOSERA
- BORDON DE PEREGRINO. POEMAS
- CORONA DE LA INMACULADA
- EUCARISTICAS. ANTOLOGIA
- LUCIA DE FATIMA DICE...
- MILAGROS DE FATIMA
- MILAGROS EUCARISTICOS Y FLORES...
- POEMAS MARIANOS
- SANTA CLARA DE ASIS. ANTOLOGIA POETICA
- STABAT MATER DOLOROSA. ANTOLOGIA DE LA SANTISIMA VIRGEN DE LOS DOLORES
- LA VIRGEN DE LAS LAGRIMAS DE SIRACUSA. RELATO HISTORICO

Corredor Garcia, Antonio (OF M) *see* HISPANIARUM REGINE. POEMAS GUADALUPENSES

LOS CORREGIDORES Y SUBDELEGADOS DEL C. / Morales Grinazu, Fernando - Madrid: Razon y Fe, 1940 - 1 - sp Bibl Santa Ana [946]

Correia, Leoncio *see* A VERDADE HISTORICA SOBRE O 15 DE NOVEMBRO

O CORREIO : JORNAL MATUTINO INDEPENDENTE - [s.l.]. 8 Jul 1913-18 Mar 1914 - 1,5,6 - bl Biblioteca [072]

O CORREIO - Sao Joao del-Rei, Brazil. Dec 1027; Jan Fob 1037; Jul, Doo 1054; Jan, Jul, Sept 1955 - 1 - bl Biblioteca [072]

CORREIO BRASILIENSE : FOLHA OFFICIAL, LITTERARIA E MERCANTIL - [s.l.]. 26 Set 1839 - 1,5,6 - bl Biblioteca [072]

CORREIO BRAZILIENSE - London, England. Jun 1808-Dec 1822 - 1 - bl Biblioteca [072]

O CORREIO BRAZILIENSE - London, England. Jun 1808-1822. 25 reels - 1 - bl Biblioteca [072]

CORREIO CARMELITANO - Monte Carmelo, Brazil. Apr 1939 - 1 - bl Biblioteca [072]

CORREIO CATOLICO - Uberaba, 13 Dec 1947; Jul, Nov 1957; Oct 1958; Jan 1959; 2 Jun 1967 - 1,5,6 - bl Biblioteca [072]

CORREIO DA BAHIA - [s.l.]. 29-31 Dez 1871; Abr-Jun, Set 1872; Jan, Ago, Out, Dez 1873; Fev, Maio 1874; Nov-Dez 1876; Jan-Dez 1877; Jan-18 Set 1878 - 1,5,6 - bl Biblioteca [072]

CORREIO DA FEIRA - Feira de Sant' Anna, BA. 8 Jan 1882 - 1,5,6 - bl Biblioteca [072]

CORREIO DA MANHA - Manaos, Amazonas. 22 Maio 1885 - 1,5,6 - bl Biblioteca [072]

CORREIO DA MANHA - Rio de Janeiro, 15 Jun 1901-Dec 1917; Apr 1918-Aug 1924; May 1925-Dec 1926; Jan-Apr, Jul-Dec 1927; Jan-Feb, May-Dec 1928; Jan 1929-Dec 1964; Jan-Jun, Sep, Dec 1965; Jan 1966-7 Jun 1974 - 1,5,6 - bl Biblioteca [072]

CORREIO DA MATTA - Rio Pomba, Brazil. Jun 1908 - 1 - bl Biblioteca [072]

CORREIO DA PALMA - Cidade de Palma, 6 Aug 1893; 13 Mar 1898 - 1,5,6 - bl Biblioteca [072]

CORREIO DA SEMANA : JORNAL INDEPENDENTE E NEUTRO EM POLITICA - Ponte Nova, 13 Jan, May 1918; Feb-Mar, 21 Dec 1919 - 1,5,6 - bl Biblioteca [072]

CORREIO DA SEMANA : ORGAO DOS INTERESSES SOCIAES - Maceio, Alagoas. 27 Out 1889 - 1,5,6 - bl Biblioteca [072]

CORREIO DA SEMANA - Queluz de Minas, 6 Apr 1913; Aug-Nov 1914; Jan 1922-Jan 1924; Jan 1931; Jul-Dec 1937; Jan-May 1938; Feb 1940; Apr 1942; 12 May 1943 - 1,5,6 - bl Biblioteca [072]

CORREIO DA TARDE : JORNAL COMMERCIAL, POLITICO, LITTERARIO E NOTICIOSO - Rio de Janeiro, Brazil. 7 Ago 1855-Dez 1858; Jan-Maio, Jul-Dez 1859; Jan-1860-31 Maio 1862 - bl Biblioteca [072]

CORREIO DA ZAMBEZIA - Quelimane: Tip do Correio, dec 1-15 1886; jan 26-feb 10 1887 - us Res Libr [072]

CORREIO D'ANNUNCIOS E SEMANARIO COMERCIAL DO MARANHAO - '(s.l.')-Sao Luiz, Brazil. 22 Apr 1845; Feb-Mar, Jun, Aug-15 Sep 1851 - 1,5,6 - bl Biblioteca [072]

CORREIO DE AFRICA - Lisboa: "Correio de Africa", [may 22-oct 13 1921; oct 27 1921-aug 1 1923; sep 10-nov 25 1924 - us Res Libr [072]

CORREIO DE ALAGOAS : ORGAO DO PARTIDO REPUBLICANO DO ESTADO - Maceio, Alagoas. 16 Set 1904 - 1,5,6 - bl Biblioteca [072]

CORREIO DE BRASILIA - Brasilia, 16 Nov 1930-16 May 1931 - 1,5,6 - bl Biblioteca [072]

CORREIO DE COIMBRA : ORGAM SEM POLITICA CONSAGRADO AOS INTERESSES DO POVO - Coimbra, 28 Feb-Mar 1927; Jun-28 Oct 1933 - 1,5,6 - bl Biblioteca [072]

O CORREIO DE ITAJUBA : O P.T.B. E UMA FORCA POLITICA A SERVICO DO BRASIL - Itajuba, 9 Jan 1949-Jan 1955; 27 Mar 1960 - 1,5,6 - bl Biblioteca [072]

CORREIO DE LIBERDADE - Liberdade, 15 Mar-May, 30 Sep 1943 - 1,5,6 - bl Biblioteca [072]

O CORREIO DE MACAU - (Filmed with: Correio macaense) - Macau: Manuel Joaquim dos Santos, jan 7, feb 18-20 1883 - us Res Libr [072]

CORREIO DE MANAOS - Manaos, Amazonas. 7 Set-Dez 1869; 26 Out 1881 - 1,5,6 - bl Biblioteca [072]

O CORREIO DE MINAS - Ouro Preto, 9 Feb-Nov 1841; Jan-27 Apr 1842 - 1,5,6 - bl Biblioteca [072]

O CORREIO DE NANUQUE - Nanuque, Brazil. Apr 1961 - 1 - bl Biblioteca [072]

CORREIO DE NOTICIAS - Feira de Sant' Anna, BA. 25 Out 1885 - 1,5,6 - bl Biblioteca [072]

CORREIO DE OBIDOS : ORGAO INDEPENDENTE - Manoas, Amazonas. 15 Nov 1912 - 1,5,6 - bl Biblioteca [072]

CORREIO DE PASSOS : SEMANARIO CONSAGRADO AOS INTERESSES GERAES - Cidade de Passos, 27 Apr, Jun 1924; Jul-24 Dec 1933 - 1,5,6 - bl Biblioteca [072]

CORREIO DE PRADOS - Prados, 2 Nov-14 Dec 1918 - 1,5,6 - bl Biblioteca [072]

CORREIO DE SERGIPE : ORGAM DOS INTERESSES MORAES E MATERIAES DO COMMERCIO - Aracaju, 12 Oct 1890; Jan, Apr, Jul 1891; 7 May 1896 - 1,5,6 - bl Biblioteca [072]

CORREIO DE SERPA - Itacoatiara, Amazonas. 1 Jan 1912-4 Dez 1913 - 1,5,6 - bl Biblioteca [072]

CORREIO DE UBERLANDIA - Uberlandia, Brazil. Apr 1939-Nov 1962. Widely scattered issues except 1943-45, 1950-51, 1954 complete - 1 - bl Biblioteca [072]

CORREIO DO ACRE : JORNAL INDEPENDENTE E NOTICIOSO - Rio Branco, Acre. 5-25 Dez 1965 - 1,5,6 - bl Biblioteca [072]

CORREIO DO ACRE - Xapury, Acre. 7 Set 1910-1 Jan 1913 - 1,5,6 - bl Biblioteca [072]

CORREIO DO BRAZIL - [s.l.]. 21 Ago 1903-Jun 1904; Jan-20 Set 1905 - 1,5,6 - bl Biblioteca [072]

CORREIO DO MADEIRA : ORGAO DO PARTIDO LIBERAL - Manicore, Amazonas. 20 Set 1885; 24 Jan 1890 - 1,5,6 - bl Biblioteca [072]

CORREIO DO NORTE : JORNAL DEDICADO AOS INTERESSES DA PROVINCIA DO AMAZONAS - Manoas, Amazonas. 21 Jun 1877 - 1,5,6 - bl Biblioteca [072]

CORREIO DO NORTE : ORGAO DO PARTIDO REVISIONISTA DO ESTADO DO AMAZONAS - Manaus, Amazonas. 21 Jan-Jul 1906; Jun 1909-2 Jul 1912 - 1,5,6 - bl Biblioteca [072]

CORREIO DO NORTE : SUPPLEMENTO ILLUSTRADO - Manaos, Amazonas. 19 Jul-13 Set 1909 - 1,5,6 - bl Biblioteca [072]

CORREIO DO OESTE : JORNAL INDEPENDENTE E NOTICIOSO - Rio Branco, Acre. 31 Dez 1965-Dez 1968; Jan, 7 Set 1969 - 1,5,6 - bl Biblioteca [072]

CORREIO DO POMBA - Rio Pomba, Brazil. Jun 1897 - 1 - bl Biblioteca [072]

CORREIO DO POVO - Maceio, Alagoas. 14,25 Ago 1892 - 1,5,6 - bl Biblioteca [072]

CORREIO DO POVO - [s.l.]. 2 Out 1891 - 1,5,6 - bl Biblioteca [072]

CORREIO DO POVO - [s.l.]. 3 Jun-31 Dez 1925 - 1,5,6 - bl Biblioteca [072]

CORREIO DO POVO - Varginha, 20 Jun 1897 - 1,5,6 - bl Biblioteca [072]

O CORREIO DO PURUS - Labrea, Amazonas. 13 Maio, Jul-Ago 1900; Nov 1904; Nov-Dez 1905; Ago-Dez 1906; Jan-Nov 1907; Mar, Dez 1908; Jan 1909-Jul 1911; Fev 1912-Ago 1914; Jan-Dez 1915; Jan, 4 Jul 1916 - 1,5,6 - bl Biblioteca [072]

CORREIO DO RIO DE JANEIRO - Rio de Janeiro, 10 Apr-Oct 1822; Aug-24 Nov 1823 - 1,5,6 - bl Biblioteca [072]

CORREIO DO RIO DOCE - Governador Valadares, 24 Jul-4 Sept 1955 - 1,5,6 - bl Biblioteca [072]

CORREIO DO SERTAO - Arassui, 1 Jun 1944 - 1,5,6 - bl Biblioteca [072]

CORREIO DO SERTAO - Santa Cruz do Rio Pardo, Brazil. Mar 1902-Dec 1903 - 1 - bl Biblioteca [072]

CORREIO DO SUL : ORGAM DO PARTIDO REPUBLICANO DE VARGINHA - Varginha, 26 Nov 1905 - 1,5,6 - bl Biblioteca [072]

CORREIO DO SUL - Santa Rita do Sapucai, Brazil. Dec 1953 - 1 - bl Biblioteca [072]

CORREIO DO SUL - Varginha, Brazil. Sept 1956-May 1979. Scattered issues - 1 - bl Biblioteca [072]

O CORREIO DO VALE - Januaria, Brazil. Apr 1960 - 1 - bl Biblioteca [072]

CORREIO ESTUDANTIL : ORGAO DO GREMIO 10. DE JUNHO - Rio Branco, Acre. 10 Out 1964; 2 Set 1967 - 1,5,6 - bl Biblioteca [072]

CORREIO EXTRAORDINARIO DO RIO DE JANEIRO - Rio de Janeiro, 23 May-Oct 1822; May-31 Jul 1823 - 1,5,6 - bl Biblioteca [072]

CORREIO GYMNASIAL : JORNAL LITTERARIO E NOTICIOSO - Manaos, Amazonas. 3 Maio-8 Out 1915 - 1,5,6 - bl Biblioteca [072]

O CORREIO MACAENSE - (Filmed with: Correio de Macau) - Macau: A de Silva Telles, nov 3 1885 - 1r - us Res Libr [072]

O CORREIO MACEIOENSE - Maceio, Alagoas. 24 Mar 1850-2 Mar 1851 - 1,5,6 - bl Biblioteca [072]

CORREIO MERCANTIL - (Cont of: O Mercantil) - Rio de Janeiro, 2 Jan 1848-15 Nov 1868 - 1,5,6 - bl Biblioteca [072]

CORREIO MERCANTIL : FOLHA OFFICIAL DE COMMERCIO E DE LITTERATURA - '(s.l.')-BA, Brazil. 10 dez 1836; abr 1938-dez 1841; jan 1843-dez 1844; jan 1847-dez 1 849; 22 maio 1854 - 1,5,6 - bl Biblioteca [072]

CORREIO MERCANTIL - Maceio, Alagoas. 2 Set 1891; Fev, 28 Abr 1895 - 1,5,6 - bl Biblioteca [072]

CORREIO MUNICIPAL - Curitiba, 29 Jun 1895-25 Apr 1896 - 1,5,6 - bl Biblioteca [072]

CORREIO OFFICIAL - Rio de Janeiro, 1 Jul 1833-147 Aug 1841 - 1,5,6 - bl Biblioteca [072]

CORREIO OFFICIAL DE MINAS - Ouro Preto, 8 Jan 1857-9 Jul 1860 - 1,5,6 - bl Biblioteca [072]

CORREIO PAULISTANO - Sao Paulo, 26 Jun 1854-Dec 1868; Feb 1869-Dec 1882; Jan 1883-Dec 1888; Jan-Jun, Aug-Dec 1889; Jan 1890-Dec 1893; Jan-Oct, Dec 1894; Jan-Dec 1895; Jan 1897-Dec 1898; Jan-Dec 1900; Jan-Jun 1902; Jan 1903-31 Jul 1963 - 1,5,6 - bl Biblioteca [072]

CORREIO PAULISTANO - Sao Paulo, Brazil. Jan-July 1908 - 1 - us Res Libr [072]

CORREIO SERGIPENSE : FOLHA OFFICIAL, POLITICA E LITERARIA - S. Christova/ Aracaju, 19 Feb-Dec 1840; Jan, Jun-Aug 1841; Jan 1842-Dec 1843; Mar-Jun 1844; Feb-May, Sep-Dec 1845; Jun, Sep 1846; Jan 1847-Dec 1864; May-Jun, Nov 1865; Jan-27 Jun 1866 - 1,5,6 - bl Biblioteca [072]

CORREIO SPORTIVO : ORGAO DE PROPAGANDA SPORTIVA - Manaus, Amazonas. 27 Mar-Jun 1910; 12 Mar 1911 - 1,5,6 - bl Biblioteca [072]

CORREIO SPORTIVO : SEMANARIO SPORTIVO E NOTICIOSO - Manaos, Amazonas. 19 Mar-3 Jun 1916 - 1,5,6 - bl Biblioteca [072]

CORREIO TRABALHISTA : ORGAO DO PARTIDO TRABALHISTA BRASILEIRO - Salvador, BA. 22 Jan-07 Maio 1946 - 1,5,6 - bl Biblioteca [072]

CORREL SMITH DIARY *see* SMITH, CORREL, DIARY, MS 3285

CORRELATION BETWEEN MUSCLE RELAXATION AND SARCOPLASMIC RETICULUM CA2+-ATPASE DURING FATIGUE : AN IN-SITU MODEL / Biedermann, Michael C & Klug, Gary A - 1992 - 1mf - $4.00 - us Microform Publ [612]

CORRELATION OF LABORATORY TESTS TO DISTANCE RUNNING PERFORMANCE DURING A CROSS-COUNTRY TRACK SEASON / Mosenthal, Teese M - 1988 - 105p 2mf - 9 - $8.00 - us Microform Publ [617]

THE CORRELATION OF THE PRE-KARROO SUCCESSION IN NORTHERN RHODESIA WITH THAT OF ADJACENT TERRITORIES / Hays, J - Lusaka 1950 - us Res Libr [960]

Correns, C E *see* UNTERSUCHUNGEN UEBER DIE VERMEHRUNG DER LAUBMOOSE DURCH BRUTORGANE UND STECKLINGE

Correns, P *see*
- DIE DEM BOETHIUS...ZUGESCHRIEBENE ABHANDLUNG DES DOM. GUNDISALVI DE UNITATE

CORRENTINO POR A : EPOPEYA DE UN DESCAMISADO / Gauna, Adrian - Buenos Aires: [A. Gauna], 1949 - 1 - CSUXAHZ7472-B - us Hoover Inst Photo [830]

CORREO ARGENTINO. EXTREMADURA - Buenos Aires, 1940. 1 numero - 5 - sp Bibl Santa Ana [073]

EL CORREO DE EDUCATION CHRISTIANA - (Lacking: no 63) - nos 42-91. 1939-47 - 1r - 1 - ATLA S0665B - us A.T.L.A. [073]

CORREO DE EXTREMADURA - Badajoz, 1891-1894 - 5 - sp Bibl Santa Ana [072]

CORREO DE LA MANANA - Badajoz, 1915. 1 numero - 5 - sp Bibl Santa Ana [073]

EL CORREO ESPANOL - Madrid, Spain. - d. 21 Sept 1914-10 Aug 1919. Imperfect. 15 reels - 1 - uk British Libr Newspaper [072]

CORREO GENERAL DE ESPANA / Nipho, Francisco Mariano - 1769 - 2mf - 9 - Pta1,500.00 - 84-7848-167-2 - sp Pentalfa [946]

CORREO LITERARIO - Madrid. Spain. -w. 15 Mar, 1 Jun 1951-Mar 1955. (3 reels) - 1 - uk British Libr Newspaper [800]

CORREO MEXICANO : EL DIARIO DE LA RAZA - Chicago, IL: Francisco Huerta, 4 sep 1926-4 mar 1927 - 1r - 1 - us Res Libr [071]

CORREO MUSICAL SUD-AMERICANO - v1. 1915 - 1r - 1 - us Ross [780]

EL CORREO PLACENTINO - Plasencia, 1901 - 5 - sp Bibl Santa Ana [073]

CORRESPONCENCE BETWEEN THE SECRETARY OF STATE FOR THE COLONIES AND THE GOVERNORS OF CANADA AND MR. W.B. FELTON, RELATIVE TO LANDS GRANTED TO THE SAID W.B. FELTON - [London, England: s.n., 1836]. SEM105P1395 - 1mf - 9 - Can$2.25 - cn Bibl Nat [333]

CORRESPONDANCE - devenu: Union pour la verite. Correspondance puis Bulletin. Paris. 1906, 1908-juin 1914, 1920-23, 1925-avr 1939 - 1 - fr A.C.R.P.P. [073]

CORRESPONDANCE / Hmae, Pasteur Apou & Leenhardt, M & Rey-Lescure, P - 1917-1946 - 9 - F70.00 - fr Ethnologie [920]

CORRESPONDANCE AGRICOLE ET POLITIQUE - Paris. juin 1898-1921 - 1 - fr A.C.R.P.P. [630]

CORRESPONDANCE AUTHENTIQUE DE LA COUR DE ROME AVEC LA FRANCE... - N.p., 1809 - 5mf - 1 - ILM-2859/1 - ne IDC [327]

CORRESPONDANCE AUTOGRAPHIEE DU BUREAU INTERNATIONAL DE LA PAIX - 1892-1940. Continued as: Correspondance bi-mensuelle; Mouvement pacifiste; Peace Movement - 85mf - 9 - $320.00 - us UPA [320]

CORRESPONDANCE DE GUERRE D'UN RURAL 1914-1917 / Raybaut, P - 9 - F70.00 - fr Ethnologie [940]

CORRESPONDANCE DE NAPOLEON 1ER : PUBLIEE PAR ORDRE DE L'EMPERERUR NAPOLEON 3RD - Paris, 1858-1898. 32v - 305mf - 2404/2 - ne IDC [944]

CORRESPONDANCE DIPLOMATIQUE... / Callery, J M - Paris, 1879 - 4mf - 9 - ILM-354/1 - ne IDC [327]

CORRESPONDANCE DIPLOMATIQUE DU COMTE POZZO DI BORGO, AMBASSADEUR DE RUSSIE EN FRANCE, ET DU COMTE DE NESSELRODE DEPUIS LA RESTAURATION..., 1814-18 / Pozzo di Borgo, Carlo Andrea, Comte - Paris: Calmann Levy, 1890-97. 2v. v1 2nd ed - 1 - us U.W. Library [940]

CORRESPONDANCE, DOCUMENTS, TEMOIGNAGES ET PROCEDES DANS L'ENQUETE DE MESSRS. LAFRENAYE ET DOHERTY – Montreal: Imp. de la Minerve, 1864. SEM105P321 – 2mf – 9 – Can$4.50 – cn Bibl Nat [323]

CORRESPONDANCE ENTRE LE BUREAU COLONIAL ET LES GOUVERNEURS DU CANADA, RELATIVE A LA TENURE SEIGNEURIALE ET FEODALE.. – Quebec: Imprimerie de E R Frechette, 1853. SEM105P254 – 1mf – 9 – Can$2.25 – cn Bibl Nat [323]

CORRESPONDANCE ENTRE LE GOUVERNEMENT FRANCAIS ET LES GOUVERNEURS ET INTENDANTS DU CANADA, RELATIVE A LA TENURE SEIGNEURIALE, DEMANDEE PAR UNE ADRESSE DE L'ASSEMBLE LEGISLATIVE, 1851 – Quebec: Imprimerie de E R Frechette..., 1853. SEM105P253 – 1mf – 9 – Can$2.25 – cn Bibl Nat [333]

CORRESPONDANCE HAVAS – Paris. 2 nov-dec 1852 – 1 – fr A.C.R.P.P. [073]

CORRESPONDANCE INEDITE(...) 5 MAI 1789 – 29 MAI 1790 / Pellerin, Joseph-Michel – Paris: Sauton, 1883 – fr Armell [944]

CORRESPONDANCE INEDITE DE NAPOLEON 1ER : CONSERVEE AUX ARCHIVES DE LA GUERRE 1804-1812 – Paris, 1912-1925 – 73mf – 2405/2 – ne IDC [944]

LA CORRESPONDANCE INTERNATIONALE – Berlin puis Vienne, Paris. oct 1921-aout 1939 – 1 – fr A.C.R.P.P. [073]

LA CORRESPONDANCE INTERNATIONALE – Berlin, Vienna, Paris. v1 no 1-v19 no 43, Oct 1921-Aug 1939. French edition of Internationale Presse-Korrespondenz – 274mf – 9 – $760.00 – us UPA [335]

CORRESPONDANCE INTERNATIONALE OUVRIERE – Paris puis Nimes. sept 1932-avr 1933 – 1 – fr A.C.R.P.P. [073]

CORRESPONDANCE MARITIME DE NANTES – Nantes. 1782. BM. Nantes 60579 – 1 – fr A.C.R.P.P. [073]

CORRESPONDANCE MATHEMATIQUE ET PHYSIQUE – Bruxelles, 1827-39 – 3 – us Readex [510]

CORRESPONDANCE OFFICIELLE DE LA COUR DE ROME AVEC LES AGENS DE BUONAPARTE,... – Lyon, 1814 – 4mf – 1 – ILM-2835/1 – ne IDC [327]

CORRESPONDANCE ON CHURCH AND RELIGION SELECTED AND ARRANGED BY D.C. LATHBURY / Gladstone, William Ewart – (Volume 1 London, 1910.-9mf; Volume 2 London, 1910.-9mf) – 8 – ne Slangenburg [240]

CORRESPONDANCE POLITIQUE DE PARIS ET DES DEPARTEMENS – no. 216-315. Paris. janv-avr 1794 (II) – 1 – fr A.C.R.P.P. [073]

CORRESPONDANCE POLITIQUE DES VERITABLES AMIS DU ROI ET DE LA PATRIE – devenu: Nouvelle correspondance politique, pour servir de suite aux LII premiers numeros de la Correspondance. Paris. janv-aout 1792 – 1 – fr A.C.R.P.P. [073]

LA CORRESPONDANCE REGIONALISTE – no. 1-4. Paris. mars-aout 1901 – 1 – fr A.C.R.P.P. [073]

CORRESPONDANCE RELATIVE A LA REUNION DES HOPITAUX D'AVILA. TEXTES EN PROSE INEDITS PUBLIES...PAR GEORGES DEMERSON / Melendez Valdes, Juan – Bordeaux: Feret and Fils, 1964 – 1 – sp Bibl Santa Ana [944]

CORRESPONDANCE SECRETE CENTRE LE COMTE A.W. KAUNITZ-RIETBERG... : ET LE BARON IGNAZ DE KOCH...1750-1752 / ed by Schlitter, H – Paris, 1899 – 5mf – 9 – ne IDC [943]

CORRESPONDANCE SECRETE DU COMTE DE MERCY-ARGENTEAU AVEC L'EMPEREUR JOSEPH 2 / ed by D'Arneth, A & Flammermont, J – Paris. 2v. 1889-1891 – 14mf – 9 – ne IDC [920]

CORRESPONDANCE SOCIALISTE INTERNATIONALE – Le mensuel de l'internationalisme militant. Dir. Marceau Pivert. no. 1-106. Paris. 1951-avr mai 1960. mq no. 1-4, 77, 80, 88-89 – 1 – fr A.C.R.P.P. [073]

CORRESPONDANCE UNIVERSELLE – Dir. Ballero. no. 4817-4885. Paris. 2 janv-11 mars 1884 – 1 – fr A.C.R.P.P. [073]

CORRESPONDANCES INTIMES DE L'EMPEREUR JOSEPH 2 AVEC SON AMI LE COMTE DE COBENZL ET SON PREMIER MINISTRE LE PRINCE DE KAUNITZ. MAYENCE / ed by Brunner, S – Paris, Bruxelles, 1871 – 2mf – 9 – ne IDC [943]

CORRESPONDANT – London, UK. 8 Aug 1873 – 1 – uk British Libr Newspaper [072]

LE CORRESPONDANT – Paris. mars 1829-fevr 1831 – 1 – fr A.C.R.P.P. [073]

LE CORRESPONDANT – puis Recueil periodique. Paris. oct 1855-sept 1870 – 1 – fr A.C.R.P.P. [073]

LE CORRESPONDANT DES DEPARTEMENTS – Paris: Maulde et Renou, apr 30 1850 – us Res Libr [944]

LE CORRESPONDANT; RELIGION, PHILOSOPHIE, POLITIQUE, HISTOIRE, SCIENCES, ECONOMIE SOCIALE, VOYAGES, LITTERATURE, BEAUX-ARTS – Paris. v. 1-333. 1843-Oct 1933 – 1 – us NY Public [073]

CORRESPONDENCE / Atchison, Topeka and Santa Fe Railroad Company – 1873-93 – 1 – us KS Hist [025]

CORRESPONDENCE / Banks, Joseph – 1766-1820 – 1 – uk Microform Academic [920]

CORRESPONDENCE / Baptist State Conventions. (Southern Baptist). Virginia – 1790-1820 – 1 – 5.00 – us Baptist [240]

CORRESPONDENCE / Beresford, John – Illustrative of the last 30 years of the Irish parliament. Selections from original papers, Edited, with notes, by Right Hon. William Beresford. London, 1854. 2v – 1 – us U.W. Library [920]

CORRESPONDENCE / Blaho, P & Srobar, V – 1905-1913 – 1 reel – 1 – us I.H.R.C. [860]

CORRESPONDENCE / Carlyle, Thomas & Welsh, Janet – 1 – uk Microform Academic [920]

CORRESPONDENCE / Cary, Orland R – 1946-53. 600p – 1 – 21.00 – us Baptist [240]

CORRESPONDENCE / Coke Family – 1595-1750. Holkham ms. 746. Holkham Hall, Norfolk, England – 1 – uk Microform Academic [920]

CORRESPONDENCE / Columbian College – Baptist Records in Library of Congress, 1822-36. 144p – 1 – 5.04 – us Baptist [240]

CORRESPONDENCE / Flamsteed, John – From Royal Society, London – 1 – uk Microform Academic [920]

CORRESPONDENCE / Furman, Richard – 1755-1825. 1,232p – 1 – 43.12 – us Baptist [240]

CORRESPONDENCE / Graton, John R – 1838-1910 – 1 – us KS Hist [920]

CORRESPONDENCE / Hill, Kate Alexander – 1896-1936 – 5 – $50.00 – us Presbyterian [920]

CORRESPONDENCE / Jackson, Sheldon – 1856-1908. Calendars – 1 – $350.00 – us Presbyterian [978]

CORRESPONDENCE / Jackson, Sheldon – 1856-1908. Orig – 1 – $800.00 – us Presbyterian [240]

CORRESPONDENCE / Jackson, Sheldon – 1856-1908. Transcripts – 1 – $250.00 – us Presbyterian [240]

CORRESPONDENCE / Koehler, Robert – 1888-1927. 1 roll including filmed inventory – 1 – $30.00r – us M.H.S. [920]

CORRESPONDENCE / Mellichamp, Joseph H – 1885-1902. 11 fiches – 9 – us South Carolina Historical [920]

CORRESPONDENCE / Mickiewicz, Adam – 1870 – 1 – us U.W. Library [920]

CORRESPONDENCE / Peel, Robert – Royal Archives. Windsor. 1841-46 – 1 – uk Microform Academic [920]

CORRESPONDENCE / Presbyterian Church in the U.S.A. Board of Foreign Missions. Furrukhabad Mission – 1839-64 – 1 – $50.00 – us Presbyterian [240]

CORRESPONDENCE / Ray, John – 1848 – 1 – uk Microform Academic [920]

CORRESPONDENCE / Richardson, Samuel – 1748-62 – 1 – uk Microform Academic [920]

CORRESPONDENCE / Sloane, Hans – British Museum, Sloane Mss 4036-4069 – 1 – uk Microform Academic [920]

CORRESPONDENCE / Wells, Edward L – 1861, 1865, 1885-1913. 7 fiches – 9 – us South Carolina Historical [025]

CORRESPONDENCE, 16 OCTOBER 1873-15 OCTOBER 1878 / Fison, Lorimer – (Access to this material is restricted) – 1r – 1 – at Pacific Mss [980]

CORRESPONDENCE, 1610-88 AND 1665-1745 / Butler, James, First Duke of OrmondeButler, James Second Duke of Ormonde – 1 – uk Microform Academic [920]

CORRESPONDENCE 1621-79 / Boyle, Roger – 1 – uk Microform Academic [920]

CORRESPONDENCE, 1697-1725 / Nicolson, William (Bishop) & Wake (Archbishop) – 1 – uk Microform Academic [240]

CORRESPONDENCE, 1729-1775 / Penn, Thomas – 10 reels, guide included. Guide available separately – 1 – 250.00r – us H.S.P. [025]

CORRESPONDENCE, 1829-92 / Manly Family – 5158p – 1 – 180.53 – us Baptist [240]

CORRESPONDENCE, 1830-1865 / Church Missionary Society. South India Mission. Madras – London: Kodak Ltd, Recordak Div, 1967 (mf ed) – 1 – us Res Libr [240]

CORRESPONDENCE 1830-1865 / South India (Madras) Mission. Church Missionary Society – London, Kodak Ltd, Recordak Division, 1967 – us Res Libr [240]

CORRESPONDENCE, 1870-1881 / Fison, Lorimer – 1r – at Pacific Mss [920]

CORRESPONDENCE 1914-1918 / Baksh, Ahmad – (Filmed with: National Archives of India: Selections from the Home Political Files jul 1914-1916, 1918 and the Army Department Files 1914-may 1919) – New Delhi, National Archives of India, 1969 – us Res Libr [950]

CORRESPONDENCE, 1943-1947 / Bengal Relief Committee – [s.l: s.n, –] – 1 – us Res Libr [950]

CORRESPONDENCE, 1964-67 / BEST (Baptist Education Study Task) – 1103p – 5 – 38.60 – us Baptist [240]

CORRESPONDENCE AND OTHER PAPERS RE BUSINESS AND FAMILY ACTIVITIES IN THE NEW HEBRIDES / Zeitler, Adolf – 1899-1935 – 1r – 1 – PMB 1091 – at Pacific Mss [920]

CORRESPONDENCE AND OTHER PAPERS RELATED TO THEIR SERVICE WITH THE METHODIST OVERSEAS MISSION / Simpson, Thomas Nevison & Simpson, Nellie – New Hanover, PNG: 1936-42 – 1r – 1 – PMB1114 – at Pacific Mss [920]

CORRESPONDENCE AND PAPERS / Hyatt, Thaddeus – (Papers. 1843-98. 1) – 1858-1901 – 1 – us KS Hist [920]

CORRESPONDENCE AND PAPERS, 1825-56 / Owen, Robert – BRRAM – 1 – uk Microform Academic [970]

CORRESPONDENCE AND PAPERS, DISTURBANCES 1812-1855 / Great Britain. Home Office – 46r – 1 – us Ross [941]

CORRESPONDENCE AND PAPERS OF DAVID NELSON / Nelson, David – 1835-1857 – 1 – $50.00 – us Presbyterian [240]

THE CORRESPONDENCE AND PUBLIC PAPERS OF JOHN JAY / ed by Johnston, Henry P – New York. 4v. 1890-93 – 1r – 1 – us Ross [920]

CORRESPONDENCE AND RECORD CARDS OF THE MILITARY INTELLIGENCE DIVISION RELATING TO GENERAL, POLITICAL, AND MILITARY CONDITIONS IN CENTRAL AMERICA, 1918-1941 – 12r – 1 – M1488 – us Nat'l Archives [355]

CORRESPONDENCE AND RECORD CARDS OF THE MILITARY INTELLIGENCE DIVISION RELATING TO GENERAL, POLITICAL, ECONOMIC, AND MILITARY CONDITIONS IN CUBA AND THE WEST INDIES, 1918-1941 – 10r – 1 – M1507 – us Nat'l Archives [355]

CORRESPONDENCE AND RECORD CARDS OF THE MILITARY INTELLIGENCE DIVISION RELATING TO GENERAL, POLITICAL, ECONOMIC, AND MILITARY CONDITIONS IN ITALY, 1918-1941 – 26r – 1 – M1446 – us Nat'l Archives [355]

CORRESPONDENCE AND RECORD CARDS OF THE MILITARY INTELLIGENCE DIVISION RELATING TO GENERAL, POLITICAL, ECONOMIC, AND MILITARY CONDITIONS IN POLAND AND THE BALTIC STATES, 1918-1941 – 10r – 1 – M1508 – us Nat'l Archives [355]

CORRESPONDENCE AND RECORDS, 1944-55 / Kiamichi Baptist Assembly. Oklahoma – 649p – 1 – us Baptist [240]

CORRESPONDENCE AND REPORTS / Presbyterian Church in the U.S.A. Board of Aid for Colleges and Academies. Henry Kendall College-University of Tulsa – 1892-1938 – 1 – $100.00 – us Presbyterian [370]

CORRESPONDENCE AND REPORTS / Presbyterian Church in the U.S.A. Board of Foreign Missions. Korea, Independence movement – 1919-20 – 1 – $50.00 – us Presbyterian [950]

CORRESPONDENCE AND REPORTS / Presbyterian Church in the U.S.A. Board of Foreign Missions. Korea, Japanese Colonial Government, Religious education controversy – 1915-19 – 1 – $50.00 – us Presbyterian [950]

CORRESPONDENCE AND REPORTS OF THE CONFEDERATE TREASURY DEPT., 1861-65 / U.S. War Department. Confederate Records – 2rolls. T1025 – 1 – us Nat'l Archives [324]

CORRESPONDENCE AND REPORTS ON MISSIONS TO THE CHINESE IN CALIFORNIA / Loomis, Augustus Ward – 1863-1873 – 1 – $50.00 – us Presbyterian [240]

CORRESPONDENCE BETWEEN ARCHBISHOP CLEARY, OF KINGSTON, AND W. R. MEREDITH, LEADER OF THE ONTARIO OPPOSITION; ALSO, THE ARCHBISHOP'S REMARKS AT TWEED, AND HIS CIRCULAR ON SEPARATE SCHOOLS, ADDRESSED TO HIS CLERGY / Cleary, James Vincent – 1890? 00680. (Pre-1900 Canadiana) – 9 – cn C.I.H.M. [240]

CORRESPONDENCE BETWEEN DONALD MOODIE..AND THE REV. JOHN PHILIP...RELATIVE TO THE PRODUCTION FOR PUBLICATION OF ALLEGED "OFFICIAL AUTHORITY" : FOR THE STATEMENT THAT IN THE YEAR 1774 THE WHOLE RACE OF BUSHMEN OR HOTTENTOTS WHO HAD NOT SUBMITTED TO SERVITUDE WAS ORDERED TO BE SEIZED OR EXTIRPATED / Moodie, Donald – Cape Town. 1841 – 1 – us Res Libr [960]

THE CORRESPONDENCE BETWEEN GREAT BRITAIN AND FRANCE...1803 – London, 1803 – 2mf – 1 – ILM-1178/1 – ne IDC [327]

CORRESPONDENCE BETWEEN SIR HENRY MCMAHON, HIS MAJESTY'S HIGH COMMISSIONER AT CAIRO, AND THE SHERIF HUSSEIN OF MECCA JUL 1915-MAR 1916 / Great Britain – London. 1939. Cmd. 5957. BJ-28-89 1 – 9 – ne IDC [956]

CORRESPONDENCE BETWEEN THE COLONIAL OFFICE AND THE GOVERNORS OF CANADA, RELATIVE TO THE SEIGNIORIAL AND FEUDAL TENURE.. / Canada – Quebec: E R Frechette, 1853. SEM105P256 – 1mf – 9 – Can$2.25 – cn Bibl Nat [323]

CORRESPONDENCE BETWEEN THE COMPANY AND THE DOMINION GOVERNMENT RESPECTING ADVANCES TO THE CANADIAN PACIFIC RAILWAY COMPANY / Grand Trunk Railway Company of Canada – 1884?. 00115. (Pre-1900 Canadiana) – 9 – cn C.I.H.M. [971]

CORRESPONDENCE BETWEEN THE FRENCH GOVERNMENT AND THE GOVERNORS AND INTENDANTS OF CANADA, RELATIVE TO THE SEIGNEURIAL TENURE.. / Canada – Quebec: E R Frechette, 1853. SEM105P255 – 9 – Can$2.25 – cn Bibl Nat [323]

CORRESPONDENCE BETWEEN THE ROMAN CATHOLIC BISHOP OF TORONTO AND THE CHIEF SUPERINTENDENT OF SCHOOLS ON THE SUBJECT OF SEPARATE COMMON SCHOOLS IN UPPER CANADA / Canada. Departement de l'Instruction Publique pour le Haut-Canada – Toronto: Printed and publ by Thomas Hugh Bentley, 1853. SEM105P332 – 1mf – 9 – Can$2.25 – cn Bibl Nat [370]

CORRESPONDENCE BETWEEN THE SECRETARY OF STATE FOR INDIA AND THE VARIOUS LOCAL GOVERNMENTS / India. Secretary of State – Parliamentary paper 1883. v. 51, paper 93-I, II and app. II. Including: Extra correspondence. BI-516 2 – 8 – ne IDC [324]

CORRESPONDENCE CONCERNING LAC QUI PARLE MISSION, DAKOTA AND SIOUX INDIANS / Riggs, Stephen R – 1837-51 – 1 – $50.00 – us Presbyterian [240]

CORRESPONDENCE DE FERNAND CORTES AVEC 1 EMPEREUR CHARLES QUINT. SUR LA CONQUETE DE MEXIQUE / Cortes, Hernando – Tradiste por M le vi comte de Flavigny. Suisse, Libraires Associes, 1779 – sp Bibl Santa Ana [350]

CORRESPONDENCE, DOCUMENTS, EVIDENCE AND PROCEEDINGS IN THE ENQUIRY OF MESSRS. LAFRENAYE AND DOHERTY...FOLLOWED BY THE REMARKS OF MESSRS. DELISLE & SCHILLER...AND THE REMARKS OF MR. BREHAUT ON THE LETTER ANNOUNCING...CAUSES OF HIS DISMISSAL.. – Montreal: M. Longmoore

& Co, 1864. SEM105P322 – 2mf – 9 – Can$4.50 – cn Bibl Nat [971]

CORRESPONDENCE, ETC., RELATING TO THE MONTREAL, OTTAWA AND GEORGIAN BAY CANAL – s.l.: s.n., 1897? (Ottawa: Printed by Paynter & Abbott). 00249. (Pre-1900 Canadiana) – 9 – cn C.I.H.M. [971]

LA CORRESPONDENCE FEDERATIVE – (Some issues missing) – 1939-44 – 1r – 1 – ATLA S0662 – us A.T.L.A. [073]

CORRESPONDENCE FILES, ALPHABETICAL SINGLE NUMBER SERIES, 1911-1914 / Kaiserliches Gouvernement Van Deutsch Neu-Guinea (Imperial Government of German New Guinea) – 11r – 1 – CRS G2 – at Archives [920]

CORRESPONDENCE FILES OF CORRESPONDING SECRETARIES, BAPTIST SUNDAY SCHOOL BOARD / Frost, J M & Bell, T P – 1889-1916. 71,273p – 1 – 2494.55 – us Baptist [240]

CORRESPONDENCE FILES, SINGLE NUMBER SERIES, 1899-1911 / Imperial Government of German New Guinea – 8r – 1 – CRS G1 – at Archives [920]

CORRESPONDENCE INEDITE DE LA COMTESSE DE SABRAN ET DU CHEVALIER DE BOUFFLERS, 1778-88 / Sabran, Francoise Eleonore – 2e ed. Paris: E Plon, 1875 – 1 – us Res Libr [960]

CORRESPONDENCE, MINUTES, CIRCULARS, CLIPPINGS, ETC / Congress of Democrats – Johannesburg, Microfile, [19–?] – us Res Libr [960]

CORRESPONDENCE OF A. D. BACHE, SUPERINTENDENT OF COAST AND GEODETIC SURVEY, 1843-65 / U.S. Coast and Geodetic Survey – 281 rolls. M642. Printed guide – 1 – us Nat'l Archives [550]

CORRESPONDENCE OF DANIEL O'CONNELL, THE LIBERATOR; ED. WITH NOTICES OF HIS LIFE AND TIMES. / O'Connell, Daniel – Ed. by W.J. Fitzpatrick.London: J. Murray, 1888. 2v – 1 – us U.W. Library [920]

CORRESPONDENCE OF FRAEULEIN GUENDERODE AND BETTINE VON ARNIM – Boston: T O H P Burnham, 1861 – 1r – 1 – us U.W. Library [920]

CORRESPONDENCE OF FREDERICK CHASE, 1861-1874 / Chase, Frederick – 3r – 1 – $215.00 – us UMI [920]

CORRESPONDENCE OF FREDERICK CHASE IN THE YEARS 1861-1874 / Chase, Frederick – 3r – 1 – $50.00 set – us Dartmouth [975]

THE CORRESPONDENCE OF ISAAC BASIRE : D.D., ARCHDEACON OF NORTHUMBERLAND AND PREBENDARY OF DURHAM IN THE REIGNS OF CHARLES 1 AND CHARLES 2 / Darnell, WN – London: John Murray, 1831 – 1mf – us A.T.L.A. [240]

CORRESPONDENCE OF RALPH W. BROWN *see* MINUTES

THE CORRESPONDENCE OF RICHARD PORSON, M.A. FORMERLY REGIUS PROFESSOR OF GREEK IN THE UNIVERSITY OF CAMBRIDGE / Porson, Richard; ed by Luard, Henry Richards – Cambridge: Deighton, Bell & Co., 1867 – 1 roll – 1 – 1-55879-732-7 – uk Libr Preservation [450]

CORRESPONDENCE OF ROBERT H. GARDINER *see* MINUTES

CORRESPONDENCE OF SECRETARY OF STATE BRYAN WITH PRESIDENT WILSON, 1913-15 / U.S. Department of State – 4rolls. T841 – 1 – us Nat'l Archives [977]

CORRESPONDENCE OF THE MENNONITE WOMAN'S MISSIONARY SOCIETY – nos1-10. 1919-21 (complete) – 1r – 1 – ATLA 1994-S038 – us A.T.L.A. [240]

CORRESPONDENCE OF THE MILITARY INTELLIGENCE DIVISION CORRESPONDENCE RELATING TO "NEGRO SUBVERSION", 1917-1941 – 6r – 1 – M1440 – us Nat'l Archives [355]

CORRESPONDENCE OF THE MILITARY INTELLIGENCE DIVISION RELATING TO GENERAL, POLITICAL, AND MILITARY CONDITIONS IN SCANDANAVIA AND FINLAND, 1918-1941 – 12r – 1 – M1497 – us Nat'l Archives [355]

CORRESPONDENCE OF THE MILITARY INTELLIGENCE DIVISION RELATING TO GENERAL, POLITICAL, ECONOMIC, AND MILITARY CONDITIONS IN CHINA, 1918-1941 – 19 rolls – 9 – $437.00 – Dist. us Scholarly Res – us L of C Photodup [355]

CORRESPONDENCE OF THE MILITARY INTELLIGENCE DIVISION RELATING TO GENERAL, POLITICAL, ECONOMIC, AND MILITARY CONDITIONS IN RUSSIA AND THE SOVIET UNION, 1918-1941 – 23r – 1 – M1443 – us Nat'l Archives [355]

CORRESPONDENCE OF THE MILITARY INTELLIGENCE DIVISION RELATING TO GENERAL, POLITICAL, ECONOMIC, AND MILITARY CONDITIONS IN SPAIN, 1918-1941 – 12r – 1 – M1445 – us Nat'l Archives [355]

CORRESPONDENCE OF THE OFFICE OF CIVIL AFAIRS IN THE DEPARTMENT OF TEXAS / U.S. Office of Civil Affairs – 1867-70. M1188 – 1 – us Nat'l Archives [324]

CORRESPONDENCE OF THE SECRETARY OF ALASKA / Alaska. Office of the Secretary – 1900-13. 20 rolls. T1201 – 1 – us Nat'l Archives [978]

CORRESPONDENCE OF THE SECRETARY OF THE NAVY RELATING TO AFRICAN COLONIZATION, 1819-1844 / U.S. Navy. Office of Naval Records and Library – M205. Printed guide – 2 rolls – 1 – us Nat'l Archives [355]

CORRESPONDENCE OF THE SECRETARY OF THE TREASURY WITH COLLECTORS OF CUSTOMS, 1789-1833 / U.S. Treasury Department – 39 rolls. M178. Printed guide – 1 – us Nat'l Archives [324]

CORRESPONDENCE OF THE SURVEYORS GENERAL OF UTAH, 1874-1916 – 86r – 1 – M1110 – us Nat'l Archives [324]

CORRESPONDENCE OF THE U.S. NAVAL ASTRONOMICAL EXPEDITION TO THE SOUTHERN HEMISPHERE, 1846-61 / U. S. Naval Observatory – T54 – 1r – 1 – us Nat'l Archives [324]

CORRESPONDENCE OF THE WAR DEPARTMENT RELATING TO INDIAN AFFAIRS, MILITARY PENSIONS, AND FORTIFICATIONS / U.S. War Department – 1791-97. 1 roll. M1062 – 1 – us Nat'l Archives [324]

CORRESPONDENCE ON CHURCH AND RELIGION OF WILLIAM EWART GLADSTONE / Gladstone, William Ewart; ed by Lathbury, D C – New York: Macmillan, 1910 – 3mf – us A.T.L.A. [240]

CORRESPONDENCE RECEIVED BY THE SURVEYORS GENERAL OF NEW MEXICO, 1854-1907 – 11r – 1 – M1288 – us Nat'l Archives [324]

CORRESPONDENCE RELATING TO THE CIVIL LIST AND MILITARY EXPENDITURE IN CANADA; AND TO THE PROJECTED RAILWAY FROM HALIFAX TO QUEBEC / Canada. Gouverneur general – London: Harrison and Son, 1851. SEM105P123 – 2mf – 9 – Can$4.50 – cn Bibl Nat [355]

CORRESPONDENCE RELATING TO THE CONFERENCE...THE HAGUE, 1910 / Great Britain. Foreign Office – London, 1910 – 3mf – 1 – ILM-3954/1 – ne IDC [327]

CORRESPONDENCE RELATING TO THE FILIBUSTERING EXPEDITION AGAINST THE SPANISH GOVERNMENT OF MEXICO, 1811-16 / U.S. Department of State – 1roll. T286 – 1 – us Nat'l Archives [975]

CORRESPONDENCE RELATING TO THE JOSEPH BARKER CASE, 1838-1869 / Barker, J – (Coll title: The People Called Methodists, Phase 3: Primary Sources, 1801-1850) – 7mf – 9 – MP-689/1 – ne IDC [240]

CORRESPONDENCE RELATING TO THE MARRIAGES OF THE QUEEN AND INFANTA OF SPAIN – London, 1847 – 4mf – 1 – ILM-2849/1 – ne IDC [327]

CORRESPONDENCE RELATIVE TO THE AFFAIRS OF CANADA, 1841 – London: Printed by William Clowes and Sons,...for Her Majesty's Stationery Office, 1841 – 1mf – 9 – Can$2.25 – cn Bibl Nat [971]

CORRESPONDENCE RELATIVE TO THE AFFAIRS OF CANADA: 1846 – London: Printed by William Clowes & Son, 1847. SEM105P119 – 1mf – 9 – Can$2.25 – cn Bibl Nat [971]

CORRESPONDENCE RELATIVE TO THE AFFAIRS OF HUNGARY : 1847-1849 – London, 1850 – 8mf – 1 – ILM-2861/1 – ne IDC [327]

CORRESPONDENCE, REPORTS / Presbyterian Church in the U.S.A. Board of Foreign Missions. Korea, Conspiracy Case, Japanese Colonial government – 1912-20 – 1 – $50.00 – us Presbyterian [950]

CORRESPONDENCE RESPECTING THE PROPOSED UNION OF THE BRITISH NORTH AMERICAN PROVINCES – London: George Edward Eyre and William Spottishwoode, 1867. SEM105P1759 – 2mf – 9 – Can$4.50 – cn Bibl Nat [324]

THE CORRESPONDENCE SERIES AND SPEECHES SERIES OF THE PERSONAL PAPERS OF JOHN FOSTER DULLES (1888-1959) / Challener, Richard – (Includes guide) – 1994 – 67r – 1 – $5,360.00 – D3300 – us L of C Photodup [320]

CORRESPONDENCE ("TOP SECRET") OF THE MANHATTAN ENGINEER DISTRICT, 1942-1946 / U.S. Office of the Chief of Engineers – RG 77. M1109. 5 rolls – 1 – us Nat'l Archives [355]

CORRESPONDENCE WITH HY. S.L. POLAK, 1917-1929?, CHARLES ROBERTS, 1917-1919, AND WILLIAM WEDDERBURN, 1904?-1918 / Natesan, Ganapati Agraharam – (Filmed with: Masani, R P: Correspondence with Reed Stanley and Drafts of two articles...Correspondence with Roberts and Wedderburn filmed later on the reel) – New Delhi: Nehru Memorial Museum & Lib, [19–?] – 1 – us Res Libr [950]

CORRESPONDENCE WITH KAISAR BAGH 1914-1917 / Mahmud, Syed – (Filmed with: Masani, R P: Correspondence...) – New Delhi, Nehru Memorial Museum and Library, [19–?] – us Res Libr [920]

[CORRESPONDENCE WITH REED STANLEY AND DRAFTS OF TWO ARTICLES, 1915-1933?] / Masani, Rustom Pestonji – New Delhi: Nehru Memorial Museum & Lib, [19–?] – 1 – us Res Libr [950]

CORRESPONDENCE WITH THE GOVERNMENT, 1926-1931 AND WITH DR CLIFFORD JAMES ON CLOTHES, 1931 / Binet, Vincent – Pt of 1r – 1 – PMB1108 – at Pacific Mss [920]

CORRESPONDENCE WITH THE PALESTINE ARAB DELEGATION AND THE ZIONIST ORGANISATION / Great Britain. Palestine – London. 1922. BJ-28-67 1 – 9 – ne IDC [956]

CORRESPONDENCE WITH WILLIAM HENRY JACKSON / Taft, Robert – undated – 1 – us KS Hist [920]

CORRESPONDENCE...CONCERNING ISSAC STEVENS' SURVEY OF A NORTHERN ROUTE FOR THE PACIFIC R.R., 1853-61 / U.S. Office of Explorations and Surveys – 1roll. M126 – 1 – us Nat'l Archives [324]

CORRESPONDENCE...RELATING TO THE ADMINSITRATION OF TRUST FUNDS FOR THE CHICKASAW AND OTHER TRIBES (S SERIES), 1834-72 / U.S. Treasury Department – 1roll. M749. Printed guide – 1 – us Nat'l Archives [324]

CORRESPONDENCE...WITH THE BRANCH MINT AT DAHLONEGA, GEORGIA, 1835-61 / U.S. Bureau of the Mint – 3rolls. T646 – 1 – us Nat'l Archives [324]

CORRESPONDENCIA CON JUAN ALCAIDE SANCHEZ / Carrasco, Castulo – Caceres: Imprenta Moderna, 1955 – 1 – sp Bibl Santa Ana [920]

LA CORRESPONDENCIA DE ESPANA – Madrid, Spain. -d. 7 Oct 1914-26 May 1916; 8 Sept 1916-9 Aug 1919. Imperfect. 20 reels – 1 – uk British Libr Newspaper [072]

CORRESPONDENCIA DEL DOCTOR BENITO ARIAS MONTANO CON EL LICENCIADO JUAN DE OVANDO / Jimenez de la Espada, Marcos – Madrid: Fortanet, 1891. B.R.A.H. 19, pp. 476-498 – sp Bibl Santa Ana [946]

CORRESPONDENCIA DIPLOMATICA CAMBIADA ENTRE EL GOBIERNO DE LOS ESTADOS UNIDOS MEXICANOS Y LOS DE VARIAS POTENCIAS EXTRANJERAS / Mexico. Secretaria de Relaciones Exteriores – Mexico. 1882-92. 6v – 1 – $46.00 – us L of C Photodup [972]

LA CORRESPONDENCIA DIPLOMATICA ENTRE LOS DUQUES DE PARMA Y SUS AGENTES O AMBAJADORES EN LA CORTE DE MADRID, DURANTE LOS SIGLOS XVI, XVII Y XVIII / Perez Bustamante, Ciriaco – Madrid. 1934 – 1 – us Res Libr [940]

CORRESPONDENCIA DIPLOMATICA SOBRE LA CUESTION DE LIMITES CON EL PERU... – Quito, 1903 – 2mf – 1 – ILM-2492/1 – ne IDC [327]

CORRESPONDENCIA ENTRE LA NUNCIATURA... / Olarra y Garmendia, Jose de et al – Madrid: Archivo Ibero Americano, 1965 – 1 – sp Bibl Santa Ana [946]

CORRESPONDENCIA EPISTOLAR DEL P. ANDRES MARCOS BURRIEL, EXISTENTE EN LA BIBLIOTECA REAL DE BRUSELAS / Reymondez del Campo, Jesus – Madrid: Est. Tip. Fortanet, 1908. B.R.A.H. Tomo 52, 1908, pp. 273-286 – 1 – sp Bibl Santa Ana [946]

CORRESPONDENCIA Y DIARIO MILITAR. 1810-1814. TOMO 3 / Iturbide, Agustin – Mexico, 1930; Madrid: Razon y Fe, 1932 – 1 – sp Bibl Santa Ana [355]

CORRESPONDENT AND ADVOCATE – Toronto, Canada. 1833-37. Also Canadian Correspondent – 2r – 1 – $136.00 – cn Library Assoc [971]

CORRESPONDENZ DES KAISERS KARL 5. / Lanz, K – Leipzig. 3v. 1844-1846 – 24mf – 9 – ne IDC [943]

CORRESPONDENZBLATT DER GENERAL-KOMMISSION DER GEWERKSCHAFTEN DEUTSCHLANDS – Berlin, 1891-1923 – 12r – 1 – DM1200.00 – gw Mikro Press [331]

CORRESPONDENZBLATT DER GENERAL-KOMMISSION DER GEWERKSCHAFTEN DEUTSCHLANDS – Berlin, 1891-1923 – 12r – 1 – Dist. gw Mikrofilm – gw Misc Inst [072]

CORRESPONDENZBLATT DES KREISES EUPEN – Eupen, Belgium. 12 Mai 1900-Dec 1907; 3 Jan 1920-29 Aug 1921 – 1 – gw Mikrofilm [949]

CORRESPONDIENTE DE LA REAL ACADEMIA DE LA HISTORIA / Prado, Eladio del – Madrid: Razon y Fe, 1926 – 1 – sp Bibl Santa Ana [946]

CORRESPONDIENTE EN CACERES DE LA R.A. DE LA HISTORIA / Acedo, Federico – Madrid: Fortanet, 1919. B.R.A.H. 74. p. 101 – 1 – sp Bibl Santa Ana [946]

CORRESPONDIENTE EN MERIDA DE LA R.A. DE LA HISTORIA / Gonzalez y Gomez de Soto, Juan Jose – Madrid: Ed. Reus, 1922. B.R.A.H. 80. p. 93 – 1 – sp Bibl Santa Ana [946]

UN CORRESPONSAL EXTRANJERO Y UNAS TEORIAS / Bayle, Constantino – Madrid: Razon y Fe, 1947 – 1 – sp Bibl Santa Ana [946]

Corrette, M *see*
- L'ART DE SE PERFECTIONNER DANS LE VIOLIN. CET OUVRAGE FAIT LA SUITE DE L'ECOLE D'ORPHEE METHODE POUR LE VIOLON
- LE MAITRE DE CLAVECIN POUR L'ACCOMPAGNEMENT, METHODE THEORIQUE ET PRATIQUE
- METHODE POUR APPRENDRE AISEMENT A JOUER DE LA FLUTE TRAVERSIERE
- METHODE, THEORIQUE ET PRATIQUE POUR APPRENDRE EN PEU DE TEMS LE VIOLONCELLE DANS SA PERFECTION
- LE PARFAIT MAITRE A CHANTER..

Correyero, M *see* 1X2 LAS QUINIELAS AL ALCANCE DE TODOS

Corri, D *see* SELECT COLLECTION OF... SONGS, ETC

CORRIEO PORTUGUES – (In Portuguese) – Canada, 1963-77 – 15r – 1 – cn Commonwealth Micro [072]

IL CORRIERE – Salerno. Italy. apr. 20-June 20, 1944 – 1 – us NY Public [072]

CORRIERE CANADESE – (In Italian) – Canada, Jun 1954-1991 – 95r – 1 – cn Commonwealth Micro [072]

CORRIERE D'AMERICA – New York, NY: Tiber Pub Corp, [1923-1934; 1935, jan 1-jul 2, dec 15,22,29; 1936-apr 18 1937 (sunday issues only] – 156r – us Res Libr [071]

CORRIERE DEL CANADA – Montreal, Canada. v1 n2. jun 1900 – 1r – 1 – Can$25.00 – cn Can Microfilming [072]

CORRIERE DEL NIAGARA – (In Italian) – Canada, 1960-68 – 6r – 1 – cn Commonwealth Micro [072]

IL CORRIERE DEL POPOLO – San Francisco, CA: Pedretti Bros, jan 13 1919-dec 30 1926 – 1 – us Res Libr [071]

IL CORRIERE DEL POPOLO – San Francisco. Calif. 1916-1962 – 1 – us UMI [071]

CORRIERE DEL QUEBEC – (In Italian) – Canada, 1960-68 – 6r – 1 – cn Commonwealth Micro [072]

CORRIERE DEL SABATO – London, UK. 19 Jun 1943-23 Sept 1944; 16 Dec 1944-21 Jul 1945 – 1 – uk British Libr Newspaper [072]

CORRIERE DEL TICINO – 1941-1964 – 2r per y – 5,6 – Sfr962.00 – sz Infoprint [072]

CORRIERE DEL TICINO – (Also available on CD-ROM) – 1894-1940 – 1r per y – 5,6 – Sfr668.00 – sz Infoprint [072]

CORRIERE DEL TICINO – (Also available on CD-ROM) – Switzerland. 1965-1995 – 3r per y – 5,6 – Sfr1,176.00 – sz Infoprint [949]
IL CORRIERE DELLA DALMAZIA – Zadar, Yugoslavia. Jul 1919-Feb 1920 – 1r – 1 – us L of C Photodup [949]
CORRIERE DELLA SERA – 1876-1901 – Annual – 1 – L420,000 – sz Infoprint [072]
CORRIERE DELLA SERA – 1902-1906 – 2 times per yr – 1 – L420,000 – sz Infoprint [072]
CORRIERE DELLA SERA – 1907-1915 – 3 times per yr – 1 – L420,000 – sz Infoprint [072]
CORRIERE DELLA SERA – 1914-1937 – 1 – us UMI [073]
CORRIERE DELLA SERA – 1916-1917 – 2 times per yr – 1 – L420,000 – sz Infoprint [072]
CORRIERE DELLA SERA – 1918 – Annual – 1 – L420,000 – sz Infoprint [072]
CORRIERE DELLA SERA – 1919-1928 – 2 times per yr – 1 – L420,000 – sz Infoprint [072]
CORRIERE DELLA SERA – 1929-1934 – 3 times per yr – 1 – L420,000 – sz Infoprint [072]
CORRIERE DELLA SERA – 1935-1942 – 2 times per yr – 1 – L420,000 – sz Infoprint [072]
CORRIERE DELLA SERA – 1943-1948 – 1 per y – 1 – L420,000 – sz Infoprint [072]
CORRIERE DELLA SERA – 1949-1953 – 2 times per yr – 1 – L420,000 – sz Infoprint [072]
CORRIERE DELLA SERA – 1954-1956 – 3 times per yr – 1 – L420,000 – sz Infoprint [072]
CORRIERE DELLA SERA – 1957-1959 – 4 times per yr – 1 – L550,000 – sz Infoprint [072]
CORRIERE DELLA SERA – 1960-1962 – 5 times per yr – 1 – L550,000 – sz Infoprint [072]
CORRIERE DELLA SERA – 1963-1987 – 6 times per y – 1 – L650,000 – sz Infoprint [072]
CORRIERE DELLA SERA – 1968-1969 – 7 times per yr – 1 – L650,000 – sz Infoprint [072]
CORRIERE DELLA SERA – 1970 – 8 times per yr – 1 – L780,000 – sz Infoprint [072]
CORRIERE DELLA SERA – 1971 – 6 times per yr – 1 – L780,000 – sz Infoprint [072]
CORRIERE DELLA SERA – 1972 – 7 times per yr – 1 – L780,000 – sz Infoprint [072]
CORRIERE DELLA SERA – 1973 – 8 times per yr – 1 – L925,000 – sz Infoprint [072]
CORRIERE DELLA SERA – 1974 – 7 times per yr – 1 – L925,000 – sz Infoprint [072]
CORRIERE DELLA SERA – 1975 – 8 times per yr – 1 – L925,000 – sz Infoprint [072]
CORRIERE DELLA SERA – 1976-1979 – 11 times per yr – 1 – L1,295,000 – sz Infoprint [072]
CORRIERE DELLA SERA – 1980 – 11 times per yr – 1 – L1,400,000 – sz Infoprint [072]
CORRIERE DELLA SERA – 1981 – 11 times per yr – 1 – L1,400,000 – sz Infoprint [072]
CORRIERE DELLA SERA – 1982-1985 – 12 times per yr – 1 – L1,400,000 – sz Infoprint [072]
CORRIERE DELLA SERA – 1986 – 14 times per y – 1 – L1,600,000 – sz Infoprint [072]
CORRIERE DELLA SERA – 1987 – 16 times per yr – 1 – L1,600,000 – sz Infoprint [072]
CORRIERE DELLA SERA – 1988-1989 – 15 times per yr – 1 – L1,600,000 – sz Infoprint [072]
CORRIERE DELLA SERA – 1990 – 18 times per yr – 1 – L1,600,000 – sz Infoprint [072]
CORRIERE DELLA SERA – 1991-1995 – 17 times per yr – 1 – L1,600,000 – sz Infoprint [072]
CORRIERE DELLA SERA – 1992-1995 – 12 times per yr – 6 – F4,600 – sz Infoprint [072]
CORRIERE DELLA SERA – Milan: [s.n, 1919-26; 1934-35; jul 1938-apr 25 1945] – 1 – us Res Libr [072]
CORRIERE DELLA SERA – (Yrly reel count varies. Index 1901-95 available 1r per yr. Newspaper also available on CD-ROM. Inquire about 16mm film) – Milano, 1876- – 1 – inquire – us Ross [072]
CORRIERE DELLA SERA – Milano: [Filli Crespi & C, may 10 1959-1985 – us Res Libr [072]
CORRIERE DELLA SERA INDEX – 1901-1975 – Annual – 1 – L250,000 – sz Infoprint [072]
CORRIERE DELLA SERA INDEX – 1976-1995 – Annual – 1 – L430,000 – sz Infoprint [072]
CORRIERE DELLA SOMALIA – Somalia Courier. Mogadiscio. Somali Republic. -d. Jan 1947-Mar 1950. (4 reels) – 1 – uk British Libr Newspaper [072]
CORRIERE DELLO SPORT – 1991-1995 – 3r per y – 5,6 – Sfr1,123.00 – sz Infoprint [790]
IL CORRIERE DI CHICAGO – Chicago, 1907, 1917 – 3r – 1 – us I.H.R.C. [978]
CORRIERE DI ROMA – Italy. -d. 8 Jun-31 Dec 1944. (Imperfect). (1 reel) – 1 – uk British Libr Newspaper [072]
CORRIERE DI SICILIA – Catania. Italy. feb. 1-Apr. 21, 1944 – 1 – us NY Public [072]
CORRIERE D'INFORMAZIONE – (Issues for 1952-may 9 1959 filmed consecutively with: Nuovo corriere dellasera; issues for may 10 1959-1962 filmed consecutively with: Corriere della sera (Milan, Italy)) – Milano: [Filli Crespi & C, may 22 1945-may 5 1946; 1952-1955; 1956-feb 1962 – us Res Libr [072]
CORRIERE DIPLOMATICO E CONSOLARE – Rome. -w. 10 Jan 1923 – 15 May 1940 – 5r – 1 – uk British Libr Newspaper [940]
CORRIERE ILLUSTRATO – (In Italian) – Canada, 1958-84 – 23r – 1 – cn Commonwealth Micro [072]
IL CORRIERE ISRAELITICO – Trieste. v. 1-53. 1862-1914. Incomplete – 1 – us NY Public [072]
CORRIERE ITALIANO / ed by Gagliardi, Alfredo – Montreal. v1 n33. 26 nov 1954-v4 n43. 25 oct 1957 – 1r – 1 – Can$50.00 – cn Can Microfilming [072]
CORRIERE ITALIANO DI LONDRA – London, UK. 6 Jan-30 Mar 1872 – 1 – uk British Libr Newspaper [072]
CORRIERE LIBERTARIO – Barre, VT, 1914-1915 (Aug. 1-March 5) – 6mf or 1r – 1 – us I.H.R.C. [978]
CORRIERE SICILIANO – New York. N.Y. v. 1-4. Mar 1931-Jun 1934 – 1 – us NY Public [071]
CORRIG SCHOOL RECORD – Victoria, B.C: Record Pub. Co., [1887?-1890?] – 9 – cn C.I.H.M. [370]
Corrigan, Ann E *see* A DESCRIPTIVE ANALYSIS OF CORPORATE HEALTH PROMOTION ACTIVITY EVALUATIONS
Corrigan, Felicia *see* SOME SOCIAL PRINCIPLES OF ORESTES A. BROWNSON
Corrivault, Blaise *see* BIBLIOGRAPHIE ANALYTIQUE DE L'HISTOIRE D'ACADIE
Corro, Antonio del *see* THE SPANISH GRAMMAR
CORROSION – v1- 1945- – 1,5,6,9 – us UMI [540]
CORROSION ABSTRACTS – (1985- . 5,6,9) – v1- . 1962- – 1 – us UMI [073]
CORROSION AND ENCRUSTATION IN WATER WELLS – 1980 – 108p – it F.A.O. [628]
CORROSION PREVENTION AND CONTROL – 1954-58 – 1 – uk Microform Academic [073]
CORROSION SCIENCE – v1- 1961- – 5,6,9 – us UMI [540]
CORROSPONDANCE/FEUILLE MARITIME DE NANTES – (The years 1783, 1784, and part of 1793 are missing) – Bimens. puis bi- ou tri-hebd., Nantes, janv. 1782-sept. 1794 (annees 1783, 1784, et une partie de 1793 manquantes) – 2r – 1 – F754.30 – fr Armell [380]
CORRY HERALD – Corry, PA. -w 1899-1900. 6 rolls – 13 – $25.00r – us I.M.R. [071]
Corry, J *see* OBSERVATIONS UPON THE WINDWARD COAST OF AFRICA
CORS JOURNAL – Canadian Operational Research Society. v1-8. 1963-70 – 1 – us UMI [500]
LE CORSAIRE – Journal des spectacles, de la litterature, des arts, des moeurs et modes.Paris.11 juil-dec 1823, 1826-8 sept 1852, 29 aout, 4 oct-14 nov 1858, n.s. 1902 – 1 – fr A.C.R.P.P. [073]
LE CORSAIRE – Paris. Red. en chef, E. Gaillet. no.1-52, 9 aout 1879-juil 1880. no.2-12, 14. 25 dec/1 janv-26 mars/3 avr 1881 – 1 – fr A.C.R.P.P. [073]
CORSARIO : PERIODICO CRITICO, SATYRICO E CHISTOSO – Rio de Janeiro, 2 Oct 1880-Oct 1883; Jan-4 Apr 1896 – 1,5,6 – bl Biblioteca [072]
CORSARIO – [s.l.]. 19, 28 Set 1886; Set, 4 Out 1888 – 1,5,6 – bl Biblioteca [072]
O CORSARIO – Manaos, Amazonas. 8 Set 1901 – 1,5,6 – bl Biblioteca [072]
O CORSO – Manaos, Amazonas. 23 Nov 1908; 10 Jan 1909 – 1,5,6 – bl Biblioteca [072]
CORSO DI DIRITTO... / Anzilotti, D – Rome, 1915 – 4mf – 9 – ILM-101/1 – ne IDC [340]
Corssen, P *see* MONARCHIANISCHE PROLOGE ZU DEN VIER EVANGELIEN (T.U.U. 1-15/1)
Corswarem, P de *see* DE LITURGISCHE BOEKEN VAN DE KOLLEGIALE KERK VAN O.L. VROUW VAN TONGEREN VOOR HET CONCILIE VAN TRENTE
Cort, C *see* WOMEN AS PREACHERS
EEN CORT, DOCH GRONDTLICK VERHAEL VANDEN TWISTIGEN HANDEL ENDE ONSCHRIFTMETIGEN ORDEEL / Philips, Dirk – 1567. BME-312 1 – 9 – ne IDC [240]
CORT ENDE CLAER BEWIJS, DAT DIE TWAELF JONGHEREN DAER D'EUANGELIST LUCAS VAN MELDET / Ries, H de – 1597. BME-339 1 – 9 – ne IDC [240]
Cortambert, Richard *see* NOUVELLE HISTORIE DES VOYAGES ET DES GRANDES DECOUVERTES GEOGRAPHIQUES DANS TOUS LES TEMPS ET DANS TOUS LES PAYS. TOME PREMIER
EENE CORTE BEKENTENISSE ENDE BELYDINGHE VANDEN EENIGEN, ALMACHTIGEN, LEUENDIGEN GOD, VADER, SOON ENDE HEYLIGE GEST, ENDE VAN DIE SCHEPPINGHE. ENDE TEN LAETSTEN VAN DAT RECHTE GEBRUYCK DES AUONTMAELS ONSES HEEREN / Philips, Dirk – 1557. BME-303 1 – 9 – ne IDC [240]
EEN CORTE BEKENTENISSE ENDE GRONDIGE AENWYSINGE WT DER H. SCHRIFT / Timmerman, H – 1577. BME-323 1 – 9 – ne IDC [240]
Corte d'Apello di Lucca *see* CAUSA SAMAMA...SENTENZA...1880
CORTE DE CUENTAS / El Salvador. Courts – San Salvador. Tomo 1. No. 1-33, no. 115. Jan 1940-Dec 1954 – 1 – us NY Public [340]
Corte di Appello di Roma *see* DICHIARAZIONE DE NULLITA DI MATRIMONIO (G GARIBALDI CONTRO G RAIMONDI)
EEN CORTE ENDE CLARE BELIJDINGHE ENDE SCHRIFTELIJCKE AENWIJSINGE. GESCHREUEN AEN. JOHAN A LASCO, MET T'SAMEN ZIJNEN MEDEHULPEREN BINNEN EMDEN / Simons, Menno – Anno. 1544. BME-285 1 – 9 – ne IDC [240]
EEN CORTE ENDE CLARE BELIJDINGHE ENDE SCHRIFTELIJCKE AENWIJSINGE. GESCHREUEN AEN. JOHAN A LASCO, MET T'SAMEN ZIJNEN MEDEHULPEREN BINNEN EMDEN / Simons, Menno – Anno. 1544. BME-286 1 – 9 – ne IDC [240]
CORTE ENDE LICHTE ONDER WIJSINGHE VAN DE PRINCIPAELSTE GRONTREGULEN DER MUSYKE – P 418. 1639 – 9 – ne IDC [780]
CORTE MADERA NEWS – Larkspur, CA. 1927-47 – 7r – 1 – $350.00 – B02339 – us Library Micro [071]
LA CORTE SUPREMA FEDERALE NEL SISTEMA COSTITUZIONALE DEGLI STATI UNITI D'AMERICA / Catinella, Salvatore – Padova, Milani, 1934. 452p. LL-226 – 1 – us L of C Photodup [340]
EEN CORTE VERMANINGHE VTH GODES WOORT VAN DIE WEDERGEBOORTE, VNDE WIE DIE GHENE SYN, DIE BELOFTE HEBBEN / Simons, Menno – BME-273 1 – 9 – ne IDC [240]
CORTE Y CORTIJO / Hurtado, Antonio – 1870 – 9 – 1.50f – sp Bibl Santa Ana [830]
CORTES AND MONTEZUME / Collis, Maurice – London: Faber and Faber, s.a. – sp Bibl Santa Ana [910]
CORTES AND THE AZTEC CONQUE CONSULTENT. GORDON ECKHOLM / Blacker, Irwir R – New York: American Heritage. Pub. Co., Inc, 1965 – sp Bibl Santa Ana [350]
CORTES AND THE CONQUEST OF MEXICO / Hamlyn, Raul – Londres: Golden Pleasure Books LTD, 1967 – sp Bibl Santa Ana [350]
Cortes, Cristobal Maria *see* ATAHUALPA. TRAGEDIA
LAS CORTES DE CADIZ Y EL OBISPO DE ORENSE (EPISODIO CURIOSO DE LAS CORTES CONSTITUYENTES / Risco, A – Madrid: Razon y Fe, 1926 – 1 – sp Bibl Santa Ana [946]
CORTES DE LA MUERTE / Carvajal, Micael & Hurtado de Mendoza, Luis – Madrid: Rivadeneyra, 1855 – 1 – sp Bibl Santa Ana [920]
Cortes, Fernando *see* LETTRES DE FERNAND CORTES A CHARLES QUINT SUR LA DECOUVERTE ET LA CONQUETE DU MEXIQUE
Cortes, Hernando *see*
- CARTA
- CARTAS Y OTROS DOCUMENTOS NOVISIMAMENTE DESCUBIERTOS EN EL ARCHIVO GENERAL DE INDIAS DE SEVILLA
- CARTAS Y RELACIONES DE HERNANDO CORTES AL EMPERADOR CARLOS V
- CORRESPONDENCE DE FERNAND CORTES AVEC 1 EMPEREUR CHARLES QUINT. SUR LA CONQUETE DE MEXIQUE
- ESTUDIOS HISPANOAMERICANOS. HOMENAJE A HERNAN CORTES
- HERNAN CORTES
- HERNAN CORTES, LETTERS FROM MEXICO
- HISTORIA DE NUEVA ESPANA...Y NOTAS DEL ILMO. D.F.A. LORENZANA..
- LETTRES DE FERNAND CORTES A CHARLES V

Cortes Vazquez, Luis *see* VIAJE LITERARIO AL NORTE CACERENO
CORTES Y LA EVANGELIZACION DE NUEVA ESPANA / Bayle, Constantino – Madrid: Ediciones Jura, 1948 – sp Bibl Santa Ana [946]
CORTES Y LA EVANGELIZACION DE NUEVA ESPANA / Bayle, Constantino – Madrid: Missionalia Hispanica, 1948 – 1 – sp Bibl Santa Ana [240]
CORTEX – (v1-9. Dfl90.00v; v10-19. Dfl120.00v) – Milan. v1-19. 1965-83 – 5,9 – Dfl2,010.00 – ne Swets [590]
Corteza Collantes, Alfonso *see* RESUMEN DE UNA DISCUSION ACERCA DE LOS HIJOS ILEGITIMOS ANTE LA SOCIEDAD Y EL DERECHO
Corthesy, F *see* ETUDE DE LA CONVENTION DE BARCELONE...
THE CORTICAL AND SUBCORTICAL EFFERENT AND AFFERENT CONNECTIONS OF A PROPOSED CINGULATE MOTOR CORTEX AND ITS TOPOGRAPHICAL RELATIONSHIP TO THE PRIMARY AND SUPPLEMENTARY MOTOR CORTICES OF THE RHESUS MONKEY / Morecraft, Robert Jet al – 1989 – 4mf – 9 – $16.00 – us Microform Publ [612]
CORTICELLI HOME NEEDLEWORK – St. Johns, Quebec: Corticelli Silk, [1899-19–] – 9 – cn C.I.H.M. [640]
O CORTICO / Azevedo, Aluizio – Paris et Rio: H. Garnier, 1896. 354p. 4 fiches. (Literature Collection) – 9 – 10.00 – fr Bibl Nationale [830]
Cortijo Valdes, A *see* BIOGRAFIA DE LEXCMO. D. VICENTE BARRANTES
Cortines, Ruiz *see* DISCURSOS... PRONUNCIADOS...1951 AL 1952
CORTLAND GAZETTE : WEEKLY GENERAL NEWSPAPER – Cortland, OH. 20 Aug 1880 – 1r – 1 – us Western Res [071]
CORTLAND HERALD – Cortland, NE. -w. Jan. 1886-Nov. 1892. Incomplete; Oct. 1895-Jul. 1899; Nov. 1899-Nov. 1900 – 1 – us NE Hist [071]
CORTLAND NEWS – Cortland, NE. -w. Apr. 1933-Jul.1976 – 1 – us NE Hist [071]
CORTLAND NEWS – Cortland, NE. -w. Jul. 1897-Jun. 1898; Feb. 1899-Sep. 1918; Mar. 1919-Jul. 1919; Sep. 1919-Dec. 1920; Sep. 1921-Apr. 1925 – 1 – us NE Hist [071]
Corts Grau, Jose *see* PERFIL ACTUAL DE DONOSO CORTES
Corvalan-Groessling, Veronica *see* THE PHYSIOLOGICAL AND PERCEIVED EFFECTS OF DRAFTING ON A GROUP OF HIGHLY TRAINED DISTANCE RUNNERS
CORVALLIS GAZETTE – (Set incl. Union Gazette (Corvallis)) – Corvallis, OR. -w. 22 Apr 1865-2 Jul 1909. – 12r – 1 – us U.O. Library [071]
CORVALLIS GAZETTE-TIMES – Corvallis, OR. -d. 1 Jan 1910-10 Oct 1978+. 205 rolls – 1 – us U.O. Library [071]
CORVALLIS TIMES – Corvallis, OR. -d. 2 Aug 1893-25 Jun 1909. 5 rolls – 1 – us U.O. Library [071]

CORVEY : FUERSTLICHE BIBLIOTHEK CORVEY / ed by Schoewerling, Rainer et al – Hildesheim, 1995 – 20000mf – 9 – DM74,000.00 diazo DM88,000.00 silver – gw Olms [072]
CORVEY – FUERSTLICHE BIBLIOTHEK CORVEY-SACHLITERATUR : MICROEDITION DER BUECHERSAMMLUNG MIT RARA UND UNIKATEN – 20,000mf – DM74,000.00 diazo DM88,000.00 silver – gw Olms [019]
Corvinus, A *see*
- DER 128TH PSALM VOM GLUECK, SEGEN, GEDEIEN DER EHELEUT...
- ACTA: HANDLUNGEN: LEGATION VND SCHRIFFTE. GESPRECHE VND DISPUTATION ANTONIJ CORUINI VND JOANNIS KYMEI, MIT DEM MUENSTERISCHEN KOENIG
- ACTA: HANDLUNGEN: LEGATION VND SCHRIFFTE: SO DURCH DEN...HERRN PHILIPSEN LANDGRAVEN ZU HESSEN ETC...
- BERICHT OB MAN ON DIE TAUFFE VND EMPFAHUNGEN DES LEIBS VND BLUTS CHRISTI ALLEIN DURCH DEN GLAUBEN KUENNE SELIG WERDEN...
- DE INTEGRO SACRAMENTO CORPORIS ET SANGUINIS DOMINI,...
- DE MISERABILI MONASTERIENSIVM ANABAPTISTARVM OBSIDIONE
- EXPOSITIO DECALOGI, SYMBOLI, APOSTOLICI, SACRAMENTORU, AND DOMINICAE PRAECATIONIS,...

Corvinus, Gottlieb S *see* NUTZBARES, GALANTES UND CURIOESES FRAUENZIMMER-LEXIKON...(HQ 14)
Corvinus, J A *see* PETRI MOLINAEI NOVI ANATOMICI MALA ENCHEIRESIS SEU CENSURA ANATOMES ARMINIANISMI
Corvinus, J M *see* HEPTACHORDUM DANICUM SEU NOVA SOLSISATIO IN QUA MUSICAE PRACTICAE USUS
Corwin, E T et al *see* THE HISTORY OF THE REFORMED CHURCH, DUTCH, THE REFORMED CHURCH, GERMAN, AND THE MORAVIAN CHURCH IN THE UNITED STATES
Corwin, Edward A *see*
- THE CONSTITUTION AND WHAT IT MEANS TODAY
- JOHN MARSHALL AND THE CONSTITUTION

Corwin, Rebecca *see* THE VERB AND THE SENTENCE IN CHRONICLES, EZRA, AND NEHEMIAH
Corwin, Robert N *see* VETTER GABRIEL
Cory, C B *see*
- THE BIRDS OF EASTERN NORTH AMERICA
- BIRDS OF THE BAHAMA ISLANDS
- THE BIRDS OF THE WEST INDIES
- CATALOGUE OF WEST INDIAN BIRDS
- A NATURALIST IN THE MAGDALEN ISLANDS: GIVING A DESCRIPTION OF THE ISLANDS AND LIST OF THE BIRDS TAKEN THERE: WITH OTHER ORNITHOLOGICAL NOTES

Cory, William Johnson *see* IONICA
THE CORYSTON FAMILY / Ward, Mary Augusta – British Fiction Archive: Unit 2 – 9 – uk Bell [830]
LA COSA GIUDICATA E LE QUESTIONI DI STATO... / Cavaglieri, A – Padova, 1909 – 3mf – 1 – ILM-2098/1 – ne IDC [327]
LA COSA RARA. OVERTURE, ARR. PIANO AND VIOLIN BY FERDINND STAES / Martin y Solar, V – (Pts. Violin part in MS., added part for violin 2) – Paris: Boyer, 1789 – 1 – us Sibley [780]
LES COSAQUES A PARIS – Paris [1848?] – us Res Libr [944]
COSAS DE MADRID: APUNTES SOCIALES DE LA VILLA Y CORTE / Chaulie, Dionisio – Madrid: M.G. Hernandez, 1884. 318p. 4 fiches. (Miscellaneous Selections) – 9 – 10.00 – fr Bibl Nationale [305]
COSAS DEL MUNDO / Hurtado, Antonio – 1846 – 9 – 1.50f – sp Bibl Santa Ana [830]
COSAS DEL TAPETE VERDE / Roso de Luna, Mario – Madrid: Editorial Atlantida, 1930 – 1 – sp Bibl Santa Ana [946]
COSAS Y GENTES DE ANTANO... / Fernandez Guardia, Ricardo – Madrid: Razon y Fe, 1941 – 1 – sp Bibl Santa Ana [240]
Cosentini, F *see*
- LA BASI DI UN CODICE PENALE INTERNAZIONALE...
- CODE PENAL INTERNATIONAL EN 1314 ARTICLES
- CODIGO CIVIL PAN-AMERICANO
- ESSAI D'UN CODE PENAL INTERNATIONAL...

Cosenza, Mario Emilio *see*
- BIOGRAPHICAL AND BIBLIOGRAPHICAL DICTIONARY OF THE ITALIAN HUMANISTS AND OF THE WORLD OF CLASSICAL SCHOLARSHIP IN ITALY, 1300-1800
- BIOGRAPHICAL AND BIBLIOGRAPHICAL DICTIONARY OF THE ITALIAN PRINTERS AND OF FOREIGN PRINTERS IN ITALY FROM THE INTRODUCTION OF THE ART OF PRINTING INTO ITALY TO 1800

COSMAE PRAGENSIS CHRONICA BOEMORUM (MGH 6: 2.BD) / ed by Bretholz, B – 1923 – Dfl28.00 – ne Slangenburg [240]
Cosman, A C *see* DE DELICTIS EXTRA CIVITATIS FINES COMMISSIS,...
Cosmann, M *see* ESSAIS DE PALEOCONCHOLOGIE
Cosmas Le Pretre *see* LE TRAITE CONTRE LES BOGOMILES
COSMETIC TECHNOLOGY – v1-5, no.2. 1979-Feb 1983 – 1,5,6,9 – us UMI [073]
COSMETIC WORLD NEWS – (v. 6-. 1979-. 5,6,9) – v. 1-. 1974- – 1 – us UMI [660]
COSMETICS – (v17 1988/89 Can$37.00y) – Toronto. v1-22. 1972/73-1994 – 9 – Can$28.00y – cn Micromedia [073]
COSMETICS AND PERFUMERY – v1-90 1906-75 1; v86-90 5,6 – us UMI [660]
COSMETICS AND TOILETRIES – (See also: Cosmetics and Perfumery) – v91- 1976- 1; v91- 5,6; v92- 1977- 9 – us UMI [660]
COSMIC CONSCIOUSNESS: A STUDY IN THE EVOLUTION OF THE HUMAN MIND / Bucke, Richard Maurice – 4th ed., cor. and re-set. New York: E.P. Dutton & Co., (1923). xviii,384p – 1 – us U.W. Library [150]
COSMIC RESEARCH – v1-32. 1963-94 – 1,5 – $100.00v – us UMI [520]
COSMIC STORIES – v1, nos. 1-3 (all publ). 1941 – 1 reel – 1 – $45.00 – us UPA [830]
COSMOGRAPHIA, ETC / Mela, Pomponius – 14th and 15th cents. Holkham Mss. 326, 329, 393. Holkham Hall, Norfolk, England – 1 – uk Microform Academic [760]
COSMOGRAPHIE DE LEVANT / Thevet, A – Lion, 1556 – 3mf – 9 – H-8291/1 – ne IDC [944]
EL COSMOPOLITA – Kansas City, KS: Cosmopolita Pub Co, [aug 22 1914-nov 15 1919] – 2r – 1 – us Res Libr [071]
COSMOPOLITAN – 1972- 1; 1975- 5,6; 1976- 9 – us UMI [073]
COSMOPOLITAN HERALD – Girard, PA., 1910-1912 – 13 – $25.00r – us I.M.R. [071]
THE COSMOPOLITE – Girard, PA., 1889-1905 – 13 – $25.00r – us I.M.R. [071]
COSMOPOLITE HERALD – Girard. Pa. -w. 1910-42, 1944- – 1 – us UMI [071]
COSMOPOLITE HERALD – Union City. Pa. 1958-1968 – 1 – us UMI [071]
COSMOPOLITE OV NOVVELLE LVMIERE DE LA PHISIQUE NATURELLE / Sendivogius, Michael – Traduit nouuellement de Latin en Francois, par le sieur De Bosnay. Paris, Charles Hulpeau, 1629 – 1 – us U.W. Library [530]
UN COSMOPOLITE SUISSE : JACQUES-HENRI MEISTER / Grubenmann, Yvonne de Athayde – (Includes bibliographical references) – Geneve: E Droz, 1954 – 1r – 1 – us U.W. Library [440]
COSMOPOLITE'S STATISTICAL CHART OF NOVA SCOTIA GOLD MINES, 1862-1866, INCLUSIVE – Halifax, N.S.: (J. Bowes), 1867 00728. (Pre-1900 Canadiana) – 9 – cn C.I.H.M. [971]
DIE COSMOPOLITISCHE UNION; THE COSMOPOLITAN UNION / Ackermann, Werner – Declaration of Principles; Declaration des Principles de l'Union Cosmopolitan, 1930 – 9 – 1.00f – at Libertarian Micro [320]
COSMOS – Pattee, University Park, PA. 1989 – 182p 7mf – 9 – $0.50f – us Lawrence Pub [720]
THE COSMOS AND THE LOGOS : BEING THE LECTURES FOR 1901-2 ON THE L.P. STONE FOUNDATION... / Minton, Henry Collin – (Includes bibliographical references and index) – Philadelphia:Westminster Press, 1902 – 1mf – 9 – 0-8370-4448-0 – 1985-2448 – us A.T.L.A. [210]
Cosneau, E *see* LES GRANDS TRAITES DE LA GUERRE DE CENT ANS
Cosnier, Henri Charles *see* L'OUEST AFRICAIN FRANCAIS
COSPAR INFORMATION BULLETIN / Committee on Space Research – 1977- – 5,6,9 – us UMI [629]
Cosquin, Emmanuel *see* ETUDES FOLKLORIQUES
COSSACK COURIER 92 *see* KAZACHI I VESTNIK
THE COSSACKS HERALD – Prague, Czechoslovakia, 1941-1945 – 2r – 1 – us I.H.R.C. [947]
COSSACKS PAMPHLET COLLECTION – 1919-1961? – 1 – CSUXANR5329-B – us Hoover Inst Photo [972]
COSSACKS PAMPHLET COLLECTION – 1919-1961? – 1 – CSUXANR3676-B – us Hoover Inst Photo [972]
Cossarin, Mark A *see* JOYRIDE
Cossette, Angele *see* BIBLIOGRAPHIE DE L'OEUVRE DE LOUIS-PHILIPPE AUDET, L. SC. DE LA SOCIETE DES ECRIVAINS CANADIENS, PROFESSEUR A L'UNIVERSITE LAVAL
Cossette, Raymond *see* MELANGES OFFERTS A ME. RAYMOND COSSETTE
Cossio, Carlos *see* LA POLITICA COMO CONCIENCIA
COSSMAN V. GRUBER – Dolchstoss-Prozess, Munich. 19 Oct-17 Nov 1925. 2 rolls. T1173 – 1 – us Nat'l Archives [340]
Cosson, E S C *see*
- EXPLORATION SCIENTIFIQUE DE L'ALGERIE
- ILLUSTRATIONES FLORAE ATLANTICAE
- NOTES SUR QUELQUES PLANTES CRITIQUES, RARES OU NOUVELLES, ET ADDITIONS A LA FLORE DES ENVIRONS DE PARIS

Cosson, E SC *see*
- COMPENDIUM FLORAE ATLANTICAE
- SYNOPSIS ANALYTIQUE DE LA FLORE DES ENVIRONS DE PARIS

COST ACCOUNTANT – (See also: Management Accounting) – 1921-1964 – 1 – us UMI [650]
COST ANALYSIS OF EDUCATIONAL INCLUSION OF MARGINALIZED POPULATIONS / Tsang, Mun C – 1994 – 106p – 9 – 92-803-1152-2 – fr UNESCO [370]
COST BENCHMARKING ALS INSTRUMENT DES KOSTENMANAGEMENTS / Baur, Thorsten – 1995 – 1mf – 9 – DM60.00 – 3-8267-2241-8 – gw Hänsel [650]
COST CONTROL IN FOREST HARVESTING AND ROAD CONSTRUCTION – 1992 – 112p – it F.A.O. [634]
COST ENGINEERING *see* AACE BULLETIN
COST ENGINEERING: A PUBLICATION OF THE AMERICAN ASSOCIATION OF COST ENGINEERS – v20-. Jul 1978- – 1,5,6,9 – us UMI [650]
COST ESTIMATING IN SAWMILLING INDUSTRIES : GUIDELINES – 1984 – 97p – it F.A.O. [338]
Costa, A *see*
- DEGLI' INSETTI CHE ATTACCANO L'ALBERO ED IL FRUTTO DELL' OLIVO
- RICERCHE ENTOMOLOGICHE SOPRA I MONTI PARTENII NEL PRINCIPATO ULTERIORE

Costa, Alcino Louis da et al *see* NEWS VALUES AND PRINCIPLES OF CROSS-CULTURAL COMMUNICATION
Costa, Avelino de Jesus da *see* LIBER FIDEI...TOMO 1. BRAGA, 1965
Costa, Carl *see* DAS ERBE DES WUCHERERS
Costa Duran, Maria *see* LAS ALAS ROTAS
Costa, I da *see* ISRAEEL EN DE VOLKEN
Costa, J *see* MESUAE MEDICI. CLARISSIMI OPERA...
Costa, M *see* ELI
Costa, M A da *see*
- BIBLIOGRAFIA GERAL DE MOCAMBIQUE...
- BIBLIOGRAFIA GERAL DE MOCAMBIQUE

Costa, Manuel G da *see* IGNACIO DE AZCUEDO...
COSTA MESA CITY DIRECTORIES – Orange Co, CA. 1931; 1939-1944; 1947-1951 – 8r – 1 – $400.00 – D070 – us Library Micro [910]
COSTA MESA DAILY PILOT – Costa Mesa, CA. 1966; 1968 – 11r – 1 – $550.00 – H03190 – us Library Micro [071]
COSTA MESA HERALD *see* BALBOA TIMES, COSTA MESA HERALD, NEWPORT BALBOA TIMES, NEWPORT NEWS
COSTA MESA NEWS – Costa Mesa, CA. 1984- – 14+ r – 1 – $900.00 ($70.00y) – HR04018 – us Library Micro [071]
Costa, O G *see* CATALOGO SISTEMATICO E RAGIONATO DE TESTACEI DELLE DUE SICILIE
COSTA RICA : ANUARIO ESTADISTICO 1883-1969 / Costa Rica. Direccion General de Estadistica y Censo – (1892, 1894-1906 not publ. 1883-87, 1890-93, 1908, 1910, 1917, 1939, 1948-50 not available. Coll title: Latin American and Caribbean Official Statistical Serials, 1821-1982) – 198mf – 9 – £1,250.00 – uk Chadwyck [972]
COSTA RICA : PLAN NACIONAL DE DESAROLLO 1990-1994: DESARROLLO SOSTENIDO CON JUSTICIA SOCIAL: RESUMEN / Ministerio de Planification Nacional y Politica Economica – San Jose, 1991 – 1mf – 9 – ne IDC [338]
Costa Rica *see*
- LA GACETA
- GACETA DIARIO OFICIAL

Costa Rica. Asociacion Nacional de Fomento Economico *see* EL MODELO EDUCATIVO COSTARRICENSE
Costa Rica. Banco de Costa Rica *see* PLAN DE FOMENTO ECONOMICO
Costa Rica. Direccion General de Estadistica y Censo *see*
- COSTA RICA
- INFORMA

Costa Rica. Ministerio de Education Publica *see* PLAN OPERATIVO ANUAL 1988
Costa Rica. Oficina de Planificacion *see*
- PLAN DE DESARROLLO ECONOMICO Y SOCIAL DE COSTA RICA. VERSION PRELIMINAR REVISADA, JUN 1965
- PLAN DE INVERSIONES PUBLICAS
- PLAN NACIONAL DE DESAROLLO
- PLAN NACIONAL DE DESARROLLO, 1974-1978. ESTRATEGIA Y PLAN GLOBAL

Costa Rica. Secretaria de Educacion Publica *see* MEMORIA
Costa y Martinez, Joaquin *see*
- LA IGNORANCIA DEL DERECHO, CON UN AMPLIO ESTUDIO PRELIMINAR
- INTRODUCCION A UN TRATADO DE POLITICA

Costadoni, A *see* ANNALES CAMALDULENSES O.S.B.
Costalius, Petrus *see* PEGMA, CUM NARRATIONIBUS PHILOSOPHICIS
Costantin, J *see* LES MUCEDINEES SIMPLES
Costarini, Vivien *see* BIOTECHNOLOGIES IN PERSPECTIVE
A COST/BENEFIT ANALYSIS OF DECLINING NUMBERS OF WOMEN COACHES : A SOCIAL EXCHANGE THEORY PERSPECTIVE / Stevens, S C – 1989 – 2mf – 9 – $8.00 – us Microform Publ [790]
Coste, Adolphe *see* HYGIENE SOCIALE CONTRE LE PAUPERISME
Coste d'Arnobat, Pierre-Nicolas *see* VOYAGE AU PAYS DE BAMBOUC SUIVI D'OBSERVATIONS INTERESSANTES SUR LES CASTES INDIENNES, SUR LA HOLLANDE ET SUR L'ANGLETERRE
Coste-Floret, Alfred *see* LES PROBLEMES FONDAMENTAUX DU DROIT
Coster, F *see*
- ENCHIRIDION CONTROVERSIARUM PRAECIPUARUM...
- LIBELLUS SODALITATIS

Costerus, W *see* AN ALTERNATIVE WAY OF EXPLAINING THE GEORGIST THEORY
Costigan, George Purcell *see* HANDBOOK ON AMERICAN MINING LAW
Costigan, John *see* LOCAL SELF-GOVERNMENT FOR IRELAND: SPEECH DELIVERED IN THE HOUSE OF COMMONS OF CANADA, THURSDAY, APRIL 20, 1882
Costigan, S P *see* DIARY
Costill, David L *see*
- EFFECT OF SODIUM AND WATER INTAKE ON PLASMA ALDOSTERONE DURING PROLONGED EXERCISE IN WARM ENVIRONMENT
- THE RELATIONSHIP BETWEEN PHYSIOLOGICAL MEASUREMENTS AND CROSS-COUNTRY RUNNING PERFORMANCE
- RELIABILITY IN THE MEASUREMENT OF MUSCLE FIBER COMPOSITION AND THE HISTOCHEMICAL STAINING FOR GLYCOGEN

LA COSTITUZIONE ETIOPICA : STUDIO SEQUITO DALLA VERSIONE DELLA COSTITUZIONE... / ed by Cerulli, Enrico – 2. ed. Roma: Instituto per l'Oriente, 1936 – 1 – us Res Libr [960]
COSTUMBRES CACERENAS. MADRID / Ramon y Fernandez, Jose – G. Bermejo Impresor, 1950. Separata de Revista de Dialectologia y Tradiciones Populares – sp Bibl Santa Ana [306]
COSTUME AND SET DESIGN *see* SHAKESPEARE AT STRATFORD-UPON-AVON
COSTUME AND SET DESIGNS : IN THE MANDER AND MITCHENSON THEATRE COLLECTION – (Includes printed index) – 1993 – 28mf – 15 – $874.00 – 1-869934-51-2 – uk Emmett [790]
THE COSTUME OF THE THEATRE / Komisarjevsky, Theodore – London: G. Bles, 1931.xii,178p. plates – 1 – us U.W. Library [740]

COSTUME PRINTS IN THE BRITISH MUSEUM : AUTHORITIES FOR ARTISTS / British Museum. London – (Over 7,200 historical fashion prints listed in chronological order (55BC- 1900)) – 1991 – 145mf – 9 – $890.00 – 0-907006-29-9 – uk Mindata [740]
LES COSTUMES DANS L'OPERA DE PEKIN / Tang, R – 9 – F50.00 – fr Ethnologie [740]
COSTUMES DU 18EME SIECLE – 1 reel. (Collections of the Department of Prints and Photographs) – 1 – $50.00 – fr Bibl Nationale [740]
COSTUMES DU REGNE DE LOUIS 14 – Engravings depicting contemporary fashions. 7 reels. (Collections of the Department of Prints and Photographs) – 1 – fr Bibl Nationale [740]
Cotallo, Jose Luis *see* LAS REALIDADES SOCIALES CONTEMPORANEAS
Cotallo Sanchez, Jose Luis *see* VIVIR EN CRISTIANO
THE COTATI CALL – Rohnert Park, CA. 1974-1977 – 2r – 1 – $100.00 – B05051 – us Library Micro [071]
COTATI CLARION *see* COTATI-THE COMMUNITY VOICE
COTATIAN – Cotati, CA. 1946-1947; 1951-1964 – 6r – 1 – $300.00 – B03589 – us Library Micro [071]
COTATI-THE COMMUNITY VOICE – (Also known as: Cotati Clarion, Central County Clarion, The Clarion) – Rohnert Park, CA. Sept 1969- – 32+ r – 1 – $1,600.00 ($50.00y) – B02726 – us Library Micro [071]
Cote, Antonia *see* BIO-BIBLIOGRAPHIE DE GEORGINA LEFAIVRE
Cote, Athanase *see* BIBLIOGRAPHIE ANALYTIQUE DES OUVRAGES DE LANGUE FRANCAISE SUR L'HISTOIRE DE LA VILLE DE QUEBEC AU 19E SIECLE
Cote, Augustin *see* JOURNAL DE QUEBEC
Cote, Berthe *see* BIO-BIBLIOGRAPHIE ANALYTIQUE DE MONSIEUR HENRI TURGEON, NOTAIRE, PROFESSEUR AGREGE A LA FACULTE DE DROIT DE QUEBEC
Cote, Chanoine V *see* CHEZ-NOUS
COTE DE LA BOURSE ET DE LA BANQUE – Journal politique, economique et financier. Paris. juil-dec 1907, juil-dec 1913 – 1 – fr A.C.R.P.P. [073]
LA COTE DEFOSSE ET TRIBUNE – 1992 – 1r per y – 5,6 – Sfr428.00 – sz Infoprint [072]
LA COTE DEFOSSE ET TRIBUNE – 1994- – 6r per y – 5,6 – Sfr1,337.00 – sz Infoprint [072]
LE COTE DES ESCLAVES ET LE DAHOMEY / Bouche, Pierre Bertrand – Paris, 1885 – 1 – us Res Libr [910]
LA COTE D'IVOIRE – Corbeil, France: E Crete, 1906 – 1 – us Res Libr [960]
LA COTE D'OR : JOURNAL POLITIQUE (...) – 5 fois par sem., puis quot., Dijon, janv. 1868-mars 1883 – 16r – 1 – F8577,15 – fr Armell [320]
Cote, Georges-Pierre *see*
- NOTICE BIOGRAPHIQUE MGR C.-E. LEGARE, PROTONOTAIRE APOSTOLIQUE A. J. P., VICAIRE GENERAL DE S. E. LE CARDINAL TASCHEREAU, ARCHEVEQUE DE QUEBEC
- NOTICE BIOGRAPHIQUE SUR LE REVEREND J. AUCLAIR: CURE DE NOTRE DAME DE QUEBEC: DECEDE LE 29 NOVEMBRE, 1887
- NOTICE BIOGRAPHIQUE SUR LE REVEREND J. AUCLAIR, CURE DE NOTRE-DAME DE QUEBEC, DECEDE LE 29 NOVEMBRE 1887
- SERMON PRONONCE A L'OCCASION DE LA BENEDICTION DES CLOCHES DE LA BASILIQUE NOTRE DAME DE QUEBEC, 4 OCTOBRE, 1891

Cote, J-P *see* LA PRESSE REGIONALE
Cote, Narcisse Omer *see* POLITICAL APPOINTMENTS, PARLIAMENTS AND THE JUDICIAL BENCH IN THE DOMINION OF CANADA, 1867 TO 1895
LA COTE NORD – Baie-Comeau, Canada. 17 oct 1957-15 jun 1976 – 12r – 1 – Can$75.00r – cn Can Microfilming [072]
COTE OCCIDENTALE D'AFRIQUE. COTE D'OR. GEOGRAPHIE. COMMERCE. MOEURS / Peuchgaric, N – (African Library). Paris. J. Rouvier. 1857 – 9 – fr Hachette [960]
Cote, Paul *see* LIVRES SUR LES BEAUX-ARTS, L'ARCHITECTURE, LA DANSE, LE DESSIN, LA MUSIQUE, LA NUMISMATIQUE, ET LA PEINTURE, PUBLIES AU CANADA DE 1750 A 1899...
Cote, Roland *see* DERNIERE HEURE
Cote, Stanislas (1846-1920) *see* LA CHASSE A L'HERITAGE
Cote, Thomas *see*
- TROIS ETUDES

COTEJO DE LAS EGLOGAS QUE HA PREMIADO LA REAL ACADEMIA DE LA LENGUA / Forner Segarra, Juan Pablo – Salamanca: CSIC, 1951 – 1 – sp Bibl Santa Ana [946]
Cotel, Pierre *see* DICTIONNAIRE FRANCAIS-BANDA ET BANDA-FRANCAIS PRECEDE D'UN ESSAI DE GRAMMAIRE BANDA
Cote-Mercier, G *see* VERS DEMAIN
Cotes, E C *see* A CATALOGUE OF THE MOTHS OF INDIA
Cotgrave, Randle *see*
- A DICTIONARIE OF THE FRENCH AND ENGLISH TONGUES

Cothenius, C A von *see* DISPOSITIO VEGETABILIUM METHODICA
THE COTNER COLLEGIAN – Bethany, NE. -w. (Every Tues. during school year). Sept 1904-26 May 1933 – 1 – us NE Hist [071]
Coton, P *see*
- DU TRES-SAINCT ET TRES-AUGUSTE SACREMENT, ET SACRIFICE DE LA MESSE
- GENEVE PLAGIAIRE, ...
- INSTITUTION CATHOLIQUE, OU EST DECLAREE ET CONFIRMEE LA VERITE DE LA FOY
- RECHEUTE DE GENEVE PLAGIAIRE

LE COTON, SON REGIME, SES PROBLEMES, SON INFLUENCE EN EUROPE / Reybaud, Louis – (Condition of 19th C. French working class series). 1867 – 9 – fr Hachette [630]
COTORRA – Montijo.1895. Solo no. 1 – 9 – 1.50f – sp Bibl Santa Ana [072]
LA COTORRA – Montijo, 1895. 1 numero – 5 – sp Bibl Santa Ana [073]
COTSWOLD STANDARD *see* NORTH COTSWOLD STANDARD
Cotta y Marquez de Prado, Fernando de *see* BIBLIOGRAFIA MANCHEGA. BIBLIOGRAFIA DE LAS PROVINCIAS DE ALBACETE, CIUDAD REAL, CUENCA Y TOLEDO
Cotta y Marquez de Prado, Fernando de et al *see* CATALOGO DE LAS LABRAS HERALDICAS DE LA CIUDAD DE VILLANUEVA DE LA SERENA (BADAJOZ)
Cotta y Marquez de Prado, Ventura de *see* FUERO DE POBLACION OTORGADO POR...DON CARLOS 3 A LAS LOCALIDADES FORMADAS EN LA SIERRA MORENA POR LA LLAMADA "COLONIZACION INTERIOR"...
COTTAGE GROVE ECHO-LEADER – (Set incl. Cottage Grove and Lemati Echo-Leader) – Cottage Grove, OR. -w. 8 Dec 1894-5 Oct 1895. – 1r – 1 – us U.O. Library [071]
COTTAGE GROVE SENTINEL – Cottage Grove, OR. -w. 24 Sep 1909-. – 1 – us U.O. Library [071]
A COTTAGE IN AN ENGAGED SPACE – Pattee, University Park, PA. 1989 – 34p 1mf – 9 – $0.50f – us Lawrence Pub [720]
COTTAGE LIFE – Toronto. v1-28. 1988-94 – 9 – Can$28.00y – cn Micromedia [640]
THE COTTAGER'S FRIEND AND GUIDE OF THE YOUNG – Toronto: Printed by T H Bentley, for J Donogh, [1854-18–?] – 9 – cn C.I.H.M. [360]
Cottam, Bart *see* COTTAM'S NEW ILLUSTRATED BOOK ON CAGE BIRDS: THEIR NECESSARY FOOD AND CARE TOGETHER WITH VALUABLE FORMULAE FOR BIRD FOODS, TREATS, MEDICINES, ETC
COTTAM'S NEW ILLUSTRATED BOOK ON CAGE BIRDS: THEIR NECESSARY FOOD AND CARE TOGETHER WITH VALUABLE FORMULAE FOR BIRD FOODS, TREATS, MEDICINES, ETC / Cottam, Bart – London, Ont.?: s.n., 1894? (London, Ont.: Advertiser Printing Co.). 05273. (Pre-1900 Canadiana) – 9 – cn C.I.H.M. [971]
COTTA'SCHE ZEITUNG *see* ALLGEMEINE ZEITUNG
Cotte, C *see* LA POLITIQUE ECONOMIQUE DE LA FRANCE EN AFRIQUE NOIRE DE 1936 A 1946
Cotte, Fremin de *see* EXPLICATION FACILE ET BREVE DES CINQ ORDRES D'ARCHITECTURE.
Cotte, Paul Vincent *see* REGARDONS VIVRE UNE TRIBU MALGACHE, LES BETSIMISARAKA.
Cotter, Charles H *see* STUDIES IN MARITIME HISTORY
Cotteret, J M et al *see* RECHERCHE SUR LE VOCABULAIRE DU GENERAL DE GAULLE
Cotterill, H B *see* TRAVELS AND RESEARCHES AMONG THE LAKES AND MOUNTAINS OF EASTERN AND CENTRAL AFRICA
Cotterill, Henry Bernard *see* ITALY FROM DANTE TO TASSO (1300-1600), ITS POLITICAL HISTORY..
Cottiaux, J *see* L'OFFICE LIEGEOIS DE LA FETE-DIEU, SA VALEUR ET SON DESTIN
Cottineau, Dom L H *see* REPERTOIRE TOPO-BIBLIOGRAPIQUE DES ABBAYES ET PRIEURES
Cottle, Joseph *see* REMINISCENCES OF SAMUEL TAYLOR COLERIDGE AND ROBERT SOUTHEY
COTTON FACTORY TIMES – 1885-1937 – 1 – uk Manchester Libr [072]
COTTON FACTORY TIMES – Manchester, Ashton-under-Lyne, England. -w. 1912, 1915-18. 3 reels – 1 – uk British Libr Newspaper [072]
Cotton, Henry *see*
- MEMOIR OF A FRENCH NEW TESTAMENT, IN WHICH THE MASS AND PURGATORY ARE FOUND IN THE SACRED TEXT...
- THE SUCCESSION OF THE PRELATES AND MEMBERS OF THE CATHEDRAL BODIES IN IRELAND, VOL 3
- THE SUCCESSION OF THE PRELATES AND MEMBERS OF THE CATHEDRAL BODIES IN IRELAND, VOL 4
- THE SUCCESSION OF THE PRELATES AND MEMBERS OF THE CATHEDRAL BODIES OF IRELAND, VOL 1

COTTON IN EGYPT / Egypt. Ministry of Agriculture – Prepared for the International Cotton Advisory Committee. 7th plenary meeting, held in Cairo, Apr 1948. BNE-4649 1 – 9 – ne IDC [630]
COTTON INDUSTRY AND TRADE IN CHINA / Fong, H D – (Industry Ser., bull. nr. 4. 2 v. Tientsin. 1932). Nankai Inst. of Economics. BCH-989 2 – 8 – ne IDC [338]
Cotton, J J *see* LIST OF INSCRIPTIONS ON TOMBS OR MONUMENTS IN MADRAS POSSESSING HISTORICAL OR ARCHAEOLOGICAL INTEREST
Cotton, John *see* GODS MERCIE MIXED WITH HIS JUSTICE, OR HIS PEOPLES DELIVERANCE IN TIMES OF DANGER
Cotton, Joseph Jr *see* CONSTITUTIONAL DECISIONS OF JOHN MARSHALL
COTTON LEAFLET / Clemson University. Agricultural Extension Division – 1970-78.1 fiches – 9 – us Spaulding [630]
COTTON LEAFLET / Clemson University. Agricultural Extension Division – n.1-7. 1962 – 1,5 – us Spaulding [630]
COTTON MARKET REPORTS – 1848-63. BRRAM – 1 – uk Microform Academic [975]
COTTON SPECIALISTS AND RESEARCH INSTITUTIONS IN SELECTED COUNTRIES – 1976 – 44p – it F.A.O. [631]
COTTON STATES – (Weekly Confederate newspaper) – Gainesville, FL. Apr 16 1864 – 1r – 1 – us Western Res [071]
COTTON STATISTICS / Egypt. Ministry of Agriculture – Prepared for the International Cotton Advisory Committee. 7th plenary meeting, Cairo, Apr 1948. BNE-4651 1 – 9 – ne IDC [630]
COTTON STATISTICS / Egypt. Ministry of Agriculture – Presented to the 18th International Cotton Congress, Cairo, Jan 1938. BNE-4652-1 – 9 – ne IDC [630]
COTTON STATISTICS / Egypt. Ministry of Agriculture – Presented to the 19th International Cotton Congress, Cairo and Alexandria, 24 Feb-3 Mar 1951.BNE-4654-1 – 9 – ne IDC [630]
COTTON VARIETIES FOR ALABAMA / Alabama. Agricultural Experiment Station – 1955-63 – 1,5,6 – us Spaulding [630]
Cotton, Walter Aidan *see* RACIAL SEGREGATION IN SOUTH AFRICA, AN APPEAL
COTTON'S WEEKLY : SOCIALIST – Cowansville, Canada. n108-6 oct 1910; n253-17 jul 1913; n254-24 jul 1913 – 1r – 1 – Can$25.00 – cn Can Microfilming [072]
Cottrell, Randall R *see* AN ANALYSIS OF THE MOTIVATIONAL IMPACT OF A HEALTH RISK APPRAISAL AND A COLLEGE HEALTH EDUCATION COURSE UTILIZING A LIFESTYLE THEME ON SELECTED HEALTH BEHAVIORS
Cottrell, Stuart P *see* PREDICTORS OF RESPONSIBLE ENVIRONMENTAL BEHAVIOR AMONG BOATERS ON THE CHESAPEAKE BAY
Couard, Ludwig *see*
- ALTCHRISTLICHE SAGEN UEBER DAS LEBEN JESU UND DER APOSTEL
- DIE RELIGIOESEN UND SITTLICHEN ANSCHAUUNGEN DER ALTTESTAMENTLICHEN APOKRYPHEN UND PSEUDEPIGRAPHEN

Couat, Auguste Henri *see* ETUDE SUR CATULLE.
Coube, Stephen *see* THE GREAT SUPPER OF GOD
Couch, J *see* A HISTORY OF THE FISHES OF THE BRITISH ISLANDS
Couch, Lorinda C *see* RESTENOSIS RATE AFTER PERCUTANEOUS TRANSLUMINAL CORONARY ANGIOPLASTY IN CARDIAC REHABILITATION PROGRAM PARTICIPANTS
THE COUCHER BOOK OF THE CISTERCIAN ABBEY OF KIRKSTALL / ed by Lancaster, W T & Baildon, W Paley – Leeds, 1904 – 8mf – 8 – Dfl30.00 – ne Slangenburg [240]
Coudert, F R *see* "REVISION OF THE LEAGUE"
Coudray, Alexandre J C du *see* FABLES ALLEMANDES ET CONTES FRANCAIS EN VERS, AVEC UN ESSAI SUR LA FABLE
Coudreau, Henri *see* VIAGEM AO TAPAJOS
Coues, E *see* KEY TO NORTH AMERICAN BIRDS
Coughlin, Dennis *see* VILLAGE SCENES: A CANADIAN POEM
Coughlin, Michael E *see* THE AMERICAN JURY
Couillard-Despres, Azarie *see*
- HISTOIRE DE LA SEIGNEURIE DE ST-OURS
- LOUIS HEBERT, PREMIER COLON CANADIEN ET SA FAMILLE
- LA PREMIERE FAMILLE FRANCAISE AU CANADA, SES ALLIES ET SES DESCENDANTS

Couissin, P *see* LES ARMES ROMAINES
Coulanges, F de *see* THE ORIGIN OF PROPERTY IN LAND
Coulet, Jules *see* ETUDES SUR L'ANCIEN POEME FRANCAIS DU VOYAGE DE CHARLEMAGNE EN ORIENT
Coulie, B *see*
- THESAURUS AMPHILOCHII ICONIENSIS
- THESAURUS PSEUDO-NONNI QUONDAM PANOPOLITANI, PARAPHRASIS EVANGELII S. IOANNIS
- THESAURUS SANCTI GREGORII NAZIANZENI

Couling, S *see* HISTORY OF SHANGHAI
Coulombe, M *see* BIO-BIBLIOGRAPHIE DU REVEREND PERE FRANCIS GOYER, S.S.S., CONSULTEUR PROVINCIAL
Coulombe, Marie-Anne *see* BIBLIOGRAPHIE ANALYTIQUE PARTIELLE DE LA COTE-NORD
Coulon, Emile *see* POETICAL LEISURE HOURS AND TORONTONIAN DESCRIPTIONS: IN FRENCH VERSE AND ENGLISH ESSAYS, FOLLOWED BY A TOKEN OF AFFECTION TO A DEPARTED AND FOND SISTER, AND A CURRICULUM VITAE
Coulon, H *see* DROIT ROMAIN
Coulon, R *see* SCRIPTORES ORDINIS PRAEDICATORUM
Couloubaly, Pascal Baba F *see* L'ENFANCE BAMBARA
Coulter, E M *see* HISTORY OF KENTUCKY
Coulter, J M *see*
- MANUAL OF THE BOTANY OF THE ROCKY MOUNTAIN REGION
- SYNOPSIS OF THE FLORA OF COLORADO

Coulton, G G *see*
- FROM ST FRANCIS TO DANTE
- A MEDIEVAL GARNER

COUNCIL AND GENERAL ASSEMBLY MINUTE BOOKS – 20r – 1 – $1,440.00 – us UMI [700]
COUNCIL BLUFFS BEILAGE – Council Bluffs, IO: [s.n.], jan 25-mar 22 1923 – 1r – us Res Libr [071]
COUNCIL BLUFFS FREIE PRESSE UND WOCHENTLICHE OMAHA TRIBUNE – Council Bluffs, IO, and Omaha, NE: Philip Andres 1920-1923. 1922-jan 3 1923 – 1r – us Res Libr [071]
COUNCIL FIRE... DEVOTED TO THE CIVILIZATION AND RIGHTS OF THE AMERICAN INDIAN – v.1-12. 1878-89. (LC lacks v.5, no.10-12) – 1 – 25.00 – us L of C Photodup [970]
COUNCIL FOR A COMPETITIVE ECONOMY – 1p leaflet – 9 – 1.00f – at Libertarian Micro [338]
COUNCIL FOR DEMOCRACY IN KOREA – 30 docs, 1980-1985 – 3mf – 9 – ne IDC [320]

COUNCIL FOR EXCEPTIONAL CHILDREN MICROFICHE LIBRARY – 1934-89. The complete collection of CEC journals: Exceptional Children and Teaching Exceptional Children. Focus on education of handicapped and gifted students. Complete, or individual components – 9 – $15.00v – us UMI [370]

Council for Monetary Reform *see* STATEMENT OF GOALS

COUNCIL FOR NATIONAL COOPERATION IN AQUATICS : ARCHIVES, RECORDS, REFERENCE MATERIAL, CONFERENCE REPORTS 1951-1972 – 32mf – 9 – $64.00 – us Microform Publ [790]

COUNCIL FOR NATIONAL COOPERATION IN AQUATICS : BIENNIAL CONFERENCE REPORTS 1974-1980 – 8mf – 9 – $16.00 – us Microform Publ [790]

Council for National Cooperation in Aquatics *see* ARCHIVES, RECORDS, REFERENCE MATERIAL AND CONFERENCE REPORTS

Council for the Investigation of Vatican Influence and Censorship *see* MEMORANDUM ON THE PENETRATION OF THE TRADES UNIONS BY ROMAN CATHOLIC GUILDS

Council for World Mission *see* ARCHIVES

COUNCIL FOR WORLD MISSION ARCHIVES 1775-1940 / School of Oriental and African Studies, London – (This collection also incorporates the archives of the London Missionary Society. Includes printed guide) – 23,343mf – 9 – ne IDC [240]

COUNCIL MINUTES, 1660-1800 / Royal Society – $295.00 – 0-89093-876-8 – us UPA [500]

Council of Action for Peace and Reconstruction *see* NEWS BULLETIN

THE COUNCIL OF ADVICE AT THE CAPE OF GOOD HOPE, 1825-1834 : A STUDY IN COLONIAL GOVERNMENT / Donaldson, Margaret E – [s.l.: s.n.], 1974 – us Res Libr [960]

COUNCIL OF ANTHROPOLOGY AND EDUCATION QUARTERLY *see* ANTHROPOLOGY AND EDUCATION QUARTERLY

Council of Constance *see* MAGNUM OECUMENICUM CONSTANTIENSE CONCILIUM.

Council of Educational Facility Planners *see* CEFP JOURNAL

Council of Europe. Directorate of Legal Affairs *see* SURVEY OF THE LAWS OF THE MEMBER STATES ON PAYMENT OF MAINTENANCE BETWEEN DIVORCED SPOUSES

Council of Georgist Organizations *see* AN INTRODUCTION TO THE GEORGIST PHILOSOPHY AND MOVEMENT

COUNCIL OF LEGAL EDUCATION CALENDAR, 1901-1925/26 / Inns of Court. England. Council of Legal Education – (The Council was established by the societies of Lincoln's Inn, the Inner Temple, the Middle Temple and Gray's Inn) – 111mf – 9 – $166.00 – LLMC 95-261 – us L.L.M.C. [340]

Council of Micronesia *see* PROCEEDINGS

Council of Pacific Teachers Organisations *see* MINUTES OF ANNUAL MEETINGS, REPORTS AND WOMEN'S NETWORK FILES

COUNCIL OF PLANNING LIBRARIANS : BIBLIOGRAPHIES – nos 1-168. 1978-1986 – 9 – $435.00 set – 0-89941-268-8 – us Hein [020]

COUNCIL OF PLANNING LIBRARIANS EXCHANGE BIBLIOGRAPHIES – Chicago: Council of Planning Librarians nos 1-1565, 1958-1978 – 9 – $2,995.00 set – 0-89941-267-X – us Hein [020]

COUNCIL OF STATE DEBATES – (Index 1921-1929) – Delhi, 1921-1947 – 638mf – I-13/2 – ne IDC [320]

COUNCIL OF STATE GOVERNMENTS PUBLICATIONS – (Annual update ca $195.00) – Lexington: Council of State Governments, 1930-1995 no 1 update – 9 – $5,475.00 set – 0-89941-271-8 – us Hein [350]

COUNCIL OF THE LAW SOCIETY ANNUAL REPORTS – (Lacking: 1903) – Law Society of Great Britain, 1896-1953 – 88mf – 9 – $132.00 – LLMC 84-452 – us L.L.M.C. [340]

COUNCIL ON CHRISTIAN MEDICAL WORK : BULLETIN / Council on Christian Medical Work – nos 37-41. Nov 1947-Oct 1948 (incomplete) – 1r – 1 – ATLA S0707E – us A.T.L.A. [073]

Council on Christian Medical Work *see* COUNCIL ON CHRISTIAN MEDICAL WORK

COUNCIL ON CONSUMER INFORMATION *see* NEWSLETTER

Council on Education. Committee *see* MINUTES AND REPORTS

COUNCIL ON ENVIRONMENTAL QUALITY ANNUAL REPORTS – 1st-19th. 1970-88 – 102mf – 9 – $153.00 – LLMC 81-221 – us L.L.M.C. [324]

COUNCIL ON FOREIGN RELATIONS : PUBLICATIONS – (Collection includes Foreign Affairs Periodicals) – New York: Council on Foreign Relations, 1928-96 no 1 monographs – 9 – $3,214.00 set – 0-89941-212-2 – us Hein [327]

COUNCIL ON HEMISPHERIC AFFAIRS (COHA) – Washington DC. 548 docs. 1980-1991 – 66mf – 9 – ne IDC [320]

Council on Library Resources *see* FIFTH ANNUAL REPORT FOR THE PERIOD ENDING 30 JUN 1961

Council on the Study of Religion *see* BULLETIN

COUNCIL ON THE STUDY OF RELIGION BULLETIN *see* JOURNAL OF THE AMERICAN ACADEMY OF RELIGION

COUNCILS, ANCIENT AND MODERN : FROM THE APOSTOLICAL COUNCIL OF JERUSALEM, TO THE OECUMENICAL COUNCIL OF NICAEA, AND TO THE LAST PAPAL COUNCIL IN THE VATICAN / Rule, William Harris – London: Hodder and Stoughton, 1870 – 1mf – us A.T.L.A. [240]

COUNCILS AND ECCLESIASTICAL DOCUMENTS RELATING TO GREAT BRITAIN AND IRELAND / Haddan, Arthur West & Stubbs, William – H-1144 2. 2 v. 1869-1878 – 9 – ne IDC [240]

COUNCILS AND ECCLESIASTICAL DOCUMENTS RELATING TO GREAT BRITAIN AND IRELAND / ed by Haddan, Arthur West & Stubbs, William – Oxford: Clarendon Press, 1869-1878 – 3mf – us A.T.L.A. [240]

COUNCILS AND ECCLESIASTICAL DOCUMENTS RELATING TO GREAT BRITAIN AND IRELAND / ed by Haddan, Arthur West & Stubbs, William – (vl 1869 13mf. v2 1873 7mf. v3 1871 12mf) – Oxford. v1-3. 1869-71 – 8 – Dfl112.00 – ne Slangenburg [240]

COUNSELING AND HUMAN DEVELOPMENT – v10-. 1977-. Continues: Focus on Guidance – 1,5,6,9 – us UMI [370]

COUNSELING AND VALUES – (1975-. 5,6,9) – v. 1-. 1956- – 1 – us UMI [370]

COUNSELING PSYCHOLOGIST – (1975-. 5,6,9) – v. 1-. 1969- – 1 – us UMI [073]

COUNSELLING PSYCHOLOGY QUARTERLY – 1988- 6v – 9 – £185.00 – 0951-5070 – uk Carfax [150]

COUNSELLOR – London. 1861 – 1 – uk Microform Academic [073]

COUNSELLOR : THE NEW YORK LAW SCHOOL LAW JOURNAL – v1-5. 1891-96 – 1 – $40.00 – us Hein [073]

THE COUNSELLOR : JOURNAL OF THE NEW YORK LAW SCHOOL – v1-5. 1891-96 (all publ) – 15mf – 9 – $22.50 – LLMC 82-918 – us L.L.M.C. [073]

COUNSELOR EDUCATION AND SUPERVISION – (1971-. 5,6,9) – v. 4- 1961- – 1 – us UMI [370]

COUNT CAMPELLO : AN AUTOBIOGRAPHY: GIVING HIS REASONS FOR LEAVING THE PAPAL CHURCH / Campello, Enrico di – London: Hodder and Stoughton, 1881 – 1mf – 9 – 0-8370-9694-4 – 1986-3694 – us A.T.L.A. [920]

COUNTDOWN TO 1997 / Goodhart et al – 1992 – sz I.C.J. [320]

COUNTEE CULLEN PAPERS – 1921-69 – 1 – $248.00 – us Amistad [010]

COUNTER-SPY – v1-8 no 4 1973 – Jun/Aug 1984 – 1,5,6,9 – us UMI [320]

THE COUNTESS EVE / Shorthouse, Joseph Henry – British Fiction Archive: Unit 1 – 9 – uk Bell [830]

THE COUNTESSE OF PEMBROKE'S ARCADIA, EXAMINED AND DISCUSSED / Harman, Edward George – London: Cecil Palmer (1924). x,233p., front., facsim – 1 – us U.W. Library [440]

COUNTIES OF LAGRANGE AND NOBLE / F.A. Battey and Co – Historical and biographical sketches. Chicago, 1882. Indiana Reel 18. (The Cox Library Collection) – 5 – us Americana [978]

COUNTIES OF MORGAN, MONROE AND BROWN / Blanchard, Charles – Historical and biographical sketches. Chicago: F.A. Battey and Co., 1884. Indiana Reel 23. (The Cox Library Collection) – 5 – us Americana [978]

COUNTIES OF PORTER AND LAKE / Goodspeed & Blanchard – Historical and biographical sketches. Chicago: F.A. Battey and Co., 1882. Indiana Reel 24. (The Cox Library Collection) – 5 – us Americana [978]

COUNTIES OF WARREN, BENTON, JASPER AND NEWTON / F.A. Battey and Co – Historical and biographical sketches. Chicago, 1883. Indiana Reel 29. (The Cox Library Collection) – 5 – us Americana [978]

COUNTIES OF WHITE AND PULASKI / F.A. Battey and Co – Historical and biographical sketches. Chicago, 1883. Indiana Reel 31. (The Cox Library Collection) – 5 – us Americana [978]

COUNTIES OF WHITELY AND NOBLE / Goodspeed & Blanchard – Historical and biographical sketches. Chicago: F.A. Battey and Company, 1882. Indiana Reel 31. (The Cox Library Collection) – 5 – us Americana [978]

COUNTRIES OF THE WORLD – Area handbooks prepared for the U.S. Department of Defense, covering over 100 countries – 9 – us UMI [306]

THE COUNTRY – Adelaide, Australia. 2 Sep 1893-5 May 1894; 12 Jan 1895-26 Dec 1896.-w. 2 reels – 1 – uk British Libr Newspaper [072]

COUNTRY ACCOUNTS / Holkham Hall. Norfolk. England – 1722-67 and 1793-1800 – 1 – uk Microform Academic [941]

THE COUNTRY ALMANAC – Woodside, CA. 1965- – 39+ r – 1 – $1,950.00 ($120.00y) – B03113 – us Library Micro [071]

"COUNTRY BEFORE PARTY" – issued by the Dominion National League. Hamilton Ont.: The League, 1878. 02735. (Pre-1900 Canadiana) – 9 – cn C.I.H.M. [971]

THE COUNTRY FROM CAPE PALMAS TO RIVER CONGO / Adams, J – 1823 – 7 – uk Microform Academic [910]

COUNTRY GENTLEMEN – Albany. N.Y. 1853-1911 – 1 – us UMI [071]

THE COUNTRY GENTLEMEN – Philadelphia. Pa. 1911-1947 – 1 – us UMI [071]

COUNTRY GUIDE : EASTERN EDITION – Winnipeg, 1980-89 – 17r – 1 – cn Commonwealth Micro [073]

COUNTRY GUIDE : WESTERN EDITION – Winnipeg, 1980-89 – 17r – 1 – cn Commonwealth Micro [073]

COUNTRY GUIDE – Winnipeg, CN. 1908-79 – 47r – 1 – cn Commonwealth Micro [073]

COUNTRY HANDCRAFTS – 1984- – 1,5,6,9 – us UMI [740]

COUNTRY LIFE PHOTOGRAPH ARCHIVE 1897-1950 – (Features over 72,000 photographs, mostly unpubl, detailing thousands of private and public buildings and their contents. Includes printed guide) – 9 – $8,330.00 – 1-869934-65-2 – uk Emmett [770]

COUNTRY LIVING – v5-. 1982- – 1,5,6,9 – us UMI [073]

COUNTRY MAGAZINE – 1985-. -m – 1 – us UMI [640]

COUNTRY MUSIC – 1986- – 1,5,6,9 – us UMI [780]

COUNTRY NEWS – Paso Robles, CA. Aug 1976-1979; 1982-93 – 32r – 1 BR03390 – $1,600.00 – us Library Micro [071]

COUNTRY PEOPLE – 1984- – 1,5,6,9 – us UMI [073]

COUNTRY PROGRAMMING DOCUMENT IN THE FORM OF A BACKGROUND PAPER (GENERAL STUDY) ON LIBYA / Libya – Tripoli. 1971. General Economic Background Information. BNE-528 1 – 9 – ne IDC [338]

COUNTRY REPORT THAILAND : FUNCTIONAL LITERACY PROGRAM IN THAILAND / Thailand. Ministry of Education – Bangkok, c. 1977 – 1mf – 9 – DE-293/1 – ne IDC [370]

COUNTRY REPORT THAILAND; ... / Pangputhipong, V – Bangkok, 1979 – 1mf – 9 – DE-297/1 – ne IDC [370]

COUNTRY REPORTS PRESENTED AT THE 5TH SESSION OF THE INDO-PACIFIC FISHERY COMMISSION WORKING PARTY OF EXPERTS ON INLAND FISHERIES AND PAPERS : CONTRIBUTED TO THE WORKSHOP ON TILAPIA IN CAPTURE AND CULTURE-ENHANCED FISHERIES IN THE INDO-PACIFIC FISHERY COMMISSION COUNTRIES BOGOR, INDONESIA, 1991 / IPFC – 1992 – 288p – it F.A.O. [338]

COUNTRYMAN – Coburg, OR. -w. 30 Mar 1971-19 Aug 1980 – 1r – 1 – us U.O. Library [071]

COUNTRYSIDE – (v68-69. 1984-85. 5,6,9) – v60-69. 1976-85 – 1 – us UMI [073]

COUNTRYSIDE AND SMALL STOCK JOURNAL – v56-60. 1972-76 – 1 – us UMI [636]

COUNTRYSIDE AND SMALL STOCK JOURNAL – v69-. 1985- – 1,5,6,9 – us UMI [636]

COUNTRYSIDE CHURCHES = HSIANG-TS'UN CHIAO-HUI – nos 1-3. Dec 1940-Dec 1942; nos 8-9. Dec 1946-Jun 1947 (complete) – 1r – 1 – ATLA S0296J – us A.T.L.A. [073]

Counts, Charlene L M *see* THE EFFECT OF SWIM TRAINING ON PLASMA SOMATOMEDIN-C LEVELS IN 8- TO 10-YEAR-OLD CHILDREN

COUNTY ACTIVIST – Redway, CA. 1984-1991 – 1r – 1 – $50.00 – B05047 – us Library Micro [071]

COUNTY AGENT AND VO-AG TEACHER *see* FARM TECHNOLOGY AND AGRI-FIELDMAN

COUNTY AND DISTRICT RECORDS: ABBEVILLE COUNTY / South Carolina. Department of Archives and History – 1872-1925. 46 reels. More details on request – 1 – $30.00r – us SC Archives [025]

COUNTY AND DISTRICT RECORDS: AIKEN (CITY) / South Carolina. Department of Archives and History – 1895-1916. Treasurer's Tax Duplicates. 1 reel – 1 – $30.00r – us SC Archives [025]

COUNTY AND DISTRICT RECORDS: AIKEN COUNTY / South Carolina. Department of Archives and History – 1872-1974. 154 reels. More details on request – 1 – $30.00r – us SC Archives [025]

COUNTY AND DISTRICT RECORDS: ANDERSON COUNTY / South Carolina. Department of Archives and History – Includes Pendleton District. 1790-1972.319 reels. More details on request – 1 – $30.00r – us SC Archives [025]

COUNTY AND DISTRICT RECORDS: BARNWELL COUNTY / South Carolina. Department of Archives and History – 1784-1954. 12 reels. More details on request – 1 – $30.00r – us SC Archives [025]

COUNTY AND DISTRICT RECORDS: BEAUFORT COUNTY / South Carolina. Department of Archives and History – 1864-1980. 60 reels. More details on request – 1 – $30.00r – us SC Archives [025]

COUNTY AND DISTRICT RECORDS: BERKELEY COUNTY / South Carolina. Department of Archives and History – 1881-1954. 17 reels. More details on request – 1 – $30.00r – us SC Archives [025]

COUNTY AND DISTRICT RECORDS: CAMDEN DISTRICT / South Carolina. Department of Archives and History – 1784-1841. 6 reels. More details on request – 1 – $30.00r – us SC Archives [025]

COUNTY AND DISTRICT RECORDS: CHARLESTON COUNTY / South Carolina. Department of Archives and History – 1735-1915. 31 reels. More details on request – 1 – $30.00r – us SC Archives [025]

COUNTY AND DISTRICT RECORDS: CHEROKEE COUNTY / South Carolina. Department of Archives and History – 1897-1960. 85 reels. More details on request – 1 – $30.00r – us SC Archives [025]

COUNTY AND DISTRICT RECORDS: CHESTER COUNTY / South Carolina. Department of Archives and History – 1785-1839. 9 reels. More details on request – 1 – $30.00r – us SC Archives [025]

COUNTY AND DISTRICT RECORDS: CHESTERFIELD COUNTY / South Carolina. Department of Archives and History – 1847-1978. 250 reels. More details on request – 1 – $30.00r – us SC Archives [025]

COUNTY AND DISTRICT RECORDS: CLARENDON COUNTY / South Carolina. Department of Archives and History – 1857-1980. 106 reels. More details on request – 1 – $30.00r – us SC Archives [025]

COUNTY AND DISTRICT RECORDS: COLLETON COUNTY / South Carolina. Department of Archives and History – 1802-1974. 91 reels. More details on request – 1 – $30.00r – us SC Archives [025]
COUNTY AND DISTRICT RECORDS: DARLINGTON COUNTY / South Carolina. Department of Archives and History – 1803-1980. 106 reels. More details on request – 1 – $30.00r – us SC Archives [025]
COUNTY AND DISTRICT RECORDS: DORCHESTER COUNTY / South Carolina. Department of Archives and History – 1757-1949. 61 reels. More details on request – 1 – $30.00r – us SC Archives [025]
COUNTY AND DISTRICT RECORDS: EAU CLAIRE (TOWN) / South Carolina. Department of Archives and History – Board of Health Minutes.1931-54. 1 reel – 1 – $30.00r – us SC Archives [025]
COUNTY AND DISTRICT RECORDS: EDGEFIELD COUNTY / South Carolina. Department of Archives and History – 1785-1976. 286 reels. More details on request – 1 – $30.00r – us SC Archives [025]
COUNTY AND DISTRICT RECORDS: FAIRFIELD COUNTY / South Carolina. Department of Archives and History – 1785-1970. 165 reels. More details on request – 1 – $30.00r – us SC Archives [025]
COUNTY AND DISTRICT RECORDS: FLORENCE COUNTY / South Carolina. Department of Archives and History – 1874-1981. 58 reels. More details on request – 1 – $30.00r – us SC Archives [025]
COUNTY AND DISTRICT RECORDS: GEORGETOWN COUNTY / South Carolina. Department of Archives and History – 1783-1963. 176 reels. More details on request – 1 – $30.00r – us SC Archives [025]
COUNTY AND DISTRICT RECORDS: GREENVILLE COUNTY / South Carolina. Department of Archives and History – 1787-1976. 281 reels. More details on request – 1 – $30.00r – us SC Archives [025]
COUNTY AND DISTRICT RECORDS: HAMPTON COUNTY / South Carolina. Department of Archives and History – 1879-1930. 33 reels. More details on request – 1 – $30.00r – us SC Archives [025]
COUNTY AND DISTRICT RECORDS: HORRY COUNTY / South Carolina. Department of Archives and History – 1803-1950. 90 reels. More details on request – 1 – $30.00r – us SC Archives [025]
COUNTY AND DISTRICT RECORDS: IRMO (TOWN) / South Carolina. Department of Archives and History – 1899-1975. Town Council Minutes. 1 reel – 1 – $30.00r – us SC Archives [025]
COUNTY AND DISTRICT RECORDS: KERSHAW COUNTY / South Carolina. Department of Archives and History – 1782-1980. 112 reels. More details on request – 1 – $30.00r – us SC Archives [025]
COUNTY AND DISTRICT RECORDS: LANCASTER COUNTY / South Carolina. Department of Archives and History – 1762-1960. 148 reels. More details on request – 1 – $30.00r – us SC Archives [025]
COUNTY AND DISTRICT RECORDS: LAURENS COUNTY / South Carolina. Department of Archives and History – 1785-1969. 286 reels. More details on request – 1 – $30.00r – us SC Archives [025]
COUNTY AND DISTRICT RECORDS: LEE COUNTY / South Carolina. Department of Archives and History – 1902-20.20 reels. More details on request – 1 – $30.00r – us SC Archives [025]
COUNTY AND DISTRICT RECORDS: LEXINGTON COUNTY / South Carolina. Department of Archives and History – 1806-1964. 237 reels. More details on request – 1 – $30.00r – us SC Archives [025]
COUNTY AND DISTRICT RECORDS: LEXINGTON (TOWN) / South Carolina. Department of Archives and History – 1917-71.Details on request. 2 reels – 1 – $30.00r – us SC Archives [025]
COUNTY AND DISTRICT RECORDS: MARION COUNTY / South Carolina. Department of Archives and History – 1790-1955. 123 reels. More details on request – 1 – $30.00r – us SC Archives [025]
COUNTY AND DISTRICT RECORDS: MARLBORO COUNTY / South Carolina. Department of Archives and History – 1785-1973. 143 reels. More details on request – 1 – $30.00r – us SC Archives [025]
COUNTY AND DISTRICT RECORDS: NEWBERRY COUNTY / South Carolina. Department of Archives and History – 1776-1953. 98 reels. More details on request – 1 – $30.00r – us SC Archives [025]
COUNTY AND DISTRICT RECORDS: NINETY SIX DISTRICT / South Carolina. Department of Archives and History – Plats. 1784-1803. 3 reels – 1 – $30.00r – us SC Archives [025]
COUNTY AND DISTRICT RECORDS: OCONEE COUNTY / South Carolina. Department of Archives and History – 1868-1959. 95 reels. More details on request – 1 – $30.00r – us SC Archives [025]
COUNTY AND DISTRICT RECORDS: ORANGEBURG COUNTY / South Carolina. Department of Archives and History – 1775-1975. 217 reels. More details on request – 1 – $30.00r – us SC Archives [025]
COUNTY AND DISTRICT RECORDS: PICKENS COUNTY / South Carolina. Department of Archives and History – 1828-1971. 81 reels. More details on request – 1 – $30.00r – us SC Archives [025]
COUNTY AND DISTRICT RECORDS: PINCKNEY DISTRICT (YORK) / South Carolina. Department of Archives and History – 1792-1872. 39 reels. More details on request – 1 – $30.00r – us SC Archives [025]
COUNTY AND DISTRICT RECORDS: RICHLAND COUNTY / South Carolina. Department of Archives and History – 1803-1962. 190 reels. More details on request – 1 – $30.00r – us SC Archives [025]
COUNTY AND DISTRICT RECORDS: SALUDA COUNTY / South Carolina. Department of Archives and History – 1896-1979. 113 reels. More details on request – 1 – $30.00r – us SC Archives [025]
COUNTY AND DISTRICT RECORDS: SPARTANBURG COUNTY / South Carolina. Department of Archives and History – 1785-1968. 275 reels. More details on request – 1 – 25.00r – us SC Archives [025]
COUNTY AND DISTRICT RECORDS: SPARTANBURG (TOWN) / South Carolina. Department of Archives and History – Town Council Ordinances, 1832-42. 1 reel – 1 – $30.00r – us SC Archives [025]
COUNTY AND DISTRICT RECORDS: ST PAUL'S PARISH / South Carolina. Department of Archives and History – Road Commissioner's Minutes, 1783-1839. 1 reel – 1 – $30.00r – us SC Archives [025]
COUNTY AND DISTRICT RECORDS: ST STEPHEN'S PARISH / South Carolina. Department of Archives and History – Road Commissioner's Minutes, 1789-99. 1 reel – 1 – $30.00r – us SC Archives [025]
COUNTY AND DISTRICT RECORDS: SUMTER COUNTY / South Carolina. Department of Archives and History – 1800-1955. 22 reels. More details on request – 1 – $30.00r – us SC Archives [025]
COUNTY AND DISTRICT RECORDS: UNION COUNTY / South Carolina. Department of Archives and History – 1785-1974. 243 reels. More details on request – 1 – $30.00r – us SC Archives [025]
COUNTY AND DISTRICT RECORDS: WILLIAMSBURG COUNTY / South Carolina. Department of Archives and History – 1806-1981. 81 reels. More details on request – 1 – $30.00r – us SC Archives [025]
COUNTY AND DISTRICT RECORDS: YORK COUNTY / South Carolina. Department of Archives and History – 1786-1974. 409 reels. More details on request – 1 – $30.00r – us SC Archives [025]
COUNTY AND REGIONAL HISTORIES AND ATLASES – Based on various bibliogs. for CA, IL, IN, MI, NY, OH, PA and WI – 1 – us Primary [978]
COUNTY ARGUS – Racine. Wis. -w. 1869-80 – 1 – us UMI [071]
THE COUNTY ATLAS OF SCOTLAND – ca 1855 – 9 – 0-7306-2387-4 – at State Libr Vic [941]
COUNTY AUDITORS' FUND RECORDS / Hancock County. Ohio. Biglick Township. Board of Education – 1868-1901 – 1r – 1 – $32.50r – us Archival [324]
COUNTY BANNER – Logan. West Virginia. 1889-1892 – 1 – us UMI [071]
COUNTY BREEZE – Sarasota. Fl. 1950-53 – 1 – us UMI [071]
COUNTY CITIZEN – McHenry. Ill. 1965- – 1 – us UMI [071]
COUNTY CLARION – Lapeer. Mich. -w. 1878-81, 1884, 1890-1900, 1906-10, 1913-23 – 1 – us UMI [071]
COUNTY COMMISSIONERS' LEGAL GUIDE, (FOR THE STATE OF TEXAS). / Texas. County Commissioners – St. Louis, Barnard 1894 340 p. LL-506 – 1 – us L of C Photodup [340]
COUNTY COURIER – Camden. N.J. 1880-1881; 1883-1889; 1893 – 1 – us UMI [071]
THE COUNTY COURT MANUAL: BEING A COLLECTION OF THE STATUTES RELATING TO THE PRACTICE, PROCEDURE AND JURISDICTION OF THE COUNTY COURTS OF NOVA SCOTIA WITH NOTES, ETC / Bingay, George – Toronto: Carswell, 1891. 00138. (Pre-1900 Canadiana) – 9 – cn C.I.H.M. [971]
COUNTY COURTS CHRONICLE AND GAZETTE OF BANKRUPTCY – London. 1847-1920. (13-20, 1860-67) wanting) – 1 – 249.00 – us L of C Photodup [941]
COUNTY DEMOCRAT – Lapeer. Mich. -w. 1879-97 – 1 – us UMI [071]
COUNTY DOWN REPORTER – Bangor, Ireland. Jun 1904-Dec 1916; 1925-79 (1930 imperfect).-w. 91mqn reels – 1 – uk British Libr Newspaper [072]
COUNTY DOWN SPECTATOR AND ULSTER STANDARD – Jun 3 1904-Dec 29 1905; 1906-16; 1925-29; Mar-Nov 1930; 1931-Dec 24 1991; 1992-Jun 1994; 1995-Dec 23 1996 – 152 1/2r – 1 – uk British Libr Newspaper [072]
COUNTY EXPRESS FOR WORCESTERSHIRE AND STAFFORDSHIRE – Stourbridge, England. 1920-39.-w. 32 reels – 1 – uk British Libr Newspaper [072]
COUNTY GAZETTE – San Mateo, CA. 1859-1931 – 16r – 1 – $800.00 – B02913 – us Library Micro [071]
COUNTY GAZETTE *see* TIMES GAZETTE
COUNTY HALL RECORDS / Glamorgan. County Council – 1719-1890 – 1 – uk Microform Academic [941]
COUNTY HERALD – Holywell, Wales. -w. 15 July 1887-Dec 1947. Lacking 1897, 1911. 48 reels – 1 – uk British Libr Newspaper [072]
COUNTY HISTORIES / Indiana – Over 900 titles for all 92 counties. Atlases, indexes by county with names, persons, firms.Individual histories and counties available – 1,5,9 – us A.G.L.L. [978]
COUNTY HOME JOURNAL / Lucas County. Ohio. Board of County Commissioners – 1956-1968 – 1r – 1 – $32.50r – us Archival [324]
COUNTY HOME RECORDS / Sandusky County. Ohio. Board of County Commissioners – 1864-1891 – 1r – 1 – $32.50r – us Archival [324]
COUNTY INDEPENDENT – Choteau. Mont. 1910-1911; 1915-1925 – 1 – us UMI [071]
COUNTY INDEPENDENT *see* INDEPENDENT
COUNTY JOURNAL – Salina. Kan. 1871-1893 – 1 – us UMI [071]
COUNTY LEADER – Fayette. Iowa. 1918-1926 – 1 – us UMI [071]
COUNTY LINE BAPTIST CHURCH. OGLETHORPE COUNTY. GEORGIA : CHURCH RECORDS – 1919-54 – 1 – 30.00 – us Baptist [240]
COUNTY LONG-TIME EXTENSION PROGRAM SUMMARY / Auburn University. Extension Service – 1947-65 – 1,5,6 – us Spaulding [630]
COUNTY NEWS – San Mateo, CA. 1937-45 – 1r – 1 – $50.00 – B02914 – us Library Micro [071]
COUNTY NEWS – Yazoo City. Miss. 1915-1931 – 1 – us UMI [071]
COUNTY NEWS (D) – San Mateo, CA. 1914-1918; 1925-1926 – 12r – 1 – $600.00 – B02915 – us Library Micro [071]
COUNTY OF BUTE 1851 CENSUS INDEX : ARGYLL AND WEST SCOTLAND CENSUS INDEX, PART 1 / Gibson, Peter & Macinnes, John – 1993 – 3mf – 9 – A$19.95 – 0-646-13250-4 – at Seanachas [920]
THE COUNTY OF HIGHLAND / Klise & Hough, Franklin B – Biographical sketches. Madison: Northwestern Historical Asso., 1902. Vols. 1-2. Mississippi Reel 4. (The Cox Library Collection) – 5 – us Americana [978]
THE COUNTY OF LOS ANGELES / American Historical Society – Chicago, 1923. California Reel 16. (The Cox Library Collection) – 5 – us Americana [978]
COUNTY OF MUSEUM ART CATALOGUE – (Individual titles not listed separately) – Los Angeles, 1932-1976 – 93 catalogues on 123mf – 9 – £775.00 – uk Chadwyck [700]
THE COUNTY OF NOBLE / ed by Martin, Frank M – A history of Noble County, Ohio, from the Earliest Days, with Special Chapter on Military Affairs, and Special Attention Given to Resources. Madison: Selwyn A. Brant, 1904. Ohio Reel 52. (The Cox Library Collection) – 5 – us Americana [978]
COUNTY OF WILLIAMS / Goodspeed & Blanchard – Historical and Biographical. Chicago: F. A. Battey and Co., 1882. Ohio Reel 67. (The Cox Library Collection) – 5 – us Americana [978]
THE COUNTY OF WILLIAMS / Shinn, William H – Historical and biographical. Madison: Historical Asso.-Northwestern, 1905. Ohio Reel 67. (The Cox Library Collection) – 5 – us Americana [978]
THE COUNTY PAPER – Antioch, CA. 1898-99 – 1r – 1 – $50.00 – B02018 – us Library Micro [071]
COUNTY POST – Litchfield. Conn. 1826-1829 – 1 – us UMI [071]
COUNTY PRESS – David City. Neb. 1892-1953 – 1 – us UMI [071]
COUNTY RECORD – Blountstown. Fl. -w. 1953. Apr. 1954- – 1 – us P.K. Yonge [071]
COUNTY RECORDER – San Mateo, CA. 1933-34 – 1r – 1 – $50.00 – B02916 – us Library Micro [071]
COUNTY RECORDS / Illinois – V141 – 1 – us A.G.L.L. [920]
COUNTY REPORTER – Napa, CA. 1862-64 – 1r – 1 – $50.00 – C02505 – us Library Micro [071]
THE COUNTY REPORTER – Fort Jones, CA. 1895-98 – 1r – 1 – $50.00 – B02239 – us Library Micro [071]
COUNTY REPORTS / Great Britain. Board of Agriculture – 1799-1815 – 7 – uk Microform Academic [630]
COUNTY SENTINEL – Asotin. Wash. 1891-1942 – 1 – us UMI [071]
COUNTY SENTINEL – Hot Springs. Mont. 1912-1920; 1922-1924 – 1 – us UMI [071]
COUNTY SUN – Merced, CA. 1891-92; 1900-03; 1906-22 – 12r – 1 – $600.00 – B02446 – us Library Micro [071]
COUNTY TIMES – Beaver. Pa. 1900- – 1 – us UMI [071]
COUNTY TIMES – Liberty. Mont. 1966- – 1 – us UMI [071]
COUNTY TIMES AND EXPRESS – Welshpool, Wales, Apr 4-Aug 29 1981; Sep 1981-Mar 1982; 1983-96 – 47r – 1 – uk British Libr Newspaper [072]
COUNTY TIPPERARY INDEPENDENT ETC – Ireland.11 Nov 1882-30 Dec 1893; 5 Jan-30 Mar, 11 May-21 Dec 1895. -d. 14 reels – 1 – uk British Libr Newspaper [072]
COUNTY TRUTH – Alma. Kan. 1893-1937 – 1 – us UMI [071]
COUNTY WEEKLY – Grenada. Miss. 1942-1953 – 1 – us UMI [071]
COUNTY-TOWNSHIP ROAD INVENTORY / Lucas County. Ohio. Engineer – 3r – 1 – $32.50r – us Archival [324]
THE COUP ATTEMPT OF THE "SEPTEMBER 30 MOVEMENT" IN INDONESIA / Nugroho, Notosusanto – SE-6394 1. 1968 – 9 – ne IDC [950]
LE COUP DE TRIQUE – Paris: Ad Blondeau, [1850]. mar-apr 1850 – us Res Libr [072]
LE COUP D'ETAT, OU, LE RENVOI DU CABINET DE BOUCHERVILLE:.. / Angers, Auguste Real – 1878. 00041. (Pre-1900 Canadiana) – 9 – cn C.I.H.M. [971]
COUP D'OEIL – Beloeil: L'Oeil regional inc, 1984-. SEM105P892 – 12mf – 9 – Can$27.00 – cn Bibl Nat [072]
COUP D'OEIL SUR LA SOCIETE EN GENERAL, EN 1792 – Chez les Directeurs de l'Imprimerie du Cercle Social. 1793 – 9 – fr Hachette [321]
COUP D'OEIL SUR L'EGLISE CATHEDRALE DE MONTREAL EN CONSTRUCTION EN 1873 – Montreal?: s.n., 1873?. 04255. (Pre-1900 Canadiana) – 9 – cn C.I.H.M. [971]
COUP D'OEIL SUR L'ESTABLISSEMENT DE COLLEGES MUNICIPAUX, POUR LES SCIENCES, ARTS ET METIERS / Dupain-Triel, Jean Louis – Paris: Cellot, 1780. 38p. 1 fiche. (Education Collection) – 9 – 6.00 – fr Bibl Nationale [370]
Coupal, Maximilien *see* FORMULAIRE DU CODE MUNICIPAL DE LA PROVINCE DE QUEBEC: SUIVI D'UNE TABLE ALPHABETIQUE ET DE TOUTES LES FORMULES NECESSAIRIES POUR L'ORGANISATION ET LE FONCTIONNEMENT DANS UNE PAROISSE, D'UNE COMPAGNIE D'ASSURANCE MUTUELLE CONTRE LE FEU

COUP-D OEIL SUR LES QUATRE DEPARTEMENTS DE LA RIVE GAUCHE DU RHIN / Rebmann, Georg F – an X – 9 – fr Hachette [944]
COUP-D'OEIL SUR LA NOUVELLE ORGANISATION DE LA STATISTIQUE GENERALE EN FRANCE, ET LES ORGANISATIONS ANTERIEURES / Heuschling, Xavier – Reprod. d'un extrait du Journal des Economistes, juin 1853. 1 fiche. (Economics Collection) – 9 – $6.00 – fr Bibl Nationale [330]
LE COUPE-PAPIER – no. 1-7. Paris. nov 1936-38 – 1 – fr A.C.R.P.P. [073]
Couperin, Francois *see*
- L'ART DE TOUCHER LE CLAVECIN
- LES GOUTS-REUNIS OU NOUVEAUX CONCERTS A L'USAGE DE TOUTES LES SORTES...
- PIECES DE CLAVECIN. PREMIER LIVRE

Coupland, R *see*
- EAST AFRICA AND ITS INVADERS FROM EARLIEST TIMES TO THE DEATH OF SEYYID SAID IN 1856
- THE EXPLOITATION OF EAST AFRICA, 1854-1890: THE SLAVE TRADE AND THE SCRAMBLE

[Couplet, P] *see* HISTOIRE D'UNE DAME CHRETIENNE DE LA CHINE,...
Couprie, L D *see* ALINARI PHOTO ARCHIVE
Couprie, LD *see* ART HISTORY
COUPS DE CRAYON / Baillairge, Frederic Alexandre – Joliette: Bureau de l'Etudiant et du Couvent, 1899. 00077. (Pre-1900 Canadiana) – 9 – cn C.I.H.M. [370]
COUPS DE GUEULE : REVUE – Montreal, oct 1965-avr 1966 – 1r – 1 – Can$25.00 – cn Can Microfilming [073]
LA COUR D'APPEL DE DIJON – AN HUIT – MILLE HUIT CENT CINQUANTE DEUX / Avril, Chantal – 2mf – 9 – 10443 – fr Atelier National [340]
COURANT – Chico. Calif. 1866-1868 – 1 – us UMI [071]
COURANT – Delphos, Ohio. 1896-1910 – 10r – 1 – $32.50r – us Archival [071]
Courant, M *see* L'ASIE CENTRALE AUX XVII-XVIII SIECLES. EMPIRE KLAMOUK OU EMPIRE MANTCHOUX
Courant, Maurice *see* BIBLIOGRAPHIE COREENNE
Courcelle, P *see* LES LETTRES GRECQUES EN OCCIDENT, DE MACROBE A CASSIODORE
Courcelle Seneuil, JG *see* TRAITE THEORETIQUE ET PRATIQUE DES OPERATIONS DE BANQUE
Courcelles, P de *see* RHETORIQUE
Courcelle-Seneuil, Jean Gustave *see*
- ADAM SMITH: RICHESSE DES NATIONS
- LA BANQUE LIBRE

Courcy, A de *see*
- QUESTION DE DROIT MARITIME
- D'UNE REFORME INTERNATIONALE DU DROIT MARITIME

Courdioux, Ph. E *see* DICTIONNAIRE ABREGE DE LA LANGUE FO-GBE OU DAHOMEENNE
Courgeau, Daniel *see* STUDY ON THE DYNAMICS, EVOLUTION AND CONSEQUENCES OF MIGRATIONS 2
COURIER – (Also known as: Weekly Courier. Cont by: Courier, Gardnerville) – Genoa, NV. 1881-99 – 7r – 1 – $315.00 – U04539 – us Library Micro [071]
COURIER – Alton. Ill. -w. 1852-59 – 1 – us UMI [071]
COURIER – Auburn. Ind. 1871-1887; 1890-1912; 1914-1917 – 1 – us UMI [071]
COURIER – Belmont, NV. 1874-1901 – 10r – 1 – $500.00 – U04415 – us Library Micro [071]
COURIER – Boston. Mass. 1795-96. and Federal Gazette. 1798. and Polar Star. 1796-97. Sold as one unit – 1,3 – us Readex [071]
COURIER – Carlin, NV. 1976 – 1r – 1 – $50.00 – N04436 – us Library Micro [071]
COURIER – Cascade. Mont. 1910-1947; 1956-1959; 1966- – 1 – us UMI [071]
COURIER – Ceres. Calif. -w. 1944-56 – 1 – us UMI [071]
COURIER – Charlevoix. Mich. -w. 1967- – 1 – us UMI [071]
COURIER – Clinton. N.Y. 1973- – 1 – us UMI [071]
COURIER – Colton. Calif. -w. 1966- – 1 – us UMI [071]
COURIER – Columbus. Kan. 1875-1902 – 1 – us UMI [071]
COURIER – Connellsville. Pa. -w. 1879-1929 – 1 – us UMI [071]
COURIER – Corona. Calif. 1896-1938 – 1 – us UMI [071]
COURIER – Covington. Ky. 1902-03 – 1 – us UMI [071]
COURIER – Crescent City. Calif. 1927-1930 – 1 – us UMI [071]
COURIER – Cupertino, CA. 1973-76 – 11r – 1 – $550.00 – B02155 – us Library Micro [071]
COURIER – Dubois. Pa. -w. 1882-86, 1892-1902 – 1 – us UMI [071]
COURIER – Eau Gallie. Fl. 1965-1967 – 1 – us UMI [071]
COURIER – Evansville. Ind. 1875- – 1 – us UMI [071]
COURIER – Georgetown, D.C. 1812; Senator. 1814. Sold as one unit – 3 – us Readex [071]
COURIER – Gering. Neb. 1887-1963 – 1 – us UMI [071]
COURIER – Germantown. Pa. 1952- – 1 – us UMI [071]
COURIER – Glasgow. Mont. 1913-1954; 1957; 1966- – 1 – us UMI [071]
COURIER – Hazelhurst. Miss. 1936-1951 – 1 – us UMI [071]
COURIER – Jacksonville, IL. 1957-84 – 1 – us UMI [071]
COURIER – Kelso. Wash. -w. 1888-89 – 1 – us UMI [071]
COURIER – Kennewick. Wash. -w. 1903-14 – 1 – us UMI [071]
COURIER – Kent. Ohio. 1886-1928 – 1 – us UMI [071]
COURIER – Kingman. Kansas. 1884-1889 – 1 – us UMI [071]
COURIER – Lincoln, NE. -w. Dec 1887-Apr 1903 – 1 – us NE Hist [071]
COURIER – Magee. Miss. 1941-1952 – 1 – us UMI [071]
COURIER – Milwaukee. Wis. 1964- – 1 – us UMI [071]
COURIER – Milwaukee. Wis. -w. 1841-46 – 1 – us UMI [071]
COURIER – Natchez. Miss. 1837-1838; 1852-1860; 1861-1865 – 1 – us UMI [071]
COURIER – New Castle. Ind. 1907-1930 – 1 – us UMI [071]
COURIER – New Castle. Ind. -w. 1860-1917 – 1 – us UMI [071]
COURIER – New York, NY. 1815-17 – 1 – us Readex [071]
COURIER – Norwich, CT. 1796-1820 – 1,3 – us Readex [071]
COURIER – Olympia. Wash. 1872-1877 – 1 – us UMI [071]
COURIER – Ottumwa. Iowa. 1931- – 1 – us UMI [071]
COURIER – Oxnard. Calif. -w. 1900-19 – 1 – us UMI [071]
COURIER – Placentia, CA. 1975-77 – 3r – 1 – $150.00 – B02629 – us Library Micro [071]
COURIER – Placentia. Calif. 1971- – 1 – us UMI [071]
COURIER – (Publ for Thomas the Druggist) – Lovelock, NV. – 1r – 1 – $50.00 – U04620 – us Library Micro [071]
COURIER – Reedsport OR. May 30 1963 + – 1 – us U.O. Library [071]
COURIER – Salisbury. Md. 1905-1910 – 1 – us UMI [071]
COURIER – Seneca. Kan. -w. 1871-75 – 1 – us UMI [071]
COURIER – Waterloo. Iowa. 1890- – 1 – us UMI [071]
COURIER – Waterloo. Iowa. -w. 1859-97 – 1 – us UMI [071]
COURIER – Winfield. Kan. -w. 1873-1919 – 1 – us UMI [071]
COURIER – Zanesville. Ohio. 1846-1883 – 1 – us UMI [071]
COURIER *see*
- DER COURIER AN DER WESER
- NEW BRUNSWICK COURIER

THE COURIER – Cincinnati, 1882-93 – 1 – £115.00 – uk Chadwyck [780]
THE COURIER – Covelo, CA. 1971 – 1r – 1 – $50.00 – B03130 – us Library Micro [071]
THE COURIER – Fenton. Mich. 1932-1946 – 1 – us UMI [071]
THE COURIER – Gardnerville, NV. 1901-09 – 4r – 1 – $200.00 – U04532 – us Library Micro [071]
THE COURIER – Lincoln. Neb. 1888-1903 – 1 – us UMI [071]
THE COURIER – London. -d. Jun 1798-Dec 1800; 1802; Jan 1818-Dec 1820; Jul 1830-Jun 1833. (19 reels) – 1 – uk British Libr Newspaper [072]
THE COURIER – Pittsburgh. New York Edition. Nov 2 1957-Apr 25 1959; Nov 7 1959-Aug 23 1969 – 1 – us NY Public [071]
THE COURIER – Upland. Ind. 1942-1968 – 1 – us UMI [071]
THE COURIER *see* HENDON COURIER
COURIER ADVOCATE – Trenton, 1926-1960 – 34r – 1 – cn Preston [971]
DER COURIER AN DER WESER – (Cont by: Courier, sep 9 1863; Bremer Courier, mar 18 1886) – Bremen, 1846-93, 1894 (incomplete), 1895-1906 – 122r – 1 – Inquire at Mikrofilmarchiv for details – gw Misc Inst [943]
DER COURIER AN DER WESER – (Since 1886: Bremer Courier) – Bremen, Germany. 1 Jan 1846-30 Dec 1906 – 1 – gw Mikrofilm [072]
COURIER AND CHURCH REFORM GAZETTE – London, UK. 4 Mar 1854-31 Jul 1855. -irr. 1 reel – 1 – uk British Libr Newspaper [072]
COURIER (BALLARAT) – 1945-4/1966 – 107r – 1 – at Corangamite [072]
COURIER BULLETIN – Belmont. Calif. 1953-54 – 1 – us UMI [071]
COURIER BULLETIN – San Carlos, CA. 1944-52 – 5r – 1 – $250.00 – C02776 – us Library Micro [071]
COURIER BULLETIN – San Carlos. Calif. 1944-52 – 1 – us UMI [071]
COURIER BULLETIN *see* CARLMONT-ENQUIRER BULLETIN
COURIER DE L'EGYPTE – Cairo. n1-116. 1798-1801 – 1r – 1 – us Ross [072]
COURIER DE L'EUROPE ECHO DU CONTINENT – London, UK. 1867. -w. 1 reel – 1 – uk British Libr Newspaper [072]
COURIER DE LONDRES – London, UK. 2 Jan 1818-30 Dec 1825 – 1 – uk British Libr Newspaper [072]
L'COURIER DE L'OUEST – Calgary, Alberta, CN. 1905-16 – 4r – 1 – cn Commonwealth Micro [072]
LE COURIER DU CANADA – Quebec, 1864 – 1r – 1 – cn Preston [971]
COURIER EXPRESS – Dubois. Pa. and predecessors. 1884- – 1 – us UMI [071]
COURIER FREE PRESS – Redding. Calif. 1906-1940 – 1 – us UMI [071]
COURIER, GARDNERVILLE *see* COURIER
COURIER HERALD – Saginaw. Mich. 1890-1918 – 1 – us UMI [071]
COURIER JOURNAL – (Also known as: Danville Journal; Contra Costa Courier) – Walnut Creek, CA. Nov 1914-1946; Apr 1948-1951 – 17r – 1 – $850.00 – B03083 – us Library Micro [073]
COURIER JOURNAL – Palmyra. N.Y. 1957-1964 – 1 – us UMI [071]
COURIER (LAVERNE; MONTCLAIR AND UPLAND COMB.) – Claremont, CA. 1983-1989 – 7r – 1 – $350.00 – R04014 – us Library Micro [071]
COURIER MAIL – Brisbane, Australia. -d. 28 Jan 1941-30 Dec 1952; 1 Jan 1969-4 Sept 1972. 1942 imperfect. 114 reels – 1 – uk British Libr Newspaper [072]
COURIER MAIL : INCLUDING MORTON BAY COURIER – Brisbane – 1 – at Pascoe [072]
COURIER MARCH FIELD DISTRICT – Los Angeles, CA. 1934-1935 – 1r – 1 – $50.00 – R04056 – us Library Micro [071]
COURIER NEWS – Blytheville. Ark. 1928- – 1 – us UMI [071]
COURIER OF BAKER – Baker, OR. -w. 19 Jun 1930-22 Oct 1931. 1 roll. Incl. Courier of Huntington – 1 – us U.O. Library [071]
COURIER OF HUNTINGTON – Huntington OR. June 19 1930-May 28 1931 – 1 – us U.O. Library [071]
COURIER OF NEW HAMPSHIRE – Concord. N.H. 1794-1805 – 1,3 – us Readex [071]
COURIER OF THE MINES – Sandhurst, Australia. Oct 1855-Oct 1857.-w. 3 reels – 1 – uk British Libr Newspaper [072]
THE COURIER OF UPPER CANADA – Toronto. v13 n13. 11 jun 1836-v13 n52. 7 jan 1837 – 1r – 1 – Can$45.00 – cn Can Microfilming [072]
COURIER OXFORD *see* OXFORD CITY COURIER
Courier, Pablo Luis *see* HISTORIA DE UNA MANCHA DE TINTA (EL MANUSCRITO DE LONGO)
COURIER POST – Hannibal. Mo. 1906- – 1 – us UMI [071]
COURIER RECORD – Blackstone. Va. 1950- – 1 – us UMI [071]
COURIER REPORTER – Kennewick. Wash. -w. 1914-49 – 1 – us UMI [071]
COURIER SOUTH OXFORDSHIRE *see* SOUTH OXFORDSHIRE COURIER
COURIER TIMES – New Castle. Ind. 1930- – 1 – us UMI [071]
COURIER WARWICK – (Also known as: Warwick Courier) – Jun 15 1990-96 – 29 1/2r – 1 – uk British Libr Newspaper [072]
Courier-Citizen Co *see* ILLUSTRATED HISTORY OF LOWELL AND VICINITY
COURIER-CRESCENT – Orrville. Ohio. -w. 1963, 1968-71 – 1 – us UMI [071]
COURIER-FREE PRESS – Redding, CA. 1900-41 (broken series) – 62r – 1 BC02670 – $3,100.00 – us Library Micro [071]
COURIER-HERALD – Kennewick. Wash. -w. 1949-50 – 1 – us UMI [071]
COURIER-ITEM – Santa Cruz, CA. 1887-89 – 2r – 1 – $100.00 – B02951 – us Library Micro [071]
COURIER-POST – Camden. N.J. 1950- – 1 – us UMI [071]
LE COURIER-SENTINELLE *see* LA SENTINELLE
COURIER-TRIBUNE – Bloomington. Ind. 1968- – 1 – us UMI [071]
COURIER-TRIBUNE – Callaway, NE. -w. Jun. 1892; Feb. 1894-Aug. 1894; Oct. 1895-Jan. 1896; May 1896-Apr. 1914 – 1 – us NE Hist [071]
COURIER-TRIBUNE – Kent. Ohio. 1929-44 – 1 – us UMI [071]
COURIER-UNION – Findlay, Ohio. 1904-07 – 4r – 1 – $32.50r – us Archival [071]
COURONNE DE MESSES REPARATRICES OFFERTES A LA T. STE VIERGE MARIE, MERE DE DIEU, UR LA CONVERSION DE PAUVRES PECHEURS – Montreal: s.n., 18?? (Montreal: Chez M. de la Rousseliere). 04256. (Pre-1900 Canadiana) – 9 – cn C.I.H.M. [971]
LE COURRIER : L'HEBDOMADAIRE DE TERREBONNE ET DE LA REGION – Saint-Eustache: La Victoire. v1 no 1 1969-. SEM35P16 – 1r – 1 – Can$20.00 – cn Bibl Nat [072]
LE COURRIER : JOURNAL DU DIMANCHE – Montreal, Canada. 10 sep 1899 – 1r – 1 – Can$25.00 – cn Can Microfilming [073]
LE COURRIER – Lawrence, MA: Wood Press, [apr 15, 1932-may 6, 1938] – 1 – us Res Libr [071]
LE COURRIER : ORGANE DES TROIS-RIVIERES – Trois-Rivieres, Canada. 3 oct-4 nov 1902 – 1r – 1 – Can$30.00 – cn Can Microfilming [072]
LE COURRIER – Orsainville, Canada. v7 n3. 21 jun 1969 – 1r – 1 – Can$25.00 – cn Can Microfilming [072]
LE COURRIER – Port-au-Prince, Haiti: Imp de l'Abeille, [1902-] sep 8-dec 26, 1902 – 1 – us Res Libr [072]
LE COURRIER : UNION NATIONALE – Montreal, Canada. 3 oct 1952-13 mar 1953 – 1r – 1 – Can$40.00 – cn Can Microfilming [072]
LE COURRIER – Windsor, Ontario. 2 avr 1908-v1 n41. 7 jan 1909 – 1r – 1 – Can$30.00 – cn Can Microfilming [072]
LE COURRIER *see* LE COURRIER DE BEAUHARNOIS
LE COURRIER ARTISTIQUE – Beaux-arts, expositions, musique, theatre, arts industriels, ventes. 15 juin 1861-nov 1865. devenu: Les Fantaisies parisiennes. Courrier artistique. Paris. dec 1865-13 mai 1866 – 1 – fr A.C.R.P.P. [073]
COURRIER BELGE – London, UK. 8, 15 May 1920 – 1 – uk British Libr Newspaper [072]
COURRIER BELGE. DE BELGISCHE KOERIER – London, UK. Organe edite pur les refugies belge en Derby. 22 Oct 1914-31 Jul 1915 – 1 – uk British Libr Newspaper [072]
COURRIER CANADIEN : JOURNAL DU DIMANCHE – Montreal, Canada. 11 mar 1900; v1 n2. 18 mar 1900 – 1r – 1 – Can$25.00 – cn Can Microfilming [072]
LE COURRIER CANADIEN / ed by Houlee, J-B – Montreal, Canada. 17 jan-28 sep 1838 – 1r – 1 – Can$35.00 – cn Can Microfilming [072]
LE COURRIER CANADIEN : LITTERATURE, SCIENCE, ARTS, ECONOMIE POLITIQUE, ETC – Montreal: G A Dumont. v1- 1889-. SEM105P667 – 1mf – 9 – Can$2.25 – cn Bibl Nat [073]

LE COURRIER CANADIEN / ed by Robillard, L-G – St-Jerome, Canada. 3 nov 1892; v1 n3. 17 nov 1892 – 1r – 1 – Can$25.00 – cn Can Microfilming [072]
COURRIER COMMERCIAL *see* COMMERCIAL COURIER/COURRIER COMMERCIAL
COURRIER CONSULAIRE DE LA HAUTE-VOLTA – [Ouagadougou], may-jun 1962; aug 1962-jul 1963; sep-oct 1963 – us Res Libr [960]
COURRIER D'AFRIQUE – 31 Dec 1959-29 Dec 1967 – 23r – 1 – ne IDC [072]
LE COURRIER D'AFRIQUE – Leopoldville: [s.n, dec 31 1955-jan 23 1970] – 43r – 1 – us Res Libr [072]
LE COURRIER D'AFRIQUE – (Issues for june-jul 22 1960 at MF-691 and Neg. MF-at lab filmed as pt of the Bartlett collection) – Leopoldville: [s.n.], [jun-jul 22 1960] – us Res Libr [072]
LE COURRIER D'AVIGNON – Avignon. oct-dec 1733, avr-dec 1734, 1736, 1756-60, 1778-83. IC. 10736 – 1 – fr A.C.R.P.P. [073]
LE COURRIER DE BEAUHARNOIS – (Cont by and filmed with: Le Courrier, Huntingdon v4 n12 3 jan 1944- 27 dec 1951. Lacking: 1943) – Beauharnois, Canada. v1 n2. 19 mai-28 dec 1942 – 2r – 1 – Can$55.00r – cn Can Microfilming [072]
LE COURRIER DE BEAUHARNOIS – (Filmed with: L'Echo de Beauharnois 8 mai 1873-31 oct 1874. L'Avenir de Beauharnois 4 fev 1875-28 dec 1876. L'Echo de Beauharnois 14 fev 1878-25 jul 1878) – Beauharnois, Canada. v1 n41. 27 fev 1868-10 mai 1872 – 1r – 1 – Can$80.00 – cn Can Microfilming [072]
LE COURRIER DE BELLECHASSE – (Cont: L'Etendard de Bellechasse) – Montmagny, Canada. v7 n3. 17 dec 1937-25 dec 1965 – 5r – 1 – Can$45.00r – cn Can Microfilming [072]
LE COURRIER DE BELLECHASSE *see* L'ETENDARD DE BELLECHASSE
LE COURRIER DE BERTHIERVILLE / ed by Milot, A-D – (Cont by: Le Courrier de Berthier 15 nov 1946-24 jul 1974. Nouvelle serie publiee par L'Echo de Louiseville) – Berthier, Canada. 15 jun 1926-8 nov 1946 – 20r – 1 – Can$60.00r – cn Can Microfilming [072]
LE COURRIER DE BERTHIERVILLE *see* LE COURRIER DE BERTHIERVILLE
LE COURRIER DE CALAIS – puis DU Pas-de-Calais. Nouvelles politiques, litteraires, de commerce et de marine. Calais. 29 juin 1794-19 avr 1795 – 1 – fr A.C.R.P.P. [073]
LE COURRIER DE CHAMBLY-ROUVILLE – Chambly, Canada. 24 nov 1971 – 1r – 1 – Can$25.00 – cn Can Microfilming [072]
LE COURRIER DE CHARLEVOIX / ed by Dallaire, Elzear – Baie St Paul, Canada. 1 mar 1895-3 sep 1897 – 1r – 1 – Can$45.00 – cn Can Microfilming [072]
COURRIER DE CHIBOUGAMAU COURIER – Chibougamau, 29 sep 1956f – 1r – 1 – Can$25.00 – cn Can Microfilming [072]
COURRIER DE FINANCES DE LONDRES – London, UK. 30 May-14 Nov 1889 – 1 – uk British Libr Newspaper [072]
COURRIER DE FINANCES DE LONDRES – London, UK. Mar 1891-Aug 1892 – 1 – uk British Libr Newspaper [072]
LE COURRIER DE FRANCE – Dir. L. Guyot-Montpayroux. 2 ed. Paris. juil-dec 1875 – 1 – fr A.C.R.P.P. [073]
LE COURRIER DE FRANCE – Journal quotidien, politique, economique et litteraire. Dir. H. Desbrousses. Paris. 4 dec 1871-2 mars 1873 – 1 – fr A.C.R.P.P. [073]
LE COURRIER DE FRASERVILLE – Riviere-du-Loup, Canada. 16 nov 1887-20 dec 1889 – 1r – 1 – Can$35.00 – cn Can Microfilming [072]
LE COURRIER DE GRAND-MERE : CONSERVATEUR-INDEPENDANT / ed by Dallaire, Elzear – Grand-Mere, Canada. v1 n14. 22 avr 1909-v3 n13. 11 mai 1911 – 1r – 1 – Can$30.00 – cn Can Microfilming [072]
LE COURRIER DE HULL – Hull, Canada. v2 n42. 7 jun 1883 – 1r – 1 – Can$25.00 – cn Can Microfilming [072]
COURRIER DE LA COLERE – puis DE LA NATION. Paris. nov 1957-oct 1958 – 1 – fr A.C.R.P.P. [073]
COURRIER DE LA COMMUNAUTE DES DIACONNESSES DE REUILLY – nos 31-114. 1974-89 (complete) – 2r – 1 – ATLA S0641 – us A.T.L.A. [073]
LE COURRIER DE LA GIRONDE – Bordeaux. juil 1870-juin 1871. BM. Bordeaux – 1 – fr A.C.R.P.P. [073]
COURRIER DE LA GUADELOUPE – Guadeloupe. French West Indies. 1881-84, 1887, 1891-1907 – 1 – us UMI [072]
COURRIER DE LA LOUISIANE – New Orleans. La. and The Courier (Le Courrier). 1810-60 – 1 – us UMI [071]
LE COURRIER DE LA NOUVELLE-CALEDONIE – Victoria, BC. 18 sep 1858 – 1r – 1 – Can$25.00 – cn Can Microfilming [072]
LE COURRIER DE LA VIENNE ET DES DEUX-SEVRES – (Some missing numbers) – Poitiers (Vienne), Dec. 1851 – May 1925 – 76r – fr Armell [944]
COURRIER DE LACHINE : JOURNAL HEBDOMADAIRE – Lachine: Lamarche & Tourigny, ca 1911-. SEM105P800 – 1mf – 9 – Can$2.25 – cn Bibl Nat [072]
LE COURRIER DE LACHUTE – Lachute, Canada. v1 n6. 18 aut 1933; v1 n7. 25 aut 1933 – 1r – 1 – Can$25.00 – cn Can Microfilming [072]
COURRIER DE L'AIR – London, UK. 6 Apr 1917-25 Jan 1918 – 1 – uk British Libr Newspaper [072]
COURRIER DE L'ART – Paris, 1881-90. 6 reels – 1 – $505.00 – us UPA [700]
LE COURRIER DE L'ASSEMBLEE NATIONALE – Paris: Impr de E Marc-Aurel, jun 4 1848 – us Res Libr [944]
COURRIER DE LAVAL – (Becomes: Hebdo Courrier de Laval 12 nov 1970-7 jun 1972. Becomes: Courrier-Laval 14 jun 1972-29 sep 1991) – Laval, Canada. v11 n28. 28 mar 1956-5 nov 1970 – 50r – 1 – Can$75.00r – cn Can Microfilming [072]
LE COURRIER DE LAVIOLETTE – Grand-Mere, Canada. 1 mai 1952-31 mar 1955; ns: 7 avr 1955-27 dec 1956 – 50r – 1 – Can$60.00r – cn Can Microfilming [072]
LE COURRIER DE LAWRENCE – Lawrence, MA: Courrier Pub [feb 1922-apr 8, 1932] – 1 – us Res Libr [071]
LE COURRIER DE LAWRENCE – Lawrence, MA: Wood Press, [may 13, 1938-aug 1946] – 1 – us Res Libr [071]
COURRIER DE L'EGYPTE – Cairo. no. 1-116. Aug 29 1798-June 8 1801 – 1 – us NY Public [072]
COURRIER DE L'EGYPTE – no. 1-116. Le Caire. aout 1798-juin 1801 – 1 – fr A.C.R.P.P. [073]
LE COURRIER DE L'EST – Montreal, Canada. v1 n9. 28 mai 1953 – 1r – 1 – Can$25.00 – cn Can Microfilming [072]
LE COURRIER DE L'EST – Nancy. 1889-sept 1892, avr-mai 1898 – 1 – fr A.C.R.P.P. [073]
COURRIER DE L'EUROPE – (Courrier de l'Europe, Semaine francaise. 5 Jan 1884-2 Feb 1889. Semaine francaise et le Courrier de l'Europe. 7 Apr-29 Dec 1883) – London, UK. 6 Jun 1840-31 Mar 1883 – 1 – uk British Libr Newspaper [072]
COURRIER DE L'EUROPE ET DES SPECTACLES – puis ET Memorial europeen reunis. Paris. 1er juin 1807-30 sept 1811 – 1 – fr A.C.R.P.P. [073]
COURRIER DE L'EUROPE, SEMAINE FRANCAISE *see* COURRIER DE L'EUROPE
LE COURRIER DE L'HYMEN, JOURNAL DES DAMES – Nos 1-2, 4-7, 19, 22, 32, 41-42, 45. Paris. Feb-Jul 1791 – 1 – fr A.C.R.P.P. [640]
LE COURRIER DE L'ISLET – (Cont by: Le Progres de L'Islet/Le Courrier de L'Islet v7 n43 17 nov 1937-v24 n2 13 mai 1961 4r Can$60.00) – Montmagny, Canada. v1 n2. 6 dec 1930-23 dec 1933 – 2r – 1 – Can$60.00r – cn Can Microfilming [072]
COURRIER DE LONDRES – London, UK. 13 May 1911-6 Dec 1912 – 1 – uk British Libr Newspaper [072]
COURRIER DE LONDRES – London, UK. 31 Oct 1885-14 May 1898 – 1 – uk British Libr Newspaper [072]
COURRIER DE LONDRES – London, UK. 6 May-3 Jul 1879 – 1 – uk British Libr Newspaper [072]
LE COURRIER DE LONDRES – London, England. v53 n7. 25 Jan 1803-v55 n53. 7 mar 1804 – 1r – 1 – Can$40.00 – cn Can Microfilming [072]
COURRIER DE LONDRES ET DE PARIS – London, UK. 15 Jul 1899-19 May 1900 – 1 – uk British Libr Newspaper [072]
COURRIER DE LONDRES ET PARIS *see* LONDRES ET PARIS
LE COURRIER DE L'OUEST – Chicago, IL. v32 n1613. 13 jul 1900; v32 n1622. 14 sep 1900 – 1r – 1 – Can$25.00 – cn Can Microfilming [071]
LE COURRIER DE L'OUEST – Edmonton, Alberta. 14 oct 1905-v11 n9. 23 dec 1915 – 3r – 1 – Can$55.00r – cn Can Microfilming [072]
LE COURRIER DE L'OUEST – Windsor, Ontario. v3 n3. 27 jun 1885-v4 n23. 7 mai 1886 – 1r – 1 – Can$35.00 – cn Can Microfilming [072]
LE COURRIER DE LOUISEVILLE – Louiseville, Canada. v9 n35. 18 nov 1886-v14 n20. 30 jul 1891 – 1r – 1 – Can$30.00 – cn Can Microfilming [072]
LE COURRIER DE LYON / Valoris, Maxime – Paris: J. Rouff, 189?. 3v – 1 – us U.W. Library [830]
LE COURRIER DE MARSEILLE COMMERCIAL ET POLITIQUE – Marseille. 1848, 1850-51 – 1 – fr A.C.R.P.P. [073]
LE COURRIER DE MASKINONGE – Louiseville, Canada. v1 n2. 14 mar 1878-v16 n1. 3 nov 1893 – 1r – 1 – Can$40.00 – cn Can Microfilming [072]
LE COURRIER DE MONTCALM – Rawdon, Canada. 14 nov 1958; v1 n17. 13 aut 1959 – 1r – 1 – Can$30.00 – cn Can Microfilming [072]
LE COURRIER DE MONTMAGNY / ed by Marquis, Maurice – (Cont by: Le Courrier de Montmagny-L'Islet 18 mai 1961-223 mai 1968. Cont by: Le Courrier Montmagny-L'Islet Kamouraska 30 mai 1968-3 nov 1971. Becomes: Nouveau Courrier de la Cote Sud 17 nov 1971-24 dec 1972. Becomes: Le Peuple-Courrier) – Montmagny, Canada. v40 n1. 12 nov 1937-31 mai 1962 – 15r – 1 – Can$75.00r – cn Can Microfilming [072]
LE COURRIER DE MONTMAGNY – Montmagny, Canada. v1 n11. 14 mar 1902-v24 n52. 27 dec 1918 – 2r – 1 – Can$60.00r – cn Can Microfilming [072]
LE COURRIER DE MONTMAGNY / ed by Toupin, JoS – Quebec, Montmagny, Canada. 15 nov 1881-v1 n45. 19 jun 1882 – 1r – 1 – Can$35.00 – cn Can Microfilming [072]
LE COURRIER DE MONTMAGNY-L'ISLET *see* LE COURRIER DE MONTMAGNY
LE COURRIER DE MONTREAL – Montreal, Canada. 17 sep 1874-6 oct 1876 – 1r – 1 – Can$35.00 – cn Can Microfilming [072]
LE COURRIER DE MONTREAL – Montreal, Canada. v1 n30. 1 jul 1879-12 avr 1883 – 3r – 1 – Can$45.00r – cn Can Microfilming [072]
LE COURRIER DE NOEL – Quebec, Canada. dec 1934 – 1r – 1 – Can$25.00 – cn Can Microfilming [072]
LE COURRIER DE PAPINEAU – Buckingham, Canada. 4 jul 1930-v1 n9. 29 aut 1930 – 1r – 1 – Can$25.00 – cn Can Microfilming [072]
LE COURRIER DE PAPINEAU – Hull, Canada. v30. 1 dec 1960-v37. n5. 27 oct 1966 – 1r – 1 – Can$50.00 – cn Can Microfilming [072]
COURRIER DE PARIS – Correspondance des journaux des departements et de l'etranger. Paris. 29 janv-31 mars 1851 – 1 – fr A.C.R.P.P. [073]
COURRIER DE PROVENCE – suite de: Lettres du Comte de Mirabeau a ses commettants. no. 1-350. Paris. mai 1789-sept 1791 – 1 – fr A.C.R.P.P. [073]
LE COURRIER DE QUEBEC – Quebec, Canada. 29 oct 1806; 3 jan 1807-31 dec 1808 – 1r – 1 – Can$35.00 – cn Can Microfilming [072]
LE COURRIER DE QUEBEC OU HERAULT FRANCOIS – Quebec, Canada. jan 1788; v1 n1. 24 nov 1788-8 dec 1788 – 1r – 1 – Can$40.00 – cn Can Microfilming [072]
LE COURRIER DE RIMOUSKI – Rimouski, Canada. 2 sep 1871-21 nov 1873 – 1r – 1 – Can$45.00 – cn Can Microfilming [072]
LE COURRIER DE SAINT-HYACINTHE : SEMI-QUOTIDIEN – St-Hyacinthe, Canada. v15 n125. 4 jan 1868-v20 n118. 31 dec 1872 – 2r – 1 – Can$70.00r – cn Can Microfilming [072]
LE COURRIER DE SAINT-HYACINTHE – St-Hyacinthe, Canada. 24 fev 1853-29 dec 1992 – 123r – 1 – Can$70.00r – cn Can Microfilming [072]
LE COURRIER DE SAINT-HYACINTHE : TABLOID – St-Hyacinthe, Canada. v7 n20. 26 jul 1872; v7 n25. 30 aut 1872; 28 mar 1873 – 1r – 1 – Can$35.00 – cn Can Microfilming [072]
LE COURRIER DE SAINT-JEAN / ed by Molleur, J E – St Jean, Canada. 1 mai 1896-5 mar 1909 – 3r – 1 – Can$55.00r – cn Can Microfilming [072]
LE COURRIER DE SAINT-JEAN – St-Jean, Canada. sep 1887 – 1r – 1 – Can$25.00 – cn Can Microfilming [072]
LE COURRIER DE SAINT-MALO – St-Malo, Canada. v3 n17. 25 avr 1953; v5 n7. 21 oct 1954 – 1r – 1 – Can$25.00 – cn Can Microfilming [072]
LE COURRIER DE SAUMUR – (Microfilming in progress. 1856 missing) – Saumur (Maine-et-Loire), May 1849 – June 1897 – 36r – fr Armell [944]
LE COURRIER DE SMYRNE – Journal politique, commercial et litteraire. Smyrne. sept 1828-aout 1830 – 1 – fr A.C.R.P.P. [073]
LE COURRIER DE SOREL / ed by Chenevert, C A – Sorel, Canada. v2 n1. 15 mar 1901-v32 n33. 13 nov 1931 – 2r – 1 – Can$75.00r – cn Can Microfilming [072]
LE COURRIER DE ST HYACINTHE – St. Hyacinthe, Canada. 1853-1900 – 41r – 1 – $2,665.00 – cn Library Assoc [971]
LE COURRIER DE ST-HYACINTHE ET JOURNAL D'AGRICULTURE – St-Hyacinthe. v13 n20. 12 jul 1878-31 dec 1880 – 1r – 1 – Can$45.00 – cn Can Microfilming [072]
LE COURRIER DE TERREBONNE : CHAMBRE DE COMMERCE / ed by Hetu, Jean – Terrebonne, Canada. v18 n20. 10 jan 1959-14 nov 1968 – 3r – 1 – cn Can Microfilming [072]
LE COURRIER DE TERREBONNE – Terrebonne: Chambre de commerce. v1-40. 1949-68. SEM35P17 – 6r – 1 – Can$301.00 – cn Bibl Nat [072]
COURRIER DE TOURCOING : JOURNAL QUOTIDIEN POLITIQUE DES DEUX CANTONS – (5 numbers are missing) – Quot., Tourcoing (Nord), mars 1882-avril 1884 (5 no. manquants) – 3r – 1 – F1425,10 – fr Armell [320]
LE COURRIER DE TROIS-PISTOLES – Trois-Pistoles, 2 jan 1980-30 dec 1991 – 14r – 1 – Can$75.00 – cn Can Microfilming [072]
LE COURRIER DE TROIS-PISTOLES ET DU TEMISCOUATA – Trois-Pistoles, Canada. v2 n12. 11 avr 1963-29 dec 1979 – 11r – 1 – Can$75.00r – cn Can Microfilming [072]
LE COURRIER DE TROIS-RIVIERES – Trois-Rivieres, Canada. 16 jan 1913-24 aut 1917 – 1r – 1 – Can$50.00 – cn Can Microfilming [072]
LE COURRIER DE VALLEYFIELD – Valleyfield, Canada. 31 jan 1907 – 1r – 1 – Can$25.00 – cn Can Microfilming [072]
LE COURRIER DE VALOIS-VILLE – Pointe-Claire, Canada. v1 n3. 5 sep 1878 – 1r – 1 – Can$25.00 – cn Can Microfilming [072]
LE COURRIER DE VAUGELAS – 1871-81 – 9 – fr I.C.S. [800]
LE COURRIER DE VERSAILLES A PARIS ET DE PARIS A VERSAILLES – devenu: Le Courrier de Paris. devenu: Le Courrier des departements. Paris. juil 1789-mai 1793 – 1 – fr A.C.R.P.P. [073]
LE COURRIER DE WOLFE – Disraeli, Canada. v2 n16. 5 mai 1958; v10 n45. 3 jul 1968 – 1r – 1 – Can$25.00 – cn Can Microfilming [072]
COURRIER DES COMPTOIRS – London, UK. 7 Nov 1883 – 1 – uk British Libr Newspaper [072]
COURRIER DES ETATS-UNIS – New York, 1849-91 – 48r – 1 – us Ross [071]
COURRIER DES ETATS-UNIS – New York. Mar 1 1828-Dec 25 1937. Not collated – 1 – us NY Public [071]
LE COURRIER DES ETATS-UNIS / ed by Gaillardet, Frederic – New York City, NY. 1 mar 1826-v1 n52. 21 fev 1829 – 1r – 1 – Can$50.00 – cn Can Microfilming [071]
LE COURRIER DES ETATS-UNIS – Ed. hebdomadaire. New York [NY: Ch Lassale, [1855-jul 1857] – 1r – us Res Libr [071]
COURRIER DES EXPOSITIONS – London, UK. Edition illustree du Courrier de Londres et de l'Europe. 23 Jun-18 Aug 1889 – 1 – uk British Libr Newspaper [072]
LE COURRIER DES LAURENTIDES – Saint-Lin, Canada. 1 oct 1887 – 1r – 1 – Can$25.00 – cn Can Microfilming [072]
COURRIER DES PLANETES – or Correspondance du cousin Jacques avec le firmament folie periodique dediee a la lune. no. 1-74. Paris. 1788-89 – 1 – fr A.C.R.P.P. [073]
COURRIER DES PROVINCES MARITIMES – Bathurst, Canada. 1885-1903 – 7r – 1 – $455.00 – cn Library Assoc [971]

COURRIER DES PROVINCES MARITIMES – Bathurst, New Brunswick. v5 n40. 31 jul 1890 – 1r – 1 – Can$25.00 – cn Can Microfilming [072]

LE COURRIER D'ESSEX – Windsor, Ontario. 8 aut 1884; v2 n8. 17 jan 1885 – 1r – 1 – Can$25.00 – cn Can Microfilming [072]

COURRIER D'ETHIOPIE – Addis Ababa, [23 aug 1929-28 apr 1936] – 1 – us Res Libr [960]

LE COURRIER D'HAIPHONG – Vietnam. -d. 19 Sep 1886-31 Dec 1922. (Imperfect). (71 reels) – 1 – uk British Libr Newspaper [072]

LE COURRIER D'ORAN – Journal politique, commercial, agricole et litteraire. no. 1-200. Oran. 24 fevr 1850-14 fevr 1852 – 1 – fr A.C.R.P.P. [073]

LE COURRIER D'OTTAWA – Ottawa, Ontario. 3 avr 1861-v4 n33. 4 nov 1864 – 1r – 1 – Can$60.00 – cn Can Microfilming [072]

LE COURRIER D'OUTAOUAIS – Ottawa, Ontario. 5 jan 1870-v6 n148. 1 avr 1876 – 6r – 1 – Can$55.00r – cn Can Microfilming [072]

LE COURRIER DU BAS-CANADA / ed by Bibaud, Michel & Delorme, V – Montreal, Canada. 9 oct-18 dec 1819 – 1r – 1 – Can$30.00 – cn Can Microfilming [072]

COURRIER DU CANADA – Quebec, Canada. 1857-73 – 18r – 1 – $1,170.00 – cn Library Assoc [971]

LE COURRIER DU CANADA : JOURNAL DES INTERETS CANADIENS / ed by Chapais, Thomas – Quebec, Canada. 2 fev 1857-10 avr 1901 – 35r – 1 – Can$50.00r – cn Can Microfilming [072]

LE COURRIER DU DIMANCHE – Journal politique, litteraire et financier. Paris. 1860-29 juil 1866 – 1 – fr A.C.R.P.P. [073]

LE COURRIER DU DIMANCHE – Quebec, Canada. v1 n2. 12 jun 1904 – 1r – 1 – Can$25.00 – cn Can Microfilming [072]

COURRIER DU GARD : JOURNAL POLITIQUE, ADMINISTRATIF ET JUDICIAIRE – (4 missing numbers) – Bi-hebd. puis quot., Nimes, oct. 1831-sept. 1837 (4 n° manq.) – 3r – 1 – F1439.33 – fr Armell [320]

LE COURRIER DU LIVRE – Quebec: L Brousseau, [1896-1901?] – 9 – cn C.I.H.M. [971]

LE COURRIER DU MAINE : JOURNAL HEBDOMADAIRE PARAISSANT LE DIMANCHE – (1 missing number) – Hebd, Laval (Mayenne), fevr 1885-oct 1944 (1 no manq) – 14r – 1 – F6925.29 – fr Armell [073]

LE COURRIER DU NORD / ed by Marquis, Maurice – La Malbaie, Canada. 28 dec 1928-3 mar 1933 – 3r – 1 – Can$60.00r – cn Can Microfilming [072]

LE COURRIER DU NORD-OUEST – Winnipeg, Canada. 31 mai 1888-v1 n7. 21 jul 1888 – 1r – 1 – Can$25.00 – cn Can Microfilming [072]

COURRIER DU NOUVEAU MONDE – Worcester, MA. v10 n590. 13 jun 1891 – 1r – 1 – Can$25.00 – cn Can Microfilming [071]

LE COURRIER DU PACIFIQUE – (Filmed consecutively with: West coast leader 1919-20) – Lima: E-A Le Roux, jun 21 1919-jun 10 1920 – us Res Libr [072]

COURRIER DU SOIR – Port-au-Prince: [s.n., [feb-dec 1919; apr 10 1920-dec 29 1921] – 27 sheets – us Res Libr [072]

LE COURRIER DU SOIR – Dernieres nouvelles de Paris jusqu'a neuf heures du soir. Paris. 21 fevr 1878-87 – 1 – fr A.C.R.P.P. [073]

LE COURRIER DU SUD = THE SOUTH SHORE COURIER – Longueuil: [s.n.] v1- 1947-. SEM35P179 – 103r – 1 – cn Bibl Nat [072]

LE COURRIER DU SUD – Les Cayes [Haiti]: Imp Ach Bonnefil, [apr 28 1890-aug 28 1891] – 2 sheets – us Res Libr [072]

COURRIER EXTRAORDINAIRE – ou Le Premier arrive. Londres, Paris. mars 1790-aout 1792 – 1 – fr A.C.R.P.P. [073]

LE COURRIER FEDERAL – Ottawa, Ontario. 21 mai 1887-v2 n16. 5 jul 1888 – 1r – 1 – Can$50.00 – cn Can Microfilming [072]

LE COURRIER FEDERAL – Ottawa, Ontario. 3 aut 1917-v8 n7. 27 mar 1925 – 2r – 1 – Can$50.00r – cn Can Microfilming [072]

COURRIER FINANCIER DE LONDRES ET DE PARIS – London, UK. 3-24 Mar 1904 – 1 – uk British Libr Newspaper [072]

LE COURRIER FRANCAIS – 3sept 1864-24 juin 1868 avec un prosp. du 8 aout 1868. suit e de: Revue de l'Empire. 14 dec 1862-27 aout 1864 – 1 – fr A.C.R.P.P. [073]

LE COURRIER FRANCAIS – Litterature, beaux-arts, theatre, medecine, finances. Paris. nov 1884-14 mars 1907, nov 1909-2 juil 1910, janv-oct 1911, janv-8 mars 1913, avr-mai 1914 – 1 – fr A.C.R.P.P. [073]

LE COURRIER FRANCAIS – Paris. 1 juil 1819-14 mars 1851. Mq: 11 mai-1 juil 1843, 1845, 1846-47 – 1 – fr A.C.R.P.P. [073]

LE COURRIER FRANCAIS – Paris. -w 16 Nov 1884-31 Dec 1893. 5 reels – 1 – uk British Libr Newspaper [072]

LE COURRIER FRANCAIS DES ETATS-UNIS – San Francisco, CA. v27 n63. 15 aut 1964 – 1r – 1 – Can$25.00 – cn Can Microfilming [071]

LE COURRIER FRANCAIS DU CANADA / ed by Sauvalle, Marc & Roode, C L de – Montreal, Canada. v1 n40. 4 fev 1911-v1 n44. 4 mar 1911 – 1r – 1 – Can$25.00 – cn Can Microfilming [072]

COURRIER FRANCAIS DU TEMOIGNAGE CHRETIEN – [Paris: s.n. n8-78. 1944?-nov 23 1945 – 1r – us Res Libr [072]

COURRIER FRANCAIS OU TABLEAU PERIODIQUE ET RAISONNE DES OPERATIONS DE L'ASSEMBLEE NATIONALE – Paris. juin-dec 1789 – 1 – fr A.C.R.P.P. [073]

LE COURRIER HAITIEN – Port-au-Prince: Imp aug A Heraux, nov 15 1920-sep 8/9,18/19/20-28/29/30, nov 18-28/29, dec 29 1922 – 16 sheets – us Res Libr [072]

LE COURRIER INTERNATIONAL – no. spec., no. 1-57. Paris. 28 nov 1866-30 juin 1867. mq no. 50 – 1 – fr A.C.R.P.P. [073]

COURRIER LA PENSEE DE BAGOT *see* LA PENSEE DE BAGOT

LE COURRIER LAURENTIEN : MENSUEL – Montreal, Canada. 5 dec 1953-5 mai 1954 – 1r – 1 – Can$35.00 – cn Can Microfilming [072]

COURRIER MAIL BRISBANE – 1 – F4,798.00 – sz Infoprint [072]

LE COURRIER METROPOLITAIN – Montreal-Nord, Canada. v2 n2. 5 fev 1969-dec 1975 – 2r – 1 – Can$60.00r – cn Can Microfilming [072]

LE COURRIER MONTMAGNY-L'ISLET KAMOURASKA *see* LE COURRIER DE MONTMAGNY

LE COURRIER NATIONAL – Lawrence, MA. v2 n5. 2 dec 1901 – 1r – 1 – Can$20.00 – cn Can Microfilming [071]

COURRIER PAYS L'EST – 1992-1995 – 15 times per yr – 9 – F2,400.00 – sz Infoprint [072]

LE COURRIER PICARD – Amiens. 1959-juil 1975, nov 1982-1991 – 1 – fr A.C.R.P.P. [073]

LE COURRIER POPULAIRE – Montreal, 15 nov 1969 – 1r – 1 – Can$25.00 – cn Can Microfilming [072]

LE COURRIER RIVIERA *see* LE RIVIERA

COURRIER ROYAL / Maison de France – Paris. dec 1934-37 – 1 – fr A.C.R.P.P. [073]

COURRIER SUD – Nicolet: Armand Bouchard. v1- 1964-. SEM35P152 – 59r – 1 – cn Bibl Nat [072]

COURRIER SUD – Toronto. 1973-76 – 1 – 185.00 – cn McLaren [971]

Courriere, C *see* HISTOIRE DE LA LITTERATURE CONTEMPORAINE EN RUSSIE

COURRIER-LAVAL *see* COURRIER DE LAVAL

LE COURRIER-SUD – Nicolet, Canada. 23 sep 1964-v4 n139. 27 dec 1967 – 1r – 1 – cn Can Microfilming [072]

COURS COMPLET DE LA LANGUE FRANCOISE / Mauvillon, E de – 1754 – 9 – fr I.C.S. [440]

COURS D'ARCHEOLOGIE UNIVERSITE LAVAL DE MONTREAL: LES INDES, L'EGYPTE, L'ASSYRIE, LA PALESTINE / Desmazures, Adam Charles Gustave – abbe Desmazures Montreal: s.n., 1890. 05250. (Pre-1900 Canadiana) – 9 – cn C.I.H.M. [971]

COURS D'ARCHITECTURE : L'ART DE BATIR / Daviler – Paris, France. 1v. 1720 – 1r – 1 – cn Can Microfilming [720]

COURS D'ARCHITECTURE ENSEIGNE DANS L'ACADEMIE ROYALE D'ARCHITECTURE / Blondel, Jacques Francois – 3v. Paris. 1771. BO-154 1 – 9 – ne IDC [720]

COURS D'ARCHITECTURE ENSEIGNE DANS L'ACADEMIE ROYALE D'ARCHITECTURE / Blondel, Jacques Francois – Paris, P. Auboin et F. Clouzier, 1675-83. 27, 799p., illus. (Architecture Series) – 9 – fr Hachette [720]

COURS D'ARCHITECTURE, OU TRAITE DE LA DECORATION, DISTRIBUTION ET CONSTRUCTION DES BATIMENTS. / Blondel, Jacques Francois – Paris. Dessaint, 1771-77. 8 fol. 6v. of text and 3 of plates. (Architecture Series) – 9 – fr Hachette [720]

COURS D'ARCHITECTURE QUI COMPREND LES ORDRES DE VIGNOLE. / Avilier, Augustin Charles d' – Part I. Paris, Y. Mariette, 1710. 97, 355p., pl. EXPLICATION DES TERMES D'ARCHITECTURE...Paris, J. Mariette, 1710. pp.357-920. (Architecture Series) – 9 – fr Hachette [720]

COURS DE CHYMIE, AUGMENTE DE LA COMPOSITION DU BAUME VERT VULNERAIRE, AVEC SON EMPLASTRE STIPTIQUE, DU FEBRIFUGE DE F. DELBOE SYLVIVS.. / Thibaut, Pierre – Paris, 1674 – 1 – us U.W. Library [540]

COURS DE CHYMIE CONTENANT LA MANIERE DE FAIRE LES OPERATIONS / Lemery, Nicolas – 11th ed. Paris: Chez Jean-Baptiste Delespine, 1730. SEM16P259 – 1r – 5 – Can$12.00 – cn Bibl Nat [540]

COURS DE CHYMIE CONTENANT LA MANIERE DE FAIRE LES OPERATIONS / Lemery, Nicolas – 8th ed. Paris: Chez Estienne Machelet, 1696. SEM16P258 – 1r – 5 – Can$9.00 – cn Bibl Nat [540]

COURS DE DROIT... / Brocher, C A – Paris, 1882-1885 – 14mf – 1 – ILM-441/1 – ne IDC [327]

COURS DE DROIT DE L'INDOCHINE / Dureteste, A – Paris, Larose Editeurs, 1938. 240 p. LL-10003 – 1 – us L of C Photodup [340]

COURS DE LANGUE FRANCAISE / Lemare, P A – 3e ed. 1835 – 9 – fr I.C.S. [440]

COURS DE PEDAGOGIE, OU PRINCIPE D'EDUCATION / Langevin, Jean – 2e ed. Rimouski: Impr. de la Voix de (sic) Golfe, 1869. SEM16P157 – 1r – 5 – Can$9.00 – cn Bibl Nat [370]

COURS DE PEINTURE PAR PRINCIPES / Piles, Roger de – O 402. 1708 – 9 – ne IDC [760]

COURS D'ELOQUENCE PARLEE D'APRES DELSARTE / Hamel, Thomas Etienne – Quebec: La Compagnie de l'Evenement, 1906. SEM105P656 – 4mf – 9 – Can$9.00 – cn Bibl Nat [440]

COURS D'ETHNOBOTANIQUE ET D'ETHNOZOOLOGIE (1969-1970) / Laboratoire d'Ethnobotanique et d'Ethnozoologie – 9 – F100.00 – fr Ethnologie [306]

COURS D'ETUDE, OU RECUEIL DES DEVOIRS DONNES DANS LES COURS DE QUATRIEME... / Pellerin, Joseph-Michel – (Rhetorique francaise donnee par le R.P. de L'Isle...Cursus philosophiae, ... 3 tomes. Essai d'un cahier de doleances pour les trois ordres de la province de Bretagne. Cahier des doleances que presentent au roi et aux Etats generaux...Lettre autographe signee de Pellerin,...) – 18th c. – fr Armell [944]

COURS D'ETUDE POUR L'INSTRUCTION DU PRINCE DE PARME / Condillac, E B de – 1780 – 9 – fr I.C.S. [370]

COURS ENTIER DE PHILOSOPHIE, OU SYSTEME GENERAL SELON LES PRINCIPES DE M. DESCARTES / Regis, P S – Amsterdam. 3v. 1691 – 22mf – 9 – CA-57/1 – ne IDC [100]

COURS ET EXERCICES POUR LES STAGES DE RECYCLAGE DES MONITEURS / Lamy, A & Berthet, P – (Africa series). 1970 – 9 – fr Hachette [621]

COURS PRATIQUE DE LANGUE MALGACHE / Rahidy, Basilide, R P – Premiere partie: grammaire; deuxieme partie: dialogues usuels et vocabulaire francais-malgache; troisieme partie: exercices et vocabulaire malgache-francais. Paris, Librairie africaine et coloniale: Joseph Andre et Cie. 1895 – 9 – $20.00 – fr Orientalistes [490]

A COURSE IN CIVIL GOVERNMENT : BASED ON THE "THE GOVERNMENT OF THE PEOPLE OF THE UNITED STATES" / Thorpe, Francis N – 2nd ed. Philadelphia: Eldredge & Bro, 1894 – 3mf – 9 – $4.50 – LLMC 96-059 – us L.L.M.C. [323]

A COURSE OF LECTURES ON ELOCUTION / Sheridan, Thomas – 1762. 293p. (English Linguistics Series 1500-1800) – 9 – us UMI [400]

A COURSE OF LECTURES ON ORATORY AND CRITICISM / Priestley, Joseph – 1777. 334p. (English Linguistics Series 1500-1800) – 9 – us UMI [400]

A COURSE OF LECTURES ON THE THEORY OF LANGUAGE, AND UNIVERSAL GRAMMAR / Priestley, Joseph – 1762. 318p. (English Linguistics Series 1500-1800) – 9 – us UMI [400]

A COURSE OF MECHANICAL, OPTICAL HYDROSTATICAL AND PNEUMATICAL EXPERIMENTS... / Hauksbee, F – London, 1730 – 1mf – 9 – ne IDC [619]

A COURSE OF SIX LECTURES ON THE CHEMICAL HISTORY OF A CANDLE : TO WHICH IS ADDED A LECTURE ON PLATINUM. DELIVERED BEFORE A JUVENILE AUDITORY AT THE ROYAL INSTITUTION OF GREAT BRITAIN... / Faraday, Michael – New York: Harper & Brothers, 1861 – 1 roll – 1 – 1-55879-376-3 – uk Libr Preservation [540]

COURSE OF THE EXCHANGE – England.1895. -w. 1/2 reel – 1 – uk British Libr Newspaper [072]

COURSE OF THE EXCHANGE – London, UK. 11 Mar 1825-1828; 1873; 1882-83; 1886-30 Jun 1908. 13 reels – 1 – uk British Libr Newspaper [072]

THE COURSE OF TRUE LOVE / Reade, Charles L – British Fiction Archive: Unit 2 – 9 – uk Bell [830]

Court, Antoine *see* LETTRE D'UN PATRIOTE SUR LA TOLERANCE CIVILE DES PROTESTANTS DE FRANCE ET SUR LES AVANTAGES QUI EN RESULTERAIENT POUR LE ROYAUME

COURT CIRCULAR & COURT NEWS – London, England. -w. Jan-Dec 1893. 1 reel – 1 – uk British Libr Newspaper [072]

[(COURT) DAILY REGISTER OF LETTERS RECEIVED], 1893-1897 / Imperial Court of Protectorate of the New Guinea Company – Eastern Jurisdiction District Journal/Gerichts – Journal – 1 reel – 1 – CRS G250 – at Archives [920]

Court de Gebelin, A *see*
- HISTOIRE NATURELLE DE LA PAROLE
- HISTOIRE NATURELLE DE LA PAROLE OU ORIGINE DU LANGAGE, DE L'ECRITURE ET DE LA GRAMMAIRE UNIVERSELLE

COURT DECISIONS RELATING TO THE NATIONAL LABOR RELATIONS ACT / U. S. Courts – (Additional vols to be filmed) – Washington: GPO. v1-38 + index. 1939-86 – 551mf – 9 – $826.00 – LLMC 79-432 – us L.L.M.C. [340]

COURT DOCKET / Paulding County. Ohio. Cecil Mayor – 1892-1978 – 1r – 1 – $32.50r – us Archival [324]

Court, Jesaias Frederik H. A. de la *see* SOAL INDONESIA. TERDJEMAHAN DAJAT HARDJAKOESOEMAH

THE COURT JOURNAL, COURT CIRCULAR AND FASHIONABLE GAZETTE – London. no. 1-4950. 1829-1925. (Scattered issues wanting) – 1 – 1,794.00 – us L of C Photodup [073]

COURT MARTIAL REPORTS – v1-50. 1951-75 – 9 – $895.00 set – us Hein [340]

COURT MARTIAL REPORTS OF THE JUDGE ADVOCATE GENERAL (JAG) OF THE AIR FORCE...THE JUDICIAL COUNCIL, AND BOARDS OF REVIEW / U.S. Army. Air Force. Office of the Judge Advocate General – (Covers: ACM 2 to ACM 2891. Cont by: Court-Martial Reports) – v1-4. 1948-51 (all publ) – 41mf – 9 – $61.50 – LLMC 82-212 – us L.L.M.C. [340]

COURT MINUTE BOOKS OF THE BOROUGH / Neath. England – 1759-1853 – 1 – uk Microform Academic [941]

COURT NETHERLEIGH / Wood, Ellen – British Fiction Archive: Unit 1 – 9 – uk Bell [830]

THE COURT OF APPEALS AND ITS RELATION TO THE METHODS BY WHICH PUBLIC SPECULATORS HAVE EVADED JUSTICE – New York, Polhemus, 1876. 53 p. LL-972 – 1 – us L of C Photodup [340]

THE COURT OF ARBITRATION: ITS ADVANTAGES AND IMPORTANCE TO BUSINESS MEN / Shepard, Elliott Fitch – New York: Press of the Chamber of Commerce, 1875. 16p. LL-1389 – 1 – us L of C Photodup [340]

COURT OF CUSTOMS APPEALS REPORTS *see* U.S. COURT OF CUSTOMS AMD PATENT APPEALS REPORTS

COURT PAPERS, JOURNAL, EXHIBITS, AND JUDGMENTS..., 1900-48 / International Military Tribunal for the Far East – 39 rolls. T918 – 1 – us Nat'l Archives [324]

COURT PAPERS, JOURNALS, EXHIBITS, AND JUDGMENTS OF THE INTERNATIONAL MILITARY TRIBUNAL FOR THE FAR EAST, 1900-1948 – 61r – $1,403.00 – T918 – us Nat'l Archives [340]
COURT RECORDS : MISC. INCLUDING COURT ORDER BOOK 1765-1766; SURVEYS 1742-1756 LAND RECORDS 1742-1770; LAND CAUSES 1788-1832 / Virginia. Fairfax County – 9 – $225.00 – us Bloch [340]
COURT RECORDS : THE NAME AND SUBJECT INDEX AND ABSTRACT / Virginia. Fairfax County – 1807-26 – 9 – $375.00 – us Bloch [340]
COURT RECORDS : THE NAME AND SUBJECT INDEX AND ABSTRACT / Virginia. Fairfax County – 1813-1816 – 9 – $225.00 – us Bloch [340]
COURT RECORDS : THE NAME AND SUBJECT INDEX AND ABSTRACT / Virginia. Fairfax County – 1863-1871 – 9 – $475.00 – us Bloch [340]
COURT RECORDS : NAME INDEX AND ABSTRACT / Virginia. Fairfax County – 1749-74 – 9 – $575.00 – us Bloch [340]
COURT RECORDS : THE NAME INDEX AND ABSTRACT / Virginia. Fairfax County – 1783-1802 – 9 – $475.00 – us Bloch [340]
COURT RECORDS : THE NAME INDEX AND ABSTRACT / Virginia. Fairfax County – 1835-1852 – 9 – $475.00 – us Bloch [340]
COURT RECORDS : NAME INDEX AND ABSTRACT / Virginia. Fairfax County – (1835-52. $375.00 (diazo); $410.00 (silver halide). 1853-60. $275.00 (diazo); $310.00 (silver halide)) – 1783-1802 – 9 – $310.00d; 345.00s – us Bloch [340]
COURT RECORDS : THE NAME INDEX AND ABSTRACT / Virginia. Fairfax County – 1853-1860 – 9 – $375.00 – us Bloch [340]
COURT RECORDS : SUBJECT INDEX AND ABSTRACT / Virginia. Fairfax County – 1749-1802 – 9 – $275.00 – us Bloch [340]
COURT RECORDS : THE SUBJECT INDEX AND ABSTRACT / Virginia. Fairfax County – 1831-1865 – 9 – $225.00 – us Bloch [340]
COURT REPORTING; A MANUAL OF LEGAL DICTATION AND FORMS FOR TEACHERS, STENOGRAPHERS AND TYPEWRITERS / Robinson, Addie M – New York: Excelsior 1904. 290p. LL-1091 – 1 – us L of C Photodup [340]
COURT REPORTS, COUNTY REPORTS 1885-1921, DISTRICT REPORTS 1892-1921, DISTRICT AND COUNTY REPORTS, 1922-50 / Pennsylvania – 51 reels – 1 – $1,290.00 – us Trans-Media [340]
COURT ROLLS / Holkham Hall. Norfolk. England – Billingford, Castleacre, Elmham, Longham, Warham, Wellingham, West Lexham – 1 – uk Microform Academic [941]
COURT ROLLS / Holkham Hall. Norfolk. England – c.1200-c.1500 – 1 – uk Microform Academic [941]
COURT ROLLS / Minster Lovell. Oxfordshire – 1560-1627 – 1 – uk Microform Academic [941]
THE COURT ROLLS OF RAMSEY, HEPMANGROVE AND BURY, 1268-1600 / ed by DeWindt, Edwin Brezette – 1990 – 5mf – 9 – Can$49.50 – 0-88844-366-8 – cn Pontif [910]
COURT STUDIES – A collection of surveys and analyses of judicial systems in the United States. Printed guide – 1 – $2,410.00 – 0-89093-650-1 – us UPA [340]
COURT SYSTEMS DIGEST – v. 1-. 1977- – 1,5,6,9 – us UMI [340]
COURT TO COURT PROCEDURE, WITH FORMS. / Smith, Frank Charles – Springfield, Ill.: Fiske, 1910. 664p. LL-1133 – 1 – us L of C Photodup [340]
Court, William B *see* THE STORY OF MY CONNECTION WITH THE CHINIQUY MOVEMENT IN MONTREAL, OF 1874-77, OR, A PRESBYTERIAN CHURCH ASSEMBLY REPORT CRITICISED
COURT-ANNEXED ARBITRATION IN TEN DISTRICT COURTS / Meierhoefer, Barbara S – Washington: FJC, 1990 – 2mf – 9 – $3.00 – LLMC 95-380 – us L.L.M.C. [340]
COURT-APPOINTED EXPERTS / Willging, Thomas E – Washington: FJC, 1986 – 1mf – 9 – $1.50 – LLMC 95-330 – us L.L.M.C. [340]
Courtat, F T *see* MONOGRAPHIE DU DICTIONNAIRE DE L'ACADEMIE
Courtauld Institute of Art *see*
- AMERICAN ARTISTS
- THE CONWAY LIBRARY
- COURTAULD INSTITUTE OF ART PERIODICALS SUBJECT INDEX
- GERMAN ARTISTS
- THE WITT LIBRARY

COURTAULD INSTITUTE OF ART PERIODICALS SUBJECT INDEX / Courtauld Institute of Art – (Brief synopses of articles on art-historical related subjects appearing in almost 200 journals from the 1930s to 1983) – 277mf – 9 – $2,250.00 – 0-907006-84-1 – uk Mindata [020]
THE COURTAULD INSTITUTE OF ART, THE UNIVERSITY OF LONDON / Conway Library – (Accompanied by a printed index.-also available separately; Architecture, Part A.-France and Italy, Midieval to 20th-century.$8,525.00.-ISBN 0-8161-1778-0; Architecture, Part B.-Europe, British Isles, South America, Asia, Islamic architecture, Africa, Medieval to 20th-century.$8,415.00.-ISBN 0-8161-1779-9; Architecture, Part C.-Drawings 14th- to 20th-century, including design and stained glass.$1,870.00.-ISBN 0-8161-1780-2; Sculpture.-15th- to 20th-century, including ivories, metalwork, seals, cameos, coins and medals.$6,380.00.-ISBN 0-8161-1781-0; Medieval Arts.-Greek to 14th-century, including Byzantine monuments.$6,215.00.-ISBN 0-8161-1782-9; Manuscripts.-Western Byzantine and Early Christian 4th- to 18th-century.$4,950.00.-ISBN 0-8161-1783-7) – 7,045mf – 9 – $26,250.00set – 0-8161-1762-4 – uk Hall [700]
Courtemanche, Joseph Israel *see* HISTOIRE DE LA FAMILLE COURTEMANCHE, 1663-1895
Courtenay, Baudouin de *see*
- DAL', V.I. TOLKOVII SLOVAR' ZHIVOGO VELIKORUSSKOGO IAZIKA
- TOLKOVYI SLOVAR' ZHIVOGO VELIKORUSSKOGO IAZYKA

COURTENAY FREE PRESS – British Columbia, CN. Jan 1927-Jul 1931 – 2r – 1 – cn Commonwealth Micro [072]
COURTENAY OF WALREDDON / Bray, Anna Eliza – British Fiction Archive: Unit 2 – 9 – uk Bell [830]
Courtenay, William Ashmead *see* COLLECTION
Courtet, M *see* ETUDE SUR LE SENEGAL.
Courteville, R *see* A SOLO FOR A FLUTE AND A BASS
COURTHOUSE CONSTRUCTION RECORD / Wood County. Ohio. Board of County Commissioners – 1893 – 1r – 1 – $32.50r – us Archival [324]
COURTHOUSE SPECIFICATIONS / Allen County. Ohio. Board of County Commissioners – 1r – 1 – $32.50r – us Archival [324]
COURT-MARTIAL REPORTS : HOLDINGS, AND DECISIONS OF THE JUDGE ADVOCATE GENERALS, BOARDS OF REVIEWS, AND THE COURT OF MILITARY APPEALS / U.S. Army. Judge Advocate General – (With index vols A (covering v1-25) and B (covering v26-50). Cont by: Military Justice Reporter, West Publ Co. v1- 1977- not offered by LLMC) – v1-50. 1951-75 – 573mf – 9 – $859.00 – LLMC 84-214 – us L.L.M.C. [340]
COURT-MARTIAL REPORTS *see* COURT MARTIAL REPORTS OF THE JUDGE ADVOCATE GENERAL (JAG) OF THE AIR FORCE...THE JUDICIAL COUNCIL, AND BOARDS OF REVIEW
Courtois, Victor Joseph *see* ELEMENTOS DE GRAMMATICA TETENSE, LINGUA CHI-NYUNGUE; IDIOMA FALLADO NO DISTRICTO DE TETE EEM TODA A VASTA REGIAO DO ZAMBEZE INFERIOR
Courtonne, J *see* TRAITE DE LA PERSPECTIVE PRATIQUE AVEC DES REMARQUES SUR L'ARCHITECTURE.
Courtot, Lieutenant-Colonel *see* DU GOLFE DES SYRTES AU GOLFE DU BENIN PAR LE LAC TCHAD
COURTROOM / Reynolds, Quentin James – London: Gollancz, 1950. 396p. LL-397 – 1 – us L of C Photodup [340]
COURTS AND LAWYERS OF ILLINOIS / Crossley, Frederic B – Chicago: American Historical Society, 1916. Vols. 1-2. Illinois Reel 7; Vol. 3. Illinois Reel 8. (The Cox Library Collection) – 5 – us Americana [978]
THE COURTS AND LEGAL PROFESSION OF IOWA. / Ebersole, Ezra Christian – Chicago, Cooper, 1907. 2 v. LL-767 – 1 – us L of C Photodup [340]
COURTS, JUDGES, AND LAWYERS OF MISSISSIPPI 1798-1935 / Rowland, Dunbar – Biographical sketches. Jackson: Mississippi Historical Society, 1935. Mississippi Reel 1. (The Cox Library Collection) – 5 – us Americana [978]
THE COURTS OF NEW JERSEY; THEIR ORIGIN, COMPOSITION AND JURISDICTION / Clevenger, William May – Plainfield: New Jersey Law Journal, 1903. 143p. LL-323 – 1 – us L of C Photodup [340]
THE COURTS OF QUEBEC: MR. CASGRAIN'S MEASURE FOR THEIR RE-ORGANIZATION: ITS PROVISION DISCUSSED: THE NEED OF IMPROVEMENT URGENT: HOW THE PROPOSED LAW WILL MEET THE WANTS OF THE CASE / Casgrain, Thomas Chase – 1893? 02541. (Pre-1900 Canadiana) – 9 – cn C.I.H.M. [971]
Cousar, Robert Moore *see* DIGEST OF THE LAWS AND DECISIONS RELATING TO THE APPOINTMENT, SALARY, AND COMPENSATION OF THE OFFICIALS OF THE UNITED STATES COURTS.
Cousens, H *see*
- LISTS OF ANTIQUARIAN REMAINS IN HIS HIGHNESS THE NIZAM'S TERRITORIES
- REVISED LISTS OF ANTIQUARIAN REMAINS IN THE BOMBAY PRESIDENCY AND THE NAT. STATES OF BARODA, PALANPUR, RADHANPUR, KATHIAWAS, KACHI, KOLHAPUR, AND THE SOUTHERN MARATHA MINOR STATES

Cousin d'Avallon *see* VOLTAIRIANA
Cousin, Jean *see*
- THE BOOK OF FORTUNE (LIBER FORTUNAE)
- LE LIVRE DE FORTUNE

Cousin, Paul *see* BOOK OF REFERENCE OF THE CITY OF QUEBEC AND VILLAGE OF SAINT SAUVEUR: ACCOMPANYING THE CADASTRAL PLAN
COUSIN PHILIP (HELENA) / Ward, Mary Augusta – British Fiction Archive: Unit 2 – 9 – uk Bell [830]
COUSIN PHILLIS / Gaskell, Elizabeth Cleghorn – London: George Bell, 1908 – 1 roll – 1 – 1-55879-940-0 – uk Libr Preservation [830]
Cousin, V *see*
- OPERA
- PETRI ABAELARDI OPERA. TOMUS 1,2

Cousin, Victor *see* THE YOUTH OF MADAME DE LONGUEVILLE, OR NEW REVELATIONS OF COURT AND CONVENT IN THE SEVENTEENTH CENTURY
Coussemaker, Charles Edmond Henri de *see* QUELQUES RECHERCHES SUR LE DIALECTE FLAMAND EN FRANCE
Cousturier, Lucie *see*
- LA FORET DU HAUT-NIGER
- MES INCONNUS CHEZ EUX

LE COUT DE LA VIE A PARIS DE 1840 A 1954 / Singer-Kerel, J – 1961 – F150.00 – fr Ethnologie [330]
Coutant, C G *see* THE HISTORY OF WYOMING
Coutlee, Louis William (1851-1917) *see* AN ALPHABETICAL INDEX OF THE CODE OF CIVIL PROCEDURE OF LOWER CANADA
COUTLEE'S SUPREME COURT CASES – (Coll of notes of unreported cases) – 1v. 1875-1906 (all publ) – 5mf – 9 – $7.50 – LLMC 81-010 – us L.L.M.C. [340]
Coutu, Debra L *see* THE EFFECT OF THE PRESENCE OF THE COACH ON PAIN PERCEPTION AND PAIN TOLERANCE OF ATHLETES
COUTUMIERS JURIDIQUES DE L'AFRIQUE OCCIDENTALE FRANCAISE – Paris: Larose, 1939 – 1 – us Res Libr [340]
COUTUMIERS LITURGIQUES DE PREMONTRE DU 13TH ET 14TH SIECLE / Lefevre, F – Louvain, 1953 – 3mf – 8 – Dfl13.00 – ne Slangenburg [240]
Couturat, Louis *see*
- L'ALGEBRE DE LA LOGIQUE
- LA LOGIQUE DE LEIBNIZ D'APRES DES DOCUMENTS INEDITES

Couture, Joseph Alphonse *see*
- CHOIX DES VACHES LAITIERES D'APRES LE SYSTEME GUENON
- PRECIS DE MEDICINE VETENNAIRE: A L'USAGE DES CULTIVATEURS
- TRAITE SUR L'ELEVAGE ET LES MALADIES DES BESTIAUX

Couture, Marguerite *see* BIBLIOGRAPHIE ANALYTIQUE DE LUC LACOURCIERE, TITULAIRE DE LA CHAIRE DE FOLKLORE, UNIVERSITE LAVAL, QUEBEC
Couture, Suzanne *see* BIBLIOGRAPHIE DE LOTBINIERE
LE COUVENT – Joliette, Quebec: F A Baillairge, 1886?-1899 – 9 – cn C.I.H.M. [971]
LE COUVENT : PUBLICATION MENSUELLE A L'USAGE DES JEUNES FILLES – Joliette: [s.n.], 1886-. SEM16P315 – 1r – 5 – Can$31.00 – cn Bibl Nat [240]
LE COUVENT OU LES VOEUX FORCES / Olympe, Gouges d' – (French Theatre Series). Paris. Vve Duchesne, Vve Bailly et chez les marchands de nouveautes. 1792 – 9 – fr Hachette [820]
LES COUVENTS PRES DE SCHAG / Monneret de Villard, Ugo – Milan, 1925 – 6mf – 8 – Dfl25.00 – ne Slangenburg [240]
Covarrubias y Leyra, D de *see* OPERA OMNIA
Covarsi, Antonio *see* NARRACIONES DE UN MONTERO Y PRACTICA DE CAZA MAYOR
COVE CREEK BAPTIST CHURCH. SHERWOOD, NORTH CAROLINA : CHURCH RECORDS – 1799-May 1963 – 1 – 46.08 – us Baptist [240]
COVE LEDGER – Cove, OR. -w. 17 Nov 1898-8 Feb 1900. 1 roll – 1 – us U.O. Library [071]
COVELO REVIEW – Covelo, CA. Dec 1904-Apr 1907 – 1r – 1 – $50.00 – B02147 – us Library Micro [071]
COVENANT, CONSTITUTION, BY-LAWS, CERTIFICATE OF INCORPORATION, DEED / Pickens County. South Carolina. Crescent Hill Baptist Church – c1956. Miscellaneous Papers – 1 – 5.00 – us Baptist [240]
COVENANT NAMES AND PRIVILEGES / Newton, Richard – New York: Robert Carter, c1882 – 1mf – 9 – 0-8370-5975-5 – 1985-3975 – us A.T.L.A. [210]
THE COVENANT OF SALT : AS BASED ON THE SIGNIFICANCE AND SYMBOLISM OF SALT IN PRIMITIVE THOUGHT / Trumbull, Henry Clay – (Includes bibliographical references & indexes) – New York: Charles Scribner, 1899 – 1mf – 9 – 0-8370-5578-4 – 1985-3578 – us A.T.L.A. [390]
COVENANT PEOPLE OF GOD (CCC324) / Wickings, H F – (In Chinese) – 1st ed. Hong Kong: Council on Christian Literature for Overseas Chinese, 1958 – 1r – 1 – 1984-6663 – us A.T.L.A. [240]
THE COVENANTERS : A HISTORY OF THE CHURCH IN SCOTLAND FROM THE REFORMATION TO THE REVOLUTION / Hewison, James King – Glasgow: J. Smith, 1913 – 3mf – us A.T.L.A. [240]
COVENT GARDEN JOURNAL – Dublin, Ireland.23 Jan 1752-10 Jun 1756. -irr. 1/2 reel – 1 – uk British Libr Newspaper [072]
COVENT GARDEN PROMPT BOOKS, 1710-1824 – (Ca 30 plays annotated by prompters) – Newberry Library Collections – 3r – 1 – $220.00 – us UMI [790]
COVENTRY EVENING TELEGRAPH – England.May 1947-1959.-d. 59 reels – 1 – uk British Libr Newspaper [072]
COVENTRY HERALD – England. -w. 1829-36. (4 reels) – 1 – uk British Libr Newspaper [072]
COVENTRY MERCURY – (Coventry Standard). England. -w. 1829-36. 3 reels – 1 – uk British Libr Newspaper [072]
COVENTRY PAPERS / Bath. Archives (Marquess). Longleat – Longleat. v1-119. With appendix, index and catalogue – 1 – uk Microform Academic [941]
COVENTRY PAPERS: CATALOGUE AND INDEX / Bath. Archives (Marquess). Longleat – 1 – uk Microform Academic [941]
COVENTRY STANDARD – England, 1940-64 – 30r – 1 – uk British Libr Newspaper [072]
COVERAGE OF AFRICAN AMERICAN BASKETBALL ATHLETES IN SPORTS ILLUSTRATED (1954 TO 1986) / Francis, Mark E – 1990 – 107p 2mf – 9 – $8.00 – us Microform Publ [305]
COVERAGE OF THE SPIRITUAL DIMENSION OF HEALTH IN PERSONAL HEALTH TEXTBOOKS IN HIGHER EDUCATION / Allen, Donna – Texas Woman's University, 1993 – 2mf – 9 – $8.00 – HE 561 – us Microform Publ [613]
COVERED EMPLOYMENT TRENDS IN NEW JERSEY BY GEOGRAPHICAL AREAS OF THE STATE / New Jersey. Dept. of Labor and Industry. Division of Planning and Research – 1944-78. 36 fiches. (Harvard Law School Library Collection.) – 9 – 1.50f – us H.U. Law [310]
COVERTACTION INFORMATION BULLETIN – n. 1-. 1978- – 1,5,6,9 – us UMI [320]

COVINA ARGUS CITIZIEN – Covina, Ca. 1921- – 100+ r – 1 – $5,000.00 ($90.00y) – R02148 – us Library Micro [071]
COVINA CITIZEN – Covina, CA. 1940-45 – 6r – 1 – $300.00 – R04019 – us Library Micro [071]
COVINA SENTINEL – Covina, CA. 1951-1979 – 28r – 1 – $1,400.00 – R04020 – us Library Micro [071]
COVINA VALLEY COURIER – Covina, CA. 1961-1980 – 3r – 1 – $150.00 – R04021 – us Library Micro [071]
COVINGTON FIRST BAPTIST CHURCH. COVINGTON, LOUISIANA : CHURCH RECORDS – 1904-72. 1338p – 1 – 60.21 – us Baptist [240]
COVJEK I PROSTOR – (Lacking: Jan, Feb 1957) – Zagreb, Yugoslavia. Feb 1954-Dec 1970 – 4r – 1 – uk British Libr Newspaper [949]
COVRS DE CHYMIE / Thibaut, Pierre – Paris, 1667 – 1 – us U.W. Library [540]
COW AND DAIRY REGISTER / Topeka. Kansas. Clerk – 1908-14. Automotive vehicle register, 1916-25 – 1 – us KS Hist [978]
COW COUNTRY COURIER – Valentine, NE. -w. May 1937-Sept 1943 – 1 – us NE Hist [071]
Cowan, Christopher *see* CHRISTOPHER COWAN PAPERS, MS 1328
Cowan, Henry *see*
- THE INFLUENCE OF THE SCOTTISH CHURCH IN CHRISTENDOM
- JOHN KNOX
- SUB CORONA

Cowan, James *see* SAMOA AND ITS STORY
Cowan, Minna G *see* THE EDUCATION OF THE WOMEN OF INDIA
Cowans, David *see* ANECDOTES OF A LIFE ON THE OCEAN: BEING A PORTION OF THE EXPERIENCES OF TWENTY-SEVEN YEARS' SERVICE IN MANY PARTS OF THE WORLD
Coward, Noel Pierce *see* PLAY PARADE
COWBOY – Dodge City. Kan. 1884-1885 – 1 – us UMI [071]
Cowdery, Jabez Franklin *see*
- COWDERY'S FORMS AND PRECEDENTS.
- COWDERY'S NEW BOOK OF FORMS...ESPECIALLY ADAPTED TO THE CODES AND STATUTES OF ALASKA, ARIZONA, CALIFORNIA, COLORADO, IDAHO, MONTANA, NEVADA, NEW MEXICO, NORTH DAKOTA, OREGON, SOUTH DAKOTA, UTAH, WASHINGTON AND WYOMING.
- THE LAW OF INSOLVENCY
- A TREATISE ON THE LAW AND PRACTICE IN JUSTICES' COURTS, AS DETERMINED BY THE STATUTES AND DECISIONS OF THE STATES OF CALIFORNIA, COLORADO, NEVADA, AND OREGON...

COWDERY'S FORMS AND PRECEDENTS. / Cowdery, Jabez Franklin – San Francisco, Bancroft-Whitney, 1895. 673 p. LL-327 – 1 – us L of C Photodup [340]
COWDERY'S NEW BOOK OF FORMS...ESPECIALLY ADAPTED TO THE CODES AND STATUTES OF ALASKA, ARIZONA, CALIFORNIA, COLORADO, IDAHO, MONTANA, NEVADA, NEW MEXICO, NORTH DAKOTA, OREGON, SOUTH DAKOTA, UTAH, WASHINGTON AND WYOMING. / Cowdery, Jabez Franklin – San Francisco, Bancroft-Whitney, 1905. 1087 p. LL-872 – 1 – us L of C Photodup [340]
Cowell, D *see* THE INTERPRETER OF WORDS AND TERMS
Cowell, John *see*
- COWELL'S LAW DICTIONARY
- THE INTERPRETER

COWELL'S LAW DICTIONARY : A LAW DICTIONARY ON THE INTERPRETATION OF LEGAL WORDS AND TERMS... WITH AN APPENDIX CONTAINING ANCIENT NAMES OF PLACES / Cowell, John – London, 1708 – 4mf – 9 – $6.00 – LLMC 95-410 – us L.L.M.C. [340]
Cowen, Esek, 1787-1844 *see* A TREATISE ON THE CIVIL JURISDICTION OF JUSTICES OF THE PEACE IN THE STATE OF NEW-YORK
Cowen, Robert Ernest *see* A BIBLIOGRAPHY OF THE HISTORY OF CALIFORNIA, 1510-1930
Cowen, Robert Grainess *see* A BIBLIOGRAPHY OF THE HISTORY OF CALIFORNIA, 1510-1930
COWETA COUNTY CHRONICLES FOR 100 YEARS – Atlanta, Stein Printing Co., 1928. Georgia Reel 3. (The Cox Library Collection) – 5 – us Americana [978]
COWETA COUNTY CHRONICLES FOR ONE HUNDRED YEARS...WITH LINEAGE PAGES – Ed. and comp. by Mary G. Jones & Lily Reynolds (1928). Item L. Indexed. 869p beginning with p570 and continuing to the end of the book. SW16-0026 – 5 – us A.G.L.L. [920]
Cowherd, Thomas *see* THE EMIGRANT MECHANIC: AND OTHER TALES IN VERSE, TOGETHER WITH NUMEROUS SONGS UPON CANADIAN SUBJECTS
Cowie, J S *see* BAND OF HOPE RITUAL
Cowing, Richard *see* RICHARD COBDEN, 1887
Cowles *see* LAND MARKS OF WAYNE COUNTY
Cowles, Albert E *see* PAST AND PRESENT OF THE CITY OF LANSING AND INGHAM COUNTY
Cowles, Edward B *see* DIRECTORY AND HISTORY OF BERRIEN COUNTY, 1871
COWLES ENTERPRISE – Cowles, NE. -w. Nov. 1907-Oct. 1908 – 1 – us NE Hist [071]
Cowles, Fleur *see*
- BLOODY PRECEDENT

Cowles, Henry *see*
- ACTS OF THE APOSTLES
- THE EPISTLE TO THE HEBREWS
- JEREMIAH AND HIS LAMENTATIONS
- LONGER EPISTLES OF PAUL: ROMANS, 1 CORINTHIANS, 2 CORINTHIANS
- MATTHEW AND MARK
- MINOR PROPHETS: WITH NOTES, CRITICAL, EXPLANATORY, AND PRACTICAL
- PENTATEUCH, IN ITS PROGRESSIVE REVELATIONS OF GOD TO MEN
- THE PENTATEUCH, IN ITS PROGRESSIVE REVELATIONS OF GOD TO MEN DESIGNED FOR BOTH PASTORS AND PEOPLE
- REVELATION OF JOHN: WITH NOTES... DESIGNED FOR BOTH PASTORS AND PEOPLE

Cowley, A E *see* CATALOGUE OF THE HEBREW MSS IN THE BODLEIAN LIBRARY
Cowley, Abraham *see* THE WORKS OF MR. ABRAHAM COWLEY
COWLEY CO. TELEGRAM – Winfield. Kan. 1876-1887 – 1 – us UMI [071]
Cowley, Edward *see* WRITERS OF GENESIS: AND RELATED TOPICS, ILLUSTRATING DIVINE REVELATION
Cowper *see*
- THE OLNEY HYMNS AND A BAPTIST HYMN BOOK
- VOYAGE EN AFRIQUE OU CINQ ANNEES DE SEJOUR

Cowper, William *see*
- THE ANATOMY OF HUMANE BODIES WITH FIGURES DRAWN AFTER THE LIFE
- THE ANATOMY OF HUMANE BODIES: WITH FIGURES DRAWN AFTER THE LIFE...AND CURIOUSLY ENGRAVEN..
- A CONCORDANCE TO THE OLNEY HYMNS OF JOHN NEWTON AND WILLIAM COWPER
- MEMOIR OF THE EARLY LIFE OF WILLIAM COPWER, ESQ. WRITTEN BY HIMSELF, AND NEVER BEFORE PUBLISHED...
- MYOTOMIA REFORMATA
- POEMS
- TABLE TALK
- THE TASK

COWRA FREE PRESS – Jan 4 1911-Dec 24 1921 – 9 – at Pascoe [072]
COWRA GUARDIAN – Jan 2 1897-Dec 31 1904 – 9 – at Pascoe [072]
Cowtan, Robert *see* A BIOGRAPHICAL SKETCH OF SIR ANTHONY PANIZZI...LATE PRINCIPAL LIBRARIAN, BRITISH MUSEUM
Cox, A F *see* A MANUAL OF THE NORTH ARCOTT DISTRICT IN THE PRESIDENCY OF MADRAS
Cox, Charles *see* ENGLISH CHURCH FURNITURE
Cox, E K *see* CHRISTIAN STEWARDSHIP, MORRISTOWN, TENN
Cox, Edward *see* THOUGHTS BY THE WAY
Cox, Edward W *see* COX'S MAGISTRATES CASES
Cox, Edward W et al *see* COX'S CRIMINAL CASES
Cox, F A *see*
- THE BAPTISTS IN AMERICA
- FEMALE SCRIPTURE BIOGRAPHY: INCLUDING AN ESSAY ON WHAT CHRISTIANITY HAS DONE FOR WOMEN

Cox, George W *see*
- THE LIFE OF JOHN WILLIAM COLENSO, D.D.
- THE LIFE OF SAINT BONIFACE

Cox, H *see* JOURNAL OF A RESIDENCE IN THE BURMHAN EMPIRE, AND MORE PARTICULARLY AT THE COURT OF AMARAPOORAH
Cox, H E *see* A HANDBOOK OF THE COLEOPTERA...OF GREAT BRITAIN AND IRELAND
Cox, Harold *see*
- ECONOMIC LIBERTY
- FREE TRADE VS PROTECTION
- LAND NATIONALIZATION AND LAND TAXATION

Cox, Isaac *see* THE ANNALS OF TRINITY COUNTY
Cox, J C *see* A MONOGRAPH OF AUSTRALIAN LAND SHELLS
Cox, Jacob Dolson *see*
- MILITARY REMINISCENCES OF THE CIVIL WAR. VOL. 1. APRIL 1861-NOVEMBER 1863
- MILITARY REMINISCENCES OF THE CIVIL WAR. VOL. 2. NOVEMBER 1863-JUNE 1865

Cox, James *see* HISTORICAL AND BIOGRAPHICAL RECORD OF THE CATTLE INDUSTRY AND THE CATTLEMEN OF TEXAS AND ADJACENT TERRITORY
Cox, John Charles *see*
- CHURCHWARDENS' ACCOUNTS
- THE ENGLISH PARISH CHURCH
- HOW TO WRITE THE HISTORY OF A PARISH
- THE PARISH REGISTERS OF ENGLAND
- PULPITS LECTERNS AND ORGANS IN ENGLISH CHURCHES
- THE SANCTUARIES AND SANCTUARY SEEKERS OF MEDIAEVAL ENGLAND

Cox, Kimberley A *see* EFFECT OF A PSYCHOLOGICAL SKILLS TRAINING PROGRAM ON COMPETITION ANXIETY AND PERFORMANCE OF SELECTED NATIONAL YOUTH SPORTS PROGRAM CAMPERS
THE COX LIBRARY COLLECTION – 4,000 v. of state and local histories. Titles being listed individually – 5 – us Americana [080]
THE COX LIBRARY COLLECTION : COUNTY, STATE AND LOCAL HISTORIES – (States listed individually) – 1 – $50.00r – us Library Micro [978]
Cox, Norman W *see* MANUSCRIPTS, PERSONAL PAPERS, PASTORAL RECORDS, PUBLISHED ARTICLES, ETC
Cox, Palmer *see*
- FRONTIER HUMOR: SOME RATHER LUDICROUS EXPERIENCES THAT BEFELL MYSELF AND MY ACQUAINTANCES AMONG FRONTIER CHARACTERS BEFORE I MADE THE ACQUAINTANCE OF MY ESTEEMED FRIENDS "THE BROWNIES"
- QUEER PEOPLE AND THEIR KWEER KAPERS: BIRDS THAT TALK, GIANTS THAT FLEE, BEASTS THAT THINK, INSECTS THAT FLIRT, SPRITES THAT DANCE, WITH THEIR VARIOUS ANTICS ILLUSTRATED

Cox, Richard J *see* THE CALVERT PAPERS
Cox, Rowland *see*
- AMERICAN TRADEMARK CASES.
- COX'S MANUAL OF TRADEMARK CASES
- A MANUAL OF TRADEMARK CASES

Cox, Samuel *see*
- THE BOOK OF ECCLESIASTES
- BOOK OF ECCLESIASTES: WITH A NEW TRANSLATION
- BOOK OF RUTH: A POPULAR EXPOSITION
- HEBREW TWINS: A VINDICATION OF GOD'S WAYS WITH JACOB AND ESAU
- MIRACLES
- MIRACLES: AN ARGUMENT AND A CHALLENGE
- THE PILGRIM PSALMS
- PILGRIM PSALMS: AN EXPOSITION OF THE SONGS OF DEGREES

Cox, W E *see* ROLE OF WATER IN SOCIOECONOMIC DEVELOPMENT
Cox, W W *see* HISTORY OF SEWARD COUNTY, NEBRASKA
Cox, Walter Smith *see*
- COMMON LAW PRACTICE IN CIVIL ACTIONS
- QUESTIONS FOR THE USE OF STUDENTS IN THE JUNIOR LAW CLASS OF COLUMBIAN UNIVERSITY

Cox, William Charles *see* THE DEVELOPMENT OF A COMPREHENSIVE PLAN FOR MINISTRY FOR FIRST BAPTIST CHURCH, NEVADA, MISSOURI
Cox, William M *see* THE SOCIAL AND CIVIL STATUS OF WOMAN
Coxe, Arthur Cleveland *see* HOLY WRIT AND MODERN THOUGHT
Coxe, D *see* ACCOUNT OF THE RUSSIAN DISCOVERIES BETWEEN ASIA AND AMERICA, TO WHICH ARE ADDED THE CONQUEST OF SIBERIA AND
Coxe, H O *see* CATALOGUS CODICUM MSS. QUI IN COLLEGIIS AULISQUE OXONIENSIBUS HODIE ADSERVANTUR EST
Coxe, Robertson D *see* LEGAL PHILADELPHIA, COMMENTS AND MEMORIES
Coxe, Tench *see* TENCH COXE PAPERS, 1638-1896
Coxe, William *see* ACCOUNT OF THE RUSSIAN DISCOVERIES BETWEEN ASIA AND AMERICA. TO WHICH ARE ADDED THE CONQUEST OF SIBERIA, AND THE HISTORY OF THE TRANSACTIONS AND COMMERCE BETWEEN RUSSIA AND CHINA
Coxey, Jacob S, Sr *see* PAPERS
COX'S CRIMINAL CASES : REPORTS OF CASES IN CRIMINAL LAW IN ALL THE COURTS OF ENGLAND AND IRELAND / Great Britain. England; ed by Cox, Edward W et al – (Add vols planned as they fall out of copyright) – v1-31. 1843-1941. London: J Crockford/Butterworth, 1846-1948 (all publ) – 215mf (only v1-25) – 9 – $322.00 – LLMC 95-285 – us L.L.M.C. [324]
COX'S MAGISTRATES CASES : REPORTS OF ALL THE CASES DECIDED BY ALL THE SUPERIOR COURTS RELATING TO MAGISTRATES, MUNICIPAL AND PAROCHIAL LAW / Great Britain. England; ed by Cox, Edward W – (Includes 1v of digest of cases for the yrs 1856-69) – London: Law Times Office. v1-27. 1862-1919 (all publ) – 205mf – 9 – $307.00 – LLMC 95-226 – us L.L.M.C. [324]
COX'S MANUAL OF TRADEMARK CASES : INCLUDES "SEBASTIAN'S DIGEST OF TRADEMARK CASES" COVERING ALL THE CASES REPORTED PRIOR TO 1879, TOGETHER WITH LEADING CASES DECIDED SINCE... / Cox, Rowland – 2nd rev enl ed. Boston: Houghton-Mifflin, 1892 (all publ) – 2mf – 9 – $9.00 – LLMC 84-339 – us L.L.M.C. [340]
Coy, Owen C *see* HUMBOLDT BAY REGION, 1850-1895
Coyer, Gabriel-Francois *see*
- CHINKI, HISTOIRE COCHINCHINOISE QUI PEUT SERVIR A D'AUTRES PAYS
- DECOUVERTE DE L'ISLE FRIVOLE
- PLAN D'EDUCATION PUBLIQUE

Coyle, Robert F *see* WORKINGMEN AND THE CHURCH
Coyne, James Henry *see* A CENTURY OF ACHIEVEMENT
COYUNTURA ECONOMICA – Bogota: Fundacion para la Educacion Superior y el Desarrollo. v18 n1-2. mar-jun 1988 – us Res Libr [330]
COYUNTURA ECONOMICA ANDINA – Bogota: Fundacion para la Educacion Superior y el Desarrollo. n9. jun 1988 – 1r – us Res Libr [330]
COZAD LOCAL – Cozad, NE. (-w. except -sw. 1897-1924 and -tw. 1954-57.) Jul. 1897-May 1902. Incomplete; Sep. 1902-Mar. 1913; Jun. 1913-Mar. 1916; May 1916-Apr. 1961; Jan. 1962-May 1971 – 1 – us NE Hist [071]
COZAD REPUBLIC – Cozad, NE. -w. Aug. 1908-Feb. 1910 – 1 – us NE Hist [071]
COZAD TRIBUNE – Cozad, NE. -w. May 1887-Jan. 1896. Incomplete; May 1896-May 1898; Jan. 1899-Jan. 1907; Mar. 1907-Nov. 1907; Sep. 1909 – 1 – us NE Hist [071]
Cozza-Luzi, J *see* NOVA PATRUM BIBLIOTHECA
CPA JOURNAL – (1971-. 5,6. 1976-. 9) – Certified Public Accountant. v1- . 1930- – 1 – us UMI [380]
CPA LETTER – (1985-. 5,6,9) – v53-. 1973- – 1 – us UMI [380]
CPC (CHRISTIAN PEACE CONFERENCE) INFORMATION / Christian Peace Conference – 1968-87 (complete) – 2r – 1 – ATLA S0474 – us A.T.L.A. [240]
CPI PURCHASING – 1983- – 1,5,6,9 – us UMI [380]
CPJ: CANADIAN PHARMACEUTICAL JOURNAL *see* THE CANADIAN PHARMACEUTICAL JOURNAL
CQ MAGAZINE – 1945- – over 900mf – 9 – $360.00 – us Buckmaster [621]
Craandijk, H *see* HET KOOPCONTRACT IN DEN OVERZEESCHEN HANDEL
CRAB ORCHARD HERALD – Crab Orchard, NE. -w. Aug. 1892; Nov. 1894-Aug. 1936 – 1 – us NE Hist [071]
Crabbe, George *see*
- POEMS
- THE WORKS OF THE REV. GEORGE CRABBE
- THE WORKS OF THE REVEREND GEORGE CRABBE, LL. B.

Crabbe, W H *see* CRABBE'S REPORTS OF CASES FOR THE EASTERN DISTRICT OF PENNSYLVANIA, 1836-1846

CRABBE'S REPORTS OF CASES FOR THE EASTERN DISTRICT OF PENNSYLVANIA, 1836-1846 / Crabbe, W H – Philadelphia: Johnson. 1v. 1853 (all publ) – 7mf – 9 – $10.50 – LLMC 81-444 – us L.L.M.C. [340]
Crabites, Pierre *see* THE WINNING OF THE SUDAN
THE CRACE COLLECTION OF LONDON VIEWS IN THE BRITISH MUSEUM / British Museum. Department of Prints and Drawings – (Almost eight thousand engravings, drawings and watercolours of London through the ages. Arranged topographically in chronological sequence, 1236-1800s. With guides and 2 extensive printed indexes) – 8r – 1 – $790.00 – 0-907006-39-6 – uk Mindata [700]
Crackanthorpe, Hubert *see* WRECKAGE, SEVEN STUDIES
CRADLE ROLL HOME – Jul 1925-46 – 1 – 24.36 – us Baptist [240]
CRADOCK : SOUTH AFRICA COLLECTED PAPERS 1929-1962 – [New Haven, CT: Yale University Library 197-?] – 13r – us Res Libr [960]
CRADOCK AFRIKANER *see* MIDDELLANDSCHE AFRIKAANDER, DE
CRADOCK NOWELL / Blackmore, Richard Doddridge – British Fiction Archive: Unit 3 – 9 – uk Bell [830]
THE CRADOCK REGISTER – Cradock, South Africa. 5 Jan 1858-29 Dec 1899. 30 reels. Title varies: Cradock News, 1858-1862; Cradock and Tarkastad Register, 1863 – 1, 16 diazo available at reduced price – sa SA Libr [072]
CRAFT HORIZONS – (v. 29-39. 1969-79 5,6. v. 30-39. 1970-79 9) – v. 1-39. 1942-79 – 1 – us UMI [740]
CRAFT HORIZONS WITH CRAFT WORLD *see* AMERICAN CRAFT
CRAFTNEWS – (v1-9 1976-84 Can$115.00) – Toronto. v1-20. 1976-95 – 1 – Can$60.00y – cn Micromedia [740]
CRAFTS – (1975- 5,6,9) – I.-1-. 1973- – 1 – us UMI [740]
CRAFTS PLUS – (Incorporates: Hands 1988) – Markham. v1-10. 1985-94 – 9 – Can$28.00y – cn Micromedia [740]
CRAFTS PLUS *see* HANDS
CRAFTS REPORT – (1978-; 5,6,9) – v1-.1975- – 1 – us UMI [740]
Crafts, Wilbur F *see* NATIONAL PERILS AND HOPES
Crafts, Wilbur F et al *see* INTOXICANTS AND OPIUM IN ALL LANDS AND TIMES
Crafts, Wilbur Fisk *see*
- MUST THE OLD TESTAMENT GO?
- THE SABBATH FOR MAN, A STUDY OF THE ORIGIN, OBLIGATION, HISTORY, ADVANTAGES AND PRESENT STATE OF SABBATH OBSERVANCE..

CRAFTSMAN – (Cont by: Ontario Craft at v6 1981) – Toronto. v1-5. 1976-80 – 9 – Can$20.00y – cn Micromedia [740]
CRAFTSMAN *see* ONTARIO CRAFT
THE CRAFTSMAN AND BRITISH AMERICAN MASONIC RECORD – (Cont by: The Craftsman and Canadian Masonic Record) – Hamilton, C W [Ont]: T & R White, 1866-1869 – 9 – cn C.I.H.M. [360]
THE CRAFTSMAN AND BRITISH AMERICAN MASONIC RECORD *see* THE CRAFTSMAN AND CANADIAN MASONIC RECORD
THE CRAFTSMAN AND CANADIAN MASONIC RECORD – (Cont: The Craftsman and British American Masonic Record. Cont by: The Canadian Craftsman and Masonic Record) – Hamilton, Ont: T & R White, 1869-1877 – 9 – cn C.I.H.M. [360]
THE CRAFTSMAN AND CANADIAN MASONIC RECORD *see* THE CRAFTSMAN AND BRITISH AMERICAN MASONIC RECORD
CRAG AND CANYON – Banff Hot Springs, Alta: I Byers, [1900-19–] – 9 – cn C.I.H.M. [072]
Cragg, Kenneth *see* THE CALL OF THE MINARET
Craib, Alexander *see* AMERICA AND THE AMERICANS: A NARRATIVE OF A TOUR IN THE UNITED STATES AND CANADA: WITH CHAPTERS ON AMERICAN HOME LIFE
Craig, Edward Thomas *see* THE IRISH LAND AND LABOUR QUESTION, ILLUSTRATED IN THE HISTORY OF RALAHINE AND CO-OPERATIVE FARMING
Craig, J A *see* ASSYRIAN AND BABYLONIAN RELIGIOUS TEXTS
Craig, J J *see* OLD COLONISTS' JUBILEE, AUCKLAND, NZ 1842-1892
Craig, Jon D *see* MACRO CONTROLS ON PUBLIC SPENDING
Craig, Maria G *see* INFORMATION RELATING TO MUNICIPAL LEGISLATION OF THE LIQUOR TRAFFIC: ALSO OF MUNICIPAL FRANCHISE FOR WOMEN
CRAIG NEWS – Craig, NE. -w. Jan. 1892-Dec. 1900. Incomplete; Jan. 1906-Sep. 1906. Incomplete; Aug. 1909-Dec. 1914; Jan. 1918-Jan. 1961 – 1 – us NE Hist [071]
Craig, R T *see* THE MAMMILLARIA HANDBOOK
Craig, Robert *see* REGENERATION
THE CRAIGHEAD FAMILY : A GENEALOGICAL MEMOIR / Craighead, JG – 1876 – 1 – $50.00 – us Presbyterian [920]
Craighead, J G *see* SCOTCH AND IRISH SEEDS IN AMERICAN SOIL
Craighead, JG *see*
- THE CRAIGHEAD FAMILY
- THE STORY OF MARCUS WHITMAN

Craigie, E J *see* THE FALLACIES OF PROTECTION
CRAIGMYLE GAZETTE – Alberta, CN. 1921-22 – 1r – 1 – cn Commonwealth Micro [072]
Craik, Dinah Maria *see*
- THE LAUREL BUSH: AN OLD FASHIONED LOVE STORY
- A WOMAN'S THOUGHTS ABOUT WOMEN

Craik, Henry *see* IMPROVED RENDERINGS OF THOSE PASSAGES IN THE ENGLISH VERSION OF THE NEW TESTAMENT...
CRAIN'S DETROIT BUSINESS – 1985-. -w – 1 – us UMI [073]
CRAIN'S ILLINOIS BUSINESS – v1-. 1982- – 1,5,6,9 – us UMI [073]
CRAIN'S NEW YORK BUSINESS – v1-. 1985- – 1,5,6,9 – us UMI [073]
Craker, Lyle E *see* JOURNAL OF HERBS, SPICES AND MEDICINAL PLANTS
Cralle, Richard K *see* A DISQUISITION ON GOVERNMENT
Cram, Ralph Adams *see*
- CHURCH BUILDING
- HEART OF EUROPE
- IMPRESSIONS OF JAPANESE ARCHITECTURE AND THE ALLIED ARTS
- THE MINISTRY OF ART

Cramer, A M *see* BIJVOEGSELEN TOT DE LEVENSBESCHRIJVING VAN DAVID JORIS
Cramer, Barbara J *see*
- SELF-ESTEEM AND ADOLESCENT PREGNANCY
- STRESS AND JOB SATISFACTION OF NURSE MANAGERS IN HOSPITAL SETTINGS

Cramer, Carl F *see*
- MAGAZIN DER MUSIK
- MUSIK VON CARL FRIEDRICH CRAMER. ERSTES VIERTELJAHR

Cramer, D *see*
- DE DISTINGVENDO DECALOGO,...
- IN NATALITIAM MEMORIAM R. PATRIS D. MARTINI LVTHERI...
- NEUN FASTEN: U. PASSIONS PREDIGTEN:...
- WOLGEGRUENDETER BEWEISS VON DER VOLLSTAENDIGKEIT UND VOLLKOMMENHEIT DER HEILIGEN BIBEL:...

Cramer, Daniel *see* EMBLEMATA MORALIA NOVA
Cramer, Floyd *see* OUR NEIGHBOR NICARAGUA
Cramer, J *see* BIBLIOTHECA REFORMATORIA NEERLANDICA
Cramer, J A *see* CATENAE GRAECORUM PATRUM IN NOVUM TESTAMENTUM
Cramer, Johann Baptist *see*
- GRANDE SONATE POUR LE PIANOFORTE
- QUINTUOR POUR PIANOFORTE, VIOLIN, ALTO, VIOLONCELLE ET BASSE, OP. 69

Cramer, Maria *see* THOMAS DE QUINCEY UND JOHN WILSON (CHRISTOPHER NORTH) IHRE LITERARISCHEN UND PERSOENLICHEN BEZIEHUNGEN
Cramer, Rose Fulton *see* AUTHOR HEADINGS FOR THE OFFICIAL PUBLICATIONS OF OKLAHOMA
Cramer, Sydney *see*
- MONUMENTAL INSCRIPTIONS AND ARMS, 1245-1959, RELATING TO MARSKE, WILTON, ST PETER, LEEDS, ST ANDREW'S UPLEATHAM
- SCOTTISH MONUMENTAL INSCRIPTIONS FROM EDINBURGH AND GLASGOW, ETC

Cramer von Clausbruch, Juliane *see* FREIWIRTSCHAFT-FUEHRT DIE GELDREFORM AUS DER KRISE
Cramer-Hamman, Buffy *see* PREDICTING SUCCESSFUL ADJUSTMENT TO DISENGAGEMENT FROM COLLEGIATE ATHLETICS
CRAMMER'S FIRST LITANY 1544 AND MERBECKE'S BOOK OF COMMON PRAYER NOTED 1550 / Hunt, J E – London, 1939 – 4mf – 8 – Dfl19.00 – ne Slangenburg [240]
CRAMMER'S LITURGICAL PROJECTS / Wickham Legg, J – 1915 – 5mf – 8 – ne Slangenburg [240]
Cramp, John Mockett *see*
- A MEMOIR OF MADAME FELLER
- A MEMOIR OF MADAME FELLER: WITH AN ACCOUNT OF THE ORIGIN AND PROGRESS OF THE GRANDE LIGNE MISSION
- THE REFORMATION IN EUROPE
- A TEXT-BOOK OF POPERY

CRAMPTON PAPERS, 1844-1856 : THE AMERICAN PAPERS OF SIR JOHN CRAMPTON (1805-1886) – 17r – 1 – uk Microform Academic [975]
Cranch, William *see* CRANCH'S REPORTS OF CASES IN THE DISTRICT OF COLUMBIA, 1804-1841
CRANCH'S REPORTS OF CASES IN THE DISTRICT OF COLUMBIA, 1804-1841 / Cranch, William – Boston: Little-Brown. v1-6. 1852-53 (all publ) – 47mf – 9 – $70.00 – LLMC 81-443 – us L.L.M.C. [340]
Crandall, John J *see* LEADING CASES, AMERICAN AND ENGLISH, ON THE LAW OF LEGAL TENDER AND MONEY.
Crandell, DR et al *see* SOURCE-BOOK FOR VOLCANIC-HAZARDS ZONATION
CRANE AMERICAN – Crane, OR. -w. 18 Aug 1916-6 Dec 1935. 2 rolls – 1 – us U.O. Library [071]
Crane, Ellery B *see*
- HISTORIC HOMES AND INSTITUTIONS AND GENEALOGICAL AND PERSON MEMOIRS OF WORCESTER COUNTY

Crane, F G *see* JOURNAL OF PROMOTION MANAGEMENT
Crane, Frank *see* THE RELIGION OF TO-MORROW
Crane, J Willard *see* 'THE ORIGIN AND CAUSE OF THE BRITISH-AMERICAN ORDER OF GOOD TEMPLARS', REVIEWED
Crane, Oliver Turnbull *see* THE TARGUMS ON THE BOOKS OF RUTH AND JONAH
Crane, R T *see* THE STATE IN CONSTITUTIONAL AND INTERNATIONAL LAW
Crane, Richard Teller *see* THE FUTILITY OF TECHNICAL, INDUSTRIAL, VOCATIONAL AND CONTINUATION SCHOOLS; A PAPER.
[Crane, Robert I] *see* CALENDAR OF ITEMS MICROFILMED AT THE INDIA OFFICE, LONDON
Crane, Stephen *see* MAGGIE, A GIRL OF THE STREETS
Crane, Walter *see* CARTOONS FOR THE CAUSE, 1886-1896
Crane, William Carey *see* COLLECTION: DIARIES, 1832-85; NOTEBOOKS, MANUSCRIPTS AND CORRESPONDENCE WITH CONTEMPORARIES
Cranfield College of Aeronautics. England *see* COLLECTION
Crankshaw, James *see*
- AN ANALYTICAL SYNOPSIS OF THE CRIMINAL CODE OF THE CANADA EVIDENCE ACT
- IN MEMORY OF THE BRAVE MEN WHO MET THEIR DEATH WHILE IN THE DISCHARGE OF THEIR DUTIES AT THE ST URBAIN STREET FIRE ON SUNDAY, APRIL 29, 1877: AND WHOSE FUNERALS ARE TO TAKE PLACE THIS DAY
- A PRACTICAL GUIDE TO POLICE MAGISTRATES AND JUSTICES OF THE PEACE: WITH AN ALPHABETICAL SYNOPSIS OF THE CRIMINAL LAW AND AN ANALYTICAL INDEX

Cranmer, Gibson L *see* HISTORY OF WHEELING CITY AND REPRESENTATIVE CITIZENS
Cranmer, Thomas *see* WRITINGS AND DISPUTATIONS
Cranswick, G H *see* A NEW DEAL FOR PAPUA
Cranswick, Kester *see* TEAMING UP, BUT ONLY JUST IN TIME
Crantz, H J N von *see*
- CLASSIS CRUCIFORMIUM EMENDATA
- INSTITUTIONES REI HERBARIAE
- STIRPES AUSTRIACAE

Cranz, D *see* HISTORIE VON GROENLAND
LE CRAPAUD – Montreal, Canada. 7 jun 1878-9 oct 1878 – 1r – 1 – Can$25.00 – cn Can Microfilming [072]
LE CRAPOUILLOT – Magazine non-conformiste. Paris. Dir., Jean Galtier-Boissiere. 1948-1993 – 1 – fr A.C.R.P.P. [073]
CRARY'S NEW YORK PRACTICE : SPECIAL PROCEEDINGS / New York. (State) – v1-2. 1866 (all publ) – 16mf – 9 – $24.00 – LLMC 80-022 – us L.L.M.C. [340]
Cras, H C *see* LAUDATIO HUGONIS GROTII
Crasset, J S J *see* LA VERITABLE DEVOTION ENVERS LA SAINTE VIERGE
Craufurd, Alexander Henry *see* CHRISTIAN INSTINCTS AND MODERN DOUBT
Crauthwaldt, S von *see*
- DER NEW MENSCH
- VON DER WIDERGEBURT VNND HERKUMMEN EYNES CHRISTEN MENSCHENS

LA CRAVACHE : SATIRIQUE – Quebec, Canada. 29 jul-v1 n4. 23 aut 1899 – 1r – 1 – Can$25.00 – cn Can Microfilming [072]
LA CRAVACHE PARISIENNE – Journal satirique illustre. Paris. sept 1881-mars 1898 – 1 – fr A.C.R.P.P. [073]
Cravath, Prosper *see* EARLY ANNALS OF WHITEWATER 1837-1867
Craven, Charles E *see* HISTORY OF LONG ISLAND'S MATTITUCK
O CRAVO : ORGAO DA MOCIDADE ITACOATIARENSE – Itacoatiara, Amazonas. 20 Out-10 Nov 1918 – 1,5,6 – bl Biblioteca [072]
CRAWDADDY – 1966- 1; 1975- 5,6; 1977- 9 – us UMI [073]
Crawford, Abraham *see* REMINISCENCES OF A NAVAL OFFICER
CRAWFORD BAPTIST CHURCH. CRAWFORD, GEORGIA : CHURCH RECORDS – 1871-Feb 1913 – 1 – 23.58 – us Baptist [240]
CRAWFORD BULLETIN – Crawford, NE. -w. Aug. 1897-Oct. 1900. Incomplete; Jan. 1901-Aug. 1904 – 1 – us NE Hist [071]
THE CRAWFORD COLLECTION OF EARLY CHARTERS AND DOCUMENTS / ed by Napier, A S & Stevenson, W H – Oxford, 1895 – 7mf – 9 – H-1258/2 – ne IDC [025]
CRAWFORD COUNTY FORUM – Bucyrus, Ohio. 1850-99 – 25r – 1 – $32.50r – us Archival [071]
CRAWFORD COUNTY NEWS – Bucyrus, Ohio. 1897-1901 – 3r – 1 – $32.50r – us Archival [071]
Crawford County. Ohio. Clerk of Courts *see*
- NATURALIZATION RECORDS
- NATURALIZATIONS, DECLARATIONS
- NATURALIZATIONS, STUB BOOKS

Crawford County. Ohio. Common Pleas. Civil Division *see*
- APPEARANCE DOCKETS
- CHANCERY RECORDS

Crawford County. Ohio. Galion *see*
- BIRTH RECORD
- DEATH RECORD
- MINUTES
- ORDINANCE RECORDS
- RESOLUTION RECORDS

Crawford. County, Ohio. Liberty Township. Board of Education *see* SCHOOL RECORD
Crawford County. Ohio. Probate Court *see* MARRIAGE RECORDS
Crawford County.Ohio. St. Paul's Lutheran Church *see* RECORDS
Crawford, D G *see* ROLL OF THE INDIAN MEDICAL SERVICE, 1615-1930
Crawford, E May Grimes *see* BY THE EQUATOR'S SNOWY PEAK
Crawford, Francis J *see* HORAE HEBRAICAE
Crawford, G *see* A TALK ABOUT WINE: WHAT IT IS, ITS USE AND ITS ABUSE
CRAWFORD GAZETTE – Crawford, NE. -w. Jun. 1892; Oct. 1893-Nov. 1894. Incomplete; Aug. 1902 – 1 – us NE Hist [071]
Crawford, Geddings H *see*
- WHO'S WHO IN SOUTH CAROLINA

Crawford, Isabella Valancy *see* 'OLD SPOOKSES' PASS": 'MALCOLM'S KATIE' AND OTHER POEMS
Crawford, J Law *see* PROPOSED SCHEME OF IMPERIAL COMMERCIAL UNION
Crawford, Mrs. John *see* SONGS OF ALL SEASONS, CLIMES AND TIMES: A MOTLEY JINGLE OF JUMBLED RHYMES
Crawford, John *see* DEBATE ON THE POINTS OF DIFFERENCE IN FAITH AND PRACTICE BETWEEN THE TWO RELIGIOUS BODIES KNOWN AS THE DICIPLES OF CHRIST AND THE REGULAR BAPTISTS
CRAWFORD JOURNAL – Meadville, PA. -w 1885-1917 – 13 – $25.00r – us I.M.R. [071]
Crawford, Kenneth C *see* FORMS OF OATHS FOR USE IN THE U.S. DISTRICT COURTS
Crawford, Mary C *see* THE ROMANCE OF OLD NEW ENGLAND CHURCHES

Crawford, Robert Henry *see* THE DAILY INDONESIAN-LANGUAGE PRESS OF DJAKARTA: ANALYSIS OF TWO RECENT CRITICAL PERIODS. (THESIS). SE-5970/1. 1967

Crawford, Tarleton P *see*
- EVOLUTION IN MY MISSION VIEWS OR GROWTH OF GOSPEL MISSION PRINCIPLES IN MY OWN MIND
- PATRIARCHAL DYNASTIES FROM ADAM TO ABRAHAM

Crawford, Tarleton Perry *see* THE PATRIARCHAL DYNASTIES FROM ADAM TO ABRAHAM

Crawford, Thomas J *see* MYSTERIES OF CHRISTIANITY

Crawford, Thomas Jackson *see* THE MYSTERIES OF CHRISTIANITY

CRAWFORD TRIBUNE – Crawford, NE. - w. Jan. 1892-Dec. 1892. Incomplete; Jul. 1896-May 1898; Jan. 1899-Dec. 1951; Jun. 1952- – 1 – us NE Hist [071]

Crawford, W S *see* SYNESIUS, THE HELLENE

Crawford, William *see* RECEIPT BOOK

CRAWFORDVILLE BAPTIST CHURCH. TALIAFERRO COUNTY. GEORGIA : CHURCH RECORDS – 1831-1900 – 1 – 14.17 – us Baptist [240]

Crawfurd, J *see*
- A DESCRIPTIVE DICTIONARY OF THE INDIAN ISLANDS AND ADJACENT COUNTRIES
- HISTORY OF THE INDIAN ARCHIPELAGO

Crawley, Alfred Ernest *see* THE TREE OF LIFE

CRAWLEY AND DISTRICT OBSERVER – England, 1948-53; 1973- – 86+ r – 1 – uk British Libr Newspaper [072]

Crawshay, R *see* THE BIRDS OF TIERRA DEL FUEGO

THE CRAYON – New York. v1-8. 1855-61 – 1r – 1 – us Ross [073]

CRE (Conference des Recteurs Europeens) *see* INFORMATION

CREA REPORTER *see* CANADIAN REAL ESTATE

CREACION DEL MUNDO / Acevedo, Alonso de – Madrid: Rivadeneyra, 1854 – 1 – sp Bibl Santa Ana [210]

CREACION FILOSOFICA Y CREACION POETICA / Frutos Cortes, Eugenio – Barcelona: Juan Flors, editor, 1958 – sp Bibl Santa Ana [810]

CREACION POETICA (J. GUILLEN, SALINAS, A. MACHADO, D. ALONSO, S.J. DE LA CRUZ, M. PINILLOS) / Frutos Cortes, Eugenio – Madrid: Edic. Jose Purrua Turanzas S.A., 1976 – sp Bibl Santa Ana [810]

Creagh, M R *see* L. SPOONER

CREAM OF THE LAW – v1-3. 1905-07 (all publ) – 94mf – 9 – $141.00 – LLMC 82-919 – us L.L.M.C. [073]

CREAM RAISING BY THE CENTRIFUGAL AND OTHER SYSTEMS:.. / Barre, SM – Montreal: Senecal, 1884.03381.(Pre-1900 Canadiana) – 9 – cn C.I.H.M. [630]

Creasy, E S *see* FIRST PLATFORM...

CREATING THE FEDERAL JUDICIAL SYSTEM / Wheeler, Russell R & Harrison, Cynthia – 2nd ed. Washington: GPO, 1994 – 1mf – 9 – $1.50 – LLMC 95-839 – us L.L.M.C. [340]

CREATING THE FEDERAL JUDICIAL SYSTEM / Wheeler, Russell R & Harrison, Cynthia – Washington: GPO, 1989 – 1mf – 9 – $1.50 – LLMC 95-344 – us L.L.M.C. [340]

CREATION : GOD IN TIME AND SPACE / Foster, Randolph Sinks – New York: Hunt & Eaton; Cincinnati: Cranston & Curts, 1895 – 1mf – us A.T.L.A. [210]

CREATION / Haydn, Joseph – An oratorio arranged as quartettos for two violins, tenor and violoncello. 179? – 9 – us Sibley [780]

CREATION : OR, THE BIBLICAL COSMOGONY IN THE LIGHT OF MODERN SCIENCE / Guyot, Arnold – New York: Charles Scribner, 1887, c1884 – 1mf – 9 – 0-8370-3435-3 – 1985-1435 – us A.T.L.A. [210]

CREATION D'UNE UNION POUR L'ETUDE DU DROIT DES GENS D'APRES LES PRINCIPES CHRETIENS – Brignais, 1912 – 1mf – 1 – ILM-4091/1 – ne IDC [327]

CREATION, INSTITUTION, FONDATION ET PRIVILEGES DE L'UNIVERSITE DE NANTES / Universite de Nantes – Nantes: s.n., s.d. (apres/after 1755) – 1 – F50.00 – fr Armell [370]

CREATION: MAN'S FALL EXPLAINED IN THE LIGHT OF MODERN SCIENCE / Benson, Lawrence Sluter – New York: Lawrence S. Benson, 1885. 1 fiche – 9 – us A.T.L.A. [240]

CREATION, OR, THE BIBLICAL COSMOSGONY IN THE LIGHT OF MODERN SCIENCE / Guyot, Arnold – New York: Charles Scribner, 1887 – 9 – us A.T.L.A. [240]

Creation Research Society *see* QUARTERLY

THE CREATION STORY / Gladstone, William Ewart – (Includes bibliographical references) – Philadelphia: Henry Altemus, c1896 – 1mf – 9 – 0-8370-9470-4 – 1986-3470 – us A.T.L.A. [220]

CREATION'S TESTIMONY TO ITS GOD: THE ACCORDANCE OF SCIENCE, PHILOSOPHY, AND REVELATION : A MANUAL OF THE EVIDENCES OF NATURAL AND REVEALED RELIGION, WITH ESPECIAL REFERENCE TO THE PROGRESS OF SCIENCE, AND ADVANCE OF KNOWLEDGE / Ragg, Thomas – (Includes bibliographical references, indexes) – 11th rev enl ed. London: Charles Griffin, 1867 – 1mf – 9 – 0-8370-4826-5 – 1985-2826 – us A.T.L.A. [210]

THE CREATION-STORY OF GENESIS 1 : A SUMERIAN THEOGONY AND COSMOGONY / Radau, Hugo – (Includes bibliographical references) – Chicago: Open Court; London: Kegan Paul, Trench, Truebner, 1902 – 1mf – 9 – 0-8370-4820-6 – 1985-2820 – us A.T.L.A. [220]

CREATIVE – 1985- – 1,5,6,9 – us UMI [073]

THE CREATIVE ATTITUDE : FUSION OF FACTS AND VALUES / Maslow, Abraham S – [New York: Ethical Culture Publications, c1966] – us Res Libr [975]

CREATIVE CHILD AND ADULT QUARTERLY – v1- 1976- – 1,5,6,9 – us UMI [306]

CREATIVE COMPUTING – v. 1-. 1974- – 1,5,6,9 – us UMI [510]

CREATIVE CRAFTS AND MINIATURES – 1972- – 9 – us UMI [740]

CREATIVE IDEAS FOR LIVING – v15-. 1984- – 1,5,6,9 – us UMI [640]

CREATIVE, THE MAGAZINE OF PROMOTION – 1985-. -bim – 1 – us UMI [073]

THE CREATIVE USE OF THE LORD'S SUPPER AS A TEACHING TOOL FOR THE DOCTRINE OF ATONEMENT / Stephens, David Ellis – 1982 – 1 – 6.16 – us Baptist [240]

CREATOR AND CREATION : OR, THE KNOWLEDGE IN THE REASON OF GOD AND HIS WORK / Hickok, Laurens Perseus – Boston: Lee and Shepard; New York: Lee, Shepard and Dillingham, 1872 – 1mf – 9 – 0-8370-4879-6 – 1985-2879 – us A.T.L.A. [210]

DES CRECHES OU MOYEN DE DIMINUER LA MISERE EN AUGMENTANT LA POPULATION / Marbeau, J BF – (Condition of 19th C. French working class series). 1845 – 9 – fr Hachette [360]

CREDENTIALS OF CARDIAC REHABILITATION PERSONNEL / Bennett, Susan B – Springfield College, 1995 – 2mf – 9 – $8.00 – HE553 – us Microform Publ [616]

CREDENTIALS OF CHRISTIANITY : A COURSE OF LECTURES DELIVERED AT THE REQUEST OF THE CHRISTIAN EVIDENCE SOCIETY / Goodwin, Harvey et al – New York: T Whittaker, 1876 – 1mf – 9 – 0-8370-2775-6 – 1985-0775 – us A.T.L.A. [230]

CREDENTIALS OF SCIENCE: THE WARRANT OF FAITH / Cooke, Joseph Parsons – New York: Appleton, 1893. 1 fiche – 9 – us A.T.L.A. [240]

THE CREDENTIALS OF THE CATHOLIC CHURCH / Bagshawe, John B – London: R Washbourne, 1885 – 1mf – 9 – 0-8370-7360-X – 1986-1360 – us A.T.L.A. [230]

THE CREDENTIALS OF THE GOSPEL : A STATEMENT OF THE REASON OF THE CHRISTIAN HOPE / Beet, Joseph Agar – London: Wesleyan Methodist Bk Rm, 1889 – 1mf – 9 – 0-8370-2248-7 – 1985-0248 – us A.T.L.A. [230]

CREDIBILITY OF THE BOOK OF THE ACTS OF THE APOSTLES / Chase, Frederic Henry – London: Macmillan, 1902.1 fiche – 9 – us A.T.L.A. [240]

THE CREDIBILITY OF THE CHRISTIAN RELIGION, OR, THOUGHTS ON MODERN RATIONALISM / Smith, Samuel – London: Hodder & Stoughton, 1873. 1 fiche – 9 – us A.T.L.A. [240]

CREDIBILITY OF THE GOSPEL NARRATIVES OF THE BIRTH AND INFANCY OF CHRIST / Scott, Thomas Lucas – Ramsgate: T. Scott, 1866. 1 fiche – 9 – us A.T.L.A. [240]

CREDIT – 1986- – 1,5,6,9 – us UMI [336]

CREDIT : ROMAN / Niemann, August – 3. Aufl. Dresden: E Pierson, 1908 – 1r – 1 – us U.W. Library [830]

LE CREDIT AGRICOLE AU MAROC / Morocco. Caisse Nationale de Credit Agricole – 1964. BNE-3019 1 – 9 – ne IDC [324]

CREDIT AND BANKING DEVELOPMENTS / Egypt. National Bank – 1958-59 – 9 – ne IDC [336]

CREDIT AND BANKING DEVELOPMENTS, 1960-1969/70 / Egypt. Central Bank of Egypt – 3v. in 3. BNE-4615 1 – 9 – ne IDC [336]

CREDIT AND FINANCIAL MANAGEMENT – v2-1905- 1; v73- 5,6; v78- 9 – us UMI [332]

LE CREDIT FONCIER / Boucher de Boucherville, George – Quebec: Imprime pour les entrepreneurs par Hunter, Rose et Lemieux, 1863. SEM105P240 – 2mf – 9 – Can$4.50 – cn Bibl Nat [332]

THE "CREDIT FONCIER" / Bas-Canada. Parlement. Chambre d'assemblee. Comite sur Cette Partie... – Quebec: Hunter, Rose & Co, 1863. SEM105P1523 – 2mf – 9 – Can$4.50 – cn Bibl Nat [971]

CREDIT FOR AGRICULTURE IN THE DEVELOPING WORLD – 1977 – 110p – it F.A.O. [338]

CREDIT INTERNATIONAL – London, UK. 12 Jun 1869-16 Jul 1870 – 1 – uk British Libr Newspaper [072]

CREDIT NATIONAL – London, UK. 28 Nov 1872-15 May 1873 – 1 – uk British Libr Newspaper [072]

CREDIT SOCIAL REGARDS – Rouyn, Canada. v4 n5. mar/avr 1963 – 1r – 1 – Can$25.00 – cn Can Microfilming [072]

THE CREDIT SYSTEM IN FRANCE, GREAT BRITAIN AND THE UNITED STATES / Carey, Henry C – 1838, 1974. 130p, Free Banking Series – 1.00f – at Libertarian Micro [335]

CREDIT UNION WAY MAGAZINE – (v1-23 1948-1970 Can$300.00 1) – Regina. v1-46. 1948-1993/94 – 5,9 – Can$20.00y – cn Micromedia [332]

Credit Valley Railway Company *see*
- APPLICATION OF THE CREDIT VALLEY RAILWAY FOR RIGHT OF WAY AND CROSSINGS AT THE CITY OF TORONTO: SECOND INTERVIEW OF THE RAILWAY DELEGATION WITH THE RAILWAY COMMITTEE OF THE PRIVY COUNCIL, OTTAWA, THURSDAY, JUNE 3RD, 1879
- LA DIFFICULTE DE L'ESPLANADE: RESPONSE DE LA COMPANIE DE CHEMIN DE FER DE CREDIT VALLEY AUX ALLEGATIONS DES COMPANIES DE FER DU GRAND TRONC ET DU NOTHERN DANS L'AFFAIRE DE LA CONTESTATION DU DROIT D'ENTREE DU PORT DE TORONTO
- THE ESPLANADE DIFFICULTY: THE REPLY OF THE CREDIT VALLEY RAILWAY COMPANY TO THE STATEMENTS OF THE GRAND TRUNK AND NORTHERN RAILWAY COMPANIES IN THE MATTER OF THE DISPUTED ENTRANCE TO TORONTO HARBOUR
- RAILWAY COMMISSION

CREDIT WORLD – v4- 1914- 1; v60- 5,6; v66- 9 – us UMI [336]

EL CREDITO EXTREMENO. ESTATUTOS Y REGLAMENTO DE EL CREDITO EXTREMENO (CAJA RURAL) SOCIEDAD DE SOCORROS MUTUOS Y CAJA DE AHORROS...ESTABLECIDO EN... / Villafranca de los Barros – Badajoz: Tipografia el Noticiero Extremeno, 1906 – 1 – sp Bibl Santa Ana [350]

CREDITO NACIONAL O SEA HACIENDA PUBLICA / Alvarez Guerra, Andres – 1820 – 9 – 1.50f – sp Bibl Santa Ana [336]

DAS CREDO DER KIRCHE UND DIE INTELLIGENZ DES ZEITGEISTES / Peip, Albert – Guetersloh: C. Bertelsmann, 1892. 1 fiche – 9 – us A.T.L.A. [240]

EL CREDO Y LA RAZON. 3RD ED. MADRID, 1928 / Elola, Jose – Madrid: Razon y Fe, 1929 – 1 – sp Bibl Santa Ana [240]

THE CREED EXPLAINED : OR, AN EXPOSITION OF CATHOLIC DOCTRINE: ACCORDING TO THE CREEDS OF FAITH AND THE CONSTITUTIONS AND DEFINITIONS OF THE CHURCH / Devine, Arthur – (Includes bibliographical references) – 4th ed. London: R & T Washbourne; New York: Benziger Bros, 1903 – 2mf – 9 – 0-8370-8336-2 – 1986-2336 – us A.T.L.A. [240]

THE CREED IN THE PULPIT / Henson, Hensley – London, New York: Hodder and Stoughton, [1912?] – 1mf – us A.T.L.A. [240]

CREED OF CHRIST / Holmes, Edmund Gore Alexander – London: John Lane, 1905.1 fiche – 9 – us A.T.L.A. [240]

CREEDS AND CHURCHES IN SCOTLAND : WITH AN APPENDIX / Moncreiff, Henry Wellwood – Edinburgh: Edmonston & Douglas, 1869 – 1mf – us A.T.L.A. [240]

THE CREEDS AND PLATFORMS OF CONGREGATIONALISM / ed by Walker, Williston – (Includes bibliographical references and index) – New York: Charles Scribner, 1893 – 2mf – 9 – 0-8370-9836-X – 1986-3836 – us A.T.L.A. [240]

THE CREEDS OF THE CHURCH : IN THEIR RELATIONS TO THE WORD OF GOD AND TO THE CONSCIENCE OF THE CHRISTIAN: THE HULSEAN LECTURES FOR THE YEAR 1857 / Swainson, Charles Anthony – Cambridge: Macmillan, 1858 – 1mf – us A.T.L.A. [240]

Creegan, Charles Cole *see*
- GREAT MISSIONARIES OF THE CHURCH
- PIONEER MISSIONARIES OF THE CHURCH

Creel, David B *see* EFFECT OF EXERCISE INTENSITY AND DURATION ON POSTEXERCISE METABOLISM IN OBESE ADULTS

CREEM – (1985-. 1,5,6) – 1976- – 9 – us UMI [073]

Creer, John W *see* DIE DARSTELLUNG DER HAFTUNG DES AMERIKANISCHEN STAATES UND DER BEAMTEN SOWIE EIN RECHTSVERGLEICHENDER UBERBLICK UBER DAS DEUTSCHE RECHT

Crehuet, Diego Maria *see*
- LA PENA DE MUERTE, COMO TEMA LITERARIO
- RESUMEN DE UNA DISCUSION ACERCA DE LOS HIJOS ILEGITIMOS ANTE LA SOCIEDAD Y EL DERECHO
- LA TUTELA...DISCURSO Y CONTESTACION...

CREIGHTON LIBERAL – Creighton, NE. -w. Jun. 1899; Sep. 1895-Jun. 1899; Aug. 1899-Jul. 1905. Incomplete; Dec. 1905-Aug. 1917 – 1 – us NE Hist [071]

Creighton, Louise *see*
- THE CHURCH AND THE NATION
- HISTORICAL LECTURES AND ADDRESSES
- LIFE AND LETTERS OF MANDELL CREIGHTON
- THOUGHTS ON EDUCATION
- UNIVERSITY AND OTHER SERMONS

Creighton, Mandell *see*
- CARDINAL WOLSEY
- THE CHURCH AND THE NATION
- HISTORICAL ESSAYS AND REVIEWS
- HISTORICAL LECTURES AND ADDRESSES
- LIFE OF SIMON DE MONTFORT
- PERSECUTION AND TOLERANCE
- QUEEN ELIZABETH
- THOUGHTS ON EDUCATION
- UNIVERSITY AND OTHER SERMONS

CREIGHTON NEWS – Creighton, NE. -w. May 1879-Jul. 1879; Dec. 1879-Mar. 1880; Sep. 1901-Apr. 1902; Oct. 1902- – 1 – us NE Hist [071]

Creizenach, M C *see*
- SCHULCHAN ARUCH ODER ENCYCLOPAEDISCHE DARSTELLUNG DES MOSAISCHEN GESETZES...
- ZIVYON

Cremazie, Octave *see* OEUVRES COMPLETES DE OCTAVE CREMAZIE

Cremer, Ernst *see* DIE STELLVERTRETENDE BEDEUTUNG DER PERSON JESU CHRISTI

Cremer, Hermann *see*
- REPLY TO HARNACK ON THE ESSENCE OF CHRISTIANITY
- WARUM KOENNEN WIR DAS APOSTOLISCHE GLAUBENSBEKENNTNIS NICHT AUFGEBEN?
- ZUM KAMPF UM DAS APOSTOLIKUM

[Cremers, E] *see* ERREURS OU SOPHISMES?

CREOLE – Guiana. 1856-1882; 1905-1907 – 1 – us UMI [072]

IL CREPUSCOLO DEI FILOSOFI / Papini, Giovanni – 4th ed., riveduta. Firenze 1921 – 1 – us U.W. Library [190]

O CREPUSCULO : PERIODICO INSTRUCTIVO E MORAL – [s.l.]: 2 Ago 1845-Fev 1847 – 1,5,6 – bl Biblioteca [072]

CRESCENT – Canadian. Tex. 1888-89 – 1 – us UMI [071]

THE CRESCENT AND THE CROSS : ROMANCE AND REALITIES OF EASTERN TRAVEL / Warburton, Eliot – 5th ed. London: H. Colburn, 1846. 2v. ill – 1 – us U.W. Library [910]
CRESCENT CITY NEWS – Crescent City, CA. 1906-1911 – 2r – 1 – $100.00 – C03590 – us Library Micro [071]
CRESCENT NEWS – Defiance. Ohio. 1917- – 1 – us UMI [071]
Crescimbeni, Giovanni Mario *see*
– L'ISTORIA DELLA BASILI CA DIACONALE COLLEGIATA, E PARROCCHIALE DI S. MARIA IN COSMEDIN DI ROMA
– LE VITE DEGLI ARCADI ILLUSTRI-SCRITTE DA DIVERSI AUTORI
Cresi, Domenico *see* DISCUSSIONI E DOCUMENTI DI STORIA FRANCESCANA...
Crespet, Pierre *see* DEUX LIVRES DE LA HAYNE DE SATHAN ET MALINS ESPRITS CONTRE L'HOMME ET DE L'HOMME CONTRE EUX
Crespo, Alfonso *see* EVA PERON
Crespo, E *see* LEGISLACION UNIFORME DE CHEQUES
Crespo, Manuel Maria *see* CATECISMO SOCIAL A SEA LA ENCICLICA "RERUM NOVARUM" DEL PAPA LEON 13 PUESTA EN PREGUNTAS Y RESPUETAS PARA SU MEJOR INTELIGENCIA
Crespo Marquez, Jose Maria *see* PREGON DE LA SEMANA SANTA CACERENA, 1976
Crespo, Nicasio *see*
– ARITMETICA, LAS CUATRO OPERACIONES FUNDAMENTALES
– NOCIONES ELEMENTALES DE ARITMETICA
Crespo, Pedro *see* EL PASO DEL GUADIANA
Crespo y Escoriaza, Benito *see*
– BRAVE RESENA DE LAS AGUAS SULFURADO-SODI CAS TERMALES DE MONTEMAYOR O BANOS
– DISCURSO INAUGURAL...ACADEMIA CIENTIFICO
Crespolani, R *see* LA CAMBIALE E IL VAGLIA CAMBIARIO...
Cress, Donald A *see* ARISTOTLE
CRESSET – Medicine Lodge. Kan. 1878-1894 – 1 – us UMI [071]
Cressolles, Loius de *see* THEATRUM VETERUM RHETORUM, ORATORUM, DECLAMATORUM, QUOS IN GRAECIA NOMINABANT...EXPOSITUM LIBRIS QUINQUE
Cresson, E T *see* SYNOPSIS OF THE FAMILIES AND GENERA OF THE HYMENOPTERA OF AMERICA, NORTH OF MEXICO
CRESSWELL'S NOTTINGHAM AND NEWARK JOURNAL – 1772-75 – 1 – uk Microform Academic [072]
Cressy, Earl H *see* CHRISTIAN HIGHER EDUCATION IN CHINA
CRESTHILL BAPTIST CHURCH. BOWIE, MARYLAND : CHURCH RECORDS – 16 Oct 1966-Jun 1979 – 1 – 17.04 – us Baptist [240]
CRESTLINE COURIER – Crestline, CA. 1967-79 – 9r – 1 – $450.00 – R02151 – us Library Micro [071]
Crestline. Ohio. First English Lutheran Church *see* RECORDS
CRESTON NEWS – Grand Rapids. Mich. 1909-1953 – 1 – us UMI [071]
CRESTON NEWS ADVERTISER INDEX – Creston, Iowa. 1869-1969. Centennial ed. 37p.SW16-0156 – 5 – us A.G.L.L. [071]
CRESTON STATESMAN – Creston, NE. -w. Aug. 1902-Jun. 1932 – 1 – us NE Hist [071]
CRESWELL CHRONICLE – Creswell, OR. -w. 17 Dec 1965-. – 1 – us U.O. Library [071]
CRESWELL CHRONICLE – Creswell, OR. -w. 30 Sep 1909-20 Dec 1917. - 2r – 1 – us U.O. Library [071]
Creswell, Creswell *see* BARNEWELL AND CRESSWELL'S REPORTS
CRESWELL NEW ERA – Creswell, OR. -w. 6 Jan 1949-30 Nov. 1950. 1 roll – 1 – us U.O. Library [071]
CRESWICK ADVERTISER – 1921-1942. CA1-21 – 21r – 1 – at Corangamite [072]
Cresz, J *see* DAS GEBET HIEREMIE DES PROPHETEN
CRETACEOUS FAUNA OF SOUTHERN INDIA / Stoliczka, F & Blanford, H F – (Palaeontologia Indica Series, 1, 3, 5, 6, 8). 4 v. Calcutta. 1865-73. BG-162 2 – 8 – ne IDC [590]
CRETE DEMOCRAT – Crete, NE. -w. Oct. 1874-Jan. 1890; Apr. 1890-Apr. 1922 – 1 – us NE Hist [071]
CRETE GLOBE – Crete, NE. -w. Jan. 1884-Jan. 1891 – 1 – us NE Hist [071]
CRETE HERALD – Crete, NE. -w. Dec. 1893-Apr. 1895; Jul. 1895-Apr. 1902 – 1 – us NE Hist [071]
CRETE NEWS – Crete, NE. -w. Mar. 1908- – 1 – us NE Hist [071]
CRETE VIDETTE – Crete, NE. -w. May 1883-Jan. 1891; Apr. 1891-Sep. 1891; Dec. 1891-Nov. 1894; Jan. 1895-Apr. 1895; Jul. 1895-Feb. 1911; Sep. 1911-Jun. 1928 – 1 – us NE Hist [071]
CRETESKY POKROK – Crete, NE. -w. Feb. 1905-Jun. 1909 – 1 – us NE Hist [071]
Creutzer, C *see* ENTOMOLOGISCHE VERSUCHE
Creuze de Lesser *see* LE SECRET DU MENAGE
Creuzer, F *see* PLOTINI ENNEADES CUM MARSILII FICINI INTERPRETATIONE CASTIG
Crevier, Jean-Baptiste-Louis *see*
– DE L'EDUCATION PUBLIQUE
– DIFFICULTES PROPOSEES A M. DE CARADEUC DE LA CHALOTAIS, SUR LE MEMOIRE INTITULE: ESSAI D'EDUCATION NATIONALE
– RHETORIQUE FRANCOISE
Crevier, Joseph Alexandre *see* LE CHOLERA
CREW AND PASSENGER LISTS, PORT OF NEWCASTLE, INWARDS AND OUTWARDS, 1865-1884 / Sub-Collector of Customs, Newcastle – 21r – 1 – CRS C667 – at Archives [920]
CREW LISTS OF VESSELS ARRIVING AT BOSTON, 1917 / U.S. Immigration and Naturalization Service – 269 rolls. T938 – 1 – us Nat'l Archives [324]
CREW LISTS OF VESSELS ARRIVING AT GLOUCESTER, 1918-43 / U.S. Immigration and Naturalization Service – 13 rolls. T941 – 1 – us Nat'l Archives [324]
CREW LISTS OF VESSELS ARRIVING AT NEW BEDFORD, 1917-1943 / U.S. Immigration and Naturalization Service – RG 85. T942. 2 rolls – 1 – us Nat'l Archives [975]
CREW LISTS OF VESSELS ARRIVING AT NEW ORLEANS, 1910-45 / U.S. Immigration and Naturalization Service – (1910-19. 311 rolls. T939) – 189 rolls. T905 – 1 – us Nat'l Archives [324]
CREW LISTS OF VESSELS ARRIVING AT SAN FRANCISCO, 1905-1954 – 174r – 1 – M1416 – us Nat'l Archives [340]
CREW LISTS OF VESSELS ARRIVING AT SEATTLE, WASHINGTON, 1903-1917 – 15r – 1 – M1399 – us Nat'l Archives [340]
CREWE AND NANTWICH CHRONICLE – Crewe, Nantwich, England. Crewe Chronicle. -w. 17 April 1875-Dec 1981. Lacking Jan-May 1897; Jan 1911-Dec 1912. 136 reels – 1 – uk British Libr Newspaper [072]
CREWE GUARDIAN – England. 25 Sep 1869-Dec 1920 (missing 1898).-w. 53 reels.) – 1 – uk British Libr Newspaper [072]
Crews, Debra J *see* EFFECT OF HEART RATE DECELERATION BIOFEEDBACK TRAINING ON GOLF PUTTING PERFORMANCE
LE CRI DE L'EST – Matane, Canada. 26 mai 1911-v1 n48. 19 avr 1912 – 1r – 1 – Can$25.00 – cn Can Microfilming [072]
CRI DE LONDRES – London, UK. 17 Aug 1914-Feb 1916 – 1 – uk British Libr Newspaper [072]
LE CRI DE L'OUVRIER – Douai. nov 1884-avr 1885 – 1 – fr A.C.R.P.P. [073]
LE CRI DE QUEBEC : JEUNESSE LIBERALE DE QUEBEC – Quebec, Canada. 23 mai 1925-27 nov 1925 – 1r – 1 – Can$35.00 – cn Can Microfilming [072]
LE CRI DE QUEBEC – Quebec, Canada. v1 n1. dec 1932 – 1r – 1 – Can$25.00 – cn Can Microfilming [072]
CRI DES COLONS CONTRE UN OUVRAGE DE M. L'EVEQUE ET SENATEUR GREGOIRE, AYANT POUR TITRE DE LA LITERATURE DES NEGRES, OU REFUTATION DES INCULPATIONS CALOMNIEUSES FAITES AUX COLONS PAR L'AUTEUR, ET PAR LES AUTRES PHILOSOPHES NEGROPHILES, TELS QUE RAYNAL / Tussac, F R de – 1810. (Slave Trade and Abolitionism in France Series) – 9 – fr Hachette [305]
LE CRI DES FLANDRES – Hazebrouck, France. -w. 1 May 1910-27 Sept 1914. 2 reels – 1 – uk British Libr Newspaper [072]
LE CRI DES JEUNES – no. 1-114. Lille. mars 1928-34. mq no. 9, 59, 79, 95, 111 – 1 – fr A.C.R.P.P. [073]
LE CRI DES NEGRES – Paris. oct 1931, juil 1933-nov 1934 – 1 – fr A.C.R.P.P. [073]
LE CRI DES NEGRES – Paris: La Cooptypography, aug 1931-jan/feb 1933; july/aug 1933-apr/may 1936 170=Filmed with Les continents and 11 other titles – us Res Libr [072]
LE CRI DU FORCAT – Lille. avr-aout 1884 – 1 – fr A.C.R.P.P. [073]
LE CRI DU NORD – Ste-Adele, Canada. 4 jul-8 aut 1930 – 1r – 1 – Can$35.00 – cn Can Microfilming [072]
LE CRI DU PEUPLE – Hebdomadaire syndicaliste revolutionnaire publie sous le controle du Comite pour l'independance du syndicalisme. Paris dec 1929-31 – 1 – fr A.C.R.P.P. [073]
LE CRI DU PEUPLE – Organe republicain. Dir. A. Ertus Beauchamps. Fort-de-France. dec 1933-mai 1934 – 1 – fr A.C.R.P.P. [073]
LE CRI DU PEUPLE – Paris. 22 fevr-23 mai 1871, 28 oct 1883-9 avr 1890, 27 janv 1891-15 dec 1896, 15 fevr-15 juil 1897, 4 juin 1898-17 sept 1899, 15 juin 1901-6 dec 1908, 15 juin, 1er nov 1910, 1er mai 1912, 25 oct 1913, 18 janv-10 juin 1914, juil-dec 1919, 30 mai, 10 juin, 20 juil 1922 – 1 – fr A.C.R.P.P. [073]
LE CRI DU PEUPLE – Verviers. Belgium. -w. 7 Jul 1878-21 Jun 1879. (14 ft) – 1 – uk British Libr Newspaper [949]
LE CRI DU PEUPLE – (Issues filmed as pt of: Commune de Paris newspapers; newspapers on these reels are filmed chronologically, not alphabetically) – Paris: Jules Valles, [mar 26-may 23 1871] – us Res Libr [072]
LE CRI DU PEUPLE DE PARIS – Fond. J. Doriot. Paris. 19 oct 1940-16 aout 1944 – 1 – fr A.C.R.P.P. [073]
LE CRI DU PEUPLE SOCIALISTE – Organe sous le controle de la Federation du Finistere. (Section francaise de l'Internationale ouvriere). Brest. oct 1908-16 – 1 – fr A.C.R.P.P. [073]
LE CRI DU SOL – Le journal de Dorgeres. Lyon. aout 1940-juil 1944 – 1 – fr A.C.R.P.P. [073]
LE CRI DU TRAVAILLEUR – Organe du Parti ouvrier de la region Nord. Lille. juil 1887-sept 1891 – 1 – fr A.C.R.P.P. [073]
LE CRI POPULAIRE – Socialisme, syndicalisme, cooperation. Bordeaux. 1929-34 – 1 – fr A.C.R.P.P. [073]
LOS CRIADEROS DE HIERRO DE BURGUILLOS (BADAJOS) / Gascon y Miramon, Antonio – Madrid: Imp. Ricardo Rojas, 1904 – 1 – sp Bibl Santa Ana [946]
Criado Valcarcel, Vicente *see* LUIS DE MORALES EN ARROYO DE LA LUZ
CRIBRUM MUSICUM ODER MUSICALISCHES SIEB / Werckmeister, A – 1700 – 9 – us Sibley [780]
CRIBRVM MVSICVM ODER MUSICALISCHES SIEB / Werckmeister, A – Quedlinburg und Leipzig. 1700. BP-773 1 – 9 – ne IDC [780]
Crichton, W J *see* THE MICROSCOPE OF THE NEW TESTAMENT
CRICKET – London. May 1882-Dec 1913.-m. 16mqn reels – 1 – uk British Libr Newspaper [072]
Cricket, J *see* SERMON REGISTERS, 1774-1803
LE CRI-CRI – Red. E. Marcellus, L. Fleury. Paris. juil 1872-juin 1873, juil-dec 1876 – 1 – fr A.C.R.P.P. [073]
CRIEFF ADVERTISER – Scotland, UK. 7 Jan-10 Jun 1865. -w. 23 feet – 1 – uk British Libr Newspaper [072]
CRIEFF HERALD – Scotland, UK. 1 Nov 1856-1862. -w. 2 reels – 1 – uk British Libr Newspaper [072]
Criegern, Hermann Ferdinand *see* JOHANN AMOS COMENIUS ALS THEOLOG
LE CRIEUR : GAZETTE DE SAINT-LAURENT / ed by Legault, Emile – Ville St-Laurent, Canada. n5. fev 1938-avr/mai 1938 – 1r – 1 – Can$25.00 – cn Can Microfilming [072]
Crigler, Sara Gossett *see* COLLECTION
CRILE, GEORGE W., PAPERS, MS 2806 – (Correspondence, telegrams, diaries and journals, memoranda books, articles, speeches, and financial papers of Dr. George W. Crile, noted surgeon, author, and co-founder of the Cleveland Clinic) – 1864-1943 – 71r – 1 – us Western Res [920]
CRIME AND DELINQUENCY – 1919-78 1; 1971-78 5,6; 1975-78 4 x 6 in. 9 – us UMI [360]
CRIME AND DELINQUENCY – (v1-30 1955-84 on reel $363.00. v31-41 1985-95 on mf $391.00. Title varies: v1-6 1955-60 as NPPA Journal) – v1-41. 1955-95 – 5,6,9 – $754.00 set – us Hein [360]
CRIME AND DELINQUENCY ABSTRACTS / U.S. Dept of Health and Human Services – (1st 3v entitled: International Bibliography on Crime and Delinquency) – HEW, National Clearinghouse for Mental Health Info. v.1-8. 1963-72 – 9 – LLMC 81-208 – us L.L.M.C. [360]
CRIME AND DELINQUENCY LITERATURE *see* CRIMINAL JUSTICE ABSTRACTS
CRIME AND JUVENILE DELIQUENCY DOCUMENTS – (Cataloging available) – Base collection to 1975; annual updates 1976- – 11,407mf complete collection to 1989; base collection 4201mf – 9 – $23,140.00 complete collection; $8820 base collection – us UMI [360]
CRIME AND PUNISHMENT / Dostoevskii, Fedor M – 1968. Trans. With an afterword by Sidney Monas. New York. New American Library. 543 p. 1 reel – 1 – us U.W. Library [830]
CRIME AND PUNISHMENT. THE MARK SYSTEM / Maconochie, Alexander – London. 1846 – 1 – us Res Libr [360]
CRIME AND SOCIAL JUSTICE – v1- 1974- 1; v5- 5,6,9 – us UMI [360]
LE CRIME COMME PRODUIT SOCIAL / Rosengart, Cecel – Paris. 1929. (La Condition Ouvriere. Part Two.) – 9 – 5.00 – fr Bibl Nationale [360]
THE CRIME CONTROL AND FINE ENFORCEMENT ACTS OF 1984 : A SYNOPSIS / Partridge, Anthony – Washington: FJC, Jan 1985 – 1mf – 9 – $1.50 – LLMC 95-393 – us L.L.M.C. [340]
CRIME CONTROL DIGEST – v1- 1967- 1; v9-1975- 5,6,9 – us UMI [360]
CRIME CRAPULEUX DE L'IMPERIALISME – [Conakry]: Impr Nationale "Partice Lumumba" 1973 – us Res Libr [960]
CRIME, CRIMINOLOGY AND CIVIL LIBERTIES, SERIES ONE / Howard League for Penal Reform. Great Britain. Archives – 1 – us Primary [360]
CRIME IN INDONESIA : AN INDEX TO SELECTED ARTICLES FROM TEMPO 1981-1985 / Zachri, Rukiah – 1986 – A$10.00 – 0-86758-197-2 – at BISA [360]
THE CRIME OF FRANCISCO FRANCO – New York, 1938? Fiche W 819. (Blodgett Collection of Spanish Civil War Pamphlets) – 9 – us H.U. College Libr [946]
THE CRIME OF GUERNICA / Spanish Information Bureau. New York – N.Y., 1937. Fiche W1200. (Blodgett Collection of Spanish Civil War Pamphlets) – 9 – us H.U. College Libr [946]
THE CRIME OF PAUL SACRISTAN: A TALE / Campbell, Alfred – Montreal: J. Lovell, 1891. 00398. (Pre-1900 Canadiana) – 9 – cn C.I.H.M. [830]
THE CRIME ON THE ROAD MALAGA-ALMERIA / Bethune, Norman – n.p. 1937? Fiche W 754. (Blodgett Collection of Spanish Civil War Pamphlets) – 9 – us H.U. College Libr [946]
CRIME PREVENTION REVIEW – v1- 1973- 1; 1976- 5,6,9 – us UMI [360]
CRIME PREVENTION REVIEW – (Available in reel only) – v1-6. 1973-79 (all publ) – 5,6 – $52.00 set – us Hein [360]
CRIME VICTIMS DIGEST *see* WASHINGTON CRIMINAL JUSTICE REPORT'S CRIME VICTIMS DIGEST
CRIMEAN WAR PAMPHLET COLLECTION – 1855? – 1 – CSUXANS1294-B – us Hoover Inst Photo [355]
UN CRIMEN DE HERNANDO CORTES. LA MUERTE DE DONA CATALINA XUARES MARCAYDA (ESTUDIO HISTORICO Y MEDICO LEGAL) / Toro, Alfonso – Mexico: Editorial Patria S.A., 2nd ed 1947 – sp Bibl Santa Ana [360]
EL CRIMEN DEL CAMINO MALAGA-ALMERIA / Bethune, Norman – n.p. 1937? Fiche W 755. (Blodgett Collection of Spanish Civil War Pamphlets) – 9 – us H.U. College Libr [946]
CRIMEN SATANOWSKY : OPERACION HOMICIDIO. OPERACION HOMICIDO – Buenos Aires [Argentina]: Editorial Verdad, 1958 – 1 – CSUXADJ1330-B – us Hoover Inst Photo [972]

CRIMENES DE LOS INVASORES NAZIS EN UNA CIUDAD RUSA : RELATO DEL PROCESO PUBLICO EN KRASNODAR (CAUCASO DEL NORTE) DEL 14 AL 17 DE JULIO DE 1943 – Mexico: Publicado po la Embajada de la Union de las Republicas Sovieticas Socialistas en Mexico, 1943 – 1 – CSUX91-B1356 – us Hoover Inst Photo [320]

CRIMENES DEL IMPERIALISMO NORTEAMERICANO / Blanco Fombona, Horacio – Mexico: D.F., Ediciones Churubusco, 1927. 144p – 1 – us U.W. Library [972]

CRIMES BY NATIONAL BANK OFFICERS AND AGENTS UNDER SECTIONS 5208 AND 5209 REVISED STATUTES OF THE UNITED STATES / Terrell, Henry – Chicago, Callaghan, 1906. 193 p. LL-1498 – 1 – us L of C Photodup [340]

LES CRIMES ET DELITS COMMIS A L'ETRANGER... / Donnedieu de Vabres, H – Paris, 1906 – 1mf – 1 – ILM-2077/1 – ne IDC [327]

CRIMINAL ABORTION AND THE NEW ENGLISH CRIMINAL EVIDENCE ACT / Bell, Clark, 1832-1918 – New York, 1898? 162-171 p. LL-1452 – 1 – us L of C Photodup [340]

CRIMINAL AND CIVIL DOCKETS / Ellis County. Kansas. Big Creek Township. Justice of the Peace – 1872-1957 – 1 – us KS Hist [978]

CRIMINAL CASE FILES OF THE U.S. CIRCUIT COURT FOR THE DISTRICT OF MARYLAND / U.S. Circuit and District Courts. Maryland – 1795-1860 – 4r – 1 – M1010 – us Nat'l Archives [324]

CRIMINAL CASE FILES OF THE U.S. CIRCUIT COURT FOR THE EASTERN DISTRICT OF PENNSYLVANIA / U.S. Circuit and District Courts. Pennsylvania – 1791-1840. 7 rolls – 1 – M986 – us Nat'l Archives [324]

CRIMINAL CASE FILES OF THE U.S. CIRCUIT COURT FOR THE SOUTHERN DISTRICT OF NEW YORK / U.S. Circuit and District Courts. New York – 1790-1853 – 6r – 1 – M885 – us Nat'l Archives [324]

CRIMINAL CODE OF THE JEWS ACCORDING TO THE TALMUD / Benny, Philip Berger – London: Smith, Elder, 1880. 1 fiche – 9 – us A.T.L.A. [270]

THE CRIMINAL CONSPIRACY IN THE JAPANESE WAR CRIMES TRIALS – (Memorandum for the Hon. Joseph B. Keenan, Chief of Counsel, acting on behalf of the US, of the International Military Tribunal for the Far East) – n.p., n.d. – 5mf – 9 – $7.50 – LLMC 97-005 – us L.L.M.C. [327]

CRIMINAL DEFENSE – (Available in reel only) – University of Houston. v1-11. 1973-84 (all publ) – 5,6 – $97.00 set – us Hein [340]

CRIMINAL DOCKET / Huron County. Ohio. Probate Court – 1853-1874 – 1r – 1 – $32.50r – us Archival [324]

CRIMINAL DOCKET / Lucas County, Ohio. Waterville Township. Justice of the Peace – (Some issues missing) – 1852-1876 – 1r – 1 – $32.50r – us Archival [324]

CRIMINAL DOCKETS / Fulton County. Ohio. Swan Creek Township. Justice of the Peace – 1881-1896 – 1r – 1 – $32.50r – us Archival [324]

CRIMINAL DOCKETS / Fulton County. Ohio. Swanton, Village. Mayor's Court – 1953-1969 – 8r – 1 – $32.50r – us Archival [324]

CRIMINAL DOCKETS / Ottawa County. Ohio. Carroll Township. Justice of the Peace – 1873-1934 – 1r – 1 – $32.50r – us Archival [324]

CRIMINAL DOCKETS / Seneca County. Ohio. Liberty Township. Justice of the Peace – 1857-1879 – 1r – 1 – $32.50r – us Archival [324]

CRIMINAL DOCKETS (INDEXED) / Ottawa County. Ohio. Carroll Township. Justice of the Peace – 1852-1876 – 1r – 1 – $32.50r – us Archival [324]

CRIMINAL FORMS FOR THE STATE OF INDIANA, COMPLETE UNDER THE CRIMINAL STATUTES OF THE STATE DOWN TO 1903 / Horner, Francis Asbury – 2d ed. Rochester: Lawyers' Co-Operative Publishing Co., 1903. 530p. LL-968 – 1 – us L of C Photodup [340]

CRIMINAL JOURNALS / Allen County. Ohio. Probate Court – 1865-1921 – 2r – 1 – $32.50r – us Archival [324]

CRIMINAL JOURNALS / Putnam County. Ohio. Probate Court – 1853-1915 – 1r – 1 – $32.50r – us Archival [324]

CRIMINAL JUSTICE – v1- 1973- 1; v4- 1976- 5,6,9 – us UMI [340]

CRIMINAL JUSTICE (ABA) – v1-10. 1986-96 – 9 – $114.00 set – us Hein [340]

CRIMINAL JUSTICE / ABA STANDARDS / MILITARY PRACTICE : REPORT OF THE AD HOC COMMITTEE, COMPARATIVE ANALYSIS OF THE ABA STANDARDS FOR THE ADMINISTRATION OF CRIMINAL JUSTICE AND MILITARY PRACTICE AND PROCEDURE – n.p. Sep 1976? – 7mf – 9 – $10.50 – LLMC 97-010 – us L.L.M.C. [340]

CRIMINAL JUSTICE ABSTRACTS – (v1-16 1968-84 on reel $332.00. v17-27 1985-95 on mf $455.00. Title varies: v2-8 1970-76 as Crime and Delinquency Literature) – v1-27. 1968-95 – 5,6,9 – $787.00 set – us Hein [340]

CRIMINAL JUSTICE AND BEHAVIOR – (v1-11 1974-84 on reel $183.00. v12-22 1985-95 on mf $369.00) – v1-22. 1974-95 – 5,6,9 – $552.00 set – us Hein [360]

CRIMINAL JUSTICE ETHICS – v1-. 1982- – 1,5,6,9 – us UMI [073]

CRIMINAL JUSTICE JOURNAL – (Cont as: San Diego Justice Journal. v1-7 1976-84 in reel $80.00. v8-14 1985-92 in mf $115.00) – Western State University. v1-14. 1976-92 – 5,6,9 – $195.00 set – us Hein [340]

CRIMINAL JUSTICE JOURNAL *see* SAN DIEGO JUSTICE JOURNAL

CRIMINAL JUSTICE NEWSLETTER – v1- 1970- 1; v7- 6; v7- 1976- 9 – us UMI [340]

CRIMINAL JUSTICE PERIODICAL INDEX – (1987- . 5,6,9) – v1- . 1975- – 1 – us UMI [340]

CRIMINAL JUSTICE: SOLUTIONS TO CONTEMPORARY MANAGEMENT PROBLEMS – v1-. 1982- – 1,5,6,9 – us UMI [650]

THE CRIMINAL LAW AND SEXUAL OFFENDERS; A REPORT / British Medical Association. Joint Committee on Psychiatry and the Law – London: British Medical Association 1954. 24p. LL-2257 – 1 – us L of C Photodup [340]

THE CRIMINAL LAW, INCLUDING THE FEDERAL PENAL CODE. / Grigsby, James Edward – Chicago: Smith, 1922. 1440p. LL-552 – 1 – us L of C Photodup [340]

THE CRIMINAL LAW MAGAZINE – Jersey City: F D Linn & Co. v1-18. 1880-96 + index 1880-94 (all publ) – 65mf – 9 – $292.00 – LLMC 82-917 – us L.L.M.C. [073]

CRIMINAL LAW MAGAZINE AND REPORTER – Jersey City. v1-18. 1880-96 – 1 – $240.00 – us Hein [073]

CRIMINAL LAW MONTHLY – (1985-. 5,6,9) – v1-. 1981- – 1 – us UMI [340]

CRIMINAL LAW QUARTERLY *see* AMERICAN CRIMINAL LAW REVIEW

CRIMINAL LAW REPORTS : BEING REPORTS OF CASES DETERMINED IN THE FEDERAL AND STATE COURTS OF TH UNITED STATES, AND IN THE COURTS OF ENGLAND, IRELAND, CANADA, ETC / Green, Nicholas John – New York: Hurd and Houghton, 1874-75. 2v. LL-329 – 1 – us L of C Photodup [340]

CRIMINAL PLEADING AND PRACTICE. / Bassett, James – 2d ed. Chicago, 1885. 563p. LL-1468 – 1 – us L of C Photodup [340]

CRIMINAL PLEADING AND PRACTICE. / Bassett, James – Chicago, Myers, 1870. 248 p. LL-1469 – 1 – us L of C Photodup [340]

CRIMINAL PROCEDURE OF UNITED STATES COURTS / Roe, Edward Thomas – Chicago: Callaghan, 1887. 274p. LL-1492 – 1 – us L of C Photodup [340]

CRIMINAL RECORDS / Fulton County. Ohio. Probate Court – 1867-1931 – 1r – 1 – $32.50r – us Archival [324]

CRIMINAL RECORDS / Huron County. Ohio. Probate Court – 1895-1928 – 1r – 1 – $32.50r – us Archival [324]

CRIMINAL STATISTICS, ENGLAND AND WALES : STATISTICS RELATING TO CRIME AND CRIMINAL PROCEEDINGS 1926-1977 – (Coll title: British Government Publications...1801-1977, Crime) – 129mf – 9 (£1,035.00 crime set of 164mf) – uk Chadwyck [360]

CRIMINAL STATISTICS, SCOTLAND : STATISTICS RELATING TO POLICE APPREHENSIONS AND CRIMINAL PROCEEDINGS 1938-1977 – (Coll title: British Government Publications....1801-1977, Crime) – 35mf – 9 (£1,035.00 crime set of 164mf) – uk Chadwyck [360]

CRIMINALES DE GUERRA / Federacion Estudiantil Universitaria – La Habana, 1945. Fiche W 820. (Blodgett Collection of Spanish Civil War Pamphlets) – 9 – us H.U. College Libr [946]

LOS CRIMINES DEL CACIQUISMO. LA TRAGEDIA DE EL POBO. DEFENSA DEL MEDICO... / Albinana Sanz, J – Madrid, 1916 – 2mf – 9 – sp Cultura [360]

CRIMINOLOGY AND LAW ENFORCEMENT – 1947-52. Continued by yPolice Chief – 1,5,6,9 – us UMI [360]

THE CRINOIDEA FLEXIBILIA / Springer, F – Z 315 2. 2 v. 1920 – 8 – ne IDC [590]

Crippen, T G *see* A POPULAR INTRODUCTION TO THE HISTORY OF CHRISTIAN DOCTRINE

CRIPPLE CREEK MAIL – Pueblo. Colo. 1895-1898 – 1 – us UMI [071]

CRIPPS THE CARRIER / Blackmore, Richard Doddridge – British Fiction Archive: Unit 3 – 9 – uk Bell [830]

CRIPPS, THE CARRIER : A WOODLAND TALE / Blackmore, Richard Doddridge – London: Sampson Low, Marston, Searle & Rivington, 1876 – 1 roll – 1 – 1-55879-219-8 – uk Libr Preservation [830]

CRIS PROGRESS REPORT / Mississippi State University. Agricultural Experiment Station – 1970-82 – 1,5 – us Spaulding [630]

CRISANA – Oradea, Romania. 1962-Jun 1980; Apr-Oct 1981; 1984-90 – 36r – 1 – us L of C Photodup [949]

Criscuolo, E *see* LA SOVRANITA DEGLI STATI SULLE ACQUE

LA CRISE DE LA MAIN D'OEUVRE AGRICOLE EN FRANCE / Souchon, Auguste – Paris. 1914. (La Condition Ouvriere. Part Two.) – 9 – 15.00 – fr Bibl Nationale [360]

LA CRISE DE L'INDUSTRIE LINIERE ET LA CONCURRENCE VICTORIEUSE DE L'INDUSTRIE COTONNIERE / Aftalion, Albert – Paris. 1904. (La Condition Ouvriere. Part Two.) – 9 – 5.00 – fr Bibl Nationale [360]

LA CRISE DU CLERGE / Houtin, Albert – (Includes bibliographical references and index) – Paris: Librairie E Nourry, 1907 – 1mf – 9 – 0-8370-8828-3 – 1986-2828 – us A.T.L.A. [240]

LA CRISE DU PARTI SOCIALISTE ET L'AVENEMENT DE GUY MOLLET (1944-1946) / Jaffre, J – F120.00 – fr Ethnologie [335]

LA CRISE DU REGIME PARLEMENTAIRE / Celles, Alfred Duclos de – (s.l., s.n.), 1887. (Montreal: Imprimerie generale). 02692. (Pre-1900 Canadiana) – 9 – cn C.I.H.M. [971]

LA CRISE MILITAIRE FRANCAISE 1945-1962 : ASPECTS SOCIOLOGIQUES ET IDEOLOGIQUES / Girardet, R – 1964 – F60.00 – fr Ethnologie [320]

LA CRISE MONTANISTE / Labriolle, Pierre de – Paris: E. Leroux, 1913 ([Bibliotheque de la Fondation Thiers; 31]) – 2mf – us A.T.L.A. [240]

UNE CRISE PAYSANNE DANS LE NORD-CAMEROUN : LE CAS DES FULBE (PEULS) / Nassourou, S – 1984 – F90.00 – fr Ethnologie [339]

LA CRISE POLITIQUE DE QUEBEC – Notes et precedents, Quebec, septembre 1879. Quebec: s.n., 1879?. 02264. (Pre-1900 Canadiana) – 9 – cn C.I.H.M. [971]

LA CRISE RELIGIEUSE DU 16E SIECLE (16) – Paris, 1950 – Dfl42.00 – ne Slangenburg [240]

LA CRISE RELIGIEUSE EN HOLLANDE : SOUVENIRS ET IMPRESSIONS / Saussaye, Chantepie de la – Leyde: De Breuk & Smits, 1860 – 1mf – us A.T.L.A. [240]

LA CRISE REVOLUTIONNAIRE, 1789-1846 (20) – Paris, 1951 – Dfl49.00 – ne Slangenburg [240]

LES CRISES PERIODIQUES DE SURPRODUCTION / Aftalion, Albert – Paris. 1913. (La Condition Ouvriere. Part Two.) – 9 – 22.50 – fr Bibl Nationale [360]

CRISIS – v1- 1910- 1; v83- 5,6; v84- 9 – us UMI [321]

CRISIS – (Excerpted articles from this Democratic newspaper, relating to the activities of Clement L Vallandigham and the Peace Democrats during the American Civil War) – Columbus, OH. jan, 1864-jan, 1865 – 1 – us Western Res [071]

CRISIS : A RECORD OF THE DARKER RACES / National Association for the Advancement of Colored People – v1-93. 1910-1986 – 26r – 1 – us Ross [360]

CRISIS! : A RECORD OF THE DARKER RACES / National Association for the Advancement of Colored People – 1-47. 1910-1940 – 173mf – 9 – $360.00 – us UPA [360]

THE CRISIS – New York. Nov 1910-1963 – 1 – us NY Public [073]

CRISIS AND NATIONAL CO-OPERATIVE TRADES UNION GAZETTE – Robert Owen. 1-4 2+20 (all publ). 1832-1834 – 11mf – 9 – $65.00 – us UPA [331]

LA CRISIS ARGENTINA / Bermann, Gregorio – [Buenos Aires?]: Editorial Proceso, [1965?] – 1 – CSUXADJ2694-B – us Hoover Inst Photo [360]

LA CRISIS ARGENTINA : COMO PODRIA RESOLVERSE / Carril, Bonifacio del – Buenos Aires: Emece, [1960] – 1 – CSUXAJA7152-B – us Hoover Inst Photo [360]

CRISIS CHRISTOLOGY – v1-5. 1943-48 (complete) – Inquire – 1 – ATLA 1993-S516 – us A.T.L.A. [073]

CRISIS DE LA CIVILIZACION. LA GUERRA EUROPEA / Trigo, Felipe – Madrid: Renacimiento, 1915 – sp Bibl Santa Ana [946]

CRISIS ESPIRITUAL DE UNAMUNO Y SU EVASION A EXTREMADURA / Sanchez Morales, Narciso – Badajoz: Imp. Diputacion Prov., 1970 – sp Bibl Santa Ana [240]

CRISIS HISTORICA DE LA CIUDAD DE BADAJOZ / Morales, Ascencio – Badajoz: Tip.y Libr. de A.Arqueros, 1908 – 1 – sp Bibl Santa Ana [360]

CRISIS HUPFELDIANA : BEING AN EXAMINATION OF HUPFELD'S CRITICISM ON GENESIS: AS RECENTLY SET FORTH IN BISHOP COLENSO'S FIFTH PART / Kay, William – (Includes appendixes) – Oxford: John Henry and James Parker, 1865 – 1mf – 9 – 0-8370-3855-3 – 1985-1855 – us A.T.L.A. [220]

THE CRISIS IN MORALS : AN EXAMINATION OF RATIONAL ETHICS IN THE LIGHT OF MODERN SCIENCE / Bixby, James Thompson – (Includes bibliographical references) – Boston: Roberts, 1891 – 1mf – 9 – 0-8370-7123-2 – 1986-1123 – us A.T.L.A. [170]

CRISIS IN PANAMA AND THE DOMINICAN REPUBLIC : NATIONAL SECURITY FILES AND NSC HISTORIES (1963-1969) / Johnson, Lyndon B – (With printed guide) – 1982 – 1 – $810.00 – 0-89093-389-8 – us UPA [972]

CRISIS IN THE CLASSROOM / Dubose, Martha – 1971, 2p – 9 – 1.00f – at Libertarian Micro [370]

CRISIS INTERVENTION AND TIME-LIMITED TREATMENT / ed by Roberts, Albert R – 9,5,1 – us Harwood [150]

CRISIS MATRIMONIALES / Perez Lozano, Jose Maria – Madrid: Edita PPC, S.A., 1965 – 1 – sp Bibl Santa Ana [306]

THE CRISIS OF MISSIONS : OR, THE VOICE OUT OF THE CLOUD / Pierson, Arthur Tappan – (Includes index) – New York: Fleming H Revell, c1886 – 1mf – 9 – 0-8370-6598-4 – 1986-0598 – us A.T.L.A. [230]

CRISIS ON THE HIGH PLAINS: A STUDY OF AMARILLO BAPTISTS, 1920 TO 1940 / Hickman, James Thomas – 1981 – 1 – 7.60 – us Baptist [240]

LA CRISIS POLITICA ARGENTINA : ENSAYO DE INTERPRETACION IDEOLOGICA / Frondizi, Silvio – Buenos Aires: [Ediciones A.D.I.], 1946 – 1 – CSUXAJB7859-B – us Hoover Inst Photo [320]

CRISIS Y PROTESTA SOCIAL CORDOBA, MAYO 1969 / Delich, Francisco Jose – Buenos Aires: Ediciones Signos, 1st ed 1970 – 1 – CSUXADP3953-B – us Hoover Inst Photo [360]

EL CRISOL – Madrid, Spain. -d. 4 April 1931-6 Jan 1932. 3 reels – 1 – uk British Libr Newspaper [072]

CRISOL DE LA VERDAD ILUSTRADO CON DIVINAS Y HUMANAS LETRAS, PADRES Y DOCTORES... : REPUESTO AL AUTO DEL MOTOMEDICATIO / Aldrete y Soto, L – Madrid, 1683 – 3mf – 9 – sp Cultura [610]
Crisp, William *see* THE BECHUANA OF SOUTH AFRICA
Crispolti, C *see* PERUGIA AUGUSTA DESCRITTA
CRISS-CROSS ART COMMUNICATIONS – n.3-1976- 1; n.6- 5,6,9 – us UMI [700]
CRISS-CROSS COMMUNICATIONS – (See also: Criss-Cross Art Communications) – n. 1-2. 1974-1975 – 1 – us UMI [700]
Crist, L M *see* HISTORY OF BOONE COUNTY
CRISTAL – Caceres, 1935 y 1936 – 5 – sp Bibl Santa Ana [073]
Cristia, Pedro Jet al *see* ARGENTINA EN LA POST GUERRA
IL CRISTIANESIMO IN EGITTO / Naldini, M – Firenze, 1968 – 9mf – 8 – Dfl32.00 – ne Slangenburg [240]
CRISTIANISMO Y SOCIEDAD – Montivideo: Iglesia y Sociedad en America Latina. v1 n1-v29 n110. 1963-1991 – 6r – us Res Libr [972]
CRISTIANOS CADA DIA / Perez Lozano, Jose Maria – Madrid: Propaganda Popular Catolica, 1962 – 1 – sp Bibl Santa Ana [240]
EL CRISTO DE LA REJA / Casquete, Antonio – Sevilla: Imp. Alvarez Gonzalez, 1924 – 1 – sp Bibl Santa Ana [240]
CRISTO REY EN MEXICO – Leon, Gto, Mexico: Centro General de Propaganda del Monumento Votivo Nacional a Cristo Rey de La Paz. v1-30 n1-4. 1953-jan/feb, mar/apr 1983 – 15r – us Res Libr [972]
CRISTOBAL COLON / Bayle, Constantino & Poch Noguer, Jose – Madrid: Razon y Fe, 1944 – 1 – sp Bibl Santa Ana [910]
CRISTOBAL COLON / Justiniano Arribas, Juan – 1897 – 9 – 1.50f – sp Bibl Santa Ana [910]
CRISTOBAL COLON Y EL DESCUBRIMIENTO DE AMERICA. 2 VOL. BARCELONA, 1945 / Ballesteros Beretta, Antonio – Madrid: Razon y Fe, 1946 – 1 – sp Bibl Santa Ana [910]
CRISTOBAL DE SAN ANTONIO, OFM...EN NOTAS BIBLIOGRAFIA FRANCISCANA / Castro, Manuel – Madrid: Graf. Calleja, 1969 – 1 – sp Bibl Santa Ana [240]
CRISTOFORO COLOMBO – New York. Jan 6-June 1891; Jan-Dec 1892; July-Dec 1893; July-Dec 1894 – 1 – us NY Public [073]
CRISTOFORO COLOMBO – New York. v4-6.1891-93 – 3r – 1 – us Ross [071]
LES CRITERES THEOLOGIQUES = CRITERI TEOLOGICI : OUVRAGE TRADUIT DE L'ITALIEN PAR UN PRETRE DE L'ORATOIRE DE RENNES SUR LA SECONDE EDITION REVUE ET AMELIOREE PAR L'AUTEUR / Bartolo, Salvatore di – (Includes bibliographical references and index) – Paris: Berche et Tralin, 1889 – 1mf – 9 – 0-8370-8418-0 – 1986-2418 – us A.T.L.A. [230]
CRITERIA OF DIVERSE KINDS OF TRUTH AS OPPOSED TO AGNOSTICISM.. / McCosh, James – 1882 – 1 – us A.T.L.A. [210]
CRITERIO – Buenos Aires. v.1-27. nos. 1-1225. March 8, 1928-December 23, 1954 – 1 – 420.00 – us L of C Photodup [073]
CRITERION – v1-23. 1962-84 (complete) – 2r – 1 – ATLA S0362 – us A.T.L.A. [240]
THE CRITERION – London. v1-18. 1922-39 – 5r – 1 – us Ross [073]
THE CRITERION – Toronto: J W Treen, [1885-18–?] – 9 – cn C.I.H.M. [072]
THE CRITERION: A QUARTERLY REVIEW – London. v. 1-18. Oct 1922-Jan 1939 – 1 – us NY Public [073]
CRITERIUM – Jogjakarta, Perguruan Tingga Agama Islam Negeri. 1954-58(8). TE 191. Lacking: 1955(4-?); 1956-57; 1958(2-7). BSE-478 1 – 9 – ne IDC [290]
CRITIC – 1- 1942- 1; v30- 5,6; v35- 9 – us UMI [073]
CRITIC – Allentown. Pa. 1883-1884; 1888-1894 – 1 – us UMI [071]
CRITIC – Johannesburg. South Africa. 1890-96 – 1 – sa State Libr [072]
CRITIC – Manila. 18 Oct 1934-. v1,no1-. Manila: M. de Gracia Concepcion, 1934- – 1 – us U.W. Library [073]
CRITIC *see*
- DAILY CRITIC
- THE WASP

THE CRITIC – (Filmed with: Daily Critic (Washington DC) jan-oct 16 1872) – Washington, DC: [The Critic], 1868-72 – 1r – 1 – us Res Libr [073]
THE CRITIC – Halifax, Canada. Canadian Colliery Guardian. -w. 27 April 1888-10 Jan 1896. 6 reels – 1 – uk British Libr Newspaper [072]
THE CRITIC – Halifax, NS: Critic Pub. Co, [1884-1894] – 9 – cn C.I.H.M. [420]
THE CRITIC – (Merger of: Pulpit Criticism; Merger of: Medical Criticism) – Toronto: [s.n., 1883-18– or 19–] – 9 – cn C.I.H.M. [072]
THE CRITIC – Wynberg. v1-5 n5. sep 1932-1939 – 1 – us Res Libr [073]
THE CRITIC *see*
- MEDICAL CRITICISM
- PULPIT CRITICISM

CRITICA – Rio de Janeiro, 24 Nov 1928-24 Oct 1930 – 1,5,6 – bl Biblioteca [072]
CRITICA DE LAS BASES TEORICAS DE LA TERAPIA FAMILIAR DE M. SELVINI / Carreras Gargallo, Alberto – 3mf – 9 – Pta2,000.00 – 84-85422-50-3 – sp Pentalfa [240]
CRITICA FASCISTA – Rome. v. 1-21. June 1923-July 15 1943 – 1 – us NY Public [073]
CRITICA LITERARIA. ENSAYO SOBRE EL CATOLICISMO...POR D. JUAN DONOSO – 1851 – 9 – $1.50f – sp Bibl Santa Ana [240]
CRITICA MUSICA / Mattheson, J – 2v. 1722-25 – 9 – us Sibley [780]
CRITICA MUSICA, D.I. GRUNDRICHTIGE UNTERSUCHUNG UND BEURTHEILUNG / Mattheson, J – P 718. 2 v. 1722-1725 – 9 – ne IDC [780]
LA CRITICA MUSICALE – v. 1-6. 1918-23 – 1 – 19.00 – us L of C Photodup [780]
CRITICA NEGATIVA / Coronado, Nicolas – Buenos Aires: "Buenos Aires" Cooperative Editorial, 1923 – 1 – us U.W. Library [440]
CRITICA SACRA / Cappel, L; ed by Cappel, J – Lutetiae Parisiorum, 1650 – 21mf – 8 – ne Slangenburg [220]
CRITICA Y COMPENDIO ESPECULATIVO-PRACTICO DE LA ARQUITECTURA CIVIL... / Losada, M – Madrid, 1740 – 11mf – 9 – sp Cultura [624]
A CRITICAL AND DOCTRINAL COMMENTARY UPON... PAUL TO THE ROMANS / Shedd, William Greenough Thayer – New York: Charles Scribner, 1879. 2 fiches – 9 – us A.T.L.A. [240]
A CRITICAL AND EXEGETICAL COMMENTARY ON DEUTERONOMY / Driver, Samuel Rolles – New York: Charles Scribner, 1895. 1 fiche – 9 – us A.T.L.A. [240]
A CRITICAL AND EXEGETICAL COMMENTARY ON THE BOOK OF ECCLESIASTES / Barton, George Aaron – New York: Scribner, 1908. xiv,212p. (The International Critical Commentary on the Holy Scriptures of the Old and New Testaments 17) – 1 – us U.W. Library [240]
A CRITICAL AND EXEGETICAL COMMENTARY ON THE BOOK OF ESTHER / Paton, Lewis Bayles – New York: C. Scribner's Sons, 1908. xvii,339p – 1 – us U.W. Library [220]
A CRITICAL AND EXEGETICAL COMMENTARY ON THE BOOK OF ESTHER / Paton, Lewis Bayles – New York: Charles Scribner, 1908. xvii,339p. 1 fiche – 9 – us A.T.L.A. [220]
A CRITICAL AND EXEGETICAL COMMENTARY ON THE BOOK OF EXODUS / Murphy, James Gracey – 1868 – 9 – $12.00 – us I.R.C. [220]
A CRITICAL AND EXEGETICAL COMMENTARY ON THE BOOK OF EXODUS / Murphy, James Gracey – Andover: Warren F. Draper, 1881.1 fiche – 9 – us A.T.L.A. [240]
A CRITICAL AND EXEGETICAL COMMENTARY ON THE BOOK OF LEVITICUS / Murphy, James Gracey – Andover: Warren F. Draper, 1874.1 fiche – 9 – us A.T.L.A. [240]
A CRITICAL AND EXEGETICAL COMMENTARY ON THE EPISTLES OF ST PETER AND ST JUDE / Bigg, Charles – Edinburgh: T. & T. Clark, 1902. xv,353p. 1 fiche – 9 – us A.T.L.A. [240]
CRITICAL AND EXEGETICAL COMMENTARY ON THE EPISTLES TO THE EPHESIANS AND... COLOSSIANS / Abbott, Thomas Kingsmill – New York: Scribner's, 1897. 1 fiche – 9 – us A.T.L.A. [240]

CRITICAL AND EXEGETICAL COMMENTARY ON THE GOSPEL ACCORDING TO ST MARK / Gould, Ezra P – New York: Charles Scribner, 1907. 1 fiche – 9 – us A.T.L.A. [240]
A CRITICAL AND EXEGETICAL COMMENTARY ON...PHILIPPIANS AND...PHILEMON / Vincent, Marvin Richardson – New York: Charles Scribner, 1897. 1 fiche. 8370-5639-X – 9 – us A.T.L.A. [240]
CRITICAL AND EXEGETICAL HANDBOOK TO THE GENERAL EPISTLES OF PETER AND JUDE / Huther, Johann Eduard – Edinburgh: T. & T. Clark, 1893. vi,440p. 2 fiches – 9 – us A.T.L.A. [240]
CRITICAL AND EXEGETICAL HANDBOOK TO...EPISTLES OF ST PAUL TO... THESSALONIANS / Luenemann, Gottlieb – Edinburgh: T. & T. Clark, 1880. 1 fiche – 9 – us A.T.L.A. [240]
A CRITICAL AND EXIGETICAL COMMENTARY ON THE BOOK OF DANIEL / Charles, R H – 1929 – 9 – $18.00 – us I.R.C. [220]
CRITICAL AND GRAMMATICAL COMMENTARY ON ST PAUL'S EPISTLE TO THE EPHESIANS / Ellicott, Charles J – Andover: Warren F Draper, 1865.1 fiche – 9 – us A.T.L.A. [240]
CRITICAL AND HISTORICAL ESSAYS CONTRIBUTED TO THE EDINBURGH REVIEW / Macaulay, Thomas Babington; ed by Montague, FC – London: Methuen and Co., 1903 – 3 rolls – 1 – 1-55879-246-5 – uk Libr Preservation [900]
A CRITICAL AND HISTORICAL INTRODUCTION TO THE CANONICAL SCRIPTURES OF THE OLD TESTAMENT / De Wette, Wilhelm Martin Leberecht – 2v. 1859 – 9 – us A.T.L.A. [240]
A CRITICAL AND PHILOSOPHICAL ENQUIRY INTO THE CAUSES OF PRODIGIES AND MIRACLES, AS RELATED BY HISTORIANS / Warburton, William – London: T. Corbett, 1727 – xxii/137p – 1 – us U.W. Library [190]
CRITICAL CARE CLINICS – v1-. Mar 1985- – 1,5,6,9 – us UMI [617]
CRITICAL CARE MEDICINE – (Also available on CD-ROM: 1984-88 $395.00) – v1-24. 1973-96 – 24r – 1,5,6,9 – $110.00r – us Williams [610]
A CRITICAL COMMENTARY ON THE BOOK OF DANIEL...FOR STUDENTS OF THE ENGLISH BIBLE / Prince, John Dyneley – Leipzig: J.C. Hinrichs, 1899. 1 fiche – 9 – us A.T.L.A. [240]
CRITICAL DIGEST – (v24-36, no.12. Apr 1972-84. 5,6. v27-36, no.12. Apr 1975-84. 9) – v2-36, no.12. Oct 1949-1984. v1 never published – 1 – us UMI [410]
CRITICAL DIGEST, NYC AND LONDON THEATRE – v36, no.13-. 1 Oct 1984- – 1,5,6,9 – us UMI [790]
CRITICAL ENQUIRIES INTO THE VARIOUS EDITIONS OF THE BIBLE / Simon, Richard – 1684 – 1 – $50.00 – us Presbyterian [240]
A CRITICAL ESSAY ON OILPAINTING; PROVING THAT THE ART OF PAINTING IN OIL WAS KNOWN BEFORE THE PRETENDED DISCOVERY OF JOHN AND HUBERT VAN EYCK / Raspe, R E – O 1177 1. 1781 – 9 – ne IDC [750]
A CRITICAL ESSAY ON THE GOSPEL OF ST LUKE / Schleiermacher, Friedrich – Trans. by Connop Thirlwall. 1825 – 9 – us A.T.L.A. [240]
CRITICAL ESSAYS ON THE PERFORMERS OF THE LONDON THEATRES, INCLUDING GENERAL OBSERVATIONS ON THE PRACTISE AND GENIUS OF THE STAGE / Hunt, Leigh – London: Printed by and for John Hunt, 1807 – 1 roll – 1 – 1-55879-445-X – uk Libr Preservation [790]
CRITICAL EXAMINATION OF SOME PASSAGES IN GENESIS 1 / Stuart, Moses – The Biblical Repository and Quarterly Observer, v7,no21, Jan 1836 – p46-106 – 9 – us A.T.L.A. [240]
A CRITICAL EXAMINATION OF...EVIDENCES FOR THE DOCTRINE OF THE VIRGIN BIRTH / Thorburn, Thomas James – London: S.P.C.K., 1908. 1 fiche – 9 – us A.T.L.A. [240]
CRITICAL EXAMINATION OF...THE TIME OF OUR SAVIOUR'S CRUCIFIXION / Aldrich, Jeremiah K – London: Rand, Avery, 1882. 1 fiche – 9 – us A.T.L.A. [240]

A CRITICAL EXPOSITION OF THE THIRD CHAPTER OF ST PAUL'S EPISTLE TO THE ROMANS / Morison, James C – London: Hamilton, Adams, 1866. 1 fiche – 9 – us A.T.L.A. [240]
CRITICAL, HISTORICAL, AND MISCELLANEOUS ESSAYS AND POEMS / Macaulay, Thomas Babington – Boston. 3v. 1884 – 1r – 1 – us Ross [080]
A CRITICAL HISTORY AND DEFENCE OF THE OLD TESTAMENT CANON / Stuart, Moses – 1845 – 9 – us A.T.L.A. [240]
CRITICAL HISTORY AND DEFENCE OF THE OLD TESTAMENT CANON / Stuart, Moses – (Includes appendix of ancient documents) – rev ed. Andover:Warren F Draper, 1872 – 1mf – 9 – 0-8370-5460-5 – 1985-3460 – us A.T.L.A. [220]
A CRITICAL HISTORY OF FREE THOUGHT IN REFERENCE TO THE CHRISTIAN RELIGION / Farrar, Adam Storey – London: J. Murray, 1862 – 2mf – us A.T.L.A. [240]
A CRITICAL HISTORY OF THE DOCTRINE OF A FUTURE LIFE IN ISRAEL, IN JUDAISM AND IN CHRISTIANITY / Charles, R H – London, 1899 – 8mf – 8 – ne Slangenburg [270]
A CRITICAL HISTORY OF THE EVOLUTION OF TRINITARIANISM AND ITS OUTCOME IN THE NEW CHRISTOLOGY / Paine, Levi Leonard – (Includes bibliographical references and index) – Boston: Houghton, Mifflin, 1900 – 1mf – 9 – 0-8370-3952-5 – 1985-1952 – us A.T.L.A. [240]
CRITICAL KIT-KATS / Gosse, Edmund – London: William Heinemann, 1896 – 1r – 1 – 1-55879-829-3 – uk Libr Preservation [420]
A CRITICAL LATIN GRAMMAR / Coleridge, John – 1772. 191p. (English Linguistics Series 1500-1800) – 9 – us UMI [450]
CRITICAL MISCELLANIES / Morley, John – London, New York: Macmillan and Co., 1886-1908 – 2 rolls – 1 – 1-55879-209-0 – uk Libr Preservation [420]
CRITICAL NOTES ON OLD TESTAMENT HISTORY : THE TRADITIONS OF SAUL AND DAVID / Cook, Stanley Arthur – (Includes index) – London; New York:Macmillan, 1907 – 1mf – 9 – 0-8370-2732-2 – 1985-0732 – us A.T.L.A. [220]
CRITICAL NOTES ON THE NEW TESTAMENT: SUPPLEMENTARY TO...GRAMMAR OF THE NEW TESTAMENT DIALECT / Green, Thomas S – London: Samuel Bagster, 1867 – 9 – us A.T.L.A. [240]
A CRITICAL PRONOUNCING DICTIONARY AND EXPOSITOR OF THE ENGLISH LANGUAGE / Walker, John – 1791. 581p. (English Linguistics Series 1500-1800) – 9 – us UMI [420]
CRITICAL QUARTERLY – (1985-. 5,6,9) – v1-. 1959- – 1 – us UMI [410]
CRITICAL REMARKS ON DR. TREGELLES' GREEK TEXT OF THE REVELATION / Tomlin, Jacob – Liverpool: Arthur Newling, 1865.1 fiche – 9 – us A.T.L.A. [240]
CRITICAL REMARKS ON THE HEBREW SCRIPTURES, CORRESPONDING WITH A NEW TRANSLATION OF THE BIBLE / Geddes, Alexander – v. 1, Continuing Remarks on the Pentateuch. 1800 – 9 – us A.T.L.A. [220]
A CRITICAL REVIEW OF CHU CHIH SIN'S "WHAT THING IS JESUS" (CCC11) = KUAN YU CHU CHIH YEH SU SHI NO TUNG SI TI TSA P'ING / Chang, I-Ching – (In Chinese) – Shanghai: China Baptist Publication Society, 1930 – 1r – 1 – 0-8370-1711-4 – 1984-608-5 – us A.T.L.A. [240]
CRITICAL REVIEW; OR ANNALS OF LITERATURE – London. v. 1-24. (3 Ser.); 1-6. (4 Ser.); 1-5. (5 Ser.). 1804-Jun 1817 – 1 – us NY Public [073]
THE CRITICAL SPELLING-BOOK / Lowe, Solomon – 1755. 214p. (English Linguistics Series 1500-1800) – 9 – us UMI [420]
CRITICAL STUDIES / Ouida – British Fiction Archive: Unit 3 – 9 – uk Bell [830]
CRITICAL STUDIES IN MASS COMMUNICATION – v1-. 1984- – 1,5,6,9 – us UMI [073]
CRITICAL STUDIES IN THE PHONETIC OBSERVATIONS OF INDIAN GRAMMARIANS / Varma, S – 1929 – 1 – uk Microform Academic [400]
A CRITICAL STUDY OF CURRENT THEORIES OF MORAL EDUCATION / Hart, Joseph Kinmont – Chicago: University of Chicago Press, 1910 – 1mf – 9 – 0-8370-8677-9 – 1986-2677 – us A.T.L.A. [370]

A CRITICAL STUDY OF THE FIRST FOUR CHAPTERS OF RETHINKING MISSIONS (CCC77) = PING HSUAN CHIAO SHIH YEH PING I CHIEN SSU CHANG / Chao, Tzu-chen – (In Chinese) – Yenching: Yenching University School of Religion, 1934 – 1r – 1 – 1984-6416 – us A.T.L.A. [240]

A CRITICAL STUDY OF THE HISTORICAL METHOD OF SAMUEL RAWSON GARDINER : WITH AN EXCURSUS ON THE HISTORICAL CONCEPTION OF THE PURITAN REVOLUTION FROM CLARENDON TO GARDINER / Usher, Roland G – [St. Louis?: Washington University?, 1915?] – 1mf – us A.T.L.A. [240]

CRITICI SACRI LIBRI 4 / Rivetus, Andr. – Ed. 4a. Genevae, 1642 – 11mf – 8 – ne Slangenburg [220]

CRITICISM – v1- 1959- 1; v13- 5,6; v17- 9 – us UMI [420]

A CRITICISM OF SYSTEMS OF HEBREW METRE : AN ELEMENTARY TREATISE / Cobb, William Henry – (Includes indexes) – Oxford: Clarendon Press, 1905 – 1mf – 9 – 0-8370-2694-6 – 1985-0694 – us A.T.L.A. [470]

THE CRITICISM OF THE FOURTH GOSPEL: EIGHT LECTURES / Sanday, William – New York: Charles Scribner, 1905. 1 fiche – 9 – us A.T.L.A. [240]

CRITICISM OF THE NEW TESTAMENT / Sanday, W., et al – London: John Murray, 1903. 1 fiche – 9 – us A.T.L.A. [240]

CRITICISMS OF THE NEUMARK TREATMENT OF THE AGRICULTURAL SECTOR IN ESTIMATING THE NATIONAL INCOME OF INDONESIA / Tan, An Djien – SE 5462 1. 1951-52 – 9 – ne IDC [630]

CRITICISMS ON ART : AND SKETCHES OF THE PICTURE GALLERIES OF ENGLAND. WITH CATALOGUES OF THE PRINCIPAL GALLERIES, NOW FIRST COLLECTED / Hazlitt, William – London: John Templeman, 1843 – 1r – 1 – 1-55879-849-8 – uk Libr Preservation [700]

CRITICISMS ON ART : WITH CATALOGUES OF THE PRINCIPAL PICTURE GALLERIES OF ENGLAND, 2D SERIES / Hazlitt, William – London: C. Templeman, 1844 – 1r – 1 – 1-55879-319-4 – uk Libr Preservation [700]

CRITICISMS ON THE RECENT FINANCIAL POLICIES OF THE UNITED STATES AND FRANCE: INCLUDING AN ATTEMPT TO EXPLAIN THE CAUSE OF THE PRESENT PROSTRATE CONDITION OF THE SOUTHERN STATES / Baird, Henry Carey – Philadelphia: H. Baird & Co., 1875. 00804. (Pre-1900 Canadiana) – 9 – cn C.I.H.M. [336]

O CRITICO : E LITTERARIO, CRITICO E NOTICIOSO – Pilar, Alagoas. 9 Jun, 11 Ago 1889 – 1,5,6 – bl Biblioteca [072]

O CRITICO – Manaos, Amazonas. 24 Fev 1925 – 1,5,6 – bl Biblioteca [072]

CRITICS OF HENRY GEORGE / Andelson, Robert V – 1979. Cover sheet and contents listing only. 4p – 9 – 1.00f – at Libertarian Micro [320]

LA CRITIQUE – Paris. avr 1895-1913. mq 1907 – 1 – fr A.C.R.P.P. [073]

LA CRITIQUE DE KANT ET LA METAPHYSIQUE DE LEIBNIZ: HISTOIRE ET THEORIE DE LEURS RAPPORTS / Nolen, Desire – Paris: G. Bailliere, 1875. iv,472p. 5 fiches. (Philosophy Collection) – 9 – $12.00 – fr Bibl Nationale [110]

CRITIQUE GENERALE DES AVENTURES DE TELEMAQUE / Gueudeville, Nicolas – (Utopias in the Enlightenment series). 1700 – 9 – fr Hachette [190]

CRITIQUE HISTORIQUE DU N.T / Lagrange, Marie Joseph – 1937 – 5mf – 8 – ne Slangenburg [220]

LA CRITIQUE INTERNATIONALE – no. 1-13. Paris. 15 mai 1902-sept 1903. devenu: Anthologie. N.S., no. 1-12. oct 1903-sept 1904 – 1 – fr A.C.R.P.P. [073]

A CRITIQUE OF DESIGN-ARGUMENTS : A HISTORICAL REVIEW AND FREE EXAMINATION OF THE METHODS OF REASONING IN NATURAL THEOLOGY / Hicks, Lewis Ezra – (Includes index) – New York: Charles Scribner, 1883 – 1mf – 9 – 0-8370-3583-X – 1985-1583 – us A.T.L.A. [210]

A CRITIQUE OF KANT / Fischer, Kuno – Trans. from the German by W.S. Hough. London: Swan Sonnenschein, Lowrey & Co., 1888. 188p – 1 – us U.W. Library [190]

A CRITIQUE OF OBJECTIVISM / Kroy, Moshe – Also: Is Ayn Rand a Kantian and does not even know it? by John Zube. 2 fiches. (24X) – 9 – 1.00f – at Libertarian Micro [320]

A CRITIQUE ON THE ETYMOLOGY OF THE WESTMINSTER GRAMMAR / Lowe, Solomon – 1723-38. 66p. (English Linguistics Series 1500-1800) – 9 – us UMI [420]

LA CRITIQUE SOCIALE – Revue des idees et des livres. Sociologie, economie politique, histoire, philosophie, droit public, demographie puis pedagogie. Mouvement ouvrier. Lettres et arts. Paraissant six fois par an. Dir. Boris Souvarine. no. 1-11. Paris. mars 1931-mars 1934 – 1 – fr A.C.R.P.P. [073]

CRITIQUE TEXTUELLE DU N.T / Lagrange, Marie Joseph – 1935 – 12mf – 8 – ne Slangenburg [220]

DER CRITISCHE MUSICUS : ESTER [-ZWEITER] THEIL / ed by Scheibe, J A – Hamburg: Thomas von Wierings Erben, 1738 – 11mf – 9 – us Sibley [780]

DER CRITISCHE MUSICUS : ESTER [-ZWEITER] THEIL / Scheibe, Johann Adolph – Hamburg: Thomas von Wierings Erben, 1738 – 11mf – 9 – us Sibley [780]

DER CRITISCHE MUSICUS, HERAUSGEGEBEN VON JOHANN ADOLPH SCHEIBE / Scheibe, Johann Adolph – Erster-Zweeter Theil. 1738-40 – 9 – us Sibley [780]

CRITISCHER MUSIKUS / Scheibe, Johann Adolph – Neue, vermehrte und verbesserte auflage. 4 v. 1745 – 9 – us Sibley [780]

CRITISCHER MUSIKUS: NEUE, VERMEHRTE UND VERBESSERTE AUFLAGE / Scheibe, Johann Adolph – Leipzig. 1745. BP-757 1 – 9 – ne IDC [780]

Critolaus *see* GROWLS FROM UGANDA

THE CRITTENDEN COMMERCIAL ARITHMETIC AND BUSINESS MANUAL... / Groesbeck, John – Philadelphia: Eldredge & Bro, 1869 – 4mf – 9 – $6.00 – LLMC 96-064 – us L.L.M.C. [650]

CRITTENDEN COUNTY TIMES – West Memphis. Ark. -w. 1931-60 – 1 – us UMI [071]

Crittenden, John Jordan *see* PAPERS

Crivellati, Cesare *see* DISCORSI MUSICALI..

CRKVA U SVIJETU – Split. 4 no. per year – 1 – us U.W. Library [240]

CRKVA U SVIJETU – v9-16; v20-25. 1974-81; 1985-90 – 4r – 1 – ATLA S0846 – us A.T.L.A. [073]

CRLS COMMITTEE MINUTES – 1967-1987. CRLS1-4 – 4r – 1 – at Corangamite [080]

LES CROATES SOUS LE JOUG MAGYAR / Hinkovic, Henrik – Paris: Plon-Nourrit, 1915. Address given on 17 Apr 1915 – 1 – us U.W. Library [943]

CROATIA – Geneva, Switzerland: Chief Committee of the Croatian Peasants' Party in Chicago, USA – us Res Libr [949]

Croatia. (Federated Republic, 1945-) Laws, Statutes, etc *see* ZAKON O SUMAMA I ZAKON O LOVU

CROATIAN NATIONALISM PAMPHLET COLLECTION – 1919?-1979 – 1 – CSUXANL5605-B – us Hoover Inst Photo [947]

Croce, Benedetto *see*
- AESTHETIC AS SCIENCE OF EXPRESSION AND GENERAL LINGUISTIC
- INDAGINI SU HEGEL, E SCHIARIMENTI FILOSOFICI

CROCIATA – v23-36. Jun 1956-1966 (complete) – 3r – 1 – ATLA S0485 – us A.T.L.A. [073]

CROCIATA MISSIONARIA – 1930-56 (complete) – 4r – 1 – ATLA S0546 – us A.T.L.A. [073]

Crocker, H G *see*
- THE EXTENT OF THE MARGINAL SEA
- THE LAWS OF LAND WARFARE...

Crocker, Hannah Mather *see* OBSERVATIONS ON THE REAL RIGHTS OF WOMEN: WITH THEIR APPROPRIATE DUTIES, AGREEABLE TO SCRIPTURE, REASON AND COMMON SENSE

Crocker, Uriel Haskell *see*
- THE HISTORY OF A TITLE
- NOTES ON COMMON FORMS: A BOOK OF MASSACHUSETTS LAW
- NOTES ON THE PUBLIC STATUTES OF MASSACHUSETTS

Crocker, William Andrew *see* STUDIES IN THE PROPHECY OF DANIEL

CROCKERY AND GLASS JOURNAL – New York: G Whittemore & Co. v2 n27-v46 n6 jul 8 1875-dec 30 1897 (7r); v122-147 (1938-50); v151-152 (jul 1952-jun 1953); v155 n1-5 (jul-nov 1954) – 31r – 1 – us Res Libr [073]

CROCKERY JOURNAL – New York: G Whittemore & Co. v1 n2-26. dec 12 1874-jul 1 1875 – 15r – us Res Libr [640]

CROCKETT CREEK BAPTIST CHURCH. MODEL, TENNESSEE : CHURCH RECORDS – 1863-Aug 1964 – 1 – 36.81 – us Baptist [240]

Crockett, David *see* NOT YOURS TO GIVE

Crockett, Walter H *see* HISTORY OF VERMONT-THE GREEN MOUNTAIN STATE

Crockett, William D *see*
- BOOKS OF THE KINGS...HARMONY OF THE BOOKS OF SAMUEL, KINGS, AND CHRONICLES
- A HARMONY OF SAMUEL, KINGS AND CHRONICLES
- THE REPUBLIC OF INDONESIA'S GRAPHIC ARTS AND ALLIED INDUSTRY CONFERENCES, 1961
- TERMINAL REPORT: RECENT U.S. DEVELOPMENTS

CROCKFORD'S CLERICAL DIRECTORY – 1858-92. English clerical biographical dictionary. Continued annually – 1 – £3,500.00 – uk World [073]

LA CROCODILE OU LA GUERRE DU BIEN ET DU MAL ARRIVEE SOUS LE REGNE DE LOUIS XV / Saint Martin, Louis Claude de – Poeme epiquo-magique en 102 chants. Paris: Cercle social, an VII. 460p. 5 fiches. (Literature Collection) – 9 – 12.00 – fr Bibl Nationale [810]

LE CROCODILE OU LA GUERRE DU BIEN ET DU MAL, ARRIVEE SOUS LE REGNE DE LOUIS XV / Saint Martin, Louis Claude de – Paris. Imprimerie-Librairie du Cercle Social. 1799 – 9 – fr Hachette [321]

Crocombe, Ron *see* LAND TENURE COURSEBOOK

Croenert, Wilhelm *see* MEMORIA GRAECA HERCULANENSIS

Croft, G *see*
- EIGHT SERMONS PREACHED BEFORE THE UNIVERSITY OF OXFORD IN THE YEAR 1786...
- THOUGHTS CONCERNING THE METHODISTS AND THE ESTABLISHED CLERGY

Croft, Herbert *see*
- A LETTER FROM GERMANY TO THE PRINCESS ROYAL OF ENGLAND
- AN UNFINISHED LETTER TO THE RIGHT HONOURABLE WILLIAM PITT

Croft, W *see* DR. CROFT'S SERVICE IN B, AND EVENING IN E

Croft-Cooke, Rupert *see* SONGS OF A SUSSEX TRAMP

Crofton, A S *see* LIST OF INSCRIPTIONS ON TOMBS OR MONUMENTS IN H.E.H. THE NIZAM'S DOMINIONS

Crofton, Francis Blake *see*
- FOR CLOSER UNION: SOME SLIGHT OFFERINGS TO A GREAT CAUSE
- HAIRBREADTH ESCAPES OF MAJOR MENDAX: HIS PERILOUS ENCOUNTERS, STARTLING ADVENTURES, AND DARING EXPLOITS WITH INDIANS, CANNIBALS, WILD BEASTS, SERPENTS, BALLONS, GEYSERS, ETC., ETC., ALL OVER THE WORLD, IN THE BOWELS OF THE EARTH, AND ABOVE THE CLOUDS

Crofton, H T *see* HISTORY OF THE ANCIENT CHAPEL OF STRETFORD

CROFTON JOURNAL – Crofton, NE. -w. Jun. 1906- – 1 – us NE Hist [071]

Crofton. Yorkshire *see* PARISH REGISTERS

Crogman, William Henry *see* THE COLORED AMERICAN FROM SLAVERY TO HONORABLE CITIZENSHIP

Croil, James *see*
- THE MISSIONARY PROBLEM: CONTAINING A HISTORY OF PROTESTANT MISSIONS IN SOME OF THE PRINCIPAL FIELDS OF MISSIONARY ENTERPRISE: TOGETHER WITH A HISTORICAL AND STATISTICAL ACCOUNT OF THE RISE AND PROGRESS OF MISSIONARY SOCIETIES IN THE NINETEENTH CENTURY
- STEAM NAVIGATION AND ITS RELATION TO THE COMMERCE OF CANADA AND THE UNITED STATES

LA CROISSANCE DES OS LONGS CHEZ LES AMPHIBIENS. SON UTILISATION COMME CRITERE D'AGE / Francillon-Vieillot, H – 9 – F65.00 – fr Ethnologie [590]

LA CROIX – 1988- – 3r per y – 5 – inquire – us Ross [072]

LA CROIX – 1988-1995 – 3r per y – 5,6 – Sfr1,123.00 – sz Infoprint [072]

LA CROIX – Montreal, Canada. 5 avr 1903-6 fev 1937 – 4r – 1 – Can$55.00r – cn Can Microfilming [072]

LA CROIX – Paris. 16 juin 1883-1993 – 1 – fr A.C.R.P.P. [073]

LA CROIX – Paris. France. Aug. 1914-Mar. 1919. Missing Feb. 14 and May 31, 1915 – 1 – 35.00r – us Hoover Inst Photo [072]

LA CROIX – Quebec: J U Begin, [1897-189- ou 19–] – 9 – cn C.I.H.M. [240]

LA CROIX – Paris: La Croix, 1953-61 – us Res Libr [072]

Croix, C la *see* THEOLOGIA MORALIS...

LA CROIX DE LA MAYENNE : SUPPLEMENT DE LA "CROIX" DE PARIS – Laval (Mayenne), Dec. 1892 – Dec. 1907 – 3r – fr Armell [944]

LA CROIX DE MONTREAL-CANADA – Montreal, Canada. 30 mai 1893-27 jul 1894 – 1r – 1 – Can$45.00 – cn Can Microfilming [072]

LA CROIX DE ROUBAIX-TOURCOING – Lille (Nord), May 1901 – August 1914 – 8r – fr Armell [944]

LA CROIX DU CANADA / ed by Denault, Amedee – Montreal, Canada. 28 jul 1894-31 mai 1895 – 1r – 1 – Can$50.00 – cn Can Microfilming [072]

Croix, Madeleine-de-la *see* BIBLIOGRAPHIE ANALYTIQUE DE MGR LOUIS-JOSEPH AUBIN, P.D., PRINCIPAL DE L'ECOLE NORMALE N.-D. DU BON-CONSEIL, CHICOUTIMI

Croix, P de la *see* HISTOIRE DE TIMUR-BEC, CONNU SOUS LE NOM DU GRAND TAMERLAN, EMPEREUR DES MONGOLS ET TARTARES

LA CROIX ROUGE EN EXTREME-ORIENT / Nagao, Ariga – Expose sur l'organisation et la fonctionnement de la societe de la Croix-Rouge du Japon. Ed. by A. Pedone. Paris. 1900 – 9 – 5.00 – fr Orientalistes [360]

Croker, Thomas Crofton *see* FAIRY LEGENDS AND TRADITIONS OF THE SOUTH OF IRELAND

CROKER'S BOSWELL AND BOSWELL. STUDIES IN THE LIFE OF JOHNSON / Fitzgerald, Percy Hetherington – London: Chapman & Hall, 1880. viii,308p – 1 – us U.W. Library [920]

Crolard, A *see* LES EAUX DU LAC LEMAN AU POINT DE VUE INTERNATIONAL

Crole, C S *see* CHINGLEPUT DISTRICT MANUAL

Croly, Jane Cunningham *see* THE HISTORY OF THE WOMEN'S CLUB MOVEMENT IN AMERICA

Cromaziano, A *see* ISTORIA CRITICA...

Crombie, J M *see* LICHENES BRITANNICI

Cromhout, Emile Henri Antoine *see* SKEIREINS AIVAGGELJONS PAIRH IOHANNEN

Crommelin, H A *see* DE VERPLICHTINGEN VAN NEDERLAND ALS NEUTRALE MOGENDHEID...

CROMOS – Bogota, Colombia. -w. 1916-81. 1930-32; 1976 imperfect. 133 1 2 reels – 1 – uk British Libr Newspaper [072]

CROMPTON AND ROYSTON CHRONICLE – Lancashire. 1959 – 1 – uk Microform Academic [072]

Crompton, Richard, 1573-99 *see* STAR CHAMBER CASES; SHOWING WHAT CASES PROPERLY BELONG TO THE COGNIZANCE OF THAT COURT

CROMWELL : EINE TRILOGIE / Raupach, Ernst Benjamin Salomon – Hamburg: Hoffmann und Campe, 1841-1844 – 1r – 1 – us U.W. Library [820]

Cromwell, Emma Guy *see* CATALOGUE OF RECORDS, DOCUMENTS, PAPERS, ETC. OF KENTUCKY GOVERNORS, 1792-1926

Cromwell, John W *see* THE NEGRO IN AMERICAN HISTORY

CROMWELL'S PLACE IN HISTORY : FOUNDED ON SIX LEXTURES / Gardiner, Samuel R – London; New York: Longmans, Green, 1897 – 1mf – us A.T.L.A. [941]

CROMWELL'S SOLDIER'S BIBLE : BEING A REPRINT, IN FACSIMILE, OF "THE SOLDIER'S POCKET BIBLE",... – Boston: Roberts, 1895 – 1mf – 9 – 0-8370-9203-5 – 1986-3203 – us A.T.L.A. [220]

CRONACA – (Eco d'Italia 1 Jul 1922-7 Jul 1928) – London, UK. 5 Jun 1920-24 Jun 1922 – 1 – uk British Libr Newspaper [072]

CRONACA BIZANTINA – Jun 1883-Dec 1884 – 1 – us Res Libr [945]

CRONACA DELLA BRIOLOGIA ITALIANA / Notaris, G de – Genova, 1866-1867. (Commentario della Societaa6 Crittogamologia Italiana, 1865-1867. v. 2.). B-5455 2 – 8 – ne IDC [580]
CRONACA SOVVERSIVA – Lynn, MA, 1917 – 3r – 1 – us I.H.R.C. [978]
CRONACA SOVVERSIVA – Lynn, MA; Barre, VT, June 6, 1903-1919, Nov. 1933 – 5r – 1 – us I.H.R.C. [978]
CRONACHE ILLUSTRATE DELLA AZIONE ITALIANA IN A.O – Roma: Tumminelli. fasc1-12. apr 25-oct 10 1936 – 1 – us Res Libr [960]
Crone, Curt *see* SONNETTE
Crone, G R *see* THE VOYAGES OF CADAMOSTO
CRONICA – Jassy, Romania. -w. 1967-70. 4 reels – 1 – uk British Libr Newspaper [949]
LA CRONICA – Badajoz, 1871-1881. Es segunda epoca de la 48 – 5 – sp Bibl Santa Ana [073]
LA CRONICA – Badajoz, 1890. 1 numero – 5 – sp Bibl Santa Ana [073]
CRONICA DE ALFONSO EL ONCENO / Cerda Rico, Francisco – 1787 – 2mf – 9 – Pta1,500.00 – 84-7848-263-6 – sp Pentalfa [440]
CRONICA DE BADAJOZ – Badajoz, 1866-1870 – 5 – sp Bibl Santa Ana [073]
CRONICA DE CAVALLERS CATALANS / Tarafa, Francisco – Barcelona, 1952-54. 2v. col. coats of arms – 1 – us U.W. Library [920]
CRONICA DE DON ALVARO DE LUNA / Flores Barrera, Jose Miguel – 1784 – 2mf – 9 – Pta1,500.00 – 84-7848-264-4 – sp Pentalfa [830]
CRONICA DE DON PEDRO NINO / Llaguno Amirola, Eugenio – 1782 – 2mf – 9 – Pta1,500.00 – 84-7848-268-7 – sp Pentalfa [946]
CRONICA DE ENRIQUE EL QUARTO / Flores Barrera, Jose Miguel – 1787 – 2mf – 9 – Pta1,500.00 – 84-7848-265-2 – sp Pentalfa [830]
CRONICA DE ISIDORO PACENSE / Martinez de Escobar, T – 1870 – 9 – 1.50f – sp Bibl Santa Ana [920]
CRONICA DE LA ORDEN DE ALCANTARA / Torres Tapia, Alfonso – 1763 – 9 – 1.50f – sp Bibl Santa Ana [946]
CRONICA DE LA PRIMERA ASAMBLEA MISIONAL DIOCESANA DE BADAJOZ CELEBRADA EN ZAFRA... / Fuertes, Damaso – Zafra: Imp. de Eulalio Morera Perez, 1924 – 1 – sp Bibl Santa Ana [240]
CRONICA DE LA PROVINCIA DE ALBACETE / Blanch e Illa, Narciso – 1867 – 9 – 1.50f – sp Bibl Santa Ana [946]
CRONICA DE LA PROVINCIA DE CACERES / Perez de Guzman, Juan – 1870 – 9 – 1.50f – sp Bibl Santa Ana [946]
CRONICA DE LA PROVINCIA DE MURCIA / Bisso, Jose – 1870 – 9 – 1.50f – sp Bibl Santa Ana [946]
CRONICA DE LA PROVINCIA FRANCISCANA DE LOS APOSTOLES SAN PEDRO Y SAN PABLO DE MICHOACAN. 2ND ED. MEXICO, 1946 / Espinosa, Isidro Felix – Madrid: Razon y Fe, 1947 – 1 – sp Bibl Santa Ana [240]
CRONICA DE LA SUBVERSION EN LA ARGENTINA – Buenos Aires (Talcahuano 494, Buenos Aires): Ediciones Depalma, 1980 – 1 – CSUXADQ6589-B – us Hoover Inst Photo [320]
CRONICA DE LA...CACERES / Perez de Guzman, Juan – 1870 – 9 – 1.50f – sp Bibl Santa Ana [946]
UNA CRONICA DE LOS MOCTEZUMA, MADRID...1954 / Cerralbo, Marques de – Hidalguia, 2, Abril-Junio, 1954 – 1 – sp Bibl Santa Ana [946]
CRONICA DE LOS REYES DE CASTILLA. TOMO 1 / Llaguno Amirola, Eugenio – 1779 – 2mf – 9 – Pta1,500.00 – 84-7848-266-0 – sp Pentalfa [920]
CRONICA DE LOS REYES DE CASTILLA. TOMO 2 / Llaguno Amirola, Eugenio – 1780 – 2mf – 9 – Pta1,500.00 – 84-7848-267-9 – sp Pentalfa [920]
LA CRONICA DE PLASENCIA – Plasencia, 1899 – 5 – sp Bibl Santa Ana [073]
LA CRONICA DE PLASENCIA – Plasencia. 1899. Solo no. 11 – 9 – 1.50f – sp Bibl Santa Ana [072]
CRONICA DE SAN PEDRO DE ALCANTARA – Madrid: Archivo Ibero Americana, 1960 – 1 – sp Bibl Santa Ana [240]
CRONICA DEL CONGRESO EUCARISTICO NACIONAL / ed by Bayle, Constantino – Madrid: Razon y Fe, 1926 – 1 – sp Bibl Santa Ana [240]
LA CRONICA DEL PERU / Cieza de Leon, Pedro de – Ediciones de la Revista Ximenez de Quesada, 1971 – 1 – sp Bibl Santa Ana [972]
LA CRONICA DI GIOVANNI VILLANI: ANNOTATA AD USO DELLA GIOVENTU / Villani, Giovanni – By Prof. Celestino Durando. Torino, 1880. 8v in 4 – 1 – us U.W. Library [945]
CRONICA DI PISA. ETC / Holkham Hall. Norfolk. England – 13th 14th century. Holkham MSS 556, 575 and 600 – 1 – uk Microform Academic [025]
CRONICA EL EMPERADOR CARLOS 5TH. EDICION DE JUAN SANCHEZ MONTES. PROLOGO DE PETER RASOW. MADRID, 1964 / Mesaguer Fernandez, J & Giron, Pedro – Madrid: Graf. Calleja, 1967 – 1 – sp Bibl Santa Ana [920]
CRONICA ET CARTULARIUM MONASTERII DE DUNIS / ed by Putte, Fvan de – Brugis, 1864-1870 – Dfl165.00 – ne Slangenburg [240]
CRONICA FRATRIS SALIMBENE DE ADAM ORDINIS MINORUM (MGH 5: 32.BD) – 1905-1913 – Dfl70.00 – ne Slangenburg [240]
CRONICA GENERAL DE ESPANA. BOOK 1-4 / Ocampo, Florian de – Camora Zamora: Juan Picardo, 1543. First ed. Includes index – 1 – us U.W. Library [946]
CRONICA INTERNA DE LA REVOLUCION LIBERTADORA / Carril, Bonifacio del – Buenos Aires, 1959 – 1 – CSUXADJ0137-B – us Hoover Inst Photo [320]
CRONICA JOHANNIS VITODURANI (MGH 6: 3.BD) / ed by Brun, B & Baethgen, F – 1924 – Dfl25.00 – ne Slangenburg [240]
CRONICA MENSUAI DE LA SECRETARIA DE TRABAJO Y PREVISION – (Includes c.1: v.1:no.5 1944: Sept.-v.3:no.22 (1946: Mar./Apr.)) – 1 – CSUXAHZ7741-S – us Hoover Inst Photo [332]
LA CRONICA MEXICANA DE HERNANDO ALVARADO TEZOZOMOC / Romero Galvan, J R – Manifestation d'une conscience de peuple conquis chez un auteur indigene du XVIe siecle – 9 – F60.00 – fr Ethnologie [306]
LA CRONICA OFICIAL DE LAS INDIAS OCCIDENTALES. LA PLATA 1934 / Carbra, Romulo D – Madrid: Razon y Fe, 1935 – 1 – sp Bibl Santa Ana [950]
CRONICA PROCESO DIOCESANO DE BEATIFICACION DE SIETE FRANCISCANOS... – Madrid: Arch. Ibero Americano, 1964 – 1 – sp Bibl Santa Ana [240]
CRONICA...BADAJOZ / Henao y Munoz, Manuel – 1870 – 9 – 1.50f – sp Bibl Santa Ana [520]
CRONICAS DE LA GUERRA / Manobens, Enrique – Valencia, 1937. Fiche W1019. (Blodgett Collection of Spanish Civil War Pamphlets) – 9 – us H.U. College Libr [946]
CRONICAS DE LA GUERRA / Zamacois, Eduardo – Recopilacion de articulos periodisticos. Valencia, 1937. Fiche W1260. (Blodgett Collection of Spanish Civil War Pamphlets) – 9 – us H.U. College Libr [946]
CRONICAS DE LOS REYES DE CASTILLA, DESDE DON ALFONSO DE SABIO, HASTA LOS CATOLICOS DON FERNANDO Y DONA ISABEL / ed by Rosell y Lopez, Cayetano – Madrid: M. Rivadeneyra, 1875-78.3v. 1220 – 1 – us U.W. Library [946]
CRONICAS DEL REY DON PEDRO Y DE DON ENRIQUE 2 / Lopez de Ayala, Pedro – Spanish manuscript on vellum in a cursive scribal hand of the early 15th century – 1 – us U.W. Library [920]
CRONICA...SAN GABRIEL / Trinidad, Juan de la – 1652 – 9 – 1.50f – sp Bibl Santa Ana [946]
CRONICL CYMRU – Bangor, Wales. -f. Jan 1866-June 1872. 2 1 2 reels – 1 – uk British Libr Newspaper [072]
CRONICON DE LA CAUSA DEL MUERTO RESUCITADO Y GUIA DE SU VISTA PUBLICA CON LA BIOGRAFIA DE LOS PROTAGONISTAS – Plasencia: Imp. Jose Hontiveros, 1888 – 1 – sp Bibl Santa Ana [920]
CRONICON...MUERTO RESUCITADO / Paredes Guillen, Vicente – 1888 – 9 – 1.50f – sp Bibl Santa Ana [830]
Cronin, H S *see* CODEX PURPUREUS PETROPOLITANUS (CODEX N OF THE GOSPELS)
Cronise, Titus Fey *see* NATURAL WEALTH OF CALIFORNIA
EL CRONISTA – Panama City, Panama. 1904-08 (incomplete) – 2r – 1 – us L of C Photodup [072]
EL CRONISTA – Serradilla, 1928-1932 – 5 – sp Bibl Santa Ana [073]
CRONISTA E HISTORIADORES DE LA CONQUISTA DE MEXICO, FONDO DE CULTURA ECONOMICA / Iglesia, Ramon – 1942 – 1 – sp Bibl Santa Ana [350]
CRONISTAS FRANCISCANOS : COLECCION DE LA REVISTA "ESTUDIOS HISTORICOS", CUADERNO 1 / Asencio, Jose Maria – Guadalajara, Mexico: Impr. Grafica, 1944 – 1mf – 9 – ne IDC [972]
CRONOLOGIA DELLA VITA DI S. FRANCESCO / Terzi, Arduino – Madrid: Archivo Ibero Americano, 1964 – 1 – sp Bibl Santa Ana [946]
CROOK COUNTY JOURNAL – Prineville, OR. -w 3 Jan 1901-7 Jul 1921. 6 rolls – 1 – us U.O. Library [071]
CROOK COUNTY NEWS – Prineville, OR. -w. 16 Apr 1937-8 Sept 1939. 1 roll – 1 – us U.O. Library [071]
Crook, J *see* DIARY, 1775-1776
Crookall, Robert *see* ECSTASY
Crooke, H *see* MIKROKOSMOGRAPHIA. A DESCRIPTION OF THE BODY OF MAN
Crooke, P *see* BASHAQRA AREA SETTLEMENTS 1963; A CASE STUDY IN VILLAGE DEVELOPMENT IN THE GEZIRA SCHEME
Crooke, W *see*
- HOBSON-JOBSON; A GLOSSARY OF COLLOQUIAL ANGLO-INDIAN WORDS AND PHRASES
- THE TRIBES AND CASTES OF THE NORTHWESTERN PROVINCES AND OUDH

THE CROOKED DISCIPLE'S REMARKS UPON THE BLIND GUIDE'S METHOD OF PREACHING FOR SOME YEARS,... / Harman, J – London, [1761] – 1mf – 9 – MP-407/1 – ne IDC [240]
CROOKED RUN BAPTIST CHURCH (CALLED CEDAR CREEK, 1826-1836). FAIRFIELD COUNTY. SOUTH CAROLINA : CHURCH RECORDS – 1834-1877, 1883-1907, 1944-72 – 1 – 43.20 – us Baptist [240]
Crooker, Joseph Henry *see*
- PROBLEMS IN AMERICAN SOCIETY
- THE UNITARIAN CHURCH

Crooks, Adam *see*
- EDUCATIONAL STATEMENT OF THE HON. ADAM CROOKS, MINISTER OF EDUCATION: ON MOVING THE ESTIMATES FOR 1880: IN COMMITTEE OF SUPPLY, HOUSE OF ASSEMBLY, PROVINCE OF ONTARIO
- REFORM GOVERNMENT IN ONTARIO: EIGHT YEARS' REVIEW: IN AN ADDRESS TO THE ELECTORS OF THE SOUTH RIDING OF OXFORD

Crooks, John Joseph *see* HISTORY OF THE COLONY OF SIERRA LEONE, WESTERN AFRICA
Crookshank, C H *see*
- HISTORY OF METHODISM IN IRELAND
- MEMORABLE WOMEN OF IRISH METHODISM IN THE LAST CENTURY

Croone, W *see* DE RATIONE MOTUS MUSCULORUM
CROP AGRONOMY AND IMPROVEMENT IN CYRENAICA / United Nations. Food and Agriculture Organization – Report to the Government of Libya. FAO nr. 1577. Rome. 1962. BNE-1027 1 – 9 – ne IDC [630]
CROP CALENDAR – 1978 – 131p – it F.A.O. [630]
CROP INSURANCE – 1989 – 54p – it F.A.O. [360]
CROP PRODUCTION LEVELS AND FERTILIZER USE – 1981 – 78p – it F.A.O. [630]
CROP RESEARCH – (Published as: Horticultural Research) – Edinburgh. v1-17. 1961-77. Continues: Horticultural Research – 5,9 – Dfl765.00; Dfl45.00v – ne Swets [631]
CROP RESIDUES AND AGRO-INDUSTRIAL BY-PRODUCTS IN ANIMAL FEEDING – 1982 2nd print 1985 – 152p – it F.A.O. [636]
CROP SCIENCE – 7710. V. 1-8. 1961-1968 – 9 – ne IDC [630]
CROP WATER REQUIREMENTS – 1981 – 156p – it F.A.O. [631]
CROPLEY'S CELESTIAL SPECTATOR AND YORK ADVERTISER – Fredericton, NB: H A Cropley, [1880?] – 9 – cn C.I.H.M. [971]
CROPS AND LIVESTOCK REPORT / Purdue University. Cooperative Extension Service – No.1-575. 1925-73 – 1,5 – us Spaulding [631]
CROPWAT *see* COMPUTER PROGRAM FOR IRRIGATION PLANNING AND MANAGEMENT
Croquer Cabezas, Emilio *see* CENTENARIO DE LA INDEPENDENCIA ESPANOLA. NOTICIA GENEALOGICA Y BIOGRAFICA Y BIOGRAFICA DEL MARISCAL CAMPO...
CROQUIS D'ARCHITECTURE – Paris, 1866-98. 3 reels – 1 – $245.00 – us UPA [720]
CROQUIS DE BROUSSE / Davesne, Andre – Paris: Editions du Sagittaire, [1946] – 1 – us Res Libr [960]
CROQUIS MONTREALAIS / Morin, Victor – Montreal, 1929. SEM105P784 – 1mf – 9 – Can$2.25 – cn Bibl Nat [971]
CROQUIS PARISIENS: A VAU L'EAU; UN OFLEMME / Huysmans, Joris Karl – Paris: P.V. Stock, 1905.332p. 4 fiches. (Literature Collection) – 9 – 10.00 – fr Bibl Nationale [830]
Cros, Charles *see* SOLUTION GENERALE DU PROBLEME DE LA PHOTOGRAPHIE DES COULEURS
Crosby *see* A HANDBOOK OF IOWA
Crosby, Alpheus *see* A GRAMMAR OF THE GREEK LANGUAGE
Crosby, Frank *see*
- EVERYBODY'S LAWYER AND COUNSELOR IN BUSINESS...
- LIFE OF ABRAHAM LINCOLN

Crosby, Howard *see*
- BUCH NEHEMIAH
- EXPOSITORY NOTES ON THE BOOK OF JOSHUA
- THE SEVEN CHURCHES OF ASIA
- SEVEN CHURCHES OF ASIA, OR, WORLDLINESS IN THE CHURCH
- SOCIAL HINTS FOR YOUNG CHRISTIANS

Crosby, J Sherwin *see* ADDRESS AT THE FUNERAL OF HENRY GEORGE
Croskery, Thomas *see*
- A CATECHISM ON THE DOCTRINES OF THE PLYMOUTH BRETHERN
- PLYMOUTH-BRETHRENISM

Croslegh, Charles *see* CHRISTIANITY JUDGED BY ITS FRUITS
CROSS – 1834 – 1 – 5.00 – us Baptist [240]
THE CROSS – Halifax [NS]: J P Walsh, [1843-1850] – 9 – cn C.I.H.M. [240]
Cross, A G *see* EIGHTEENTH CENTURY RUSSIAN STUDIES
CROSS AND CROWN – v. 1. 1855-1856 – 1 – us UMI [240]
THE CROSS AND THE CALUMET – 1962-70. (American Indian Periodicals in the Princeton University Library). 2 fiches – 9 – $45.00 – us UPA [305]
THE CROSS AND THE DRAGON : OR, LIGHT IN THE BROAD EAST / Henry, Benjamin Couch – New York: Anson D F Randolph, c1885 – 2mf – 9 – 0-8370-6263-2 – 1986-0263 – us A.T.L.A. [950]
THE CROSS AND THE KINGDOM : AS VIEWED BY CHRIST HIMSELF AND IN THE LIGHT OF EVOLUTION / Walker, William Lowe – (Includes index) – Edinburgh: T & T Clark, 1902 – 1mf – 9 – 0-8370-5685-3 – 1985-3685 – us A.T.L.A. [240]
Cross, Arthur Lyon *see*
- THE ANGLICAN EPISCOPATE AND THE AMERICAN COLONIES
- A HISTORY OF ENGLAND AND GREATER BRITAIN

THE CROSS: BEING A COURSE OF SERMONS PREACHED IN HOLY TRINITY CHURCH, HALIFAX, ON THE SUNDAY EVENINGS IN LENT, 1879 / Ancient, William Johnson – Halifax: W. Macnab, 1879. 06168. (Pre-1900 Canadiana) – 9 – cn C.I.H.M. [240]
CROSS CANADA WRITERS' QUARTERLY – (Cont: Cross-Canada Writers' Magazine at v10 1988) – Stratford. v1-9. 1980-87 – 9 – Can$20.00y – cn Micromedia [420]
CROSS CANADA WRITERS' QUARTERLY *see* CROSS-CANADA WRITERS' MAGAZINE
CROSS CREEK BAPTIST CHURCH. CUMBERLAND ASSOCIATION. STEWART COUNTY. TENNESSEE : CHURCH RECORDS – 1851-1969 – 1 – 21.69 – us Baptist [240]
CROSS CURRENTS – v1- 1950- 1; v20- 5,6; v26- 9 – us UMI [240]
Cross, Ethelbert F H *see* FIRE AND FROST: STORIES, DIALOGUES, SATIRES, ESSAYS, POEMS, ETC

Cross, F L *see*
- STUDIA EVANGELICA, VOL 2 (TUU 5-87)
- STUDIA EVANGELICA, VOL 4 (TUU 5-102)
- STUDIA EVANGELICA, VOL 5 (TUU 5-103)
- STUDIA PATRISTICA
- STUDIA PATRISTICA, VOL 3 PT 2 (TUU 5-88)
- STUDIA PATRISTICA, VOL 3 (TUU 5-78)
- STUDIA PATRISTICA, VOL 5 (TUU 5-80)
- STUDIA PATRISTICA, VOL 6 (TUU 5-81)
- STUDIA PATRISTICA, VOL 7 (TUU 5-92)
- STUDIA PATRISTICA, VOL 8 (TUU 5-93)
- STUDIA PATRISTICA, VOL 9 (TUU 5.94)
- STUDIA PATRISTICA, VOL 10 (TUU 5-107)
- STUDIA PATRISTICA, VOL 11 (TUU 5-108)

Cross Family *see* PAPERS

Cross, FL *see* STUDIA PATRISTICA, VOL 4 (TUU 5-79)

Cross, Frank M *see* EARLY HEBREW ORTHOGRAPHY

THE CROSS IN THE LAND OF THE TRIDENT / Beach, Harlan Page – (Includes bibliographies and statistical appendixes) – New York: Fleming H Revell, c1895 – 1mf – 9 – 0-8370-6644-1 – 1986-0644 – us A.T.L.A. [950]

THE CROSS IN THE OLD TESTAMENT / Robinson, H Wheeler – SCM. 1955 – 9 – $10.00 – us I.R.C. [240]

THE CROSS IN THE OLD TESTAMENT / Wheeler Robinson, H – London, 1955 – Dfl19.00 – ne Slangenburg [220]

CROSS INDEX TO THE CENTRAL FILES OF THE ADJUTANT GENERAL'S OFFICE / U.S. War Department. Adjutant General's Office – 1917-39. 1956 rolls. T822 – 1 – us Nat'l Archives [324]

Cross, John A *see*
- INTRODUCTORY HINTS TO ENGLISH READERS OF THE OLD TESTAMENT
- SOME NOTES ON THE BOOK OF PSALMS

Cross, Kimball Allyn *see* A TREATISE, ANALYTICAL, CRITICAL AND HISTORICAL, ON SUCCESSIONS

THE CROSS OF JESUS, OR, HEAVEN ON EARTH TO ME / Thompson, David – New York: Carlton & Porter, 1865. 1 fiche – 9 – us A.T.L.A. [240]

CROSS REFERENCE – v.1-2. 1978-79 – 1 – us UMI [073]

CROSS REPORT / Great Britain. Commissioners Appointed to Enquire into the Elementary Education Acts in England and Wales – 1886-88 – 1 – uk Microform Academic [324]

CROSS RIVER NATIVES : BEING SOME NOTES ON THE PRIMITIVE PAGANS OF OBUBURA HILL DISTRICT, SOUTHERN NIGERIA / Partridge, Charles – (Including a description of the circles of upright sculptured stones on the left bank of the Aweyong River) – London: Hutchinson, 1905 – 1 – us Res Libr [305]

CROSS ROADS BAPTIST CHURCH. CHESTERFIELD COUNTY. RUBY, SOUTH CAROLINA : CHURCH RECORDS – 1877-1900, 1947-1977 – 1 – 29.88 – us Baptist [240]

CROSS ROADS BAPTIST CHURCH. NEWBERRY COUNTY. SOUTH CAROLINA : CHURCH RECORDS – 1839-59, 1859-1925, 1872-77 – 1 – 349.74 – us Baptist [240]

CROSS ROADS BAPTIST CHURCH. PICKENS COUNTY. EASLEY, SOUTH CAROLINA : CHURCH RECORDS – 1838-1977 – 1 – 43.61 – us Baptist [240]

CROSS ROADS BAPTIST CHURCH. ROTAN, TEXAS : CHURCH RECORDS – 1909-78. 1050p – 1 – 47.25 – us Baptist [240]

Cross, Thomas *see* THE COLONIES AND INDIA IN LONDON: READ BEFORE THE LITERARY AND SCIENTIFIC SOCIETY OF OTTAWA, 5TH APRIL, 1887

CROSS-BENCH VIEWS OF CURRENT CHURCH QUESTIONS / Henson, H Hensley – London: Edward Arnold, 1902 – 1mf – us A.T.L.A. [240]

CROSSBRED DAIRY CATTLE PRODUCTIVITY IN ARSI REGION, ETHIOPIA = PRODUCTIVITE DE BOVINS LAITIERS METIS DANS LA REGION D'ARSI EN ETHIOPIE / Kiwuwa, G H et al – 1983 – 9 – $7.00 – 92-9053-115-0 – et ILRI [636]

CROSSBREEDING BOS INDICUS AND BOS TAURUS FOR MILK PRODUCTION IN THE TROPICS – 1987 – 93p – it F.A.O. [636]

CROSS-CANADA WRITERS' MAGAZINE – (Cont: Cross Canada Writers' Quarterly at v10 1988. Cont by: Paragraph – the Fiction Magazine at v12 n2 1990) – Stratford. v10. 1988- – 9 – Can$20.00y – cn Micromedia [073]

CROSS-CANADA WRITERS' MAGAZINE *see*
- CROSS CANADA WRITERS' QUARTERLY
- PARAGRAPH

A CROSS-CULTURAL ANALYSIS OF ACHIEVEMENT MOTIVATION IN ANGLO AMERICAN AND JAPANESE MARATHON RUNNERS / Hayashi, CT – 1991 – 2mf – 9 – $8.00 – us Microform Publ [150]

A CROSS-CULTURAL ANALYSIS OF CHILDREN'S ATTITUDES TOWARD PHYSICAL ACTIVITY AND PATTERNS OF PARTICIPATION / Liu, Z – 1990 – 1mf – 9 – $4.00 – us Microform Publ [150]

CROSS-CULTURAL BROADCASTING / Contreras, Eduardo et al – repr 1982 – 49p – 9 – 92-3-101353-X – fr UNESCO [380]

Crosse, Gordon *see* A DICTIONARY OF ENGLISH CHURCH HISTORY

CROSS-EDUCATION FOLLOWING SINGLE-LIMB ECCENTRIC AND CONCENTRIC TRAINING ON THE BIODEX ISOKINETIC DYNAMOMETER / Mahler, Erik B – 1994 – 1mf – $4.00 – us Microform Publ [617]

Crosskill, Herbert *see* NOVA SCOTIA, ITS CLIMATE, RESOURCES AND ADVANTAGES: BEING A GENERAL DESCRIPTION OF THE PROVINCE FOR THE INFORMATION OF INTENDING EMIGRANTS

Crosskill, William Hay *see* PRINCE EDWARD ISLAND, GARDEN PROVINCE OF CANADA: ITS HISTORY, INTERESTS AND RESOURCES, WITH INFORMATION FOR TOURISTS, ETC

Crossley, Frederic B *see* COURTS AND LAWYERS OF ILLINOIS

Crossley, Hugh Thomas *see*
- A PRACTICAL DISCUSSION OF THE PARLOR DANCE, THE THEATRE, THE CARDS
- PRACTICAL TALKS ON IMPORTANT THEMES: TO YOUNG CONVERTS, OLDER CHRISTIANS AND THE UN-CONVERTED

Crosta, Clino *see* L'ASSUNTA NELL'ODIERNA TEOLOGIA CATTOLICA

Croston, J *see* THE MIRROUR OF MAIESTIE

Croswell, Simon Greenleaf *see*
- CROSWELL'S COLLECTION OF PATENT CASES IN THE U.S. COURTS
- A TREATISE ON THE LAW RELATING TO ELECTRICITY

Crosweller, William Thomas *see* OUR VISIT TO TORONTO, THE NIAGRA FALLS AND THE UNITED STATES OF AMERICA: BEING A SHORT ACCOUNT OF A TOUR IN CONNECTION WITH THE MEETING OF THE BRITISH ASSOCIATION FOR THE ADVANCEMENT OF SCIENCE, HELD AT TORONTO, CANADA, AUGUST 18 TO 25, 1897

CROSWELL'S COLLECTION OF PATENT CASES IN THE U.S. COURTS / Croswell, Simon Greenleaf – Boston: Little-Brown. 1v. 1888 (all publ) – 3mf – 9 – $4.50 – LLMC 84-326 – us L.L.M.C. [340]

Crotch, G R *see*
- CHECKLIST OF THE COLEOPTERA OF AMERICA, NORTH OF MEXICO
- A REVISION OF THE COLEOPTEROUS FAMILY COCCINELLIDAE

Crotch, William *see* SUBSTANCE OF SEVERAL COURSES

Crottet, Alexandre *see* COLLECTION

Crotty, R *see* TAXING LAND AND ECONOMIC DEVELOPMENT

Crouan, H M *see* FLORULE DU FINISTERE

Crouan, PL *see* FLORULE DU FINISTERE

Crouch, FN *see* SHEILA! MY DARLING COLLEEN

Crouch, Joseph *see* PURITANISM AND ART

Crough, E A *see* AN ILLUSTRATED INTRODUCTION TO LAMARCK'S CONCHOLOGY

Crousle, L *see* BOSSUET ET LA PROTESTANTISME

Crouter, John Wesley *see*
- BOILED-DOWN ESSAYS
- HUMAN TRAITS OF CHARACTER: IN RHYME
- MY POLICY FOR THE CONSTRUCTION OF THE CANADA PACIFIC RAILWAY: AS A GOVERNMENT WORK, WITH IRREFUTABLE ARGUMENTS IN FAVOR OF THIS POLICY
- PROF. J. W. CROUTER'S NEW AND IMPROVED PHRENOLOGICAL CHART

Crouzat, Henri *see* AZIZAH DE NIAMKOKO

Crowder, Todd A *see* THE EFFECTS OF VARIOUS EXERCISE MODALITIES ON SERUM CHOLESTEROL AND TRIGLYCERIDE CONCENTRATIONS

Crowe, Catherine *see*
- THE NIGHT-SIDE OF NATURE; OR, GHOSTS AND GHOST SEERS
- SUSAN HOPLEY

Crowe, Eyre Evans *see* HISTORY OF THE REIGNS OF LOUIS XVIII AND CHARLES X

Crowe, Frederick *see* THE GOSPEL IN CENTRAL AMERICA, PUBLISHED IN LONDON IN 1850

Crowe, James W *see* SMOKELESS TOBACCO USE AMONG BIG TEN WRESTLERS AND FACTORS ASSOCIATED WITH USE

Crowe, S E *see* THE BERLIN WEST AFRICAN CONFERENCE, 1884-1885

Crowe, Sophia Bennett *see* DIARY

Crowell, Fred E *see* NEW ENGLANDERS IN NOVA SCOTIA

Crowest, Frederick J *see* THE STORY OF THE ART OF MUSIC

Crowfoot, J W *see*
- THE BUILDINGS AT SAMARIA
- CHURCHES AT BOSRA AND SAMARIA-SEBASTE
- CHURCHES AT JERASH
- EARLY CHURCHES IN PALESTINE
- EARLY IVORIES FROM SAMARIA
- EXPLORATIONS IN THE TYROPOEON VALLEY

Crowley, Jeremiah J *see* THE PAROCHIAL SCHOOL

THE CROWN OF LIFE / Gissing, George Robert – London: Methuen, 1899 – 1 roll – 1 – 1-55879-470-0 – uk Libr Preservation [890]

CROWN OF THORNS: A STORY OF THE TIME OF CHRIST / Carus, Paul – Chicago: Open Court, 1901. 1 fiche – 9 – us A.T.L.A. [240]

THE CROWN OF WILD OLIVE : THREE LECTURES ON WORK, TRAFFIC AND WAR / Ruskin, John – London: Smith, Elder, 1866 – 1 roll – 1 – 1-55879-490-5 – uk Libr Preservation [850]

CROWN SERVANTS : SERIES ONE: THE PAPERS OF THOMAS WENTWORTH 1ST EARL OF STRAFFORD, 1593-1641, FROM SHEFFIELD ARCHIVES – Marlborough: Adam Matthew Publications, 1994 – 20r – 1 – $2,400.00 – uk Matthew [355]

CROWN THEOLOGICAL LIBRARY, VOL 16 *see* HEBREW RELIGION TO THE ESTABLISHMENT OF JUDAISM UNDER EZRA

CROWN VS. ADAMS AND 29 OTHERS / Adams, Faried – Documents introduced in evidence in the trial for treason in a special criminal court, Pretoria, 1959-1961 – 1 – us Res Libr [960]

CROWN VS. ADAMS AND 29 OTHERS; PREPARATORY EXAMINATION ON A CHARGE OF HIGH TREASON, IN THE MAGISTRATE'S COURT OF JOHANNESBURG, 1956-1958 / Adams, Faried – 1 – us Res Libr [960]

CROWNED IN PALM-LAND. A STORY OF AFRICAN MISSION LIFE / Nassau, Robert Hamill – Philadelphia: J. Lippincott & Company, 1874. 390p. front. plates, map – us U.W. Library [920]

Crowther, Bryan *see* PRACTICAL REMARKS ON INSANITY: TO WHICH IS ADDED A COMMENTARY ON THE DISSECTION OF THE BRAINS OF MANIACS; WITH SOME ACCOUNT OF DISEASES INCIDENT TO THE INSANE

Crowther, J *see* A PORTRAITURE OF METHODISM; OR, THE HISTORY OF THE WESLEYAN METHODISTS, SHOWING THEIR RISE, PROGRESS AND PRESENT STATE; BIOGRAPHICAL SKETCHES...

Crowther, Samuel Adjai *see* A VOCABULARY OF THE YORUBA LANGUAGE, ETC ETC

CROYDON CHRONICLE – London. -w. Jul 1855-Jul 1869. (7 reels) – 1 – uk British Libr Newspaper [072]

CROYDON TIMES – London, England. -w. 1885-90. 8 reels – 1 – uk British Libr Newspaper [072]

Crozier, William Armstrong *see* GENERAL ARMORY

DE LA CRUAUTE RELIGIEUSE – (D'Holbach series). 1769 – 9 – fr Hachette [240]

Cruchet, Rene *see* LA CONQUETE PACIFIQUE DU MAROC ET DU TAFILALET

THE CRUCIAL RACE QUESTION, OR, WHERE AND HOW SHALL THE COLOR LINE BE DRAWN 101: BROWN, WILLIAM MONTGOMERY – Little Rock, Ark.: Arkansas Churchman's Pub. Co., 1907 – 1mf – us A.T.L.A. [305]

THE CRUCIALITY OF THE CROSS / Forsyth, Peter Taylor – New York: Eaton & Mains; Cincinnati: Jennings & Graham, [19–] – 1mf – 9 – 0-8370-3848-0 – 1985-1848 – us A.T.L.A. [240]

THE CRUCIBLE – Journal of the Board for Social Responsibility of the Church of England – 1 – uk Microform Academic [240]

CRUCIFIXION / Osborne, John H – Syracuse: Wolcott & West, 1897. 1 fiche – 9 – us A.T.L.A. [240]

Cruciger, G *see* HARMONIA LINGUARUM QUATUOR CARDINALIUM; HEBRAICAE, GRAECAE, LATINAE ET GERMANICAE

LA CRUE – 1963-64. SEM35P195 – 1r – 1 – Can$23.00 – cn Bibl Nat [073]

Crueger, J *see*
- D.M. LUTHERS WIE AUCH ANDERER GOTTSELIGEN UND LENTE GEISTLICHE LIEDER UND PSALMEI WIE SIE BISHER IN EVANENSCHEN KIRCHEN DIESER LANDEN GEBRAUCHT WERDEN...
- PSALMODIA SACRA, DAS IST, DES KOENIGS AND PROPHETEN DAVIDS GEISTREICHE PSALMEN...

Cruikshank, B *see*
- EIGHTEEN YEARS ON THE GOLD COAST
- EIGHTEEN YEARS ON THE GOLD COAST OF AFRICA, INCLUDING AN ACCOUNT OF THE NATIVE TRIBES, AND THEIR INTERCOURSE WITH EUROPEANS

Cruikshank, Ernest Alexander *see*
- THE ADMINISTRATION OF LIEUT. GOVERNOR SIMCOE VIEWED IN HIS OFFICIAL CORRESPONDENCE
- THE BATTLE OF LUNDY'S LANE, 1814: AN ADDRESS DELIVERED BEFORE THE LUNDY'S LANE HISTORICAL SOCIETY, OCTOBER 10TH, 1888
- A CENTURY OF MUNICIPAL HISTORY, 1792-1892. PART 1, 1792-1841
- A CENTURY OF MUNICIPAL HISTORY: PART 2, 1841-1893
- THE EMPLOYMENT OF INDIANS IN THE WAR OF 1812
- THE FIGHT IN THE BEECHWOODS: A STUDY IN CANADIAN HISTORY
- QUEENSTON HEIGHTS: A THRILLING NARRATIVE OF THE FAMOUS BATTLE WHERE GENERAL BROCK DIED DEFENDING HIS COUNTRY: A LECTURE DELIVERED AT DRUMMONDVILLE, ONT., DEC 18, 1889

THE CRUISE OF THE ALBATROSS, OR WHEN WAS WEDNESDAY THE TENTH? : A STORY OF THE SOUTH PACIFIC / Allen, Grant – Boston: Lothrop, 1898. 05020. (Pre-1900 Canadiana) – 9 – cn C.I.H.M. [830]

THE CRUISE OF THE ALICE MAY IN THE GULF OF ST LAWRENCE AND ADJACENT WATERS / Benjamin, Samuel Greene Wheeler – New York: D. Appleton, 1885. c1884. 00134. (Pre-1900 Canadiana) – 9 – cn C.I.H.M. [910]

THE CRUISE OF THE BROOKLYN. A JOURNAL OF THE PRINCIPAL EVENTS OF A THREE YEARS' CRUISE...IN THE SOUTH ATLANTIC STATION / Beehler, William Henry – Descriptions of places in South America, Africa and Madagascar. Philadelphia: Lippincott, 1885. 341p.front., plates, double map – 1 – us U.W. Library [910]

CRUISE OF THE U.S. REVENUE MARINE STEAMER BEAR / Jackson, Sheldon – 1894-1896 – 1 – $50.00 – us Presbyterian [240]

A CRUISE ON THE EOTHEN, 1872 / Brassey, Annie – London, 1873. 00848. (Pre-1900 Canadiana) – 9 – cn C.I.H.M. [910]

CRUISE TRAVEL MAGAZINE – 1981- – 9 – us UMI [910]

Cruise, William *see* A DIGEST OF THE LAW OF REAL PROPERTY

CRUISING WORLD – (1982-. 1,5,6,9) – v1-. 1974- – 1 – us UMI [073]

Crum, W E *see*
- THE CANONS OF ATHANASIUS OF ALEXANDRIA
- THE MONASTERY OF EPIPHANIUS AT THEBES

Crum, WE *see* CATALOGUE OF THE COPTIC MANUSCRIPTS IN THE BRITISH MUSEUM

CRUMBLING IDOLS: TWELVE ESSAYS ON ART AND LITERATURE / Garland, Hamlin – 1894 – 9 – 15.00 – us Scholars' Facs [420]

Crummell, Alexander *see* A SELECTION OF WORKS

Crump, J, Fr. *see* PNEUMA IN THE GOSPELS

Crumrine, Boyd *see* HISTORY OF WASHINGTON COUNTY

A CRUSADE OF BROTHERHOOD : A HISTORY OF THE AMERICAN MISSIONARY ASSOCIATION / Beard, Augustus Field – 1909 – 1r – 1 – us Ross [240]

A CRUSADE OF BROTHERHOOD: A HISTORY OF THE AMERICAN MISSIONARY ASSOCIATION / Beard, Augustus Field – Boston: Pilgrim Press, 1909. xii,334p. 1 fiche – 9 – us A.T.L.A. [240]
CRUSADE OR CLASS WAR? / Gallegos Rocafull, Jose Manuel – Washington, DC. 193? Fiche W 904. (Blodgett Collection of Spanish Civil War Pamphlets) – 9 – us H.U. College Libr [946]
CRUSADE OR CLASS WAR? THE SPANISH MILITARY REVOLT / Gallegos Rocafull, Jose Manuel – London, 1937. Fiche W 905. (Blodgett Collection of Spanish Civil War Pamphlets) – 9 – us H.U. College Libr [946]
THE CRUSADE THAT LASSOED SPANISH HEARTS / Whitten, Indy – 1 – 5.00 – us Baptist [240]
CRUSADER – East St. Louis. Ill. 1963- – 1 – us UMI [071]
THE CRUSADER – Gary. Ind. 1962- – 1 – us UMI [071]
THE CRUSADER – Negro Labor Relations League. Chicago. June 16, 1945; Apr. 10, 17; Nov. 1954 – 1 – us NY Public [073]
THE CRUSADER – New York. Jan.-Feb.; Nov. 1921 – 1 – us NY Public [071]
CRUSADER AND MISSION *see* AMERICAN BAPTIST
THE CRUSADERS IN THE EAST : A BRIEF HISTORY OF THE WARS OF ISLAM WITH THE LATINS IN SYRIA DURING THE TWELFTH AND THIRTEENTH CENTURIES / Stevenson, W B – Cambridge: University Press; New York: Putnam [distributor], 1907 – 1mf – us A.T.L.A. [900]
CRUSADERS OF THE TWENTIETH CENTURY : OR, THE CHRISTIAN MISSIONARY AND THE MUSLIM / Rice, Walter Ayscoughe – (Includes bibliographical references and index) – London: W A Rice, 1910 – 2mf – 9 – 0-8370-6696-4 – 1986-0696 – us A.T.L.A. [230]
Cruse, Henri Pierre *see* DIE OPHEFFING VAN DIE KLEURLINGBEVOLKING
Crusell, Bernhard H *see* DIVERTIMENTO PER L'OBOE CON ACCOMPAGNAMENTO DI 2 VIOLINI, VIOLA, ET VIOLONCELLO
Crusenius, N O E S A *see* MONASTICON AUGUSTINIANUM
Crusius, M *see* TVRCOGRAECIAE LIBRI OCTO A'MARTINO CRVSIO, IN ACADEMIA TYBINGENSI GRAECO ET LATINO PROFESSORE, VTRAQUE LINGUA EDITA
CRUSOE'S ISLAND : A RAMBLE IN THE FOOTSTEPS OF ALEXANDER SELKIRK WITH SKETCHES OF ADVENTURE IN CALIFORNIA AND WASHOE, NEVADA / Browne, J Ross – 1864 – 1 – $15.00 – us Library Micro [978]
CRUSTACEANA – Leiden. v1-58. 1960-90 – 5,9 – Dfl5,220.00; Dfl90.00v – ne Swets [590]
Cruttenden, R *see* THE PRINCIPLES AND PREACHING OF THE METHODISTS CONSIDERED IN A LETTER TO THE REVEREND MR. ****
Cruttwell, Charles Thomas *see* A LITERARY HISTORY OF EARLY CHRISTIANITY
Cruttwell, CT *see*
– THE SAXON CHURCH AND THE NORMAN CONQUEST
– SIX LECTURES ON THE OXFORD MOVEMENT
Crutwell, Clement *see* A CONCORDANCE OF PARALLELS
Cruz Brocarte, Antonio de la *see* MEDULA DE LA MUSICA THEORICA..
CRUZ DE MALTA : ORGAM LYRICO-PIEGAS, CARNAVALESCO – Itajuba, 12 Apr 1884 – 1,5,6 – bl Biblioteca [072]
Cruz, Eddy Diaz de *see* STELLA ME ABRIU A PORTA
LA CRUZ EN AMERICA, CON NOTICIA BIOGRAFICA DEL AUTOR POR ERNESTO MORALES ET PROLOGO DE SAMUEL A. LAFONE QUEVEDO / Quiroga, Adan – Buenos-Aires: Editorial americana, 1942 – 1 – F170.78 – fr Armell [920]
LA CRUZ EN LA CONQUISTA DE AMERICA / Bayle, Constantino – Madrid: Razon y Fe, 1933 – 1 – sp Bibl Santa Ana [910]
Cruz, Guillermo Feliu *see* IMAGENES DE CHILE VIDA Y COSTUMBRES CHILENAS EN LOS SIGLOS 18 Y 19 A TRAVES DE...
Cruz Guzman, Emilio *see* LOS PASTOS. SU IMPORTANCIA A TRAVES DEL TIEMPO
Cruz, L M *see* A MULTI-CASE STUDY OF BEGINNING PHYSICAL EDUCATION TEACHERS AT THE ELEMENTARY SCHOOL LEVEL
Cruz Marin, Eugenio de la *see* FLORES Y FRUTOS DE MI CORAZON DEDICACDOS A TI
Cruz Rebosa, Maximo *see* HOMENAJE AL MAESTRO DON..., CABALLERO DE LA ORDEN DE ALFONSO 10TH EL SABIO SEPTIEMBRE, 1958
Cruz, San Juan de la *see* CARTAS (SIECLE 16)
Cruz Valero, Antonio *see* PONENCIA ACERCA DE "PROCEDIMIENTOS DE ELABORACION DE ACEITES DE OLIVAS EN SUS DISTINTOS ASPECTOS"
A CRUZADA : CRITICA, LITTERARIA E CHISTOSA – [s.l.]. 6 Jun 1889 – 1,5,6 – bl Biblioteca [072]
A CRUZADA : DIARIO POLITICO-RELIGIOSO, LITTERARIO, COMMERCIAL E NOTICIOSO – Sao Luis, Oct-Nov 1890; Jan-Dec 1891; Jan-Apr, Sep-Dec 1892 – 1,5,6 – bl Biblioteca [072]
A CRUZADA : PERIODICO LITTERARIO E CENSORIO – Maceio, Alagoas. 25 Jun 1882 – 1,5,6 – bl Biblioteca [072]
A CRUZADA – Queluz de Minas, 28 Apr, Jul-Sep 1930 – 1,5,6 – bl Biblioteca [072]
A CRUZADA – Sao Joao del-Rei, Brazil. Jun-Dec 1925; 1926; Jan-Jun 1927 – 1 – bl Biblioteca [072]
LAS CRUZADAS DEL CORAZON DE JESUS / Alcaniz, Florentino – Badajoz: Tip. J. Sanchez, s.a. – 1 – sp Bibl Santa Ana [240]
EL CRUZADO EXTREMENO – Plasencia, 1903 – 5 – sp Bibl Santa Ana [073]
LOS CRUZADOS DEL CORAZON DE JESUS. AVISOS PRACTICOS PARA SU FUNDACION Y ORGANIZACION / Alcaniz, Florentino – Badajoz: Tip. Grafica Corporativa, 1938 – 1 – sp Bibl Santa Ana [240]
CRUZEIRO – San Luiz, 28 Jan, May, Jul 1884. 12-27 Jan 1885 – 1,5,6 – bl Biblioteca [072]
O CRUZEIRO : DECICADO A RELIGIAO E A PATRIA – [s.l.]. 6 Ago 1874 – 1,5,6 – bl Biblioteca [072]
O CRUZEIRO – Penedo, Alagoas. 29 Jul-17 Dez 1909 – 1,5,6 – bl Biblioteca [072]
O CRUZEIRO DO SUL : ORGAO DO DEPARTEMENTO DO ALTO JURUA – Alto Jurua, Acre. 3 Maio 1906-Fev 1910; Abr, Jul, Out-Dez 1910; Jan-Abr, Jun-Ago 1911; Jan 1912-20 Dez 1917 – 1,5,6 – bl Biblioteca [072]
O CRUZEIRO DO SUL : QUINZENARIO MUNICIPAL – Cruzeiro do Sul, Acre. 6 Abr 1975 – 1,5,6 – bl Biblioteca [072]
CRUZERIO DO NORTE – Maceio, Alagoas. 1 Nov 1890; Jan-Dez 1891; Jan-Dez 1892; 24 Jan 1893 – 1,5,6 – bl Biblioteca [072]
O CRUZILIENSE – Cruzilia, Brazil. Jan 1957 – 1 – bl Biblioteca [072]
A CRY FROM THE LAND OF CALVIN AND VOLTAIRE : A SEQUEL TO "THE WHITE FIELDS OF FRANCE" / McAll, Robert Whitaker – London: Hodder and Stoughton, 1887 – 1mf – us A.T.L.A. [240]
CRYOGENICS – (1982-. 1,5,6,9) – v1-. 1960- – 1 – us UMI [073]
CRYOSCOPIE / Raoult, Francois Marie – Evreux: C. Herissey, 1901. xiii,106p. 2 fiches. (Science Collection) – 9 – 6.00 – fr Bibl Nationale [530]
CRYPTOLOGIA – v.1. 1977 – 1,5,6,9 – us UMI [500]
CRYSTAL LATTICE DEFECTS AND AMORPHOUS MATERIALS – 1970- – 1,5,9 – us Gordon [540]
CRYSTAL SPRINGS FIRST BAPTIST CHURCH. CRYSTAL SPRINGS, MISSISSIPPI : CHURCH RECORDS; DIRECTORY – 1908 – 1 – 5.00 – us Baptist [240]
Crystal Springs, Mississippi *see* MISCELLANEOUS EARLY NEWSPAPERS
CRYSTALLOGRAPHY REPORTS – v1- 1956- – 1,5,6 – us A.I.P. [530]
CRYSTALLOGRAPHY REVIEWS / ed by Moore, Moreton – 9,5,1 – us Gordon [540]
C-S *see* LA LIBERTE DES MERS
CSA (CANADIAN STANDARDS ASSOCIATION) – Printed index. Updates every 60 days – 6,9 – us Info Handling [380]
Csaky, Susan D *see* A COLLECTION OF TRIALS ON MICROFICHE
CSNA BULLETIN – California State Nurses Association. v55-57. 1959-61 – 1 – us UMI [073]
Csoma, Alexandre, de Koros *see* ANALYSE DU KANDJOUR
Csoma de Koeroes, A *see* ESSAY TOWARDS A DICTIONARY, TIBETAN AND ENGLISH
CSONGRAD MEGYEI HIRLAP – Hodmezovasarhely, Hungary. 1962-68 – 14r – 1 – us L of C Photodup [072]
C.S.S. Florida (Confederate Ship) *see* RECORDS OF AND RELATING TO THE C.S.S. FLORIDA, 1862-64
C.T. Mitchell & Co. Charleston, South Carolina *see* RECORDS
CTA MICROFICHE / Canadian Telebook Agency – (Information for identifying and ordering English language books from Canadian sources) – Contains Author and Title sets – 11 issues per yr – 9 – cn Telebook [020]
CTAL WHITE AND BLUE BOOK : IN DEFENSE OF THE ARGENTINE PEOPLE AND AGAINST THE FASCIST REGIME OPPRESSING IT / Confederacion de Trabajadores de America Latina – Mexico City, 1946 – 1 – CSUXAJA7164-B – us Hoover Inst Photo [320]
CTI (COOLING TOWER INSTITUTE) – Printed index. Updated every 60 days – 6,9 – us Info Handling [620]
CUADERNILLO DE MIGUEL PICAZO, MANUSCRITO / Garcia Lorca, Federico – 9 – sp Cultura [440]
CUADERNO DE ACTIVIDADES – 1961. 70p – 1 – 5.00 – us Baptist [240]
CUADERNO DE CONCORDANCIAS Y ORACIONES GRAMATICALES LATINAS PARA USO PARTICULAR DE LOS ESTUDIANTES DE DICHA LENGUA / Romero de Castilla, Pedro – Badajoz: Tip. El Progreso, 1880 – sp Bibl Santa Ana [440]
CUADERNO DE LENGUAJE 4-1 – Plasencia: Editorial Sanchez Rodrigo, S.A., 1970 – 1 – sp Bibl Santa Ana [440]
CUADERNO DE LENGUAJE CURSO 2-1. OTONO / Hijosa del Valle, Gregorio – (Tambien Nos 1-3) – Plasencia: Edit. Sanchez Rodrigo, S.A. 1971 – 1 – sp Bibl Santa Ana [440]
CUADERNO DE LENGUAJE. CURSO NO 2. PT. 2 / Hinojosa del Valle, Gregorio – Plasencia: Editorial Sanchez Rodrigo, S.A., 1971 – 1 – sp Bibl Santa Ana [440]
CUADERNO DE LENGUAJE NO 4, 2 – Plasencia, Caceres: Editorial Sanchez Rodrigo, S.A., 1970 – 1 – sp Bibl Santa Ana [440]
CUADERNO DE MATEMATICAS 3 NO 2 – (Tambien no3; 3-no4; 3-no1) – Plasencia: Edit. Sanchez Rodrigo S.A., 1970 – 1 – sp Bibl Santa Ana [510]
CUADERNO DE MATEMATICAS 4TH 2 / Serradillo Calvo, Martin & Serrano, A – Plasencia: Ed. Sanchez Rodrigo, s.a. – 1 – sp Bibl Santa Ana [510]
CUADERNO DE MATEMATICAS. CURSO 1ST / Rivera Casas, Francisco Moises – (Plasencia): Editorial Sanchez Rodrigo, 1970 – sp Bibl Santa Ana [510]
CUADERNO DE MATEMATICAS NO 1 / Rivera Casas, Francisco Mioses – Plasencia: Edit. Sanchez Rodrigo, S.A. 1971 – 1 – sp Bibl Santa Ana [510]
CUADERNO DE MATEMATICAS NO 3, 1 – Plasencia: Edit. Sanchez Rodrigo, 1971 – 1 – sp Bibl Santa Ana [530]
CUADERNO DE MATEMATICAS NO 4. 1 / Serradilla Calvo, Martin & Serrano, A – Plasencia, Caceres: Editorial Sanchez Rodrigo, S.A., 1971 – 1 – sp Bibl Santa Ana [510]
CUADERNO DE MATEMATICAS NO 4 B / Serradilla Calvo, Martin & Serrano, A – Plasencia, Caceres: Editorial Sanchez Rodrigo, S.A., 1971 – 1 – sp Bibl Santa Ana [510]
CUADERNO DE UNIDADES DIDACTICAS 1-3 / Rojo Cerezo, Virgilio – (Tambien Nos 1-4) – Plasencia: Edit. Sanchez Rodrigo, 1971 – 1 – sp Bibl Santa Ana [370]
CUADERNO DE UNIDADES DIDACTICAS NO 3 – (Tambien no4) – Plasencia: Edit. Sanchez Rodrigo S.A., 1970 – 1 – sp Bibl Santa Ana [370]
CUADERNO DE UNIDADES DIDACTICAS NO 4. NATURALEZA 1 / Garcia Carrasco, Francisco A & Garcia Carrasco, Florencio – Plasencia, Caceres: Editorial Sanchez Rodrigo, S.A., 1970 – 1 – sp Bibl Santa Ana [500]
CUADERNO DE UNIDADES DIDACTICAS NO 4 NATURALEZA 2 / Garcia Carrasco, Francisco A & Garcia Carrasco, Florencio – Plasencia, Caceres: Editorial Sanchez Rodrigo, S.A., 1970 – 1 – sp Bibl Santa Ana [500]
CUADERNO DE UNIDADES DIDACTICAS NO 4 NATURALEZA 3 / Garcia Carrasco, Francisco A & Garcia Carrasco, Florenico – Plasencia, Caceres: Editorial Sanchez Rodrigo, S.A., 1970 – 1 – sp Bibl Santa Ana [500]
CUADERNO DE UNIDADES DIDACTICAS NO 4. VIDA SOCIAL 1 / Garcia Carrasco, Francisco A & Garcia Carrasco, Florencio – Plasencia, Caceres: Editorial Sanchez Rodrigo, S.A., 1970 – 1 – sp Bibl Santa Ana [301]
CUADERNO DE UNIDADES DIDACTICAS NO 4 VIDA SOCIAL 2 / Garcia Carrasco, Francisco A & Garcia Carrasco, Florencio – Plasencia, Caceres: Editorial Sanchez Rodrigo, S.A., 1970 – 1 – sp Bibl Santa Ana [301]
CUADERNO DE UNIDADES DIDACTICAS NO 4 VIDA SOCIAL 3 / Garcia Carrasco, Francisco A & Garcia Carrasco, Florencio – Plasencia, Caceres: Editorial Sanchez Rodrigo, S.A., 1970 – 1 – sp Bibl Santa Ana [301]
CUADERNOS DE ESCRITURA ESCOLAR – Plasencia: Edit. Sanchez Rodrigo, 1975 – 1 – sp Bibl Santa Ana [946]
CUADERNOS DE ESCRITURA ESCOLAR – Plasencia: Edit. Sanchez Rodrigo, S.A. 1976 – 1 – sp Bibl Santa Ana [370]
CUADERNOS DE ESCRITURA ESCOLAR. ADAPTADOS AL METODO RAYAS – Plasencia: Ed. Sanchez Rodrigo, 1961. – Nos 3,4,5,6 – 1 – sp Bibl Santa Ana [370]
CUADERNOS DE HISTORIA DEL PERU... / Barrenechea, Raul Porras – Madrid: Razon y Fe, 1941 – sp Bibl Santa Ana [972]
CUADERNOS DE LA CATEDRA FEIJOO (1 A 24) (CATEDRA FEIJOO-CENTRO DE ESTU DIOS DEL SIGLO XVIII) / Varios – Libros en Microficha no. 02 – 8mf – 9 – Pta4,500.00 – 84-85422-27-9 – sp Pentalfa [900]
CUADERNOS DE LA REALIDAD NACIONAL – Santiago, CL. 1969-1972 – 2r – $100.00 – R04190 – us Library Micro [300]
CUADERNOS DE TEOLOGIA – [Buenos Aires: s.n.] v1-11. 1970-91 – 2r – us Res Libr [200]
CUADERNOS DE TESTIMONIO PARA REUNIONES COMUNITARIAS – (No 1 filmed with: Testimonio (Santiago, Chile), dec 1968-1987) – [Santiago, Chile: Conferencia de Superiores Mayores Religiosos de Chile 1968?- – 1r – us Res Libr [200]
CUADERNOS DEL TERZER MUNDO – Mexico City, MX. 1977-1985 – 5r – $250.00 – R04220 – us Library Micro [072]
CUADERNOS MONASTICOS – Buenos Aires, Argentina: Conferencia de Comunidades Monasticas del Cono Sur. v7 n22 jul/sep 1972; v8 n25 apr/jun 1973; v9 n29 apr/jun 1974; v10 n33/34-v31 n119 apr/sep 1975-oct/dec 1996 – us Res Libr [240]
CUADERNOS POLITICOS – Mexico City, MX. 1974-1975 – 2r – $100.00 – R04221 – us Library Micro [320]
CUADERNOS...GRAMATICALES...ESTUDIANTES / Romero de Castilla, Pedro – 1880 – 9 – 1.50f – sp Bibl Santa Ana [440]
Cuadrado Ceballos, Juan *see* LA VOZ DE DIOS
Cuadrado Retamosa, Joaquin *see* CARTILLA AGRARIA EN VERSO PARA USO DE LAS ESCUELAS DE PRIMERA ENSENANZA
CUADRO GENERAL DEL COMERCIO EXTERIOR DE ESPANA CON SUS POSESIONES DE ULTRAMAR Y POTENCIAS ESTRANGERAS EN 1849-1855 – Madrid, 1852-1856 – 51mf – 9 – sp Cultura [380]
CUADROS DE VIAJE / Heine, Heinrich – Madrid: Calpe, 1920- – 1 – us U.W. Library [890]
CUADROS SINOPTICOS DE TEOLOGIA MORAL / Serrano Serrano, Ildefonso – Segura de Leon: Imp. Ntra. Sra. de Gracia, 1927 – 1 – sp Bibl Santa Ana [290]
CUANDO EL ESTADO GASTA / Bogliolo, Romulo – Buenos Aires: Editorial La Vanguardia, 1st ed 1951 – 1 – CSUXAHZ3587-B – us Hoover Inst Photo [972]
CUANDO LOS MILITARES TENEMOS RAZON / Gazzoli, Luis – Buenos Aires: Plus Ultra, [1973] – 1 – CSUXADJ0206-B – us Hoover Inst Photo [355]
CUANDO PINTO ZURBARAN LOS CUADROS DE LA CARTUJA DE JEREZ DE LA FRONTERA? / Bravo, Luis & Peman, Cesar – Badajoz: Imp. Diput. Provincial, 1963 – sp Bibl Santa Ana [946]
CUANDO Y DONDE SE ORDENO BARTOLOME DE LAS CASAS / Bayle, Constantino – Madrid: Missionalia Hispanica, 1944 – 1 – sp Bibl Santa Ana [240]

CUARESMA Y SEMANA SANTA / Sanchez Aliseda, Casimiro – Madrid: Art. G. Euroamerica, 1957 – 1 – sp Bibl Santa Ana [946]

CUARTA CONFERENCIA INTERNACIONAL SOBRE LA EDUCACION DE ADULTOS, PARIS, 19-29 DE MARZO DE 1985 : EL DESARROLLO DE LA EDUCACION DE ADULTOS, ASPECTOS Y TENDENCIAS / UNESCO – Paris, 1985 – 2mf – 9 – DE-137/1 – ne IDC [370]

Cuartero, Baltasar *see* INDICE DE LA COLECCION SALAZAR, TOMOS 20, 8-37. MADRID, 1961-1966

CUARTERO, BALTASAR Y VARGAS ZUNIGA, ANTONIO. INDICE DE LA COLECCION SALAZAR. TOMOS 23-27. MADRID, 1959-1960 / Uribe, Angel – Madrid: Graf. Calleja, 1967 – 1 – sp Bibl Santa Ana [946]

CUARTILLAS / Groizard y Coronado, Carlos – 1886 – 9 – 1.50f – sp Bibl Santa Ana [810]

CUARTO CENTENARIO DEL NACIMIENTO DE D. BENITO ARIAS MONTANO / Perez Goyena, A – Madrid: Razon y Fe, 1927 – 1 – sp Bibl Santa Ana [946]

CUARTO PLANO DIRECTOR, 1969-73 / Brazil. Superintendencia do Desenvolvimento do Nordeste – 2v. Recife. 1968. BD-654 1 – 9 – ne IDC [338]

CUARTO PLANO DIRECTOR DE DESENVOLVIMENTO ECONOMICO E SOCIAL DO NORDESTE / Brazil – D-910 1. 1969-1973 – 9 – ne IDC [338]

CUATRO ANOS BAJO LA MEDIA LUNA... / Nogales, Rafael de – Madrid: Razon y Fe, 1940 – 1 – sp Bibl Santa Ana [946]

CUATRO ARTICULOS / Aguirre Camara, Jose – Buenos Aires, [1944] – 1 – CSUXAJA7346-B – us Hoover Inst Photo [972]

LOS CUATRO CAMINOS DEL TOREO / Mahizflor – Badajoz: Tip. Vda. de Arqueros, 1947 – 1 – sp Bibl Santa Ana [946]

CUATRO DECRETOS BASICOS PARA EL DESARROLLO AGRARIO DE LA PROVINCIA / Duputacion Provincial – Caceres: Imprenta Diputacion Provincial, 1973 – 1 – sp Bibl Santa Ana [630]

CUATRO LEYENDAS CACERENAS / Arias Corrales, Juan – Caceres: Tip. El Noticiero hacia, 1973 – 1 – sp Bibl Santa Ana [946]

CUATRO MESES DE BARBARIE, MALLORCA BAJO EL TERROR FASCISTA / Perez, Manuel – Valencia, 1937. Fiche W1102. (Blodgett Collection of Spanish Civil War Pamphlets) – 9 – us H.U. College Libr [946]

LOS CUATRO PERONISMOS : ENSAYO CRITICO / Horowicz, Alejandro – Buenos Aires: Editorial Legasa, 1985 – 1 – CSUXAHZ7493-B – us Hoover Inst Photo [320]

CUATRO REVOLUCIONES ARGENTINAS / Zorraquin Becu, Horacio [et al] – Buenos Aires: Ediciones del Club Nicolas Avellaneda, [1960] – 1 – CSUXAJA7157-B – us Hoover Inst Photo [972]

CUATROCIENTAS ESPINELAS / Sanchez Arjona, Vicente – Sevilla: Graficas T., 1952 – 1 – sp Bibl Santa Ana [810]

CUBA : ANUARIO 1972-1974 / Cuba. Direccion Central de Estadistica – (Coll title: Latin American and Caribbean Official Statistical Serials, 1821-1982) – 20mf – 9 – £7.00f (set £450.00 61mf) – uk Chadwyck [972]

CUBA : ANUARIO ESTADISTICO DE CUBA 1952, 1956-1957 / Cuba. Direccion General de Estadistica – (Coll title: Latin American and Caribbean Official Statistical Serials, 1821-1982) – 22mf – 9 – £7.00f (set £450.00 61mf) – uk Chadwyck [972]

CUBA : BOLETIN ESTADISTICO 1964-1965, 1968, 1971 / Cuba. Direccion General de Estadistica – (Coll title: Latin American and Caribbean Official Statistical Serials, 1821-1982) – 15mf – 9 – £7.00f (set £450.00 61mf) – uk Chadwyck [972]

CUBA : COMPENDIO ESTADISTICO DE CUBA 1965-1966, 1968, 1976 / Cuba. Direccion Central de Estadistica – (Coll title: Latin American and Caribbean Official Statistical Serials, 1821-1982) – 4mf – 9 – £7.00f (set £450.00 61mf) – uk Chadwyck [972]

Cuba *see*
- GACETA DE LA HABANA
- GACETA OFICIAL
- PLAN TRIENAL DE CUBA

CUBA, 1930-45 / U.S. Department of State – (Pt 1: 1930-39. 61r $6,715.00; Pt 2: 1940-45. 63r $6,935.00. With printed guides. See also series listing) – Series: Confidential U.S. Diplomatic Post Records: Central America and the Caribbean – 1 – us UPA [972]

Cuba. Consejo Nacional de Economica *see* PROGRAMA NACIONAL DE ACCION ECONOMICA

Cuba. Direccion Central de Estadistica *see* – CUBA

Cuba. Direccion General de Estadistica *see* – CUBA

CUBA ESPANOLA / Reverter Delmas, Emilio – 6v. 1896-99 – 1 – 45.00 – us L of C Photodup [972]

CUBA INTERNACIONAL – Havana, Cuba. -m. Sept 1969-April 1970. 1 reel – 1 – uk British Libr Newspaper [072]

Cuba. Junta central de Planificacion *see* RESUMEN DEL PLAN DE DESARROLLO ECONOMICO DE CUBA PARA 1962'

CUBA NEWS – Havana. v2-4. 1913-15 – 1r – 1 – us Ross [072]

Cuba. Oficina Panamericana *see* CATALOGO DE OBRAS DE DERECHO INTERNACIONAL...

Cuba. Programa Nacional de Accion Economica. (Primera Revision) *see* EL PROGRAMA ECONOMICO DE CUBA

CUBA RESOURCE CENTER NEWSLETTER – NY City, NY. 1972-1973 – 1r – 1 – $50.00 – R04922 – us Library Micro [071]

Cuba. Secretaria de Hacienda *see* INFORME DIRIGIDO AL HONORABLE SENOR PRESIDENTE DE LA REPUBLICA [...] POR EL SECRETARIO DE HACIENDA [...] SOBRE LOS TRABAJOS REALIZADOS POR EL DEPARTAMENTO DESDE EL [...]

CUBA SOCIALISTA – Havana. Sept. 1961-Feb. 1967 and index – 1 – 35.00r – us Hoover Inst Photo [972]

Cuba. Superindendencia de Escuelas *see* INFORME DEL SUPERINTENDENTE DE ESCUELAS DE CUBA

CUBA: THE POLITICAL CONTENT OF ADULT EDUCATION / Fagen, Richard – 77 p. Stanford, Calif.: Hoover Institution on War, Revolution and Peace, Stanford University, 1964 – 1 – 35.00r – us Hoover Inst Photo [370]

THE CUBAN MISSILE CRISIS, 1962 – (With 2-vol printed guide & index £630.00) – 586mf – 9 – £2,940.00 – uk Chadwyck [327]

CUBAN NEWS – Miami. Fl. 1. Feb-Apr 1935 – 1 – us P.K. Yonge [071]

CUBAN REVIEW – NY City, NY. 1974-1979 – 1r – 1 – $50.00 – R04923 – us Library Micro [071]

Cuban Revolutionary Armed Forces *see* VERDE OLIVO

Cubie, Juan Bautista *see* LAS MUGERES VINDICADAS DE LAS CALUMNIAS DE LOS HOMBRES

Cubieres-Palmezeaux, M de *see* LA VENGEANCE DE PLUTON, OU SUITE DES MUSES RIVALES

LE CUBILOT – Journal international d'education, d'organisation et de lutte ouvriere. no. 37-40, 42-44. Colonie d'Aiglemont (Ardennes). nov-dec 1907 – 1 – fr A.C.R.P.P. [335]

CUBISM : SUBJECT COLLECTIONS – (Individual titles not listed separately) – 117 catalogues on 145mf – 9 – £915.00 – uk Chadwyck [700]

Cuboni, G *see* ANNUARIO DELLA R. STAZIONE DI PATOLOGIA VEGETALE DI ROMA

Cuchesne, L *see* THE BEGINNINGS OF THE TEMPORAL SOVEREIGNTY OF THE POPES, A.D. 754-1073

Cucheval, Victor *see* CICERON ORATEUR: ANALYSE ET CRITIQUE DES DISCOURS DE CICERON

A CUCKOO IN KENYA : THE REMINISCENCES OF A PIONEER POLICE OFFICER IN BRITISH EAST AFRICA / Foran, William Robert – London: Hutchinson, [1936] – 1 – us Res Libr [960]

Cucuel, Ernst *see* DIE EINGANGSBUECHER DES PARZIVAL UND DAS GESAMTWERK

Cudell, C A *see* UDINJI (CHEZ LES RIVERAINS DE LA BUSCHIMAIE)

THE CUDGEL – Bowmanville [Ont: s.n., 1859?-18–?] – 9 – cn C.I.H.M. [072]

Cudworth, W *see*
- A DIALOGUE BETWEEN A PREACHER OF INHERENT RIGHTEOUSNESS AND A PREACHER OF GOD'S RIGHTEOUSNESS, REVEAL'D FROM FAITH TO FAITH;...
- A PRESERVATIVE IN PERILOUS TIMES, IN THREE LETTERS
- TRUTH DEFENDED AND CLEARED FROM MISTAKES AND MISREPRESENTATIONS, IN A DIALOGUE BETWEEN ONE MISINFORMED AND AN ADVOCATE FOR THE TRUTH,...

CUE JOURNAL – (Publ delay at v10 1991) – Vancouver. v713. 1987/88-1994 – 9 – Can$20.00y – cn Micromedia [073]

Cuellar Grajera, Antonio *see*
- LA FORMACION PROFESIONAL DEL JURISTA
- LA INTERVENCION DEL ABOGADO EN LA CONSTITUCION DE LAS SOCIEDADES MERCANTILES
- EL PROBLEMA DE LA DEFENSA DE LOS DERECHOS E INTERESES LEGITIMOS DE LAS MINORIAS DE ACCIONISTAS EN LAS SOCIEDADES MERCANTILES

CUENCO COLLECTION – Manila, Philippines: Microfilm Corporation of the Philippines, 1983 – 9r – us Res Libr [950]

CUENTA DETALLADA Y DOCUMENTADA QUE PRESENTA EL MINISTRO DE HACIENDA E INDUSTRIA CIUDADANO PEDRO GARCIA, COMO AJENTE FINANCIERO EN EL EXTERIOR, NOMBRADO POR EL SUPREMO GOBIERNO DE BOLIVIA – La Paz: Impr de La Libertad, 1872 – us Res Libr [972]

CUENTA GENERAL DE RENTAS Y GASTOS Y CUENTA DE GASTOS DEL DEPARTMENTO DE HACIENDA / Venezuela. Ministerio de Hacienda – Caracas. 1912 13-1940 41 – 1 – 253.00 – us L of C Photodup [972]

CUENTA QUE EL ALCALDE...DE 1850 / Badajoz – 1851 – 9 – 1.50f – sp Bibl Santa Ana [946]

CUENTA QUE PRESENTA AL CONGRESO NACIONAL DE LOS ESTADOS UNIDOS DE VENEZUELA EL MINISTRO DE HACIENDA EN ... – Caracas: Impr de la "Gaceta oficial," 1880-1881 – us Res Libr [972]

CUENTA QUE PRESENTA AL CONGRESO NACIONAL DE LOS ESTADOS UNIDOS DE VENEZUELA EN... – Caracas: Impr de la vapor de "la opinion nacional," 1882-90 – us Res Libr [972]

CUENTA...MEMORIAS CRITICAS Y APOLOGETICAS...CARLOS 4 DE BORBON / Godoy, Manuel – 1838 – 9 – $1.50f – sp Bibl Santa Ana [946]

CUENTAS DE PROPIOS (ANNO 1511-1555) – Caceres – 1r – 5,6 – sp Cultura [946]

EL CUENTO DE TRISTAN DE LEONIS – Edited from the unique ms. Vatican 6428 by George Tyler Northup. Chicago: University of Chicago Press, 1928. ix,298p. (The Modern Philology Monographs of the University of Chicago.) – 1 – us U.W. Library [390]

CUENTOS / Hauff, Wilhelm – Madrid, Barcelona: Calpe, 1920 – 1r – 1 – us U.W. Library [830]

CUENTOS DE LA ABUELITA / Gallardo de Alvarez, Isabel – Madrid: Sociedad de Educacion Atenas S.A., Tomo 1 – 1 – sp Bibl Santa Ana [946]

CUENTOS DE LA ABUELITA / Gallardo de Alvarez, Isabel – Madrid: Sociedad de Educacion Atenas S.A., Tomo 2. 1947 – 1 – sp Bibl Santa Ana [370]

CUENTOS INGENUOS / Trigo, Felipe – Madrid: Renacimiento, 1920 – sp Bibl Santa Ana [946]

CUENTOS POPULARES...EXTREMADURA / Hernandez de Soto, Sergio – 1886 – 9 – 1.50f – sp Bibl Santa Ana [830]

CUENTOS REALISTAS / Villalba Dieguez, Fernando – Caceres: Imprenta Mordena, 1954 – sp Bibl Santa Ana [946]

CUENTOS Y CHASCARRILLOS ANDALUCES – 1898 – 1 – us I.U. Libraries [390]

EL CUERDO EN SU CASA / Vega Carpio, Lope de – Madrid: Rivadeneyra, 1857 – 1 – sp Bibl Santa Ana [946]

CUERPO DE DOCUMENTOS DEL SIGLO 16 SOBRE LOS DERECHOS DE ESPANA EN LAS INDIAS Y LAS FILIPINAS DESCUBIERTOS Y CONTADOS POR... / Hanke, Lewis – Madrid: Missionalia Hispanica, 1947 – 1 – sp Bibl Santa Ana [946]

CUERPO DE DOCUMENTOS DEL SIGLO 17 SOBRE LOS DERECHOS DE ESPANA EN LAS INDIAS Y LAS FILIPINAS, DESCUBIERTOS Y ANOTADOS POR LEWIS HANKE...MEXICO, 1943 / Hanke, Lewis – Madrid: Razon y Fe, 1947 – 1 – sp Bibl Santa Ana [946]

Cuervo, Fray usto *see* BIOGRAFIA DE FR. LUIS DE GRANADA...DEMUESTRA...AUTOR DEL LIBRO DE ORACION

Cuervo, Justo OP *see* FR. LUIS DE GRANADA, VERDADERO Y UNICO AUTOR DEL LIBRO DE LA ORACION

Cuesta, M *see* MADRID. BIBLIOTECA NACIONAL. CATALOGO DE OBRAS DE IBEROAMERICA Y FILIPINAS

CUESTION DE ACTUALIDAD / Castel, Joaquin – 1899 – 9 – 1.50f – sp Bibl Santa Ana [000]

LA CUESTION DE TEHUANTEPEC – Nueva-York, 1852 – 1mf – 1 – ILM-2380/1 – ne IDC [327]

LA CUESTION ELECTORAL / Pastor Diaz, Nicomedes – 1839 – 9 – 1.50f – sp Bibl Santa Ana [946]

CUESTION INTERNACIONAL : "ES EXTRANJERO EL HIJO DEL EXTRANJERO" / Fombona, E – Caracas, 1868 – 1mf – 1 – ILM-3732/1 – ne IDC [327]

LA CUESTION RELIGIOSA EN AMERICA / Bayle, Constantino – Madrid: Razon y Fe, 1922 – 1 – sp Bibl Santa Ana [240]

LA CUESTION ROMANA Y EL MARQUES DE COMILLAS / ed by Bayle, Constantino – Madrid: Razon y Fe, 1927 – 1 – sp Bibl Santa Ana [946]

LA CUESTION SOCIAL EN DICIEMBRE DE 1839 Y ENERO DE 1840 / Pastor Diaz, Nicomedes – Caceres: Imprenta de Don Lucas de Burgos, 1839 – 1 – sp Bibl Santa Ana [946]

LA CUESTION SOCIAL EN EXTREMADURA A LA LUZ DE LAS ENCICLICAS RERUM NOVARUM Y QUADREGESIMO ANNO / Fernandez Santana, Ezequiel – Los Santos de Maimona: Imprenta Boletin Parroquial, 1935 – sp Bibl Santa Ana [946]

CUESTIONARIO RESUMEN DE LAS ORDENES Y CIRCULARES SOBRE ENLACES SINDICALES Y JUNTAS DE JURADOS. CARTILLAS DEL ENLACE SINDICAL (SECCIONES SINDICALES) / Delegacion Provincial de SindicatosVicesecretaria Provincial de Ordenacion Social – Caceres: Tip. El Noticiero, 1944 – sp Bibl Santa Ana [946]

CUESTIONES ACTUALES DE DOCTRINA Y PRACTICA. BUENOS AIRES, 1927 / Macklin, J M – Madrid: Razon y Fe, 1930 – 1 – sp Bibl Santa Ana [240]

CUESTIONES DE DERECHO INTERNACIONAL PRIVADO (EL DIVORCIO) / Calandrelli, A – Buenos Aires, 1923 – 4mf – 1 – ILM-3724/1 – ne IDC [327]

THE CUESTONIAN – San Luis Obispo, CA: Cuesta College, Feb 1966-May 1982 – 3r – 1 – $150.00 – B02902 – us Library Micro [370]

Cuevas, Manuel *see* TESTAMENTO DE HERNAN CORTES

Cuevas, Mariano *see* LA VIRGEN DE GUADALUPE EN MEJICO

THE CUGACH ESKIMO / Birket-Smith, K – BN 140 2. 1953 – 8 – ne IDC [970]

Cugnet, Francois Joseph *see* AN ABSTRACT OF THE SEVERAL ROYAL EDICTS AND DECLARATIONS, AND PROVINCIAL REGULATIONS AND ORDINANCES, THAT WERE IN FORCE IN THE PROVINCE OF QUEBEC IN THE TIME OF THE FRENCH GOVERNMENT..

CUIHUA XUEBAO – (1980-81, 1984 $4.50f; 1983 $3.50f) – Journal of Catalysis. In Chinese but English abstracts to the main articles. F p87 – 9 – cc Microforms [073]

CUISINE – (1982- 1,5,6,9) – v8- 1979- – 1 – us UMI [640]

CUISINE – (v11-13 no 12 1982-84 5,6,9) – v8-13 no 12 1979-84 – 1 – us UMI [640]

Cuisinier, Jeanne *see* LES MU'O'NG

Cuisset, Octave *see* LE PERE COULANGE OU ENTRETIENS SUR LA CULTURE ET LA PREPARATION DU TABAC

LE CUIVRE / Federation Nationale des Syndicats du Cuivre et Similaires – nos 1-105. Lyon. Oct 1894 – Apr 1903 – 1 – fr A.C.R.P.P. [622]

CUK NA PAL'CI – Buenos Aires, Argentina, 1930 – 1mf or 1 reel – 9,1 – us I.H.R.C. [972]

CULBERTSON BANNER – Culbertson, NE. -w. Jan. 1908-May 1921 – 1 – us NE Hist [071]

CULBERTSON ERA – Culbertson, NE. -w. Oct. 1895-Jul. 1898; Sep. 1898-Dec. 1898. Incomplete; Jan. 1899-Sep. 1900; Nov. 1900-Dec. 1900. Incomplete; Apr. 1901-Dec. 1904 – 1 – us NE Hist [071]

CULBERTSON PROGRESS – Culbertson, NE. -w. Jul. 1920-Aug. 1965 – 1 – us NE Hist [071]

CULBERTSON SUN – Culbertson, NE. -w. Jul. 1880; Feb. 1883-Aug. 1884 – 1 – us NE Hist [071]

CULCAIRN SHIRE ADVERTISER – Sep 10 1909-Mar 29 1912 – 9 – at Pascoe [072]

THE CULDEES OF THE BRITISH ISLANDS AS THEY APPEAR IN THE HISTORY / Reeves, W – Dublin, 1864 – Dfl30.00 – ne Slangenburg [240]

Culen, Konstantin *see*
- DEJINY SLOVAKOV V AMERIKE, VOLS 1 AND 2
- J. SLOVENSKY

Culligan, C T *see* EXERCISE ADHERENCE

Cullinan, Bernice E *see* RESEARCH ON CHILDREN'S AND YOUNG ADULT LITERATURE

Cullom Association. North Carolina. Warrenton Baptist Church *see* CHURCH MINUTES

Cullum, George Washington *see*
- BIOGRAPHICAL REGISTER OF THE OFFICERS AND GRADUATES OF THE U.S. MILITARY ACADEMY AT WEST POINT, NY FROM ITS ESTABLISHMENT IN 1802, TO 1890
- CAMPAIGNS OF THE WAR OF 1812-15, AGAINST GREAT BRITAIN, SKETCHED AND CRITICISED: WITH BRIEF BIOGRAPHIES OF THE AMERICAN ENGINEERS
- MAJOR-GENERAL RICHARD MONTGOMERY

Culmann, Hellmut *see* TEUFELSMUELLER

CULMER ZEITUNG – Culm (Chelmno), Poland. 13 Oct 1925-24 Dec 1926, 8 Feb-9 Sept 1927, 16 Jul-19 Sept 1928 – 1 – gw Mikrofilm [072]

CULP. (CALIFORNIA UNION LIST OF PERIODICALS) / CLASS. (Cooperative Library Agency for Systems and Services) – A finding list for serials in California libraries – 9 – us CLASS [073]

Culpeper, N *see*
- A DIRECTORY FOR MIDWIVES
- THE ENGLISH PHYSITIAN
- PHARMACOPOEIA LONDINENSIS...
- SEMEIOTICA URANICA OR AN ASTROLOGICAL JUDGMENT OF DISEASES...

Culpepper, James Edward *see* INDUCTIVE PREACHING: AN ANALYSIS OF CONTEMPORARY THEORY AND PRACTICE

Culross, James *see*
- RESURRECTION AND THE LIFE, OR, LAZARUS REVISITED
- THE RESURRECTION AND THE LIFE, OR, LAZARUS REVIVED
- THE THREE RYLANDS: A HUNDRED YEARS OF VARIOUS CHRISTIAN SERVICE

LE CULTE CATHOLIQUE, OU, EXPOSITION DE LA FOI DE L'EGLISE ROMAINE:.. / Begin, Louis Nazaire – Quebec: A. Cote, 1875. 02334. (Pre-1900 Canadiana) – 9 – cn C.I.H.M. [240]

LE CULTE DE SAINTE ANNE EN AMERIQUE OU SAINTE-ANNE DE BEAU ET SA FILIATION DANS LE NOUVEAU MONDE / Charland, Paul Victor – (Levis; Quebec: Mercier). 00580. (Pre-1900 Canadiana) – 9 – cn C.I.H.M. [240]

LE CULTE DES SAINTS DANS LA BRENNE / Galvan Soto, F – 9 – F70.00 – fr Ethnologie [240]

UN CULTE DYNASTIQUE AVEC EVOCATION DES MORTS CHEZ LES SAKALAVES DE MADAGASCAR, LE "TROMBA" / Rusillon, Henry – Paris: A Picard, 1912 – 1 – us Res Libr [960]

LES CULTES POPULAIRES EN VENDEE / Riviere, G – 9 – F60.00 – fr Ethnologie [306]

THE CULTIC DEITIES OF THE INUIT (ESKIMO) / Thalbitzer, W – BN 416 2. 1928 – 8 – ne IDC [290]

CULTIVATED FERNS, OR A CATALOGUE OF EXOTIC AND INDIGENOUS FERNS CULTIVATED IN BRITISH GARDENS / Smith, J – 7262. 1857 – 9 – ne IDC [580]

LE CULTIVATEUR : HEBDO DE LA PATRIE – (16 nov 1911-28 sep 1933f 14r Can$50.00) – Montreal, 10 dec 1892-17 nov 1906 – 7r – 1 – Can$50.00 – cn Can Microfilming [072]

LE CULTIVATEUR : HEBDO DU CANADIEN DE QUEBEC – Montreal, Canada. v8 n22. 19 nov 1881-30 dec 1882 – 1r – 1 – Can$50.00 – cn Can Microfilming [072]

LE CULTIVATEUR INDEPENDANT – Trois-Rivieres, Canada. v1 n5. 7 oct-18 nov 1854 – 1r – 1 – Can$25.00 – cn Can Microfilming [072]

CULTIVATION, MANURING AND WATERING "SAWAH-RICE" (RICE GROWN IN FLOODED FIELDS) / Indonesia. Institute for the Research of Rice at Bogor – 1962 – 9 – SE-8512 1 – ne IDC [630]

CULTIVATION OF FISH FRY AND ITS LIVE FOOD / ed by Styczynska-Jurewicz, E et al – 1979 – xii/534p – 9 – Bf950.00 (Bf1,200.00 for non-EAS/WAS members) – be E.A.S. [639]

THE CULTIVATION OF PISTACHIO IN LIBYA / Libya. Ministry of Agriculture and Livestock – Pamphlet nr.35. Jul 1963. BNE-1030 1 – 9 – ne IDC [630]

EL CULTO A LA EUCARISTIA EN LA ESPANA ROJA / Bayle, Constantino – Burgos: Razon y Fe, 1938 – 1 – sp Bibl Santa Ana [240]

EL CULTO A MA-BELLONA EN LA ESPANA ROMANA / Garcia y Bellido, Antonio – Madrid, 1956 – 1 – sp Bibl Santa Ana [946]

EL CULTO AL EMPERADOR EN NUMIDIA. DE AUGUSTO A DIOCLECIANO / Cid Lopez, Rosa Maria – 3mf – 9 – Pta2,000.00 – 84-85422-60-0 – sp Pentalfa [290]

CULTO ANTIGUO DE SAN MASONA METROPOLITANO DE MERIDA / Smedt, C de – Madrid: Fortanet, 1885. B.R.A.H. vi/pp. 141-142 – 1 – sp Bibl Santa Ana [240]

CULTOS EMERITENSES DE SERAPIS Y DE MITHRAS / Melida, Jose Ramon – Madrid: Tip. Fortanet, 1914. B.R.A.H. LIV, pp. 439-456 – sp Bibl Santa Ana [946]

CULTOS EN HONOR DE LA SANTISIMA VIRGEN DE ARGEME. PATRONA DE LA CIUDAD DE CORIA Y CONSAGRACION DE SU NUEVO SANTUARIO / Coria. Ayuntamiento – Plasencia: Imp. La Victoria, 1972 – 1 – sp Bibl Santa Ana [240]

Cultru, P *see* HISTOIRE DU SENEGAL DU XVE SIECLE A 1870

CULTURA – Rio de Janeiro, BL. 1951-1954 – 2r – $100.00 – R04170 – us Library Micro [072]

CULTURA – Tegucigalpa. v.1-11. July 1939-Dec 1951 – 1 – 69.00 – us L of C Photodup [370]

CULTURA CIUDADANA : EL JUSTICIALISMO SOCIAL, EL JUSTICIALISMO ECONOMICO, LA POLITICA JUSTICIALISTA / Gonzalez Trillo, Enrique & Behety, Luis Ortiz – [Buenos Aires: s.n.], 1953 – 1 – CSUXADH8448-B – us Hoover Inst Photo [360]

CULTURA E FE – Porto Alegre, Brasil: Instituto de Desenvolvimento Cultural. v1-12 n51. apr/jun 1978-90 – us Res Libr [972]

CULTURA EN LA ESPANA REPUBLICANA / Marinello, Juan – N.Y., 1937. Fiche W 1501. (Blodgett Collection of Spanish Civil War Pamphlets) – 9 – us H.U. College Libr [946]

LA CULTURA EN MEXICO – (Suppl to: Siempre (Mexico City, Mexico). Filmed with main title) – [Mexico: Editorial Siempre! n1-814. feb 21 1962-sep 30 1977 (81r); n827-1342 1978-1987 (32r) – us Res Libr [972]

LA CULTURA ESPANOLA MEDIEVAL : DATOS BIO-BIBLIO-GRAFICOS PARA SU HISTORIA, TOMO 1, A-G / Vera, Francisco – Madrid: Imprenta Gongora, 1933 – 1 – sp Bibl Santa Ana [946]

LA CULTURA ESPANOLA MEDIEVAL : DATOS BIO-BIBLIOGRAFICOS PARA SU HISTORIA. TOMO 2. H-Z / Vera, Francisco – Madrid: Imprenta Gongora, 1934 – 1 – sp Bibl Santa Ana [946]

CULTURA HOJE : BOLETIM EDITADO PELA COORDENADORIA DE COMUNICACAO SOCIAL DA CULTURA – [s.l.], 19 Maio 1985-Jun 1986; Jan-Dez 1987 – 1 – bl Biblioteca [072]

CULTURA PARA EL PUEBLO / Argentina. Direccion General de Relaciones Culturales y Difusion – [Buenos Aires?, 1950?] – 1 – CSUXADM8380-B – us Hoover Inst Photo [306]

CULTURA TURCICA – Ankara, 1964-1967. v1-4 – 21mf – NE-114/2 – ne IDC [490]

LA CULTURA Y LA IMPRENTA EUROPEAS EN EL JAPON DURANTE LOS SIGLOS 16 Y 17. LA INICIATIVA ESPANOLA BASE DE LA IMPORTANTE GESTA (1548-1616) / Vindel, Francisco – Madrid: Razon y Fe, 1944 – 1 – sp Bibl Santa Ana [306]

A CULTURAL AND HISTORICAL STUDY OF SELECTED WOMEN'S DANCE FROM HERAT, AFGANISTAN : 1970-1980 / St John, Katherine – 1993 – 3mf – $12.00 – us Microform Publ [790]

CULTURAL ANTHROPOLOGY AND EDUCATION / Camilleri, C – 1986 – 171p – 9 – 92-3-102339-X – Co-published with Kogan Page Ltd, London, who have exclusive sales rights in the United Kingdom – fr UNESCO [306]

THE CULTURAL BACKGROUND OF INDONESIAN POLITICS / Zoetmulder, Petrus Josephus – SE 6182 1. 1967 – 9 – ne IDC [306]

CULTURAL CHRONOLOGY OF THE GULF OF CHIRIQUI, PANAMA / Linares de Sapir, Olga – 1968 – 4mf – 9 – $5.00f – us Ross [520]

CULTURAL CREATIONS. / Comite Tecnico de Ayuda a los Espanoles en Mexico – Mexico, 1940. Fiche W 821. (Blodgett Collection of Spanish Civil War Pamphlets) – 9 – us H.U. College Libr [946]

CULTURAL DEVELOPMENT : EXPERIENCE AND POLICIES / Giraud, Augustin – 2nd rev ed 1983 – 189p – 9 – 92-3-102020-X – fr UNESCO [303]

CULTURAL DEVELOPMENT : SOME REGIONAL EXPERIENCES – 1981 – 477p – 9 – 92-3-101667-9 – fr UNESCO [303]

CULTURAL DEVELOPMENT AND ENVIRONMENT / Tohme, Georges – 1992 – 120p – 9 – 92-3-102787-5 – fr UNESCO [370]

CULTURAL DIMENSION OF DEVELOPMENT : TOWARDS A PRACTICAL APPROACH – 1995 – 229p – 9 – 92-3-103043-4 – fr UNESCO [306]

CULTURAL DIVERSITY PROGRAM / Human Relations Area Files – 1988. 46 cultural files constituting a teaching sample – 9 – 7000.00; apply – us H.R.A.F. [306]

THE CULTURAL EAST – (Filmed with: Eastern Buddhist) – v1 nos 1-2. Jul 1946-Aug 1947 (complete) – 1r – 1 – ATLA S0068B – us A.T.L.A. [270]

THE CULTURAL EAST *see* EASTERN BUDDHIST

CULTURAL INDUSTRIES : A CHALLENGE FOR THE FUTURE OF CULTURE – 1982 – 236p – 9 – 92-3-102003-X – fr UNESCO [301]

CULTURAL NOTES – Libertarian Alliance, London, nos.1-7,9,11. 22p – 9 – 1.00f – at Libertarian Micro [335]

CULTURAL POLICY : A PRELIMINARY STUDY – 1969 – 51p – 9 – 92-3-100775-0 – fr UNESCO [350]

CULTURAL POLICY IN ARGENTINA / Harvey, Edwin R – 1979 – 9 – 92-3-101547-8 – fr UNESCO [972]

CULTURAL POLICY IN CZECHOSLOVAKIA / Marek, Miroslav et al – 2nd ed 1986 – 9 – 92-3-100853-6 – fr UNESCO [943]

CULTURAL POLICY IN ECUADOR / Moreira, Dario – 1979 – 9 – 92-3-101549-4 – fr UNESCO [972]

CULTURAL POLICY IN THE KINGDOM OF SAUDI ARABIA / Almani, Muhammad Abdullah & Assbit, Abdul-Rahman – 1981 – 9 – 92-3-101772-1 – fr UNESCO [956]

CULTURAL POLICY IN THE MONGOLIAN PEOPLE'S REPUBLIC – 1982 – 9 – 92-3-101985-6 – fr UNESCO [950]

CULTURAL POLICY IN THE PEOPLE'S REPUBLIC OF CHINA – 1983 – 9 – 92-3-102153-2 – fr UNESCO [950]

CULTURAL POLICY IN THE REPUBLIC OF PANAMA / National Institute of Culture – 1978 – 9 – 92-3-101529-X – fr UNESCO [972]

CULTURAL POLICY IN THE UNITED KINGDOM / Abercrombie, Nigel – 1982 – 9 – 92-3-102018-8 – fr UNESCO [941]

CULTURAL POLICY IN THE YEMEN ARAB REPUBLIC / Al-Haddad, Abdul-Rahman – 1982 – 9 – 92-3-101976-7 – fr UNESCO [956]

CULTURAL SITUATION IN SOCIALIST ETHIOPIA / Eshete, Aleme – 1982 – 56p – 9 – 92-3-101981-3 – fr UNESCO [306]

CULTURAL SURVIVAL – Cambridge. 96 docs. 1980-1991 – 105mf – 9 – ne IDC [320]

CULTURAL TRIANGLE OF SRI LANKA – 1993 – 200p – 9 – 92-3-102874-X – Co-published with the Central Cultural Fund (CCF) – fr UNESCO [306]

CULTURAL TYPES PROGRAM / Human Relations Area Files – 1988. Modules of 3 to 6 cultural files each. Limited to two-year colleges – 9 – us H.R.A.F. [306]

CULTURE : REVUE TRIMESTRIELLE; SCIENCES RELIGIEUSES ET PROFANES AU CANADA / Association des recherches sur les sciences religieuses et profanes au Canada – Quebec. v5-32. 1940-71. SEM16P260 – 5r – 5 – Can$151.00 – cn Bibl Nat [073]

LA CULTURE – Montreal, Canada. 4 nov 1876-v1 n3. 2 dec 1876 – 1r – 1 – Can$25.00 – cn Can Microfilming [072]

CULTURE AND CIVILIZATION OF ALSACE-LORRAINE PAMPHLET COLLECTION – 1914-1918 – 1 – CSUXANR9454-B – us Hoover Inst Photo [306]

CULTURE AND RELIGION IN SOME OF THEIR RELATIONS / Shairp, John Campbell – New York: Hurd and Houghton; Cambridge: Riverside Press, 1872 – 1mf – 9 – 0-8370-5240-8 – 1985-3240 – us A.T.L.A. [306]

CULTURE AND THE GOSPEL, OR, A PLEA FOR THE SUFFICIENCY OF THE GOSPEL / McCall, Salmon – New York: A.D.F. Randolph, 1871.1 fiche – 9 – us A.T.L.A. [240]

LA CULTURE DU TABAC – Montreal: E. Senecal, 1882. 02233. (Pre-1900 Canadiana) – 9 – cn C.I.H.M. [971]

CULTURE ET CIVILISATION KHMERES / Universite Buddhique Preah Sihanouk Raj – Phnom Penh, 1962. Nos 1-7. Lacking: No 6 – 6mf – 9 – ne IDC [950]

LA CULTURE FRANCAISE EN RUSSIE (1700-1900) / Haumant, E – Ed. 2. Paris. 1913. BR-6182 2 – 8 – ne IDC [947]

CULTURE, MEDICINE AND PSYCHIATRY – (v8-. 1984-. 5,6,9) – v1-. Apr 1977- – 1 – us UMI [616]

THE CULTURE OF JUSTICE : A MODE OF MORAL EDUCATION AND OF SOCIAL REFORM / Du Bois, Patterson – (Includes bibliographical references and index) – New York: Dodd, Mead, 1907 – 1mf – 9 – 0-8370-8504-7 – 1986-2504 – us A.T.L.A. [230]

THE CULTURE OF SIMPLICITY / McLeod, Malcolm James – 4th ed. New York: Fleming H Revell, c1904 – 1mf – 9 – 0-8370-6333-7 – 1986-0333 – us A.T.L.A. [240]

THE CULTURE OF THE BEST : AND THE MANUFACTURE OF BEET SUGAR / Child, David Lee – Boston: Weeks, Jordan, 1840 – 1 – us Res Libr [631]

LA CULTURE PHYSIQUE DE LA FEMME / Parnet, Max – Paris: Nilsson, 1913. vi,129p. (Les Femmes Collection) – 2mf – 9 – $6.00 – fr Bibl Nationale [790]

CULTURE PROBLEMS IN NORTHEASTERN NORTH AMERICA / Speck, F G – BN 395 2. 1926 – 8 – ne IDC [971]

CULTURE VIVANTE / Quebec. (Province). Ministere des Affaires Culturelles – Quebec. nos 1-29/30. 1966-73. SEM35P147 – 1r – 1 – Can$48.00 – cn Bibl Nat [971]

CULTURES AND CIVILIZATIONS / Reid, Struan – 1994 – 48p – 9 – 92-3-102927-4 – fr UNESCO [900]

LES CULTURES POPULAIRES – (Textes d'orientation. Programme et conclusions generales. 1mf. F20.00. Commission 1. Les Cultures populaires comme cultures du travail. 5mf. F70.00. Commission 2. Cultures populaires et cultures politiques. 4mf. F60.00. Commission 3. Les Cultures populaires comme cultures de groupes sociaux ou territoriaux specifiques. 4mf. F60.00. Commission 4. Les Cultures populaires dans leurs systemes d'expression. 5mf. F70.00) – Colloque de la Societe d'Ethnologie Francaise et de la Societe Francaise de Sociologie – 9 – F220.00 – fr Ethnologie [306]

LE CULTURISTE – Montreal, Canada. 11 dec 1912 – 1r – 1 – Can$25.00 – cn Can Microfilming [073]

Culver, April D *see* COMPARISON OF BEHAVIOR MODIFICATION TECHNIQUES USED IN PHYSICAL EDUCATION WITH INSTITUTIONALIZED PROFOUNDLY MENTALLY RETARDED STUDENTS AT DIFFERENT AGES

CULVER CITY – 1947-48; 1972-92 – 27r – 1 – $1,350.00 – P00022 – us Library Micro [910]

CULVER CITY INDEPENDENT – Culver City, CA. Oct 1957- – 270+ r – 1 – $13,500.00 ($120.00) – R02154 – us Library Micro [071]

CULVER CITY NEWS – Culver City, CA. 1958- – 144+ r – 1 – $7,200.00 ($200.00y) – H04041 – us Library Micro [071]

CULVER CITY STAR NEWS – (Various titles including: Crenshaw-News, Hawthorne-Press Tribune, Inglewood-News, La Brea/Inglewood-The Daily News, Lawndale-Tribune, Lennox-Citizen, Rancho-Chevoit Hills-News, Torrance-News, Venice-Vanguard, Westchester-Star News) – Culver City, CA. 1941-1985 – 394r – 1 – $19,700.00 – H03195 – us Library Micro [071]
CULVER SITY/MARINA DEL REY – 1993- – 2+ r – 1 – $100.00 – P00023 – us Library Micro [910]
Culwick, A T *see* GOOD OUT OF AFRICA
CUMBERLAND, 1820 : BRITISH ISLES CENSUS DIRECTORIES PROJECT, ENGLAND – (In prep) – at Vine [941]
CUMBERLAND, 1828 : BRITISH ISLES CENSUS DIRECTORIES PROJECT, ENGLAND – (In prep) – at Vine [941]
CUMBERLAND, 1834 : BRITISH ISLES CENSUS DIRECTORIES PROJECT, ENGLAND – (In prep) – at Vine [941]
CUMBERLAND, 1847 : BRITISH ISLES CENSUS DIRECTORIES PROJECT, ENGLAND. VOL 149 – 4mf – 9 – A$27.00 – at Vine [941]
CUMBERLAND, 1855 : BRITISH ISLES CENSUS DIRECTORIES PROJECT, ENGLAND – at Vine [941]
CUMBERLAND, 1879 : BRITISH ISLES CENSUS DIRECTORIES PROJECT, ENGLAND. VOL 110 – 3mf – 9 – A$21.00 – at Vine [941]
CUMBERLAND, 1897 : BRITISH ISLES CENSUS DIRECTORIES PROJECT, ENGLAND. VOL 112 – 7mf – 9 – A$45.00 – at Vine [941]
CUMBERLAND, 1901 : BRITISH ISLES CENSUS DIRECTORIES PROJECT, ENGLAND – at Vine [941]
CUMBERLAND AND CARLISLE JOURNAL – 1966 and 1967 – 1 – uk Microform Academic [072]
CUMBERLAND AND REG. – Camp Hill, PA., 1805-1809 – 13 – $25.00r – us I.M.R. [071]
CUMBERLAND AND WESTMORELAND, ANCIENT AND MODERN / Sullivan, Jeremiah – 1857 – 1 – us I.U. Libraries [390]
The Cumberland and Westmoreland Antiquarian and Archaeological Society *see* TRANSACTIONS
Cumberland, Barlow *see* A SKETCH OF HOW "THE DIAMOND ANTHEM" WAS SUNG AROUND THE WORLD THROUGH THE COLONIES OF THE EMPIRE ON THE 20TH JUNE, 1897: THE 60TH ANNIVERSARY OF THE ACCESSION DAY OF HER MAJESTY QUEEN VICTORIA
CUMBERLAND (CARLISLE), 1837 : BRITISH ISLES CENSUS DIRECTORIES PROJECT, ENGLAND. VOL 199 – 1mf – 9 – A$9.00 – at Vine [941]
CUMBERLAND (CARLISLE AND WHITEHAVEN), 1805 : BRITISH ISLES CENSUS DIRECTORIES PROJECT, ENGLAND. VOL 171 – 1mf – 9 – A$9.00 – at Vine [941]
CUMBERLAND CITY FIRST BAPTIST CHURCH. CUMBERLAND CITY, TENNESSEE : CHURCH RECORDS – 1914-64 – 1 – 8.82 – us Baptist [240]
CUMBERLAND (EAST), 1884 : BRITISH ISLES CENSUS DIRECTORIES PROJECT, ENGLAND – at Vine [941]
CUMBERLAND EVENING NEWS *see* CUMBERLAND NEWS (EVENING ED)
CUMBERLAND EVENING NEWS AND STAR *see* CUMBERLAND NEWS (EVENING ED)
Cumberland, G *see* THOUGHTS ON OUTLINE, SCULPTURE, AND THE SYSTEM THAT GUIDED THE ANCIENT ARTISTS IN COMPOSING THEIR FIGURES AND GROUPES
CUMBERLAND ISLANDER – British Columbia, CN. Jan 1910-Jul 1931 – 9r – 1 – cn Commonwealth Micro [072]
CUMBERLAND MAPS / Windsor Castle. Royal Archives – 1 – uk Microform Academic [910]
THE CUMBERLAND MAPS / Royal Library. Windsor Castle – (Over 4,500 military maps and documents from 15th-19th C. Printed chronological and geographical indexes.) – 1987 – 692 colour mf – 15 – $10,900.00 – 0-907716-19-9 – uk Mindata [910]
CUMBERLAND MAPS: CATALOGUE AND INDEX / Windsor Castle. Royal Archives – 1 – uk Microform Academic [941]
Cumberland, Maryland *see* MISCELLANEOUS EARLY NEWSPAPERS
CUMBERLAND METROPOLITAN – Carlisle, PA., 1823 – 13 – $25.00r – us I.M.R. [071]
CUMBERLAND NEWS – Carlisle, England. Jun 1910-1913; 1973- – 85+ r – 1 – uk British Libr Newspaper [072]
CUMBERLAND NEWS – Jul 1910-Dec 1972 – 1 – uk Microform Academic [072]
CUMBERLAND NEWS (EVENING ED) – (Also known as: Cumberland Evening News; Cumberland Evening News and Star; News and Star) – Aug 12 1914-68; 1979-Feb 1983; Nov 1984-90; Jan 4 1991-92; Jan 2-Dec 1993; Jan 4 1994-Jul, Aug-Nov (incl Sunday News), Dec 1995-Jun 1997 – 293r – 1 – uk British Libr Newspaper [072]
CUMBERLAND PACQUET – Or Ware's Whitehaven Advertiser, Great Britain. 1774-1783 – 1 – uk Microform Academic [072]
CUMBERLAND PAPERS / Windsor Castle. Royal Archives – 1745-65 – 1 – uk Microform Academic [920]
CUMBERLAND PAPERS, INDEX / Windsor Castle. Royal Archives – 1 – uk Microform Academic [920]
CUMBERLAND PRESBYTERIAN CHURCH : MINUTES / Cumberland Presbyterian Church – 1966-90 (complete) – Inquire – 1 – ATLA S0509 – us A.T.L.A. [240]
Cumberland Presbyterian Church *see* CUMBERLAND PRESBYTERIAN CHURCH
Cumberland Presbyterian Church. General Assembly *see* MINUTES, 1848-1942
Cumberland. Presbytery (Cum. Pres. Ch.) *see* MINUTES, 1810-13; CUMBERLAND. SYNOD
Cumberland, R *see*
- ANECDOTES OF EMINENT PAINTERS IN SPAIN, DURING THE 16TH AND 17TH CENTURIES
- ANECDOTES OF EMINENT PAINTERS IN SPAIN, DURING THE SIXTEENTH AND SEVENTEENTH CENTURIES...

CUMBERLAND REGISTER – Carlisle, PA. -w 1805-09. 1 roll – 13 – $25.00r – us I.M.R. [071]
Cumberland, Richard *see* SANCHONIATHO'S PHOENICIAN HISTORY
CUMBERLAND VALLEY JOURNAL – Mechanicsburg, PA. -w 1860-63. 1 roll – 13 – $25.00r – us I.M.R. [071]
CUMBERLAND (WHITEHAVEN), 1883 : BRITISH ISLES CENSUS DIRECTORIES PROJECT, ENGLAND – (In prep) – at Vine [941]
CUMBERLANDS – v14-19, no.2. Fall 1977-Fall-Winter 1982 – 1,5,6,9 – us UMI [410]
CUMBERNAULD NEWS AND KILSYTH CHRONICLE – 1 – £42.00r – uk Scot News [072]
CUMHURIYET – Iskece, Greece. Siyasi Tuerkce gazetedir. Sahibi ve Mesul Mueduerue: Ibrahim Demir. No. 1 (2 Subat 1934) – 9 – $20.00 – us MEDOC [956]
CUMHURIYET – Istanbul: Cumhuriyet, 1956- – 1 – us Res Libr [949]
CUMHURIYET – Istanbul. Turkey. 1924-1942 – 1 – us UMI [072]
CUMHURIYET – (Yrly reel count varies) – [Turkey], 1980- – 1 – inquire – us Ross [072]
CUMING COUNTY ADVERTISER – West Point, NE. -w. Apr 1889-Nov 1900 – 1 – us NE Hist [071]
CUMING COUNTY DEMOCRAT – West Point, NE. -w. Aug 1876-Mar 1877, scattered issues missing; Oct 1877-Nov 1886; Jun-Sep 1902; Jan 1907; Aug 1909-Dec 1974 – 1 – us NE Hist [071]
Cuming, G J *see* THE DURHAM BOOK, BEING THE FIRST DRAFT OF THE REVISION OF THE BOOK OF COMMON PRAYER IN 1661
Cumming, James Elder *see* THROUGH THE ETERNAL SPIRIT
Cumming, Jed *see* REVEALING INDIA'S PAST
Cumming, John *see*
- BENEDICTIONS
- FORESHADOWS
- MOSES RIGHT, AND BISHOP COLENSO WRONG

Cumming, Robert Cushing *see*
- THE ANNOTATED CORPORATION LAWS OF ALL THE STATES, GENERALLY APPLICABLE TO STOCK CORPORATIONS
- THE INSURANCE LAWS OF THE STATE OF NEW YORK.
- THE LAWS OF NEW YORK STATE RELATING TO GENERAL, RELIGIOUS AND NON-BUSINESS CORPORATIONS, TAXATION AND EXEMPTION, SUNDAY OBSERVANCE, MARRIAGE AND DIVORCE

Cumming, W P *see* THE REVELATIONES OF SAINT BIRGITTA
Cummings, Ephraim Chamberlain *see* NATURE IN SCRIPTURE
Cummings, John N *see* LETTERS
Cummings-Danson, G *see* THE DIFFERENCES IN EDUCATIONAL PREPARATION AND ATHLETIC EXPERIENCE BETWEEN DIVISION 1 AND DIVISION 2 ATHLETIC DIRECTORS OF NATIONAL COLLEGIATE ATHLETIC ASSOCIATION MEMBER INSTITUTIONS
CUMMINGTON 1751-1902 – (Mf 1-6: Town & Vital Records 1762-1856. Mf 7: Proprietors 1762-79. Mf 8-12: Vital Records 1744-1844. Mf 13-18: Town & Vital Records 1770-1835. Mf 19-20: B,M,D 1844-52. Mf 21-23: Index to Intentions 1780-1986. Mf 24-28: Intentions of Marriage 1780-1986. Mf 29: Rebellion Records 1861-65. Mf 30-31: Index to Births 1853-1986. Mf 32-33: Index to Marriages 1853-1986. Mf 34-35: Index to Deaths 1853-1986. Mf 36-40: Deaths 1853-1987. Mf 41: Marriages 1853-94. Mf 42-43: Births 1853-1902) – (mf ed 1988) – 43mf – 9 – 0-87623-083-4 – us Holbrook [920]
Cummins, James Sheldon *see* STATE AND TERRITORIAL GENERAL STATUTES RELATING TO THE USE OF STREETS AND HIGHWAYS BY STREET RAILWAY, GAS, WATER AND ELECTRIC LIGHT COMPANIES
CUMMINS' TERRITORY REPORTS / Idaho. Supreme Court – (A Pre-NRS title) – 1v. 1866-1867 (all publ) – 3mf – 9 – $4.50 – LLMC 91-031 – us L.L.M.C. [340]
CUMNOCK CHRONICLE AND MUIRKIRK ADVERTISER – 1 – £42.00r – uk Scot News [072]
Cumont, Franz *see*
- ASTROLOGY AND RELIGION AMONG THE GREEKS AND ROMANS
- THE MYSTERIES OF MITHRA
- THE ORIENTAL RELIGIONS IN ROMAN PAGANISM
- TEXTES ET MONUMENTS FIGURES RELATIFS AUX MYSTERES DE MITRA PUBLIES AVEC UNE INTRODUCTION CRITIQUE

EL CUMPLIMIENTO DE LAS OGLIGACIONES / Lumbreras Valiente, Pedro – Valencia, 1974 – 1 – sp Bibl Santa Ana [946]
THE CUMULATED INDEX KEWENSIS / Royal Botanical Gardens. Kew – (Consolidation of over 1 million taxonomic entries in the Index Kewensis published in printed form from 1893-1975) – 484mf – 9 – $2,000.00 – 1-900853-25-6 – uk Mindata [580]
CUMULATED INDEX MEDICUS – 1960- 1; 1970- 5,6; 1975- 4 x 6 in. 9 – us UMI [610]
CUMULATED INDEX MEDICUS – v1-23. 1960-82.Continues: Index Medicus; Quarterly Cumulative Index to Current Medical Literature; Quarterly Cumulative Index Medicus; Current List of Medical Literature – 1,5,6 – us Princeton Micro [610]
CUMULATED MAGAZINE SUBJECT INDEX, 1907-1949 / F.W. Faxon Company. Boston – 1964 – 2r – 1 – $675.00 – 0-8161-1513-3 – uk Hall [073]
CUMULATED SUBJECT INDEX TO PSYCHOLOGICAL ABSTRACTS, 1927-1960 / G.K. Hall and Co. – (First Supplement, 1961-1965, 1968. 125,000 entries 1 reel. $310.00 export $375.00. – ISBN 0-8161-1295-5; Second Supplement, 1966-1968, 1971. 176,000 entries on 2 reels. $410.00 export $495.00. – ISBN 0-8161-1289-4) – 1966. 350,000 entries on 2 reels – $745.00 export $900.00 – 0-8161-1352-1 – uk Hall [150]
THE CUMULATIVE ANNUAL INDEX TO THE CURRENT DIGEST OF THE POST-SOVIET PRESS – v28 1976-v50 1998 – 9,1 – $295.00v diazo $10.00 extra for silver – us Current [072]
CUMULATIVE BIBLIOGRAPHY OF AFRICAN STUDIES : AUTHOR CATALOG / International African Institute. London – 1973 – 4r – 1 – $200.00 export $240.00 – 0-8161-1252-5 – uk Hall [960]
CUMULATIVE BIBLIOGRAPHY OF AFRICAN STUDIES : CLASSIFIED CATALOG / International African Institute. London – 1973 – 6r – 1 – $300.00 export $360.00 – 0-8161-1253-3 – uk Hall [960]
CUMULATIVE BIBLIOGRAPHY OF AFRICAN STUDIES / International African Institute. London – (Author Catalog, 1973.-55,700 entries 4 reels. $220.00 ISBN: 0-8161-1252-5; Classified Catalog, 1973.-51,600 entries 6 reels. $330.00 ISBN: 0-8161-1253-3) – Card index-2 parts: author and classified (geographically with subdivisions by subjects, peoples and languages) – 1 – uk Hall [960]
CUMULATIVE BIBLIOGRAPHY OF ASIAN STUDIES, 1966-70 / Association for Asian Studies – (Subject Bibliography, 1966-70.-1972.-68,500 entries 6 reels. $455.00 ISBN: 0-8161-1326-2) – 1972.-76,200 entries 3 reels.-ISBN: 0-8161-1488-9 – 1 – $455.00 – uk Hall [950]
CUMULATIVE BULLETIN / U.S. Internal Revenue Service – v1-. 1919-95 – 9 – $1,770.00 set – us Hein [324]
CUMULATIVE BULLETIN, INCOME TAX RULINGS / U.S. Treasury Department – (Cont by: IRS Cumulative Bulletin) – Bureau of Internal Revenue. Weekly, irregular – 21mf – 9 – $31.50 – LLMC 82-707 – us L.L.M.C. [324]
CUMULATIVE DOCUMENT RETRIEVAL INDEX (DRI) / U.S. National Institute of Justice NCJRS – 1972-89. Annotated descriptions of more than 105,000 documents in the NCJRS collection, indexed, in binder – 9 – $99.00 – us N.C.J.R.S. [360]
THE CUMULATIVE EFFECTS OF MULTIPLE EXERCISE BOUTS OF EQUAL CALORIC EXPENDITURE ON EXCESS POST-EXERCISE OXYGEN CONSUMPTION / Williams, Jeffrey P – 1989 – 64p 1mf – 9 – $4.00 – us Microform Publ [612]
CUMULATIVE INDEX TO A SELECTED LIST OF PERIODICALS : ANNUAL – v1-3. 1896-98 (complete) – 1r – 1 – ATLA S0926 – us A.T.L.A. [020]
CUMULATIVE INDEX TO A SELECTED LIST OF PERIODICALS : MONTHLY – v4-8. 1899-1903 (incomplete) – 2r – 1 – ATLA S0927 – us A.T.L.A. [020]
CUMULATIVE INDEX TO ENGLISH TRANSLATIONS, 1948-1968, UNESCO / UNESCO. Paris – 1973. 44,000 entries on 2 reels – 1 – $429.00 export $515.00 – 0-8161-1467-6 – uk Hall [420]
CUMULATIVE INDEX TO NURSING LITERATURE – (See also: Cumulative Index to Nursing and Allied Health Literature) – v1-21 1956-76 1; 1974-76 5,6; v20-21 1975-76 9 – us UMI [610]
CUMULATIVE INDEX TO NURSING LITERATURE AND ALLIED HEALTH LITERATURE – v. 22-. 1977- – 1,5,6,9 – us UMI [610]
CUMULATIVE INDEX TO THE NCJRS MICROFICHE COLLECTION / U.S. National Institute of Justice NCJRS – 9 – 1985 $117.00; 1986 $117.00; 1987 $168.00; 1988 $100.00; 1989 $35.00; 1990 $64.00; 1991 $68.00 – us N.C.J.R.S. [360]
Cunard, Nancy *see* NEGRO ANTHOLOGY 1931-1933
THE CUNEIFORM INSCRIPTIONS FROM WESTERN ASIA / Rawlinson, H C – (G. Smith, Pinches, E. Norris). v1-4. 1861-1875 – 9 – ne IDC [930]
CUNEIFORM TEXTS FROM BABYLONIAN TABLETS – (C. J. Cadd). v. 36. London. 1921. BNE-20,059 1 – 9 – ne IDC [930]
Cuneo, Dardo *see*
- COMPORTAMIENTO Y CRISIS DE LA CLASE EMPRESARIA
- EL DESENCUENTRO ARGENTINO, 1930-1955
- OLIGARQUIA Y PODER EN LA ARGENTINA

Cuneo-Vidal, Romulo *see*
- EL CAPITAN DON GONZALO PIZARRO, PADRE DE PIZARRO HERNANDO, JUAN Y GONZALO PIZARRO, CONQUISTADORES DEL PERU
- DONA INES MUNOZ, LA MUJER EXTREMENA, CUNADA DE FRANCISCO PIZARRO, QUETRAJO EL TRIGO Y EL OLIVO AL PERU
- LOS HIJOS AMERICANOS DE LOS PIZARROS DE LA CONQUISTA
- LAS LEYENDAS GEOGRAFICAS DEL PERU DE LOS INCAS
- VIDA DEL CONQUISTADOR DEL PERU DON FRANCISCO PIZARRO Y DE SUS HERMANOS HERNANDO, JUAN Y GONZALO PIZARRO Y FRANCISCO MARTIN DE ALCANTARA

Cuni y Martorell, M *see* CATALOGOMETODICO Y RAZONADO DE LOS COLEOPTEROS OBSERVADOS IN CATALUNA
Cuninggim, J L *see* A PLAN FOR BETTER RELIGIOUS INSTRUCTION IN THE SOUTHERN METHODIST CHURCH
Cuningham, Granville Carlyle *see* REPORT ON THE SYSTEM OF ELECTRIC STREET CARS FOR THE CITY OF TORONTO
Cunningham, Allan *see*
- THE LIFE AND CORRESPONDENCE OF ROBERT BURNS
- SONGS CHIEFLY IN THE RURAL LANGUAGE OF SCOTLAND

Cunningham, D D *see* ON THE PHENOMENA OF FERTILIZATION IN FICUS ROXBURGHII WALL
Cunningham, George Godfrey *see* LIVES OF EMINENT AND ILLUSTRIOUS ENGLISHMEN: FROM ALFRED THE GREAT TO THE LATEST TIMES, ON AN ORIGINAL PLAN.
Cunningham, J F *see* UGANDA AND ITS PEOPLES
Cunningham, J T *see*
- THE NATURAL HISTORY OF THE MARKETABLE MARINE FISHES OF THE BRITISH ISLANDS
- A TREATISE ON THE COMMON SOLE (SOLEA VULGARIS)

Cunningham, John *see*
- THE CHURCH HISTORY OF SCOTLAND
- THE GROWTH OF THE CHURCH IN ITS ORGANIZATION AND INSTITUTIONS
- THE QUAKERS

Cunningham, K M *see* ST SEGMENT CHANGES DUE TO HANDRAIL SUPPORT DURING GRADED EXERCISE TREADMILL TESTING
Cunningham, Lynda F *see* FACTORS ASSOCIATED WITH THE RECALL OF PHYSICAL ACTIVITY
Cunningham, Thomas *see* A NEW AND COMPLETE LAW DICTIONARY, OR, GENERAL ABRIDGMENT OF THE LAW:...
Cunningham, Thomas J *see* THE BLUE BOOK OF THE STATE OF WISCONSIN
Cunningham, William *see*
- CHRISTIAN CIVILISATION
- CHRISTIANITY AND ECONOMIC SCIENCE
- CHRISTIANITY AND POLITICS
- CHRISTIANITY AND SOCIAL QUESTIONS
- DISCUSSIONS ON CHURCH PRINCIPLES
- THE REFORMERS AND THE THEOLOGY OF THE REFORMATION

Cunningham, William Bennett *see* LAW OF FORCIBLE ENTRY AND DETAINER, IN THE STATE OF ILLINOIS
Cuoq, Jean A *see* LEXIQUE DE LA LANGUE ALGONQUINE
CUORE – 1992-1995 – 1r per y – 5,6 – Sfr401.00 – sz Infoprint [944]
CUORE E CRITICA – (See also series: Important Periodicals of Italian and International Socialism, 1868-1917) – Savona, Bergamo. v1,no1-v4,no24. 1887-90. 12 fiches – 9 – $55.00 – us UPA [335]
CUP OF BLESSING (CCC152) / Ho, Shih-ming – (In Chinese) – 1st ed. Hong Kong: Council on Christian Literature for Overseas Chinese, 1957 – 1r – 1 – 1984-B500 – us A.T.L.A. [240]
Cuperi, G *see* TRACTATUS DE PATRIARCHIS CONSTANTINOPOLITANIS (CBH 32)
CUPIDOOS MENGELWERKEN OF MINNESPIEGEL DER DEUGDEN, BESTAANDE UIT STIGHTELYKE ZINNEBEELDEN / Hesman, Gerrit – Amsterdam, 1728 – 2mf – 9 – O-3081/1 – ne IDC [760]
CUPIDO'S LUSTHOF ENDE DER AMOUREUSE BOOGAERT BEPLANT ENDE VERCIERT MEET 22 SCHOONE COPERE FIGUIREN... / Breughel, G H van – Amsterdam, 1613 – 2mf – 9 – ne IDC [700]
Cuq, M E *see* LA NATIONALITE DES SOCIETES
EL CURA DE SANTA CRUZ. SAN SEBASTIAN, 1928 / Urquijo, Julio de La Cruz de Sangre; ed by Bayle, Constantino – Madrid: Razon y Fe, 1928 – 9 – sp Bibl Santa Ana [946]
EL CURA SANTA CRUZ / ed by Bayle, Constantino – Madrid: Razon y Fe, 1926 – 1 – sp Bibl Santa Ana [946]
CURA Y MIL VECES CURA. BARCELONA, 1928 / Merino, Eugenio; ed by Bayle, Constantino – Madrid: Razon y Fe, 1929 – 9 – sp Bibl Santa Ana [240]
Curacao. (Netherlands) *see* TIENJARENPLAN 1962-1971
DE CURACAOSCHE COURANT – Netherlands West Indies. 1812-1948 – 1 – us UMI [072]
DE CURACAOSCHE COURANT / Netherlands West Indies. Curacao – v157 + suppls. 1969 – 2r – 1 – us Ross [072]
DE CURACAOSCHE COURANT – (Willemstad). July 1853-Aug. 1893; 1949-69 – 1 – us NY Public [972]
Curado Garcia, Blas *see* ABC DEL ALCOHOLISMO
Curaeus, J *see* EXEGESIS PERSPICVA ET FERME INTEGRA CONTRAVERSIAE DE SACRA COENA,...
LOS CURAS / Aradillas Agudo, Antonio – Barcelona: Dopesa, 1978 – 1 – sp Bibl Santa Ana [946]
Curatorium der Zunz-Stiftung *see* JUBELSCHRIFT ZUM NEUNZIGSTEN GEBURTSTAG DES DR. L. ZUNZ
Curatulo, Giacomo Emilio *see* IL DISSIDIO TRA MAZZINI E GARIBALDI: LA STORIA SENZA VELI
Curci, Carlo Maria *see* IL VATICANO REGIO
Cure, B F *see* PROGRESSIVE MEN OF IOWA
A CURE FOR CANTING : OR, THE GRAND IMPOSTORS OF ST. STEPHEN'S AND OF SURREY CHAPELS UNMASKED,... / Woolley, W – London, 1794 – 1mf – 9 – MP-587/1 – ne IDC [240]
LE CURE LABELLE (1833-1891) / Baudoncourt, Jacques de – Bar-le-Duc France, 1892. 04077. (Pre-1900 Canadiana) – 9 – cn C.I.H.M. [920]
CURED FISH : MARKET PATTERNS AND PROSPECTS – 1983 – 151p – it F.A.O. [650]
CURENTUL – Bucuresti: Imp "Curentul" SAR, apr 16 1939-1942 – 10r – 1 – us Res Libr [072]
Cureton, Kirk J *see*
- PEAK OXYGEN DEFICIT AS A PREDICTOR OF SPRINT AND MIDDLE-DISTANCE TRACK PERFORMANCE
- VALIDATION OF FITNESSGRAM ONE-MILE RUN/WALK CRITERION-REFERENCED STANDARDS IN MEN AND WOMEN 18 TO 25 YEARS OF AGE

Cureton, Stephen *see* PERSEVERANCE WINS: THE CAREER OF A TRAVELLING CORRESPONDENT: ENGLAND, CANADA, UNITED STATES, HAWAIIAN ISLANDS, NEW ZEALAND, AUSTRALIA, EGYPT, ITALY
Cureton, Thomas Kirk *see* HOW TO TEACH SWIMMING AND DIVING
Cureton, William *see*
- ANCIENT SYRIAC DOCUMENTS RELATIVE TO THE EARLIEST ESTABLISHMENT OF CHRISTIANITY IN EDESSA AND THE NEIGHBOURING COUNTRIES
- SPICILEGIUM SYRIACUM
- THE THIRD PART OF THE ECCLESIASTICAL HISTORY OF JOHN, BISHOP OF EPHESUS
- VINDICIAE IGNATIANAE, OR, THE GENUINE WRITINGS OF ST IGNATIUS

CURIAE SIGILLI SECRETI (ANNO 1479-1516) / Fernando 2 – Barcelona – 1r – 5,6 – sp Cultura [946]
Curie, P *see* EXPOSITION DE LA RELIGION SAINT-SIMONIENNE
CURIEUSE BIBLIOTHEC, ODER FORTSETZUNG DER MONATLICHEN UNTERREDUNGEN – Frankfurt, Leipzig, 1704-1706. Repositorium 1-3 (mf ed 1993) – 13mf – 9 – DM380.00 – 3-89131-087-0 – gw Fischer [020]
CURIEUSER AVISEN- ODER ZEITUNGS-SCHLUESSEL [...] – Braunschweig, 1725 – 9 – Inquire at Mikrofilmarchiv for details – gw Misc Inst [943]
Curio, C A *see*
- CAELII AVGVSTINI CVRIONIS SARRACENICAE HISTORIAE LIBRI TRES, ...
- HISTORIAE LIBRI TRES, AB AUTORE INNUMERIS LOCIS EMENDATI ATQUE EXPOLITI. IN QVIBVS SARRACENORUM, TURCARUM, ALIARUMQUE; GENITUM ORIGINES ET RES PER ANNOS SEPTIN GENTOS GESTAE, CONTINENTUR
- A NOTABLE HISTORIE OF THE SARACENS. BRIEFLY AND FAITHFULLY DESCRYBING THE ORIGINALL BEGINNING CONTINUAUNCE AND SUCCESSE ASWELL OF THE SARACENS, AS ALSO OF TURKES, SOULDANS, MAMALUKES, ASSASSINES, TARTARIANS AND SOPHIANS

CURIOSIDADES GRAMATICALES, GRAMATICA AMPLIADA DEL IDIOMA ESPANOL Y SUS DIALECTOS / Martinez Garcia, Ramon – 3rd ed. corrected and ampl. with 3rd part. Madrid: Viuda de Hernando, 1896 – 1 – us U.W. Library [440]
CURIOSIDADES: NOTICIAS E VARIEDADES HISTORICAS BRAZILEIRAS / Moreira de Azevedo, Manuel Duarte – Rio de Janeiro: B.L. Garnier, 1873. 214p – 1 – us U.W. Library [972]
CURIOSITES LINGUISTIQUES... / Doucere, Victor – Lyon, Paris: Vitte, 1936 – 1 – F55.03 – fr Armell [400]
CURIOSITEZ FRANCOISES / Oudin, A – 1640 – 9 – fr I.C.S. [440]
THE CURIOSITIES AND LAW OF WILLS / Proffatt, John – San Francisco: Whitney, 1876. 216p. LL-1023 – 1 – us L of C Photodup [340]
THE CURIOSITIES OF ALE AND BEER: AN ENTERTAINING HISTORY / Cook, Charles Henry – London: Swan Sonnenschein, 1889.xii,449p. illus – 1 – us U.W. Library [390]
CURIOSITIES OF LAW AND LAWYERS / James, Croake – (Lacking: p178) – New York: Funk & Wagnalls Co, 1899 – 9mf – 9 – $13.50 – LLMC 95-151 – us L.L.M.C. [340]
CURIOSITIES OF LAW AND LAWYERS / James, Croake – London: Sampson, Low, Marston, Searle & Rivington, 1891 – 9mf – 9 – $13.50 – LLMC 91-063 – us L.L.M.C. [340]
CURIOSITIES OF THE LAW REPORTERS / Heard, Franklin Fiske – San Francisco: Bancroft, 1876. 212p. LL-1670 – 1 – us L of C Photodup [340]
CURIOSITIES OF THE LAW REPORTERS / Heard, Franklin Fiske – San Francisco: Sumner Whitney & Co, 1885 – 3mf – 9 – $4.50 – LLMC 95-164 – us L.L.M.C. [340]
EL CURIOSO AVERIQUADOR – Valencia de Alcantara, 1907-1909 – 5 – sp Bibl Santa Ana [073]
EL CURIOSO EXTREMENO – Llerena, 1905-1906 – 5 – sp Bibl Santa Ana [073]
UN CURIOSO MANUSCRITO SOBRE EL CONVENTO DE SAN ONOFRE DE LA LAPA (BADAJOZ) (SU BIBLIOTECA Y SACRISTIA EN EL SIGLO 16) / Alvarez, Arturo – Badajoz: Dip. Prov., 1958. Sep. REE – sp Bibl Santa Ana [946]
CURIOSO TRATADO DE LA NATURALEZA Y CALIDAD...DEL CHOCOLATE... / Colmenero Ledesma, A – Madrid, 1631 – 1mf – 9 – sp Cultura [630]
CURIOUS CASES : A COLLECTION OF AMERICAN AND ENGLISH DECISIONS SELECTED FOR THEIR READABILITY / Milburn, Benjamin Arrell – Charlottesville: Michie, 1902 – 5mf – 9 – $7.50 – LLMC 95-048 – us L.L.M.C. [340]
CURIOUS CASES; A COLLECTION OF AMERICAN AND ENGLISH DECISIONS, SELECTED FOR THEIR READABILITY / Milburn, Benjamin Arrell – Charlottesville, VA: Michie Co., 1902. 441p. LL-567 – 1 – us L of C Photodup [340]
CURIOUS FACTS, MYTHS, LEGENDS, AND SUPERSTITIONS CONCERNING CHRIST / Wright, John W – Cincinnati: Cranston & Curts, 1894. 1 fiche – 9 – us A.T.L.A. [240]
CURIOUS QUESTIONS / Brann, Henry A – Newark, N.J.: J.J. O'Connor, 1866 – 1mf – us A.T.L.A. [240]
Curipeschitz, B *see*
- EIN DISPUTATION ODER BESPRECH ZWAYER STALBUBEN
- WEGRAYSZ KEYSERLICHER MAIESTAT LEGATION MIT 32. JAR ZU DEM TURCKEN GESCHICKT WIE VND WAS GESTALT SIE HINEIN VND WIDERUMB HERAUSZ KOMEN I..

Curle, J *see* A ROMAN FRONTIER POST AND ITS PEOPLE. THE FORT OF NEWSTEAD
Curley, Jeffrey J *see* THE EFFECTS OF PLYOMETRIC TRAINING ON SPRINTING PERFORMANCE OF COLLEGIATE MALES
O CURRALINHENSE – Villa do Curralinho, BA. 7 Dez 1882; Maio, 25 Out 1884 – 1,5,6 – bl Biblioteca [072]
Curran, Edward Lodge *see* FRANCO: WHO IS HE, WHAT DOES HE FIGHT FOR?
Curran, J J *see* DEBATE ON LOUIS RIEL [SIC]
THE CURRENCY AND THE BANKING LAW OF THE DOMINION OF CANADA: CONSIDERED WITH REFERENCE TO CURRENCY REFORM IN THE UNITED STATES / Cornwell, William Caryl – New York: G. Putnam, 1895. 00245. (Pre-1900 Canadiana) – 9 – cn C.I.H.M. [332]
CURRENCY EXCHANGE SURVEY; SURVEY REPORT / U.S. Agency for International Development – SE 11,629 1. 1963 – 9 – ne IDC [324]
CURRENCY LAD – Sydney, 1832-33 – 1r – 1 – A$31.00 silver A$27.00 vesicular – at Pascoe [072]
CURRENT – v1-248 1960-82 1; v125-248 5,6,9 – us UMI [073]
CURRENT – North Platte, NE. -w. Jan-Aug 1890; Nov 1890 – 1 – us NE Hist [071]
CURRENT ADVANCES IN APPLIED MICROBIOLOGY AND BIOTECHNOLOGY; A SECTION OF CURRENT AWARENESS IN BIOLOGICAL SCIENCES – v1- 1983- – 5,6,9 – us UMI [576]
CURRENT ADVANCES IN CANCER RESEARCH; A SECTION OF CURRENT AWARENESS IN BIOLOGICAL SCIENCES – v1- 1988- – 5,6,9 – us UMI [616]
CURRENT ADVANCES IN CELL AND DEVEOLPMENTAL BIOLOGY; A SECTION OF CURRENT AWARENESS IN BIOLOGICAL SCIENCES – v1- 1983- – 5,6,9 – us UMI [574]
CURRENT ADVANCES IN CLINICAL CHEMISTRY; A SECTION OF CURRENT AWARENESS IN BIOLOGICAL SCIENCES – v1- 1974- – 5,6,9 – us UMI [615]
CURRENT ADVANCES IN ECOLOGICAL AND ENVIRONMENTAL SCIENCES; A SECTION OF CURRENT AWARENESS IN BIOLOGICAL SCIENCES – v1- 1975- – 5,6,9 – us UMI [574]
CURRENT ADVANCES IN ENDOCRINOLOGY AND METABOLISM; A SECTION OF CURRENT AWARENESS IN BIOLOGICAL SCIENCES – v1- 1984- – 5,6,9 – us UMI [612]
CURRENT ADVANCES IN GENETICS AND MOLECULAR BIOLOGY; A SECTION OF CURRENT AWARENESS IN BIOLOGICAL SCIENCES – (Continues: Current Advances in Genetics) – v1- 1976- – 5,6,9 – us UMI [575]
CURRENT ADVANCES IN IMMUNOLOGY AND INFECTIOUS DISEASES; A SECTION OF CURRENT AWARENESS IN BIOLOGICAL SCIENCES – v1- 1984- – 5,6,9 – us UMI [616]
CURRENT ADVANCES IN NEUROSCIENCE; A SECTION OF CURRENT AWARENESS IN BIOLOGICAL SCIENCES – v1- 1984- – 5,6,9 – us UMI [610]
CURRENT ADVANCES IN PLANT SCIENCE; A SECTION OF CURRENT AWARENESS IN BIOLOGICAL SCIENCES – v1- 1972- – 5,6,9 – us UMI [580]
CURRENT ADVANCES IN PROTEIN BIOCHEMISTRY; A SECTION OF CURRENT AWARENESS IN BIOLOGICAL SCIENCES – v1- 1984- – 5,6,9 – us UMI [540]
CURRENT ADVANCES IN TOXICOLOGY; A SECTION OF CURRENT AWARENESS IN BIOLOGICAL SCIENCES – v1- 1984- – 5,6,9 – us UMI [615]
CURRENT AFFAIRS – (Issues for may 31 1978-mar 2 1981 filmed with: Comment (South African Broadcasting Corporation), mar 3 1981-jun 21 1982) – Johannesburg: Broadcast House, jan-may 30 1978, 1977, 1976, 1975, 1974, jan 29-dec 1973 (2r); may 31 1978-mar 2 1981 (1r) – us Res Libr [070]
CURRENT AFFAIRS TRANSLATIONS BULLETIN – 1976 – 1,5,6,9 – us UMI [073]
CURRENT AFFAIRS TRANSLATIONS BULLETIN – (Cont: Indonesian Current Affairs Translation Bulletin) – Jakarta, 1976 1,5*,9* – 1,5,9 – D9950.01 – us UMI [490]
CURRENT AFFAIRS TRANSLATIONS BULLETIN *see* INDONESIAN CURRENT AFFAIRS TRANSLATION BULLETIN
CURRENT ANTHROPOLOGY – v1- 1960- 1; v12- 5,6 – us UMI [301]
CURRENT AWARENESS IN BIOLOGICAL SCIENCES (CABS) – (Formerly: Int'l. Abstracts of Biological Sciences. Database combining the following 12 titles: Current Advances in Applied Microbiology and Biotechnology; Current Advances in Cancer Research; Current Advances in Cell and Developmental Biology; Current Advances in Clinical Chemistry; Current Advances in Ecological and Environmental Sciences; Current Advances in Endocrinology and Metabolism; Current Advances in Genetics and Molecular Biology; Current Advances in Immunology and Infectious Diseases; Current Advances in Neuroscience; Current Advances in Plant Science; Current Advances in Protein Biochemistry; Current Advances in Toxicology) – v1- 1954- – 5,6,9 – us UMI [574]
CURRENT BACKGROUND / U.S. Consulate General. Hong Kong – 13 Jun 1950-74 – 1 – $32.00y $503.00 – us L of C Photodup [950]
CURRENT BIBLIOGRAPHICAL SOURCES IN EDUCATION – (English/French/Spanish) – 2nd ed 1984 – xv/53p – 9 – 92-3-002192-X – fr UNESCO [370]
CURRENT CLINICAL CANCER – 1995, Vol 3 – £256.00 – uk Carfax [616]
CURRENT COIN / Haweis, Hugh Reginald – 1876 – 9 – us A.T.L.A. [240]

CURRENT COMMENT AND LEGAL MISCELLANY – v1-3. 1889-91 (all publ) – 20mf – 9 – $30.00 – LLMC 82-920 – us L.L.M.C. [073]
CURRENT CONCEPTS OF CEREBROVASCULAR DISEASE: STROKE – v1- 1966- 1; v11- 5,6,9 – us UMI [616]
CURRENT CONSUMER – v. 1-6. 1976-82 – 1,5,6,9 – us UMI [380]
CURRENT CONSUMER AND LIFE STUDIES – v7-. 1982- – 1,5,6,9 – us UMI [073]
CURRENT DECISIONS...WITH NOTES AND DIGEST / U.S. Supreme Court – B. R. Curtis, 1790-1854, Boston, Little, 1855-56, 22 vols., (cited as Cur. Dec.) 81-421 – 9 – $116.00 – us L.L.M.C. [340]
CURRENT DEVELOPMENTS IN THE SOVIET UNION – Munich, DE. 1971 – 1r – $50.00 – R63613 – us Library Micro [072]
THE CURRENT DIGEST OF THE POST-SOVIET PRESS – (Cont: The Current Digest of the Soviet Press) – v45- feb 1992- – 1r, 28mf – 1,9 – $295.00v diazo $10.00 extra for silver – us Current [072]
THE CURRENT DIGEST OF THE POST-SOVIET PRESS *see* THE CURRENT DIGEST OF THE SOVIET PRESS
THE CURRENT DIGEST OF THE SOVIET PRESS – (Annual compilation of weekly translations and or abstracts of significant articles from numerous Russian-language publications (publ in English). Quarterly and annual indexes in hard copy available separately. Cont as: The Current Digest of the Post-Soviet Press) – v1-44. 1949-92 – 1,9 – $295.00v $10.00v extra for silver – us Current [072]
THE CURRENT DIGEST OF THE SOVIET PRESS *see* THE CURRENT DIGEST OF THE POST-SOVIET PRESS
CURRENT DOCUMENTS *see* AMERICAN FOREIGN POLICY SERIES
CURRENT ENERGY AND ECOLOGY – v. 1-. 1978- – 1,5,6,9 – us UMI [333]
CURRENT GENETICS – Eukaryotes with emphasis on yeasts, fungi, mitochondria, plastids. v.1-4, 1980-81. ISSN: 0172-8083 – 1,5,6,9,13 – 80.00v – us UMI [575]
CURRENT GUIDE : GUIDE TO THE CONTENTS OF THE PUBLIC RECORD OFFICE / Public Record Office – London; PRO Publications, 1996 – 27mf – 9 – £75.00 institutions, "50.00 individuals – 1-873162-29-4 – uk G.B.P.R.O. [941]
CURRENT HEALTH – v. 1-3 1974-Feb. 1977 – 1. ; 5,6,9 – apply; v.3 – us UMI [610]
CURRENT HEALTH ONE – v. 1-. 1977- – 1,5,6,9 – us UMI [610]
CURRENT HEALTH TWO – v. 3-. March 1977- – 1,5,6,9 – us UMI [610]
CURRENT HISTORY – 1916-1936. All published – 1 – us Princeton Micro [900]
CURRENT HISTORY – (v. 54- 1968- 5,6. v. 58- 1970- 9) – 1- 1941- – 1 – us UMI [900]
CURRENT HISTORY AND FORUM – 1-53. 1914-1941 – 1 – us UMI [900]
CURRENT INDEX TO JOURNALS IN EDUCATION (CIJE) – (1981-82. $112.00 in North America, $115.00 elsewhere. 1983. $112.00y in North America, $115.00y elsewhere) – 1969-80. Main Entry Section – 9 – $869.00 in North America, $886.00 elsewhere – us Oryx [370]
THE CURRENT INDONESIAN NATIONAL ARMY'S ROLE IN THE REPUBLIC OF INDONESIA / Indonesia. Angkatan Darat – SE-11,654 1. 1961? – 9 – ne IDC [324]
CURRENT ISSUES IN HIGHER EDUCATION – 1947- 1; 1975- 5,6; 1976- 9 – us UMI [370]
CURRENT LAW : A COMPLETE ENCYCLOPAEDIA OF LAW – St Paul: West Publ Co. v1-16. 1903-11 (all publ) – 100mf – 9 – $492.00 – LLMC 84-382 – us L.L.M.C. [340]
CURRENT LEFT AND LABOUR PRESS – 9 – uk Microform Academic [073]
CURRENT LEGAL THOUGHT – New York. v1-14. 1935-48 (all publ) – 31mf – 9 – $139.00 – LLMC 84-453 – us L.L.M.C. [073]
CURRENT LIFESTUDIES – v. 1-5. 1977-82 – 1,5,6,9 – us UMI [370]
CURRENT LIST OF MEDICAL LITERATURE – v. 1-36. 1941-59 – 1,5,6 – us Princeton Micro [610]
CURRENT LITERATURE IN FAMILY PLANNING – 1984- – 1,5,6,9 – us UMI [310]
CURRENT LITERATURE ON AGING *see* ABSTRACTS IN SOCIAL GERONTOLOGY
CURRENT MEDIA – v. 1-. 1978- – 1,5,6,9 – us UMI [380]
CURRENT MICROBIOLOGY – v.1-6, 1978-81. ISSN: 0343-8651 – 1,5,6,9,13 – 55.00v – us UMI [073]
CURRENT NATIONAL STATISTICAL COMPENDIUMS ON MICROFICHE – (Key data from national governments around the world. May be purchased either as a complete coll or select world-region subsets. A printed bibliography is included with purchase) – Groups 1- 1970- – 9 – Apply for prices – us CIS [310]
CURRENT PROBLEMS IN AMERICAN SAMOA : HEARING BEFORE THE SUBCOMMITTEE ON TERRITORIAL AND INSULAR AFFAIRS OF THE HOUSE COMMITTEE ON INTERIOR AND INSULAR AFFAIRS / American Samoa. US Congress – 93rd Congress 2nd sess 2 Apr 1974. Washington: GPO, 1974 – 2mf – 9 – $3.00 – LLMC 82-100C Title 16 – us L.L.M.C. [327]
CURRENT PROBLEMS IN ANESTHESIA AND CRITICAL CARE MEDICINE – 1977-78 – 1 – us UMI [617]
CURRENT PROBLEMS IN CANCER – v1-3. 1976-79 – 1 – us UMI [616]
CURRENT PROBLEMS IN CARDIOLOGY – v1-3. 1976-79 – 1 – us UMI [616]
CURRENT PROBLEMS IN DIAGNOSTIC RADIOLOGY – v6-9. 1976-79 – 1 – us UMI [616]
CURRENT PROBLEMS IN OBSTETRICS AND GYNECOLOGY – v1-3. 1977-79 – 1 – us UMI [618]
CURRENT PROBLEMS IN PEDIATRICS – v1-10. 1970-79 – 1 – us UMI [618]
CURRENT PROBLEMS IN RADIOLOGY – v1-5. 1971-75 – 1 – us UMI [616]
CURRENT PROBLEMS IN SURGERY – v1-17. 1964-80 – 1 – us UMI [617]
CURRENT PSYCHOLOGICAL RESEARCH AND REVIEW – 1985- – 1 – us UMI [073]
CURRENT PUBLICATIONS / Ontario – 1973- – 9 – cn Micromedia [971]
CURRENT PUBLICATIONS / Quebec – 1973- – 9 – cn Micromedia [971]
CURRENT PUBLICATIONS / Saskatchewan – 1973- – 9 – cn Micromedia [971]
CURRENT RELIGIOUS PERILS: WITH...ADDRESSES ON LEADING REFORMS / Cook, Joseph – Boston: Houghton, Mifflin, 1888.2 fiches – 9 – us A.T.L.A. [240]
CURRENT RELIGIOUS THOUGHT – v1 nos 1-16; v2 nos 1-2; v3 no 1. 1941-60 (complete) – 6r – 1 – ATLA S0167 – us A.T.L.A. [073]
CURRENT RESEARCH IN LITERACY : LITERACY STRATEGIES IN THE COMMUNITY MOVEMENT / ed by Hautecœur, Jean-Paul – 1993 – 472p – 9 – 92-820-1061-9 – fr UNESCO [370]
CURRENT RESEARCHES IN ANESTHESIA AND ANALGESIA – v1-35. 1922-56 – 1 – us UMI [073]
CURRENT REVIEW OF AGRICULTURAL CONDITIONS – (Cont by: Canadian Farm Economics, 1966) – Ottawa. v1-26. 1940/41-1965 – 9 – Can$20.00y – cn Micromedia [630]
CURRENT RULE LISTINGS OF NEW MEXICO STATE AGENCIES / Ortiz, Vickie J – New Mexico State Records Center and Archives, 1984-85; 1988-89; 1991; 1995-96 – 8mf – 5,9 – $0.35f – us NM Archives [324]
CURRENT STATE OF CATALOG CARD REPRODUCTION – 22 papers. 1973. RLMS Micro-File Series, v. 1 – 9 – $13.00 – us L of C Photodup [020]
CURRENT STATE OF CATALOG CARD REPRODUCTION: SUPPLEMENT 1 – 9 papers. 1974. RLMS Micro-File Series, v. 1, suppl. 1 – 1 – $8.00 – us L of C Photodup [020]
CURRENT STATE OF KNOWLEDGE ON PROSOPIS TAMARUGO : PAPERS PRESENTED AT THE INTERNATIONAL ROUND TABLE ON PROSOPIS TAMARUGO PHIL. ARICA, CHILE, 1984 – 1985 – 464p – it F.A.O. [630]
CURRENT SURGERY – v49-53. 1992-1996 – 1,5,6,9 – $80.00r – us Williams [617]
CURRENT TOPICS IN RADIATION RESEARCH – v7-12. 1970-76.Ceased publication – 1,5,6,13 – sz Elsevier [073]
CURRENT TRENDS IN EDUCATIONAL POLICY / Swaziland. Ministry of Education – Mbabane, 1976 – 1mf – 9 – DE-481/1 – ne IDC [370]
CURRENT TRENDS IN THE RECONSTRUCTION AND REHABILITATION OF THE ANTERIOR CRUCIATE LIGAMENT / Bovee, Kristin K & Thorland, William G – 1993 – 1mf – $4.00 – us Microform Publ [617]
CURRENT U.S. ECONOMIC ASSISTANCE TO INDONESIA / Indonesia – SE-6185 1. 1967 – 9 – ne IDC [950]
CURRENT WORLD LEADERS – (1982-. 1,5,6,9) – v21-. 1978- – 1 – us UMI [073]
CURRENTS : INTERNATIONAL TRADE LAW JOURNAL – v1-3. 1991-1994 – 9 – $24.00 set – us Hein [340]
CURRICULA AND LIFELONG EDUCATION / Busshoff, L et al – 1981 – 360p – 9 – 92-3-101615-6 – fr UNESCO [370]
CURRICULA AND SYLLABI IN HYDROLOGY / Chandra, Satish et al – 2nd ed 1983 – 111p – 9 (92-3-102106-0) – fr UNESCO [550]
CURRICULUM – v.1. 1980 – 1,5,6,9 – us UMI [073]
Curriculum Advisory Service *see* CURRICULUM REVIEW
CURRICULUM AND EXAMINATIONS IN THE SECONDARY SCHOOL / Great Britain. Committee of the Secondary School Examination Council – Norwood Report. 1943 – 9 – uk Microform Academic [324]
CURRICULUM BULLETIN – (Cont by: Education Manitoba 1974/75) – Winnipeg. v1-7. 1967-73 – 5 – Can$100.00 – cn Micromedia [370]
CURRICULUM BULLETIN 1974/75 *see* EDUCATION MANITOBA
THE CURRICULUM DEVELOPMENT CENTRE OF THAILAND : STUDY PREPARED FOR THE ASIAN CENTRE OF EDUCATIONAL INNOVATION FOR DEVELOPMENT / Thailand. Ministry of Education – Bangkok, UNESCO, 1980 – 1mf – 9 – DE-281/1 – ne IDC [370]
CURRICULUM DEVELOPMENT FOR EXERCISE BEHAVIORAL CHANGE / Rehor, Peter R & Jewett, Ann E – 1991 – 2mf – 9 – $8.00 – us Microform Publ [150]
CURRICULUM DEVELOPMENT IN PRIMARY EDUCATION, PAPUA NEW GUINEA SITUATION / Papua New Guinea; ed by Isoiamo, A – Konedobu, 1973 – 1mf – 9 – DE-231/1 – ne IDC [370]
CURRICULUM DEVELOPMENT IN ZAMBIA, THE SEARCH FOR RELEVANCE 1964-1974 : A SPECIAL REPORT PUBLISHED ... IN CONJUNCTION WITH THE INSPECTORATE / Zambia. Ministry of Education. Curriculum Development Centre – Lusaka, 1974 – 1mf – 9 – DE-501/1 – ne IDC [370]
CURRICULUM FOR THE TRAINING OF AQUACULTURISTS IN THE ASIAN AQUACULTURE NETWORK – 1980 – 41p – it F.A.O. [370]
CURRICULUM GUIDES IN MICROFICHE COLLECTION *see* NEW YORK STATE CURRICULUM DOCUMENTS
CURRICULUM GUIDES OF CANADA – 1976- – 9 – cn Micromedia [370]
CURRICULUM INQUIRY – (See also: Curriculum Theory Network) – v6-. 1976- – 1,5,6,9 – us UMI [370]
CURRICULUM PHILOSOPHIAE PERIPATETICAE... / Cornaeus, M – Herbipoli, 1657 – 12mf – 9 – CA-13/1 – ne IDC [100]
CURRICULUM REVIEW / Curriculum Advisory Service – v. 15- 1976- – 1,5,6,9 – us UMI [370]
CURRICULUM REVIEW – LATE 1973 / Papua New Guinea. Department of Education – Konedobu, 1974 (Curriculum and Research Bulletin n1) – 1mf – 9 – DE-239/1 – ne IDC [370]
CURRICULUM THEORY AND CONSTRUCTION / Israel. Ministry of Education and Culture – Proceedings of an international seminar 1974. By Giselher Tiegel and Uriel Simri. 1975. 205 p. In cooperation with the Deutsche Sporthochschule Koeln – 9 – 5.00 – is I.T.T.I. [324]
CURRICULUM THEORY NETWORK – (See also: Curriculum Inquiry) – v1-5. 1968-1976 – 1,5,6,9 – us UMI [370]
CURRICULUM; UPPER DIVISION / Indonesia. Bandung – 13th and 14th grades, Lower division 10th, 11th, and 12th grades. SE-2058 1. 1955 – 9 – ne IDC [370]
Currie, David P *see* JUDICIAL REVIEW UNDER THE CLEAN AIR ACT AND FEDERAL WATER POLLUTION CONTROL ACT
Currie, George Graham *see* HOW I ONCE FELT: SONGS OF LOVE AND TRAVEL
Currie, James *see* JOURNAL
Currie, John Allister *see* A QUARTETTE OF LOVERS
Currie, Margaret A *see* THE LETTERS OF MARTIN LUTHER
Currie, Margaret Gill *see* JOHN SAINT JOHN AND ANNA GREY: A ROMANCE OF OLD NEW BRUNSWICK
Currier, Charles Warren *see* HISTORY OF RELIGIOUS ORDERS
CURRUS TRIUMPHALES ADVENTUM CLARISSIMORUM MOSCHOVIAE PRINCIPUM PAUL PETROVITZ ET MARIAE THEODOROWNAE CONJUGIS...IN DIVI MARCI VENETIARUM FORO DIE 22. JANUARII ANNO MDCCLXXXII / Fossatis, G & Fossatis, D – Venezia, 1782. BO-1123 1 – 9 – ne IDC [947]
CURRUS TRIUMPHALIS / Yonge, J – M 428. 1679 – 9 – ne IDC [610]
Curry *see* REGISTER OF OHIO SOCIETY OF SONS OF THE AMERICAN REVOLUTION 1917-18-19-20-21
CURRY COUNTY REPORTER – Gold Beach OR. Dec 6 1923 + – 1 – us U.O. Library [071]
CURRY COUNTY REPORTER – (Set incl. Gold Beach Reporter) – Gold Beach, OR. -w. 6 Dec 1923-. – 1 – us U.O. Library [071]
Curry, Fred S *see* REMINISCENCES
Curry, J L M *see* LETTERS
Curry, J LM *see*
– THE SOUTHERN STATES OF THE AMERICAN UNION
– VIRGINIA BAPTISTS, STRUGGLES AND TRIUMPHS
Curry, Peter *see* YOUNG EMU AND ITS FAMILY LIFE IN CAPTIVITY
Curry, W L *see*
– HISTORY OF JEROME TOWNSHIP, UNION COUNTY
– HISTORY OF UNION COUNTY ITS PEOPLE, INDUSTRIES AND INSTITUTIONS
Curry, William L *see* PAPERS
Curschmann, KF *see* CURSCHMANN-ALBUM: SAMMTLICHE LIEDER UND GESANGE...
CURSCHMANN-ALBUM: SAMMTLICHE LIEDER UND GESANGE... : AUSGABE FUR SOPRAN ODER TENOR / Curschmann, KF – Berlin: Schlesinger, 1871 – 1 – us Sibley [780]
THE CURSE OF KEHAMA / Southey, Robert – London: Longman, Hurst, Rees, Orme, and Brown, 1810 – 1 roll – 1 – 1-55879-435-2 – uk Libr Preservation [810]
THE CURSE OF ROME : A FRANK CONFESSION OF A CATHOLIC PRIEST, AND A COMPLETE EXPOSE OF THE IMMORAL TYRANNY OF THE CHURCH OF ROME / MacGrail, Joseph F – [S.l.: s.n.], c1907 (New York City: Nyvall Press) – 1mf – 9 – 0-8370-8358-3 – 1986-2358 – us A.T.L.A. [240]
CURSE YE MEROZ : LETTERS WRITTEN ON OCCASION OF THE OPPOSITION TO A LATE BILL FOR LIBERTY OF CONSCIENCE,... – Halifax, [1773] – 1mf – 9 – MP-489/1 – ne IDC [240]
CURSILLO SOBRE EXPLOTACIONES OVINAS EN SU ASPECTO DE PRODUCCION DE LANA / Junta Provincial de Fomento Pecuario. Badajoz – Madrid: Ed. Espasa-Calpe, 1947. Publ. no 9 – sp Bibl Santa Ana [946]
CURSO DE GEOMETRIA Y MATEMATICAS / Ciruelo, P – SL, SA – 4mf – 9 – sp Cultura [510]
CURSO DE HISTORIA DE ESPANA / Arenas Lopez, Anselmo – 1892 – 9 – 1.50f – sp Bibl Santa Ana [946]
CURSO DE HISTORIA DE ESPANA. TOMO 1 / Arenas Lopez, Anselmo – 1881 – 9 – $1.50f – sp Bibl Santa Ana [946]
CURSO DE HISTORIA GENERAL / Arenas Lopez, Anselmo – 1886 – 9 – 1.50f – sp Bibl Santa Ana [900]
CURSO DE INSTRUCTORES EN HIGIENE Y SEGURIDAD DEL TRABAJO / Hidroelectrica Espanola – (Tambien 1974) – Caceres: Imp. La Minerva, 1973 – 1 – sp Bibl Santa Ana [360]
CURSO DE INSTRUCTORES EN HIGIENE Y SEGURIDAD DEL TRABAJO. 199TH CURSO DE MONITORES DE H.E. GABRIEL Y GALAN. CACERES, JULIO 1977 / Hidroelectrica Espanola – Plasencia: Graf. Sandoval, 1977 – 1 – sp Bibl Santa Ana [360]
CURSO DE INTRODUCCION A LA HISTORIA DE CUBA.. – Habana: Municipio de la Habana, 1938. 463p. Includes bibliogs.1 reel. 1173 – 1 – us U.W. Library [972]

CURSO DE LENGUA GRIEGA / Morillo Trivino, Santiago – Cadiz: Establec. Ceron. Libreria Cervantes, 1942 – 1 – sp Bibl Santa Ana [450]
CURSO DE LENGUA GRIEGA / Morillo Trivino, Santiago – Madrid: Edit. Garcia Enciso, 1941 – 1 – sp Bibl Santa Ana [946]
CURSO DE LENGUA GRIEGA. MORFOLOGIA. FASCICULO 1 : PRECEPTIVA GRAMATICAL. TRATADO DE ETMOLOGIA / Morillo Trivino, Santiago – Cadiz: Establec. Ceron y Libreria Cervantes, 2nd ed 1943 – 1 – sp Bibl Santa Ana [946]
CURSO DE LENGUA GRIEGA. MORFOLOGIA. FASCICULO 2. EJERCICIO Y ANTOLOGIA : LIBRO DEL ALUMNO / Morillo Trivino, Santiago – Cadiz: Establecimiento Ceron y Libreria Cervantes, 1942 – 1 – sp Bibl Santa Ana [946]
CURSO DE LENGUA GRIEGA. MORFOLOGIA. FASCICULO 2. EJERCICIOS Y ANTOLOGIA : LIBRO DEL MAESTRO / Morillo Trivino, Santiago – Cadiz: Establ. Ceron y Libreria Cervantes, 1942 – 1 – sp Bibl Santa Ana [946]
CURSO DE MATEMATICAS : TRATADO OCTAVO DE ARQUITECTURA CIVIL / Martel, C – Barcelona, 1778. MS – 3mf – 9 – sp Cultura [510]
CURSO DE POLITICA ECONOMICA PERONISTA : [DICTADO EN EL ANO 1951 EN LA ESCUELA SUPERIOR PERONISTA] / Gomez Morales, Alfredo – [Buenos Aires?], 1951 – 1 – CSUXADQ3402-B – us Hoover Inst Photo [330]
CURSO DE TEOLOGIA PASTORAL. BARCELONA, 1933 / Lithard, Victor – Madrid: Razon y Fe, 1934 – 1 – sp Bibl Santa Ana [240]
CURSO ELEMENTAL DE BOTANICA : PARTE PRACTICA / Gomez Ortega, Casimiro – 1795 – 1mf – 9 – Pta1,000.00 – 84-7848-133-8 – sp Pentalfa [580]
CURSO ELEMENTAL DE BOTANICA : PARTE TEORICA / Gomez Ortega, Casimiro – 1795 – 1mf – 9 – Pta1,000.00 – 84-7848-132-X – sp Pentalfa [580]
CURSO GENERAL DE DIDACTICA (METODOLOGIA Y ORGANIZACION ESCOLAR) / Floriano Cumbreno, Antonio C – Oviedo: Editorial Supra, 1947 – 1 – sp Bibl Santa Ana [370]
CURSO GENERAL DE PALEOGRAFIA Y DIPLOMATICA ESPANOLAS (TEXTO) / Doriano Cumbreno, Antonio C – Oviedo: Universidad, 1946 – 1 – sp Bibl Santa Ana [440]
CURSO GENERAL DE PALEOGRAFIA Y DIPLOMATICA ESPANOLES. SELECCION DIPLOMATICA / Floriano Cumbreno, Antonio C – Oviedo: Universidad, 1946 – 1 – sp Bibl Santa Ana [440]
CURSORY REMARKS ON THE MEDITATED ATTACK ON NORWAY;... – London, n.d. – 2mf – 1 – ILM-727/1 – ne IDC [327]
CURSOS DE LENGUA PANAYANA / Lozano, Raymundo – Manila: Impr del Colegio de Santo Tomas, 1876 – 1 – us Res Libr [490]
CURSUS FHILOSOPHIU TOMUS SECUNDUS PARTIS SECUNDAE / San Pedro de Alcantara, Domingo de – 1 – sp Bibl Santa Ana [100]
CURSUS OSTEOLOGICUS; BEING A COMPLEAT DOCTRINE OF THE BONES / Baker, R – M297. 1697 – 9 – ne IDC [611]
CURSUS PHILOSOPHICI / San Pedro de Alcantara, Domingo de – 1729 $1.50f; 1731 $1.50f; 1734 $1.50f – 9 – sp Bibl Santa Ana [190]
CURSUS PHILOSOPHICUS / Arriaga, R de – Antverpiae, 1632 – 17mf – 9 – CA-2/1 – ne IDC [100]
CURSUS PHILOSOPHICUS... / Lingen, B – Ed.3. Coloniae Agrippinae, 1718 – 12mf – 9 – CA-22/1 – ne IDC [100]
CURSUS PHILOSOPHICUS AD USUM STUDENTIUM TOTIUS ORDINIS MINORAM / Petrus a S Catharina & Thomas a S Joseph – Venetiis. 3v. 1732 – 24mf – 9 – CA-30/1 – ne IDC [100]
CURSUS PHILOSOPHICUS THOMISTICUS, SECUNDUM EXACTAM, VERAM ET GENUINAM ARISTOTELIS... / Johannes a S Thoma – Lugdoni, 1663 – 19mf – 9 – CA-20/1 – ne IDC [100]
CURSUS QUATTOR MATHEMATICORUM ARTIUM LIBERALIUM / Ciruelo, P – 4mf – 9 – sp Cultura [510]
CURSUS THEOLOGICI IN PRIMAM SECUNDAM PARTEM D. THOMAE / Johannes a S Thoma – Lugduni. 4v. 1663 – 68mf – 9 – CA-21/1 – ne IDC [240]
CURSUSSEN OVER DE ISLAM / Salim, Agus – Contents: 1. Tauhid. Se 6094 1. v. 1 only. 1935- – 9 – ne IDC [260]
CURTAIN CALL – Toronto. v. 1-13. 1929-41 – 1 – 140.00 – cn McLaren [790]
Curteis, G H *see* BISHOP SELWYN OF NEW ZEALAND AND OF LICHFIELD
Curteis, George Herbert *see* THE SCIENTIFIC OBSTACLES TO CHRISTIAN BELIEF
Curtin, Jeremiah *see* MYTHS AND FOLK-LORE OF IRELAND
Curtis, Alfred *see* THE CHRISTIAN FAITH
Curtis, B R *see*
– CURTIS' DECISIONS
– CURTIS' REPORTS OF CASES IN THE FIRST CIRCUIT, 1851-1856
Curtis, Benjamin Robbins *see* JURISDICTION, PRACTICE, AND PECULIAR JURISPRUDENCE OF THE COURTS OF THE UNITED STATES
Curtis, C *see* A CATALOGUE OF THE FLOWERING PLANTS AND FERNS FOUND GROWING WILD IN THE ISLAND OF PENANG
Curtis, Charles Ticknor *see*
– EQUITY PRECEDENTS, 4TH ED
– A TREATISE ON THE LAW OF PATENTS FOR USEFUL INVENTIONS, AS ENACTED AND ADMINISTERED IN THE UNITED STATES OF AMERICA
CURTIS COURIER – Curtis, NE. -w. except -sw. 1896. Jun. 1892; Dec. 1895-May 1898; Jan. 1899-Jan. 1901; Apr. 1901-Dec. 1903; Jan. 1905-Nov. 1916 – 1 – us NE Hist [071]
CURTIS' DECISIONS : REPORTS OF DECISIONS OF THE SUPREME COURT OF THE U.S., 1790-1854 / Curtis, B R – (With notes and digest) – Boston: Little Brown. v1-21. 1855-56 (all publ) – 171mf – 9 – $256.00 – LLMC 81-421 – us L.L.M.C. [340]
CURTIS ENTERPRISE – Curtis, NE. -d. Jul. 1892-Dec. 1897. Incomplete; Jan. 1898-Jan. 1910; Mar. 1910-Oct. 1910. Incomplete; May 1911-May 1965 – 1 – us NE Hist [071]
Curtis, Gates *see* ST. LAWRENCE: OUR COUNTY AND ITS PEOPLE
Curtis, George Ticknor *see*
– THE AMERICAN CONVEYANCER; CONTAINING A LARGE VARIETY OF LEGAL FORMS AND INSTRUMENTS, ADAPTED TO POPULAR WANTS AND PROFESSIONAL USE THROUGHOUT THE UNITED STATES.
– CONSTITUTIONAL HISTORY OF THE UNITED STATES
– EQUITY PRECEDENTS; SUPPLEMENTARY TO MR. JUSTICE STORY'S TREATISE ON EQUITY PLEADINGS
– HISTORY OF THE ORIGIN, FORMATION AND ADOPTION OF THE CONSTITUTION OF THE UNITED STATES
Curtis, J *see*
– BRITISH ENTOMOLOGY
– FARM INSECTS, BEING THE NATURAL HISTORY AND ECONOMY OF THE INSECTS
Curtis, Neil *see* A MULTI-CASE STUDY OF FIRST YEAR ATHLETIC TRAINERS AT THE HIGH SCHOOL LEVEL
Curtis, Olin Alfred *see* ELECTIVE COURSE OF LECTURES IN SYSTEMATIC THEOLOGY
CURTIS POSTER – Portland OR. Oct 18 1937-Feb 21 1938 – 1 – us U.O. Library [071]
Curtis, R *see* PARTICULARS OF THE COUNTRY OF LABRADORE
CURTIS REPORTER – Curtis, NE. -w. Jan. 1914-May 1917 – 1 – us NE Hist [071]
CURTIS' REPORTS OF CASES IN THE FIRST CIRCUIT, 1851-1856 / Curtis, B R – Boston: Little-Brown. v1-2. 1854-56 (all publ) – 14mf – 9 – $21.00 – LLMC 81-445 – us L.L.M.C. [324]
Curtis, Thomas *see* BRIEF BIOGRAPHICAL SKETCH OF DR. THOMAS CURTIS FOUNDER FOR LIMESTONE COLLEGE
Curtis, Thomas F *see* HUMAN ELEMENT IN THE INSPIRATION OF THE SACRED SCRIPTURES
Curtis, W *see*
– BOTANICAL MAGAZINE
– A CATALOGUE OF THE PLANTS GROWING WILD IN THE ENVIRONS OF LONDON
– FLORA LONDINENSIS
Curtis, William A *see* A HISTORY OF CREEDS AND CONFESSIONS OF FAITH IN CHRISTENDOM AND BEYOND
CURTIS'S BOTANICAL MAGAZINE – Illustrations of roses. 7677 2 – 8 – ne IDC [580]
Curtiss, George Lewis *see* ARMINIANISM IN HISTORY, OR, THE REVOLT FROM PREDESTINATIONISM
Curtiss, Samuel Ives *see*
– DATE OF OUR GOSPELS IN THE LIGHT OF THE LATEST CRITICISM
– THE DATE OF OUR GOSPELS IN THE LIGHT OF THE LATEST CRITICISM
– DE AARONITICI SACERDOTII ATQUE THORAE ELOHISTICAE ORIGINE
– THE LEVITICAL PRIESTS
Curtiss-Wedge, Franklyn *see*
– HISTORY OF DAKOTA AND GOODHUE COUNTIES
– HISTORY OF FILMORE COUNTY
– HISTORY OF FREEBORN COUNTY
– HISTORY OF MCLEOD COUNTY
– HISTORY OF MOWER COUNTY
– THE HISTORY OF REDWOOD COUNTY
– HISTORY OF RENVILLE COUNTY
– HISTORY OF RICE COUNTY AND STEELE COUNTY
– HISTORY OF WABASHA COUNTY
Curtius, Georg *see* GRIECHISCHE SCHULGRAMMATIK
Curtius, Q. *see* RES GESTAE ALEXANDRI MAGNI
O CURUPIRA : JORNAL LITTERARIO E INSTRUCTIVO – Rio de Janeiro, 3 Oct 1852-Mar 1853 – 1,5,6 – bl Biblioteca [072]
Curwen, John Spencer *see*
– AN ACCOUNT OF THE TONIC SOL-FA METHOD OF TEACHING TO SING
– STUDIES IN WORSHIP MUSIC. FIRST SERIES
– STUDIES IN WORSHIP MUSIC. SECOND SERIES
Curwen, Maskell E *see* A MANUAL UPON THE SEARCHING OF RECORDS AND THE PREPARATION OF ABSTRACTS OF TITLE TO REAL PROPERTY
Curzon, Sarah Anne *see*
– CANADA IN MEMORIAM, 1812-14: HER DUTY IN THE ERECTION OF MONUMENTS IN MEMORY OF HER DISTINGUISHED SONS AND DAUGHTERS
– LAURA SECORD, THE HEROINE OF 1812: A DRAMA: AND OTHER POEMS
– THE STORY OF LAURA SECORD, 1813
Cusack, Mary *see*
– LIFE INSIDE THE CHURCH OF ROME
– WOMAN'S WORK IN MODERN SOCIETY
Cusanus, N *see* DE AUCTORITATE PRESIDENDI IN CONCILIO GENERALI
Cushing, Caleb *see*
– A DISCOURSE ON THE SOCIAL INFLUENCE OF CHRISTIANITY
– THE RIGHT OF THE NATIONAL LIFE INSURANCE CO. TO ESTABLISH AGENCIES IN THE STATE OF NEW YORK
– THE TREATY OF WASHINGTON
Cushing, Lemuel *see* THE GENEALOGY OF THE CUSHING FAMILY
Cushing, Luther Stearns *see*
– AN INTRODUCTION TO THE STUDY OF ROMAN LAW
– AN INTRODUCTION TO THE STUDY OF THE ROMAN LAW
– MANUAL OF PARLIAMENTARY PRACTICE
Cushing, William B *see* JOURNAL
CUSHING'S CONTROVERTED ELECTION REPORTS – 1v. 1780-1852 – 3mf – 9 – $13.50 – LLMC 84-155 – us L.L.M.C. [340]
CUSHING'S ELECTION CASES / Massachusetts. Supreme Court – 1v. 1780-1852 (all publ) – 3mf – 9 – $13.50 – LLMC 84-155 – us L.L.M.C. [340]
Cushny, A R *see* THE ACTION AND USES IN MEDICINE OF DIGITALIS
Cuspinianus, J *see*
– ...DE CAESARIBUS ATQUE IMPERATORIBUS ROMANIS OPUS INSIGNE
– DE TVRCORVM ORIGINE, RELIGIONE, AC IMMANISSIMA EORUM IN CHRISTIANOS TYRANNIDE, ...
Cussy, F de Cornot *see*
– DICTIONNAIRE,...
– DICTIONNAIRE, OU, MANUEL-LEXIQUE DU DIPLOMATIE ET DU CONSUL
– PHASES ET CAUSES...
– PRECIS HISTORIQUE...
– REGLEMENTS CONSULAIRES...
Cust, Robert Needham *see*
– CLOUDS ON THE HORIZON
– ESSAY ON THE COMMON FEATURES WHICH APPEAR IN ALL FORMS OF RELIGIOUS BELIEF
– ESSAY ON THE PREVAILING METHODS OF THE EVANGELIZATION OF THE NON-CHRISTIAN WORLD
– THE GOSPEL MESSAGE
– NORMAL ADDRESSES ON BIBLE-DIFFUSION FOR THE USE OF YOUNGER CLERGY, AND LAY-SPEAKERS IN GENERAL MEETINGS, TRAINING COLLEGES, AND SCHOOLS
– NOTES ON MISSIONARY SUBJKECTS
– THE SHRINES, OR, CHIEF PLACES OF PILGRIMAGE OF THE ADHERENTS OF THE CHURCH OF ROME
– A SKETCH OF THE MODERN LANGUAGES OF AFRICA
– THREE LISTS OF BIBLE-TRANSLATIONS ACTUALLY ACCOMPLISHED
Custance, Reginald Neville *see* THE SHIP OF THE LINE IN BATTLE
CUSTAR NEWS – Custar, Ohio, 1897-1928 – 1r – 1 – $32.50r – us Archival [978]
CUSTER BATTLEFIELD NATIONAL MONUMENT, MONTANA / Utley, Robert M – 1969 – 2mf – 9 – $5.00f – us Ross [975]
CUSTER COUNTY CHIEF – Broken Bow, NE. -sw. Apr 1892 – 1 – us NE Hist [071]
CUSTER COUNTY CHIEF – Broken Bow. Neb. 1893-1961 – 1 – us UMI [071]
CUSTER COUNTY INDEPENDENT – Callaway, NE. -w. Nov.1888-Oct. 1891 – 1 – us NE Hist [071]
CUSTER COUNTY REPUBLICAN – Broken Bow, NE. -w. Jun 1882-1916. Incomplete – 1 – us NE Hist [071]
CUSTER COUNTY REPUBLICAN – Broken Bow. Neb. 1895-1920 – 1 – us UMI [071]
Custer, Elizabeth B *see* COLLECTION
Custer, George Armstrong *see* CUSTER IN TEXAS
CUSTER IN TEXAS / Custer, George Armstrong – undated, Records of the Department of Texas, 2nd Cavalry Division, and general court-martial of Lt. Col. Nicholas H. Dale, 2nd Wisconsin Cavalry, at Rolla, Missouri, during the Civil War – 1 – us KS Hist [350]
Custine, Astolphe de *see* LA RUSSIE
Custis, Eleanor *see* COLLECTION OF EARLY AMERICAN MUSIC PUBLISHED AND MANUSCRIPT, VARIOUS PUBLISHERS
Custodio, E et al *see* GROUNDWATER PROBLEMS IN COASTAL AREAS
Custodio, M *see* DISERTACION EUCARISTICA SOBRE LA PRECISA OBLIGACION DE RECIBIR TODO ENFERMO LA SAGRADA EUCARISTIA EN AYUNO
CUSTOM HOUSE PAPERS, PORT OF PHILADELPHIA, 1704-1789 – (With Guide) – ca 5r – 1 – ca $425.00 – S3361 – Co-publ with the Historical Society of Pennsylvania. Available Spring, 1997 – us Scholarly Res [380]
CUSTOMARY LAND LAW IN AFRICA : WITH REFERENCE TO LEGISLATION AIMED AT ADJUSTING CUSTOMARY TENURES TO THE NEEDS OF DEVELOPMENT / Mifsud, Frank M – 1967 2nd print 1985 – 96p – it F.A.O. [340]
CUSTOMARY OF THE BENEDICTINE MONASTERIES OF ST AUGUSTINE, CANTERBURY AND ST PETER, WESTMINSTER, VOL 1 / Thompson, E M – 1902 – 7mf – 8 – Dfl28.00 – ne Slangenburg [240]
CUSTOMARY OF THE BENEDICTINE MONASTERIES OF ST AUGUSTINE, CANTERBURY AND ST PETER, WESTMINSTER, VOL. 2 / Thompson, E M – 1904 – 6mf – 8 – Dfl25.00 – ne Slangenburg [240]
THE CUSTOMARY OF THE CATHEDRAL CHURCH OF NORWICH / Tolhurst, J B L – 1948 – 5mf – 8 – ne Slangenburg [240]
CUSTOMS 3. 1696-1780 / Great Britain. Public Record Office – Vols. 1-82 Brram – 1 – uk Microform Academic [970]
CUSTOMS 16 AMERICA 1768-72 / Great Britain. Public Record Office – BRRAM – 1 – uk Microform Academic [975]
CUSTOMS 17 / Great Britain. Public Record Office – 1772-1808. Commerce, Navigation, Finance. BRRAM – 1 – uk Microform Academic [380]
CUSTOMS AND EXCISE TARIFF – With list of warehousing parts in the Dominion, sterling exchange, franc, German nxmark, and the principal foreign currencies at Canadian customs values, also a table of the value of francs in English money. Montreal: Morton, Phillips & Bulmer, 1883. 04196. (Pre-1900 Canadiana) – 9 – cn C.I.H.M. [971]
CUSTOMS AND MANNERS OF THE WOMEN OF PERSIA / Qulsum Nani – 1832 – 1 – uk Microform Academic [950]

CUSTOMS AND TRADITIONS OF PALESTINE: ILLUSTRATING THE MANNERS OF... ANCIENT HEBREWS / Pierotti, Ermete – Cambridge: Deighton, Bell, 1864.1 fiche – 9 – us A.T.L.A. [270]

CUSTOMS BULLETIN : 1967-1986 – v1-26 – 198mf – 9 – $297.00 – LLMC 78-234B – us L.L.M.C. [340]

CUSTOMS BULLETIN *see* TREASURY DECISIONS, 1899-1966

CUSTOMS, EXCISE AND COMMERCIAL LAWS OF CANADA / Canada. Laws, Statutes, etc – Toronto: Printed by Stewart Derbishire & George Desbarats, 1859. SEM105P201 – 3mf – 9 – Can$6.75 – cn Bibl Nat [324]

CUSTOMS JOURNALS. / Virgin Islands. Danish Government – 22 r – 1 – T39 – us Nat'l Archives [324]

THE CUSTOMS OF PRIMITIVE CHURCHES / Edwards, Morgan – 1774 – 1 – 5.00 – us Baptist [240]

CUSTOMS PASSENGER LISTS OF VESSELS ARRIVING AT PORT TOWNSEND AND TACOMA, WASHINGTON, 1894-1909 – 1r – 1 – M1484 – us Nat'l Archives [340]

CUSTOMS PASSENGER LISTS OF VESSELS ARRIVING AT SAN FRANCISCO, 1903-1918 – 13r – 1 – M1412 – us Nat'l Archives [340]

CUSTOMS TARIFF, EXCISE AND EXPORT DUTIES, REGULATIONS, ETC.. / Barry, James – Montreal: Montreal Print. & Pub., 1870. 02435. (Pre-1900 Canadiana) – 9 – cn C.I.H.M. [336]

THE CUT AND ENGRAVED GLASS OF CORNING, 1868-1940 / Spillman, Jane Shadel & Farrar, Estelle Sinclaire – 1977. 101p. 112 illus. 2 fiches. Fiche no. 4455 – 9 – $5.00 – us Corning Mus [740]

CUT BANK PIONEER PRESS – Helena. Mont. 1911-1950 – 1 – us UMI [071]

CUT BY THE COUNTY / Braddon, Mary Elizabeth – Includes: One Thing Needful. British Fiction Archive: Unit 5 – 9 – uk Bell [830]

Cutforth, Nicholas J *see* POLICIES AND PROVISIONS FOR ADAPTED PHYSICAL EDUCATION IN THE ORDINARY SCHOOL: A CROSS-CULTURAL COMPARISON BETWEEN THE UNITED STATES OF AMERICA AND ENGLAND AND WALES

Cuthbert F *see* ESSAYS ON CEREMONIAL BY VARIOUS AUTHORS

Cuthbert, Ross *see*
- AN APOLOGY FOR GREAT BRITAIN: IN ALLUSION TO A PAMPHLET ENTITLED 'CONSIDERATIONS ETC. PAR UN CANADIEN, M.P.P.'
- L'AREOPAGE

Cuthbert, W N *see* CUTHBERT'S PRIMARY NUMBER-WORK AND COMPANION TO THE COMMON-SENSE ARITHMETICAL CALCULATOR

CUTHBERT'S PRIMARY NUMBER-WORK AND COMPANION TO THE COMMON-SENSE ARITHMETICAL CALCULATOR / Cuthbert, W N – Toronto: Copp, Clark, 1896. 02253. (Pre-1900 Canadiana) – 9 – cn C.I.H.M. [971]

Cuthbertson, Sandy *see* MOVING TO A FREE-TRADE ZONE OR A TRADE-FREE ZONE

Cuthbertus Butler, D OSB *see* BENEDICTI REGULA MONASTERIORUM, SANCTI

Cutler, J *see* THE LAW OF NATURALIZATION,...

Cutler, James E *see* LYNCH-LAW

CUTLER OROSI COURIER – Orosi, CA. 1932-54 – 15r – 1 – $750.00 – C02566 – us Library Micro [071]

CUTLER OROSI COURIER – Orosi. Calif. -w. 1944-56 – 1 – us UMI [071]

Cutright, W B *see* HISTORY OF UPSHUR COUNTY

Cutter, William Richard *see*
- GENEALOGICAL AND FAMILY HISTORY OF CENTRAL NEW YORK
- GENEALOGICAL AND FAMILY HISTORY OF NORTHERN NEW YORK
- GENEALOGICAL AND FAMILY HISTORY OF WESTERN NEW YORK

CUTTING TOOL ENGINEER – (v.31. 1979 5,6,9) – 1967 – 1 – us UMI [073]

CUTTINGS NOTEBOOKS RELATING TO ENGLISH ARTISTS / Whitley, W T – From Dept. of Prints and Drawings, British Museum – 1 – uk Microform Academic [700]

Cutts, Edward L *see*
- AUGUSTINE OF CANTERBURY
- CHARLEMAGNE
- CONSTANTINE THE GREAT
- HISTORY OF EARLY CHRISTIAN ART
- PARISH PRIESTS AND THEIR PEOPLE IN THE MIDDLE AGES IN ENGLAND
- SAINT AUGUSTINE
- SAINT JEROME
- SCENES AND CHARACTERS OF THE MIDDLE AGES
- TURNING POINTS OF ENGLISH CHURCH HISTORY

Cutts, Edwards L *see* CHRISTIANS UNDER THE CRESCENT IN ASIA

Cuvelier de Trie et Mittie *see*
- L'ANNIVERSAIRE OU LA FETE DE LA SOUVERAINETE
- C'EST LE DIABLE OU LA BOHEMIENNE

Cuvelier, J *see*
- ACTES DES ETATS GENERAUX DES ANCIENS PAYS-BAS
- CARTULAIRE DE L'ABBAYE DU VAL-BENOIT

Cuvier, Georges *see*
- DICTIONNAIRE DES SCIENCES NATURELLES DANS LEQUEL ON TRAITE METHODIQUEMENT DES DIFFERENT ETRES DE LA NATURE
- DISCOURS SUR LES REVOLUTIONS DE LA SURFACE DU GLOBE, AVEC DES NOTES ET UN APPENDICE
- DISCOURS SUR LES REVOLUTIONS DE LA SURFACE DU GLOBE ET SUR LES CHANGEMENTS QU'ILS ONT PRODUITS DANS LE REGNE ANIMAL
- ELOGE HISTORIQUE DE M. A. THOUIN
- HISTOIRE NATURELLE DES POISSONS
- LETTRES DE GEORGES CUVIER A C.M. PFAFF SUR L'HISTOIRE NATURELLE, LA POLITIQUE ET LA LITTERATURE, 1788-1792
- RECHERCHES SUR LES OSSEMENTS FOSSILES DE QUADRUPEDES
- RECUEIL DES ELOGES HISTORIQUES LUS DANS LES SEANCES PUBLIQUES DE FRANCE
- RECUEIL DES ELOGES HISTORIQUES LUS DANS LES SEANCES PUBLIQUES DE L'INSTITUTE DE FRANCE
- LE REGNE ANIMAL

Cuvillier, Louis Andrew *see* VIEWS IN REFERENCE TO THE SIMPLIFICATION OF CIVIL PRACTICE IN THE COURTS OF NEW YORK STATE

CUXHAVENER NACHRICHTEN – Cuxhaven, West Germany. 1977- – ca 5r per yr – 1 – gw Mikrofilm [072]

CUYAHOGA COUNTY AUDITOR'S TAX DUPLICATE – (Contains record of real estate taxes levied in Cleveland and other municipalities, and certain information on companies and corporations enumerated for assessment, icluding real and personal property values) – 1819-69 – 56r – 1 – us Western Res [978]

CUYAHOGA COUNTY MARRIAGE INDEX – (Name index to the Cuyahoga Co. Marriage Records) – 1810-1973 – 27r – 1 – us Western Res [978]

CUYAHOGA COUNTY MARRIAGE RECORDS – (Chronological record of filing of marriage returns with the County) – 1810-1949 – 110r – 1 – us Western Res [978]

Cuyahoga County. Ohio. Auditor *see* TAX DUPLICATES

Cuyahoga County. Ohio. Probate Court *see* MARRIAGE RECORDS

CV ZEITUNG – Berlin. May 4 1922-Nov 3 1938 – 1 – us NY Public [072]

CVA JOURNAL / Canadian Vocational Association – v1-2. Jan 1965-Spring 1967 – 1 – us UMI [073]

CVRAE POSTERIORES DE BARBARISMIS ET IDIOTISMIS SERMONIS LATINI / Cellarius, C – Ed5. Ienae, 1709 – 6mf – 9 – ne IDC [450]

C-V-ZEITUNG : CENTRAL-VEREIN DEUTSCHER STAATSBUERGER JUEDISCHEN GLAUBENS – Berlin, 1922-38 – 7r – 1 – Dist. gw Mikrofilm – gw Misc Inst [943]

CWA NEWS / Communications Workers of America – v. 34-. 1975- – 1 – us UMI [330]

CWA NEWS – Communications Workers of America. v1-29. 1949-70 – 3r – 1 – us Ross [331]

CWAC NEWS LETTER (CANADIAN WOMEN'S ARMY CORPS) / Ottawa. Department of National Defence – v.1-2, no.7; Jan 1944-Oct 1945 – 1 – 75.00 – cn McLaren [971]

CYANIDES: DECOMPOSITION AND DETERMINATION / Israel. Prime Minister's Office – By I. Gilath and L. Cohen. Aug 1977. 36 p. Bibliog – 9 – 2.00 – is I.T.T.I. [540]

CYANKALI [PARAGRAPH SYMBOL] 218 / Wolf, Friedrich – (Publ as v1 of the series Das neue Drama; v2 never publ) – Berlin: Internationaler Arbeiter-Verlag, 1929 – 1r – 1 – us U.W. Library [430]

CYANOPHYCEES DES COTES D'EUROPE / Fremy, P – (Mem. Soc. Nat. et Math. Cherbourg). v. 41. Saint-Lo. 1933. B-665 2 – 8 – ne IDC [580]

LA CYBELLINE : A NEW DANCE FOR A GIRL / Firbank, Mr. – London: Pemberton, 173- – 1 – us Sibley [780]

CYBERNETICS AND SYSTEMS ANALYSIS – v1-30. 1965-94 – 1,5 – $120.00v – us UMI [000]

CYBERNETICS IN THE U.S.S.R / U.S. Foreign Broadcast Information Service – 1966-Aug 1974 – 1 – 202.00 – us L of C Photodup [947]

Cybichowski, S *see* STUDIEN ZUM INTERNATIONALEN RECHT

CYCLE CANADA – Toronto. v11-24. 1981-94 – 1 – Can$28.00y – cn Micromedia [790]

CYCLE WORLD – v1- 1962- 1; v19- 6; v15-1976- 9 – us UMI [790]

CYCLING – Toronto: W H Miln, C B Robinson, [1890-189- or 19–] – 9 – cn C.I.H.M. [790]

CYCLING FOR OLD AND YOUNG – 187?. 07020. (Pre-1900 Canadiana) – 9 – cn C.I.H.M. [790]

THE CYCLISTS' ROAD GUIDE OF CANADA / ed by Fred Bryers – Toronto: W. Miln – 9 – cn C.I.H.M. [910]

CYCLONE OCCASIONAL – Reno, NV. May 1891 – 1r – 1 – $50.00 – U04664 – us Library Micro [073]

CYCLOPAEDIA / Chambers, Ephraim – London. 5v. 1728-88 – 52mf – 9 – subsc: DM300.00 diazo DM400.00 silver – gw Olms [030]

THE CYCLOPAEDIA : OR UNIVERSAL DICTIONARY OF ARTS, SCIENCES AND LITERATURE... / ed by Rees, A – London. v1-39. [1802]-1819-1820 – 1074mf – 9 – 495/2 – ne IDC [030]

CYCLOPAEDIA (AEL, ABT.1;2) : OR, AN UNIVERSAL DICTIONARY OF ARTS AND SCIENCES / Chambers, Ephraim – 1st ed. London. 2v. 1728 (mf ed 1992) – 22mf – DM220.00 – 3-89131-053-6 – gw Fischer [030]

A CYCLOPAEDIA OF CANADIAN BIOGRAPHY BEING CHIEFLY MEN OF THE TIME / ed by Rose, George Maclean – Toronto: Rose Publishing Co., 1886. Canada reel 1. (Cox Library Collection) – 5 – us Americana [971]

CYCLOPAEDIA OF ENGLISH LITERATURE / Chambers, Robert – v1-2. 1853 – 9 – $60.00 – us Opus [420]

LE CYCLOPE – Quebec, Canada. 8 nov 1865-v1 n4. 6 dec 1865 – 1r – 1 – Can$25.00 – cn Can Microfilming [072]

CYCLOPEDIA OF DELAWARE COUNTY / Wiley, Samuel T – New York, Gresham Publ. Co., 1894. Pennsylvania Reel 20. (The Cox Library Collection) – 5 – us Americana [978]

CYCLOPEDIA OF GEORGIA / Candler, Allen D & Evans – Historical and biographical sketches. Atlanta, State Historical Asso., 1906. Vol. 1. Georgia Reel 1; Vols. 2-3 and Vol. 4, Supplement. Georgia Reel 2. (The Cox Library Collection) – 5 – us Americana [978]

CYCLOPEDIA OF INDIANA AND ARMSTRONG COUNTIES / Wiley, Samuel T – Philadelphia, John M. Gresham and Co., 1891. Pennsylvania Reel 24. (The Cox Library Collection) – 5 – us Americana [978]

CYCLOPEDIA OF LAW AND PROCEDURE / ed by Mack, William et al – (With annotations vol in 4 sections, and 1st + 2nd "Permanent Annotations" vols covering 1901-13 and 1914-18) – New York, London: American Law Book Co/Butterworths. v1-40 + index. 1901-18 (all publ) – 762mf – 9 – $1,143.00 – LLMC 82-509 – us L.L.M.C. [340]

A CYCLOPEDIA OF MISSIONS : CONTAINING A COMPREHENSIVE VIEW OF MISSIONARY OPERATIONS THROUGH OUT THE WORLD / Newcomb, Harvey – (Includes index) – New York: Charles Scribner, 1858, c1854 – 2mf – 9 – 0-8370-6233-0 – 1986-0233 – us A.T.L.A. [240]

CYCLOPEDIA OF NEW ZEALAND – (v1: Wellington Province 17mf ISBN 0-908797-05-2 NZ$44.00. v2: Auckland Province 12mf ISBN 0-908797-03-6 NZ$32.00. v3: Canterbury Province 13mf ISBN 0-908797-06-0 NZ$34.00. v4: Otago and Southland Province 13mf ISBN 0-908797-07-9 NZ$34.00. v5: Nelson, Marlborough and Westland Provinces 7mf ISBN 0-908797-04-4 NZ$19.00. v6: Taranaki, Hawkes' Bay and Wellington Provinces 9mf ISBN 0-908797-02-8 NZ$24.00) – Christchurch, 1897-1906 – 9 – NZNB c1958-c1964 – nz BAB [980]

CYCLOPEDIA OF TASMANIA – Maitland & Krone, Hobart, 1900 – 13mf – 9 – A$35.00 – at State Libr Vic [030]

THE CYCLOPEDIA OF THE COLORED BAPTISTS OF ALABAMA / Boothe, Charles Octavius – 1895. 280p – 1 – 9.80 – us Baptist [240]

CYCLOPEDIA OF VICTORIA / ed by Smith, James – Melbourne: Cyclopedia Company, 1903-5. 3v – 24mf – 9 – A$55.00 – at State Libr Vic [030]

CYCLOPEDIA OF WISCONSIN / Peck, George W – Madison: Western Historical Asso., 1906. Wisconsin Reel 3. (The Cox Library Collection) – 5 – us Americana [978]

CYCLOPEDIC MANUAL OF THE UNITED PRESBYTERIAN CHURCH OF NORTH AMERICA : COMPRISING A BRIEF HISTORY OF HER ANCESTRAL BRANCHES, MINISTRY, CONGREGATIONS, INSTITUTIONS, COURTS, BOARDS, MISSIONS, PERIODICALS,... / Glasgow, William Melancthon – Pittsburgh: United Presbyterian Board of Publication, 1903 – 2mf – us A.T.L.A. [240]

LE CYCLORAMA UNIVERSEL : ILLUSTRE – Montreal, Canada. 21 sep 1895-10 jul 1897 – 2r – Can$60.00r – cn Can Microfilming [073]

LE CYCLORAMA UNIVERSEL : JOURNAL D'ILLUSTRATIONS – Montreal: [s.n.] v1-4. 1895-97. SEM16P338 – 2r – 5 – Can$54.00 – cn Bibl Nat [073]

Y CYMRO – Bangor, Wales. Jan 1849-Feb 1866 – 5r – 1 – uk British Libr Newspaper [072]

CYPERACEAE ET GRAMINEAE SICULAE / Presl, K B – Prague. 1820. B-415 2 – 8 – ne IDC [580]

CYPRESS BAPTIST CHURCH. CYPRESS, FLORIDA : CHURCH RECORDS – 1888-1965 – 1 – 37.89 – us Baptist [240]

CYPRESS NEWS – Cypress, CA. 1993-1994 – 6r – 1 – $300.00 – R04022 – us Library Micro [071]

CYPRIAN : HIS LIFE, HIS TIMES, HIS WORK / Benson, Edward White – London; New York: Macmillan, 1897 – 2mf – us A.T.L.A. [240]

CYPRIAN UND DER ROEMISCHE PRIMAT (T.U.U. 3-35/1) / Koch, H – Leipzig, 1910 – 3mf – 9 – ne Slangenburg [240]

CYPRIAN VON KARTHAGO UND DIE VERFASSUNG DER KIRCHE : EINE KIRCHENGESCHICHTLICHE UND KIRCHENRECHTLICHE UNTERSUCHUNG / Ritschl, Otto – Goettingen: Vandenhoeck & Ruprecht, 1885 – 1mf – us A.T.L.A. [240]

DIE CYPRIANISCHE BRIEFSAMMLUNG : GESCHICHTE IHRER ENTSTEHUNG UND UEBERLIEFERUNG / Soden, Hans, Freiherr von – Leipzig: J.C. Hinrichs, 1904. (Texte und Untersuchungen zur Geschichte der altchristlichen Literatur; der ganzen Reihe 25. Bd., Heft 3. n.F., 10. Bd., 3. Heft) – 1mf – us A.T.L.A. [240]

DIE CYPRIANISCHE BRIEFSAMMLUNG : GESCHICHTE IHRER ENTSTEHUNG UND UEBERLIEFERUNG (T.U.U. 2-25/2) / Soden, Hans, Freiherr von – Leipzig, 1904 – 4mf – 9 – ne Slangenburg [240]

CYPRIANISCHE UNTERSUCHUNGEN : ARBEITEN ZUR KIRCHENGESCHICHTE 4 / Koch, H – Bonn, 1926 – 9mf – 8 – ne Slangenburg [240]

Cyprianus *see* DE LAPSIS (FLOR. PATR., 21)

CYPRIVM BELLVM, INTER VENETOS, ET SELYMVM TVRCARVM IMPERATOREM... / Bizari, P – Basle, 1573 – 4mf – 9 – H-8342/1 – ne IDC [945]

CYPRUS CRISIS OF 1974 PAMPHLET COLLECTION – 1974 – 1 – CSUXANL2908-B – us Hoover Inst Photo [947]

CYPRUS GAZETTE – Nicosia, 1956-60 – 5r – 1 – us Ross [324]

CYPRUS MAIL – Nicosia: The "Cyprus Mail" Co, 1956- – 1 – us Res Libr [949]

Cyprus. Planning Bureau *see*
- THE SECOND FIVE-YEAR PLAN (1967-1971)
- THE THIRD FIVE-YEAR PLAN (1972-1976)

Cyprus. President *see* FIVE-YEAR PROGRAMME OF ECONOMIC DEVELOPMENT AN ADDRESS OF THE PRESIDENT, 21 AUG 1961
Cyprus. Secretariat *see* A TEN YEAR PROGRAMME OF DEVELOPMENT
CYRANO DE BERGERAC; A PLAY IN FIVE ACTS / Rostand, Edmond – Trans. from the French by Gladys Thomas and Mary F. Guillemard. New York: R.H. Russell, 1899. 294p – 1 – us U.W. Library [820]
THE CYRENAICA GAZETTE / Cyrenaica. Territory under British Occupation – Benghazi. 1944-1954 – 1 – us NY Public [956]
Cyrenaica. Territory under British Occupation *see* THE CYRENAICA GAZETTE
CYRIL WHYMAN'S MISTAKE / Harris, Carrie Jenkins – Toronto: W. Bryce, c1894. 05375. (Pre-1900 Canadiana) – 9 – cn C.I.H.M. [830]
CYRILL UND METHODIUS : DIE LEHRER DER SLAVEN / Bonwetsch, G N – Erlangen: A. Deichert, 1885 – 1mf – us A.T.L.A. [240]
CYRILLE ET METHODE : ETUDE HISTORIQUE SUR LA CONVERSION DES SLAVES AU CHRISTIANISME / Leger, Louis – Paris: A. Franck, 1868 – 1mf – us A.T.L.A. [240]
CYRILLIC UNION CATALOG / U.S. Library of Congress – 3 – us Readex [025]
Cyrillus, D *see*
- PLANTARUM RARIORUM REGNI NEAPOLITANI
- TABULAE BOTANICAE ELEMENTARES QUATOR PRIORES SIVE ICONES PARTIUM
Cyrillus, Patriarch of Alexandria *see*
- COMMENTARY ON THE GOSPEL ACCORDING TO ST. JOHN
- FIVE TOMES AGAINST NESTORIUS
DIE CYROPAEDIE IN WIELANDS WERKEN / Herchner, Hans – Berlin: R Gaertner. 2v in 1. 1892 – 1 – us U.W. Library [430]
CYRPIAN UND DAS PAPSTTUM / Ernst, Johann – Mainz, 1912 – 3mf – 8 – ne Slangenburg [240]
Cyrus, Enoch *see*
- LIGHT OF THE SUN AS REVEALED IN THE BOOK OF GENESIS
- THE LIGHT OF THE SUN AS REVEALED IN THE BOOK OF GENESIS
CYTOGENETICS AND CELL GENETICS – v14-. 1975- – 1,5,9 – us UMI [574]
CYTOLOGIA – v. 1-35. 1929-70 – 1,5,6 – us Princeton Micro [574]
Czarnikow-Rionda Company, New York *see* WEEKLY SUGAR REPORT
CZAS – (1990-98 4r per y $340y) – Warsaw, 1999- – 4r per y – 1 – $320.00 standing order – us Ross [072]
CZAS – Krakow, Poland. 28 Dec 1918-1 Jan 1919; 1929; Aug 1939 – 3r – 1 – us L of C Photodup [947]
CZAS = TIMES: THE OFFICIAL ORGAN OF THE POLISH ALLIANCE IN BROOKLYN : ORGAN URZEDOWY ZJEDNOCZENIA POLSKO NARODOWEGO W BROOKLYNIE – Brooklyn, NY: Czas Pub Assoc, 1906-29; 1931-aug 29 1975 – 37r – 1 – us Res Libr [071]
CZAS – Warszawa: Drukarnia Polska, jan, mar, may-jun 1939 – 4r – 1 – us Res Libr [947]
CZASOPISMO SKARBOWE – Warsaw. v11-12. 1936-37 – 1r – 1 – us Ross [072]
Czechoslovak Academy of Sciences. Prague *see* CZECHOSLOVAK ECONOMIC PAPERS
CZECHOSLOVAK ECONOMIC PAPERS / Czechoslovak Academy of Sciences. Prague – v. 1-11. 1959-69 – 9 – 345.00; 4.50v – uk Dawson [330]
CZECHOSLOVAK MUSIC PAMPHLET COLLECTION – 1919-1945 – 1 – CSUXANL5042-B – us Hoover Inst Photo [780]
CZECHOSLOVAK REPUBLIC PRESS REVIEW / Great Britain. Embassy. Prague – Jul 1958-1976 – 1 – us L of C Photodup [943]
Czechoslovak Society of America. Cleveland, Ohio *see* RECORDS, MS P.P.
CZECHOSLOVAK WAR LITERATURE PAMPHLET COLLECTION – 1915-1946 – 1 – CSUXANL4883-B – us Hoover Inst Photo [355]
CZECHOSLOVAKIA : ANNUAIRE STATISTIQUE DE LA REPUBLIQUE TCHECOSLOVAQUE 1934-1938 / Czechoslovakia. L'Office Statistique de La Republique Tchecoslovaque – (Coll title: European Official Statistical Serials, 1841-1984) – 22mf – 9 – £7.00f (set £870.00 138mf) – uk Chadwyck [947]
CZECHOSLOVAKIA : MANUEL STATISTIQUE DE LA REPUBLIQUE TCHECOSLOVAQUE 1920-1932 / Czechoslovakia. L'Office Statistique d'Etat – (Coll title: European Official Statistical Serials, 1841-1984) – 24mf – 9 – £7.00f (set £870.00 138mf) – uk Chadwyck [943]
CZECHOSLOVAKIA : STATISTICKA ROCENKA CESKOSLOVENSKE SOCIALISTICKE REPUBLIKY 1957-1970 / Czechoslovakia. Federalni Statisticky Urad, Cesky Statisticky Urad, Slovensky Statisticky Urad – (Coll title: European Official Statistical Serials, 1841-1984) – 92mf – 9 – £6.00f (set £870.00 138mf) – uk Chadwyck [943]
Czechoslovakia *see*
- THE FIRST CZECHOSLOVAK ECONOMIC FIVE-YEAR PLAN ACT
- THE FIRST CZECHOSLOVAK ECONOMIC FIVE-YEAR PLAN, ACT AND GOVERNMENT MEMORANDUM
- THE FIRST CZECHOSLOVAK ECONOMIC PLAN
- LE PLAN ECONOMIQUE QUINQUENNAL TCHECOSLOVAQUE TEXTE DE LA LOI
- SBIRKA ZAKONU A ZARIZENI STATU REPUBLIKY CESKOSLOVENSKEHO
CZECHOSLOVAKIA AND FOREIGN RELATIONS WITH THE SOVIET UNION PAMPHLET COLLECTION – 1920-1948 – 1 – CSUXANL4492-B – us Hoover Inst Photo [320]
Czechoslovakia. Federalni Statisticky Urad, Cesky Statisticky Urad, Slovensky Statisticky Urad *see* CZECHOSLOVAKIA
Czechoslovakia. Hospodarske Rady *see*
- PRUBEH PLNENI HOSPODARSKEHO PLANU 1948
- PRUBEH PLNENI HOSPODARSKEHO PLANU ROK 1947
Czechoslovakia. Justicni Statisticka Rocenha *see* CAST TRESTNI, 1967
Czechoslovakia. L'Office Statistique de La Republique Tchecoslovaque *see* CZECHOSLOVAKIA
Czechoslovakia. L'Office Statistique d'Etat *see* CZECHOSLOVAKIA
Czechoslovakia. Narodni shromazdeni Poslanecka snemova *see*
- TISKY K TESNOPISECKYM ZPRAVAM O SCHUZICH POSLANECKE SNEMOVNY NARODNIHO SHROMAZDONI..
- ZAPISY O SCHUZICH
Czechoslovakia. Narodni shromazdeni. Senat *see*
- TESNOPISECKE ZPRAVY O SCHUZICH
- TISKY K TESNOPISECKYM ZPRAVAM O SCHUZICH
Czechoslovakia. Statni Urad Statisticky *see*
- CENOVE ZPRAVY
- MESICNI PREHLED ZAHRANICNIHO OBCHODU
- MITTEILUNGEN DES STATISITSCHEN STAATSAMTES DER CECHOSLOVAKISCHEN REPUBLIK
- RESULTS OF THE FULFILLMENT OF THE STATE PLAN OF DEVELOPMENT OF THE NATIONAL ECONOMY FOR THE YEAR 1955
CZECHOSLOVAKIAN DIARY: 1980 : 23 GLASSMAKERS / Buechner, Thomas S & Warmus, William – 1981. 16p. 52 b w illus. 1 fiche. Fiche no. 6664 – 9 – $2.50 – us Corning Mus [740]
CZECHOSLOVAKIAN GLASS: 1350-1980 – 1981. 176p. 108 objects illus: 69 color, 39 b w. 4 fiches. Fiche no. 6663 – 9 – $7.50 – us Corning Mus [740]
CZECHOSLOVAKIA'S FOREIGN RELATIONS PAMPHLET COLLECTION – 1921-1946 – 1 – CSUXANL4482-B – us Hoover Inst Photo [320]
Czechowski, Michael Belina *see* THRILLING AND INSTRUCTIVE DEVELOPMENTS
CZECH/SLOVAKIAN PERIODICALS / ed by Obrman, Jan – (Titles also listed separately) – 5180mf – 9 – ne IDC [943]
CZECH/SLOVAKIAN PERIODICALS *see*
- LUD
- MLADA FRONTA
- NOVA MYSL
- SMENA
- ZIVOT STRANY
Czermak, Wilhelm *see* ZUR SPRACHE DER EWE-NEGER
CZERNOWITZER ALLGEMEINE ZEITUNG – Czernowitz (Cernauti), Rumaenien. 26 Okt 1920-6 Jul 1932 – 19r – 1 – gw Mikrofilm [949]
CZERNOWITZER DEUTSCHE TAGESPOST – Czernowitz (Cernauti), Rumaenien. 1 Feb 1924-28 Jun 1940 – 22r – 1 – gw Mikrofilm [949]
CZERNOWITZER MORGENBLATT – Czernowitz, Rumaenien. 4 Jan 1921-31 Mar 1933 – 22r – 1 – gw Mikrofilm [949]
CZERNOWITZER SONN- UND MONTAGSZEITUNG – Czernowitz, Rumaenien. 2 Mar-17 Aug 1930 – 1r – 1 – gw Mikrofilm [949]
CZERWONY SZTANDAR : ORGAN SOCIALDEMOKRACJI KROLESTWA POLSKIEGO I LITWY: ORGANE CENTRAL DE LA SOCIALDEMOCRATIE DE POLOGNE ET LITHUANIE – Warszawa, Zuerich, Krakow, 1917-18, 191-195- – 1 – us Hoover Inst Photo [335]
CZERWONY SZTANDAR – Vilna, U.S.S.R. -d. Jan 1957-Dec 1958. 6 reels – 1 – uk British Libr Newspaper [947]
CZESCI MOWY ODMIENIAJACE SIE PRZEZ PRZYPADKI / Zochowski, F – Warsaw, 1838 – 8 – BR-8014 2 – ne IDC [943]
Czestochowski, Joseph S *see* THE WORKS OF ARTHUR B. DAVIES
Czikann, Johann *see* OESTERREICHISCHE NATIONAL-ENZYKLOPAEDIE ODER ALPHABETISCHE DARLEGUNG DER WISSENSWUERDIGSTEN EIGENTHUEMLICHKEITEN DES OESTERREICHISCHEN KAISERTUMS (AEL, ABT.1;10)
Czin r, M, OSB *see* MONASTERIOLOGIAE REGNI HUNGARIAE
Czubatynski, Uwe *see* KIRCHLICHER ZENTRALKATALOG BEIM EVANGELISCHEN ZENTRALARCHIV IN BERLIN
CZYTANIA DLA SZKOL POWSZECHNYCH / Zlobicka, Jadwiga – Wyd. 2. Lwow, 1933. 124p – 1 – us U.W. Library [947]
D A BURGERZEITUNG : ORGAN DES D A BURGERBUNDES – Chicago: Beobachter Publ Co, [apr 10 1920-dec 30 1921] – 1r – 1 – us Res Libr [071]
D and J Sadlier and Co *see* CATALOGUE OF SCHOOL BOOKS, STATIONERY, ETC
D. CHIPMAN'S REPORTS / Chipman, D – (A Pre-NRS title) – v1-2. 1789-1825 (all publ) – 8mf – 9 – $12.00 – LLMC 90-308 – us L.L.M.C. [340]
D F de Viu *see* COLECCION DE INSCRIPCIONES Y ANTIGUEDADES DE EXTREMADURA
D. FRANCISCO DE ROJAS, EMBAJADOR DE LOS REYES CATOLICOS / Rodriguez Villa, Antonio – Madrid: Fortanet, 1896, pp. 180-202, 295-339, 364-402, 440-474 y 1896, pp. 5-36. Boletin Real Academie de la Historia 28 y 29, 1896 – 1 – sp Bibl Santa Ana [320]
D. FRANCISCO FERNANDEZ DE LA CUEVA / Fernandez Duro, Cesareo – 1885 – 9 – 1.50f – sp Bibl Santa Ana [920]
D. IOANNES AEPINI IN PSALMUM 26 COMMENTARIU,... / Aepinus, J – Francofvrti, [1544] – 1mf – 9 – ne IDC [240]
D JC *see* CATECISMO POLITICO...MONARQUIA ESPANOLA
D. JOHANNES HINRICH WICHERNS LEBENSWERK IN SEINER BEDEUTUNG FUER DAS DEUTSCHE VOLK / Henning, M – Hamburg 1908 – 1mf – 9 – DM76.00 – 3-89349-659-9 – gw Hänsel [943]
D. JUAN MELENDEZ VALDES CORRESPONDANCE...HOPITAUX D'AVILA...BORDEAUX, 1964 / Demerson, Georges – Madrid: Graf. Calleja, 1964 – 1 – sp Bibl Santa Ana [946]
D. MAGNI AUSONII OPUSCULA (MGH 1: 5.BD. 2.TEIL) / ed by Schenkl, C – 1883 – Dfl35.00 – ne Slangenburg [240]
D. Mason and Co *see* HISTORY OF LIVINGSTON COUNTY
D. N. MAMIN-SIBIRIAK. RUKOPISI I PEREPISKA / Mamin-Sibiriak, D N & Udintsev, B; ed by Bonch-Bruevich, Vladimir Dmitrievich – (Katalog fondov Gosuddarstvennogo literaturnogo muzeia, nr. 8). M. 1949. BR-10,810 1 – 9 – ne IDC [920]
D. PETRI DORLANDI DIESTENSIS O. CART. : CHRONICON CARTUSIENSE – Col. Agrippinae, 1608 – 7mf – 8 – ne Slangenburg [240]
D, Susie *see* MAPLE LEAVES
DA GONG BAO – Changsha, Hunan, China. Da Gong Daily, Changsha ed. Jan 1917-Feb 1927. M B1 – 26r – 1 – $1,170.00 – cc Microforms [072]
DA GONG BAO – Chongqing, China. Da Gong Daily Chongquing ed. Dec 1938-Nov 1949. M B2 – 21r – 1 – $1,050.00 – cc Microforms [072]
DA MENSCH MUASS A FREUD HABN : BOEHMERWAELDER SCHNADERHUEPFELN / Jungbauer, Gustav – Reichenberg: E Ullmann, [194-?] – 1r – 1 – us U.W. Library [810]
Da Vella, O *see* LA NAVE IN ALTO MARE;...
DA ZDRAVSTVUET EMIGRATSIIA / Goldenveizer-Liubimov, Nikolai – Parizh: Goldenveizer-Liubimov, 1929 – 1 – CSUX89-B6484 – us Hoover Inst Photo [947]
DA ZHONG HUA RI BAO – China. 1916-17 – 9 – 215.00 – cc Globe [072]
DA ZHONG RI BAO – Shan Dong Province, China. 51 ill. DL17f – 9 – 175.00 – cc Globe [072]
DABA GUANCE YU TUGONG CESHI – Dam Observation and Geotechnical Tests. In Chinese but English abstracts to the main articles. F p106 – 9 – 4.00f – cc Microforms [073]
DABALAKA. RECENSEMENT DEMOGRAPHIQUE / Ancey, G – v. 1: Resultats Commentes. v. 2: Tableaux De Base. (Africa series). Jan. 1969 – 9 – fr Hachette [310]
Dabbs, Norman H *see* DAWN OVER THE BOLIVIAN HILLS
DABER-I SAHIH / Mazhar, Mehmed Fevzi Elhac Kureysizade – Istanbul, 1290-1293 – 5v 31mf – 9 – $63.00 – us MEDOC [949]
Dabin, Jean *see*
- THEORIE GENERALE DU DROIT
- A TREATISE ON THE LAW OF NEGOTIABLE INSTRUMENTS, INCLUDING BILLS OF EXCHANGE; PROMISSORY NOTES; NEGOTIABLE BONDS AND COUPONS.
DABISTAN – Baku. Numrah-'i 1 (4 Rabi' al-avval 1324 [16 Apr 1906]) – 1 reel – 1 – $10.00 – us MEDOC [950]
DABISTAN – Mashhad. Sal-i 1, shumarah-i 1-12 (1 Rabi al-Sani 1341-1 Rabi al-Avval 1342 [21 November 1922-12 October 1923]) – 1 reel – 1 – $175.00 – us MEDOC [950]
DABISTAN – Trans. by D. Shea and A. Troyer. 1843, 1844 – 1 – uk Microform Academic [950]
Dabney, M *see* TWELVE MINUETS AND TWELVE DANCES FOR A VIOLIN, HAUTBOY, AND HARPSICHORD
Dabney, Robert Lewis *see*
- THE BELIEVER BORN OF ALMIGHTY GRACE
- A DEFENCE OF VIRGINIA
Dabry de Thiersant, Philibert *see* DE L'ORIGINE DES INDIENS DU NOUVEAU MONDE ET DE LEUR CIVILISATION
DEN DABSKE KONEBAADS-EXPEDITION TIL GRONLANDS OSTKUST / Holm, G & Garde, V – Kjobenhavn. 1887. BN-253 2 – 8 – ne IDC [910]
DABT AL-NASL : ABADUHU WA-ATHARUHU AL-DIMUGHRAFIYAH WA-AL-IQTISADIYAH WA-AL -IJTIMAIYAH 101=ABD AL-QADIR SALIH, HASAN – al-Kuwayt: [s.n.], 1981 – us Res Libr [956]
THE DACCA GAZETTE / Pakistan. East – Dacca. 1961-1966 – 1 – us NY Public [072]
DACCA NEWS – India. 1856-58 – 1 – uk Microform Academic [072]
d'Achery, L *see* ACTA SANCTORUM O.S.B.
d'Achery, L, Mabillon, J *see* ACTA SANCTORUM O.S.B.
Dacheux, L *see* JEAN GEILER DE KAYSERSBERG, PREDICATEUR A LA CATHEDRALE DES STRASBOURG, 1478-1510
DACIA – Bucharest, Romania. -d. 31 Jan-24 May 1920. Imperfect. 1 reel – 1 – uk British Libr Newspaper [949]
D'Acres, R *see* ART OF WATER DRAWING
LE DACTYLOGRAPHE CANADIEN : METHODE FRANCAISE ET ANGLAISE LA PLUS RATIONNELLE ET LA PLUS EFFICACE POUR APPRENDRE FACILEMENT LA DACTYLOGRAPHIE EN PEU DE TEMPS PAR LE FRAPPE DES DIX DOIGTS OU LE TOUCHER DES AVEUGLES / Nadeau, Wilfrid – 4e ed. [Quebec (Province)?]: en vente chez tous les libraires; Ste-Marie: ou chez l'auteur, [1926?] ([Beauceville: Imp. l'"Eclaireur", ltee). SEM105P1774 – 1mf – 9 – Can$2.25 – cn Bibl Nat [650]
DER DADA – Berlin-Charlottenburg, jul 1917-sep 1921 – 1 – fr A.C.R.P.P. [700]
DADAISMUS UND RELIGION : HUGO BALLS "WEG ZU GOTT!" / Steinbrenner, Manfred – Frankfurt a.M., 1983 – 2mf – DM62.00 – 3-89349-880-X – gw Hänsel [943]
DA-DERECH = THE WAY – (In Hebrew) – Frankfurt, DE. v1 no1 Sep 1912-v1 no11 Jul 1914 – 1r – 1 – $25.00 – cn Can Microfilming [072]

DADIANJI JISHU – Large Electric Machine & Hydraulic Turbine. 1983. F- – 9 – 4.00f – cc Microforms [073]
Dadie, Bernard Binlin *see* LEGENDES AFRICAINES
DADOS – Rio de Janeiro, BL. 1966-1972 – 1r – $50.00 – R04171 – us Library Micro [072]
DAE RESEARCH REPORT / Louisiana State University. Agricultural Extension Service. Department of Agricultural Economics and Agribusiness – No.397-631. 1969-84 – 1,5 – us Spaulding [630]
DAEDALUS – v1- 1846- 1; v102- 5,6; v104- 9 – us UMI [073]
Daemmrich *see* THE CHALLENGE OF GERMAN LITERATURE
DAEMONENTAENZER DER URZEIT : EIN ROMAN AUS DEN WILDNISSEN DER ZWEITEN EISENZEIT / Achermann, Franz Heinrich – 5. Aufl. Olten (Switzerland): Otto Walter, c1935 – 1r – 1 – us U.W. Library [830]
DAEMONOLOGIA SACRA; OR, A TREATISE OF SATAN'S TEMPTATIONS / Gilpin, Richard – in three parts. Edinburgh: J. Nichol, 1867. lvi,480p – 1 – us U.W. Library [290]
DAENEMARK UND WIR / Scheel, Otto – Tuebingen: Kloeres, 1915. 32p – 1 – us U.W. Library [943]
DIE DAENISCHE BELTSPERRE 1914-1918... / Brueel, E – Leipzig, 1938 – 2mf – 1 – ILM-1816/1 – ne IDC [327]
DAERAH TAK BERTUAN; SEBUAH EPOS REVOLUSI / Toha, Mohtar – SE 4498 1. 1963 – 9 – ne IDC [950]
DAF YOMI REVIEW – Staten Island, NY. Kesubos, Nedorim, Nozir, Sotah, Gitin, Kiddushin, Bava Kama, Minachos – 1 – us A.J.P.C. [071]
Daffy, A *see* ELIXIR SALUTIS
DAFNIS I KHLOA / Merezhkovskii, Dimitrii – Povest'-Lotusa. Spb. 1904. BR-759 2 – 8 – ne IDC [460]
Daftary, Ali Akkbar Khan *see* GESCHICHTE UND SYSTEM DES IRANISCHEN STRAFRECHTS
I DAG – Goeteborg, 1990-95 – 1 – sw Kungliga [072]
I DAG – Malmoe, 1990-95 – 1 – sw Kungliga [072]
DAGARCIK – Istanbul: Muharriri: Ahmed Midhat, 1872-1873. – Nos 1-10. 1872-1873 – 5mf – 9 – $75.00 – us MEDOC [949]
HET DAGBLAD – Batavia, 1945-1949. Lacking: 1946(June 5,20); 1948(Nov 20,Dec 17) – 7r – 9 – ne IDC [072]
HET DAGBLAD – Paarl, South Africa. 31 Jan 1883-30 Sept 1898. 22 reels. Title varies: Paarl District Advertentieblad 1883-91; De Paarl 1891-96. Absorbed by: De Kolonist – 1, 16 diazo available at reduced price – sa SA Libr [072]
DAGBLADET – 1990- – 24r per y – 1 – inquire – us Ross [072]
DAGBLADET – Copenhagen, Denmark. -d. 11 Aug 1859-31 Dec 1863. 9 reels – 1 – uk British Libr Newspaper [072]
DAGBLADET – Harnosand, Sweden. 1979- – 1 – sw Kungliga [072]
DAGBLADET *see* DAGBLADET NYA SAMHALLET
DAGBLADET NYA SAMHALLET – (Nya Samhallet, 1900-54. Dagbladet, 1955-78) – Sundsvall, Sweden – 438r – 1 – sw Kungliga [072]
DAGBOAGER / Glahn, H C – H. Ostermann (ed.). Koabenhavn, 1921. (Det groanl. Selsk. Skr. Bd.). 247 pp., index. BN-223 2 – 8 – ne IDC [910]
DAGBOAGER FRA HANS REJSER I GROANLAND 1739-1753 / Walloaep, O – Kobenhavn 1927. (Groanlandske Selskabs Skrifter Bd. v. 127 pp.). BN-446 2 – 8 – ne IDC [910]
DAGBOK OA5FVER EN OA5STENDISK RESA AA'REN 1750-1752 / Osbeck, P – Stockholm, 1757. 376, 16 pp., 12 pls. B-247 2 – 8 – ne IDC [910]
DAGEN – Stockholm, Sweden. 1888-89. 2 reels; 1896-1915. 58 reels – 1 – sw Kungliga [072]
DAGEN – Stockholm, Sweden. 1945- – 1 – sw Kungliga [072]
D'Agen, Boyer *see* INTRODUCTION AUX MELODIES GREGORIENNES
Dagenais, Gerard *see* LE JOURNAL DE WATERLOO
DAGENHAM POST – London. 1928-30, 1932-35.-w. 7 reels – 1 – uk British Libr Newspaper [072]
DAGENS INDUSTRI – Stockholm, Sweden. 1983- – 1 – sw Kungliga [072]
DAGENS NAERINGSLIV – 1994- – 12r per y – 1 – us Ross [072]
DAGENS NYHETER – (Ed. A-B.1875-1900. 20 reels. Ed. B. 1875-1966. 600 reels. Ed. A. Newsbills. 1924-63. 34 reels. Ed. B. Newsbills. 1931-52. 14 reels. Semiweekly ed. 1913-24.19 reels) – Stockholm, Sweden. Ed. A., 1864-1978. 1481 reels – 1 – sw Kungliga [072]
DAGENS NYHETER – (Filmed from Uppl. A (Stockholms-uppl.)) – Stockholm: Dagens Nyheters Tryckeri, 1952 – 1 – us Res Libr [072]
DAGENS NYHETER – Stockholm, Sweden. 1979- – 1 – sw Kungliga [072]
DAGERAAD – London, UK. Jun 1918-15 Feb 1919 – 1 – uk British Libr Newspaper [072]
DAGEROTIP – Periodicheskoe izdanie. nr. 1-11. Spb. 1842. BR-2270 2 – 8 – ne IDC [073]
DAGESTANSIK FILIAL, MAKHACH-KALA / Akademiia Nauk. SSSR – Institut Istorii, Yazyka I Literatury. Uchenyye Zapiski. Makhach-Kala. v. 1-13, 15-18. 1956-1968 – 1 – us NY Public [490]
Daget, S *see* LA FRANCE ET L'ABOLITION DE LA TRAITE DES NOIRS DE 1814 A 1831
Dagg, John L *see* AUTOBIOGRAPHY AND OTHER MATERIALS BY HIM
THE DAGGER / ed by Dixon, John – Quebec, Canada. v1 n3. 14 nov 1863-v1 n20. 12 mar 1864 – 1r – 1 – Can$25.00 – cn Can Microfilming [072]
THE DAGGER – Quebec: [s.n., 1863-1864] – 9 – cn C.I.H.M. [072]
Daggett, L H *see* HISTORICAL SKETCHES OF WOMEN'S MISSIONARY SOCIETIES IN AMERICA AND ENGLAND
DAGLIGT ALLEHANDA – Stockholm, Sweden. 1767-1830 – 57r – 1 – sw Kungliga [072]
Dagnino, Carlos *see* TERRITORIO ACTUAL Y DIVISION POLITICA DE LA NACION ARGENTINA
Dagny Enterprises *see* FREE MARKET YELLOW PAGES
Dagny, Sharon *see* FREENETWORK ECONOMIC SYSTEM
DAGOBERT : ROI DES FRANCS / Barroux, R – Paris, 1938 – Dfl19.00 – ne Slangenburg [240]
DAGSPOSTEN – Stockholm, 1941-51 – 9 – sw Kungliga [072]
THE DAGUERREIAN JOURNAL/HUMPHREY'S JOURNAL – 1 Nov 1850-Jul 1870. 20v. 6 reels – 1 – $450.00 – us UPA [700]
D'Aguilar, George C D *see* OBSERVATIONS ON THE PRACTICE AND FORMS OF DISTRICT, REGIMENTAL AND DETACHMENT COURTS-MARTIAL
Daguin, C *see* DE L'AUTORITE ET DE L'EXECUTION DES JUGEMENTS ETRANGERS...EN FRANCE...
Daguin, D *see* DE L'AUTORITE ET DE L'EXECUTION DES JUGEMENTS ETRANGERS...EN FRANCE...
Daguin, F *see* RAPPORT PRESENTE A LA SOCIETE DE LEGISLATION COMPAREE
DAGVERHAAL DER HANDELINGEN / Nationale Vergadering representeerende het Volk van Nederland – In de Haage, 7 maart 1796-4 mei 1798. 9v – 84mf – H-2501A/1 mf. 1-84 – ne IDC [949]
DAGVERHAAL DER HANDELINGEN / Vertegenwoordigend en Intermediair Wetgevend Lichaam des Bataffschen volks – In de Haage, 4 mei 1798-18 september 1801. 13v – 127mf – H-2501/1 mf. 1-127 – ne IDC [949]
DAHEIM – Chicago: Free Press Printing Co, feb 11-may 26 1872 – 1r – 1 – us Res Libr [071]
DAHEIM – Chicago: [s.n.] 1891-jun 2 1901 – us Res Libr [071]
DAHEIM – Leipzig, Germany. Apr-Sep 1892 – 1r – 1 – gw Mikrofilm [072]
DAHIEL, DER KONVERTIT : ROMAN / Voss, Richard – Stuttgart: Deutsche Verlags-Anstalt, 1889 – 1r – 1 – us U.W. Library [830]
DAHIR-AL'UMAR SHALLIT HA-GALIL / Heyd, U – Jerusalem. 1942. BJ-27-27 1 – 9 – ne IDC [270]
Dahiya, Bhim S *see* THE HERO IN HEMINGWAY: A STUDY IN DEVELOPMENT
Dahl, A *see* OBSERVATIONES BOTANICAE
Dahl, G *see* COLEOPTERA UND LEPIDOPTERA: EIN SYSTEMATISDIES VERZEICHNISS
Dahl, H V *see* EESTI BAPTISMI AJALUGU: I. ARKAMISE AEG
Dahlan, Nursiah *see* TIGA PUTERA MEMBELA IBU DAN TANAH AIR; TJERITA DIMASA PERDJUANGAN KEMERDEKAAN UNTUK ANAK-ANAK BERUMUR 12 TAHUN KEATAS
Dahlbom, A G *see*
- CLAVIS NOVI HYMENOPTERORUM SYSTEMATIS
- DISPOSITIO METHODICA SPECIERUM SCANDINAVICARUM AD FAMILIAS HYMENOPTERORUM NATURALES PERTINENTIUM
- EXERCITATIONES HYMENOPTEROLOGICAE
- HYMENOPTERA EUROPAEA PRAECIPUE BOREALIA
- KORT UNDERRAETTELSE OM SKANDINAVISKA INSEKTERS ALLMAENNARE SKADA OCH NYTTA I HUSHALLNINGEN
- PRODROMUS HYMENOPTEROLOGIAE SCANDINAVICAE
- SYNOPSIS HYMENOPTEROLOGIAE SCANDINAVICAE

Dahlmann, FC *see*
- THE HISTORY OF THE ENGLISH REVOLUTION
- VOM RECHTE DES WIDERSTANDES

Dahlmann, Friedrich Wilhelm *see* PHILOSOPHIE DES SICHSELBSTBEWUSSTEN
Dahmen, Hans *see* E.T.A. HOFFMANNS WELTANSCHAUUNG
Dahmen, J A *see* TROIS TRIOS FOR VIOLON, ALTO ET VIOLONCELLE
Dahn, F *see*
- EINE LANZE FUER RUMAENIEN
- VOELKERRECHTLICHE UND STATSRECHTLICHE STUDIEN

Dahn, Felix *see*
- ATTILA
- DIE BATAVER
- BISSULA
- DICHTUNGEN
- FELIX DAHN'S SAEMTLICHE WERKE POETISCHEN INHALTS
- FREDIGUNDIS
- GEDICHTE
- JULIAN DER ABTRUENNIGE
- EIN KAMPF UM ROM
- KLEINE NORDISCHE ERZAEHLUNGEN
- KLEINE ROMANE AUS DER VOELKERWANDERUNG
- ROMANE
- SCHAUBUEHNE
- DIE SCHLIMMEN NONNEN VON POITIERS

Dahnke, Hans-Dietrich *see* ERBE UND TRADITION IN DER LITERATUR
LE DAHOME : SOUVENIRS DE VOYAGE ET DE MISSION / Laffitte, J – 4e ed. Tours: A Mame, 1876 – 1 – us Res Libr [960]
Dahomey *see*
- ECONOMIE ET PLAN DE DEVELOPPEMENT
- JOURNAL OFFICIEL
- JOURNAL OFFICIEL DE LA REPUBLIQUE DU DAHOMEY
- PLAN DE DEVELOPPEMENT ECONOMIQUE ET SOCIAL, 1966-1970
- PLAN DE DEVELOPPEMENT ECONOMIQUE ET SOCIAL 1966-1970. EDITION PROVISOIRE. PROJET SOUMISA L'ASSEMBLEE NATIONALE

LE DAHOMEY – Corbeil, France: E Crete, 1906 – 1 – us Res Libr [960]
LE DAHOMEY : HISTOIRE, GEOGRAPHIE, MOEURS, COUTUMES, COMMERCE, INDUSTRIE, EXPEDITIONS FRANCAISES, 1891-1894 / Foa, Edouard – Paris: A Hennuyer, 1895 – 1 – us Res Libr [960]
LE DAHOMEY, A L'ASSAUT DU PAYS DES NOIRS / Grandin, Leonce – Paris: R Haton, 1895 – 1 – us Res Libr [960]
DAHOMEY AND THE DAHOMANS / Forbes, F E – 2v. London. 1851. BA-306 2 – 8 – ne IDC [960]
LE DAHOMEY, HISTOIRE, GEOGRAPHIE, MOEURS, COUTUMES, COMMERCE, INDUSTRIE, EXPEDITIONS FRANCAISES / Foa, Edouard – Paris, A. Hennuyer. 1895 – 9 – 12.50 – fr Orientalistes [960]
Dahomey. Porto Novo *see* JOURNAL OFFICIEL
Dahomey. Societe Generale d'Etudes et de Planification, Paris *see* PLAN DE DEVELOPPEMENT ECONOMIQUE ET SOCIAL DU DAHOMEY, 1962-65
DAI NIPPON / Villaret, E de – (Le Japon). Paris: Librairie Ch. Delagrave. 1889 – 9 – 12.50 – fr Orientalistes [950]
DAI NIPPON ORHANISASI KEBUN PERTARUHAN KELUARKAN SAJUR-SAJURAN DAN LAIN-LAIN HASIL BUMI : KEMA'MOERAN MASJARAKAT KAOEM TANI INDONESIA. PERSATOEAN BALATENTARA DAN RA'JAT. MEMBANTOE PEMBANGOENAN ASIA RAJA – Djakarta ? Dai Nippon Orhanisasi P.K.S., Bagian Propaganda, 2602. folder (2p) – 208mf – 9 – ne IDC [950]
DAI VIET TAP CHI – I, no. 1-7. Saigon. janv-juil 1918; n.s., no. 1-33. 1er oct 1942-16 fevr 1944 – 1 – fr A.C.R.P.P. [073]
Daigle, Louise *see* BIBLIOGRAPHIE ANALYTIQUE DE L'OEUVRE DE M. EMILE CASTONGUAY
Daignan, Guillaume *see* TABLEAU DES VARIETES DE LA VIE HUMAINE: AVEC LES AVANTAGES ET LES DESAVANTAGES DE CHAQUE CONSTITUTION ET DES AVIS.
Daigneault, Pierre *see* LES AVENTURES ETRANGES DE L'AGENT 9E-13
Daille, Jean *see*
- EXPOSITION OF THE EPISTLE OF SAINT PAUL TO THE COLOSSIANS
- EXPOSITION OF THE EPISTLE OF SAINT PAUL TO THE PHILIPPIANS
- SERMONS DE JEAN DAILLE SUR L'EPITRE DE L'APOTRE S. PAUL AUX COLOSSIANS

Daille, John *see* A TREATISE ON THE RIGHT USE OF THE FATHERS IN THE DECISION OF CONTROVERSIES EXISTING AT THIS DAY IN RELIGION
DAILY – Muncie. Ind. and Evening Times. 1880-1905 – 1 – us UMI [071]
DAILY ADVANCE – Dover. N.J. 1903- – 1 – us UMI [071]
DAILY ADVANCE – Lynchburg. Va. 1951- – 1 – us UMI [071]
DAILY ADVERTISER – Auburn. N.Y. 1846-1913 – 1 – us UMI [071]
DAILY ADVERTISER – Creston. Iowa. 1921-1928 – 1 – us UMI [071]
DAILY ADVERTISER – Kingston. Jamaica. -d. 1 Jan-29 Dec 1790. (1 reel) – 1 – uk British Libr Newspaper [072]
DAILY ADVERTISER – New York, 1801-35 – 12r – 1 – us Ross [071]
DAILY ADVERTISER – New York, NY. 1785-1806 – 3 – us Readex [071]
DAILY ADVERTISER – New York, NY. 1817-1820 – 1,3 – us Readex [071]
DAILY ADVERTISER – Newark. N.J. 1884-1892 – 1 – us UMI [071]
DAILY ADVERTISER – Philadelphia, PA. -d. 7 Feb-11 Sept 1797. 1 reel – 1 – uk British Libr Newspaper [071]
DAILY ADVERTISER – Tiffin, Ohio. 1886-1932 – 73r – 1 – $32.50r – us Archival [071]
DAILY ADVERTISER – Wagga Wagga, Jan 1 1951-Dec 31 1968 – 9 – at Pascoe [072]
DAILY ADVERTISER *see* THE PORT ELIZABETH ADVERTISER
THE DAILY ADVERTISER – (First daily publ in British North America) – Montreal, Canada. 14 mai 1833-n147. 31 oct 1833 – 1r – 1 – Can$45.00 – cn Can Microfilming [072]
THE DAILY ADVERTISER – Hongkong: H P C Lassen, [oct 2-30 1871] – 1r – 1 – us Res Libr [072]
THE DAILY ADVERTISER AND SHIPPING GAZETTE – Hongkong: H P C Lassen, jan 2 1872-apr 30 1873 – 3r – 1 – us Res Libr [072]
DAILY ADVOCATE – Baton Rouge. Louisiana. 1845- – 1 – us UMI [071]
DAILY ADVOCATE – Manistee. Mich. 1896-1898; 1903-1914 – 1 – us UMI [071]
THE DAILY ALASKA EMPIRE – Juneau, Alaska: Empire Printing Co, jan 2 1952-60; jul 1963-jul 21 1964 – us Res Libr [071]
DAILY ALHAMBRA ADVOCATE *see* POST-ADVOCATE
DAILY ALJAMIAT – Delhi, India. 1965-Jun 1966 – 2r – 1 – us L of C Photodup [072]
DAILY AMERICAN – Reno, NV. Jul 1908 – 1r – 1 – $50.00 – U04665 – us Library Micro [071]
DAILY AMERICAN FLAG – San Francisco, CA. 1864; 1867 – 1r – 1 – $50.00 – C03476 – us Library Micro [071]
DAILY AMERICAN REPUBLIC – Poplar Bluff. Mo. 1893-1915; 1923- – 1 – us UMI [071]
DAILY AND SUNDAY GLEANER – Kingston, Jamaica, 1956-67 – 66r – 1 – us Ross [072]
DAILY APPEAL – (Index available) – Marysville, CA. 1860-1916; 1918-23; 1926-27 – 123r – 1 BC02426 – $6,150.00 – us Library Micro [071]
DAILY APPEAL – Memphis. Tenn. 1847-1870; 1871-1890 – 1 – us UMI [071]
DAILY APPEAL – Petersburg. Va. 1872-73 – 1 – us UMI [071]
DAILY ARBOR STATE – Wymore, NE. -w. Oct 1895-Oct 1896, scattered issues missing – 1 – us NE Hist [071]

DAILY ARGONAUT – Elko, NV. 1897; 1898-99 – 2r – 1 – $100.00 – U04493 – us Library Micro [071]
DAILY ARGOSY – Georgetown. Guyana. -d. 1 Oct 1908-31 Jul 1917; 13 Nov 1919-31 May 1940; 23 Feb 1941-18 Aug 1963. (215 reels) – 1 – uk British Libr Newspaper [072]
DAILY ARGUS – Easton. Pa. 1879-1916 – 1 – us UMI [071]
DAILY ARGUS – Goldsboro. N.C. 1890-1929 – 1 – us UMI [071]
DAILY ARGUS – Mount Vernon. N.Y. 1892- – 1 – us UMI [071]
DAILY ARGUS – Petaluma. Calif. 1899-1909 – 1 – us UMI [071]
DAILY ARGUS – Stockton, CA. 1857-1862 – 18r – 1 – $900.00 – C03655 – us Library Micro [071]
DAILY ARGUS *see*
– ALAMEDA TIMES STAR
– SANTA CLARA ARGUS
DAILY ARGUS OBSERVER – Ontario OR. Nov 23 1970 + – 1 – us U.O. Library [071]
DAILY ARIZONA REPUBLICAN – Phoenix. Ariz. 1910-30 – 1 – us UMI [071]
DAILY ASTORIAN – Astoria, OR. 25 Jan 1961-19 Oct 1976+. 47 rolls – 1 – us U.O. Library [071]
DAILY ATLAS – Toronto. v1 n3. 12 July 1858; v1 n14. 24 jul 1858 – 1r – 1 – Can$25.00 – cn Can Microfilming [072]
DAILY AVALANCHE – Memphis. Tenn. 1861-1895 – 1 – us UMI [071]
DAILY BANNER – Mt. Vernon. Ohio. 1898-1904; 1906-1935 – 1 – us UMI [071]
DAILY BEACON – North Baltimore, Ohio. 1889-90 – 1r – 1 – $32.50r – us Archival [071]
DAILY BEE – Omaha. Neb. (evening). 1872-1927 – 1 – us UMI [071]
DAILY BEE – Omaha. Neb. (morning). 1872-1927 – 1 – us UMI [071]
DAILY BEE – Portland. Or. 1876-1879 – 1 – us UMI [071]
DAILY BEE – Portland OR. Nov 2 1875-Dec 31 1879 – 1 – us U.O. Library [071]
DAILY BEE – Sacramento, CA. 1857-74 – 40r – 1 – $2,000.00 – R04100 – us Library Micro [071]
DAILY BEE – San Diego. Calif. 1887-88 – 1 – us UMI [071]
DAILY BONANZA – Tonopah, NV. 1906-11; 1928-29 (broken series) – 7r – 1 – $350.00 – U04763 – us Library Micro [071]
DAILY BREEZE – South Bay, CA. 1909 – 2040+ r – 1 – $102,000.00 ($1,200.00y) – H04067 – us Library Micro [071]
DAILY BRISTOL TIMES AND MIRROR – Bristol, England. Jan-Dec 1865 – 4r – 1 – uk British Libr Newspaper [072]
DAILY BRITISH COLONIST – Victoria, Australia. Mar 1864-Jun 1904; Apr 1911-Dec 1921 – 121r – 1 – uk British Libr Newspaper [072]
DAILY BULLETIN – Ireland.1922-23 – 1 – ie Microforms [072]
DAILY BULLETIN – North Platte. Neb. 1939-1946 – 1 – us UMI [071]
DAILY BULLETIN – Odessa. Tex. 1938-39 – 1 – us UMI [071]
DAILY BULLETIN – Portland, OR. 5 Aug 1870; 2-31 Jan 1917 1-14 Feb 1917; 16 Jan, 11 Feb, 21-22 May 1874; 16 June, 10, 13, 15, 22. Oct 1874 – 1 – us U.O. Library [071]
DAILY BULLETIN – Portland OR. July 1-5 1916 – 1 – us U.O. Library [071]
DAILY BULLETIN – Rhyolite, NV. 1907-09 – 3r – 1 – $150.00 – U04729 – us Library Micro [071]
DAILY BUTTE RECORD – Oroville, CA. 1856-58 – 4r – 1 – $200.00 – B02569 – us Library Micro [071]
DAILY CALIFORNIA – El Cajon. Calif. 1965- – 1 – us UMI [071]
DAILY CALIFORNIA CHRONICLE – San Francisco, CA. Nov 1853-Jun 1855; 1856-1857 – 5r – 1 – $250.00 – C02808 – us Library Micro [071]
DAILY CALIFORNIA EXPRESS – Marysville, CA. 1858-65 – 11r – 1 – $550.00 – B02427 – us Library Micro [071]
DAILY CALIFORNIAN – (Also known as: Inland Empire Daily Californian. Formerly: Valley News) – El Cajon, CA. 1974- – 192+ r – 1 RC02193 – $9,600.00 ($480.00y) – us Library Micro [071]
DAILY CALIFORNIAN – Berkeley, CA: UC of Berkeley, 1897-1908; 1910-18; 1920-58 – 61r – 1 – $3,050.00 – C02056 – us Library Micro [071]
DAILY CALIFORNIAN – Berkeley. Calif. 1943-58 – 1 – us UMI [071]
DAILY CALL – Lincoln. Neb. 1888-1898 – 1 – us UMI [071]
DAILY CALL – Piqua. Ohio. 1883-1895; 1896-1897; 1898-1910; 1968- – 1 – us UMI [071]
DAILY CALL AND POST – San Francisco. Calif. 1913-1929 – 1 – us UMI [071]
DAILY CAMPAIGN – McMinnville, OR. 3 Apr 1886-11 Jun 1886. 1 roll – 1 – us U.O. Library [071]
DAILY CASSET – Denison. Tex. 1875-1877 – 1 – us UMI [071]
THE DAILY CAYMANIAN COMPASS *see* CAYMANIAN COMPASS
DAILY CENTRAL CITY REGISTER – Central City, CO: Collier & Hall, feb 9 1869-jan 5 1870; dec 9 1870-nov 5 1871 – 2r – 1 – us Res Libr [071]
DAILY CHAMPION – Atchison. Kan. 1877-1887 – 1 – us UMI [071]
DAILY CHIEF – Upper Sandusky, Ohio. 1906-37 – 65r – 1 – $32.50r – us Archival [071]
DAILY CHIEF UNION – Upper Sandusky, Ohio. 1938- – 31r – 1 – $32.50r – us Archival [071]
DAILY CHRONICLE – Bozeman. Mont. 1891-1900; 1902- – 1 – us UMI [071]
DAILY CHRONICLE : DAILY NEWSPAPER – Warren, OH. 17 July 1868 – 1r – 1 – us Western Res [071]
DAILY CHRONICLE – Guiana. 1957- – 1 – us UMI [072]
DAILY CHRONICLE – Kingston, Jamaica. 29 Jun 1914-29 Dec 1917 (imperfect) – 42r – 1 – uk British Libr Newspaper [072]
DAILY CHRONICLE – Knoxville. Tenn. 1870-73; 1883-86 – 1 – us UMI [071]
DAILY CHRONICLE – London, Jul-Dec 1888; Jan 1890-May 1921 – 182r – 1 – uk British Libr Newspaper [072]
DAILY CHRONICLE – Nairobi: P P Sheth, 1956-mar 1959; may 1959-may 1962 – 3r – 1 – us Res Libr [072]
DAILY CHRONICLE – Santa Paula, CA. 1890- – 186+ r – 1 RC02972 – $9,300.00 ($240.00y) – us Library Micro [071]
DAILY CHRONICLE – Willimantic. Conn. 1891- – 1 – us UMI [071]
DAILY CHRONICLE *see* DEMERARA DAILY CHRONICLE
DAILY CHRONICLE AND SENTINEL – (Lacking: all of 1856. The run also has Apr 15,16,18 & 25 1865 issues) – Augusta, FL. Jan 3 1855-Jun 30 1857 – 4r – 1 – us Western Res [071]
DAILY CHRONICLE & GENERAL ADVERTIZER – Philadelphia, PA. 1841-43 – 1 – us Readex [071]
DAILY CINCINNATI ATLAS – Cincinnati. Nov. 1, 1843-May 2, 1844 – 1 – us NY Public [071]
DAILY CINCINNATI COMMERCIAL – Cincinnati: J W S Browne & Co, 1846-54 – us Res Libr [071]
DAILY CITIZEN – Ambridge. Pa. 1904-1959 – 1 – us UMI [071]
DAILY CITIZEN – Centerville. Iowa. 1897-1899; 1910 – 1 – us UMI [071]
DAILY CITIZEN – (London ed: 8 Oct 1913-13 Mar 1915 3r) – Manchester, England. 8 Oct 1912-13 Mar 1915 – 10r – 1 – uk British Libr Newspaper [072]
DAILY CITIZEN – Searcy. Ark. 1956- – 1 – us UMI [071]
DAILY CITIZEN – Tucson. Ariz. 1940- – 1 – us UMI [071]
DAILY CITIZEN – Urbana. Ohio. 1883-1890; 1891 – 1 – us UMI [071]
DAILY CLASS REGISTER / Ottawa County. Ohio. Board of Education – 1874-1879 – 1r – 1 – $32.50r – us Archival [324]
DAILY CLEVELAND HERALD : DAILY WHIG AND REPUBLICAN NEWSPAPER – Cleveland, OH. 23 Jun 1857-31 Dec 1868 – 23r – 1 – us Western Res [071]
DAILY CLEVELAND HERALD : DAILY WHIG NEWSPAPER – Cleveland, OH. 11 Apr 1853-20 Jul 1856 – 7r – 1 – us Western Res [071]
DAILY CLEVELAND HERALD : DAILY WHIG NEWSPAPER, THE FIRST DAILY PUBLISHED IN CLEVELAND – Cleveland, OH. 30 May 1835-21 Mar 1837 – 2r – 1 – us Western Res [071]
DAILY CLEVELAND HERALD – (Evening ed of this daily Republican newspaper) – Cleveland, OH. Jan 2 1869-Dec 31 1870 – 4r – 1 – us Western Res [071]
DAILY CLEVELAND HERALD – (Evening ed of this daily Republican newspaper) – Cleveland, OH. Jul 1 1873-May 30 1874 – 2r – 1 – us Western Res [071]
DAILY CLINTONIAN – Clinton. Ind. 1955- – 1 – us UMI [071]
DAILY COAST MAIL BULLETIN – Marshfield OR. Apr 23-June 22 1898 – 1 – us U.O. Library [071]
DAILY COLLEGIAN – University Park. Pa. 1962- – 1 – us UMI [071]
DAILY COLLEGIAN *see* THE COLLEGIAN
DAILY COLONIST – Victoria, Canada. 1858-71. Also British Colonist – 13r – 1 – $845.00 – cn Library Assoc [971]
THE DAILY COLONIST – Toronto. n1910. 7 Jan 1858-n2103. 20 aut 1858 – 1r – 1 – Can$45.00 – cn Can Microfilming [072]
THE DAILY COLUMBIAN – Chicago, Illinois. May-Oct 1993 – 2r – 1 – us L of C Photodup [072]
DAILY COLUSA SUN – Colusa. Calif. 1904-1917; 1919-1934; 1957- – 1 – us UMI [071]
DAILY COMMERCE – Los Angeles, CA. 1980 – 84+ r – 1 – $4,200.00 ($300.00y) – H04050 – us Library Micro [071]
DAILY COMMERCIAL – Louisville. Ky. 1869-1902 – 1 – us UMI [071]
THE DAILY COMMERCIAL – Cincinnati: Curtiss & Hastings, oct 2 1843-sep 28 1844; [feb 11 1845-may 9 1846] – us Res Libr [071]
DAILY COMMERCIAL NEWS – Los Angeles, CA. 1976-1993 – 63r – 1 – $3,150.00 – R03288 – us Library Micro [071]
DAILY COMMERCIAL NEWS – San Francisco, CA. 1946-86 – 141r – 1 BC02809 – $7,050.00 – us Library Micro [071]
DAILY COMMERCIAL REGISTER – Sandusky. Ohio. 1851-67 – 1 – us UMI [071]
DAILY COMMONWEALTH – Fond Du Lac. Wis. 1912-13 – 1 – us UMI [071]
DAILY COMPASS – New York. N.Y. 1950-1952 – 1 – us UMI [071]
DAILY COMPASS – New York. v1-4.1949-52 – 11r – 1 – us Ross [071]
DAILY CONSERVATIVE – Leavenworth. Kan. 1867-68 – 1 – us UMI [071]
DAILY CONSTRUCTION JOURNAL / Atchison, Topeka and Santa Fe Railroad Company – 1887 – 1 – us KS Hist [380]
DAILY CORINTHIAN – Corinth. Miss. 1903; 1946- – 1 – us UMI [071]
DAILY COURANT *see* HARTFORD COURANT
DAILY COURIER – (1993.-24r; 1904-1976.-134r) – Kelowna, 1977-1992 – 229r – 1 – cn Preston [971]
DAILY COURIER – Charleston. S.C. 1803-1873 – 1 – us UMI [071]
DAILY COURIER – Connellsville. Pa. 1879- – 1 – us UMI [071]
DAILY COURIER – Grants Pass. Or. 1929-1952 – 1 – us UMI [071]
DAILY COURIER – Lafayette. Ind. 1859; 1861-1863; 1872; 1874-1875; 1916-1919 – 1 – us UMI [071]
DAILY COURIER – Louisville. Ky. 1844-1861; 1866-1868 – 1 – us UMI [071]
DAILY COURIER – Oxnard. Calif. 1909-1940 – 1 – us UMI [071]
DAILY COURIER – Saginaw. Mich. 1870-1889 – 1 – us UMI [071]
DAILY COURIER – San Bernardino. Calif. 1887-1894 – 1 – us UMI [071]
DAILY COURIER – Winfield. Kan. 1885-1912 – 1 – us UMI [071]
THE DAILY COURIER – San Bernardino, CA. 1886-1894 – 18r – 1 – $900.00 – R03450 – us Library Micro [071]
DAILY CRITIC – (Filmed with: Critic (Washington, DC) oct 17-dec 1872) – Washington, DC: Ringwalt, Hack & Co, 1872-81 – 1r – 1 – us Res Libr [071]
DAILY CRITIC *see* THE CRITIC
DAILY CYPRESS – Monterey, CA. 1907-12; 1914-22 – 24r – 1 – $1,080.00 – B02480 – us Library Micro [071]
DAILY DELTA – Visalia, CA. 1892-1909 – 21r – 1 CB03073 – $1,050.00 – us Library Micro [071]
DAILY DEMOCRAT – Beatrice, NE. Oct. 1886-Oct. 1887; Nov. 1888-Oct. 1889; Mar. 1892-Jun. 1892 – 1 – us NE Hist [071]
DAILY DEMOCRAT – Boyertown, PA., 1890-1891 – 13 – $25.00r – us I.M.R. [071]
DAILY DEMOCRAT – Corning. N.Y. 1885-1888 – 1 – us UMI [071]
DAILY DEMOCRAT – Davenport. Iowa. 1856-1939 – 1 – us UMI [071]
DAILY DEMOCRAT – El Reno. Okl. 1901-1929 – 1 – us UMI [071]
DAILY DEMOCRAT – Greenville. Miss. 1904-1916 – 1 – us UMI [071]
DAILY DEMOCRAT – Hamilton. Ohio. 1887-1896 – 1 – us UMI [071]
DAILY DEMOCRAT – Huntington. Ind. 1886-1897 – 1 – us UMI [071]
DAILY DEMOCRAT – Kenton, Ohio. 1898-1919 – 40r – 1 – $32.50r – us Archival [071]
DAILY DEMOCRAT – Louisville. Ky. 1862; 1865 – 1 – us UMI [071]
DAILY DEMOCRAT – Ottumwa. Iowa. 1881-1885; 1888-1891; 1901-1904 – 1 – us UMI [071]
DAILY DEMOCRAT – Santa Rosa, CA. 1883-90 – 6r – 1 – $300.00 – B02976 – us Library Micro [071]
DAILY DEMOCRAT – Santa Rosa. Calif. 1889-1890 – 1 – us UMI [071]
DAILY DEMOCRAT – Seymour. Ind. 1884-1901 – 1 – us UMI [071]
DAILY DEMOCRAT – Tulsa. Okl. 1904-1919 – 1 – us UMI [071]
DAILY DEMOCRAT *see* EVENING DEMOCRAT
THE DAILY DEMOCRAT – Doylestown, PA. -d 1891-1893 – 13 – $25.00r – us I.M.R. [071]
DAILY DEMOCRAT TRIBUNE – Jefferson City. Mo. 1910-1922; 1924 – 1 – us UMI [071]
DAILY DEMOCRAT-TIMES – Greenville. Miss. 1917-1938 – 1 – us UMI [071]
DAILY DIARY OF PRESIDENT JOHNSON (1963-69) / Johnson, Lyndon B – 1980 (Presidential Documents Series) – 1 – $1,380.00 – 0-89093-359-6 – us UPA [977]
DAILY DIGEST OF THE ARABIC PRESS – Cairo: USIS, News Dep, [jan 5 1945-oct 1946] – 3r – 1 – us Res Libr [072]
DAILY DISPATCH – 1900-1955 – 1 – uk Manchester Libr [072]
DAILY DISPATCH – Brainerd. Minn. 1901-1914; 1950- – 1 – us UMI [071]
DAILY DISPATCH – East London, South Africa. 1920-81 – 1 – sa State Libr [072]
DAILY DISPATCH – East London, South Africa: East London Daily Dispatch Ltd, jan 2-mar 1925; jul 1925-nov 1966 – 1 – us Res Libr [960]
DAILY DISPATCH – Oneida. N.Y. 1927- – 1 – us UMI [071]
DAILY DISPATCH – Pittsburgh. Pa. 1847-1864; 1892-1923 – 1 – us UMI [071]
THE DAILY DISPATCH – (1 Dec 1981-31 Aug 1995 filmed currently) – East London, South Africa, 10 Sept 1872-30 June 1920 – 280+ r – 1,16 diazo available – sa SA Libr [072]
DAILY DROVERS TELEGRAM – Kansas City. Mo. 1885-1960 – 1 – us UMI [071]
DAILY EAGLE – Enid. Okl. 1904-05; 1908-48; 1950-1964 – 1 – us UMI [071]
DAILY EAGLE – Lancaster. Ohio. 1915-1935 – 1 – us UMI [071]
DAILY EAGLE – Poughkeepsie. N.Y. 1860-1914 – 1 – us UMI [071]
DAILY EAGLE – Traverse City. Mich. 1903-1909 – 1 – us UMI [071]
DAILY ECHO – Accra: Independent Press Ltd, [mar 20-dec 1954] – us Res Libr [072]
DAILY ECHO – Moundsville. West Virginia. 1896-1909; 1921; 1935-1947; 1951-65- – 1 – us UMI [071]
THE DAILY ECHO – (Library has incomplete holdings from between June 24, 1946 and Feb. 17, 1954) – Accra, Ghana: Daily Echo, 193u – 1 – CSUX86-S90 – us Hoover Inst Photo [960]
DAILY ENQUIRER – Grand Rapids. Mich. and pred. 1855-61 – 1 – us UMI [071]
DAILY ENTERPRISE – Allegheny. Pa. 1851-1852 – 1 – us UMI [071]
DAILY ENTERPRISE – Chico. Calif. 1905-1935 – 1 – us UMI [071]
DAILY ENTERPRISE – Phoenix. Ariz. 1898-1905 – 1 – us UMI [071]
DAILY ENTERPRISE – Riverside, CA. 1891-1987 – 888r – 1 – $44,400.00 – R04091 – us Library Micro [071]
THE DAILY ENTERPRISE – Harlan. Ky. 1969- – 1 – us UMI [071]
THE DAILY ENTERPRISE *see* PRESS ENTERPRISE
DAILY EVENING BULLETIN – San Francisco, 9 Oct 1855-29 Nov 1871 – 33r – 1 – uk British Libr Newspaper [073]
DAILY EVENING CHIEF – Red Cloud, NE. Nov 1887-Apr 1888; Jun 1888 – 1 – us NE Hist [071]

DAILY EVENING CRESCENT – Reno, NV. 1868-1874; 1875 – 2r – 1 – $100.00 – U04663 – us Library Micro [071]
DAILY EVENING EXPOSITOR – Fresno, CA. 1883-1889; 1892-98 – 29r – 1 – $1,450.00 – B02260 – us Library Micro [071]
DAILY EVENING HERALD – Carson City, NV. Aug-Sep 1875 – 1r – 1 – $50.00 – U04451 – us Library Micro [071]
DAILY EVENING HERALD – Huntington. Ind. 1883-1887 – 1 – us UMI [071]
DAILY EVENING HERALD – Marysville, CA. Aug-Nov 1853 – 1r – 1 – $50.00 – B02428 – us Library Micro [071]
DAILY EVENING HERALD – St. Joseph. Mich. 1881-1882 – 1 – us UMI [071]
DAILY EVENING HERALD – Stockton, CA. 1865-1874; 1881 – 11r – 1 – $550.00 – C03539 – us Library Micro [071]
(DAILY) (EVENING) JOURNAL – Portland, OR. 19 Apr 1875-3 Jan 1876. 1 roll – 1 – us U.O. Library [071]
DAILY EVENING LEADER – Stockton, CA. 1873-1875 – 1r – 1 – $50.00 – C03540 – us Library Micro [071]
DAILY EVENING MAIL – Stockton, CA. 1880-1918 – 67r – 1 – $3,350.00 – B03009 – us Library Micro [071]
DAILY EVENING NEWS – Modesto, CA. 1884-1925 – 100r – 1 BC02469 – $5,000.00 – us Library Micro [071]
DAILY EVENING NEWS – Sacramento, CA. 1890-92; Jan-Sept 1893; 1909-16 – 11r – 1 – $550.00 – B03425 – us Library Micro [071]
DAILY EVENING PICAYUNE – San Francisco, CA. 1851-1852 – 1r – 1 – $40.00 – C05067 – us Library Micro [071]
DAILY EVENING POST – San Francisco, CA. 1872-1913 – 125r – 1 – $6,250.00 – C03477 – us Library Micro [071]
DAILY EVENING RECORD – Reno, NV. Aug-Nov 1878 – 1r – 1 – $50.00 – U04666 – us Library Micro [071]
DAILY EVENING STANDARD – Portland, OR. -d. 1876-77 – 1 – $24.00 – us Oregon Hist [071]
DAILY EVENING SUN – Red Cloud. Neb. 1887-1888 – 1 – us UMI [071]
DAILY EVENING TELEGRAM – Portland OR. Apr 5 1882-Jan 31 1883 – 1 – us U.O. Library [071]
DAILY EVENING TELEPHONE – (Also known as: Weekly Telephone) – Arcata, CA. 1881-1882 – 2r – 1 – $100.00 – B02021 – us Library Micro [071]
DAILY EVENING TIMES MOUNTAINEER – The Dalles OR. Apr 8 1889, May 13 1889-Sep 28 1889 – 1 – us U.O. Library [071]
DAILY EVENING TRANSCRIPT – Boston, MA: Dutton & Wentworth, jul-dec 1845 – 1 – us Res Libr [071]
DAILY EVENING TRIBUNE – Portsmouth. Ohio. 1856-1857 – 1 – us UMI [071]
DAILY EVERGREEN – Pullman. Wash. (Wash. St. U.). 1892- – 1 – us UMI [071]
DAILY EXAMINER – Bellefontaine. Ohio. 1891- – 1 – us UMI [071]
DAILY EXAMINER – Charlottetown, 1901-1922 – 48r – 1 – cn Preston [971]
DAILY EXAMINER *see* ULSTER EXAMINER
THE DAILY EXCHANGE – Baltimore, Maryland. Feb 22 1958-Sept 14 1961 – 8r – 1 – us L of C Photodup [071]
THE DAILY EXPERIENCES OF OLDER ADULTS RESIDING IN INSTITUTIONAL ENVIRONMENTS / Voelkl, Judith E – 1989 – 209p 3mf – 9 – $12.00 – us Microform Publ [305]
DAILY EXPOSITOR – Adrian. Mich. 1860-1862 – 1 – us UMI [071]
DAILY EXPRESS – (Daily Confederate newspaper) – Petersburg, VA. sept 7, 1861-june 16, 1865 – 1r – 1 – us Western Res [071]
DAILY EXPRESS – Easton. Pa. 1855-1918 – 1 – us UMI [071]
DAILY EXPRESS – Fed. of Malaysia. Jesselton. 1963-1966 – 1 – us UMI [072]
DAILY EXPRESS – London, Apr 1900-70; Oct 1973; Feb 1974; Mar 1975; May,Nov 1977; May 1978; May,Jul,Sep,Oct 1980; May 1981; Mar,May,Dec 1982; Feb,Apr 1983; Jul 1985; 1986- – 700+ r – 1 – uk British Libr Newspaper [072]
DAILY EXPRESS – London, Great Britain. 1954- – 1 – us UMI [072]
DAILY EXPRESS – Montreal, 1 nov 1971-v1 n44. 30 dec 1971 – 1r – 1 – Can$25.00 – cn Can Microfilming [072]
DAILY EXPRESS *see*
– POPULAR NEWSPAPERS DURING WORLD WAR 1
– POPULAR NEWSPAPERS DURING WORLD WAR 2
DAILY EXPRESS AND ORANGE FREE STATE ADVERTISER – Bloemfontein. South Africa. 1882-1900 – 1 – sa State Libr [072]
DAILY FACTS – Redlands, CA. 1890-97; 1919-54 – 150r – 1 RC02679 – $7,500.00 – us Library Micro [071]
DAILY FACTS – Redlands. Calif. 1891-1892; 1940- – 1 – us UMI [071]
DAILY FORUM – Philadelphia. Oct. 12, 1843, Oct. 10, 28, Nov. 2, 1844 – 1 – us NY Public [071]
DAILY FORUM *see* NEVADA FORUM
DAILY FREE PRESS – Atchison. Kan. 1865-1868 – 1 – us UMI [071]
DAILY FREE PRESS – Beloit. Wis. 1897-1915 – 1 – us UMI [071]
DAILY FREE PRESS – Carbondale. Ill. 1899-1953 – 1 – us UMI [071]
DAILY FREE PRESS – Easton. Pa. 1866-1926 – 1 – us UMI [071]
DAILY FREE PRESS – Elko. Nev. 1949- – 1 – us UMI [071]
DAILY FREE PRESS – Kinston. N.C. 1898-1904; 1914- – 1 – us UMI [071]
DAILY FREE PRESS – Quakertown. Pa. 1958- – 1 – us UMI [071]
DAILY FREE PRESS – Redding, CA. 1896-1900 – 4r – 1 – $200.00 – B02672 – us Library Micro [071]
DAILY FREE PRESS – Streator. Ill. 1881-1926 – 1 – us UMI [071]
DAILY FREE TRADER – Ottawa. Ill. 1890; 1915 – 1 – us UMI [071]
DAILY FREEMAN JOURNAL – Webster City. Iowa. 1920- – 1 – us UMI [071]
DAILY GAZETTE – Beaumont. Calif. 1965-1966 – 1 – us UMI [071]
DAILY GAZETTE – Berkeley. Calif. 1912-1944; 1949- – 1 – us UMI [071]
DAILY GAZETTE – Bowling Green, Ohio. 1888 – 1r – 1 – $32.50r – us Archival [071]
DAILY GAZETTE – Burlington. Iowa. and pred. 1837-40, 1848-59, 1867-1907 – 1 – us UMI [071]
DAILY GAZETTE – Lancaster. Ohio. 1916; 1926; 1936 – 1 – us UMI [071]
DAILY GAZETTE – Lawrence. Kan. 1884-85; 1893-95 – 1 – us UMI [071]
DAILY GAZETTE – Martinez, CA. 1905-57 – 129r – 1 – $6,450.00 – B02422 – us Library Micro [071]
DAILY GAZETTE – Pittsburgh. Pa. 1833-1841; 1844-1927 – 1 – us UMI [071]
DAILY GAZETTE – Utica. N.Y. 1842-1855 – 1 – us UMI [071]
DAILY GLEANER – Fredericton, Canada. 7 Oct 1914-29 Jun 1940; 17 Mar 1941-19 Jan 1943; 5 Jun 1943-4 Dec 1952 – 223r – 1 – uk British Libr Newspaper [072]
DAILY GLEANER – Fredericton. New Brunswick. Canada. Ja 1976- – 1 – cn Commonwealth Micro [072]
DAILY GLEANER – Jamaica. 1950-1956 – 1 – us UMI [072]
DAILY GLEANER – Kingston, Jamaica. 10 Sep 1879-31 Dec 1888; 19 Aug 1891-Dec 1899 – 52r – 1 – uk British Libr Newspaper [072]
DAILY GLEANER – Phenix. R.I. 1892-1893 – 1 – us UMI [071]
THE DAILY GLEANER – Kingston, Jamaica: Gleaner Co Ltd, 1902-1956-dec 6 1992 – 1 – us Res Libr [072]
DAILY GLOBE – Washington. D.C. 1857-1858; 1864 – 1 – us UMI [071]
THE DAILY GLOBE – Washington, DC: Francis P Blair, John Rives, James C Pickett, dec 5 1871-jun 19 1872 – 2r – 1 – us Res Libr [071]
DAILY GRAPHIC – 1948-1953 – 1 – uk Manchester Libr [072]
DAILY GRAPHIC – Accra: West African Graphic, 1956-dec 30 1982 – 1 – us Res Libr [072]
DAILY GRAPHIC – Accra: West African Graphic, -1982. [may 24 1954-sep 25 1965] – us Res Libr [072]
DAILY GRAPHIC – New York. v1-50. 1873-89 – 35r – 1 – us Ross [071]
THE DAILY GRAPHIC – New York. Mar 4 1873-Sept 23 1889. v. 1-50 no. 5129 – 1 – us NY Public [071]
DAILY GUARDIAN – (Lacking: July-Dec 1946. Jan-June 1954. Feb-May 1958) – Freetown, Sierra Leone. Jan 1941-Aug 1958 – 17r – 1 – uk British Libr Newspaper [072]
DAILY GUERNSEY TIMES – Cambridge. Ohio. 1890-91; 1905-1917 – 1 – us UMI [071]
DAILY HAMPSHIRE INDEPENDENT *see* HAMPSHIRE INDEPENDENT
THE DAILY HEBREW JOURNAL – Toronto, Canada. v21 n7547. apr 7 1931-n16, 842. 4 apr 1962 – 8 – 1 – Can$65.00 – cn Can Microfilming [072]
DAILY HERALD – Adelaide, Australia. Sep 1912-Aug 1916 – 21r – 1 – uk British Libr Newspaper [072]
DAILY HERALD – Beacon. N.Y. 1913-1927 – 1 – us UMI [071]
DAILY HERALD – Biloxi-Gulfport. Miss. 1898- – 1 – us UMI [071]
DAILY HERALD – Carlisle, PA., 1889 – 13 – $25.00r – us I.M.R. [071]
DAILY HERALD – Carroll. Iowa. 1871-1941 – 1 – us UMI [071]
DAILY HERALD – Chambersburg, PA., 1886 – 13 – $25.00r – us I.M.R. [071]
DAILY HERALD – Dayton. Ohio. and Empire. 1874-76 – 1 – us UMI [071]
DAILY HERALD – Delphos, Ohio. 1894-1910 – 19r – 1 – $32.50r – us Archival [071]
DAILY HERALD – Fredonia. Kan. 1973- – 1 – us UMI [071]
DAILY HERALD – Gulfport. Miss. 1969 – 1 – us UMI [071]
DAILY HERALD – London, 1911-64 – 268r – 1 – uk British Libr Newspaper [072]
DAILY HERALD – London, 1912-19, 1938-45 – 1 – $35.00r – us Hoover Inst Photo [072]
DAILY HERALD – London: "Limited" Print. & Pub Co, 1939-55; 1956-sep 14 1964 – 1 – us Res Libr [072]
DAILY HERALD – Middletown. N.Y. 1919-1926 – 1 – us UMI [071]
DAILY HERALD – Monongahela, PA., 1970-1972 – 13 – $25.00r – us I.M.R. [071]
DAILY HERALD – Monongahela. Pa. 1973- – 1 – us UMI [071]
DAILY HERALD – Nanaimo, Canada. Apr 1913-Nov 1920 – 20r – 1 – uk British Libr Newspaper [072]
DAILY HERALD – Newton. Iowa. 1902-1903 – 1 – us UMI [071]
DAILY HERALD – Oskaloosa. Iowa. 1968- – 1 – us UMI [071]
DAILY HERALD – Palestine. Tex. 1942- – 1 – us UMI [071]
DAILY HERALD – Rutland. Vt. 1861-1905; 1908- – 1 – us UMI [071]
DAILY HERALD – Stratford, 1887-1923 – 72r – 1 – cn Preston [971]
DAILY HERALD – Thunder Bay, 1885-1886 – 2r – 1 – cn Preston [971]
DAILY HERALD – Vicksburg. Miss. 1864-1881 – 1 – us UMI [071]
DAILY HERALD – Wellsburg. West Virginia. 1900-1909; 1929-1955; 1958-1970 – 1 – us UMI [071]
DAILY HERALD – Wilmington. N.C. 1854-60 – 1 – us UMI [071]
THE DAILY HERALD – Somerset. Pa. 1929-36 – 1 – us UMI [071]
DAILY HERALD AND GAZETTE : DAILY WHIG NEWSPAPER – Cleveland, OH. 22 Mar 1837-5 Aug 1839 – 4r – 1 – us Western Res [071]
DAILY HERALD-TELEPHONE – Bloomington. Ind. and Sun. Herald Times. 1948- – 1 – us UMI [071]
DAILY HOTEL AND COMMERCIAL ADVERTISER – Portland OR. Dec 26 28 1888 – 1 – us U.O. Library [071]
DAILY HUMBOLDT TIMES – Eureka, CA. Jan 1874-Dec 1951 – 223r – 1 BC02213 – $11,150.00 – us Library Micro [071]
DAILY HUSTLER – Three Rivers. Mich. 1905-09 – 1 – us UMI [071]
DAILY IBERIAN – New Iberia. La. 1965- – 1 – us UMI [071]
DAILY ILLINOIS COURIER – Jacksonville. Ill. 1882-1911 – 1 – us UMI [071]
DAILY ILLUSTRATED HERALD – San Francisco, CA. 1923-1926 – 15r – 1 – $750.00 – C03666 – us Library Micro [071]
DAILY INDEPENDENT – Corona. Calif. 1906- – 1 – us UMI [071]
DAILY INDEPENDENT – Delphos, Ohio. 1894 – 1r – 1 – $32.50r – us Archival [071]
DAILY INDEPENDENT – Kannapolis. N.C. 1938- – 1 – us UMI [071]
DAILY INDEPENDENT – Murphysboro. Ill. 1923-49 – 1 – us UMI [071]
DAILY INDEPENDENT – Salem OR. Mar 18-May 30 1893 – 1 – us U.O. Library [071]
DAILY INDEPENDENT – Stockton, CA. 1861-1905; 1907-40 – 149r – 1 – $7,450.00 – B03010 – us Library Micro [071]
DAILY INDEPENDENT – Stockton. Calif. 1865-1926 – 1 – us UMI [071]
DAILY INDEPENDENT – Virginia City, NV. 1875 – 1r – 1 – $50.00 – N04784 – us Library Micro [071]
DAILY INDEPENDENT *see* WEEKLY ELKO INDEPENDENT
THE DAILY INDEPENDENT – (Title varies: The Independent, 1875-79; 1893) – Kimberley, South Africa.29 Sept 1875-30 Jun 1893 – 46r – 1,16 diazo available at reduced price – sa SA Libr [072]
DAILY INDEPENDENT (CORONA/NORCO) – Corona, CA. 1969- – 129+ r – 1 – $6,450.00 ($340.00y) – R02143 – us Library Micro [071]
DAILY INDEPENDENT TIMES – Streator. Ill. 1914-1926 – 1 – us UMI [071]
DAILY INDEX – Carson City, NV. 1863-64 (scats); 1880-87 – 8r – 1 – $400.00 – U04450 – us Library Micro [071]
DAILY INDEX – (Cont by: Index Journal) – Salinas, CA. 1894-1928 – 54r – 1 – $2,700.00 – B02750 – us Library Micro [071]
DAILY INDEX – Moberly. Mo. 1906-17 – 1 – us UMI [071]
DAILY INDEX – Salinas. Calif. 1897-1905 – 1 – us UMI [071]
DAILY INDEX APPEAL – Petersburg. Va. 1873-1878 – 1 – us UMI [071]
DAILY INDIANIAN – Warsaw. Ind. 1881-1882 – 1 – us UMI [071]
THE DAILY INDONESIAN-LANGUAGE PRESS OF DJAKARTA: ANALYSIS OF TWO RECENT CRITICAL PERIODS. (THESIS). SE-5970/1. 1967 / Crawford, Robert Henry – 9 – ne IDC [380]
DAILY INLAND EMPIRE – Hamilton, NV. 1869-70 – 2r – 1 – $100.00 – U04573 – us Library Micro [071]
DAILY INTELLIGENCER – Augusta, GA. Oct 7 1858-Dec 31 1864 – 6r – 1 – us Western Res [071]
DAILY INTELLIGENCER – Baltimore. Md. 1793-1794 – 1,3 – us Readex [071]
DAILY INTELLIGENCER – Belleville, Ontario, CN. Oct 1913-Nov 1915 – 11 1/2r – 1 – uk British Libr Newspaper [072]
THE DAILY INTER OCEAN – Chicago: Inter Ocean Pub Co, 1879-1902. jan 4 1882; apr 30, may 3-6,13,20, aug 10-31 1893 – us Res Libr [071]
DAILY IOWEGIAN – Centerville. Iowa. 1921-1935. 1936-1941; 1949- – 1 – us UMI [071]
DAILY ITEM – Great Bend. Kan. 1900-1908 – 1 – us UMI [071]
DAILY ITEM – Steelton, PA. -d 1883-1885 – 13 – $25.00r – us I.M.R. [071]
DAILY ITEM – Sumter. S.C. 1961- – 1 – us UMI [071]
DAILY ITEM – Sunbury. Pa. 1954- – 1 – us UMI [071]
DAILY JEFFERSONIAN – Cambridge. Ohio. 1892- – 1 – us UMI [071]
DAILY JEFFERSONIAN – Findlay, Ohio. 1880-85 – 5r – 1 – $32.50r – us Archival [071]
THE DAILY JEWISH COURIER – Chicago. Ill. 1893; 1906-47 – 1 – us A.J.P.C. [071]
DAILY JEWISH EXPRESS – London. 1908-1922 – 1 – us NY Public [072]
DAILY JEWISH PRESS – Chicago. Ill. 1913 – 1 – us A.J.P.C. [071]
DAILY JOURNAL – Antigo. Wis. 1904-1952 – 1 – us UMI [071]
DAILY JOURNAL – Billings. Mont. 1907-1908 – 1 – us UMI [071]
DAILY JOURNAL – Clinton. Ill. and Public. 1950- – 1 – us UMI [071]
DAILY JOURNAL – Coffeyville. Kan. 1880; 1893-1961 – 1 – us UMI [071]
DAILY JOURNAL – Corning. N.Y. 1892-1910 – 1 – us UMI [071]
DAILY JOURNAL – Elizabeth. N.J. 1882- – 1 – us UMI [071]
DAILY JOURNAL – Fairbury. Neb. 1892-1963 – 1 – us UMI [071]
DAILY JOURNAL – Franklin. Ind. 1963- – 1 – us UMI [071]
DAILY JOURNAL – Jacksonville. Ill. 1875-1877; 1891- – 1 – us UMI [071]
DAILY JOURNAL – Lawrence. Kan. 1879-1911 – 1 – us UMI [071]

DAILY JOURNAL – Los Angeles, CA. 1888 – 1000+ r – 1 – $50,000.00 ($800.00y) – HC02392 – us Library Micro [073]
DAILY JOURNAL – Louisville. Ky. 1830-1868 – 1 – us UMI [071]
DAILY JOURNAL – McComb. Miss. 1937-1945 – 1 – us UMI [071]
DAILY JOURNAL – Mansfield. Ohio. 1924-1927 – 1 – us UMI [071]
DAILY JOURNAL – Mechanicsburg, PA. -d 1901-11. 12 rolls – 13 – $25.00r – us I.M.R. [071]
DAILY JOURNAL – Moundsville. West Virginia. 1910-1922; 1925-1945 – 1 – us UMI [071]
DAILY JOURNAL – Napa, CA. 1890-1949 – 77r – 1 – $3,850.00 – B02506 – us Library Micro [071]
DAILY JOURNAL – Napa. Calif. 1913-1920 – 1 – us UMI [071]
DAILY JOURNAL – Providence. R.I. 1858-65 – 1 – us UMI [071]
DAILY JOURNAL – Salem OR. June 30 1899-Nov 25 1903 – 1 – us U.O. Library [071]
DAILY JOURNAL – Salinas. Calif. 1889-1897 – 1 – us UMI [071]
DAILY JOURNAL – San Francisco, CA. 1988 – 144+ r – 1 – $7,200.00 ($1,200.00y) – H04062 – us Library Micro [071]
DAILY JOURNAL – Stevens Point. Wis. 1895-1940; 1953- – 1 – us UMI [071]
DAILY JOURNAL – Turlock, CA. 1972 – 132+ r – 1 – $6,600.00 ($300.00y) – H04075 – us Library Micro [071]
DAILY JOURNAL – Turlock. Calif. 1905-1907; 1911-1914; 1919-1920; 1923-1940; 1942-1943; 1950- – 1 – us UMI [071]
DAILY JOURNAL – Ukiah. Calif. 1950- – 1 – us UMI [071]
DAILY JOURNAL – Wilmington. N.C. 1851-77 – 1 – us UMI [071]
DAILY JOURNAL OF COMMERCE – Portland, OR. 1 Oct 1925-14 May 1985; 2 Nov 1987-. – 1 – us U.O. Library [071]
DAILY JOURNAL WORLD – Lawrence. Kan. 1911- – 1 – us UMI [071]
DAILY JOURNALS / U.S. Weather Bureau. Station 85, Alpena, Michigan – 1872-1917 – 2r – 1 – $32.50r – us Archival [550]
THE DAILY LANTER – Reno, NV. 1907-1928 – 1r – 1 – $50.00 – U04675 – us Library Micro [071]
DAILY LAW BULLETIN – Chicago. Ill. 1871- – 1 – us UMI [071]
DAILY LAW RECORD – Chicago. Ill. 1871-73 – 1 – us UMI [071]
DAILY LEADER – Bluefield. West Virginia. 1906-1910 – 1 – us UMI [071]
DAILY LEADER – Davenport. Iowa. 1892-1904 – 1 – us UMI [071]
DAILY LEADER – Eureka, NV. 1878-85 – 8r – 1 – $400.00 – U04509 – us Library Micro [071]
DAILY LEADER – Galion. Ohio. 1891-94; 1910-1917 – 1 – us UMI [071]
DAILY LEADER – Marion. Ind. 1894-1912 – 1 – us UMI [071]
DAILY LEADER – Mount Clemens. Mich. 1921-42 – 1 – us UMI [071]
DAILY LEADER – Piqua. Ohio. 1889-1892 – 1 – us UMI [071]
DAILY LEADER – Pontiac. Ill. 1959- – 1 – us UMI [071]
DAILY LEADER TIMES – Kittanning. Pa. 1957- – 1 – us UMI [071]
DAILY LEDGER – Canton. Ill. 1962- – 1 – us UMI [071]
DAILY LEDGER – Fairfield. Ohio. 1940-1947 – 1 – us UMI [071]
DAILY LEDGER – Noblesville. Ind. 1913- – 1 – us UMI [071]
DAILY LEGAL NEWS AND CLEVELAND RECORDER – Cleveland. On film: v48, no. 131-v75, no.313; Ju 1935-Dec 1962. LL-04 – 1 – us L of C Photodup [340]
DAILY LEVER – Seymour. Ind. 1880-1883 – 1 – us UMI [071]
DAILY LIVE WIRE – Portland OR. Sep 28 1912 – 1 – us U.O. Library [071]
DAILY LOCAL LEVER – Seymour. Ind. 1881 – 1 – us UMI [071]
DAILY LOCAL NEWS – West Chester. Pa. 1873- – 1 – us UMI [071]
DAILY LODE – Delamar, NV. Mar-Jun 1898 – 1r – 1 – $50.00 – U04487 – us Library Micro [071]
DAILY LOKMAT – Nagpur, India. 5 May-7 Dec 1950; 2 Jan-9 Dec 1951; Jan-12 Dec 1952; 1953 – 4r – 1 – us L of C Photodup [072]
DAILY MAIL – 1896- – 12r per y – 1 – inquire – us Ross [072]
DAILY MAIL – 1973 – 1 – $148.50 – us African Imprint [960]
DAILY MAIL – Anderson. S.C. 1945-49 – 1 – us UMI [071]
DAILY MAIL – Anderson. S.C. 1973- – 1 – us UMI [071]
DAILY MAIL – Brisbane, Australia. Oct 1903-Nov 1916; May 1920-Jun 1922; Oct 1926-Aug 1933 (imperfect) – 163r – 1 – uk British Libr Newspaper [072]
DAILY MAIL – London. 1896-to date – 1 – uk Microform Academic [072]
DAILY MAIL – London, Feb 1896-1979; 1986- – 833+ r – 1 – uk British Libr Newspaper [072]
DAILY MAIL – Nevada. Mo. 1883- – 1 – us UMI [071]
DAILY MAIL – Olney. Ill. 1952- – 1 – us UMI [071]
DAILY MAIL – Silver jubilee issue. London, England. 6 May 1935 – 3ft – 1 – uk British Libr Newspaper [072]
DAILY MAIL AND EMPIRE – Toronto, Canada. Sept-Oct 1918 – 2r – 1 – uk British Libr Newspaper [072]
DAILY MERCURY – (1993.-14r; 1901-1976.-388r) – Guelph, 1977-1992 – 204r – 1 – cn Preston [971]
DAILY MERCURY *see* MERCURY
DAILY MESSENGER – Astoria, OR. 1 Feb 1931-16 Jan 1934. – 5r – 1 – us U.O. Library [071]
DAILY MESSENGER – Homestead. Pa. 1898- – 1 – us UMI [071]
THE DAILY MESSENGER – Canadaigua. N.Y. 1922- – 1 – us UMI [071]
DAILY MIDWAY DRILLER – Taft. Calif. 1910- – 1 – us UMI [071]
DAILY MINER – Butte. Mont. 1876-1878; 1879-1890; 1894-1925 – 1 – us UMI [071]
DAILY MINER AND NEWS – (1920-1992.-180r) – Kenora, 1993 – 4r – 1 – cn Preston [971]
THE DAILY MINER TRANSCRIPT – Nevada City, CA. Jul 1904-Dec 1905 – 3r – 1 – $150.00 – B02515 – us Library Micro [071]
DAILY MINING JOURNAL – Marquette. Mich. 1896- – 1 – us UMI [071]
DAILY MIRROR – Manila-Philippines. 1951-1966 – 1 – us UMI [072]
DAILY MIRROR – (Mirror, 1985) – London, Jul 1903- – 744+ r – 1 – uk British Libr Newspaper [072]
DAILY MIRROR – New York. N.Y. 1924-1963 – 1 – us UMI [071]
DAILY MIRROR – Sydney, Australia. May-Sept 3 1945; Jan-Aug 1946 – 5r – 1 – us L of C Photodup [072]
DAILY MIRROR *see*
– POPULAR NEWSPAPERS DURING WORLD WAR 1
– POPULAR NEWSPAPERS DURING WORLD WAR 2
DAILY MOON. (OR NIGHTLY MOON) – Battle Creek. Mich. 1880-1914 – 1 – us UMI [071]
DAILY MORNING ASTORIAN – Astoria, OR. 3 Jan 1884-29 Dec 1904. – 1 – us U.O. Library [071]
THE DAILY MORNING CALL – (Also known as: The Call and Post) – San Francisco, CA. 1863-1929 – 596r – 1 – $29,800.00 – C02810 – us Library Micro [071]
DAILY MORNING CHRONICLE – Concord. N.H. 1853-1855; 1865 – 1 – us UMI [071]
DAILY MORNING JOURNAL – Oakland, CA. 1867 – 1r – 1 – $50.00 – C03361 – us Library Micro [071]
DAILY MORNING NEWS – Parkersburg. West Virginia. 1898-1905 – 1 – us UMI [071]
DAILY MORNING POST – Carson City, NV. Mar, Apr 1865 – 1r – 1 – $50.00 – U04452 – us Library Micro [071]
DAILY MORNING STANDARD – Williamsport, PA., 1872 – 13 – $25.00r – us I.M.R. [071]
DAILY MORNING TIMES – (Also known as: Times Star) – San Jose, CA. 1879-83; Jul-Dec 1884; 1906-09 – 21r – 1 – $1,050.00 – B02875 – us Library Micro [071]
DAILY MORNING TIMES MOUNTAINEER – The Dalles OR. Apr 10-May 12 1889 – 1 – us U.O. Library [071]
DAILY MORNING TRIBUNE – Portland, OR. 4 Dec 1897-7 Jun 1898. 1 roll – 1 – us U.O. Library [071]
DAILY MORNING UNION *see* THE UNION
DAILY MOUNTAINEER – The Dalles, OR. 20 Feb 1864-7 Jun 1866. 1 roll – 1 – us U.O. Library [071]
DAILY MUSALMAN – Madras, India. 2 Jul 1944-Dec 1965 – 17r – 1 – us L of C Photodup [072]
DAILY NATION – Nairobi: East African Newspapers Ltd, jun 1962. mon-sat issues filmed only – 1 – us Res Libr [072]
DAILY NATIONAL *see* NEVADA NATION
DAILY NATIONAL DEMOCRAT – Marysville, CA. 1858-61 – 6r – 1 – $300.00 – B02429 – us Library Micro [071]
DAILY NATIONAL GAZETTE – Nevada City, CA. Apr-Dec 1870; Jan-Oct 1871 – 2r – 1 – $100.00 – B02516 – us Library Micro [071]
DAILY NATIONAL INTELLIGENCER – Washington, DC. v8,11,19,43,44. 1820-56 – 5r – 1 – us Ross [071]
DAILY NATIONAL JOURNAL – Washington, DC. Aug 9 1824-Dec 31 1831 – 13r – 1 – us L of C Photodup [071]
DAILY NATIONAL JOURNAL – Washington, DC, jan-jun 1831 – 1r – 1 – us Res Libr [071]
DAILY NAWAN ZAMANA – Jullundur, India. Jul-Sept 1966 – 1r – 1 – us L of C Photodup [072]
DAILY NEBRASKA HERALD – Plattsmouth, NE. Jun-Nov 1872 – 1 – us NE Hist [071]
DAILY NEBRASKAN – Lincoln. Neb. 1901-1914 – 1 – us UMI [071]
DAILY NEVADA DEMOCRAT – Reno, NV. Jun-Aug 1875 – 1r – 1 – $50.00 – U04667 – us Library Micro [071]
DAILY NEW ERA – Lancaster. Pa. 1884-1939; 1945-1960 – 1 – us UMI [071]
THE DAILY NEW ERA – Lancaster, PA., 1884 – 13 – $25.00r – us I.M.R. [071]
DAILY NEWS – (1878 ends) – Durban, South Africa. 1 Jan 1879- – 1073r – 1 – sa Microfile [960]
DAILY NEWS – (1976-1992.-204r) – Truro, 1993 – 12r – 1 – cn Preston [971]
DAILY NEWS – (1978 Nevada Day edition) – Goldhill, NV. 1867-82 (scats) – 1r – 1 – $50.00 – U04567 – us Library Micro [071]
DAILY NEWS – (1980-1991.-186r) – Halifax, 1993 – 24r – 1 – cn Preston [971]
DAILY NEWS – Anadarko. Okl. 1951-1960 – 1 – us UMI [071]
DAILY NEWS – Anaheim, CA. 1959 – 2r – 1 – $100.00 – R04002 – us Library Micro [071]
DAILY NEWS – Anchorage. Alaska. 1971- – 1 – us UMI [071]
DAILY NEWS – Arlington. Tex. 1958-1964; 1968- – 1 – us UMI [071]
DAILY NEWS – Beloit. Wis. 1897- – 1 – us UMI [071]
DAILY NEWS – Boone. Iowa. 1888-1891 – 1 – us UMI [071]
DAILY NEWS – Canton. Ohio. 1913-1930 – 1 – us UMI [071]
DAILY NEWS – Danville. Ill. 1876-1903 – 1 – us UMI [071]
DAILY NEWS – Dayton. Ohio. 1899- – 1 – us UMI [071]
DAILY NEWS – Dowagiac. Mich. 1897-1919; 1933-1936; 1956 – 1 – us UMI [071]
DAILY NEWS – Elk City. Okl. 1953- – 1 – us UMI [071]
DAILY NEWS – Flint. Mich. 1884-1905 – 1 – us UMI [071]
DAILY NEWS – Fort Lauderdale. Fl. Feb 1946-Jan 1952 – 1 – us P.K. Yonge [071]
DAILY NEWS – Fremont, Ohio. -d. 1887-1938 – 1 – us Hayes [071]
DAILY NEWS – Garland. Tex. 1908-1939; 1946- – 1 – us UMI [071]
DAILY NEWS – Geelong, Australia. 6 May 1858-30 Jun 1859.-d 3mqn reels – 1 – uk British Libr Newspaper [072]
DAILY NEWS – Goldfield, NV. 1909-10; 8 Mar 1911 – 2r – 1 – $100.00 – U04550 – us Library Micro [071]
DAILY NEWS – Grand Prairie. Tex. 1970- – 1 – us UMI [071]
DAILY NEWS – Greensboro. N.C. 1909- – 1 – us UMI [071]
DAILY NEWS – Greensburg. Ind. 1918- – 1 – us UMI [071]
DAILY NEWS – Hamilton, 1954-1955 – 18r – 1 – cn Preston [971]
DAILY NEWS – Hamilton. Ohio. 1880-1897; 1919-1933 – 1 – us UMI [071]
DAILY NEWS – Harrisonburg. Va. 1901-1913 – 1 – us UMI [071]
DAILY NEWS – Havre. Mont. 1925- – 1 – us UMI [071]
DAILY NEWS – Hillsdale. Mich. 1963- – 1 – us UMI [071]
DAILY NEWS – Hinton. West Virginia. 1902-1940; 1952-1966 – 1 – us UMI [071]
DAILY NEWS – Huntingdon. Pa. 1959- – 1 – us UMI [071]
DAILY NEWS – Huntingdon, PA. -d 1922-1990; 1959-1970; 1983-1984 – 13 – $25.00r – us I.M.R. [071]
DAILY NEWS – Inglewood, CA. 1916-80 (broken series) – 203r – 1 HC02306 – $10,150.00 – us Library Micro [071]
DAILY NEWS – Inglewood. Calif. 1960-1966 – 1 – us UMI [071]
DAILY NEWS – Irving. Tex. 1954-1958; 1970- – 1 – us UMI [071]
DAILY NEWS – Jackson. Miss. 1902- – 1 – us UMI [071]
DAILY NEWS – Jacksonville. N.C. 1970- – 1 – us UMI [071]
DAILY NEWS – Kenton, Ohio. 1890-91 – 2r – 1 – $32.50r – us Archival [071]
DAILY NEWS – Ketchikan. Alaska. 1961- – 1 – us UMI [071]
DAILY NEWS – Kingston, Canada. 1862-73 – 16r – 1 – $1,040.00 – cn Library Assoc [971]
DAILY NEWS – Logan. Ohio. 1936- – 1 – us UMI [071]
DAILY NEWS – London. (News Chronicle). -d. Jan 1846-Oct 1960. (581 reels) – 1 – uk British Libr Newspaper [072]
DAILY NEWS – Lorain. Ohio. 1904-18 – 1 – us UMI [071]
DAILY NEWS – Los Angeles, CA. 1870-1872 – 3r – 1 – $150.00 – C03289 – us Library Micro [071]
DAILY NEWS – Ludington. Mich. 1913-1953 – 1 – us UMI [071]
DAILY NEWS – Manistee. Mich. 1894-1914 – 1 – us UMI [071]
DAILY NEWS – Marshfield. Wis. 1921-1927 – 1 – us UMI [071]
DAILY NEWS – Mauch Chunk, PA., 1914 – 13 – $25.00r – us I.M.R. [071]
DAILY NEWS – Milwaukee. Wis. 1855-1881; 1887-1915; 1918-1939 – 1 – us UMI [071]
DAILY NEWS – Milwaukee. Wis. and Review. 1889-91 – 1 – us UMI [071]
DAILY NEWS – Minot. N.D. 1968- – 1 – us UMI [071]
DAILY NEWS – Montreal, Canada. ns: v1 n118. 18 mai 1867-v10 n13. 16 jan 1872 – 1r – 1 – Can$25.00 – cn Can Microfilming [072]
DAILY NEWS – Mount Vernon. N.Y. 1956-1958 – 1 – us UMI [071]
DAILY NEWS – Nelson, Canada. -d. Jan 1905-June 1922. 59 reels – 1 – uk British Libr Newspaper [072]
DAILY NEWS – New York. N.Y. (All Editions). 1919- – 1 – us UMI [071]
DAILY NEWS – Newburgh. N.Y. 1857-1861 – 1 – us UMI [071]
DAILY NEWS – Newport. R.I. 1892-1949 – 1 – us UMI [071]
DAILY NEWS – Norfolk. Neb. 1886- – 1 – us UMI [071]
DAILY NEWS – Oakland, CA. Jan 1862-76 – 6r – 1 – $300.00 – B02541 – us Library Micro [071]
DAILY NEWS – Omaha. Neb. 1899-1927 – 1 – us UMI [071]
DAILY NEWS – Orange. Calif. 1953-1960 – 1 – us UMI [071]
DAILY NEWS – Palatka. Fl. 1884-1888, 1902-1917, 1930-1956 – 1 – us P.K. Yonge [071]
DAILY NEWS – Palm Beach. Fl. 1933-1938, 1940-1941, 1949-1954 – 1 – us P.K. Yonge [071]
DAILY NEWS – Pasadena, CA. 1901-15 (broken series) – 51r – 1 – $2,550.00 – C02611 – us Library Micro [071]
DAILY NEWS – Pasadena. Calif. 1898-1902; 1905-1910 – 1 – us UMI [071]
DAILY NEWS – Passaic. N.J. 1877-1932 – 1 – us UMI [071]
DAILY NEWS – Pensacola. Fl. 1889-1905 – 1 – us P.K. Yonge [071]
DAILY NEWS – Perth, Australia. Jul 1882-Dec 1888.-w. 13 reels – 1 – uk British Libr Newspaper [072]
DAILY NEWS – Pittsburgh. Pa. 1896-1900 – 1 – us UMI [071]
DAILY NEWS – Port Clinton, Ohio. 1956-69 – 17r – 1 – $32.50r – us Archival [071]
DAILY NEWS – Port Clinton. Ohio. 1967- – 1 – us UMI [071]
DAILY NEWS – Portland. Or. 1883-1887; 1907-1931 – 1 – us UMI [071]

DAILY NEWS – Prince Rupert, Canada. -d. June 1912-June 1922. 30 1 2 reels – 1 – uk British Libr Newspaper [072]
DAILY NEWS – Quebec, 1865-1867 – 3r – 1 – cn Preston [971]
DAILY NEWS – Red Bluff, CA. 1892-95; 1897-1908; 1926-71 – 136r – 1 BC02656 – $6,800.00 – us Library Micro [071]
DAILY NEWS – Red Bluff. Calif. 1943- – 1 – us UMI [071]
DAILY NEWS – Richardson. Tex. 1963- – 1 – us UMI [071]
DAILY NEWS – Richmond, CA. 1914-20 – 9r – 1 – $450.00 – B02691 – us Library Micro [071]
DAILY NEWS – Salem OR. Sep 27 1916 – 1 – us U.O. Library [071]
DAILY NEWS – Salisbury. Rhodesia. Feb 1962-Aug 1964. Weekend editions only. Missing v. 2, no. 19 – 1 – 35.00r – us Hoover Inst Photo [072]
DAILY NEWS – Santa Barbara. Calif. 1875-1927 – 1 – us UMI [071]
DAILY NEWS – Shamokin. Pa. 1931-1933 – 1 – us UMI [071]
DAILY NEWS – Sidney. Ohio. 1973- – 1 – us UMI [071]
DAILY NEWS – Springfield. Ohio. 1905- – 1 – us UMI [071]
DAILY NEWS – St. John's. Canada. -d. Jan 1911-Dec 1913, Jan 1917-Jun 1940; 18 Mar 1941-25 Aug 1948; 21 Mar 1949-7 Feb 1953; 26 Sept 1957-25 Sept 1967. (327 reels) – 1 – uk British Libr Newspaper [072]
DAILY NEWS – St. John's, Newfoundland, Canada. 1894-1920 – 70r – 1 – $4,550.00 – cn Library Assoc [971]
DAILY NEWS – St. John's, Newfoundland, Canada. Trailer reel (issues that were originally missing for 1908-20) – 1r – 1 – $68.00 – cn Library Assoc [971]
DAILY NEWS – Starkville. Miss. 1902-1918; 1937- – 1 – us UMI [071]
DAILY NEWS – Staunton. Va. 1912-1913 – 1 – us UMI [071]
DAILY NEWS – Tiffin, Ohio. 1896-1900 – 6r – 1 – $32.50r – us Archival [071]
DAILY NEWS – Virgin Islands. 1950-1961 – 1 – us UMI [072]
DAILY NEWS – Welch. West Virginia. 1924-29; 1932-1940; 1947-1970 – 1 – us UMI [071]
DAILY NEWS – Welland, De1922-1923Ap – 1r – 1 – cn Preston [971]
DAILY NEWS – Wheeling. West Virginia. 1904-1935 – 1 – us UMI [071]
DAILY NEWS – Whittier, CA. 1983- – 156+ r – 1 – $7,800.00 ($380.00y) – R03100 – us Library Micro [071]
DAILY NEWS – Williamson. West Virginia. 1913-1916; 1935-1945 – 1 – us UMI [071]
DAILY NEWS – Wilmington. Ohio. 1915-19 – 1 – us UMI [071]
DAILY NEWS – Winona. Minn. 1954- – 1 – us UMI [071]
DAILY NEWS – Wooster. Ohio. 1906-1913; 1917-1918 – 1 – us UMI [071]
DAILY NEWS – Gaborone: [s.n.], sep 17 1975-81 – us Res Libr [071]
THE DAILY NEWS – Athens, PA., 1889-1890 – 13 – $25.00r – us I.M.R. [071]
THE DAILY NEWS – Camarillo/Port Huneme, CA. 1967-1981; 1982- – 179+ r – 1 – $8,950.00 ($360.00y) – H03171 – us Library Micro [071]
THE DAILY NEWS – Sherbrooke, Canada. n92. 21 aut 1908 – 1r – 1 – Can$25.00 – cn Can Microfilming [072]
DAILY NEWS ADVERTISER – Vancouver, Canada. Jul-Aug 1912; Jul-Aug 1917.-d. 3 reels – 1 – uk British Libr Newspaper [072]
DAILY NEWS ALMANAC AND POLITICAL REGISTER *see* WHIG ALMANAC AND POLITICIAN'S REGISTER, 1834-1914/ THE DAILY NEWS ALMANAC AND POLITICAL REGISTER, 1885-1937
THE DAILY NEWS ALMANAC AND POLITICAL REGISTER – 1885-1937 – 9 – us UMI [030]
DAILY NEWS BULLETIN – New York, NY. 7 Nov 1923-15 Oct 1924. Incomplete – 1 – us A.J.P.C. [071]
DAILY NEWS BULLETIN / Jewish Telegraphic Agency, Inc – New York: The Agency. [v4 n248-v6 n300. 1924-26] – 2r – us Res Libr [071]
DAILY NEWS BULLETIN = WAKALAT AL-ANBA AL-QATARIYAH – Qatar: The Agency, aug 4 1986-apr 18 1987 – 1r – 1 – us Res Libr [072]
DAILY NEWS DEALER – Wilkes-Barre. Pa. 1890-1898 – 1 – us UMI [071]
DAILY NEWS DEMOCRAT – Huntington. Ind. 1897-1911 – 1 – us UMI [071]
DAILY NEWS DIGEST – Bangkok. Thailand. 1958- – 1 – us UMI [072]
DAILY NEWS DIGEST – Huntington. West Virginia. 1952-54 – 1 – us UMI [071]
DAILY NEWS ERA – Boyertown, PA., 1908-1915 – 13 – $25.00r – us I.M.R. [071]
THE DAILY NEWS HISTORY OF BUCHANAN COUNTY AND ST JOSEPH / St. Joseph Publishing Co – Biographical sketches of noted citizens living and dead.St. Joseph, 1898. Missouri Reel 10. (The Cox Library Collection) – 5 – us Americana [978]
DAILY NEWS HUNTINGDON SAXON – Mount Union, PA., 1982 – 13 – $25.00r – us I.M.R. [071]
DAILY NEWS INDIO – Indio, CA. 1928-90 – 106r – 1 RH02304 – $5,300.00 – us Library Micro [071]
DAILY NEWS MINER – Fairbanks. Alaska. 1943-1950; 1970- – 1 – us UMI [071]
DAILY NEWS MT. CARMEL – Mount Carmel, PA., 1892-1912 – 13 – $25.00r – us I.M.R. [071]
DAILY NEWS PROMOTER – Havre. Mont. 1925-1968 – 1 – us UMI [071]
DAILY NEWS RECORD – Harrisonburg. Va. 1880-1950- – 1 – us UMI [071]
DAILY NEWS RECORD – New York, 1917- – 1 – $330y – us Fairchild Micro [670]
DAILY NEWS REVIEW – Vienna, Austria. -d. 21 June 1949-31 March 1950. 2 reels – 1 – uk British Libr Newspaper [072]
DAILY NEWS SEARCHLIGHT – Bremerton, WA. 1922-45 – 53r – 1 – $2,650.00 – R05401 – us Library Micro [071]
DAILY NEWS TEXAN – Mid Cities. Tex. 1962- – 1 – us UMI [071]
DAILY NEWS-CHIEF – Winter Haven. Fl. 1931-1977 – 1 – us P.K. Yonge [071]
DAILY NEXUS – Santa Barbara, CA. UC Santa Barbara: 1990-1994 – 10r – 1 – $500.00 – B06074 – us Library Micro [370]
DAILY NORTHERN ARGUS – Rockhampton, Australia. Apr 1872-Dec 1888; May 1894-Dec 1896.-d. 34 reels – 1 – uk British Libr Newspaper [072]
DAILY NORTHERN STATESMAN – Marysville, CA. Jun-Jul 1867 – 1r – 1 – $50.00 – B02430 – us Library Micro [071]
DAILY NORTHWEST – Missoula. Mont. 1928-1929 – 1 – us UMI [071]
DAILY NORTHWESTERN – Oshkosh. Wis. 1876-1940; 1952- – 1 – us UMI [071]
DAILY NOTES – Cannonsburg. Pa. 1973- – 1 – us UMI [071]
DAILY NOTES – Canonsburg, PA. 1879-1973 – 13 – $25.00r – us I.M.R. [071]
DAILY OBSERVER – Newport. R.I. 1888-1894 – 1 – us UMI [071]
DAILY OBSERVER – Utica. N.Y. 1839-1843; 1848-1850; 1858-1921 – 1 – us UMI [071]
DAILY OKLAHOMAN – Oklahoma City. Okl. 1963- – 1 – us UMI [071]
DAILY OLD PIUTE – Virginia City, NV. 1864 – 1r – 1 – $50.00 – U04785 – us Library Micro [071]
DAILY ONTARIO – Belleville, 1910-1929 – 59r – 1 – cn Preston [971]
(DAILY) OREGON HERALD – Portland, OR. 17 Mar 1866-4 Apr 1873. 6 rolls – 1 – us U.O. Library [071]
DAILY OROVILLE REGISTER – Oroville, CA. 1895-1927 – 56r – 1 – $2,800.00 – B02570 – us Library Micro [071]
DAILY OUTLOOK – Beloit. Wis. 1881-1882 – 1 – us UMI [071]
DAILY PALLADIUM – Benton Harbor. Mich. 1886-1903 – 1 – us UMI [071]
THE DAILY PALO ALTO – (Cont: Stanford Daily) – Stanford, CA. Stanford University: 1892-1926 – 18r – 1 – $900.00 – C03007 – us Library Micro [370]
THE DAILY PALO ALTO – (See Stanford) – Palo Alto, CA: Stanford Univeristy, 1902-04 – 3r – 1 – $150.00 – B02595 – us Library Micro [071]
DAILY PANTAGRAPH – Bloomington. Ill. 1853- – 1 – us UMI [071]
DAILY PATRIOT – Woonsocket. R.I. 1876-1881 – 1 – us UMI [071]
DAILY PATRIOT. (DAILY WISCONSIN PATRIOT.-WISCONSIN DAILY PATRIOT) – Madison, Wisconsin. 1 Nov 1854-31 Dec 1858; 31 Mar 1859-9 Nov 1864.-d. 24 reels – 1 – uk British Libr Newspaper [071]
DAILY PEOPLE – New York, 1900-22 – 30r – 1 – us Ross [071]
DAILY PEOPLES CAUSE – (See also: Weekly Peoples Cause) – Red Bluff, CA. 1878-81; 1896-1902; 1904-06; 1908-17 – 23r – 1 – $1,150.00 – B02657 – us Library Micro [071]
DAILY PHOENIX – Canada. Saskatoon Phoenix. -d. Jan 1912-June 1922. Imperfect. 65 reels – 1 – uk British Libr Newspaper [072]
DAILY PHOENIX – Saskatoon. Canada. Oct 1902-Sept 1928 – 1 – cn Commonwealth Micro [072]
THE DAILY PILOT – Montreal, Canada. 12 fev 1884-v1 n3. 14 fev 1884 – 1r – 1 – Can$25.00 – cn Can Microfilming [072]
DAILY PIONEER – Bemidji. Minn. 1903-1907; 1950-1966- – 1 – us UMI [071]
DAILY PLACER TIMES AND TRANSCRIPT – San Francisco, CA. 1853-1855 – 6r – 1 – $300.00 – C03667 – us Library Micro [071]
DAILY PLEBIAN – New York. Jun. 27, 1842-May 12, 1845 – 1 – us NY Public [071]
DAILY POCONO RECORD – Stroudsburg. Pa. 1950- – 1 – us UMI [071]
DAILY POST – Bangalore, India. -d. 1887-1888. 6 reels – 1 – uk British Libr Newspaper [072]
DAILY POST – Camden. N.J. 1876-1897 – 1 – us UMI [071]
DAILY POST – Hobart, Australia, Jan 1910-Feb 1917.-d. 28 reels – 1 – uk British Libr Newspaper [072]
DAILY POST – Plattsmouth, NE. Mar-May 1898; Jan 1899-Dec 1900 – 1 – us NE Hist [071]
DAILY POST – Providence. R.I. 1850-1867 – 1 – us UMI [071]
DAILY POST – Yaquina City OR. Mar 28 1886 – 1 – us U.O. Library [071]
THE DAILY POST – Pittsburgh, PA., 1869 – 13 – $25.00r – us I.M.R. [071]
DAILY POST TRIBUNE – LaSalle. Ill. 1926-1947 – 1 – us UMI [071]
THE DAILY PRATAP – Jullundur, India. Jul 1966-1980 – 52r – 1 – us L of C Photodup [072]
DAILY PRESS – (1993.-24r; 1933-1972.-225r) – Timmins, 1973-1992 – 235r – 1 – cn Preston [971]
DAILY PRESS – Adrian. Mich. 1873-1876 – 1 – us UMI [071]
DAILY PRESS – Clarksdale. Miss. 1922-1949 – 1 – us UMI [071]
DAILY PRESS – Detroit. Mich. (Strike Paper). 1964 – 1 – us UMI [071]
DAILY PRESS – Elwood. Ind. 1893-1896 – 1 – us UMI [071]
DAILY PRESS – Martinez, CA. Jan-Mar 1905 – 1r – 1 – $50.00 – B02423 – us Library Micro [071]
DAILY PRESS – Middletown. N.Y. 1881-1906 – 1 – us UMI [071]
DAILY PRESS – Nebraska City. Neb. 1859-1864; 1912-1913 – 1 – us UMI [071]
DAILY PRESS – Newburgh. N.Y. 1889-1904 – 1 – us UMI [071]
DAILY PRESS – Newport News. Va. 1898-1899; 1905- – 1 – us UMI [071]
DAILY PRESS – Oklahoma City. Okl. 1893 – 1 – us UMI [071]
DAILY PRESS – Piqua. Ohio. 1916-1918 – 1 – us UMI [071]
DAILY PRESS – Riverside. Calif. 1878-1880; 1886-1910; 1939-1953 – 1 – us UMI [071]
DAILY PRESS – St. Joseph. Mich. 1905-1916 – 1 – us UMI [071]
DAILY PRESS – St. Marys. Pa. 1911-1940; 1959- – 1 – us UMI [071]
DAILY PRESS – Utica. N.Y. 1882- – 1 – us UMI [071]
DAILY PRESS – Victorville, CA. 1993 – 59+ r – 1 – $2,950.00 ($1,200.00y) – R04131 – us Library Micro [071]
DAILY PRESS – White Plains. N.Y. 1929-1932 – 1 – us UMI [071]
DAILY PRESS *see* SANTA BARBARA NEWS PRESS
THE DAILY PRESS – Paso Robles. Calif. 1969- – 1 – us UMI [071]
DAILY PROGRESS – Charlottesville. Va. 1954- – 1 – us UMI [071]
DAILY PROGRESS – Claremore. Okl. 1921-1927 – 1 – us UMI [071]
DAILY PROGRESS – Hattiesburg. Miss. 1902-1903 – 1 – us UMI [071]
DAILY PROGRESS – Petersburg. Va. 1872; 1903-22 – 1 – us UMI [071]
DAILY PROMOTER – Havre. Mont. 1909-1924 – 1 – us UMI [071]
DAILY PUBLIC BALANCE – San Francisco, CA. 1850-1851 – 1r – 1 – $50.00 – C03478 – us Library Micro [071]
DAILY RANGE – Raton, NM. 1881-1982 – 1 – us UMI [071]
DAILY RECORD – Dunn. N.C. 1955-1956; 1969- – 1 – us UMI [071]
DAILY RECORD – Elwood. Ind. 1896-1911 – 1 – us UMI [071]
DAILY RECORD – Lebanon. Missouri. 1978- – 1 – us UMI [071]
DAILY RECORD – Los Angeles, CA. Mar 1895-1905 – 21r – 1 RC02378 – $1,050.00 – us Library Micro [071]
DAILY RECORD – Middletown. N.Y. 1956-1959 – 1 – us UMI [071]
DAILY RECORD – Newton. Iowa. 1898 – 1 – us UMI [071]
DAILY RECORD – Niagara Falls, 1908-1917 – 9r – 1 – cn Preston [971]
DAILY RECORD – Omaha, NE. Oct 1908 to date – 1 – us NE Hist [071]
DAILY RECORD – Peoria. Ill. 1966- – 1 – us UMI [071]
DAILY RECORD – Pioche, NV. 1872-76 (scats) – 5r – 1 – $250.00 – U04641 – us Library Micro [071]
DAILY RECORD – Richmond. Va. 1916-46 – 1 – us UMI [071]
DAILY RECORD – Rockhampton, Australia. Jan 1897-Nov 1922.-d. 84 reels – 1 – uk British Libr Newspaper [072]
DAILY RECORD – San Jose, CA. Jul 1890-Jun 1893 – 1r – 1 – $50.00 – B02876 – us Library Micro [071]
DAILY RECORD – Stroudsburg, PA. -d 1909-1920; 1943-1950 – 13 – $25.00r – us I.M.R. [071]
DAILY RECORD – Titusville. Pa. 1865-1866 – 1 – us UMI [071]
DAILY RECORD – Wooster. Ohio. 1920- – 1 – us UMI [071]
THE DAILY RECORD – Baltimore. Md. 1889-1970 – 1 – us UMI [071]
DAILY RECORD ABSTRACT – Portland, OR. 13 Jan 1928-27 Jul 1928. 1 roll – 1 – us U.O. Library [071]
DAILY RECORD ABSTRACT – Portland OR. July 6 1916-Sep 30 1925 – 1 – us U.O. Library [071]
THE DAILY RECORD AND JUDICIAL NEWS – Montreal: J Daoust and Fulton and Richard, [1889?-189- or 19–] – 9 – cn C.I.H.M. [340]
DAILY RECORD HERALD – Wausau. Wis. 1908-1940; 1951- – 1 – us UMI [071]
DAILY RECORDER – Sacramento. Calif. 1946-1962; 1963- – 1 – us UMI [071]
DAILY RECORDER *see* PORTERVILLE PAPERS
THE DAILY RECORDER – (Cont: The Wesleyan Daily Recorder) – Toronto: [s.n., 1874-18– or 19–] – 9 – cn C.I.H.M. [240]
THE DAILY RECORDER – Sacramento, CA. 1911- – 211+ r – 1 CH03426 – $10,550.00 ($810.00y) – us Library Micro [071]
THE DAILY RECORDER *see* THE WESLEYAN DAILY RECORDER
DAILY REFLECTOR – Abilene. Kan. 1887-1911 – 1 – us UMI [071]
DAILY REFLECTOR – Norwalk. Ohio. 1882-1913 – 1 – us UMI [071]
DAILY REGISTER – Clarksdale. Miss. 1915-1949 – 1 – us UMI [071]
DAILY REGISTER – Mobile. Ala. 1822-1868; 1869-1969 – 1 – us UMI [071]
DAILY REGISTER – Napa, CA. 1878-80; 1883-84; 1885-96; 1926-38 – 48r – 1 CB02509 – $2,400.00 – us Library Micro [071]
DAILY REGISTER – New York. N.Y. 1872-1888 – 1 – us UMI [071]
DAILY REGISTER – Newburgh. N.Y. 1886; 1888-1889; 1891; 1893-1908 – 1 – us UMI [071]
DAILY REGISTER – Sandusky. Ohio. 1867-1941 – 1 – us UMI [071]
DAILY REPORT – Stockton, CA. 1916 – 1r – 1 – $50.00 – C03656 – us Library Micro [071]
DAILY REPORT *see* LONDON STOCK MARKET REPORT
DAILY REPORT: SUPPLEMENT / U.S. Foreign Broadcast Information Service – 1960-69 – 1 – 202.00 – us L of C Photodup [324]
(DAILY) REPORTER – Sumpter, OR. 20 Aug 1902-31 Oct 1902. 1 roll – 1 – us U.O. Library [071]
DAILY REPORTER – Coldwater. Mich. 1895-1900; 1960- – 1 – us UMI [071]
DAILY REPORTER – Dover. Ohio. 1905-1967 – 1 – us UMI [071]

DAILY REPORTER – Lincoln. Neb. 1934- – 1 – us UMI [071]
DAILY REPORTER – Logansport. Ind. 1889-1912 – 1 – us UMI [071]
DAILY REPORTER – McMinnville, OR. 1 Sept. 1886-13 Aug 1887. 1 roll – 1 – us U.O. Library [071]
DAILY REPORTER – Napa, CA. 1866-67 – 1r – 1 – $50.00 – B02510 – us Library Micro [071]
DAILY REPORTER – Wellsville. N.Y. 1880- – 1 – us UMI [071]
DAILY REPORTER – Wellsville. N.Y. 1881- – 1 – us UMI [071]
DAILY REPORTER – White Plains. N.Y. 1925-1937 – 1 – us UMI [071]
DAILY REPORTS / U.S. Foreign Broadcast Information Service – 4Sep 1941-Mar 1974. Scattered issues wanting – 1 – 8,576.00 – us L of C Photodup [324]
DAILY REPUBLIC – Ottawa. Kan. 1902-14 – 1 – us UMI [071]
THE DAILY REPUBLIC – Fairfield, CA. 1962- – 357+ r – 1 – $17,850.00 ($570.00y) – B02228 – us Library Micro [071]
THE DAILY REPUBLIC – San Luis Obispo, CA. 1884-90 – 6r – 1 – $300.00 – B02904 – us Library Micro [071]
DAILY REPUBLICAN – Belvidere. Ill. 1900- – 1 – us UMI [071]
DAILY REPUBLICAN – Corning, CA. 1926-1956 – 11r – 1 – $550.00 – B02139 – us Library Micro [071]
DAILY REPUBLICAN – Corvallis, OR. 2 Jan 1915-19 Feb 1915; 4 Sept 1912; 3July 1914. – 1r – 1 – us U.O. Library [071]
DAILY REPUBLICAN – Davenport. Iowa. 1895-1904 – 1 – us UMI [071]
DAILY REPUBLICAN – El Dorado. Kan. 1885-1887; 1895-1919 – 1 – us UMI [071]
DAILY REPUBLICAN – Eureka, NV. 1877-78; Feb-Apr 1878 (scats) – 3r – 1 – $150.00 – U04510 – us Library Micro [071]
DAILY REPUBLICAN – Hamilton. Ohio. 1892-1895; 1908 – 1 – us UMI [071]
DAILY REPUBLICAN – Hastings. Neb. 1892-1915 – 1 – us UMI [071]
DAILY REPUBLICAN – Indianapolis. Ind. 1916-1930 – 1 – us UMI [071]
DAILY REPUBLICAN – Meriden. Conn. 1868-1899 – 1 – us UMI [071]
DAILY REPUBLICAN – Millville. N.J. 1923- – 1 – us UMI [071]
DAILY REPUBLICAN – Milwaukee. Wis. and News. 1881-82 – 1 – us UMI [071]
DAILY REPUBLICAN – Mitchell. S.D. 1886- – 1 – us UMI [071]
DAILY REPUBLICAN – Monongahela, PA. -d 1881-1970 – 13 – $25.00r – us I.M.R. [071]
DAILY REPUBLICAN – Mount Carmel. Ill. Register. 1964- – 1 – us UMI [071]
DAILY REPUBLICAN – Omaha. Neb. 1864-1890 – 1 – us UMI [071]
DAILY REPUBLICAN – Parsons. Kan. 1880-81 – 1 – us UMI [071]
DAILY REPUBLICAN – Pawnee City, NE. Jun-Nov 1894 – 1 – us NE Hist [071]
DAILY REPUBLICAN – Rochester. Ind. 1910-1923 – 1 – us UMI [071]
DAILY REPUBLICAN – Saginaw. Mich. 1874-1878 – 1 – us UMI [071]
DAILY REPUBLICAN – Wooster. Ohio. 1890-1895; 1917-1919 – 1 – us UMI [071]
DAILY REPUBLICAN *see* MORNING REPUBLICAN
THE DAILY REPUBLICAN – (Filmed with: Charleston Daily Republican) – Charleston: [s.n.], aug 19 1869-sep 8 1871 – 3r – us Res Libr [071]
DAILY REPUBLICAN NEWS – Hamilton. Ohio. 1898-1919 – 1 – us UMI [071]
DAILY REPUBLICAN-NEWS – Hamilton, OH. 9 Oct 1915-6 Sept 1919 – 1r – 1 – us Western Res [071]
DAILY REVIEW – Decatur. Ill. 1878-1931 – 1 – us UMI [071]
DAILY REVIEW – Milwaukee. Wis. 1887-1889 – 1 – us UMI [071]
DAILY REVIEW – Ottumwa. Iowa. 1909-1920 – 1 – us UMI [071]
DAILY REVIEW – Pacific Grove, CA. 1906-1914; 1915 (2 issues only); 1916-1919 – 10r – 1 – $500.00 – B02587 – us Library Micro [071]
THE DAILY REVIEW – Hayward, CA. 1895-1902; 1909-12; 1925- – 830+ r – 1 BC02287 – $41,500.00 ($700.00y) – us Library Micro [071]
THE DAILY REVIEW : SUNRISE EDITION – Hayward, CA. 1978 – 106+ r – 1 – $5,300.00 ($700.00y) – B02288 – us Library Micro [071]
THE DAILY REVIEW – Towanda, PA. -d 1944-79; 1972-76. 18 rolls – 13 – $25.00r – us I.M.R. [071]
DAILY REVIEW OF THE ARABIC PRESS / U.S. Embassy. United Arab Republic – 1956-61. 10 reels. Scattered issues lacking – 1 – 227.00 – us L of C Photodup [956]
DAILY REVIEW OF THE ARABIC PRESS – Cairo: American Embassy, 1947-nov 23 1954 – 12r – us Res Libr [072]
DAILY REVIEW OF THE BAGHDAD PRESS – Baghdad: Embassy of the USA, sep 1-12, sep 30-dec 19 1951; jan 30-feb 18, mar 2-3 1952; sep 14,16,18-20,22 1954 – 1r – us Res Libr [072]
DAILY RICHMOND WHIG – Richmond: J H Pleasants, M Smith and W Ramsay, mar 3 1829-feb 10 1831 – 2r – us Res Libr [071]
DAILY RUSTLER – Great Bend. Kan. 1904-1908 – 1 – us UMI [071]
DAILY SAN DIEGAN – San Diego. Calif. 1887-88 – 1 – us UMI [071]
DAILY SANDUSKIAN – Sandusky. Ohio. 1849-1851 – 1 – us UMI [071]
DAILY SCIOTO GAZETTE – (Daily edition of this Whig, later Republican newspaper) – Chillicothe, OH. feb 18, 1850-feb 28, 1857 – 13r – 1 – us Western Res [071]
DAILY SCOTSMAN – Edinburgh. Scotland. -d. 1855-59. (11 reels) – 1 – uk British Libr Newspaper [072]
DAILY SENATOR – Scottsbluff, NE. -w. Aug 1936-Mar 1937 – 1 – us NE Hist [071]
DAILY SENTINEL – Bowling Green. Ohio. 1890-1910 – 1 – us UMI [071]
DAILY SENTINEL – Lemars. Iowa. 1959- – 1 – us UMI [071]
DAILY SENTINEL – Rome. N.Y. 1853-1855; 1882- – 1 – us UMI [071]
DAILY SENTINEL – Thunder Bay, 1882-1892 – 10r – 1 – cn Preston [971]
DAILY SENTINEL – Vicksburg. Miss. 1838-1852 – 1 – us UMI [071]
DAILY SENTINEL-REVIEW – (1993.-12r; 1900-1975.-313r) – Woodstock, 1976-1992 – 166r – 1 – cn Preston [971]
DAILY SENTINEL-TRIBUNE – Bowling Green, Ohio. 1960- – 70r – 1 – $32.50r – us Archival [071]
DAILY SERVICE – Lagos, Nigeria. -d. 1 Jan-15 May 1954; 1 Jan 1955-17 Sept 1960. Imperfect. 19 reels – 1 – uk British Libr Newspaper [072]
THE DAILY SERVICE – (Issues filmed as pt of: St Clair Drake collection of Africana (apr 22 1954; aug 20, sep 5 1955; oct 18 1957; dec 8,12-13,30 1958)) – Lagos [Nigeria]: Service Press Ltd., [-1960] – us Res Libr [071]
DAILY SHEET – Ireland.25 Oct-22 Dec 1923 – 1 – ie Microforms [072]
DAILY SHIELD – Mansfield. Ohio. 1888-1919 – 1 – us UMI [071]
DAILY SHIPPING AND COMMERCIAL NEWS – Shanghai, China. -d. 27 Jan-13 Dec 1862. 23 ft – 1 – uk British Libr Newspaper [072]
(DAILY) SHIPPING NEWS – Portland, OR. 2 Jan 1964-. – 23r – 1 – us U.O. Library [071]
DAILY SHIPPING NEWS – Portland. Or. (Marine Guide). -d. 1941-63 – 1 – us UMI [071]
DAILY SIGNAL – Middletown. Ohio. 1890-1905 – 1 – us UMI [071]
DAILY SILVER STATE *see* SILVER STATE
DAILY SISKIYOU REPORTER – Yreka, CA. 1898-99 – 1r – 1 – $50.00 – B03117 – us Library Micro [071]
DAILY SKETCH – London, England. Daily Graphic & Daily Sketch. 2 March 1909-Dec 1949. 198 reels – 1 – uk British Libr Newspaper [072]
DAILY SOUTHERN ARGUS – Norfolk. Va. 1848-1860 – 1 – us UMI [071]
THE DAILY SOUTHERN CRISIS – Jackson, MS: Jones, Wisely & Co, jan 2-mar 30 1863 – 1r – 1 – us Res Libr [071]
THE DAILY SPECTATOR AND JOURNAL OF COMMERCE – Hamilton, Ontario. v6 n216. 21 jan 1858-v7 n87. 20 aut 1858 – 1r – 1 – Can$35.00 – cn Can Microfilming [072]
DAILY SPECTATOR. (THE SPECTATOR) – Hamilton, Canada. Oct-Dec 1875; Jul-Dec 1876; Jan-Nov 1877; 2-28 Apr 1883.-d. 5 reels – 1 – uk British Libr Newspaper [072]
DAILY SPOKESMAN – Shelton. Wash. 1938-1939 – 1 – us UMI [071]
DAILY STAGE – Virginia City, NV. 9 Oct 1878; Sep-Nov 1880 – 1r – 1 – $50.00 – U04786 – us Library Micro [071]
DAILY STANDARD – Bridgeport. Conn. 1861-1893; 1908-1910; 1912 – 1 – us UMI [071]
DAILY STANDARD – Eureka, CA. Apr-Dec 1876 – 1r – 1 – $50.00 – B02214 – us Library Micro [071]
DAILY STANDARD – Portland. Or. 1876-1880 – 1 – us UMI [071]
DAILY STANDARD – Regina, Canada. -d. Dec 1906-Sept 1913. 39 reels – 1 – uk British Libr Newspaper [072]
DAILY STAR – Alameda, CA. 1908 – 1r – 1 – $50.00 – B06002 – us Library Micro [071]
DAILY STAR – Gettysburg. Pa. and Sentinel. 1914-17 – 1 – us UMI [071]
DAILY STAR – Logansport. Ind. 1874-1875 – 1 – us UMI [071]
DAILY STAR – Niles. Mich. 1906- – 1 – us UMI [071]
DAILY STAR – Shelby. N.C. 1902-1906; 1917- – 1 – us UMI [071]
DAILY STAR HERALD – Scottsbluff. Neb. 1962- – 1 – us UMI [071]
DAILY STAR JOURNAL – Sandusky. Ohio. 1904-1911 – 1 – us UMI [071]
DAILY STAR PROGRESS – La Habra, CA. 1927- – 281+ r – 1 – $14,050.00 ($840.00y) – R02331 – us Library Micro [071]
DAILY STATE DEMOCRAT – Lincoln. Neb. 1879-88 – 1 – us UMI [071]
DAILY STATE JOURNAL – Parkersburg. West Virginia. 1883-1916 – 1 – us UMI [071]
DAILY STATE REGISTER – Carson City. Nev. 1871-1872 – 1 – us UMI [071]
DAILY STATE REGISTER – Carson City, NV. Dec 1870-72 – 3r – 1 – $150.00 – U04454 – us Library Micro [071]
DAILY SUMMARY OF THE JAPANESE PRESS / U.S. Embassy. Tokyo, Japan – Feb 2, 1952- – 1 – us L of C Photodup [324]
DAILY SUN – Beatrice. Neb. 1902-1914; 1915-26; 1929- – 1 – us UMI [071]
DAILY SUN – Colusa, CA. Jul 1919-1932 – 27r – 1 – $1,350.00 – C02130 – us Library Micro [071]
DAILY SUN – Gainesville. Fl. 1903-1981 – 1 – us P.K. Yonge [071]
DAILY SUN – Omaha, South, NE. Nov-Dec 1895; Apr 1896-Feb 1897; Apr 1897-Jan 1901; Apr-May 1901 – 1 – us NE Hist [071]
DAILY SUN – Saint John, Canada. 1878-1910 – 113r – 1 – $7,345.00 – cn Library Assoc [971]
DAILY SUN – San Diego. Calif. 1881-1883; 1888 – 1 – us UMI [071]
DAILY SUN – Warner Robins. Ga. 1970- – 1 – us UMI [071]
DAILY SUN – West Memphis. Ark. 1955-56 – 1 – us UMI [071]
DAILY SUN – Yuma. Ariz. 1936- – 1 – us UMI [071]
THE DAILY SUN – San Bernardino, CA. 1894-1951 – 289r – 1 – $14,450.00 – R03452 – us Library Micro [071]
DAILY SUN TELEGRAM – Richmond. Ind. 1897-1905 – 1 – us UMI [071]
THE DAILY SUNDIAL – Northridge, CA: CSU Northridge, Aug 1977- – 20+ r – 1 – $1,000.00 ($90.00y) – B02531 – us Library Micro [370]
DAILY SUN-GAZETTE – Fulton. Mo. 1963- – 1 – us UMI [071]
DAILY SUN-POST – San Clemente, CA. 1969 – 100+ r – 1 – $5,000.00 ($200.00y) – H04061 – us Library Micro [071]
DER DAILY TELEGRAF – New York. N.Y. The daily telegraph. 1894 – 1 – us A.J.P.C. [071]
DAILY TELEGRAM – Bluefield. West Virginia. 1896- – 1 – us UMI [071]
DAILY TELEGRAM – Clarksburg. West Virginia. 1902-1961 – 1 – us UMI [071]
DAILY TELEGRAM – Columbus, NE. (-d. except -w. 1874-80, 1883-1921.) Feb. 1874-Oct. 1880; Jan. 1883- – 1 – us NE Hist [071]
DAILY TELEGRAM – Columbus. Neb. and pred. 1874- – 1 – us UMI [071]
DAILY TELEGRAM – Eau Claire. Wis. 1952-1970 – 1 – us UMI [071]
DAILY TELEGRAM – Temple. Tex. 1907-1911; 1912- – 1 – us UMI [071]
DAILY TELEGRAMS – Port Blair, India. Nov 1968-JUl 1994 – 43r – 1 – us L of C Photodup [072]
DAILY TELEGRAPH – 1869-1881. DT1-32 – 32r – 1 – at Corangamite [072]
DAILY TELEGRAPH – Bluefield. West Virginia. 1896- – 1 – us UMI [071]
DAILY TELEGRAPH – Lagos, 1963-67 – 4r – 1 – us Ross [072]
DAILY TELEGRAPH – Lagos, Nigeria. -d. 12 July 1958-31 Dec 1959; 2 Jan 1963-31 Dec 1965. Imperfect. 11 reels – 1 – uk British Libr Newspaper [072]
DAILY TELEGRAPH – London. -d. 1855-1927. (491 reels) – 1 – uk British Libr Newspaper [072]
DAILY TELEGRAPH – Melbourne, Australia. Feb 1869-May 1892.-d. 55mqn reels – 1 – uk British Libr Newspaper [072]
DAILY TELEGRAPH – Napier. New Zealand. -d. Jan 1902-Sep 1915. (56 reels) – 1 – uk British Libr Newspaper [072]
DAILY TELEGRAPH – North Platte. Neb. 1936-1941 – 1 – us UMI [071]
DAILY TELEGRAPH – Quebec, 1877-1884 – 4r – 1 – cn Preston [971]
DAILY TELEGRAPH – Sharon. Pa. 1893-1903; 1909-1915 – 1 – us UMI [071]
DAILY TELEGRAPH – Sydney, 1879-Apr 1963 – 462r – 1 – at Pascoe [072]
THE DAILY TELEGRAPH – London. England. 1945- – 1 – us Primary [072]
THE DAILY TELEGRAPH – (Numeros speciaux (11) dont le 20e ann 1895-1937 1r Can$75.00) – Quebec, 2 jan 1894-9 nov 1894 – 1r – 1 – Can$50.00 – cn Can Microfilming [072]
THE DAILY TELEGRAPH – Quebec. v1 n5. 13 nov 1875-29 dec 1876 – 1r – 1 – Can$50.00 – cn Can Microfilming [072]
THE DAILY TELEGRAPH AND DAILY WITNESS – Montreal. 13-v2 n22. 12 jul 1927 jan 1914f – 3r – 1 – Can$65.00 – cn Can Microfilming [072]
DAILY TELEGRAPH AND WITNESS – Montreal, 1913-1914Ja – 4r – 1 – cn Preston [971]
DAILY TELEGRAPH AND WITNESS. (DAILY TELEGRAPH) – Montreal, Canada. Jul 1913-Jan 1914.-d. 6mqn reels – 1 – uk British Libr Newspaper [072]
DAILY TELEGRAPH COLOUR SUPPLEMENT – London, UK. 25 Sept 1964-1969; 1974. -w. 26 reels – 1 – uk British Libr Newspaper [072]
DAILY TELEGRAPH (DAILY TELEGRAPH NEWS PICTORIAL) – Launceston, Australia. -d. 1883-1928. 122 1 2 reels – 1 – uk British Libr Newspaper [072]
DAILY TELEGRAPH MIRROR – 1 – F4,625.00 – sz Infoprint [072]
DAILY TELEGRAPH/SUNDAY TELEGRAPH – 1 – F7,072.00 – sz Infoprint [072]
DAILY TELEGRAPH/SUNDAY TELEGRAPH – 1945-1956 – 1 – F2,881.00 – sz Infoprint [072]
DAILY TELEGRAPH/SUNDAY TELEGRAPH – 1957-1958 – 1 – F5,544.00 – sz Infoprint [072]
DAILY TELEGRAPH/SUNDAY TELEGRAPH – 1959-1971 – 1 – F6,941.00 – sz Infoprint [072]
DAILY TELEGRAPH/SUNDAY TELEGRAPH – 1972-1977 – 1 – F8,818.00 – sz Infoprint [072]
DAILY TELEGRAPH/SUNDAY TELEGRAPH – 1978-1994 – 1 – F9,473.00 – sz Infoprint [072]
DAILY TERRITORIAL ENTERPRISE – Virginia City. Nev. 1865-1916 – 1 – us UMI [071]
DAILY TIMES – Alameda, CA. 1908 – 1r – 1 – $50.00 – B06003 – us Library Micro [071]
DAILY TIMES – Beatrice. Neb. 1892-1902 – 1 – us UMI [071]
DAILY TIMES – Brazil. Ind. 1969- – 1 – us UMI [071]
DAILY TIMES – Charleston. Ill. 1967- – 1 – us UMI [071]
DAILY TIMES – Colusa, CA. 1916-17; Jan-Mar 1933; Jul 1933-52 – 28r – 1 – $1,260.00 – B02132 – us Library Micro [071]
DAILY TIMES – Coshocton. Ohio. 1908-14 – 1 – us UMI [071]
DAILY TIMES – Danville. Ill. 1877-79 – 1 – us UMI [071]
DAILY TIMES – Ely. Nev. 1949- – 1 – us UMI [071]
DAILY TIMES – Geneva. N.Y. 1895- – 1 – us UMI [071]
DAILY TIMES – Grand Rapids. Mich. 1870-1885 – 1 – us UMI [071]

DAILY TIMES – Harrison, AR. 1920-84 – 1 – us UMI [071]
DAILY TIMES – Kittanning. Pa. 1898-1911 – 1 – us UMI [071]
DAILY TIMES – Lagos: The Nigerian Print. & Pub Co Ltd, [1949-jan 2 1956-] – 1 – us Res Libr [072]
DAILY TIMES – Marietta. Ohio. 1864-71; 1898- – 1 – us UMI [071]
DAILY TIMES – Middletown. N.Y. 1891-1906 – 1 – us UMI [071]
DAILY TIMES – Parkersburg. West Virginia. 1865-1872 – 1 – us UMI [071]
DAILY TIMES – Portland OR. Nov 7 Dec 6 1861, Mar 26 1862, Sep 26 1863 – 1 – us U.O. Library [071]
DAILY TIMES – Richmond. Va. 1886-1903 – 1 – us UMI [071]
DAILY TIMES – San Francisco, CA. 1859-1861 – 5r – 1 – $250.00 – C03668 – us Library Micro [071]
DAILY TIMES – Sioux City. Iowa. 1870-1883 – 1 – us UMI [071]
DAILY TIMES – Stroudsburg, PA. -d 1894-1908 – 13 – $25.00r – us I.M.R. [071]
DAILY TIMES – Tonopah, NV. 1916-30 – 13r – 1 – $650.00 – us Library Micro [071]
DAILY TIMES – Valdosta. Ga. 1906-1915; 1925- – 1 – us UMI [071]
DAILY TIMES – Vallejo, CA. 1910-23; 1951-63 – 184r – 1 – $9,200.00 – B03059 – us Library Micro [071]
DAILY TIMES – Vicksburg. Miss. 1866-1871 – 1 – us UMI [071]
DAILY TIMES – Visalia, CA. 1892-1901; 1909-32 – 71r – 1 – $3,550.00 – B03074 – us Library Micro [071]
DAILY TIMES – Visalia. Calif. 1892-1928 – 1 – us UMI [071]
DAILY TIMES – Watertown. N.Y. 1850- – 1 – us UMI [071]
DAILY TIMES – Weirton. West Virginia. 1935-1938; 1951- – 1 – us UMI [071]
DAILY TIMES – Wilson. North Carolina. 1951- – 1 – us UMI [071]
DAILY TIMES – York. Neb. 1891-1893; 1895-1898 – 1 – us UMI [071]
DAILY TIMES *see* TIMES
THE DAILY TIMES – Lehighton, PA. -d 1921-26 – 13 – $25.00r – us I.M.R. [071]
THE DAILY TIMES – Mauch Chunk, PA. -d 1913-1915. 1 roll – 13 – $25.00r – us I.M.R. [071]
THE DAILY TIMES – Narragansett. R.I. 1895-1904; 1949-1951 – 1 – us UMI [071]
DAILY TIMES ADVOCATE – Escondido. Calif. 1912-1931- – 1 – us UMI [071]
DAILY TIMES AND BONANZA *see* TIMES-BONANZA AND GOLDFIELD NEWS
DAILY TIMES HERALD – Carroll. Iowa. 1870-1929; 1941- – 1 – us UMI [071]
DAILY TIMES INDEX – San Bernardino, CA. 1888-1906 – 34r – 1 – $1,700.00 – R02761 – us Library Micro [071]
DAILY TIMES JOURNAL – Fort William, Canada. -d. 2 March 1914-30 June 1922. Imperfect. 48 reels – 1 – uk British Libr Newspaper [072]
DAILY TIMES LEADER – West Point. Miss. 1929-1943; 1946-47; 1951- – 1 – us UMI [071]
DAILY TIMES NEWS – Burlington. N.C. 1923- – 1 – us UMI [071]
DAILY TIMES-INDEX – San Bernardino. Calif. 1896-1905 – 1 – us UMI [071]
DAILY TIMES-MAIL – Bedford. Ind. and Sunday Herald Times. 1968- – 1 – us UMI [071]
DAILY TITAN – (Also known as: Titan Times) – Fullerton, CA: CSU Fullerton, 1994 – 20r – 1 – $1,000.00 – R02263 – us Library Micro [370]
DAILY TRANSCRIPT – Concord. Calif. 1905; 1907; 1911-1939; 1945-1954; 1962- – 1 – us UMI [071]
DAILY TRANSCRIPT – Oakland, CA. 1869-Jul 1870 (broken file); Apr 1871-77. – 8r – 1 – $400.00 – B02542 – us Library Micro [071]
DAILY TRANSCRIPT – Providence. R.I. 1847-1849; 1855-1857 – 1 – us UMI [071]
DAILY TRANSCRIPT – San Diego. Calif. 1965- – 1 – us UMI [071]
DAILY TRIBUNE : DAILY NEWSPAPER – Warren, OH. 1 Dec 1885 – 1r – 1 – us Western Res [071]
DAILY TRIBUNE – Davenport. Iowa. 1887-93; 1895 – 1 – us UMI [071]
DAILY TRIBUNE – El Reno. Okl. 1929- – 1 – us UMI [071]
DAILY TRIBUNE – Fairfield. Iowa. 1879-1913 – 1 – us UMI [071]
DAILY TRIBUNE – Gary. Ind. 1908-21 – 1 – us UMI [071]
DAILY TRIBUNE – Goldfield, NV. 1906-30 – 27r – 1 – $1,350.00 – U04551 – us Library Micro [071]
DAILY TRIBUNE – Great Bend. Kan. 1908- – 1 – us UMI [071]
DAILY TRIBUNE – Greensburg. Pa. 1952-55 – 1 – us UMI [071]
DAILY TRIBUNE – Hastings. Neb. 1892- – 1 – us UMI [071]
DAILY TRIBUNE – LaSalle. Ill. 1906-1926 – 1 – us UMI [071]
DAILY TRIBUNE – Nebraska City, NE. May 1901-May 1902; Sep 1902-Nov 1907 – 1 – us NE Hist [071]
DAILY TRIBUNE – Omaha, South, NE. Jun 1892; Jan 1896-May 1901 – 1 – us NE Hist [071]
DAILY TRIBUNE – Peru. Ind. 1967- – 1 – us UMI [071]
DAILY TRIBUNE – Providence. R.I. 1853-1859 – 1 – us UMI [071]
DAILY TRIBUNE – Royal Oak. Mich. 1925- – 1 – us UMI [071]
DAILY TRIBUNE – South Haven. Mich. 1899- – 1 – us UMI [071]
DAILY TRIBUNE – Tahoe. Calif. 1961- – 1 – us UMI [071]
DAILY TRIBUNE – Westerly. R.I. 1889; 1894-1898 – 1 – us UMI [071]
DAILY TRIBUNE AND HERALD – Tiffin, Ohio 1887-1933 – 96r – 1 – $32.50r – us Archival [071]
DAILY TRIBUNE INDEX – New York. N.Y. 1875-1906 – 1 – us UMI [071]
DAILY TRUE AMERICAN – Trenton. N.J. 1880-1914 – 1 – us UMI [071]
THE DAILY TRUTH – Williamsport, PA., 1898 – 13 – $25.00r – us I.M.R. [071]
DAILY UNION – Ottawa, Canada. 1861-66 – 7r – 1 – $455.00 – cn Library Assoc [971]
DAILY UNION – Pasadena. Calif. 1887-1889 – 1 – us UMI [071]
DAILY UNION – Salina. Kan. 1917-18 – 1 – us UMI [071]
DAILY UNION – Upper Sandusky, Ohio. 1890-1929 – 19r – 1 – $32.50r – us Archival [071]
DAILY UNION – Warsaw. Ind. 1904-1935; 1940-1949 – 1 – us UMI [071]
DAILY VARIETY – Hollywood, CA. 1972-84 – 35r – 1 – $1,750.00 – R02298 – us Library Micro [071]
DAILY VIDETTE – Valparaiso. Ind. 1894; 1906-1915; 1925-1927 – 1 – us UMI [071]
DAILY WATCHTOWER – Adrian. Mich. 1853-1863 – 1 – us UMI [071]
DAILY WHIG – Vicksburg. Miss. 1839-1860; 1862-1865 – 1 – us UMI [071]
DAILY WILMINGTON JOURNAL – Wilmington, CA. 1925-1932 – 28r – 1 – $1,400.00 – R04136 – us Library Micro [071]
DAILY WISCONSIN – Milwaukee. Wis. 1847-1868 – 1 – us UMI [071]
DAILY WITNESS – Montreal, Canada. 1862-79 – 35r – 1 – $2,275.00 – cn Library Assoc [971]
DAILY WITNESS – Montreal, Canada. -d. 3 Jan 1873; 10 Jan 1878; 4 Oct 1884; 20 April 1885; 2 Jan 1886-11 July 1913. 189 1 2 reels – 1 – uk British Libr Newspaper [072]
DAILY WONDER – Parsons. Kan. 1879-1880 – 1 – us UMI [071]
DAILY WORKER – London, England. -d. Jan 1930-Dec 1945. 59 1 2 reels – 1 – uk British Libr Newspaper [072]
DAILY WORKER – New York. N.Y. 1936-58 – 1 – us UMI [071]
DAILY WORKER – New York, NY. -d. 1 Feb 1943-2 Dec 1944; 11 April 1945-29 Dec 1955. Imperfect. 35 reels – 1 – uk British Libr Newspaper [071]
THE DAILY WORKER : 1941-1949 – 9 – $5,670.00 – us UPA [320]
THE DAILY WORKER *see* THE WORKER, 1922 : THE DAILY WORKER, 1923-1924
THE DAILY WORKER, 1924-1940 – 9 – $3,850.00 – us UPA [320]
THE DAILY WORKER, 1950-1957 – 9 – $4,955.00 – us UPA [320]
DAILY WORKER; MORNING STAR – London, 1930-93. Continued annually – 1 – £8,195.00 – uk World [072]
DAILY WORLD – Atlanta. Ga. 1932; 1934-1964; 1970-1973 – 1 – us UMI [071]
DAILY WORLD – Girard. Kan. 1894-1895 – 1 – us UMI [071]
DAILY WORLD – Martinsburg. West Virginia. 1891-93 – 1 – us UMI [071]
DAILY WORLD – Omaha. Neb. 1885-1889 – 1 – us UMI [071]
DAILY WORLD – Tulsa. Okl. 1967- – 1 – us UMI [071]
THE DAILY WORLD : 1978-1986 – 9 – $2,575.00 – us UPA [320]
THE DAILY WORLD, 1968-1977 – 9 – $2,430.00 – us UPA [320]
Dain, C *see* DE L'ABOLITION DE L'ESCLAVAGE
Daines, Simon *see* ORTHOPIA ANGLICANA: OR, THE FIRST PRINCIPALL PART OF THE ENGLISH GRAMMAR
DAINIK ASHA – (Oriya language) – Cuttack, India. 18 Sept 1946-1950 – 5r – 1 – us L of C Photodup [072]
DAINIK JAGRAN – Kanpur, India. Jul-Sept 1966 – 1r – 1 – us L of C Photodup [072]
DAINIK MARATHA – Bombay, India. Jul-Sept 1966 – 1r – 1 – us L of C Photodup [072]
DAINIK SAMBAD – Agartala, India. 1974-93 – 40r – 1 – us L of C Photodup [072]
DAINIK VIR PRATAP – Jullundur, India. Jul-Sept 1966 – 1r – 1 – us L of C Photodup [072]
DAINIKA ASAMA – (Assamese language) – Gauhati, India. 1968-1993 – 64r – 1 – us L of C Photodup [072]
DAINIPPON-TEIKOKU NAIMUSHO TOKEI-HOKOKU = STATISTICAL ABSTRACTS OF JAPANESE EMPIRE – 1st-52nd reports, 1884-1942 – 26r – 1 – Y207,000 – ja Yushodo [950]
DAINIPPON-TEIKOKU TOKEI-TEKIYO = STATISTICAL REPORTS OF THE DEPARTMENT OF THE INTERIOR OF JAPANESE EMPIRE – 1st-53rd reports. 1887-1939 – 13r – 1 – Y110,000 – ja Yushodo [950]
Dainskii, Ivan *see* KAK PROIZOSHLA RUSSKAIA REVOLIUTSIIA
DAIRY AND FOOD SANITATION – v1- 1981 – 1,5,6,9 – us UMI [660]
DAIRY IMPORTS INTO SUB-SAHARAN AFRICA = LES IMPORTATIONS LAITIERES EN AFRIQUE SUBSAHARIENNE: PROBLEMES, POLITIQUES ET PERSPECTIVES : PROBLEMS, POLICIES AND PROSPECTS / Massow, VH von – 1989 – 9 – $12.50 – 92-9053-120-7 – et ILRI [636]
DAIRY MARKETING IN ETHIOPIA = COMMERCIALISATION DU LAIT ET DES PRODUITS LAITIERS EN ETHIOPIE: PREMIERS DE BOUCHES ET CIRCUITS DE COMMERCIALISATION UTILSES PAR LES PRODUCTEURS : MARKETS OF FIRST SALE AND PRODUCERS' MARKETING PATTERNS / Debrah, Siegfried & Anteneh, Berhanu – 1991 – 9 – $7.50 – et ILRI [338]
DAIRY MARKETING IN SUB-SAHARAN AFRICA : PROCEEDINGS OF A SYMPOSIUM HELD AT ILCA, ADDIS ABABA, ETHIOPIA, 26-30 NOVEMBER 1990 / ed by Brokken, R F & Seyoum, Senait – 1992 – 9 – $30.00 – 92-9053-244-0 – et ILRI [650]
DAIRY PRODUCT TESTING ANNUAL SUMMARY / Auburn University. Extension Service – 1961-62. 1 fiche – 9 – us Spaulding [636]
DAIRY PROFITS BY BETTER FEEDING / Virginia. Polytechnic Institute. Extension Division – 1fiche – 9 – us Spaulding [636]
DAIRY PROGRESS REPORT / Louisiana State University. Agricultural Experiment Station. North Louisiana Experiment Station, Calhoun – 1889-1978. 1 reel – 1,5 – us Spaulding [636]
DAIRY RECORD – (v82- 1981- 5,6,9) – v1-1900- – 1 – us UMI [636]
DAIRY RECORD *see* AMERICAN DAIRY REVIEW
DAIRY REPORT / Wisconsin. College of Agricultural and Life Sciences. Dept. of Dairy Science – Dec 1960-Dec 1969 – 1,5 – us Spaulding [636]
DAIRY RESEARCH SERIES / Clemson University. Agricultural Experiment Station – No.54-67. 1970-84. 1 reel – 1,5 – us Spaulding [630]
DAIRY RESEARCH SERIES / South Carolina. Agricultural Experiment Station. Clemson – n.1-53 – 1,5 – us Spaulding [636]
DAIRY SCIENCE EXTENSION LEAFLET / Clemson University. Agricultural Extension Division – No.4-65.1970-82. 1 reel – 1,5 – us Spaulding [636]
DAIRY SHORT COURSE PROCEEDINGS / Texas A & M University. Agricultural Extension Service – 1958-82.12 fiches – 9 – us Spaulding [636]
DAIRY TEACHING, RESEARCH AND EXTENSION AT NEW MEXICO STATE UNIVERSITY / New Mexico State University. Department of Animal and Range Sciences – May 1979. 1 reel – 1,5 – us Spaulding [636]
DAIRY WORLD – (1986-. 1,5,6) – 1983- – 9 – us UMI [636]
DAIRYING INSTITUTE PROCEEDINGS / Washington. Agricultural College Experiment Station – Nos 4-35 1931-70 – 1,5,6 – us Spaulding [636]
THE DAIRYMAN – Bellows Falls, VT. 30 apr 1884 – 1r – 1 – Can$25.00 – cn Can Microfilming [071]
THE DAIRYMAN – Montreal: J Cheesman, [1885?-1886?] – 9 – cn C.I.H.M. [630]
DAIRYMEN'S ASSOCIATION OF THE PROVINCE OF QUEBEC *see* BULLETIN DE LA SOCIETE D'INDUSTRIE LAITIERE DE LA PROVINCE DE QUEBEC
Dairymen's Association of the Province of Quebec *see* BULLETIN OF THE DAIRYMEN'S ASSOCIATION OF THE PROVINCE OF QUEBEC
Daish, John Broughton *see*
– MEMORANDUM. THE WRITE OF CERTIORARI IN THE DISTRICT OF COLUMBIA IN RELATION TO THE INTERSTATE COMMERCE COMMISSION
– PROCEDURE IN INTERSTATE COMMERCE CASES, WITH ILLUSTRATIVE PRECEDENTS AND FORMS
DAISY FIRST BAPTIST CHURCH. DAISY, TENNESSEE : CHURCH RECORDS – 1878-1906 – 1 – 5.00 – us Baptist [240]
Daitokyu Memorial Library. Tokyo *see* EDO BUNGAKU SOKWAN
DAJACKSCH-DEUTSCHES WOERTERBUCH / Hardeland, A – Amsterdam, 1859 – 13mf – ne IDC [490]
DAJACKSCH-DEUTSCHES WOERTERBUCH / Hardeland, A – SE-1621 1. 1859 – 9 – ne IDC [430]
DAKOTA CONFLICT OF 1862 MANUSCRIPTS COLLECTIONS – 4r – 1 – $120.00 $30.00r – us M.H.S. [978]
DAKOTA CONNECTION – Bismarck, North Dakota: Dakota Southern Baptist Fellowship, 1987-91 – 1 reel – 1 – $14.40 – us Baptist [240]
DAKOTA COUNTY HERALD – Dakota City, NE. -w. Dec. 1899-Apr. 1904. Incomplete; Sep. 1906-Feb. 1965 – 1 – us NE Hist [071]
DAKOTA COUNTY RECORD – South Sioux City, NE. -w. Oct 1895-May 1898; Mar 1899-Dec 1900; Apr-Dec 1901; Feb-Sep 1902; Nov 1908-Dec 1916; Feb 1917-Mar 1919 – 1 – us NE Hist [071]
DAKOTA FARMER *see* FARMER
DAKOTA FREIE PRESSE – Aberdeen, SD. -w. 8 Apr 1909-19 Sep 1916 – 1 – us NE Hist [071]
DAKOTA LAND; OR, THE BEAUTY OF ST PAUL / Hankins, Col – New York: Hankins & Sons, Publ., 1868. Minnesota Reel 10. (The Cox Library Collection) – 5 – us Americana [978]
DAKOTA LAW REVIEW – North Dakota School of Law. v1-4. 1927-32 (all publ) – 6mf – 9 – $27.00 – LLMC 84-454 – us L.L.M.C. [073]
THE DAKOTA REPORTS / Dakota. Territory – (Pre-NRS: v1 1867-77 6mf $9.00. Cont by: North Dakota and South Dakota official reports series) – v1-6. 1867-89 (all publ) – 36mf – 9 – $54.00 – LLMC 81-801 – us L.L.M.C. [340]
DAKOTA TERRITORY – 1862-1889 – 9 – $118.75 set – us Hein [975]
Dakota. Territory *see*
– THE DAKOTA REPORTS
– RECORDS
– REPORTS, PRE-NRS
DAKOTA ZEPHYR / South Dakota. Agricultural Extension Service. State College of Agriculture and Mechanic Arts – v.1-8. 1935-44 – 1,5,6 – us Spaulding [630]
DAL' – Zhurnal kul'turno-prosvetitel'nyi. nr. 1-3. Spb. 1908-09. BR-2269 2 – 8 – ne IDC [073]
DAL PROTEZIONISMO AL SINDACALISMO / Ricci, Umberto – Bari: G. Laterza, 1926 – 1 – us U.W. Library [945]
Dal', V I *see* TOLKOVYI SLOVAR' ZHIVOGO VELIKORUSSKOGO IAZYKA

DAL', V.I. TOLKOVII SLOVAR' ZHIVOGO VELIKORUSSKOGO IAZIKA = VLDIMIR DAL'S EXPLANATORY DICTIONARY OF THE LIVING GREAT RUSSIAN LANGUAGE / ed by Courtenay, Baudouin de – 4th ed. St Petersburg, Moscow: M Wolf Publ. v1-4. 1912 – 44mf – 9 – $290.00 – us Ross [460]

DALABYGDEN – Borlange, Sweden. 1979- – 1 – sw Kungliga [072]

DALADEMOKRATEN – Falun, Sweden. 1917-78 – 388r – 1 – sw Kungliga [072]

DALADEMOKRATEN – Falun, Sweden. 1979- – 1 – sw Kungliga [072]

Dalager, L *see* GRONLANDSKE RELATIONER

Dalam, Jusuf Muda *see* THE BANK AND THE PRESS

Daland, William C *see* SONG OF SONGS TRANSLATED FROM THE HEBREW WITH OCCASIONAL NOTES

Dalayrac, N *see*
- [ADOLPHE ET CLARE] D'UN EPOUX CHERI
- LE CHATEAU DE MONTENERO
- [LA DOT] OVERTURE, ARR. PIANO OR HARPSICHORD AND VIOLIN AD. LIB.
- GULISTAN OU LE HULLA DE SAMARCANDE
- UNE HEURE DE MARIAGE
- LA MAISON A VENDRE
- [NINA] AIR DE NINA
- [NINA] OVERTURE
- PICAROS ET DREGO, OU LA FOLLE SOIREE
- LA SOIREE ORAGEUSE, COMEDIE ET UN ACTE ET EN PROSE, OP. 12

Dalayrac, Nicolas *see* L'ANTHICHAMBRE OU LES VALETS CHEZ EUX

Dalberg, Johann F H von *see*
- BLICKE EINES TONKUENSTLER IN DIE MUSIK DER GEISTER
- BLICKE EINES TONKUENSTLERS IN DIE MUSIK DER GEISTER
- UNTERSUCHUNGEN UEBER DEN URSPRUNG DER HARMONIE UND IHRE ALLMAEHLIGE AUSBILDUNG

Dalby, Henry *see* THE ARGUS

THE DALCASSIAN – Ireland.1 Nov 1919 – 1 – ie Microforms [072]

Dale, A M *see* THE ILA-SPEAKING PEOPLES OF NORTHERN RHODESIA

Dale, Daphne *see* THE STORY OF THE BIBLE IN POETRY AND SONG

Dale, Edgar Thorniley *see* CANADIAN WORKMEN'S COMPENSATION ACTS AND CASES, CONTAINING COMPARATIVE TABLES AND REFERENCES TO THE ACTS OF BRITISH COLUMBIA, ALBERTA, MANITOBA AND SASKATCHEWAN.

Dale, J *see* SELECTION OF...COUNTRY DANCES AND REELS ETC., WITH THEIR PROPER FIGURES FOR THE HARP, HARPSICHORD AND VIOLIN

Dale, Robert William *see*
- CHRISTIAN DOCTRINE: A SERIES OF DISCOURSES
- ESSAYS AND ADDRESSES
- THE JEWISH TEMPLE AND THE CHRISTIAN CHURCH
- JEWISH TEMPLE AND THE CHRISTIAN CHURCH: DISCOURSES ON THE EPISTLE TO THE HEBREWS
- THE LIFE AND LETTERS OF JOHN ANGELL JAMES
- LIVING CHRIST AND THE FOUR GOSPELS
- A MANUAL OF CONGREGATIONAL PRINCIPLES
- PROTESTANTISM
- TEN COMMANDMENTS
- THE TEN COMMANDMENTS

Dale, Thomas Nelson *see* OUTSKIRTS OF PHYSICAL SCIENCE: ESSAYS

D'Alembert *see* ENCYCLOPEDIE OU DICTIONNAIRE RAISONNE DES SCIENCES, DES ARTS ET DES METIERS (AEL, ABT 1;34)

D'Alembert, J Le Rond *see* ENCYCLOPEDIE OU DICTIONNAIRE RAISONNE DES SCIENCES, DES ARTS ET DES METIERS

d'Alembert M *see* ENCYCLOPEDIE, OU DICTIONNAIRE RAISONNE DES SCIENCES...

Dalens, H *see* L'OEUVRE ISOPODOLOGIQUE D'ALBERT VANDEL

D'Ales, A *see*
- L'EDIT DE CALLISTE

Dalgado, D G *see* FLORA DE GOA E SAVANTVADI

Dalgarno, George *see*
- ARTS SIGNORUM
- DIDASCALOCOPHUS...
- DIDASCALOCOPHUS: OR, THE DEAF AND DUMB MANS TUTOR

D'ALGER A TOMBOUCTOU : DES RIVES DE LA LOIRE AUX RIVES DU NIGER, AVEC UNE CARTE / More, Rene la – Paris, Plon-Nourrit, 1913 – us Res Libr [900]

DALGETY'S REVIEW – Sydney, Australia. Sep 1898-Sep 1916.-m. 33mqn reels – 1 – uk British Libr Newspaper [072]

DALGETY'S REVIEW (AUSTRALASIA) – Sydney, Australia. 13 Feb 1920-30 Jun 1933 (missing Jan 1923-Jun 1925; Apr-Dec 1927).-w. 5mqn reels – 1 – uk British Libr Newspaper [072]

THE DALHOUSIE MUNIMENTS – 1748-1759. BRRAM – 1 – uk Microform Academic [025]

DALHOUSIE REVIEW – (v1-62 1921-82 Can$115.00 1. v63-65 1983-85 Can$60.00 1) – Halifax. v1-74. 1921/22-1994/95 – 1,9 – Can$28.00y – cn Micromedia [420]

DALIAN GONGXUEYUAN XUEBAO – Journal of Dalian Institute of Technology. In Chinese but English abstracts to the main articles. F p192 – 9 – 4.00f – cc Microforms [073]

DALIAN RIBAO – Dalian Daily. 1985-. M D89 – 1 – $55.00r – cc Microforms [072]

DALKA – Mogadishu: Yousuf Jama Ali Duhul. v1 n2-v2 n10 aug 1 1965-apr 1 1967. Ser 2: v1 n1-2 oct 1-15 1969. Special issues: jul 1, oct 21 1981 – us Res Libr [073]

DALKEITH ADVERTISER – 1 – £42.00r – uk Scot News [072]

DALKEITH ADVERTISER – Scotland. Jul 1869-Dec 1953.-w. 31 reels – 1 – uk British Libr Newspaper [072]

Dall, Caroline H *see* CAROLINE H. DALL PAPERS, 1811-1917

Dall, Caroline Wells Healey *see* FOG BELLS

Dall, W H *see*
- THE MOLLUSCA OF PORTO RICO
- A MONOGRAPH OF WEST AMERICAN PYRAMIDELLID MOLLUSKS
- ON MASKS, LABRETS, AND CERTAIN ABORIGINAL CUSTOMS
- ON SOME PECULIARITIES OF THE ESKIMO DIALECT
- ON THE REMAINS OF LATER PRE-HISTORIC MAN IN THE CATHERINE ARCHIPELAGO, ALASKA TERRITORY
- REPORTS ON THE RESULTS OF DREDGING BY THE UNITED STATES COAST SURVEY STEAMER BLAKE, 15
- REPORTS ON THE RESULTS OF DREDGING BY THE U.S. COAST SURVEY STEAMER BLAKE.29
- SCIENTIFIC RESULTS OF EXPLORATIONS BY THE U.S. FISH COMM. STEAMER ALBATROSS
- SYNOPSIS OF THE FAMILY TELLINIDAE AND OF THE NORTH AMERICAN SPECIES

Dalla Torre, K W von *see*
- FLORA DER GEFUERSTETEN GRAFSCHAFT TIROL, DES LANDES VORARLBERG, UND DES FUERSTENTHUMES LIECHTENSTEIN
- GENERA SIPHONOGAMARUM

Dallaeus, Ion. *see*
- DE CULTIBUS RELIGIOSIS LATINORUM
- DE IMAGINIBUS LIBRI 4

Dallaire, Elzear *see*
- LE COURRIER DE CHARLEVOIX
- LE COURRIER DE GRAND-MERE

DALLAM'S REPORTS / Texas. Supreme Court – (A Pre-NRS title) – 1v. 1840-1844 (all publ) – 6mf – 9 – $9.00 – LLMC 94-039 – us L.L.M.C. [340]

DALLAS / Baptist Association. Texas – 1980-87 – 1 – 78.48 – us Baptist [240]

Dallas, Angus *see*
- THE EDUCATIONAL CHART: BEING A COMPARATIVE ABSTRACT OF TWO ANTAGONISTIC SYSTEMS OF EDUCATION, THE MATHEMATICAL AND THE AESTHETIC
- LATIN LANGUAGE AND GRAMMAR ADAPTED TO THE CAPACITIES OF CHILDREN AND FOR THE USE OF PARENTS IN THE WORK OF HOME EDUCATION

DALLAS COUNTY / Cochran, John H – Record of its pioneers and progress. Dallas: Service Publ. Co., 1948. Texas Reel 11.(The Cox Library Collection) – 5 – us Americana [978]

DALLAS FIRST BAPTIST CHURCH. DALLAS, TEXAS : CHURCH RECORDS – 1877-1913 – 1 – 53.10 – us Baptist [240]

Dallas, George *see* A BIOGRAPHICAL MEMOIR OF THE LATE SIR PETER PARKER, BARONET, CAPTAIN OF HIS MAJESTY'S SHIP MENELAUS, OF 38 GUNS, KILLED IN ACTION WHILE STORMING THE AMERICAN CAMP AT BELLAIR, NEAR BALTIMORE, ON THE THIRTY-FIRST OF AUGUST, 1814

DALLAS' REPORTS / Pennsylvania. Superior Court – (A Pre-NRS title) – v1-4. 1754-1806 (all publ) – 24mf – 9 – $36.00 – LLMC 84-191 – us L.L.M.C. [340]

Dallas, Robert Charles *see* RECOLLECTIONS OF THE LIFE OF LORD BYRON, FROM THE YEAR 1808 TO THE END OF 1814...

DALLAS TIMES$HERALD – Dallas. Texas1886- – 1 – us UMI [071]

Dallas, W.S *see* ELEMENTS OF ENTOMOLOGY

Dallemand, Henry *see* LA FRANCE

THE DALLES CHRONICLE – The Dalles, OR. 15 Dec 1890-31 Dec 1901, 10 rolls; 1 Apr 1921-30 Jun 1921, 1 roll; 2 Jan 1953-7 Nov 1978+, 76 rolls – 1 – us U.O. Library [071]

THE DALLES CHRONICLE – The Dalles, OR. -sw, w. 1901-47 and The Dalles Chronicle. -d. 1947-52. Incomplete – 1 – 792.00 – us Oregon Hist [071]

THE DALLES OPTIMIST – The Dalles OR. June 19 1906-Mar 10 1966 – 1 – us U.O. Library [071]

THE DALLES OPTIMIST MID-COLUMBIAN – (Set incl. The Dalles Optimist) – The Dalles, OR. -w. 17 Mar 1966-19 Feb 1970. – 20r – 1 – us U.O. Library [071]

THE DALLES TIMES-MOUNTAINEER – (Set incl. Daily Evening Times-Mountaineer (The Dalles)) – The Dalles, OR. -d. 29 Oct 1882-8 Oct 1892; 25 Aug 1883-24 Aug 1889 – 6r – 1 – us U.O. Library [071]

THE DALLES WEEKLY CHRONICLE – The Dalles, OR. 20 Dec 1890-29 Dec 1900. 3 rolls – 1 – us U.O. Library [071]

Dallet, C *see* HISTOIRE DE L'EGLISE DE COREE

Dallin, David J *see* MENSHEVIZM V PERIOD SOVETSKOI VLASTI

Dallinger, William Henry *see* SERMON AND LECTURE: DELIVERED IN THE ST JAMES STREET CHURCH, AND THE JAMES FARRIER HALL, THEOLOGICAL COLLEGE, DURING THE SESSION OF THE BRITISH ASSOCIATION AT MONTREAL, AUGUST, 1884

Dallmann, William Henry *see* TEN COMMANDMENTS EXPLAINED IN SERMONIC LECTURES

d'Almada, Andre Alvares *see* RELACAO E DESCRIPCAO DE GUINE

Dalman, G H *see* DER LEIDENDE UND DER STERBENDE MESSIAS DER SYNAGOGE IM ERSTEN NACHCHRISTLICHEN JAHRTAUSEND

Dalman, Gustaf *see*
- GRAMMATIK DES JUEDISCH-PALAESTINISCHEN ARAMAEISCH
- JESAJA 53
- DER LEIDENDE UND DER STERBENDE MESSIAS DER SYNAGOGE
- STUDIEN ZUR BIBLISCHEN THEOLOGIE
- WORDS OF JESUS

Dalman, J W *see*
- EPHEMERIDES ENTOMOLOGICAE
- PRODROMUS MONOGRAPHIAE CASTNIAE, GENERIS LEPIDOPTERORUM

Dalmatia. Laws, Statutes, etc *see* SVEUCILISTNI ZAKONI I PROVEDBENA NAREDBA O DRZAVNIM ISPITIMA

DALMATIA PAMPHLET COLLECTION – 1917-1919 – 1 – CSUXANL5616-B – us Hoover Inst Photo [947]

LA DALMAZIA – Sibenik, Yugoslavia. Feb-May 1919 – 1r – 1 – us L of C Photodup [949]

LA DALMAZIA LA VOCE DALMATICA – Zadar, Yugoslavia. Jun 1919-Feb 1920 – 1r – 1 – us L of C Photodup [949]

Dalmer, Johannes *see*
- DER BRIEF PAULI AN DIE GALATER
- DIE ERWAEHLUNG ISRAELS NACH DER HEILSVERKUENDIGUNG DES APOSTELS PAULUS

DALMIRO Y SILVANO / Salas, Francisco Gregorio de – 1780 – 9 – 1.50f – sp Bibl Santa Ana [810]

Dalmond *see* VOCABULAIRE ET GRAMMAIRE POUR LES LANGUES MALGACHES, SAKALAVE ET BETSIMITSARA

DAL'NEVOSTOCHNAIA KOOPERATSIIA – Khabarovsk, 1928-29 n2 – 20mf – 9 – COR-581/1 – ne IDC [334]

DALNEVOSTOCHNY I KAZAK : IZDANIE SOI UZA KAZAKOV NA DALNEM VOSTOKI E – (Includes: c.1: 1936:Mar.17/30) – Kharbin: Soi uz, 19uu – 1 – CSUXANR1701-S – us Hoover Inst Photo [947]

DALNI I VOSTOK / Borisov, B – Viena: Izd. "Novo i Rossii", 1921 – 1 – CSUX88-B7680 – us Hoover Inst Photo [947]

Dalnii, V *see* VOINA I KRASNOE ZNAMIA

DAL'NIIA MOLNII / Gorodetskii, S – Razskazy. Petrograd. 1916. BR-1121 2 – 8 – ne IDC [460]

DALRYMPLE CHART INDEX DIXON LIBRARY – (Apply to publ for details) – 9 – at Pascoe [020]

Dalrymple, J *see* MEMOIRS OF GREAT BRITAIN AND IRELAND

Dalrymple, S E *see* REPORT ON THE PUTATAN SUB-DISTRICT FOR THE EIGHT MONTHS ENDING 31 DEC 1884

DALS DAGBLAD *see* BOHUSLANINGEN

DALSOVNARKOM, 1917-1918 GG : SBRONIK DOKUMENTOV I MATERIALOV / ed by Flerov, V S – Khabarovsk, 1969 – 1 – CSUX90-B1870 – us Hoover Inst Photo [947]

DALTON 1772-1849 – (Mf 1T: Marriage Intentions 1782-1802; Births 1772-1820; Marriages 1787-1816; Births 1843-46. Mf 2T: Births 1846-49; Marriages, Deaths 1843-49) – (mf ed 1996) – 2mf – 9 – 0-87623-235-7 – us Holbrook [920]

Dalton & Co *see* THE SAN FRANCISCO BUSINESS DIRECTORY

Dalton, Deborah S *see* NEGOTIATED RULEMAKING SOURCEBOOK

DALTON DELEGATE – Dalton, NE. -w. May 1919-Oct. 1919; Dec. 1919-Sep. 1942; Mar. 1946-Sep. 1951 – 1 – us NE Hist [071]

Dalton, Hermann *see*
- BEITRAEGE ZUR GESCHICHTE DER EVANGELISCHEN KIRCHE IN RUSSLAND
- DIE EVANGELISCHE KIRCHE IN RUSSLAND
- EVANGELISCHE STROEMUNGEN IN DER RUSSISCHEN KIRCHE DER GEGENWART
- FERIENREISE EINES EVANGELISCHEN PREDIGERS
- JOHANNES GOSSNER
- JOHN A LASCO
- LASCIANA NEBST DEN AELTESTEN EVANGELISCHEN SYNODALPROTOKOLLEN POLENS 1555-1561
- NATHANAEL: VORTRAEGE UEBER DAS CHRISTENTHUM, DEN GEBILDETEN IN DER GEMEINDE
- ON RELIGIOUS LIBERTY IN RUSSIA
- REISEBILDER AUS GRIECHENLAND UND KLEINASIEN

Dalton, J N *see*
- ORDINALE EXON
- ORDINALE EXON, VOL. 3

Dalton, L H *see* TWO SWORDS

Dalton, Lawrence *see* HISTORY OF RANDOLPH COUNTY, ARKANSAS

Dalton, O M *see* NOTES ON AN ETHNOGRAPHICAL COLLECTION FROM THE WEST COAST OF NORTH AMERICA FORMED DURING THE VOYAGE OF CAPT. VANCOUVER, 1790

Dalton, Richard B *see* EFFECTS OF EXERCISE AND VITAMIN B12 SUPPLEMENTATION ON THE DEPRESSION SCALE SCORES OF A WHEELCHAIR CONFINED POPULATION

DALTON'S SAN FRANCISCO, OAKLAND, ALAMEDA BUSINESS DIRECTORIES – Alameda Co, CA. 1880; 1887-1888 – 4r – 1 – $200.00 – D003 – us Library Micro [978]

DALTON'S SAN FRANCISCO, OAKLAND, ALAMEDA BUSINESS DIRECTORIES – San Francisco Co, CA. 1880; 1887-1888 – 4r – 1 – $200.00 – D003 – us Library Micro [380]

Daluz, Eusebio T *see* FILIPINO-ENGLISH VOCABULARY, WITH PRACTICAL EXAMPLES OF FILIPINO AND ENGLISH GRAMMARS

Daly, C P *see* NATURALIZATION

Daly, Cesar *see*
- L'ARCHITECTURE PRIVEE AU 19E SIECLE (SOUS NAPOLEON 3)
- NOS DOCTRINES.

Daly, Charles Patrick *see* THE COMMON LAW; ITS ORIGIN, SOURCES, NATURE AND DEVELOPMENT, AND WHAT THE STATE OF NEW YORK HAS DONE TO IMPROVE UPON IT

DALY CITY RECORD – Daly City, CA. 1913- – 86+ r – 1 – $4,300.00 ($120.00y) – B02158 – us Library Micro [071]

Daly, Malachy Bowes *see* REMINISCENCES OF WINTER IN THE SOUTH OF FRANCE: A LECTURE ON THE PYRENEES, PAU, LOURDES, ETC., DELIVERED AT HALIFAX, N. S. IN AID OF THE FUNDS OF THE SOCIETY OF ST VINCENT DE PAUL

Daly, Thomas G *see* THE RELATIONSHIP BETWEEN MUSCLE FIBER TYPE AND SERUM LACTATE DEHYDROGENASE

Daly's Fifth Avenue Theatre. New York *see*
- BILL OF THE PLAY
- COLLECTION OF PROGRAMS
- SCRAPBOOKS

Dalzel, A *see* THE HISTORY OF DAHOMEY
Dalzell, Georg W *see* THE LAW OF THE SEA
Dalzell, N A *see* THE BOMBAY FLORA
Dam, D C van *see* RECHERCHES SUR LA FAUNE DE MADAGASCAR
DAM DESIGN AND OPERATION TO OPTIMIZE FISH PRODUCTION IN IMPOUNDED RIVER BASINS – 1984 – 103p – it F.A.O. [338]
Dam, Z Antonist *see* MASALAH SEPATU MILITER
DAMAGE ASSESSMENT REPORTS, 1945 – 1993 – 17r – 1 – $391.00 set in US $30.00r outside – M1721 – us Nat'l Archives [355]
DAMAGES IN INTERNATIONAL LAW / Whiteman, Marjorie M – Washington: GPO. 3v. 1937-43 (all publ) – 25mf – 9 – $37.50 – LLMC 80-910 – us L.L.M.C. [340]
Damais, Louis Charles *see* CENT DEUX POEMES INDONESIENS (1925-1950)
DAMALS IN WEIMAR : ERINNERUNGEN UND BRIEFE / Schopenhauer, Johanna; ed by Houben, Heinrich Hubert – (Includes bibliographical references and index) – Leipzig: Klinkhardt & Biermann, 1924 – 1r – 1 – us U.W. Library [943]
Damanskaia, Avgusta Filippovna *see* KARTOCHNYE DOMIKI SOVIETSKAGO STROITELSTVA
Dama-ntsoha *see* DICTIONNAIRE ETYMOLOGIQUE DE LA LANGUE MALGACHE
Damantsoha *see* LA LANGUE MALGACHE ET LES ORIGINES MALGACHES-RAZAFINTSAMALA
Damariscotta Mills, Maine. Damariscotta Mills Baptist Church *see* RECORDS
Damarjian, Nicole M *see* EFFECT OF HEART RATE DECELERATION BIOFEEDBACK TRAINING ON GOLF PUTTING PERFORMANCE
DAMAR-WULAN – The story of Damar-Wulan, the most popular legend of Indonesia and, Lady of the South Sea – 9 – ne IDC [390]
DAMASKIN SEMENOV-RUDNEV, OPISKOP NIZHEGORODSKII (1737-1795) : EGO ZHIZN' I TRUDY / Gorozhanskii, Ia. I – Kiev, 1894 – 8 – BR-6036 2 – ne IDC [947]
DAMASO DE LA PRESENTACION. VIDA DEL P. JOSE MA DEL MONTECARMELO / Bayle, Constantino – Burgos, 1931; Madrid: Razon y Fe, 1933 – 1 – sp Bibl Santa Ana [920]
DAMAYANTI; TJARITANE RESHI BHRIGADDHASWA MARANG JUDISTHIRA NALIKANE PANDAWA NEMAHI PAPA SANGSARA ING SATENGAHING WANAWASA / Sedah, Mpu – SE 5010 1. 1963 – 9 – ne IDC [950]
Damberger, Christian F *see*
- TRAVELS IN THE INTERIOR OF AFRICA FROM THE CAPE OF GOOD HOPE TO MOROCCO
- VOYAGE DANS L'INTERIEUR DE L'AFRIQUE

Damberqer, Christian F *see* VOYAGE DANS L'INTERIEUR DE L'AFRIQUE DEPUIS LE CAP DE BONNE ESPERANCE, A TRAVERS LA CAFRERIE, LES ROYAUMES DE MATAMAM, D'ANGOLA, DE MASSI, DE MONOEMUGI, DE MUSCHAKO, ETC. EN CONTINUANT PAR LE DESERT DU SAHARA ET LA PARTIE SEPTENTRIONALE DE LA BARBARIE
LA DAME BLANCHE: OPERA COMIQUE EN TROIS ACTES / Boieldieu, Adrien – Paroles de E. Scribe, musique de Boieldieu. Montreal: E. Lavigne, 1878. 02843. (Pre-1900 Canadiana) – 9 – cn C.I.H.M. [780]
DAME EUROPA'S REMOSTRANCE AND HER ULTIMATUM / Endean, James Russell – by the author of "Dame Europa's school". Toronto: Belford, 1877. 02915. (Pre-1900 Canadiana) – 9 – cn C.I.H.M. [971]
DIE DAME IN SCHWARZ / Langewiesche, Marianne – Muenchen: Deutscher Volksverlag, 1942 – 1r – 1 – us U.W. Library [830]
DIE DAME MIT DER MASKE / Auernheimer, Raoul – Wien: Wiener Verlag, [1905?] – 1r – 1 – us U.W. Library [820]
Damen, Arnold *see* REPONSES AUX OBJECTIONS POPULAIRES CONTRE LA RELIGION CATHOLIQUE: CONFERENCE DONNEE A LA CATHEDRALE D'OTTAWA
DAMEN-CONVERSATIONS-LEXIKON (HQ 13) / ed by Herloßsohn, C – 1834-1838 (mf ed 1993) – 20mf – 9 – DM420.00 – 3-89131-125-7 – gw Fischer [305]
Dames, W *see* PALAEONTOLOGISCHE ABHANDLUNGEN
DAMIAN, ODER, DAS GROSSE SCHERMESSER : ROMAN / Stehr, Hermann – Leipzig: P List, c1944 – 1r – 1 – us U.W. Library [830]
Damianus, J *see* IANIDA MIANI SENENSIS AD LEONEM 10. PONT. MAX. DE EXPEDITIONE IN TURCAS ELEGEIA, CU ARGUTISSIMIS
D'Amico, Silvio *see* SCOPERTA DELL'AMERICA CATTOLICA
Damiron, P *see* DE L'INCOMPETENCE...
Dammertz, V *see* DAS VERFASSUNGSRECHT DER BENEDIKTINISCHEN MOENKSKONGREGATION
Damonte Taborda, Raul *see*
- A DONDE VA PERON?
- EL ANTIPERONISMO COMO NEGOCIO

DAS DAMPFBOOT *see* DANZIGER DAMPFBOOT
DAS DAMPFSCHIFF – Bremen, apr 1-oct 7 1838 (incomplete) – 1r – 1 – Inquire at Mikrofilmarchiv for details – gw Misc Inst [072]
DAS DAMPFSCHIFF – Bremen, Germany. 1 Apr-7 Okt 1838 – 1r – 1 – gw Mikrofilm [072]
Dampier, Margaret G *see*
- HISTORY OF THE ORTHODOX CHURCH IN AUSTRIA-HUNGARY
- THE ORGANIZATION OF THE ORTHODOX EASTERN CHURCHES

DAMSKII MIR – St Petersburg, 1909-1912; 1913 n9; 1914 n3,4,7; 1915 n11; 1916; 1917 n1-10 – 71mf – 9 – $490.00 – us Hoss [305]
Damson, R L *see* THE EFFECT OF DAILY BEAN INGESTION ON THE LIPID PROFILES OF NORMOCHOLESTEROLEMIC COLLEGE STUDENTS
Damste, Onno *see*
- NEDERLAND EN INDONESIE IN DE 20STE

DAN BAO – no. 2-14. Hanoi. 2-16 mai 1927 – 1 – fr A.C.R.P.P. [073]
DAN CHUNG – Saigon. South Vietnam. 1964-1967 – 1 – us UMI [072]
DAN DE VERE'S COMIC AND SENTIMENTAL SONG-BOOK: HUDSON'S CALIFORNIAN AND NORTH AND SOUTH AMERICAN CIRCUS / De Vere, Dan – s.l.: s.n., 1873 (Quebec: Le Canadien). 04280. (Pre-1900 Canadiana) – 9 – cn C.I.H.M. [971]
DIE DAN, EIN BAUERNVOLK IM WESTAFRIKANISCHEN URWALD: ERGEBNIS DREIER VOELKERKUNDLICHER EXP. 1949/50, 1952/53, 1955/56 / Himmelheber, H & Himmelheber, U – Stuttgart. 1958. BA-577 2 – 8 – ne IDC [306]
Dan, F *see* RABOCHIE DEPUTATY V I-OI GOSUDARSTVENNOI DUME
Dan, Fedor *see* NAROZHDENIE NOVOI ROSSII
DANA – 1904-05.12 issues. 4 fiches – 9 – Ir£5.00 – ie Microforms [800]
DANA 1801-1849 – (Mf 1T: Marriage Intentions 1801-18. Mf 2T: Marriage & Intentions 1817-31. Mf 3T: Marriages & Intentions 1831-43. Mf 4T: Births, Marriages 1843-49; Deaths 1844-47) – (mf ed 1996) – 4mf – 9 – 0-87623-236-5 – us Holbrook [920]
DANA 1801-1890 – (Mf 1: Marriages & Intentions 1801-18. Mf 2-3: Marriages & Intentions 1818-36. Mf Marriages & Intentions 1837-43. Mf 5-6: B,M,D 1843-67. Mf 7-10: B,M,D 1855-93. Mf 11-21: Index to Births 1843-1938. Mf 22-29: Index to Marriage Intentions 1801-1938. Mf 30-46: Index to Marriages 1801-1938. Mf 47-57: Index to Deaths 1844-1938. Mf 58: B,M,D 1891-93) – (mf ed 1984) – 57mf – 9 – 0-931248-72-8 – us Holbrook [920]
Dana, Alexander Hamilton *see* ENIGMAS OF LIFE, DEATH, AND THE FUTURE STATE
DANA: AN IRISH MAGAZINE OF INDEPENDENT THOUGHT – Dublin. v. 1 no. 1-12. May 1904-Apr 1905 – 1 – us NY Public [073]
Dana, Charles A *see* PROUDHON AND HIS BANK OF THE PEOPLE
Dana, Daniel *see* MEMOIRS OF EMINENTLY PIOUS WOMEN
Dana, James Dwight *see*
- THE GENESIS OF THE HEAVENS AND THE EARTH AND ALL THE HOST OF THEM
- GENESIS OF THE HEAVENS AND THE EARTH AND ALL THE HOST OF THEM

Dana Montano, Salvador M *see* JUSTICIA SOCIAL Y REFORMA CONSTITUCIONAL
DANA POINT NEWS – South Co, CA. 1993 – 4+ r – 1 – $200.00 ($100.00y) – R04118 – us Library Micro [071]
DANAB = BULLETIN OF SOMALI LIBERATION FRONTS : WARSIDAHA JABHADAHA GOBANIMADOONKA SOOMAALIYEED – Mogadisho: WSLF: SALF. n16-376 jan 2-sep 27 1978. n519,577,614 mar 21, sep 27, nov 15 1979 – 1r – 1 – us Res Libr [320]
Danailov, G T *see* LES EFFETS DE LA GUERRE EN BULGARIE
Danbury, New Hampshire. Danbury Baptist Church *see* RECORDS
DANBURY NEWS – Danbury, NE. -w. Sep. 1895-Feb. 1896; Apr. 1896-Oct. 1896; Jun. 1900-Jul. 1901; Aug. 1902-Aug. 1910; Mar. 1911-Dec. 1912; Dec. 1913-Sep. 1922 – 1 – us NE Hist [071]
Danbury. Ohio. St. Paul Lutheran Church *see* RECORDS
Danby, Herbert *see* THE MISHNAH
Danby, John *see* LA GUIDA ALLA MUSICA VOCALE. OP. 2
DANCE AND LITERATURE IN JAVA / Kuntjaraningrat – SE-2957 1. 1959 – 9 – ne IDC [790]
DANCE COLLECTION / ed by Hul, Dick van den – (Dance History and Aesthetics: 152mf. Dance Methods: 97mf. Dance Music: 95mf. Collection includes a printed guide) – 344mf – 9 – PDA-1-120/1 – ne IDC [790]
THE DANCE FESTIVALS OF THE ALASKAN ESKIMO / Hawkes, E W – N 244. 1914 – 9 – ne IDC [390]
DANCE HISTORY AND COMPUTER COURSEWARE : THE DESIGN, DEVELOPMENT, AND PRODUCTION OF INTERDISCIPLINARY MULTIMEDIA COURSEWARE FOR INTRODUCTORY-LEVEL INSTRUCTION IN LATE RENAISSANCE EUROPEAN COURT DANCE / Manning, Keitha D – Temple University, 1996 – 3mf – 9 – $12.00 – PE 3663 – us Microform Publ [790]
DANCE IN CANADA – (Ceased no 61 1989) – Toronto. nos 1-61. 1973-1989 – 9 – Can$20.00y – cn Micromedia [790]
DANCE IS...?: A LECTURE DEMONSTRATION FOR CHILDREN / Raabe, Julie L – 1981 – 2mf – 9 – $8.00 – us Microform Publ [790]
DANCE MAGAZINE – v1- . 1927- – 1,5,6,9 – us UMI [790]
Dancer, T *see* CATALOGUE OF PLANTS, EXOTIC AND INDIGENOUS, IN THE BOTANICAL GARDEN, JAMAICA, 1792
THE DANCER'S QUEST; ESSAYS ON THE AESTHETIC OF THE CONTEMPORARY DANCE / Selden, Elizabeth S – Berkeley, CA: Univ. of CA. Press, 1935. xv,215p. illus – 1 – us U.W. Library [790]
DANCES AND MARCHES, TWELVE, IN CHARACTER, FOR THE QUADRILLE, AT THE CLOSE OF THE BERLIN CARNIVAL, 1799 / Righini, V – Adapted for the harp or pianoforte. Comp. by. Righini. 180-? – 5,15 – us Sibley [780]
DANCES OF DEATH / ed by Dongen, Wim van – 35 titles – 9 – ne IDC [790]
DANCING AND ITS RELATIONS TO EDUCATION AND SOCIAL LIFE / Dodworth, Allen – New and enl. ed.New York: Harper, 1888. vi,302p. illus – 1 – us U.W. Library [790]
DANCING IN DIXIE'S LAND : THEATRICAL DANCE IN NEW ORLEANS, 1860-1870 / Akins, Ann S & LaPointe-Crump, Janice D – 1991 – 4mf – $16.00 – us Microform Publ [790]
THE DANCING-MASTER: OR, THE WHOLE ART AND MYSTERY OF DANCING EXPLAINED; AND THE MANNER OF PERFORMING ALL STEPS IN BALL-DANCING MADE SHORT AND EASY / Rameau, Pierre – London: J Brotherton, [1731] – 1 – us Sibley [780]
THE DANDELION – Nos. 1-11. Spring '77 – Fall '79. 308p. Cont'd. 1 fiche (29x) – 9 – 1.00f – at Libertarian Micro [320]
THE DANDELION – v.1-. 1977- – 9 – 1.00f – at Libertarian Micro [320]
DANDERYDS TIDNING *see* NORRORT
Dandeu, Jean-Pierre *see* INTERNATIONAL JOURNAL OF BIO-CHROMATOGRAPHY
Dandouau, Andre *see*
- CONTES POPULAIRES DES SAKALAVA ET DES TSIMIHETY DE LA REGION D'ANALALAVA
- HISTOIRE DES POPULATIONS DE MADAGASCAR

DANDRIDGE BAPTIST CHURCH. JEFFERSON COUNTY. TENNESSEE : CHURCH RECORDS – 1786-1966 – 1 – 45.54 – us Baptist [240]
DANDRIDGE FIRST BAPTIST CHURCH. JEFFERSON COUNTY. DANDRIDGE, TENNESSEE : CHURCH RECORDS – 1786-1966 – 1 – 45.54 – us Baptist [240]
Dandurand, J L *see* LE CINEMA CANADIEN
Dandurand, Josephine *see*
- CE QUE PENSENT LES FLEURS: SAYNETE ENFANTINE
- RANCUNE: COMEDIE EN UN ACTE ET EN PROSE

Dandurand, Raoul *see* MANUEL DU JUGE DE PAIX: COMPRENANT LA NATURE DES FONCTIONS DU JUGE DE PAIX, LA PROCEDURE REGULIERE AT LA PROCEDURE SOMMAIRE, LA RESPONSABILITE DES JUGES DE PAIX...ETC.
Dandurand, Therese *see* BIO-BIBLIOGRAPHIE DE MONSIEUR LE CHANOINE VICTOR TREMBLAY, PRESIDENT DE LA SOCIETE HISTORIQUE DU SAGUENAY ET MEMBRE DE LA SOCIETE DES ECRIVAINS CANADIENS-FRANCAIS
Dane, Nathan *see* DANE'S GENERAL ABRIDGEMENT OF LAW AND EQUITY
Daneau, Lambert *see* DEUX TRAITEZ NOUVEAUX TRES UTILES POUR CE TEMPS
LE DANEMARK. SES TRESORS, SON ART / Reunion des musees nationaux. Paris – 1965. 43 illus. 2 fiches – 9 – fr Réunion [700]
Daneri, Alberto *see* CARTA ABIERTA DE UN PERONISTA A UN CONFUNDIDO
DANE'S GENERAL ABRIDGEMENT OF LAW AND EQUITY / Dane, Nathan – Boston, MA: Cummins, Hilliard & Co. v1-8. 1823-1824 (all publ) – 64mf – 9 – $96.00 – LLMC 81-404 – us L.L.M.C. [073]
Danes, John *see* A LIGHT TO LILIE
DANESBURY HOUSE / Wood, Ellen – British Fiction Archive: Unit 1 – 9 – uk Bell [830]
Danet, P *see* GRAND DICTIONNAIRE FRANCOIS ET LATIN
Danevskii, V P *see* SISTEMATI POLITICHESKOGO RAVNOVESIIA I LEGITIMIZMA I NACHALO NATSIONAL'NOSTI V IKH VZAIMNOI SVIAZI
Danford, J *see* DIARY OF THE SIEGE OF QUEBEC, 1775
Danforth *see* DIRECTORY AND REFERENCE BOOK OF SCHOHARIE COUNTY
d'Anfreville de la salle *see* SUR LA COTE D'AFRIQUE
Dangeau, L de Courcillon de *see* LES PRINCIPES DU BLAZON
D'Angel, Arnaldo *see* SAN VICENTE PAUL, DIRECTOR DE CONCIENCIA
DANGEROUS PROPERTIES OF INDUSTRIAL MATERIALS REPORT – v1-. 1980- – 1,5,6,9 – us UMI [670]
LES DANGERS ET INCONVENIENS QUE LA PAIX FAIRE...1585 – N.p., n.d. – 1mf – 1 – ILM-1236/1 – ne IDC [327]
DANGERS OF THE APOSTOLIC AGE / Moorhouse, James – New York: Thomas Whittaker, 1891. 1 fiche – 9 – us A.T.L.A. [240]
DANGERS OF THE DAY / Vaughan, John Stephen – Notre Dame, IN: Ave Maria Press, 1909 – 1mf – 9 – 0-8370-7197-6 – 1986-1197 – us A.T.L.A. [240]
Dani, Ahmad Hasan *see* HISTORIC CITY OF TAXILA
Dani, Ahmad Hassan *see*
- HISTORY OF CIVILIZATIONS OF CENTRAL ASIA
- RECENT ARCHAEOLOGICAL DISCOVERIES IN PAKISTAN

DANIEL : AN EXPOSITION OF THE HISTORICAL PORTION OF THE WRITINGS OF THE PROPHET DANIEL / Payne Smith, Robert – Cincinnati: Cranston & Curts; New York: Hunt & Eaton, [18-?] – 1mf – 9 – 0-8370-9725-8 – 1986-3725 – us A.T.L.A. [220]
DANIEL : HIS LIFE AND TIMES / Deane, Henry – New York:Anson D.F. Randolph, [1888] – 1mf – 9 – 0-8370-2855-8 – 1985-0855 – us A.T.L.A. [220]
DANIEL / Tiefenthal, Fr. Salesius – Paderbornae: Ferd. Schoeningh, 1895. 1 fiche. 8370-5533-4 – 9 – us A.T.L.A. [240]
DANIEL AND ITS CRITICS : BEING A CRITICAL AND GRAMMATICAL COMMENTARY / Wright, Charles Henry Hamilton – (Includes indexes) – London: Williams and Norgate, 1906 – 1mf – 9 – 0-8370-6550-X – 1986-0550 – us A.T.L.A. [220]
DANIEL AND THE PROPHET: NINE LECTURES DELIVERED IN THE DIVINITY SCHOOL OF THE UNIVERSITY OF OXFORD / Pusey, E B – 2nd ed. 1868 – 9 – us A.T.L.A. [240]

DANIEL CASPER VON LOHENSTEIN'S TRAUERSPIELE : MIT BESONDERER BERUECKSICHTIGUNG DER CLEOPATRA: BEITRAG ZUR GESCHICHTE DES DRAMAS IM XVII. JAHRHUNDERT / Kerckhoffs, August – (Includes bibliographical references) – Paderborn: F Schoeningh, 1877 – 1r – 1 – us U.W. Library [430]
Daniel, Charles *see* ONE OF THE JESUITS: ALEXIS CLERC, SAILOR AND MARTYR
DER DANIEL DER ROEMERZEIT : EIN KRITISCHER VERSUCH ZUR DATIERUNG EINER WICHTIGEN URKUNDE DES SPAETJUDENTUMS / Hertlein, Eduard – Leipzig: M Heinsius Nachfolger, 1908 – 1mf – 9 – 0-8370-3573-2 – 1985-1573 – us A.T.L.A. [220]
DANIEL DERONDA / Eliot, George – Edinburgh: William Blackwood, 1876 – 2 rolls – 1 – 1-55879-213-9 – uk Libr Preservation [830]
Daniel, F de F *see* HISTORY OF KATSINA
Daniel, Francois *see*
– LES FRANCAIS DANS L'AMERIQUE DE NORD, OU, HISTOIRE DES PRINCIPALES FAMILLES DU CANADA. SUPPLEMENT
– NOTICE SUR LA FAMILLE GUY: ET SUR QUELQUES AUTRES FAMILLES
Daniel, H A *see* CODEX LITURGICUS ECCLESIAE UNIVERSA
DANIEL IN THE CRITIC'S DEN : A REPLY TO PROFESSOR DRIVER OF OXFORD AND THE DEAN OF CANTERBURY / Anderson, Robert – (Includes appendixes. Includes indexes) – NY: Fleming H Revell, [19-?] – 1mf – 9 – 0-8370-2095-6 – 1985-0095 – us A.T.L.A. [220]
Daniel, J *see*
– COLEOPTEREN-STUDIEN
– DIE LEHRE VON DER UNFEHLBARKEIT DES PAPSTES AUS DER GESCHICHTE
Daniel, J C *see* A HISTORY OF THE BAPTISTS OF HILL COUNTY, TEXAS
Daniel, J F *see*
– LECONS DE FRANCAIS A L'USAGE DE L'ACADEMIE FRANCAISE
– RECREATIONS GRAMMATICALES
Daniel, John Warwick *see* THE LAW AND PRACTICE OF ATTACHMENT, UNDER THE CODE OF VIRGINIA.
Daniel, K *see* COLEOPTEREN-STUDIEN
DANIEL QUORM, AND HIS RELIGIOUS NOTIONS / Pearse, Mark Guy – 1875 – 9 – us A.T.L.A. [240]
DANIEL QUORM, AND HIS RELIGIOUS NOTIONS: SECOND SERIES / Pearse, Mark Guy – 1890 – 9 – us A.T.L.A. [240]
DANIEL THE BELOVED / Taylor, William MacKergo – (Includes bibliographical references and index) – New York: Harper, c1878 – 1mf – 9 – 0-8370-9311-2 – 1986-3311 – us A.T.L.A. [920]
DANIEL WEBSTER / Lodge, Henry Cabot – Boston & NY: Houghton, Mifflin & Co, 1899 – 5mf – 9 – $7.50 – LLMC 96-030 – us L.L.M.C. [975]
Danieli, G *see* LE SOCIETA STRANIERE IN ITALIA
Daniell, L E *see* TEXAS: THE COUNTRY AND ITS MEN
Daniell, Samuel (drawings) *see* SKETCHES REPRESENTING THE NATIVE TRIBES, ANIMALS AND SCENERY OF SOUTHERN AFRICA
Danielowski, Emma *see* RICHARDSONS ERSTER ROMAN
Daniels, A *see* QUELLENBEITRAEGE U. UNTERS. Z. GESCH. DER GOTTESBEWEISE IM DREIZEHNTEN JAHRHT.
Daniels, Augustus Thatcher *see* DIARY
DANIELS COUNTY LEADER – Scobey. Mont. 1966- – 1 – us UMI [071]
DANIEL'S GREAT PROPHECY: THE EASTERN QUESTION: THE KINGDOM / West, Nathaniel – New York: Hope of Israel, 1898. 1 fiche. 8370-5800-7 – 9 – us A.T.L.A. [240]
Daniels, W H *see* A SHORT HISTORY OF 'THE PEOPLE CALLED METHODISTS', FROM THE DAYS OF THE WESLEYS TO THE METHODIST OECUMENICAL CONFERENCE HELD AT...
Danielson, Vernon J *see* MORMONISM EXPOSED
DANIK BASUMATI – Calcutta, India. 14 Oct 1946-4 Sept 1947; Sept 1950-Aug 1952; 12 Sept 1953-57; 1960-Aug 1966; Aug 1968-Sept 1970; Sept 1971-76; May 1977-Aug 1992 – 103r – 1 – us L of C Photodup [072]
Danilenko, Boris *see*
– CHURCH SLAVONIC AND RUSSIAN HAGIOGRAPHIES
– RUSSIAN NECROPOLIS
Danilov, I Uri i Nikiforovich *see* ROSSIIA V MIROVOI VOINIE 1914-1915 G
Danilov, M V *see* ZAPISKI NAPISANNYE V 1771 GODU
Danilova, E *see* ZAKONODATEL'STVO O TRUDOVYKH ARTELIAKH
Danilovaia, E N *see* TRUDOVYE ARTELI
Danish Baptist General Conference of America *see* PAPERS
DANISH CANADIAN NEWS *see* DANSK CANADISK TIDENDE
DANISH CENTER OF HUMAN RIGHTS – Copenhagen. 33 docs. 1987-1990 – 68mf – 9 – ne IDC [320]
THE DANISH CO-OPERATIVE MOVEMENT / Ravnholt, Henning – In Indonesian. SE-5743 1. 1954 – 9 – ne IDC [360]
DANISH HERALD OF CANADA *see* DANSKE HEROLD
DANISH MEDICAL BULLETIN – v.1-25. 1952-78 – 1,5,6 – 22138.00 – us Princeton Micro [610]
DANISH-AMERICAN DIPLOMACY 1776-1920 / Fogdall, S J M P – Iowa city, n.d. – 2mf – 1 – ILM-1748/1 – ne IDC [327]
DANISHKADAH – Isfahan. Sal-i 1, shumarah-i 2-5, 7 (2 Hut va Hamal 1304-4 Bahman 1305 [22 Mar 1925-17 Jan 1926]), Sal-i 2, shumarah-i 1-5 (31 Tir 1313-Farvardin 1314 [22 July 1934-Mar 1935]) – 9 – $125.00 – us MEDOC [956]
DANISHKADAH – (Sumarah 1-11/12[21 Apr 1918-20 Apr 1919]) – Tehran, 1918 – 1 reel – 1 – $35.00 – us MEDOC [950]
DANISHNAMAH – Tehran. Shumarah-i 2 (Aban 1326 [October 1947]) – 1 reel – 1 – $45.00 – us MEDOC [950]
DANK UND DIENST : REDEN UND AUFSAETZE / Alverdes, Paul – Muenchen: A Langen/G Mueller, 1939 – 1r – 1 – us U.W. Library [943]
DER DANKBARE PATIENT / Penzoldt, Ernst – 7.-9. Aufl. Berlin: S Fischer, 1940 – 1r – 1 – us U.W. Library [880]
Dankevich, Vladimir *see* POUCHENYA V OGRAZHDENIE PRAVOSLAVNYKH OT SHTUNDISTSKIKH ZABLUZHDENI
Danko, Mykola *see* IAK PRYISHLO V ROSII DO REVOLIUTSII
Danky, James P *see* LABOR UNION PERIODICALS, PART 3
DANMARK EKSPEDITIONEN TIL GRONLANDS NORDOSTKYST / Friis, A – BH-467 2. 1909 – 8 – ne IDC [910]
DANMARK I FEST OG GLAEDE – v1-6. 1935-36 – 1 – us I.U. Libraries [390]
DANMARKS LANGTIDSPROGRAM, 1948/49-1952/53 / Denmark – Kobenhavn. 1948 – 9 – ne IDC [338]
DANNEBROG NEWS – Dannebrog, NE. -w. Oct. 1908-Jan. 1959 – 1 – us NE Hist [071]
Danner, John *see* OLD LANDMARKS OF CANTON AND STARK COUNTY
Danner, Tracy *see* RUNNING ECONOMY FOLLOWING AN INTENSE CYCLING BOUT IN TRAINED FEMALE DUATHLETES AND TRIATHLETES
Dannevic, A *see* CANADIAN FISH-EGGS AND LARVAE
DANNEVIRKE – 1880-1951 (complete) – 35r – 1 – ATLA S0199 – us A.T.L.A. [073]
DANNEVIRKE – Cedar Falls, IA. -w. 20 Jan 1885-30 Oct 1895. In Danish – 1 – us NE Hist [071]
Danou et al *see* RECUEIL DES HISTORIENS DES GAULES ET DE LA FRANCE
DANS LA HAUTE-GAMBIE : VOYAGE D'EXPLORATION SCIENTIFIQUE, 1891-1892 / Rancon, Andre – Paris: Societe d'Editions Scientifiques, 1894 – 1 – us Res Libr [910]
DANS LE BROUSSE : SENSATIONS DU SOUDAN / Bonnetain, Paul – Paris, New York: A Lemerre, 1895 – 1 – us Res Libr [910]
DANS LE DESERT, OP. 15 / Paderewski, Ignace Jan – Berlin: Bote & Book, 188- – 1 – us Sibley [780]
DANS LES TENEBRES DE L'AFRIQUE, RECHERCHE, DELIVRANCE ET RETRAITE D'EMIN PACHA / Stanley, Henry Morton – Paris, Hachette. 1890 – 9 – 30.00 – fr Orientalistes [960]
DANS L'OUEST AFRICAIN / Segonzac, M R de – In "Revue des deux mondes". 1891. Paris. 1891 – 1 – us Res Libr [960]
DANS NOTRE EMPIRE NOIR : PREFACE DU GENERAL DE TRENTINIAN / Rondet-Saint, Maurice – Paris: Societe d'Editions Geographiques, Maritimes et Coloniales, 1929 – 1 – us Res Libr [960]
DANS OG KVADDIGINING PAA FAEROERNE / Thuren, Hjalmar – 1901 – 1 – us I.U. Libraries [390]
DANSBESKRIVNINGAR – 1938 – 1 – us I.U. Libraries [390]
DANSE MACABRE : ARRANGED FOR ORGAN / Saint-Saens, Camille & LeMare, Edwin – New York: Schirmer, [c1919] – 1 – us Sibley [780]
Dansereau, Clement Arthur *see*
– REPONSE A UNE ADRESSE DE L'ASSEMBLEE LEGISLATIVE, EN DATE DU 18 MARS 1885, DEMANDANT UNE LISTE DETAILLEE DES LIVRES ACHETES POUR LA BIBLIOTHEQUE DU PARLEMENT
– LES RUINES LIBERALES: QUELQUES PAGES DE POLITIQUE
LES DANSES DT LES BALS: SERMONS, NOTES ET DOCUMENTS / Auclair, Joseph – Quebec: Brousseau, 1879. 00056. (Pre-1900 Canadiana) – 9 – cn C.I.H.M. [971]
DANSES MASQUEES ET JEUX DE MARIONNETTES EN COREE / Chong Pyong-Hi – 1975 – 9 – fr Orientalistes [790]
LES DANSEURS KACHINE HOPI / Laniel-Le Francois, M – 9 – F180.00 – fr Ethnologie [306]
DANSK BOTANISK ARKIV = DANSK BOTANISK FORENING – Kjobenhavn, 1913-1915. v1; 1914-1921. v2; 1915-1920. v3 – 22mf – 7414/2 – ne IDC [580]
DANSK CANADISK TIDENDE = DANISH CANADIAN NEWS – Montreal. 1931 – 1 – $35.00 – cn McLaren [072]
DANSK LUTHERSK KIRKEBLAD – Blair, NE. -w. 1 Jan 1879-29 Dec 1920 – 1 – us NE Hist [071]
DANSK LUTHERSK KIRKEBLAD – v1-25. 1869-1920 (complete) – 8r – 1 – ATLA S0285 – us A.T.L.A. [073]
DANSK MISSIONSBLAD – (Lacking: 1914-70) – 1884-1989 – Inquire – 1 – ATLA S0567 – us A.T.L.A. [073]
DANSK ORNITHOLOGISK FORENINGS TIDSSKRIFT / ed by Helms, O et al – Kjobenhavn, 1906-1942. v1-36 – 152mf – Z-2017c/2 – ne IDC [590]
DANSK TIDENDE – Chicago: Dansk Tidende, mar 20 1931-mar 1952 – 11r – us Res Libr [072]
DANSK TIDENDE OG REVYEN – Chicago: Dansk Tidende, Inc, 1921-31. 1925-mar 13 1931 – 7r – us Res Libr [072]
DET DANSKE BIBELSELSKABS ARBOG – (Cont by: Nyt Fra Bibelselskabet) – 1966-92 (complete) – Inquire – 1 – ATLA S0746 – us A.T.L.A. [073]
DEN DANSKE DIAKONISSESTIFTELSES ARBOG – 1962-86 (complete) – 2r – 1 – ATLA S0869 – us A.T.L.A. [073]
DANSKE DIATOMEER / Oestrop, E – Kjobenhavn. 1910. B-6440 1 – 9 – ne IDC [580]
DE DANSKE DOMKAPITLER : DERES OPRINDELSE, INDRETNING OG VIRKSOMHED, FOR REFORMATIONEN: EN HISTORISK SKILDRING / Helveg, Ludvig – Kjobenhavn: C.G. Iversen, 1855 – 1mf – us A.T.L.A. [240]
DANSKE FOLKEMAAL – v1-20. 1927-75 – 1 – us I.U. Libraries [390]
DE DANSKE GJODNINGSSVAMPE / Hansen, E C – (Fungi fimicoli Danici). (Medd. Vidensk. Natyrh. Foeren. Kobenhavn. 1876. Lacking: pls. 4-9. B-103 2 – 8 – ne IDC [580]
DANSKE HEROLD = DANISH HERALD OF CANADA – Kentville, N.S. v1-8. 1932-1939 – 1 – $175.00 – cn McLaren [072]
DANSKE KIRKELOVE SAMT UDVALG AF ANDRE BESTEMMELSER VEDRORENDE KIRKEN, SKOLEN OG DE FATTIGES FORSORGELSE FRA REFORMATIONEN INDTIL CHRISTIAN V'S DANSKE LOV, 1536-1683 / ed by Rordam, Holger Frederik – Kjobenhavn, 1883-89. 3v – 1 – us U.W. Library [340]
DANSKE KIRKETIDENDE – (Lacking some pgs) – v1-144. 1845-1992 – Inquire – 1 – ATLA S0368 – us A.T.L.A. [073]
DEN DANSKE PIONEER – Omaha, NE. -w. (-bw 1956-59). Nov 1887; Aug 1888; Jan 1894-Dec 1923; Jan 1926-Jul 1958; Oct 1958-Feb 1959 – 1 – us NE Hist [071]
DANSKE TRACTATER : 1751-1800 – Copenhagen, 1882 – 5mf – 1 – ILM-2298/1 – ne IDC [327]
DANSKE TRAKTATER EFTER 1800 – Copenhagen. 2v. 1874-85 – 15mf – 1 – ILM-2445/1 – ne IDC [327]
Danske Videnskabernes selskab. Copenhagen *see*
– DET KONGELIGE DANSKE VIDENSKABERS SELSKABS SKRIVETER
– NYE SAMLING AF DET KONGELIGE DANSKE VIDENSKABERNES SELSKABS SKRIFTER
– SKRIFTER, SOM UDI DET KIOBENHAVNSKE SELSKAB AF LAERDOMS OG RIDENSKABERS ELSKERE, ERE FREMLAGTE OG OPLAESTE
DANSKEREN – Blair, NE. v1-25. 9 Jun 1892-1920 (complete) – 12r – 1 – ATLA S0287 – us A.T.L.A. [073]
DANSKEREN – Blair, NE. -w, sw. 20 Apr 1899-29 Dec 1920 – 1 – us NE Hist [071]
DANSK-GROENLANDSK ORDBOG / Kjer, J & Rasmussen, C – (Supplement) – Kjoebenhavn, 1893 – 14mf – ne IDC [430]
DANSK-GROENLANDSK ORDBOG, PLUS SUPPL / Kjer, J & Rasmussen, C – BH-181 2. 1893 – 8 – ne IDC [910]
Danson, John Towne *see* OUR COMMERCE, IN WAR; AND HOW TO PROTECT IT
DANTE / Merezhkovskii, Dimitrii – 2v. Paris. 1939. BR-760 2 – 8 – ne IDC [440]
Dante Alighieri *see*
– DE VULGARI ELOQUENTIA, SIVE IDIOMATE. AVEC COMMENTAIRES ET PREFACE
– DIVINA COMMEDIA
Dante, Alighieri *see*
– IL CONVIVIO: THE BANQUET OF DANTE ALIGHIERI
– DIVINA COMMEDIA
– THE VISION
DANTE AND AQUINAS : BEING THE SUBSTANCE OF THE JOWETT LECTURES OF 1911 / Wicksteed, Philip Henry – London: J.M. Dent; New York: E.P. Dutton, 1913 – 1mf – us A.T.L.A. [240]
Dante Society *see* ANNUAL REPORTS
Danton, George H *see* TIECK'S ESSAY ON THE BOYDELL SHAKESPEARE GALLERY
Dantz, Antonie *see* GOETHE UND DIE WIRTSCHAFT
Dantzig, A van *see* DUTCH DOCUMENTS RELATING TO THE GOLD COAST AND TRANSLATIONS OF LETTERS AND PAPERS COLLECTED IN THE ALGEMEEN RIJKS ARCHIEF (ARA), STATE ARCHIVES OF THE NETHERLANDS AT THE HAGUE
LE DANUBE / Baicoianu, Cl – Paris, 1917 – 4mf – 9 – ILM-334/1 – ne IDC [340]
THE DANUBE / Chamberlain, J P – Washington, 1918 – 2mf – 1 – ILM-2282/1 – ne IDC [327]
THE DANUBE;... / Hajnal, H – The Hague, 1920 – 2mf – 1 – ILM-1853/1 – ne IDC [327]
LE DANUBE ET LES INTER-TS ECONOMIQUES DE L'EUROPE – Paris, 1920 – 1mf – 1 – ILM-2280/1 – ne IDC [327]
Danusugondo, Purwanto *see* BAHASA INDONESIA FOR BEGINNERS
DANVERS 1652-1849 – (Mf 1T-6T: Births & Deaths 1652-1835. Mf 6T-7T: Marriages 1752-73. Mf 7T-10T: Vital Records 1720-1857. Mf 10T-15T: Vital Records 1695-1860. Mf 15T-17T: Marriages 1752-1818. Mf 17T: Out-of-Town Marriages 1752-99; Marriage Intentions 1752-1819. Mf 17T-19T: Marriages 1773-1828. Mf 19T-20T: Marriage Intentions 1819-49. Mf 20T-21T: Marriages 1827-49. Mf 22T-24T: Births 1843-49. Mf 24T: Marriages 1774-1849. Mf 25T-26T: Deaths 1830-49) – (mf ed 1996) – 26mf – 9 – 0-87623-237-3 – us Holbrook [920]
THE DANVERS JEWELS / Cholmondeley, Mary – British Fiction Archive: Unit 3 – 9 – uk Bell [830]
Danvers, Massachusetts. Danvers Baptist Church *see* RECORDS
DANVILLE BAPTIST CHURCH. VERMONT : CHURCH RECORDS – 1792-1842 – 1 – 6.32 – us Baptist [240]
THE DANVILLE COURIER – Richmond, Canada. v1 n7. 28 sep 1865 – 1r – 1 – Can$25.00 – cn Can Microfilming [072]
DANVILLE INTELLIGENCER – Danville, PA. -w 1904-1907 – 13 – $25.00r – us I.M.R. [071]
DANVILLE JOURNAL *see* COURIER JOURNAL
DANVILLE, PENNSYLVANIA / Brower, D H B – Historical and biographical sketches. Harrisburg, Lane S. Hart, Printer, 1881. Pennsylvania Reel 33. (The Cox Library Collection) – 5 – us Americana [978]
DANVILLE UNION – Danville, Canada. v1 n47. 6 fev 1869 – 1r – 1 – Can$20.00 – cn Can Microfilming [072]

DANVILLER HEROLD UND ZEITUNG – Danville, IL. jul 1917-jul 13 1919 – 3r – us Res Libr [071]

Danylchuk, Karen *see* MARKETING STRUCTURES, ACTIVITIES AND OUTCOMES AMONGST SELECTED NATIONAL SPORT ORGANIZATIONS

Danzel, Theodor Wilhelm *see* UEBER GOETHE'S SPINOZISMUS

DANZHONG RIBAO – Popular Daily. China. In Chinese. Current subscription. Annual delivery. Backfiles supplied on request. M D17 – 1 – $55.00r – cc Microforms [072]

Danzi, F *see*
- DUOS, TRIOS, POUR ALTO ET VIOLONCELLE
- QUATORS, TROIS, OP. 7
- QUATUORS, TROIS, OP. 6
- QUATUORS, TROIS, OP. 44
- QUATUORS, TROIS, OP. 55
- QUATUORS, TROIS, POUR FLUTE, VIOLON, ALTO ET VIOLONCELLE, OP. 56
- QUINTETTE, TROIS, OP. 66

Danzig. Regierungsbezirk *see* AMTSBLATT DER KOENIGLICHEN REGIERUNG ZU DANZIG

DANZIGER ALLGEMEINE ZEITUNG – Danzig (Gdansk), Poland. 2 Jan 1924-29 Sept 1934 – 19r – 1 – gw Mikrofilm [943]

DANZIGER DAMPFBOOT – (Since 1838: Das Dampfboot) – Danzig (Gdansk), Poland. Nov 1831-1832; 1835; Jan-Jun 1838 – 6r – 1 – gw Mikrofilm [943]

DANZIGER ECHO – Danzig (Gdansk), Poland. 1934-1936 – 1r – 1 – gw Mikrofilm [072]

Danziger, Kurt *see* PSYCHOLOGI DAN MASJARAKAT

DANZIGER LANDES-ZEITUNG – Danzig (Gdansk), Poland. 1927-34 – 16r – 1 – gw Mikrofilm [943]

DANZIGER NACHRICHTEN – Danzig (Gdansk), Poland. 1752-57 – 3r – 1 – gw Mikrofilm [943]

DANZIGER NEUESTE NACHRICHTEN – Danzig (Gdansk), Poland. 1924-43 – 69r – 1 – gw Mikrofilm [943]

DANZIGER NEUESTE NACHRICHTEN – Gdansk, Poland. Jan-Aug 1944 (scattered issues) – 1r – 1 – us L of C Photodup [943]

DANZIGER SONNTAGS-ZEITUNG – Danzig (Gdansk), Poland. 1930-42 – 26r – 1 – gw Mikrofilm [943]

DANZIGER VOLKSSTIMME – Danzig (Gdansk), Poland. 16 Apr 1924-1936 (incomplete) – 32r – 1 – gw Mikrofilm [335]

DANZIGER VOLKS-ZEITUNG – Danzig (Gdansk), Poland. 1935 (incomplete); 1936-37 – 13r – 1 – gw Mikrofilm [943]

DANZIGER VORPOSTEN – (Some missing issues) – Gdansk, Poland. Jan-Mar 1938; 1940-Jun 1943; Apr 1944-Mar 1945 – 10r – 1 – us L of C Photodup [943]

DER DANZIGER VORPOSTEN – Danzig (Gdansk), Poland. 1933-44 (incomplete) – 33r – 1 – gw Mikrofilm [943]

DANZIGER ZEITUNG – Danzig (Gdansk), Poland. 1796-1801; 1921-22 (incomplete); 1924-30 (incomplete) – 35r – 1 – gw Mikrofilm [943]

DANZIG-WESTPREUSSISCHER KIRCHENBRIEF – nos 1-154. 1948-86 – 1r – 1 – ATLA S0840 – us A.T.L.A. [073]

DAO DARA YUK SAYAM – Bangkok, Thailand. 1974-76 – 14r – 1 – us L of C Photodup [072]

Daoulas abbaye *see* ACTES RELATIFS A LA RECONSTRUCTION DE L'ABBAYE DE DAOULAS (15 AVRIL 1722-18 AOUT 1723

Daoust, C Roger *see* CENT-VINGT JOURS DE SERVICE ACTIF

DAPHNE, OR, MARRIAGE A LA MODE / Ward, Mary Augusta – British Fiction Archive: Unit 2 – 9 – uk Bell [830]

Dapontes, C *see* EPHEMERIDES DACES

DAPOTNA PABIDANGKON DOHOT PABAGASHON; BUKU PARSIADJARAN HATA BATAK IU ANGKA SEKOLAH LANDJUTAN / Sihombing gelar Sutan Mulia Parlinggoman, T M – SE 4378 1. v. 1 only. 1960? – 9 – ne IDC [950]

Dapper, O *see*
- DESCRIPTION DE L'AFRIQUE
- HISTORISCHE BESCHRYVING DER STADT AMSTERDAM: WAER IN DE VOORNAEMITE GEICHIEDENIFFEN..
- NAUKEURIGE BESCHRIJVINGE DER AFRIKAENSCHE GEWESTEN; VAN EGYPTEN, BARBARYEN, LIBYEN, BILEDULGERID, NEGROSLANT, GUINEA, ETHIOPIEN, ABYSSINIE

DAPPIM AL HALUKKAT HOVOT HA-YEHUDIM BI-YERUSHALAYIM BA-MEAH HA-18 / Hirschberg, H Z – Erez-Yisra'el. v. 1. 1951. BJ-27-72 1 – 9 – ne IDC [956]

DAPPIM BODEDIM / Rivkind, I – Ed. by le-Zekher A. M. Luncz, E. L. Sukenik and J. Peres. Yerushalayim. 1928. BJ-27-58 1 – 9 – ne IDC [270]

DAPPIM BODEDIM / Rivkind, I – v. 5. Ziyyon. 1933. BJ-27-57 1 – 9 – ne IDC [270]

DAQI KEXUE – (1983, 1986- $4.50f; 1984 $3.50f) – Atmospherica Sinica. In Chinese but English abstracts to the main articles. F p82 – 9 – cc Microforms [073]

DAQING LICHAO SHILU – Historical Records of Qing Dynasty, 1644-1911. 122 reels. M G2B – 5 – $4,270.00 – cc Microforms [950]

DAR MDO'I GSAR 'GYUR – Kangting, China. July-Oct 1956 – 1r – 1 – us L of C Photodup [072]

DARA SHUKOH / Qanungo, Kalika-Ranjan – Foreward by Dr. R.C. Majumdar. 2nd ed. Calcutta: S.C. Sarkar, 1952- – 1 – us U.W. Library [920]

DARAH DAN PELUH: KUMPULAN SADJAK / Ukur, Fridolin – SE 4391 1. 1962 – 9 – ne IDC [950]

DARAH, KERINGAT DAN AIRMATA; KUMPULAN KISAH-PERANG / Daulay, Is – SE-4749 1. 1963 – 9 – ne IDC [950]

DARBAR – Ajmer, India. 6 Apr 1944-53; 1957-60; 1962-63 – 8r – 1 – us L of C Photodup [072]

DARBAS = LABOR – New York, NY, Jan. 4, 1929-Dec. 6, 1930 – 1r – 1 – us I.H.R.C. [978]

D'Arbelles, Salvador *see* CORINTO A TRAVES DE LA HISTORIA (1514-1933). CORINTO (NICARAGUA)

DARBININKAS : AMERIKOS LIETUVIU R K SVENTO JUOZAPO DARBININKU SAJUNGA – South Boston: 1919-20 – 2r – us Res Libr [071]

Darbishire, O V *see* MONOGRAPHIA ROCCOLEORUM

D'Arbois de Jubainville, MH *see* ETUDES SUR L'ETAT INTERIEUR DES ABBAYES CISTERCIENNES ET PRINCIPALEMENT DE CLAIRVAUX AU 12TH ET AU 13TH SIECLE

Darby, Douglas *see* THE NEW RAT TRACK

Darby, John N *see* NOTES ON THE BOOK OF REVELATIONS TO ASSIST INQUIRERS IN SEARCHING INTO THAT BOOK

Darby, W E *see*
- MODERN SPECIFIC SETTLEMENTS...
- THE PEACE CONFERENCE...

D'Arcy, Charles Frederick *see*
- CHRISTIAN ETHICS AND MODERN THOUGHT
- CHRISTIANITY AND THE SUPERNATURAL
- GOD AND FREEDOM IN HUMAN EXPERIENCE
- IDEALISM AND THEOLOGY
- RULING IDEAS OF OUR LORD
- A SHORT STUDY OF ETHICS

Darcy, J *see* FRANCE ET ANGLETERRE...

Dard, J *see*
- DICTIONNAIRE FRANCAIS-WOLOF ET FRANCAIS-BAMBARA, SUIVI DU DICTIONNAIRE WOLOF-FRANCAIS
- GRAMMAIRE WOLOFE OU METHODE POUR ETUDIER LA LANGUE DES NOIRS QUI HABITENT LES ROYAUMES DE BOURBA-YOLOF

EL DARDO – Plasencia, 1901-1904 – 5 – sp Bibl Santa Ana [073]

Dardy, Cl. *see* REPARATEUR DE PORCELAINE

DAREKHEI NO'AM / Ibn Habib, M; ed by Heidenheim, W – Roedelheim. 1806. BJ-421-84 1 – 9 – ne IDC [470]

Dares Phrygius *see* DARETIS PHRYGII DE EXCIDIO TROIAE HISTORIA, RECENSUIT FERDINANDUS MEISTER

DARETIS PHRYGII DE EXCIDIO TROIAE HISTORIA, RECENSUIT FERDINANDUS MEISTER / Dares Phrygius – Lipsiae, in aedibus B. G. Teubneri, 1873. 67 p. (Bibliotheca scriptorum graecorum et romanorum Teubneriana) Film Mas 8376 – 1 – us H.U. Library [450]

DARFUR AL-JADIDAH = DARFUR AL-GADIDA – Sudan: s.n., jul 4 1992-aug 28 1993 – 1r – us Res Libr [072]

Dargan, Edwin Charles *see*
- THE DOCTRINES OF OUR FAITH: A CONVENIENT HANDBOOK
- ECCLESIOLOGY
- A HISTORY OF PREACHING
- PAPERS AND SERMONS OF E.C. DARGAN
- SOCIETY, KINGDOM, AND CHURCH

DARI IR. SOEKARNO SAMPAI KE PRESIDEN SOEKARNO / Tan Malaka – SE 6317 1. 1966 – 9 – ne IDC [920]

DARI LIMA ZAMAN PENDJADJAHAN MENUDJU ZAMAN KEMERDEKAAN; BUKU PELADJARAN SEDJARAH INDONESIA UNTUK SEKOLAH MENEGAH ATAS BAGIAN A.B. DAN C / Sutjipto Wirjosuparto, R M – SE 4314 1. 1956 – 9 – ne IDC [950]

DARI PERBENDAHARAAN LAMA / Amrullah, Abdul Malik Karim – SE-5291 1. 1963 – 9 – ne IDC [950]

DARI SEKOLAH KEMEDAN PERANG / Takato, A – (Microfiche Nos 174-175) – Djakarta: Poesat Keboedajaan, 2604 – 2mf – 9 – SE-2002/1 – ne IDC [950]

DARI SUN YAT SEN KE MAO TZE TUNG / Arifin, Bey – SE-4082 1. 1953? – 9 – ne IDC [950]

Darias y Padron, Dacio V *see* A PROPOSITO DE LOS CONDES DE LA GOMERA "FUE ANTANO REGULAR LA SUCESION DE ESTE TITULO"

DARIEL / Blackmore, Richard Doddridge – British Fiction Archive: Unit 3 – 9 – uk Bell [830]

DARIEN RECORDS / Royal Bank of Scotland. Archives – BRRAM – 1 – uk Microform Academic [941]

Dario Alessandro, Julio *see* CONCIONERO DE JUAN PERON Y EVA PERON

Darjanto *see* CHASIAT, RATJUN DAN MASAKAN KETELA POHON

Darjes, J G *see*
- DISCOURS...
- OBSERVATIONS IURIS NATURALIS,...

Dark, M *see* A DICTIONARY OF THE KILENGE OF NEW BRITAIN

Dark, P *see* A DICTIONARY OF THE KILENGE OF NEW BRITAIN

Dark, Phillip John Crosskey *see* BUSH NEGRO ART

DARK ROAD AHEAD OF LABOR / Buenacasa, Manuel – 1951. 2p – 9 – 1.00f – at Libertarian Micro [335]

DARKENOE – Velsen, 1939-1940. Nos 1-6 – 3mf – J-261-23/1 – ne IDC [073]

DARKEST ENGLAND GAZETTE / Salvation Army – (The Social Gazette). Official newspaper of the social operations of the Salvation Army. London. -w. Jul. 1893-Mar. 1917. 9 reels – 1 – uk British Libr Newspaper [072]

DARKHEI HA-MISHNAH / Frankel, Zacharias – Leipzig. 1859. BJ-32-2 1 – 9 – ne IDC [470]

DARKHEI ZIYYON – Amsterdam? Prague? 1650. BJ-43-14 1 – 9 – ne IDC [470]

DARKROOM PHOTOGRAPHY – v. 1-. 1979- – 1,5,6,9 – us UMI [770]

Darland, Lloyd *see* THE EMPEROR'S CLOTHES COST TWENTY DOLLARS

DARLEGUNG DER DICHTERISCHEN TECHNIK UND LITTERARHISTORISCHEN STELLUNG VON GOETHES ELEGIE "ALEXIS UND DORA" / Kassewitz, Joseph – Leipzig: G Fock, 1893 – 1r – 1 – us U.W. Library [430]

Darley, George *see*
- THE COMPLETE POETICAL WORKS...
- SYLVIA

Darley, George Marshall *see* PIONEERING IN THE SAN JUAN

Darling, Charles John Darling *see* SCINTILLAE JURIS

Darling, Charles William *see* HISTORICAL ACCOUNT OF SOME OF THE MORE IMPORTANT VERSIONS AND EDITIONS OF THE BIBLE

DARLING DOWNS GAZETTE – Toowoomba, Australia. 16 Jun 1864; 14 Oct 1865; 4 Jan, 30 Oct 1866; 6 Jul, 12 Sep, 24 Dec 1867, 11 Jan, 4, 11-16, 23, 25 Apr 1868; 14 Apr 1875; 30 May 1877; 6 Feb 1888-1 Jul 1891 (imperfect).-w. 5 reels – 1 – uk British Libr Newspaper [072]

Darling, Hon. Mr. Justice *see* SCINTILLAE JURIS

Darling, Sharon S *see* DECORATIVE AND ARCHITECTURAL ARTS IN CHICAGO, 1871-1933

DARLINGTON FIRST BAPTIST CHURCH. DARLINGTON, SOUTH CAROLINA : CHURCH RECORDS – Deacons' Meetings. 1856-96, 1923-52 – 1 – 108.32 – us Baptist [240]

THE DARLINGTON NEWS – Pawtucket. R.I. 1907-1909 – 1 – us UMI [071]

Darlington. South Carolina. St. Matthew's Protestant Episcopal Church *see* REGISTERS

DARLINGTON & STOCKTON TIMES – Darlington, Stockton, England. -w. 1847-54. 3 reels – 1 – uk British Libr Newspaper [072]

Darlington, W *see* FLORA CESTRICA

Darmester, James *see* LES PROPHETES D'ISRAEL

Darmesteter, Arsene *see* THE TALMUD

Darmon, R *see* DES CONFLITS DE LOIS EN MATIERE D'AVARIES...

DARMSTAEDTER ECHO – Darmstadt, West Germany. 1968- – ca 11r per yr – 1 – gw Mikrofilm [072]

DARMSTAEDTER FRAG- UND ANZEIGEBLATT *see* DARMSTAEDTISCHES FRAG- UND ANZEIGUNGS-BLAETTGEN

DARMSTAEDTER JOURNAL – Darmstadt, Germany. Jan 1843-Sept 1845; 12 Mar 1848-Jun 1852 – 6r – 1 – gw Mikrofilm [072]

DARMSTAEDTER NEUE PRESSE *see* DARMSTAEDTISCHES FRAG- UND ANZEIGUNGS-BLAETTGEN

Darmstaedter, P *see* GESCHICHTE DER AUFTEILUNG...AFRIKAS...

DARMSTAEDTER TAGBLATT – Darmstadt, West Germany. May-Jun 1964; 1 Sept 1978- – ca 8r per yr – 1 – gw Mikrofilm [072]

DARMSTAEDTER TAGBLATT *see*
- DARMSTAEDTISCHES FRAG- UND ANZEIGUNGS-BLAETTGEN

DARMSTAEDTER WOCHENBLATT *see* DARMSTAEDTISCHES FRAG- UND ANZEIGUNGS-BLAETTGEN

DARMSTAEDTER ZEITUNG – Darmstadt, Germany. 1848-49 – 4r – 1 – gw Mikrofilm [072]

DARMSTAEDTER ZEITUNG *see* HESSEN-DARMSTAEDTISCHE PRIVILEGIRTE LANDES-ZEITUNG

DARMSTAEDTISCHES FRAG- UND ANZEIGUNGS-BLAETTGEN – (Title change: Darmstaedter Frag- und Anzeigeblatt, 26 Sep 1835; Darmstaedter Tagblatt, 1 Jan 1874; Darmstaedter Wochenblatt, 18 Dec 1949; Darmstaedter Neue Presse, 30 May 1950; Darmstaedter Tagblatt, 1 Jul 1950) – Darmstadt, Germany. 1848-49 – 1r – 1 – gw Mikrofilm [072]

Darnell, Ermina Jett *see* FORKS OF ELKHORN CHURCH

Darnell, WN *see* THE CORRESPONDENCE OF ISAAC BASIRE

D'Arneth, A *see* CORRESPONDANCE SECRETE DU COMTE DE MERCY-ARGENTEAU AVEC L'EMPEREUR JOSEPH 2

Daron, E Acoghih de *see* HISTOIRE UNIVERSELLE

Darques, F Martin *see* MISCELLANEOUS MANUSCRIPTS, 1968-1983

Darrach *see* A STANDARD HISTORY OF JASPER AND NEWTON COUNTIES

Darracott, Charles R 3. *see* RATINGS OF PERCEIVED EXERTION AS A DETERMINANT OF PHYSICAL ACTIVITY IN 9 TO 11 YEAR-OLD CHILDREN

Darragh, Patricia M *see* THE RELATIONSHIP OF FAT PATTERNING TO PERIPHERAL RESISTANCE FOLLOWING SUPINE SUBMAXIMAL EXERCISE

Darras, Maxime *see* LE NOUVEAU CODE CIVIL DU TONKIN.

DARRELL ST CLAIRE, SENATE SERVICE 1933-1939, 1949-1977 : ASSISTANT SECRETARY TO THE SENATE – 3mf – 9 – $15.00 – us Scholarly Res [320]

Darrington. Yorkshire *see* PARISH REGISTERS

Darrouzes, J *see* LITTERATURE ET HISTOIRE DES TEXTES BYZANTINS. (1950-1965)

Darrow, Clarence S *see*
- AN EYE FOR AN EYE
- PLEA IN DEFENCE OF LOEB AND LEOPOLD
- RESIST NOT EVIL

Darsono *see* THE INDONESIAN COMMUNIST PARTY

DIE DARSTELLUNG DER HAFTUNG DES AMERIKANISCHEN STAATES UND DER BEAMTEN SOWIE EIN RECHTSVERGLEICHENDER UBERBLICK UBER DAS DEUTSCHE RECHT / Creer, John W – n.p. 1969. 166 p. LL-4207 – 1 – us L of C Photodup [340]

DIE DARSTELLUNG DES WAHNSINNS IM ENGLISCHEN DRAMA BIS ZUM ENDE DES 18. JAHRHUNDERTS / Berghaeuser, Wilhelm – Mainz, 1915 – 2mf – DM62.00 – 3-8267-3099-2 – gw Hänsel [420]

DARSTELLUNG UND EIGENSCHAFTEN DER METAGERMANATE DES MANGANS, EISENS UND KOBALTS / Forwerg, Walter – Frankfurt a.M., 1962 – 1mf – 9 – DM48.00 – 3-89349-655-6 – gw Hänsel [540]

DARSTELLUNG UND KRITIK DER LEHRE DES DESCARTES VON DER BILDUNG DES UNIVERSUMS / Kratzmoeller, Wilhelm – Rostock, 1903 – 1mf – DM48.00 – 3-8267-3105-0 – gw Hänsel [110]

DARSTELLUNG UND KRITIK DER VON HERDER GEGEBENEN ERGAENZUNG UND FORTBILDUNG DER ANSICHTEN LESSINGS IN SEINEM LAOKOON / Hoffmann, G F – (Includes bibliographical references) – Augsburg: Reichel, 1901 – 1r – 1 – us U.W. Library [430]
DIE DARSTELLUNGSWEISE LESSINGS IN SEINEN PROSAISCHEN SCHRIFTEN : SCHULNACHRICHTEN VON DEM DIREKTOR DER ANSTALT HEINRICH VOCKERADT / Mummenhoff, Wilhelm – Recklinghausen: J Bauer, 1903 – 1r – 1 – us U.W. Library [430]
DARTMOOR PRISON. / Rhodes, Albert John – London. 1933 – 1 – us Res Libr [941]
DARTMOUTH 1650-1849 – (Mf 1T-6T: Vital Records 1650-1791. Mf 1T: Marriage Intentions 1727, 1739-44. Mf 7T-8T: Births 1710-80. Mf 7T-9T: Marriages 1722-88. Mf 7T-15T: Marriage Intentions 1742-1821. Mf 15T-20T: Marriages 1749-1844. Mf 17T: Marriage Intentions 1787-88. Mf 20T: Out-of-Town Marriages 1698-1799. Mf 20T-23T: Marriage Intentions 1821-50. Mf 23T-26T: Births & Deaths 1722-1847. Mf 26T-27T: Births 1843-49. Mf 27T-28T: Marriages 1843-49. Mf 28T: Deaths 1848-49) – (mf ed 1996) – 28mf – 9 – 0-87623-238-1 – us Holbrook [920]
DARTMOUTH 1650-1900 – (Mf 1-13: Vital Records 1650-1847. Mf 14-19: Vitals 1667-1788. Mf 20-23: Vitals 1722-1864. Mf 24-30: Town, Vitals 1674-1779. Mf 31-48: Town Records 1777-1844. Mf 49-58: Town Records 1789-1867. Mf 59-60: Taxes 1882, 1883, 1885. Mf 61-74: Marrs & Ints 1699-1850. Mf 75-76: Town & Marrs 1829-39. Mf 77-78: Ints Index 1848-77+. Mf 79-81: Intentions 1848-77. Mf 82: Baptist Records 1831-78. Mf 83-85: Birth Index 1843-1922. Mf 86-88: Marr Index 1844-91. Mf 89-91: Death Index 1850-1923. Mf 92-94: Births 1843-64. Mf 95: Marriages 1844-55, 1869. Mf 95-96: Deaths 1848-51. Mf 97-98: Births 1843-64. Mf 98: Marriages 1844-55. Mf 98-99: Deaths 1848-61. Mf 100-102: Deaths 1862-91. Mf 103-105: Marriages 1855-91. Mf 106-107: Births 1865-95. Mf 108-109: Deaths 1892-1903. Mf 110-111: Marriages 1892-1906) – (mf ed 1992) – 111mf – 9 – 0-87623-147-4 – us Holbrook [920]
Dartmouth College. Library *see*
- DICTIONARY CATALOG OF THE STEFANSSON COLLECTION ON THE POLAR REGIONS
- THE LIBRARY OF JEREMIAH SMITH

DARTMOUTH COLLEGE LIBRARY BULLETIN – 1931-53; 1957-69. 1 reel, index inc – 1 – $15.00 – us Dartmouth [020]
DARTMOUTH PAPERS : THE AMERICAN PAPERS OF THE SECOND EARL OF DARTMOUTH – 16r – 1 – uk Microform Academic [975]
Darton. Yorkshire *see* PARISH REGISTERS
Dartt *see* HISTORY OF THE TOWN OF SPRINGFIELD
DAR'UEL-ELHAN MECMUASI – Istanbul: Evkaf-i Islamiyye Matbaasi, 1924-1926 – 9 – $85.00 – us MEDOC [956]
DAR'UES-S'AFAKA – Nos 1-12. – 1325-1326 – 10mf – 9 – $47.00 – us MEDOC [949]
Darussalam, Banda Atjah, Lembaga Penjelidikan Ekonomi dan Sosial, Fakultas Ekonomi Universitas Sjiah Kuala *see* BULLETIN FAKTA-FAKTA EKONOMI DAERAH ISTIMEWA ATJAH
Darut, J A *see* DE L'EXPULSION DES ETRANGERS;...
Darveau, C *see* SPECIMEN DE PHOTO-GRAVURE DE L'IMPRIMERIE C. DARVEAU
Darveau, L M *see* L'OBSERVATEUR
DARWIN AND THE HUMANITIES / Baldwin, James Mark – Baltimore: Review Pub., 1909 – 1mf – us A.T.L.A. [100]
Darwin, Charles *see*
- THE 18 NOTEBOOKS WRITTEN DURING THE VOYAGE OF THE BEAGLE
- THE DIARY AND CORRESPONDENCE OF... WRITTEN DURING THE VOYAGE OF THE BEAGLE
- THE EXPRESSION OF THE EMOTIONS IN MAN AND ANIMALS
- EXPRESSION OF THE EMOTIONS IN MAN AND ANIMALS
- THE FORMATION OF VEGETABLE MOULD
- THE FOUNDATIONS OF THE ORIGIN OF SPECIES
- A MONOGRAPH OF THE FOSSIL LEPADIDAE, OR PEDUNCULATED CIRRIPEDES OF GREAT BRITAIN
- A MONOGRAPH OF THE SUB-CLASS CIRRIPEDIA: THE BALANIDAE, THE VERRUEIDAE ETC
- A MONOGRAPH OF THE SUB-CLASS CIRRIPEDIA: THE LAPADIDAE OR PODUNCULATED CIRRIPEDES
- A MONOGRAPH ON THE FOSSIL BALANIDAE AND VERRUCIDAE OF GREAT BRITAIN
- A MONOGRAPH ON THE SUBCLASS CIRRIPEDIAE: 1, THE BALANTIDAE; 2, THE VERRICIDAE
- THE ORIGIN OF SPECIES BY MEANS OF NATURAL SELECTION, OR, THE PRESERVATION OF FAVOURED RACES IN THE STRUGGLE FOR LIFE

Darwin, Erasmus *see* COMMONPLACE BOOK
Darwin, Francis *see* THE FOUNDATIONS OF THE ORIGIN OF SPECIES
DARWIN, HUXLEY AND THE NATURAL SCIENCES – (Units 1 and 2: Scientific Papers and Correspondence of T.H. Huxley, c1843-1895, from the Imperial College of Science, Technology and Medicine, London; Units 3, 4, 5: The Darwin Papers from the Cambridge University Library) – 1 – us Primary [500]
DARWIN INQUEST BOOK 1875-1905 – 9 – A$5.00 – 0-949124-64-8 – item 29 – at G.S.N.T. [920]
DARWINISCHEN THEORIEN UND IHRE STELLUNG ZUR PHILOSOPHIE, RELIGION UND MORAL = THE THEORIES OF DARWIN AND THEIR RELATION TO PHILOSOPHY, RELIGION, AND MORALITY / Schmid, Rudolf – (In English. Includes bibliographical references) – Chicago:Jansen, McClurg, 1883, c1882 – 1mf – 9 – 0-8370-5107-X – 1985-3107 – us A.T.L.A. [210]
DIE DARWINISCHEN THEORIEN UND IHRE STELLUNG ZUR PHILOSOPHIE, RELIGION UND MORAL / Schmid, Rudolf – (Includes bibliographical references) – Stuttgart:Paul Moser, 1876 – 1mf – 9 – 0-8370-5105-3 – 1985-3105 – us A.T.L.A. [210]
DARWINISM / Benson, Lawrence Sluter – New York: Serial Science Soc., 1876. 1 fiche – 9 – us A.T.L.A. [240]
DARWINISM IN MORALS : AND OTHER ESSAYS / Cobbe, Frances Power – London: Williams and Norgate, 1872 – 1mf – us A.T.L.A. [170]
Das, Devandra Nath *see* SKETCHES OF HINDOO LIFE
Das, Sarat Chandra *see*
- TIBETAN-ENGLISH DICTIONARY
- A TIBETAN-ENGLISH DICTIONARY WITH SANSKRIT SYNONYMS

Das Socialistische Bund *see* TURN-ZEITUNG
DASAR2 BAHASA DJEPANG / Badaruttamam Akasah – 2V. SE-4088 1. 1962 – 9 – ne IDC [950]
DASAR-DASAR LENINISME / Stalin, Iosif – SE 6100 1. 1948? – 9 – ne IDC [335]
DASAR-DASAR UMUM TATANEGARA / Sunarko, R – SE 4901 1. 1961 – 9 – ne IDC [950]
DASA-WARSA PERDJUANGAN PERBANA, 1952-1962 / Perhimpunan Bank-Bank Nasional Indonesia – SE-6038 1. 1962 – 9 – ne IDC [336]
D'Asbeck, M *see* LA MYSTIQUE DE RUYSBROECK L'ADMIRABLE. UN ECHO DU NEOPLATONISME AU 14TH SIECLE
Dascovici, N *see*
- LA QUESTION DE BOSPHORE...
- LA QUESTION DU BOSPHORE...

DASE CUENTA DEL ESTADO DE LO SUCEDIDO EN LOS PLEYTOS DE LA RELIGION DE NUESTRA PADRE S. GERONIMO DESDE 22 DE OCTUBRE DE 1641 HASTA 16 DE ABRIL DE 1642 / Davila, Andres – S.l., s.i., s.a. 1642 – 1 – sp Bibl Santa Ana [946]
DAS DASEIN GOTTES WISSENSCHAFTLICH BEWIESEN / Kroenig, Gottlieb – Milwaukee: G. Kroening, 1907. 1 fiche – 9 – us A.T.L.A. [240]
"DASEIN HEISST EINE ROLLE SPIELEN" : STUDIEN ZUR DEUTSCHEN LITERATURGESCHICHTE / Burger, Heinz Otto – (Includes bibliographical references) – Muenchen: C Hanser Verlag, c1963 – 1r – 1 – us U.W. Library [430]
DASEINSANGST ALS URSPRUNG MENSCHLICHEN FEHLVERHALTENS / Schumacher, Stefan – 1992 – 107p – 9 – DM98.00 – 3-89349-562-2 – gw Hänsel [150]
Dasent, A I *see* THE SPEAKERS OF THE HOUSE OF COMMONS FROM THE EARLIEST TIMES TO THE PRESENT DAY
Dashar, M *see* THE REVOLUTIONARY MOVEMENT IN SPAIN
Dashkevich, Leonid Viacheslavovich *see*
- GOSUDARSTVENNYE IZBIRATELNYE ZAKONY
- REFORMA VOLOSTI

Daskova, E R *see* ZAPISKI
Dasmann, R F *see* PLANET IN PERIL?
THE DASSENAIKE FAMILY OF HAPITIGAM KORALE / Dassenaike, Louis Arthur – Colombo: Colombo Apothecaries, 1923 – 1 – us Res Libr [950]
Dassenaike, Louis Arthur *see* THE DASSENAIKE FAMILY OF HAPITIGAM KORALE
Dassler, Charles Frederick William *see* DASSLER'S BOOK OF FORMS, AND CONVEYANCERS' MANUAL
DASSLER'S BOOK OF FORMS, AND CONVEYANCERS' MANUAL / Dassler, Charles Frederick William – Topeka, Kan., Crane, 1894. 446 p. LL-768 – 1 – us L of C Photodup [340]
Dasta Notes Staff *see* TELESALES SCRIPT PRESENTATIONS DIRECTORY
DASTAN HAZRAT AMIR HAMZAH RAZI ALLAH ANAH KI – Bamba'i: Khoja, Khanmahamui Rahm, 1269 A H [1852?]. v2-4 – 1r – us Res Libr [956]
DATA ARCHIVES FOR THE SOCIAL SCIENCES : PURPOSES, OPERATIONS AND PROBLEMS – 1973 – 126p – 9 – 92-3-101052-2 – fr UNESCO [301]
DATA BOOK OF THE NOLACHUCKY BAPTIST ASSOCIATION / Reeves, Thomas H – Morristown, Tennessee. 1914. 242p – 1 – 8.47 – us Baptist [240]
DATA CHANNELS – (v.6 .1979 5,6,9) – v.1. 1975 – 1 – us UMI [073]
DATA COMMUNICATIONS – v1- 1972- 1; v3-6; v4- 1975- 9 – us UMI [621]
DATA FROM HIS PAPERS ON BAPTIST INTERNATIONAL YOUTH CONFERENCE, 1931-1947 / Leavell, Frank H – 1 – $5.00 – us Baptist [240]
DATA INPUT FOR PUBLISHERS. STATE OF THE ART REPORT / Buckland, Lawrence F – ED 244-594 – 9 – 0.91 – us EDRS [070]
DATA MANAGEMENT – Superseded by DM Data Management – v1-12 1963-74 1; v7-5,6; v13- 9 – us UMI [650]
DATA NEEDS FOR ASSESSING THE NUTRITIONAL EFFECTS OF AGRICULTURAL AND RURAL DEVELOPMENT PROJECTS : A PAPER FOR PROJECT PLANNERS – 1983 – 68p – it F.A.O. [640]
Data Notes Staff *see*
- BREAD PUDDING ENCYCLOPEDIA
- INCORPORATING FORM SAMPLES OR INFORMATION FOR THE 50 STATES
- INCORPORATING IN THE CAYMAN ISLANDS, UNITED KINGDOM, HONG KONG, DELAWARE AND OTHERS

THE DATA OF ETHICS / Spencer, Herbert – 1907. 270p. 1 fiche (24x) – 9 – 1.00f – at Libertarian Micro [320]
THE DATA OF ETHICS / Spencer, Herbert – New York: Hurst, [1879?] – 1mf – 9 – 0-8370-6411-2 – 1986-0411 – us A.T.L.A. [170]
THE DATA OF JURISPRUDENCE / Miller, William G – Edinburgh/London: William Green & Sons, 1903 – 6mf – 9 – $9.00 – LLMC 95-174 – us L.L.M.C. [340]
THE DATA OF MODERN ETHICS EXAMINED / Ming, John Joseph – (Includes bibliographical references) – New York: Benziger, 1894 – 1mf – 9 – 0-8370-6284-5 – 1986-0284 – us A.T.L.A. [170]
DATA ON FISHING VESSELS AND GEAR IN THE MEDITERRANEAN – 1977 rev ed 1986 – 188p – it F.A.O. [639]
DATA SHEETS TO MICROFILMED CAPTURED GERMAN RECORDS / National Archives Trust Fund Board. Washington, D.C – 34r – 1 – T176 – us Nat'l Archives [350]
DATABASE PROJECT ON PALESTINIAN HUMAN RIGHTS – Chicago, Jerusalem. 53 docs. 1986-1990 – 54mf – 9 – ne IDC [320]
DATABASE PROJECT ON PALESTINIAN HUMAN RIGHTS *see* PALESTINE HUMAN RIGHTS INFORMATION CENTRE (PHRIC)
DATABASE TECHNOLOGY *see* INFORMATION SYSTEMS
DATA-BASED TEACHING IN THE SOCIAL SCIENCES – 1983 – 46p – 9 – 92-3-102113-3 – fr UNESCO [370]
DATABOOK ON ENDANGERED TREE AND SHRUB SPECIES AND PROVENANCES – 1986 – 540p – it F.A.O. [634]
DATAMATION – (v. 13- 1967- 5,6. v. 21-1975- 9) – v. 4- 1958- – 1 – us UMI [600]
DATANEWS – (1985-. 5,6,9) – 1976- – 1 – us UMI [510]
Date, Elizabeth *see* COMPARISON OF THE LOCATABILITY OF VOCALISATIONS OF BELL MINERS AND NOISY MINERS IN RELATION TO DIFFERENCES IN HABITAT
Date, Henry Harrington *see*
- LES DIALBES ROUGES
- SONG OF THE U.E. LOYALIST AND YORK PIONEER

DATE OF OUR GOSPELS IN THE LIGHT OF THE LATEST CRITICISM / Curtiss, Samuel Ives – Chicago: Revell, 1881. 1 fiche – 9 – us A.T.L.A. [240]
THE DATE OF OUR GOSPELS IN THE LIGHT OF THE LATEST CRITICISM / Curtiss, Samuel Ives – Chicago: F H Revell, 1881 – 1mf – 9 – 0-8370-2794-2 – 1985-0794 – us A.T.L.A. [220]
THE DATE OF THE EXODUS IN THE LIGHT OF EXTERNAL EVIDENCE / Jack, J W – T. & T. Clark, 1925 – 9 – $12.00 – us I.R.C. [270]
DATE PALM – Indio, CA. 1912-59 – 32r – 1 – $1,600.00 – R02305 – us Library Micro [071]
DATE PRODUCTION AND PROTECTION : WITH SPECIAL REFERENCE TO NORTH AFRICA AND THE NEAR EAST – 1982 – 313p – it F.A.O. [338]
Date, S R *see* BHAGANAGAR STRUGGLE
DATED EVENTS OF THE OLD TESTAMENT / Beecher, Willis Judson – Philadelphia: Sunday School Times, 1907.1 fiche – 9 – us A.T.L.A. [220]
THE DATED EVENTS OF THE OLD TESTAMENT : BEING A PRESENTATION OF OLD TESTAMENT CHRONOLOGY / Beecher, Willis Judson – (Includes appendix and index. Includes chronological tables comparing Near East events with Israelite history) – Philadelphia: Sunday School Times Company, c1907 – 1mf – 9 – 0-8370-2239-8 – 1985-0239 – us A.T.L.A. [220]
DATELINE WORLD JEWRY – (Missing: June 1990) – (New York, NY), May 1988-December 1993 – 25ft – us A.J.P.C. [270]
DATEN DEUTSCHER DICHTUNG : CHRONOLOGISCHER ABRISS DER DEUTSCHEN LITERATURGESCHICHTE VON DEN ANFAENGEN BIS ZUR GEGENWART / Frenzel, Herbert Alfred – (Includes index) – Koeln: Kiepenheuer & Witsch, [1959, c1953] – 1r – 1 – us U.W. Library [430]
DATES : HANDLING, PROCESSING AND PACKING / Dowson, VH W & Aten, A – 2nd printing 1978 – 392p – it F.A.O. [338]
DATES AND EVENTS / Spanish Committee in Defense of Democracy – Washington, DC, 1936? Fiche W1198. (Blodgett Collection of Spanish Civil War Pamphlets) – 9 – us H.U. College Libr [946]
THE DATES OF GENESIS : A COMPARISON OF THE BIBLICAL CHRONOLOGY WITH THAT OF OTHER ANCIENT NATIONS: WITH AN APPENDIX ON CHRONOLOGICAL ASTRONOMY / Jones, Frederick Augustus – London: Kingsgate Press, 1909 – 1mf – 9 – 0-8370-3795-6 – 1985-1795 – us A.T.L.A. [220]
DATES OF GENESIS: A COMPARISON / Jones, Frederick Augustus – London: Kingsgate Press, 1909. 1 fiche – 9 – us A.T.L.A. [240]
Dati, C R *see* VITE DE PITTORI ANTICHI...
DIE DATIERUNG DER PSALMEN SALOMOS: EIN BEITRAG ZUR JUEDISCHEN GESCHICHTE / Frankenberg, Wilhelm – Giessen: J. Ricker, 1896. 1 fiche – 9 – us A.T.L.A. [220]
Datillo, John P *see* ATTITUDES OF THERAPEUTIC RECREATION PROFESSIONALS TOWARD PERSONS WITH AIDS AND THE RELATIONSHIP OF THEIR ATTITUDE TO THEIR KNOWLEDGE OF AIDS
DATO Y SU VIDA : NOTAS RECOPILADAS / Peris, Ramon – Madrid: Razon y Fe, 1926 – 1 – sp Bibl Santa Ana [324]
DATOS ESTADISTICOS / Argentine Republic. Direccion de Economica Rural y Estadistica – 2v. 1898-1900 – 1 – 23.00 – us L of C Photodup [310]
DATOS INEDITOS PARA LA BIOGRAFIA DEL CAPITAN ARMANDO DE MONTENEGRO, COMPANERO DE PIZARRO EN LA CONQUISTA DEL PERU / Rafal, Marques de – Madrid: Tip. de Archivos, 1932. B.R.A.H. 100, pp.801-813 – sp Bibl Santa Ana [350]

DATOS INFORMATIVOS / Subsecretaria de turismo – Badajoz: Imp. Campini, 1964 – sp Bibl Santa Ana [338]
DATOS PARA EL ESTUDIO DE LAS ANTIGUEDADES DE MERIDA / Alvarez Saenz de Buruaga, Jose – Badajoz: Imprenta Provincial, 1950 – 1 – sp Bibl Santa Ana [946]
Datta, Surendra Kumar *see* THE DESIRE OF INDIA
Dattilo, John P *see* THE RELATIONSHIP BETWEEN SHARED FAMILY RECREATION TIME AND EXPRESSED PARENT-ADOLESCENT CONFLICT
DATUS / Finn, George – (A chronology of NZ from the time of the Moa. Account of important events in history from c925AD-1910) – 2mf – 9 – NZ$8.00 – 0-908797-13-3 – nz BAB [980]
Daubanton, L J M *see* DU DEPLACEMENT DE LA POPULATION DE PARIS
Daube, Anna *see* DER AUFSTIEG DER MUTTERSPRACHE IM DEUTSCHEN DENKEN DES 15. UND 16. JAHRHUNDERTS
Daube, D *see* STUDIES IN BIBLICAL LAW
Daube, J F *see*
- ANLEITUNG ZUR ERFINDUNG DER MELODIE UND IHRER FORTSETZUNG...ERSTER [ZWEYTER] THEIL
- GENERAL-BASS IN DREY ACCORDEN
- DER MUSIKALISCHE DILLETTANT

Daube, Julie *see* LA FEMME PAUVRE AU XIXE SIECLE
Daubigny, Eugene *see* CHOISEUL ET LA FRANCE D'OUTRE-MER APRES LE TRAITE DE PARIS: ETUDE SUR LA POLITIQUE COLONIALE AU XVIIIE SIECLE, AVEC UN APPENDICE SUR LES ORIGINES DE LA QUESTION DE TERRE-NEUVE
Daubney, William Heaford *see*
- USE OF THE APOCRYPHA IN THE CHRISTIAN CHURCH
- THE USE OF THE APOCRYPHA IN THE CHRISTIAN CHURCH

Dauchy, Luc J E *see* STATISTIQUE DU DEPARTEMENT DE L'AISNE
Daudet, E *see* VINGT-CINQ ANS A PARIS (1826-1850)
Daudin, F M *see* HISTOIRE NATURELLE, GENERALE ET PARTICULIERE DES REPTILES
DIE DAUER DER OEFFENTLICHEN WIRKSAMKEIT JESU / Fendt, Leonhard – Muenchen: J.J. Lentner, 1906. 1 fiche – 9 – us A.T.L.A. [240]
DIE DAUER DER OEFFENTLICHEN WIRKSAMKEIT JESU / Zellinger, Johann B – (Includes bibliographical references and index) – Muenster i.W.: Aschendorff, 1907 – 1mf – 9 – 0-8370-9356-2 – 1986-3356 – us A.T.L.A. [240]
A DAUGHTER OF HETH : A NOVEL / Black, William – London: Sampson Low, Marston, Searle & Rivington, 19th ed 1885 – 1 roll – 1 – 1-55879-391-7 – uk Libr Preservation [830]
A DAUGHTER OF HETH: A NOVEL / Black, William – British Fiction Archive: Unit 4 – 9 – uk Bell [830]
A DAUGHTER OF TODAY: A NOVEL / Duncan, Sara Jeannette – By Mrs. Everard Cotes. Toronto: Toronto News, 1894. 05291. (Pre-1900 Canadiana) – 9 – cn C.I.H.M. [830]
DAUGHTERS OF AMERICA, OR, WOMEN OF THE CENTURY / Hannaford, Phebe Ann Coffin – 1883 – 9 – us A.T.L.A. [240]
Daughters of American Revolution. Kansas City Chapter *see* VITAL HISTORICAL RECORDS OF JACKSON COUNTY
DAUGHTERS OF SARAH – (1985-. 5,6,9) – v1- 1974- – 1 – us UMI [640]
DAUGHTERS OF SARAH – v3-13. 1977-87 (incomplete) – 2r – 1 – ATLA S0468 – us A.T.L.A. [240]
Daughters of the American Revolution *see*
- CATALOGUE OF THE GEORGIA SOCIETY D.A.R. LIBRARY
- HISTORICAL COLLECTIONS OF THE GEORGIA CHAPTERS
- LINEAGE BOOK OF THE NATIONAL SOCIETY

DAUGHTERS OF VIENNA / Adolph, Karl – London, New York: The International Editor, c1922 – 1r – 1 – us U.W. Library [430]
Daukes, Wilfred H *see* ANGLO-INDONESIAN PLANTATIONS
Daulay, Is *see* DARAH, KERINGAT DAN AIRMATA; KUMPULAN KISAH-PERANG
Daulby, D *see* A DESCRIPTIVE CATALOGUE OF THE WORKS OF REMBRANDT, AND HIS SCHOLARS, BOL, LIEVENS AND VAN VLIET,...
Dauley, Patricia A *see* THE EFFECTS OF ACUTE EXERCISE OF VARYING INTENSITIES ON SUBJECTS WITH TYPE 1 DIABETES MELLITUS
Daum, H *see* ZIVILE RECHTSHILFEERSUCHEN...
Daumas, F *see* RELATION D'UN VOYAGE D'EXPLORATION AU NORD-EST DE LA COLONIE DU CAP DU BONNE-ESPERANCE EN 1836
Daumas, Gal Eugene *see* LE GRAND DESERT, OU ITINERAIRE D'UNE CARAVANE DU SAHARA AU PAYS DES NEGRES...
Daunou, Pierre Claude Francois *see* PLAN D'EDUCATION, PRESENTE A L'ASSEMBLEE NATIONALE, AU NOM DES INSTITUTEURS PUBLICS DE L'ORATOIRE
Dauphin, B P *see* EMISSION ET CIRCULATION DES TITRES DE SOCIETES ETRANGERES EN FRANCE
Dauphin-Tinturier, A M *see*
- LE PERSONNAGE DU LION A TRAVERS QUELQUES CONTES BEMBA RECUEILLIS DANS LA (LUAPALA PROVINCE) ET LA (NORTHERN PROVINCE) (ZAMBIE)
- PIEGE POUR UN LION

Daurets, N P *see* SEMENOVSKIE ZASTENKI
Daurignac, J M S *see* HISTOIRE DU BIENHEUREUX PIERRE CLAVER DE LA COMPAGNIE DE JESUS
Daus, E *see* DIE LUFTSCHIFFAHRT...
Dauth, Gaspard *see* LE DIOCESE DE MONTREAL A LA FIN DU DIX-NEUVIEME SIECLE
Dautriche, Gregoire *see* LE PROCES DAUTRICHE
Dauvin, J C *see* DYNAMIQUE D'ECOSYSTEMES MACROBENTHIQUES DES FONDS SEDIMENTAIRES DE LA BAIE DE MORLAIX ET LEUR PERTURBATION PAR LES HYDROCARBURES DE L'AMOCO CADIZ
Dauzat, A *see* DU ROLE DES CHAMBRES...
Dauzats, Andre *see*
- ELEMENTS DE LANGUE PEULE DU NORD-CAMEROUN
- LEXIQUE FRANCAIS-PEUL ET PEUL-FRANCAIS

Daval, Nicola *see* THE SUM OF THE PARTS: SHARING THE RESPONSIBILITY FOR BIBLIOGRAPHIC CONTROL
DAVAR – 1979- – 6mf per y – 9 – $430.00y – us Ross [072]
DAVAR / Achdut Haawoda Poale Zion/ Histradut – Tel Aviv, 1925-76 – 1,9 – BJ-91-94 3 – ne IDC [072]
DAVAR / Achdut Haawoda Poale Zion/ Histradut – Tel Aviv. nos 1-89. 1929-31 (Engl suppl) – 1 – us Hoover Inst Photo [072]
DAVAR = THE WORD – (In Hebrew) – Tel-Aviv, IS. v23 no6946. 16 May 1948 (Birth of Israel Issue) – 1r – 1 – $25.00 – cn Can Microfilming [072]
DAVAR LAGOLA = WORD TO THE DIASPORA – (In Hebrew. Weekly suppl) – Tel-Aviv, IS. v1 no35 27 Sep 1939-v2 no79 31 Jul 1940 – 1r – 1 – $35.00 – cn Can Microfilming [072]
DAVAR LATZOFEH – New York, NY. Nov 1945-Jun 1946 – 1 – us A.J.P.C. [071]
DA'VAT AL-ISLAM – Bombay, India: Anjuman-i Da'vat al-Islam. Sal-i 1, shumarah-'i 1-24 (Ramazan 1324-Sha'ban 1325 [Oct 1906-Sep 1907]) – 1 reel – 1 – $35.00 – us MEDOC [950]
Davatts, Vladimir Khristianovich *see*
- GODY
- NA MOSKVU
- RUSSKAIA ARMIIA NA CHUZHBINIE

Davaux, J B *see*
- QUATUOR CONCERTANS, TROIS, OP. 17
- QUINTETTOS, SIX, OP. 9

Davenant, C *see* ESSAYS UPON:...
Davenant, John *see* A TREATISE ON JUSTIFICATION, OR THE DISPUTATIO DE JUSTITIA HABITUALI ET ACTUALI
Davenport, Mrs. *see* JOURNAL OF A FOURTEEN DAYS' RIDE THROUGH THE BUSH FROM QUEBEC TO LAKE ST JOHN
Davenport, Charles Benedict *see* BODY-BUILD AND ITS INHERITANCE
DAVENPORT DUNN : A MAN OF OUR DAY / Lever, Charles James – London: Chapman and Hall, 1859 – 1 roll – 1 – 1-55879-842-0 – uk Libr Preservation [920]
Davenport, Frances G *see*
- GUIDE TO THE MANUSCRIPT MATERIALS FOR THE HISTORY OF THE UNITED STATES TO 1783 IN THE BRITISH MUSEUM, MINOR LONDON ARCHIVES AND THE LIBRARIES OF OXFORD AND CAMBRIDGE
- GUIDE TO THE MANUSCRIPT MATERIALS FOR THE HISTORY OF THE UNITED STATES TO 1793, IN THE BRITISH MUSEUM, IN MINOR LONDON ARCHIVES, AND IN THE LIBRARIES OF OXFORD AND CAMBRIDGE

Davenport, Frederick Morgan *see*
- PRIMITIVE TRAITS IN RELIGIOUS REVIVALS
- PRIMITIVE TRAITS IN RELIGIOUS REVIVALS: A STUDY IN MENTAL AND SOCIAL EVOLUTION

Davenport, Iowa *see* MISCELLANEOUS EARLY NEWSPAPERS
DAVENPORT IOWA, PAST & PRESENT; INCLUDING THE EARLY HISTORY & PERSONAL & ANECDOTAL REMINISCENCES OF DAVENPORT – By Franc B. Wilkie. 1858. Biog. & hist. sketches. 6 fiches. F-0140 – 9 – us A.G.L.L. [920]
Davenport, John M *see* PAPAL INFALLIBILITY: "CATHOLIC'S REPLIES TO 'CIEOPHAS,' REFUTING THE VATICAN DOGMA: WITH PREFACE AND COPIOUS APPENDIX
DAVENPORT LANCET – Davenport, NE. -w. Jul. 1888-Jan. 1891 – 1 – us NE Hist [071]
Davenport, Montague *see* UNDER THE GRIDIRON: A SUMMER IN THE UNITED STATES AND THE FAR WEST, INCLUDING A RUN THROUGH CANADA
DAVENPORT NEWS – Davenport, NE. -w. Aug. 1951-Jul. 1953 – 1 – us NE Hist [071]
DAVENPORT PAST AND PRESENT / Wilkie, Franc Bangs – Davenport: Luse, Lane & Co., 1858. Iowa Reel 37. (The Cox Library Collection) – 5 – us Americana [978]
DAVENTRIAE ILLUSTRATAE SIVE HISTORIAE URBIS DAVENTRIENSIS, LIBRI SEX / Revius, J – Lugduni Batavorum, 1651 – Dfl60.00 – ne Slangenburg [240]
Davesne, Andre *see* CROQUIS DE BROUSSE
Davey, F H *see* A TENTATIVE LIST OF THE FLOWERING PLANTS, FERNS, ETC., KNOWN TO OCCUR IN. CORNWALL, INCLUDING THE SCILLY ISLES
DAVEY MIRROR – Davey, NE, -w. Dec. 1892; Oct. 1894; Dec. 1895-Jul. 1899; Mar. 1908-Dec. 1921 – 1 – us NE Hist [071]
Davey, William G *see* A VALIDATION STUDY OF THE Q-PLEX 1 CARDIOP-ULMONARY EXERCISE SYSTEM
Davey, William Harrison *see* ARTICULI ECCLESIAE ANGLICANAE
David, A *see* LES OISEAUX DE LA CHINE
THE DAVID BAILIE WARDEN PAPERS / ed by Marks, Bayly Ellen – (Guide sold separately $10.00) – 1972 – 8r – 1 – $680.00 – S1623 – us Scholarly Res [360]
DAVID BAPTIST CHURCH. KINGS MOUNTAIN, NORTH CAROLNA : CHURCH RECORDS – 1938-63 – 1 – 5.00 – us Baptist [240]
David ben Joseph Kimhi *see* SEFER HA-SHORASHIM
DAVID BEN-GURION: 1886-1973 / Israel. Jerusalem Municipality – An exhibition on his life and deeds. Binyanei Ha'Ooma. 47 p – 9 – 2.00 – is I.T.T.I. [920]
DAVID BRAINERD, THE APOSTLE TO THE NORTH AMERICAN INDIANS / Page, Jesse – 18–? – 1 – us A.T.L.A. [240]
DAVID CITY NEWS – David City, NE. -w. Sep. 1895-May 1901 – 1 – us NE Hist [071]
DAVID CITY TRIBUNE – David City, NE. -w. Jan. 1884-Nov. 1892. Incomplete – 1 – us NE Hist [071]
DAVID COBB PAPERS, 1708-1833 / Cobb, David – Massachusetts Historical Society – 3r – 1 – $230.00 – us UMI [920]
DAVID D'ASHBY AUTEUR MECONNU DES FAITS DES TARTARES / Brunel, C – In Romania. U 707. 1958 – 9 – ne IDC [920]
David, F *see* METHODE NOUVELLE OU PRINCIPES GENERAUX POUR APPRENDRE FACILEMENT LA MUSIQUE ET L'ART DE CHANTER
DAVID GEORGEN AUSZ HOLAND DESZ ERTZKAETZERS WARHAFFTIGE HISTORI, SEINES LEBENS, VNND VERFUERISCHEN LEER – Basel, H. Curio. 1559. BME-265 1 – 9 – ne IDC [240]
DAVID, HOY / Aradillas Agudo, Antonio – Madrid: Ediciones Studium, 1963 – 1 – sp Bibl Santa Ana [946]
DAVID HUDSON FAMILY PAPERS *see* HUDSON, DAVID, FAMILY PAPERS, MS 3893
DAVID HUME / Calderwood, Henry – Edinburgh: Oliphant Anderson & Ferrier, (1898?) – 1mf – us A.T.L.A. [190]
DAVID HUNTER MILLER PAPERS – (Legal adviser to American Commission to Negotiate Peace and to post-World War I German Government) – 6r – 9 – $440.00 – us UMI [920]
David, I *see* OCCASIO ARREPTA, NEGLECTA, HUIUS COMMODA; ILLIUS INCOMMODA
David, J *see*
- CHRISTELIICKEN WAERSEGGHER, DE PRINCIPALE STUCKEN VAN T'CHRISTEN GELOOF EN LEVEN INT CORT BEGRIJPENDE
- VERIDICUS CHRISTIANUS

David, Jakob Julius *see* ANZENGRUBER
DAVID JORIS / Burckhardt, P – Basel. 1900. BME-426 1 – 9 – ne IDC [240]
DAVID JORIS VON DELFT. SEIN LEBEN, SEINE LEHRE UND SEINE SECTE / Nippold, Friedrich – Gotha. 1863-1864. BME-422 1 – 9 – ne IDC [240]
DAVID JORIS. WIEDERTAEUFER UND KAEMPFER FUER TOLERANZ IM 16. JAHRHUNDERT / Bainton, R H – (Archiv fuer Reformationsgeschicht; Ergaenzungro). Leipzig. 1937. BME-392 1 – 9 – ne IDC [240]
DAVID JORIS WT HOLLANDT DES ERTZKETTERS WAERAFFTIGHE HISTORIE – 1559. BME-266 1 – 9 – ne IDC [240]
David, Laurent Oliver *see*
- LE BIEN PUBLIC
- LA TRIBUNE

David, Laurent Olivier *see*
- BIOGRAPHIE AVEC PORTRAIT DE M. L'ABBE MERCIER
- LE CLERGE CANADIEN: SA MISSION, SON OEUVRE
- LE COLONEL C. M. DE SALABERRY
- LES DEUX PAPINEAU
- L'HONORABLE LS. JOSEPH PAPINEAU
- MES CONTEMPORAINS
- LES PATRIOTES DE 1837-1838
- LES PATRIOTES DE 1837-38
- L'UNION DES DEUX CANADAS, 1841-1867

David, M *see* DIE ADOPTION IM ALTBABYLONISCHEN RECHT
DAVID OU L'HISTOIRE DE L'HOMME SELON LE COEUR DE DIEU – (D'Holbach Series). 1768 – 9 – fr Hachette [190]
DAVID OUTLAW PAPERS / Outlaw, David – 1847-66. University of North Carolina Library. Guide – 1 – $18.00 – us U.N.C. Southern Hist [920]
David, P *see* LES MONASTERES DU DIOCESE DE GRENOBLE A L'EPOQUE MEROVINGIENNE
David, R P F *see* LA PECHE MARITIME...
THE DAVID ROBISON COLLECTION OF MATERIALS RELATED TO THE WAR IN THE SOUTHERN SUDAN – Chicago: U of Chicago, Photodup Dep, 1972 (mf ed) – us Res Libr [355]
David, Siegfried *see* AUGUST WILHELM IFFLANDS SCHAUSPIELKUNST BIS ZUM ABSCHLUß DER MANNHEIMER ZEIT (1796)
DAVID WORTHINGTON SIMON : M.A., PH.D. (TUEBINGEN) D.D. (EDINBURGH)... / Powicke, Frederick J – London, New York: Hodder and Stoughton, [1912?] – 1mf – us A.T.L.A. [240]
DAVID ZEISBERGER'S HISTORY OF THE NORTHERN AMERICAN INDIANS / ed by Schwarze, William Nathaniel & Schwarze, Hulbert – [Columbus?]: Ohio State Archaeological and Historical Society, [1910?] – 1mf – us A.T.L.A. [305]
Davidenko, Vasilii *see* SOVREMENNOE SOSTOYANIE RAKOLO SEKTANTSTVA V KHARKOVSKOI EPARKII
Davidenkova, N K *see* SPRAVOCHNIK. ESTESTVENNYE I FIZIKOMATEMATICHESKIE NAUKI
DAVIDIS GEORGII HOLANDI HAERESIARCHAE UITA ET DOCTRINA – Basilaae, H. Cvrio. 1559. BME-264 1 – 9 – ne IDC [240]
DAVIDIS REGIS...PSALMI / Arias Montano, Benito – 1574 – 9 – 1.50f – sp Bibl Santa Ana [240]
DE DAVID-JORISCHEN GHEEST IN LEVEN ENDE LEERE, S'-GRAVENHAGE / Emmius, Ubbo – Hillebrandt Jacobszoon. 1603. BME-412 1 – 9 – ne IDC [240]
DER DAVID-JORITEN-PROZESS IN TOENNING 1642 / Hansen, R – Kiel. 1900. BME-425 1 – 9 – ne IDC [240]
DAVID'S BLESSED MAN, OR, A SHORT EXPOSITION ON THE FIRST PSALM / Smith, Samuel – Edinburgh: James Nichol, 1868. 1 fiche – 9 – us A.T.L.A. [240]
DAVID'S HARP NEW TUNES *see* HYMN AND TUNE COLLECTION FROM LIBRARY OF EDMOND D. KEITH

Davids, Thomas William *see* ANNALS OF EVANGELICAL NONCONFORMITY IN THE COUNTY OF ESSEX
Davidson, Alexander *see* A COMPLETE HISTORY OF ILLINOIS FROM 1673 TO 1873: EMBRACING THE PHYSICAL FEATURES OF THE COUNTRY, ITS EARLY EXPLORATIONS, ABORIGINAL INHABITANTS..
Davidson, Andrew Bruce *see*
- BIBLICAL AND LITERARY ESSAYS
- THE BOOK OF THE PROPHET EZEKIEL: IN THE REVISED VERSION
- THE BOOKS OF NAHUM, HABAKKUK AND ZEPHANIAH
- CALLED OF GOD
- A COMMENTARY, GRAMMATICAL AND EXEGETICAL, ON THE BOOK OF JOB, VOL 1
- THE EPISTLE TO THE HEBREWS
- HEBREW SYNTAX
- AN INTRODUCTORY HEBREW GRAMMAR
- OUTLINES OF HEBREW ACCENTUATION, PROSE AND POETICAL
- THE THEOLOGY OF THE OLD TESTAMENT

Davidson, Basil *see* THE AFRICAN AWAKENING
Davidson, Charles Peers *see* A COMPILATION OF THE STATUTES PASSED SINCE CONFEDERATION RELATING TO BANKS AND BANKING: GOVERNMENT AND OTHER SAVINGS BANKS, PROMISSORY NOTES AND BILLS OF EXCHANGE, AND INTEREST AND USURY IN NEW BRUNSWICK AND NOVA SCOTIA
Davidson, Dana *see* JOURNAL OF RELIGION IN DISABILITY AND REHABILITATION
DAVIDSON DISPATCH – Lexington. N.C. 1890-1902 – 1 – us UMI [071]
Davidson, Donna Morris *see* "THE MORRISES AS PIONEERS"
Davidson, G *see* THE ALASKA BOUNDARY
Davidson, George *see* THE ALASKA BOUNDARY
Davidson, Grace Gillan *see* EARLY RECORDS OF GEORGIA
Davidson, H S *see* DE LAGARDE'S AUSGABE DER ARABISCHEN UEBERSETZUNG DER GENESIS SEMITISTISCHE STUDIEN
Davidson, I *see* PARODY IN JEWISH LITERATURE
Davidson, John *see*
- BALLADS AND SONGS
- A SECOND SERIES OF FLEET STREET ECLOGUES
- THE TESTAMENT OF JOHN DAVIDSON

Davidson, Judson France *see* MUSE WHANGS: POEMS, AMOROUS, BACCHANALIAN, POLITICAL, MEMORIAL, HUMOROUS AND MISCELLANEOUS
Davidson, Randall Thomas *see*
- CAPTAINS AND COMRADES IN THE FAITH
- THE CHARACTER AND CALL OF THE CHURCH OF ENGLAND
- THE CHRISTIAN OPPORTUNITY
- KIKUYU
- THE LAMBETH CONFERENCES OF 1867, 1878, AND 1888

Davidson, Robert *see*
- HISTORY OF THE PRESBYTERIAN CHURCH IN THE STATE OF KENTUCKY
- LECTURES ON GRAMMAR, RHETORIC

Davidson, Samuel *see*
- AUTOBIOGRAPHY AND DIARY OF SAMUEL DAVIDSON, WITH AN ACCURATE ACCOUNT OF THE CONTROVERSY OF 1857
- THE CANON OF THE BIBLE
- DOCTRINE OF THE LAST THINGS CONTAINED IN THE NEW TESTAMENT
- AN INTRODUCTION TO THE NEW TESTAMENT
- AN INTRODUCTION TO THE STUDY OF THE NEW TESTAMENT
- THE TEXT OF THE OLD TESTAMENT CONSIDERED
- VORLESUNGEN UEBER DIE APOKALYPSE

Davidson, Thomas *see* GIORDANO BRUNO AND THE RELATION OF HIS PHILOSOPHY TO FREE THOUGHT; A LECTURE...NEW YORK LIBERAL CLUB, OCT. 30, 1885
Davidson, W *see* UEBER DIE BUERGERLICHE VERBESSERUNG DER JUDEN
Davidsson, Ake *see* MUSICOLOGY GENERAL CATALOGUE
Davidts, Hermann *see* DIE ERSTLINGSNOVELLEN HEINRICH VON KLEIST
Davie, John G *see* INTRODUCTION TO THE SOLUTION OF THE PROBLEMS OF THE PYRAMID
Davies, Charles Maurice *see*
- HETERODOX LONDON, OR, PHASES OF FREE THOUGHT IN THE METROPOLIS
- MYSTIC LONDON, OR, PHASES OF OCCULT LIFE IN THE METROPOLIS

Davies, Courtney C *see* A STUDY OF THE RELATIONSHIP BETWEEN SELFREPORTED STRESS-RELATED PHYSICAL SYMPTOMOLOGY AND SPIRITUAL WELLNESS
Davies, Edward Owen *see*
- PROLEGOMENA TO SYSTEMATIC THEOLOGY
- THEOLOGICAL ENCYCLOPAEDIA

Davies, Gerald Stanley *see* ST. PAUL IN GREECE
Davies, H W *see* BERNHARD VON BREYDENBACH AND HIS JOURNEY TO THE HOLY LAND, 1843-4
Davies, J *see* DICTIONARIUM DUPLEX
Davies, J G *see* THE BIU BOOK
Davies, J Lewis O *see* BIBLE ENGLISH: CHAPTERS ON OLD AND DISUSED EXPRESSIONS IN THE AV
Davies, John *see*
- ANTIQUAE LINGUAE BRITANNICAE NUNC COMMUNITER
- ANTIQUAE LINGUAE BRITANNICAE, NUNC VULGO
- DAVIES' PATENT CASES

Davies, John B *see* ADDICTION RESEARCH
Davies, John Llewelyn *see*
- THE CHRISTIAN CALLING
- EPISTLES OF ST PAUL TO THE EPHESIANS, COLOSSIANS, AND PHILEMON

Davies, M J *see* A BIBLIOGRAPHY OF NINETEENTH-CENTURY LEGAL LITERATURE
Davies, Michael J *see* GENDER DIFFERENCES IN RUNNING ECONOMY
DAVIES' PATENT CASES : 1624-1816 (BRITISH AND AMERICAN) / Davies, John – London, 1816 (all publ) – 5mf – 9 – $7.50 – LLMC 84-324 – us L.L.M.C. [340]
Davies, Robert *see* EXTRACTS FROM THE MUNICIPAL RECORDS OF THE CITY OF YORK, DURING THE REIGNS OF EDWARD 4, EDWARD 5 AND RICHARD 3, WITH NOTES.
Davies, Roy *see* "MARCHING RULE"
Davies, S J J F *see* METHODS OF CENSUSING BIRDS IN AUSTRALIA
Davies, Samuel *see* SELECTED WORKS, MANUSCRIPT AND PUBLISHED
Davies, Stephen *see*
- AGAINST THE PROFESSIONS
- STUDIES OF THE BEHAVIOUR OF CERTAIN STREPTOPLIA DOVES AND THEIR HYBRIDS

Davies, Thomas Alfred *see*
- AM I A JEW OR GENTILE? READ AND SEE
- ANSWER TO HUGH MILLER AND THEORETIC GEOLOGISTS
- GENESIS DISCLOSED

Davies, Thomas Lewis Owen *see* BIBLE ENGLISH
Davies, Thomas Witton *see* EZRA, NEHEMIAH AND ESTHER
Davila, Andres *see*
- CONSULTA...SOBRE ASUNTO P. CACERES Y RESPUESTA DE ANDRES BARBOSA
- DASE CUENTA DEL ESTADO DE LO SUCEDIDO EN LOS PLEYTOS DE LA RELIGION DE NUESTRA PADRE S. GERONIMO DESDE 22 DE OCTUBRE DE 1641 HASTA 16 DE ABRIL DE 1642
- INFORME AJUSTADO AL NUNCIO POR PARTE DEL P. GENERAL (CACERES) EN EL PLEYTO CON LOS PADRES DIPUTADOS

Davila Garibi, Jose Ignacio *see* LA SOCIEDAD DE ZACATECAS EN LOS ALBORES DEL REGIMEN COLONIAL
Davila, Vicente *see*
- DON SANCHO BRICENO, SU MONUMENTO EN TRUJILLO. EL ARBOL DE LOS BRICENOS. CARACAS, 1929
- ENCOMIENDAS. TOMO 1. CARACAS, 1927
- INVESTIGACIONES HISTORICAS. TOMO 2. CARACAS, 1927

Davila y Figueroa, Marino *see* CATALOGO DE LAS OBRAS
Davila y Heredia, A *see* PARECER DE D. ANDRES DAVILA...QUE NO HAY MEDICINA UNIVERSAL...
Daviler *see* COURS D'ARCHITECTURE
Davin, Nicholas Flood *see*
- ALBUM VERSES AND OTHER POEMS
- IRELAND AND THE EMPIRE: A SPEECH DELIVERED BEFORE THE ST PATRICK'S SOCIETY, IN NORDHEIMER'S HALL, MONTREAL, ON ST PATRICK'S DAY, 1885
- THE IRISHMAN IN CANADA
- REMARKS SUGGESTED BY PRESIDENT GARFIELD'S DEATH
- SPEECH OF MR. N. F. DAVIN, M.P., ON HOME RULE FOR IRELAND, DELIVERED IN THE HOUSE OF COMMONS, OTTAWA, APRIL 22ND AND 26TH, 1887
- SPEECH OF N. F. DAVIN, M.P., ON THE ADDRESS, OTTAWA, FRIDAY 24TH MARCH, 1899
- SPEECH OF NICHOLAS FLOOD DAVIN, M.P., ON THE REVIEW OF THE FINANCIAL SITUATION: OTTAWA, TUESDAY, JULY 10, 1900
- SPEECH ON THE BUDGET: DELIVERED IN THE HOUSE OF COMMONS, JULY 22ND., 1891
- SPEECH ON THE BUDGET: DELIVERED IN THE HOUSE OF COMMONS, OTTAWA, MARCH 29TH, 1892
- "THE SPRINGS OF NATIONAL PROGRESS": A SPEECH IN THE OPERA HOUSE, BRANDON, FRIDAY, NOVEMBER 4TH, 1892, ON THE OCCASION OF A BANQUET TO THE HON. T. MAYNE DALY

Davis *see*
- THE ENCYCLOPEDIA OF TEXAS
- A HISTORY OF BLAIR COUNTY

Davis, Abraham N *see* PROTECTING THE LAMBS
Davis, Andrew Jackson *see* THE PRINCIPLES OF NATURE, HER DIVINE REVELATIONS, AND A VOICE TO MANKIND.
Davis, C K *see* LECUTRES ON INTERNATIONAL LAW
Davis, Carlyle C *see* OLDEN TIMES IN COLORADO
Davis, Charles F *see* MONROVIA BLUE BOOK
Davis, Cynthia M *see* THE RELATIONSHIP BETWEEN KNOWLEDGE AND EXPERTISE IN BREASTSTROKE SWIMMING
Davis, Daniel *see* A PRACTICAL TREATISE UPON THE AUTHORITY AND DUTY OF JUSTICES OF THE PEACE IN CRIMINAL PROSECUTIONS.
Davis, Douglas *see* RAGING INFLATION FORCES ISRAELI CURRENCY CHANGE
Davis, Ellis A *see* PACIFIC SOUTHWEST, DAVIS' COMMERCIAL ENCYCLOPEDIA
THE DAVIS ENTERPRISE – Davis, CA. 1898- – 229+ r – 1 – $11,450.00 ($400.00y) – B02164 – us Library Micro [071]
Davis, Frederick W *see* PREDICTORS OF OVERALL JOB SATISFACTION AMONG PUBLIC SCHOOL PHYSICAL EDUCATORS
Davis, G B *see*
- THE LAWS AND USAGES OF MARITIME WARFARE
- OUTLINES OF INTERNATIONAL LAW...

Davis, George B *see* THE ELEMENTS OF INTERNATIONAL LAW
Davis, George Edward *see* A HANDBOOK OF CHEMICAL ENGINEERING
Davis, George H *see* WATER AND ENERGY
Davis, George T B *see*
- DWIGHT L. MOODY
- TWICE AROUND THE WORLD WITH ALEXANDER, PRINCE OF GOSPEL SINGERS

Davis, George Thompson Brown *see* KOREA FOR CHRIST
Davis, H *see* AMONG THE WORLD'S PEACEMAKERS;...
Davis, J *see*
- HISTORY OF THE WELSH BAPTISTS, FROM THE YEAR 1763 TO THE YEAR 1770
- THE VOYAGES AND WORKS OF

Davis, J F *see*
- LA CHINE, OU DESCRIPTION GENERALE...
- THE CHINESE

Davis, Jefferson *see* PAPERS
Davis, John *see*
- NOSCE TE IPSUM
- PAPERS OF JOHN DAVIS
- THE POST-CAPTAIN; OR, THE WOODEN WALLS WELL MANNED, COMPREHENDING A VIEW OF NAVAL SOCIETY AND MANNERS

Davis, John A *see* CHOH LIN
Davis, John Chandler Bancroft *see* THE COMMITTEES OF THE CONTINENTAL CONGRESS, CHOSEN TO HEAR AND DETERMINE APPEALS FROM COURTS OF ADMIRALTY
Davis, John D *see* GENESIS AND SEMITIC TRADITION
DAVIS' LAND COURT CASES / Massachusetts. Supreme Court – 1v. 1898-1908 – 4mf – 9 – $6.00 – LLMC 84-158 – us L.L.M.C. [340]
Davis, Lynn M, Jr *see* DECADE OF PROGRESS
Davis, M *see*
- STOCHASTICS
- THOUGHTS ON DANCING OCCASIONED BY SOME LATE TRANSACTIONS AMONG THE PEOPLE CALLED METHODISTS

Davis, Minnie K *see* THE LOLLARD; A STORY OF THE WICLIFITES
Davis, Noah *see*
- CONCISE ACCOUNT OF THE LATE REV. NOAH DAVIS
- REPORT OF HON. NOAH DAVIS, REFEREE, TO THE SURROGATE'S COURT, CITY AND COUNTY OF NEW YORK, ON THE AMERICAN SURETY COMPANY, OF NEW YORK

Davis, Noah Knowles *see* ELEMENTS OF ETHICS
Davis, Ozora S *see*
- JOHN ROBINSON
- THE PILGRIM FAITH

Davis, Ozora Stearns *see* VOCABULARY OF NEW TESTAMENT WORDS
Davis, Robert Henry *see* THE CANADIAN MILITIA: ITS ORGANIZATION AND PRESENT CONDITION
Davis, Samuel T *see* CARIBOU SHOOTING IN NEW FOUNDLAND: WITH A HISTORY OF ENGLAND'S OLDEST COLONY FROM 1001 TO 1895
Davis, Stephen Brooks *see* THE LAW OF RADIO COMMUNICATION
Davis, T B *see* TORREY AND ALEXANDER
Davis, Thomas Osborne *see* LITERARY AND HISTORICAL ESSAYS
Davis, Warren Jefferson *see* PUTTING LAWS OVER WINGS
Davis, William J *see*
- A DICTIONARY OF THE KAFFIR LANGUAGE
- SACRAMENTO COUNTY

Davis, William Stearns *see* THE INFLUENCE OF WEALTH IN IMPERIAL ROME
Davis, William W *see*
- HISTORY OF BUCKS COUNTY
- HISTORY OF WHITESIDE COUNTY

Davis, Winfield J *see* HISTORY OF POLITICAL CONVENTIONS IN CALIFORNIA
Davison, Annie *see* GEORGIA BAPTIST ASSOCIATION
Davison, C S *see* THE FREEDOM OF THE SEAS
DAVISON INDEX – Flint. Mich. 1932-1969 – 1 – us UMI [071]
Davison, John *see* DISCOURSES ON PROPHECY
Davison, Newman and Co., Ltd *see* PAPERS
Davisson, William *see* LES ELEMENS DE LA PHILOSOPHIE DE L'ART DU FEU OU CHEMIE
Davitt, Michael *see* THE IRISH CAUSE: A LECTURE DELIVERED IN THE ADELAIDE STREET RINK, ON SATURDAY EVENING, NOVEMBER 20TH, 1886
Davity, Pierre *see* DESCRIPTION GENERALE DE L'AFRIQUE, SECOND PARTIE DU MONDE
Davoust, M *see* NOUVELLES DONNEES HISTORIQUES DANS L'EPIGRAPHIE MAYA
DAVUL – (In French and Ottoman) – Nos 1-24. – 1325 [1908/09] – 8mf – 9 – $42.00 – us MEDOC [870]
Davydova, Natalia *see* POLGODA V ZAKLI UCHENII
Dawani, Jalal-al-Din *see* PRACTICAL PHILOSOPHY OF THE MUHAMMADAN PEOPLE
Dawe, Charles G *see* ESSAYS AND SPEECHES
Dawkins, W B et al *see* A MONOGRAPH OF THE BRITISH PLEISTOCENE MAMMALIA
DAWN – A Baptist Magazine. Apr, Jul, Oct 1916, Jan 1917 – 1 – 5.00 – us Baptist [240]
DAWN – Blantyre: GrafoPrint Works, jul 27, aug 19/23, aug 31/sep 6-oct 24, dec 1 1995; apr 20-29 1996 – 1r – 1 – us Res Libr [072]
DAWN – Delhi, India. 26 Oct 1941-3 Sept 1947 – 13r – 1 – us L of C Photodup [072]
DAWN – Ellensburg. Wash. 1900-1913 – 1 – us UMI [071]
DAWN – Karachi: Pakistan Herald Press by A A Khan, 1951-66 – 1 – us Res Libr [072]
DAWN – Sydney, 1888-1905 – 3r – 1 – A$235.00 silver A$203.00 vesicular – at Pascoe [072]
DAWN *see*
- RASSVET (CHICAGO, ILL.)
- RASSVET (NEW YORK, N.Y.)

THE DAWN = AL-FAJR – (Missing: 1981(83, 84); 1982/1983(139); 1983(161); 1983/1984(191); 1984/1985(243); 1986(343-346); 1990, V.11) – Jerusalem, 1980(April 23)-1991. V.1-12. Index 1980-1985 – 11r – 1 – j-91-117/3 – ne IDC [072]
THE DAWN / ed by Butler, Josephine E – (Missing: 1895(28)) – London, 1888-1896 – 13mf – W-17/1 – ne IDC [073]

THE DAWN – v5-33. May 1934-Feb 1962 (complete) – 1r – 1 – ATLA S0524 – us A.T.L.A. [073]
DAWN BAPTIST CHURCH. DAWN, MISSOURI : CHURCH RECORDS – 1865-1968 – 1 – 15.30 – us Baptist [240]
DAWN GINSBURGH'S REVENGE / Perelman, Sidney Joseph – New York: H. Liveright, (c1929).viii,11+239p. Illus. 1 reel.1285 – 1 – us U.W. Library [830]
DAWN IN THE DARK CONTINENT : OR, AFRICA AND ITS MISSIONS / Stewart, James – (Includes bibliographical references and index) – Edinburgh: Oliphant Anderson & Ferrier, 1903 – 1mf – 9 – 0-8370-6618-2 – 1986-0618 – us A.T.L.A. [240]
THE DAWN OF CHRISTIANITY, OR, STUDIES OF THE APOSTOLIC CHURCH / Vedder, Henry Clay – Philadelphia: Amer. Bap. Pub. Soc., 1894. 1 fiche – 9 – us A.T.L.A. [240]
THE DAWN OF CIVILIZATION; EGYPT AND CHALDAEA / Maspero, Gaston – Ed. by A.H. Sayce, trans. by M.L. McClure. London: Society for Promoting Christian Knowledge; New York, Toronto: Macmillan Co., 1922. xiv,800p. illus.maps – 1 – us U.W. Library [900]
THE DAWN OF MAGIC / Pauwels, Louis – London: A. Gibbs & Phillips c1963 – 1 – us U.W. Library [150]
THE DAWN OF MODERN ENGLAND : BEING A HISTORY OF THE REFORMATION IN ENGLAND, 1509-1525 / Lumsden, Carlos B – London; New York: Longmans, Green, 1910 – 2mf – us A.T.L.A. [240]
THE DAWN OF THE CATHOLIC REVIVAL IN ENGLAND, 1781-1803 / Ward, Bernard – London, New York: Longmans, Green, 1909 – 2mf – us A.T.L.A. [240]
THE DAWN OF TOMORROW – the national Negro weekly devoted to the interests of the darker races. 1923-72 – 1 – 265.00 – cn McLaren [305]
DAWN ON THE HILLS OF T'ANG : OR, MISSIONS IN CHINA / Beach, Harlan Page – (Includes indexes) – New York: Student Volunteer Movement for Foreign Missions, 1898 – 1mf – 9 – 0-8370-6561-5 – 1986-0561 – us A.T.L.A. [240]
DAWN OVER THE BOLIVIAN HILLS / Dabbs, Norman H – 286p – 1 – 10.01 – us Baptist [240]
THE DAWN, SOCIALISM – Ilkeston, England. -m. Jan 1902-Feb 1905. 13 ft – 1 – uk British Libr Newspaper [072]
THE DAWNING OF MUSIC IN KENTUCKY, OR THE PLEASURES OF HARMONY IN THE SOLITUDE OF NATURE / Heinrich, Anthony Philipp – Opera prima. Philadelphia: Bacon & Hart, 1820. A miscellaneous collection of piano, vocal and instrumental music. MUSIC 136, Item 2 – 1 – us L of C Photodup [780]
DAWNINGS OF LIGHT IN THE EAST : WITH BIBLICAL, HISTORICAL, AND STATISTICAL NOTICES OF PERSONS AND PLACES VISITED DURING A MISSION TO THE JEWS, IN PERSIA, COORDISTAN, AND MESOPOTAMIA / Stern, Henry A – London: C.H. Purday, 1854 – 1mf – us A.T.L.A. [240]
Dawson, Aeneas McDonell *see*
– THE CATHOLICS OF SCOTLAND: FROM 1593, AND THE EXTINCTION OF THE HIERARCHY IN 1603, TILL THE DEATH OF BISHOP CARRUTHERS IN 1852
– DOMINION DAY: CARACTACUS, MALCOLM AND MARGARET POEMS
– THE LAST DEFENDER OF JERUSALEM
– ZENOBIA, QUEEN OF PALMYRA: A POEM
Dawson, Benjamin *see* PROLEPSIS PHILOLOGIAE ANGLICANAE
Dawson, Charles *see* PIONEER TALES OF THE OREGON TRAIL
Dawson, Christopher *see* LOS ORIGENES DE EUROPA. TRADUCCION DE FRANCISCO ELIAS DE TEJADA. MADRID, 1945
DAWSON COUNTY ENTERPRISE – Lexington, NE. -w. Oct-Nov 1895; May 1896-Jan 1897 – 1 – us NE Hist [071]
DAWSON COUNTY HERALD – Lexington, NE. -w. (-sw 1953-64). May 1902; Aug 1902-Oct 1904; Jan 1905-Dec 1915; Jan 1918 to date – 1 – us NE Hist [071]
DAWSON COUNTY PIONEER – Lexington, NE. -w. May 1874-Jun 1894, scattered issues missing; Aug 1895-Oct 1897; Jan-Aug 1898; Oct 1898-Aug 1900; Oct 1900-Aug 1903; Oct 1903; Jan 1904-Dec 1918; Feb 1920-Aug 1937 – 1 – us NE Hist [071]
DAWSON COUNTY REVIEW – Glendive. Mont. 1898-1921; 1926-1949 – 1 – us UMI [071]
DAWSON CREEK STAR – Dawson Creek, British Columbia, CN. Nov 1949-Nov 1962 – 9r – 1 – cn Commonwealth Micro [072]
Dawson, Francis Warrington *see* LETTERS
Dawson, George M *see*
– GLACIATION OF HIGH POINTS IN THE SOUTHERN INTERIOR OF BRITISH COLUMBIA
– NOTES ON THE COLES AND LIGNITES OF THE CANADIAN NORTH-WEST: CHIEFLY DERIVED FROM THE REPORTS OF THE GEOLOGICAL SURVEY OF CANADA
– NOTES ON THE LOCUST INVASION OF 1874, IN MANITOBA AND THE NORTH-WEST TERRITORIES
– NOTES ON THE OCCURENCE OF MAMMOTH-REMAINS IN THE YUKON DISTRICT OF CANADA AND IN ALASKA
– ON FORAMINIFERA FROM THE GULF AND RIVER ST LAWRENCE
– ON THE SUPERFICIAL GEOLOGY OF BRITISH COLUMBIA
– RAPP. SUR UN VOYAGE D'EXPL. FAIT DANS LA REGION DU YUKON. EN 1887
– REPORT ON THE CLIMATE AND AGRICULTURAL VALUE, GENERAL GEOLOGICAL FEATURES, AND MINERALS OF ECONOMIC IMPORTANCE OF PART OF THE NORTHERN PORTION OF BRITISH COLUMBIA, AND OF THE PEACE RIVER COMPANY
Dawson, Grace D *see* GERONTOLOGY AND GERIATRICS EDUCATION
DAWSON HERALD – Dawson, NE. -w. May 1921-Oct. 1947 – 1 – us NE Hist [071]
Dawson, J M *see* COLLECTION, FIVE NOTEBOOKS.
Dawson, John E *see* THE LIFE AND SERVICES OF JOHN E. DAWSON
Dawson, John William *see*
– ADDRESS TO THE BRITISH ASSOCIATION FOR THE ADVANCEMENT OF SCIENCE
– APPENDIX TO MEMORANDA OF JUNE, 1892, ON THE SUBJECT OF FREE TUITIONS IN THE FACULTY OF ARTS: EXEMPTIONS FROM FEES IN FAVOUR OF STUDENTS OF AFFILIATED THEOLOGICAL COLLEGES
– ASSOCIATION OF PROTESTANT TEACHERS OF THE PROVINCE OF QUEBEC: MONTREAL MEETING, 1886
– THE CANADIAN ICE AGE: BEING NOTES ON THE PLEISTOCENE GEOLOGY OF CANADA, WITH ESPECIAL REFERENCE TO THE LIFE OF THE PERIOD AND ITS CLIMATAL CONDITIONS
– THE CHAIN OF LIFE IN GEOLOGICAL TIME: A SKETCH OF THE ORIGIN AND SUCCESSION OF ANIMALS AND PLANTS
– THE CONSTITUTION OF MCGILL UNIVERSITY: BEING THE ANNUAL UNIVERSITY LECTURE IN THE SESSION OF 1888-89
– CONTINENTAL AND ISLAND LIFE, A REVIEW OF WALLACE: WITH REFERENCE TO THE BEARING OF GEOLOGICAL FACTS AND THEORIES OF EVOLUTION ON THE DISTRIBUTION OF LIFE
– EDEN LOST AND WON
– EGYPT AND SYRIA: THEIR PHYSICAL FEATURES IN RELATION TO BIBLE HISTORY
– FACTS AND FANCIES IN MODERN SCIENCE
– FOSSIL MEN AND THEIR MODERN REPRESENTATIVES: AN ATTEMPT TO ILLUSTRATE THE CHARACTERS AND CONDITIONS OF PRE-HISTORIC MEN IN EUROPE, BY THOSE OF THE AMERICAN RACES
– THE FUTURE OF MCGILL UNIVERSITY: ANNUAL UNIVERSITY LECTURE, SESSION 1880-81
– HANDBOOK OF GEOLOGY: FOR THE USE OF CANADIAN STUDENTS
– HANDBOOK OF ZOOLOGY: WITH EXAMPLES FROM CANADIAN SPECIES, RECENT AND FOSSIL: PART 1 – INVERTEBRATA
– THE HIGHER EDUCATION OF WOMEN, IN CONNECTION WITH MCGILL UNIVERSITY
– THE HISTORICAL DELUGE
– LOYALTY: A LETTER TO MCGILL STUDENTS FROM THE PRINCIPAL
– MCGILL UNIVERSITY: ANNUAL UNIVERSITY LECTURE OF THE SESSION 1884-5
– MEMORANDA AND STATEMENTS RELATING TO BENEFACTORS' EXEMPTIONS AND FREE TUITIONS TO THEOLOGICAL STUDENTS IN MCGILL UNIVERSITY
– MODERN IDEAS OF EVOLUTION AS RELATED TO REVELATION AND SCIENCE
– MODERN SCIENCE IN BIBLE LANDS
– NATURE AND THE BIBLE
– NOTES ON PREHISTORIC MAN EGYPT AND THE LEBANON: BEING A PAPER READ BEFORE A MEETING OF THE VICTORIA INSTITUTE, HELD AT THE HOUSE OF THE SOCIETY OF ARTS, MAY 6, 1884
– NOTES ON THE PHOSPHATES OF THE LAURENTIAN AND CAMBRIAN ROCKS OF CANADA
– NOTES ON THE POST-PLIOCENE GEOLOGY OF CANADA: WITH ESPECIAL REFERENCE TO THE CONDITIONS OF ACCUMULATION OF THE DEPOSITS AND THE MARINE LIFE OF THE PERIOD
– NOTES ON TREES ON THE GROUNDS OF MCGILL UNIVERSITY
– THE ORIGIN OF THE WORLD, ACCORDING TO REVELATION AND SCIENCE
– THE RELATION OF MCGILL UNIVERSITY TO LEGAL EDUCATION: LETTER
– RELICS OF PRIMEVAL LIFE: BEGINNING OF LIFE IN THE DAWN OF GEOLOGICAL TIME
– SCIENCE EDUCATION ABROAD: A LECTURE, BEING THE ANNUAL UNIVERSITY LECTURE OF THE SESSION 1870-71, DELIVERED IN THE WILLIAM MOLSON HALL, NOV. 18, 1870
– SOME SALIENT POINTS IN THE SCIENCE OF THE EARTH
– THE STORY OF THE EARTH AND MAN
– THE UNIVERSITY IN RELATION TO PROFESSIONAL EDUCATION: BEING THE ANNUAL UNIVERSITY LECTURE OF MCGILL UNIVERSITY, MONTREAL, IN THE SESSION OF 1887-8
Dawson, Miles M *see* ELEMENTS OF LIFE INSURANCE
DAWSON NEWS – Dawson, Canada. 1899-1954 – 76r – 1 – $4,940.00 – cn Library Assoc [971]
DAWSON NEWS BOY – Dawson, NE. -w. Jun. 1888-Sep. 1896. Incomplete; Nov. 1896-Apr. 1909 – 1 – us NE Hist [071]
Dawson, PK *see* EFFECTS OF TRAINING ON RESTING BLOOD PRESSURE IN MEN AT RISK FOR CORONARY HEART DISEASE
DAWSON REPORTER – Dawson, NE. -w. Jul. 1914-Apr. 1920 – 1 – us NE Hist [071]
Dawson, Samuel Edward *see*
– CHAMPLAIN
– THE DISCOVERY OF AMERICA BY JOHN CABOT IN 1497, BEING EXTRACTS FROM THE PROCEEDINGS OF THE ROYAL SOCIETY OF CANADA RELATIVE TO A CABOT CELEBRATION IN 1897
– HANDBOOK FOR THE CITY OF MONTREAL AND ITS ENVIRONS: WITH A PLAN OF THE CITY AND A GEOLOGICAL MAP OF THE SURROUNDING COUNTRY
– HAND-BOOK FOR THE DOMINION OF CANADA: PREPARED FOR THE MEETING OF THE BRITISH ASSOCIATION FOR THE ADVANCEMENT OF SCIENCE, AT MONTREAL, 1884
– A STUDY: WITH CRITICAL AND EXPLANATORY NOTES OF ALFRED TENNYSON'S POEM THE PRINCESS
– THE VOYAGES OF THE CABOTS IN 1497 AND 1498: WITH AN ATTEMPT TO DETERMINE THEIR LANDFALL AND TO IDENTIFY THEIR ISLAND OF ST JOHN
Dawson, Simon James *see* RAPPORT SUR L'EXPLORATION DE LA CONTREE SITUEE ENTRE LE LAC SUPERIEUR ET LA COLONIE DE LA RIVIERE ROUGE, ET ENTRE CE DERNIER ENDROIT ET LES RIVIERES ASSINIBOINE ET SASKATCHEWAN
DAWSON SPRINGS FIRST BAPTIST CHURCH. DAWSON SPRINGS, KENTUCKY : CHURCH RECORDS – November 1909-May 1989. 1,666p – 1 – $74.97 – us Baptist [240]
Dawson Turner, A M *see*
– FUCI SIVE PLANTARUM FUCORUM GENERI A BOTANIIS ASCRIPTARUM IEONES DESCRIPTIONES ET HISTORIA
– SYNOPSIS OF THE BRITISH FUCI
Dawson, Walter Robert *see* EQUIPPING THE LAITY AS WORSHIP LEADERS IN THE MINISTRY OF BIG BETHEL BAPTIST CHURCH
Dawson, William Bell *see* THE EASTERN CANAL OF FRANCE: FOR ESTABLISHING A LINE OF WATER COMMUNICATION FROM THE SAONE TO THE MEUSE
Dawson, William Francis *see* CHRISTMAS..
DAY – London, UK. 1809. -d. 2 1/2 reels – 1 – uk British Libr Newspaper [072]
DAY – London, UK. 19 Mar-4 May 1867. 1/2 reel – 1 – uk British Libr Newspaper [072]
DAY – New London. Conn. 1881- – 1 – us UMI [071]
THE DAY – New York, NY. 1914-57 – 1 – us A.J.P.C. [071]
THE DAY – New York. N.Y. Der tog. 1952-57 – 1 – us A.J.P.C. [071]
Day, A *see* A TREATISE ON HARMONY
Day, Angel *see* THE ENGLISH SECRETORIE
Day, Barbara Bruehl *see* THINKING AND DOING
DAY BOOK / Indian Home Guards. First Regiment – 1862-63 – 1 – us KS Hist [978]
DAY BOOK / Miami Trading Post – 1847-49 – 1 – us KS Hist [978]
THE DAY BOOK – (The Evening Day Book). New York. Jan 19-Dec 1852; Jan-Nov 1856; Jan-June, Oct-Dec 1857; Apr 1858-June 1860; and Jan-Aug 1861. Not collated – 1 – us NY Public [073]
DAY BOOK OF THE REGISTER'S OFFICE OF THE TREASURY, 1789-91 / U.S. Register of the Treasury – 1roll – 1 – T964 – us Nat'l Archives [336]
DAY CARE AND EARLY EDUCATION – v. 1-. 1973- – 1,5,6,9 – us UMI [370]
Day, Clarence B *see*
– CHINESE PEASANT CULTS
DAY DAWN IN AFRICA : OR, PROGRESS OF THE PROTESTANT EPISCOPAL MISSION AT CAPE PALMAS, WEST AFRICA / Scott, Anna Miller – New York: Protestant Episcopal Society for the Promotion of Evangelical Knowledge, 1858 – 1mf – 9 – 0-8370-6369-8 – 1986-0369 – us A.T.L.A. [240]
Day, F *see*
– THE FISHES OF GREAT BRITAIN AND IRELAND
– THE FISHES OF INDIA. BURMA AND CEYLON
– THE FISHES OF MALABAR
– THE SEA-FISHES OF INDIA AND BURMA
Day, Francis A *see* DIARY, MS P.P.
A DAY IN CAPERNAUM / Delitzsch, Franz – New York: Funk & Wagnalls, 1892.1 fiche – 9 – us A.T.L.A. [240]
DAY IN COURT : OR THE SUBTLE ARTS OF GREAT ADVOCATES / Wellmann, Francis L – New York: The Macmillan Co, 1910 – 3mf – 9 – $4.50 – LLMC 92-181 – us L.L.M.C. [340]
DAY IN COURT; OR, THE SUBTLE ARTS OF GREAT ADVOCATES / Wellman, Francis Lewis – New York, Macmillan, 1914. 257 p. LL-1568 – 1 – us L of C Photodup [340]
THE DAY JEWISH JOURNAL *see* THE DAY
Day, John *see* THE VALLEY PEOPLE
Day, Lal Behari *see* BENGAL MAGAZINE
Day, Mary A *see* LETTERS
DAY STAR – Cincinnati, OH. Feb 1845-Jul 1847 – 1 – us Western Res [071]
DAY STAR / Cincinnati, Ohio – (Publ as: Western Midnight Cry 1843-44) – Cincinnati, OH. 1843-47 – 1 – us Western Res [071]
Day, W A *see* THE RUSSIAN GOVERNMENT IN POLAND
Day, Warren *see* LETTERS
THE DAY WILL COME / Braddon, Mary Elizabeth – British Fiction Archive: Unit 5 – 9 – uk Bell [830]
THE DAYA-CRANA-SANGRAHA, AN ORIGINAL TREATISE ON THE HINDOO LAW OF INHERITANCE / Tarkalankara, Krsna – Calcutta, Pereira, 1818. 138 p. LL-29 – 1 – us L of C Photodup [340]
DAYBOOK / McClish Family – 1908-1922 – 1r – 1 – $32.50r – us Archival [920]
DAYBOOK / Western Bakery. Lawrence, Kansas – 1861 – 1 – us KS Hist [380]
DAYBOOK AND ACCOUNTS / Malpuss, Samuel – 1854-56, 1867-68. 5 fiches – 9 – us South Carolina Historical [025]
DAYBOOK OF THE DEPARTMENT OF STATE FOR MISCELLANEOUS AND CONTINGENT EXPENSES / U.S. Department of State – Feb 1, 1978 – Nov 3, 1980. 1 roll. T903 – 1 – us Nat'l Archives [975]
DAYBREAK: A POEM / Beck, George Fairley – Toronto, 1873. 03536. (Pre-1900 Canadiana) – 9 – cn C.I.H.M. [810]
DAYBREAK IN KOREA : A TALE OF TRANSFORMATION IN THE FAR EAST / Baird, Annie Laurie Adams – New York: Fleming H Revell, c1909 – 1mf – 9 – 0-8370-6642-5 – 1986-0642 – us A.T.L.A. [950]
DAYBREAK IN LIVINGSTONIA : THE STORY OF THE LIVINGSTONIA MISSION, BRITISH CENTRAL AFRICA / Jack, James W – Edinburg: Oliphant, Anderson & Ferrier, 1901 – 1mf – us A.T.L.A. [240]
DAYBREAK IN THE DARK CONTINENT / Naylor, Wilson Samuel – (Includes bibliographical references and index) – New York: Laymen's Missionary Movement, c1908 – 1mf – 9 – 0-8370-6286-1 – 1986-0286 – us A.T.L.A. [240]

DAYKIN HERALD – Daykin, NE. -w. May 1900-Mar. 1902; Aug. 1928; Oct. 1928-Dec. 1954 – 1 – us NE Hist [071]
Dayringer, Richard *see* AMERICAN JOURNAL OF PASTORAL COUNSELING
DAYS OF BLESSING IN INLAND CHINA : BEING AN ACCOUNT OF MEETINGS HELD IN THE PROVINCE OF SHAN-SI / Taylor, James Hudson – 2nd ed. London: Morgan & Scott, 1887 – 1mf – 9 – 0-8370-6533-X – 1986-0533 – us A.T.L.A. [240]
DAY'S REPORTS / Connecticut. Supreme Court – (A Pre-NRS title) – v1-5. 1830-1833 (all publ) – 30mf – 9 – $45.00 – LLMC 90-004 – us L.L.M.C. [340]
DAY-STAR – v. 8. 1845-1846 – 1 – us UMI [240]
Dayton, A C *see*
- GOSPEL HOLINESS
- HOW CHILDREN MAY BE BROUGHT TO CHRIST
- PERSEVERANCE OF ALL SAINTS

DAYTON HERALD – Dayton, OR. -w. 1893-1906 – 1 – 72.00 – us Oregon Hist [071]
DAYTON J.C.C. NEWS – (Vol. 27, no. 11 (1 July 1970); v. 28, no. 1 (1 Sept. 1970); v. 28, no 10 (1 June 1971); v. 28, no. 12 (2 Aug. 1971); comes on a reel with other titles) – Dayton, Ohio – 1 – us A.J.P.C. [978]
DAYTON JEWISH CHRONICLE – Dayton. Ohio. 1964-68 – 1 – us A.J.P.C. [071]
THE DAYTON JEWISH LIFE – Dayton, OH. 1918 – 1 – us A.J.P.C. [071]
Dayton. Presbytery (Pres. Ch. in the U.S.A.) *see* RECORDS, 1838-1917
DAYTON TRIBUNE – Dayton, OR. -w. 5 Jan 1912-. – 1 – us U.O. Library [071]
DAYTONA BEACH OBSERVER – Daytona Beach. Fla. Dec 1934-68, 1970-73 – 1 – us P.K. Yonge [071]
DAYTONA GAZETTE NEWS – Daytona Beach. Fl. -w. 1901- 1903, 1904-10, 1912, 1915 – 1 – us P.K. Yonge [071]
DAZHONG RIBAO – China. Mass Daily, Shandong ed.1939-42. M/B14 – 3r – 1 – $135.00 – cc Microforms [072]
DAZHONG RIBAO = POPULAR DAILY – (1980-1991 Consists of 1 reel for each year) – 1992- – $55.00r – cc Microforms [950]
DAZHONG SHENGHUO – Life of the Masses. -w. Nov 1935-36. 6 fiches. F C52 – 9 – $27.00 – cc Microforms [073]
d'Azyr, Felix Vicq *see* ENCYCLOPEDIE METHODIQUE
D.B. Lewis & Co *see* FEDERAL INCOME TAX RECORD FOR INDIVIDUALS
D.C. BAR JOURNAL *see* JOURNAL OF THE BAR ASSOCIATION OF THE DISTRICT OF COLUMBIA
DD – Mitteilungsblatt der Arbeitsgemeinschaft "Demokratisches Deutschland." Basel, Switzerland. Sept 1945-Jan 1949 – 1r – 1 – gw Mikrofilm [072]
D.D. BREVIS INTRODUCTIO IN HISTORIAM.. / Wallerius, Johan Gottschalk – Holmiae: In Officinis Libr. Reg. Ac. Biblop. M. Swederi, 1779. 194,(4)p. Bibliog. and index.1 reel. 1230 – 1 – us U.W. Library [500]
D.D. EISENHOWER HOME AND FAMILY / Endacott, J Earl – 1 – us KS Hist [920]
DDR: DREIHUNDERT FRAGEN, 300 ANTWORTEN / Germany. Democratic Republic. Ausschuss fuer Deutsche Einheit – Berlin, 1959. 223p. illus – 1 – us U.W. Library [943]
DDR-LANDTAGSPROTOKOLLE – (Sachsen Jun 1946-49. Mecklenburg Nov 1946-49. Brandenburg Nov 1946-49. Sachsen-Anhalt Nov 1946-48) – Thueringen, 21 Nov 1946-1948 – 4r – 1 – DM300.00 – gw Mikro Press [072]
DE 6 PERCUSSIONIS LIBER / Borelli, Giovanni Alfonso – Bologna, 1667. Ill. – 1 – us U.W. Library [530]
DE 1867 A 1871 – s.l.: s.n., 1872?. 03780. (Pre-1900 Canadiana) – 9 – cn C.I.H.M. [971]
DE AARONITICI SACERDOTII ATQUE THORAE ELOHISTICAE ORIGINE : DISSERTATIO HISTORICO-CRITICA / Curtiss, Samuel Ives – Lipziae [Leipzig]: J C Hinrichs, 1878 – 1mf – 9 – 0-8370-2795-0 – 1985-0795 – us A.T.L.A. [270]
DE ACCENTIBUS ET ORTHOGRAPHIA, LINGUAE HEBRAICAE / Reuchlin, J – 1518 – 9 – us Sibley [470]
DE ACIDO VEGETABILI / Scepin, C – Lugduni Batavorum. 1758. B-5711 2 – 8 – ne IDC [580]
DE AEDIFICIIS DN. IUSTINIANI LIBRI 6 (CBH 3,2) / Caesariensis, Procopii; ed by Maltret, C L – Parisiis, 1663 – Dfl25.00 – ne Slangenburg [930]
DE AEQUALITATE IN CONTRACTIBUS PRAESERTIM ONEROSIS... / Gendt, W G J van – Leiden, 1782 – 2mf – 1 – ILM-669/1 – ne IDC [327]
DE AETERNA PRAEDESTINATIONE FILIORVM DEI AD SALVTEM PROPOSITIONES THEOLOGICAE:... / Hunnius, A – Francoforti ad Moenvm, 1594 – 1mf – ne IDC [240]
DE AFFLICTIONE TAM CAPTIVORVM QUAM ETIAM SUB TURCAE TRIBUTO VIUENTIUM CHRISTIANORUM,... / Bartholomaeus, G – Antverpiae, 1544 – 1mf – 9 – H-8270/1 – ne IDC [956]
DE ALCAEI ET SAPPHONIS COPIA VOCABULORUM / Gerstenhauer, Arthurius – (Includes bibliographical references and index) – Halis Saxonum: Max Niemeyer, 1894 – 1mf – 9 – 0-8370-9286-8 – 1986-3286 – us A.T.L.A. [450]
DE ALEXANDRINAE INTERPRETATIONIS LIBRI DANIELIS / Bludau, August – Aschendorf: Monasterii Gueste, 1891. 1 fiche – 9 – us A.T.L.A. [240]
DE ALLII GENERE NATURALI LIBELLUS / Haller, Albrecht von – Gottingae. 1745. B-6190 2 – 8 – ne IDC [580]
DE AMICITIA, ETC / Cicero, Marcus Tullius – 15th cent. Holkham ms. 375, 383, 386. Holkham Hall, Norfolk, England – 1 – uk Microform Academic [760]
DE ANABAPTISMO / Wigandus, J – Lispiae, G. Defnerus. 1582. BME-238 1 – 9 – ne IDC [240]
DE ANIMA BRUTORUM / Willis, Thomas – M 423. 1672 – 9 – ne IDC [590]
DE ANNABAPTISMI EXORDIO, ERRORIBVS, HISTORIIS ABOMINANDIS / Gastius, I – Basiliae, R. Winter. 1544. BME-132 1 – 9 – ne IDC [240]
DE ANTIQUIS ECCLESIAE RITIBUS / Martene, Edmond – Antverpiae. v1-4. 1763-64 – 71mf – 8 – Dfl249.00 – ne Slangenburg [240]
DE ANTIQUIS MONACHORUM RITIBUS / Martene, Edmond – Antverpiae, 1764 – 20mf – 8 – Dfl70.00 – ne Slangenburg [240]
DE ANTIQUITATE BENEDICTINORUM IN REGNO ANGLIAE / Reynerus, Cl. OSB – Duaci, 1626 – Dfl91.00 – ne Slangenburg [240]
DE APELLIS GNOSI MONARCHICA : COMMENTATIO HISTORICA / Harnack, Adolf von – Lipsiae: E. Bidder, 1874 – 1mf – us A.T.L.A. [240]
DE AQUATILIBUS LIBRI DUO : CUM EICONIBUS AD VIVAM IPSORUM EFFIGIEM... / Bélon, P – Parisiis, 1553 – 12mf – 9 – ne IDC [610]
DE ARCANIS CATHOLICI VERITATIS LIBRI 12 / Galatinus, P – Barii, 1603 – 14mf – 8 – ne Slangenburg [240]
DE ARCHITECTURA / Vitruvio, M – SL, SA – 5mf – 9 – sp Cultura [720]
DE ARCHITECTURA, ALCALA DE HENARES, 1582 / Vitruvio, M – Alcala de Henares, 1582 – 7mf – 9 – sp Cultura [720]
DE ARK GODS : HET OUD-ISRAELITISCHE HEILIGDOM / Sevensma, Tietse Pieter – (In Dutch) – Amsterdam:J Clausen, 1908 – 1mf – 9 – 0-8370-5233-5 – 1985-3233 – us A.T.L.A. [220]
DE ARMIS ILLICITIS / Birckholtz, J G – Francofurti ad Viadrum, 1698 – 1mf – 9 – ILM-1122/1 – ne IDC [327]
DE ARMIS ROMANIS... / Gentili, A – Hanoviae, 1612 – 4mf – 1 – ILM-2590/1 – ne IDC [327]
DE ARTE CANENDI / Heyden, S – 1540 – 9 – us Sibley [780]
DE ARTE CHYMIAE SCRIPTA. CVI ACCESSERVNT OPUSCULA ALIA EIUSDEM AUTHORIS / Bacon, Roger – Francofurti, 1603 – 1 – us U.W. Library [540]
DE ARTE CURATIVA LIBRI QUATOR QUIBUS SANANDI MORBOS BRENIS TRADITUR SATIS... / Lopez de Corella, A – Estella, 1555 – 8mf – 9 – sp Cultura [610]
DE ARTE DICENDI / Aristotle – Paris, 1549. Unclassified Holkham ms. Holkham Hall, Norfolk, England – 1 – uk Microform Academic [180]
DE ARTICULARI MORBO COMMENTARIUS / Laguna, A de – Roma, 1551 – 1mf – 9 – sp Cultura [610]
DE AUCTORITATE PRESIDENDI IN CONCILIO GENERALI / Cusanus, N; ed by Kallen, G – 1935 – 3mf – 8 – ne Slangenburg [290]
DE AURE HUMANA TRACTATUS / Valsalva, A M – M 270. 1704 – 9 – ne IDC [610]
DE AUXILIIS DIVINAE GRATIAE / Alvares, Didac – Col. Agrippinae, 1621 – 9mf – 8 – ne Slangenburg [240]
DE BAPTISMO INFANTIVM, TESTIMONIA VETERUM ECCLESIASTICARUM SCRIPTORUM / Cassander, G – Coloniae, haer. A. Birckmanni. 1563. BME-195 1 – 9 – ne IDC [240]
De Bary, Richard *see* THE SPIRITUAL RETURN OF CHRIST WITHIN THE CHURCH
DE BAZUIN – (Missing: 1962(52)) – Kampen, 1853-1964 – 567mf – 9 – H-2030/1 – ne IDC [073]
De Beers Consolidated Mines *see* ANNUAL REPORT
...DE BELLO A CHRISTIANIS CONTRA BARBAROS GESTO PRO CHRISTI SEPVLCHRO ET 4 DAEA RECVPERANDIS / Accolti, B – Venetius, 1532 – 2mf – 9 – H-8240/1 – ne IDC [956]
DE BELLO ET PACE OPUSCULUM... : REPRODUCCION FOTOTIPOGRAFICA EDITADA POR EL MARQUES DE OLIVART / Clichtouei, J – Parisiis, 1523; Madrid, 1914 – 2mf – 1 – ILM-1109/1 – ne IDC [327]
DE BELLO ET PACE OPUSCULUM, CHRISTIANOS PRINCIPES AD SEDANOS BELLORUM TUMULTUS ET PACEM COMPONENDAM EXHORTANS... / Clichtouei, J – Paris, 1523 – 2mf – 1 – ILM-4088/1 – ne IDC [327]
DE BELLO MELITENSI, ET EIUS EUENTU FRANCIS IMPOSITO, AD CAROLUS CAESAREM 5. NICOLAI / Durand de Villegagnon, N – Parisiis, 1553 – 1mf – 9 – H-8286/1 – ne IDC [945]
DE BELLO MELITENSI HISTORIA / Viperanus, J A – Pervsiae, 1567 – 1mf – 9 – H-8307/1 – ne IDC [956]
DE BELLO PANNONICO, PER ILVSTRISSIMVM PRINCIPEM DOMINUM AC DOMINUM FREDERICUM COMITEM... / Soiterus, M – Vindelicorum, 1538 – 2mf – 9 – H-8255/1 – ne IDC [956]
DE BELLO RHODIO, LIBRI TRES, CLEMENTI 7. PONT. MAX. DEDICATI... / Fontanus, J – Haganoae, 1527 – 2mf – 9 – H-8236/1 – ne IDC [240]
DE BELLO TURCIS INFERENDO, ORATIO / Sadoleto, J – Basileae, 1538 – 3mf – 9 – H-8254/1 – ne IDC [956]
DE BELLO TURCIS INFERENDO, ORATIO GRAUISSIMA, ... / Callimachus, P – Haganoae, 1533 – 2mf – 9 – H-8241/1 – ne IDC [956]
DE BENEDICTIONIBUS PATRIARCHARUM JACOB ET MOYSI / Radbertus, Pascasius – 1993 – 4mf – 9 – Bf1,300.00 – 2-503-63962-3 – be Brepols [450]
DE BENGUELLA AS TERRAS DO IACCA.. / Capello, Hermenegildo Carlos de Brito – Lisboa: Imprensa nacional, 1881.2v. illus – 1 – us U.W. Library [910]
DE BERGREDE / Oort, Henricus – Assen: L Hansma, 1905 – 1mf – 9 – 0-8370-4619-X – 1985-2619 – us A.T.L.A. [220]
DE BIBLIORUM SACRORUM VULGATAE EDITIONIS GRAECITATE / Saalfeld, Guenther Alexander – Quedlinburgi [Germany (East)]: Christianus Fridericus, 1891 – 1mf – 9 – 0-8370-5011-1 – 1985-3011 – us A.T.L.A. [450]
DE BONIS ECCLESIAE TEMPORALIBUS / Vromant, G – Bruxelles, 1953 – 6mf – 8 – ne Slangenburg [240]
DE BONONIENSI SCIENTIARUM ET ARTIUM INSTITUTO ATQUE ACADEMIA COMMENTARII / Accademia delle scienze dell'Instituto di Bologna – Bononiae, 1731-91 – 3 – us Readex [500]
DE BOSPORO THRACIO LIBRI 3 / Gilles, P – Lvgdvni, 1561 – 3mf – 9 – H-8297/1 – ne IDC [956]
de Brahm, William Gerard *see* PARTIAL TRANSCRIPT REPORT
de Bunsen, Ernest *see*
- CHRONOLOGY OF THE BIBLE CONNECTED WITH CONTEMPORANEOUS EVENTS
- THE CHRONOLOGY OF THE BIBLE, CONNECTED WITH CONTEMPORANEOUS EVENTS IN THE HISTORY OF BABYLONIANS, ASSYRIANS, AND EGYPTIANS

...DE CAESARIBUS ATQUE IMPERATORIBUS ROMANIS OPUS INSIGNE / Cuspinianus, J – [Strasburg], 1540 – 14mf – 9 – H-8262/1 – ne IDC [945]
DE CALIFORNIA A ALASKA. MADRID, 1945 / Ibarra y Berge, Javier de – Madrid: Razon y Fe, 1947 – 1 – sp Bibl Santa Ana [975]
DE CANTU ET MUSICA SACRA A PRIMA ECCLESIAE AETATE USQUE AD PRAESENS TEMPUS / Gerbert, Martin – 2v. 1774 – 9 – us Sibley [780]
DE CANTU ET MUSICA SACRA A PRIMA ECCLESIAE AETATE USQUE PRAESENS TEMPUS AUCTORE MARTINO GERBERTO / Gerbert, Martin – S. 1. v. 1-2. 1774. BP-293 1 – 9 – ne IDC [780]
DE CAPTA CONSTANTINOPOLI, ANNO 1453 : ORATIO RECITATA CUM DECERNERETUR GRADUS DOCTORIS REUERENDO D. PAULO AB EIZEN / Meier, G – VVitebergae, 1556 – 1mf – 9 – H-8290/1 – ne IDC [956]
DE CAPTIS IN BELLO,... / Groot, O O – Holmiae, 1751 – 1mf – 1 – ILM-1088/1 – ne IDC [327]
DE CAPTIVIS, ET POSTLIMINIO REVERSIS / Baysius, L – Lutetiae, 1549 – 4mf – 9 – ILM-809/1 – ne IDC [327]
De Cass, Anthonius de P *see* EXPOSITE IN TERENTIUM, ETC
DE CASUARINEARUM / Loew, E – Berolini. 1865. B-5137 2 – 8 – ne IDC [580]
DE CAUSIS DIVERSITATIS LINGVARUM DISSERTATIO / Borrichius, O – Hafniae, 1675 – 1mf – 9 – ne IDC [400]
DE CAUSIS LINGUAE LATINAE / Scaliger, Julius Cesar – In French. (Linguistic series). 1598 – 9 – fr Hachette [450]
DE CAUSIS MAGNITUDINIS IMPERII TVRCICI, ET VIRTVTIS AC FELICITATIS TVRCARUM IN BELLIS PERPETUAE:... / Foglietta, U – Rostochi, 1594 – 1mf – 9 – H-8381/1 – ne IDC [956]
DE CERTALDO INSIGNIS OPUS DE CLARIS MULIERIBUS / Boccaccio, G – O 1013 1. 1539 – 9 – ne IDC [450]
DE CHIMIE ET D'HISTOIRE NATURELLE *see* OBSERVATIONS ET MEMOIRES SUR LA PHYSIQUE, SUR L'HISTOIRE NATURELLE ET SUR LES ARTS...
DE CIUILI ET BELLICA FORTITUDINE LIBER, EX MYSERIIS POETAE VERGILII NEUNE PRIMUM DEPROMPTUS... / Balbi, G – Roma, [1526] – 2mf – 9 – H-8232/1 – ne IDC [450]
DE CIVITATE DISCRETA / Duppe, S E – Berolini, 1874 – 1mf – 1 – ILM-1552/1 – ne IDC [327]
DE CLERICO MEDICO CURIOSA DISCEPTATIO, SIVE INTERPRETATIO AD TESTUM... / Tristan Valentin, G – Valencia, 1606 – 4mf – 9 – sp Cultura [610]
DE CODICE SANCTI EVANGELII, LIBRI 3 / Josepho Catalano Presbytero – Roma, 1738 – 5mf – 8 – ne Slangenburg [240]
DE COLEOPTERIS NOVIS AC RARIORIBUS MINUSUE COGNITIS PROVINCIAE NOVOCOMI / Comolli, A – Ticini-Regii, 1837. 54p. Z-1141/2 – 8 – ne IDC [590]
DE COMMUNIBUS OMNIUM RERUM NATURALIUM PRINCIPIIS ET AFFECTIONIBUS / Pererius, B – Romae, 1576 – 10mf – 9 – CA-28/1 – ne IDC [100]
DE COMO O MULATO PORCIUNCULA DESCARREGOU SEU DEFUNTO / Amado, Jorge – Lisboa: Distribuicao da Editorial Organizacoes, 1962 – us Res Libr [072]
DE COMPOSICIONE CANTUS / Galliculus. Isagoge Ioannis Gallicvli – Lipsiae, apud Valentinum Schumannu. An. Christi. 1520. BP-681 1 – 9 – ne IDC [780]
DE CONCEPTU ET GENERATIONE HOMINIS / Rueff, J – Tiguri, 1554 – 4mf – 9 – ne IDC [611]
DE CONCHIS MINUS NOTIS LIBER / Plancus, J – Z-720 2. 1739 – 8 – ne IDC [560]
De Concilio, Januarius *see*
- CATHOLICITY AND PANTHEISM: ALL TRUTH OR NO TRUTH
- THE ELEMENTS OF INTELLECTUAL PHILOSOPHY

DE CONCORDIA ECCLESIAE OCCID. ET ORIENTALIS / Arcudius, P – Parisiis, 1626 – 29mf – 8 – ne Slangenburg [240]
DE CONCORDIA ECCLESIAE OCCID. ET ORIENTALIS / Arcudius, P – Parisiis, 1626 – 29mf – 8 – ne Slangenburg [240]
DE CONFOEDERATIONIBUS LIBERARUM... / Fels, I – Jena, 1752 – 1mf – 1 – ILM-443/1 – ne IDC [327]
DE CONGREGATIONIBUS CLERICORUM IN COMMUNI VIVENTIUM / Miraeus, A – Colonia Agrippina, 1632 – 4mf – 8 – Dfl22.00 – ne Slangenburg [240]
DE CONSOLATIONE PHILOSOPHIAE / Boethius – 14th Century Ms. Holkham Ms 402 – 1 – uk Microform Academic [180]

DE CONSTANTINO IMPERATORE, PONTIFICO MAXIMO : DISSERTATIONEM / Aube, Benjamin – Lutetiae: F. Didot: A. Durand, 1861 – 1mf – us A.T.L.A. [240]

DE CONSTRUCTIONE LIBRI 2 / Priscianus – 14th cent. Holkham ms. 405. Holkham Hall, Norfolk, England – 1 – uk Microform Academic [760]

DE CONSTRUCTIONE OCTO PARTIUM ORATIONIS LIBER / Alvarez, Emmanuel – Hispali Seville: Alonsi a Barrera, 1590. 54 leaves. With: Principios de la grammatica latina compuestos por Juan Sanchez. 1589 – 1 – us U.W. Library [400]

DE CONTINUITATIS LEGE ET EJUS CONSECTARIIS PERTINENTIBUS AD PRIMA MATERIAE ELEMENTA EORUMQUE VIRES / Boskovich, Rudzer J – Roma, 1754, lxxx p. et 1 depl. Histoire des Sciences XVIIe-XIXe Siecles. 7982 – 9 – fr Hachette [530]

DE' CORPI MARINI, CHE SU' MONTI SI TROVANO / Vallisnieri, A – 2545 2. Ed. 2. 1728 – 8 – ne IDC [590]

DE COSAS EXTREMENAS Y DE ALGO MAS / Sancho y Gonzalez, Javier – Badajoz: Vicente Rodriguez, 1912 – 1 – sp Bibl Santa Ana [946]

De Costa, Benjamin Franklin *see*
- VERRAZANO THE EXPLORER: BEING A VINDICATION OF HIS LETTER AND VOYAGE: WITH AN EXAMINATION OF THE MAP OF HIERONIMO DE VERRAZANO: AND A DISSERATION UPON THE GLOBE OF VLPIUS: TO WHICH IS PREFIXED A BIBLIOGRAPHY OF THE SUBJECT
- THE VOYAGE OF PIERRE ANGIBAUT. KNOWN AS CHAMPDORE: CAPTAIN IN THE MARINE OF NEW FRANCE: MADE TO THE COAST OF MAINE, 1608

De Courcy, B W *see* A GENEALOGICAL HISTORY OF THE MILESIAN FAMILIES OF IRELAND, WITH THE MONUMENT TO BRIAN BOROIMHE: THE CHART OF THE ARMORIAL BEARINGS OF THE SAME FAMILIES

DE CRITICAE SACRAE ARGUMENTO E LINGUAE LEGIBUS REPETITO...GENESEOS CAPP, 1 / Koenig, Eduard – Leipzig: J.C. Hinrichs, 1879. 1 fiche – 9 – us A.T.L.A. [240]

DE CRITICIS VET. GR. ET LATINIS / Estienne, Henri – 16th Century – 1 – uk Microform Academic [450]

DE CULTIBUS RELIGIOSIS LATINORUM / Dallaeus, Ion. – Genevae, 1671 – 23mf – 8 – ne Slangenburg [240]

DE CULTU ADORATIONIS LIBRI TRES / Vazquez, Gabr. S J – Compluti, 1594 – 11mf – 8 – ne Slangenburg [240]

DE CULTU ADORATIONIS LIBRI TRES / Vazquez, Gabr. S J – Compluti, 1594 – 11mf – 8 – ne Slangenburg [240]

DE CYMBALIS VETERUM LIBRI TRES / Lampe, Friedrich A – 1703 – 2,9 – us Sibley [780]

DE CYMBALIS VETERUM; LIBRI TRES / Lampe, Friedrich A – P-355. 1703 – 9 – ne IDC [780]

DE DANICAE LINGUAE,... COMMENTARIOLUS / Sperling, O – Hafniae, 1694 – 2mf – 9 – ne IDC [490]

DE DELICTIS EXTRA CIVITATIS FINES COMMISSIS,... / Cosman, A C – Amsterdam, 1829 – 1mf – 1 – ILM-726/1 – ne IDC [327]

DE DELICTIS EXTRA REGNI TERRITORIUM ADMISSIS / Asch van Wijk, H A M van – Trajecti ad Rhenum, 1839 – 3mf – 9 – ILM-2549/1 – ne IDC [340]

DE DEO : DISPUTATIONES METAPHYSICAE: QUAS EXCIPIT DISSERTATIO DE MENTE SANCTI ANSELMI IN PROSLOGIO / Piccirelli, Josephus M – (Includes bibliographical references) – Lutetiae Parisiorum: Victorem Lecoffre, 1885 – 2mf – 9 – 0-8370-7252-2 – 1986-1252 – us A.T.L.A. [210]

DE DESERTORIBUS ET TRANSFUGIS... / Duvernoy, P – Jena, 1714 – 1mf – 1 – ILM-976/1 – ne IDC [327]

DE DIGAMIA EPISCOPORUM : EIN BEITRAG ZUR LUTHERFORSCHUNG / Kawerau, Gustav – Kiel: E. Homann, 1889 – 1mf – us A.T.L.A. [240]

DE DIPHTHONGIS / Gataker, Thomas – 1646. 78p. (English Linguistics Series 1500-1800) – 9 – us UMI [400]

DE DISTINGVENDO DECALOGO,... / Cramer, D – VVitebergae, 1598 – 2mf – 9 – ne IDC [240]

DE DISTRIBUTIONE GEOGRAPHICA PLANTARUM / Humboldt, Alexander von – Lutetiae Parisiorum. 1817. B-5971 2 – 8 – ne IDC [580]

DE DIVINA PRAEDESTINATIONE / Scottus, Iohannes – 1982 – 3mf – 9 – Bf675.00 – 2-503-60502-8 – be Brepols [240]

DE DIVINO...JESUS...ORATIONEM / Martinez Siliceo, Juan – 1551 – 9 – 1.50f – sp Bibl Santa Ana [240]

DE DOCTRINA CHRISTIANA / Augustinus, St – 1982 – 4mf – 9 – Bf775.00 – 2-503-60322-X – be Brepols [240]

DE' DOVERI DE' PRINCIPI NEUTRALI... / Galiani, F – [Milan], 1782 – 6mf – 1 – ILM-526/1 – ne IDC [327]

DE DUBIO SOLVENDO IN RE MORALI / Waffelaert, Gustave Joseph – (Includes bibliographical references) – Lovanii: Valinthout, [1880?] – 1mf – 9 – 0-8370-6535-6 – 1986-0535 – us A.T.L.A. [230]

DE DVABVS NATVRIS IN CHRISTO.. / Chemnitz, Martin – 1580 – 1 – us A.T.L.A. [240]

DE DVABVS NATVRIS IN CHRISTO. DE HYPOSTATICA EARVM VNIONE... / Chemnitz, Martin – Lipsiae, 1578 – 7mf – 9 – ne IDC [240]

DE DVABVS NATVRIS IN CHRISTO, EARVMQVE VNIONE HYPOSTATICA TRACTATVS / Hesshusen, T – Magdebvrgi, 1590 – 4mf – ne IDC [240]

DE ECCLESIA = THE CHURCH / Huss, John – New York: Scribner, 1915 – 1mf – us A.T.L.A. [240]

DE ECCLESIA CHRISTI : PRAELECTIONES NOVAE IN SEMINARIO SANCTI SULPITII HABITAE: CUM MULTIS ANNOTATIONIBUS IN ULTERIORA CUJUSQUE STUDIA ET PRAEDICTIONIS USUS PROFUTURIS / Brugere, Lud-Fred – (In Latin and French. Includes bibliographical references and index) – ed nova. Parisiis: A Roger et F Chernoviz, 1878 – 2mf – 9 – 0-8370-8408-3 – 1986-2408 – us A.T.L.A. [240]

DE ECCLESIAE OCCIDENTALIS ET ORIENTALIS PERPETUA CONSENSIONE / Allatius, L – 1648 – 18mf – 8 – ne Slangenburg [240]

DE ECCLESIASTICIS OFFICIIS / Hispalensis, Isidorus episcopus – 1989 – 3mf – 9 – Bf1,125.00 – 2-503-61132-X – be Brepols [240]

DE ECCLESIASTICIS OFFICIIS (CCSL 113) / Isidorus Hispalensis – 1989 – 2mf – 9 – Bf1,125.00 – 2-503-71132-4 – be Brepols [240]

DE ECCLESIASTICIS OFFICIIS, FRAGMENTOS (SIECLE 9-10) / Isidore de Seville, Saint – Barcelona – 1r – 5,6 – sp Cultura [240]

DE EEKBOOM *see* UNS EEKBOOM

DE EL REMEDIO DE EL AMOR IMPURO / Ovidio Nason, P – 1732 – 9 – 1.50f – sp Bibl Santa Ana [450]

DE L'ELECTRISATION LOCALISEE ET DE SON APPLICATION... / Duchenne de Boulogne, G B A – Paris, 1855 – 17mf – 9 – ne IDC [611]

DE ELOHISTAE PENTATEUCHICI SERMONE : COMMENTATIO HISTORICO-CRITICA / Ryssel, Victor – (In Latin. Includes index of Hebrew words) – Lipsiae [Leipzig]: L Fernau, 1878 – 1mf – 9 – 0-8370-5009-X – 1985-3009 – us A.T.L.A. [220]

DE EL...!SIGLO PASADO! / Sanchez Arjona, Vicente – Sevilla: Graficas Tirvia, 1954 – 1 – sp Bibl Santa Ana [810]

DE L'EMANCIPATION DES ESCLAVES, LETTRES A M. DE LAMARTINE / Cassagnac, Granier de – (Slave Trade and Abolitionism in France series). 1840 – 9 – fr Hachette [360]

DE L'EMANCIPATION DES NOIRS OU LETTRES A M. LE DUC DE BROGLIE SUR LES DANGERS DE CETTE MESURE, SUIVIES DE CONSIDERATIONS SUR LE DROIT DE VISITE / Petit de Barancourt – (Slave Trade and Abolitionism in France series). 1845 – 9 – fr Hachette [305]

DE L'EMANCIPATION DES SERFS EN RUSSIE. ETUDE SUR LA QUESTION AU 16 MARS 1861. EXPOSE ET CRITIQUES DU PROJET DU COMITE DE REDACTION. AVEC UNE CARTE ET TABLEAUX STATISTIQUES / Jourdier, Auguste – (Russia – 19th C.). 1861 – 9 – fr Hachette [360]

DE EMENDATA STRUCTURA LATINI SERMONIS LIBRI SEX / Linacre, Thomas – 1524. 397p. (English Linguistics Series 1500-1800) – 9 – us UMI [450]

DE ENUNTIATIONIBUS RELATIVIS SEMITICIS. PARS PRIOR, PRAEMISSO IBN JAOI SI IN ZAMACH SARII, DE PRONOMINIBUS RELATIVIS LOCUM COMMENTARIO, DE ENUNTIATIONIBUS RELATIVIS ARABICIS AGENS = SHARH AL-MUFASSAL : DISSERTATIO LINGUISTICA / Ibn Yaoish, Abu al-Baqa Yaoish ibn Ali – (Text in Arabic; notes in Latin. No more publ. Includes bibliographical references) – Bonnae ad Rhenum: Tobiae Habichtii, 1868 – 1mf – 9 – 0-8370-7324-3 – 1986-1324 – us A.T.L.A. [470]

DE ENUNTIATIS FINALIBUS APUD GRAECORUM RERUM SCRIPTORES POSTERIORIS EATATIS / Diel, Heinrich – Muenchen: J Fuller, 1895 – 1mf – 9 – 0-8370-9226-4 – 1986-3226 – us A.T.L.A. [450]

DE EO QUOD EST JUSTUM... / Dorn, J C – Jena, [1716] – 1mf – 1 – ILM-508/1 – ne IDC [327]

DE EO QUOD IUSTUM E.. / Bachoff von Echt, J F – Jena, 1730 – 1mf – 9 – ILM-330/1 – ne IDC [340]

DE ESCULTURA E IMAGENERIA / Perez Comendador, Enrique – Madrid: (Blas), 1957 – sp Bibl Santa Ana [946]

DE ESPANA AL JAPON / Oteyza, Luis de – Madrid: Editorial Pueyo, S.L., 1927 – sp Bibl Santa Ana [946]

DE L'ESSENCE DES PASSIONS. ETUDE PSYCHOLOGIQUE ET MORALE / Maillet, Eugene – (French Precursors of Psychiatry Series). Paris. Hachette. 1877 – 9 – fr Hachette [170]

...DE ESSENTIA ORIGINALIS IVSTITIAE ET INIVSTITIAE SEU IMAGINIS DEI ET CONTRARIAE,... / Flacius Illyricus d.A E, M – Basileae, 1568 – 4mf – 9 – ne IDC [240]

DE L'ETAT DES OUVRIERS ET DE SON AMELIORATION PAR L'ORGANISATION DU TRAVAIL / Boyer, Adolphe – (Condition of 19th C. French working class series). 1841 – 9 – fr Hachette [360]

DE EUCHARISTIAE SIVE COENAE DOMINICAE SACRAMENTO LIBRI TRES / Albertinus, Edm. – Daventriae, 1655 – 27mf – 8 – ne Slangenburg [240]

DE EUPHORBIACEARUM GENERIBUS MEDICIQUE EARUNDEM VIRIBUS TENTAMEN / Jussieu, A H L de – Paris. 1824. B-5982 2 – 8 – ne IDC [580]

DE EXEMTIONIBUS TERRITORIORUM GERMANIAE / Carrach, I P – N.p., 1752 – 2mf – 1 – ILM-940/1 – ne IDC [327]

DE FACULTATIBUS NATURALIBUS DISPUTATIONES MEDICAE ET PHYLOSOPHICAE / Fernandez, F – Granada, 1619 – 7mf – 9 – sp Cultura [610]

DE FEBRIUM DIFFERENTIIS... / Mercado, P – Granada, 1581 – 6mf – 9 – sp Cultura [610]

DE FIDE : SYNOPSIS PRAELECTIONUM, QUAS IN C.R. UNIVERSITATE OENIPONTANA / Stentrup, Ferdinandus Aloisius – Oeniponte [Innsbruck]: Feliciani Rauch, 1890 – 1mf – 9 – 0-8370-7022-8 – 1986-1022 – us A.T.L.A. [240]

DE FIDE HOSTI A PRIVATO DATA SERVANDA / Furstenau, J A – Jena, 1705 – 1mf – 1 – ILM-1123/1 – ne IDC [327]

DE FIDE INTER HOSTES,... / Chastelein, C P – Leiden, 1769 – 1mf – 1 – ILM-665/1 – ne IDC [327]

DE FIDE, SPE ET CARITATE / Radbertus, Pascasius – 1990 – 4mf – 9 – Bf2,175.00 – 2-503-63972-0 – be Brepols [240]

DE FILICIBUS VERIS HUNGARIAE, TRANSSYLVANIAE, CROATIAE ET LITORALIS HUNGARICI / Sadler, J – Budae. 1830. B-7254 1 – 9 – ne IDC [580]

DE FOEDERIBUS FINIUM DISPUTATIO / Carlowitz, K W von – Lipsiae, 1763 – 1mf – 1 – ILM-366/1 – ne IDC [327]

DE FOEDERIS NOTIONE JEREMIANA / Guthe, Hermann – Leipzig: J.C. Hinrichs, 1877 – 9 – us A.T.L.A. [220]

DE FOEDERUM JURE: ... / Besoldus, C – Argentorati, 1622 – 1mf – 9 – ILM-1086/1 – ne IDC [327]

DE FOIX / Bray, Anna Eliza – British Fiction Archive: Unit 2 – 9 – uk Bell [830]

De Fonblanque, Edward Barrington *see* POLITICAL AND MILITARY EPISODES IN THE LATTER HALF OF THE EIGHTEENTH CENTURY: DERIVED FROM THE LIFE AND CORRESPONDENCE OF THE RIGHT. HON. JOHN BURGOYNE, GENERAL, STATESMAN, DRAMATIST

DE FONSEKA FAMILY OF KALUTARA (CEYLON) / Abeyesooriya, Samson – Colombo: Independent Press, [n.d.] – 1 – us Res Libr [950]

DE FORNICATIONE CAVENDA ADMONITIO... 1698. VWITH / Beverland, Adriaan – De peccato originali...1679. AND De stolatae virginitatis jure lucubratio academica...1680 – 1 – us A.T.L.A. [240]

DE FORO LEGATORUM... / Bynkershoek, C van – Leiden, 1721 – 3mf – 1 – ILM-448/1 – ne IDC [327]

DE FRANCISCAE LINGUAE RECTA PRONUNTATIONE / Beze, Th. de – 1584 – 9 – fr I.C.S. [440]

DE FRENTE – (Includes c.1: no.1;n.s.v.1:no.1 1974:May 2-; n.s.v.1:no.11 1974:July 25) – Buenos Aires – 1 – CSUXAHZ5147-S – us Hoover Inst Photo [972]

DE FRENTE – (Includes c.1: v.1:no.11 1945:Aug. 29) – 1 – CSUXAHZ5142-S – us Hoover Inst Photo [972]

DE FRONDIZIA ALFONS IN : LA TRADICION POLITICA DEL RADICALISMO / Acuna, Marcelo Luis – Buenos Aires: Centro Editor de America Latina, c1984. 2v – 1 – CSUXADP5039-B – us Hoover Inst Photo [320]

DE FRUCTIBUS ET SEMINBUS PLANTARUM / Gaertner, J – 1788-1805 – 7 – uk Microform Academic [580]

DE FRUCTIBUS ET SEMINIBUS PLANTARUM / Gaertner, J – 2v. Stuttgartiae-Tuebingen. 1788-91. Contains also: Gaertner, C. F. von. Supplementum carpologicae seu continuati operis J. Gaertner: De fructibus. v. 3. Leipzig. 1805-07. B-425 2 – 8 – ne IDC [580]

DE GASPE ET GARNEAU / Casgrain, Henri Raymond – 1924. SEM105P749 – 2mf – 9 – Can$4.50 – cn Bibl Nat [920]

DE GENERICIS QUIBUSDAM PLANTARUM / Cartheuser, J F – Ed. 3. Francofurti a. V. 1764 – 8 – ne IDC [580]

DE GENTES DEL OTRO MUNDO / Roso de Luna, Mario – Madrid: Libreria Viuda de Pueyo, 1917 – 1 – sp Bibl Santa Ana [240]

DE GEOGRAPHIA VNIUERSALI / Muhammad ibn Muhammad, al-Idrisi – Rome, 1592 – 4mf – 9 – H-8434/1 – ne IDC [956]

DE GESTIS PONTIFICUM ANGLORUM LIBRI QUINQUE (RS52) / Wilhelmi Malmesbiriensis; ed by Hamilton, N E S A – 1870 – Dfl42.00 – ne Slangenburg [240]

DE GESTIS REGUM ANGLORUM LIBRI QUINQUE : HISTORIAE NOVELLAE LIBRI TRES (RS90) / Willelmi Malbesbiriensis; ed by Stubbs, W – (v1 1887 Dfl30.00. v2 1889 Dfl32.00) – ne Slangenburg [240]

DE GESTIS SICULORUM SUB FREDERICO 2 REGE / Specialis, Nicolaus – 15th Century. Holkham Ms 495 – 1 – uk Microform Academic [900]

DE GIBRALTAR A LISBOA. VIAJE HISTORICO / Espronceda, Jose de – 1852 – 9 – 1.50f – sp Bibl Santa Ana [910]

DE GILLES DE RAIS A GUILLAUME APOLLINAIRE / Fleuret, Fernand – Paris: Mercure de France, 1933 – 1 – F149.91 – fr Armell [944]

DE GODSDIENST UIT PLICHTBESEF EN DE GELOOFSVOORSTELLING UIT DICHTENDE VERBEELDING GEBOREN? : BEDENKINGEN TEGEN DR. L.W.E. RAUWENHOFF'S WIJSBEGEERTE VAN DEN GODSDIENST / Cannegieter, Tjeerd – Leiden:E J Brill, 1890 – 1mf – 9 – 0-8370-2582-6 – 1985-0582 – us A.T.L.A. [240]

DE GRAMINIBUS PANICEIS / Trinius, Carl Bernhard – Petropoli, 1826 – 5mf – 9 – ne IDC [580]

DE GRATIA DEI IUSTIFICANTE NOS PROPTER CHRISTUM, PER SOLAM FIDEM ABSQUE OPERIBUS BONIS, FIDE INTERIM EXUBERANTE IN OPERA BONA LIBRI 4....1554 / Bullinger, Heinrich – 1 – us A.T.L.A. [240]

DE HAERESIS ANGLICANAE INTRUSIONE ET PROGRESSU / Rinuccini, Giovani B – 17th cent. Holkham ms. 200. Holkham Hall, Norfolk, England – 1 – uk Microform Academic [760]

DE HARMONIA MUSICORUM INSTRUMENTORUM OPUS / Gaffurio, Franchino – 1518 – 2 – us Sibley [780]

de Hart, William Chetwood *see* OBSERVATIONS ON MILITARY LAW, AND THE CONSTITUTION AND PRACTICE OF COURTS MARTIAL.

DE HEBRAEA ET ADFINIBVS ORIENTIS LINGVIS A GRAECA DERIVANDIS / Michaelis, C B & Baumgarten, S I – Halae, [1726] – 1mf – 9 – ne IDC [450]

DE HISTORIA DE BADAJOZ / Lozano Rubio, Tirso – Badajoz: Ed.Arqueros, Tomo 2(Mateos). 1930 – 1 – sp Bibl Santa Ana [946]

DE HISTORIA. RELACIONES DE BADAJOZ CON LA CORTE Y CON DON MANUEL GODOY DURANTE EL VALIMIENTO DE ESTE / Guerra Guerra, Arcadio – Badajoz: Imp. Dip. Provincial, 1958 – sp Bibl Santa Ana [946]

DE HISTORIAE BYZANTINAE SCRIPTORIBUS EMITTENDIS PROTREPTICON : APPARATUS HISTORIAE BYZANTINAE DELINEATIO PRIMA (CBH 1,1) / Labbe, Ph. – Parisiis, 1648 – Dfl13.00 – ne Slangenburg [220]

DE HISTORIAS AMERICANAS / Bayle, Constantino – Madrid: Razon y Fe, 1925 – 1 – sp Bibl Santa Ana [972]

DE HOLLANDSCHE AMERIKAAN – Kalamazoo: Dalm Print Co, [-1945]. Dec 31 1928-1942 – 14r – 1 – us Res Libr [071]

DE HONORE GENTIUM... / Brand, C L de – Francofurti ad Viadrum, 1748 – 1mf – 1 – ILM-347/1 – ne IDC [327]

DE HUMANI CORPORIS FABRICA / Vesalius, A – M 77. 1543 – 9 – ne IDC [611]

DE HYDROPHOBIAE NATURA, CAUSIS ATQUE MEDELA... / Bravo de Piedrahita, J – Salamanca, 1571 – 4mf – 9 – sp Cultura [610]

DE IIS, QUAE IN TESTAMENTO VETERE COMMEMORANTUR, PROPHETARUM SOCIETATIBUS / Kranichfeld, Rudolph – Berolini: Gust. Schlawitz, 1861.1 fiche – 9 – us A.T.L.A. [240]

DE ILLUSTRATIONE URBIS FLORENTIAE / Verino, U – O 1056 1790 – 9 – ne IDC [945]

DE IMAGINIBUS LIBRI 4 / Dallaeus, Ion. – Lugd. Batavorum, 1642 – 6mf – 8 – ne Slangenburg [240]

DE IMPEDIMENTIS MAGNORUM AUXILIORUM IN MORBORUM CURATIONE, LIBRI 3 / Ponce de Santa Cruz, A – Madrid, 1629 – 4mf – 9 – sp Cultura [610]

DE IMPERATORUM CONSTANTINOPOLITANO-RUM SEU DE INFERIORIS AEVI : VEL IMPERII NUMISMATIBUS DISSERTATIO / Cange, C du – Parisiis, 1766 – Dfl22.00 – ne Slangenburg [240]

DE IMPERIO ET REBUS GESTIS IUSTINIANI (CBH 4) / Scholastici, Agathiae; ed by Vulcanii, B – Parisiis, 1660 – Dfl35.00 – ne Slangenburg [240]

DE INCANTAMENTIS NONNULLIS SUMERICO-ASSYRIIS / Jensen, Petrus – (Text in Latin and Sumerian; preface and notes in Latin) – Monachii: F Straub, [1884?] – 1mf – 9 – 0-8370-7640-4 – 1986-1640 – us A.T.L.A. [230]

DE INCARNATIONE FILII DEI ITEM DE OFFICIO ET MAIESTATE CHRISTI TRACTUS : MARTINI CHEMNICII DE INCARNATIONE FILII DEI ITEM DE OFFICIO ET MAIESTATE CHRISTI TRACTATUS / Chemnitz, Martin – (Includes index) – Berolini:Gust. Schlawitz, 1865 – 1mf – 9 – 0-8370-3222-9 – 1985-1222 – us A.T.L.A. [240]

DE INDIAE UTRIUSQUE RE NATURALI ET MEDICA / Piso, G – Amstelaedami, 1658 – 14mf – 9 – ne IDC [615]

DE INITERE SVO CONSTANTINOPOLITANO, EPISTOLA / Dousa, G – Lugduno Batavae, 1599 – 2mf – 9 – H-8405/1 – ne IDC [956]

DE INSECTORUM SYSTEMATE NATURALI / Burmeister, C H C – Halis Saxonum, 1829 – [IV], 40[3]p – 8 – ne IDC [590]

DE INSPIRATIONE SCRIPTURAE SACRAE QUID STATUERINT PATRES APOSTOLICI ET APOLOGETAE SECUNDI SAECULI : COMMENTATIO DOGMATICO-HISTORICA / Delitzsch, Johannes – (Includes bibliographical references and index) – Lipsiae [Leipzig]:Prostat apud A. Lorentz Bibliopolam, 1872 – 1mf – 9 – 0-8370-2883-3 – 1985-0883 – us A.T.L.A. [220]

DE INSTITUTIONIS THEOLOGICAE VIA AC RATIONE : ORATIO ACADEMICA SOLEMNIS, QUAM PRO ANNI SCHOLASTICI CURSU FAUSTE FINIENDO AUSPICIIS REV. EPISCOPI PADERBORNENSIS IN AUDITORIO ALMAE SCHOLAE THEODORIANAE MAXIMO / Oswald, H – Paderbornae: Apud Ferdinandum Schoeningh, 1850 – 1mf – 9 – 0-8370-8461-X – 1986-2461 – us A.T.L.A. [240]

DE INTEGRO SACRAMENTO CORPORIS ET SANGUINIS DOMINI,... / Corvinus, A – [Hannoverae, 1544] – 2mf – 9 – ne IDC [240]

DE INVENTIONE RHETORICA / Cicero, Marcus Tullius – 12th century commentary. From York Minster Library. Ms. XVI. M7 – 1 – uk Microform Academic [760]

DE IRIDIBUS DOCTRINA ARISTOTELIS ET VITELLIONIS.. / Fleischer, Johannes – Wittenberg, 1571 – 1 – us U.W. Library [180]

DE ISIDORI PELUSIOTAE VITA, SCRIPTIS ET DOCTRINA COMMENTATIO, HISTORICA THEOLOGICA / Niemeyerus, H A – Halae, 1825 – 5mf – 8 – ne Slangenburg [240]

DE ISRAELIET – (Missing: 1880-1884. v1-5) – Rotterdam, 1880-1896. v1-17 – 70mf – 9 – J-261-126/1 – ne IDC [073]

DE ISTVUI USHCHEE ZAKONODATELSTVO O TRUDE : R.S.F.S.R. NARODNY I KOMISSARIAT TRUDA / Russian S.F.S.R. – (Includes c.1: v.1 1922) – Moskva: Voprosy truda, 1922- – 1 – CSUXAKZ6922-S – us Hoover Inst Photo [947]

DE IURE BELLI... / Asmuth, J D – Goettingen, 1747 – 1mf – 9 – ILM-415/1 – ne IDC [340]

DE IURE BELLI, LIBRI III / Gentili, A – Hanover, 1612 – 9mf – 1 – ILM-530/1 – ne IDC [327]

DE IURE CEREMONIALI CIRCA LEGATOS / Gasser, S P – Magdeburg, 1700 – 1mf – 1 – ILM-1120/1 – ne IDC [327]

DE IURE ET OFFICIIS BELLICIS ET DISCIPLINA MILITARI : LIBRE TRES / Ayala, Balthazar – Antverpiae, 1597 – 5mf – 9 – ILM-326/1 – ne IDC [340]

DE IURE GENTIS AUSTRIACAES IN REGNUM HISPANIAE / Buddeus, I F – N.p., 1702 – 1mf – 1 – ILM-2567/1 – ne IDC [327]

DE IURE NEUTRALITATIS STATUUM... / Gonne, J G – Erlangae, Lipsiae, 1746 – 1mf – 1 – ILM-885/1 – ne IDC [327]

DE IURE PRAECEDENDI... / Dewitz, B C de – Jena, 1758 – 1mf – 1 – ILM-1118/1 – ne IDC [327]

DE IURE SACRORUM / Becerra y Valcarzel, Diego – 1673. 2 tomas – 9 – 1.50f – sp Bibl Santa Ana [240]

DE IUSTIFICATIONE DOCTRINA UNIVERSA / Vega, Andr. de – Coloniae, 1572 – 39mf – 8 – ne Slangenburg [240]

DE IUSTO IMPERIO... / Freitas, S de – Valladolid, 1925 – 8mf – 1 – ILM-523/1 – ne IDC [327]

DE JAERFSCHOPP : ERZAEHLUNG IN MUENSTERLAENDER MUNDART / Wibbelt, Augustin – Essen: Fredebeul & Koenen, [1911?] – 1r – 1 – us U.W. Library [390]

DE JEAN-JACQUES ROUSSEAU / Corancez, Olivier de – Paris: Bureau du Journal de Paris; Desenne; Maradan, (an VI). 1797 – 9 – fr Hachette [190]

DE J.J. ROUSSEAU, CONSIDERE COMME L'UN DES PREMIERS AUTEURS DE LA REVOLUTION / Mercier, Louis S – 2v. Paris, Buisson juin. 1791 – 9 – fr Hachette [190]

DE JOHANNEISKA SMAABREFVENS URSPRUNG : UNDERSOEKT MED SAERSKILD HAENSYN TILL PRESBYTERHYPOTESEN: AKADEMISK AFHANDLING / Hjelt, Arthur – (Bibliography) – Helsingfors [Helsinki]: Frenckellska Tryckeri-Aktiebolaget, 1901 – 1mf – 9 – 0-8370-3600-3 – 1985-1600 – us A.T.L.A. [220]

DE JURE EORUM, QUI INAEQUALI FOEDERI JUNCTI SUNT / Gevers, P – Leiden, 1761 – 1mf – 1 – ILM-735/1 – ne IDC [327]

DE JURE ET JUDICE LEGATORUM DIATRIBE... / Cassius, S – Francofurti, 1717 – 2mf – 1 – ILM-1074/1 – ne IDC [327]

DE JURE ET OFFICIIS BELLICIS,... / Ayala, B – Madrid, 1793 – 5mf – 9 – ILM-717/1 – ne IDC [340]

DE JURE ET OFFICIIS BELLICIS,... / Ayala, B – Antwerp. 2v. 1597 – 9mf – 9 – ILM-418/1 – ne IDC [340]

DE JURE ET OFFICIIS BELLICIS ET DISCIPLINA MILITARI, LIBRI 3 / Ayala, Balthazar – Washington: Carnegie Endowment. 2v. 1912 – 9mf – 9 – $13.50 – LLMC 88-108 – us L.L.M.C. [340]

DE JURE SOCIETATIS ARMORUM ... / Berber, G – Erfurt, 1711 – 1mf – 9 – ILM-1101/1 – ne IDC [327]

DE JURE VICTORIS IN PERSONAM ET BONA HOSTIS,... / Brauw, O G S de – Lugduni Batavorum, 1830 – 2mf – 1 – ILM-950/1 – ne IDC [327]

DE JUSTES PRETENTIONS DU ROY SUR L'EMPIRE / Aubery, Antoine – Paris: A. Bertier, 1667 – 1 – us U.W. Library [944]

DE JUSTINI MARTYRIS SCRIPTIS ET DOCTRINA / Otto, J CT – Jenae: F. Maukium, 1841 – 1mf – us A.T.L.A. [240]

DE KALB CHRONICLE SOUVENIR / J.F. Glidden Publishing Co – De Kalb, 1899. Illinois Reel 21. The Cox Library Collection – 5 – us Americana [978]

DE KLEINE STAD IN VLAANDEREN (14DE - 16DE EEUW) / Stabel, P – 1995 – 320p + 2mf – 9 – Bf1,600.00 – 90-6569-625-3 – be Academie Royale [949]

DE KOULIKORO A TOMBOUCTOU A BORD DU "MAGE", 1889-1890 / Jaime, G – Paris: E Dentu, [1892] – 1 – us Res Libr [960]

DE KRUYS-LEER TER ZALIGHEYDT / Meyster, E – O 693. 1658 – 9 – ne IDC [700]

DE LA CARACTEROLOGIA INDIVIDUAL A LA COLECTIVA / Frutos Cortes, Eugenio – Badajoz: Imp. Dip. Provincial, 1960. Sep. Revista de Estudios Extremenos – sp Bibl Santa Ana [946]

DE LA COMPETENCE DES TRIBUNAUX FRANCAIS EN MATIERE DE SUCCESSION / Barbarina, P – Paris, 1895 – 2mf – 9 – ILM-3510/1 – ne IDC [340]

DE LA COMPLICITE... / Deprez, M – Paris, 1913 – 3mf – 1 – ILM-506/1 – ne IDC [327]

DE LA COMPOSITION DES PAYSAGES OU DES MOYENS D'EMBELLIR LA NATURE AUTOUR DES HABITATIONS / Girardon, Rene Louis de – Geneva; Paris. Delaguette, 1777. 8 fol., xix, 166p. (Architecture Series) – 9 – fr Hachette [720]

DE LA CONCLUSION DES TRAITES INTERNATIONAUX D'APRES LE DROIT PUBLIC ROMAIN / Coqueugniot, G – Paris, 1891 – 3mf – 1 – ILM-1040/1 – ne IDC [327]

DE LA CONDITION... / Chehpeliades, M G – Paris, 1887 – 3mf – 1 – ILM-450/1 – ne IDC [327]

DE LA CONDITION DES CLASSES PAUVRES A LA CAMPAGNE, DES MOYENS LES PLUS EFFICACES DE L'AMELIORER / Dutouquet, H E – (Condition of 19th C. French working class series). 1846 – 9 – fr Hachette [360]

DE LA CONDITION DES OUVRIERS DE PARIS DE 1789 JUSQU'EN 1841. AVEC QUELQUES IDEES SUR LA POSSIBILITE DE L'AMELIORER / Durand – (Condition of 19th C. French working class series). 1841 – 9 – fr Hachette [360]

DE LA CONDITION JURIDIQUE DES SOCIETES COMMERCIALES ETRANGERES EN FRANCE / Drouin, L – Paris, 1897 – 3mf – 1 – ILM-3274/1 – ne IDC [327]

DE LA CONDITION JURIDIQUE DES SOCIETES ETRANGERES EN FRANCE ... / Boullay, G – Paris, 1899 – 5mf – 9 – ILM-3273/1 – ne IDC [327]

DE LA CONDITION SOCIALE DES FEMMES AU TEMPS PRESENT / Rameau, Marcel – Asnieres: La Revue des Independants, 1927. 160p. (Les Femmes Collection) – 2mf – 9 – $6.00 – fr Bibl Nationale [360]

DE LA CONJURATION CONTRE LES FINANCES ET DES MESURES A PRENDRE POUR EN ARRETER LES EFFETS / Claviere, Etienne – Paris. Chez les Directeurs du Cercle Social. 1792 – 9 – fr Hachette [321]

DE LA CROYANCE EN DIEU / Piat, Clodius – (Includes bibliographical references) – 3e ed. Paris: Felix Alcan, [1908?] – 1mf – 9 – 0-8370-5459-1 – 1985-3459 – us A.T.L.A. [210]

De la Cruz Napoli, Jose *see* CHANGES IN BLOOD RESISTIVITY OVER A SUB-MAXIMAL EXERCISE BOUT

DE LA DECLARATION DE GUERRE;... / Bruyas, N – Lyons, 1899 – 3mf – 1 – ILM-445/1 – ne IDC [327]

DE LA DELIMITATION DU DOMAINE PUBLIC MARITIME... / Baratoux, J – Paris, 1902 – 3mf – 9 – ILM-2327/1 – ne IDC [340]

DE LA DISTRIBUTION DES MAISONS DE PLAISANCE ET DE LA DECORATION DES EDIFICES EN GENERAL / Blondel, Jacques Francois – 2v. Paris. 1737-38. BO-153 1 – 9 – ne IDC [720]

DE LA DIVISION DU TRAVAIL SOCIAL : ETUDE SUR L'ORGANISATION DES SOCIETES SUPERIEURES / Durkheim, Emile – Paris: F. Alcan, 1893 – 2mf – us A.T.L.A. [335]

DE LA EXTRATERRITORIALIDAD DE LA PERSONA JURIDICA / Cacici, A S – Buenos Aires, 1917 – 3mf – 1 – ILM-3628/1 – ne IDC [327]

DE LA FIN DU 2E SIECLE A LA PAIX CONSTANTINIENNE (2) – Paris, 1935 – Dfl46.00 – ne Slangenburg [240]

DE LA GVERRA DI GIUSTINIANO IMPERATORE CONTRA I PERSIANI... / Procopius, of Caeserea – Vinegia, 1547 – 5mf – 9 – H-8278/1 – ne IDC [956]

De La Hunt, Thomas J *see* HISTORY OF PERRY COUNTY

DE LA JURIDICTION FRANCAISE... / Feraud-Giraud, L J D – Paris, 1871 – 12mf – 1 – ILM-515/1 – ne IDC [327]

DE LA JUSTICE ... / Bouquie, J – Brussels, 1884 – 8mf – 9 – ILM-435/1 – ne IDC [327]

DE LA LAMENTACION DE LA VIRGEN MARIA / Bravo Riesco, Agustin – Salamanca: Imp. Calatrava, 1954 – 1 – sp Bibl Santa Ana [240]

DE LA LATINITE DES SERMONS DE SAINT AUGUSTIN / Regnier, Louis-Adolphe – Paris: Hachette, 1886 – 1mf – us A.T.L.A. [240]

DE LA LEGISLACION ROMANA EN LAS RELACIONES CON LA DE LOS PUEBLOS EUROPEOS / Chaves y Manso, Rafael – Madrid, 1851 – 1 – sp Bibl Santa Ana [350]

DE LA LEGISLATION FONCIERE OTTOMANE / Padel, Wilhelm – Paris: Pedone, 1904. 350p. LL-12029 – 1 – us L of C Photodup [340]

DE LA LIBERTE DES MERS / Gerard de Reyneval, J M – Paris, 1811 – 7mf – 1 – ILM-174/1 – ne IDC [327]

DE LA LIQUIDATION ET DU PARTAGE DES SUCCESSIONS EN DROIT INTERNATIONAL / Demey, J – Paris, 1926 – 1mf – 1 – ILM-3120/1 – ne IDC [327]

DE LA LITTERATURE DES NEGRES / Gregoire, Henri Baptiste – Paris, Maradan. 1808 – 9 – $10.00 – fr Orientalistes [490]

DE LA LITTERATURE DES NEGRES, OU RECHERCHES SUR LEURS FACULTES INTELLECTUELLES, LEURS QUALITES MORALES ET LEUR LITTERATURE: SUIVIES DE NOTICES SUR LA VIE ET LES OUVRAGES DES NEGRES QUI SE SONT DISTINGUES DANS LES SCIENCES, LES LETTRES ET LES ARTS / Gregoire, Henri Baptiste – (Slave Trade and Abolitionism in France series). 1808 – 9 – fr Hachette [305]

DE LA LITTERATURE DU NIDI (SIC) DE L'EUROPE / Simonde de Sismondi, Jean Charles Leonar – 3rd. ed. rev. and corr. Paris: Chez Treuttel et Wurtz, 1829. 4v – 1 – us U.W. Library [440]

DE LA LOI DU CONTRASTE SIMULTANE DES COULEURS... / Chevreul, Eugene – Paris: Pitois-Levraut, 1839 – 1 – F371.93 – fr Armell [540]

DE LA LONGA ET ASTRA GUERRA DE GOTHI / Procopius, of Caeserea – Venetia, 1544 – 6mf – 9 – H-8273/1 – ne IDC [945]

DE LA LYCANTHROPIE, TRANSFORMATION, EXTASE DES SORCIERS / Nynauld, I de – Paris. 1615 – 9 – fr Hachette [360]

DE LA MANIERE D'APPRENDRE ET D'ENSEIGNER / Jouvancy, Joseph de – Paris: Hachette, 1892. xiv,138p. 2 fiches. (Education Collection) – 9 – 6.00 – fr Bibl Nationale [370]

DE LA MANIERE DE NEGOCIER AVEC LES SOUVERAINS,... / Callieres, F de – Amsterdam, 1716 – 3mf – 1 – ILM-355/1 – ne IDC [327]

DE LA MEDECINE AU TEMPS DE MME. SEVIGNE (SUIVI DE) DU THEATRE A BESANCON / Druhen, Ignace – Besancon, Dodiverz, 1883, 31 p. 1 fiche. (Statistics Series: Medical Studies) – 9 – 6.00 – fr Bibl Nationale [310]

DE LA MEDIATION... / Fourchault, C – Paris, 1900 – 5mf – 1 – ILM-522/1 – ne IDC [327]

DE LA MISERE, DE SES CAUSES, DE SES REMEDES / Esterno, FC P d' – (Condition of 19th C. French working class series). 1842 – 9 – fr Hachette [150]

DE LA MISERE DES CLASSES LABORIEUSES EN ANGLETERRE ET EN FRANCE. DE LA NATURE DE LA MISERE, DE SON EXISTENCE, DE SES EFFETS, DE SES CAUSES ET DE L'INSUFFISANCE DES REMEDES QU'ON LUI A OPPOSES JUSQU'ICI : AVEC L'INDICATION DES MOYENS PROPRES A EN AFFRANCHIR LES SOCIETES / Buret, Eugene – (Condition of 19th C. French working class series). 1840 – 9 – fr Hachette [360]

DE LA MISERE DES OUVRIERS ET DE LA MARCHE A SUIVRE POUR Y REMEDIER / Morogues, Bigot de – (Condition of 19th C. French working class series). 1832 – 9 – fr Hachette [360]
DE LA MODERATION POLITIQUE / Laurent, Paul-Mathieu – Revue encyclopedique. Paris, 1831, 28 p. Les Saint-Simoniens, 1825-1834. 6885 – 9 – fr Hachette [335]
DE LA MONARCHIE PONTIFICALE A PROPOS DU LIVRE DE MGR. L'EVEQUE DE SURA = DIE HOECHSTE LEHRGEWALT DES PAPSTES / Gueranger, Prosper – (In German. Includes bibliographical references) – Mainz: Franz Kirchheim, 1870 – 1mf – 0-8370-8515-2 – 1986-2515 – us A.T.L.A. [240]
DE LA MORT DE THEODOSE A L'ELECTION DE GREGOIRE LE GRAND (4) – Paris, 1937 – Dfl56.00 – ne Slangenburg [240]
DE LA MORTALITE DANS LES DIVERS QUARTIERS DE LA VILLE DE PARIS ET DES CAUSES QUI LA RENDENT TRES DIFFERENTE DANS PLUSIEURS D'ENTRE EUX / Villerme, Louis Rene – Reprod. d'un extrait des Annales d'Hygiene publique et de Medecine legale. v3, 1830. p294-339. 1 fiche. (Statistics Series: Medical Studies) – 9 – 6.00 – fr Bibl Nationale [310]
DE LA MORTALITE D'ENFANS-TROUVES CONSIDEREE DANS SES RAPPORTS AVEC LE MODE D'ALLAITEMENT, ET SUR L'ACCROISSEMENT DE LEUR NOMBRE EN FRANCE / Villerme, Louis Rene – Reprod. d'un extrait des Annales d'Hygiene publique et de Medecine legale. v19, 1838. p47-60. 1 fiche.(Statistics Series: Medical Studies) – 9 – 6.00 – fr Bibl Nationale [310]
DE LA MORTALITE DES ENFANTS TROUVES EN FRANCE ET A ROUEN EN PARTICULIER – Reprod. de l'ed. de Rouen: Vve. A. Surville, 1851. 39p. tabl. 1 fiche.(Statistics Series: Medical Studies) – 9 – 6.00 – fr Bibl Nationale [310]
DE LA MORTALITE DES NOURRISSONS EN FRANCE: SPECIALEMENT DANS L'ARRONDISSEMENT DE NOGENT-LE-ROTROU / Brochard, Andre Theodore – Paris: J.B. Bailliere et fils, 1866. xiv,161p. 2 fiches. (Statistics Series: Medical Studies) – 9 – 6.00 – fr Bibl Nationale [310]
DE LA MORTALITE DES NOUVEAU-NES ET DES MOYENS DE DIMINUER / Lober, Cesar – Paris, O. Doin, s.d., xiv, 88 p. 2 fiches. (Statistics Series: Medical Series) – 9 – 6.00 – fr Bibl Nationale [310]
de la Motte Fouque, Georg Doering *see* FRAUENTASCHENBUCH (HQ, 22)
DE LA MUSIQUE A NANTES, DEPUIS LES TEMPS LES PLUS RECULES JUSQU'A NOS JOURS / Mellinet, Camille – Nantes: Mellinet, 1837 – fr Armell [780]
DE LA MUSIQUE EN ITALIE PAR LE PRINCE DE BELOSELSKY, DE L'INSTITUT DE BOLOGNE / Beloselsky, A – A. La Haye. 1778. BP-639 1 – 9 – ne IDC [780]
DE LA MUSIQUE RELIGIEUSE. / Vroye, Theodore J de – PAR T. J. de Vroye, et X. van Elewyck.... 1866 – 9 – us Sibley [780]
DE LA NATIONALITE DANS L'EMPIRE OTTOMAN SPECIALEMENT EN EGYPTE / Arminjon, P – Paris, 1901 – 1mf – 9 – ILM-3435/1 – ne IDC [340]
DE LA NATIONALITE DES NAVIRES / Cantillon de Tramont, P – Montaubon, 1907 – 3mf – 1 – ILM-1779/1 – ne IDC [327]
DE LA NATIONALITE SUIVANT LA LEGISLATION SERBE / Peric, Zivojin M, 1868-1953 – Paris: Marchal & Billard, 1900. 37p. With: Les Croates sous le joug Magyar xH. Hinkovic – 1 – us U.W. Library [949]
DE LA NATURAL HISTORIA DE LAS INDIAS / Fernandez de Oviedo Valdes, Gonzalo – 1526. Libros en Microficha no. 10 – 1mf – 9 – Pta1,000.00 – 84-85422-35-X – sp Pentalfa [574]
DE LA NATURAL HISTORIA DE LAS INDIAS. SUMARIO DE HISTORIA NATURAL DE LAS INDIAS. CON UN ESTUDIO PRELIMINAR Y NOTAS POR ENRIQUE ALVAREZ LOPEZ / Fernandez de Oviedo Valdes, Gonzalo – Madrid: Editorial S., 1942 – 1 – sp Bibl Santa Ana [950]
DE LA NATURE JURIDIQUE DU PROTECTORAT... / Hachenburger, M – Paris, 1896 – 2mf – 1 – ILM-1955/1 – ne IDC [327]
DE LA NAVIGATION DE L'AMAZONE... / Angelis, Pedro de – Montevideo, 1854 – 3mf – 9 – ILM-2292/1 – ne IDC [340]
DE LA NECESSITE D'UNE REPRESENTATION SPECIALE POUR LES PROLETAIRES / Reynaud, Jean – Paris, Revue encyclopedique, 1832, 20 p. Lds Saint-Simoniens, 1825-1834. 6887 – 9 – fr Hachette [305]
DE LA NOTION DE CONTREBANDE... / Flourens, M – Paris, 1907 – 2mf – 1 – ILM-519/1 – ne IDC [327]
DE LA PAIX CONSTANTINIENNE A LA MORT DE THEODOSE (3) – Paris, 1936 – Dfl49.00 – ne Slangenburg [240]
DE LA PAIX DE DIEU A LA PAIX DE FER / Duval, F – Paris, 1923 – 2mf – 1 – ILM-4096/1 – ne IDC [327]
DE LA PETITE VEROLE : MEMOIRES CONCERNANT L'HISTOIRE, LES SCIENCES...DES CHINOIS... – Paris, 1776-1783 – 1mf – 9 – ne IDC [616]
DE LA PIROTECHNIA LIBRI 10 / Biringuccio, V – O-1031 1. 1540 – 9 – ne IDC [790]
DE LA PRECELLENCE DU LANGAGE FRANCOIS / Estienne, Henri – 1896 – 9 – fr I.C.S. [440]
DE LA PRIMAUTE EN L'EGLISE / Blondel, D – Genève, 1641 – 23mf – 9 – CA-115/1 – ne IDC [240]
DE LA PROCEDURE SUIVIE ... / Berney, J – Basle, 1889 – 2mf – 9 – ILM-429/1 – ne IDC [327]
DE LA PRODUCTION ET DE LA CONSOMMATION DES BOISSONS ALCOOLIQUES EN FRANCE / Lunier, Jules Joseph Ludger – Paris: F. Savy, 1877. 230p. 3 fiches. (Miscellaneous Selections) – 9 – 8.00 – fr Bibl Nationale [310]
DE LA PRONONCIATION FRANCAISE DEPUIS LE COMMENCEMENT DU XVIE / Thurot, Ch – Siecle. 1881-83 – 9 – fr I.C.S. [440]
DE LA PROPRIETE PRIVEE ... / Boeck, C de – Paris, 1882 – 9mf – 9 – ILM-430/1 – ne IDC [327]
DE LA PROSTITUTION DANS LA VILLE DE PARIS??: CONSIDEREE SOUS LE RAPPORT DE L'HYGIENE PUBLIQUE, DE LA MORALE ET DE L'ADMINISTRATION / Parent-Duchatelet, Alexandre Jean Baptiste – Paris et Londres: J.B. Bailliere, 1836. 2v. 13 fiches.(Statistics Series: Medical Studies) – 9 – 32.00 – fr Bibl Nationale [310]
DE LA PROTECTION DES ENFANTS DU PREMIER AGE / Guillemin, Julien – Paris. 1901. (La Condition Ouvriere. Part Two.) – 9 – 7.50 – fr Bibl Nationale [360]
DE LA QUALITE... / Bressonnet, M – Paris, 1902 – 2mf – 1 – ILM-439/1 – ne IDC [327]
DE LA REPARATION DES ACCIDENTS DE TRAVAIL (RESPONSABILITE, GARANTIE, ASSURANCE). BIBLIOGRAPHIE DES TRAVAUX EN LANGUE FRANCAISE / Losseau, Leon – (Condition of 19th C. French working class series). 1897 – 9 – fr Hachette [360]
DE LA REPETITION DANS LES TEXTES LITTERAIRES SITUATION HISTORIQUE ET APPROCHE STRUCTURALE / Grajon, Nicole – 2mf – 9 – 10039 – fr Atelier National [440]
DE LA REPRESSION... / Gence, E – Paris, 1906 – 2mf – 1 – ILM-528/1 – ne IDC [327]
DE LA REPUBLIQUE, OU UN ROI EST-IL NECESSAIRE A LA CONSERVATION DE LA LIBERTE? / Condorcet, Marie Jean Antoine Nicolas de – Paris. Imp. du Cercle Social. s.d – 9 – fr Hachette [321]
DE LA REPVBLIQUE DES TURCS : ET LA OU L'OCCASION S'OFFRERA, DES MEURS ET LOYS DE TOUS MUHAMEDISTES, ... / Postel, G – Poitiers. 3pts. [1565] – 4mf – 9 – H-8303/1 – ne IDC [956]
DE LA RESPONSABILITE DES PATRONS VIS-A-VIS DES OUVRIERS DANS LES ACCIDENTS INDUSTRIELS / Sauzet, Marc – Paris. 1883. (La Condition Ouvriere. Part Two.) – 9 – 2.50 – fr Bibl Nationale [360]
DE LA SANTE DES OUVRIERS EMPLOYES DANS LES FABRIQUES DE SOIE, DE COTON ET DE LAINE / Villerme, Louis Rene – Reprod. d'un extrait des Annales d'Hygiene publique et de Medecine legale. 1839.p338-420. 1 fiche. (Statistics Series: Medical Studies) – 9 – 6.00 – fr Bibl Nationale [310]
DE LA SENEGAMBIE FRANCAISE / Carrere, Frederic & Holle, Paul – Paris: F Didot, 1855 – 1 – us Res Libr [960]
DE LA SOCIETE SAINT-SIMONIENNE ET DES CAUSES QUI ONT AMENE SA DISSOLUTION / Reynaud, Jean – Paris, Everat, 1832, 32 p. Les Saint-Simoniens, 1825-1834. 6962 – 9 – fr Hachette [335]
DE LA SUCCESSION LEGITIME ET TESTAMENTAIRE... / Antoine, C F – Nancy, 1876 – 2mf – 9 – ILM-3513/1 – ne IDC [340]
DE LA SUCCESSION LEGITIME ET TESTAMENTAIRE... / Antoine, C F – Paris, 1876 – 3mf – 9 – ILM-411/1 – ne IDC [340]
DE LA TIERRA Y EL CIELO. POESIAS LIRICAS Y RELIGIOSAS. CACERES, 1925 / Lopez Cruz, Lorenzo – Madrid: Razon y Fe, 1930 – 1 – sp Bibl Santa Ana [810]
DE LA TIRANIA A LA DEMOCRACIA SOCIAL / Ghioldi, Americo – Buenos Aires: Ediciones Gure, [1956] – 1 – CSUXAHZ2506-B – us Hoover Inst Photo [320]
DE LA TOLERANCE DANS LA RELIGION OU DE LA LIBERTE DE CONSCIENCE. L'INTOLERANCE CONVAINCUE DE CRIME ET DE FOLIE – (D'Holbach series). 1769 – 9 – fr Hachette [360]
DE LA TRAITE DES ESCLAVES EN AFRIQUE ET DES MOYENS D'Y REMEDIER / Buxton, Thomas Fowell – Traduction de l'Anglais. Paris, Arthus Bertrand. 1840 – 9 – 20.00 – fr Orientalistes [305]
DE LA TRAITE ET DE L'ESCLAVAGE DES NOIRS ET DES BLANCS, PAR UN AMI DES HOMMES DE TOUTES LES COULEURS / Gregoire, Henri Baptiste – (Slave Trade and Abolitionism in France series). 1815 – 9 – fr Hachette [305]
DE LA TRAITE ET D'ESCLAVAGE... – Paris, 1815 – 1mf – 1 – ILM-1203/1 – ne IDC [327]
DE LA TRANQUILLITE D'ESPRIT, LIVRE SINGULIER / Le Caron, Louis – Paris. 1588 – 9 – fr Hachette [360]
DE LA TRESHEVREVSE VICTOIRE DES CHRESTIENS A L'ENCONTRE DE L'ARMEE DU GRAND TURC – Anuers, 1571 – 1mf – 9 – H-8176/1 – ne IDC [956]
DE LA VACCINE ET DE SES HEREUX RESULTATS: DEMONTRES PAR DES VISITES FAITES AU DOMICILE DES INDIVIDUS DECEDES A PARIS...EN 1825 / Brunet, Jacques Louis Dubreuil & Charmont, J – Paris, Roret, Delaunay et Guitel, 1826. 172 p. 2 fiches. (Statistics Series: Medical Studies) – 9 – 6.00 – fr Bibl Nationale [310]
DE LA VENDEE / Chateaubriand, Francois-Rene de – (Extr. du journal "Le Conservateur") – Paris: Le Normant, 1820 – 1 – F50.00 – fr Armell [944]
DE LA VERITABLE ELOQUENCE / Gibert, B – 1703 – 9 – fr I.C.S. [400]
DE LA VERITE DANS L'HISTOIRE DU CHRISTIANISME: LETTRES D'UN LAIQUE SUR JESUS / Ruelle, Charles – Paris: C. Reinwald, 1866. 1 fiche – 9 – us A.T.L.A. [240]
DE LA VIDA, SENTIRES Y SABERES DE D. JOSE MORENO NIETO / Rodriguez y Rivero, Jose – Sevilla: Imp. J. Peralto, 1929, 1 lam – sp Bibl Santa Ana [920]
DE L'ABOLITION DE L'ESCLAVAGE / Dain, C – Paris, 1836 – 1mf – 1 – ILM-1208/1 – ne IDC [327]
DE L'ABOLITION DES DROITS FEODAUX ET SEIGNEURIAUX DU CANADA, ET SUR LE MEILLEUR MODE A EMPLOYER POUR ACCORDER UNE JUSTE INDEMNITE AUX SEIGNEURS / Dumesnil, Clement – Montreal: Imp. J Starke et cie, 1849. SEM105P247 – 1mf – 9 – Can$2.25 – cn Bibl Nat [971]
DE L'ABOLITION DU REGIME FEODAL EN CANADA, ET DE L'INDEMNITE DUE AUX SEIGNEURS POUR LA SUPPRESSION DES DROITS ET DEVOIRS FEODAUX.. – Quebec: Typographie d'Augustin Cote, 1855. SEM105P275 – 2mf – 9 – Can$4.50 – cn Bibl Nat [323]
DE LACONDITION PHYSIQUE ET MORALE DES JEUNES OUVRIERS ET DES MOYENS DE L'AMELIORER / Ducpetiaux, Edouard – (Condition of 19th C. French working class series). 1843 – 9 – fr Hachette [360]
DE LACTEIS THORACICIS IN HOMINE BRUTISQUE NUPERRIME OBSERVATIS,... / Bartholin, T – Londini, 1652 – 2mf – 9 – ne IDC [611]
DE L'AFFRANCHISSMENT DES ESCLAVES ET DE SES RAPPORTS AVEC LA POLITIQUE ACTUELLE / Gasparin, Agenor de – (Slave Trade and Abolitionism in France Series). 1839 – 9 – fr Hachette [360]
DE LAGARDE'S AUSGABE DER ARABISCHEN UEBERSETZUNG DER GENESIS SEMITISTISCHE STUDIEN / Davidson, H S – (Leipziger semitische studien. v. 3, pt. 5. Leipzig. 1920). Leipzig. 1919. BNE-20,115 1 – 9 – ne IDC [290]
DE LAGARDES AUSGABE DER ARABISCHEN UEBERSETZUNG DES PENTATEUCHS / Hughes, J C – (Leipziger semitistische studien. v. 7, pt. 3. Leipzig. 1915). Leipzig. 1920. BNE-20,120 1 – 9 – ne IDC [220]
DE L'ALLEMAGNE / Enfantin, BP – Paris, Duverger, 1836, 24 p. Les Saint-Simoniens, 1825-1834. 6970 – 9 – fr Hachette [335]
De Lancey, Edward Floyd *see*
– HISTORY OF THE TOWN OF MAMARONECK IN THE COUNTY OF WESTCHESTER AND STATE OF NEW YORK
– NEW YORK AND ADMIRAL SIR PETER WARREN AT THE CAPTURE OF LOUISBOURG, 1745: AN ADDRESS AT THE INAUGURATION OF THE MONUMENT AT LOUISBOURG, ON THE ONE HUNDRED AND FIFTIETH ANNIVERSARY OF ITS CAPTURE BY THE SOCIETY OF COLONIAL WARS, 1895
– PHILIP FRENEAU, THE HUGUENOT PATRIOT-POET OF THE REVOLUTION AND HIS POETRY
DE L'APPLICATION DU ... ENTRE LA FRANCE ET LA SARDAIGNE ... / Bourdelles, R de – Paris, 1882 – 1mf – 9 – ILM-2018/1 – ne IDC [327]
DE L'APPLICATION INTERNATIONALE DE LA REGLE "NON BIS IN IDEM"... / Barbey, A – Lausanne, 1930 – 3mf – 9 – ILM-2032/1 – ne IDC [340]
DE LAPSIS (FLOR. PATR., 21) / Cyprianus – 1930 – 2mf – 8 – ne Slangenburg [240]
DE L'ART DE PARLER / Lamy, B – (Linguistic series). 1675 – 9 – fr Hachette [440]
DE L'ART DES DEVISES. AVEC DIVERS RECUEILS DE DEVISES DU MESME AUTHEUR / Moyne, Pierre 1e – O 668. 1666 – 9 – ne IDC [760]
DE LAS ANDANZAS DE UNAMUNO POR TIERRAS EXTREMENAS / Garcia Blanco, Manuel – Madrid, 1956 – 1 – sp Bibl Santa Ana [946]
DE LAS CINCO ORDENES DE ARCHITECTURA / Vignola, J – Madrid, 1593 – 1mf – 9 – sp Cultura [720]
DE LAS DEUDAS AMORTIZABLES...CUPONES / Bravo Murillo, Juan – 1864 – 9 – 1.50f – sp Bibl Santa Ana [336]
DE LAS ORDENES MILITARES DE CALATRAVA, ALCANTARA Y MONTESA / Guillamas, Manuel de – 1852 – 9 – 1.50f – sp Bibl Santa Ana [355]
DE LAS SIETE PALABRAS...DE MANUEL BENITEZ SANCHEZ CORTES / Perez Embrid, Florentino – Madrid: Arbor, 1949 – 1 – sp Bibl Santa Ana [240]
DE L'ASILE ACCORDE AUX VAISSEAUX DE GUERRE ... / Boullier, J – Paris, 1912 – 2mf – 9 – ILM-1094/1 – ne IDC [327]
DE L'ASSIETTE DE L'IMPOT. EXAMEN CRITIQUE / Pereire, Emile – Paris, Revue encyclopedique, 1832, 72 p. Les Saint-Simoniens, 1825-1834. 6888 – 9 – fr Hachette [336]
DE L'ASSISTANCE JUDICIAIRE DES ETRANGERS EN FRANCE / Guerard, H – Paris, 1910 – 2mf – 1 – ILM-2230/1 – ne IDC [327]
DE L'ATLANTIQUE AU NIGER PAR LE FOUTAH-DJALLON : CARNET DU VOYAGE / Olivier, Aime, Vicomte de Sanderval – Paris: P Ducrocq, 1882 – 1 – us Res Libr [960]
DE L'ATLANTIQUE AU NIGER PAR LE FOUTAH-DJALLON / Sanderval, Aime Olivier – Carnet de voyage. Paris, P. Ducrocq. 1882 – 9 – 12.50 – fr Orientalistes [910]
DE LAUBENFIL'S SPONGE FILE / Allan Hancock Foundation – 1965 – 18r – 1 – $360.00 – us Microfilm [590]
DE L'AUDITION EN MATIERE CRIMINELLE... / Bregeault, J – Paris, 1878 – 1mf – 1 – ILM-2056/1 – ne IDC [327]
DE L'AUSCULTATION MEDIATE / Laennec, R T H – Paris, 1819. 2v – 19mf – 9 – ne IDC [610]
DE L'AUTORITE ET DE L'EXECUTION DES JUGEMENTS ETRANGERS...EN FRANCE... / Daguin, C – Paris, 1887 – 6mf – 1 – ILM-2019/1 – ne IDC [327]
DE L'AUTORITE ET DE L'EXECUTION DES JUGEMENTS ETRANGERS...EN FRANCE... / Daguin, D – Paris, 1887 – 5mf – 1 – ILM-2023/1 – ne IDC [327]

DE L'AUTORITE QUE POSSEDENT EN FRANCE LES JUGEMENTS ETRANGERS / Cabannes, A – Nancy, 1914 – 2mf – 1 – ILM-2092/1 – ne IDC [327]

DE L'AUTRE RIVE / Herzen, Aleksandr I – (Russia – 19th C. series). 1870 – 9 – fr Hachette [360]

DE L'ECONOMIE DU SALUT : ETUDE SUR LE DOGME DANS SES RAPPORTS AVEC LA MORALE / Weber, Alfred – Strasbourg: Treuttel et Wurtz, 1864 – 1mf – 9 – 0-8370-5720-5 – 1985-3720 – us A.T.L.A. [210]

DE L'EDIT DE NANTES EXECUTE SELON... / Meynier, B – Paris, 1670 – 2mf – 9 – CA-140/1 – ne IDC [240]

DE L'EDUCATION / Halma, Nicolas B – 1791. 6764 – 9 – fr Hachette [370]

DE L'EDUCATION: CONFERENCE FAITE EN FEVRIER 1881 DEVANT LE CERCLE CATHOLIQUE DE QUEBEC / Boucher de la Bruere, Pierre – St. Hyacinthe: Presses du Courrier, 1881. 00194. (Pre-1900 Canadiana) – 9 – cn C.I.H.M. [370]

DE L'EDUCATION DES COLLEGES / Philipon de La Madelaine, Louis – Londres. 1784. 6780 – 9 – fr Hachette [370]

DE L'EDUCATION DES FEMMES / Choderlos de Laclos, P AF – Paris: L. Vanier, 1903. 146p. (Les Femmes Collection) – 2mf – 9 – $6.00 – fr Bibl Nationale [370]

DE L'EDUCATION PUBLIQUE – Aout 1790 – 9 – fr Hachette [370]

DE L'EDUCATION PUBLIQUE / Crevier, Jean-Baptiste-Louis – Amsterdam. 1762 – 9 – fr Hachette [370]

DE L'EDUCATION PUBLIQUE, ET DES MOYENS D'EN REALISER LA REFORME PROJETEE DANS LA DERNIERE ASSEMBLEE DU CLERGE / Proyart, Lievin-Bonaventure – Paris. Herissant et Barrois. 1785 – 9 – fr Hachette [370]

DE LEER VAN HET MESSIASRIJK BIJ DE EERSTE CHRISTENEN : VOLGENS DE HANDELINGEN DER APOSTELEN.... / Blom, Abraham Herman – (Includes index) – Dordrecht:P K Braat, 1863 – 1mf – 9 – 0-8370-2382-3 – 1985-0382 – us A.T.L.A. [220]

DE L'EFFET DU CHANGEMENT DU STATUT PERSONNEL... / Ambelouis, R – Paris, [1928] – 2mf – 9 – ILM-3006/1 – ne IDC [340]

DE L'EFFICACITE EXTRATERRITORIALE... / Gidel, G C – Paris, 1905 – 2mf – 1 – ILM-537/1 – ne IDC [327]

DE L'EGALITE DES DEUX SEXES, DISCOURS PHYSIQUE ET MORALE OU L'ON VOIT L'IMPORTANCE DE SE DEFAIRE DES PREJUGEZ / La Barre, Francois Poullain de – Paris: Jean du Pais, 1676. 221p. (Les Femmes Collection) – 3mf – 9 – $8.00 – fr Bibl Nationale [306]

DE L'EGALITE OU PRINCIPES GENERAUX SUR LES INSTITUTIONS CIVILES, POLITIQUES ET RELIGIEUSES / Escherny, Francois L d' – Basle: J. Decker, 1796 – 9 – fr Hachette [190]

DE LEGATIONIBUS LIBRI TRES... / Gentili, A – Hanover, 1607 – 3mf – 1 – ILM-532/1 – ne IDC [327]

DE LEGATIONUM JURE,... / Arosinus, H J – Ubsaliae, 1659 – 1mf – 9 – ILM-969/1 – ne IDC [340]

DE LEGATIS PRINCIPUM,... / Germoni, A – Rome, 1627 – 5mf – 1 – ILM-534/1 – ne IDC [327]

DE LEGATO PACIS GRATIA... / Goessell, I C – Rintelii, 1736 – 1mf – 1 – ILM-1084/1 – ne IDC [327]

DE LEGIBUS O TRATADO DE LEYES... / Leon, Luis de – Madrid: Arch. Ibero Americano, 1964 – 1 – sp Bibl Santa Ana [946]

DE L'EMBAUMEMENT AVANT ET APRES JESUS CHRIST / Rosemont, Louis Reutter de – Avec analyses de masses resineuses. Paris: Vigot Freres, (1912?) – 1 – us U.W. Library [610]

DE L'ENSEIGNEMENT PROFESSIONNEL / Corbon, Anthime – (Condition of 19th C. French working class series). 4e ed – 9 – fr Hachette [370]

DE L'ENSEIGNEMENT PUBLIC / Mathias, principal du college de Langres – Paris, 1776. xvi,125p. 2 fiches. (Education Collection) – 9 – 6.00 – fr Bibl Nationale [370]

DE LEON FIRST BAPTIST CHURCH. DE LEON, TEXAS : CHURCH RECORDS – 1877-1942 – 1 – 59.04 – us Baptist [240]

DE L'EPOPEE ANCIENNE ET MODERNE / Bazy, Jean Pierre Antoine – Paris: Ve. Thuan, 1883. 39p. 1 fiche. (Literature Collection) – 9 – 6.00 – fr Bibl Nationale [440]

DE L'ESCLAVAGE DES NOIRS ET DE LA LEGISLATION COLONIALE / Schoelcher, Victor – (Slave Trade and Abolitionism in France series). 1833 – 9 – fr Hachette [305]

DE L'ESCLAVAGE ET DES COLONIES / Du Puynode, Gustave – (Slave Trade and Abolitionism in France Series). 1847 – 9 – fr Hachette [360]

DE L'ESPRIT DES RELIGIONS / Bonneville, Nicolas de – Paris. Imp. du Cercle Social. 1792 – 9 – fr Hachette [321]

DE L'ETABLISSEMENT DES CONNOISSANCES HUMAINES, ET DE L'INSTRUCTION PUBLIQUE DANS LA CONSTITUTION FRANCAISE / Lacretelle, Pierre-Louis – Paris. Desenne. 1791. 6767 – 9 – fr Hachette [323]

DE L'ETAT DES NEGRES RELATIVEMENT A LA PROSPERITE DES COLONIES FRANCAISES ET DE LEUR METROPOLE – 1789 – 9 – 5.00 – fr Orientalistes [305]

DE L'EXCELLENCE DE LA LANGUE FRANCOISE / Charpentier, Fr – 1683 – 9 – fr I.C.S. [440]

DE L'EXECUTION DES JUGEMENTS ET ACTES AUTHENTIQUES ETRANGERS... / Garat, M J – Paris, 1896 – 3mf – 1 – ILM-2266/1 – ne IDC [327]

DE L'EXECUTION DES JUGEMENTS ETRANGERS... / Constant, C – Paris, 1883 – 1mf – 1 – ILM-2024/1 – ne IDC [327]

DE L'EXECUTION DES JUGEMENTS ETRANGERS DANS LES DIVERS PAYS / Constant, C – Ed 2. Paris, 1890 – 3mf – 1 – ILM-2008/1 – ne IDC [327]

DE L'EXERCISE DE LA MEDICINE EN PROVINCE AU XIXE SIECLE / Hamon, Louis – Paris. 1868. (La condition Ouvriere. Part Two.) – 9 – 5.00 – fr Bibl Nationale [360]

DE L'EXISTANCE DE DIEU / Lagneau, Jules – Paris. 1925. vi, 156p. (Religion series) – 9 – 6.00 – fr Bibl Nationale [240]

DE L'EXPULSION DES ETRANGERS;... / Darut, J A – Aix, 1902 – 3mf – 1 – ILM-465/1 – ne IDC [327]

DE L'EXTRADITION / Bonafos-Lazerme, H – Lyon, 1866 – 2mf – 9 – ILM-432/1 – ne IDC [327]

DE LEYTE DE CAVALLEROS...CAVALLOS / Maestre de San Juan, Lucas – 1735 – 9 – 1.50f – sp Bibl Santa Ana [340]

DE L'HYPOTHEQUE LEGALE DE LA FEMME MARIEE / Dufoussat, Henry – Paris: Rousseau, 1898. 316p. (Les Femmes Collection) – 4mf – 9 – $10.00 – fr Bibl Nationale [305]

DE LIBERTATE COMMERCIORUM EX STATU COMMUNIONIS PRIMAEVAE DERIVANDA / Bruistens, J – Groningae, 1770 – 1mf – 1 – ILM-719/1 – ne IDC [327]

DE L'IMPOSTURE SACERDOTALE OU RECUEIL DE PIECES SUR LE CLERGE – (D'Holbach series). 1767 – 9 – fr Hachette [240]

DE L'INCERTITUDE, VANITE, ET ABUS DES SCIENCES / Agrippa, Henricus Cornelius – Reprod. d'une ed. s.l., s.n., 1630. xxii,526p. 6 fiches. (Science Collection) – 9 – 15.00 – fr Bibl Nationale [500]

DE L'INCOMPETENCE... / Damiron, P – Paris, 1908 – 2mf – 1 – ILM-457/1 – ne IDC [327]

DE L'INFECONDITE DE CERTAINES POPULATIONS INDUSTRIELLES. / Dumont, Arsene – Reprod. de l'extrait du Journal de la Ste. Stat. de Paris, no.10, 1900. p321-69. 1 fiche. (Statistics Series: Medical Studies) – 9 – 6.00 – fr Bibl Nationale [310]

DE L'INFLUENCE DES SAISONS SUR LA MORTALITE AUX DIFFERENS AGES DANS LA BELGIQUE / Quetelet, Adolphe Lambert Jacques – Bruxelles, M. Hayez, 1838, 42 p., tableaux. 1 fiche. (Statistics Series: Medical Studies) – 9 – 6.00 – fr Bibl Nationale [310]

DE L'INFLUENCE DU DIALECTE GASCON / Lanusse, M – 1893 – 9 – fr I.C.S. [440]

DE L'INITIATIVE CONSULAIRE EN FAIT DE TUTTELLE ET DE CURATELLE... / Flaischlen, G G – Paris, 1891 – 1mf – 1 – ILM-3441/1 – ne IDC [327]

DE L'INSTRUCTION PUBLIQUE OU CONSIDERATIONS MORALES ET POLITIQUES SUR LA NECESSITE, LA NATURE ET LA SOURCE DE CETTE INSTRUCTION / LeMercier de La Riviere – Stockholm et Paris. Didot. 1775. 6768 – 9 – fr Hachette [170]

DE L'INTERET DE LA FRANCE A L'EGARD DE LA TRAITE DES NEGRES / Sismondi, Leonard Simonde de – (Slave Trade and Abolitionism in France series). 1814 – 9 – fr Hachette [360]

DE L'INTERVENTION DE LA SOCIETE POUR PREVENIR ET SOULAGER LA MISERE / Melun, Armand de – (Condition of 19th C. French working class series). 1849 – 9 – fr Hachette [360]

DE LISTIGE ONSTANTVASTIGHEYT DES WERELTS / Vermeren, M F – O 792 1. 1745 – 9 – ne IDC [999]

DE LITERIS ET LINGUA GETARUM, SIUE GOTHORUM... / De Smet, B – Lvgdvni Batavorvm, 1597 – 2mf – 9 – ne IDC [400]

DE LITURGIA GALLICANA LIBRI 3 / Mabillon, Jean – Parisiis, 1685 – 9mf – 8 – Dfl32.00 – ne Slangenburg [240]

DE LO PASADO : ESTAMPAS BREVES / Pineda, Ramon – Badajoz: Imp. Ind. Graficas, 1958 – sp Bibl Santa Ana [946]

DE L'OCCUPATIO BELLICA.... / Delalande, E – Paris, 1875 – 3mf – 1 – ILM-493/1 – ne IDC [327]

DE L'ORGANISATION – 3rd ed. Conakry: Imp nationale Patrice Lumumba, [1970] – us Res Libr [072]

DE L'ORGUE ET DE SON ARCHITECTURE / Cavaille-Coll, Aristide – (Deuxieme tirage, revu et augmente) – Paris: Ducher et Sie, 1872 – 1 – us Sibley [780]

DE L'ORIENT A TOULON SUR MER ET SUR TERRE / Bernard, Marius (de Cannes) – Paris. 1887. 235p. (Travel series) – 9 – 6.00 – fr Bibl Nationale [910]

DE L'ORIGINE DES INDIENS DU NOUVEAU MONDE ET DE LEUR CIVILISATION / Dabry de Thiersant, Philibert – Paris: E. Leroux. 1883. 02254. (Pre-1900 Canadiana) – 9 – cn C.I.H.M. [971]

DE L'ORIGINE DU LANGAGE / Renan, Ernest – 2e ed. 1858 – 9 – fr I.C.S. [400]

DE L'ORIGINE ET DES FONCTIONS DES CONSULS / Borel, F – Spb, 1807 – 4mf – 9 – ILM-133/1 – ne IDC [327]

DE LOS CAMINOS O VIAS MILITARES FABRICADAS POR LOS ROMANOS EN ESPANA / Morales, Ambrosio – Madrid: Oficina de D. Benito Cano, 1792 – 1 – sp Bibl Santa Ana [946]

DE LOS MALEFICIOS Y LOS DEMONIOS / Montoto, Jose Maria – 1884 – 1 – sp Bibl Santa Ana [946]

DE LOS NOMBRES ATRIBUIDOS A TRUJILLO / Acedo, Federico – Caceres: Tip. Enc. y Lib. de N.M. Jimenez, 1900 – 1 – sp Bibl Santa Ana [946]

DE L'OUBANGHI A FACHODA : MARCHAND ET LA MISSION CONGO-NIL. OUVRAGE ORNE DE GRAVURES / Poirier, Jules – Paris: J Lefort, [1899] – 1 – us Res Libr [960]

DE LS *see* CATALOGO DE LOS LIBROS... CACERES

DE L'UNIFICATION... : CONFLITS DE LOIS EN MATIERE DE LETTRES DE CHANGE ET DE BILLETS A ORDRE / Bayssat, F – Paris, 1932 – 3mf – 9 – ILM-3603/1 – ne IDC [327]

DE L'UNIFICATION DU DROIT RELATIF A LA LETTRE DE CHANGE ET AU BILLET A ORDRE / Bouteron, J – Paris, 1912 – 4mf – 9 – ILM-3496/1 – ne IDC [327]

DE L'UNIVERSALITE DU DELUGE / Schoebel, Charles – (Includes bibliographical references) – Paris: Benjamin Duprat, 1858 – 1mf – 9 – 0-8370-4634-3 – 1985-2634 – us A.T.L.A. [220]

DE MACARIO MAGNETE ET SCRIPTIS EJUS / Duchesne, Louis – Parisiis: Fr. Klincksieck, 1877 – 1mf – us A.T.L.A. [240]

DE MADRID A LISBOA / Diaz Perez, Nicolas – 1887 – 9 – 1.50f – sp Bibl Santa Ana [910]

DE MAGNO SIVE HALECUM PISCATU BELGICO,... / Gevers Deynoot, W T – Lugduni Batavorum, 1829 – 2mf – 1 – ILM-840/1 – ne IDC [327]

DE MANICHAEISMO APUD LATINOS QUINTO SEXTOQUE SAECULO : ATQUE DE LATINIS APOCRYPHIS LIBRIS / Dufourcq, Albertus – Paris: A. Fontemoing, 1900 – 1mf – us A.T.L.A. [240]

DE MARSEILLE A TAMATAVE / Brunet, Louis – Paris. 1898. 239p. (Travel series) – 9 – 9.00 – fr Bibl Nationale [910]

DE MASSUA A SAATI : NARRAZIONE DELLA SPEDIZIONE ITALIANA DEL 1888 IN ABISSINIA – (Con un' appendice contenente il testo completo del Libro Verde presentado al parlamento, la relazione ufficiale sul combattimento di Saganeiti e tutte le note crispi e goblet sull' incidente di Massua) – Milan, Treves, 1888 – 1 – us Res Libr [960]

...DE MEDENDIS HUMANI CORPORIS. ENCHIRIDION VULGO VENI MECUM... / Bayro, P – Coimbra, 1689 – 14mf – 9 – sp Cultura [610]

DE MENTE DOGMATICA LOCI PAULINI AD ROM. 5, 12 SQ / Fricke, Gustav Adolfus – Lipsiae: J.C. Hinrichs, 1880. 1 fiche – 9 – us A.T.L.A. [240]

DE METALLICIS LIBRI TRES ANDREA CAESALPINO ARETINO / Cesalpino, Andrea – 1602. 222p. With: Dispvtationvm de medicina nova Philippi Paracelsi para prima, by T. Erastus – 1 – us U.W. Library [530]

DE MI ALBUM DE FIRMA. SEMBLANZAS DE ILUTRES VARONES / Sanchez Arjona, Vicente – Sevilla: Imprenta Zambrano, Tomos 1-3. 1956 – 1 – sp Bibl Santa Ana [810]

DE MI VIDA; MEMORIAL POLITICAS / Reyes, Rodolfo – Madrid. 1929-30. 2 vols – 1 – us Res Libr [320]

DE MI VIEJA EXTREMADURA (PAGINAS MONTANCHEGAS) / Galan y Galan, FG – Sevilla: Tip. Divina Pastora, 1935 – 1 – sp Bibl Santa Ana [946]

DE MICHAEL ET ANDROICO PALAEOLOGIS LIBRI 13 (CSHB 24, 25) / Pachymeris, Georgii; ed by Bekkerus, Imm – Bonnae. v1-2. 1835 – Dfl102.00 – ne Slangenburg [240]

DE MICHAELIS SERVETI DOCTRINA : COMMENTATIONUM DOGMATICO-HISTORICAM / Puenjer, Georg Christian Bernhard – Jenae: Sumptibus Hermanni Dufft, 1876 – 1mf – us A.T.L.A. [240]

De Mille, Alban Bertram *see* LITERATURE IN THE CENTURY

De Mille, James *see*
- THE AMERICAN BARON: A NOVEL
- BEHIND THE VEIL: A POEM
- THE "B.O.W.C.": A BOOK FOR BOYS
- THE DODGE CLUB, OR ITALY IN 1859
- THE LADY OF THE ICE: A NOVEL
- THE LILY AND THE CROSS: A TALE OF ACADIA

DE MINNENDE SIELE GHESCHONCKEN AEN ALLE LIEF-HEBBERS GODTS VOOR EEN NIEUW-IAER / Smidt, A de – Antwerpen, 1665 – 1mf – 9 – ne IDC [700]

DE MIRACULIS LIBRI DUO / Cluniacensis abbas, Petrus – 1988 – 5mf – 9 – Bf1,350.00 – 2-503-63832-5 – be Brepols [240]

DE MIS CANTARES INEDITOS / Sanchez Arjona, Vicente – Sevilla: Imprenta Carlos Acuna, Tomo 1. 1948 – 1 – sp Bibl Santa Ana [810]

DE MIS OCHO MIL CONETOS / Sanchez Arjona, Vicente – Sevilla: Imprenta Alvarez, 1955 – 1 – sp Bibl Santa Ana [810]

DE MIS POESIAS INEDITAS / Sanchez Arjona, Vicente – Sevilla: Imp. Carlos Acuna, Tomo 1. 1948 – 1 – sp Bibl Santa Ana [810]

DE MIS POESIAS INEDITAS / Sanchez-Arjona, Vicente – Sevilla: Imp. Carlos Acuna, Tomo 2. 1949 – 1 – sp Bibl Santa Ana [810]

DE MIS SOLEDADES VENGO / Sanchez-Arjona, Vicente – Sevilla: Imprenta Alvarez, 1959 – 1 – sp Bibl Santa Ana [810]

DE MIS VEINTE MIL CANTARES / Sanchez-Arjona, Vicente – Sevilla: Editorial Franciscana San Antonio, 1950 – 1 – sp Bibl Santa Ana [810]

DE MISERABILI MONASTERIENSIVM ANABAPTISTARVM OBSIDIONE / Corvinus, A – Vitebergae, G. Rhau. 1536. BME-160 1 – 9 – ne IDC [240]

DE MISSIONE LEGATORVM IAPONENSIUM AD ROMANAM CURIAM / Saude, E de – Macaensi, 1590 – 5mf – 9 – H-8425/1 – ne IDC [956]

DE MONACHICO STATU IUXTA DICIPLINAM BYZANTINAM / Meester, Placidus de – Romae, 1942 – 18mf – 8 – Dfl63.00 – ne Slangenburg [240]

de Montfaucon, D Bern *see* COLLECTIO NOVA PATRUM ET SCRIPTORUM GRAECORUM

DE MONTREAL A LOURDES – Montreal: s.n., 1883. 04223. (Pre-1900 Canadiana) – 9 – cn C.I.H.M. [910]
DE MORALI PRINCIPIS INSTITUTIONE / Belvacensis, Vincentius – 1995 – 4mf – 9 – Bf1,400.00 – 2-503-64372-8 – be Brepols [450]
DE MORBIS ACUTIS INFANTUM / Harris, W – M-173 2. 1698 – 8 – ne IDC [610]
DE MORBIS CAPITIS / Pemell, R – M 388. 1650 – 9 – ne IDC [610]
DE MORBIS VENEREIS LIBRI SEX / Astruc, Jean – M-82. 1736 – 9 – ne IDC [610]
DE MORBO POSTULATO SIVE CENTICVLARI / Lopez de Corella, A – Zaragoza, 1574 – 4mf – 9 – sp Cultura [610]
DE MOTU MUSCULORUM... / Bernouilli, J – Venetiis, Ed.2 1721 – 3mf – 9 – ne IDC [610]
DE MOZAEISCHE OORSPRONG VAN DE WETTEN IN DE BOEKEN EXODUS, LEVITICUS EN NUMERI : LEZINGEN OVER DE MODERNE SCHRIFT-CRITIEK DES OUDEN TESTAMENTS / Hoedemaker, Philippus Jacobus – (Includes bibliographical references and indexes) – Leiden:D.A. Daamen, 1895 – 1mf – 9 – 0-8370-3611-9 – 1985-1611 – us A.T.L.A. [220]
DE MULIERUM ORGANIS GENERATIONI INSERVIENTIBUS / Graaf, R de – Lugduni Batavorum, 1672 – 8mf – 9 – ne IDC [612]
DE MULTRO, TRADITIONE ET OCCISIONE GLORIOSI KAROLI COMITIS FLANDRIARUM / Brugensis, Galbertus Notarius – 1995 – 5mf – 9 – Bf1,400.00 – 2-503-64312-4 – be Brepols [450]
De Mundi Universitate libri duc, sive Megacosmus et microcosmus *see* BERNARDI SILVESTRIS
DE MUSCULIS ET GLANDULIS OBSERVATIONUM SPECIMEN / Stensen, N – Hafniae, 1664 – 2mf – 9 – ne IDC [611]
DE MYCETOGENESI / Ehrenberg, CG – Bonnae. 1820. B-5097 2 – 8 – ne IDC [580]
DE NATURA FIDEI APUD PAULUM APOSTOLUM: MYSTICANE IN EA CONTINEANTUR ELEMENTA, NECNE / Vernes, Maurice – Strasbourg: Ed. Heitzii, 1871. 1 fiche – 9 – us A.T.L.A. [240]
DE NATURA NOVI ORBIS LIBRI DUO ET DE PROMULGATIONE EVANGELI APUD... / Acosta, J – Salamanca, 1589 – 11mf – 9 – sp Cultura [240]
DE NATURA POPULORUM... / Besold, C – Tvbingae, 1632 – 2mf – 9 – ne IDC [400]
DE NATURIS RERUM / Neckham, A – 1863 – 7 – uk Microform Academic [120]
...DE NEUTRALITATE TEMPORE BELLI / Constant Rebeque, C T J de – Lugduni Batavorum, 1829 – 2mf – 1 – ILM-1068/1 – ne IDC [327]
[DE NOMI CORDE DEL MONOCHORDO] / Mei, G – Italy: Ms, late 16th C – 1 – us Sibley [780]
DE NOMINUM ANALOGIA : DE CONCEPTU ENTIS / Caietanus, Thomas de Vio Cardinalis – Romae, 1952 – 3mf – 8 – ne Slangenburg [240]
DE NOMINUM ANALOGIA - DE CONCEPTU ENTIS / Cajetanus – Roma, 1934 – 2mf – 8 – ne Slangenburg [290]
DE NONNULLI PORPHYRII...SCHOLAE / Sanchez de las Brozas, Francisco – 1597 – 9 – 1.50f – sp Bibl Santa Ana [450]
DE NONULLIS PORPLIYRY, ALRIORUMQ; IN DIALECTICA ER RORIBUS SCHOLA DIALECTTICA / Sanchez de las Brozas, Francisco – Salamanca: Miguel Serrona de Vargas, 1588 – 1 – sp Bibl Santa Ana [946]
DE NUEVO ACERCA DEL CONDADO DE LA GOMERA / Regulo Perez, Juan – Madrid, s.i., 1956 – 1 – sp Bibl Santa Ana [946]
DE NUEVO EN LA ACCION / Repetto, Nicolas – [Buenos Aires]: Bases, 1958 – 1 – CSUXADH1694-B – us Hoover Inst Photo [972]
DE NUPTIIS ET SEXU PLANTARUM / Linnaeus, Carl – Ed. by J. A. Afzelius. Upsaliae. 1828. B-162 2 – 8 – ne IDC [580]
DE OFFICIIS ECCLESIASTICIS DE JEAN D'ARVRANCHES / Delmare, R Le. – Paris, 1923 – 5mf – 8 – Dfl22.00 – ne Slangenburg [240]
DE OFFICIIS MAGNAE ECCLESIAE ET AULAE CONSTANTINOPO- LITANAE (CBH 18) / Codini, Georgii; ed by Gretser, J & Goar, J – Parisiis, 1648 – Dfl70.00 – ne Slangenburg [240]
DE OMNIBUS ILLIBERALIBUS SIVE MECHANICIS ARTIBUS / Schopperus, H – O 1009 1. 1574 – 9 – ne IDC [760]
DE ONTOLOGICAE DEI EXISTENTIS ARGUMENTATIONIS 6 / Johanny, Erichio – Vienna: C.A. Mueller, 1883. 1 fiche – 9 – us A.T.L.A. [240]
DE OPTIMA LEGENDORUM ECCLESIAE PATRUM METHODO / Bonaventura Argonensis O – Augustae Taurinorum, 1742 – 8mf – 8 – ne Slangenburg [240]
DE OPTIMO IMPERIO SIVE JOSUAE / Arias Montano, Benito – 1583 – 9 – 1.50f – sp Bibl Santa Ana [240]
DE ORACULIS SIBYLLINIS A IUDAEIS COMPOSITIS, PARS 1 / Badt, Benno Guilelmus – (In Latin) – Vratislaviae [Wroclaw]: Henricus Lindner, [1869?] – 1mf – 9 – 0-8370-2147-2 – 1985-0147 – us A.T.L.A. [240]
DE ORBE NOVO / Angleria, Pedro Martir – 1587 – 9 – 1.50f – sp Bibl Santa Ana [970]
DE ORBE NOVO / Angleria, Pedro Martir – v. 1-2. 1892 – 9 – 1.50f – sp Bibl Santa Ana [970]
DE ORBIS TERRAE CONCORDIA LIBRI QUATUOR, ... / Postel, G – Basle, 1544 – 8mf – 9 – H-8272/1 – ne IDC [956]
DE ORCHIDEIS EUROPAEIS ANNOTATIONES / Richard, L C M – Parisiis. 1817. B-5677 2 – 8 – ne IDC [580]
DE L'ORGANISATION DE LA JUSTICE REPRESSIVE AUX PRINCIPALES EPOQUES HISTORIQUES / Becot, Joseph – Paris, Durand, 1860. 308 p. LL-4065 – 1 – us L of C Photodup [340]
DE L'ORGANISATION DE LA STATISTIQUE DU TRAVAIL ET DU PLACEMENT DES OUVRIERS / Hennequin, Amedee – (Condition of 19th C. French working class series). 1848 – 9 – fr Hachette [310]
DE L'ORGANISATION DES SOCIETES DE PREVOYANCES OU DE SECOURS MUTUEL / Hubbard, G – (Condition of 19th C. French working class series). 1852 – 9 – fr Hachette [360]
DE L'ORGANISATION D'UN ETAT MONARCHIQUE / Salaville, Jean-Baptiste – 1789 – 9 – fr Hachette [321]
DE L'ORIGINE DE LA FRANC-MACONNERIE / Paine, Thomas – Ouvrage posthum.Traduit par Nicolas de Bonneville. Paris: C.F. Patris, 1812 – 9 – fr Hachette [321]
DE L'ORIGINE DES PRINCIPES RELIGIEUX / Meister, Jacques-Henri – (D'Holbach series). 1768 – 9 – fr Hachette [240]
DE ORIGINE ET AVTORITATE UERBI DEI, AND QUAE PONTIFICUM, PATRUM AND CONCILIORUM...ADMONITIO HOC TEMPORE, QUO DE CONCILIO CONGREGANDO AGITUR, UALDE NECESSARIA / Major, G – VVittembergae, 1550 – 2mf – ne IDC [240]
DE ORIGINE ET GESTIS FRANCORUM COMPENDIUM : IMPR. LUGDUNIS IMPENSIS JOH. TRECHSL ALEMANNI ET DILIGENTI ACCURATIONE JODOCI BADII ASCENSII / Robertus Gaguinus – 1491 – Dfl28.00 – ne Slangenburg [240]
DE ORIGINE ET PVERITIA LATINAE LINGVAE, LIBRI DVO... ACCEDIT SPICILEGIVM LITERARIVM, ET INDEX... / Funck, J N – Marburgi Cattorum, 1735 – 5mf – 9 – ne IDC [450]
DE ORIGINE GERMANORUM... / Eckhardt, J G von – Goettingae, 1750 – 6mf – 9 – ne IDC [430]
DE ORIGINE HAERESIVM NOSTRI TEMPORIS / Hosius, Stanislaus – Lovanii, P. S. Tiletanus. 1559. BME-356 2 – 8 – ne IDC [240]
DE ORIGINE JURISDICTIONUM LIBER : TRACTATUS DE LEGIBUS / Durandas de S Portiano OP – Parisiis, 1506 – Dfl13.00 – ne Slangenburg [240]
DE ORIGINE LINGUARUM VARIARUM... / Muhle, H – Kiloni, 1692 – 3mf – 9 – ne IDC [400]
DE ORIGINIBUS LINGUAE SORABICAE / Frenzel, A – Budisinae Lusatorum. 2v. 1693-1696 – 9mf – 9 – ne IDC [400]
...DE ORIGINIBUS SEU DE HEBRAICAE LINGUAE ET GENTIS ANTIQUITATE, ... / Postel, G – N.p., 1538 – 1mf – 9 – H-8253/1 – ne IDC [956]
DE ORIGINIBUS SEU DE HEBRAICAE LINGUAE ET GENTIS ANTIQUITATE, ATQUE VARIARUM LINGUARUM AFFINITATE / Postel, G – In French. (Linguistic series). 1538 – 9 – fr Hachette [470]
DE ORIGINIBUS, SEV, DE VARIA ET POTISSIMUM ORBI LATINO AD HANC DIEM INCOGNITA, AUT INCOSYDERATA HISTORIA, QUU TOTIUS ORIENTIS, TUM MAXIME TARTARORUM, PERSARUM, TURCARUM / Postel, G – Basileae, [1553] – 2mf – 9 – H-8414/1 – ne IDC [956]
DE ORTHO SEU MATUTINO BYZANTINO / Mateos, J – 3mf – 8 – Dfl13.00 – ne Slangenburg [240]
DE ORTU ET OCCASU LINGUAE LATINAE / Niess, J – Dilingae, 1627 – 6mf – 9 – ne IDC [450]
DE ORTU ET PROGRESSU ORDINIS...DE MONTE CARMELO / Trithemius, J & Miraeus A – Colonia Agrippina, 1643 – 8mf – 8 – Dfl30.00 – ne Slangenburg [240]
DE PACTIS ANNO 1556... / Duruy, G – Paris, 1883 – 2mf – 1 – ILM-512/1 – ne IDC [327]
De Paepe, N *see* HADEWIJCH'S STROPHISCHE GEDICHTEN
DE PARIS AU NIAGARA / Bigot, Charles – Paris: A. Dupret, 1887. 00135. (Pre-1900 Canadiana) – 9 – cn C.I.H.M. [910]
DE PARTU VIRGINIS : DE ASSUMPTIONE SANCTAE MARIAE / Radbertus, Paschasius – 1985 – 3mf – 9 – Bf800.00 – 2-503-30568-7 – be Brepols [240]
DE PASSAUER ANONYMUS (MGH SCHRIFTEN..: 22.BD) : EIN SAMMELWERK UEBER KETZER, JUDEN, ANTICHRIST AUS DER MITTE DES 13. JAHRHUNDERTS / Patschovsky, A – 1968 – Dfl22.00 – ne Slangenburg [240]
DE PASTILLIS VIPERINIS THERIACAE... / Monsalvo, O – SL, SA – 2mf – 9 – sp Cultura [616]
DE PASTOR VON DRIEBECK : ERZAEHLUNG IN NIEDERDEUTSCHER MUNDART / Wibbelt, Augustin – 3. Aufl. Essen (Ruhr): Fredebeul & Koenen, 1920 – 1 – us U.W. Library [830]
UNE DE PERDUE, DEUX DE TROUVEES / Boucher de Boucherville, George – Montreal: E Senecal. 2v. 1874. SEM16P111 – 1r – 5 – Can$9.00 – cn Bibl Nat [830]
De Peyster, John Watts *see*
– MILITARY (1776-79) TRANSACTIONS OF MAJOR, AFTERWARDS COLONEL, 8TH OR KING'S FOOT, ARENT SCHUYLER DE PEYSTER
– SIR JOHN JOHNSON, THE FIRST AMERICAN BORN BARONET: AN ADDRESS DELIVERED BEFORE THE NEW YORK HISTORICAL SOCIETY, AT ITS ANNUAL MEETING, TUESDAY, JANUARY 6TH, 1880
DE PHILIPPI MELANCHTHONIS ORTV, TOTIVS VITAE CVRRICVLO ET MORTE,... / Camerarius, J – Lipsiae, [1566] – 5mf – 9 – ne IDC [240]
DE PHILOSOPHIA MORALI : PRAELECTIONES QUAS IN COLLEGIO GEORGIOPOLITANO SOC. JESU ANNO 1889-90 / Russo, Nicolaus – (Includes index) – Ed altera. Neo-Eboraci [New York]: Benziger, 1891 – 1mf – 9 – 0-8370-6361-2 – 1986-0361 – us A.T.L.A. [170]
DE PHRYNICHO SOPHISTA / Kaibel, George – (Discussion in Latin; citations in Greek) – Gottingae: Vandenhoeck et Ruprecht, [1899?] – 1mf – 9 – 0-8370-9798-3 – 1986-3798 – us A.T.L.A. [450]
DE PICTURA VETERUM LIBRI TRES / Junius, Franciscus – O-317. 1694 – 9 – ne IDC [760]
DE PLACITIS HIPPOCRATIS ET PLATONIS LIBRI NOVEM / Galenus – Recensu1t et explanavit Iwanus Mueller. Lipsiae, in aedibus B. G. Teubneri, 1874. vii, 824 p. Generally known as: De decretis Hippocratis et Platonis. Film Mas 8374 – 1 – us H.U. Library [180]
DE POEMATUM CANTU ET VIRIBUS RYTHMI / Vossius, I – Oxonii. 1673. BP-502 1 – 9 – ne IDC [780]
DE POENITENTIA / Medina, Ioannes – Brixiae, 1606 – 9mf – 8 – ne Slangenburg [240]
De Poorter, A *see* LE TRAITE "ERUDITIO REGUM ET PRINCIPUM" DE GUIBERT DE TOURNAI
DE PRAEDESTINATIONE SALUANDORUM, AND HUIC OPPOSITA REPROBATIONE DAMNANDORUM, DISPUTATIO... / Hunnius, A – Marpurgi, 1588 – 1mf – ne IDC [240]
DE PRAESCRIPTIONE JURIS GENTIUM,... / Geyr, M H J A de – Alma, 1735 – 1mf – 1 – ILM-1052/1 – ne IDC [327]
DE PRAESTANTIA MUSICAE VETERIS LIBRI TRES TOTIDEM DIALOGIS COMPREHENSI / Doni, G B – 1647 – 2,9 – us Sibley [780]
DE PRINCIPI DELL'ARMONIA MUSICALE CONTENUTA NEL DIATONICO GENERE / Tartini, G – 1767 – 9 – us Sibley [780]
DE PRINCIPIIS JURIS NATURAE,... / Finetti, G F – Venice, 1764 – 8mf – 1 – ILM-516/1 – ne IDC [327]
DE PRINCIPIIS JURIS NATURAE,... / Finettus, I F – Neapoli. 2v. 1780 – 6mf – 1 – ILM-1030/1 – ne IDC [327]
DE PROBATIS SANCTORUM HISTORIIS / Surius, L – Coloniae. v1-6. 1570-75 – 266mf – 8 – Dfl931.00 – ne Slangenburg [240]
DE PROBATIS SANCTORUM. HISTORIIS, PARTIM EX TOMIS ALOYSII LIPOMANI / Laurentium, F – Coloniae, 1573. 5 vols. BH.P-30 – 9 – ne IDC [240]
DE PROBATIS SANCTORUM. HISTORIIS, PARTIM EX TOMIS ALOYSII LIPOMANI / Surius, L – Coloniae, 1570-1575. 6 vols. BH.P-30 – 9 – ne IDC [700]
DE PROBLEMAS FILOSOFICOS... / Huerta, J – Madrid, 1628 – 6mf – 9 – sp Cultura [100]
DE PROFETISCHE BOEKEN DES OUDEN VERBONDS / Kuenen, Abraham – (Includes bibliographies) – 2. geheel omgewerkte uitg. Leiden: P Engels en Zoon, 1889 – 2mf – 9 – 0-8370-9710-X – 1986-3710 – us A.T.L.A. [220]
DE PROFUNDIS / Wilde, Oscar – London: Methuen, [1905] – 1 roll – 1 – 1-55879-402-6 – uk Libr Preservation [420]
DE PRONUNTIATIONE LINGUAE GALICAE / Desainliens, Claude – 1580. 188p. (English Linguistics Series 1500-1800) – 9 – us UMI [490]
DE PRONUNTIATIONE LINGUAE GALLICAE LIBRI DUO / Sainliens, Cl. de – 1580 – 9 – fr I.C.S. [440]
DE PROPRIETATIBUS RERUM / Bartholomaeus, A – London, 1535 – 21mf – 9 – ne IDC [580]
DE PROSODIA LIBELLUS / Buchanan, George – 1590. 40p. (English Linguistics Series 1500-1800) – 9 – us UMI [400]
DE PROVERBIORUM QUAE DICUNTUR AGURI ET LEMUELIS ORIGINE ATQUE INDOLE HENRICUS FERDINANDUS MUEHLAU / Muehlau, Ferdinand – Lipsiae [Leipzig]:Metzger & Wittig, [ca. 1869] – 1mf – 9 – 0-8370-4521-5 – 1985-2521 – us A.T.L.A. [220]
DE PROVINCIA REMENSI 1 (GC 9) – Parisiis, 1751 – Dfl116.00 – ne Slangenburg [240]
DE PROVINCIA REMENSI 2 (GC 10) – Parisiis, 1751 – Dfl112.00 – ne Slangenburg [240]
DE PUERTAS ADENTRO / Sanchez Arjona, Vicente – Sevilla: Graficas T., Tomo 2. 1954 – 1 – sp Bibl Santa Ana [810]
DE PUERTAS ADENTRO / Sanchez Arjona, Vicente – Sevilla: Graficas Tirvia, Tomo 4. 1954 – 1 – sp Bibl Santa Ana [810]
DE PUERTAS ADENTRO / Sanchez Arjona, Vicente – Sevilla: Graficas Tirvia, Tomo 5. 1954 – 1 – sp Bibl Santa Ana [810]
DE PUERTAS ADENTRO / Sanchez Arjona, Vicente – Sevilla: Imprenta Crufer, Tomo 7-8. 1958 – 1 – sp Bibl Santa Ana [810]
DE PUERTAS ADENTRO / Sanchez Arjona, Vicente – Sevilla: Vda. de J. Mejias. Impresor, Tomo 6. 1956 – 1 – sp Bibl Santa Ana [810]
DE PUERTAS ADENTRO. POESIAS INTIMAS / Sanchez Arjona, Vicente – Sevilla: Imprenta San Antonio, Tomo 1. 1954 – 1 – sp Bibl Santa Ana [810]
DE PUERTAS ADENTRO (TODO EN BROMA) / Sanchez Arjona, Vicente – Sevilla: Graficas Tirvia, Tomo 3. 1954 – 1 – sp Bibl Santa Ana [810]
DE QUATTORDECIM REGIONIBUS URBIS ROMAE EARUMDEMQUE AEDIFICIIS / P ANCIROLUS, G – Lugduni, 1608 – Dfl22.00 – ne Slangenburg [240]
DE QUATTUTOR ARTIBUS POPULARIBUS: GRAMMATICA. MUSICA / Vossius, G J – Amstelaedami. 1650. BP-503 1 – 9 – ne IDC [780]
...DE QUE EL AFORISMO PRIMERO DE HIPOCRATES...SIRVE A LA MILICIA COMO A LA MEDICINA... / Gomez, M – Antverpiae, 1643 – 3mf – 9 – sp Cultura [610]
De Quincey, Thomas *see* CONFESSIONS OF AN ENGLISH OPIUM-EATER
DE RACHITIDE SIVE MORBO PUERILI, QUI VULGO THE RICKETS DICITUR / Glisson, F – Londini, 1650 – 8mf – 9 – ne IDC [616]

DE RATIONE COMMUNI OMNIUM LINGUARUM ET LITTERARUM COMMENTARIUS / Bibliander – In French. (Linguistics series). 1548 – 9 – fr Hachette [400]

DE RATIONE MOTUS MUSCULORUM / Croone, W – M 332. 1664 – 9 – ne IDC [612]

DE RE AEDIFICATORIA / Alberti, L B – Firenze. O-105 1. 1485 – 9 – ne IDC [700]

DE RE BIBLIOGRAPHICA : LA AUTOBIBLIOGRAFIA DE JUAN ANTONIO MUNOZ GALLARDO / Fernandez Serrano, Francisco – Badajoz: Dip. Provincial, 1975. Sep. REE – 1 – sp Bibl Santa Ana [920]

DE RE DIPLOMATICA LIBRI / Mabillon, D J – 6 rev ed. Luteciae Parisiorum. 1709 – 37mf – 8 – Dfl130.00 – ne Slangenburg [240]

DE RE LITERARIA SINENSIUM COMMENTARIUS,... / Spitzel, T G – Lugd. Batavorum, [1660] – 4mf – 9 – ne IDC [480]

DE RE METRICA HEBRAEORUM / Gietmann, Gerhard – (Includes index) – Friburgi Brisgoviae: Herder, 1880 – 1mf – 9 – 0-8370-3276-8 – 1985-1276 – us A.T.L.A. [470]

DE RE METRICA VETERUM HEBRAEORUM: DISPUTATIO IN UNIVERSITATE VINDOBONENSI / Schloegl, Nivardus – Vienna: Mayer, 1899. 1 fiche – 9 – us A.T.L.A. [240]

DE RE MILITARI ET BELLO TRACTATUS / Belli, Piero – Washington: Carnegie Endowment for International Peace, Division of International Law. 2v. 1936 – 9mf – 9 – $13.50 – LLMC 88-029 – us L.L.M.C. [340]

DE REBUS CONSTANTINOPOLITANIS LIBRI 4 (CBH30,1) / Genesius, J – Venetiis, 1733 – Dfl19.00 – ne Slangenburg [930]

DE REBUS FIDEI HOC TEMPORE... / Valentia, Greg. De – Lugduni, 1591 – 42mf – 8 – ne Slangenburg [240]

DE REBUS HISPANIAE MEMORABILI / Marineo Siculo, Lucio – 1533? – 9 – 1.50f – sp Bibl Santa Ana [946]

DE REBUS INTER IOANNEM ET... / Becker, P W – Copenhagen, 1835 – 9 – 2mf – ILM-427/1 – ne IDC [327]

DE REBUS OCEANICIS & ORBE NOVO DECADA TRES / Angleria, Pedro Martir – 1533 – 9 – 1.50f – sp Bibl Santa Ana [970]

DE REBUS OCEANICIS & ORBE NOVO DECADA TRES / Angleria, Pedro Martir – 1553 – 9 – 1.50f – sp Bibl Santa Ana [970]

DE REBUS TURCARU... / Richier, C – 2mf – 9 – H-8265/1 – ne IDC [956]

DE REBVS; EMMANVELIS, LVSITANIAE REGIS INVICTISSIMI, VIRTVTE ET AVSPICIO, ... / Osorio da Fonesca, J – Coloniae, 1586 – 10mf – 9 – H-8422/1 – ne IDC [956]

DE REBVS NATVRALIBVS LIBRIS XXX: QVIBUS QVAESTIONES.... / Zabarella, Giacomo – (WITH: DISPVTATIONVM DE MEDICINA NOVA PHILIPPI PARACELSI PARS PRIMA/ THOMAS ERASTUS) – 4th ed 1602 – 16p. 1076 columns, 30p – 1 – us U.W. Library [574]

DE REBVS TVRCICIS COMMENTARII DVO ACCVRATISSIMI / Camerarius, J – Francofvrti, 1598 – 3mf – 9 – H-8396/1 – ne IDC [956]

DE REBVS TVRCICIS LIBER / Balbi, G – Romae, 1526 – 1mf – 9 – H-8233/1 – ne IDC [945]

DE RECLUSIS/SPECULUM HUMANAE SALVATIONIS / Hilton, W – York Minster Library Ms XVI. K5 – 1 – uk Microform Academic [240]

DE RECTA ET EMENDATA LINGUAE ANGLICAE SCRIPTIONE, DIALOGUS / Smith, Thomas – 1568. 97p. (English Linguistics Series 1500-1800) – 9 – us UMI [420]

DE REGE ET REGENDI RATIONE / Lopez Bravo, Mateo – 1616 – 9 – 1.50f – sp Bibl Santa Ana [321]

DE REGIONIBUS MARINIS / Oersted, A S – Z-2123 2. 1844 – 8 – ne IDC [910]

DE RERUM CREATIONE EX NIHILO / Hoonacker, Albin van – (Includes bibliographical references) – Lovanii: VanLinthout, 1886 – 1mf – 9 – 0-8370-3815-4 – 1985-1815 – us A.T.L.A. [210]

DE RERUM INVENTORIBUS LIBRI 8 / Polydorus, Vergilius – Basileae, 1525 – 7mf – 8 – ne Slangenburg [240]

DE RERUM USU ET ABUSU / Furmer, B G – O 615. 1575 – 9 – ne IDC [999]

DE RERVM VARIETATE LIBRI 17 / Cardano, Girolamo – Basileae, 1557. Folio. Imperfect: Wants all leaves of index after leaf 006 – 1 – us U.W. Library [900]

DE RESTITUTIONE ET CONTRACTIBUS / Medina, Ioannes – Brixiae, 1606 – 8mf – 8 – ne Slangenburg [240]

DE RITIBUS ET INSTITUTIS ECCLESIAE TIGURINAE OPUSCULUM / Lavater, Ludwig – 1559 – 1 – us A.T.L.A. [240]

DE ROMANIS PISCIBUS LIBELLUS / Giovio, P – 1524. B-2128 2 – 8 – ne IDC [590]

De Ruyter, John A *see* THE STAR OF THE TWENTIETH CENTURY

DE RVSSORVM MOSCOVITARVM ET TARTARORVM RELIGIONE, SACRIFICIIS, ... – N.p., 1582 – 4mf – 9 – H-8202/1 – ne IDC [956]

DE SACRA POESI HEBRAEORUM / Lowth, Robert – 1758 – 1 – us A.T.L.A. [270]

DE SACRA PRAEDICATIONES IN O.F.M... / Belluco, Bartolome – Madrid: Archivo Ibero Americano, 1960 – 1 – sp Bibl Santa Ana [240]

DE SACRA TRADITIONE CONTRA NOVAM HAERESIM EVOLUTIONISMI / Billot, Ludovico – Romae: A.S. Iosepho, 1904. 1 fiche – 9 – us A.T.L.A. [240]

DE SACRAMENTO EUCHARISTIAE CONTRA OECOLAMPADIUM OPUSCULUM... / Clichtove, J – Parisiis, 1526 – 4mf – 9 – CA-82/1 – ne IDC [240]

DE SACRAMENTO EXTREMAE UNCTIONIS : TRACTATUS DOGMATICUS / Kern, Josephus – (Includes index) – Ratisbonae [Regensburg]; Neo Eboraci [New York]: Friderici Pustet, 1907 – 1mf – 9 – 0-8370-9162-4 – 1986-3162 – us A.T.L.A. [240]

DE SACRI ROM. IMPERII LIBERA CIVITATE NORIBERGENSI COMMENTATIO / Wagenseil, Johann C – Altdorfi Noricorum. 1697. BP-507 1 – 9 – ne IDC [780]

...DE SACRI ROMANI IMPERII LIBERA CIVITATE NORIBERGENSI COMMENTATIO.. / Wagenseil, Johann C – 1697 – 2 – us Sibley [780]

DE SACRIS NOTIS ET SCULPTURIS LIBRI DUO / Horus Apollo – O 303. 1551 – 9 – ne IDC [730]

DE SACRIS RHODIORUM COMMENTATIO / Dittenberger, Wilhelm – 2 parts.1886-87 – 1 – us U.W. Library [250]

DE SACRO FOEDERE IN SELIMVM. LIBRI QUATTOR / Foglietta, U – Genvae, 1587 – 4mf – 9 – H-8368/1 – ne IDC [956]

DE SAINT-LOUIS A SIERRA-LEONE / Bouteiller, J – Huit ans de navigation dans les rivieres du sud. Paris, Augustin Challamel. 1891 – 9 – 10.00 – fr Orientalistes [910]

DE SAINT-LOUIS A TRIPOLI PAR LE LAC TCHAD / Monteil, P L – Paris. 1896. BA-180 2 – 8 – ne IDC [910]

DE SAINT-LOUIS A TRIPOLI PAR LE LAC TCHAD, VOYAGE AU TRAVERS DU SOUDAN ET DU SAHARA ACCOMPLI PENDANT LES ANNEES 1890-91-92 / Monteil, P L – Paris, Felix Alcan. 1895 – 9 – 12.50 – fr Orientalistes [910]

DE SANCTO MATRIMONII SACRAMENTO DISPVTATIONVM; TOMI TRES.. / Sanchez, Tomas Antonio – 1669. SEM35P230 – 1r – 1 – Can$42.00 – cn Bibl Nat [240]

DE SANTO TOMAS A KRAUSE? / Fernandez Valbuena, Ramiro – 1882 – 9 – 1.50f – sp Bibl Santa Ana [240]

DE' SECRETI DEL R. D. ALESSIO PIEMONTESE / Ruscelli, Girolamo – Venetia: Appresso Angelo Bodio, 1674 – 1 – us U.W. Library [615]

DE SEDIBUS, ET CAUSIS MORBORUM PER ANATOMEN INDAGATIS / Morgagni, G B – 1761 – 9 – ne IDC [610]

DE SEVILLA A BATALHA. EXCURSION... DE SEVILLA A MERIDA Y BADAJOZ.. / Cascales Munoz, Jose – 1892 – 9 – 1.50f – sp Bibl Santa Ana [910]

DE SEVILLA A GUADALUPE. BREVES APUNTES TOMADOS A VUELA PLUMA / Gestoso y Perez, Jose – Sevilla: Oficina del Correo de Andalucia, 1913 – 1 – sp Bibl Santa Ana [946]

DE SIGNIS...MORBI SUFFOCANTIS... / Villarreal, J – Alcala de Henares, 1611 – 5mf – 9 – sp Cultura [610]

de Silva Barahona e Costa, Henrique Cesar *see* APONTAMENTOS PARA A HISTORIA DE GUERRA DE ZAMBEZIA, 1871-1875

De Smet, B *see* DE LITERIS ET LINGUA GETARUM, SIUE GOTHORUM...

DE SOTO COUNTY NEWS – Olive Branch. Miss. 1940-1944 – 1 – us UMI [071]

De Soyres, John *see* THE CHILDREN OF WISDOM AND OTHER SERMONS PREACHED IN CANADIAN PULPITS

De Soysa, A H T *see* ANCIENT KAURAWA FLAGS

THE DE SOYSA CHARITAYA : OR, THE LIFE OF CHARLES HENRY DE SOYSA, ESQ, J P / Bastian, C Don – Colombo: "Sinhalese Daily News" Press, 1904 – 1 – us Res Libr [950]

DE SPECIEBUS GENERIBUSQUE NONNULLIS NOVIS EX ALGARUM ET FUNGORUM CLASSE / Reinsch, P F – Frankf. a.M. 1866-67. B-6401 2 – 8 – ne IDC [580]

DE SPORARUM EQUISETORUM GERMINATIONE / Milde, J – Vratislaviae, 1850. 20 pp., 2 pls. B-7228 1 – 9 – ne IDC [580]

DE SQUAMIS LEPIDOPTERORUM / Kettelhoit, T – Dissertatio Zoologica. Bonnae, 1860. 29p. 1 pl. Z-1388/2 – 8 – ne IDC [590]

DE SS. SACRAMENTIS SECUNDUM RITUM AETHIOPICUM / Abba Tecle Mariam Semhary Selam – Romae, 1931 – 3mf – 8 – Dfl13.00 – ne Slangenburg [240]

DE STATU RELIGIONIS CHRISTIANAE / Miraeus, A – Colonia Agrippina, 1619 – 5mf – 8 – Dfl22.00 – ne Slangenburg [240]

DE STIRPIUM... / Gessner, C (Hieronymus Tragus) – (Available: Preface and list of botanical writers) – Argentorati, Excudebat Wendelinus Rihelius, 1552 – 1mf – ne IDC [580]

DE STRUNZ : NE INDUSTRIE- UN BUERN-GESCHICHT UT'N MOENSTERLANNE / Wibbelt, Augustin – 4. Aufl. Essen (Ruhr): Fredebeul & Koenen, 1920 – 1 – us U.W. Library [830]

DE STUDIIS SINICIS... / Montucci, A – Berolini, 1808 – 1mf – 9 – ne IDC [480]

DE SUPREMA ROMANI PONTIFICIS IN ECCLESIAM POTESTATE DISPUTATIO QUADRIPARTITA / Val, Andr. du – Parisiis, 1614 – 14mf – 8 – ne Slangenburg [240]

DE SUPREMA ROMANI PONTIFICIS IN ECCLESIAM POTESTATE DISPUTATIO QUADRIPARTITA / Val, Andr. du – Parisiis, 1614 – 14mf – 8 – ne Slangenburg [240]

DE SYMBOLIS HEROCIS. LIBRI / Pietrasancta, S – 9. O 717. 1634 – 9 – ne IDC [760]

DE SYMBOLISCHE SHRIFTEN DER NED. HERV. KERK / Toornenbergen, J J van – Utrecht, 1869 – 5mf – 8 – ne Slangenburg [290]

DE TARTARIS DIARIVM / Brussius, G – Francofvrti, 1598 – 1mf – 9 – H-8395/1 – ne IDC [950]

DE TELEGRAAF – Paterson, NJ: [Cornelius Poeistra, dec 1917-1921] – us Res Libr [071]

DE TEMPLO, ET DE IIS QUAE AD TEMPLUM PERTINENT, LIBRI QUINQUE / Ribera, F – Antverpiae, 1593 – 30mf – 8 – ne Slangenburg [220]

DE THEOLOGIA GENTILI ET PHYSIOLOGIA CHRISTIANA : SIVE DE ORIGINE AC PROGRESSU IDOLOLATRIAE... / Vossius, G J – Amsterdami. 4v. 1641 – 22mf – 9 – CA-154/1 – ne IDC [240]

DE THOMA BRADWARDINO COMMENTATIO / Lechler, Gotthard Victor – Lipsiae: Apud A. Edelmannum, 1862 – 1mf – us A.T.L.A. [240]

DE TODOS : ORGANO DE DIFUSION DE LA FEDERACION ARGENTINA DE IGLESIAS EVANGELICAS – Buenos Aires: La Federacion, n1-17. aug 1987-1992 – 1r – 1 – us Res Libr [240]

De Toni *see* SYLLOGE ALGARUM

DE TOPOGRAPHIA CONSTANTINOPOLEOS, ET DE ILLIVS ANTIQVITATIBVS LIBRI QVATVOR / Gilles, P – Lvgdvni, 1561 – 3mf – 9 – H-8298/1 – ne IDC [956]

de Totanes, Sebastian *see* ARTE DE LA LENGUA TAGALA; Y, MANUAL TAGALOG

DE TRANSLATIONE IMPERII ROMANI AD GERMANOS... / Flacius Illyricus d.A E, M – Basileae, 1566 – 8mf – 9 – ne IDC [240]

DE TRIBORD A BABORD: TROIS CROISIERES DANS LE GOLFE SAINT LAURENT: NORD ET SUD / Faucher de Saint-Maurice, Narcisse – Montreal: Duvernay et Dansereau, 1877. 03063. (Pre-1900 Canadiana) – 9 – cn C.I.H.M. [910]

DE TRIBUS GENERIBUS INSTRUMENTORUM MUSICAE VETERUM ORGANICAE DISSERTATIO / Bianchini, F – 1742 – 9 – us Sibley [780]

DE TRIBUS GENERIBUS INSTRUMENTORUM MUSICAE VETERUM ORGANICAE DISSERTATIO / Blanchinus, F Francisci Blanchini – Romae. 1742. BP-171 1 – 9 – ne IDC [780]

DE TRIBUS HISTORICIS CONCILII TRIDENTINI / Aquilinius, C – Amstelodami, 1662 – 2mf – 8 – ne Slangenburg [240]

DE TRIGINTA SEX DECANIS / Trismegistus, Hermes – 1994 – 4mf – 9 – Bf1,300.00 – 2-503-64442-2 – be Brepols [450]

DE TRINITATE : PRAEFATIO, LIBRI 1-6 / Hilarius Pictaviensis; ed by Smulders, P – 1979 – 12mf – 9 – Bf3,500.00 – 2-503-00621-3 – be Brepols [240]

DE TRITONIDE LACU, THESES DIVIONONSI LITTERARUM FACULTATI PROPONETRE, EX TYPIS J.E. RABUTOT / Tissot, Charles Joseph – 1863. 39p. 1 fiche. (Literature Collection) – 9 – 6.00 – fr Bibl Nationale [450]

DE TURCARUM ORIGINE, MORIBUS, ET REBUS GESTIS COMMENTARIUS / Cervarius Tubero, L – Florentiae, 1590 – 2mf – 9 – H-8424/1 – ne IDC [956]

DE TURCARUM RITV ET CAEREMONIIS,... / Bartholomaeus, G – Antverpiae, 1544 – 1mf – 9 – H-8271/1 – ne IDC [956]

DE TUTTE L'OPERE DEL R. M. GIOSEFFO ZARLINO DA CHIOGGIA / Zarlino, G – 4v. Venetia. 1589. BP-527 1 – 9 – ne IDC [780]

DE TVRCARVM MORIBVS EPITOME / Bartholomaeus, G – Lvgdvni, 1567 – 3mf – 9 – H-8306/1 – ne IDC [945]

DE TVRCORVM ORIGINE, RELIGIONE, AC IMMANISSIMA EORUM IN CHRISTIANOS TYRANNIDE, ... / Cuspinianus, J – Antverpiae, 1541 – 3mf – 9 – H-8267/1 – ne IDC [956]

DE UNA ESPECIE DE GARROTILLO O ESQUILENCIA MORTAL / Figueroa, F – Lima, 1616 – 1mf – 9 – sp Cultura [616]

DE URIJE PERS – Surabaja. Indonesia. 1949-1954 – 1 – us UMI [072]

DE L'USAGE DE L'ARTILLERIE NOUVELLE. / Du Teil, Jean – Metz. Marchal. 1778. vi, 130p. pl. (Strategy of War Series) – 9 – fr Hachette [355]

DE USU ASTROLABI COMPENDIUM, SCHEMATIBUS COMMODISSIMIS ILLUSTRATUM / Poblacion, Juan Martinez – Parisiis: Ioannis Barbaei, 1546. SEM105P878 – 2mf – 9 – Can$4.50 – cn Bibl Nat [623]

DE UTRAQUE POTESTATE PAPALI ET REGALI / Johannes Parisiensis – Parisiis, 1506 – Dfl19.00 – ne Slangenburg [240]

DE VARIA COMMESURACION PARA LA ESCULPTURA Y ARCHITECTURA / Arfe y Villafane, J – Sevilla, 1585 – 4mf – 9 – sp Cultura [720]

DE VARIA REPUBLICA SIVE COMMENTARIA IN LIBRUM JUDICUM / Arias Montano, Benito – 1592 – 9 – 1.50f – sp Bibl Santa Ana [320]

DE VARIOLIS ET MORBILIS...CUM NONNULIS EUISDEM ARGUMENTI / Rhazes – Londini, 1766 – 6mf – 9 – ne IDC [616]

DE VARIOS COLORES / Sanchez Arjona, Vicente – Sevilla: Imp. Zambrano, 1955 – 1 – sp Bibl Santa Ana [810]

De Veiga Beirao, F A *see* DE LETTRA DE CAMBIO...

DE VENERATIONE SANCTORUM, OPUSCULUM DUOS LIBROS COPLECTENS / Clichtove, J – Parisiis, 1523 – 3mf – 9 – CA-86/1 – ne IDC [240]

DE VERA RELIGIONE : PRAELECTIONES NOVAE IN SEMINARIO SANCTI SULPITII HABITAE: CUM MULTIS ANNOTATIONIBUS IN ULTERIORA CUJUSQUE STUDIA ET PRAEDICATIONIS USUS PROFUTURIS / Brugere, Lud-Fred – (In Latin and French. Includes bibliographical references and index) – ed nova. Parisiis: A Roger et F Chernoviz, 1878 – 1mf – 9 – 0-8370-8409-1 – 1986-2409 – us A.T.L.A. [240]

De Vere, Dan *see* DAN DE VERE'S COMIC AND SENTIMENTAL SONG-BOOK: HUDSON'S CALIFORNIAN AND NORTH AND SOUTH AMERICAN CIRCUS

DE VERI PRECETTI DELLA PITTURA / Armenini, G B – O-129 1. 1587 – 9 – ne IDC [760]

DE VETERIS LATINAE ECCLESIASTICI CAPITIBUS I-XLIII / Herkenne, Heinrich – Leipzig: J.C. Hinrichs, 1899. 1 fiche – 9 – us A.T.L.A. [240]

DE VETERIS RECENTISQ. ECCLESIAE HYMNO / Tentzel, W – Te Deum laudamus. Wittenbergae. 1686. BP-485 1 – 9 – ne IDC [780]

DE VETERUM MUSICA / Alard, L – P-120. 1636 – 9 – ne IDC [780]

DE VI ET USU PRAEPOSITIONUM EPI, META, PARA, PERI, PROS, HUPO APUD ARISTOPHANEM / Iltz, Johannes – (Includes bibliographical references) – Halis Saxonum: Formis Kaemererianis, 1890 – 1mf – 9 – 0-8370-9159-4 – 1986-3159 – us A.T.L.A. [450]

THE DE VINCK COLLECTION – The Revolution of 1830 and the July Monarchy. Cartoons, posters, billboards, public announcements, etc.4 reels. (Collections of the Department of Prints and Photographs) – 1 – fr Bibl Nationale [080]

DE VIRIS ILLUSTRIBUS URBIS ROMAE, A ROMULO AD AUGUSTUM: AD USUM SEXTAE SCHOLAE / Lhomond, Charles F – Quebec: apud Joannem Neilson, 1809. SEM16P56 – 1r – 5 – Can$9.00 – cn Bibl Nat [930]

DE VISCERUM STRUCTURA EXERCITATIO ANATOMICA / Malpighi, M – Londini, 1669 – 4mf – 9 – ne IDC [611]

DE VISIBILI MONARCHIA ECCLESIAE LIBRI OCTO / Sanderus, Nic. – Lovanii, 1571 – 37mf – 8 – ne Slangenburg [240]

DE VITA ET HONESTATE CLERICORUM / Fabrotus, C A – Parisiis, 1651 – Dfl19.00 – ne Slangenburg [240]

DE VITA ET MORIBUS SACERDOTUM OPUSCULUM... / Clichtove, J – [Parisiis], 1519 – 2mf – 9 – CA-79/1 – ne IDC [240]

DE VITA ET SCRIPTIS APHRAATIS, SAPIENTIS PERSAE / Forget, J – Lovanii, 1882 – Dfl28.00 – ne Slangenburg [240]

DE VITA MORIBVS AC REBVS PRAECIPVE ADVERSVS TVRCAS, ... / Barletius, M – Argentorati, 1537 – 7mf – 9 – H-8247/1 – ne IDC [956]

DE VITA RECESSUOLI... / Bluma, Daciano – Madrid: Arch. Ibero Americano, 1963 – 1 – sp Bibl Santa Ana [240]

DE VOCABVLO FIDEI ET ALIIS QVIBVSDAM VOCABVLIS, EXPLICATIO UERA ET UTILIS, SUMTA EX FONTIBUS EBRAICIS / Flacius Illyricus d.A E, M – Vitebergae, 1549 – 3mf – 9 – ne IDC [240]

DE VOITIA ET SYSTYLIO / Hornschuch, C F – Erlangae. 1818. B-5967 2 – 8 – ne IDC [580]

DE VOLKSKRANT – Amsterdam: NV de Volkskrant, oct 1970- – us Res Libr [072]

De Vreesse, W *see* BIJDRAGEN TOT DE KENNIS VAN HET LEVEN EN DE WERKEN VAN JAN VAN RUUSBROEC

De Vriese, Dozy *see* NEDERLANDSCH KRUIDKUNDIG ARCHIEF

DE VULGARI ELOQUENTIA, SIVE IDIOMATE. AVEC COMMENTAIRES ET PREFACE / Dante Alighieri – (Linguistics series). 1878 – 9 – fr Hachette [450]

DE WERKEN DER MARNIX-VEREENIGING *see* BRIEVEN UIT ONDERSCHEIDENE KERKELIJKE ARCHIEVEN (DE WERKEN..3,5)

De Wesselow, Charles Hare Simpkinson *see* THOMAS HARRISON, REGICIDE AND MAJOR-GENERAL

De Wette, Wilhelm Martin Leberecht *see*
- A CRITICAL AND HISTORICAL INTRODUCTION TO THE CANONICAL SCRIPTURES OF THE OLD TESTAMENT
- EINE IDEE UEBER DAS STUDIUM DER THEOLOGIE
- THEODORE

DE WIELINGEN... / Brugmans, H – Amsterdam, 1920 – 1mf – 1 – ILM-1885/1 – ne IDC [327]

De Windt, Harry *see* THROUGH THE GOLD-FIELDS OF ALASKA TO BERING STRAITS

De Witt, John *see*
- THE PSALMS: A NEW TRANSLATION WITH INTRODUCTORY ESSAY AND NOTES
- WHAT IS INSPIRATION?: A FRESH STUDY OF THE QUESTION

DEACONESS ADVOCATE – (Title varies) – v1-29 no 2. 1886-Feb 1914 (complete) – 3r – 1 – ATLA S0292 – us A.T.L.A. [073]

DEACONESSES: BIBLICAL, EARLY CHURCH, EUROPEAN, AMERICAN: WITH THE STORY OF THE CHICAGO TRAINING SCHOOL FOR CITY, HOME, AND FOREIGN MISSIONS AND THE CHICAGO DEACONESS HOME / Meyer, Lucy R – c1889 – 9 – us A.T.L.A. [240]

DEACONESSES IN EUROPE: AND THEIR LESSONS FOR AMERICA / Robinson, Jane Marie Bancroft – 1890 – 9 – us A.T.L.A. [240]

THE DEACONESSS AND HER VOCATION / Thoburn, James Mills – New York: Hunt & Eaton; Cincinnati: Cranston & Curtis, 1893 – 1mf – us A.T.L.A. [240]

DEACONS' AND TRUSTEES' MINUTES / Anna. Illinois. First Baptist Church – (Deacons' Minutes: Oct 1942-Nov 1984. Trustees' Minutes: Jul 1946-Jan 1952 (scattered); Feb 1960-Nov 1984) – 1942-84 – 1 – us UMI [240]

THE DEAD CITIES OF THE ZUYDER ZEE: A VOYAGE TO THE PICTURESQUE SIDE OF HOLLAND / Havard, Henry – Annie Wood, trans. Illus. by Havard and van Beest. London: R. Bentley & son, 1875. xii, 363p. 9 pl – 1 – us U.W. Library [949]

DEAD LOVE HAS CHAINS / Braddon, Mary Elizabeth – British Fiction Archive: Unit 5 – 9 – uk Bell [830]

DEAD MARCH AND MONODY / Carr, Benjamin – Performed in the Lutheran Church, Philadelphia, on Thursday, 26 December 1799, being part of the music selected for funeral honours to our late illustrious cheif General George Washington. Baltimore: J. Carr 1799-1800. MUSIC 3082, Item 2 – 1 – us L of C Photodup [780]

DEAD MEN'S SHOES / Braddon, Mary Elizabeth – British Fiction Archive: Unit 5 – 9 – uk Bell [830]

DEAD MOUNTAIN ECHO – Oakridge, OR. -w. 29 Aug 1973-. – 1 – us U.O. Library [071]

THE DEAD PULPIT / Haweis, Hugh Reginald – 1896 – 9 – us A.T.L.A. [240]

DEAD SEA FRUIT / Braddon, Mary Elizabeth – British Fiction Archive: Unit 5 – 9 – uk Bell [830]

THE DEAD SEA SCROLLS / ed by Tov, Emanuel – (A printed catalogue by S.A. Reed comes with the microfiches) – 134mf – 9 – ne IDC [240]

THE DEAD SEA SCROLLS ON MICROFICHE / ed by Tov, Emanuel & Pfann, S J – (Prices and data are subject to change without prior notice) – 1992 – ca 100mf – 9 – Dfl850.00 – ne Brill [200]

Deady, M P *see* DEADY'S REPORTS OF CASES IN THE NINTH CIRCUIT, 1859-1869

DEADY'S REPORTS OF CASES IN THE NINTH CIRCUIT, 1859-1869 / Deady, M P – San Francisco: Bancroft. 1v. 1872 (all publ) – 8mf – 9 – $12.00 – LLMC 81-447 – us L.L.M.C. [340]

THE DEAF AND DUMB MAN'S DISCOURSE / Sibscota, George – 1670. 101p. (English Linguistics Series 1500-1800) – 9 – us UMI [400]

Deahl, Anthony *see* 20TH CENTURY HISTORICAL AND BIOGRAPHICAL RECORD OF ELKHART

DEAK ELETE / Ferenczi, Z – 3v. Budapest. 1904. BR-5295 2 – 8 – ne IDC [999]

Deak, F von *see* EIN BEITRAG ZUM UNGARISCHEN STAATSRECHT

DEAL MAGAZINE – Reno, NV. 1994 – 2+ r – 1 – $100.00 ($90.00y) – U04880 – us Library Micro [071]

Dean *see*
- HISTORY OF DAVIESS COUNTY
- HISTORY OF GRUNDY COUNTY
- HISTORY OF LINN COUNTY

Dean, B *see*
- A BIBLIOGRAPHY OF FISHES...
- A BIBLIOGRAPHY OF FISHES
- FISHES, LIVING AND FOSSIL

DEAN BIBLIOGRAPHY OF FISHES – 1916-69. 39 fiches – 9 – 99.00 – us Updata [639]

DEAN CHURCH / Lathbury, D C – Oxford: A.R. Mowbray, 1905 (Leaders of the church, 1800-1900) – 1mf – us A.T.L.A. [240]

Dean, Maurice B *see* A DIGEST OF CORPORATION CASES

DEAN SWAMP. BARNWELL COUNTY. SOUTH CAROLINA : CHURCH RECORDS – 1880-1921, 1932-44 – 1 – 20.79 – us Baptist [240]

Dean, William *see* THE CHINA MISSION

Dean, William B *see* NATURAL BANK CURRENCY AND NATIONAL BANK CURRENCY

Deane, H B *see* THE LAW OF BLOCKADE:...

Deane, Henry *see* DANIEL

Deane, J P *see*
- EFFECT OF WAR...
- THE LAW OF BLOCKADE,...

Deane, William John *see*
- PSEUDEPIGRAPHA
- SAMUEL AND SAUL; THEIR LIVES AND TIMES

THE DEANERY MAGAZINE – (Cont: Kingston Deanery Magazine; The Diocesan Magazine) – Sussex, NB: C Medley, [1889] – 9 – cn C.I.H.M. [240]

THE DEANERY MAGAZINE *see* KINGSTON DEANERY MAGAZINE

DEAN'S GRANGE CEMETERY MONUMENTAL INSCRIPTIONS / Blackrock. Ireland – 1 – uk Microform Academic [920]

DEAPRTMENT OF STATE TREATY PUBLICATIONS *see*
- MALLOY'S TREATIES
- TREATIES AND OTHER INTERNATIONAL ACTS OF THE UNITED STATES

DEAR FAUSTINA: A NOVEL / Broughton, Rhoda – British Fiction Archive: Unit 4 – 9 – uk Bell [830]

Dearden, James S *see* SALE AND EXHIBITION CATALOGUES RELATING TO JOHN RUSKIN

Dearing, F *see* WESLEYAN AND TRACTARIAN WORSHIP

Dearmer, Percy *see*
- BODY AND SOUL
- RELIGIOUS PAMPHLETS
- THE STORY OF THE PRAYER-BOOK IN THE OLD AND NEW WORLD AND THROUGHOUT THE ANGLICAN CHURCH

DEATH AND BURIAL LORE IN THE ENGLISH AND SCOTTISH POPULAR BALLADS / Wimberley, Lowry Charles – 1927 – 1 – us I.U. Libraries [390]

THE DEATH AND RESURRECTION OF JESUS CHRIST / Stapfer, Edmond – New York: Charles Scribner, 1898. 1 fiche – 9 – us A.T.L.A. [240]

DEATH BY WRONGFUL ACT...2ND ED / Tiffany, Francis Buchanan – Kansas City, Mo., Vernon, 1913. 646 p. LL-1317 – 1 – us L of C Photodup [340]

DEATH CERTIFICATES / Putnam County, Ohio. General Health District – 1909-1995 – 4r – 5 – $32.50r – us Archival [324]

DEATH CERTIFICATES / Wood County. Ohio. Middletown Township. Township Clerk – (Incomplete) – 1909-1951 – 1r – 1 – $32.50r – us Archival [324]

DEATH EDUCATION – v1-8,no.6. 1977-84 – 1,5,6,9 – us UMI [360]

DEATH EDUCATION AND DEATH ANXIETY IN STUDENT NURSE AIDES / Kienow, Nancy L & Heit, Philip – 1992 – 2mf – 9 – $8.00 – us Microform Publ [613]

DEATH LISTS AND LOT REGISTERS / Shawnee Center Cemetery, Shawnee County, KS – 1875-1990 – 1 – us KS Hist [920]

THE DEATH OF CHRIST : ITS PLACE AND INTERPRETATION IN THE NEW TESTAMENT / Denney, James – (Includes index) – 5th ed. New York:A.C. Armstrong, 1907 – 1mf – 9 – 0-8370-2889-2 – 1985-0889 – us A.T.L.A. [220]

DEATH OF CHRIST: ITS PLACE AND INTERPRETATION IN THE NEW TESTAMENT / Denny, James – New York: A.C. Armstrong, 1907. 1 fiche – 9 – us A.T.L.A. [240]

THE DEATH OF OENONE : AKBAR'S DREAM, AND OTHER POEMS / Tennyson, Alfred, Lord – London, New York: Macmillan, 1892 – 1 roll – 1 – 1-55879-459-X – uk Libr Preservation [810]

THE DEATH OF THE GOOD MAN...REV. JOHN BROWN / Blythe, James – 1804 – 1 – $50.00 – us Presbyterian [240]

THE DEATH OF THE VERBAL THEORY AND THE UNVEILING OF CHRIST / MacInnes, George – Sydney: George Robertson, 1894. 1 fiche – 9 – us A.T.L.A. [240]

DEATH PENALTY REPORTER – (Available in reel only) – 1980-81 (all publ) – 5,6 – $40.00 – us Hein [340]

THE DEATH PROBLEM IN THE LIFE AND WORKS OF GERHART HAUPTMANN / Klemm, Frederick Alvin – (Includes bibliographical references) – Philadelphia: [s.n.], 1939 – 1r – 1 – us U.W. Library [430]

DEATH RECORD / Crawford County. Ohio. Galion – 1880-1898 – 1r – 1 – $32.50r – us Archival [324]

DEATH RECORDS / Defiance County, Ohio. Probate Court – (Some issues missing) – 1856-1908 – 1r – 1 – $32.50r – us Archival [324]

DEATH RECORDS / Hardin County, Ohio. Probate Court – 1868-1908 – 1r – 1 – $32.50r – us Archival [920]

DEATH RECORDS / Huron County. Ohio. County Home – 1884-1925 – 1r – 1 – $32.50r – us Archival [324]

DEATH RECORDS / Monroe County. Mich, Bedford Township. Board of Trustees – 1888-1889 – 1r – 1 – $32.50r – us Archival [324]

DEATH RECORDS / Putnam County. Ohio. Probate Court – 1867-1920 – 1r – 1 – $32.50r – us Archival [324]

DEATH RECORDS / Van Wert County. Ohio. Probate Court – 1867-1908 – 2r – 1 – $32.50r – us Archival [324]

DEATH RECORDS / Wood County. Ohio. Probate Court – 1867-1908 – 2r – 1 – $32.50r – us Archival [324]

DEATH RECORDS / Wyandot County. Ohio. County Home – 1882-1896 – 1r – 1 – $32.50r – us Archival [324]

THE DEATH SONG OF AN INDIAN CHIEF, FROM "OUABI." / Gram, Hans – Printed as supplement to the March, 1791, number of "The Massachusetts Magazine." According to Sonneck, the first orchestral score published in the U.S. MUSIC 1117 – 1 – us L of C Photodup [780]

DEATH STUDIES – v9-. 1985- – 1,5,6,9 – us UMI [073]

DEATH VALLEY GATEWAY GAZETTE – Pahrump, NV. 1983 – 6+ r – 1 – $300.00 ($60.00y) – N03702 – us Library Micro [071]

DEATH VALLEY MAGAZINE – Rhyolite, NV. 1908 – 1r – 1 – $50.00 – U04895 – us Library Micro [071]

DEATH VALLEY PROSPECTOR – Rhyolite, NV. 9 Dec 1907 – 1r – 1 – $50.00 – U04730 – us Library Micro [071]

Deatherage, Charles P *see* EARLY HISTORY OF GREATER KANSAS CITY, MISSOURI AND KANSAS

DEATHLESS BOOK / Mears, David Otis – Boston: D. Lothrop, 1888. 1 fiche – 9 – us A.T.L.A. [240]

DEATHS / Delaware: Census – (Delaware Manuscript Census Schedules. V11-0001. Dover & Murderkill Hundred to Mispillion Hundred, 1860. V11-0001. Insane Schedules, 1880. V11-0003. Regular Census, 1860-70. V11-0001. Social Statistical Schedules, 1850-60. V11-0003) – 1850-1880. V11-0003 – 1 – us A.G.L.L. [920]

LA DEBACLE – Brussels. Belgium. -m. 7 Jan-6 Aug 1893. (14 ft) – 1 – uk British Libr Newspaper [949]

DEBACLE GENERALE DU COMITE DE LA RUE DE POITIERS AVEC LA BIOGRAPHIE DE SES CANDIDATS AVORTES – Paris [1848?] – us Res Libr [940]

DeBacy, Diane L *see* DEVELOPMENT OF A CHILD INJURY DATA BASE FOR USE IN BIOMECHANICS RESEARCH

Debar, C C *see* VINGT QUATRE VARIATIONS

Debartzch, P D *see* L'ECHO DU PAYS

LE DEBAT COMMERCIAL – Quebec, Canada. v1 n8. sep 1878; v1 n10. nov 1878 – 1r – 1 – Can$25.00 – cn Can Microfilming [072]

DEBAT SUR L'ADRESSE, NOVEMBRE 1896-DISCOURS DE M.F.X. LEMIEUX / Lemieux, Francois Xavier – 1896?. 02620. (Pre-1900 Canadiana) – 9 – cn C.I.H.M. [971]

EL DEBATE – Madrid. Spain. -d. 1-31 Jan 1915, 1 Jan 1917-19 Jul 1936. (76 reels) – 1 – uk British Libr Newspaper [072]

O DEBATE : O DEBATE DOS DISCENTES DO CURSO CIENTIFICO DO C.E.A. IGUALDADE E FRATERNIDADE – [s.l.] 2-19 Jun 1945 – 1,5,6 – bl Biblioteca [072]

O DEBATE – Maceio, Alagoas. 2 Abr 1893 – 1,5,6 – bl Biblioteca [072]

O DEBATE : ORGAO POPULAR – Manaos, Amazonas. 27 Abr-Maio 1901; Jan, Jun 1902; Abr-12 Jul 1903 – 1,5,6 – bl Biblioteca [072]

EL DEBATE CONSTITUCIONAL. DISCURSOS EN LA ASAMBLEA 1931-1933. LIMA 1933 / Belaunde, Victor Andres – Madrid: Razon y Fe, 1934 – 1 – sp Bibl Santa Ana [320]

DEBATE ON LOUIS RIEL [SIC] : SPEECH BY MR. J.J. CURRAN,... IN THE HOUSE OF COMMONS, OTTAWA, ON MONDAY THE 15TH OF MARCH, 1886 / Curran, J J – [s.l.]: [s.n.], 1886. SEM105P35 – 1mf – 9 – Can$2.25 – cn Bibl Nat [971]

DEBATE ON THE POINTS OF DIFFERENCE IN FAITH AND PRACTICE BETWEEN THE TWO RELIGIOUS BODIES KNOWN AS THE DICIPLES OF CHRIST AND THE REGULAR BAPTISTS : EMBRACING THE SUBJECT OF CALVINISM AND THE DESIGN OF BAPTISM, HELD IN THE VILLAGE OF SPRINGFIELD IN THE COUNTY OF ELGIN, ONTARIO, FROM THE 10TH TO THE 12TH SEPTEMBER, 1874 / Crawford, John – between Prof. Crawford and John S. Sweeny; reported by Geo. Eyvel. Toronto: Sheppard, 1875. 02125. (Pre-1900 Canadiana) – 9 – cn C.I.H.M. [971]

EL DEBATE SOBRE EL SEGUNDO PLAN QUINQUENAL EN LA CAMERA DE DIPUTADOS DE LA NACION : DISCURSOS PRONUNCIADOS PRO LOS SENORES DIPUTADOS: RODOLFO A. WEIDMANN [ET. AL.] EN LAS SESIONES DEL 15, 16, 17, 18, 19 DE DICIEMBRE DE 1952 / Union Civica Radical – Buenos Aires, 1953 – 1 – CSUXADQ3370-B – us Hoover Inst Photo [320]

EL DEBATE SOBRE LA ENSENANZA RELIGIOSA : DISCURSOS PRONUNCIADOS POR SILVANO SANTANDER [ET AL.] EN LAS SESIONES DEL 6/7, 7, 12, 13 Y 13/14 DE MARZO DE 1947 / Argentina. Congreso de la Nacion. Camara de Diputados de la Nacion – Buenos Aires, 1947 – 1 – CSUXADQ2048-B – us Hoover Inst Photo [320]

DEBATES / Assam. India (State). Legislative Council – v. 1-11. 1937-47. BI-64 2 – 8 – ne IDC [324]

DEBATES / Bombay. India. Legislative Assembly – v. 1-7. Bombay. 1937-39. BI-29 2 – 8 – ne IDC [324]

DEBATES / Bombay. India. Legislative Council – v. 1-8. Bombay. 1937-39. BI-28 2 – 8 – ne IDC [324]

DEBATES / Canada. Parliament – 1846-74. (Recorded in newspapers) – 5r – 1 – $325.00 – cn Library Assoc [971]

DEBATES / Canada. Parliament. House of Commons – 28th Parliament, 1970- – 9 – cn Micromedia [324]

DEBATES / Canada. Parliament. Senate – (1983- . 32nd Parliament- . 9) – 28th-32nd Parliaments, 1970-82 – 5 – cn Micromedia [324]

DEBATES / Gold Coast. Legislative Council – (Legislative Assembly Debates). 1928-1957. Missing: 1933, 1942, 1954, and other scattered issues – 1 – 35.00r – us Hoover Inst Photo [324]

DEBATES / Great Britain. Parliament – 199 v. Fourth series. 1892-1908. (Hansard) – 3 – us Readex [324]

DEBATES / Great Britain. Parliament – 25 v. Second series. 1820-30. (Hansard) – 3 – us Readex [324]

DEBATES / Great Britain. Parliament – 356 v. Third series. 1830-91. (Hansard) – 3 – us Readex [324]

DEBATES / Great Britain. Parliament – 36 v. 1066-1803. (Hansard) – 3 – us Readex [324]

DEBATES / Great Britain. Parliament – 41 v. First series. 1803-20. (Hansard) – 3 – us Readex [324]

DEBATES / Great Britain. Parliament – Series 4: v78-151. 1900-05 (Hansard) – 29r – 1 – us Ross [941]

DEBATES / Great Britain. Parliament. House of Commons – 111 v. Fifth series. 1909-18. (Hansard) – 3 – us Readex [324]

DEBATES / Great Britain. Parliament. House of Commons – 1919-28. (Hansard) – 3 – us Readex [324]

DEBATES / Great Britain. Parliament. House of Commons – 1928 29-1937 38. (Hansard) – 3 – us Readex [324]

DEBATES / Great Britain. Parliament. House of Commons – 1938 39-1948. (Hansard) – 3 – us Readex [324]

DEBATES / Great Britain. Parliament. House of Commons – 1948 49-1957 58. (Hansard) – 3 – us Readex [324]

DEBATES / Great Britain. Parliament. House of Commons – 1958 59-1967 68. (Hansard) – 3 – us Readex [324]

DEBATES / Great Britain. Parliament. House of Commons – 1968 69-1974. (Hansard) – 3 – us Readex [324]

DEBATES / Great Britain. Parliament. House of Commons – 1974-75 76. (Hansard) – 3 – us Readex [324]

DEBATES / Great Britain. Parliament. House of Commons – 1976 77-1979 80. (Hansard) – 3 – us Readex [323]

DEBATES / Great Britain. Parliament. House of Lords – (1972; 73-1979; 80. 3) – 1909-1971 72. (Hansard) – 3 – us Readex [324]

DEBATES / India. Coorg. Lesiglative Council – v. 1-2. Bangalore. 1924-38; Index. 1924-26. BI-53 2 – 8 – ne IDC [324]

DEBATES / Madras. India. Legislative Assembly – v. 1-14. 1937-39. BI-35 2 – 8 – ne IDC [323]

DEBATES / Nigeria. Eastern Region. House of Assembly – 11 Jul 1952-30 Nov 1965 – 1 – 121.00 – us L of C Photodup [960]

DEBATES / Nigeria. House of Representatives – Jan 1952-May 1965 – 1 – 243.00 – us L of C Photodup [960]

DEBATES / Nigeria. Legislative Council – Feb 1924-Aug 1951 – 1 – 142.00 – us L of C Photodup [960]

DEBATES / Nigeria. Western Provinces. House of Assembly – 1947-50 – 1 – 19.00 – us L of C Photodup [960]

DEBATES / Nigeria. Western Region. House of Assembly – 1st-7th sessions. 1952-59 – 1 – us Res Libr [960]

DEBATES / Nigeria. Western Region. House of Chiefs – 2nd, 4th-6th sessions. 1953, 1956-58 – 1 – us Res Libr [960]

DEBATES / Orissa. India (State). Legislative Assembly – v. 1-10. 1937-44. BI-51 2 – 8 – ne IDC [324]

DEBATES / Rhodesia. (Northern). Legislative Council – May 1924-Dec 1945 – 1 – 160.00 – us L of C Photodup [324]

DEBATES / Rhodesia. Southern. Legislative Council (later Legislative Assembly) – 1899-1964 65. Lacking only fourth session of the third council for 1907 – 1 – 1,101.00 – us L of C Photodup [960]

DEBATES / Sierra Leone. Legislative Council – 1925-56.7 reels – 1 – 276.50 – us African Imprint [960]

DEBATES / South Africa. Parliament. House of Assembly – 19 Jan. 1940-17 Feb. 1967. (Hansard) – 55r – 1 – sa Microfile [324]

DEBATES, 1937-1939 / Bihar. India (State). Legislative Assembly – v. 1-5. Bihar-Patna. 1937-39. BI-47 2 – 8 – ne IDC [324]

DEBATES, 1937-1943 / Bengal. India (State). Legislative Council – Alipore. 1937-44. Lacking: 1940, v. 1-3; 1941, v. 1-2. BI-23 2 – 8 – ne IDC [324]

DEBATES, 1937-1946 / North West Frontier Province. India. Legislative Assembly – v. 1-11. 1937-46. Lacking: v. 1; v. 11. BI-69 2 – 8 – ne IDC [324]

DEBATES, 1937-1947 / Assam. India (State). Legislative Assembly – Shillong. 1937-47. BI-65 2 – 8 – ne IDC [324]

THE DEBATES IN THE FEDERAL CONVENTION OF 1789 : WHICH FRAMED THE CONSTITUTION OF THE UNITED STATES / Madison, James; ed by Hunt, Galliard & Scott, James B – Buffalo, NY: Prometheus Books. 2v. 1987 – 8mf – 9 – $12.00 – LLMC 90-360 – us L.L.M.C. [323]

THE DEBATES IN THE SEVERAL STATE CONVENTIONS ON THE ADOPTION OF THE FEDERAL CONSTITUTION, AS RECOMMENDED BY THE GENERAL CONVENTION AT PHILADELPHIA, IN 1787 / Elliot, Jonathan – 2d ed. Philadelphia, Lippincott, 1896. 5 v. LL-166 – 1 – us L of C Photodup [340]

DEBATES OF BOTH HOUSES OF PARLIAMENTS – Cape Town: Printed & publ under contract with the Union Parliament by Cape Times, sep 9/14 1914 – us Res Libr [324]

DEBATES OF THE ASSAM LEGISLATIVE ASSEMBLY – Shillong, 1937-1947 – 332mf – I-65/2 – ne IDC [340]

DEBATES OF THE EUROPEAN PARLIAMENT : ANNEX TO THE OFFICIAL JOURNAL OF THE EC (IRREGULAR) / Euroepan Parliament – (Available in 9 languages. Annual indexes included) – 9 – ECU190.00 subsc – AX-AA-96-000-EN-A – lu EEC [340]

DEBATES OF THE FEDERAL CONSTITUTION : IN THE SEVERAL STATE CONVENTIONS – 2nd ed. Philadelphia: Lippincott. v1-5. 1836 – 33mf – 9 – $49.50 – LLMC 84-243 – us L.L.M.C. [323]

DEBATES OF THE HOUSE OF COMMONS IN THE YEAR 1774 ON THE BILL FOR MAKING MORE EFFECTUAL PROVISION FOR THE GOVERNMENT OF THE PROVINCE OF QUEBEC / Cavendish, Henry – London, Ridgway, Piccadilly, 1839. SEM105P86 – 4mf – 9 – Can$9.00 – cn Bibl Nat [323]

DEBATES: OFFICIAL REPORT / Nigeria. North-Central States Legislature. House of Assembly – Feb 1952-Aug 1959 – 6 – $40.00 – us L of C Photodup [960]

DEBATS / European Coal and Steel Community. Common Assembly – Luxemburg. Sept 10 13 1952-Feb 28 1958. Incomplete – 1 – us NY Public [324]

DEBATS / France. Assemblee consultative provisoire – Algers puis Paris. 4 nov 1943-20 oct 1945 – 1 – fr A.C.R.P.P. [323]

DEBATS / France. Assemblee de l'Union francaise – 10 dec 1947-29 mai 1958 – 1 – fr A.C.R.P.P. [323]

DEBATS / France. Assemblee puis Nationale Constituante – 7nov 1945-27 nov 1946 – 1 – fr A.C.R.P.P. [323]

DEBATS / Ubangi-Shari. Assemblee territoriale – 1947-May 1956 complete – 1 – 35.00r – us Hoover Inst Photo [324]

LES DEBATS – (Filmed with: Le Combat v4 n203 11 oct 1903-24 jan 1904. L'Action v1 n1. 31 jan 1904) – Montreal, Canada. v1 n1. 3 dec 1899-v4 n202. 4 oct 1903 – 1r – 1 – Can$40.00 – cn Can Microfilming [072]

LES DEBATS : JOURNAL PARLEMENTAIRE – Quebec, Canada. 22 mar-10 jun 1862 – 1r – 1 – Can$40.00 – cn Can Microfilming [971]

LES DEBATS – Montreal, Canada. 1899-1904 – 2r – 1 – $136.00 – cn Library Assoc [971]

LES DEBATS – Quebec, Canada. 28 oct-2 dec 1854 – 1r – 1 – Can$25.00 – cn Can Microfilming [072]

LES DEBATS – Port-au-Prince: [s.n.], [1951-]. [1 annee, n1-6 annee, n203 1er mai 1951-23 dec 1956] – us Res Libr [072]

DEBATS DANS L'ASSEMBLEE LEGISLATIVE SUR LA TENURE SEIGNEURIALE / Canada. Parlement. Assemblee Legislative – Quebec: E R Frechette..., 1853. SEM105P263 – 1mf – 9 – Can$2.25 – cn Bibl Nat [340]

DEBATS DE L'ASSEMBLEE NATIONALE / France. Assemblee Nationale – (1881-1910 F2,400.00; 1911-1940 F3,000.00; 1944-1973 F10,000.00; 1881-1973 F13,500.00) – 1974-. Approx. 200 fiches per year – 9 – F650.00y – fr Journal Officiel [944]

DEBATS DE L'ASSEMBLEE NATIONALE *see* LE JOURNAL OFFICIEL

DEBATS DU SENAT / France. Senat – (1881-1910 F2,200.00; 1911-1940 F2,800.00; 1947-1976 F9,800.00; 1881-1976 F13,500.00) – 1977-. Approx. 140 fiches per year – 9 – F470.00y – fr Journal Officiel [944]

DEBATS DU SENAT *see* LE JOURNAL OFFICIEL

DEBATS DU SENAT 1881 A 1900 – F1,600.00 – fr Journal Officiel [944]

DEBATS DU SENAT 1901 A 1920 – F1,600.00 – fr Journal Officiel [944]

DEBATS DU SENAT 1921 A 1940 – F1,600.00 – fr Journal Officiel [944]

DEBATS PARLEMENTAIRES / France. Assemblee Nationale – 29 nov 1946-85 – 1 – fr A.C.R.P.P. [323]

DEBATS PARLEMENTAIRES / France. Chambre des Deputes – 1881-10 JUIL 1940 – 1 – fr A.C.R.P.P. [323]

DEBATS PARLEMENTAIRES / France. Conseil de la Republique – 26 dec 1946-58 – 1 – fr A.C.R.P.P. [323]

DEBATS PARLEMENTAIRES / France. Senat – 1881-10 juil 1940 – 1 – fr A.C.R.P.P. [323]

DEBATS PARLEMENTAIRES / France. Senat – 1959-86 – 1 – fr A.C.R.P.P. [323]

DEBATS PARLEMENTAIRES / France. Senat – Compte rendu in extenso des comites secrets des 14 mars et 16 avr 1940. no. special du 2 aout 1948 – 1 – fr A.C.R.P.P. [323]

DEBATS PARLEMENTAIRES SUR LA QUESTION DE LA CONFEDERATION DES PROVINCES A L'AMERIQUE BRITANNIQUE DU NORD / Canada. Parliament – Quebec: Hunter, Rose et Lemieux, 1865. SEM105P391 – 11mf – 9 – Can$24.75 – cn Bibl Nat [323]

DEBATS...SUR LA TENURE SEIGNEURIALE / Canada. Parliament. Legislative Assembly – Quebec: E R Frechette, 1853. SEM105P263 – 1mf – 9 – Can$2.25 – cn Bibl Nat [323]

Debect, H *see* LA QUESTION SIAMOISE...

DEBEN DEROGARSE LOS ESCRITOS DE REPLICA, DUPLICA Y EXTRACTO DE LITIS DEL CODIGO DE PROCEDIMIENTOS CIVILES DEL ESTADO DE LA BAJA CALIFORNIA / Guerrero Meza, Hector Emilio – Guadalajar Mexico Universidad Autonoma de Guadalajara, 1969. 52 3 p. LL-8026 – 1 – us L of C Photodup [340]

EL DEBER DEL ESTADO CON RELACION A LA RIQUEZA INTELECTUAL DE UN PUEBLO / Perez Bueno, Fernando – Madrid: Est. Tip. de Jaime Rates, 1917 – sp Bibl Santa Ana [946]

EL DEBER Y LA PASION / Solar y Taboada, Antonio – Badajoz: Tip. del Nuevo Diario s.a. – 1 – sp Bibl Santa Ana [946]

Debidour, Antonin *see*
- L'EGLISE CATHOLIQUE ET L'ETAT SOUS LA TROISIEME REPUBLIQUE (1870-1906)
- HISTOIRE DES RAPPORTS DE L'EGLISE ET DE L'ETAT EN FRANCE DE 1789 A 1870

DeBillo, Francis D *see* PROTESTANT MISSION WORK AMONG ITALIANS IN BOSTON

DEBIT AND CREDIT = SOLL UND HABEN / Freytag, Gustav – New York: W Abbatt, 1909 – 1r – 1 – us U.W. Library [430]

DEBIT CARD NEWS *see* POS NEWS

Deblois, Charles J *see* JOURNAL OF CHARLES J. DEBLOIS, CAPTAIN'S CLERK, ABOARD THE U.S.S. MACEDONIAN

Deblois, Isidore Gregoire *see* THEORETICAL AND PRACTICAL SYSTEM OF BOOK-KEEPING BY SINGLE AND DOUBLE ENTRY: CONTAINING SEVEN SETS FULLY ILLUSTRATED: PRESENTING A GOOD COURSE OF MERCANTILE TRAINING: WITH NUMEROUS EXERCISES AND USEFUL FORMS FOR PRACTICAL USE

DIE DEBORAH – Cincinnati. Ohio. 1855-1900 – 1 – us A.J.P.C. [071]

DEBORAH AND BARAK. AN ORATORIO FOR SOLO VOICES, CHORUS, AND ORCHESTRA / Greene, M – (Never published) – Manuscript score, 1732? – 1 – us Sibley [780]

Deborogii-Mokrievich, Vladimir Karpovich *see* 14 MIESIATSEV VO VLASTI BOLSHEVIKOV

DEBOUT! / ed by Boisseau, Fernand – Montreal, Canada. 31 mar 1935-28 mar 1937 – 1r – 1 – Can$45.00 – cn Can Microfilming [072]

Debout *see* VIE DE SAINT CAMILLE DE LELLIS...PARIS, 1932

Debout, Jacques *see* D'APRES LES PARABOLES HISTOIRES VRAIES...

Debrah, Siegfried *see* DAIRY MARKETING IN ETHIOPIA

DEBRECEN – Debrecen, Hungary. 1 Feb-30 Apr 1950 – 1r – 1 – us L of C Photodup [072]

DEBRETT'S BARONETAGE AND KNIGHTAGE,... INFORMATION RESPECTING THE IMMEDIATE FAMILY CONNECTIONS OF BARONETS / ed by Mair, Robert H – London: Dean, 1880. xxxi,616p. – 1 – us U.W. Library [920]

Debs, Eugene V *see* PAPERS OF EUGENE V. DEBS, 1834-1945

DEB'S MAGAZINE – Chicago. v. 1 no. 2-v. 2 no. 20. Sept 1921-Apr 1923. Incomplete – 1 – us NY Public [073]

DEBS MAGAZINE – 1-2 (all publ). 1921-1923 – 5mf – 9 – $40.00 – us UPA [335]

DEBS MAGAZINE – Chicago. v1-2. 1921-23 – 1r – 1 – us Ross [073]

Debu, K I *see* KOLLECTIVNOE ISPOL'ZOVANIE SEL'SKOKHOZIAISTVENNYKH MASHIN I ORUDII

Deburaux, Edouard *see* DU TCHAD AU DAHOMEY EN BALLON.

Debussy, Claude *see* MARCHE DES ANCIENS COMTES DE ROSS...MARCHE POUR PIANO A QUATRE MAINS....MARCHE ECOSSAISE

DEBUT GUYANE – French Guiana. 1957-1962 – 1 – us UMI [072]

LES DEBUTS DE L'OEUVRE AFRICAINE DE LEOPOLD 2 1875-1879 / Roeykens, Auguste – Bruxelles, 1955 – 1 – us Res Libr [960]

LES DEBUTS DE M. J. A. OUIMET AU BARREAU – Montreal?: s.n., 1873. 03782. (Pre-1900 Canadiana) – 9 – cn C.I.H.M. [971]

Deby, J *see* ANALYSIS OF THE DIATOMACEOUS GENUS CAMPYLODISCUS

DEC PROFESSIONAL – (1986-. 1,5,6) – v1-. 1982- – 9 – us UMI [510]

DEC TODAY – v1-. 1986- – 1,5,6,9 – us UMI [510]

UNA DECADA DE PROGRESO EN BADAJOZ / Duarte Insua, Lino – Badajoz: Dip. Provincial, 1945 – 1 – sp Bibl Santa Ana [946]

LA DECADA PERONISTE / Bearn, Georges – Paris: Gallimard, 1975 – 1 – CSUXADJ7757-B – us Hoover Inst Photo [320]
LA DECADE EGYPTIENNE – Journal litteraire de l'Economie politique. Caire: Imp. nationale, 1798-1800. 3v. 12 fiches. (Selected Periodicals) – 9 – 30.00 – fr Bibl Nationale [073]
LA DECADE EGYPTIENNE – Journal litteraire et d'economie politique. Le Caire. 1799-1800 (I-III) – 1 – fr A.C.R.P.P. [073]
DECADE FOR WOMEN, UN WORLD CONFERENCE : COPENHAGEN – 1980 – (Includes printed index) – 9 – $185.00 – us UNIFO [305]
DECADE FOR WOMEN, UN WORLD CONFERENCE : NAIROBI, KENYA (JULY 1985) – (Includes printed index) – ca 60mf/2,600p – 9 – $185.00 – 0-89111-023-2 – us UNIFO [305]
A DECADE OF GLASS COLLECTING: SELECTIONS FROM MELVIN BILLUPS COLLECTION – 1962. 64p. 100 illus. 2 fiches. No.1037 – 9 – $5.00 – us Corning Mus [740]
DECADE OF PROGRESS / Davis, Lynn M, Jr – A history of the State Convention of Baptists in Ohio. 1954-64 – 1 – 5.00 – us Baptist [240]
LA DECADENCE ARTISTIQUE ET LITTERAIRE – no. 1-3. Paris. oct 1886. mq no. 4. Supplement de: Le Scapin voir a ce titre – 1 – fr A.C.R.P.P. [800]
DECADENCE OF POLITICAL SOCIALISM / Alaiz, Felipe – 1951. 7p – 9 – 1.00f – at Libertarian Micro [320]
LE DECADENT LITTERAIRE ET ARTISTIQUE – Dir. A. Baju. no. 1-35. avr-dec 1886. devenu: Le Decadent. Revue litteraire bimensuelle. 2e s., no. 1-32. dec 1887-avr 1889. devenu: La France litteraire. Philosophie, critique, sociologie. n.s., no. 33-35. Paris. mai 1889 – 1 – fr A.C.R.P.P. [800]
Decaisne, J *see* DESCRIPTION D'UN HERBIER DE L'ILE DE TIMOR,...
DECAMERONE / Boccaccio G – 15th century illuminated MS. Holkham 531. Holkham Hall, Norfolk, England – 1 £20.00 14 £35.00 – uk Microform Academic [830]
Decamps, Henri *see* ECOLOGY AND MANAGEMENT OF AQUATIC-TERRESTRIAL ECOTONES
Decanver, H C pseud. [i.e. Curtis H Cavender] *see* CATALOGUE OF WORKS IN REFUTATION OF METHODISM, FROM ITS ORIGIN IN 1729 TO THE PRESENT TIME,...
DECAS GENERUM NOVORUM / Ventenat, E P – Parisiis. 1808. B-5261 2 – 8 – ne IDC [580]
DECAS PRIMA ET SECUNDA. PLANTARUM RARIORUM HORTI UPPSALIENSIS / Linnaeus, Carl – Stockholmiae. 1762. B-5504 2 – 8 – ne IDC [580]
DECATUR ADVERTISER – Decatur, NE. -w. Jul. 1955-Mar. 1960 – 1 – us NE Hist [071]
Decatur Baptist College. Decatur, Texas *see* CATALOGS AND COLLEGE RECORDS
DECATUR COUNTY NEWS – Oberlin. Kan. 1911-1912 – 1 – us UMI [071]
DECATUR HERALD – Decatur, NE. -w. Aug. 1902-Dec. 1942 – 1 – us NE Hist [071]
Decatur, Illinois *see* MISCELLANEOUS NEWSPAPERS
DECATUR NEWS – Decatur, NE. -w. Apr. 1947-Oct. 1947 – 1 – us NE Hist [071]
DECATUR NEWS – Decatur, NE. -w. Jun. 1895-Sep. 1896 – 1 – us NE Hist [071]
DECATUR NEWS – Greensburg. Ind. -w. 1878-85 – 1 – us UMI [071]
DECATUR PRESS – Greensburg. Ind. -w. 1868-70 – 1 – us UMI [071]
DECATUR REPUBLICAN – Greensburg. Ind. -w. 1857-63 – 1 – us UMI [071]
DECAYING WITH THE DINOSAURS, U.S. FUTURE IS IN NIMBLER FIRMS, NOT MERGER-CRAZED GIANTS / Burck, Arthur – 1982. 1p – 9 – 1.00f – at Libertarian Micro [335]
DECCAN CHRONICLE – Secunderabad, India. 1962-Nov 1994 – 199r – 1 – us L of C Photodup [072]
Deccan College. Research Institute *see* BULLETIN
DECCAN HERALD – Bangalore, India. Mar 1949-Jul 1995 – 247r – 1 – us L of C Photodup [072]
DECCAN HERALD – Poona, India. Daily Telegraph & Deccan Herald. -d. 1876-1889. 45 reels – 1 – uk British Libr Newspaper [072]
DECCAN TIMES – Madras, India. 16 Apr 1944-8 Jul 1956 – 4r – 1 – us L of C Photodup [072]
THE DECCAN TIMES – Madras: Deccan Print and Pub Co, 1949 – us Res Libr [072]
THE DECCAN TIMES – Madras: Deccan Print & Pub Co, 1949 – us Res Libr [072]
DeCelles, Alfred Duclos *see*
– A LA CONQUETE DE LA LIBERTE
– CARTIER ET SON TEMPS
– LES CONSTITUTIONS DU CANADA
– LES ETATS UNIS: ORIGINE, INSTITUTIONS, DEVELOPPEMENT
– LES ETATS-UNIS
– LAFONTAINE ET SON TEMPS
– LAURIER ET SON TEMPS
– PAPINEAU, 1786-1871
– THE PATRIOTES OF '37
– SCENES DE MOEURS ELECTORALES
DECENNIAL CENSUS 1980 : POPULATION AND HOUSING / U.S. Bureau of the Census – (PC(1)-A: Number of Inhabitants. PC(1)-B: General Population Characteristics. PC(1)-C: General and Social Economic Characteristics. PC(1)-D: Detailed Population Characteristics. HC(1)-A: General Housing Characteristics. HC(1)-B: Detailed Housing Characteristics) – 9 – $5.00f – us Ross [310]
DECENNIAL CENSUS PUBLICATIONS: POPULATION / U.S. Bureau of the Census – 1790-1890, 1900, 1910, 1920, 1930, 1940, 1950, 1960, 1970, 1980 – 1 – us Primary [310]
DECENTRALIST, MONEY- AND LAND REFORMER, FREE TRADER, PEACE LOVER AND FOUNDER OF THE SCHOOL OF LIVING / Borsodi, Ralph – 1fiche – 9 – 1.00f – at Libertarian Micro [320]
DECENTRALIZATION OF AGRICULTURAL PLANNING SYSTEMS IN LATIN AMERICA – 1990 – 68p – it F.A.O. [630]
DECHADO Y REFORMACION DE TODAS LAS MEDICINAS COMPUESTAS, RENALES... / Jubera, A – Valladolid, 1578 – 12mf – 9 – sp Cultura [610]
Dechambre, A *see* DICTIONNAIRE ENCYCLOPEDIQUE DES SCIENCES MEDICALES (AEL, ABT 3;15)
DECHENIANA – Title varies. v1-62, 1844-1905; index 1844-83 – 13r – 1 – $270.00; outside North America add $1.25r – us L of C Photodup [574]
Dechent, Hermann *see* GOETHES SCHOENE SEELE SUSANNA KATHARINA V. KLETTENBERG
Dechet, Arlette *see* STRATEGIE POUR L'ENSEIGNEMENT DE L'ANGLAIS DE L'INFORMATIQUE
DECHIARATIONE DI VN SALMO FATTO SOPRA LA FELISSIMA VITTORIA DE L'ARMATA CHRISTIANA; ... – N.p., [1571] – 1mf – 9 – H-8182/1 – ne IDC [956]
DECIDING CASES WITHOUT ARGUMENT : A DESCRIPTION OF PROCEDURES IN COURTS OF APPEALS / Cecil, Joe S & Steinstra, Donna – Washington: FJC, 1985 – 1mf – 9 – $1.50 – LLMC 95-323 – us L.L.M.C. [340]
DECIDING CASES WITHOUT ARGUMENT : AN EXAMINATION OF FOUR COURTS OF APPEALS / Cecil, Joe S & Steinstra, Donna – Washington: FJC, 1987 – 3mf – 9 – $4.50 – LLMC 95-334 – us L.L.M.C. [340]
DECIMAS EN HONOR...DE LA VIRGEN / Barco Perez, Paulina – 188? – 9 – 1.50f – sp Bibl Santa Ana [946]
DECIMOCTAVO DE JULIO *see* 18 DE JULIO; DOS ANOS DE GUERRA
DECIMOS – Caceres, 1933-1934 – 5 – sp Bibl Santa Ana [073]
LA DECISION POLITIQUE EN BELGIQUE : LE POUVOIR ET LES GROUPES / Meynaud, Jet al – 1965 – F100.00 – fr Ethnologie [320]
DECISION SCIENCES – (1982-. 1,5,6,9) – v1-. 1970- – 1 – us UMI [500]
DECISION SUPPORT SYSTEMS FOR THE MANAGEMENT OF GRAZING LAND : EMERGING ISSUES – 9 – 92-3-102835-9 – fr UNESCO [333]
LA DECISION...CONCERNANT LES ILES D'ALAND / Colyn, H A – Amsterdam, 1923 – 3mf – 1 – ILM-923/1 – ne IDC [327]
DECISIONES DEL TRIBUNAL DE CONTRIBUCIONES DE PUERTO RICO : (TAX COURT) 13 AUGUST 1943 TO 12 DECEMBER 1947 – San Juan: Govt Press. v1-5. 1946-51 – 56mf – 9 – $84.00 – LLMC 92-411 – us L.L.M.C. [340]
DECISIONES S. ROTAE ROMANAE. OPERA OMNIA / Gutierrez, Juan – 1730 – 9 – 1.50f – sp Bibl Santa Ana [240]
DECISION-MAKING PROCESSES IN FOUR WEST JAVANESE VILLAGES / Hofsteede, W M F – Nijmegen 1971 – 3mf – 9 – ne IDC [302]
DECISIONS / California. Public Utilities Commission – v1-. Jan. 1, 1911-75. 818 fiches. (Harvard Law School Library Collection.) – 9 – $1.50f – us H.U. Law [336]
DECISIONS / Pennsylvania. Public Utility Commission – Jul 26, 1913-78. 495 fiches. (Harvard Law School Library Collection.) – 9 – $1.50f – us H.U. Law [336]
DECISIONS / U.S. Board of Tax Appeals – v. 1-47. 1924-42 – 1,5,6 – us Princeton Micro [336]
DECISIONS / U.S. Bureau of Labor Statistics – 1912-32 – 9 – us UMI [324]
DECISIONS / U.S. Department of the Interior – 1881-1971 – 1,5,6 – us Princeton Micro [323]
DECISIONS / U.S. Employee's Compensation Appeals Board – v1-33 plus 9 suppl and index vols. 1946-82. 81-219 – 9 – 216.00 – us L.L.M.C. [324]
DECISIONS / U.S. Indian Claims Commission – v1-43. 1948-78.80-510 – 9 – 324.00 – us L.L.M.C. [324]
DECISIONS / U.S. Patent Office. Commissioner – v.1-100, 1869-1968. 80-700 – 9 – 456.00 – us L.L.M.C. [324]
DECISIONS / U.S. Tax Court – (Formerly: U.S. Board of Tax Appeals). v. 1-62. 1942-74 – 1,5,6 – us Princeton Micro [336]
DECISIONS / Wisconsin. Employment Relations Board – No1-8879, 1939-67. 130 fiches. (Harvard Law School Library Collection.) – 9 – $1.50f – us H.U. Law [330]
DECISIONS AND ORDERS / U.S. National Labor Relations Board – v1-196. 1935-72 – 1,5,6 – us Princeton Micro [324]
DECISIONS CONSTITUCIONALES DE LOS TRIBUNALES FEDERALES DE ESTADOS UNIDOS DESDE 1789. / Bump, Orlando Franklin – 2ed. Buenos Aires, Klingelfuss, 1887. 2 v. in 1. LL-157 – 1 – us L of C Photodup [340]
DECISIONS OF THE ADMINISTRATOR OF VETERANS' AFFAIRS *see* PENSION AND BOUNTY-LAND CLAIMS DECISIONS
DECISIONS OF THE AGRICULTURAL LABOR RELATIONS BOARD OF THE STATE OF CALIFORNIA (ALRB) : 1975-PRESENT – (Included in coll: Case Digest which is a summary of cases arranged by topical classification number with cross reference to ALRB citation number; an alphabetical case table and other cross references. Coll also includes: Subsequent History Table listing decisions affected by a new decision by the Board or by a State Court ruling on appeal) – v1-20. 1975-94 – 9 – $750.00 set ($55.00y update service) – B50572 – us Library Micro [340]
DECISIONS OF THE APPELLAT SPORTS, AND FACILITIES OF THE STATE OF WASHINGTON / Maynard, D N – 1992 – 2mf – 9 – $8.00 – us Microform Publ [790]
DECISIONS OF THE COMPTROLLER GENERAL OF THE U.S. *see* COMPTROLLER OF THE TREASURY DECISIONS
THE DECISIONS OF THE COURT OF SESSION OF SCOTLAND / Scotland. Court of Session – Arranged by subject, this collection includes decisions of the most important Scottish court, covering the years 1540-1800. v1-24. 1801-23 – 1 – $860.00 – 0-89093-029-5 – us UPA [941]
DECISIONS OF THE DEPARTMENT OF INTERIOR IN CASES RELATED TO PUBLIC LANDS *see* DECISIONS OF THE DEPARTMENT OF THE INTERIOR
DECISIONS OF THE DEPARTMENT OF THE INTERIOR / U.S. Department of the Interior – (v1-52 entitled: Decisions of the Department of Interior in Cases Related to Public Lands. Updates planned) – Washington: GPO. v1-100. 1881-1993 – 746mf – 9 – $1,119.00 – LLMC 78-020 – us L.L.M.C. [324]
DECISIONS OF THE DEPARTMENT OF THE INTERIOR *see*
– DEPARTMENT OF THE INTERIOR ANNUAL REPORTS
– INDEX/DIGESTS OF DECISIONS OF THE DEPARTMENT OF THE INTERIOR
DECISIONS OF THE INTERIOR DEPARTMENT IN PUBLIC LAND CASES AND LAND LAWS PASSED, 1838-1870 / Lester, William W – Philadelphia: Small. 2v. 1860; 1870 – 13mf – 9 – $19.50 – LLMC 82-101-2 – us L.L.M.C. [340]
DECISIONS OF THE SPEAKERS OF THE LEGISLATIVE ASSEMBLY AND HOUSE OF COMMONS OF CANADA, FROM 1841 TO JUNE 1872. / Lapierre, Augustin – Ottawa: Times Printing and Publishing Co, 1872. SEM105P439 – 3mf – 9 – Can$6.75 – cn Bibl Nat [971]
DECISIONS OF THE SPEAKERS OF THE LEGISLATIVE ASSEMBLY AND HOUSE OF COMMONS OF CANADA, FROM 1841 TO JUNE 1872 WITH AN APPENDIX CONTAINING THE SPEAKERS' DECISIONS ON ELECTION PETITION RECOGNIZANCES / Laperriere, Augustin – Ottawa: Printed by Times Printing and Publishing Company..., 1872. SEM105P439 – 3mf – 9 – Can$6.75 – cn Bibl Nat [324]
DECISIONS OF THE SUPREME COURT OF LIBERIA, 1861-1898 – 1r – $49.50 – us African Imprint [340]
DECISIONS OF THE TREASURY DEPARTMENT, 1857-1865 – (Publ as suppl to: Synopsis of Sundry Decisions of the Treasury Department, 1868-1898) – Washington: GPO. 1v. 1876 (all publ) – 4mf – 9 – $6.00 – LLMC 84-365A – us L.L.M.C. [340]
DECISIONS OF THE TREASURY DEPARTMENT ON APPEALS, 1865-1867 – (Publ as suppl to: Synopsis of Sundry Decisions of the Treasury Department, 1868-1898) – Washington: GPO. 1v (all publ) – 2mf – 9 – $3.00 – LLMC 84-365B – us L.L.M.C. [340]
DECISIONS ON THE LAW OF PATENTS FOR INVENTIONS RENDERED BY ENGLISH COURTS (V.1-3) AND BY THE U.S. SUPREME COURT (V.4-20) / U.S. Supreme Court – 1662-1890. Washington: GPO, 1887-92, C.R. Brodix. 81-420 – 9 – $96.00 – us L.L.M.C. [340]
DECISIONS...ON APPEAL FROM COURTS OF REQUESTS. PT. 1 / Ceylon. Supreme Court – Kandy: Industrial School, 1871? 39p. L.C. copy imperfect: cover title wanting. LL-8 – 1 – us L of C Photodup [340]
THE DECISIVE HOUR OF CHRISTIAN MISSIONS / Mott, John Raleigh – (Includes index) – New York: Laymen's Missionary Movement, 1910 – 1mf – 9 – 0-8370-6687-5 – 1986-0687 – us A.T.L.A. [240]
Deck, Louis *see* SYPHILIS ET REGLEMENTATION DE LA PROSTITUTION
Decker, A *see* DIE PASSION DES HERRN NACH DEN VIER EVANGELIEN SYNOPTISCH DARGESTELLT FUER DIE GEBILDETEN IN DER GEMEINDE
Decker, P *see* COLLECTION OF AUTOGRAPH FIRST EDITIONS
Deckert, Emil *see* DIE NEUE WELT: REISESKIZZEN AUS DEM NORDEN UND SUEDEN DER VEREINIGTEN STAATEN SOWIE AUS KANADA UND MEXICO
DECLAMATIO, DE BELLO TURCIS INFERENDO / Nannius, P – Lovanii, 1536 – 1mf – 9 – H-8244/1 – ne IDC [956]
DECLAMATION CONTRE L'ERREUR EXECRABLE DES MALEFICIERS, SORCIERS, ENCHANTEURS, MAGICIENS / Node, P Le – Paris. 1578 – 9 – fr Hachette [360]
DECLAMATIONES IN OMNES SOLEMNITATES... / Orozco, Alfonso de – Salamanca: Simonis Portonarys, 1573 – 1 – sp Bibl Santa Ana [946]
DECLAMATIONES QUADRAGESIMALES. / Alfonso de Orozco, Beato – 1576 – 9 – 1.50f – sp Bibl Santa Ana [890]
DECLAMATIONES VINTIGINQUE IN EVANGELIA. / Orozco, Alfonso de – 1571 – 9 – 1.50f – sp Bibl Santa Ana [240]
DECLAMATIONES...DOMINICIS / Orozco, Alfonso de – (1573 ed.1.50f; 9) – 1571 – 9 – 1.50f – sp Bibl Santa Ana [240]
DECLARACION BREVE...Y SUMARIA DEL VALOR DEL ORO... / Gallo, A – Madrid, 1613 – 3mf – 9 – sp Cultura [330]
DECLARACION FUNEBRE...CLERIGOS / Lozano, Antonio – 1742 – 9 – 1.50f – sp Bibl Santa Ana [240]

DECLARACION MAGISTRAL SOBRE LOS EMBLEMAS DE ANDRES ALCIATO. / Lopez, Diego – 1655 – 9 – 1.50f – sp Bibl Santa Ana [946]
DECLARACION MAGISTRAL SOBRE LOS EMBLEMAS DE ANDRES ALCIATO. / Lopez, Diego – 1670 – 9 – 1.50f – sp Bibl Santa Ana [946]
DECLARACION...EMBLEMAS DE ANDRES ALCIATO / Lopez, Diego – (1670 $1.50f) – 1655 – 9 – $1.50f – sp Bibl Santa Ana [740]
DECLARACIONES DEL PATER NOSTER Y AVE MARIA / Martinez Siliceo, Juan – Toledo, 1551 – 1 – sp Bibl Santa Ana [240]
DECLARACIONES...NOSTER / Martinez Siliceo, Juan – 1551 – 9 – 1.50f – sp Bibl Santa Ana [240]
DECLARACION...SATIRAS DE IUVENAL / Lopez, Diego – 1642 – 9 – 1.50f – sp Bibl Santa Ana [450]
DECLARACION...SOBRE LAS SATIRAS DE.. / Iuvenal – 1642 – 9 – 1.50f – sp Bibl Santa Ana [410]
DECLARATIO, OFT OPENBARE VERTOONINGE, ENDE NOOTELICKE VERCLARINGE, TEGHEN / Meulen, I P vander – Alckmaer, J. de Meester. 1600. BME-259 1 – 9 – ne IDC [240]
DECLARATION / Boulet, J B – 1883? 02538. (Pre-1900 Canadiana) – 9 – cn C.I.H.M. [971]
DECLARATION DE LA DIGNITE DES PLANETES [...] / Thibault, Jehan – Paris: Nyverd, 1543 – fr Armell [520]
LA DECLARATION DES ABUS QUE L'ON COMMET EN ESCRIVANT / Rambaud, H – 1578 – 9 – fr I.C.S. [440]
LA DECLARATION DU DROIT... / Chevalley, L – Le Caire, Barbey, [1912] – 2mf – 1 – ILM-451/1 – ne IDC [327]
LA DECLARATION DU GUERRE;... / Defourny, P – Paris, 1887 – 1mf – 1 – ILM-487/1 – ne IDC [327]
DECLARATION DU ROY CONTRE LES CORSAIRES ENNEMIS – Paris, 1691 – 1mf – 1 – ILM-1226/1 – ne IDC [327]
A DECLARATION OF FAITH OF THE ENGLISH PEOPLE / Helwys, Thomas – From York Minster Library, 17th century – 1 – uk Microform Academic [941]
A DECLARATION OF HIS ELECTORAL HIGHNESS THE DUKE OF BRANDENBURGH... – London, 1689 – 1mf – 1 – ILM-670/1 – ne IDC [327]
THE DECLARATION OF INDEPENDENCE : ILLUSTRATED STORY OF ITS ADOPTION, WITH BIOGRAPHIES AND PORTRAITS OF THE SIGNERS / Casey, Robert E – Fredericksburg, VA: printed for the Citizen's Guild of Washington's Boyhood Home, n.d. – 2mf – 9 – $3.00 – LLMC 92-193 – us L.L.M.C. [340]
DECLARATION OF INTENT / Palau Political Status Commission – Koror: Political Status Commission, mar 1977 – 1mf – 9 – $1.50 – LLMC 82-100G, Title 14 – us L.L.M.C. [323]
DECLARATION OF LONDON / Cohen, A – London, 1911 – 2mf – 1 – ILM-454/1 – ne IDC [327]
THE DECLARATION OF PARIS OF 1856 / Bowles, T G – London, 1900 – 3mf – 1 – ILM-342/1 – ne IDC [327]
DECLARATION OF RIGHTS / Equal Rights Advocates and Anti-Monopolists of N.Y – 8 points, 1836 – 9 – 1.00f – at Libertarian Micro [335]
THE DECLARATION OF THE TRUE PRESBYTERIANS WITHIN THE KINGDOM OF SCOTLAND CONCERNING MR. GEORGE WHITEFIELD AND THE WORK AT CAMBUSLANG – Glasgow, 1742 – 1mf – 9 – MP-296/1 – ne IDC [240]
DECLARATIONS BY MR. IRUJO – n.p. 1937. Fiche W 824. (Blodgett Collection of Spanish Civil War Pamphlets) – 9 – us H.U. College Libr [946]
DECLARATIONS OF INDENTION / Putnam County. Ohio. Common Pleas. Probate Division – 1833-1915 – 1r – 1 – us Archival [324]
DECLARATIONS OF INTENTION / Ottawa County. Ohio. Probate Court – 1907-1935 – 1r – 1 – $32.50r – us Archival [324]
Declareuil, Jean *see* LES SYSTEMES DE TRANSPORTATION ET DE MAIN-D'OEUVRE PENALE AUX COLONIES DANS LE DROIT FRANCAIS
DECLASSIFIED DOCUMENTS REFERENCE SYSTEM – Annual collections, 1975- . Full text of documents on fiche with bimonthly catalogs of abstracts and one cumulative annual subject index – 9 – us Primary [324]
DECLASSIFIED DOCUMENTS REFERENCE SYSTEM – Retrospective Collection. With two abstracts volumes and combined (with 1975) cumulative subject index volume – 9 – us Primary [324]
THE DECLINE AND FALL OF KEEWATIN, OR, THE FREE TRADE REDSKINS – A satire. Illustrated by J. W. Bengough. Toronto: Grip, 1876. 02695. (Pre-1900 Canadiana) – 9 – cn C.I.H.M. [971]
DECLINING BREEDS OF MEDITERRANEAN SHEEP – 1978 – 68p – it F.A.O. [636]
DECOLONIZATION : SPECIAL ISSUE ON AMERICAN SAMOA / U.N. Dept of Political Affairs, Trusteeship & Colonization – Oct 1978 – 1mf – 9 – $1.50 – LLMC 82-100C Title 40 – us L.L.M.C. [340]
DECOLONIZATION : A SPECIAL ISSUE ON THE TRUST TERRITORY OF THE PACIFIC ISLANDS / U.N. Dept of Political Affairs, Trusteeship and Decolonization – no 16. Apr 1880 – 1mf – 9 – $1.50 – LLMC 82-100F Title 101 – us L.L.M.C. [324]
DECOLONIZATION OF AFRICA : SOUTHERN AFRICA AND THE HORN OF AFRICA – 1981 – 163p – 9 – 92-3-101834-5 – fr UNESCO [960]
DECORATING AND CRAFT IDEAS – (1984-. 5,6,9) – 1976-84 – 1 – us UMI [740]
DECORATING AND CRAFT IDEAS MADE EASY – 1970-76 – 1 – us UMI [740]
DECORATING AND REMODELING *see* AMERICAN HOMESTYLE
DE LA DECORATION APPLIQUEE AUX EDIFICES. / Viollet-Le-Duc, Eugene Emmanuel – Paris, Ballue, 1880. 45p., ill. (Architecture Series) – 9 – fr Hachette [720]
DECORATIVE AND ARCHITECTURAL ARTS IN CHICAGO, 1871-1933 : AN ILLUSTRATED GUIDE TO THE CERAMICS AND GLASS EXHIBITION / Darling, Sharon S – 1982 – 4 color mf – 15 – $78.00f – 0-226-68884-4 – us Chicago [740]
DECORATIVE ART / Caisse Nationale des Monuments Historiques et des Sites. Paris – (Major collections from the Louvre and the Musee Cluny, and the oriental collections from the Musee Guimet are included. Over 2000 tapestries. Over 9000 reproductions) – 153mf – 9 – $780.00 – 0-907006-75-2 – uk Mindata [740]
DECORATIVE ART IN THE VICTORIA AND ALBERT MUSEUM / Victoria and Albert Museum. London – (Pictorial record of the principal objects in the Museum, in 5 sections. Also listed separately) – 9 – $3,800.00 complete coll – 0-907006-30-2 – uk Mindata [700]
DECORATIVE ART IN THE VICTORIA AND ALBERT MUSEUM *see*
- ARCHITECTURE AND SCULPTURE COLLECTION
- CERAMICS COLLECTION
- FURNITURE AND WOODWORK COLLECTION
- METALWORK
- TEXTILES

THE DECORATOR AND FURNISHER – v. 1-32. Oct 1882-Aug 1898 – 1 – 113.00 – us L of C Photodup [740]
DECORATOR AND PAINTER FOR AUSTRALIA AND NEW ZEALAND *see* AUSTRALASIAN DECORATOR AND PAINTER
DECORMAG : MAGAZINE DE LA DECORATION – Montreal. v1 n1. aut 1972-v4 n4. dec 1975 – 1r – 1 – Can$60.00 – cn Can Microfilming [072]
DeCosta, Benjamin Franklin *see* THE MOABITE STONE
Decourcelle, J *see* LA CONDITION DES JUIFS DE NICE AUX 17E ET 18E SIECLES
Decourdemanche, A *see*
- AUX INDUSTRIELS
- EST-CE LEGALEMENT QUE LE GOUVERNMENT A FAIT SUSPENDRE L'EXERCISE DU CULTE SAINT-SIMONIEN?

Decourt, Fernand *see* LA FAMILLE KERDALEC AU SOUDAN
DECOUVERTE DE L'AMERIQUE PAR LES NORMANDS AU 10E SIECLE / Gravier, Gabriel – Rouen: E Cagniard, 1874. SEM35P66 – 1r – 1 – Can$15.00 – cn Bibl Nat [970]
LA DECOUVERTE DE L'EMPIRE DE CANTAHAR / Varennes de Mondasse – (Utopias of the Enlightenment series). 1730 – 9 – fr Hachette [830]
DECOUVERTE DE L'ISLE FRIVOLE / Coyer, Gabriel-Francois – (Utopias in the Enlightenment series). 1751 – 9 – fr Hachette [830]
LA DECOUVERTE DU MISSISSIPI: POEME / Frechette, Louis H – Quebec: s.n., 1873?. 04329. (Pre-1900 Canadiana) – 9 – cn C.I.H.M. [810]
DECOUVERTE ET EVOLUTION CARTOGRAPHIQUE DE TERRE NEUVE ET DES PAYS CIRCONVOISINS 1497-1501-1769: ESSAIS.. / Harrisse, Henry – Paris: Welter, 1890. 05390. (Pre-1900 Canadiana) – 9 – cn C.I.H.M. [910]
DECOUVERTES SUR LE FEU, L'ELECTRICITE ET LA LUMIERE CONSTATEES PAR UNE SUITE D'EXPERIENCES NOUVELLES QUI VIENNENT D'ETRE VERIFEES PAR MM. LES COMMISSAIRES DE L'ACAD. DES SC / Marat, Jean-Paul – Paris, Clousier, 1779, iv, 38 p. Histoire des Sciences XVIIe-XIXe Siecles. 7987 – 9 – fr Hachette [510]
Decraene, P *see* TABLEAU DES PARTIS POLITIQUES DE L'AFRIQUE AU SUD DU SAHARA
DECREES AND JUDGEMENTS IN ANTITRUST CASES *see* FEDERAL ANTITRUST DECISIONS, 1890-1931
DECREES CONCERNING THE STATE OF EMERGENCY / Indonesia. Laws, Statutes, etc – In English. SE-4617 1 – 9 – ne IDC [324]
DECRETALES CUM GLOSSIS (SIECLE 14) / Gregorio 10 – Barcelona – 1r – 5,6 – sp Cultura [240]
DECRETALES ET CONSTITUCIONES PAPALES (SIECLE 14) – Barcelona – 1r – 5,6 – sp Cultura [240]
DECRETO DE 25 DE ABRIL DE 1938 Y REGLAMENTO DEL MIS MO MES, REORGANIZANDO EL SERVICIO DEL SUBSIDIO AL COMBATIENTE / Comision Provincial de subsidio el Combatiente – Instrucciones sobre Inspeccion. Caceres: Imp. Moderna, 1938 – 1 – sp Bibl Santa Ana [060]
EL DECRETO DE 25 DE JUNIO DE 1856,O SEA, ECSAMEN SOBRE LA LEGALIDAD Y CONVENIENCIA DE LA LLAMADA, LEY DE DESAMORTIZACION DE BIENES RAICES DE LAS CORPORACIONES CIVILES Y ECLESIASTICAS : COLECCION DE ARTICULOS PUBLICADOS POR EL LIC. SABINO FLORES EN "LA NACIONALIDAD", PERIODICO OFICIAL DEL GOBIERNO DE ESTADO DE GUANAJUATO – Mexico: Impr de I Cumplido, 1856 – us Res Libr [972]
DECRETO Y RESOLUCION DE LA DIRECCION GENERAL DE EXPANSION COMERCIAL SOBRE ORGANIZACION DEL REGISTRO GENERAL DE EXPORTADORES Y DE LOS REGISTROS ESPECIALES / Camara Oficial de Comercio e Industria de Badajoz – Badajoz: Tip. A. Mangas Cuenda, 1966 – sp Bibl Santa Ana [380]
DECRETS ET STATUTS SYNODAUX DU DIOCESE DE NANTES... / Diocese de Nantes – Nantes: Doriou, 1642 – 1 – F139.47 – fr Armell [240]
DAS DECRETUM GELASIANUM (T.U.U. 3-38/4) / Dobschuetz, E V – Leipzig, 1912 – 6mf – 9 – ne Slangenburg [240]
Decroix, J -J-M *see* L'AMI DES ARTS OU JUSTIFICATION DE PLUSIERS GRANDS HOMMES...
Dede, Galib *see* HUESN VE ASK
Dederich, Hermann *see* LUDWIG UHLAND ALS DICHTER UND PATRIOT
THE DEDHAM HISTORICAL REGISTER – v. 1-14. 1890-1903 – 1 – 19.00 – us L of C Photodup [978]
DEDICATIONS AND PATRON SAINTS OF ENGLISH CHURCHES: ECCLESIASTICAL SYMBOLISM : SAINTS AND THEIR EMBLEMS / Bond, Francis – London; New York: Oxford University Press, 1914 – 1mf – us A.T.L.A. [240]
DEDICATORIAS DE MIS LIBROS / Sanchez Arjona, Vicente – Sevilla: Graficas Tirvia, Tomo 1. 1956 – 1 – sp Bibl Santa Ana [810]
DEDICATORIAS DE MIS LIBROS / Sanchez Arjona, Vicente – Sevilla: Graficas Tirvia, Tomo 2. 1956 – 1 – sp Bibl Santa Ana [810]
DEDICATORIAS EN MIS LIBROS / Sanchez Arjona, Vicente – Sevilla: Imprenta Alvarez, Tomo 4-10. 1957 – 1 – sp Bibl Santa Ana [810]
O DEDO DE DEOS – [s.l.]. 1879 – 1,5,6 – bl Biblioteca [072]
Dedreux, R *see* DER SUEZKANAL
Dee, John *see*
- A LETTER, CONTAINING A MOST BRIEFE DISCOURSE APOLOGETICALL..
- A TRUE AND FAITHFUL RELATION..

DEED RECORD / Fulton County. Ohio. Recorder – 1835-1857 – 1r – 1 – $32.50r – us Archival [324]
DEED RECORD / Ottawa County. Ohio. Recorder – 1863-1868 – 1r – 1 – us Archival [340]
DEED RECORD / Ottawa County. Ohio. Recorder – 1863-1868 – 1r – 1 – $32.50r – us Archival [324]
DEED RECORDS / Allen County. Ohio. Recorder – 1831-1835 – 1r – 1 – $32.50r – us Archival [324]
DEED RECORDS / Henry County. Ohio. Recorder – 1872-1896 – 10r – 1 – $32.50r – us Archival [324]
DEED RECORDS / Van Wert County. Ohio. Auditor – 1829-1883 – 1r – 1 – $32.50r – us Archival [324]
DEED RECORDS / Wyandot County. Ohio. Recorder – 1880-1886 – 4r – 1 – $32.50r – us Archival [324]
DEED RECORDS, FIRELANDS / Huron County. Ohio. Recorder – 1795-1809 – 3r – 1 – $32.50r – us Archival [324]
DEEDS AND LAND SALES / Wood County. Ohio. Common Pleas. Civil Divison – 1818-1860s – 1r – 1 – $32.50r – us Archival [324]
DEEDS, MS 3193 / Ashland County & Wayne County. Ohio – 1833-93 Ashland County 1853-93; Wayne County 1833-41 Excerpts – 1r – 1 – us Western Res [920]
DEEDS OF THE BOROUGH / Neath. England – 1566-1826 – 1 – uk Microform Academic [941]
DEEDS OF VALOR / ed by Beyer, Walter Frederick & Keydel, Oscar F – Detroit. 2v. 1903 – 1r – 1 – us Ross [970]
DE DEELNAME DER MARRANEN IN HET OPRICHTINGSKAPITAAL DER OOST-INDISCHE COMPAGNIE / Vaz Dias, A M – Jaarboek Amstelodamum. XXXII. 1936. BJ-262-67 1 – 9 – ne IDC [950]
Deems, Charles Force *see* THE GOSPEL OF COMMON SENSE
DEENBHANDHU – Poona, India. 14 Mar 1947-19 Dec 1950; 7 Jan 1951-4 Dec 1953; Feb 1950-7 Jul 1978 – 24r – 1 – us L of C Photodup [072]
DEEP SEA RESEARCH : PART 1: OCEANOGRAPHIC RESEARCH PAPERS; PART 2: TOPICAL STUDIES IN OCEANOGRAPHY – (Pt 2 is also available separately) – v1-1953- – 5,6,9 – us UMI [550]
DEEP SEA RESEARCH AND OCEANOGRAPHIC LITERATURE REVIEW – (See also individual titles) – v1- 1953- – 5,6,9 – us UMI [550]
DEEP THINGS OF THE BIBLE...EXPOSITION OF THE FUNDAMENTAL DOCTRINES / Farmer, A H – Youngstown: H. Syxbe, 1886. 1 fiche – 9 – us A.T.L.A. [240]
A DEEP WATER PIER AT FATHER POINT, ON THE LOWER ST LAWRENCE, BADLY NEEDED – Montreal?: s.n., 1886?. 03788. (Pre-1900 Canadiana) – 9 – cn C.I.H.M. [971]
DEEPIKA – Kottayam, India. Apr 1944-Apr 1948; Apr 1949-1953; Mar-Sept 1966 – 12r – 1 – us L of C Photodup [072]
DEEP-SEA CHALLENGE : THE JOHN MURRAY/ MABAHISS EXPEDITION TO THE INDIAN OCEAN (1933-34) / ed by Rice, A L – 1986 – 301p – 9 – 92-3-102400-0 – fr UNESCO [910]
DEEPWATER, VEGETABLE CREEK AND CASTLERAG MINER – Aug 9 1890-May 30 1891 – 9 – at Pascoe [072]
DEER FARMING – 1982 – 60p – it F.A.O. [636]
DEERFIELD 1675-1898 – (Mf 1: Index to Births & Deaths 1675-1844 (A). Mf 2: Births & Deaths 1675-1844 (A-C). Mf 3: Births & Deaths 1675-1844 (C-H). Mf 4: Births & Deaths 1675-1844 (J-S). Mf 5: Births & Deaths 1675-1844 (S-W). Mf 5-6: Marriages 1689-1844. Mf 7: Births 1844-60. Mf 8: Births 1861-63; Marriages/Deaths 1844-54. Mf 9: Deaths 1855-59. Mf 10-12: Births 1864-97. Mf 13-15: Marriages 1853-97. Mf 15-18: Deaths 1860-98) – (mf ed 1987) –

18mf – 9 – 0-87623-039-7 – us Holbrook [920]

DEERFIELD 1676-1849 – (Mf 1T-7T: Births & Deaths by Family 1676-1865. Mf 7T-8T: Marriages 1689-1833. Mf 8T-11T: Intentions of Marriage 1752-1850. Mf 10T: Out-of-Town Marriages 1703-99. Mf 10T-11T: Marriages 1832-1843. Mf 12T: B,M,D 1844-49) – (mf ed 1996) – 12mf – 9 – 0-87623-239-X – us Holbrook [920]

DEESIDE AND BUCKLEY LEADER. (MOLD, DEESIDE & BUCKLEY LEADER) – Mold, Wales. 8 Dec 1922-Dec 1933.-w. 14 reels – 1 – uk British Libr Newspaper [072]

DEESIDE PIPER AND HERALD – 1 – £42.00r – uk Scot News [072]

LA DEESSE ANAT. / Virolleaud, Ch. – Paris, 1938 – 5mf – 8 – Dfl22.00 – ne Slangenburg [270]

Deetjen, Werner et al *see* FUNDE UND FORSCHUNGEN

DEEWA ROKA MANA DSIHWE, 1904-1928 = GOD'S HAND IN MY LIFE, 1904-1928 / Lauberts, Peter – Liepaja: P. Lauberts, 1928. Publ. No. 6349 c. One of trhee items on reel – 1 – us Baptist [240]

DEFENCE AND PEACE ECONOMICS : THE POLITICAL ECONOMY OF DEFENCE DISARMAMENT AND PEACE / ed by Hartley, Keith – 9,5,1 – us Harwood [330]

LA DEFENCE, ET L'ILLUSTRATION DE LA LANGUE FRANCOISE / Du Bellay, J – 1904 – 9 – fr I.C.S. [440]

DEFENCE FOR CHILDREN INTERNATIONAL – New York. 154 docs. 1980-1991 – 74mf – 9 – ne IDC [320]

DEFENCE OF FORT M'HENRY-STAR-SPANGLED BANNER / Key, Francis Scott – Broadside, 1814. First printed edition of the words with the tune indicated (Anacreon in Heaven). MUSIC 1121 – 1 – us L of C Photodup [780]

A DEFENCE OF LIBERAL CHRISTIANITY / Norton, Andrews – (The General Repository and Review, v. 1, Jan. 1812, p. 1-25) – 9 – us A.T.L.A. [240]

A DEFENCE OF "OUR FATHERS" AND OF THE ORIGINAL ORGANIZATION OF THE METHODIST EPISCOPAL CHURCH AGAINST THE REV. ALEXANDER M'CAINE AND OTHERS : WITH HISTORICAL AND CRITICAL NOTICES OF EARLY AMERICAN METHODISM / Emory, John – New York: T Mason and G Lane for the Methodist Episcopal Church, 1838 – 1mf – us A.T.L.A. [240]

A DEFENCE OF THE CATHOLIC FAITH = DEFENSIO FIDEI CATHOLICAE DE SATISFACTIONE CHRISTI : CONCERNING THE SATISFACTION OF CHRIST AGAINST FAUSTUS SOCINUS / Grotius, Hugo – (In English. Includes indexes) – Andover: Warren F Draper, 1889 – 1mf – 9 – 0-8370-3847-2 – 1985-1847 – us A.T.L.A. [240]

A DEFENCE OF THE ELKHORN ASSOCIATION IN SIXTEEN LETTERS, ADDRESSED TO ELDER HENRY TOLER, ENTITLED UNION-NO UNION / Fishback, James – 1822 – 1 – 6.65 – us Baptist [240]

DEFENCE OF THE ROMAN CHURCH AGAINST FATHER GRATRY = DEFENSE DE L'EGLISE ROMAINE / Gueranger, Prosper – London: R Washbourne, 1870 – 1mf – 9 – 0-8370-8577-2 – 1986-2577 – us A.T.L.A. [240]

A DEFENCE OF VIRGINIA : (AND THROUGH HER, OF THE SOUTH), IN RECENT AND PENDING CONTESTS AGAINST THE SECTIONAL PARTY / Dabney, Robert Lewis – 1867 – 1r – 1 – us Ross [976]

A DEFENCE OF VIRGINIA : AND THROUGH HER, OF THE SOUTH, IN RECENT AND PENDING CONTESTS AGAINST THE SECTIONAL PARTY / Dabney, Robert Lewis – New York: E.J. Hale, 1867 – 1mf – us A.T.L.A. [978]

DEFENCES TO CRIME. THE ADJUDGED CASES IN THE AMERICAN AND ENGLISH REPORTS WHEREIN THE DIFFERENT DEFENCES TO CRIMES ARE CONTAINED – San Francisco, Whitney, 1874-92. 6 v. LL-667 – 1 – us L of C Photodup [340]

DEFENDER – (1975-. 5,6. 1977-. 9) – v. 1-. 1926- – 1 – us UMI [240]

DEFENDER – Louisville. Ky. -w. 1951- – 1 – us UMI [071]

DEFENDER – Wichita. Kansas. 1926-1952 – 1 – us UMI [071]

THE DEFENDER – Scranton, PA. -w 1904-1905 – 13 – $25.00r – us I.M.R. [071]

DEFENDER LA INDEPENDENCIA DE LA PATRIA / Spain. Presidencia del Consejo de Ministros – Barcelona, 19?? Fiche W825. (Blodgett Collection of Spanish Civil War Pamphlets) – 9 – us H.U. College Libr [946]

DEFENDERS OF NEW ZEALAND / Gudgeon, T W – (Publ in 1887 as "Defenders of New Zealand and Maori History of the War". Contains biographies, lists recipients of the War Medal and members of colonial forces killed 1860-70) – 5mf – 9 – NZ$20.00 – 0-908797-69-9 – NZNB 2371 – nz BAB [355]

DEFENSA CIUDADANA / Juez, Antonio – Badajoz: Tip.Vda.de A.Arqueros, 1936 – 1 – sp Bibl Santa Ana [350]

DEFENSA DE BADAJOZ – Badajoz.1887-89. No. sueltos – 9 – 1.50f – sp Bibl Santa Ana [072]

DEFENSA DE D. LUIS CALDERON...PRESOS DE CONFESION / Calzado Pedrilla, Felipe – 1836 – 9 – 1.50f – sp Bibl Santa Ana [946]

DEFENSA DE DON FERNANDO PEREZ – 1790. Por un amigo de Don Fernando – 9 – $1.50f – sp Bibl Santa Ana [920]

DEFENSA DE DON FERNANDO PEREZ... PARACUELLOS / Forner Segarra, Juan Pablo – 1790 – 9 – $1.50f – sp Bibl Santa Ana [946]

DEFENSA DE LA ASTROLOGIA Y CONJETURAS / Aldrete y Soto, L – Madrid, 1861 – 1mf – 9 – sp Cultura [130]

DEFENSA DE LA CHINA Y VERDADERA RESPUESTA A LAS FALSAS RAZONES OVE PARA SU REPROBACION TRAE EL DOCTOR DON JOSE COLMENERO : CHINA Y VERDADERA RESPUESTA A LAS FALSAS RAZONES... / Fernandez, T – Madrid, 1689 – 3mf – 9 – sp Cultura [610]

DEFENSA DE LA HISPANIDAD / Maeztu, Ramiro de – Madrid: Razon y Fe, 1934 – 1 – sp Bibl Santa Ana [946]

EN DEFENSA DE LA LIBERTAD : CRONICA DE UN MOVIMIENTO TERRORISTA / Cerro Fernandez, Patricio – Buenos Aires, [n.d.] – 1 – CSUXADQ2926-B – us Hoover Inst Photo [303]

DEFENSA DE LA NATURALEZA / Carrion Marquez, Jesus – Caceres: Imp. D. Rodriguez, 1972 – 1 – sp Bibl Santa Ana [946]

DEFENSA DE LA POESIA (SIECLE 17) / Sidney, Philip – Madrid – 1r – 5,6 – sp Cultura [090]

EN DEFENSA DE LOS VASCOS – Santiago de Chile, 1937. Fiche W 858. (Blodgett Collection of Spanish Civil War Pamphlets) – 9 – us H.U. College Libr [946]

DEFENSA DE MADRID. RELATO HISTORICO / Lopez Fernandez, Antonio et al – Mejico: Editorial A.P. Marquez, 1945 – 1 – sp Bibl Santa Ana [355]

DEFENSA ORAL...MANUEL BLANCO / Valcarcel, Joaquin, Ma – 1850 – 9 – 1.50f – sp Bibl Santa Ana [946]

LA DEFENSA PERUANA / Cornejo M, P – Quito, 1909 – 2mf – 1 – ILM-2479/1 – ne IDC [327]

DEFENSA Y RESPUESTA...DE LA MEDICINA RACIONAL Y PHILOSOPHICA...CONTRA... / Delgado de Vera, J – Madrid, 1687 – 5mf – 9 – sp Cultura [610]

DEFENSA Y VERDADERO MANIFIESTO DE LA VIA CURATIVA QUE D. MANUEL PELLAZ Y ESPINOSA... / Pellaz y Espinosa, Manuel – SL, SA – 1mf – 9 – sp Cultura [610]

DEFENSA...DIOCESIS DE PLASENCIA...VICARIO CAPITULAR / Ros Biosca, Godofredo – 1872 – 9 – 1.50f – sp Bibl Santa Ana [240]

DEFENSA...FERNANDO PEREZ...PARACUELLOS / Sanchez, Tomas Antonio – 1790 – 9 – 1.50f – sp Bibl Santa Ana [440]

DEFENSA...ORDEN DE ALCANTARA / Valencia y Bravo, Alonso – 1818 – 9 – 1.50f – sp Bibl Santa Ana [946]

DEFENSAS OMITIDAS EN EL MEMORIAL AJUSTADO HECHO POR EL RELATOR EN LA CAUSA DE DON JUAN DE OVANDO... / Consejo de Hacienda – 1 – sp Bibl Santa Ana [946]

DEFENSE *see* VICTORY BULLETIN

LA DEFENSE – Alger. 1934-aout 1939 – 1 – fr A.C.R.P.P. [073]

LA DEFENSE – puis organe du secours populaire de France. Paris. 1933-juil 1934 – 1 – fr A.C.R.P.P. [073]

LA DEFENSE / ed by Tremblay, U. & Tardivel, Paul – Chicoutimi, Canada. 18 jan 1898-2 fev 1905 – 2r – 1 – Can$70.00r – cn Can Microfilming [072]

LA DEFENSE – Windsor, Ontario. 7 mar 1918 – 1r – 1 – Can$25.00 – cn Can Microfilming [072]

LA DEFENSE – Woonsocket, RI. v1 n2. 20 dec 1928 – 1r – 1 – Can$25.00 – cn Can Microfilming [071]

DEFENSE 80 – Title carries year's designation – 1,5,6,9 – us UMI [073]

DEFENSE COUNSEL JOURNAL – (v1-51 1934-84 on reel $577.00. v52-62 1985-95 on mf $334.00. Title varies: v1-53 1934-85 as Insurance Counsel Journal) – v1-62. 1934-95 – 5,6,9 – $911.00 set – us Hein [340]

DEFENSE DE LA FRANCE – Paris, France. -m. 15 Dec 1942-June 1944. Imperfect. 10 ft – 1 – uk British Libr Newspaper [072]

LA DEFENSE DE LA POESIE ET DE LA LANGUE FRANCOISE / Desmarets de Saint-Sorlin, J – 1675 – 9 – fr I.C.S. [440]

DEFENSE DES NOUVEAUX CHRESTIENS ET DES MISSIONARES DE LA CHINE... / Le Tellier, M – Paris, 1687 – 7mf – 9 – HTM-227/1 – ne IDC [240]

DEFENSE DU CULTE EXTERIEUR DE L'EGLISE / Brueys, D-A – Ed.2. Paris, 1686 – 6mf – 9 – CA-118/1 – ne IDC [240]

LA DEFENSE DU POEME HEROIQUE / Desmarets de Saint Sorlin, J – 1674 – 9 – fr I.C.S. [410]

DEFENSE ELECTRONICS – v11-. 1979- . Continues Electronic Warfare-Defense Electronics – 1,5,6,9 – us UMI [621]

DEFENSE HISTORY PROGRAM STUDIES PREPARED DURING THE KOREAN WAR PERIOD / U.S. Office of Price Stabilization – 3rolls. T460 – 1 – us Nat'l Archives [324]

Defense Metals Information Center *see* INDEX

Defense Metals Information Center. Battelle Memorial Institute *see* THE DMIC METALLURGY COLLECTION

DEFENSE MONITOR – 1972-82 – 10mf – 9 – $55.00 – us UPA [355]

DEFENSE NATIONALE – London, UK. 21 Nov 1870 – 1 – uk British Libr Newspaper [072]

LA DEFENSE NATIONALE DANS LE NORD EN 1870-1871 / Levi, Camille – Paris, etc., H. Charles-Lavauzelle, 1904-21.4v. Film Mas 9396 – 1 – us H.U. Library [944]

DEFENSE NEWS – v1-. 1986- – 1,5,6,9 – us UMI [355]

DEFENSE OF CHRISTIANITY AGAINST THE WORK OF GEORGE B. ENGLISH / Everett, Edward – 1814 – 9 – us A.T.L.A. [240]

A DEFENSE OF JUDAISM VERSUS PROSELYTIZING CHRISTIANITY / Wise, Isaac Mayer – Cincinnati: American Institute, 1889 – 1mf – 9 – 0-8370-6467-8 – 1986-0467 – us A.T.L.A. [270]

DEFENSE OF PHILOSOPHIC DOUBT / Balfour, Arthur James – London: Macmillan, 1879.1 fiche – 9 – us A.T.L.A. [240]

A DEFENSE OF POETRY / Shelley, Percy Bysshe; ed by Cook, Albert S – Boston: Ginn & Co., 1891 – 1 roll – 1 – 1-55879-725-4 – uk Libr Preservation [420]

DEFENSE OF THE JESSEY RECORDS AND KIFFIN MANUSCRIPT WITH A REVIEW OF DR. JOHN T. CHRISTIAN'S WORK ENTITLED: "BAPTIST HISTORY VINDICATED" / Lofton, George A – 1899 – 1 – 5.11 – us Baptist [240]

LA DEFENSE SOCIALE – Organe de la Federation socialiste de la Vienne (S.F.I.O.). Chatellerault. 1916-17 – 1 – fr A.C.R.P.P. [335]

LA DEFENSE SOCIALE DE SAONE-ET-LOIRE – Journal bihebdomadaire liberal. Dir. P. Prost. Chalon-sur-Saone. nov 1904-05 – 1 – fr A.C.R.P.P. [073]

DEFENSE SYSTEMS MANAGEMENT REVIEW – (1979 5,6,9) – 1976 – 1 – us UMI [073]

DEFENSES DE LOUIS MEIGRET / Meigret, Louis – 1550 – 9 – fr I.C.S. [440]

LE DEFENSEUR – Holyoke, MA. v7 n343. 1 jul 1891 – 1r – 1 – Can$20.00 – cn Can Microfilming [071]

LE DEFENSEUR DE LA PATRIE, FAISANT SUITE A L'AMI DU PEUPLE – no. 1-54. Paris. juin-aout 1799 – 1 – fr A.C.R.P.P. [073]

DEFENSIO CONFESSIONIS MINISTRORVM IESV CHRISTI, ECCLESIAE ANTUERPIENSIS, QUAE AUGUSTANAE CONFESSIONI ADSENTITUR, CONTRA IVDOCI TILETANI UARIA SOPHISMATA / Flacius Illyricus d.A E, M – Basileae, 1567 – 4mf – 9 – ne IDC [240]

DEFENSIO SANAE DOCTRINAE DE ORIGINALI IVSTITIA AC INIUSTITIA, AUT PECCATO,... / Flacius Illyricus d.A E, M – Basileae, 1570 – 2mf – 9 – ne IDC [240]

DEFENSIO VERAE SEMPERQVE IN ECCLESIA RECEPTAE DOCTRINAE DE CHRISTI DOMINI INCARNATIONE, ADUERSUS MENNONEM SIMONIS / Lasco, Johannes a – Bonnae, Laur. Mylius. 1545. BME-325 1 – 9 – ne IDC [240]

DEFENSIO VERITATIS HEBRAICAE SACRARUM SCRIPTURARUM / Levita, Iohannes Isaac – Coloniae, 1559 – 4mf – 8 – ne Slangenburg [220]

DEFENSIO, WT DE HEYLIGHE GODLIJCKE SCHRIFTUERE / Meulen, I P vander – Alcmaer, J. de Meester. 1599. BME-341 1 – 9 – ne IDC [240]

DEFENSIONES THEOLOGIAE DIVI THOMAE AQUINATIS / Capreolus, Johannes; ed by Paban, C & Pegues, T – Turonibus. Tomes 1-7. 1900-1908 – 94mf – 8 – ne Slangenburg [240]

DEFENSIONES THEOLOGIAE DIVI THOMAE AQUINATIS. VOL 1-7 / Capreolus, Johannes; ed by Paban, C & Pegues, T – Turonibus, 1900-1908 – 94mf – 8 – ne Slangenburg [240]

EL DEFENSOR DE LA VERDAD – Valencia de Alcantara, 1911 – 5 – sp Bibl Santa Ana [073]

EL DEFENSOR DE SU AGRAVIO. NOTICIA SATIRICA SOBRE LA PESTE EN EL PUERTO DE SANTA MARIA / Diez de Leiva, F – S.L., S.A. – 1mf – 9 – sp Cultura [616]

O DEFENSOR DO POVO : JORNAL POLITICO, INTERESSANTE A TODOS OS HOMENS LIVRES DO BRASIL – [s.l.]. 16 Maio, Nov 1835; Jan-Fev, Dez 1836 – 1,5,6 – bl Biblioteca [072]

A DEFESA : ORGAM INDEPENDENTE – Manaos, Amazonas. Jan 1938 – 1,5,6 – bl Biblioteca [072]

A DEFESA : ORGAO DOS INTERESSES GERAIS DO MUNICIPIO DE PALMA – Cidade de Palma, 6 Mar 1932; Nov, 20 Dec 1953 – 1,5,6 – bl Biblioteca [072]

A DEFESA : SEMANARIO INDEPENDENTE – Oliveira, 29 Jan, Oct-Dec 1933; Jan 1934-24 Mar 1935 – 1,5,6 – bl Biblioteca [072]

A DEFESA – S Tome: H J Assumpcao, sep 25 oct 25-dec 25 1915; jan 8-mar 10 1916 – us Res Libr [072]

DEFFENSE DE LA LANGUE FRANCOISE / Charpentier, Fr – 1676 – 9 – fr I.C.S. [440]

Deffke, Paul *see* DER LAEROVERKS-LEHRER

Deffontaines, Pierre *see*
- EL BRASIL. LA TIERRA Y EL HOMBRE, SEGUIDO DE UN ESTUDIO HISTORICO DE JOAQUINA COMAS ROS. BARCELONA
- LES HOMMES ET LEURS TRAVAUX DANS LES PAYS DE LA MOYENNE GARONNE.

DEFI / ed by Dupuis, Yvon – Montreal. 16 avr 1971-4 nov 1973 – 2r – 1 – Can$60.00r – cn Can Microfilming [072]

Defiance County. Ohio. Auditor *see*
- BLIND RELIEF RECORDS
- ENUMERATIONS OF DEAF, DUMB...
- MILITIA ROLLS
- MOTHERS' PENSION DISBURSEMENTS
- MOTHERS' PENSION DOCKETS
- SOLDIERS' RELIEF DISBURSEMENTS

Defiance County, Ohio. Board of County Commissioners *see*
- COMMISSIONERS JOUR.-CO HOME
- COMMISSIONERS' JOURNALS

Defiance County, Ohio. Board of Elections *see*
- ABSTRACT OF VOTES (HARDIN CO)
- ABSTRACT OF VOTES (PAULDING CO)
- POLL BOOKS AND TALLY SHEETS

Defiance County. Ohio. Clerk of Courts *see* QUADRENNIEL ENUMERATIONS

Defiance County. Ohio. Common Pleas. Civil Division *see*
- NATURALIZATION RECORDS
- NATURALIZATIONS, DECLARATIONS

Defiance County, Ohio. Common Pleas. Criminal Div. *see* CORONER'S INQUESTS

Defiance County, Ohio. County Home *see*
- MINUTES
- VISITOR'S REGISTER

Defiance County, Ohio. Hicksville, Village. Village Council *see* ORDINANCES AND RESOLUTIONS

Defiance County, Ohio. Probate Court *see*
- BIRTH RECORDS
- BIRTH/DEATH RECORDS
- BIRTH/DEATH STATEMENTS
- DEATH RECORDS
- ENUMERATION RECORDS
- INDEX TO MARRIAGE RECORDS
- MARRIAGE FEES
- MARRIAGE RECORDS
- NATURALIZATION RECORDS
- REGISTRY/RETURN OF MARRIAGES
- STATEMENTS OF BIRTHS
- STATEMENTS OF DEATHS

Defiance County. Ohio. Recorder *see* SOLDIERS' DISCHARGE RECORDS

Defiance County. Ohio. Sheriff *see* JAIL REGISTERS

DeFilippo, G J *see* EFFECT OF TRAINING FREQUENCY ON CERVICAL ROTATION STRENGTH

Defilippo, Rodolfo Antonio *see* UN PUEBLO EN MARCHA

DEFINICIONES DE LA ORDEN Y CAVALLERIA DE ALCANTARA – 1663 – 9 – 1.50f – sp Bibl Santa Ana [946]

DEFINICIONES DEL JUSTICIALISMO : SELECCION Y PRESENTACION DE ALBERTO J. PLA – Buenos Aires: Nueva Vision, 1968 – 1 – CSUXADH8410-B – us Hoover Inst Photo [360]

DEFINICIONES Y ESTABLECIMIENTOS DE LA ORDEN DE ALCANTARA – Madrid: Luis Sanchez, 1609 – 1 – sp Bibl Santa Ana [240]

DEFINING AND LIMITING THE JURISDICTION OF COURTS SITTING IN EQUITY: HEARING. / U.S. Congress. Senate. Committee on the Judiciary – Washington, Govt. Print. Off., 1930. 36 p. LL-1358 – 1 – us L of C Photodup [340]

DEFINITION AND CLASSIFICATION OF FISHERY VESSEL TYPES – 1985 – 70p – it F.A.O. [623]

DEFINITION AND CLASSIFICATION OF FISHING GEAR CATEGORIES – 1990 – 107p – it F.A.O. [790]

DEFINITION DU FOLKLORE / Varagnac, Andre – 1938 – 1 – us I.U. Libraries [390]

DEFINITIONES GENERUM PLANTARUM / Ludwig, C G – ed. 2. Lipsiae, 1747. B-6044 2 – 8 – ne IDC [580]

DEFINITIONES GENERUM PLANTARUM IN USUM AUDITORUM / Ludwig, C G – ed. 3. Lipsiae, 1760. 516, 44 pp. B-6045 2 – 8 – ne IDC [580]

DEFINITIONS GEOMETRIQUES : SUIVIES DES ELEMENTS D'ARCHITECTURE ET D'HISTOIRE NATURELLE APPLIQUES AU DESSIN LINEAIRE A MAIN LEVEE: PARTIE DE L'ELEVE – Montreal: Soeurs de la Congregation de Notre Dame de Montreal?, c1879. 02700. (Pre-1900 Canadiana) – 9 – cn C.I.H.M. [510]

DEFINITIONS OF RARE OR HITHERTO UNDESCRIBED AUSTRALIAN PLANTS / Mueller, Ferdinand Jakob Heinrich von – Melbourne, 1855. 53 pp. B-6462 1 – 9 – ne IDC [580]

DEFINITIONUM MEDICARUM LIBRI 24 LITERIS GRAECIS DISTINCTI (AEL, ABT 3;1) / Gorraeus, Ioannis – Paris, 1564 (mf ed 1993) – 27mf – 9 – DM150.00 – 3-89131-145-1 – gw Fischer [610]

THE DEFINITIVE TREATY OF PEACE,...SIGNED AT AMIENS THE 27TH OF MARCH 1802 – London, 1802 – 3mf – 1 – ILM-1204/1 – ne IDC [327]

Defoe, Daniel *see* DEFOE PAPERS

DEFOE PAPERS / Defoe, Daniel – (Ca 500 of Defoe's books, tracts, pamphlets, letters, etc. Based on John R. Moore's Checklist of the Writings of Daniel Defoe) – 39r – us UMI [800]

Defourny, P *see*
- LA DECLARATION DU GUERRE;...
- JEANNE D'ARC ET LE DROIT DES GENS
- TROIS QUESTIONS CAPITALES:...

Defoy, Henri *see*
- JESUS ET L'OUVRIER: DISCOURS PRONONCE A L'EGLISE ST SAUVEUR, QUEBEC, FETE DU TRAVAIL, 4 SEPTEMBRE 1893
- LE PATRON ET L'OUVNER

Defoy, Louisa *see* BIBLIOGRAPHIE ANALYTIQUE DE MONSIEUR YVON THERIAULT, CONSEILLER EN RELATIONS PUBLIQUES

LE DEFRICHEUR / ed by Dorion, J-B E & Laurier, Wilfrid – L'Avenir, Canada. 27 dec 1862-15 aut 1866; v4 n2. 13 dec 1866-v5 n15. 21 mar 1867 – 1r – 1 – Can$50.00 – cn Can Microfilming [072]

LE DEFRICHEUR DU LAC ST-JEAN / ed by Bernier, C-E – Roberval, Canada. 24 oct 1901-v1 n28. 1 mai 1902 – 1r – 1 – Can$30.00 – cn Can Microfilming [072]

DEFUNIAK HERALD – DeFuniak Springs, Florida. -w. 1940-41, Sept. 1945- – 1 – us P.K. Yonge [071]

Degand, M *see* LA REPARATION DES DOMMAGES...

DEGAS. PORTRAITISTE-SCULPTEUR / Reunion des musees nationaux. Paris – 1931. 16 illus. 2 fiches – 9 – fr Réunion [750]

Degenhart, Friedrich *see* STUDIEN UEBER ZACHARIAS WERNERS STIL

DEGGENDORFER ZEITUNG : BA DER PASSAUER NEUEN PRESSE – Deggendorf, West Germany. 1 Sept 1978- – ca 9r per yr – 1 – gw Mikrofilm [072]

D'Eggville *see* THE FUTURE GREAT STATE – CINCINNATI AND CLEVELAND

DEGLI' INSETTI CHE ATTACCANO L'ALBERO ED IL FRUTTO DELL' OLIVO / Costa, A – Napoli, 1857. 197p. 10 pls. Z-1148/2 – 8 – ne IDC [590]

Deglin, H *see* ETUDE SUR LE CONTRAT DE MARIAGE...

Degot, Vladimir Aleksandrovich *see* POD ZNAMENEM BOLSHEVIZMA

DIE DEGRADATIONSHYPOTHESE UND DIE ALTTESTAMENTLICHE GESCHICHTE / Giesebrecht, Friedrich – Leipzig: A Deichert, 1905 – 1mf – 9 – 0-8370-3272-5 – 1985-1272 – us A.T.L.A. [220]

Degranthe *see* ABUS DE L'ANCIENNE EDUCATION, DEVOILES ET REFORMES PAR LES PROGRES DE LA RAISON

Deguilleville, Guillaume de *see*
- LE PELERINAGE DE VIE HUMAINE
- THE PILGRIMAGE OF THE LIFE OF MAN

Deguise, Charles *see*
- LE CAP AU DIABLE: LEGENDE
- HELIKA: MEMOIRE D'UN VIEUX MAITRE D'ECOLE

DEH NUMI PIETOSI = GLI GIOCHI D'AGRIGENTO / Gederici, V – London: T Skillern, 1793 – 1 – us Sibley [780]

Dehaisnes, C C A *see* DOCUMENTS ET EXTRAITS DIVERS CONCERNANT L'HISTOIRE DE L'ART DANS LA FLANDRE, L'ARTOIS ET LE HAINAUT AVANT LE XVE SIECLE

DeHart, R P *see* PAST AND PRESENT OF TIPPECANOE COUNTY

DEHAVEN MEMORIAL BAPTIST CHURCH. OLDHAM COUNTY. LAGRANGE, KENTUCKY : CHURCH RECORDS – March 1867-May 1977 – 1 – 101.07 – us Baptist [240]

Deherpe, L *see* ESSAI SUR LE DEVELEOPPEMENT...

Deheza, Jose A *see*
- ISABEL PERON
- QUIENES DERROCARON A ISABEL PERON

Dehio, G G *see* DIE KIRCHLICHE BAUKUNST DES ABENDLANDES, HISTORISCH UND SYSTEMATISCH DARGESTELLT

Dehn, Joe *see* LIBERTY BUCKS PROVE SUCCESSFUL

Dehn, Paul *see* UNFALLSTATISTISCHES ZUR UNFALL VERSICHERUNG

Dehn, Siegfried Wilhelm *see* CAECILIA

Dehri *see* DIVANCE

DEI APOLOGIE DES ARISTIDES (T.U.U. 1-4/3) / Hennecke, E – Leipzig, 1893 – 2mf – 9 – ne Slangenburg [240]

DEI ATELNOST SNK I STO, SVODNYE MATERIALY / Soviet Union, Sovet narodnykh komissarov – (Includes c.1: 1928/1929) – Moskva: Otdel pechati i informatsii SNK SSSR i STO, 1929- – 1 – CSUXAKY6398-S – us Hoover Inst Photo [340]

DEIANIIA PETRA VELIKAGO, MUDRAGO PREOBRAZITELIA ROSSII, SOBRANNYIA IZ DOSTOVERNYKH ISTOCHNIKOV I RAZPOLOZHENNYI PO GODAM / Golikov, I I – Ed 2. v1-15. 1837-43 – 8 – BR-6033 2 – ne IDC [947]

DEIANIIA ZNAMENITYKH POLKOVODTSEV I MINISTROV SLUZHIVSHIKH V TSARSTVOVANIE GOSUDARIA IMPERATORA PETRA VELIKOGO / Bantysh-Kamenskii, N – v. 1-2. 1821. BR-5980 2 – 8 – ne IDC [947]

DEIATEL'NOST' MOSKOPROMSOIUZA V 1924-25 GODU – M., 1926 – 1mf – 9 – COR-421/1 – ne IDC [334]

DEIATELNOST PRODOVOLSTVENNOI ORGANIZATSII : PODANNYM CHREZVYCHAINOI REVIZII SOVETA OBORONY / Mashkovich, A G – Moskva: [s.n.], 1919 – 1 – CSUX90-B5586 – us Hoover Inst Photo [947]

DEIATELNOST SNK I STO, SVODNYE MATERIALY ZA...APR./II UN 1924/25-1927/28 *see* SVODNYE MATERIALY O DEIATELNOSTI SOVETA NARODNYKH KOMISSAROV SSSR I SOVETA TRUDA I OBORONY ZA...

Deibel, Franz *see* GOETHE IM GESPRAECH

LES DEICIDES : EXAMEN DE LA VIE DE JESUS ET DES DEVELOPPEMENTS DE L'EGLISE CHRETIENNE DANS LEURS RAPPORTS AVEC LE JUDAEISME / Cohen, Joseph – (Includes bibliographical references) – new ed. Paris: Michel Levy, 1864 – 1mf – 9 – 0-8370-9690-1 – 1986-3690 – us A.T.L.A. [240]

THE DEICIDES : ANALYSIS OF THE LIFE OF JESUS, AND OF THE SEVERAL PHASES OF THE CHRISTIAN CHURCH IN THEIR RELATION TO JUDAISM / Cohen, Joseph – London: Simpkin, Marshall, 1872 – 1mf – 9 – 0-8370-2703-9 – 1985-0703 – us A.T.L.A. [230]

Deile, Gotthold *see* GOETHE ALS FREIMAURER

Deimann, Wilhelm *see*
- HERMANN LOENS

Deimier, P de *see* L'ACADEMIE DE L'ART POETIQUE

Deindoerfer, Johannes *see* GESCHICHTE DER EVANGEL.-LUTH. SYNODE VON IOWA UND ANDEREN STAATEN

Deinhardstein, Johann Ludwig *see* GEDICHTE

Deissmann, Gustav Adolf *see*
- BEITRAEGE ZUR WEITERENTWICKLUNG DER CHRISTLICHEN RELIGION
- BIBELSTUDIEN
- BIBLE STUDIES
- DEUTSCHER SCHWERTSEGEN
- DER KRIEG UND DIE RELIGION
- DER LEHRSTUHL FUER RELIGIONSGESCHICHTE
- A LIGHT FROM THE ANCIENT EAST
- NEUE BIBELSTUDIEN
- DIE NEUTESTAMENTLICHE FORMEL ST "IN CHRISTO JESU"

THE DEIST OR MORAL PHILOSOPHER – Being an impartial inquiry after moral and theological truths: selected from the writings of the most celebrated authors in ancient and modern times. 3 v. 1819-26 – 1 – us A.T.L.A. [210]

DEISTER- UND WESERZEITUNG – Hameln, West Germany. 1969- – ca 8r per yr – 1 – gw Mikrofilm [072]

DEISTVUIUSHCHEE KOOPERATIVNOE ZAKONODATEL'STVO : SISTEMATICHESKII, KHRONOLOGICHESKII I PREDMETNYI UKAZATEL' ZAKONOV O KOOPERATSII / Berdichevskii, N G – Moscow. 2v. 1926-27 – 7mf – 9 – COR-712/1 – ne IDC [334]

DEISTVUIUSHCHEE KOOPERATIVNOE ZAKONODATELSTVO : SISTEMATICHESKII KHRONOLOGICHESKII I PREDMETNYI UKAZATEL ZAKONOV O KOOPERATSII / Berdichevskii, N G – Moskva: Izd. T Sentrosoi uza, 1926-1927. 2v – 1 – CSUX91-B266 – us Hoover Inst Photo [947]

DEISTVUIUSHCHEE ZAKONODATEL'STVO O NALOGAKH : V1. GOSUDARSTVENNO-PODOKHODNYI NALOG I PODOKHODNYI NALOG S GOSUDARSTVENNYKH I KOOPERATIVNYKH PREDPRIIATII... – Ed 2. Khar'kov, 1924 – 4mf – 9 – COR-714/1 – ne IDC [334]

DEISTVUIUSHCHEE ZAKONODATELSTVO O PECHATI : SISTEMATICHESKII SBORNIK / Fogelevich, LG – Izd. 2-e. Moskva: Izd-vo Narkomtorgov SSSR i RSFSR, 1929 – 1 – CSUX91-B239 – us Hoover Inst Photo [947]

DEISTVUIUSHCHEE ZAKONODATEL'STVO O POTREBITEL'SKOI KOOPERATSII / Berdichevskii, N G – Rostov n/D., 1925 – 1mf – 9 – COR-287/1 – ne IDC [334]

DEISTVUIUSHCHEE ZAKONODATELSTVO PO SOTSIALNOMU STRAKHOVANIIU (S KOMMENTARII AMI) / Baevskii, IL – 2-oe perer. dop. izd. [Moskva]: Voprosy truda, 1928 – 1 – CSUX90-B6241 – us Hoover Inst Photo [947]

DEISTVUIUSHCHIE RASPORIAZHENIIA PO KOMMUNALNOMU KHOZIAISTVU / Smirnov, A; ed by Anokhina, A V – Moskva: Izd-vo Narodnogo komissariata vnutrennikh del RSFSR, 1928 – 1 – CSUX91-B29 – us Hoover Inst Photo [947]

DEISTVUIUSHCHIE RASPORIAZHENIIA PO MILITSII.. / ed by Kiselev, I F – Moscow, 1928. 775p. Second and larger ed. of collected prevailing RSFSR laws and regulations of a nonsecret nature relating to police. BR-9612/1 – 9 – ne IDC [340]

THE DEITY OF CHRIST : AN ADDRESS DELIVERED AT NORTHFIELD, WITH THREE SUPPLEMENTARY NOTES / Speer, Robert Elliott – NY: Fleming H Revell, c1909 – 1mf – 9 – 0-8370-5394-3 – 1985-3394 – us A.T.L.A. [240]

THE DEITY OF JESUS CHRIST ACCORDING TO THE GOSPEL OF ST JOHN / Pratt, Samuel Wheeler – Philadelphia: Sun. Sch. Times, 1907. 1 fiche – 9 – us A.T.L.A. [240]

"DEIXAI VIR A MIM OS PEQUENINOS" : SEMINARIO ECUMENICO SOBRE OS PROBLEMAS DOS MENORES CARENTES E MARGINALIZADOS E A PARTICIPACAO DAS IGREJAS NA SUA SOLUCAO, SAO PAULO, 20 A 26 DE JUNHO DE 1980 – Rio de Janeiro: Centro Ecumenico de Documentacao e Informacao, 1982 – us Res Libr [972]

DEIXIS : CIBLES ET ORDRE DES OPERATIONS DANS LA STRUCTURATION DE L'ENONCE EN ANGLAIS CONTEMPORAIN / Augustin, Catherine – 1mf – 9 – 10007 – fr Atelier National [420]

Dejean, P F M A *see* CATALOGUE DE LA COLLECTION DE COLEOPTERES DE M. LE BARON DEJEAN

Dejean, PF M A *see* SPECIES GENERAL DES COLEOPTERES DE LA COLLECTION DE M. LE COMTE DEJEAN

DEJINY CECH A MORAVY NOVE DOBY / Rezek, Antonin – 1892-93.2v. (Historical Studies Series) – 9 – 33.00 – fr Bibl Nationale [900]

DEJINY SLOVAKOV V AMERIKE, VOLS 1 AND 2 / Culen, Konstantin – 1942 – 1r – 1 – us I.H.R.C. [947]

DEKABRIST NIKITA MURAV'EV / Druzhinim, N M – M. 1933. BR-245 2 – 8 – ne IDC [947]

DEKABRISTY I IKH VREMIA. MATERIALY I SOOBSHCHENIIA / ed by Alekseev, M P & Meilakh, B S – Leningrad, 1951. 383p. BR-11,051/1 – 9 – ne IDC [947]

DEKADENSTVO I MISTICHESKII REALIZM / Berdiaev, N A – Russkaia Mysl'. 1907. BR-3249 2 – 8 – ne IDC [700]

Dekalb County Historical Society *see* PAPERS

DEKALB DEMOCRAT – Auburn. Ind. 1865-1866 – 1 – us UMI [071]

Dekalb Historical Society *see* COLLECTIONS

DER DEKALOG ALS KATECHETISCHES LEHRSTUCK / Achelis, Ernst Christian – Giessen: Alfred Toppelmann, 1905 – 9 – 0-8370-2035-2 – 1985-0035 – us A.T.L.A. [220]

DER DEKALOG: EINE KRITISCHE STUDIE: TEIL I: DER DEKALOG IM HEXATEUCH / Meisner, Oskar – Halle a.S.: Waisenhauses, 1893. 1 fiche – 9 – us A.T.L.A. [240]

Dekker, C et al *see* ALBUM PALEOGRAPHICUM 17 PROVINCIARUM

Dekker, R M *see* EGO DOCUMENTS FROM THE NETHERLANDS, 16TH CENTURY-1814

DEKON; DEKLARASI EKONOMI, DISAMPAIKAN TGL. 28 MARET 1963 / Sukarno, Pres. Indonesia – SE 6772 1 – 9 – ne IDC [025]

DEKORATIVE KUNST – Muenchen, DE. 1898-99 – 1r – 1 – gw Mikrofilm [072]

DEKRET O POTREBITEL'SKOI KOOPERATSII, 20 MAIA 1924 G. : PRAK. POST. KOMMENT / Berdichevskii, N G – Ed 2. M., 1925 – 1mf – 9 – COR-288/1 – ne IDC [334]

DEKRETY O SUDIE RABOCHAGO I KRESTIANSKAGO PRAVITELSTVA – Petrograd: [Petrogradskii Soviet rabochikh i krasnoarme iskikh deputatov], 1918 – 1 – CSUX90-B9578 – us Hoover Inst Photo [947]

DEKRETY SOVETSKOI VLASTI – Moskva: Gos. izd-vo polit. lit-ry, 1957- – 1 – CSUX90-B9141 – us Hoover Inst Photo [947]

DEKRIT PRESIDEN, UNDANG-UNDANG DASAR 1945 / Indonesia. Constitution – SE-10,802 1. 1963 – 9 – ne IDC [323]

DEL 4 PLENO DEL CONSEJO ECONOMICO SINDICAL PROVINCIAL / Organizacion Sindical – Badajoz: Graficas Jimenez, 1964 – sp Bibl Santa Ana [330]

DEL ANARQUISMO AL PERONISMO : HISTORIA DEL MOVIMIENTO OBRERO ARGENTINO / Belloni, Alberto – [Buenos Aires]: A. Pena Lillo, Editor, [1960] – 1 – CSUXAHZ2926-B – us Hoover Inst Photo [320]

DEL ARBOL DE LAS HESPERIDES / Roso de Luna, Mario – Madrid: Editorial Pueyo, 1923 – 1 – sp Bibl Santa Ana [240]

DEL BLOCCO MARITTIMO / Carnazza Amara, G – Catania, 1897 – 3mf – 1 – ILM-368/1 – ne IDC [327]

DEL CERCADO AJENO / Diez-Canedo, Enrique – (Versiones poeticas) – Madrid: M. Perez. Villavicencio, Editor, 1907 – 1 – sp Bibl Santa Ana [810]

DEL ESTADO DE SALUD Y ENFERMEDAD Y SUS CONSECUENCIAS JURIDICO-SOCIALES; MEMORIA DE PRUEBA PARA OPTAR AL GRADO DE LICENCIADO EN LA FACULTAD DE CIENCIAS JURIDICAS Y SOCIALES DE LA UNIVERSIDAD DE CHILE / Perez Grille, Ramon – Santiago de Chile: Carrera, 1936. 101 6p. LL-4081 – 1 – us L of C Photodup [340]

DEL FORO COMPETENTE PER LE AZIONI SUCCESSORIE ... / Bottino, L – Napoli, 1891 – 1mf – 9 – ILM-3937/1 – ne IDC [327]

DEL FRAUDE A LA SOBERANIA POPULAR : 1938-1946 / Ferrero, Roberto A – Buenos Aires: La Bastilla, 1976 – 1 – CSUXADM9256-B – us Hoover Inst Photo [320]

DEL KERESZTJE – Sydney, Australia. Fueggetlen Magyarorszag. -f. 11 March 1951-Oct 1967. 4 reels – 1 – uk British Libr Newspaper [072]

DEL NORTE, LASSEN, MODOC, PLUMAS, SHASTA, SIERRA, SISKYOU, TEHAMA AND TRINITY COUNTIES – Del Notre Co, CA. 1885 – 1r – 1 – $50.00 – D015 – us Library Micro [978]

DEL NORTE, LASSEN, MODOC, PLUMAS, SHASTA, SIERRA, SISKYOU, TEHAMA AND TRINITY COUNTIES – Lassen Co, CA. 1885 – 1r – 1 – $50.00 – D015 – us Library Micro [978]

DEL NORTE, LASSEN, MODOC, PLUMAS, SHASTA, SIERRA, SISKYOU, TEHAMA AND TRINITY COUNTIES – Modoc Co, CA. 1885 – 1r – 1 – $50.00 – D015 – us Library Micro [978]

DEL NORTE, LASSEN, MODOC, PLUMAS, SHASTA, SIERRA, SISKYOU, TEHAMA AND TRINITY COUNTIES – Plumas Co, Ca. 1885 – 1r – 1 – $50.00 – D015 – us Library Micro [978]

DEL NORTE, LASSEN, MODOC, PLUMAS, SHASTA, SIERRA, SISKYOU, TEHAMA AND TRINITY COUNTIES – Shasta Co, CA. 1885 – 1r – 1 – $50.00 – 015 – us Library Micro [978]

DEL NORTE, LASSEN, MODOC, PLUMAS, SHASTA, SIERRA, SISKYOU, TEHAMA AND TRINITY COUNTIES – Sierra Co, CA. 1885 – 1r – 1 – $50.00 – D015 – us Library Micro [978]

DEL NORTE, LASSEN, MODOC, PLUMAS, SHASTA, SIERRA, SISKYOU, TEHAMA AND TRINITY COUNTIES – Tehama Co, CA. 1885 – 1r – 1 – $50.00 – D015 – us Library Micro [978]

DEL NORTE, LASSEN, MODOC, PLUMAS, SHASTA, SIERRA, SISKYOU, TEHAMA AND TRINITY COUNTIES – Trinity Co, CA. 1885 – 1r – 1 – $50.00 – D015 – us Library Micro [978]

DEL NORTE RECORD – Crescent City, CA. 1891-1911 – 6r – 1 – $300.00 – C03192 – us Library Micro [071]

DEL ORIGEN, Y PRINCIPIO DE LA LENGVA CASTELLANA O ROMACE QUE OI SE USA EN ESPANA / Aldrete, B – Roma, 1606 – 5mf – 9 – ne IDC [440]

DEL PAIS DE LA QUIMERA. HISTORIAS Y PAISAJES / Manzano de Garias, Antonio – Madrid: Patr.Social de Buenas Lecturas S.A. Bib.de Cultura Popular. Tomo 40 – 1 – sp Bibl Santa Ana [946]

DEL PASADO Y DEL PRESENTE / Sanchez Arjona, Vicente – Sevilla: Graficas Sevillanas, 1954 – 1 – sp Bibl Santa Ana [810]

DEL PERIODO MARXISTA / Sanchez Arjona, Vicente – Sevilla: Imprenta Alvarez, 1958 – 1 – sp Bibl Santa Ana [810]

DEL PERIODO MARXISTA / Sanchez Arjona, Vicente – Sevilla: Imprenta de la Divina Pastora, 1938 – 1 – sp Bibl Santa Ana [810]

DEL PRINCIPIO DI NON INTERVENTO... / Castelmola, di – Firenze, 1882 – 1mf – 1 – ILM-1221/1 – ne IDC [327]

Del Rosario, Marissa E *see* BAGONG AKLAT SA PILIPINO: AKLAT-SANAYAN

DEL SIGLO 17 EXTREMENO. CONTIENDA ENTRE TORRE DE MIGUEL SESMERO Y ALMENDRAL / Rodriguez Amaya, Esteban – Badajoz: Dip. Provincial, 1948. Sep. REE – 1 – sp Bibl Santa Ana [946]

DEL TIEMPO EN QUE FUISTEIS ANGELES / Sanchez Arjona, Vicente – Sevilla: Imprenta Carlos Acuna, 1953 – 1 – sp Bibl Santa Ana [810]

DEL UNICO MODO DE ATRAER A TODOS LOS PUEBLOS A LA VERDADERA RELIGION. ADVERTENCIA...MEXICO, 1942 / Casas, Bartolome de las – Madrid: Razon y Fe, 1947 – 1 – sp Bibl Santa Ana [200]

DEL UNICO MODO DE ATRAER TODOS LOS PUEBLOS A LA VERDADERA RELIGION / Casas, Bartolome de las – Mejico, 1942; Madrid: Missionalia Hispanica, 1947 – 1 – sp Bibl Santa Ana [240]

DEL VIAGGIO DI TERRA SANTA : DA VENETIA, A TRIPOLI, DI SORIA PER MARE, ET DI LA PER TERRA A GIERUSALEME, ... / Alcarotti, G F – Novara, 1596 – 4mf – 9 – H-8384/1 – ne IDC [945]

DELA I DNI – Istoricheskii zhurnal. v. 1-3. Spb. 1920-22. BR-2327 2 – 8 – ne IDC [947]

DELA I DNI – Petrograd. 1920-1922 complete – 1 – 35.00r – us Hoover Inst Photo [073]

DELA REPVBLIQUE DES TURCS, ... / Postel, G – Poitiers. 3pts. 1560 – 2mf – 9 – H-8407/1 – ne IDC [956]

Delachet-Guillon, C *see* LA MATERNITE, LA NAISSANCE ET LEURS RITUELS EN BIRMANIE

Delafond, O *see* TRAITE PRATIQUE D'ENTOMOLOGIE ET DE PATHOLOGIE COMPAREES DE LA PSORE

Delafons, John *see* TREATISE ON NAVAL COURTS-MARTIAL

Delafosse, Maurice *see*
- LES AGNI
- CHRONIQUES DE FOUTA SENEGALAIS DE SIRE-ABBAS-SOH
- ENQUETE COLONIALE DANS L'AFRIQUE FRANCAISE OCCIDENTALE ET EQUATORIALE SUR L'ORGANISATION DE LA FAMILLE INDIGENE, LES FINANCAILLES, LE MARIAGE
- ESSAI DE MANUEL PRATIQUE DE LA LANGUE MANDE OU MANDINGUE
- LES FRONTIERES DE LA COTE D'IVOIRE, DE LA COTE D'OR ET DU SOUDAN
- LE GANA ET LE MALI
- HAUT SENEGAL NIGER
- HAUT-SENEGAL-NIGER (SOUDAN FRANCAIS)
- LA LANGUE MANDINGUE ET SES DIALECTES (MALINKE, BAMBARA, DIOULA)
- MANUEL DAHOMEEN GRAMMAIRE-CHRESTOMATHIE
- LE PEUPLE SIENA OU SENOUFO
- TRADITIONS HISTORIQUES ET LEGENDAIRES DU SOUDAN OCCIDENTAL
- VOCABULAIRES COMPARATIFS DE PLUS DE 60 LANGUES OU DIALECTES PARLES A LA COTE D'IVOIRE ET DANS LES REGIONS LIMITROPHES

Delair, Paul *see* THEATRE INEDIT-LE ROSSIGNOL, RABELAIS, CRETE-ROUGE HELENE

Delaistre, Guillaume J *see* STATISTIQUE DU DEPARTEMENT DE LA CHARENTE

Delalande, E *see* DE L'OCCUPATIO BELLICA....

Delalande, P *see* PRECIS D'UN VOYAGE AU CAP DE BONNE-ESPERANCE

DELAMAR LODE – Lincoln, NV. 1854-1905 – 1r – 1 – $50.00 – U04618 – us Library Micro [071]

Delamarre, C *see* LA SITUATION ECONOMIQUE DE L'ESPAGNE

Deland, Charles Edmund *see* ANNOTATED STATUTES AND RULES OF TRIAL PRACTICE AND APPELLATE PROCEDURE IN SOUTH DAKOTA AND NORTH DAKOTA.

DELAND SUN NEWS – Deland. Fla. 1948-1980 – 1 – us P.K. Yonge [071]

Delangle *see* PROCES VERBAL DE MR. LE PENITENCIER D'EVREUX, DE CE QUI LUY EST ARRIVE DANS LA PRISON

DELANO BAPTIST CHURCH. DELANO, TENNESSEE : CHURCH RECORDS – (Formerly Prendergast Baptist Church. 826p) – Sept 1923-Sept 1979 – 1 reel – 1 – $37.17 – us Baptist [240]

Delano, Charles G *see* OUTLINE OF THE LAW OF LANDLORD AND TENANT IN MASSACHUSETTS

Delano, Isaac O *see* THE SINGING MINISTER OF NIGERIA

Delany, Selden Peabody *see* DIFFICULTIES OF FAITH

DELAPIDATION SIC DES FONDS PUBLICS: 12,000 POUR LA FAMILLE JOLY. JOB HONTEUX / Tarte, Joseph Israel – 18–?. 02587. (Pre-1900 Canadiana) – 9 – cn C.I.H.M. [971]

DeLaporte, J *see* ANECDOTES DRAMATIQUES

Delaporte, Y *see*
- JEUX DE FICELLE LAPONS
- LA SIIDA LAPONE
- TERMES DE PARENTE DANS UNE POPULATION SCOLARISEE DE LA BANLIEUE PARISIENNE
- LA VIE SOCIALE ET ECONOMIQUE DES LAPONS DE KAUTOKEINO

Delapree, Louis *see*
- LE MARTYRE DE MADRID, TEMOIGNAGES INEDITS
- DAS MARTYRIUM VON MADRID; EIN UNVEROEFFENTLICHTES ZEUGNIS

Delarbre, A *see* FLORA D'AUVERGNE

Delarc, Odon *see* L'EGLISE DE PARIS PENDANT LA REVOLUTION FRANCAISE, 1789-1801

Delaroche, F *see* ERYNGIORUM NEC NON GENERIS NOVI ASCLEPIDEAE HISTORIA

Delashmit, S J *see* THE EFFECTS OF GAME STRESS SITUATIONS ON THE HEART RATES OF SELECTED HIGH SCHOOL FOOTBALL COACHES

LE DELASSEMENT DE MONTCEAU-LES-MINES ET DU CANTON – no. 1-4. Paris. oct-nov 1889 – 1 – fr A.C.R.P.P. [073]

LES DELASSEMENTS MILITARIES. THE FAVORITE DIVERTISMENT COMPOSED BY MON. GALLET AS DANCED AT THE KING'S THEATRE / Mazzinghi, J – (Adapted for the pianoforte by Joseph Mazzinghi) – London, [1797] – 1 – us Sibley [780]

Delaunay *see* GRAMMAIRE KISWAHILI

DELAVEC – Chicago, 1926, 1927 – 3mf or 1 reel – 9,1 – us I.H.R.C. [975]

DELAVEC – Detroit, MI, 1928 – 1mf or 1 reel – 9,1 – us I.H.R.C. [975]

Delavignette, Robert Louis *see* LES PAYSANS NOIRS

Delaville le Roulx, Joseph M A *see* CARTULAIRE DE L'ORDRE DES HOSPITALIERS DE SAINT-JEAN DE JERUSALEM (1100-1310)

DELAVSKA ENOTNOST – Ljubljana, Yugoslavia. -w. 1958-70. 16 reels – 1 – uk British Libr Newspaper [949]

DELAVSKA POLITIKA – Maribor, Yugoslavia. Sept 1939 – 1r – 1 – us L of C Photodup [949]

DELAVSKA SLOVENIJA – Milwaukee, WI. 1922, 1925, 1926 – 3mf or 1r – 9,1 – us I.H.R.C. [975]

DELAWARE : SESSION LAWS OF AMERICAN STATES AND TERRITORIES – 1776-1994 – 9 – $1,187.00 set – us Hein [340]

Delaware *see*
- 1800 CENSUS
- DELAWARE CHANCERY REPORTS
- OPINIONS (A-G)
- REPORTS, POST-NRS
- REPORTS, PRE-NRS

Delaware and Shawnee Indian Tribes *see* REGISTERS, ROLLS, AND PUBLICATIONS

DELAWARE AND THE EASTERN SHORE / Vallandigham, Edward N – Philadelphia, J. B. Lippincott Co., 1922. Delaware Reel 2. (The Cox Library Collection) – 5 – us Americana [978]

DELAWARE ATTORNEY GENERAL REPORTS AND OPINIONS – (6 1963-1977 $105.00. 9 1978-1995 $110.00) – 1963-1995 – 6,9 – $215.00set – us Hein [340]

Delaware: Census *see* DEATHS

DELAWARE CHANCERY REPORTS / Delaware – (Add vols planned) – v1-9. 1814-1912 – 60mf – 9 – $90.00 – LLMC 84-128 – us L.L.M.C. [340]

DELAWARE CODE ANNOTATED – St Paul: West Pub Co, 1953-Feb 1996 update – 9 – $925.00 set – us Hein [340]

THE DELAWARE CONTINENTALS 1776-1783 / Ward, Christopher L – Wilmington, The Historical Society of Delaware, 1941. Delaware Reel 1. (The Cox Library Collection) – 5 – us Americana [978]

DELAWARE COUNTY AMERICAN – Media, PA. -w 1890-1912 – 13 – $25.00r – us I.M.R. [071]

DELAWARE COUNTY DAILY TIMES – Chester. Pa. 1876- – 1 – us UMI [071]

DELAWARE COUNTY VOICE – Media. Pa. -w. 1973- – 1 – us UMI [071]

Delaware. Courts *see* RULES OF THE SUPERIOR COURT, COURT OF CHANCERY, ORPHANS' COURT, COURT OF GENERAL SESSIONS, AND SUPREME COURT OF THE STATE OF DELAWARE

DELAWARE JOURNAL OF CORPORATE LAW – v1-19. 1976-94 – 1,5,6 – $495.00 – us Hein [073]

DELAWARE JOURNAL OF CORPORATE LAW – Widener University, v1-20. 1976-95 – 9 – $388.00 set – us Hein [340]

DELAWARE LAWYER – v1-13. 1982-95 – 9 – $123.00 set – us Hein [340]

THE DELAWARE LOYALISTS / Hancock, H B – Wilmington, Historical Society of Delaware, 1940. Delaware Reel 1. (The Cox Library Collection) – 5 – us Americana [978]

DELAWARE REPUBLICAN – Wilmington, DE: Allerdice, Jeandell & Miles, jan 2 1860-jun 1865 – 2r – 1 – us Res Libr [071]

DELAWARE SETTLERS, 1693 – Item R 4p SW16-0093 – 5 – us A.G.L.L. [920]

DELAWARE STATE NEWS – Dover. Del. 1946- – 1 – us UMI [071]

Delaware. Supreme Court *see* DELAWARE SUPREME COURT REPORTS

DELAWARE SUPREME COURT REPORTS / Delaware. Supreme Court – (Pre-NRS: v1-11 1832-85 80mf $120.00. Updates planned) – v1-30. 1832-1920 – 223mf – 9 – $334.00 – LLMC 84-127 – us L.L.M.C. [340]

DELAWARE SUPREME COURT REPORTS *see* DELAWARE CHANCERY REPORTS

DELAWARE VALLEY ADVANCE – Langhorne. Pa. -w. 1958- – 1 – us UMI [071]

DELAWARE VALLEY ADVANCE – Langhorne, PA. -w 1972 – 13 – $25.00r – us I.M.R. [071]

DELAYED ONSET MUSCLE SORENESS AND DAMAGE IN RELATION TO ELECTROMYOGRAPHIC ACTIVITY DURING CONCENTRIC AND ECCENTRIC CONTRACTION / Harper, Elizabeth – 1988 – 173p 2mf – 9 – $8.00 – us Microform Publ [612]

De-Lazari, Aleksandr Nikolaevich *see* MIROVAIA VOINA 1914-1918

Delbrueck, Hans *see* NUMBERS IN HISTORY: HOW THE GREEKS DEFEATED THE PERSIANS, THE ROMANS CONQUERED THE WORLD, THE TEUTONS OVERTHREW THE ROMAN EMPIRE, AND WILLIAM THE NORMAN TOOK POSSESSION OF ENGLAND

DELBURNE TIMES – Alberta, CN. 1912-67 – 12r – 1 – cn Commonwealth Micro [072]

Delcoitre, Patrick Antoine *see* VANUA SCOPE

Delecaille, A *see* DROIT ROMAIN

DELECTUS OPUSCULORUM BOTANICORUM / Usteri, P – 2v. Strasbourg. 1790-93. B-5784 2 – 8 – ne IDC [580]

DELECTUS SEMINUM IN HORTO BOTANICO. DORPATENSIS / Bunge, A A von – Dorpat. 1836-66. Lacking: 1837-38, 1845-56. B-5542 2 – 8 – ne IDC [580]

Delefortrie-Soubeyroux, N *see* LES DIRIGEANTS DE L'INDUSTRIE FRANCAISE

Delegacion de Deportes *see* 2ND GALA DEL DEPORTE COMARCAL

Delegacion de la Juventud *see* AVENTURA 77

Delegacion de Mutualidades Laborales *see* MEMORIA, 1974

Delegacion Local de la Juventud *see* SEMANA DE LA JUVENTUD. MADRONERA, 20 AL 27 MAYO 1972

Delegacion Nacional de la Juventud *see* COMPROMISO Y RESPONSABILIDAD. CAMPAMENTO NACIONAL "FRANCISCO FRANCO". CAVALEDA (SORIA) 74

Delegacion Nacional de Prensa, Propaganda y Radio *see* ESPANA Y FRANCISCO FRANCO. 25 ANIVERSARIO DE LA EXALTACION A LA JEFATURA DEL ESTADO

Delegacion Nacional de Sindicatos de FET y de las JONS *see* REGLAMENTO DEL GRUPO SINDICAL DE COLONIZACION NO 2049 DE GABRIEL Y GALAN

Delegacion Prov. de la Org.Sindical *see* CONVENIO COLECTIVO SINDICAL PROVINCIAL PARA LAS INDUSTRIAS DEL ACEITE Y SUS DERIVADOS DE BADAJOZ
Delegacion Provincial Consejo Superior de Deportes *see* 16TH GALA DEL DEPORTE PROVINCIAL
Delegacion Provincial de Educacion Fisica y Deportes *see* 13TH GALA DEL DEPORTE PROVINCIAL. 1977. HOMENAJE A LA EXCMA. DIPUTACION PROVINCIAL
Delegacion Provincial de Educacion y Ciencia *see* MEMORIA 1974
Delegacion Provincial de Juventudes *see* NORMAS Y ORIENTACIONES PARA LA ENSENANZA PRIMARIA
Delegacion Provincial de la Juventud *see*
- 4TH JUEGOS NACIONALES DE LA EDUCACION GENERAL BASICA
- 10TH CERTAMEN DE EXPERIENCIAS TEATRALES PARA LA JUVENTUD
- CAMPAMENTOS 1971. CACERES
- CAMPANA DE CAMPAMENTOS 1974
- FIESTAS DE LA JUVENTUD. CACERES 26 ABRIL 30 MAYO 1973

Delegacion Provincial de Ministerio de Informacion y Turismo *see* CARRO DE LA ALEGRIA EN LAS LOCALIDADES DE HERVAS, JARANDILLA...
Delegacion Provincial de Mutualidades Laborales (de Badajoz) *see* MEMORIA DE ACTIVIDADES
Delegacion Provincial de Sindicatos *see*
- 1 CONSEJO SINDICAL COMARCAL. DELEGACION COMARCAL DE AZUAGA
- 2 CONGRESO SINDICAL AGRARIO DE EXTREMADURA
- CICLO
- CONVENIO COLECTIVO SINDICAL DE TRABAJO AGRICOLA, APROBADO Y SUSCRITO POR LOS REPRESENTANTES...DE VILLAMIEL (CACERES)
- CONVENIO COLECTIVO SINDICAL DE TRABAJO AGRICOLA DE ALCANTARA (CACERES) Y SUS AGREGADOS DE ESTORNINOS Y PIEDRAS ALBAS
- CONVENIO COLECTIVO SINDICAL DE TRABAJO AGRICOLA...DE CASAS DE MILLAN CACERES
- CONVENIO COLECTIVO SINDICAL DE TRABAJO AGRICOLA...DE GUADALUPE
- CONVENIO COLECTIVO SINDICAL DE TRABAJO...DE LA EMPRESA TEXTIL LANERA SOBRINO DE BENITO MATAS EN HERVAS (CACERES)
- ESTATUTOS DE LA COOPERATIVA DE VIVIENDAS DE PROTECCION OFICIAL "SAN CARLOS BARROMERO" DEL SINDICATO PROVINCIAL DE BANCA, BOLSA Y AHORRO DE CACERES
- PRIMER CONSEJO COMARCAL SINDICAL DE OLIVENZA. CONCLUSIONES DEFINITIVAS
- PRIMER CONSEJO SINDICAL COMARCAL DE DON BENITO
- PRIMER CONSEJO SINDICAL COMARCAL. DELEGACION COMARCAL DE FREGENAL DE LA SIERRA
- PROYECTO DE REGLAMENTO DE LAS CASAS SINDICALES COMARCALES DEPENDIENTES DE LA DELEGACION PROVINCIAL SINDICAL DE CACERES

Delegacion Provincial de Sindicatos de FET y de las JONS *see* PRIMER CONSEJO SINDICAL COMARCAL. DELGACION COMARCAL DE CASTUERA
Delegacion Provincial de SindicatosVicesecretaria Provincial de Ordenacion Social *see* CUESTIONARIO RESUMEN DE LAS ORDENES Y CIRCULARES SOBRE ENLACES SINDICALES Y JUNTAS DE JURADOS. CARTILLAS DEL ENLACE SINDICAL (SECCIONES SINDICALES)
Delegacion Provincial del Frente de Juventudas, Seccion de Centros de Trabajo *see* 2 CONCURSO PROVINCIAL DE FORMACION PROFESIONAL, MAYO 1948
Delegacion Provincial del Frente de Juventudes *see*
- DIA DE LA CANCION
- NORMAS QUE HA DE TENER EN CUENTA EL QUE MANDA
- PLAN DE TRABAJO DE EDUCACION PRELIMINAR PARA LOS MESES DE FEBRERO Y MARZO

Delegacion Provincial del Frente de Juventudes. Caceres *see* FORMACION DE LAS FALANGES JUVENILES DE FRANCO
Delegacion Provincial e Sindicatos *see* OBRA SINDICAL DE COLONIZACION. GRANJA ESCUELA SINDICAL AGRARIA. NUESTRA SENORA DE BOTOA
Delegacon Provincial de Sindicatos *see* CONVENIO COLECTIVO SINDICAL DE TRABAJO AGRICOLA, APROBADO Y SUSCRITO POR LOS REPRESENTANTES...DE CORIA
DELEGATE ARGUS – Jan 15 1914-Dec 20 1917 – 9 – at Pascoe [072]
DELEGATE PROPOSALS : N1-162 – (Various pagination) – Saipan, n.p, 1975 – 6mf – 9 – $9.00 – LLMC 82-100F, Title 90 – us L.L.M.C. [323]
DELEGATION DIRECTORY – (Incl biographies; unpag) – Saipan, n.p, 1975 – 2mf – 9 – $3.00 – LLMC 82-100F, Title 89 – us L.L.M.C. [323]
DELEGATION EN FRANCE DE LA SOCIETE SAINT-JEAN-BAPTISTE ET DE LA SOCIETE HISTORIQUE DE MONTREAL / Thomas Cook et fils – Montreal, 1926?. SEM105P813 – 1mf – 9 – Can$2.25 – cn Bibl Nat [971]
La Delegation Syro-Palestinienne. aupres de la Societe des Nations *see* LA NATION ARABE
DELEGATKA – (Library has: Nov./Dec. 1934) – Moskva: otd. rabotnit s MK. RKP., 1923-1931. 9v – 1 – CSUX89-S874 – us Hoover Inst Photo [947]
DELEGATKA – Moscow, 1923-31 – 98mf – 9 – $590.00 – us Ross [305]
Delegorgue, Adolphe *see* VOYAGE DANS L'AFRIQUE AUSTRALE
LE DELEGUE DU LUXEMBOURG – [Paris]: Typ F Malteste et cie. n1. may 1849 – us Res Libr [072]
Delehaye, Hippolyte *see*
- THE LEGENDS OF THE SAINTS
- LES ORIGINES DU CULTE DES MARTYRS

Delesalle, Paul *see* LES CONDITIONS DE TRAVAIL CHEZ LES OUVRIERS EN INSTRUMENTS DE PRECISION DE PARIS
Deleseluse, A *see* CHARTES INEDITES DE L'ABBAYE D'ORVAL
Delessert, B *see* ICONES SELECTAE PLANTARUM
Deletang, Luis F *see* CONTRIBUCION AL ESTUDIO DE NUESTRA TOPONIMIA
Delevaque, Charles *see* LA MARINE AU CANADA: RAPPORT DE MISSION
Delevsky, J *see* MOLODAIA ROSSIIA
DELEYTE DE CAVALLEROS Y PLACER DE LOS CAVALLOS / Maestre de San Juan, Lucas – Madrid: Franciso Martin Abad, 1736 – 1 – sp Bibl Santa Ana [946]
Delfau, Guillaume *see* ANNUAIRE STATISTIQUE DU DEPARTEMENT DE LA DORDOGNE POUR L'AN XII DE LA REPUBLIQUE
Delfendahl, B *see* LES DIEUX DANS LES CHAMPS D'UN VILLAGE DU MAHARASHTRA (INDE)
Delfino, C *see* L'ESECUTORIETA DELLE SENTENZE CIVILI STRANIERE IN ITALIA
Delgado, Antonio *see* MEMORIA HISTORICA... HISTORIA
Delgado de Vera, J *see* DEFENSA Y RESPUESTA...DE LA MEDICINA RACIONAL Y PHILOSOPHICA...CONTRA...
Delgado del Pino, Francisco *see* DISCURSO
Delgado Fernandez, Manuel *see*
- MENSAJES DE SOL Y LUNA
- ROMANCERO DEL CORONEL VILLALBA

Delgado Fernandez, Rufino *see* BREVIARIO SENTIMENTAL
Delgado Gomez, Enrique *see* LA IGLESIA Y LA PATRIA. LA ACCION CATOLICA
Delgado, Jose *see* RELATO OFICIAL DE LA MENTISIMA EXPEDICION CARLISTA DIRIGIDA POR EL GENERAL ANDALUZ, DON MIGUEL GOMEZ...
Delgado, Jose Matias *see* HISTORIA GERAL DAS GUERRAS ANGOLANAS, 1680
Delgado Moreno, Mateo *see* INSTRUCCION PASTORAL ESTABLECIDAS..
Delgado, P J OS A *see* EN PLENA POLEMICA...
Delgado Solis, Sebastian *see*
- EL BUHO DEL RIBERO
- YO HE VISITADO FRAGOSA, EL GASCO Y MARTILANDRAN (HURDES)

Delhaise, Arnould M L *see* AMEDRA
Delhaye, P *see* SIGER DE BRABANT, QUESTIONS SUR LA PHISIQUE D'ARISTOTE
DELHI / India. Preservation of National Monuments; ed by Cole, H H – Calcutta, 1884. BI-683 2 – 8 – ne IDC [720]
DELHI EXPRESS – Delhi, CA. 1967- – 14+ r – 1 – $700.00 ($50.00y) – B02168 – us Library Micro [071]
DELHI GAZETTE – Agra, India. Delhi Gazette & North-West Englishman. -w. Jan 1837-May 1857; 1859; 1877-1889. 118 reels – 1 – uk British Libr Newspaper [072]
DELHI GAZETTE / Delhi. India. (State) – 1958-1966. Incomplete – 1 – us NY Public [950]
Delhi. India. (State) *see* DELHI GAZETTE
DELHI MISSION NEWS – London. 1895-1918. Lacking: 1886 (2-4) – 33mf – 8 – ne IDC [073]
DELHI RECORD – Delhi, CA. 1926-1932 – 3r – 1 – $150.00 – B06019 – us Library Micro [071]
DELI COURANT – [Medan]: J Deen, mar 28 1885-mar 16 1940 – 142r – 1 – us Res Libr [072]
DELI HIRLAP – Budapest, Hungary. -d. 1 Feb 1918-29 March 1919. Imperfect. 2 reels – 1 – uk British Libr Newspaper [072]
DELI HIRLAP – Timisoara. Rumania. -d. 1 Jan-20 Aug 1944. (Imperfect). (1 reel) – 1 – uk British Libr Newspaper [949]
DELI IN WOORD EN BEELD – Medan, 1925-1933. Lacking: 1926(9,19-21,46-49); 1927(2,17,22,32,35); 1928 (7,20); 1929(8,10-11,29,32-33); 1930(1-52); 1931(50); 1932(14,51); 1933(11,16) – 73mf – 9 – ne IDC [950]
DELI NIU – Bangkok, Thailand. 1976 – 5r – 1 – us L of C Photodup [072]
DELIA BLANCHFLOWER / Ward, Mary Augusta – British Fiction Archive: Unit 2 – 9 – uk Bell [830]
D'Elia, Paschal *see* CHUNG-KUO T'IEN CHU CHIAO CH'UAN CHIAO SHIH (CCC121)
DELIBAZIONE / Angelia Mangano, E de – Milano, 1905 – 1mf – 9 – ILM-2264/1 – ne IDC [340]
Delicado, Juan M *see* CARTAS SOBRE QUINTOS
Delich, Francisco Jose *see* CRISIS Y PROTESTA SOCIAL CORDOBA, MAYO 1969
DELICIAE GALLO-BELGICAE SILVESTRES / Necker, N J de – Argentorati, 1768. 2 vols. 568 pp. B-5145 2 – 8 – ne IDC [580]
DELICIAE PRAGENSES, HISTORIAM NATURALEM SPECTANTES / Presl, J S & Presl, K B – v. 1. Pragae. 1822. B-276 2 – 8 – ne IDC [580]
Deligny, Lucien *see* DES EPIDEMIES ET EN PARTICULIER DE LA GRANDE PESTE DU XVIIEME SIECLE EN LORRAINE
Delile, A R *see*
- DESCRIPTION DE L'EGYPTE. HISTOIRE NATURELLE
- FRAGMENTS D'UNE FLORE DE L'ARABIE PETREE

DELINEATIO IURIS DIVINI, ... / Beyerus, G – Lipsiae, 1726 – 3mf – 9 – ILM-627/1 – ne IDC [327]
DELINEATIONS OF EXOTICK PLANTS CULTIVATED IN THE ROYAL GARDEN AT KEW / Bauer, F A – London. 1796-1803. B-6129 2 – 8 – ne IDC [580]
THE DELINEATOR – Toronto: Delineator Pub. Co, [1849?-19–] – 9 – cn C.I.H.M. [640]
LE DELIRE OU LES SUITE D'UNE ERREUR / Saint-Cyr, Reveroni & Berton – French Theatre Series. Paris. Du Pont de Nemours, an VIII. 1799 – 9 – fr Hachette [820]
Delise, D F *see* HISTOIRE DES LICHENS
Delisle, L *see* CATALOGUE DES ACTES DE PHILIPPE AUGUSTE
Delitzsch, Franz *see*
- ASSYRISCHES HANDWOERTERBUCH
- BEITRAEGE ZUR ASSYRIOLOGIE UND VERGLEICHENDEN SEMITISCHEN SPRACHWISSENSCHAFT
- COMMENTARY ON THE SONG OF SONGS AND ECCLESIASTES
- A DAY IN CAPERNAUM
- DOCUMENTE DER NATIONAL-JUEDISCHEN CHRISTGLAEUBIGEN BEWEGUNG IN SUEDRUSSLAND
- DIE GENESIS
- DAS HOHELIED
- JUEDISCH-ARABISCHE POESIEN AUS VORMUHAMMEDISCHER ZEIT
- DIE LESE- UND SCHREIBFEHLER IM ALTEN TESTAMENT, NEBST DEN DEM SCHRIFTTEXTE EINVERLEIBTEN RANDNOTEN KLASSIFIZIERT
- MESSIANIC PROPHECIES
- MESSIANISCHE WEISSAGUNGEN IN GESCHICHTLICHER FOLGE
- NEUESTE TRAUMGESCHICHTE DES ANTISEMITISCHEN PROPHETEN
- NEW COMMENTARY ON GENESIS
- OLD TESTAMENT HISTORY OF REDEMPTION
- PAULUS DES APOSTELS BRIEF AN DIE ROEMER
- TAG IN KAPERNAUM
- VIER BUECHER VON DER KIRCHE
- ZUR GESCHICHTE DER JUEDISCHEN POESIE

Delitzsch, Friedrich *see*
- ASSYRISCHE GRAMMATIK
- BABEL AND BIBLE
- WO LAG DAS PARADIES?

Delitzsch, Johannes *see*
- DE INSPIRATIONE SCRIPTURAE SACRAE QUID STATUERINT PATRES APOSTOLICI ET APOLOGETAE SAECULI
- DAS GRUNDDOGMA DES ROMANISMUS

Delius, W *see* GESCHICHTE DER IRISCHEN KIRCHE VON ANFANG BIS ZUM 12. JH.
DELIVERANCE : THE FREEING OF THE SPIRIT IN THE ANCIENT WORLD / Taylor, Henry Osborn – New York: Macmillan, 1915 – 1mf – us A.T.L.A. [240]
DELIVERY AND DEVELOPMENT OF CHRISTIAN DOCTRINE / Rainy, Robert – Edinburgh: T. & T. Clark, 1874. 1 fiche – 9 – us A.T.L.A. [240]
LA DELIVRANCE : NUMERO SPECIAL – Montreal, Canada. 21 nov 1935 – 1r – 1 – Can$25.00 – cn Can Microfilming [072]
DELIVRANCE ET CONVIVIALITE / Mahias, M C – Le systeme culinaire des Jaina de Delhi – 9 – F130.00 – fr Ethnologie [306]
DELL ISTORIA DELLA COMPAENIA DI GESU. L'ASIA. PARTES PRIMA ET SECUNDA / Bartoli, D – 1507 2. 1825 – 8 – ne IDC [240]
DELL' ORIGINE E DELLE REGOLE DELLA MUSICA COLLA STORIA DEL SUO PROGRESSO, DECADENZA, E RINNOVAZIONE / Eximeno, Antonio – In Roma, nella stamperia di Michel' Angelo Barbiellini nel Palazzo Massimi. 1774. BP-257 1 – 9 – ne IDC [780]
Dell, William *see* TESTIMONY FROM THE WORD AGAINST DIVINITY DEGREES IN THE UNIVERSITY
DELLA ARCHITETTURA CON CENTOSESSANTA FIGURE DISSEGNATE DAL MEDESIMO, SECONDO I PRECETTI DI VITRUVIO / Rusconi, G A – Venetia, 1590 – 9 – ne IDC [720]
DELLA ARCHITETTURA CON CENTOSESSANTA FIGURE DISSEGNATE DAL MEDESIMO, SECONDO I PRECETTI DI VITRUVIO / Rusconi, G A – Venetia. 1590. BO-1029 1 – 9 – ne IDC [720]
DELLA DESCRIZIONE UNIVERSALE MENTOVATA DA SAN LUCA / Patrizi, Francesco Saverio – 1876 – 1 – us A.T.L.A. [240]
DELLA DIVISIONE DEL TEMPO NELLA MUSICA / Sacchi, B G – 1770 – 9 – us Sibley [780]
DELLA FORZA DEI GIUDICATI... / Amadei, M – Roma, 1888 – 1mf – 9 – ILM-2417/1 – ne IDC [340]
Della Gatta, Marco *see* BREVE RAGGUAGLIO DELLE PRINCIPALI REGOLE DEL CANTO FERMO GREGORIANO..
DELLA GIURISDIZIONE PENALE...AL REATI COMMESSI ALL'ESTERO / Fiore, P – Pisa, 1875 – 1mf – 1 – ILM-2057/1 – ne IDC [327]
DELLA GVERRA DI RHODI LIBRI 3. AGGIUNTA LA DISCRITTIONE DELL' ISOLA DI MALTA CONCESSA A CAUALIERI, DOPO CHE RHODI FU PRESO / Fontanus, J – Vinegia, 1545 – 2mf – 9 – H-8274/1 – ne IDC [956]
DELLA HISTORIA...DELLE COSE DELL' IMPERIO DI CONSTANTINOPOLI LIBRI 7 / Nicetas, A C – Venetia, [1562] – 3mf – 9 – H-8300/1 – ne IDC [956]
DELLA LETTERATURA DE TURCHI... / Donado, G – Venetia, per Andrea Poletti, 1688 – 1 – us Sibley [780]
DELLA NATURA E PERFEZIONE DELLA ANTICA MUSICA DE' GRECI / Sacchi, BG – 1778 – 9 – us Sibley [780]
DELLA NATURA E PERFEZIONE DELLA ANTICA MUSICA DE' GRECI. DISSERTAZIONI 3 / Sacchi, BG – Milano, 1778. BP-460/1 – 9 – ne IDC [780]
DELLA NECESSITA DI UN NUOVO DIRITTO INFORMAZIONALE... / Cimbali, E – Roma, 1904 – 1mf – 1 – ILM-452/1 – ne IDC [327]
DELLA PERSONALITA GIURIDICA DEI CORPI MORALI... / Fiore, P – Torino, 1895 – 1mf – 1 – ILM-3666/1 – ne IDC [327]
DELLA PITTURA VENEZIANA E DELLE OPERE PUBBLICHE DE' VENEZIANI MAESTRI / Zanetti, A M – O 1067. 1771 – 9 – ne IDC [760]
DELLA PRATTICA MUSICA VOCALE ET INSTRUMENTALE. / Cerreto, Scipione – 1601 – 2 – us Sibley [780]

DELLA REALTA, AND PERFETTIONE DELLE IMPRESE / Tasso, H – O 1271 1. 1614 – 9 – ne IDC [760]
DELLA REPARAZIONE... / Funaioli, G B – Prato, 1916 – 1mf – 1 – ILM-524/1 – ne IDC [327]
DELLA VITA DI ANTONIO ROSMINI-SERBATI : MEMORIE / Paoli, Francesco – (Includes bibliographical references) – Torino: Accademia di Rovereto: G B Paravia, 1880 – 2mf – 9 – 0-8370-6928-9 – 1986-0928 – us A.T.L.A. [920]
DELLE ACVTEZZE, CHE ALTRIMENTI SPIRITI, VIVEZZE, E CONCETTI, VOLGARMENTE SI APPELLANO, TRATTATO. IN QUESTA SECONDA IMPRESSIONE DALL AUTORE RIUISTE, E MIGLIORATE / Pellegrini, Matteo – Genova, Presso C. Ferroni, 1639. Bound with the author's Politica Massima. Genova, 1641 – 1 – us U.W. Library [440]
DELLE AGGREGAZIONI LEGITTIME... / Fiore, P – Torino, 1879 – 1mf – 1 – ILM-1974/1 – ne IDC [327]
DELLE BENEMERENZE DI S. TOMMASO D'AQUINO VERSO LE ARTI BELLE / Marchese, V – O-992 1. 1874 – 9 – ne IDC [180]
DELLE CINQUE PIAGHE DELLA SANTA CHIESA = OF THE FIVE WOUNDS OF THE HOLY CHURCH / Rosmini, Antonio; ed by Liddon, H P – (In English) – London: Rivingtons, 1883 – 1mf – 9 – 0-8370-8466-0 – 1986-2466 – us A.T.L.A. [240]
DELLE CONDIZIONI IMPOSTE ALLO STRANIERO IN ITALIA... / Franca Cannizzo, S la – Napoli, 1908 – 2mf – 1 – ILM-3556/1 – ne IDC [327]
DELLE COSE DE TVRCHI : LIBRI TRE – Vinegia, 1541 – 1mf – 9 – H-8147/1 – ne IDC [956]
DELLE COSE GENTILESCHE E PROFANE TRASPORTATE AD USO ET ADORNAMENTO DELLE CHIESE / Marangoni, G – Roma. 1744. BO-359 1 – 9 – ne IDC [720]
DELLE DEMOSTRATIONI DEGLI ERRORI DELLA SETTA MACOMETTANA LIBRI CINQUE / Pientini da Corsignano, A – Firenze, 1588 – 5mf – 9 – H-8372/1 – ne IDC [956]
DELLE IMPRESE / Capaccio, Giulio Cesare – O-578. 1592 – 9 – ne IDC [760]
DELLE IMPRESE SACRE. CON UTILI E DILETTEUOLI DISCORSI ACCOMPAGNATE LIBRO PRIMA / Aresi, P – Verona, 1615. BO-856 1 – 9 – ne IDC [760]
DELLE NAVIGATIONI ET VIAGGI RACCOLTE DA M. GIO. BATTISTA RAMUSIO IN TRE VOLUMI DIVISE / Ramusio, Giovanni Battista – Venetia: Appresso i Giunti, 1606. SEM105P879 – 27mf – 9 – Can$60.75 – cn Bibl Nat [910]
DELLE POSSIBILI CONSEQUENZE DEL POSITIVISMO PENALE... / Fedozzi, P – Torino, 1897 – 1mf – 1 – ILM-2415/1 – ne IDC [327]
DELLE QUINTE SUCCESSIVE NEL CONTRAPPUNTO E DELLE REGOLE DEGLI ACCOMPAGNAMENTI / Sacchi, B G – 1780 – 9 – us Sibley [780]
DELLE QUINTE SUCCESSIVE NEL CONTRAPPUNTO E DELLE REGOLE DEGLI ACCOMPAGNAMENTI / Sacchi, B G – Lettera. Milano. 1780. BP-461 1 – 9 – ne IDC [780]
DELLE SUCCESSIONI NEL DIRITTO INTERNAZIONALE CIVILE ITALIANO / Ansaldi, C F – Roma, 1908 – 1mf – 9 – ILM-2972/1 – ne IDC [340]
DELLE TORRI GENTILIZIE DI BOLOGNA E DELLA FAMIGLIE ALLE QUALI PRIMA APPARTENNERO / Gozzadini, Giovanni – Bologna: N. Zanichelli, 1875. 772p. 9 fiches. (Miscellaneous Selections) – 9 – 22.00 – fr Bibl Nationale [305]
DELLE TRE SONTUOSE CAPELLE MEDICEE SITUATE NELL' IMP. BASILICA DI S. LORENZO DESCRIZIONE ISTORICO-CRITICA / Moreni, D – Firenze. 1813. BO-963 1 – 9 – ne IDC [700]
DELL'EFFICACIA DEL DIRITTO DI PEGNO... / Cavagnari, V W – Genova, 1882 – 1mf – 1 – ILM-3659/1 – ne IDC [327]
DELL'EFFICACIA IN ITALIA DELLA SENTENZA ESTERA DI DIVORZIO / Fusinato, G – Venezia, 1892 – 1mf – 1 – ILM-3103/1 – ne IDC [327]
Deller, F J *see* SIX SONATAS FOR 2 VIOLINS AND A VIOLONCELLO, WITH A THOROUGH-BASS FOR HARPSICHORD
DELL'ESECUTORIETA IN ITALIA DELLE SENTENZE STRANIERE DI DIVORZIO / Ansaldi, C F – Firenze, 1904 – 1mf – 9 – ILM-3104/1 – ne IDC [340]
Delling, G *see*
– BIBLIOGRAPHIE ZUR JUEDISCH-HELLENISTISCHEN UND INTERTESTAMENTARISCHEN LITERATUR 1900-1965 (T.U.U. 5-106)
– PAULUS' STELLUNG ZU FRAU UND EHE
DELL'OPERA IN MUSICA TRATTATO / Planelli, A – Napoli. 1772. BP-431 1 – 9 – ne IDC [780]
DELL'ORGINE E DELLE REGOLE DELLA MUSICA / Eximeno, Antonio – 1774 – 9 – us Sibley [780]
DELL'UNIONE... / Conestaggio, G F di – Genoa, 1585 – 5mf – 1 – ILM-456/1 – ne IDC [327]
DEL-MAGYARORSZAG – Szeged, Hungary. 1962-79 – 36r – 1 – us L of C Photodup [072]
Delmare, R Le. *see* DE OFFICIIS ECCLESIASTICIS DE JEAN D'ARVRANCHES
DELMENHORSTER KREISBLATT – Delmenhorst, West Germany. 1977- – ca 9r per yr – 1 – gw Mikrofilm [072]
DELMENHOSTER KURIER : BA DES BREMER WESER-KURIER – Bremen, Germany.16 Dec 1971- – 1 – gw Mikrofilm [072]
Delmonico Hotel. Dodge City, Kansas *see* REGISTER OF GUESTS
DELNICKA BESIDKA – 1900-1909 inc. – 1 – us I.U. Libraries [073]
DELO – 1958-1995 – 1 – F1,397.00 – sz Infoprint [947]
DELO – (Backfile 1958-95 $85.00r) – Slovenia, 1999- – 2r per y – 1 – $160.00 standing order – us Ross [072]
DELO – Belgrade, Serbia. v1-72, 1894-1915 – 1 – us I.U. Libraries [073]
DELO – Ljubljana, 1976-1992ff – 90r – 1 – DM6,750.00 – gw Mikro Press [949]
DELO – Ljubljana, Yugoslavia. May 1959-1976 – 92r – 1 – us L of C Photodup [949]
DELO – (Yrly reel count varies (approx 2r/y)) – [Slovenia], 1958- – 1 – inquire – us Ross [072]
DELO – Zhurnal ucheno-literaturnyi. Spb. 1867-88. Lacking: 1868 (3); 1881 (12); 1884 (7-12); 1886 (9-12); 1887 (7-12). B-1704 2 – 8 – ne IDC [073]
DELO I OTDYKH – Chtenie dlia mal'chikov i devochek vsekh soslovii. Spb. 1864-66. Lacking: 1864, v. 7-9. BR-2349 2 – 8 – ne IDC [073]
DELO NARODA – (Delo narodnoe Delo narodov Delo Dela naroda). Leningrad. USSR. -d. 2 May 1917-30 Jan 1918. (Imperfect). (1 reel) – 1 – uk British Libr Newspaper [947]
DELO NARODA / Sotsialistov-Revoliutsionerov Partii – Petrograd. Mar. 15-Dec. 30, 1917. Missing: 8 scattered issues – 1 – 35.00r – us Hoover Inst Photo [335]
DELO O VOSSTANII NA EKATERININSKO I ZH. D / Anisimov, Sergei Sergeevich – Moskva: "Istproftran," Izd. T SKZHD, 1926 – 1 – CSUX88-B846 – us Hoover Inst Photo [947]
DELO ZHIZNI – Ezhenedel'nyi, populiarnyi, literaturnyi i nauchnyi zhurnal. nr. 1-16. M. 1907. Available: nr. 1-4. BR-8135 2 – 8 – ne IDC [073]
Deloche, M *see* DU PRINCIPE DES NATIONALITES
DELOG-POST – Berlin. oct 1916-17 – 1 – gw Mikrofilm [073]
Delomier, D *see* LES ADJECTIFS DE QUALITE PHYSIQUE RELATIFS A L'ESPACE EN FRANCAIS MODERNE: ETUDE MORPHO-SYNTAXIQUE
Delommeau, P *see* LEX MAXIMES GENERALES DU DROICT FRANCOIS
Deloncle, L *see* STATUT INTERNATIONAL DU MAROC
DELOPROIZVODSTVO I KORRESPONDENTSIIA SEL'SKOKHOZIAISTVENNYKH KOOPERATIVNYKH ORGANIZATSII / Khudiakov, P – M., 1930 – 2mf – 9 – COR-523/1 – ne IDC [334]
Delorme, Philibert *see*
– NOUVELLES INVENTIONS POUR BIEN BASTIR ET A PETIT FRAIS.
– LE PREMIER TOME DE L'ARCHITECTURE
Delorme, V *see* LE COURRIER DU BAS-CANADA
Delormois *see* INSTRUCTION GENERALE POUR LA TEINTURE DES LAINES ET MANUFACTURES DE LAINES DE TOUTES COULEURS, & POUR LA CULTURE DES DROGUES OU INGREDIENS QU'ON Y EMPLOYE
Deloume, A *see* PRINCIPES GENERAUX DU DROIT INTERNATIONAL EN MATIERE CRIMINELLE
DELOVOI MIR – Moscow: Delovoi mir, 1990- – 4mf per year – 9 – $299.95y – us East View [330]
DELOVOI SPRAVOCHNIK "MOSKVA" / Rudometov, N M – M., 1922 – 2mf – 9 – COR-293/1 – ne IDC [334]
DELOYNES COLLECTION *see* COLLECTION DELOYNES
Delozier, Eric P *see* HEALTH CARE ON THE INTERNET
Delpech, Henri *see* LA TACTIQUE AU TREIZIEME SIECLE
Delpech, J *see* LA NOUVELLE CONVENTION DE GENEVE (6 JUILLET 1906)...
Delprat, Charles *see* LE JAPON ET LA QUESTION JAPONAISE
Delprat, G H M *see* VERHANDELING OVER DE BROEDERSCHAP VAN G. GROOTE EN OVER DEN INVLOED DER FRATERHUIZEN
DELTA – Buckhannon. West Virginia. 1872-1892; 1899-1928 – 1 – us UMI [071]
DELTA ATLAS – Delta, Ohio. 1885- – 56r – 1 – $32.50r – us Archival [071]
DELTA DEMOCRAT – Tunica. Miss. 1902-1909 – 1 – us UMI [071]
DELTA DEMOCRAT TIMES – Greenville. Miss. 1938- – 1 – us UMI [071]
DELTA FARM PRESS – Clarksdale. Miss. -w. 1944- – 1 – us UMI [071]
DELTA FIRST BAPTIST CHURCH. DELTA, MISSOURI : CHURCH RECORDS – 1900-Oct 1921 – I – 5.76 – us Baptist [240]
DELTA HERALD – Rio Vista, CA. 1946-48 – 1r – 1 – $50.00 – C02703 – us Library Micro [071]
DELTA HERALD – Rio Vista. Calif. -w. 1946-48 – 1 – us UMI [071]
DELTA KAPPA GAMMA BULLETIN – (v.48-. 1981-. 5,6,9) – v.1-. 1934- – 1 – us UMI [370]
DELTA NEWS – Isleton, CA. 1929-1944 – 7r – 1 – $350.00 – C03256 – us Library Micro [071]
DELTA STAR – Greenville. Miss. 1937-1938 – 1 – us UMI [071]
Delta Woman's Club. Delta, Ohio *see* RECORDS
Delteil, H L *see* LE PEINTRE-GRAVEUR ILLUSTRE
DELTION PLEROPHORION – (In French, German, Italian and English) – Athens, Greece. 3 Jul-4 Oct 1940 (imperfect) – 1r – 1 – uk British Libr Newspaper [949]
DELUGE IN THE IZDUBAR EPIC AND IN THE OLD TESTAMENT / Kellner, Maximilian – Cambridge: Church Review, 1888. 1 fiche – 9 – us A.T.L.A. [220]
Deluz, A *see* CORPUS D'ARCHIVES HISTORIQUES DE L'ETHNIE GURO
Delvaille, C *see* GUIA HIGIENICA Y MEDICA DEL MAESTRO
Delvau, A *see*
– DICTIONNAIRE DE LA LANGUE VERTE
– DICTIONNAIRE EROTIQUE MODERNE
D'Elvert, C *see* DIE BESTRAFUNG DER BOEHMISCHEN REBELLION, INSBESONDERE DIE CORRESPONDENZ FERDINAND 2 MIT DEM FUERSTEN LIECHTENSTEIN
DELVIN ESTATE PAPERS, 1812-38 – Leeward Islands – 1 – uk Microform Academic [025]
DEM. REP. AND FARMERS MUSEUM – Carlisle, PA., 1824 – 13 – $25.00r – us I.M.R. [071]
"DEM TRAUM FOLGEN" : INNERE RAEUME UND EIGENE FREMDHEIT IN DEN BILDERN DES ANDEREN BEI JEAN-JAQUES ROUSSEAU, JOSEPH CONRAD UND KARL MAY / Trinkaus, Stephan – 1995 – 3mf – 9 – DM98.00 – 3-8267-2170-5 – gw Hänsel [410]
Demachi, G *see* SEI QUARTETTI, OP. 9
Demachy, Jacques Francois *see*
– INSTITUTS DE CHYMIE, OU PRINCIPES ELEMENTAIRES DE CETTE SCIENCE
– RECUEIL DE DISSERTATIONS PHYSICO-CHYMIQUES, PRESENTEES A DIFFERENTES ACADEMIES
DEMAGOGIA, INFLACION Y ARMAMENTISMO / Aguirre Camara, Jose – Buenos Aires, [1944] – 1 – CSUXAJA7354-B – us Hoover Inst Photo [350]
EL DEMAGOGO / Ferraris, Agustin – [Buenos Aires]: Editorial Catedra Lisandro de la Torre, 1958 – 1 – CSUXAJA7160-B – us Hoover Inst Photo [240]
DEMAIN – Journal socialiste et de defense syndicaliste. no. 1-91. Alger. avr 1919-fevr 1921 – 1 – fr A.C.R.P.P. [073]
DEMAIN – Lyons, France. 27 Oct 1905-26 Jul 1907 – 1r – 1 – uk British Libr Newspaper [072]
DEMAIN – Pages et documents. Organe du groupe communiste francais de Moscou. Dir. Henri Guilbeaux. no. 1-31. Geneve. 1916-sept 1919 – 1 – fr A.C.R.P.P. [073]
THE DEMAK PROJECT / Indonesia – SE-8480 1. 1967 – 9 – ne IDC [950]
DEMAND FOR PRIMARY SCHOOL TEACHERS 1975-1985 / Papua New Guinea. Manpower Planning Unit – 1976 – 1mf – 9 – DE-218/1 – ne IDC [370]
DEMAND PROSPECTS FOR RICE AND OTHER FOODGRAINS IN SELECTED ASIAN COUNTRIES – 1991 – 129p – it F.A.O. [338]
DEMAND STUDY FOR THE TEXTILE AND CLOTHING INDUSTRY IN LIBYA, A GENERAL OUTLINE / Hemmersbach, H – Tripoli. Dec 6 1966. Appendix I and II. BNE-1209 1 – 9 – ne IDC [338]
DEMANDES A FAIRE A CHAQUE ADMINISTRATION DE DEPARTEMENT / France – P., Prault, an VI – 9 – fr Hachette [944]
Demandre, A *see* DICTIONNAIRE DE L'ELOCUTION FRANCOISE
LOS DEMANES EN LA CONQUISTA DE AMERICA, BUENOS AIRES, 1943 / Bayle, Constantino & Arcimegas, German – Madrid: Razon y Fe, 1944 – 1 – sp Bibl Santa Ana [972]
Demanet *see*
– NOUVELLE HISTOIRE DE L'AFRIQUE FRANCAISE ENRICHIE DE CARTES ET D'OBSERVATIONS ASTRONOMIQUES ET GEOGRAPHIQUES, DE REMARQUES SUR LES USAGES LOCAUX, LES MOEURS, LA RELIGION ET LA NATURE DU COMMERCE DE CE PAYS
– NOUVELLE HISTOIRE DE L'AFRIQUE FRANCOISE
Demangeat, C *see* HISTOIRE DE LA CONDITION CIVILE...
Demantius, C *see* TIRADES, SIONIAE INTROTIUM MISSARUM EX PROSARUM...
Demantius, J C *see*
– ISAGOGE ARTIS MUSICAE, AD INCIPIENTIUM CAPTUM MAXIME ACCOMMODATA
– ISAGOGE ARTIS MUSICAE AD INCIPIENTIUM CAPTUM MAXIME ACCOMMODATA
Demar, Claire *see* APPEL D'UNE FEMME DU PEUPLE, SUR L'AFFRANCHISSEMENT DE LA FEMME
Demare, Sophie *see* LA FEMME DANS LE DROIT PENAL DU PROCHE-ORIENT ANCIEN
Demarest, David D *see* THE REFORMED CHURCH IN AMERICA
Demarest, John Terhune *see* A COMMENTARY ON THE SECOND EPISTLE OF THE APOSTLE PETER
Demassieux, G *see* LE CHANGEMENT DE NATIONALITE DES SOCIETES COMMERCIALES
Demay *see*
– INVENTAIRE DES SCEAUX DE LA FLANDRE
– INVENTAIRE DES SCEAUX DE LA NORMANDIE
– INVENTAIRE DES SCEAUX DE L'ARTOIS ET DE LA PICARDIE
Demay, G *see* INVENTAIRE DES SCEAUX DE LA COLLECTION CLAIRAM BAULT A LA BIBLIOTHEQUE NATIONALE
Dembele, P C *see* L'IDEOLOGIE DU CONTE CHEZ LES BWA DU MALI
Dembo, Isaak Aleksandrovich *see* JEWISH METHOD OF SLAUGHTER COMPARED WITH OTHER METHODS
Dembovskii, Kazimir Bronislavovich *see* PROMYSHLENNAIA ORGANIZATSIIA
Dembski, V *see* EUROPE AND THE NEW SEA LAW;...
Demchenko, I Akov Grigorevich *see*
– PO POVODU NASHEI SMUTY I VYSOCHAISHAGO UKAZA 12 DEKABRIA 1904 G
– PROTIVORIECHIIA I NESOOBRAZNOSTI V NASHEI VNUTRENNEI POLITIKIE
Dement'ev, A *see* RUSSKAIA SOVETSKAIA LITERATURA
Dement'ev, B A *see* TRUDOVYE ARTELI
DEMENTIA – v1-. 1990- – 1,5,9 – us UMI [616]
DEMERARA DAILY CHRONICLE – Georgetown, Guyana. Nov 1881-Jun 1922; 1930-51; 1958-Apr 1966 – 292 1/2r – 1 – uk British Libr Newspaper [072]

THE DEMERARA MARTYR : MEMOIRS OF THE REV. JOHN SMITH, MISSIONARY TO DEMERARA / Wallbridge, Edwin Angel – London: C. Gilpin, 1848 – 1mf – us A.T.L.A. [240]
Demers, Benjamin *see* NOTES SUR LA PAROISSE DE ST FRANCOIS DE LA BEAUCE
Demers, Jerome *see* INSTITUTIONES PHILOSOPHICAE AD USUM STUDIOSAE JUVENTUTIS
Demersay, Alfred *see* ETUDE ECONOMIQUE SUR LE MATE OU THE DU PARAGUAY
Demerson, Georges *see* D. JUAN MELENDEZ VALDES CORRESPONDANCE...HOPITAUX D'AVILA...BORDEAUX, 1964
DEMETER AND OTHER POEMS / Tennyson, Alfred, Lord – London, New York: Macmillan, 1889 – 1 roll – 1 – 1-55879-460-3 – uk Libr Preservation [810]
DEMETRIO RAMOS PEREZ. EL TRATADO DE LIMITES DE 1750 Y LA EXPEDICIONS DE ITURIAGA AL ORINOCO... / Mateos, Francisco – Madrid: Missionalia Hispanica, 1950 – 1 – sp Bibl Santa Ana [240]
DEMETRIUS : GESCHICHTLICHES TRAUERSPIEL IN VIER AUFZUEGEN / Schiller, Friedrich von – (Includes bibliographical references) – 1r – 1 – us U.W. Library [820]
DEMETRIUS / Grimm, Hermann Friedrich – Leipzig: S Hirzel, 1854 – 1r – 1 – us U.W. Library [430]
DEMETRIUS : ROMAN / Worms, Carl – Stuttgart: J G Cotta, 1919 – 1r – 1 – us U.W. Library [830]
DEMETRIUS : TRAUERSPIEL IN FUENF ACTEN / Schiller, Friedrich von – Dresden: E Pierson, 1897 – 1r – 1 – us U.W. Library [820]
DEMETRIUS / Worms, Carl – 1.-3. Aufl. Stuttgart: J G Cotta, 1919 – 1 – us U.W. Library [830]
Demeunier, J N *see* L'ESPRIT DES USAGES ET DES COUTUMES DES DIFFERENTS PEUPLES OU OBSERVATIONS TIREES DES VOYAGEURS ET DES HISTORIENS
Demey, J *see* DE LA LIQUIDATION ET DU PARTAGE DES SUCCESSIONS EN DROIT INTERNATIONAL
LE DEMI-CONGE – Montreal, Canada. avr 1907; v1 n5. 8 jun 1907 – 1r – 1 – Can$25.00 – cn Can Microfilming [072]
Demilt, A P *see* STORY OF AN OLD TOWN
Deming, Eleanor *see* HANDBOOK FOR CANOEING COUNCILLORS
Demitropulos, Libertad *see* EVA PERON
A DEMOCRACIA : ORGAO DEDICADO AOS INTERESSES ESTADOAES, MUNICIPAES, DO COMMERCIO E DA AGRICULTURA – Oliveira, 21 Jun 1896 – 1,5,6 – bl Biblioteca [072]
A DEMOCRACIA : ORGAO POPULAR – Maceio, Alagoas. 14 Jun, 26 Out 1878 – 1,5,6 – bl Biblioteca [072]
LA DEMOCRACIA : DIARIO DEL PARTIDO FILIPINO FEDERAL – (Filmed with other miscellaneous titles from Duke University) – Manila: [s.n.], jan 16 1901 – us Res Libr [072]
LA DEMOCRACIA – Manila: [s.n.], aug 11 1899 – us Res Libr [072]
DEMOCRACIA COLECTIVISTA. LECCIONES DE SOCIOLOGIA SOBRE UNA NUEVA POLITICA A LA ANTIGUA ESPANOLA...POR... / Cascales Munoz, Jose – Madrid: Sociedad Espanola de Libreria, s.a. – 1 – sp Bibl Santa Ana [320]
DEMOCRACIA, LUJAN, ARGENTINE REPUBLIC *see* AQUELLO SE LLAMO JUSTICIALISMO
DEMOCRACY – Bangkok, Thailand. Jan 1946-47 – 1r – 1 – uk British Libr Newspaper [072]
DEMOCRACY – London. 1901 – 1 – uk Microform Academic [073]
DEMOCRACY – v.1-. 1981- – 1,5,6,9 – us UMI [320]
DEMOCRACY AND DIPLOMACY : A PLEA FOR POPULAR CONTROL OF FOREIGN POLICY / Ponsonby, Arthur Ponsonby – London: Methuen, (1915). xxiii,198p – 1 – us U.W. Library [327]
DEMOCRACY IN SPAIN / Dingle, Reginald James – London. I937. Fiche W 840. (Blodgett Collection of Spanish Civil War Pamphlets) – 9 – us H.U. College Libr [946]
DEMOCRACY INTERNATIONAL COMMITTEE TO AID DEMOCRATIC DISSIDENTS IN YUGOSLAVIA (CADDY) – New York. 71 docs. 1980-1990 – 11mf – 9 – ne IDC [320]
DEMOCRACY NOT SUITED TO INDIA / Allahabad, Oudh – (Filmed with: A historical sketch of Fyzabad Tehsil/P Carnegy. Lucknow, 1870) – Pioneer Press, 1888 – us Res Libr [321]
THE DEMOCRACY OF CHRISTIANITY : OR, EQUALITY IN THE DEALINGS OF GOD WITH MEN / White, Lorenzo – NY: Hunt & Eaton, 1892 – 1mf – 9 – 0-8370-5759-0 – 1985-3759 – us A.T.L.A. [240]
DEMOCRACY OR REVOLUTION IN SPAIN? / Matteo, Johan – London, 1937. Fiche W 1033. (Blodgett Collection of Spanish Civil War Pamphlets) – 9 – us H.U. College Libr [946]
DEMOCRAT – (Also known as: Dungannon Democrat (N. Ireland)) – Feb 5 1919-Dec 24 1920; 1921; 1923; 1986-87; Jan 7-Jun 16 1988; Sep 8 1988; Sep 15 1988-Jan 5 1989; Jan 12-Jun 29 1989; Jul 6 1989-Jan 4 1990; Jan 11 1990-Dec 1990; Jan 10-Jan 27 1991; Jul 4 1991-92; Jan 14-Jun 24 1993; Jul 1993-Jan 6 1994; Jan 13-Dec 1994; Jan 12-Jun 29 1995; Jul 6-Dec 21 1995; 1996 – 25 1/2r – 1 – uk British Libr Newspaper [072]
DEMOCRAT – Bainville. Mont. 1934-1947 – 1 – us UMI [071]
DEMOCRAT – Bedford. Va. -w. 1929- – 1 – us UMI [071]
DEMOCRAT – Belle Plaine. Kan. 1873-1874 – 1 – us UMI [071]
DEMOCRAT – Brookhaven. Miss. 1883-1884 – 1 – us UMI [071]
DEMOCRAT – Brookville. Ind. 1852-1936; 1938-1939 – 1 – us UMI [071]
DEMOCRAT – Burlington. Kan. 1907-1910 – 1 – us UMI [071]
DEMOCRAT – Camden. N.J. 1859-1908 – 1 – us UMI [071]
DEMOCRAT – Canada. v1-9. Nov. 1961-Oct. 1969 – 1 – cn Precision [320]
DEMOCRAT – Carrollton. Mo. 1958-1969 – 1 – us UMI [071]
DEMOCRAT – Centralia. Ill. -w. 1867-70, 1885-87 – 1 – us UMI [071]
DEMOCRAT – Chester. Mont. 1916-1921 – 1 – us UMI [071]
DEMOCRAT – Clarion. Pa. -w. 1958-65 – 1 – us UMI [071]
DEMOCRAT – Columbus. Mont. 1913-1914 – 1 – us UMI [071]
DEMOCRAT – Corning. N.Y. 1857-1888 – 1 – us UMI [071]
DEMOCRAT – Coshocton. Ohio. 1843-1859; 1862-1901 – 1 – us UMI [071]
DEMOCRAT – Coshocton. Ohio. and Standard. 1882-1906 – 1 – us UMI [071]
DEMOCRAT – Decatur. Ind. 1950- – 1 – us UMI [071]
DEMOCRAT – Dodge City. Kan. 1884-1905 – 1 – us UMI [071]
DEMOCRAT – Ellensburg. Wash. 1914-1915 – 1 – us UMI [071]
DEMOCRAT – Ellsworth. Kan. 1885-1891 – 1 – us UMI [071]
DEMOCRAT – Elyria. Ohio. 1887-1916 – 1 – us UMI [071]
DEMOCRAT – Emporia. Kan. -w. 1882-99 – 1 – us UMI [071]
DEMOCRAT – Estherville. Iowa. 1895-1927 – 1 – us UMI [071]
DEMOCRAT – Everett. Wash. -w. 1895-96 – 1 – us UMI [071]
DEMOCRAT – Ewing. Neb. 1888-1892 – 1 – us UMI [071]
DEMOCRAT – Forsyth. Mont. 1915-1917; 1919-1920 – 1 – us UMI [071]
DEMOCRAT – Fort Madison. Iowa. -w. 1877-1915, 1920, 1922-25 – 1 – us UMI [071]
DEMOCRAT – Fostoria, Ohio. 1875-96 – 7r – 1 – $32.50r – us Archival [071]
DEMOCRAT – Franklin. Ind. -w. 1852-1942 – 1 – us UMI [071]
DEMOCRAT – Fulton. Pa. 1955-1967 – 1 – us UMI [071]
DEMOCRAT – Galesburg. Ill. 1858-60 – 1 – us UMI [071]
DEMOCRAT – Glasgow. Mont. -w. 1909-10, 1914-18 – 1 – us UMI [071]
DEMOCRAT – Glenville. West Virginia. -w. 1905-41. 1944-68 – 1 – us UMI [071]
DEMOCRAT – Grand Rapids. Mich. -w. 1868-83, 1885-97, 1899 – 1 – us UMI [071]
DEMOCRAT – Hamlin. West Virginia. 1917-1962 – 1 – us UMI [071]
DEMOCRAT – Huntington. Ind. -w. 1861-62, 1878-83, 1886-97 – 1 – us UMI [071]
DEMOCRAT – Indiana. Pa. 1862-1897 – 1 – us UMI [071]
DEMOCRAT – Johnstown. Pa. 1893-1952 – 1 – us UMI [071]
DEMOCRAT – Johnstown. Pa. -w. 1863-1912 – 1 – us UMI [071]
DEMOCRAT – Kenton, Ohio, 1857-1935 – 26r – 1 – us Archival [978]
DEMOCRAT – Logan. West Virginia. 1911-1918 – 1 – us UMI [071]
DEMOCRAT – Manistee. Mich. -w. 1882-91 – 1 – us UMI [071]
DEMOCRAT – Marion. Va. 1925-1940 – 1 – us UMI [071]
DEMOCRAT – Moberly. Mo. -w. 1896, 1903-15 – 1 – us UMI [071]
DEMOCRAT – Natchez. Miss. 1882-1884; 1902- – 1 – us UMI [071]
DEMOCRAT – Natchez. Miss. -w. 1865-76 – 1 – us UMI [071]
DEMOCRAT – Neosho. Mo. 1905-1952 – 1 – us UMI [071]
DEMOCRAT – New Castle. Ind. -w. 1887-1924 – 1 – us UMI [071]
DEMOCRAT – Niagara. N.Y. 1886-1895 – 1 – us UMI [071]
DEMOCRAT – Noblesville. Ind. 1889-1903 – 1 – us UMI [071]
DEMOCRAT – Paulding, Ohio. 1874-1949 – 29r – 1 – $32.50r – us Archival [071]
DEMOCRAT – Perrysburg, Ohio. 1857-58 – 1r – 1 – $32.50r – us Archival [071]
DEMOCRAT – Petersburg. Va. 1854-1856 – 1 – us UMI [071]
DEMOCRAT – Phoenix. Ariz. 1911-12; 1931 – 1 – us UMI [071]
DEMOCRAT – Piqua. Ohio. 1866-1867 – 1 – us UMI [071]
DEMOCRAT – Providence. R.I. 1879-1894 – 1 – us UMI [071]
DEMOCRAT – Racine. Wis. 1857-60 – 1 – us UMI [071]
DEMOCRAT – Redwood City, CA. 1889-1931 – 14r – 1 CB02680 – $700.00 – us Library Micro [071]
DEMOCRAT – Reno, NV. 1883-84 – 1r – 1 – $50.00 – U04668 – us Library Micro [071]
DEMOCRAT – Sedalia. Mo. 1871-83; 1912- – 1 – us UMI [071]
DEMOCRAT – Shelbyville. Ind. -d. 1919-47 – 1 – us UMI [071]
DEMOCRAT – St. Louis. Mo. 1843-44 – 1 – us UMI [071]
DEMOCRAT – Urbana. Ohio. 1887-1922 – 1 – us UMI [071]
DEMOCRAT – Wahoo. Neb. 1893-1964 – 1 – us UMI [071]
DEMOCRAT – Washington. Ind. 1952-1954 – 1 – us UMI [071]
DEMOCRAT – Washington. Iowa. -w. 1878-1927 – 1 – us UMI [071]
DEMOCRAT – Weston. West Virginia. 1936-1968 – 1 – us UMI [071]
DEMOCRAT – Wilmington. Ohio. and Herald. 1836-40 – 1 – us UMI [071]
DEMOCRAT – Woodland. Calif. 1890-1914; 1917- – 1 – us UMI [071]
DEMOCRAT – Woodland. Calif. (Davis ed.). -d. 1968- – 1 – us UMI [071]
DEMOCRAT – Woodsdale. Kan. -w. 1887-89 – 1 – us UMI [071]
DEMOCRAT – Wooster. Ohio. -w. 1840-49 – 1 – us UMI [071]
DEMOCRAT – Yakima. Wash. -w. 1897-1909 – 1 – us UMI [071]
DEMOCRAT – York. Neb. 1890-1924 – 1 – us UMI [071]
THE DEMOCRAT – Basseterre, St. Kitts. -w. 10 Jan 1959-22 Oct 1966; 28 Jan 1967-14 Dec 1968; 2 Jan 1971-27 Oct 1973. Imperfect. 6 reels – 1 – uk British Libr Newspaper [072]
THE DEMOCRAT – Kuala Lumpur. Malaysia. -w. 9 Mar-26 May 1946. (17 ft) – 1 – uk British Libr Newspaper [072]
THE DEMOCRAT – Lilongwe: [s.n.], 1994. jul 20/27-nov 21; dec 6-21; 1995: jan-mar 10, 23-apr 6, 21-28; may 11-Jul 21; aug 5, 18-nov 24; dec 21; 1996: jan 13-apr 9, 19-27; may 10-jun 15; jul-aug 2 – 2r – us Res Libr [071]
DEMOCRAT AND ARGUS – Easton, PA., 1833-1841 – 13 – $25.00r – us I.M.R. [071]
DEMOCRAT AND CHRONICLE – Rochester. N.Y. 1871- – 1 – us UMI [071]
DEMOCRAT AND LABOUR ADVOCATE – Birmingham, England. -w. 3 Nov-8 Dec 1855. 3 ft – 1 – uk British Libr Newspaper [072]
DEMOCRAT AND REGISTER-START DEMOCRAT – Mifflintown, PA. -w 1889-1906 – 13 – $25.00r – us I.M.R. [071]
DEMOCRAT BANNER – Mount Vernon. Ohio. -w. 1852-94 – 1 – us UMI [071]
DEMOCRAT HERALD – Butler, PA., 1889-1898 – 13 – $25.00r – us I.M.R. [071]
DEMOCRAT HERALD – Charleston. Miss. 1903-1905 – 1 – us UMI [071]
DEMOCRAT KONGOLAIS – Leopoldville: G Masiala, aug-sep 1961 – us Res Libr [072]
THE DEMOCRAT. (LABOUR WORLD.-SUNDAY WORLD) – London. Nov 1884-May 1891.-w,m. 2mqn reels – 1 – uk British Libr Newspaper [072]
DEMOCRAT MESSENGER – Waynesburg. Pa. 1958-1972; 1973- – 1 – us UMI [071]
DEMOCRAT NEWS – Niagara. N.Y. 1890-1895 – 1 – us UMI [071]
DEMOCRAT PRESS – Reading, PA., 1835-1840 – 13 – $25.00r – us I.M.R. [071]
DEMOCRAT SENTINEL – Logan. Ohio. 1910-1935 – 1 – us UMI [071]
DEMOCRAT SENTINEL – Sedalia. Mo. 1907-11 – 1 – us UMI [071]
DEMOCRAT STATE JOURNAL – Harrisburg, PA., 1835-1836 – 13 – $25.00r – us I.M.R. [071]
DEMOCRAT UNION – Harrisburg, PA., 1853-1855 – 13 – $25.00r – us I.M.R. [071]
DEMOCRATA : ORGAO DEFENSOR DO POVO – Jaragua, Alagoas. 14 Nov 1891 – 1,5,6 – bl Biblioteca [072]
EL DEMOCRATA – Mexico, 1916-19 – 8r – 1 – us Res Libr [072]
EL DEMOCRATA – Mexico City, 1917-18 – 2r – 1 – us Ross [072]
EL DEMOCRATA – Mexico. -d. 12 May 1916-10 April 1917; 2-31 March, 21 Oct-31 Dec 1918. 3 reels – 1 – uk British Libr Newspaper [072]
O DEMOCRATA – Formiga, 13 Jul, Sep 1890; Jul, 30 Aug 1891 – 1,5,6 – bl Biblioteca [072]
O DEMOCRATA : HEBDOMADARIO ORGAO PROPAGANDISTA, CRITICO-SOCIAL E COMMERCIAL – Manaos, Amazonas. Dez 1912 – 1,5,6 – bl Biblioteca [072]
O DEMOCRATA : JORNAL LITTERARIO, NOTICIOSO E DEFFENSOR DOS INTERESSES DA PROVINCIA – Aracaju, 9-24 Jul 1879; Feb 1880; Jan, Jul-Nov 1881; Jan-Dec 1882; Jan-Dec 1883; Jan-14 Jun 1884 – 1,5,6 – bl Biblioteca [072]
O DEMOCRATA : ORGAO DO PARTIDO DEMOCRATA DO SUL DE ALAGOAS – Penedo, Alagoas. 30 Out 1892 – 1,5,6 – bl Biblioteca [072]
O DEMOCRATA : ORGAO DO PARTIDO DEMOCRATA MUNICIPAL DE LAFAYETTE E DE QUELUZ, FILIADO, AO P.R. MINEIRO – Lafayette, 26 Aug 1923-20 Aug 1924 – 1,5,6 – bl Biblioteca [072]
O DEMOCRATA : ORGAO DO P.S.D. DO ACRE – Rio Branco, Acre. 7 Nov 1957 – 1,5,6 – bl Biblioteca [072]
O DEMOCRATA – '(s.l'). 7 dez 1833; fev-mar, out-nov 1834; dez 1835; jan-7 maio 1836 – 1,5,6 – bl Biblioteca [072]
O DEMOCRATA – [s.l.]. 7 Set 1871 – 1,5,6 – bl Biblioteca [072]
O DEMOCRATA FEDERAL – Sao Paulo, 24 Mar-10 Dec 1895 – 1,5,6 – bl Biblioteca [072]
EL DEMOCRATA FRONTERIZO – Laredo, TX: J Cardenas, dec 8 1917-jun 6 1919 – 1 – us Res Libr [071]
LE DEMOCRATE – Le Paysan libre. suite de: Le Paysan libre. Le democrate de Tarn-et-Garonne. Montauban. juin 1966-67 – 1 – fr A.C.R.P.P. [073]
LE DEMOCRATE – Montreal, Canada. v3 n2. mai 1966-v4 n6. sep/oct 1967 – 1r – 1 – Can$25.00 – cn Can Microfilming [072]
LE DEMOCRATE – Cap-Haitien: Impr National – us Res Libr [072]
LE DEMOCRATE EGALITAIRE – [Paris]: Impr d'Ed Bautruche, apr 1848 – 1r – us Res Libr [072]
LE DEMOCRATE VENDEEN – Journal politique, agricole, commercial et d'annonces. La Roche-sur-Yon. 14 dec 1850-20 dec 1851. mq no. 1-3, 8, 18, 60, 101, 106 – 1 – fr A.C.R.P.P. [073]
DEMOCRAT-HERALD – Albany. Or. 1966- – 1 – us UMI [071]
DEMOCRAT-HERALD – Baker, OR. -d. 1 Feb 1929-14 Apr 1977+. 92 rolls – 1 – us U.O. Library [071]
DEMOCRATIC ADVOCATE – Westminster, Maryland. 1866-1928 – 1 – us MD Archives [071]
DEMOCRATIC AGE/THE AGE – York, PA., 1889 – 13 – $25.00r – us I.M.R. [071]

DEMOCRATIC BANNER – Williamsport, PA., 1874-1876 – 13 – $25.00r – us I.M.R. [071]
THE DEMOCRATIC BANNER – Sonora, CA. 1885-95; 1898-1908 – 6r – 1 – $300.00 – B03000 – us Library Micro [071]
DEMOCRATIC BLADE – Valentine, NE. -w. Sept 1885-Sept 1888 – 1 – us NE Hist [071]
DEMOCRATIC CITIZEN – (Weekly Democratic newspaper) – Lebanon, OH. aug 25, 1859-aug 8, 1862 – 1r – 1 – us Western Res [071]
DEMOCRATIC COURIER – Findlay, Ohio. 1846-48 – 1r – 1 – $32.50r – us Archival [071]
DEMOCRATIC CULTURE AND GOVERNANCE : LATIN AMERICA ON THE THRESHOLD OF THE THIRD MILLENNIUM / ed by Albala-Bertrand, Luis – 1993 – 159p – 9 – 92-3-102858-8 – Co-published with Hispamerica – fr UNESCO [320]
THE DEMOCRATIC DAILY STATE JOURNAL – Sacramento, CA. 1852-1857 – 7r – 1 – $350.00 – B03427 – us Library Micro [073]
DEMOCRATIC DIGEST – Washington. D.C. 1953-1960 – 1 – us UMI [071]
DEMOCRATIC ENQUIRER – Bedford, PA. -w 1827-1833 – 13 – $25.00r – us I.M.R. [071]
DEMOCRATIC ENQUIRER – Muscatine. Iowa. 1850-1853 – 1 – us UMI [071]
DEMOCRATIC ERA – Portland OR. Apr 21 1871-Apr 11 1872 – 1 – us U.O. Library [071]
DEMOCRATIC EXPOSITOR – Wauseon County, Ohio. 1875-1929 – 22r – 1 – $32.50r – us Archival [071]
DEMOCRATIC FRONT FOR THE LIBERATION OF PALESTINE PUBLICATIONS – (Filmed by the University of Chicago Library Photoduplication Laboratory for the Middle Eastern Microfilm Project at the Center for Research Libraries, 1994) – Chicago – us Res Libr [071]
DEMOCRATIC GUIDE – Wilber, NE. -w. Nov 1888-Feb 1890 – 1 – us NE Hist [071]
DEMOCRATIC HERALD – Eugene OR. -w. 5 Jun 1860; Feb 1861. – 1r – 1 – us U.O. Library [071]
DEMOCRATIC LEFT / Democratic Socialist Organizing Committee – New York, 1982-85 (incompl) – 1 – us Hoover Inst Photo [335]
DEMOCRATIC MESSENGER – Fremont. Ohio. 1871-73 – 1 – us UMI [071]
THE DEMOCRATIC MESSENGER – Waynesburg, PA. -d 1972-76. 16 rolls – 13 – $25.00r – us I.M.R. [071]
DEMOCRATIC NEWS – Jacksonville OR. May 1-June 12 1869, May 1-Aug 28 1869, Aug 13-Oct 22 1870 + – 1 – us U.O. Library [071]
DEMOCRATIC NEWS – Jacksonville, OR. -w. 1 May 1869-21 Oct 1870. – 1r – 1 – us U.O. Library [071]
DEMOCRATIC NEWS : WEEKLY DEMOCRATIC NEWSPAPER – Warren, OH. 17 Feb 1938-22 May 1941 – 1r – 1 – us Western Res [071]
DEMOCRATIC NORTHWEST – Napoleon, Ohio. 1881-1906 – 6r – 1 – $32.50r – us Archival [071]
DEMOCRATIC NORTHWEST – (Weekly Democratic newspaper) – Napoleon, OH. may 8, 1869-jan 11, 1894 – 11r – 1 – us Western Res [071]
DEMOCRATIC NORTHWEST AND HENRY COUNTY NEWS – Napoleon, Ohio. 1894-1905 – 6r – 1 – $32.50r – us Archival [071]
DEMOCRATIC NORTHWEST & HENRY CO. NEWS – (Weekly Democratic newspaper) – Napoleon, OH. jan 18, 1894-jan 26, 1905 – 6r – 1 – us Western Res [071]
Democratic Party. National Convention *see* OFFICIAL REPORT OF THE PROCEEDINGS
DEMOCRATIC PHAROS – Logansport. Ind. 1858-1859; 1869-1871 – 1 – us UMI [071]
DEMOCRATIC PIONEER – Upper Sandusky, Ohio. 1845-50 – 1r – 1 – $32.50r – us Archival [071]
DEMOCRATIC PRESS – Port Townsend. Wash. -w. 1877-81 – 1 – us UMI [071]
DEMOCRATIC PRESS – York, PA. 1 Jul 1839-31 Dec 1862 – 5r – 1 – us L of C Photodup [071]
DEMOCRATIC RECORD : WEEKLY DEMOCRATIC NEWSPAPER – Chardon, OH. 19 May 1888-26 Dec 1891 – 1r – 1 – us Western Res [071]
DEMOCRATIC REPUBLICAN AND AGRICULTURE REGISTER – Carlisle, PA. -w 1829-30. 1 roll – 13 – $25.00r – us I.M.R. [071]
DEMOCRATIC REVIEW – Jacksonville OR. May 25 June 1 15 1872 – 1 – us U.O. Library [071]
DEMOCRATIC SENTINEL – Kittanning, PA. -w 1889-1910. 7 rolls – 13 – $25.00r – us I.M.R. [071]
DEMOCRATIC SENTINEL – Rensselaer. Ind. 1877-1898 – 1 – us UMI [071]
DEMOCRATIC SOCIALISM : BEING THE MANIFESTO OF THE ACTION GROUP OF NIGERIA FOR AN INDEPENDENT NIGERIA – [Lagos]: Action Group Bureau of Information, 1960 – us Res Libr [960]
Democratic Socialist Organizing Committee *see* DEMOCRATIC LEFT
DEMOCRATIC STANDARD – Eureka, CA. 1877-83 – 1r – 1 – $50.00 – B02215 – us Library Micro [071]
DEMOCRATIC STANDARD – Holidaysburg, PA. -w 1889-1912 – 13 – $25.00r – us I.M.R. [071]
DEMOCRATIC STANDARD – Leavenworth. Kan. 1880-1883; 1885-1886; 1897-1903 – 1 – us UMI [071]
DEMOCRATIC STANDARD – Portland. Or. 1855-1859 – 1 – us UMI [071]
DEMOCRATIC STANDARD – Portland, OR. 27 Sept 1854-11 May 1859. 1 roll – 1 – us U.O. Library [071]
DEMOCRATIC STANDARD – Portland, OR. -w. 1854-59 – 1 – 24.00 – us Oregon Hist [071]
DEMOCRATIC STANDARD – San Luis Obispo, CA. 1870-1872 – 1r – 1 – $50.00 – C03679 – us Library Micro [071]
DEMOCRATIC TEST – New Bloomfield, PA., 1860 – 13 – $25.00r – us I.M.R. [071]
DEMOCRATIC TIMES – Hays. Kan. 1888-1891 – 1 – us UMI [071]
DEMOCRATIC TIMES – Jacksonville, OR. -w. 7 Oct 1871-15 Aug 1907. 3 rolls – 1 – us U.O. Library [071]
DEMOCRATIC TIMES – Lima, Ohio. 1879-1889 – 3r – 1 – $32.50r – us Archival [071]
DEMOCRATIC VINDICATOR – Tionesta, PA. -w 1904-1912 – 13 – $25.00r – us I.M.R. [071]
DEMOCRATIC VINDICATOR – Upper Sandusky, Co. 1855-57 – 1r – 1 – $32.50r – us Archival [071]
DEMOCRATIC VISTAS AND OTHER PAPERS / Whitman, Walt – London: Routledge; New York: Dutton, 1906? – 1 – us U.W. Library [810]
DEMOCRATIC VOICE – Salem OR. Apr 14 1950 – 1 – us U.O. Library [071]
DEMOCRATIC WATCHMAN – Bellefonte, PA. -w 1861-1932 – 13 – $25.00r – us I.M.R. [071]
DEMOCRATIC WATCHMAN – Bellefonte. Pa. -w. 1861-63, 1889-1932 – 1 – us UMI [071]
DEMOCRATIC WEEKLY DISPATCH – Ukiah, CA. 1879-81 – 1r – 1 – $50.00 – B03047 – us Library Micro [071]
LA DEMOCRATIE – Dir. Marc Sangnier. Paris. 17 aout 1910-2 aout 1914 – 1 – fr A.C.R.P.P. [073]
LA DEMOCRATIE CHRETIENNE – puis Revue sociale d'etudes et d'action. Lille. mai 1894-1908 – 1 – fr A.C.R.P.P. [073]
LE DEMOCRATIE DE LA GUADELOUPE – Guadeloupe. French West Indies. 1900-1906 – 1 – us UMI [072]
LA DEMOCRATIE JURASSIENNE – Journal politique et litteraire puis Journal de la revolution sociale. Salins. 31 dec 1848-30 juil 1850 – 1 – fr A.C.R.P.P. [073]
DEMOCRATIE NOUVELLE : REVUE MENSUELLE DE POLITIQUE MONDIALE / ed by Duclos, J – Paris. 1947-59 – 1 – fr A.C.R.P.P. [320]
La Democratie Socialiste des Arrondissements de Saint-Claude (Jura) et de Nantua (Ain) *see* LE MONTAGNARD
La Democratie Socialiste du XXe Arrondissement *see* PARIS-DEMAIN
DEMOCRATIES – [Dakar?]: Impr Tandian-Yoff, [feb 1992-apr 1993] – 1r – 1 – us Res Libr [320]
DEMOCRAT-INDEPENDENT – Washington. Iowa. -w. 1927-41 – 1 – us UMI [071]
DEMOCRATIZING THE WEALTH OF NATIONS FROM NEW MONEY SOURCES AND PROFIT MOTIVES / Turnbull, Shann – 1975. With: Monetary Freedom Proposals. 2 fiches (24x) – 9 – 1.00f – at Libertarian Micro [320]
DEMOGRAFIE VAN DE JODEN IN NEDERLAND / Boekman, E – Amsterdam. 1936. BJ-262-9 1 – 9 – ne IDC [310]
DEMOGRAPHIC CHARACTERISTICS OF THE POPULATION / Israel. Prime Minister's Office – Part 1. Age, sex and marital status. Data from Stage A of the Census. Jerusalem, 1975. 27, 239, 57 p. (Population and Housing Census 1972, series no. 6). Text also in Hebrew – 9 – 6.00 – is I.T.T.I. [310]
DEMOGRAPHIC DATA : PART 1 – 3v. 1963 – 1r – $49.50 – us African Imprint [304]
DEMOGRAPHIC DATA : PART 2 – 1966-1969 – 1r – $49.50 – us African Imprint [304]
DEMOGRAPHICS, EMPLOYMENT STATUS, AND EMPLOYMENT SATISFACTION OF GRADUATES FROM NATA APPROVED UNDERGRADUATE ATHLETIC TRAINING PROGRAMS IN THE STATE OF PENNSYLVANIA / Marks, Melissa A – 1994 – 2mf – $8.00 – us Microform Publ [370]
DEMOGRAPHY FOR AGRICULTURAL PLANNERS – 1979 – 196p – it F.A.O. [630]
LA DEMOISELLE EN OR / Mendes, Catulle – Paris, s.d. 3v.6 fiches. (Literature Collection) – 9 – 15.00 – fr Bibl Nationale [830]
DEMOKRACIJA – Trieste. Italy. -f. 1 Sep 1958-17 May 1963. (1 reel) – 1 – uk British Libr Newspaper [949]
DEMOKRASI – (Weekly. Missing: 1950(18,21-22,25-27); 1951(31,34-36,39-41)) – Surabaja. nos 1-42/43. 1950-1951 – 11mf – 9 – SE-1398/1 – ne IDC [320]
DEMOKRASI DAN ADJARAN ISLAM / Sjaf'at – Indonesian or Arabic. SE 10,886 1. 1963.m – 9 – ne IDC [320]
DEMOKRASI KITA / Hatta, Mohammad – SE-2231 1. 1960 – 9 – ne IDC [300]
DEMOKRASI POLITIK DALAM ISLAM / Usman, Sjarif – SE 10,061 1 – 9 – ne IDC [320]
DEMOKRASI SOSIALIS DALAM PEKERDJAAN PERADILAN DAN PEMBUATAN UNDANGUNDANG / Adjitorop, Jusuf – SE-3975 1. 1962 – 9 – ne IDC [950]
DER DEMOKRAT – Mecklenburg. Dec. 1945-Dec. 1949. Missing: scattered issues – 1 – 35.00r – us Hoover Inst Photo [072]
DER DEMOKRAT – Mitteilungsblatt der Demokratischen Volkspartei. Stuttgart, West Germany. 14 Jun 1946-51 – 1 – gw Mikrofilm [072]
DER DEMOKRAT – Rostock and Schwerin, East Germany. 3 Jan-Dec 1947; 2 Aug 1954-1990 – 60r – 1 – gw Mikrofilm [072]
DER DEMOKRAT – Rostock, Schwerin, 1947 – 1 – DM80.00 – gw Mikro Press [072]
DEMOKRATICHNA UKRAINA – (Backfile through 1998 $85.00r) – Ukraine, 1999- – 2r per y – 1 – $160.00 standing order – us Ross [072]
DEMOKRATICKE HLASY – Zvolen, Czechoslovakia. Jul-Nov 1945 – 1r – 1 – us L of C Photodup [072]
DEMOKRATIJA – Belgrade, Yugoslavia. Sept-Nov 1945 – 1r – 1 – us L of C Photodup [949]
DAS DEMOKRATISCHE DEUTSCHLAND – Berlin, 1920, 1923 – 1 – Dist. gw Mikrofilm – gw Misc Inst [072]
DIE DEMOKRATISCHE GEMEINDE – Hannover, Bonn, West Germany. Oct 1949-1950 – 1r – 1 – gw Mikrofilm [072]
DIE DEMOKRATISCHE GEMEINDE – Hannover/Bonn, Oct 1949-50 – 1r – 1 – DM80.00 – gw Mikro Press [072]
DEMOKRATISCHE POST : ORGANO DE LOS ALEMANES DEMOCRATAS DE MEXICO Y CENTRO-AMERICA – Mexico City, Mexico. 15 Aug 1943-Feb Mar 1952 – 1r – 1 – gw Mikrofilm [072]
DIE DEMOKRATISCHE REPUBLIK – Heidelberg, Germany. 1 May-6 Jun 1849 – 1r – gw Mikrofilm [072]
DEMOKRATISCHE RUNDSCHAU – Berlin, may 4-nov 23 1919 – 1r – 1 – Dist. gw Mikrofilm – gw Misc Inst [072]
DEMOKRATISCHE ZEITUNG – Berlin, oct 1 1871-72 – 1r – 1 – Dist. gw Mikrofilm – gw Misc Inst [072]
DEMOKRATISCHES WOCHENBLATT – Leipzig, 1868-1869 – 1r – 1 – DM110.00 – gw Mikro Press [072]
DEMOKRATISCHES WOCHENBLATT – (Title change: Der Volksstaat, 2 Oct 1869; Vorwaerts, 1 Oct 1876) – Leipzig, Germany. 1868-21 Oct 1878 – 1 – gw Mikrofilm [072]
Demokratisch-Zionistische Fraktion *see* PROGRAMM UND ORGANISATIONS-STATUT
DEMOKRATSIIA – 1990-1995 – 1 – sz Infoprint [072]
DEMOKRATSIIA – (Backfile through 1998 $85.00r) – Bulgaria, 1999- – 4r per y – 1 – $320.00 standing order – us Ross [072]
Demonchau, C *see* TRIO POUR LE FORTE PIANO AVEC ACCOMP. DE VIOLON ET VIOLONCELLE OBLIGEE, OP. 2
Demonferrand, Jean Baptiste Firmin *see* ESSAI SUR LES LOIS DE LA POPULATION ET DE LA MORTALITE EN FRANCE
DEMONIC POSSESSION IN THE NEW TESTAMENT...HISTORICAL, MEDICAL, AND THEOLOGICAL / Alexander, William – Edinburgh: T. & T. Clark, 1902. 1 fiche – 9 – us A.T.L.A. [240]
LA DEMONOMANIE DE LOUDUN – La Fleche. 1634 – 9 – fr Hachette [360]
DEMONSTRACION Y VINDICACION DE LAS INJUSTICIAS...POR ACUSACION DEL DELATOR DON JOAQUIN RODRIGUEZ LEAL / Ceresoles, Mauricio – 1841 – 9 – $1.50f – sp Bibl Santa Ana [360]
DEMONSTRATIO FALLACIARUM JOHANNIS CALVINI, IN DOCTRINA DE COENA DOMINI QVIBVS VSVS EST IN LIBRO INSTITUTIONIS CHRISTIANAE, AND EX QUO SUUM CALVINISMUM IN OMNEM EGURGITAVIT CHRISTIANUM ORBEM / Huber, S – VVitebergae, 1593 – 1mf – ne IDC [240]
DEMONSTRATIO, IDIOMA UNGARORUM ET LAPPONUM INDEM ESSE / Sajnovics, J – Hafniae, 1770 – 1mf – 9 – ne IDC [470]
DEMONSTRATION DU PRINCIPE DE L'HARMONIE / Rameau, Jean-Phillippe – 1750 – 9 – us Sibley [780]
DEMONSTRATION PHILOSOPHIQUE DU CATHOLICISME : A TOUS CEUX QUI TIENNENT A LA VERITE, A LEURS SEMBLABLES, A LEUR PATRIE / Polge, Abbe – (Includes bibliographical references) – Paris: Jacques Lecoffre, 1851 – 1mf – 9 – 0-8370-8371-0 – 1986-2371 – us A.T.L.A. [240]
DEMONSTRATIONES EVIDENTISSIMAE DOCTRINAE DE ESSENTIA IMAGINIS DEI AND DIABOLI,... / Flacius Illyricus d.A E, M – Basileae, [1507] – 5mf – 9 – ne IDC [240]
DEMONSTRATIONS CATHOLIQUES, OU L'ART DE REUNIR LES PRETENDUS REFORMEZ / Regourd, A – Paris, 1630 – 11mf – 9 – CA-144/1 – ne IDC [240]
DEMONSTRATOR: A PERIODICAL OF FACT, THOUGHT, AND COMMENT – v1-5. no. 14. (all publ). 1903-1908 – 1 reel – 1 – $65.00 – us UPA [335]
DEMOREST'S NEW YORK ILLUSTRATED NEWS – New York. v1-10. 1859-64 – 3r – 1 – us Ross [071]
Demorgny, G *see*
– LA QUESTION DU DANUBE,...
– LA QUESTION PERSANE...
DEMOS, A STORY OF ENGLISH SOCIALISM / Gissing, George Robert – London: Smith, Elder, 1886 – 2 rolls – 1 – 1-55879-215-5 – uk Libr Preservation [320]
DEMOSTRACION CRITICO-APOLOGETICA. TOMO 1 / Sarmiento, Martin – 1732 – 2mf – 9 – Pta1,500.00 – 84-7848-020-X – sp Pentalfa [440]
DEMOSTRACION CRITICO-APOLOGETICA. TOMO 2 / Sarmiento, Martin – 1732 – 2mf – 9 – Pta1,500.00 – 84-7848-021-8 – sp Pentalfa [440]
DEMOSTRACION...ENGANO...FRAY MARCOS DE ALCALA...FUNDACION DESCALZAS / Velasco, Matias – 1737 – 9 – 1.50f – sp Bibl Santa Ana [240]
DEMOSTRACTIONES PALMARIAS.. / Bachiller Reganadientes – 1787 – 9 – 1.50f – sp Bibl Santa Ana [946]
Demoustier *see* LE TOLERANT OU LA TOLERANCE MORALE ET RELIGIEUSE
Demoz de la Salle *see* METHODE DE MUSIQUE..
Dempf, A *see* DAS UNENDLICHE IN DER MITTELALTERLICHEN METAPHYSIK UND IN DER KANTISHEN DIALEKTIK
Dempsey, James M *see* SURVEY OF INDONESIA FOR LONG VEGETABLE FIBER DEVELOPMENT
Dempsey, Richard *see* MAGISTRATE'S HAND-BOOK
Dempwolff, Otto *see* PAPERS REGARDING PACIFIC LINGUISTICS, 1897-1938

THE DEMURRER: OR, PROOFS OF ERROR IN THE DECISION OF THE SUPREME COURT OF THE STATE OF NEW YORK, REQUIRING FAITH IN PARTICULAR RELIGIOUS DOCTRINES AS A LEGAL QUALIFICATION OF WITNESSES. / Herttell, Thomas – New York: Conrad, 1828. 158p. LL-624 – 1 – us L of C Photodup [340]

Demus, Otto *see* THE MEDIEVAL MOSAICS OF SAN MARCO, VENICE

Demyk, M *see*
- A PROPOS DE LA DEFINITION DE L'INDIEN AU GUATEMALA
- LEXIQUE ESPAGNOL-KI-CHE ET KI-CHE-ESPAGNOL
- MISERY AGE MAYA

DEN' – 1869-71. Vodessa. Russian – 1 – us NY Public [073]

DEN = DAY – New York: Orient Publ Co, dec 30 1922-feb 5 1926 – 1 – us Res Libr [071]

DEN – Sofia, Bulgaria. Aug 1945-Apr 1946 – 1r – 1 – us L of C Photodup [949]

Den, Vladimir Eduardovich *see* POLOZHENIE ROSSII V MIROVOM KHOZIAISTVE

Denault, Amedee *see*
- L'AMI DU COLON
- LE BON CINEMA
- LA CROIX DU CANADA
- LE JOURNAL DU PEUPLE
- LES PETITES LECTURES CANADIENNES
- LE PIONNIER

Denault, Jean-Marc *see* LE CANADIEN LIBERAL

DENBIGH, RUTHIN AND VALE OF CLWYD FREE PRESS – Denbigh, Wales. Denbighshire Free Press. -w. 11 Nov 1882-Dec 1920. Lacking 1896, 1897. 33 reels – 1 – uk British Libr Newspaper [072]

Denck, H *see*
- VON DEM GSATZ GOTTES
- VON DER WAREN LIEB
- WAS GEREDT SEY, DAS DIE SCHRIFFT SAGT, GOTT THUE VND MACHE GUTS VND BOESES
- WER DIE WARHAIT WARLICH LIEB HAT, MAG SICH HIERINNE BRUFEN IM ERKANDTNUSZ SEYNES GLAUBENS

Dencker, K *see* DER RANG DER "ALLGEMEIN ANERKANNTEN REGELN..."

DENDANG MELAJU DELI MODEREN; DIHIASI DENGAN SADJAK DAN GUBAHAN SERTA GAMBER2 PENGGEMARNJA / Arbie Zairany, Agus – v. 1 ONLY. SE-4329 1. 1959 – 9 – ne IDC [950]

DENDERAH. DESCRIPTION GENERALE DU GRAND TEMPLE DE CETTE VILLE / Mariette, A – 5v. Paris. 1870-75. BNE-365 1 – 9 – ne IDC [930]

DENDEREH (MEES VOL 17) / Flinders Petrie, W M – London, 1900 – 10mf – 8 – Dfl35.00 – ne Slangenburg [930]

Dendy DR *see* THE USE OF LIGHTS IN CHRISTIAN WORSHIP

DENE HOLLOW / Wood, Ellen – British Fiction Archive: Unit 1 – 9 – uk Bell [830]

Denecke, Rolf *see* GESTALTEN DEUTSCHER DICHTUNG

Denefle, S *see* LES FONTAINES EN BRETAGNE

DENEZHNOE OBIAZATEL'STVO V GRAZHDANSKOM I KOLLIZIONNOM PRAVE KAPITALISTICHESKIKH STAN. M / Lunts, L A – 1948. R-9675 1 – 9 – ne IDC [947]

DENEZHNOE OBRASHCHENIE I DENEZHNYE ZNAKI DAL'NEGO VOSTOKA ZA PERIOD VOINY I REVOLIUTSII (1914-1924) / Pogrebetskii, A I – Harbin, 1924 – 1 – 35.00r – us Hoover Inst Photo [947]

Dengel, DR *see* EFFECTS OF DEHYDRATION ON RATINGS OF PERCEIVED EXERTION AT THE LACTATE AND VENTILATORY THRESHOLDS

Dengk, H *see*
- ALLE PROPHETEN NACH HEBRAISCHER SPRACH VERTEUETSCHT
- ALLE PROPHETENN NACH HEBRIESCHER SPRACH VERDEUETSCHT

Denham, D *see*
- NARRATIVE OF TRAVELS AND DISCOVERIES IN NORTHERN AND CENTRAL AFRICA IN THE YEARS 1822, 1823 AND 1824
- TRAVELS AND DISCOVERIES IN AFRICA
- TRAVELS AND DISCOVERIES IN NORTHERN AND CENTRAL AFRICA
- VOYAGES ET DECOUVERTES DANS LE NORD ET LES PARTIES CENTRALES DE L'AFRIQUE

Denham, Oudney *see* VOYAGES ET DECOUVERTES DANS LE NORD ET LES PARTIES CENTRALES DE L'AFRIQUE

Denham, W *see* A SECOND ANSWER TO MR. JOHN WESLEY, BEING A SUPPLEMENT TO THE LETTER OF AMERICANUS,...

Deniel, E *see* THE PANAMA CANAL

Denifle, Heinrich *see*
- AUCTARIUM CHARTULARII UNIVERSITATIS PARISIENSIS
- CHARTULARIUM UNIVERSITATIS PARISIENSIS
- HUMANITY
- LUTHER IN RATIONALISTISCHER UND CHRISTLICHER BELEUCHTUNG
- LUTHER UND LUTHERTUM IN DER ERSTEN ENTWICKELUNG
- TAULERS BEKEHRUNG
- DIE UNIVERSITAETEN DES MITTELALTERS BIS 1400
- LES UNIVERSITES FRANCAISES AU MOYEN-AGE

Denikin, Anton Ivanovich *see*
- OCHERKI RUSSKOI SMUTY
- OFITSERY, OCHERKI

Denikin, Anton Ivanovich et al *see* FRANTSUZY V ODESSE

DENIKIN, I UDENICH, VRANGEL : MEMUARY: DENIKIN, LUKOMSKI I, RAKOVSKI I, VORONOVICH, SKOBT SOV, OBOLENSKI I, VALENTINOV, GORN I DR – 2-e izd. Moskva: Gos. sotsialno- ekon. izd-vo, 1931 – 1 – CSUX88-B5075 – us Hoover Inst Photo [947]

DENIKIN, I UDENICH, VRANGEL – Moskva: Gos. izd-vo, 1927 – 1 – CSUX88-B5079 – us Hoover Inst Photo [947]

Denis, A-M *see* CONCORDANCE LATINE DES PSEUDEPIGRAPHES D'ANCIEN TESTAMENT

Denis, E *see*
- LA BOHEME DEPUIS LA MONTAGNE BLANCHE
- FIN DE L'INDEPENDENCE BOHEME

Denis, Hector *see* LE MOUVEMENT DE LA POPULATION ET SES CONDITIONS ECONOMIQUES

DENISE DE MONTMIDI : ROMAN / Ompteda, Georg, Freiherr von – Berlin, Wien: Ullstein, [1910?] – 1r – 1 – us U.W. Library [830]

Denisiuk, N F *see* KUSTARNAIA ROSSIIA

Denison, George Anthony *see*
- FIFTY YEARS AT EAST BRENT
- MR. GLADSTONE
- NOTES OF MY LIFE, 1805-1878
- SUPPLEMENT TO "NOTES OF MY LIFE" 1879, AND "MR. GLADSTONE", 1886

Denison, George Taylor *see*
- THE BRITISH EMPIRE LEAGUE IN CANADA: SPEECH DELIVERED BY THE PRESIDENT, GEORGE T. DENISON, IN MOVING THE ADOPTION OF THE ANNUAL REPORT AT THE ANNUAL MEETING OF THE LEAGUE
- A CHRONICLE OF ST JOHN'S CEMETARY ON THE HUMBER
- A HISTORY OF CAVALRY FROM THE EARLIEST TIMES, WITH LESSONS FOR THE FUTURE

Denison, John Hopkins *see* BESIDE THE BOWERY

Denison, John Ledyard *see* AN ILLUSTRATED HISTORY OF THE NEW WORLD: CONTAINING A GENERAL HISTORY OF ALL THE VARIOUS NATIONS, STATES AND REPUBLICS OF THE WESTERN CONTINENT...AND A COMPLETE HISTORY OF THE UNITED STATES TO THE PRESENT TIME.

Denison, Louisa Evelyn *see* FIFTY YEARS AT EAST BRENT

Denison Ross, E *see* POLYGLOT LIST OF BIRDS IN TURKI, MANCHU AND CHINESE

Denison, S D *see* A HISTORY OF THE FOREIGN MISSIONARY WORK OF THE PROTESTANT EPISCOPAL CHURCH

Denjean, Georges *see* L'ASSURANCE CONTRE LE CHOMAGE

Denjoy, Paul *see* ETUDE PRATIQUE DE LA LEGISLATION CIVILE ANNAMITE

DENKEN UND SPRECHEN BEI GEISTIG BEHINDERTEN KINDERN / Gangkofer, Manfred D – 1991 – 96p – 9 – DM98.00 – 3-89349-434-0 – gw Hänsel [360]

DENKMACHER DEUTSCHER TONKUNST – 1folge. Herausgegeben von der Musikgeschichtlichen Kommission. Leipzig. 65 v. 1892-1931. (Called "Erste Folge" from bd. 4, 1900) – 1 – 199.00 – us L of C Photodup [780]

DENKMAELER AUS AEGYPTEN UND AETHIOPIEN / ed by Lepsius, C R – Berlin, 1849-1913. v.1-13 – 172mf – 8 – ne IDC [930]

DENKMAELER DER ENTSTEHUNGSGESCHICHTE DES BYZANTINISCHEN RITUS / Baumstark, Anton – 1927 – 1mf – 8 – Dfl6.00 – ne Slangenburg [240]

DENKSCHREIBEN UEBER DIE REORGANISIRUNG DES NIEDERL / Duenners, J H – Israelitischen Seminars in Amsterdam vom 29 Jan 1862. Amsterdam. 1917. BJ-262-21 1 – 9 – ne IDC [290]

DENKSCHRIFT / Verband der Steinsetzer, Pflasterer und Berufsgenossen Deutschlands. Berlin – v4. 1914. Berlin. (Serial publications of German trade unions in the Memorial Library, University of Wisconsin-Madison.) – 1 – us U.W. Library [330]

DENKSCHRIFT UEBER DAS VERHAELTNISS DES STAATES ZU DEN SAETZEN DER PAEPSTLICHEN CONSTITUTION VOM 18. JULI 1870: GEWIDMET DEN REGIERUNGEN DEUTSCHLANDS UND OESTERREICHS / Schulte, Johann Friedrich von – Prag: Friedrich Tempsky, 1871 – 1mf – 9 – 0-8370-8382-6 – 1986-2382 – us A.T.L.A. [240]

DENKSCHRIFT ZUR EINWEIHUNG DES KNAPPSCHAFTS-VERWALTUNGSGEBAUDES AM 18. JUNI 1910 – 1 – DM30.00 – gw Mikro Press [330]

DENKSCHRIFT ZUR HUNDERTSTEN WIEDERKEHR SEINES TODESTAGES / Lavater, Johann Caspar – (Includes bibliographical references) – Zuerich: A Mueller, 1902 – 1r – 1 – us U.W. Library [100]

DENKSCHRIFTEN DER KAISERLICHEN AKADEMIE DER WISSENSCHAFTEN : MATHEMATISCH-NATURWISSENSCHAFTLICHE KLASSE – (Index) – Wien, 1850-1941. v1-104 – 2,029mf – H-1070c/2 – ne IDC [500]

DENKSCHRIFTEN DER KAISERLICHEN AKADEMIE DER WISSENSCHAFTEN : PHILOSOPHISCH-HISTORISCHE KLASSE – Wien, 1896. v44 – 15mf – H-632/2 – ne IDC [500]

DENKSCHRIFTEN DER KOENIGLICH-BAIERISCHEN BOTANISCHEN GESELLSCHAFT IN REGENSBURG – Regensburg, 1815-1931. v1-12 – 60mf – 8566/1 – ne IDC [580]

DENKSCHRIFTEN MILITAERISCH-POLITISCHEN INHALTS... / Radetzky, J J W – Stuttgart, Augsburg, 1858 – 6mf – 9 – ne IDC [355]

DENKWUERDIGKEITEN / Menzel, Wolfgang; ed by Menzel, Konrad – Bielefeld, Leipzig, 1977 – viii/591p – 9 – DM75.00 – 3-89349-102-3 – gw Hänsel [100]

DENKWUERDIGKEITEN AUS DEM LEBEN DER FUERSTIN AMALIA VON GALLITZIN / Katerkamp, Theodor – Muenster, 1828 – 9 – DM48.00 – 3-89349-206-2 – gw Hänsel [920]

DENKWUERDIGKEITEN DER SCHARFRICHTERFAMILIE SANSON / ed by Sanson, Henry – Muenchen: Rosl & Cie, 1924 – us Res Libr [920]

DENKWUERDIGKEITEN DES EIGENEN LEBENS / Varnhagen von Ense, Karl August; ed by Leutner, Karl – (Includes index) – 3. erw. Aufl. Berlin: Verlag der Nation, [1954] – 1r – 1 – us U.W. Library [920]

DENKWUERDIGKEITEN EINER REISE NACH DEM RUSSISCHEN AMERIKA / Kittlitz, F H von – BN 281 2. 2 v. 1858 – 8 – ne IDC [910]

DENKWUERDIGKEITEN UND VERMISCHTE SCHRIFTEN / Varnhagen von Ense, Karl August – 2. Aufl. Leipzig: F Brockhaus. 9v. 1843-59 – 1 – us U.W. Library [800]

DENMARK : BUREAU DE STATISTIQUE / Denmark. Statistiske Bureau – (Coll title: European Official Statistical Serials, 1841-1984) – 2mf – 9 – £7.00f (set £1,490.00 284 mf) – uk Chadwyck [948]

DENMARK : SAMMENDRAG AF STATISTISKE OPLYSNINGER ANGAAENDE KONGERIGET DANMARK 1869-1893 / Denmark. Statistiske Bureau – (Coll title: European Official Statistical Serials, 1841-1984) – 16mf – 9 – £7.00f (set £1,490.00 284mf) – uk Chadwyck [948]

DENMARK = STATISTICAL YEARBOOK 1896-1965 : STATISTISK ARBOG 1896-1965 / Denmark. Statistiske Bureau – (Coll title: European Official Statistical Serials, 1841-1984) – 266mf – 9 – £4.00f (set £1,490.00 284mf) – uk Chadwyck [948]

Denmark *see*
- DANMARKS LANGTIDSPROGRAM, 1948/49-1952/53
- LONG-RANGE ECONOMIC PLAN (1971-1985?)
- THE LONG-TERM PROGRAM OF DENMARK
- PERSPEKTIVPLAN-REDEGORELSE 1972-1987
- STATSTIDENDE

Denmark, Maine. First Free Will Baptist Church *see* RECORDS

Denmark. National Archives *see* RECORDS RELATING TO THE DANISH WEST INDIES, 1672-1860, RECEIVED FROM THE DANISH NATIONAL ARCHIVES

Denmark. Organization for European Economic Cooperation *see* REPORT TO THE ECONOMIC COOPERATION ADMINISTRATION ON THE 1949/50 PROGRAMME

Denmark. Statistiske Bureau *see*
- DENMARK

Dennery, R *see*
- LE PARTAGE EN DROIT INTERNATIONAL PRIVE FRANCAIS...

Denney, James *see*
- THE DEATH OF CHRIST
- THE EPISTLE TO THE THESSALONIANS
- THE EPISTLES TO THE THESSALONIANS
- JESUS AND THE GOSPEL: CHRISTIANITY JUSTIFIED IN THE MIND OF CHRIST
- THE SECOND EPISTLE TO THE CORINTHIANS

DENNI POKROK – Omaha, NE. -d. 1 Nov 1915-23 May 1920 – 1 – us NE Hist [071]

DENNI POKROK – Omaha, NE. -w. Nov-Dec 1915; Feb 1916-May 1920 – 1 – us NE Hist [071]

DENNICA = MORNING STAR : URADNY ORGAN EVANJELICKEJ SLOVENSKEJ ZENSKEJ JEDNOTY V AM – Pittsburgh, PA: Jednota, sep 15 1924-1930, 1932-33, 1935-45 – 3r – 1 – us Res Libr [071]

DENNICE NOVOVEKU : WEEKLY CZECH LANGUAGE, FREE THINKER NEWSPAPER – Cleveland, OH. Oct 1877-Oct 1913 – 1 – us Western Res [071]

Dennie, Joseph *see* THE LAY PREACHER

Denning, Margaret Beahm *see* MOSAICS FROM INDIA

DENNIS 1710-1890 – (Mf 1-4: Births & Deaths 1710-1855 Pt 1. Mf 5-8: Births & Deaths 1710-1855 Pt 2. Mf 9-16: Births & Deaths Early 1700's-1890. Mf 17-22: Index to Births & Deaths 1710-1855. Mf 23-24: Marriage Records 1814-55. Mf 25-27: B,M,D 1855-62. Mf 28-29: Index to B,M,D 1855-62. Mf 30-31: Births 1862-90 Bk 2. Mf 32-33: Marriage Record 1863-90 Bk 2. Mf 34-35: Deaths 1863-90 Bk 2. Mf 36-40: Index to B,M,D 1863-1966) – (mf ed 1986) – 40mf – 9 – 0-931248-98-1 – us Holbrook [920]

Dennis, D *see* THE CHRONOLOGY OF EFFECTS OF CAFFEINE DURING PROLONGED CYCLE ERGOMETRY

Dennis, James Shepard *see*
- CHRISTIAN MISSIONS AND SOCIAL PROGRESS: A SOCIOLOGICAL STUDY
- FOREIGN MISSIONS AFTER A CENTURY
- THE MESSAGE OF CHRISTIANITY TO OTHER RELIGIONS
- THE MODERN CALL OF MISSIONS
- THE NEW HOROSCOPE OF MISSIONS
- SOCIAL EVILS OF THE NON-CHRISTIAN WORLD

Dennis, John *see* STUDIES IN ENGLISH LITERATURE

Dennison, George Taylor *see* CANADA AND HER RELATIONS TO THE EMPIRE

Dennstedt, A W *see*
- NOMENCLATOR BOTANICUS ENUMERATIO ALPHABETICA OMNIUM HUCUSQUE COGNITORUM VEGETABILIUM ADJECTIS PRAECIPUIS SYNONYMIS
- SCHLUESSEL ZUM HORTUS INDICUS MALABARICUS

Denny, H *see* MONOGRAPHIA ANOPLURORUM BRITANNIAE

DENNY HLAS = DAILY VOICE – Cleveland: John Pankuch, -1925. dec 1917-jun 1918; 1924 – 5r – 1 – us Res Libr [071]

Denny, James *see* DEATH OF CHRIST: ITS PLACE AND INTERPRETATION IN THE NEW TESTAMENT

Denny, Karen L *see* A BIOMECHANICAL ANALYSIS OF THE EFFECTS OF HAND WEIGHTS ON THE ARM-SWING WHILE WALKING AND RUNNING

Denolf, Prosper *see* AAN DE RAND DE DIBESE

DENOMBREMENT CONSTITUTIONNEL DE LA FRANCE. CONCORDANCE PROVINCES-DEPARTEMENTS-DISTRICS-CANTONS – Paris, 1791 – 1mf – 9 – F30.00 – fr F.F.G. [323]

Denoncourt, Louise *see* BIO-BIBLIOGRAPHIE DE YVES LECLERC, 1953-1961

DeNotaris, G *see* PRODROMUS BRYOLOGIAE MEDIOLANENSIS
Dent, John Charles *see*
- CANADIAN NOTABILITIES VOL.1
- CANADIAN NOTABILITIES VOL.2
- THE GERRARD STREET MYSTERY AND OTHER WEIRD TALES
- THE STORY OF THE UPPER CANADIAN REBELLION, LARGELY DERIVED FROM ORIGINAL SOURCES AND DOCUMENTS. VOL. 01
- THE STORY OF THE UPPER CANADIAN REBELLION, LARGELY DERIVED FROM ORIGINAL SOURCES AND DOCUMENTS. VOL. 02

Dent. Yorkshire *see* PARISH REGISTERS
DENTAL ECONOMICS – (v. 57- 1967- 5,6. v. 60- 1970- 9) – v. 1- 1911- – 1 – us UMI [617]
DENTAL HEALTH ATTITUDES AND KNOWLEDGE LEVELS OF RURAL AND SUBURBAN TEXAS / Russell, Linda M & Cissell, William B – 1991 – 1mf – $4.00 – us Microform Publ [613]
DENTAL HYGIENE – v. 47- 1973- – 1,5,6,9 – us UMI [617]
DENTAL HYGIENISTS' KNOWLEDGE, ATTITUDES AND INFECTION CONTROL PRACTICES IN RELATION TO AIDS AND AIDS PATIENTS / Snyder, Gail A & Levy, Marvin R – 1992 – 2mf – 9 – $8.00 – us Microform Publ [613]
DENTAL MANAGEMENT – v24-. Dec 1984- – 1,5,6,9 – us UMI [073]
DENTAL PRACTICE – (v. 17 1970 5,6,9) 1968- – 1 – us UMI [073]
DENTAL STUDENT – (1975-. 5,6,9) – v. 1-. 1923- – 1 – us UMI [073]
LA DENTELLE A L'AIGUILLE EN BASSE-NORMANDIE / Moulinet, Jean – Argentan. 1912. (La Condition Ouvriere. Part Two.) – 9 – 7.50 – fr Bibl Nationale [360]
DENTON BAPTIST CHURCH. GREENUP ASSOCIATION. DENTON, KENTUCKY : CHURCH RECORDS – Oct 1965-73 and scattered Feb 1974-May 1987 – 1 – 5.00 – us Baptist [978]
Denton, John *see* ACCOUNT OF COUNTY OF CUMBERLAND
Denton, S F *see* MOTHS AND BUTTERFLIES OF THE UNITED STATES
LE DENTURO / Association des denturologistes du Quebec – (Including Bulletin des Denturologistes du Quebec (1970)) – Montreal: l'Association. v1-10. 1970-79. SEM35P219 – 1r – 1 – Can$25.00 – cn Bibl Nat [617]
LE DENTURO / Association des denturologistes du Quebec – Montreal: l'Association. v20 no 1- 1989. SEM16P180 – 1r – 5 – Can$10.00 – cn Bibl Nat [617]
DENTURO PLUS – Montreal: le Syndicat. v11-19. 1980-85. SEM16P351 – 1r – 5 – Can$19.00 – cn Bibl Nat [617]
DENVER JOURNAL OF INTERNATIONAL LAW AND POLICY – (v10- 1980- 5,6,9) – v1- 1971- – 1 – us UMI [340]
DENVER JOURNAL OF INTERNATIONAL LAW AND POLICY – (v1-13 1971-84 on reel $148.00. v14-23 1985-95 on mf $201.00. With 10-yr index) – v1-23. 1971-95 – 5,6,9 – $349.00 set – us Hein [340]
DENVER LAW CENTER JOURNAL *see*
- DENVER UNIVERSITY LAW REVIEW
- DICTA

DENVER LAW JOURNAL *see*
- DENVER UNIVERSITY LAW REVIEW
- DICTA

THE DENVER LAW JOURNAL – v1-2. 1883-84 – 9 – $8.00 – LLMC 82-921 – us L.L.M.C. [073]
DENVER LEGAL NEWS – v1-2. 1887-89 – 1 – $40.00 – us Hein [073]
DENVER POST – 1979- With index – 1 – us UMI [071]
Denver Public Library *see* CATALOG OF THE CONSERVATION LIBRARY
Denver. Public Library *see* CATALOG OF THE WESTERN HISTORY DEPARTMENT
THE DENVER STAR – Denver. Colo. aug. 7, 1926; Feb. 14, 1942 – 1 – us NY Public [071]
DENVER UNIVERSITY LAW REVIEW – (v1-62 1923-85 on reel $700.00. v63-72 1986-95 on mf $239.00. Title varies: v1-39, 1923-62 as Dicta. v40-42 1963-65 as Denver Law Center Journal. v43-61 1966-83 as Denver Law Journal) – v1-72. 1923-95 – 5,6,9 – $939.00 set – us Hein [340]
DENVER UNIVERSITY LAW REVIEW *see* DICTA
Deny, J *see* GRAMMAIRE DE LA LANGUE TURQUE
DENZ STUDENTA – (Includes c.1: 1930:Dec.) – Kharbin: Izd. Russkago studencheskago obshchestva, 1930- – 1 – CSUXANR2034-S – us Hoover Inst Photo [370]
DENZIL PLACE : A STORY IN VERSE / Fane, Violet – London: Chapman and Hall, 1875 – 1 roll – 1 – 1-55879-689-4 – uk Libr Preservation [830]
DENZIL QUARRIER : A NOVEL / Gissing, George Robert – London: Lawrence and Bullen, 1892 – 1 roll – 1 – 1-55879-755-6 – uk Libr Preservation [830]
Depambour, J *see* DES EFFETS DE L'OCCUPATION...
Deparcieux, M *see* ESSAY ON THE PROBABILITIES OF THE DURATION OF HUMAN LIFE
O DEPARTAMENTO – Cidade de Seabra, Acre. 15 Nov 1914-2 Abr 1916 – 1,5,6 – bl Biblioteca [072]
Departemen Perindustrian *see* BERITA INDUSTRI
LE DEPARTEMENT DE LA MEURTHE: STATISTIQUE, HISTORIQUE ET ADMINISTRATIVE / Lepage, Henri – Nancy: Peiffer, 1843. 2v. 12 fiches. (Statistics Series: Topography) – 9 – 30.00 – fr Bibl Nationale [944]
Departement de sociologie, Universite Laval *see* RECHERCHES SOCIOGRAPHIQUES
Departement des Manuscrits *see* BIBLIOTHEQUE NATIONALE DEPARTEMENT DES MANUSCRITS
Departement Evangelique Francais d'Action Apostolique (DEFAP), Paris *see*
- DOCUMENTARY HISTORY OF THE BASOTHO (LESOTHO)
- PARIS EVANGELICAL MISSIONARY SOCIETY ARCHIVES 1822-1935

DEPARTMENT BULLETINS / U.S. Department of Agriculture – Nos. 1-1500. 1913-29. 1611 fiches – 9 – $2000.00 – us Updata [630]
Department of Defence 1 *see* NOMINAL ROLLS OF BATTALIONS FOR SERVICE IN SOUTH AFRICA, 1902-1902
Department of Defence, Victoria *see*
- ENROLMENTS FORMS OF VICTORIAN CONTINGENTS, 1899-1900
- NOMINAL ROLL OF BETHUNE'S MOUNTED INFANTRY FOR SERVICE IN THE BOER WAR, 1899-1901
- NOMINAL ROLLS OF VICTORIAN CONTINGENTS FOR SOUTH AFRICA, 1900-1900

Department of External Affairs 1, Melbourne *see* VOLUMES OF DUPLICATE CERTIFICATES OF NATURALIZATION, 1904-1917
DEPARTMENT OF HEALTH, EDUCATION AND WELFARE (1963-1969) / U.S. Department of Health, Education and Welfare – (Part 1: History $580.0; Part 2: Documents $1,060.00) – 1983. (Presidential Documents Series) – 1 – 0-89093-390-1 – us UPA [360]
DEPARTMENT OF HEALTH, EDUCATION AND WELFARE ANNUAL REPORTS / U.S. Department of Health and Human Services – (Agencies within HEW publ reports subsequent to 1970) – 1953-70 (all publ) – 71mf – 9 – $106.00 – LLMC 81-207 – us L.L.M.C. [360]
Department of Home and Territories, Central Office *see*
- DUPLICATE CERTIFICATES OF NATURALISATION, 'A' SERIES, 1917-1921
- DUPLICATE CERTIFICATES OF NATURALISATION, 'AA' SERIES, 1921-1937
- DUPLICATE CERTIFICATES OF NATURALISATION, 'B' SERIES, 1917-1921
- DUPLICATE CERTIFICATES OF NATURALISATION, 'BB' SERIES, 1921-1937
- DUPLICATE CERTIFICATES OF NATURALISATION, 'C' SERIES, 1918-1921
- DUPLICATE CERTIFICATES OF NATURALISATION, 'CC' SERIES, 1921-1937
- DUPLICATE CERTIFICATES OF NATURALISATION, 'D' SERIES, 1921-1936
- DUPLICATE CERTIFICATES OF NATURALISATION, 'E' SERIES AND 'F' SERIES, 1921-1936

DEPARTMENT OF HORTICULTURE RESEARCH SERIES / Clemson University. Agricultural Experiment Station – No.126-209. 1970-82 – 1,5 – us Spaulding [580]
DEPARTMENT OF HOUSING AND URBAN DEVELOPMENT ANNUAL REPORTS / U.S. Department of Housing and Urban Development – (Updates planned) – 1st-18th. 1965-82 – 25mf – 9 – $37.50 – LLMC 81-210 – us L.L.M.C. [360]
Department of Justice, Office of Information & Privacy *see* FREEDOM OF INFORMATION CASELIST
Department of Justice, Office of Justice Programs *see* TASK FORCE ON FELON IDENTIFICATION IN FIREARM SALES REPORT TO THE A.G.
DEPARTMENT OF LABOR ANNUAL REPORTS / U.S. Department of Labor – 1913-80 – 9 – LLMC 80-620 – us L.L.M.C. [331]
DEPARTMENT OF SEED CERTIFICATION RESEARCH SERIES / Clemson University. Agricultural Experiment Station – No.4. 1971. 1 reel – 1,5 – us Spaulding [631]
DEPARTMENT OF STATE BULLETIN / U.S. Department of State – (Includes indexes nos 1-2141. Cont by: Department of State Dispatch) – v1-89. 1939-89 (all publ) – 1029mf – 9 – $1,543.00 – LLMC 79-446 – us L.L.M.C. [324]
DEPARTMENT OF STATE BULLETIN *see* DEPARTMENT OF STATE DISPATCH
DEPARTMENT OF STATE DISPATCH – (Cont: Department of State Bulletin. Updates planned) – v1-3. 1990-92 – 55mf – 9 – $82.00 – LLMC 79-446B – us L.L.M.C. [340]
DEPARTMENT OF STATE DISPATCH *see* DEPARTMENT OF STATE BULLETIN
DEPARTMENT OF STATE OFFICE OF THE LEGAL ADVISER : OPINIONS AND REPORTS, 1866-1950 – 1992- – 39r – 5 – $2,925.00 set – us Hein [327]
DEPARTMENT OF STATE TREATY PUBLICATIONS *see*
- BEVAN'S TREATIES
- MILLER'S TREATIES
- TREATIES AND CONVENTIONS CONCLUDED BETWEEN THE U.S. AND OTHER POWERS SINCE JULY 4 1776
- THE TREATY SERIES
- UNITED STATES TREATIES AND OTHER INTERNATIONAL AGREEMENTS

THE DEPARTMENT OF TEACHER TRAINING : ITS WORK AND ORGANIZATION / Thailand. Ministry of Education – Bangkok, 1973 – 1mf – 9 – DE-282/1 – ne IDC [370]
DEPARTMENT OF THE ARMY PAMPHLETS / U.S. Army. Office of Military History – 7rolls. T1108 – 1 – us Nat'l Archives [355]
DEPARTMENT OF THE INTERIOR ANNUAL REPORTS – 9 – LLMC 94-297 – us L.L.M.C. [340]
DEPARTMENT REPORT / Nebraska. College of Agriculture. Dept. of Agricultural Economics – n.1-16. 1967-69 – 1,5 – us Spaulding [630]
DEPARTMENT REPORTS OF THE STATE OF NEW YORK : CONTAINING DECISIONS, OPINIONS AND RULINGS OF THE STATE OFFICERS, DEPARTMENTS, BOARDS AND COMMISSIONS AND MESSAGES OF THE GOVERNOR / New York State. Executive Branch – (Indexes for v1-4 (1931)) – Albany: Lyon Co/State. v1-74. 1914-1954 – 636mf – 9 – $954.00 – LLMC 94-108 – us L.L.M.C. [340]
DEPARTMENTAL BULLETIN / Wisconsin. College of Agriculture. Dept. of Dairy Science – n.1-2. Jun 1964-Jun 1966 – 1,5 – us Spaulding [630]
DEPARTMENTAL COOPERATION IN STATE GOVERNMENT / Ellingwood, Albert R – New York: The Macmillan Co, 1918 – us Res Libr [350]
DEPARTMENTAL INFORMATION REPORT / Texas A & M University. College of Agriculture.Department of Agricultural Economics – 70-1 – 82-2. 1970-82 – 1,5 – us Spaulding [630]
DEPARTMENTAL INFORMATION REPORT / Texas A & M University. Department of Poultry Science – 1-6M. 1964-68. 2 fiches – 9 – us Spaulding [630]
DEPARTMENTAL INFORMATION REPORT / Texas A & M University. Department of Recreation and Parks – No.1-8. 1970-77. 4 fiches – 9 – us Spaulding [630]
DEPARTMENTAL INFORMATION REPORT; DEPARTMENTAL TECHNICAL REPORT; PROGRESS REPORT / Texas A & M University. Department of Soil and Crop Sciences – No.1-81/12. 1964-82. 34 fiches – 9 – us Spaulding [630]
DEPARTMENTAL SERIES / Auburn University. Agricultural Experiment Station – No.1-77.1971-81 – 1, 5 – us Spaulding [630]
DEPARTMENTAL TECHNICAL REPORT / Texas A & M University. College of Agriculture.Department of Agricultural Economics – 70-1 – 82-2. 1970-82 – 1,5 – us Spaulding [630]
DEPARTMENTAL TECHNICAL REPORT / Texas A & M University. Department of Animal Science – No.2-103. 1965-77. 8 fiches – 9 – us Spaulding [630]
DEPARTMENTAL TECHNICAL REPORT / Texas A & M University. Department of Entomology – No1-24. 1964-75. 11 fiches – 9 – us Spaulding [630]
DEPARTMENTAL TECHNICAL REPORT / Texas A & M University. Department of Recreation and Parks – No.1-6. 1969-74. 4 fiches – 9 – us Spaulding [630]
DEPAUL BUSINESS LAW JOURNAL – v1-7. 1989-1995 – 9 – $84.00 set – us Hein [340]
DEPAUL LAW REVIEW – (v1-34 1951-84 on reel $470.00. v35-45 1985-95 on mf $219.00) – v1-45. 1951-95 – 5,6,9 – $689.00 set – us Hein [340]
DePauw, Karen P *see*
- THE EFFECTS OF GLASNOST AND PERESTROIKA ON THE SOVIET SPORT SYSTEM
- FEMININITY AND MASCULINITY

DEPECHE – London, UK. 23 Sept 1914-28 Jan 1915 – 1 – uk British Libr Newspaper [072]
LA DEPECHE AFRICAINE – no. 8-9, 11-14. Paris. oct 1928-avr 1932 – 1 – fr A.C.R.P.P. [073]
LA DEPECHE AFRICAINE – (Filmed with Les continents and 11 other titles) – Paris: Maurice Satineau, feb 1928-jul 1931; feb 1932; jan 1938 – 1r – us Res Libr [072]
LA DEPECHE ALGERIENNE – Alger. 1908-21 – 1 – fr A.C.R.P.P. [073]
LA DEPECHE COLONIALE – puis et maritime. suite de: Tablettes coloniales. devenu: France – Outre-mer. Paris. aout 1896-juin 1940 – 1 – fr A.C.R.P.P. [073]
DEPECHE COLONIALE ILLUSTREE – 1903-1905 – 1 – us Res Libr [073]
LA DEPECHE DE CONSTANTINE – Constantine. 15 nov 1908-fevr 1914, 1915, 28-29 nov 1920, juil 1922-1939, 1954-62 – 1 – fr A.C.R.P.P. [949]
DEPECHE DE LONDRES – London, UK. 5 Jul 1903 – 1 – uk British Libr Newspaper [072]
LA DEPECHE DE TAHITI – Papeete.Dir., Ph. Mazellier. aout 1964-1993 – 1 – fr A.C.R.P.P. [073]
LA DEPECHE DE TOULOUSE – Toulouse. 1885-1940 – 1 – fr A.C.R.P.P. [073]
LA DEPECHE (DEMOCRATIQUE) : GRAND JOURNAL REGIONAL D'INFORMATION – Quot., Saint-Etienne (Loire); plusieurs ed. locales; janv. 1946-dec. 1956 – 51r – 1 – F38,895.11 – fr Armell [073]
LA DEPECHE DEMOCRATIQUE – Saint-Etienne. 4 sept 1944-45 – 1 – fr A.C.R.P.P. [073]
LA DEPECHE DU MIDI – Toulouse. avr 1969-1987 – 1 – fr A.C.R.P.P. [072]
LA DEPECHE DU MIDI – Toulouse: [s.n.], 1953-mar 1969 – 130r – 1 – us Res Libr [072]
LA DEPECHE MAROCAINE – Tangier, Morocco. -d. 5 Aug 1916-23 Dec 1918. Imperfect. 4 reels – 1 – uk British Libr Newspaper [072]
LES DEPECHES – Montreal, Canada. 28 avr 1907 – 1r – 1 – Can$25.00 – cn Can Microfilming [072]
DEPECHES DU SECRETAIRE DE SA MAJESTE POUR LES COLONIES ET AUTRES DOCUMENTS RELATIFS A L'UNION FEDERALE DES COLONIES BRITANIQUES DE L'AMERIQUE DU NORD. / Canada. Parliament. Legislative Assembly – Toronto: Imprime par Stewart Derbishire et George Desbarats, 1859. SEM105P165 – 1mf – 9 – Can$2.25 – cn Bibl Nat [324]
DEPECHES DU SECRETAIRE DE SA MAJESTE POUR LES COLONIES, ET AUTRES DOCUMENTS RELATIFS AU SIEGE DU GOUVERNEMENT. / Canada. Parliament. Legislative Assembly – Toronto: Imprime par Stewart Derbishire & George Desbarats, 1859. SEM105P164 – 1mf – 9 – Can$2.25 – cn Bibl Nat [324]
DEPECHOS LEGALES...TIERRA SANTA / Garcia, Manuel – 1814 – 9 – 1.50f – sp Bibl Santa Ana [340]
LES DEPENDANCES DE L'ABBAYE DE SAINT-GERMAIN-DES-PRES / Anger, D – Tom. 1: Seine et Seine-et-Marne, 1906 – Dfl30.00 – ne Slangenburg [240]

LES DEPENDANCES DE L'ABBAYE DE SAINT-GERMAIN-DES-PRES / Anger, D – Tom. 2: Seine-et-Oise. Paris, 1907 – Dfl28.00 – ne Slangenburg [240]
LES DEPENDANCES DE L'ABBAYE DE SAINT-GERMAIN-DES-PRES / Anger, D – Tome 2. 1909 – Dfl35.00 – ne Slangenburg [240]
DEPENDENCE, OR, THE INSECURITY OF THE ANGLICAN POSITION / Rivington, Luke – London: K. Paul, Trench, 1889 – 1mf – us A.T.L.A. [240]
EL DEPENDIENTE EXTREMENO – Merida, 1921. 1 numero – 5 – sp Bibl Santa Ana [073]
DIE DEPESCHEN DES NUNTIUS ALEANDER VOM WORMSER REICHSTAGE 1521 / Aleandro, Girolamo; ed by Kalkoff, Paul – Halle: Verein fuer Reformationsgeschichte, 1886. ([Schriften des Vereins fuer Reformationsgeschichte; Bd. 17]) – 1mf – us A.T.L.A. [240]
Depew, Chauncy M *see* MY MEMORIES OF EIGHTY YEARS
DePeyster, John Watts *see*
- THE LIFE AND MISFORTUNES AND THE MILITARY CAREER OF BRIGADE GENERAL SIR JOHN JOHNSON, BART
- WATERLOO: THE CAMPAIGN AND BATTLE
DePiano, Frank *see* JOURNAL OF CHILD AND ADOLESCENT SUBSTANCE ABUSE
Depinay, J *see* LE REGIME DOTAL...
Depince, M Ch *see* COMPTE-RENDU DES TRAVAUX
Depitre, M *see*
- ESSAI SUR LE SYSTEME ANGLAIS DE CONFLITS DE LOIS EN MATIERE DE SUCCESSIONS
Deplace, G M *see* OBSERVATIONS GRAMMATICALES
Depoin, J *see*
- HISTOIRE ET CARTULAIRE DE L'ABBAYE DEMALBUISSON
- RECUEIL DE CHARTES ET DOCUMENTS DE SAINT-MARTIN-DES-CHAMPS
- RECUEIL DE CHARTRES ET DOCUMENTS DE SAINT-MARTIN-DES-CHAMPS
DEPORTATIONS FROM BELGIUM DURING WORLD WAR 1 PAMPHLET COLLECTION – 1916-1918 – 1 – CSUXANL5296-B – us Hoover Inst Photo [360]
DEPORTATIONS FROM LITHUANIA DURING WORLD WAR 2 PAMPHLET COLLECTION – 1981 – 1 – CSUXANL3588-B – us Hoover Inst Photo [360]
DEPORTATIONS FROM POLAND DURING WORLD WAR 1 PAMPHLET COLLECTION – 1943-1979 – 1 – CSUXANL3602-B – us Hoover Inst Photo [360]
EL DEPOSITO DE MUJER CASADA EXTRANJERA... / Garcia Herreros, E – Madrid, 1906 – 1mf – 1 – ILM-3374/1 – ne IDC [327]
Deppe, Oskar *see* SCHILLERS "XENIEN" UND "TABULAE VOTIVAE" IM MUSENALMANACH FUER 1797
Deppert, Fritz *see* SCHULD UND UEBERWINDUNG DER SCHULD IN DEN DRAMEN ERNST BARACHS
Depres, Josquin *see*
- MISSARUM JOSQUIN LIBER PRIMUS
- MISSARUM JOSQUIN LIBER SECUNDUS
- MISSARUM JOSQUIN LIBER TERTIUS
DEPRESSIONS: THEIR CAUSE AND CURE / Rothbard, Murray N – 1fiche (29x) – 9 – 1.00f – at Libertarian Micro [320]
Deprez, M *see* DE LA COMPLICITE...
Dept. Penerangan IPNU wil. Djk. Raya *see* CHAZANAH; SUARA SANTRI DAN SISWA PROGESIP
DEPTFORD AND PECKHAM MERCURY – London, England. -w. April-Dec 1981. 2 reels – 1 – uk British Libr Newspaper [072]
AO DEPUTADO MONTEIRO DE SOUSA : HOMENAGEM – Manaos, Amazonas. Jan 1910 – 1,5,6 – bl Biblioteca [072]
LE DEPUTE EN BLOUSE / Montuses, Ernest – Nevers. 1913. (La Condition Ouvriere. Part Two.) – 9 – 2.50 – fr Bibl Nationale [360]
LES DEPUTES A L'ASSEMBLEE LEGISLATIVE DE 1791 / Kuscinski, Auguste – Paris, 1900. Ste de l'histoire de la Revolution francaise – 1mf – 9 – F30.00 – fr F.F.G. [323]
LES DEPUTES AUX CORPS LEGISLATIFS, CONSEIL DES CINQ CENTS, CONSEIL DES ANCIENS DE L'AN 4 A L'AN 7 / Kuscinski, Auguste – Paris, 1905. Ste de l'histoire de la Revolution francaise – 2mf – 9 – F60.00 – fr F.F.G. [944]
DEPUTY KEEPERS' REPORTS 1869-1931 – 96mf – 1 – Ir£100.00 – ie Microforms [350]
Der Nersessian, S *see* MANUSCRITS ARMENIENS ILLUSTRES DES 12E, 13E ET 14E SIECLES DE LA BIBLIOTHEQUE DES PERES MEKHITARISTES DE VENISE
Deraismes, Maria *see*
- LES DROITS DE L'INFANT
- EPIDEMIE NATURALISTE
- EVE DANS L'HUMANITE
Deramey, J-P *see* PRECIS DU MOUVEMENT CATHOLIQUE-LIBERAL DANS LE JURA BERNOIS, 1873-74
Derand, Francois *see* L'ARCHITECTURE DES VOUTES, OU L'ART DES TRAITS ET COUPE DE VOUTES.
Derbes, A *see* MEMOIRE SUR QUELQUES POINTS DE LA PHYSIOLOGIE DES ALGUES
DERBY CLUB : ORGAM SOCIEDADE – Manaus, Amazonas. 23 Jul 1910; 2 Jun 1911 – 1,5,6 – bl Biblioteca [072]
Derby, Elias Hasket *see*
- THE CATHOLIC
- LETTER TO THE HON. WILLIAM H. SEWARD, SECRETARY OF STATE: IN ANSWER TO ONE FROM HIM ON THE RESOLUTION OF THE SENATE AS TO THE RELATIONS OF THE UNITED STATES WITH THE BRITISH PROVINCES: AND THE ACTUAL CONDITION OF THE QUESTION OF THE FISHERIES
DERBY EXPRESS – 1889; Oct 22-Dec 1894; Sep 1924; Jun 19-Dec 25 1986; Jan 8-Jun 25 1987; Jul 1987-96 – 38r – 1 – uk British Libr Newspaper [072]
Derby, George Horatio *see* PHOENIXIANA; OR, SKETCHES AND BURLESQUES
Derby, John Sayward *see* A LEGAL MONOGRAPH UPON PROVISIONAL REMEDIES UNDER THE CODE
DERBYSHIRE, 1822 : BRITISH ISLES CENSUS DIRECTORIES PROJECT, ENGLAND – (In prep) – at Vine [941]
DERBYSHIRE, 1835 : BRITISH ISLES CENSUS DIRECTORIES PROJECT ENGLAND, VOL 44 – 1mf – 9 – A$9.00 – at Vine [941]
DERBYSHIRE, 1848 : BRITISH ISLES CENSUS DIRECTORIES PROJECT, ENGLAND – at Vine [941]
DERBYSHIRE, 1850 : BRITISH ISLES CENSUS DIRECTORIES PROJECT, ENGLAND – at Vine [941]
DERBYSHIRE, 1857 : BRITISH ISLES CENSUS DIRECTORIES PROJECT ENGLAND, VOL 83 – 5mf – 9 – A$33.00 – at Vine [941]
DERBYSHIRE, 1888 : BRITISH ISLES CENSUS DIRECTORIES PROJECT, ENGLAND – at Vine [941]
DERBYSHIRE, 1895 : BRITISH ISLES CENSUS DIRECTORIES PROJECT ENGLAND, VOL 42 – 6mf – 9 – A$39.00 – at Vine [941]
DERBYSHIRE, 1908 : BRITISH ISLES CENSUS DIRECTORIES PROJECT, ENGLAND – at Vine [941]
DERBYSHIRE, 1916 : BRITISH ISLES CENSUS DIRECTORIES PROJECT, ENGLAND – at Vine [941]
DERBYSHIRE AND LEICESTERSHIRE EXAMINER – Derby, Burton-on-Trent and Wolverhampton. England. -w. 13 Sep 1873-17 Aug 1877. (3 reels) – 1 – uk British Libr Newspaper [072]
Derbyshire Archaeological and Natural History Society *see* JOURNAL OF THE DERBYSHIRE ARCHAEOLOGICAL AND NATURAL HISTORY SOCIETY
DERBYSHIRE (CHESTERFIELD), 1849 : BRITISH ISLES CENSUS DIRECTORIES PROJECT, ENGLAND – (In prep) – at Vine [941]
DERBYSHIRE (CHESTERFIELD AND DERBY), 1805 : BRITISH ISLES CENSUS DIRECTORIES PROJECT, ENGLAND. VOL 173 – 1mf – 9 – A$9.00 – at Vine [941]
DERBYSHIRE COURIER – Chesterfield, England. 12 Dec 1829; 1 Jan 1831-Dec 1853.-w. 8 reels – 1 – uk British Libr Newspaper [072]
DERBYSHIRE (FAR NORTH WEST), 1832 : BRITISH ISLES CENSUS DIRECTORIES PROJECT, ENGLAND. VOL 192 – 1mf – 9 – A$9.00 – at Vine [941]
DERBYSHIRE (GLOSSOP), 1825 : BRITISH ISLES CENSUS DIRECTORIES PROJECT, ENGLAND. VOL 148 – 1mf – 9 – A$9.00 – at Vine [941]
DERBYSHIRE (NORTH), 1852 : BRITISH ISLES CENSUS DIRECTORIES PROJECT, ENGLAND. VOL 257 – 2mf – 9 – A$15.00 – at Vine [941]
DERBYSHIRE (NORTH), 1868 : BRITISH ISLES CENSUS DIRECTORIES PROJECT ENGLAND, VOL 24 – 1mf – 9 – A$9.00 – at Vine [941]
HET DERDE BOECK DER CHRISTLIJCKER SENDBRIEVEN / Joris, David – Brieven van 1542-56. 1611. BME-384 1 – 9 – ne IDC [240]
DERECH LETSION – Eindhoven, 1930. Nos 1-3 – 1mf – J-261-24/1 – ne IDC [073]
EL DERECHO DE BELIGERANCIA. LA VOZ DEL ESTADO ESPANOL CONTRA LA MEDIACION. NO CABE MEDIACION EN LA GUERRA ESPANOLA. JUGANDO CON FUEGO – n.p. 1938. Fiche W 828. (Blodgett Collection of Spanish Civil War Pamphlets) – 9 – us H.U. College Libr [946]
EL DERECHO DE CONQUISTA... / Guzman, S V – Buenos Aires, 1881 – 3mf – 1 – ILM-543/1 – ne IDC [327]
DERECHO DE PRENSA : ENSAYO SISTEMATICO SOBRE LA LIBERTAD DE IMPRENTA / Ballester, Eliel C – Buenos Aires: El Ateneo, 1947 – 1 – CSUXADJ9183-B – us Hoover Inst Photo [070]
DERECHO DEL TRABAJO; REVISTA CRITICA MENSUAL DE JURISPRUDENCIA – Buenos Aires. Ano. 2, no. 1-4, no. 3; Ano. 7-26. Jan 1942-Mar 1944; 1947-1966 & Repertorio 1956 65 – 1 – us NY Public [073]
DERECHO DIPLOMATICO... / Albertini, L E – Paris, 1866 – 5mf – 9 – ILM-410/1 – ne IDC [340]
DERECHO DIPLOMATICO Y... / Guesalaga, A – Buenos Aires, 1900 – 5mf – 1 – ILM-542/1 – ne IDC [327]
EL DERECHO FLUVIAL INTERNACIONAL / Carlomagno, J C – Buenos Aires, 1913 – 3mf – 1 – ILM-2349/1 – ne IDC [327]
DERECHO HISPANICO Y "COMMON LAW" EN PUERTO RICO / Mouchet, Carlos – Buenos Aires: Perrot, 1953. 134p. LL-8017 – 1 – us L of C Photodup [340]
DERECHO INTERNACIONAL / Gerardo Marquez, D – Puebla, 1875 – 2mf – 1 – ILM-3726/1 – ne IDC [327]
DERECHO INTERNACIONAL CONVENCIONAL / Arbo, H – Asuncion, 1928 – 3mf – 9 – ILM-2299/1 – ne IDC [340]
DERECHO INTERNACIONAL MARITIMO / Benites, J E – N.p, 1932 – 3mf – 9 – ILM-1622/1 – ne IDC [327]
DERECHO INTERNACIONAL PRIVADO : BOLILLAS 17 Y 18 – Buenos Aires, 1908 – 1mf – 1 – ILM-3805/1 – ne IDC [327]
DERECHO MARITIMO... / Chucarro, E M – Montevideo, 1931 – 9mf – 1 – ILM-2576/1 – ne IDC [327]
DERECHO MERCANTIL DE ESPANA / Carreras y Gonzalez, M & Revilla, L Gonzalez – Ed 7. Madrid, 1910 – 6mf – 1 – ILM-3976/1 – ne IDC [327]
DERECHO PENAL INTERNACIONAL / Diaz, M P – Madrid, 1911 – 3mf – 1 – ILM-2271/1 – ne IDC [327]
DERECHO PENAL ISLAMICO, ESCUELA MALEKITA / Arevalo, Rafael – Tanger, F. Erola, 1939. 188 p. LL-12021 – 1 – us L of C Photodup [340]
EL DERECHO PUBLICO... / Esteva Ruiz, R A – Mexico, 1911 – 1mf – 1 – ILM-379/1 – ne IDC [327]
DERECHO SINDICAL Y CORPORATIVO / Cabanellas, Guillermo – Buenos Aires: Editorial Atalaya, [1946] – 1 – CSUXAJL9747-B – us Hoover Inst Photo [338]
LOS DERECHOS DEL TRABAJADOR / Consoli, Maximiliano – [Buenos Aires]: Editorial Viracocha, 1948 – 1 – CSUXADQ0645-B – us Hoover Inst Photo [331]
DERECHOS HUMANOS Y SERVICIOS LEGALES EN EL CAMPO – 1988 – sz I.C.J. [340]
Derenboug, H *see* MELANGES
Derenbourg, Hartwig *see*
- LES MANUSCRITS ARABES DE L'ESCURIAL
- OUSAMA IBN MOUNKIDH
- QUELQUES OBSERVATIONS SUR L'ANTIQUITE DE LA DECLINAISON DANS LES LANGUES SEMITIQUES
Derenbourg, J *see* MASSA EREZ YISRA'EL. SPB., 1896-1897
Derenbourg, Joseph *see* MANUEL DU LECTEUR, D'UN AUTEUR INCONNU
Derendinger, L *see* AUTOUR DE MELFI. LES IAL-NAS
Derennes, Gustave *see* LE DRAPEAU DE CANADA
Derevenko, N N *see* GOD RABOTY PO SNABZHENIIU ZHELEZNYKH DOROG TOPLIVOM
DEREVENSKAI A BI EDNOTA – (Includes c.1: 1917:Nov.9, Dec.1, 5-9; 1918:Jan.11) – [Petrograd]: Voennai a organizat sii a pri t s.k.r.s.-d.r.p., 19uu – 2r – 1 – CSUXANR2400-S – us Hoover Inst Photo [947]
DEREVENSKAI A BI EDNOTA I TRUDOVOE KAZACHESTVO *see* DEREVENSKAI A BI EDNOTA
DEREVENSKAI A PRAVDA – (Includes c.1: 1921:Nov.7) – Petrograd: Izd. Petrogradskogo gubernskogo komiteta Rossi isko i kommunistichesko i partii, 1921-1922 – 1 – CSUXAHZ5890-S – us Hoover Inst Photo [947]
DEREVENSKAIA KOOPERATSIIA – Ivano-Voznesensk, 1925-26 n1 – 8mf – 9 – COR-582/1 – ne IDC [334]
DEREVENSKAIA KOOPERATSIIA / Kulyzhnyi, A E – (Vzaimnaia pomoshch 'pod. red. I. Gorbunova – Posadova. Pt 12. 274p) – M., [1909] – 3mf – 9 – COR-55/1 – ne IDC [334]
DEREVENSKAYA BEDNOTA – Leningrad. USSR. -d. 9, 17 Nov-14 Dec 1917. (1 reel) – 1 – uk British Libr Newspaper [947]
DEREVENSKI I KOMMUNAR : ORGAN GRI AZOVET SKOGO UEZDNOGO KOMITETA PARTII KOMMUNISTOV-BOLSHEVIKOV – (Includes c.1: 1917:Nov.7; 1922:Mar.11) – Gri azovet s: Komitet, 19uu – 1 – CSUXANR2270-S – us Hoover Inst Photo [335]
DERGAH – Istanbul, 1.-4. cilt, nos 1-42. – 15 Nisan 1337-5 Kanunisani 1339 [April 1921-Jan. 1924] – 14mf – 9 – $100.00 – us MEDOC [949]
Derham, Walter *see* A VISIT TO CAPE COLONY AND NATAL IN 1879
De'Ricci, Caterina, Saint *see* LE LETTERE DI SANTA CATERINA DE'RICCI
Derigo, G A *see* BIOGRAPHY OF WILLIAM SHERMAN WILEY
Dering, Richard *see* MUSIC PART BOOKS
Derive, J *see* LE FONCTIONNEMENT SOCIOLOGIQUE DE LA LITTERATURE ORALE
Derleth, Kurt *see* DIE RELIGIOESE ENTWICKLUNG GOTTFRIED KELLERS IM HINBLICK AUF DEN NATUR-KULTUR-BEGRIFF SEINES GEREIFTEN WELTBILDES
Dermassen, Bern *see* VERTRIEB ANARCHISTISCHER LITERATUR
DERMATOLOGIC CLINICS – 1983- – 1,5,6,9 – us UMI [616]
DERMATOLOGICA – v79-109.1939-54 – 1,5,6 – us Princeton Micro [616]
DERMATOLOGY – v150-. 1975- – 1,5,9 – us UMI [616]
LA DERNIER ANNEAU DE LA QUEUE DE ROBESPIERRE – Paris: Imp de Lacour, 1848 – us Res Libr [944]
LE DERNIER CHANT DES SERINS SIC DE LAVAL / Beausoleil, Joseph Maxime – Montreal, 1890. 03529. (Pre-1900 Canadiana) – 9 – cn C.I.H.M. [971]
LA DERNIER CONSEIL DU PERE DUCHESNE AUX ELECTEURS – Montmartre: Imp Pilloy freres et Ce, 1849 – us Res Libr [944]
LE DERNIER CRI DE LA VERITE SUR LA REVOLUTION FRANCAISE / Thiery, Avocat – La Haye; Paris. 1791 – 9 – fr Hachette [944]
LE DERNIER DES MARTYRS / Frechette, Louis-Honore – s.l.: s.n., 1885?. 03229. (Pre-1900 Canadiana) – 9 – cn C.I.H.M. [971]
DERNIER MOT SUR LA PRESIDENCE : OR, CANDIDATURE COMPARES DE MM BONAPARTE ET CAVAIGNAC – Paris, [1848?] – us Res Libr [944]
UN DERNIER MOT SUR L'EMANCIPATION DES SERFS EN RUSSIE / Tourgueniev, Nicolas Ivanovitch – (Russia – 19th C. series). 1860 – 9 – fr Hachette [305]
UN DERNIER MOT SUR LES BIENS DES JESUITES – Montreal: s.n, 1888. SEM105P454 – 1mf – 9 – Can$2.25 – cn Bibl Nat [240]
LE DERNIER MOT SUR LES FEMMES...CONNAIS-TOI TOI-MEME / Larcher, Louis Julien – Paris: Achille Faure, 1864. 96p. (Miscellaneous Selections) – 2mf – 9 – $6.00 – fr Bibl Nationale [360]
LE DERNIER RAPPORT D'UN EUROPEEN SUR GHAT ET LES TOUAREG DE L'AIR : JOURNAL DE VOYAGE D'ERWIN DE BARY, 1876-1877 / Bary, Erwin de – Paris: Librarie Fischbacher, 1898 – 1 – us Res Libr [910]

DERNIERE HEURE / ed by Cote, Roland – Montreal, Canada. 3 oct 1965-15 jan 1984 – 28r – 1 – Can$65.00r – cn Can Microfilming [072]

DERNIERE HEURE – Montreal, Canada. v1 n2. 8 jun 1945 – 1r – 1 – Can$25.00 – cn Can Microfilming [072]

LA DERNIERE JOURNEE DE SAPPHO / Faure, Gabriel – Paris: Mercure de France, 1901. 212p. (Les Femmes Collection) – 3mf – 9 – $8.00 – fr Bibl Nationale [830]

DERNIERES DECOUVERTES DANS L'AMERIQUE SEPTENTRIONALE DE M. DE LA SALLE / Tonti, Henri de – Paris au Palais: Jean Guignard, 1697. SEM105P17 – 4mf – 9 – Can$9.00 – cn Bibl Nat [910]

LES DERNIERES EXPLORATIONS DU DOCTEUR ALFRED PENEY DANS LA REGION DU HAUT FLEUVE BLANC / Malte-Brun, Victor Adolphe – Paris, Imprimerie de E. Martinet. 1863 – 9 – 5.00 – fr Orientalistes [910]

LES DERNIERES NOUVELLES D'ALSACE – (Bilingue. Toutes eds. 1959-81. 1. Strasbourg-ville. 1969-81. 1) – Strasbourg, France. Toutes eds.21 dec 1944-1987 – 1 – fr A.C.R.P.P. [072]

LES DERNIERES NOUVELLES DU LUNDI – Strasbourg, France. Toutes eds.1961-84 – 1 – fr A.C.R.P.P. [072]

LES DERNIERES PERSECUTIONS DU TROISIEME SIECLE (GALLUS, VAKERIEN, AURELIEN) / Allard, Paul – Paris: V. Lecoffre, 1907 – 2mf – us A.T.L.A. [240]

DERNIERS ADIEUX DE GRAZIELLA: SUIVIS DE QUELQUES AUTRES POESIES DETACHEES / Baillairge, Maurice – Quebec: Typographie de C. Darveau, 1879.00091.(Pre-1900 Canadiana) – 9 – cn C.I.H.M. [810]

DERNIERS AVIS A SES JEUNES PRETRES. / Bourget, Ignace – Montreal: J. Holland, 1877. 00212. (Pre-1900 Canadiana) – 9 – cn C.I.H.M. [240]

LES DERNIERS BARBARES : CHINE, TIBET, MONGOLIE... / Ollone, Charles-A – 4e ed. Paris. Lafitte, 1911 – 1 – F192.61 – fr Armell [305]

LES DERNIERS JOURS – Cahier politique et litteraire. Redige par Pierre Drieu la Rochelle et Emmanuel Berl. no. 1-7. Paris. fevr-juil 1927 – 1 – fr A.C.R.P.P. [073]

LES DERNIERS JOURS DE L'ACADIE, 1748-1758 – Correspondances et memoires: extraits du portefeuille de M. Le Courtois de Surlaville...mis en order et annotes par Gaston Du Boscq de Beaumont. Paris: E. Lechevalier, 1899. 02781. (Pre-1900 Canadiana) – 9 – cn C.I.H.M. [971]

LES DERNIERS PAYSANS / Souvestre, Emile – Paris. 1851. (La Condition Ouvriere. Part Two.) – 9 – 17.50 – fr Bibl Nationale [360]

DERNIERS PORTRAITS / Larroumet, Gustave – Paris: Hachette, 1904. 281p. 3 fiches.(Literature Collection) – 9 – 8.00 – fr Bibl Nationale [830]

Derouet, Camille *see*
- LES METIS CANADIENS-FRANCAIS
- LA RENAISSANCE DE LA NATIONALITE FRANCAISE EN ACADIE

Derouin, Barbara *see* ADMINISTRATIVE STRUCTURE OF ATHLETIC DEPARTMENTS AND THE IMPACT OF TITLE IX

DeRouyn, Solange *see* BIBLIOGRAPHIE SUR LE CENTRE DE SERVICE SOCIAL DU DIOCESE DES TROIS-RIVIERES

DERRICK – Bloomdale, Ohio. 1918-48 – 11r – 1 – $32.50r – us Archival [071]

DERRICK – Gibsonburg, Ohio. 1970-77 – 16r – 1 – $32.50r – us Archival [071]

DERRICK – Oil City. Pa. 1956- – 1 – us UMI [071]

DERRICK – Oil City. Pa. and Blizzard. 1871-1956 – 1 – us UMI [071]

THE DERRICK – Gibsonburg. Ohio. 1960- – 1 – us UMI [071]

DERRINALLUM NEWS AND NATTER – 1982-1992. DNN1 – 2r – 5 – at Corangamite [072]

Derrion, M *see* CONSTITUTION DE L'INDUSTRIE ET ORGANISATION PACIFIQUE DU COMMERCE ET DU TRAVAIL OU TENTATIVE D'UN FABRICANT DE LYON

A DERROCADA – Ouro Preto, 16 Nov 1893; Jun-22 Sept 1894 – 1,5,6 – bl Biblioteca [072]

LA DERROTA DE LOS PEDANTES / Fernandez de Moratin, Leandro – 1799 – 1mf – 9 – Pta1,000.00 – 84-7848-192-3 – sp Pentalfa [946]

DERROTERO...COSTAS DE ESPANA...ATLANTICO / Tofino de San Miguel, Vicente – 1849 – 9 – 1.50f – sp Bibl Santa Ana [910]

DERRY JOURNAL *see* LONDONDERRY JOURNAL

DERRY STANDARD *see* LONDONDERRY STANDARD

DERTLI – Bolu, 1919-19? – 9 – $20.00 – us MEDOC [956]

Dertli *see* DIVAN

Derumaux, M *see* ETUDE HISTORIQUE SUR L'EXTRATERRITORIALITE DE LA LOI PENALE...

Derwein, Herbert *see* HOFFMANN VON FALLERSLEBEN UND JOHANNA KAPP

DERWENT PATENT INDEXES ON MICROFICHE (COM) – (General. 1974-91. Mechanical. 1974-91. Electrical. 1974-91. Chemical. 1963-91) – Pre-1974, 1975-79, 1980-89, 1990-91, depending on subject covered. Cumulative quarterly updates. Five million patent specifications from 29 countries.Indexed by Patentee; Subject; Patent Number; Derwent Accession Number; Priority – 17 – uk Derwent [340]

Dery, Marie-Claire *see* BIBLIOGRAPHIE DE MME MARTHE LEMAIRE-DUGUAY

DERZHAVIN / Khodasevich, V – Paris. 1931. BR-694 2 – 8 – ne IDC [460]

Derzhavin, N S *see* SLAVIANE V DREVNOSTI; KUL'TURNO-ISTORICHESKII OCHERK

Des Abbayes, H *see* REVISION MONOGRAPHIQUE DES CLADONIA DU SOUS-GENRE CLADINA

DES ADELARD VON BATH TRAKTAT DE EODEM ET DIVERSO / Wilner, H – Muenster, 1903 – 2mf – 8 – Dfl3.50ea – ne Slangenburg [100]

DES AUGSBURGER PATRICIERS PHILIPP HAINHOFER BEZIEHUNGEN ZUM HERZOG PHILIPP 2 VON POMMERN-STETTIN / ed by Doering, O – (Quellenschriften fuer kunstgeschichte. n.s. v. 6. Wien. 1894). BO-517u 1 – 9 – ne IDC [700]

Des Autels, G *see* REPLIQUE AUX FURIEUSES DEFENSES DE LOUIS MEIGRET

DES BONS MOTS ET DES BONS CONTES / Callieres, F de – 1692 – 9 – fr I.C.S. [880]

DES CHAMPIGNONS AU POINT DE VUE DE LEURS CARACTERES USUELS, CHIMIQUES ET TOXICOLOGIQUES... / Boudier, E – Paris, 1866 – 136p, 2pls – 8 – ne IDC [580]

DES COLONIES ET DE LA TRAITE DES NEGRES / Belu, C – (Slave Trade and Abolitionism in France Series). 1800 – 9 – fr Hachette [360]

DES CONDITIONS D'ACCROISSEMENT DE LA POPULATION FRANCAISE COMPAREE AUX AUTRES POPULATIONS EUROPEENES / Legoyt, Alfred – Reprod. des extraits du Journal de la Societe Statistique de Paris, 1867. p166-79; 221-40. 1 fiche. (Statistics Series: Demography) – 9 – 6.00 – fr Bibl Nationale [310]

DES CONDITIONS REQUISES... / Garin, J – Paris, 1876 – 4mf – 1 – ILM-527/1 – ne IDC [327]

DES CONFLITS DE LOIS EN MATIERE DE MARIAGE AU MAROC / Franchassin, L – Toulouse, 1936 – 2mf – 1 – ILM-3011/1 – ne IDC [327]

DES CONVENTIONS NATIONALES / Condorcet, Marie Jean Antoine Nicolas de – Paris. Imprimerie du Cercle Social. 1791 – 9 – fr Hachette [321]

DES CRITISCHEN MUSICUS AN DER SPREE ESTER BAND / Marpug, Friedrich Wilhelm – Berlin: A Haude und J C Spener, 1750 – 10mf – 9 – us Sibley [780]

DES DEUTSCHEN SPIESSERS WUNDERHORN : GESAMMELTE NOVELLEN / Meyrink, Gustav – Muenchen: A Langen, 1913 – 1r – 1 – us U.W. Library [830]

DES DIFFERENTS SYSTEMES DE REPRESSION DES CRIMES ET DELITS COMMIS EN PAYS ETRANGERS... / Dumas, R – Paris, 1913 – 3mf – 1 – ILM-2060/1 – ne IDC [327]

DES DROITS ET DES DEVOIRS... / Hautefeuille, L B – Paris, 1868 – 15mf – 1 – ILM-193/1 – ne IDC [327]

Des Ecorres, Charles *see*
- EXPEDITIONS AUTOUR DE MA TENTE: BOUTADES MILITAIRES
- SAINT MAIXENT: SOUVENIRS D'ECOLE MILITAIRE

DES ELEMENTS CONSTITUTIFS DE LA SCIENCE DOGMATIQUE / Lichtenberger, Frederic – Strasbourg: Treuttel & Wurtz, 1860 – 1mf – 9 – us A.T.L.A. [240]

DES ERREURS ET DES PREJUGES / Salgues, Jacques B – Paris. 3v. 1818-25 – 1r – 1 – us Ross [370]

Des Etangs, G *see* L'ASSOLEMENT SIDERAL DE M. G. VILLE ET LA BETTERAVE A SUCRE AU CANADA: PETIT PRECIS D'AGRICULTURE PRATIQUE A L'USAGE SPECIAL DE LA PROVINCE DE QUEBEC

DES GLOBULAIRES AU POINT DE VUE BOTANIQUE ET MEDICAL / Planchon, [F]G – Montpellier, 1859 – 1mf – 9 – ne IDC [615]

DES H. EUSTATHIUS BEURTHEILING DES ORIGENES (T.U.U. 1-2/4) / Jahn, A – Leipzig, 1886 – 2mf – 9 – ne Slangenburg [240]

DES H. HIPPOLYTUS VON ROM COMMENTAR ZUM BUCHE DANIEL / Bardenhewer, Otto – Freiburg Brsg., 1877 – 2mf – 8 – ne Slangenburg [220]

DES HALLUCINATIONS OU HISTOIRE RAISONNEE DES APPARITIONS, DES VISIONS, DES SONGES, DE L'EXTASE, DU MAGNETISME ET DU SOMNAMBULISME / Brierre de Boismont, Alexandre Jacques Francois – (French Precursors of Psychiatry Series). Paris. Germer Bailliere. 1845 – 9 – fr Hachette [150]

DES HEILIGEN EPIPHANIUS VON SALAMIS. / Epiphanius, Saint, Bishop of Constantia in Cyprus – 1919. Trans. by Joseph Hoermann – 1 – us U.W. Library [240]

DES HEILIGEN HIPPOLYTUS VON ROM COMMENTAR ZUM BUCHE DANIEL : EIN LITERARGESCHICHTLICHER VERSUCH / Bardenhewer, Otto – Freiburg im Breisgau; St. Louis, Mo.: Herder, 1877 – 1mf – us A.T.L.A. [220]

DES HEILIGEN IRENAEUS SCHRIFT ZUM ERWEISE DER APOSTOLISCHEN VERKUENDIGUNG : EIS EPIDEIXIN TOU APOSTOLIKOU KERYGMATOS. IN ARMENISCHER VERSION ENTDECKT / Ter-Mekerttschian, Karapet & Ter-Minassiantz, Erwand – Leipzig: J.C. Hinrichs, 1907. (Texte und Untersuchungen zur Geschichte der altchristlichen Literatur; der ganzen Reihe 31. Bd., Heft 1. Reihe, 1. Bd., Heft 1) – 1mf – us A.T.L.A. [240]

DES HEILIGEN IRENAEUS SCHRIFT ZUM ERWEISE DER APOSTOLISCHEN VERKUENDIGUNG (T.U.U. 3-31/1) / Ter-Mekerttschian, K – Leipzig, 1907 – 3mf – 9 – ne Slangenburg [240]

DES JACINTHES, DE LEUR ANATOMIE, REPRODUCTION ET CULTURE / Saint-Simon, M H de – Amsterdam. 1768. B-5709 2 – 8 – ne IDC [580]

DES LANGST GEWUNSCHTEN UND VERSPROCHENEN CHYMISCH-PHILOSOPHISCHEN PROBIER-STEINS, ERSTE CLASSE, IN WELCHER DER WAHREN UND ACHTEN ADEPTORUM UND ANDERER WURDIG ERFUNDENEN SCHRIFFTEN... / Fictuld, Hermann – Dresden: Hilscher, 1784 – 1 – us U.W. Library [540]

DES LOIS PROTECTRICES DU TRAVAIL, CE QU'ELLES SONT, CE QU'ELLES DEVRAIENT ETRE / Guesde, Jules – Lille. 1896. (La Condition Ouvriere. Part Two.) – 9 – 2.50 – fr Bibl Nationale [360]

DES MALADIES MENTALES CONSIDEREES SOUS LES RAPPORTS MEDICAL, HYGIENIQUE ET MEDICO-LEGAL / Esquirol, Jean Etienne Dominique – (French Precursors of Psychiatry Series). Paris. J. B. Bailliere. 1838 – 9 – fr Hachette [616]

DES MALADIES MENTALES ET DES ASILES D'ALIENES. LECONS CLINIQUES ET CONSIDERATIONS GENERALES / Falret, Jean Pierre – (French Precursors of Psychiatry Series). Paris. Bailliere. 1864 – 9 – fr Hachette [616]

Des Marchais, Etienne Renaud *see* JOURNAL DE NAVIGATION DU VOYAGE DE LA COSTE DE GUINEE.

DES MOINES COURIER – Ottumwa. Iowa. 1849-1853 – 1 – us UMI [071]

DES MOINES TOGETHER WITH THE HISTORY OF POLK COUNTY / Brigham, Johnson – Chicago: S. J. Clarke Publ. Co., 1911. Vol. 1, Iowa Reel 34; Vol. 2, Iowa Reel 35. (The Cox Library Collection) – 5 – us Americana [978]

DES MOINES VALLEY WHIG – Keokuk. Iowa. and Keokuk Register. 1849-51, 1855-61 – 1 – us UMI [071]

DES NAISSANCES ILLEGITIMES EN EUROPE / Legoyt, Alfred – Reprod. d'un extrait du Journal des Economistes: Revue de la Science economique, 3eme serie, v10, mai 1868, p177-205. 1 fiche. (Statistics Series: Medical Studies) – 9 – 6.00 – fr Bibl Nationale [310]

Des Pepliers, J R *see* NOUVELLE ET PARFAITE GRAMMAIRE ROYALE FRANCOISE ET ALLEMANDE

DES PHRASES NON DES FAITS – Madrid, 193? Fiche W 829. (Blodgett Collection of Spanish Civil War Pamphlets) – 9 – us H.U. College Libr [946]

DES PRINCIPES DE LA GUERRE / Foch, Ferdinand – Paris. Berger-Levrault. 1903. vi, 339 p. maps. (Strategy of War Series) – 9 – fr Hachette [355]

DES PRINCIPES DE L'ARCHITECTURE / Felibien, A – 1676 – 9 – fr I.C.S. [720]

DES PRINCIPES DE L'ARCHITECTURE, DE LA SCULPTURE, DE LA PEINTURE. / Felibien, Andre – Paris, J. B. Coignard, 1690. 4v. 24, 797p., ill. (Architecture Series) – 9 – fr Hachette [700]

DES PRISONNIERS, DE L'EMPRISONNEMENT ET DES PRISONS / Ferrus, Guillaume Marie Andre – (French Precursors of Psychiatry Series). Paris. Germer Bailliere. 1850 – 9 – fr Hachette [150]

DES PRISONS, TELLES QU'ELLES SONT ET TELLES QU'ELLES DEVRAIENT ETRE PAR RAPPORT A L'HYGIENE, A LA MORALE ET A L'ECONOMIE / Villerme, Louis Rene – (Condition of 19th C. French working class series). 1820 – 9 – fr Hachette [360]

DES PROGRES DE LA PUISSANCE RUSSE DEPUIS SON ORIGINE JUSQU'AU COMMENCEMENT DU 19E SIECLE / Lesur – 1812. (Russia-19th c. Series) – 9 – fr Hachette [574]

Des Rochers, Guy *see* BIO-BIBLIOGRAPHIE ANALYTIQUE DE MARCEL TRUDEL

DES SAMUEL AL-MAGREBI ABHANDLUNG UEBER...PFLICHTEN DER PRIESTER UND RICHTER / Al-Magrebi, Samuel – Berlin: H. Itzkowski, 1907. 1 fiche – 9 – us A.T.L.A. [270]

DES SOCIETES ANONYMES EN DROIT INTERNATIONAL PRIVE / Anspach, L & Houbotte, E – Bruxelles, 1896 – 1mf – 9 – ILM-3920/1 – ne IDC [340]

DES SOCIETES DE BIENFAISANCE MUTUELLE : OU DES MOYENS D'AMELIORER LE SORT DES CLASSES OUVRIERES / Cerfbeer, Auguste-Edouard – (Condition of 19th C. French working class series). 1836 – 9 – fr Hachette [360]

DES SOCIETES DE PREVOYANCES OU DE SECOURS MUTUELS: RECHERCHES SUR L'ORGANISATION DE CES INSTITUTIONS / Villerme, Louis Rene – Reprod. d'un extrait des Annales d'Hygiene publique et de Medecine legale. 1845.p94-111. 1 fiche. (Statistics Series: Medical Studies) – 9 – 6.00 – fr Bibl Nationale [310]

DES SOCIETES POPULAIRES CONSIDEREES COMME UNE BRANCHE ESSENTIELLE DE L'INSTRUCTION PUBLIQUE / Lanthenas, Francois X. – Paris. Chez les Directeurs de l'Imprimerie du Cercle Social. 1792 – 9 – fr Hachette [321]

DES VERWEGENEN CHIRURGUS WELTBERUEHMBT WUNDER-DOKTOR JOHANN ANDREAS EISENBART : ZAHNBRECHERS, BAENKELSAENGERS, OKULISTEN,... / Winckler, Josef – Berlin: Deutsche Buch-Gemeinschaft, 1933 – 1 – us U.W. Library [617]

DES VOIES D'EXECUTION DES JUGEMENTS A ROME / Lemoine, Charles Amedee – Nancy, Crepin-Leblond. 1881. 344p. LL-4042 – 1 – us L of C Photodup [340]

DES WERELDTS PROEF-STEEN OFTE DE YDELHEYDT DOOR DE WAERHEYD BESCHULDIGHT ENDE OVERTUYGHT VAN VALSCHEYDT / Burgundia, A – 1st ed. Antwerpen, 1643 – 5mf – 9 – ne IDC [700]

DESABHIMANI VARIKA – Cochin, India. Jul-Sept 1966; 1981-May 1995 – 30r – 1 – us L of C Photodup [072]

DESABRATI – Calcutta, India. Jul 1968-Apr 1970 – 3r – 1 – us L of C Photodup [072]

Desache, Gaetan *see* SOUVENIR DE MON VOYAGE AUX ETATS-UNIS AT AU CANADA

DESAFIO A LA REVOLUCION ARGENTINA / Gentiluomo, Federico A – Buenos Aires: [S.n.], 1969 – 1 – CSUXADH9256-B – us Hoover Inst Photo [320]

DESAFIOS Y RETOS DE VARIOS CABALLEROS DEL SIGLO 15 – Madrid, Biblioteca Nacional [19–] – us Res Libr [072]
A DESAFRONTE – [Sao Tome]: Tip do Anunciador, feb 9 1924-sep 3 1925 – us Res Libr [072]
Desai, Yunus *see* FROM 'COOLIE LOCATION' TO GROUP AREA
Desainliens, Claude *see*
- DE PRONUNTIATIONE LINGUAE GALICAE
- A DICTIONARIE FRENCH AND ENGLISH
- THE FRENCH LITTELTON
- THE FRENCH SCHOOLE-MAISTER

Desaivre, Leo *see* L'ELECTION DE NIERT AU XVIIIE SIECLE: NOTES ET DOCUMENTS
DESALINATION – v1-52. 1966-84 – 1,5,6,13 – sz Elsevier [073]
LA DESAMORTIZACION DE LAS PROPIEDADES...VALENCIA DE ALCANTARA / Garcia Perez, Juan – 9 – 1.50f – sp Bibl Santa Ana [336]
DESA-RAPPORTEN CHERIBON, MODJOKERTO, SEMARANG, SURABAJA, PROBOLINGGO, KRAKSAAN, VERZAMELD DOOR J.W. MEYER RANNEFT, 1898-1923 – BSD-109/1 mf.1-6 – 9 – ne IDC [950]
DESARROLLO ECONOMICO DE GUATEMALA / Guatemala. Con. Nac. de Plan. Econ – D-1317 1. Plan 1955-1960 – 9 – ne IDC [338]
DESARROLLO ECONOMICO Y SOCIAL DE MEXICO, 1966-1970. BORRADOR PARA DISUSION / Mexico. Comision Intersecretarial para formular Planes Nacionales de Desarrollo Economico y Social – (Economic and social development of Mexico, 1966-1970. Draft for discussion). 1966 – 9 – ne IDC [330]
DESARROLLO Y BIENESTAR, O CONTRACCION, MISERIA Y DICTADURA : RECOPILACION DE ENSAYOS Y CONFERENCIAS SOBRE POLITCA ECONOMICA / Frigerio, Rogelio – [Buenos Aires: Editorial Concordia, 1962] – 1 – CSUXAHZ5794-B – us Hoover Inst Photo [330]
Desaubrys, J P *see* ...SONATES FOR 2 VIOLINS AND VIOLONCELLO, OP. 1
Desaugiers, M *see* AIR DES DEUX JUMEAUX DE BERGAME...
Desaulniers, Abraham Lesieur *see* DICTIONNAIRE DE DROIT ET DE PROCEDURE D'APRES LE CODE CIVIL DU BAS-CANADA: CELUI DE PROCEDURE CIVILE ET LEURS AMENDEMENTS, JUSQU'A LA FIN DE LA DERNIERE SESSION DU PARLEMENT, CONTENANT DIVERSES FORMULES USITEES DANS LA PRACTIQUE
Desaulniers, Francois Lesieur *see*
- NOTES HISTORIQUES SUR LA PAROISSE DE SAINT-GUILLAUME D'UPTON AVEC LA GENEALOGIE DES FAMILLES DE SERRE, VANASSE...
- REUNION DES PAROISSIENS D'YAMACHICHE, OU, LE 18 OCTOBRE 1876
- LES VIEILLES FAMILLES D'YAMACHICHE
- LES VIELLES FAMILLES D'YAMACHICHE, TOME PREMIER: DIX GENEALOGIES COMPRENANT LES BLAIS, LACERTE, LAMY..
- LES VIELLES FAMILLES D'YAMACHICHE, TOME QUATRIEME: VINGT-TROIS GENEALOPES COMPRENANT LES AUCOIN, BETTEZ, BOISVERT..
- LES VIELLES FAMILLES D'YAMACHICHE, TOME TROISIEME: VINGT-CINQ GENEALOGIES COMPRENANT LES LESIEUR, HEROUX, MILETTE..

Desaulniers, G *see* LE NATIONAL
Desault, P J *see* OEUVRES CHIRURGICALES
DeSaussure, Wilmot Gibbes *see*
- HISTORICAL NOTES
- PAPERS OF WILMOT GIBBES DESAUSSURE

DESAUSSURE'S CASES IN EQUITY / South Carolina. Supreme Court – (A Pre-NRS title) – v1-4. 1784-1816 (all publ) – 29mf – 9 – $44.00 – LLMC 94-026 – us L.L.M.C. [340]
Desautels, Adrien *see* BIBLIOGRAPHIE DES OEUVRES LITTERAIRES PUBLIEES AU CANADA DE ROBERT RUMILLY, ECRIVAIN, MEMBRE DE L'ACADEMIE CANADIENNE-FRANCAISE, TRADUCTEUR AU SENAT CANADIEN A OTTAWA
Desbarats Co *see* THE FAVORITE
Desbarats, G E *see* DOMINION ILLUSTRATED MONTHLY
Desbarats, George *see* THE HEARTHSTONE
Des-Barres, Antoine *see* L'ESTAT PRESENTE DE L'ARCHIPEL
Desbois, R *see* LA CONVENTION FRANCO-BADOISE...1846...
Descallar, R *see* ANARCHISM AND LEGAL RULES
DESCAMISADA – 1 – CSUXADM8402-S – us Hoover Inst Photo [073]
Descamps, Jean Baptiste *see*
- LA VIE DES PEINTRES FLAMANDS, ALLEMANDS ET HOLLANDOIS...
- VOYAGES PITTORESQUES DE LA FLANDRE ET DU BRABANT

Descartes, Rene *see*
- EXCELLENT COMPENDIUM OF MUSICK
- KORT BEGRYP DER ZANG KUN IN DE LATIJNSCHE TAAL BESCHREVEN EN VAN J.H. GLAZEMAKER VERTAALT
- RENE DESCARTES

Descastes, Francois *see* DES ALPES AU NIGER
Descemet, Louis *see* RECUEIL D'ENVIRON 1200 PHRASES FRANCAIS USUELLES AVEC LEUR TRADUCTION. EN OUOLOF DE SAINT-LOUIS
THE DESCENDANTS OF JOHN ELIOT FROM 1598-1905 / Emerson, Wilimena H – 1905 – 1r – 1 – $50.00 – B50010 – us Library Micro [920]
DESCENDANTS OF PHILIP HENRY / Lawrence, Sarah – 1844 – 1 – $50.00 – us Presbyterian [920]
DESCENDENTS OF THE LATE QUEEN VICTORIA / McNaughton, A – 7 – uk Microform Academic [920]
THE DESCENT INTO HELL : WITH AN ANALYSIS AND NOTES; TO WHICH ARE ADDED, URIEL, A FRAGMENT, AND THREE ODES / Heraud, John Abraham – London: James Fraser, 2nd rev ed 1835 – 1 roll – 1 – 1-55879-655-X – uk Libr Preservation [810]
Deschamps *see* SAUL
Deschamps, Clement E *see*
- LISTE DES MUNICIPALITES DANS LA PROVINCE DE QUEBEC
- MUNICIPALITES ET PAROISSES DANS LA PROVINCE DE QUEBEC

Deschamps, Dercy *see* OSSIAN OU LES BARDES
Deschamps, Edouard *see* AFRICA
Deschamps, Emile Felix *see* CARNET D'UN VOYAGEUR AU PAYS DES VEDDAS, CEYLAX
Deschamps, Enrique *see* LA REPUBLICA DOMINICANA; DIRECTORIO Y GUIA GENERAL
Deschamps, Hubert *see* THE SLAVE TRADE AND ABOLITIONISM IN FRANCE: 1744-1848
Deschamps, Lesueur *see* OSSIAN OU LES BARDES
Deschenes, Jean-Claude *see* BIBLIOGRAPHIE DE L'OEUVRE DU REVEREND PERE HECTOR-L. BERTRAND, S.J., FONDATEUR DU COMITE DES HOPITAUX DU QUEBEC...
Deschler, Lewis et al *see* DESCHLER'S PRECEDENTS OF THE HOUSE OF REPRESENTATIVES
DESCHLER'S PRECEDENTS OF THE HOUSE OF REPRESENTATIVES / Deschler, Lewis et al – (Updates planned) – Washington: GPO. v1-10. 1965- – 17mf (1:42) 43mf (1:24) – 9 – $141.00 – LLMC 84-108 – us L.L.M.C. [324]
DESCHUTES ECHO – Bend, OR. -w. 30 Aug 1902-25 Jun 1904. 1 roll – 1 – us U.O. Library [071]
DeSchweinitz, LD *see* CONSPECTUS FUNGORUM IN LUSATIAE SUPERIORIS AGRO NISKIENSI CRESCENTIUM
Descloitres, R *see* COMMUNE ET SOCIETE RURALE EN ALGERIE: ADMINISTRATION LOCALE ET PARTICIPATION AU DEVELOPPEMENT DANS L'AURES
O DESCOBRIDOR DE VERDADES – '(s.l.'). 28 Ago-13 Set 1832 – 1 – bl Biblioteca [072]
DESCOBRIMENTO DA ILHA DE SAM THOME – (Filmed with Pinto, M R Relacas) – [S.l: s.n., 19–?] – us Res Libr [072]
Descolins *see* DESCRIPTION ABREGEE DU DEPARTEMENT DE L'AUBE
UN DESCONOCIDO CEDULARIO DEL SIGLO 16. MEXICO, 1944 / Carreno, Alberto Maria – Madrid: Razon y Fe, 1947 – 1 – sp Bibl Santa Ana [972]
Descourtilz, M E *see* FLORE [PITTORESQUE ET] MEDICALE DES ANTILLES
LA DESCOUVERTE DES FAUX POSSEDEZ / Pithois, P Claude Le – Chalons. 1621 – 9 – fr Hachette [360]
O DESCRIDO : PERIODICO CRITICO E LITTERARIO – Aracaju, 15 Oct, Dec 1881; Jan-3 Oct 1882 – 1,5,6 – bl Biblioteca [072]
DESCRIPCAO DE SERRA-LEOA E SEUS CONTORNOS : ESCRIPTA EM DOZE CARTAS, A QUAL SE AJUNTAO OS TRABALHOS DA COMMISSAO-MIXTA PORTUGUEZA E INGLEZA, ESTABELECIDA NAQUELLA COLONIA – Lisbon: J Baptista Morando, 1822 – 1 – us Res Libr [960]
DESCRIPCAO HISTORICA, TOPOGRAPHICA E ETHNOGRAPHICA DO DISTRICTO DE S. JOAO BAPTISTA D'AJUDIA E DO REINO DE DAHOME NA COSTA DA MINA / Bettencourt Vasconcellos Corte Real do Canto, Vital de – Lisboa: Typographia Universal de T Q Antunes, 1869 – 1 – us Res Libr [910]
DESCRIPCION DE LA CANADA... MONTEMOLIN – 1856 – 9 – 1.50f – sp Bibl Santa Ana [971]
DESCRIPCION DE LA CIUDAD Y OBISPADO DE PLASENCIA POR... / Toro, Luis de – Plasencia: La Victoria, 1961 – 1 – sp Bibl Santa Ana [240]
DESCRIPCION DE LAS INDIAS OCCIDENTALES... / Herrera, Antonio de – Madrid: Imprenta Real, 1601 – 1 – sp Bibl Santa Ana [950]
DESCRIPCION DE LAS ISLAS BALEARES / Vargas Ponce, Jose – 1787 – 1mf – 9 – Pta1,000.00 – 84-7848-338-1 – sp Pentalfa [910]
DESCRIPCION DE LAS PLANTAS / Cavanilles, A J – Madrid, 1802 – 13mf – 9 – ne IDC [580]
DESCRIPCION E HISTORIA DEL PARAGUAY. TOMO 2 / Azara, Felix – 1847 – 1mf – 9 – Pta1,000.00 – 84-7848-032-3 – sp Pentalfa [972]
DESCRIPCION GEOGRAFICA DE LOS REINOS DE LA NUEVA GALICIA... / Motay Escobar, Alonso – Madrid: Razon y Fe, 1940 – sp Bibl Santa Ana [910]
DESCRIPCION PROCLAMA...BADAJOZ...AL TRONO...REY D. FERNANDO 6 / Gallardo Bonilla, Leandro – 1747 – 9 – $1.50f – sp Bibl Santa Ana [946]
DESCRIPCION Y DISENO DEL TRILLO / Alvarez Guerra, Andres – 1815 – 9 – 1.50f – sp Bibl Santa Ana [621]
DESCRIPCION...CASA DE AGUALLO / Ramos, Antonio – 1781 – 9 – 1.50f – sp Bibl Santa Ana [946]
DESCRIPCION...CORRIDAS DE TOROS...CACERES / Sevillano, Casimiro – 1846 – 9 – 1.50f – sp Bibl Santa Ana [790]
DESCRIPCION...DE LAS ENFERMEDADES MAS COMUNES DEL EXERCITO CON UN NUEVO METODO DE CURAR EL MAL VENEREO / Van Swieten – Madrid, 1761 – 5mf – 9 – sp Cultura [616]
DESCRIPCION...DEL ESTANDARTE REAL – 1700 – 9 – $1.50f – sp Bibl Santa Ana [920]
DESCRIPCION...DEL SANTUARIO...DE GUADALUPE EN EXTREMADURA. – 1878 – 9 – 1.50f – sp Bibl Santa Ana [946]
DESCRIPCIONES DE INDIAS OCCIDENTALES / Herrera, Antonio de – 1730 – 9 – 1.50f – sp Bibl Santa Ana [972]
DESCRIPTIO AC DELINEATIO GEOGRAPHICA DETECTIONIS FRETI, SIVE, TRANSITUS AD OCCASUM, SUPRA TERRAS AMERICANAS, IN CHINAM ARQ;... / ed by Gerritsz, Hessell – Amsterdam, 1612. SEM105P881 – 1mf – 9 – Can$2.25 – cn Bibl Nat [910]
DESCRIPTIO ET ADUMBRATIO MICROSCOPICOANALYTICA MUSCORUM FRONDOSORUM / Hedwig, J – 4v. Lipsiae. 1787-97. B-578 2 – 8 – ne IDC [580]
DESCRIPTIO ET ADUMBRATIO PLANTARUM E CLASSE CRYPTOGAMICA LINNAEI QUAE LICHENS DICUNTUR / Hoffmann, G F – 3v. Lipsaie. 1790-1801. B-813 2 – 8 – ne IDC [580]
DESCRIPTIO ICONIBUS ILLUSTRATA PLANTARUM NOVARUM E FLORA HISPANICA / Lange, J M C – Havniae. 1864-66. B-5560 2 – 8 – ne IDC [580]
DESCRIPTIO MAGNAE ECCLESIAE SEU SANCTAE SOPHIAE (CBH 11,2) / Silentiarii, Pauli; ed by Gange, C du – Parisiis, 1670 – Dfl25.00 – ne Slangenburg [240]
DESCRIPTIO NOVI GENERIS PLANTAE / Heister, L – Brunsvigae. 1753. B-5252 2 – 8 – ne IDC [580]
DESCRIPTIO TEMPLI SANCTAE SOPHIAE (CSHB 32) : GEORGII PISIDAE, EXPEDITIO PERSICA, BELLUM AVARICUM, HERACLIAS SANCTI NICEPHORI PATRIARCHAE CP., BREVIARIUM RERUM POST MAURICIUM GESTARUM / Silentiarii, Pauli; ed by Bekkerus, Imm – Bonnae, 1837 – Dfl39.00 – ne Slangenburg [240]
DESCRIPTION ABREGEE DE L'EMPIRE DE LA CHINE,... / PDB – (Supplement) – Maestricht, 1776-1780 – 1mf – 9 – ne IDC [950]
DESCRIPTION ABREGEE DU DEPARTEMENT DE LA MEURTHE / Lecreulx, Francois M – an VII – 9 – fr Hachette [944]
DESCRIPTION ABREGEE DU DEPARTEMENT DE LA VENDEE / Cavoleau, Jean A – 9 – fr Hachette [944]
DESCRIPTION ABREGEE DU DEPARTEMENT DE L'AUBE / Descolins – an VII – 9 – fr Hachette [944]
DESCRIPTION ABREGEE DU DEPARTEMENT DE L'ORNE, REDIGEE PAR LE LYCEE D'ALENCON / Orne. France (Department) – an IX – 9 – fr Hachette [944]
DESCRIPTION ABREGEE DU DEPARTEMENT DE LOT ET GARONNE / Saint Amand, Jean F B de – an VIII – 9 – fr Hachette [944]
DESCRIPTION ABREGEE DU DEPARTEMENT DES HAUTES-ALPES / Farnaud, Pierre A – 9 – fr Hachette [944]
DESCRIPTION ABREGEE DU DEPARTEMENT DES LANDES / Landes. France (Department) – an VII – 9 – fr Hachette [944]
DESCRIPTION ABREGEE DU DEPARTEMENT DU GARD / Grangent, Stanislas V – an VIII – 9 – fr Hachette [944]
DESCRIPTION ABREGEE DU DEPARTEMENT DU MORBIHAN / Morbihan. France (Department) – an VII – 9 – fr Hachette [944]
DESCRIPTION ABREGEE DU DEPARTEMENT DU VAR / Fauchet, Joseph H A – an IX – 9 – fr Hachette [944]
DESCRIPTION AND HISTORY OF VIENNA PAMPHLET COLLECTION – 1957-1978 – 1 – CSUXANQ3121-B – us Hoover Inst Photo [943]
DESCRIPTION AND ILLUSTRATIONS OF THE MYOPORINOUS PLANTS OF AUSTRALIA. 2. LITHOGRAMS / Mueller, Ferdinand Jakob Heinrich von – Melbourne. 1886. B-8047 1 – 9 – ne IDC [580]
DESCRIPTION AND TRAVEL IN ALBANIA PAMPHLET COLLECTION – 1970-1976 – 1 – CSUXANQ7737-B – us Hoover Inst Photo [910]
DESCRIPTION AND TRAVEL IN BULGARIA PAMPHLET COLLECTION – 1923-1964 – 1 – CSUXANL7370-B – us Hoover Inst Photo [910]
DESCRIPTION AND TRAVEL IN CYPRUS PAMPHLET COLLECTION – 1939-1965 – 1 – CSUXANR0391-B – us Hoover Inst Photo [910]
DESCRIPTION AND TRAVEL IN CZECHOSLOVAKIA PAMPHLET COLLECTION – 1918-1985 – 2r – 1 – CSUXANL4430-B – us Hoover Inst Photo [910]
DESCRIPTION AND TRAVEL IN GREECE PAMPHLET COLLECTION – 1987 – 1 – CSUXANL5825-B – us Hoover Inst Photo [910]
DESCRIPTION AND TRAVEL IN HUNGARY PAMPHLET COLLECTION – 1910-1953 – 1 – CSUXANL5670-B – us Hoover Inst Photo [910]
[DESCRIPTION AND TRAVEL IN IRELAND PAMPHLET COLLECTION] – 1977 – 1 – CSUXANQ2016-B – us Hoover Inst Photo [910]
[DESCRIPTION AND TRAVEL IN ISTANBUL PAMPHLET COLLECTION] – 1946? – 1 – CSUXANR0529-B – us Hoover Inst Photo [910]
[DESCRIPTION AND TRAVEL IN NORTHERN IRELAND PAMPHLET COLLECTION] – 1984 – 1 – CSUXANQ2302-B – us Hoover Inst Photo [910]
[DESCRIPTION AND TRAVEL IN NORTHERN IRELAND PAMPHLET COLLECTION] – 1984 – 1 – CSUXANQ2022-B – us Hoover Inst Photo [910]
[DESCRIPTION AND TRAVEL IN POLAND COLLECTION] – 1917-1956 – 2r – 1 – CSUXANL6553-B – us Hoover Inst Photo [910]
[DESCRIPTION AND TRAVEL IN ROMANIA PAMPHLET COLLECTION] – 1881-1949 – 1 – CSUXANL8093-B – us Hoover Inst Photo [910]
[DESCRIPTION AND TRAVEL IN THE SOVIET UNION PAMPHLET COLLECTION] – 1920?-1960 – 2r – 1 – CSUXANR6105-B – us Hoover Inst Photo [910]

[DESCRIPTION AND TRAVEL IN TURKEY PAMPHLET COLLECTION] – 1916-1966 – 2r – 1 – CSUXANQ7754-B – us Hoover Inst Photo [910]
[DESCRIPTION AND TRAVEL IN YUGOSLAVIA PAMPHLET COLLECTION] – 1925-1952? – 1 – CSUXANQ5264-B – us Hoover Inst Photo [910]
DESCRIPTION DE LA BASLLIQUE DE ST PIERRE A ROME, MODELE DE LA CATHEDRALE DE MONTREAL – sl: sn, 189? (Montreal: J. Chapleau). 02681. (Pre-1900 Canadiana) – 9 – cn C.I.H.M. [720]
DESCRIPTION DE LA CHINE : PREVOST D'EXILES, A.F. HISTOIRE GENERALE DES VOYAGES... – Paris. v21-23. 1749-1761 – 16mf – 9 – ne IDC [950]
DESCRIPTION DE LA COLONIE CANADIENNE DU COMTE DE POLK, PAR UN COMITE DE CANADIENS FRANCAIS – Crookston, Minn.: s.n., 1883. 04282. (Pre-1900 Canadiana) – 9 – cn C.I.H.M. [306]
DESCRIPTION DE LA DEFAICTE DES TVRCZ ESTANS ENTREZ DANS L'ISLE DE MALTE – Paris, 1565 – 1mf – 9 – H-8165/1 – ne IDC [956]
DESCRIPTION DE LA FLORE FOSSILE / Zeiller, C R – Etudes des Gites Mineraux de la France. 2573 2. 1886-1888 – 8 – ne IDC [560]
DESCRIPTION DE LA NIGRITIE / Pruneau de Pommegorge, Antoine E – Amsterdam. 1789. BA-119 2 – 8 – ne IDC [960]
DESCRIPTION DE LA NIGRITIE / Pruneau de Pommegorge, Antoine E – Amsterdam, Paris, Maradan. 1789 – 9 – 10.00 – fr Orientalistes [305]
DESCRIPTION DE L'AFRIQUE : CONTENANT LES NOMS, LA SITUATION ET LES CONFINS DE TOUTES SES PARTIES, LEURS RIVIERES,... / Dapper, O – Amsterdam: Wolfgang, Waesberge, Boom & van Someren, 1686 – 1 – us Res Libr [960]
DESCRIPTION DE L'AFRIQUE / Dapper, O – Amsterdam, Waesberge, Boom et van Someren. 1686 – 9 – 20.00 – fr Orientalistes [910]
DESCRIPTION DE L'AFRIQUE SEPTENTRIONALE / Bakri, Abd Allah ibn' Abd al-Aziz, Abu Ubaid, al – Traduite par MacGuckin de Slane. Alger, A. Jourdan. 1913. BA-274 1 – 9 – ne IDC [960]
DESCRIPTION DE L'ART DE FABRIQUER LES CANONS / Monge, Gaspard – Paris: Impr. du Comite de Salut public, (1794) – 2p/leaf/viii/231p. 70 folding plates, 4 folding tables – 1 – us U.W. Library [623]
DESCRIPTION DE L'EGYPTE. HISTOIRE NATURELLE / Delile, A R – 78 2. v. 2. 1812 – 8 – ne IDC [550]
DESCRIPTION DE L'UNIVERS CONTENANT LES DIFFERENTS SYSTEMS DU MONDE, LES CARTES GENERALES ET PARTICULIERES DE LA GEOGRAPHIE ANCIENNE ET MODERNE : LES PLANS ET LES PROFILS DES PRINCIPALES VILLES ET DES AUTRES LIEUX PLUS CONSIDERABLES DE LA TERRE. LES MOEURS, RELIGIONS, GOUVERNEMENTS / Manesson-Mallet, Allain – (African Library). 1683 – 9 – fr Hachette [910]
DESCRIPTION DE TOVTE L'ISLE DE CYPRE, ET DES ROYS, PRINCES, ET SEIGNEURS, TANT PAYENS QUE CHRESTIENS, ... / Lusignano, S di – Paris, 1580 – 7mf – 9 – H-8356/1 – ne IDC [956]
DESCRIPTION DES ANIMAUX FOSSILES DU GROUPE NUMMULITIQUE DE L'INDE / Archiac, E J & Haime, J – Paris. 1853. BG-156 2 – 8 – ne IDC [560]
DESCRIPTION DES ARTS ET METIERS / Academie Royale des Sciences – (Including printed guide) – Paris, 1761-1788. 74v – 453mf – O-2126/1 – ne IDC [700]
DESCRIPTION DES BAINS DE TITUS, OU COLLECTION DES PEINTURES TROUVEES DANS LES RUINES DES THERMES DE CET EMPEREUR / Ponce, M – O 415. 1786 – 9 – ne IDC [930]
DESCRIPTION DES CRUSTACES DE LA FAMILLE DES GALATHEIDES / Edwards, A M & Bouvier, E L – Z-232 2. 1897 – 8 – ne IDC [590]
DESCRIPTION DES PLANTES DE L'AMERIQUE / Plumier, C – Paris. 1693. B-938 2 – 8 – ne IDC [580]
DESCRIPTION DES PLANTES NOUVELLES ET PEU CONNUES. DANS LE JARDIN DE J. M. CELS / Ventenat, E P – Paris. 1800-02. B-706 2 – 8 – ne IDC [580]
DESCRIPTION DES PLANTES QUI CROISSENT AUX ENVIRONS DE MONTAUBAN / Gateau – Montauban. 1789. B-6455 2 – 8 – ne IDC [580]
DESCRIPTION DES PLANTES RARES CULTIVEES A MALMAISON ET A NAVARRE / Bonpland, A J A – Paris. 1812-1813-17. B-5856 2 – 8 – ne IDC [580]
DESCRIPTION DU CAP DE BONNE ESPERANCE / Kolb, Peter – Amsterdam, Jean Catuffe. 1743 – 9 – 30.00 – fr Orientalistes [910]
DESCRIPTION DU CAP DE BONNE-ESPERANCE. / Kolb, Peter – Amsterdam. 1741 – 1 – us Res Libr [960]
DESCRIPTION DU CAP DE BONNE-ESPERANCE: OU L'ON TROUVE TOUT CE QUI CONCERNE L'HISTOIRE NATURELLE DU PAYS; ET L'ETABLISSEMENT DES HOLLANDAIS / Kolbe, Pierre – (African Library). 3 v. 1741 – 9 – fr Hachette [910]
DESCRIPTION DU DEPARTEMENT DE L'AVEIRON / Monteil, Amans A – an X – 9 – fr Hachette [944]
DESCRIPTION DU DEPARTEMENT DE L'OISE / Cambry, Jacques – 1803 – 9 – fr Hachette [944]
DESCRIPTION DU DEPARTEMENT DU CHER / Lucay, Jean Baptiste C L – an X – 9 – fr Hachette [944]
DESCRIPTION DU DEPARTEMENT DU SIMPLON OU DE LA CI-DEVANT REPUBLIQUE DU VALAIS / Schiner, Hildebrand – 1812 – 9 – fr Hachette [944]
DESCRIPTION DU JUBILE DE SEPT CENS ANS DE S. MACAIRE, PATRON PARTICULIER CONTRE LA PESTE... – Gent, 1767 – 2mf – 9 – ne IDC [700]
DESCRIPTION DU PARNASSE FRANCOIS / Titon du Tillet, Evrard – 1732. (Contains also: Suite du Parnasse Francois Jusqu'en 1743 and at the end, "Remarques sur la poesie et la musique. "; Second supplement du Parnasse Francois. 1743-1755; Description du Parnasse Francois... Third supplement. Premiere -seconde partie, 1760) – 9 – us Sibley [780]
DESCRIPTION D'UN HERBIER DE L'ILE DE TIMOR,... / Decaisne, J – Paris, 1835 – 2mf – 9 – ne IDC [580]
DESCRIPTION E HISTORIA DEL PARAGUAY, TOMO 1 / Azara, Felix – 1847 – 1mf – 9 – Pta1,000.00 – 84-7848-031-5 – sp Pentalfa [972]
DESCRIPTION ET DETAILS DES ARTS DU MEUNIER, DU VERMICELIER ET DU BOULANGER / Malouin, Paul J – Paris: Saillant et Nyon, 1767. SEM35P116 – 1r – 5 – Can$16.00 – cn Bibl Nat [660]
DESCRIPTION ET HISTOIRE NATURELLE DU GROENLAND / Egede, H – H-473 2. 1763 – 8 – ne IDC [580]
DESCRIPTION GENERALE DE L'AFRIQUE.. / Avity, Pierre d' – 1 – us Res Libr [910]
DESCRIPTION GENERALE DE L'AFRIQUE, SECOND PARTIE DU MONDE / Davity, Pierre – Paris, nouvelle edition Jean-Baptiste de Rocoles. 1660 – 9 – 20.00 – fr Orientalistes [910]
DESCRIPTION GENERALE DE L'AFRIQUE SECONDE PARTIE DU MONDE, AVEC TOUS SES EMPIRES, ROYAUMES, ETATS ET REPUBLIQUE. OU SONT DEDUITS ET TRAITES PAR ORDRE LEURS NOMS, ASSIETTE, CONFINS MOEURS, RICHESSES, FORCES, GOUVERNEMENTS ET RELIGION / Avity, Pierre d' – (African Library series). 1637 – 9 – fr Hachette [960]
DESCRIPTION GENERALE DU DEPARTEMENT DE LA VIENNE / Cochon de Lapparent, Charles – an X – 9 – fr Hachette [944]
DESCRIPTION GENERALE DU DEPARTEMENT DE L'ISERE / Perrin-Dulac, F M – 1806 – 9 – fr Hachette [944]
DESCRIPTION GEOGRAPHIQUE, HISTORIQUE,... DE L'EMPIRE DE LA CHINE ET DE LA TARTARIE CHINOISE / DuHalde, J B – Paris. 4v. 1735 – 75mf – 9 – ne IDC [950]
DESCRIPTION GEOGRAPHIQUE, PHYSIQUE ET POLITIQUE DU DEPARTEMENT DE SEINE-ET-OISE / Garnier, Germain – an X – 9 – fr Hachette [944]
DESCRIPTION OF A COLLECTION OF FOSSIL SHELLS, CORALS, ETC. FROM SUMATRA, OBTAINED BY R.D.M. VERBEEK / Woodward, H – London, 1879 – 1mf – 9 – Z-885/2 – ne IDC [590]
[DESCRIPTION OF ALSACE-LORRAINE PAMPHLET COLLECTION] – 1917 – 1 – CSUXANQ7764-B – us Hoover Inst Photo [910]
DESCRIPTION OF AN UNRECORDED ARDISIA OF NEW GUINEA / Mueller, Ferdinand Jakob Heinrich von – 1886. B-8048 1 – 9 – ne IDC [580]
[DESCRIPTION OF AND TRAVEL IN AQUITAINE PAMPHLET COLLECTION] – 1971? – 1 – CSUXANQ5641-B – us Hoover Inst Photo [910]
[DESCRIPTION OF AND TRAVEL IN BERLIN: PAMPHLET COLLECTION] – 1959-1988 – 1 – CSUXANS8682-B – us Hoover Inst Photo [910]
[DESCRIPTION OF AND TRAVEL IN CORSICA PAMPHLET COLLECTION] – 1978 – 1 – CSUXANQ5648-B – us Hoover Inst Photo [910]
[DESCRIPTION OF AND TRAVEL IN EAST GERMANY: PAMPHLET COLLECTION] – 1955-1986 – 2r – 1 – CSUXANS3641-B – us Hoover Inst Photo [910]
[DESCRIPTION OF AND TRAVEL IN FRANCE, 1871 TO 1944, PAMPHLET COLLECTION] – 1892?-1944 – 1 – CSUXANQ3138-B – us Hoover Inst Photo [910]
[DESCRIPTION OF AND TRAVEL IN FRANCE, 1945 TO THE PRESENT, PAMPHLET COLLECTION] – 1946-1984 – 1 – CSUXANQ3146-B – us Hoover Inst Photo [910]
[DESCRIPTION OF AND TRAVEL IN GERMANY PAMPHLET COLLECTION] – 1913-1917 – 1 – CSUXANQ7818-B – us Hoover Inst Photo [910]
[DESCRIPTION OF AND TRAVEL IN GERMANY–1919 TO 1944–PAMPHLET COLLECTION] – 1919-193? – 1 – CSUXANQ7826-B – us Hoover Inst Photo [910]
[DESCRIPTION OF AND TRAVEL IN GERMANY–1945 TO THE PRESENT–PAMPHLET COLLECTION] – 1946-1961 – 1 – CSUXANQ7830-B – us Hoover Inst Photo [910]
[DESCRIPTION OF AND TRAVEL IN PARIS PAMPHLET COLLECTION] – 1918-1972 – 1 – CSUXANQ7769-B – us Hoover Inst Photo [910]
[DESCRIPTION OF AND TRAVEL IN PRUSSIA: PAMPHLET COLLECTION] – 1933-1947 – 1 – CSUXANS5602-B – us Hoover Inst Photo [910]
[DESCRIPTION OF AND TRAVEL IN RUSSIA PAMPHLET COLLECTION] – 1988-1899? – 2r – 1 – CSUXANR6042-B – us Hoover Inst Photo [910]
[DESCRIPTION OF AUSTRIA PAMPHLET COLLECTION] – 1958-1973 – 1 – CSUXANQ2246-B – us Hoover Inst Photo [910]
DESCRIPTION OF CENSUS ENUMERATION DISTRICTS, 1900 / U.S. Bureau of the Census – 10 rolls. T1210 – 1 – us Nat'l Archives [310]
DESCRIPTION OF RUNIC STONES FOUND NEAR YARMOUTH, NOVA SCOTIA / Brown, R Balfour – 1898? 02280. (Pre-1900 Canadiana) – 9 – cn C.I.H.M. [730]
DESCRIPTION OF STRAYS / Hancock County. Ohio. Biglick Township. Township Clerk – 1897 – 1r – 1 – $32.50r – us Archival [324]
THE DESCRIPTION OF SWEDLAND, GOTLAND, AND FINLAND / North, George – 1561 – 9 – 10.00 – us Scholars' Facs [910]
DESCRIPTION OF THE BURMESE EMPIRE / Sangermano, V – 1833 – 1 – uk Microform Academic [900]
A DESCRIPTION OF THE CAUSAL ATTRIBUTIONS MADE TO PERCEIVED TEACHING BEHAVIOR ACROSS THREE ELEMENTARY PHYSICAL EDUCATION CONTEXTS / Mros, M – 1990 – 2mf – 9 – $8.00 – us Microform Publ [150]
DESCRIPTION OF THE COAST OF GUINEA / Bosman, Willem – 1907 – 7 – uk Microform Academic [910]
A DESCRIPTION OF THE COASTS OF NORTH AND SOUTH GUINEA / Barbot, J – London. 1746. BA-128 2 – 8 – ne IDC [960]
A DESCRIPTION OF THE EAST AND SOME OTHER COUNTRIES / Pococke, R – H 314 2. v. 1-2. 1743-45 – 8 – ne IDC [940]
A DESCRIPTION OF THE EMPIRE OF CHINA AND CHINESE-TARTARY, TOGETHER WITH THE KINGDOMS OF KOREA AND TIBET:... / DuHalde, J B – (Index) – London. 2v. 1738-1741 – 36mf – 9 – ne IDC [950]
DESCRIPTION OF THE FOSSIL REMAINS OF MOLLUSCA FOUND IN THE CHALK OF ENGLAND, (CEPHALOPODA) / Sharpe, D – London. 1853-1909. BG-216 2 – 8 – ne IDC [560]
A DESCRIPTION OF THE GENUS PINUS / Lambert, A B – 2v. London. 1803-24. B-5559 2 – 8 – ne IDC [580]
DESCRIPTION OF THE PROVINCE OF FARS IN PERSIA / Ibn-al-Balkhi – 1912 – 1 – uk Microform Academic [910]
A DESCRIPTION OF THE SCENERY OF THE LAKES IN THE NORTH OF ENGLAND... / Wordsworth, William – London: Longman, Hurst, Rees, Orme, and Brown, 3rd ed 1822 – 1 roll – 1 – 1-55879-868-4 – uk Libr Preservation [910]
DESCRIPTION OF THE WILTON HOUSE DIPTYCH, CONTAINING A CONTEMPORARY PORTRAIT OF KING RICHARD THE SECOND / Scharf, George – (London): Printed for the Arundel Society, 1882.vi,(7),99p. ill – 1 – us U.W. Library [760]
A DESCRIPTION OF TRENDS EMERGING DURING YEARS THREE AND FOUR OF THE WISCONSIN COMPREHENSIVE ELEMENTARY HEALTH EDUCATION PILOT PROJECT / Knutson-Kaske, Jill A – University of Wisconsin-La Crosse, 1995 – 1mf – 9 – $4.00 – HE556 – us Microform Publ [370]
DESCRIPTION PHYSIQUE ET HISTORIQUE DES CAFRES / Alberti, Louis – Amsterdam, E. Maaskamp. 1811 – 9 – 7.50 – fr Orientalistes [910]
DESCRIPTION PHYSIQUE ET POLITIQUE DU DEPARTEMENT DU RHONE / Verninac de Saint-Maur, Raymond de – an X – 9 – fr Hachette [944]
DESCRIPTION TOPOGRAPHIQUE DE LA PROVINCE DU BAS-CANADA = A TOPOGRAPHICAL DESCRIPTION OF LOWER CANADA / Bouchette, Joseph – England, 1815 – 1r – 1 – Can$50.00 – cn Can Microfilming [971]
DESCRIPTION TOPOGRAPHIQUE DE LA PROVINCE DU BAS-CANADA, AVEC DES REMARQUES SUR LE HAUT-CANADA / Bouchette, Joseph – Londres: W Faden, 1815. SEM35P58 – 1r – 1 – Can$26.00 – cn Bibl Nat [971]
DESCRIPTION TOPOGRAPHIQUE DU DEPARTEMENT DE LA MARNE / Jessaint, Claude LB – an X – 9 – fr Hachette [944]
DESCRIPTION TOPOGRAPHIQUE ET HISTORIQUE DE BOUKHARA / Nerchakhy, Mohammed – Texte persan publie par Ch. Schefer. 1892 – 9 – fr Orientalistes [910]
DESCRIPTION TOPOGRAPHIQUE ET STATISTIQUE / Peuchet, Jacques & Chanlaire, Pierre G – 1810 – 9 – fr Hachette [944]
DESCRIPTION TOPOGRAPHIQUE, PHYSIQUE, CIVILE, POLITIQUE ET HISTORIQUE DE LA PARTIE FRANCAISE DE L'ISLE SAINT-DOMINGUE / Moreau de Saint-Mery, Mederic Louis Elie – Paris. 2v. 1875 – 1r – 1 – us Ross [972]
DESCRIPTION TRIPARTITA MEDICO-ASTRONOMICA QUE TOCA... SOBRE LA CONSTITUCION EPIDEMICA... DE ESPANA, CON ESPECIALIDAD EN LA VILLA DE ORGAZ EN 1735 Y 1737 / Aranda y Marzo, J – Madrid, 1737 – 4mf – 9 – sp Cultura [610]
DESCRIPTIONES ET ICONES PLANTARUM RARIORUM HUNGARIAE / Waldstein, F de et al – 3v. Viennae. 1802-12. B-676 2 – 8 – ne IDC [580]
DESCRIPTIONES PLANTARUM EX CAPITE BONAE SPEI / Bergius, P J – Stockholmiae. 1767. B-2232 2 – 8 – ne IDC [580]
DESCRIPTIONES PLANTARUM QUARANDAM SURINAMENSIUM / Rottboll, C F – Hafniae. 1778. B-2260 2 – 8 – ne IDC [580]
DESCRIPTIONES PLANTARUM RARIORUM ICONIBUS ILLUSTRANDAS / Rottboll, C F – Hauniae. 1772. B-5694 2 – 8 – ne IDC [580]
DESCRIPTIONS AND FIGURES OF SOME NEW LEPIDOPTEROUS INSECTS. CHIEFLY FROM NEPAL / Gray, G R – London. 1846. BZ-1306 2 – 8 – ne IDC [590]
DESCRIPTIONS AND FIGURES OF TWO HUNDRED FISHES; COLLECTED AT VIZAGAPATAM ON THE COAST OF COROMANDEL / Russell, P – 2v. London. 1803. BZ-289 2 – 8 – ne IDC [590]

DESCRIPTIONS ET FIGURES DES PLANTES NOUVELLES ET RARES DU JARDIN BOTANIQUE DE L'UNIVERSITE DE LEIDE / Vriese, W H de – Leide, Leipzig. 1847-51. B-5796 2 – 8 – ne IDC [580]

DESCRIPTIONS OF CENSUS ENUMERATION DISTRICTS, 1830-90 AND 1910-50 / U.S. Bureau of the Census – 146 rolls. T1224 – 1 – us Nat'l Archives [310]

DESCRIPTIONS OF MALAYAN PLANTS / Jack, W – Malayan Miscellanies. v. 1, nr. 1. Bencoolen. 1820; v. 2, nr. 7. 1822. B-5081 2 – 8 – ne IDC [580]

DESCRIPTIONS OF NEW INDIAN LEPIDOPTEROUS INSECTS / Hewitson, W C – Calcutta. 1879. BZ-1437 2 – 8 – ne IDC [590]

DESCRIPTIONS OF SOME RARE AND CURIOUS PLANTS / Wallich, N – (Transact. Medical and Physical Soc.). v. 7. Calcutta. 1834. B-6483 2 – 8 – ne IDC [580]

DESCRIPTIONUM ET ICONUM RAIORES / Rottboll, C F – Hafniae. 1773. B-2259 2 – 8 – ne IDC [580]

A DESCRIPTIVE ANALYSIS OF CORPORATE HEALTH PROMOTION ACTIVITY EVALUATIONS / Corrigan, Ann E & Kaplan, Leah E – 1992 – 2mf – $8.00 – us Microform Publ [613]

A DESCRIPTIVE ANALYSIS OF SPORTS COMMISSIONS IN THE UNITED STATES / Pennell, BL – 1990 – 1mf – 9 – $4.00 – us Microform Publ [790]

A DESCRIPTIVE AND HISTORICAL ACCOUNT OF THE GODAVIRY DISTRICT / Morris, H – London. 1878. BI-150-17 2 – 8 – ne IDC [950]

DESCRIPTIVE AND PREDICTIVE DISCRIMINANT ANALYSIS OF THE GOLF ABILITY OF COLLEGE MALES / Joyner, A Barry & Baumgartner, Ted A – 1992 – 1mf – 9 – $4.00 – us Microform Publ [790]

DESCRIPTIVE CATALOG AND PRICE LIST OF PHOTOGRAPHIC APPARATUS / Anthony and Co. – 1892, 1895. Reel 13 – 1 – $50.00 – us UPA [760]

DESCRIPTIVE CATALOGUE OF A COLLECTION OF THE ECONOMIC MINERALS OF CANADA, AND OF ITS CRYSTALLINE ROCKS / Canada. Exploration Geologique – Montreal: John Lovell, 1862. SEM105P228 – 1mf – 9 – Can$2.25 – cn Bibl Nat [550]

DESCRIPTIVE CATALOGUE OF MATERIALS RELATING TO THE HISTORY OF GREAT BRITAIN AND IRELAND TO THE END OF THE REIGN OF HENRY 7 (RS26) / Hardy, T D – (v1,1 + v1,2 1862 Dfl67.00. v2 1865 Dfl42.00. v3 1871 Dfl42.00) – 3v – ne Slangenburg [941]

A DESCRIPTIVE CATALOGUE OF MSS IN MITHILA – Patna. 4v. 1927-1940 – 23mf – 9 – ne IDC [090]

A DESCRIPTIVE CATALOGUE OF SAMSKRTA AND PRAKRTA MSS IN THE LIBRARY OF THE BOMBAY BRANCH OF THE ROYAL ASIATIC SOCIETY – Bombay. 4 pts. 1925-1930 – 7mf – 9 – ne IDC [490]

DESCRIPTIVE CATALOGUE OF SANSKRIT MSS IN THE ADYAR LIBRARY – (Missing: v2-4. v7-8 have not been published) – Adyar. v1-10. 1942-1966 – 31mf – 9 – ne IDC [490]

A DESCRIPTIVE CATALOGUE OF SANSKRIT MSS IN THE GOVERNMENT ORIENTAL MSS. LIBRARY, MADRAS – Madras. v1-31. 1901-1951 – 139mf – 9 – ne IDC [490]

A DESCRIPTIVE CATALOGUE OF SANSKRIT MSS IN THE LIBRARY OF THE CALCUTTA SANSKRIT COLLEGE – Calcutta. v1-10(3). 1895-1917 – 37mf – 9 – ne IDC [490]

A DESCRIPTIVE CATALOGUE OF THE CHINESE COLLECTION IN PHILADELPHIA / Dunn, N – Philadelphia, 1839 – 2mf – 9 – ne IDC [950]

A DESCRIPTIVE CATALOGUE OF THE CHINESE COLLECTION, NOW EXHIBITING AT ST GEORGE'S PLACE, HYDE PARK CORNER, LONDON,... / Langdon, W B – London, 1842 – 2mf – 9 – ne IDC [950]

A DESCRIPTIVE CATALOGUE OF THE FIRST EDITIONS IN BOOK FORM OF THE WRITINGS OF PERCY BYSSHE SHELLEY : BASED ON A MEMORIAL EXHIBITION HELD AT THE GROLIER CLUB... / Granniss, Ruth Shepard – New York: The Grolier Club, 1923 – 1 roll – 1 – 1-55879-873-0 – uk Libr Preservation [014]

DESCRIPTIVE CATALOGUE OF THE REPTILES OF BRITISH INDIA / Theobald, W – Z 294 2. 1876 – 8 – ne IDC [590]

A DESCRIPTIVE CATALOGUE OF THE SAMSKRTA AND PRAKRTA MSS IN THE LIBRARY OF THE UNIVERSITY OF BOMBAY : BHAGVATSINGHJI COLLECTION AND H.M. BHADHAMKAR COLLECTION – Bombay. 2v. 1944 – 10mf – 9 – ne IDC [490]

A DESCRIPTIVE CATALOGUE OF THE SANSKRIT MSS ACQUIRED FOR AND DEPOSITED IN THE GOVERNMENT SANSKRIT COLLEGE IN THE SANSKRIT UNIVERSITY LIBRARY, (SARASVATI BHAVANA), BANARAS (VARANASI), DURING THE YEARS 1791-1950 – (Missing: v1-7) – Benares. v8-12. 1962-1965 – 22mf – 9 – ne IDC [490]

A DESCRIPTIVE CATALOGUE OF THE SANSKRIT MSS IN THE GOVERNMENT ORIENTAL LIBRARY, MYSORE – Mysore. 2v. 1937-1944 – 12mf – 9 – ne IDC [490]

A DESCRIPTIVE CATALOGUE OF THE SANSKRIT MSS IN THE TANJORE MAHARAJA SERFOJI'S SARASVATI MAHAL LIBRARY, TAJORE – Srirangan. v1-19. 1928-1934 – 114mf – 9 – ne IDC [490]

DESCRIPTIVE CATALOGUE OF THE SPIDERS OF BURMA / Thorell, T T T – Z 2201 2. 1895 – 8 – ne IDC [590]

A DESCRIPTIVE CATALOGUE OF THE WESTERN MEDIAEVAL MANUSCRIPTS IN EDINBURGH UNIVERSITY LIBRARY / Borland, C R – Edinburgh, 1916 – 11mf – 8 – ne Slangenburg [090]

A DESCRIPTIVE CATALOGUE OF THE WORKS OF REMBRANDT, AND HIS SCHOLARS, BOL, LIEVENS AND VAN VLIET,... / Daulby, D – Liverpool, 1796 – 5mf – ne IDC [750]

DESCRIPTIVE COMMENTARIES FROM THE MEDICAL HISTORIES OF POSTS / U.S. Army – 5 rolls.M903 – 1 – us Nat'l Archives [324]

A DESCRIPTIVE DICTIONARY OF THE INDIAN ISLANDS AND ADJACENT COUNTRIES / Crawfurd, J – London, 1856 – 5mf – 9 – ne IDC [950]

DESCRIPTIVE HANDBOOK OF THE CAPE COLONY: ITS CONDITION AND RESOURCES / Noble, John – Cape Town: J.C. Juta, 1875. 315p. illus – 1 – us U.W. Library [960]

DESCRIPTIVE INVENTORY OF THE ARCHIVES OF THE STATE OF ILLINOIS – (Includes suppl 1985 and index 1990) – 1978 – 34mf – 9 – $20.00 – us IL Archives [324]

DESCRIPTIVE LIST OF THE HEBREW AND SAMARITAN MSS IN THE BRITISH MUSEUM / Margoliouth, G – London, 1893 – 2mf – ne IDC [470]

DESCRIPTIVE NOTES ON PAPUAN PLANTS / Mueller, Ferdinand Jakob Heinrich von – pt. 1-10. Melbourne. 1875-90. Lacking: (pt.10) 1890. B-8049 1 – 9 – ne IDC [580]

A DESCRIPTIVE STUDY EXAMINING TWENTY YEARS OF FOOTBALL RELATED INJURY RESEARCH AT THE HIGH SCHOOL AND COLLEGE LEVELS / Peters, Arlene L – University of North Carolina at Chapel Hill, 1995 – 2mf – 9 – $8.00 – PE3617 – us Microform Publ [617]

A DESCRIPTIVE STUDY OF SEXUAL HEALTH ATTITUDES AND PRACTICES AMONG ADOLESCENT AND YOUNG ADULT MALE COUNTY HEALTH DEPARTMENT CLIENTS / Robbins, R D – 1991 – 2mf – 9 – $8.00 – us Microform Publ [613]

DESCRITTIONE DE GLI APPARATI FATTI IN BOLOGNA PER LA VENUTA DI N.S. PAPA CLEMENTE VIII / Benacci, V – O-1036 1. 1598 – 9 – ne IDC [240]

DESCRITTIONE DI TUTTA ITALIA / Alberti, Fra Leandro – O-103 1. 1550 – 9 – ne IDC [945]

DESCRIZIONE DEGL'ISTROMENTI ARMONICI D'OGNI GENERE DEL PADRE BONANNI / Bonanni, F – Seconda edizione rivedvta. Roma. 1776. Text in Italian and French. BP-643 1 – 9 – ne IDC [780]

DESCRIZIONE DEI FUNGHI MANGERECCI PIU COMUNI DELL' ITALIA E DE VELENOSI CHE POSSONO CO' MEDESIMI CONFONDERSI / Vittadini, C – Milano. 1835. B-6334 1 – 9 – ne IDC [580]

DESCRIZIONE DELL'IMPERIALE GIARDINO DI BOBOLI / Cambiagi, G – Firenze. 1757. BO-961 1 – 9 – ne IDC [700]

DESCRIZIONE REGIONATA DELLA GALLERIA DORIA PRECEDUTA DA UN BREVE SAGGIO DI PITTURA / Tonci, S – Roma. 1794. BO-1051 1 – 9 – ne IDC [700]

DESCRIZIONE STORICA DELLE PITTURE DEL REGIO-DUCALE PALAZZO DEL TE FUORI DELLA PORTA DI MANTOVA DETTA PUSTERLA / Bottani, G – Mantova, 1783 – 2mf – ne IDC [700]

DESCRIZZIONE DELLE IMMAGINI DIPINTE DA RAFAELLE D'URBINO NELLE CAMERE DEL PALAZZO APOSTOLICO VATICANO / Bellori, Giovanni Pietro – O 143. 1695 – 9 – ne IDC [760]

DESCUBRIDORES JESUITAS DEL AMAZONAS / Bayle, Constantino – Madrid: Instituto Gonzalo Fernandez de Oviedo, 1940 – 1 – sp Bibl Santa Ana [240]

DESCUBRIDORES JESUITAS DEL AMAZONAS, BREVE DESCRIPCION / Bayle, Constantino – Madrid: Revista de Indias, 1940 – 1 – sp Bibl Santa Ana [972]

DESCUBRIMIENTO DE LOS RESTOS DE FREY NICOLAS DE OVANDO, PRIMER GOVERNADOR DE LAS INDIAS / Munoz de San Pedro, Miguel – Sevilla, 1948. Separata del T.V. del Anuario de Est. Americanos – 1 – sp Bibl Santa Ana [946]

DESCUBRIMIENTO DEL RIO AMAZONAS / Carvajal, Gaspar de – 1895 – 9 – 1.50f – sp Bibl Santa Ana [910]

DESCUBRIMIENTO Y CONQUISTA DE CHILE / Carrasco, Adolfo – 1892 – 9 – 1.50f – sp Bibl Santa Ana [972]

DESCUBRIMIENTO Y CONQUISTA DE CHILE. BARCELONA, 1946 / Estave Barba, Francisco – Madrid: Razon y Fe, 1948 – 1 – sp Bibl Santa Ana [972]

DESCUBRIMIENTO Y CONQUISTA DEL PERU / Reyna y Reyna, Tomas de la – 1892 – 9 – 1.50f – sp Bibl Santa Ana [972]

DESCUBRIMIENTO...MINAS / Sabido y Martinez, Antonio – 1875 – 9 – 1.50f – sp Bibl Santa Ana [972]

DESCUBRIMIENTOS GEOMETRICOS / Molina Cano, Juan A – 1598 – 9 – 1.50f – sp Bibl Santa Ana [510]

EL DESCUENTO DE LAS CLASES PRIVADAS / Diaz Perez, Nicolas – 1879 – 9 – 1.50f – sp Bibl Santa Ana [300]

DESDE LA FORMACION PROFESIONAL A LAS FACULTADES O ESCUELAS UNIVERSITARIAS E INDUSTRIAS Y SERVICIOS / Caceres. Delegacion Provincial del Ministerio, de Educacion – Aldea Moret: Imp. Linea 21, 1981 – 1 – sp Bibl Santa Ana [370]

DESDE MI TONEL / Barrantes Molina, Luis – Madrid: Razon y Fe, 1934 – 1 – sp Bibl Santa Ana [972]

DESDE QUE GRIT E VIVA PERON! / Cafiero, Antonio Francisco – Buenos Aires: Pequen Ediciones, 1983 – 1 – CSUXADQ7069-B – us Hoover Inst Photo [320]

Desdevises du Dezert, Georges *see* L'EGLISE ET L'ETAT EN FRANCE

Desdevises du Dezert, Theophile *see* L'AMERIQUE AVANT LES EUROPEENS

DESEMPENO AL METODO RACIONAL EN LA CURACION DE LAS CALENTURAS TERCIANAS / Flores, S L de – Sevilla, 1698 – 3mf – 9 – sp Cultura [616]

EL DESENCUENTRO ARGENTINO, 1930-1955 / Cuneo, Dardo – Buenos Aires: Ediciones Pleamar, [1965] – 1 – CSUXADQ3335-B – us Hoover Inst Photo [972]

DESENGANO AL TEATRO ESPANOL / Fernandez de Moratin, Nicolas – s.a. – 1mf – 9 – Pta1,000.00 – 84-7848-147-8 – sp Pentalfa [790]

DESENGANO DEL ABUSO DE LA SANGRIA... / Romero, L – Tarragona, 1623 – 6mf – 9 – sp Cultura [610]

DESERT – Reno, NV. 1936 – 1 – 1 – $50.00 – B06065 – us Library Micro [071]

DESERT BARNACLE – Coachella, CA. 1945-Mar 1952 – 3r – 1 – $150.00 – R02120 – us Library Micro [071]

DESERT DISPATCH – Barstow, CA. 1971- – 92+ r – 1 RC02048 – $4,600.00 ($170.00y) – us Library Micro [071]

DESERT GAZE – Las Vegas, NV. 1983-1984 – 1r – 1 – $50.00 – U04853 – us Library Micro [071]

THE DESERT OF THE EXODUS / Palmer, Edward Henry – Journeys On Foot In The Wilderness of the Forty Years' Wanderings; Undertaken in Connexion with the Ordinance Survey of Sinai, and the Palestine exploration fund.... 1871 – 1 – us A.T.L.A. [270]

DESERT RANCHER – Coachelle, CA. 1969-1986 – 4r – 1 – $200.00 – R03184 – us Library Micro [071]

DESERT RAT – Palm Springs, CA. 1936-1981 – 1r – 1 – $50.00 – R03382 – us Library Micro [071]

THE DESERT SCORPION – (Also known as: Sibert Scorpion) – Boulder City, NV. 1941-1943 – 2r – 1 – $100.00 – U04425 – us Library Micro [071]

DESERT SENTINEL – Desert Hot Springs, CA. 1946- – 40+ r – 1 – $2,000.00 ($90.00y) – R02169 – us Library Micro [071]

DESERT SHOPPER – Boulder City, NV. 1948 – 1r – 1 – $50.00 – U04832 – us Library Micro [071]

THE DESERT SUN – Las Vegas, NV. 1931 – 1r – 1 – $50.00 – U04854 – us Library Micro [071]

DESERT SUN (COACHELLA VALLEY) – Palm Springs, CA. 1990 – 121+ r – 1 – $6,050.00 ($1,215.00y) – RH04088 – us Library Micro [071]

DESERT TRAIL – Twentynine Palms, CA. 1984 – 33+ r – 1 – $1,650.00 ($240.00y) – R03557 – us Library Micro [071]

DESERT WINGS – Moraco. Calif. 1955-1967 – 1 – us UMI [071]

THE DESERTED DAUGHTER : A COMEDY / Holcroft, T – London, 3rd ed 1795 – 1mf – 9 – ne IDC [820]

LE DESERTEUR : DRAME EN TROIS ACTES / Monsigny, P-A – Paris: C Herisant, 1769 – 1 – us Sibley [780]

O DESESPERO – [s.l.]. Maio 1878 – 1,5,6 – bl Biblioteca [072]

LE DESESPOIR DE JOCRISSE OU LES FOLIES D'UNE JOURNEE / Doin, Ernest – Montreal: Librairie Beauchemin..., 1908. SEM105P460 – 1mf – 9 – Can$2.25 – cn Bibl Nat [830]

Desessart *see* PENSEES POLITIQUES ET RELIGIEUSES DU SAINT-SIMONIEN

Desfontaines, Pierre-Francois Guyot *see*
- LE NOUVEAU GULLIVER, OU VOYAGE DE JEAN GULLIVER, FILS DU CAPITAINE GULLIVER, TRADUIT D'UN MANUSCRIT ANGLOIS
- RACINE VENGE OU EXAMEN DES REMARQUES GRAMMATICALES DE M. L'ABBE D'OLIVET SUR LES OEUVRES DE RACINE

Desfontaines, R L *see*
- CATALOGUS PLANTARUM HORTI REGII PARISIENSIS
- CHOIX DE PLANTES DU COROLLAIRE DES INSTITUTS DE TOURNEFORT
- FLORA ATLANTICA
- HERBARIUM
- TABLEAU DE L'ECOLE DE BOTANIQUE DU MUSEUM D'HISTOIRE NATURELLE

Desgouttes, Zacharie H *see* TABLEAU STATISTIQUE DU DEPARTEMENT DES VOSGES

Desgranges, J *see* PETIT DICTIONNAIRE DU PEUPLE

Desgrouais *see* LES GASCONISMES CORRIGES

DESHASHEH (MEES VOL 15) / Flinders Petrie, W M – London, 1898 – 6mf – 8 – Dfl25.00 – ne Slangenburg [930]

Deshayes de Courmenin, Louis *see* VOIAGE DE LEVANT FAIT PAR LE COMMANDEMENT DU ROY EN L'ANNEE 1621

DESHDOOT – Allahabad, India. 3 Oct 1948-18 Jun 1950 – 1r – 1 – us L of C Photodup [072]

DESHLER CITIZEN – Deshler, NE. -w. Nov. 1895-Mar. 1897 – 1 – us NE Hist [071]

DESHLER FLAG – Deshler, Ohio. 1897- – 35r – 1 – $32.50r – us Archival [071]

DESHLER RUSTLER – Deshler, NE. -w. Jun. 1899-Feb. 1905; Jul. 1905-Jun. 1906; Nov. 1906-Aug. 1918; Jan. 1919- – 1 – us NE Hist [071]

Deshoulieres, Antoinette du L de la G *see* OEUVRES DE MADAME ET DE MADEMOISELLE DESHOULIERES

Deshusses, J *see* LE SACRAMENTAIRE GREGORIEN

DESIAT LET SOVETSKOGO STROITELSTVA : SBORNIK STATE I / ed by Riabinina L – [Moskva]: Ogonek, 1927 – 1 – CSUX88-B1561 – us Hoover Inst Photo [947]

DESIAT' LET SOVETSKOI KOOPERATSII / Tikhomirov, V A – M., 1927 – 1mf – 9 – COR-190/1 – ne IDC [334]

DESIAT' LET SOVETSKOI PROMYSLOVOI KOOPERATSII, 1917-27 / Frommett, B R – M., 1927 – 1mf – 9 – COR-454/1 – ne IDC [334]

DESIATICHNAIA MEZHDUNARODNAIA KLASSIFIKATSII A KNIG : SOKRASHCHENNYE TABLITSY, SOSTAVLENNYE OSOBOI KOMISSIE I PRI GLAVPOLITPROSVETE DLIA OBIAZATELNOGO UPOTREBLENIIA V BIBLIOTEKAKH R.S.F.S.R – [Gomel]: Gos. izd-vo, 1921 – 1 – CSUX91-B814 – us Hoover Inst Photo [020]

DESIAT'LET NA KOOPERATIVNOI RABOTE : VOLOGOD. OBSHCHESTVO SEL'SKOGO KHOZIALISTVA (1908-1918) / Shevtsov, A – Vologda, 1918 – 1mf – 9 – COR-143/1 – ne IDC [334]

IL DESIDERIO OVERO DE' CONCERTI DI VARII STRUMENTI MUSICALI.. / Bottrigari, Ercole – 1594 – 9 – us Sibley [780]

DESIDERIUS ERASMUS : CONCERNING THE AIM AND METHOD OF EDUCATION / Woodward, William Harrison – Cambridge: University Press, 1904 – 1mf – 9 – 0-8370-7599-8 – 1986-1599 – us A.T.L.A. [370]

DESIDERIUS ERASMUS OF ROTTERDAM / Emerton, Ephraim – New York: G.P. Putnam, c1899. (Heroes of the Reformation; [v3]) – 2mf – us A.T.L.A. [240]

DESIGN – (1972-. 5,6. 1976-. 9) – England. v. 1- 1949- – 1 – us UMI [760]

DESIGN – (v. 69- 1967- 5,6. v. 71- 1969- 9) – 1- 1899- – 1 – us UMI [760]

DESIGN / Victoria and Albert Museum. London – (10,000 captioned photographs of designs for buildings, furniture, costume. Fashion plates. Theatrical designs. Bookbinding. With printed index) – 172mf – 9 – $945.00 – uk Mindata [700]

DESIGN ABSTRACTS: INTERNATIONAL – 1977- – 5,6,9 – us UMI [030]

THE DESIGN AND IMPLEMENTATION OF A PROGRAM OF MINISTRY TO NON-PARTICIPATING RESIDENT MEMBERS OF BEREA BAPTIST CHURCH / Jenkins, Floyd Thomas, jr – 1981 – 1 – 5.00 – us Baptist [240]

DESIGN AND OPERATION OF COLD STORES IN DEVELOPING COUNTRIES – 1984 – 89p – it F.A.O. [631]

DESIGN AND OPERATION OF IRRIGATION SYSTEMS FOR SMALLHOLDER AGRICULTURE IN SOUTH ASIA – 1986 – 153p – it F.A.O. [627]

DESIGN AND OPTIMIZATION OF IRRIGATION DISTRIBUTION NETWORKS – 1988 – 261p – it F.A.O. [631]

DESIGN BY MOTLEY : THEATRE SET AND COSTUME DESIGNS FROM 1932-1976 / Illinois University – (Coll of over 4,700 outstanding theatre set and costume designs from the design team consisting of Margaret Harris, Sophia Harris and Elizabeth Montgomery. Includes printed catalogue) – 1992 – 58mf – 15 – $1,330.00 – 1-869934-49-0 – uk Emmett [790]

DESIGN CENTRE SELECTION / The Design Council – (7000 British-made products, from baths and benches to television and tools. Names, specifications, dimensions, prices, manufacturers and designers. Includes Design Council Awards since 1973. Printed index by product type) – 1984 – 159mf – 9 – $630.00 – 1-900853-16-7 – uk Mindata [740]

DESIGN COST AND DATA FOR BUILDING DESIGN MANAGEMENT – v25-. 1981- – 1,5,6,9 – us UMI [720]

The Design Council *see* DESIGN CENTRE SELECTION

DESIGN DRAFTING AND REPROGRAPHICS – v6. 1982 – 1 – us UMI [073]

DESIGN ENGINEERING – (v1-16 1955-70 Can$415.00) – Toronto. v1-39. 1955-93 – 1 – Can$60.00y – cn Micromedia [620]

DESIGN ENGINEERING – v1-53 1955-82 – 1,5,6,9 – us UMI [620]

A DESIGN FOR DEVELOPMENT IN WEST IRIAN; REPORT / United Nations. Development Programme – SE 6542 1. 1968 – 9 – ne IDC [338]

DESIGN GRAPHICS WORLD – v7-. 1983- – 1,5,6,9 – us UMI [073]

DESIGN HORIZONS – 1985-. -q – 1 – us UMI [073]

DESIGN INTERCONNECTIONS – Pattee, University Park, PA. 1989. 178p. In progress – 9 – $0.50f – us Lawrence Pub [720]

DESIGN MANUAL ON BASIC WOOD HARVESTING TECHNOLOGY – 1989 – 126p – it F.A.O. [634]

DESIGN OF AGRICULTURAL INVESTMENT PROJECTS – 1989 – 102p – it F.A.O. [332]

DESIGN QUARTERLY – (1971-. 5,6. 1975-. 9) – v. 1- 1946- – 1 – us UMI [760]

DESIGN TODAY – 1985-. -q – 1 – us UMI [073]

DESIGN VON LOCUS- UND GEWEBESPEZIFISCHEN RETROVIRALEN VEKTOREN FUER EINE IN VIVO GENTHERAPIE / Saller, Robert Michael – 1995 – 2mf – 9 – DM80.00 – 3-8267-2151-9 – gw Hänsel [574]

DESIGNING PROCEDURES FOR THE PROVISION OF NEW FACILITIES FOR CENTRAL BAPTIST ASSOCIATION / Overton, Carl McKinely – 1982 – 1 – 5.00 – us Baptist [240]

DESIGNS FOR SHOP-FRONTS AND DOOR-CASES / Taylor, L & Taylor, J – O 1142 1 – 9 – ne IDC [380]

LE DESIR DE VOIR L'HOSTIE ET LES ORIGINES DE LA DEVOTION AU SAINT-SACREMENT / Dumoutet, E – Paris, 1926 – 2mf – 8 – Dfl9.00 – ne Slangenburg [240]

THE DESIRE OF INDIA / Datta, Surendra Kumar – (Includes index) – London: Young People's Missionary Movt [1908] – 1mf – 9 – 0-8370-6103-2 – 1986-0103 – us A.T.L.A. [240]

THE DESIRE OF THE EYES AND OTHER STORIES / Allen, Grant – New York: R.F. Fenno, c1895. 05021. (Pre-1900 Canadiana) – 9 – cn C.I.H.M. [830]

Desjardins, A *see* LE CONGRES INTERNATIONAL DE DROIT MARITIME DE G-NES (SEMPTEMBRE 1892)

Desjardins, E *see* THE WEEK SANCTIFIED BY THE DEVOTION TO THE SACRED HEART OF JESUS

Desjardins, J F *see* SIXIEME RAPPORT ANNUEL SUR LES TRAVAUX DE LA SOCIETE D'HISTOIRE NATURELLE DE L'ILE MAURICE

Desjardins, Jeannette *see* BIBLIOGRAPHIE ANALYTIQUE DE L'OEUVRE DU DOCTEUR JEAN-BAPTISTE JOBIN, PRESIDENT DU COLLEGE DES MEDECINS ET CHIRURGIENS DE LA PROVINCE DE QUEBEC

Desjardins, Joseph *see* GUIDE PARLEMENTAIRE HISTORIQUE DE LA PROVINCE DE QUEBEC, 1792 A 1902

Desjardins, Louis Georges *see* DISCOURS DE M. L. G. DESJARDINS, DEPUTE DU DISTRICT ELECTORAL DE MONTMORENCY, SUR LES FINANCES DE LA PROVINCE DE QUEBEC, FAIT A L'ASSEMBLEE LEGISLATIVE, A LA SEANCE DU MARDI LE 11 MAI 1886

Desjardins, Ls. E *see* EXPOSE SOMMAIRE DES AFFAIRES RELATIVES A L'INTERPRETATION DES DECRETS DE FEVRIER 1876 ET 1883

Desjardins, Paul *see* CATHOLICISME ET CRITIQUE

Desjardins, Soeur *see* ESQUISSE BIO-BIBLIOGRAPHIQUE DE MONSIEUR LE NOTAIRE LEONIDAS BACHAND, PRESIDENT DE L'ALLIANCE FRANCAISE DE SHERBROOKE

DESJARDIN'S SPEAKER'S DECISIONS / Canada. Quebec – 1v. 1867-1901; L'Assemblee Legislative, 1902 (all publ) – 13mf – 9 – $19.50 – LLMC 81-072 – us L.L.M.C. [324]

DESK BOOK FOR CHIEF JUDGES OF U.S. DISTRICT COURTS / Wheeler, Russell R – (Including revision pages through Nov. 1985) – Washington: FJC, 1984 – 3mf – 9 – $4.50 – LLMC 95-809 – us L.L.M.C. [340]

DESK DIARIES / Lansing, Robert – 1915-22 – 1 – $59.00 – us L of C Photodup [920]

DESKTOP COMPUTING – v1-3. 1981-83 – 1,5,6,9 – us UMI [510]

Deslandes, Germain *see* CLIMATOLOGIE, PEDOLOGIE ET ECOLOGIE FORESTIERES AU CANADA, 1937-1956

Deslauriers, Francoise *see* BIO-BIBLIOGRAPHIE ANALYTIQUE DE M. AIME PLAMONDON

Desloge, T *see* ETUDES SUR LA SIGNIFICATION DES CHOSES LITURGIQUES

Desmarais, Odilon *see* PLAIDOYER DE M. O. DESMARAIS L'AFFAIRE DE NAPOLEON DEMERS

Desmarest, Henri *see* LA FEMME FUTURE

Desmarets de Saint-Sorlin, J *see*
- LA COMPARAISON DE LA LANGUE ET DE LA POESIE FRANCOISE AVEC LA GRECQUE ET LA LATINE
- LA DEFENSE DE LA POESIE ET DE LA LANGUE FRANCOISE
- LA DEFENSE DU POEME HEROIQUE

Desmarets, P *see* HISTOIRE DE MAGDELAINE BAVENT, RELIGIEUSE DU MONASTERE DE SAINT LOUIS DE LOUVIERS

Desmaze, Ch *see* RAPPORTS A SON EXCELLENCE LE MINISTRE DE L'INTERIEUR SUR L'EMIGRATION: ANNEES 1857 ET 1858

Desmazieres, J B H J *see*
- AGROSTOGRAPHIE DES DEPARTEMENTS DU NORD DE LA FRANCE
- CATALOGUE DES PLANTES OMISES DANS LA BOTANOGRAPHIE BELGIQUE ET DANS LES FLORES DU NORD DE LA FRANCE

Desmazures, Adam Charles Gustave *see*
- COLBERT ET LE CANADA
- COURS D'ARCHEOLOGIE UNIVERSITE LAVAL DE MONTREAL: LES INDES, L'EGYPTE, L'ASSYRIE, LA PALESTINE
- M. FAILLON, PRETREDE ST SULPICE: SA VIE ET SES OEUVRES
- M. FLAVIEN MARTINEAU, PRETRE DE ST SULPICE: ESQUISSE BIOGRAPHIQUE

Desmond, Humphrey J *see*
- THE A.P.A. MOVEMENT
- MOOTED QUESTIONS OF HISTORY

Desmousseaux, Antoine F *see* TABLEAU STATISTIQUE DU DEPARTEMENT DE L'OURTHE

Desnoyers, Paul-Henri *see* LE PATRONAGE, OEUVRE DE FORMATION POUR LA JEUNESSE

LE DESOEUVRE OU L'ESPOIN DU BOULEVARD DU TEMPLE: CHRONIQUE SCANDALEUSE DES PETITS THEATRES... AU XVIIIE SIECLE / Mayeur de Saint Paul, Francois Marie – Paris: E. Sansot, 1907. 155p. 2 fiches. (Literature Collection) – 9 – 6.00 – fr Bibl Nationale [440]

LES DESORDRES DE L'AMOUR / Villedieu, Marie C H des Jardins – 1676 – 1 – uk Microform Academic [810]

DESORMAIS : HEBDO DU NOUVEAU QUEBECOIS – Outremont, Canada. avr 1966 – 1r – 1 – Can$25.00 – cn Can Microfilming [072]

Desormonts, M *see* LES SYSTEMES DE REPRESENTATION DANS LES CONTES DU VETALA

DESOTO PILOT – DeSoto, NE. -w. May 1857-May 1858 – 1 – us NE Hist [071]

Despagnet, F *see* ESSAI SUR LES PROTECTORATS

DESPATCH *see* THE UITENHAGE TIMES

DESPATCHES AND OTHER DOCUMENTS ON THE SUBJECT OF THE INTERCOLONIAL RAILWAY – Quebec: Hunter, Rose & Lemieux, 1863. SEM105P647 – 1mf – 9 – Can$2.25 – cn Bibl Nat [971]

DESPATCHES FROM U.S. CONSULAR REPRESENTATIVES IN PUERTO RICO, 1821-99 / U.S. Department of State – 31r – 1 – M76 – us Nat'l Archives [975]

DESPATCHES FROM U.S. CONSULS IN AARAU, SWITZERLAND, 1898-1902 / U.S. Department of State – 1r – 1 – T502 – us Nat'l Archives [977]

DESPATCHES FROM U.S. CONSULS IN ACAPULCO, MEXICO, 1823-1906 / U.S. Department of State – Printed Guide – 8r – 1 – M143 – us Nat'l Archives [972]

DESPATCHES FROM U.S. CONSULS IN ADEN, 1880-1906 / U.S. Department of State – 3r – 1 – T503 – us Nat'l Archives [956]

DESPATCHES FROM U.S. CONSULS IN AGUASCALIENTES, MEXICO, 1901-1906 / U.S. Department of State – Printed Guide – 1r – 1 – M285 – us Nat'l Archives [972]

DESPATCHES FROM U.S. CONSULS IN AIX-LA-CHAPELLE GERMANY, 1849-1906 / U.S. Department of State – 11r – 1 – $253.00 – T356 – us Nat'l Archives [327]

DESPATCHES FROM U.S. CONSULS IN ALEPPO, SYRIA, 1835-1840 / U.S. Department of State – 1r – 1 – T188 – us Nat'l Archives [956]

DESPATCHES FROM U.S. CONSULS IN ALEXANDRETTA, TURKEY, 1896-1906 / U.S. Department of State – 1r – 1 – T504 – us Nat'l Archives [956]

DESPATCHES FROM U.S. CONSULS IN ALEXANDRIA, EGYPT, 1835-73 / U.S. Department of State – 7r – 1 – T45 – us Nat'l Archives [960]

DESPATCHES FROM U.S. CONSULS IN ALGIERS, ALGERIA, 1785-1906 / U.S. Department of State – 19r – 1 – M23 – us Nat'l Archives [960]

DESPATCHES FROM U.S. CONSULS IN ALICANTE, SPAIN, 1788-1905 / U.S. Department of State – 3r – 1 – T357 – us Nat'l Archives [946]

DESPATCHES FROM U.S. CONSULS IN ALTONA GERMANY, 1838-1869 / U.S. Department of State – 5r – 1 – $115.00 – T358 – us Nat'l Archives [327]

DESPATCHES FROM U.S. CONSULS IN AMAPALA, HONDURAS, 1873-1886 / U.S. Department of State – See also: Tegucigalpa, Honduras, 1871-94 (Rolls 1-4) – 1r – 1 – T589 – us Nat'l Archives [972]

DESPATCHES FROM U.S. CONSULS IN AMHERSTBURG, CANADA, 1882-1906 / U.S. Department of State – 2r – 1 – T590 – us Nat'l Archives [971]

DESPATCHES FROM U.S. CONSULS IN AMOOR RIVER, RUSSIA, 1856-74 / U.S. Department of State – 2r – 1 – T111 – us Nat'l Archives [947]

DESPATCHES FROM U.S. CONSULS IN AMOY, CHINA, 1844-1906 / U.S. Department of State – 15r – 1 – M100 – us Nat'l Archives [950]

DESPATCHES FROM U.S. CONSULS IN AMSTERDAM, NETHERLANDS, 1790-1906 / U.S. Department of State – 7r – 1 – M446 – us Nat'l Archives [949]

DESPATCHES FROM U.S. CONSULS IN ANCONA, ITALY, 1840-74 / U.S. Department of State – 2r – 1 – T359 – us Nat'l Archives [945]

DESPATCHES FROM U.S. CONSULS IN ANNABERG GERMANY, 1882-1906 / U.S. Department of State – 3r – 1 – $69.00 – T592 – us Nat'l Archives [327]

DESPATCHES FROM U.S. CONSULS IN ANTIGUA, LEEWARD ISLANDS, BRITISH WEST INDIES, 1794-1906 / U.S. Department of State – 9r – 1 – T327 – us Nat'l Archives [972]

DESPATCHES FROM U.S. CONSULS IN ANTOFAGASTA, CHILE, 1893-1906 / U.S. Department of State – 1r – 1 – T505 – us Nat'l Archives [972]

DESPATCHES FROM U.S. CONSULS IN ANTUNG, MANCHURIA, CHINA / U.S. Department of State – 1904-06. 1 roll – 1 – M447 – us Nat'l Archives [950]

DESPATCHES FROM U.S. CONSULS IN ANTWERP, BELGIUM, 1802-1906 / U.S. Department of State – 14r – 1 – T181 – us Nat'l Archives [949]

DESPATCHES FROM U.S. CONSULS IN APIA, SAMOA, 1843-1906 / U.S. Department of State – 27r – 1 – T27 – us Nat'l Archives [980]

DESPATCHES FROM U.S. CONSULS IN ARCHANGEL, RUSSIA, 1833-61 / U.S. Department of State – (Printed guide) – 1r – 1 – M481 – us Nat'l Archives [947]

DESPATCHES FROM U.S. CONSULS IN ARICA, CHILE, 1849-1906 / U.S. Department of State – 2r – 1 – T328 – us Nat'l Archives [972]

DESPATCHES FROM U.S. CONSULS IN ASUNCION, PARAGUAY, 1844-1906 / U.S. Department of State – 6r – 1 – T329 – us Nat'l Archives [972]

DESPATCHES FROM U.S. CONSULS IN ATHENS, GREECE, 1837-1906 / U.S. Department of State – 8r – 1 – T362 – us Nat'l Archives [949]

DESPATCHES FROM U.S. CONSULS IN AUGSBURG GERMANY, 1846-1873 / U.S. Department of State – 1r – 1 – $23.00 – T361 – us Nat'l Archives [327]

DESPATCHES FROM U.S. CONSULS IN AUX CAYES, HAITI, 1797-1874 / U.S. Department of State – 4r – 1 – T330 – us Nat'l Archives [972]

DESPATCHES FROM U.S. CONSULS IN BAGHDAD, IRAQ, 1888-1906 / U.S. Department of State – 2r – 1 – T509 – us Nat'l Archives [956]

DESPATCHES FROM U.S. CONSULS IN BAHIA, BRAZIL, 1850-1906 / U.S. Department of State – 8r. (See St. Salvador, Brazil, for earlier despatches) – 1 – T331 – us Nat'l Archives [972]

DESPATCHES FROM U.S. CONSULS IN BAMBERG GERMANY, 1892-1906 / U.S. Department of State – 1 – $23.00 – T510 – us Nat'l Archives [327]

DESPATCHES FROM U.S. CONSULS IN BANGKOK, SIAM / U.S. Department of State – 1856-1906. 6 rolls – 1 – M448 – us Nat'l Archives [950]

DESPATCHES FROM U.S. CONSULS IN BARACOA, CUBA, 1827-46; 1878-99 / U.S. Department of State – 3r – 1 – T511 – us Nat'l Archives [972]

DESPATCHES FROM U.S. CONSULS IN BARBADOS, BRITISH WEST INDIES, 1823-1906 / U.S. Department of State – 17r – 1 – T333 – us Nat'l Archives [972]

DESPATCHES FROM U.S. CONSULS IN BARCELONA, SPAIN, 1797-1906 / U.S. Department of State – 15r – 1 – T121 – us Nat'l Archives [946]

DESPATCHES FROM U.S. CONSULS IN BARRANQUILLA, COLOMBIA, 1883-1906 / U.S. Department of State – (See Sabanilla, Colombia, for earlier despatches) – 6r – 1 – T512 – us Nat'l Archives [972]

DESPATCHES FROM U.S. CONSULS IN BASLE, SWITZERLAND, 1830-1906 / U.S. Department of State – 9r – 1 – T364 – us Nat'l Archives [949]

DESPATCHES FROM U.S. CONSULS IN BATAVIA, JAVA, NETHERLANDS, EAST INDIES / U.S. Department of State – 1818-1906. 6 rolls – 1 – M449 – us Nat'l Archives [324]

DESPATCHES FROM U.S. CONSULS IN BATHURST, GAMBIA, BRITISH AFRICA, 1857-89 / U.S. Department of State – 2r – 1 – T365 – us Nat'l Archives [960]

DESPATCHES FROM U.S. CONSULS IN BATUM, U.S.S.R., 1890-1906 (SIC) / U.S. Department of State – Printed guide – 1r – 1 – M482 – us Nat'l Archives [949]

DESPATCHES FROM U.S. CONSULS IN BAY OF ISLANDS AND AUCKLAND, NEW ZEALAND, 1839-1906 / U.S. Department of State – 13r – 1 – T49 – us Nat'l Archives [980]

DESPATCHES FROM U.S. CONSULS IN BAYONNE, FRANCE, 1835-65 / U.S. Department of State – 1r – 1 – T366 – us Nat'l Archives [944]

DESPATCHES FROM U.S. CONSULS IN BEIRUT, LEBANON, 1836-1906 / U.S. Department of State – 23r – 1 – T367 – us Nat'l Archives [956]

DESPATCHES FROM U.S. CONSULS IN BELFAST, UNITED KINGDOM, 1796-1906 / U.S. Department of State – 11r – 1 – T368 – us Nat'l Archives [941]

DESPATCHES FROM U.S. CONSULS IN BELGRADE, SERBIA, 1883-1906 / U.S. Department of State – 1r – 1 – T513 – us Nat'l Archives [949]

DESPATCHES FROM U.S. CONSULS IN BELIZE, BRITISH HONDURAS, 1847-1906 / U.S. Department of State – 8r – 1 – T334 – us Nat'l Archives [972]

DESPATCHES FROM U.S. CONSULS IN BELLEVILLE, CANADA, 1878-1906 / U.S. Department of State – 2r – 1 – T514 – us Nat'l Archives [971]

DESPATCHES FROM U.S. CONSULS IN BERGEN, NORWAY, 1821-1906 / U.S. Department of State – 4r – 1 – T369 – us Nat'l Archives [948]

DESPATCHES FROM U.S. CONSULS IN BERLIN GERMANY, 1865-1906 / U.S. Department of State – 27r – 1 – $621.00 – T163 – us Nat'l Archives [327]

DESPATCHES FROM U.S. CONSULS IN BERMUDA, BRITISH WEST INDIES, 1818-1906 / U.S. Department of State – 11r – 1 – T262 – us Nat'l Archives [972]

DESPATCHES FROM U.S. CONSULS IN BERNE, SWITZERLAND, 1882-1906 / U.S. Department of State – 3r – 1 – T528 – us Nat'l Archives [949]

DESPATCHES FROM U.S. CONSULS IN BILBAO, SPAIN, 1791-1875 / U.S. Department of State – 1r – 1 – T183 – us Nat'l Archives [946]

DESPATCHES FROM U.S. CONSULS IN BIRMINGHAM, UNITED KINGDOM, 1869-1906 / U.S. Department of State – 6r – 1 – T247 – us Nat'l Archives [941]

DESPATCHES FROM U.S. CONSULS IN BOGOTA, COLOMBIA, 1851-1906 / U.S. Department of State – 4r – 1 – T116 – us Nat'l Archives [972]

DESPATCHES FROM U.S. CONSULS IN BOMA, CONGO, 1888-95 / U.S. Department of State – 2r – 1 – T47 – us Nat'l Archives [960]

DESPATCHES FROM U.S. CONSULS IN BOMBAY, INDIA, 1838-1906 / U.S. Department of State – Printed guide – 8r – 1 – M168 – us Nat'l Archives [950]

DESPATCHES FROM U.S. CONSULS IN BORDEAUX, FRANCE, 1783-1906 / U.S. Department of State – 13r – 1 – T164 – us Nat'l Archives [944]

DESPATCHES FROM U.S. CONSULS IN BOULOGNE, FRANCE, 1866-74 / U.S. Department of State – 1r – 1 – T413 – us Nat'l Archives [944]

DESPATCHES FROM U.S. CONSULS IN BRADFORD, UNITED KINGDOM, 1865-1906 / U.S. Department of State – 8r – 1 – T165 – us Nat'l Archives [941]

DESPATCHES FROM U.S. CONSULS IN BREMEN GERMANY, 1794-1906 / U.S. Department of State – 21r – 1 – $483.00 – T184 – us Nat'l Archives [327]

DESPATCHES FROM U.S. CONSULS IN BREMEN GERMANY, 1868-1906 / U.S. Department of State – T363 – 6r – 1 – $204.00 – us Scholarly Res [327]

DESPATCHES FROM U.S. CONSULS IN BRESLAU, POLAND, 1878-1906 (SIC) / U.S. Department of State – 3r – 1 – T532 – us Nat'l Archives [943]

DESPATCHES FROM U.S. CONSULS IN BRINDISI, ITALY, 1864-76 / U.S. Department of State – 1r – 1 – T370 – us Nat'l Archives [945]

DESPATCHES FROM U.S. CONSULS IN BRISTOL, UNITED KINGDOM, 1792-1906 / U.S. Department of State – 16r – 1 – T185 – us Nat'l Archives [941]

DESPATCHES FROM U.S. CONSULS IN BROCKVILLE, CANADA, 1885-1906 / U.S. Department of State – 1r – 1 – T530 – us Nat'l Archives [971]

DESPATCHES FROM U.S. CONSULS IN BRUNEI, BORNEO, 1862-68 / U.S. Department of State – 1r – 1 – T110 – us Nat'l Archives [972]

DESPATCHES FROM U.S. CONSULS IN BRUNSWICK (BRAUNSCHWEIG) GERMANY, 1858-1906 / U.S. Department of State – 6r – 1 – $138.00 – T371 – us Nat'l Archives [327]

DESPATCHES FROM U.S. CONSULS IN BRUSA (BROUSA), TURKEY, 1837-40 / U.S. Department of State – 1r – 1 – T711 – us Nat'l Archives [956]

DESPATCHES FROM U.S. CONSULS IN BRUSSELS, BELGIUM, 1863-1906 / U.S. Department of State – 4r – 1 – T166 – us Nat'l Archives [949]

DESPATCHES FROM U.S. CONSULS IN BUCHAREST, RUMANIA, 1866-85; 1892-1906 / U.S. Department of State – 3r – 1 – T285 – us Nat'l Archives [947]

DESPATCHES FROM U.S. CONSULS IN BUDAPEST HUNGARY, 1876-1906 / U.S. Department of State – 4r – 1 – $92.00 – T531 – us Nat'l Archives [327]

DESPATCHES FROM U.S. CONSULS IN BUENAVENTURA, COLOMBIA, 1867-85 / U.S. Department of State – 1r – 1 – M140 – us Nat'l Archives [972]

DESPATCHES FROM U.S. CONSULS IN BUENOS AIRES, ARGENTINA, 1811-1906 / U.S. Department of State – 25r – 1 – M70 – us Nat'l Archives [972]

DESPATCHES FROM U.S. CONSULS IN BURSLEM, UNITED KINGDOM, 1905-6 / U.S. Department of State – 1r – 1 – T533 – us Nat'l Archives [941]

DESPATCHES FROM U.S. CONSULS IN BUTARITARI, GILBERT ISLANDS, 1888-92 / U.S. Department of State – 1r – 1 – T89 – us Nat'l Archives [980]

DESPATCHES FROM U.S. CONSULS IN CADIZ, SPAIN, 1791-1904 / U.S. Department of State – 20r – 1 – T186 – us Nat'l Archives [976]

DESPATCHES FROM U.S. CONSULS IN CAGLIARI, ITALY, 1802-25 / U.S. Department of State – 1r – 1 – T187 – us Nat'l Archives [945]

DESPATCHES FROM U.S. CONSULS IN CAIRO, EGYPT, 1864-1906 / U.S. Department of State – 24r – 1 – T41 – us Nat'l Archives [960]

DESPATCHES FROM U.S. CONSULS IN CALAIS, FRANCE, 1804-1906 / U.S. Department of State – 1r – 1 – T373 – us Nat'l Archives [944]

DESPATCHES FROM U.S. CONSULS IN CALCUTTA, INDIA / U.S. Department of State – 1792-1906. 7 rolls – 1 – M450 – us Nat'l Archives [950]

DESPATCHES FROM U.S. CONSULS IN CALLAO, PERU, 1854-1906 / U.S. Department of State – Printed guide – 17r – 1 – M155 – us Nat'l Archives [972]

DESPATCHES FROM U.S. CONSULS IN CAMARGO, MEXICO, 1870-80 / U.S. Department of State – Printed guide – 1r – 1 – M288 – us Nat'l Archives [972]

DESPATCHES FROM U.S. CONSULS IN CAMPBELLTON, CANADA, 1897-1906 / U.S. Department of State – 1r – 1 – T535 – us Nat'l Archives [971]

DESPATCHES FROM U.S. CONSULS IN CAMPECHE, MEXICO, 1820-80 / U.S. Department of State – Printed guide – 1r – 1 – M286 – us Nat'l Archives [972]

DESPATCHES FROM U.S. CONSULS IN CANDIA, CRETE, GREECE, 1836-41 / U.S. Department of State – 1r – 1 – T374 – us Nat'l Archives [949]

DESPATCHES FROM U.S. CONSULS IN CANEA, CRETE, GREECE, 1832-74 / U.S. Department of State – (See also: Cyprus) – 2r – 1 – T190 – us Nat'l Archives [949]

DESPATCHES FROM U.S. CONSULS IN CANNES, FRANCE, 1891 / U.S. Department of State – 1r – 1 – T537 – us Nat'l Archives [944]

DESPATCHES FROM U.S. CONSULS IN CANTON, CHINA, 1790-1906 / U.S. Department of State – Printed guide – 20r – 1 – M101 – us Nat'l Archives [950]

DESPATCHES FROM U.S. CONSULS IN CAP HAITIEN, HAITI, 1797-1906 / U.S. Department of State – 17r – 1 – M9 – us Nat'l Archives [972]

DESPATCHES FROM U.S. CONSULS IN CAPE GRACIAS A DIOS, NICARAGUA, 1903-6 / U.S. Department of State – 1r – 1 – T538 – us Nat'l Archives [972]

DESPATCHES FROM U.S. CONSULS IN CAPE TOWN, UNION OF SOUTH AFRICA, 1800-1906 / U.S. Department of State – 22r – 1 – T191 – us Nat'l Archives [960]

DESPATCHES FROM U.S. CONSULS IN CARACAS, VENEZUELA, 1868-85 / U.S. Department of State – 1r – 1 – T599 – us Nat'l Archives [972]

DESPATCHES FROM U.S. CONSULS IN CARDENAS, CUBA, 1843-45; 1879-98 / U.S. Department of State – 5r – 1 – T583 – us Nat'l Archives [972]

DESPATCHES FROM U.S. CONSULS IN CARDIFF, UNITED KINGDOM, 1861-1906 / U.S. Department of State – 6r – 1 – T375 – us Nat'l Archives [941]

DESPATCHES FROM U.S. CONSULS IN CARLISLE, UNITED KINGDOM, 1867-69 / U.S. Department of State – 1r – 1 – T639 – us Nat'l Archives [941]

DESPATCHES FROM U.S. CONSULS IN CARLSBAD CZECHOSLOVAKIA, 1902-1906 / U.S. Department of State – 1r – 1 – $23.00 – T540 – us Nat'l Archives [327]

DESPATCHES FROM U.S. CONSULS IN CARLSRUHE (KARLSRUHE) GERMANY, 1854-74 / U.S. Department of State – 3r – 1 – $69.00 – T541 – us Nat'l Archives [327]

DESPATCHES FROM U.S. CONSULS IN CARRARA, ITALY, 1852-81 / U.S. Department of State – 1r – 1 – T376 – us Nat'l Archives [945]

DESPATCHES FROM U.S. CONSULS IN CARTAGENA, COLOMBIA, 1822-1906 / U.S. Department of State – 14r – 1 – T192 – us Nat'l Archives [972]

DESPATCHES FROM U.S. CONSULS IN CARTAGENA, SPAIN / U.S. Department of State – 1863-1906. 1 roll – 1 – 377 – us Nat'l Archives [946]

DESPATCHES FROM U.S. CONSULS IN CASTELLAMARE DI STABIA, ITALY, 1878-1906 / U.S. Department of State – 3r – 1 – T543 – us Nat'l Archives [945]

DESPATCHES FROM U.S. CONSULS IN CATANIA, ITALY, 1883-1906 / U.S. Department of State – 4r – 1 – T544 – us Nat'l Archives [945]

DESPATCHES FROM U.S. CONSULS IN CAYENNE, FRENCH GUIANA, 1801-97 / U.S. Department of State – 1r – 1 – T378 – us Nat'l Archives [972]

DESPATCHES FROM U.S. CONSULS IN CETTE, FRANCE, 1802-40 / U.S. Department of State – 1r – 1 – T379 – us Nat'l Archives [944]

DESPATCHES FROM U.S. CONSULS IN CHARLOTTETOWN, CANADA, 1857-1906 / U.S. Department of State – 5r – 1 – T462. (See also: Pictou, Canada) – us Nat'l Archives [971]

DESPATCHES FROM U.S. CONSULS IN CHATHAM, CANADA, 1879-1906 / U.S. Department of State – 3r – 1 – T546 – us Nat'l Archives [971]

DESPATCHES FROM U.S. CONSULS IN CHAUDIERE JUNCTION, CANADA, 1898-1905 / U.S. Department of State – 1r – 1 – T547 – us Nat'l Archives [971]

DESPATCHES FROM U.S. CONSULS IN CHEFOO, CHINA, 1863-1906 / U.S. Department of State – Printed guide – 9r – 1 – M102 – us Nat'l Archives [950]

DESPATCHES FROM U.S. CONSULS IN CHEMNITZ GERMANY, 1867-1906 / U.S. Department of State – 8r – 1 – $184.00 – T380 – us Nat'l Archives [327]

DESPATCHES FROM U.S. CONSULS IN CHIHUAHUA, MEXICO, 1830-1906 / U.S. Department of State – Printed guide – 3r – 1 – M289 – us Nat'l Archives [972]

DESPATCHES FROM U.S. CONSULS IN CHINKIANG, CHINA, 1864-1902 / U.S. Department of State – (See Nanking, China, for later despatches) – 7r – 1 – M103 – us Nat'l Archives [950]

DESPATCHES FROM U.S. CONSULS IN CHIOS, GREECE, 1862-71 / U.S. Department of State – 1r – 1 – T669 – us Nat'l Archives [949]

DESPATCHES FROM U.S. CONSULS IN CHRISTIANIA, NORWAY, 1869-1906 (SIC) / U.S. Department of State – 5r – 1 – T122 – us Nat'l Archives [948]

DESPATCHES FROM U.S. CONSULS IN CHRISTIANSUND, NORWAY, 1810-91 / U.S. Department of State – 1r – 1 – T235 – us Nat'l Archives [948]

DESPATCHES FROM U.S. CONSULS IN CHUNGKING, CHINA, 1896-1906 / U.S. Department of State – 1r – 1 – M104 – us Nat'l Archives [950]

DESPATCHES FROM U.S. CONSULS IN CIENFUEGOS, CUBA, 1876-1906 / U.S. Department of State – (See also Trinidad, Cuba, for earlier despatches) – 8r – 1 – T548 – us Nat'l Archives [950]

DESPATCHES FROM U.S. CONSULS IN CIUDAD BOLIVAR, VENEZUELA, 1850-93 / U.S. Department of State – 3r – 1 – T335 – us Nat'l Archives [972]

DESPATCHES FROM U.S. CONSULS IN CIUDAD DEL CARMEN, MEXICO, 1830-72 / U.S. Department of State – 1r – 1 – M308 – us Nat'l Archives [972]

DESPATCHES FROM U.S. CONSULS IN CIUDAD JUAREZ (PASO DEL NORTE), MEXICO, 1850-1906 / U.S. Department of State – 6r – 1 – M184 – us Nat'l Archives [972]

DESPATCHES FROM U.S. CONSULS IN CLIFTON, CANADA, 1864-1906 / U.S. Department of State – 7r – 1 – T549 – us Nat'l Archives [971]

DESPATCHES FROM U.S. CONSULS IN COATICOOK, CANADA, 1864-1906 / U.S. Department of State – 4r – 1 – T550 – us Nat'l Archives [971]

DESPATCHES FROM U.S. CONSULS IN COBIJA, BOLIVIA, 1854-74 / U.S. Department of State – 1r – 1 – T381 – us Nat'l Archives [972]

DESPATCHES FROM U.S. CONSULS IN COBURG GERMANY, 1898-1906 / U.S. Department of State – 2r – 1 – $46.00 – T551 – us Nat'l Archives [327]

DESPATCHES FROM U.S. CONSULS IN COGNAC, FRANCE, 1883-98 / U.S. Department of State – (See also La Rochelle, France) – 2r – 1 – T552 – us Nat'l Archives [944]

DESPATCHES FROM U.S. CONSULS IN COLLINGWOOD, CANADA, 1879-1906 / U.S. Department of State – 3r – 1 – T553 – us Nat'l Archives [971]

DESPATCHES FROM U.S. CONSULS IN COLOGNE (KOELN) GERMANY, 1876-1906 / U.S. Department of State – 5r – 1 – $115.00 – T555 – us Nat'l Archives [327]

DESPATCHES FROM U.S. CONSULS IN COLOMBO, CEYLON / U.S. Department of State – 1850-1906. 4 rolls – 1 – M451 – us Nat'l Archives [950]

DESPATCHES FROM U.S. CONSULS IN COLON, PANAMA, 1852-1906 / U.S. Department of State – 19r – 1 – T193 – us Nat'l Archives [972]

DESPATCHES FROM U.S. CONSULS IN COLONIA, URUGUAY, 1870-1906 / U.S. Department of State – 1r – 1 – T556 – us Nat'l Archives [972]

DESPATCHES FROM U.S. CONSULS IN CONSTANTINOPLE, TURKEY, 1820-1906 / U.S. Department of State – 24r – 1 – T194 – us Nat'l Archives [956]

DESPATCHES FROM U.S. CONSULS IN COPENHAGEN, DENMARK, 1792-1906 / U.S. Department of State – 11r – 1 – T195 – us Nat'l Archives [948]

DESPATCHES FROM U.S. CONSULS IN COQUIMBO, CHILE, 1850-98 / U.S. Department of State – (See Valparaiso, Chile, for later despatches) – 1r – 1 – T332 – us Nat'l Archives [972]
DESPATCHES FROM U.S. CONSULS IN CORDOBA, ARGENTINA, 1870-1906 / U.S. Department of State – 1r – 1 – T557 – us Nat'l Archives [972]
DESPATCHES FROM U.S. CONSULS IN CORK, IRELAND, 1800-1906 / U.S. Department of State – 12r – 1 – T196 – us Nat'l Archives [941]
DESPATCHES FROM U.S. CONSULS IN CORNWALL, CANADA, 1901-6 / U.S. Department of State – 2r – 1 – T558 – us Nat'l Archives [971]
DESPATCHES FROM U.S. CONSULS IN CORUNNA, SPAIN, 1867-1906 / U.S. Department of State – 2r – 1 – T450 – us Nat'l Archives [946]
DESPATCHES FROM U.S. CONSULS IN CREFELD (KREFELD) GERMANY, 1878-1906 / U.S. Department of State – 5r – 1 – $115.00 – T559 – us Nat'l Archives [327]
DESPATCHES FROM U.S. CONSULS IN CURACAO, NETHERLANDS WEST INDIES, 1793-1906 / U.S. Department of State – 13r – 1 – T197 – us Nat'l Archives [972]
DESPATCHES FROM U.S. CONSULS IN CYPRUS, 1835-78 / U.S. Department of State – 2r – 1 – T463 – us Nat'l Archives [949]
DESPATCHES FROM U.S. CONSULS IN DAWSON CITY, CANADA, 1898-1906 / U.S. Department of State – 4r – 1 – T560 – us Nat'l Archives [971]
DESPATCHES FROM U.S. CONSULS IN DENIA, SPAIN, 1852-98 / U.S. Department of State – 2r – 1 – T382 – us Nat'l Archives [946]
DESPATCHES FROM U.S. CONSULS IN DRESDEN GERMANY, 1837-1906 / U.S. Department of State – 6r – 1 – $138.00 – T383 – us Nat'l Archives [327]
DESPATCHES FROM U.S. CONSULS IN DUBLIN, IRELAND, 1790-1906 / U.S. Department of State – 11r – 1 – T199 – us Nat'l Archives [941]
DESPATCHES FROM U.S. CONSULS IN DUCHY OF NASSAU GERMANY, 1854-69 / U.S. Department of State – 1r – 1 – $23.00 – T473 – us Nat'l Archives [327]
DESPATCHES FROM U.S. CONSULS IN DUESSELDORF GERMANY, 1881-1906 / U.S. Department of State – 3r – 1 – $69.00 – T562 – us Nat'l Archives [327]
DESPATCHES FROM U.S. CONSULS IN DUNDEE, UNITED KINGDOM, 1834-1906 / U.S. Department of State – 8r – 1 – T200 – us Nat'l Archives [941]
DESPATCHES FROM U.S. CONSULS IN DUNFERMLINE, UNITED KINGDOM, 1877-1906 / U.S. Department of State – 3r – 1 – T561 – us Nat'l Archives [941]
DESPATCHES FROM U.S. CONSULS IN DURANGO, MEXICO, 1886-1906 / U.S. Department of State – Printed guide – 1r – 1 – M290 – us Nat'l Archives [972]
DESPATCHES FROM U.S. CONSULS IN EDINBURGH, UNITED KINGDOM, 1893-1906 / U.S. Department of State – (See Leith, United Kingdom for earlier despatches) – 1r – 1 – T602 – us Nat'l Archives [941]
DESPATCHES FROM U.S. CONSULS IN EIBENSTOCK GERMANY, 1902-6 / U.S. Department of State – 1r – 1 – $23.00 – T565 – us Nat'l Archives [327]
DESPATCHES FROM U.S. CONSULS IN ELBERFELD, LUBECK, AND ROSTOCK GERMANY, 1804-49; 1883-89 / U.S. Department of State – 2r – 1 – $46.00 – T566 – us Nat'l Archives [327]
DESPATCHES FROM U.S. CONSULS IN ELSINORE, DENMARK, 1792-1874 / U.S. Department of State – 6r – 1 – T201 – us Nat'l Archives [948]
DESPATCHES FROM U.S. CONSULS IN ENSENADA, MEXICO, 1888-1906 / U.S. Department of State – Printed Guide – 1r – 1 – M291 – us Nat'l Archives [972]
DESPATCHES FROM U.S. CONSULS IN ERFURT GERMANY, 1892-94 / U.S. Department of State – 1r – 1 – $23.00 – T563 – us Nat'l Archives [327]
DESPATCHES FROM U.S. CONSULS IN ERZERUM, TURKEY, 1895-1904 / U.S. Department of State – 2r – 1 – T568 – us Nat'l Archives [956]
DESPATCHES FROM U.S. CONSULS IN FALMOUTH, BRITISH WEST INDIES, 1790-1905 / U.S. Department of State – 12r – 1 – T202 – us Nat'l Archives [972]
DESPATCHES FROM U.S. CONSULS IN FAYAL, AZORES, 1795-1897 / U.S. Department of State – 11r – 1 – T203 – us Nat'l Archives [949]
DESPATCHES FROM U.S. CONSULS IN FLORENCE, ITALY, 1824-1906 / U.S. Department of State – 10r – 1 – T204 – us Nat'l Archives [943]
DESPATCHES FROM U.S. CONSULS IN FOOCHOW, CHINA, 1849-1906 / U.S. Department of State – Printed guide – 10r – 1 – M105 – us Nat'l Archives [950]
DESPATCHES FROM U.S. CONSULS IN FORT ERIE, CANADA, 1865-1906 / U.S. Department of State – 3r – 1 – T465 – us Nat'l Archives [971]
DESPATCHES FROM U.S. CONSULS IN FRANKFURT ON THE MAIN GERMANY, 1829-1906 / U.S. Department of State – 30r – 1 – $690.00 – M161 – us Nat'l Archives [327]
DESPATCHES FROM U.S. CONSULS IN FREIBURG GERMANY, 1892-1906 / U.S. Department of State – 2r – 1 – $46.00 – T569 – us Nat'l Archives [327]
DESPATCHES FROM U.S. CONSULS IN FUERTH GERMANY, 1890-98 / U.S. Department of State – 1r – 1 – $23.00 – T689 – us Nat'l Archives [327]
DESPATCHES FROM U.S. CONSULS IN FUNCHAL, MADEIRA, PORTUGAL, 1793-1906 / U.S. Department of State – 9r – 1 – T205 – us Nat'l Archives [946]
DESPATCHES FROM U.S. CONSULS IN GABOON, 1856-88 / U.S. Department of State – 1r – 1 – T466 – us Nat'l Archives [960]
DESPATCHES FROM U.S. CONSULS IN GALATZ, RUMANIA, 1858-69 / U.S. Department of State – (See also Bucharest, Rumania) – 1r – 1 – T384 – us Nat'l Archives [947]
DESPATCHES FROM U.S. CONSULS IN GALVESTON, TEXAS, 1832-46 / U.S. Department of State – 2r – 1 – T151 – us Nat'l Archives [978]
DESPATCHES FROM U.S. CONSULS IN GALWAY, IRELAND, 1834-63 / U.S. Department of State – 1r – 1 – T570 – us Nat'l Archives [941]
DESPATCHES FROM U.S. CONSULS IN GARRUCHA, SPAIN, 1877-97 / U.S. Department of State – 1r – 1 – T571 – us Nat'l Archives [946]
DESPATCHES FROM U.S. CONSULS IN GASPE BASIN, CANADA / U.S. Department of State – 1856-1906. 6 rolls – 1 – T467 – us Nat'l Archives [971]
DESPATCHES FROM U.S. CONSULS IN GEESTEMUENDE GERMANY, 1867-82 / U.S. Department of State – 1r – 1 – $23.00 – T385 – us Nat'l Archives [327]
DESPATCHES FROM U.S. CONSULS IN GENEVA, SWITZERLAND, 1855-1906 / U.S. Department of State – 6r – 1 – T387 – us Nat'l Archives [949]
DESPATCHES FROM U.S. CONSULS IN GENOA, ITALY, 1799-1906 / U.S. Department of State – 13r – 1 – T64 – us Nat'l Archives [945]
DESPATCHES FROM U.S. CONSULS IN GEORGETOWN, DEMERARA, BRITISH GUIANA, 1827-1906 / U.S. Department of State – 23r – 1 – T336 – us Nat'l Archives [972]
DESPATCHES FROM U.S. CONSULS IN GHENT, BELGIUM, 1860-1906 / U.S. Department of State – 6r – 1 – T388 – us Nat'l Archives [949]
DESPATCHES FROM U.S. CONSULS IN GIBRALTAR, SPAIN, 1791-1906 / U.S. Department of State – 17r – 1 – T206 – us Nat'l Archives [946]
DESPATCHES FROM U.S. CONSULS IN GLASGOW, UNITED KINGDOM, 1801-1906 / U.S. Department of State – 12r – 1 – T207 – us Nat'l Archives [941]
DESPATCHES FROM U.S. CONSULS IN GLAUCHAU GERMANY, 1891-1906 / U.S. Department of State – 2r – 1 – $46.00 – T572 – us Nat'l Archives [327]
DESPATCHES FROM U.S. CONSULS IN GLOUCESTER, UNITED KINGDOM, 1879-86 / U.S. Department of State – 1r – 1 – T539 – us Nat'l Archives [941]
DESPATCHES FROM U.S. CONSULS IN GODERICH, CANADA,1865-1906 / U.S. Department of State – 4r – 1 – T468 – us Nat'l Archives [971]
DESPATCHES FROM U.S. CONSULS IN GOREE DAKAR, FRENCH AFRICA, 1883-1906 / U.S. Department of State – 2r – 1 – T573 – us Nat'l Archives [960]
DESPATCHES FROM U.S. CONSULS IN GOTHENBURG, SWEDEN, 1800-1906 / U.S. Department of State – 4r – 1 – T276 – us Nat'l Archives [948]
DESPATCHES FROM U.S. CONSULS IN GRAND BASSA, LIBERIA, 1868-82 / U.S. Department of State – 1r – 1 – M171 – us Nat'l Archives [960]
DESPATCHES FROM U.S. CONSULS IN GRENOBLE, FRANCE, 1893-1906 / U.S. Department of State – 1r – 1 – T574 – us Nat'l Archives [944]
DESPATCHES FROM U.S. CONSULS IN GRENVILLE, CANADA, 1904-6 / U.S. Department of State – 1r – 1 – T575 – us Nat'l Archives [971]
DESPATCHES FROM U.S. CONSULS IN GUADELOUPE, FRENCH WEST INDIES, 1802-1906 / U.S. Department of State – 8r – 1 – T208 – us Nat'l Archives [972]
DESPATCHES FROM U.S. CONSULS IN GUAM, 1854-1856 / U. S. Department of State – 1r – 1 – M1306 – us Nat'l Archives [327]
DESPATCHES FROM U.S. CONSULS IN GUATEMALA CITY, GUATEMALA, 1824-1906 / U.S. Department of State – 15r – 1 – T337 – us Nat'l Archives [972]
DESPATCHES FROM U.S. CONSULS IN GUAYAQUIL, ECUADOR, 1826-1906 / U.S. Department of State – 13r – 1 – T209 – us Nat'l Archives [972]
DESPATCHES FROM U.S. CONSULS IN GUAYMAS, MEXICO, 1832-96 / U.S. Department of State – Printed guide – 5r – 1 – M284 – us Nat'l Archives [972]
DESPATCHES FROM U.S. CONSULS IN GUELPH, CANADA, 1883-1906 / U.S. Department of State – 2r – 1 – T578 – us Nat'l Archives [971]
DESPATCHES FROM U.S. CONSULS IN GUERRERO, MEXICO, 1871-88 / U.S. Department of State – Printed guide – 1r – 1 – M292 – us Nat'l Archives [972]
DESPATCHES FROM U.S. CONSULS IN HAKODATE, JAPAN / U.S. Department of State – 1856-78. 1 roll – 1 – M452 – us Nat'l Archives [950]
DESPATCHES FROM U.S. CONSULS IN HALIFAX, CANADA, 1833-1906 / U.S. Department of State – 18r – 1 – T469 – us Nat'l Archives [971]
DESPATCHES FROM U.S. CONSULS IN HAMBURG GERMANY, 1790-1906 / U.S. Department of State – 35r – 1 – $805.00 – T211 – us Nat'l Archives [327]
DESPATCHES FROM U.S. CONSULS IN HAMILTON, CANADA, 1867-1906 / U.S. Department of State – (See also Montreal, Canada) – 8r – 1 – T470 – us Nat'l Archives [971]
DESPATCHES FROM U.S. CONSULS IN HANGCHOW, CHINA, 1904-6 / U.S. Department of State – 1r – 1 – M106 – us Nat'l Archives [950]
DESPATCHES FROM U.S. CONSULS IN HANKOW, CHINA, 1861-1906 / U.S. Department of State – Printed guide – 8r – 1 – M107 – us Nat'l Archives [950]
DESPATCHES FROM U.S. CONSULS IN HANOVER GERMANY, 1854-67; 1893-1906 / U.S. Department of State – 2r – 1 – $46.00 – T372 – us Nat'l Archives [327]
DESPATCHES FROM U.S. CONSULS IN HARPUT, TURKEY, 1895-1906 / U.S. Department of State – 1r – 1 – T579 – us Nat'l Archives [956]
DESPATCHES FROM U.S. CONSULS IN HAVANA, CUBA, 1783-1906 / U.S. Department of State – 133r – 1 – T20 – us Nat'l Archives [972]
DESPATCHES FROM U.S. CONSULS IN HELSINGFORS, FINLAND, 1851-1906 / U.S. Department of State – Printed guide – 1r – 1 – M483 – us Nat'l Archives [948]
DESPATCHES FROM U.S. CONSULS IN HERMOSILLO, MEXICO, 1905-6 / U.S. Department of State – Printed guide – 1r – 1 – M293 – us Nat'l Archives [972]
DESPATCHES FROM U.S. CONSULS IN HESSE-CASSEL GERMANY, 1835-69 / U.S. Department of State – 3r – 1 – $69.00 – T213 – us Nat'l Archives [327]
DESPATCHES FROM U.S. CONSULS IN HESSE-DARMSTADT GERMANY, 1854-71 / U.S. Department of State – 4r – 1 – $92.00 – T390 – us Nat'l Archives [327]
DESPATCHES FROM U.S. CONSULS IN HESSE-HOMBURG GERMANY, 1854-66 / U.S. Department of State – 1r – 1 – $23.00 – T391 – us Nat'l Archives [327]
DESPATCHES FROM U.S. CONSULS IN HILO, HAWAII, 1853-72 / U.S. Department of State – 4r – 1 – T133 – us Nat'l Archives [978]
DESPATCHES FROM U.S. CONSULS IN HOBART, AUSTRALIA, 1842-1906 / U.S. Department of State – 4r – 1 – T127 – us Nat'l Archives [980]
DESPATCHES FROM U.S. CONSULS IN HONG KONG, 1844-1906 / U.S. Department of State – Printed guide – 21r – 1 – M108 – us Nat'l Archives [950]
DESPATCHES FROM U.S. CONSULS IN HONOLULU, HAWAII, 1820-1903 / U.S. Department of State – Printed guide – 22r – 1 – M144 – us Nat'l Archives [978]
DESPATCHES FROM U.S. CONSULS IN HORGEN, SWITZERLAND, 1882-98 / U.S. Department of State – 3r – 1 – T591 – us Nat'l Archives [949]
DESPATCHES FROM U.S. CONSULS IN HUDDERSFIELD, UNITED KINGDOM, 1890-1906 / U.S. Department of State – 1r – 1 – T593 – us Nat'l Archives [941]
DESPATCHES FROM U.S. CONSULS IN HULL, UNITED KINGDOM, 1879-1906 / U.S. Department of State – 4r – 1 – T594 – us Nat'l Archives [941]
DESPATCHES FROM U.S. CONSULS IN ILOILO, PHILIPPINE ISLANDS, 1878-86 / U.S. Department of State – 1r – 1 – T109 – us Nat'l Archives [980]
DESPATCHES FROM U.S. CONSULS IN IQUIQUE, CHILE, 1877-1906 / U.S. Department of State – 5r – 1 – T595 – us Nat'l Archives [972]
DESPATCHES FROM U.S. CONSULS IN JALAPA ENRIQUEZ, MEXICO, 1905-6 / U.S. Department of State – Printed guide – 1r – 1 – M294 – us Nat'l Archives [972]
DESPATCHES FROM U.S. CONSULS IN JEREZ DE LA FRONTERA, SPAIN, 1903-6 / U.S. Department of State – 1r – 1 – T596 – us Nat'l Archives [946]
DESPATCHES FROM U.S. CONSULS IN JERUSALEM, PALESTINE / U.S. Department of State – 1856-1906. 5 rolls – 1 – M453 – us Nat'l Archives [956]
DESPATCHES FROM U.S. CONSULS IN KANAGAWA, JAPAN, 1861-97 / U.S. Department of State – 22r – 1 – M135 – us Nat'l Archives [950]
DESPATCHES FROM U.S. CONSULS IN KEHL GERMANY, 1882-1906 / U.S. Department of State – 5r – 1 – $115.00 – T597 – us Nat'l Archives [327]
DESPATCHES FROM U.S. CONSULS IN KINGSTON, CANADA, 1864-1906 / U.S. Department of State – 5r – 1 – T472 – us Nat'l Archives [971]
DESPATCHES FROM U.S. CONSULS IN KINGSTON, JAMAICA, BRITISH WEST INDIES, 1796-1906 / U.S. Department of State – 40r – 1 – T31 – us Nat'l Archives [972]
DESPATCHES FROM U.S. CONSULS IN KOENIGSBERG (FORMERLY EAST PRUSSIA GERMANY, NOW KALININGRAD U.S.S.R.), 1879-81 / U.S. Department of State – 1r – 1 – $23.00 – T598 – us Nat'l Archives [327]
DESPATCHES FROM U.S. CONSULS IN LA CEIBA, HONDURAS, 1902-6 / U.S. Department of State – 1r – 1 – T545 – us Nat'l Archives [972]
DESPATCHES FROM U.S. CONSULS IN LA GUAIRA, VENEZUELA, 1810-1906 / U.S. Department of State – 23r – 1 – M84 – us Nat'l Archives [972]
DESPATCHES FROM U.S. CONSULS IN LA PAZ, BOLIVIA, 1869-1901 / U.S. Department of State – 2r – 1 – T338 – us Nat'l Archives [972]
DESPATCHES FROM U.S. CONSULS IN LA PAZ, MEXICO / U.S. Department of State – 1855-1906. 5 rolls – 1 – M282 – us Nat'l Archives [972]
DESPATCHES FROM U.S. CONSULS IN LA ROCHELLE, FRANCE, 1794-1906 / U.S. Department of State – 8r – 1 – T394 – us Nat'l Archives [944]
DESPATCHES FROM U.S. CONSULS IN LA UNION, EL SALVADOR, 1854-87 / U.S. Department of State – 1r – 1 – T395 – us Nat'l Archives [972]

DESPATCHES FROM U.S. CONSULS IN LAHAINA, HAWAII, 1850-71 / U.S. Department of State – 3r – 1 – T101 – us Nat'l Archives [978]
DESPATCHES FROM U.S. CONSULS IN LAMBAYEQUE, PERU, 1860-88 / U.S. Department of State – 3r – 1 – T393 – us Nat'l Archives [972]
DESPATCHES FROM U.S. CONSULS IN LAUTHALA, FIJI ISLANDS, 1844-90 / U.S. Department of State – 7r – 1 – T25 – us Nat'l Archives [980]
DESPATCHES FROM U.S. CONSULS IN LE HAVRE, FRANCE, 1789-1906 / U.S. Department of State – 21r – 1 – T212 – us Nat'l Archives [944]
DESPATCHES FROM U.S. CONSULS IN LEEDS UPON HULL, UNITED KINGDOM, 1797-1906 / U.S. Department of State – 14r – 1 – T474 – us Nat'l Archives [941]
DESPATCHES FROM U.S. CONSULS IN LEGHORN, ITALY, 1793-1906 / U.S. Department of State – 10r – 1 – T214 – us Nat'l Archives [945]
DESPATCHES FROM U.S. CONSULS IN LEIPZIG GERMANY, 1826-1906 / U.S. Department of State – 12r – 1 – $276.00 – T215 – us Nat'l Archives [327]
DESPATCHES FROM U.S. CONSULS IN LEITH, UNITED KINGDOM, 1798-1893 / U.S. Department of State – 8r – 1 – T396 – us Nat'l Archives [941]
DESPATCHES FROM U.S. CONSULS IN LEVUKA AND SUVA, FIJI ISLANDS, 1891-1906 / U.S. Department of State – 1r – 1 – T108 – us Nat'l Archives [980]
DESPATCHES FROM U.S. CONSULS IN LIBEREC CZECHOSLOVAKIA, 1886-1906 / U.S. Department of State – 3r – 1 – $69.00 – T664 – us Nat'l Archives [327]
DESPATCHES FROM U.S. CONSULS IN LIEGE, BELGIUM, 1863-1906 / U.S. Department of State – 6r – 1 – T397 – us Nat'l Archives [949]
DESPATCHES FROM U.S. CONSULS IN LIMA, PERU, 1823-54 / U.S. Department of State – Printed guide – 6r – 1 – M154 – us Nat'l Archives [972]
DESPATCHES FROM U.S. CONSULS IN LIMOGES, FRANCE, 1887-1906 / U.S. Department of State – 4r – 1 – T601 – us Nat'l Archives [944]
DESPATCHES FROM U.S. CONSULS IN LINDSAY, CANADA, 1891-92 / U.S. Department of State – 1r – 1 – T603 – us Nat'l Archives [971]
DESPATCHES FROM U.S. CONSULS IN LISBON, PORTUGAL, 1791-1906 / U.S. Department of State – 11r – 1 – T180 – us Nat'l Archives [946]
DESPATCHES FROM U.S. CONSULS IN LIVERPOOL, UNITED KINGDOM, 1790-1906 / U.S. Department of State – 55r – 1 – M141 – us Nat'l Archives [941]
DESPATCHES FROM U.S. CONSULS IN LONDON, ONTARIO, 1885-1906 / U.S. Department of State – 2r – 1 – T604 – us Nat'l Archives [971]
DESPATCHES FROM U.S. CONSULS IN LONDON, UNITED KINGDOM, 1790-1906 / U.S. Department of State – 64r – 1 – T168 – us Nat'l Archives [941]
DESPATCHES FROM U.S. CONSULS IN LONDONDERRY, UNITED KINGDOM, 1835-76 / U.S. Department of State – 3r – 1 – T216 – us Nat'l Archives [941]
DESPATCHES FROM U.S. CONSULS IN LOURENCO MARQUES, MOZAMBIQUE, PORTUGUESE AFRICA, 1854-1906 / U.S. Department of State – 6r – 1 – T171 – us Nat'l Archives [327]
DESPATCHES FROM U.S. CONSULS IN LUCERNE, SWITZERLAND, 1902-6 / U.S. Department of State – 1r – 1 – T605 – us Nat'l Archives [949]
DESPATCHES FROM U.S. CONSULS IN LUDWIGSHAFEN AM RHEIN GERMANY, 1858-74 / U.S. Department of State – 1r – 1 – $23.00 – T585 – us Nat'l Archives [327]
DESPATCHES FROM U.S. CONSULS IN LUXEMBOURG CITY, LUXEMBOURG, 1893-96 / U.S. Department of State – 1r – 1 – T607 – us Nat'l Archives [949]
DESPATCHES FROM U.S. CONSULS IN LYON, FRANCE, 1829-1906 / U.S. Department of State – 14r – 1 – T169 – us Nat'l Archives [944]
DESPATCHES FROM U.S. CONSULS IN MACAO, CHINA, 1849-69 / U.S. Department of State – Printed guide – 2r – 1 – M109 – us Nat'l Archives [950]
DESPATCHES FROM U.S. CONSULS IN MAGDEBURG GERMANY, 1890-1906 / U.S. Department of State – 2r – 1 – $46.00 – T633 – us Nat'l Archives [327]
DESPATCHES FROM U.S. CONSULS IN MAHE, SEYCHELLES ISLANDS, INDIAN OCEAN / U.S. Department of State – 1868-88. 1 roll – 1 – M454 – us Nat'l Archives [950]
DESPATCHES FROM U.S. CONSULS IN MALAGA, SPAIN, 1793-1906 / U.S. Department of State – 17r – 1 – T217 – us Nat'l Archives [946]
DESPATCHES FROM U.S. CONSULS IN MALTA, 1801-1906 / U.S. Department of State – 13r – 1 – T218 – us Nat'l Archives [949]
DESPATCHES FROM U.S. CONSULS IN MANAGUA, NICARAGUA, 1884-1906 / U.S. Department of State – 5r – 1 – T634 – us Nat'l Archives [972]
DESPATCHES FROM U.S. CONSULS IN MANCHESTER, UNITED KINGDOM, 1847-1906 / U.S. Department of State – 7r – 1 – T219 – us Nat'l Archives [941]
DESPATCHES FROM U.S. CONSULS IN MANILA, PHILIPPINE ISLANDS / U.S. Department of State – 1817-99. 6 rolls – 1 – M455 – us Nat'l Archives [950]
DESPATCHES FROM U.S. CONSULS IN MANNHEIM GERMANY, 1874-1906 / U.S. Department of State – 7r – 1 – $161.00 – T582 – us Nat'l Archives [327]
DESPATCHES FROM U.S. CONSULS IN MANZANILLO, CUBA, 1844-46 / U.S. Department of State – 1r – 1 – T613 – us Nat'l Archives [972]
DESPATCHES FROM U.S. CONSULS IN MANZANILLO, MEXICO, 1855-1906 / U.S. Department of State – Printed guide – 2r – 1 – M295 – us Nat'l Archives [972]
DESPATCHES FROM U.S. CONSULS IN MAORIO, SPAIN, 1882-84; 1891-1906 / U.S. Department of State – 2r – 1 – T632 – us Nat'l Archives [946]
DESPATCHES FROM U.S. CONSULS IN MARACAIBO, VENEZUELA, 1824-1906 / U.S. Department of State – 20r – 1 – T62 – us Nat'l Archives [972]
DESPATCHES FROM U.S. CONSULS IN MARANHAM (MARANHAO), BRAZIL, 1817-76 / U.S. Department of State – 3r – 1 – T398 – us Nat'l Archives [972]
DESPATCHES FROM U.S. CONSULS IN MARSEILLES, FRANCE, 1790-1906 / U.S. Department of State – 20r – 1 – T220 – us Nat'l Archives [944]
DESPATCHES FROM U.S. CONSULS IN MATAMORAS, MEXICO, 1826-1906 / U.S. Department of State – Printed guide – 12r – 1 – M281 – us Nat'l Archives [972]
DESPATCHES FROM U.S. CONSULS IN MATANZAS, CUBA, 1820-99 / U.S. Department of State – 17r – 1 – T339 – us Nat'l Archives [972]
DESPATCHES FROM U.S. CONSULS IN MAYENCE (MAINZ) GERMANY, 1871-1906 / U.S. Department of State – T635 – 7r – 1 – $238.00 – us Scholarly Res [327]
DESPATCHES FROM U.S. CONSULS IN MAZATLAN, MEXICO, 1826-1906 / U.S. Department of State – Printed guide – 7r – 1 – M159 – us Nat'l Archives [972]
DESPATCHES FROM U.S. CONSULS IN MEDAN-PADANG, SUMATRA, NETHERLANDS EAST INDIES, 1853-98 / U.S. Department of State – T106 – 2r – 1 – us Nat'l Archives [976]
DESPATCHES FROM U.S. CONSULS IN MEDELLIN, COLOMBIA, 1859-1902 / U.S. Department of State – 1r – 1 – T341 – us Nat'l Archives [972]
DESPATCHES FROM U.S. CONSULS IN MELBOURNE, AUSTRALIA, 1852-1906 / U.S. Department of State – 16r – 1 – T102 – us Nat'l Archives [980]
DESPATCHES FROM U.S. CONSULS IN MERIDA, 1843-97, AND PROGRESO, MEXICO, 1897-1906 / U.S. Department of State – Printed guide – 4r – 1 – M287 – us Nat'l Archives [972]
DESPATCHES FROM U.S. CONSULS IN MESSINA, ITALY, 1822-1906 / U.S. Department of State – 7r – 1 – T399 – us Nat'l Archives [945]
DESPATCHES FROM U.S. CONSULS IN MEXICO CITY, MEXICO, 1822-1906 / U.S. Department of State – Printed guide – 15r – 1 – M296 – us Nat'l Archives [972]
DESPATCHES FROM U.S. CONSULS IN MIER, MEXICO, 1870-78 / U.S. Department of State – Printed guide – 1r – 1 – M297 – us Nat'l Archives [972]
DESPATCHES FROM U.S. CONSULS IN MILAN, ITALY, 1874-1906 / U.S. Department of State – 4r – 1 – T170 – us Nat'l Archives [945]
DESPATCHES FROM U.S. CONSULS IN MINATITLAN, MEXICO, 1853-81 / U.S. Department of State – Printed guide – 2r – 1 – M298 – us Nat'l Archives [972]
DESPATCHES FROM U.S. CONSULS IN MONCTON, CANADA, 1885-1905 / U.S. Department of State – 2r – 1 – T636 – us Nat'l Archives [971]
DESPATCHES FROM U.S. CONSULS IN MONROVIA, LIBERIA, 1852-1906 / U.S. Department of State – 7r – 1 – M169 – us Nat'l Archives [960]
DESPATCHES FROM U.S. CONSULS IN MONTEREY, UPPER CALIFORNIA, 1834-48 / U.S. Department of State – 1r – 1 – M138 – us Nat'l Archives [978]
DESPATCHES FROM U.S. CONSULS IN MONTERREY, MEXICO, 1849-1906 / U.S. Department of State – Printed guide – 7r – 1 – M165 – us Nat'l Archives [972]
DESPATCHES FROM U.S. CONSULS IN MONTEVIDEO, URUGUAY, 1821-1906 / U.S. Department of State – 15r – 1 – M71 – us Nat'l Archives [972]
DESPATCHES FROM U.S. CONSULS IN MONTREAL, CANADA, 1850-1906 / U.S. Department of State – 22r – 1 – T222 – us Nat'l Archives [971]
DESPATCHES FROM U.S. CONSULS IN MORRISBURG, CANADA, 1882-1901 / U.S. Department of State – 1r – 1 – T637 – us Nat'l Archives [971]
DESPATCHES FROM U.S. CONSULS IN MOSCOW, U.S.S.R., 1857-1906 (SIC) / U.S. Department of State – Printed guide – 2r – 1 – M456 – us Nat'l Archives [947]
DESPATCHES FROM U.S. CONSULS IN MUKDEN, MANCHURIA, CHINA / U.S. Department of State – 1904-06. 1 roll – 1 – M457 – us Nat'l Archives [950]
DESPATCHES FROM U.S. CONSULS IN MUNICH (MUENCHEN) GERMANY, 1833-1906 / U.S. Department of State – 13r – 1 – $299.00 – T261 – us Nat'l Archives [327]
DESPATCHES FROM U.S. CONSULS IN MUSCAT, OMAN, 1880-1906 / U.S. Department of State – 2r – 1 – T638 – us Nat'l Archives [956]
DESPATCHES FROM U.S. CONSULS IN NAGASAKI, JAPAN, 1860-1906 / U.S. Department of State – 7r – 1 – M131 – us Nat'l Archives [950]
DESPATCHES FROM U.S. CONSULS IN NANKING, CHINA, 1902-6 / U.S. Department of State – 1r – 1 – M110 – us Nat'l Archives [950]
DESPATCHES FROM U.S. CONSULS IN NANTES, FRANCE, 1790-1906 / U.S. Department of State – 8r – 1 – T223 – us Nat'l Archives [944]
DESPATCHES FROM U.S. CONSULS IN NAPLES, ITALY, 1796-1906 / U.S. Department of State – 12r – 1 – T224 – us Nat'l Archives [945]
DESPATCHES FROM U.S. CONSULS IN NAPOLEON-VENDEE, FRANCE, 1800-70 / U.S. Department of State – 1r – 1 – T415 – us Nat'l Archives [944]
DESPATCHES FROM U.S. CONSULS IN NASSAU, BRITISH WEST INDIES, 1821-1906 / U.S. Department of State – 24r – 1 – T475 – us Nat'l Archives [972]
DESPATCHES FROM U.S. CONSULS IN NEW ORLEANS, LOUISIANA, 1798-1807 / U.S. Department of State – 1r – 1 – T225 – us Nat'l Archives [978]
DESPATCHES FROM U.S. CONSULS IN NEWCASTLE, AUSTRALIA, 1887-1906 / U.S. Department of State – 6r – 1 – T92 – us Nat'l Archives [980]
DESPATCHES FROM U.S. CONSULS IN NEWCASTLE UPON TYNE, UNITED KINGDOM, 1854-1906 / U.S. Department of State – 10r – 1 – T416 – us Nat'l Archives [941]
DESPATCHES FROM U.S. CONSULS IN NEWCHWANG, MANCHURIA, CHINA, 1865-1906 / U.S. Department of State – Printed guide – 7r – 1 – M115 – us Nat'l Archives [950]
DESPATCHES FROM U.S. CONSULS IN NICE, FRANCE, 1819-1906 / U.S. Department of State – 7r – 1 – T417 – us Nat'l Archives [944]
DESPATCHES FROM U.S. CONSULS IN NINGPO, CHINA, 1853-96 / U.S. Department of State – 7r – 1 – M111 – us Nat'l Archives [950]
DESPATCHES FROM U.S. CONSULS IN NOGALES, MEXICO, 1889-1906 / U.S. Department of State – Printed guide – 4r – 1 – M283 – us Nat'l Archives [972]
DESPATCHES FROM U.S. CONSULS IN NOTTINGHAM, UNITED KINGDOM, 1877-1906 / U.S. Department of State – 3r – 1 – T641 – us Nat'l Archives [941]
DESPATCHES FROM U.S. CONSULS IN NOUMEA, NEW CALEDONIA ISLAND, 1887-1905 / U.S. Department of State – 2r – 1 – T91 – us Nat'l Archives [980]
DESPATCHES FROM U.S. CONSULS IN NOVOROSSISK, U.S.S.R., 1883-84 (SIC) / U.S. Department of State – Printed guide – 1r – 1 – M458 – us Nat'l Archives [947]
DESPATCHES FROM U.S. CONSULS IN NUERNBERG, 1846-1906 / U. S. Department of State – T418 – 9r – 1 – $306.00 – us Scholarly Res [327]
DESPATCHES FROM U.S. CONSULS IN NUEVITAS, CUBA, 1842-47; 1892-98 / U.S. Department of State – 1r – 1 – T588 – us Nat'l Archives [972]
DESPATCHES FROM U.S. CONSULS IN NUEVO LAREDO, MEXICO, 1871-1906 / U.S. Department of State – Printed guide – 4r – 1 – M280 – us Nat'l Archives [972]
DESPATCHES FROM U.S. CONSULS IN NUREMBERG, GERMANY, 1846-1906 / U.S. Department of State – 9r – 1 – T418 – us Nat'l Archives [943]
DESPATCHES FROM U.S. CONSULS IN OAXACA, MEXICO, 1869-78 / U.S. Department of State – Printed guide – 1r – 1 – M328 – us Nat'l Archives [972]
DESPATCHES FROM U.S. CONSULS IN ODESSA, U.S.S.R., 1831-1906 (SIC) / U.S. Department of State – Printed guide – 7r – 1 – M459 – us Nat'l Archives [947]
DESPATCHES FROM U.S. CONSULS IN OLDENBURG GERMANY, 1856-69 / U.S. Department of State – 2r – 1 – $46.00 – T419 – us Nat'l Archives [327]
DESPATCHES FROM U.S. CONSULS IN OMOA, TRUJILLO, AND RUATAN, HONDURAS, 1831-93 / U.S. Department of State – 6r – 1 – T477 – us Nat'l Archives [972]
DESPATCHES FROM U.S. CONSULS IN OPORTO, PORTUGAL, 1821-77 / U.S. Department of State – 5r – 1 – T342 – us Nat'l Archives [946]
DESPATCHES FROM U.S. CONSULS IN ORILLIA, CANADA, 1893-1906 / U.S. Department of State – 1r – 1 – T642 – us Nat'l Archives [971]
DESPATCHES FROM U.S. CONSULS IN OSAKA AND HIOGO (KOBE), JAPAN / U.S. Department of State – 1868-1906. 6 rolls – 1 – M460 – us Nat'l Archives [950]
DESPATCHES FROM U.S. CONSULS IN OTRANTO, ITALY, 1861-67 / U.S. Department of State – 1r – 1 – T542 – us Nat'l Archives [945]
DESPATCHES FROM U.S. CONSULS IN OTTAWA, CANADA, 1877-1906 / U.S. Department of State – 12r – 1 – T643 – us Nat'l Archives [971]
DESPATCHES FROM U.S. CONSULS IN PADANG, SUMATRA, NETHERLANDS, EAST INDIES / U.S. Department of State – 1853-98. 1 roll – 1 – M461 – us Nat'l Archives [324]
DESPATCHES FROM U.S. CONSULS IN PAITA, PERU, 1833-74 / U.S. Department of State – 3r – 1 – T600 – us Nat'l Archives [972]
DESPATCHES FROM U.S. CONSULS IN PALERMO, ITALY, 1803-1906 / U.S. Department of State – 11r – 1 – T420 – us Nat'l Archives [945]
DESPATCHES FROM U.S. CONSULS IN PALMERSTON, CANADA, 1892-1900 / U.S. Department of State – 1r – 1 – T647 – us Nat'l Archives [971]
DESPATCHES FROM U.S. CONSULS IN PANAMA CITY, PANAMA,1823-1906 / U.S. Department of State – 27r – 1 – M139 – us Nat'l Archives [972]
DESPATCHES FROM U.S. CONSULS IN PARA, BRAZIL, 1831-1906 / U.S. Department of State – 9r – 1 – T478 – us Nat'l Archives [972]
DESPATCHES FROM U.S. CONSULS IN PARAMARIBO, BRAZIL, 1799-1897 / U.S. Department of State – T226 – 8r – 1 – us Nat'l Archives [972]
DESPATCHES FROM U.S. CONSULS IN PARIS, FRANCE, 1790-1906 / U.S. Department of State – 32r – 1 – T1 – us Nat'l Archives [944]

DESPATCHES FROM U.S. CONSULS IN PATRAS, GREECE, 1874-1906 / U.S. Department of State – 4r – 1 – T648 – us Nat'l Archives [949]
DESPATCHES FROM U.S. CONSULS IN PERNAMBUCO, BRAZIL, 1817-1906 / U.S. Department of State – 17r – 1 – T344 – us Nat'l Archives [972]
DESPATCHES FROM U.S. CONSULS IN PETERBOROUGH, CANADA, 1905-6 / U.S. Department of State – 1r – 1 – T649 – us Nat'l Archives [971]
DESPATCHES FROM U.S. CONSULS IN PETROPAVLOVSK, RUSSIA, 1875-78 / U.S. Department of State – 1r – 1 – T104 – us Nat'l Archives [947]
DESPATCHES FROM U.S. CONSULS IN PICTOU, CANADA, 1837-97 / U.S. Department of State – 6r – 1 – T479 – us Nat'l Archives [971]
DESPATCHES FROM U.S. CONSULS IN PIEDRAS NEGRAS, MEXICO, 1868-1906 / U.S. Department of State – 5r – 1 – M299 – us Nat'l Archives [972]
DESPATCHES FROM U.S. CONSULS IN PIRAEUS, GREECE, 1864-74 / U.S. Department of State – 3r – 1 – T534 – us Nat'l Archives [949]
DESPATCHES FROM U.S. CONSULS IN PLAUEN GERMANY, 1887-1906 / U.S. Department of State – 3r – 1 – $69.00 – T536 – us Nat'l Archives [327]
DESPATCHES FROM U.S. CONSULS IN PLYMOUTH, UNITED KINGDOM, 1793-1906 / U.S. Department of State – 7r – 1 – T228 – us Nat'l Archives [941]
DESPATCHES FROM U.S. CONSULS IN PONAPE, CAROLINE ISLANDS, 1890-92 / U.S. Department of State – 1r – 1 – T90 – us Nat'l Archives [980]
DESPATCHES FROM U.S. CONSULS IN PORSGRUND (PORSGRUNN), NORWAY, 1861-69 / U.S. Department of State – 1r – 1 – T421 – us Nat'l Archives [948]
DESPATCHES FROM U.S. CONSULS IN PORT ANTONIO, BRITISH WEST INDIES, 1895-1906 / U.S. Department of State – 1r – 1 – T650 – us Nat'l Archives [972]
DESPATCHES FROM U.S. CONSULS IN PORT AU PRINCE, HAITI, 1835-1906 / U.S. Department of State – 10r – 1 – T346 – us Nat'l Archives [972]
DESPATCHES FROM U.S. CONSULS IN PORT HOPE, CANADA, 1882-1906 / U.S. Department of State – 2r – 1 – T651 – us Nat'l Archives [971]
DESPATCHES FROM U.S. CONSULS IN PORT LIMON, COSTA RICA, 1902-06 / U.S. Department of State – 1r – 1 – T656 – us Nat'l Archives [972]
DESPATCHES FROM U.S. CONSULS IN PORT LOUIS, MAURITIUS, MASCARENE ISLANDS, INDIAN OCEAN / U.S. Department of State – 1794-1805, 1817-1906. 8 r – 1 – M462 – us Nat'l Archives [950]
DESPATCHES FROM U.S. CONSULS IN PORT MAHON, SPAIN, 1803-76 / U.S. Department of State – 4r – 1 – T422 – us Nat'l Archives [946]
DESPATCHES FROM U.S. CONSULS IN PORT ROWAN, CANADA, 1882-1906 / U.S. Department of State – 1r – 1 – T657 – us Nat'l Archives [971]
DESPATCHES FROM U.S. CONSULS IN PORT SAID, EGYPT, 1870-76 / U.S. Department of State – 1r – 1 – T658 – us Nat'l Archives [960]
DESPATCHES FROM U.S. CONSULS IN PORT STANLEY, CANADA, AND ST THOMAS, CANADA / U.S. Department of State – 1878-1906. 4 rolls – 1 – T659 – us Nat'l Archives [971]
DESPATCHES FROM U.S. CONSULS IN PORT STANLEY, FALKLAND ISLANDS, 1851-1906 / U.S. Department of State – 4r – 1 – T480 – us Nat'l Archives [972]
DESPATCHES FROM U.S. CONSULS IN PORTO PRINCIPE AND XIBARA, CUBA, 1828-43 / U.S. Department of State – 1r – 1 – T567 – us Nat'l Archives [972]
DESPATCHES FROM U.S. CONSULS IN PRAGUE CZECHOSLOVAKIA, 1869-1906 / U.S. Department of State – 4r – 1 – $92.00 – T663 – us Nat'l Archives [327]
DESPATCHES FROM U.S. CONSULS IN PRESCOTT, CANADA, 1864-1906 / U.S. Department of State – 5r – 1 – T481 – us Nat'l Archives [971]
DESPATCHES FROM U.S. CONSULS IN PRETORIA, UNION OF SOUTH AFRICA, 1898-1906 / U.S. Department of State – 3r – 1 – T660 – us Nat'l Archives [960]
DESPATCHES FROM U.S. CONSULS IN PUERTO CABELLO, VENEZUELA, 1823-1906 / U.S. Department of State – 12r – 1 – T229 – us Nat'l Archives [972]
DESPATCHES FROM U.S. CONSULS IN PUERTO CORTER, HONDURAS, 1902-6 / U.S. Department of State – 2r – 1 – T661 – us Nat'l Archives [972]
DESPATCHES FROM U.S. CONSULS IN PUERTO PLATA, DOMINICAN REPUBLIC, 1875-1906 / U.S. Department of State – 3r – 1 – T662 – us Nat'l Archives [972]
DESPATCHES FROM U.S. CONSULS IN QUEBEC, CANADA, 1861-1906 / U.S. Department of State – 7r – 1 – T482 – us Nat'l Archives [971]
DESPATCHES FROM U.S. CONSULS IN REVAL, ESTONIA, 1859-70 / U.S. Department of State – Printed guide – 1r – 1 – M484 – us Nat'l Archives [947]
DESPATCHES FROM U.S. CONSULS IN RHEIMS, FRANCE, 1867-1906 / U.S. Department of State – 3r – 1 – T424 – us Nat'l Archives [944]
DESPATCHES FROM U.S. CONSULS IN RIGA, LATVIA, 1811-72; 1890-1906 / U.S. Department of State – Printed guide. (See also St. Petersburg, U.S.S.R.) – 1r – 1 – M485 – us Nat'l Archives [947]
DESPATCHES FROM U.S. CONSULS IN RIMOUSKI, CANADA, 1897-1906 / U.S. Department of State – 1r – 1 – T666 – us Nat'l Archives [971]
DESPATCHES FROM U.S. CONSULS IN RIO DE JANEIRO, BRAZIL, 1811-1906 / U.S. Department of State – 33r – 1 – T172 – us Nat'l Archives [972]
DESPATCHES FROM U.S. CONSULS IN RIO GRANDE DO SUL, BRAZIL, 1829-97 / U.S. Department of State – 7r – 1 – T145 – us Nat'l Archives [972]
DESPATCHES FROM U.S. CONSULS IN RIO MACHA, COLOMBIA, 1835-83 / U.S. Department of State – 1r – 1 – T425 – us Nat'l Archives [972]
DESPATCHES FROM U.S. CONSULS IN ROME, ITALY, 1801-1906 / U.S. Department of State – 20r – 1 – T231 – us Nat'l Archives [945]
DESPATCHES FROM U.S. CONSULS IN ROSARIO, ARGENTINA, 1858-1906 / U.S. Department of State – 3r – 1 – T343 – us Nat'l Archives [972]
DESPATCHES FROM U.S. CONSULS IN ROTTERDAM, NETHERLANDS, 1802-1906 / U.S. Department of State – 13r – 1 – T232 – us Nat'l Archives [949]
DESPATCHES FROM U.S. CONSULS IN ROUBAIX, FRANCE, 1890-1906 / U.S. Department of State – 2r – 1 – T667 – us Nat'l Archives [944]
DESPATCHES FROM U.S. CONSULS IN ROUEN, FRANCE, 1790; 1878-1906 / U.S. Department of State – 4r – 1 – T668 – us Nat'l Archives [944]
DESPATCHES FROM U.S. CONSULS IN SABANILLA, COLOMBIA, 1856-84 / U.S. Department of State – 5r – 1 – T426 – us Nat'l Archives [972]
DESPATCHES FROM U.S. CONSULS IN SAGUA LA GRANDE, CUBA, 1878-1900 / U.S. Department of State – 6r – 1 – T678 – us Nat'l Archives [972]
DESPATCHES FROM U.S. CONSULS IN SAIGON, VIETNAM, 1889-1906 / U.S. Department of State – 1r – 1 – T103 – us Nat'l Archives [950]
DESPATCHES FROM U.S. CONSULS IN SALONICA, GREECE, 1832-40 / U.S. Department of State – 1r – 1 – T414 – us Nat'l Archives [949]
DESPATCHES FROM U.S. CONSULS IN SALTILLO, MEXICO, 1876-1906 / U.S. Department of State – Printed guide – 1r – 1 – M300 – us Nat'l Archives [972]
DESPATCHES FROM U.S. CONSULS IN SAMANA, DOMINICAN REPUBLIC, 1873-1905 / U.S. Department of State – 2r – 1 – T670 – us Nat'l Archives [972]
DESPATCHES FROM U.S. CONSULS IN SAN ANDRES, COLOMBIA, 1870-78 / U.S. Department of State – 1r – 1 – T554 – us Nat'l Archives [972]
DESPATCHES FROM U.S. CONSULS IN SAN BLAS, MEXICO, 1837-92 / U.S. Department of State – Printed Guide – 1r – 1 – M301 – us Nat'l Archives [972]
DESPATCHES FROM U.S. CONSULS IN SAN DIMAS, MEXICO, 1871-73 / U.S. Department of State – Printed guide – 1r – 1 – M442 – us Nat'l Archives [972]
DESPATCHES FROM U.S. CONSULS IN SAN JOSE, COSTA RICA, 1852-1906 / U.S. Department of State – 7r – 1 – T35 – us Nat'l Archives [972]
DESPATCHES FROM U.S. CONSULS IN SAN JUAN DE LOS REMEDIOS, CUBA, 1844-46; 1879-98 / U.S. Department of State – 2r – 1 – T584 – us Nat'l Archives [972]
DESPATCHES FROM U.S. CONSULS IN SAN JUAN DEL NORTE, NICARAGUA, 1851-1906 / U.S. Department of State – 21r – 1 – T348 – us Nat'l Archives [972]
DESPATCHES FROM U.S. CONSULS IN SAN JUAN DEL SUR, NICARAGUA, 1847-81 / U.S. Department of State – 4r – 1 – T152 – us Nat'l Archives [972]
DESPATCHES FROM U.S. CONSULS IN SAN LUIS POTOSI, MEXICO, 1869-86 / U.S. Department of State – Printed guide – 1r – 1 – M302 – us Nat'l Archives [972]
DESPATCHES FROM U.S. CONSULS IN SAN SALVADOR, EL SALVADOR, 1868-1906 / U.S. Department of State – 10r – 1 – T237 – us Nat'l Archives [972]
DESPATCHES FROM U.S. CONSULS IN SANTA CATARINA, BRAZIL, 1831-74 / U.S. Department of State – 2r – 1 – T483 – us Nat'l Archives [972]
DESPATCHES FROM U.S. CONSULS IN SANTA FE, NEW MEXICO, 1830-46 / U.S. Department of State – Printed guide – 1r – 1 – M199 – us Nat'l Archives [978]
DESPATCHES FROM U.S. CONSULS IN SANTA MARTA, COLOMBIA, 1823-83 / U.S. Department of State – 2r – 1 – T427 – us Nat'l Archives [972]
DESPATCHES FROM U.S. CONSULS IN SANTANDER, SPAIN, 1862-92 / U.S. Department of State – 1r – 1 – T433 – us Nat'l Archives [946]
DESPATCHES FROM U.S. CONSULS IN SANTIAGO, CAPE VERDE ISLANDS, 1818-98 / U.S. Department of State – 7r – 1 – T434 – us Nat'l Archives [949]
DESPATCHES FROM U.S. CONSULS IN SANTIAGO DE CUBA, CUBA, 1799-1906 / U.S. Department of State – 17r – 1 – T55 – us Nat'l Archives [972]
DESPATCHES FROM U.S. CONSULS IN SANTO DOMINGO, DOMINICAN REPUBLIC, 1837-1906 / U.S. Department of State – 19r – 1 – T56 – us Nat'l Archives [972]
DESPATCHES FROM U.S. CONSULS IN SANTOS, BRAZIL, 1831-1906 / U.S. Department of State – 6r – 1 – T351 – us Nat'l Archives [972]
DESPATCHES FROM U.S. CONSULS IN SARNIA, CANADA, 1864-1906 / U.S. Department of State – 4r – 1 – T488 – us Nat'l Archives [971]
DESPATCHES FROM U.S. CONSULS IN SAULT STE. MARIE, CANADA, 1891-1906 / U.S. Department of State – 1r – 1 – T679 – us Nat'l Archives [971]
DESPATCHES FROM U.S. CONSULS IN SCHWERIN GERMANY, 1862-69 / U.S. Department of State – 1r – 1 – $23.00 – T435 – us Nat'l Archives [327]
DESPATCHES FROM U.S. CONSULS IN SEOUL, KOREA, 1886-1906 / U.S. Department of State – 2r – 1 – M167 – us Nat'l Archives [950]
DESPATCHES FROM U.S. CONSULS IN SEVILLE, SPAIN, 1859-1906 / U.S. Department of State – 2r – 1 – T436 – us Nat'l Archives [946]
DESPATCHES FROM U.S. CONSULS IN SHANGHAI, CHINA, 1847-1906 / U.S. Department of State – Printed guide – 53r – 1 – M112 – us Nat'l Archives [950]
DESPATCHES FROM U.S. CONSULS IN SHEFFIELD, UNITED KINGDOM, 1864-1906 / U.S. Department of State – 12r – 1 – T248 – us Nat'l Archives [941]
DESPATCHES FROM U.S. CONSULS IN SHERBROOKE, CANADA, 1879-1906 / U.S. Department of State – 3r – 1 – T680 – us Nat'l Archives [971]
DESPATCHES FROM U.S. CONSULS IN SIERRA LEONE, BRITISH AFRICA, 1858-1906 / U.S. Department of State – 5r – 1 – T438 – us Nat'l Archives [960]
DESPATCHES FROM U.S. CONSULS IN SINGAPORE, STRAITS SETTLEMENTS / U.S. Department of State – 1833-1906. 16 rolls – 1 – M464 – us Nat'l Archives [950]
DESPATCHES FROM U.S. CONSULS IN SIVAS, TURKEY, 1886-1906 / U.S. Department of State – 2r – 1 – T681 – us Nat'l Archives [956]
DESPATCHES FROM U.S. CONSULS IN SMYRNA, TURKEY, 1802-1906 / U.S. Department of State – 15r – 1 – T238 – us Nat'l Archives [956]
DESPATCHES FROM U.S. CONSULS IN SOFIA, BULGARIA, 1901-4 / U.S. Department of State – 1r – 1 – T682 – us Nat'l Archives [949]
DESPATCHES FROM U.S. CONSULS IN SOLINGEN GERMANY, 1898-1905 / U.S. Department of State – 2r – 1 – $46.00 – T683 – us Nat'l Archives [327]
DESPATCHES FROM U.S. CONSULS IN SONNEBERG GERMANY, 1851-98 / U.S. Department of State – 7r – 1 – $161.00 – T439 – us Nat'l Archives [327]
DESPATCHES FROM U.S. CONSULS IN SONSONATE, EL SALVADOR, 1868-87 / U.S. Department of State – 1r – 1 – T440 – us Nat'l Archives [972]
DESPATCHES FROM U.S. CONSULS IN SOREL, CANADA, 1882-98 / U.S. Department of State – 1r – 1 – T684 – us Nat'l Archives [971]
DESPATCHES FROM U.S. CONSULS IN SOUTHAMPTON, UNITED KINGDOM, 1790-1906 / U.S. Department of State – 10r – 1 – T239 – us Nat'l Archives [941]
DESPATCHES FROM U.S. CONSULS IN SPEZIA, ITALY, 1856-69 / U.S. Department of State – 3r – 1 – T441 – us Nat'l Archives [945]
DESPATCHES FROM U.S. CONSULS IN ST BARTHOLOMEW, FRENCH WEST INDIES, 1799-1899 / U.S. Department of State – 3r – 1 – M72 – us Nat'l Archives [972]
DESPATCHES FROM U.S. CONSULS IN ST CHRISTOPHER, WEST INDIES FEDERATION, 1800-1906 / U.S. Department of State – 3r – 1 – T234 – us Nat'l Archives [972]
DESPATCHES FROM U.S. CONSULS IN ST CROIX, VIRGIN ISLANDS, 1791-1876 / U.S. Department of State – 8r – 1 – T233 – us Nat'l Archives [972]
DESPATCHES FROM U.S. CONSULS IN ST DENIS, REUNION ISLAND, MASCARENE ISLANDS, AND INDIAN OCEAN / U.S. Department of State – 1880-92. 1 roll – 1 – M463 – us Nat'l Archives [950]
DESPATCHES FROM U.S. CONSULS IN ST ETIENNE, FRANCE, 1877-1906 / U.S. Department of State – 3r – 1 – T672 – us Nat'l Archives [944]
DESPATCHES FROM U.S. CONSULS IN ST EUSTATIUS, NETHERLANDS WEST INDIES, 1793-1838 / U.S. Department of State – 1r – 1 – T236 – us Nat'l Archives [972]
DESPATCHES FROM U.S. CONSULS IN ST GALL, SWITZERLAND, 1878-1906 / U.S. Department of State – 6r – 1 – T673 – us Nat'l Archives [949]
DESPATCHES FROM U.S. CONSULS IN ST GEORGE, BRITISH WEST INDIES, 1878-1906 / U.S. Department of State – 1r – 1 – T173 – us Nat'l Archives [972]
DESPATCHES FROM U.S. CONSULS IN ST HELENA, BRITISH WEST AFRICA, 1831-1906 / U.S. Department of State – 20r – 1 – T428 – us Nat'l Archives [960]
DESPATCHES FROM U.S. CONSULS IN ST HYACINTHE, CANADA, 1882-1906 / U.S. Department of State – 2r – 1 – T674 – us Nat'l Archives [971]
DESPATCHES FROM U.S. CONSULS IN ST JOHN, NEW BRUNSWICK, CANADA, 1835-1906 / U.S. Department of State – 10r – 1 – T485 – us Nat'l Archives [971]
DESPATCHES FROM U.S. CONSULS IN ST JOHN'S, NEWFOUNDLAND, CANADA, 1852-1906 / U.S. Department of State – 9r – 1 – T129 – us Nat'l Archives [971]
DESPATCHES FROM U.S. CONSULS IN ST JOHNS, QUEBEC, CANADA, 1864-1906 / U.S. Department of State – 3r – 1 – T484 – us Nat'l Archives [971]
DESPATCHES FROM U.S. CONSULS IN ST MARC, HAITI, 1861-91 / U.S. Department of State – 1r – 1 – T486 – us Nat'l Archives [972]
DESPATCHES FROM U.S. CONSULS IN ST MARTIN, NETHERLANDS WEST INDIES, 1848-1906 / U.S. Department of State – 3r – 1 – T429 – us Nat'l Archives [972]
DESPATCHES FROM U.S. CONSULS IN ST MICHAEL ISLAND, AZORES, 1897-1906 / U.S. Department of State – 1r – 1 – T675 – us Nat'l Archives [949]
DESPATCHES FROM U.S. CONSULS IN ST PAUL DE LOANDA, PORTUGUESE AFRICA, 1854-93 / U.S. Department of State – 5r – 1 – T430 – us Nat'l Archives [960]

DESPATCHES FROM U.S. CONSULS IN ST PETERSBURG, RUSSIA, 1803-1906 / U.S. Department of State – Printed guide – 18r – 1 – M81 – us Nat'l Archives [947]

DESPATCHES FROM U.S. CONSULS IN ST PIERRE AND MIQUELON, 1850-1906 / U.S. Department of State – 4r – 1 – T487 – us Nat'l Archives [970]

DESPATCHES FROM U.S. CONSULS IN ST PIERRE, MARTINIQUE, FRENCH WEST INDIES, 1790-1906 / U.S. Department of State – 11r – 1 – T431 – us Nat'l Archives [972]

DESPATCHES FROM U.S. CONSULS IN ST SALVADOR, BRAZIL, 1808-49 / U.S. Department of State – 4r – 1 – T432 – us Nat'l Archives [972]

DESPATCHES FROM U.S. CONSULS IN ST STEPHEN, CANADA, 1882-1906 / U.S. Department of State – 2r – 1 – T676 – us Nat'l Archives [971]

DESPATCHES FROM U.S. CONSULS IN ST THOMAS, VIRGIN ISLANDS, 1804-1906 / U.S. Department of State – 17r – 1 – T350 – us Nat'l Archives [972]

DESPATCHES FROM U.S. CONSULS IN ST UBEC, PORTUGAL, 1835-42 / U.S. Department of State – 1r – 1 – T564 – us Nat'l Archives [946]

DESPATCHES FROM U.S. CONSULS IN STANBRIDGE STATION, CANADA, 1878-1906 / U.S. Department of State – 2r – 1 – T685 – us Nat'l Archives [971]

DESPATCHES FROM U.S. CONSULS IN STAVANGER, NORWAY, 1905-6 / U.S. Department of State – 1r – 1 – T686 – us Nat'l Archives [948]

DESPATCHES FROM U.S. CONSULS IN STETTIN GERMANY, 1830-1906 / U.S. Department of State – T59 – 10r – 1 – $340.00 – us Scholarly Res [327]

DESPATCHES FROM U.S. CONSULS IN STOCKHOLM, SWEDEN, 1810-1906 / U.S. Department of State – 9r – 1 – T230 – us Nat'l Archives [948]

DESPATCHES FROM U.S. CONSULS IN STRASBOURG, FRANCE, 1866-72 / U.S. Department of State – 1r – 1 – T442 – us Nat'l Archives [944]

DESPATCHES FROM U.S. CONSULS IN STRATFORD, CANADA, 1887-1906 / U.S. Department of State – 2r – 1 – T687 – us Nat'l Archives [971]

DESPATCHES FROM U.S. CONSULS IN STUTTGART GERMANY, 1830-1906 / U.S. Department of State – 8r – 1 – $184.00 – T443 – us Nat'l Archives [327]

DESPATCHES FROM U.S. CONSULS IN SWANSEA, UNITED KINGDOM, 1892-1906 / U.S. Department of State – 1r – 1 – T688 – us Nat'l Archives [941]

DESPATCHES FROM U.S. CONSULS IN SWATOW, CHINA, 1860-81 / U.S. Department of State – 4r – 1 – M113 – us Nat'l Archives [950]

DESPATCHES FROM U.S. CONSULS IN SYDNEY, AUSTRALIA, 1836-1906 / U.S. Department of State – Printed guide – 18r – 1 – M173 – us Nat'l Archives [980]

DESPATCHES FROM U.S. CONSULS IN SYDNEY, CANADA, 1838-1906 / U.S. Department of State – 2r – 1 – T490 – us Nat'l Archives [971]

DESPATCHES FROM U.S. CONSULS IN TABASCO, MEXICO, 1832-74 / U.S. Department of State – Printed guide – 2r – 1 – 303 – us Nat'l Archives [972]

DESPATCHES FROM U.S. CONSULS IN TAHITI, SOCIETY ISLANDS, FRENCH OCEANIA / U.S. Department of State – 1836-1906. 5 rolls – 1 – M465 – us Nat'l Archives [980]

DESPATCHES FROM U.S. CONSULS IN TALCAHUANO, CHILE, 1836-95 / U.S. Department of State – 5r – 1 – T115 – us Nat'l Archives [972]

DESPATCHES FROM U.S. CONSULS IN TAMATAVE, MADAGASCAR, 1853-1906 / U.S. Department of State – 11r – 1 – T60 – us Nat'l Archives [960]

DESPATCHES FROM U.S. CONSULS IN TAMPICO, MEXICO, 1824-1906 / U.S. Department of State – Printed guide – 8r – 1 – M304 – us Nat'l Archives [972]

DESPATCHES FROM U.S. CONSULS IN TAMSUI, FORMOSA, 1898-1906 / U.S. Department of State – 1r – 1 – M117 – us Nat'l Archives [950]

DESPATCHES FROM U.S. CONSULS IN TANGIER, MOROCCO, 1797-1906 / U.S. Department of State – 27r – 1 – T61 – us Nat'l Archives [960]

DESPATCHES FROM U.S. CONSULS IN TARANTO, ITALY, 1861-76 / U.S. Department of State – 1r – 1 – T444 – us Nat'l Archives [943]

DESPATCHES FROM U.S. CONSULS IN TEGUCIGALPA, HONDURAS, 1860-1906 / U.S. Department of State – 8r – 1 – T352 – us Nat'l Archives [972]

DESPATCHES FROM U.S. CONSULS IN TEHERAN, IRAN, 1883-1906 / U.S. Department of State – 2r – 1 – T305 – us Nat'l Archives [950]

DESPATCHES FROM U.S. CONSULS IN TEHUANTEPEC, MEXICO, 1850-67 / U.S. Department of State – Printed guide – 1r – 1 – M305 – us Nat'l Archives [972]

DESPATCHES FROM U.S. CONSULS IN TENERIFFE, CANARY ISLANDS, 1795-1906 / U.S. Department of State – 10r – 1 – T690 – us Nat'l Archives [946]

DESPATCHES FROM U.S. CONSULS IN TETUAN, MOROCCO / U.S. Department of State – 1877-88 – 1r – 1 – T156 – us Nat'l Archives [960]

DESPATCHES FROM U.S. CONSULS IN TEXAS, 1825-44 / U.S. Department of State – 1r – 1 – T153 – us Nat'l Archives [978]

DESPATCHES FROM U.S. CONSULS IN THREE RIVERS, CANADA, 1881-1906 / U.S. Department of State – 3r – 1 – T691 – us Nat'l Archives [971]

DESPATCHES FROM U.S. CONSULS IN TIENTSIN, CHINA, 1868-1906 / U.S. Department of State – Printed guide – 8r – 1 – M114 – us Nat'l Archives [950]

DESPATCHES FROM U.S. CONSULS IN TORONTO, CANADA, 1864-1906 / U.S. Department of State – 9r – 1 – T491 – us Nat'l Archives [971]

DESPATCHES FROM U.S. CONSULS IN TREBIZOND, TURKEY, 1904-6 / U.S. Department of State – 1r – 1 – T700 – us Nat'l Archives [956]

DESPATCHES FROM U.S. CONSULS IN TRIESTE, ITALY, 1800-1906 / U.S. Department of State – 13r – 1 – T242 – us Nat'l Archives [945]

DESPATCHES FROM U.S. CONSULS IN TRINIDAD, CUBA, 1824-76 / U.S. Department of State – 9r – 1 – T699 – us Nat'l Archives [972]

DESPATCHES FROM U.S. CONSULS IN TRINIDAD, WEST INDIES FEDERATION, 1824-1906 / U.S. Department of State – 11r – 1 – T148 – us Nat'l Archives [972]

DESPATCHES FROM U.S. CONSULS IN TRIPOLI, LIBYA, 1796-1885 / U. S. Department of State – 7r – 1 – M466 – us Nat'l Archives [327]

DESPATCHES FROM U.S. CONSULS IN TUMBES, PERU, 1852-74 / U.S. Department of State – 2r – 1 – T353 – us Nat'l Archives [972]

DESPATCHES FROM U.S. CONSULS IN TUNIS, TUNISIA, 1797-1906 / U.S. Department of State – 12r – 1 – T303 – us Nat'l Archives [960]

DESPATCHES FROM U.S. CONSULS IN TUNSTALL, UNITED KINGDOM, 1869-1905 / U.S. Department of State – 3r – 1 – T445 – us Nat'l Archives [941]

DESPATCHES FROM U.S. CONSULS IN TURIN, ITALY, 1877-1906 / U.S. Department of State – 2r – 1 – T174 – us Nat'l Archives [945]

DESPATCHES FROM U.S. CONSULS IN TURKS ISLAND, BRITISH WEST INDIES, 1818-1906 / U.S. Department of State – 18r – 1 – T446 – us Nat'l Archives [972]

DESPATCHES FROM U.S. CONSULS IN TUXPAN, MEXICO, 1879-1906 / U.S. Department of State – Printed guide – 2r – 1 – M306 – us Nat'l Archives [972]

DESPATCHES FROM U.S. CONSULS IN UTILA, HONDURAS, 1894-1906 / U.S. Department of State – 2r – 1 – T701 – us Nat'l Archives [972]

DESPATCHES FROM U.S. CONSULS IN VALENCIA, SPAIN, 1816-1906 / U.S. Department of State – 4r – 1 – T447 – us Nat'l Archives [946]

DESPATCHES FROM U.S. CONSULS IN VALPARAISO, CHILE, 1812-1906 / U.S. Department of State – Printed guide – 14r – 1 – M146 – us Nat'l Archives [972]

DESPATCHES FROM U.S. CONSULS IN VANCOUVER, CANADA, 1890-1906 / U.S. Department of State – 5r – 1 – T114 – us Nat'l Archives [971]

DESPATCHES FROM U.S. CONSULS IN VENICE, ITALY, 1830-1906 / U.S. Department of State – 7r – 1 – M153 – us Nat'l Archives [945]

DESPATCHES FROM U.S. CONSULS IN VERACRUZ, MEXICO, 1822-1906 / U.S. Department of State – Printed guide – 18r – 1 – M183 – us Nat'l Archives [972]

DESPATCHES FROM U.S. CONSULS IN VICTORIA, CANADA, 1862-1906 / U.S. Department of State – 16r – 1 – T130 – us Nat'l Archives [971]

DESPATCHES FROM U.S. CONSULS IN VIENNA, AUSTRIA, 1830-1906 / U.S. Department of State – 20r – 1 – $460.00 – T243 – us Nat'l Archives [327]

DESPATCHES FROM U.S. CONSULS IN VIGOR, SPAIN, 1852-62 / U.S. Department of State – 1r – 1 – T449 – us Nat'l Archives [946]

DESPATCHES FROM U.S. CONSULS IN VLADIVOSTOK, RUSSIA, 1898-1906 / U.S. Department of State – Printed guide – 1r – 1 – M486 – us Nat'l Archives [947]

DESPATCHES FROM U.S. CONSULS IN WALLACEBURG, CANADA, 1888-1905 / U.S. Department of State – 1r – 1 – T702 – us Nat'l Archives [971]

DESPATCHES FROM U.S. CONSULS IN WARSAW, POLAND, 1871-1906 / U.S. Department of State – Printed guide – 3r – 1 – M467 – us Nat'l Archives [943]

DESPATCHES FROM U.S. CONSULS IN WAUBAUSHENE, CANADA, 1890-93 / U.S. Department of State – 1r – 1 – T704 – us Nat'l Archives [971]

DESPATCHES FROM U.S. CONSULS IN WEIMAR GERMANY, 1893-1906 / U.S. Department of State – 1r – 1 – $23.00 – T705 – us Nat'l Archives [327]

DESPATCHES FROM U.S. CONSULS IN WINDSOR, NOVA SCOTIA, CANADA, 1872-1906 / U.S. Department of State – 3r – 1 – T706 – us Nat'l Archives [971]

DESPATCHES FROM U.S. CONSULS IN WINDSOR, ONTARIO, CANADA, 1864-1906 / U.S. Department of State – 4r – 1 – T492 – us Nat'l Archives [971]

DESPATCHES FROM U.S. CONSULS IN WINNIPEG, CANADA, 1869-1906 / U.S. Department of State – 10r – 1 – T24 – us Nat'l Archives [971]

DESPATCHES FROM U.S. CONSULS IN WOODSTOCK, CANADA, 1882-1906 / U.S. Department of State – 1r – 1 – T707 – us Nat'l Archives [971]

DESPATCHES FROM U.S. CONSULS IN YARMOUTH, CANADA, 1886-1906 / U.S. Department of State – 3r – 1 – T708 – us Nat'l Archives [971]

DESPATCHES FROM U.S. CONSULS IN YOKOHAMA, JAPAN, 1897-1906 / U.S. Department of State – 5r – 1 – M136 – us Nat'l Archives [950]

DESPATCHES FROM U.S. CONSULS IN ZACATECAS, MEXICO, 1860-84 / U.S. Department of State – Printed guide – 1r – 1 – M307 – us Nat'l Archives [972]

DESPATCHES FROM U.S. CONSULS IN ZANTE, GREECE, 1853-62 / U.S. Department of State – 3r – 1 – T451 – us Nat'l Archives [949]

DESPATCHES FROM U.S. CONSULS IN ZANZIBAR, BRITISH AFRICA / U.S. Department of State – 1836-1906 – 5r – 1 – M468 – us Nat'l Archives [960]

DESPATCHES FROM U.S. CONSULS IN ZITTAU, GERMANY, 1897-1906 / U.S. Department of State – 1r – 1 – T709 – us Nat'l Archives [943]

DESPATCHES FROM U.S. CONSULS IN ZURICH, SWITZERLAND, 1852-1906 / U.S. Department of State – 8r – 1 – T452 – us Nat'l Archives [949]

DESPATCHES FROM U.S. CONSULS TO ZITTAU, 1897-1906 / U. S. Department of State – T709 – 1r – 1 – $34.00 – us Scholarly Res [327]

DESPATCHES FROM U.S. MINISTERS TO ARGENTINA, 1817-1906 / U.S. Department of State – Printed Guide – 40r – 1 – M69 – us Nat'l Archives [972]

DESPATCHES FROM U.S. MINISTERS TO AUSTRIA, 1838-1906 / U.S. Department of State – 51r – 1 – T157 – us Nat'l Archives [972]

DESPATCHES FROM U.S. MINISTERS TO AUSTRIA, 1838-1906 / U.S. Department of State – 51r – 1 – $1,734.00 – us Scholarly Res [327]

DESPATCHES FROM U.S. MINISTERS TO BELGIUM, 1832-1906 / U.S. Department of State – 37r – 1 – M193 – us Nat'l Archives [949]

DESPATCHES FROM U.S. MINISTERS TO BOLIVIA, 1848-1906 / U.S. Department of State – 22r – 1 – T51 – us Nat'l Archives [972]

DESPATCHES FROM U.S. MINISTERS TO BRAZIL. 1809-1906 / U.S. Department of State – Printed guide – 74r – 1 – M121 – us Nat'l Archives [972]

DESPATCHES FROM U.S. MINISTERS TO CENTRAL AMERICA, 1824-1906 / U.S. Department of State – 93r – M219 – us Nat'l Archives [972]

DESPATCHES FROM U.S. MINISTERS TO CHILE, 1823-1906 / U.S. Department of State – 52r – 1 – M10 – us Nat'l Archives [972]

DESPATCHES FROM U.S. MINISTERS TO CHINA, 1843-1906 / U.S. Department of State – Printed guide – 131r – 1 – M92 – us Nat'l Archives [950]

DESPATCHES FROM U.S. MINISTERS TO COLOMBIA, 1820-1906 / U.S. Department of State – 64r – 1 – T33 – us Nat'l Archives [972]

DESPATCHES FROM U.S. MINISTERS TO CUBA, 1902-6 / U.S. Department of State – 18r – 1 – T158 – us Nat'l Archives [972]

DESPATCHES FROM U.S. MINISTERS TO DENMARK, 1811-1906 / U.S. Department of State – 28r – 1 – M41 – us Nat'l Archives [948]

DESPATCHES FROM U.S. MINISTERS TO ECUADOR / U.S. Department of State – 1848-1906. 19 rolls – 1 – T50 – us Nat'l Archives [972]

DESPATCHES FROM U.S. MINISTERS TO FRANCE, 1789-1906 / U.S. Department of State – 128r – 1 – M34 – us Nat'l Archives [944]

DESPATCHES FROM U.S. MINISTERS TO GREAT BRITAIN, 1791-1906 / U.S. Department of State – Printed guide – 200r – 1 – M30 – us Nat'l Archives [941]

DESPATCHES FROM U.S. MINISTERS TO GREECE, 1868-1906 / U.S. Department of State – 18r – 1 – T159 – us Nat'l Archives [949]

DESPATCHES FROM U.S. MINISTERS TO HAITI, 1862-1906 / U.S. Department of State – 47r – 1 – M82 – us Nat'l Archives [972]

DESPATCHES FROM U.S. MINISTERS TO HAWAII, 1843-1900 / U.S. Department of State – 34r – 1 – T30 – us Nat'l Archives [978]

DESPATCHES FROM U.S. MINISTERS TO JAPAN, 1855-1906 / U.S. Department of State – Printed guide – 82r – 1 – M133 – us Nat'l Archives [950]

DESPATCHES FROM U.S. MINISTERS TO KOREA, 1883-1905 / U.S. Department of State – Printed guide – 22r – 1 – M134 – us Nat'l Archives [950]

DESPATCHES FROM U.S. MINISTERS TO LIBERIA, 1863-1906 / U.S. Department of State – 14r – 1 – M170 – us Nat'l Archives [960]

DESPATCHES FROM U.S. MINISTERS TO MEXICO, 1823-1906 / U.S. Department of State – 179r – 1 – M97 – us Nat'l Archives [972]

DESPATCHES FROM U.S. MINISTERS TO MONTENEGRO, 12 MAR 1905-14 JUN 1906 / U.S. Department of State – 1r – 1 – T525 – us Nat'l Archives [949]

DESPATCHES FROM U.S. MINISTERS TO MOROCCO, 1905-6 / U.S. Department of State – 1r – 1 – T725 – us Nat'l Archives [960]

DESPATCHES FROM U.S. MINISTERS TO PANAMA, 1903-06 / U.S. Department of State – 5r – 1 – T726 – us Nat'l Archives [972]

DESPATCHES FROM U.S. MINISTERS TO PARAGUAY AND URUGUAY, 1858-1906 / U.S. Department of State – 19r – 1 – M128 – us Nat'l Archives [972]

DESPATCHES FROM U.S. MINISTERS TO PERSIA, 1883-1906 / U.S. Department of State – Printed guide – 11r – 1 – M223 – us Nat'l Archives [950]

DESPATCHES FROM U.S. MINISTERS TO PERU, 1826-1906 / U.S. Department of State – 66r – 1 – T52 – us Nat'l Archives [972]

DESPATCHES FROM U.S. MINISTERS TO PORTUGAL, 1790-1906 / U.S. Department of State – 41r – 1 – M43 – us Nat'l Archives [946]

DESPATCHES FROM U.S. MINISTERS TO RUMANIA, 1880-1906 / U.S. Department of State – 5r – 1 – T727 – us Nat'l Archives [947]
DESPATCHES FROM U.S. MINISTERS TO RUSSIA, 1808-1906 / U.S. Department of State – 66r – 1 – M35 – us Nat'l Archives [947]
DESPATCHES FROM U.S. MINISTERS TO SERBIA, 5 JUL 1900-31 JUL 1906 / U.S. Department of State – 1r – 1 – T630 – us Nat'l Archives [949]
DESPATCHES FROM U.S. MINISTERS TO SIAM, 1882-1906 / U.S. Department of State – Printed guide – 9r – 1 – M172 – us Nat'l Archives [950]
DESPATCHES FROM U.S. MINISTERS TO SPAIN, 1792-1906 / U.S. Department of State – Printed guide – 134r – 1 – M31 – us Nat'l Archives [946]
DESPATCHES FROM U.S. MINISTERS TO SWEDEN AND NORWAY, 1813-1906 / U.S. Department of State – 28r – 1 – M45 – us Nat'l Archives [948]
DESPATCHES FROM U.S. MINISTERS TO SWITZERLAND, 1853-1906 / U.S. Department of State – 35r – 1 – T98 – us Nat'l Archives [949]
DESPATCHES FROM U.S. MINISTERS TO TEXAS, 1836-45 / U.S. Department of State – 2r – 1 – T728 – us Nat'l Archives [978]
DESPATCHES FROM U.S. MINISTERS TO THE DOMINICAN REPUBLIC, 1883-1906 / U.S. Department of State – 15r – 1 – M93 – us Nat'l Archives [972]
DESPATCHES FROM U.S. MINISTERS TO THE GERMAN STATES AND GERMANY, 1799-1801; 1835-1906 / U.S. Department of State – 107r – 1 – $2,461.00 – M44 – us Nat'l Archives [327]
DESPATCHES FROM U.S. MINISTERS TO THE ITALIAN STATES, 1832-1906 / U.S. Department of State – 44r – 1 – M90 – us Nat'l Archives [945]
DESPATCHES FROM U.S. MINISTERS TO THE NETHERLANDS, 1794-1906 / U.S. Department of State – 46r – 1 – M42 – us Nat'l Archives [949]
DESPATCHES FROM U.S. MINISTERS TO TURKEY, 1818-1906 / U.S. Department of State – M46 – 77r – 1 – us Nat'l Archives [956]
DESPATCHES FROM U.S. MINISTERS TO VENEZUELA, 1835-1906 / U.S. Department of State – 60r – 1 – M79 – us Nat'l Archives [972]
DESPATCHES RECEIVED BY THE DEPT. OF STATE FROM THE U.S. COMMISSION TO CENTRAL AND SOUTH AMERICA, 14 JULY 1884-26 DEC 1885 / U.S. Department of State – T908 – 1r – 1 – us Nat'l Archives [972]
D'Espence, C *see* OPERA OMNIA QUAE SUPERSTES ADHUC EDITIT
O DESPERTADOR : DIARIO COMMERICAL, POLITICO, SCIENTIFICO E LITTERARIO – Rio de Janeiro, 27 Mar 1838-Dec 1840; Apr-18 Oct 1841 – 1,5,6 – bl Biblioteca [072]
O DESPERTADOR : JORNAL POLITICO E LITTERARIO – '(s.l.')-Sao Luis, Brazil. 1 Jul-Sept 1852. Nov 1853-22 Apr 1854 – 1,5,6 – bl Biblioteca [072]
O DESPERTADOR : ORGAO DOS INTERESSES GERAES DO MUNICIPIO E DA PROVINCIA – S. Luiz do Quitunde, Alagoas. 7 Jan 1888 – 1,5,6 – bl Biblioteca [072]
O DESPERTADOR CONSTITUCIONAL – '(s.l.')-Sao Luis, Brazil. 14 Aug 1828 – 1,5,6 – bl Biblioteca [072]
DESPERTADOR CONSTITUCIONAL EXTRAORDINARIO – Rio de Janeiro, 1-25 Feb, May 1825; Jan 1826; May 1927; 1 May 1828 – 1,5,6 – bl Biblioteca [072]
EL DESPIDO DE OBREROS Y LAS DEMAS CAUSAS DE DETERMINACION DEL CONTRATO DE TRABAJO / Menayo Garcia, Alfonso – Badajoz: Imp. Campini, 1958 – 1 – sp Bibl Santa Ana [331]
EL DESPIDO DEL TRABAJADOR (COMENTARIOS DEL DECRETO DE 26 DE OCTUBRE DE 1956). MANUAL DE LA EMPRESA. 1 / Elias Perez, Alberto – Madrid: Editorial Pizarro, 2nd ed 1957 – sp Bibl Santa Ana [331]
Despine, Prosper *see* ETUDE SCIENTIFIQUE SUR LE SOMNAMBULISME, SUR LES PHENOMENES QU'IL PRESENTE ET SUR SON ACTION THERAPEUTIQUE DANS CERTAINES MALADIES NERVEUSES
Despins, Simonne *see* ESSAI BIBLIOGRAPHIQUE
Desplagnes, Louis *see*
– ETUDE SUR LES TUMULI DU KILLI
– LE PLATEAU CENTRAL NIGERIEN
LE DESPOTISME DECRETE PAR L'ASSEMBLEE NATIONALE / Fauchet, Joseph – Londres. 1790 – 9 – fr Hachette [321]
Despreaux de la Condamine, S *see* SOIREES DE FERNEY, OU, CONFIDENCES DE VOLTAIRE
Despres *see* SAUL
DESPUES DE LA GUERRA... / Alvarez, Arturo – Buenos Aires, 1942 – 6mf – 9 – ILM-2491/1 – ne IDC [340]
DESPUTATIONES PHYSIOLOGICO-THEOLOGICAE : DE HUMANAE GENERATIONIS OECONOMIA: DE EMBRYOLOGIA SACRA: DA ABORTU MEDICALI ET DE EMBRYOTOMIA: DE COLENDA CASTITATE / Eschbach, Alphons – (Includes bibliographical references) – Parisiis: Vict Palme, 1884 – 2mf – 9 – 0-8370-7040-6 – 1986-1040 – us A.T.L.A. [240]
Desridelieres-Leroux *see* JOURNAL DE MES VOYAGES [SUIVI DE] LETTRES DE DESRIDELIERES-LEROUX FAITES A SON PERE ET A DIVERSES AUTRES PERSONNES
Desrochers-Leduc, Lucienne *see* BIBLIOGRAPHIE ANALYTIQUE DE LA RELIURE AU CANADA FRANCAIS
Desroches, J Israel *see*
– CATECHISM OF PRIVATE AND PUBLIC HYGIENE
– CATECHISME D'HYGIENE PRIVEE
– CATECHISME D'HYGIENE PRIVEE ET PUBLIQUE
– L'HYGIENE DANS L'EDUCATION: CONFERENCE FAITE DEVANT L'UNION CATHOLIQUE DE MONTREAL, LE 15 MARS 1891
– TRAITE ELEMENTAIRE D'HYGIENE PRIVEE
Desruisseaux, Paul *see* LA TRIBUNE
Dessaulles, L A *see* A SA GRANDEUR MONSIGNEUR CHARLES LAROCQUE, EVEQUE DE ST HYACINTHE
LE DESSIN FRANCAIS DE FOUQUET A CEZANNE / Reunion des musees nationaux. Paris – 1950. 16 illus. 2 fiches – 9 – fr Réunion [700]
DESSINS D'ARCHITECTURE DU 15 AU 19 SIECLE / Musee du Louvre. Paris – 1972 – 9 – fr Réunion [720]
DESSINS DE GUSTAVE MOREAU / Musee Gustave Moreau. Paris – 54 fiches reproduisant l'ensemble des 4831 dessins repertoires au catalogue – 9 – fr Réunion [740]
DESSINS DE MICHEL-ANGE, 1475-1564 / Reunion des musees nationaux. Paris – 1922. 1 fiche – 9 – fr Réunion [740]
DESSINS FRANCAIS DU MILIEU DU XVIIE SIECLE / Reunion des musees nationaux. Paris – 1929. 1 fiche – 9 – fr Réunion [740]
DESSINS ITALIENS. 14E, 15E ET 16E SIECLES / Reunion des musees nationaux. Paris – 1931. 16 illus. 2 fiches – 9 – fr Réunion [740]
Dessoir, Max *see*
– KARL PHILIPP MORITZ ALS AESTHETIKER
– OUTLINES OF THE HISTORY OF PSYCHOLOGY
LES DESSOUS DU CONGRES DE VIENNE / Weil, M H – Paris. 2v. 1917 – 19mf – 9 – HQ-74/1 – ne IDC [943]
Dessureau, Robert M *see* HISTORY OF LANGLADE COUNTY
DESTAILLEUR COLLECTION – France. 18th and 19th cent. drawings. 6 reels.(Collections of the Department of Prints and Photographs) – 1 – fr Bibl Nationale [760]
D'Ester, Carl *see* DAS ZEITUNGSWESEN IN WESTFALEN VON DEN ERSTEN ANFAENGEN BIS ZUM JAHRE 1813
LE DESTIN SOCIAL D'UNE FAMILLE PAYSANNE BRETONNE (FIN DU XIXE SIECLE-1985) / Rouvrais, A – 9 – F80.00 – fr Ethnologie [306]
THE DESTINATION AND EARLY CAREER PERFORMANCE OF SECONDARY SCHOOL GRADUATES IN COLOMBIA : FINDINGS FROM THE 1978 COHORT / Psacharopoulos, G & Zabalza, A – Washington, 1984 (World Bank Staff working papers n653) – 3mf – 9 – DE-139/1 – ne IDC [370]
LES DESTINEES DU CONGO BELGE / Vermeersch, Arthur – Bruxelles: A Dewit, 1906 – 1 – us Res Libr [960]
Destinon, Justus Von *see* DIE CHRONOLOGIE DES JOSEPHUS
THE DESTINY OF MAN VIEWED IN THE LIGHT OF HIS ORIGIN / Fiske, John – Boston: Houghton, Mifflin, 1889, c1884 – 1mf – us A.T.L.A. [120]
Destray, Paul *see* CORPORATIONS ET METIERS DE CLAMECY A LA FIN DU 18E SIECLE
Destree, Jules *see* LE SOCIALISME EN BELGIQUE
[DESTRUCTION AND PILLAGE AS A RESULT OF WORLD WAR 2 PAMPHLET COLLECTION] – 1940-1987 – 1 – CSUXANN2537-B – us Hoover Inst Photo [355]
[DESTRUCTION AND PILLAGE DURING WORLD WAR 1 PAMPHLET COLLECTION] – 1918-1919 – 2r – 1 – CSUXANL5306-B – us Hoover Inst Photo [355]
[DESTRUCTION CAUSED BY WORLD WAR 2 IN EASTERN EUROPE PAMPHLET COLLECTION] – 1944 – 1 – CSUXANL3556-B – us Hoover Inst Photo [355]
DESTRUCTIVE AND POOR MAN'S CONSERVATIVE – London, UK. 1833-34 – 1r – 1 – uk British Libr Newspaper [072]
Destutt de Tracy, Antoine Louis Claude *see* ELEMENTS D'IDEOLOGIE
Desty, Robert *see*
– A COMPENDIUM OF AMERICAN CRIMINAL LAW
– A MANUAL OF PRACTICE IN THE COURTS OF THE UNITED STATES
– THE REMOVAL OF CAUSES FROM STATE TO FEDERAL COURTS
Desvaux, A N *see*
– JOURNAL DE BOTANIQUE, APPLIQUEE A L'AGRICULTURE, A LA PHARMACIE, A LA MEDECINE...
– JOURNAL DE BOTANIQUE, REDIGE PAR UNE SOCIETE DE BOTANISTES
– PRODROME DE FAMILLE DES FOUGERES
Desvergers, Noel *see* ABYSSINIE
DESVIOS DE LA NATURALEZA O TRATADO DEL ORIGEN DE LOS MONSTRUOS A QUEVA ANADIDO SU COMPENDIO DE CURACIONES CHYRURGICAS... / Rivilla y Bonet y Pueyo, J – Lima, 1695 – 5mf – 9 – sp Cultura [610]
Desy, Edouard *see* LA PERLE JAUNE, OU, LA VIERGE DE L'HINDOUSTAN
Deszkiewicz, J N *see* GRAMMATYKA JEZYKA POLSKIEGO
DETAILED PLAN FOR ECONOMIC AND SOCIAL DEVELOPMENT FOR THE FIFTH YEAR 1964/65, OF THE FIVE YEAR PLAN / United Arab Republic. Ministry of Planning – Cairo. BD-1774 1 – 9 – ne IDC [338]
DETATOM : ROMAN / Sieg, Paul Eugen – Berlin: Scherl, 1944 – 1r – 1 – us U.W. Library [830]
DETECTIVE – Issue Nos. 11-15 Jan 1938-May 1938 – 5mf – 15 – $31,95 – us Comics [760]
DETECTIVE – Issue Nos. 1-5 Mar 1937-Jul 1937 – 5mf – 15 – $31,95 – us Comics [760]
DETECTIVE – Issue Nos. 16-20 Jun 1938-Oct 1938 – 5mf – 15 – $31,95 – us Comics [760]
DETECTIVE – Issue Nos. 21-25 Nov 1938-Mar 1939 – 5mf – 15 – $31,95 – us Comics [760]
DETECTIVE – Issue Nos. 26-30 Apr 1939-Aug 1939 – 5mf – 15 – $31,95 – us Comics [760]
DETECTIVE – Issue Nos. 31-35 Sept 1939-Jan 1940 – 5mf – 15 – $31,95 – us Comics [760]
DETECTIVE – Issue Nos. 36-40 Feb 1940-Jun 1940 – 5mf – 15 – $31,95 – us Comics [760]
DETECTIVE – Issue Nos. 41-45 Jul 1940-Nov 1940 – 5mf – 15 – $31,95 – us Comics [760]
DETECTIVE – Issue Nos. 46-50 Dec 1940-Apr 1941 – 5mf – 15 – $31,95 – us Comics [760]
DETECTIVE – Issue Nos. 51-55 May 1941-Sept 1941 – 5mf – 15 – $31.95 – us Comics [760]
DETECTIVE – Issue Nos. 56-60 Oct 1941-Feb 1942 – 5mf – 15 – $31.95 – us Comics [760]
DETECTIVE – Issue Nos. 6-10 Aug 1937-Dec 1937 – 5mf – 15 – $31,95 – us Comics [760]
DETECTIVE – Issue Nos. 61-65 Mar 1942-Jul 1942 – 5mf – 15 – $31.95 – us Comics [760]
DETECTIVE – Issue Nos. 66-70 Aug 1942-Dec 1942 – 5mf – 15 – $31.95 – us Comics [760]
DETECTIVE – Issue Nos. 71-75 Jan 1943-May 1943 – 5mf – 15 – $31.95 – us Comics [760]
DETECTIVE – Issue Nos. 76-80 Jun 1943-Oct 1943 – 5mf – 15 – $31.95 – us Comics [760]
DETECTIVE – Issue Nos. 81-85 Nov 1943-Mar 1944 – 5mf – 15 – $31.95 – us Comics [760]
DETECTIVE – Issue Nos. 86-90 Apr 1944-Aug 1944 – 5mf – 15 – $31.95 – us Comics [760]
DETECTIVE – Issue Nos. 91-95 Sept 1944-Jan 1945 – 5mf – 15 – $31.95 – us Comics [760]
DETECTIVE – Issue Nos. 96-100 Feb 1945-Jun 1945 – 5mf – 15 – $31.95 – us Comics [760]
THE DETECTOR – Dublin. Ireland. -w. 30 Jan-20 May 1800. (3 ft) – 1 – uk British Libr Newspaper [072]
DETENTION HOME REGISTER / Allen County. Ohio. Common Pleas. Juvenile Div – 1938-1945 – 1r – 1 – $32.50r – us Archival [324]
Detering, Soeren *see* TECHNIKUNTERSTUETZUNG FUER VIRTUELLE UNTERNEHMEN 1500 1995
DETERMINANTS OF CRITICAL POWER AND ANAEROBIC WORK CAPACITY IN YOUNG AND ELDERLY MEN / Overend, T J – 1992 – 2mf – 9 – $8.00 – us Microform Publ [612]
DETERMINATIO COMPENDIOSA DE IURISDICTIONE IMPERII AUCTORE ANONYMO UT VIDETUR THOLOMEO LUCENSI O.P. (MGH LEGES 4: 1.BD) – 1909 – Dfl9.00 – ne Slangenburg [240]
LA DETERMINATION DE LA LOI APPLICABLE AU REGIME MATRIMONIAL / Bateman, H – Aire sur la Lys, 1938 – 3mf – 9 – ILM-3009/1 – ne IDC [340]
DETERMINATION DES INSECTES PIQUEURS ET SUCEURS DE SANG / ed by Sergent, E – Paris, 1909 – [1], 308p – 8 – ne IDC [590]
DETERMINATION OF GROWTH IN BONY FISHES FROM OTOLITH MICROSTRUCTURE – 1992 – 57p – it F.A.O. [639]
A DETERMINATION OF MEMBER SATISFACTION AT THREE DIFFERENT TYPES OF FITNESS CENTER / Streff, L L – 1991 – 2mf – 9 – $8.00 – us Microform Publ [790]
DETERMINATION OF OCCUPATIONAL STRESS AND COPING STRATEGIES OF MEDIATORS UTILIZING THE DELPHI TECHNIQUE / Arabyazdi, Behjat – 1989 – 139p 2mf – 9 – $8.00 – us Microform Publ [150]
DETERMINATION OF POLYCHLORINATED BIPHENYLS IN OPEN OCEAN WATERS – 1984 – 48p – 9 – 92-3-102262-8 – fr UNESCO [540]
DETERMINATION OF THE PRECISION, ACCURACY AND RESOLUTION OF A VIDEO-BASED MOTION ANALYSIS SYSTEM / Wisner, David M & Widule, Carol J – 1992 – 1mf – 9 – $4.00 – us Microform Publ [612]
DETERMINING MINISTRY PRIORITIES FOR MACEDONIA BAPTIST CHURCH DURING A TRANSITIONAL PERIOD / Duvall, Terry Glenn – 1982 – 1 – 6.56 – us Baptist [240]
DETERMINING THE ESSENTIAL ELEMENTS OF GOLF SWINGS USED BY ELITE GOLFERS / Fujimoto-Kanatani, Koichiro – Oregon State University, 1995 – 8mf – 9 – $32.00 – PE 3643 – us Microform Publ [612]
DETERMINING THE VALIDITY AND RELIABILITY OF THE NICHOLAS MANUAL MUSCLE TESTER AS A MEASURE OF ISOMETRIC STRENGTH IN WOMEN WITH ARTHRITIS / Sierra, Nelson – Oregon State University, 1995 – 1mf – 9 – PH 1508 – us Microform Publ [612]
DETERMINING TYPES AND TYPAL PROFILES OF ADULT AMATEUR THEATRE PARTICIPANTS THROUGH Q-TECHNIQUE / Haner, Janet A S – 1989 – 129p 2mf – 9 – $8.00 – us Microform Publ [790]
DETERMINISTIC MODELS IN HYDROLOGY – 1979 – 85p – it F.A.O. [627]
Detert, Richard A *see* THE RELATIONSHIP BETWEEN PERSONALITY TYPE PREFERNCES AND LEVELS OF COPING RESOURCES AMONG CARDIAC REHABILITATION PARTICIPANTS AT THE UNIVERSITY OF WISCONSIN-A CROSSE

Detlefsen, Hans *see* DIE NAMENGEBUNG IN DEN DRAMEN DER VORGAENGER SHAKESPEARES
DETLEV LILIENCRON / Remer, Paul – Berlin: Schuster and Loeffler, [1904] – 1r – 1 – us U.W. Library [920]
DETLEV VON LILIENCRON : VORTRAG GEHALTEN IN DER LITERARHISTORISCHEN GESELLSCHAFT IM JANUAR 1910 / Litzmann, Berthold – Bonn: F Cohen, [1910?] – 1r – 1 – us U.W. Library [430]
Detmers, Arthur C Jr *see* PETER B. PORTER PAPERS
Detours, J *see* LA SITUATION ECONOMIQUE DE L'ALGERIE
DETRAS DE LA CRISIS : APORTES Y REFLEXIONES DE UN ESTUDIO DE LA ENFERMEDAD ARGENTINA / Barraco Aguirre, Rodolfo – Buenos Aires: Editorial Los Andes, 1st ed 1976 – 1 – CSUXADNO103-B – us Hoover Inst Photo [972]
DETRESSE DES OUVRIERS AU XIXE SIECLE / Burgy, Jules – Paris. 1848. (La Condition Ouvriere. Part Two.) – 9 – 2.50 – fr Bibl Nationale [360]
DETROICKI DZIENNIK LUDOWY – Detroit; Chicago: The Polish Peoples Pub Co, 1919-feb 1923 – 13r – us Res Libr [071]
DETROIT CITY DIRECTORY 1857-58 / Johnson, James D – Detroit: Fisher, Fleming and Co., Printer, 1857. Michigan Reel 23. The Cox Library Collection – 5 – us Americana [978]
DETROIT COLLEGE OF LAW OF MICHIGAN STATE UNIVERSITY ENTERTAINMENT AND SPORTS LAW JOURNAL – v1. 1994 – 9 – $10.00 – us Hein [340]
DETROIT COLLEGE OF LAW REVIEW – (1975-84 on reel $185.00. 1985-94 on mf $186.00) – 1975-94 – 5,6,9 – $371.00 set – us Hein [340]
LE DETROIT DE MAGELLAN... / Abribat, J M – Paris, 1902 – 4mf – 9 – ILM-311/1 – ne IDC [340]
LE DETROIT ET LA BAIE D'HUDSON / Baillairge, George F – 1888. 02488. (Pre-1900 Canadiana) – 9 – cn C.I.H.M. [910]
DETROIT GAY LIBERATOR – v1,no.5-v1,no.10. Sept-Oct 1970-Mar 1971. Detroit: Gay Liberation Front of Detroit, 1970-71. Continued by: Gay Liberator – 1 – us U.W. Library [305]
THE DETROIT JEWISH CHRONICLE – Detroit. Mich. 1916-51 – 1 – us A.J.P.C. [071]
DETROIT JEWISH HERALD – Detroit. Mich. 1927-28 – 1 – us A.J.P.C. [071]
DETROIT LAW JOURNAL – Detroit. On film: 1906-17. Incomplete. LL-015 – 1 – us L of C Photodup [340]
DETROIT LAW REVIEW – Detroit College of Law. v1-9. 1931-48 – 8mf – 9 – $36.00 – LLMC 84-456 – us L.L.M.C. [073]
DETROIT LAWYER – (Temporarily suspended with v59 no 2 1992) – v1-59. 1931-92 – 9 – $482.00 set – us Hein [340]
DETROIT LEGAL NEWS – (Lacking: v1-2) – v1-23. 1895-1916. Devoted to Michigan Court Opinions, Supreme and Lower Courts – 267mf – 9 – $400.00 – LLMC 84-457 – us L.L.M.C. [073]
DETROIT NEWS – Detroit, Michigan. 1873- – 1 – us UMI [071]
DETROIT NEWS INDEX – Detroit. Michigan. 1976- – 1 – us UMI [071]
Detroit Public Library *see*
– THE AUTOMOTIVE HISTORY COLLECTION OF THE DETROIT PUBLIC LIBRARY
– CATALOG OF THE E. AZALIA HACKLEY MEMORIAL COLLECTION OF NEGRO MUSIC, DANCE, AND DRAMA..
Detroit. Public Library. Automotive History Collection *see* A SIMPLIFIED GUIDE TO THE HOLDINGS..
Detroit Urban League *see* THE DETROIT URBAN LEAGUE PAPERS
THE DETROIT URBAN LEAGUE PAPERS / Detroit Urban League; ed by McNitt, William – (With printed guide) – Bentley Historical Library, Univ of Michigan, 1974 – 35r – 1 – $2,975.00 – D3155 – us Scholarly Res [360]
DETROITER – 1976- – 9 – us UMI [073]
DETROITER ABEND-POST – Detroit, MI. 1972 – 1 – gw Mikrofilm [071]
DETROITER VOKHENBLAT = DETROIT WEEKLY – Detroit, MI. no 8,9. 1917 – 1r – Can$25.00 – cn Can Microfilming [071]
DETROITI MAGYAR UJSAG = DETROIT HUNGARIAN NEWS – Detroit: Metropolitan Hungarian News, Inc, sep 1971-75 – 5r – us Res Libr [071]
DETROITI UJSAG = DETROIT HUNGARIAN NEWS – Detroit, MI: Julius Fodor, nov 17 1933-aug 1971 – 1 – us Res Libr [071]
DETSKAIA ENTSIKLOPEDIIA = THE CHILDREN'S ENCYCLOPEDIA / ed by Vagner, Y et al – Moscow: I Sytin Publ. v1-10. 1914 – 31mf – 9 – $200.00 – us Ross [030]
DETSKII MUZYKAL'NYI MIROK – Odessa, 1887-88 – 6mf – 9 – us Ross [780]
DETSKII RAI / Lur'e, A – Vozdushnye Puti. III. 1963. BR-3676 2 – 8 – ne IDC [460]
O DETSKIKH KNIGAKH, KRITIKO-BIBLIOGRAFICHESKII UKAZATEL' KNIG, VYSHEDSHIKH DO 1 IANVARIA 1907 G – Rekomenduemykh dlia chteniia detiam v vozraste ot 7-mi do 16 let. M. 1908. BR-7195 2 – 8 – ne IDC [010]
DETSKOE CHTENIE – Spb. 1869-74 (6). Lacking: 1869, v. 7-8; 1871, v. 12. BR-2271 2 – 8 – ne IDC [947]
DETSKOE CHTENIE DLIA SERDTSA I RAZUMA – v. 1-18. M. 1819. BR-1581 2 – 8 – ne IDC [073]
DETTAER ZEITUNG – Detta (Deta), Rumaenien. 2 Okt 1921-11 Nov 1939 – 4r – 1 – gw Mikrofilm [949]
Detwiler, Justice B *see* WHO'S WHO IN CALIFORNIA, 1928-1929
Deuber, Walter *see* REALISMUS DER ARBEITERLITERATUR
DEUCALION : COLLECTED STUDIES OF THE LAPSE OF WAVES, AND LIFE OF STONES, VOLUME 1 / Ruskin, John – Sunnyside, Orpington, Kent: G. Allen, 1879 – 1 roll – 1 – 1-55879-410-7 – uk Libr Preservation [700]
DEUDA SAGRADA / Sanchez Arjona, Vicente – Fregenal de la Sierra (Badajoz): Imprenta de Angel Verde, 1924 – 1 – sp Bibl Santa Ana [810]
DEUDA SAGRADA / Sanchez Arjona, Vicente – Sevilla: Imprenta Alvarez, 1960 – 1 – sp Bibl Santa Ana [810]
DEUGDEN-SPOOR / Baardt, P – Leeuwarden, 1645 – 5mf – 9 – ne IDC [700]
DEUGDEN-SPOOR; IN DE ON-DEUGHDEN DES WERELTS AFF-GEBEELDT / Baardt, P – Leeuwarden, 1645 – 4mf – 9 – ne IDC [700]
DEUS SERMONS SUR LA PAIX... / Drelincourt, L & Gaches, R – Paris. 7pts in 1. 1659 – 6mf – 1 – ILM-1031/1 – ne IDC [327]
DEUS SUPER "HAMMONIA"! / Arantes, T C B – N.p., n.d. – 1mf – 9 – ILM-2467/1 – ne IDC [340]
Deusinger, Ingrid M *see* UNTERSUCHUNGEN ZUM PROBLEM DER NORMVORSTELLUNG
Deussen, Paul *see*
– ALLGEMEINE GESCHICHTE DER PHILOSOPHIE
– ERINNERUNGEN AN FRIEDRICH NIETZSCHE
– DIE PHILOSOPHIE DER GRIECHEN
DEUTEROJESAIA : HEBRAEISCH UND DEUTSCH MIT ANMERKUNGEN / Klostermann, August – (Includes index of Hebrew words) – Muenchen: C H Beck, 1893 – 1mf – 9 – 0-8370-3927-4 – 1985-1927 – us A.T.L.A. [220]
DAS DEUTERONOMIUM: SEIN INHALT UND SEINE LITERARISCHE FORM / Staerk, Willy – Leipzig: J.C. Hinrichs, 1894 – 9 – us A.T.L.A. [240]
DAS DEUTERONOMIUM UND DER DEUTERONOMIKER : UNTERSUCHUNGEN ZUR ALTTESTAMENTLICHEN RECHTS- UND LITERATURGESCHICHTE / Kleinert, Paul – (Includes indexes) – Bielefeld: Velhagen & Klasing, 1872 – 1mf – 9 – 0-8370-3920-7 – 1985-1920 – us A.T.L.A. [220]
DEUTERONOMY = DEUTERONOMIUM : OR, THE FIFTH BOOK OF MOSES / Schroeder, Friedrich Wilhelm Julius – (In English) – New York:Charles Scribner, 1900, c1879 – 1mf – 9 – 0-8370-4529-0 – 1985-2529 – us A.T.L.A. [220]
DEUTERONOMY: THE PEOPLE'S BOOK: ITS ORIGIN AND NATURE: A DEFENCE / Sime, James – London: Daldy, Isbister, 1877. 1 fiche – 9 – us A.T.L.A. [240]
DEUTSCH ALS FREMDSPRACHE – v. 13-. 1976- – 1,5,6 – us UMI [430]
Deutsch, Gotthard *see* PHILOSOPHY OF JEWISH HISTORY
Deutsch, Karl *see* ECOSOCIAL SYSTEMS AND ECOPOLITICS
DEUTSCH KIRCHENAMPT : ALSO CONTAINS: SO MAN JTZUNDT (GOOTT ZU LOB)INN DEN KIRCHEN ZU SINGEN/GEDRUCKT ZU ERFFURDT/DURCH MERTEN VON DOLGEN/ZU DEN DREYEN GULDEN KRONEN/BEY SANCT JORGEN – [1550] – us Sibley [780]
Deutsch, Lev Grigorevich *see*
– ROL EVREEV V RUSSKOM REVOLIUTSIONNOM DVIZHENII
– SIXTEEN YEARS IN SIBERIA
Deutsch, Mario et al *see* EVA PERON
Deutsch, Martin *see* DREI ACTENSTUECKE ZUR GESCHICHTE DES DONATISMUS
Deutsch, S M *see*
– LEHRBUCH DER KIRCHENGESCHICHTE
– PETER ABAELARD
Deutsch, Solomon *see* A NEW PRACTICAL HEBREW GRAMMAR
DEUTSCH-AMERIKANISCHE BAECKER ZEITUNG – New York: H Weismann. v11, n1-4. may 1895] – us Res Libr [071]
DEUTSCH-AMERIKANISCHE BUCHDRUCKER-ZEITUNG / Deutsch-Amerikanischen Typographie – Offizielle Organ. New York. Jahrg. 2, no. 22; 4, no. 1-67, no. 13. 15 May 1875; 1 Jul 1876-Jul 1940 – 1 – us NY Public [073]
DEUTSCH-AMERIKANISCHE BURGER-ZEITUNG : OFFIZIELLES ORGAN DES DEUTSCH-AMERIKANISCHEN BURGERBUNDES – Forest Park, IL: H Kaul, feb 8 1924-nov 1 1927; feb 16, mar 13, jun 3-oct 1 1929: jan-aug 30 1930; nov 1930-aug 1 1931 – 1r – 1 – us Res Libr [071]
Deutsch-Amerikanischen Typographie *see* DEUTSCH-AMERIKANISCHE BUCHDRUCKER-ZEITUNG
DEUTSCH-AMERIKANISCHER FARMER – n.p. n.d – 1 – us NE Hist [071]
DEUTSCH-AMERIKANISCHES CONVERSATIONS-LEXICON : MIT SPEZIELLER RUECKSICHT AUF DAS BEDUERFNIS DER IN AMERIKA LEBENDEN DEUTSCHEN (AEL, ABT 1;11) / Schem, Alexander J – New York. 11 bde. 1869-74 (mf ed 1993) – 55mf – 9 – DM968.00 – 3-89131-075-7 – gw Fischer [040]
DEUTSCH-AMERIKANISCHES HAND-LEXIKON DES ALLGEMEINEN WISSENS (AEL, ABT 1;12) / ed by Zickel, S – New York, 1874-75 (mf ed 1996) – 21mf – 9 – DM240.00 – 3-89131-098-6 – gw Fischer [030]
DEUTSCH-BELGISCHE RUNDSCHAU – Bruessel, Belgium. 1 Jul 1931-15 Dez 1934/35 – 1 – gw Mikrofilm [949]
DEUTSCH-BELGISCHE RUNDSCHAU – Bruessel, jul 1 1931-dec 15 1935? – 1 – Inquire at Mikrofilmarchiv for details – gw Misc Inst [949]
DEUTSCH-CHINESISCHE NACHRICHTEN – Tientsin, China. Oct 1930-Dec 1930; 1931-1 Oct 1939 – 22r – 1 – gw Mikrofilm [072]
DEUTSCH-CHINESISCHEN NACHRICHTEN – Tientsin. 1 Oct 1930-1 Oct 1939. KCHF-10-3 – 1 – ne IDC [072]
DER DEUTSCHE : TAGESZEITUNG DER CHRISTLICHEN GEWERKSCHAFTSBEWEGUNG – Berlin. apr 1921-jan 31 1935 – 29r – 1 – gw Mikrofilm [072]
DER DEUTSCHE AAR – (Cont by: Der Nationalsozialist, mar 21 1925. Thueringische Staatszeitung, apr 1 1933. Thueringer Gauzeitung, jan 18 1936. Thueringer Gauzeitung-Der Nationalsozialist, jan 2 1937. Publ in Ilmenau until mar 28 1925) – Weimar, jul 1 1935-jun 30 1940. oct 1 1940-mar 31 1941. oct 1 1941-44 – 29r – 1 – gw Mikrofilm [943]
DEUTSCHE ACTA ERUDITORUM : ODER GESCHICHTE DER GELEHRTEN, WELCHE DEN GEGENWAERTIGEN ZUSTAND DER LITTERATUR IN EUROPA BEGREIFEN – Leipzig. 20v. 1712-39 – 9 – subsc: DM2,500.00 – gw Olms [073]
DEUTSCHE ACTA ERUDITORUM, ODER GESCHICHTE DER GELEHRTEN, WELCHE DEN GEGENWAERTIGEN ZUSTAND DER LITTERATUR IN EUROPA BEGREIFFEN / ed by Rabener, Justus Gotthard et al – Leipzig. bd 1-20. 1712-1739 (mf ed 1993) – 76mf – 9 – DM2,100.00 – 3-89131-095-1 – gw Fischer [410]
Deutsche Akademie der Naturforscher *see*
– ACTA PHYSICO-MEDICA ACADEMIAE
– EPHEMERIDES
– MISCELLANEA CURIOSA
– MISCELLANEA CURIOSA SIVE EPHEMERIDUM MEDICO-PHYSICARUM GERMANICARUM ACADEMIAE NATURAE CURIOSORUM
Deutsche Akademie der Wissenschaften zu Berlin, Institut fuer deutsche Sprache und Literatur *see* STUDIENAUSGABEN ZUR NEUEREN DEUTSCHEN LITERATUR
DEUTSCHE AKADEMIKER ZEITUNG – Berlin, 1931-dec 12 1936 – 1r – 1 – Dist. gw Mikrofilm – gw Misc Inst [072]
DEUTSCHE ALLGEMEINE HANDWERKS-ZEITUNG *see* NORDWESTDEUTSCHE HANDWERKS-ZEITUNG
DEUTSCHE ALLGEMEINE ZEITUNG : BEILAGE: BILDER CHRONIK – Duesseldorf. 1921-dec 3, 1922 – 1r – 1 – gw Mikrofilm [072]
DEUTSCHE ALLGEMEINE ZEITUNG – Berlin, Germany. 1914-34 – 79r – 1 – us L of C Photodup [072]
DEUTSCHE ALLGEMEINE ZEITUNG – Berlin: Norddeutsche Buchdruckerei und Verlagsanstalt, [1922-] Reichsausg. nov 10 1939-mar 9 1945 – 1 – us Res Libr [072]
DEUTSCHE ALLGEMEINE ZEITUNG – Leipzig, Germany. -d. Jan 1850-June 1879. 68 reels – 1 – uk British Libr Newspaper [072]
DEUTSCHE ALLGEMEINE ZEITUNG *see*
– NORDDEUTSCHE ALLGEMEINE ZEITUNG
DEUTSCHE ALLGEMEINE ZEITUNG – Berlin: Deutscher Verlag, mar 13-apr 19 1945 – us Res Libr [072]
DEUTSCHE ALLGEMEINE ZEITUNG DER RUSSLANDDEUTSCHEN *see* FREUNDSCHAFT
Deutsche Angestelltenschaft *see*
– RECHENSCHAFTSBERICHT
– SCHRIFTEN DES DHV
Deutsche Angestelltenschaft. Gau Bayern *see* STANDES-RUNDSCHAU UND JAHRESBERICHT
Deutsche Angestelltenschaft. Gau Brandenburg-Pommern *see* JAHRESBERICHT
DEUTSCHE APOTHEKER-ZEITUNG – v91-95. 1951-55 – 1,5,6 – us Princeton Micro [073]
DEUTSCHE ARBEIT – Berlin, 1936-37 (incomplete), 1939-40 (incomplete), 1942 n11-12 – 1 – Dist. gw Mikrofilm – gw Misc Inst [072]
DER DEUTSCHE ARBEITER – Chicago. 1869-70 – 1r – 1 – gw Mikrofilm [071]
DER DEUTSCHE ARBEITER IN POLITIK UND WIRTSCHAFT – Berlin. no. 1-4. 1925 – 1 – us NY Public [331]
DEUTSCHE ARBEITER-ZEITUNG – Berlin, apr 8-jun 24 1848 – 1r – 1 – Dist. gw Mikrofilm – gw Misc Inst [943]
DEUTSCHE ARBEITER-ZEITUNG – (Scattered issues) – Duchcov, Czechoslovakia. Aug 1922-Apr 1924 – 1r – 1 – us L of C Photodup [072]
DEUTSCHE ARBEITER-ZEITUNG – Usti Nad Labem, Czechoslovakia. 1904-05 – 1r – 1 – us L of C Photodup [072]
DEUTSCHE ARBEITER-ZEITUNG – Winnipeg. 1930-37 – 1 – 125.00 – cn McLaren [072]
DEUTSCHE ARBEITGEBER-ZEITUNG : ZENTRALBLATT DER DEUTSCHEN ARBEITGEBER-VERBAENDE – Berlin, Oct 1905-06; 1909; 1911-Sep 1922 – 8r – 1 – DM640.00 set DM80.00r – gw Mikro Press [072]
DEUTSCHE ARBEITGEBER-ZEITUNG : ZENTRALBLATT DER DEUTSCHEN ARBEITGEBER-VERBAENDE – Berlin, Oct 1905-Sep 1922; 1928-32 – 1 – gw Mikrofilm [331]
DIE DEUTSCHE ARBEITGEBER-ZEITUNG : ZENTRALBLATT DER DEUTSCHEN ARBEITGEBER-VERBAENDE – Berlin, oct 1 1905-sep 24 1922 – 1 – Dist. gw Mikrofilm – gw Misc Inst [072]
DEUTSCHE AUSSENPOLITIK (ERSCHIENEN BIS 1983) – 1956-1983 – 1,015mf – 1 – DM5,785.50 – gw Mikro Press [943]
DEUTSCHE AUSWANDERER-ZEITUNG – (Also available: Suppl 1856-58, 1r) – Bremen, 1852-67 (incomplete), 1869-75 – 6r – 1 – Inquire at Mikrofilmarchiv for details – gw Misc Inst [943]
DEUTSCHE AUSWANDERER-ZEITUNG – Bremen, Germany. 1852-67 (incomplete); 1869-1875 – 6r – 1 – gw Mikrofilm [072]
DEUTSCHE BALLADEN / Miegel, Agnes – Jena: E Diederichs, 1939, c1935 – 1r – 1 – us U.W. Library [780]
DER DEUTSCHE BAUERKRIEG / Engels, Friedrich – Leipzig, 1875 – 1 – DM30.00 – gw Mikro Press [335]
DEUTSCHE BAUERNSTIMME – Apatin, jan 5-oct 26 1939 – 1r – 1 – Dist. gw Mikrofilm – gw Misc Inst [949]
DEUTSCHE BAUERN-ZEITUNG – Koeln, West Germany. 2 Jul 1959-20 Dec 1974 – 1 – gw Mikrofilm [630]
DEUTSCHE BAUZEITUNG – (With Suppl and Year Indexes) – Berlin, 1867-1942. v1-76 – 1,357mf – OA-300/1 – ne IDC [624]

DIE DEUTSCHE BEICHTE VOM 9. JAHRHUNDERT BIS ZU REFORMATION / Zimmermann, Charlotte – Weida, 1934 – 9 – DM48.00 – 3-89349-270-4 – gw Hänsel [240]

DEUTSCHE BERG- UND HUETTENARBEITER-ZEITUNG – (Title changes: Deutsche Bergarbeiter Zeitung, 1903; Bergarbeiter-Zeitung, 1905; Die Bergbau-Industrie, 1931; Der Deutsche Bergknappe, 1933. 16 Mar 1889-1933) – Bochum, Germany. – 13r – 1 – gw Mikrofilm [622]

DEUTSCHE BERG- UND HUETTENARBEITER-ZEITUNG *see*
- GLUECKAUF!
- GLUECKAUF

DEUTSCHE BERG- UND HUETTEN-ARBIETER-ZEITUNG – (Ab 1903: Deutsche Bergarbeiter-Zeitung. Ab 1905: Bergarbeiter-Zeitung. Ab 1931: Die Bergbau-Industrie. Ab 1933: Der Deutsche Bergknappe) – Bochum, 1889-1933 – 13r – 1 – DM1,040.00 set DM80.00r – gw Mikro Press [072]

DEUTSCHE BERGARBEITER ZEITUNG *see* DEUTSCHE BERG- UND HUETTENARBEITER-ZEITUNG

DEUTSCHE BERGARBEITER-ZEITUNG *see*
- DEUTSCHE BERG- UND HUETTEN-ARBIETER-ZEITUNG
- GLUECKAUF!
- GLUECKAUF

DER DEUTSCHE BERGKNAPPE *see*
- DEUTSCHE BERG- UND HUETTENARBEITER-ZEITUNG
- DEUTSCHE BERG- UND HUETTEN-ARBIETER-ZEITUNG
- GLUECKAUF!
- GLUECKAUF

DEUTSCHE BERGWERKS-ZEITUNG – (Publ in Duesseldorf since sep 1, 1927) – Essen. sep 1, 1929-aug 31, 1944 – 1 – gw Mikrofilm [622]

DEUTSCHE BERGWERKSZEITUNG – Bochum, 1924-25; Jul 1929; 1931-32 – 6r – 1 – DM480.00 – gw Mikro Press [072]

DEUTSCHE BERGWERKSZEITUNG – Bochum, Germany. 1924-25; Jul 1929 (Jubilaeumsausgabe); 1931-32 – 6r – 1 – gw Mikrofilm [622]

DEUTSCHE BESKIDENZEITUNG – Friedek-Friedberg (Frydek-Mistek), Czechoslovakia. 14 Apr 1934-Feb 1937 – 1r – 1 – gw Mikrofilm [072]

DIE DEUTSCHE BIBEL VOR LUTHER : SEIN VERHAELTNISS ZU DERSELBEN UND SEINE VERDIENSTE UM DIE DEUTSCHE BIBELUEBERSETZUNG / Krafft, Wilhelm – Bonn: Carl Georgi, 1883 – 1mf – 9 – 0-8370-3990-8 – 1985-1990 – us A.T.L.A. [220]

DIE DEUTSCHE BIBELUEBERSETZUNG DES MITTELALTERLICHEN WALDENSER IN DEM CODEX TEPLENSIS UND DER ERSTEN GEDRUCKTEN DEUTSCHEN BIBEL NACHGEWIESEN : MIT BEITRAEGEN ZUR KENNTNIS DER ROMANTISCHEN BIBELUEBERSETZUNG UND DOGMENGESCHICHTE DER WALDENSER / Haupt, Herman – (Includes index & appendixes) – Wuerzburg: Stahel, 1885 – 1mf – 9 – 0-8370-3528-7 – 1985-1528 – us A.T.L.A. [220]

DEUTSCHE BLAETTER – Fuer ein Europaeisches Deutschland-gegen ein Deutsches Europa. Santiago de Chile. 1943-46 – 2r – 1 – gw Mikrofilm [072]

DAS DEUTSCHE BLATT – (Incl suppl) – Berlin, 1891-97, apr 1898-sep 1903, 1904-sep 1907, 1908-mar 1910, jul 1910-sep 1911, 1912-14, apr-sep 1915, 1916-18, may-aug 1919, 1920-apr 1921, sep 1921-mar 1924, sep 1924-jun 1927, oct-dec 1927, jul 1928-jun 1932, oct 1932-sep 1933, 1934-jun 1936, oct 1936-jun 1937, oct 1937-38, apr 1939-feb 1943 (incomplete) – 149r – 1 – Dist. gw Mikrofilm – gw Misc Inst [072]

DEUTSCHE BOETTCHER-ZEITUNG – Bremen, 1913-16 – 2r – 1 – Inquire at Mikrofilmarchiv for details – gw Misc Inst [680]

DEUTSCHE BOETTCHER-ZEITUNG – Bremen, Germany. 1913-16 – 2r – 1 – gw Mikrofilm [072]

DER DEUTSCHE BOTANIKER / Reichenbach, Heinrich G L – v. 1: Das Herbarienbuch. Dresden, Leipzig. 1841. v. 2: Flora Saxonica. Dresden, Leipzig. 1842. B-5665 1 – 9 – ne IDC [580]

DEUTSCHE BOTANISCHE MONATSSCHRIFT – Berlin, Arnstadt, 1883-1912. v1-23 – 67mf – 7471/2 – ne IDC [580]

DER DEUTSCHE BOTE – Klattau (Klatovy), Czechoslovakia. May-Dec 1942 – 1r – 1 – gw Mikrofilm [072]

DEUTSCHE BRUESSELER ZEITUNG – Bruessel, 1847-feb 27 1848 – 1r – 1 – Inquire at Mikrofilmarchiv for details – gw Misc Inst [949]

DEUTSCHE BRUESSELER ZEITUNG – Bruessel (Bruxelles), Belgium. 3 Jan 1847-27 Feb 1848 – 1r – 1 – gw Mikrofilm [949]

DEUTSCHE BRUESSELER ZEITUNG – Brussels, Jan 1847-Feb 1848 – 1r – 1 – DM80.00 – gw Mikro Press [949]

DAS DEUTSCHE BUCH – Porto Alegre, Brazil. Ersatzpublikation fuer die Zeitschrift Aktion, Porto Alegre. May-Jul 1937 – 1r – 1 – gw Mikrofilm [072]

DEUTSCHE BUCHBINDERZEITUNG – Leipzig, Germany. 1880-85 – 1 – gw Mikrofilm [072]

Deutsche Buecherei, Leipzig *see* LITERARISCHES ZENTRALBLATT FUER DEUTSCHLAND 1850-1945

DEUTSCHE CONSTITUTIONELLE ZEITUNG – Muenchen, Jul 1848-7 Oct 1849 – 3r – 1 – gw Mikrofilm [072]

Deutsche Demokratische Partei *see* BERICHT UBER DIE VERHANDLUNGEN DES ORDENTLICHEN PARTEITAGES

DEUTSCHE DICHTUNG : EINE DARSTELLUNG IHRER GESCHICHTE / Vogelpohl, Wilhelm; ed by Hafner, Gotthilf – (Includes index) – Stuttgart: E Klett, [1957] – 1r – 1 – us U.W. Library [430]

DEUTSCHE DICHTUNG / ed by George, Stefan & Wolfskehl, Karl – 3. Aufl. Berlin: G Bondi, 1923-1932 – 1r – 1 – us U.W. Library [810]

DEUTSCHE DICHTUNG : KURZGEFASSTE LITERATURGESCHICHTE / Mueller, Friedrich von & Valentin, G – (Includes indexes) – Paderborn: F Schoeningh, 1957 – 1r – 1 – us U.W. Library [430]

DIE DEUTSCHE DICHTUNG : GRUNDRISS DER DEUTSCHEN LITERATURGESCHICHTE / Heinemann, Karl – (Includes index) – Leipzig: A Kroener, 1927 – 1 – us U.W. Library [430]

DIE DEUTSCHE DICHTUNG : GRUNDRISS DER DEUTSCHEN LITERATURGESCHICHTE / Heinemann, Karl – (Includes index) – Leipzig: Kroener, [1930] – 1 – us U.W. Library [430]

DIE DEUTSCHE DICHTUNG 1936-1937 / ed by Elsner, Richard – Berlin: West-Ost-Verlag, 1936-1937 – 1r – 1 – us U.W. Library [790]

DIE DEUTSCHE DICHTUNG IN DER SCHULE : GESCHICHTE UND PROBLEME 1750-1860 / Boehnke, Frieda – Frankfurt a.M., 1967 – 3mf – 9 – DM76.00 – 3-89349-697-1 – gw Hänsel [430]

DIE DEUTSCHE DICHTUNG IN IHREN SOZIALEN, ZEIT- UND GEISTESGESCHICHTLICHEN BEDINGUNGEN : EINE SKIZZE / Kleinberg, Alfred – (Includes bibliographical references and indexes) – Berlin: J H W Dietz, 1927 – 1r – 1 – us U.W. Library [430]

DEUTSCHE DICHTUNG VON DER AELTESTEN BIS AUF DIE NEUESTE ZEIT / Menzel, Wolfgang; ed by Garber, Klaus – Stuttgart. 3v. 1858-59 – 16mfiches – 9 – DM120.00 – gw Olms [430]

DEUTSCHE DIENSTBOTENZEITUNG – Berlin, 1909-10 – 1r – 1 – Dist. gw Mikrofilm – gw Misc Inst [640]

DEUTSCHE DRUCKE DES BAROCK 1600-1720. MIT DEN ERGAENZUNGEN POLNISCHE DRUCKE UND POLONICA 1501-1700 SOWIE UNGARISCHE DRUCKE UND HUNGARICA 1480-1720 : KATALOG DER HERZOG AUGUST BIBLIOTHEK WOLFENBUETTEL / ed by Bircher, Martin et al – (Also sold individually: Hungarica DM298.00. Polonica DM450.00) – 1996 – 157mf (1:24) + 4 index vols – 9 – silver DM4,980.00 – 3-598-32187-2 – gw Saur [430]

DEUTSCHE EINHEIT – Bonn, Muenchen, DE. 6 Oct 1956-19 Dec 1975 – 1 – gw Mikrofilm [072]

DEUTSCHE EINHEIT – Bonn, Muenchen. oct 6 1956-may 1988 – 1 – Inquire at Mikrofilmarchiv for details – gw Misc Inst [072]

DER DEUTSCHE EISENBAHNER – semimonthly. illus. 15 Aug 1948- – 1 – us U.W. Library [380]

DEUTSCHE ENCYCLOPAEDIE ODER ALLGEMEINES REALWOERTERBUCH ALLER KUENSTE UND WISSENSCHAFTEN, (AEL, ABT 1;2) / ed by Koester, H M G & Roos, J F – Frankfurt. 23v. 1778-1807 (mf ed 1992) – 212mf – DM1,420.00 – 3-89131-052-8 – gw Fischer [700]

DEUTSCHE ERZAEHLUNGEN / Varnhagen von Ense, Karl August – 2. Aufl. Stuttgart: J G Cotta, 1879 – 1r – 1 – us U.W. Library [830]

DEUTSCHE EVANGELISCHE KIRCHENZEITUNG – (Lacking: 5(1891)-7(1893)) – 1(1887)-16(1902) – 240mf – 9 – Dfl840.00 – ne Slangenburg [073]

DEUTSCHE EVANGELISCHE KIRCHENZEITUNG – (Missing: v5-7 1891-1893) – Berlin. v1-16. 1887-1902 – 240mf – 9 – ne IDC [240]

DEUTSCHE EXCURSIONS-MOLLUSKEN FAUNA / Clessin, S – Z-474 2. 1876 – 8 – ne IDC [910]

DEUTSCHE FESTE UND VOLKSBRAUCHE / Fehrle, Eugen – 1920 – 1 – us I.U. Libraries [390]

DER DEUTSCHE FILM IN WORT UND BILD – Muenchen, 1919 n7,11. oct 7, nov 25, dec 9, dec 17 1920. jan 28-dec 30 1921 (incomplete). jan 13-mar 24 1922 (incomplete) – 1r – 1 – gw Mikrofilm [790]

DEUTSCHE FILMZEITUNG – (Cont: Sueddeutsche Filmzeitung) – Muenchen, nov 10 1922-41 – 10r – 1 – gw Mikrofilm [790]

DEUTSCHE FINANZPOLITIK / Baumgarten, Dietrich – 1924-28 – 1 – DM35.00 – gw Mikro Press [336]

DEUTSCHE FINANZWIRTSCHAFT – v1-23, Jun 1947-Jun 1969. Berlin. -m, Jun 1947-Sept 1949; semimonthly, Oct 1949-69 – 1 – us U.W. Library [073]

DEUTSCHE FORSCHUNGEN / ed by Panzer, Friedrich Wilhelm & Petersen, Julius – (v1 was publ in 1925. Cf. Union list of serials. Each vol also has a distinctive title) – Frankfurt am Main: M Diesterweg. 33v. 1921-40 – 1 – us U.W. Library [943]

DEUTSCHE FREIHEIT : EINZIGE UNABHAENGIGE TAGESZEITUNG DEUTSCHLANDS – Saarbruecken, Germany. 21 Jun 1933-17 Jan 1935 – 3r – 1 – gw Mikrofilm [072]

DEUTSCHE FREIHEIT – La Liberte allemande. Paris. 3 Dec 1937-Apr 1939 – 1 – gw Mikrofilm [072]

DEUTSCHE FRONT – Saarbrucken, Germany. Nov 1934-Jan 1935 – 1r – 1 – us L of C Photodup [072]

DER DEUTSCHE FRONTSOLDAT : MYTHOS UDN GESTALT / Kalkschmidt, Till – (Includes bibliographical references) – Berlin: Junker und Duennhaupt, 1938 – 2r – 1 – us U.W. Library [943]

DEUTSCHE FUEHRERBRIEFE – Berlin, feb 2-aug 19, oct 27 1928, 1929, 1930-33 – 2r – 1 – Dist. gw Mikrofilm – gw Misc Inst [072]

DAS DEUTSCHE FUEHRERLEXIKON 1934-35 – Berlin: Otto Stollberg, c1934. 552,148,7,(1)p – 1 – us U.W. Library [920]

DAS DEUTSCHE FUNKPROGRAMM – (1934 n56 publ as Fachfunk) – Berlin, 1933 n4-1936 n180 – 5r – 1 – Dist. gw Mikrofilm – gw Misc Inst [790]

DEUTSCHE GAERTNERPOST – (Cont by: Gaertnerpost, 1975) – Berlin, 1955-90 – 1 – Dist. gw Mikrofilm – gw Misc Inst [630]

DEUTSCHE GARTENZEITUNG / ed by Moeller, L – Erfurt, 1886-1920. v1-35 – 635mf – 7360/2 – ne IDC [630]

DEUTSCHE GASSENLIEDER / Hoffmann von Fallersleben, August Heinrich – Zuerich: Literarisches Comptoir, 1843 – 1r – 1 – us U.W. Library [780]

DER DEUTSCHE GEDANKE BEI JAKOB GRIMM : IN GRIMMS EIGNEN WORTEN / Grimm, Jacob – Leipzig: R Voigtlaender, 1915 – 1r – 1 – us U.W. Library [943]

DEUTSCHE GEGENWART – New York. 1947-48. Ein Informationsbrief – 1 – gw Mikrofilm [073]

DEUTSCHE GEISTER : AUFSAETZE / Braun, Felix – Wien: Rikola Verlag, 1925 – 1r – 1 – us U.W. Library [430]

DEUTSCHE GESCHICHTE / Lamprecht, Karl – Berlin: R. Gaertner, 1902-04. 2v in 3 – 1 – us U.W. Library [943]

[DEUTSCHE GESELLSCHAFT FUER AUSWAERTIGE POLITIK PAMPHLET COLLECTION] – 1968-1987 – 1 – CSUXANS2493-B – us Hoover Inst Photo [320]

Deutsche Gesellschaft, Leipzig *see* BEYTRAEGE ZUR CRITISCHEN HISTORIE DER DEUTSCHEN SPRACHE, POESIE UND BEREDSAMKEIT

DEUTSCHE GESELLSCHAFT ZUR ERFORSCHUNG AEQUATORIALAFRIKAS : CORRESPONDENZBLATT DER AFRIKANISCHEN GESELLSCHAFT. 1. BD. BERLIN 1873-76, 2. BD. DRESDEN 1877-1878 – Berlin, 1873-76, Dresden, 1877-78 (mf ed 1994) – 5mf – 9 – DM120.00 – 3-89131-175-3 – gw Fischer [960]

DEUTSCHE GESELLSCHAFT ZUR ERFORSCHUNG AEQUATORIALAFRIKAS : MITTHEILUNGEN DER AFRIKANISCHEN GESELLSCHAFT IN DEUTSCHLAND 1.1878-79 BIS 5.1886-89 – 1878-1889 (mf ed 1994) – 17mf – 9 – DM260.00 – 3-89131-176-1 – gw Fischer [960]

DEUTSCHE GEWERBEZEITUNG – Leipzig, Germany. 1845-46 – 1r – 1 – gw Mikrofilm [072]

DEUTSCHE GRENZSTIMMEN – Tachau (Tachov), Czechoslovakia. 8 Jul-30 Sept 1938 – 1r – 1 – gw Mikrofilm [072]

DEUTSCHE GRENZWACHT – Landskron (Lanskroun), Czechoslovakia. Jan 1922-Sept 1924 – 1r – 1 – gw Mikrofilm [072]

DEUTSCHE GRENZWACHT – Lanskroun, Czechoslovakia. Dec 1940-Mar 1941 – 1r – 1 – us L of C Photodup [072]

DEUTSCHE HANDELS-ARCHIV – Berlin. Jan 1856-June 1939 – 1 – 2668.00 – us L of C Photodup [380]

DIE DEUTSCHE HELDENSAGE DES MITTELALTERS / Gunther, Ernst A W – 1870 – 1 – us I.U. Libraries [390]

DEUTSCHE HELDENSAGEN DES MITTELALTERS – 1877 – 1 – us I.U. Libraries [390]

DEUTSCHE HOBELSPAENE : STOSSSEUFZER UND STAMMBUCHBLAETTER / Vierordt, Heinrich – Heidelberg: C Winter, 1909 – 1r – 1 – us U.W. Library [943]

DER DEUTSCHE HUGENOTT – 1952-93 (complete) – Inquire – 1 – ATLA S0619 – us A.T.L.A. [073]

DEUTSCHE HUTMACHER-ZEITUNG – Berlin, 1922-28 – 11r – 1 – uk British Libr Newspaper [072]

DEUTSCHE ILLUSTRIERTE – Berlin, Wien. jul 4 1939-may 18 1940 – 1 – Dist. gw Mikrofilm – gw Misc Inst [072]

DEUTSCHE ILLUSTRIERTE ZEITUNG – Berlin, 1884-86; 1887 (incomplete) – 1 – gw Mikrofilm [072]

DEUTSCHE ILLUSTRIRTE ZEITUNG – Berlin, aug 23 1884-aug 7 1886, 1887 (incomplete) – 1 – Dist. gw Mikrofilm – gw Misc Inst [072]

DER DEUTSCHE IN ARGENTINIEN – Buenos Aires, 1938-39 (incomplete) – 1 – Inquire at Mikrofilmarchiv for details – gw Misc Inst [972]

DER DEUTSCHE IN CANADA – Hamilton, Ont: Marrhausen'schen Buchhandlung, [1872-18– or 19–] – 9 – cn C.I.H.M. [971]

DER DEUTSCHE IN POLEN – (In 1934 also titled: Schlesiche Warte mit Anzeiger fuer den Kreis Pless) – Wochenzeitung fuer christliche Politik, Kultur, und Wirtschaft. Kattowitz (Katowice), Poland. 4 Feb 1934-27 Aug 1939 – 5r – 1 – gw Mikrofilm [072]

DEUTSCHE INDUSTRIE-ZEITUNG – Chemnitz, 1870-86 – 9r – 1 – gw Mikrofilm [072]

DEUTSCHE INDUSTRIE-ZEITUNG : ORGAN DES CENTRALVERBANDES DEUTSCHER INDUSTRIELLER – Berlin, jul 18 1901-05; 1908-aug 6 1914 – 7r – 1 – DM525.00 – gw Mikro Press [072]

DEUTSCHE INDUSTRIE-ZEITUNG : ORGAN DES CENTRALVERBANDES DEUTSCHER INDUSTRIELLER – Berlin, jul 18 1901-aug 6 1914 – 1 – Dist. gw Mikrofilm – gw Misc Inst [338]

DEUTSCHE INFORMATIONEN – Journal periodique paraissant trois fois par semaine. Herausgegeben von Heinrich Mann, Rudolf Breitscheid, Max Braun, Bruno Frei. Paris. mars 1936-mars 1937 – 1 – fr A.C.R.P.P. [073]

DEUTSCHE INFORMATIONEN – Paris. 6 Mar 1936-2 Sept 1939 – 3r – 1 – gw Mikrofilm [072]

DEUTSCHE INNERLICHKEIT / Ulrich, Christoffel – (Includes bibliographical references) – Muenchen: R Piper, c1940 – 1r – 1 – us U.W. Library [430]

DEUTSCHE INSTRUMENTENBAU-ZEITUNG – Berlin. 1933-41. Lacking: v.34; 42, n.6-8. 2 reels – 1 – 47.00 – us L of C Photodup [780]

DEUTSCHE JUGENDBEWEGUNG UND JUGENDARBEIT IN POLEN 1919-1939 / Nasarski, Peter Emil – (Includes bibliographical references and indexes) – Wuerzburg: Holzner-Verlag, 1957 – 10r – 1 – us U.W. Library [320]

DEUTSCHE JUSTIZ : AUSGABE A – Berlin, 1933-40, 1941-45 (incomplete) – 1 – Dist. gw Mikrofilm – gw Misc Inst [340]

DEUTSCHE KINO-RUNDSCHAU – Berlin, 1915 – 1r – 1 – gw Mikrofilm [790]

DEUTSCHE KINO-RUNDSCHAU – Muenchen, 1914, n1, 20-32 – 1 – gw Mikrofilm [790]

DIE DEUTSCHE KLASSIK UND DIE FRANZOESISCHE REVOLUTION / Mehring, Franz; ed by Raddatz, Fritz J – (Includes bibliographical references and index) – Darmstadt, Neuwied: Luchterhand, 1974 – 1r – 1 – us U.W. Library [430]

DEUTSCHE KOLONIALZEITUNG – Frankfurt. Berlin. Jan 1884-Sep 1922 – 1 – 35.00r – us Hoover Inst Photo [072]

DEUTSCHE KOLONIALZEITUNG – Muenchen, DE. 1884-87; 1889-93; 1901-03; 1905; 1911 – 7r – 1 – gw Mikrofilm [072]

DEUTSCHE KOLONIALZEITUNG – v. 1-39, no. 5. Jan 1884-15 Sep 1922 – 1 – 408.00 – us L of C Photodup [943]

DEUTSCHE KOLONISATION IN OSTAFRIKA. : AUS BRIEFEN UND TAGEBUECHERN DES AM 24. SEPTEMBER 1888 ZU KILWA UMGEFOMMENEN BEAMTEN DER DEUTSCH-OSTAFRIKANISCHEN GESELLSCHAFT HEINRICH HESSEL / Hessel, Karl – Bonn: E Weber, 1889 – 1 – us Res Libr [960]

DEUTSCHE KOMMENTARE – Heidelberg, Stuttgart and Berlin. Germany. -w. 3 Oct 1949-27 Oct 1956. (8 reels) – 1 – uk British Libr Newspaper [072]

DEUTSCHE KOMMENTARE, HEIDELBERG *see* DIE BUECHER-KOMMENTARE

DIE DEUTSCHE KOMOEDIE UNTER DER EINWIRKUNG DES ARISTOPHANES : EIN BEITRAG ZUR VERGLEICHENDEN LITERATURGESCHICHTE / Hille, Curt – Leipzig: Quelle & Meyer, 1907 – 1 – us U.W. Library [410]

DEUTSCHE KORRESPONDENZ – (Allgemeine Correspondenz. 1 Apr 1913-5 Aug 1914) – London, UK. 15 Nov 1901-31 Mar 1913 – 1 – uk British Libr Newspaper [072]

DER DEUTSCHE KRIEG 1870-71 : EIN HELDENGEDICHT AUS DEM NACHLASS DES SELIGEN PHILIPP ULRICH SCHARTENMAYER / Vischer, Friedrich Theodor – 4. verm. Aufl. Noerdlingen: C H Beck, 1874 – 1r – 1 – us U.W. Library [810]

DEUTSCHE KRIEGSOPFER-ZEITUNG – Bonn, nov 1951-88 – 1 – Inquire at Mikrofilmarchiv for details – gw Misc Inst [360]

DEUTSCHE KRIEGSOPFER-ZEITUNG – Bonn, West Germany. Nov 1951-75 – 1 – gw Mikrofilm [072]

DEUTSCHE KRITIK – 1-30. Oct 1924-Dec 1925 – 1 – 23.00 – us L of C Photodup [780]

DEUTSCHE KULTUR-WACHT – Berlin. 1932-33 – 1/2r – 1 – gw Mikrofilm [072]

DEUTSCHE KUNST-THEATER-MUSIK-FILM-WOCHE – Muenchen, mar-apr? 1919 – 1 – gw Mikrofilm [790]

DEUTSCHE LANDHEIMAT – Leitmeritz (Litomerice), Czechoslovakia. 23 May 1928-Mar 1931 (incomplete) – 3r – 1 – gw Mikrofilm [072]

DIE DEUTSCHE LANDNAHME / Voigt, Bernhard – Potsdam: L Voggenreiter, 1936 – 1 – us U.W. Library [830]

DIE DEUTSCHE LANDNAHME / Voigt, Bernhard – Potsdam: L Voggenreiter, 1936 – 1r – 1 – us U.W. Library [943]

DEUTSCHE LANDPOST – Boehmisch-Leipa (Ceska Lipa), Czechoslovakia. Jan-Mar 1923 – 1 – gw Mikrofilm [072]

DEUTSCHE LANDPOST – Boehmisch-Leipa, jan-mar 1923 – 1 – Inquire at Mikrofilmarchiv for details – gw Misc Inst [943]

DEUTSCHE LANDPOST – Prag (Praha), Czechoslovakia. 4 Apr 1923-31 Mar 1938 – 29r – 1 – gw Mikrofilm [072]

DEUTSCHE LANDWIRTSCHAFTSZEITUNG : BEILAGE: BILDER DER WOCHE – Berlin. 1935-37 – 1r – 1 – gw Mikrofilm [072]

DEUTSCHE LA-PLATA-ZEITUNG – Buenos Aires, 1895-1916 (single issues only), jul 6 1919-nov 1939 (incomplete), apr 3-sep 2 1941 (incomplete) – 107r – 1 – Inquire at Mikrofilmarchiv for details – gw Misc Inst [972]

DEUTSCHE LEHRERINNENZEITUNG *see* DIE LEHRERIN

DEUTSCHE LEHRERZEITUNG – Apr 1954-. semiweekly, -w – 1 – us U.W. Library [073]

DEUTSCHE LEHRERZEITUNG – Berlin, 1914, 1923 – 1r – 1 – Dist. gw Mikrofilm – gw Misc Inst [370]

DEUTSCHE LEHRERZEITUNG – Berlin, apr 3 1954-90 – 20r – 1 – Dist. gw Mikrofilm – gw Misc Inst [370]

DEUTSCHE LEIPAER ZEITUNG – Boehmisch-Leipa, aug 24-nov 1938 – 1 – Inquire at Mikrofilmarchiv for details – gw Misc Inst [943]

DEUTSCHE LEIPAER ZEITUNG – Boehmisch-Leipa (Ceska Lipa), Czechoslovakia. 24 Aug-Nov 1938 – 1 – gw Mikrofilm [072]

DIE DEUTSCHE LIBRARY – 1881-1892. 244 issues – 1 – $293.00 – us L of C Photodup [430]

DEUTSCHE LICHENEN GESAMMELT UND MIT ANMERKUNGEN HERAUSGEGEBEN / Floerke, H G – 3pts. Berlin. 1815. B-455 2 – 8 – ne IDC [580]

DER DEUTSCHE LICHTBILDTHEATER-BESITZER – (1911: Deutscher Lichtspieltheater-Besitzer) – Berlin. jan 6, 1910-jun 29, 1911 – 2r – 1 – gw Mikrofilm [073]

DEUTSCHE LICHTSPIEL-ZEITUNG – Muenchen/Berlin, jun 7-26 1919, 1920-21 – 2r – 1 – gw Mikrofilm [790]

DEUTSCHE LIEBE : AUS DEN PAPIEREN EINES FREMDLINGS / Mueller, Friedrich Max – 11. Aufl. Leipzig: F A Brockhaus, 1898 – 1r – 1 – us U.W. Library [430]

DEUTSCHE LIEDER / Matthaey, Heinrich – Winterthur: Hegner, 1847 – 1r – 1 – us U.W. Library [810]

DEUTSCHE LIEDER AUS ITALIEN / Jacoby, Leopold – Muenchen: M Poessl, 1892 – 1r – 1 – us U.W. Library [780]

DEUTSCHE LITERATUR : EINE GESCHICHTLICHE DARSTELLUNG IHRER HAUPTGESTALTEN / Clauss, Walter – (Includes bibliographical references and index) – 3., durchgesehene Aufl. Zuerich: Schulthess & Co., 1945 – 1r – 1 – us U.W. Library [430]

DIE DEUTSCHE LITERATUR : GESCHICHTE UND HAUPTWERKE IN DEN GRUNDZUEGEN / Schulze, Erich; ed by Henning, Hans – (Includes bilbiographical references and index) – Wittenberg: A Ziemsen Verlag, [1923] – 1r – 1 – us U.W. Library [430]

DIE DEUTSCHE LITERATUR / Menzel, Wolfgang; ed by Garber, Klaus – Stuttgart. 2pts. 1828 – 7mf – 9 – DM70.00 – gw Olms [430]

DIE DEUTSCHE LITERATUR / Menzel, Wolfgang – Stuttgart: Gebrueder Franckh. 2v. 1828 – 1 – us U.W. Library [430]

DIE DEUTSCHE LITERATUR DES BAROCK : EINE EINFUEHRUNG / Szyrocki, Marian – (Includes bibliographical references and index) – Reinbek bei Hamburg: Rowohlt Taschenbuch Verlag, 1968 – 1r – 1 – us U.W. Library [430]

DIE DEUTSCHE LITERATUR UND DIE REVOLUTION VON 1848 / Mehring, Franz; ed by Raddatz, Fritz J – (Includes index) – Darmstadt: Luchterhand, 1975, c1974 – 1 – us U.W. Library [430]

DEUTSCHE LITERATURGESCHICHTE / Biese, Alfred – (Includes index) – 25. Aufl. Muenchen: C H Beck, c1930 – 2r – 1 – us U.W. Library [430]

DEUTSCHE LITERATURGESCHICHTE : IN ZWEI BAENDEN / Biese, Alfred – Muenchen: C H Beck, 1907-1911 – 1r – 1 – us U.W. Library [430]

DEUTSCHE LITERATURGESCHICHTE – (Includes index) – [Leipzig?: s.n., 187-] – 1r – 1 – us U.W. Library [430]

DEUTSCHE LITERATURGESCHICHTE / Krell, Leo & Fiedler Leonhard – (Includes bibliographical references and index) – Bamberg: C C Buchners Verlag, 1960 – 1 – us U.W. Library [430]

DEUTSCHE LITERATURGESCHICHTE / Storck, Karl; ed by Rockenbach, M – Stuttgart: J B Metzler, 1926 – 1r – 1 – us U.W. Library [430]

DEUTSCHE LITERATURGESCHICHTE DES NEUNZEHNTEN JAHRHUNDERTS : DARGESTELLT NACH GENERATIONEN / Kummer, Friedrich – (Includes index) – Dresden: C Reissner, 1909 – 1 – us U.W. Library [430]

DEUTSCHE LITERATURGESCHICHTE DES NEUNZEHNTEN JAHRHUNDERTS / Kummer, Friedrich – (Includes index) – Dresden: C Reissner, 1909, c1905 – 1 – us U.W. Library [430]

DEUTSCHE LITERATURGESCHICHTE IN EINER STUNDE : VON DEN AELTESTEN ZEITEN BIS ZUR GEGENWART / Klabund – Leipzig: Duerr & Weber, 1923 – 1r – 1 – us U.W. Library [430]

DEUTSCHE LITERATURGESCHICHTE IN TABELLEN / Schmitt, Fritz – (Includes bibliographical references and indexes) – Bonn: Athenaeum-Verlag. 3v. 1949-52 – 1 – us U.W. Library [430]

DEUTSCHE LITERATURKRITIK DER GEGENWART *see* DEUTSCHE LITERATURKRITIK IM ZWANZIGSTEN JAHRHUNDERT

DEUTSCHE LITERATURKRITIK IM ZWANZIGSTEN JAHRHUNDERT : KAISERREICH, ERSTER WELTKRIEG UND ERSTE NACHKRIEGSZEIT (1889-1933) / Mayer, Hans – (Includes bibliographical references and index. Continues chronologically the author's Meisterwerke deutscher Literaturkritik. Cont by: Deutsche Literaturkritik der Gegenwart) – Stuttgart: Govert, 1965 – 1 – us U.W. Library [430]

DEUTSCHE LITERATURKRITIK IM ZWANZIGSTEN JAHRHUNDERT *see* MEISTERWERKE DEUTSCHER LITERATURKRITIK

DIE DEUTSCHE LITTERATUR UND DIE UNSITTLICHKEIT *see* MODERNE REALISTISCHE LITTERATUR IM LICHTE DER ETHIK UND AESTHETHIK

DEUTSCHE LODZER ZEITUNG – Lodz, Poland. 24 Sept-29 Dec 1939 – 1r – 1 – gw Mikrofilm [072]

DEUTSCHE LODZER ZEITUNG – Lodz, Poland. May 1915-Oct 1916; Sept-Oct 1939 – 3r – 1 – us L of C Photodup [943]

DEUTSCHE LONDONER ZEITUNG – London. -w. Apr 1845-Feb 1851. (3 reels) – 1 – uk British Libr Newspaper [072]

DAS DEUTSCHE MAERCHENDRAMA / Kober, Margarete – (Includes bibliographical references) – Frankfurt am Main: M Diesterweg, 1925 – 1r – 1 – us U.W. Library [430]

DEUTSCHE MALERERZAEHLUNGEN : DIE ART DES SEHENS BEI HEINSE, TIECK, HOFFMANN, STIFTER UND KELLER / Harnisch, Kaethe – (Includes bibliographical references) – Berlin: Junker und Duennhaupt, 1938 – 1 – us U.W. Library [430]

Deutsche Mathematiker-Vereinigung. Bielefeld *see* JAHRESBERICHT

DEUTSCHE MEDIZINISCHE WOCHENSCHRIFT – v. 75-86. 1950-61 – 1,5,6 – us Princeton Micro [610]

DER DEUTSCHE MERKUR : LITERARISCHE UND POLITISCHE ZEITSCHRIFT / ed by Wieland, Christoph Martin – Weimar, 1773-1805 – 446mf – 9 – DM2,100.00 – gw Mikro Press [072]

DER DEUTSCHE MERKUR, WEIMAR 1773-1789; DER NEUE TEUTSCHE MERKUR, WEIMAR 1790-1810 / ed by Wieland, Christoph Martin – (Ab Febr 1773: Der Teutsche Merkur; mit "Anzeiger 1783-1787", "Intelligenzblatt" 1800-1808, Beilage "Monatsberichte" 1805-1808) – Weimar 1773-1810 (mf ed 1993) – 201mf – 9 – DM5,400.00 – 3-89131-100-1 – gw Fischer [072]

DER DEUTSCHE METALLARBEITER : ORGAN DES CHRISTLICH-SOZIALEN METALLARBEITERVERBANDES – Duisburg, 1903-04; 1906-1933 – 9r – 1 – DM675.00 – gw Mikro Press [072]

DER DEUTSCHE METALLARBEITER : ORGAN DES CHRISTLICH-SOZIALEN METALLARBEITERVERBANDES DEUTSCHLANDS – Duisburg, Germany. 1906-8 Jul 1933 – 1 – gw Mikrofilm [072]

DEUTSCHE METALLARBEITERZEITUNG – Nuernberg, 1883-1933 – 14r – 1 – DM1,400.00 – gw Mikro Press [072]

DEUTSCHE METALLARBEITERZEITUNG – (Title change: Metallarbeiter-Zeitung, 1903) – Nuernberg, Germany. 1883-1933 – 14r – 1 – gw Mikrofilm [072]

DEUTSCHE METALLARBEITERZEITUNG – (Title change: Metallarbeiter-Zeitung, 1903) – Nuernberg-Stuttgart-Berlin, Germany. 1883-1933 – 14r – 1 – gw Mikrofilm [072]

DER DEUTSCHE MILITARISMUS / Blume, Wilhelm von – Tuebingen: Kloeres, 1915. 26p – 1 – us U.W. Library [943]

DEUTSCHE MITTEILUNGEN – Paris. 10 Feb 1938-7 May 1940 – 3r – 1 – gw Mikrofilm [072]

DEUTSCHE MONATSSCHRIFT/NEUE DEUTSCHE MONATSSCHRIFT / ed by Fischer, Gottlob Nathanael & Gentz, Friedrich von – (Neue Deutsche Monatsschrift; Berlin, 1795. Hildesheim, 1980) – Berlin, 1790-94. Leipzig, 1795-99 – 152mf – 9 – DM1,100.00 diazo DM1,300.00 silver – gw Olms [430]

DEUTSCHE MONTAGS-ZEITUNG – Berlin, 1910-16 – 2r – 1 – Dist. gw Mikrofilm – gw Misc Inst [072]

DEUTSCHE MONTAGS-ZEITUNG – Berlin, 1910-16 – 2r – 1 – DM180.00 – gw Mikro Press [072]

Deutsche Morgenlaendische Gesellschaft *see*
- ZEITSCHRIFT FUER INDOLOGIE UND IRANISTIK
- ZEITSCHRIFT FUER SEMITISTIK UND VERWANDTE GEBIETE

DEUTSCHE MUSIKBIBLIOGRAPHIE – Leipzig. 1873-1975. 19 reels – 1 – 381.00 – us L of C Photodup [780]

DEUTSCHE MUSIKER-ZEITUNG – Berlin. v. 1-27, 63-64. Apr 1870-1896; Jan 2 1932-May 6 1933 – 1 – us NY Public [073]

Die Deutsche Musikgesellschaft *see* ZEITSCHRIFT FUER MUSIKWISSENSCHAFT

DEUTSCHE MYTHOLOGIE / Grimm,J – 3. Ausgabe. Goettingen. bd 1-2. 1854 – Dfl81.00 – ne Slangenburg [390]

DEUTSCHE NACHRICHTEN – Bielitz-Biala, jul 1-aug 15 1939 – 1 – Inquire at Mikrofilmarchiv for details – gw Misc Inst [947]

DEUTSCHE NACHRICHTEN – Budapest, Hungary. 3 Jan-25 Dez 1942 – 1r – 1 – gw Mikrofilm [072]

DEUTSCHE NACHRICHTEN – Budapest, jan 3-dec 25 1942 – 1r – 1 – Inquire at Mikrofilmarchiv for details – gw Misc Inst [943]

DEUTSCHE NACHRICHTEN – Hannover, West Germany. 1960-73 – 1 – gw Mikrofilm [072]

DEUTSCHE NACHRICHTEN – Posen (Poznan), Poland. Nov 1934-36; Mar-Jun 1937; Sept 1937-Jun 1939 – 7r – 1 – gw Mikrofilm [943]

DEUTSCHE NACHRICHTEN – Pressburg (Bratislava), Czechoslovakia. 20 Oct 1923-14 Nov 1925 – 1r – 1 – gw Mikrofilm [072]

DEUTSCHE NACHRICHTEN – (Title change: Wochenzeitung fuer deutsche Fluechtlinge aus dem Ostgebieten in Daenemark, Jul 1945) – Copenhagen, Denmark. Antifaschistische Monats- bzw. Halbmonatsschrift. Aug 1943-15 Nov 1948 (incomplete) – 1r – 1 – gw Mikrofilm [072]

DEUTSCHE NACHRICHTEN AUS KULTUR, WIRTSCHAFT UND POLITIK – London, UK. Oct 1946-Mar-Apr 1947 – 1r – 1 – gw Mikrofilm [072]

DEUTSCHE NACHRICHTEN FUER LITAUEN – Kauen (Kaunas, Kowno), U.S.S.R. 1931-37; 1939-40 – 3r – 1 – gw Mikrofilm [943]

DEUTSCHE NACHRICHTEN IN GRIECHENLAND – Athen, 1942-jun 30 1944 – 1 – Dist. gw Mikrofilm – gw Misc Inst [949]

DEUTSCHE NAMENKUNDE; UNSERE FAMILIENNAMEN NACH IHRER ENTSTEHUNG UND BEDEUTUNG / Gottschald, Max – Muenchen: J.F. Lehmanns verlag, 1932. 423p – 1 – us U.W. Library [920]

DEUTSCHE NATIONAL- UND SOLDATENZEITUNG – (1993- DM80.00y) – Muenchen, 1951-92 – 30r – 1 – DM2,250.00 – gw Mikro Press [072]

DEUTSCHE NATIONAL- UND SOLDATENZEITUNG *see* DEUTSCHE NATIONAL-ZEITUNG

Deutsche National-Literatur *see* HISTORISCH-KRITISCHE AUSGABE

DIE DEUTSCHE NATIONALLITTERATUR DES NEUNZEHNTEN JAHRHUNDERTS : LITTERARHISTORISCH UND KRITISCH DARGESTELLT / Gottschall, Rudolf von – 3. verm. und verb. Aufl. Breslau: E Trewendt, 1872 – 1r – 1 – us U.W. Library [430]

DEUTSCHE NATIONAL-ZEITUNG – (Also known as: Deutsche National- und Soldatenzeitung) – Passau, Muenchen, DE. 1954-72 – 1 – gw Mikrofilm [072]
DEUTSCHE NATIONAL-ZEITUNG – (Lacking: 1969. July-Dec 1971. July, Dec 1972) – Munich, DE. 12 Jan 1968-Dec 1976 – 7r – 1 – uk British Libr Newspaper [072]
DER DEUTSCHE OEKONOMIST – Berlin, 1893, 1914 – 1 – Dist. gw Mikrofilm – gw Misc Inst [072]
Deutsche Pharmazeutsche Gesellschaft *see* BERICHTE
DER DEUTSCHE PIONIER : ERINNERUNGEN AUS DEM PIONIERLEBEN DER DEUTSCHEN IN AMERIKA – Cincinnati: Deutschen Pionier-Verein, 1869- . v6 mar 1874-feb 1875 – 1r – 1 – us Res Libr [305]
DEUTSCHE POLITIK SEIT BISMARCKS ENTLASSUNG 1890-1892 / Wiermann, Heinrich (Hermann Robolsky) – Berlin. 1893. 333p. (Historical Studies Series) – 9 – 12.00 – fr Bibl Nationale [900]
DEUTSCHE POST – Lodz, Poland. 19 Jul 1915-10 Nov 1918 – 1r – 1 – gw Mikrofilm [072]
DEUTSCHE POST – Troppau (Opava), Czechoslovakia. Jan 1923-Dec 1933 – 33r – 1 – gw Mikrofilm [072]
DEUTSCHE PRESSE – Belgrad, oct 9-dec 11 1938 – 1r – 1 – Dist. gw Mikrofilm – gw Misc Inst [949]
DEUTSCHE PRESSE – Berlin. oct 13, 1913-44 – 8r – 1 – gw Mikrofilm [073]
DEUTSCHE PRESSE – London, UK. 5 Jun 24 Jul 1841 – 1 – uk British Libr Newspaper [072]
DEUTSCHE PRESSE *see*
– CLEVELAND ANZEIGER AND DEUTSCHE PRESSE
– DER ZEITUNGS-VERLAG
DER DEUTSCHE PRIMAS : EINE UNTERSUCHUNG ZUR DEUTSCHEN KIRCHENGESCHICHTE IN DER ERSTEN HAELFTE DES NEUNZEHNTEN JAHRHUNDERTS / Becher, Hubert – Kolmar, ca. 1945 – 339p – 9 – DM48.00 – 3-89349-079-5 – gw Hänsel [240]
DER DEUTSCHE PROTESTANTENVEREIN : UND SEINE BEDEUTUNG IN DER GEGENWART / Schenkel, Daniel – Wiesbaden: C.W. Kreidel, 1868 – 1mf – us A.T.L.A. [240]
DER DEUTSCHE REDNER FUER RECHT UND FREIHEIT – (Cont by: Oeffentlicher Anzeiger fuer den Kreis Bochum, aug 1850) – Bochum, apr 1849-sep 14 1850 – 1 – Inquire at Mikrofilmarchiv for details – gw Misc Inst [943]
DER DEUTSCHE REDNER FUER RECHT UND FREIHEIT – (Title change Aug 1850: Oeffentlicher Anzeiger) – Bochum, Germany. Apr 1849-19 Jul 1850, 28 Aug-14 Sept 1850 – 1 – gw Mikrofilm [072]
DIE DEUTSCHE REFORM : POLITISCHE ZEITUNG FUER DAS CONSTITUTIONELLE DEUTSCHLAND – Berlin, oct 16 1848-mar 10 1851 – 1 – Dist. gw Mikrofilm – gw Mikrofilm [072]
DIE DEUTSCHE REFORMATION / Kahnis, Karl Friedrich August – Leipzig: Doerffling und Franke, 1872 – 1mf – us A.T.L.A. [240]
DER DEUTSCHE REICHSTAG WAEHREND DES OESTERREICHISCHEN ERBFOLGEKRIEGES (1740-1748) / Meisenburg, Friedrich – 1995 – 2mf – 9 – DM62.00 – 3-8267-3165-4 – gw Hänsel [943]
DEUTSCHE REICHSTAGS-ZEITUNG – Frankfurt-Main, Germany. 1 Oct 1848-2 Apr 1849 – 1r – 1 – gw Mikrofilm [072]
DEUTSCHE REICHS-ZEITUNG – (Cont: Zeitung fuer das deutsche Volk, -jun 1848) – Braunschweig, mar 20 1848-aug 2 1866 – 36r – 1 – Inquire at Mikrofilmarchiv for details – gw Misc Inst [943]
DEUTSCHE REICHS-ZEITUNG – (In 1848 also known as: Zeitung fuer das deutsche Volk) – Braunschweig, Germany. 1848-2 Aug 1866. – 36r – 1 – gw Mikrofilm [072]
DEUTSCHE REICHSZEITUNG – (Cont by: Mittelrheinische Landeszeitung, oct 1 1934) – Bonn, dec 17 1871-may 31 1941 – 1 – Inquire at Mikrofilmarchiv for details – gw Misc Inst [943]
DEUTSCHE REICHSZEITUNG – (Title change: Mittelrheinische Landeszeitung, 1 Oct 1934) – Bonn, Germany. 17 Dec 1871-21 Mar 1941. – 134r – 1 – gw Mikrofilm [072]
DEUTSCHE REICHSZEITUNG *see* GODESBERGER VOLKSZEITUNG
DEUTSCHE REPUBLIK – Frankfurt, Germany. 1926-33 – 5r – 1 – gw Mikrofilm [072]
DEUTSCHE REPUBLIK – Frankfurt. v. 1-7 no. 39. Nov 1926-June 25 1933 – 1 – us NY Public [073]
DEUTSCHE REPUBLIK – v1-7. 1926-33 – 5r – 1 – us Ross [943]
DEUTSCHE REVOLUTION : EINE SAMMLUNG ZEITGEMASSER SCHRIFTEN – Leipzig, 1919-20 – 1r – 1 – us Ross [943]
DIE DEUTSCHE REVOLUTION : ORGAN DER SCHWARZEN FRONT – Prag (Praha), Czechoslovakia. 13 May 1934-15 Nov 1937 – 1r – 1 – gw Mikrofilm [072]
DEUTSCHE REVUE : EINE MONATSSCHRIFT – Stuttgart and Leipzig. v1-47. 1877-1922; and Adolf Bastian. Spiritisten und Theosophen. Breslau. 1885. (Wanting scattered issues) – 1 – $512.00 – us L of C Photodup [073]
DER DEUTSCHE RUNDFUNK – Berlin. oct 14, 1923-may 25, 1941 – 23r – 1 – gw Mikrofilm [380]
DEUTSCHE RUNDSCHAU – (Also known as: Ostdeutsche Rundschau; Deutsche Rundschau in Polen) – Bromberg (Bydgoszcz), Poland. 1921-43 – 1 – gw Mikrofilm [943]
DEUTSCHE RUNDSCHAU – Berlin. 1874-1905 – 1 – us UMI [072]
DEUTSCHE RUNDSCHAU – Bydgoszcz. Poland. -d. Apr-Dec 1942, May-Sep 1944. (Imperfect). (2 reels) – 1 – uk British Libr Newspaper [943]
DEUTSCHE RUNDSCHAU – Bydgoszcz, Poland. Sept-Oct 1939 – 1r – 1 – us L of C Photodup [943]
DEUTSCHE RUNDSCHAU *see*
– DEUTSCHE RUNDSCHAU IN POLEN
– OSTDEUTSCHE RUNDSCHAU
DEUTSCHE RUNDSCHAU 1874-1942 / ed by Rodenberg, Julius – Berlin, Leipzig, 1874-1942 (mf ed 1993) – 951mf – 9 – DM10,200.00 – 3-89131-157-5 – gw Fischer [100]
DEUTSCHE RUNDSCHAU IN POLEN – (Cont: Bromberger Tageblatt, 1877?-sep 1919; Ostdeutsche Rundschau, -1920? Cont by: Deutsche Rundschau, sep 2 1939) – Bromberg, 1920 (incomplete), 1921-43 – 1 – Inquire at Mikrofilmarchiv for details – gw Misc Inst [943]
DEUTSCHE RUNDSCHAU IN POLEN *see* DEUTSCHE RUNDSCHAU
DEUTSCHE RUSTUNGSPOLITIK VOM BEGINN DER GENFER ABRUSTUNGSKONFERENZ BIS ZUR WIEDEREINFUEHRUNG DER ALLGEMEINEN WEHRPFLICHT / Rautenberg, Hans Juergen – 1932-1935 – 1 – DM50.00 – gw Mikro Press [943]
DEUTSCHE SAGEN / Richter, Albert – 1878 – 1 – us I.U. Libraries [390]
DEUTSCHE SALONLIEDER / Hoffmann von Fallersleben, August Heinrich – Zuerich: Verlag des literarischen Comptoirs, 1844 – 1r – 1 – us U.W. Library [780]
DEUTSCHE SATIRIKER DES 16. JAHRHUNDERTS / Geiger, Ludwig – Berlin: C Habel, 1878 – 1r – 1 – us U.W. Library [430]
DIE DEUTSCHE SCHALLFORM DER LETZTEN BLUETEZEIT UND IHRER AUSLAUFER IN DICHTUNG UND PROSA / Bluemel, Rudolf – Halle, 1923 – 2mf – DM62.00 – 3-8267-3020-8 – gw Hänsel [430]
DEUTSCHE SCHAUSPIELER UND SCHAUSPIELKUNST / Kirchbach, Wolfgang – Kiel: Lipsius und Tischer, 1892 – 1r – 1 – us U.W. Library [790]
DEUTSCHE SCHRIFTEN / Seuse, Heinrich; ed by Bihlmeyer, K – Stuttgart, 1907 – 17mf – 8 – ne Slangenburg [290]
DEUTSCHE SCHRIFTTAFELN DES 9. BIS 16. JAHRHUNDERTS AUS HANDSCHRIFTEN DER K. HOF- UND STAATSBIBL. IN MUENCHEN / Petzet, Erich & Glauning, O – 5v. 1910-1930 – 22mf – 9 – ne IDC [090]
DAS DEUTSCHE SCHRIFTTUM BIS ZUM AUSGANG DES MITTELALTERS / Wolff, Ludwig – (Includes bibliographical references and index) – Goettingen: Vandenhoeck und Ruprecht, 1951 – 1r – 1 – us U.W. Library [430]
DEUTSCHE SCHUETZEN- UND WEHR-ZEITUNG – Bremen, 1866-84 (incomplete), apr 1890-1915 (incomplete), jan 14 1920-nov 1922 (incomplete), 1924-28, 1929 (incomplete), 1930-32, 1935 – 21r – 1 – Inquire at Mikrofilmarchiv for details – gw Misc Inst [355]
DEUTSCHE SCHULZEITUNG – Berlin, 1876-80, 1885-86, 1891-92, 1905 – 1r – 1 – Dist. gw Mikrofilm – gw Misc Inst [370]
DIE DEUTSCHE SCHWEIZERBEGEISTERUNG IN DEN JAHREN 1750-1815 / Ziehen, Eduard – (Includes bibliographical references) – Frankfurt am Main: M Diesterweg, 1922 – 1r – 1 – us U.W. Library [943]
DER DEUTSCHE SEEHANDEL... / Allman, E – Muenchen, 1900 – 1mf – 9 – ILM-1799/1 – ne IDC [340]
DER DEUTSCHE SENDER – Berlin. oct 3, 1930-jun 7, 1936 – 9r – 1 – gw Mikrofilm [380]
DEUTSCHE SHANGHAI-ZEITUNG – Shanghai. 1932-35. KCHF-3-3 – 1 – ne IDC [072]
DEUTSCHE SHANGHAI-ZEITUNG – Shanghai, China. 4-9 Dec 1932, 31 Dec 1933-35 – 6r – 1 – gw Mikrofilm [072]
DEUTSCHE SIPPENNAMEN, ABLEITENDES WOERTERBUCH DER DEUTSCHEN FAMILIENNAMEN / Brechenmacher, Josef Karlmann – Goerlitz: C.A. Starke, 1936. 5v – 1 – us U.W. Library [400]
DIE DEUTSCHE SOLDATEN-ZEITUNG/SOLDAT IM VOLK – Passau, DE. 1954-72 – 1 – gw Mikrofilm [072]
DEUTSCHE SONDERRENAISSANCE IN DEUTSCHER PROSA : STRUKTURANALYSE DEUTSCHER PROSA IM SECHZEHNTEN JAHRHUNDERT / Gumbel, Hermann – (Includes bibliographical references) – 1 – us U.W. Library [430]
DER DEUTSCHE, SONST WANDSBECKER BOTHE *see* DER WANDSBECKER BOTHE
Deutsche sozialdemokratische Arbeiter-partei in der CSR *see* DER SOZIALDEMOKRAT
DEUTSCHE STAATSBUERGER ZEITUNG *see* DER JUNG-DEUTSCHE ORDEN
DEUTSCHE STIMMEN – Berlin, 1919-28 – 4r – 1 – DM480.00 set DM120.00r – gw Mikro Press [072]
DEUTSCHE STIMMEN – Berlin, DE. 1919-28 – 4r – 1 – gw Mikrofilm [072]
DEUTSCHE STIMMEN – Berlin, mar 23 1904, apr 2 1904-dec 22 1906 – 1r – 1 – Dist. gw Mikrofilm – gw Misc Inst [072]
DEUTSCHE STIMMEN – Bratislava, Czechoslovakia. Jan-Jun 1943 – 1r – 1 – us L of C Photodup [072]
DEUTSCHE STIMMEN – Pressburg (Bratislava), CS. Jan 1936-Dec 1943 – 4r – 1 – gw Mikrofilm [072]
DEUTSCHE STUDIEN : 3. DRAMEN UND DRAMATIKER / Scherer, Wilhelm – Wien: In Commission bei Karl Gerold's Sohn, 1878 – 1r – 1 – us U.W. Library [430]
DEUTSCHE SUDPOLAR-EXPEDITION 1901-1903 / Drygalski, E C von – 2831 2. v. 2, Geographie und Geologie. 1912 – 8 – ne IDC [910]
DAS DEUTSCHE TABU : SUNFUZIUS UND DER WIND DES 21. JAHRHUNDERTS UND DER NEUE PREUSSENZYKLUS UND DIE ELITEDAEMMERUNG / Schuermeyer, Manfred – 1994 – 2mf – 9 – DM80.00 – 3-89349-876-1 – gw Hänsel [320]
DEUTSCHE TAGESPOST – Hermannstadt (Sibiu), Rumaenien. 6 Dez 1919-15 Nov 1925 – 8r – 1 – gw Mikrofilm [949]
DEUTSCHE TAGESPOST – Wuerzburg, West Germany. 1 Jun 1953- – 1 – gw Mikrofilm [072]
DEUTSCHE TAGESZEITUNG – Berlin, DE. 22 Jan 1916-11 Aug 1919 – 27r – 1 – uk British Libr Newspaper [072]
DEUTSCHE TAGESZEITUNG – Berlin, sep 1 1894-aug 1898, oct 1898-1914 (incomplete) – 135r – 1 – Dist. gw Mikrofilm – gw Misc Inst [943]
DEUTSCHE TAGESZEITUNG – Berlin, Sep 1914-Apr 1934 – 103r – 1 – gw Mikro Press [072]
DEUTSCHE TAGESZEITUNG – Hermannstadt (Sibiu), RM. 2 Oct 1934-14 Jul 1939 – 6r – 1 – gw Mikrofilm [949]
DEUTSCHE TAGESZEITUNG – Karlsbad (Karlovy Vary), CS. 4 Oct-Dec 1938 – 1r – 1 – gw Mikrofilm [072]
DEUTSCHE TAGESZEITUNG IN POLEN – Posen (Poznan), PL. Dec 1934-29 Aug 1939 – 8r – 1 – gw Mikrofilm [072]
DEUTSCHE TAGEZEITUNG – Berlin, 1914-1934 – 103r – 1 – DM7,725.00 – gw Mikro Press [072]
DEUTSCHE TASCHEN-ENCYKLOPAEDIE ODER HANDBIBLIOTHEK DES WISSENSWUERDIGSTEN IN HINSICHT AUF NATUR UND KUNST, STAAT UND KIRCHE, WISSENSCHAFT UND SITTE (AEL, ABT 1;21) : 4 THEILE MIT 50 KUPFERN – Leipzig, Altenburg, 1816-1820 (mf ed 1994) – 16mf – 9 – DM340.00 – 3-89131-171-0 – gw Fischer [030]
DER DEUTSCHE TELESCOPE *see* DER FROEHLICHE BOTSCHAFTER
DEUTSCHE TOEPFER-ZEITUNG – Leipzig, Germany. Jan 1892-Oct 1898; Jul 1899-Feb 1902 (imperfect).-w. 8 reels – 1 – uk British Libr Newspaper [072]
DIE DEUTSCHE TREUE : VORTRAG, GEHALTEN IN DER AULA DER ANNEN-REALSCHULE ZU DRESDEN AM 23. APRIL, DEM GEBURTSTAGE SR. MAJESTAET, DES KOENIGS VON SACHSEN / Dolch, Oskar – (Includes bibliographical references) – Dresden: R v Zahn, 1879 – 1r – 1 – us U.W. Library [943]
DIE DEUTSCHE TREUE IN SAGE UND POESIE : VORTRAG, GEHALTEN AM GEBURTSTAGE SEINER KOENGLICHEN HOHEIT DES GROSSHERZOGS VON MECKLENBURG-SCHWERIN FRIEDRICH FRANZ AM 28. FEBRUAR 1867 / Bartsch, Karl – Leipzig: F C W Vogel, 1867 – 1 – us U.W. Library [430]
DEUTSCHE TURN-ZEITUNG : BLAETTER FUER DIE INTERESSEN DES GESAMTEN TURNWESENS – Leipzig, July 1856-1943 – 32r – 1 – DM2,400.00 – gw Mikro Press [370]
DEUTSCHE TURNZEITUNG : BLAETTER FUER DIE INTERESSEN DES GESAMTEN TURNWESENS – Leipzig, Germany. Jul 1856-1943 – 32r – 1 – gw Mikrofilm [072]
DEUTSCHE TURNZEITUNG FUER FRAUEN : ORGAN FUER DIE FRAUEN- TURN- SPIEL- UND SPORTVEREINIGUNGEN – Krefeld, 1899-1902 – 1r – 1 – DM75.00 – gw Mikro Press [790]
DEUTSCHE UKRAINE-ZEITUNG – Lutsk. USSR. -w. 1 Jul 1943-7 Jan 1944. (Imperfect). (1 reel) – 1 – uk British Libr Newspaper [072]
DAS DEUTSCHE VATERLAND – Muenchen, DE. 1884-88 (incomplete) – 1r – 1 – gw Mikrofilm [072]
DEUTSCHE VERGANGENHEIT IN DEUTSCHER DICHTUNG : DEUTSCHE RENAISSANCE: REDE BEI UEBERNAHME DES REKTORATS DER SCHLESISCHEN FRIEDRICH WILHELMS-UNIVERSITAET ZU BRESLAU, AM 30. SEPTEMBER 1918 / Koch, Max – (Includes bibliographical references ("Literaturnachweise")) – Stuttgart: Metzler, 1919 – 1r – 1 – us U.W. Library [430]
DEUTSCHE VERGANGENHEIT IN DEUTSCHER DICHTUNG : REDE BEI UEBERNAHME DES REKTORATS DER SCHLESISCHEN FRIEDRICH WILHELMS-UNIVERSITAET ZU BRESLAU, AM 30. SEPTEMBER 1918 / Koch, Max – (Includes bibliographical references) – Stuttgart: Metzler, 1919 – 1 – us U.W. Library [850]
DEUTSCHE VERKEHRSZEITUNG – Hamburg, West Germany. 10 Jul 1947-77 – 1 – gw Mikrofilm [072]
DER DEUTSCHE VOLKSERZIEHER – Berlin, 1935-39 (incomplete) – 1 – Dist. gw Mikrofilm – gw Misc Inst [370]
DEUTSCHE VOLKSGEMEINSCHAFT – Kattowitz, (Katowice), Poland. 19 Jan 1934-5 Apr 1935; 10 Apr 1936-5 Aug 1939 (incomplete) – 2r – 1 – gw Mikrofilm [072]
DIE DEUTSCHE VOLKSGRUPPE IN DAENEMARK UND DAS NATIONAL-SOZIALISTISCHE DEUTSCHLAND 1933-1939 / Lenzine, Hilke – 1 – DM40.00 – gw Mikro Press [943]
DEUTSCHE VOLKSHALLE *see*
– RHEINISCHE VOLKSHALLE
– RHEINISCHE VOLKSHALLE/DEUTSCHE VOLKSHALLE
DEUTSCHE VOLKSKUNDE AUS DEM OESTLICHEN BOEHMEN – v1-7, 8-12. 1901-1907; 1908-12 – 1 – us I.U. Libraries [390]
DAS DEUTSCHE VOLKSLIED – (Missing: 1931. v33) – Wien, 1899-1933. v1-35 – 69mf – P-577/1 – ne IDC [780]
DEUTSCHE VOLKSSCHAUSPIELE, IN STEIERMARK GESAMMELT – 1891 – 1 – us I.U. Libraries [390]
DEUTSCHE VOLKSSTIMME – Duchcov, Czechoslovakia. Feb 1912-Jul 1914 (scattered issues) – 1r – 1 – us L of C Photodup [072]
DEUTSCHE VOLKSWACHT – (With Suppl: Der Hessische Bauer; and: Spinnstube) – Friedberg. oct 3, 1894-dec 11, 1907 – 7r – 1 – gw Mikrofilm [072]
DEUTSCHE VOLKSWEHR – Friedek-Friedberg (Frydek-Mistek), Czechoslovakia. 24 24 May 1930-Dec 1933 – 3r – 1 – gw Mikrofilm [072]

DER DEUTSCHE VOLKSWIRT – Berlin, oct 1 1926-apr 17 1943 – 33r – 1 – DM2,475.00 – gw Mikro Press [330]

DIE DEUTSCHE VOLKSWIRTSCHAFT – Berlin, 1932-44 (incomplete) – 1 – Dist. gw Mikrofilm – gw Misc Inst [330]

DEUTSCHE VOLKS-ZEITUNG : EINZIGES UNABHAENGIGES WOCHENBLATT ALLER WERKTAETIGEN – Saarbruecken, Germany. 15 Feb-31 Dec 1934 – 1r – 1 – gw Mikrofilm [072]

DEUTSCHE VOLKS-ZEITUNG – Prague, Czechoslovakia. Dec 1936-1937 – 1r – 1 – us L of C Photodup [072]

DEUTSCHE VOLKS-ZEITUNG – Prigrevica, Yugoslavia. Jan-Apr 1941 – 1r – 1 – us L of C Photodup [949]

DEUTSCHE VOLKSZEITUNG : AUSGABE SUEDHANNOVER – Goettingen. mar 25, 1947-aug 23, 1949 – 2r – 1 – gw Mikrofilm [072]

DEUTSCHE VOLKSZEITUNG – Berlin, 1945-1946 – 1 – DM80.00 – gw Mikro Press [072]

DEUTSCHE VOLKSZEITUNG – Berlin, jun 13 1945-apr 21 1946 – 1 – Dist. gw Mikrofilm – gw Misc Inst [943]

DEUTSCHE VOLKSZEITUNG – (Cont by: Deutsche Volkszeitung/die tat, 1983; Der Sonntag, Berlin, 9 Nov 1990) – Duesseldorf, West Germany. 12 May 1953-30 Sept 1983 – 1 – gw Mikrofilm [072]

DEUTSCHE VOLKSZEITUNG – (Cont by: Tagblatt Bruexer Volkszeitung) – Bruex, apr 1929-38 – 1 – Inquire at Mikrofilmarchiv for details – gw Misc Inst [943]

DEUTSCHE VOLKSZEITUNG – Czernowitz (Cernauti), Rumaenien. 28 Mai 1921-11 Mar 1922 – 1r – 1 – gw Mikrofilm [949]

DEUTSCHE VOLKSZEITUNG – East Berlin, Germany. 17 Jun 1945-19 Apr 1946 – 1r – 1 – gw Mikrofilm [072]

DEUTSCHE VOLKSZEITUNG – Karlsbad (Karlovy Vary), Czechoslovakia. Apr-Dec 1938 – 1r – 1 – gw Mikrofilm [072]

DEUTSCHE VOLKSZEITUNG – Prague, Paris, Bale puis Copenhague. 1934, 1936-38 – 1 – fr A.C.R.P.P. [073]

DEUTSCHE VOLKSZEITUNG – Saaz (Zatec), Czechoslovakia. Apr 1936-Mar 1938 – 1r – 1 – gw Mikrofilm [072]

DEUTSCHE VOLKSZEITUNG – (Title change: Tagblatt Bruexer Volkszeitung, Jan 1938) – Bruex (Most), Czechoslovakia. Apr 1929-1938 – 1 – gw Mikrofilm [072]

DEUTSCHE VOLKSZEITUNG : WOCHENZEITUNG FUER "FREIHEIT UND RECHT, FRIEDEN DEM DEUTSCHEN VOLK" – Prague-Paris-Basel-Copenhagen. 22 Mar 1936-27 Aug 1939 – 1r – 1 – gw Mikrofilm [072]

DEUTSCHE VOLKSZEITUNG *see*
- DER GEGEN-ANGRIFF
- DIE TAT

DEUTSCHE VOLKSZEITUNG FUER DAS KUHLAENDCHEN – (Title changes: Deutsche Zeitung fuer das Kuhlaendchen, Jan 1930; Neu-Titscheiner Zeitung, Jan 1934) – Neu-Titschein (Novy Jicin), CS. Nov 1922-Dec 1938 – 10r – 1 – gw Mikrofilm [072]

DEUTSCHE VOLKSZEITUNG IN POLEN *see* VOLKSZEITUNG

DEUTSCHE VOLKSZEITUNG/DIE TAT *see* DEUTSCHE VOLKSZEITUNG

DEUTSCHE VOLKSZEITUNG/FREITAG – Duesseldorf, 1975- – 1 – DM75.00 – gw Mikro Press [072]

DEUTSCHE VOLKZEITUNG – Berlin, Germany. Jun 1945-Apr 1946 – 1r – 1 – us L of C Photodup [072]

DEUTSCHE WACHT – Hohenstadt (Zabreh), Czechoslovakia. Aug 1929-18 May 1934 – 3r – 1 – gw Mikrofilm [072]

DEUTSCHE WACHT : WOCHENSCHRIFT DER DEUTSCHEN VEREINIGUNG – Bonn, 1908-1922 – 3r – 1 – DM280.00 – gw Mikro Press [943]

DEUTSCHE WACHT : WOCHENSCHRIFT DER DEUTSCHEN VEREINIGUNG – Bonn, Germany. 26 Jan 1908-10 Dec 1922 (Inc. no. 2-6, 1921, of Suppl. Westdeutsche Waehlerzeitung.) – 3r – 1 – gw Mikrofilm [072]

DEUTSCHE WACHT : WOCHENSCHRIFT DER DEUTSCHEN VEREINIGUNG – (Suppl available: Westdeutsche Waehlerzeitung, jan 30-feb 19 1921) – Bonn, jan 26 1908-dec 10 1922 – 3r – 1 – Inquire at Mikrofilmarchiv for details – gw Misc Inst [072]

DEUTSCHE WARSCHAUER ZEITUNG – Warsaw, Poland. Jan-Nov 1916 – 1r – 1 – us L of C Photodup [072]

DEUTSCHE WARSCHAUER ZEITUNG – Warsaw (Waszawa), Poland. 10 Aug 1915-16 – 3r – 1 – gw Mikrofilm [943]

DEUTSCHE WARTE – (Incl suppl) – Berlin, oct 1 1890-jun 1894, oct 1894-1901, apr-dec 1902, apr 1903-04, apr-dec 1905, apr-sep 1906, jan-mar 1907, jul 1907-sep 1909, jan-sep 1910, jan-mar 1911, oct 1911-12, apr 1913-14, apr 1915-mar 1916, jul 1916-apr 1918, sep 1918-apr 1919, sep 1919-20, may 1921-22 – 107r – 1 – Dist. gw Mikrofilm – gw Misc Inst [072]

DER DEUTSCHE WEG : KATHOLISCHE WOCHENZEITUNG – Oldenzaal, Netherlands. 12 Aug 1934-5 May 1940 – 1 – gw Mikrofilm [949]

DER DEUTSCHE WEG – Lodz, Poland. 1935-28 May 1937 – 1r – 1 – gw Mikrofilm [072]

DER DEUTSCHE WEG – Moenchengladbach, jul 1 1928-jun 26 1930, oct 2 1930-jun 11 1931 – 2r – 1 – gw Mikrofilm [072]

DER DEUTSCHE WEGWEISER – Lodz, Poland. Jan-27 Aug 1939 – 1r – 1 – gw Mikrofilm [072]

DEUTSCHE WEHR – Eger (Cheb), Czechoslovakia. Mar 1930-10 Apr 1932 – 1r – 1 – gw Mikrofilm [072]

DEUTSCHE WEHRZEITUNG – Coburg, Germany. 1864 (incomplete) – 1r – 1 – gw Mikrofilm [072]

DEUTSCHE WEHRZEITUNG – (Since 1850: Preussische Wehr-Zeitung. Since 1852 publ in Potsdam) – Berlin. jul 7, 1848-jun 29, 1854 – 4r – 1 – gw Mikrofilm [355]

DEUTSCHE WELLE / DW FUNK – Berlin. 1926-sep 23, 1932 – 10r – 1 – gw Mikrofilm [380]

DIE DEUTSCHE WERBUNG *see* DIE REKLAME

DEUTSCHE WESTBOEHMISCHE STIMMEN – Plan (Plana), CS. 16 May 1928-May 1933 – 4r – 1 – gw Mikrofilm [072]

DEUTSCHE WISSENSCHAFT, ERZIEHUNG UND VOLKSBILDUNG – Berlin, 1935-44 n16 – 1 – Dist. gw Mikrofilm – gw Misc Inst [370]

DEUTSCHE WISSENSCHAFT, ERZIEHUNG UND VOLKSBILDUNG – Berlin. v.1-10, 1935-44. Incomplete. Film Mas C 629 – 1 – us H.U. Library [324]

DEUTSCHE WISSENSCHAFTLICHE ZEITSCHRIFT IM WARTHELAND – Posen. v. 1-3, 1940-42. Film Mas 9225 – 1 – us H.U. Library [500]

DEUTSCHE WOCHE – Troppau (Opava), CS. Jan-Dec 1938 – 1r – 1 – gw Mikrofilm [072]

DEUTSCHE WOCHENSCHAU – Berlin, 1925-35 – 2r – 1 – Dist. gw Mikrofilm – gw Misc Inst [072]

DEUTSCHE WOCHENZEITUNG – Berlin, may 26 1940-apr 22 1945 – 1 – Dist. gw Mikrofilm – gw Misc Inst [072]

DEUTSCHE ZEITSCHRIFT FUER DIE GESAMTE GERICHTLICHE MEDIZIN *see* ZEITSCHRIFT FUER RECHTSMEDIZIN

DEUTSCHE ZEITSCHRIFT FUER NERVENHEILKUNDE *see* ZEITSCHRIFT FUER NEUROLOGIE

DEUTSCHE ZEITSCHRIFT FUER PHILOSOPHIE – 1953-1989 – 1,209mf – 1 – DM6,891.30 – gw Mikro Press [100]

DEUTSCHE ZEITSCHRIFT FUER PHILOSOPHIE – Berlin. v1-25. 1953-77 – 5,9 – Dfl3,750.00; Dfl150.00v – ne Swets [100]

DEUTSCHE ZEITSCHRIFTEN DES 18./19. JAHRHUNDERTS – Hildesheim: Georg Olms Verlag, seit 1994 – ca 20,000mf – 9 – DM34,800.00 diazo DM44,800.00 silver – gw Olms [073]

DEUTSCHE ZEITUNG – (Beilagen: Deutsche Wehr, 1919-20 (incomplete). Deutscher Herold, 1917-18 (incomplete). Das junge Deutschland, oct 4-dec 27 1919. Rundschau, 1896-97. Zeitbilder, Ausgabe A, jun 2 1918, nov 6 1918-nov 25 1919. Zeitbilder, Ausgabe B, aug 8 1918, dec 12, dec 31 1919. Most of these suppl are only available from other sources, inquire Mikrofilmarchiv Dortmund) – Berlin, 1898-1934 (incomplete) – 184r – 1 – Dist. gw Mikrofilm – gw Misc Inst [943]

DEUTSCHE ZEITUNG – Berlin. apr 2, 1917-sep 30, 1922. jan 2-dec 30 1934 – 25r – 1 – gw Mikrofilm [072]

DEUTSCHE ZEITUNG – Budapest, Hungary. 20 Okt 1940 31 Doc 1943 – 7r – 1 – gw Mikrofilm [072]

DEUTSCHE ZEITUNG – Budapest, oct 20 1940-apr 30 1943, jul 1 1943-apr 30 1944 – 1 – Inquire at Mikrofilmarchiv for details – gw Misc Inst [943]

DEUTSCHE ZEITUNG – Celje, Yugoslavia. Feb 1929-1931; Jul-Dec 1932; Jul-Dec 1934 – 4r – 1 – us L of C Photodup [072]

DEUTSCHE ZEITUNG – Cilli (Celje), Jugoslawien. 5 Jan-29 Jun 1930, 7 Jan 1932-7 Mai 1936 – 3r – 1 – gw Mikrofilm [949]

DEUTSCHE ZEITUNG – Gablonz-Neisse (Jablonec nad Nisou), Czechoslovakia. 21 Oct 1933-13 Oct 1934 – 1r – 1 – gw Mikrofilm [072]

DEUTSCHE ZEITUNG – Heidelberg/Frankfurt, 1847-1850 – 12r – 1 – DM900.00 – gw Mikro Press [072]

DEUTSCHE ZEITUNG – Heidelberg-Frankfurt a.M.-Mannheim-Leipzig, Germany. 1 Jul 1847-31 Dec 1850 – 12r – 1 – gw Mikrofilm [072]

DEUTSCHE ZEITUNG – Indianapolis. Ind. 1875-1876 – 1 – us UMI [071]

DEUTSCHE ZEITUNG – Klausenburg (Cluj), Rumaenien. 9 Okt 1931-29 Mar 1941; 13 Jun 1942-18 Dez 1943 – 3r – 1 – gw Mikrofilm [949]

DEUTSCHE ZEITUNG – Novi Sad, Yugoslavia. Dec 1931-Sept 1940 – 9r – 1 – us L of C Photodup [072]

DEUTSCHE ZEITUNG – Olmuetz (Olomouc), Czechoslovakia. 3 Aug 1920-31 Dec 1933 – 33r – 1 – gw Mikrofilm [072]

DEUTSCHE ZEITUNG – Pressburg (Bratislava), Czechoslovakia. May 1922-1932 – 1r – 1 – gw Mikrofilm [072]

DEUTSCHE ZEITUNG – Riga, Latvia. 1 Mar-15 May 1933 – 1r – 1 – gw Mikrofilm [943]

DEUTSCHE ZEITUNG – San Diego, CA. 1887-1939 – 37r – 1 RC02780 – $1,850.00 – us Library Micro [071]

DEUTSCHE ZEITUNG – San Diego. Calif. 1887-1891 – 1 – us UMI [071]

DEUTSCHE ZEITUNG – Sao Paulo, Brazil. 1974-1976; 24 Apr 1982- – 1 – gw Mikrofilm [072]

DEUTSCHE ZEITUNG – Sombor, Yugoslavia. Jul-Nov 1931 – 1r – 1 – us L of C Photodup [072]

DEUTSCHE ZEITUNG – Stuttgart, Germany. 1972-79 – 15r – 1 – us L of C Photodup [072]

DEUTSCHE ZEITUNG – Troppau (Opava), Czechoslovakia. Nov 1921-Nov 1922 – 3r – 1 – gw Mikrofilm [072]

DEUTSCHE ZEITUNG – Wien: Druck von Kreisel & Groger, 1895-98; 1905-06 – 26r – 1 – us Res Libr [072]

DEUTSCHE ZEITUNG *see*
- CILLIER ZEITUNG
- DEUTSCHE ZEITUNG/CHRIST UND WELT
- DIRSCHAUER ZEITUNG
- DORPATER ZEITUNG

DEUTSCHE ZEITUNG / CHRIST UND WELT – Bonn, 1970-1980 – 1 – DM100.00y – gw Mikro Press [240]

DEUTSCHE ZEITUNG FUER CHINA – Shanghai. 1917.KCHF-7-3 – 1 – ne IDC [072]

DEUTSCHE ZEITUNG FUER CHINA – Shanghai, China. 2 Jan-21 May 1917 – 1r – 1 – gw Mikrofilm [072]

DEUTSCHE ZEITUNG FUER DAS KUHLAENDCHEN *see* DEUTSCHE VOLKSZEITUNG FUER DAS KUHLAENDCHEN

DEUTSCHE ZEITUNG FUER DEN LEITMERITZER KREIS – (Title change: Leitmeritzer Tagblatt, 4 May 1920) – Leitmeritz (Litomerice), Czechoslovakia. 7 Apr-Jul 1920 – 1r – 1 – gw Mikrofilm [072]

DEUTSCHE ZEITUNG FUER SPANIEN – (Cont: Deutsche Zeitung von Spanien, -1916) – Barcelona, jan 27 1916-dec 25 1934, jan 10-aug 25 1936, jan 10-dec 25 1942 – 1 – Dist. gw Mikrofilm – gw Misc Inst [946]

DEUTSCHE ZEITUNG IM OSTLAND – Riga, Latvia (U.S.S.R.). 1941-43 – 1 – gw Mikrofilm [943]

DEUTSCHE ZEITUNG IM OSTLAND – Riga. USSR. -d. 7 Jan 1942-20 Jan 1943, 19 Apr-25 Jul 1944. (Imperfect). (5 reels) – 1 – uk British Libr Newspaper [072]

DEUTSCHE ZEITUNG IN DEN NIEDERLANDEN – Amsterdam, 1941-44 (incomplete) – 1 – gw Misc Inst [949]

DEUTSCHE ZEITUNG IN DEN NIEDERLANDEN – Amsterdam, oct 24 1940-mar 27 1945. (incomplete) – 14r – 1 – uk British Libr Newspaper [949]

DEUTSCHE ZEITUNG IN GROSSBRITANNIEN – London. 12 Feb 1938-26 Aug 2 Sep 1939.-w. 1 reel – 1 – uk British Libr Newspaper [072]

DEUTSCHE ZEITUNG IN KROATIEN – Zagreb. Yugoslavia. -d. 1 Jan 1942-22 Mar 1945. (Imperfect). (12 reels) – 1 – uk British Libr Newspaper [949]

DEUTSCHE ZEITUNG IN NORDCHINA – Tientsin. 1939-41. KCHF-8-3 – 1 – ne IDC [072]

DEUTSCHE ZEITUNG IN NORDCHINA – Tientsin, China. 2 Oct-24 Dec 1939; 8 Jan 1940-2 May 1941 – 3r – 1 – gw Mikrofilm [072]

DEUTSCHE ZEITUNG VON SPANIEN *see* DEUTSCHE ZEITUNG FUER SPANIEN

DEUTSCHE ZEITUNG/CHRIST UND WELT – (Cont: Wirtschaftszeitung, may 10 1946-aug 31 1949. Deutsche Zeitung, sep 1 1949-mar 31 1959. Christ und Welt, apr 1 1959-apr 8 1971. Cont by: Rheinischer Merkur, Koblenz 1 Jan 1980) – Stuttgart, Koeln, Koblenz. jan 1 1975-dec 21 1979 – 9r – 1 – gw Mikrofilm [072]

DEUTSCHE ZEITUNG/CHRIST UND WELT *see* RHEINISCHER MERKUR

DEUTSCHE ZEITUNGEN VON DEN ANFAENGEN BIS ZUR MITTE DES 19. JAHRHUNDERTS *see*
- ALLGEMEINE ZEITUNG
- DER BOTE AUS THUERINGEN
- HAMBURGISCHER UNPARTHEYISCHER CORRESPONDENT
- RHEINISCHE ZEITUNG
- SCHLESISCHE PRIVILEGIRTE ZEITUNG
- SUEDPREUSSISCHE ZEITUNG
- DER WANDSBECKER BOTHE
- WOECHENTLICHE ZEITUNG AUSS MEHRERLEY OERTHER
- ZEITUNG AUS DEM FELDLAGER
- ZEITUNG FUER STAEDTE, FLECKEN UND DOERFER, INSBESONDERHEIT FUER DIE LIEBEN LANDSLEUTE JUNG UND ALT

DEUTSCHE ZEITUNGEN VON DEN ANFAEGEN BIS ZUR MITTE DES 19. JAHRHUNDERTS *see* RHEINISCHER MERKUR

DEUTSCHE ZEITUNG/TAGESZEITUNG *see* DEUTSCHE ZENTRAL-ZEITUNG (DZZ)

DEUTSCHE ZENTRAL-ZEITUNG (DZZ) : ORGAN DER DEUTSCHEN WERKTAETIGEN IN DER UDSSR – (Title change 26 Aug 1938-28 Febr 1939: Deutsche Zeitung/Tageszeitung) – Moscow, U.S.S.R. 1935-12 Jul 1939 – 1 – gw Mikrofilm [943]

DEUTSCHE ZUKUNFT – Berlin. oct 15, 1933-jun 2, 1940 – 8r – 1 – gw Mikrofilm [072]

DEUTSCHE ZUKUNFT *see* DIE BRUECKE

DIE DEUTSCHEN BISCHOEFE UND DER ABERGLAUBE : EINE DENKSCHRIFT / Reusch, Franz Heinrich – Bonn: P Neusser, 1879 – 1mf – 9 – 0-8370-8705-8 – 1986-2705 – us A.T.L.A. [240]

DIE DEUTSCHEN DOMINIKANER IM KAMPFE GEGEN LUTHER (1518-1563) / Paulus, Nikolaus – Freiburg im Breisgau, St. Louis, Mo.: Herder, 1903 – 1mf – us A.T.L.A. [240]

Deutschen Freiheitspartei *see* DAS WAHRE DEUTSCHLAND

DIE DEUTSCHEN IM BRASILISCHEN URWALD / Zoeller, Hugo – Berlin, Stuttgart: W. Spemann, 1883. 2v. illus. map – 1 – us U.W. Library [972]

DIE DEUTSCHEN MITTELALTERLICHEN HANDSCHRIFTEN DER UNIVERSITAETSBIBLIOTHEK MUENCHEN – (Gesamtedition: Die Handschriften der Universitaetsbibliothek Muenchen) – 1994 – 401mf – 9 – DM7,400.00 – 3-89131-201-6 – gw Fischer [090]

DIE DEUTSCHEN, OESTERREICHISCHEN UND UNGARISCHEN ACTIEN-GESELLSCHAFTEN IM FRANZOESISCHEN RECHT / Goirand, L – Wien, 1902 – 2mf – 1 – ILM-3305/1 – ne IDC [327]

DIE DEUTSCHEN PAEPSTE : NACH HANDSCHRIFTLICHEN UND GEDRUCKTEN QUELLEN / Hoefler, Karl Adolf Constantin, Ritter von – Regensburg: G.J. Manz, 1839 – 2mf – us A.T.L.A. [240]

DIE DEUTSCHEN PERSONENNAMEN / Baehnisch, Alfred – Leipzig: B.G. Teubner, 1914. viii,126p – 1 – us U.W. Library [920]

DIE "DEUTSCHEN SAGEN" DER BRUEDER GRIMM : EIN BEITRAG ZU IHRER ENTSTEHUNGSGESCHICHTE, UNTER BESONDERER BERUECKSICHTIGUNG DES WESTFAELISCHEN ANTEILS / Erfurth, Fritz – Muenster, 1937 – 1mf – 9 – DM48.00 – 3-89349-354-9 – gw Hänsel [430]

DIE DEUTSCHEN SCHRIFTSTELLERINNEN DES 19. JAHRHUNDERTS / Schindel, Carl Wilhelm Otto August von – Leipzig, 1823-25. Hildesheim, 1983 – 14mf – 9 – DM85.00 diazo DM100.00 silver – gw Olms [430]
Deutschen Schulvereines Sua5dmark *see* GRENZLAND
DIE DEUTSCHEN SCHUTZGEBIETE IN AFRIKA / ed by Eschner, Max – Leipzig, 1910 – 1mf – DM48.00 – 3-8267-3094-1 – gw Hänsel [960]
DIE DEUTSCHEN VOLKSNAMEN DER PFLANZEN / Pritzel, G A – Hannover: P. Cohen, 1882. viii,701p. illus – 1 – us U.W. Library [580]
DEUTSCH-ENGLISCHE HEFTE – Berlin, 1936-39 (incomplete) – 1 – Dist. gw Mikrofilm – gw Misc Inst [072]
DEUTSCHENSPIEGEL UND AUGSBURGER SACHSENSPIEGEL (MGH LEGES 3: 3.BD) – 1930 – Dfl25.00 – ne Slangenburg [240]
DEUTSCHE-OSTAFRIKANISCHE ZEITUNG – Morogoro. Aug 1914-Jun 1916 gaps – 1 – 35.00r – us Hoover Inst Photo [072]
DEUTSCHER ADEL : EINE ERZAEHLUNG / Raabe, Wilhelm Karl – Braunschweig: G Westermann, 1880 – 1r – 1 – us U.W. Library [830]
Deutscher Alpenverein *see* MITTHEILUNGEN
Deutscher Arbeiter-Kongress *see* BERICHT UEBER DIE VERHANDLUNGEN..
Deutscher Arbeitgeberbund fuer das Baugewerbe *see* GESCHAEFTSBERICHT
Deutscher Arbeitsnachweis-Kongress *see* PROCEEDINGS
Deutscher Arbeitverein *see* BERICHT UEBER DIE VERHANDLUNGEN..
Deutscher Bauarbeiterverband. Hamburg *see*
- JAHRBUCH
- PROTOKOLL UEBER DIE VERHANDLUNGEN..

Deutscher Baugewerksbund *see*
- JAHRBUCH
- NIEDERSCHRIFTEN UEBER DIE VERHANDLUNGEN..

DEUTSCHER BEOBACHTER – Windhoek, South West Africa. 1939-43 – 1 – sa Stato Libr [072]
DEUTSCHER BEOBACHTER ODER PRIVILEGIRTE HANSEATISCHE ZEITUNG – (Publ in Hamburg since 1814) – Bremen, apr-may 1813, jan-jul 1814, 1815, 1817-19 – 1 – Inquire at Mikrofilmarchiv for details – gw Misc Inst [943]
DEUTSCHER BLAETTER – Leipzig, Germany. 14 Okt 1813-7 Mar 1814 – 2r – 1 – gw Mikrofilm [072]
DEUTSCHER BOTE – (Cont by: Ostboehmens Deutscher Bote, mar 1936) – Braunau, nov 1922-38 – 14r – 1 – Inquire at Mikrofilmarchiv for details – gw Misc Inst [943]
DEUTSCHER BOTE – Klausenburg (Cluj), Rumaenien. 5 Jan 1924-31 Dec 1930 – 2r – 1 – gw Mikrofilm [949]
DEUTSCHER BOTE – Libau (Liepaja), Latvia. 1 Apr 1938-22 Jun 1939 – 2r – 1 – gw Mikrofilm [943]
DEUTSCHER BOTE – Mitau (Jelgava), Latvia. 27 Mar 1924-25 – 1r – 1 – gw Mikrofilm [943]
DEUTSCHER BOTE – Riga, Latvia. 1 Apr 1926-18 Sept 1936 – 3r – 1 – gw Mikrofilm [943]
DEUTSCHER BOTE – (Title change: Ostboehmens Deutscher Bote, Mar 1936) – Braunau (Broumov), Czechoslovakia. Nov 1922-Dec 1938 – 14r – 1 – gw Mikrofilm [072]
DEUTSCHER BUEHNEN- ALMANACH *see* ALMANACH FUER FREUNDE DER SCHAUSPIELKUN JAHRGANG (1)-(6), JAHRGANG 7-10
DEUTSCHER BUEHNEN-ALMANACH – Berlin. Jahrg. 18-55; 1854-91. Continues Almanach fuer Freunde der Schauspielkunst. Title varies. Film Mas C 487 – 1 – us H.U. Library [790]
DEUTSCHER BUEHNENVEREIN *see* DAS MAGAZIN
DEUTSCHER BUHNENSPIELPLAN MIT UNTERSTUTZUNG DES DEUTSCHEN BUHNENVEREINS – Leipzig. 1896-1941. Lacking: v.19; 25; 28 and scattered ns. 16, 17, 21, 22, 29. 10 reels – 1 – 188.00 – us L of C Photodup [780]
Deutscher Eisenbahner-Verband *see* PROTOKOLL DER GENERALVERSAMMLUNG
Deutscher Gewerkschaftsbund *see* BETRIEBSRATEPOST
Deutscher Gewerkschaftsbund. (British Zone). Zonen jugendkonferenz *see* BERICHT DER..
DEUTSCHER GRENZBOTE FUER POLNISCH-SCHLESIEN – Teschen (Cieszyn), Poland. 1922-33; 1935 – 2r – 1 – gw Mikrofilm [943]
Deutscher Handels- und Industrieangestellten-Verband *see*
- GESCHAEFTSBERICHT
- RECHENSCHAFTSBERICHT

Deutscher Handwerks- und Gewerbekammertag. Koenigsberg *see* STENOGRAPHISCHER BERICHT UEBER DIE VERHANDLUNGEN..
Deutscher Holzarbeiter-Verband *see*
- PROTOKOLL...

Deutscher Holzarbeiter-Verband. Berlin *see*
- JAHRBUCH
- PROTOKOLL DES KONGRESSES..
- TARIFVERTRAGE DES DEUTSCHEN..
- VERHANDLUNGEN DER KONFERENZ..
- VERHANDLUNGSBERICHT UEBER DIE REICHSKONFERENZ DER BURSTEN- UND PINSELMACHER

DEUTSCHER KAEMPFER – Recife, 2 Ago 1875 – 1,5,6 – bl Biblioteca [072]
EIN DEUTSCHER KOLONIALHELD : DER FALL PETERS IN PSYCHOLOGISCHER BELEUCHTUNG / Giesebrecht, Franz – 2. Aufl. Zürich: C Schmidt, 1897 – us Res Libr [920]
DEUTSCHER KURIER – Berlin, DE. 3 Sep 1916-30 Jun 1919 (imperfect) – 6r – 1 – uk British Libr Newspaper [072]
DEUTSCHER KURIER *see* LDP-KURIER
DEUTSCHER KURIERDIENST – Herausgegeben von Friedrich Stampfer. Prague. sept 1935-juin 1936 – 1 – fr A.C.R.P.P. [073]
DEUTSCHER KURIERDIENST – Prag (Praha), Czechoslovakia. 4 Sept 1935-25 Jun 1936 – 1r – 1 – gw Mikrofilm [072]
DEUTSCHER KURZWELLENSENDER : IBEROAMERIKA-PROGRAMM – Berlin, may-sep 1939 – 1r – 1 – Dist. gw Mikrofilm – gw Misc Inst [790]
DEUTSCHER KURZWELLENSENDER : MITTEL- UND SUEDAMERIKA-PROGRAMM – Berlin, apr 1938-apr 1939 – 1r – 1 – Dist. gw Mikrofilm – gw Misc Inst [790]
DEUTSCHER KURZWELLENSENDER : SUEDAMERIKA-PROGRAMM – Berlin, apr 1938-sep 1939 – 1r – 1 – Dist. gw Mikrofilm – gw Misc Inst [790]
Deutscher Landarbeiter-Verband *see* BERICHT
DEUTSCHER LANDBOTE – Karlsbad (Karlovy Vary), Czechoslovakia. Apr 1929-Mar 1938 – 7r – 1 – gw Mikrofilm [072]
DEUTSCHER LANDRUF – Bruenn (Brno), Czechoslovakia. Oct 1923 (incomplete)-Mar 1938 – 6r – 1 – gw Mikrofilm [072]
DEUTSCHER LANDRUF – Bruenn, oct 1923-mar 1938 (incomplete) – 6r – 1 – Inquire at Mikrofilmarchiv for details – gw Misc Inst [943]
DEUTSCHER LANDRUF – Eger (Cheb), Czechoslovakia. Jul 1925-31 Dec 1932 – 3r – 1 – gw Mikrofilm [072]
Deutscher Lederarbeiter-Verband *see*
- JAHRBUCH
- JAHRESBERICHT UEBER DIE TAETIGKEIT DES ZENTRALVORSTUNDES
- PROTOKOLL...

Deutscher Lehrerverein *see* JAHRBUCH
DEUTSCHER LICHTSPIELTHEATER-BESITZER *see* DER DEUTSCHE LICHTBILDTHEATER-BESITZER
DEUTSCHER LITERATURKALENDER 1883-1902 *see* ALLGEMEINER DEUTSCHER LITERATURKALENDER, 1879-1882
Deutscher Maschinensetzerkongress *see* PROTOKOLL
DEUTSCHER MERKUR – (Missing: 1876. v7) – Muenchen, Bonn. v1-46. 1870-1915 – 438mf – 9 – ne IDC [240]
DEUTSCHER MERKUR : ORGAN FUER DIE KATHOLISCHE REFORMBEWEGUNG – (Formely: Rheinischer Merkur. Lacking: 7(1876)) – Muenchen-Bonn, 1(1870)-46(1915) – 366mf – 9 – Df1,533.00 – ne Slangenburg [073]
DEUTSCHER METALLARBEITER VERBAND VERWALTUNGSTELLE BERLIN – (Jahresberichte) – 1920-1923 – 1r – 1 – DM75.00 – gw Mikro Press [331]
DEUTSCHER METALLARBEITER-VERBAND : DMV JAHR- UND HANDBUCH FUER VERBANDSMITGLIEDER – 1914-1923 – 2r – 1 – DM150.00 – gw Mikro Press [331]
DEUTSCHER METALLARBEITER-VERBAND : JAHRESBERICHTE – Berlin, Stuttgart. 1920-23 – 1r – 1 – gw Mikro Press [072]
Deutscher Metallarbeiterverband *see*
- JAHR- UND HANDBUCH
- DER ORDENTLICHE VERBANDSTAG; PROTOKOLL, ETC
- PROTOKOLL DER KONFERENZ DES REICHSBEIRATS DER PETRIEBSRATE UND KONZERNVERTRETER DER METALLINDUSTRIE. BERLIN. V10. 1931. (SERIAL

Deutscher Metallarbeiterverband. Verwaltungsstelle. Berlin *see* JAHRESBERICHT FUER DAS GESCHAFTSJAHR
Deutscher Nahrungs- und Genussmitterlarbeiter-verband *see*
- JAHRBUCH
- PROTOKOLL UEBER DIE VERHANDLUNGEN DES VERBANDSTAGES

DEUTSCHER OEKONOMIST – Berlin, DE. 1884-89; 1893; 1914 – 1 – gw Mikrofilm [072]
DEUTSCHER REICHSANZEIGER UND KOENIGLICH PREUSSISCHER STAATS-ANZEIGER – (Teil 1 1819-71 102r DM7,650.00. Teil 2 1871-96 145r DM10,875.00. Teil 3 1897-1918 167r DM12,525.00. Teil 4 93r DM6,975.00: Teil 5 1933-45 46r DM3,450.00) – Berlin, 1819-1945 – 553r – 1 – DM41,475.00 – gw Mikro Press [943]
DEUTSCHER REICHS-ANZEIGER UND PREUSSISCHER STAATS-ANZEIGER – Berlin. 1875-1943. Incomplete – 1 – us NY Public [073]
DEUTSCHER REICHS-ANZEIGER UND PREUSSISCHER STAATS-ANZEIGER / Germany – Berlin. 1875-1943 – 1 – us NY Public [073]
DEUTSCHER REICHSANZEIGER UND PREUSSISCHER STAATSANZEIGER *see*
- ALLGEMEINE PREUSSISCHE STAATS-ZEITUNG

Deutscher Sattler-, Tapezierer- und Portefeuiller-Verband *see* JAHRBUCH
DEUTSCHER SCHWERTSEGEN : KRAEFTE DER HEIMAT FUERS REISIGE HEER / Deissmann, Gustav Adolf – Stuttgart: Deutsche Verlags-Anstalt, 1915 – 1mf – us A.T.L.A. [943]
Deutscher Seefischereiverein *see* ABHANDLUNGEN
DEUTSCHER SPRACHSCHATZ GEORDNET NACH BEGRIFFEN ZUR LEICHTEN AUFFINDUNG UND AUSWAHL DES PASSENDEN AUSDRUCKS / Sanders, Daniel – Hamburg, Hoffmann & Campe, 1873-77. 2 v. Film Mas 8709 – 1 – us H.U. Library [430]
Deutscher Tabakarbeiter-Verband *see*
- JAHRESBERICHT
- PROTOKOLL UEBER DIE VERHANDLUNGEN DER GENERALVERSAMMLUNG

Deutscher Textilarbeiter-Verband *see*
- JAHRBUCH
- PROTOKOLL UEBER DIE KONFERENZ...IM VOLKSHAUS ZU LEIPZIG AM SONNTAG, 28 JUNI. BERLIN. 1925. 77P. (SERIAL PUBLICATIONS OF GERMAN TRADE UNIONS IN THE MEMORIAL LIBRARY, UNIVERSITY OF WISCONSIN-MADISON.)
- PROTOKOLL VOM KONGRESS..
- VERHANDLUNGSBERICHT DER KONFERENZ..

Deutscher Transportarbeiter-Kongress. First *see* PROTOKOLL DER VERHANDLUNGEN
Deutscher Transportarbeiter-Verband *see* JAHRBUCH
Deutscher Verkehrsbund *see*
- JAHRBUCH
- JAHRESBERICHT UEBER DAS GESCHAFTSJAHR

DEUTSCHER VOLKSBOTE – Budapest, 1936-43 (dec-issue always missing) – 1r – 1 – Inquire at Mikrofilmarchiv for details – gw Misc Inst [943]
DEUTSCHER VOLKSBOTE – Budapest, Hungary. 1936-43 – 1r – 1 – gw Mikrofilm [072]
DEUTSCHER VOLKSBOTE – Lodz, Poland. 28 Apr-25 Dec 1935 – 1r – 1 – gw Mikrofilm [072]
DEUTSCHER VOLKSFREUND – (Also known as: Volksbote, Freiwaldau/Jaegerndorf) – Freiwaldau (Jesenik), Czechoslovakia. 20 Apr 1929-1938 – 6r – 1 – gw Mikrofilm [072]
DEUTSCHER VOLKSFREUND : DER VOLKSFREUND FUER STADT UND LAND – Breslau, 1881-84 – 4r – 1 – Inquire at Mikrofilmarchiv for details – gw Misc Inst [072]
DEUTSCHER VOLKSFREUND – Vrsac, Yugoslavia. Apr-Dec 1921; 1924; 1928-39 – 5r – 1 – us L of C Photodup [949]
DEUTSCHER VOLKSFUEHRER – Altoona, PA. jan 12 1923-sep 5 1940 (incomplete) – 5r – 1 – Dist. gw Mikrofilm – gw Misc Inst [072]
DEUTSCHER VOLKSRAT – Teschen (Cieszyn), Czechoslovakia. Jan-Nov 1919 – 1r – 1 – gw Mikrofilm [072]
Deutscher Webertag. 1st. Glauchau *see* AUSFUHRLICHER BERICHT UEBER DIE VERHANDLUNGEN..
Deutscher Webertag. 2nd. Berlin *see* STENOGRAPHISCHER BERICHT UEBER..
Deutscher Werkmeister-Verband *see*
- GESCHAEFTSBERICHT
- STENOGRAPHISCHER BERICHT
- STENOGRAPHISCHER BERICHT..

Deutscher Werkmeister-verband *see* STENOGRAPHISCHER BERICHT..
DEUTSCHER WESTERN – Lincoln, NE. 8 Dec 1894-23 Feb 1895 – 1 – us NE Hist [071]
DEUTSCHER WETTERDIENST / Germany. Federal Republic – Monatlicher Witterungsbericht. Bad Kissingen, etc.. v. 1-17. 1953-1969, and Indexes – 1 – us NY Public [943]
Deutscher Wirtschaftsbund fuer das Baugewerbe *see* GESCHAEFTSBERICHT
DEUTSCHER ZUSCHAUER – (Incl "falscher Zuschauer", jul 8-28 1848) – Mannheim, Basel, Dornach, Neustadt a d Haardt, New York. nov 21, dec 12 1846, jan2-dec 24 1847, jan 1-7, 28-oct 15 1848, jun 13 1849, jul 9-dec 31 1851 – 1r – 1 – gw Mikrofilm [943]
DEUTSCHES AGRARBLATT – Prag (Praha), Czechoslovakia. Jul 1920-Dec 1923 – 3r – 1 – gw Mikrofilm [630]
DEUTSCHES ALLGEMEINES SONNTAGSBLATT – 1975-1994 – 2 times per yr – 1 – DM140.00 – sz Infoprint [072]
DEUTSCHES ALLGEMEINES SONNTAGSBLATT – Hamburg, 1975-1994 – 30r – 1 – DM2,250.00 (DM150.00y 1995ff) – gw Mikro Press [943]
DEUTSCHES ALLGEMEINES SONNTAGSBLATT – Hamburg. 1979- – 22125.00y; CPC; 9 – gw Alpha Com [072]
DEUTSCHES ALLGEMEINES SONNTAGSBLATT – Hamburg, West Germany. 1954- – 1 – gw Mikrofilm [072]
DEUTSCHES ALLGEMEINES SONNTAGSBLATT – (Lacking some issues. Title varies) – v1-45. 1948-92 – Inquire – 1 – ATLA S0155 – us A.T.L.A. [073]
Deutsches Archaeologisches Institut *see*
- JAHRBUCH
- JAHRBUCH: ERGAENZUNGSHEFT

Deutsches Archaeologisches Institut. Roemische Abteilung *see* MITTHEILUNGEN
Deutsches Archaeologisches Institut. Rome *see* INDEX DER ANTIKEN KUNST UND ARCHITEKTUR
Deutsches Archaeologisches Institut. Rome. *see*
- KATALOGE DER BIBLIOTHEK DES DEUTSCHEN ARCHAEOLOGISCHEN INSTITUTES

Deutsches Auslandswissenschaftliches Institut *see* JAHRBUCH DER WELTPOLITIK
DEUTSCHES BUEHNEN-JAHRBUCH – Berlin etc. Jahrg. 1-20; 1890-1909. Title varies: 1890-1914. Neuer Theater-Almanach. Supersedes Gettke's Buehnen-Almanach. Film Mas C 469 – 1 – us H.U. Library [790]
DEUTSCHES FAMILIENBLATT – (Filmed also as a suppl of Fulda-Werra-Zeitung and of Schaumburger Wochenblatt) – Berlin, 1880-87, 1890, 1893-94 n13 – 1 – Dist. gw Mikrofilm – gw Misc Inst [072]
DEUTSCHES HANDWERK : KAMPFBLATT DES DEUTSCHEN HANDWERKS, GEWERBES UND EINZELHANDELS – Muenchen, DE. 1932-1933 – 1r – 1 – DM80.00 – gw Mikro Press [380]
DEUTSCHES HANDWERK : KAMPFBLATT DES DEUTSCHEN HANDWERKS, GEWERBES UND EINZELHANDELS – Muenchen, DE. 2 Apr 1932-33 – 1r – 1 – gw Mikrofilm [072]
DEUTSCHES HANDWERKSBLATT – Bonn, 1954-56, 1957-67 (incomplete) – 1 – Inquire at Mikrofilmarchiv for details – gw Misc Inst [072]
DEUTSCHES KOLONIALBLATT – Berlin, apr 1890-1901, 1903-jan 6 1921 – 1 – Dist. gw Mikrofilm – gw Misc Inst [960]
DEUTSCHES KOLONIALBLATT – Berlin. Apr. 1890-Dec. 1896- Jan. 1900-Dec. 1901; Jan. 1903-Jan. 1921. Missing vols. 8-10, 1902 – 1 – 35.00r – us Hoover Inst Photo [072]

DEUTSCHES LANDBLATT – Berlin, 1991 – 4r – 1 – DM300.00 – gw Mikro Press [943]
DEUTSCHES LANDBLATT – Berlin, jan 2-jul 31 1992 – 1 – Dist. gw Mikrofilm – gw Misc Inst [072]
DEUTSCHES MAGAZIN FUER GARTEN- UND BLUMENKUNDE / ed by Neubert, W – Stuttgart. 1848-81; v.1-34. 1870. Index (1848-1869). Continued as Neubert's Deutsches Gartenmagazin. N.S. Stuttgart, etc. v.35-52 1882-99 – 447mf – 8 – ne IDC [631]
DEUTSCHES MAGAZIN ZUR UNTERHALTUNG UND BELEHRUNG – Berlin, 1863 – 1r – 1 – Dist. gw Mikrofilm – gw Misc Inst [072]
DEUTSCHES MONATSBLATT – (Cont as: Union 1990) – Bonn, ab 1979 – 1 – DM75.00y – gw Mikro Press [943]
DEUTSCHES MONATSBLATT : ORGAN DER CDU – (Cont by: Union) – Bonn, 1954- – 1 – Inquire at Mikrofilmarchiv for details – gw Misc Inst [320]
DEUTSCHES MONATSBLATT : ORGAN DER CDU – (Title change: Union) – Bonn, West Germany. 1979- – 1 – gw Mikrofilm [072]
DEUTSCHES MONTAGSBLATT – Berlin, jul 2 1877-88 – 6r – 1 – Dist. gw Mikrofilm – gw Misc Inst [072]
DEUTSCHES MUSEUM / ed by Boie, Heinrich Christian – (Forts: Neues Deutsches Museum, 1789-91. Hildesheim, 1979) – Leipzig, 1776-88 – 212mf – 9 – DM1,550.00 diazo DM1,750.00 silver – gw Olms [430]
DEUTSCHES MUSEUM – Leipzig, 1776-1788 – 3 – us Readex [943]
DEUTSCHES MUSEUM, BILDARCHIV = GERMAN MUSEUM PICTURE ARCHIVE / ed by Deutsches Museum, Muenchen – (Subject catalogue) – 1987-1996 – 480 fiches (1:24) – 9 – silver DM12,400.00 – 3-598-30403-X – gw Saur [700]
Deutsches Museum, Muenchen *see* DEUTSCHES MUSEUM, BILDARCHIV
DEUTSCHES PFARRERBLATT – 1936-91 (complete) – 21r – 1 – ATLA S0755 – us A.T.L.A. [073]
DEUTSCHES RECHT – Berlin, 1931-33 (incomplete), 1934-44 – 1 – Dist. gw Mikrofilm – gw Misc Inst [340]
DEUTSCHES SCHRIFTSTELLER-LEXIKON *see* LEXIKON DEUTSCHSPRACHIGER SCHRIFTSTELLER VON DEN ANFAENGEN BIS ZUR GEGENWART
DEUTSCHES SPORTECHO – Berlin, may 31 1954-90 – 48r – 1 – Dist. gw Mikrofilm – gw Misc Inst [790]
DEUTSCHES TAGEBLATT – Berlin, apr-jun, oct-dec 1881, oct 1883-mar 1884, apr-jun 1888, apr-jun 1889 – 6r – 1 – Dist. gw Mikrofilm – gw Misc Inst [943]
DEUTSCHES TAGEBLATT FUER WESTBOEHMEN – Eger (Cheb), Czechoslovakia. Oct-Dec 1933 – 1 – gw Mikrofilm [072]
DEUTSCHES THEATRUM CHEMICUM, AUF WELCHEM DER BERUEHMTESTEN PHILOSOPHEN UND ALCHYMISTEN SCHRIFFTEN,... – Nuremberg: Felszecker. 2v. 1728 – 13mf – ne IDC [540]
Deutsches UEbersee-Institut Hamburg *see* LAENDERKATALOG AFRIKA DER UEBERSEE-DOKUMENTATION HAMBURG, 1971-1984
DEUTSCHES UND AMERIKANISCHES / Knortz, Karl – Glarus: Vogel, 1894 – 1r – 1 – us U.W. Library [400]
DEUTSCHES VOLKSBLATT – Bremen, Germany. 1892-94 – 1 – gw Mikrofilm [072]
DEUTSCHES VOLKSBLATT – Komotau (Chomutov), Czechoslovakia. 7 Sept 1922-31 Dec 1938 – 35r – 1 – gw Mikrofilm [072]
DEUTSCHES VOLKSBLATT – Novi Sad. Yugoslavia. -d. Jan 1935-Aug 1937. (17 reels) – 1 – uk British Libr Newspaper [949]
DEUTSCHES VOLKSBLATT – Novi Sad, Yugoslavia. Feb 1920-Oct 1944 (incomplete) – 36r – 1 – us L of C Photodup [949]
DEUTSCHES VOLKSBLATT – Stuttgart, Germany. 1849 – 1 – gw Mikrofilm [072]
DEUTSCHES VOLKSBLATT – Vienna, Austria. -d. June 1916-March 1919. Imperfect. 11 reels – 1 – uk British Libr Newspaper [072]
DEUTSCHES VOLKSBLATT – Zagreb. Yugoslavia. -d. 12 May 1940-17 Mar 1941. (Imperfect). (4 reels) – 1 – uk British Libr Newspaper [949]
DEUTSCHES VOLKSBLATT *see* DER UNABHAENGIGE
DEUTSCHES VOLKSBLATT FUER GALIZIEN – Lemberg (Lwow), U.S.S.R. 10 Nov 1911 – 1 – gw Mikrofilm [943]
DEUTSCHES VOLKSECHO – (Cont by: Deutsch-Kanadische Volks-Zeitung) – New York. 20 Feb 1937-16 Sept 1939 – 1r – 1 – gw Mikrofilm [071]
DEUTSCHES VOLKSTUM IN GLAUBEN UND ABERGLAUBEN / Pfister, Friedrich – 1936 – 1 – us I.U. Libraries [390]
DEUTSCHES VOLKSTUM IN MAERCHEN UND SAGE, SCHWANK UND RAETSEL / Peuckert, Will Erich – 1938 – 1 – us I.U. Libraries [390]
DEUTSCHES VOLKSTUM IN SITTE UND BRAUCH / Geiger, Paul – 1936 – 1 – us I.U. Libraries [390]
DEUTSCHES VOLKSTUM IN VOLKSKUNST UND VOLKSSTRACHT / Lehmann, Otto – 1938 – 1 – us I.U. Libraries [390]
DEUTSCHES VOLKSTUM IN VOLKSSCHAUSPIEL UND VOLKSTANZ / Moser, Hans – 1938 – 1 – us I.U. Libraries [390]
DEUTSCHES WOCHENBLATT – Berlin, 1893, 1895 – 1 – Dist. gw Mikrofilm – gw Misc Inst [072]
DEUTSCHES WOCHENBLATT : ORGAN DER DEUTSCHEN VOLKSPARTEI – Mannheim, 1864-1867 – 1r – 1 – DM80.00 – gw Mikro Press [943]
DEUTSCHES WOCHENBLATT : ORGAN DER DEUTSCHEN VOLKSPARTEI – Mannheim, DE. 1865-22 Sep 1867 – 1r – 1 – gw Mikrofilm [072]
DEUTSCHES WOLLEN – Berlin, feb 1 1935-apr 9 1936 – 1r – 1 – Dist. gw Mikrofilm – gw Misc Inst [072]
DEUTSCHE-VOLKS-ZEITUNG – Prague. Mar 22 1936-Aug 27 1939. Incomplete – 1 – us NY Public [072]
DEUTSCHE-VOM STURME VERWEHT – Article in Deutsche Wochenzeitung Christ und Welt. Stuttgart, 21 Jun 1956. 8p – 1 – 5.00 – us Baptist [240]
DEUTSCH-GABLER ZEITUNG – Deutsch Gabel (Jablonne Podjestedi), Czechoslovakia. 20 Aug-31 Dez 1938 – 1r – 1 – gw Mikrofilm [072]
DEUTSCH-INDISCHE GEISTESBEZIEHUNGEN / Alsdorf, Ludwig – (Includes bibliographical references) – Heidelberg, Berlin, Magdeburg: K Vowinckel, 1942 – 1 – us U.W. Library [430]
DEUTSCH-KANADISCHE VOLKS-ZEITUNG *see* DEUTSCHES VOLKSECHO
DEUTSCH-KANADISCHE VOLKSZEITUNG – Toronto. 1937 – 1 – 45.00 – cn McLaren [072]
DEUTSCHLAND, DEUTSCHLAND UEBER ALLES! : EIN LEBENSBILD DES DICHTERS HOFFMANN VON FALLERSLEBEN / Gerstenberg, Heinrich – Muenchen: C H Beck, 1916 – 1r – 1 – us U.W. Library [920]
DEUTSCHLAND FLORA / Sturm, J W – 7 – uk Microform Academic [580]
DEUTSCHLAND IM JAHRE 2000 / Erman, G – Kiel: Lipsius und Tischer, 1891 – 1r – 1 – us U.W. Library [943]
DEUTSCHLAND IM KAMPF – (Official Nazi War Journal). (German language). 1939-44 – 1 – us UMI [324]
DEUTSCHLAND MUSS LEBEN! / Lersch, Heinrich – Jena: E Diederichs, 1943, c1935 – 1r – 1 – us U.W. Library [810]
DEUTSCHLAND (NUEVA ALEMANIA) *see* FREIES DEUTSCHLAND
DEUTSCHLAND UND DIE NATIONALSOZIALISTEN IN DEN VEREINIGTEN STAATEN VON AMERIKA / Graessner, Gernot Heinrich Willi – 1933-1939 – 1 – DM40.00 – gw Mikro Press [977]
DEUTSCHLAND UND POLEN, 1772-1945 / ed by Fechner, Helmuth – (Includes bibliographical references) – Wuerzburg: Holzner, Verlag, 1964 – 1r – 1 – us U.W. Library [327]
DEUTSCHLAND UND RUSSLAND / Haller, Johannes – Tuebingen: Kloeres, 1915. 32p – 1 – us U.W. Library [943]
DEUTSCHLAND-BERICHT DER SOPADE. PRAG – Jahrg. 1-3; Aug Sept. 1934-Dec. 1936 (incomplete). Issued in two parts: Teil A, Nachrichten und Berichte; Teil B, Uebersichten. Ceased with issue for Dec. 1936. Continued by Deutschland-Berichte der Sozialdemokratischen Partei Deutschlands. Film Mas C 683. Includes Deutschland-Bericht der Sozialdemokratischen Partei Deutschlands) – 1 – us H.U. Library [073]
DEUTSCHLANDBERICHTE DER SOPADE – (Title change: Deutschland-Berichte der Sozialdemokratischen Partei Deutschlands (SoPaDe)) – Prag (Praha), Paris. Apr-May 1934-Apr 1940 – 8r – 1 – gw Mikrofilm [072]
DEUTSCHLAND-BRIEF – Berchtesgaden, 1951-54 (incomplete) – 1 – Dist. gw Mikrofilm – gw Misc Inst [943]
DEUTSCHLANDS ERNEUERUNG – Muenchen, DE. 1920-22 – 1r – 1 – gw Mikrofilm [072]
DEUTSCHLANDS FLORA / Roehling, J C – ed. 2. 3 v. Frankfurt am Main. 1812-13. B-5242 2 – 8 – ne IDC [580]
DEUTSCHLANDS FLORA. NACH EINEM VERAENDERTEN UND ERWEITERTEN PLANE BEARBEITET VON F. C. MERTENS UND W. D. J. KOCH / Roehling, J C – 5v. Frankfurt am Main. 1823-39. B-5581 2 – 8 – ne IDC [580]
DEUTSCHLANDS FLORA ODER BOTANISCHES TASCHENBUCH FUER 1800 (1804) / Hoffmann, G F – Erlangen. 1800-04. B-5554 2 – 8 – ne IDC [580]
DEUTSCHLANDS FLORA ODER BOTANISCHES TASCHENBUCH FUER DAS JAHR 1791 UND FUER DAS JAHR 1795 / Hoffmann, G F – Erlangen. 1791, 1796. B-1206 2 – 8 – ne IDC [580]
DEUTSCHLANDS GESCHICHTSQUELLEN IM MITTELALTER / Wattenbach, W – Berlin, 1858 – Dfl32.00 – ne Slangenburg [240]
DEUTSCHLANDS INSEKTENFAUNE ODER ENTOMOLOGISCHES TASCHENBUCH FUER DAS JAHR 1795 / Panzer, G W F – Nuernberg, 1795, 370p, 14 pls.Z-1528/2 – 8 – ne IDC [590]
DEUTSCHLANDS KRYPTOGAMISCHE GEWAECHSE / Schkuhr, C – 3Hefte. pt. 2. Leipzig. 1810-47. B-5714 2 – 8 – ne IDC [580]
DEUTSCHLANDS MOOSE / Mueller, K A F W – Halle, 1853. 512 pp. B-5317 2 – 8 – ne IDC [580]
DEUTSCHLANDS POLITISCHE PARTEIEN UND DAS MINISTERIUM BISMARK / Parisius, L – 1878 – 1 – uk Microform Academic [943]
DEUTSCHLANDS SCHMETTERLINGE, MIT BERUECKSICHTIGUNG SAEMMTLICHER EUROPAEISCHER ARTEN / Kayser, J C – Leipzig, 1852-59. viii,608p. 153 pls. Z-1385/2 – 8 – ne IDC [943]
DEUTSCHLANDS STIMME – Berlin, 1948 – 1r – 1 – Dist. gw Mikrofilm – gw Misc Inst [072]
DEUTSCHLANDS TRAUM, KAMPF UND SIEG : GEHARNISCHTE SONETTE NEBST EINEM ANHANG VATERLAENDISCHER GESAENGE / Minckwitz, Johannes – Leipzig: M G Priber, 1870 – 1 – us U.W. Library [780]
DEUTSCHLANDSENDER *see* NACHRICHTENDIENST DES DEUTSCHLANDSENDERS
DIE DEUTSCH-LETTISCHEN BEZIEHUNGEN... – Leipzig, 1916 – 1mf – 1 – ILM-1156/1 – ne IDC [327]
DIE DEUTSCH-LETTISCHEN BEZIEHUNGEN... – Leipzig, 1916 – 1mf – 9 – ne IDC [947]
DEUTSCH-MANDSCHURISCHE NACHRICHTEN – Harbin. 1929-30 – 1 reel – 1 – ne IDC [072]
DEUTSCH-MANDSCHURISCHE NACHRICHTEN – Harbin (Pingkiang), China. Einzige Deutsche Tageszeitung in China und Japan. 8 Dec 1919-9 Jul 1930 – 1r – 1 – gw Mikrofilm [072]
DEUTSCH-OESTERREICHISCHE THEATERZEITUNG – Berlin, 1891-93 – 1r – 1 – Dist. gw Mikrofilm – gw Misc Inst [790]
DEUTSCH-OSTAFRIKA : GEOGRAPHIE UND GESCHICHTE DER COLONIE / Forster, Brix – Leipzig: F A Brockhaus, 1890 – 1 – us Res Libr [960]
DEUTSCH-OSTAFRIKA : GESCHICHTE DER GESELLSCHAFT FUER DEUTSCHE KOLONISATION UND DER DEUTSCH-OSTAFRIKANISCHEN GESELLSCHAFT NACH DEN AMTLICHEN QUELLEN / Wagner, J – Berlin: Verlag der Engelhardt'schen Landkartenhandlung, 1886 – 1 – us Res Libr [960]
DEUTSCH-OSTAFRIKA UNVERLOREN! : ERZAEHLUNG AUS DEN DEUTSCHEN KOLONIALKAEMPFEN IM WELTKRIEG / Viera, Josef – 4. Aufl. Stuttgart: Loewes, 1936 – 1 – us U.W. Library [960]
DER DEUTSCH-POLNISCHE STAATSVERTRAG... / Haase, B – Berlin, 1925 – 1mf – 1 – ILM-3693/1 – ne IDC [327]
DEUTSCH-RUSSISCHE HANDELSVERTRAEGE DES MITTELALTERS / Goetz, L K – Hamburg, 1916 – 5mf – 1 – ILM-1782/1 – ne IDC [327]
DEUTSCH-RUSSISCHES VERTRAGSWERK... 1925 / Glanz, R – Berlin, 1926 – 3mf – 1 – ILM-1754/1 – ne IDC [327]
DIE DEUTSCHSPRACHIGEN FREIMAURER-ZEITSCHRIFTEN DES 18. UND 19. JAHRHUNDERTS / Haensel-Hohenhausen, Markus – (1. Lieferung: S. 1-1251. DM 400,00: ISBN 3-89349-279-8; 2. Lieferung: S. 1252-2067. DM 300,00: ISBN 3-89349-280-1; 3. Lieferung: S. 2068-3032. DM 300,00: ISBN 3-89349-281-X) – Egelsbach, Koeln, New York, 1993 – 9 – DM1,000.00 set – 3-89349-282-8 – gw Hänsel [943]
DEUTSCH-SUDWEST AFRIKA. AMTSBLATT = SOUTH WEST AFRICA. OFFICIAL GAZETTE – (Only available as diazo) – Windhoek, Namibia, 1910-1968 – 1506mf – 9 – sa SA Libr [324]
DEUTSCH-SUDWESTAFRIKA : DREI JAHRE IM LANDE NENDRIK WITBOOIS: SCHILDERUNGEN VON LAND UND LEUTEN / Bulow, Franz Josef von – 2. Aufl. Berlin: E S Mittler, 1897 – 1 – us Res Libr [910]
DEUTSCH-SUDWESTAFRIKA SEIT DER BESITZERGREIFUNG, DIE ZUGE UND KRIEGE GEGEN DIE EINGEBORENEN / Bulow, Heinrich von – Berlin: W Susserott, 1904 – 1 – us Res Libr [960]
DEUTSCH-SUEDWESTAFRIKANISCHE ZEITUNG – Swakopmund, South West Africa. 1898-1914 – 1 – sa State Libr [072]
DAS DEUTSCHTUM IM AUSLAND: VIERTELJAHRSHEFTE DES VEREINS FUER DAS DEUTSCHTUM IM AUSLAND (ALLG. DEUTSCHER SCHULVEREIN.) – Berlin. Heft 1-41 42; 1909-19. Film Mas C 619 – 1 – us H.U. Library [073]
DEUTSCH-UNGARISCHER BOTE = GERMAN-AMERICAN HERALD – Cincinnati: Deutsch-Ungarischer Bote Co, jan-may 23, 1918 – 1r – us Res Libr [071]
DEUTSCHUNTERRICHT FUER AUSLAENDER – (cont: Zielsprache Deutsch) – Muenchen. v1-18. 1951-68 – 5,9 – Dfl450.00; Dfl25.00v – ne Swets [430]
DEUTSCHUNTERRICHT FUER AUSLAENDER *see* ZIELSPRACHE DEUTSCH
DEUTUNGEN UND BEKENNTNISSE : AUSGEWAEHLTE TEXTE ZUR DEUTSCHEN LITERATUR / ed by Schubert & Hoefer, Karl-Heinz – (Includes bibliographical references and index) – Leipzig: Verlag Enzyklopaedie, c1986 – 1r – 1 – us U.W. Library [430]
DEUX ABRIS DECORES DE LA SERRA NOVA, REGION DE SAO RAIMUNDO NONATO, ETAT DU PIAUI, BRESIL / Guidon, N et al – 9 – F90.00 – fr Ethnologie [930]
DEUX ANS DE VACANCES / Verne, Jules – Paris: J. Hetzel, 1888. 2v. 9 fiches. (Literature Collection) – 9 – 22.00 – fr Bibl Nationale [830]
DEUX CAMPAGNES AU SOUDAN FRANCAIS, 1886-1888 / Gallieni, Joseph-Simon – Paris: Hatchette, 1891 – 1 – us Res Libr [960]
LES DEUX COCHERS DE QUEBEC: SOUVENIRS HISTORIQUES / Evanturel, Francois – Montreal-Oeil, cocher de nuit s.l.: s.n., 1886 (Quebec: C. Darveau). 02930. (Pre-1900 Canadiana) – 9 – cn C.I.H.M. [971]
DEUX COPAINS: REPLIQUE A MM. FRECHETTE ET SAUVALLE / Chapman, William – Quebec: L. Brousseau, 1894. 00572. (Pre-1900 Canadiana) – 9 – cn C.I.H.M. [971]
DES DEUX COTES DE LA BARRICADE – Paris [1848?] – us Res Libr [072]
DEUX COTES DU DETROIT *see* COMMUNIQUE DE LA CHAMBRE DE COMMERCE FRANCAISE DE LONDRES
DEUX DETROITS; QUELQUES REFLEXIONS SUR LA PHASE ACTUELLE DE LA QUESTION D'ORIENT – Stockholm, 1879 – 2mf – 1 – ILM-2877/1 – ne IDC [327]
DEUX DIALOGUES DU NOUVEAU LANGAGE FRANCOIS / Estienne, Henri – 1885 – 9 – fr I.C.S. [440]
DEUX DISCOURS / Alvarez del Vayo, Julio – Paris, 1938. Fiche W 714. (Blodgett Collection of Spanish Civil War Pamphlets) – 9 – us H.U. College Libr [946]
DEUX ET DEUX FONT QUATRE / Coler, Bird S – Montreal: imprime au Devoir, [1919 ?]. SEM105P1555 – 3mf – 9 – Can$6.75 – cn Bibl Nat [971]

LES DEUX GRAMMAIRES FRANSAIZES / Milleran, R – 1694 – 9 – fr I.C.S. [440]
LES DEUX JOURNEES / Bouilly, Jean Nicolas & Cherubini – French Theatre Series. Paris. Andre, an VIII. 1800 – 9 – fr Hachette [820]
DEUX LETTRES A UN VIEIL AMI SUR LES DOMESTIQUES / Eichthal, Gustave d' – Paris, Pillet, s. d., 14 p. Doctrine de Saint-Simon. Des sentiments de famille et d'amitie. Paris, Pillet, s. d., 19 p. A un catholique, sur la vie et le caractere de Saint-Simon. Paris, Everat, 1830, 13 p. plus 12 p. manuscrites. Les Saint-Simoniens, 1825-1834. 6856 – 9 – fr Hachette [240]
DEUX LIVRES DE LA HAYNE DE SATHAN ET MALINS ESPRITS CONTRE L'HOMME ET DE L'HOMME CONTRE EUX / Crespet, Pierre – Paris. 1590 – 9 – fr Hachette [360]
DEUX MODES SATIRIQUES OU LE CHOIX FAIT PAR BUTLER DANS HUDIBRAS ET SWIFT DANS A TALE OF A TUB (LE CONTE DU TONNEAU) / Aniq Filali, Rabea – 2mf – 9 – 10556 – fr Atelier National [420]
LES DEUX MOUSQUETAIRES / Berton, H – Paris: Dufaut et Dubois, 1824 – 1 – us Sibley [780]
DEUX NOCTURNES POUR HARPE & HAUTBOIS, OEUV. 51, NO. 1 / Bocha, R – (Score and parts) – Paris: Dufaut et Dubois, [182-] – 1 – us Sibley [780]
LES DEUX PAPINEAU / David, Laurent Olivier – Montreal: E. Senecal, 1896. 02513. (Pre-1900 Canadiana) – 9 – cn C.I.H.M. [971]
DEUX PROCEDES – n.p. 193? Fiche W830. (Blodgett Collection of Spanish Civil War Pamphlets) – 9 – us H.U. College Libr [946]
DEUX RECITS DE CHASSE : BANMANA NDORONKELEN ET BANI-NYENEMA / Sidibe, Fode Moussa Balla – 1984 – us Res Libr [960]
DEUX SERMONS : LA GRACE DE DIEU, LE PARDON DES OFFENSES / Rabaut, Paul – Paris: Grassart, 1886 – 1mf – us A.T.L.A. [240]
DEUX SIECLES DE L'HISTOIRE DE FRANCE ET CENTENAIRE DU MUSEE DE VERSAILLES / Reunion des musees nationaux. Paris – 1937. 25 illus. 2 fiches – 9 – fr Réunion [700]
DEUX SONATES POUR LE PIANOFORTE AVEC D'UN VIOLON OU FLUTE ET VIOLONCELLE / Gyrowetz, Adalbert – (Folio, parts) – Augsbourg: Gombert, 180- – 1 – us Sibley [780]
LES DEUX TESTAMENTS / Thibault, Anna-Marie Duval – Fall River, Massachusetts, 1888. SEM105P18 – 2mf – 9 – Can$4.50 – cn Bibl Nat [830]
LES DEUX THEOLOGIES NOUVELLES DANS LE SEIN DU PORTESTANTISME FRANCAIS : ETUDE HISTORICO-DOGMATIQUE / Astie, J F – Paris: Meyrueis, 1862 – 1mf – us A.T.L.A. [240]
DEUX TRAITEZ NOUVEAUX TRES UTILES POUR CE TEMPS / Daneau, Lambert – Le premier touchant les sorciers. Gien. 1579 – 9 – fr Hachette [360]
DEUX VOYAGES SUR LE SAINT MAURICE / Caron, Napoleon – Trois Rivieres, Quebec: P. V. Ayotte, 1889. 00467. (Pre-1900 Canadiana) – 9 – cn C.I.H.M. [910]
LA DEUXIEME ANNEE DE GEOGRAPHIE, PREMIER QUARTIER, NOTIONS PRELIMINAIRES, OU, LA TERRE A VOL D'OISEAU / Baillairge, Frederic Alexandre – Joliette, Imp. generale, 1898. 00075. (Pre-1900 Canadiana) – 9 – cn C.I.H.M. [910]
DEUXIEME CENTENAIRE DE LA FONDATION DE L'INSTITUT DES FRERES DES ECOLES CHRETIENNES: SERMON PRONONCE DANS L'EGLISE ST JEAN BAPTISTE DE QUEBEC LE 20 OCTOBRE 1880 / Bruchesi, Louis Joseph Paul Napoleon – Quebec: C. Darveau, 1880. 03735. (Pre-1900 Canadiana) – 9 – cn C.I.H.M. [240]
DEUXIEME ESQUISSE DU PLAN QUINQUENNAL DE DEVELOPPEMENT 1971-1975 / Ivory Coast. Ministere du Plan – (Second Draft of the Five-Year Development Plan 1971-1975). Jun 1970. BD-1106 1 – 9 – ne IDC [338]
DEUXIEME LETTRE AUX ELECTEURS DU COMTE DE LOTBINIERE / Amyot, Guillaume – 187?. 00798. (Pre-1900 Canadiana) – 9 – cn C.I.H.M. [971]
DEUXIEME LETTRE AUX TRAVAILLEURS – (Signe Ch. Noiret, ouvrier de Rouen). Rouen. 1841. (La Condition Ouvriere. Part Two.) – 9 – 2.50 – fr Bibl Nationale [360]
DEUXIEME PLAN DE DEVELOPPEMENT ECONOMIQUE ET SOCIAL / Mauritania. Ministere de la Planification et du Developpement Rural – D-1123 1. 1970-1973 – 9 – ne IDC [338]
DEUXIEME PLAN DE DEVELOPPEMENT ECONOMIQUE ET SOCIAL 1970-1973 / Mauritania. Direction du Plan – (Second Economic and Social Development 1970-1973 Plan). Nouakchott. 1971. BD-1692 1 – 9 – ne IDC [338]
DEUXIEME PLAN DE DEVELOPPEMENT ECONOMIQUE ET SOCIAL, 1971-1975 / Gabon. Republique Gabonaise – (Second economic and social development plan, 1971-1975). Libreville. 1972 – 9 – ne IDC [338]
DEUXIEME PLAN DE MODERNISATION ET D'EQUIPEMENT (1954-1957) / France – (Second modernization and equipment plan (1954-1957). Annex to Projet de Loi portant approbation du deuxieme plan de modernisation et d'equipement. Assemblee Nationale. No. 8555. Session de 1954. Paris. 1954 – 9 – ne IDC [338]
DEUXIEME PLAN DE MODERNISATION ET D'EQUIPEMENT 1954-1957 (LOI NO. 56-342 DU 27 MAR 1956) / France – Paris. 1956 – 9 – ne IDC [338]
DEUXIEME PLAN QUADRIENNAL DE DEVELOPPEMENT ECONOMIQUE ET SOCIAL, 1965-1969 / Senegal – 3v. Paris. 1965. BD-184 1 – 9 – ne IDC [338]
DEUXIEME PLAN QUINQUENNAL, 1962-1966 / Vietnam. South. Direction Generale du Plan – Saigon. 1962 – 9 – ne IDC [338]
DEUXIEME PLAN QUINQUENNAL DE DEVELOPPEMENT ECONOMIQUE ET SOCIALD-1009/1. 2 V. JUL. 1966-JUNE. 1971 / Cameroon. Ministere des Affaires Economiques et du Plan – 9 – ne IDC [338]
DEUXIEME PLAN QUINQUENNAL PREAH NORODNOM SURAMARIT 1968-1972 / Cambodia. Ministere du Plan – BD-1008 – 9 – ne IDC [338]
DEUXIEME PROGRAMME D'EXPANSION ECONOMIQUE, 1966-1970 LES SECTEURS DE PRODUCTION / Belgium. Bureau de Programmation Economique – Bruxelles. 1968. BD-389 1 – 9 – ne IDC [338]
DEUXIEME PROGRAMME D'EXPANSION ECONOMIQUE PROGRAMME GENERAL DE CADRE 1966-1970 / Belgium. Ministere des Affaires Economiques – (Senat. Session 1967-68). Bruxelles. 1967 – 9 – ne IDC [338]
DEUXIEME QUINTUOR POUR LA FLUTE, 2 ALTO ET VIOLONCELLE, OP. 60 / Brandl, J – (Parts) – Bonn: Simrock, ca 1812 – 1 – us Sibley [780]
DEUXIEME RAPPORT DE LA COMMISSION CHARGEE DE REVISER ET DE MODIFIER LE CODE DE PROCEDURE CIVILE DU BAS-CANADA / Quebec Province – Quebec: imprime par Leger Brousseau, 1894. SEM105P1514 – 3mf – 9 – Can$6.75 – cn Bibl Nat [340]
DEUXIEME RAPPORT SUR L'EXECUTION DU PLAN QUINQUENNAL, 1964-1968 / Malagasy Republic. Commissariat General au Plan – Tananarive. 1966 – 9 – ne IDC [338]
LA DEUXIEME REPUBLIQUE ESPAGNOLE 1931-1936 : ESSAI D'INTERPRETATION / Becarud, J – F50.00 – fr Ethnologie [946]
DEV / University of Kentucky. Cooperative Extension Service – No.1-3. 1973-75 – 1mf – 9 – us Spaulding [630]
DeValinger, Leon *see* RECONSTRUCTED 1790 CENSUS OF DELAWARE
AL DEVAR AVODAH U-MELAKHAH VE-YISHUV HA-AREZ / Pines, Y M – (Havazzelet, Jerusalem, 5635). 1875. BJ-27-203 1 – 9 – ne IDC [270]
AL DEVAR HEVRAT MEYASSEDEI HA-YISHUV / Krieger, Y – Havazzelet. Jerusalem. 20 Elul 5641. 1881. BJ-27-213 1 – 9 – ne IDC [900]
AL DEVAR YISHUV EREZ-YISRA'EL – (Ha-Levanon, 5636). 1876. BJ-27-227 1 – 9 – ne IDC [956]
DEVARENU = OUR WORDS – (In Hebrew. Monthly) – Vienna, AU. v1 no1 Mar 1930-v2 no1-2 Oct/Nov 1931 – 1r – 1 – $30.00 – cn Can Microfilming [072]
Devas, Charles Stanton *see* L'EGLISE ET LE PROGRES DU MONDE
Devas, Raymund *see* THE DOMINICAN REVIVAL IN THE NINETEENTH CENTURY
DEVEKUSU – Trabzon. Sahib ve Sermuharriri: Cemal Riza. No. 5 (17 Eyluel 1341 [1925]) – 9 – $20.00 – us MEDOC [956]
Devel', T M *see* OBOZRENIE KOLLEKTSII SOBRANIIA FOTOARKHIVA INSTITUTA ISTORII MATERIAL'NOI KUL'TURY IM. N. IA. MARRA AN SSSR
Develle, P *see* LA CONCESSON EN DROIT INTERNATIONAL
DEVELOPING A MERCHANT MARINE OFFICER CORPS FOR INDONESIA : PICTORIAL PRESENTATION / U.S. AID Mission to Indonesia – SE 11,626 1 – 9 – ne IDC [370]
DEVELOPING A MERCHANT MARINE OFFICER CORPS FOR INDONESIA : A PICTORIAL REPRESENTATION / Indonesia. Akademi Ilmu Pelajaran – SE-10,308 1. 1963? – 9 – ne IDC [950]
DEVELOPING A MINISTRY OF LAY EVANGELISM AT THE FIRST BAPTIST CHURCH OF ROANOKE, VIRGINIA / Peverall, Albert Arthur – 1982 – 1 – 7.36 – us Baptist [240]
DEVELOPING A PROGRAM OF FAMILY MINISTRY BY THE DEACONS OF FIRST BAPTIST CHURCH, HODGENVILLE, KENTUCKY / McDonald, Isaac Burkhalter – 1981 – 1 – 5.60 – us Baptist [240]
DEVELOPING PUBLIC LIBRARY SYSTEMS AND SERVICES : A GUIDE TO THE ORGANIZATION OF NATIONAL AND REGIONAL PUBLIC LIBRARY SYSTEMS AS A PART OF OVERALL NATIONAL INFORMATION SERVICE PLANNING / Campbell, H C – 1983 – 186p – 9 – 92-3-101995-3 – fr UNESCO [020]
DEVELOPING THE SPACE FRONTIER – (v52 1983, Advances) – 1983 – 9 – $45.00 – us Univelt [380]
DEVELOPMENT : THOUGHTS ON BISHOP GORE'S "ROMAN CATHOLIC CLAIMS" / Rickaby, Joseph – London: Catholic Truth Society, 1905 – 1mf – 9 – 0-8370-7096-1 – 1986-1096 – us A.T.L.A. [240]
THE DEVELOPMENT... / Bulter, G & Maccoby, S – London, 1928 – 7mf – 1 – ILM-142/1 – ne IDC [327]
DEVELOPMENT AND CHANGE / Institute of Social Studies. The Hague – 1969. BH-1806 1 – 9 – ne IDC [300]
DEVELOPMENT AND CHANGES, PRIMARY CURRICULUM 1972 / Papua New Guinea. Department of Education – Konedobu, 1972 – 1mf – 9 – DE-240/1 – ne IDC [370]
DEVELOPMENT AND COMPARATIVE IMMUNOLOGY – v.1- 1977- – 5,6,9 – us UMI [073]
DEVELOPMENT AND EDUCATION IN THE MWANZA DISTRICT (TANZANIA) / Heynen, J D – (Thesis). A-677 2. 1968 – 8 – ne IDC [370]
DEVELOPMENT AND EVALUATION OF A LEISURE EDUCATION MODULE FOR USE IN A COLLEGE RESOURCE CENTER / Fierle, Karen M – 1982 – 2mf – 9 – $8.00 – us Microform Publ [790]
DEVELOPMENT AND EVALUATION OF AN INTERPRETIVE NINETEENTH CENTURY AMERICAN CHILDREN'S GAMES PROGRAM : KNOWLEDGE AND SATISFACTION ATTAINED THROUGH PROGRAM PARTICIPATION / Bakke, P Q – 1991 – 3mf – 9 – $12.00 – us Microform Publ [790]
DEVELOPMENT AND EVOLUTION : INCLUDING PSYCHOPHYSICAL EVOLUTION, EVOLUTION BY ORTHOPLASY, AND THE THEORY OF GENETIC MODES / Baldwin, James Mark – New York: Macmillan Co, 1902 – 1 – us Res Libr [575]
DEVELOPMENT AND FOREST RESOURCES IN THE ASIA AND FAR EAST REGION : TRENDS AND PERSPECTIVES 1961-1991 – 1979 – 99p – it F.A.O. [634]
THE DEVELOPMENT AND IMPLEMENTATION OF A COMPUTER-ASSISTED INSTRUCTION SERIES TO BE UTILIZED AS AN AID TO CURRICULUM METHODOLOGY IN PHYSICAL EDUCATION / Lease, Barbara J – 1981 – 2mf – 9 – $8.00 – us Microform Publ [790]
DEVELOPMENT AND LEGAL SERVICES IN AFRICA – 1983 – sz I.C.J. [340]
DEVELOPMENT AND THE RULE OF LAW, PREVENTION VERSUS CURE AS A HUMAN RIGHTS STRATEGY – 1981 – sz I.C.J. [340]
DEVELOPMENT AND VALIDATION OF A MAXIMAL TESTING PROTOCOL FOR THE NORDICTRACK CROSS-COUNTRY SKI SIMULATOR / Haug, Rhea C – University of Wisconsin-La Crosse, 1995 – 1mf – 9 – PH 1495 – us Microform Publ [612]
DEVELOPMENT AND VALIDATION OF A QUESTIONNAIRE FOR ASSESSING HABITUAL PHYSICAL ACTIVITY OF SIXTH-GRADE STUDENTS / Koehler, Karen M – 1988 – 131p 2mf – 9 – $8.00 – us Microform Publ [370]
DEVELOPMENT AND VALIDATION OF THE WELLNESS KNOWLEDGE, ATTITUDE, AND BEHAVIOR INSTRUMENT / Dinger, Mary K & Watts, Parris – 1993 – 2mf – $8.00 – us Microform Publ [613]
DEVELOPMENT BUDGET, 1965/1966-1968/1969 / Libya. Economic Social Development (incl. Planning, Literacy) – 4v. BNE-719 1 – 9 – ne IDC [338]
DEVELOPMENT BUDGETS / Sudan – 13 v. in 3. 1956 57-1970 71. (lacking 1969 71). BNE-7687 1 – 9 – ne IDC [332]
DEVELOPMENT BUDGETS ESTIMATES, 1946/1951 AND 1951/1956 PROGRAMMES / Sudan. Finance Department – 6v. in 1. BNE-7634 1 – 9 – ne IDC [336]
DEVELOPMENT CO-OPERATION SIERRA LEONE : 1989 UNDP REPORT / Sierra Leone. Office of the Resident Representative – [Freetown], 1991 – 3mf – 9 – ne IDC [338]
DEVELOPMENT FINANCE, 1955-56 (INTERIM DEVELOPMENT PLAN) / Nigeria – Lagos. 1955. BD-720 1 – 9 – ne IDC [332]
DEVELOPMENT FORUM / UN – (Nos 1-150 1973-90 mf: F.55) – v1-18. 1973-1990 – E.57 – 9 – us U.N. Pubs [340]
DEVELOPMENT, HUMAN RIGHTS AND THE RULE OF LAW – 1981 – sz I.C.J. [320]
THE DEVELOPMENT HYPOTHESIS, IS IT SUFFICIENT? / McCosh, James – New York: Robert Carter, 1876. 1 fiche – 9 – us A.T.L.A. [240]
DEVELOPMENT IN INDONESIA / Dipokusumo, S – SE-11,532 1 – 9 – ne IDC [338]
DEVELOPMENT IN THE FEDERATION OF SOUTH ARABIA (1963-1966) / South Arabia. Ministry of Finance – Al-Ittihad. 1965 – 9 – ne IDC [336]
DEVELOPMENT ISSUES, NATIONAL OBJECTIVES AND EDUCATIONAL POLICIES 1982-1986 / Thailand. Ministry of Education. Planning Division – Bangkok, [1981] – 1mf – 9 – DE-588/1 – ne IDC [370]
DEVELOPMENT OF A CHILD INJURY DATA BASE FOR USE IN BIOMECHANICS RESEARCH / Kelleher-Walsh, Barbara J & DeBacy, Diane L – 1992 – 1mf – 9 – $4.00 – us Microform Publ [612]
DEVELOPMENT OF A COLLEGIATE LICENSING ADMINISTRATIVE PARADIGM / Irwin, R L – 1990 – 3mf – 9 – $12.00 – us Microform Publ [370]
THE DEVELOPMENT OF A COMPREHENSIVE PLAN FOR MINISTRY FOR FIRST BAPTIST CHURCH, NEVADA, MISSOURI / Cox, William Charles – 1981 – 1 – 6.00 – us Baptist [240]
THE DEVELOPMENT OF A CRITERION-REFERENCED HEALTH KNOWLEDGE INSTRUMENT FOR GRADES FOUR, FIVE, AND SIX / Massey, MS – 1991 – 3mf – 9 – $12.00 – us Microform Publ [613]
THE DEVELOPMENT OF A MANUAL FOR RECREATION LEADERS IN SOUTHERN BAPTIST ASSOCIATIONS / Smith, Frank Hart – 1982 – 1 – 6.64 – us Baptist [240]
THE DEVELOPMENT OF A MINISTRY AT THE IMMANUEL BAPTIST CHURCH, TORONTO, CANADA, TO INTEGRATE MULTICULTURAL PEOPLES, WITH SPECIAL REFERENCE TO WEST INDIAN IMMIGRANTS / Baxter, Samuel John – 1982 – 1 – 5.60 – us Baptist [240]
DEVELOPMENT OF A PREDICTIVE EQUATION FOR MAXIMAL OXYGEN CONSUMPTION ON THE STEPTREADMILL / Carroll, K K – 1991 – 1mf – 9 – $4.00 – us Microform Publ [612]
THE DEVELOPMENT OF A PROGRAM OF STUDENT FINANCIAL ASSISTANCE FOR EAST COAST BIBLE COLLEGE / Bell, Kenneth Ray – 1982 – 1 – 5.44 – us Baptist [240]
THE DEVELOPMENT OF A PROGRAM OF SUPPLEMENTAL PASTORAL CARE FOR WHITSITT CHAPEL BAPTIST CHURCH / Nail, Marvin Powell – 1982 – 1 – 5.00 – us Baptist [240]
THE DEVELOPMENT OF A VIDEO-BASED MOTION ANALYSIS SYSTEM / Bothner, Krisanne E & Widule, Carole J – 1992 – 1mf – 9 – $4.00 – us Microform Publ [612]

DEVELOPMENT OF ADMINISTRATIVE AND MANAGEMENT PERSONNEL FOR INDONESIA'S PUBLIC SERVICE: APPROACHES AND PROBLEMS / Jones, Garth N – SE-11,288 1. 1961 – 9 – ne IDC [350]

THE DEVELOPMENT OF AMERICAN COMMERCE / Frederick, John Hutchinson – New York, London: D. Appleton and Company, c1932. xx,390p. Illus. Maps, tables, diagrams. With: Lehrbuch der Mechanischen Naturlehre by E.G. Fisher. 1 reel. 1292 – 1 – us U.W. Library [380]

THE DEVELOPMENT OF AMERICAN HYMNODY, 1620-1900 / Burnett, Madeline L – 1946 – 1 – 5.04 – us Baptist [240]

DEVELOPMENT OF AN ANTHROPOMETRIC REGRESSION EQUATION TO PREDICT BODY DENSITY IN AFRICAN AMERICAN WOMEN / Irwin, Melinda L – 1994 – 2mf – $8.00 – us Microform Publ [612]

THE DEVELOPMENT OF AN INSTRUMENT TO ASSESS THE ATTITUDES TOWARD CULTURAL DIVERSITY AND CULTURAL PLURALISM AMONG PRESERVICE PHYSICAL EDUCATION MAJORS / Stanley, Linda S et al – 1992 – 2mf – 9 – $8.00 – us Microform Publ [150]

DEVELOPMENT OF AN INVENTORY TO ASSESS MULTICULTURAL EDUCATION ATTITUDES, COMPETENCIES AND KNOWLEDGE OF PHYSICAL EDUCATION PROFESSIONALS / Woods, Lydia A & Jewett, Ann E – 1992 – 3mf – 9 – $12.00 – us Microform Publ [150]

THE DEVELOPMENT OF BANTU EDUCATION IN THE NORTH-WESTERN CAPE, 1840-1947 : A HISTORICAL SURVEY / Lekhela, Ernest Plaelo – Pretoria, 1958 – us Res Libr [370]

THE DEVELOPMENT OF BELLIGERENT OCCUPATION / Conner, J E – N.p., n.d. – 1mf – 1 – ILM-1023/1 – ne IDC [327]

THE DEVELOPMENT OF CHRISTIANITY IN TAIWAN (CCC301) = CHI-TU-CHIAO TSAI TAI-WAN TE FA-CHAN / Tung, Hsien-Kuang – (In Chinese) – [s.l: s.n, 19–?] – 1r – 1 – 1984-6640 – us A.T.L.A. [240]

DEVELOPMENT OF COMMUNICATION IN THE ARAB STATES : NEEDS AND PRIORITIES / Bakr, Yahya Abu et al – 1985 – 60p – 9 – 92-3-102082-X – fr UNESCO [380]

DEVELOPMENT OF COMMUNITY RECREATION PROGRAMS / U.S. Congress. House. Committee on Education and Labor – 1946 – 2mf – 9 – $12.00 – us Microform Publ [790]

THE DEVELOPMENT OF COMPETENCY GUIDELINES FOR RIDING INSTRUCTORS AND EQUESTRIAN COACHES / Harris, Johanna L – University of North Carolina at Chapel Hill, 1995 – 2mf – 9 – $8.00 – PE3596 – us Microform Publ [790]

THE DEVELOPMENT OF DOCTRINE / Dewart, Edward Hartley – by E. H. Dewart, The work of Christ. by E. A. Stafford. Toronto: Methodist Conference Printing Office, 1879. 02647. (Pre-1900 Canadiana) – 9 – cn C.I.H.M. [971]

THE DEVELOPMENT OF DOCTRINE FROM THE EARLY MIDDLE AGES TO THE REFORMATION / Banks, John Shaw – London: Charles H. Kelly, 1901 – 1mf – us A.T.L.A. [240]

THE DEVELOPMENT OF DOCTRINE IN THE EARLY CHURCH / Banks, John Shaw – London: C.H. Kelly, 1900 – 1mf – us A.T.L.A. [240]

THE DEVELOPMENT OF DOCTRINE IN THE EPISTLES / Henderson, Charles Richmond – (Includes index) – Philadelphia: American Baptist Publ Soc, 1896 – 1mf – 9 – 0-8370-3558-9 – 1985-1558 – us A.T.L.A. [220]

DEVELOPMENT OF EDUCATION 1988-1990. MALDIVES COUNTRY REPORT : INTERNATIONAL CONFERENCE ON EDUCATION, 42ND SESSION, GENEVA, 1990 / Maldives. Ministry of Education – Male, 1990 – 1mf – 9 – DE-672/1 – ne IDC [370]

DEVELOPMENT OF EDUCATION IN BAHRAIN DURING 1983/84-1985/86 : A REPORT SUBMITTED TO THE 40TH SESSION...INTERNATIONAL CONFERENCE... GENEVA, 2-11 DEC 1986/... / Bahrain. Educational Documentation Section – (In Englich and Arabic) – [Manama], 1986 – 4mf – 9 – DE-615/1 – ne IDC [370]

DEVELOPMENT OF EDUCATION IN INDONESIA / Indonesia. Kementerian Pendidikan – SE-476 1. 1955-1957 – 9 – ne IDC [324]

DEVELOPMENT OF EDUCATION IN QATAR (1982/83-1983/84) : REPORT SUBMITTED TO THE 39TH SESSION...INTERNATIONAL CONFERENCE... IBE, GENEVE, 16-25 OCT 1984 / Qatar. Ministry of Education – 1984 – 2mf – 9 – DE-636/1 – ne IDC [370]

DEVELOPMENT OF EDUCATION IN THE BECHUANALAND PROTECTORATE (1824-1944) : AN HISTORICAL SURVEY / Seboni, Michael Ontefetse Martinus – 1946 – us Res Libr [370]

DEVELOPMENT OF EDUCATION IN THE KINGDOM OF SAUDI ARABIA 1403-1406 A.H./1983-1986 A.D. : PRESENTED TO THE INTERNATIONAL CONFERENCE...40TH SESSION, GENEVA, DEC 1986 A.D. / Saudi Arabia. Ministry of Education. Educational Development – Riyadh, 1986 – 2mf – 9 – DE-633/1 – ne IDC [370]

THE DEVELOPMENT OF ENGLISH THEOLOGY IN THE NINETEENTH CENTURY, 1800-1860 / Storr, Vernon F – London, New York: Longmans, Green, 1913 – 2mf – us A.T.L.A. [240]

THE DEVELOPMENT OF HIGHER EDUCATION IN SOUTH AFRICA, 1873-1927 / Metrowich, F C – Cape Town: M Miller, 1929 – 1 – us Res Libr [960]

THE DEVELOPMENT OF INDUSTRIAL CREDIT IN EGYPT / Egypt. Industrial Bank – Statute and complementary laws. 1956. BNE-4633 1 – 9 – ne IDC [332]

THE DEVELOPMENT OF IRON AND STEEL TECHNOLOGY IN CHINA / Needham, J – 7 – uk Microform Academic [950]

THE DEVELOPMENT OF LONG-RANGE GOALS FOR THE FIRST BAPTIST CHURCH OF FAIRFIELD, OHIO / Copeland, Edward Brent – 1982 – 1 – 5.04 – us Baptist [240]

THE DEVELOPMENT OF MEDICAL SCIENCE IN INDONESIA / Sardjito, K – SE 3636 1 – 9 – ne IDC [610]

THE DEVELOPMENT OF MODERN PHILOSOPHY : WITH OTHER LECTURES AND ESSAYS / Adamson, Robert; ed by Sorley, W R – Edinburgh: W. Blackwood, 1903 – 2mf – us A.T.L.A. [100]

THE DEVELOPMENT OF NATIVE EDUCATION IN THE BECHUANALAND PROTECTORATE (1840-1946) : AN HISTORICAL SURVEY – BC Thema, 1947 – us Res Libr [370]

THE DEVELOPMENT OF NAVIES DURING THE LAST HALF-CENTURY / Wilmot, Sydney Marow Eardley – 1892 – 9 – uk Libr Preservation [941]

DEVELOPMENT OF NON-FORMAL EDUCATION IN INDONESIA / Indonesia. Office of Educational Development – 1976 – 1mf – 9 – DE-558/1 – ne IDC [370]

DEVELOPMENT OF PRIMARY EDUCATION IN NEPAL / Nepal. Ministry of Education. Planning, Statistics and Research Division – Kathmandu, 1967 – 1mf – 9 – DE-563/1 – ne IDC [370]

DEVELOPMENT OF PUBLIC FINANCE IN LIBRARY, 1944-1963 / Libya. Bank of Libya – BNE-628 1 – 9 – ne IDC [336]

THE DEVELOPMENT OF RELIGIOUS LIBERTY IN CONNECTICUT / Greene, M Louise – Boston: Houghton, Mifflin, 1905 – 2mf – us A.T.L.A. [240]

THE DEVELOPMENT OF SECONDARY AND TERTIARY EDUCATION / Hong Kong – Hong Kong, 1978 – 1mf – 9 – DE-147/1 – ne IDC [370]

DEVELOPMENT OF SECONDARY EDUCATION IN NEPAL / Nepal. Ministry of Education. Planning, Statistics and Research Division – Kathmandu, 1969 – 1mf – 9 – DE-564/1 – ne IDC [370]

THE DEVELOPMENT OF SENIOR SECONDARY AND TERTIARY EDUCATION / Hong Kong. Education Department – Hong Kong, 1978 – 1mf – 9 – DE-174/1 – ne IDC [370]

THE DEVELOPMENT OF SPIRITUAL HEALTH INSTRUCTIONAL STRATEGIES USING A SYSTEMS APPROACH MODEL / Larsen, Michelle H – Brigham Young University, 1994 – 1mf – 9 – HE 568 – us Microform Publ [613]

DEVELOPMENT OF THE ATHLETE SATISFACTION QUESTIONNAIRE / Riemer, Harold A – Ohio State University, 1995 – 6mf – 9 – $24.00 – PSY1858 – us Microform Publ [150]

DEVELOPMENT OF THE ATTITUDES TOWARD THE DISABLED IN PHYSICAL EDUCATION SCALE / Gantz, J L – 1991 – 1mf – 9 – $4.00 – us Microform Publ [150]

DEVELOPMENT OF THE CANAANITE DIALECTS / Harris, Z S – 1939 – 9 – $10.00 – us I.R.C. [470]

THE DEVELOPMENT OF THE HYMN AMONG SPANISH SPEAKING EVANGELICALS / McConnell, Harry C – 1952 – 1 – $13.44 – us Baptist [780]

THE DEVELOPMENT OF THE LOGICAL METHOD IN ANCIENT CHINA / Hu, Shih – 2nd ed. Introd. by Hyman Kublin. New York: Paragon Book Reprint Corp., 1963 – 187p – 1 – us U.W. Library [180]

THE DEVELOPMENT OF THE MOTIVE OF PROTESTANT MISSIONS TO CHINA, 1807-1928 / Workman, George Bell – 1 – us A.T.L.A. [240]

THE DEVELOPMENT OF THE SUNDAY-SCHOOL, 1780-1905 : THE OFFICIAL REPORT OF THE 11TH INTERNATIONAL SUNDAY-SCHOOL CONVENTION, TORONTO, CANADA, JUNE 23-27, 1905 / ed by International Sunday-School Convention of the United States and British American Provinces – Boston, Mass.: Executive Committee of the International Sunday-School Association, 1905 – 2mf – us A.T.L.A. [240]

THE DEVELOPMENT OF THE TEACHING OF LAW IN THE UNIVERSITY OF EDINBURGH / Coldstream, John Phillips – Edinburgh, Morrison & Gibb, 1884. 20 p. LL-2250 – 1 – us L of C Photodup [340]

THE DEVELOPMENT OF THE TEACHING OF READING IN INDONESIA / Gana, Ujeng S – SE-2725 1. 195? – 9 – ne IDC [370]

THE DEVELOPMENT OF THE TRANSPORTATION PATTERN IN GHANA / Gould, Peter R – Evanston: Dept of Geography, Northwestern University, 1960 – us Res Libr [380]

DEVELOPMENT OF THE WESTERN REGION OF NIGERIA, 1955-1960 / Nigeria. Western – (Sessional Paper no. 4 of 1955). Ibadan. 1955 – 9 – ne IDC [338]

THE DEVELOPMENT OF THEOLOGY IN GERMANY SINCE KANT AND ITS PROGRESS IN GREAT BRITAIN SINCE 1825 = ENTWICKLUNG DER PROTESTANTISCHEN THEOLOGIE IN DEUTSCHLAND SEIT KANT UND IN GROSSBRITANNIEN SEIT 1825 / Pfleiderer, Otto – (Includes bibliographical references and index) – 2nd ed. London: Swan Sonnenschein; New York: Macmillan, 1893 – 2mf – 9 – 0-8370-8701-5 – 1986-2701 – us A.T.L.A. [240]

THE DEVELOPMENT OF TRINITARIAN DOCTRINE IN THE NICENE AND ATHANASIAN CREEDS : A STUDY IN THEOLOGICAL DEFINITION / Bishop, William Samuel – New York: Longmans, Green, 1910 – 1mf – us A.T.L.A. [240]

THE DEVELOPMENT OF WEIGHT-ADJUSTED ESTIMATES OF CALORIC EXPENDITURES FOR THE NORDIC TRACK / Bowes, Michelle L – 1989 – 95p 1mf – 9 – $4.00 – us Microform Publ [612]

THE DEVELOPMENT OF WEIGHTBEARING SKILLS : A LONGITUDINAL STUDY OF INFANTS FOUR TO SEVEN MONTHS OF AGE / Roncesvalles, Maria N C – 1993 – 2mf – $8.00 – us Microform Publ [150]

THE DEVELOPMENT OF WELL INTEGRATED RURAL COMMUNITIES IN LAND SETTLEMENT AND LAND REFORM AREAS / United Nations. Economic and Social Office for the Middle East. Development Center on Land Policy and Settlement for the Near East – Tripoli, Libya. 16 to 28 Oct 1965. S. Abd (Regional Community Development Adviser). BNE-1007 1 – 9 – ne IDC [338]

DEVELOPMENT PLAN / North Borneo. (United Kingdom). Development Committee – D-1142 1. 1959-1964 – 9 – ne IDC [338]

DEVELOPMENT PLAN / Tonga – D 1221 1965-1970 – 9 – ne IDC [338]

DEVELOPMENT PLAN, 1 JUL 1961 TO 30 JUN 1965 – Lusaka. 1962. BD-200 1 – 9 – ne IDC [338]

THE DEVELOPMENT PLAN, 1951: FOR ECONOMIC AND SOCIAL DEVELOPMENT OF THE GOLD COAST 1951-1956 / Gold Coast – D 1306 1 – 9 – ne IDC [338]

DEVELOPMENT PLAN, 1948-1960 ESTIMATES, 1957 / Fiji – (Legislative Council Paper No. 37, 1956). Suva. 1956. BD-704 1 – 9 – ne IDC [338]

DEVELOPMENT PLAN, 1955-1960 – Aden. 1956 – 9 – ne IDC [338]

DEVELOPMENT PLAN, 1955-1960 / Barbados – Bridgetown. 1955. BD-122 1 – 9 – ne IDC [338]

DEVELOPMENT PLAN, 1955-1960 CAPITAL WORKS PROGRAMME – Dar es Salaam. 1955 – 9 – ne IDC [338]

DEVELOPMENT PLAN, 1960-1964 – 1960. D-9201 – 9 – ne IDC [338]

DEVELOPMENT PLAN, 1960-1964 / Swaziland. United Kingdom – D 1206 1. 1960 – 9 – ne IDC [338]

DEVELOPMENT PLAN, 1960-1964AND – draft colonial development and welfare schemes 1960-1964. D-950 1 – 9 – ne IDC [360]

DEVELOPMENT PLAN, 1960-1965 / Barbados – Bridgetown. 1960 – 9 – ne IDC [338]

DEVELOPMENT PLAN, 1960-64 / Zanzibar – Sessional Paper No. 24 of 1959. Zanzibar. 1959. BD-699 1 – 9 – ne IDC [338]

DEVELOPMENT PLAN, 1961-65 / Fiji – Legislative Council Paper 6 of 1961. Suva. 1961 – 9 – ne IDC [338]

DEVELOPMENT PLAN, 1962-1965 – Zomba. 1962. BD-111 1 – 9 – ne IDC [338]

DEVELOPMENT PLAN, 1962-65 / Barbados – Bridgetown. 1962. BD-183 1 – 9 – ne IDC [338]

DEVELOPMENT PLAN, 1962-68 / Nigeria. Northern. Ministry of Economic Planning – Kaduna. 1962. BD-681 1 – 9 – ne IDC [338]

DEVELOPMENT PLAN, 1963-1968 – Bulawayo. 1963 – 9 – ne IDC [338]

DEVELOPMENT PLAN, 1963-1970 / British Honduras – 4v. D-968 1 – 9 – ne IDC [338]

DEVELOPMENT PLAN, 1964-1968 (DEVELOPMENT PLAN 4) / Fiji – (Legislative Council Paper 33 of 1963). Suva. 1963. BD-141 1 – 9 – ne IDC [338]

DEVELOPMENT PLAN, 1964-1970 / Honduras. British – Belize City. 1964 – 9 – ne IDC [338]

DEVELOPMENT PLAN, 1964-1970 / Kenya – Nairobi. 1964 – 9 – ne IDC [338]

DEVELOPMENT PLAN, 1965-1969 / Malawi – Zomba. 1964. BD-228 1 – 9 – ne IDC [338]

DEVELOPMENT PLAN, 1965-68 / Barbados – Bridgetown. 1965. BD-129 1 – 9 – ne IDC [338]

DEVELOPMENT PLAN, 1966-1969 / Seychelles – Victoria. 1965. BD-349 1 – 9 – ne IDC [338]

DEVELOPMENT PLAN, 1966-1970 DEVELOPMENT PLANNING REVIEW / Fiji. Central Planning Office – Suva. 1966. BD-586 1 – 9 – ne IDC [338]

DEVELOPMENT PLAN, 1966-1970 OUTLINE AND PUBLIC EXP / Fiji. Central Planning Office – Suva. 1966 – 9 – ne IDC [338]

DEVELOPMENT PLAN, 1966-70 / Montserrat – Plymouth. 1966. BD-407 1 – 9 – ne IDC [338]

DEVELOPMENT PLAN, 1969-1972 / Barbados – D-946 1 – 9 – ne IDC [338]

DEVELOPMENT PLAN, 1970-1972 / Gilbert and Ellice Islands Colony – D-1082 1. 1970 – 9 – ne IDC [338]

DEVELOPMENT PLAN 1970-74 / Nigeria. Mid-Western State of Nigeria, Ministry of Economic Development and Reconstruction – Benin City. BD-1714 1 – 9 – ne IDC [338]

DEVELOPMENT PLAN 1970-74 / Nigeria. Western State of Nigeria, Ministry of Economic Planning and Reconstruction – Ibadan. BD-1713 1 – 9 – ne IDC [338]

DEVELOPMENT PLAN, 1971-1975 / Fiji. Central Planning Office – Sixth. 1970. D-1050 1 – 9 – ne IDC [338]

DEVELOPMENT PLAN 1990/91-1992/93 / Swaziland. Economic Planning Office – Mbabane, 1990 – 4mf – 9 – ne IDC [338]

DEVELOPMENT PLAN 1991/92-1993/94 / Swaziland. Economic Planning Office – Mbabane, 1991 – 6mf – 9 – ne IDC [338]

DEVELOPMENT PLAN 1992/93-1994/95 / Swaziland. Economic Planning Office – Mbabane, 1992 – 7mf – 9 – ne IDC [338]

DEVELOPMENT PLAN A.H. 1390 (1970-1974?) / Saudi Arabia. Central Planning Organization – D 1189 1. 1970 – 9 – ne IDC [338]

DEVELOPMENT PLAN, FIRST FIVE YEARS (1963-1967), 1963 ANNUAL PROGRAM / Turkey. State Planning Organization – Ankara. 1963. BD-1765 1 – 9 – ne IDC [338]

DEVELOPMENT PLAN FOR MALTA, 1973-1980 / Malta. Office of the Prime Minister – Malta. 1974 – 9 – ne IDC [338]

DEVELOPMENT PLAN FOR PUERTO RICO, TECHNICAL PAPER NO. 1 / Puerto Rico. Planning, Urbanizing and Zoning Board – D 1444 1. 1944 – 9 – ne IDC [338]

DEVELOPMENT PLAN FOR THE MALTESE ISLANDS, 1959-64 / Malta – Valletta. 1959. BD-142 1 – 9 – ne IDC [338]

DEVELOPMENT PLAN FOR THE MALTESE ISLANDS, 1964-69 / Malta – Valletta. 1964. BD-182 1 – 9 – ne IDC [338]

DEVELOPMENT PLAN FOR THE NATIONAL ECONOMY 1971-1975 / Israel. Economic Planning Authority – Assumptions, targets, guidelines. Jerusalem. Nov 1969 – 9 – ne IDC [338]

DEVELOPMENT PLAN FOR THE PERIOD 1974 TO 1978 / Kenya. Ministry for Finance and Planning – 2pts. Nairobi. 1974. BD-2022 1 – 9 – ne IDC [336]

DEVELOPMENT PLAN FOR THE PERIOD 1965/66 TO 1969/70 / Kenya – Nairobi. 1966. BD-218 1 – 9 – ne IDC [338]

DEVELOPMENT PLAN, PART 3 (1955-60) / Honduras. British – Belize. 1955 – 9 – ne IDC [338]

DEVELOPMENT PLAN PROPOSALS, 1965-1968 / Swaziland. (United Kingdom) – D 1208 1. 1966 – 9 – ne IDC [338]

THE DEVELOPMENT PLAN REPORT FOR THE YEAR 1947 / Tanganyika – Dar es Salaam. 1947 – 9 – ne IDC [338]

THE DEVELOPMENT PLAN REPORT FOR THE YEAR 1948 / Tanganyika – Dar es Salaam. 1948. Bd-825 1 – 9 – ne IDC [338]

DEVELOPMENT PLANNING COMMITTEE REPORT, 1947-1956 / British Honduras – D-1246 1 – 9 – ne IDC [324]

DEVELOPMENT PLANS / Ireland – 9 – ne IDC [338]

DEVELOPMENT PLANS / Kenya – Report of the Development Committee (1946-1955). D-1350; 1. 2v. 1946. SF 21.00; 9. Report of the Planning Committee (1951-1955). D-1351; 1. 1951. SF 10.00; IDC; 9. The Development Programme 1957-1960. D-1110; 1. 1957. SF 10.00; IDC; 9. Development plan for 1970-1974. D-881; 1. 1969. SF 23.00; IDC; 9 – ne IDC [338]

DEVELOPMENT PLANS / Nigeria – Revised plan of development and welfare for Nigeria, 1951-1956. D-1395; 1. 1951. SF 12.00; 9. Economic programme of the government, 1955-1960. D-1396; 1. 1956. SF 8.00; IDC; 9. Federal government development programme, 1962-68. D-1397; 1. 1962. SF 8.00; IDC; 9. Second national development plan, 1970-74. D-1141; 1. 1970. SF 14.00; IDC; 9 – ne IDC [338]

DEVELOPMENT PLANS / Sarawak – (Revised development plan, 1951-1957. D 1469; 1. 1951. SF 8.00; 9. Development plan, 1955-1960. D 1185; 1. 1954. SF 12.00; IDC; 9. Revision of 1955-1960 development plan. D 1186; 1. 1957. SF 8.00; IDC; 9. Development plan, 1959-1963. D 1187; 1. 1959. SF 8.00; IDC; 9. Development plan, 1964-1968. (To be absorbed into first Malaysian Development Plan, 1966-1970, with revisions as desirable). D 1188; 1. 1963. SF 10.00; IDC; 9) – ne IDC [338]

DEVELOPMENT PLANS / Turkey. Basbakanlik Devlet Planlama Teskilati – Basbakanlik Devlet Planlama Teskilati. 1971 Yili Programi. Kalkinma Plani Ikinci Bes Yil 1968-1972. D 1507; 1. 1971. SF 25.00; 9. State Planning Organization. Development plan, first five year, 1963-1967. 1964 annual program. D 1504; 1. 1963. SF 14.00; IDC; 9. State Planning Organization. Development plan, first five year, 1963-1967. 1965 annual program. D 1505; 1. 1964. SF 16.00; IDC; 9 – ne IDC [338]

DEVELOPMENT PLANS: / Laos – (Plan De Developpement Social, 1959; 64. D-220; 1. 1959. SF 16.00; 9. Commissariat au Plan. Plan De Developpement Economique Et Social. Etat Des Realisations Effectuees Au Cours De La Premiere Annee 1959-1960 Et Programme Pour La Deuxieme Annee. Annee 1960-61. D-1363; 1. SF 12.00; IDC; 9. Commissariat au Plan, Plan Cadre de Developpement economique et social, 1969-1974. D-872; 1. SF 16.00; IDC; 9) – ne IDC [360]

DEVELOPMENT PLANS, 1954-1957 / Federation of Rhodesia and Nyasaland – D-1293 1. 4v. 1953 – 9 – ne IDC [338]

DEVELOPMENT PLANS, 1957-1961 / Federation of Rhodesia and Nyasaland – 1957. D-1044 1 – 9 – ne IDC [338]

DEVELOPMENT PLANS, 1962-1965 / Federation of Rhodesia and Nyasaland – 1962. D-1047 1 – 9 – ne IDC [338]

DEVELOPMENT PLANS: DEUXIEME PLAN QUADRIENNAL DE DEVELOPPEMENT ECONOMIQUE ET SOCIAL 1965-1969 / Senegal – (Minist. du Devel. et du Plan. Programme Interimaire De Devel. De La Region Du Fleuve Senegal. D 899; 1. 1960. SF 23.00; 9. Minist. du Plan et de l'Indust. Troisieme Plan Quadriennal De Devel. Econ. Et Soc., 1969-73. D 895; 1. 1969. SF 21.00; IDC; 9) – D 1191 1. 1967 – 9 – ne IDC [338]

DEVELOPMENT PLANS. PRODUCTIVIDAD ANEXO A1 PLAN 1964-1967. D 1200/1. 1964 / Spain. Comisaria del Plan de Desarrollo Economico y Social – (Economic and social development program for Spain, 1964-1967. D 1202; 1. 1965. SF 23.00; 9. 2nd Plan De Desarrollo Economico Y Social (1968-1971). D 1203; 1. 1969. SF 496.00; IDC; 9. 3rd Plan De Desarrollo Economico Y Social 1972-1975. D 1553; 1. 1972. SF 21.00; IDC; 9. 3rd Plan De Desarrollo Economico Y Social 1972-1975. Annex 1-18. D 1554; 1. 1972. SF 191.00; IDC; 9) – 9 – ne IDC [338]

DEVELOPMENT POLICIES AND PLANS / Malawi. Ministry of Natural Resources – D-896 1. 1965-69 – 9 – ne IDC [960]

DEVELOPMENT POLICY AND INTERIM EXPENDITURE PROGRAMME 1961-1963 / British Honduras – D-1247 1 – 9 – ne IDC [338]

DEVELOPMENT POTENTIAL AND CONSTRAINTS / Chad – A World Bank Country Economic Report. 1974. BD-1856 1 – 9 – ne IDC [338]

DEVELOPMENT PROGRAMME / Nyasaland – Zomba. 1947. BD-401 1 – 9 – ne IDC [338]

DEVELOPMENT PROGRAMME (1 JUL 1960 TO 30 JUN 1961) / Pakistan. Planning Commission – Karachi. Jun 1960. BD-1411 1 – 9 – ne IDC [338]

DEVELOPMENT PROGRAMME. (1 JUL 1961 TO 30 JUN 1962) AS APPROVED BY THE ECONOMIC COUNCIL / Pakistan. Planning Commission – Aug 1961. BD-1412 1 – 9 – ne IDC [338]

DEVELOPMENT PROGRAMME (1 JUL 1962 TO 30 JUN 1963) / Pakistan. Planning Commission – Karachi. 1962. BD-1414 1 – 9 – ne IDC [338]

DEVELOPMENT PROGRAMME. (1 JUL 1963 TO 30 JUN 1964) 1 AS APPROVED BY THE NATIONAL ECONOMIC COUNCIL / Pakistan. Planning Commission – Aug 1963. Karachi. 1963. BD-1415 1 – 9 – ne IDC [338]

THE DEVELOPMENT PROGRAMME, 1954-57 / Kenya – Nairobi. 1955. BD-332 – 9 – ne IDC [338]

DEVELOPMENT PROGRAMME, 1956-1960 / British Guiana – D-963 1 – 9 – ne IDC [338]

DEVELOPMENT PROGRAMME, 1959-1964 / Dominica – Roseau. 1959 – 9 – ne IDC [338]

DEVELOPMENT PROGRAMME, 1960-1964 / British Guiana – D-964 1 – 9 – ne IDC [338]

THE DEVELOPMENT PROGRAMME, 1964-1965 / Ceylon. Department of National Planning – Colombo. 1964. BD-366 1 – 9 – ne IDC [338]

DEVELOPMENT PROGRAMME, 1964-65 / Pakistan. Planning Commission – Karachi. 1964. BD-1416 1 – 9 – ne IDC [338]

DEVELOPMENT PROGRAMME 1965-66 (1 JUL 1965 TO 30 JUN 1966). AS APPROVED BY THE NATIONAL ECONOMIC COUNCIL / Pakistan. Planning Commission – Jun 1965. Karachi. 1965. BD-1417 1 – 9 – ne IDC [338]

DEVELOPMENT PROGRAMME, 1966-1972 / Guyana – D-885 1 – 9 – ne IDC [338]

THE DEVELOPMENT PROGRAMME, 1966-67 / Ceylon. Ministry of Planning and Economic Affairs – Colombo. 1966. BD-304 1 – 9 – ne IDC [338]

DEVELOPMENT PROGRAMME, 1966-76 / Pakistan. Planning Commission – Karachi. 1966. BD-860 1 – 9 – ne IDC [338]

DEVELOPMENT PROGRAMME 1967-68 / Pakistan. Planning Commission – Jun 1967. BD-1720 1 – 9 – ne IDC [338]

DEVELOPMENT PROGRAMME, 1968-70 / Malawi. Ministry of Economic Affairs – Budget Document No. 6. Zomba. 1968 – 9 – ne IDC [338]

DEVELOPMENT PROGRAMME 1969-70 / Pakistan. Planning Commission – Jun 1969. BD-1721 1 – 9 – ne IDC [338]

DEVELOPMENT PROGRAMME 1970-1971 (1 JUL 1970 TO 30 JUN 1971) / Pakistan. Planning Commission – Karachi. Aug 1970 – 9 – ne IDC [338]

DEVELOPMENT PROGRAMME 1970-1972/73 / Malawi – 2v. Zomba. May 1970. BD-1374 1 – 9 – ne IDC [338]

DEVELOPMENT PROGRAMME 1971-1973 / Somali Republic. Planning and Coordination Committee – Mogadishu. 1971. BD-1849 1 – 9 – ne IDC [338]

THE DEVELOPMENT PROGRAMME IN EDUCATION FOR SIERRA LEONE, 1964-1970 / Sierra Leone. UNESCO Educational Planning Mission – Freetown, 1964 – 9 – DE-702/1 – ne IDC [370]

THE DEVELOPMENT PROGRAMME IN EDUCATION FOR THE GAMBIA, 1965-1975 / UNESCO Educational Planning Mission – (Sessional Paper n8 of 1966). Bathurst, 1965 – 9 – DE-428/1 – ne IDC [370]

Development Projects Consulting Service (Indonesia) *see*
- INDUSTRIAL METAL WORKING SHOPS
- PRETASK ORDER REPORTS
- PROGRESS REPORT NO. 1

DEVELOPMENT REPORT / Libya – BNE-503 1 – 9 – ne IDC [338]

DEVELOPMENT SCHEMES IN THE FIRST FIVE YEAR PLAN / India. Planning Commission – New Delhi. 1952 – 9 – ne IDC [338]

DEVELOPMENT, SEEDS OF CHANGE, VILLAGE THROUGH GLOBAL ORDER – 1981- – 1,5,6,9 – us UMI [073]

DEVELOPMENT STRATEGIES FOR THE RURAL POOR – 1984 – 117p – it F.A.O. [338]

DEVELOPMENT STRATEGIES IN EDUCATION TOWARD THE FUTURE INDUSTRIAL SOCIETY / Korea. Korean Educational Development Institute – Seoul, 1988 – 2mf – 9 – DE-657/1 – ne IDC [370]

DEVELOPMENT STRATEGY 1971-1980 / Mauritius – D-1537 1. 1970 – 9 – ne IDC [338]

DEVELOPMENT STRATEGY 1979-1980 / Mauritius. Ministry of Economic Planning and Development – Port Louis. Dec 1970. BD-1693 1 – 9 – ne IDC [338]

DEVELOPMENTAL AND COMPARATIVE IMMUNOLOGY – v1- 1977- – 5,6,9 – us UMI [610]

DEVELOPMENTAL AND SITUATIONAL FACTORS AFFECTING LITTLE LEAGUE PARTICIPATION / McAndrews, M R – 1991 – 1mf – 9 – $4.00 – us Microform Publ [150]

DEVELOPMENTAL BRAIN DYSFUNCTION – v1-. 1988- – 1,5,9 – us UMI [073]

DEVELOPMENTAL IMMUNOLOGY / ed by Scollay, Roland – 9,5,1 – us Harwood [616]

DEVELOPMENTAL MEDICINE AND CHILD NEUROLOGY – (1971-. 5,6. 1976-. 9) – 1-1958- – 1 – us UMI [618]

DEVELOPMENTAL NEUROSCIENCE – v1-. 1978- – 1,5,9 – us UMI [073]

DEVELOPMENTAL PSYCHOBIOLOGY – v. 1-. 1968- – 1,5,6,9 – us UMI [574]

DEVELOPMENTAL PSYCHOLOGY – v1- 1969- 1,5,6; v11- 9 – us UMI [150]

DEVELOPMENTAL PSYCHOLOGY – v1-19. 1969-83 – 1,5,6 – us Princeton Micro [150]

DEVELOPMENTAL RELATIONSHIPS BETWEEN THROWING AND STRIKING: A PRE-LONGITUDINAL TEST OF MOTOR STAGE THEORY / Langendorfer, Stephen – 1982 – 3mf – 9 – $12.00 – us Microform Publ [790]

DEVELOPMENT-PROGRESS REPORT / Fiji – (Legislative Council Paper No. 57, 1948). Suva. 1948. BD-701 1 – 9 – ne IDC [338]

DEVELOPMENTS IN MARKETING SCIENCE *see* ACADEMY OF MARKETING SCIENCE

DEVELOPPEMENT, CROISSANCE ET REGENERATION DES ECAILLES D'HEMICHROMIS BIMACULATUS (GILL, 1862) (PERCIFORMES CICHLIDES) / Sire, J Y – 9 – F50.00 – fr Ethnologie [590]

LE DEVELOPPEMENT DE LA FABRIQUE ET LE TRAVAIL A DOMICILE DANS LES INDUSTRIES DE L'HABILLEMENT / Aftalion, Albert – Paris. 1906. (La Condition Ouvriere. Part Two.) – 9 – 10.00 – fr Bibl Nationale [360]

LE DEVELOPPEMENT DE LA PENSEE RELIGIEUSE DE LUTHER JUSQU'EN 1517 : D'APRES DES DOCUMENTS INEDITS / Jundt, Andre – Paris: Fischbacher, 1906 – 1mf – us A.T.L.A. [240]

DEVELOPPEMENT DU CHONDROCRANE ET DES VAISSEAUX SANGUINS CEPHALIQUES CHEZ LE BROCHET, ESOX LUCIUS L / Amouzou-Medina, M – 9 – F60.00 – fr Ethnologie [580]

LE DEVELOPPEMENT ECONOMIQUE ET SOCIAL DE LA PROVINCE DE FES / Morocco. Division de la Coordination Economique et du Plan – 1961. BNE-3039 1 – 9 – ne IDC [338]

DEVELOPPEMENT ET CROISSANCE EMBRYONNAIRE DE L'OURSIN INCUBANT ABATUS CORDATUS (ECHINOIDEA: SPATANGOIDA) / Schatt, P – 9 – F60.00 – fr Ethnologie [590]

LE DEVELOPPEMENT RURAL – Conakry: PDG, 1970 – us Res Libr [600]

DEVELOPPEMENT-QUEBEC / Quebec. (Province). Office de Planification et de Developpement du Quebec – Quebec: l'O.P.D.Q. v1-8. 1973-83. SEM16P302 – 5 – Can$38.00 – cn Bibl Nat [310]

DEVENIR – no. 1-5. Paris. fevr-juil 1944 – 1 – fr A.C.R.P.P. [073]

LE DEVENIR SOCIAL – Revue internationale d'economie, d'histoire et de philosophie. Paris. avr 1895-98 – 1 – fr A.C.R.P.P. [073]

Deventer, H van *see* OPERATIONES CHIRURGICAE NOVUM LUMEN EXHIBENTES OBSTETRICANTIBUS

O DEVER : ORGAO LITTERARIO, SCIENTIFICO E NOTICIOSO – Maceio, Alagoas. 5-19 Jun, Set-Out 1887; 23 Ago 1896 – 1,5,6 – bl Biblioteca [072]

Dever, M *see* WOMEN IN THE PULPIT

DEVEREUX PAPERS / Bath. Archives (Marquess). Longleat – 1533-1664. v1-10. Boxes 1-16 and index. Longleat – 1 – uk Microform Academic [941]

Deveria, G *see*
- LA FRONTIERE SINO-ANNAMITE
- HISTOIRE DES RELATIONS DE LA CHINE AVEC L'ANNAM-VIETNAM DU XIVE AU XIXE SIECLE

DEVIANT BEHAVIOR – (1984-. 5,6,9) – v1-. 1979- – 1 – us UMI [073]

DEVIATOE IANVARI A 1905-1925 : KHRESTOMATIIA DLIA AGITATOROV / Anatolev, P – [Moskva]: "Proletari i", 1925 – 1 – CSUX88-B820 – us Hoover Inst Photo [947]

DEVIATY I VAL : K DESI ATILETII U OSVOBOZHDENII A IZ T SARSKO I KATORGI I SSYLKI / ed by Vilenskogo, V et al – Moskva: Izd-vo Vses. ob-va politkatorzhan i ssylno-poselent sev, 1927 – 1 – CSUX88-B3944 – us Hoover Inst Photo [947]

DEVIATY I VAL : VI ESTNIK ROSSI ISKAGO NATSIONAL-SOTSIALISTICHESKAGO DVIZHENII A – (Includes c.1: 1935:Jan., June, Oct) – Berlin: RNSD, 1935- – 1 – CSUXAHZ2927-S – us Hoover Inst Photo [947]

DEVIATY I VAL (BERLIN, GERMANY) *see* DEVIATY I VAL

Devienne, Francois *see*
- NEUVIEME CONCERTO DE FLUTE PRINCIPALE, DEUX VIOLONS, ALTO, BASSE, CORS ET HAUTBOIS
- SIX DUOS POUR DEUX FLUTES

Devienne, Jean Baptiste d'Agneaux, dit Dom *see* PLAN D'EDUCATION ET LES MOYENS DE L'EXECUTER

THE DEVIL AND THE DEEP SEA / Broughton, Rhoda – British Fiction Archive: Unit 4 – 9 – uk Bell [830]

THE DEVIL IN THE CHURCH : HIS SECRET WORKS EXPOSED AND HIS SNARES LAID TO DESTROY OUR PUBLIC SCHOOLS – 3rd ed. Beaver Springs, PA: American Pub Co, c1902 – 2mf – 9 – 0-8370-8709-0 – 1986-2709 – us A.T.L.A. [240]

Deville, D *see* RECHERCHES SUR LE RANPORT EXISTANT ENTRE LE NOMBRE DES MORT-NES ET CELUI DES DECES, A PARIS, PENDANT TREIZE ANNEES, DE 1846 A 1858.

Deville, Edouard *see* EXAMPLES OF ASTRONOMIC AND GEODETIC CALCULATIONS FOR THE USE OF LAND SURVEYORS

Devillers, James *see* SAR AND QSAR IN ENVIRONMENTAL RESEARCH

THE DEVIL'S DIE: A NOVEL / Allen, Grant – New York: F. M. Lupton, 189?. 05022. (Pre-1900 Canadiana) – 9 – cn C.I.H.M. [830]

THE DEVIL'S MOTOR / Corelli, Marie – British Fiction Archive: Unit 1 – 9 – uk Bell [830]
THE DEVIL'S PARABLES : AND OTHER ESSAYS / Hannon, John – (Includes bibliographical references) – London: R & T Washbourne; New York: Benzinger, 1910 – 1mf – 9 – 0-8370-6816-9 – 1986-0816 – us A.T.L.A. [230]
THE DEVIL'S SHADOW / Thiess, Frank – New York: A A Knopf, 1928 – 1 – us U.W. Library [430]
Devin, J *see* LA PROPRIETE IMMOBILIERE DES ETRANGERS EN FRANCE
DEVINDEX BOTSWANA : INDEX TO LITERATURE ON ECONOMIC AND SOCIAL DEVELOPMENT IN BOTSWANA / Monageng, Stella B & Moahi, Kgomotso H – 1990 No. 3 – bs U.B. Nat'l Inst [338]
DEVINDEX BOTSWANA : INDEX TO LITERATURE ON ECONOMIC AND SOCIAL DEVELOPMENT IN BOTSWANA / Monageng, Stella B & Moahi, Kgomotso H – 1990 No. 4 – bs U.B. Nat'l Inst [338]
DEVINDEX BOTSWANA : INDEX TO LITERATURE ON ECONOMIC AND SOCIAL DEVELOPMENT IN BOTSWANA / Monageng, Stella B & Moahi, Kgomotso H – 1990 Nos. 2 – 66p – bs U.B. Nat'l Inst [338]
Devine, Arthur *see* THE CREED EXPLAINED
Devine, Carl Thomas *see* READINGS IN ACCOUNTING THEORY
Devine, Pius *see* EUTROPIA
Devine, Thomas *see* ATLAS
DEVIR / Eliasewich, H Z – Vilna. 1864. BJ-422-11 1 – 9 – ne IDC [920]
DEVIR / Eliasewich, H Z – Vilna. 3v. 1844-1864 – 7mf – 9 – ne IDC [947]
DEVIR / Ginzburg, M A – 2v. Warsaw. 1884. BJ-290-8 1 – 9 – ne IDC [920]
DEVIR / ed by Guenzburg, M A – Vilna. 2v. 1883-1884 – 5mf – 9 – ne IDC [947]
DEVIS DE LA LANGUE FRANCOYSE / Matthieu, A – 1559-60 – 9 – fr I.C.S. [440]
DEVISES ET EMBLEMES D'AMOUR ANCIENS ET MODERNES MORALISEZ ET EXPLIQUEZ EN SEPT SORTES DE LANGUES (LATIN, ITALIAN, FRENCH, SPANISH, DUTCH, ENGLISH AND GERMAN) / Pallavicini – O 705. 1696 – 9 – ne IDC [760]
DEVISES ET EMBLESMES D'AMOUR / Flamen, Albert – O-256. 1658 – 9 – ne IDC [760]
Devitt, Edward J *see* YOUR HONOR
DEVIZES AND WILTSHIRE GAZETTE – (Wiltshire Gazette, 1909-56) – Devizes, England. 1897; 1913 – 2r – 1 – uk British Libr Newspaper [072]
DEVLET SALNAMES : SALNAME-I DEVLET-I ALIYYE-I OSMANIYYE – (1263, 3 fiche. $21.00; 1264, 2 fiche. $21.00; 1265, 2 fiche. $21.00; 1266, 1 fiche. $21.00; 1267, 2 fiche. $21.00; 1268, 2 fiche. $21.00; 1269, 2 fiche. $15.75; 1270, 2 fiche. $21.00; 1271, 2 fiche. $21.00; 1272, 2 fiche. $21.00; 1273, 2 fiche. $21.00; 1274, 3 fiche. $21.00; 1275, 3 fiche. $21.00; 1276, 3 fiche. $21.00; 1277, 3 fiche. $21.00; 1278, 2 fiche. $21.00; 1279, 2 fiche. $21.00; 1280, 3 fiche. $26.25; 1281, 3 fiche. $26.25; 1282, 3 fiche. $26.25; 1283, 3 fiche. $26.25; 1284, 3 fiche. $26.25; 1285, 2 fiche. $26.25; 1286, 3 fiche. $26.25; 1287, 3 fiche. $26.25; 1288, 5 fiche. $26.25; 1289, 8 fiche. $26.25; 1290, 6 fiche. $26.25; 1291, 5 fiche. $26.25; 1292, 5 fiche. $26.25; 1293, 7 fiche. $26.25; 1294, 10 fiche. $26.25; 1295, 6 fiche. $26.25; 1296, 7 fiche. $26.25; 1297, 4 fiche. $39.00; 1298, 12 fiche. $36.75; 1299, 10 fiche. $36.75; 1300, 10 fiche. $36.75; 1301, 14 fiche. $39.00; 1302, 10 fiche. $39.00; 1303, 10 fiche. $39.00; 1304, 11 fiche. $39.00; 1305, 11 fiche. $28.75; 1306, 11 fiche. $36.75; 1307, 7 fiche. $42.00; 1308, 9 fiche. $42.00; 1309, 8 fiche. $44.00; 1310, 9 fiche. $42.00; 1311, 9 fiche. $42.00; 1312, 10 fiche. $44.00; Dates correspond to Islamic Calendar) – 1993 – 9 – us MEDOC [320]
DEVLET-I ALIYE OSMANIYENIN 1318 SENESI MUVAZENE UMUMIYE HULASASI – Dersaadet [Istanbul]: Matbaa-yi Osmaniye, 1318 [1902] – 9 – $20.00 – us MEDOC [350]
DEVLET-I ALIYENIN DOKSAN SENESI MUVAZENE DEFTERIDIR – Istanbul: Matbaa-yi Amire, 1291 [1875] – 9 – $20.00 – us MEDOC [350]
DEVLET-I 'OSMANIYYE' NIN BUETCESI – (1327 M[1911].-3mf. $35.00; 1328 M[1911].-2mf. $35.00; 1330 M[1913].-3mf. $35.00; 1331 M[1914].-3mf. $35.00; 1332 M[1915].-4mf. $35.00; 1334 M[1917].-4mf. $35.00) – us MEDOC [650]
DEVLETLER HUSUSI HUKUKU / Birsen, K – (v2 is missing) – Istanbul. 2v. 1936 – 4mf – 9 – ILM-3386/1 – ne IDC [327]
LA DEVOCION AL PAPA : CARTA PASTORAL / Perez Munoz, Adolfo – Badajoz: Uceda Hnos, 1914 – 1 – sp Bibl Santa Ana [240]
DEVOCIONES ANTONIANAS / Corredor, Antonio – Caceres: Ediciones Cruzada mariana. Tip. La Minerva, 1958 – sp Bibl Santa Ana [240]
DEVOCIONES ANTONIANAS / Corredor, Antonio – Plasencia: Graf. Sandoval, 9th ed 1979 – 1 – sp Bibl Santa Ana [240]
LAS DEVOCIONES DE MI PUEBLO, LAS SANTAS RELIQUIAS, EL SANTUARIO... ALBURQUERQUE / Duarte Insua, Lino – Badajoz: Dip. Prov, 1947 – 1 – sp Bibl Santa Ana [240]
LE DEVOIR – Montreal, Canada. 10 jan 1910-31 dec 1992 – 265r – 1 – Inquire – cn Can Microfilming [072]
LE DEVOIR – Muskegon, MI. v1 n10. 17 jul 1890-v1 n26. 6nov 1890 – 1r – 1 – Can$25.00 – cn Can Microfilming [071]
LE DEVOIR – Port-au-Prince: Impr de l'Abeille, [1902-]. [1re annee, n1-2e annee, n2. 10 avril 1902-24 juin 1903] – 3r – 9 – us Res Libr [072]
LE DEVOIR ECONOMIQUE – Montreal, 18 jan 1985-jun 1990f – 2r – 1 – Can$75.00 – cn Can Microfilming [072]
LE DEVOIR INDEX : "LE DOCUMENT" – Montreal, Canada. 1931 – 1r – 1 – Can$25.00 – cn Can Microfilming [030]
DEVOIRS GENERAUX DES DOMESTIQUES DE L'UN ET DE L'AUTRE SEXE, ENVERS DIEU ET LEURS MAITRES ET MAITRESSES. – Paris. 1713. (La Condition Ouvriere. Part Two.) – 9 – 7.50 – fr Bibl Nationale [360]
DEVON AND CORNWALL RECORD SOCIETY – (Coll title: Publications of the English Record Societies, 1835-1972...) – v1-25. 1906-54 – 162mf – 9 – £1,020.00 – uk Chadwyck [941]
DEVON AND CORNWALL RECORD SOCIETY NEW SERIES – (Coll title: Publications of the English Record Societies, 1835-72...) – v26-39. 1955-70 – 39mf – 9 – £330.00 – uk Chadwyck [941]
DEVON COMMISSION 1845 : REPORT ON THE STATE AND PRACTICE OF LAND OCCUPATION IN IRELAND – 43 mf – Ir£30.00 – ie Microforms [333]
DEVON COMMISSION REPORT / Great Britain. Parliament. House of Commons – 1845. 42 fiches – 9 – Ir£50.00 – ie Microforms [941]
DEVONSHIRE, 1823 : BRITISH ISLES CENSUS DIRECTORIES PROJECT, ENGLAND. VOL 222 – 1mf – 9 – A$9.00 – at Vine [941]
DEVONSHIRE, 1830 : BRITISH ISLES CENSUS DIRECTORIES PROJECT, ENGLAND. VOL 52 – 1mf – 9 – A$9.00 – at Vine [941]
DEVONSHIRE, 1844 : BRITISH ISLES CENSUS DIRECTORIES PROJECT, ENGLAND. VOL 269 – 4mf – 9 – at Vine [941]
DEVONSHIRE, 1850 : BRITISH ISLES CENSUS DIRECTORIES PROJECT, ENGLAND. VOL 62 – 5mf – 9 – A$33.00 – at Vine [941]
DEVONSHIRE, 1852 : BRITISH ISLES CENSUS DIRECTORIES PROJECT, ENGLAND. VOL 153 – 3mf – 9 – A$21.00 – at Vine [941]
DEVONSHIRE, 1878 : BRITISH ISLES CENSUS DIRECTORIES PROJECT, ENGLAND – at Vine [941]
DEVONSHIRE, 1889 : BRITISH ISLES CENSUS DIRECTORIES PROJECT, ENGLAND – at Vine [941]
DEVONSHIRE, 1890 : BRITISH ISLES CENSUS DIRECTORIES PROJECT, ENGLAND. VOL 159 – 15mf – 9 – A$93.00 – at Vine [941]
DEVONSHIRE, 1902 : BRITISH ISLES CENSUS DIRECTORIES PROJECT, ENGLAND – at Vine [941]
DEVONSHIRE, 1910 : BRITISH ISLES CENSUS DIRECTORIES PROJECT, ENGLAND. VOL 161 – 15mf – 9 – A$93.00 – at Vine [941]
DEVONSHIRE, 1923 : BRITISH ISLES CENSUS DIRECTORIES PROJECT, ENGLAND. VOL 264 – 15mf – 9 – A$93.00 – at Vine [941]
DEVONSHIRE (EXETER, PLYMOUTH AND TIVERTON), 1805 : BRITISH ISLES CENSUS DIRECTORIES PROJECT, ENGLAND. VOL 177 – 1mf – 9 – A$9.00 – at Vine [941]
DEVONSHIRE FREEHOLDER – Plymouth, England. 18 Sept 1824-31 May 1828. -w. 1 reel – 1 – uk British Libr Newspaper [072]
DEVONSHIRE REPORT / Great Britain. Royal Commission for the Advancement of Science – 1871-75 – 9 – uk Microform Academic [324]
Devot, J *see* LA NATIONALITE ET SON INFLUENCE...
DEVOTA CORONA...A LA VIRGEN MARIA – 1855 – 9 – 1.50f – sp Bibl Santa Ana [240]
A DEVOTEE / Cholmondeley, Mary – British Fiction Archive: Unit 3 – 9 – uk Bell [830]
DEVOTION TO THE BLESSED VIRGIN : BEING THE SUBSTANCE OF ALL THE SERMONS FOR MARY'S FEASTS TROUGHOUT THE YEAR / Bossuet, Jacques Benigne – London; New York: Longmans, Green, 1903 – 1mf – 9 – 0-8370-6886-X – 1986-0886 – us A.T.L.A. [240]
IL DEVOTISSIMO VIAGGIO DIE GIERVSALEMME / Zuallart, H – Roma, 1595 – 4mf – 9 – H-8383/1 – ne IDC [956]
DEVUSHKI BOSIKOM / Kamenskii, V – Stikhi. 1917. Izd. "Progress." Tiflis. 1916. BR-939 2 – 8 – ne IDC [460]
DEVX LIVRES, L'VN DE LA PUISSANCE & SAPIENCE DE DIEU, L'AUTRE DE LA VOLONTE DE DIEU / Hermes Trismegistus – Le tout Traduit de Grec en Francois par Gabriel du Preau. Paris, 1557 – 1 – us U.W. Library [240]
DEW DROPS – Toronto: W Briggs, [1897-19–] – 9 – cn C.I.H.M. [240]
DEWAN GEREDJA-GEREDJA DI INDONESIA: TEMPAT PERMUSJAWARATAN DAN USAHA BERSAMA MENUDJU KE-ESAAN GEREDJA DI INDONESIA – SE-4247 1 – 9 – ne IDC [950]
DEWAN NORMALISASI INDONESIA. PERATURAN TJAT INDONESIA – SE-4599 1. 1961 – 9 – ne IDC [950]
DEWAN PERWAKILAN RAKJAT DAERAH GOTONG ROJONG. LAPORAN HASIL SIDANG SEKSI A. / Batang, Indonesia (Kabupaten) – Batang, 1970 – 2mf – 9 – SE-1342/1 – ne IDC [950]
Dewantara, Ki Hadjar *see* TAMAN-INDRYA, KINDERGARTEN
Dewar, D *see* BOMBAY DUCKS
Dewar, Daniel *see* THE HOLY SPIRIT: HIS PERSONALITY, DIVINITY, OFFICE AND AGENCY, IN THE REGENERATION AND SANCTIFICATION OF MAN
DEWAR HATSOFEH – Amsterdam, 1938-1939 – 1mf – J-261-25/1 – ne IDC [073]
DEWAR HECHALOETS – Amsterdam, 1935-1939. v1-5 – 19mf – J-261-26/1 – ne IDC [073]
Deward, D *see* A HAND-BOOK TO THE ENGLISH PRE-MUTINY RECORDS IN THE GOVERNMENT RECORD ROOMS OF THE UNITED PROVINCES OF AGRA AND OUDH
Dewart, Edward Hartley *see*
- THE DEVELOPMENT OF DOCTRINE
- ESSAYS FOR THE TIMES: STUDIES OF EMINENT MEN AND IMPORTANT LIVING QUESTIONS
- THE FALLS OF NIAGARA
- JESUS THE MESSIAH IN PROPHECY AND FULFILMENT: A REVIEW AND REFUTATION OF THE NEGATIVE THEORY OF MESSIANIC PROPHECY
- SONGS OF LIFE: A COLLECTION OF POEMS
- WAYMARKS, OR COUNSEL AND ENCOURAGEMENT FOR PENITENT SEEKERS OF SALVATION

DEWEESE BOOSTER – Deweese, NE. -w. Apr. 1915-May 1918; Jul. 1918-Sep. 1918 – 1 – us NE Hist [071]
Dewey, Davis R *see* FINANCIAL HISTORY OF THE UNITED STATES
Dewey, Fred Perkins *see* SOME CANADIAN IRON ORES
Dewey John *see* ETHICS
Dewey, John *see*
- THE INFLUENCE OF DARWIN ON PHILOSOPHY, AND OTHER ESSAYS IN CONTEMPORARY THOUGHT
- LEIBNIZ'S NEW ESSAYS CONCERNING THE HUMAN UNDERSTANDING
- MORAL PRINCIPLES IN EDUCATION

Dewey, Lyster Hoxie *see* LEGISLATION AGAINST WEEDS
Dewey, Melvil *see* KLASIFIKASI PERSEPULUNAN DEWEY AND INDEKS RELATIF
Dewey, Orville *see*
- DISCOURSES AND DISCUSSIONS IN EXPLANATION AND DEFENCE OF UNITARIANISM
- DISCOURSES ON HUMAN LIFE
- DISCOURSES ON VARIOUS SUBJECTS
- MORAL VIEWS OF COMMERCE, SOCIETY AND POLITICS
- THE OLD WORLD AND THE NEW
- THE PROBLEM OF HUMAN DESTINY
- THE TWO GREAT COMMANDMENTS
- THE UNITARIAN'S ANSWER

Dewey, Thomas Henry *see* A TREATISE ON CONTRACTS FOR FUTURE DELIVERY AND COMMERCIAL WAGERS, INCLUDING "OPTIONS," "FUTURES," AND "SHORT SALES."
DEWI ANGGRAENI: WANITA BERNASIB MALANG / Badjaranputera – SE-4513 1. 1962 – 9 – ne IDC [950]
Dewick, E S *see*
- CORONATION BOOK OF CHARLES 5 OF FRANCE
- FACSIMILES OF HORAE DE B.M.V. 11TH CENTURY
- THE LEOFRIC COLLECTAR, VOL. 1
- THE MARTILOGE IN ENGLYSSHE AFTER THE USE OF THE CHURCH OF SALISBURY AND AS IT REDDE IN SYON. WITH ADDICYONS

DeWindt, Edwin Brezette *see* THE COURT ROLLS OF RAMSEY, HEPMANGROVE AND BURY, 1268-1600
DEWITT ADVERTISER – DeWitt, NE. -bw. May 1874-Sep. 1874 – 1 – us NE Hist [071]
DEWITT EAGLE – DeWitt, NE. -w. Aug. 1894-Aug. 1895. Incomplete; Oct. 1895-Aug. 1902; Jan. 1903-Sep. 1907 – 1 – us NE Hist [071]
DEWITT NEWS – DeWitt, NE. -w. Aug. 1902-May 1903 – 1 – us NE Hist [071]
DEWITT REPUBLICAN – DeWitt, NE. -w. Jan. 1904-Sep. 1904 – 1 – us NE Hist [071]
DEWITT TIMES-NEWS – DeWitt, NE. -w. Sep. 1881-Dec. 1890; Jun. 1892; Mar. 1893-Mar. 1894; May 1894-Apr. 1900; Jun. 1900-Oct. 1900; Dec. 1900- – 1 – us NE Hist [071]
DEWITT'S BASE-BALL GUIDE – New York. 1869-1885 – 1 – us NY Public [790]
DEWITT'S BASEBALL GUIDE – 1869-85 – 1r – 1 – us Ross [790]
Dewitz, B C de *see* DE IURE PRAECEDENDI...
DeWolf, Charles Wesley *see* DIARY
Dewolfe, Harry F *see* DIARY
Dewora, Viktor Joseph *see* BRIEFE UND GESPRAECHE VERANLASST DURCH DIE ENTFUEHRUNG UND GEFANGENSCHAFTSREISE DES HEILIGEN VATERS PIUS DES SIEBENTEN, VON ROM NACH SAWONNA IM JULI UND AUGUST 1809, GESAMMELT UND ZUR BELEHRUNG UND ERBAUUNG SEINER MITCHRISTEN
DEWSBURY REPORTER – England. -w. 1869-84. (15 reels) – 1 – uk British Libr Newspaper [072]
Dewsbury. Yorkshire *see* PARISH REGISTERS
Dexippi et al *see* HISTORIARUM QUAE SUPERSUNT (CSHB 14)
Dexter, Henry M *see* THE MORAL INFLUENCE OF MANUFACTURING TOWNS
Dexter, Henry Martyn *see*
- AS TO ROGER WILLIAMS AND HIS 'BANISHMENT' FROM THE MASSACHUSETTS PLANTATION
- THE ENGLAND AND HOLLAND OF THE PILGRIMS
- A GLANCE AT THE ECCLESIASTICAL COUNCILS OF NEW ENGLAND
- A HANDBOOK OF CONGREGATIONALISM
- THE TRUE STORY OF JOHN SMYTH, THE SE-BAPTIST

Dexter, Morton *see* THE ENGLAND AND HOLLAND OF THE PILGRIMS
DEXTER SMITH'S MUSICAL, LITERARY, DRAMATIC AND ART PAPER – Boston. v1-14. 1872-78 – 2r – 1 – £115.00 – uk Chadwyck [780]
Dexter-Fogarty, Tracey *see* THE EFFECTIVENESS OF THE HINGED GOLF CLUB AS A TRAINING AID TO DEVELOP CONSISTENCY IN NOVICE GOLFERS
DEXTER-SMITH'S – Boston. 1-14, 1872-78. Incomplete – 1 – 23.00 – us L of C Photodup [780]
Dey, Sushil Kumar *see* GOTONGROYONG,OR
Deycks, Ferdinand *see* FRIEDRICH HEINRICH JACOBI IM VERHAELTNIS ZU SEINEN ZEITGENOSSEN, BESONDERS ZU GOETHE
Deyo *see* ILLUSTRATED HISTORY OF KENNEBEC COUNTY

Dez. J *see* AD VIRUM NOBILEM DE CULTU CONFUCII PHILOSOPHI ET PROGENITORUM APUD SINAS

Dezallier d'Argenville, A J *see* ABREGE DE LA VIE DES PLUS FAMEUX PEINTRES...

Dezallier d'Argenville, AN *see* VIES DES FAMEUX ARCHITECTES [ET SCULPTEURS] DEPUIS LA RENAISSANCE DES ARTS...

Dezallier d'Argenville, Antoine Joseph *see*
- ABREGE DE LA VIE DES PLUS FAMEUX PEINTRES
- LA THEORIE ET LA PRATIQUE DU JARDINAGE

Dezeimeris, Jean E *see* DICTIONNAIRE HISTORIQUE DE LA MEDECINE ANCIENNE ET MODERNE (AEL, ABT 3;17)

Dezell, Robert *see* LOST TRACK OF A DAY: A STRICTURE ON SEVENTH DAY TEACHING AND SABBATH DESECRATION

DEZENOVE DE DEZEMBRO – Curitiba, 1 Apr 1854-15 Feb 1890 – 1,5,6 – bl Biblioteca [072]

DEZESEIS DE JULHO : FOLHA POLITICA E LITTERARIA – Rio de Janeiro, 4 Jul-Oct, Dec 1869; Jan-2 Jul 1870 – 1,5,6 – bl Biblioteca [072]

D.F. STRAUSS' DAS LEBEN JESU / Parker, Theodore – Christian Examiner, 28, 1840; und, The Relation of the Bible to the Soul. Western Messenger, 8. 1840-41 – 9 – us A.T.L.A. [240]

D'Hainaut, L *see* EDUCATIONAL SYSTEMS REGULATION

Dhalla, Maneckji Nusservanji *see*
- NYAISHES OR ZOROASTRIAN LITANIES
- ZOROASTRIAN THEOLOGY: FROM THE EARLIEST TIMES TO THE PRESENT DAY

THE DHAMMAPADA / ed by Mueller, Friedrich Max – (Translated from Pali by F. Max Mueller, and The Sutta-Nipata. Translated from Pali by V. Fausboell; being Canonical Books of the Buddhists) – 1881 – 7mf – 8 – ne Slangenburg [280]

DHARMA WORLD – 1974-89 – 6r – 1 – us A.T.L.A. [280]

D'Hautel *see* DICTIONNAIRE DU BAS LANGAGE

Dhauteville, J *see* LE FRANCAIS ALSACIEN

DHESA NESAN WEEKLY – Penang, Malaysia. In Tamil. -w. 9 April 1933-28 Feb 1940. 5 reels – 1 – uk British Libr Newspaper [072]

d'Hoop, F-G *see* RECEUIL DES CHARTES DU PRIEURE DE SAINT-BERTIN A POPERINGHE, ET DE SES DEPENDANCES

Dhorme, P *see* LE LIVRE JOB. ETB

DI BRUKLIN BRONZVIL POST = THE E.N.Y. AND BROWNSVILLE POST – Brooklyn [NY]: E N Y, Brooklyn and Brownsville Post Publ Co, dec 1917-1919 – 1r – us Res Libr [071]

Di Bruno, Joseph Fa a *see* CATHOLIC BELIEF

DI CAIT – Vilnius, 1924-37 – 22r – 1 – $1,650.00 – us Ross [072]

DI ELO ROSSII (NEWSPAPER) – (Includes c.1: 1920:Mar.20-26, Apr.5-May 18, July 10-16) – Tokio: A.I A. Gutman (A. Gan), 1920- – 1 – CSUXANR1952-S – us Hoover Inst Photo [947]

Di Tella, Guido *see*
- ARGENTINA UNDER PERON, 1973-76
- ARGENTINA UNDER PERON, 1973-76. SPANISH PERON-PERON, 1973-1976

EL DIA – Mexico D.F., MX. 1967-1977 – 40r – $2,000.00 – R04225 – us Library Micro [072]

EL DIA – Tegucigalpa, Honduras: J L Pineda, [jan, apr, jun 1954] – 1 – us Res Libr [072]

EL DIA – Tegucigalpa, Honduras: J L Pineda, jan, apr, jun 1954 – us Res Libr [072]

O DIA : DIARIO DO COMMERCIO, INDUSTRIA E LAVOURA – Juiz de Fora, 9, 10 Oct 1918; Dec 1919; Apr 1921; 12 Nov 1922 – 1,5,6 – bl Biblioteca [072]

O DIA – Lisbon. Nos.1-1251; 11 Dec 1975-14 Feb 1980. Incomplete. (Portuguese Revolution of 1974. Newspapers from Portugal publ. from 21 Feb 1971-15 Feb 1980, collected and filmed by University of Wisconsin-Madison Libraries.) – 1 – us U.W. Library [072]

EL DIA DE COLON Y DE LA PAZ. 12 DE OCTUBRE DE 1492-12 DE OCTUBRE DE 1918 2ND ED OVIEDO, 1933 / Gonzales, Jose Maria – Madrid: Razon y Fe, 1934 – 1 – sp Bibl Santa Ana [946]

EL DIA DE COLON Y LA PAZ. MADRID, 1930 / Gonzales, Jose Maria – Madrid: Razon y Fe, 1930 – 1 – sp Bibl Santa Ana [946]

DIA DE LA CANCION / Delegacion Provincial del Frente de Juventudes – Badajoz: Tip. Vda. A. Arqueros, 1942 – sp Bibl Santa Ana [780]

DIA DE LA RECONQUISTA : DISCURSOS PRONUNCIADOS EN EL FUERTE DE BARRAG AN POR EL EXCMO. SR. GOBERNADOR DE BUENOS AIRES DON CARLOS ALOE Y EL CONTRALMIRANTE DON ROLANDO A. ESTEVERANA EL 12 DE AGOSTO DE 1953 / Aloe, Carlos – [n.p.] Eva Peron, 1953 – 1 – CSUXAJA8428-B – us Hoover Inst Photo [370]

DIA DEL SEMINARIO / Plasencia. Seminario Diocesano – Plasencia: La Victoria, 1960 – sp Bibl Santa Ana [240]

EL DIA FAMILIAR / Sanchez Arjona, Vicente – Sevilla: Imprenta Alvarez, 1956 – 1 – sp Bibl Santa Ana [810]

DIA FESTIVO...GUADALUPE...PROCESION / Zafra, Manuel de – 1755 – 9 – 1.50f – sp Bibl Santa Ana [240]

EL DIA HISTORICO. CARACAS, 1929 / Machado, Jose E – Madrid: Razon y Fe, 1930 – 1 – sp Bibl Santa Ana [946]

DIABETES – v1-5. 1952-56 – 1,5,6 – us Princeton Micro [616]

DIABETES CARE – (v.3-. 1980-. 5,6,9) – v.1-. 1978- – 1 – us UMI [616]

DIABETES FORECAST *see* ADA FORECAST

DIABETES LITERATURE INDEX – v.5-9. 1970-74 – 1,5,6 – 22161.00 – us Princeton Micro [610]

DIABETES MELLITUS IM ALTER / Naurath, Hans Joachim – 1995 – 4mf – 9 – DM112.00 – 3-8267-2102-0 – gw Hänsel [616]

DIABETES-METABOLISM REVIEWS – 1985- – 1,5,6,9 – us UMI [616]

DIABETIC JOURNAL – 1935-59 – 1 – uk Microform Academic [616]

DIABETIC MEDICINE: A JOURNAL OF THE BRITISH DIABETIC ASSOCIATION – v1-. 1984- – 1,5,6,9 – us UMI [616]

DIABETOLOGIA – v. 1-19. 1965-80 – 1,5,9 – 1682.00 – us UMI [073]

DIABINHO : JORNAL CRITICO E LITTERARIO – Manaos, Amazonas. 18 Out-8 Nov 1885 – 1,5,6 – bl Biblioteca [072]

O DIABINHO : ORGAO DEMOCRATICO E CRITICO – Antonio Dias, 22 Dec 1884-Dec 1885; May 1887; May-Jun, Aug-Oct, Dec 1888; Jan-Mar, May-5 June 1889 – 1,5,6 – bl Biblioteca [072]

LE DIABLE A BRUXELLES / Hymans, Louis Salomon & Rousseau, Jean-Baptist – Bruxelles. 1853. 2v. 272p. (Historical Studies Series) – 9 – 18.00 – fr Bibl Nationale [240]

LE DIABLE A QUATRE – Quebec, Canada. 9 nov 1878 – 1r – 1 – Can$25.00 – cn Can Microfilming [072]

LE DIABLE BLEU – Montreal, Canada. 8 nov 1843; v1 n8. 28 dec 1843 – 1r – 1 – Can$25.00 – cn Can Microfilming [072]

LE DIABLE EST AUX VACHES : ET VIE DE JEUNESSE DE JOHNNY CASSEPINETTE / La Glebe, Jean de – Quebec: [s.n.], 1923. SEM105P1309 – 2mf – 9 – Can$4.50 – cn Bibl Nat [420]

LE DIABLE ET LES ELECTIONS – Paris, [1848?] – us Res Libr [320]

LE DIABLE ROSE – [Paris]: Imp de Bureau. [n1-3. jun 15-29 1848] – us Res Libr [072]

DIABLO BEACON – Concord, CA. 1949; 1951-1967 – 5r – 1 – $250.00 – B03588 – us Library Micro [071]

EL DIABLO MUNDO / Espronceda, Jose de – (1849 ed.1.50f; 9. 1852 ed.1.50f; BSA; 9. 1875 ed.1.50f; BSA; 9) – 1841 – 9 – 1.50f – sp Bibl Santa Ana [830]

EL DIABLO MUNDO / Espronceda, Jose de – Buenos Aires: Emece, editores, s.a. 1942 – 1 – sp Bibl Santa Ana [946]

O DIABO : CRITICO LITTERARIO JOCO-SERIO – Maceio, Alagoas. 13 Dez 1891 – 1,5,6 – bl Biblioteca [072]

O DIABO – Lisbon. Nos.1-161; 10 Feb 1976-29 Jan 1980. Incomplete. (Portuguese Revolution of 1974. Newspapers from Portugal publ. from 21 Feb 1971-15 Feb 1980, collected and filmed by University of Wisconsin-Madison Libraries.) – 1 – us U.W. Library [072]

O DIABO – Passo de Camaragibe, Alagoas. 23 Jun, 15 Ago 1896 – 1,5,6 – bl Biblioteca [072]

O DIABO : PERIODICO CRITICO, CHISTOSO E MORALISADOR – [s.l.]. 25 Ago 1889 – 1,5,6 – bl Biblioteca [072]

DIABO AZUL : PERIODICO LITTERARIO, CRITICO E CHISTOSO – Curityba, 2-9 Jun 1878 – 1,5,6 – bl Biblioteca [072]

Diabouniotis, C *see* HIPPOLYTS SCHRIFT UEBER DIE SEGNUNGEN JAKOBS (T.U.U. 3-38/1A)

O DIABRETE : CRITICO, LITTERARIO E NOTICIOSO – [s.l.]. 23 Ago, Set, 15 Out 1885 – 1,5,6 – bl Biblioteca [072]

D'iachenko, G *see* POLNYI TSERKOVNO-SLAVIANSKII SLOVAR'

Diachkov-Tarasov, V *see* O NOVOI SILIE V REVOLIUTSIONNYKH KADRAKH

DIACONI CASINENSIS IN SANCTAM REGULAM COMMENTARIUM / Warnefridi, Pauli – Monte Casino, 1880 – 15mf – 8 – Dfl53.00 – ne Slangenburg [240]

Diaconi, Leonis *see* HISTORIA SCRIPTORESQUE ALII AD RES BYZANTINAS PERTINENTES (CBH 39)

Diacono, Paulo *see* LIBER DE VITA ET MIRACLES

Diaconus, Paulus *see* HISTORIA, ETC

Diadichenko, A N *see* STATISTICHESKII SPRAVOCHNIK

Diagne, M *see* L'ENCEPHALE DES CHONDROSTEENS

DIAGNOSE DES TECHNISCHEN ZUSTANDES UND DES INNENRAUMZUSTANDES VON GASLEITUNGEN UNTER DER BEDINGUNG UNVOLLSTAENDIGER INFORMATION / Heymer, Juergen – 1993 – 2mf – 9 – DM98.00 – 3-89349-674-2 – gw Hänsel [670]

DIAGNOSES LICHENUM SOCOTRENSIUM NOVORUM A PARTICIBUS EXPEDITIONUM BAYLEY BALFOUR ET SCHWEINFURTH LECTORUM / Mueller, J A – Edinburgh, 1882. B-5387 2 – 8 – ne IDC [580]

DIAGNOSES PHYCOLOGICAE / Montagne, J P F C – Ann. Sci. Nat. s. 3, 1852, v. 18. p. 302-319. B-5076 2 – 8 – ne IDC [580]

DIAGNOSES PLANTARUM NOVARUM HISPANICARUM / Boissier, E P & Reuter, G F – Geneve. 1842. B-5540 2 – 8 – ne IDC [580]

DIAGNOSES PLANTARUM ORIENTALIUM NOVARUM / Boissier, E P – 3v. Geneve etc. 1842-59; (S.1 (1-3). 2 v. Leipzig. 1842-54; S.2 (1-6). 1 v. Leipzig. Paris. 1854-59). B-5407 2 – 8 – ne IDC [580]

DIAGNOSIS – v.1. 1979 – 1,5,6,9 – us UMI [616]

THE DIAGNOSIS AND TREATMENT OF POSTURAL DEFECTS / Phelps, Winthrop M & Kiphuth, R – 1932 – 4mf – 9 – $12.00 – us Microform Publ [610]

DIAGNOSIS AND VACCINATION FOR THE CONTROL OF BRUCELLOSIS IN THE NEAR EAST – 1982 – 45p – it F.A.O. [636]

DIAGNOSIS OF THE MENTAL HYGIENE PROBLEMS OF COLLEGE WOMEN BY MEANS OF PERSONALITY RATINGS / Rice, Mary Berenice – Washington, 1937 – 2mf – DM62.00 – 3-8267-3093-3 – gw Hänsel [616]

DIAGNOSTIC AND THERAPEUTIC ENDOSCOPY / ed by Kato, Harubumi – 9,5,1 – us Harwood [617]

DIAGNOSTIC GYNECOLOGY AND OBSTETRICS *see* AMERICAN JOURNAL OF DIAGNOSTIC GYNECOLOGY AND OBSTETRICS

DIAGNOSTIC IMAGING – (1982-. 1,5,6,9) – v1-. 1979- – 1 – us UMI [616]

DIAGNOSTIC MEDICINE – v.1. 1978 – 1,5,6,9 – us UMI [616]

DIAGNOSTIC ONCOLOGY – v3-. 1993- – 1,5,9 – us UMI [616]

DIAGNOSTIC STATISTICS OF HOSPITALIZED PATIENTS 1971 / Israel. Prime Minister's Office. Central Bureau of Statistics – Jerusalem. 1975. 17, 241, 17 p. (Special Series no. 482). In cooperation with the Ministry of Health. Text also in Hebrew – 9 – 6.00 – is I.T.T.I. [310]

DIAGNOSTIQUE – (v.6. 1980 5,6,9) – v.1. 1975 – 1 – us UMI [073]

DIAGRAMMES ET SURFACES THERMODYNAMIQUES / Gibbs, Josiah Willard – Evreux: C. Herissey, 1903. 86p.1 fiche. (Science Collection) – 9 – 6.00 – fr Bibl Nationale [530]

DIAKONIA : A QUARTERLY DEVOTED TO ADVANCING ORTHODOX-CATHOLIC DIALOGUE – 1(1966)-8(1973) – 72mf – 9 – Dfl252.00 – ne Slangenburg [073]

DIAKONIE, FESTFREUDE UND ZELOS IN VERBINDUNG MIT DER ALTCHRISTLICHEN AGAPENFEIER / Reicke, B – Uppsala, 1951 – 9mf – 8 – ne Slangenburg [240]

DIAKONIE UND DIAKINIE IM RHEINLAND – 1964-90 (complete) – 13r – 1 – ATLA S0767 – us A.T.L.A. [073]

D'lakonov, M M *see* RUKOPISI SHAKH-NAME V LENINGRADSKIKH SOBRANIIAKH

Diakonova, Elizaveta Aleksandrovna *see* DNEVNIK ELIZAVETY DIAKONOVO I: NA VYSSHIKH ZHENSKIKH KURSAKH (1895-1899 G.)

D"iakov, FB *see* PRAVOVYE OSNOVY PROMYSLOVOINOGO KONTROLIA

DIAL – 1-86. 1880-1929 – 1 – us UMI [073]

DIAL – 1980 – 1,5,6,9 – us UMI [073]

THE DIAL – Chicago. v1-86. 1880-1929 – 27r – 1 – us Ross [073]

THE DIAL : A MAGAZINE FOR LITERATURE, PHILOSOPHY AND RELIGION – Boston. v1-4. 1840-44 – 1r – 1 – us Ross [073]

DIAL BAPTIST CHURCH. HONEY GROVE, TEXAS : CHURCH RECORDS – 1893-1954. Formerly Pleasant Hill Baptist Church. Name changed Jul 1904. 342p – 1 – 15.39 – us Baptist [240]

LES DIALBES ROUGES / Date, Henry Harrington – s.l.: s.n., 1890 (Montreal: L'Etendard). 02689. (Pre-1900 Canadiana) – 9 – cn C.I.H.M. [971]

LES DIALECTES BELGO-ROMANS – Bruxelles, 1937-1939. v1-3 – 12mf – H-10028/1 – ne IDC [440]

LES DIALECTES NEO-ARAMEENS DE SALAMAS : TEXTES SUR L'ETAT ACTUEL DE LA PERSE ET CONTES POPULAIRES – (Text in Aramaic and French; introduction in French. Includes bibliographical references) – Paris: F Vieweg, 1883 – 1mf – 9 – 0-8370-7627-7 – 1986-1627 – us A.T.L.A. [470]

DIALECTICAL ANTHROPOLOGY – v1-9. 1976-84 – 1,5,6,13 – sz Elsevier [301]

DIALECTICS – 1-9 (all publ). 1937-1939 – 4mf – 9 – $35.00 – us UPA [430]

LA DIALECTIQUE / Launay, G de – 1673 – 9 – fr I.C.S. [160]

LA DIALECTIQUE / Ramus, Peter – 1577 – 9 – fr I.C.S. [440]

DER DIALEKT IN DEN DORFGESCHICHTEN BERTHOLD AUERBACHS UND MELCHIOR MEYRS / Glueck, Hermann – (Includes bibliography) – Tuebingen: H Laupp, 1914 – 1r – 1 – us U.W. Library [430]

DIALEKTIKE ISKUSSTVA / Chuzhak, N K – Teoreticheski-polemicheskie stat'i. Chita. 1921. BR-2044 2 – 8 – ne IDC [460]

DIALEKTOLOGICHESKI SEKTOR / Akademiia Nauk. SSSR Institut Russkovo Yazyka – Moscow 1947-49. Byulleten'. Vyp. 1-6 – 1 – us NY Public [073]

DIALEKTOLOGICHNYI BIULETEN' – Kiev, 1949-1960. v. 1-7. Lacking: v. 4. BR-1721 2 – 8 – ne IDC [073]

DER DIALOG BEI DEN CHRISTLICHEN SCHRIFTSTELLERN DER ERSTEN VIER JAHRHUNDERTE (T.U.U. 5-96) / Hoffmann, M – Berlin, 1966 – 4mf – 9 – ne Slangenburg [240]

DIALOGI DI MESSER DELLA INVENTIONE POETICA / Lionardi, Allesandro – 1554. British Museum – 1 – uk Microform Academic [410]

EL DIALOGO CON LOS HIJOS / Perez Lozano, Jose Maria – Madrid: PPC, 1966 – 1 – sp Bibl Santa Ana [946]

DIALOGO CON UN TURISTA. REPORTAJE GRAFICO-HISTORICO SOBRE SAN PEDRO DE ALCANTARA. MADRID, 1969 / Corredor, Antonio – Madrid: Graf. Calleja, 1969 – 1 – sp Bibl Santa Ana [240]

DIALOGO DE LA INFANCIA Y ADOLESCENCIA / Montero y Santaren, Eulogio – 1892 – 9 – 1.50f – sp Bibl Santa Ana [370]

DIALOGO DELL'IMPRESE MILITARI ET AMOROSE / Giovio, Paolo – O-271. 1574 – 9 – ne IDC [760]

DIALOGO DELL'IMPRESE MILITARI ET AMOROSE, DI MONSIGNOR GIOVIO VESCOVO DI NOCERA / Giovio, Paolo – O 267. 1556 – 9 – ne IDC [760]

DIALOGO DI CARACOSA, E CARONTE, IL QUALE GLI NEGA IL PASSO DELLA SUA BARCA / Caracosa – Venetia, [1572] – 1mf – 9 – H-8416/1 – ne IDC [945]

DIALOGO DI VINCENTIO GALILEI NOBILE FIORENTINO DELLA MUSICA ANTICA, ET DELLA MODERNA / Galilei, V – 1581 – 9 – us Sibley [780]

EL DIALOGO SEXUAL / Aradillas Agudo, Antonio – Madrid: A.Q. Ediciones, S.A., 1976 – 1 – sp Bibl Santa Ana [306]

DIALOGO SOPRA LA MIRACOLOSA VITTORIA OTTENVTA DALL' ARMATA DELLA SANTISSIMA LEGA CHRISTIANA, CONTRA LA TURCHESCA / Meduna, B – Venetia, 1572 – 1mf – 9 – H-8332/1 – ne IDC [956]
DIALOGO TEOLOGICO – 1973. No. 1 & No. 2. 202p – 1 – 7.07 – us Baptist [240]
DIALOGO TEOLOGICO – Buenos Aires, Argentina: Asociacion Bautista de Instituciones Teologicas Hispanoamericanas: distribuido por la Casa Bautista de Publicaciones. n1-34. 1973-89 – 2r – 1 – us Res Libr [072]
DIALOGORUM DE LINGUAE GALLICAE ORIGINE... / Perionius, J – Parisiis, 1555 – 4mf – 9 – ne IDC [440]
DIALOGOS CON FRONDIZI / Frondizi, Arturo – [Buenos Aires]: Editorial Desarrollo, [1963] – 1 – CSUXADJ8397-B – us Hoover Inst Photo [972]
DIALOGOS DE LA CONQUISTA...DIOS / Juan de los Angeles – 1595 – 9 – 1.50f – sp Bibl Santa Ana [240]
DIALOGOS DE LA PINTURA / Carducho, Vincencio – O-190. 1633 – 9 – ne IDC [760]
DIALOGOS DE LOS MUERTOS DE LUCIANO / Franco y Lozano, Francisco – 1882 – 9 – 1.50f – sp Bibl Santa Ana [946]
DIALOGOS MORALES DE LUCIANO / Lucian; ed by Herrera Maldonado, Francisco – 1796 – 9 – 1.50f – sp Bibl Santa Ana [450]
DIALOGOS PARA EL FUTURO / Estrella Estralla, Jose Emilio – Madrid: Graf. Menor, 1966 – sp Bibl Santa Ana [946]
DIALOGOS SINDICALES ENTRE PERONISTAS Y COMUNISTAS / Iscaro, Rubens – Buenos Aires: Editorial Fundamentos, 1974 – 9 – us Hoover Inst Photo [320]
DIALOGUE – (1986-. 1,5,6) – 1978- – 9 – us UMI [073]
DIALOGUE – A journal of Mormon thought – v1- 1966- 1; v10- 5,6,9 – us UMI [240]
A DIALOGUE BETWEEN A GENTLEMAN OF LONDON...AND AN HONEST ALDERMAN OF THE COUNTRY PARTY / Fielding, Henry – London: Printed for M. Cooper, 1747. SEM16P231 – 1r – 5 – Can$9.00 – cn Bibl Nat [941]
A DIALOGUE BETWEEN A PREACHER OF INHERENT RIGHTEOUSNESS AND A PREACHER OF GOD'S RIGHTEOUSNESS, REVEAL'D FROM FAITH TO FAITH;... / Cudworth, W – London, 1745 – 1mf – 9 – MP-323/1 – ne IDC [240]
A DIALOGUE BETWEEN THE PULPIT AND READING DESK / Green, William – London, 1767 – 1mf – 9 – MP-444/1 – ne IDC [240]
DIALOGUE DE LA LYCANTHROPIE OU TRANSFORMATION D'HOMMES EN LOUP / Prieur, P Claude Le – Louvain. 1596 – 9 – fr Hachette [360]
DIALOGUE DE L'ORTHOGRAPHE E PRONONCIATION FRANCOESE / Peletier du Mans, J – 1550 – 9 – fr I.C.S. [440]
DIALOGUE ENTRE DEUX MONDES / Catalogne, Gerard de – Paris. 1931 – 1 – fr A.C.R.P.P. [900]
DIALOGUE ENTRE VICTOR ET LE PERE ANDRE SUR LA RELIGION SAINT-SIMONIENNE / Morainville – Nantes, impr. d'Herault, s.d., 16 p. Explication de la religion Saint-Simonienne. Nantes, impr. V. Mangin, s.d., 12 p. Foi Nouvelle. Nantes, impr. V. Mangin, 1833, 8 p. Rene-Eugene: A Dieux a la Famille de Paris. Lettre aux Mayennais. Paris, Johanneau, 1834, 36 p. Les Saint-Simoniens, 1825-1834. 6936 – 9 – fr Hachette [335]
A DIALOGUE ON CHRISTIANITY FOR MY CHINESE FRIENDS (CCC1) / Adams, Archibald G – (In Chinese) – Shanghai: Publication Dept., National Committee, YMCAs of China, 1922 – 1r – 1 – 0-8370-1701-7 – 1984-6090 – us A.T.L.A. [240]
DIALOGUE SUR LA MUSIQUE DES ANCIENS / Chateauneuf, Francois de Castagneres, Abbe de – P 210. 1725 – 9 – ne IDC [930]
DIALOGUE SUR LA MUSIQUE DES ANCIENS: A MONSIEUR DE / Chateauneuf, Francois de Castagneres, Abbe de – Paris: N Pissot, 1725 – 1 – us Sibley [780]
DIALOGUE DE LA PAIX, ET DE LA GUERRE – Paris, 1649 – 1mf – 1 – ILM-998/1 – ne IDC [327]
DIALOGUES D'UN SAINT-SIMONIEN SUR LA RELIGION SAINT-SIMONIENNE / Neveux – Paris, impr. de Setier, s.d., 8 p. Les Saint-Simoniens, 1825-1834. 6992 – 9 – fr Hachette [335]
DIALOGUES ENTRE CHARLES QUINT ET FRANCOIS PREMIER... – N.p., n.d. – 1mf – 1 – ILM-2892/1 – ne IDC [327]
DIALOGUES FAMILIERS SUR LES PRINCIPALES OBJECTIONS DES MISSIONNAIRES DE CE TEMPS / Drelincourt, C – N.p., 1648 – 4mf – 9 – CA-125/1 – ne IDC [240]
DIALOGUES PAR UN MINISTRE SUISSE / Vernes, Jacob – s.l.: s.n; 1763 – 1 – us U.W. Library [949]
DIALOGUES SUR LA MUSIQUE / Villers, C de – 1774 – 9 – us Sibley [780]
DIALOGUS DE GESTIS SANCTORUM FRATRUM MINORUM AUCTORE FR. THOMA DE PAPIA / Thomas de Papia – 1923 – 1 – us A.T.L.A. [240]
DIALOGUS DE IMPERIO ET PONTIFICA POTESTATE / Occam, Guillelmus de – Lyon, 1494 – 18mf – 8 – ne Slangenburg [240]
DIALOGUS MALEGRANATUM / Gallus A Koenigsaal, O Cist. – Argentorati, 1474 – 24mf – 8 – Dfl84.00 – ne Slangenburg [240]
DIALOGUS MIRACULORUM / Heisterbach, Caesarius; ed by Strange, J – Keulen, 1851.-2v – 12mf – 8 – ne Slangenburg [290]
EIN DIALOGUS ODER GESPRAECH ETLICHER PERSONEN VOM INTERIM... / Alber, E – [Augsburg, 1557] – 2mf – 9 – ne IDC [240]
DIALOGUS U. GRUENDL. BERICHTUNG GEHALTENER DISPUTATION ZU HOLSTEIN VOM NACHTMAL / (Hoffmann, M) – Strassb. 1529. Title page lacking. BME-176 1 – 9 – ne IDC [240]
A DIALOGVE PHILOSOPHICALL / Tymme, Thomas – 1612 – 72p 1r – 1 – us U.W. Library [190]
DIALOGVS. EIN GOETTLICH VND CHRISTLICH GESPRECK, MIT DEN WEDDERDOEPEREN, SACRAMENTEREREN, VND ANDEREN SECTEN MEHR IM NEDDERLANDE / Vossenholivs, A – Hamborch, N. Wegener. 1575. BME-211 1 – 9 – ne IDC [240]
DIALOGVS ODER. EIN GESPRECHE EINES ESELS VND BERGKNECHTS...DEM SYNODO AUIUM ZU LIEB GESCHRIEBEN / Magdeburg, J – [Luebeck], 1557 – 1mf – 9 – ne IDC [240]
DIALOQUE SUR LA MUSIQUE DES ANCIENS: A MONSIEUR DE *** / Chateauneuf, Francois de Castagneres, Abbe de – Paris: Ches N Pissot, 1725 – 1 – us Sibley [780]
DE DIAMANTBEWERKERS VAN AMSTERDAM / Heertje, H – Amsterdam. 1936. BJ-262-25 1 – 9 – ne IDC [333]
Diamante, Juan Bautista *see* VALOR NO TIENE EDAD Y SANSON DE EXTREMADURA. EL
THE DIAMOND FIELD – Kimberley, South Africa.13 Oct 1870-20 Jul 1877. 2 reels – 1, 16 diazo available at reduced price – sa SA Libr [072]
DIAMOND FIELDS ADVERTISER – Kimberley, South Africa. 23 Mar 1878- – 431r – 1 – sa Microfile [960]
DIAMOND FIELDS ADVERTISER – Kimberley, South Africa. -d. 1906-40. 189 reels – 1 – uk British Libr Newspaper [072]
DIAMOND FIELDS ADVERTISER – (These dates supplement the product offered by Microfile Ltd., Johannesburg) – Kimberley, South Africa. 4 Jan-31 Dec 1884. 4r; 4 Jan 1887-31 Jan 1890. 7r – 1, 16 diazo available at reduced price – sa SA Libr [072]
THE DIAMOND FIELDS EXPRESS – Kimberley, South Africa.18 Jan 1886-12 May 1888. 4 reels – 1, 16 diazo available at reduced price – sa SA Libr [072]
THE DIAMOND FIELDS HERALD – Beaconsfield, South Africa. 1 Jan-31 Dec 1885. 1 reel – 1, 16 diazo available at reduced price – sa SA Libr [072]
THE DIAMOND FIELDS MAIL – Kimberley, South Africa. 9 Jul-1 Sept 1888 – 1r – 1, 16 diazo available at reduced price – sa SA Libr [072]
THE DIAMOND FIELDS MINING NEWS – Kimberley, South Africa.21 Nov 1896-7 Apr 1897. 1 reel – 1, 16 diazo available at reduced price – sa SA Libr [072]
THE DIAMOND FIELDS TIMES – Kimberley, South Africa. 1 Oct 1884-13 Aug 1885 – 3r – 1, 16 diazo available at reduced price – sa SA Libr [072]
DIAMOND FIELDS WITNESS *see* THE DIAMOND FIELDS TIMES
THE DIAMOND MINES OF SOUTH AFRICA : SOME ACCOUNT OF THEIR RISE AND DEVELOPMENT / Williams, Gardner F – 1902 – 1r – 1 – us Ross [622]
THE DIAMOND NEWS – Kimberley, South Africa. 16 Oct 1870-7 Feb 1884 – 19r – 1, 16 diazo available at reduced price – sa SA Libr [072]
DIAN – Djakarta. Incomplete. SE-712 1. 1953-1969 – 9 – ne IDC [073]
DIAN JIAGONG – Electromachining. 1985.F/P 285 – 9 – $4.50f – cc Microforms [073]
DIAN YIN CUANG ZUO – Mainly film scripts. 1959, 1961. 37 ill. LIT67f – 9 – 130.00 – cc Globe [073]
DIANA MALLORY / Ward, Mary Augusta – British Fiction Archive: Unit 2 – 9 – uk Bell [830]
LA DIANA O ARTE DE LA CAZA / Fernandez de Moratin, Nicolas – 1765 – 1mf – 9 – Pta1,000.00 – 84-7848-146-X – sp Pentalfa [946]
Diana, Pierre *see* UN CAS DE CONSCIENCE
DIANA TEMPEST / Cholmondeley, Mary – British Fiction Archive: Unit 3 – 9 – uk Bell [830]
DIANE LA BELLE AVENTURIERE – 303 nos. 1956-1962. SEM16P320 – 4r – 5 – Can$12.00 – cn Bibl Nat [971]
DIANGONG JISHU – Electrotechnics. 1982-. F P250 – 9 – $4.50f – cc Microforms [073]
DIANGONG JISHU ZAZHI – Electrotechnical Journal. 1986.F/P 295 – 9 – $4.50f – cc Microforms [073]
DIANLI XITONG ZIDONGHUA – Automation of Electric Power Systems. In Chinese but English abstracts to the main articles. F p96 – 9 – $4.50f – cc Microforms [073]
Diannyere, Antoine *see* ESSAIS D'ARITHMETIQUE POLITIQUE
DIANXIN JISHU – Telecommunications Technology. 1981-. F P243 – 9 – $4.50f – cc Microforms [073]
DIANXIN KUAIBAO – Telecommunications Information. 1981-. F P237 – 9 – $4.50f – cc Microforms [073]
DIANZI KEXUE JISHU – Electronic Science and Technology. 1981-. F P244 – 9 – $4.50f – cc Microforms [073]
DIANZI KEXUE XUEKAN – Journal of Electronics. In prep. F/P 310 – 9 – 4.00f – cc Microforms [073]
DIANZI XUEBAO – Acta Electronica Sinica. In Chinese but English abstracts to the main articles. F p67 – 9 – 4.00f – cc Microforms [073]
DIANZIXUE TONGXUN – Journal of Electronics. In Chinese but English abstracts to the main articles. F p95 – 9 – 4.00f – cc Microforms [073]
DIAPASON – (v. 70- 1978- 5,6,9) – v. 1-. 1909- – 1 – us UMI [780]
THE DIARI / Reuther, John G – 1981 – 4417p on 49mf – 9 – A$14.70 – at Aboriginal [305]
DIARIES / Alele, Joseph – (English translation from Roviana original) – oct 1940-mar 1943 – 1r – 1 – PMB1100 – at Pacific Mss [920]
DIARIES / Anderson, Chandler P – 1914-28, 1934 – 1 – 72.00 – us L of C Photodup [920]
DIARIES / Bartholomew, Elam – 1871-1934 – 1 – us KS Hist [920]
DIARIES / Bocker Family – 1895-1952 – 1 – us KS Hist [978]
DIARIES / Bonekemper, Johannes – 1 – 29.40 – us Baptist [240]
DIARIES / Brewer, Mandane Williamson – 1854-60 – 1 – us KS Hist [920]
DIARIES / Bridwell, Arthur – 1903-44 – 1 – us KS Hist [920]
DIARIES / Byers, George D – 1907-24.Incomplete – 1 – $50.00 – us Presbyterian [920]
DIARIES / Dimond, Susan B – 1870-73 – 1 – us KS Hist [920]
DIARIES / Fry, Elizabeth – 1797-1845. With printed index – 1 – £325.00 – uk World [920]
DIARIES / Kelsey, Dandridge E – 1853-1903, Relate to Indiana; Shawnee county, KS; and Salida, Colorado – 1 – us KS Hist [920]
DIARIES / Madden, Frederick – Bodleian Library, Oxford. 1801-73 – 1 – £750.00 – uk World [920]
DIARIES / Nassau, Robert Hamill – 1880-1919 – 1 – $100.00 – us Presbyterian [920]
DIARIES / Ngatu, Ishmael – (English transls and some originals) – 1927-54 – r1-3 – 1 – PMB1109 – at Pacific Mss [920]
DIARIES / Norton Family – 1876-1895, Accounts of life in early Pawnee County, KS. Included are many references to the fort and city of Larned. Most of the entries pertain to agricultural work. Copied and annotated by Helen Norton Starr – 1 – us KS Hist [920]
DIARIES / Parkerson, Harriet – 1891-1900, Diaries of the adopted daughter of Isaac Goodnow – 1 – us KS Hist [920]
DIARIES / Riddle, L H – 1887-1891 – 1 – us KS Hist [978]
DIARIES / Ringi, Daniel – (Photocopy of Roviana original and English transl) – 1951-56 (irreg) – 1r – 1 – PMB1103 – at Pacific Mss [920]
DIARIES / Spotts, David L – 1868-69. Letters received, 1924-28 – 1 – us KS Hist [978]
DIARIES / Thompson, James – 1873-74 – 1 – us KS Hist [978]
DIARIES / Thornton, Anna Maria (Brodeau) – 1793-1863 – 1 – 45.00 – us L of C Photodup [920]
DIARIES / Tozaka, Job – (Photocopy of Roviana originals and English transl) – jun 1925; feb 1936; apr 1937; mar-sep 1942; jan-mar 1946; may-dec 1950 – 1r – 1 – PMB1102 – at Pacific Mss [920]
DIARIES / Trego, Joseph Harrington – 1844-59 – 1 – us KS Hist [978]
DIARIES / Wheeler, John H – 1854-72. Includes material relating to Nicaragua – 1 – 85.00 – us L of C Photodup [920]
DIARIES / Wiberg, Anders – v1-15. 1844-87. 5849p – 1 – 204.71 – us Baptist [240]
DIARIES / Williams, Alice Tapp – 1914-1918. Women's History – 1r – 1 – $32.50r – us Archival [920]
DIARIES, 1767, 1772-1786, 1788-1791 / Bosanquet, M – (Coll title: The People Called Methodists, Phase 2: Primary Sources 1738-1800) – 4mf – 9 – MP-619/1 – ne IDC [240]
DIARIES, 1892, 1899, 1900, 1904 / Banks, Charles W – Rarotonga – 1r – 1 – PMB1068 – at Pacific Mss [920]
DIARIES, 1877-8 NOV 1912 / Rennolds, Edwin Hansford – 2893p – 1 – 101.25 – us Baptist [240]
DIARIES, 1701-1714 / Nicolson, William – 1 – uk Microform Academic [240]
DIARIES, 1742-1744 [FRAGMENTS], 1747-1754 / Bennet, J – (Coll title: The People Called Methodists, Phase 2: Primary Sources 1738-1800) – 2mf – 9 – MP-614/1 – ne IDC [240]
DIARIES, 1777-1815 / Dugdale, B – (Coll title: The People Called Methodists, Phase 2: Primary Sources 1738-1800) – 17mf – 9 – MP-627/1 – ne IDC [240]
DIARIES, 1779-1781, 1784-1797, 1805-1809, 1817-1825 / Yewdall, Z – (Coll title: The People Called Methodists, Phase 2: Primary Sources 1738-1800) – 21mf – 9 – MP-670/1 – ne IDC [240]
DIARIES, 1788-1790, 1805, 1810, 1815-1819, 1821-1828, 1831-1836 / Reece, R – (Coll title: The People Called Methodists, Phase 3: Primary Sources, 1801-1850) – 40mf – 9 – MP-678/1 – ne IDC [240]
DIARIES, 1825-1858 / Woodcock, I – (Coll title: The People Called Methodists, Phase 3: Primary Sources, 1801-1850; Transcript for 1825-1844; Manuscript for 1845-1858) – 7mf – 9 – MP-682/1 – ne IDC [240]
DIARIES, 1845-1846, 1848, 1850, 1852-1858, 1861, 1863, 1867 / Lea, W – (Coll title: The People Called Methodists, Phase 3: Primary Sources, 1801-1850) – 21mf – 9 – MP-688/1 – ne IDC [240]
DIARIES, 1881-1932 / Plunkett, Horace – 1 – uk Microform Academic [920]
DIARIES, 1896-1946 : A DESCRIPTION. COLLECTION EMORY UNIVERSITY / Haden, T H – n.d. – 1mf – 9 – ne IDC [880]
DIARIES, 1897-1898 / Banks, Charles W – Rarotonga – 1r – 1 – PMB1067 – at Pacific Mss [920]
DIARIES, 1914-1919 / Russell, Charles Edward – Washington, DC: Library of Congress Photodup Service, 1979 – us Res Libr [320]
DIARIES, 1934-1966 / Lee, Ada – r1-2 – 1 – PMB1098 – at Pacific Mss [920]
DIARIES, 1953-61 / Eisenhower, Dwight D – 28 reels with printed guide – 1 – $3,080.00 – 0-89093-889-X – us UPA [920]

DIARIES AND ACCOUNT BOOKS / Oakley, Edward Ellsworth - 1859-61 - 1 - us KS Hist [978]
DIARIES AND ACCOUNTS / Stephenson Family - 1881-1948, Diaries and account books of several members of this Osborne County, KS, farm family - 1 - us KS Hist [920]
DIARIES AND CORRESPONDENCE / Carter, Merle - 1946-50 - 1r - 1 - PMB1107 - at Pacific Mss [920]
DIARIES AND MEMOIRS / Brown, George A - 1811-70. BRRAM - 1 - uk Microform Academic [920]
DIARIES AND PAPERS OF BERTHA AND HERMAN BENKE / Benke, Bertha & Benke, Herman C - 1886-93 - 1 - us KS Hist [978]
DIARIES AND PAPERS OF JULIA AND CHARLES LOVEJOY / Lovejoy, Julia L & Lovejoy, Charles H - 1828-64 - 1 - us KS Hist [978]
DIARIES AND POCKET-BOOKS, 1772, 1805, 1809-1810, 1815, 1817, 1822 / Wesley, Charles - (Coll title: The People Called Methodists, Phase 2: Primary Sources 1738-1800) - 11mf - 9 - MP-648/1 - ne IDC [240]
DIARIES AND RECORDS, 1838-1967 / St. Mary's College. St. Mary's, Kansas - 1 - us KS Hist [370]
DIARIES, CORRESPONDENCE AND MISCELLANEOUS PAPERS, 1882-1937 / Gray, William - 3r - at Pacific Mss [920]
DIARIES, CORRESPONDENCE AND RELATED PAPERS, 1945-1947 / Luxton, Clarence T J - Pt of 1r - 1 - PMB1099 - at Pacific Mss [920]
DIARIES OF CAPTAIN JOHN GREGORY BOURKE / Bourke, John Gregory - (124v covering 1872-96) - 10r - 1 - $735.00 - us UMI [976]
DIARIES OF MISS SARAH HALE, MISSIONARY FOR MANY YEARS TO MEXICO / Hale, Sarah - 612p - 1 - 21.42 - us Baptist [240]
THE DIARIES OF WILLIAM MICHAEL ROSSETTI / Rossetti, William Michael - (Part of the Angeli-Dennis Collection) - Vancouver, BC: University of British Columbia Library, 1995 - 3r - 1 - Can$100.00r - cn U.B.C. Preserve [920]
DIARIO / Portugal. Cortes. Camara dos deputados - 1885-1911 12. 1889, v. 1; 1895 wanting - 1 - 605.00 - us L of C Photodup [946]
EL DIARIO - La Paz: [s.n.], 1956- - 1 - us Res Libr [072]
EL DIARIO - New York. N.Y. (Spanish Language). 1962- - 1 - us UMI [071]
EL DIARIO - La Paz: [s.n.], [1956-] - us Res Libr [072]
DIARIO CARIOCA - Rio de Janeiro, 17 Jul 1928-Dec 1942; Mar 1943-Dec 1962; Mar 1963-31 Dec 1965 - 1,5,6 - bl Biblioteca [072]
DIARIO CONSTITUCIONAL - '(s.l'). 8 Fev-3 Abr 1822 - 1 - bl Biblioteca [072]
DIARIO DA ASSEMBLEA LEGISLATIVA PROVINCIAL DE MINAS GERAIS - Ouro Preto, 8 Apr-18 Oct 1850 - 1,5,6 - bl Biblioteca [972]
DIARIO DA ASSEMBLEIA GERAL, CONSTITUINTE E LEGISLATIVA DO IMPERIO DO BRASIL - Rio de Janeiro, May-Nov 1823 - 1,5,6 - bl Biblioteca [072]
DIARIO DA BAHIA : JORNAL MERCANTIL, POLITICO E LITTERARIO - [s.l.]. 20 Mar-Maio, Jul 1833; Fev, Nov 1835; Nov 1837; Jan-Fev 1838 - 1,5,6 - bl Biblioteca [072]
DIARIO DA CACHOEIRA - Cachoeira, BA. 8 Out 1880 - 1,5,6 - bl Biblioteca [072]
DIARIO DA CAMARA MUNICIPAL DA CIDADE DO RIO DE JANEIRO - Rio de Janeiro, Jan-Dec 1830 - 1,5,6 - bl Biblioteca [072]
DIARIO DA JUSTICA / Minas Gerais. Brazil - 1945-1946 - 1 - us NY Public [972]
DIARIO DA JUSTICA / Pernambuco. Brazil (State). Courts - Diario Oficial Suplemento. Racife. 1962-1963 - 1 - us NY Public [972]
DIARIO DA JUSTICA AND APENSO JURISPRUDENCIA / Brazil. Courts - 1958-1962 - 1 - us NY Public [324]
DIARIO DA MANHA - Juiz de Fora, 1 Mar-3 Apr 1891 - 1,5,6 - bl Biblioteca [072]
DIARIO DA MANHA - Lisbon. Portugal. -d. 2 Aug 1941-25 May 1945, 1 Jan-31 Aug 1946. (Imperfect). (19 reels) - 1 - uk British Libr Newspaper [072]
DIARIO DA MANHA - Maceio, Alagoas. 17 Jan, Maio-Ago 1882; Jan-Fev, Nov-Dez 1883; Dez 1884; Jun 1887; 5 Jan 1889 - 1,5,6 - bl Biblioteca [072]
DIARIO DA REPUBLICA : ORGAO OFICIAL DA REPUBLICA DE ANGOLA - Luanda. [1s nov 11 1975-1977; mar 17 1981-aug 13 1984; 1s, 2s, 3s: 1978-1980] - 9r - us Res Libr [072]
DIARIO DA TARDE - Belo Horizonte, Brazil. Sept-Dec 1977; 1978; Jan-May 1979 - 1 - bl Biblioteca [072]
DIARIO DA TARDE : ORGAO DOS DIARIOS ASSOCIADOS - Juiz de Fora, 25 Mar-Apr 1954; 10 May 1962 - 1,5,6 - bl Biblioteca [072]
DIARIO DAS ALAGOAS - Maceio, Alagoas. 9 Abr 1860; Fev 1868; Dez 1876; Mar 1878; Nov 1880; Nov 1883; Abr 1885; Out-Nov 1888; Set, 17 Dez 1889 - 1,5,6 - bl Biblioteca [072]
DIARIO DAS PETAS - [s.l.]. 1 Abr 1878 - 1,5,6 - bl Biblioteca [072]
DIARIO DE ASSEMBLEIA / Parana. Brazil. Assembleia - 1957-1958 - 1 - us NY Public [972]
DIARIO DE BADAJOZ - Badajoz, 1883-1886 y 1888-1892 - 5 - sp Bibl Santa Ana [072]
DIARIO DE BADAJOZ - Badajoz.1830-1900 - 9 - 1.50f - sp Bibl Santa Ana [072]
DIARIO DE BADAJOZ - (Numeros sueltos. Estan relacionados otros anos en el numero 9, ya enviado) - Badajoz, 1882 - 5 - sp Bibl Santa Ana [073]
DIARIO DE CACERES - Caceres, 1903-1935. Incomp - 5 - sp Bibl Santa Ana [073]
DIARIO DE CACERES - Caceres, 1910-1921 - 5 - sp Bibl Santa Ana [072]
DIARIO DE CATAGUAZES - Cataguazes, 26 Apr-20 Jun 1914 - 1,5,6 - bl Biblioteca [072]
DIARIO DE CENTRO AMERICA - (Also: 1991-12r/y $80r) - Guatemala City. v130-191. 1950-71 - 45r - 1 - $3,600.00 coll - us Ross [324]
DIARIO DE CENTRO AMERICA - Guatemala: [s.n.], dec 31 1955-feb 1972 - 65r - 1 - us Res Libr [072]
DIARIO DE CENTRO AMERICA. GUATEMALA / Guatemala - On film: Ag. 1972-. LL-02115 - 1 - us L of C Photodup [340]
DIARIO DE COSTA RICA - San Jose: J V Coto, 1956-sep 29 1964 - 53r - 1 - us Res Libr [072]
EL DIARIO DE HOY - San Salvador, El Salvador: N V Altamirano, R Membreno, 1936-56- - 1 - us Res Libr [072]
DIARIO DE LA MARINA - Cuba. 1947-May 1961 - 1 - us UMI [972]
DIARIO DE LAS SESSIONES DE CORTES - (Indices, 1914-1919/1920 and appendices) - Madrid, 1914-1919/1920 - 1,219mf - H-1022/2 - ne IDC [340]
DIARIO DE MADRID - Anos 1808-1809 (16-IV/31-I) - 12mf - 9 - sp Cultura [946]
DIARIO DE MANAOS - Manaos, Amazonas. 10 Dez 1890-22 Mar 1894 - 1,5,6 - bl Biblioteca [072]
DIARIO DE MANILA - Manila: Ramirez y Giraudier, Suppl to nov 7 1897; nov 12 18, dec 30 1897; jan 5,11-12,17,28, mar 11,26, apr 12, may 4,16,26 1898 - us Res Libr [072]
DIARIO DE MONTES CLAROS - Montes Claros, Brazil. Aug 1964 - 1 - bl Biblioteca [072]
DIARIO DE NOTICIAS - Aracaju, 11-24 Jun, Oct 1886; 9 Aug 1887 - 1,5,6 - bl Biblioteca [072]
DIARIO DE NOTICIAS - (Cont as: Fusao da Folha Nova e Brasil) - Rio de Janeiro, 7 Jun 1885-Oct 1889; Jan 1890-30 Sep 1895 - 1,5,6 - bl Biblioteca [072]
DIARIO DE NOTICIAS - Rio de Janeiro, 12 Jun 1930-10 Nov 1976 - 1,5,6 - bl Biblioteca [072]
DIARIO DE NOTICIAS - [s.l.]. 2 Set, Nov 1876; Set 1877; Jan 1878; Abr, Jun-Jul 1880; Out-Nov 1881; Maio 1882; Abr 1883; Ago 1884; Fev 1885; Jan 1886; Nov 1888; Jun 1893; Fev-Mar 1895; Nov 1897; Maio 1900; Mar 1903; 6 Ago 1909 - 1,5,6 - bl Biblioteca [072]
O DIARIO DE NOTICIAS - Manaos, Amazonas. 14 Mar 1900 - 1,5,6 - bl Biblioteca [072]
EL DIARIO DE NUEVA YORK = NEW YORK'S SPANISH DAILY - Brooklyn: El Diario Publ Co, 1948-1963. feb 25 1950-mar 11 1952 - 15r - us Res Libr [071]
DIARIO DE PANAMA - Panama. 1915-Oct. 1917 - 1 - us UMI [072]
DIARIO DE PANAMA/PANAMA JOURNAL - Panama City, Panama. 14 Apr 1905-9 Sept 1914. 21 Oct 1921-33 (incomplete) - 43r - 1 - us L of C Photodup [072]
DIARIO DE PERNAMBUCO - Recife, 7 Nov 1835- - 1,5,6 - bl Biblioteca [072]
DIARIO DE PETAS - [s.l.]. 7 Mar 1886 - 1,5,6 - bl Biblioteca [072]
DIARIO DE POCOS DE CALDAS - Pocos de Caldas, 28 Apr 1954; Sept 1956; Oct 1958; 5 Mar 1959 - 1,5,6 - bl Biblioteca [072]
DIARIO DE SANTOS - Santos, Brazil. 1879-81 - 1 - bl Biblioteca [072]
DIARIO DE SAO PAULO : JORNAL DIARIO E LIVRE - Sao Paulo, 8 Aug 1865-18 Aug 1878 - 1,5,6 - bl Biblioteca [072]
DIARIO DE SERGIPE : ORGAO DA LAVOURA E DO COMMERCIO - Aracaju, 20-31 Jan, Feb, May-8 Aug 1877 - 1,5,6 - bl Biblioteca [072]
DIARIO DE SESIONES : ENERO 24-MARZO 16, 1949 / Argentina. Convencion Nacional Constituyente - Buenos Aires: [La Convencion, 1949] - 1 - CSUXADJ0081-B - us Hoover Inst Photo [340]
DIARIO DE SESIONES DE LAS CORTES CONSTITUYENTES / Spain. Cortes, 1836-1837 - v. 1-10. 1870-77 - 1 - 105.00 - us L of C Photodup [946]
DIARIO DE SESIONES DE LAS CORTES CONSTITUYENTES / Spain. Cortes Constituyentes, 1869-1871 - v. 1-15, Nos. 1-332. 1870-71 - 1 - 155.00 - us L of C Photodup [946]
DIARIO DE UN INGENIERO / Sanchez Arjona, Vicente - Sevilla: Imprenta Carlos Acuna, 1954 - 1 - sp Bibl Santa Ana [810]
DIARIO DE UN MINISTRO DE LA MONARQUIA / Areilza, Jose Maria de - Barcelona: Planeta, 1st ed c1977 - 1 - CSUXADQ2497-B - us Hoover Inst Photo [350]
DIARIO DE UN PADRE DE FAMILIA / Perez Lozano, Jose Maria - Madrid: Propaganda Popular Catolica, 1959 - 1 - sp Bibl Santa Ana [920]
DIARIO DEL CARIBE - Barranquilla, Colombia. 1990-May 1991 - 17r - 1 - us L of C Photodup [072]
DIARIO DES LAS SESIONES DEL CONGRESO DE LOS DIPUTADOS / Spain. Congreso de los Diputados - v. 1-523. 1837 38-1936 - 1 - 5,678.00 - us L of C Photodup [946]
DIARIO DO ABAIXO PIQUES : DIARIO SEMINALE DI GRANDE IMPURTANZA - Zanbaolo, Brazil. Maio-Out 1933 - 1 - bl Biblioteca [072]
DIARIO DO ACRE - Rio Branco, Acre. 11 Maio 1982-8 Jan 1984 - 1,5,6 - bl Biblioteca [072]
DIARIO DO AMAZONAS - Manaos, Amazonas. 5 Jan-Mar, Nov 1873; Jan-31 Mar 1874 - 1,5,6 - bl Biblioteca [072]
DIARIO DO AMAZONAS : ORGAO DO PARTIDO REPUBLICANO - Manaos, Amazonas. 22 Fev-30 Jun 1910 - 1,5,6 - bl Biblioteca [072]
DIARIO DO ARACAJU - Aracaju, 11-12 Mar-Apr, Jul, 18-20 Oct 1885 - 1,5,6 - bl Biblioteca [072]
DIARIO DO COMERCIO - Sao Joao del-Rei, Brazil. Apr 1939; Jan 1941; Jul-Aug 1954 - 1 - bl Biblioteca [072]
DIARIO DO COMMERCIO - Maceio, Alagoas. 12 Abr, Maio, 10 Jun 1896 - 1 - bl Biblioteca [380]
DIARIO DO COMMERCIO : ORGAO DA LAVOURA, INDUSTRIA E COMMERCIO - Belo Horizonte, 2 Nov 1927; Jan-10 Feb 19287 - 1,5,6 - bl Biblioteca [072]
DIARIO DO CONGRESSO NACIONAL / Brazil. Congresso - 1957-66 - 78r - 1 - us Ross [324]
DIARIO DO GOVERNO - (Also under title: Diario Fluminense) - Rio de Janeiro, 2 Jan 1823-28 Jun 1833 - 1,5,6 - bl Biblioteca [072]
DIARIO DO GOVERNO - Lisbao, 1962-69 - 14r - 1 - us Ross [324]
DIARIO DO GOVERNO *see* DIARIO FLUMINENSE
DIARIO DO OESTE : MATUTINO, NOTICIOSO E INDEPENDENTE - Divinopolis, 18-19 Oct 1958; May 1961; 1 Jun 1962 - 1,5,6 - bl Biblioteca [072]
DIARIO DO PODER LEGISLATIVO / Pernambuco. Brazil (State). Assemblea Legislativo - 1959-1963 - 1 - us NY Public [972]
DIARIO DO POVO - Juiz de Fora, 24 Sept 1914 - 1,5,6 - bl Biblioteca [072]
DIARIO DO POVO : ORGAO DO CLUB CENTRO POPULAR REPUBLICANO DE MACEIO - Maceio, Alagoas. 10 Jan-16 Abr 1890 - 1,5,6 - bl Biblioteca [072]
DIARIO DO POVO : ORGAO DO PARTIDO REPUBLICANO CONSERVADOR - Maceio, Alagoas. 19 Set 1916-25 Dez 1917 - 1,5,6 - bl Biblioteca [072]
DIARIO DO POVO : POLITICO, LITTERARIO, NOTICIOSO E COMMERCIAL - Rio de Janeiro, 2 Jul 1867-30 Apr 1869 - 1,5,6 - bl Biblioteca [072]
DIARIO DO POVO - Salvador, BA. 2 Jan-31 Out 1889 - 1,5,6 - bl Biblioteca [072]
DIARIO DO RIO DE JANEIRO - Rio de Janeiro, 1 Jun 1821-Dec 1844; Jan-Jun, Aug-Dec 1845; Jan 1846-31 Oct 1878 - 1,5,6 - bl Biblioteca [072]
DIARIO DO RIO DOCE - Governador Valadares, 4 Feb, Aug 1959; 19 May 1960 - 1,5,6 - bl Biblioteca [072]
DIARIO DO TRIANGULO - Uberaba, 5 Dec 1953 - 1,5,6 - bl Biblioteca [072]
DIARIO ECLESIASTICO, E CIVIL, DO ANNO DE 1838 - [s.l.]. 1837 - 1,5,6 - bl Biblioteca [072]
DIARIO FLUMINENSE : CRITICO, LITTERARIO, RECREATIVO E NOTICIOSO - (Also under title: Diario do Governo) - Rio de Janeiro, 1 Jul-21 Oct 1884 - 1,5,6 - bl Biblioteca [072]
DIARIO FLUMINENSE *see* DIARIO DO GOVERNO
DIARIO LATINO - San Salvador, El Salvadore. 1956 - 6r - 1 - us L of C Photodup [072]
DIARIO MERCANTIL - Juiz de Fora, Brazil. Sept 1912-Jun 1979. very scattered issues - 1 - bl Biblioteca [072]
DIARIO MERCANTIL - Rio de Janeiro, 3 Nov 1824-Oct 1825; Jan 1826-31 Oct 1827 - 1,5,6 - bl Biblioteca [072]
DIARIO MUNICIPAL / Rio de Janeiro. Federal District. Camara Legislativa - 1957-Apr. 20, 1960 - 1 - us NY Public [324]
DIARIO MUNICIPAL AND SUPPLEMENTS / Rio de Janeiro. Federal District. Prefeitura - Nov. 14, 1957-Apr. 1960 - 1 - us NY Public [324]
EL DIARIO NACIONAL - Panama City, Panama. 16 Jun 1920-11 Aug 1921 - 2r - 1 - us L of C Photodup [072]
DIARIO OFFICIAL - Manaos, Amazonas. 15 Nov 1893-25 Dez 1900 - 1,5,6 - bl Biblioteca [072]
DIARIO OFICIAL - Bogata. v92-102. 1956-66 - 20r - 1 - us Ross [324]
DIARIO OFICIAL / Brazil - 1823-36, 1892-1969 - 1 - 17,250.00 - us L of C Photodup [324]
DIARIO OFICIAL / Brazil - Rio de Janeiro. 1900-1949 - 1 - us NY Public [324]
DIARIO OFICIAL / Brazil - (Section 1, Part 2. 1971-. 1. Section 4. 1973-. 1) - Section 1, Part 1. 1971- - 1 - us L of C Photodup [972]
DIARIO OFICIAL - Brazil, 1964-70 - 41r - 1 - us Ross [324]
DIARIO OFICIAL / Chile - 1877-1969 - 1 - 7751.00 - us L of C Photodup [324]
DIARIO OFICIAL / Chile - Santiago. 1952-1960 - 1 - us NY Public [324]
DIARIO OFICIAL / Colombia - 1821-1969 - 1 - $6,615.00 - us L of C Photodup [340]
DIARIO OFICIAL / Colombia - Bogota. On film: 1970-. LL-02086 - 1 - us L of C Photodup [340]
DIARIO OFICIAL - El Salvador. v218-229. 1968-70 - 16r - 1 - us Ross [324]
DIARIO OFICIAL / Mexico - 1821-1945 - 1 - us NY Public [972]
DIARIO OFICIAL / Mexico - 1954-59, 1970- - 1 - $501.00 - us L of C Photodup [340]
DIARIO OFICIAL - Mexico City, 1939-70 - 49r - 1 - us Ross [324]
DIARIO OFICIAL / Parana. Brazil - Curitiba. 1946-Feb. 1969- - 1 - us NY Public [324]
DIARIO OFICIAL / Pernambuco. Brazil (State) - Feb. 1947-1963 - 1 - us NY Public [972]
DIARIO OFICIAL / El Salvador - San Salvador. 1944-Nov 1948, 1958-1967 - 1 - us NY Public [972]
DIARIO OFICIAL / El Salvador - San Salvador. 1970- - 1 - us L of C Photodup [340]
DIARIO OFICIAL / El Salvador - (Supplement. 1847-1969) - 1847-1969 - 1 - $7,070.00 - us L of C Photodup [340]
DIARIO OFICIAL - Santiago. v75-93. 1952-70 - 28r - 1 - us Ross [324]

DIARIO OFICIAL / Yucatan. Mexico (State) – Merida. 1946-1960 – 1 – us NY Public [972]
DIARIO OFICIAL – Yucatan, Mexico. v61-66. 1961-66 – 5r – 1 – us Ross [324]
DIARIO OFICIAL. 1890- / Uruguay – 1 – us L of C Photodup [972]
DIARIO OFICIAL DE LA REPUBLICA DE CHILE / Chile – Santiago. On film: 1970-. LL-02085 – 1 – us L of C Photodup [340]
DIARIO OFICIAL DEL GOBIERNO DEL ESTADO DE YUCATAN / Yucatan. Mexico (State) – Merida. On film: 1821-1969. LL-02040 – 1 – us L of C Photodup [340]
DIARIO OFICIAL DO ESTADO DE SAO PAULO / Sao Paulo. (State). Brazil – (Jan 1975-May 1981. 5) – May 1891-Sept 1892 – 1 – bl Biblioteca [072]
DIARIO OFICIAL DO ESTADO DO RIO DE JANEIRO / Rio de Janeiro. (State). Brazil – Jul 1931-1950; 1975-81 – 1 – bl Biblioteca [324]
DIARIO OFICIAL. SECCION AVISOS / Uruguay – 1906-69, 1970- – 1 – $10,902.00 – us L of C Photodup [972]
DIARIO OFICIEL / Montevideo. Uruguay – Seccion Avisos. Oct 1959-68 – 1 – us NY Public [972]
DIARIO POPULAR : FOLHA CONSAGRADA AOS INTERESSES DA PROVINCIA – (Cont by: Jornal Popular) – Aracaju, 6 Feb, 13, 27 Mar 1879 – 1,5,6 – bl Biblioteca [072]
DIARIO POPULAR : ORGAM POLITICO E NOTICIOSO – [s.l.]. 1 Jun-8 Out 1914 – 1,5,6 – bl Biblioteca [072]
O DIARIO POPULAR *see* JORNAL POPULAR
DIARIO Y NOTAS AUTOBIOGRAFICAS / Reboucas, Andre – Rio de Janeiro. 1938 – 1 – us Res Libr [920]
DIARIUM SPIRITUALE. ROMAN OM EN ROEST / Gyllensten, Lars Johan Wictor – Stockholm: Bonnier, 1968. 182p – 1 – us U.W. Library [830]
DIARY / Alexander, Thomas P – 1883-1913 – 1 – us KS Hist [920]
DIARY / Atsumaro, Konoe, Prince – 1 – 35.00r – us Hoover Inst Photo [920]
DIARY / Baptist, Edward – May 1790-May 1860. 41p – 1 – 5.00 – us Baptist [240]
DIARY / Barnett, William T – 1899-1900 – 1 – us KS Hist [920]
DIARY / Bensley, A A – (Original & typescript) – may 1926-dec 1934 – 1r – 1 – PMB1101 – at Pacific Mss [920]
DIARY / Berle, Adolf A – 1937-71. 8 rolls. Available by individual roll – 1 – us Roosevelt [920]
DIARY / Billard, Louis Phillip – 1917-18 – 1 – us KS Hist [920]
DIARY / Bolton, C S – 1861-62 – 1 – us KS Hist [920]
DIARY / Bragg, John – 1771-94. BRRAM – 1 – uk Microform Academic [920]
DIARY / Bragg, Thomas – 1861-62. Guide – 1 – $18.00 – us U.N.C. Southern Hist [920]
DIARY / Brownfield, J M – Ione, Arkansas, 1921. 108p – 1 – 5.00 – us Baptist [920]
DIARY / Carter, Elizabeth (Simerwell) – 1852-61 – 1 – us KS Hist [920]
DIARY / Chaudoin, William – 1858-59. 76p – 1 – 5.00 – us Baptist [920]
DIARY / Cole, Isaac – 1759-1870 – 1 – 23.17 – us Baptist [240]
DIARY / Comer, John & Barrows, E C & Willmarth, J W – 1892 – 1 – 15.19 – us Baptist [240]
DIARY / Converse, John Melvin – Jan 1863-Dec 1864 – 1 – us KS Hist [920]
DIARY / Cool, Amanda & Cool, J – 1879-85 – 1 – us KS Hist [920]
DIARY / Copas, J V – Apr-Sept 1912 – 1 – us KS Hist [978]
DIARY / Costigan, S P – 1874-77 – 1 – us KS Hist [978]
DIARY / Crowe, Sophia Bennett – 1874 – 1 – us KS Hist [920]
DIARY / Daniels, Augustus Thatcher – 1865-1921 – 1 – us KS Hist [920]
DIARY / DeWolf, Charles Wesley – undated, Civil War diary of a Kansas soldier in Arkansas – 1 – us KS Hist [976]
DIARY / Dewolfe, Harry F – Dec 1862-May 1863 – 1 – us KS Hist [920]
DIARY / Dimond, W W – 1865 – 1 – us KS Hist [920]
DIARY / Durban, E S – 1871-73.Plantation manager. Diary of his stay at White House near Toogoodoo River, Charleston County, SC. 2 fiches – 9 – us South Carolina Historical [978]
DIARY / Evans, Eliza (Pruitt) – 1884-92 – 1 – us KS Hist [920]
DIARY / Fenn, Courtenay Hughes – (1866-1953) for The Period 1866-1927 – 1 – us A.T.L.A. [920]
DIARY / Folliot, George – 1765-66. BRRAM – 1 – uk Microform Academic [920]
DIARY / Fouquet, Leon Charles – 1880-82 – 1 – us KS Hist [920]
DIARY / Gailland, Maurice, S J – 1848-77 – 1 – us KS Hist [920]
DIARY / Guthrie, James H – 1861-65 – 1 – us KS Hist [920]
DIARY / Hall, Cyrus – 1861-64 – 1 – us KS Hist [920]
DIARY / Hammond, OT – 1834-37. 284p – 1 – 9.94 – us Baptist [920]
DIARY / Hand, Julia – 1872-75 – 1 – us KS Hist [920]
DIARY / Hinson, William G – 1864-65. 2 fiches – 9 – us South Carolina Historical [976]
DIARY / Holman, Charles – 1863-64, 1866-67 – 1 – us KS Hist [920]
DIARY / Holmes, Henry S – 1895-1903. 4 fiches – 9 – us South Carolina Historical [978]
DIARY / Honyman, Robert – 1 – 20.00 – us L of C Photodup [920]
DIARY / Kelly, Edward – Pioneer Baptist Minister, Corn Island, Nicaragua. 1903-1913 – 1 – 5.00 – us Baptist [240]
DIARY / Kevisi, John (?) – (Photocopy of Roviana original) – jan-apr 1937 – Pt of 1r – 1 – PMB1105 – at Pacific Mss [920]
DIARY / McCoy, Joseph Geating – Jun 1880-Jan 1881 – 1 – us KS Hist [978]
DIARY / McKechnie, Archie – 1882-83 – 1 – us KS Hist [978]
DIARY / Martin, George – 1779-1800. BRRAM – 1 – uk Microform Academic [920]
DIARY / Peelle, Will J – 1879-84, 1902 – 1 – us KS Hist [978]
DIARY / Pomeroy, Henry H – 1r – 1 – $50.00 – C40020 – us Library Micro [920]
DIARY / Price, Henry E – 1842-48. BRRAM – 1 – uk Microform Academic [920]
DIARY / Raymond, Henry Hubert – 1870-72 – 1 – us KS Hist [978]
DIARY / Raymond, J M – 1862-65 – 1 – us KS Hist [978]
DIARY / Reynolds, Richard – 1763 – 1 – uk Microform Academic [920]
DIARY / Richards, James C – 1867 – 1 – us KS Hist [978]
DIARY / Riley, B F – 1894, 1898, 1904. 150p – 1 – 5.25 – us Baptist [240]
DIARY / Ruffin, Edmund – 1856-65 – 1 – 148.00 – us L of C Photodup [636]
DIARY / Scott, Cyrus McNeely – 1867-1915 – 1 – us KS Hist [978]
DIARY / Smith, Margaret A – 1878-81 – 1 – $50.00 – us Presbyterian [240]
DIARY / Smith, William M – 1864 – 1 – us KS Hist [978]
DIARY / Snyder, Edwin – 1 Dec 1864-30 Jun 1865 – 1 – us KS Hist [978]
DIARY / Snyder, S J H – 1848 – 1 – us KS Hist [978]
DIARY / Spooner, E A – 1849-50 – 1 – us KS Hist [978]
DIARY / Stafford, Alfred – 1864 – 1 – us KS Hist [978]
DIARY / Stewart, James R – 1855-60 – 1 – us KS Hist [978]
DIARY / Tichenor, Isaac Taylor – 1850. 486p – 1 – 17.01 – us Baptist [240]
DIARY / Trego, Joseph Harrington – 1861-63 – 1 – us KS Hist [978]
DIARY / Voeta, David – (Roviana original and English transl) – may 1935-jan 1936 – Pt of 1r – 1 – PMB1104 – at Pacific Mss [920]
DIARY / Watson, Sidney O – 1899-1901 – 1 – us KS Hist [978]
DIARY / Welch, James E – 1832-59 – 1 – $50.00 – us Presbyterian [920]
DIARY / Woods, Walter Hastings – 1858-59 – 1 – us KS Hist [978]
DIARY / Hamlin, Charles – Washington, DC: Library of Congress Photodup Service. v2-16. 1913-1929 – us Res Libr [320]
THE DIARY / Losh, James – 1796-1815 – 1 – uk Microform Academic [920]
DIARY, 1755-1757 / Grimshaw, W – (Coll title: The People Called Methodists, Phase 2: Primary Sources 1738-1800) – 1mf – 9 – MP-630-1 – ne IDC [240]
DIARY, 1775-1776 / Crook, J – (Coll title: The People Called Methodists, Phase 2: Primary Sources 1738-1800) – 1mf – 9 – MP-626/1 – ne IDC [240]
THE DIARY. 1788-1821 / Farington, Joseph – (typescript). Royal Archives, Windsor. Original Ms. un-indexed or fully indexed – 1 – uk Microform Academic [920]
DIARY, 1794-1805 / Rogers, J – (Coll title: The People Called Methodists, Phase 2: Primary Sources 1738-1800) – 2mf – 9 – MP-635/1 – ne IDC [240]
DIARY, 1825-1827, 1831-1834, 1836-1838, 1840, 1842, 1845, 1848, 1855, 1857-1864 / O'Bryan, W – (Coll title: The People Called Methodists, Phase 3: Primary Sources, 1801-1850) – 19mf – 9 – MP-694/1 – ne IDC [240]
DIARY, 1832-1917 / Littleberry, J Haley – 170p – 1 – 5.95 – us Baptist [240]
DIARY, 1845-46 / Smith, Thomas – 1 – 6.09 – us Baptist [240]
DIARY, 1848-1852 / Officer, M – With His African Bible pictures. 1859 – 1 – us A.T.L.A. [920]
DIARY, 1911-20 / Lockett, BL – 500p – 1 – 17.50 – us Baptist [240]
THE DIARY AND CORRESPONDENCE OF... WRITTEN DURING THE VOYAGE OF THE BEAGLE / Darwin, Charles – 1831-1836 – 1 – uk Microform Academic [574]
DIARY AND FINANCIAL ACCOUNTS : THE BRIG HENRICUS / Piper, Richard; ed by Rowson, A H – (v1 1807-10 3mf. v2 1815-20 4mf) – Liverpool: The Athenaeum, 1994 – 7mf – 9 – £14.00 – uk Athenaeum [920]
DIARY AND INDEX : TOGETHER WITH CORRESPONDENCE, PRESS CUTTINGS AND OTHER DOCUMENTS, 1942-1978, INCLUDING, REV J R METCALFE, "THE GIZO SCUTTLE" / Farland, Merle – dec 1938-mar 1940; nov 1941-feb 1943 – 1r – PMB1106 – at Pacific Mss [920]
DIARY AND JOURNAL KEPT AT IOWAY MISSION IN KANSAS / Irvin, Samuel M – 1841-49 – 1 – us KS Hist [920]
THE DIARY AND JOURNAL OF HIS GRACE, THE ARCHBISHOP OF YORK / Mathew, Toby – 1583-1622. From York Minster Library – 1 – uk Microform Academic [240]
DIARY AND LETTERS / Landon, R B – 1881-1916 – 1 – us KS Hist [978]
DIARY AND LETTERS...ED. BY HER NIECE CHARLOTTE BARRETT / Arblay, Frances Burney; ed by Barrett, Charlotte – 7v. London: H. Colburn, 1854 – 1 – us U.W. Library [920]
DIARY AND MEMORANDA BOOK, 1730-1759 / Wesley, Martha – (Coll title: The People Called Methodists, Phase 2: Primary Sources 1738-1800) – 1mf – 9 – MP-653/1 – ne IDC [240]
DIARY AND PERSONAL RECORDS / Younker, Bowman H – 1867-68 – 1 – us KS Hist [978]
DIARY AND TRANSCRIPT, 1942-1943 / Odgers, Len – 1r – 1 – PMB1061 – at Pacific Mss [920]
DIARY AND TRAVELOGUE / Dill, Jacob Smiser – 1879-81. 420p – 1 – 14.70 – us Baptist [910]
DIARY DURING A TRIP FROM PAPAR TO KIMANIS VIA TAMBUNAN, LOBO AND LIMBAWAN, 1882 / Donop, L B von – 1 – uk Microform Academic [920]
DIARY DURING AN EXCURSION ACROSS NORTH BORNEO FROM MARUDA BAY TO SANDAKAN / Witti, Francis X – 1881 – 1 – uk Microform Academic [910]
DIARY, MS 4 / Brown, Lucinda White – Mar 20-Sept 20 1854 – 1r – 1 – us Western Res [920]
DIARY, MS P.P. / Day, Francis A – Apr-Dec 1864 – 1r – 1 – us Western Res [976]
DIARY, MS P.P. / Mills, Henry A – 1862-65 – 1r – 1 – us Western Res [976]
DIARY OF A BUCCANEER / Sharp, Bartholomew – 1680 – 1 – uk Microform Academic [920]
"DIARY OF A BUFFALO HUNTER, 1872-73." / Raymond, Henry Hubert – 1 – us KS Hist [978]
DIARY OF A JOURNEY THROUGH UPPER CANADA AND SOME OF THE NEW ENGLAND STATES, 1819 / Goldie, John – Toronto: W. Tyrrell, 1897. 03461. (Pre-1900 Canadiana) – 9 – cn C.I.H.M. [910]
THE DIARY OF AN EXILED NUN – 2nd ed. St Louis, MO: B Herder, 1911, c1910 – 1mf – 9 – 0-8370-7293-X – 1986-1293 – us A.T.L.A. [920]
DIARY OF AN ITALIAN COMMANDER KILLED AT GUADALAJARA – n.p. 1937? Fiche W 831. (Blodgett Collection of Spanish Civil War Pamphlets) – 9 – us H.U. College Libr [946]
DIARY OF BEATRICE WEBB 1873-1943 / Webb, Beatrice – (With index £30.00) – 237mf – 9 – £1,040.00 – uk Chadwyck [920]
THE DIARY OF DR. JOHN WILLIAM POLIDORI, 1816 : RELATING TO BYRON, SHELLEY, ETC / Polidori, John William; ed by Rossetti, William Michael – London: E. Matthews, 1911 – 1 roll – 1 – 1-55879-876-5 – uk Libr Preservation [420]
DIARY OF HANS FRANK / U. S. World War Two Crimes Records – T992 – 12r – 5 – us Nat'l Archives [943]
DIARY OF HIS JOURNEY TO THE LOW COUNTRIES / Smeaton, John – 1755 – 7 – uk Microform Academic [910]
DIARY OF JOHN COMER / Barrows, E C & Willmarth, J W – 1892. 434p – 1 – 15.19 – us Baptist [240]
DIARY OF OPERATIONS DIVISION, WAR DEPARTMENT GENERAL STAFF, 1942-1946 / U.S. Army – 4r – 1 – $340.00 – S1677 – Co-publ with the Center of Military History – us Scholarly Res [355]
DIARY OF THE SIEGE OF QUEBEC, 1775 / Danford, J – British Library Add. Ms. 46840 – 1 – uk Microform Academic [920]
DIARY; PAPERS / Grinell, DeWitt Clinton – 1867-77 – 1 – us KS Hist [920]
Dias, Demosthenes de Oliveira *see* FORMACAO TERRITORIAL DO BRASIL; ORIGEM E EVOLUCAO
Dias, Marco Antonio Rodriguez et al *see* NATIONAL COMMUNICATION POLICY COUNCILS
DIAS PARA LA HISTORIA, 9 Y 10 DE JULIO DE 1953 – Buenos Aires: [Servicio Internacional Publicaciones Argentinas, 1953?] – 1 – CSUXADL7058-B – us Hoover Inst Photo [972]
DIAS SIN SOL / Barrantes Moreno, Vicente – 1875 – 9 – 1.50f – sp Bibl Santa Ana [946]
Dias, Walter Patrick *see* SHAKESPEARE: HIS TRAGIC WORLD
THE DIATESSARON OF TATIAN: A PRELIMINARY STUDY / Harris, James Rendel – London: C.J. Clay, 1890.1 fiche – 9 – us A.T.L.A. [240]
THE DIATESSARON OF TATIAN AND THE SYNOPTIC PROBLEM / Hobson, Alphonzo Augustus – Chicago: University of Chicago Press, 1904. 1 fiche – 9 – us A.T.L.A. [240]
LES DIATOMEES D'AUVERGNE / Heribaud, J – Clermont-Ferrand. Paris. 1893. B-6373 2 – 8 – ne IDC [580]
DIATOMEES DU MIDI DE LA FRANCE / Peragallo, H – (Bull. Soc. Hist. Nat. Toulouse). v. 18. 1884. B-6389 2 – 8 – ne IDC [580]
DIATOMEES MARINES DE FRANCE ET DES DISTRICTS MARITIMES VOISINS / Peragallo, H & Peragallo, M – Paris. 1897-1908. B-6391 2 – 8 – ne IDC [580]
DIATRIBAE DUAE MEDICOPHILOSOPHICAE,...DE FERMENTATIONE...DE FEBRIBUS, ...DE URINIS / Willis, Thomas – London, 1659 – 8mf – 9 – ne IDC [610]
DIAVOLA : OR, NOBODY'S DAUGHTER / Braddon, M E – New York: Dick & Fitzgerald, [188-?] – us Res Libr [920]
Diaz Alejandro, Carlos Federico *see* ENSAYOS SOBRE LA HISTORIA ECONOMICA ARGENTINA
Diaz Araujo, Enrique *see* LA CONSPIRACION DEL '43; EL GOU
Diaz Bordenave, Juan E *see* COMMUNICATION AND RURAL DEVELOPMENT
Diaz Bustamante y Quijano, Alfonso *see* LA UNIVERSIDAD DE EXTREMADURA (RAZONES QUE ABANDONAN SU ESTABLECIMIENTO)
Diaz Cisneros, S *see* ESTUDIOS DE DERECHO INTERNACIONAL PUBLICO
Diaz Daza, A *see* LIBRO DE LOS PROVECHOS Y DANOS...POR BEBIDA DEL AGUA...
Diaz de Entresotos, Baldomero *see* SEIS MESES DE ANARQUIA EN EXTREMADURA
Diaz de Isla, R *see* TRACTADO CONTRA EL MAL SERPENTINO QUE VULGARMENTE EN ESPANA ES LLAMADO BUBAS
Diaz de la Carrera, Diego *see* ORIGEN Y PRINCIPIO...ALCANTARA
Diaz de la Cruz, Felipe *see* EL ASUNTO DE PLASENCIA

Diaz de Montalvo, A *see* EL FUERO REAL DE ESPANA HECHO POR ALFONSO 9
Diaz de Vargas, Francisco *see*
- DISCURSO. GUERRA DE PORTUGAL
- DISCURSO Y SUMARIO DE LA GUERRA EN PORTUGAL

Diaz de Villar y Martinez, Juan M *see* TRATADO ELEMENTAL DE HIGIENE COMPARADA DEL HOMBRE Y LOS ANIMALES DOMESTICOS
Diaz del Castillo, Bernal *see*
- LA CONQUISTA DE MEJICO
- HISTOIRE DE LA NOUVELLE ESPAGNE
- HISTORIA DE LA CONQUISTA DE NUEVA ESPANA
- HISTORIA DE LA...NUEVA ESPANA
- HISTORIA VERDADERA DE LA CONQUISTA DE LA NUEVA ESPANA
- HISTORIA VERDADERA DE LA CONQUISTA DE LA NUEVA ESPANA...
- HISTORIA VERDADERA DE LA CONQUISTA DE LA NUEVA ESPANA
- HISTORIA VERDADERA DE LA CONQUISTA DE LA NUEVA ESPANA...
- HISTORIA VERDADERA DE LA CONQUISTA DE LA NUEVA ESPANA
- HISTORIA VERDADERA DE LA CONQUISTA DE LA NUEVA ESPANA. UNICA EDICION HECHA SEGUN EL CODICE AUTOGRAFO
- HISTORIA VERDADERA DE LA CONQUISTA DE LA NUEVA ESPANA
- THE TRUE HISTORY OF THE CONQUEST OF NEW SPAIN
- VERDADERA HISTORIA DE LOS SUCESOS DE LA CONQUISTA DE LA NUEVA ESPANA
- VERDADERA Y NOTABLE RELACION DEL DESCUBRIMIENTO Y CONQUISTA DE GUATEMALA
- VERDADERA Y NOTABLE RELACION DEL DESCUBRIMIENTO Y CONQUISTA DE LA NUEVA ESPANA Y GUATEMALA
- VERDADERA...NUEVA ESPANA
- VERIDIQUE...NOUVELLE HISTOIRE

Diaz, Fanor *see* CONVERSACIONES CON ROGELIO FRIGERIO SOBRE LA CRISIS POLITICA ARGENTINA
Diaz, Jose *see*
- ESPANA Y LA GUERRA IMPERIALISTA
- POR LA UNIDAD, HACIA LA VICTORIA
- TRES ANOS DE LUCHA

Diaz, M P *see* DERECHO PENAL INTERNACIONAL
Diaz Maciaz, Jose *see*
- FABIANELO
- LOS HIJOD DEL MAR
- LA HUELGA
- VIRTUD Y CIENCIA

Diaz Montilla, Rafael *see* LA ALIMENTACION RACIONAL DEL GANADO
Diaz Montilla, Rafael et al *see* 1ST CONGRESO SINDICAL AGRARIO DE EXTREMADURA. PONENCIA 5 MUTUALIDADES AGRICOLAS
Diaz Moreno, Juan *see* VIGENCIA DEL FRENTE E JUVENTUDES EN EL PRESENTE Y EN EL FUTURO DE ESPANA
Diaz Perez, Nicolas *see*
- BANOS DE BANOS
- LAS BIBLIOTECAS DE ESPANA...PUBLICAS
- CATALOGO DE LOS OBJETOS...EXPOSICION
- DE MADRID A LISBOA
- EL DESCUENTO DE LAS CLASES PRIVADAS
- DICCIONARIO HISTORICO...EXTREMENOS ILUSTRES
- ECOS PERDIDOS
- LA EMIGRACION EN BALEARES Y CANARIAS
- EXTREMADURA
- LA FRANCMASONERIA ESPANOLA
- HISTORIA DE TALAVERA LA REAL...
- HISTORIA DE TALAVERA LA REAL
- INFLUENCIA DE EXTREMADURA EN LA LITERATURA ESPANOLA
- JOSE MAZZINI. ENSAYO ITALIA
- NOTICIA HISTORICA DE...BADAJOZ
- EL PLUTARCO EXTREMENO
- EL PODER TEMPORAL DE LOS PAPAS EN EL S. 19
- RECUERDOS DE EXTREMADURA

Diaz Tanco, Vasco *see*
- JARDIN DEL ALMA CRISTIANA
- PALINODIA

Diaz Villar Martinez, Juan Manuel *see*
- MANUAL DE FISIOLOGIA EXPERIMENTAL
- PROFILAXIS DE LA FIEBRE CARBUNCOSA
- PROFILAXIS DE LAS ENFERMEDADES INFECCIOSAS DEL GANADO DE CERDA
- TRATADO ELEMENTAL DE HIGIENE
- TRATADO ELEMENTAL DE HIGIENE COMPARADA DEL HOMBRE Y DE LOS ANIMALES DOMESTICOS

Diaz Villar y Martinez, Juan M *see* MANUAL DE FISIOLOGIA EXPERIMENTAL
Diaz y Perez, Nicolas *see*
- HISTORIA DE TALAVERA LA REAL
- HISTORIA DEL PUEBLO DE ALANGE

Diaz-Ambrona, Adolfo *see* DISCURSO DEL..., EN DEFENSA DE LOS DICTAMENES DE LOS SIGUIENTES PROYECTOS DE LEY: 1° DE MONTES VECINALES EN MANO COMUN. 2° DE ORDENACION RURAL. 3° REGIMEN DE TIERRAS DEL INSTITUTO NACIONAL DE COLONIZACION
DIBATTIMENTI *see* JOURNAUX DIVERS
DIBAWAH BENDERA REVOLUSI / Sukarno, Pres. Indonesia – SE 10,978 1. 1964 – 9 – ne IDC [335]
DIBAWAH BENDERA REVOLUSI / Sukarno, Pres. Indonesia – SE 1215 1. 1959 – 9 – ne IDC [335]
Dibble, R A *see* JOHN H. NEWMAN
Dibdin, Charles *see*
- THE MUSICAL TOUR OF MR. DIBDIN, IN WHICH PREVIOUS TO HIS EMBARKATION FOR INDIAN HE FINISHED HIS CAREER AS A PUBLIC CHARACTER..
- THE PADLOCK

Dibelius, Martin *see*
- A FRESH APPROACH TO THE NEW TESTAMENT
- DIE GEISTERWELT IM GLAUBEN DES PAULUS

DIBHRE HAY-YAMIM = WORDS OF THE DAY – (Dibre Hayomim. May 1896-Nov/Dec 1909) – London, UK. Jan-Apr 1896 – 1 – uk British Libr Newspaper [072]
DIBRE HAYOMIM *see* DIBHRE HAY-YAMIM
DICCIONARIO BIBLIOGRAPHICO BRAZILEIRO / Blake, A V – Rio de Janeiro, 1883 – 38mf – 9 – ne IDC [972]
DICCIONARIO BIOGRAFICO DEL CLERO SECULAR DE CHILE, 1535-1918 / Prieto del Rio, LF – Santiago de Chile: Impr. Chile, 1922 – 8mf – 9 – ne IDC [920]
DICCIONARIO BOTANICO... / Roig y Mesa, J T – Habana. 3pts. 1928 – 12mf – ne IDC [580]
DICCIONARIO CHINA-PORTUGUEZ / Goncalves, J A – Macao, 1833 – 14mf – ne IDC [040]
DICCIONARIO CHOROGRAPHICO, HISTORICO E ESTATISTICO DE PERNAMBUCO / Galvao, S de Vasconcellos – Rio de Janeiro: Imprensa Nacional. 4v. 1908 – 22mf – 9 – ne IDC [972]
DICCIONARIO CRITICO-BURLESCO DEL QUE SE TITULA – Madrid: Imprenta de Repulles, 1812 – 1 – sp Bibl Santa Ana [050]
DICCIONARIO DE BOTANICA BRASILEIRA... / Pinto, J de A – Rio de Janeiro, 1873 – 9mf – ne IDC [580]
DICCIONARIO DE DERECHO MARITIMO / Garcia-Parreno y Lopez, G – Cartagena, 1908 – 16mf – 9 – ILM-1662/1 – ne IDC [340]
DICCIONARIO DE GOBIERNO Y LEGISALCION DE INDIAS...TOMO 4, VOL 1 / Ayala, Manuel Jose de – Madrid: Razon y Fe, 1929 – 1 – sp Bibl Santa Ana [340]
DICCIONARIO DE LA LENGUA CASTELLANA. TOMO 1 / Academia de la Lengua – 1726 – 6mf – 9 – Pta3,500.00 – 84-7848-204-0 – sp Pentalfa [040]
DICCIONARIO DE LA LENGUA CASTELLANA. TOMO 2 / Academia de la Lengua – 1729 – 6mf – 9 – Pta3,500.00 – 84-7848-205-9 – sp Pentalfa [040]
DICCIONARIO DE LA LENGUA CASTELLANA. TOMO 3 / Academia de la Lengua – 1732 – 6mf – 9 – Pta3,500.00 – 84-7848-206-7 – sp Pentalfa [040]
DICCIONARIO DE LA LENGUA CASTELLANA. TOMO 4 / Academia de la Lengua – 1734 – 5mf – 9 – Pta3,000.00 – 84-7848-207-5 – sp Pentalfa [040]
DICCIONARIO DE LA LENGUA CASTELLANA. TOMO 5 / Academia de la Lengua – 1737 – 5mf – 9 – Pta3,000.00 – 84-7848-208-3 – sp Pentalfa [040]
DICCIONARIO DE LA LENGUA CASTELLANA. TOMO 6 / Academia de la Lengua – 1739 – 5mf – 9 – Pta3,000.00 – 84-7848-209-1 – sp Pentalfa [040]
DICCIONARIO DE LA MUSICA ILLUSTRADO – Barcelona. 1927-29. 2v – 1 – 23.00 – us L of C Photodup [780]
DICCIONARIO DE LAS NOBLES ARTES / Rejon de Silva, Diego A – 1788 – 1mf – 9 – Pta1,000.00 – 84-7848-350-0 – sp Pentalfa [700]
DICCIONARIO DE TERMINOS COMUNES TAGALO-CASTELLANO / Serrano, Rosalio – Manila: Imprenta de Ramirez y Giraudier, 1858 – us Res Libr [040]
DICCIONARIO GENERAL DE AMERICANISMO. 3 VOL. MEXICO, 1943 / Santamaria, Francisco – Madrid: Razon y Fe, 1946 – 1 – sp Bibl Santa Ana [972]
DICCIONARIO GEOGRAPHICO, HISTORICO E ESTATISTICO : RIO GRANDE DO SUL. / Faria, OA – Porto Alegre: Livr. Do Globo, 1914 – 5mf – 9 – ne IDC [972]
DICCIONARIO HISPANO-TAGALOG / Laktaw, Pedro Serrano – Manila: Estab tip "La Opinion" a cargo de G Bautista. v1. 1889-1914 – 2r – us Res Libr [040]
DICCIONARIO HISTORICO DE LOS MAS ILLUSTRES PROFESORES DE LAS BELLAS ARTES EN ESPANA / Cean Bermudez, Juan A – Madrid. 6v. 1800 – 24mf – ne IDC [700]
DICCIONARIO HISTORICO DE LOS MAS ILLUSTRES PROFESORES DE LAS BELLAS ARTES EN ESPANA / Cean Bermudez, Juan A – O-979. 6 v. 1800 – 9 – ne IDC [920]
DICCIONARIO HISTORICO-BIOGRAFICO DEL PERU. 2ND ED. TOMOS 9, 10 Y 11. LIMA 1934-1935 / Mendiburu, Manuel de – Madrid: Razon y Fe, 1935 – 1 – sp Bibl Santa Ana [972]
DICCIONARIO HISTORICO-BIOGRAFICO DEL PERU...2ND ED. PUBLICADA POR EVARISTO SANCRISTOVAL / Mendiburu, Manuel de – Madrid: Razon y Fe, v6-8. 1935 – 1 – sp Bibl Santa Ana [972]
DICCIONARIO HISTORICO...EXTREMENOS ILUSTRES / Diaz Perez, Nicolas – 2v. 1884 – 9 – 1.50f – sp Bibl Santa Ana [940]
DICCIONARIO IBANAG-ESPANOL / Bugarin, Jose – Manila: Impr de los Amigos del Pais, 1854 – 1 – us Res Libr [490]
DICCIONARIO MANUAL DE TERMINOS COMUNES ESPANOL-TAGALO / Serrano, Rosalio – 2nd ed. Manila: J. Martinez, 1913. 400p – 1 – us U.W. Library [040]
DICCIONARIO MUY COPIOSO DE LA LENGUA ESPANOLA Y FRANCESA, DICTIONNAIRE TRES AMPLE DE LA LANGUE FRANÇOISE ET ESPAGNOLE (AEL, ABT 2;15) / Pallet, Jean – 1st ed. Paris, 1604 (mf ed 1995) – 7mf – 9 – DM160.00 – 3-89131-198-2 – gw Fischer [040]
DICCIONARIO POPULAR DE HISTORIA DE LA REPUBLICA O. DEL URUGUAY. DESDE LA EPOCA DEL DESCUBRIMIENTO DE SU TERRITORIO, HASTA LA DE SU INDEPENDENCIA / Araujo, O – Montevideo: Impr. Artistica, de Dornalecha y Reyes. 3v. 1901-1903 – 14mf – 9 – ne IDC [972]
DICCIONARIO PORTUGUEZ-CHINA... / Goncalves, J A – Macao, 1831 – 10mf – ne IDC [040]
DICCIONARIO TIRURAY-ESPANOL / Bennasar, P Guillermo – Manila: Tipo-litog de Chofre, [1892-1893]. v1. 1892 – 1r – us Res Libr [040]
Dicey, A V *see*
- THE LAW OF DOMICIL...
- LE STATUT PERSONNEL ANGLAIS OU LA LOI DU DOMICILE

Dicey, Albert Venn *see* A TREATISE ON THE RULES FOR THE SELECTION OF THE PARTIES TO AN ACTION
DICHIARAZIONE DE NULLITA DI MATRIMONIO (G GARIBALDI CONTRO G RAIMONDI) / Corte di Appello di Roma – Roma, 1879 – 3mf – 1 – ILM-3966/1 – ne IDC [327]
DICHT-, SING- UND SPIEL-KUN.. / Til, S van – Leipzig: Matthias Groot, 1706 – 14 cards – 2 – us Sibley [780]
DIE DICHTER DES ALTEN BUNDES / Ewald, Heinrich – 3v in 2.1854-67 – 1 – us A.T.L.A. [220]
DER DICHTER DES OBERON / Seuffert, Bernhard – Prag: Verlag des deutschen Vereins zur Verbreitung gemeinnutziger Kenntnisse in Prag, 1900 – 1r – 1 – us U.W. Library [430]
DER DICHTER J.M.R. LENZ IN LIVLAND : EINE MONOGRAPHIE NEBST EINER BIBLIOGRAPHISCHEN PARALLELE ZU M. BERNAY'S JUNGEM GOETHE VON 1766-1768: UNBEKANNTE JUGENDDICHTUNGEN VON LENZ AUS DERSELBEN ZEIT ENTHALTEND / Falck, P T – (Includes bibliographical references) – Winterthur: J Westfehling, 1878 – 1r – 1 – us U.W. Library [920]
DER DICHTER SIEGFRIED LIPINER (1856-1911) / Hartungen, Hartmut von – (Includes bibliographical references) – Munich: s.n., 1932? – 1r – 1 – us U.W. Library [920]
DER DICHTER VOR DER GESCHICHTE : HOELDERLIN, NOVALIS / Schneider, Reinhold – 2. Aufl. Heidelberg: F H Kerle, 1946 – 1r – 1 – us U.W. Library [430]
DICHTERISCHE ARBEITEN / Winkler, Eugen Gottlob – Leipzig-Markkleeberg: Karl Rauch Verlag, 1937 – 1 – us U.W. Library [430]
DIE DICHTERISCHE ENTWICKLUNG J.F.W. ZACHARIAS / Kirchgeorg, Otto Hermann – (Includes bibliographical references) – Greifswald: J Abel, 1904 – 1 – us U.W. Library [430]
DER DICHTERISCHE ESSAY, DIE PROSAFORM DER ENGLISCHEN ROMANTIK / Egner, Fritz – Marburg, 1931 – 1mf – DM48.00 – 3-8267-3039-9 – gw Hänsel [420]
DIE DICHTERISCHE SELBSTDARSTELLUNG IM ROMAN DES JUNGEN DEUTSCHLAND / Greatwood, Edward Albert – 1995 – 2mf – 9 – DM62.00 – 3-8267-3203-0 – gw Hänsel [430]
DICHTERKLAENGE AUS SPANIENS BESSEREN TAGEN / Sulzbach, A – Ed. 2. Frankfurt a.M. 1903. BJ-421-20 1 – 9 – ne IDC [810]
DICHTERTUM UND FUEHRERSCHAFT : GEDENKREDE GEHALTEN AN DER GOETHEFEIER DES LEHRERVEREINS BERN-STADT / Schaeffner, Georg – Bern: A Francke, 1932 – 1r – 1 – us U.W. Library [430]
DICHTKUNDIGE BESPIEGELINGEN OP 57 GEPASTE IN KOPER GEBRAGTE ZINNEBEELDEN / Houbraken, Arnold – Amsterdam, 1782 – 4mf – 9 – O-3089/1 – ne IDC [760]
DICHTLIEVENDE VERLUSTIGINGEN, VAN BERNARDUS DE BOSCH / Bosch, B de – 1st ed. Amsterdam, 1742-1788 – 4mf – 9 – ne IDC [700]
DICHTUNG, SPRACHE, GESELLSCHAFT : AKTEN DES 4. INTERNATIONALEN GERMANISTEN-KONGRESSES / ed by Internationaler Germanisten-Kongress – (German and English. Includes bibliographical references) – Frankfurt/M: Athenaeum Verlag, c1971 – 1 – us U.W. Library [430]
DICHTUNG UND ARETE : UNTERSUCHUNEN ZUR BEDEUTUNG DER MUSISCHEN ERZIEHUNG BEI PLATO / Harth, Helene – Frankfurt a.M., 1965 – 3mf – 9 – DM76.00 – 3-89349-679-3 – gw Hänsel [180]
DICHTUNG UND DICHTER DER ZEIT : EINE SCHILDERUNG DER DEUTSCHEN LITERATUR DER LETZTEN JAHRZEHNTE / Soergel, Albert – 20. Auflage, 67. bis 71. Tausend. Leipzig: R Voigtlaender, 1928 – 1 – us U.W. Library [430]
DICHTUNGEN / Dahn, Felix – Leipzig: Breitkopf & Haertel, 1898 – 1 – us U.W. Library [810]
DICHTUNGEN DER DROSTE / ed by Castelle, Friedrich – 2. Aufl. Moenchengladbach: Volksvereins-Verlag, 1923 – 1 – us U.W. Library [810]
DICIONARIO BIO-BIBLIOGRAFICO BRASILEIRO / Velho Sobrinho, J F – Rio de Janeiro. 2v. 1937-1940 – 15mf – 9 – ne IDC [972]
DICK AND JANE'S ADVENTURES ON SABLE ISLAND / Ashley, Barnas Freeman – Chicago: Laird & Lee, 1896?. 06156. (Pre-1900 Canadiana) – 9 – cn C.I.H.M. [830]
Dick, Robert P *see* HEBREW POETRY: SUNDAY AFTERNOON LECTURES
Dick, Wenceslas E *see* LE ROI DES ETUDIANTS
Dickason, Elizabeth L *see* USE OF THE HEALTH BELIEF MODEL IN DETERMINING MAMMOGRAPHY SCREENING PRACTICE IN OLDER WOMEN
Dicke, F *see* DE OPLEIDING VAN DE BOUWKUNDIG INGENIEUR OF ARCHITECT IN INDONESIE
Dickens, Charles *see*
- L'AMI COMMUN
- THE BATTLE OF LIFE
- THE CHIMES
- THE HAUNTED MAN AND THE GHOST'S BARGAIN
- MANUSCRIPT LETTERS
- THE MANUSCRIPT OF 'GREAT EXPECTATIONS'
- ORIGINAL MSS. AND ANNOTATED PROOFS
- ORIGINAL MSS. AND OTHER PAPERS
- THE POEMS AND VERSES OF CHARLES DICKENS
- SPEECHES, LITERARY AND SOCIAL. NOW FIRST COLLECTED

THE DICKENS COUNTRY : WITH FIFTY FULL-PAGE ILLUSTRATIONS MOSTLY FROM PHOTOGRAPHS BY T.W. TYRRELL / Kitton, Frederic George – London: Adam and Charles Black, 1905 – 1 roll – 1 – 1-55879-326-7 – uk Libr Preservation [420]

DICKENS DICTIONARY : A KEY TO THE CHARACTERS AND PRINCIPAL INCIDENTS IN THE TALES OF CHARLES DICKENS / Pierce, Gilbert A – Boston: Osgood, 1872 – 1 roll – 1 – 1-55879-848-X – uk Libr Preservation [420]

DICKENS PLAYBILLS IN THE BODLEIAN LIBRARY – (Includes guide) – 9mf – 9 – $57.50 – us UMI [790]

THE DICKENSIAN – 1905-74 – 9 – us Primary [420]

Dickerhoff, Hans *see* DIE ENTSTEHUNG DER JOBSIADE

DICKER'S MINING RECORD. (MINING RECORD OF VICTORIA, AUSTRALIA, AND PUBLIC COMPANIES GAZETTE) – Melbourne, Australia. 23 Nov 1861-14 Jun 1870. - w – 3r – 1 – uk British Libr Newspaper [622]

Dickerson, S H *see* THE BRITISH COLONIST

Dickey, Samuel *see* THE POSITION OF GREEK IN THE THEOLOGICAL EDUCATION OF TODAY

Dickie, G *see* FLORA ABREDONENSIS

Dickinson County. Kansas. Board of Commissioners *see* JOURNALS

DICKINSON COUNTY NEWS – Abilene. Kan. 1888-1918 – 1 – us UMI [071]

Dickinson, Emily *see*
- THE COMPLETE POEMS..
- POEMS

Dickinson, F H *see* MISSALE AD USUM INSIGNIS ET PRAECLARAE ECCLESIAE SARUM

Dickinson, G Lowes *see* RELIGION AND IMMORTALITY

Dickinson, Goldsworthy Lowes *see* RELIGION

Dickinson, H W *see* WATER SUPPLY OF GREATER LONDON

DICKINSON INTERNATIONAL LAW ANNUAL *see* DICKINSON JOURNAL OF INTERNATIONAL LAW

Dickinson, John P *see* SCIENCE AND SCIENTIFIC RESEARCHERS IN MODERN SOCIETY

Dickinson, Jonathan *see* A SERMON...SEPTEMBER 19, 1722

DICKINSON JOURNAL OF INTERNATIONAL LAW – (v1-3 1982-85 on reel $52.00. v4-13 1985-95 on mf $207.00. Title varies: v1-2 no 1 1982-83 as Dickinson International Law Annual) – v1-13. 1982-95 – 5,6,9 – $261.00 set – us Hein [340]

DICKINSON LAW REVIEW – (v1-12 1897-1912 are titled "The Forum") – Dickinson Law School. v1-24. 1897-1919/20 – 75mf – $112.00 – LLMC 84-446 – us L.L.M.C. [073]

DICKINSON LAW REVIEW – (v1-89 1897-85 on reel $830.00. v90-99 1985-95 on mf $253.00. Title varies: v1-12 1897-1909 as The Forum) – v1-99. 1897-1999 – 5,6,9 – $1,083.00 set – us Hein [340]

Dickinson, Marguerite *see* HOLMES COUNTY, OHIO, CEMETERY RECORDS

THE DICKINSON PAPERS – 1675-1849. From the Jamaica Plantation Records. BRRAM – 1 – uk Microform Academic [972]

Dickinson, Richard William *see* THE RESURRECTION OF JESUS CHRIST HISTORICALLY AND LOGICALLY VIEWED

Dickius, L *see* ADVERSVS IMPIOS ANABAPTISTARVM ERRORES. IUDITIUM

Dickmann, Fritz *see* DIE NOTWENDIGKEIT DES RELIGIONSUNTERRICHTS IN DER STAATSSCHULE

Dickson, Alexander *see* ALL ABOUT JESUS

Dickson, Andrew F *see*
- PLANTATION SERMONS..
- PLANTATION SERMONS, OR, PLAIN AND FAMILIAR DISCOURSES FOR THE INSTRUCTION OF THE UNLEARNED

Dickson, J *see* PLANTARUM CRYPTOGAMICARUM BRITANNIAE

Dickson, James *see* CAMPING IN THE MUSKOKA REGION

Dickson, James A R *see* WORKING FOR JESUS

Dickson, Richard W *see* JOHN HOWARD AND THE PRISON WORLD OF EUROPE

Dickson, William K L *see* HISTORY OF THE KINETOGRAPH, KINETOSCOPE AND KINETOPHONOGRAPH

DICP *see* ANNALS OF PHARMACOTHERAPY

DICTA – (Title changes: v40 1963: The Denver Law Center Journal. v43 1966: The Denver Law Journal. v62 1985: Denver University Law Review. For copyright reasons only the Dicta portion of the title can be offered by LLMC) – Denver Bar Association. v1-39. 1923-62 – 172mf – 9 – $258.00 – LLMC 84-458 – us L.L.M.C. [073]

DICTA *see* DENVER UNIVERSITY LAW REVIEW

DICTA BEATI AEGIDII ASSISIENSIS / Aegidius, of Assisi – 2nd ed., 1939 – 1 – us A.T.L.A. [240]

LA DICTADURA PERONISTA / Alonso Pineiro, Armendo – [Buenos Aires]: Editorial "Prestigio", 1955 – 1 – CSUXADH2081-B – us Hoover Inst Photo [972]

EL DICTAMEN – Veracruz: [s.n. 1920-47] – 99R – 1 – us Res Libr [072]

DICTAMEN DE LAS ACADEMIA...DE BARCELONA...SOBRE LA FRECUENCIA DE LAS MUERTES...REPENTINAS Y APOPLEJIAS – Barcelona, 1748 – 2mf – 9 – sp Cultura [616]

DICTAMEN FISCAL...OFICIALES GENERALES – 1816 – 9 – 1.50f – sp Bibl Santa Ana [336]

DICTAMEN SOBRE LA CONSTRUCCION DE UNA LINEA FERREA...HA TOMADO LA EXPRESADA CORPORACION – 1867 – 9 – $1.50f – sp Bibl Santa Ana [380]

DICTAMEN SOBRE LA UTILIDAD...DE LA EXCAVACION DEL POZO-AIRON...PARA EVITAR TERREMOTOS / Vaca de Guzman, O – Granada, 1779 – 2mf – 9 – sp Cultura [946]

DICTAMEN TORREMOCHA – 1894 – 9 – 1.50f – sp Bibl Santa Ana [946]

DICTATOR - DEMOCRAT / Singer, Ignatius – Pamphlet. 1 fiche (29x) – 9 – 1.00f – at Libertarian Micro [320]

DICTATOR-DEMOCRAT / Berens, Lewis H & Singer, I – 1fiche (29x) – 9 – 1.00f – at Libertarian Micro [320]

DICTATUM CHRISTIANUM / Arias Montano, Benito – 1575 – 9 – 1.50f – sp Bibl Santa Ana [240]

DICTEES GRADUEES ET ANALYSES : 1ER MANUEL: DEUX CENTS DICTEES POUR COURS PREPARATOIRE, 1ERE ET 2EME ANNEES / Theodule, Fr – Montreal: les freres du Sacre-Coeur, [1932?]. SEM105P1618 – 1mf – 9 – Can$2.25 – cn Bibl Nat [440]

DICTEES GRADUEES ET ANALYSES : 3E MANUEL: DEUX CENT CINQUANTE DICTEES POUR COURS PRIMAIRE, 5E ET 6E ANNEES / Freres du Sacre-Coeur – Montreal: les freres du Sacre-Coeur, [1932?]. SEM105P1612 – 3mf – 9 – Can$6.75 – cn Bibl Nat [440]

DICTIONAIRE DE MUSIQUE... / Brossard, S de – Paris, 1703 – 3mf – ne IDC [780]

DICTIONAIRE DES SCIENCES MEDICALES (AEL, ABT 3;16) / Jourdan, A J L – Paris, 1820-1825 (mf ed 1994) – 27mf – 9 – DM420.00 – 3-89131-184-2 – gw Fischer [055]

DICTIONAIRE ETYMOLOGIQUE... / Menage, G – Paris, 1694 – 15mf – ne IDC [400]

DICTIONAIRE FRANCOIS ALLEMAND ET ALLEMAND FRANCOIS; DICTIONARIUM TEUTSCH FRANTZOESISCH UND FRANTZOESISCH TEUTSCH (AEL, ABT.5;5) / Hulsius, Levinus – 1. Ausgabe Nuernberg, 1596, 3. Ausgabe Nuernberg, 1607 – 21mf – 9 – DM210.00 – 3-89131-065-X – gw Fischer [054]

DICTIONAIRE FRANCOIS LATIN / Thierry, J – 1564 – 9 – fr I.C.S. [450]

DICTIONAIRE FRANCOIS-FLAMENG / Mellema, E – 1602 – 9 – fr I.C.S. [440]

DICTIONAIRE HARMONIQUE OU GUIDE SUR POUR LA VRAI MODULAISON = DICTIONARIUM HARMONICUM OF ZEEKERE WEGWYZER TOT DE WAARE MODULATIE / Geminiani, Francesco – Amsterdam, 1756 – 1mf – ne IDC [780]

DICTIONAIRE HARMONIQUE OU GUIDE SUR POUR LA VRAIE MODULAISON / Geminiani, Francesco – 1756 – 9 – us Sibley [780]

DICTIONAIRE (SIC) DE L'ANCIEN DROIT DU CANADA / McCarthy, Justin – Quebec: J Neilson, 1809. SEM16P181 – 1r – 5 – Can$9.00 – cn Bibl Nat [971]

DICTIONAIRE UNIVERSEL CONTENANT GENERALEMENT TOUT LES MOTS FRANCOIS TANT VIEUX QUE MODERNES, ET LES TERMES DE TOUTES LES SCIENCES ET DES ARTS (AEL, ABT 2; 1/) : EDITION DER AUSGABEN 1690, 1691, 1694, 1701, 1702, 1708, 1725, 1727 / Furetiere, Antoine – Den Haag/Rotterdam. 1690-1727 (mf ed 1997) – 243mf – 9 – DM2,300.00 – 3-89131-226-1 – gw Fischer [440]

A DICTIONARIE FRENCH AND ENGLISH / Desainliens, Claude – 1593. 512p. (English Linguistics Series 1500-1800) – 9 – us UMI [440]

A DICTIONARIE IN SPANISH AND ENGLISH : [...]HEREUNTO IS ANNEXED AN AMPLE ENGLISH DICTIONAIRE ALPHABETICALLY... / Percyvall, Richard & Minsheu, John – London, 1599 (mf ed 1993) – 8mf – 9 – DM184.00 – 3-89131-066-8 – gw Fischer [040]

A DICTIONARIE OF THE FRENCH AND ENGLISH TONGUES / Cotgrave, Randle – 1611 – 9 – fr I.C.S. [440]

A DICTIONARIE OF THE FRENCH AND ENGLISH TONGUES / Cotgrave, Randle – 1611, 977p. (English Linguistics Series 1500-1800) – 9 – us UMI [420]

DICTIONARIES – 9 – ne IDC [050]

DICTIONARIES AND VOCABULARIES 1966-1981 IN THE TERMINOLOGY AND REFERENCE LIBRARY / F.A.O. – 1983 – 232p – it F.A.O. [010]

DICTIONARIES AND VOCABULARIES 1982-1985 IN THE TERMINOLOGY AND REFERENCE LIBRARY / F.A.O. – 1986 – 72p – it F.A.O. [010]

DICTIONARIOLUM PUERORUM TRIBUS LINGUIS LATINA, GALLICA ET GERMANICA CONSCRIPTUM... / Stephanus, R & Fries, J – Tiguri: Froschouer, 1548 – 7mf – ne IDC [450]

DICTIONARIUM ANGLO-BRITANNICUM: OR, A GENERAL ENGLISH DICTIONARY / Kersey, John – 1708. 736p. (English Linguistics Series 1500-1800) – 9 – us UMI [420]

DICTIONARIUM DUPLEX : ANTIQUAE LINGUAE BRITTANICAE... / Davies, J – Londini, 1632 – 5mf – ne IDC [420]

DICTIONARIUM FRANTZOESICSH-TEUTSCH UND TEUTSCH-FRANTZOESISCHES WOERTERREGISTER UEBER KRAMERS DICTIONNAIRE (AEL, ABT.2;1) / Kramer, Matthias – Nuernberg. 5v. 1712, 1715 (mf ed 1992) – 30mf – 9 – DM270.00 – 3-89131-057-9 – gw Fischer [050]

DICTIONARIUM GROENLANDICO-DANICO-LATINUM / Egede, P – Hafnaie, 1750 – 6mf – ne IDC [430]

DICTIONARIUM LATINO LUSITANICUM / Calepinus, A – Amacusa, 1595 – 10mf – 9 – H-8426/1 – ne IDC [450]

DICTIONARIUM LATINO-ARMENUM SUPER SACRAM SCRIPTURAM / Nierszesovicz, Deodatus (Astuatsatur) – Romae, 1695 – 7mf – ne IDC [450]

DICTIONARIUM LATINO-GERMANICUM... : EDITIO NOVA... / Fries, J – Tiguri: Christoph Froschouer, 1556 – 15mf – ne IDC [450]

DICTIONARIUM LINGUAE LATINAE ET ANGLICANAE / Thomas, Thomas – 1587. 1017p. (English Linguistics Series 1500-1800) – 9 – us UMI [450]

DICTIONARIUM MEDICUM, VEL EXPOSITIONES VOCUM MEDICINALIUM AD VERVUM EXCERPTAE ES HIPPOCRATE, ARETEO ETC. (AEL, ABT 3;21) / Estienne, Henri – Paris, 1564 (mf ed 1996) – 7mf – 9 – DM140.00 – 3-89131-217-2 – gw Fischer [610]

DICTIONARIUM SAXONICA-LATINO-ANGLICUM / Somner, William – 1659. 460p. (English Linguistics Series 1500-1800) – 9 – us UMI [420]

DICTIONARIUM SINENSE-LATINUM SUN-KIAM A M D G 1847 / Brueyre, B – Sun-Kiam, 1847. [10] 1192 – 13mf – ne IDC [040]

DICTIONARIUM SYRIACO-LATINUM / Brun, J – Beryti Phoeniciorum: Typographia PP Soc Jesu, 1911 – 2mf – 9 – 0-8370-9765-7 – 1986-3765 – us A.T.L.A. [470]

DICTIONARIUM TEUTSCH-ITALIAENISCH UND ITALIAENISCH-TEUTSCH (AEL, ABT.2;7) / Hulsius, Levinus – Frankfurt, 1605 (mf ed 1992) – 6mf – 9 – DM84.00 – 3-89131-067-6 – gw Fischer [054]

DICTIONARIVM ARMENO-LATINVM / Rivola, F – Paris, 1633 – 9mf – ne IDC [460]

DICTIONARIVM HEBRAICVM NOVVM,... / Forster J G A – Basileae, 1557 – 17mf – ne IDC [470]

DICTIONARIVM, SEV LATINAE LINGUAE THESAURUS,... / ed by Stophanuc, R – Parisiis. 2v. 1536 – 31mf – ne IDC [450]

DICTIONARIVM TRILINGVE, IN QVO SCILICET LATINIS VOCABVLIS...RESPONDENT GRAECA ET HEBRAICA / Muenster, S – Basileae, 1562 – 5mf – 9 – H-8409/1 – ne IDC [040]

DICTIONARUM GERMANICO LATINUM... / Gessner, C Josua Maler – Tiguri: Excudebat Christophorus Froschoverus, 1561 – 1mf – ne IDC [430]

DICTIONARUM SIVE THESAURI LINGUAE JAPONICAE / Collado, Fr. Diego – 1632 – 9 – 1.50f – sp Bibl Santa Ana [480]

THE DICTIONARY / Elyot, Thomas – 1538. 424p. (English Linguistics Series 1500-1800) – 9 – us UMI [420]

DICTIONARY AND AUCTION CATALOGS OF THE LIBRARY / American Numismatic Society. New York. Library – (Dictionary Catalog 108,000 cards 6r $655.00 ISBN: 0-8161-149-73; Auction Catalog, 1962 15,300 cards 1r $110 ISBN: 0-8161-1426-9; 2nd Suppl 1973 17,200 cards 1r $120.00 ISBN: 0-8161-1427-7; 3rd Suppl 1978 29,100 cards 4r $225.00 ISBN: 0-8161-1375-0) – 1962 – 1 – $695.00 – uk Hall [730]

DICTIONARY AND GRAMMAR OF THE CHAMORRO LANGUAGE OF THE ISLAND OF GUAM / Preissig, E von – Washington, 1918 – 4mf – ne IDC [490]

A DICTIONARY CARNATACA AND ENGLISH / Reeve, William – Madras: Printed at Govt Gazette Press, 1832 – 1 – us Res Libr [040]

DICTIONARY CATALOG / Bernice P. Bishop Museum. Honolulu – (First suppl., 1967.-14,100 cards 1 reel. $130.00 ISBN: 0-8161-1448-X; Second suppl., 1969.-5000 cards 1 reel. $120.00 ISBN: 0-8161-1449-8) – uk Hall [975]

DICTIONARY CATALOG / Columbia University. Law Library – (First Suppl., 1973.-107,000 cards 7 reels. $1035.00 ISBN: 0-8161-1501-X; Second Suppl., 1977.- 50,700 cards 8 reels $500.00) – 1969, 690,000 cards 28 reels ISBN: 0-8161-1495-1 – 1 – $3145.00 – uk Hall [013]

DICTIONARY CATALOG / Columbia University. Teachers College Library – (Second Suppl., 1973.-39,200 cards 4 reels. $300.00 ISBN: 0-8161-1376-9; Third Suppl., 1977.-135,000 cards 10 reels. $1205.00 ISBN: 0-8161-1452-8) – uk Hall [013]

DICTIONARY CATALOG / Hebrew Union College. Jewish Institute of Religion. Klau Library – 1964.-451,000 cards 59 reels ISBN: 0-8161-1374-2 – 1 – $2425.00 – uk Hall [012]

DICTIONARY CATALOG / Massachusetts Horticultural Society. Library – 1962.-43,700 cards 6 reels.-ISBN: 0-8161-1368-8 – 1 – $285.00 – uk Hall [016]

DICTIONARY CATALOG / Michigan. University. Robert Vincent Voice Library – 1975.-6700 cards 1 reel.-ISBN: 0-8161-1444-7 – 1 – $85.00 – uk Hall [410]

DICTIONARY CATALOG / Missionary Research Library. New York – 1968.-273,000 cards 34 reels.-ISBN: 0-8161-1378-5 – 1 – $1850.00 – uk Hall [012]

DICTIONARY CATALOG / New York Public Library.Schomburg Collection – (First Suppl., 1967.-37,100 cards 4 reels.-ISBN: 0-8161-1260-2) – 1960.-177,000 entries 17 reels.-ISBN: 0-8161-1259-2 – 1 – $915.00 – uk Hall [017]

DICTIONARY CATALOG / Racquet and Tennis Club.New York. Library of Sports – With special collections on tennis, lawn tennis and early American sport, 1970.-34,700 cards 2 reels.-ISBN: 0-8161-1386-6 – 1 – $220.00 – uk Hall [017]

DICTIONARY CATALOG AND SHELF LIST OF THE SPENCER COLLECTION OF ILLUSTRATED BOOKS AND MANUSCRIPTS AND FINE BINDINGS / New York Public Library. Research Libraries – 1971.-34,100 catalog cards and 5000 Shelf List cards 2 reels.-ISBN: 0-8161-1504-4 – 1 – $220.00 – uk Hall [010]

DICTIONARY CATALOG OF THE APPLIED LIFE STUDIES LIBRARY / Illinois. University at Urbana-Champaign – 1977.-52,300 cards 8 reels – 8r – 1 – $375.00 export $450.00 – 0-8161-1233-9 – uk Hall [015]

DICTIONARY CATALOG OF THE ARCHIVES / University of California at Berkeley. Water Resources Center – Fifth suppl., 1976.-21,000 cards 4 reels.-ISBN: 0-8161-1266-5 – 1 – uk Hall [333]

DICTIONARY CATALOG OF THE COLUMBIA UNIVERSITY LAW LIBRARY / Columbia University. Law Library – (First Supplement, 1973. 107,000 cards 7 reels. $940.00 export $1135.00. – ISBN 0-8161-1501-X; Second Supplement, 1977. 50,700 cards 8 reels. $500.00 export $605.00. – ISBN 0-8161-1272-X) – 1969. 690,000 cards on 28 reels – 1 – $2,860.00 export $3,435.00 – 0-8161-1495-1 – uk Hall [340]

DICTIONARY CATALOG OF THE DEPARTMENT LIBRARY / U.S. Department of Housing and Urban Development. Library and Information Division – (First Suppl., 1974.-30,100 cards 4 reels. $240.00 ISBN: 0-8161-1250-9; Second Suppl., 1975.-26,100 cards 2 reels. $240.00 ISBN: 0-8161-1492-7) – 1972.-294,000 cards 19 reels.-ISBN: 0-8161-1491-9 – 1 – $2070.00 – uk Hall [013]

DICTIONARY CATALOG OF THE DEPARTMENT LIBRARY / U.S. Department of the Interior – (First Suppl.-1969.-64,000 cards 8 reels.$245.00 export $295.00.-ISBN 0-8161-1254-1; Second Suppl.-1971.-30,300 cards 4 reels.$180.00 export $220.00.-ISBN 0-8161-1255-X; Fourth Suppl.- 1975.-116,000 cards.$825.00 export $998.00.-all are available on microfilm by request) – 1 – uk Hall [013]

DICTIONARY CATALOG OF THE EDWARD E. AYER COLLECTION OF AMERICANA AND AMERICAN INDIANS / Newberry Library. Chicago – 1961.-169,000 cards – 1 – uk Hall [019]

DICTIONARY CATALOG OF THE G. ROBERT VINCENT VOICE LIBRARY / Michigan State University. Robert Vincent Voice Library – 1975. 6700 cards on 1 reel – 1 – $78.00 export $95.00 – 0-8161-1444-7 – uk Hall [010]

DICTIONARY CATALOG OF THE GIANNINI FOUNDATION OF AGRICULTURAL ECONOMICS LIBRARY / University of California at Berkeley. Giannini Foundation of Agricultural Economics – (Available on microfilm by request) – 1971. 420,000 cards – 1 – $1,185.00 export $1,435.00 – uk Hall [330]

DICTIONARY CATALOG OF THE GIANNINI FOUNDATION OF AGRICULTURAL ECONOMICS LIBRARY UNIVERSITY OF CALIFORNIA AT BERKELEY / Giannini Foundation of Agricultural Economics – 1971. 42.000 cards on 12 reels – 1 – $1,305.00 export $1,580.00 – 0-8161-1563-X – uk Hall [330]

DICTIONARY CATALOG OF THE HARRIS COLLECTION OF AMERICAN POETRY AND PLAYS / Brown University. Library – (First Suppl., 1977.-46,200 cards 3 reels. $365.00 ISBN: 0-8161-1453-6) – 1972.-337,000 cards 13 reels ISBN: 0-8161-1497-8 – 1 – $1860.00 – uk Hall [018]

DICTIONARY CATALOG OF THE HENRY W. AND ALBERT A. BERG COLLECTION OF ENGLISH AND AMERICAN LITERATURE : SECOND SUPPLEMENT / New York Public Library. Research Libraries – 1983. 16,537 cards on 1 reel – 1 – $150.00 export $180.00 – 0-8161-1471-4 – uk Hall [420]

DICTIONARY CATALOG OF THE JEWISH COLLECTION / New York Public Library. Reference Department – (First suppl.- 1975.-117,000 cards 8 reels $875.00) – 1960.-254,000 cards 14 reels.-ISBN: 0-8161-1457-9 – 1 – $1365.00 – uk Hall [012]

DICTIONARY CATALOG OF THE KLAU LIBRARY / Hebrew Union College-Jewish Institute of Religion. Cincinnati – 1964. 451,000 cards on 59 reels – 1 – $2,205.00 export $2,665.00 – 0-8161-1374-2 – uk Hall [270]

DICTIONARY CATALOG OF THE LIBRARY / Pontifical Institute of Mediaeval Studies. Toronto – (First Suppl., 1979.-13,400 cards 1 reel. $145.00 ISBN: 0-8161-1528-1) – 1973.-89,700 cards 10 reels.-ISBN: 0-8161-1257-6 – 1 – $555.00 – uk Hall [010]

DICTIONARY CATALOG OF THE LIBRARY / Smithsonian Institution.Washington, DC. Library of the Freer Gallery of Art – 1967.-89,200 cards 6 reels.-ISBN: 0-8161-1521-4 – 1 – $610.00 – uk Hall [017]

DICTIONARY CATALOG OF THE LIBRARY OF THE BERNICE P. BISHOP MUSEUM : FIRST SUPPLEMENT / Bernice P. Bishop Museum. Honolulu – (Second Supplement, 1969. 5000 cards, 1 reel. $110.00 export $135.00. – ISBN 0-8161-1449-8) – 1967. 14,100 cards on 1 reel – 1 – $120.00 export $145.00 – 0-8161-1448-X – uk Hall [978]

DICTIONARY CATALOG OF THE LIBRARY OF THE CENTER FOR APPLIED LINGUISTICS / Center for Applied Linguistics. Washington, D.C. – (Available on microfilm by request) – 1974. 53,100 cards – 1 – $410.00 export $490.00 – 0-8161-1114-6 – uk Hall [410]

DICTIONARY CATALOG OF THE LIBRARY OF THE FREER GALLERY OF ART; SMITHSONIAN INSTITUTION 2ND ENLARGED EDITION / Freer Gallery of Art, Smithsonian Institution – Boston, G.K. Hall and Co., 1991 – 195,839 cards on 252mf, with printed index – 9 – $995.00 US; export $1095.00 – 0-8161-1791-8 – uk Hall [017]

DICTIONARY CATALOG OF THE LIBRARY OF THE MASSACHUSETTS HORTICULTURAL SOCIETY / Massachusetts Horticultural Society. Boston – 1962. 43,700 cards on 6 reels – 1 – $260.00 export $315.00 – 0-8161-1368-8 – uk Hall [580]

DICTIONARY CATALOG OF THE LIBRARY, THE MARINERS MUSEUM / The Mariners Museum. Newport News, Virginia – (Available on microfilm by request; $980.00 export $1190.00. – ISBN 0-8161-0674-6) – 1964. 144,000 cards – 1 – uk Hall [380]

DICTIONARY CATALOG OF THE LOCAL HISTORY AND GENEALOGY DIVISION / New York Public Library. Research Libraries – 1974. 320,000 cards on 18 reels – 1 – $1,600.00 export $1,935.00 – 0-8161-1468-4 – uk Hall [920]

DICTIONARY CATALOG OF THE MANUSCRIPT DIVISION / New York Public Library, Research Libraries – 1967.-24,000 cards 2 reels.-ISBN: 0-8161-1450-1 – 1 – $170.00 – uk Hall [010]

DICTIONARY CATALOG OF THE M.C. MIGEL MEMORIAL LIBRARY, AMERICAN FOUNDATION FOR THE BLIND / American Foundation for the Blind. M.C. Migel Memorial Library, New York City – (Available on microfilm by request) – 1966. 22,000 cards – 9 – $170.00 export $210.00 – 0-8161-0705-X – uk Hall [010]

DICTIONARY CATALOG OF THE MUSIC COLLECTION / Boston Public Library – (First suppl., 1976.-56,000 cards 4 reels. $485.00 ISBN: 0-8161-1419-6) – 1972.-328,000 cards 20 reels.-ISBN: 0-8161-1514-1 – 1 – $2175.00 – uk Hall [017]

DICTIONARY CATALOG OF THE MUSIC COLLECTION / New York Public Library. Reference Department – 1964.-532,824 cards 66 reels.-ISBN: 0-8161-1308-4 – 1 – $2750.00 – uk Hall [017]

DICTIONARY CATALOG OF THE NEGRO COLLECTION OF THE FISK UNIVERSITY LIBRARY / Fisk University Libary. Nashville – (Available on microfilm by request) – 1974. 57,000 cards – 1 – $560.00 export $675.00 – 0-8161-1055-7 – uk Hall [305]

DICTIONARY CATALOG OF THE ORIENTAL COLLECTION / New York Public Library. Research Libraries – 1960.-318,000 cards 30 reels.-ISBN: 0-8161-1282-7 – 1 – $1320.00 – uk Hall [019]

DICTIONARY CATALOG OF THE PRINCETON UNIVERSITY PLASMA PHYSICS LABORATORY LIBRARY / Princeton University. Firestone Library. Plasma Physics Laboratory Library – (First Supplement, 1972. 18,300 cards. $175.00 export $215.00. – ISBN 0-8161-1032-8. Available on microfilm by request) – 1970. 62,000 cards – 1 – $435.00 export $525.00 – 0-8161-0881-1 – uk Hall [530]

DICTIONARY CATALOG OF THE RARE BOOK DIVISION / New York Public Library. Research Libraries. Astor, Lenox & Tilden Foundations – (First Suppl., 1973.-15,600 entries 2 reels. $125.00 ISBN: 0-8161-1258-4) – 1 – uk Hall [010]

DICTIONARY CATALOG OF THE RESEARCH LIBRARIES / New York Public Library. Research Libraries – 1911-71.-800 reels.-ISBN: 0-8191-0327-5 – 1 – $24,000.00 – uk Hall [010]

DICTIONARY CATALOG OF THE SCHOMBURG COLLECTION OF NEGRO LITERATURE AND HISTORY / New York Public Library. Schomburg Collection – (First Supplement, 1967. 37,100 cards on 4 reels. $120.00 export $145.00. – ISBN 0-8161-1260-6) – 1962. 177,000 cards on 17 reels – 1 – $830.00 export $1,005.00 – 0-8161-1259-2 – uk Hall [305]

DICTIONARY CATALOG OF THE SLAVONIC COLLECTION, SECOND EDITION REVISED AND ENLARGED / New York Public Library. Research Libraries – 1974.-727,000 cards 88 reels.-ISBN: 0-8161-1264-9 – 1 – $4355.00 – uk Hall [014]

DICTIONARY CATALOG OF THE STEFANSSON COLLECTION ON THE POLAR REGIONS / Dartmouth College. Library – 1967.-115,000 cards 16 reels – 1 – $720.00 export $870.00 – 0-8161-1357-2 – uk Hall [910]

DICTIONARY CATALOG OF THE TEACHERS COLLEGE LIBRARY : SECOND SUPPLEMENT / Columbia University. Teachers College Library – (Additional supplements appear annually as the Bibliographic Guide to Education) – 1973. 39,200 cards on 4 reels – 1 – $270.00 export $325.00 – 0-8161-1376-9 – uk Hall [370]

DICTIONARY CATALOG OF THE TEACHERS COLLEGE LIBRARY : THIRD SUPPLEMENT / Columbia University. Teachers College Library – 1977. 135,000 cards on 10 reels – 1 – $1,095.00 export $1,325.00 – 0-8161-1452-8 – uk Hall [370]

THE DICTIONARY CATALOG OF THE UNITED STATES DEPARTMENT OF HOUSING AND URBAN DEVELOPMENT LIBRARY AND INFORMATION DIVISION / U.S. Department of Housing and Urban Development. Library and Information Division. Washington, D.C. – (First Supplement, 1974. 30,100 cards 4 reels. $220.00 export $265.00. – ISBN 0-8161-1250-9; Second Supplement, 1975. 26,100 cards 2 reels. $220.00 export $265.00. – ISBN 0-8161-1492-7) – 1972. 294,000 cards on 19 reels – 1 – $1,880.00 export $2,275.00 – 0-8161-1491-9 – uk Hall [360]

DICTIONARY CATALOG OF THE WATER RESOURCES CENTER ARCHIVES : FIFTH SUPPLEMENT / University of California at Berkeley. Water Resources Center – 1976. 21,000 cards on 4 reels – 1 – $145.00 export $175.00 – 0-8161-1266-5 – uk Hall [333]

DICTIONARY CATALOG OF THE WATER RESOURCES CENTER ARCHIVES : SIXTH SUPPLEMENT / University of California at Berkeley. Water Resources Center – 1978. 26,500 cards on 2 reels – 1 – $260.00 export $315.00 – 0-8161-1456-0 – uk Hall [333]

DICTIONARY CATALOG OF THE WILLIAM ANDREWS CLARK MEMORIAL LIBRARY / California. University. Los Angeles – 1974.-242,000 cards 30 reels.-ISBN: 0-8161-1330-0 – 1 – $1545.00 – uk Hall [010]

DICTIONARY CATALOG ON DEAFNESS AND THE DEAF / Gallaudet College. Washington, DC – 1970.-35,300 cards 4 reels.-ISBN: 0-8161-1248-7 – 1 – $190.00 – uk Hall [616]

DICTIONARY CATALOGUE / American Numismatic Society. New York – 108,000 cards onr – 1 – $595.00 export $720.00 – 0-8161-1489-7 – uk Hall [730]

DICTIONARY CATALOGUE OF THE BYZANTINE COLLECTION / Harvard University. Dumbarton Oaks Research Library. Washington, DC – 1975.-174,000 cards 12 reels.-ISBN: 0-8161-1502-8 – 1 – $1530.00 – uk Hall [940]

DICTIONARY CATALOGUE OF THE HISTORY OF PRINTING FROM THE JOHN M. WING FOUNDATION / Newberry Library. Chicago – 1961.-127,000 cards 11 reels.-ISBN: 0-8161-1479-X – 1 – $655.00 – uk Hall [010]

DICTIONARY CATALOGUE OF THE LIBARY OF THE PONTIFICAL INSTITUTE OF MEDIAEVAL STUDIES / Pontifical Institute of Mediaeval Studies. Toronto – (First Supplement, 1979. 13,400 cards. 1 reel. $130.00 export $160.00. – ISBN 0-8161-1528-1) – 1972. 89,700 cards on 10 reels – 1 – $505.00 export $610.00 – 0-8161-1257-6 – uk Hall [200]

A DICTIONARY CATALOGUE OF THE LIBRARY OF SPORTS IN THE RACQUET AND TENNIS CLUB, WITH SPECIAL COLLECTIONS ON TENNIS, LAWN TENNIS, AND EARLY AMERICAN SPORT / Racquet and Tennis Club. Library of Sports, New York – 1970. 34,700 cards on 2 reels – 1 – $200.00 export $240.00 – 0-8161-1386-6 – uk Hall [790]

DICTIONARY CATALOGUE OF THE LIBRARY OF THE PROVINCIAL ARCHIVES OF BRITISH COLUMBIA / Provincial Archives. Victoria, British Columbia – (Available on microfilm by request) – 1971. 176.000 cards – 1 – $790.00 export $955.00 – uk Hall [010]

A DICTIONARY ENGLISH, GERMAN AND FRENCH UND TEUTSCH-ENGLISCHES LEXICON (AEL, ABT.2;4) / Ludwig, Christian – Leipzig, 1706, 1716 (mf ed 1992) – 23mf – 9 – DM230.00 – 3-89131-064-1 – gw Fischer [054]

A DICTIONARY ENGLISH-ARMENIAN AND ARMENIAN-ENGLISH / Awgerian, Y & Brand, Y – Venice. 2v. 1821-25 – 18mf – 9 – AR-1701/1 – ne IDC [040]

DICTIONARY ENGLISH-INDONESIA / Hadat, D – SE-10,084 1. 1951 – 9 – ne IDC [490]

A DICTIONARY IN ENGLYSHE AND WELSHE / Salesbury, William – 1547. 170p. (English Linguistics Series 1500-1800) – 9 – us UMI [490]

DICTIONARY OF ARCHITECTURE – 1852-92 – 30mf – 9 – £170.00 – uk Chadwyck [720]

A DICTIONARY OF ASSYRIAN CHEMISTRY AND GEOLOGY / Thompson, R C – Oxford, 1936 – 4mf – 9 – ne IDC [055]

A DICTIONARY OF BIRDS / Newton, A – Z-1871 2. 1893-1896 – 8 – ne IDC [590]

DICTIONARY OF BOOKS RELATING TO AMERICA / Sabin, Joseph – 29 V. 1868-1936 – 3 – us Readex [010]

DICTIONARY OF DOCTRINAL AND HISTORICAL THEOLOGY / Blunt, John Henry – London: Rivingtons, 1872 – 2mf – us A.T.L.A. [240]

THE DICTIONARY OF EDUCATION AND INSTRUCTION: A REFERENCE BOOK AND MANUAL ON THE THEORY AND PRACTICE OF TEACHING. / ed by Kiddle, Henry – 3rd ed. New York: E. Steiger & Co., 1882. 332p – 1 – us U.W. Library [370]

A DICTIONARY OF ENGLISH AND WELSH SURNAMES / Bardsley, C W – 1901 – 1 – uk Microform Academic [420]

A DICTIONARY OF ENGLISH CHURCH HISTORY / ed by Ollard, Sidney Leslie & Crosse, Gordon – London: A.R. Mowbray; Milwaukee: The Young Churchman, 1912. 2 maps. xvi, 672p – 1 – us U.W. Library [240]

DICTIONARY OF INDIAN BIOGRAPHY / Buckland, C E – London, 1906 – 9mf – 9 – ne IDC [950]

A DICTIONARY OF LONDON / Harben, H – 1918 – 1 – uk Microform Academic [941]

A DICTIONARY OF MALAYALAM PHRASES AND IDIOMS = MALAYALA SAILINGHANTU / Pillai, T Ramalingam – Trivandrum: R S Pillai. v1. 1930 – 1 – us Res Libr [490]

A DICTIONARY OF MIRACLES : IMITATIVE, REALISTIC, AND DOGMATIC / Brewer, E Cobham – Philadelphia: J.B. Lippincott, 1884 – 2mf – us A.T.L.A. [240]

DICTIONARY OF NATIONAL BIOGRAPHY – Oxford, 1885-1900 – 422mf – 9 – $1335.00 – us UMI [920]

DICTIONARY OF NAUTICAL TERMS / LaDage, John H – In Indonesian. SE-3013 1. 1962 – 9 – ne IDC [623]

DICTIONARY OF OLD ENGLISH : FASCICLE A – 1994 – 8mf – 9 – Can$12.00 – 0-88844-922-4 – cn Pontif [420]

DICTIONARY OF OLD ENGLISH : FASCICLE B – 1991 – 9mf – 9 – Can$13.50 – 0-88844-924-0 – cn Pontif [420]

DICTIONARY OF OLD ENGLISH : FASCICLE C – 1988 – 6mf – 9 – Can$8.95 – 0-88844-925-9 – cn Pontif [420]

DICTIONARY OF OLD ENGLISH : FASCICLE D – 1986 – 4mf – 9 – Can$5.95 – 0-88844-926-7 – cn Pontif [420]

DICTIONARY OF OLD ENGLISH : FASCICLE E – 1996 – 6mf – 9 – Can$8.95 – 0-88844-927-5 – cn Pontif [420]

THE DICTIONARY OF OLD ENGLISH : FASCICLE AE; BEON – 1992 – 4mf – 9 – Can$11.00 – 0-88844-923-2 – cn Pontif [420]

A DICTIONARY OF PRACTICAL MEDICINE (AEL, ABT 3;14) / Copland, James – London. v3. 1858 (mf ed 1995) – 36mf – 9 – DM790.00 – 3-89131-182-6 – gw Fischer [610]

A DICTIONARY OF TERMS IN ART / Fairholt, FW – O-248 1. 1854 – 9 – ne IDC [700]

A DICTIONARY OF TERMS IN ART... WITH 500 ENGRAVINGS ON WOOD / Fairholt, FW – London, 1854 – 6mf – ne IDC [700]

DICTIONARY OF THE AMHARIC LANGUAGE / Isenberg, CW – London. 2pts. 1841 – 5mf – ne IDC [470]

A DICTIONARY OF THE CHINESE LANGUAGE IN THREE PARTS... / Morrison. R – Macao, 1815-1823 – 88mf – ne IDC [480]

A DICTIONARY OF THE ECONOMIC PRODUCTS OF INDIA / ed by Watt, G – Calcutta. 6v. 1885-1893 – 99mf – 9 – ne IDC [338]

A DICTIONARY OF THE ECONOMIC PRODUCTS OF THE MALAY PENINSULA... / Burkill, IH – London. 2v. 1935 – 43mf – 9 – ne IDC [338]

DICTIONARY OF THE ENGLISH AND BENGA LANGUAGES – 1879 – 1 – $50.00 – us Presbyterian [490]

A DICTIONARY OF THE ENGLISH AND MALABAR LANGUAGES – Reprod. de l'ed. de Vepery, 1786. 3 fiches. (Language Collection) – 9 – 8.00 – fr Bibl Nationale [420]

A DICTIONARY OF THE ENGLISH LANGUAGE CONTAINING ALL ENGLISH WORDS AND PHRASES NOW IN USE, WITH THEIR MEANINGS, SYNONYMS, AND TAMIL EQUIVALENTS / Pillay, A Mootootamby – Jaffna: Navalar Press, 1907 – 1 – us Res Libr [490]

DICTIONARY OF THE FAVORLANG DIALECT OF THE FORMOSAN LANGUAGE / Happart, G – Batavia, 1840 – 4mf – ne IDC [490]

DICTIONARY OF THE GALLA LANGUAGE / Tutschek, C – Munich, 1844 – 5mf – ne IDC [470]

DICTIONARY OF THE HAUSA LANGUAGE. : WITH APPENDICES OF HAUSA LITERATURE / Schoen, James Frederick – London: Church Missionary House, 1876 – 1 – us Res Libr [470]

A DICTIONARY OF THE HOK-KEEN DIALECT OF THE CHINESE LANGUAGE : ACCORDING TO THE READING AND COLLOQUIAL IDIOMS: CONTAINING ABOUT 12,000 CHARACTERS,... / Medhurst, W H – Macao, 1832 – 16mf – ne IDC [480]

A DICTIONARY OF THE KAFFIR LANGUAGE / Davis, William J – Including The Xosa and Zulu dialects. Part 1. Kaffir-English. 1872 – 1 – us A.T.L.A. [490]

A DICTIONARY OF THE KILENGE OF NEW BRITAIN / Dark, P & Dark, M – Leiden, 1977 – 10mf – ne IDC [420]

A DICTIONARY OF THE LANGUAGE OF BUGOTU, SANTA ISOBEL ISLAND, SOLOMON ISLANDS / Ivens, W G – 1940 – 1 – uk Microform Academic [490]

A DICTIONARY OF THE MALAGASY LANGUAGE IN TWO PARTS : PT 1: ENGLISH AND MALAGASY / Freeman, J J – Tananarive: R Kitching: Press of the London Missionary Society, 1835 – 1 – us Res Libr [490]

A DICTIONARY OF THE NORMAN OR OLD FRENCH LANGUAGE : WITH THE LAWS OF WILLIAM THE CONQUEROR / Kelham, R – London, 1779 – 4mf – ne IDC [440]

A DICTIONARY OF THE TARGUMIM / Jastrow, Morris – 1903 – 9 – $57.00 – us I.R.C. [270]

A DICTIONARY OF THE TARGUMIM, THE TALMUD BABLI AND YERUSHALMI, AND THE MIDRASHIC LITERATURE : WITH AN INDEX OF SCRIPTURAL QUOTATIONS / Jastrow, Marcus – (Includes index) – London: Luzac; New York: G P Putnam. 2v. 1903 – 5mf – 9 – 0-8370-7394-4 – 1986-1394 – us A.T.L.A. [470]

A DICTIONARY OF THE TIV LANGUAGE / Abraham, Roy Clive – London: Crown Agents for the Colonies, 1940 – 1 – us Res Libr [490]

DICTIONNAIRE,... / Cussy, F de Cornot – Leipzig, 1846 – 9mf – 1 – ILM-158/1 – ne IDC [327]

DICTIONNAIRE ABREGE DE LA LANGUE FO-GBE OU DAHOMEENNE / Courdioux, Ph. E – Paris, Ernest Leroux. 1879 – 9 – $5.00 – fr Orientalistes [490]

DICTIONNAIRE AMARIGNA-FRANCAIS, SUIVI D'UN VOCABULAIRE FRANCAIS-AMARIGNA / Baeteman, J – Dire-Dadona, 1929 – 11mf – 9 – NE-20317/1 – ne IDC [040]

DICTIONNAIRE ANALOGIQUE DE LA LANGUE FRANCAISE / Boissiere, P – 1862 – 9 – fr I.C.S. [440]

DICTIONNAIRE BELEP-FRANCAIS / Dubois, M J – (Nouvelle-Caledonie) – 9 – F100.00 – fr Ethnologie [040]

DICTIONNAIRE BIBLIOGRAPHIQUE DES OUVRAGES RELATIFS A LA PENINSULE INDOCHINOISE / Bibliotheca Indosinica; ed by Cordier, Henri – (Index) – Paris. 4v. 1912-1915 – 32mf – 9 – ne IDC [950]

DICTIONNAIRE BIOGRAPHIQUE DE MUSICIENS ET VOCABULAIRE DE TERMES MUSICAUX / Soeurs de Sainte-Anne – Lachine: Mont Sainte-Anne, 1922. SEM16P207 – 1r – 5 – Can$9.00 – cn Bibl Nat [920]

DICTIONNAIRE CAMBODGIEN – 5th ed 1968 – 38mf – $40.00 – us I.A.S.W.R. [950]

DICTIONNAIRE CAMBODGIEN – Cambodian-Cambodian. 2v. 38 fiches – 9 – $40.00 – us I.A.S.W.R. [490]

DICTIONNAIRE CANADIEN-FRANCAIS / Clapin, Sylvia – 1894 – 9 – fr I.C.S. [440]

DICTIONNAIRE CANADIEN-FRANCAIS OU LEXIQUE-GLOSSAIRE DES MOTS, EXPRESSIONS ET LOCUTIONS NE SE TROUVANT PAS DAN LES DICTIONNAIRES COURANTS ET DONT L'USAGES APPARTIENT SURTOUT AUX CANADIENS-FRANCAIS / Clapin, Sylvia – Montreal: C. Beauchemin, 1894?. 03198. (Pre-1900 Canadiana) – 9 – cn C.I.H.M. [440]

DICTIONNAIRE CHINOIS, FRANCAIS ET LATIN,... / Brollo, B de Glemona – Paris. 2v. 1813 – 22mf – ne IDC [040]

DICTIONNAIRE CLASSIQUE D'HISTOIRE NATURELLE / ed by Bory de Saint-Vincent, J B C M – Paris, 1822-1831. 17v – 124mf – 8330/1 – ne IDC [500]

DICTIONNAIRE COMIQUE, SATYRIQUE, CRITIQUE, BURLESQUE, ETC / Le Roux, Ph.J – 1786 – 9 – fr I.C.S. [440]

DICTIONNAIRE COMPLET DES LANGUES FRANCAISE ET ALLEMANDE / Mozin, Abbe – 1842-46 – 9 – fr I.C.S. [440]

DICTIONNAIRE CRITIQUE DE BIOGRAPHIE ET D'HISTOIRE / Jal – Paris, 1872. 2nd ed – 4mf – 9 – F120.00 – fr F.F.G. [920]

DICTIONNAIRE CRITIQUE DE LA LANGUE FRANCAISE / Feraud, Abbe – 1787 – 9 – fr I.C.S. [440]

DICTIONNAIRE CRITIQUE ET RAISONNE DU LANGAGE VICIEUX / Platt, L – 1835 – 9 – fr I.C.S. [440]

DICTIONNAIRE D'ARCHEA1OLOGIE CHRETIENNE ET DE LITURGIE / Cabrol, F & Leclerq, H – Paris. 1907-1928, v. 1-8(1); 1929-1953, v. 8(2)-15. BOC-186 2 – 8 – ne IDC [930]

DICTIONNAIRE D'ARCHITECTURE CIVILE / Aviler, A – 1755 – 9 – fr I.C.S. [720]

DICTIONNAIRE DE BIBLIOGRAPHIE HAITIENNE / Bissainthe, M – Washington, D.C.: Scarecrow Press, 1951 – 12mf – 9 – ne IDC [972]

DICTIONNAIRE DE BOTANIQUE / Baillon, H E – Paris. 4v. 1876-1892 – 94mf – ne IDC [580]

DICTIONNAIRE DE DROIT... / Calvo, C – Paris, 1885 – 10mf – 9 – Dfl 69 – ILM-143/1 – ne IDC [340]

DICTIONNAIRE DE DROIT ET DE PROCEDURE D'APRES LE CODE CIVIL DU BAS-CANADA: CELUI DE PROCEDURE CIVILE ET LEURS AMENDEMENTS, JUSQU'A LA FIN DE LA DERNIERE SESSION DU PARLEMENT, CONTENANT DIVERSES FORMULES USITEES DANS LA PRACTIQUE / Desaulniers, Abraham Lesieur – Montreal: J. Lovell, 1878. 02678. (Pre-1900 Canadiana) – 9 – cn C.I.H.M. [971]

DICTIONNAIRE DE GEOGRAPHIE ANCIENNE ET MODERNE A L'USAGE DU LIBRAIRE ET DE L'AMATEUR DE LIVRES / Brunet, Jacques Charles – Paris – 21mf – 8 – ne Slangenburg [900]

DICTIONNAIRE DE LA BIBLE : SUPPLEMENT / ed by Pirot et al – Paris. v1-6. 1928-1960 – Dfl315.00 – ne Slangenburg [220]

DICTIONNAIRE DE LA BIBLE / ed by Vigouroux et al – Paris. v1-5. 1895-1912 – Dfl431.00 – ne Slangenburg [220]

DICTIONNAIRE DE LA LANGUE DENE-DINDJIE / Petitot, E – Paris, 1876 – 27mf – ne IDC [490]

DICTIONNAIRE DE LA LANGUE FRANCOISE / Richelet, P – Nouv. ed. 1732 – 9 – fr I.C.S. [440]

DICTIONNAIRE DE LA LANGUE VERTE / Delvau, A – 1866 – 9 – fr I.C.S. [440]

DICTIONNAIRE DE LA LANGUE VERTE / Delvau, A – Nouv. ed. 1883 – 9 – fr I.C.S. [440]

DICTIONNAIRE DE L'ACADEMIE / Academie Francaise – (2nd ed. 1718. 9. 3rd ed. 1740. 9. 4th ed. 1762. 9. 5th ed. 1798. 9. 6th ed. 1835. 9. 7th ed. 1879. 9) – 1694 – 9 – fr I.C.S. [000]

DICTIONNAIRE DE L'ANCIEN DEPARTEMENT DE LA MOSELLE / Neree Quepat – Paris, 1887 – 2mf – 9 – F60.00 – fr F.F.G. [944]

DICTIONNAIRE DE L'ANCIENNE LANGUE FRANCAISE / Godefroy, FE – 1880-90 – 9 – fr I.C.S. [440]

DICTIONNAIRE DE L'ANCIENNE LANGUE FRANCAISE DU IXEME AU XVEME SIECLE / Godefroy, Frederic – Paris, 1881-1902. 10v – 20mf – 9 – F780.00 – fr F.F.G. [040]

DICTIONNAIRE DE L'ELOCUTION FRANCOISE / Demandre, A – 1769 – 9 – fr I.C.S. [440]

DICTIONNAIRE DE MUSIQUE / Brossard, S de – 1703 – 9 – us Sibley [780]

DICTIONNAIRE DE MUSIQUE / Brossard, S de – P 185. 1703 – 9 – ne IDC [780]

DICTIONNAIRE DE MUSIQUE / Rousseau, Jean-Jacques – 1768 – 9 – us Sibley [780]

DICTIONNAIRE DE MUSIQUE / Rousseau, Jean-Jacques – Paris, 1768 – 9mf – ne IDC [780]

DICTIONNAIRE DE NOMS HIEROGLYPHIQUES EN ORDRE GENEALOGIQUE ET ALPHABETIQUE / Lieblein, J D C – Christiania, Leipzig. 2v. 1871, 1892 – 13mf – ne IDC [920]

DICTIONNAIRE DE NOS FAUTES CONTRE LA LANGUE FRANCAISE / Rinfret, Raoul – 1896 – 9 – fr I.C.S. [440]

DICTIONNAIRE DE NOS FAUTES CONTRE LA LANGUE FRANCAISE / Rinfret, Raoul – Montreal: C O Beauchemin et fils, [1897?]. SEM105P1346 – 4mf – 9 – Can$9.00 – cn Bibl Nat [440]

DICTIONNAIRE DES ARTISTES, DONT NOUS AVONS DES ESTAMPES / Heinecken, KH V – O 995. 4 v. 1778-1790 – 9 – ne IDC [700]

DICTIONNAIRE DES ARTISTES, DONT NOUS AVONS DES ESTAMPES... / Heinecken, KH V – Leipzig. 4v. (A-Di). 1778-1790 – 38mf – ne IDC [700]

DICTIONNAIRE DES ARTS DE PEINTURE, SCULPTURE ET GRAVURE / Watelet, Claude H de & Levesque, P C – O 1182 1. 5 v. 1792 – 9 – ne IDC [700]

DICTIONNAIRE DES ARTS DE PEINTURE, SCULPTURE ET GRAVURE / Watelet, Claude H de & Levesque, P C – Paris. 5v. 1792 – 45mf – ne IDC [700]

LE DICTIONNAIRE DES ARTS ET DES SCIENCES / Corneille, Th – 1694 – 9 – fr I.C.S. [000]

DICTIONNAIRE DES CONSTITUANTS, LISTE DES DEPUTES ET DES SUPPLEANTS ELUS A L'ASSEMBLEE CONSTITUANTE DE 1789 / Brette, Armand – Paris, 1897 – 1mf – 9 – F30.00 – fr F.F.G. [320]

DICTIONNAIRE DES CONVENTIONNELS, STE D'HISTOIRE DE LA REVOLUTION FRANCAISE / Kuscinski, Auguste – Paris, 1919 – 2mf – 9 – F60.00 – fr F.F.G. [944]

DICTIONNAIRE DES DEVISES ECCLESIASTIQUES / Tausin, H – Paris, Lechevalier, 1907 – 4mf – 9 – ne IDC [240]

DICTIONNAIRE DES EXPRESSIONS VICIEUSES / Michel, J F – 1807 – 9 – fr I.C.S. [440]

DICTIONNAIRE DES FIEFS, SEIGNEURIES... DE L'ANCIENNE FRANCE / Gourdon de Genouillac – Paris, 1862 – 2mf – 9 – F60.00 – fr F.F.G. [944]

DICTIONNAIRE DES FIGURES HERALDIQUES / Renesse – Bruxelles, 1894-1903. 7v – 12mf – 9 – F360.00 – fr F.F.G. [920]

LE DICTIONNAIRE DES HALLES / Artaud (ou Furetiere) – 1696 – 9 – fr I.C.S. [440]

DICTIONNAIRE DES INSTITUTIONS DE LA FRANCE / Cheruel, A – Paris, 1874 – 4mf – 9 – F120.00 – fr F.F.G. [306]

DICTIONNAIRE DES LOCUTIONS VICIEUSES / Munier, F – 3e ed. 1829 – 9 – fr I.C.S. [440]

DICTIONNAIRE DES LOCUTIONS VICIEUSES LES PLUS REPANDUES DANS LA SOCIETE / Sauger-Preneuf, F – 2E ED. 1838 – 9 – fr I.C.S. [440]

DICTIONNAIRE DES LOCUTIONS VICIEUSES USITEES DANS LE MIDI DE LA FRANCE / Sauger-Preneuf, F – 1825 – 9 – fr I.C.S. [440]

DICTIONNAIRE DES NOMS ANCIENS ET MODERNES DES VILLES ET ARRONDISSEMENTS... DANS L'EMPIRE CHINOIS... / Biot, E C – Paris, 1842 [4] – 4mf – 9 – ne IDC [910]

DICTIONNAIRE DES NOMS DE BAPTEME / Beleze, G – 1863 – 9 – fr I.C.S. [240]

DICTIONNAIRE DES NOMS DE LIEUX HABITES DU DEPARTEMENT DE L'ALLIER / Chazaud – Moulins, 1881 – 1mf – 9 – F30.00 – fr F.F.G. [944]

DICTIONNAIRE DES NOMS GEOGRAPHIQUES CONTENUS DANS LES TEXTES HIEROGLYPHIQUES / Gauthier, H – Caire. v1-7. 1925 – 23mf – 9 – ne IDC [930]

DICTIONNAIRE DES NOMS GEOGRAPHIQUES CONTENUS DANS LES TEXTES HIEROGLYPHIQUES / Gauthier, H – v. 1-7. Caire, 1925. B-461 1 – 9 – ne IDC [910]

DICTIONNAIRE DES NOMS MALGACHES DE VEGETAUX / Boiteau, P – 9 – F450.00 – fr Ethnologie [580]

DICTIONNAIRE DES NOMS PROPRES DE BELEP / Dubois, M J – 9 – F30.00 – fr Ethnologie [490]

DICTIONNAIRE DES NOMS PROPRES DE L'ILE DES PINS / Dubois, M J – 9 – F50.00 – fr Ethnologie [490]

DICTIONNAIRE DES PARALLELES, CONCORDANCES ET ANALOGIES BIBLIQUES – Paris, Strasbourg, 1856. xii, 300p. (Religion series) – 9 – 12.00 – fr Bibl Nationale [240]

DICTIONNAIRE DES PARLEMENTAIRES FRANCAIS, COMPRENANT TOUS LES MEMBRES DES ASSEMBLEES FRANCAISES ET TOUS LES MINISTRES FRANCAIS DEPUIS LE 1. MAI 1789 JUSQU'AU 1. MAI 1889... / Robert, Adolphe et al – Paris: Bourloton, 1891 – 1 – us Res Libr [944]

DICTIONNAIRE DES PAROISSES DU RESSORT DU PARLEMENT DE PARIS – Paris, 1776 – 2mf – 9 – F60.00 – fr F.F.G. [944]

DICTIONNAIRE DES RICHESSES DE LA LANGUE FRANCOISE / Alletz, Pons Augustin – 1770 – 9 – fr I.C.S. [440]

DICTIONNAIRE DES RIMES / Richelet, P – Nouv. ed. 1692 – 9 – fr I.C.S. [440]

DICTIONNAIRE DES RIMES / Richelet, P – Nouv. ed. 1749 – 9 – fr I.C.S. [440]

DICTIONNAIRE DES RIMES DE RICHELET. AN 7 / Wailly, N F – 1799 – 9 – fr I.C.S. [440]

DICTIONNAIRE DES RIMES FRANCOISES / Le Fevre, J – 1588 – 9 – fr I.C.S. [440]

LE DICTIONNAIRE DES RIMES FRANCOISES / La Noue, O de – 1596 – 9 – fr I.C.S. [440]

DICTIONNAIRE DES SCIENCES MEDICALES, PAR UNE SOCIETE DE MEDECINS ET DE CHIRURGIENS (AEL, ABT.3;5) : MM ADELON, ALARD, ALIBERT (ET AL.) / Adelon, Alard, Alibert et al – Paris, 1812-1822 (mf ed 1993) – 299mf – 9 – DM2,900.00 – 3-89131-143-5 – gw Fischer [610]

DICTIONNAIRE DES SCIENCES NATURELLES DANS LEQUEL ON TRAITE METHODIQUEMENT DES DIFFERENT ETRES DE LA NATURE / ed by Cuvier, Georges – Paris. 60v. 1816-1830 – 621mf – 9 – ne IDC [500]

DICTIONNAIRE DES SCIENCES POLITIQUES ET SOCIALES / Ott, A – 1854-55 – 9 – fr I.C.S. [300]

DICTIONNAIRE DES TERMES DE DROIT, D'ECONOMIE POLITIQUE ET D'ADMINISTRATION / Appert, Georges – Yokohama: Imprimerie de S. Salabelle. 1885 – 9 – 5.00 – fr Orientalistes [300]

DICTIONNAIRE DES TERMES DU VIEUX FRANCOIS / Borel, P – Nouv. ed. 1750 – 9 – fr I.C.S. [440]

DICTIONNAIRE DES VERBES IRREGULIERS ET DEFECTIFS DE LA LANGUE FRANCAISE / Baillairge, Frederic Alexandre – 1887. 00079. (Pre-1900 Canadiana) – 9 – cn C.I.H.M. [440]

DICTIONNAIRE D'HOMONYMES, RIMES, ETC., DE M. R. LE. C. BAILLAIRGE – s.l.: s.n., 1888?. 02662. (Pre-1900 Canadiana) – 9 – cn C.I.H.M. [971]

DICTIONNAIRE D'HYGIENE PUBLIQUE ET DE SALUBRITE (AEL, ABT 3;24) / Tardieu, Ambroise – Paris. 3 Bde. 1852-54 (mf ed 1995) – 21mf – 9 – DM340.00 – 3-89131-220-2 – gw Fischer [610]

DICTIONNAIRE DIPLOMATIQUE, OU ETYMOLOGIES DES TERMES DES BAS SIECLES / Montignot – Nancy: De l'imprimerie de C S Lamort, 1787. SEM16P299 – 1r – 5 – Can$9.00 – cn Bibl Nat [327]

DICTIONNAIRE DJAGHATAI-TURC / Veliaminof-Zernof, V de – Spb, 1869 – 8mf – ne IDC [400]

DICTIONNAIRE DU BAS LANGAGE / D'Hautel – 1808 – 9 – fr I.C.S. [440]

DICTIONNAIRE DU BON LANGAGE / Carpentier, N J – 1860 – 9 – fr I.C.S. [440]

DICTIONNAIRE DU LANGAGE DES NOMBRES...: AVEC UNE INTRODUCTION CONTENANT LES PRINCIPES D'UNE METHODE DE REDUCTION ET L'USAGE QUE L'ON EN PEUT FAIRE POUR ABREGER LES CORRESPONDANCES TELEGRAPHIQUES ET AUTRES / Boucherville, Georges Boucher de – Premiere edition. Quebec: C. Darveau, 1889. 00889. (Pre-1900 Canadiana) – 9 – cn C.I.H.M. [050]

DICTIONNAIRE ELEMENTAIRE DE BOTANIQUE,... / Bulliard, J BF – Paris, 1783 – 6mf – ne IDC [580]
DICTIONNAIRE ENCYCLOPEDIQUE DES SCIENCES MEDICALES (AEL, ABT 3;15) / Dechambre, A & Raige-Delorme, J – Paris. 100 bde. 1864-1889 (mf ed 1994) – 450mf – 9 – DM7,600.00 – 3-89131-183-4 – gw Fischer [610]
DICTIONNAIRE EROTIQUE MODERNE / Delvau, A – Nouv. ed. s.d – 9 – fr I.C.S. [440]
DICTIONNAIRE ETYMOLOGIQUE / Menage, G – 1694 – 9 – fr I.C.S. [440]
DICTIONNAIRE ETYMOLOGIQUE DE LA LANGUE FRANCOISE / Menage, G – 1750 – 9 – fr I.C.S. [440]
DICTIONNAIRE ETYMOLOGIQUE DE LA LANGUE MALGACHE / Dama-ntsoha – [Tananarive]: Ny antsiva, 1953 – 1 – us Res Libr [490]
DICTIONNAIRE ETYMOLOGIQUE DE LA LANGUE WALLONNE / Grandgagnage, Ch. – 1850-1880 – 9 – fr I.C.S. [440]
DICTIONNAIRE ETYMOLOGIQUE, HISTORIQUE, ET ANECDOTIQUE DES PROVERBES / Quitard, P M – 1842 – 9 – fr I.C.S. [440]
DICTIONNAIRE FRANCAIS-ARMENIEN-TURC / Awgerian, Y – Venice, 1840 – 8mf – 9 – AR-1700/1 – ne IDC [040]
DICTIONNAIRE FRANCAIS-BANDA ET BANDA-FRANCAIS PRECEDE D'UN ESSAI DE GRAMMAIRE BANDA / Cotel, Pierre – Brazzaville, Mission catholique. 1907 – 9 – $5.00 – fr Orientalistes [040]
DICTIONNAIRE FRANCAIS-BELEP / Dubois, M J – 9 – F60.00 – fr Ethnologie [040]
DICTIONNAIRE FRANCAIS-ILE DES PINS / Dubois, M J – 9 – F60.00 – fr Ethnologie [440]
DICTIONNAIRE FRANCAIS-MALGACHE / Malzac, R P – Tananarive, Imprimerie de la Mission catholique. 1893 – 9 – $20.00 – fr Orientalistes [490]
DICTIONNAIRE FRANCAIS-PONGOUE / Missionnaires de la Congregation du Saint-Esprit – Paris, Maisonneuve et Cie. 1877 – 9 – $10.00 – fr Orientalistes [040]
DICTIONNAIRE FRANCAIS-VOLOF / Guy-Grand, V J – 3e rev aug ed. Saint Joseph de Negasobil: Impr de la Mission, 1890 – 1 – us Res Libr [040]
DICTIONNAIRE FRANCAIS-VOLOF / Guy-Grand, VJ – St-Joseph de Ngasobil, Imprimerie de la Mission. 1890 – 9 – $22.50 – fr Orientalistes [040]
DICTIONNAIRE FRANCAIS-WOLOF ET FRANCAIS-BAMBARA, SUIVI DU DICTIONNAIRE WOLOF-FRANCAIS / Dard, J – Paris, Imprimerie Royale. 1825 – 9 – $10.00 – fr Orientalistes [040]
DICTIONNAIRE FRANCAIS-WOLOF ET WOLOF-FRANCAIS / Missionnaires de la Congregation du Saint-Esprit – Dakar, Imprimerie de la Mission, nouvelle ed. 1855 – 9 – $10.00 – fr Orientalistes [040]
DICTIONNAIRE FRANCAIS-WOLOF ET WOLOF-FRANCAIS – Nouv ed. Dakar: Impr de la Mission, 1855 – 1 – us Res Libr [490]
DICTIONNAIRE FRANCOIS CONTENANT LES MOTS ET LES CHOSES, PLUSIEURS NOUVELLES REMARQUES SUR LA LANGUE FRANCOISE / Richelet, P – 1680 – 9 – fr I.C.S. [440]
DICTIONNAIRE FRANCOIS CONTENANT LES MOTS ET LES CHOSES, VERSCH. AUSGABEN (AEL, ABT 2;16) / Richelet, Cesar-Pierre – mf ed 1996 – 104mf – 9 – DM1,290.00 – 3-89131-225-3 – gw Fischer [440]
DICTIONNAIRE FRANCOIS ET ITALIEN / Canal, P – 2e ed. 1603 – 9 – fr I.C.S. [440]
DICTIONNAIRE FRANCOIS-ALEMAND ET ALEMAND-FRANCOIS / Hulsius, Levinus – 1602 – 9 – fr I.C.S. [440]
DICTIONNAIRE FRANCOIS-LATIN / Dupuys, J – 1573 – 9 – fr I.C.S. [450]
DICTIONNAIRE FRANCOIS-LATIN / Estienne, R – 1540 – 9 – fr I.C.S. [450]
DICTIONNAIRE FRANCOIS-LATIN / Estienne, Robert – 1549 – 9 – fr I.C.S. [450]
DICTIONNAIRE GENEALOGIQUE DES FAMILLES CANADIENNES DEPUIS LA FONDATION DE LA COLONIE JUSQU'A NOS JOURS / Tanguay, Cyprien – Province de Quebec (Montreal): E Senecal..., 1871-1890. SEM35P175 – 2r – 1 – Can$82.00 – cn Bibl Nat [920]
DICTIONNAIRE GENERAL DE LA LANGUE FRANCAISE / Raymond, F – 2e ed. 1835 – 9 – fr I.C.S. [440]
DICTIONNAIRE GENERAL DE LA POLITIQUE / Block, M – 1863-64 – 9 – fr I.C.S. [320]
DICTIONNAIRE GENERAL ET CURIEUX / Rochefort, C de – 1685 – 9 – fr I.C.S. [440]
DICTIONNAIRE GEOGRAPHIQUE DE L'EMPIRE OTTOMAN / Mostras, C – Spb., 1873 – 3mf – 9 – ne IDC [956]
DICTIONNAIRE GEOGRAPHIQUE ET ADMINISTRATIF UNIVERSEL D'HAITI / Rouzier, S – N.p. 4v. 1891-1927 – 19mf – 9 – ne IDC [972]
DICTIONNAIRE GRAMMATICAL DE LA LANGUE FRANCOISE / Feraud, Abbe – 1768 – 9 – fr I.C.S. [440]
DICTIONNAIRE GRAMMATICAL DU MAUVAIS LANGAGE, AN 11 / Molard, E – 1803 – 9 – fr I.C.S. [440]
DICTIONNAIRE HERALDIQUE / Grandmaison, Charles – Paris, 1861 – 2mf – 9 – F60.00 – fr F.F.G. [920]
DICTIONNAIRE HISTORICO-ARTISTIQUE DU PORTUGAL... / Raczynski, A – Paris, 1847 – 9 – ne IDC [700]
DICTIONNAIRE HISTORICO-ARTISTIQUE DU PORTUGAL... / Raczynski, A – Paris, 1847 – 3mf – ne IDC [700]
DICTIONNAIRE HISTORIQUE D'ARGOT / Larchey, L – 7e ed. 1878 – 9 – fr I.C.S. [440]
DICTIONNAIRE HISTORIQUE D'ARGOT / Larchey, L – 8e ed. 1880 – 9 – fr I.C.S. [440]
DICTIONNAIRE HISTORIQUE DE LA MEDECINE ANCIENNE ET MODERNE (AEL, ABT 3; 19) / Eloy, F J Nicholas – 4 Bde. 1778 (mf ed 1996) – 29mf – 9 – DM320.00 – 3-89131-191-5 – gw Fischer [610]
DICTIONNAIRE HISTORIQUE DE LA MEDECINE ANCIENNE ET MODERNE (AEL, ABT 3;17) / Dezeimeris, Jean E & Ollivier, Charles P – Paris. 1828-1839 (mf ed 1994) – 31mf – 9 – DM540.00 – 3-89131-185-0 – gw Fischer [610]
DICTIONNAIRE HISTORIQUE DE L'ANCIEN FRANCOIS / La Curne de Sainte Palaye – 9 – fr I.C.S. [440]
DICTIONNAIRE HISTORIQUE DE L'ARGOT PARISIEN / Larchey, L – 6e ed. 1872 – 9 – fr I.C.S. [440]
DICTIONNAIRE HISTORIQUE DES CANADIENS ET DES METIS FRANCAIS DE L'OUEST / Morice, Adrien G – 2e ed. augm d'un suppl. Quebec: Garneau, 1912. SEM16P267 – 1r – 5 – Can$9.00 – cn Bibl Nat [971]
DICTIONNAIRE HISTORIQUE ET CRITIQUE / Bayle, P – 1697 – 9 – fr I.C.S. [440]
DICTIONNAIRE HISTORIQUE ET CRITIQUE / Bayle, P – Nouv. ed. 1820-24 – 9 – fr I.C.S. [440]
DICTIONNAIRE HISTORIQUE ET GEOGRAPHIQUE DES PAROISSES, MISSIONS ET MUNICIPALITES DE LA PROVINCE DE QUEBEC / Magnan, Hormidas – Arthabaska: Imp. d'Arthabaska Inc, 1925. SEM105P386 – 8mf – 9 – Can$18.00 – cn Bibl Nat [971]
DICTIONNAIRE HISTORIQUE ET GEOGRAPHIQUE DU CANADA – Montreal: Beauchemin & Valois, 1885. 02661. (Pre-1900 Canadiana) – 9 – cn C.I.H.M. [971]
DICTIONNAIRE HISTORIQUE ET GEOGRAPHIQUE DU DEPARTEMENT DE LA CREUSE – Aubusson, 2nd ed 1882 – 1mf – 9 – F30.00 – fr F.F.G. [944]
DICTIONNAIRE, ICONOGRAPHIQUE DES CHAMPIGNONS SUPERIEURS... / Laplanche, M C de – Autun, Paris, 1894 – 11mf – ne IDC [580]
DICTIONNAIRE ICONOLOGIQUE / Prezel, L de – Paris. O 1260 1. 1779 – 9 – ne IDC [760]
DICTIONNAIRE ICONOLOGIQUE... / Prezel, L de – Gotha, 1758 – 4mf – ne IDC [700]
DICTIONNAIRE ICONOLOGIQUE... / Prezel, L de – Paris, 1756 – 3mf – ne IDC [700]
DICTIONNAIRE ICONOLOGIQUE... / Prezel, L de – Paris, 1779 – 6mf – ne IDC [700]
DICTIONNAIRE ICONOLOGIQUE, OU INTRODUCTION A LA CONNOISSANCE DES PEINTURES, SCULPTURES, ESTAMPES, MEDAILLES, PIERRES GRAVEES, EMBLEMES, DEVISES ET C. / Lacombe de Prezel, H – Paris: de Hansy, 1756 – 4mf – ne IDC [700]
DICTIONNAIRE ILE DES PINS-FRANCAIS / Dubois, M J – 9 – F120.00 – fr Ethnologie [440]
DICTIONNAIRE INFERNAL; REPERTOIRE UNIVERSEL DES ETRES, DES PERSONNAGES, DES LIVRES, DES FAITS ET DES CHOSES QUI TIENNENT AUX ESPRITS. / Collin de Plancy, J A S – 6eme ed. augm. de 800 articles nouv., illus. Paris: H. Plon, 1863. 723p – 1 – us U.W. Library [150]
DICTIONNAIRE KIKINGO-FRANCAIS, AVEC UNE ETUDE PHONETIQUE DECRIVANT LES DIALECTES LES PLUS IMPORTANTS DE LA LANGUE DITE KIKONGO / Laman, Karl Eduard – [Bruxelles: G van Campenhout, 1936] – 1 – us Res Libr [490]
DICTIONNAIRE LANGUEDOCIEN-FRANCOIS / Boissier de Sauvages, P A – 1785 – 9 – fr I.C.S. [440]
DICTIONNAIRE LATIN-FRANCAIS DES NOMS PROPRES DE LIEUX / Chevin – Bar le Duc, 1897 – 2mf – 9 – F60.00 – fr F.F.G. [920]
DICTIONNAIRE NATIONAL DE LA LANGUE FRANCAISE / Bescherelle, LN – 1887 – 9 – fr I.C.S. [440]
DICTIONNAIRE ORDOS / Mostaert, R P A – Peking. v1-2. 1941-1944 – 31mf – ne IDC [480]
DICTIONNAIRE, OU, MANUEL-LEXIQUE DU DIPLOMATIE ET DU CONSUL / Cussy, F de Cornot – Leipzig, 1846 – 9mf – ne IDC [320]
DICTIONNAIRE PONGOUE-FRANCAIS PRECEDE DES PRINCIPES DE LA LANGUE PONGOUEE / Missionnaires de la Congregation du Saint-Esprit – Paris, Maisonneuve et Cie. 1881 – 9 – $10.00 – fr Orientalistes [040]
DICTIONNAIRE PORTATIF DE L'INGENIEUR ET DE L'ARTILLEUR / Belidor, Bernard Forest de – Nouvelle ed. Paris, 1768. 8 fol., vi, 746p. (Architecture Series) – 9 – fr Hachette [720]
DICTIONNAIRE PORTATIF ET ABREGE DES LOIX ET REGLES DU PARLEMENT PROVINCIAL DU BAS-CANADA, DEPUIS SON ETABLISSEMENT...JUSQUES ET COMPRIS L'AN DE NOTRE SEIGNEUR, 1805 / Perrault, Joseph Francois – Quebec: John Neilson, 1806. SEM16P76 – 1r – 5 – Can$9.00 – cn Bibl Nat [971]
DICTIONNAIRE RAISONNE DE L'ARCHITECTURE FRANCAISE DU 11 AU 16 SIECLE / Viollet-Le-Duc, Eugene Emmanuel – Paris. 10v. 1854-1870 – 69mf – ne IDC [720]
DICTIONNAIRE RAISONNE DE L'ARCHITECTURE FRANCAISE DU XIE AU XVIE SIECLES / Viollet-Le-Duc, Eugene Emmanuel – 1854-68 – 9 – fr I.C.S. [720]
DICTIONNAIRE RAISONNE UNIVERSEL D'HISTOIRE NATURELLE / Valmont de Bomare, J C – 1764 – 9 – fr I.C.S. [500]
DICTIONNAIRE ROUCHI-FRANCAIS / Hecart, G A J – 3e ed. 1834 – 9 – fr I.C.S. [440]
DICTIONNAIRE TAMOUL-FRANCAIS = TAMIL PORANCU AKARATI / Mousset, Louis Marie – 3rd. ed. Pondichery. 1938-1942. 2 vols – 1 – us Res Libr [490]
DICTIONNAIRE TARTARE-MANTCHOU FRANCOIS... / Amiot, J J M – Paris. 3v. 1789-90 – 18mf – 9 – HT-1069/1 – ne IDC [040]
DICTIONNAIRE TCHOUKTCHE-RUSSE / Bogoraz, V G – 1937 – 9 – fr Orientalistes [040]
DICTIONNAIRE TOPOGRAPHIQUE, ARCHEOLOGIQUE ET HISTORIQUE DE LA CREUSE / Lecler, A – Limoges, 1902 – 2mf – 9 – F60.00 – fr F.F.G. [910]
DICTIONNAIRE TOPOGRAPHIQUE DE DEPARTEMENT DE L'YONNE: COMPRENANT LES NOMS DE LIEU ANCIENS ET MODERNES / Quantin, Maximilen – Paris, Impr. Imp., 1862. xxii, 167 p. 4 fiches. (Statistics Series: Topography) – 9 – 10.00 – fr Bibl Nationale [944]
DICTIONNAIRE TOPOGRAPHIQUE DE L'ANCIEN DEPARTEMENT DE LA MOSELLE: COMPRENANT LES NOMS DE LIEU ANCIENS ET MODERNES / Bouteiller, Ernest de – Paris, Impr. nationale, 1874. lv, 316 p. 7 fiches. (Statistics Series: Topography) – 9 – 17.50 – fr Bibl Nationale [944]
DICTIONNAIRE TOPOGRAPHIQUE DU DEPARTEMENT DE CANTAL / Ame, Emile – Paris: Imp. nationale, 1897. 630p. 12 fiches. (Statistics Series: Topography) – 9 – 30.00 – fr Bibl Nationale [944]
DICTIONNAIRE TOPOGRAPHIQUE DU DEPARTEMENT DE HAUT-RHIN / Stoffel, Georges – Paris: Imp. Imperiale, 1868. xxiv,260p.5 fiches. (Statistics Series: Topography) – 9 – 12.00 – fr Bibl Nationale [944]
DICTIONNAIRE TOPOGRAPHIQUE DU DEPARTEMENT DE LA MEURTHE / Lepage, Henri – Paris: Imp. Imperiale, 1862. xxvii,213p. 3 fiches. (Statistics Series: Topography) – 9 – 8.00 – fr Bibl Nationale [944]
DICTIONNAIRE TOPOGRAPHIQUE DU DEPARTEMENT DE LA MEUSE: COMPRENANT LES NOMS DE LIEU ANCIENS ET MODERNES / Lienard, Felix – Paris, Impr. nat., 1872, xliv, 297 p. 6 fiches. (Statistics Series: Topography) – 9 – 15.00 – fr Bibl Nationale [944]
DICTIONNAIRE TOPOGRAPHIQUE DU DEPARTEMENT DE LA NIEVRE: COMPRENANT LES NOMS DE LIEU ANCIENS ET MODERNES / Soultrait, Georges de – 5 fiches. (Statistics Series: Topography) – 9 – 12.00 – fr Bibl Nationale [944]
DICTIONNAIRE TOPOGRAPHIQUE DU DEPARTEMENT DE L'AUBE / Boutiot, Theophile & Socard, Emile – Paris: Impr. nationale, 1874. 6 fiches.(Statistics Series: Topography) – 9 – 15.00 – fr Bibl Nationale [944]
DICTIONNAIRE TOPOGRAPHIQUE DU DEPARTEMENT DE L'EURE / Blosseville, Ernest Poret – Paris, Impr. nationale, 1877. xl, 179 p. 6 fiches. (Statistics Series: Topography) – 9 – 15.00 – fr Bibl Nationale [944]
DICTIONNAIRE TOPOGRAPHIQUE DU DEPARTEMENT DES BASSES-PYRENEES / Raymond, Paul – Paris: Imp. imperiale, 1863. xx,208p. 4 fiches. (Statistics Series: Topography) – 9 – 10.00 – fr Bibl Nationale [944]
DICTIONNAIRE TOPOGRAPHIQUE DU DEPARTEMENT DES HAUTS-ALPES / Roman, M J – Paris, 1884 – 1mf – 9 – F30.00 – fr F.F.G. [910]
DICTIONNAIRE TOPOGRAPHIQUE DU DEPARTEMENT D'EURE-ET-LOIR: COMPRENANT LES NOMS DE LIEU ANCIENS ET MODERNES / Merlet, Lucien – Paris, Impr. Imp., 1801. xxiv, 254 p. 5 fiches. (Statistics Series: Topography) – 9 – 12.00 – fr Bibl Nationale [944]
DICTIONNAIRE TOPOGRAPHIQUE, HISTORIQUE ET STATISTIQUE DU HAUT ET DU BAS RHIN / Baquol & Ristelhuber P – Strasbourg, 3rd ed 1865 – 2mf – 9 – F60.00 – fr F.F.G. [910]
DICTIONNAIRE TOPOGRAPHIQUE, HISTORIQUE, GENEALOGIQUE ET BIBLIOGRAPHIQUE DU MAINE / Le Paige – Mayenne, 1895. 2v – 4mf – 9 – F120.00 – fr F.F.G. [910]
DICTIONNAIRE TURC-FRANCAIS / Meynard, Barbier de – 1885, 1886 – 9 – fr Orientalistes [040]
DICTIONNAIRE TURK-ORIENTAL / Pavet de Courteille, M – Paris, 1870 – 10mf – ne IDC [460]
DICTIONNAIRE UNIVERSEL / Furetiere, Antoine – 1690 – 9 – fr I.C.S. [000]
DICTIONNAIRE UNIVERSEL, CONTENANT GENERALMENT TOUS LES MOTS FRANCOIS, TANT VIEUX QUE MODERNES, ET LES TERMES DES SCIENCES ET DES ARTS / Furetiere, Antoine – Publiee a la Haye: Chez Pierre Husson, 1727. SEM35P187 – 2r – 1 – Can$124.00 – cn Bibl Nat [440]
DICTIONNAIRE UNIVERSEL D'AGRICULTURE ET DE JARDINAGE / Aubert de la Chesnaye des Bois, Fr. A – 1751 – 9 – fr I.C.S. [630]
DICTIONNAIRE UNIVERSEL DE LA FRANCE ANCIENNE ET MODERNE, ET DE LA NOUVELLE FRANCE – Paris: Chez Saugrain, 1726. SEM35P184 – 2r – 1 – Can$88.00 – cn Bibl Nat [944]
DICTIONNAIRE UNIVERSEL DE LA LANGUE FRANCAISE / Boiste, P CV – 8e ed. 1834 – 9 – fr I.C.S. [440]
DICTIONNAIRE UNIVERSEL DE MEDECINE (AEL, ABT.3;3.2) / James, Robert – Paris, 1746-1748 (mf ed 1993) – 57mf – 9 – DM520.00 – 3-89131-153-2 – gw Fischer [610]
DICTIONNAIRE UNIVERSEL DES SYNONYMES DE LA LANGUE FRANCAISE – 1824 – 9 – fr I.C.S. [440]
DICTIONNAIRE UNIVERSEL FRANCOIS ET LATIN / Trevoux – 1704 – 9 – fr I.C.S. [450]
DICTIONNAIRE UNIVERSEL FRANCOIS ET LATIN / Trevoux – 2e ed. 1721 – 9 – fr I.C.S. [450]
DICTIONNAIRE UNIVERSEL FRANCOIS ET LATIN / Trevoux – 3e ed. 1732 – 9 – fr I.C.S. [450]

DICTIONNAIRE UNIVERSEL FRANCOIS ET LATIN / Trevoux – 5e ed. 1752 – 9 – fr I.C.S. [450]
DICTIONNAIRE UNIVERSEL FRANCOIS ET LATIN / Trevoux – 6e ed. 1771 – 9 – fr I.C.S. [450]
DICTIONNAIRE VERIDIQUE DES ORIGINES DES MAISONS NOBLES OU ANOBLIES DU ROYAUME DE FRANCE / Laine, PL – Paris, 1818-1819. 2v – 3mf – 9 – F90.00 – fr F.F.G. [920]
DICTIONNAIRE VOLOF-FRANCAIS / Kobes, Alois – Nouv. ed. Dakar. 1923 – 1 – us Res Libr [490]
DICTIONNAIRE VOLOF-FRANCAIS / Kobes, Mgr – Nouv ed. Dakar, Senegal: Mission Catholique, 1923 – us Res Libr [040]
DICTIONNAIRES ABENAQUIS (AUBERY), GRAMMAIRE MIC-MAC (MAILLARD) ET "RADICUM..." (NUDENAS) / Seminaire de Nicolet. Odanak (Canada). Archives – Odanak, Canada – 2r – 1 – cn Can Microfilming [490]
DICTIONNAIRES ALGONQUINS, HURONS, ETC / College Sainte-Marie. Montreal. Archives – Montreal, Canada – 1r – 1 – cn Can Microfilming [490]
DICTIONNAIRES, GRAMMAIRES, LEXIQUES ALGONQUINS, ABENAQUIS, HURONS, IROQUOIS / Seminaire de Quebec. Archives – Quebec, Canada – 6r – 1 – cn Can Microfilming [490]
DICTIONNAIRES, GRAMMAIRES, LEXIQUES, ETC (CUOQ, GUICHART, MATHEVET, MARCOUX, ETC) / Seminaire Saint Sulpice de Montreal. Archives – Oka, Canada – 10r – 1 – cn Can Microfilming [490]
DICTIONNAIRES IROQUOIS (MARCOUX) ETC – Kanawague, Canada – 1r – 1 – cn Can Microfilming [490]
DICTONARIUM NOVUM LATINO-ARMENIUM... / Villotte, J – Roma, 1714 – 22mf – ne IDC [450]
DICURSO...MAL DE URINA SEA EL QUE PADECE DIEGO ENRIQUEZ LEON... / Sanchez de Oropesa, F – Sevilla, 1594 – 4mf – 9 – sp Cultura [610]
DID CHRIST CLAIM TO BE SON OF GOD? / Hiller, H Croft – Manchester: H Croft Hiller, 1907 – 1mf – 9 – 0-8370-3588-0 – 1985-1588 – us A.T.L.A. [240]
DID THE FIRST CHURCH OF SALEM ORIGINALLY HAVE A CONFESSION OF FAITH DISTINCT FROM THEIR COVENANT? / Felt, Joseph B – Boston: Edward L. Balch, 1856 – 1mf – us A.T.L.A. [240]
DID THE LOUISIANA PURCHASE EXTEND TO THE PACIFIC OCEAN? AND OUR TITLE TO OREGON / Anderson, John Jacob – New York: Clark & Maynard, 1881. 00799. (Pre-1900 Canadiana) – 9 – cn C.I.H.M. [971]
DIDASCALIA – The Apostolic Constitutions (Coptic text) with English translation. 1848. Royal Asiatic Society – 1 – uk Microform Academic [240]
DIDASCALIA – The Apostolic Constitutions (Ethiopic Version) with English translations. Royal Asiatic Society. 1823 – 1 – uk Microform Academic [240]
DIDASCALIAE APOSTOLORUM CANONUM ECCLESIASTICORUM TRADITIONIS APOSTOLICAE : VERSIONES LATINAE. RECENSUIT E. TIDNER (T.U.U. 5-75) / Tidner, E – Berlin, 1963 – 4mf – 9 – ne Slangenburg [240]
DIDASCALOCOPHUS... / Dalgarno, George – Oxford, 1680 – 3mf – 9 – ne IDC [617]
DIDASCALOCOPHUS: OR, THE DEAF AND DUMB MANS TUTOR / Dalgarno, George – 1680. 153p. (English Linguistics Series 1500-1800) – 9 – us UMI [400]
DIDASKALOS – (v8. 1977. 5,6,9) – v1. 1970 – 1 – us UMI [073]
DIDCOT POST – England. Jul 1933-Sep 1935.-w. 1men reels – 1 – uk British Libr Newspaper [072]
Dide, Auguste *see*
- HERETIQUES ET REVOLUTIONNAIRES
- J.-J. ROUSSEAU

DI/DECISIONS INFORMATION – (Mf available to 1986 only) – Ottawa. nos 43-60. 1981-86 – 9 – Can$20.00y – cn Micromedia [650]
Diderot *see* ENCYCLOPEDIE OU DICTIONNAIRE RAISONNE DES SCIENCES, DES ARTS ET DES METIERS (AEL, ABT 1;34)
Diderot, D *see*
- ENCYCLOPEDIE. 6 LUTHERIE
- ENCYCLOPEDIE. 6 MUSIQUE
- ENCYCLOPEDIE OU DICTIONNAIRE RAISONNE DES SCIENCES, DES ARTS ET DES METIERS

Diderot, Denis *see*
- (ENCYCLOPEDIE)
- ENCYCLOPEDIE
- EST-IL BON? EST-IL MECHANT?
- NOUVEAU DICTIONNAIRE POUR SERVIR DE SUPPLEMENT AUX DICTIONNAIRES DES SCIENCES, DES ARTS ET DES METIERS
- RECUEIL DE PLANCHES SUR LES SCIENCES, LES ARTS LIBERAUX ET LES ARTS MECHANIQUES AVEC LEUR EXPLICATION
- LA RELIGIEUSE
- TABLE ANALYTIQUE ET RAISONNEE DE L'ENCYCLOPEDIE

Diderot, M *see* ENCYCLOPEDIE, OU DICTIONNAIRE RAISONNE DES SCIENCES...
DIDJEMPUT MAMAKNJA / Amrullah, Abdul Malik Karim – SE-3978 1. 1962 – 9 – ne IDC [950]
DIDO IN DER DEUTSCHEN DICHTUNG / Semrau, Eberhard – (Includes bibliographical references) – Berlin: W de Gruyter & Co, 1930 – 2r – 1 – us U.W. Library [430]
Didon, H *see* BELIEF IN THE DIVINITY OF JESUS CHRIST
[DIDONE ABBANDONATA] AH NON LASCIARM / Mortellari, M – (Full Score) – London: Longman & Broderip, 1786 – 1 – us Sibley [780]
[DIDONE ABBANDONATA] OMBRA CARA, OMBRA TRADITA / Schuster, J – (Full score) – London: Longman & Broderip, 1786 – 1 – us Sibley [780]
[DIDONE ABBANDONATA] SON REGINA E SONO AMANTE / Sacchini, A M – (Full score) – London: Longman & Broderip, [1786] – 1 – us Sibley [780]
Didot, Ambr *see* FRAGMENTA HISTORICORUM GRAECORUM
DIDSBURY PIONEER – Alberta, CN. 1903 – 1r – 1 – cn Commonwealth Micro [072]
DIDYME L'AVEUGLE / Bardy, Gustave – Paris: G. Beauchense, 1910 – 1mf – us A.T.L.A. [240]
DIDYMUS DER BLINDE VON ALEXANDRIA / Leipoldt, Johannes – Leipzig: J.C. Hinrichs, 1905. (Texte und Untersuchungen zur Geschichte der altchristlichen Literatur; der ganzen Reihe 29. Bd., Heft 3: n.F., 14. Bd., Heft 3) – 1mf – us A.T.L.A. [240]
DIDYMUS, DER BLINDE VON ALEXANDRIA (T.U.U. 2-29/3) / Leipoldt, Johannes – Leipzig, 1905 – 3mf – 9 – ne Slangenburg [240]
DIE AND BE DAMNED : OR, AN ANTIDOTE AGAINST EVERY SPECIES OF METHODISM AND ENTHUSIASM / Mortimer, T – (Revised and enlarged edition) – London, 2nd ed 1758 – 1mf – 9 – MP-375/1 – ne IDC [240]
DIECASTING AND METAL MOULDING – v1- 1964- 1; v12- 1975- 5,6,9 – us UMI [670]
DIECIOCHO DE JULIO – n.p. 1938. Fiche W 836. (Blodgett Collection of Spanish Civil War Pamphlets) – 9 – us H.U. College Libr [946]
DIECISIETE MESES DE ALCALDIA / Martinez Montero, Emilio – 1898 – 9 – 1.50f – sp Bibl Santa Ana [830]
Dieckhoff, A W *see*
- DER ABLASSSTREIT
- LUTHERS LEHRE IN IHRER ERSTEN GESTALT
- DIE WALDENSER IM MITTELALTER
- ZUR LEHRE VON DER BEKEHRUNG UND VON DER PRAEDESTINATION

Dieckhoff, August Wilhelm *see* JUSTIN, AUGUSTIN, BERNHARD UND LUTHER
DIEDERICH VON DEM WERDER : EIN BEITRAG ZUR DEUTSCHEN LITTERATURGESCHICHTE DES SIEBZEHNTEN JAHRHUNDERTS / Witkowski, Georg – (Includes bibliographical references) – Leipzig: Veit, 1887 – 1r – 1 – us U.W. Library [430]
Diederichs, Joern *see* ESPANOL – CASTELLANO
Diefenbach, L *see* GLOSSARIUM LATINO-GERMANICUM MEDIAE ET INFIMAE AETATIS
Diego de Madrid *see*
- VIDA...DE...SAN PEDRO DE ALCANTARA... SACADA A LA LUZ JUAN DE LA CALZADA... TOMO 4...
- VIDA...SAN PEDRO DE ALCANTARA

DIEGO GARCIA DE PAREDES. HERCULES Y SANSON DE ESPANA / Munoz de San Pedro, Miguel – Madrid: Espasa-Calpe, S.A., 1946 – 1 – sp Bibl Santa Ana [946]
DIEGO GARCIA DE PAREDES, HERCULES Y SANTON DE ESPANA. MADRID, 1946 / Munoz de San Pedro, Miguel – Madrid: Razon y Fe, 1948 – 1 – sp Bibl Santa Ana [946]
Diego, Sandalio *see*
- EN EL 4TH CENTENARIO DEL DOCTOR ARIAS MONTANO. LA VERSION METRICOLATINA DEL SALTERIO HEBRAICO
- LA VERSION METRICA DEL SALTERIO DE BENITO ARIAS MONTANO

Diehl, Charles *see*
- L'AFRIQUE BYZANTINE
- BYZANTINE PORTRAITS

Diehl, E *see* INSCRIPTIONES LATINAE CHRISTIANAE VETERES
Diehl, Ernst *see* POMPEIANISCHE WANDINSCHRIFTEN UND VERWANDTES
Diehl, H *see* DIE ZWANGSVOLLSTRECKUNG AUSLAENDISCHER URTEILE...
Diehl, W et al *see* FESTGRUSS BERNHARD STADE
Diehl Wilhelm *see* LANDGRAF PHILIPP VON HESSEN
DIEISTVIIA IAPONII V PRIAMURSKOM KRAIE : SBORNIK OFFITSIALNYKH DOKUMENTOV, OTNOSIASHCHIKHSIA K INTERVENTSII DERZHAV V PREDIELAKH PRIAMURIA / Golos rodiny (Vladivostok, RSFSR) – Vladivostok: Izd. t-va izd. svobodnai a Rossii a, 1921 – 1 – CSUX88-B7725 – us Hoover Inst Photo [947]
Diekmann, Rudolf *see* ZACHARIAS WERNERS DRAMEN
Diel, Heinrich *see* DE ENUNTIATIS FINALIBUS APUD GRAECORUM RERUM SCRIPTORES POSTERIORIS EATATIS
DIELA NARODA – (Library's copy imperfect: n3 has several articles cut out. Filmed with: Dielo naroda, Dielo narodov, Dielo, Dielo narodnoe, Diela narodnyia) – Petrograd: P K P s-r, 1918. n1-6. feb 12-feb 19 1918 – us Res Libr [072]
DIELA NARODNYIA – (Library's copy imperfect: issue has several articles cut out. Filmed with: Dielo naroda, Dielo narodnoe, Dielo narodov, Dielo, Diela naroda) – Petrograd: Petrogradskii komitet Partii sotsialistov-revoliutsionerov. n1. feb 21 1918 – us Res Libr [072]
DIELLI – (Albanian language) – Boston, MA. Feb 15 1908-1977; Jan 16 1984-Dec 1991 – 31r – 1 – us L of C Photodup [071]
DIELO – v. 1-21, no. 1 3. Oct 1866-Apr Mar 1888. wanting v. 21, no. 1 3, Jan Mar 1888 – 1 – 1,049.00 – us L of C Photodup [460]
DIELO – (Filmed with: Dielo naroda, Dielo narodnoe, Dielo narodov, Diela naroda, Diela narodnyia) – Petrograd: P K P s-r, 1918. n1. jan 23 1918 – us Res Libr [072]
DIELO NARODA – Petrograd: redaktor-izdatel S P Postnikov, 1917-1918 (Tip "Viestnika Vremennago pravitelstva"). [n25-216. apr 15 1917-nov 22 1917]; [n230-251. dec 12 1917-jan 26 1918] – us Res Libr [072]
DIELO NARODA – Petrograd: T-vo s-r v litsie D F Rakova, [1918-]. [n8-50. mar 30 1918-jun 22 1918] – us Res Libr [072]
DIELO NARODNOE – (Filmed with: Dielo naroda, Dielo narodov, Dielo, Diela naroda, diela narodnyia) – Petrograd: TSK Partii sotsialistov-revoliutsionerov, 1918. [n1-2. jan 14-16 1918] – us Res Libr [072]
DIELO NARODOV PETROGRAD: TSK P S-R, 1918. [N1-3. JAN 17-JAN 20 1918] – (Filmed with: Dielo naroda, Dielo narodnoe, Dielo, Diela naroda, Diela narodnyia) – us Res Libr [072]
DIELO O VYBORGSKOM VOZZVANII V PRAVITELSTVUI USHCHEM SENATIE : PRIGOVOR PALATY, KASSATIONNYIA ZHALOBY, STENOGRAFICHESKII OTCHETI OPREDIELENIE SENATA – S.-Peterburg: Tip. t-va "Obshchestvennai a polza, 1908 – 1 – CSUX89-B7066 – us Hoover Inst Photo [947]
DIELO SUKHOMLINOVA – Petrograd: "T Sentropechat", [1917] – 1 – CSUX89-B7315 – us Hoover Inst Photo [947]
Diels, Hermann *see* SIBYLLINISCHE BLAETTER
DIEMAKING, DIECUTTING AND CONVERTING *see* PACKAGE PRINTING AND DIECUTTING
DIEMENSIONEN DER ALTERUNG IM SOZIALSTAAT : SOZIALPOLITISCHE UND SOZIALGERONTOLOGISCHE UNTERSUCHUNG DES POLITIKFELDES ALTERNSPOLITIK / Baur, Tobias – 1995 – 2mf – 9 – DM80.00 – 3-8267-2178-0 – gw Hänsel [350]
DIENA = THE DAY – 1991 – 3r – 1 – Sfr360.00 – sz Infoprint [947]
DIENA = THE DAY – (1991 3r $255. 1992 4r $340. 1993 5r $425. 1994-98 6r per y $510y) – Latvia, 1999- – 6r per y – 1 – $480.00 standing order – us Ross [072]
DIENA = THE DAY – 1992-1995 – 4 times per yr – Sfr480.00 – sz Infoprint [947]
Diena, G *see*
- CONDIZIONE GIURIDICA DELLA VEDOVA...
- CONSIDERAZIONI CRITICHE SU ALCUNE TEORIE DEL DIRITTO INTERNAZIONALE...
- DES DROITS DE SUCCESSION...
- I CONTRATTI DIFFERENZIALI...
- I DIRITTO REALI CONSIDERATI NEL DIRITTO INTERNAZIONALE PRIVATO
- TRATTATO DI DIRITTO COMMERCIALE INTERNAZIONALE...

Dieng, M Samba *see* L'EPOPEE D'EL HADJ OMAR
DE DIENST DER BAALIM IN ISRAEL: NAAR AANLEIDING VAN...R. DOZY, DE ISRAELIETEN TE MEKKA / Oort, Henricus – Leiden: P. Engels, 1864.1 fiche – 9 – us A.T.L.A. [270]
DER DIENST DER FRAU IN DEN ERSTEN JAHRHUNDERTEN DER CHRISTLICHEN KIRCHE / Zscharnack, Leopold – Goettingen: Vandenhoeck & Ruprecht, 1902 – 1mf – us A.T.L.A. [305]
DER DIENST DER FRAU IN DER CHRISTLICHEN KIRCHE : GESCHICHTLICHER UEBERBLICK MIT EINER SAMMLUNG VON URKUNDEN / Goltz, Eduard von der – Potsdam: Stiftungsverlag, 1914 – 2mf – us A.T.L.A. [240]
DAS DIENSTBOTEN-BUCH ODER BEISPIELE DES GUTEN – Augsburg, 1832, 1835, 1838 – 1r – 1 – Dist. gw Mikrofilm – gw Misc Inst [640]
DIENSTBOTENZEITUNG – Berlin, DE. 1909 – 1r – 1 – gw Mikrofilm [072]
DIENSTLEISTNGEN DER INFORMATIONS/ AUSKUNFTSBANK / Buch, Ricarda – Entwurf, c1985. 4p – 9 – 1.00f – at Libertarian Micro [335]
DIEN-XA TAP CHI – no. 1-63. Saigon. 4 fevr 1928-8 juin 1929 – 1 – fr A.C.R.P.P. [073]
Diepenbrock, Irmgard *see* QUANTITATIVE ELASTIZITAETSMESSUNG DER HAUT UND IHRE AUSWERTUNG
[DIEPPE RAID PAMPHLET COLLECTION] – 1942 – 1 – CSUXANM8182-B – us Hoover Inst Photo [355]
Dierbach, J H *see* ABHANDLUNG UEBER DIE ARZNEIKRAEFTE DER PFLANZEN,...
DIEREN, SPANKEREN EN LAAG-SOEREN IN VROEGER TIJDEN / Zadelhoff, F van – Rheden, 1958 – Dfl9.00 – ne Slangenburg [240]
Diereville, N *see* VOYAGE DU SIEUR DE DIEREVILLE EN ACADIE: PRECEDE D'UNE INTRODUCTION ET SUIVI DE NOTES ET D'EXTRAITS
DIES BLATT GEHOERT DER HAUSFRAU : BEILAGE: MODENHEFT – Berlin, Wiesbaden, Wien. oct 1906-mar 24, 1907 – 1 – gw Mikrofilm [640]
DIES BLATT GEHOERT DER HAUSFRAU – (Incl Beilagen, Wiener und Schweizer Ausgabe. Cont by: Ullsteins Blatt der Hausfrau. 1929/30: Das Blatt gehört der Hausfrau. oct 1932: Das Blatt der Hausfrau (since n1 1934/35: Ausgabe A ohne Schnittmusterbogen)) – Berlin, Wiesbaden, Wien. oct 1891-sep 22, 1894. n27 1902-mar 28, 1909. oct 2, 1910-sep 24, 1911. oct 1, 1916-sep 28, 1919. oct 1923-n26 1936. 1938/39-sep 1941. nov 1941. mar-jun 1942. jun 1943. feb-may 1944 – 39r – 1 – gw Mikrofilm [640]
DIES BLATT GEHOERT DER HAUSFRAU : SCHWEIZER AUSGABE – Berlin, Wiesbaden, Wien. 1924 – 1 – gw Mikrofilm [640]
DIES BLATT GEHOERT DER HAUSFRAU : WIENER AUSGABE – Berlin, Wiesbaden, Wien. oct 1924-sep 1931 – 1 – gw Mikrofilm [640]
Diesel Engineers and Users Associations. Including Gas Turbines *see* TRANSACTIONS
Diestensis, D Petri Dorlandi *see* CHRONICON CARTUSIENSE
DIET COMPOSITION AND BODY FAT : A MULTIVARIATE STUDY OF 203 ADULT MALES / Nelson, Lisa H – 1994 – 2mf – $8.00 – us Microform Publ [612]
DIET COMPOSITIONAL CHANGES DURING MOUNTAINEERING AT HIGH ALTITUDE IN COLD WEATHER / Schneider, Allison K – University of North Carolina at Chapel Hill, 1995 – 1mf – 9 – $4.00 – PH1474 – us Microform Publ [612]

DIETARY ADEQUACY AND CHANGES IN THE NUTRITIONAL STATUS OF APPALACHIAN TRAIL THROUGH-HIKERS / Lutz, Karen L – 1982 – 1mf – 9 – $4.00 – us Microform Publ [612]

DIETARY FAT AND CARBOHYDRATE IN RELATION TO BODY FATNESS IN LEAN AND OBESE MEN AND WOMEN / Niederpruem, Michael G & Miller, Wayne C – 1992 – 1mf – 9 – $4.00 – us Microform Publ [613]

DIETARY FATS AND OILS IN HUMAN NUTRITION – 1980 – 102p – it F.A.O. [640]

DIETER UND DIE FRAUEN : EIN ROMAN VON MUSIK, FREUNDSCHAFT UND LIEBE / Reichelt, Johannes – Dresden: Wodni & Lindecke, 1941 – 1r – 1 – us U.W. Library [830]

Dieterich, Karl *see* UNTERSUCHUNGEN ZUR GESCHICHTE DER GRIECHISCHEN SPRACHE

Dieterichs, Mikhail Konstantinovich *see* UBIISTVO TSARSKOI SEMII CHLENOV DOMA ROMANOVYKH NA URALIE

Dieterici, Wilhelm *see* DER WAHRE INWENDIGE UND AUSWENDIGE CHRIST, VORGESTELLET IN ZWEYEN THEILEN

DIETHNES EPHEMERIS TES NOMIMATIKES ARCHAIOLOGIAS = JOURNAL INTERNATIONAL D'ARCHEOLOGIE NUMISMATIQUE – (Text in Greek and French) – Athens, 1898-1920/21. v.1-20 – 134mf – 8 – ne IDC [730]

DIETI EMIGRATSII : SBORNIK STATE I / ed by Zienkovskago, V V – Praga: Izd. Pedagogicheskago bi uro po di elam sredne i i nizshe i russko i shkoly zagranit se i, 1925 – 1 – CSUX89-B3723 – us Hoover Inst Photo [947]

DIETI I VOINA : SBORNIK STATE I – Kiev: Izd. Kievskago frebelevskago ob-va, 1915 – 1 – CSUX89-B1661 – us Hoover Inst Photo [947]

Dietrich, A G *see* FLORA REGNI BORUSSICI

Dietrich, D N F *see* SYNOPSIS PLANTARUM

DIETRICH ECKART PAMPHLET COLLECTION – 1934-1976 – 1 – CSUXANR9516-B – us Hoover Inst Photo [943]

Dietrich, Veit *see* WIE MAN DAS VOLCK ZUR BUSS VND ERNSTLICHEM GEBET WIDER DEN TUERCKEN AUFF DER CANTZEL VERMANEN SOL..

DIETRICH VON BERN IN DER NEUEREN LITERATUR / Altaner, Bruno – (Includes bibliographical references) – Breslau: F Hirt, 1912 – 1 – us U.W. Library [430]

Dietrick, Ellen Battelle *see* WOMEN IN THE EARLY CHRISTIAN MINISTRY

DIETSCHE WARANDE EN BELFORT – 10(1909) – 9 – Dfl32.00 – ne Slangenburg [073]

Diettenhofer, J *see* THE CELEBRATED CANON NON NOBIS DOMINE

Dietterlin, W *see* ARCHITECTURA VON AUSSTHEILUNG/SYMMETRIA UND PROPORTION DER FUNFF SEULEN

Diettrich, Gustav *see* EIN APPARATUS CRITICUS ZUR PESITTO ZUM PROPHETEN JESAIA

Dietz, Theodor *see* AUFBAU, AUFGABEN UND ERGEBNISSE DER INTERNATIONALEN ARBEITSORGANISATION

Dietze, Walter *see*
- REDEN, VORTRAEGE, ESSAYS
- SCHRIFTEN ZUR DEUTSCHEN LITERATUR

Dietzsch, August *see* ADAM UND CHRISTUS

LE DIEU AU COEUR QUI RAYONNE. PARIS, 1928 / Anizan, Felix – Madrid: Razon y Fe, 1930 – 1 – sp Bibl Santa Ana [944]

DIEU LE TAM THOI VE CHE DO HOP DONG KINH TE = PROVISIONAL REGULATIONS ON ECONOMIC CONTRACTS / Central Arbitration Council – 1963 – 2mf – 9 SEL-112/1 – ne IDC [340]

LE DIEU MALGRE LUI OU LE CLUB SOUS UN CLOCHER / Lepine, de – Brignoles, impr. Perreymond, 1832, 176 p. Les Saint-Simoniens, 1825-1834. 6993 – 9 – fr Hachette [335]

Dieudonne, Christophe *see* STATISTIQUE DU DEPARTEMENT DU NORD

LES DIEUX DANS LES CHAMPS D'UN VILLAGE DU MAHARASHTRA (INDE) / Delfendahl, B – Essai d'ethnographie religieuse – 9 – F160.00 – fr Ethnologie [290]

DIEZ ANOS DE LA CRISIS ARGENTINA / Frigerio, Rogelio – Buenos Aires, Argentina: Sudamericana/Planeta, c1983 – 1 – CSUXADQ4264-B – us Hoover Inst Photo [360]

DIEZ ANOS DE ORGANIZACION SINDICAL : [VERSIONES TAQUIGRAFICAS Y ACTAS DE LOS DIEZ PRIMEROS CONGRESOS DE LA FEDERACION ARGENTINA DE PERIODISTAS] / Palazzolo, Octavio – Buenos Aires: [s.n.], 1949 – 1 – CSUXADJ2909-B – us Hoover Inst Photo [320]

DIEZ ANOS DE POLITICA LIBERAL, 1892-1902 / Rodriguez Pineres, Eduardo – Bogota. 1945 – 1 – us Res Libr [972]

DIEZ BLANCO, ALEJANDRO EVOLUCION DEL PENSAMIENTO FILOSOFICO. TOMO 1 : DESDE TALES DE MILETO A MARTIN HEIDEGGER, 1942 / Marquez, Gabino – Madrid: Razon y Fe, 1943 – 1 – sp Bibl Santa Ana [100]

Diez Canedo, Enrique *see*
- ALGUNOS VERSOS
- EL ARTE EN LA GRAN BRETANA E IRLANDA
- EPIGRAMAS AMERICANOS
- IMAGENES (VERSIONES POETICAS) ROSAS DEL TIEMPO ANTIGUO. MIES DE LOGRONO
- JUAN RAMON JIMENEZ EN SU OBRA
- ORACION DE LOS DEBILES AL COMENZAR EL ANO POR...
- UNIDAD Y DIVERSIDAD DE LAS LETRAS HISPANICAS
- LA VISITA DEL SOL

Diez Coronel, Diego Manuel *see* POR D. JOAQUIN TOPETE, AFRONTE...POR SI Y POR SUS HIJOS...

Diez Daza, A *see*
- AVISOS Y DOCUMENTOS PARA LA PRESERVACIN Y CURA DE LA PESTE
- LIBRI TRES DE RATIONE COGNOSCENDI CAUSAS ET SIGNA TAM IN PROSPERA QUAM ADVERSA VALITUDINE, URINARIUM

Diez de Leiva, F *see*
- ANTIAXIOMAS MORALES, MEDICOS...
- EL DEFENSOR DE SU AGRAVIO. NOTICIA SATIRICA SOBRE LA PESTE EN EL PUERTO DE SANTA MARIA

Diez de Medina, E *see* APUNTES SOBRE TOPICOS INTERNACIONALES

Diez, F *see* ETYMOLOGISCHES WOERTERBUCH DER ROMANISCHEN SPRACHEN

Diez, Genadius *see* SPAIN'S STRUGGLE AGAINST ANARCHISM AND COMMUNISM

Diez Gomez, Adolfo *see* UNA MUJER ARGENTINA

Diez, J *see* NOCIONES GENERALES SOBRE LAS OBLIGACIONES CONVENCIONALES...

LOS DIEZ LIBROS DE ARCHITECTURA / Alberti, L B – SL, 1582 – 7mf – 9 – sp Cultura [720]

Diez Lopez, Juan *see*
- DISCURSO PRONUNCIADO POR EL OBRERO EN EL CIRCULO CATOLICO DE VILLAFRANCA DE LOS BARROS EL DIA 8 DE DICIEMBRE DE 1906
- SUENO MISTICO EXPLICACION

Diez, M *see* LIBRO DE ALBEITERIA

Diez Mieres, A *see* LAS SUCESIONES EN EL DERECHO INTERNACIONAL PRIVADO... REPUBLICA ARGENTINA

Diez Olivares, J Ma *see* COMPENDIO DE GRAMATICA CASTELLANA

DIEZ PRIVILEGIOS PARA MUJERES PRENADAS...CON UN DICCIONARIO MEDICO / Alonso y de los Ruizes de Fontecha, J – Alcala de Henares, 1606 – 14mf – 9 – sp Cultura [610]

Diez-Canedo, Enrique *see* DEL CERCADO AJENO

DIFA' AZ ZINDANIYAN-I SIYASI-YI IRAN – [S.l.]: Jibhah-'i Milli-i Iran. Shumarah-'i 1-2 (Isfand 1344-Farvardin 1345 [Feb/Mar 1966-Mar 1966]) – 1 reel – 1 – $25.00 – us MEDOC [950]

LA DIFESA – Chicago, May 1 Nov 23 1918 – 1r – 1 – us I.H.R.C. [978]

LA DIFESA – Lawrence, MA. Aug 28 1920-Sept 1922 – 1r – 1 – us I.H.R.C. [071]

THE DIFFERENCE BETWEEN PARTICIPATION IN INTERCOLLEGIATE ATHLETICS AND ACADEMIC PERFORMANCE BASED ON TIME USE / Kartschoke, Christopher – University of Wisconsin-La Crosse, 1995 – 1mf – 9 – PSY 1891 – us Microform Publ [150]

THE DIFFERENCE BETWEEN WORDS / Trusler, John – 1766. 494p. (English Linguistics Series 1500-1800) – 9 – us UMI [420]

THE DIFFERENCE IN COACH ROLE MODEL BEHAVIORS FOR MALE AND FEMALE ATHLETES / Killmer, Karen J – 1993 – 2mf – $8.00 – us Microform Publ [150]

DIFFERENCES BETWEEN OLD AND NEW SCHOOL PRESBYTERIANS / Cheeseman, Lewis – Rochester: E. Darrow, 1848 – 1mf – us A.T.L.A. [240]

DIFFERENCES IN COMPETITIVE ANXIETY AND PERCEIVED COMPETENCE FOR HIGH AND LOW LEVEL COMPETITIVE YOUTH SWIMMERS / McNamara, Catherine M – Springfield College, 1995 – 2mf – 9 – $8.00 – PSY1853 – us Microform Publ [150]

THE DIFFERENCES IN EDUCATIONAL PREPARATION AND ATHLETIC EXPERIENCE BETWEEN DIVISION 1 AND DIVISION 2 ATHLETIC DIRECTORS OF NATIONAL COLLEGIATE ATHLETIC ASSOCIATION MEMBER INSTITUTIONS / Cummings-Danson, G – 1991 – 1mf – 9 – $4.00 – us Microform Publ [790]

DIFFERENCES IN MOVEMENT SPEED BETWEEN SIX YEAR OLD CHILDREN AND ADULTS ON THREE MOTOR TASKS / McMillan, Monique C & Zelaznik, Howard – 1992 – 1mf – 9 – $4.00 – us Microform Publ [150]

DIFFERENCES IN PEAK BLOOD LACTATE VALUES IN LONG COURSE VERSUS SHORT COURSE SWIMMING / Lowensteyn, I – 1991 – 1mf – 9 – $4.00 – us Microform Publ [612]

DIFFERENCES IN PHYSICAL ACTIVITY ATTITUDES AND FITNESS KNOWLEDGE BETWEEN HEALTH FITNESS STANDARD, SEX, AND GRADE GROUP / Bocket, Thomas J – 1994 – 2mf – $8.00 – us Microform Publ [306]

DIFFERENCES IN PHYSIOLOGICAL AND MECHANICAL PROPERTIES OF STAIR CLIMBING ON THREE DIFFERENT APPARATUS / Aiello, Kimberly A – Springfield College, 1995 – 2mf – 9 – $8.00 – PE1450 – us Microform Publ [612]

DIFFERENCES OF CO-DEPENDENCY AND SELF-ESTEEM IN COLLEGE AGE MALE AND FEMALE ATHLETES AND NONATHLETES / Mau, Robert E – Springfield College, 1995 – 2mf – 9 – $8.00 – PSY1852 – us Microform Publ [150]

LA DIFFERENCIATION SEXUELLE DANS LES RITES DE PASSAGE DE LA VIE QUOTIDIENNE EN ARIEGE / Tievant, S – 9 – F30.00 – fr Ethnologie [306]

DIFFERENT CONCEPTIONS OF PRIESTHOOD AND SACRIFICE : A REPORT OF A CONFERENCE HELD AT OXFORD, DEC 13 AND 14, 1899 / ed by Sanday, William – London; New York: Longmans, Green, 1900 – 1mf – 9 – 0-8370-9816-5 – 1986-3816 – us A.T.L.A. [240]

DIFFERENTIAL EFFECTIVENESS OF RELAXATION PROCEDURES IN ATTENUATING COMPONENTS OF ANXIETY IN SHOOTERS / Doyle, Lauren A – 1981 – 2mf – 9 – $8.00 – us Microform Publ [616]

DIFFERENTIAL EFFECTS OF STRENGTH TRAINING AND ENDURANCE TRAINING ON PARAMETERS REALTED TO RESISTANCE TO GRAVITATIONAL FORCES / Kim, H D – 1991 – 2mf – 9 – $8.00 – us Microform Publ [613]

DIFFERENTIAL EQUATIONS – v. 1- 1965- – 1,5,6 – us UMI [510]

DIFFERENTIAL EQUATIONS – v1-29. 1965-93 – 1,5 – $180.00v – us UMI [510]

DIFFERENTIATION – v. 1-6. 1973-76 – 1,5,9 – 311.00 – us UMI [073]

DIFFERENTIATION OF ETHNIC CULTURE REGIONS USING LABAN MOVEMENT ANALYSIS : A STUDY OF BULGARIAN DANCE / Kerr, Kathleen A & Lockhart, Aileene – 1991 – 3mf – $12.00 – us Microform Publ [790]

DIFFERENTSIATSIIA ZARABOTNOI PLATY V FABRICHNO-ZAVODSKOI PROMYSHLENNOSTI SOIUZA SSR ZA 1927 I 1928 – Moskva: Stat. izd-vo T SSU SSSR, 1929 – 1 – CSUX89-B6601 – us Hoover Inst Photo [947]

DIFFERENZIERTE BETRACHTUNGEN DES EINSATZES VON LYRIK UND KARIKATUREN BEI DER BILDUNG VON UMWELTRELEVANTEN EINSTELLUNGEN IM UNTERRICHT DER KLASSENSTUFEN 7 BIS 10 / Schilling, Kerstin – 1992 – vi/198p – 9 – DM98.00 – 3-89349-628-9 – gw Hänsel [370]

LA DIFFICULTE DE L'ESPLANADE: RESPONSE DE LA COMPANIE DE CHEMIN DE FER DE CREDIT VALLEY AUX ALLEGATIONS DES COMPANIES DE FER DU GRAND TRONC ET DU NOTHERN DANS L'AFFAIRE DE LA CONTESTATION DU DROIT D'ENTREE DU PORT DE TORONTO / Credit Valley Railway Company – s.l.: s.n., 1880 (Ottawa: A. Bureau). 05276. (Pre-1900 Canadiana) – 9 – cn C.I.H.M. [971]

DIFFICULTE SCOLAIRE DE MANITOBA PAR QUESTIONS ET REPONSES A LA PORTEE DE TOUS / Lacasse, Zacharie – s.l.: s.n., s.d. SEM105P458 – 1mf – 9 – Can$2.25 – cn Bibl Nat [370]

LES DIFFICULTES DE CROIRE / Brunetiere, Ferdinand – (Includes bibliographical references) – Paris: Librairie Academique, 1904 – 1mf – 9 – 0-8370-2494-3 – 1985-0494 – us A.T.L.A. [210]

DIFFICULTES PROPOSEES A M. DE CARADEUC DE LA CHALOTAIS, SUR LE MEMOIRE INTITULE: ESSAI D'EDUCATION NATIONALE / Crevier, Jean-Baptiste-Louis – Paris. 1763. 6745 – 9 – fr Hachette [944]

DIFFICULTIES OF FAITH / Delany, Selden Peabody; ed by Grafton, Charles Chapman – Milwaukee: Young Churchman, 1906 – 1mf – 9 – 0-8370-2863-9 – 1985-0863 – us A.T.L.A. [240]

THE DIFFICULTIES OF THE NEW HYPOTHESIS / Streibert, Jacob – (Includes bibliographical references) – New York: Funk & Wagnalls, 1888 – 1mf – 9 – 0-8370-5783-3 – 1985-3783 – us A.T.L.A. [220]

LA DIFFUSION DU COTON ALLEN DANS LA ZONE DENSE A L'OUEST DE BOUAKE / Michotte, J – (Africa series) – 9 – fr Hachette [380]

DIFICULTADES VENCIDAS...PARA LA LIMPIEZA Y ASEO DE LAS CALLES DE ESTA CORTE / Arce, Joan C – Madrid, 1735 – 3mf – 9 – sp Cultura [614]

DIFUSI ON DE LA DOCTRINA PERONISTA Y DEL PLAN ECONOMICO DE 1952 : BANCO DE LA PROVINCIA DE BUENOS AIRES – [Buenos Aires]: El Banco, [19–]-[19–] – 1 – CSUXADH9055-S – us Hoover Inst Photo [332]

Digard, J P *see* TECHNIQUES ET CULTURE DES NOMADES BAXTYARI D'IRAN

DIGBY COURIER – Digby, Canada. 1874-1948. And Digby Record. 1908-09 – 28r – 1 – $1,820.00 – cn Library Assoc [971]

Digby, K *see*
- CHOICE AND EXPERIMENTED RECEIPTS IN PHYSICK AND CHIRURGERY
- OF THE SYMPATHETICK POWDER

Digby, M *see* AGRICULTURAL COOPERATIVE MARKETING

Digby, William *see* THE BRITISH INVASION FROM THE NORTH: THE CAMPAIGNS OF GENERALS CARLETON AND BURGOYNE FROM CANADA, 1776-1777, WITH THE JOURNAL OF LIEUT. WILLIAM DIGBY, OF THE 53RD, OR SHROPSHIRE REGIMENT OF FOOT

DIGEST... / [Cadwalader, J L] – Washington D C, 1877 – 4mf – 1 – ILM-148/1 – ne IDC [327]

DIGEST OF ACTS AND DELIVERANCES / Presbyterian Church in the U.S.A. General Assembly – 1820-1976. 53v. and supplements – 1 – $550.00 – us Presbyterian [240]

A DIGEST OF ALL THE DECISIONS OF ALL THE COURTS RELATING TO NATIONAL BANKS, REPORTED FROM 1864 TO APRIL 1, 1898 / Smith, Hal Horace – Chicago: Flood, 1899. 326p. LL-1118 – 1 – us L of C Photodup [340]

A DIGEST OF AND INDEX TO THE REPORTS OF CASES DECIDED IN THE SUPREME COURT OF THE GOLD COAST COLONY. 1844-1931 / Griffith, William Brandford – Accra, the government printer, 1935. 194col. LL-12041 – 1 – us L of C Photodup [340]

A DIGEST OF CASES: DETERMINED BY THE SUPREME COURT OF CANADA FROM THE ORGANIZATION OF THE COURT IN 1875 TO THE 1ST DAY OF MAY, 1893: COMPRISING THE CASES RECORDED IN VOLUMES 1 TO 21. / Cassels, Robert – Toronto: Carswell, 1893. 00759. (Pre-1900 Canadiana) – 9 – cn C.I.H.M. [971]

A DIGEST OF CASES...RELATING TO RECOGNITION OF GOVERNMENT / Fraenkel, O K – N.p., 1925 – 1mf – 1 – ILM-1528/1 – ne IDC [327]

A DIGEST OF CORPORATION CASES / Dean, Maurice B – New York, Banks, 1906. 1087 p. LL-1142 – 1 – us L of C Photodup [340]

A DIGEST OF CRIMINAL LAW OF CANADA (CRIMES AND PUNISHMENTS): FOUNDED BY PERMISSION ON SIR JAMES FITZJAMES STEPHEN'S DIGEST OF THE CRIMINAL LAW / Burbidge, George Wheelock – Toronto: Carswell, 1890. 00331. (Pre-1900 Canadiana) – 9 – cn C.I.H.M. [340]

A DIGEST OF DECISIONS IN CRIMINAL CASES, CONTAINED IN THE REPORTS OF THE FEDERAL COURTS. / Waterman, Thomas Whitney – New York, Baker, Voorhis, 1877. 816 p. LL-1643 – 1 – us L of C Photodup [340]

DIGEST OF DECISIONS OF LAW AND PRACTICE IN THE PATENT OFFICE AND THE UNITED STATES AND STATE COURTS IN PATENTS, TRADE-MARKS, COPYRIGHTS, AND LABELS / Hart, Amos Winfield – Chicago: Callaghan, 1898. 385p. LL-408 – 1 – us L of C Photodup [340]

DIGEST OF DECISIONS OF LAW AND PRACTICE IN THE PATENT OFFICE AND THE UNITED STATES COURTS IN PATENTS, TRADEMARKS, COPYRIGHTS AND LABELS, 1912-1919 / Pollard, Willard Lacy – Washington, D.C.: Byrne, 1920. 119p. LL-1616 – 1 – us L of C Photodup [340]

DIGEST OF DECISIONS OF THE COURTS AND THE INTERSTATE COMMERCE COMMISSION...UNDER THE ACT TO REGULATE COMMERCE / Pierce, Edward B – 1887-1908. Chicago, 1908 – 4mf – 9 – $18.00 – LLMC 84-392 – us L.L.M.C. [340]

DIGEST OF DECISIONS OF THE DEPARTMENT OF THE INTERIOR IN CASES RELATED TO PUBLIC LANDS – Washington: GPO. 2pts. 1913 (all publ) – 10mf – 9 – $15.00 – LLMC 88-007 – us L.L.M.C. [340]

DIGEST OF DECISIONS OF THE DEPARTMENT OF THE INTERIOR IN CASES RELATING TO THE PUBLIC LANDS (INDIAN MATTERS INCLUDED) / U.S. Department of the Interior – v52-61 pt 1. 1927-1954, 1962 – 9 – $5.00f – us Ross [970]

DIGEST OF DECISIONS RELATING TO THE NATIONAL BANKS / U.S. Comptroller of the Currency – Washington: GPO. v1-5. 1864-1936 – 28mf – 9 – $42.00 – LLMC 84-394 – us L.L.M.C. [340]

DIGEST OF DECISIONS UNDER THE CUSTOMS REVENUE LAWS / U.S. Treasury Department. Division of Customs – (Covers Treasury Dept Board of General Appraisers and US Court Decisions) – Washington: GPO. 2v. 1918 (all publ) – 6mf – 9 – $27.00 – LLMC 84-366 – us L.L.M.C. [336]

DIGEST OF EDUCATION STATISTICS ... 1977/78-1984/85 / Nigeria. Bendel State. Statistics Office – Benin City, 1988 – 3mf – 9 – DE-643/1 – ne IDC [370]

DIGEST OF EDUCATIONAL STATISTICS [1986]-1987(1-4) / Mauritius. Ministry of Economic Planning and Development – (Missing: v1-3[1986]) – Port Louis – 2mf – 9 – DE-450/1 – ne IDC [370]

A DIGEST OF FEDERAL DECISIONS AND STATUTES, FROM THE EARLIEST PERIOD 1789 TO THE YEAR 1880 / Rapalje, Stewart – Jersey City, Linn, 1880. 793 p. LL-1472 – 1 – us L of C Photodup [340]

DIGEST OF INCOME TAX RULINGS : DIGEST A, APRIL 1919-DECEMBER 1930 / U.S. Treasury Department – Washington: GPO, 1932 – 5mf – 9 – $7.50 – LLMC 82-708 – us L.L.M.C. [324]

A DIGEST OF INTERNATIONAL LAW / Moore, John Bassett – Washington, 1906. 8v – 3r – 1 – $100.00 – us Trans-Media [340]

DIGEST OF INTERNATIONAL LAW / Hackworth, G H – Washington. 8v. 1940-44 – 66mf – 1 – ILM-182/1 – ne IDC [327]

DIGEST OF INTERNATIONAL LAW / Hackworth, Green Haywood – 1904-44 – 3r – 1 – $100.00 – us Trans-Media [340]

DIGEST OF MARYLAND STATUTES AND DECISIONS ON CRIMINAL LAW / Gans, Edgar Hilary – Baltimore: Murphy, 1884. 170p. LL-723 – 1 – us L of C Photodup [340]

A DIGEST OF MISSISSIPPI RAILWAY DECISIONS FROM VOL. 1 TO AND INCLUDING VOL. 71, MISSISSIPPI REPORTS / Harris, James Bowmar – Galveston: Clarke & Courts, 1894. 191p. LL-953 – 1 – us L of C Photodup [340]

DIGEST OF NEUROLOGY AND PSYCHIATRY – (1975-. 5,6. 1976-. 9) – v. 1-. 1932- – 1 – us UMI [616]

DIGEST OF NEW HAMPSHIRE SCHOOL LAW : ADAPTED TO THE GENERAL LAWS AND AMENDMENTS THERETO – Concord: J B Sanborn, 1881 – 2mf – 9 – $3.00 – LLMC 96-046 – us L.L.M.C. [340]

A DIGEST OF PAROCHIAL RETURNS / Great Britain. Select Committee into the Education of the Poor – 1819 – 9 – uk Microform Academic [324]

DIGEST OF PATENT AND TRADE-MARK CASES DECIDED BY THE COURT OF APPEALS OF THE DISTRICT OF COLUMBIA. / Torbert, William Sydenham – Washington, Byrne, 1909. 291 p. LL-1345 – 1 – us L of C Photodup [340]

A DIGEST OF PATENT CASES : DECIDED IN THE FEDERAL AND STATE COURTS FROM 1789-1888 / Simonds, William Edgar – New York: Strouse & Co, 1888 – 3mf – 9 – $4.50 – LLMC 84-336 – us L.L.M.C. [340]

DIGEST OF "PRECEDENTS OR DECISIONS" BY SELECT COMMITTEES APPOINTED TO TRY THE MERITS OF UPPER CANADA CONTESTED ELECTIONS, FROM 1824 TO 1849 / Patrick, Alfred – Montreal: Printed by Lovell and Gibson, 1849. SEM105P135 – 2mf – 9 – Can$4.50 – cn Bibl Nat [971]

DIGEST OF PUBLIC GENERAL BILLS AND RESOLUTIONS / U.S. Congress – 75th-101st Congress. 1937-90 – 1044mf – 9 – $1,566.00 – LLMC 80-036 – us L.L.M.C. [323]

DIGEST OF PUBLIC LAND LAWS OF THE UNITED STATES – (Prepared for the Public Land Law Review Commission by Shepard's Citations) – Washington: GPO, 1968 – 12mf – 9 – $18.00 – LLMC 85-301 – us L.L.M.C. [324]

DIGEST OF REPORTED CASES TOUCHING THE CRIMINAL LAW OF CANADA. / Foran, Thomas Patrick – Toronto: Carswell, 1889. 252p. LL-2377 – 1 – us L of C Photodup [340]

DIGEST OF REPORTED CASES TOUCHING THE CRIMINAL LAW OF CANADA: WITH REFERENCES TO THE STATUTES AND AN INDEX / Foran, Thomas Patrick – Toronto: Carswell, 1889. 03146. (Pre-1900 Canadiana) – 9 – cn C.I.H.M. [971]

DIGEST OF REPORTS OF CASES DECIDED IN THE COURT OF CHANCERY, IN THE COURT OF ERROR & APPEAL, ON APPEAL FROM THE COURT OF CHANCERY, AND IN CHANCERY CHAMBERS. / Cooper, Charles William – Toronto: Blackburn's, 1868-73. 2v in 1. LL-2304 – 1 – us L of C Photodup [340]

DIGEST OF STATE LAWS REGULATING FRATERNAL BENEFICIARY SOCIETIES / Landis, Abb – (Supplement. 1922? 28 p. Washington, D.C. LL-1486. Supplement. With rev. to 1924. Washington, D.C., 1924. 86 p. LL-1486) – Washington, D.C., Rogers, 1921 239 p. LL-1486 – 1 – us L of C Photodup [340]

DIGEST OF STATUTES AND LEGAL DECISIONS RELATING TO OFFICIAL STENOGRAPHERS / National Shorthand Reporters' Association – New Haven, Conn.: Mac, 1906. 242p. LL-1259 – 1 – us L of C Photodup [340]

A DIGEST OF STATUTES, EQUITY RULES, AND DECISIONS, UPON THE JURISDICTION, PLEADINGS, AND PRACTICE OF THE CIRCUIT COURTS OF THE UNITED STATES / Thatcher, Erastus – Boston, Little, Brown, 1883. 976 p. LL-1406 – 1 – us L of C Photodup [340]

A DIGEST OF STATUTES, RULES, AND DECISIONS RELATIVE TO THE JURISDICTION AND PRACTICE OF THE SUPREME COURT OF THE UNITED STATES 1790-1879 / Thatcher, Erastus – (2d ed. Boston, Little, Brown, 1883. 602 p. LL-1454. 1) – Boston, Little, Brown, 1882. 520 p. LL-1180 – 1 – us L of C Photodup [340]

DIGEST OF STUDIES AND LECTURES IN THEOLOGY – Auburn: Wm. J. Moses, 1866. 1 fiche – 9 – us A.T.L.A. [240]

DIGEST OF THE AMERICAN AND ENGLISH ANNOTATED CASES – New York: Thompson Co. 1v. 1912 (all publ) – 20mf – 9 – $30.00 – LLMC 84-695D – us L.L.M.C. [340]

A DIGEST OF THE DECISIONS OF THE DEPARTMENT OF THE INTERIOR AND THE GENERAL LAND OFFICE IN CASES RELATING TO THE PUBLIC LANDS, FROM JULY, 1881 TO DECEMBER, 1887 / Matthews, William Baynham – Washington, D.C.: Wilson, 1888. 579p. LL-189 – 1 – us L of C Photodup [340]

DIGEST OF THE DECISIONS...IN CASES RELATED TO PUBLIC LANDS / Heselman, George J – pts 1-2, covering v1-40 of the Dec. of the Dept. of the Int.... Washington: GPO, 1913 – 10mf – 9 – $15.00 – LLMC 88-007 – us L.L.M.C. [324]

DIGEST OF THE DICISIONS OF THE COMPTROLLER OF THE TREASURY – 1894-1920 (all publ) – 26mf – 9 – $39.00 – LLMC 90-373 – us L.L.M.C. [340]

A DIGEST OF THE HISTORY, POLITY AND DOCTRINES OF THE PRIMITIVE METHODISTS,... / Parrott, J – London, 1866 – 2mf – 9 – ne IDC [240]

DIGEST OF THE INTERNATIONAL LAW OF THE UNITED STATES / Wharton, Francis A – Washington. 1886. 3v – 1 – $50.00 – us Trans-Media [340]

A DIGEST OF THE LAW OF EVIDENCE IN CRIMINAL CASES / Roscoe, Henry – Philadelphia: Johnson, 1852. 993 (i.e.929)p. LL-1168 – 1 – us L of C Photodup [340]

A DIGEST OF THE LAW OF EVIDENCE...FROM THE 15TH ED. (1899)...WITH BOTH GENERAL AMERICAN NOTES AND NOTES ESPECIALLY ADAPTED TO THE STATE OF OHIO / Stephen, James Fitzjames – (From the 5th ed. (1899) with both general American notes and notes especially adapted to the states of Illinois, Indiana, and Michigan. Hartford, Conn., Bissell, 1903. 719 p. LL-961) – Hartford, Conn., Dissell, 1902. 579 p. LL-886 – 1 – us L of C Photodup [340]

DIGEST OF THE LAW OF IMPEACHMENT / Todd, Hiram C – n.p. 1913. 3 p., 2-41 numb. LL-1367 – 1 – us L of C Photodup [340]

DIGEST OF THE LAW OF MINES AND MINERALS AND OF ALL CONTROVERSIES INCIDENT TO THE SUBJECT-MATTER OF MINING / Morrison, Robert Stewart – San Francisco: Bancroft, 1878. 448p. LL-578 – 1 – us L of C Photodup [622]

A DIGEST OF THE LAW OF PARTNERSHIP. / Montagu, Basil – 1st Amer. ed. from the 2nd and last London ed. of 1822. New York: Lamson and Collins & Hannay, 1824. 2v. LL-511 – 1 – us L of C Photodup [340]

A DIGEST OF THE LAW OF REAL PROPERTY / Cruise, William – v1-7. 1856-57 – 1 – $95.00 – 0-89093-032-5 – us UPA [941]

A DIGEST OF THE LAW RELATING TO DISTRICT COUNCILS. / Chambers, George Frederick – 9th ed. London: Stevens, 1895. 283p. LL-108 – 1 – us L of C Photodup [340]

A DIGEST OF THE LAW RELATING TO PUBLIC HEALTH AND LOCAL GOVERNMENT. / Chambers, George Frederick – 8th ed. London: Stevens, 1881 i.e. 1884?. 556p. LL-1451 – 1 – us L of C Photodup [340]

DIGEST OF THE LAWS AND DECISIONS RELATING TO THE APPOINTMENT, SALARY, AND COMPENSATION OF THE OFFICIALS OF THE UNITED STATES COURTS. / Cousar, Robert Moore – Washington, Govt. Print. Off., 1895. 300 p. LL-1171 – 1 – us L of C Photodup [340]

A DIGEST OF THE LAWS OF ENGLAND / Comyns, John – v1-8. 1822 – 1 – $200.00 – 0-89093-025-2 – us UPA [324]

DIGEST OF THE LAWS OF VIRGINIA OF A CIVIL NATURE / Matthews, James Muscoe – Richmond: Randolph, 1856-57. 2v. LL-634 – 1 – us L of C Photodup [340]

DIGEST OF THE LAWS OF VIRGINIA, OF A CRIMINAL NATURE / Matthews, James Muscoe – (2nd ed. Richmond: Randolph and English, 1871. 376p. Supplement. Richmond, 1878. 57p. LL-683. 3rd ed. Richmond: Randolph and English, 1890. 421p. LL-887) – Richmond: West & Johnston, 1861. 320p. LL-815 – 1 – us L of C Photodup [340]

A DIGEST OF THE MECHANICS' LIEN LAW OF ILLINOIS / Scott, Adolphus G – Chicago: Stansbury, 1896. 23, 3p. LL-97 – 1 – us L of C Photodup [340]

A DIGEST OF THE MILITARY AND NAVAL LAWS OF THE CONFEDERATE STATES : FROM THE COMMENCEMENT OF THE PROVISIONAL CONGRESS TO THE END OF THE FIRST CONGRESS UNDER PERMANENT CONSTITUTION, ANALYTICALLY ARRANGED / Lester, W W & Bromwell, William J – Columbia: Evans & Cogswell, 1864 – 4mf – 9 – $6.00 – LLMC 96-091 – us L.L.M.C. [340]

A DIGEST OF THE MINUTES, INSTITUTIONS, POLITY, DOCTRINES, ORDINANCES AND LITERATURE OF THE METHODIST NEW CONNEXION / Baggaly, W – London, 1862 – 3mf – 9 – ne IDC [240]

A DIGEST OF THE MINUTES, INSTITUTIONS, POLITY, DOCTRINES, ORDINANCES AND LITERATURE OF THE METHODIST NEW CONNEXION / Baggaly, W – London, 1862. 253p – 3mf – 9 – ne IDC [060]

A DIGEST OF THE MINUTES OF THE METHODIST CONFERENCES, FROM THE FIRST,... BY THE LATE REV. JOHN WESLEY,... 1744, TO THE YEAR 1826 / Garrett, P – Halifax, 1827 – 4mf – 9 – ne IDC [240]

A DIGEST OF THE NOVA SCOTIA COMMON LAW, EQUITY, VICE-ADMIRALTY AND ELECTION REPORTS: WITH NOTES OF MANY UNREPORTED CASES AND OF CASES APPEALED TO THE PRIVY COUNCIL AND SUPREME COURT OF CANADA FROM NOVA SCOTIA / Congdon, Frederick Tennyson – Containing also rules of court, and an index of the Imperial, Dominion and Nova Scotia statutes...Toronto: Carswell, 1890. 00743. (Pre-1900 Canadiana) – 9 – cn C.I.H.M. [971]

DIGEST OF THE PRINCIPAL ACTS AND DELIVERANCES / United Presbyterian Church of North America – 1878-1952 – 1 – $50.00 – us Presbyterian [240]

A DIGEST OF THE REPORTED DECISIONS OF THE COURTS OF THE UNITED STATES OF AMERICA, AND OF GREAT BRITAIN AND HER COLONIES, RELATING TO THE RIGHTS AND LIABILITIES OF GAS COMPANIES / Greenough, Charles Pelham – Boston: Little, Brown, 1883. 307p. LL-170 – 1 – us L of C Photodup [340]

A DIGEST OF THE RULES, REGULATIONS AND USAGES OF THE PEOPLE DENOMINATED BIBLE CHRISTIANS,... / Bible Christians – 6th ed. London, 1892. xvi/147p – 2mf – 9 – ne IDC [240]

A DIGEST OF THE RULES, REGULATIONS AND USAGES OF THE PEOPLE DENOMINATED BIBLE CHRISTIANS,... / Bible Christians – 7th ed. London, 1902. xvi/176p – 3mf – 9 – ne IDC [240]

A DIGEST OF THE RULES, REGULATIONS AND USAGES OF THE PEOPLE DENOMINATED BIBLE CHRISTIANS,... / Bible Christians – London, [1882] – 2mf – 9 – ne IDC [240]

DIGEST OF UNITED KINGDOM ENERGY STATISTICS 1948/49-1977 – (Coll title: British Government Publications...1801-1977, Energy) – 73mf – 9 – £535.00 – uk Chadwyck [333]

DIGEST OPERASI DAILY BULLETIN – Indonesia. Djakarta. 1966- – 1 – us UMI [072]

DIGEST SOCIALE *see* BIEN-ETRE SOCIAL CANADIEN

DIGEST TO AMERICAN NEGLIGENCE CASES AND REPORTS – (Covers both American Negligence Cases and American Negligence Reports) – Chicago: Callaghan. 1v. 1912 (all publ) – 18mf – 9 – $27.00 – LLMC 84-699F – us L.L.M.C. [340]

DIGEST TO AMERICAN NEGLIGENCE CASES AND REPORTS – New York: Remick & Schilling. 1v. 1902 (all publ) – 7mf – 9 – $10.50 – LLMC 84-699A – us L.L.M.C. [340]

DIGEST TO AMERICAN NEGLIGENCE REPORTS – (Covers v1-20 of American Negligence Reports) – New York: Remick & Schilling. 1v. 1909 (all publ) – 18mf – 9 – $27.00 – LLMC 84-699B – us L.L.M.C. [340]

DIGESTA MALACOLOGICA / Sykes, E R – Z 828 2. Nos. 1-2. 1901-1903 – 8 – ne IDC [590]

DIGESTE SOCIAL – (Cont: Bien-etre social canadien 1974. Cont by: Perception 1977-78) – Ottawa, v26-29 1974-77 – 5 – Can$100.00 – cn Micromedia [073]

DIGESTE SOCIAL *see* PERCEPTION

DIGESTED SUMMARY & ALPHABETICAL LIST OF PRIVATE CLAIMS...FROM THIRTY-SECOND TO THE FORTY-FIRST CONGRESS, INCLUSIVE – Land claims, 1852-71. 1873. 526p. V300-0041 – 1 – us A.G.L.L. [978]

DIGESTED SUMMARY & ALPHABETICAL LIST OF PRIVATE CLAIMS...PRESENTED TO THE HOUSE OF REPRESENTATIVES FROM FIRST TO THIRTY-FIRST CONGRESS, INCLUSIVE – Land claims, 1789-1851. 1853. 3v. V300-0043/45 – 1 – us A.G.L.L. [920]

LE DIGESTEUR = THE DIGESTOR – Grand-Mere, Canada. 20 mar 1918-v4 n10. 7 sep 1921 – 1r – 1 – Can$45.00 – cn Can Microfilming [072]

DIGESTION – v12-. 1975- – 1,5,9 – us UMI [073]

DIGESTIVE DISEASES – v1-. 1983- – 1,5,9 – us UMI [616]

DIGESTIVE DISEASES AND SCIENCES – v10-39. 1965-94 – 1,5 – $225.00v – us UMI [616]

DIGESTIVE DISEASES AND SCIENCES *see* AMERICAN JOURNAL OF DIGESTIVE DISEASES
DIGESTIVE SURGERY – v1-. 1984- – 1,5,9 – us UMI [073]
DIGESTO CONSTITUCIONAL DE LA NACION ARGENTINA / Argentina. Congreso de la Nacion. Camara de Diputados de la Nacion – Buenos Aires: Impr. del Congreso de la Nacion, 1950 – 1 – CSUXADH9205-B – us Hoover Inst Photo [340]
DIGESTS AND DECISIONS: LAW AND PRACTICE IN THE PATENT OFFICE – in 3 bks: Bk. 1, by D.H. Rice & L.C. Rice, 1869-80, publ. in 1880; Bk. 2, by E.S. Beach, 1880-90, publ. in 1890; Bk. 3, by L.H. Rice, 1890-1900, publ. in 1900; George B. Reed, Boston.84-331 – 9 – $12.00 – us L.L.M.C. [340]
DIGESTS OF INTERNATIONAL LAW SERIES – (Original Monograph Series: Cadwalader 1v 1877. Wahrton 3v 1887. Moore 8v 1906. Hackworth 9v 1940-44. Whiteman 15v 1963-73. These occasional studies followed by annuals: Digests of US Practice in International Law: Rovine v1-2 1973-1974. McDowell v3-4 1975-1976. Boyd v5 1977. Cumulative index for 1973-1980) – 411mf – 9 – $617.00 – LLMC 79-444 – us L.L.M.C. [340]
DIGESTS OF U.S. PRACTICE IN INTERNATIONAL LAW *see* DIGESTS OF INTERNATIONAL LAW SERIES
DIGGER'S FRIEND – Bloemhof, South Africa. 9 Jan-21 Aug 1914. 1 reel – 1, 16 diazo available at reduced price – sa SA Libr [072]
DIGGER'S NEWS – Bloemhof, South Africa. 16 Jan-8 May 1914. 1 reel – 1, 16 diazo available at reduced price – sa SA Libr [072]
DIGGERS' NEWS AND WITWATERSRAND ADVERTISER – Johannesburg. South Africa. -w. 2 Feb 1888-28 Dec 1889. (1 reel) – 1 – uk British Libr Newspaper [072]
Digges, D *see* THE COMPLEAT AMBASSADOR
DIGHTON 1695-1890 – (Mf 1-5: Vital Records 1687-1792. Mf 6-7: Vitals Index 1687-1792. Mf 8-15: Vital Records 1695-1859. Mf 16-17: Births 1844-54. Mf 17: Marriages 1844-54. Mf 17-18: Deaths 1844-55. Mf 19-21: Births 1855-91. Mf 21-23: Marriages 1855-90. Mf 23-25: Deaths 1855-89. Mf 26-28: Vitals Index 1695-1859. Mf 29-30: Births Index 1855-1900. Mf 30-32: Marriages 1841-1900. Mf 32-33: Deaths 1855-1900. Mf 34-38: Births 1700-1899. Mf 39-40: Brides 1700-1899. Mf 41-43: Grooms 1700-1899. Mf 44-51: Deaths 1700-1980. Mf 52-54: Deaths by Maiden Names) – (mf ed 1984) – 54mf – 9 – 0-931248-64-7 – us Holbrook [920]
DIGITAL DESIGN – (1982-. 1,5,6,9) – v1-. 1971- – 1 – us UMI [073]
DIGITAL NEWS *see* HARDCOPY
DIGITAL REVIEW – v1-. 1983- – 1,5,6,9 – us UMI [073]
DIGITAL SYSTEMS FOR INDUSTRIAL AUTOMATION – v.1. 1981 – 5,6,9 – us UMI [073]
DIGNIDAD DEL TRABAJO / Ganduglia, Santiago – Buenos Aires: Subsecretaria de Informaciones de la Presidencia de la Nacion, 1950?] – 1 – CSUXADQ0938-B – us Hoover Inst Photo [331]
DIGNITE NOUVELLE – (Issues for mar 19-Apr 2 1961 filmed as pt of: Herbert C Weiss collection on the Belgian Congo) – Bukavu: Ramazani-Ngongo, Joseph M, [1961-]. mar 19-apr 2 1961 – us Res Libr [072]
THE DIGNITY OF LABOR: LECTURE TO THE YOUNG / Christie, Robert – Delivered... January, 1879, Hamilton, Ont.: A. Lawson, 1879. 00637. (Pre-1900 Canadiana) – 9 – cn C.I.H.M. [331]
DIGUO ZHUYI YU ZHONGGUO HAIGUAN (DIBABIAN: ZHONGGUO HAIGUAN YU ING-DE XUJIE KUAN) – Series of reference materials on the economic history of modern China: Imperialism and the Chinese Customs, Part VIII-The Chinese Customs and Additional Loans from Great Britain and Germany. Comp. by the Head Office of the Customs of the People's Republic of China. 1 fiche. F/H162 – 9 – $4.50f – cc Microforms [950]
DIGUO ZHUYI YU ZHONGGUO HAIGUAN (DIJIUBIAN: ZHONGGUO HAIGUAN YU YIHETUAN) – Series of Reference Materials on the Economic History of Modern China: Imperialism and the Chinese Customs, Part IX-The Chinese Customs and the Boxer Rebellion. Comp. by the Head Office of the Customs of the People's Republic of China. 2 fiches. F H163 – 9 – $9.00 – cc Microforms [950]
DIGUO ZHUYI YU ZHONGGUO HAIGUAN (DILIUBIAN: ZHONGGUO HAIGUAN YU ZHONG-PU LISIBEN CAOYUE) – Series of Reference Materials on the Economic History of Modern China: Imperialism and the Chinese Customs, Part VI-The Chinese Customs and the Sino-Portuguese Lisbon Draft Treaty. Comp. by the Head Office of the Customs of the People's Republic of China. 2 fiches. F H160 – 9 – $9.00 – cc Microforms [950]
DIGUO ZHUYI YU ZHONGGUO HAIGUAN (DIQIBIAN: ZHONGGUO HAIGUAN YU ZHONG-RI ZHANZHENG) – Series of Reference Materials on the Economic History of Modern China: Imperialism and the Chinese Customs, Part VII-The Chinese Customs and the Sino-Japanese War. Comp. by the Head Office of the Customs of the People's Republic of China. 3 fiches. F H161 – 9 – $13.50 – cc Microforms [950]
DIGUO ZHUYI YU ZHONGGUO HAIGUAN (DISHIBIAN: ZHONGGUO HAIGUAN GENGZI PEIKUAN) – Series of Reference Materials on the Economic History of Modern China: Imperialism and the Chinese Customs, Part X-The Chinese Customs and the War Indemnity of 1900. Comp. by the Head Office of the Customs of the People's Republic of China. 3 fiches. F H164 – 9 – $13.50 – cc Microforms [950]
DIGUO ZHUYI YU ZHONGGUO HAIGUAN (DISHIERBIAN: ZHONGGUO HAIGUAN YU YOUZHENG) – Series of Reference Materials on the Economic History of Modern China: Imperialism and the Chinese Customs, Part XII-The Chinese Customs and Postal Services. Comp. by the Head Office of the Customs of the People's Republic of China. 3 fiches. F H165 – 9 – $13.50 – cc Microforms [950]
DIGUO ZHUYI YU ZHONGGUO HAIGUAN (DISHISANBIAN: ZHONGGUO HAIGUAN YU XINHAI GEMING) – Series of Reference Materials on the Economic History of Modern China: Imperialism and the Chinese Customs, Part XIII-The Chinese Customs and the Revolution of 1911. Comp. by the Head Office of the Customs of the People's Republic of China. 5 fiches. F H166 – 9 – $22.50 – cc Microforms [950]
DIGUO ZHUYI YU ZHONGGUO HAIGUAN (DISHIWUBIAN: YI-JIU-SAN-BA NIAN YING RI HUANYU ZHONGGUO HAIGUAN DE FEIFA XIEDING) – Series of Reference Materials on the Economic History of Modern China: Imperialism and the Chinese Customs, Part XV-The Illegal Agreement Between Great Britain and Japan on the Chinese Customs in 1938. Comp. by the Head Office of the Customs of the People's Republic of China. 3 fiches. F H167 – 9 – $13.50 – cc Microforms [950]
DIGUO ZHUYI YU ZHONGGUO HAIGUAN (DISIBIAN: ZHONGGUO HAIGUAN YU ZHONG-FA ZHANZHENG) – Series of Reference Materials on the Economic History of Modern China: Imperialism and the Chinese Customs, Part IV-The Chinese Customs and the Sino-French War. Comp. by the Head Office of the Customs of the People's Republic of China. 3 fiches. F H158 – 9 – $13.50 – cc Microforms [950]
DIGUO ZHUYI YU ZHONGGUO HAIGUAN (DIWUBIAN: ZHONGGUO HAIGUAN YU CHUCANG WENTI) – Series of Reference Materials on the Economic History of Modern China: Imperialism and the Chinese Customs, Part V-The Chinese Customs and the Problem of Burma and Tibet. Comp. by the Head Office of the Customs of the People's Republic of China. 3 fiches. F H159 – 9 – $13.50 – cc Microforms [950]
Dihkhuda, Ali Akbar *see* LUGHATNAMAH
Dijkstra, Harmen *see* DUISTERNIS EN LICHT
Dijon *see* BULLETIN MUNICIPAL
DIKAIA PORFIRA / Zenkevich, M – Spb. 1912. BR-1237 2 – 8 – ne IDC [460]
DIKAIA VOLIA / Gorodetskii, S – Stikhi i skazki. Spb. 1908. BR-1122 2 – 8 – ne IDC [460]
DIKDUKEI SOFERIM / Rabbinovicz, R N N – 16 v. Munich, Przemysl. 1867-97. BJ-32-14 1 – 9 – ne IDC [270]
Dikgof-Derental, Aleksandr Arkadevich *see* V NASHI DNI
Dikovics, John *see* TWENTY-FIVE YEARS OF PRESBYTERIAN...HUNGARIANS; OUR MAGYAR PRESBYTERIANS
Dikshit, Kiranmani A et al *see* RURAL RADIO
DIKSIYONARYO NG WIKANG PILIPINO – Rosendo Ignacio. Quezon City: Samar Pub Co, 1958 – 1 – us Res Libr [072]
"DIKTATURA PROLETARIATA" V ROSSII : NABROSKI S NATURY I U.K. ART SYBUSHEVA: POLITICHESKIE DI EI ATELI NA ZASI EDANII AKH SOVIETOV RAB., SOLD. I KREST. DEPUTATOV, UCHREDITELNAGO SOBRANII A, KRESTI ANSKIKH SI EZDOV I PROCH. V DEKABRI E 1917 I V IANVARI E 1918 G.G. / Artsybushev, U K – Moskva: Izd. t-va I. Knebel, [1918?] – 1 – CSUX89-B1087 – us Hoover Inst Photo [320]
DILADANG; PILIHAN TJERPEN2 BULGARIA / Arimami, tr – SE-5333 1. 1961 – 9 – ne IDC [949]
DILECTISSIMA NOBIS – 3Jun 1933. English. Encyclical on Spain. New York, 1937. Fiche W 786. (Blodgett Collection of Spanish Civil War Pamphlets) – 9 – us H.U. College Libr [946]
THE DILEMMA OF HUMANITARIAN MODERNISM / Calhoun, Robert L – 1937 – 1 – us A.T.L.A. [240]
DILETTANTEN – Sundsvall, Sweden. 1853-58 – 1 – sw Kungliga [072]
DILI XUEBAO – Acta Geographica Sinica. In Chinese but English abstracts to the main articles. F p107 – 9 – 4.00f – cc Microforms [073]
DILI ZHISHI – Geographical Knowledge. 1984-85. F/P 300 – 9 – $4.50f – cc Microforms [073]
Dill, Augustus *see* THE BROWNIES' BOOK; A MONTHLY MAGAZINE FOR NEGRO CHILDREN
Dill, Jacob Smiser *see* DIARY AND TRAVELOGUE
Dill, Samuel *see*
- ROMAN SOCIETY FROM NERO TO MARCUS AURELIUS
- ROMAN SOCIETY IN THE LAST CENTURY OF THE WESTERN EMPIRE

DILLALIYA – (Filmed with Zaruma and other Hausa newspapers) – Lagos: Shu-Aibu Paiko, nov 7 1969 – us Res Libr [072]
Dillen, J G van *see* VREEMDELINGEN TE AMSTERDAM IN DE EERSTE HELFT DER ZEVENTIENDE EEUW
Dillen, J J *see*
- HISTORIA MUSCORUM
- HISTORIA MUSCORUM: A GENERAL HISTORY OF LAND AND WATER
- HORTI ELTHAMENSIS PLANTARUM RARIORUM ICONES ET NOMIA
- HORTUS ELTHAMENSIS

Dillenback *see* HISTORY AND DIRECTORY OF KENT COUNTY, MICHIGAN
DILLER RECORD – Diller, NE. -w. Mar. 1887-Oct. 1950; Dec. 1951-Jan. 1954 – 1 – us NE Hist [071]
Dillinger, Stefan *see* SYSTEMISCHES DENKEN
Dillmann, August *see*
- DIE BUECHER EXODUS UND LEVITICUS
- DIE BUECHER NUMERI, DEUTERONOMIUM UND JOSUE
- CATALOGUS CODICUM MANUSCRIPT BIBLIOTHECAE BODLEIANAE OXONIENSIS
- CHRESTOMATHIA AETHIOPICA EDITA ET GLOSSARIO EXPLANATA
- CHRESTOMATHIA AETHIPICA EDITA ET GLOSSARIO EXPLANATA
- DIE GENESIS
- GENESIS, CRITICALLY AND EXEGETICALLY EXPOUNDED
- HANDBUCH DER ALTTESTAMENTLICHEN THEOLOGIE
- HIOB FUER DIE DRITTE AUFLAGE NACH L. HIRZEL UND J. OLSHAUSEN
- LEXICON LINGUAE AETHIOPICAE
- DER PROPHET JESAIA
- UEBER DIE GRIECHISCHE UEBERSETZUNG DES QOHELETH

Dillon, E J *see* THE SHADE OF THE BALKANS: A COLLECTION OF BULGARIAN FOLKSONGS AND PROVERBS
Dillon, Emile Joseph *see* A SCRAP OF PAPER
DILLON FIRST BAPTIST CHURCH. DILLON COUNTY. SOUTH CAROLINA : CHURCH RECORDS – 1891-1902, 1905-16, 1924-41, 1947-89 – 1 – $63.59 – us Baptist [240]
Dillon, John Forest *see* DILLON'S REPORTS OF CASES IN THE EIGHTH CIRCUIT, 1870-1880
Dillon, John Forrest *see*
- COMMENTARIES ON THE LAW OF MUNICIPAL CORPORATIONS
- JOHN MARSHALL; LIFE, CHARACTER AND JUDICIAL SERVICES.
- THE LAWS AND JURISPRUDENCE OF ENGLAND AND AMERICA
- PROPERTY; ITS RIGHTS AND DUTIES IN OUR LEGAL AND SOCIAL SYSTEMS
- REMOVAL OF CAUSES FROM STATE COURTS TO FEDERAL COURTS.

Dillon, John M *see* JOHN MARSHALL
DILLON'S REPORTS OF CASES IN THE EIGHTH CIRCUIT, 1870-1880 / Dillon, John Forest – Davenport, IA: Griggs. v1-5. 1871-80 (all publ) – 35mf – 9 – $52.00 – LLMC 81-448 – us L.L.M.C. [340]
Dills, R S *see*
- HISTORY OF FAYETTE COUNTY
- HISTORY OF GREENE COUNTY

Dillwyn, L W *see*
- BRITISH CONFERVAE
- FUCI SIVE PLANTARUM FUCORUM GENERI A BOTANIIS ASCRIPTARUM IEONES DESCRIPTIONES ET HISTORIA
- HORTUS COLLINSONIANUS
- MEMORANDA RELATING TO COLEOPTEROUS INSECTS FOUND IN THE NEIGHBORHOOD OF SWANSEA
- A REVIEW OF THE REFERENCES TO THE HORTUS MALABARICUS

DILL-ZEITUNG – Dillenburg, West Germany. 1976- – ca 7r per yr – 1 – gw Mikrofilm [072]
Dilnot, George *see* THE STORY OF SCOTLAND YARD
Dilthey, Wilhelm *see*
- LEBEN SCHLEIERMACHERS
- LE MONDE DE L'ESPRIT

DILUCIDATIO IN GENERALI CAPITULO ORDINO D. HYERONYMI A.. / Caceres, Diego de – 1641 – 9 – 1.50f – sp Bibl Santa Ana [240]
O DILUCULO – Ouro Preto, Jun-Dec 1896; Jan-Feb, 26 Sep 1897 – 1,5,6 – bl Biblioteca [072]
Dilworth, John *see* PICTORIAL DESCRIPTION OF THE TABERNACLE IN THE WILDERNESS
Dilworth, Thomas *see* A NEW GUIDE TO THE ENGLISH TONGUE
Diman, Jeremiah Lewis *see* THE THEISTIC ARGUMENT
DIMANCHE-MATIN : HEBDO, INDEPENDANT / ed by Francoeur, Jacques – Montreal, Canada. 18 jan 1953-17 nov 1985 – 94r – 1 – Can$70.00r – cn Can Microfilming [072]
DIMANCHE-MATIN – Montreal, Canada. (Including 'Perspectives'). 20 Mar 1966-28 Dec 1969.-w. 23 reels – 1 – uk British Libr Newspaper [072]
DIMANCHE-QUEBEC : PUBLIEE DURANT LA GREVE DES EMPLOYES DU "SOLEIL" – Quebec, 12 mar-4 jun 1978 – 1r – 1 – Can$30.00 – cn Can Microfilming [072]
DIMANCHE-TURF – Paris. oct 1948-avr 1958 – 1 – fr A.C.R.P.P. [073]
DIMBOOLA SHIRE COUNCIL MINUTES – 1885-1995 SOD1-10 – 13r – 1,5 – at Corangamite [910]
DIMBOOLA SHIRE COUNCIL RATES – 1886-1947 SODR1-3 – 8r – 1 – at Corangamite [910]
DIMBOOLA SHIRE WHOLE COUNCIL MINUTES – 1990-1995 – 1 – at Corangamite [910]
DIME BASEBALL PLAYER – 1860-81 – 1r – 1 – us Ross [790]
THE DIME BASE-BALL PLAYER – New York. 1860-1862, 1864-1881 – 1 – us NY Public [790]
DIME NOVELS – 1 – us L of C Photodup [830]
DIME NOVELS – (3117 titles published by Beadle and Adams, New York, 1840s to early 1900s. Cataloging available. Units available separately, each with index: Unit 1 Dime Novels $1350; Unit 2 Pocket Novels $980; Unit 3 Starr's NY Library and Dilme Library $1350; Unit 4 Boys Octavo/Quarto, Ivers Boys $395; Unit 5 Pocket Library $560; Unit 6 Half Dime Library, Deadwood Dick $395.00; Unit 7 Frontier and Biographical $960) – 73r – 1 – $5990.00 – us UMI [830]
DIMENSIONS : JOURNAL OF PASTORAL CONCERN – v1-10. 1969-1978 (complete) – 2r – 1 – ATLA S0899 – us A.T.L.A. [073]
DIMENSIONS IN EDUCATION *see* ONTARIO EDUCATION DIMENSIONS

DIMENSIONS OF CRITICAL CARE NURSING: DCCN – v1-. 1982- – 1,5,6,9 – us UMI [073]
Dimes, Louis Thomas *see* ARTICLES ON MODERN ART
DIMINEATA – Bucharest, Romania. -d. 30 Jan-22 May 1920. Imperfect. 1 reel – 1 – uk British Libr Newspaper [949]
DAS DIMINUTIV IN DER DEUTSCHEN ORIGINALLITERATUR DES 12. UND 13. JAHRHUNDERTS / Hastenpflug, Fritz – Marburg, 1914 – 2mf – DM 62.00 – 3-8267-3107-7 – gw Hänsel [430]
DIMITRIJE V. LJOTIC PAMPHLET COLLECTION – 1953 – 1 – CSUXANQ9778-B – us Hoover Inst Photo [949]
Dimitrov, Georgi *see*
- LAS LECCIONES DE ALMERIA
- TWO YEARS OF HEROIC STRUGGLE OF THE SPANISH PEOPLE

DIMITROVGRADSKA PRAVDA – (Lacking: 1964-65) – Dimitrovgrad, Bulgaria. Dec 1954-1966 – 2r – 1 – us L of C Photodup [949]
DIMITROVSKO ZNAME – (Lacking: 1965-66) – Pernik, Bulgaria. 1964-1970 – 4r – 1 – us L of C Photodup [949]
DIMITROVSKO ZNAME – (Missing: 1964) – Dimitrovo, Bulgaria. 1955-66 – 5r – 1 – us L of C Photodup [949]
DIMMITT FIRST BAPTIST CHURCH. DIMMITT, TEXAS : CHURCH RECORDS – 1891-1963 – 1 – 55.17 – us Baptist [240]
Dimock, J F *see*
- GIRALDI CAMBRENSIS OPERA, VOLS 5-7 (RS21)
- MAGNA VITA S. HUGONIS, EPISCOPI LINCOLNIENSIS (RS37)

Dimock, Marshall Edward *see* CONGRESSIONAL INVESTIGATING COMMITTEES
Dimock, Nathaniel *see*
- THE DOCTRINE OF THE DEATH OF CHRIST
- THE DOCTRINE OF THE SACRAMENTS IN RELATION TO THE DOCTRINES OF GRACE

Dimon, Denise *see* LATIN AMERICAN BUSINESS REVIEW
Dimond, Susan B *see* DIARIES
Dimond, W W *see* DIARY
DIMONSTRATIONI HARMONICHE / Zarlino, G – Venetia. Francesco dei Franceschi Senese. 1571. BP-526 1 – 9 – ne IDC [780]
DIMOSTRATIONI HARMONICHE.. / Zarlino, G – 1571 – 2 – us Sibley [780]
Dimsdale, T *see* THE PRESENT METHOD OF INOCULATING FOR THE SMALL-POX
DIN (DEUTSCHES INSTITUT FUER NORMUNG) – German updated every 30 days. English updated every 60 days. Printed index – 6,9 – us Info Handling [380]
THE DINA I MAINU I KHYRAT, OR THE RELIGIOUS DECISIONS OF THE SPIRIT OF WISDOM / ed by Peshotan, D D – Bombay, 1895 – 2mf – NE-20156/1 – ne IDC [290]
DINAMANI – Madras, India. 17 Aug 1950-1959; Jul-Sept 1966 – 24r – 1 – us L of C Photodup [072]
DINAMIKA IZMENENIIA POLOZHENIIA DAGESTANSKOI ZHENSHCHINY I SEMIA / Gadzhieva, S – (Filmed with various others) – Moskva: In-t konkretnykh sotsialnykh issledovanii AN SSSR, 1972 – us Res Libr [947]
DINAMIKA IZMENENIIA POLOZHENIIA ZHENSHCHINY I SEMIA / Sovetskaia sotsiologicheskaia assotsiatsiia & Institut konkretnykh sotsialnykh issledovanii AN SSSR & Orgkomitet XII Mezhdunarodnogo seminara po issledovaniiu semi – (Filmed with: Dinamika izmeneniia polozheniia dagestanskoi zhenshchiny i semia/S Gadzheiva) – Moskva: the Institute, 1972 – us Res Libr [947]
DINAMIKA IZMENENIIA POLOZHENIIA ZHENSHCHINY I SEMIA / Sovetskaia sotsiologicheskaia assotsiatsiia & Institut konkretnykh sotsialnykh issledovanii AN SSSR & XII Mezhdunarodnyi seminar po issledovaniiu semi – (Filmed with: Dinamika izmeneniia polozheniia dagestanskoi zhenshchiny i semia/S Gadzhieva) – Moskva: the Institute, 1972 – us Res Libr [947]
DINAMIKA IZMENENIIA POLOZHENIIA ZHENSHCHINY I SEMIA / Sovetskaia sotsiologicheskaia assotsiatsiia & Institut konkrotnykh sotsialnykh issledovanii SSSR & Orgkomitet XII Mezhdunarodnogo seminara po issledovaniiu semi – (Filmed with: Dinamika izmeneniia polozheniia dagestanskoi zhenshchiny i semia/S Gadzhieva) – Moskva: the Institute, 1972 – us Res Libr [947]
DINAMIKA PROIZVODITELNOSTI TRUDA I EE VAZHNE ISHIKH FAKTOROV V 1924-25 I 1925-26 G.G. = THE MOVEMENT OF THE PROUCTIVENESS OF LABOUR AND OF ITS CHIEF FACTORS DURING 1924-25 AND 1925-26 (OCTOBER 1924 TO OCTOBER 1926) / Central Statistical Administration of the USSR, Department of Industrial Statistics – Moskva: Izd. T SSU, 1927 – 1 – CSUX91-B1064 – us Hoover Inst Photo [331]
DINAMIS; ORGANO OFICIAL DEL SINDICATO DE LUZ Y FUERZA (PERIODICAL) EVA PERON : MARTIR DEL TRABAJO – [Buenos Aires]: Editado en colaboracion con la federacion Argentina de Trabajadores de Luz y Fuerza, 1952 – 1 – CSUXADJ1063-B – us Hoover Inst Photo [331]
Dinas Humas Pusat *see* BULLETIN PERTAMINA
DINASARI – Madras, India. 1947-51 – 9r – 1 – us L of C Photodup [072]
Y DINASYDD CYMREIG – London, England. 3 Jan-28 Feb 1885 – 7ft – 1 – uk British Libr Newspaper [072]
Dincklage-Campe, Friedrich, Freiherr von *see* ANKER GESCHLIPPT
Dindas, J H *see* HISTORY OF NEMAHA COUNTY
Dindorfii, GuiL *see*
- CORPUS SCRIPTORUM HISTORIAE BYZANTINAE (CSHB 12, 13)
- CORPUS SCRIPTORUM HISTORIAE BYZANTINAE (CSHB 18-20

Dindorfius, L *see*
- CHRONICON PASCHALE AD EXEMPLAR VATICANUM (CSHB 16, 17)
- CHRONOGRAPHIA (CSHB 15)

D'Indy, V *see* THEME D'HARMONIE, 100
DINE BAA-HANI – 1969-72. (American Indian Periodicals in the Princeton University Library). 15 fiches – 9 – $65.00 – us UPA [305]
Dinekov, P *see* BALGARSKA LIRIKA
DINER EN MUSIQUE : FANTAISIE GASTRONOMICO-MUSICALE EN DEUX ACTES...3 FEVRIER 1930 / Morin, Victor – Montreal, 1930. SEM105P787 – 1mf – 9 – Can$2.25 – cn Bibl Nat [790]
DINER EN MUSIQUE: FANTAISIE GASTRONOMICO-MUSICALE EN DEUX ACTES.. / Morin, Victor – Montreal, 1931. SEM105P786 – 1mf – 9 – Can$2.25 – cn Bibl Nat [790]
DINER EN MUSIQUE: FANTAISIE GASTRONOMICO-MUSICALE EN DEUX ACTES:... 28 NOVEMBRE 1935 / Morin, Victor – Montreal, 1935. SEM105P790 – 1mf – 9 – Can$2.25 – cn Bibl Nat [790]
DINER OFFERT A L'HONORABLE ADELARD TURGEON...A L'OCCASION DE SON DEPART POUR QUEBEC AU CLUB DE GARNISON, JEUDI LE 26 SEPTEMBRE 1901 – Levis: s.n., 1901. SEM105P462 – 1mf – 9 – Can$2.25 – cn Bibl Nat [920]
DINER – OPERETTE EN DEUX ACTES : FANTAISIE GASTRONOMICO-MUSICALE OFFERTE PAR LA SOCIETE SAINT JEAN BAPTISTE DE MONTREAL...3E CENTENAIRE DE MONTREAL / Morin, Victor – 7e ed. Montreal, 1942. SEM105P789 – 1mf – 9 – Can$2.25 – cn Bibl Nat [790]
DINER – OPERETTE EN DEUX ACTES : FANTAISIE GASTRONOMICO-MUSICALE OFFERTE PAR LA SOCIETE SAINT JEAN BAPTISTE DE MONTREAL...LE TROISIEME CONGRES DE LA LANGUE FRANCAISE AU CANADA / Morin, Victor – Montreal, 1952. SEM105P788 – 1mf – 9 – Can$2.25 – cn Bibl Nat [790]
DINER – OPERETTE EN DEUX ACTES : A GASTRONOMICO-MUSICAL FANTASY OFFERED TO THE FELLOWS...ROYAL SOCIETY OF CANADA...1939 / Morin, Victor – Montreal, 1939. SEM105P791 – 1mf – 9 – Can$2.25 – cn Bibl Nat [790]
EL DINERO DE SAN PEDRO. CARTA PASTORAL QUE...ADOLFO PEREZ MUNOZ DIRIGE AL CLERO Y FIELES DE SU DIOCESIS / Perez Munoz, Adolfo – Badajoz: Tip. Uceda Hnos, 1915 – 1 – sp Bibl Santa Ana [240]
Dingel, F *see* ERRICHTUNG UND AUFHEBUNG LETZTWILLIGER VERFUEGUNGEN...
Dingelstedt, Franz, Freiherr von *see*
- AUS DER BRIEFMAPPE EINES BURGTHEATERDIREKTORS
- DIE NEUEN ARGONAUTEN

Dingelstedt, Franz von *see* SAEMMTLICHE WERKE
DIE DINGELSTOCKS : DER WEG EINER SIPPE: ROMAN / Wurtz, Johann – Belgrad: Verlags- und Vertriebs- A G "Suedost", 1943 – 1r – 1 – us U.W. Library [830]
Dinger, Mary K *see* DEVELOPMENT AND VALIDATION OF THE WELLNESS KNOWLEDGE, ATTITUDE, AND BEHAVIOR INSTRUMENT
Dingle, Reginald James *see*
- DEMOCRACY IN SPAIN
- RUSSIA'S WORK IN SPAIN
- SECOND THOUGHTS ON DEMOCRACY IN SPAIN

Dingler, Johann Gottfried *see*
- POLYTECHNISCHES JOURNAL
- POLYTECHNISCHES JOURNAL 1. 1820-211. 1874. DINGLERS POLYTECHNISCHES JOURNAL 212.1874-346. 1931

DINGOLFINGER ANZEIGER – Dingolfing, Germany. 1 Jun 1983- – ca 9r per yr – 1 – gw Mikrofilm [072]
DINGWALL AND SURROUNDS 1851 CENSUS INDEX : ARGYLL AND WEST SCOTLAND CENSUS INDEX, PART 10 / Macinnes, John & Gibson, Peter – 1996 – 2mf – 9 – A$19.95 – 0-9586638-0-7 – at Seanachas [920]
Dini, Nh *see* DUA DUNIA
THE DIN-I-ILAHI: OR, THE RELIGION OF AKBAR / Roychoudhury, Makhanlal, Sastri – 2nd ed. Calcutta: Das Gupta, 1952. xxxiii,222p. ill – 1 – us U.W. Library [260]
DINIM VE-SEDER – Venice. 1601-02. BJ-43-15 1 – 9 – ne IDC [956]
DINI-NA-MILA – v1-7. 1965-75 (incomplete) – 1r – 1 – ATLA S0725A – us A.T.L.A. [073]
DINING AT THE WHITE HOUSE : TWO CENTURIES OF PRESIDENTIAL TABLEWARE: CHECK LIST / Spillman, Jane Shadel – Corning, NY: The Corning Museum of Glass, 1989 – 1mf – 9 – $2.50 plus $0.50 postage and handling plus N.Y. State tax as applicable – us Corning Mus [740]
Diniz, A *see* O NAVIO PESSOA DE DIREITO INTERNACIONAL PUBLICO
DINKARD / ed by Behramjee, P & Sunjana, P D B – (The originla Pehlwi text; the same transliterated in Zend characters; translations of the text in the Gujarati and English languages; a commentary and a glossary of select terms; Available: 1874-1883. V. 1-4) – Bombay, 1874-1928. 19v – 15mf – NE-20149/1 – ne IDC [490]
DINNA FORGET : A SOUVENIR OF PRIMITIVE METHODIST SOUL-WINNING PERSONALITIES / Pearce, J – Leomister, 1932 – 2mf – 9 – ne IDC [240]
THE DINNER HORN – Paris. Tex. 1925-1926; 1929-1933; 1934-1966 – 1 – us UMI [071]
Dino, Charles Maurice Camille de Talleyrand-Perigord *see* ETUDE SUR LA REPUBLIQUE DES ETAS-UNIS D'AMERIQUE
Dinschel, Kimberly M *see* THE INFLUENCE OF AGILITY ON THE MILE RUN AND PACER TESTS OF AEROBIC ENDURANCE IN FOURTH- AND FIFTH-GRADE SCHOOL CHILDREN
Dinshaw, Carolyn *see* GLQ
Dinsmore, Charles Allen *see*
- AIDS TO THE STUDY OF DANTE
- THE TEACHINGS OF DANTE

THE DINUBA ADVOCATE – Dinuba, CA. 1907-1915 – 5r – 1 – $250.00 – B06020 – us Library Micro [071]
DINUBA SENTINEL – Dinuba, CA. 1909-17; 1919-36; 1938-39; Jan-Dec 1948; 1952-79; 1981- – 85+ r – 1 BC02170 – $4,250.00 ($50.00y) – us Library Micro [071]
DINUBA TRIBUNE : ALTA DISTRICT SPECIAL EDITION – Dinuba, CA. 15 Mar 1906 – 1r – 1 – $50.00 – B02171 – us Library Micro [071]
Dinur, B *see*
- ME-ARKHIYYONO SHEL HE-HAKHAM BASHI
- SEFER DINABURG
- TOLEDOT HA-YISHUV U-MEKOMAN BA-HISTORIYYAH HA-YISRE'ELIT HA-KELALIT

Diobounioits, C *see* DER SCHOLIEN-KOMMENTAR DAS ORIGENES ZUR APOKALYPSE JOHANNIS (T.U.U. 3-38/3)
Diobouniotis, C *see* HIPPOLYTS DANIELCOMMENTAR (T.U.U. 3-38/1B)
THE DIOCESAN AND PARISH MAGAZINE, VICTORIA, B.C. – Victoria [BC: s.n., 1887?-189- or 19-] – 9 – cn C.I.H.M. [240]
DIOCESAN ARCHIVES / Rarotonga and Niue. Catholic Church Diocese – Rarotonga, Cook Islands, 1891-1993 – 53r – 1 – PMB1064 – at Pacific Mss [240]
Diocesan Association for Western China *see* THE FOUR STREAMS
THE DIOCESAN MAGAZINE *see* THE DEANERY MAGAZINE
LE DIOCESE DE MONTREAL A LA FIN DU DIX-NEUVIEME SIECLE / Dauth, Gaspard – Montreal: Eusebe Senecal et Cie, 1900. SEM16P366 – 1r – 6 – Can$15.00 – cn Bibl Nat [240]
Diocese de Nantes *see* DECRETS ET STATUTS SYNODAUX DU DIOCESE DE NANTES...
LE DIOCESE DE NANTES PENDANT LA REVOLUTION / Lallie, Alfred – 2v. Nantes: Cier, 1893 – 1 – F500.02 – fr Armell [240]
Diocesis *see*
- CALENDARIO Y PLAN DE ESTUDIOS DEL CURSO ACADEMICO 1975-76. SEMINARIO MAYOR DIOCESANO
- MEMORIA DEL EJRCICIO MISIONAL DE 1968
- MEMORIA-INFORME 1970

LA DIOCESIS DE BADAJOZ. ESTADISTICA DE 1970 / Badajoz. Diocesis – Badajoz: Imp. Espanola, 1970 – 1 – sp Bibl Santa Ana [240]
DIODOR VAN TARSUS : VIER PSEUDOJUSTINISCHE SCHRIFTEN ALS EIGENTUM DIODORS (T.U.U. 2-21/4) / Harnack, Adolf von – Leipzig, 1901 – 4mf – 9 – ne Slangenburg [240]
DIE DIOECESANSYNODE / Phillips, George – Freiburg im Breisgau: Herder, 1849 – 1mf – us A.T.L.A. [240]
DIOECESES BRIXINENSIS, FRISINGENSIS, RATISBONENSIS (MGH ANTIQUITATES 2: 3.BD) – 1905 – Dfl49.00 – ne Slangenburg [240]
DIOECESIS AUGUSTENSIS, CONSTANTIENSIS, CURIENSIS (MGH ANTIQUITATES 2: 1.BD) – 1888 – Dfl74.00 – ne Slangenburg [240]
DIOECESIS PATAVIENSIS (MGH ANTIQUITATES 2: 4.BD) : PARS 1. 1: DIOECESIS PATAVIENSIS REGIO BAVARICA. 2: DIOECESIS PATAVIENSIS REGIO AUSTRIACA NUNC LENTENSIS – 1920 – Dfl74.00 – ne Slangenburg [240]
DIOECESIS PATAVIENSIS (MGH ANTIQUITATES 2: 5.BD) : PARS 2: AUSTRIA INFERIOR 1913 – Dfl70.00 – ne Slangenburg [240]
DIOECESIS SALISBURGENSIS (MGH ANTIQUITATES 2: 2.BD) – 1904 – Dfl74.00 – ne Slangenburg [240]
DIOGENE SANS-CULOTTE – Paris: E Bautruche, jun 18/22-22/25 1848 – us Res Libr [072]
DIOGENES : ILLUSTRE – Montreal, Canada. 13 nov 1868-21 jan 1870 – 1r – 1 – Can$45.00 – cn Can Microfilming [072]
DIOGENES – Madison, Wisc. v. 1 no. 1-2. Oct Nov 1940-Dec 1940 Jan 1941 – 1 – us NY Public [073]
DIOGENES – Montreal. v. 1-3. 1868-70 – 1 – 60.00 – cn McLaren [800]
Diogenes, Laertius *see* THE LIVES AND OPINIONS OF EMINENT PHILOSOPHERS
Dion, J O *see*
- NOTES ARCHEOLOGIQUES: LE FORT DE CHAMBLY, 1709 A 1760
- ST. LIN ET SA JOURNEE DU 9 OCTOBRE 1872

Dionigi, M *see* PRIMI TUONI OVERO INTRODUZIONE DEL CANTO FERMO CON L'AGGIUNTA D'ALTRI TUONI DEL SIGNOR DOTTOR MARCO DIONIGI...
DIONIS I PRADIONISIISTVO / Ivanov, V – Baku. 1923. BR-736 2 – 8 – ne IDC [460]
DIONISO – Siracusa. v1-22. 1929-59 – 5,9 – Dfl1,540.00; Dfl70.00v – ne Swets [100]
Dionne, Narcisse Eutrope *see*
- L'ABBE GABRIEL RICHARD, CURE DE DETROIT
- LES CERCLES AGRICOLES DANS LA PROVINCE DE QUEBEC
- LES ECCLESIASTIQUES ET LES ROYALISTES FRANCAIS REFUGIES AU CANADA A L'EPOQUE DE LA REVOLUTION 1791-1802
- FETE NATIONALE DES CANADIENS-FRANCAIS CELEBREE A WINDSOR, ONTARIO LE 25 JUIN 1883
- GALERIE HISTORIQUE
- INVENTAIRE CHRONOLOGIQUE
- INVENTAIRE CHRONOLOGIQUE DES LIVRES, BROCHURES, JOURNEAUX ET REVUES PUBLIES EN DIVERSES LANGUES DANS ET HORS LA PROVINCE DE QUEBEC
- JACQUES CARTIER
- LE PARLER POPULAIRE DES CANADIENS FRANCAIS OU LEXIQUE DES CANADIANISMES, ACADIANISMES, ANGLICISMES, AMERICANISMES, MOTS ANGLAIS LES PLUS EN USAGE AU SEIN DES FAMILLES CANADIENNES ET ACADIENNES FRANCAISES

- SAINTE ANNE DE LA POCATIERE, 1672-1900
- SERVITEURS ET SERVANTES DE DIEU EN CANADA; QUARANTE BIOGRAPHIES
- THE SIEGE OF QUEBEC AND THE BATTLE OF THE PLAINS OF ABRAHAM
- TRAVAUX HISTORIQUES PUBLIES DEPUIS TRENTE ANS PAR LE DR. N.E. DIONNE..

DIONYS-BACSI : DREI NOVELLEN / Schaukal, Richard von – Braunschweig: G Westermann, 1922 – 1r – 1 – us U.W. Library [830]

Dionysius, Cart. *see* OPERA OMNIA

Dionysius of Halicarnassus *see* HIERARCHIES

DIONYSIUS THE PS.-AREOPAGITE: THE ECCLESIASTICAL HIERARCHY / Campbell, T L – Washington, D.C., 1955 Nr. 83 – 2mf – 8 – ne Slangenburg [240]

DIONYSOS AND IMMORTALITY; THE GREEK FAITH IN IMMORTALITY AS AFFECTED BY THE RISE OF INDIVIDUALISM / Wheeler, Benjamin Ide – Boston, New York: Houghton, Mifflin, 1899. (Ingersoll Lectures on Immortality) – 1 – us U.W. Library [250]

Diop, Birago *see* LES CONTES D'AMADOU-KOUMBA

DIOS ESTA AQUI / Jesus, Gabriel de – Madrid, 1933 – 1 – sp Bibl Santa Ana [240]

DIOS IMMORTAL.. / Stanihursto, Guillermo – 1826. Francisco P. Berguizas, trans – 9 – 1.50f – sp Bibl Santa Ana [240]

DIOS INMORTAL...PASION DE CRISTO / Stanihursto, Guillermo – 1826 – 9 – 1.50f – sp Bibl Santa Ana [240]

DIOS SOBRE TODO / Spinola de Gironza, Araceli – Ediciones Ritmo, S, L. Madrid, 1940 – 1 – sp Bibl Santa Ana [946]

Dios Trias, D J de *see*
- CONSTITUCION POLITICA...DEL PRINCIPADO DE ANDORRA
- PROGRAMA DE LAS LECCIONES DE DERECHO INTERNACIONAL PUBLICO

DIOS Y ESPANA: O SEA ENSAYO DE LO QUE DEBE A LA R. CATOLICA / Amado, Manuel – v. 1-2. 1831 – 9 – 1.50f – sp Bibl Santa Ana [240]

Diosay, Marian Po *see* PHILIPPINE ETHNOGRAPHIC SERIES

DIOSCORO PATRIARCHA ALEXANDRINO / Caceres, Diego de – S.l., s.i., s.a. Hacia 1641 – 1 – sp Bibl Santa Ana [240]

DIOSPOLIS PARVA (MEES VOL 20) : THE CEMETRIES OF ABADIYEH AND HU / Flinders Petrie, W M – London, 1901 – 7mf – 8 – Dfl28.00 – ne Slangenburg [930]

DIOTREPHES AND STENTOR : A NEW FARCE, ACTED NEAR MOORFIELDS – London, 1765 – 1mf – 9 – MP-435/1 – ne IDC [820]

Dioum, Abdoulaye *see* LES EXPLOITS DE MASIRE ISSE DIEYE

DIPALU ARUS REVOLUSI, KISSAH NJATA / Elias, H B – SE-4756 1. 1958? – 9 – ne IDC [950]

DIPANAGARA PANGERANNJA : BABAD DIPONAGORO. SERAT BABAD DIPA NAGARA KARANGANI PUN SWARGIPIJAMBAH...INGKANG ANGEDALAKEN ADMINISTRATIE DJAWI KANDO – (Javanese text) – Soerakarta, 1909 – 3mf – 9 – ne IDC [950]

DIPANDA – Brazzaville, nov 1963-oct 10 1967; special issue 1967 – 1 – us Res Libr [072]

[DIPLOMACY AND NEUTRALITY (AND ITS VIOLATION) IN BELGIUM DURING WORLD WAR 1 PAMPHLET COLLECTION] – 1914-1918 – 2r – 1 – CSUXANL3024-B – us Hoover Inst Photo [320]

[DIPLOMACY AND NEUTRALITY DURING WORLD WAR 1 PAMPHLET COLLECTION] – 1915-1919 – 2r – 1 – CSUXANL2830-B – us Hoover Inst Photo [320]

[DIPLOMACY AND NEUTRALITY IN NETHERLANDS DURING WORLD WAR 1 PAMPHLET COLLECTION] – 1914-1919 – 1 – CSUXANL3035-B – us Hoover Inst Photo [320]

[DIPLOMACY AND NEUTRALITY IN SPAIN DURING WORLD WAR 1 PAMPHLET COLLECTION] – 1915-1917 – 1 – CSUXANL3038-B – us Hoover Inst Photo [320]

[DIPLOMACY AND NEUTRALITY IN SWITZERLAND DURING WORLD WAR 1 PAMPHLET COLLECTION] – 1914-1957 – 1 – CSUXANL3041-B – us Hoover Inst Photo [320]

THE DIPLOMACY OF THE BALKAN WARS 1912-1913 / Helmreich, E C – BR-3869 2 – 8 – ne IDC [949]

UM DIPLOMATA NA CORTE DE INGLATERRA / Mendonca, Renato – Sao Paulo, 1942 – 9mf – 8 – ne Slangenburg [327]

DIPLOMATA REGUM FRANCORUM E STIRPE MEROVINGICA (MGH DIPLOMATA 1: 1.BD) – 1872 – Dfl42.00 – ne Slangenburg [240]

DIPLOMATES ET PUBLICISTES / Verge, Ch. – (Collected biographical sketches of Maurice d'Hauterue, de Gentz, Pinheiro-Ferreira, Ancillon D'Entraigues, Sieyes, Chateaubriand, and Mignet) – Paris, 1856 – 3mf – 9 – ILM-300/1 – ne IDC [920]

DIPLOMATIC AND CONSULAR INSTRUCTIONS... 1791-1801 / U.S. Department of State – 5r – 1 – M28 – us Nat'l Archives [976]

DIPLOMATIC AND CONSULAR LIST / Indonesia. Kementerian Luar Negeri – SE-616 1. 1957-1971. Lacking: 1959, 1962, 1965, 1967 – 9 – ne IDC [950]

DIPLOMATIC CORRESPONDENCE OF BRITISH MINISTERS TO THE RUSSIAN COURT AT ST PETERSBURG 1704-1776 – (With printed index) – 15v. 1867-1916 – 100mf – 9 – £510.00 – uk Chadwyck [941]

DIPLOMATIC FLY-SHEETS – [London], 1886-90 – 7mf – 1 – ILM-3842/1 – ne IDC [327]

[DIPLOMATIC HISTORY DURING WORLD WAR 2 PAMPHLET COLLECTION] – 1941-1944 – 1 – CSUXANM8154-B – us Hoover Inst Photo [320]

[DIPLOMATIC HISTORY IN FRANCE DURING WORLD WAR 2 PAMPHLET COLLECTION] – 19?? – 1 – CSUXANM8161-B – us Hoover Inst Photo [320]

[DIPLOMATIC HISTORY IN GREAT BRITAIN DURING WORLD WAR 2 PAMPHLET COLLECTION] – 1941 – 1 – CSUXANM8157-B – us Hoover Inst Photo [320]

A DIPLOMATIC HISTORY OF BULGARIA, 1870-1886 / Hyde, A M – Urbana. 1928. Br-3870 2 – 8 – ne IDC [949]

[DIPLOMATIC HISTORY OF EASTERN EUROPE PAMPHLET COLLECTION] – 1939-1948 – 1 – CSUXANL3013-B – us Hoover Inst Photo [320]

[DIPLOMATIC HISTORY OF GREECE DURING WORLD WAR 1 PAMPHLET COLLECTION] – 1906-1917? – 1 – CSUXANL2942-B – us Hoover Inst Photo [320]

DIPLOMATIC HISTORY OF THE AMERICAN REVOLUTION / U.S. Department of State; ed by Wharton, Francis A – (Suppl to Wharton's Digest of the International Law of the U.S.) – 9 – LLMC 82-979 – us L.L.M.C. [976]

A DIPLOMATIC HISTORY OF THE CONGO FREE STATE / Muller, George F – Washington, DC, 1948 – us Res Libr [960]

DIPLOMATIC HISTORY OF THE PANAMA CANAL : CORRESPONDENCE RELATING TO THE NEGOTIATION AND APPLICATION OF CERTAIN TREATIES ON THE SUBJECT OF THE CONSTRUCTION OF AN INTEROCEANIC CANAL AND ACCOMPANYING PAPERS – Senate doc no 474. 63rd Congress 2nd sess. Washington: GPO, 1914 – 7mf – 9 – $10.50 – LLMC 82-100D Title 19 – us L.L.M.C. [324]

DIPLOMATIC INSTRUCTIONS REGARDING AUSTRIA, 1837-1906 – M77 – 5r – $170.00 – us Scholarly Res [327]

DIPLOMATIC INSTRUCTIONS REGARDING THE GERMAN STATES AND GERMANY, 1835-1906 – M77 – 10r – $340.00 – us Scholarly Res [320]

DIPLOMATIC INSTRUCTIONS...1801-1906 / U.S. Department of State – Printed guide – 175r – 1 – M77 – us Nat'l Archives [975]

DIPLOMATIC LIST / U.S. Department of State – 1930-75 – 1,5,6 – us Princeton Micro [977]

DIPLOMATIC PAPERS OF JOHN MOORS CABOT, 1929-78 – (Pt 1, Latin America: 5r $480.00 ISBN 0-89093-477-0; Pt 2, Europe: 6r $580.00 ISBN 0-89093-478-9; Pt 3, General Political and Diplomatic Materials: 6r $580.00 ISBN 0-89093-479-7; Pt 4, Diaries: 5r $480.00 ISBN 0-89093-480-0. All with printed guides) – 1 – us UPA [920]

DIPLOMATIC PETREL / Hohler, Thomas Beaumont – 1st ed. London: J Murray, [1942] – 1 – us Res Libr [960]

[DIPLOMATIC RELATIONS BETWEEN THE CATHOLIC CHURCH AND YUGOSLAVIA PAMPHLET COLLECTION] – 1937 – 1 – CSUXANL2811-B – us Hoover Inst Photo [320]

THE DIPLOMATIC REMINISCENCES OF LORD AUGUSTUS LOFTUS...1837-62 / Loftus, Augustus William Frederick Spencer, Lord – London: Cassell & Co., Ltd., 1892. 2v – 1 – us U.W. Library [941]

DIPLOMATIC REVIEW – 1-25 2+1 with supplement nos. 1-61 (all publ). 1855-1881 – 6r – 1 – $280.00 – us UPA [940]

DIPLOMATICHESKIE SNOSHENIIA ROSSII S ZAPADNOIU EVROPOIU VO VTOROI POLOVINE XVII-GO VEKA / Kapustin, MN – Moscow, 1852. 152p. Documents Russia's attitudes and practices toward the law of nations in the late 17th cent. BR-9478/1 – 9 – ne IDC [947]

DIPLOMATICHESKII SLOVAR' – M., 1948-1950. 2 vols – 17mf – 9 – R-8551/1 – ne IDC [340]

LA DIPLOMATIE / Cambon, J M – Paris, 1926 – 2mf – 1 – ILM-356/1 – ne IDC [327]

LA DIPLOMATIE : REVUE BI-MENSUELLE INTERNATIONALE – Paris. 2v. 1897-98 – 18mf – 1 – ILM-3923/1 – ne IDC [327]

LA DIPLOMATIE FRANCAISE... / Auerbach, Berthold – Paris, 1888 – 6mf – 9 – ILM-322/1 – ne IDC [340]

DIPLOMATISCHE CORRESPONDENZEN AUS DER REVOLUTIONSZEIT 1791-1797 / ed by Herrmann, E – Gotha, 1867 – 8mf – 9 – ne IDC [943]

DIPLOMATUM BELGICORUM NOVA COLLECTIO / Miraeus, A; ed by Foppens, J F – Bruxellis, 1734-1748 – Dfl235.00 – ne Slangenburg [240]

DIPLOME DE CABALEUR POUR LES ELECTIONS, DELIVRE PAR LE COMITE ANTI-NATIONAL – Paris, 1849 – us Res Libr [320]

LES DIPLOMES *see* L'ACTION UNIVERSITAIRE

Dipokusumo, S *see*
- DEVELOPMENT IN INDONESIA
- KEARAH KEMAKMOERAN DAN KEADILAN SOSIAL DI LAPANGAN EKONOMI

DIPTERA SVECIAE / Fallen, C F – 2466 2. 2 v. 1814-1827 – 8 – ne IDC [590]

DIPTERENFAUNA VON BOSNIEN, HERCEGOVINA UND DALMATIEN / ed by Strobl, P G – Wien, 1900. 120p. Wissensch. Mitthl. Bosnien und Hercegovina. v7 – 8 – ne IDC [590]

DIPTERES EXOTIQUES NOUVEAUX OU PEU CONNUS / Macquart, P J M – Paris, 1838-85. 2v.,suppl. 1-5.Z-1449/2 – 8 – ne IDC [590]

DIPTERES NOUVEAUX OU PEU CONNUS / Bigot, J M F – v. 1-37. 2464 2. 1874-1892 – 8 – ne IDC [610]

Diputacion Provincial *see*
- EXPOSICION DE REPRODUCCIONES EN COLOR DE LA UNESCO 90 ANOS DE PINTURA UNIVERSAL. CATALOGO
- MEMORIA, ANO DE 1978
- OFICINA PROVINCIAL DE INVERSIONES INFORME ANUAL. DICIEMBRE DE 1978
- ORDENANZA FISCAL, NUM. 3 PARA LA EXACCION DE DERECHOS Y TASAS POR PRESTACIONES DE SERVICIOS...SANITARIOS...1968
- PRESUPUESTO ORDINARIO DE GASTOS E INGRESOS. EJERCICIO 1966
- PRESUPUESTO ORDINARIO DE GASTOS E INGRESOS. EJERCICIO DE 1963
- PRESUPUESTO ORDINARIO DE GASTOS E INGRESOS. EJERCICIO DE 1967
- PRESUPUESTO ORDINARIO DE GASTOS E INGRESOS. EJERCICIO DE 1968
- PRESUPUESTO ORDINARIO DE INGRESOS Y GASTOS. EJERCICIO DE 1960
- PRESUPUESTO ORDINARIO DE INGRESOS Y GASTOS. EJERCICIO DE 1969
- PRESUPUESTO ORDINARIO DE INGRESOS Y GASTOS. EJERCICIO DE 1971
- PRESUPUESTO ORDINARIO DE INGRESOS Y GASTOS PARA EL EJERCICIO DE 1973...
- REGLAMENTO DE LA CAJA DE CREDITO PROVINCIAL
- REGLAMENTO DE LOS SERVICIOS BENEFICO-SANITARIOS
- REGLAMENTO DEL CENTRO DE ESTUDIOS EXTREMENOS
- REGLAMENTO PARA LA CONCESION DE BECAS DE ESTUDIOS QUE ESTABLECE ESTA CORPORACION
- SSMM LOS REYES DE ESPANA EN LA DIPUTACION DE CACERES

DIPUTADOS PINTADOS POR SUS HECHOS... – Madrid, 1870 – 29mf – 9 – sp Cultura [946]

DIPUTATIONES IN UNIVERSAM ARISTOTELIS LOGICAM / Peinado, I – Alcala de Henares, 1721 – 1mf – 9 – sp Cultura [160]

DIQIU HUAXUE – Geochemica. In Chinese but English abstracts to the main articles. F p89 – 9 – 4.00f – cc Microforms [073]

DIQIU WULI XUEBAO – Acta Geophysica Sinica. In Chinese but English abstracts to the main articles. F p39 – 9 – $4.50f – cc Microforms [073]

Diradja, D M *see* KISAH NABI ADAM

DIRASAT ASKARIYAH – [Lebanon?: Harakat al-Tahrir al-Watani al-Filastini, "Fath", 1970. [n1-2. jun-jul 1970] – 1r – us Res Libr [072]

Dircks, H *see* A BIOGRAPHICAL MEMOIR OF SAMUEL HARTLIB

DIRECCION GENERAL DE ARCHIVOS Y BIBLIOTECAS : EXPOSICION... / Barrado Manzano, Arcangel – Madrid: Archivo Ibero-Americano, 1959 – 1 – sp Bibl Santa Ana [020]

Direccion General de Estadistica *see*
- NOMENCLATOR DE LAS CIUDADES, VILLAS, LUGARES, ALDEAS Y DEMAS ENTIDADES DE POBLACION DE ESPANA...CON REFERENCIA AL 31-12-1940. PROVINCIA DE BADAJOZ
- NOMENCLATURA DE LAS CIUDADES, VILLAS, LUGARES, ALDEAS Y DEMAS ENTIDADES DE POBLACION DE ESPANA...CON REFERENCIA AL 31-12-1940. PROVINCIA DE CACERES

Direccion General de Estadistica, Ministerio de Trabajo *see* CENSO DE LAS POBLACIONES DE ESPANA SEGUN LA INSCRIPCION DE 31 DE DICIEMBRE DE 1940

Direccion General de Ganaderia. Junta Provincial de Fomento Pecuario de Badajoz *see* CARTILLA DIVULGADORA. SOBRE EXPLOTACION OVINA EN SU FACETA DE LANA

Direccion General de Turismo *see* BREVE RESENA DE BADAJOZ

DIRECT AND FUNDAMENTAL PROOFS OF THE CHRISTIAN RELIGION / Knox, George William – New York: Scribner, 1903. 1 fiche – 9 – us A.T.L.A. [240]

DIRECT CURRENT – June 1952-58 – 1 – uk Microform Academic [073]

DIRECT FROM CUBA – Havana, CU. 1976-1978 – 3r – $150.00 – R04199 – us Library Micro [072]

DIRECT TRADE BETWEEN THE DOMINION OF CANADA AND THE EMPIRE OF BRAZIL, ETC / Bentley, W Darley – 1880. 02307. (Pre-1900 Canadiana) – 9 – cn C.I.H.M. [971]

DIRECTION – Los Angeles, CA.Winter 1973/74-Summer 1985. Many issues missing. In English – 1 – us A.J.P.C. [071]

DIRECTION DE CONSCIENCE: LETTRE A UNE SUPERIEUR RELIGIEUSE AU SUJECT D'UN RECENT DECRET PONTIFICAL / Franco, Secondo – Traduit de l'italien par A. E. Gauthier. 3e ed. Montreal: Cadieux & Derome, 1893. 04330. (Pre-1900 Canadiana) – 9 – cn C.I.H.M. [971]

DIRECTION DE L'ENSEIGNEMENT PRIMAIRE. RAPPORT SUR L'ORGANISATION ET LA SITUATION DE L'ENSEIGNEMENT PRIMAIRE PUBLIC EN FRANCE / France. Ministere de l'Instruction Publique et des Beaux-Arts – Paris. 1900 – 1 – fr A.C.R.P.P. [324]

DIRECTION DES ETUDES DE DEVELOPPEMENT. POPULATION RURALE ET URBAINE PAR DEPARTEMENT ET PAR SOUSPREFECTURE / Baillon, D – (Africa series). 1970 – 9 – fr Hachette [310]

DIRECTION DES ETUDES DU DEVELOPPEMENT / Office de la Recherche Scientifique et Technique Outre Mer (ORSTROM) – (v1 – Esquisse Regionalisee Des Objectifs De Production. v2 – Resultats Par Region. v3.Superficie necessaire a la Realisation des Objectifs agricoles) – (Africa Series) – 9 – fr Hachette [025]

LA DIRECTION GENERALE...19 NOVEMBRE 1802 / Musee Central des Arts. Paris – 1952. 1 fiche – 9 – fr Réunion [700]

DIRECTIONS – A magazine for the survivalist. Sample issue, v9, no.8, Mar 1986. 4p – 9 – 1.00f – at Libertarian Micro [335]

DIRECTIONS AND FORMS FOR THE EXECUTION AND ACKNOWLEDGEMENT OF DEEDS TO BE USED OR RECORDED IN OTHER STATES / Butts, Isaac Ridler – Boston, Butts, 1857. 108 p. LL-275 – 1 – us L of C Photodup [340]

DIRECTIONS DE NAVIGATION POUR L'ILE DE TERRENEUVE ET LA COTE DU LABRADOR ET POUR LE GOLFE ET LE FLEUVE ST LAURENT / Bayfield, Henry Wolsey – Quebec: Imp. Elzear Vincent, 1864. SEM105P309 – 3mf – 9 – Can$6.75 – cn Bibl Nat [910]

DIRECTIONS DIVERSES DONNEES PAR LA REV. MERE CARON, SUP. GEN. DES SOEURS DE LA PROVIDENCE POUR AIDER SES SOEURS A FORMER DE BONNES CUISINIERES / Caron, Mere – Montreal, 1878. 02193. (Pre-1900 Canadiana) – 9 – cn C.I.H.M. [640]

DIRECTIONS GIVEN TO THE CLERGY OF THE DIOCESE OF LONDON IN THE YEAR 1724 BY THE RIGHT REVEREND FATHER IN GOD, EDMUND LORD BISHOP OF LONDON;... / Gibson, E – London, 1744 – 2mf – 9 – MP-317/1 – ne IDC [240]

DIRECTIONS OF CHANGE IN SOUTH AFRICAN POLITICS / ed by Randall, Peter – Johannesburg, Study Project on Christianity in Apartheid Society, 1971 – us Res Libr [320]

DIRECTIVES FOR THE FIVE YEAR PLAN FOR ECONOMIC DEVELOPMENT OF THE USSR FOR 1966-1970 / Kosygin, A – D 1227 1. Apr. 5, 1966 – 9 – ne IDC [338]

DIRECTIVES OF THE FIVE YEAR ECONOMIC DEVELOPMENT PLAN OF THE USSR FOR 1971-1975 / Kosygin, A – D 1511 1. 1971 – 9 – ne IDC [338]

DIRECTOIRE DE JOLIETTE, ST JACQUES, ST LIN, ST JEROME, TERREBONNE, ST EUSTACHE, L'ASSOMPTION, STE. THERESE, ETC – (Only 1877 ed) – Montreal, 1877-. SEM105P822 – 5mf – 9 – Can$11.25 – cn Bibl Nat [971]

DIRECTORATE GENERAL OF PLANNING AND COORDINATION – Annual programme. D-1539 1. 1972 – 9 – ne IDC [330]

DIRECTORIES – 340p. Spectrum, Australian Spectrum, Freenetwork Directory, Anarchist Association of the Americas, Directory of Libertarian periodicals, Index of Liberty (Petterson, 1985), Green Alliance directory, Sydney Bio-regional Resource Guide, Free Market Yellow Pages, E-Mail Directory, Libertarians who use computers – 9 – 1.00f – at Libertarian Micro [335]

DIRECTORIES, FREEDOM ADDRESSES – Compiled by John Zube. 4 fiches (29x) – 9 – 1.00f – at Libertarian Micro [320]

DIRECTORIO CATHECHISTICO...ROIPALDA / Ortiz Cantero, Jose – (v2. 1727. 1.50f; 9. v2. 1766. 1.50f; BSA; 9) – 1705 – 9 – 1.50f – sp Bibl Santa Ana [240]

DIRECTORIO CATHEQUISTICO DEL CHRISTIANO ILUSTRADO EN LA FE CON LA GLOSA UNIVERSAL DE LA DOCTRINA CHRISTIANA... / Ortiz Cantero, Jose – Madrid: Antonio Perez de Soto, 1766.-v1 – 1 – sp Bibl Santa Ana [240]

DIRECTORIO OFICIAL DE SENADO Y DE LA CAMARA DE REPRESENTATES / Philippines. Legislature – 1917. Manila: Bureau of Printing – 1 – us U.W. Library [950]

DIRECTORIO PARRAQUIAL / Ortiz Cantero, Jose – (1796 ed.1.50f; 9) – 1727 – 9 – 1.50f – sp Bibl Santa Ana [240]

DIRECTORIO PARROQUIAL, PRACTICA DE CONCURSOS Y DE CURAS... / Ortiz Cantero, Jose – Madrid: Antonio Perez de Soto, 1769 – 1 – sp Bibl Santa Ana [240]

DIRECTORIUM AD DIVINUM OFFICIUM...MELCHIORE GRANADOS ET ORTIZ – Don Benito: D. Amalio Gallardo Valades, 1871 – 1 – sp Bibl Santa Ana [946]

DIRECTORIUM ANNUALE DIVINUM OFFICIUM... PACENSIS – 1828 – 9 – 1.50f – sp Bibl Santa Ana [946]

DIRECTORIUM ANNUALE DIVINUM OFFICIUM... PACENSIS – 1829 – 9 – 1.50f – sp Bibl Santa Ana [946]

DIRECTORIUM ANNUALE DIVINUM OFFICIUM... PACENSIS – 1838 – 9 – 1.50f – sp Bibl Santa Ana [946]

DIRECTORS AND BOARDS – (v.4. 1979 5,6,9) – v.1. 1976 – 1 – us UMI [650]

DIRECTORS ANNUAL REPORT / Jordan. Jordan Development Bank – 1951-67. BNE-9781 1 – 9 – ne IDC [336]

DIRECTORS' MINUTES OF MEETINGS / St Francis' Boys Home. Kansas – 1945-69 – 1 – us KS Hist [360]

DIRECTORY / Phi Delta Phi – 8th ed. Galesburg, IL: Mail, 1909. 320p. LL-454 – 1 – us L of C Photodup [340]

DIRECTORY 1908 : NEW WESTMINSTER CITY AND THE MUNICIPALITIES OF THE FRASER VALLEY,.... – New Westminster: James Davis Taylor, 1908 – 1r – 1 – cn U.B.C. Preserve [910]

DIRECTORY 1909 : NEW WESTMINSTER CITY AND THE MUNICIPALITIES OF THE FRASER VALLEY – New Westminster: James Davies Taylor, 1909 – 1r – 1 – cn U.B.C. Preserve [910]

DIRECTORY AND HISTORY OF BERRIEN COUNTY, 1871 / Cowles, Edward B – Buchanan: Record Steam Print House, 1871. Michigan Reel 5. (The Cox Library Collection) – 5 – us Americana [978]

DIRECTORY AND REFERENCE BOOK OF SCHOHARIE COUNTY / Mallery & Danforth – Middleburgh, Pierre W. Danforth, 1899. New York Reel 33. (The Cox Library Collection) – 5 – us Americana [978]

DIRECTORY AND SOLDIER'S REGISTER OF WAYNE COUNTY / ed by Power, J C – Richmond: W.H. Lanthum and Co., 1865. Indiana Reel 29. (The Cox Library Collection) – 5 – us Americana [978]

A DIRECTORY FOR MIDWIVES / Culpeper, N – London, 1684 – 4mf – 9 – ne IDC [618]

DIRECTORY OF ADMINISTRATIVE HEARING FACILITIES / Administrative Conference of the U.S. (ACUS) – 1st ed Feb 1981. Acus: np. nd. (all publ) – 3mf – 9 – $4.50 – LLMC 94-343A – us L.L.M.C. [340]

DIRECTORY OF ADMINISTRATIVE HEARING FACILITIES / Administrative Conference of the U.S. (ACUS) – 2nd ed Nov 1984. Washington: GPO, 1984 (all publ) – 3mf – 9 – $4.50 – LLMC 94-343B – us L.L.M.C. [340]

DIRECTORY OF ADULT EDUCATION DOCUMENTATION AND INFORMATION SERVICES – (English/French/Spanish) – 3rd ed 1984 – 76p – 9 – 92-3-002188-1 – fr UNESCO [370]

DIRECTORY OF CHAMBLY BASIN, CHAMBLY CANTON, ST JEAN BAPTISTE, ST CESAIRE, ROUGEMONT, ST HILAIRE, BELOEIL, ST BRUNO, MARIEVILLE, LAPRAIRIE, AND ST EDOUARD FOR...1877-78 – Montreal: Lovell Printing and Publ Co, 1877/78. SEM105P666 – 4mf – 9 – Can$9.00 – cn Bibl Nat [971]

DIRECTORY OF COMPUTER SOFTWARE / U.S. National Technical Information Service – Annual listing of thousands of mainframe and microcomputer software. More than 1700 programs. Full indexes by subject, hardware, language, and sponsoring agency. PB88-190962 – 9 – us N.T.I.S. [000]

DIRECTORY OF COMPUTERIZED DATAFILES / U.S. National Technical Information Service – Annual listing of thousands of mainframe and microcomputer datafiles. 27 subject headings. PB89-191761 – 9 – us N.T.I.S. [000]

DIRECTORY OF DOCUMENTATION, LIBRARIES AND ARCHIVES SERVICES IN AFRICA / Zidouemba, Dominique & Grolier, Eric de – 2nd red ed 1978 – 311p – 9 – 92-3-001479-6 – fr UNESCO [020]

DIRECTORY OF EDUCATIONAL DOCUMENTATION AND INFORMATION SERVICES / ed by International Bureau of Education – (English/French/Spanish) – 5th ed 1988 – x/114p – 9 – 92-3-002518-6 – fr UNESCO [370]

DIRECTORY OF EDUCATIONAL INSTITUTIONS 1983-1984 / Jamaica. Ministry of Education – [Kingston] – 2mf – 9 – DE-521/1 – ne IDC [370]

DIRECTORY OF EDUCATIONAL INSTITUTIONS 1983/84-1984/85 / Nigeria. Bendel State. Ministry of Finance and Economic Planning. Statistics Office – Benin City – 4mf – 9 – DE-454/1 – ne IDC [370]

DIRECTORY OF EDUCATIONAL RESEARCH INSTITUTIONS – (English/French/Spanish) – 2nd ed 1986 – xx/428p – 9 – 92-3-002405-8 – fr UNESCO [370]

DIRECTORY OF ENGINEERING EDUCATION INSTITUTIONS : AFRICA, ARAB STATES, ASIA, LATIN AMERICA AND THE CARIBBEAN – (English/French/Spanish) – 3rd ed 1986 – xiv/303p – 9 – 92-3-002393-0 – fr UNESCO [370]

DIRECTORY OF FOOD AND NUTRITION INSTITUTIONS IN THE NEAR EAST – 1987 – 92p – it F.A.O. [640]

DIRECTORY OF HUNTINGDON, BEAUHARNOIS, ST JEAN CHRYSOSTOME, CHATEAUGUAY, ST THIMOTHEE, VALLEYFIELD, DURHAM, HOWICK, HEMMINGFORD, STE. MARTINE, LACOLLE, ST REMI AND NAPIERVILLE – Montreal: Lovell Printing & Publ Co, 1987-. SEMP105P821 – 5mf – 9 – Can$11.25 – cn Bibl Nat [971]

DIRECTORY OF JAPANESE TECHNICAL RESOURCES / U.S. National Technical Information Service – U.S. sources of Japanese high-technology information. PB89-158869 – 9 – us N.T.I.S. [000]

DIRECTORY OF LABOR ORGANIZATIONS / Massachusetts. Dept. of Labor and Industries. Division of Statistics – Aug. 1902-78. 50 fiches. (Harvard Law School Library Collection.) – 9 – 1.50f – us H.U. Law [324]

DIRECTORY OF LIBERTARIAN PERIODICALS – Comp. by Jim Stumm, Aug 1985 – 9 – 1.00f – at Libertarian Micro [335]

DIRECTORY OF NAMES / Wood County. Ohio. Lake Township. Township Clerk – 1905 – 1r – 1 – $32.50r – us Archival [324]

DIRECTORY OF POST-PRIMARY INSTITUTIONS IN THE EAST CENTRAL STATE OF NIGERIA / Nigeria. East Central State. Ministry of Education – Enugu, 1971 – 1mf – 9 – DE-101/1 – ne IDC [370]

DIRECTORY OF POST-PRIMARY INSTITUTIONS IN THE EAST CENTRAL STATE OF NIGERIA 1973 / Nigeria. East Central State. Ministry of Education – 1974 – 2mf – 9 – DE-102/1 – ne IDC [370]

DIRECTORY OF PREBLE COUNTY 1875 / Morgan, B F – Historical Sketches and Biographies of Eminent Pioneers. Eaton: 1875. Ohio Reel 54. (The Cox Library Collection) – 5 – us Americana [978]

DIRECTORY OF PRINCIPAL CHINESE BUSINESS FIRMS IN SAN FRANCISCO – San Francisco Co, CA. 1878 – 1r – 1 – $50.00 – D086 – us Library Micro [380]

DIRECTORY OF SCHOOLS 1974-1975 / Bahamas. Ministry of Education and Culture – Nassau – 2mf – 9 – DE-511/1 – ne IDC [370]

DIRECTORY OF SOCIAL SCIENCE INFORMATION COURSES – (Trilingual: English/French/Spanish) – 1988 – xxxii/167p – 9 – 92-3-002525-9 – Co-published with Berg – fr UNESCO [301]

DIRECTORY OF SPECIAL LIBRARIES IN INDONESIA, INCLUDING PROVINCIAL LIBRARIES / Prawirasumantri, Kosasih – SE-6039 1. 1966 – 9 – ne IDC [020]

DIRECTORY OF ST JOHNS, WEST FARNHAM, GRANBY, WEST SHEFFORD, WATERLOO, ROXTON FALLS, ETC – Montreal: Lovell Printing & Publ Co, 1876. SEM105P635 – 4mf – 9 – Can$9.00 – cn Bibl Nat [910]

DIRECTORY OF ST SCHOLASTIQUE, LACHUTE, HULL ETC – Montreal: Printed by Lovell Printing & Publ Co, 1878. SEM105P173 – 5mf – 9 – Can$11.25 – cn Bibl Nat [910]

DIRECTORY OF THE ANCESTRAL HEADS OF NEW ENGLAND FAMILIES, 1620-1700 – Comp. by Frank R. Holmes, 1964. Orig. publ., 1923. Alphabetically by surname. 4 fiches. F-0864 – 9 – us A.G.L.L. [978]

DIRECTORY OF THE BAR OF NEW JERSEY / Pierson, Leslie Cook – 4th ed. Trenton: MacCrellish & Quigley, 1888. 42p. LL-459 – 1 – us L of C Photodup [340]

DIRECTORY OF THE BRETHREN IN CHRIST : COMMONLY CALLED RIVER BRETHREN – 1880-86 (complete) – 1r – 1 – ATLA 1993-S026 – us A.T.L.A. [030]

DIRECTORY OF THE CHURCH OF THE BRETHREN IN CHRIST – 1899 (complete) – 1r – 1 – ATLA 1993-S028 – us A.T.L.A. [030]

DIRECTORY OF THE CITY OF FAIRFIELD AND JEFFERSON COUNTY FOR 1899 / Waltz, George B; ed by Waltz, George B – Fairfield: 1899. Iowa Reel 23. (The Cox Library Collection) – 5 – us Americana [978]

DIRECTORY OF THE CITY OF NEVADA AND GRASS VALLEY / Thompson, Hugh H – Nevada Co, 1861 – 1r – 1 – $50.00 – B40247 – us Library Micro [978]

THE DIRECTORY OF THE DEVOUT LIFE : MEDITATIONS ON THE SERMON ON THE MOUNT / Meyer, Frederick Brotherton – New York: Fleming H Revell, 1904 – 1mf – 9 – us A.T.L.A. [240]

DIRECTORY OF THE MEMBERS AND OFFICIALS OF THE BRETHREN IN CHRIST CHURCH – 1903 (complete) – 1r – 1 – ATLA 1993-S029 – us A.T.L.A. [030]

DIRECTORY OF THE MEMBERS OF THE BAR IN PRACTICE IN NEW JERSEY. / Honeyman, Abraham Van Doren – Somerville, N.J.: Honeyman, 1888. 64p. LL-1101 – 1 – us L of C Photodup [340]

DIRECTORY OF THE NEVADA TERRITORY – State of Nevada. 1862-1863; 1868-1869 – 3r – 1 – $150.00 – D115 – us Library Micro [978]

A DIRECTORY OF THE NORTHERN PART OF THE SAANICH PENINSULA / St-Barbe, Charles – Sidney, B.C.: Sidney Printing & Publishing Co, 1914 – 1r – 1 – cn U.B.C. Preserve [971]

DIRECTORY OF VANCOUVER ISLAND AND ADJACENT ISLANDS FOR 1909 – Victoria, B.C.: Provincial Publishing Co, 1909 – 1r – 1 – cn U.B.C. Preserve [910]

THE DIRECTORY OF VICTORIA CITY AND VANCOUVER ISLAND FOR 1914 : CONTAINING A COMPLETE STREET DIRECTORY OF THE CITY OF VICTORIA AND SUBURBAN DISTRICTS,... – Victoria, B.C.: Tregillus-Thompson Ltd., 1914 – 1r – 1 – cn U.B.C. Preserve [910]

DIRECTORY OF VICTORIAN SOLICITORS 1937-1986 – 4mf – 9 – A$30.00 – at State Libr Vic [340]

A DIRECTORY TO COLLECTIVE BARGAINING AGREEMENTS: PRIVATE SECTOR – 1981- – 9 – us UMI [331]

A DIRECTORY TREATISE / Martin, Charles Hynes – Jacksonville, Texas: Small, 1886. 42p. LL-496 – 1 – us L of C Photodup [340]

O DIREITO : PERIODICO SCIENTIFICO E DEMOCRATA – [s.l.]. 25 Ago 1883 – 1,5,6 – bl Biblioteca [072]

O DIREITO – S. Felix, BA. 8-12, 19 Abr 1886 – 1,5,6 – bl Biblioteca [072]

DIREKTIVY 23 S'EZDA KPSS PO PIATILETNEMU PLANU RAZVITIIA NARODNOGO KHOZIAISTVA SSSR NA 1966-1970 GODY / U.S.S.R. – D 1226 1. 1966 – 9 – ne IDC [338]

DIREKTIVY GLAVNOGO KOMANDOVANIIA KRASNOI ARMII, 1917-1920 : SBORNIK DOKUMENTOV / Viunova, N M et al – Moskva: Voenizdat, 1969 – 1 – CSUX90-B5041 – us Hoover Inst Photo [355]

DIREKTIVY KOMANDOVANIIA FRONTOV KRASNOI ARMII, 1917-1922 : SBORNIK DOKUMENTOV – Moskva: Voennoe izd-vo, 1971-1978. 4v – 1 – CSUX90-B4733 – us Hoover Inst Photo [355]

DIREKTIVY KPSS I SOVETSKOGO PRAVITEL'STVA PO KHOZIAISTVENNYM VOPROSAM, 1917-1957 GODY / Russia. (1923-U.S.S.R.). Laws, Statutes, etc – Moscow, 1957-1958. 4 vols – 1 – 35.00r – us Hoover Inst Photo [324]

DIREKTIVYPO SHESTOMU PIATILETNEMU PLANU 1956-1960 GG / U.S.S.R. Kommunisticheskaia Partiia Sovetskogo Soiuza – M. 1956. BD-246 1 – 9 – ne IDC [947]

Direktorat Bahasa dan Kesusasteraan, DitDjen Kebudajaan, Departmen P. dan K. *see* BAHASA DAN KESUSASTERAAN

Direktorat Djenderal Koperasi *see* BULLETIN KOPERASI

Direktorat Djenderal Minjak dan Gas Bumi *see* BULLETIN BULANAN INDUSTRI MINJAK DAN GAS BUMI INDONESIA

Direktorat Pembinaan Wilajah Direktorat Djendral Padjak *see* BERITA PADJAK

DIREKTORIIA, KOLCHAK I INTERVENTY; VOSPOMINANIIA (IZ TSIKLA "SHEST'LET" 1917-1922 GG) / Boldyrev, V G – Novonikolaevsk, 1925 – 1 – 35.00r – us Hoover Inst Photo [335]

DIRETRIZES – Rio de Janiero. n. 1-207. 1938-44. and Suplemento literario diretrizes. 1939-41. (Wanting n. 1-7, 33-34, 131, 144-207) – 1 – 85.00 – us L of C Photodup [972]

DIRETTORIO MONASTICO DI CANTO FERMO / Banchieri, A – 1615-16 – 9 – us Sibley [780]

LES DIRIGEANTS DE L'INDUSTRIE FRANCAISE / Delefortrie-Soubeyroux, N – 1961 – F70.00 – fr Ethnologie [338]

DIRIGIDO POR HERMANAS CARMELITAS DE LA CARIDAD LEGALMENTE RECONOCIDO PARA ENSENANZA MEDIA / Colegio de Santa Cecilia de Caceres – Caceres: Tip. Vda. de Floriano, s.a. – 1 – sp Bibl Santa Ana [946]

Dirin, P *see* VELIKAIA KNIAGINIA EKATERINA ALEKSEEVNA 1729-1761 G. ISTORICHESKII OCHERK

IL DIRITO INTERNAZIONALE NEI GIUDIZI INTERNI / Anzilotti, D – Bologna, 1905 – 4mf – 9 – ILM-3144/1 – ne IDC [340]
DIRITTI SUI TERRITORIAL ALTRUI... / Cavarretta, G – Palermo, 1905 – 1mf – 1 – ILM-1963/1 – ne IDC [327]
IL DIRITTO – New York, 1918-1919 (Dec 20-June) – 6mf or 1r – 1 – us I.H.R.C. [978]
IL DIRITTO – Rome, Italy. -d. 1 Jan 1872-31 Dec 1895. 47 reels – 1 – uk British Libr Newspaper [072]
DIRITTO CAMBIARIO INTERNAZIONALE... / Esperson, P – Firenze, 1870 – 2mf – 1 – ILM-3232/1 – ne IDC [327]
DIRITTO CAMBIARIO INTERNAZIONALE... / Esperson, P – Florence, 1870 – 2mf – 1 – ILM-513/1 – ne IDC [327]
IL DIRITTO CIVILE INTERNAZIONALE NELLA CODIFICAZIONE FRANCESE ED ITALIANA – Napoli, etc 1881 – 1mf – 1 – ILM-3942/1 – ne IDC [327]
IL DIRITTO COMMERCIALE E LA PARTE GENERALE DELLE OBBLIGAZIONI. – Pisa. On film: v1-58; 1883-1939. Missing: v40 & 48; 1921 & 1929. LL-0284 – 1 – us L of C Photodup [340]
IL DIRITTO D'ALBINAGGIO... / Guerra, P – Firenze, 1900 – 2mf – 1 – ILM-3321/1 – ne IDC [327]
IL DIRITTO DELLA NATURA... / Ferrante, S – Naples, 1763 – 2mf – 1 – ILM-733/1 – ne IDC [327]
IL DIRITTO DI ESTRADIZIONE / Castori, C – Torino, 1886 – 2mf – 1 – ILM-372/1 – ne IDC [327]
IL DIRITTO DI FRATERNA NELLA GIURISPRUDENZA DA ACCURSIO ALLA CODIFICAZIONE / Fumagalli, Camillo – Torino etc.: Fratelli Bocca, 1912. 178p. LL-4099 – 1 – us L of C Photodup [340]
IL DIRITTO EREDITARIO INTERNAZIONALE... / Contuzzi, F P – Milano, 1908 – 7mf – 1 – ILM-3649/1 – ne IDC [327]
IL DIRITTO INTERNAZIONALE COMMERCIALE / Cavaglieri, A – Padova, 1936 – 6mf – 1 – ILM-3065/1 – ne IDC [327]
DIRITTO INTERNAZIONALE E ... / Bigliati, F G – Torino, 1904 – 4mf – 9 – ILM-1594/1 – ne IDC [327]
DIRITTO INTERNAZIONALE E DIRITTO CRIMINALE / Carnevale, E – Messina, n.d. – 1mf – 1 – ILM-2072/1 – ne IDC [327]
IL DIRITTO INTERNAZIONALE E LA SUA CRISI / Caristia, C – Milano, 1925 – 1mf – 1 – ILM-3132-1 – ne IDC [327]
IL DIRITTO INTERNAZIONALE IN ITALIA... / Cimbali, E – Roma, 1914 – 2mf – 1 – ILM-3636/1 – ne IDC [327]
DIRITTO INTERNAZIONALE OPPRESSORE E GUERRESCO... / Cimbali, E – Catania, 1933 – 2mf – 1 – ILM-3637/1 – ne IDC [327]
DIRITTO INTERNAZIONALE PENALE / Adinolfi, S – Milano, 1913 – 4mf – 9 – ILM-2059/1 – ne IDC [340]
DIRITTO MARITTIMO... / Feichtinger de B Nadasd, A – Fiume, 1894 – 6mf – 1 – ILM-1638/1 – ne IDC [327]
IL DIRITTO PENALE INTERNAZIONALE... / Baldassarri, A – Roma, 1928 – 1mf – 9 – ILM-2063/1 – ne IDC [340]
Dirr, A *see* MANUEL PRATIQUE DE LA LANGUE HAOUSSA
DIRSCHAUER ZEITUNG – (Title change 8 Sept-3 dec 1939: Deutsche Zeitung) – Dirschau (Tczew), Poland. 28 Nov-30 Dec 1922; 8 Sept 1939-17 Jan 1940 – 1 – gw Mikrofilm [943]
DIRSOS...!TENGO MADRE! COSAS DE UN RECLUTA / Galan, Leocadio – Caceres: Tip. El Noticiero, 1972 – 1 – sp Bibl Santa Ana [946]
DIRT RIDER – (1986-. 1,5,6) – 1984- – 9 – us UMI [790]
Diruta, Girolamo *see* IL TRANSILVANO DIALOGO SOPRA IL VERO MODO DI SONAR ORGANI, E ISTROMENTI DA PENNA
DIRVA – (Weekly Lithuanian language newspaper) – Cleveland, OH. 25 Aug 1971-20 Dec 1990 – 15r – 1 – us Western Res [071]
DIRVA = FIELD – Cleveland: Ohio Lithuanian Pub Co, 1958-65 – 14r – us Res Libr [071]
DIRVA-THE-FIELD – Cleveland. Ohio. (Lithuanian). 1952-57 – 1 – us UMI [071]
DISABILITY ALLOWANCE RECORDS / Allen County. Ohio. Soldiers Relief Commission – 1887-1926 – 2r – 1 – $32.50r – us Archival [324]
DISABILITY APPEALS IN SOCIAL SECURITY PROGRAMS / Liebman, Lance – Washington: FJC, 1985 – 1mf – 9 – $1.50 – LLMC 95-375 – us L.L.M.C. [340]
DISABILITY, HANDICAP AND SOCIETY – 1986- 8v – 9 – £141.00 – 0267-4645 – uk Carfax [360]
DISABILITY LAW IN THE UNITED STATES : A LEGISLATIVE HISTORY OF THE AMERICANS WITH DISABILITY ACT OF 1990, PUBLIC LAW 101-336 / Reams, Bernard N & Schultz, Jon S – 6v – 9 – $186.00set – LC 92-28981 – us Hein [340]
Disabled American Veterans. Fulton County Chapter no. 78 *see* RECORDS
DiSalle, Michael V *see* PAPERS OF THE OFFICE OF PRICES STABILIZATION
DISANCI GUONEI GEMING ZHANZHENG GAIKUANG (ZHONGUO XIANDAISHI ZILIAO CONGKAN) – Series of Materials on Contemporary Chinese History: A General History of the Third Revolutionary Civil War. Comp. by Renmin Chubanshe. 3 fiches. F H131 – 9 – 4.00f – cc Microforms [950]
Disandro, Carlos A *see* LA TERCERA POSICION Y LA NEUTRALIZACION ARGENTINA
DISARMAMENT AND DISBANDMENT OF THE GERMAN ARMED FORCES / U.S. Army. Office of the Chief Historian, European Command – 1947 – 1 – $19.00 – us L of C Photodup [943]
[DISARMAMENT AND WORLD WAR 2 PAMPHLET COLLECTION] – 1942 – 1 – CSUXANP1495-B – us Hoover Inst Photo [320]
DISARMAMENT CAMPAIGNS – Hague, Netherlands. ill. 11 issues yearly. 1980?- – 1 – us U.W. Library [327]
DISASTERS, THE INTERNATIONAL JOURNAL OF DISASTER STUDIES AND PRACTICE – v.1- 1977- – 5,6,9 – us UMI [360]
DISC AND MUSIC ECHO/MUSIC MIRROR – London. 1958-75. 20 reels – 1 – 358.00 – us L of C Photodup [780]
DISCAR – Dog Information Storage Control and Retrieval. v. 1-. 1975- – 1,5,6,9 – us UMI [636]
DISCH DESIGNS – For Vehicles, muscle and solar powered. German leaflet, 2p – 9 – 1.00f – at Libertarian Micro [600]
DISCHARGE OF SELECTED RIVERS OF THE WORLD – 9 – fr UNESCO [550]
THE DISCIPLE OF CHRIST AND CANADIAN EVANGELIST – (Cont: The Canadian Evangelist. Cont by: The Canadian Evangelist and Disciple of Christ) – Hamilton, Ont: G Munro, [1895-1896] – 9 – cn C.I.H.M. [240]
THE DISCIPLES OF CHRIST / Gates, Errett – New York: Baker & Taylor, 1905. (The story of the churches) – 1mf – us A.T.L.A. [240]
DISCIPLESHIP / Morgan, George Campbell – New York: Fleming H Revell, c1897 – 1mf – 9 – 0-8370-7313-8 – 1986-1313 – us A.T.L.A. [240]
DISCIPLESHIP: THE SCHEME OF CHRISTIANITY – London: Williams & Norgate, 1894. 1 fiche – 9 – us A.T.L.A. [240]
DISCIPLINA ORDINIS CARTUSIENSIS TRIBUS LIBRIS DISTRIBUTA / Le Masson, Dom Inn. O Cart. – Monstrolii, 1894 – Dfl74.00 – ne Slangenburg [240]
DISCIPLINA UNIDAD TRIUMFO / Largo Caballero, Francisco – n.p., 1937. Fiche W991. (Blodgett Collection of Spanish Civil War Pamphlets) – 9 – us H.U. College Libr [946]
LA DISCIPLINE – Port-au-Prince: Impr de l'Abeille, jan 27-apr 3 1909; apr 28 1909-mar 12, apr 9 1910 – 3r – 9 – us Res Libr [072]
LA DISCIPLINE PENITENTIELLE EN GAULE DES ORIGINES A LA FIN DU 7TH SIECLE / Vogel, C – Paris, 1952 – 4mf – 8 – Dfl19.00 – ne Slangenburg [240]
DISCIPLINE-BASED DANCE EDUCATION : A TRANSLATION AND INTERPRETATION OF DISCIPLINE-BASED ART EDUCATION FOR THE DISCIPLINE OF DANCE / Hong-Joe, Christina M & Hanstein, Penelope – 1991 – 1mf – $4.00 – us Microform Publ [790]
O DISCIPULO : ORGAO CATHOLICO LITTERARIO – Ouro Preto, 7 Mar-15 Apr 1897 – 1,5,6 – bl Biblioteca [072]
DISCONTENT AND AUTHORITY 1820-40 / Great Britain. Public Record Office – Rewards, Pardons and Secret Service 1820-40. (PRO Class H064. Boxes 1-19) – 1 – us Primary [941]
THE DISCOPHILE : THE MAGAZINE FOR RECORD INFORMATION – Nos. 1-61 (all publ). Aug 1948-Dec 1958. (Jazz Periodicals) – 1 reel – 1 – $120.00 – us UPA [780]
LAS DISCORDANCIAS ENTRE ALBERDI Y SUS ADVERSARIOS, SOBRE LA CULTURA PUBLICA / Victoria, Maximio S – Tucuman. 1925 – 1 – us Res Libr [972]
(LA DISCORDIA FORTUNATA] AH MIA CARA / Paisiello, G – (Full score) – London: Skillern/Goulding, 179- – 1 – us Sibley [780]
DISCORSI DELLA MUSICA.. / Chiavelloni, Vincenzo – 1668 – 9 – us Sibley [780]
DISCORSI MUSICALI.. / Crivellati, Cesare – 1624 – 9 – us Sibley [780]
DISCORSI SOPRA L'ANTICHITA DI ROMA / Scamozzi, V – Venetia, 1582 – 9 – ne IDC [700]
DISCORSO DI VICENTIO GALILEI NOBILE FIORENTINO. ET ALTRI INPORTANTI PARTICOLARI ATTENENTI ALLA MUSICA / Galilei, V – 1589 – 9 – us Sibley [780]
DISCORSO DI VINCENTIO GALILEI, INTORNO ALL' OPERE DI MESSER GIOSEFFO ZARLINO DA CHIOGGIA / Galilei, V – P 281 1589 – 9 – ne IDC [780]
DISCORSO INTERNE ALLA SCOLTURA ET PITTURA / Lamo, A – O-1024 1. 1584 – 9 – ne IDC [730]
DISCOURS... / Darjes, J G – Jena, 1762-63 – 16mf – 1 – ILM-462/1 – ne IDC [327]
DISCOURS: 21 AOUT 1804: DISCOURS PRONONCES A L'UNIVERSITE DE JURISPRUDENCE / Gin, Pierre L C – Paris: Garnery, Artur-Bertrand, Royez, 1805. 25p. 1 fiche. (Law Collection) – 9 – 6.00 – fr Bibl Nationale [340]
DISCOURS A LA CHAMBRE SUR LA TRAITE DES NOIRS, DES 27 JUIN 1821, 4 AVRIL ET 31 JUILLET 1822 / Constant, Benjamin – (Slave Trade and Abolitionism in France Series). 1827 – 9 – fr Hachette [360]
DISCOURS ADMIRABLE D'UN MAGICIEN DE LA VILLE DE MOULINS – Paris. 1623 – 9 – fr Hachette [360]
DISCOURS AU SUJET DE LA PROPOSITION DEMANDANT LA DEUXIEME LECTURE DU BILL CONSTITUANT EN CORPS LEGAL L'ORDRE DES ORANGISTS, 17 MARS 1884 / Blake, Edward – Prononce par l'Honorable Edward Blake, M. P., dans la Chambre des communes du Canada. 1884? 00160. (Pre-1900 Canadiana) – 9 – cn C.I.H.M. [971]
DISCOURS DE LA LYCANTHROPIE OU DE LA TRANSFORMATION DES HOMMES EN LOUPS / Chauvincourt, Beauvois de – Paris. 1599 – 9 – fr Hachette [360]
DISCOURS DE L'HON. M. BEAUBIEN A L'INAUGURATION DE L'ECOLE D'INDUSTRIE LAITIERE DE ST HYACINTHE, LE 11 MARS 1893 / Beaubien, Louis – 1893? 02967. (Pre-1900 Canadiana) – 9 – cn C.I.H.M. [971]
DISCOURS DE L'HON. M. MERCIER, PREMIER MINISTRE DE LA PROVINCE DE QUEBEC DEVANT UNE ASSEMBLEE A LA SALLE BONSECOURS A MONTREAL, LE 9 FEVRIER, 1891 / Mercier, Honore – Quebec, 1891. 03182. (Pre-1900 Canadiana) – 9 – cn C.I.H.M. [971]
DISCOURS DE L'HON. SOLLICITEUR-GENERAL ANGERS: EXPOSANT LA POLITIQUE DU GOUVERNEMENT RELATIVE A LA CONSTRUCTION D'UN CHEMIN DE FER PROVINCIAL SUR LA RIVE NORD DU SAINT-LAURENT: SEANCE DU 10 DECEMBRE 1875 / Angers, Auguste Real – Quebec: 1875. 00817. (Pre-1900 Canadiana) – 9 – cn C.I.H.M. [971]
DISCOURS DE L'HON. W. S. FIELDING, M.P., MINISTRE DES FINANCES. SIR RICHARD CARTWRIGHT, M.P., MINISTRE DU COMMERCE ET L'HON. WILLIAM PATERSON, M.P., MINISTRE DES DOUANES, CHAMBRE DES COMMUNES, OTTAWA, 5, 12 & 13 AVRIL 1898 / Fielding, William Stevens – Ottawa?: s.n., 1898? 03102. (Pre-1900 Canadiana) – 9 – cn C.I.H.M. [971]
DISCOURS DE L'HONORABLE A.W. ATWATER...ET DE FELIX CARBRAY...SUR LE BUDGET / Atwater, Albert William – Quebec: L. Demers, 1899.04481.(Pre-1900 Canadiana) – 9 – cn C.I.H.M. [971]
DISCOURS DE L'HONORABLE E. J. FLYNN, DEPUTE DE GASPE, PRONONCE A LA SEANCE DE L'ASSEMBLEE LEGISLATIVE DU 22 JANVIER 1883 / Flynn, Edmund James – s.l.: s.n., 1883?. 03114. (Pre-1900 Canadiana) – 9 – cn C.I.H.M. [971]
DISCOURS DE L'HONORABLE E. J. FLYNN, DEPUTE DE GASPE, SUR LES RESOLUTIONS DE LA CONFERENCE INTERPROVINCIALE, PRONONCE DEVANT L'ASSEMBLEE LEGISLATIVE A SA SEANCE DU LUNDI LE 21 MAI 1888 / Flynn, Edmund James – Quebec: s.n.. 1888. 03115. (Pre-1900 Canadiana) – 9 – cn C.I.H.M. [971]
DISCOURS DE L'HONORABLE L. BEAUBIEN, COMMISSAIRE DE L'AGRICULTURE..., PRONONCE A L'ASSEMBLEE LEGISLATIVE LE 26 DECEMBRE 1893:.. / Beaubien, Louis – Montreal: E. Senecal, 1894. 02286. (Pre-1900 Canadiana) – 9 – cn C.I.H.M. [630]
DISCOURS DE M. L. G. DESJARDINS, DEPUTE DU DISTRICT ELECTORAL DE MONTMORENCY, SUR LES FINANCES DE LA PROVINCE DE QUEBEC, FAIT A L'ASSEMBLEE LEGISLATIVE, A LA SEANCE DU MARDI LE 11 MAI 1886 / Desjardins, Louis Georges – s.l.: s.n., 1886?. 02159. (Pre-1900 Canadiana – 9 – cn C.I.H.M. [971]
DISCOURS DE M. P.W. ELLIS...A LA CONVENTION ANNUELLE, TENUE A MONTREAL, MARDI ET MERCREDI 5-6 NOVEMBRE 1901 / Ellis, PW – SEM105P469 – 1mf – 9 – Can$2.25 – cn Bibl Nat [971]
DISCOURS DE SIR RICHARD CARTWRIGHT, PRONONCE A TORONTO LE 24 AOUT 1899: UN EXPOSE MAGISTRAL DE LA SITUATION FINANCIERE DU PAYS / Cartwright, Richard – Quebec: Soleil, 1899. 00501. (Pre-1900 Canadiana) – 9 – cn C.I.H.M. [971]
DISCOURS DE SIR WILFRED LAURIER-ALFRED D. DECELLES / Laurier, Wilfred – Montreal, 1920. SEM105P540 – 6mf – 9 – Can$13.50 – cn Bibl Nat [971]
DISCOURS DE...DANS LES CORTES / Donoso Cortes, Juan Francisco – 1851 – 9 – $1.50f – sp Bibl Santa Ana [946]
DISCOURS DES MARQUES DES SORCIERS ET DE LA REELLE POSSESSION QUE LE DIABLE PREND SUR LE CORPS DES HOMMES / Fontaine, Jacques – Paris. 1611 – 9 – fr Hachette [360]
DISCOURS D'OUVERTURE DU C N R DE LABE : PARTI DEMOCRATIQUE DE GUINEE – [Conakry]: Imp Nationale "P Lumumba", 1968 – us Res Libr [320]
DISCOURS D'OUVERTURE DU COURS DE PHILOSOPHIE POSITIVE / Comte, Auguste – Revue Encyclopedique, nov 1829, 39 p. Les Saint-Simoniens, 1825-1834. 6883 – 9 – fr Hachette [335]
DISCOURS D'OUVERTURE DU PRESIDENT AHMED SEKOU TOURE : 12E SESSION DE LA CONFERENCE DES MINISTRES AFRICAINS DU TRAVAIL – 2nd aug ed. [Conakry]: Impr nationale "Patrice-Lamumba", 18 mars 1974 – us Res Libr [320]
DISCOURS DU SONGE DE POLIPHILE / Colonna, F – O-1037 1. 1546 – 9 – ne IDC [760]
LE DISCOURS DU VOYAGE DE CONSTANTINOBLE, ... – Lyon, 1542 – 1 mf – 9 – H-8149/1 – ne IDC [956]
DISCOURS D'UN NEGRE A UN EUROPEEN / Doigni – Paris, 1775 – 1mf – 1 – ILM-1211/1 – ne IDC [327]
DISCOURS ET CONFERENCES / Chapais, Thomas – (Quebec: L. J. Demers), 1897. 00561. (Pre-1900 Canadiana) – 9 – cn C.I.H.M. [971]
DISCOURS ET ELOGES ACADEMIQUES / Dumas, J B – Paris, Gauthier-Villars, 1885, t. I, 315 p; t. II, 319 p. Histoire des Sciences XVIIe-XIXe Siecles. 7925 6 – 9 – fr Hachette [500]
DISCOURS ET VOTES DE JACQUES BUREAU CONTRE LA CONSCRIPTION EN 1917 / Bureau, Jacques – [Trois-Rivieres ?]: [s.n.], [1921 ?]. SEM105P1440 – 1mf – 9 – Can$2.25 – cn Bibl Nat [971]
DISCOURS EXECRABLE DES SORCIERS: ENSEMBLE LEUR PROCEZ FAITS DEPUIS DEUX ANS EN CA EN DIVERS ENDROITS DE LA FRANCE / Boguet, Henri – Paris. 1603 – 9 – fr Hachette [360]
DISCOURS HISTORIQUE SUR L'APOCALYPSE / Abauzit (Firmin) – (D'Holbach series). 1770 – 9 – fr Hachette [240]
DISCOURS LE 10 JUILLET 1888, AU CONSEIL LEGISLATIF SUR LA QUESTION DES BIENS DE JESUITES / Archambault, Horace – 1888. 02475. (Pre-1900 Canadiana) – 9 – cn C.I.H.M. [971]

DISCOURS MERVEILLEUX ET VERITABLE, D'UN CAPITAINE DE LA VILLE DE LYON QUE SATHAN A ENLEVE DANS SA CHAMBRE – Paris. 1613 – 9 – fr Hachette [360]

DISCOURS OU ORAISON FUNEBRE PRONONCE(...)AU SERVICE SOLENNEL DU MARQUIS DE LA ROCHE-JACQUELIN(...) / Chaffault, Silvestre-F du – (Le Drapeau blanc : ronde militaire, chant royal. – Nantes: Mellinet-Malassis,[s.d.]; Nouveau chansonnier breton : n°ler. – Nantes: Mellinet-Malassis,[s.d.]) – Nantes: Busseuil, 1816 – fr Armell [944]

DISCOURS PHISIQUE DE LA PAROLE / Cordemoy, G de – 1668 – 9 – fr I.C.S. [400]

DISCOURS PRODIGIEUX ET ESPOUVANTABLE DU THRESORIER ET BANQUIER DU DIABLE ET SON FILS QUI ONT ETE BRUSLES A VESOUL – Lyon. 1610 – 9 – fr Hachette [360]

DISCOURS PROGRAMME...AU COMITE CENTRAL DU PARTI CONSERVATEUR A MONTREAL, 10 FEVRIER 1891 / Chapleau, Joseph Adolphe – 189?. 00612. (Pre-1900 Canadiana) – 9 – cn C.I.H.M. [971]

DISCOURS...: PRONONCE A LA GRANDE ASSEMBLEE TENUE A LEVIS, DIMANCHE, 10 MARS / Chapleau, Joseph Adolphe – 18??. 00567. (Pre-1900 Canadiana) – 9 – cn C.I.H.M. [971]

DISCOURS PRONONCE A LA SALLE WINDSOR, MONTREAL, LE 16 FEVRIER 1892, SUR LES AFFAIRES FINANCIERES DE LA PROVINCE ET CRITIQUE DE L'ADMINISTRATION MERCIER / Hall, John Smythe – 1892?. 05338. (Pre-1900 Canadiana) – 9 – cn C.I.H.M. [336]

DISCOURS PRONONCE A LA SEANCE DU 3 JUIN 1892 DE L'ASSEMBLEE LEGISLATIVE DE LA PROVINCE DE QUEBEC / Beaubien, Louis – 1892. 03315. (Pre-1900 Canadiana) – 9 – cn C.I.H.M. [630]

DISCOURS PRONONCE A L'ASSEMBLEE DE MESSIEURS LES ELECTEURS DU DISTRICT DE CLISSON, LE 10 MAI 1790 / Duboueix, Michel – Nantes: Malassis, [1790] – 1 – F50.00 – fr Armell [320]

DISCOURS PRONONCE A NICOLET LE 4 OCTOBRE 1896 / Beaubien, Louis – Montreal, E. Senecal, 1896. 03319. (Pre-1900 Canadiana) – 9 – cn C.I.H.M. [971]

DISCOURS PRONONCE LE 31 MAI 1880: DANS L'ASSEMBLEE LEGISLATIVE DE QUEBEC EN SECONDANT L'ADRESSE EN REPONSE AU DISCOURS DU TRONE / Wuertele, Jonathan Saxton Campbell – Paris, 1880. 02584. (Pre-1900 Canadiana) – 9 – cn C.I.H.M. [971]

DISCOURS PRONONCE LORS DE L'INAUGURATION DU MONUMENT CARTIER-BREBEUF LE 24 JUIN 1889; DONNACORNA: POESIE / Chauveau, Pierre J O – Montreal: C. Beauchemin, 1889. 00590. (Pre-1900 Canadiana) – 9 – cn C.I.H.M. [810]

DISCOURS PRONONCE PAR L'HONORABLE A.T. GALT,...EN PRESENTANT LE BUDGET / Canada. Departement des finances – Ottawa: G E Desbarats, 1866. SEM105P298 – 1mf – 9 – Can$2.25 – cn Bibl Nat [350]

DISCOURS PRONONCE PAR M.G. AMYOT, DEPUTE DE BELLECHASSE AUX COMMUNES DU CANADA: EN REPONSE A CELUI DE DR. RINFRET...LE 3 AVRIL 1883.. / Amyot, Guillaume – Quebec, 1883?. 02399. (Pre-1900 Canadiana) – 9 – cn C.I.H.M. [971]

DISCOURS PRONONCE...AU BANQUET DES OUVRIERS A OTTAWA, LE 18 OCTOBRE 1888 / Chapleau, Joseph Adolphe – Ottawa?, 1888. 02864. (Pre-1900 Canadiana) – 9 – cn C.I.H.M. [971]

DISCOURS PRONONCES A L'ASSEMBLEE LEGISLATIVE DE LA PROVINCE DE QUEBEC AL L'APPUI DES RESOLUTIONS JOLY – par les Honbles, Joly, Mercier, Ross et Irvine et par Mm. Flynn. Racicot et Chs. Langelier, tresorier provincial. Compiles par P. Aug. Choquette. Quebec: Levy & Blouchard, 1879. 03049. (Pre-1900 Canadiana) – 9 – cn C.I.H.M. [971]

DISCOURS PRONONCES DANS L'ACADEMIE FRANCAISE, LE 4 MARS 1979 / Ducis, V F & Le Radonvilliers, P – Paris. Demonville. 1779 – 9 – fr Hachette [440]

DISCOURS PRONONCES PAR FELIX HOUPHOUET-BOIGNY / Ivory Coast. Ministry of Information – 1957-71 – 2r – 1 – $99.00 – us African Imprint [320]

DISCOURS QUI A REMPORTE LE PRIX, PAR LE JUGEMENT DE L'ACADEMIE DES JEUX FLORAUX EN L'ANNEE 1763, SUR CES PAROLES, QUE SEROIT EN FRANCE LE PLAN D'ETUDE LE PLUS AVANTAGEUX? / Navarre, Jean – 1763. 6777 – 9 – fr Hachette [360]

DISCOURS RELIGIEUX / Pressense, Edmond de – Paris: Ch. Meyrueis, 1859 – 1mf – us A.T.L.A. [240]

DISCOURS...: SUBVENTIONS AUX CHEMINS DE FER: RECLAMATIONS DE LA PROVINCE DE QUEBEC (COMPTE RENDU OFFICIEL), CHAMBRE DES COMMUNES, 12 AVRIL 1884 / Chapleau, Joseph Adolphe – (Ottawa: MacLean, Roger), 1884. 02164. (Pre-1900 Canadiana) – 9 – cn C.I.H.M. [971]

DISCOURS SUR LA CASTRAMETATION ET DISCIPLINE MILITAIRE DES ROMAINS; ... / Du Choul, G – Lyon, 1555 – 3mf – 9 – H-8289/1 – ne IDC [355]

DISCOURS SUR LA GUERRE DES FLANDRES / Coligny, Gaspard de – Leyde. A. Maire. 1596. 43p. (Strategy of War Series) – 9 – fr Hachette [355]

DISCOURS SUR LA LOI DE L'INSTRUCTION PUBLIQUE: PRONONCE...DEVANT LE CONSEIL LEGISLATIF, LE 10 JANVIER 1898 / Chapais, Thomas – Quebec?, 1898. 02867. (Pre-1900 Canadiana) – 9 – cn C.I.H.M. [971]

DISCOURS SUR LA LOI DE L'INSTRUCTION PUBLIQUE: PRONONCE...DEVANT LE CONSEIL LEGISLATIF, LES 2 ET 3 MARS 1899 / Chapais, Thomas – Quebec?, 1899. 02866. (Pre-1900 Canadiana) – 9 – cn C.I.H.M. [971]

DISCOURS SUR LA NECESSITE DE L'ETUDE DE L'ARCHITECTURE. / Blondel, Jacques Francois – Paris, Jombert, 1754. 8 fol., 99p. (Architecture Series) – 9 – fr Hachette [720]

DISCOURS SUR LA PEINTURE ET SUR L'ARCHITECTURE. / Du Perron – Paris, Prault, 1758. 8 fol., viii, 75. 4p. (Architecture Series) – 9 – fr Hachette [720]

DISCOURS SUR LA QUESTION DE LA CONFEDERATION, PRONONCE A LA SEANCE DE L'ASSEMBLEE LEGISLATIVE DU 2 MARS 1865 / Cauchon, Joseph – Quebec, 1865? SEM16P121 – 1r – 5 – Can$9.00 – cn Bibl Nat [971]

DISCOURS SUR LA QUESTION RIEL, PRONONCE LE 22 MARS 1886 A LA CHAMBRE DES COMMUNES / Thompson, John S D – SEM35P81 – 1r – 1 – Can$15.00 – cn Bibl Nat [971]

DISCOURS SUR LA SCIENCE DES ETYMOLOGIES / Besnier, Pierre – Paris, 1694 – 1mf – 9 – ne IDC [400]

DISCOURS SUR LA STRUCTURE DES FLEURS / Vaillant, S – Leiden. 1718. B-7329 2 – 8 – ne IDC [580]

DISCOURS SUR L'ART DE NEGOCIER – Paris, 1737 – 3mf – 1 – ILM-897/1 – ne IDC [327]

DISCOURS SUR L'EDUCATION / Vanier, Ignace – Suive de Second Discours sur l'Education. Paris, 1760-63. 6792 – 9 – fr Hachette [370]

DISCOURS SUR LES CONVENTIONS NATIONALES PRONONCE A L'ASSEMBLEE DES AMIS DE LA CONSTITUTION SEANTE AUX JACOBINS LE 7 AOUT 1791 / Condorcet, Marie Jean Antoine Nicolas de – Paris. Imp. du Cercle Social – 9 – fr Hachette [321]

DISCOURS SUR LES DIFFERENTES FIGURES DES ASTRES AVEC UNE EXPOSITION DES SYSTEMES DE MM. DESCARTES ET NEWTON / Maupertuis, Pierre-Louis M de – Paris, 1732, 83 p. Histoire des Sciences XVIIe-XIXe Siecles. 7969 – 9 – fr Hachette [510]

DISCOURS SUR LES MIRACLES DE JESUS-CHRIST / Woolston, Thomas – (D'Holbach series). 1769 – 9 – fr Hachette [240]

DISCOURS SUR LES REVOLUTIONS DE LA SURFACE DU GLOBE, AVEC DES NOTES ET UN APPENDICE / Cuvier, Georges – 2552 2. 1850 – 8 – ne IDC [520]

DISCOURS SUR LES REVOLUTIONS DE LA SURFACE DU GLOBE ET SUR LES CHANGEMENTS QU'ILS ONT PRODUITS DANS LE REGNE ANIMAL / Cuvier, Georges – Ed. 5. 2551 2. 1828 – 8 – ne IDC [550]

DISCOURS SUR L'ESCLAVAGE DES NEGRES ET SUR L'IDEE DE LEUR AFFRANCHISSEMENT DANS LES COLONIES, PAR UN COLON DE SAINT-DOMINGUE / Duval Sanadon, David – (Slave Trade and Abolitionism in France Series). 1786 – 9 – fr Hachette [360]

DISCOURS SUR L'ETUDE PHILOSOPHIQUE DES LANGUES / Chasseboeuf, Comte de Volney – 1819 – 9 – fr I.C.S. [190]

DISCOURS SUR L'HARMONIE / Gresset, J -B – 1737 – 9 – us Sibley [780]

DISCOURS SUR L'ORIGINE DE LA POESIE / Frain du Tremblay, J – 1713 – 9 – fr I.C.S. [410]

DISCOURS SUR L'OUVRIER PRONONCE PAR LE REVEREND M. COLIN DEVANT L'INSTITUT DES ARTISANS CANADIENS LE 2 AVRIL 1869 / Colin, Frederic Louis de Gonzague – Montreal, 1869. SEM105P39 – 1mf – 9 – Can$2.25 – cn Bibl Nat [331]

DISCOURS SUR L'UNIVERSALITE DE LA LANGUE FRANCAISE / Rivarol, Antoine – Paris: Librairie Hatier, [1929]. SEM105P1156 – 1mf – 9 – Can$2.25 – cn Bibl Nat [440]

DISCOURS TRES-VERITABLE D'UN INSIGNE VOLEUR QUI CONTRE-FAISOIT LE DIABLE – Bayonne. 1609 – 9 – fr Hachette [360]

LE DISCOURS VERITABLE DE LA PRAISE DE LA VILLE DE MAHOMETTE PAR LES CHEVALLIERS DE MALTE – Paris. 1602. 13p. (Historical Studies Series) – 9 – 3.00 – fr Bibl Nationale [900]

DISCOURS VERITABLE DES PROPOS TENUS PAR MONSIEUR LE PRINCE DE CONDE, AUEC LES SEIGNEURS DEPUTEZ PAR LE ROY: CONTENANT LES CAUSES GUI ONT CONTRAINT LEDICT SEIGNEUR PRINCE & AUTRES DE SA COPAGNIE A PRENDRE LES ARMS / Conde, Louis 1st Prince of Bourbon – s.l.: s.n., 1567 – 1 – us U.W. Library [944]

DISCOURS VERITABLE SUR LA FAICT DE MARTHE BROSSIER DE ROMORANTIN / Marescot, Michel – Paris. 1599 – 9 – fr Hachette [360]

DISCOURS...ACCOMPAGNES DE NOTICES PAR JOSEPH TASSE / Cartier, Georges Etienne – Montreal: E. Senecal, 1893. 00497. (Pre-1900 Canadiana) – 9 – cn C.I.H.M. [971]

A DISCOURSE / Eliot, William G – Boston: Crosby, Nichols, 1855 – 1mf – us A.T.L.A. [240]

A DISCOURSE / Grew, N – M-361 2. 1675 – 8 – ne IDC [580]

A DISCOURSE : ON THE INCARNATION OF THE WORD OF GOD / Athanasius, Patriarch of Alexandria – With an English translation and copious analysis by James Ridgway. 1880 – 1 – us A.T.L.A. [240]

DISCOURSE COMMEMORATIVE OF REV. RUFUS ANDERSON, D.D., LL.D. : LATE CORRESPONDING SECRETARY OF THE AMERICAN BOARD OF COMMISSIONERS FOR FOREIGN MISSIONS: TOGETHER WITH ADDRESSES AT THE FUNERAL / Thompson, A C – Boston: American Board of Commissioners for Foreign Missions, 1880 – 1mf – us A.T.L.A. [240]

A DISCOURSE: COMMEMORATIVE OF THE HISTORY OF THE CHURCH OF CHRIST IN YALE COLLEGE / Fisher, George Park – 1858 – 9 – us A.T.L.A. [240]

DISCOURSE DE L'HON. J.A. CHAPLEAU A L'OCCASION DE LA MOTION CENSURANT LE MINISTERE POUR AVOIR PERMIS L'EXECUTION DE LOUIS RIEL / Chapleau, Joseph Adolphe – Montreal: Imp. Generale, 1886. SEM105P40 – 1mf – 9 – Can$2.25 – cn Bibl Nat [971]

DIE DISCOURSE DER MAHLERN / ed by Bodmer, Johann Jakob & Breitinger, Johann Jakob – Zuerich, 1721-23. Hildesheim, 1977 – 11mf – 9 – DM100.00 diazo DM120.00 silver – gw Olms [430]

A DISCOURSE, INVESTIGATING THE DOCTRINE OF WASHING THE SAINTS' FEET / Brookes, Iveson L – 1830. 28p – 1 – us Baptist [240]

A DISCOURSE OF THE COMMON WEAL OF THIS REALM OF ENGLAND / Lamond, Elizabeth – (First printed in 1581 and commonly attributed to "W.S.", this manuscript describes legal and social conditions in Elizabethan England) – Cambridge: at the University Press, 1929 – 3mf – 9 – $4.50 – LLMC 92-150 – us L.L.M.C. [340]

A DISCOURSE OF THE KINGDOM OF CHINA... / Purchas, S – London. v3. 1625-1625 – 2mf – 9 – ne IDC [950]

A DISCOURSE OF THE PLAGUE / Harvey, G – M 367. 1665 – 9 – ne IDC [610]

A DISCOURSE OF THE WHOLE ART OF CHYRURGERIE / Lowe, P – M 376. Ed. 2. 1612 – 9 – ne IDC [617]

A DISCOURSE ON OCCASION OF THE DEATH OF THE REVEREND WILBUR FISK / Bangs, Nathan – 1839 – 9 – us A.T.L.A. [240]

DISCOURSE ON THE HISTORY, CHARACTER, AND PROSPECTS OF THE WEST / Drake, Daniel – 1834 – 9 – 5.00 – us Scholars' Facs [978]

A DISCOURSE ON THE LIFE AND SERVICES OF PROFESSOR MOSES STUART / Adams, William – New York: J.F. Trow, 1852 – 1mf – us A.T.L.A. [240]

A DISCOURSE ON THE LOVE OF OUR COUNTRY, DELIVERED ON NOV. 4, 1789,... / Price, R – London, 1789 – 2mf – 9 – MP-565/1 – ne IDC [240]

A DISCOURSE ON THE SOCIAL INFLUENCE OF CHRISTIANITY / Cushing, Caleb – Andover: Printed by Gould and Newman, 1839 – 1mf – us A.T.L.A. [240]

A DISCOURSE ON THE TRANSIENT AND PERMANENT IN CHRISTIANITY / Parker, Theodore – 1841 – 9 – us A.T.L.A. [240]

A DISCOURSE ON THEOLOGICAL EDUCATION / Howe, George – New York: Leavitt, Trow, 1844 – 1mf – us A.T.L.A. [240]

A DISCOURSE ON TRADE, AND OTHER MATTERS RELATIVE TO IT... / Cary, J – London, 1745 – 3mf – 9 – ne IDC [380]

A DISCOURSE SHEWING THE NATURE OF THE GOUT / Atkins, W – M-289. 1694 – 9 – ne IDC [610]

DISCOURS...EN PROPOSANT LA VENTE DU CHEMIN DE FER QUEBEC, MONTREAL, OTTAWA ET OCCIDENTAL A L'ASSEMBLEE LEGISLATIVE, SEANCES DES 27 ET 28 MARS 1882 / Chapleau, Joseph Adolphe – (Quebec: A. Cote), 1882. 00568. (Pre-1900 Canadiana) – 9 – cn C.I.H.M. [971]

DISCOURSES / Jackson, Abner – 1875 – 9 – us A.T.L.A. [240]

DISCOURSES AND ADDRESSES / Douglas, George – Toronto: W. Briggs, 1894. 02742. (Pre-1900 Canadiana) – 9 – cn C.I.H.M. [971]

DISCOURSES AND DISCUSSIONS IN EXPLANATION AND DEFENCE OF UNITARIANISM / Dewey, Orville – 1840 – 9 – us A.T.L.A. [240]

DISCOURSES AND ESSAYS / Shedd, William Greenough Thayer – (Includes bibliographical references) – [2nd ed]. Andover: Warren F Draper, c1862 – 1mf – 9 – 0-8370-5346-3 – 1985-3346 – us A.T.L.A. [240]

DISCOURSES IN AMERICA / Arnold, Matthew – London: Macmillan, 1885 – 1mf – us A.T.L.A. [240]

DISCOURSES IN AMERICA / Arnold, Matthew – London: Macmillan, 1885 – 1 roll – 1 – 1-55879-165-5 – uk Libr Preservation [800]

DISCOURSES ON HUMAN LIFE / Dewey, Orville – 1841 – 9 – us A.T.L.A. [240]

DISCOURSES ON PHILIPPIANS / Noble, Frederick Alphonso – Chicago: Fleming H Revell, c1896 – 1mf – 9 – 0-8370-4594-0 – 1985-2594 – us A.T.L.A. [220]

DISCOURSES ON PROPHECY : IN WHICH ARE CONSIDERED ITS STRUCTURE, USE AND INSPIRATION: BEING THE SUBSTANCE OF TWELVE SERMONS PREACHED IN THE CHAPEL OF LINCOLN'S INN, IN THE LECTURE FOUNDED BY THE RIGHT REVEREND WILLIAM WARBURTON, BISHOP OF GLOUCESTER / Davison, John – (Includes bibliographical references) – new ed. Oxford: James Parker, 1875 – 1mf – 9 – 0-8370-9458-5 – 1986-3458 – us A.T.L.A. [220]

DISCOURSES ON SOME THEOLOGICAL DOCTRINES AS RELATED TO THE RELIGIOUS CHARACTER / Park, Edwards Amasa – (Includes index) – Andover: Warren F Draper, 1885 – 1mf – 9 – 0-8370-3974-6 – 1985-1974 – us A.T.L.A. [240]

DISCOURSES ON THE UNITY OF GOD, AND OTHER SUBJECTS / Eliot, William G – St. Louis: Printed at the Republican Office, 1852 – 1mf – us A.T.L.A. [240]

DISCOURSES ON VARIOUS SUBJECTS / Dewey, Orville – 1838 – 9 – us A.T.L.A. [240]

DISCOURSES UPON SENECA THE TRAGEDIAN / Cornwallis, William – 1601 – 9 – 10.00 – us Scholars' Facs [450]

DISCOURS...PRONONCE A L'ASSEMBLEE DE SAINT-LAURENT, COMTE DE JACQUES-CARTIER, LE 6 SEPTEMBRE 1883 / Chapleau, Joseph Adolphe – (Montreal: La Minerve), 1883. 00569. (Pre-1900 Canadiana) – 9 – cn C.I.H.M. [971]

DISCOURS...PRONONCE A STE.THERESE, LE 3 NOVEMBRE 1881 / Chapleau, Joseph Adolphe – Montreal, 1881. 02585. (Pre-1900 Canadiana) – 9 – cn C.I.H.M. [971]

DISCOURS...SUR L'EXECUTION DE LOUIS RIEL: CHAMBRE DES COMMUNES, 24 MARS 1886 / Chapleau, Joseph Adolphe – Ottawa: MacLean, Roger, 1886. 00613. (Pre-1900 Canadiana) – 9 – cn C.I.H.M. [971]

DISCOVER MAGAZINE – v.1. 1980 – 1,5,6,9 – us UMI [500]

THE DISCOVERIE OF WITCHCRAFT...BEING A REPRINT OF THE FIRST EDITION PUBLISHED IN 1584 / Scot, Reginald – Ed. with explanatory notes, glossary and introd. by Brinsley Nicholson. London: E. Stock, 1886. xlvii,xxxviii,589p. illus – 1 – us U.W. Library [150]

DISCOVERIES IN ANATOLIA / Von der Osten, Hans Henning – 1933 – 9 – $10.00 – us I.R.C. [930]

THE DISCOVERIES OF THE NORSEMEN IN AMERICA / Fischer, J – 2223 2. 1903 – 8 – ne IDC [910]

DISCOVERY – (Ceased v10 1989) – Colborne. v1-10. 1980-89 – 9 – Can$28.00y – cn Micromedia [073]

DISCOVERY – v. 1-19. 1920-38. N.S. V. 1-27. 1938-66 – 1,5,6 – us Princeton Micro [910]

THE DISCOVERY : A COMEDY / Sheridan, F – London, 1792 – 2mf – 9 – ne IDC [820]

THE DISCOVERY AND CONQUEST OF THE NEW WORLD, CONTAINING THE LIFE AND VOYAGES OF CHRISTOPHER COLUMBUS / Irving, Washington – Toronto: Rose, 1892. 02719. (Pre-1900 Canadiana) – 9 – cn C.I.H.M. [970]

THE DISCOVERY AND CONQUESTS OF THE NORTHWEST : INCLUDING THE EARLY HISTORY OF CHICAGO, DETROIT, VINCENNES, ST. LOUIS, FT. WAYNE, PRAIRIE DU CHIEN, MARIETTA, CINCINNATI, CLEVELAND, ETC. AND INCIDENTS OF PIONEER LIFE IN THE REGION OF THE GREAT LAKES AND THE MISSISSIPPI VALLEY / Blanchard, Rufus – Chicago: Cushing, Thomas, 1880. 00180. (Pre-1900 Canadiana) – 9 – cn C.I.H.M. [978]

DISCOVERY AND EXPLORATION OF THE MISSISSIPPI VALLEY : WITH THE ORIGINAL NARRATIVES OF MARQUETTE, ALLOUEZ, MEMBRE, HENNEPIN, AND ANASTASE DOUAY / Shea, John Dawson Gilmary – New York: Redfield, 1852 – 1mf – us A.T.L.A. [975]

THE DISCOVERY AND EXPLORATION OF THE PELLY (YUKON) RIVER / Campbell, Robert, 1808-94 – 18?? 02020. (Pre-1900 Canadiana) – 9 – cn C.I.H.M. [971]

THE DISCOVERY, CONQUEST, AND ORGANIZATION OF SPANISH AMERICA AND OCEANIA – 239mf – 9 – $720.00 – us UPA [972]

THE DISCOVERY OF A WORLD IN THE MOONE / Wilkins, John – 1638 – 9 – 10.00 – us Scholars' Facs [520]

THE DISCOVERY OF AMERICA AND ISLANDS ADJACENT – 1582. Hakluyt Society – 7 – uk Microform Academic [910]

THE DISCOVERY OF AMERICA BY JOHN CABOT IN 1497, BEING EXTRACTS FROM THE PROCEEDINGS OF THE ROYAL SOCIETY OF CANADA RELATIVE TO A CABOT CELEBRATION IN 1897 : AND, THE VOYAGES OF THE CABOTS, A PAPER FROM THE TRANSACTIONS OF THE SOCIETY IN 1896, WITH APPENDICES ON KINDRED SUBJECTS / Dawson, Samuel Edward – Ottawa?: s.n., 1896 (Ottawa: J. Hope). 02612. (Pre-1900 Canadiana) – 9 – cn C.I.H.M. [971]

THE DISCOVERY OF CHINA'S EARLIEST STORY OF JESUS CHRIST (CCC214) = YEH SU CHI TU TSAI CHUNG-KUO KU CHI CHUNG CHIH FA HSIEN / Li, Sheng-hua & Liu, Ch'u-t'ang – (In Chinese) – [s.l: s.n, 1960] – 1r – 1 – 1984-B500 – us A.T.L.A. [240]

THE DISCOVERY OF LAKE SUPERIOR: A STUDY FROM THE JESUITS JOURNALS / Harvey, Arthur – 1885?. 05251. (Pre-1900 Canadiana) – 9 – cn C.I.H.M. [910]

DISCOVERY OF LAKES RUDOLF AND STEFANIE : A NARRATIVE OF COUNT SAMUEL TELEKI'S EXPLORING AND HUNTING EXPEDITION IN EASTERN EQUATORIAL AFRICA IN 1887 AND 1888 / Hohnel, Ludwig, Ritter von – London. 2v. 1894 – 1r – 1 – us Ross [960]

A DISCOVERY OF THE BARMUDAS / Jourdain, Silvester – 1610 – 9 – 5.00 – us Scholars' Facs [972]

DISCOVERY OF THE EMPIRE OF GUIANA / Raleigh, Walter – 1595. Hakluyt Society Extra Series v. 3 – 7 – uk Microform Academic [910]

THE DISCOVERY OF THE NORTHWEST PASSAGE / MacClure, Robert John Le Mesurier – BN 302 2. 1856 – 8 – ne IDC [910]

THE DISCOVERY OF THE NORTH-WEST PASSAGE BY H.M.S. INVESTIGATOR / MacClure, Robert John Le Mesurier – Ed. by S. Osborn from the logs and journals of Capt. R. Le Mesurier MacClure. 4th ed. 1865 – 9 – 20.00 – uk Libr Preservation [910]

DISCOVERY OF TRIPOLI OR POLISHING POWDER NEAR ST JOHN:. / Allison, L C – 1881?. 05936. (Pre-1900 Canadiana) – 9 – cn C.I.H.M. [580]

DISCOVERY PROBLEMS IN CIVIL CASES / Ebersole, Joseph L & Burke, Barlow – Washington: FJC, Apr 1980 – 2mf – 9 – $3.00 – LLMC 95-822 – us L.L.M.C. [340]

DISCOVERY REPORTS / Institute of Oceanographic Sciences. (Great Britain) – 7,9 – uk Microform Academic [910]

DISCOVERY REPORTS / National Institute of Oceanography – 7,9 – uk Microform Academic [910]

DISCOVRS, DE LA BATAILLE NOVVELLEMENT PERDVE PAR LE TVRC, CONTRE LE ROY DE PERSE, 1586 – 1mf – 9 – H-8205/1 – ne IDC [956]

DISCOVRS DE LA GRANDE ET PVISSANTE ARMEE DE SOLTAN SOLYMAN GRAND EMPEREUT DES TURCZ, ... – Paris, 1565 – 1mf – 9 – H-8166/1 – ne IDC [956]

DISCOVRS SVR LA CHRESTIENNE ET GENEREUSE ENTREPRISE DE HAULT ET PUISSANT PRINCE MONSEIGNEUR CHARLES DE LORRAINE, ... CONTRE LE GRAND TURC, EN L'AN 1572 – Paris, 1572 – 1mf – 9 – H-8191/1 – ne IDC [956]

DISCOVRS VERITABLE DES VISIONS ADVENVES AV PREMIER ET SECOND IOUR D'AOUST 1589 A LA PERSONNE DE L'EMPEREUR DES TURCS SULTAN AMURAT, EN LA VILLE DE CONSTANTINOPLE – Paris, [1589] – 1mf – 9 – H-8208/1 – ne IDC [956]

DISCRETE APPLIED MATHEMATICS – v1-9. 1979-84 – 1,5,6,13 – sz Elsevier [073]

DISCRETE MATHEMATICS – v1-52. 1971-84 – 1,5,6,13 – sz Elsevier [073]

DISCURSO / Chaves y Manso, Rafael – Universidad literaria de.... 1851 – 9 – 1.50f – sp Bibl Santa Ana [440]

DISCURSO / Delgado del Pino, Francisco – 1835 – 9 – 1.50f – sp Bibl Santa Ana [946]

DISCURSO.. / Olabarrieta, Francisco de – 1834 – 9 – 1.50f – sp Bibl Santa Ana [890]

DISCURSO ANTISOFISTICO EXTRACTADO DEL HOMBRE / Forner Segarra, Juan Pablo – 1787 – 9 – 1.50f – sp Bibl Santa Ana [840]

DISCURSO DE CLAUSURA PRONUNCIADO POR EL EXCMO. SR. OBISPO DE BADAJOZ EL... 1907 / Soto y Mancera, Felix – Badajoz: Tip. Lit. y Enc. de Uceda Hnos – 1 – sp Bibl Santa Ana [240]

DISCURSO DE COSAS AROMATICAS...DE LAS INDIAS...PARA USO DE MEDICINAS / Fragoso, J – Madrid, 1572 – 8mf – 9 – sp Cultura [615]

DISCURSO DE LA RAZON / Pizarro de Aragon, Juan – Madrid: Francisco Martinez, 1629 – 1 – sp Bibl Santa Ana [100]

DISCURSO DE RECEPCION...EN LA ACADEMIA DE LA HISTORIA : TEMA: EL CONQUISTADOR ESPANOL, LOS FUNDADORES DE NUESTRA SENORA DE LA PAZ, DE TRUJILLO. CACERES, 1930 / Briceno-Iregorry, Mario – Madrid: Razon y Fe, 1930 – 1 – sp Bibl Santa Ana [240]

DISCURSO DE S.S....ALAS CONFERENCIAS DE SAN VICENTE DE PAUL (EN LA AUDIENCIA DE 27 DE ABRIL DE 1952) – Caceres: Tip. Extremadura, s.a. – 1 – sp Bibl Santa Ana [240]

DISCURSO DE...AUDIENCIA DE CACERES / Penalver, Nicolas – 1853 – 9 – 1.50f – sp Bibl Santa Ana [340]

DISCURSO DEL COMETA DEL ANO 1680 / Aldrete y Soto, L – Madrid, S.A. – 1mf – 9 – sp Cultura [100]

DISCURSO DEL COMETA INOCENTE... / Gamez, A – Napoles, 1681 – 2mf – 9 – sp Cultura [100]

UN DISCURSO DEL DR. GOEBBELS, MINISTRO DE PROPAGANDA DE ALEMANIA / Goebbels, Joseph – n.p. 193? Fiche W922. (Blodgett Collection of Spanish Civil War Pamphlets) – 9 – us H.U. College Libr [946]

DISCURSO DEL..., EN DEFENSA DE LOS DICTAMENES DE LOS SIGUIENTES PROYECTOS DE LEY: 1° DE MONTES VECINALES EN MANO COMUN. 2° DE ORDENACION RURAL. 3° REGIMEN DE TIERRAS DEL INSTITUTO NACIONAL DE COLONIZACION / Diaz-Ambrona, Adolfo – Madrid: Suc. Rivadeneyra, 1959 – sp Bibl Santa Ana [946]

DISCURSO DEL GENERALISIMO. NO CABE TRANSACCION IDEALOGICA / Spain. Ministerio del Interior – n.p., 1938. Fiche W843. (Blodgett Collection of Spanish Civil War Pamphlets) – 9 – us H.U. College Libr [946]

DISCURSO DEL PAPA A 20000 OBREROS EL 13 DE JUNIO, DIA DE PENTECOSTES. PLASENCIA / Pio 12. – Ediciones J.D. de A.C., Imprenta La Victoria, s.a. – sp Bibl Santa Ana [240]

DISCURSO DEL PRESIDENTE DEL CONSEJO Y MINISTRO DE DEFENSA, PRONUNCIADO EN MADRID, EL 18 DE JUNIO DE 1938 / Negrin, Juan – Madrid, 1938. Fiche W 1071. (Blodgett Collection of Spanish Civil War Pamphlets) – 9 – us H.U. College Libr [946]

DISCURSO EN EL "GRAN PRICE" DE BARCELONA, EL DIA 17 DE ENERO DE 1937 / Tomas, Pascual – Barcelona, 1937? Fiche W1230. (Blodgett Collection of Spanish Civil War Pamphlets) – 9 – us H.U. College Libr [946]

DISCURSO FILOSOFICO, MEDICO E HISTORIAL...EN DEFENSA DE LA MEDICINA DOGMATICA Y SU SANGRIA... / Gamez, A – Madrid, 1683 – 2mf – 9 – sp Cultura [610]

DISCURSO. GUERRA DE PORTUGAL / Diaz de Vargas, Francisco – 1644 – 9 – 1.50f – sp Bibl Santa Ana [946]

DISCURSO INAUGURAL / Remon de Moncada y Calderon, Jesus – 1856 – 9 – 1.50f – sp Bibl Santa Ana [440]

DISCURSO INAUGURAL PRONUNCIADO POR D. JESUS REUNION DE MONCADA Y CALDERON / Ramon de Moncada y Calderon, Jesus – Badajoz: Geronimo Orduna, 1856 – 1 – sp Bibl Santa Ana [946]

DISCURSO INAUGURAL...ACADEMIA CIENTIFICO / Crespo y Escoriaza, Benito – 1857 – 9 – $1.50f – sp Bibl Santa Ana [500]

DISCURSO LEIDO EN LA APERTURA DEL CURSO ACADEMICO 1943-44 / Hernandez Pacheco, Francisco – Madrid: Estades-Artes Graficas, 1943 – sp Bibl Santa Ana [370]

DISCURSO LEIDO EN LA SOLEMNE INAUGURACION DEL CURSO ACADEMICO 1912 A 1913 / Rivas Mateos, Marcelo – Madrid: Imp. Colonial, 1912 – 1 – sp Bibl Santa Ana [370]

DISCURSO LEIDO POR...ARTES Y OFICIOS DE FREGENAL EN LA SOLEMNE INAUGURACION DE LA MISMA / Real, Enrique – Fregenal: Imp. Indalecio Blanco, s.a. – sp Bibl Santa Ana [946]

DISCURSO MEDICINAL...EN EL QUE SE DECLARA LA HORDEN...PARA PRESERVARSE DE LA PESTE / Franco, M – Cordoba, 1601 – 1mf – 9 – sp Cultura [614]

DISCURSO MEDICO SOBRE EL VERDADERO METODO DE CURAR LAS VIRUELAS... / Adami, A – Sevilla, S.A. – 1mf – 9 – sp Cultura [616]

DISCURSO PARLAMENTARIO / Donoso Cortes, Juan Francisco – Madrid: Imprenta Espn., 1915 – 1 – sp Bibl Santa Ana [350]

DISCURSO PARTICULAR Y PRESERVATIVO DE LA GOTA, EN QUE SE DESCUBRE SU NATURALEZA Y SE PONE SU PROPIA CURA / Cornejo, J – Madris, S.A. – 2mf – 9 – sp Cultura [600]

DISCURSO POLITICO SOBRE LA IMPORTANCIA DE LOS HOSPICIOS, CASAS DE EXPOSITOS CON Y HOSPITALES / Murcia, P J de – Madrid, 1798 – 3mf – 9 – sp Cultura [360]

DISCURSO PRONUNCIADO : EN EL ACTO DE LA ENTREGA DEL DESPACHO POR EL CUAL SE PROMUEVE AL GRADO DE GENERAL DE DIVISION AL EXCMO. SENOR PRESIDENTE DE LA NACION, GENERAL JUAN PERON / Campora, Hector Jose – Buenos Aires: [s.n.], 1950 – 1 – CSUXADH8395-B – us Hoover Inst Photo [320]

DISCURSO PRONUNCIADO 8 NOVIEMBRE DE 1888 / Canovas del Castillo, Antonio – Madrid, 1888 – 1 – us Res Libr [946]

DISCURSO PRONUNCIADO EN LA COLABORACION DE GRADOS DE LICENCIADOS EN JURISPRUDENCIA... / Gomez Jara, Francisco – Sevilla: Imprenta del Regalo, 1850 – 1 – sp Bibl Santa Ana [340]

DISCURSO PRONUNCIADO EN LA SOCIEDAD PATRIOTICA CONSTITUCIONAL DE BADAJOZ EL DIA 9 DE JULIO DE 1820 / Rocha, Manuel de la – Badajoz: Imp. de Capitania General, 1820 – 1 – sp Bibl Santa Ana [350]

DISCURSO PRONUNCIADO POR EL EXCMO. SR. GOBERNADOR CIVIL-PRESIDENTE...EN LA REUNION...25 DE FEBRERO DE 1950 / Ruiz de la Serna, Manuel – Badajoz: Graficas Iberia, 1950 – 1 – sp Bibl Santa Ana [320]

DISCURSO PRONUNCIADO POR EL OBRERO EN EL CIRCULO CATOLICO DE VILLAFRANCA DE LOS BARROS EL DIA 8 DE DICIEMBRE DE 1906 / Diez Lopez, Juan – Villafranca de los Barros: Imp. Ventura Rodriguez, 1906 – 1 – sp Bibl Santa Ana [240]

DISCURSO PRONUNCIADO POR EL PRESIDENTE DEL CONSEJO ECONOMICO NACIONAL EN LA LIGA POR LOS DERECHOS DEL TRABAJADOR, BUENOS AIRES, AGOSTO 5, 1949 / Cereijo, Ramon Antonio – [Buenos Aires, 1949?] – 1 – CSUXADM9637-B – us Hoover Inst Photo [320]

DISCURSO PRONUNCIADO POR LUIS COMPANYS EL DIA 27 DE DICIEMBRE DE 1936 EN EL PALACIO DE BELLAS ARTES DE BARCELONA, CON MOTIVO DEL 3 ANIVERSARIO DEL FALLICIMIENTO DE FRANCISCO MACIA / Companys, Lluis – Barcelona, 1937? Fiche W1503. (Blodgett Collection of Spanish Civil War Pamphlets) – 9 – us H.U. College Libr [946]

DISCURSO PRONUNCIADO POR...EL 30 DE NOVIEMBRE DE 1881 EN EL ATENEO CIENTIFICO Y LITERARIO DE MADRID CON MOTIVO DE LA APERTURA DE SUS CATEDRAS / Moreno Nieto, Jose – Madrid: Imp. Central a cargo de Victor Saiz, 1881 – 1 – sp Bibl Santa Ana [946]

DISCURSO PRONUNCIADO POR...EL DIA 8 DE NOVIEMBRE DE 1877 EN EL ATENEO CIENTIFICO LITERARIO DE MADRID, CON MOTIVO DE LA APERTURA DE SUS CATEDRAS / Moreno Nieto, Jose – Madrid: Empresa del Boletin Oficial del Ateneo, 1877 – 1 – sp Bibl Santa Ana [946]

DISCURSO PRONUNCIADO POR...EL DIA 10 DE NOVIEMBRE DE 1880 EN EL ATENEO CIENTIFICO Y LITERARIO DE MADRID CON MOTIVO DE LA APERTURA DE SUS CATEDRAS / Moreno Nieto, Jose – Madrid: Imp. Central a cargo de V. Saiz, 1880 – 1 – sp Bibl Santa Ana [946]

DISCURSO PRONUNCIADO POR...EL DIA 31 DE OCTUBRE DE 1878 EN EL ATENEO CIENTIFICO Y LITERARIO DE MADRID CON MOTIVO DE LA APERTURA DE SUS CATEDRAS / Moreno Nieto, Jose – Madrid: Empresa del Bol. del Ateneo, 1878 – 1 – sp Bibl Santa Ana [946]

DISCURSO PRONUNCIADO...SOBRE EL PROYECTO DE REFORMA AGRARIA / Teixeira, Antonio – 1931 – 1 – sp Bibl Santa Ana [630]

DISCURSO QUE...PRONUNCIO EL 23 DE ABRIL. / Alvarado, Manuel – 1821 – 9 – 1.50f – sp Bibl Santa Ana [946]

DISCURSO SOBRE ALGUNAS PROPOSICIONES DEL DOCTOR LUYS DE MERCADO / Lopez Coronel, P – SL, 1611 – 1mf – 9 – sp Cultura [610]

DISCURSO SOBRE EL CHARLATANISMO MEDICO Y QUIRURGICO... / Arguello Castrillo, A – Valladolid, 1796 – 3mf – 9 – sp Cultura [610]

DISCURSO SOBRE EL FOMENTO DE LA INDUSTRIA POPULAR / Rodriguez Campomanes, Pedro – 1774 – 1mf – 9 – Pta1,000.00 – 84-7848-348-9 – sp Pentalfa [338]

DISCURSO SOBRE LA EDUCACION POPULAR DE LOS ARTESANOS / Rodriguez Campomanes, Pedro – 1775 – 2mf – 9 – Pta1,500.00 – 84-7848-349-7 – sp Pentalfa [370]

DISCURSO SOBRE LAS PENAS CRIMINALES EN ESPANA / Lardizabal Uribe, Manuel – 1782 – 1mf – 9 – Pta1,000.00 – 84-7848-315-2 – sp Pentalfa [360]

DISCURSO SOBRE QUE LOS NINOS EXPOSITOS CONSIGAN EN LAS INCLUSAS EL FIN DE ESTOS ESTABLECIMIENTOS / Trespalacios y Mier, J – Madrid, 1798 – 1mf – 9 – sp Cultura [360]

DISCURSO Y SUMARIO DE LA GUERRA EN PORTUGAL / Diaz de Vargas, Francisco – Zaragoza: Pedro Vargas, 1644 – 1 – sp Bibl Santa Ana [946]

DISCURSO...6 NOVIEMBRE DE 1822...APERTURA DE LA UNIVERSIDAD...BADAJOZ / Rocha, Manuel de la – Imp. de la comandancia general, 1822 – 1 – sp Bibl Santa Ana [946]

DISCURSO...ACADEMIA DE LA HISTORIA / Barrantes Moreno, Vicente – 1872 – 9 – 1.50f – sp Bibl Santa Ana [946]

DISCURSO...ACADEMIA DE LA HISTORIA / Barrantes Moreno, Vicente – 1874 – 9 – 1.50f – sp Bibl Santa Ana [946]

DISCURSO...APERTURA DE CURSO SOBRE LA IMPORTANCIA DEL CATOLICISMO / Guillen y Flores, Agustin – 1857 – 9 – 1.50f – sp Bibl Santa Ana [240]

DISCURSO...APERTURA DE CURSO...CACERES / Ollero, Meliton – 1849 – 9 – 1.50f – sp Bibl Santa Ana [440]

DISCURSO...AUDIENCIA...CACERES. .BI.-1838 / Miguel Sanchez & Paula, Francisco de – 9 – 1.50f – sp Bibl Santa Ana [850]

DISCURSO...CATEDRAS / Moreno Nieto, Jose – 1876 – 9 – 1.50f – sp Bibl Santa Ana [440]

DISCURSO...CIENCIAS MORALES / Fernandez de Soria, Rafael – 1862 – 9 – 1.50f – sp Bibl Santa Ana [170]

DISCURSO...CURSO / Muela, Jose de la – 1848 – 9 – 1.50f – sp Bibl Santa Ana [440]

DISCURSO...DE LAS SESIONES DEL ANO 1853 EN LA REAL ACADEMIA DE MEDICINA... / Nieto y Serrano, M – Madrid, 1853 – 1mf – 9 – sp Cultura [610]

DISCURSO...DEL SARAMPION Y VIRUELAS... / Samillan, L – Montilla, 1626 – 1mf – 9 – sp Cultura [616]

DISCURSO...DISTRIBUCION DE PREMIOS / Redondo y Poblacion, Pedro – 1892 – 9 – 1.50f – sp Bibl Santa Ana [946]

DISCURSO..."EL TRATAMIENTO ANTIPARASITO DE LA TUBERCULOSIS Y LA LINFA DE KOCH" / Miguel y Guerra, Regino de – Badajoz: Tip. Lit. y Enc. La Industria, 1891 – 1 – sp Bibl Santa Ana [616]

DISCURSO...NOBLEZA...ESPANA / Moreno de Vargas, Bernabe – (1659 ed.1.50f; 9. 1795 ed.1.50f; BSA; 9) – 1622 ed – 9 – 1.50f – sp Bibl Santa Ana [946]

DISCURSO...PEDRO CALDERON / Fuertes Acevedo, Maximo – 1881 – 9 – $1.50f – sp Bibl Santa Ana [440]

DISCURSO-POLITICO...COLERO NORBO / Gomez, Florencio – 1834 – 9 – 1.50f – sp Bibl Santa Ana [946]

DISCURSOS / Elviro Meseguer, Francisco – Toledo: Dip. Provincial, 1961 – sp Bibl Santa Ana [946]

DISCURSOS / Fernandez-Ouesta, Raimundo – Gijon. 1939? Fiche W 880. (Blodgett Collection of Spanish Civil War Pamphlets) – 9 – us H.U. College Libr [946]

DISCURSOS / Tenorio Cordero de Santoyo, Miguel – 1841, 1843 – 9 – 1.50f – sp Bibl Santa Ana [946]

DISCURSOS.. / Moreno Nieto, Jose – 1877 – 9 – 1.50f – sp Bibl Santa Ana [440]

DISCURSOS.. / Moreno Nieto, Jose – 1879 – 9 – 1.50f – sp Bibl Santa Ana [440]

DISCURSOS.. / Moreno Nieto, Jose – 1880 – 9 – 1.50f – sp Bibl Santa Ana [440]

DISCURSOS.. / Moreno Nieto, Jose – 1881 – 9 – 1.50f – sp Bibl Santa Ana [440]

DISCURSOS, 1973-74 *see* TODOS SUS DISCURSOS, MENSAJES Y CONFERENCIAS COMPLETOS, 1973-1974

DISCURSOS A LOS ASTURIANOS DE AMERICA – Buenos Aires, 1937. Fiche W 844. (Blodgett Collection of Spanish Civil War Pamphlets) – 9 – us H.U. College Libr [946]

DISCURSOS A LOS VASCOS DE AMERICA / Ibarguren, Carlos – Buenos Aires, 1937. Fiche W952. (Blodgett Collection of Spanish Civil War Pamphlets) – 9 – us H.U. College Libr [946]

DISCURSOS ACADEMICOS DEL.. / Moreno Nieto, Jose – 1882 – 9 – 1.50f – sp Bibl Santa Ana [440]

DISCURSOS DE LA NOBLEZA DE ESPANA / Moreno de Vargas, Bernabe – Corregidos y anadidos por el mismo autor. Madrid, Imprenta de Don Antonio Espinosa, 1795 – 1 – sp Bibl Santa Ana [946]

DISCURSOS DE LA NOBLEZA DE ESPANA / Moreno de Vargas, Bernabe – Madrid: Jose Fernandez Buendia, 1659 – 1 – sp Bibl Santa Ana [946]

DISCURSOS DE...SOBRE CUESTIONES DE CARACTER POLITICO...LEGISLATURA DE 1864-65 / Claros, Jose Ma de – 1865 – 9 – 1.50f – sp Bibl Santa Ana [320]

DISCURSOS ELOCUENTES Y POLITICOS / Nipho, Francisco Mariano – 1755 – 1mf – 9 – Pta1,000.00 – 84-7848-165-6 – sp Pentalfa [320]

DISCURSOS EN DEFENSA DE LA RELIGION CATHOLICA / Farfan de los Godos, Antonio – 1623 – 9 – 1.50f – sp Bibl Santa Ana [240]

DISCURSOS ERUDITOS DE INGENIOS ESPANOLES / Nipho, Francisco Mariano – 1764 – 1mf – 9 – Pta1,000.00 – 84-7848-166-4 – sp Pentalfa [946]

DISCURSOS EVANGELICOS / Gomez, Antonio – (1698 ed.1.50f; 9) – 1688 – 9 – 1.50f – sp Bibl Santa Ana [240]

DISCURSOS FILOSOFICOS SOBRE EL HOMBRE / Forner Segarra, Juan Pablo – 1787 – 2mf – 9 – Pta1,500.00 – 84-7848-196-6 – sp Pentalfa [100]

DISCURSOS FILOSOFICOS SOBRE EL HOMBRE / Forner Segarra, Juan Pablo – 1787 – 9 – $1.50f – sp Bibl Santa Ana [190]

DISCURSOS FORENSES / Malendez Valdes, Juan – 1821 – 9 – 1.50f – sp Bibl Santa Ana [340]

DISCURSOS LEIDOS ANTE LA REAL ACADEMIA DE LA HISTORIA EN LA RECEPCION...EL 14 DE ENERO DE 1872 CON UN BIOGRAFIA DE ESTE / Barrantes Moreno, Vicente – Madrid: Imp. Julian Pena, 3rd ed. 1873 – 1 – sp Bibl Santa Ana [946]

DISCURSOS LEIDOS ANTE LA REAL ACADEMIA ESPANOLA EN LA RECEPCION PUBLICA DE.... : NOTICIAS SOBRE DON LUIS ZAPATA, CONTESTACION DE DON FRANCISCO RODRIGUEZ MARIN / Menendez Pidal, Juan – Madrid: Tip. Rev. Arch. B. y Museos, 1915 – 1 – sp Bibl Santa Ana [370]

DISCURSOS LEIDOS ANTE LA REAL ACADEMIA SEVILLANA DE BUENAS LETRAS EL 3 DE ENERO DE 1897 / Perez de Guzman y Boza, Manuel & Rodriguez Marin, Francisco – Sevilla: Imp. E. Rasco, 1897 – 1 – sp Bibl Santa Ana [370]

DISCURSOS LEIDOS EN EL ACTO DE REPARTO DE PREMIOS...ORGANIZADO POR EL EXCMO. AYUNTAMIENTO / Villafranca de los Barros – Villafranca de los Barros: Ventura Rodriguez, impresor, 1928 – 1 – sp Bibl Santa Ana [946]

DISCURSOS LEIDOS...CIENCIAS MORALES Y POLITICAS / Concha Castaneda, Juan de la – 1888 – 9 – $1.50f – sp Bibl Santa Ana [170]

DISCURSOS LEIDOS...SAN BENITO DE VILLANUEVA / Fernandez Valbuena, Ramiro – 1886 – 9 – 1.50f – sp Bibl Santa Ana [240]

DISCURSOS MERCURIALES, NO 7 AL 13 / Graef, Juan Enrique – 1756 – 2mf – 9 – Pta1,500.00 – 84-7848-181-8 – sp Pentalfa [660]

DISCURSOS PATRIOS...BADAJOZ / Dosma Delgado, Rodrigo – (1870 ed.1.50f; 9) – 1601 – 9 – 1.50f – sp Bibl Santa Ana [946]

DISCURSOS PHYSICO-MEDICO, POLITICO-MORAL QUE TRATAN SER TODA CALENTURA HECTICA CONTAGIOSA / Cerdan, F – Valencia, 1752 – 4mf – 9 – sp Cultura [610]

DISCURSOS POLITICOS Y MORALES EN CARTAS APOLOGETICAS CONTRA LOS QUE DEFIENDEN EL VSO DE LA COMEDIAS MODERNAS QUE SE REPRESENTAN EN ESPANA, EN COMPARACION DEL TEATRO ANTIGUO... / Navarro Castellanos, Gonzalo – Madrid: Impr. Real, 1684- – 1 – us U.W. Library [440]

DISCURSOS...ACADEMIA ESPANOLA / Barrantes Moreno, Vicente – 1876 – 9 – 1.50f – sp Bibl Santa Ana [946]

DISCURSOS...ACADEMIA SEVILLANA DE BUENAS LETRAS / Perez de Guzman, Juan – 1897 – 9 – 1.50f – sp Bibl Santa Ana [440]

DISCURSOS...ACADEMIA...MANUEL DE LO PALACIO / Barrantes Moreno, Vicente – 9 – 1.50f – sp Bibl Santa Ana [946]

DISCURSOS...CONGRESO DE LOS DIPUTADOS.. / Bravo Murillo, Juan – 1858 – 9 – 1.50f – sp Bibl Santa Ana [946]

DISCURSOS...DE LA REAL ACADEMIA DE MEDICINA Y CIRUGIA DE MADRID EN EL ANO. 1861 / Nieto y Serrano, M – Madrid, 1861 – 1mf – 9 – sp Cultura [610]

DISCURSO...SEGUNDA ENSENANZA DE CACERES / Sergio Sanchez, Luis – 1846 – 9 – 1.50f – sp Bibl Santa Ana [920]

DISCURSOS...NOBLEZA / Moreno de Vargas, Bernabe – 1636 – 9 – 1.50f – sp Bibl Santa Ana [946]

DISCURSO...SOBRE LA EPIDEMIA DE PAMPLONA / Ortiz, M – Pamplona, 1789 – 4mf – 9 – sp Cultura [614]

DISCURSO...SOCIEDAD...BADAJOZ / Rocha, Manuel de la – 1820 – 9 – 1.50f – sp Bibl Santa Ana [440]

DISCURSOS...PRONUNCIADOS...1951 AL 1952 / Cortines, Ruiz – 1 – us Res Libr [972]

DISCURSO...TRATAMIENTO...TUBERCULOSIS / Miguel y Guerra, Regino de – 1891 – 9 – 1.50f – sp Bibl Santa Ana [610]

DISCURSO...UNIVERSIDAD.. / Rocha, Manuel de la – 1822 – 9 – 1.50f – sp Bibl Santa Ana [440]

DISCURSUS...MYSTERIA FIDEI / Ovando, Juan de – 1593 – 9 – 1.50f – sp Bibl Santa Ana [240]

DISCUSSING CHRISTIANITY WITH CHAN AND TSEN (CCC12) = YU CH'EN TU-SIU SHEN HSUAN-LU PIEN TAO / Chang, I-Ching – (In Chinese) – Canton: China Baptist Publication Society, 1923 – 1r – 1 – 0-8370-1712-2 – 1984-6091 – us A.T.L.A. [240]

DISCUSSION – A journal for free spirits. Ed., Laurance Labadie. v1,no.6-7, 1937. 38p. Extensive monetary freedom discussion – 9 – 1.00f – at Libertarian Micro [335]

A DISCUSSION OF THE CONSTITUTIONALITY OF THE ACT OF CONGRESS OF MARCH 2, 1867, AUTHORIZING THE SEIZURE OF BOOKS AND PAPERS FOR ALLEGED FRAUDS UPON THE REVENUE. / Eaton, Sherburne Blake – New York, Chamber of Commerce, 1874. 56 p. LL-56 – 1 – us L of C Photodup [340]

DISCUSSION PAPER / Wisconsin. Land Tenure Center – 1963-Aug 1965. n.1-5 – 1,5 – us Spaulding [630]

DISCUSSIONE – 1987-1995 – 1r per y – 5,6 – Sfr401.00 – sz Infoprint [072]

DISCUSSIONI E DOCUMENTI DI STORIA FRANCESCANA... / Cresi, Domenico – Madrid: Arch. Ibero Americano, 1959 – 1 – sp Bibl Santa Ana [240]

DISCUSSIONS / Faraday Society. London – v1-58 1947-74 – 1,5,6 – us Princeton Micro [500]

DISCUSSIONS AND ARGUMENTS ON VARIOUS SUBJECTS / Newman, John Henry – London: Pickering, 1873 – 1mf – us A.T.L.A. [240]

DISCUSSIONS IN CHURCH POLITY : FROM THE CONTRIBUTIONS TO THE "PRINCETON REVIEW" / Hodge, Charles – New York: Scribner, c1878 – 2mf – us A.T.L.A. [240]

DISCUSSIONS IN HISTORY AND THEOLOGY / Fisher, George Park – New York: Scribner, 1880 – 2mf – us A.T.L.A. [240]

DISCUSSIONS ON CHURCH PRINCIPLES : POPISH, ERASTIAN, AND PRESBYTERIAN / Cunningham, William – Edinburgh: T.& T. Clark, 1863. (The Works of William Cunningham / edited by his literary executors; v.4) – 2mf – us A.T.L.A. [240]

DISCUTION UNIVERSELLE DE TOUS LES ARTICLES DU TRAITE DE LA BARRIERE DES PAYS-BAS... – Anvers, 1715, 1716 – 1mf – 1 – ILM-1206/1 – ne IDC [327]

DISEASE CONTROL IN SEMEN AND EMBRYOS – 1981 – 103p – it F.A.O. [616]

DISEASE MARKERS – 1983- – 1,5,6,9 – us UMI [616]

THE DISEASE OF GOVERNMENT / Ferns, H S – 1978. 1 fiche (29x) – 9 – 1.00f – at Libertarian Micro [320]

DISEASE OF THE COLON AND RECTUM – v1-17. 1958-74. 1; v18-33. 1975-90. 5,6,9 – us UMI [616]

DISEASES OF THE BIBLE / Bennet, James Risdon – London: Religious Tract Society, 1891. 1 fiche – 9 – us A.T.L.A. [240]

DISEASES OF THE COLON AND RECTUM – v34-39. 1991-96 – 6r – $95.00r – us Williams [616]

DISEASES OF THE HEART AND AORTA / Stokes, W – M 76. 1854 – 9 – ne IDC [610]

DISEASES OF THE NERVOUS SYSTEM – (v25-38. 1964-77 5,6. v31-38. 1970-77. 9. See also: Journal of Clinical Psychiatry) – v1-38. 1940-77 – 1 – us UMI [616]

DISEASES OF THE TEETH: THEIR DIAGNOSES AND TREATMENT / Marshall, John Albert – 1926 – 1 – us Res Libr [617]

DISEBERANG DJEMBATAN EMAS; DONGENG MODEREN / Gazaldun – SE-5066 1. 1963 – 9 – ne IDC [950]

DISEGNO PARTITO IN PIU RAGIONAMENTI, NE QUALI SI TRATTA DELLA SCOLTURA ET PITTURA / Doni, A F – O-1034 1. 1549 – 9 – ne IDC [730]

DISERTACION CHIRURGICA RELATIVA AL GOBIERNO POLITICO EN LA QUE SE PROPONEN LOS DANOS DE LA CASTRACION VULGAR SEGUN SE PRACTICA PARA CURAR NINOS QUEBRADOS / Arguello Castrillo, A – Madrid, 1775 – 1mf – 9 – sp Cultura [617]

DISERTACION EUCARISTICA SOBRE LA PRECISA OBLIGACION DE RECIBIR TODO ENFERMO LA SAGRADA EUCARISTIA EN AYUNO / Custodio, M – Sevilla, 1779 – 1mf – 9 – sp Cultura [240]

DISERTACION FISICO-LEGAL DE LOS SITIOS... PARA SEPULTURAS / Fernandez, F – Madrid, 1783 – 3mf – 9 – sp Cultura [614]

DISERTACION FISICO-MEDICA..., PARA PRESERVAR...DE VIRUELA / Gil, F – Madrid, 1784 – 3mf – 9 – sp Cultura [616]

DISERTACION PHYSICO-MEDICA DE LAS VIRTUDES MEDICINALES, USO Y ABUSO DE LAS AGUAS TERMALES DE LA VILLA DE ARCHENA / Cerdan, F – Orihuela, 1760 – 8mf – 9 – sp Cultura [610]

DISERTACIONES HISTORICAS SOBRE LOS TEMPLARIOS / Rodriguez Campomanes, Pedro – 1747 – 1mf – 9 – Pta1,000.00 – 84-7848-352-7 – sp Pentalfa [780]

DISESTABLISHMENT IN FRANCE / Sabatier, Paul – London: T.F. Unwin, 1906 – 1mf – us A.T.L.A. [944]

Dishman, Rodney K *see*
- THE EFFECT OF ACUTE EXERCISE ON STATE ANXIETY AND ACOUSTIC STARTLE EYEBLINK RESPONSE IN PHYSICALLY ACTIVE AND INACTIVE MEN
- RATINGS OF PERCEIVED EXERTION AS A DETERMINANT OF PHYSICAL ACTIVITY IN 9 TO 11 YEAR-OLD CHILDREN
- THE RELATIONSHIP OF AEROBIC FITNESS, TYPE A BEHAVIOR PATTERN, AND HOSTILITY TO BAROREFLEX RESPONSES AND CARDIOVASCULAR REACTIVITY TO NONEXERTIONAL STRESSORS

THE DISINTEGRATION OF CANADA / Bender, Prosper – Boston, 18??. 03570. (Pre-1900 Canadiana) – 9 – cn C.I.H.M. [971]

DISKRIMINIERUNG AM ARBEITSMARKT : AUSGEWAEHLTE ERKLAERUNGSANSAETZE MIT BESONDERER BERUECKSICHTIGUNG DER FRAUENDISKRIMINIERUNG / Djumena, Sascha – 1993 – 1mf – 9 – DM60.00 – 3-89349-774-9 – gw Hänsel [331]

DISKUSSII A 1925 GODA : MATERIALY I DOKUMENTY / ed by Popova, K A – Moskva: Gos. izd-vo, 1929 – 1 – CSUX89-B1103 – us Hoover Inst Photo [947]

DISKUSSIONY I LISTOK : ROSSI ISKAI A KOMMUNISTICHESKAI A PARTII A (BOLSHEVIKOV) – (Library has: Jan., Feb. 1921) – Moskva: Izd. T S.K.R.K.P. (b)., 19uu – 1 – CSUX90-S346 – us Hoover Inst Photo [320]

DISLEXIAS : CONCEPTOS FUNDAMENTALES CLINICA / Gutierrez Gomez, Diego & Pelaez Lorenzo, Luis – Badajoz: Imprenta Provincial, 1969. Ponencia a la V Reunion anual de la Sociedad espanola de neuropsiquiatria infantil – sp Bibl Santa Ana [616]

THE DISMAL STATE OF THE NATION : WITH REMARKS ON THE ARTICLES OF GERTRUYDENBERG AND UTRECHT – London, 1715 – 1mf – 1 – ILM-2338/1 – ne IDC [327]

DISPARERI IN MATERIA D'ARCHITETTURA ET PERSPETTIVA / Bassi, M – O-1003 1. 1572 – 9 – ne IDC [730]

DES DISPARITES REGIONALES ET ETHNIQUES DANS L'ENSEIGNEMENT SUPERIEUR RWANDAIS : ESSAI DE CORRECTION / Rwanda. Ministere de l'Enseignement Superieur et de la Recherche Scientifique – Kigali, 1988 – 1mf – 9 – DE-623/1 – ne IDC [370]

DISPATCH – Brainerd. Minn. -w. 1883-1901 – 1 – us UMI [071]

DISPATCH – Clay Center. Kan. -d. 1956- – 1 – us UMI [071]

DISPATCH – Clay Center. Kan. -w. 1876-1917 – 1 – us UMI [071]

DISPATCH – Cordele, GA. 1950-84 – 1 – us UMI [071]

DISPATCH – Dufur. Or. 1910-1941 – 1 – us UMI [071]

DISPATCH – Gilroy. Calif. 1949-58 – 1 – us UMI [071]

DISPATCH – Hiawatha. Kan. 1876-1882 – 1 – us UMI [071]

DISPATCH – Hoisington. Kan. 1889-1930 – 1 – us UMI [071]

DISPATCH – Keokuk. Iowa. -w. 1854-55 – 1 – us UMI [071]

DISPATCH – Lexington. Ky. 1890- – 1 – us UMI [071]

DISPATCH – Moline. Ill. 1897- – 1 – us UMI [071]

DISPATCH – New Kensington. Pa. 1892- – 1 – us UMI [071]

DISPATCH – Oneida. N.Y. -w. 1900-28 – 1 – us UMI [071]

DISPATCH – Peterborough, 1845-1852 – 2r – 1 – cn Preston [971]

DISPATCH – Pittsburg. Calif. 1917-18; 1923-30 – 1 – us UMI [071]

DISPATCH – Richmond. Va. 1852-1903 – 1 – us UMI [071]

DISPATCH – Richton. Miss. 1936-1944; 1946-1952 – 1 – us UMI [071]

DISPATCH – Sparks, NV. 1905 – 1r – 1 – $50.00 – U04744 – us Library Micro [071]

DISPATCH – Wadsworth, NV. 1892-1904 – 13r – 1 – $650.00 – U04801 – us Library Micro [071]

DISPATCH – Wytheville. Va. 1884-1898 – 1 – us UMI [071]

THE DISPATCH – Lexington. N.C. 1903- – 1 – us UMI [071]

DISPATCH DEMOCRAT – Ukiah, CA. 1900-20; 1933 – 7r – 1 – $350.00 – B03048 – us Library Micro [071]

DISPATCH NEWS – Parkersburg. West Virginia. 1909-1914 – 1 – us UMI [071]

DISPATCH NEWS – Staunton. Va. 1908-1909; 1912 – 1 – us UMI [071]

DISPATCHER – San Francisco. Calif. -w. 1952-66 – 1 – us UMI [071]

THE DISPATCHER – San Francisco, CA. 1942- – 12+ r – 1 – $600.00 ($50.00y) – C02811 – us Library Micro [071]

THE DISPATCHES AND LETTERS OF VICE ADMIRAL LORD VISCOUNT NELSON, WITH NOTES BY SIR N.H. NICOLAS / Nelson, Horatio – 7v. 1844-46 – 9 – $280.00 – uk Libr Preservation [920]

DISPERSION AND SELF-PURIFICATION OF POLLUTANTS IN SURFACE WATER SYSTEMS : A CONTRIBUTION TO THE INTERNATIONAL HYDROLOGICAL PROGRAMME / Whitehead, PG & Lack, T – 1982 – 98p – 9 – 92-3-102049-8 – fr UNESCO [628]

DISPERSION AND UNITY – 1969-74. Superseded by Forum on the Jewish People, Zionism and Israel – 1 – us UMI [290]

DISPLACED PERSONS / U.S. Army. Office of the Chief Historian, European Command – 1947 – 1 – 18.00 – us L of C Photodup [940]

DISPLAY AND IMAGING / ed by Archambault, R T et al – 1,5,9 – in prep – us Gordon [073]

A DISPLAY OF THE BAD PRINCIPLES OF THE METHODISTS, IN CERTAIN ARTICLES PROPOSED TO THE SERIOUS CONSIDERATION OF THE WORSHIPFUL COMPANY OF SALTERS IN LONDON / Free, J – London, 2nd ed 1759 – 1mf – 9 – MP-377/1 – ne IDC [240]

A DISPLAY UNIT – Pattee, University Park, PA. 1989 – 56p 3mf – 9 – $0.50f – us Lawrence Pub [720]

DISPLAY WORLD *see* VISUAL MERCHANDISING

DISPOSAL REGISTERS / U.S. National Archives and Records Service – 3rolls. T820 – 1 – us Nat'l Archives [324]

DISPOSICIONES COMPLEMENTARIAS DE LAS LEYES DE INDIAS / Spain. Laws, Statutes, etc – 1930 – 1 – us U.W. Library [946]

DISPOSITIEN DER MERKWAARDIGSTE KERK-ORGELEN, WELKEN IN DE PROVINCIE FRIESLAND, GRONINGEN EN ELDERS AANGETROFFEN WORDEN / Knock, N A – Kunnende dit werk verstrekken tot een vervolg van het werk van den heer J. Hess. Groningen. 1788. BP-348 1 – 9 – ne IDC [780]

DISPOSITIEN DER MERKWAARDIGSTE KERK-ORGELEN, WELKEN IN DE ZEVEN VEREEENIGDE PROVINCIEN ALS MEDE IN DUYTSLAND EN ELDERS AANGETROFFEN WORDEN / Hess, J – Gouda. 1774. BP-696 1 – 9 – ne IDC [780]

DISPOSITIO METHODICA SPECIERUM SCANDINAVICARUM AD FAMILIAS HYMENOPTERORUM NATURALES PERTINENTIUM / Dahlbom, A G – Lundae, 1842. Pt.1, iv,16p. 1 pl. Pt.2-4, Lundae, 1845. 20p. Z-1170/2 – 8 – ne IDC [590]

DISPOSITIO SYSTEMATICA MUSCORUM FRONDOSORUM SUECIAE / Swartz, O P – Erlangae, 1799. 112 pp., 9 pls. B-5005 2 – 8 – ne IDC [580]

DISPOSITIO VEGETABILIUM METHODICA / Cothenius, C A von – Berolini. 1790. B-853 2 – 8 – ne IDC [580]

DISPOSITION METHODIQUE DES ESPECES DE MOUSSES / Walker-Arnott, G A – Paris. 1825. B-5322 2 – 8 – ne IDC [580]

DISPUTATIO, CONTRA ANABAPTISTAS, DE REGNO CHRISTI, DEF. IOH. HONOLD / Hafenrefferus, M – Tubingae, J. Kircherus. 1595. BME-248 1 – 9 – ne IDC [240]

DISPUTATIO DE NATURA FEBRIS / Rodriguez Guerrero, D – Sevilla, 1606 – 3mf – 9 – sp Cultura [616]

DISPUTATIO INAUGURALIS DE GENERIS HUMANI VARIETATE / Prichard, James Cowles – Edinburgi, Excudebant Abernethy & Walker, 1808 – 1 – us U.W. Library [572]

DISPUTATIO INAUGURALIS MEDICA DE LOLIO TEMULENTO / Camerarius, R J – 7675 2. 1710 – 8 – ne IDC [610]

DISPUTATIO MUSICA / Carolus, Sebastian – 3v. 1609 (-1610) – 9 – us Sibley [780]

DISPUTATIO MUSICA PRIMA (-TERTIA). / Carolus, Sebastian – Complete. 1609 (-10) – 5 – us Sibley [780]

EIN DISPUTATION ODER BESPRECH ZWAYER STALBUBEN : SO MIT KUENIGLICHER MAYE BOTSCHAFFT BEY DEM TUERCKISCHEN KEYSER ZU CONSTANTINOPEL GEWESEN... / Curipeschitz, B – Constantinopolis, 1531 – 1mf – 9 – H-8415/1 – ne IDC [956]

DISPUTATIONES DE CONTROVERSIIS CHRISTIANAE FIDEI, ADVERSUS HUIUS TEMPORIS HAERETICOS... / Bellarmin, R – Ingolstadii. 8v. 1599 – 66mf – 9 – CA-87/1 – ne IDC [240]

DISPUTATIONES DE UNIVERSA PHILOSOPHIA / Hurtado de Mendoza, Publio – Lugduni, 1617 – 15mf – 9 – CA-19/1 – ne IDC [100]

DISPUTATIONES IN...ARISTOTELIS DE ANIMA / Alfonso, Francisco – 1640 – 9 – $1.50f – sp Bibl Santa Ana [120]

DISPUTATIONES MEDICAE DE ANGINORUM ... / Alonso y de los Ruizes de Fontecha, J – Alcala de Henares, 1611 – 8mf – 9 – sp Cultura [616]

DISPUTATIONES META PHYSICAE... / Pasqualigus, Z – Romae. 2v. 1634-36 – 29mf – 9 – CA-27/1 – ne IDC [110]

DISPUTATIONES THEOLOGICAE. IN PRIMAN PARTEM DIVI THOMAE. TOMUS SECUNDUS / Godoy, Pedro de – Burgo de Osma: Imp. Episcopal, 1670 – 9 – sp Bibl Santa Ana [240]

DISPUTATIONES THEOLOGICAE IN TERTIAM PARTEM DIVI THOMAE / Godoy, Pedro de – Burgo de Osma: Imprenta Episcopal, 1966 – 1 – sp Bibl Santa Ana [290]

DISPUTATIONES THEOLOGICAE INTERTIAM PARTEM DIVI THONAE... / Godoy, Pedro de – Burgo de Osma: Imprenta Episcopal, 1668 – 1 – sp Bibl Santa Ana [290]

DISPUTATIONES THEOLOGICAE INTERTIAN PASTEM DIVI THONAE... / Godoy, Pedro de – Burgo de Osma: Imprenta Episcopal, 1667 – 1 – sp Bibl Santa Ana [290]

DISPUTATIONES...THOMAE EIDEM ANGELICO / Godoy, Manuel – 1669, 1671, 1672. 3v – 9 – 1.50f – sp Bibl Santa Ana [946]

DISPUTATIONUM DE SANCTO MATRIMONII SACRAMENTUM / Sanchez, Tomas Antonio – Antverpiae. 3v. 1626 – 25mf – 9 – CA-68/1 – ne IDC [240]

DISPUTATIONUM THEOLOGICARUM... TOMUS PRIMUS : DE DEO UNO / Smising, T – Antverpiae, 1627 – 17mf – 9 – CA-38/1 – ne IDC [240]

DISPUTATIO...QUA HUGONIS GROTII MEMORIA VINDICATUR... / Gratama, H – Groningae, 1820 – 1mf – 1 – ILM-736/1 – ne IDC [327]

DISPUTA...Y AVERIGUACIONES DE LA ENFERMEDAD PESTILENTE... / Valdes, F – Sevilla, 1599 – 1mf – 9 – sp Cultura [616]

DISPUTE RESOLUTION SLIM / U.S. National Institute of Justice – 1985. 155 documents – 9 – $126.00 – us N.C.J.R.S. [360]

THE DISPUTED WATERS OF THE JORDAN / Smith, C G – Oxford: Institute of British Geographers, 1966 – us Res Libr [956]

DISPVTATIO SECVNDA CONTRA CALVINISTAS, AND PRAESERTIM SYNOPSIN KIMEDONCIJ... / Huber, S – VVitebergae, [1593] – 1mf – ne IDC [240]

DISPVTATIO TERTIA CONTRA CALVINISTAS. QVOD FACIANT DEVM AVTOREM PECCATI... / Huber, S – VVitebergae, 1593 – 1mf – ne IDC [240]

EINE DISPVTATION VON MITTELDINGEN VND VON DEN ITZIGEN VERENDERUNGN IN KIRCHEN DIE CHRISTLICH VND WOL GEORDENT SIND... / Gallus, N – [Magdeburg, 1550] – 1mf – 9 – ne IDC [240]

DISPVTATIONVM DE MEDICINA NOVA PHILIPPI PARACELSI PARS PRIMA: IN QVA, QVAE DE REMEDIIS.. / Erastus, Thomas – Basileae: Apud Petrvm Pernam, 1572. With: solis e pvteo emergentis. by J. Rhenanus; de rebvs natvralibvs libri XXX. by G. Zabarella; de metalicis libri tres. by A. Cesalpini – 1 – us U.W. Library [610]

DISQUALIFICATION OF FEDERAL JUDGES BY PEREMPTORY CHALLENGE / Chaset, Alan J – Washington: FJC, Feb 1981 – 1mf – 9 – $1.50 – LLMC 95-307 – us L.L.M.C. [340]

LE DISQUE VERT – n.s., I, no. 1-6. Bruxelles. dec 1952 (no. hors serie sur Proust), avr 1953-54, 1955 (no. special sur Jung) – 1 – fr A.C.R.P.P. [800]

LE DISQUE VERT – sous ce titre sont regroupees les revues suivantes: Signaux de France et de Belgique. Revue mensuelle de litterature. no. 1-11 12. Anvers, Paris. 1er mai 1921-mars juin 1922. Le Disque vert. Revue mensuelle de litterature. I, no. 1-6. Bruxelles, Paris. mai-oct 1922. Ecrits du Nord. Revue mensuelle de litterature. I, 2e s., no. 1-3. Bruxelles et Paris. nov 1922-janv 1923. Le Disque vert. Revue mensuelle de litterature. I, 2e s., no. 4 5 6. 1923; II, 3e s., no. 1-4 5, no. special Charlie Chaplain et no. special Freud et la psychanalyse, oct 1923-24; III, 4e s., no. 1-3, no. special Le Cas Lautreamont, 1925. Nord. Cahiers litteraires trimestriels. no. 1-4. Bruxelles. avr 1929-nov 1930. Au Disque vert. no. 1. 1934. Ecrits du Nord. Revue mensuelle de litterature, d'art et de critique. no. 1-2. juin-juil 1935. Le Disque vert. Revue mensuelle de litterature. I, n.s., no. 1. 15 juil 1941. et collection privee – 1 – fr A.C.R.P.P. [800]

DISQUISICIONES AMERICANAS 2. DON MARTIN CORTES Y DON DIEGO COLON, CABALLEROS DE SANTIAGO / Fita, Fidel – Madrid: Fortanet, 1892. B.R.A.H. 21, pp. 374-377 – sp Bibl Santa Ana [970]

DISQUISICIONES BIBLIOGRAFICAS: AUTORES, LIBROS, BIBLIOTECAS, ARTES GRAFICAS / Iguiniz, J B – Mexico: El colegio de Mexico, 1943 – 4mf – 9 – ne IDC [010]

DISQUISICION...INSTITUCION...MONTES DE PIEDAD / Texeyro de Valcarcel, Francisco J – 1746 – 9 – 1.50f – sp Bibl Santa Ana [240]

A DISQUISITION ON GOVERNMENT / Calhoun, John C; ed by Cralle, Richard K – New York: Peter Smith, 1853 repr 1943 – 2mf – 9 – $3.00 – LLMC 95-073 – us L.L.M.C. [323]

DISRUPTIONS AND SECESSIONS IN METHODISM : THEIR CAUSES, CONSEQUENCES AND LESSONS / Swallow, T – London, 1880. viii/215p – 3mf – 9 – ne IDC [240]

Dissel, Karl *see* PHILIPP VON ZESEN UND DIE DEUTSCHGESINNTE GENOSSENSCHAFT

DISSEMINATOR – Brandon. Miss. 1845-1846 – 1 – us UMI [071]

DISSEMINATOR – Harrisburg, OR. -w. 27 May 1882-9 Aug 1884. 1 roll – 1 – us U.O. Library [071]

DISSENT – v1- 1954- 1; 1971- 5,6; v24- 9 – us UMI [360]

DISSENT – Salisbury, Rhodesia: T Ranger and J Reed. [n1-24. mar 26 1959-mar 2 1961] – us Res Libr [072]

[DISSENTERS IN EASTERN EUROPE PAMPHLET COLLECTION] – 1983 – 1 – CSUXANL4388-B – us Hoover Inst Photo [320]

DISSENTING ACADEMIES IN ENGLAND : THEIR RISE AND PROGRESS AND THEIR PLACE AMONG THE EDUCATIONAL SYSTEMS OF THE COUNTRY / Parker, Irene – Cambridge: University Press; New York: G.P. Putnam [distributor], 1914 – 1mf – us A.T.L.A. [370]

DISSERTATIO DE FABRICA ET USU ANTENNARUM IN INSECTIS / Erichson, G F – Z 1217. 1847 – 9 – ne IDC [590]

DISSERTATIO DE ORIGINE GERMANICA LATINAE LINGUAE / Prasch, J L – Ratisbonae, 1686 – 1mf – 9 – ne IDC [430]

DISSERTATIO EPISTOLICA DE FORMATIONE PULLI... / Malpighi, M – Londini, 1673 – 1mf – 9 – ne IDC [612]

DISSERTATIO HISTORICO-CRITICA DE DOGMATICES CHRISTIANAE FONTIBUS EORUMQUE USU PUBLICO OMNIUM EXAMINI OFFERT ALBERTUS GOSWINUS BOON / Boon, Albertus Goswinus – Groningae:K de Waard, [c1860] – 1mf – 9 – 0-8370-2415-3 – 1985-0415 – us A.T.L.A. [240]

DISSERTATIO INAUGURALIS MEDICA DE SAGU / Steck, A – Argentorati, 1757. 44 pp. B-5753 2 – 8 – ne IDC [610]

DISSERTATIO MEDICA INAUGURALIS DE CARYOPHYLLIS AROMATICIS / Thunberg, C P – Upsaliae. 1788. B-5766 2 – 8 – ne IDC [580]

DISSERTATION ABSTRACTS – (See also: Dissertation Abstracts. International Section A and B) – v1-26. 1938-66 – 1,5,6 – us UMI [080]

DISSERTATION ABSTRACTS INTERNATIONAL – (v.39. 1978 5,6,9) – Section C.v.37. 1976 – 1 – us UMI [073]

DISSERTATION ABSTRACTS. INTERNATIONAL – Section A.Humanities and Social Science Section – v27- 1966- 1,5,6; v36- 9 – us UMI [300]

DISSERTATION ABSTRACTS. INTERNATIONAL – Section B.Science and Engineering Section – v27- 1966- 1,5,6; v36- 9 – us UMI [600]

DISSERTATION CRITIQUE SUR L'ILIADE D'HOMERE / Terrasson, Jean – Paris: F. Fournier et A.U. Coustelier, 1715. 2v. 13 fiches. (Literature Collection) – 9 – 32.00 – fr Bibl Nationale [450]

DISSERTATION DE SYRORUM FIDE ET DISCIPLINA IN RE EUCHARISTICA / Lamy, Thomas Josephus – Lovanii, 1859 – 5mf – 8 – Dfl22.00 – ne Slangenburg [240]

DISSERTATION HISTORIQUE ET POLITIQUE; SUR LA TRAITE FAIT ENTRE LE ROY ET LE DUC CHARLES,... – N.p., 1662 – 1mf – 1 – ILM-729/1 – ne IDC [327]

A DISSERTATION ON ENTHUSIASM, SHEWING THE DANGER OF ITS LATE INCREASE AND THE GREAT MISCHIEFS IT HAS OCCASIONED, BOTH IN ANCIENT AND MODERN TIMES;... / Green, T – London, 1755 – 3mf – 9 – MP-366/1 – ne IDC [240]

A DISSERTATION ON ORIENTAL GARDENING / Chambers, V – O-1061 1. 1772 – 9 – ne IDC [710]

A DISSERTATION ON THE CAUSES OF THE DIFFICULTIES WHICH OCCUR IN LEARNING THE ENGLISH TONGUE / Sheridan, Thomas – 1761. 45p. (English Linguistics Series 1500-1800) – 9 – us UMI [420]

A DISSERTATION ON THE ENGLISH VERB / Pickbourn, James – 1789. 279p. (English Linguistics Series 1500-1800) – 9 – us UMI [420]

A DISSERTATION ON THE EPISTLE OF S. BARNABAS – including a discussion of its date and authorship. By William Cunningham. 1877 – 1 – us A.T.L.A. [240]

A DISSERTATION ON THE GOUT / Cadogan, W – M 85. 1771 – 9 – ne IDC [610]

A DISSERTATION ON THE LAW OF NATURE : TOGETHER WITH SOME OBSERVATIONS ON THE ROMAN CIVIL LAW IN PARTICULAR; TO WHICH IS ADDED, BY WAY OF AN APPENDIX, A CURIOUS CATALOG OF BOOKS, VERY USEFUL TO THE STUDENTS OF THESE SEVERAL LAWS, TOGETHER WITH THE CANON LAW – London: J Roberts, 1723 – 2mf – 9 – $3.00 – LLMC 95-200 – us L.L.M.C. [340]

A DISSERTATION ON THE PHILOSOPHY OF ARISTOTLE, IN FOUR BOOKS : IN WHICH HIS PRINCIPAL PHYSICAL AND METAPHYSICAL DOGMAS ARE UNFOLDED / Taylor, Thomas – London: White, Cochrane, Black, Parry, 1812 (London: Robert Wilks) – 1 roll – 1 – 1-55879-355-0 – uk Libr Preservation [180]

DISSERTATION SUR LA MUSIQUE MODERNE / Rousseau, Jean-Jacques – 1743 – 9 – us Sibley [780]

DISSERTATION SUR LA NATURE ET PROPAGATION DE FEU / Chatelet-Lomont, Gabrielle Emilie du – Paris: Prault, 1744 – 1 – us U.W. Library [530]

DISSERTATION SUR LA QUESTION: S'IL EST PERMIS D'AVOIR EN SA POSSESSION DES ESCLAVES ET DE S'EN SERVIR COMME TELS, DANS LES COLONIES DE L'AMERIQUE / Firman, Philippe – (Slave Trade and Abolitionism in France Series). 1770 – 9 – fr Hachette [360]

DISSERTATION SUR LA TRAITE ET LE COMMERCE DES NEGRES / Bellon de Saint-Quentin – (Slave Trade and Abolitionism in France Series). 1764 – 9 – fr Hachette [380]

DISSERTATION SUR L'AETHER, DANS LAQUELLE ON EXAMINE LES DIFFERENS PRODUITS DU MELANGE DE L'ESPRIT DE VIN AVEC LES ACIDES MINERAUX / Baume, Antoine – Paris, 1757 – 1 – us U.W. Library [640]

DISSERTATION SUR LES DIFFERENTES METHODES D'ACCOMPAGNEMENT POUR LE CLAVECIN OU POUR L'ORGUE / Rameau, Jean-Philippe – ca.1766 – 9 – us Sibley [780]

DISSERTATION SVR LA CONDEMNATION DES THEATRES / Aubignac, Francois Hedelin – Paris, 1666 – 1 – us U.W. Library [790]

DISSERTATIONEN-KATALOG DER UNIVERSITAET TUEBINGEN, 1500-1981 = CATALOGUE OF DISSERTATIONS OF THE UNIVERSITY OF TUEBINGEN – 1983 – 370 fiches (1:42) – 9 – silver DM3,400.00 – 3-598-30449-8 – Published by Norbert Gaertner, FRG – gw Saur [020]

DISSERTATIONES ACADEMICAE UPSALIAE HABITAE / Thunberg, C P – 3v. Gottingae. 1799-1801. B-5765 2 – 8 – ne IDC [080]

DISSERTATIONES ACADEMICAE VARII ARGUMENTI IN SUMMAN REDACTAE... / Cellarius, C – Lipsiae. 2pts. 1712 – 11mf – 9 – ne IDC [400]

DISSERTATIONES BOTANICAE / Thunberg, C P – 2v. Uppsala. 1781-1825. B-619 2 – 8 – ne IDC [580]

DISSERTATIONES PHILOLOGAE VINDOBONENSES / Vienna. Universitaet – Lipsiae, etc. Bd. 1-12; 1887-1918. Film Mas C 283 – 1 – us H.U. Library [370]

DISSERTATIONES PHILOLOGICAE ARGENTORATENSES SELECTAE – Argentorati, 1879-1910. v1-14 – 102mf – H-359/2 – ne IDC [400]

DISSERTATIONS ON NETHERLANDS INDIES LAW 1850-1945 / Van Vollenhoven Institute, University of Leiden – (Individual titles available) – 360mf – 9 – ne IDC [340]

DISSERTATIONS ON SUBJECTS RELATING TO THE "ORTHODOX" OR "EASTERN-CATHOLIC" COMMUNION / Palmer, William P – London: J. Masters, 1853 – 1mf – us A.T.L.A. [240]

DISSERTATIONS ON THE APOSTOLIC AGE / Lightfoot, Joseph B – London: Macmillan, 1892.1 fiche – 9 – us A.T.L.A. [240]

DISSERTATIONS ON THE ENGLISH LANGUAGE / Webster, Noah – 1789 – 9 – 25.00 – us Scholars' Facs [420]

DISSERTATIONS ON THE ENGLISH LANGUAGE / Webster, Noah – 1789. 414p. (English Linguistics Series 1500-1800) – 9 – us UMI [420]

DISSERTATIONS READ TO THE / Edinburgh Royal Medical Society – 1750-1970 – 1. ; 7 – uk Microform Academic [500]

DISSERTATIONS SUR LA POESIE ET LA MUSIQUE DES ANCIENS EN GENERAL, ET DES HEBREUX EN PARTICULIER : AVEC LES FIGURES DES INSTRUMENTS DE MUSIQUE... / Calmet, A – Amsterdam, 1723 – 3mf – ne IDC [780]

DISSERTATIONS SUR LE POEME EPIQUE / Barre, Vatry de la – Reprod. de 4 articles extraits de Memoires de Litterature, p228-304. Histoire de l'Academie royale des Inscriptions et Belles Lettres, v9, 1731-33. Paris, 1736.1 fiche. (Literature Collection) – 9 – 6.00 – fr Bibl Nationale [410]

DISSERTATIONS SUR PLUSIEURS ESPECES DE FUCUS / Lamouroux, J V F – Agen, Paris. 1805. B-6005 2 – 8 – ne IDC [580]

DISSERTAZIONE SOPRA IL QUESITO DIMONSTRARE CHE COSA FOSSE E QUANTA PARTE AVESSE LA MUSICA NELL' EDUCAZIONE DE 'GRECI / Colle, F M – Mantova. 1775. BP-221 1 – 9 – ne IDC [780]

DISSERTAZIONE SOPRA LI PREGGI DEL CANTO GREGORIANO / Belli, L V – 1788 – 9 – us Sibley [780]

THE DISSIDENT PRESS OF REVOLUTIONARY IRAN : A UNIQUE COLLECTION / Behn, Wolfgang & Hoefig, Willi – (With handbook and explicit descriptions) – 1981-82 – 19r – 1 – DM1,900.00 – gw Mikro Press [956]

IL DISSIDIO TRA MAZZINI E GARIBALDI: LA STORIA SENZA VELI / Curatulo, Giacomo Emilio – Documenti inediti. Milano: A. Mondadori, 1928. 431p. illus., ports – 1 – us U.W. Library [945]

DISSIPATIVNYE SVOISTVA METALLOV I METALLICHESKIKH SPLAVOV : O RASCHETAKH I PROGNOZIROVANII SVOISTV ZHIDKOSTEI I GAZOV TERMODINMIACHESKIE I PERENOSNYE SVOISTVA ZHIDKOSTEI V METASTABILNOM SOSTOIANII / Novikov, I I & Filippov, L P et al; ed by Filippova, L P – Moskva: In-t vysokikh temperatur AN SSSR, 1980 – us Res Libr [072]

DISTANCE EDUCATION – (1983-. 5,6,9) – 1980- – 1 – us UMI [073]

DISTANCE EDUCATION SYSTEMS – 1990 – 77p – it F.A.O. [370]

DISTILLER'S MAGAZINE AND SPIRIT TRADE NEWS. (DISTILLERS' AND BREWERS' MAGAZINE.-DISTILLERS', BREWERS' AND SPIRIT MERCHANTS' MAGAZINE) – Glasgow, Scotland. Apr 1897-Apr 1905. -m – 4r – 1 – uk British Libr Newspaper [660]

DISTILLERY, RECTIFYING AND WINE WORKERS INTERNATIONAL JOURNAL : 1942-1947 / Distillery, Rectifying and Wine Workers' International Union of America – (Coll title: Labor Union Periodicals, Pt 3) – 1996 – 1r – 1 – $135.00 – 1-55655-616-0 – us UPA [331]

Distillery, Rectifying and Wine Workers' International Union of America *see* DISTILLERY, RECTIFYING AND WINE WORKERS INTERNATIONAL JOURNAL

DISTINCTIONES PHILOSOPHICAE / Reeb, Georg – Duaci, 1637 – 5mf – 9 – CA-33/1 – ne IDC [100]

DISTINCTIVE CHARACTERISTICS AND COMMON FEATURES OF AFRICAN CULTURAL AREAS SOUTH OF THE SAHARA – 1986 – 149p – 9 – 92-3-102316-0 – fr UNESCO [305]

THE DISTINCTIVE DOCTRINES AND USAGES OF THE GENERAL BODIES OF THE EVANGELICAL LUTHERAN CHURCH IN THE UNITED STATES / Loy, M – Philadelphia, P.: Lutheran Publication Society, c1914 – 1mf – us A.T.L.A. [240]

DISTINGUISHED 100: THE BOOK OF EMINENT ALUMNI OF THE UNIVERSITY OF THE PHILIPPINES / Gwekoh, Sol H – Manila: Apo Book Co., c1939. 147p. ill – 1 – us U.W. Library [920]

LES DISTIQUES POPULAIRES DU NIPPON – Traducteur by Leon de Rosny. Traduction du japonais. Paris: Maisonneuve. 1878 – 9 – 5.00 – fr Orientalistes [950]

Distler, J *see*
– SIX QUATUORS...OP. 6, LIV. 2
– TROIS QUATUORS...OP. 1

DISTRIBUTABLE UNION CATALOG / Harvard College. Library – Author, title and subject entries for computerized cataloging, produced by Harvard libraries since Jul 1977. Includes entries for works on order and works received but not yet cataloged. 360 fiches – 9 – 75.00 – us H.U. College Libr [010]

DISTRIBUTABLE UNION CATALOG / Harvard University. Library – 2nd ed. Approx. 400 COM fiches. 4 parts: author title; author title supplements; subject (LC headings); medical subject (NLM headings). Cumulative – 17 – 95.00 – us H.U. Library [010]

DISTRIBUTED SYSTEMS ENGINEERING – UK: 10P Publishing, 1993.-v1 – 1,5,6,9 – £76.00 – Copublished by the British Computer Society – uk I.O.P. [621]

DISTRIBUTION *see* WAREHOUSING MANAGEMENT

DISTRIBUTION AND IMPACT OF HELMINTH DISEASES OF LIVESTOCK IN DEVELOPING COUNTRIES – 1992 – 227p – it F.A.O. [636]

DISTRIBUTION AND IMPORTANT BIOLOGICAL FEATURES OF COASTAL FISH RESOURCES IN SOUTHEAST ASIA – 1986 – 89p – it F.A.O. [333]

THE DISTRIBUTION OF AFRICAN POPULATION, NATIVE AND IMMIGRANT, IN BUGANDA / Fortt, J M – (Filmed with: Language teaching in Kikuyu schools/L J Beecher, and various others) – 1953 – us Res Libr [960]

THE DISTRIBUTION OF CANADIAN FOREST TREES IN ITS RELATION TO CLIMATE AND OTHER CAUSES: A PAPER READ BEFORE THE BRITISH ASSOCIATION FOR THE ADVANCEMENT OF SCIENCE, MONTREAL, SEPT. 2ND, 1884 / Drummond, Andrew Thomas – Montreal: Dawson, 1885. 02767. (Pre-1900 Canadiana) – 9 – cn C.I.H.M. [971]

THE DISTRIBUTION OF ESTATES OF DECEASED PERSONS IN MASSACHUSETTS / Newhall, Guy – 2d ed. Boston: Jackson, 1915. 12p. LL-393 – 1 – us L of C Photodup [340]

THE DISTRIBUTION OF KINSHIP SYSTEMS IN NORTH AMERICA / Spier, Leslie – BN 397 2. 1925 – 8 – ne IDC [304]

THE DISTRIBUTION OF POWER TO REGULATE INTERSTATE CARRIERS BETWEEN THE NATION AND THE STATES / Reynolds, George Greenwood – New York: Columbia, 1928. 434p. LL-1298 – 1 – us L of C Photodup [340]

DISTRIBUTIQUE – (1985-. 5,6,9) – 1983- – 1 – us UMI [073]

THE DISTRIBUTIVE INTERMEDIATE TRADE OF THE CHINESE ON JAVA / Liem, Twan Djie – Trans. by E. P. Wittermans.m SE-10,366 1. 1964 – 9 – ne IDC [380]

THE DISTRICT ASSOCIATION A REVIEW AND A PLEA / Ryland, Charles H – 18p – 1 – 5.00 – us Baptist [240]

DISTRICT CENSUS STATISTICS / Northwestern Provinces and Oudh. India – 1891. Budaun, Bahraich, Bara Banki, Bijnor, Cawnpore, Gorakhpur, Jhansi, Lucknow, Moradabad, Rae Bareli, Saharanpur and Shahjahanpur districts – 1 – us Res Libr [310]

DISTRICT CENSUS STATISTICS / Northwestern Provinces and Oudh. India – 1911. Budaun, Bahraich, Dehra Dun, Etah, Farrukhabad, Hamirpur, Jalaun, Lucknow, Manipuri, Partabgarh and Sitapur districts – 1 – us Res Libr [310]

THE DISTRICT COUNCILS ELECTIONS PROCLAMATION, 1959 – [S.l: s.n., 1959?] – us Res Libr [320]

THE DISTRICT COURT EXECUTIVE PILOT PROGRAM : A REPORT / Eldridge, William B – Washington: FJC, 1984 – 1mf – 9 – $1.50 – LLMC 95-316 – us L.L.M.C. [340]

DISTRICT COURT IMPLEMENTATION OF AMENDED CIVIL RULE 16 : A REPORT / Weeks, Nancy – Washington: FJC, Apr 1984 – 1mf – 9 – $1.50 – LLMC 95-317 – us L.L.M.C. [340]

LE DISTRICT DE MACHECOUL, 1788-1793... / Lallie, Alfred – Nantes: Forest et Grimaud, 1869 – 1 – F228.66 – fr Armell [944]

THE DISTRICT GAZETTEERS OF BRITISH INDIA : A BIBLIOGRAPHY / Scholberg, Henry – Zug, 1970 – 2mf – 9 – ne IDC [950]

DISTRICT LAWYER – (Superseded by: Washington Lawyer v1-10. 1976-1986) – 9 – $110.00 set – us Hein [340]

DISTRICT LAWYER *see* WASHINGTON LAWYER

DISTRICT MINER – Bullion, NV. Jul 1907 – 1r – 1 – $50.00 – U04427 – us Library Micro [071]

DISTRICT NEWS – LaGrande, OR. -w,-sw. 27 Mar 1925-28 Aug 1931. 2 rolls – 1 – us U.O. Library [071]

DISTRICT NEWS – Whittier. Calif. 1924 – 1 – us UMI [071]

DISTRICT OF BEDFORD TIMES AND GENERAL ADVERTISER – Sweetsburg, Canada. v1 n4. 24 aut 1866-24 sep 1869 (ns: v4 n8 "whole n162") – 1r – 1 – Can$40.00 – cn Can Microfilming [072]

DISTRICT OF COLUMBIA – 3r – 1 – $240.00 – us Scholarly Res [370]

DISTRICT OF COLUMBIA : SESSION LAWS OF AMERICAN STATES AND TERRITORIES – 1975-86 – 9 – $160.00 set – us Hein [340]

District of Columbia *see*
– CENSUS: MORTALITY SCHEDULES
– RECORDS OF THE CITY OF GEORGETOWN, DC, 1800-79
– REPORTS, PRE-NRS

DISTRICT OF COLUMBIA APPEALS CASES / U.S. Courts. District of Columbia – (A Pre-NRS title) – v1-48. 1893-1919 (all offered) – 353mf – 9 – $529.00 – LLMC 81-481 – us L.L.M.C. [340]

District of Columbia. Board of Commissioners for the Emancipation of Slaves *see* RECORDS, 1862-63

DISTRICT OF COLUMBIA CODE – 1981-Feb 1996 update – 9 – $935.00 set – us Hein [340]

DISTRICT OF COLUMBIA LAW REVIEW – v1-3. 1992-95 – 9 – $51.00 set – us Hein [340]

DISTRICT OF COLUMBIA LAWS AND RESOLUTION – 1975-1986 – 9 – $160.00 set – us Hein [340]

District of Columbia. Laws, Statutes, etc *see* THE ALCOHOLIC BEVERAGE LAWS OF THE DISTRICT OF COLUMBIA, REV. TO JANUARY 1, 1948

DISTRICT OF INVERNESS 1851 CENSUS INDEX : ARGYLL AND WEST SCOTLAND CENSUS INDEX, PART 2 / Gibson, Peter & Macinnes, John – 1994 – 3mf – 9 – A$21.95 – 0-646-17260-3 – at Seanachas [920]

DISTRICT OF SHANGHAI NEWSLETTER – v18-19. 1932-33 (incomplete) – 1r – 1 – ATLA S0703A – us A.T.L.A. [073]

DISTRICT SILVER ADVOCATE – Vale OR. Oct 27 Nov 24 1897 – 1 – us U.O. Library [071]

O DISTRICTO DE LOURENCO MARQUES E A AFRICA DO SUL / Eduardo de Noronha. Lisboa: Imprensa Nacional, 1895 – us Res Libr [072]

O DISTRICTO DE LOURENCO MARQUES, NO PRESENTO E NO FUTURO / Casrilho Barreto e Noronha, Augusto Vidal de – (Filmed with: Apontamentos para historia de guerra de Zambezia 1871-75 et al) – Lisboa: Soc de Geographia, 1880 – 1 – us Res Libr [946]

EL DISTRITO – Jerte, 1914. Numeros sueltos – 5 – sp Bibl Santa Ana [073]

DISTURBANCES IN MAY, 1921 / Great Britain. Colonial Office. Palestine – Report of the Commission of Inquiry with correspondence relating thereto. Presented to Parliament by command of His Majesty. London. Oct 1921. BJ-28-63 1 – 9 – ne IDC [956]

DISTURBED IRELAND; BEING THE LETTERS WRITTEN DURING THE WINTER OF 1880-81 / Becker, Bernard Henry – London: Macmillan, 1881.ix,338p. 2 maps. Republished from the London Daily News – 1 – us U.W. Library [941]

Disturnell, John *see*
– SAILING ON THE GREAT LAKES AND RIVERS OF AMERICA: EMBRACING A DESCRIPTION OF LAKES ERIE, HURON, MICHIGAN & SUPERIOR, AND RIVERS ST MARY, ST CLAIR, DETROIT, NIAGARA & ST LAWRENCE; ALSO, THE COPPER AND SILVER REGION OF LAKE SUPERIOR
– THE TRAVELLER'S GUIDE TO THE HUDSON RIVER, SARATOGA SPRINGS, LAKE GEORGE, FALLS OF NIAGARA AND THOUSAND ISLANDS

DISWEEK – Belize City, Belize. June 24 1983-Feb 15 1985 – 1r – 1 – us L of C Photodup [072]

DISZ BIECHLIN ZAIGT AN DIE FALSCHEN PROPHETEN / Greyffenberger, H – 1524. BME-25 1 – 9 – ne IDC [240]

DISZ IST AIN ANZAYG:. DES SACRAMENT VND ANNDERS BETREFFEND / Langenmantel, E H – BME-58 1 – 9 – ne IDC [240]
DIT IS EEN SEER SCHOON CHRISTELIJCKE ONDERWIJSINGHE VANDEN DOOPSEL, TEGHEN DIE WEDERDOOPERS, PAPISTEN EN ALLE VALSCHE SECKTEN / Alberus, E – Magnus van den Merberghe van Oesterhout. BME-216 1 – 9 – ne IDC [240]
DITCH ASSESSMENT RECORDS / Fulton County. Ohio. Swan Creek Township. Board of Trustees – 1877-1920 – 1r – 1 – $32.50r – us Archival [324]
DITCH CARDS / Lucas County. Ohio. Engineer – 2r – 1 – $32.50r – us Archival [324]
DITCH JOURNALS / Hancock County. Ohio. Biglick Township. Board of Trustees – 1867-1917 – 1r – 1 – $32.50r – us Archival [324]
DITCH JOURNALS / Ottawa County. Ohio. Carroll Township. Board of Trustees – 1874-1933 – 2r – 1 – $32.50r – us Archival [324]
DITCH JOURNALS / Seneca County. Ohio. Liberty Township. Board of Trustees – 1879-1917 – 1r – 1 – $32.50r – us Archival [324]
DITCH PAPERS / Ottawa County. Ohio. Carroll Township. Board of Trustees – 1903-1958 – 1r – 1 – $32.50r – us Archival [324]
DITCH PLATS AND SURVEYS / Hancock County. Ohio. Biglick Township. Board of Trustees – 1875-1876 – 1r – 1 – $32.50r – us Archival [324]
DITCH RECORD / Hancock County. Ohio. Marion Township. Board of Trustees – 1866-1883 – 1r – 1 – $32.50r – us Archival [324]
DITCH RECORDS / Allen County. Ohio. Engineer – 1887-1903 – 1r – 1 – $32.50r – us Archival [324]
DITCH RECORDS / Fulton County. Ohio. Engineer – 1866-1870 – 2r – 1 – $32.50r – us Archival [324]
Ditchfield, P H *see*
– THE CHURCH IN THE NETHERLANDS
– THE OLD-TIME PARSON
– THE PARISH CLERK
– SYMBOLISM OF THE SAINTS
– THE VILLAGE CHURCH
DITHMARSCHER LANDESZEITUNG – Heide, West Germany. 1969- – ca 7r per yr – 1 – gw Mikrofilm [072]
DITIA ALLAKHA / Gumilev, Nikolai Sepanovich – Arabskaia skazka. Berlin. 1922. BR-3616 2 – 8 – ne IDC [460]
Ditiatin, I *see* USTROISTVO I UPRAVLENIE GORODOV ROSSII
DITJELAH-TJELAH KEHIDUPAN NABI MUHAMMAD S.A.W / Abbas, Hassan – SE-5324 1. 1964 – 9 – ne IDC [950]
DITJERITAKAN KEMBALI / Valmiki, Ramayana – 1962 – 9 – SE 4502 1 – ne IDC [950]
Ditmar, Nikolai Fedorovich fon- *see* ZADACHI PROMYSHLENNOSTI V SVIAZI S VOINOI
Dito, O *see* LA STORIA CALABRESE E LA DIMORA DEGLI EBREI IN CALABRIA
LES DITS DE LA NUIT. CONTES TENDA, SENEGAL ORIENTAL / Ferry, M P – 8 fiches – 9 – F120.00 – fr Ethnologie [306]
Ditson, Oliver *see* CATALOGS OF VOCAL MUSIC
Ditte, M *see* DES CONVENTIONS CONSULAIRES...
Dittenberger, Wilhelm *see*
– DE SACRIS RHODIORUM COMMENTATIO
– OBSERVATIONIS DE SACRIS AMPHIARAI THEBANIS ET OROPIIS
Ditterich, F G *see* COMPENDIUM JURIS NATURAE
Ditters von Dittersdorf, C *see* THE PERIODICAL OVERTURE, K. 19, C MAJOR
Dittmar, Manuela *see*
– BIBLIOGRAFIA SOBRE LOS MIXTECAS (1719-1991)
– ZUR GENETIK DER WAHRNEHMUNGS-GESCHWINDIGKEIT
Dittrich, Franz *see* GASPARO CONTARINI, 1483-1542
Diuperron, G A *see* BIBLIOGRAFIIA SPORTA I FIZICHESKAGO RAZVITIIA
DIUTISKA : AN HISTORICAL AND CRITICAL SURVEY OF THE LITERATURE OF GERMANY, FROM THE EARLIEST PERIOD TO THE DEATH OF GOETHE / Solling, Gustav – London: Truebner and Co, 1863 – 1r – 1 – us U.W. Library [430]
DIUTURNITY : OR, THE COMPARATIVE AGE OF THE WORLD: SHOWING THAT THE HUMAN RACE IS IN THE INFANCY OF ITS BEING, AND DEMONSTRATING A REASONABLE AND RATIONAL WORLD, AND ITS IMMENSE FUTURE DURATION / Abbey, Richard – Cincinnati: Applegate, 1866 – 1mf – 9 – ATLA 1985-0003 – us A.T.L.A. [230]
Diuvernua, A *see* MATERIALY DLIA SLOVARIA DREVNERUSSKOGO IAZYKA
Diuvernua, N L *see* ISTOCHNIKI PRAVA I SUDA V DREVNEI ROSSII
DIUZHINA NOZHEI V SPINU REVOLIUTSII : 12 NOVYKH RAZSKAZOV / Averchenko, Arkadii – Paris: Bibliothe'que universelle, 1921 – 1 – CSUX88-B5098 – us Hoover Inst Photo [460]
DIVAGAR... / Sanchez Arjona, Vicente – Sevilla: Imprenta Carlos Acuna, Tomo 1. 1948 – 1 – sp Bibl Santa Ana [810]
DIVAGAR... / Sanchez Arjona, Vicente – Sevilla: Imprenta Carlos Acuna, Tomo 3. 1949 – 1 – sp Bibl Santa Ana [810]
DIVAGAR...(DE MIS ARCHIVOS) / Sanchez Arjona, Vicente – Sevilla: Carlos Acuna Imprenta, Tomo 2. 1948 – 1 – sp Bibl Santa Ana [810]
DIVAN / Abduelkadir, Gulami – Istanbul, 1291 – 2mf – 9 – $12.00 – us MEDOC [949]
DIVAN / Aczi – Istanbul, 1290 – 2mf – 9 – $12.00 – us MEDOC [949]
DIVAN / Agribozli Nu'man Mahir, Beg – Istanbul, 1288 – 2mf – 9 – $12.00 – us MEDOC [949]
DIVAN / Ahmed, Muesellem – Istanbul, 1326 – 3mf – 9 – $18.00 – us MEDOC [949]
DIVAN / A'ma Yusuf Garibi, Efendi – Istanbul, n.d. – 2mf – 9 – $12.00 – us MEDOC [949]
DIVAN / Arif – Bulak, 1258 – 4mf – 9 – $24.00 – us MEDOC [949]
DIVAN / Asik Oemer – Istanbul, 1341 – 1mf – 9 – $6.00 – us MEDOC [949]
DIVAN / Avni – Istanbul, 1303 – 1mf – 9 – $6.00 – us MEDOC [949]
DIVAN / Ayni – Istanbul, 1258 – 8mf – 9 – $48.00 – us MEDOC [949]
DIVAN / Azbi – Istanbul, 1286 – 2mf – 9 – $12.00 – us MEDOC [949]
DIVAN / Baki – Istanbul, 1276 – 4mf – 9 – $24.00 – us MEDOC [949]
DIVAN / Beg, Leskofceli Galib – Istanbul, 1335 – 2mf – 9 – $12.00 – us MEDOC [810]
DIVAN / Belig – Istanbul, 1258 – 2mf – 9 – $12.00 – us MEDOC [949]
DIVAN / Celaleddin – Istanbul, 1317 – 6mf – 9 – $36.00 – us MEDOC [949]
DIVAN / Dertli – Istanbul, 1329 – 1mf – 9 – $6.00 – us MEDOC [949]
DIVAN / Ebue-l'Kemal – Istanbul, 1324 – 2mf – 9 – $12.00 – us MEDOC [949]
DIVAN / Emrah – Istanbul, 1332 – 1mf – 9 – $6.00 – us MEDOC [949]
DIVAN / Enis, Dede – Edirne, 1307 – 2mf – 9 – $12.00 – us MEDOC [949]
DIVAN / Es'ad – Istanbul, 1337 – 1mf – 9 – $6.00 – us MEDOC [949]
DIVAN / Esrar Dede, Efendi – Istanbul, 1257 – 3mf – 9 – $18.00 – us MEDOC [949]
DIVAN / Esrefoglu Abdulah, Al-Rumi – Istanbul, 1869 – 2mf – 9 – $12.00 – us MEDOC [949]
DIVAN / Fatin – Istanbul, 1288 – 2mf – 9 – $12.00 – us MEDOC [949]
DIVAN : FITNAT (1) – Istanbul, 1264 – 1mf – 9 – $6.00 – us MEDOC [949]
DIVAN : FITNAT (2) – Istanbul, 1286 – 1mf – 9 – $6.00 – us MEDOC [949]
DIVAN : FITNAT (3) – Istanbul, 1291 – 3mf – 9 – $18.00 – us MEDOC [949]
DIVAN : FITNAT DANIM (4) – n.p., n.d. – 2mf – 9 – $12.00 – us MEDOC [949]
DIVAN : FUZULI (1) – Bulak, 1256 – 3mf – 9 – $18.00 – us MEDOC [949]
DIVAN : FUZULI (2) – Istanbul, 1268 – 3mf – 9 – $18.00 – us MEDOC [949]
DIVAN : FUZULI (3) – Tabriz, 1266 – 2mf – 9 – $12.00 – us MEDOC [949]
DIVAN : FUZULI (4) – Istanbul, 1308 – 5mf – 9 – $30.00 – us MEDOC [949]
DIVAN : FUZULI (5) – Istanbul, 1328 – 6mf – 9 – $36.00 – us MEDOC [949]
DIVAN / Halet, Efendi – Istanbul, 1258 – 1mf – 9 – $6.00 – us MEDOC [949]
DIVAN / Halid – Istanbul, 1260 – 2mf – 9 – $12.00 – us MEDOC [949]
DIVAN / Halim Giray, Sultan – Istanbul, 1257 – 1mf – 9 – $6.00 – us MEDOC [949]
DIVAN / Hasmet – Bulak, 1257 – 3mf – 9 – $18.00 – us MEDOC [949]
DIVAN / Hazik, Efendi – Istanbul, 1318 – 2mf – 9 – $12.00 – us MEDOC [949]
DIVAN / Hersekli Arif Hikmet, Beg – Istanbul, 1334 – 4mf – 9 – $24.00 – us MEDOC [949]
DIVAN / Hikmet Arif, Seyhuelislam – Istanbul, 1283 – 6mf – 9 – 24.00 – us MEDOC [949]
DIVAN : HILMI (1) – Istanbul, 1274 – 1mf – 9 – $6.00 – us MEDOC [949]
DIVAN : HILMI (2) – Istanbul, 1293 – 1mf – 9 – $6.00 – us MEDOC [810]
DIVAN : HIZIR AGAZADE SA'ID BEY (1) – Istanbul, 1257 – 1mf – 9 – $6.00 – us MEDOC [810]
DIVAN : HIZIR AGAZADE SEYYID BEY (2) – n.p., 1289 – 1mf – 9 – $6.00 – us MEDOC [810]
DIVAN / Hudayi 'Aziz Mahmud, Efendi – n.p., n.d. – 2mf – 9 – $12.00 – us MEDOC [810]
DIVAN / Huzni – np., 1312 – 2mf – 9 – $12.00 – us MEDOC [810]
DIVAN / Ihsan (Hamamizade) – Istanbul, 1347 – 2mf – 9 – $12.00 – us MEDOC [810]
DIVAN / Isma'il, Hakki – Istanbul, 1288 – 3mf – 9 – $18.00 – us MEDOC [810]
DIVAN / Ismet – Istanbul, 1291 – 1mf – 9 – $6.00 – us MEDOC [810]
DIVAN – Istanbul, 1273 – 1mf – 9 – $6.00 – us MEDOC [810]
DIVAN / Izzet – Bulak, 1255 – 7mf – 9 – $42.00 – us MEDOC [810]
DIVAN / Izzet Beg – Istanbul, 1258 – 2mf – 9 – $12.00 – us MEDOC [810]
DIVAN / Kai, Burhaneddin – Istanbul, 1338 – 1mf – 9 – $6.00 – us MEDOC [810]
DIVAN / Kayguli, Sultan – n.p., n.d. – 2mf – 9 – $12.00 – us MEDOC [810]
DIVAN / Kaygulu, Efendi – n.p., 1272 – 1mf – 9 – $6.00 – us MEDOC [810]
DIVAN : KAZIM PASA (1) – n.p., n.d. – 1mf – 9 – $6.00 – us MEDOC [810]
DIVAN : KAZIM PASA (2) – Istanbul, 1328 – 2mf – 9 – $12.00 – us MEDOC [810]
DIVAN / Kemalpasazade – Istanbul, 1313 – 3mf – 9 – $18.00 – us MEDOC [810]
DIVAN / Kethudazade 'Arif – Istanbul, 1271 – 1mf – 9 – $6.00 – us MEDOC [810]
DIVAN : KUDDUSI (1) – Istanbul, 1322 – 3mf – 9 – $18.00 – us MEDOC [810]
DIVAN : KUDDUSI (2) – Istanbul, 1325 – 3mf – 9 – $18.00 – us MEDOC [810]
DIVAN : KUDDUSI (3) – Istanbul, 1326 – 3mf – 9 – $18.00 – us MEDOC [810]
DIVAN : LEYLA HANIM (1) – Bulak, 1260 – 2mf – 9 – $12.00 – us MEDOC [810]
DIVAN : LEYLA HANIM (2) – Bulak, 1267 – 2mf – 9 – $12.00 – us MEDOC [810]
DIVAN : LEYLA HANIM (3) – Istanbul, 1299 – 2mf – 9 – $12.00 – us MEDOC [810]
DIVAN / Mehmed 'Ali Hilmi Dede, Baba – Istanbul, 1327 – 2mf – 9 – $12.00 – us MEDOC [810]
DIVAN / Mehmed Emin, Iffet – Istanbul, 1257 – 2mf – 9 – $12.00 – us MEDOC [810]
DIVAN / Mehmed, Sebateddin – Istanbul, 1310 – 1mf – 9 – $6.00 – us MEDOC [810]
DIVAN / Muestak, Efendi – Istanbul, 1264 – 2mf – 9 – $12.00 – us MEDOC [810]
DIVAN / Muhibbi – Istanbul, 1308 – 4mf – 9 – $24.00 – us MEDOC [810]
DIVAN / Munif – Istanbul, 1266 – 2mf – 9 – $12.00 – us MEDOC [810]
DIVAN / Murad, Emri – Bursa, 1329 – 2mf – 9 – $12.00 – us MEDOC [810]
DIVAN / Mustafa Nyzuli, Al-Kulavi – Istanbul, 1331 – 2mf – 9 – $12.00 – us MEDOC [810]
DIVAN : NABI (1) – Bulak, 1257 – 10mf – 9 – $60.00 – us MEDOC [810]
DIVAN : NABI (2) – Istanbul, 1292 – 9mf – 9 – $54.00 – us MEDOC [810]
DIVAN / Na'ili – Bulak, 1253 – 2mf – 9 – $12.00 – us MEDOC [810]
DIVAN / Naim – Istanbul, 1257 – 8mf – 9 – $48.00 – us MEDOC [810]
DIVAN / Necmi – Istanbul, 1287 – 2mf – 9 – $12.00 – us MEDOC [810]
DIVAN / Nedim – Istanbul, 1338/40 – 6mf – 9 – $36.00 – us MEDOC [810]
DIVAN / Nef'i – Istanbul, 1269 – 4mf – 9 – $24.00 – us MEDOC [810]
DIVAN / Nes'et, Efendi – Bulak, 1252 – 2mf – 9 – $12.00 – us MEDOC [810]
DIVAN : NESIMI (1) – Istanbul, 1260 – 3mf – 9 – $18.00 – us MEDOC [810]
DIVAN : NESIMI (2) – Istanbul, 1286 – 3mf – 9 – $18.00 – us MEDOC [810]
DIVAN / Nevres – Istanbul, 1290 – 5mf – 9 – $30.00 – us MEDOC [810]
DIVAN : NIYAZI (1) – Istanbul, 1291 – 2mf – 9 – $12.00 – us MEDOC [810]
DIVAN : NIYAZI (2) – Istanbul, 1325 – 2mf – 9 – $12.00 – us MEDOC [810]
DIVAN : NIYAZI (3) – Istanbul, 1254 – 2mf – 9 – $12.00 – us MEDOC [810]
DIVAN / 'Oerfi ve 'Avnuellah, Al-Kazimi – Istanbul, 1327 – 2mf – 9 – $12.00 – us MEDOC [810]
DIVAN / Pertev, Pasa – Istanbul, 1256 – 2mf – 9 – $12.00 – us MEDOC [810]
DIVAN : RAGIB (1) – n.p., 1253 – 3mf – 9 – $18.00 – us MEDOC [810]
DIVAN : RAGIB PASA (2) – Bulak, 1252 – 2mf – 9 – $12.00 – us MEDOC [810]
DIVAN / Refi'i, Kalayi – Istanbul, 1284 – 2mf – 9 – $12.00 – us MEDOC [810]
DIVAN : REVUE LITTERAIRE – Paris, 1909-1941 – 211mf – H-403c/2 – ne IDC [440]
LE DIVAN – Paris. 1909-31 – 1 – fr A.C.R.P.P. [073]
DIVAN SHEL SHELOMOH BEN MESHULLAM DA PIERRA / Bernstein, Simon – pt. 1, Shirei Hol. New York. 1942. BJ-421-82 1 – 9 – ne IDC [890]
DIVANCE / Dehri – Istanbul, 1330 – 2mf – 9 – $12.00 – us MEDOC [949]
DIVANCE / Es'ad Pasa – Istanbul, 1268 – 1mf – 9 – $6.00 – us MEDOC [949]
DIVANCE / Fazil – Istanbul, 1329 – 2mf – 9 – $12.00 – us MEDOC [949]
DIVANCE / Fehim, Sueleyman – Istanbul, 1262 – 1mf – 9 – $6.00 – us MEDOC [949]
DIVANCE / Hanyevi Sefik, Efendi – Istanbul, 1293 – 1mf – 9 – $6.00 – us MEDOC [949]
DIVANCE / Hasimi – Istanbul, 1329 – 1mf – 9 – $6.00 – us MEDOC [949]
DIVANCE / Izzet – Istanbul, 1257 – 1mf – 9 – $6.00 – us MEDOC [949]
DIVANCE / Kazim – n.p., n.d. – 1mf – 9 – $6.00 – us MEDOC [949]
DIVANCE / Lutfi, Vak'anuevis Ahmed – Istanbul, 1302 – 2mf – 9 – $12.00 – us MEDOC [949]
DIVANCE / Naim – Istanbul, 1308 – 1mf – 9 – $6.00 – us MEDOC [949]
DIVANCE / Pasa, Ragib – n.p., 1276 – 1mf – 9 – $6.00 – us MEDOC [949]
DIVANCE / Sinaver – Istanbul, 1330 – 2mf – 9 – $12.00 – us MEDOC [949]
DIVANCE / Tevfik – Cairo, 1283 – 1mf – 9 – $6.00 – us MEDOC [949]
DIVANELIKLERIM / Hamid, Abduelhak – Istanbul, 1303 – 1mf – 9 – $6.00 – us MEDOC [949]
DIVAN-I GUELZAR / Sa'di – Istanbul, 1284 – 3mf – 9 – $18.00 – us MEDOC [949]
DIVAN-I OERFI VE AVNULLAH KAZIMI / Kazimi, Avnullah [Mehmet Selim] – Dersaadet [Istanbul]: Nuemune-i Tabaat Matbaasi, 1327 [1909] – $25.00 – us MEDOC [956]
Diver, Maud *see* KABUL TO KANDAHAR
DIVERS – BIBLIOTHEQUE OSLER CATALOG NO. 107-7636 / Bibliotheque Osler. Montreal – Montreal, Canada – 36r – 1 – cn Can Microfilming [020]
DIVERS – CATALOG NO. 1839-1881 AND COLLECTION OF M. HERSHEY – CATALOG NO. 1882-1914 / Societe de Numismatique et d'Archeologie. Chateau de Ramesay. Archives – Montreal, Canada – 1r – 1 – cn Can Microfilming [730]
DIVERS DOCUMENTS ADDRESSED TO THE HONORABLE LOUIS JOSEPH PAPINEAU... / Viger, Denis Benjamin – [S.l.: s.n., 1834 ?]. SEM105P1374 – 4mf – 9 – Can$9.00 – cn Bibl Nat [971]
DIVERS DOCUMENTS ADRESSES A L'HONORABLE LOUIS JOSEPH PAPINEAU... / Viger, Denis Benjamin – [S.l.: s.n., 1834 ?]. SEM105P1375 – 4mf – 9 – Can$9.00 – cn Bibl Nat [971]
DES DIVERS MODES DE PAIEMENTS INTERNATIONAUX / Caris, H E – Paris, 1913 – 3mf – 1 – ILM-2981/1 – ne IDC [327]
DIVERS, OU, LES ENSEIGNEMENTS DE LA VIE / Bailairge, Charles – Quebec: C. Darveau, 1898. 00049. (Pre-1900 Canadiana) – 9 – cn C.I.H.M. [370]

DIVERS OUVRAGES DE MATHEMATIQUE ET DE PHYSIQUE PAR MESSIEURS DE L'ACADEMIE ROYALE DES SCIENCES / Roberval, Gilles de – Paris, imprimerie royale, 1693, p. 65-302. Historie des Sciences XVIIe-XIXe Siecles. 7963 – 9 – fr Hachette [510]

DIVERS, RE: RIVIERE ROUGE (1820) (MANITOBA) / Quebec. Archbishop. Archives – Quebec, Canada – 5r – 1 – cn Can Microfilming [240]

DIVERSE PIECES / Willermoz, J B – N.p., n.d. – 10mf – ne IDC [900]

DIVERSES ACTES DE LA HERENCIA DEL DUCH DE CALABRIA (SIECLE 16) – Valencia – 2r – 5,6 – sp Cultura [945]

DIVERSES PIECES POUR LA DEFENSE DE LA ROYNE, MERE DU ROY LOUIS 13TH... / Morgues, Mathieu de – Anvers: [s.n.], 1643 – fr Armell [944]

THE DIVERSIONS OF PURLEY / Tooke, John Horne – 1798. 2v. (English Linguistics Series 1500-1800) – 9 – us UMI [400]

DIVERSORUM (ANNO 1479-1516) / Fernando 2 – Barcelona – 1r – 5,6 – sp Cultura [946]

DIVERSORUM...LOCOS DE REGIA.. / Weijers, Henrico E – 1839 – 9 – 1.50f – sp Bibl Santa Ana [240]

DIVERTIMENTO PER L'OBOE CON ACCOMPAGNAMENTO DI 2 VIOLINI, VIOLA, ET VIOLONCELLO / Crusell, Bernhard H – Op. 9. 183-? – 9 – us Sibley [780]

DIVERTIMENTOS, A SECOND SET OF THREE, FOR THE PIANOFORTE CONSISTING OF MARCHES, SCOTTISH [SIC] AIRS FOR SLOW MOVEMENTS, AND ORIGINAL GERMAN WALTZES WITH AN ACCOMP. FOR TAMBOURINO AND TRIANGLE AD LIB, OP. 18 / Haig, T – London: Birchall, [ca. 1800] – 1 – us Sibley [780]

DIVERTING POST – Dublin, Ireland. -w. 18 25 Oct-15 22 Nov 1725. Lacking 1 8 Nov. 3 ft – 1 – uk British Libr Newspaper [072]

DIVIDE CITY TIMES – Virginia City, NV. 1919 – 1r – 1 – $50.00 – U04490 – us Library Micro [071]

Divilkovskii, A *see*
– POMOGA I STROIT SOVETSKUIU VLAST
– TRETIA GODOVSHCHINA OKTIABRSKOI REVOLIUTSII

DIVINA COMMEDIA / Dante, Alighieri – 1474. Holkham MS. 518. Holkham Hall, Norfolk, England – 1 – uk Microform Academic [810]

DIVINA COMMEDIA / Dante Alighieri – 14th, 15th century MS. Holkham 513, 515, 516, 517. Holkham Hall, Norfolk, England – 1 – uk Microform Academic [810]

DIVINA COMMEDIA / Dante Alighieri – Late 14th century. Holkham MS. 514. Holkham Hall, Norfolk, England – 1,14 – uk Microform Academic [810]

DIVINA PROPORTIONE / Pacioli, L – O-1006 1. 1509 – 9 – ne IDC [760]

DIVINAE INSTITUTIONES, ETC / Lactantius Placidus – 14th and 15th cents. Holkham mss. 120, 389, 391. Holkham Hall, Norfolk, England – 1 – uk Microform Academic [760]

LA DIVINATION A LA COTE DES ESCLAVES ET A MADAGASCAR : LE VODOU FA, LE SIKIDY / Trautmann, Rene – Paris: E Larose, 1940 – 1 – us Res Libr [306]

THE DIVINE AUTHORITY OF HOLY SCRIPTURE ASSERTED, FROM ITS ADAPTATION TO THE REAL STATE OF HUMAN NATURE IN EIGHT SERMONS PREACHED BEFORE THE UNIVERSITY OF OXFORD IN THE YEAR MDCCCXVII / Miller, John – 1817 – 9 – us A.T.L.A. [240]

THE DIVINE AUTHORITY OF THE BIBLE / Wright, George Frederick – Boston: Congregational S.-S. Pub., 1884.1 fiche – 9 – us A.T.L.A. [240]

THE DIVINE AUTHORITY OF THE SCRIPTURES OF THE OLD TESTAMENT / McIntyre, David – 1917 – 9 – us A.T.L.A. [240]

LA DIVINE CABALLE OU EST CONTENU LES FIGURES DES DIVINS SECRETS DE L'ART DE LA NATURE, LA SCIENCE DU FEU ET DE L'EAU ET DES TROIS REGNES DE LA NATURE – 19th c. – fr Armell [100]

THE DIVINE COMPANION *see* HYMN AND TUNE COLLECTION FROM LIBRARY OF EDMOND D. KEITH

DIVINE DISCIPLINE OF ISRAEL...LECTURES ON THE GROWTH OF IDEAS IN THE OLD TESTAMENT / Gray, George Buchanan – London: A.&C. Black, 1900 – 9 – us A.T.L.A. [220]

THE DIVINE DRAMA: THE MANIFESTATION OF GOD IN THE UNIVERSE / Pike, Granville Ross – New York: Macmillan, 1898. 1 fiche. 8370-4756-0 – 9 – us A.T.L.A. [240]

DIVINE EMBLEMS / Abricht, J – O-534 1. 1838 – 9 – ne IDC [240]

THE DIVINE ENTERPRISE OF MISSIONS : A SERIES OF LECTURES / Pierson, Arthur Tappan – (Includes index) – New York: Baker & Taylor, c1891 – 1mf – 9 – 0-8370-6599-2 – 1986-0599 – us A.T.L.A. [240]

THE DIVINE FORCE IN THE LIFE OF THE WORLD / McKenzie, Alexander – Boston: Houghton, Mifflin, 1899.1 fiche – 9 – us A.T.L.A. [240]

THE DIVINE GLORY OF CHRIST / Brown, Charles J – London, New York: T Nelson, 1868 – 1mf – 9 – 0-8370-2998-8 – 1985-0998 – us A.T.L.A. [240]

THE DIVINE GOVERNMENT / Smith, Southwood – 5th ed. Philadelphia: J B Lippincott, 1866 – 1mf – 9 – 0-8370-5169-X – 1985-3169 – us A.T.L.A. [240]

DIVINE GUIDANCE, OR, THE HOLY GUEST: A DISCUSSION OF THE BELIEVER'S PRIVILEGE IN CHRIST JESUS: THE HOLY SPIRIT AS GUIDE INTO ALL TRUTH: THE PENTECOSTAL BAPTISM, PHYSICAL RELIGIOUS MANIFESTATIONS, INDWELLING SIN. / Burns, Nelson – Brantford, Ont.: Book and Bible House, 1889. 00347. (Pre-1900 Canadiana) – 9 – cn C.I.H.M. [240]

DIVINE HARMONY : 6 SELECTED ANTHEMS FOR A VOICE [TREBEL OR TENOR] ALONE WITH A THOROW BASS FOR THE ORGAN, HARPSICHORD OR ARCH-LUTE / Weldon, J – (Score) – London: Walsh, 1716 – 1 – us Sibley [780]

DIVINE HEALING OF SOUL AND BODY / Byrum, Enoch Edwin – 1892 – 1 – us A.T.L.A. [240]

THE DIVINE HUMAN IN THE SCRIPTURES / Lewis, Tayler – New York: Robert Carter, 1860 – 1mf – 9 – 0-8370-4100-7 – 1985-2100 – us A.T.L.A. [220]

DIVINE IMMANENCE:...ON THE SPIRITUAL SIGNIFICANCE OF MATTER / Illingworth, J Richardson – New York: Macmillan, 1898. 1 fiche – 9 – us A.T.L.A. [240]

THE DIVINE INDWELLING / Brown, Edmund Woodward – New York:Fleming H. Revell, c1895 – 1mf – 9 – 0-8370-3020-X – 1985-1020 – us A.T.L.A. [210]

THE DIVINE LIBRARY OF THE OLD TESTAMENT : ITS ORIGIN, PRESERVATION, INSPIRATION AND PERMANENT VALUE: FIVE LECTURES / Kirkpatrick, Alexander Francis – London, NY: Macmillan, 1891 – 1mf – 9 – 0-8370-3905-3 – 1985-1905 – us A.T.L.A. [220]

DIVINE LIBRARY OF THE OLD TESTAMENT: ITS ORIGIN...AND PERMANENT VALUE / Kirkpatrick, Alexander F – London: Macmillan, 1891.1 fiche – 9 – us A.T.L.A. [240]

THE DIVINE LIBRARY: SUGGESTIONS HOW TO READ THE BIBLE / Smyth, John Paterson – New York: James Pott, 1896. 1 fiche – 9 – us A.T.L.A. [240]

DIVINE MAN: FROM THE NATIVITY TO THE TEMPTATION / Boardman, George Dana – New York: Appleton, 1888. 1 fiche – 9 – us A.T.L.A. [240]

DIVINE OR CIVIL OBEDIENCE? / Brown, Brian et al – Johannesburg, Ravan [n.d.] – us Res Libr [321]

LA DIVINE PASTORALE : DIX LINOS D'ANT. DE VINCK – Bruxelles: Editions du Marais, 1952-55 – 1 – us Res Libr [490]

THE DIVINE PEDIGREE OF MAN : OR, THE TESTIMONY OF EVOLUTION AND PSYCHOLOGY TO THE FATHERHOOD OF GOD / Hudson, Thomson Jay – (Includes bibliographical references) – Chicago: A C McClurg, 1899 – 1mf – 9 – 0-8370-3685-2 – 1985-1685 – us A.T.L.A. [210]

THE DIVINE PERSONALITY : BEING A CONSIDERATION OF THE ARGUMENTS TO PROVE THAT THE AUTHOR OF NATURE A BEING ENDUED WITH LIBERTY AND CHOICE / Pearson, John Batteridge – (Includes bibliographical references) – Cambridge: Deighton, Bell; London: Bell and Daldy, 1865 – 1mf – 9 – 0-8370-4688-2 – 1985-2688 – us A.T.L.A. [210]

DIVINE REVELATION EXPLAINED AND VINDICATED : A COURSE OF LECTURES FOR THE TIMES / Fairbairn, Patrick et al – Glasgow: David Bryce, 1866 – 1mf – 9 – 0-8370-2925-2 – 1985-0925 – us A.T.L.A. [240]

THE DIVINE RIGHT OF KINGS / Figgis, John Neville – Cambridge: University Press, 1914 – 1mf – us A.T.L.A. [240]

THE DIVINE RIGHT OF MISSIONS : OR, CHRISTIANITY THE WORLD-RELIGION AND THE RIGHT OF THE CHURCH TO PROPAGATE IT / Mabie, Henry Clay – Philadelphia: Griffith & Rowland Press, 1908 – 1mf – 9 – 0-8370-6211-X – 1986-0211 – us A.T.L.A. [230]

THE DIVINE SATISFACTION:...WHAT SHOULD... BE THOUGHT ABOUT THE ATONEMENT / Whiton, James Morris – London: James Clarke, 1889. 1 fiche – 9 – us A.T.L.A. [240]

THE DIVINE SOCIETY, OR, THE CHURCH'S CARE OF LARGE POPULATIONS : SIX LECTURES ON PASTORAL THEOLOGY / Jacob, Edgar – London: S.P.C.K.; New York: E.S. Gorham, 1903 – 1mf – us A.T.L.A. [240]

THE DIVINE UNITY OF SCRIPTURE / Saphir, Adolph – London: Hodder & Stoughton, 1896. 1 fiche – 9 – us A.T.L.A. [240]

THE DIVINE WORKER IN CREATION AND PROVIDENCE / Dykes, James Oswald – Edinburgh: T &T. Clark, 1909. 1 fiche – 9 – us A.T.L.A. [240]

DIVINE WORSHIP IN ENGLAND IN THE THIRTEENTH AND FOURTEENTH CENTURIES CONTRASTED WITH AND ADAPTED TO THAT IN THE NINETEENTH / Chambers, John David – New ed. rev. with additions. London: B.M. Pickering, 1877. xviii,432,x/vi,9p. illus – 1 – us U.W. Library [240]

THE DIVINITY OF CHRIST / Ames, Edward Scribner – Chigago: Bethany Press, c1911 – 1mf – us A.T.L.A. [240]

THE DIVINITY OF JESUS CHRIST : AN EXPOSITION OF THE ORIGIN AND REASONABLENESS OF THE BELIEF OF THE CHRISTIAN CHURCH – Boston: Houghton, Mifflin; Cambridge: Riverside Press, 1894, c1893 – 1mf – 9 – 0-8370-5388-9 – 1985-3388 – us A.T.L.A. [240]

EL DIVINO AMOR / Willemenot, Luis G – Jerez de los Caballeros: Talleres Tipograficos Horizonte, 1957 – sp Bibl Santa Ana [946]

DIVINO...GARCIA GOLFIN DE CARVAJAL. MANIFIESTO / Olivas y Frances, Francisco – 1744 – 9 – 1.50f – sp Bibl Santa Ana [240]

DIVINOPOLIS-JORNAL – Divinopolis, 24 Jan 1943-Dec 1944; Jan, Dec 1945; Jan, Aug-Dec 1946; Jan-Dec 1947; Jan-Feb, 20 Jun 1948 – 1,5,6 – bl Biblioteca [072]

DIVISION BIPARTITA DE LA PROVINCIA FRANCISCANA DE SAN MIGUEL DE EXTREMADURA / Barrado Manzano, Arcangel – Separata del Archivo Ibero-Americano. 19, Julio-Septiembre 1959 – 1 – sp Bibl Santa Ana [946]

DIVISION IN THE PROTESTANT HOUSE / Hoge, Dean R – Technical supplement. 1976 – 1 – us A.T.L.A. [240]

DIVISION LISTS / Great Britain. Parliament. House of Commons – 1880-92 – 1 – us Res Libr [324]

DIVISION LISTS, 1836-1909 / ed by Torrington, F W – (Includes indexes for 1836-75) – 1981 – 517mf – 9 – £2,120.00 – uk Chadwyck [324]

DIVISION OF HUMAN RIGHTS / UN Commission on Human Rights – E.11 F.11 R.3 S.6 – 9 – ST/HR.1-4 – us U.N. Pubs [340]

Division of Statistics on Culture and Communication. Office of Statistics *see* LATEST STATISTICS ON RADIO AND TELEVISION BROADCASTING

THE DIVISION-VIOLIST OR AN INTRODUCTION TO THE PLAYING UPON A GROUND: DIVIDED INTO TWO PARTS / Simpson, Christopher – 1659 – 9 – us Sibley [780]

THE DIVORCE AND SEPARATION OF ALIENS IN FRANCE / Bates, LT – New York, 1929 – 4mf – 9 – ILM-3005/1 – ne IDC [340]

DIVORCE CASES / Wood County. Ohio. Common Pleas. Civil Division – 1837-1875 – 2r – 1 – $32.50r – us Archival [324]

LE DIVORCE DU TAILLEUR: PIECE ARCHICOMIQUE EN UN ACTE / Doin, Ernest – Montreal: C. Payette, 1873. 04292. (Pre-1900 Canadiana) – 9 – cn C.I.H.M. [820]

LE DIVORCE ET LA SEPARATION DE CORPS ... / Bouseus, F – Paris, 1930 – 3mf – 9 – ILM-3004/1 – ne IDC [327]

LE DIVORCE ET LA SEPARATION DE CORPS: THESE / Fremont, Joseph – Quebec: A. Cote, 1886. 03255. (Pre-1900 Canadiana) – 9 – cn C.I.H.M. [971]

DIVORCE LAW IN OHIO / May, Geoffrey – Baltimore: Johns Hopkins Press, 1932. 76p. LL-1391 – 1 – us L of C Photodup [340]

THE DIVORCE OF CATHERINE OF ARAGON : THE STORY AS TOLD BY THE IMPERIAL AMBASSADORS RESIDENT AT THE COURT OF HENRY 8 / Froude, James Anthony – New York: Scribner, 1891 – 2mf – us A.T.L.A. [941]

THE DIVORCE QUESTION : THE DIVORCE LAWS OF EVERY STATE IN THE UNITED STATES AND POSSESSIONS / Collins, William A – Chicago, Penn, 1926. 104p. LL-854 – 1 – us L of C Photodup [340]

DIVORCIARSE EN ESPANA MERCADO NEGRO Y CORRUPCION / Aradillas Agudo, Antonio – Madrid: Angel Herrero Fernandez, 1977 – 1 – sp Bibl Santa Ana [306]

DIVORCIAS? !LAGARTO! / Merchan Vargas, Regina – Toro: Imp. Siris, 1936 – 1 – sp Bibl Santa Ana [946]

EL DIVORCIO A LA LUZ DEL DERECHO INTERNACIONAL... / Gonzalez, F A – (Missing: p7-10) – Mexico, 1901 – 1mf – 1 – ILM-3106/1 – ne IDC [327]

EL DIVORCIO ANTE EL DERECHO INTERNACIONAL PRIVADO... / Calandrelli, A – Buenos Aires, 1923 – 4mf – 1 – ILM-3725/1 – ne IDC [327]

DIVORCIO EN ESPANA / Aradillas Agudo, Antonio – Barcelona: Luis de Caralt, Editor, S.A., 1977 – 1 – sp Bibl Santa Ana [306]

EL DIVORCIO, ESTUDIO DE LEGISLACION COMPARADA: ESPANA Y SUDAMERICA / Guzman Gundian, Lucila – Santiago de Chile, 1936. 222 p. LL-8011 – 1 – us L of C Photodup [306]

IL DIVORZIO NEI RAPPORTI INTERNAZIONALI... / Esperson, P – Roma, 1901 – 1mf – 1 – ILM-3670/1 – ne IDC [327]

DIVREI RIVOT / Satanow, I – 2v. Constantinople. n.d. approx. 1799-1800. BJ-422-73 1 – 9 – ne IDC [290]

DIVREI SHALOM VE-EMET / Rapoport, S J L – Prague. 1861. BJ-32-4 1 – 9 – ne IDC [270]

DIVREI SHALOM VE-EMET / Wessely, N H – Warsaw. 1866. BJ-422-97 1 – 9 – ne IDC [470]

DIVREI SOFERIM / Rubinstein, S M – Kovno. 1930. BJ-32-8 1 – 9 – ne IDC [270]

DIVTTI – (Konkani language) – Margao, India. 1968-Oct 1971 – 5r – 1 – us L of C Photodup [072]

DIVULGACION HISTORICA FRANCISCO PIZARRO / Tena Fernandez, Juan – Trujillo: Tip. Sobrino de B. Pena, 1925 – 1 – sp Bibl Santa Ana [920]

DIVULGCAO MARXISTA – Rio de Janeiro, BL. 1946-1947 – 1r – $50.00 – R04172 – us Library Micro [072]

DIVUS THOMAS – Freiburg Schw., 1(1914)-24(1946) – 205mf – 9 – Dfl718.00 – ne Slangenburg [073]

DIVUS THOMAS – Freiburg, Schweiz, etc. S2 v1-9. 1914-1922; S3 v10-24. 1923-1946 – 205mf – 9 – ne IDC [240]

DIWAN DES JEHUDA HALEVI / Karpeles, Gustav – Leipzig. 1907. BJ-421-50 1 – 9 – ne IDC [470]

DIWAN R. YEHUDAH HA-LEVI / Luzzatto, S D – Lyck. 1864. BJ-421-53 1 – 9 – ne IDC [470]

DIWEN WULI – (1981 $3.50f; 1980-82 $4.50f) – Physics of Low Temperature. In Chinese but English abstracts to the main articles. F p131 – 9 – cc Microforms [073]

DIWREI CHALOETSIEM – Amsterdam, 1940-1941. V.1(1-4) – 2mf – J-261-27/1 – ne IDC [073]

DIX ANNEES EN EQUATORIA / Casati, Gaetano – Le retour d'Emin Pacha et l'expedition Stanley. Paris, Didot. 1892 – 9 – 17.50 – fr Orientalistes [910]

Dix, Arthur *see* GEOGRAFIA POLITICA. BARCELONA, 1929

LE DIX DECEMBRE – 15 avr 1849-18 juin 1850. continue par: Le Pouvoir. Dir. M. Guillonet. Paris. 19 juin 1850-15 janv 1851 – 1 – fr A.C.H.P.P. [073]

DIX DISCOURS DE G. HERVE SARRAUTE MILLERAND JEAN JAURES BAUDOT RENAUDEL DE PRESSENSE PREFACE DE ROUANET / Congres du Parti Socialiste Francais, Jauressistes. Congres socialiste de Bordeaux, 12 au 14 avril 1903 – l'Emancipatrice, Paris. 1903. 160 p. 5689 – 9 – fr Hachette [335]
Dix, G *see* THE THEOLOGY OF CONFORMATION IN THE RELATION TO BAPTISM
DIX INSCRIPTIONS CHINOISES DE L'ASIE CENTRALE D'APRES LES ESTAMPAGES DE M. C.E. BONIN / Chavannes, E – (Memoires presentes. Inscriptions et belles-lettres). Ser 1 v11(2). Paris, 1904. BU-802 2 – 8 – ne IDC [410]
LES DIX LIVRES D'ARCHITECTURE DE VITRUVE / Perrault, M – Paris, France. 1v. 1684 – 1r – 1 – cn Can Microfilming [720]
LES DIX LIVRES D'ARCHITECTURE DE VITRUVE / Vitruve, Marc – Par Claude Perrault. Paris, J. B. Coignard, 1673. 16, 325p., ill. (Architecture Series) – 9 – fr Hachette [720]
DIX LIVRES DE LA CHIRURGIE, AVEC LE MAGASIN DES INSTRUMENS NECESSAIRES A ICELLE / Pare, A – Paris, 1564 – 10mf – 9 – ne IDC [617]
Dix, Morgan *see*
- THE GOSPEL AND PHILOSOPHY
- LECTURES ON THE CALLING OF A CHRISTIAN WOMAN, AND HER TRAINING TO FULFIL IT
- LECTURES ON THE FIRST PRAYER BOOK OF KING EDWARD 6TH
- LECTURES ON THE PANTHEISTIC IDEA OF AN IMPERSONAL-SUBSTANCE-DEITY
- LECTURES ON THE TWO ESTATES
- THREE GUARDIANS OF SUPERNATURAL RELIGION

DIX NEUVIEME SIECLE *see* LE 19E SIECLE
LE DIX NEUVIEME SIECLE TABLEAUX DES PREMIERES ANNEES *see* LE 19. SIECLE: TABLEAUX DES PREMIERES ANNEES
DIXIA GONGCHENG – Underground Engineering Projects. 1981-. F P232 – 9 – $4.50f – cc Microforms [624]
DIXIANA BAPTIST CHURCH. LEXINGTON COUNTY. SOUTH CAROLINA : CHURCH RECORDS – 1969-72 – 1 – 5.00 – us Baptist [240]
DIXIE COIN AND STAMP NEWS – 1955-1956 – 1 – us P.K. Yonge [730]
DIXIE COUNTY ADVOCATE – Cross City. Fla. Oct 1946-47, 1949- – 1 – us P.K. Yonge [071]
DIXIE GUIDE – Gulfport. Miss. -w, m. 1938-65 – 1 – us UMI [071]
DIXIE PRESS – West Point. Miss. 1902-1907 – 1 – us UMI [071]
Dixon *see* HEROES OF SAN JACINTO
Dixon, A C *see* LIGHTS AND SHADOWS OF AMERICAN LIFE
Dixon, Amzi Clarence *see*
- EVANGELISM OLD AND NEW
- THE GOD MAN

Dixon, Benjamin Homer *see*
- THE BIBLE AND THE PRAYER BOOK: MISTRANSLATIONS, MUTILATIONS AND ERRORS WITH REFERENCES TO PAGANISM
- THE EAST IN PRAYER

DIXON COUNTY ADVOCATE – Ponca, NE. -w. Dec 1917-Dec 1928 – 1 – us NE Hist [071]
DIXON COUNTY LEADER – Ponca, NE. -w. Nov-Dec 1895; Feb-Aug 1896; Apr 1901-Feb 1902; Apr 1908-Mar 1913 – 1 – us NE Hist [071]
Dixon, Frederick Augustus *see*
- FIFINE, THE FISHER MAID, OR, THE MAGIC SHRIMPS
- LITTLE NOBODY: A FAIRY TALE FOR FAIRY PEOPLE
- MAIDEN MONA THE MERMAID: A FAIRY PLAY FOR FAIRY PEOPLE
- YE LAST SWEET THING IN CORNERS: BEING YE FAITHFUL DRAMA OF YE ARTISTS' VENDETTA

Dixon, George *see* THE BARD OF WAR IN TWO VOLUMES
Dixon, H N *see*
- REPORT ON THE MOSSES OF THE ABOR EXPEDITION, 1911-1912
- REPORTS ON THE MOSSES COLLECTED BY MR. C. E. C. FISCHER A.O. FROM SOUTH INDIA AND CEYLON
- STUDIES IN THE BRYOLOGY OF NEW ZEALAND

Dixon, Henry *see* THE ENGLISH INSTRUCTOR
Dixon, Hepworth *see* JOHN HOWARD AND THE PRISON-WORLD OF EUROPE
Dixon, John *see* THE DAGGER
DIXON JOURNAL – Dixon, NE. -w. Jan. 1920-Sep. 1921; Jan. 1925-May 1942 – 1 – us NE Hist [071]
Dixon, Richard Watson *see*
- CHRIST'S COMPANY AND OTHER POEMS
- THE CLOSE OF THE TENTH CENTURY OF THE CHRISTIAN ERA

Dixon, S F *see* SUBSTITUTED LIABILITIES
Dixon, Sam Houston *see* MEN WHO MADE TEXAS FREE
DIXON SPRINGS SHEEPDAY: PROCEEDINGS: ROBBS / Illinois. Agricultural Experiment Station – n.1-5. 1960-64 – 1, 5 – us Spaulding [636]
DIXON TRIBUNE – Dixon, CA. 1883- – 68+ r – 1 BC02172 – $3,400.00 ($120.00y) – us Library Micro [071]
Dixon, W A *see* THE PLANTS OF NEW SOUTH WALES
Dixon-Gottschild, Brenda *see* AESTHETIC STANDARDS IN OLD TIME DANCING IN SOUTHWEST VIRGINIA
DIYARBEKIR – Diyarbekir: Vilayet Matbaasi, 1869-?. No. 319 (22 Eyluel 1927) – 9 – $20.00 – us MEDOC [956]
DIYICI GUONEI GEMING ZHANZHENG SHIQI DE GONGREN YUNDONG (ZHONGGUO XIANDAISHI ZILIAO CONGSHU) – Series of Materials on Contemporary Chinese History: The Workers' Movement in the Period of the First Revolutionary Civil War. Comp. by Renmin Chubanshe, 1954. 7 fiches. F H127 – 9 – $27.00 – cc Microforms [950]
DIYICI GUONEI GEMING ZHANZHENG SHIQI DE NONGMIN YUNDONG (ZHONGGUO XIANDAISHI ZILIAO CONGSHU) – Series of Materials on Contemporary Chinese History: The Peasant Movement in the Period of the First Revolutionary Civil War. Comp. by Renmin Chubanshe, 1953. 5 fiches. F H126 – 9 – $22.50 – cc Microforms [950]
DIYOJEN – Istanbul, 1-3 sene, nos 1-183. – 12 Tesrin 2 1286-12 Kanun 1 1288 [26 Nov. 1869-12 Jan. 1872] – 13mf – 9 – $65.00 – us MEDOC [949]
DIZ ANS A LA COTE D'IVOIRE / Clozel, Francois Joseph – Paris: Augustin Challamel, 1906 – 1 – us Res Libr [910]
DIZHEN DIZHI – Seismology and Geology. In Chinese but English abstracts to the main articles. F p136 – 9 – 4.00f – cc Microforms [073]
DIZHEN GONGCHENG YU GONGCHENG ZHENDONG – Earthquake Engineering and Engineering Vibration. In Chinese, with English abstracts of the main articles. p94 – 9 – $4.50f – cc Microforms [624]
DIZHEN XUEBAO – Acta Seismologica Sinica. 1982-. F P247 – 9 – $4.50f – cc Microforms [073]
DIZHI DIQIU HUAXUE – Geology-Geochemistry. 1981-. F P227 – 9 – $4.50f – cc Microforms [073]
DIZHI KEXUE – Scientia Geologica Sinica. In Chinese but English abstracts to the main articles. F p63 – 9 – 4.00f.00 – cc Microforms [073]
DIZHI LUN-PING – Geological Review. In Chinese but English abstracts to the main articles. F p102 – 9 – $4.50f – cc Microforms [073]
DIZHI XUEBAO – Acta Geologica Sinica. In Chinese but English abstracts to the main articles. F p32 – 9 – 4.00f – cc Microforms [073]
DIZIONARIO ARMENO-ITALIANO / Ciakciak, E – Venice, 1837 – 17mf – ne IDC [040]
DIZIONARIO DEL PITTORI DAL RINNOVAMENTO DELLO BELLE ARTI FINO AL 1800 / Ticozzi, S – Milano. 2v. 1818 – 10mf – ne IDC [700]
...DIZIONARIO DELLA LINGUA ITALIANA E NUBIANA / Carradori, Arcangelo – Uppsala, 1931 – 1 – us Res Libr [040]
DIZZIONARIO DEI PITTORI DAL RINNEVAMENTO DELLE BELLE ARTI FINO AL 1800 / Ticozzi, S – O 1081. 2 v. 1818 – 9 – ne IDC [760]
DIZZIONARIO ITALIANO-TEDESCO : NEUES TEUTSCH-ITALIENISCHES WOERTERBUCH 1732 (AEL, ABT 2;10) / Leys, Franz Jacob – Handschrift aus der Universitaetsbibliothek Erlangen-Nuernberg (mf ed 1993) – 63mf – 9 – DM1,450.00 – 3-89131-084-6 – gw Fischer [040]
DJADIKAN INDONESIA POROS THE NEW EMERGING FORCES / Sukarno, Pres. Indonesia – SE 5019 1. 1964 – 9 – ne IDC [950]
DJADILAH BANGSA JANG "AEROSPACE-MINDED" / Djuanda, Raden – 1962. SE-10,463-1 – 9 – ne IDC [629]
Djadji Darmowijono, R *see* URAIAN MANIPOL (GARISGARIS BESAR HALUAN NEGARA) JOGJAKARTA, MADJELIS LUHUR TAMAN SISWA
DJAGOENG. SING NDJAWAKAKE WASIR REKSAWARDAJA. TJAP2AN KAPINDO / Sanif, Sutan – (Microfiche No 151) – Djakarta: Guneikanbu Kokumin Tosyokyoku (Balai Poestaka), 2604 – 1mf – 9 – SE-2002/1 – ne IDC [950]
DJAGUNG / Sukadis Sosroprawiro, R – SE 4898 1. 1958? – 9 – ne IDC [950]
Djajadiningrati, Raden Mas Arja *see* MARGOWIRJO. SERAT MARGAWIRJA...KA-ETAP INGKANG KAPING 2
DJAJAPRANA. KLUNGKUNG, TOKO BUKU MURNI – (Indonesian and Balinese) – 9 – SE-5180 1 – ne IDC [950]
DJAKA TINGKIR, DITJERITAKAN KEMBALI / Rukiah Kertapati, S – SE-4836 1. 1962 – 9 – ne IDC [950]
Djakarta, Biro Penerangan Ekonomi *see* BULLETIN EKONOMI KEUANGAN
DJAKARTA CHARTER OBLIGATES THE LAW OF SHARIAT UPON ITS ADHERENTS / Sukarno, Pres. Indonesia – Speech on Juli 5, 1963. SE 5320 1. 1964? – 9 – ne IDC [324]
THE DJAKARTA CHARTER; THE SPIRIT OF THE CONSTITUTION OF 1945 / Indonesia. Departemen Agama – Trans. by Amiruddin Djamil. SE-10,573 1. 1964 – 9 – ne IDC [323]
DJAKARTA DISPATCHES – (Some vols missing) – Washington, 1959-1961 – 23mf – SE-526/1 – ne IDC [070]
DJAKARTA GUIDE; A YEAR-ROUND VACATION CITY / Harjati – SE-3151 1. 1962 – 9 – ne IDC [950]
DJAKARTA, INDONESIA'S NATIONAL CAPITAL / Indonesia – SE-3400 1 – 9 – ne IDC [950]
DJAKARTA PRESS SUMMARY / Jakarta – 1961-1965. (Irregular publication. Incomplete). Title varies; also called: Indonesian Language Press Summary. SE-527 1 – 9 – ne IDC [072]
DJAKARTA PRESS SUMMARY *see* INDONESIAN LANGUAGE PRESS SUMMARY
THE DJAKARTA TIMES – Djakarta: Djakarta Times Foundation, sep 1966-sep 1972 – 15r – 1 – us Res Libr [072]
DJAKARTA-KEBAJORAN. LIST OF STREET NAMES / Latif, Chalid – SE-4678 1. 1962 – 9 – ne IDC [950]
Djakasuria *see* LINTASAN REPOLUSI
DJALWN RINGKAS KE BAHASA INGGERIS / Sardjito, K – v1 only. 1951- – 9 – SE-4470 1 – ne IDC [370]
Djamaloedin Bin Moh. Rasad, B *see* BOEAH PIKIRAN
DJANGAN MENDERITA TANI-PHOBI / Sukarno, Pres. Indonesia – SE 5450 1. Sept. 7, 1964 – 9 – ne IDC [324]
Djanin, Arief *see* TEORI EKONOMI NASIONAL; KUMPULAN BATJAAN
DJASA JANG TA'DILOEPAKAN : TJETAKAN 2 – Djakarta, Gunseikanbu Kokumin Tosyokyoku (2603). 40p – 31mf – 9 – ne IDC [370]
DJAWA / Java Instituut – (Index 1921-1940) – Weltevreden, etc., 1921-1941. v1-21 – 252mf – SE-86/1 – ne IDC [073]
DJAWA TENGAH DALAM ANGKA / Central Java (Province) – (Annual. Missing: 1970) – Semarang, 1969-1971 – 36mf – 9 – SE-1377/1 – ne IDC [950]
DJAWATAN PENERANGAN / Jogjakarta. Indonesia – Daerah istimewa Jogjakarta. 1958-62. TEN 1147.BSE-1721/1 – 9 – ne IDC [950]
Djawatan Perikanan Darat/Laut *see* BERITA PERIKANAN
AL- DJAZAIR – Alger. n1-19, dec 1904-avr 1905. mq. n3-4, 12 – 1 – fr A.C.R.P.P. [073]
DJAZAIR *see* AL- DJAZAIR
DJEDJAK DYNAMICA MASJARAKAT / Suprapti, I N – SE 4071 1. 1946? – 9 – ne IDC [950]
DJEM – Istanbul, nos 1-33. – 15 Kanun 1 1927-2 Agustos 1928 [15 Dec. 1927-2 Aug. 1928] – 9mf – 9 – $57.00 – us MEDOC [949]
Djenen *see* GEOGRAFI INDONESIA
Djevalikian, Raffi *see* THE RELATIONSHIP BETWEEN ASYMMETRICAL LEG POWER AND CHANGE OF RUNNING DIRECTION
DJIKA MALAM DIPADANG PASIR / Kasim Sutan Mohammed Sjah – Djakarta, Balai Pustaka.1950. For voice and orchestra. SEM-5232/1 – 9 – ne IDC [780]
LES DJIMINI. ELEMENTS D'ORGANISATION SOCIALE / Thoret, Jean-Claude – (Africa series). 1969 – 9 – fr Hachette [300]
LE DJIN [CIN] – Istanbul, 1928-?; Sahib-i Imtiyaz ve Mueduer-i Mes'ul: Ahmed Cemaleddin, No 1.-16 Mai 1918 – 1mf – 9 – $12.00 – us MEDOC [949]
DJIWA ISLAM – (Lacking: 1946, V.1(1,4)) – Jogjakarta: G.P.I.I., 1946 – 3mf – 9 – ne IDC [260]
Djojoadhiningrat, Abdulmadjid *see* DER PRESSEZUSTAND IN INDONESIEN
DJOJOBOJO – (Lacking: 1945 v1(1,3,4,8-14). 1947 v2(5,6,9-?). 1948 v3(1-13,16-19)) – Kediri, 1945-1948 – 12mf – 9 – ne IDC [950]
Djojohadikusumo, Sumitro *see*
- REPORT ON THE P.R.R.I. REBELLION
- SEARCHLIGHT ON INDONESIA

Djoko Santoso *see* SOME ASPECTS OF SPONTANEOUS TRANSMIGRATION IN INDONESIA
Djuanda, Raden *see* DJADILAH BANGSA JANG "AEROSPACE-MINDED"
Djumena, Sascha *see* DISKRIMINIERUNG AM ARBEITSMARKT
DJURSHOLMS TIDNING – Stockholm, Sweden. 1895-1957 – 24r – 1 – sw Kungliga [072]
Djurusan Antropologi, Fakultas Sastra, Universitas Indonesia *see* BERITA ANTROPOLOGI
Djurusan Bahasa dan Sastra Sunda Fakultas Keguruan *see* BENDE RANTJAGE
D.L.I. *see* OB OZHIDOVLENII BYVSHE I GOSUDARSTV. DUMY
DLIA CHEGO NUZHNA SEL'SKOKHOZIAISTVENNAIA I PROMYSLOVAIA KOOPERATSIIA I KAK EE ORGANIZOVAT' V DEREVNE / Kisliakov, E N – Tula, 1922 – 1mf – 9 – COR-423/1 – ne IDC [334]
DLIA CHEGO NUZHNY SOVIETY KRESTIANSKIKH DEPUTATOV / Bykhovskii, Naum I Akovlevich – Petrograd: Partii a sotsialistov-revoliutsionerov, 1917 – 1 – CSUX89-B7303 – us Hoover Inst Photo [947]
DLIA LEGKAGO CHTENIIA – Povesti, rasskazy, komedii, puteshestviia i stikhotvoreniia sovremennykh russkikh pisatelei. v. 1-9. Spb. 1856-59. BR-3482 2 – 8 – ne IDC [460]
DM DATA MANAGEMENT – v.13- 1975- – 1,5,6,9 – us UMI [650]
D.M. LUTHERS WIE AUCH ANDERER GOTTSELIGEN UND LENTE GEISTLICHE LIEDER UND PSALMEI WIE SIE BISHER IN EVANENSCHEN KIRCHEN DIESER LANDEN GEBRAUCHT WERDEN... / Crueger, J – (Tenor partbook) – Berlin: Christoff Runge, 1657 – us Sibley [780]
DM NEWS – (Direct Marketing).1979 – 1,5,6,9 – us UMI [073]
D.M. THORNTON : A STUDY IN MISSIONARY IDEALS AND METHODS / Gairdner, William Henry Temple – London; New York: Hodder and Stoughton, [1908?] – 1mf – 9 – 0-8370-6494-5 – 1986-0494 – us A.T.L.A. [920]
DMA WEEKLY NEWS LETTER *see* AIR FORCE MAGAZINE
THE DMIC METALLURGY COLLECTION / Defense Metals Information Center. Battelle Memorial Institute – 1952-71 – 9 – 1000.00 – us Updata [660]
Dmitrenko, I I *see* OPIS' KAZACH'IKH DEL MOSKOVSKOGO OTDELENIIA OBSHCHEGO ARKHIVA GLAVNOGO SHTABA
DMITRI I LEONIDOVICH KHORVAT / [Vatrantsev..., B D et al] – [Vladivostok: s.n., 1918] – 1 – CSUX89-B2677 – us Hoover Inst Photo [947]
DMITRI IWANOWITSCH : DRAMA / Wilhelmi, Adolph – Leipzig: I M Gebhardt's Verlag, 1869 – 1r – 1 – us U.W. Library [820]
Dmitriev, A M *see* UKAZATEL' LITERATURY PO TRAVOSEIANIIU I LUGOVODSTVY NA RUSSKOM IAZYKE
Dmitriev, I I *see* SOCHINENIIA
Dmitriev, M A *see* MELOCHI IZ ZAPASA MOEI PAMIATI
Dmitriev, N *see* OT VOLGI DO BAIKALA
Dmitrieva, Valentina Iovovna *see* TAK BYLO
Dmitriev-Mamanov, A I *see*
- PECHAT' Y TOBOL'SKOM NAMESTNICHESTVE V KONTSE 18 STOLETIIA
- PUGACHEVSKII BUNT V ZAURAL'E I SIBIRI

DMITRII MEREZHKOVSKII / Gippius-Merezhkovskaia, Z – YMCA-Press. Paris. 1951. BR-713 2 – 8 – ne IDC [920]
Dmitrovskii, N V *see* KATALOG KNIG RUSSKAGO OTDELENIIA TURKESTANSKOI PUBLICHNOI BIBLIOTEKI
Dmowski, R *see* LA QUESTION POLONAISE
DN NORD SOLLENTUNA/VASBY – Stockholm, Sweden. 1988 – 1 – sw Kungliga [072]
DN NORD SOLNA/SUNDBYBERG – Stockholm, Sweden. 1988 – 1 – sw Kungliga [072]
DN NORDOST TABY – Stockholm, Sweden. 1988 – 1 – sw Kungliga [072]
DN NORDVAST JARFALLA – Stockholm, Sweden. 1988 – 1 – sw Kungliga [072]
DN NORDVAST VALLINGBY – Stockholm, Sweden. 1988 – 1 – sw Kungliga [072]
DN SODERMALM – Stockholm, Sweden. 1988 – 1 – sw Kungliga [072]
DN STOCKHOLMSSPORTEN – Stockholm, Sweden. 1988 – 1 – sw Kungliga [072]
DN SYD FARSTA – Stockholm, Sweden. 1988 – 1 – sw Kungliga [072]
DN SYD HANINGE – Stockholm, Sweden. 1988 – 1 – sw Kungliga [072]
DN SYDOST – Stockholm, Sweden. 1988 – 1 – sw Kungliga [072]
DN SYDVAST – Stockholm, Sweden. 1988 – 1 – sw Kungliga [072]
DNA NEWSLETTER – 1968-75. (American Indian Periodicals in the Princeton University Library). 6 fiches – 9 – $45.00 – us UPA [305]
DNA SEQUENCE : THE JOURNAL OF DNA SEQUENCING AND MAPPING / ed by Barrell & Bart – 9,5,1 – us Harwood [575]
Dneprovskii, S P *see*
– KAK SOSTAVIT' PLAN DEIATEL'NOSTI SEL'SKOGO OBSHCHESTVA POTREBITELEI
– PRIMERNAIA REVIZIIA I PLAN DEIATEL'NOSTI SEL'SKOGO KOOPERATIVA
DNES – Sofia, Bulgaria.May 1941-Jun 1944 (scattered issues) – 4r – 1 – us L of C Photodup [949]
DNESEK – v1-2. 1946-1948 – 1 – us I.U. Libraries [073]
DNESTR – Kishiniev, 1948-62. v1-15. Lacking: 1948-59 (1-5); 1960, v13 (12). BR-10,387/1 – 9 – ne IDC [947]
DNEVNIK – Novi Sad, Yugoslavia. Jan 1953-1970 – 61r – 1 – us L of C Photodup [949]
DNEVNIK – Sofia, Bulgaria. Oct 1942-1943 – 2r – 1 – us L of C Photodup [949]
DNEVNIK ALEKSI EI A BUDBERGA / Budberg, Aleksei Pavlovich Baron – Berlin: "Slovo", 1923-1924. 4v – 1 – CSUX88-B8949 – us Hoover Inst Photo [947]
DNEVNIK ARTISTA – Prilozhenie k zhurnalu "Artist". v. 1-10. M. 1892-93. B-1705 2 – 8 – ne IDC [073]
DNEVNIK ELIZAVETY DIAKONOVO I: NA VYSSHIKH ZHENSKIKH KURSAKH (1895-1899 G.) / Diakonova, Elizaveta Aleksandrovna – 2-e izd. S.Peterburg: Tip. M.P.S. (T-va I.N. Kushnerev), 1905 – 1 – CSUX88-B9128 – us Hoover Inst Photo [370]
DNEVNIK PISATELIA – Ezhemesiachnoe izdanie D. V. Averkieva. Spb. 1885-86. B-1706 2 – 8 – ne IDC [460]
DNEVNIK PISATELIA – Ezhemesiachnoe obshchedostupnoe izdanie. Izd. A. V. Kruglova. M. 1907-09. B-1707 2 – 8 – ne IDC [460]
DNEVNIK POETA / Aseev, N – L. 1929. BR-898 2 – 8 – ne IDC [460]
DNEVNIK PORUCHIKA VASIL'EVA – Prodolzhenie vremeni 1774, 1775, 1776, i 1777 godov. Spb. 1896. BR-6017 2 – 8 – ne IDC [073]
DNEVNIK V STIKHAKH / Otsup, N – Paris. 1950. BR-1214 2 – 8 – ne IDC [460]
DNEVNITZI / Bulgaria. Obiknoveno Narodno Subraniye – Sofia. Feb 10 1879-Mar 28 1943. Incomplete – 1 – us NY Public [324]
DNI – Berlin puis Paris. en russe. oct 1922-juin 1933 – 1 – fr A.C.R.P.P. [073]
DNI – Ezhednevniaia gazeta. (Cont. as ezhenedel'nik) pod red. A. F. Kerenskago. Berlin, Paris. 1922-33. Available: 1928-32. BR-8269 2 – 8 – ne IDC [073]
DNI – (Library has: no. 802-1465 (Sept. 16, 1925-June 30, 1928)) – Berlin: "Dni", 1922-1928 – 1 – CSUX87-S196 – us Hoover Inst Photo [947]
DNI LIUBVI / Gorodetskii, S – Razskazy. Spb. 1914. BR-1123 2 – 8 – ne IDC [460]
DNI REVOLIUTSII : PAMI ATKA NARODU – Moskva: "Voli a", [1917] – 1 – CSUX88-B6483 – us Hoover Inst Photo [335]
DNI SOLDATSKO I SHKOLY *see* GAZETA DEVI ATAGO OKTI ABRI A
DNIPRO – Kiev, 1944-72. Lacking issues. BR-10,388/1 – 9 – ne IDC [947]
DNIPRO / Ukrainian Orthodox Church of America – Trenton, NJ. Official organ. -w. 17 May 1924-March 1942. Lacking Dec 1926-Dec 1927. 4 reels – 1 – uk British Libr Newspaper [073]
Do Chi, T *see* MODELES CINETIQUES ET STRUCTURAUX EN DYNAMIQUE DES POPULATIONS EXPLOITEES: APPLICATION AUX SQUILLES; SQUILLA MANTIS (L.) (CRUSTACE STOMATOPODE) DU GOLFE DU LION
DO ESP AND MICROGRAPHICS HAVE ANYTHING IN COMMON? / Zube, John – Together with: Letter on Super Computer Club and L.M.P. and Editorial Note on Apjohn: Cobden and Difficulties and techniques of libertarian propaganda. 1 fiche (29x) – 9 – 1.00f – at Libertarian Micro [320]
THE "DO NOT FILE" FILE / ed by Theoharis, Athan – With printed guide – 2r – 1 – $225.00 – 1-55655-134-7 – us UPA [324]
"DO NOT SAY" : OR, THE CHURCH'S EXCUSES FOR NEGLECTING THE HEATHEN: WITH A STATEMENT AND AN APPEAL / Horsburgh, J Heywood – [3rd ed]. New York: Fleming H Revell, c1892 – 1mf – 9 – 0-8370-7156-9 – 1986-1156 – us A.T.L.A. [230]
DO YOU THINK YOU CAN GOVERN YOURSELF CHEAPER THAN YOU CAN HIRE IT DONE? / Barnhill, J B – 1p leaflet, 1919 in favour of Henry Replogle's writings – 9 – 1.00f – at Libertarian Micro [335]
DOA RESTU P.J.M. PRESIDEN R.I. PADA UPATJARA PENTJANGKULAN PERTAMA DALAM USAHA SELF-SUPPORTING BERAS DI RENGASDENGKLOK, KRAWANG / Sukarno, Pres. Indonesia – SE 4383 1. 1961 – 9 – ne IDC [025]
Doan, Frank Carleton *see* RELIGION AND THE MODERN MIND
Doane, A N *see*
– ANGLO-SAXON GOSPELS
– ANGLO-SAXON MANUSCRIPTS IN MICROFICHE FACSIMILE, VOL 1
Doane, William Croswell *see* MANIFESTATIONS OF THE RISEN JESUS
Dobayashi, Yoichi *see* THE HERMENEUTICAL PROBLEM OF YAHWEH WAR IN THE BOOK OF JOSHUA 1-12
Dobbek, Wilhelm *see*
– HERDER
– J.G. HERDERS HUMANITAETSIDEE ALS AUSDRUCK SEINES WELTBILDES UND SEINER PERSOENLICHKEIT
Dobbriner, Paul *see* "ERITIS SICUT DEUS", EIN BEITRAG ZUR GESCHICHTE DES RELIGIOESEN ROMANS
Dobbs, Archibald Edward *see* PHILOSOPHY AND POPULAR MORALS IN ANCIENT GREECE
Dobbs, Hugh J *see* HISTORY OF GAGE COUNTY
Dobell, Richard Reid *see* LECTURE ON IMPERIAL FEDERATION, DECEMBER 1888
Dobiash-Rozhdestvenskaia, O A *see* SREDNEVEKOV'E V RUKOPISIAKH PUBLICHNOI BIBLIOTEKI
Dobie, Robert *see*
– IN THE QUEEN'S BENCH: IN APPEAL FROM SUPERIOR COURT, MONTREAL: REVEREND ROBERT DOBIE, PETIONER-APPELLANT VS. BOARD FOR THE MANAGEMENT OF THE TEMPORALITIES FUND OF THE PRESBYTERIAN CHURCH OF CANADA...
– IN THE SUPERIOR COURT: THE REVEREND ROBERT DOBIE, PETITIONER, VS. BOARD FOR THE MANAGEMENT OF THE TEMPORALITIES' FUND OF THE PRESBYTERIAN CHURCH OF CANADA, IN CONNECTION WITH THE CHURCH OF SCOTLAND. ET AL., RESPONDENTS
Doble, G H *see*
– ORDINALE EXON, VOL 4
– PONTIFICALE LANALETENSE
DOBLESTNAI A ZASHCHITA PETROGRADA V OKTIABRE 1919 GODA : PO MATERIALAM POLEVOGO SHTABA REVVOENSOVETA RESPUBLIKI – Moskva: Gos. izd-vo, 1921 – 1 – CSUX88-B3681 – us Hoover Inst Photo [947]
DOBRI VESTI = GOOD NEWS / ed by Angelov, Vasil G – Bulgaria. v1-2, no 10, Sept. 1946-June 1948 – 1r – 1 – $17.28 – us Baptist [240]
Dobrof, Rose *see* JOURNAL OF GERONTOLOGICAL SOCIAL WORK
DOBROGEA NOUA – Constanta, Romania. 1962-81 – 28r – 1 – us L of C Photodup [949]
Dobroklonskii, Aleksandr Pavlovich *see* PREP. FEODOR, ISPOVEDNIK I IGUMEN STUDIISKII
Dobroklonskii, S *see* KRATKAIA ISTORIIA ROSSIISKOI DIPLOMATII
Dobroliubov, IV *see* BIBLIOGRAFICHESKII SLOVAR' PISATELEI, UCHENYKH I KHUDOZHNIKOV UROZHENTSEV (PREIMUSHCHESTVENNO) RIAZANSKOI GUBERNII
Dobroliubov, N A *see* PERVOE POLNOE SOBRANIE SOCHINENII
DOBROVOLET S : IZDANIE SOI UZA DOBROVOLT SEV: LE VOLONTAIRE – (Includes c.1: 1937:Feb.; 1938:Feb) – Paris: Soi uz, 19uu – 1 – CSUXAKG5982-S – us Hoover Inst Photo [947]
DOBROVOLET S (PARIS, FRANCE) *see* DOBROVOLET S
Dobrowolski, Augustinus *see* PARADISUS EUCHARISTICUS
DOBRUCA SADASI – Koestence (Konstanza): Dobruca Muesuelman Te'emin-i Maarif Cemiyeti. Sahib-i Imtiyaz ve Mueduer-i Mes'ul: Sueleyman Abduelhamid, 1910-19? – 9 – $25.00 – us MEDOC [956]
DOBRUDZHANSKA TRIBUNA – Tolbukhin, Bulgaria. 1955-1969 – 10r – 1 – us L of C Photodup [949]
DOBRUJA PAMPHLET COLLECTION – 1917-1928 – 1 – CSUXANQ5199-B – us Hoover Inst Photo [999]
Dobrynin, G *see* ISTINNOE POVESTVOVANIE ILI ZHIZN' GAVRIILA DOBRYNINA
Dobrynin, V *see* DON V BORBI E S KOMMUNO I NA DONT SI E I MANYCHI E FEVRALMA I 1919 G
Dobschuetz, E V *see*
– CHRISTUSBILDER
– DAS DECRETUM GELASIANUM (T.U.U. 3-38/4)
– DAS KERYGMA PETRI (T.U.U. 1-11/1)
Dobschuetz, Ernst von *see*
– PROBLEME DES APOSTOLISCHEN ZEITALTERS
– STUDIEN ZUR TEXTKRITIK DER VULGATA
Dobson, George H *see* OCEAN ROUTES AND MODERN TRANSPORTATION: CANADA'S SPLENDID OPPORTUNITY
DOCE ANOS DE POLITICA / Frondizi, Silvio – Buenos Aires: [Ediciones Praxis], 2nd ed 1958 – 1 – CSUXADQ0031-B – us Hoover Inst Photo [320]
DOCE NOS... / Sanchis Alventosa, Joaquin – Barcelona, 1965: Madrid: Graf. Calleja, 1966 – 1 – sp Bibl Santa Ana [946]
Dochez, L *see* NOUVEAU DICTIONNAIRE DE LA LANGUE FRANCAISE
LE DOCKER NOIR / Sembene, Ousmane – Paris, Editions Debresse [1956] – us Res Libr [072]
DOCKET / Coldwater. Kansas. Police Court – 1884-1915 – 1 – us KS Hist [360]
DOCKET / Dodge City. Kansas. Police Court – 1885-1906 – 1 – us KS Hist [978]
THE DOCKET – Toronto: Docket Publishing Co, [1889?-18– or 19–] – 9 – cn C.I.H.M. [971]
THE DOCKET – v1-2 no 5. 1897-98 – 1mf – 9 – $4.50 – LLMC 82-922 – us L.L.M.C. [073]
DOCKET BOOKS / U.S. Indian Claims Commission – 41 fiches – 9 – $135.00 – us UPA [305]
DOCKET OF COUNTY HOME BILLS / Allen County. Ohio. Auditor – 1905-1912 – 1r – 1 – $32.50r – us Archival [324]
DOCKETS / Erie County. Ohio. Milan Township. Justice of the Peace – 1857-1955 – 1r – 1 – $32.50r – us Archival [324]
DOCKETS / Erie County. Ohio. Vermilion Township. Justice of the Peace – 1849-1935 – 2r – 1 – $32.50r – us Archival [324]
DOCKETS / Hays. Kansas. Police Court – 1912-41 – 1 – us KS Hist [978]
DOCKETS / Monroe County. Mich, Bedford Township. Justice of the Peace – 1871-1950 – 1r – 1 – $32.50r – us Archival [324]
DOCKETS, 1791-1950 / U.S. Supreme Court – 27 rolls. Printed guide – 1 – M216 – us Nat'l Archives [340]
Docking, Virginia *see* LETTERS RECEIVED FROM PROMINENT INDIVIDUALS
Dockwray, T *see* THE OPERATIONS OF THE HOLY SPIRIT IMPERCEPTIBLE, AND HOW MEN MAY KNOW WHEN THEY ARE UNDER THE GUIDANCE AND INFLUENCE OF THE SPIRIT:...
DOCTEUR D. SAQUET : 7 BROCHURES MICROFILMEES ENSEMBLE / Saquet, D – (Action trophique locale du massage abdominal leger...) – 1 – F72.11 – fr Armell [615]
THE DOCTOR / Southey, Robert – London: Longman, Rees, Orme, Brown, Green and Longman, 1834-1847 – 4 rolls – 1 – 1-55879-143-4 – uk Libr Preservation [810]
EL DOCTOR ALEM Y EL RADICALISMO / Castellanos, Joaquin – Buenos Aires, n.d – 1 – us Res Libr [335]
DOCTOR BALTHASAR HUBMAIER UND DIE ANFAENGE DER WIEDERTAUFE IN MAEHREN : AUS GLEICHZEITIGEN QUELLEN UND MIT BENUETZUNG DES WISSENSCHAFTLICHEN NACHLASSES DES HOFRATHES DR. JOSEF RITTER V. BECK / Loserth, Johann – Bruenn: Verlag der Hist.-Statist. Section, 1893 – 1mf – us A.T.L.A. [240]
DOCTOR CRISP'S GHOST : OR, A CHECK UPON CHECKS, BEING A BRIDLE FOR ANTINOMIANS AND A WHIP FOR PELAGIAN AND ARMINIAN METHODISTS – London, 1773 – 1mf – 9 – MP-491/1 – ne IDC [240]
DOCTOR CUPID: A NOVEL / Broughton, Rhoda – British Fiction Archive: Unit 4 – 9 – uk Bell [830]
DOCTOR DOBB'S JOURNAL OF COMPUTER CALISTHENICS AND ORTHODONTIA – v1-1976- 1; v3- 1978- 5,6,9 – us UMI [617]
DOCTOR, FAMILY PHYSICIAN & MEDICAL ANSWERS – London, UK. 1906. -irr. 8 feet – 1 – uk British Libr Newspaper [072]
DR. JOHN R. MOTT; PELOPOR PEKABARAM INDJIL DAN KESATUAN KRISTEN / Fransz, A L – SE-5818 1. 1960 – 9 – ne IDC [920]
DR. JOHN WALKER AND THE SUFFERINGS OF THE CLERGY / Tatham, Geoffrey Bulmer – Cambridge: University Press, 1911 – 1mf – us A.T.L.A. [240]
DOCTOR KERKHOVEN / Wassermann, Jakob – New York: H Liveright, c1932 – 1r – 1 – us U.W. Library [830]
Doctor, M *see* DIE PHILOSOPHIE DES JOSEF (IBN) ZADDIK
DR. MARTIN LUTHER'S SMALL CATECHISM / Reu, Johann M – 1929 – 1 – us A.T.L.A. [240]
DAS DOCTOR MARTINUS KEIN ADIAPHORIST GEWESEN I.. / Amsdorff, N von – Magdeburg, 1550 – 1mf – 9 – ne IDC [240]
DOCTOR OF TANGANYIKA / White, Paul Hamilton Hume – Sydney: G.M. Dash, publisher's note 1943. 244p. ill – 1 – us U.W. Library [610]
DAS DOCTOR POMER VND DOCTOR MAIOR MIT IREN ADIAPHORISTEN ERGERNIS VNND ZURTRENNUNG ANGERICHT VNND DEN KIRCHEN CHRISTI VNUEBERWINTLICHEN SCHADEN GETHAN HABEN / Amsdorff, N von – [Magdeburg], 1551 – 1mf – 9 – ne IDC [240]
DOCTOR SYNTAX, HIS THREE TOURS IN SEARCH OF THE PICTURESQUE, OF CONSOLATION, OF A WIFE / Combe, William – London: F. Warne & Co., (n.d.). 376p – 1 – us U.W. Library [830]
DOCTOR TUCKER, PRIEST-MUSICIAN : A SKETCH WHICH CONCERNS THE DOINGS AND THINKINGS OF THE REV. JOHN IRELAND TUCKER, S.T.D.... / Knauff, Christopher W – New York: A.D.F. Randolph, 1897 – 1mf – us A.T.L.A. [240]
DOCTORAL DISSERTATIONS ACCEPTED BY AMERICAN UNIVERSITIES – (Superseded by: American Doctoral Dissertations) – v1-22. 1933-55 – 1 – us UMI [000]
DOCTORAL DISSERTATIONS ACCEPTED BY AMERICAN UNIVERSITIES *see* AMERICAN DOCTORAL DISSERTATIONS
DOCTORIS SUBTILIS ET MARIANI JOANNIS DURIS SCOTI (OFM). OPERA OMNIA... / Barrado Manzano, Arcangel – Madrid: Arch. Ibero Americano, 1965 – 1 – sp Bibl Santa Ana [780]
DOCTORIS...JOANNIS DIUS SCOTI...OPERA OMNIA / Barrado Manzano, Arcangel – Madrid: Graf. Calleja, 1966 – 1 – sp Bibl Santa Ana [780]
EL DOCTOR...MEDICO DE SEVILLA / Saavedra, J – Malaga, SA: S. 17 – 1mf – 9 – sp Cultura [610]

THE DOCTOR'S DAUGHTER – Ottawa: A.S. Woodburn, 1885. 00557. (Pre-1900 Canadiana) – 9 – cn C.I.H.M. [830]

THE DOCTOR'S WIFE / Braddon, Mary Elizabeth – British Fiction Archive: Unit 5 – 9 – uk Bell [830]

THE DOCTOR'S WIFE / Braddon, Mary Elizabeth – London: John Maxwell, 4th ed 1864 – 3v 2 rolls – 1 – 1-55879-217-1 – uk Libr Preservation [830]

DOCTRINA CRISTIANA CANTADA Y AMENIZADA, DEDICADA A CORTIJOS, ESCUELAS RURALES, BARRIADAS, ETC / Lopez de Sosoaga y Borinaga, Benigno – Badajoz: Imp. Comercial, 1968 – 1 – sp Bibl Santa Ana [240]

DOCTRINA DE LA IGLESIA SOBRE EL DERECHO DE ENSENAR / Marquez, Gabino – Madrid: Ed. Studium de Cultura, 1951 – 1 – sp Bibl Santa Ana [240]

DOCTRINA DE LA REVOLUCION DEL 4 DE JUNIO : BASES PARA LA ORGANIZACION ECONOMICA Y SOCIAL DE LA REPUBLICA ARGENTINA / Barboza, Emiliano M & Sosa, Estelredo J – Buenos Aires: Editorial Yunque, 1946 – 1 – CSUXADQ4918-B – us Hoover Inst Photo [320]

DOCTRINA DEL ESTOICO...EPICTETO... ENCHIRIDION / Sanchez de las Brozas, Francisco – 1612 – 9 – $1.50f – sp Bibl Santa Ana [180]

DOCTRINA DEL NACIONALISMO : EDITADA POR EL AUTOR COMO CONTRIBUCION A LA OBRA DEL NACIONALISMO ARGENTINO / Feria, Salvador – Florida [Argentine Republic], 1947 – 1 – CSUXADH7738-B – us Hoover Inst Photo [320]

DOCTRINA NACIONAL – Buenos Aires: Presidencia de la Nacion, Secretaria de Prensa y Difusion, 1955 – 1 – CSUXAJA7266-B – us Hoover Inst Photo [320]

LA DOCTRINA NACIONAL JUSTICIALISTA : EL ESTADO DE DERECHO JUSTICIALISTA. LOS PERONISTAS, LA IGLESIA Y LAS FF. AA / Centro de Documentacion Justicialista – Buenos Aires, 1st ed 1973 – 1 – CSUXADQ2933-B – us Hoover Inst Photo [320]

LA DOCTRINA QUE...INFALIBIDAD DE LA RAZON.. / Romero de Castillay Perosso, Francisco – 1879 – 9 – 1.50f – sp Bibl Santa Ana [140]

DOCTRINA...ANTONIO GOMEZ...DIEGO GOMEZ CORNEJO / Perez Villamil, Juan – 1776 – 9 – 1.50f – sp Bibl Santa Ana [890]

DOCTRINAL DE UN HEROE Y HOMBRE DE ESTADO / Mola Y Vidal, Emilio – Pensamientos y juicios del caudillo del ejercito del norte. Bilbao, 1937. Fiche W 1054. (Blodgett Collection of Spanish Civil War Pamphlets) – 9 – us H.U. College Libr [946]

THE DOCTRINAL SYSTEM OF ST JOHN... AS EVIDENCE FOR THE DATE OF HIS GOSPEL / Lias, John James – London: George Bell, 1875. 1 fiche – 9 – us A.T.L.A. [240]

DOCTRINAL THOUGHTS / Seely, Amos W – New York: Frank McElroy, 1861 – 1mf – 9 – 0-8370-5361-7 – 1985-3361 – us A.T.L.A. [240]

LAS DOCTRINAS POLITICAS DE EUGENIO MARIA DE HOSTOS / Elias de Tejada, Francisco – Madrid: Ediciones de Cultura Hispanica, 1949 – sp Bibl Santa Ana [320]

LAS DOCTRINAS POLITICAS EN PORTUGAL (EDAD MEDIA) / Elias de Tejada Spinola, Francisco – Madrid: Escelicer, S.L., 1943 – sp Bibl Santa Ana [320]

DOCTRINAS SOCIALES, SUPERADAS POR... / Almendrallucas, Bernardo – Caceres: Tip. El Noticiero, s.a. (1950) – sp Bibl Santa Ana [946]

DOCTRINE AND LIFE : A STUDY OF SOME OF THE PRINCIPAL TRUTHS OF THE CHRISTIAN RELIGION IN THEIR RELATION TO CHRISTIAN EXPERIENCE / Stevens, George Barker – (Include index) – New York: Silver, Burdett, 1895 – 1mf – 9 – 0-8370-2898-1 – 1985-0898 – us A.T.L.A. [240]

LA DOCTRINE ASCETIQUE DE SAINT BASILE DE CESAREE / Humbertclaude, P – Paris, 1932 – 6mf – 8 – ne Slangenburg [240]

LA DOCTRINE CURIEUSE DES BEAUX ESPRITS DE CE TEMPS... / Garasse, F – Paris, 1624 – 12mf – 9 – CA-112/1 – ne IDC [240]

LA DOCTRINE DE LA CREATION DANS L'ECOLE DE CHARTRES / Parent, J M – Paris, 1938 – 4mf – 8 – ne Slangenburg [210]

LA DOCTRINE DE LA MATIERE CHEZ AVICEBRON / Brunner, F – 1956, los artikel – 1mf – 8 – ne Slangenburg [100]

DOCTRINE DE LA SAINTE CÈNE: ESSAI DOGMATIQUE *see* COLLECTED WORKS

DOCTRINE DE L'EXPIATION ET SON EVOLUTION HISTORIQUE = THE DOCTRINE OF THE ATONEMENT AND IST HISTORICAL EVOLUTION / Sabatier, Auguste – (In English. Includes bibliographical references) – New York: G P Putnam; London: Williams & Norgate, 1904 – 1mf – 9 – 0-8370-5268-8 – 1985-3268 – us A.T.L.A. [240]

LA DOCTRINE DE MALHERBE / Brunot, F – 1891 – 9 – fr I.C.S. [190]

DOCTRINE DE SAINT-SIMON: EXPOSITION, DEUXIEME ANNEE – Paris, l'Organisateur. 1830. 172 p. Les Saint-Simoniens, 1825-1834. 6848 – 9 – fr Hachette [335]

DOCTRINE DE SAINT-SIMON: EXPOSITION, PREMIERE ANNEE, 1829 – Paris, l'Organisateur. 1830. 327 p. Les Saint-Simoniens, 1825-1834. 6847 – 9 – fr Hachette [335]

DOCTRINE DE SAINT-SIMON: LA MARSEILLAISE / Chevalier, Michel – Paris, Everat. s.d. 8 p. Les Saint-Simoniens, 1825-1834. 6860 – 9 – fr Hachette [335]

DOCTRINE DES FONCTIONS MÉDIATRICES DU SAUVEUR *see* COLLECTED WORKS

THE DOCTRINE OF CY PRES AS APPLIED TO CHARITIES / McGrath, Robert Hunter, jr – Philadelphia, Johnson, 1887. 74 p. LL-310 – 1 – us L of C Photodup [340]

THE DOCTRINE OF ELECTION : AND ITS CONNECTION WITH THE GENERAL TENOR OF CHRISTIANITY / Erskine, Thomas – 2nd ed. Edinburgh: David Douglas, 1878 – 1mf – 9 – 0-8370-3723-9 – 1985-1723 – us A.T.L.A. [240]

THE DOCTRINE OF ELECTION : NEITHER DEROGATORY TO GOD, NOR DISCOURAGING TO MAN / Boardman, Henry Augustus – Philadelphia: Presbyterian Bd of Publ, 1860 – 1mf – 9 – 0-8370-2713-6 – 1985-0713 – us A.T.L.A. [240]

THE DOCTRINE OF ENDLESS PUNISHMENT / Shedd, William Greenough Thayer – (Includes bibliographical references) – New York: Charles Scribner, 1886, c1885 – 1mf – 9 – 0-8370-9821-1 – 1986-3821 – us A.T.L.A. [240]

THE DOCTRINE OF EQUITY / Adams, John Coleman – 5th American ed. Phila., Johnson, 1868. 811 p. LL-729 – 1 – us L of C Photodup [340]

THE DOCTRINE OF GRACE : OR, THE OFFICE AND OPERATIONS OF THE HOLY SPIRIT VINDICATED FROM THE INSULTS OF INFIDELITY AND THE ABUSES OF FANATICISM,...IN THREE BOOKS / Warburton, W – London, 2nd ed 1763 – 3mf – 9 – MP-419/1 – ne IDC [240]

THE DOCTRINE OF GRACE IN OUR APOSTOLIC FATHERS / Torrance, Thomas F – 1947 – 9 – $10.00 – us I.R.C. [240]

THE DOCTRINE OF GRACE IN THE APOSTOLIC FATHERS / Torrance, Thomas F – 1959 – 9 – $10.00 – us I.R.C. [240]

THE DOCTRINE OF INSPIRATION : AN OUTLINE HISTORICAL STUDY / Hopkins, Theodore Weld – (Includes bibliographical references and index) – Rochester, NY: Printed for the author, 1881 – 1mf – 9 – 0-8370-3654-2 – 1985-1654 – us A.T.L.A. [220]

THE DOCTRINE OF INTERNATIONAL EXCHANGES: THE LIMITS OF FREE TRADE AND THE PROTECTIVE SYSTEM / Bowen, Francis – 20p – 9 – 1.00f – at Libertarian Micro [335]

THE DOCTRINE OF INTERVENTION / Hodges, Henry G – Princeton: The Banner Press, 1915 – us Res Libr [321]

THE DOCTRINE OF MERITS IN OLD RABBINICAL LITERATURE / Marmorstein, Arthur – London, 1920 – 4mf – 8 – ne Slangenburg [270]

THE DOCTRINE OF MODERNISM AND ITS REFUTATION / Godrycz, John A – Philadelphia: John Joseph McVey, 1908 – 1mf – 9 – 0-8370-8427-X – 1986-2427 – us A.T.L.A. [240]

THE DOCTRINE OF PREDESTINATION DEFENDED, IN ANSWER TO MR. JOHN WESLEY'S BOOK ENTITULED 'FREE GRACE', WHEREIN HIS SELF-CONTRADICTIONS ARE SHEWN;... / Birt, W – London, 1746 – 1mf – 9 – MP-331/1 – ne IDC [240]

THE DOCTRINE OF PREDESTINATION STATED AND SET IN THE SCRIPTURE-LIGHT, IN OPPOSITION TO MR. WESLEY'S 'PREDESTINATION CALMLY CONSIDER'D',... / Gill, J – London, 1752 – 1mf – 9 – MP-358/1 – ne IDC [240]

THE DOCTRINE OF PROXIMATE CAUSE AND LAST CLEAR CHANGE / Peck, Melville – Richmond, Va.: Peck 1914. 181p. LL-1153 – 1 – us L of C Photodup [340]

THE DOCTRINE OF REPROBATION / Ross, Frederick Augustus – Nashville, TN: Cumberland Presbyterian Publ House, 1881 – 1mf – 9 – 0-8370-5274-2 – 1985-3274 – us A.T.L.A. [240]

THE DOCTRINE OF SACRED SCRIPTURE : A CRITICAL, HISTORICAL AND DOGMATIC INQUIRY INTO THE ORIGIN AND NATURE OF THE OLD AND NEW TESTAMENTS / Ladd, George Trumbull – (Includes bibliographical references, indexes) – New York:Charles Scribner. 2v. 1883 – 4mf – 9 – 0-8370-5846-5 – 1985-3846 – us A.T.L.A. [220]

THE DOCTRINE OF SACRIFICE DEDUCED FROM THE SCRIPTURES / Maurice, Frederick Denison – 1879 – 1 – us A.T.L.A. [240]

THE DOCTRINE OF SAINT JOHN: AN ESSAY IN BIBLICAL THEOLOGY / Lowrie, Walter – New York: Longmans, Green, 1899.1 fiche – 9 – us A.T.L.A. [240]

DOCTRINE OF SALVATION IN THE CHINESE LANGUAGE (CCC136) / Gutzlaff, Karl Friedrich August – (In Chinese) – [s.l: s.n, 1836] – 1r – 1 – 1984-B500 – us A.T.L.A. [240]

THE DOCTRINE OF SCRIPTURE CONCERNING THE HOLY GHOST, IN ITS RELATIONS TO MINISTERIAL EDUCATION / Williams, William R – (A discourse) – 1 – 5.00 – us Baptist [240]

DOCTRINE OF THE AGES / Cameron, Robert – New York: F.H. Revell, 1896. 1 fiche – 9 – us A.T.L.A. [240]

THE DOCTRINE OF THE AGES BY ROBERT CAMERON / Cameron, Robert – New York:Fleming H. Revell, c1896 – 1mf – 9 – 0-8370-2574-5 – 1985-0574 – us A.T.L.A. [230]

DOCTRINE OF THE APOCALYPSE / Gebhardt, Hermann – Edinburgh: T.&T. Clark, 1878 – 9 – us A.T.L.A. [240]

THE DOCTRINE OF THE CHURCH OF ENGLAND : AS STATED IN ECCLESIASTICAL DOCUMENTS SET FORTH BY AUTHORITY OF CHURCH AND STATE IN THE REFORMATION PERIOD BETWEEN 1536 AND 1662 – (Includes index) – London: Rivingtons, 1868 – 1mf – 9 – 0-8370-8729-5 – 1986-2729 – us A.T.L.A. [240]

THE DOCTRINE OF THE DEATH OF CHRIST : IN RELATION TO THE SIN OF MAN, THE CONDEMNATION OF THE LAW, AND THE DOMINION OF SATAN / Dimock, Nathaniel – London: E. Stock, 1903 – 1mf – us A.T.L.A. [240]

THE DOCTRINE OF THE DIVINE FATHERHOOD IN RELATION TO THE ATONEMENT / Brown, James Baldwin – (Includes bibliographical references) – London:Ward, [1860] – 1mf – 9 – 0-8370-2869-8 – 1985-0869 – us A.T.L.A. [220]

DOCTRINE OF THE LAST THINGS CONTAINED IN THE NEW TESTAMENT / Davidson, Samuel – London: Kegan Paul, Trench, 1882. 1 fiche – 9 – us A.T.L.A. [240]

THE DOCTRINE OF THE PASTORATE, OR, THE DIVINE INSTITUTION, RELIGIOUS RESPONSIBILITIES, AND SCRIPTURAL CLAIMS OF THE CHRISTIAN MINISTRY : CONSIDERED WITH SPECIAL REFERENCE TO WESLEYAN METHODISM / Smith, George Adam – London: Printed for the author, 1851 – 1mf – us A.T.L.A. [240]

DOCTRINE OF THE PERSON OF CHRIST : AN HISTORICAL SKETCH / Glover, Octavius – Cambridge: Deighton, Bell; London: Bell and Daldy, 1867 – 1mf – 9 – 0-8370-4928-8 – 1985-2928 – us A.T.L.A. [240]

THE DOCTRINE OF THE PROPHETS / Kirkpatrick, Alexander Francis – (Includes bibliographical references and index) – 3rd ed. London; New York: Macmillan, 1901 – 2mf – 9 – 0-8370-9395-3 – 1986-3395 – us A.T.L.A. [220]

THE DOCTRINE OF THE SACRAMENTS IN RELATION TO THE DOCTRINES OF GRACE : AS CONTAINED IN THE SCRIPTURES, TAUGHT IN OUR FORMULARIES, AND UPHELD BY OUR REFORMERS / Dimock, Nathaniel – London, New York: Longmans, Green, 1908 – 1mf – us A.T.L.A. [240]

THE DOCTRINE OF THE SAINTS FINAL PERSEVERANCE ASSERTED AND VINDICATED, IN ANSWER TO A LATE PAMPHLET CALLED 'SERIOUS THOUGHTS' ON THAT SUBJECT / Gill, J – London, 1752 – 1mf – 9 – MP-357/1 – ne IDC [240]

THE DOCTRINE OF THE SAINT'S PERSEVERANCE, VINDICATED AND ESTABLISHED, 1820 / Tyler, Bennet – 1 – 5.00 – us Baptist [240]

THE DOCTRINE OF THE TRINITY : APOLOGETICALLY CONSIDERED / Illingworth, John Richardson – London:Macmillan, 1907 – 1mf – 9 – 0-8370-4502-9 – 1985-2502 – us A.T.L.A. [210]

DOCTRINE SAINT-SIMONIENNE: RESUME GENERAL DE L'EXPOSITION FAITE EN 1829 ET EN 1830 – Paris, l'Organisateur. 1831. 45 p. Les Saint-Simoniens, 1825-1834. 6849 – 9 – fr Hachette [335]

THE DOCTRINES OF GRACE / Maclaren, Ian – London: Hodder and Stoughton, 1900 – 1mf – 9 – 0-8370-5707-8 – 1985-3707 – us A.T.L.A. [240]

THE DOCTRINES OF METHODISM EXAMINED AND CONFUTED – London, 1765 – 1mf – 9 – MP-433/1 – ne IDC [240]

THE DOCTRINES OF OUR FAITH: A CONVENIENT HANDBOOK / Dargan, Edwin Charles – Nashville: Sunday School Board, Southern Baptist Convention, 1905. 1 fiche – 9 – us A.T.L.A. [240]

DOCUMENT / Committee to Frame a World Constitution – Chicago: The Committee. Description based on Doc. no.2, 16 Sept 1975 – 1 – us U.W. Library [320]

DOCUMENT / European Coal and Steel Community. Common Assembly – Luxemburg. Jan 1953-1957 58. Incomplete – 1 – us NY Public [324]

DOCUMENT CATALOG : CATALOG OF THE PUBLIC DOCUMENTS OF THE CONGRESS AND OF ALL DEPARTMENTS / U.S. Government Printing Office – (Superior to Monthly Catalog and Document Index for time frame duplicated) – Washington: GPO. 53rd-76th Congresses. v1-25. 1893-1940 (all publ) – 530mf – 9 – $795.00 – LLMC 81-405 – us L.L.M.C. [324]

DOCUMENT DELIVERY IN THE UNITED STATES: A REPORT / Boss, Richard W & McQueen, Judy – ED 244-626 – 9 – 0.91 – us EDRS [380]

DOCUMENT FROM THE HONORABLE DENIS BENJAMIN VIGER, DATED 25TH OCTOBER, 1832 / Viger, Denis Benjamin – [S.l.: s.n., 1832 ?]. SEM105P1376 – 1mf – 9 – Can$2.25 – cn Bibl Nat [324]

DOCUMENT SERIES..., 1933-36 / U.S. National Recovery Administration – 186 rolls. M213. Printed guide – 5 – us Nat'l Archives [324]

DOCUMENTA HISTORICA : OFFICII NOCTURNI ET MATUTINI / Mateos, J – 2mf – 8 – Dfl9.00 – ne Slangenburg [240]

DOCUMENTA TECHNICA *see* POLYTECHNISCHES JOURNAL

DOCUMENTA TECHNICA, REIHE 2 *see*
– PHYSIKALISCH-OEKONOMISCHE BIBLIOTHEK
– TECHNOLOGISCHES WOERTERBUCH ODER ALPHABETISCHE ERKLAERUNGEN ALLER NUETZLICHEN MECHANISCHEN KUENSTE, MANUFAKTUREN..

DOCUMENTA TECHNICA, REIHE 3 *see* BEITRAEGE ZUR GESCHICHTE DER TECHNIK UND INDUSTRIE

DOCUMENTACION, AUTORES Y COMPLICES DE LAS IRREGULARIDADES COMETIDAS DURANTE LA SEGUNDA TIRANIA / Argentina. Comision Nacional de Investigaciones – Buenos Aires, 1958. 5v – 1 – CSUXAGN1654-B – us Hoover Inst Photo [972]

DOCUMENTACION CELAM / Consejo Episcopal Latinoamericano, Secretariado General – Bogota, Colombia: El Consejo. [v1-v8 n37/38. 1976-83] – 4r – us Res Libr [210]

DOCUMENTACION DE LA CAPELLANIA Y ENTERRAMIENTO DEL PRESIDENTE DON JUAN DE OVANDO / Martinez Quesada, Juan – Badajoz: Imp. Dip. Provincial, 1958. Sep. REE – sp Bibl Santa Ana [320]

DOCUMENTACION HISTORICA DE DIEGO GARCIA DE PAREDES / Munoz San Pedro, Miguel – Badajoz: Imp. de la Diputacion Prov., 1949. Sep. Rev. Est. Extremenos – 1 – sp Bibl Santa Ana [946]

DOCUMENTACION SOCIAL CATOLICA LATINOAMERICANA DOCLA / Instituto Latinoamericano de Doctrina y Estudios Sociales – Santiago, Chile: El Instituto, [1974-]. [v1 n1-v20 n106. oct 1972-92] – 3r – 1 – us Res Libr [210]

LE DOCUMENTAIRE : REVUE – Quebec, Canada. v1 n10. mai 1939 – 1r – 1 – Can$25.00 – cn Can Microfilming [073]

DOCUMENTARY ANNALS OF THE REFORMED CHURCH OF ENGLAND : BEING A COLLECTION OF INJUNCTIONS, DECLARATIONS, ORDERS, ARTICLES OF INQUIRY, AND C. FROM THE YEAR 1546 TO THE YEAR 1716 / Cardwell, Edward – Oxford: University Press, 1844 – 3mf – us A.T.L.A. [240]

DOCUMENTARY HISTORY OF RECONSTRUCTION : POLITICAL, MILITARY, SOCIAL, RELIGIOUS, EDUCATIONAL AND INDUSTRIAL, 1865 TO THE PRESENT TIME / Fleming, Walter L – Cleveland. 2v. 1906-07 – 1r – 1 – us Ross [976]

DOCUMENTARY HISTORY OF THE AMERICAN COMMITTEE ON REVISION : PREPARED BY ORDER OF THE COMMITTEE FOR THE USE OF THE MEMBERS – New York: [s.n.], 1885 – 1mf – 9 – 0-8370-9201-9 – 1986-3201 – us A.T.L.A. [220]

DOCUMENTARY HISTORY OF THE BASOTHO (LESOTHO) / Departement Evangelique Francais d'Action Apostolique (DEFAP), Paris – (Includes printed guide) – 60mf – 9 – ne IDC [960]

THE DOCUMENTARY HISTORY OF THE CAMPAIGN ON THE NIAGARA FRONTIER IN 1814 – Edited for the Lundy's Lane Historical Society by E. Cruikshank. s.l.: The Society, 1896? (Welland: Tribune). 05281. (Pre-1900 Canadiana) – 9 – cn C.I.H.M. [971]

THE DOCUMENTARY HISTORY OF THE CAMPAIGN UPON THE NIAGARA FRONTIER IN 1812-4, DECEMBER 1813 TO MAY, 1814, VOL. IX – Collected and edited for the Lundy's Lane Historical Society by E. Cruikshank. s.l.: The Society, 1908 (Welland: Tribune). 05289. (Pre-1900 Canadiana) – 9 – cn C.I.H.M. [971]

THE DOCUMENTARY HISTORY OF THE CAMPAIGN UPON THE NIAGARA FRONTIER IN THE YEAR 1812 – Collected and edited for the Lundy's Lane Historical Society by E. Cruikshank. s.l.: the Society, 1899. (Welland: Tribune). 05283. (Pre-1900 Canadiana) – 9 – cn C.I.H.M. [971]

THE DOCUMENTARY HISTORY OF THE CAMPAIGN UPON THE NIAGARA FRONTIER IN THE YEAR 1812 – Collected and edited for the Lundy's Lane Historical Society by E. Cruikshank. s.l.: The Society, 1900. (Welland: Tribune). 05284. (Pre-1900 Canadiana) – 9 – cn C.I.H.M. [971]

THE DOCUMENTARY HISTORY OF THE CAMPAIGN UPON THE NIAGARA FRONTIER IN THE YEAR 1813, PART 2 (1813), JUNE TO AUGUST, 1813 – Collected and edited for the Lundy's Lane Historical Society by E. Cruikshank. s.l.: The Society, 1903? (Welland: Tribune). 05286. (Pre-1900 Canadiana) – 9 – cn C.I.H.M. [971]

THE DOCUMENTARY HISTORY OF THE CAMPAIGN UPON THE NIAGARA FRONTIER IN THE YEAR 1813, PART 3 (1813), AUGUST TO OCTOBER, 1813 – Collected and edited for the Lundy's Lane Historical Society by E. Cruikshank. s.l.: The Society, 1905 (Welland: Tribune). 05287. (Pre-1900 Canadiana) – 9 – cn C.I.H.M. [971]

THE DOCUMENTARY HISTORY OF THE CAMPAIGN UPON THE NIAGARA FRONTIER IN THE YEAR 1813, PART 4 (1813), OCTOBER TO DECEMBER, 1813, WITH ADDITIONAL DOCUMENTS, JUNE TO OCTOBER, 1813 – Collected and edited for the Lundy's Lane Historical Society by E. Cruikshank. s.l.: The Society, 1907 (Welland: Tribune). 05288. (Pre-1900 Canadiana) – 9 – cn C.I.H.M. [971]

THE DOCUMENTARY HISTORY OF THE CAMPAIGN UPON THE NIAGARA FRONTIER IN THE YEAR 1813, PART I (1813), JANUARY TO JUNE, 1813 – Collected and edited for the Lundy's Lane Historical Society by E. Cruikshank. s.l.: The Society, 1902 (Welland: Tribune). 05285. (Pre-1900 Canadiana) – 9 – cn C.I.H.M. [971]

THE DOCUMENTARY HISTORY OF THE CAMPAIGN UPON THE NIAGARA FRONTIER IN THE YEAR 1814 – Edited for the Lundy's Lane Historical Society by E. Cruikshank. s.l.: The Society, 1897. (Welland: Tribune). 05282. (Pre-1900 Canadiana) – 9 – cn C.I.H.M. [971]

DOCUMENTARY HISTORY OF THE PROTESTANT EPISCOPAL CHURCH IN THE UNITED STATES OF AMERICA. SOUTH CAROLINA / Hawks, Francis L – New York: J. Pott, 1862 – 1mf – us A.T.L.A. [240]

DOCUMENTATIE OVER KOLONISCHE ONDERWERPEN: INDONESIE (OOST-INDIE), 1819-1933; EN WEST INDIE, 1815-1929 = DOCUMENTATION REGISTER TO COLONIAL SUBJECTS: EAST INDIES AND WEST INDIES / Netherlands. General State Archives – (Indonesia (Oost Indie), 1819-1933.-142mf.Dfl1540.00; West Indie (West Indies), 1815-1929.-15mf.Dfl155.00) – 157mf – 9 – Dfl1695.00 silver – ne MMF Publ [324]

DOCUMENTATION CONCERNING JEWS IN THE BERLIN DOCUMENTS CENTER / Germany. Berlin Documents Center – 14r – 1 – T457 – us Nat'l Archives [324]

DOCUMENTATION DES OBLATS DE MARIE IMMACULEE – (Issues for 1943-1944, fasc 11 filmed with: Petites annales des Missionaires oblats de Marie Immaculee (1926), 1940-jan/feb 1942; and: Du pole et tropiques; and: Petites annales des Missionaires oblats de Marie Immaculee (1926) (cont), dec 1944-jan 1953; and: Petites annales, pole et tropiques, mar 1953-jul 1957) – Paris: OMI, 1943-1944, fasc 11 – us Res Libr [210]

DOCUMENTATION DU 1ER CONGRES: FEDERATION NATIONALE DES SYNDICATS DES OUVRIERS ET DES EMPLOYES AU LIBAN / Lebanon. Federation Nationale des Syndicats des Ouvriers et des Employes au Liban – 1970. BNE-19.703 1 – 9 – ne IDC [331]

DOCUMENTATION ET BIBLIOTHEQUES / Association pour l'Avancement des Sciences et des Techniques de la Documentation – Montreal: ASTED, 1955-1990. SEM16P221 – 4r – 5 – Can$113.00 – cn Bibl Nat [073]

DOCUMENTATION GENERALE SUR LE CONGO ET LE RUANDA-URUNDI, 1953-1955 / Heyse, Theodore – (Cahiers Belges et Congolais; no. 26). Bruxelles. 1956. BA-497 2 – 8 – ne IDC [960]

DOCUMENTATION OF THE COLLECTION I.R.E.S / Congo. Kwango – Kwango, Popokaba, Kasongo-Lunda.BA-569/2 – 8 – ne IDC [960]

Documentation Office for East European Law (DBOER), University of Leiden *see* SYSTEMATIC CARD CATALOGUE

DOCUMENTATION REFUGIES (CENTRE INTERASSOCIATIF FRANCOPHONE D'INFORMATION ET DE DOCUMENTATION SUR LE DROIT D'ASILE ET LES REFUGIES – Paris. 169 docs. 1987-1991 – 82mf – 9 – ne IDC [320]

DOCUMENTATION REFUGIES (CENTRE INTERASSOCIATIF FRANCOPHONE D'INFORMATION ET DE DOCUMENTATION SUR LE DROIT D'ASILE ET LES REFUGIES) – Paris. 133 docs. 1987-1991 – 62mf – 9 – ne IDC [320]

DOCUMENTATION SCIENTIFIQUE – Revue bimestrielle des laboratoires et des industries chimiques. no. 1-75. Paris. fevr 1932-juil aout 1939 – 1 – fr A.C.R.P.P. [073]

DOCUMENTE DER NATIONAL-JUEDISCHEN CHRISTGLAEUBIGEN BEWEGUNG IN SUEDRUSSLAND / Delitzsch, Franz – Erlangen: A. Deichert, 1884 – 1mf – us A.T.L.A. [240]

DOCUMENTI ARMONICI / Berardi, A – 1687 – 9 – us Sibley [780]

DOCUMENTO – Rio Branco, Acre. Ago-Dez 1985 – 1,5,6 – bl Biblioteca [072]

DOCUMENTO INEDITO...MANUEL GOMEZ / Venegas, Francisco Javier – (1888 ed.1.50f; 9) – 1886 – 9 – 1.50f – sp Bibl Santa Ana [946]

DOCUMENTOS AUTOGRAFOS E INEDITOS / Venegas, Francisco Javier – Sevilla: Imp. E. Rasco, 1888 – 1 – sp Bibl Santa Ana [946]

DOCUMENTOS AUTOGRAFOS E INEDITOS / Venegas, Francisco Javier – Sevilla: Sociedad del Archivo Hispalense, 1886 – 1 – sp Bibl Santa Ana [946]

DOCUMENTOS DE 1584 A 1595, RELATIVOS A DON LUIS ZAPATA DE CHAVES, EXISTENTES EN EL ARCHIVO MUNICIPAL DE LLERENA / Carrasco, Antonio – Badajoz: Dip. Provincial, 1969 – sp Bibl Santa Ana [946]

DOCUMENTOS DE CARLOS 5 (ANNO 1529) – Caceres – 1r – 5,6 – sp Cultura [946]

DOCUMENTOS DE LA COMPANIA DE JESUS EN EL ARCHIVO HISTORICO NACIONAL / Guglieri, A – Madrid; 1967 – 10mf – 9 – sp Cultura [240]

DOCUMENTOS DE LA CURIA ROMANA (ANNO 1238-1517) – Zamora – 1r – 5,6 – sp Cultura [240]

DOCUMENTOS DE LAS FUNDACIONES RELIGIOSAS Y BENEFICAS DE LA VILLA DE ALMONTE, POR LORENZO CRUZ DE FUENTES / T'Serclaes, Duque de – Madrid: Fortanet, 1913. B.R.A.H. 63, pp. 162-164 – sp Bibl Santa Ana [240]

DOCUMENTOS DEL CABILDO (ANNO 1045-1600) – Calahorra – 1r – 5,6 – sp Cultura [946]

DOCUMENTOS DEL CABILDO (ANNO 1276-1312) – Calahorra – 1r – 5,6 – sp Cultura [946]

DOCUMENTOS DEL CABILDO (SIECLE 13-15) – Calahorra – 1r – 5,6 – sp Cultura [946]

DOCUMENTOS DEL CABILDO (SIECLE 13-16) – Calahorra – 1r – 5,6 – sp Cultura [946]

DOCUMENTOS DEL CABILDO (SIECLE 1312-1436) – Calahorra – 1r – 5,6 – sp Cultura [946]

DOCUMENTOS EPISCOPALES (ANNO 1199-1260) – Zamora – 1r – 5,6 – sp Cultura [240]

DOCUMENTOS HISTORICOS COLECCIONADOS PO...SECCION GEOGRAFIA... / Grenon, P; ed by Bayle, Constantino – Madrid: Razon y Fe, 1928 – 9 – sp Bibl Santa Ana [900]

DOCUMENTOS HISTORICOS REFERENTES A EXTREMADURA / Archivo Extremeno – Badajoz: Tip.y Lib.de Antonio Arqueros, Tomo 1. 1908 – 1 – sp Bibl Santa Ana [946]

DOCUMENTOS HISTORICOS. TESTAMENTO DE DON BARTOLOME MARTINEZ, OBISPO DE PANAMA Y ARZOBISPO DE SANTA FE / Rodriguez Amaya, Esteban – Badajoz: Dip. Provincial, 1948. Sep. REE – 1 – sp Bibl Santa Ana [920]

DOCUMENTOS INEDITOS O MUY RAROS PARA LA HISTORIA DE MEXICO – Mexico. 1905-11. 36v – 1 – 529.00 – us L of C Photodup [972]

DOCUMENTOS. LO QUE HAN VISTO EN MADRID LOS PARLAMENTARIOS INGLESES / Spain. Ministerio de Estado – Valencia, 1936? Fiche W1188. (Blodgett Collection of Spanish Civil War Pamphlets) – 9 – us H.U. College Libr [946]

DOCUMENTOS PARA LA BIBLIOGRAFIA DE D. MANUEL JOSE QUINTANA / Perez de Guzman, Juan – Madrid: Fortanet, 1910. B.R.A.H. 57, 1910. pp. 376-381 – sp Bibl Santa Ana [010]

DOCUMENTOS PARA LA HISTORIA ARGENTINA : TOMO 20, IGLESIA... / Bayle, Constantino – Buenos Aires, 1929; Madrid: Razon y Fe, 1931 – 1 – sp Bibl Santa Ana [240]

DOCUMENTOS PARA LA HISTORIA ARGENTINA. TOMO 20, IGLESIA. CARTAS ANTIGUAS DE LA PROVINCIA DEL PARAGUAY, AVILA Y TUCUMAN DE LA COMPANIA DE JESUS (1609-1614). BUENOS AIRES, 1927 / Bayle, Constantino – Madrid: Razon y Fe, 1929 – 1 – sp Bibl Santa Ana [946]

DOCUMENTOS PARA LA HISTORIA DE LA GUERRA DE SUCESION EN EXTREMADURA / Munoz de San Pedro, Miguel – Badajoz: Diputacion Prov. de Badajoz, 1948. Sep. Revista Estudios Extremanos – 1 – sp Bibl Santa Ana [946]

DOCUMENTOS PARA LA HISTORIA DE LA VIDA PUBLICA DEL LIBERTADOR DE COLOMBIA, PERU, Y BOLIVIA / Blanco, Jose Felix – Caracas. 1875-78. 14v – 1 – $161.00 – us L of C Photodup [972]

DOCUMENTOS PARTICULARES Y PONTIFICOS (SIECLE 13-18) – Albarracin – 1r – 5,6 – sp Cultura [240]

DOCUMENTOS PONTIFICIOS (ANNO 1210-1616) – Zamora – 1r – 5,6 – sp Cultura [240]

DOCUMENTOS PONTIFICIOS (ANNO 1468-1572) – Zamora – 1r – 5,6 – sp Cultura [240]

DOCUMENTOS REALES (ANNO 1260) – Avila – 1r – 5,6 – sp Cultura [946]

DOCUMENTOS REALES (ANNO 1520-1558) : NO 1-185 – Avila – 1r – 5,6 – sp Cultura [946]

DOCUMENTOS REALES (ANNO 1558-1584) : NO 185-215 – Avila – 1r – 5,6 – sp Cultura [946]

DOCUMENTOS REALES (ANNO 1636-1653) : NO 1-7 – Avila – 1r – 5,6 – sp Cultura [946]

DOCUMENTOS REALES, ECLESIASTICOS T PARTICULARES EN PERGAMINO (SIECLE 11-17) – Valencia – 1r – 5,6 – sp Cultura [240]

DOCUMENTOS REALES. EJECUTORIAS...(SIECLE 15-16) : NO 1-30 – Avila – 1r – 5,6 – sp Cultura [946]

DOCUMENTOS REALES (SIECLE 15-16) : NO 1-264 – Avila – 1r – 5,6 – sp Cultura [946]

DOCUMENTOS REALES (SIECLE 16-17) – Avila – 1r – 5,6 – sp Cultura [946]

DOCUMENTOS REFERENTES A LA CREACION DE BOLIVIA... / Lecuna, Vicente – Madrid: Razon y Fe, 1926 – 1 – sp Bibl Santa Ana [972]

DOCUMENTOS REFERENTES A LA FAMILIA TOPETE (ANNO 1292-1613) – Caceres – 1r – 5,6 – sp Cultura [920]

DOCUMENTOS SOBRE LA EXPULSION DE LOS MORISCOS DE DENIA (ANNO 1596-1621) – Almeria – 1r – 5,6 – sp Cultura [946]

DOCUMENTOS SOBRE LA PUEBLA DE ARGANZON (SIECLE 13-15) – Calahorra – 1r – 5,6 – sp Cultura [946]

DOCUMENTOS VARIOS (ANNO 1138-1593) – Avila – 1r – 5,6 – sp Cultura [946]

DOCUMENTOS VARIOS (ANNO 1260-1518). INVENTARIO DE ESCRITURAS (ANNO 1585) – Agreda – 1r – 5,6 – sp Cultura [946]

DOCUMENTOS VARIOS (ANNO 834-1566) : NO 1-314 – Calahorra – 1r – 5,6 – sp Cultura [946]

DOCUMENTOS VARIOS (SIECLE 12) – Caceres – 1r – 5,6 – sp Cultura [946]

DOCUMENTOS VARIOS (SIECLE 13-16) – Caceres – 1r – 5,6 – sp Cultura [946]

DOCUMENTOS VARIOS (SIECLE 15-16) – Caceres – 1r – 5,6 – sp Cultura [946]

DOCUMENTOS Y MONUMENTOS EPIGRAFICOS DEL MUSEO PROVINCIAL DE BADAJOZ / Carrasco Lianes, Virgilio – Badajoz: Imp. Dip. Provincial, 1976. Sep. Revista de Estudios Extremenos – sp Bibl Santa Ana [060]

DOCUMENTS – Doctrines, archeologie, beaux-arts, ethnographie. Dir. Georges Bataille. I, no. 1-7; II, no. 1-8, 3e s., no. 1; 4e s., no. 1. Paris. 1929-30, 1933-34 – 1 – fr A.C.R.P.P. [073]

DOCUMENTS / Evangelical Alliance for the U.S. – New York. v1-42. 1867-1900 – 1r – 1 – us Ross [240]

DOCUMENTS / Federation des Ouvriers des Metaux et Similaires de France. 4e-6e Congres National – 1919-23 – 1 – fr A.C.R.P.P. [331]

DOCUMENTS / France. Assemblee consultative provisoire – 7nov 1944-5 oct 1946 – 1 – fr A.C.R.P.P. [323]

DOCUMENTS / France. Assemblee de l'Union francaise – 10 dec 1947-29 mai 1958 : 1 – fr A.C.R.P.P. [323]

DOCUMENTS / Universities' Mission to Central Africa – 'A' series. 1857-1929 – 1 – uk Microform Academic [240]

DOCUMENTS 1-701 / Maritime Law Association of the United States – (Lacking: Doc nos 129B,146,147. Updated regularly) – 1899-1996 – 294mf – 9 – $441.00 – LLMC 85-100 – us L.L.M.C. [340]

DOCUMENTS ADMINISTRATIFS / France – 1905-86 – 1 – fr A.C.R.P.P. [323]

DOCUMENTS ADMINISTRATIFS / France – (1906-41 F950.00; 1945-80 F950.00; 1906-80 F1,800.00) – 1981- – F280.00y – fr Journal Officiel [350]

DOCUMENTS ALGERIENS – (Serie Economique: n1-125 oct 15 1945-sep 30 1957. Serie Militaire: n1-11 sep 8 1946-mar 20 1953. Serie Monographie: n1-21 jun 20 1948-may 10 1953. Serie Politique: [n1-30] sep 1 1945-aug 1 1957. Serie Sociale: [n1-49] jan 5 1946-aug 15 1956) – Serie culturelle. [Alger]: Service d'information du cabinet du gouverneur general. [n1-81]. mar 25 1946-sep 25 1957 – 1 – us Res Libr [080]

DOCUMENTS AND BIOGRAPHY PERTAINING TO THE SETTLEMENT OF AND PROGRESS OF STARK COUNTY / Leeson, M A – Chicago: M. A., Leeson and Co., 1887. Illinois Reel 55. (The Cox Library Collection) – 5 – us Americana [978]
DOCUMENTS AND CORRESPONDENCE RELATING TO PALESTINE, AUG 1939-MAR 1940 / Jewish Agency for Palestine. London – 1940. BJ-28-141 1 – 9 – ne IDC [956]
DOCUMENTS AND NEWSPAPERS FROM THE COLLECTION OF B. ABAYOMI CASSELL / Cassell, B Abayomi – 10r – 1 – $495.00 – us African Imprint [960]
DOCUMENTS AND OFFICIAL RECORDS / United Nations – 1946-53, 1982-86 – 3,9 – us Readex [900]
DOCUMENTS AND OFFICIAL RECORDS / United Nations – (1982. 9) – 1954-81 – 3 – us Readex [900]
DOCUMENTS AND OFFICIAL RECORDS / United Nations. Conference on International Organizations, 1945. San Francisco – 3,9 – us Readex [900]
DOCUMENTS AND OFFICIAL RECORDS / United Nations. Preparatory Commission of the United Nations, 1945-46. London – 3,9 – us Readex [900]
DOCUMENTS AND RECORDS RELATING TO NEW HAMPSHIRE 1776-1783 – 1874. Vol. 8, New Hampshire Reel 8. (The Cox Library Collection) – 5 – us Americana [978]
DOCUMENTS AND STUDIES ON THE JAPANESE FREE BALLOONS OF WORLD WAR 2 / U.S. Army – 5items. 1945-? – 1 – $26.00 – us L of C Photodup [950]
DOCUMENTS ARABES RELATIFS A L'HISTOIRE DU SOUDAN / Abd al-Rahman ibn' Abd Allah – 2v. Tarikhes-Soudan. Paris. 1898-1900. BA-265 2 – 8 – ne IDC [960]
DOCUMENTS CAMEROUNAIS – 1960-70.-2r – 1 – $49.50 – us African Imprint [330]
DOCUMENTS CONCERNANT LE CONGRES NATIONAL DE NANCY 4E ET LE CONGRES INTERNATIONAL DE STUTTGARD (AOUT 1907) / Congres National du Parti Socialiste (S.F.I.O.). Federation de la Seine – Paris, au siege de la federation de la Seine, 1907. 39p 5693 – 9 – fr Hachette [335]
DOCUMENTS DE L'ASSEMBLEE NATIONALE / France. Assemblee Nationale – (IIIe Republique, 3e a 16e legislature (1881-1940) F5,300.00; Assemblee provisoire, Assemblee constituante (1943-1946), IVe Republique, 1re a 3e legislature (1946-1958) F1,600.00; Ve Republique, 1re a 4e legislature (1958-1973) F2,300.00; Ve Republique, 5e legislature (1973-1978) F3,000.00; Ve Republique, 6e legislature (1978-1981) F2,000.00; Ve Republique, 7e legislature (1981-1986) F3,600.00; Ve Republique, 8e legislature (1986-1988) F1,600.00; L'ensemble IIIe a Ve Republique (1881-1988) F16,000.00) – 1988- Approx. 300mf per year – 9 – F600.00y – fr Journal Officiel [944]
DOCUMENTS DE L'ASSEMBLEE NATIONALE *see* LE JOURNAL OFFICIEL
DOCUMENTS DE L'ASSEMBLEE NATIONALE 1881 A 1940 – F5,300.00 – fr Journal Officiel [944]
DOCUMENTS DE L'ASSEMBLEE NATIONALE 1943 A 1958 – F1,600.00 – fr Journal Officiel [944]
DOCUMENTS DE L'ASSEMBLEE NATIONALE 1958 A 1973 – F2,300.00 – fr Journal Officiel [944]
DOCUMENTS DE L'ASSEMBLEE NATIONALE 1973 A 1978 – F3,000.00 – fr Journal Officiel [944]
DOCUMENTS DE L'ASSEMBLEE NATIONALE 1978 A 1981 – F2,000.00 – fr Journal Officiel [944]
DOCUMENTS DE L'ASSEMBLEE NATIONALE 1981 A 1986 – F3,600.00 – fr Journal Officiel [944]
DOCUMENTS DE L'ASSEMBLEE NATIONALE 1986 A 1988 – F1,600.00 – fr Journal Officiel [944]
DOCUMENTS DE SOLA / Famille Miller – 1r – 1 – Can$50.00 – cn Can Microfilming [920]
DOCUMENTS DIPLOMATIQUES: AFFAIRES DE TERRE-NEUVE / France. Ministere des Affaires Etrangeres – Paris: s.n., 1891 (Paris: Impr. nationale). 05604. (Pre-1900 Canadiana) – 9 – cn C.I.H.M. [971]
DOCUMENTS DIPLOMATIQUES. CONFERENCE INTERNATIONALE DE LA HAYE (1910)... / France. Ministere des Affaires Etrangeres – Paris, 1910 – 2mf – 1 – ILM-3953/1 – ne IDC [327]
DOCUMENTS DIPLOMATIQUES FRANCAIS / France – 1871-1914 – 1 – us UMI [944]
DOCUMENTS DIPLOMATIQUES FRANCAIS 1871-1914 / France. Ministere des Affaires Etrangeres – Paris, S.1, 1929-39. v.1-9; S.2, 1930-38. v.1-8; S.3, 1929-36. v.1-11 – 356mf – 8 – ne IDC [944]
DOCUMENTS DU CONGRES / Federation nationale des Travailleurs du Sous-Sol – 1920, 1925-26, 1929, 1931-32, 1934, 1938, 1946, 1950 – 1 – fr A.C.R.P.P. [331]
LES DOCUMENTS DU PROGRES – Revue internationale dirigee par le Dr. Rodolphe Broda. Paraissant tous les mois a Paris, Berlin, Londres, Budapest, Madrid. dec 1907-janv 1914 – 1 – fr A.C.R.P.P. [073]
DOCUMENTS DU SENAT / France. Senat – (1881-1940 F2,200.00; 1946-1970 F4,700.00; 1881-1970 F6,300.00) – 1971- Approx. 250mf per year – F400.00y – fr Journal Officiel [944]
DOCUMENTS DU SENAT *see* LE JOURNAL OFFICIEL
DOCUMENTS DU SENAT 1881 A 1940 – F2,200.00 – fr Journal Officiel [944]
DOCUMENTS DU SENAT 1946 A 1970 – F4,700.00 – fr Journal Officiel [944]
DOCUMENTS EMANES DU SAINT-SIEGE SUR LA CONDUITE DU CLERGE DANS LA POLITIQUE, L'INFLUENCE INDUE ET L'UNIVERSITE LAVAL, 13 SEPTEMBRE 1881 – s.l.: s.n., 1881?. 04289. (Pre-1900 Canadiana) – 9 – cn C.I.H.M. [971]
DOCUMENTS ET EXTRAITS DIVERS CONCERNANT L'HISTOIRE DE L'ART DANS LA FLANDRE, L'ARTOIS ET LE HAINAUT AVANT LE XVE SIECLE / Dehaisnes, C C A – Lille, 1886. 2v. BO-221-1 – 9 – ne IDC [700]
DOCUMENTS FROM THE ARCHIVE OF THE STATES OF HOLLAND, C. 1445-1572 – 74r – 1 – Dfl16,650.00 – ne MMF Publ [949]
DOCUMENTS GENEALOGIQUES SUR LES FAMILLES DE TOURAINE / Lambron de Lignim, H de – 19th cent. 3v – 1 – F373.83 – fr Armell [920]
DOCUMENTS GRATZ AND JOSEPH / Famille Joseph – 8r – 1 – cn Can Microfilming [920]
DOCUMENTS ICONOGRAPHIQUES SUR SAN ANDRES SAJCABAJA : LA VIE DU VILLAGE PRESENTEE PAR LES DESSINS DES ENFANTS ET DES PHOTOGRAPHIES / Hocquenghem, Anne Marie & Schlupmann, Klaus – 15 – F280.00 – fr Ethnologie [305]
DOCUMENTS ILLUSTRATIVE OF ENGLISH CHURCH HISTORY / Gee, Henry & Hardy, John – London, New York: Macmillan, 1896 – 2mf – us A.T.L.A. [240]
DOCUMENTS ILLUSTRATIVE OF ENGLISH HISTORY IN THE 13TH AND 14TH CENTURIES / ed by Cole, H OF LA HOGUE – (v2: Letters From The French Ambassadors to Their Court London, 1773) – Dfl67.00 – ne Slangenburg [941]
DOCUMENTS ILLUSTRATIVE OF THE BURMESE WAR / Wilson, H H – (Government Gazette Press). Calcutta. 1827. BSE-67 2 – 8 – ne IDC [950]
DOCUMENTS ILLUSTRATIVE OF THE CONTINENTAL REFORMATION / Kidd, B J – Oxford: Clarendon Press, 1911 – 2mf – us A.T.L.A. [240]
DOCUMENTS ILLUSTRATIVE OF THE FORMATION OF THE UNION OF THE AMERICAN STATES : SELECTED, ARRANGED AND INDEXED / Tansil, Charles C – Washington: GPO, 1927 – 12mf – 9 – $18.00 – LLMC 90-361 – us L.L.M.C. [323]
DOCUMENTS ILLUSTRATIVE OF THE HISTORY OF THE SLAVE TRADE TO AMERICA / ed by Donnan, E – Washington, D.C., 1930-35. 4 vols – 47mf – 9 – ne IDC [976]
DOCUMENTS INEDITS POUR SERVIR A L'HISTOIRE ECCLESIASTIQUE DE LA BELGIQUE / Berliere, Ursmer – Maredsous: Abbaye de Saint-Beonit, 1894 – 1mf – us A.T.L.A. [240]
DOCUMENTS INEDITS SUR LE COLONEL DE LONGUEUIL – Annotes et publies par monongahela de Beaujeu. Montreal: M. de Beaujeu, 1891. 02977. (Pre-1900 Canadiana) – 9 – cn C.I.H.M. [971]
DOCUMENTS INTERNATIONAUX DE L'ESPRIT NOUVEAU – Paul Dermee, Michel Seuphor. no. 1. Paris. printemps 1927. Collection privee – 1 – fr A.C.R.P.P. [073]
DOCUMENTS LE CONCERNANT CONSERVES A LA BIBLIOTHEQUE MUNICIPALE DE NANTES / Talleyrand, Henri de – 1 – F224.87 – fr Armell [920]
Documents Mangareviens *see*
– JOURNAL ADMINISTRATIF DE 1939 A 1943
– REGISTRE DES DELIBERATIONS DU GRAND CONSEIL MANGAREVIEN
DOCUMENTS NON CONFIDENTIELS CONCERNANT LE LOI DE 1885 RELATIVES AUX ASILES D'ALIENE DANS LA PROVINCE DE QUEBEC: – (48 Vict., chap. 34). Montreal: s.n., 1886 (Montreal: L'Etendard). 04290. (Pre-1900 Canadiana) – 9 – cn C.I.H.M. [971]
DOCUMENTS OF THE FIRST CENTRAL COUNCIL MEETING, DJAKARTA, 3-4 FEB., 1966. SE-6613/1. 1966 / Africa-Asia Islamic Organization. Central Council – 9 – ne IDC [260]
DOCUMENTS OF THE INTERDIVISIONAL COUNTRY AND AREA COMMITTEE / U.S. Department of State – 1943-46. 6 rolls. T1221 – 1 – us Nat'l Archives [977]
DOCUMENTS OF THE INTERNATIONAL CONFERENCES ON EDUCATION, 1979-1986 : CUMULATIVE CATALOGUE – (Trilingual: English/French/Spanish) – 1988 – xiv/147p – 9 – 92-3-002554-2 – fr UNESCO [370]
DOCUMENTS OF THE NATIONAL SECURITY COUNCIL *see* MINUTES OF MEETINGS OF THE NATIONAL SECURITY COUNCIL
DOCUMENTS OF THE NATIONAL SECURITY COUNCIL, 1947-1977 / US. National Security Council – (Supplements: 1st 3r $375.00 ISBN 0-89093-310-3. 2nd 3r $375.00 ISBN 0-89093-536-X. 3rd 3r $375.00 ISBN 0-89093-569-6. 4th 7r $875.00 ISBN 0-89093-192-5. 5th 4r $505.00 ISBN 1-55655-161-4. 6th 10r $1,250.00 ISBN 1-55655-473-7. 7th 7r $875.00 ISBN 1-55655-592-X. All with printed guides) – 1980 – 5r – 1 – $690.00 – 0-89093-311-1 – us UPA [977]
DOCUMENTS OF THE POST WAR PROGRAMS COMMITTEE, 1944 / U.S. Department of State – 4 rolls.T1222 – 1 – us Nat'l Archives [977]
DOCUMENTS OF THE PREPARATORY CONFERENCE FOR THE GANEFO HELD 27, 28 AND 29TH APRIL, 1963 / Games of the New Emerging Forces. Preparatory Conference, Djakarta, 1963 – SE-4335 1 – 9 – ne IDC [790]
DOCUMENTS OF THE U.N. CONFERENCE ON INTERNATIONAL ORGANIZATION, SAN FRANCISCO 1945 / UN – (V3,17-18,21 mf: E.46; v4,19-20,22 mf: F.51) – v1-2, 5-16 – E/F.175 – 9 – us U.N. Pubs [340]
DOCUMENTS OF THE U.N. ENVIRONMENT PROGRAMME : GOVERNING COUNCIL, 1973-1977 / UN – 1st-5th sess – E.147 – 9 – UNEP/GC.1-106 – us U.N. Pubs [340]
DOCUMENTS ON ASIA, AFRICA, OCEANIA AND SOUTH AMERICA / Missionary Archives. Council for World Mission, 1775-1940. London – Zug, 1977. BH-2127-2131/1 – 9 – ne IDC [240]
DOCUMENTS ON DISARMAMENT, 1945-1959 / U.S. Department of State – 2v. 1960-79 (all publ?) – 210mf – 9 – $315.00 – LLMC 80-911 – us L.L.M.C. [327]
DOCUMENTS ON DISARMAMENT, 1945-1982 – (With printed guide) – 11r – 1 – $1,105.00 – 0-89093-195-X – us UPA [327]
DOCUMENTS ON EDUCATION DEVELOPMENT – 508 titles – 9 – ne IDC [370]
DOCUMENTS ON PREPARATIONS OF THE FIRST GANEFO AND CONFERENCE OF THE PREPARATORY COMMITTEE IN DJAKARTA / Games of the New Emerging Forces. 1st, Djakarta, 1963 – SE-5714 1. Nov. 1963 – 9 – ne IDC [790]
DOCUMENTS ON SOVIET MILITARY LAW AND ADMINISTRATION / ed by Berman, Harold J & Kerner, Miroslav – Cambridge: Harvard University Press, 1955 – 1 – CSUX90-B4225 – us Hoover Inst Photo [355]
DOCUMENTS ON THE CONSTITUTIONAL HISTORY OF PUERTO RICO – (Contains: Spanish Constitution of 1876, the Self-Government Constitution of 1897, the Treaty of Paris of 1898, the Military Government of 1898-1900, among others) – Washington: Office of Puerto Rico, n.d. – 2mf – 9 – $3.00 – LLMC 92-404 – us L.L.M.C. [324]
DOCUMENTS ON TIME REFORM / American Society of Civil Engineers – 1884? 00790. (Pre-1900 Canadiana) – 9 – cn C.I.H.M. [624]
DOCUMENTS ON UNIVERSITY APARTHEID AND ON CHRISTIAN NATIONAL EDUCATION POLICIES : PRINTED AND MIMEOGRAPHED REPORTS, ETC [1931?-63] – [S.l: s.n., 19–?] – us Res Libr [370]
DOCUMENTS PARA LA HISTORIA ECONOMICA DE MEXICO – Mexico: Secretaria de la Economia Nacional, 1933-36. 11v – 1 – us U.W. Library [972]
DOCUMENTS PARLEMENTAIRES / France. Assemblee Nationale – 28 nov 1946-23 mars 1971 – 1 – fr A.C.R.P.P. [323]
DOCUMENTS PARLEMENTAIRES / France. Chambre des Deputes – 1881-1938 – 1 – fr A.C.R.P.P. [323]
DOCUMENTS PARLEMENTAIRES / France. Conseil de la Republique – 26 decembre 1946-sept 1957 – 1 – fr A.C.R.P.P. [323]
DOCUMENTS PARLEMENTAIRES / France. Senat – 1881-1938 – 1 – fr A.C.R.P.P. [323]
DOCUMENTS PERTAINING TO THE POLITICAL AND ECONOMIC RELATIONS BETWEEN SYRIA AND LEBANON 1943-1950 / Syria – 1950. BNE-9732 1 – 9 – ne IDC [327]
DOCUMENTS PERTAINING TO THE RULE OF NASIR AL-DIN SHAH QAJAR – 1mf – 9 – $10.00 – us MEDOC [324]
DOCUMENTS RECUEILLIS POUR REMANIER LE RECUEIL DE CHANTS POPULAIRES DU COMTE NANTAIS..., T.1-5 / Gueraud, Armand – 19th cent – 4r – 1 – F2,298.00 – fr Armell [944]
THE DOCUMENTS REFERRED TO IN THE KAMINSTEIN LEGISLATIVE HISTORY PROJECT – (Includes a hard copy pamphlet with calendar of events and list of materials filmed. For use in conjunction with: Kaminstein Legislative History Project: A Compendium and Analytical Index of Materials Leading to the Copyright Act of 1976. Available in hard copy 6v at $570) – 9 – $475.00 – us Hein [323]
DOCUMENTS RELATED TO KHRUSCHEV'S VISIT TO INDONESIA IN 1960 / Indonesia. Departemen Penerangan – In English. SE-4608 1 – 9 – ne IDC [950]
DOCUMENTS RELATIFS AUX EGLISES DE L'ORIENT ET A LEURS RAPPORTS AVEC ROME / Avril, Adolphe d' – (Includes bibliographical references) – 3e ed, rev et augm. Paris: Challamel Aine, 1885 – 1mf – 9 – 0-8370-7602-1 – 1986-1602 – us A.T.L.A. [240]
DOCUMENTS RELATIFS AUX ETATS – GENERAUX DE 1789 : BAS-POITOU / Etats Generaux de 1789 – Fontenay: Robuchon, 1850 – fr Armell [944]
DOCUMENTS RELATING TO APPOINTMENT AND CAREER OF REGINALD ARTHUR ROBERTS, AS JUDICIAL OFFICER (VICE CONSUL, SENIOR RESIDENT) OF THE NIGER COAST PROTECTORATE, LATER ONITSHA PROVINCE, 1895-1928 – Oxford: Oxford University Press, [19–?] – us Res Libr [920]
DOCUMENTS RELATING TO THE AMERICAN REVOLUTION / National Maritime Museum. London – 1775-83. BRRAM – 1 – uk Microform Academic [025]
DOCUMENTS RELATING TO THE COLONIAL HISTORY OF THE STATE OF NEW YORK / Broadhead, J R & O'Callaghan, E B – Albany, NY. v1-2 + index. 1856 – 1r – 1 – Can$50.00 – cn Can Microfilming [978]
DOCUMENTS RELATING TO THE CONSTRUCTION OF THE PARLIAMENTARY AND DEPARTMENTAL BUILDINGS AT OTTAWA / Canada. Ministere des Travaux Publics – Quebec: s.n, 1862. SEM105P310 – 5mf – 9 – Can$11.25 – cn Bibl Nat [336]
DOCUMENTS RELATING TO THE DEMAND OF THE PROVINCE OF QUEBEC FOR A RE-ADJUSTMENT OF THE SUBSIDY – Quebec: s.n., 1883 (Quebec: "Morning Chronicle"). 04291. (Pre-1900 Canadiana) – 9 – cn C.I.H.M. [971]
DOCUMENTS RELATING TO THE MILITARY AND NAVAL SERVICE OF BLACKS AWARDED THE CONGRESSIONAL MEDAL OF HONOR FROM THE CIVIL WAR TO THE SPANISH AMERICAN WAR – RG 24, 25, 94, 107, 153, 391, and 393. 4 rolls. M929 – 1 – us Nat'l Archives [324]
DOCUMENTS RELATING TO THE NEGOTIATION OF RATIFIED AND UNRATIFIED TREATIES WITH VARIOUS INDIAN TRIBES, 1801-69 / U.S. Bureau of Indian Affairs – 10 rolls. T494 – 1 – us Nat'l Archives [324]

DOCUMENTS RELATING TO THE SETTLEMENT OF THE CHURCH OF ENGLAND BY THE ACT OF UNIFORMITY OF 1662 : WITH AN HISTORICAL INTRODUCTION / Gould, George – London: W. Kent, 1862 – 2mf – us A.T.L.A. [240]

DOCUMENTS STATISTIQUES SUR LE COMMERCE EXTERIEUR DE L'ALGERIE / Algeria. Direction Nationale des Douanes – 1947-68. (lacking 1961). BNE-8638 1 – 9 – ne IDC [380]

DOCUMENTS SUBMITTED TO THE COMMITTEE OF GOOD OFFICES BY THE NETHERLANDS DELEGATION IN THE PERIOD FROM THE BEGINNING OF THE NEGOTIATIONS UP TO JAN., 1948 / United Nations. Security Council. Representative from the Netherlands – SE 12,161 1 – 9 – ne IDC [950]

DOCUMENTS SUR L'HISTOIRE, LA GEOGRAPHIE ET LE COMMERCE DE L'AFRIQUE ORIENTALE / Guillain, M – Paris: A Bertrand, [1856] – 1 – us Res Libr [910]

DOCUMENTS TO THE PEOPLE – v1-2. 1972-74 – 1 – us UMI [073]

Dodd, C H *see*
– THE APOSTOLIC PREACHING AND ITS DEVELOPMENT
– THE EPISTLE OF PAUL TO THE ROMANS
– THE JOHANNINE EPISTLES

Dodd, Peter *see* AUSTRALIAN TAKEOVERS: THE EVIDENCE

Dodd, W *see*
– CAUTIONS AGAINST METHODISM
– A CONFERENCE BETWEEN A MYSTIC, AN HUTCHINSONIAN, A CALVINIST, A METHODIST, A MEMBER OF THE CHURCH OF ENGLAND...

Dodd, William *see* A FULL AND CIRCUMSTANTIAL ACCOUNT OF THE TRIAL OF THE REV. DOCTOR DODD, AT THE SESSIONS HOUSE IN THE OLD BAILEY, ON SATURDAY THE 22ND OF FEBRUARY, 1777.

DODDRIDGE COUNTY REPUBLICAN – West Union. West Virginia. 1912-42 – 1 – us UMI [071]

DODEKACHORDON / Glareanus, H L – Basileae. 1547. BP-298 1 – 9 – ne IDC [780]

DAS DODEKAPROPHETON / Marti, Karl – (Includes bibliographies and index) – Tuebingen: J C B Mohr (Paul Siebeck), 1904 – 2mf – 9 – 0-8370-9804-1 – 1986-3804 – us A.T.L.A. [220]

Doderer, Otto *see* BRENTANOS IM RHEINGAU

Dodge City. Kansas. City Council *see* RECORDS

Dodge City. Kansas. Police Court *see* DOCKET

THE DODGE CLUB, OR ITALY IN 1859 / De Mille, James – New York: Harper, 1869. 02630. (Pre-1900 Canadiana) – 9 – cn C.I.H.M. [830]

DODGE CRITERION – Dodge, NE. -w. Sep. 1895-Jul. 1899; Sep. 1899- – 1 – us NE Hist [071]

Dodge, David Low *see*
– MEMORIAL OF MR. DAVID L. DODGE
– WAR INCONSISTENT WITH THE RELIGION OF JESUS CHRIST

Dodge, Jim *see* LIVING BY LIFE

Dodge, Martin Herbert *see* THE GOVERNMENT OF THE CITY OF FRANKFORT-ON-THE-MAIN

Dodge, Mary Mapes *see* THE IRVINGTON STORIES

Dodge, Norman *see* MONTH AT GOODSPEED'S, 1929-1969

Dodge, Orvil *see* PIONEER HISTORY OF COOS COUNTY AND CURRY COUNTY

Dodge, R *see* PSYCHOLOGISCHE UNTERSUCHUNGEN UEBER DAS LESEN AUF EXPERIMENTELLER GRUNDLAGE

Dodoens, R *see* A NEW HERBAL

Dods, Marcus *see*
– THE BIBLE, ITS ORIGIN AND NATURE
– THE BOOK OF GENESIS
– EARLY LETTERS OF MARCUS DODS, D.D.: (LATE PRINCIPAL OF NEW COLLEGE, EDINBURGH) (1850-1864)
– THE EPISTLES OF OUR LORD TO THE SEVEN CHURCHES OF ASIA
– ERASMUS AND OTHER ESSAYS
– THE FIRST EPISTLE TO THE CORINTHIANS
– THE GOSPEL OF ST JOHN
– AN INTRODUCTION TO THE NEW TESTAMENT
– LATER LETTERS OF MARCUS DODS, D.D. : (LATE PRINCIPAL OF NEW COLLEGE, EDINBURGH) (1895-1909)
– THE PARABLES OF OUR LORD
– PARABLES OF OUR LORD (SECOND SERIES): THE PARABLES RECORDED BY ST LUKE
– THE POST-EXILIAN PROPHETS

Dodwell *see*
– ALPHABETICAL LIST OF THE BOMBAY CIVIL SERVANTS, 1798-1839
– ALPHABETICAL LIST OF THE MADRAS CIVIL SERVANTS, 1780-1838
– ALPHABETICAL LIST OF THE OFFICERS OF THE INDIAN ARMY, 1760-1837

Dodwell, H *see*
– A TREATISE CONCERNING THE LAWFULNESS OF INSTRUMENTAL MUSICK IN HOLY OFFICES

Dodworth, Allen *see*
– DANCING AND ITS RELATIONS TO EDUCATION AND SOCIAL LIFE
– DODWORTH'S BRASS BAND SCHOOL: CONTAINING INSTRUCTIONS IN THE FIRST PRINCIPLES OF MUSIC;...TOGETHER WITH A NUMBER OF PIECES OF MUSIC, ARRANGED FOR A FULL BRASS BAND

DODWORTH'S BRASS BAND SCHOOL: CONTAINING INSTRUCTIONS IN THE FIRST PRINCIPLES OF MUSIC;...TOGETHER WITH A NUMBER OF PIECES OF MUSIC, ARRANGED FOR A FULL BRASS BAND / Dodworth, Allen – New York: H. B. Dodworth & Co. 1853. In score, playable by 6-12 instruments.MUSIC 1978 – 1 – us L of C Photodup [780]

Doe, Walter P *see*
– IMPORTANT RELIGIOUS TRUTHS
– REVIVALS

Doederlein, Julius *see* GOTTES DASEIN BEWIESEN AM WISSEN UND SEIN

Doedes, Jacobus Izaak *see*
– ENCYCLOPEDIE DER CHRISTELIJKE THEOLOGIE
– DE LEER VAN GOD

Doehring, K *see* INDISCHE KUNST

Doelger, Frans J *see* ANTIKE UND CHRISTENTUM

Doell, Heinrich *see* GOETHE UND SCHOPENHAUER

Doell, J C *see* FLORA DES GROSSHERZOGTHUMS BADEN

Doell, M *see*
– DIE BENUETZUNG DER ANTIKE IN WIELANDS MORALISCHEN BRIEFEN
– DIE EINFLUESSE DER ANTIKE IN WIELANDS HERMANN
– WIELAND UND DIE ANTIKE

Doelle, H W *see* APPLIED MICROBIOLOGY

Doeller, Johannes *see*
– GEOGRAPHISCHE UND ETHNOGRAPHISCHE STUDIEN ZUM 3. UND 4. BUCHE DER KOENIGE
– RHYTHMUS, METRIK UND STROPHIK IN DER BIBLISCH-HEBRAEISCHEN POESIE

Doellinger, Ignaz von *see*
– ADDRESSES ON HISTORICAL AND LITERARY SUBJECTS
– BEITRAEGE ZUR SEKTENGESCHICHTE DES MITTELALTERS
– THE CHURCH AND THE CHURCHES, OR, THE PAPACY AND THE TEMPORAL POWER
– THE FIRST AGE OF CHRISTIANITY AND THE CHURCH
– KIRCHE UND KIRCHEN, PAPSTTHUM UND KIRCHENSTAAT
– LECTURES ON THE REUNION OF THE CHURCHES
– DIE LEHRE VON DER EUCHARISTIE IN DEN DREI ERSTEN JAHRHUNDERTEN
– STUDIES IN EUROPEAN HISTORY
– UEBER DIE WIEDERVEREINIGUNG DER CHRISTLICHEN KIRCHEN

Doellinger, Johann Joseph Ignaz von *see*
– BRIEFE UND ERKLAERUNG VON J. VON DOELLINGER UEBER DIE VATICANISCHEN DECRETE, 1869-87
– BRIEFE UND ERKLAERUNGEN VON J. VON DOELLINGER UEBER DIE VATICANISCHEN DECRETE, 1869-87
– GESCHICHTE UND KIRCHE
– THE POPE AND THE COUNCIL

Doering, O *see*
– DER AUGSBURGER PATRICIERS PHILIPP HAINHOFER REISEN NACH INNSBRUCK UND DRESDEN
– DES AUGSBURGER PATRICIERS PHILIPP HAINHOFER BEZIEHUNGEN ZUM HERZOG PHILIPP 2 VON POMMERN-STETTIN

DOERPTISCHE BEITRAEGE FUER FREUNDE DER PHILOSOPHIE, LITERATUR UND KUNST – Dorpat, Leipzig, 1813-1814 – 17mf – R-1751/2 – ne IDC [100]

Doerrer, Anton *see* BOZNER BUERGERSPIELE

Doerries et al *see* DIE 50 GEISTLICHEN HOMILIEN DES MARKARIOS

Doerries, H *see*
– SYMEON VON MESOPOTANIEN (T.U.U. 4-55/1)
– DIE VITA ANTONII ALS GESCHICHTSQUELLE NACHRICHTEN D. AKADEMIE D. WISSENSCHAFTEN IN GOETTINGEN

Doersam, Edgar *see* TECHNISCHE HOCHSCHULE DARMSTADT

DOES BODY TEMPERATURE MEDIATE ANXIOLYTIC EFFECTS AF ACUTE EXERCISE / Youngstedt, S D – 1991 – 2mf – 9 – $8.00 – us Microform Publ [150]

DOES GOD CARE FOR ME? (CCC191) / Koh, Roland – (In Chinese) – 1st ed. Hong Kong: Bible Book and Tract Depot, 1953 – 1r – 1 – 1984-B500 – us A.T.L.A. [210]

DOES HELLENISM CONTRIBUTE CONSTITUENT ELEMENTS TO PAUL'S CHRISTOLOGY / Bailey, John W – Chicago: G.K. Hazlitt, 1905. 1 fiche – 9 – us A.T.L.A. [240]

DOES INTERCOSTAL STRETCH AFFECT RESPIRATORY MUSCLE ACTIVITIES / Puckree, T – 1992 – 1mf – 9 – $4.00 – us Microform Publ [612]

DOES VITAMIN E SUPPLEMENTATION ATTENUATE EXERCISE-INDUCED SKELETAL MUSCLE INJURY / Warren, J A – 1991 – 1mf – 9 – $4.00 – us Microform Publ [612]

DOES WOMAN REPRESENT GOD? / Easton, Peter Zaccheus – 1895 – 9 – us A.T.L.A. [240]

Doetsch, Carlos *see*
– BENITO ARIAS MONTANO. EXTRACTOS DE SU VIDA
– ICONOGRAFIA DE BENITO ARIAS MONTANO
– LA PENA (RETIRO PREDILECTO DE MONTANO)

THE DOG CRUSOE: A TALE OF THE WESTERN PRAIRIES / Ballantyne, Robert Michael – Boston: Crosby and Nichols, 1862. 07468. (Pre-1900 Canadiana) – 9 – cn C.I.H.M. [830]

DOG FANCY – 1976- – 1 – us UMI [590]

A DOG OF FLANDERS / Ouida – British Fiction Archive: Unit 3 – 9 – uk Bell [830]

A DOG OF FLANDERS, AND OTHER STORIES / Ouida – London: Chapman and Hall, 1872 – 1 roll – 1 – uk Libr Preservation [830]

Dogadov, Vasilii Mikhailovich *see*
– OCHERKI TRUDOVOGO PRAVA
– PRAVOVOE POLOZHENIE PROFESSIONALNYKH SOIUZOV SSSR

Dogan, M *see* LES FRANCAISES FACE A LA POLITIQUE. COMPORTEMENT POLITIQUE ET CONDITION SOCIALE

Dogan, M. et al *see* LE REFERENDUM DE SEPTEMBRE ET LES ELECTIONS DE NOVEMBRE 1958

Dogan, Selami *see* A BIOMECHANICAL ANALYSIS OF CANINE GAIT BEFORE AND AFTER UNILATERAL CEMENTED TOTAL HIP REPLACEMENT

Doggett, L L *see*
– HISTORY OF THE YOUNG MEN'S CHRISTIAN ASSOCIATION. VOLUME 1, THE FOUNDING OF THE ASSOCIATION, 1844-1855
– LIFE OF ROBERT R. MCBURNEY

DOGMA AND DUTY / Awde, James – Toronto: W. Briggs, 1885. 02448. (Pre-1900 Canadiana) – 9 – cn C.I.H.M. [971]

DOGMA AND HISTORY : THE ESSEX HALL LECTURE / Krueger, Gustav – London: Philip Green, 1908 – 1mf – us A.T.L.A. [240]

DAS DOGMA DER ALTEN KIRCHE / Baur, Ferdinand Christian – Leipzig: Fues, 1865-1866. (Vorlesungen ueber die christliche Dogmengeschichte / von Ferdinand Christian Baur; 1. Bd.) – 3mf – us A.T.L.A. [240]

DAS DOGMA DER NEUEREN ZEIT / Baur, Ferdinand Christian – Leipzig: Fues, 1867. (Vorlesungen ueber die christliche Dogmengeschichte / von Ferdinand Christian Baur; 3. Bd.) – 2mf – us A.T.L.A. [240]

DAS DOGMA DES MITTELALTERS / Baur, Ferdinand Christian – Leipzig: Fues, 1866. (Vorlesungen ueber die christliche Dogmengeschichte / von Ferdinand Christian Baur; 2. Bd.) – 2mf – us A.T.L.A. [240]

DOGMA IN RELIGION AND CREEDS IN THE CHURCH / Kinross, John – Edinburgh: James Thin, 1897. 1 fiche – 9 – us A.T.L.A. [240]

DOGMA UND SCHULMEINUNG : DENKSCHRIFT IN SACHEN DER SOGENANNTEN "ERHEBUNG" VON LEHRANSICHTEN ZU "NEUEN GLAUBENSWAHRHEITEN" / Liano, Heinrich St A von – (Includes bibliographical references) – Muenchen: J J Lentner, 1869 – 1mf – 9 – 0-8370-8919-0 – 1986-2919 – us A.T.L.A. [240]

DAS DOGMA UND SEINE BEURTEILUNG IN DER NEUEREN DOGMENGESCHICHTE / Stange, Carl – Berlin: Reuther & Reichard, 1898. 1 fiche – 9 – us A.T.L.A. [240]

DAS DOGMA VOM NEUEN TESTAMENT / Krueger, Gustav – (Includes bibliographical references) – Giessen: Curt von Muenchow, 1896 – 1mf – 9 – 0-8370-4417-0 – 1985-2417 – us A.T.L.A. [220]

DAS DOGMA VON DER DREIEINIGKEIT UND GOTTMENSCHHEIT IN SEINER GESCHICHTLICHEN ENTWICKLUNG / Krueger, Gustav – (Includes index) – Tuebingen: J C B Mohr (Paul Siebeck), 1905 – 1mf – 9 – 0-8370-4416-2 – 1985-2416 – us A.T.L.A. [240]

DAS DOGMA VON DER SICHTBAREN UND UNSICHTBAREN KIRCHE : EIN HISTORISCH-KRITISCHER VERSUCH / Muenchmeyer, AF O – Goettingen: Vandenhoeck und Ruprecht, 1854 – 1mf – us A.T.L.A. [240]

DOGMAS DEL DERECHO... / Aspiazu, A – New York, 1872 – 4mf – 9 – ILM-416/1 – ne IDC [340]

DOGMATIC FAITH: AN INQUIRY INTO...REVELATION AND DOGMA / Garbett, Edward – London: Rivingtons, 1879. 1 fiche – 9 – us A.T.L.A. [240]

DOGMATICHESKOW ZNACHENIE SED'MAGO VSELENSKAGO SOBORA: NAUCHNO ISTORICHESKOW IZSLENOVANIE VAZHNOSTI I NEOPKHODIMOSTI.. / Ostroumov, G – St. Petersburg, 1884 – 1 – 9.96 – us Baptist [240]

DIE DOGMATIK DES NEUNZEHNTEN JAHRHUNDERTS : IN IHREM INNEREN FLUSSE UND IM ZUSAMMENHANG MIT DER ALLGEMEINEN THEOLOGISCHEN, PHILOSOPHISCHEN UND LITERARISCHEN ENTWICKLUNG DESSELBEN / Muecke, Albert – (Includes indexes) – Gotha: Friedrich Andreas Perthes, 1867 – 2mf – 9 – 0-8370-8845-3 – 1986-2845 – us A.T.L.A. [240]

DOGMATIKA MASAKINI / Niftrik, Gerrit Cornelis van – (Free translation of Kleine Dogmatiek,BY B. J. Boland. SE-6743 1. 1967 – 9 – ne IDC [240]

DOGMATISCHE STUDIEN / Frank, Franz Hermann Reinhold – Erlangen:Andr. Deichert (Georg Boehme), 1892 – 1mf – 9 – 0-8370-3177-X – 1985-1177 – us A.T.L.A. [240]

DOGME DE LA NAISSANCE MIRACULEUSE DU CHRIST *see* COLLECTED WORKS

LE DOGME DE LA REDEMPTION / Riviere, Jean – 1905 – 1 – us A.T.L.A. [240]

DOGME ET CRITIQUE / Le Roy, Edouard – (Includes bibliographical references and index) – 4e ed. Paris: Bloud, 1907 – 1mf – 9 – 0-8370-9486-0 – 1986-3486 – us A.T.L.A. [200]

DOGME ET RITUAL DE LA HAUTE MAGIE / Constant, Alphonse Louis – Paris. 1856. 2v. 284,324p. (Religion Series) – 9 – $21.00 – fr Bibl Nationale [130]

LE DOGME GREC / Bois, Henri – (Includes bibliographical references) – Paris: Librairie Fischbacher, 1893 – 1mf – 9 – 0-8370-7446-0 – 1986-1446 – us A.T.L.A. [250]

DIE DOGMENGESCHICHTE DES MITTELALTERS VON CHRISTOLOGISCHE STANDPUNKTE, ODER, DIE MITTELALTERLICHE CHRISTOLOGIE VOM ACHTEN BIS SECHZEHNTEN JAHRHUNDERT / Bach, Joseph – Wien: W. Braumueller, 1873-1875 – 3mf – us A.T.L.A. [240]

DOGMENGESCHICHTE DES PROTESTANTISMUS / Ritschl, Otto – H 128 2. 4 v. 1908-1927 – 8 – ne IDC [240]

Dognin, P *see* NOTE SUR LA FAUNE DES LEPIDOPTERES DE LOJA (EQUATEUR) ET DESCRIPTIONS D'ESPECES NOUVELLES

Dognon, Paul *see* LES INSTITUTIONS POLITIQUES ET ADMINISTRATIVES DU PAYS DE LANGUEDOC DU 13E SIECLE AUX GUERRES DE RELIGION.

Doherty, Patrick John *see*
– L'ABBE DOHERTY: SES PRINCIPAUX ECRITS EN FRANCAIS: PRECEDES D'UN PORTRAIT ET D'UNE NOTICE BIOGRAPHIQUE
– PRINCIPAL ENGLISH WRITINGS OF THE LATE REV. P. J. DOHERTY: PREFACED BY A SKETCH OF HIS LIFE

Doherty, Robert J *see* THE COMPLETE PHOTOGRAPHIC WORK OF JACOB A. RIIS

Dohm, CW *see* UEBER DIE BUERGERLICHE VERBESSERUNG DER JUDEN

Dohms, Evelyn *see* DIE BESTIMMUNG DES FACHLICHKEITSGRADES VON TEXTEN DER INDUSTRIESOZIOLOGIE DES ENGLISCHEN UND DEUTSCHEN
Dohn, Walter *see* DAS JAHR 1848 IM DEUTSCHEN DRAMA UND EPOS
Doiarenko, A G *see* PUTI K PODNIATIIU UROZHAINOSTI OZIMYKH KHLEBOV
Doige, Thomas *see* ALPHABETICAL LIST OF MERCHANTS, TRADERS AND HOUSEKEEPERS RESIDING IN MONTREAL
Doigni *see* DISCOURS D'UN NEGRE A UN EUROPEEN
Doin, Ernest *see*
- LE CONSCRIT OU LE RETOUR DE CRIMEE
- LE DESESPOIR DE JOCRISSE OU LES FOLIES D'UNE JOURNEE
- LE DIVORCE DU TAILLEUR: PIECE ARCHICOMIQUE EN UN ACTE
- JOACHIM MURAT ROI DES DEUX SICILIES
- TROIS PIECES COMIQUES: PROPRES A ETRE JOUEES DAN LES COLLEGES, MAISONS D'EDUCATION, ET SUR TOUT THEATRE

DOING IT – (See also: Humanizing City Life) – n. 1-8. 1976-1977 – 1 – us UMI [300]
DOINGS – Dresden. Ohio. 1875-1878; 1879 – 1 – us UMI [071]
DOIS MUNDOS – Nanuque, Brazil. Nov-Dec 1967; 1968; Jan-May, Jul-Aug 1969; Aug-Oct 1970 – 1 – bl Biblioteca [072]
DOIS PAULISTAS INSIGNES / Ennes, Ernesto – Sao Paulo, 1944 – 9mf – 8 – ne Slangenburg [999]
Doisy, M *see* LE ROYAUME DE FRANCE ET LES ETATS DE LORRAINE
Doka, C *see* DER BODENSEE IM INTERNATIONALEN RECHT
Doka, Carl *see* SWITZERLAND'S FOUR NATIONAL LANGUAGES
Doke, Clement Martin *see*
- THE LAMBAS OF NORTHERN RHODESIA: A STUDY OF THEIR CUSTOMS AND BELIEFS
- TEXT BOOK OF LAMBA GRAMMAR

DOKLAD O ZHURNALAKH "ZVEZDA" I "LENINGRAD" / Zhdanov, A – 1952. BR-2230 2 – 8 – ne IDC [073]
DOKLAD OBSHCHEPLANOVOI GOSUDARSTVENNOI KOMISSII IV SEZDU SOVNARKHOZOV – [Moskva: Vysshi i sovet narodnogo khozi a istva, Otdel redatsionno-izdatelski i, 1921?] – 1 – CSUX91-B3347 – us Hoover Inst Photo [947]
DOKLAD PO KONSTITUTSIONNYM VOPROSAM NA 7 S"EZD SOVETOV SOIUZA SSR. 5 FEVRALIA 1935 G / Enukidze, Avel'Sofronovich – Moskva Partizdat TsK VKP (b), 1935. 28. 4p LL-4013 – 1 – us L of C Photodup [340]
DOKLAD PREDSEDATELIA CHEREPOVETSKOGO GUB. SOV. NARODN. KHOZIAISTVA TOV. VASINOVA K V-MU OCHEREDNOMU GUBERNSKOMU SEZDU SOVETOV : 27-GO SENTIABRIA, 1919 GODA. GUBERNSKII SOEZD SOVETOV (5TH: 1919: CHEREPOVET S, R.S.F.S.R.) / Cherepovet ski i gubernski i sovet narodnogo khozi a istva – [Cherepovets: s.n., 1919] – 1 – CSUX91-B1109 – us Hoover Inst Photo [947]
DOKLAD SOVETA NARODNYKH KOMISSAROV BSSR SOVETU NARODNYKH KOMISSAROV SSSR : MATERIALY K DOKLADU T. ADAMOVICHA – Minsk: Upravlenie delami Soveta Narodnykh Komissarov BSSR, 1926 – 1 – CSUX91-B2429 – us Hoover Inst Photo [947]
DOKLAD TSENTROSOIUZA SOVETU NARODNYKH KOMISSAROV SSSR – M., 1929 – 2mf – 9 – COR-325/1 – ne IDC [334]
DOKLADNA 23RD CHREZVYCHAINOI LENINGRADSKOI GUBERNSKOI KONFERENTSII VKP(B) / Bukharin, Nikolai Ivanovich – Moskva: Gos. izd-vo, 1926 – 1 – CSUX89-B3777 – us Hoover Inst Photo [947]
DOKLADNAIA ZAPISKA TSENZORA SPB-GO TSENZURNOGO KOMITETA N. SOKOLOVA O TSIRKULIARNYKH RASPORIAZHENIIAKH PO DELAM PECHATI S 1 SENTIABRIA 1865 G. PO 1 IANVARIA 1900 G – Spb. 1900. BR-10,513 1 – 9 – ne IDC [947]
DOKLADY / Akademiia Nauk. SSSR – Comptes Rendus. Russian ed. v1-213. 1933-73 – 1,5,6 – us Princeton Micro [500]
DOKLADY / Akademiia Nauk. SSSR – (Comptes Rendus). Russian Edition. Series A: Science Section. 1926-1933 – 1,5,6 – us Princeton Micro [540]
DOKLADY / Akademiia Nauk. SSSR – Earth Science Section. Jan 1959-73 – 1 – us UMI [550]
DOKLADY BIOCHEMISTRY – v154-333. 1964-93 – 1,5 – $65.00y – us UMI [540]
DOKLADY BIOLOGICAL SCIENCES – v142-333. 1962-93 – 1,5 – $85.00y – us UMI [574]
DOKLADY BIOPHYSICS – v154-333. 1964-93 – 1,5 – $35.00y – us UMI [530]
DOKLADY BOTANICAL SCIENCES – v154-333. 1964-93 – 1,5 – $35.00y – us UMI [580]
DOKLADY CHEMICAL TECHNOLOGY – v106-333. 1956-93 – 1,5 – $35.00y – us UMI [660]
DOKLADY CHEMISTRY – v106-333. 1956-93 – 1,5 – $85.00y – us UMI [540]
DOKLADY I SOOBSHCHENIIA – Ikutsk: IAkutskoe knizhnoe izd-vo, 1973-1975. [v3,5. 1973] – us Res Libr [072]
DOKLADY I SOOBSHCHENIIA INSTITUTA ISTORII / Akademiia Nauk. SSSR – Akademiia nauk SSSR. v. 9-12. M. 1956-57. BR-1739 2 – 8 – ne IDC [500]
DOKLADY PHYSICAL CHEMISTRY – v112-333. 1957-93 – 1,5 – $95.00y – us UMI [540]
DOKLADY.EARTH SCIENCE SECTION – (v280-. 1984-. 5,6,9) – v208-. Mar 1974- – 1 – us UMI [550]
DOKLADY.SOIL SCIENCE – 1964-68 – 1 – us UMI [631]
DOKTER ZHIVAGO / Pasternak, B – SE-2914 1. 2 v. 1960 – 9 – ne IDC [830]
DER DOKTOR = THE DOCTOR – (In Yiddish) – Warsaw, PL. no8(108) 19 Apr 1932 – 1r – 1 – $25.00 – cn Can Microfilming [610]
DOKTOR POMERANUS, JOHANNES BUGENHAGEN : EIN LEBENSBILD AUS DER ZEIT DER REFORMATION / Hering, Hermann – Halle: Verein fuer Reformationsgeschichte, 1888. (Schriften des Vereins fuer Reformationsgeschichte; 6. Jahrg., 1. Stueck, Nr. 22) – 1mf – us A.T.L.A. [240]
DOKUKA I BALAGUR'E. RUSSKIIA SKAZKI / Remizov, A – 1914. BR-820 2 – 8 – ne IDC [460]
DOKUMEN 1966-1968; LAPORAN UMUM PROGRAM KERDJA 1968 / Indonesia. Direktorat Film – SE-8565 1. 1968 – 9 – ne IDC [790]
DOKUMEN DARI 'MALAYSIA.' SE-10,766/1. 1964 / Muis, A – 9 – ne IDC [950]
DOKUMENTARISCHE INFORMATION-PANORAMA DDR – Berlin: Panorama DDR. Continued by: Dokumentation (Panorama DDR) – 1 – us U.W. Library [073]
DOKUMENTASI PEMUDA: SEKITAR PROKLAMASI INDONESIA MERDEKA – SE-4755 1. 1948 – 9 – ne IDC [950]
DOKUMENTATION – Evangelischer Pressedienst. Zentralredaktion. -w – 1 – us U.W. Library [073]
DOKUMENTATION DER ZEIT (ERSCHIENEN BIS 1972) – 1949-1972 – 750mf – 1 – DM4,275.00 – gw Mikro Press [900]
DOKUMENTATION, EIN INFORMATIONSDIENST – 1971-73; 1978-86 – 1 – us A.T.L.A. [240]
DOKUMENTATION ZUR JUEDISCHEN KULTUR IN DEUTSCHLAND 1840-1940, ABT. 1 : DIE ZEITUNGSAUSSCHNITTSAMMLUNG STEININGER. TEIL 1: BILDENDE KUENSTLER. TEIL 2: DARSTELLENDE KUENSTLER – 101mf – 9 – DM4,980.00 – 3-598-33317-X – gw Saur [306]
DOKUMENTATION ZUR JUEDISCHEN KULTUR IN DEUTSCHLAND 1840-1940, ABT. 2 : MUSIK – 1996/97 – ca 120mf in 3 installments (1:24) – 9 – silver DM4,980.00 – 3-598-33322-6 – gw Saur [780]
DOKUMENTATIONEN ZUM PARLAMENTARISMUS – (See individual titles: Protokolle der deutschen Bundesversammlung 1816-1866. Stenographische Berichte ueber die Verhandlungen des deutschen Reichstages des norddeutschen Bundes. Stenographischer Bericht ueber die Verhandlungen der deutschen constituirenden Nationalversammlung zu Frankfurt 1848-49. Stenographische Berichte des Reichstags der Weimarer Republik 1919-33. Stenographische Protokolle ueber die Sitzungen des Herrenhauses des oesterreichischen Reichsrates 1861-1918. Stenographische Protokolle ueber die Sitzungen des Hauses der Abgeordneten des oesterreichischen Reichsrates 1861-1918. Stenographische Protokolle, Sitzungen der provisorischen Nationalversammlung. Stenographische Protokolle der Landtage des Koenigreichs Sachsen) – 15,288mf – 9 – DM21,000.00 diazo DM25,200.00 silver – gw Olms [320]
DOKUMENTATIONEN ZUM PARLAMENTARISMUS *see*
- PROTOKOLLE DER DEUTSCHEN BUNDESVERSAMMLUNG 1816-1866
- STENOGRAPHISCHE BERICHTE DES REICHSTAGS DER WEIMARER REPUBLIK 1919-1933
- STENOGRAPHISCHE BERICHTE UEBER DIE VERHANDLUNGEN DES DEUTSCHEN REICHSTAGES, DES NORDDEUTSCHEN BUNDES, BZW. AB 1871 DES DEUTSCHEN REICHSTAGES 1867-1918
- STENOGRAPHISCHE PROTOKOLLE
- STENOGRAPHISCHE PROTOKOLLE DER LANDTAGE DES KOENIGREICHS SACHSEN SOWIE DES SPAETEREN FREISTAATES SACHSEN 1833-1933
- STENOGRAPHISCHE PROTOKOLLE UEBER DIE SITZUNGEN DES HAUSES DER ABGEORDNETEN DES OESTERREICHISCHEN REICHSRATES 1861-1918
- STENOGRAPHISCHE PROTOKOLLE UEBER DIE SITZUNGEN DES HERRENHAUSES DES OESTERREICHISCHEN REICHSRATES 1861-1918
- STENOGRAPHISCHER BERICHT UEBER DIE VERHANDLUNGEN DER DEUTSCHEN CONSTITUIERENDEN NATIONALVERSAMMLUNG ZU FRANKFURT 1848-49

DOKUMENTE DES FORTSCHRITTS – Berlin. Nov. 1907-July 1918. Missing Jan. 1915 – 1 – 35.00r – us Hoover Inst Photo [073]
DOKUMENTE ZUM ABLASSSTREIT VON 1517 / Koehler, Walther E – Tuebingen: Mohr, 1902 (Sammlung ausgewaehlter kirchen- und dogmengeschichtlicher Quellenschriften; 2. Reihe, 3. Heft) – 1mf – us A.T.L.A. [240]
DOKUMENTE ZUM WELTKRIEG 1914 / Bernstein, Eduard – Berlin: Buchhandlung Vorwaerts, 1914 – 1 – us U.W. Library [940]
DOKUMENTY DLIA ISTORII DIPLOMATICHESKIKH SNOSHENII ROSSII S ZAPADNYMI DERZHAVAMI EVROPEISKIMI OT ZAKLIUCHENIIA VSEOBSHCHAGO MIRA V 1814 G. DO KONGRESSA V VERONE V 1822 GODU – (In French and Russian) – 1823-1825. 2v – 34mf – R-9471/1 – ne IDC [320]
DOKUMENTY I MATERIALY PO ISTORII VELIKOI OKTIABR SKOI SOTSIAL-ISTICHESKOI REVOLIUTSII / Astrakhantseva, I F et al – Moscow, 1969. 49p. BR-11,063 1 – 9 – ne IDC [947]
DOKUMENTY PO ISTORII PRIBALTIKI SHVEDSKOGO PERIODA V ARKHIVAKH RIGI / Ensh, G A – (Skandinavskii sbornik Skandinavia kogumik (Tallinn). 1958). Latvian version: "Zviedru perioda dokumentalie materiali Latvijas PSR valsts archivo (Fondu vesture un dokumentalo materialu apskats). Vestures problemas. 1958. BR-14.091 1 – 9 – ne IDC [947]
DOKUMENTY SOTSIALISTICHESKO I REVOLIUTSII : SBORNIK MATERIALOV – Moskva: Sov. mir, 1919- – 1 – CSUX88-B8389 – us Hoover Inst Photo [320]
DOKUMENTY TSGIA SSSR V LENINGRADE V RABOTAKH SOVETSKIKH ISSLEDOVATELEI – Bibliograficheskii ukazatel'. Pt.1, 1917-57, 282p, Leningrad, 1960. Pt.2, 1958-62, 327p, Leningrad, 1966. BR-10,724- – 9 – ne IDC [010]
DOKUMENTY VNESHNE I POLITIKI SSSR / Ministerstvo inostrannykh del SSSR – Moskva: Izd-vo polit. lit-ry, 1957- – 1 – CSUX90-B5352 – us Hoover Inst Photo [320]
DOKUMENTY ZBRODNI I MECZENSTWA, KOLEGIUM REDAKCYJNE / ed by Borwicz, Michal Maksymilian – Krakow: Centralny Komitet Zydow Polskich, 1945. xv,214p – 1 – us U.W. Library [940]
Dol *see* ISTORIIA KRASNOGO OKTIABRIA
DOLBEAU JOURNAL – (Includes: La Voie du Nord, Dolbeau v3 n25 17 avr 1948-24 dec 1949f) – Dolbeau, 2 nov 1945-10 avr 1948 – 2r – 1 – Can$70.00 – cn Can Microfilming [072]
Dolbey, Robert Valentine *see* SKETCHES OF THE EAST AFRICA CAMPAIGN
Dolch, A *see* DIE VERBREITUNG OBERLAENDISCHER MYSTIKERWERKE IM NIEDERLAENDISCHEN
Dolch, Oskar *see* DIE DEUTSCHE TREUE
Dold, A *see* DIE VOM MISSALE ROMANUM ABWEICHENDEN LESETEXTE FUER DIE MESZFEIERN NACH DEN NOTIERUNGEN DES AUS MONTE-CASINO STAMMENDEN CODEX VAT. LAT. 6082
DIE DOLDENBLUETLER ALS HEILPFLANZEN IM MITTELALTER : EIN MEDIZINHISTORISCHER VERGLEICH / Wemmer, Dagmar – 1994 – 1mf – DM60.00 – 3-8267-2054-7 – gw Hänsel [615]
Dole, Artemus Wood *see* AUTOBIOGRAPHY
Dole, Charles Fletcher *see*
- JESUS AND THE MEN ABOUT HIM
- THE THEOLOGY OF CIVILIZATION
- WHAT WE KNOW ABOUT JESUS

Doleschall, A *see*
- BUENTETOEJOG A NEMZETKOEZI JOGBAN...
- A HONOSSAQ A BUENTETOE JOGBAN

Dolet, E *see* LA MANIERE DE BIEN TRADUIRE
Dolgoff, Sam *see* LAISSEZ FAIRE LIBERTARIANISM VERSUS ANARCHISM
Dolgoroukov *see* LA VERITE SUR LA RUSSIE
Dolgorukov, I M *see* POVEST'O ROZHDENII MOEM, PROISKHOZDENII I VSEI ZIZNI, 1764-1800
Dolgorukov, P D *see* POLITICHESKII STROI SOVREMENNYKH GOSUDARSTV
Dolgorukov, P V *see* ROSSIISKAIA RODOSLOVNAIA KNIGA
DOLGOZOK LAPJA – Tatabanya, Hungary. 1962-68; 1970-Mar 1980 – 30r – 1 – us L of C Photodup [072]
Dolinin, A S *see*
- AKMEIZM
- OTRESHENNYI

Dolitzki, M M *see*
- KOL SHIREI
- MIBAYIT UMIHUZ

DOLLAR AND SENSE – Washington, DC. 1977-83 – 2r – 1 – $100.00 – R05501 – us Library Micro [071]
DOLLAR DEMOCRAT – Grenada. Miss. 1841-1846 – 1 – us UMI [071]
DOLLAR DOOMSDAY / Riegel, E C – 1fiche. (24x) – 9 – 1.00f – at Libertarian Micro [320]
THE DOLLAR NEWSPAPER – Philadelphia, PA: A H Simmons, 1860; [1861-63] – 2r – 1 – us Res Libr [071]
DOLLAR WEEKLY NEWS – Wilkes Barre. Pa. 1884-1899 – 1 – us UMI [071]
DOLLARD NEWS/ECHO DE DOLLARD – Montreal, 27 mar 1958f – 1r – 1 – Can$25.00 – cn Can Microfilming [072]
DOLLARS AND DECISIONS / Vermont. Agricultural Extension Service – v. 1-6. 1964-70 – 1,5,6 – us Spaulding [630]
DOLLARS AND SENSE – 1978- – 1,5,6,9 – us UMI [650]
Dollier de Casson, Francois *see*
- HISTOIRE DU MONTREAL
- HISTOIRE DU MONTREAL, 1640-1672

Dolling, Robert R *see* TEN YEARS IN A PORTSMOUTH SLUM
Dollinger, Hermann *see* DIE DRAMATISCHE HANDLUNG IN KLOPSTOCKS "DER TOD ADAMS" UND GERSTENBERGS "UGOLINO"
Dolly Svobodny *see* RESEARCH ON CHILDREN'S AND YOUNG ADULT LITERATURE
Dolmatovskii, A M *see*
- NOVYE ZAKONY O KOOPERATSII
- ZAKONY O KOOPERATSII

Dolmetsch, Arnold *see* DOLMETSCH LIBRARY OF EARLY MUSIC
DOLMETSCH LIBRARY OF EARLY MUSIC / Dolmetsch, Arnold – (260 vols of printed and manuscript music and related documents from 1581-1840. With printed catalogue) – 488mf – 9 – $2,812.00 – 1-869934-40-7 – uk Emmett [780]
DOLO I BLOKADU! : K DVUKHLI ETII U BOLSHEVITSKO I REVOLIUTSII V ROSSII – Chikago: Izd. obl. kom-ta, Chikagskago ra iona, Russko i federatsii Kommunistichesko i partii Ameriki, [1919?] – 1 – CSUX88-B7700 – us Hoover Inst Photo [320]
DOLO I POLITIKU! : KNIZHKADLI A BESPARTI INYKH / Urmanskii, Ivan – Moskva: Gos. izdvo, 1921 – 1 – CSUX88-B6364 – us Hoover Inst Photo [320]
DOLOI NEGRAMOTNOST : BUKVAR DLIA VZROSLYKH / Elkina, D et al – Moskva: Gos. izd-vo, 1920 – 1 – CSUX91-B747 – us Hoover Inst Photo [947]
DOLOMITE IN INDONESIA / Johannas – 1963. 22p. maps (7 fold. in pocket). SEM-13096/1 – 9 – ne IDC [910]
DOLOMITEN : TAGBLATT DER SUEDTIROLER – Bozen, 1954- – 1 – Inquire at Mikrofilmarchiv for details – gw Misc Inst [072]

DOLOMITEN : TAGBLATT DER SUEDTIROLER – Bozen (Bolzano), Italy. 1 Jul 1954-77; 1979 – 1 – gw Mikrofilm [072]
DOLOR BOHEMIO / Ruiz de Silva, Enrique – Badajoz: Tipografia Correo de la Manana, 1916 – 1 – sp Bibl Santa Ana [946]
EL DOLOR SUPREMO / Oton, Alfonso y Zaldivar, Ignacio – Caceres: Imp. Santos Floriano, S.A. – sp Bibl Santa Ana [946]
Dolores y Santa Marta, Felix *see* ORACION FUNEBRE
DOLOROSO NOVENARIO...JESUS, DE LA SOLEDAD DE BADAJOZ – 1805 – 9 – 1.50f – sp Bibl Santa Ana [240]
DOLTON POINTER – Chicago. Ill. 1932-1963 – 1 – us UMI [071]
DOM A SKOLA – Ruzomberok, Slovakia, 1886-1897 – 3r – 1 – us I.H.R.C. [947]
DOM CASMURRO – Rio de Janeiro, 13 May 1937-May 1946; Dec 1946 – 1,5,6 – bl Biblioteca [072]
DES DOM. GUNDISSALINUS SCHRIFT 'VON DER UNSTERBLICHKEIT DER SEELE' : BGPHMA 2/3 / Buelow, G – Muenster, 1897 – 3mf – 9 – ne Slangenburg [240]
DES DOM. GUNDISSALINUS SCHRIFT 'VON DER UNSTERBLICHKEIT DER SEELE' / Buelow, G – Muenster, 1897 – 3mf – 8 – ne Slangenburg [120]
DOM IN SVET – Chicago, IL, 1929 – 3mf or 1 reel – 9,1 – us I.H.R.C. [972]
Dom Literatorov. Leningrad *see* LETOPIS'
DOM PETRUS, BIBLIORUM SACRORUM LATINAE VERSIONES ANTIQUAE, SEU VETUS ITALICA / Sabatier, Paul – Remis. Tomi 1. 1743 – 139mf – 8 – ne Slangenburg [220]
DER DOM VON KOELN UND DAS MUENSTER VON STRASSBURG / Goerres, Joseph – Regensburg, 1842 – 136p – 9 – DM48.00 – 3-89349-071-X – gw Hänsel [720]
DOMACHNII OCHAG – Semeinyi illiustrirovannyi zhurnal. v. 1-24. Spb. 1907. BR-3398 2 – 8 – ne IDC [073]
DOMACI NOVINY – Clarkson, NE. -w. 27 Aug 1909-25 Mar 1924. In Czech – 1 – us NE Hist [071]
THE DOMAIN OF BELIEF / Coke, Henry John – London: Macmillan, 1910 – 1mf – us A.T.L.A. [240]
LE DOMAINE COLONIAL DE LA FRANCE, SES RESOURCES ET SES BESOINS : GUIDE PRATIQUE DE L'ALGERIE, DES COLONIES, DES PAYS DE PROTECTORAT ET TERRITOIRES A MANDAT... – Paris: F Alcan, 1922 – 1 – us Res Libr [960]
LA DOMAINE RESERVE / Feifer, E – Paris, 1937 – 2mf – 1 – ILM-2178/1 – ne IDC [327]
Doman, Andrew S *see* HEALTH INSURANCE AND EFFICIENT HEALTH SERVICE DELIVERY
Domanig, Karl *see* DIE FREMDEN
Domanski, B *see* DIE PSYCHOLOGIE DES NEMESIUS
DOMASHNIAIA BESEDA DLIA NARODNAGO CHTENIIA – Spb. 1858-77. Lacking: v. 10-31, 1863; v. 27-52, 1864; v. 29, 1867; v. 19, 1872; 1874-77. BR-1583 2 – 8 – ne IDC [073]
DOMASHNIAIA BIBLIOTEKA – Romany i povesti russkikh i inostrannykh pisatelei. Ezhemesiachnoe izdanie. Spb. 1895-99. Lacking: 1896 (1, 3). B-1709 2 – 8 – ne IDC [460]
DOMASHNIAIA BIBLIOTEKA – v. 1-12. Spb. 1869-71. BR-1584 2 – 8 – ne IDC [460]
DOMASHNIE PTITSY, UKHOD ZA NIMI I SPOSOBY SOKHRANENIIA IAITS : KRATKOE RUKOVODSTVO DLIA MELKIKH KHOZIAISTV / Gratsianov, PK – [Moskva]: Gos. izd-vo, 1921 – 1 – CSUX91-B2466 – us Hoover Inst Photo [339]
DOMASI COMMUNITY DEVELOPMENT SCHEME, 1949-54 / Thomson, T D – Zomba, Govt Print [1955] – us Res Libr [072]
Dombart, B *see* ZUR TEXTGESCHICHTE DER CIVITAS DEI AUGUSTINS (T.U.U. 3-32/2A)
DOMENICA DEL CORRIERE – 1988-1989 – 2 times per yr – 6 – L2,200 – sz Infoprint [072]
Domenzain, Moises *see* EL JAPON SU EVOLUCION, CULTURA, RELIGIONES
Domergue, U *see* GRAMMAIRE FRANCOISE SIMPLIFIEE
DOMESDAY BOOK AND BEYOND / Maitland, Frederic William – Cambridge. 1907 – 1 – us Res Libr [941]
DOMESDAY BOOK AND BEYOND : THREE ESSAYS IN THE EARLY HISTORY OF ENGLAND / Maitland, Frederick William – Cambridge: University Press, 1897 – 1 roll – 1 – 1-55879-915-X – uk Libr Preservation [941]
THE DOMESDAY BOROUGHS / Ballard, A – H-1218 2. 1904 – 8 – ne IDC [941]
THE DOMESDAY INQUEST / Ballard, A – H-1166 2. 1906 – 8 – ne IDC [941]
DOMESDAY STUDIES / ed by Dove, P E & Wheatley, H B – H-1161 2. 2 v. 1888, 1891 – 8 – ne IDC [941]
Domeslius, P *see* EEN KORTE EN KLARE INSTRUCTIE OFTE ONDERWYSINGHE DER MUSYCKE
DOMESTIC ACCOUNTS / Holkham Hall. Norfolk. England – 1719-92 – 1 – uk Microform Academic [941]
DOMESTIC DUTIES OF THE FAMILY / Bailey, Rufus W – 1 – $50.00 – us Presbyterian [240]
DOMESTIC LETTERS OF THE DEPT. OF STATE, 1784-1906 / U.S. Department of State – 171 rolls. M40 – 1 – us Nat'l Archives [975]
DOMESTIC LIFE IN PALESTINE / Rogers, Mary Eliza – Cincinnati: Poe & Hitchcock, 1867 – 1mf – 9 – 0-8370-6357-4 – 1986-0357 – us A.T.L.A. [956]
THE DOMESTIC SLAVE TRADE OF THE SOUTHERN STATES / Collins, Winfield Hazlitt – New York, 1904 – 1 – us Res Libr [305]
DOMESTIC STYLE – Toronto: New York Domestic Fashion, [1877?-189- or 19–] – 9 – cn C.I.H.M. [640]
DOMESTIC UTENSILS (TIAM, PT 5) – (With printed catalogue ISBN: 0-914146-70-X £30) – 30mf – 15 – £570.00 – uk Chadwyck [640]
DOMESTIQUES. OBJETS DOMESTIQUES DES PROVINCES DE FRANCE DANS LA VIE FAMILIALE ET LES ARTS MENAGERS / Reunion des musees nationaux. Paris – 1953. 19 illus. 1 fiche – 9 – fr Réunion [740]
Domett, Alfred *see* POEMS
LE DOMICILE DES ETRANGERS EN FRANCE / Bennet, L – Pau, 1923 – 2mf – 9 – ILM-3426/1 – ne IDC [327]
DOMINACION Y GUERRAS DE ESPANA EN LOS PAISES BAJOS / Barrado Font, Francisco – Madrid: Est. Tip. El Trabajo, 1902. Rev. Tecnica de Infanteria y Caballeria – sp Bibl Santa Ana [946]
THE DOMINAT (DOMINANT) – v1-32. Feb 1893-Jan 1925 – 1 – 995.00 – us Opus [073]
DOMINATION OR SHARING : ENDOGENOUS DEVELOPMENT AND THE TRANSFER OF KNOWLEDGE / Ribes, Bruno et al – 1981 – 288p – 9 – 92-3-101842-6 – fr UNESCO [000]
O DOMINGO : HEBDOMADARIO LITERARIO E DE CRITICA HUMORISTICA – Manaos, Amazonas. 12-19 Abr, 8-22 Nov 1908 – 1,5,6 – bl Biblioteca [072]
O DOMINGO : SEMANARIO CRITICO E LITTERARIO – '(s.l.')-Sao Luis, Brazil. 21 Jul 1872-15 Mar 1874 – 1,5,6 – bl Biblioteca [072]
O DOMINGO – [s.l.]. 24 mar 1889 – 1,5,6 – bl Biblioteca [072]
DOMINGO CRESI... / Barrado Manzano, Arcangel – Madrid: Archivo Ibero-Americano, 1959 – 1 – sp Bibl Santa Ana [240]
Domingo de San Pedro de Alcantara *see* CELESTIAL LIRIO
Dominguez Berrueta, Juan *see* SANTA TERESA DE JESUS. MADRID 1934
Dominguez, Francisco *see* EL APOSTOL DE LA MENTIRA JUAN PERON
Dominguez, Manuel *see* INSTITUTO DE SEGUNDA ENSENANZA DE MERIDA. MEMORIA DEL CURSO 1934-35
Dominguez Peaz, Fidel *see*
– DUQUES DE LA TORRE
– RASGOS BIBLIOGRAFICOS DE SANTA TERESA DE JESUS
Dominguez, Rafael *see*
– GALERIA UNIVERSITARIA. TOMO 1. CARACAS, 1934
– JOSE MARIA VARGAS
Dominguez Villagra, David *see* ODONTOLOGIA SANITARIA POR...
Dominica *see* DEVELOPMENT PROGRAMME, 1959-1964
Dominica. British West Indies *see* OFFICIAL GAZETTE
DOMINICA CHRONICLE – 1909-July 1962 – 1 – us UMI [072]
DOMINICA GUARDIAN – Roseau, Dominica. -w. 1 July 1893-15 Dec 1921. 1914-19 very imperfect. 9 reels – 1 – uk British Libr Newspaper [072]
DOMINICA HERALD – Roseau, Dominica. -w. 10 Jan 1959-7 Jan 1967. 4 reels – 1 – uk British Libr Newspaper [072]
DOMINICA TRIBUNE – Roseau. Dominica. -w. 2 Jan 1930-5 May 1951. (Wanting Jan-Jun 1933; Aug-Dec 1938; Dec 1944-May 1945; Jul-Sep 1946). (14 reels) – 1 – uk British Libr Newspaper [072]
DOMINICAL GOSPELS AND THE PATERNOSTER WITH WYCLIFFITE COMMENTARY – Late 14th century. Ms. xvi. D2 York Minster Library – 1 – uk Microform Academic [240]
DOMINICAN – Dominica. 1842-1907 – 1 – us UMI [072]
DOMINICAN PROVINCE OF SAINT JOSEPH : JUSTICE STUDIES – 1977-80 (complete) – 1r – 1 – ATLA S0458 – us A.T.L.A. [073]
DOMINICAN PROVINCE OF SAINT JOSEPH : NEWS DIGEST – v1-23. Nov 1858-1982 (complete) – 1R – 1 – ATLA S0457 – us A.T.L.A. [240]
Dominican Province of Saint Joseph *see*
– JUSTICE STUDIES
– NEW DIGEST
DOMINICAN REPUBLIC : 21 ANOS DE ESTADISTICAS DOMINICANAS 1936-1956 / Dominican Republic. Direccion General de Estadistica y Censos – (Coll title: Latin American and Caribbean Official Statistical Serials, 1821-1982) – 6mf – 9 – £7.00f (set £1,340.00 213mf) – uk Chadwyck [972]
DOMINICAN REPUBLIC : ANUARIO ESTADISTICO 1936-1954 / Dominican Republic. Direccion General de Estadistica y Censos – (Coll title: Latin American and Caribbean Official Statistical Serials, 1821-1982) – 199mf – 9 – £5.00f (set £1,340.00 213mf) – uk Chadwyck [972]
DOMINICAN REPUBLIC : REPUBLICA DOMINICANA EN CIFRAS 1964-1969 / Dominican Republic. Oficina Nacional de Estadistica – (1966 not available. Coll title: Latin American and Caribbean Official Statistical Serials, 1821-1982) – 8mf – 9 – £7.00f (set £1,340.00 213mf) – uk Chadwyck [972]
Dominican Republic *see*
– ADAPTIVE AGRICULTURAL RESEARCH PROJECT, 1981-1985
– GACETA OFICIAL
Dominican Republic. Direccion General de Estadistica y Censos *see*
– DOMINICAN REPUBLIC
Dominican Republic. Laws, Statutes, etc *see* CODIGO CIVIL DE LA REPUBLICA DOMINICANA.
Dominican Republic. Oficina Nacional de Estadistica *see* DOMINICAN REPUBLIC
Dominican Republic. Oficina Nacional de Planificacion *see*
– PLAN NACIONAL DE DESARROLLO
– PLATAFORMA PARA EL DESARROLLO ECONOMICO Y SOCIAL DE LA REPUBLICA DOMINICANA (1968-1985)
THE DOMINICAN REVIVAL IN THE NINETEENTH CENTURY : BEING SOME ACCOUNT OF THE RESTORATION OF THE ORDER OF PREACHERS THROUGHOUT THE WORLD UNDER FR. JANDEL THE SEVENTY-THIRD MASTER-GENERAL / Devas, Raymund – London; New York: Longmans, Green, 1913 – 1mf – us A.T.L.A. [240]
DOMINICANS IN EARLY FLORIDA / O'Daniel – New York, 1930; Madrid, 1931 – 1 – sp Bibl Santa Ana [240]
Dominick, Mary F *see* HUMAN RIGHTS, EUROPEAN POLITICS, AND THE HELSINKI ACCORD
Dominicus de Flandria *see*
– IN 12 LIBROS METAPHYSICAE ARISTOTELIS
– IN D. THOMAE AQ. COMMENTARIA SUPER LIBROS POSTERIORUM ANALYTICORUM ARISTOTELIS
Dominicus, F C *see* HET HUISELIK EN MAATSCHAPPELIK LEVEN VAN SE ZUID-AFRIKANER IN DE EERSTE HELFT DER 18DE EEUW
Dominicus, Foort Cornelius *see* HET HUISELIK EN MAA SCHAPPELIK LEVEN VAN DE ZUID-AFRIKANER IN DE EERSTE HELFT DER 18DE EEUW
DIE DOMINIKANERMISSIONEN DES 13 JAHRHUNDERTS / Altaner, Bruno – Habelschwerdt, 1924. xxiii, 248p. BU-715 2 – 8 – ne IDC [240]
THE DOMINION – Wellington, 1991- – 12r per y – 1 – us Ross [072]
DOMINION BAZAAR – Yorkville [Toronto]: Dominion Bazaar Co, [1877?-1881?] – 9 – cn C.I.H.M. [760]
DOMINION CHURCH OF ENGLAND TEMPERANCE JOURNAL – Toronto: A C Winton, [1886-18– or 19–] – 9 – cn C.I.H.M. [170]
Dominion Commercial Travellers' Association *see* CONSTITUTION...MONTREAL, INSTITUTED A.D. 1875: ALSO BY-LAWS, AS REVISED AT ANNUAL MEETING, DECEMBER 23RD, 1880
DOMINION DAY: CARACTACUS, MALCOLM AND MARGARET POEMS / Dawson, Aeneas McDonell – Ottawa: s.n., 1886 (Ottawa: C. Mitchell). 02603. (Pre-1900 Canadiana) – 9 – cn C.I.H.M. [810]
DOMINION DENTAL JOURNAL – Toronto: Dominion Dental Journal Pub. Co, [1889-1934] – 9 – cn C.I.H.M. [617]
DOMINION ELECTIONS 1891 – Compliments of the Canadian Pacific Railway Company's telegraph. s.l.: s.n., 1891?. 05705. (Pre-1900 Canadiana) – 9 – cn C.I.H.M. [971]
DOMINION ILLUSTRATED – Special Numbers. 1891-92 – 1 – 35.00 – cn McLaren [971]
DOMINION ILLUSTRATED – v. 1-7. 1888-1891 – 1 – 265.00 – cn McLaren [073]
DOMINION ILLUSTRATED MONTHLY / ed by Desbarats, G E – Montreal, Canada. 7 jul 1888-fev 1893 – 3r – 1 – Can$50.00r – cn Can Microfilming [073]
DOMINION ILLUSTRATED MONTHLY, AND FINANCIAL AND COMMERCIAL REVIEW – 1892-1893 – 1 – 125.00 – cn McLaren [073]
THE DOMINION IN 1983 / Centennius, Ralph – Peterborough, Ont.: Toker, c1883. 00529. (Pre-1900 Canadiana) – 9 – cn C.I.H.M. [971]
DOMINION MECHANICAL AND MILLING NEWS – Toronto: Beaver Pub. Co, [1884?-1889?] – 9 – cn C.I.H.M. [621]
THE DOMINION MONTHLY JOURNAL OF MUSIC AND GENERAL MISCELLANY – Toronto: Sargant & Eldridge, [1876?-18– or 19–] – 9 – cn C.I.H.M. [780]
THE DOMINION MUSICAL JOURNAL – Toronto: Timms, [1891?-189 or 19–] – 9 – cn C.I.H.M. [780]
DOMINION ODDFELLOW – Napanee, Ont: Templeton and Beeman, [1881?-189- or 19–] – 9 – cn C.I.H.M. [360]
THE DOMINION OF CANADA / Eden, Charles Henry – Published under the direction of the Committee of General Literature and Education, appointed by the Society for Promoting Christian Knowledge. Enlarged and corrected. London: The Society, 1873. 02640. (Pre-1900 Canadiana) – 9 – cn C.I.H.M. [971]
THE DOMINION OF CANADA – With Newfoundland and an excursion to Alaska: handbook for travellers. By Karl Baedeker. Leipsic Germany?: Karl Baedeker, 1894. 00076. (Pre-1900 Canadiana) – 9 – cn C.I.H.M. [971]
THE DOMINION OF CANADA: A STUDY OF ANNEXATION / Aitken, William Benford – New York: Van Sielen, 1890?. 02282. (Pre-1900 Canadiana) – 9 – cn C.I.H.M. [971]
DOMINION OF CANADA AND NEWFOUNDLAND GAZETTEER AND CLASSIFIED BUSINESS DIRECTORY-1922 / Canadian Gazetteer Publishing Co – Toronto, 1922. Canada reel 2. (Cox Library Collection) – 5 – us Americana [072]
THE DOMINION OF CANADA: AS IT WILL APPEAR TO THE MEMBERS OF THE BRITISH ASSOCIATION FOR THE ADVANCEMENT OF SCIENCE IN 1884: A PAPER READ BEFORE THE SOCIETY OF ARTS, TUESDAY, JANUARY 29, 1884 / Colmer, Joseph Grose – (London: McCorquodale), 1884. 00717. (Pre-1900 Canadiana) – 9 – cn C.I.H.M. [910]
THE DOMINION OF CHRIST : THE CLAIMS OF FOREIGN MISSIONS IN THE LIGHT OF MODERN RELIGIOUS THOUGHT AND A CENTURY OF EXPERIENCE / Pierce, William – (Includes indexes) – London: H R Allenson, 1895 – 1mf – 9 – 0-8370-6597-6 – 1986-0597 – us A.T.L.A. [240]
THE DOMINION PHILATELIST – Bellevile, Ont: H F Ketcheson, [1889?-189-?] – 9 – cn C.I.H.M. [760]
DOMINION PRESBYTERIAN – Montreal: Mount Royal Pub. Co, 1898-[1910] – 9 – cn C.I.H.M. [240]

DOMINION PRINTER – Montreal, Canada. jul 1873-v5 n1. avr 1879 – 1r – 1 – Can$30.00 – cn Can Microfilming [073]

DOMINION PROHIBITORY LIQUOR LAW CONVENTION (1875: MONTREAL) – Report of proceedings, list of members, societies represented: with a resume of Report of Commissioners appointed by the Dominion Government 1874, and other evidence in favor of prohibition. Montreal: s.n., 1875 (Montreal: J. Wilson). 03427. (Pre-1900 Canadiana) – 9 – cn C.I.H.M. [971]

THE DOMINION REVIEW – Montreal: W. Drysdale, v1 no 1 (July 15 1882)- – 9 – cn C.I.H.M. [971]

THE DOMINION REVIEW – Toronto: C.M. Ellis, v1 no 1 (Mar 1896)- – 9 – cn C.I.H.M. [971]

DOMINION SANITARY JOURNAL *see* MAN

THE DOMINION STATIST – Ottawa: Citizen Print and Pub, [1890-189-or-19–] – 9 – cn C.I.H.M. [073]

DOMINION VON CANADA INDUSTRIEN UND MANUFAKTUREN – Ottawa: s.n., 1886?. 04298. (Pre-1900 Canadiana) – 9 – cn C.I.H.M. [971]

THE DOMINION WATCHMAN – (Cont by: The Dominion Watchman and National Reformer) – Hamilton, Ont.: G.D. Griffin, [1876?-187-?] – 9 – cn C.I.H.M. [971]

THE DOMINION WATCHMAN AND NATIONAL REFORMER – Hamilton [Ont.]: G.D. Griffin, [187-or 18–18–] – 9 – cn C.I.H.M. [971]

DOMINION-NEWS – Morgantown, West Virginia. 1897- – 1 – us UMI [071]

DOMINIQUE DE FLANDRE : SA METAPHYSIQUE / Mahieu, L – Paris, 1942 – 10mf – 8 – ne Slangenburg [110]

Dominique, Joseph Biancolelli *see* NOUVEAU THEATRE ITALIEN

Dominique, L C *see* UN GOUVERNEUR GENERAL DE L'ALGERIE, L'AMIRAL DE GUEYDON

Domin-Petrushevecz, A de *see* PRECIS D'UN CODE DU DROIT INTERNATIONAL

Domke, M *see* INTERNATIONALER SCHUTZ VON ANLEIHEGLAEUBIGERN

DOMMER SELV! : TIL SELVPROVELSE: SAMTIDEN ANBEFALET: ANDEN RAEKKE / Kierkegaard, Soren – Kjobenhavn: C.A. Reitzels, 1876 – 1mf – us A.T.L.A. [190]

DOMOVINA – New York, Jan. 7, 1916-Oct. 26, 1917 – 2r – 1 – us I.H.R.C. [975]

DON – Ezhemesiachnyi illiustrirovannyi istoriko literaturnyi zhurnal. Novocherkassk. 1887-88. Lacking: 1888 (1-12). B-1710 2 – 8 – ne IDC [460]

Don Alvaro *see* PROGRAMA OFICIAL DE CULTOS Y FESTEJOS EN HONOR DE LA SANTA CRUZ

DON ALVARO DE SANDE CRONISTA DEL DESASTRE DELOS GELVES / Munoz, Pedro de san – Badajoz: Diputacion Provincial de Badajoz, 1955 – 1 – sp Bibl Santa Ana [946]

DON ALVARO DE SANDE Y LA ORDEN DE MALTA / Serrablo Aguareles, Eugenio – Madrid: Revista de Archivos, Bibliotecas y Museos, 1955 – 1 – sp Bibl Santa Ana [240]

DON ANDRES MANJON Y LA LIBERTAD DE ENSENANZA / Marquez, Gabino – Madrid: Razon y Fe, 1940 – 1 – sp Bibl Santa Ana [946]

DON ANDRES MANJON Y LA LIBERTAD DE ENSENANZA (CONCLUSION) / Marquez, Gabino – Madrid: Razon y Fe, 1940 – sp Bibl Santa Ana [946]

DON BARTOLOME JOSE GALLARDO Y LA CRITICA LITERARIA DE SU TIEMPO / Sainz y Rodriguez, Pedro – New-York, Paris. 1921. Extracto de Revue Hispanique, tome 49 – sp Bibl Santa Ana [440]

Don Benito *see*
- FERIA Y FIESTAS. 1967
- FERIAS Y FIESTAS, 1945
- FOLLETO PRIMERO DON BENITO...
- ORDENANZAS MUNICIPALES PARA EL REGIMEN Y GOBIERNO DE DON BENITO. ANO DE 1928

DON BENITO MARIA DE MOXO Y DE FRANCOLI, ARZOBISPO DE CHARCAS / Vargas Ugarte, Ruben – Buenos Aires, 1931; Madrid: Razon y Fe, 1931 – 1 – sp Bibl Santa Ana [240]

Don Benito. Spain. Ayuntamiento *see* ORDENANZAS MUNICIPALES

DON BERNARDO MARQUEZ DE LA VEGA / Chaves, Manuel – 1896 – 9 – $1.50f – sp Bibl Santa Ana [920]

DON BOSCO / Bayle, Constantino & Joergen, Juan – Madrid: Razon y Fe, 1944 – 1 – sp Bibl Santa Ana [946]

DON BOSCOCON DIOS / Ceria, E – Madrid: Razon y Fe, 1933 – 1 – sp Bibl Santa Ana [920]

DON CALASCIONE : THE FAVORITE SONGS IN THE OPERA / Lattila, G – (Orchestral score) – London: I Walsh, 1784 – 1 – us Sibley [780]

DON CARLOS / Maurenbrecher, Wilhelm – (Includes bibliographical references. Includes handwritten contents at end) – Berlin: C Habel, 1876 – 1 – us U.W. Library [430]

DON CARLOS / Schiller, Friedrich von; ed by Ibel, Rudolf – (Includes bibliographical references) – Frankfurt am Main: M Diesterweg, [between 1957 and 1960] – 1 – us U.W. Library [430]

DON CARLOS UND HAMLET / Thomas, Anneliese – (Includes bibliographical references) – Bonn a. Rh.: L Roehrscheid, 1933 – 1r – 1 – us U.W. Library [400]

DON CONSTITUYENTES DEL ANO 1824. BIOGRAFIAS DE DON MIGUEL RAMOS ARIZPE Y D. LORENZO ZAVALA, MEXICO. MUSEO NACIONAL DE ARQUEOLOGIA, 1925 / Toro, Alfonso; ed by Bayle, Constantino – Madrid: Razon y Fe, 1928 – 9 – sp Bibl Santa Ana [920]

Don, D *see*
- PRODROMUS FLORAE NEPALENSIS

DON DIEGO CAMACHO Y AVILA... / Rubio Merino, Pedro – Madrid: Archivo Ibero Americano, 1960 – 1 – sp Bibl Santa Ana [920]

DON DIEGO HURTADO DE MENDOZA NO FUE EL AUTOR DE "LA GUERRA DE GRANADA". APUNTES PARA UN LIBRO / Torre Yfranco Romero, Lucas de – Madrid: Fortanet, 1914. B.R.A.H. 64 y 65, pp. 461-501, 557-596 y 1915, pp. 28-47, 273-302 y 369-415 – sp Bibl Santa Ana [440]

DON DIEGO QUIJADA... / Schols, France V & Adams, Elenor B – Madrid: Razon y Fe, 1940 – 1 – sp Bibl Santa Ana [946]

DON DORRIGO GAZETTE – Jan 8 1910-Sep 28 1918 – 9 – at Pascoe [072]

DON EUGENIO ESCOBAR PRIETO. APUNTES DE SU VIDA / Solar y Taboada, Antonio – Badajoz: Imp. La Minerva Extremena, 1916 – 1 – sp Bibl Santa Ana [920]

DON FRANCISCO DE NAVARRA, OBISPO DE BADAJOZ (1545-1556). SUS INTERVENEIONES EN TRENTO SOBRE LA OBLIGACION EPISCOPAL DE RESIDIR / Camacho Macias, Aquilino – Badajoz: Dip. Provincial, 1968 – sp Bibl Santa Ana [240]

DON FRANCISCO DE PAULA ROMERO Y PALOMEQUE / Risco, Alberto – Jerez de la Frontera: Tip. de Salido Hermanos, 1916 – 1 – sp Bibl Santa Ana [920]

DON FRANCISCO DE TOLEDO, SUPREMO ORGANIZADOR DEL PERU. 1515-1585. MADRID, 1935 / Levillier, Roberto – Madrid: Razon y Fe, 1935 – 1 – sp Bibl Santa Ana [972]

Don, G *see*
- A GENERAL HISTORY OF THE DICHLAMYDEOUS PLANTS
- A MONOGRAPH OF THE GENUS ALLIUM

DON GESUALDO / Ouida – British Fiction Archive: Unit 3 – 9 – uk Bell [830]

DON HERNANDO CORTES, MARQUES DEL VALLE DE OAJACE / Solana y Gutierrez, Mateo – Madrid: Razon y Fe, 1940 – sp Bibl Santa Ana [240]

DON HERNANDO CORTES...MARQUES DEL VALLE DE OCIJACA / Solana y Gutierrez, Mateo – Mexico: Ediciones Botas, 1938 – sp Bibl Santa Ana [920]

DON ISAAC ABARBANEL / Landau, J L – Newark. 1919. BJ-422-41 1 – 9 – ne IDC [830]

DON JUAN DE AUSTRIA : PRINCIPE DE LA CRISTIANDAD / Cordero Marina, Pedro – Plasencia: Imp. La Victoria, 1978 – 1 – sp Bibl Santa Ana [943]

DON JUAN DE CARVAJAL. UN ESPANOL AL SERVICIO DE LA SANTA SEDE. MADRID, 1947 / Cereada, F & Gomez Canedo, Lino – Madrid: Razon y Fe, 1948 – 1 – sp Bibl Santa Ana [920]

DON JUAN DECADENTE / Melida, Jose Ramon – 1894 – 9 – $1.50f – sp Bibl Santa Ana [830]

DAS DON JUAN-PROBLEM IN DER NEUEREN DICHTUNG / Heckel, Hans – (Includes bibliographical references ("Die Bearbeitungen des Don Juan-Stoffes") – Stuttgart: Metzler, 1915 – 1r – 1 – us U.W. Library [430]

DON KARLOS IN DER GESCHICHTE UND IN DER POESIE / Pappritz, Richard – (Includes bibliographical references) – Naumburg a.S.: H Sieling, 1913 – 1r – 1 – us U.W. Library [430]

DON LORENZO SUAREZ DE FIGUEROA Y DE MENDOZA. NOTAS SOBRE SU DESCENDENCIA / Solar y Taboada, Antonio – Badajoz: Ediciones Arqueros, 1929 – 1 – sp Bibl Santa Ana [920]

DON MANUEL RUIZ ZORRILLA...NOTICIAS SOBRE.. / Perez, Miguel – 1883 – 9 – $1.50f – sp Bibl Santa Ana [920]

DON NARCISO DIAZ DE ESCOVAR. APUNTES DE SU VIDA / Solar y Taboada, Antonio – Badajoz: Imp. La Constancia s.a. – 1 – sp Bibl Santa Ana [920]

DON PEDRO DE ALVARADO, CONQUISTADOR DEL REINO DE GUATEMALA. MADRID, 1927 / Altolaguirre, Angel de; ed by Bayle, Constantino – Madrid: Razon y Fe, 1928 – 9 – sp Bibl Santa Ana [972]

DON PEDRO DE ALVARADO. OBRA POSTUMA REVISADA POR ANTONIO FERNANDEZ DEL CASTILLO / Fernandez del Castillo, Francisco – Guatemala: Editorial Cultura, 1945 – sp Bibl Santa Ana [920]

DON PEDRO DE VALDIVIA CONQUISTADOR DE CHILE / Arciniega, Rosa – Santiago de Chile: Editorial Nascimento, 1925 – 1 – sp Bibl Santa Ana [972]

DON PEDRO DE VALDIVIA...BADAJOZ, 1928 / Rujula, Solar y Manzano; ed by Bayle, Constantino – Madrid: Razon y Fe, 1928 – 9 – sp Bibl Santa Ana [910]

DON PLACIDO...DOVE CERCASI.. / Sacchi, Giovenale – 1786 – 2 – us Sibley [780]

DON QUIJOTE EN AMERICA / Febres Cordero, Julio – Caracas, 1930; Madrid: Razon y Fe, 1931 – 1 – sp Bibl Santa Ana [440]

DON RODRIGO DE BASTIDAS / Navarro, Nicolas – Caracas, 1931; Madrid: Razon y Fe, 1931 – 1 – sp Bibl Santa Ana [920]

DON RODRIGO DE TORRES, PRIMER MARQUES DE MATALLANA / Solar y Taboada, Antonio – Badajoz: Arqueros – 1 – sp Bibl Santa Ana [920]

DON SANCHO BRICENO, SU MONUMENTO EN TRUJILLO. EL ARBOL DE LOS BRICENOS. CARACAS, 1929 / Davila, Vicente – Madrid: Razon y Fe, 1930 – 1 – sp Bibl Santa Ana [946]

DON V BORBI E S KOMMUNO I NA DONT SI E I MANYCHI E FEVRALMA I 1919 G / Dobrynin, V – Praga: Ispolneno "Slavi anskim izd-vom", 1922 – 1 – CSUX88-B7737 – us Hoover Inst Photo [947]

DON VASCO DE QUINOGA... / Aquayo Spencer, Rafael – Madrid: Razon y Fe, 1940 – sp Bibl Santa Ana [920]

DONA CAROLINA CORONADO / Castelar, Emilio – 1869 – 9 – $1.50f – sp Bibl Santa Ana [920]

DONA INES MUNOZ, LA MUJER EXTREMENA, CUNADA DE FRANCISCO PIZARRO, QUETRAJO EL TRIGO Y EL OLIVO AL PERU / Cuneo-Vidal, Romulo – Madrid: Tip. de la Rev. de Bib. Archivos y Museos, 1928 – 1 – sp Bibl Santa Ana [946]

DONA MENCIA DE LOS NIDOS / Cidoncha, Marques de & Solar y Taboada, Antonio – Badajoz: Arqueros, 1943 – 1 – sp Bibl Santa Ana [920]

Donado, G *see* DELLA LETTERATURA DE TURCHI...

DONAGHADEE CEMETERY, MONUMENTAL INSCRIPTIONS / Copeland Island. Co. Down. Ireland – 1 – uk Microform Academic [920]

Donaghey, Richard H *see* ECOLOGY AND EVOLUTION OF BOWERBIRD MATING SYSTEMS

Donaire Fernandez, Maria Luisa *see* ESTRUCTURA DE LA EPICA FRANCESA Y LOS PERSONAJES FEMENINOS

DONALD J. DETWILER, SENATE SERVICE 1917-18 : SENATE PAGE – 1mf – 9 – $5.00 – us Scholarly Res [320]

DONALD RECORD – Donald, OR. -w. 16 Jun 1916-1 Mar 1918. 1 roll – 1 – us U.O. Library [071]

DONALD ROSS OF HEIMRA / Black, William – British Fiction Archive: Unit 4 – 9 – uk Bell [830]

DONALD'S BAPTIST CHURCH. ABBEVILLE COUNTY. SOUTH CAROLINA : CHURCH RECORDS – (141p) – 1876-1912 – 1 reel – 1 – $6.35 – us Baptist [240]

Donaldson, G *see* THE MAKING OF THE SCOTTISH PRAYER BOOK OF 1637

Donaldson, James *see*
- THE WESTMINSTER CONFESSION OF FAITH AND THE THIRTY-NINE ARTICLES OF THE CHURCH OF ENGLAND
- WOMAN
- WOMAN: HER POSITION AND INFLUENCE IN ANCIENT GREECE AND ROME, AND AMONG THE EARLY CHRISTIANS

Donaldson, John William *see* A COMPARATIVE GRAMMAR OF THE HEBREW LANGUAGE

Donaldson, Margaret E *see* THE COUNCIL OF ADVICE AT THE CAPE OF GOOD HOPE, 1825-1834

Donaldson, Stuart Alexander *see* CHURCH LIFE AND THOUGHT IN NORTH AFRICA A.D. 200

Donaldson, Thomas *see*
- PRELIMINARY BIBLIOGRAPHY ON LONGEVITY DRUGS, WITH 2 PAPERS ON CRYONICS
- THE PUBLIC DOMAIN, ITS HISTORY...AND DISPOSITION TO 1880

DONANMA [DONANMA MECMUASI] – (Sahibi: Donanma-i Osmani Muavenet-i Milliye Cemiyeti Merkez-i Umumisi, Nos. 1, 16/64, 31/79, 83-84, 86, 102-103, 80/129-143/192. – Mart 1326-1 Nisan 1335[1910-1919]. – Published monthly 1910-1913 as Donanma, then weekly 1914-1919 as Donanma Mecmuasi) – Istanbul: Matbaa-i Hayriye ve Suerekasi, Matbaa-i Ahmet Ihsan, 1910-1913, 1914-1919 – 30mf – 9 – $350.00 – us MEDOC [949]

Donat, Walter FW K *see* DIE LANDSCHAFT BEI TIECK UND IHRE HISTORISCHEN VORAUSSETZUNGEN

Donatelle, Rebecca J *see*
- COMPARATIVE ANALYSIS OF FACTORS INFLUENCING PARTICIPATION IN AN EMPLOYEE HEALTH PROMOTION PROGRAM, INCLUDING CHARACTERIZATIONS OF PARTICIPANTS AND NONPARTICIPANTS
- EFFECTIVENESS OF SELECTED COMPONENTS IN BEHAVIORAL WEIGHT-LOSS INTERVENTIONS

DONATELLO, SEINE ZEIT UND SCHULE / Semper, Hans – O 517i. 1875 – 9 – ne IDC [730]

DONATELLO, SEINE ZEIT UND SCHULE / Semper, Hans – (Quellenschriften fuer Kunstgeschichte...Wien, 1875, v9) – 9 – ne IDC [730]

DONATION PAUL JAMOT / Reunion des musees nationaux. Paris – 1941. 9 illus. 1 fiche – 9 – fr Réunion [700]

Donato, Baldassare *see* CANTO DI BALDASSARE DONATO IL PRIMO LIBRO DI MADRIGALI A CINQUE E A SEI VOCI CON TRE DIALOGHI A SETTE NOVAMENTE PER ANTONIO GARDANO

Donatus Ortigraphus *see*
- ARS GRAMMATICA (CCCM 40D)

DIE DONAU – Apatin, jan 6-oct 31 1940 – 1r – 1 – Dist. gw Mikrofilm – gw Misc Inst [949]

DIE DONAU – Apatin, Yugoslavia. 1938-39; 1941-43 – 2r – 1 – us L of C Photodup [949]

DONAU-BODENSEE-ZEITUNG – (Title change: Schwaebische Zeitung, 18 Dec 1945) – Sigmaringen-Friedrichshafen-Leutkirch, Germany. 1977- – ca 6r per yr – 1 – gw Mikrofilm [072]

DONAU-BODENSEE-ZEITUNG *see*
- ANZEIGER VOM OBERLAND
- WUERTTEMBERGISCHES SEEBLATT

DONAU-BULGARIEN UND DER BALKAN / Kanitz, FP – Historisch-geographisch-etnographische Reisestudien aus den Jahren 1860-1879. Ed. 2. 3 v. Leipzig. 1882. BR-3879 2 – 8 – ne IDC [910]

DONAU-KURIER – Budapest, Hungary. 15 Nov 1933-1939/40 (incomplete) – 1r – 1 – gw Mikrofilm [072]

DONAU-KURIER – Budapest, nov 15 1933-1939/40 (incomplete) – 1r – 1 – Inquire at Mikrofilmarchiv for details – gw Misc Inst [943]

DONAU-KURIER – Ingolstadt, West Germany. 1969- – ca 9r per yr – 1 – gw Mikrofilm [072]

DONAUSCHWAEBISCHE RUNDSCHAU – Aalen, nov 25 1951-aug 31 1956 – 1 – Dist. gw Mikrofilm – gw Misc Inst [072]

DONAU-ZEITUNG – Augsburg, 1954-sep 27 1974, 1987- – 1 – Dist. gw Mikrofilm – gw Misc Inst [072]

DONAU-ZEITUNG – Passau, Germany. 1849 – 1r – 1 – gw Mikrofilm [072]

DONAUZEITUNG – Belgrad, aug 12 1941-25 jul 25 1944, jan 12-mar 24 1945 (incomplete) – 13r – 1 – uk British Libr Newspaper [949]
DONAUZEITUNG – Belgrad, jul 15 1941-jun 29 1944 – 1 – Dist. gw Mikrofilm – gw Misc Inst [949]
Doncel, Fernando *see* FELIPE 5 EN MORALEJA, ANO DE 1704
Doncel y Ordaz, Jose *see*
- ESCRITOS ANEJOS. SERIOS Y HUMURISTICOS
- FABULAS MORALES SATIRICAS Y..

Doncker, Hendrick *see* ZEE-ATLAS OFTE WATER WAERELD
DONDE DESEMBOCARA LA SITUACION POLITICA ARGENTINA? : DISCURSO PRONUNDCIADO EN EL 11TH CONGRESO DEL PARTIDO COMUNISTA, REALIZDO EN BUENOS AIRES DESDE EL 14 AL 18 DE AGOSTO DE 1946 / Codovilla, Victorio – [s.l.: s.n., 1946?] – 1 – CSUXADQ1408-B – us Hoover Inst Photo [320]
DONDE ESTUVO? : EL PUEBLO QUE EL 17 DE OCTUBRE PREGUNTABA AL CORONEL PERON CON GRAN INSISTENCIA ?DONDE ESTUVO? TIENE AQUI UNA AMPLIA RESPUESTA / Caledonia, Bill de – Buenos Aires: [s.n., 1945?] – 1 – CSUXADL5910-B – us Hoover Inst Photo [320]
DONDE ESTUVO? REFUTANDO CON LOS HECHOS UN PANFLETO INSIDIOSO Y ANONIMO : EL PUEBLO QUE EL 17 DE OCTUBRE PREGUNTABA AL CORONEL PERON, CON GRAN INSISTENCIA: DONDE ESTUVO?, TIENE AQUI UNA AMPLIA RESPUESTA / Caledonia, Bill de – [Buenos Aires?, 1949?] – 1 – CSUXADJ1849-B – us Hoover Inst Photo [320]
Doneaud, A *see* NOTIONS PRATIQUES DE DROIT MARITIME INTERNATIONAL ET COMMERCIAL
Donegal. Presbytery (Pres. Ch. in the U.S.A.) *see* MINUTES
Donegal. Presbytery (Pres. Ch. in the U.S.A. Old School) *see* MINUTES, 1843-1870
Donehoo, James Ramsey *see* THE NEW TESTAMENT VIEW OF THE OLD TESTAMENT
Donelson, Andrew J *see* PAPERS
DONELSON VIEW BAPTIST CHURCH. NASHVILLE, TENNESSEE : CHURCH RECORDS – Feb 1922-Sept 1956. Formerly Seventh Baptist Church, name changed 1962 – 1 – 35.10 – us Baptist [240]
DONG BEI RI BAO – China. Nov 1945-Sept 1949. DL8 – 9 – 490.00 – cc Globe [072]
DONG DU'O'NG TAP CHI – Dir. F. H. Schneider. n.s., no. 186-231. Hanoi, Saigon. 11 aout 1er sept 1918-15 juin 1919 – 1 – fr A.C.R.P.P. [073]
DONG-A ILBO – 1920-1995 – 12 times per yr – 1 – F2,473.00 – sz Infoprint [072]
DONGBEI GONGXUEYUAN XUEBAO – Journal of Northeast Institute of Technology. In Chinese but English abstracts to the main articles. F p194 – 9 – $4.50f – cc Microforms [073]
DONGBEI LIN XUEYUAN XUEBAO – Journal of North-Eastern Forestry Institute. In Chinese but English abstracts to the main articles. F p198 – 9 – 4.00f – cc Microforms [073]
DONGBEI SHI DA XUEBAO – (1977-1982 $4.50f; 1983-84 $3.50f) – Shehui Kexue Ban. Journal of Northeast Normal University, Social Sciences. In Chinese but Table of Contents in English in each issue. F p218 – 9 – cc Microforms [073]
DONGBEI YIHETUAN DANGAN SHILIAO – Archival Materials on the Boxer Rebellion in Northeast China. Comp. by the Liaoning Provincial Archives, Institute of History, Liaoning Academy of Social Sciences. 8 fiches. F H87 – 9 – $40.50 – cc Microforms [950]
Dongen, Wim van *see*
- DANCES OF DEATH
- EMBLEM BOOKS
- SHIPS OF FOOLS

DONGENG-DONGENG SASAKALA, KENGING NGEMPELKEUN MOH. AMBRI / Ambri, M – Balai Poestaka 2604. 2v. (B.P. 1517). v1, 32p – 5mf – 9 – ne IDC [950]
DONGOLA FIRST BAPTIST CHURCH. DONGOLA, ILLINOIS : CHURCH RECORDS – 1892-Jan 1981. 2304p – 1 – 103.68 – us Baptist [240]
DONG-PHAP THO'I-BAO – Saigon. mai 1923-28 – 1 – fr A.C.R.P.P. [073]
DONGWU FENLEI XUEBAO – Acta Zootaxonomica Sinica. In Chinese but English abstracts to the main articles. F p70 – 9 – 4.00f – cc Microforms [073]
DONGWU XUEBAO – Acta Zoologica Sinica. In Chinese but English abstracts to the main articles. F p37 – 9 – $3.50f – cc Microforms [073]
DONGWUXUE YANJIU – Zoologicia Research. In Chinese but English abstracts to the main articles. F p144 – 9 – 4.00f – cc Microforms [073]
Doni, A F *see*
- DISEGNO PARTITO IN PIU RAGIONAMENTI, NE QUALI SI TRATTA DELLA SCOLTURA ET PITTURA
- I MARMI
- PITTURE NELLE QUALI SI MOSTRA DI NUOVA INVENTIONE: AMORE, FORTUNA, TEMPO, CASTITA, RELIGIONE, SDEGNO, RIFORMA, MORTE, SONNO E SOGNO, HUOMO, REPUBLICA, E MAGNANIMITA

Doni, G B *see* DE PRAESTANTIA MUSICAE VETERIS LIBRI TRES TOTIDEM DIALOGIS COMPREHENSI
DONIEL BUKH – Prague. 1609. BJ-43-16 1 – 9 – ne IDC [956]
DONIPHAN ENTERPRISE – Doniphan, NE. -w. Jul. 1914-Aug. 1921 – 1 – us NE Hist [071]
DONIPHAN HERALD – Doniphan, NE. -w. Aug. 1923-Aug. 1937 – 1 – us NE Hist [071]
DONIPHAN HERALD – Doniphan, NE. -w. Aug. 1971- – 1 – us NE Hist [071]
DONIPHAN INDEX – Doniphan, NE. -w. Jul. 1896-Jan. 1897; Mar. 1897-Oct. 1897 – 1 – us NE Hist [071]
Donisthorpe. Wordsworth *see*
- INDIVIDUALISM, A SYSTEM OF POLITICS
- LAW IN A FREE STATE

Donle, L *see* UEBER INTERNATIONALE EHESCHLIESSUNG...
Donn, J *see* HORTUS CANTABRIGIENSIS
LA DONNA DEL LAGO / Rossini, G – Riduzione per Canto con Accomp. di Pianoforte di Luigi Truzzi. 185-? – 9 – us Sibley [780]
Donnan, E *see* DOCUMENTS ILLUSTRATIVE OF THE HISTORY OF THE SLAVE TRADE TO AMERICA
Donnant, Denis Francois *see* THEORIE ELEMENTAIRE DE LA STATISTIQUE
Donnedieu de Vabres, H *see*
- LES CRIMES ET DELITS COMMIS A L'ETRANGER...
- INTRODUCTION A L'ETUDE DE DROIT PENAL INTERNATIONAL
- LES PRINCIPES MODERNES DU DROIT PENAL INTERNATIONAL

Donnell, Courtney Graham *see* TWENTIETH-CENTURY EUROPEAN PAINTINGS
Donnelly *see* HISTORY OF GREENE COUNTY
Donnelly, Eleanor C *see* GIRLHOOD'S HAND-BOOK OF WOMAN
Donnelly, Eleanor Cecilia *see* A KLONDIKE PICNIC: THE STORY OF A DAY
Donnelly, Ignatius *see*
- THE CIPHER IN THE PLAYS, AND ON THE TOMBSTONE
- PAPERS
- RAGNAROK: THE AGE OF FIRE AND GRAVEL

Donnelly, Loyd and Co *see*
- HISTORY OF LOGAN COUNTY
- HISTORY OF MORGAN COUNTY ITS PAST AND PRESENT

Donnenfeld, J *see* ETUDE D'UN MARCHE URBAIN AFRICAIN
Donner, E O *see* DER SEEFRACHTVERTRAG IM INTERNATIONALEN PRIVATRECHT
Donner, K *see* UEBER DAS ALTER DER OSTJAKISCHEN UND WOGULISCHEN RENNTIERZUCHT
Donnet, Alexis *see* ARCHITECTONOGRAPHIE DES THEATRES DE PARIS OU PARALLELE HISTORIQUE ET CRITIQUE DE CES EDIFICES.
Donnet, Gaston *see* EN SAHARA A TRAVERS LE PAYS DES MAURES NOMADES
Donohoe, Thomas *see* THE IROQUOIS AND THE JESUITS: THE STORY OF THE LABORS OF CATHOLIC MISSIONARIES AMONG THESE INDIANS
Donohue, E B *see* RESCUING THE ECONOMY IS YOUR CONCERN-YOU ARE THE TRUE ECONOMISTS
Donohue, Mary *see* OCCUPATIONAL THERAPY IN MENTAL HEALTH
Donop, L B von *see* DIARY DURING A TRIP FROM PAPAR TO KIMANIS VIA TAMBUNAN, LOBO AND LIMBAWAN, 1882
DONOSO CORTES / Blanco Garcia, Francisco – Madrid: Saenz de Jubera. 1909 – 1 – sp Bibl Santa Ana [920]
DONOSO CORTES / Donoso Cortes, Juan Francisco – Ediciones Fe, 1940 – 1 – sp Bibl Santa Ana [946]
DONOSO CORTES / Galindo Herrero, Santiago – Madrid: Publicaciones espanolas, 1953 – sp Bibl Santa Ana [920]
DONOSO CORTES : SU POSICION EN LA HISTORIA DE LA FILOSOFIA DEL ESTADO EUROPEO / Schmitt, Carl – Madrid, 1930; Madrid: Razon y Fe, 1931 – 1 – sp Bibl Santa Ana [190]
DONOSO CORTES : SU SENTIDO TRASCENDENTE DE LA VIDA / Armas, Gabriel – Madrid: Edit. E.T. Coleccion Alamo, 1953 – sp Bibl Santa Ana [200]
Donoso Cortes *see* SELECCION DE ANTONIO TOVAR
DONOSO CORTES, EL PROFETA DE LA HISPANIDAD / Gutierrez Lasanta, Francisco – Imprenta Torroba, 1953-1954 – 1 – sp Bibl Santa Ana [946]
DONOSO CORTES EN LA PROBLEMATICA DE LA ESPIRITUALIDAD (ESBOZO DE BIOGRAFIA MISTICA) / Armas, Gabriel – Las Palmas de Gran Canaria: Tip. Minerva, 1950 – sp Bibl Santa Ana [240]
DONOSO CORTES EN LA ULTIMA ETAPA DE SU VIDA / Galindo Herrero, Santiago – Madrid: Arbor, 1953 – 1 – sp Bibl Santa Ana [320]
DONOSO CORTES, EN SU TIEMPO Y EN EL NUESTRO / Silio, Francisco Javier – Madrid: Arbor, 1950 – 1 – sp Bibl Santa Ana [320]
Donoso Cortes, Juan Francisco *see*
- ACIVILICAO CATOLICA E OS ERROS MODERNOS
- AFRICA EN EL PENSAMIENTO DE DONOSO CORTES
- COLECCION...LA DIPLOMACIA
- COLECCION...PROYECTO DE LEY
- CONSIDERACIONES SOBRE LA DIPLOMACIA
- DISCOURS DE...DANS LES CORTES
- DISCURSO PARLAMENTARIO
- DONOSO CORTES
- DONOSO CORTES Y LA CUESTION SOCIAL
- ENSAYO SOBRE EL CATOLICISMO, EL LIBERALISMO Y EL SOCIALISMO
- ENSAYO SOBRE EL CATOLICISMO LIBERALISMO
- LOS ERRORES DE NUESTRO TIEMPO
- ESSAY ON CATHOLICISM, LIBERALISM AND SOCIALISM
- LECCIONES DE DERECHO POLITICO
- LA LEY ELECTORAL
- MEMORIA SOBRE...MONARQUIA
- OBRAS
- OBRAS ESCOGIDAS
- EL PENSAMIENTO POLITICO HISPANOAMERICANO...
- PROYECTO DE LEY SOBRE ESTADOS EXCEPCIONALES
- RAPPEL
- SAGGIO SUL CATTOLICESIMO, IL LIBERALISMO E IL SOCIALISMO
- LA VENIDA DE CRISTINA

DONOSO CORTES, JUAN. OBRAS COMPLETAS RECOPILADAS POR...2 VOL. MADRID, 1946 / Errandonea, Ignacio – Madrid: Razon y Fe, 1947 – 1 – sp Bibl Santa Ana [946]
Donoso Cortes y Donoso Cortes, E et al *see* 1ST CONGRESO SINDICAL AGRARIO DE EXTREMADURA, PONENCIA I ESTRUCTURA Y FINES DEL SINDICALISMO AGRARIO
DONOSO CORTES Y LA CUESTION SOCIAL / Donoso Cortes, Juan Francisco – Barcelona: Casa Subirana, 1934 – 1 – sp Bibl Santa Ana [301]
DONOSO CORTES Y LA DICTADURA / Sevilla Andres, Diego – Madrid: Arbor, 1953 – 1 – sp Bibl Santa Ana [320]
Donoso, Ricardo *see* UN LETRADO DEL SIGLO 18, EL DCOTOR JOSE PERFECTO DE SALAS. BUENOS AIRES, 1963
Donovan, Carolyn M *see* HEALTH ATTITUDES AND THEIR RELATION TO COMPLIANCE AND MEASURED CHOLESTEROL LEVELS
Donovan, E *see*
- EPITOME OF THE INSECTS OF ASIA
- AN EPITOME OF THE NATURAL HISTORY OF THE INSECTS OF CHINA
- AN EPITOME OF THE NATURAL HISTORY OF THE INSECTS OF INDIA
- AN EPITOME OF THE NATURAL HISTORY OF THE INSECTS OF NEW HOLLAND, NEW ZEALAND, NEW GUINEA
- THE NATURAL HISTORY OF BRITISH BIRDS
- THE NATURAL HISTORY OF BRITISH FISHES, INCLUDING SCIENTIFIC AND GENERAL DESCRIPTIONS OF THE MOST INTERESTING SPECIES, AND AN EXTENSIVE SELECTION OF ACCURATELY FINISHED COLOURED PLATES
- THE NATURAL HISTORY OF BRITISH INSECTS

Donovan, Joseph Wesley *see*
- SKILL IN TRIALS: CONTAINING A VARIETY OF CIVIL AND CRIMINAL CASES WON BY THE ART OF ADVOCATES.
- TACT IN COURT

Donovan, Karen S *see* THE RELATIONSHIP BETWEEN HEART RATE AND RATE OF PERCEIVED EXERTION AMONG PHASE 2 CARDIAC REHABILITATION PATIENTS WITH VARIOUS MODES OF EXERCISE
Donovan, R J et al *see*
- LASER CHEMISTRY
- MOLECULAR CRYSTALS AND LIQUID CRYSTALS

DONSIDE PIPER AND HERALD – 1 – £42.00r – uk Scot News [072]
DONSKAI A RI ECH – (Includes c.1: 1919:Dec.16) – Utrennee izd. Rostov n-D.: "Donskai a ri ech", 19uu – 1 – CSUXANR2820-S – us Hoover Inst Photo [947]
Donskoe pravitelstvo (1921) *see* OTCHET O DIEIATELNOSTI DANSKOGO PRAVITELSTVA ZA GRANITSE I PO 25 SENTIABRIA 1921 G
DONSKOI PRODOVOL'STVENNIK I KOOPERATOR – Rostov n/D, 1920 n1 – 1mf – 9 – COR-583/1 – ne IDC [334]
DON'T CONFUSE THOSE YEARS AT SCHOOL WITH EDUCATION / Connors, Lyndsay – 1972. 1p – 9 – 1.00f – at Libertarian Micro [370]
Dont, J *see* 24 VIOLIN EXERCISES, OP. 37
DONTVENYTAR / Hungary. Courts – v1-101; 1870-1906 – 1 – 299.00 – us L of C Photodup [340]
Donzellini, G *see* EPISTOLAE PRINCIPVM, RERVMPVBLICARVM, AC SAPIENTVM VIRORVM
DOOKOLA SWIATA – Warsaw, Poland. -w. June 1954-Dec 1958. 5 reels – 1 – uk British Libr Newspaper [947]
DEN DOOLHOF VAN DE DWALENDE GHEESTEN WAER IN DEN AENVANG, VOORTGANG, VRUCHTEN... – Amsterdam, [c. 1620] – 1mf – 9 – ne IDC [700]
Doolittle, James R *see* PAPERS
DOOM OF DOGMA AND DAWN OF TRUTH / Frank, Henry – New York: G.P. Putnam, 1901. 1 fiche – 9 – us A.T.L.A. [240]
THE DOOM OF DOGMA AND THE DAWN OF TRUTH / Frank, Henry – (Includes index) – New York:G.P. Putnam, 1901 – 1mf – 9 – 0-8370-3179-6 – 1985-1179 – us A.T.L.A. [140]
DOOMED RELIGIONS : A SERIES OF ESSAYS ON GREAT RELIGIONS OF THE WORLD / Reid, J M – New York: Phillips & Hunt; Cincinnati: Walden & Stowe, 1884 – 2mf – us A.T.L.A. [240]
DOOPSGEZINDE BIJDRAGEN – Leiden, 1861-1919 – 135mf – H-3063/1 – ne IDC [073]
DOOPSGEZING JAARBOEKJE – (Lacking: 1944-48. 1952 p132-36. Some original pgs damaged) – v1-80. 1902-86 – 7r – 1 – ATLA S0759 – us A.T.L.A. [073]
DOORGRAVING DER LANDENGTE VAN SUEZ,... / Bake, R W JC – Haarlem, 1857 – 2mf – 9 – ILM-1817/1 – ne IDC [340]
DOORLUGTE VOORBEELDEN DER OUDEN / Leuve, R van – O 341. 1725 – 9 – ne IDC [999]
Doorn, Robert J *see* INDIVIDUAL RIGHTS
Doorninck, J van *see* GESLACHTKUNDIGE AANTEEKENINGEN
Doornink, Adam van *see* BIJDRAGE TOT DE TEKSTKRITIEK VAN RICHTEREN 1-16
Dooyeweerd, H *see*
- TRANSCENDENTAL PROBLEMS OF PHILOSOPHICAL THOUGHT
- DE WIJSBEGEERTE DER WETSIDEE

DOPOLNENIE VTOROE K PODROBNOMU SISTEMATICHESKOMU UKAZATELIU KNIG D. S. PONOMAREVA. GODA 1892-1894 / Gintse, G E – Khar'kov. 1895. BR-5900 2 – 8 – ne IDC [460]
DOPOLNENIIA K AKTAM ISTORICHESKIM / Russia. Arkheograficheskaia Kommissiia – v. 1-12. 1846-1872 – 1 – 35.00r – us Hoover Inst Photo [930]
DOPOLNENIIA K ISTORII MASONSTVA V ROSSII V 18 STOLETII / Pekarskii, P P – Spb. 1869. BR-7751 2 – 8 – ne IDC [947]
DOPOVIDI AKADEMII NAUK UKRAINS'KOI RSR – Kiev.1956-64. Lacking: 1958 v11-12. BR-1746 2 – 8 – ne IDC [500]

DIE DOPPELBEARBEITUNGEN DER "RAEUBER", DES "FIESCO" UND DES "DON CARLOS" VON SCHILLER : EINE LITTERARHISTORISCHE STUDIE / Tischler, Hermann – (Includes bibliographical references) – Leipzig: E Herrmann, 1888 – 1 – us U.W. Library [430]

Dopper, C *see*
- BLASERSTUCK
- PRELUDE, SCHERZION, IMPROMPTU

Doppler, Josef *see* PATER WENZEL HOCKE

DOPRAVA A SPOJE – Prague. Czechoslovakia. -w. Jan 1959-Dec 1968. (2 reels) – 1 – uk British Libr Newspaper [072]

DOR HA-YOM = GENERATION OF TO-DAY – (In Hebrew) – Netanya, IS. v1. 8 Jul 1937 – 1r – 1 – $25.00 – cn Can Microfilming [072]

DOr, OL *see* KRASNYI CHASOVOI KRONSHTADT

LOS DORADOS INGLESES / Bayle, Constantino – Madrid: Razon y Fe, 1930 – 1 – sp Bibl Santa Ana [240]

Dorais, O Emile *see* TABLES GIVING THE NUMBER OF DAYS FROM ONE DATE TO ANOTHER

Doran, Joseph I *see* OUR FISHERY RIGHTS IN THE NORTH ATLANTIC

Dorat des Monts, Roger *see* LA CAUSE IMMORALE, ETUDE DE JURISPRUDENCE

DORCHESTER 1631-1869 – (Mf 1-4: B,M,D 1631-83. Mf 5-6: B,M,D 1684-1744/45. Mf 7-11: B,M,D 1745-1825. Mf 12: B,M,D 1826-44. Mf 13-22: B,M,D 1631 1844. Mf 23-31: First Church Dorchester 1729-1845. Mf 32-39: B,M,D 1843-49. Mf 40-43: Index to B,M,D 1631-1849. Mf 44-45: Publishments of Marriages 1799-1849. Mf 46-55: Births 1850-69; Index to Births. Mf 56-64: Intentions, Marriages, Indexes 1850-69. Mf 65-72: Deaths 1850-69; Index to Deaths) – (mf ed 1986) – 72mf – 9 – 0-931248-85-X – us Holbrook [920]

DORCHESTER AND SHERBOURNE JOURNAL AND WESTERN ADVERTISER – Dorchester, Sherbourne, England. -w. 21 Jan, 4 Feb, 11 March, 8, 22, 29 April, 13 May, 3, 10, 24 June, 23 Sept 1791. 9 ft – 1 – uk British Libr Newspaper [072]

DORCHESTER BOOSTER – Dorchester, NE. -w. Aug. 1941-Dec. 1946 – 1 – us NE Hist [071]

Dorchester, Daniel *see*
- CHRISTIANITY VINDICATED BY ITS ENEMIES
- THE PROBLEM OF RELIGIOUS PROGRESS
- ROMANISM VERSUS THE PUBLIC SCHOOL SYSTEM
- THE WHY OF METHODISM

DORCHESTER LEADER – Dorchester, NE. -w. Jun. 1934-Jul. 1941 – 1 – us NE Hist [071]

Dorchester. South Carolina. Independent Congregational Church *see* MINUTES

DORCHESTER STAR – Dorchester, NE. -w. Sep. 1881-Sep. 1883. Incomplete; Nov. 1883-Apr. 1889; Aug. 1889-Oct. 1890. Incomplete; Dec. 1890-Apr. 1895; Jul. 1895-Sep. 1907; Jan. 1908-May 1968 – 1 – us NE Hist [071]

Dordevic, Andra *see* PORODICNO PRAVO NASLEDA U DANASNJIM ROMANSKIM I GERMANSKIM DRZAVAMA

Dore, Ronald *see* COMMUNITY DEVELOPMENT

Doreian, Patrick *see* JOURNAL OF MATHEMATICAL SOCIOLOGY

Doren, J B J van *see* THOMAS MATULESIA, HET HOOFD DER OPSTANDELINGEN OP HET EILAND HONIMOA, NA DE OVERNAME VAN HET BESTUUR DER MOLUKKEN DOOR DEN LANDVOOGD J.A. VAN MIDDELKOOP IN 1817

Dorer-Egloff, Edward *see* J.M.R. LENZ UND SEINE SCHRIFTEN

DAS DORF AM MEER : ROMAN / Swars, Ewald – Karlsbad: A Kraft, 1944 – 1r – 1 – us U.W. Library [830]

DORF IM KAUKASUS : ROMAN / Strobl, Karl Hans – Budweis: Verlagsanstalt Moldavia, 1944 – 1r – 1 – us U.W. Library [830]

DAS DORF IN DER TAIGA / Velter, Joseph M – Leipzig: W Goldmann, 1944, c1936 – 1r – 1 – us U.W. Library [830]

DER DORFBOTE – Budweis, 1933-feb 9 1936, 1937, 1939-oct 17 1942 – 1 – Inquire at Mikrofilmarchiv for details – gw Misc Inst [072]

DER DORFBOTE – Budweis (Ceske Budejovice), Czechoslovakia. 1933-9 Feb 1936; 1937; 1939-17 Oct 1942 – 1 – gw Mikrofilm [072]

DORFSCHWALBEN AUS OESTERREICH : FRISCHER FLUG / Silberstein, August – Breslau: S Schotlaender, 1881 – 1r – 1 – us U.W. Library [390]

Doriano Cumbreno, Antonio C *see* CURSO GENERAL DE PALEOGRAFIA Y DIPLOMATICA ESPANOLAS (TEXTO)

Dorion, F X. J *see* LA BICYCLETTE

Dorion, J-B E *see* LE DEFRICHEUR

DORION'S DECISIONS ON APPEAL / Canada. Quebec – v1-4. 1881-84 (all publ) – 20mf – 9 – $30.00 – LLMC 81-073 – us L.L.M.C. [340]

Doris, Charles, de Bourges *see* AN APPEAL TO THE BRITISH NATION ON THE TREATMENT EXPERIENCED BY NAPOLEON BUONAPARTE IN THE ISLAND OF ST HELENA

DORMANT AND EXTINCT PEERAGES / Burke, J B – 1846 – 1 – uk Microform Academic [920]

Dormoy, Jean *see* RAPPORTS ET RESOLUTIONS DES CONGRES OUVRIERS DE 1876 A 1883

Dorn, B *see*
- NACHTRAEGE ZU DER ABHANDLUNG UEBER DIE MUENZEN DER ILEKE
- UEBER DIE MUENZEN DER ILEKE ODER EHEMALIGEN CHANE VON TURKISTAN

Dorn, B A *see*
- DAS ASIATISCHE MUSEUM DER KAISERLICHEN AKADEMIE DER WISSENSCHAFTEN ZU ST PETERSBURG
- CATALOGUE DES MANUSCRITS ET XYLOGRAPHES ORIENTAUX DE LA BIBLIOTHEQUE IMPERIALE PUBLIQUE DE ST PETERSBOURG

Dorn, Gerhard *see* SCHLUESSEL DER CHIMISTISCHEN PHILOSOPHIE

Dorn, J C *see* DE EO QUOD EST JUSTUM...

Dornemann, Timothy M *see* THE EFFECT OF A WEIGHT TRAINING PROGRAM ON THE BONE DENSITY OF WOMEN AGED 40-50 YEARS

DER DORNENWEG : ROMAN / Wilbrandt, Adolf von – 4. Aufl. Stuttgart: J G Cotta, 1901 – 1r – 1 – us U.W. Library [830]

Dorner, Isaak August *see*
- AUGUSTINUS: SEIN THEOLOGISCHES SYSTEM
- DIE CHRISTLICHE LEHRE
- DORNER ON THE FUTURE STATE
- GRUNDRISS DER ENCYCLOPAEDIE DER THEOLOGIE
- HISTORY OF PROTESTANT THEOLOGY
- SYSTEM OF CHRISTIAN ETHICS

DORNER ON THE FUTURE STATE : BEING A TRANSLATION OF THE SECTION OF HIS SYSTEM OF CHRISTIAN DOCTRINE COMPRISING THE DOCTRINE OF THE LAST THINGS / Dorner, Isaak August – New York: Scribner, 1883 – 1mf – us A.T.L.A. [240]

Dornin, Thomas A *see* THE JOURNALS OF THOMAS A. DORNIN, U.S. NAVY

DORNROSEN ERSTLINGSBLUETHEN DEUTSCHER LYRIK IN AMERIKA / Steiger, Ernst – New York, 1871. vi,159p – 1 – us U.W. Library [430]

Doroshenko, V V *see* LITERATURA UKRAINOVEDENIIA ZA 1912

DOROTHEA ANGERMANN : SCHAUSPIEL / Hauptmann, Gerhart – Berlin: S Fischer, c1926 – 1r – 1 – us U.W. Library [820]

DOROTHY SOUTH: A LOVE STORY OF VIRGINIA JUST BEFORE THE WAR / Eggleston, George Cary – Illus. by C.D. Williams.Boston: Lothrop Pub. Co., (1902). 453p – 1 – us U.W. Library [830]

DOROTHYE G. SCOTT, SENATE SERVICE 1945-1977 : ADMINISTRATIVE ASSISTANT TO THE DEMOCRATIC SECRETARY AND THE SECRETARY OF THE SENATE – 4mf – 9 – $20.00 – us Scholarly Res [320]

DORPATER NACHRICHTEN – Dorpat (Tartu), Estonia. 1921-24 – 1 – gw Mikrofilm [943]

DORPATER TAGESBLATT – Dorpat. nov 21, dec 10, dec 15, 1862. 1863-jul 20, 1864 – 3r – 1 – gw Mikrofilm [943]

DORPATER ZEITUNG – (Title change: Deutsche Zeitung, Oct 1934) – Dorpat (Tartu), U.S.S.R. Jul 1925-1929; Jul 1930-8 Sep 1939 – 1 – gw Mikrofilm [072]

Dorpius, H *see* WARHAFFTIGE HISTORIE, WIE DAS EUANGELIUM ZU MUENSTER ANGEFANGEN, VND DARNACH DURCH DIE WIDDERTEUFFER, WIDDER AUFFGEHOERT HAT

Dorrego, Alejandro *see* EL CASO ARGENTINO

Dorris, Charles Ellis *see* A PROGRAM OF OUTREACH THROUGH RECREATION AT THE HUFFMAN BAPTIST CHURCH

THE DORRIS TIMES – Dorris, CA. 1915-19 – 2r – 1 – $100.00 – B02175 – us Library Micro [071]

Dorsch, Anton-Joseph *see* STATISTIQUE DU DEPARTEMENT DE LA ROER

Dorschel, Gotthold *see* MARIA THERESIAS STAATS- UND LEBENSANSCHAUUNG

DORSET, 1823 : BRITISH ISLES CENSUS DIRECTORIES PROJECT, ENGLAND. VOL 221 – 1mf – 9 – A$9.00 – at Vine [941]

DORSET, 1830 : BRITISH ISLES CENSUS DIRECTORIES PROJECT, ENGLAND. VOL 53 – 1mf – 9 – A$9.00 – at Vine [941]

DORSET, 1844 : BRITISH ISLES CENSUS DIRECTORIES PROJECT, ENGLAND. VOL 270 – 3mf – 9 – at Vine [941]

DORSET, 1852 : BRITISH ISLES CENSUS DIRECTORIES PROJECT, ENGLAND. VOL 151 – 2mf – 9 – A$15.00 – at Vine [941]

DORSET, 1867 : BRITISH ISLES CENSUS DIRECTORIES PROJECT, ENGLAND. VOL 90 – 4mf – 9 – A$27.00 – at Vine [941]

DORSET, 1875 : BRITISH ISLES CENSUS DIRECTORIES PROJECT, ENGLAND. VOL 104 – 5mf – 9 – A$33.00 – at Vine [941]

DORSET, 1895 : BRITISH ISLES CENSUS DIRECTORIES PROJECT, ENGLAND – at Vine [941]

DORSET, 1903 : BRITISH ISLES CENSUS DIRECTORIES PROJECT, ENGLAND – (In prep) – at Vine [941]

DORSET, 1927 : BRITISH ISLES CENSUS DIRECTORIES PROJECT, ENGLAND – at Vine [941]

DORSET AND SOMERSET PAPERS 18TH AND 19TH CENTURY / Dorset & Somerset, England – Various dates from 4 Apr 1748-3 Mar 1797 (14 feet) and 25 Apr 1806-18 Jul 1822 (34 feet) – 1 – uk British Libr Newspaper [072]

DORSET COUNTY CHRONICLE – Dorchester, England. -w. 1830-62. 17 1 2 reels – 1 – uk British Libr Newspaper [072]

DORSET DAILY ECHO AND WEYMOUTH DISPATCH – Weymouth, England. 1955-83. -d. 187 reels – 1 – uk British Libr Newspaper [072]

DORSET (SHERBORN), 1805 : BRITISH ISLES CENSUS DIRECTORIES PROJECT, ENGLAND. VOL 184 – 1mf – 9 – A$9.00 – at Vine [941]

Dorset & Somerset, England *see* DORSET AND SOMERSET PAPERS 18TH AND 19TH CENTURY

Dorsey, G A *see* CERTAIN GAMBLING GAMES OF THE KLAMATH INDIANS

"DORT DRUEBEN IN WESTFALEN" : HOELDERLINS REISE NACH BAD DRIBURG MIT WILHELM HEINSE UND DIOTIMA / Hock, Erich – (Includes bibliographical references) – Muenster: Regensberg, 1949 – 1r – 1 – us U.W. Library [910]

Dortch, John Douglas *see* AN ANALYSIS OF THE HERMENEUTIC OF THE SOUTHERN BAPTIST CONVENTION SERMON IN SELECTED PERIODS OF BIBLICAL CONTROVERSY: 1925, 1963, 1970

DORTMUNDER ANZEIGER – (Cont by: Dortmunder Zeitung) – Dortmund, Germany. 26 May 1847-31 Jun 1874 – 1 – gw Mikrofilm [072]

DORTMUNDER WOCHENBLATT – (Title changes: Dortmunder Anzeiger, 26 May 1847; Dortmunder Zeitung, 1 Jul 1874) – Dortmund, Germany. 26 May 1847-30 May 1877; 1878-Jun 1884; 1885; Jul 1886-1905; Apr 1906-Oct 1934; Dec 1934-30 Apr 1939 – 236r – 1 – gw Mikrofilm [072]

DORTMUNDER ZEITUNG *see* DORTMUNDER ANZEIGER

THE DORVAL REPORTER – Dorval, Canada. 19 sep 1957-v10 n21. 26 mai 1965 – 1r – 1 – Can$25.00 – cn Can Microfilming [072]

Dorweiler, Joachim *see* KARL VON RAUMER UND SEIN BEITRAG ZUR VOLKSBILDUNG IM 19. JAHRHUNDERT

Dory, Alphonse *see* RETOUR AU CHRISTIANISME DE LA PART D'UN SAINT-SIMONIEN

Dory, I *see* WALLONISMES

DORY NEWS – Pacific City OR. Jan 31 1963 – 1 – us U.O. Library [071]

UNO EN DOS – Medellin, CK. 1971-1972 – 1r – $50.00 – R04195 – us Library Micro [320]

DOS ANOS DE GUERRA *see* 18 DE JULIO; DOS ANOS DE GUERRA

LOS DOS ARTISTAS / Lopez de Ayala, Adelardo – 1882 – 9 – 1.50f – sp Bibl Santa Ana [820]

LAS DOS CIUDADES / Pla y Deniel, Enrique – Salamanca. 1936 – 1 – us Res Libr [240]

DOS DISCURSOS AL SERVICIO DE LA CAUSA POPULAR / Marinello, Juan – Paris, 1937. Fiche W 1025. (Blodgett Collection of Spanish Civil War Pamphlets) – 9 – us H.U. College Libr [946]

DOS FECHAS, 4 DE JUNIO-24 DE FEBRERO / Ghioldi, Americo – Buenos Aires: Editorial "La Vanguardia", 1946 – 1 – CSUXAHZ7763-B – us Hoover Inst Photo [972]

DOS FOLK = THE PEOPLE – (In Yiddish) – Warsaw, PL. v3 no14 16 Jun 1922-v3 no24 Aug 1922 – 1r – 1 – $25.00 – cn Can Microfilming [072]

DOS FOLK = THE PEOPLE – (In Yiddish. Semi-monthly) – London, GB. v1 no1 15 Nov 1899-v1 no5 1 Feb 1900 – 1r – 1 – $25.00 – cn Can Microfilming [072]

LOS DOS GUZMANES / Lopez de Ayala, Adelardo – 1851 – 9 – 1.50f – sp Bibl Santa Ana [820]

DOS HEMISFERIOS – London, UK. 2 Apr, 1 May 1883 – 1 – uk British Libr Newspaper [072]

DOS HISTORIAS, LA UNA DE LA SANCTA CASA DE NUESTRA SENORA DE GUADALUPE, Y SU PRINICPIO Y FUNDACION Y COSAS NOTABLES DELLAS : Y LA OTRA DEL PRINCIPIO Y FUNDACION DE LA CASA DEL SENOR SANCTIAGO DE GALIZIA, PATRON DE ESPANIA Y DE LAS COSAS NOTABLES DESTA SANCTA CASA – Valencia: Art. Graf. Soler, 1965 – 1 – sp Bibl Santa Ana [946]

DOS INFORMAZIONES: UNA DIRIJIDA AL EMPERADOR CARLOS 5 / Sleidanus, Johannes – Madrid, Impr. de Alegria, 1857. Various pagings – 1 – us U.W. Library [946]

DOS MEDICOS EXTREMENOS DE AYER / Enriquez Anselmo, Juan – Badajoz: Dip. Provincial, 1970 – 1 – sp Bibl Santa Ana [610]

DOS MISIONEROS FRANCISCANOS HERMANOS EN EL COLEGIO DE CHILLAN (CHILE) / Barrado Manzano, Arcangel – Madrid: Archivo Ibero-Americano, 1959 – 1 – sp Bibl Santa Ana [240]

DOS OBRAS...FIEL CRISTIANO / Pedro de Vitoria, Fray – 1626 – 9 – 1.50f – sp Bibl Santa Ana [240]

DOS PALABRAS SOBRE EL PRESENTE NUMERO-HOMENAJE. BENITO ARIAS MONTANO / Fernandez de Castro, Eduardo Felipe – Malaga, 1928 – 1 – sp Bibl Santa Ana [946]

DOS PALOS STAR – Dos Palos, CA. 1911-22; 1923- – 50+ r – 1 – $2,500.00 ($50.00y) – B02177 – us Library Micro [071]

LAS DOS PARTIDAS DE BAUTISMO DE DON LUIS DE SALAZAR Y CASTRO / Siete Iglesias, Antonio de – Madrid: Hidalguia, 1958. Aparte Rev. Hidalguia. Marzo-Abril 1958. no 27 – 1 – sp Bibl Santa Ana [946]

Dos Passos, Benjamin Franklin *see* THE LAW OF COLLATERAL AND DIRECT INHERITANCE, LEGACY AND SUCCESSION TAXES, EMBRACING ALL AMERICAN AND MANY ENGLISH DECISIONS.

Dos Passos, John Randolph *see*
- THE INTER-STATE COMMERCE ACT; AN ANALYSIS OF ITS PROVISIONS
- A TREATISE ON THE LAW OF STOCK-BROKERS AND STOCK EXCHANGES.

LAS DOS REPUBLICAS: EL 11 DE FEBRERO Y EL 14 DE ABRIL / Castrovido, Roberto – Barcelona, 1938? Fiche W 782. (Blodgett Collection of Spanish Civil War Pamphlets) – 9 – us H.U. College Libr [946]

DOS ROBINSONES – 1860. 2v – 9 – 1.50f – sp Bibl Santa Ana [830]

LAS DOS ROMAS : IMPRESIONES DE UN PEREGRINO EN EL ANO SANTO / Ruano, Jesus Maria – Madrid: Razon y Fe, 1926 – 1 – sp Bibl Santa Ana [910]

DOS TESIS Y UN CANAL / Aristizabal Llano, N – Bogota, 1914 – 2mf – 9 – ILM-2360/1 – ne IDC [340]

DOS TESTIGOS ABRUMADORES CONTRA LOS NACIONALES / Bayle, Constantino – Burgos: Razon y Fe, 1938 – 1 – sp Bibl Santa Ana [946]

DOSA KITA SEMUA; SEBUAH ROMAN / Motinggo, Busje – SE-4635 1. 1963 – 9 – ne IDC [950]

Dosch, Margaret *see* THE EFFECTS OF ACQUAINTANCE RAPE PREVENTION PROGRAMMING ON MALE ATHLETES' SEXUAL AND DATING ATTITUDES

DOSCIENTAS OBRAS...!EN UNA! / Sanchez Arjona, Vicente – Sevilla: Imprenta Zambrano, 1957 – 1 – sp Bibl Santa Ana [810]

Dosker, Nina Ellis *see* PIONEER PREACHER IN THE TREASURE STATE

Dosma Delgado, Rodrigo *see* DISCURSOS PATRIOS...BADAJOZ

Doss, Lal Mohun *see* THE LAW OF RIPARIAN RIGHTS, ALLUVION AND FISHERY

UN DOSSIER / Congres du Parti Ouvrier Socialiste Revolutionnaire, Allemanistes. Congres National (14e), septembre 1896, Paris – 14 feuillets, coupures de press (Musee social). 5672 – 9 – fr Hachette [335]

DOSSIER DE QUEIQUES LIBERAUX – Ce que l'on trouve dans les comptes publics. s.l.: s.n., 189?. 03191. (Pre-1900 Canadiana) – 9 – cn C.I.H.M. [971]

DOSSIER DEL ORDRE DE LA PENITENCE... / Meersseman, G G – Madrid: Archivo Ibero Americano, 1963 – 1 – sp Bibl Santa Ana [240]

DOSSIER D'ETHNOLOGIE PROVENCALE, NO. 3. LES JARDINS OUVRIERS CODER, 1941-79, MARSEILLE ST MARCEL / Seyer, N – 9 – F40.00 – fr Ethnologie [306]

DOSSIER D'ETHNOLOGIE PROVENCALE, NO. 4. "LES QUATRE SAISONS" / Schippers, T K – 9 – F40.00 – fr Ethnologie [306]

DOSSIERS DE L'AGITATEUR – Paris. v. 1-3 no. 7. Nov 1933-July 1935 – 1 – us NY Public [073]

LES DOSSIERS DE L'AGITATEUR – Supplement aux Cahiers du bolchevisme. Paris. juin 1933-juin 1935 – 1 – fr A.C.R.P.P. [073]

DOSSIERS D'ETHNOLOGIE PROVENCALE, NO. 1. LA CUISINE EN BASSE PROVENCE RURALE / Bouverot, A – 9 – F30.00 – fr Ethnologie [640]

DOSSIERS D'ETHNOLOGIE PROVENCALE, NO. 2. CULTES ET REPRESENTATIONS DE SAINT-JOSEPH EN PROVENCE / Grava, S – 9 – F70.00 – fr Ethnologie [306]

LES DOSSIERS DU TEVECOIS *see* LE TEVECOIS

DOSSIERS EXPRESS – 1991-1995 – 1r per y – 5,6 – F800.00 – sz Infoprint [944]

DOSSIERS LIBERATION – 1973-1992 – 1 times per yr – 6 – F2,500.00 – sz Infoprint [072]

DOSSIERS LIBERATION – 1992 – 1r per y – 5,6 – Sfr668.00 – sz Infoprint [944]

Doster, Frank *see* PAPERS

Dostert, Klaus *see* PRINZIPIEN DER INFORMATIONSUEBERTRAGUNG UEBER ELEKTRISCHE ENERGIEVERSORGUNGSNETZE

DOSTIZHENIIA SOVETSKOI BELORUSSII ZA 40 LET : STATISTICHESKI I SBORNIK / T SU SSSR, Statisticheskoe upravlenie Belorussko i SSR – Minsk: Gos. izd-vo, 1958 – 1 – CSUX91-B2376 – us Hoover Inst Photo [947]

Dostoevskaia, A *see*
- BIBLIOGRAFICHESKII UKAZATEL'SOCHINENII I PROIZVEDENII ISKUSSTVA OTNOSIASHCHIKHSIA K ZHIZNI I DEIATEL'NOSTI F. M. DOSTOEVSKOGO 1846-1903
- MUZEI PAMIATI F.M. DOSTOEVSKAGO V IMP. ROSSIISKOM ISTORICHESKOM MUZEE IM. IMPERATORA ALEKSANDRA 3 V MOSKVE, 1846-1903 GG

Dostoevskii, Fedor M *see* CRIME AND PUNISHMENT

[LA DOT] OVERTURE, ARR. PIANO OR HARPSICHORD AND VIOLIN AD. LIB. / Dalayrac, N – (Violin part lacking) – Paris: Boyer, 179- – 1 – us Sibley [780]

Dothel, Nicholas *see*
- SEI DUETTI NOTTURNI PER DUE FLAUTI...3 OEUVRE
- SONATES POUR UNE FLUTE TRAVERSIERE ET UN VIOLINCELLE.

LA DOTTRINA DELLA SUCCESSIONE DI STATO A STATO... / Cavaglieri, A – Pisa, 1910 – 2mf – 1 – ILM-3161/1 – ne IDC [327]

Doty, James Duane *see* JAMES DUANE DOTY PAPERS, MS 1090

Doty, Lockwood L *see* HISTORY OF LIVINGSTON COUNTY

DOU ZHENG – China. News Daily of the Central Committee of the Communist Party. Feb 1933-Sept 1943. 15 ill. DL10f – 9 – 75.00 – cc Globe [072]

Douai Abbey *see*
- NOBILITY OF ENGLAND WITH THEIR DESCENT
- WELDON PAPERS: BENEDICTINE RECORDS FROM DOUAI ABBEY

DOUBLE BLIND CLINICAL EFFICACY STUDY OF DEXAMETHASONE-LIDOCAINE PULSED PHONOPHORESIS ON PERCEIVED PAIN ASSOCIATED WITH SYMPTOMATIC TENDINITIS / Penderghest, Caroline E – Temple University, 1995 – 1mf – 9 – $4.00 – PE3616 – us Microform Publ [617]

DOUBLE BRANCHES BAPTIST CHURCH. LINCOLNTON, GEORGIA : CHURCH RECORDS – 1826-Jun 1952. Lacking: Oct 1923-Jul 1938 – 1 – 33.39 – us Baptist [240]

DOUBLE FORTRESSE SACRAMENTALE DE FOY / Roscius, L – 1590 – 1 – uk Microform Academic [025]

THE DOUBLE MARRIAGE, OR, WHITE LIES / Reade, Charles L – British Fiction Archive: Unit 2 – 9 – uk Bell [830]

DOUBLE SHOALS BAPTIST CHURCH. SHELBY, NORHT CAROLINA : CHURCH RECORDS – 1954-62 – 1 – 5.00 – us Baptist [240]

DOUBLE SPRINGS BAPTIST CHURCH. SHELBY, NORTH CAROLINA : CHURCH RECORDS – 1854-1963 – 1 – 82.40 – us Baptist [240]

DOUBLE UPROOTED: DUTCH INDONESIAN REFUGEES IN THE UNITED STATES / American Immigration and Citizenship Conference. Committee on Integration – SE-5175 1. 1965 – 9 – ne IDC [975]

Doubleday, E *see* THE GENERA OF DIURNAL LEPIDOPTERA

DOUBLE-DEALER – New Orleans. v1-8. 1921-26 – 1r – 1 – us Ross [073]

THE DOUBLE-DEALER : A COMEDY / Congreve, William – London, [1720] – 2mf – 9 – ne IDC [820]

THE DOUBLE-DEALER – New Orleans. v. 1-8. 1921-May 1926 – 1 – us NY Public [073]

Doublier, Roger *see* LA PROPRIETE FONCIERE EN A.O.F. REGIME EN DROIT PRIVE

A DOUBTER'S DOUBTS ABOUT SCIENCE AND RELIGION / Anderson, Robert – 2nd ed. London: Kegan Paul, Trench, Truebner, 1894 – 1mf – 9 – 0-8370-2096-4 – 1985-0096 – us A.T.L.A. [210]

DOUBTER'S DOUBTS ABOUT SCIENCE AND RELIGION / Anderson, Robert – London: Kegan Paul, Trench, Tru., 1894. 1 fiche – 9 – us A.T.L.A. [240]

Doucere, Victor *see* CURIOSITES LINGUISTIQUES...

Doudiet, Charles A *see* FUNERAL SERMON OF THE LATE JOHN MELVILLE: LOCOMOTIVE DEPARTMENT OF G.T.R.: FOR MANY YEARS A MEMBER OF ST MATTHEWS'S CHURCH, POINT ST CHARLES: PREACHED IN ST MATTHEW'S CHURCH, ON SUNDAY, 24TH JUNE, 1874

DOU-EL-FAKAR – Red. A. Assanhadji. Alger. 1913-14 – 1 – fr A.C.R.P.P. [073]

Douence, J C *see* LA MISE EN PLACE DES INSTITUTIONS ALGERIENNES

Dougall, Lily *see*
- THE CHRIST THAT IS TO BE
- PRO CHRISTO ET ECCLESIA

THE DOUGHERTY COLLECTION OF MILITARY NEWSPAPERS – (Comes with guide) – 58r – 1 – $4,640.00 in the U.S. $5,336.00 outside U.S. – us UMI [350]

Dougherty County. Georgia *see* INVENTORY OF THE COUNTY ARCHIVES

Dougherty, Peter *see* LETTERS

Doughty, Arthur G *see* THE FORTRESS OF QUEBEC 1608-1903

Doughty, Charles Montagu *see* ADAM CAST FORTH

Doughty, Oswald *see* THE CASTLE OF OTRANTO

DOUGLAS 1718-1890 – (Mf 1-4: B,M,D 1718-1843. Mf 5-7: B,M,D 1844-60. Mf 8-10: Births 1860-90. Mf 11-13: Index to Births 1844-1939. Mf 14-15: Marriages 1860-90. Mf 16-17: Index to Marriages 1844-1938. Mf 18-19: Deaths 1860-90. Mf 20-21: Index to Deaths 1844-1939) – (mf ed 1986) – 21mf – 9 – 0-87623-004-4 – us Holbrook [920]

DOUGLAS 1724-1849 – (1T-5T: Births & Deaths 1724-1825. Mf 1T: Out-of-Town Marriages 1759-75. Mf 1T-3T: Marriage Intentions 1751-90; Marriages 1748-97. Mf 5T-9T: Marriages & Intentions 1789-1849. Mf 9T-10T: Births 1841-49. Mf 10T: Marriages, Deaths 1844-49) – (mf ed 1996) – 10mf – 9 – us Holbrook [920]

Douglas, Ben *see* HISTORY OF WAYNE COUNTY

Douglas, C E *see* PURITAN MANIFESTOES

Douglas, C R *see* SUMMARY JUDGEMENT PRACTICE IN THREE DISTRICT COURTS

Douglas, Charles H *see* THE GOVERNMENT OF THE PEOPLE IN THE STATE OF CONNECTICUT

Douglas, Christopher *see* REVIEW OF RECENT PUBLICATIONS, REGARDING THE PROPOSED REFORM OF THE BANKRUPTCY LAWS OF SCOTLAND

DOUGLAS CITY GAZETTE – Douglas, CA. May 1861-Apr 1862 – 1r – 1 – $50.00 – B02178 – us Library Micro [071]

DOUGLAS COUNTY BANNER – Genoa, NV. Oct-Dec 1865 – 1r – 1 – $50.00 – U04537 – us Library Micro [071]

DOUGLAS COUNTY GAZETTE – Waterloo, NE. -w. Mar 1895-Jun 1898; Sept-Dec 1898, scattered issues missing; Feb 1899 to date – 1 – us NE Hist [071]

DOUGLAS COUNTY PRESS – Waterville. Wash. -w. 1902-09 – 1 – us UMI [071]

DOUGLAS COUNTY TIMES – Roseburg, OR. 3 May 1934-13 Jun 1936; 3 May-28 Dec 1934; 8 Jan-30 Apr 1935 – 2r – 1 – us U.O. Library [071]

DOUGLAS ENTERPRISE – Douglas, NE. -w. Mar. 1889-Apr. 1899; Sep. 1901-Mar. 1921; Mar. 1922-Sep. 1934 – 1 – us NE Hist [071]

Douglas, George *see*
- DISCOURSES AND ADDRESSES
- THOU ART THE MAN

Douglas, George Brisbane *see* JAMES HOGG

Douglas, George C M *see*
- ISAIAH ONE AND HIS BOOK ONE
- SAMUEL AND HIS AGE: A STUDY IN THE CONSTITUTIONAL HISTORY OF ISRAEL

Douglas, George Cunningham Monteath *see*
- THE BOOK OF JOSHUA
- THE BOOK OF JUDGES
- WHY I STILL BELIEVE THAT MOSES WROTE DEUTERONOMY

DOUGLAS INDEPENDENT – Roseburg OR. Sep 17 1881, Dec 25 1880, Jan 20 1883, July 22 1876 (part), July 20 1883 + – 1 – us U.O. Library [071]

Douglas, J W *see*
- THE BRITISH HEMIPTERA
- A CATALOGUE OF BRITISH HEMIPTERA
- THE WORLD OF INSECTS: A GUIDE TO ITS WONDERS

Douglas, James *see*
- CANADIAN INDEPENDENCE, ANNEXATION AND BRITISH IMPERIAL FEDERATION
- FACTS AND REFLECTIONS BEARING ON ANNEXATION, INDEPENDENCE AND IMPERIAL FEDERATION
- A MEMOIR OF THOMAS STERRY HUNT

DOUGLAS JERROLD'S WEEKLY NEWSPAPERS – London, UK. Jul 1846-1848. -w.3 reels – 1 – uk British Libr Newspaper [072]

Douglas, Kenneth C *see* MANUSCRIPTS RELATING TO PAPUA NEW GUINEA, (1943)

Douglas, Robert S *see* HISTORY OF SOUTHEAST MISSOURI

DOUGLAS SLATE QUARRYING COMPANY OF NOVA SCOTIA – Prospectus of the.... Halifax, N.S.?: s.n., 1868?. 02749. (Pre-1900 Canadiana) – 9 – cn C.I.H.M. [971]

Douglass, Benjamin *see* FOUR SHORT LECTURES ON THE BOOK OF REVELATION

Douglass, Frederick *see*
- LIFE OF FREDERICK DOUGLASS
- MY BONDAGE AND MY FREEDOM
- PAPERS
- A SELECTION OF WORKS

Douglass, Harlan Paul *see*
- CHRISTIAN RECONSTRUCTION IN THE SOUTH
- THE NEW HOME MISSIONS

Douglass, Jacqueline A *see* AN EXAMINATION OF TWO THEORETICAL DISTRIBUTIONS USING THREE METHODS OF SCORING CRITERION-REFERENCED MEASURES OF MOTOR PERFORMANCE

DOUGLASS' MONTHLY – 1-5 (all publ). 1858-1863 – 9mf – 9 – $70.00 – us UPA [335]

DOUGLASS' MONTHLY – Rochester, NY. v1-5. 1859-63 – 1r – 1 – us Ross [071]

Douglass, Truman O *see* THE PILGRIMS OF IOWA

DOUGLASVILLE FIRST BAPTIST CHURCH. DOUGLASVILLE, GEORGIA : CHURCH RECORDS – Nov 1944-88. 4,258p – 1 – 191.61 – us Baptist [240]

Douin, Georges *see*
- HISTOIRE DE REGNE DU KHEDIVE ISMAIL. L'EMPIRE AFRICAIN. TOME 3, LE ET 2E PARTIES
- HISTOIRE DU REGNE DU KHEDIVE ISMAIL

Doumenc, D A *see* ETUDE DE L'ORGANOGENESE DE L'ACTINIE ACOUTIAIRE CEREUS PEDUNCULATUS PENNANT

Doumergue, Emile *see*
- CALOMNIES ANTI-PROTESTANTES
- CALVIN AND THE REFORMATION
- CALVIN, LE PREDICATEUR DE GENEVE
- ESSAI SUR L'HISTOIRE DU CULTE REFORME PRINCIPALEMENT AU 16E ET AU 19E SI'ECLE
- GENEVA, PAST AND PRESENT
- LA HONGRIE CALVINISTE
- ICONOGRAPHIE CALVINIENNE
- LA PIETE REFORMEE D'APRES CALVIN
- LA VEILLE DE LA LOI DE L'AN 10, 1763-1802

Doumon, Genevieve *see* GUIDE FOR THE COLLECTION OF TRADITIONAL MUSICAL INSTRUMENTS

Dours, J A *see* CATALOGUE SYNONYMIQUE DES HYMENOPTERES DE FRANCE

Dousa, G *see* DE INITERE SVO CONSTANTINOPOLITANO, EPISTOLA

DOUTES SUR LA LANGUE FRANCOISE / Bouhours, D – 1674 – 9 – fr I.C.S. [440]

DOUTES SUR LA RELIGION SUIVIS DE L'ANALYSE DU TRAITE THEOLOGI-POLITIQUE DE SPINOSA – (D'Holbach series). 1767 – 9 – fr Hachette [240]

Douthwaite, William R *see* GRAY'S INN

Doutre, A *see* L'ARGUS MUNICIPAL

Doutre, Gonzalve *see* LE PRINCIPE DES NATIONALITES

Doutre, Joseph *see*
- CONSTITUTION OF CANADA THE BRITISH NORTH AMERICA ACT, 1867; ITS INTERPRETATION.
- CONSTITUTION OF CANADA: THE BRITISH NORTH AMERICA ACT, 1867: ITS INTERPRETATION, GATHERED FROM THE DECISIONS OF COURTS, THE DICTA OF JUDGES, AND THE OPINIONS OF STATESMEN AND OTHERS
- LES FIANCES DE 1812

A DOUTRINA : ORGAO DA FEDERACAO ESPIRITA DO PARANA – Curitiba, Jan, Mar-Jun, Aug-Nov 1906 – 1,5,6 – bl Biblioteca [072]

Doutte, Edmond *see* L'ISLAM ALGERIEN EN L'AN 1900

Douville, Jean-Baptiste *see*
- VOYAGE AU CONGO ET DANS L'INTERIEUR DE L'AFRIQUE EQUINOXALE
- VOYAGE AU CONGO ET DANS L'INTERIEUR DE L'AFRIQUE EQUINOXIALE

Douville, Raymond *see* LE MAURICIEN

Douwes, C *see* GRONDIG ONDERSOEK VAN DE TOONEN DER MUSIJK

DOUZE ANS DANS LA HAUTE-ETHIOPIE (ABYSSINIE) / Abbadie, Arnauld d' – (African Library). v1. Paris. Hachette. 1868 – 9 – fr Hachette [960]

DOUZE BACCHANALES POUR LE FORTE-PIANO AVEC ACCOMPAGNEMENT DE TAMBOURIN.. / Steibelt, Daniel – ca. 1800 – 9 – us Sibley [780]

DOUZE EVENTAILS DE BONZE SIAMOIS. ANALYSE ET DESCRIPTION / Hemmet, C – 9 – F20.00 – fr Ethnologie [740]

DOUZE ROMANCES AVEC ACCOMP. DU PIANO / Baumbach, F – 1790 – 1 – us Sibley [780]

LES DOUZE TRAVAUX D'HERCULE – 1mf – 15 – F60.00 – fr C.R.D.P. [390]

DOUZHENG – Struggle. Feb 1933-Sept 1934. 1 reel. M/C 84 – 1 – $55.00 – cc Microforms [073]

THE DOVE; OR, PASSAGES OF COSMOGRAPHY; A POEM...REPRINTED FROM THE ORIGINAL ED. OF 1613. / Zouch, Richard – Memoir, notes, coll. and arr. by Richard Walker.Oxford: H. Slatter; London: T. Rodd, 1839.xiiii,82p. incl. geneal. tab – 1 – us U.W. Library [920]

Dove, P E *see* DOMESDAY STUDIES

DOVER 1753-1849 – (Mf 1T-2T: Births by Family 1753-1844. Mf 2T: Marriages 1785-1844. Mf 2T-3T: Deaths 1774-1844. Mf 3T-4T: Intentions 1786-1849. Mf 5T: Births 1843-49; Marriages, Deaths 1844-49) – 5mf – 9 – 0-87623-241-1 – us Holbrook [920]

Dover Baptist Association. Virginia *see* CHURCH DISCIPLINE

DOVER BAPTIST CHURCH. LAGRANGE, MISSOURI : CHURCH RECORDS – 1838-1965 – 1 – 46.80 – us Baptist [240]

DOVER BAPTIST CHURCH. SHELBY, NORTH CAROLINA : CHURCH RECORDS – 1934-63 – 1 – 27.81 – us Baptist [240]

DOVER BAPTIST CHURCH. TENNESSEE : CHURCH RECORDS – 1924-58 – 1 – 16.65 – us Baptist [240]

Dover, New Hampshire. Dover Free Will Baptist Church *see* RECORDS

Dover. Ohio. Baptist Church *see* CHURCH RECORDS, MS 668

THE DOVER SELECTION OF SPIRITUAL SONGS / Broadus, Andrew – Philadelphia, 1828 – 1 – 14.56 – us Baptist [240]

Dover, Thomas Birkett *see*
- HIDDEN WORD: THIRTY DEVOTIONAL STUDIES OF THE PARABLES OF OUR LORD
- THE MINISTRY OF MERCY

DOVER WEEKLY ARGUS – New Philadelphia. Ohio. 1880-1882 – 1 – us UMI [071]

DOVOLNO NASILI I!!! : BRATSTVO "SVOBODY I PORI ADKA" RUSSKOMU NARODY / Bratstvo svobody i pori adka – [S.l.: s.n.], 1905 (S.-Peterburg: T-vo R. Golike i A. Vilborg) – 1 – CSUX88-B1239 – us Hoover Inst Photo [947]

DOW AIR STRIP – Bangor, ME. dec 20 1951-jun 13 1952 – 1 – us Res Libr [071]

DOW FIELD OBSERVER – Bangor, ME. jul 4 1942-1945; jan 9,30 1946 – 1 – us Res Libr [071]

DOW THUNDERJET – Bangor, ME. [jan 30-dec 17 1948]; jan 12-sep 26 1949 – 1 – us Res Libr [071]

DOW THUNDERSTREAK *see* THUNDERSTREAK

Dowbiggin, Herbert *see* CONFIDENTIAL REPORT ON THE NORTHERN RHODESIA POLICE

Dowbor-Musnicki, Josef *see* KROTKI SZKIS DO HISTORJI 1-GO POLSKIEGO KORPUSU

Dowden, Edward *see*
- NEW STUDIES IN LITERATURE
- PURITAN AND ANGLICAN:
- TRANSCRIPTS AND STUDIES

Dowden, John *see*
- THE ANNOTATED SCOTTISH COMMUNION OFFICE
- THE CELTIC CHURCH IN SCOTLAND
- THE CHURCH YEAR AND KALENDAR
- FURTHER STUDIES IN THE PRAYER BOOK
- THE MEDIEVAL CHURCH IN SCOTLAND
- THE WORKMANSHIP OF THE PRAYER BOOK IN ITS LITERARY AND LITURGICAL ASPECTS

Dowding, W C *see* THE LIFE AND CORRESPONDENCE OF GEORGE CALIXTUS

Dowe, WA *see* THE PLACE OF MONEY IN A FREE SOCIETY

Dowell, Linus J *see* THE EFFECT OF THE LEAD LEG PLANT ON FACTORS AFFECTING DISTANCE ON KICKOFFS IN FOOTBALL

Dowie, John A *see* OUR SECOND YEAR'S HARVEST

Dowkontt, George D *see* MURDERED MILLIONS

Dowling, Joannis Goulter *see* NOTITIA SCRIPTORUM SS. PATRUM ALIORUMQUE VETERIS ECCLESIAE MONUMENTORUM

Dowling, John *see* THE JUDSON OFFERING

Dowling, John Goulter *see* INTRODUCTION TO THE CRITICAL STUDY OF ECCLESIASTICAL HISTORY

Dowling, Theodore Edward *see*
- THE ABYSSINIAN CHURCH
- THE EGYPTIAN CHURCH
- GAZA, A CITY OF MANY BATTLES
- HELLENISM IN ENGLAND
- SKETCHES OF CAESAREA (PALESTINAE): BIBLICAL, MEDIAEVAL, MODERN
- SKETCHES OF GEORGIAN CHURCH HISTORY

DOWN BEAT – v4 1937- 1; v38- 5,6; v42- 9 – us UMI [073]

DOWN IN WATER STREET: A STORY OF SIXTEEN YEARS...IN WATER STREET MISSION / Hadley, Samuel Hopkins – New York: Fleming H. Revell, 1906. 254p. 1 fiche – 9 – us A.T.L.A. [240]

DOWN RIVER – 1974-79 – 1 – us UMI [073]

Down, T C *see* THE TEETOTAL TYRANT: BEING ILLUSTRATIONS OF TEETOTAL METHODS UNDER A PROHIBITORY LIQUOR LAW: TOGETHER WITH REMARKS ON THE PRESENT POSITION IN GREAT BRITAIN

DOWN THE ST LAWRENCE & GULF / Balmoral Hotel. Montreal, Quebec – Presented by Balmoral Hotel, Montreal, 18??. 03361. (Pre-1900 Canadiana) – 9 – cn C.I.H.M. [910]

DOWNEASTER – Bangor. Maine. Dow A.F. Base. 1959-1968 – 1 – us UMI [071]

DOWNEASTER – Bangor, ME. [feb 1960-apr 13 1962] – 1 – us Res Libr [071]

Downer, Harry E *see* HISTORY OF DAVENPORT AND SCOTT COUNTY

Downes, J *see* METHODISM EXAMINED AND EXPOSED

DOWNEY – 1931; 1933; 1935-52; 1955-74 – 61r – 1 – $3,050.00 – P00024 – us Library Micro [910]

DOWNEY/NORWALK – 1984 – 2r – 1 – $100.00 – P00025 – us Library Micro [910]

Downie, David *see* THE LONE STAR, THE HISTORY OF THE TELUGU MISSION OF THE AMERICAN BAPTIST MISSIONARY UNION

Downie, William *see* HUNTING FOR GOLD: REMINISENCES (SIC) OF PERSONAL EXPERIENCE AND RESEARCH IN THE EARLY DAYS OF THE PACIFIC COAST FROM ALASKA TO PANAMA

Downing, Hugh Urquhart *see* CASES IN GEORGIA REPORTS THAT HAVE BEEN OVERRULED, DOUBTED, CRITICISED, OR MODIFIED

Downing, William *see* OBSERVATIONS ON THE CONSTITUTION, CUSTOMS, AND USAGE OF MIDDLE TEMPLE

DOWNPATRICK RECORDER – Dec 31 1836-Dec 28 1839; 1840-77; Jan 5 1878-Dec 24 1880; 1881-1929; 1931-33; Jan 6 1934-Dec 19 1936; 1937-47; Jan 3 1948-Dec 24 1949; 1950; Jan 6 1951-Dec 24 1953; Jan 9 1954-Dec 24 1955; 1956-Sep 1990, Oct 3-Dec 19 1990; 1991-Dec 22 1992; Jan-Sep 1993; Oct 6-Dec 22 1993; Jan-Dec 21 1994; Jan-Dec 20 1995; 1996 – 121r – 1 – uk British Libr Newspaper [072]

Downs *see* CHAUTAUQUA COUNTY AND ITS PEOPLE

DOWNSHIRE CHRONICLE – Downpatrick. Ireland. -w. 2 Feb 1839-13 Jun 1840. (44 ft) – 1 – uk British Libr Newspaper [072]

DOWNSIDE : THE HISTORY OF ST. GREGORY'S SCHOOL FROM ITS COMMENCEMENT AT DOUAY TO THE PRESENT TIME / Birt, Henry Norbert – London: K. Paul, Trench, Truebner, 1902 – 1mf – us A.T.L.A. [240]

THE DOWNSIDE REVIEW – 1(1880)-91(1973) – 623mf – 9 – Dfl2,181.00 – ne Slangenburg [073]

THE DOWNSIDE REVIEW – (1920 has not been publ) – Bath. v1-91. 1880-1973 – 623mf – 9 – ne IDC [240]

DOWNTOWN NEWS – Los Angeles, CA. 1972-1992 – 1r – 1 – $550.00 – R04057 – us Library Micro [071]

DOWNTOWN REVIEW – Portland OR. Aug 4 1932 – 1 – us U.O. Library [071]

DOWNTOWN SHOPPING GUIDE *see* GUIDE

Dowson, VH W *see* DATES

Doyle, Andrew *see* EXTRAORDINARY GEOMETRICAL DISCOVERY: TRISECTION OF ANY RECTILINEAL ANGLE BY ELEMENTARY GEOMETRY: AND SOLUTIONS OF OTHER PROBLEMS CONSIDERED IMPOSSIBLE EXCEPT BY AID OF THE HIGHER GEOMETRY

Doyle, Arthur Conan *see*
- THE GREEN FLAG AND OTHER STORIES OF WAR AND SPORT
- THE HOUND OF THE BASKERVILLES
- THE MEMOIRS OF SHERLOCK HOLMES
- THE RETURN OF SHERLOCK HOLMES
- THE SIGN OF FOUR
- SIR NIGEL

Doyle, James William Edmund *see* THE OFFICIAL BARONAGE OF ENGLAND, SHOWING THE SUCCESSION, DIGNITIES, AND OFFICES OF EVERY PEER FROM 1066 TO 1885

Doyle, Joseph B *see* 20TH CENTURY HISTORY OF JEFFERSON COUNTY AND REPRESENTATIVE CITIZENS

Doyle, Lauren A *see* DIFFERENTIAL EFFECTIVENESS OF RELAXATION PROCEDURES IN ATTENUATING COMPONENTS OF ANXIETY IN SHOOTERS

Doyle, Sherman Hoadley *see* PRESBYTERIAN HOME MISSIONS

Doyle, William B *see* CENTENNIAL HISTORY OF SUMMIT COUNTY AND REPRESENTATIVE CITIZENS

DOYLESTOWN DEMOCRAT – Doylestown, PA. -w 1889-1912 – 13 – $25.00r – us I.M.R. [071]

DOZE ESTUDOS / Rosenfeld, Anatol – (Includes bibliographical references and index) – Sao Paulo: Conselho Estadual de Cultura, Commissao de Literatura, [1959] – 1r – 1 – us U.W. Library [440]

Dozon, A *see* BALGARSKI NARODNI PESNI

Dozy, F *see*
- BRYOLOGIA JAVANICA...
- MUSCI FRONDOSI INEDITI ARCHIPELAGI INDICI...
- MUSCORUM FRONDOSORUM NOVAE SPECIES EX ARCHIPELAGO INDICO ET JAPONICA
- NOVAE FUNGORUM SPECIES IN BELGIO SEPTENTRIONALI

Dozy, R *see*
- COMMENTAIRE HISTORIQUE SUR LE POEME D'IBN-ABDOEN
- THE HISTORY OF THE ALMOHADES
- NOTICES SUR QUELQUES MANUSCRITS ARABES

DR. ABBOTT AND CHRISTIAN EVOLUTION: I...CONFLICT BETWEEN TWO WORLD-THEORIES / Savage, Minot Judson – Boston: George H. Ellis, 1892. 1 fiche – 9 – us A.T.L.A. [240]

DR. ALI SASTROAMIDJOJO OF INDONESIA; A PICTURE STORY OF THE INDONESIAN PRIME MINISTER / Sastroamidjojo, Ali – SE-10,527 1. 1955? – 9 – ne IDC [920]

DR. AMBROSIUS MOIBANUS : EIN BEITRAG ZUR GESCHICHTE DER KIRCHE UND SCHULE SCHLESIENS IM REFORMATIONSZEITALTER / Konrad, P – Halle: Verein fuer Reformationsgeschichte, 1891. ([Schriften des Vereins fuer Reformationsgeschichte; Bd. 34]) – 1mf – us A.T.L.A. [240]

DR. CHINIQUY TO SENATOR TASSE AND MGR. LYNCH: ARCHBISHOP OF TORONTO / Chiniquy, Charles – 1884? 00610. (Pre-1900 Canadiana) – 9 – cn C.I.H.M. [971]

DR. CODEX'S PASTORAL LETTER VERSIFIED, BY WAY OF CAUTION AGAINST LUKEWARMNESS ON ONE HAND AND ENTHUSIASM ON THE OTHER;... – London, 1739 – 1mf – 9 – MP-262/1 – ne IDC [240]

DR. CROFT'S SERVICE IN B, AND EVENING IN E / Croft, W – Manuscript, [1748] – 1 – us Sibley [780]

DR. E.L.TH. HENKE'S NACHGELASSENE VORLESUNGEN UEBER LITURGIK UND HOMILETIK / Henke, Ernst Ludwig Theodor; ed by Zschimmer, W – Halle a/S.: Lippert, 1876 – 2mf – us A.T.L.A. [240]

DR. FERDINAND HITZIG'S VORLESUNGEN UEBER BIBLISCHE THEOLOGIE...DES ALTEN TESTAMENTS / Hitzig, Ferdinand – Karlsruhe: H. Reuther, 1880. 1 fiche – 9 – us A.T.L.A. [240]

DR. FILETO PIRES – Manaos, Amazonas. 16 Mar 1897 – 1,5,6 – bl Biblioteca [072]

DR. FOOTE'S HEALTH MONTHLY – New York: Murray Hill Pub Co, [1876?-18– or 19–] – 9 – cn C.I.H.M. [613]

DR. FREE'S EDITION OF THE REV. MR. JOHN WESLEY'S FIRST PENNY-LETTER,... / Free, J – London, 2nd ed 1759 – 1mf – 9 – MP-379/1 – ne IDC [240]

DR. FREE'S EDITION OF THE REV. MR. JOHN WESLEY'S SECOND LETTER, WITH PROLEGOMENA FOR THE BETTER INFORMATION OF THE STUDIOUS ENGLISH READER AND A PERPETUAL COMMENT UPON THE ORIGINAL TEXT;... / Free, J – London, 1759 – 1mf – 9 – MP-380/1 – ne IDC [240]

DR. FREE'S REMARKS UPON MR. JONES'S LETTER AND THE AFFIDAVITS RELATIVE TO THE COMPOSING,... / Free, J – London, 1759 – 1mf – 9 – MP-381/1 – ne IDC [240]

DR. FRIEDRICH BLEEKS VORLESUNGEN UEBER DIE BRIEFE (KOLOSSER, PHILEMON, EPHESIER) / Bleek, Friedrich – Berlin: Georg Reimer, 1865. 1 fiche – 9 – us A.T.L.A. [240]

DR. GILMAN FROST'S GENEALOGICAL RECORDS OF HANOVER, NEW HAMPSHIRE / Frost, Gilman Dubois – Dartmouth College Library Collections – 15r – 1 – $1050.00 – us UMI [920]

DR. GILMAN FROST'S GENEALOGICAL RECORDS OF HANOVER, NEW HAMPSHIRE *see* GENEALOGICAL RECORDS OF HANOVER, NEW HAMPSHIRE

DR. GIRARDEAU'S ANTI-EVOLUTION: THE LOGIC OF HIS REPLY / Martin, James L – Columbia: Presb. Pub. House, 1889. 1 fiche. 8370-4299-2 – 9 – us A.T.L.A. [240]

DR. GRANT AND THE MOUNTAIN NESTORIANS / Laurie, Thomas – Boston: Gould and Lincoln, 1853 – 1mf – us A.T.L.A. [240]

DR. HEINR. ANDR. CHRI HAEVERNICKS VORLESUNGEN UEBER DIE THEOLOGIE DES A.T / Haevernick, Heinr. A C – Frankfurt a.M.: Heyder & Zimmer, 1863. 1 fiche – 9 – us A.T.L.A. [240]

DR. J.A. MOEHLER'S, ERNANNTEN DOMDECANS ZU WUERZBURG UND RITTERS, DES KGL. BAYER. ST MICHAEL-ORDENS, EHEDEM ORD. PROFESSORS DER THEOLOGIE AN DER UNIVERSITAET MUENCHEN, PATROLOGIE, ODER, CHRISTLICHE LITERAERGESCHICHTE / Moehler, Johann Adam; ed by Reithmayr, F X – Regensburg: G.J. Manz, 1839-1840 – 3mf – us A.T.L.A. [240]

DR. JAMES ROBB: THE FIRST PROFESSOR OF CHEMISTRY AND NATURAL HISTORY IN KING'S COLLEGE, FREDERICTON: A SKETCH OF HIS LIFE AND LABOURS / Bailey, Loring Woart – St. John, N.B., Barnes, 1898. 00810. (Pre-1900 Canadiana) – 9 – cn C.I.H.M. [920]

DR. LIDDON / Russell, George W E – London: A.R. Mowbray, 1905 – 1mf – us A.T.L.A. [240]

DR. MACKENZIE'S PAPERS – (Case history) – 7r – 1 – sa Microfile [960]

DR. MARTIN LUTHERS KRANKHEITEN UND DEREN EINFLUSS AUF SEINEN KOERPERLICHEN UND GEISTIGEN ZUSTAND / Ebstein – Stuttgart, 1908 – 9 – DM48.00 – 3-89349-204-6 – gw Hänsel [240]

DR. MOLEMA PAPERS – 1 reel – 1 – sa Microfile [960]

DR. ROBINSON'S VOICE IN THE WILDERNESS – 1-3 2+2 (all publ). 1917-1920 – 5mf – 9 – $40.00 – us UPA [335]

DR. RYERSON: A REVIEW AND A STUDY / Allen, Joseph Antisell – Toronto: s.n., 1884?. 00783. (Pre-1900 Canadiana) – 9 – cn C.I.H.M. [920]

Dr. Williams's Library *see* HENRY CRABB ROBINSON DIARIES, TRAVEL JOURNALS AND REMINISCENCES 1790-1867

Drabkin, S *see* GRAZHDANSKIE KODEKSY SOIUZNYKH RESPUBLIK

Drabkina, Elizaveta *see* GRUZINSKAIA KONTR-REVOLIUTSIIA

Drach, Margaret *see* PRINCIPES GUIDANT L'ELABORATION D'UNE METHODE D'ENSEIGNEMENT DU FRANCAIS ORAL POUR DES ETUDIANTS ANGLOPHONES

Drachkovitch, M M *see*
- THE COMINTERN: HISTORICAL HIGHLIGHTS
- MARXIST IDEOLOGY IN THE CONTEMPORARY WORLD: ITS APPEALS AND PARADOXES

DRACONTI CARMINA / Arevalo, Faustino – 1791 – 9 – 1.50f – sp Bibl Santa Ana [780]

DRACUT 1687-1849 – (Mf 1T: Marriage Intentions 1710-22. Mf 1T-4T: Births & Deaths 1687-1822. Mf 2T: Marriages 1730-38. Mf 2T-7T: Marriage Intentions 1736-1822. Mf 4T-8T: Marriages 1765-1822. Mf 8T: Births & Deaths 1776-1825. Mf 9T: Births 1801-40. Mf 9T-10T: Deaths 1796-1840. Mf 10T: Marriages 1822-40. Mf 10T-11T: Marriage Intentions 1822-40. Mf 11T-13T: Births 1843-49. Mf 13T: Marriages 1844-49. Mf 14T: Deaths 1844-49) – (mf ed 1996) – 14mf – 9 – 0-87623-242-X – us Holbrook [920]

DRACUT 1697-1900 – (Mf 1: Proprietors 1710-34. Mf 2-7: Town & Vitals 1697-1751. Mf 8-9: Vitals Index 1710-1840. Mf 10-57: Town Records 1710-1822. Mf 13-15: Intentions 1715-51. Mf 13-15: Births, Deaths 1715-50. Mf 20-21: Births, Deaths 1722-1820. Mf 23-23,25: Intents, Marriages 1749-90. Mf 31-32: Births, Deaths 1756-1821. Mf 33: Marriages & Intents 1785-94. Mf 41-46: Births, Deaths 1757-1822. Mf 42,45-48: Marriages, Intents 1786-1822. Mf 51-53: Births, Deaths 1757-1822. Mf 53-56: Marriages, Intents 1800-22. Mf 58-59: Births, Deaths 1776-1840. Mf 63-64: Marriages, Intents 1822-32. Mf 65-72: Town Records 1835-50. Mf 71-72: Marriages, Intents 1831-40. Mf 73-75: Military 1807-19, 1862. Mf 75-76: Paupers 1855-1900. Mf 77-80: Vitals Index 1848-1905. Mf 81-84: Vitals 1840-61. Mf 85-86: Deaths 1861-96. Mf 87-88: Marriages 1853-1900. Mf 89: Deaths 1896-1905. Mf 90-92: Births 1861-1900) – (mf ed 1995) – 92mf – 9 – 0-87623-379-5 – us Holbrook [920]

Draeger, Otto *see* THEODOR MUNDT UND SEINE BEZIEHUNGEN ZUM JUNGEN DEUTSCHLAND

Draeseke, J *see* APOLLINARIOS VON LAODICEA (T.U.U. 1-7/3.4.)

Draeseke, Johannes *see*
- APOLLINARIOS VON LAODICEA
- DER BRIEF AN DIOGNETOS
- GESAMMELTE PATRISTISCHE UNTERSUCHUNGEN
- JOHANNES SCOTUS ERIGENA UND DESSEN GEWAEHRSMAENNER IN SEINEM WERKE DE DIVISIONE NATURAE LIBRI V

DER DRAEUMLING / Raabe, Wilhelm Karl – 2. Aufl. Berlin: Otto Janke, 1893 – 1r – 1 – us U.W. Library [830]

DRAFT ANALYSIS OF THE U.S. JOINT RESOLUTION FOR APPROVAL OF THE COMPACT OF FREE ASSOCIATION : ADDRESSED BY THE CHIEF SECRETARY AND ADVISER TO THE PRESIDENT AND CABINET TO THE PRESIDENT, THE CABINET, THE NITIJELA, AND THE DEPARTMENT SECRETARIES / Marshall Islands – 9 Jan 1986 – 1mf – 9 – $1.50 – LLMC 82-100I Title 4 – us L.L.M.C. [324]

DRAFT AND MILITARY LAW COLLECTION – 188mf – 9 – $715.00 – us UMI [340]

DRAFT CIVIL AND COMMERCIAL CODE FOR THE KINGDOM OF SIAM. BOOK ON OBLIGATIONS / Thailand. Laws, Statutes, etc – Bangkok, Bangkok Daily Mail, 1914. 5 p. l., 284, lxxiii p. LL-10016 – 1 – us L of C Photodup [340]

DRAFT COMPACT OF FREE ASSOCIATION : PRESENTED BY THE JOINT COMMITTEE ON FUTURE STATUS TO THE CONG OF MICRONESIA. 4TH CONG, 2ND SPEC SESS, AUG 1972 / Joint Committee on Future Status [TTPI (U.S.)] – (Various pagination) – n.p, n.d. – 1mf – 9 – $1.50 – LLMC 82-100F, Title 45 – us L.L.M.C. [323]

DRAFT CONSTITUTIONS. ALTERNATIVES 1 AND 2 / Constitutional Convention, Koror – (Various pagination) – Koror: Constitutional Convention, may 30, 1975 – 2mf – 9 – $3.00 – LLMC 82-100G, Title 11 – us L.L.M.C. [323]

DRAFT DEVELOPMENT PLAN, 1963-1968 / Bechuanaland Protectorate – 1963. BD-1616 1 – 9 – ne IDC [338]

DRAFT DEVELOPMENT PLAN OF THE FEDERATION OF MALAYA / Malaya – Kuala Lumpur. 1950. BD-120 1 – 9 – ne IDC [338]

DRAFT DEVELOPMENT PROGRAMME, 1970 / Trinidad and Tobago – Trinidad. 1969. BD-1758 1 – 9 – ne IDC [338]

DRAFT DEVELOPMENT PROGRAMME, 1971 / Trinidad and Tobago – Trinidad. 1971. BD-1759 1 – 9 – ne IDC [338]

DRAFT DIRECTIVES OF THE NINTH CONGRESS OF THE RUMANIAN COMMUNIST PARTY ON THE DEVELOPMENT OF THE NATIONAL ECONOMY ON THE 1966-1970 PERIOD / Romania – Bucharest. 1965. BD-1741 1 – 9 – ne IDC [338]

DRAFT ENVIRONMENTAL IMPACT STATEMENT FOR THE COMPACT OF FREE ASSOCIATION / Micronesia. (U.S.) – (Covers FSM, RMI and Palau) – Washington: Office for Micronesian Status Negotiations, 1984 – 2mf – 9 – $3.00 – LLMC 82-100F Title 16 – us L.L.M.C. [324]

DRAFT FIFTH FIVE YEAR PLAN 1974-1979 / India. Planning Commission – 2v. New Delhi. 1973. BD-1808 1 – 9 – ne IDC [338]

DRAFT FIRST FIVE-YEAR ECONOMIC PLAN, 1962-1966 / Korea. South. Economic Planning Board – D-1356 1. 1961 – 9 – ne IDC [338]

DRAFT FIVE YEAR PLAN, A SYNOPSIS / Nepal – Kathmandu. 1956. BD-132 1 – 9 – ne IDC [338]

DRAFT FIVE YEAR PLAN OF ECONOMIC AND SOCIAL DEVELOPMENT, 1 JUL 1966-30 JUN 1971 / Sierra Leone – Nov 1965 – 9 – ne IDC [338]

DRAFT FOURTH PLAN MATERIAL AND FINANCIAL BALANCES, 1964-65, 1970-71 AND 1975-76 / India. Planning Commission – New Delhi. 1966 – 9 – ne IDC [338]

THE DRAFT GUAM COMMONWEALTH ACT : PREPARED FOR THE HOUSE COMMITTEE ON INTERNATIONAL AND INSULAR AFFAIRS / Zafren, Daniel H – Washington: Library of Congress, Congressional Research Service, 27 May 1986 – 1mf – 9 – $1.50 – LLMC 82-100B Title 29 – us L.L.M.C. [324]

DRAFT MAPS / Lucas County. Ohio. Engineer – 2r – 1 – $32.50r – us Archival [324]

DRAFT NATIONAL DEVELOPMENT PLAN, 1967-1970 / Liberia. Dept. of Planning and Economic Affairs – D-1368 1. 1967 – 9 – ne IDC [338]

DRAFT OF AN ACT DESIGNED TO SIMPLIFY AND IMPROVE TRANSFERS OF LAND AND TITLES IN MASSACHUSETTS AND TO ENLARGE THE JURISDICTION OF THE LAND COURT / Rackemann, Charles Sedgwick – Boston, Mudge, 1908. 35 p. LL-1378 – 1 – us L of C Photodup [340]

DRAFT OF FIVE YEAR PLAN OF INDONESIA / Indonesia. Departemen Penerangan – SE-8481 1. 1968 – 9 – ne IDC [338]

DRAFT OF THE FIVE-YEAR ECONOMIC DEVELOPMENT PLAN (1966-1970) / Greece. Center of Planning and Economic Development, Athens – 1965 – 9 – ne IDC [338]

DRAFT OF THE STATE BUDGET; STATEMENT BY THE MINISTER OF THE TREASURY / Egypt. Ministry of Treasury – 6v. 1961-67. (lacking 1962 63). BNE-4671 1 – 9 – ne IDC [336]

A DRAFT PAPER ON DEVELOPMENT PLANS FOR HIGHER EDUCATION IN RAJASTHAN 1968/69 TO 1985/86, WITH SPECIAL REFERENCE TO THE FOURTH FIVE YEAR PLAN / India. Rajasthan. Directorate of Education – Jaipur, [1969] – 1mf – 9 – DE-553/1 – ne IDC [370]

DRAFT PLAN FOR EDUCATIONAL DEVELOPMENT IN TRINIDAD AND TOBAGO 1968-1983 / Trinidad and Tobago – Port of Spain, 1968 – 2mf – 9 – DE-527/1 – ne IDC [370]

DRAFT PROGRAM FOR 1962 FOR TRANSITION INTO THE PLAN-PERIOD / Turkey. Devlet Planlama Teskilati – Ankara. 1961 – 9 – ne IDC [338]

DRAFT PROGRAM FOR THE YEAR 1962 FOR TRANSITION INTO THE PLAN-PERIOD IMPLEMENTATION PLAN / Turkey. Devlet Planlama Teskilati – Ankara. 1961. BD-466 1 – 9 – ne IDC [338]

DRAFT PROPOSAL FOR SYLLABUS DEVELOPMENT FOR GRADE 7 OF THE PROPOSED 8 YEAR COMMUNITY SCHOOL / Papua New Guinea. Department of Education – 1974 – 1mf – 9 – DE-251/1 – ne IDC [370]

DRAFT REPORT ON COPYRIGHT – s.l.: s.n., 189?. 00451. (Pre-1900 Canadiana) – 9 – cn C.I.H.M. [971]

DRAFT SECOND DEVELOPMENT PLAN, 1972-1976 / Guyana. Ministery of Economic Development – Georgetown. 1972. BD-1661 1 – 9 – ne IDC [338]

DRAFT SECOND FIVE-YEAR PLAN, 1964-1968 / Trinidad and Tobago. National Planning Commission – Port-of-Spain. 1963 – 9 – ne IDC [338]

DRAFT THIRD FIVE YEAR PLAN OF EDUCATION FOR CENTRAL AND CENTRALLY SPONSORED SCHEMES : EXCLUDING SCHEMES OF THE UNIVERSITY GRANTS COMMISSION / India. Ministry of Education – 1960 – 2mf – 9 – DE-544/1 – ne IDC [370]

DRAFT THIRD FIVE-YEAR PLAN, 1969-1973 / Trinidad and Tobago – Port of Spain. 1968. BD-837 1 – 9 – ne IDC [338]

DRAFTING AND REPRO DIGEST – v3-5. 1979-81 – 1 – us UMI [073]

DRAFTING FEDERAL GRANT STATUTES / Administrative Conference of the U.S. (ACUS) – Acus study. no90-1. n.p. 1990? (all publ) – 4mf – 9 – $6.00 – LLMC 94-351 – us L.L.M.C. [340]

DRAFTING OF INDIAN WILLS COVERING TRUST AND RESTRICTED PROPERTY / U.S. Department of the Interior. Office of Hearings and Appeals – 2nd ed. Washington, OHA, 1988 – 2mf – 9 – $3.00 – LLMC 88-001 – us L.L.M.C. [324]

DRAG RACING – (1986-. 1,5,6) – 1984- – 9 – us UMI [790]

Draganov, P D *see*
- GRAF L. N. TOLSTOI KAK PISATEL' VSEMIRNYI I RASPROSTRANENIE EGO PROIZVEDENII V ROSSII I ZA GRANITSEI
- PIATIDESIATIIAZYCHNYI PUSHKIN, T.E. PEREVODY A. S. PUSHKINA NA 50 IAZYKOV I NARECHII MIRA

Drage *see* ACCOUNT OF A VOYAGE FOR THE DISCOVERY OF A NORTHWEST PASSAGE

Dragendorff, Georg *see* DIE HEILPFLANZEN DER VERSCHIEDENEN VOELKER UND ZEITEN

Drago, L M *see* COBRO COERCITIVO...

Drago, Mariano Jose *see* EL JUICIO POLITICO COMO INSTRUMENTO DE OPRESION

Dragomiretskii, VS *see* CHEKHOSLOVAKI V ROSSII, 1914-1920

Dragomirov, M I *see*
- "GUERRE ET PAIX" DE TOLSTOI AU POINT DE VUE MILITAIRE
- PRINCIPES ESSENTIELS POUR LA CONDUITE DE LA GUERRE. CLAUZEWITZ INTERPRETE

DRAGONS AND DRAGON SLAYERS / Hackwood, Frederick William – Illus. by Gordon Brown. London: Religious Tract Society, n.d. 175p – 1 – us U.W. Library [240]

DRAGT – 1941 – 1 – us I.U. Libraries [390]

Drahomaniv, Mykhailo Petrovych *see* ROZVIDKY MYKHAILA DRAHOMANOVA PRO UKRAINS KU NARODNIU SLOVESNIST I PIS MENSTVO

DRAIN ECHO – Drain, OR. -w. 17 Dec 1885-21 Oct 1889. 1 roll – 1 – us U.O. Library [071]

DRAIN ENTERPRISE – Drain, OR. -w. 1922-53 – 1 – 240.00 – us Oregon Hist [071]

DRAIN ENTERPRISE – Drain, OR. -w. 3 Jan 1952-. 3 Aug 1922-10 Nov 1953. – 8r – 1 – us U.O. Library [071]

DRAIN WATCHMAN – Drain, OR. -w. 22 Feb 1900-29 Aug 1901. 1 roll – 1 – us U.O. Library [071]

DRAINAGE DESIGN FACTORS : 28 QUESTIONS AND ANSWERS BASED ON THE EXPERT CONSULTATION ON DRAINAGE DESIGN FACTORS, ROME, 1979 – 1980 – 58p – it F.A.O. [627]

DRAINAGE MATERIALS – 1976 – 126p – it F.A.O. [627]

DRAINAGE TESTING – 1976 – 185p – it F.A.O. [627]

DRAKARD'S PAPER – (The Champion The Investigator). London. -w. Jan 1813-Jul 1822. (12 reels) – 1 – uk British Libr Newspaper [072]

Drake, Allison Emery *see* THE AUTHORSHIP OF THE WEST SAXON GOSPELS

Drake, Charles Daniel *see*
- ADDRESS, DELIVERED MAY 8, 1878, AT THE ANNUAL COMMENCEMENT OF THE CINCINNATI LAW SCHOOL
- A TREATISE ON THE LAW OF SUITS BY ATTACHMENT IN THE UNITED STATES

Drake, Daniel *see* DISCOURSE ON THE HISTORY, CHARACTER, AND PROSPECTS OF THE WEST

Drake del Castillo, E *see*
- HISTOIRE NATURELLE DES PLANTES
- ILLUSTRATIONES FLORAE INSULARUM MARIS PACIFICI

Drake, Durant *see* PROBLEMS OF CONDUCT

DRAKE LAW REVIEW – v1-42. 1951-93 – 1,5,6 – $630.00 – us Hein [073]

Drake, N M *see* THE HISTORY OF ENGLISH GLASS PAINTING

Drake, Samuel Adams *see*
- BURGOYNE'S INVASION OF 1777: WITH AN OUTLINE SKETCH OF THE AMERICAN INVASION OF CANADA, 1775-76
- THE MAKING OF THE GREAT WEST, 1512-1883
- NOOKS AND CORNERS OF THE NEW ENGLAND COAST
- THE PINE-TREE COAST
- THE TAKING OF LOUISBURG, 1745

Drake, Samuel G *see*
- ANNALS OF WITCHCRAFT IN NEW ENGLAND
- FOUNDERS OF NEW ENGLAND

Drakon *see* AL'MANAKH STIKHOV

Dralet *see*
- PLAN DETAILLE DE TOPOGRAPHIE
- PLAN DETAILLE DE TOPOGRAPHIE, SUIVI DE LA TOPOGRAPHIE DU DEPARTEMENT DU GERS

Dralse de Grandpierre *see* RELATION DE DIVERS VOYAGES FAITS DANS L'AFRIQUE, L'AMERIQUE ET AUX INDES OCCIDENTALES. LA DESCRIPTION DU ROYAUME DE JUDA ET QUELQUES PARTICULARITES TOUCHANT LA VIE DU ROI REGNANT

DRAMA – (1971-. 5,6. 1975-. 9) – England. v. 1- 1919- – 1 – us UMI [790]

DRAMA : QUARTERLY THEATRE REVIEW – London. New Series. 1952-71 – 5,9 – Dfl1,000.00; Dfl50.00v – ne Swets [790]

THE DRAMA : ADDRESSES / Irving, Henry – Boston: Joseph Knight, [c1892] – 1 roll – 1 – 1-55879-543-X – uk Libr Preservation [890]

THE DRAMA – London. v. 1-2 no. 1-17, 24, 27, 30. Sept. 13-Dec. 27 1883; Jan 3, Feb 21, Mar 13, Apr 3 1884 – 1 – us NY Public [790]

THE DRAMA – v1-2. 1883-84 – 1r – 1 – us Ross [790]

DRAMA CHANG FU TANG / Slametmuljana, R B – SE 10,239 1. 1948 – 9 – ne IDC [950]

EL DRAMA DE LA VIDA / Henao y Munoz, Manuel – 1878 – 9 – 1.50f – sp Bibl Santa Ana [830]

DAS DRAMA HEINRICH VON KLEISTS / Meyer-Benfey, Heinrich – (Includes bibliographical references and index) – Goettingen: O Hapke, 1911-13 – 1 – us U.W. Library [430]

A DRAMA IN MUSLIN : A REALISTIC NOVEL / Moore, George – London: Vizetelly & Co., 1886 – 1 roll – 1 – 1-55879-686-X – uk Libr Preservation [830]

DRAMA NEGERI DI PARANG TRITIS – SE-4330 1 – 9 – ne IDC [950]

THE DRAMA OF SPAIN FROM THE PROCLAMATION OF THE REPUBLIC TO THE CIVIL WAR, 1931-36 / Ramos-Oliveira, Antonio – London, 1936? Fiche W1127. (Blodgett Collection of Spanish Civil War Pamphlets) – 9 – us H.U. College Libr [946]

THE DRAMA OF THE APOCALYPSE IN RELATION TO THE LITERARY AND POLITICAL CIRCUMSTANCES OF ITS TIME / Palmer, Frederic – (Includes appendix) – New York: Macmillan, 1903 – 1mf – 9 – 0-8370-4659-9 – 1985-2659 – us A.T.L.A. [220]

DRAMA OF THE NINETEENTH CENTURY – Ed. by Profs. James Ellis and Joe Donohue. Monthly – 3,9 – us Readex [420]

DRAMA ON THE WORLD STAGE: PROMPT BOOKS AND PERFORMANCE RECORDS, 1608-1926 – Series 1: The Folger Shakespeare Library, Washington, DC – 1 – us Primary [790]

DRAMA REVIEW – (1972-. 5,6. 1976-. 9) – v. 1- 1955- – 1 – us UMI [790]

DAS DRAMA RICHARD WAGNER'S : EINE ANREGUNG / Chamberlain, Houston Stewart – 3. Aufl. Leipzig: Breitkopf & Haertel, 1908 – 1r – 1 – us U.W. Library [790]

DRAMA V INDONEZII / Hnilicky, Martin – 1966 – 9 – SE-6373 1 – ne IDC [490]

DAS DRAMA ZACHARIAS WERNERS : ENTWICKLUNG UND LITERATURGESCHICHTLICHE STELLUNG / Stuckert, Franz – (Includes bibliographical references) – Frankfurt am Main: M Diesterweg, 1926 – 1 – us U.W. Library [430]

THE DRAMAS AND DRAMATIC DANCES OF NON-EUROPEAN RACES IN SPECIAL REFERENCE TO THE ORIGIN OF GREEK TRAGEDY.. / Ridgeway, William – With an appendix on the origin of Greek comedy. Cambridge: The University Press, 1915. xv,448p. illus – 1 – us U.W. Library [450]

DRAMATIC AND MUSICAL LAW. / Strong, Albert Ambrose – London, "The Era," 1898. 155 p. LL-129 – 1 – us L of C Photodup [340]

DRAMATIC IDYLS / Browning, Robert – London: Smith, Elder, 1879 – 1 roll – 1 – 1-55879-184-1 – uk Libr Preservation [820]

DRAMATIC MIRROR – New York. v1-85. 1879-1922 – 35r – 1 – us Ross [790]

DRAMATIC SPECTATOR – n1-10. 1837 – 1r – 1 – us Ross [790]

DRAMATIC TIMES – London. -w. Feb-Sep 1895, Apr-Jul 1919. (1 reel) – 1 – uk British Libr Newspaper [790]

THE DRAMATIC WORKS OF SAMUEL TAYLOR COLERIDGE / Coleridge, Samuel Taylor; ed by Coleridge, Derwent – London: E. Moxon, 1852 – 1 roll – 1 – 1-55879-347-X – uk Libr Preservation [820]

DRAMATICHESKII SBORNIK – Spb. 1858-62. Lacking: 1858 59 (5-6); 1859 (8-10, 12); 1860 (1-12); 1862 (7-12). B-1711 2 – 8 – ne IDC [460]

DRAMATICHESKII SLOVAR' – (1787). Spb. 1880. BR-6020/2 – 3mf – 8 – ne IDC [460]

DRAMATIS PERSONAE / Browning, Robert – London: Chapman and Hall, 1864 – 1 roll – 1 – 1-55879-183-3 – uk Libr Preservation [820]

DRAMATISCHE DICHTUNGEN : ERNST VON SCHWABEN; LUDWIG DER BAIER / Uhland, Ludwig – Heidelberg: C F Winter, 1846 – 1r – 1 – us U.W. Library [810]

DRAMATISCHE EINDRUECKE : AUS DEM NACHLASSE / Auerbach, Berthold – (Includes index) – Stuttgart: J G Cotta, 1893 – 1r – 1 – us U.W. Library [430]

DRAMATISCHE ELEMENTE IN HEBBELS JUGENDBALLADEN, 1829-1839 : EINE STUDIE ZUR ENTWICKLUNGSGESCHICHTE FRIEDRICH HEBBELS / Jahn, Walter – (Includes bibliographical references) – Halle: H John, 1915 – 1r – 1 – us U.W. Library [430]

DIE DRAMATISCHE HANDLUNG IN GERHART HAUPTMANNS WEBERN / Rabl, Hans – (Includes bibliographical references) – Halle (Saale): M Niemeyer, 1928 – 1r – 1 – us U.W. Library [430]

DIE DRAMATISCHE HANDLUNG IN KLOPSTOCKS "DER TOD ADAMS" UND GERSTENBERGS "UGOLINO" / Dollinger, Hermann – (Includes bibliographical references) – Halle: Niemeyer, 1930 – 1r – 1 – us U.W. Library [790]

DIE DRAMATISCHE HANDLUNG IN SOPHOKLES' "KOENIG OIDIPUS" UND KLEISTS "DER ZERBROCHENE KRUG" / Gordon, Wolff von – Halle: M Niemeyer, 1926 – 1r – 1 – us U.W. Library [430]

DRAMATISCHE HANDLUNG UND AUFBAU IN HEBBELS HERODES UND MARIAMNE / Weichenmayr, Franz – (Includes bibliographical references) – Halle (Saale): M Niemeyer, 1929 – 1r – 1 – us U.W. Library [430]

DIE DRAMATISCHEN VERSUCHE DES JUNGEN GRILLPARZER : AUF IHRE ENTSTEHUNG GEPRUEFT UND IN ZUSAMMENHANG GEBRACHT MIT DER INNEREN ENTWICKELUNG DES DICHTERS / Keidel, Heinrich – (Includes bibliographical references) – Muenster i.W.: Theissing, 1911 – 1r – 1 – us U.W. Library [430]

DRAMATISCHES / Gugler, Julius – Milwaukee: Selbstverlag des Verfassers, c1892 – 1r – 1 – us U.W. Library [830]

DRAMATISIS OF THE RESTORATION / ed by Maidment, James & Logan, William Hugh – Edinburgh u. London, 1872-1979 – 5332p on 66mf – 9 – DM330.00 diazo DM400.00 silver – gw Olms [420]

DRAMATURGISCHE BLAETTER *see* DAS MAGAZIN

LE DRAME DE DANKORI : MISSION VOULET-CHANOINE, MISSION JOALLAND-MEYNIER / Joalland, Jules – Paris: Editions Argo, [1930] – 1 – us Res Libr [960]

LE DRAME LYRIQUE D'ALEXANDRE BLOK / Bonneau, S – Paris, 1946 – 8 – ne IDC [460]

DRAMENFORMEN DES BAROCK : DIE FUNKTION VON ROLLEN, REYEN UND BUEHNE BEI JOH. CHR. HALLMANN (1640-1704) / Beheim-Schwarzbach, Eberhard – (Includes bibliographical references) – Jena: [s.n.], 1931 – 1r – 1 – us U.W. Library [430]

DRAMES DE LA VIE REELE : GRAND ROMAN CANADIEN / Barthe, Georges Isidore – s.l., s.n, 1896. SEM105P378 – 1mf – 9 – Can$2.25 – cn Bibl Nat [830]

DRAMES DE LA VIE REELLE: ROMAN CANADIEN / Barthe, Georges Isidore – Quebec: J. Chenevert, c1896. 03023. (Pre-1900 Canadiana) – 9 – cn C.I.H.M. [830]

DRAMMATURGIA. ACCRESCIUTA E CONTINUATA FINO ALL'ANNO 1755 / Allacci, L – P-126. 1755 – 9 – ne IDC [440]

DRAMY I POEMY ALEKSANDRA BLOKA / Medvedev, P – Pisatelei v Leningrade. L. 1928. BR-1419 2 – 8 – ne IDC [460]

Drane, Augusta Theodosia *see*
- THE HISTORY OF ST. DOMINIC
- THE MORALITY OF TRACTARIANISM
- THE THREE CHANCELLORS, OR, SKETCHES OF THE LIVES OF WILLIAM OF WYKEHAM, WILLIAM OF WAYNFLETE, AND SIR THOMAS MORE

Dranitsyn, Sergei Nikanorovich *see*
- KONSTITUTSII A ROSSI ISKO I SOTSIALISTICHESKO I FEDERATIVNO I SOVETSKO I RESPUBLIKI V OTVETAKH NA VOPROSY

Draparnaud, Jacques PR *see* HISTOIRE NATURELLE DES MOLLUSQUES TERRESTRES ET FLUVIATILES DE LA FRANCE.

LE DRAPEAU – Chicoutimi. v1 n4. 8 mai 1916-19 mai 1916 – 1r – 1 – Can$25.00 – cn Can Microfilming [072]

LE DRAPEAU – Montreal, Canada. 15 fev 1914-15 jun 1914 – 1r – 1 – Can$25.00 – cn Can Microfilming [072]

LE DRAPEAU – Paris, France. -w. 29 Dec 1881-25 Dec 1886. 3 reels – 1 – uk British Libr Newspaper [072]

LE DRAPEAU : REVUE – Montreal, Canada. sep-dec 1889 – 1r – 1 – Can$25.00 – cn Can Microfilming [073]

LE DRAPEAU – Revue hebdomadaire illustree. Tir, gymnastique, secours aux blesses, sauvetage, escrime, equitation, histoire militaire, etc. Paris. Le sous-titre et la periodicite varient. 29 dec 1881-88, 1898-99, 11 mai-9 dec 1901, 1917-20 nov 1927, 31 oct 1930, 20 sept 1931, 1932, mars-nov 1933, mai-nov 1935 – 1 – fr A.C.R.P.P. [073]

LE DRAPEAU – Port-au-Prince: [s.n.], aug 14-nov 6, dec 6-13, 1897 – 2r – 9 – us Res Libr [072]

LE DRAPEAU BLANC – Dir. Martainville. Paris. 16 juin 1819-1er fevr 1827, 1er juin 1829-28 juil 1830. A paru sous le titre: Democrate. 1er juin-15 juil 1829 – 1 – fr A.C.R.P.P. [073]

LE DRAPEAU DE CANADA / Derennes, Gustave – Illustrations de F. Masse. Paris: Libairie Picard, 18??. 04226. (Pre-1900 Canadiana) – 9 – cn C.I.H.M. [971]

LE DRAPEAU DE LEVIS – Levis, Canada. 3 nov 1864-v1 n1. 24 nov 1864 – 1r – 1 – Can$25.00 – cn Can Microfilming [072]

LE DRAPEAU DE L'UNION – Bulletin interieur de l'Union de la jeunesse democratique algerienne. no. 1-2. Alger. avr 1953-janv fevr 1954 – 1 – fr A.C.R.P.P. [073]

Drapeau, Julien *see* ESSAI DE BIBLIOGRAPHIE SUR LE REGIME MUNICIPAL DANS LA PROVINCE DE QUEBEC

LE DRAPEAU LIBERAL – Montreal, Canada. 9 dec 1893 – 1r – 1 – Can$25.00 – cn Can Microfilming [072]

LE DRAPEAU NATIONAL – Ottawa, Ontario. 28 fev 1891-v1 n4. 4 mar 1891 – 1r – 1 – Can$25.00 – cn Can Microfilming [072]

LE DRAPEAU NATIONAL – Windsor, Ontario. nov 1891; v1 n9. 29 avr 1892 – 1r – 1 – Can$30.00 – cn Can Microfilming [072]

LE DRAPEAU NATIONAL – Port-au-Prince: [s.n.], dec 21-dec 24?, 1877; jan 11-mar 8, apr 5-aug 16, 1878; jan 11, feb 5-21, 1879 – 2r – 9 – us Res Libr [072]

DRAPEAU ROUGE – Journal communiste puis marxiste revolutionnaire. Red. en chef Andre Ferrat. no. 1. n.s., no. 16 33. Paris. 11 dec 1936-1er sept 1937 – 1 – fr A.C.R.P.P. [073]

LE DRAPEAU ROUGE – Brussels. Belgium. -w. 6 Sep 1944-9 Aug 1946, 1 Jan 1947-2 Jan 1948. (6 reels) – 1 – uk British Libr Newspaper [949]

Drapeau, Stanislas *see*
- BIOGRAPHIE DE SIR N.F. BELLEAU: CHEVALIER COMMANDEUR DE L'ORDRE DE SAINT-MICHEL ET DE SAINT-GEORGES, ET PREMIER LIEUTENANT-GOUVERNEUR DE LA PROVINCE DE QUEBEC, SOUS LA CONFEDERATION DES PROVINCES DE L'AMERIQUE DU NORD
- CANADA: LE GUIDE DU COLON FRANCAIS, BELGE, SUISSE, ETC.: BROCHURE PREPAREE ET PUBLIEE
- COMMERCIAL COURIER/COURRIER COMMERCIAL
- HISTOIRE DES INSTITUTIONS DE CHARITE DE BIENFAISANCE ET D'EDUCATION DU CANADA: DEPUIS LEUR FONDATION JUSQU'A NOS JOURS
- LE JOURNAL DE QUEBEC ET LE TOMBEAU DE CHAMPLAIN

DRAPELUL ROSU – Timisoara, Romania. 1962-1985 – 33r – 1 – us L of C Photodup [949]

Draper Collection *see* MANUSCRIPTS

Draper, John William *see*
- HISTORY OF THE CONFLICT BETWEEN RELIGION AND SCIENCE
- HISTORY OF THE INTELLECTUAL DEVELOPMENT OF EUROPE

DRAPER MANUSCRIPT, 24 NOV. 1842-27 OCT. 1869 / Peck, J M & Piggott, Isaac N & Reynolds, J – 364p – 1 – us Baptist [240]

THE DRAPER MANUSCRIPTS – (Pts available separately. Also listed individually) – 123r – 1 – £7,115.00 coll – uk Chadwyck [090]

DRAPER OF AUSTRALASIA – Sydney, Australia. 27 Jul 1903-10 Feb 1965.-w. 68 reels – 1 – uk British Libr Newspaper [072]

Draper, Warwick Herbert *see* ALFRED THE GREAT: A SKETCH AND SEVEN STUDIES

Draper, William George *see* THE RULES OF THE COURTS OF QUEEN'S BENCH AND COMMON PLEAS, THE MUNICIPAL COUNCIL RULES, THE COUNTY COURTS' EQUITY EXTENSION AND THE NEW DIVISION COURT RULES.

DRAPER'S UPPER CANADA KING'S BENCH REPORTS / Ontario. Canada – 1v. 1829-31 (all publ) – 6mf – 9 – $9.00 – LLMC 81-043 – us L.L.M.C. [340]

DIE DRAU – Osijek, Yugoslavia. Oct 1923-Jun 1928; Jun 1932-Nov 1933 (scattered issues) – 5r – 1 – us L of C Photodup [949]

DRAUGAS = LITHUANIAN DAILY FRIEND – Chicago, IL: Draugas Pub Co Inc, [jul-dec 1909; 21 nov 1917-17 jul 1929; jan-apr 15 1931; 1936; 1940; jul 1945-1955] – 1 – us Res Libr [071]

DRAUGAS / Wilkes-Barre: Draugas, 1909-1916 – 1r – us Res Libr [072]

THE DRAVIDIAN ELEMENT IN INDIAN CULTURE / Slater, Gilbert – Foreward by H.J. Fleure.London: E. Benn, 1924 – 1 – us U.W. Library [900]

DRAVIDIAN GODS IN MODERN HINDUISM.. / Elmore, Wilber T – 1915 – 1 – us A.T.L.A. [280]

Drawert, Ernst Arno *see* MOERIKES MALER NOLTEN

DRAWINGS : SUBJECT COLLECTIONS – (Individual titles not listed separately) – 241 catalogues on 284mf – 9 – £1,490.00 – uk Chadwyck [700]

DRAWINGS AND PLANS FOR HOLKHAM HALL, NORFOLK / Kent, William – c. 1729 – 1 – uk Microform Academic [720]

DRAWINGS AND SPECIFICATIONS / Mills, Robert – ca.1804. Proposal for a Protestant Episcopal church bldg. for John's Island, SC. 1 fiche – 9 – us South Carolina Historical [720]

DRAWINGS AND WATERCOLOURS / Turner, John Mallord William – In the Fitzwilliam Museum, Cambridge – 14 – uk Microform Academic [740]

DRAWINGS IN PROVINCIAL AND OTHER MUSEUMS / Caisse Nationale des Monuments Historiques et des Sites. Paris – (Over 7,500 reproductions) – 126mf – 9 – $635.00 – 0-907006-70-1 – uk Mindata [740]

DRAWINGS IN THE LOUVRE AND NATIONAL MUSEUMS / Caisse Nationale des Monuments Historiques et des Sites. Paris – (Over 7,500 reproductions) – 128mf – 9 – $650.00 – 0-907006-65-5 – uk Mindata [740]

DRAWINGS OF ARACEAE / Schott, H W – (The microfiches are supplied in a single plastic binder, kept together with the printed book by D.H. Nicolson: H.W. Schott. Icones Aroideae et Reliquiae. Alphabetical Index. Zug, 1984, iv, 29p) – Vienna – 123mf – 9 – 8801/1 – ne IDC [580]

DRAWINGS OF JOHAN TOBIAS SERGEL / Nationalmuseum, Stockholm; ed by Bjurstrom, Per – (68p accompanying text) – 1979 – 1 color 3 b/w mf – 15 – $48.00f – 0-226-69420-8 – us Chicago [740]

THE DRAWINGS OF RAPHAEL IN THE ASHMOLEAN MUSEUM / Ashmolean Museum. – (The largest and most representative collection of Raphael's drawings. With printed index) – 1986 – 4 colour mf – 15 – $140.00 – 0-907716-12-1 – uk Mindata [740]

THE DRAWINGS OF ROBERT AND JAMES ADAM IN SIR JOHN SOANE'S MUSEUM / London. Sir John Soane's Museum – (Includes catalogue 1r £63.00) – 2r col + 10r b/w – 1 – £1,380.00 – uk Chadwyck [740]

Drayton Family *see* MISCELLANEOUS RECORDS

Drayton, John *see*
- CAROLINIAN FLORIST
- A VIEW OF SOUTH CAROLINA

DRAYTON VALLEY WESTERN REVIEW – Drayton Valley, Alberta, CN. 1980-89 – 25r – 1 – cn Commonwealth Micro [072]

Drayton, William *see* JUDICIAL DIARY

DRAZA MIHAILOVICH PAMPHLET COLLECTION – 1945?-1971? – 1 – CSUXANQ5677-B – us Hoover Inst Photo [949]

DRC (DUTCH REFORMED CHURCH) AFRICA NEWS – v1-10. 1976-85 (complete) – 1r – 1 – ATLA S0786 – us A.T.L.A. [073]

THE DREAD VOYAGE: POEMS / Campbell, Wilfred – Toronto: W. Briggs; Montreal: C. W. Coates; Halifax: S. F. Huestis, 1893. 00407. (Pre-1900 Canadiana) – 9 – cn C.I.H.M. [810]

A DREAM: DESERTED: AND THE FROLICSOME SNOW / Branson, Isaac Reichelderfer – Toronto: W. Briggs, 1899. 00246. (Pre-1900 Canadiana) – 9 – cn C.I.H.M. [830]

THE DREAM OF DANTE / Henderson, Henry F – 1903 – 9 – us A.T.L.A. [240]

A DREAM OF JOHN BALL; AND, A KING'S LESSON / Morris, William – London: Reeves & Turner, 1888 – 1 roll – 1 – 1-55879-589-8 – uk Libr Preservation [830]

DREAM PSYCHOLOGY / Nicoll, Maurice – 2nd ed. London: H. Frowde; Hodder & Stoughton, 1920. xv,194p – 1 – us U.W. Library [150]

DREAMERS OF THE GHETTO / Zangwill, Israel – New York, London: Harper & Brothers, 1898 – 1 roll – 1 – 1-55879-710-6 – uk Libr Preservation [830]

DREAMS / Bergson, Henri – New York: B.W. Huebsch, 1914 – 1mf – us A.T.L.A. [240]

DREAMWORKS – 1980 – 1,5,6,9 – us UMI [073]

Drechsler, Moritz *see* DIE UNWISSENSCHAFTLICHKEIT IM GEBIETE DER ALTTESTAMENTLICHEN KRITIK

Dreesen, Willrath *see* ROMANTISCHE ELEMENTE BEI THEODOR STORM

DREI ABHANDLUNGEN ZUR GESCHICHTE DER ALTEN PHILOSOPHIE UND IHRES VERHAELTNISSES ZUM CHRISTENTUM / Baur, Ferdinand Christian; ed by Zeller, Eduard – Leipzig: Fues, 1876 – 2mf – us A.T.L.A. [240]

DREI ACTENSTUECKE ZUR GESCHICHTE DES DONATISMUS / Deutsch, Martin – Berlin: W. Weber, 1875 – 1mf – us A.T.L.A. [240]

DIE DREI BRIEFE DES APOSTEL JOHANNES / Weiss, Bernhard – Goettingen: Vandenhoeck & Rup., 1899. 1 fiche – 9 – us A.T.L.A. [240]

DREI BRIEFE DES APOSTELS JOHANNES = THE EPISTLES GENERAL OF JOHN / Braune, Karl – (In English. Includes bibliographies) – New York: Charles Scribner, c1867 – 1mf – 9 – 0-8370-6724-3 – 1986-0724 – us A.T.L.A. [220]

DIE DREI ERSTEN KAPITEL DES ROEMERBRIEFS / Bleibtrau, Walter – Goettingen: Vandenhoeck & Rup., 1884 – 9 – us A.T.L.A. [240]

DIE DREI FASSUNGEN VON WIELANDS AGATHON / Freise, Otto – (Includes bibliographical references) – Goettingen: W Fr Kaestner, 1910 – 1 – us U.W. Library [430]

DIE DREI FASSUNGEN VON WIELANDS AGATHON / Freise, Otto – (Includes bibliographical references) – Goettingen: W Fr Kaestner, 1910 – 1r – 1 – us U.W. Library [430]

DREI FEDERN / Raabe, Wilhelm Karl – 2. Aufl. Berlin: Otto Janke, 1895 – 1r – 1 – us U.W. Library [830]

DREI FRAUEN : NOVELLEN / Musil, Robert – Zuerich: Pegasus Verlag, 1944 – 1r – 1 – us U.W. Library [830]

DREI GEORGISCH ERHALTENE SCHRIFTEN VON HIPPOLYTUS : DER SEGEN JAKOBS, DER SEGEN MOSES, DIE ERZAEHLUNG VON DAVID UND GOLIATH (T.U.U. 2-26/1A) / Bonwetsch, G N – Leipzig, 1904 – 2mf – 9 – ne Slangenburg [240]

DIE DREI GERECHTEN KAMMACHER / Keller, Gottfried – Stuttgart: J G Cotta'sche Buchhandlung Nachfolger, [1903] – 1 – us U.W. Library [830]

DREI GOETHE-REDEN / Koch, Franz – (Includes bibliography of the author's works) – Weimar: H Boehlau, 1932 – 1r – 1 – us U.W. Library [430]

DIE DREI LACHENDEN GESCHICHTEN / Grimm, Hans – Muenchen: A Langen/G Mueller, 1939 – 1r – 1 – us U.W. Library [830]

DIE DREI MOTIVE UND GRUENDE DES GLAUBENS / Fechner, Gustav Theodor – Leipzig: Breitkopf und Haertel, 1863 – 1mf – us A.T.L.A. [240]

DREI PSYCHOLOGISCHE FRAGEN ZUR SPANISCHEN THRONKANDIDATUR LEOPOLDS VON HOHENZOLLERN, MIT GEHEIMDEPESCHEN BISMARCKS / Hesselbarth, Hermann – Leipzig: B.G. Teubner, 1913. 130p – 1 – us U.W. Library [920]

DREI REDEN JAKOB GRIMMS : FRIEDRICH SCHILLER; UEBER DAS ALTER; WILHELM GRIMM / Grimm, Jacob; ed by Mendheim, Max – Leipzig: P Reclam, [19–?] – 1r – 1 – us U.W. Library [850]

DREI SCHAUSPIELE VOM STERBENDEN MENSCHEN : DAS MUENCHNER SPIEL VON 1510; MACROPEDIUS, HECASTUS, 1539; [UND] NAOGEORGUS, MERCATOR, 1540 / ed by Bolte, Johannes – (First play and editorial matter in German; the other plays in Latin. Includes bibliographical references) – Leipzig: K W Hiersemann, 1927 – 1 – us U.W. Library [820]

DIE DREI URSPRUENGLICHEN, NOCH UNGESCHRIEBENEN EVANGELIEN : ZUR SYNOPTISCHEN FRAGE / Holsten, Carl – Karlsruhe, 1883 – 2mf – 8 – ne Slangenburg [220]

DREI WENIG BEACHTETE CYPRIANISCHE SCHRIFTEN UND DIE "ACTA PAULI" (T.U.U. 2-19/3B) / Harnack, Adolf von – Leipzig, 1899 – 1mf – 9 – ne Slangenburg [240]

Dreier, Vladimir Nikolaevich fon *see* KRESTNYI PUT VOIMIA RODINY

DREIGUDS UN NOSCHENS / Fuchs, Meik – Milwaukee, Wis.: M H Wiltzius, 1898 – 1r – 1 – us U.W. Library [830]

DREIHEIT UND DREIFACHE WIEDERHOLUNG IM DEUTSCHEN VOLKSMAERCHEN : EIN BEITRAG ZUR TECHNIK DES MAERCHENS UEBERHAUPT / Lehmann, Alfred – Leipzig, 1914 – 1mf – DM48.00 – 3-8267-3106-9 – gw Hänsel [390]

DREISSIG JAHRE PROTESTANTISCHER MISSION IN JAPAN = A HISTORY OF PROTESTANT MISSIONS IN JAPAN / Ritter, H; ed by Greene, Daniel Crosby – (In English) – Tokyo: Methodist Pub House, 1898 – 2mf – 9 – 0-8370-6771-5 – 1986-0771 – us A.T.L.A. [240]

Dreisziger, N F *see* MOBILIZATION FOR TOTAL WAR

DREIZEHNLINDEN / Weber, Friedrich Wilhelm – 120. Aufl. Paderborn: F Schoningh, 1904 – 1 – us U.W. Library [890]

Drelincourt, C *see*
- AVERTISSEMENT SUR LES DISPUTES ET LE PROCEDE DES MISSIONNAIRES
- DIALOGUES FAMILIERS SUR LES PRINCIPALES OBJECTIONS DES MISSIONNAIRES DE CE TEMPS
- TRAITTE DES IUSTES CAUSES DE LA SEPARATION DES PROTESTANS D'AVEC L'EGLISE ROMAINE

Drelincourt, L *see* DEUS SERMONS SUR LA PAIX...

Dremina, G A *see*
- IZ ISTORII TSENTRAL'NOGO GOSUDARSTVENNOGO ARKHIVA DREVNIKH AKTOV SSSR
- TSENTRAL'NYI GOSUDARSTVENNYI ISTORICHESKII ARKHIV SSSR V G. LENINGRADE. UCHEBNOE POSOBIE

Dremsa, Catherine J *see* HANDRAIL SUPPORT VERSUS FREE ARM WING TREADMILL FITNESS TEST

Drennan, Meredith L *see* INCENTIVE MOTIVATION OF FEMALE BASKETBALL PLAYERS ACROSS THREE AGE LEVELS

[DRESDEN: PAMPHLET COLLECTION] – 1985? – 1 – CSUXANS9171-B – us Hoover Inst Photo [943]

DIE DRESDENER ROMANTIK UND HEINRICH VON KLEIST / Luetteken, Anton – (Includes bibliographical references) – [S.l.: s.n.], 1917 – 1r – 1 – us U.W. Library [430]

DRESDNER NACHRICHTEN – Dresden, Germany. -d. 1 Sept 1916-8 Aug 1919. Imperfect. 15 reels – 1 – uk British Libr Newspaper [072]

DRESDNER VOLKSZEITUNG *see* SAECHSISCHE ARBEITER-ZEITUNG

Dresner, Edgar *see* BAGAIMANA MENGETAHUI SERANGGA2 PERTANIAN

DRESS & VANITY FAIR *see* VANITY FAIR

Dresser, Frank Farnum *see* THE EMPLOYERS' LIABILITY ACTS AND THE ASSUMPTION OF RISKS IN NEW YORK, MASSACHUSETTS, INDIANA, ALABAMA, COLORADO, AND ENGLAND

Dresser, H E *see*
- EGGS OF THE BIRDS OF EUROPE
- A HISTORY OF THE BIRDS OF EUROPE

Dresser, Horatio W *see* HEALTH AND THE INNER LIFE

Dressler, E C *see* FRAGMENTE EINIGER GEDANKEN DES MUSIKALISCHEN ZUSCHAUERS DIE BESSERE AUFNAME DER MUSIK IN DEUTSCHLAND BETREFFEND

Dreves, G M *see*
- ANALECTA HYMNICA MEDII AEVI
- EIN JAHRTAUSEND LATEINISCHER HYMNENDICHTUNG

Dreves, Guido Maria *see* CANTIONES BOHEMICAE

DREVNE RUSSKAIA MINIATIURA / Vladimirov, M & Georgievskii, G P – M. 1933. BR-10,069 1 – 9 – ne IDC [490]

DREVNEE RUSSKOE PORUCHITEL'STVO / Kapustin, S Ia – Kazan, 1955. 64p. Inquiry into the institution of guarantee in ancient Russian law. BR-9745/1 – 9 – ne IDC [340]

DREVNE-RUSSKIE RUKOPISI PUSHKINSKOGO DOMA (OBZOR FONDOV) – V.I. Malyshev, comp. Moscow, Leningrad, 1965. 230p. BR-10,961/1 – 9 – ne IDC [460]

DREVNIAIA I NOVAIA ROSSIIA – Illiustrirovannyi ezhemesiachnyi istoricheskii sbornik. v. 1. Spb. 1875-81. B-1712 2 – 8 – ne IDC [073]

DREVNIAIA I NOVAIA ROSSIIA: SISTEMATICHESKII UKAZATEL' STATEI – 1875-1881. St. Petersburg, 1893 – 1 – us NY Public [073]

DREVNIAIA ISTORIIA IUZHNOI SIBIRI / Kiselev, S V – Ed. 2. M. 1951. BU-515 2 – 8 – ne IDC [947]

DREVNIAIA ROSSIISKAIA VIVLIOFIKA, IZDANNAIA NIKOLAEM NOVIKOVYM – v. 1-10. Spb. 1773-75. BR-286 2 – 8 – ne IDC [947]

DREVNIAIA RUSSKAIA ISTORIIA DO MONGOL'SKAGO IGA / Pogodin, M P – M. 1871. BR-8303 2 – 8 – ne IDC [947]

DREVNIE ROSSIISKIE STIKHOTVORENIIA, SOBRANNYE KIRSHEIU DANILOVYM – Izd. Akademii nauk SSR. M., L. 1958. BR-6144 2 – 8 – ne IDC [947]

DREVNII SLAVIANSKII PEREVOD PSALTYRI. IZSLEDOVANIE EGO TEKSTA I IAZYKA PO RUKOPISIAM 11-14 V / Sreznevskii, 6 – St. Petersburg, 1877. BR-10,063/2 – 8 – ne IDC [460]

DREVNIIA RUSSKIIA KNIAZHESTVA S 1054 PO 1240 GOD / Pogodin, M P – Spb. 1848. BR-8302 2 – 8 – ne IDC [947]

DREVNOSTI – Moskow. v1-25. 1865-1916 – 403mf – 8 – ne IDC [930]

DREVNOSTI – Trudy Komissii po sokhranenii drevnikh pamiatnikov Moskovskogo arkheologicheskogo obshchestva. Moscow, 1907-15, v1-6. B/1428/2 – 8 – ne IDC [930]

DREVNOSTI : TRUDY MOSKOVSKOGO ARKHEOLOGICHESKOGO OBSHCHESTVA – M. v1-25. 1865-1916 – 403mf – 9 – ne IDC [930]

DREVNOSTI – Trudy Slavianskoi Kommissi Moskovskago arkheologicheskago obshchestva. v. 1-5. M. 1895-1911. B-1219 2 – 8 – ne IDC [930]

DREVNOSTI GERODOTOVOI SKIFII; SBORNIK – v. 1-2. Spb. 1866-72. BR-3357 2 – 8 – ne IDC [073]

DREVNOSTI ROSSIISKAGO GOSUDARSTVA, IZDANNYIA PO VYSOCHAISHEMY POVELENIIU – M. 1849-53. BR-10,060 1 – 9 – ne IDC [460]

DREVNOSTI VOSTOCHNYIA – Trudy Vostochnoi Kommissii arkheologicheskago obshchestva. v. 1-5. M. 1889-1915. B-1220 2 – 8 – ne IDC [930]

Drews, Arthur *see*
- DER IDEENGEHALT VON RICHARD WAGNERS DRAMATISCHEN DICHTUNGEN
- THE WITNESSES TO THE HISTORICITY OF JESUS

Drews, Paul *see*
- BEITRAEGE ZU LUTHERS LITURGISCHEN REFORMEN
- DAS KIRCHLICHE LEBEN DER EVANGELISCH-LUTHERISCHEN LANDESKIRCHE DES KOENIGREICHS SACHSEN
- PETRUS CANISIUS
- UNTERSUCHUNGEN UEBER DIE SOGEN. CLEMENTINISCHE LITURGIE IM 8. BUCH DER APOSTOLISCHEN KONSTITUTIONEN
- WILIBALD PIRKHEIMERS STELLUNG ZUR REFORMATION
- ZUR ENTSTEHUNGSGESCHICHTE DES KANONS IN DER ROEMISCHEN MESSE

Drexelius, H *see* DE SONNE-BLOEME, OFTE OVEREENKOMINGE VAN DEN MENSCHELIJKEN WILLE MET DEN GODTLIJCKEN

DREY CHRISTLICHE VND IN GOTTES WORT VND DER ALTEN LEHRER SCHRIFFTEN WOLGEGRUENDTE PREDIGTEN / Gedik, S – Magdeburg, 1591 – 2mf – ne IDC [240]

DREY SCHRIFFTEN: 1. PROTESTATION SAMUEL HUBERS DOCTOR VND PROFESSORS DER H. SCHRIFFT ZU WITTEMBERG : WIDER JOHAN WILHELM STUCK D. JOHAN JACOB GRYNEUM JOHAN JETZLERN WELCHE FUER ABRAHAM MAEUSSLEIN VND PETER HYBENER IN JRER LEGATION ZU BERN HABEN FALSCHE KUNDTSCHAFFT GEREDT... / Huber, S – Wittemberg, 1593 – 1mf – ne IDC [240]

DREY SONATEN DEN LIEBHABERN DES KLAVIERS VERFERTIGET VON JOHANN CHRISTOPH RITTER...ERSTER THEIL [OP.1] / Ritter, J – Nuernberg: J U Haffner, (178-?] – 1 – us Sibley [780]

DREY UND DREISSIG PREDIGEN VON DEN FUERNEMMSTEN SPALTUNGEN IN DER CHRISTLICHEN RELIGION / Andree, J – Th.I-V. Von newen widerumb vbersehen vnd mit 6 Predigen gemehret. Tuebingen. 1573. BME-138 1 – 9 – ne IDC [240]

DREY VND DREISSIG PREDIGEN VON DEN FUERNEMBSTEN SPALTUNGEN IN DER CHRISTLICHEN RELIGION... / Andreae d.A E, J – Tuebingen, 1568 – 10mf – 9 – ne IDC [240]

Dreyer, Aloys *see*
- FRANZ VON KOBELL

Dreyer, J L E *see* TYCHO BRAHE'S SCIENTIFIC ACHIEVEMENTS

Dreyer, Karl *see*
- DIE RELIGIOESE GEDANKENWELT DES SALOMO IBN GABIROL

Dreyer, Otto *see*
- UNDOGMATISCHES CHRISTENTUM
- ZUR UNDOGMATISCHEN GLAUBENSLEHRE: VORTRAEGE UND ABHANDLUNGEN

THE DREYFUS AFFAIR – 1996 – ca 60r – 1 – us Primary [944]

Dreyfus, Alfred *see*
- L'AFFAIRE DREYFUS
- LA REVISION DU PROCES DREYFUS

Dreyfus, D.Levi-Strauss, C. *see* ETHNOGRAPHIE BORORO, OBJETS PROVENANT DU VILLAGE DE KEJARA (BRESIL)

Dreyfuss, Robert H *see* TECHNOLOGY AND COPYRIGHT: SOURCES AND MATERIALS

DREYHUNDERT AUSERLESENE AMERIKANISCHE GEWAECHSE NACH LINNEISCHER ORDNUNG / Jacquin, N J von – v. 1-3. Nuernberg. 1785-88. B-1190 2 – 8 – ne IDC [580]

Drezen, A K *see* BURZHAZIIA I POMESHCHIKI V 1917 GODU

DRIED SALTED MEATS : CHARQUE AND CARNE-DE-SOL – 1985 – 35p – it F.A.O. [636]

Driesch, Hans *see* THE PROBLEM OF INDIVIDUALITY

Driessen, Helmut *see* ERMITTLUNG VON GRUNDLAGEN ZUR ULTRAFILTRATION

DRIFT DODGER – Arcata, CA. 1982-1988 – 1r – 1 – $50.00 – B05026 – us Library Micro [071]

DRIFTED IN / Carleton, Will – New York: Moffat, Yard and Co., 1908 – 1 – us U.W. Library [830]

DRIFTNET FISHERIES AND THEIR IMPACTS ON NON-TARGET SPECIES : A WORLDWIDE REVIEW – 1991 – 122p – it F.A.O. [639]

Drijarkara, N *see*
- PERTJIKAN FILSAFAT
- SOSIALITAS SEBAGAI EKSISTENSIAL

DRILL AND RIFLE INSTRUCTION FOR THE CORPS OF RIFLE VOLUNTEERS – Quebec: printed by Stewart Derbishire and George Desbarats, 1862. SEM105P1791 – 2mf – 9 – Can$4.50 – cn Bibl Nat [355]

DRILL BIT – v33-34. 1984-85 – 1,5,6,9 – us UMI [073]

Drinker, Henry Sandwith *see* LEGAL ETHICS

Drinkwater-Bethune, C R *see* SIR RICHARD HAWKINS: OBSERVATIONS IN HIS VOYAGE INTO THE SOUTH SEAS, 1593

Drinov, M S *see*
- ISTORIKCHESKI PREGLED NA BULGARSKATA TS'RKVA
- SACHINENIIA

DRISCHATH ZION ODER ZIONS HERSTELLUNG / Kalischer, H – Ed. 2. Berlin. 1905. BJ-72-506 1 – 9 – ne IDC [956]

DRITA – 1976- – 1r per y – 1 – inquire – us Ross [072]

DRITA – 1976-1995 – 1 – sz Infoprint [072]

DRITA – Albanien, 1976-1992ff – 17r – 1 – DM1,275.00 – gw Mikro Press [949]

DAS DRITTE GESCHLECHT – Berlin, 1928-29 n5 – 1r – 1 – Dist. gw Mikrofilm – gw Mico Inst [073]

DAS DRITTE REICH : DOCUMENTARISCHE AUFSTELLUNG DES AUFBAUS DER NATION OHNE ORTSBEZEICHNUNG – 1933-1938 – 2r – 1 – DM150.00 – gw Mikro Press [943]

DRITTER THEIL DER CLAVIER UEBUNG BESTEHEND IN VERSCHIEDENEN VORSPIELEN UEBER DIE CATECHISMUS- UND ANDERE GESAENGE, VOR DIE ORGEL... : CONTAINS: PRELUDE AND FUGUE, S. 522, EB MAJOR; CHORALE PRELUDES, S. 669-689; DUETS, HARPSICHORD, S. 802-805 / Bach, Johann Sebastian – (1sr edition) – Leipzig: In Verlegung des Aucthoris, [1739] – 1 – us Sibley [780]

Driver, G R *see*
- THE ASSYRIAN LAWS
- BABYLONIAN LAWS
- CANAANITE MYTHS AND LEGENDS
- PROBLEMS OF THE HEBREW VERBAL SYSTEM
- SEMITIC WRITING

Driver, Samuel Rolles *see*
- ADDITIONS AND CORRECTIONS TO THE BOOK OF GENESIS
- THE BOOK OF DANIEL
- THE BOOK OF EXODUS
- THE BOOK OF GENESIS
- THE BOOK OF JOB IN THE REVISED VERSION
- THE BOOK OF LEVITICUS: ENGLISH TRANSLATION
- THE BOOK OF THE PROPHET JEREMIAH
- THE BOOKS OF JOEL AND AMOS
- A CRITICAL AND EXEGETICAL COMMENTARY ON DEUTERONOMY
- HEBREW TENSES
- THE HIGHER CRITICISM
- ISAIAH, HIS LIFE AND TIMES AND THE WRITINGS WHICH BEAR HIS NAME
- MODERN RESEARCH AS ILLUSTRATING THE BIBLE
- NOTES ON THE HEBREW TEXT OF SAMUEL
- SERMONS ON SUBJECTS CONNECTED WITH THE OLD TESTAMENT
- A TREATISE ON THE USE OF THE TENSES IN HEBREW AND SOME OTHER SYNTACTICAL QUESTIONS

Driver, Samuel Rolles et al *see* THE INTERNATIONAL CRITICAL COMMENTARY ON THE OLD AND NEW TESTAMENTS

DRIVER/OWNER – (1985- . 5,6,9) – v12,no.5- . 1984- – 1 – us UMI [073]

DRIVER/OWNER – Toronto, v13- 1985- – 9 – Can$20.00y – cn Micromedia [790]

Drobnitzky, Bettina *see* EIN VERGLEICH DER BUCH- UND FILMFASSUNGEN VON SHAFFERS EQUUS UND AMADEUS

Drobnitzky-Eickhoff, Barbara *see*
- HEILPAEDAGOGISCHE MOEGLICHKEITEN DER MUSIK IN DER SONDERPAEDAGOGIK
- STRUKTUR UND AUFBAU AUSGEWAEHLTER STUECKE DARSTELLENDER MUSIK (TIERDARSTELLUNGEN) IN VERBINDUNG MIT INSTRUMENTENKUNDE

Droese, Miss *see* INDIAN GEMS FOR THE MASTER'S GROWN

DROGHEDA CONSERVATIVE JOURNAL – Ireland. -w. 24 Jun 1837-30 Dec 1848. (4 reels) – 1 – uk British Libr Newspaper [072]

DROGHEDA INDEPENDENT – Ireland.1890-96. -w. 7 reels – 1 – uk British Libr Newspaper [072]

DROGHEDA JOURNAL – Ireland. -w. 1 Jan 1823-4 Mar 1843. (18 reels) – 1 – uk British Libr Newspaper [072]

DROGHEDA SENTINEL – Ireland. -w. 19 Apr-15 Jul 1834. (10 ft) – 1 – uk British Libr Newspaper [072]

DROGI EMIGRACJI / Gliwicowna, Marja – Poznan-Warszawa, 1936 – 2r – 1 – us I.H.R.C. [304]

Drogin, E B *see* EVALUATING THE BOATER EXPERIENCE

LES DROGUES SIMPLES D'ORIGINE VEGETALE / Planchon, [F]G – Paris, 1895 – 20mf – 9 – ne IDC [615]

DIE DROHENDE SICHEL / Nord, F R – 7.-9. Aufl. Leipzig: P List, 1935 – 1r – 1 – us U.W. Library [830]

LES DROICTS, AVTORITEZ ET PREROGATIVES QVE PRETENDENT AU ROYAUME DE HIERUSALEM / Lusignano, S di – Paris, 1586 – 1mf – 9 – H-8367/1 – ne IDC [956]

LE DROIT – Bulletin des tribunaux. Paris. dec 1836-juin 1837, 15 oct-31 dec 1845, 1848, 1850-51, 1853-54, janv-juin 1856, juil 1857-juin 1860, 1865-juin 1867, juil 1868-juin 1869, 1870-73, juil 1880-81, 1888, 1891, 1894-95 – 1 – fr A.C.R.P.P. [073]

LE DROIT – Ottawa, 15 jan 1913-31 dec 1992 – 731r – 1 – Can$70.00 – cn Can Microfilming [072]

LE DROIT – Port-au-Prince: [s.n.], [1892-]. [1re annee, n1-2e annee, n26 25. fevr 1892-19 aout 1893] – 6r – 9 – us Res Libr [072]

DROIT CIVIL INTERNATIONAL DU MARIAGE... / Barraud, P – Paris, 1893 – 1mf – 9 – ILM-3071/1 – ne IDC [340]

LE DROIT CRIMINEL BELGE... / Goddyn, M & Mahiels, E – Bruxelles, Paris, 1880 – 5mf – 1 – ILM-2003/1 – ne IDC [327]

LE DROIT DE FAMILLE CHINOIS / Moellendorff, PG von – Paris, 1896 – 2mf – 9 – CH-934/2 – ne IDC [340]

LE DROIT DE LA GUERRE ET DE LA PAIX, NOUVELLE TRADUCTION PAR JEAN BARBEYRAC / Groot, Hugo de – Amsterdam. P. de Coup. 1724. 2v. xliii, 1001p. Portrait. (Strategy of War Series) – 9 – fr Hachette [355]

LE DROIT DE LA NATURE ET DES GENS / Puffendorf, Samuel von – Trad. par Jean Barbeyrac. London. J. Nours. 1740. (Strategy of War Series) – 9 – fr Hachette [355]

LE DROIT DE L'ART ET DES LETTRES / Savatier, Rene – Paris: Librairie generale de droit et de jurisprudence, 1953. 224p. LL-4116 – 1 – us L of C Photodup [340]

LE DROIT DE PREEMPTION EN MATIERE CIVILE ET COMMERCIALE. / Mauzac, Louis – Montpellier, 1935. 151p. LL-4047 – 1 – us L of C Photodup [340]

LE DROIT DE VIVRE / ed by Larose, ArT – Montreal, Canada. 17 nov 1936-v1 n2. 1936 – 1r – 1 – Can$25.00 – cn Can Microfilming [072]

LE DROIT DES ETRANGERS A LA PROPRIETE COMMERCIALE / Bichon, S – Marseille, 1934 – 2mf – 9 – ILM-3040/1 – ne IDC [327]

LE DROIT DES FEMMES – Revue politique, litteraire et d'economie sociale. Red. en chef Leon Richer. Paris. 1869-91. A paru sous le titre de: L' Avenir des femmes de 1871 a 1879 – 1 – fr A.C.R.P.P. [320]

LE DROIT DES GENS... / Chaveau, M E – Paris, 1891 – 2mf – 1 – ILM-723/1 – ne IDC [327]

LE DROIT DES GENS OU PRINCIPES DE LA LOI NATURELLE APPLIQUES A LA CONDUITE ET AUX AFFAIRES DES NATIONS ET DES SOUVERAINS / Vattel, Emer de – London 1758. xxvi, 541, 375p. (Strategy of War Series) – 9 – fr Hachette [340]

LE DROIT DES NATIONALITES / Baie, E – Paris, 1915 – 2mf – 9 – ILM-1926/1 – ne IDC [340]

LE DROIT DES NEUTRES SUR MER / Gessner, L – Ed 2. Berlin, Paris, 1876 – 5mf – 1 – ILM-1067/1 – ne IDC [327]

LE "DROIT D'OBLAT" / Marchal, J – 1955 – Dfl28.00 – ne Slangenburg [240]

LE DROIT DU DANUBE INTERNATIONAL / Hajnal, H – La Haye, 1929 – 4mf – 1 – ILM-2291/1 – ne IDC [327]

LE DROIT DU PEUPLE – Journal des interets sociaux. Red. en chef Jean-Jacques Danduran. no. spec. Paris. fevr 1850 – 1 – fr A.C.R.P.P. [073]

LE DROIT DU SUND ET LE COMMERCE DU MONDE – Stettin, 1854 – 1mf – 1 – ILM-2335/1 – ne IDC [327]

DROIT ET LIBERTE – Contre le racisme et l'antisemitisme, et pour la paix. Dir. Ch. Lederman. Paris. 20 fevr 1946-juil 1974 – 1 – fr A.C.R.P.P. [073]

DROIT ET SCIENCE DANS LA PENSEE DE HANS KELSEN (CONTRIBUTION A LA THEORIE PURE DU DROIT) / Acka, Sohuily Felix – 2mf – 9 – 10212 – fr Atelier National [320]

LE DROIT INTERNATIONAL ... / Bluntschli, J K – Paris, 1895 – 7mf – 9 – ILM-137/1 – ne IDC [327]

LE DROIT INTERNATIONAL... / Calvo, C – Paris, 1887-1888 – 43mf – 1 – ILM 149/1 – ne IDC [327]

LE DROIT INTERNATIONAL... / Fiore, P – Paris, 1911 – 10mf – 1 – ILM-165/1 – ne IDC [327]

LE DROIT INTERNATIONAL... / Heffter, A G – Paris, 1883 – 7mf – 1 – ILM-195/1 – ne IDC [327]

LE DROIT INTERNATIONAL AMERICAIN... / Alvarez, Arturo – Paris, 1910 – 5mf – 9 – ILM-2118/1 – ne IDC [340]

LE DROIT INTERNATIONAL DE LA NAUFRAGE DU "TITANIC" / Boeck, C de – Paris, 1913 – 1mf – 9 – ILM-3367/1 – ne IDC [327]

LE DROIT INTERNATIONAL DE L'ACCES AUX MARCHES MONDIAUX / Balasko, A – Paris, 1927 – 3mf – 9 – ILM-1819/1 – ne IDC [340]

LE DROIT INTERNATIONAL DE L'AVENIR / Alvarez, Arturo – Washington, DC. 1916 – 2mf – 9 – ILM-1701/1 – ne IDC [340]

DROIT INTERNATIONAL ET SOUVERAINETE EN URSS / Calvez, J Y – L'evolution de l'ideologie juridique sovietique depuis la Revolution d'Octobre – 6mf – 9 – F90.00 – fr Ethnologie [340]

LE DROIT INTERNATIONAL PRIVE... / Buzzati, G C – Paris, 1911 – 6mf – 1 – ILM-447/1 – ne IDC [327]

LE DROIT INTERNATIONAL PRIVE;... / Fiore, P – Paris, 1907 – 29mf – 1 – ILM-517/1 – ne IDC [327]

LE DROIT INTERNATIONAL PUBLIC... / Alessandri – Paris, 1920 – 2mf – 9 – ILM-1893/1 – ne IDC [340]

LE DROIT INTERNATIONAL PUBLIC DE LA MER... / Gidel, G – Chateauroux, 1932 – 11mf – 1 – ILM-2453/1 – ne IDC [327]

LE DROIT INTERNATIONAL PUBLIC MARITIME ... / Bourdelles, R de – Paris, 1906 – 1mf – 9 – ILM-1609/1 – ne IDC [327]

LE DROIT MARITIME... / Cauchy, E F – Paric, 1862 – 12mf – 1 – ILM-150/1 – ne IDC [327]

DROIT MARITIME DE L'EUROPE / Azuni, D A – Paris, 1805 – 12mf – 9 – ILM-327/1 – ne IDC [340]

LE DROIT MARITIME FRANCAIS – Paris. 1949-67 – 1 – fr A.C.R.P.P. [340]

LE DROIT MUSULMAN EXPLIQUE / Savvas, Pasha – Paris: Marchal et Billard, 1896. 161p. LL-12030 – 1 – us L of C Photodup [340]

DROIT ROMAIN : DES CONDITIONS ESSENTIELLES POUR LA FORMATION DU MUTUUM... / Basilesco, N – Paris, 1884 – 3mf – 9 – ILM-3613/1 – ne IDC [340]

DROIT ROMAIN : DES CONSEQUENCES DE L'EVICTION DANS LA VENTE... / Enault, E – Paris, 1891 – 3mf – 1 – ILM-3598/1 – ne IDC [327]

DROIT ROMAIN : DE LA CITE ROMAINE... / Astor, J – Paris, 1887 – 4mf – 9 – ILM-3612/1 – ne IDC [340]

DROIT ROMAIN : DE LA FIDUCIE... / Glard, I – Paris, 1894 – 5mf – 1 – ILM-3597/1 – ne IDC [327]

DROIT ROMAIN : DU CONSTITUT DEBITI ALIENI... / Coulon, H – Poitiers, 1889 – 4mf – 1 – ILM-3599/1 – ne IDC [327]

DROIT ROMAIN : DU DROIT DE CITE A ROME... / Delecaille, A – Paris, 1893 – 4mf – 1 – ILM-3621/1 – ne IDC [327]

DROIT ROMAIN : THEORIE DES ACTIONS POPULAIRES... / Chervet, G – Paris, 1886 – 3mf – 1 – ILM-3600/1 – ne IDC [327]

DROIT ROMAIN: DE L'ACTION DE DOL ... / Bossion, A – Paris, 1884 – 4mf – 9 – ILM-3602/1 – ne IDC [327]

DROIT ROMAIN: DETERMINATION DES ELEMENTS DU LITIGE ... / Bossy, A – Paris, 1888 – 4mf – 9 – ILM-2558/1 – ne IDC [327]

DROIT ROMAIN: DU LEGS DE LA DOT ET EN GENERAL DE LA CHOSE DUE... / Centner, E – Paris, 1893 – 3mf – 1 – ILM-3601/1 – ne IDC [327]

DROIT SOCIAL – Textes et documents annotes concernant les rapports professionnels et l'organisation de la production. Paris. 1938-40 – 1 – fr A.C.R.P.P. [073]

LE DROIT SOCIAL – no. 1. Marseille. mai 1885 – 1 – fr A.C.R.P.P. [073]

LES DROITS DE LA FEMME DEVANT LA LOI FRANCAISE / Neulat, L – Paris: Librairie mondiale, 1907. vii,143p. (Les Femmes Collection) – 2mf – 9 – $6.00 – fr Bibl Nationale [340]

LE DROITS DE LA LANGUE FRANCAISE MECONNUS – s.l.: s.n., 1879?. 03187. (Pre-1900 Canadiana) – 9 – cn C.I.H.M. [971]

LES DROITS DE LA LANGUE FRANCAISE MECONNUS – Humilante position de la province de Quebec. s.l.: s.n., 1880?. 02293. (Pre-1900 Canadiana) – 9 – cn C.I.H.M. [971]

LES DROITS DE L'HOMME – Journal politique et quotidien. Paris. 1898-17 mars 1900, 27 oct-8 dec 1901, 8 juin-5 nov 1910 – 1 – fr A.C.R.P.P. [073]

LES DROITS DE L'HOMME – Liberte, egalite, fraternite. Paris. 11 fevr 1876-15 fevr 1877, 25 mars-3 juin 1878 – 1 – fr A.C.R.P.P. [073]

LES DROITS DE L'HOMME – Paris: Blondeau, jan 1849 – us Res Libr [072]

LES DROITS DE L'INFANT / Deraismes, Maria – Paris: E. Dentu, 1887. 96p. 2 fiches. (Literature Collection) – 9 – 6.00 – fr Bibl Nationale [300]

DES DROITS DE SUCCESSION... / Diena, G – Paris – 1mf – 1 – ILM-2994/1 – ne IDC [327]

LES DROITS DES OUVRIERS. ETUDE SUR L'ORDRE DANS L'INDUSTRIE / Laboulaye, Charles – (Condition of 19th C. French working class series). 1873 – 9 – fr Hachette [323]

LES DROITS DU PEUPLE SUR L'ASSEMBLEE NATIONALE / La Vicomterie de Saint-Sanson – Paris, Paquet; Lyon, Prud'homme. 1791 – 9 – fr Hachette [321]

DROITS ET DEVOIRS DES NEUTRES... / Garachanine, W – Paris, 1910 – 3mf – 1 – ILM-675/1 – ne IDC [327]

LES DROITS INTERNATIONAUX DE L'HOMME / Gramain, P – Paris, 1933 – 3mf – 1 – ILM-1557/1 – ne IDC [327]

Droixhe, D *see* HARMONIA LINGUARUM

Drolet, Bernadette *see* BIBLIOGRAPHIE ANALYTIQUE DE LA FEDERATION DES GUIDES CATHOLIQUES DE LA PROVINCE DE QUEBEC

DROMORE LEADER – 1978-79; Jan 4-Dec 19 1980; 1981-84; Jan 9-Jun 25 1986; Jan-Aug 1987; Sep 2-Dec 22 1987; 1988-Jun 1989; Jul 5-Dec 20 1989, Jan-Jun 1990; Jul 4-Dec 19 1990; Jan 2-Jun 26 1991; Jul 3-Dec 18 1991; Jan-Oct 14 1992; Oct 21-Dec 30 1992; 1993; Jan 5-Feb 23 1994; Mar 1994-Jun 1996; Jul 3-Dec 1996 – 35r – 1 – uk British Libr Newspaper [072]

DROMORE WEEKLY TIMES – Ireland. 13 May 1905-4 Oct 1952 (missing 1930).-w. 31mqn reels – 1 – uk British Libr Newspaper [072]

Droop, Fritz *see* EMIL GOETTS VERMAECHTNIS

THE DROP-OUT PROBLEM IN THAILAND : A CASE STUDY REPORT / Bhumirat, C – 1982 – 1mf – 9 – DE-594/1 – ne IDC [370]

DROSCHAK : ORGANE DU PARTI SOCIALISTE REVOLUTIONNAIRE ARMENIEN – Geneve, London, Paris, 1890-1901 – 1 – us Hoover Inst Photo [335]

Drost, Willi *see* GOETHE ALS ZEICHNER

Droste, Kathy *see*
- LIBRARY OF CONGRESS CLASSIFICATION SCHEDULES
- LIBRARY OF CONGRESS CLASSIFICATION SCHEDULES, COMBINED WITH ADDITIONS AND CHANGES THROUGH 1989

Droste, Kristy *see*
- LIBRARY OF CONGRESS CLASSIFICATION SCHEDULES THROUGH 1993

Droste-Huelshoff, Annette von *see*
- GEDICHTE
- SAEMTLICHE WERKE

Drouilleau, A *see* ETHNO-ESTHETIQUE DU GOLFE DE PAPOUASIE

Drouin, L *see* DE LA CONDITION JURIDIQUE DES SOCIETES COMMERCIALES ETRANGERES EN FRANCE

DROVERS JOURNAL – Omaha. Neb. 1891-1912 – 1 – us UMI [071]

Droysen, H *see* EUTROPI BREVIARIUM AB URBE CONDITA CUM VERSIONIBUS GRAECIS ET PAULI LANDOLFIQUE ADDITAMENTIS (MGH 1: 2. BD)

Droysen, Johann Gustav *see* GESCHICHTE DES HELLENISMUS

Drozdov, Aleksandr *see* RASPIATIE

DIE DRUCKE DER BACHSOEHNE DER HOBOKEN-SAMMLUNG MUSIKALISCHER ERST- UND FRUEHDRUCKE / Oesterreichische Nationalbibliothek Wien. Musiksammlung – 107mf – 9 – DM1,200.00 diazo DM1,400.00 silver – gw Olms [780]

Drucker, Aaron P *see* TRIAL OF JESUS: FROM JEWISH SOURCES

Drucker Ernest *see* ADDICTION RESEARCH

Drucker, P *see* DIE RECHTFERTIGUNG DES VOELKERRECHTS AUS DEM STAATSWILLEN

Drueke, Petra *see* STADTSANIERUNG KOELN-SEVERINSVIERTEL

Druener, Hans *see* UNTERSUCHUNGEN UEBER JOSEPHUS

Druery, C T *see* BRITISH FERNS AND THEIR VARIETIES

DRUG ABUSE AND ALCOHOLISM NEWSLETTER – (1980 5,6,9) – 1971 – 1 – us UMI [073]

DRUG ABUSE: APPEARANCE, REALITY AND TREATMENT / Anderton, Paul – 1986. LA Political Notes, No.30. 4p – 9 – 1.00f – at Libertarian Micro [320]

DRUG AND ALCOHOL DEPENDENCE – v1-14. 1975-84 – 1,5,6,13 – sz Elsevier [073]

DRUG AND ALCOHOL REVIEW – 1992- 12v – 9 – £172.00 – 0959-5236 – uk Carfax [360]

DRUG AND ALCOHOL USE BY FRESHMAN AT SIUSLAW HIGH SCHOOL AND THEIR OPINIONS REGARDING POTENTIALLY EFFECTIVE DRUG AND ALCOHOL EDUCATION PROGRAMS / Byrd, Marcia J – Oregon State University, 1995 – 1mf – 9 – HE 564 – us Microform Publ [613]

DRUG AND CHEMICAL TOXICOLOGY – (v7-. 1984-. 5,6,9) – v1-. 1977- – 1 – us UMI [073]

DRUG AND COSMETIC INDUSTRY – v135-. Dec 1984- – 1,5,6,9 – us UMI [073]

DRUG AND COSMETIC INDUSTRY – v1-77. 1914-55.Continues: Drug Markets – 1,5,6 – us Princeton Micro [338]

DRUG DESIGN AND DISCOVERY / ed by Saunders, John & Olson, Gary L – 9,5,1 – us Harwood [615]

DRUG DEVELOPMENT AND INDUSTRIAL PHARMACY – (1984-. 5,6,9) – v3-. 1977- – 1 – us UMI [073]

DRUG DEVELOPMENT COMMUNICATIONS – v1-2. 1974-76 – 1 – us UMI [073]

DRUG DIGESTS FROM THE FOREIGN LANGUAGE LITERATURE – Jerusalem. v. 2-3. 1966-68 – 1,5,6 – us Princeton Micro [610]

DRUG ENFORCEMENT – (1976-. 5,6,9) – v. 1-1973- – 1 – us UMI [360]

DRUG ENFORCEMENT / U.S. Bureau of Narcotics and Dangerous Drugs – (Lacking: v10 no 1. Cont: BNDD Bulletin. Updates available) – v1-12. 1973-85 – 26mf – 9 – $39.00 – LLMC 82-200 – us L.L.M.C. [360]

DRUG LAW REPORTER – (Available in reel only) – National College, Houston. v1. 1981-1982 (all publ) – 5,6 – $45.00 – us Hein [340]

DRUG MERCHANDISING – (1985- . 5,6,9) – v6- . 1925- – 1 – us UMI [073]

DRUG MERCHANDISING – (v1-51 1919-1969 Can$900.00 5. Previous title: Druggists' Weekly. Ceased v74 no 7 1993) – Toronto. v1-74. 1919-93 – 5,9 – Can$28.00y – cn Micromedia [650]

DRUG METABOLISM AND DISPOSITION – v1-24. 1973-96 – 22r – 1,5,6,9 – $110.00r – us Williams [150]

DRUG METABOLISM REVIEWS – (1984-. 5,6,9) – v1-. 1972- – 1 – us UMI [073]

DRUG NARODA *see* DRUG NARODA (PETROGRAD, R.S.F.S.R.)

DRUG NARODA (PETROGRAD, R.S.F.S.R.) – (Includes c.1: 1917:Nov.4-5) – [Petrograd: s.n., 1917- – 1 – CSUXADQ1634-S – us Hoover Inst Photo [947]

DRUG PROSVESHCHENIIA – Zhurnal literatury, nauk i khudozhestv. M. 1804-06. B-1411 2 – 8 – ne IDC [073]

DRUG STORE NEWS – v1-. 1979- – 1,5,6,9 – us UMI [073]

DRUG USAGE BY ATHLETES RELATED TO PERFORMANCE / Master, Ronald R – 1978 – 1mf – 9 – $4.00 – us Microform Publ [790]

DRUG ZHENSHCHIN – Zhurnal literaturnyi nauchnyi. M. 1883-84. B-1714 2 – 8 – ne IDC [073]

DRUGDEX SYSTEM – Referenced drug information system for health professionals who prescribe, order, dispense, or administer medication. Republished quarterly – 9 – us Micromedex [610]

DRUGGISTS' WEEKLY – v1-5. 1920-24 – 1 – us UMI [073]

DRUGGISTS' WEEKLY *see* DRUG MERCHANDISING

DRUGS : EDUCATION, PREVENTION AND POLICY – 1995, Vol 2 – £179.00 – uk Carfax [360]

DRUGS AND SOCIETY / ed by Segal, Bernard – v1- 1986- – 1, 9 ($175.00 in US $245.00 outside hardcopy subsc) – us Haworth [360]

DRUGS, BRAIN AND BEHAVIOR / Israel. Prime Minister's Office – Survey on the state of psychology and psychopharmacology in Israel. By Amiram Carmon and Daniel Dagan. Jerusalem, 1976. 129 p – 9 – 5.00 – is I.T.T.I. [615]

DRUGS DEMYSTIFIED : DRUG EDUCATION / Nowlis, Helen – 2nd impr 1980 – 92p – 9 – 92-3-101231-2 – fr UNESCO [615]

DRUGS: SPECIAL STUDIES, 1972-86 – 14r with printed guide – 1 – $1,540.00 – 0-89093-990-X – us UPA [360]

DRUGS UNDER EXPERIMENTAL AND CLINICAL RESEARCH – (v.5 .1979. 5,6,9) – v1-. 1977- – 1 – us UMI [073]

Druhen, Ignace *see* DE LA MEDECINE AU TEMPS DE MME. SEVIGNE (SUIVI DE) DU THEATRE A BESANCON

Druk, D *see* TSU DER GESHIKHTE FUN DER YIDISHER PRESE

DRUM *see* AFRICAN DRUM

DRUM NOU – Brasov, Romania. 1962-1989 – 38r – 1 – us L of C Photodup [949]

Drumgoole, Edward *see* EDWARD DRUMGOOLE PAPERS

DRUMHELLER MAIL – Alberta, CN. 1918-95 – 49r – 1 – cn Commonwealth Micro [072]

DRUMHELLER REVIEW – Alberta, CN. 1914-40 – 4r – 1 – cn Commonwealth Micro [072]

DRUMHELLER SUN – Alberta, CN. 1978-79 – 2r – 1 – cn Commonwealth Micro [072]

Drummond, A L *see* EDWARD IRVING AND HIS CIRCLE, INCLUDING SOME CONSIDERATION OF THE "TONGUES" MOVEMENT IN THE LIGHT OF MODERN PSYCHOLOGY

Drummond, Andrew Thomas *see*
- CANADIAN TIMBER TREES: THEIR DISTRIBUTION AND PRESERVATION
- THE DISTRIBUTION OF CANADIAN FOREST TREES IN ITS RELATION TO CLIMATE AND OTHER CAUSES: A PAPER READ BEFORE THE BRITISH ASSOCIATION FOR THE ADVANCEMENT OF SCIENCE, MONTREAL, SEPT. 2ND, 1884
- FOREST PRESERVATION IN CANADA
- THE GREAT LAKE BASINS OF THE ST LAWRENCE
- RAILWAY ACCIDENTS
- SOME NOTES ON THE RIDEAU CANAL: THE SOURCES OF ITS WATER SUPPLY, AND ITS EARLY HISTORY
- SOME STATISTICAL FEATURES OF THE FLORA OF ONTARIO & QUEBEC: AND A COMPARISON WITH THOSE OF THE UNITED STATES FLORA

Drummond, Henry *see*
- THE IDEAL LIFE: ADDRESSES HITHERTO UNPUBLISHED
- THE LOWELL LECTURES ON THE ASCENT OF MAN
- NATURAL LAW IN THE SPIRITUAL WORLD
- PROGRAMME OF CHRISTIANITY: AND OTHER ADDRESSES
- STONES ROLLED AWAY, AND OTHER ADDRESSES TO YOUNG MEN

Drummond, James *see*
- THE EPISTLES OF PAUL THE APOSTLE TO THE THESSALONIANS, CORINTHIANS, GALATIANS, ROMANS AND PHILIPPIANS
- INTRODUCTION TO THE STUDY OF THEOLOGY
- THE JEWISH MESSIAH: A CRITICAL HISTORY OF THE MESSIANIC IDEA AMONG THE JEWS
- PHILO JUDAEUS; OR THE JEWISH-ALEXANDRIAN PHILOSOPHY IN ITS DEVELOPMENT AND COMPLETION
- SOME THOUGHTS ON CHRISTOLOGY
- TRANSMISSION OF THE TEXT OF THE NEW TESTAMENT

Drummond, Lewis Henry *see* THE JESUITS: A REPLY TO THE REV. J. J. ROY, OF WINNIPEG, DELIVERED AT ST PATRICK'S CHURCH, OTTAWA, MONDAY, MARCH 25TH, 1889

Drummond, Robert James *see* THE RELATION OF THE APOSTOLIC TEACHING TO THE TEACHING OF CHRIST

Drummond, William *see* OEDIPUS JUDAICUS

Drummond, William Henry *see* THE HABITANT: AND OTHER FRENCH-CANADIAN POEMS

DRUMS : 1972-75 – $45.00 – us UPA [305]

DRUM-TAPS (1865) AND SEQUEL TO DRUM-TAPS (1865-66) / Whitman, Walt – 9 – 10.00 – us Scholars' Facs [810]

DRUMUL SOCIALISMULUI – Deva, Romania. 1962-Jul 1979 – 28r – 1 – us L of C Photodup [949]

Drury, A W *see*
- HISTORY OF DAYTON AND MONTGOMERY COUNTY
- THE LIFE OF REV. PHILIP WILLIAM OTTERBEIN
- OUTLINES OF DOCTRINAL THEOLOGY

Drury, B Paxson *see* A FRUITFUL LIFE

Drury, Clifford Merril *see*
- CHRISTIAN MISSIONS AND FOREIGN RELATIONS IN CHINA,AN HISTORICAL STUDY
- FOUR HUNDRED YEARS OF WORLD PRESBYTERIANISM

Drury, D *see* ILLUSTRATIONS OF NATURAL HISTORY, WHEREIN ARE EXHIBITED... FIGURES OF EXOTIC INSECTS

Drury, H *see*
- HAND-BOOK OF THE INDIAN FLORA
- THE USEFUL PLANTS OF INDIA

Drury, James Westbrook *see* CHANGES MADE BY THE 1951 LEGISLATURE IN KANSAS LIBRARY LAWS

DRURY LANE UNDER SHERIDAN, 1776-1812 – Manuscript plays and managerial correspondence from the British Library, London – 1 – us Primary [790]

DRUSTVENI PLAN, 1964 / Yugoslavia – Beograd. 1964. BD-1786/1 – 9 – ne IDC [330]

Druyanov, A *see* KETAVIM LE-TOLEDOT HIBBAT ZIYYON

DRUZHBA – Pekin, China. -d. 27 Feb-29 Sept 1957. Imperfect. 1 reel – 1 – uk British Libr Newspaper [072]

DRUZHBA – Sofia, Bulgaria. Oct 1946-1947 – 1r – 1 – us L of C Photodup [949]

DRUZHBA NARODOV – Moscow. 1939-72. Lacking some issues. BR-10,393/1 – 9 – ne IDC [335]

Druzhinim, N M *see* DEKABRIST NIKITA MURAV'EV

Druzhinin, Nikolai Petrovich *see* MI ESHCHANSKOE DVIZHENIE 1906-1917 G.G.

Druzhinina, E I *see*
- KIUCHUK-KAINARDZHIISKII MIR 1774 GODA
- SEVERNOE PRICHERNOMOR'E V 1775-1800 GG

DRY CREEK BAPTIST CHURCH. EDGEFIELD COUNTY. SOUTH CAROLINA : CHURCH RECORDS – 1825-58, 1880-1924 – 1 – 17.96 – us Baptist [240]

Dry, Wakeling *see* WAGNER'S DIE MEISTERSINGER

Dryander, J *see* CATALOGUS BIBLIOTHECA HISTORICO NATURALIS JOSEPHI BANKS

Y DRYCH – (In Welsh) – Utica, NY. 1908, 1911, 1915-21 (incomplete) – 1 – us A.B.H.S. [071]

DRYCH *see* Y DRYCH

Y DRYCH A'R COLUMBIA – Utica, NY, Chicago, IL: Thomas J Griffiths, jan 1-dec 30 1926; jan 13 1927-dec 27 1928; jan 3-dec 26 1929 – 1 – us Res Libr [071]

Drygalski, E C von *see* DEUTSCHE SUDPOLAR-EXPEDITION 1901-1903

DRYING TECHNOLOGY – v1-. 1983- – 1,5,6,9 – us UMI [073]

Drysdale, Alexander Hutton *see*
- EARLY BIBLE SONGS
- HISTORY OF THE PRESBYTERIANS IN ENGLAND

DIE DSCHINN, TEUFEL UND ENGEL IM KORAN / Eichler, P A – 3mf – 8 – ne Slangenburg [260]

DTTP: DOCUMENTS TO THE PEOPLE – (1983-. 1,5,6,9) – v3-. 1974- – 1 – us UMI [073]

Du Bartas, Guillaume de Salluste *see* BARTAS: HIS DEVINE WEEKES AND WORKES

Du Bellay, Guillaume *see* INSTRUCTIONS SUR LE FAICT DE LA GUERRE

Du Bellay, J *see* LA DEFENCE, ET L'ILLUSTRATION DE LA LANGUE FRANCOISE

DU BLOCUS MARITIME / Fauchille, P – Paris, 1882 – 5mf – 1 – ILM-920/1 – ne IDC [327]

DU BOIS COUNTY DAILY HERALD – Jasper. Ind. 1951- – 1 – us UMI [071]

DU BOIS NEWSPAPER CLIPPING BOOKS / Schomburg Center for Research in Black Culture – No. 77-4. One reel – 1 – 15.00 – us Partington [920]

Du Bois, Patterson *see* THE CULTURE OF JUSTICE

DU BOIS RESEARCH NOTES – Research notes made by Prof. Francis L. Broderick during his study in the Du Bois Papers. No. 81-1. 1 reel – 1 – 20.00 – us Partington [920]

Du Bois, W E B *see*
- SHALL THE NEGRO BE ENCOURAGED TO SEEK CULTURAL EQUALITY?
- WORKS, 1883-1922

Du Bois, WE B *see*
- JEFFERSON DAVIS AS A REPRESENTATIVE OF CIVILIZATION
- PAPERS OF W.E.B. DU BOIS
- THE SUPPRESSION OF THE AFRICAN SLAVE-TRADE TO THE UNITED STATES OF AMERICA, 1638-1870

Du Bois-Reymond, Emil Heinrich *see*
- GOETHE UND KEIN ENDE
- UEBER DAS NATIONGEFUEHL; FRIEDRICH 2 UND JEAN-JACQUES ROUSSEAU

DU BORNAGE EN DROIT ROMAIN / Thiault, M – Paris, 1878 – 3mf – 9 – ILM-3604/1 – ne IDC [327]

Du Bos, J B *see* REFLEXIONS CRITIQUES SUR LA POESIE ET SUR LA PEINTURE

Du Bose, William Porcher *see*
- GOSPEL ACCORDING TO SAINT PAUL
- SOTERIOLOGY OF THE NEW TESTAMENT

Du Calvet, Pierre *see* THE CASE OF PETER DU CALVET, ESQ. OF MONTREAL IN THE PROVINCE OF QUEBEC

Du Cange, Charles d. Fresne *see*
- GLOSSARIUM MEDIAE ET INFIMAE LATINATIS CONDITUM A CARCLO DU FRESNE
- GLOSSARIUM MEDIAE ET INFIMAE LATINITATIS

Du Cellier, Florent *see* LES CLASSES OUVRIERES EN FRANCE DEPUIS 1789

Du Chaillu, Paul Belloni *see*
- L'AFRIQUE SAUVAGE, NOUVELLES EXCURSIONS AU PAYS DES ASHANGOS
- EXPLORATIONS AND ADVENTURES IN EQUATORIAL AFRICA
- THE LAND OF THE MIDNIGHT SUN: SUMMER AND WINTER JOURNEYS THROUGH SWEDEN, NORWAY, LAPLAND AND NORTHERN FINLAND. ..BI.NEW YORK: HARPER AND BROTHERS, 1881. 2V. ILLUS. MAP. WITH: THE GERMANS BY I.A.R. WYLIE. 1 REEL. 1260
- VOYAGES ET AVENTURES DANS L'AFRIQUE EQUATORIALE

DU CHASTEAU-SE OU CASTRUM SEIUM... / Bizeul, Louis-Jacques-Marie – 19th c. – fr Armell [944]

Du Chatelet-Lomont, Gabrielle Emilie *see* REPONSE DE MADAME A LA LETTRE QUE M. DE MAIRAN, SECRETAIRE PERPETUEL DE L'ACADEMIE ROYALE DES SCIENCES LUI A ECRITE LE 18 FEVRIER 1741: SUR LA QUESTION DES FORCES VIVES

Du Choul, G *see* DISCOURS SUR LA CASTRAMETATION ET DISCIPLINE MILITAIRE DES ROMAINS; ...

Du Contant de La Molette, P *see* TRAITE SUR LA POESIE ET LA MUSIQUE DES HEBREAUX

DU CREDIT ET DES BANQUES / Coquelin, Ch – 1848. 420p – 9 – 1.00f – at Libertarian Micro [332]

DU CULTE DES DIEUX FETICHES, OU PARALLELE DE L'ANCIENNE RELIGION DE L'EGYPTE AVEC LA RELIGION ACTUELLE DE LA NIGRITIE / Brosses, Charles de – 1760 – 9 – 7.50 – fr Orientalistes [290]

DU DECROISSEMENT DE LA POPULATION DAN LE DEPARTEMENT DES BASSES-PYRENEES / O'Quin, Patrick – Reprod. de l'ed. de Pau: E. Vignan cour., 1856. 68p. – 1mf – 9 – fr Bibl Nationale [310]

DU DEPLACEMENT DE LA POPULATION DE PARIS / Daubanton, L J M – Paris, Carilian-Geoury, 1843. 54 p. 1 fiche. (Statistics Series: Demography) – 9 – 6.00 – fr Bibl Nationale [310]

DU DEVELOPPEMENT DES IDEES REVOLUTIONNAIRES EN RUSSIE PAR A. ISCANDER / Herzen, Aleksandr I – (Russia – 19th C. series). 1851 – 9 – fr Hachette [335]

DU DOMICILE EN DROIT INTERNATIONAL PRIVE / Grinberg-Vinaver, S – Paris, 1930 – 1mf – 1 – ILM-3425/1 – ne IDC [327]

DU DROIT AU TRAVAIL ET DE L'ORGANISATION DU TRAVAIL / Lamartine, Alphonse M – Macon. n.d. (La Condition Ouvriere. Part Two.) – 9 – 2.50 – fr Bibl Nationale [360]

DU DROIT DE CITE A ROME / Lesterpt de Beauvais, Henri – Poitiers, Oudin, 1882. 175 p. LL-4045 – 1 – us L of C Photodup [340]

DU DROIT DE LA GUERRE SUR TERRE ... / Billard de Saint-Laumer, J – Paris, 1910 – 2mf – 9 – ILM-1099/1 – ne IDC [327]

DU DROIT INTERNATIONAL CONCERNANT... D'EAU / Caratheodory, E – Leipzig, 1861 – 3mf – 1 – ILM-1035/1 – ne IDC [327]

DU DROIT INTERNATIONALE: DISCOURS PRONONCE A L'UNIVERSITE LAVAL, A MONTREAL, LE 22 JUIN 1886 / Chapleau, Joseph Adolphe – Ottawa: "Canada", 1888. 02863. (Pre-1900 Canadiana) – 9 – cn C.I.H.M. [971]

DU GOLFE DES SYRTES AU GOLFE DU BENIN PAR LE LAC TCHAD : JOURNAL DE MARCHE DE LA MISSION TUNIS-TCHAD / Courtot, Lieutenant-Colonel – Tunis: A Guenard, 1926 – 1 – us Res Libr [960]

DU GOUVERNEMENT ARABE ET DE L'INSTITUTION QUI DOIT L'EXERCER / Richard, Charles Louis Florentin – Alger: Bastide, 1848 – 1 – us Res Libr [960]

DU IUGE DES CONTROVERSES / Du Moulin, P – Sedan, 1630 – 8mf – 9 – CA-129/1 – ne IDC [240]

Du Lac de La Tour d'Aurec, Hector *see* PRECIS HISTORIQUE ET STATISTIQUE DU DEPARTEMENT DE LA LOIRE (FOREST)

Du Laurens, Henri-Joseph *see* LE PORTE-FEUILLE D'UN PHILOSOPHE, OU MELANGE DE PIECES PHILOSOPHIQUES, POLITIQUES, CRITIQUES, SATYRIQUES ET GALANTES

DU LIVRET D'OUVRIER / Arnaud, Camille – (Condition of 19th C. French working class series). 1856 – 9 – fr Hachette [305]

Du Manoir, G *see* LE MARIAGE DE LA MUSIQUE AVEC LA DANCE

DU MARIAGE DES ROUMAINS A L'ETRANGER... / Busdugan, C N – Bucarest, 1900 – 4mf – 1 – ILM-3077/1 – ne IDC [327]

Du Maroussem, P *see*
- LA PETITE INDUSTRIE. SALAIRES ET DUREES DU TRAVAIL
- LA QUESTION OUVRIERE

Du Marsais, C *see*
- LOGIQUE ET PRINCIPES DE GRAMMAIRE
- DES TROPES

DU MEIN VATERLAND : WORTE UND GEDICHTE / Arndt, Ernst Moritz – Leipzig: Reclam, 1944 – 1r – 1 – us U.W. Library [943]

"DU, MEIN VOLK" : BEKENNTNIS UND ZWIESPRACHE / Kremer, Hannes – 4. Aufl. Muenchen: F Eher, 1943 – 1r – 1 – us U.W. Library [840]

Du Mesnil *see* ARMORIAL HISTORIQUE DE LA BRESSE, BUGEY, DOMBES

Du Mesnil de Maricourt, Rene *see* SOUVENIRS D'UN GARIBALDIEN: CAMPAIGNE DE 1870-71

Du Mesnil et Mangenot *see* ETUDE D'HYGIENE ET D'ECONOMIE SOCIALE. ENQUETE SUR LES LOGEMENTS, PROFESSIONS, SALAIRES ET BUDGETS

Du Mesnil, O *see* L'HYGIENE A PARIS. L'HABITATION DU PAUVRE

DU MODE DE FILIATION DES RACINES SEMITIQUES ET DE L'INVERSION / Cazet, Cl – Paris: Maisonneuve, 1882 – 1mf – 9 – 0-8370-8493-8 – 1986-2493 – us A.T.L.A. [470]

Du Monceaux, Alexis *see*
- EXERCICE TRES DEVOT ENVERS S. ANTOINE DE PADOUE LE THAUMATURGE
- EXERCICE TRES DEVOT ENVERS S. ANTOINE DE PADOUE LE THAUMATURGE, DE L'ORDRE SERAPHIQUE DE S. FRANCOIS, AVEC UN PETIT RECUEIL DE QUELQUES PRINCIPAUX MIRACLES
- EXERCICE TRES DEVOT ENVERS ST-ANTOINE DE PADOUE LE THAUMATURGE

Du Moulin, Gabriel *see*
- LES CONQUESTES ET LES TROPHEES DES NORMANDS-FRANCOIS AUX ROYAUMES DE NAPLES ET DE SICILE, AUX DUCHEZ DE CALABRE, D'ANTIOCHE, DE GALILEE.
- HISTOIRE GENERALE DE NORMANDIE CONTENANT LES CHOSES MEMORABLES ADVENUES DEPUIS LES PREMIERES COURSES DES NORMANDS PAYENS, TANT EN FRANCE QU'AUX AUTRE PAYS

Du Moulin, P *see*
- ACCOMPLISSEMENT DES PROPHETIES...
- DU IUGE DES CONTROVERSES

DU MOUVEMENT DE LA POPULATION DANS LA VILLE DE VERDUN, D'APRES LES REGISTRES DE L'ETAT CIVIL / Neucourt, F – Reprod. d'un extrait des Memoires de la Societe philomatique de Verdun. Impr. Lallemant, 1850.v4, p165-94. 1 fiche.(Statistics Series: Demography) – 9 – 6.00 – fr Bibl Nationale [310]

DU NIGER AU GOLFE DE GUINEE PAR LE PAYS DE KONG ET LE MOSSI (1887-1888) / Binger, Louis Gustave – Paris, Hachette. 1892 – 9 – 27.00 – fr Orientalistes [910]
DU NIGER AU GOLFE DE GUINEE PAR LE PAYS DE KONG ET LE MOSSI, 1887-1889 / Binger, Louis Gustave – 2v. A-278 2. 1892 – 8 – ne IDC [960]
DU NIGER AU GOLFE DE GUINEE PAR LE PAYS DE KONG ET LE MOSSI PAR LE CAPITAINE BINGER (1887-1889) / Binger, Louis Gustave – (African Library). Paris. Hachette. 1892 – 9 – fr Hachette [960]
DU NIGER AU GOLFE DE GUINEE PAR LE PAYS DE KONG ET LE MOSSI / Binger, Louis Gustave – Paris, 1892 – 1 – us Res Libr [910]
DU NIGER, DU FLEUVE DE TIMBOUCTOU, DE SON EMBOUCHURE ET DE LA COMMUNICATION DES GRANDS FLEUVES D'AFRIQUE / Chauvet – (Extrait de la vRevue vEncyclopedique). Paris. 1829 – 9 – 5.00 – fr Orientalistes [960]
DU NOUVEL ORDRE SOCIAL / Bancal Des Issarts, Jean-Henri – Paris. Imp. du Cercle Social. 1792 – 9 – fr Hachette [321]
DU PAUPERISME / Marchand, PR – (Condition of 19th C. French working class series). 1845 – 9 – fr Hachette [360]
DU PAUPERISME, CE QU'IL ETAIT DANS L'ANTIQUITE ET CE QU'IL EST DE NOS. JOURS / Chamborant, CG de – (Condition of 19th C. French working class series). 1842 – 9 – fr Hachette [360]
DU PAUPERISME, DE LA MENDICITE ET DES MOYENS D'EN PREVENIR LES FUNESTES EFFETS / Morogues, Bigot de – (Condition of 19th C. French working class series). 1834 – 9 – fr Hachette [360]
DU PAUPERISME EN FRANCE ET DES MOYENS DE LE DETRUITE / Monaco, Prince de – (Condition of 19th C. French working class series). 1839 – 9 – fr Hachette [360]
DU PAUPERISME EN FRANCE ET DES MOYENS D'Y REMEDIER, OU PRINCIPES D'ECONOMIE CHARITABLE / Marbeau, J BF – (Condition of 19th C. French working class series). 1847 – 9 – fr Hachette [360]
DU PAUPERISME EN FRANCE. ETAT ACTUEL CAUSES, REMEDES POSSIBLES / Modeste, Victor – (Condition of 19th C. French working class series). 1858 – 9 – fr Hachette [360]
Du Paz, Augustin *see* HISTOIRE GENEALOGIQUE DE PLUSIEURS MAISONS ILLUSTRES DE BRETAGNE...AVEC L'HISTOIRE CHRONOLOGIQUE DES EVESQUES DE TOUS LES DIOCESES DE BRETAGNE...
Du Perron *see* DISCOURS SUR LA PEINTURE ET SUR L'ARCHITECTURE.
Du Perron, J D *see* REPLIQUE A LA RESPONSE DU SERENISSIME ROY DE LA GRANDE BRETAGNE
Du Perron, JD *see* TRAITTE DU SAINCT SACREMENT DE L'EUCHARISTIE,...
Du Petit-Thouars, L M A A *see*
- EXTRAIT DE TROIS MEMOIRES. DES PLANTES ORCHIDEES DES ISLES AUSTRALES D'AFRIQUE
- GENERA NOVA MADAGASCARIENSIA
- HISTOIRE DES VEGETAUX RECUEILLIS DANS LES ISLES AUSTRALES D'AFRIQUE
- HISTOIRE DES VEGETAUX RECUEILLIS SUR LES ISLES DE FRANCE, LA REUNION (BOURBON) ET MADAGASCAR
- HISTOIRE PARTICULIERE DES PLANTES ORCHIDEES RECUEILLIES SUR LES TROIS ISLES D'AFRIQUE, DE FRANCE, DE BOURBON ET DE MADAGASCAR

Du Plessis, Johannes *see*
- EVANGELISATION OF PAGAN AFRICA
- THE EVANGELISATION OF PAGAN AFRICA: HISTORY OF CHRISTIAN MISSIONS TO THE PAGAN TRIBES OF CENTRAL AFRICA

Du Plessis, P *see* MEMOIRES DE MESSIRE PHILIPPE DE MORNAY
DU POLE ET TROPIQUES – (Vols for 1942 filmed with: Petites annales des Missionaires oblats de Marie Immaculee (1926), 1940-jan/feb 1942; and: Documentation des Oblats de Marie Immaculee, 1943-1944, n11; and: Petites annales des Missionaires oblats de Marie Immaculee (1926) (cont), dec 1944-Jan 1953; and: Petites annales, pole et tropiques, mar 1953-jul 1957) – Paris: OMI, 1942 – 2r – 1 – us Res Libr [072]
Du Pont, G *see* ART ET SCIENCE DE RHETORIQUE METRIFFIEE
Du Pont, Samuel Francis *see* THE SAMUEL FRANCIS DU PONT PAPERS
DU PREMIER CONCILE DU LATRAN A L'AVENEMENT D'INNOCENT 3, 1123-1198 (9) – Paris, 1946 – Dfl53.00 – ne Slangenburg [240]
DU PREMIER ESPRIT DE L'ORDRE DE CISTEAUX / Paris, D Julian – Paris, 1664 – 23mf – 8 – Dfl81.00 – ne Slangenburg [240]
DU PRINCIPE DE LA LIBERTE DES MERS ET DE SES APPLICATIONS... / Castel, B – Toulouse, 1900 – 3mf – 1 – ILM-370/1 – ne IDC [327]
DU PRINCIPE DES NATIONALITES / Deloche, M – Paris, 1860 – 2mf – 1 – ILM-497/1 – ne IDC [327]
DU PRINCIPE FEDERATIF / Proudhon, Pierre-Joseph – 1868. Together with: Men Over Industry, by Paul Derrick; The Study Of Political Economy, by Henry George, 1947; and Verlagsprogramm, (Libertad Verlag), 1980 81. 1 fiche (24x) – 9 – 1.00f – at Libertarian Micro [320]
DU PROBLEME DE LA MISERE ET DE SA SOLUTION CHEZ LES PEUPLES ANCIENS ET MODERNES. TOME 3: PEUPLES MODERNES / Moreau-Christophe, L M – (Condition of 19th C. French working class series). v. 1 and 2 not published. 1851 – 9 – fr Hachette [360]
DU PROBLEME DES TROIS CORPS / Condorcet, Marie Jean Antoine Nicolas de – Paris: Imp. Didot, 1767.83p. 1 fiche.(Science Collection) – 9 – 6.00 – fr Bibl Nationale [500]
DU PROGRES ALARMANT DE LA MORTALITE DANS LE DEPARTEMENT DE LOT-ET-GARONNE ET EN PARTICULIER DANS LA COMMUNE D'AGEN / Bourrousse de Laffore, Pierre Jules de – Agen, P. Noubel, 1847. 108 p. 3 fiches. (Statistics Series: Medical Studies) – 9 – 8.00 – fr Bibl Nationale [310]
DU PROGRES DES AGGLOMERATIONS URBAINES ET DE L'EMIGRATION RURALE: EN EUROPE ET PARTICULIEREMENT EN FRANCE / Legoyt, Alfred – Marseille: Typ Cayer, 1867. 280p. 3 fiches. (Statistics Series: Demography). (La Condition Ouvriere. Part Two) – 9 – 8.00 – fr Bibl Nationale [310]
DU PROTESTANTISME AU CATHOLICISME: JOHN-HENRY NEWMAN, 1801-1845 : NOTES PSYCHOLOGIQUES / Gout, Raoul – Geneve: J.-H. Jeheber, 1906 – 1mf – us A.T.L.A. [240]
Du Puigaudeau, Odette *see* LA PISTE: MAROC-SENEGAL
Du Puynode, Gustave *see* DE L'ESCLAVAGE ET DES COLONIES
DU RECRUTEMENT DES GENS DE MER; ETUDE HISTORIQUE ET CRITIQUE / Zoete, Robert – Bordeaux, Impr. de l'Universite, 1919. 160 p. LL-4007 – 1 – us L of C Photodup [340]
DU REGIME CONVENTIONNEL DES FLEUVES INTERNATIONAUX / Engelhardt, E – Paris, 1879 – 3mf – 1 – ILM-1850/1 – ne IDC [327]
DU RESPECT DE LA... / Cauchy, E F – Paris, 1866 – 2mf – 1 – ILM-145/1 – ne IDC [327]
DU REVE A LA REALITE / Jaloux, Edmond – Paris: Editions R-A Correa, 1932 – 1r – 1 – us U.W. Library [430]
Du Roizel-Marlier, M C *see* HISTOIRE RURALE DU COMTE DE DAMMARTIN-EN-GOELE AU DEBUT DE LA RENAISSANCE. RECHERCHES SUR LA RECONSTRUCTION APRES LA GUERRE DE CENT ANS
DU ROLE DES CHAMBRES... / Dauzat, A – Paris, 1899 – 3mf – 1 – ILM-467/1 – ne IDC [327]
Du Roullet, Francois L *see* LETTRES SUR LES DRAMES-OPERA
DU STYLE GOTHIQUE AU DIX-NEUVIEME SIECLE / Viollet-le-Duc, Eugene Emmanuel – Paris. Didron, 1846. 4 fol., 31p. (Architecture Series) – 9 – fr Hachette [720]
DU SUICIDE ET DE LA FOLIE SUICIDE CONSIDERES DANS LEURS RAPPORTS AVEC LA STATISTIQUE, LA MEDECINE ET LA PHILOSOPHIE / Brierre de Boismont, Alexandre Jacques Francois – (French Precursors of Psychiatry Series). Paris. Germer Bailliere. 1856 – 9 – fr Hachette [150]
DU SYSTEME SOCIAL ET DES LOIS QUI LE REAGISSENT / Quetelet, Adolphe Lambert Jacques – Paris: Fuillaumin, 1848.v,360p. 4 fiches. (Law Collection) – 9 – 10.00 – fr Bibl Nationale [320]
DU TCHAD AU DAHOMEY EN BALLON. : VOYAGE AERIEN AU LONG COURS / Deburaux, Edouard – nouvelle ed. Paris: Hachette, 1903 – 1 – us Res Libr [910]
Du Teil, Jean *see* DE L'USAGE DE L'ARTILLERIE NOUVELLE.
DU THEATRE ITALIEN / Ortique, Joseph Louis d' – 1840 – 9 – us Sibley [780]
DU TRAITEMENT MORAL DE LA FOLIE / Leuret, Francois – (French Precursors of Psychiatry Series). Paris. J. B. Bailliere. 1840 – 9 – fr Hachette [170]
DU TRAVAIL DES ENFANTS QU'EMPLOIENT LES ANTELIERS, LES USINES ET LES MANUFACTURES, CONSIDERE DANS LES INTERETS MUTUELS DE LA SOCIETE, DES FAMILLES ET DE L'INDUSTRIE / Dupin, Charles – (Condition of 19th C. French working class series). 1840-47 – 9 – fr Hachette [331]
DU TRES-SAINCT ET TRES-AUGUSTE SACREMENT, ET SACRIFICE DE LA MESSE / Coton, P – Avignon, 1600 – 7mf – 9 – CA-124/1 – ne IDC [240]
DU UND DEUTSCHLAND / Schwarz, Hans – Breslau: W G Korn, c1933 – 1r – 1 – us U.W. Library [810]
DU VERBE INCARNE (AGNUS DEI) / Boulgakof, S – Paris, 1943 – 7mf – 8 – ne Slangenburg [290]
Du Wes, Giles *see* AN INTRODUCTORIE FOR TO LERNE TO REDE TO PRONOUNCE, AND TO SPEKE FRENCHE TREWLY
DUA DUNIA / Dini, Nh – SE-4922 1. 1961 – 9 – ne IDC [950]
DUA HATI JANG TAK PERNAH PUAS / Gazaldun – SE-5067 1. 1963 – 9 – ne IDC [950]
DUA KERINDUAN DAN TJERITA PENDEK LAINNJA / Tjahjaningsih, S – SE 5156 1. 1963 – 9 – ne IDC [950]
DUA TOKOH ASIA-AFRIKA: DR. IR. HADJI SOEKARNO – DR. RAJENDRA PRASAD / Indonesia. Kementerian Penerangan – SE-5373 1. 1958 – 9 – ne IDC [950]
DER DUALISMUS LUDWIG TIECKS ALS DRAMATIKER UND DRAMATURG / Kaiser, Oscar – (Includes bibliographical references) – Leipzig: Sturm und Koppe, 1885 – 1r – 1 – us U.W. Library [430]
LA DUALITE POLITIQUE CHEZ LES TEKE DE L'OUEST / Dupre, M C – Pouvoir Tsaayi et pouvoir nzineke – 9 – F70.00 – fr Ethnologie [306]
Duane, W J *see* THE LAW OF NATIONS, INVESTIGATED...
DUARTE DISPATCH – Duarte, CA. 1950-1956 – 5r – 1 – $250.00 – H04006 – us Library Micro [071]
Duarte, Erminda *see* MI HERMANA EVITA
Duarte, Fausto *see* AUA: NOVELA NEGRA
Duarte Insua, Lino *see*
- LAS ALCABOLAS DE ALBURQUERQUE O LOS CELEBRES BALDIOS
- ANTIGUEDADES EXTREMENAS. LA AUDIENCIA TERRITORIAL DE EXTREMADURA
- UNA DECADA DE PROGRESO EN BADAJOZ
- LAS DEVOCIONES DE MI PUEBLO, LAS SANTAS RELIQUIAS, EL SANTUARIO...ALBURQUERQUE
- HISTORIA DE ALBURQUERQUE
- LA PROPIEDAD EN ALBURQUERQUE
- VALENCIA DEL REY

Duarte, Teofilo *see* O REI DE TIMOR
DUARTEAN – Duarte, CA. 1963-1973 – 11r – 1 – $550.00 – H04007 – us Library Micro [071]
DUARTEAN – Duarte. Calif. -w. 1973- – 1 – us UMI [071]
DUARTE-BRADBURY JOURNAL – Duarte, CA. 1966-1967 – 2r – 1 – $100.00 – H04005 – us Library Micro [073]
Dubarle, E *see* STATISTIQUE DE DEPARTEMENT DE SEINE-ET-MARNE
DUBBIO DI DON ANTONIO EXIMENO SOPRA IL SAGGIO FONDAMENTALE PRATICO DI CONTRAPPUNTO / Eximeno, Antonio – 1775 – 9 – us Sibley [780]
DUBBO DISPATCH – Jan 1942-Dec 25 1942 – 9 – at Pascoe [072]
DUBBO LIBERAL – Jan 3 1928-Dec 30 1948; Jan 2 1951- Dec 31 1954; Jan 4 1960-Dec 30 1960 – 9 – at Pascoe [072]
Dubbs, Joseph Henry *see*
- HISTORIC MANUAL OF THE REFORMED CHURCH IN THE UNITED STATES
- LEADERS OF THE REFORMATION
- THE REFORMED CHURCH IN PENNSYLVANIA

Dube, J -E *see* LA SITUATION HOSPITALIERE A MONTREAL
Dubeau, Jean *see* BIO-BIBLIOGRAPHIE ANALYTIQUE DE REINE MALOUIN, MEMBRE DE LA SOCIETE DES ECRIVAINS CANADIENS
Dubee, Bernard *see* NUN'S ISLAND TRIBUNE DE L'ILE DES SOEURS
Dubenetskii, N O *see* USLOVII A I KHOD PROIZROSTANII A KHLEBOV UROZHAI A 1918-1919 S.-KH. G. V KIEVSKO I GUB
DuBerger, C C *see* MURRAY BAY ATLAS AND MAPS OF ITS ENVIRONS
Duberstein, Murray W *see* OUTLINE OF THE LAW OF WILLS, BASED ON NEW YORK CASES AND STATUTES
Dubin, Martin *see* INTERNATIONAL TERRORISM
DUBIN STRIKE NEWS – Ireland.Aug-Sept 1929 – 1 – ie Microforms [072]
Dublin *see* CALENDAR OF ANCIENT RECORDS OF DUBLIN: IN THE POSSESSION OF THE MUNICIPAL CORPORATION OF THAT CITY
DUBLIN, 1838 : BRITISH ISLES CENSUS DIRECTORIES PROJECT, IRELAND. VOL 7 – 5mf – 9 – A$33.00 – at Vine [941]
Dublin Abbey Of St Thomas The Martyr *see* REGISTER OF THE ABBEY OF ST THOMAS THE MARTYR, DUBLIN (RS94)
THE DUBLIN AND NEW YORK FENIAN PAPERS – 1 – ie Microforms [941]
DUBLIN BUILDER – Ireland. Irish Builder. -m, -w. Jan 1859-Dec 1900. 18 reels – 1 – uk British Libr Newspaper [072]
Dublin Castle. Ireland. Records, 1880-1921 *see* THE BRITISH IN IRELAND
DUBLIN CHRONICLE – Ireland. -w. 1 Jan 1816-20 Apr 1817. (1 reel) – 1 – uk British Libr Newspaper [072]
DUBLIN COURANT – Ireland.1 reel – 1 – ie Microforms [072]
DUBLIN COURANT – Ireland.24 Apr 1744-30 Dec 1746. -d. 1 reel – 1 – uk British Libr Newspaper [072]
DUBLIN DAILY ADVERTISER – Ireland. -d. 14 Oct-2 Dec 1736. 14 ft – 1 – uk British Libr Newspaper [072]
DUBLIN DIRECTORY 1904 *see* THOM'S OFFICIAL DUBLIN DIRECTORY
DUBLIN (DUBLIN), 1805 : BRITISH ISLES CENSUS DIRECTORIES PROJECT, IRELAND. VOL 10 – 1mf – 9 – A$9.00 – at Vine [941]
DUBLIN EVENING HERALD – Ireland. -d. 30 Jan 1821-29 Jan 1822. (1 reel) – 1 – uk British Libr Newspaper [072]
DUBLIN EVENING MAIL – Ireland. -d. 1897-1907. 33 reels – 1 – uk British Libr Newspaper [072]
DUBLIN EVENING POST – Dublin. Ireland. -d. 1780; 1829; 1860-65; 1870. (10 reels) – 1 – uk British Libr Newspaper [072]
DUBLIN GAZETTE – Ireland.7 reels – 1 – ie Microforms [072]
DUBLIN INTELLIGENCE – Ireland. -sw. 10, 31 Aug, 11 Sept 1708; 4 Jan 1709-30 Dec 1712. Imperfect. 1 reel – 1 – uk British Libr Newspaper [072]
DUBLIN INTELLIGENCE – Ireland.1 reel – 1 – ie Microforms [072]
DUBLIN INTELLIGENCE (SUPPLEMENTS) – Ireland.21 Mar 1722-21 May 1724. -irr. 9 feet – 1 – uk British Libr Newspaper [072]
DUBLIN INTELLIGENCER – Ireland. 17 June 1756. 1 ft – 1 – uk British Libr Newspaper [072]
DUBLIN LABOUR BULLETIN – Ireland.May 1926 – 1 – ie Microforms [072]
DUBLIN LOCAL ADVERTISER – Ireland.Sept 1858-Mar 1861. -w. 1 reel – 1 – uk British Libr Newspaper [072]
THE DUBLIN MAGAZINE – Dublin. Aug 1923-1958. 81 fiches – 9 – PS400.00 – ie European Micro [410]
DUBLIN MERCANTILE ADVERTISER – Ireland.1851-Jan 1865.-w. 5 reels – 1 – uk British Libr Newspaper [072]
DUBLIN MERCURY – (Hoey's Dublin Mercury). Ireland. -sw. 18 Mar 1766-1 Apr 1773. (5 reels) – 1 – uk British Libr Newspaper [072]
DUBLIN MERCURY – Ireland. -sw. 23 Jan-25 Sep 1742. Imperfect. (25 ft) – 1 – uk British Libr Newspaper [072]
DUBLIN MONITOR – Ireland. -w. 6 Nov 1838-11 Jul 1845. (7 reels) – 1 – uk British Libr Newspaper [072]
DUBLIN MORNING PRESS – Ireland. -d. 9 Feb-2 Apr 1842. (30 ft) – 1 – uk British Libr Newspaper [072]
DUBLIN NEWS – Ireland.23 Nov-16 Dec 1922 – 1 – ie Microforms [072]
DUBLIN NEWSLETTER – 1 reel – 1 – ie Microforms [941]

DUBLIN NEWSLETTER OR DUBLIN GAZETTE – Ireland.31 Jan 1743-7 Apr 1744. -irr.1 reel – 1 – uk British Libr Newspaper [072]

DUBLIN PENNY JOURNAL – Dublin, Ireland.1832-36 – 1 – Ir£25.00 – ie Microforms [072]

THE DUBLIN PHILOSOPHICAL JOURNAL AND SCIENTIFIC REVIEW – Dublin, 1825-26 – 3 – us Readex [100]

DUBLIN PICTORIAL ADVERTISER *see* KINGSTOWN AND BRAY OBSERVER

DUBLIN POST-MAN – Ireland. -sw. 14 Dec 1724, 4, 11, 15 Mar, 12 Apr, 13 May, 14 Jun, 29 Jul, 27 Aug, 2, 23 Sep, 10 Nov, 1, 2, 16, 20 Dec 1725. (4 ft) – 1 – uk British Libr Newspaper [072]

THE DUBLIN QUARTERLY JOURNAL OF SCIENCE: CONTAINING PAPERS READ BEFORE THE ROYAL DUBLIN SOCIETY; THE ROYAL IRISH ACADEMY; THE GEOLOGICAL SOCIETY OF DUBLIN; AND THE NATURAL HISTORY SOCIETY OF DUBLIN – Dublin, 1861-66 – 3 – us Readex [500]

DUBLIN REVIEW – 1-242. 1836-1969 – 1 – us UMI [073]

Dublin, St Mary's Abbey *see* CHARTULARIES OF ST MARY'S ABBEY, DUBLIN (RS80)

DUBLIN SPORTING NEWS – Ireland.Feb 1889-Oct 1891. -w. 3 reels – 1 – uk British Libr Newspaper [072]

DUBLIN STANDARD – Ireland. -sw. 4 Oct 1836-4 Aug 1837. (1 reel) – 1 – uk British Libr Newspaper [072]

DUBLIN STRIKE NEWS – Dublin, Ireland, Aug.-Sept. 1929 – 1 – ie Microforms [941]

DUBLIN TIMES – Ireland.5 Feb-8 May 1845; 22 Mar-1 Sept 1858. -w. 1 1/2 reels – 1 – uk British Libr Newspaper [072]

Dublin. University. Magnetical and Meteorological Observatory *see* OBSERVATIONS MADE AT THE MAGNETICAL AND METEOROLOGICAL OBSERVATORY AT TRINITY COLLEGE, DUBLIN

DUBLIN WEEKLY HERALD – Ireland. -w. 10 Nov 1838-2 Apr, 14-28 May 1842. (2 reels) – 1 – uk British Libr Newspaper [072]

DUBLIN WEEKLY JOURNAL – Ireland.1 reel – 1 – ie Microforms [072]

DUBNO RABBATI / Margulies, H S – Warsaw. 1918. BJ-290-14 1 – 9 – ne IDC [940]

Dubnov, S *see*
- PINKAS MEDINAT LITA
- SIMON DUBNOV, L'HOMME ET SON OUEVRE

Dubnov, S M *see* HISTORY OF THE JEWS IN RUSSIA AND POLAND

Dubnow, Simon *see* EVREI V TSARSTVOVANIE NIKOLAIA 2, 1894-1914

DuBoccage, Anne Marie *see*
- LA COLOMBIADE OU LA FOI PORTEE AU NOUVEAU MONDE
- LA MORT D'ABEL: POEME
- LE PARADIS TERRESTRE: POEME IMITE DE MILTON

Dubofsky, Melvyn *see* LABOR UNION PERIODICALS, PART 3

DuBois, A *see* SYNOPSIS AVIUM. NOUVEAU MANUEL D'ORNITHOLOGIE

Dubois, A *see* LES LEPIDOPTERES DE LA BELGIQUE, LEURS CHENILLES ET LEURS CHRYSALIDES, DECRITS ET FIGURES D'APRES NATURE

Dubois, CF *see* LES LEPIDOPTERES DE LA BELGIQUE, LEURS CHENILLES ET LEURS CHRYSALIDES, DECRITS ET FIGURES D'APRES NATURE

Dubois, F N A *see* METHODE EPROUVEE AVEC LAQUELLE ON PARVIENT FACILEMENT, ET SANS MAITRE, A CONNAITRE LES PLANTES

Dubois, Felix *see* NOTRE BEAU NIGER

Dubois Fontanelle, J G *see* ANECDOTES AFRICAINES, DEPUIS L'ORIGINE OU LA DECOUVERTE DES DIFFERENTS ROYAUMES QUI COMPOSENT L'AFRIQUE, JUSQU'A NOS JOURS

Dubois, H M *see* MONOGRAPHIE DES BETSILEO (MADAGASCAR)

Dubois, M J *see*
- BELEP, SYNTHESE HISTORIQUE D'APRES LES TRADITIONS
- LES CHEFFERIES DE MARE
- CORPUS DE TEXTES DE BELEP
- CORPUS DE TEXTES DE L'ILE DES PINS
- DICTIONNAIRE BELEP-FRANCAIS
- DICTIONNAIRE DES NOMS PROPRES DE BELEP
- DICTIONNAIRE DES NOMS PROPRES DE L'ILE DES PINS
- DICTIONNAIRE FRANCAIS-BELEP
- DICTIONNAIRE FRANCAIS-ILE DES PINS
- DICTIONNAIRE ILE DES PINS-FRANCAIS
- GENEALOGIES DE BELEP
- GENEALOGIES DE L'ILE DES PINS
- GENEALOGIES DE MARE
- GEOGRAPHIE MYTHIQUE ET TRADITIONELLE DE L'ILE DE MARE, ILES LOYAUTE, NOUVELLE-CALEDONIE
- INITIATION A LA LANGUE DE L'ILE DES PINS, NOUVELLE-CALEDONIE
- INITIATION A LA LANGUE DE MARE
- NOTES D'ETHNO-BOTANIQUE SUR L'ILE DES PINS, NOUVELLE-CALEDONIE

DUBOIS PAPER – DuBois, NE. -w. Mar. 1941-Jun. 1942 – 1 – us NE Hist [071]

Dubois, Philip *see* ADMINISTRATIVE STRUCTURE IN LARGE DISTRICT COURTS

DUBOIS TIMES – DuBois, NE. -w. Sep. 1895-apr. 1900 – 1 – us NE Hist [071]

DuBois, W E B *see* THE HORIZON: A JOURNAL OF THE COLOR LINE

DuBois, W E Burghard *see* THE BROWNIES' BOOK; A MONTHLY MAGAZINE FOR NEGRO CHILDREN

Dubois, W E Burghard *see* MOON ILLUSTRATED WEEKLY

DuBois, WE B *see* THE PHILADELPHIA NEGRO

DuBois, WE Burghard *see*
- PAPERS OF W.E.B. DUBOIS, 1877-1965
- THE SOULS OF BLACK FOLK

DUBOIS WEEKLY PRESS – DuBois, NE. -w. Jan. 1912-Sep. 1937; Nov. 1937-Jun. 1938; Aug. 1938-Mar. 1939, incomplete – 1 – us NE Hist [071]

Dubois-Goibaud, P *see* CONFORMITE DE LA CONDUITE DE L'EGLISE DE FRANCE...AVEC CELLE DE L'EGLISE D'AFFRIQUE...

DuBose, Hampden C *see* MEMOIRS OF REV. JOHN LEIGHTHON WILSON

DUBOSE HEYWARD / Durham, Frank – ca.1954. 4 fiches – 9 – us South Carolina Historical [920]

Dubose, Martha *see* CRISIS IN THE CLASSROOM

DuBose, William Porcher *see*
- HIGH PRIESTHOOD AND SACRIFICE: AN EXPOSITION OF THE EPISTLE TO THE HEBREWS
- THE REASON OF LIFE

Duboueix, Michel *see* DISCOURS PRONONCE A L'ASSEMBLEE DE MESSIEURS LES ELECTEURS DU DISTRICT DE CLISSON, LE 10 MAI 1790

Dubourg *see* LE MESSIE: POEME: SUIVI DE QUELQUES POESIES MELEES

Duboys, Jacques *see* RECUEIL DES REGLEMENTS, DECLARATIONS ET ARRETS, CONCERNANT LE COMMERCE, L'ADMINISTRATION DE LA JUSTICE ET LA POLICE DES COLONIES FRANCAISES DE L'AMERIQUE ET LES ENGAGES. AVEC LE CODE NOIR, ET L'ADDITION AUDIT CODE

Dubreuil, Joseph Fereol *see* INDEX TO THE CRIMINAL & PENAL STATUTES OF CANADA, AS AFFECTING THE PROVINCE OF QUEBEC.

Dubroca, L *see* TRAITE DE LA PRONONCIATION

Dubrovin, N F *see*
- PRISOEDENENIE KRYMA K ROSII
- PUGACHEV I EGO SOOBSHCHNIKI

Dubruel, Marc *see* EN PLEIN CONFICT

Dubrujeaud, A *see* DES CONFLITS DE LOIS... DU TESTAMENT SOUS-SEING PRIVE

Dubuque, Iowa *see* MISCELLANEOUS EARLY NEWSPAPERS

Dubut, Louis Ambroise *see* ARCHITECTURE CIVILE

Duby, J E *see* BOTANICON GALLICUM

Ducancel *see* L'INTERIEUR DES COMITES REVOLUTIONNAIRES OU LES ARISTIDES MODERNES

Ducarne, M *see* L'ESCAUT...

Ducasse, Angel Braulio *see* ESTRINDENCIAS POESIAS

DuCasteleier *see* PLAN D'EDUCATION NATIONALE

Duceppe, Jean *see* MIROIR DU QUEBEC

Ducharme, Camille *see* LE BERTHELAIS

Ducharme, Charles Marie *see* RIS ET CROQUIS

Duchartre, P E S *see* REVUE BOTANIQUE

Duchatel, MT *see* LA CHARITE DANS SES RAPPORTS AVEC L'ETAT MORAL ET LE BIEN-ETRE DES CLASSES INFERIEURES DE LA SOCIETE

Duchaussois, P *see* FEMMES HEROIQUES!

DUCHAUSSOIS, ROSE DU CANADA... / Bayle, Constantino – Paris, 1932; Madrid: Razon y Fe, 1933 – 1 – sp Bibl Santa Ana [999]

Duche, Emile *see* QUELQUES PARTICULARITES SUR LE MOUVEMENT DE LA POPULATION DANS LE DEPARTEMENT DE L'YONNE

Duchene, John D *see* L'ELEVAGE DU CHEVAL EN CANADA

Duchenet, Edouard *see* HISTOIRES SOMALIES

Duchenne de Boulogne, G B A *see*
- DE L'ELECTRISATION LOCALISEE ET DE SON APPLICATION...
- PHYSIOLOGIE DES MOUVEMENTS DEMONTEE A L'AIDE...

Duchenois, J *see* LE REGIME FISCAL DES SOCIETES ETRANGERES EN FRANCE

Duchesne *see*
- COMPENDIO DE HISTORIA DE ESPANA. TOMO 1
- COMPENDIO DE HISTORIA DE ESPANA. TOMO 2

Duchesne, Andre *see*
- HISTOIRE GENEALOGIQUE DE LA MAISON DE BETHUNE
- HISTOIRE GENEALOGIQUE DE LA MAISON DE MONTMORENCY
- HISTORIAE FRANCORUM SCRIPTORES COAETANEI

Duchesne, Antoine Nicolas *see*
- MANUEL DE BOTANIQUE
- SUR LA FORMATION DES JARDINS

Duchesne, J *see* L'EXPEDITION DE MADAGASCAR

Duchesne, Louis *see*
- THE CHURCHES SEPARATED FROM ROME
- DE MACARIO MAGNETE ET SCRIPTIS EJUS
- EARLY HISTORY OF THE CHRISTIAN CHURCH FROM ITS FOUNDATION TO THE END OF THE FIFTH CENTURY
- EARLY HISTORY OF THE CHRISTIAN CHURCH FROM ITS FOUNDATION TO THE END OF THE THIRD CENTURY
- EGLISES SEPAREES
- ETUDES SUR LE LIBER PONTIFICALIS
- FASTES EPISCOPAUX DE L'ANCIENNE GAULE, TOME 1
- FASTES EPISCOPAUX DE L'ANCIENNE GAULE, TOME 2
- FASTES EPISCOPAUX DE L'ANCIENNE GAULE, TOME 3
- LIBER PONTIFICALIS
- LE LIBER PONTIFICALIS

Ducis *see*
- ABUFAR OU LA FAMILLE ARABE
- OTHELLO OU LE MORE DE VENISE

Ducis, C A *see* OCCUPATIONS NEUTRALITE MILITAIRE ET ANNEXION DE LA SAVOIE

Ducis, V F *see* DISCOURS PRONONCES DANS L'ACADEMIE FRANCAISE, LE 4 MARS 1979

Duckett, Kenneth W *see* BENJAMIN TAPPAN PAPERS

DUCKETT'S DISPATCH – (Duckett's Paper). London. -w. 4 Jan-3 May 1818. (18 ft) – 1 – uk British Libr Newspaper [072]

Duckworth, H T F *see*
- THE CHURCH OF CYPRUS
- GREEK MANUALS OF CHURCH DOCTRINE
- SOME PAGES OF LEVANTINE HISTORY

Duclos, C P *see* MEMOIRES SUR L'ORIGINE ET LES REVOLUTIONS DES LANGUES CELTIQUE ET FRANCAISE. LEBER. LEBER [J.M.] C. COLLECTION DES MEILEURES DISSERTATIONS, NOTICES ET TRAIT ES PARTICULIERS RELATIFS A L'HISTOIRE DE FRANCE

Duclos, Charles Pinot *see* CONFESSIONS D'UNE ROUE DE LA REGENCE

Duclos, J *see* DEMOCRATIE NOUVELLE

Duclos, L Jet al *see* LES NATIONALISMES MAGHREBINS

Duclot, C *see* ANALYSE DE L'EVOLUTION DE LA TRADITION CERAMIQUE DE METEPEC, VILLAGE DE L'ETAT DE MEXICO

Ducpetiaux, Edouard *see* DE LACONDITION PHYSIQUE ET MORALE DES JEUNES OUVRIERS ET DES MOYENS DE L'AMELIORER

Ducros, A *see*
- ETUDE ANTHROPO-BIOLOGIQUE DES GROUPES HMONG DE GUYANE, ENQUETE PRELIMINAIRE. RAPPORT DE MISSION CNRS
- L'EXECUTION D'UN MANDAT

Ducros, J *see* ETUDE ANTHROPO-BIOLOGIQUE DES GROUPES HMONG DE GUYANE, ENQUETE PRELIMINAIRE. RAPPORT DE MISSION CNRS

Ducros, J.Ducros, A. *see* ASPECTS SOCIO-DEMOGRAPHIQUES DU VILLAGE DE MACAYE: INTRODUCTION A L'ETUDE ANTHROPO-BIOLOGIQUE

Ducuing, Fr *see* LA GUERRE DE MONTAGNE (NAVARRE 1834-35 ET KABYLIE 1841-47): LES DOMINATIONS FRANCAISES-SYRIE, CANADA, INDE, MOREE, EGYPTE, PLATA

Duda, Joan L *see* PSYCHOLOGICAL ANTECEDENTS OF THE FREQUENCY AND INTENSITY OF FLOW IN GOLFERS

Duda-Dziewierz, Krystyna *see*
- "WIES"
- WIES MALOPOLSKA A EMIGRACJA AMERIKANSKA

Duden, K *see* DER RECHTSERWERB VOM NICHTBERECHTIGTEN

Dudenhausen, Wolfgang *see* BUERGSCHAFT UND GARANTIEVERTRAG UNTER BESONDERER BERUECKSICHTIGUNG DER BANKPRAXIS

Dudenhofen, Petra *see* RECHTSEXTREMISMUS IN DER BUNDESREPUBLIK DEUTSCHLAND – NEUE RECHTE UND REPUBLIKANER

Dudin, K *see* ORGANIZATSIIA SNABZHENCHESKOI RABOTY V SISTEME SEL'SKOKHOZIAISTVENNOI KOOPERATSII I VOPROSY PROIZVODSTVENNOGO KOOPERIROVANIIA

DUDLEY 1725-1849 – (Mf 1T-5T: Vital Records 1725-1812. Mf 5T-9T: Births & Deaths 1728-1849. Mf 9T: Out-of-Town Marriages 1732-99. Mf 9T-10T: Births 1844-49. Mf 10T: Marriages, Deaths 1844-49. Mf 10T-12T: Intentions 1796-1849. Mf 12T-13T: Marriages 1796-1843. Mf 13T: Colored Intents & Marriages 1821-27) – (mf ed 1996) – 13mf – 9 – 0-87623-243-8 – us Holbrook [920]

DUDLEY 1725-1891 – (Mf 1-4: Births & Deaths 1725-1849. Mf 5-8: Vital & Land Records 1725-1887. Mf 9-12: Marriage Intentions 1788-1882. Mf 13-14: Index to Intentions 1788- 1882. Mf 15-16: B,M,D 1844-54. Mf 17-21: Births 1854-91. Mf 22-23: Marriages 1854-91. Mf 24-27: Deaths 1854-91. Mf 28-32: Index to Births 1844-91. Mf 33-37: Index to Marriages 1844-91. Mf 38-40: Index to Deaths 1844-91. Mf 41: Soldiers & Officers 1861-65) – (mf ed 1986) – 41mf – 9 – 0-87623-010-9 – us Holbrook [920]

DUDLEY AND DISTRICT NEWS – England. -w. 3 Jan 1880-10 Jan 1885. (5 reels) – 1 – uk British Libr Newspaper [072]

DUDLEY AND EAST WORCESTERSHIRE GAZETTE – England. -w. 3 Jul-25 Sep 1869. (9 ft) – 1 – uk British Libr Newspaper [072]

DUDLEY AND MIDLAND COUNTIES EXPRESS – England. -w. 19 Sep 1857-21 Aug 1858. (1 reel) – 1 – uk British Libr Newspaper [072]

DUDLEY CHRONICLE – England. -w. 1 Jan 1910-4 Apr 1935. (25 reels) – 1 – uk British Libr Newspaper [072]

DUDLEY CHRONICLE – England. -w. 14 Feb-11 Jul 1885. (28 ft) – 1 – uk British Libr Newspaper [072]

DUDLEY GUARDIAN – England. -w. 24 Jul 1865-24 Jul 1875. (4 reels) – 1 – uk British Libr Newspaper [072]

DUDLEY HERALD – England. -w. 1912-20. (Wanting 1914). (8 reels) – 1 – uk British Libr Newspaper [072]

DUDLEY MERCURY – England. -w. 5 Feb 1887-8 Feb 1890. (2 reels) – 1 – uk British Libr Newspaper [072]

DUDLEY NEWS – England. -w. 20 Aug-1 Oct 1857. (5 ft) – 1 – uk British Libr Newspaper [072]

DUDLEY PAPERS / Dudley, Robert – 1559-90. Correspondence of Robert Dudley, Earl of Leicester – 1 – uk Microform Academic [920]

Dudley, Robert *see* DUDLEY PAPERS

DUDLEY WEEKLY TIMES – (Dudley Times). England. -w. 20 Dec 1856-18 Dec 1858. (1 reel) – 1 – uk British Libr Newspaper [072]

DUDLEY'S CASES IN EQUITY / South Carolina. Supreme Court – (A Pre-NRS title) – 1v. 1837-1838 (all publ) – 3mf – 9 – $4.50 – LLMC 94-031 – us L.L.M.C. [340]

DUDLEY'S LAW REPORTS / South Carolina. Supreme Court – (A Pre-NRS title) – 1v. 1837-1838 (all publ) – 9mf – 9 – $13.50 – LLMC 94-019 – us L.L.M.C. [340]

DUDLEY'S REPORTS / Georgia. Supreme Court – (A Pre-NRS title) – 1v. 1821-1833 (all publ) – 4mf – 9 – $6.00 – LLMC 91-022 – us L.L.M.C. [340]

Dudon, P *see* LE GNOSTIQUE DE CLEMENT D'ALEXANDRIE. OPUSCULE INEDIT DE FENELON

DUE LEZIONI, NELLA PRIMA DELLE QUALI SI DICHIARA UN SONETTO DI M. MICHELAGNOLO BUONAROTTI. NELLA SECONDA SI DISPUTA QUALE SIA PIU NOBILE ARTE LA SCULTURA, O LA PITTURA / Varchi, Benedetto – BO 1025 1. 1549 – 9 – ne IDC [700]

LE DUE REGOLE DELLA PROSPETTIVA PRATICA / Vignola, J – O 1027 1. 1583 – 9 – ne IDC [700]
LE DUE REGOLE DELLA PROSPETTIVA PRATICA / Vignola, J – Roma, 1583 – 3mf – 9 – sp Cultura [720]
DUE TRATTATI UNO INTORNO ALLE OTTO PRINCIPALI ARTI DELL' OREFICERIA. L'ALTRO IN MATERIA DELL' ARTE DELLA SCULTURA / Cellini, B – Fiorenza. 1568. BO-197 1 – 9 – ne IDC [700]
Dueerkob, Monika *see* TRAUERN
Duehring, Eugen *see* DER ERSATZ DER RELIGION DURCH VOLLKOMMENERES UND DIE ABSTREIFUNG ALLES ASIATISMUS
Duehring, Eugen Karl *see* DIE JUDENFRAGE
Duehring, Hans *see* DAS GYMNASIUM MARIENWERDER
DUEL *see* TROIS ETUDES
UN DUEL A POUDRE: COMEDIE EN TROIS ACTES / Fontaine, Raphael Ernest – s.l.: s.n., 1868 (St. Hyacinthe Quebec: Journal de St. Hyacinthe). 03141. (Pre-1900 Canadiana) – 9 – cn C.I.H.M. [820]
Duelfer, E *see* OPERATIONAL EFFICIENCY OF AGRICULTURAL COOPERATIVES IN DEVELOPING COUNTRIES
DUELING (A SERMON) / Kendrick, J R – 1853 – 1 – 5.00 – us Baptist [240]
Duemichen, J *see*
- ALTAEGYPTISCHE TEMPELINSCHRIFTEN IN DEN JAHREN 1863-1865 AN ORT UND STELLEN GESAMMELT
- DER GRABPALAST DES PATUAMENAP IN DER THEBANISCHEN NEKROPOLIS

[THE DUENNA] HAD I A HEART. IRISH AIR OF GRAMACHRE / Linley, T – Philadelphia: B Carr & Co, 179- – 1 – us Sibley [780]
Duenners, J H *see* DENKSCHREIBEN UEBER DIE REORGANISIRUNG DES NIEDERL
Duentzer, Heinrich *see*
- ABHANDLUNGEN ZU GOETHES LEBEN UND WERKEN
- AUS GOETHE'S FREUNDESKREISE
- AUS HERDERS NACHLASS
- BRIEFWECHSEL ZWISCHEN GOETHE UND STAATSRATH SCHULTZ
- CHARLOTTE VON STEIN, GOETHE'S FREUNDIN
- CHARLOTTE VON STEIN UND CORONA SCHROETER
- FRAUENBILDER AUS GOETHE'S JUGENDZEIT
- FREUNDESBILDER AUS GOETHES LEBEN
- FRIEDERIKE VON SESENHEIM IM LICHTE DER WAHRHEIT
- GOETHE, KARL AUGUST UND OTTOKAR LORENZ
- GOETHE UND KARL AUGUST
- SCHILLERS LYRISCHE GEDICHTE
- UHLANDS DRAMEN UND DRAMENENTWUERFE
- WIELANDS OBERON

DUENYAYA IKINCI GELIS YAHUT ISTANBUL'DA NELER OLMUS / Cevdet, Mehmed – Istanbul: Sark Matbaasi, 1921 – $40.00 – us MEDOC [470]
Duer, John *see* A LECTURE ON THE LAW OF REPRESENTATIONS IN MARINE INSURANCE.
Duerbeck, Ernst *see* KURSACHSEN UND DIE DURCHFUEHRUNG DES PRAGER FRIEDENS 1635
Dueren, Wilhelm *see* UEBER GOETHE UND SPENGLER
DUERENER ZEITUNG : BA DER AACHENER VOLKSZEITUNG – Dueren, West Germany. 1992- – ca 7r per yr – 1 – gw Mikrofilm [072]
Duerer, Albrecht *see*
- ETLICHE UNDERRICHT
- UNDERWEYSUNG DER MESSUMG MIT DEM ZIRKEL UND RICHTSCHEYT IN LINIEN EBNEN UND GANTZEN CORPOREN ZU SAMEN GEZOGE UND ZU NUTZ ALLE KUNST-LIEBHABENDEN MIT ZU GEHOERIGEN FIGUREN IN TRUCK GEBRACHT
- VIER BUECHER VON MENSCHLICHER PROPORTION

Duerer-Bund *see* DIE WASSERSNOT IM EMMENTAL AM 13. AUGUST 1837
DUERERS BRIEFE, TAGEBUECHER UND REIME / Thausing, Moriz – O 517c. 1872 – 9 – ne IDC [760]
DUERFEN WIR NOCH CHRISTEN BLEIBEN? : KRITISCHE BETRACHTUNGEN ZUR THEOLOGIE DER GEGENWART / Heinrici, Carl Friedrich Georg – Leipzig: Duerr, 1901 – 1mf – 9 – 0-8370-2080-8 – 1985-0080 – us A.T.L.A. [240]
Duerkop, K *see* DIE INTERNATIONALISIERUNG DER ELBE
Duerksen, Rosella R *see* HYMODY OF THE 16TH CENTURY ANABAPTISTS
LES DUES JUMELLES OU LA MEPRISE / Bossi, C – (Ballet arr. for piano with violin accomp. Title page signed by the composer) – London: Goulding, Phipps & d'Almaine, 1799 – 1 – us Sibley [780]
DUESSELDORFER GENERAL-ANZEIGER – Germany. Duesseldorfer Nachrichten. -d. 1 Sept 1916-6 Aug 1919. 16 reels – 1 – uk British Libr Newspaper [072]
DUESSELDORFER JOURNAL *see* DUESSELDORFER KREISBLATT UND TAEGLICHER ANZEIGER
DUESSELDORFER JOURNAL UND KREISBLATT *see* DUESSELDORFER KREISBLATT UND TAEGLICHER ANZEIGER
DUESSELDORFER KREISBLATT UND TAEGLICHER ANZEIGER – (Title changes, no.120, 1848: Duesseldorfer Journal und Kreisblatt; Duesseldorfer Journal, 1 Jan 1856; Niederrheinische Volks-Zeitung, 12 Sep 1860; Rheinische Zeitung, 1863 no.238, Koeln) – Duesseldorf, Germany. 1848-49 – 2r – 1 – gw Mikrofilm [072]
DUESSELDORFER ZEITUNG – Duesseldorf, Germany. 1848-49 – 4r – 1 – gw Mikrofilm [072]
DUET FOR TWO PERFORMERS ON ONE GRAND PIANOFORTE, [K.521] / Mozart, Wolfgang Amadeus – London: Monzani & Cimador, [180-?] – 1 – us Sibley [780]
DUET, MOZART'S FIRST, FOR VIOLIN AND TENOR [KOECH. VERZ.423] / Mozart, Wolfgang Amadeus – (Separate parts) – London: Printed for Monzani & Cimador, [1802] – 1 – us Sibley [780]
DUETTINOS, 12 ORIGINAL FOR TWO GERMAN FLUTES OR FLUTE AND VIOLIN, OP.12 / Monzani, T – London: Clementi & Co, 180- – 1 – us Sibley [780]
Duez, N *see* LE VRAY ET PARFAIT GUIDON DE LA LANGUE FRANCOISE
Dufays, Felix *see* JOURS TROUBLES, PAGES D'EPOPEE AFRICAINE
Duff, Alexander *see* INDIA AND INDIA MISSIONS
Duff, Archibald *see*
- HINTS ON OLD TESTAMENT THEOLOGY
- THEOLOGY AND ETHICS OF THE HEBREWS

Duff, David *see* THE EARLY CHURCH
Duff, E C *see* GAZETTEER OF THE KONTAGORA PROVINCE
Duff, Mrs. E S *see* REDEEMED BY THE BLOOD
DUFF GREEN PAPERS / Green, Duff – 1810-1902. University of North Carolina Library. Guide – 1 – $450.00 – us U.N.C. Southern Hist [920]
Duff, William *see* AN ESSAY ON ORIGINAL GENIUS AND ITS VARIOUS MODES OF EXERTION IN PHILOSOPHY AND THE FINE ARTS, PARTICULARLY IN POETRY
Duff, William A *see* HISTORY OF NORTH CENTRAL OHIO
Dufferin, Ava, Hamilton-Temple-Blackwood, Frederick *see* A YACHT VOYAGE: LETTERS FROM HIGH LATITUDES, BEING SOME ACCOUNT OF A VOYAGE IN THE SCHOONER YACHT "FOAM", 85 O.M., TO ICELAND, JAN MAYEN, AND SPITZBERGEN, IN 1856
Dufferin, Earl of *see* A YACHT VOYAGE: LETTERS FROM HIGH LATITUDES, BEING SOME ACCOUNT OF A VOYAGE IN THE SCHOONER YACHT "FOAM", 85 O.M., TO ICELAND, JAN MAYEN, AND SPITZBERGEN, IN 1856
Dufferin, Lord *see* UN VOYAGE EN YACHT: LETTRES DE HAUTES LATITUDES: RECIT D'UN VOYAGE FAIT EN 1856, SUR LE YACHT LE "FOAM", EN ISLANDE, A JAN-MAYEN ET AU SPITZBERG
Duffield, Samuel Willoughby *see*
- ENGLISH HYMNS
- THE LATIN HYMN-WRITERS AND THEIR HYMNS

Duffy, Charles Gavan *see*
- FOUR YEARS OF IRISH HISTORY, 1845-1849
- THOMAS DAVIS: THE MEMOIRS OF AN IRISH PATRIOT, 1840-1846

Duffy, Ward E *see* WHO'S WHO IN CONNECTICUT
Dufort, Giovanni Battista *see* TRATTO DEL BALLO NOBILE DI GIAMBATISTA DUFORTE INDIRIZZATO ALL'ECCELENZE DELLE SIGNORE DAME, E DE'SIGNORI CAVALERI, NAPOLETANI
Dufour, Charles *see* LETTRE A UN DOCTEUR DE SORBONNE SUR LE SUJET DE PLUSIEURS ESCRITS COMPOSEZ DE LA VIE ET DE L'ETAT DE MARIE DES VALES, DU DIOCESE DE COUTANCES
Dufour, Helene *see* MARIE-CLAIRE BLAIS
Dufour, L *see*
- EXCURSION ENTOMOLOGIQUE AUX DUNES DE BASCARROSSE ET D'ARCACHON
- EXCURSION ENTOMOLOGIQUE DANS LES MONTAGNES DE LA VALLEE D'OSSAU

Dufourcq, Albertus *see* DE MANICHAEISMO APUD LATINOS QUINTO SEXTOQUE SAECULO
Dufourq-Lagelouse, L *see* LES BANQUES ETRANGERES EN FRANCE
Dufoussat, Henry *see* DE L'HYPOTHEQUE LEGALE DE LA FEMME MARIEE
Dufresne, F *see* QUATUOR BRILLIANT, OP. 20, NO. 1
Dufresne, Guy *see* KEBEC
Dufresne, J-A *see* L'INDUSTRIEL
Dufresne, Lise *see* L'INSTITUTION DES SOURDS-MUETS DE MONTREAL (1848-1948)
Dufresne, P *see* HISTOIRE NATURELLE ET MEDICALE DE LA FAMILLE DES VALERIANEES
Dufriche-Foulaines, F N *see* CODE DES PRISES ET DU COMMERCE DE TERRE ET DE MER
DUFUR DISPATCH – Dufur, OR. -w. 1910-41 – 1 – 168.00 – us Oregon Hist [071]
DUFUR DISPATCH – Dufur, OR. -w. 22 Oct 1892-12 Jun 1907. 1 roll – 1 – us U.O. Library [071]
DUGA – Belgrade, Yugoslavia. -w. Jan-Dec 1960. 2 reels – 1 – uk British Libr Newspaper [949]
Dugard, William *see*
- THE ENGLISH RUDIMENTS OF THE LATINE TONGUE
- RHETORICA ELEMENTA QUESTIONIBUS ET RESPONSIONIBUS EXPLICATA

Dugas, Georges *see*
- HISTOIRE DE L'OUEST CANADIEN DE 1822 A 1869
- HISTORIE DE LA PAROISSE DE SAINTE-ANNE DES PLAINES, ERIGEE SOUS MGR HUBERT, EVEQUE DE QUEBEC, EN L'ANNEE 1787
- QUELQUES ERREURS HISTORIQUES A CORRIGER

Dugast-Matifeux, Charles *see* COLLECTION DE DOCUMENTS IMPR. OU MANUS. CONCERNANT DIVERS PERSONNAGES DE L'EPOQUE REVOLUTIONNAIRE
Dugat, PD *see* LA MORT D'AZAIL OU LE RAPT EN DINA
Dugdale, B *see* DIARIES, 1777-1815
Dugdale, William *see* ORIGINES JURIDICIALES
Duggan, J *see* LIFE OF CHRIST
Duguay, Camille *see*
- LE MINEUR
- LE NICOLETAIN
- LE REGARD

Duguay, Camille et al *see* LA PAROLE
Duguay, M *see*
- LE NICOLETAIN
- LE VOIX DES BOIS-FRANCS

Duguay, P H Ernest *see* LE R. P. LOUIS SACHE DE LA COMPAGNIE DE JESUS
Dugue, M, L'abbe *see* ARIETTE
Duguet, Ch *see* SALUT AU NOVEAU MONDE
Duguit, L *see* CONGRES DE DROIT INTERNATIONAL D'ANVERS
DuHalde, J B *see*
- DESCRIPTION GEOGRAPHIQUE, HISTORIQUE,... DE L'EMPIRE DE LA CHINE ET DE LA TARTARIE CHINOISE
- A DESCRIPTION OF THE EMPIRE OF CHINA AND CHINESE-TARTARY, TOGETHER WITH THE KINGDOMS OF KOREA AND TIBET:...

Duhamel du Monceau, H L *see* TRAITE DES ARBRES ET ARBUSTES
Duhamel du Monceau, Henri Louis *see*
- ART DU CIRIER
- ELEMENS DE L'ARCHITECTURE NAVALE OU TRAITE PRATIQUE DE LA CONSTRUCTION DES VAISSEAUX
- TRAITE DES ARBRES ET ARBUSTES

Duhamel du Monceau, M *see*
- ART DU COUVREUR
- L'ART DU TUILIER ET DU BRIQUETIER
- TRAITE DES ARBRES FRUITIERS: CONTENANT LEUR FIGURE, LEUR DESCRIPTION, LEUR CULTURE...

Duhamel, Georges *see*
- ICHTYOFAUNE DES SECTEURS INDIEN OCCIDENTAL ET ATLANTIQUE ORIENTAL DE L'OCEAN AUSTRAL: BIOGEOGRAPHIE, CYCLES BIOLOGIQUES ET DYNAMIQUE DES POPULATIONS
- LA LANGOUSTE DES ILES ST PAUL ET AMSTERDAM (JASUS PAULENSIS, HELLER 1862). BIOLOGIE ET PECHE

Duhamel-Jouve, A *see* INFLUENCE DES FACTEURS PHYSICO-CHIMIQUES DE L'ENVIRONNEMENT SUR LES ACTIVITES RESPIRATOIRES ET VENTILATOIRES D'UN ORGANISME INTERTIDAL: LE CRABE CARCINUS MAENAS (L.)
DUHAUTCOURS OU LE CONTRAT D'UNION / Picard – (French Theatre Series). Paris. Huet et Charon, an IX. 1801 – 9 – fr Hachette [820]
DuHays, Charles *see* L'EMPLOI DU LOISIR
Duhigg, Barthelomew Thomas *see* A LETTER TO THE RIGHT HON. LORD MANNERS, &C. &C. &C. ON THE EXPEDIENCY OF AN IMMEDIATE AND SEPARATE RECORD COMMISSION, TO INVESTIGATE, ILLUSTRATE, AND ARRANGE THE RECORDS OF IRELAND.
Duhm, Bernhard *see*
- DAS BUCH HABAKUK: TEXT, UEBERSETZUNG UND ERKLAERUNG
- DAS BUCH HIOB
- DAS BUCH JEREMIA
- DIE GOTTGEWEIHTEN IN DER ALTTESTAMENTLICHEN RELIGION
- DIE PSALMEN
- DIE THEOLOGIE DER PROPHETEN ALS GRUNDLAGE FUER...DER ISRAELITISCHEN RELIGION

Duhm, Hans *see* DIE BOESEN GEISTER IM ALTEN TESTAMENT
Duhr, Bernhard *see*
- JESUITEN-FABELN
- DIE STUDIENORDNUNG DER GESELLSCHAFT JESU

Duhr, J *see* APERCUS SUR L'ESPAGNE CHRETIENNE DU 4TH SIECLE OU LE "DE LAPSO" DE BACHIARIUS
Duignan, Peter *see*
- AMERICANS IN BLACK AFRICA UP TO 1865
- A CHECKLIST OF SERIALS FOR AFRICAN STUDIES
- MADAGASCAR

Duis, E *see* THE GOOD OLD TIMES IN MC LEAN COUNTY
Duisberg, Adolf von *see* PRIMER OF KANURI GRAMMAR
DUISTERNIS EN LICHT / Dijkstra, Harmen – De zending in Oost-Afrika en op Madagaskar geschetst. 1886 – 1 – us A.T.L.A. [240]
DUITSCHE LIER, DRAAYENDE VEEL VAN DE NIEUWSTE, DEFTIGE, EN DERTELENDE TOONEN : BEVAT IN TIEN VERDEELINGEN, EN VERCIERT MET KOPERE PLAATEN. TWEEDE DRUK. VERMEERDERT MET HET LEEVEN VAN DEN AUTHEUR / Luyken, J – Den Haag, 1783 – 2mf – 9 – O-3238/1 – ne IDC [760]
Dujardin, Edouard *see* LES PREDECESSEURS DE DANIEL: RECHERCHES SUR LA TRACE DE FAITS ET D'IDEES
Dujarric, Gaston *see*
- L'ETAT MAHDISTE DU SOUDAN
- LA VIE DU SULTAN RABAH; LES FRANCAIS AU TCHAD

A DUKE AND NO DUKE / Tate, N – A farce as it is acted by their majesties servants. Written by N. Tate. With the several songs set to music, with thorow basses for the theorbo, or bass viol. 1685 – 9 – us Sibley [780]
DUKE BAR ASSOCIATION JOURNAL – Duke Law School, Student Bar Association Proceedings and Notes and Comments on current Decisions. v1-10. 1933-42 – 18mf – 9 – $27.00 – LLMC 84-459 – us L.L.M.C. [073]
DUKE DIVINITY SCHOOL BULLETIN / REVIEW – (Lacking: summer 1969) – v1-46. 1936-83 – 9r – 1 – ATLA S0747 – us A.T.L.A. [240]
Duke, Edward *see* BENEATH THE SURFACE, OR, PHYSICAL TRUTHS...SHOWN TO BE LATENT IN...HOLY SCRIPTURES
DUKE ENVIRONMENTAL LAW AND POLICY FORUM – v1-5. 1991-95 – 9 – $51.00 set – us Hein [340]
DUKE INDIAN ORAL HISTORY COLLECTION – (Index 8r $640) – 310mf – 9 – $5.00f – us Ross [975]
DUKE LAW JOURNAL – (v1-7 1959-84 in reel $610.00. 1985-v45 in mf $366.00. Includes index) – v1-7 1959-v44 1951-95 – 5,6,9 – $976.00 set – us Hein [340]
Duker, A C *see*
- GISBERTUS VOETIUS

Dukes, J L *see* GINZEI OXFORD

Dukes, L *see*
- MOSES BEN ESRA AUS GRANADA
- ZUR KENNTNISS DER NEUHEBRAEISCHEN RELIGIOESEN POESIE

DUKH KHRISTIANINA : DUKHOVNO-LITERATURNYI ZHURNAL – (Lackings v2 n1 1861) – v2 n1-7, 9-12 1861; n1-3 1865 – 2r – 1 – ATLA S0193C – us A.T.L.A. [073]

DUKHOVNAIA BESEDA, EZHENEDEL'NO IZDAVAEMAIA PRI SANKT PETERBURGSKOI DUKHOVNOI SEMINARII – Spb. 1858-76. Lacking: 1863, v. 20; 1865; 1866, v. 1; 1867, v. 2; 1869 (2)-1876. BR-1586 2 – 8 – ne IDC [947]

DUKHOVNAIA BESIEDA – n1,16-43,46-55. 1866 (complete) – 1r – 1 – ATLA S0193D – us A.T.L.A. [073]

DUKHOVNAIA POLITSIIA V ROSSII / Reisner, Mikhail Andreevich – Spb. 1907. BR-10,090 1 – 9 – ne IDC [240]

DUKHOVNYE SHKOLY V ROSSII DO REFORMY 1808 GODA / Znamenskii, P – Kazan'. 1881. BR-7988 2 – 8 – ne IDC [947]

DUKHOVNYI VESTNIK – Khar'kov. 1862-67. BR-3399 2 – 8 – ne IDC [073]

DUKUN AS REFERRER OF FAMILY PLANNING ACCEPTORS : A STUDY IN EAST JAVA / Pardoko, R H & Soemodinoto, Soekanto – Surabaya: National Institute of Public Health, [1972-1975] – us Res Libr [300]

Dulac, J *see* FLORE DU DEPARTEMENT DES HAUTES-PYRENEES

Dulaney, N M *see* THE EFFECTS OF A FLEXIBILITY TRAINING PROGRAM ON FLEXIBILITY TEST SCORES IN ELEMENTARY SCHOOL CHILDREN

Dulard, Paul Alexandre *see* OEUVRES DIVERSES

DuLaurens, Henri J *see* IMIRCE, OU LA FILLE DE LA NATURE

DULCE DOMUM : GEORGE MOBERLY (D.C.L., HEADMASTER OF WINCHESTER COLLEGE, 1835-1866, BISHOP OF SALISBURY, 1869-1885), HIS FAMILY AND FRIENDS / Moberly, C A E – London: J. Murray, 1911 – 1mf – us A.T.L.A. [240]

Dulfer, K *see* ZWEI JAHRE ARCHIVARBEIT IM REICHSKOMMISSARIAT OSTLAND

Dulikravich, G S *see* INVERSE PROBLEMS IN ENGINEERING

Duling, Anton *see* CITHERA MELICA, VEL OPUS MUSICUM PLANE NOVUM... VOCIBUS 12, 10 AND 8

Dulken, G van *see*
- HET GEREINIGT HERTE DOOR 'T GELOOF

Dulles, John Foster *see* THE PAPERS OF JOHN FOSTER DULLES AND OF CHRISTIAN A. HERTER, 1953-61

DULUTH AND THE COUNTY OF ST LOUIS / Van Brunt, Walter – Chicago: American Historical Society, 1921. 3v.Minnesota Reel 14. (The Cox Library Collection) – 5 – us Americana [978]

DULUTH VOLKSFREUND – Duluth, MN: Josef Grahamer, jul 1894-mar 17 1898 – 2r – us Res Libr [071]

DULWICH PICTURE GALLERY / Dulwich Picture Gallery. London – (The complete collection of this fine but little known gallery. 750 paintings illustrated, with 250 details) – 1987 – 14 colour mf – 15 – \$580.00 – 0-907716-22-9 – uk Mindata [750]

Dulwich Picture Gallery. London *see* DULWICH PICTURE GALLERY

DUMA – 1990- – 1 – sz Infoprint [947]

DUMA – (Backfile through 1998 \$85/r. Cont of: Rabotnichesko delo) – Bulgaria, 1999- – 4r per y – 1 – \$320.00 standing order – us Ross [072]

DUMA *see* RABOTNICESKO DELO

Dumais, A *see* INDEX ALPHABETIQUE DES NOMS DE 3400 FAMILLES DE DOUZE ENFANTS VIVANTS

Dumarsais, Cesar-Chesneau *see* ANALYSE DE LA RELIGION CHRETIENNE

Dumas, A-J *see* L'ART DE LA MUSIQUE ENSEIGNE ET PRATIQUE

Dumas, Alexandre *see*
- CELEBRATED CRIMES
- EL CONDE DE MONTECRISTO

Dumas, Gabriel-Marie *see* BIBLIOGRAPHIE ANALYTIQUE DE L'OEUVRE DU REVEREND PERE ALEXIS DE BARBEZIEUX, CAPUCIN

Dumas, J *see* LES SANCTIONS DE L'ARBITRAGE...

Dumas, J B *see* DISCOURS ET ELOGES ACADEMIQUES

Dumas, Petrus *see* VIRIDARIUM HUMILITATIS

Dumas, R *see* DES DIFFERENTS SYSTEMES DE REPRESSION DES CRIMES ET DELITS COMMIS EN PAYS ETRANGERS...

Dumas, Rollande *see* BIBLIOGRAPHIE ANALYTIQUE DE LA PSYCHOLOGIE INFANTILE, 1948 A 1952

Dumazedier, Joffre *see* TELEVISION AND RURAL ADULT EDUCATION

Dumbar, Gerhard *see* HET KERKELYK EN WERELTLYK DEVENTER

Dumbarton Oaks Collection *see* PRE-COLUMBIAN ART

DUMBARTONSHIRE, 1837 : BRITISH ISLES CENSUS DIRECTORIES PROJECT, SCOTLAND. VOL 35 – 1mf – 9 – A\$9.00 – at Vine [941]

Dumeril, A M C *see*
- CONSIDERATIONS GENERALES SUR LA CLASSE DES INSECTES
- ENTOMOLOGIE ANALYTIQUE

Dumesnil, Clement *see* DE L'ABOLITION DES DROITS FEODAUX ET SEIGNEURIAUX DU CANADA, ET SUR LE MEILLEUR MODE A EMPLOYER POUR ACCORDER UNE JUSTE INDEMNITE AUX SEIGNEURS

Dumesnil, Octave *see* RAPPORT GENERAL A M. LE MINISTRE DE L'INTERIEUR SUR LE SERVICE DES ALIENES EN 1874 PAR LES INSPECTEURS GENERAUX DU SERVICE

Dumestre, G *see* ATLAS LINGUISTIQUE DE COTE D'IVOIRE

DUMFRIESSHIRE, 1837 : BRITISH ISLES CENSUS DIRECTORIES PROJECT, SCOTLAND. VOL 36 – 1mf – 9 – A\$9.00 – at Vine [941]

DUMFRIESSHIRE, 1852 : BRITISH ISLES CENSUS DIRECTORIES PROJECT, SCOTLAND. VOL 2 – 1mf – 9 – A\$9.00 – at Vine [941]

DUMFRIESSHIRE (DUMFRIES AND ANNAN), 1820 : BRITISH ISLES CENSUS DIRECTORIES PROJECT, SCOTLAND. VOL 61 – 1mf – 9 – A\$9.00 – at Vine [941]

Dumke, Charles L *see* PROTECTIVE MECHANISM OF ESTRADIOL ON ECCENTRICALLY INDUCED MUSCLE DAMAGE

DER DUMME GARTNER, ODER DIE BEYDEN ANTON, EIN COMISCHES SINGSPIEL IN ZWEY AUFZUGEN FURS CLAVIER GESETZT / Neefe, CG – Bonn: N Simrock, [1795?] – 1 – us Sibley [780]

Dumolard, Henry *see* LE JAPON POLITIQUE ECONOMIQUE ET SOCIAL

Dumont *see* PARALLELE DE PLANS DES PLUS BELLES SALLES DE SPECTACLES D'ITALIE ET DE FRANCE AVEC DES DETAILS DE MACHINES THEATRALES

Dumont, A A *see* LES HABITATIONS OUVRIERES DANS LES GRANDS CENTRES INDUSTRIELS ET PLUS PARTICULIEREMENT DANS LA REGION DU NORD

Dumont, Arsene *see*
- DE L'INFECONDITE DE CERTAINES POPULATIONS INDUSTRIELLES.
- ESSAI SUR LA NATALITE DANS LE CANTON DE BEAUMONT-HAGUE
- LA NATALITE A SAINT-PIERRE-DE-CLAIRAC (LOT-ET-GARONNE): ESSAI DE SOCIOLOGIE CONCRETE

Dumont de Courset, G L M *see*
- LE BOTANISTE CULTIVATEUR
- LE BOTANISTE CULTIVATEUR OU DESCRIPTION, CULTURE ET USAGE

Dumont d'Urville, J S C *see* ENUMERATIO PLANTARUM QUAS IN INSULIS ARCHIPELAGI AUT LITTORIBUS PONTI-EUXINI, ANNIS 1819 ET 1820, COLLEGIT

Dumont, Emile *see* LES CONDITIONS DE L'SENSEIGNEMENT RELIGIEUX DANS LES EGLISES NATIONALES DE LA SUISSE ROMANDE

Dumont, Georges A *see* NOTES SUR L'IRLANDE

Dumont, J *see* NOUVEAU RECUEIL DE TRAITEZ,...

Dumortier, B C J *see*
- ANALYSE DES FAMILLES DES PLANTES
- COMMENTATIONES BOTANICAE
- FLORULA BELGICA
- HEPATICAE EUROPAE
- SYLLOGE JUNGERMANNIDEARUM EUROPAE INDIGENARUM

Dumoulard, H F *see* MEMOIRES ET CORRESPONDANCE. ET PRECEDES D'UNE NOTICE HISTORIQUE, REDIGEES SUR PIECES AUTHENTIQUES ET ORIGINALES

Dumoulin, Stephane *see* LE TONKIN: EXPLORATION DU MEKONG

Dumoutet, E *see* LE DESIR DE VOIR L'HOSTIE ET LES ORIGINES DE LA DEVOTION AU SAINT-SACREMENT

DUMPFE TROMMEL UND BERAUSCHTES GONG : NACHDICHTUNGEN CHINESISCHER KRIEGSLYRIK / Klabund – Leipzig: Insel-Verlag, 1915 – 1r – 1 – us U.W. Library [480]

DUMPLIN CREEK BAPTIST CHURCH. JEFFERSON COUNTY. TENNESSEE : CHURCH RECORDS – 1797-1938 – 1 – 43.65 – us Baptist [240]

DUMY BEDNI AKA : ORGAN MSTISLAVSKOGO UEZDN. KOMITETA R.K.P. (BOLSHEVIKOV) – (Includes c.1: 1921:Nov.7) – Mstislavl: Izd. Smolenskogo gubernskogo upravlenii a izdatelskim delom, 191u – 1 – CSUXAKG0822-S – us Hoover Inst Photo [947]

DUMY KOOPERATORA – Penza, 1920 n1 – 1mf – 9 – COR-584/1 – ne IDC [334]

DUMY VEKA – Literaturno-nauchno-populiarnyi. Zhurnal. v. 1-2. Spb. 1907. BR-3975 2 – 8 – ne IDC [947]

DUNA ZEITUNG – (In German) – Riga, Latvia, 1888-1908 – 38r – 1 – \$2,600.00 – us Ross [072]

Dunal, M F *see*
- HISTOIRE NATURELLE MEDICALE ET ECONOMIQUE DES SOLANUM,...
- MONOGRAPHIE DE LA FAMILLE DES ANONACEES
- SOLANORUM GENERUMQUE AFFINIUM SYNOPSIS

DUNAMIS MAGAZINE – Sept 1972-1992. Continued annually – 1 – uk World [073]

Dunan, C *see* THEORIE PSYCHOLOGIQUE DE L'ESPACE

DUNANTULI NAPLO – (Cont as: Uj Dunantuli Naplo as of 3 Apr 1990) – Pecs, Hungary. 1962-Jun 1991 – 60r – 1 – us L of C Photodup [072]

DUNAVSKA PRAVDA – Ruse, Bulgaria. 1951-Jul 1990 – 55r – 1 – us L of C Photodup [949]

DUNAVSKI OTECHESTVEN FRONT – Ruse, Bulgaria. Feb-Aug 1945 – 1r – 1 – us L of C Photodup [949]

Dunbar, Leo *see* WHAT EVERY GOOD LIBERAL NEEDS TO KNOW: THE ECONOMICS OF FRIEDRICH VON HAYEK

Dunbar, Paul Laurence *see*
- PAPERS
- THE PAUL LAURENCE DUNBAR COLLECTION
- A SELECTION OF WORKS BY AND ABOUT PAUL L. DUNBAR

DUNBAR REVIEW – Dunbar, NE. -w. Oct 1900-Jan. 1901; Apr. 1901-Sep. 1902; Aug. 1909-May 1913; Sep. 1915-May 1917; Feb. 1935-Jun. 1935, incomplete – 1 – us NE Hist [071]

Dunbarton, New Hampshire. Dunbarton Baptist Church *see* RECORDS

Duncalf, Frederic *see* PARALLEL SOURCE PROBLEMS IN MEDIEVAL HISTORY

Duncan *see* HISTORY OF ALLEN AND WOODSON COUNTIES

Duncan, Andrew *see* LATINAE GRAMMATICAE

Duncan, Bruce *see* TO PARTICIPATE – NOT JUST YOUR RIGHT BUT YOUR DUTY

Duncan, Daniel *see* A NEW ENGLISH GRAMMAR

Duncan, Daniel Wendell *see* THE EFFECT OF A STUDY OF THE BIBLICAL CONCEPT OF CHURCH ON ESTABLISHING LONG RANGE PLANNING GOALS

Duncan, David *see* THE LIFE AND LETTERS OF HERBERT SPENCER

Duncan, Francis *see* THE ROYAL PROVINCE OF NEW SCOTLAND AND HER BARONETS

Duncan, George *see* THE EPISTLE OF PAUL TO THE GALATIANS

Duncan, Isadora *see* MY LIFE

Duncan, J *see* ENTOMOLOGY

Duncan, J T *see* CONTAGIOUS DISEASES OF CATTLE: PRIZE ESSAY

Duncan, John *see* LE BON SECOURS

Duncan, L Wallace *see* HISTORY OF NEOSHA AND WILSON COUNTIES

Duncan, P M *see*
- AN ABSTRACT OF THE GEOLOGY OF INDIA
- A MONOGRAPH OF THE BRITISH FOSSIL CORALS
- TERTIARY AND UPPER CRETACEOUS FAUNA OF WESTERN INDIA

Duncan, Peter *see* A NARRATIVE OF THE WESLEYAN MISSION TO JAMAICA

Duncan, Robert Adam Haldane Philips *see* ADMIRAL DUNCAN

Duncan, Sara Jeannette *see*
- AN AMERICAN GIRL IN LONDON
- A DAUGHTER OF TODAY: A NOVEL
- HIS HONOUR AND A LADY
- THE PATH OF A STAR
- THE SIMPLE ADVENTURES OF A MEMSAHIB
- A SOCIAL DEPARTURE: HOW ORTHODOCIA AND I WENT AROUND THE WORLD BY OURSELVES
- THE STORY OF SONNY SAHIB
- A VOYAGE OF CONSOLATION: BEING IN THE NATURE OF A SEQUEL TO THE EXPERIENCES OF "AN AMERICAN GIRL IN LONDON"

Duncan, Susan C *see* THE ROLE OF COGNITIVE APPRAISAL AND FRIENDSHIP PROVISIONS IN CHILDREN'S EXPERIENCE OF AFFECT IN PHYSICAL ACTIVITY

Duncan, William *see* THE ELEMENTS OF LOGICK

Duncan, William C *see* TEARS OF JESUS OF NAZARETH

Duncan, William Wallace *see* A NEW HEBREW GRAMMAR

DUNCANNON RECORD – Duncannon, PA. 1825-1942; 1942-1975 – 13 – \$25.00r – us I.M.R. [071]

DUNCAN'S ICONOCLAST – Portland OR. Oct 22 1921 – 1 – us U.O. Library [071]

Duncanus, M *see*
- ANABAPTISTICAE HAERESEOS CONFVTATIO, ET VERE CHRISTIANI BAPTISMI
- VAN DIE KINDERDOOP, HET DERDE BOECK. VERCLARENDE DATMEN DIE KINDEREN MOET DOOPEN

THE DUNCIAD, IN FOUR BOOKS, PRINTED ACCORDING TO THE COMPLETE COPY FOUND IN THE YEAR 1742, WITH THE PROLEGOMENA OF SCRIBLERUS AND NOTES VARIORUM;... / Pope, A – London, 1743 – 3mf – 9 – MP-302/1 – ne IDC [240]

Duncker, Dora *see* ERNST VON WILDENBRUCH

Duncker, Maximilian Wolfgang *see* GESCHICHTE DES ALTERTHUMS

DUNDALK DEMOCRAT – Dundalk. Ireland. -w. 20 Oct 1849-Dec 1860. (10 reels) – 1 – uk British Libr Newspaper [072]

DUNDALK HERALD – Ireland.1869-78; 1880-86; 1888-90; 1892-95. -w. 15 reels – 1 – uk British Libr Newspaper [072]

DUNDALK & NEWRY EXPRESS – Ireland. Dundalk Express. -w. 30 June 1860-1 Jan 1870. 4 1 2 reels – 1 – uk British Libr Newspaper [072]

DUNDALK PATRIOT – Ireland. -w. 11 Dec 1847-19 Aug 1848. (23 ft) – 1 – uk British Libr Newspaper [072]

Dundas, Charles *see* PROBLEM TERRITORIES OF SOUTHERN AFRICA

Dundas, Henry *see* A FAIR STATEMENT OF THE REAL GRIEVANCES EXPERIENCED BY THE OFFICERS AND SAILORS IN THE NAVY OF GREAT BRITAIN WITH A PLAN OF REFORM... IN A LETTER TO H[ENRY] D[UNDAS]. BY A NAVAL OFFICER

DUNDAS STAR-JOURNAL – (1993.-1r; 1859-1885.-7r) – Dundas, 1893-1992 – 57r – 1 – cn Preston [971]

Dundee. Balgay Cemetery *see* REGISTERS

Dundee, Scotland *see* HOWFF BURIAL GROUND: MONUMENTAL INSCRIPTIONS WITH INDEX

Dundee. Scotland. St. Andrew's Roman Catholic Cathedral *see* TRANSCRIPTS OF RECORDS

DUNDEE WARDER – Scotland, UK. 9 Feb 1841-45 – 2r – 1 – uk British Libr Newspaper [072]

DUNDY COUNTY PIONEER – Benkelman, NE. -w. Apr. 1885-Jan. 1888; Aug. 1892 – 1 – us NE Hist [071]

DUNFERMLINE HERALD – 1 – £42.00r – uk Scot News [072]

DUNFERMLINE PRESS – 1 – £42.00r – uk Scot News [072]

DUNGANNON DEMOCRAT (N. IRELAND) *see* DEMOCRAT

DUNGANNON NEWS AND COUNTY TYRONE ADVERTISER – Ireland, 1880-89; 1891-1920; 1922- – 129+ r – 1 – uk British Libr Newspaper [072]

Dunghen, Henry *see* OPERA

DUNGOG CHRONICLE – Jun 12 1888-Dec 20 1968 – 9 – at Pascoe [072]

Dungs, H *see* SECHS HAAGER ABKOMMEN UEBER INTERNATIONALES PRIVATRECHT

Duni, E *see* MINUETTI E CONTRIDANZE...

DUNIA INTERNASIONAL – Djakarta. Incomplete. SE-528 1. 1950 51-1959 – 9 – ne IDC [073]

DUNIA MARITIM – Djakarta. Incomplete. SE-586 1. 1950-1971 – 9 – ne IDC [073]

DUNIA WANITA – Medan. Incomplete. SE-880 1. 1949-1966 – 9 – ne IDC [073]

DUNIGAN'S AMERICAN CATHOLIC ALMANAC AND LIST OF THE CLERGY, FOR THE YEAR OF OUR LORD... – New York: Edward Dunigan and Brother, 1858-59 – 1r – 1 – $40.00r – us U.N.D. Archives [240]
Dunikowski, Emil Habdank *see* WSROD POLONII W AMERYCE
Dunin-Gorkavich, Aleksandr Aleksandrovich *see* NEOBKHODIMOST OTKRYTIIA PORTO-FRANKO V USTIAKH RI EK OBI I ENISEI A
Dunkin, Christopher *see* SPEECH DELIVERED IN THE LEGISLATIVE ASSEMBLY DURING THE DEBATE ON THE SUBJ
EIN DUNKLES LOOS : VOLKSERZAEHLUNG / Bechstein, Ludwig – Nuernberg: F Korn. 3v. 1850 – 1 – us U.W. Library [830]
Dunkley, G R A *see* RATING IN SOUTH AFRICA: A QUEST FOR STABILITY THROUGH LAND TENURE AND TAXATION
DUNKLIN DEMOCRAT – Kennett. Mo. 1956- – 1 – us UMI [071]
Dunkmann, Karl *see* SYSTEM THEOLOGISCHER ERKENNTNISLEHRE
Dunlap, Samuel Fales *see* VESTIGES OF THE SPIRIT-HISTORY OF MAN
Dunlap, Susan *see* LETTERS
DUNLAP'S AMERICAN DAILY ADVERTISER – Philadelphia. Pa. 1791-1795 – 1,3 – us Readex [071]
Dunlevie, Horace G *see* THE GUIDE OR COMPANION TO THE NEW ARMY LIST
Dunlop, John *see* MEMORIES OF GOSPEL TRIUMPHS AMONG THE JEWS DURING THE VICTORIAN ERA
DUNMUNKLE STANDARD – 1921-1974. DS1-24 – 24r – 1 – at Corangamite [072]
Dunn, Henry *see*
- THE KINGDOM OF GOD, OR, WHAT IS THE GOSPEL?
- LIBER LIBRORUM

Dunn, Jacob Pratt *see*
- GREATER INDIANAPOLIS
- INDIANA AND INDIANANS

Dunn, Lewis R *see* SERMONS ON THE HIGHER LIFE
Dunn, N *see* A DESCRIPTIVE CATALOGUE OF THE CHINESE COLLECTION IN PHILADELPHIA
Dunn, Oscar *see*
- GLOSSAIRE FRANCO-CANADIEN
- GLOSSAIRE FRANCO-CANADIEN ET VOCABULAIRE DE LOCUTIONS VICIEUSES USITEES AU CANADA
- GLOSSAIRE FRANCO-CANADIEN: ET VOCABULAIRE DE LOCUTIONS VICIEUSES USITEES AU CANADA
- POURQUOI NOUS SOMMES FRANCAIS

Dunn, ST *see* FLORA OF KWANTUNG AND HONGKONG (CHINA)
Dunnam, N J *see* HISTORY OF JERAULD COUNTY
Dunne, Edward F *see* THE HEART OF THE NATION
Dunne, John P *see* EDMUND BURKE: A LECTURE, DELIVERED IN DE LA SALLE INSTITUTE ON APRIL 30TH, 1880
Dunning, Albert E *see* CONGREGATIONALISTS IN AMERICA
Dunning, McLeod, Henry *see* THE SCIENCE OF ECONOMICS AND ITS RELATION TO FREE EXCHANGE AND SOCIALISM
Dunning, William A *see* A HISTORY OF POLITICAL THEORIES FROM LUTHER TO MONTESQUIEU
Dunnington *see* MUSIC PART BOOKS
DUNNUNKLE SHIRE COUNCIL MINUTES – 1877-1995 – 8r – 5 – at Corangamite [910]
DUNNVILLE CHRONICLE – (1993.-1r; Se1896-1974.-44r) – Dunville, 1976-1992 – 23r – 1 – cn Preston [971]
DUNOLLY AND BETBETSHIRE EXPRESS – Australia, Jun 1875-Jun 1917 (imperfect) – 41r – 1 – uk British Libr Newspaper [072]
DUNOON OBSERVER – 1 – £42.00r – uk Scot News [072]
Dunoyer, Anne Marguerite *see* MEMOIRES DE MME. DUNOYER ECRITS PAR ELLE-MEME
DUN'S REVIEW – v. 1-29. 1893-1921 – 1 – 296.00 – us L of C Photodup [073]
DUN'S REVIEW – (v. 91- 1968- 5,6. v. 95-1970- 9) – v. 6- 1898- – 1 – us UMI [380]
DUNS SCOTUS...PER UNIVERSAM PHILOSOPHIAM,...CONTRA ADVERSANTES DEFENSUS / Baro, B Fr. Joan – Coloniae Agrippinae, 1664 – 17mf – 9 – CA-6/1 – ne IDC [100]
DUNSMUIR DISPATCH – Dunsmuir, CA. 1910-11 – 1r – 1 – $50.00 – B02184 – us Library Micro [071]
DUNSMUIR NEWS – Dunsmuir, CA. 1890-1917; 1919- – 38+ r – 1 – $3,400.00 ($90.00y) – B02187 – us Library Micro [071]
DUNSTABLE 1679-1900 – (Mf 1-4: Vital Records 1679-1847. Mf 5-6: Vital Records 1724-1802. Mf 6-15: Town Records 1743-1790. Mf 10,20: Marriages 1757-1773. Mf 14-15: Vitals 1724-1801. Mf 16-24: Town Records 1743-90. Mf 25-32: Town Records 1790-1822. Mf 35-36: Town Records 1792-1823. Mf 33: Out-of-Town Marriages 1682-1799. Mf 33: Intentions 1888-90. Mf 33-36: Vitals 1724-1847. Mf 37-42: Town Records 1823-53. Mf 43-48: Town Records 1824-88. Mf 49-55: Taxes 1800-18. Mf 56-62: Taxes 1819-38. Mf 63-70: Taxes 1839-58. Mf 71-79: Accounts 1785-1880. Mf 80-86: Accounts 1800-78. Mf 87-88: Voters 1884-1915. Mf 89-93: Church Records 1834-98. Mf 93: Vital Records 1834-84. Mf 94: Marriages 1790-1843. Mf 94-95: Intentions 1826-87. Mf 96: Births 1830-92. Mf 97-98: Marriages, Deaths 1844-92. Mf 99: Vital Records 1893-1900) – (mf ed 1995) – 99mf – 9 – 0-87623-380-9 – us Holbrook [920]
DUNSTABLE 1681-1849 – (Mf 1T: Births & Deaths 1679-1746. Mf 1T-2T: Marriages 1680-1839. Mf 2T-4T: Births 1730-1847. Mf 4T: Deaths 1742-1821. Mf 4T-5T: Marriages 1779-84, 1843-44. Mf 5T-9T: Births & Deaths 1724-1848. Mf 6T: Out-of-Town Marriages 1682-1799. Mf 9T: Marriages 1757-73. Mf 9T-10T: Marriages & Intentions 1790-1849. Mf 10T: Births & Deaths 1757-1804; Births 1830-49. Mf 11T: Marriages & Deaths 1844-49) – (mf ed 1996) – 11mf – 9 – 0-87623-244-6 – us Holbrook [920]
DUNSTABLE CHRONICLE – Dunstable, England. 5 Jan 1856-28 Jul 1860 – 1 1/2r – 1 – uk British Libr Newspaper [072]
Dunstane, William *see* HISTORY OF WYANDOTTE, BUTTE COUNTY, CALIFORNIA
DUNYA – (Dawrah-'i 2: sal-i 2, 1-4; sal-i 3, 1-4; sal-i 4, 3-4; sal-i 6, 1-4; sal-i 7, 1-4 (Bahar 1340-Zimistan 1345[Spring 1961-Winter 1966/67])) – [Tehran]: Hizb-i Tudah-'i Iran, 1941-1946/47 – 2r – 1 – $85.00 – us MEDOC [950]
DUNYA – (Dawrah-'i 3, sal-i 1, shumarah-'i 2-sal-i 5, shumarah-'i 12 (Murdad 1353-Isfand 1357[Jul 1974-Mar 1979]); which includes Sal-i 1: 2, 3, 5-8; Sal-i 2:1, 2-5, 8-10, 12; sal-i 3:1-2, 4-5, 8-10, 12; Sal-i 4:1-3, 5-8; Sal-i 5:5, 8-12. Missing issues: sal-i 1:4, 9-12; sal-i 2:6-7, 11; sal-i 3:3, 6-7, 11; sal-i 4:4, 9-12; sal-i 5:1-4, 6-7) – Stockholm: Kumitah-'i Markazi-i Hizb-i Tudah-'i Iran, 1974-1979 – 2r – 1 – $75.00 – us MEDOC [950]
DUNYA-YI SUKHAN – (Missing issues: 14, 21) – Tehran. Dawrah-'i jadid, Sal-i 1, shumarah-i 1-26 (Bahman 1364-Urdibihisht 136) – 1 reel – 1 – $25.00 – us MEDOC [950]
DUO, 6, A DEUX VIOLONS, OP. 8 / Campioni, C – Paris, ca 1770 – 1 – us Sibley [780]
DUO CONCERTANT POUR COR ET VIOLA / Makaweczky – Leipzig: Breitkopf & Hartel, 179- – 1 – us Sibley [780]
DUO POUR DEUX PIANOS. D'APRES LES DUOS POUR PIANO ET ORGUE : NO. 1: FANTASIE ET FUGUE: NO. 2: CHORAL; NO. 3: SCHERZO; NO. 4: FINAL / Saint-Saens, Camille – (Score and 2nd piano part) – Paris: Girod, [ca 1898] – 1 – us Sibley [780]
DUO. POUR LE VIOLON ET VIOLA / Kambra, K – (MS) – Leipsic: Breitkopf & Hartel, 1816 – 1 – us Sibley [780]
DUOC NHA NAM – Saigon. 26 sept 1928-juil 1937. N'a probablement pas paru entre le 29 oct 1929, no. 153 et le 16 avr 1930, no. 1 – 1 – fr A.C.R.P.P. [073]
DUOC-TUE – Hanoi. dec. 1935-aout 1945 – 1 – fr A.C.R.P.P. [073]
DUOS CONCERTANS, TROIS, POUR VIOLIN ET VIOLONCELLE. OEUVRE 8 / Schoeneberk, CS – (2 parts) – Paris: Janet et Cotelle, No. 1425 [179-?] – 1 – us Sibley [780]
DUOS, TRIOS, POUR ALTO ET VIOLONCELLE / Danzi, F – Paris: Richault, 1820 – 1 – us Sibley [780]
DUPAGE COUNTY TIMES – Wheaton. Ill. 1964- – 1 – us UMI [071]
Dupain-Triel, Jean Louis *see*
- COUP D'OEIL SUR L'ESTABLISSEMENT DE COLLEGES MUNICIPAUX, POUR LES SCIENCES, ARTS ET METIERS
- LA FRANCE CONNUE SOUS SES PLUS UTILES RAPPORTS OU NOUVEAU DICTIONNAIRE UNIVERSEL DE LA FRANCE DRESSE D'APRES LA CARTE EN 180 FEUILLES DE CARSIGNY

Dupanloup, Felix *see*
- THE CHILD
- CONVENTION DU 15 SEPTEMBRE ET L'ENCYCLIQUE DU 8 DECEMBRE

Dupasquier, S *see* SUMMA PHILOSOPHIAE SCHOLASTICAE ET SCOTISTICAE...
Dupaty *see* L'ANTHICHAMBRE OU LES VALETS CHEZ EUX
DuPaty de Clam, Antoine Amedee *see* FASTES CHRONOLOGIQUES DE LA VILLE DE SFAKS
Duperrey, M L I *see* VOYAGE AUTOUR DU MONDE SUR LA CORVETTE "LA COQUILLE" 1822-25
DUPES ET DEMAGOGUES: A SOUVENIR / Albyn – 1879. 05826. (Pre-1900 Canadiana) – 9 – cn C.I.H.M. [971]
Dupetit-Mere, Frederic *see* LA FAMILLE SIRVEN
Dupeux, G *see* LE FRONT POPULAIRE ET LES SELECTIONS DE 1936
Dupin, Andre Marie Jean Jacques *see*
- CONSULTATION DE M. DUPIN, AVOCAT A LA COUR ROYALE DE PARIS, POUR LE SEMINAIRE DE MONTREAL, EN CANADA
- JESUS DEVANT CAIPHE ET PILATE: OU, PROCES DE JESUS-CHRIST

Dupin, Charles *see*
- DU TRAVAIL DES ENFANTS QU'EMPLOIENT LES ANTELIERS, LES USINES ET LES MANUFACTURES, CONSIDERE DANS LES INTERETS MUTUELS DE LA SOCIETE, DES FAMILLES ET DE L'INDUSTRIE
- DES FORCES PRODUCTIVES ET COMMERCIALES DE LA FRANCE
- VIEW OF THE HISTORICAL AND ACTUAL STATE OF THE MILITARY FORCE OF GREAT BRITAIN

Dupin, Claude FE *see*
- MEMOIRE STATISTIQUE DU DEPARTEMENT DES DEUX-SEVRES
- SECOND MEMOIRE SUR LA STATISTIQUE DU DEPARTEMENT DES DEUX-SEVRES
- STATISTIQUE DU DEPARTEMENT DES DEUX-SEVRES

Dupin, M *see* PRINCIPIA JURIS CIVILIS TUM ROMANI TUMGALLICI...
Dupire, M *see* PEULS NOMADES
DUPLA DEFESA, RESPOSTA AO PAMPHLETO / Humphrey, Henry M – 1897 – 1 – $50.00 – us Presbyterian [240]
Duplatre, Louis *see* ESSAI SUR LA CONDITION DE LA FEMME AU SIAM
Dupleix, Scipion *see*
- HISTOIRE DE LOUIS LE JUSTE, 13E DU NOM, ROI DE FRANCE ET DE NAVARRE
- LIBERTE DE LA LANGUE FRANCOISE

Duplessis, Claude *see* OEUVRES DE MR. DUPLESSIS, ANCIEN AVOCAT DU PARLEMENT
DUPLESSIS DONNE A SA PROVINCE UNE SAINE LEGISLATION AGRICOLE – [Quebec (Province): Union nationale, 1948 ?]. SEM105P1659 – 1mf – 9 – Can$2.25 – cn Bibl Nat [340]
Duplessis, Francois-Xavier *see* LETTRES DU P. F. X. DUPLESSIS DE LA COMPAGNIE DE JESUS: ACCOMPAGNEES D'UNE NOTICE BIOGRAPHIQUE ET D'ANNOTATIONS
Duplessis, G *see* LE LIVRE DES PEINTRES ET GRAVEURS
Duplessis, T *see* BIBLIOGRAPHIE NECROLOGIQUE DES RELIGIEUSES HOSPITALIERES DE SAINT-JOSEPH, PROVINCE DE NOTRE-DAME DE L'ASSOMPTION, VALLEE-LOURDES, N.B.
Duplessix, E *see* LA LOI DES NATIONS
DUPLICATE CERTIFICATES OF NATURALISATION, 'A' SERIES, 1917-1921 : STATUS OF APPLICANT: UNMARRIED / Department of Home and Territories, Central Office – 1 – CRS A227 – at Archives [920]
DUPLICATE CERTIFICATES OF NATURALISATION, 'AA' SERIES, 1921-1937 : STATUS OF APPLICANT: UNMARRIED / Department of Home and Territories, Central Office – 25r – 1 – CRS A240 – at Archives [920]
DUPLICATE CERTIFICATES OF NATURALISATION, 'B' SERIES, 1917-1921 : STATUS OF APPLICANT: MARRIED / Department of Home and Territories, Central Office – 1 reel – 1 – CRS A228 – at Archives [920]
DUPLICATE CERTIFICATES OF NATURALISATION, 'BB' SERIES, 1921-1937 : STATUS OF APPLICANT: MARRIED / Department of Home and Territories, Central Office – 20r – 1 – CRS A241 – at Archives [920]
DUPLICATE CERTIFICATES OF NATURALISATION, 'C' SERIES, 1918-1921 : STATUS OF APPLICANT: MARRIED WITH CHILDREN / Department of Home and Territories, Central Office – 1 reel – 1 – CRS A229 – at Archives [920]
DUPLICATE CERTIFICATES OF NATURALISATION, 'CC' SERIES, 1921-1937 : STATUS OF APPLICANT: MARRIED WITH CHILDREN / Department of Home and Territories, Central Office – 6r – 1 – CRS A242 – at Archives [920]
DUPLICATE CERTIFICATES OF NATURALISATION, 'D' SERIES, 1921-1936 : STATUS OF APPLICANT: PREVIOUS NATURALISATION / Department of Home and Territories, Central Office – 1 reel – 1 – CRS A243 – at Archives [920]
DUPLICATE CERTIFICATES OF NATURALISATION, 'E' SERIES AND 'F' SERIES, 1921-1936 : STATUS OF APPLICANT: DOUBTFUL BRITISH NATIONALITY; MINORS / Department of Home and Territories, Central Office – 1 reel – 1 – CRS A244 – at Archives [920]
THE DUPLICATE LETTERS, THE FISHERIES AND THE MISSISSIPI... / ed by Adams, John Quincy – Washington, 1822 – 3mf – 9 – ILM-2854/1 – ne IDC [340]
Duponchel, L *see* EXERCICES STRUCTURAUX
Duponchel, P A J *see* CATALOGUE METHODIQUE DES LEPIDOPTERES D'EUROPE
Dupont *see* LES OUVRIERS, HISTOIRE POPULAIRE ILLUSTREE DES TRAVAILLEURS AU XIXE SIECLE
Dupont, Jacques *see* LIBRE NATION
Dupont, Jean Baptiste *see* TOPOGRAPHIE HISTORIQUE, STATISTIQUE ET MEDICALE DE L'ARRONDISSEMENT DE LILLE
Dupont, Jerry *see* THE LAW LIBRARY TO THE YEAR 2000
Dupont, P *see* PRINCIPES DE VIOLON PAR DEMANDES..
Dupont-White, Charles *see* ESSAI SUR LES RELATIONS DU TRAVAIL AVEC LE CAPITAL
Duport, J H *see* OUTLINES OF A GRAMMAR OF THE SUSU LANGUAGE.
Duport, J L *see* NOCTURNES, TROIS, EN DUO POUR PIANO ET VIOLONCELLE (OU VIOLON)...1ER LIVRE
Duport, Pierre Landrin *see*
- COLLECTION OF TUNES, DANCES AND MARCHES, CA. 1780-1834
- U.S. COUNTRY DANCES WITH FIGURES

Duppa, R *see* ILLUSTRATIONS OF THE LOTUS OF THE ANCIENTS AND TAMARA OF INDIA
Duppe, S E *see* DE CIVITATE DISCRETA
Dupraz, E *see* EXECUTION EN SUISSE DES...
Dupre, M C *see* LA DUALITE POLITIQUE CHEZ LES TEKE DE L'OUEST
Duproix, Paul *see* KANT ET FICHTE ET LE PROBLEME DE L'EDUCATION
Dupuis, J *see*
- JOURNAL OF A RESIDENCE IN ASHANTEE
- JOURNAL OF A RESIDENCE IN ASHANTI

Dupuis, Monique *see* BIBLIOGRAPHIE ANALYTIQUE DE LA CHANSON DE FOLKLORE
Dupuis, Yvon *see* DEFI
Duputacion Provincial *see* CUATRO DECRETOS BASICOS PARA EL DESARROLLO AGRARIO DE LA PROVINCIA
Dupuy, D *see* HISTOIRE NATURELLE DES MOLLUSQUE TERRESTRES ET D'EAU DOUCE QUI VIVENT EN FRANCE
Dupuy, M *see* L'ETAT DE GUERRE...
Dupuy, Paul *see*
- LES ILLUSTRATIONS CANADIENNES: PREMIERE SERIE, 1494-1676
- TROIS HEROS DE LA COLONIE DE MONTREAL
- VILIEMARIE: PETITES FLEURS RELIGIEUSES DE VIEUX MONTREAL

Dupuy, Starke *see* HYMNS AND SPIRITUAL SONGS
Dupuys, J *see* DICTIONNAIRE FRANCOIS-LATIN
DUQUE DE T'SERCLAES TOMA POSESION ACADEMICO NUMERO REAL DE LA HISTORIA. NOTICIAS / Fita, Fidel & Rodriguez Villa, Antonio – Madrid: Fortanet, 1909. B.R.A.H. 54, 1909, p. 438 – sp Bibl Santa Ana [946]
Duque Fuentes, Martin *see*
- PROGRAMA DE LATIN 1ER.CURSO
- PROGRAMA DE LATIN 2ND CURSO
- PROGRAMA DE LATIN 3RD CURSO

Duquenne, Lucien *see* L'ARGENTINE DE PERON
DUQUES DE LA TORRE / Dominguez Peaz, Fidel – 1883 – 9 – 1.50f – sp Bibl Santa Ana [946]
DUQUESNE LAW REVIEW – (v1-23 1963-85 on reel $366.00. v24-33 1985-95 on mf $187.00) – v1-33. 1963-95 – 5,6,9 – $553.00 set – us Hein [340]
DuQuesne, Terence *see* ILLICIT DRUGS: MYTH AND REALITY
Duquet, J-N *see* LES ETRENNES
Duquet, Joseph Norbet *see* UNE FETE A L'IMPRIMERIE DU CANADIEN
DUQUOIN FIRST BAPTIST CHURCH. DUQUOIN, ILLINOIS : CHURCH RECORDS – 30 May 1857-1966 – 1 – 157.77 – us Baptist [240]
DUR UND MOLL – v1-10. 1922-32 – 1 – $40.00 – us L of C Photodup [780]
THE DURABILITY OF PERONISM / Baily, Samuel L – Buffalo: Council on International Studies, State University of New York at Buffalo, 1975 – 1 – CSUXAJB7742-B – us Hoover Inst Photo [320]
Duran de Montijo, Juan *see*
- ADVIENTO Y SERMONES VARIOS
- SANTORAL SERAPHICO
- SERMONES DE CUARESMA...SIETE SABIOS DE GRECIA
- SERMONES PANEGIRICOS DE SANTOS

Duran i Jorda, Frederic *see* THE SERVICE OF BLOOD TRANSFUSION AT THE FRONT
Duran Munoz Garcia y, Alonso Buron Francisco *see* RAMON Y CAJAL, TOMO 1
Duran Ramas, Maria de los Angeles *see* ARIAS MONTANO Y SU TRATADO "DE OPTIMO IMPERIO"
Duranczyk, Denise M *see* MECHANICAL ENERGY ANALYSIS OF WALKING IN ELDERLY MEN
Durand *see* DE LA CONDITION DES OUVRIERS DE PARIS DE 1789 JUSQU'EN 1841. AVEC QUELQUES IDEES SUR LA POSSIBILITE DE L'AMELIORER
Durand, A *see*
- TROIS AIRS VARIES POUR LE VIOLON AVEC ACCOMPAGNEMENT DE BASSE
- TROIS DUOS CONCERTANTS POUR DEUX VIOLONS...

Durand, Charles *see* REMINISCENCES OF CHARLES DURAND OF TORONTO, BARRISTER
Durand de Villegagnon, N *see* DE BELLO MELITENSI, ET EIUS EUENTU FRANCIS IMPOSITO, AD CAROLUS CAESAREM 5. NICOLAI
Durand, Guillaume *see* DURANDUS ON THE SACRED VESTMENTS
Durand, Jean Nicolas Louis *see*
- PRECIS DES LECONS D'ARCHITECTURE DONNEA1ES A L'ECOLE POLYTECHNIQUE
- RECUEIL ET PARALLELE DES EDIFICES DE TOUT GENRE ANCIENS ET MODERNES... AVEC UN TEXTE...PAR J.G. LEGRAND

Durand, Jean-Baptiste-Leonard *see*
- ATLAS POUR SERVIR AU VOYAGE DU SENEGAL
- VOYAGE AU SENEGAL

Durand, L *see* ESSAI DE DROIT INTERNATIONAL PRIVE,...
Durand, U *see*
- THESAURUS NOVUS ANECDOTORUM
- VETERUM SCRIPTORUM ET MONUMENTORUM HISTORICORUM, DOGMATICORUM, MORALIUM AMPLISSIMA COLLECTIO

Durand, W F *see* AERODYNAMICS THEORY
Durandal, Pierre *see* LE VENGEUR DE MONTCALM
Durandas de S Portiano OP *see* DE ORIGINE JURISDICTIONUM LIBER
Durandus de S Porciano *see* IN SENTENTIAS THEOLOGICAS PETRI LOMBARDI COMMENTARIUM LIBRI QUATTUOR 1556
Durandus, Gulielmus *see* RATIONALE DIVINORUM OFFICIORUM
DURANDUS ON THE SACRED VESTMENTS = RATIONALE DIVINORUM OFFICIORUM. BOOK 3 : AN ENGLISH RENDERING OF THE THIRD BOOK OF THE RATIONALE DIVINORUM OFFICIORUM OF DURANDUS, BISHOP OF MENDE, A.D. 1287 / Durand, Guillaume – (In English. Includes bibliographical references and index) – London: Thomas Baker, [1899?] – 1mf – 9 – 0-8370-6898-3 – 1986-0898 – us A.T.L.A. [240]
DURANGO, 1937 – n.p., 1937. Fiche W 848. (Blodgett Collection of Spanish Civil War Pamphlets) – 9 – us H.U. College Libr [946]
DURANGO, MARTYRSTADEN; ETT TYSKT BOMBARDEMANG DESS ORSAKER OCH VERKNINGAR – Stockholm, 1937. Fiche W 849. (Blodgett Collection of Spanish Civil War Pamphlets) – 9 – us H.U. College Libr [946]
Durango. Mexico (State) *see*
- PERIODICO OFICIAL
- PERIODICO OFICIAL DEL GOBIERNO DEL ESTADO DE DURANGO

DURANGO, VILLE MARTYRE; CE QUE FURENT LES BOMBARDEMENTS DE LA VILLE DE DURANGO PAR LES AVIONS ALLEMANDS / Comite Franco-Espagnole – Paris, 1937? Fiche W 809-810. (Blodgett Collection of Spanish Civil War Pamphlets) – 9 – us H.U. College Libr [946]
DURANT FIRST BAPTIST CHURCH. DURANT, OKLAHOMA : CHURCH RECORDS; BULLETINS – 1942-47 – 1 – $52.74 – us Baptist [240]
DURANT LE PREMIER...SOVIETIQUE (1917-1920). PARIS / Vidal, J M Moscou – Madrid: Razon y Fe, 1934 – 1 – sp Bibl Santa Ana [946]
DURANTE EL SEMESTRE PASADO FALLECIERON...TAMBIEN D. PEDRO MARIA PLANO, EN MERIDA... / Fita, Fidel & Rodriguez Villa, Antonio – Madrid: Est.Tip. Fortanet, 1901. B.A.R.H. 38, 1901, p. 75 – sp Bibl Santa Ana [946]
Duray, Nicholas A *see* AGE OF INTRODUCTION AND CURRENT FREQUENCY OF PARTICIPATION IN LEAGUE AND CASUAL BOWLERS
DURBAN : FIFTY YEARS' MUNICIPAL HISTORY / Henderson, W P M – Durban: Robinson and Co, 1904 – us Res Libr [978]
DURBAN ADVOCATE AND GENERAL ADVERTISER – Durban, South Africa. 1852-54 – 1 – sa State Libr [072]
Durban, E S *see* DIARY
DURBAN FREE PRESS – Durban, South Africa. Oct 1905 – 1 – sa State Libr [072]
DURBAN OBSERVER – Durban, South Africa. 1851-52 – 1 – sa State Libr [072]
DURBAN STAR AND NATAL EVENING NEWS – Durban, South Africa. 1897 – 1 – sa State Libr [072]
DURCH DAS DRAMA HAUPTMANNS / Bab, Julius – Berlin: Oesterheld, [1922?] – 1r – 1 – us U.W. Library [430]
DURCH KAMPF ZUM FRIEDEN – Tuebingen. Heft 1-16. 1914-17.-irr. Each vol. has distinctive title – 1 – us U.W. Library [940]
DURCH NACHT ZUM LICHT *see* THROUGH NIGHT TO LIGHT
DURCH STURM UND NOT : ROMAN / Baudissin, Ida, Graefin – Reutlingen: Ensslin & Laiblin, [19–?] – 1r – 1 – us U.W. Library [830]
DURCHBRUCH ANNO ACHTZEHN : EIN FRONTERLEBNIS / Wittek, Erhard – 36. Aufl. Stuttgart: Franckh, c1933 – 1r – 1 – us U.W. Library [830]
DURCHFLUSSZYTOMETRISCHE UNTERSUCHUNGEN VON STOSSWELLENINDUZIERTEN ZELLSCHAEDEN / Endl, Elmar – 1994 – 2mf – DM80.00 – 3-89349-897-4 – gw Hänsel [530]
Durdenevski i, Vsevolod *see* OPYT BIBLIOGRAFII OBSHCHESTVENNYKH NAUK ZA REVOLIUTSIONNOE TREKHLETIE (1918-1920)
Durdent, R J *see* HISTOIRE LITTERAIRE ET PHILOSOPHIQUE DE VOLTAIRE
Durell, Fletcher *see* A NEW LIFE IN EDUCATION
Durelli, Augusto J *see*
- FORMA Y SENTIDO DE LA RESISTENCIA UNIVERSITARIA DE OCTUBRE 1945
- LA MOCHILA DEL CORONEL

Duren, Charles *see* WOMAN'S PLACE IN RELIGIOUS MEETINGS
Duret, C *see* THRESOR DE L'HISTOIRE DES LANGUES DE CEST UNIVERS
Duret, Theodore *see* LIVRES ET ALBUMS ILLUSTRES DU JAPON
Dureteste, A *see* COURS DE DROIT DE L'INDOCHINE
Durey de Noinville, J -B *see*
- HISTOIRE DU THEATRE DE L'ACADEMIE ROYALE DE MUSIQUE
- HISTOIRE DU THEATRE DE L'OPERA EN FRANCE DEPUIS L'ETABLISSEMENT DE L'ACADEMIE ROYALE DE MUSIQUE, JUSQU'A PRESENT. EN DEUX PARTIES
- HISTOIRE DU THEATRE DE L'OPERA EN FRANCE DEPUIS L'ETABLISSEMENT DE L'ACADEMIE ROYALW DE MUSIQUE JUSQU'A PRESENT

Durfee, Thomas *see* SOME THOUGHTS ON THE CONSTITUTION OF RHODE ISLAND
DURHAM, 1820 : BRITISH ISLES CENSUS DIRECTORIES PROJECT, ENGLAND – (In prep) – at Vine [941]
DURHAM, 1828 : BRITISH ISLES CENSUS DIRECTORIES PROJECT, ENGLAND. VOL 54 – 1mf – 9 – A$9.00 – at Vine [941]
DURHAM, 1834 : BRITISH ISLES CENSUS DIRECTORIES PROJECT, ENGLAND – (In prep) – at Vine [941]
DURHAM, 1848 : BRITISH ISLES CENSUS DIRECTORIES PROJECT, ENGLAND – at Vine [941]
DURHAM, 1855 : BRITISH ISLES CENSUS DIRECTORIES PROJECT, ENGLAND – at Vine [941]
DURHAM, 1856 : BRITISH ISLES CENSUS DIRECTORIES PROJECT, ENGLAND. VOL 80 – 6mf – 9 – A$39.00 – at Vine [941]
DURHAM, 1879 : BRITISH ISLES CENSUS DIRECTORIES PROJECT, ENGLAND. VOL 243 – 7mf – A$45.00 – at Vine [941]
DURHAM, 1894 : BRITISH ISLES CENSUS DIRECTORIES PROJECT, ENGLAND. VOL 136 – 14mf – 9 – A$87.00 – at Vine [941]
DURHAM, 1906 : BRITISH ISLES CENSUS DIRECTORIES PROJECT, ENGLAND. VOL 246 – 9mf – 9 – A$57.00 – at Vine [941]
Durham and Northumberland Parish Register Society *see* TRANSACTIONS
THE DURHAM BOOK, BEING THE FIRST DRAFT OF THE REVISION OF THE BOOK OF COMMON PRAYER IN 1661 / ed by Cuming, G J – London, 1961 – 9mf – 8 – Dfl32.00 – ne Slangenburg [240]
Durham Cathedral Library *see* CODICUM MANUSCRIPTORUM ECCLESIAE CATHEDRALIS DUNELMENSIS CATALOGUS CLASSICUS
DURHAM CHRONICLE – Durham. England. -w. 1832-33; 1860-65. (7 reels) – 1 – uk British Libr Newspaper [072]
DURHAM COUNTY, UK HISTORY, TOPOGRAPHY AND DIRECTORY – (Historical and descriptive sketches of the city, diocese, all wards, towns etc with lists of residents) – 1894 – 10mf – 9 – NZ$40.00 – 0-908989-24-5 – nz BAB [910]
Durham, Earl of *see*
- REPORT ON THE AFFAIRS OF BRITISH NORTH AMERICA
- RETURN OF APPOINTMENTS MADE BY THE EARL OF DURHAM SINCE HIS ARRIVAL IN CANADA

DURHAM (FAR NORTH EAST), 1928 : BRITISH ISLES CENSUS DIRECTORIES PROJECT, ENGLAND – at Vine [941]
Durham, Frank *see* DUBOSE HEYWARD
DURHAM (GATESHEAD AND SUNDERLAND), 1805 : BRITISH ISLES CENSUS DIRECTORIES PROJECT, ENGLAND. VOL 183 – 1mf – 9 – A$9.00 – at Vine [941]
Durham, J H *see* THE REVIVAL IN ST CATHARINES: A BRIEF HISTORY OF THE GREAT WORK, FROM ITS INCEPTION TO ITS CLOSE, UNDER THE LEADERSHIP OF THE REV. E. P. HAMMOND, AND THE PASTORS OF THE METHODIST, PRESBYTERIAN AND BAPTIST CHURCHES, AIDED BY THE POWER OF THE HOLY SPIRIT
Durham, John Pinckney *see* BAPTIST BUILDERS IN LOUISIANA
Durham, John Wyatt *see* CORALS FROM THE GULF OF CALIFORNIA AND THE NORTH PACIFIC COAST OF AMERICA
Durham, N W *see* CITY OF SPOKANE AND SPOKANE COUNTY
DURHAM NEWS – Durham, CA. Feb 1969-Aug 1969 – 1r – 1 – $50.00 – B02190 – us Library Micro [071]
Durham, North Carolina. -Duke University: Perkins Library *see* THE FRANK BAKER COLLECTION OF MANUSCRIPTS, MANUSCRIPT DEPARTMENT, PERKINS LIBRARY, DUKE UNIVERSITY [HANDLISTED BY JOHN ASHLEY VICKERS]
DURHAM RESEARCH REVIEW – Nos. 1-46. 1950-Spring 1980 – 9 – uk Microform Academic [073]
Durham, Timothy L *see* PLASMA FREE FATTY ACIDS AT REST AND EXHAUSTION FOLLOWING THEOBROMINE INGESTION
DURHAM UNIVERSITY ACT 1861: REPORT ON THE ADVANCEMENT OF HIGHER EDUCATION IN LONDON / Great Britain. Selbourne Commission – 1889. Command Nos. 3173 and 5709 – 1 – uk Microform Academic [370]
DURHARTS BAPTIST CHURCH. JEFFERSON COUNTY. LOUISVILLE, GEORGIA : CHURCH RECORDS – Louisville. Jefferson County. Georgia.Durharts Baptist Church – 1 – 24.12 – us Baptist [240]
Duric, Ladislav *see* ESSENTIALS OF EDUCATIONAL PSYCHOLOGY
DURING HER MAJESTY'S PLEASURE / Braddon, Mary Elizabeth – British Fiction Archive: Unit 5 – 9 – uk Bell [830]
Durkheim, Emile *see*
- DE LA DIVISION DU TRAVAIL SOCIAL
- EDUCATION ET SOCIOLOGIE
- THE ELEMENTARY FORMS OF THE RELIGIOUS LIFE

DURNFORD AND EAST'S REPORTS : TERM REPORTS IN THE COURT OF KING'S BENCH / Durnford, Charles & East, Edward H – (New ed with references to subsequent cases. Also called: Durnford and East's Term Reports) – v1-8. 1785-1800. London: J Butterworth, 1817 (all publ) – 70mf – 9 – $105.00 – LLMC 84-767 – us L.L.M.C. [324]
DURNFORD AND EAST'S TERM REPORTS *see* DURNFORD AND EAST'S REPORTS
Durnford, Charles *see* DURNFORD AND EAST'S REPORTS
Durocher, Georges *see* BIO-BIBLIOGRAPHIE DU REVEREND PERE PAUL-EMILE BRETON, O.M.I., JOURNALISTE ET ECRIVAIN
Duroselle, J -B *see* LA POLITIQUE ETRANGERE ET SES FONDEMENTS
Durrant, Earlene *see*
- EFFECTS OF ADHESIVE SPRAY AND PREWRAP ON TAPED ANKLE INVERSION BEFORE AND AFTER EXERCISE
- SEASONAL CHANGES IN SELECTED PHYSIOLOGICAL VARIABLES OF FEMALE BASKETBALL PLAYERS

Durrett, M *see* INFARED INTERACTANCE
DURRUTI UN ANARQUISTA INTEGRO / Gilabert, A G – Barcelona, 193? Fiche W916. (Blodgett Collection of Spanish Civil War Pamphlets) – 9 – us H.U. College Libr [946]
Durruty, Celia *see* CLASE OBRERA Y PERONISMO
Duruy, G *see* DE PACTIS ANNO 1556...
Durville, Georges *see* JEANNE D'ARC ET SES COMPAGNONS D'ARMES DU PAYS NANTAIS...
Dury, John *see* THE REFORMED-SCHOOL
DURZHAVEN VESTNIK – (Missing: 1879-1880, V.1-2; 1884, V.6(18); 1885, V.7(80, 110); 1886, V.8(62-76); 1889, V.11(136); 1895, V.17(141-163); 1898, V.20(151); 1908, V.30(73-141); 1920, V.42(223); 1945(184); 1947(153, 246); 1948(54, 221, 293, 301-302); 1949(76-77, 83, 157-158, 165-166, 169, 172, 176, 180-183, 210-211, 213, 216-217, 220-226, 232-238, 240, 297); 1950-1952; 1957; 1963(4); Supplemented: 1988-1990. 85mf) – Sofiia, 1879-1990 – 9 – H-1113/1 – ne IDC [947]
Duschak, Moritz *see*
- DIE BIBLISCH-TALMUDISCHE GLAUBENSLEHRE...BEILAGE UEBER STAAT UND KIRCHE
- GESCHICHTE UND DARSTELLUNG DES JUEDISCHEN CULTUS
- DIE MORAL DER EVANGELIEN UND DES TALMUD

DUSHA FUTURIZMA / Ivanov-Razumnik, R I – Kniga i revoliutsiia. nr. 7. 1921. BR-3563 2 – 8 – ne IDC [335]
DUSHA KOOPERATSII / Armand, L M – M., 1917 – 1mf – 9 – COR-5/1 – ne IDC [334]
DUSHEPOLEZNOE CHTENIE – Ezhemesiachnoe izdanie dukhovnago soderzhaniia. M. 1860-1917. Lacking: 1860(4)-91; 1892 (3); 1895-1900; 1901 (2); 1902 (1, 2); 1904-05; 1909; 1916-17. BR-2288 2 – 8 – ne IDC [947]
DUSHPASTYR – New York: Zachary Orun, 1909-10 – us Res Libr [071]
THE DUSK OF THE GODS = GOETTERDAEMMERUNG : MUSIC-DRAMA IN THREE ACTS AND A PRELUDE / Wagner, Richard – (German and English) – Boston: O Ditson, c1888 – 1r – 1 – us U.W. Library [790]

Duss, Le R P *see*
- FLORE PHANEROGAMIQUE DES ANTILLES FRANCAISES
- FLORE PLANEROGAMIQUE DES ANTILLES FRANCAISES

Dussault, J D *see* GUIDE DU JEUNE PIANISTE

Dussault, Joseph *see* REPONSE AU "MATIN" DU 2 FEVRIER

Dussek, J L *see*
- AIRS CONNUS VARIES, RECUEIL D'. OP. 71
- ALLA TEDESCA, ARR. AS A RONDO FOR PIANO
- A CONCERTO FOR THE GRAND OR SMALL PIANOFORTE WITH ACCOMPANIMENT...AIR OF THE "PLOUGH BOY", OP. 15
- CONCERTO [NO. 9]...OP. 50
- CONCERTO, PIANO, OP. 14, F MAJOR
- CONCERTO POUR CLAVECIN OU FORTEPIANO, OP. 17
- CONCERTO, THIRD GRAND IN C
- THE GRAND MILITARY CONCERTO FOR THE PIANOFORTE, OP. 40
- PARTANT POUR LA SYRIE. TROUBADOR ROMANCE WITH VARIATIONS, OP. 74
- SECOND GRAND CONCERTO IN F..
- SONATE FAVORITE POUR LE FORTEPIANO AVEC ACCOMP. DE VIOLON ET VIOLONCELLE, OP. 37
- SONATE, GRANDE, POUR PIANOFORTE, OP. 44
- SONATES, DEUX, POUR FORTEPIANO AVEC ACCOMP. DE VIOLON ET BASSE, OEUVRE POSTHUME
- SONATES, DEUX, POUR LE PIANOFORTE AVEC VIOLON ET BASSE, OP. 34
- SONATES, TROIS GRANDES, POUR PIANO, OP. 35
- SONATES, TROIS, OP. 29
- SONATES, TROIS, (PIANO SOLO) ET TROIS PRELUDES POUR LE PIANOFORTE AVEC ACCOMP. DE FLUTE, VIOLA ET VIOLONCELLO, OP. 31
- SONATES, TROIS, POUR LE CLAVECIN OU FORTEPIANO AVEC VIOLON AD LIB., OP. 13
- SONATES, TROIS, POUR LE CLAVECIN OU LE FORTEPIANO AVEC ACCOMPAGNEMENT DE VIOLON, OP. 10
- SONATES, TROIS, POUR LE PIANOFORTE AVEC VIOLON ET VIOLONCELLE, OP. 21

[DUSSELDORF: PAMPHLET COLLECTION – 1937 – 1 – CSUXANS9174-B – us Hoover Inst Photo [943]

Dussieux, Louis *see* NOTICES HISTORIQUES SUR LES GENERAUX ET MARINS DU 18E SIECLE

Dustin *see* HISTORY OF DWIGHT

Dusuzeau, J *see* ESSAI DE CLASSIFICATION DES LEPIDOPTERES PRODUCTEURS DE SOIE

DUTA MASJARAKAT – Djakarta. Indonesia. 1956-July 1957. 1959- – 1 – us UMI [072]

DUTCH AND FLEMISH SCHOOL – 119mf – 9 – $645.00 – 0-907006-96-5 – uk Mindata [750]

DUTCH DOCUMENTS RELATING TO THE GOLD COAST AND TRANSLATIONS OF LETTERS AND PAPERS COLLECTED IN THE ALGEMEEN RIJKS ARCHIEF (ARA), STATE ARCHIVES OF THE NETHERLANDS AT THE HAGUE / Dantzig, A van – 1971 – 1 – us Res Libr [960]

Dutch East Indies *see* INDONESIA: ANNUAL REPORT 1948 TO THE FOOD AND AGRICULTURE ORGANIZATION OF THE UNITED NATIONS

Dutch East Indies. Algemeen Regeerings-commissariaat voor Borneo en de Grote Oost *see* DEN PASAR-PONTIANAK, LAHIRNJA DOEA NEGARA

Dutch East Indies. Centraal Kantoor voor de Statistiek *see* STATISTICAL POCKETBOOK OF INDONESIA, 1941

Dutch East Indies. Departement van Economische Zaken *see* TRADE DIRECTORY OF INDONESIA

Dutch East Indies. Departement van Opvoeding, Kunsten en Wetenschappen *see* KOERSOES GOEROE NORMALIS JANG 2 TAHOEN LAMANJA

Dutch East Indies. Dept. van Onderwijs en Eredienst *see* DE NIEUWE 2-JARIGE KWEEKSCHOOL

Dutch East Indies. Dienst van den Mijnbouw *see* BULLETIN OF THE BUREAU OF MINES AND THE GEOLOGICAL SURVEY IN INDONESIA

Dutch East Indies. Laws, statutes, etc *see* ORDINANCE OF REGULATION CO-OPERATIVE SOCIETIES 1949

Dutch East Indies. Regeeringsvoorlichtings-Dienst *see* THE INDONESIAN PROBLEM. FACTS AND FACTORS; WHAT HAPPENED SINCE THE END OF THE PACIFIC WAR

DUTCH FORK BAPTIST CHURCH. RICHLAND COUNTY. SOUTH CAROLINA : CHURCH RECORDS – 1958-72 – 1 – 5.13 – us Baptist [240]

DUTCH INTERNATIONAL LAW... / Slooten, T R van – 's-Gravenhage, 1936 – 2mf – 9 – ILM-3220/1 – ne IDC [327]

DUTCH LEGISLATIVE SERIES – 5 titles – 9 – ne IDC [340]

DUTCH PAMPHLETS, 1486-1750 / Knuttel Collection, Royal Library. The Hague – (Part 1: 1486-1648 2,097mf Dfl11,580.00; Part 2: 1649-1750 3,574mf Dfl19,940.00. A printed catalogue by W.P.C. Knuttel is avail. Dfl1,970.00) – 9 – ne IDC [943]

THE DUTCH PRESS ON MICROFICHE – (Catalogue available on request) – 9 – ne MMF Publ [072]

THE DUTCH REFORMED CHURCH IN SOUTH AFRICA : WITH NOTICES OF THE OTHER DENOMINATIONS: AN HISTORICAL SKETCH / M'Carter, John – Edinburgh: W. & C. Inglis, 1869 – 1mf – us A.T.L.A. [240]

THE DUTCH SCHOOLE MASTER / LeMayre, Marten – 1606. 115p. (English Linguistics Series 1500-1800) – 9 – us UMI [430]

DUTCH SONG-BOOKS / ed by Selm, B van – (Individual titles available) – 258mf – 9 – ne IDC [780]

DUTCH THEATRE POSTERS, 1853-1926 / Municipal Archives Rotterdam – (With printed guide and concordance) – 1997 – 386mf – 9 – Dfl2,295.00 – ne MMF Publ [790]

THE DUTCH UNDERGROUND PRESS, 1940-1945 / State Institute for War Documentation, Amsterdam – (Includes a printed guide) – 1,831mf – 9 – ne IDC [355]

Dutcher, Salem *see* EXPRESSIONS OF LAW AND FACT CONSTRUED BY THE COURTS OF GEORGIA

Dutchess. Presbytery (Pres. Ch. in the U.S.A.) *see* MINUTES, 1762-1795

THE DUTCH-INDONESIAN CONFLICT / Leimena, Johannes – SE-11,976 1. 1949 – 9 – ne IDC [950]

DUTCH-LANGUAGE INDONESIAN NEWSPAPERS, 1810-1940 – (Includes: Bataviasche Koloniale Courant, cont. by Java Government Gazette, cont. by Bataviasche Courant. 1810-1827. 145mf. Dfl880.00; Javasche Courant. 1828-1940. 5,451mf. Dfl35,640.00; Soerabaiasch Handelsblad. 1866-1917. 2,067mf. Dfl12,870.00; Algemeen Dagblad van Nederlandsch Indie. 1873-1886. 323mf. Dfl1,760.00; Bataviaasch Nieuwsblad. 1885-1926. 2,746mf. Dfl17,710.00; Sumatra Post. 1898-1940. 2,764mf. Dfl16,280.00. Subsets also avail) – 9 – ne MMF Publ [072]

THE DUTCH-TUTOR – Anon. 1659. 108p. (English Linguistics Series 1500-1800) – 9 – us UMI [430]

Dutczak, B *see* DIE FESTSTELLUNG DER RUMAENISCHEN STAATSANGEHOERIGKEIT

Dutens, J M *see* ESSAI COMPARATIF SUR LA FORMATION ET LA DISTRIBUTION DU REVENU DE LA FRANCE EN 1815 ET 1835

DUTIES AND FUNCTIONS OF KENTUCKY COUNTY GOVERNMENT / Kentucky – 1938. 2 fiches.F-0506 – 9 – us A.G.L.L. [323]

THE DUTIES OF JUDGE ADVOCATES... / Hughes, R M – London: Smith, Elder & Co, 1845 – 3mf – 9 – $4.50 – LLMC 89-035 – us L.L.M.C. [340]

DUTIES OF SHERIFFS AND CONSTABLES, AS DEFINED BY THE LAWS, AND INTERPRETED BY THE SUPREME COURT, OF THE STATE OF CALIFORNIA / Harlow, William Sturtevant – San Francisco: Whitney, 1884. 549p. LL-83 – 1 – us L of C Photodup [340]

DUTIES OF SHERIFFS AND CONSTABLES PARTICULARLY UNDER THE PRACTICE IN CALIFORNIA, AND THE PACIFIC STATES AND TERRITORIES / Harlow, William Sturtevant – 2d ed. San Francisco: Bancroft-Whitney, 1895. 588p. LL-82 – 1 – us L of C Photodup [340]

THE DUTIES OF THE HEART / ibn Pakuda, Bahya ben Joseph – New York: E.P. Dutton, 1909. 1 fiche – 9 – us A.T.L.A. [240]

DUTIES ON TRADE AT CHARLESTON, 1784-1789 – (With guide) – South Carolina Department of Archives and History, 1995 – 1r – 1 – $85.00 – D3313 – us Scholarly Res [976]

DUTIES ON TRADE AT CHARLESTON, 1784-89 / South Carolina. Department of Archives and History – 1r. M-6 – 1 – $75.00r – Out-of-state orders: us Scholarly Res – us SC Archives [380]

DUTIES, POWERS, AND LIABILITY OF NATIONAL BANK DIRECTORS / A.S. Pratt and Sons. Washington, D.C – Washington, 1908 – 1 – LL-1366 – us L of C Photodup [340]

Dutilleux, A *see* HISTOIRE ET CARTULAIRE DE L'ABBAYE DEMALBUISSON

DUTOITSPAN HERALD AND BULTFONTEIN ADVERTISER – Dutoitspan, South Africa. 26 Oct 1882-30 Dec 1884. 1 reel. Continued by: Vryburg Advocate; Dec 1882-Aug 1883 missing – 1, 16 diazo available at reduced price – sa SA Libr [072]

Dutouquet, H E *see* DE LA CONDITION DES CLASSES PAUVRES A LA CAMPAGNE, DES MOYENS LES PLUS EFFICACES DE L'AMELIORER

Dutrochet, R J Henri *see*
- MEMOIRES POUR SERVIR L'HISTOIRE ANATOMIQUE ET PHYSIOLOGIQUE DES ANIMAUX ET DES VEGETAUX
- RECHERCHES ANATOMIQUES ET PHYSIOLOGIQUES SUR LA STRUCTURE INTIME DES ANIMAUX ET DES VEGETAUX, ET SUR LEUR MOTILETE

Dutt, Manmatha Nath *see* OUTLINES OF HINDU METAPHYSICS

Dutt, Surendra Nath *see* THE LIFE OF BENOYENDRA NATH SEN

Dutton, A *see* LETTERS TO THE REVEREND MR. JOHN WESTLEY, AGAINST PERFECTION AS NOT ATTAINABLE IN THIS LIFE

DUTTON ADVANCE – Ontario Prov., Canada. Feb 1889- – 1 – cn Commonwealth Micro [072]

Dutton, E *see* BASUTO OF BASUTOLAND

DUTTON ENTERPRISE – Ontario Prov., Canada. Dec 1881-1889 – 1 – cn Commonwealth Micro [072]

THE DUTY AND THE LIMITATIONS OF CIVIL DISOBEDIENCE : A DISCOURSE / Bartlett, Samuel Colcord – Manchester, N.H.: Abbott, Jenks, 1853 – 1mf – us A.T.L.A. [320]

Duval *see*
- EDOUARD EN ECOSSE OU LA NUIT D'UN PROSCRIT
- FORME GENERALE ET PARTICULIERE DE LA CONVOCATION ET DE LA TENUE DES ASSEMBLEES NATIONALES OU ETATS GENERAUX DE FRANCE, JUSTIFIEE PAR PIECES AUTHENTIQUES
- RECUEIL DE PIECES ORIGINALES ET AUTHENTIQUES CONCERNANT LA TENUE DES ETATS GENERAUX: D'ORLEANS EN 1560 SOUS CHARLES 9; DE BLOIS EN 1576 SOUS HENRI 3; DE BLOIS EN 1588 SOUS HENRI 3; DE PARIS EN 1614 SOUS LOUIS 13
- LE TYRAN DOMESTIQUE OU L'INTERIEUR D'UNE FAMILLE

Duval, A *see* LA VIE ADMIRABLE DE SOEUR MARIE DE L'INCARNATION

Duval, Alexandre *see*
- LE CHEVALIER D'INDUSTRIE
- LES HUSSITES OU LE SIEGE DE NAUMBOURG
- MONTONI OU LE CHATEAU D'UDOLPHE

Duval, F *see* DE LA PAIX DE DIEU A LA PAIX DE FER

Duval, G *see*
- L'ECHO DE LA PAROISSE JACQUES-CARTIER
- L'ECHO DE QUEBEC

Duval, J *see* TROIS QUATUORS

Duval, J B *see* L'ESCHOLE FRANCOISE

Duval, Mehul *see* LES HUSSITES OU LE SIEGE DE NAUMBOURG

Duval, Paul Alexandre Martin *see*
- BUVEURS D'AMES
- MAISON POUR DAMES

Duval, Rubens *see* LA LITTERATURE SYRIAQUE

Duval Sanadon, David *see* DISCOURS SUR L'ESCLAVAGE DES NEGRES ET SUR L'IDEE DE LEUR AFFRANCHISSEMENT DANS LES COLONIES, PAR UN COLON DE SAINT-DOMINGUE

Duval-Jouve, J *see* HISTOIRE NATURELLE DES EQUISETUM DE FRANCE

Duvall, Terry Glenn *see* DETERMINING MINISTRY PRIORITIES FOR MACEDONIA BAPTIST CHURCH DURING A TRANSITIONAL PERIOD

Duverger, Maurice *see* PARTIS POLITIQUES ET CLASSES SOCIALES EN FRANCE

Duverger, Maurice et al *see*
- LES ELECTIONS DU 2 JANVIER, 1956
- L'INFLUENCE DES SYSTEMES ELECTORAUX SUR LA VIE POLITIQUE

Duvernay, Ludger *see*
- L'AMI DE LA RELIGION ET DU ROY
- L'ARGUS
- LE CONSTITUTIONNEL
- LA GAZETTE DES TROIS-RIVIERES

Duvernay, Ludger et al *see* LA MINERVE

Duvernet, T I *see* LA VIE DE VOLTAIRE

Duvernoy, F *see*
- FANTASIE, DEUXIEME, POUR PIANO ET COR OU VIOLON
- FANTASIE, QUATRIEME, POUR LE PIANO, COR OU VIOLON
- FANTASIE, TROISIEME, POUR PIANO, COR OU VIOLON
- REVIEL DE J.J. ROUSSEAU. SIXEME FANTASIE POUR PIANO ET COR OU VIOLON
- SONGE DE J.J. ROUSSEAU. NOCTURNE POUR PIANO, COR OU VIOLON

Duvernoy, P *see* DE DESERTORIBUS ET TRANSFUGIS...

Duveyrier, Charles *see*
- AUX CHRETIENS
- LA VILLE NOUVELLE OU LE PARIS DES SAINT-SIMONIENS

Duveyrier, Henri *see*
- LA CONFRERIE MUSULMANE DE SIDI MOHAMMED BEN 'ALI ES SENOUSI ET SON DOMAINE GEOGRAHIQUE EN L'ANNEE 1300 DE L'HEGIRE
- JOURNAL DE ROUTE DE HENRI DUVEYRIER, PUBLIE ET ANNOTE PAR CH. MAUNOIR ET H. SCHIRMER; PRECEDE D'UNE BIOGRAPHIE DE H. DUVEYRIER...

Duvillars, Pierre *see* L'EROTISME AU CINEMA: PIN-UP

Duvivier, U *see* BIBLIOGRAPHIE GENERALE ET METHODIQUE D'HAITI

DUX – (Library has: v7, no. 20, 30/31, 33, 37-38, 40-48, 54 (1946: 21 June, 21 Nov.; 1947: 7 Jan., 7-21 March, 21 April-21 Aug., 21 Nov) – Amisano, Ghana: St. Teresa's Seminary, 19uu – 1 – CSUX86-S78 – us Hoover Inst Photo [240]

DUX CHRISTUS : AN OUTLINE STUDY OF JAPAN / Griffis, William Elliott – New York: Publ for the Central Committee on the United Study of Missions [by] Macmillan, 1904 – 1mf – 9 – 0-8370-6501-1 – 1986-0501 – us A.T.L.A. [950]

DUX GRAMMATICUS TYRONEM SCHOLASTICUM / Clarke, John – 1633. 367p. (English Linguistics Series 1500-1800) – 9 – us UMI [450]

DUXBURY 1681-1849 – (Mf 1T-2T: B,M,D 1644-1799. Mf 3T: Births & Deaths 1733-85, 1835; Marriages 1751-75, 1791, 1817, 1822. Mf 3T-7T: Births & Deaths 1704-1867. Mf 7T-8T: Births 1645-1786. Mf 8T. Marriages 1644-1849. Mf 8T-9T: Out-of-Town Marriages 1682-1798. Mf 9T: Deaths 1652-1847, 1880. Mf 10T: Births 1843-49; Marriages 1842-49. Mf 11T: Deaths 1843-49) – (mf ed 1996) – 11mf – 9 – 0-87623-245-4 – us Holbrook [920]

DUXER ZEITUNG – Dux (Duchcov), Czechoslovakia. Nov 1928-1938 – 8r – 1 – gw Mikrofilm [072]

DUX-GONG : TITEL UND FUNKTION DES HERZOGS IM FRANKENREICH DER MEROWINGER UND IM CHINA DER ZHOU-DYNASTIE / Holzinger, Regina – 1995 – 2mf – 9 – DM80.00 – 3-8267-2197-7 – gw Hänsel [944]

HET DUYFKEN IN DE STEEN-ROTSE... / Piorters, A – Antwerpen, 1665 – 5mf – 9 – ne IDC [700]

HET DUYFKEN IN DE STEEN-ROTSE DAT IS, EENE MEDE-LYDENDE SIELE OP DE BITTERE PASSIC JESU CHRISTI MEDITERENDE GEMAECKT DOOR EENEN PRIESTER DER SOCIETEYT JESU 7. DRUCK RYCKER VAN STOFFE, VAN BEELDEN, EN VAN POESIE / Poirters, Adrianus – Antwerpen, [c1713] – 4mf – 9 – O-3147/1 – ne IDC [760]

HET DUYFKEN IN DE STEEN-ROTSE DAT IS, EENE MEDE-LYDENDE ZIELE, OP DE BITTERE PASSIE JESU CHRISTI MEDITERENDE : GEMAEKT DOOR EENEN PRIESTER DER SOCIETEYT JESU. DEN 9. DRUK. RYKER VAN STOFFE, VAN BEELDEN, EN VAN POESIE / Poirters, Adrianus – Antwerpen, [c1787] – 4mf – 9 – O-3255/1 – ne IDC [760]

DUYGU – Izmir. Sahib-i Imtiyaz: Hueseyin Rezmi. Sermuharriri: Haydar Ruesdi. No. 298 (21 Mayis 1339 [1923]) – 9 – $20.00 – us MEDOC [956]
DUYTSE LIER, DRAAYENDE VEEL VAN DE NIEUWSTE, DEFTIGE, EN DARTELENDE TOONEN, BEVAT IN TIEN VERDEELINGEN, EN VERCIERT MET KOPERE PLATEN / Luyken, J – Amsterdam, 1729 – 2mf – 9 – O-3237/1 – ne IDC [760]
DUYTSE LIER, DRAYENDE VEEL VAN DE NIEUWSTE, DEFTIGE, EN DARTELENDE TOONEN, BEVAD IN TIEN VERDEELINGEN, EN VERCIERT MET KOPERE PLATEN : NOOYT VOOR DEZEN GEDRUKT / Luyken, J – 1st ed. Amsterdam, 1671 – 2mf – 9 – O-3110/1 – ne IDC [760]
DUYTSE LIER, DRAYENDE VEEL VAN DE NIEUWSTE, DEFTIGE, EN DARTELENDE TOONEN, BEVAT IN TIEN VERDEELINGEN, EN VERCIERT MET KOPERE PLATEN / Luyken, J – Amsterdam, 1708 – 2mf – 9 – O-3111/1 – ne IDC [760]
DVA GADY NATSYIANALNA I RABOTY U BSSR : ZBOR PRAMO U, ARTYKULA U IREZALIUTSY I NA NATSYI ANALNYM PYTANNI – Mensk: Vydanne Nat syi analna i kamisii T SVK BSSR, 1929 – 1 – CSUX91-B1597 – us Hoover Inst Photo [330]
DVA GODA DIKTATURY PROLETARIATA, 1917-1919 – [Moskva]: Otdel redaktsionno-izdatelski i, [1920?] – 1 – CSUX91-B2676 – us Hoover Inst Photo [320]
DVA GODA RABOTY : MATERIALY K OTCHETU PRAVITELSTVA RSFSR NA PIATNADT SATOM VSEROSSIISKOM SEZDE SOVETOV / ed by Lebed, D Z – [Moskva?]: Sov. zakonodatelstvo, 1931 – 1 – CSUX91-B378 – us Hoover Inst Photo [330]
DVA GODA RABOTY POTREBITEL'SKOI KOOPERATSII / Liubimov, IE – M., 1929 – 2mf – 9 – COR-331/1 – ne IDC [334]
DVA GODA RABOTY PRAVITELSTVA RSFSR – (Includes c.1 1924/1926) – Moskva: Izd. VT SIK i SNK RSFSR, 1927 – 1 – CSUXAKZ3528-S – us Hoover Inst Photo [947]
DVA KRASNYKH GODA, NOI ABR 1917 G.-NOI ABR 1919 G : KHRONOLOGIIA PROLETARSKOI DIKTATURY / Gurko-Kriazhin, Vladimir Aleksandrovich & Pavlov, B – Moskva: [s.n.], 1919 (N.-Novgorod: Tip. Narkomvoen.) – 1 – CSUX88-B6878 – us Hoover Inst Photo [947]
DVA PUTI : K POSTANOVKE VOPROSA O VZAIMOOTNOSHENIIAKH MEZHDU POTREBITEL'SKIKH I SEL'SKOKHOZIAISTVENNYKH KOOPERATSIEI / Fishgendler, Abram Markovich – M., 1923 – 1mf – 9 – COR-365/1 – ne IDC [334]
DVA STIKHOTVORENIIA / Akhmatova, A – Vosdushnye Puti. New York. 1963. BR-1094 2 – 8 – ne IDC [460]
DVADT SATY I VI EK *see* DVADT SATY I VI EK (SAINT PETERSBURG, RUSSIA: 1906)
DVADT SATY I VI EK (SAINT PETERSBURG, RUSSIA: 1906) – (Library has: Mar. 25-28, 30-31, Apr. 4,6,8,10, 1906) – S.-Petersburg: M.M. Koi alovich, 1906- – 1 – CSUX87-S186 – us Hoover Inst Photo [947]
DVADTSATSHESTTI UREM I POBIEG S SOLOVKOV / Bezsonov, I Urii Dmitrievich – Paris: Izd. Impr. de Navarre, 1928 – 1 – CSUX88-B3509 – us Hoover Inst Photo [947]
DVADTSATYI VEK – Ezhenedel'nyi khudozhestvennoliteraturnyi zhurnal. Spb. 1911-16. Available: 1914 (47-50); 1915 (8-11, 23, 25-26, 31, 44, 46, 50-52). B-1715 2 – 8 – ne IDC [947]
DVE INTELLIGENTSII (I DRUGIE OCHERKI) / Vipper, S – M. 1912. BR-2198 2 – 8 – ne IDC [460]
DVE TAINY RUSSKOI POEZII / Merezhkovskii, Dimitrii – Nekrasov i Tiutchev. Petrograd. 1915. BR-761 2 – 8 – ne IDC [460]
DVENADTSAT / Blok, Aleksandr Aleksandrovich – [S.l.]: Molodai a gvardii a, 1929 – 1 – CSUX88-B3546 – us Hoover Inst Photo [947]
DVI ENADT SAT SMERTNIKOV : SUD NAD SOT SIALISTAMI-REVOLIUTSIONERAMI V MOSKVI E – Berlin: Izd. Zagranichno i delegatsii P.S.R., 1922 – 1 – CSUX89-B7319 – us Hoover Inst Photo [320]
DVINSK I I GOLOS *see* NASH DAUGAVPILSK I I GOLOS
DVISTI SVIDKIV / Tel'man, I – Kyiv, 1953 – 1 reel – 1 – us I.H.R.C. [947]
DVIZHENIE DEKABRISTOV / Nechkina, M V – v. 1-2. M. 1955. BR-8095 2 – 8 – ne IDC [460]
DVOR CHUDES / Odoevsteva, I – Stikhi (1920-1921 g). Petrograd. 1922. BR-1223 2 – 8 – ne IDC [460]
DVOR I TSARSTVOVANIE PAVLA I / Golovkin, F – Portrety, vospominaniia i anekdoty. M. 1912. BR-6034 2 – 8 – ne IDC [920]
Dvorak, A *see* STRING QUARTET, B. 75 IN D MINOR, OP. 34
DVORIANSTVO I EGO SOSLOVNOE UPRAVLENIE ZA STOLIETIE 1762-1855 GODOV / Korff, Sergei Aleksandrovich – C.-Peterburg, Tip. Trenke i Fiusno, 1906. 720 p. LL-4010 – 1 – us L of C Photodup [340]
Dvornik, F *see* LES SLAVES, BYZANCE ET ROME AU 9 S
DVUKHSOTLETIE GRAZHDANSKAGO SHRIFTA 1708-MART 1908 – Doklady sdelanny 8 marta 1908 g. na obshchem sobranii Russkago Bibliograficheskago Obshchestva pri Imp. Moskovskom Universitete, i obzor ustroennoi togda-zhe vystavki. M. 1910. BR-4569 2 – 8 – ne IDC [947]
DVUKHSOTLETIE RUSSKOI GRAZHDANSKOI AZBUKI – 1708-1908. M. 1908. BR-4570 2 – 8 – ne IDC [947]
DVUM / Kuzmin, M – Petrograd. 1918. BR-1190 2 – 8 – ne IDC [460]
D.W. Ensign and Company *see*
- HISTORY OF ALLEGAN AND BARRY COUNTIES
- HISTORY OF BERRIEN AND VAN BUREN COUNTIES
- HISTORY OF COLUMBIANA COUNTY

DW FUNK *see* DEUTSCHE WELLE / DW FUNK
D.W. GRIFFITH PAPERS / Griffith, D W – 1897-1954. With printed guide and index – 36r – 1 – $3,750.00 – 0-89093-687-0 – us UPA [920]
Dwelle *see* HISTORY OF MITCHELL AND WORTH COUNTIES
DWI KOMANDO RAKJAT – Djakarta. Incomplete. SE-532 1955?-1965 – 9 – ne IDC [073]
Dwidjasusana, R I W *see* AMONG DJIWA, SADURAN
Dwidjo Sewojo, MN G *see* DE NOODZAKELIJKHEID VAN DE INSTELLING EENER INDISCHE VOLKSVERTEGENWOORDIGING MET WETGEVENDE MACHT
Dwight, Benjamin W *see* THE HIGHER CHRISTIAN EDUCATION
Dwight, Charles Abbott Schneider *see* CARPENTER
"DWIGHT D. EISENHOWER MATERIAL." / Endacott, J Earl – 1 – us KS Hist [920]
DWIGHT DOODLES – Dwight, Butler County, NE: May 1, 1971-Dec 15, 1987 – us NE Hist [978]
Dwight, H GO *see* CHRISTIANITY REVIVED IN THE EAST, OR, A NARRATIVE OF THE WORK OF GOD AMONG THE ARMENIANS OF TURKEY
Dwight, Henry Edwin *see* THE LIFE AND WRITINGS OF HON. VINCENT L. BRADFORD
DWIGHT L. MOODY : THE MAN AND HIS MISSION / Davis, George T B – Chicago: Monarch, c1900 – 1mf – us A.T.L.A. [240]
DWIGHT L. MOODY MATERIALS CONCERNING RUTLAND BAPTIST CHURCH / Mount Juliet. Tennessee. Rutland Baptist Church – (Church Records, 1821-1910, Nov 1933-Sept 1945. 616p. 29.64; 1) – 19p – 1 – 5.00 – us Baptist [240]
Dwirnyk, J *see* ROLE DE L'ICONOSTASE DANS LE CULTE DIVIN
Dwoden, John *see* OUTLINES OF THE HISTORY OF THE THEOLOGICAL LITERATURE OF THE CHURCH OF ENGLAND
Dworzak, L W *see* L'APPLICATION DE LA LOI PENALE...
Dwyer, Gregory B *see* GLYCOSYLATED HEMOGLOBIN AND THE OXYGEN KINETICS IN INDIVIDUALS WITH TYPE 2 DIABETES
Dyar, H G *see* A LIST OF NORTH AMERICAN LEPIDOPTERA AND KEY TO THE LITERATURE OF THIS ORDER OF INSECTS
Dybenko, Pavel Efimovich *see* IZ NEDR T SARSKOGO FLOTA K VELIKOMU OKTI ABRI U
Dyche, Thomas *see* A GUIDE TO THE ENGLISH TONGUE
Dyer, David *see* TESTS OF TRUTH:...ON THE TEACHINGS OF NATURE AND REVEALED RELIGION
Dyer, E Jerome *see*
- THE GOLD FIELDS OF CANADA AND HOW TO REACH THEM: BEING AN ACCOUNT OF THE ROUTES AND MINERAL RESOURCES OF NORTH-WESTERN CANADA
- THE ROUTES AND MINERAL RESOURCES OF NORTH WESTERN CANADA

Dyer, Helen S *see*
- A LIFE FOR GOD IN INDIA
- PANDITA RAMABAI
- REVIVAL IN INDIA

Dyer, Isaac Watson *see* MAINE CORPORATION LAW
Dyer, Samuel *see* DYER'S NEW SELECTION OF SACRED MUSIC
Dyer, Sidney *see*
- DYER'S PSALMIST
- THE SOUTH WESTERN PSALMIST

DYER'S NEW SELECTION OF SACRED MUSIC / Dyer, Samuel – 1834. 3rd ed – 1 – 9.31 – us Baptist [240]
DYER'S PSALMIST / Dyer, Sidney – A collection of hymns and sacred songs. 1851 – 1 – 16.10 – us Baptist [240]
DYER'S PSALMIST / Dyer, Sidney – Revised and corrected. 1853 – 1 – 15.60 – us Baptist [240]
DYES AND PIGMENTS – v1-5. 1980-84 – 1,5,6,13 – sz Elsevier [073]
Dyja-Ruelland, S *see* IMAGES DE LA FEMME DANS LES LITTERATURES ORALES ASHANTI ET FON
Dyke, Paul van *see* THE AGE OF THE RENASCENCE
Dykes, J W B *see* SALEM, AN INDIAN COLLECTORATE
Dykes, James Oswald *see*
- BEATITUDES OF THE KINGDOM
- THE DIVINE WORKER IN CREATION AND PROVIDENCE
- GOSPEL ACCORDING TO ST PAUL: STUDIES IN THE FIRST EIGHT CHAPTERS OF... ROMANS
- LAWS OF THE KINGDOM
- THE RELATIONS OF THE KINGDOM TO THE WORLD
- RELATIONS OF THE KINGDOM TO THE WORLD (MATTHEW 6.19-7.27)

Dykmans, M *see* OBITUAIRE DU MONASTERE DE GROENENDAEL DANS LA FORET DE SOIGNES
DYLAN THOMAS, CONCORDANCES TO THE POEMS – 5mf – 9 – us UMI [420]
Dyle. France (Department) *see* TABLEAU STATISTIQUE
Dymond, J *see* AN INQUIRY INTO THE ACCORDANCE OF WAR...
Dymond, Jonathan *see* ESSAYS ON THE PRINCIPLES OF MORALITY
DYN: THE REVIEW OF MODERN ART – Mexico. no. 1-6. Apr May 1942-Nov 1944 – 1 – us NY Public [073]
DYNAMIC FUNCTIONAL ASSESSMENT OF THE LOWER EXTREMITY IN THE NON-VARSITY ATHLETIC POPULATION / Groves, Michelle D – 1994 – 1mf – $4.00 – us Microform Publ [612]
THE DYNAMIC OF CHRISTIANITY / Chapman, Edward Mortimer – Boston: Houghton, Mifflin, 1904.1 fiche – 9 – us A.T.L.A. [240]
DYNAMIC SCIENCE STORIES – v1, nos. 1-2 (all publ). 1939 – 1 reel – 1 – $45.00 – us UPA [830]
DYNAMICS AND STABILITY OF SYSTEMS – 1995, Vol 10 – £212.00 – uk Carfax [621]
DYNAMICS OF ATMOSPHERES AND OCEANS – v1-8. 1976-84 – 1,5,6,13 – sz Elsevier [073]
DYNAMICS OF MEDITATION: (TWELVE INTERVIEW-DISCOURSES ON THE VARIOUS ASPECTS OF MEDITATION) / Rajneesh, Bhagwan Shree; ed by Prem, Ma Ananda – 1st ed. Bombay: Jeevan Jagriti Kendra, 1972. Ma Yoga Laxmi, comp. 285p. 1 reel. 1190 – 1 – us U.W. Library [280]
THE DYNAMICS OF RELIGION : AN ESSAY IN ENGLISH CULTURE HISTORY / Wiseman, M W – London: University Press, 1897 – 1mf – us A.T.L.A. [306]
DYNAMICS OF RURAL POVERTY – 1986 – 240p – it F.A.O. [360]
DYNAMICS OF SMALL VERTEBRATES IN RELATION TO FIRE IN BANKSIA WOODLAND NEAR PERTH, WESTERN AUSTRALIA / Bamford, Michael J – (PhD Thesis) – 1986 – 9 – A$15.00 – at R.A.O.U. [590]
DYNAMICS OF TUNA MOVEMENTS : AN EVALUATION OF PAST AND FUTURE RESEARCH – 1986 – 84p – it F.A.O. [639]
LE DYNAMIQUE DE LA MAURICIE – St-Tite, Canada. 5 jun 1964-26 fev 1970 – 2r – 1 – Can$50.00r – cn Can Microfilming [072]
DYNAMIQUE D'ECOSYSTEMES MACROBENTHIQUES DES FONDS SEDIMENTAIRES DE LA BAIE DE MORLAIX ET LEUR PERTURBATION PAR LES HYDROCARBURES DE L'AMOCO CADIZ / Dauvin, J C – 9 – F180.00 – fr Ethnologie [574]
DYNAMIQUE DES POPULATIONS D'ANGUILLES, ANGUILLA ANGUILLA (L.), DES LAGUNES DU BASSIN D'ARCACHON / Lee, T W – Montpellier. 1979. 218p – 9 – F70.00 – fr Ethnologie [574]
DYNAMISME DES SYMBOLES DANS LES CULTES VODUN / Brand, R – 9 – F130.00 – fr Ethnologie [306]
LES DYNAMISMES SOCIO-POLITIQUES ET ECONOMIQUES DANS LA TRANSFORMATION DES PAYSAGES AGRAIRES DU KAYOR CENTRAL ET SEPTENTRIONAL, SENEGAL / La Masseliere, B de – 9 – F120.00 – fr Ethnologie [306]
DYNAMITE – 1974- 1; 1977- 5,6,9 – us UMI [305]
DYNAMITE FOR A DOUBTING CASTLE, THE NECESSITY FOR THE TIMES, OR, IS THE JESUITE SIC RIGHT? / Asinus – Toronto: Presbyterian Print. and Pub. Co., 1893. 02459. (Pre-1900 Canadiana) – 9 – cn C.I.H.M. [240]
LA DYNASTIE DES BOURBONS / Hoog, Simone – (Recueil de portraits gravea1s). 1979 – 9 – fr Réunion [760]
DYNASTIES OF MEDIAEVAL ORISSA / Misra, Binayak – Forward by Ramaprasad Chanda. Calcutta: K.N. Chatterji, 1933.111p – 1 – us U.W. Library [950]
THE DYNASTY OF THEODOSIUS, OR, EIGHTY YEARS' STRUGGLE WITH THE BARBARIANS : A SERIES OF LECTURES / Hodgkin, Thomas – Oxford: Clarendon Press, 1889 – 1mf – us A.T.L.A. [240]
Dyne, F van *see*
- CITIZENSHIP OF THE UNITED STATES
- A TREATISE ON THE LAW OF NATURALIZATION OF THE UNITED STATES

Dyrlund, Folmer *see* TATERE OG NATMANDSFOLK I DANMARK
Dysart, Dinah *see*
- ART AND ASIAPACIFIC
- ART AND AUSTRALIA

Dyson *see* HISTORICAL SKETCHES AND REMINISCENCES OF MADISON COUNTY
Dyson, C C *see* MADAME DE MAINTENON, HER LIFE AND TIMES 1635-1719
Dyte, C E *see* REPORT OF THE F.A.O. GLOBAL SURVEY OF PESTICIDE SUSCEPTIBILITY OF STORED GRAIN PESTS
D'Yvoire, J *see* LE MAGHREB ET LA COMMUNAUTE ECONOMIQUE EUROPEENNE
Y DYWYSOGAETH – Rhyl, Wales. Apr 1870-Oct 1881 – 4 1/2r – 1 – uk British Libr Newspaper [072]
DZEN-HSI / Lowe, J – A catalog of the Official Gazetteers of China in the University of Washington. (Bibliotheca Asiatica. v. 1). Zug. 1966. BCH-1004 1 – 9 – ne IDC [310]
Dzerzhinskii, Felix Edmundovich *see* OCHEREDNYE ZADACHI PROMYSHLENNO I POLITIKI
DZHANGAR – 1940. The Dzhan'g'r tale, national epic of the Kalmyk – 1 – us I.U. Libraries [390]
Dzhangveladze, G A *see* BANKROTSTVO ANTIPROLETARSKIKH PARTII V GRUZII
Dzhanumova, Elena F *see* MOI VSTRECHI S GR. RASPUTINYM
DZHGA-6 CHASA VECHER'TA – Sofia, Bulgaria. 15 Sept-Dec 1944 – 1r – 1 – us L of C Photodup [949]
Dzhorov, Stolian *see* PERSPEKTIVY GRIADUSHCHEI MEZHDUNARODNOI REVOLIUTSII
DZIEJE EDUCACYJNE POLAKOW NA OBZYZNIE / Karbowiak, Antoni – Lwow, 1910 – 1r – 1 – us I.H.R.C. [370]
DZIEJE FLOTY POLSKIEJ / Lepszy, K – Gdansk, Torun. 1947. BR-5510 2 – 8 – ne IDC [943]
DZIEJE KULTURY POLSKIEJ / Brueckner, Aleksander – Krakow: W.L. Anczyc Spolka, 1931-46. 4v – 1 – us U.W. Library [943]
DZIEJE WOJEN I WOJSKOWOSCI W POLSCE / Korzon, R – Krakow. 1912. BR-5511 2 – 8 – ne IDC [947]
DZIENNIK BALTYCKI – Gdansk, Poland. Oct 1945-1993 – 86r – 1 – us L of C Photodup [947]

DZIENNIK CHICAGOSKI = CHICAGO DAILY NEWS – (In Polish) – Chicago: Spolka Naklad. Wydawn. Polsk, 1890-[dec 15 1890-1942] – 1 – us Res Libr [071]
DZIENNIK LITERACKI – Cracow. Poland. -w. 28 Mar 1947-31 Dec 1950. (2 reels) – 1 – uk British Libr Newspaper [947]
DZIENNIK LODZKI – Lodz, Poland. Jul-Sept 1945; Apr 1948-Aug 1953; Nov 1956-1992 – 72r – 1 – us L of C Photodup [943]
DZIENNIK LUDOWY – Warsaw, Poland. 1962-89 – 63r – 1 – us L of C Photodup [943]
DZIENNIK LUDOWY – Warsaw. Poland. -d. 29 Aug 1945-Nov 1949. (17 reels) – 1 – uk British Libr Newspaper [943]
DZIENNIK LUDOWY – Chicago: [s.n.], mar 16 1907-apr 21 1925 – 45r – us Res Libr [071]
DZIENNIK NARODOWY = NATIONAL POLISH DAILY – Chicago. apr 4 1908-jun 1909; jul 1913-1914; jul-dec 1915; sep 10 1917-jun 29 1918; jan 1920-sep 1923 – us Res Libr [071]
DZIENNIK POLSKI – (Backfile through 1998 $85/r) – Poland, 1999- – 6r per y – 1 – $480.00 standing order – us Ross [072]
DZIENNIK POLSKI – Cracow, Poland. -d. 22 June 1946-31 Oct 1951. 22 reels – 1 – uk British Libr Newspaper [943]
DZIENNIK POLSKI – Krakow, Poland. Apr 1945-1992 – 79r – 1 – us L of C Photodup [943]
DZIENNIK POLSKI – London, UK. 1986- – 40+ r – 1 – uk British Libr Newspaper [072]
DZIENNIK POLSKI – THE POLISH DAILY – Detroit, MI: Polish American Pub Co, mar 1904-jul 27 1905; dec 1905-jun 19–?; 1913-jun 1923; 1924-jun 1941; sunday suppls for 1936-37 + for jul 1938-jun 1939 – 1 – us Res Libr [071]
DZIENNIK POWSZECHNY – Warsaw, Poland. Jan-Feb 1919 – 1r – 1 – us L of C Photodup [943]
DZIENNIK POZNANSKI – Poznan, Poland. Mar-Apr 1923 – 1r – 1 – us L of C Photodup [943]
DZIENNIK USTAV POLSKIEJ RZECZYPOSPOLITEJ LUDOWEJ : OFFICIAL GAZETTE OF THE PEOPLE'S REPUBLIC OF POLAND / Poland – (Suppl: 1989; 1991 53mf Dfl327.00. Missing: 1987 (36). 1990) – Lublin, Warzawa. 1944-91 – 746mf – 8 – BR-9048 1 – ne IDC [947]
DZIENNIK USTAW – Paris, London. Oct. 31, 1939-July 3, 1945 – 1 – 35.00r – us Hoover Inst Photo [073]
DZIENNIK ZACHODNI – Katowice, Poland. Aug 1945; Oct 1947 (scattered issues); Oct 1949-1992 – 92r – 1 – us L of C Photodup [943]
DZIENNIK ZJEDNOCZENIA – (Issues for sep-dec 1921 filmed consecutively with: Dziennik zjednoczenia (Chicago: City ed)) – Chicago: Polish RCU of America, sep 1921-sep 1922; jan-jun 1927. (Country ed) – 7 – us Res Libr [071]
DZIENNIK ZJEDNOCZENIA (CITY EDITION) – (Filmed consecutively with: Dziennik zjednoczenia (country ed) sep 1921-nov 1939) – Chicago, IL: Polish RCU of America. City ed sep-dec 1921 – 80r – 1 – us Res Libr [071]
DZIENNIK ZWIAKOWY – Chicago. Jan 3 1911-July 1934; Apr 5 1935-Dec 31 1946. Incomplete – 1 – us NY Public [071]
DZIENNIK ZWIAZKOWY – Chicago, IL: Polish National Alliance of US of NA, 1908-jan 1 1977 – 1 – us Res Libr [071]
"DZIENNIKARSTWO POLSKIE" / Nagiel, Henryk – 1894 – 1r – 1 – us I.H.R.C. [947]
DZIS I JUTRO – Warsaw, Poland. 10 Sep 1950-13 May 1956 – 6r – 1 – uk British Libr Newspaper [947]
DZVIN – Zhurnal-misiachnyk literatury i nauky. v. 1-12, 1-6. Kyiv. 1913-14. BR-8035 2 – 8 – ne IDC [947]
E A *see* DIE CHRONOLOGIE DER GENESIS (1. MOSES) IM EINKLANG MIT DER PROFANEN
E AND M NEWSLETTER – (Ceased no 45 1988/89) – Toronto. nos 42-45. 1985/86-1988/89 – 9 – Can$20.00y – cn Micromedia [073]
E AU AKOANGA NO NGA TUMU TUATUA I KITEA I ROTO I TE TUTUA NA TE ATUA = THEOLOGICAL LECTURES / Bogue, David – (Transl into Raratongan by A Buzacott) – Cook Islands: London Missionary Soc, 1857 – 1r – 1 – PMB Doc409 – at Pacific Mss [240]
E. BARRAULT, APOTRE, A MR. NAUDIN – Troyes, 1832, 1p. De la suspension des conferences publiques sur la doctrine Saint-Simonienne. Versailles, impr. Allois, 1831, 7p. Les Saint-Simoniens, 1825-1834 – 9 – fr Hachette [880]
E CU *see* ANTISOFISMA
E Cumont *see* STUDIA PONTICA
E F *see* ST. BASIL AND HIS RULE
E K–v *see* AVANTI URY KERENSKAGO I KO
E PROS ROMAIOUS EPISTOLE = ST PAUL'S EPISTLE TO THE ROMANS : NOTES / Vaughan, Charles John – (Includes index of Greek words) – 6th ed. London: Macmillan, 1885 – 1mf – 9 – 0-8370-5624-1 – 1985-3624 – us A.T.L.A. [220]
E. RACICOT'S SPEECH TO HIS CONSTITUENTS: AT WEST FARNHAM, SATURDAY, NOV. 1ST, 1879 / Racicot, Ernest – 1879?. 02292. (Pre-1900 Canadiana) – 9 – cn C.I.H.M. [971]
E. T. A. HOFFMANNS ELIXIERE DES TEUFELS UND C. V. BRENTANOS ROMANZEN VOM ROSENKRANZ / Reiz, Elizabeth – Bonn 1920 – 1 – DM30.00 – gw Mikro Press [430]
E UND M : ELEKTROTECHNIK UND MASCHINENBAU – v63-67. 1946-50; v70. 1953; v72-81. 1955-64. v83-98. 1966-81 – 1,5,6,9,13 – $90.00v – us UMI [073]
Eadie, John *see*
– A COMMENTARY ON THE GREEK TEXT OF THE EPISTLE OF PAUL TO THE COLOSSIANS
– A COMMENTARY ON THE GREEK TEXT OF THE EPISTLE OF PAUL TO THE PHILIPPIANS
– A COMMENTARY ON THE GREEK TEXT OF THE EPISTLES OF PAUL TO THE THESSALONIANS
– PAUL THE PREACHER; OR, A POPULAR AND PRACTICAL EXPOSITION OF HIS DISCOURSES AND SPEECHES, AS RECORDED IN THE ACTS OF THE APOSTLES
Eadmer *see* EADMERI HISTORIA NOVORUM IN ANGLIA (RS81)
EADMERI HISTORIA NOVORUM IN ANGLIA (RS81) : ET OPUSCULA DUO DE VITA SANCTI ANSELMI ET QUIBUSDAM MIRACULIS EJUS / Eadmer; ed by Rule, M – 1884 – Dfl35.00 – ne Slangenburg [240]
Eads, Harvey L *see* TAILOR'S SYSTEM FOR CUTTING SHAKER GARMENTS
EAF: JOURNAL OF EDUCATIONAL ADMINISTRATION AND FOUNDATIONS *see* JOURNAL OF EDUCATIONAL ADMINISTRATION AND FOUNDATIONS
Eager, John Howard *see* ROMANISM IN ITS HOME
EAGLE – Brooklyn. N.Y. 1960-1963 – 1 – us UMI [071]
EAGLE – Bryan. Tex. 1896- – 1 – us UMI [071]
EAGLE – Butler. Pa. 1903- – 1 – us UMI [071]
EAGLE – Butler. Pa. -w. 1873-1910 – 1 – us UMI [071]
EAGLE – Dothan. Ala. -w. 1905-27 – 1 – us UMI [071]
EAGLE – East Providence. R.I. 1882-1887; 1895-1919 – 1 – us UMI [071]
EAGLE – Ekalaka. Mont. 1909-1949; 1956-1959; 1966- – 1 – us UMI [071]
EAGLE – Eldred. Pa. -w. 1888- – 1 – us UMI [071]
EAGLE – Fallon. Nev. -w. 1949-58 – 1 – us UMI [071]
EAGLE – Grand Rapids, MI. Also: Sunday Morning Eagle and pred. 1856-60, 1863-93 – 1 – us UMI [071]
EAGLE – Jackson. Mich. -w. 1862-66 – 1 – us UMI [071]
EAGLE – Marinette and Peshtigo. Wis. and pred. 1871-1909 – 1 – us UMI [071]
EAGLE – Maysville, KY. 1814-20.Also: Globe, Richmond, KY, 1809-10; Instructor, Paris, KY, 1818; Kentucky Journal, Frankfort, KY, 1795; People's Friend, Danville, KY, 1818-19; Political Theatre, Lancaster, KY, 1808-10; Republican Auxiliary, Washington, KY, 1806-10; Telegraph, Georgetown, KY, 1811-13; Weekly Messenger, Russellville, KY, 1814-20; Union, Washington, KY, 1814-20. Sold as one unit – 3 – us Readex [071]
EAGLE – Milton. Or. -w. 1901-48 – 1 – us UMI [071]
EAGLE – Oklahoma City. Okl. 1953-54 – 1 – us UMI [071]
EAGLE – Oxford. Miss. 1936- – 1 – us UMI [071]
EAGLE – Skamokawa. Wash. 1899-1934 – 1 – us UMI [071]
EAGLE – South Sioux City, NE. -w. Oct 1877; Sep 1879; Jul 1890; Sep-Dec 1890; Feb-Apr 1891; Nov 1891-Dec 1958 – 1 – us NE Hist [071]
EAGLE – Wichita. Kan. -w. 1872-1919 – 1 – us UMI [071]
THE EAGLE – Chadron, Dawes County, NE: Chadron State College, Sept 22, 1920-Feb 7, 1991 – us NE Hist [978]
THE EAGLE AND LAGOS CRITIC – Lagos, Nigeria. Mar 1883-Oct 1888 – 33ft – 1 – uk British Libr Newspaper [072]
EAGLE BOOSTER – Salem OR. Feb 5 1935 – 1 – us U.O. Library [071]
EAGLE EAGLET – Eagle, NE. -w. Sep. 1890-Aug. 1894; Nov. 1894; Jan. 1896-Aug. 1896. Incomplete; Sep. 1896-Apr. 1898; May 1891-Jul. 1899. Incomplete – 1 – us NE Hist [071]
EAGLE GAZETTE – Lancaster. Ohio. 1936- – 1 – us UMI [071]
EAGLE NEWS – Poughkeepsie. N.Y. 1914-42 – 1 – us UMI [071]
EAGLE ROCK NEWS HERALD – Los Angeles, CA. 1957 – 1 – us UMI [071]
EAGLE ROCK REPORTER AND SENTINEL – Los Angeles. Calif. 1925-1930 – 1 – us UMI [071]
EAGLE ROCK SENTINEL – Los Angeles. Calif. -w. 1910-1919; 1923; 1925-64; 1967-68 – 1 – us UMI [071]
EAGLE STANDARD – Fallon, CA. 1949-1985 – 53r – 1 – $2,650.00 – N04526 – us Library Micro [071]
EAGLE STANDARD – Fallon. Nev. -w. 1959- – 1 – us UMI [071]
EAGLE STAR – Marinette. Wis. 1888- – 1 – us UMI [071]
EAGLE TRADE JOURNAL – Marinette. Wis. 1936-37 – 1 – us UMI [071]
EAGLE VALLEY NEWS – Richland, OR. -w. 18 Jun 1914-10 Jul 1919. 1 roll – 1 – us U.O. Library [071]
Eagle, Walter *see* AMERICAN NEGLIGENCE DIGEST
THE EAGLE'S EYE – 1970-79. (American Indian Periodicals in the Princeton University Library). 12 fiches – 9 – $50.00 – us UPA [305]
EAGLESHAM PARISH CHURCH YARD MONUMENTAL INSCRIPTIONS / Eaglesham, Scotland – 1 – uk Microform Academic [941]
Eaglesham, Scotland *see* EAGLESHAM PARISH CHURCH YARD MONUMENTAL INSCRIPTIONS
EAGLET TIMES *see* TEMPLETON TIMES
Eaglin, James B *see*
– AN EVALUATION OF THE PROBABLE IMPACT OF SELECTED PROPOSALS FOR IMPOSING MANDATORY MINIMUM SENTENCES IN THE FEDERAL COURTS
– THE IMPACT OF THE FEDERAL DRUG AFTERCARE PROGRAM
– THE PRE-ARGUMENT CONFERENCE PROGRAM IN THE SIXTH CIRCUIT COURT OF APPEALS
– A PROCESS-DESCRIPTIVE STUDY OF THE DRUG AFTERCARE PROGRAM FOR DRUG-DEPENDENT FEDERAL OFFENDERS
– SENTENCING FEDERAL OFFENDERS FOR CRIMES COMMITTED BEFORE NOVEMBER 1, 1987
– A VALIDATION AND COMPARATIVE EVALUATION OF FOUR PREDICTIVE DEVICES FOR CLASSIFYING FEDERAL PROBATION CASELOADS
E.A.H.C. *see* ANNUAL DEPARTMENTAL REPORTS
EALING AND ACTON GAZETTE *see* MIDDLESEX COUNTY TIMES
Eamer, E H *see* CATALOGUE OF THE FLOWERING PLANTS AND FERNS OF CONNECTICUT
Eames, Charles M *see* HISTORIC MORGAN AND CLASSIC JACKSONVILLE
EAR AND HEARING – (Formerly: Journal of the American Auditory Society. v1-5 1975-79 5r) – v1-17. 1975-96 – 1,5,6,9 – $80.00r – us Williams [610]
EAR, NOSE, AND THROAT JOURNAL – v. 55-. 1976- – 1,5,6,9 – us UMI [617]
Eardley-Wilmot, Sidney *see* OUR JOURNAL IN THE PACIFIC
THE EARL BROWDER PAPERS, 1891-1975 – 36r – 1 – $2650.00 – us UMI [335]
EARL CONRAD/HARRIET TUBMAN COLLECTION : FROM THE HOLDINGS OF THE SCHOMBURG CENTER FOR RESEARCH IN BLACK CULTURE, MANUSCRIPTS, ARCHIVES AND RARE BOOKS DIVISION: THE NEW YORK PUBLIC LIBRARY, ASTOR, LENOX AND TILDEN FOUNDATIONS – (Guide which covers all coll under "Antebellum America and Slavery" sold separately for $20.00 D3305.G2) – 1995 – 2r – 1 – $170.00 – D3305P06 – Dist. us Scholarly Res – us L of C Photodup [976]
Earl, Edward Curtis *see* THE SCHOOLHOUSE
Earl, G W *see* THE EASTERN SEAS, ON VOYAGES AND ADVENTURES IN THE INDIAN ARCHIPELAGO, IN 1832-33-34
EARL RANKIN COLLECTION ON CLOZE PROCEDURE / Rankin, Earl & Svobodny, Dolly – 1900-86. 1000 titles on 250mf. Printed card indexes included. Annual supplements – 9 – us A.T.B.I. [370]
Earle, A B *see*
– BRINGING IN SHEAVES
– REVIVAL HYMNS
Earle, Alice Morse *see* THE SABBATH IN PURITAN NEW ENGLAND
THE EARLIEST ENGLISH VERSION OF THE FABLES OF BIDPAI, THE MORALL PHILOSOPHIE OF DONI / Bidpai – By Sir Thomas North; ed. and introd. by Joseph Jacobs. London: D. Nutt, 1888. Reprint of the first ed., 1570 – 1 – us U.W. Library [390]
THE EARLIEST GOSPEL: A HISTORICAL STUDY OF THE GOSPEL ACCORDING TO MARK / Menzies, Allan – London: Macmillan, 1901.1 fiche. 8370-4389-1 – 9 – us A.T.L.A. [240]
THE EARLIEST VERSION OF THE BABYLONIAN DELUGE STORY AND THE TEMPLE LIBRARY OF NIPPUR / Hilprecht, Hermann Vollrat – (Includes bibliographical references) – Philadelphia: University of Pennsylvania, 1910 – 1mf – 9 – 0-8370-7067-8 – 1986-1067 – us A.T.L.A. [930]
EARLY ADOLESCENTS' KNOWLEDGE OF AND ATTITUDES TOWARD HIV AND AIDS / Blackwell, G F – 1991 – 2mf – 9 – $8.00 – us Microform Publ [616]
EARLY AGROMETEROLOGICAL CROP YIELD ASSESSMENT – 1986 – 158p – it F.A.O. [550]
EARLY ALINARI ARCHIVES : ART AND ARCHITECTURE IN ITALY – (Representative selection of important buildings, churches and monuments in towns by perhaps the finest art and architectural photographers in Italy during the 19th C. Also extensive coverage of works in museums and galleries. Over 7,000 reproductions) – 122mf – 9 – $630.00 – 0-907006-54-X – uk Mindata [770]
EARLY AMERICAN – 1968-76. (American Indian Periodicals in the Princeton University Library). 8 fiches – 9 – $45.00 – us UPA [305]
EARLY AMERICAN – Modesto, CA. 1968-90 – 12r – 1 – $600.00 – R02467 – us Library Micro [071]
EARLY AMERICAN CHILDREN'S BOOKS IN MICROFICHE – (With guidebook) – 906mf – 9 – $5.00f – us Ross [070]
EARLY AMERICAN CHURCHES / Embury, Aymar – Garden City, N.Y.: Doubleday, Page, 1914 – 1mf – us A.T.L.A. [240]
EARLY AMERICAN HERBARIA AND RELATED DRAWINGS / British Museum (Natural History) – (William Bartram Herbarium 4mf £86.00. Samuel Dale Herbarium 2mf £24.00. John Leonard Riddell Herbarium 4mf £47.00. Thomas Walter Herbarium 2mf £24.00. William Young Herbarium 4mf £70.00) – Collection includes 5 herbaria – 4 colour and 13 b/w mf – 9,15 – £220.00 set – uk Chadwyck [580]
EARLY AMERICAN HISTORY RESEARCH REPORTS FROM THE COLONIAL WILLIAMSBURG FOUNDATION LIBRARY / Colonial Williamsburg Foundation – (Pt 1 £1,775.00. Pt 2 £920.00. Pt 3 £1,145.00. Pt 4 £1,655.00. Guide £37.00) – 1,372mf – 9 – £5,230.00 – uk Chadwyck [975]
EARLY AMERICAN IMPRINTS, 1639-1800 / ed by Shipton, Clifford K – Every existent book, pamphlet, and broadside printed in the U.S. from 1639 to 1800. Keyed to Evans' American Bibliography. 42,000 titles – 3,9 – us Readex [010]
EARLY AMERICAN IMPRINTS, 1801-1819 / ed by Shipton, Clifford K – Second series. Based on Shaw-Shoemaker. Now complete through 1818 – 3,9 – us Readex [010]

EARLY AMERICAN INDEX TO PERIODICALS TO 1860 – 3 – us Readex [010]

EARLY AMERICAN MEDICAL IMPRINTS, 1668-1820 – Titles from the Robert B. Austin bibliography – 1 – us Primary [610]

EARLY AMERICAN NEWSPAPERS – 1704-1820 – 3,9 – us Readex [071]

EARLY AMERICAN ORDERLY BOOKS, 1748-1817 – (The French and Indian War through the War of 1812) – From the holdings of the New York Historical Society – 1 – us Primary [975]

EARLY AMERICAN PHILOSOPHERS / Jones, Adam Leroy – New York: Macmillan, 1898 – 1mf – us A.T.L.A. [190]

EARLY AND CENTRAL MIDDLE AGES, C650-1200 : THE MANUSCRIPT RECORD – (Part 2: Manuscripts from Cambridge University Library, Section B (MSS Hh-Mm, Additional Mss. and the Ely Chapter of 974)) – Part 1: Manuscripts from Cambridge University Library, Section A (MSS Dd-Gg) – 1 – us Primary [900]

EARLY AND LATE PAPERS. HITHERTO UNCOLLECTED / Thackeray, William Makepeace – Boston: Ticknor and Fields, 1867 – 1 roll – 1 – 1-55879-619-3 – uk Libr Preservation [880]

EARLY ANNALS OF WHITEWATER 1837-1867 / Cravath, Prosper – Whitewater: The Whitewater Federation of Women's Clubs, 1906. Wisconsin Reel 20. (The Cox Library Collection) – 5 – us Americana [978]

EARLY ARABIC PERIODICALS – (Also available seperately) – 212mf – 9 – ne IDC [260]

THE EARLY BAPTISTS OF VIRGINIA : AN ADDRESS / Howell, Robert Boyte C – Philadelphia: Press of the Society, 1857 – 1mf – us A.T.L.A. [240]

EARLY BIBLE SONGS / Drysdale, Alexander Hutton – London: Religious Tract Society, 1890. 1 fiche – 9 – us A.T.L.A. [240]

EARLY BRITISH FICTION: PRE-1750 – Based on William McBurney's Checklist of English Prose Fiction, 1700-1739, and Jerry Begsley's Check List of Prose Fiction published in England, 1740-1749 – 1 – us Primary [830]

EARLY BRITISH PERIODICALS 1 AND 2, 1681-1921 – (Reproduces 169 periodicals. AACR1 cataloging available) – 902r (31 units) – 1 – $58,900.00 – us UMI [073]

EARLY CANADIANA : PRE-1900 ANNUALS – (Directories Collection subset with 4,135 fiches available separately for Can$8,395 including printed cat. Cat. alone Can$45.00) – 16,595 microfiche – 9 – Can$33,690 including printed cat. Cat. Can$45.00. CANMARC tapes Can$60.00. COM cat. Can$385.00 – cn C.I.H.M. [971]

EARLY CANADIANA : PRE-1900 MONOGRAPHS – (Set includes COM and CANMARC tapes. Subject sub-sections available separately. Apply to publisher) – 57,480 titles on 122,800 microfiche – 9 – Can$259,700 COM alone Can$385 – cn C.I.H.M. [971]

EARLY CANADIANA : PRE-1900 PERIODICALS – Units 1-7, 42,850 issues including cumulative printed cat. Cat alone $45 – 9 – Can$86,900 (standing order unit price – units 8,9 – Can$12,180) – cn C.I.H.M. [971]

EARLY CHAPTERS OF CAYUGA HISTORY: JESUIT MISSIONS IN GOI-O-GOUEN, 1656-1684: ALSO...THE SULPITIAN MISSION AMONG THE EMIGRANT CAYUGAS...1668 / Hawley, Charles – Auburn, NY: Knapp & Peck, 1879. 05519. (Pre-1900 Canadiana) – 9 – cn C.I.H.M. [240]

EARLY CHILD DEVELOPMENT AND CARE / ed by Evans, R – 1971- – 1,5,9 – us Gordon [640]

EARLY CHILDHOOD EDUCATION – (v1-8 1967-1974/75 Can$37.00) – Edmonton. v1-28. 1967-95 – 9 – Can$20.00y – cn Micromedia [370]

EARLY CHILDHOOD EDUCATION PROGRAMME / Jamaica. Ministry of Education – Kingston, 1983 – 1mf – 9 – DE-523/1 – ne IDC [370]

EARLY CHILDREN'S LITERATURE : THE BIRMINGHAM CENTRAL LIBRARY COLLECTION TO 1830 – (Printed contents list included) – 1085mf – 9 – $9,956.00 – 1-869934-63-6 – uk Emmett [020]

EARLY CHRISTIAN BAPTISM AND THE CREED : A STUDY IN ANTE-NICENE THEOLOGY / Chrehan, J – London, 1950 – 4mf – 8 – Dfl19.00 – ne Slangenburg [240]

THE EARLY CHRISTIAN CHURCH AS FORESHADOWED IN OLD TESTAMENT PROPHECY / Chisholm, Murdoch – Halifax: Nova Scotia Print., 1892. 03052. (Pre-1900 Canadiana) – 9 – cn C.I.H.M. [240]

EARLY CHRISTIAN ETHICS IN THE WEST : FROM CLEMENT TO AMBROSE / Scullard, Herbert Hayes – (Includes indexes of names and subjects) – London: Williams & Norgate, 1907 – 1mf – 9 – 0-8370-6371-X – 1986-0371 – us A.T.L.A. [230]

THE EARLY CHRISTIAN MARTYRS AND THEIR PERSECUTIONS / Herkless, John – London: Dent; Philadelphia: J.B. Lippincott, [1904?] – 1mf – us A.T.L.A. [240]

EARLY CHRISTIAN MISSIONS OF IRELAND, SCOTLAND AND ENGLAND / Charles, Elizabeth Rundle – London: S.P.C.K.; New York: E.& J.B. Young, 1893 – 1mf – us A.T.L.A. [240]

EARLY CHRISTIAN NUMISMATICS AND OTHER ANTIQUARIAN TRACTS / King, CW – London: Bell & Daldy, 1873 – 1mf – us A.T.L.A. [730]

EARLY CHRISTIANITY AND PAGANISM : A.D. 64 TO THE PEACE OF THE CHURCH IN THE FOURTH CENTURY: A NARRATION MAINLY BASED UPON CONTEMPORARY RECORDS AND REMAINS / Spence, H Donald M – New York: E.P. Dutton, [1901?] – 2mf – us A.T.L.A. [240]

EARLY CHRISTIANITY IN ARABIA : A HISTORICAL ESSAY / Wright, Thomas – London, 1855 – 4mf – 8 – Dfl19.00 – ne Slangenburg [240]

EARLY CHRISTIANITY IN ARABIA / Wright, Thomas – 9 – $10.00 – us I.R.C. [240]

EARLY CHRISTIANITY OUTSIDE THE ROMAN EMPIRE : TWO LECTURES DELIVERED AT TRINITY COLLEGE, DUBLIN / Burkitt, FC – Cambridge: University Press; New York: Macmillan [distributor], 1899 – 1mf – us A.T.L.A. [240]

THE EARLY CHRISTIANS IN ROME / Spence, H Donald M – London: Methuen, 1910 – 2mf – us A.T.L.A. [240]

THE EARLY CHURCH / First Congregational Church, Emporia KS – 1857-1926, Additional church records through 1958 – 1 – us KS Hist [240]

THE EARLY CHURCH : A HISTORY OF CHRISTIANITY IN THE FIRST SIX CENTURIES / Duff, David – Edingurgh: T. & T. Clark, 1891 – 2mf – us A.T.L.A. [240]

EARLY CHURCH HISTORY : TO THE DEATH OF CONSTANTINE / Backhouse, Edward; ed by Tylor, Charles – London: Simpkin, Marshall, Hamilton, Kent, 1892 – 1mf – us A.T.L.A. [240]

EARLY CHURCH HISTORY TO A.D. 313 / Gwatkin, Henry Melvill – London: Macmillan, 1912 – 2mf – us A.T.L.A. [240]

THE EARLY CHURCH IN THE LIGHT OF THE MONUMENTS : A STUDY IN CHRISTIAN ARCHAEOLOGY / Barnes, Arthur Stapylton – London; New York: Longmans, Green, 1913. (The Westminster library) – 1mf – us A.T.L.A. [240]

EARLY CHURCH: STUDIES IN THE ACTS OF THE APOSTLES / Burrell, David James – New York: American Tract Soc., 1897. 1 fiche – 9 – us A.T.L.A. [240]

EARLY CHURCHES IN PALESTINE / Crowfoot, J W – 9 – $10.00 – us I.R.C. [240]

THE EARLY CHURCHES OF CONSTANTINOPEL : ARCHITECTURE AND LITURGY / Mathews, Thomas – University Park/London, 1971 – 6mf – 8 – Dfl25.00 – ne Slangenburg [720]

THE EARLY CONFLICTS OF CHRISTIANITY / Kip, William Ingraham – New York: D. Appleton, 1850, c1849 – 1mf – us A.T.L.A. [240]

EARLY COURT RECORDS / Columbia County.Georgia – Copied by Mrs. F.F. Baker. Indexed plus index of marriages. 4 fiches. F-0679 – 9 – us A.G.L.L. [920]

EARLY CRITICAL ESSAYS 1820-1822 / Cooper, James Fenimore – 9 – 10.00 – us Scholars' Facs [840]

EARLY CZECH NEWSPAPERS OF TEXAS / Institute of Texan Cultures. Library – Svobodan (La Grange) and Obzorn (Halletsville). 17 rolls – 1 – $400.00 – us TX Culture [071]

THE EARLY DAWN – Bonthe, Sierra Leone. Jan 1885-Jun 1892 (imperfect) – 56ft – 1 – uk British Libr Newspaper [072]

EARLY DAYS IN GREENBUSH / Snapp, William L – Springfield: H. W. Rokker Co., 1905. Illinois Reel 59. (The Cox Library Collection) – 5 – us Americana [978]

THE EARLY DAYS OF CHRISTIANITY / Farrar, Frederic William – (Includes bibliographical references and indexes) – New York: Funk & Wagnalls, 1883 – 2mf – 9 – 0-8370-6327-2 – 1986-0327 – us A.T.L.A. [220]

THE EARLY DAYS OF MY EPISCOPATE / Kip, William Ingraham – New York: T. Whittaker, 1892 – 1mf – us A.T.L.A. [240]

EARLY DRAWINGS AND ILLUMINATIONS : AN INTRODUCTION TO THE STUDY OF ILLUSTRATED MANUSCRIPTS: WITH A DICTIONARY OF SUBJECTS IN THE BRITISH MUSEUM / Birch, Walter de Gray & Jenner, Henry – London: S. Bagster, 1879 – 1mf – us A.T.L.A. [740]

EARLY EASTERN CHRISTIANITY : ST. MARGARET'S LECTURES, 1904, ON THE SYRIAC-SPEAKING CHURCH / Burkitt, F Crawford – London: John Murray, 1904 – 1mf – us A.T.L.A. [240]

EARLY EIGHTEENTH CENTURY ARCHIVES / Society for Promoting Christian Knowledge – With printed index – 1 – £1,675.00 – uk World [240]

EARLY ENGLISH BOOKS 1 (POLLARD AND REDGRAVE, STC 1), 1475-1640 – (Volume equivalent 28,335 titles; 28,320 volumes. Catalog cards (cataloging according to AACR2) for Units 1-21 available from UMI; for Units 22-48, available from University of Michigan; for units 49-61, from UMI) – 1979r (61 units complete) – 1 – $121,355.00 complete – us UMI [090]

EARLY ENGLISH BOOKS 2 (WING, STC 2), 1641-1700 – (AACR2 cataloging on OCLC available) – 1982r (through Unit 79) – 1 – $162,345.00 through Unit 79 – us UMI [090]

EARLY ENGLISH COURTESY BOOKS, 1571-1773 – Newberry Library Collections – 19r – 1 – $1405.00 – us UMI [941]

THE EARLY ENGLISH DISSENTERS IN THE LIGHT OF RECENT RESEARCH (1550-1641) / Burrage, Champlin – Cambridge: University Press; New York: Putnam [distributor], 1912 – 2mf – us A.T.L.A. [240]

EARLY ENGLISH NEWSPAPERS – Based on the holdings of the Burney Collection and others at the British Library – 1 – us Primary [072]

EARLY ENGLISH TEXT SOCIETY – Extra Series. 1867-1920. v.1-125 – 618mf – 8 – ne IDC [800]

EARLY ENGLISH TEXT SOCIETY – Original Series. 1864-1904. v.1-128 – 618mf – 8 – ne IDC [080]

EARLY FEDERAL NOMINATIVE REPORTS – (Individual titles also listed separately) – 1180mf – 9 – $1,770.00 coll – us L.L.M.C. [340]

EARLY FEDERAL NOMINATIVE REPORTS *see*
- ABBOTT'S REPORTS OF CASES IN ADMIRALTY FOR THE SOUTHERN DISTRICT OF NEW YORK
- ABBOTT'S REPORTS OF U.S. CIRCUIT AND DISTRICT COURT DECISIONS
- BALDWIN'S REPORTS OF CASES IN THE THIRD CIRCUIT, 1828-1833
- BEE'S REPORTS OF CASES IN THE DISTRICT COURT OF SOUTH CAROLINA, 1792-1805
- BENEDICT'S REPORTS OF CASES IN THE DISTRICT COURTS OF THE U.S. (2ND CIRCUIT), 1865-1879
- BISSELL'S REPORTS OF CASES IN THE SEVENTH CIRCUIT, 1851-1883
- BLATCHFORD AND HOWLAND'S REPORTS OF CASES IN THE SOUTHERN DISTRICT COURT OF NEW YORK, 1827-1837
- BLATCHFORD'S PRIZE CASES IN THE SECOND CIRCUIT, 1861-1865
- BLATCHFORD'S REPORTS OF CASES IN THE SECOND CIRCUIT, 1845-1887
- BOND'S REPORTS OF CASES IN THE SIXTH CIRCUIT, 1856-1871
- BROCKENBROUGH'S REPORTS OF CASES IN THE FOURTH CIRCUIT, 1802-1833
- BROWN'S REPORTS OF ADMIRALTY AND REVENUE CASES IN THE SIXTH CIRCUIT
- BRUNNER'S REPORTS OF CASES IN THE CIRCUIT COURTS OF THE U.S., 1789-1879
- CADWALADER'S CASES IN THE DISTRICT COURT OF PENNSYLVANIA, 1858-1879
- CHASE'S REPORTS OF CASES IN THE FOURTH CIRCUIT, 1865-1869
- CLIFFORD'S REPORTS OF CASES IN THE FIRST CIRCUIT, 1858-1878
- CRABBE'S REPORTS OF CASES FOR THE EASTERN DISTRICT OF PENNSYLVANIA, 1836-1846
- CRANCH'S REPORTS OF CASES IN THE DISTRICT OF COLUMBIA, 1804-1841
- CURTIS' REPORTS OF CASES IN THE FIRST CIRCUIT, 1851-1856
- DEADY'S REPORTS OF CASES IN THE NINTH CIRCUIT, 1859-1869
- DILLON'S REPORTS OF CASES IN THE EIGHTH CIRCUIT, 1870-1880
- FISHER'S PRIZE CASES IN PENNSYLVANIA
- FLIPPEN'S REPORTS OF CASES IN THE SIXTH CIRCUIT, 1859-1881
- GALLISON'S REPORTS OF CASES IN THE FIRST CIRCUIT, 1812-1815
- GILPIN'S REPORTS OF CASES IN THE EASTERN DISTRICT OF PENNSYLVANIA, 1828-1826
- HASKELL'S JUDGEMENTS OF THE HONORABLE EDWARD FOX FOR THE MAINE DISTRICT AND FIRST CIRCUIT, 1866-1881
- HEMPSTEAD'S REPORTS OF CASES IN THE ARKANSAS DISTRICT AND CIRCUIT COURTS, 1836-1856
- HOFFMAN'S REPORTS OF CASES IN THE DISTRICT COURT FOR NORTHERN CALIFORNIA, 1853-1858
- HOLMES' REPORTS OF CASES IN THE FIRST CIRCUIT, 1870-1875
- HUGHES' REPORTS OF CASES IN THE FOURTH CIRCUIT, 1792-1883
- LOWELL'S JUDGEMENTS IN THE U.S. COURT FOR THE DISTRICT OF MASSACHUSETTS, 1865-1877
- MACALLISTER'S REPORTS OF CASES IN THE NINTH CIRCUIT, 1855-1859
- MASON'S REPORTS OF CASES IN THE FIRST CIRCUIT, 1816-1830
- MCCRARY'S REPORTS OF CASES IN THE EIGHTH CIRCUIT, 1877-1883
- MCLEAN'S REPORTS OF CASES IN THE SEVENTH CIRCUIT, 1839-1855
- NEWBERRY REPORTS OF ADMIRALTY CASES IN THE DISTRICT COURTS OF THE U.S., 1842-1957
- OLCOTT'S REPORTS OF CASES IN THE DISTRICT COURT FOR THE SOUTHERN DISTRICT OF NEW YORK, 1843-1847
- PAINE'S REPORTS OF CASES IN THE SECOND CIRCUIT, 1810-1840
- PETERS' ADMIRALTY DECISIONS IN THE DISTRICT COURT FOR PENNSYLVANIA, 1780-1807
- PETERS' REPORTS OF CASES IN THE THIRD CIRCUIT, 1803-1818
- SAWYER'S REPORTS OF CASES IN THE NINTH CIRCUIT, 1870-1891
- SPRAGUE'S ADMIRALTY AND MARITIME DECISIONS IN THE DISTRICT OF MASSACHUSETTS, 1841-1864
- STORY'S REPORTS OF CASES IN THE FIRST CIRCUIT, 1839-1845
- SUMNER'S REPORTS OF CASES IN THE FIRST CIRCUIT, 1829-1839
- TANEY'S REPORTS OF CASES IN THE FOURTH CIRCUIT, 1836-1851
- VAN NESS' REPORTS OF TWO CASES IN THE PRIZE COURT OF THE NEW YORK DISTRICT
- WALLACE JUNIOR'S REPORTS OF CASES IN THE THIRD CIRCUIT, 1842-1862
- WALLACE SENIOR'S REPORTS OF CASES IN THE THIRD CIRCUIT
- WARE'S REPORTS OF CASES IN THE DISTRICT COURTS FOR MAINE AND MASSACHUSETTS, 1822-1874
- WASHINGTON'S REPORTS OF CASES IN THE THIRD CIRCUIT, 1803-1827
- WOODBURY AND MINOT'S REPORTS OF CASES IN THE FIRST CIRCUIT, 1845-1847
- WOODS' REPORTS OF CASES IN THE FIFTH CIRCUIT, 1870-1883
- WOOLWORTH'S REPORTS OF CASES IN THE EIGHTH CIRCUIT, 1863-1869

EARLY FRIENDS IN GRANT COUNTY, INDIANA 1825-1913 / Society of Friends – By Elwood O. Ellis. Item N. 26p. SW16-0093 – 5 – us A.G.L.L. [240]

EARLY FRIENDS OF UPPER BUCKS WITH SOME ACCOUNT OF THEIR DESCENDANTS / Roberts, C V – Historical and genealogical. Philadelphia, published by the compiler, 1925. Pennsylvania Reel 44. (The Cox Library Collection) – 5 – us Americana [978]

EARLY GERMAN ART / Burlington Fine Arts Club. London – 1906 – 9 – 14.70 – uk Chadwyck [700]

EARLY HEBREW LIFE: A STUDY IN SOCIOLOGY / Fenton, John – London: Trubner, 1880 – 9 – us A.T.L.A. [270]

EARLY HEBREW ORTHOGRAPHY / Cross, Frank M – 1952 – 9 – $10.00 – us I.R.C. [470]

THE EARLY HISTORY OF AMERICA MICROFORM: OUTLINE OF A SERIES OF LECTURES DELIVERED UNDER THE AUSPICES OF THE LADIES' EDUCATION ASSOCIATION OF MONTREAL DURING THE SESSION 1881-82 / Campbell, John – Montreal: Mitchell & Wilson, 1882. 00373. (Pre-1900 Canadiana) – 9 – cn C.I.H.M. [770]

AN EARLY HISTORY OF FAYETTE COUNTY / Weyand & Wade – La Grange: Journal Plant, 1936. Texas Reel 11. (The Cox Library Collection) – 5 – us Americana [978]

EARLY HISTORY OF GREATER KANSAS CITY, MISSOURI AND KANSAS / Deatherage, Charles P – 12 Oct 1492-1870. Kansas City: Inter-State Publ. Co., 1927. Missouri Reel 21. (The Cox Library Collection) – 5 – us Americana [978]

EARLY HISTORY OF MICHIGAN / Thorp & Godfrey – Biographies of state officers, members of Congress, judges, etc. Lansing, 1888.Michigan Reel 2. (The Cox Library Collection) – 5 – us Americana [978]

EARLY HISTORY OF MOBILE BAPTISTS / Kennedy, Gladys – Unpub. mss. 192p – 1 – 6.72 – us Baptist [240]

EARLY HISTORY OF THE CHRISTIAN CHURCH FROM ITS FOUNDATION TO THE END OF THE FIFTH CENTURY / Duchesne, Louis – London: John Murray, 1912 – v2, 2mf – us A.T.L.A. [240]

EARLY HISTORY OF THE CHRISTIAN CHURCH FROM ITS FOUNDATION TO THE END OF THE THIRD CENTURY / Duchesne, Louis – London: J. Murray, 1909. (Early history of the Christian church from its foundation to the end of the fifth century / by Louis Duchesne; v1) – 2mf – us A.T.L.A. [240]

THE EARLY HISTORY OF THE CHURCH MISSIONARY SOCIETY FOR AFRICA AND THE EAST TO THE END OF A.D. 1814 / Hole, Charles – London: Church Missionary Society, 1896 – 2mf – us A.T.L.A. [240]

EARLY HISTORY OF THE DISCIPLES IN THE WESTERN RESERVE, OHIO : WITH BIOGRAPHICAL SKETCHES OF THE PRINCIPAL AGENTS IN THEIR RELIGIOUS MOVEMENT / Hayden, A S – Cincinnati: Chase & Hall, 1875 – 2mf – us A.T.L.A. [240]

EARLY HISTORY OF THE FEDERAL SUPREME COURT / Muller, William Henry – Boston: Chipman, 1922. 117p. LL-1283 – 1 – us L of C Photodup [340]

THE EARLY HISTORY OF THE TOWN OF ELLICOTT / Hazeltine, Gilbert W – Jamestown, Journal Printing Co., 1887. New York Reel 10. (The Cox Library Collection) – 5 – us Americana [978]

EARLY HISTORY OF THE TOWN OF HOPKINTON / Sanford, Carlton E – Genealogical records of 60 pioneer families. Boston, Bartless Press, 1903. New York Reel 33. (The Cox Library Collection) – 5 – us Americana [978]

EARLY HUMAN DEVELOPMENT – v1-11. 1977-84 – 1,5,6,13 – sz Elsevier [073]

EARLY IMPRINT PUBLICATIONS ON PALESTINE, 1921-1939 – Chicago: The Middle Eastern Microfilm Project, 1993 – 1 – us Res Libr [956]

EARLY INTERVENTION AND CULTURE PREPARATION FOR LITERACY : THE INTERFACE BETWEEN THEORY AND PRACTICE / ed by Eldering, Lotty & Leseman, Paul – 1993 – 352p – 9 – 92-3-102937-1 – fr UNESCO [302]

EARLY IRISH LAWS AND INSTITUTIONS / MacNeill, John – Dublin, Burns, Oates and Washbourne 1934 152 p. LL-2272 – 1 – us L of C Photodup [340]

EARLY ISRAEL AND THE SURROUNDING NATIONS / Sayce, Archibald Henry – New York: E R Herrick, 1899 – 1mf – 9 – 0-8370-9739-8 – 1986-3739 – us A.T.L.A. [270]

EARLY IVORIES FROM SAMARIA / Crowfoot, J W – PEF. 1938 – 9 – $10.00 – us I.R.C. [930]

EARLY LATIN HYMNARIES : AN INDEX OF HYMNS IN HYMNARIES BEFORE 1100 : WITH AN APPENDIX FROM LATER SOURCES / Mearns, James – Cambridge [Engl.]: University Press, 1913 – 1mf – us A.T.L.A. [240]

EARLY LAWS OF MISSOURI PERTAINING TO WOMEN : PROJECT OF HISTORICAL ACTIVITIES COMMITTEE, 1966-1968 / Ingersoll, Mrs. Albert Converse – St. Louis National Society of Colonial Dames in the State of Missouri. 1969? 37p LL-285 – 1 – us L of C Photodup [340]

EARLY LEAVING: REPORT OF THE CENTRAL ADVISORY COUNCIL FOR EDUCATION / Great Britain. Central Advisory Council for Education – 1954 – 9 – uk Microform Academic [324]

THE EARLY LETTERS AND CLASSIFIED PAPERS, 1660-1740 / Royal Society – $2,530.00 – 1-55655-171-1 – us UPA [080]

EARLY LETTERS OF MARCUS DODS, D.D.: (LATE PRINCIPAL OF NEW COLLEGE, EDINBURGH) (1850-1864) / Dods, Marcus – London: Hodder & Stoughton, [1910?] – 1mf – us A.T.L.A. [240]

EARLY LIFE AMONG THE INDIANS: REMINISCENCES FROM THE LIFE OF BENJ. G. ARMSTRONG: TREATIES OF 1835, 1837, 1842, AND 1854: HABITS AND CUSTOMS OF THE RED MEN OF THE FOREST: INCIDENTS, BIOGRAPHICAL SKETCHES, BATTLES, ETC. / Armstrong, Benjamin G – Ashland, Wis., A. Bowron, c1891. 02470. (Pre-1900 Canadiana) – 9 – cn C.I.H.M. [306]

EARLY LIFE AND TIMES IN BOONE COUNTY / Harden & Spahr – Biographical sketches. Lebanon: 1887. Indiana Reel 6. (The Cox Library Collection) – 5 – us Americana [978]

THE EARLY LIFE OF ABRAHAM LINCOLN.. / Tarbell, Ida Minerva – New York: S.S. McClure, 1896. 240p. illus. ports. (McClure's Magazine Library, no. 3) – 1 – us U.W. Library [920]

EARLY LIFE OF OUR LORD / Brough, Joshua – New York: E.P. Dutton, 1897. 1 fiche – 9 – us A.T.L.A. [240]

THE EARLY LIFE OF SAMUEL ROGERS / Clayden, Peter William – London: Smith, Elder, and Co., 1887 – 1 roll – 1 – 1-55879-631-2 – uk Libr Preservation [920]

EARLY LYRICS OF SO CHONG JU / Midang – 1993 – 9 – 92-3-102889-8 – Co-published with Forest Books – fr UNESCO [480]

THE EARLY MANUSCRIPT COLLECTION / Westminster Abbey. Library – With printed catalogue – 1 – £595.00 – uk World [025]

EARLY METHODIST PHILANTHROPY / North, Eric McCoy – New York: Methodist Book Concern, c1914 – 1mf – us A.T.L.A. [240]

EARLY MISCELLANEOUS DUNDAS NEWSPAPERS – Dundas, 1826-1862 – 1r – 1 – cn Preston [971]

EARLY MISSIONS TO AND WITHIN THE BRITISH ISLANDS / Hole, Charles – London: S.P.C.K.; New York: E. & J.B. Young, [1888?] – 1mf – us A.T.L.A. [240]

EARLY MUSIC : PART 1: THE PEMBROKE CHOIR BOOKS AND OTHER MUSIC MANUSCRIPTS FROM PEMBROKE COLLEGE, CAMBRIDGE – (Guide included) – Marlborough: Adam Matthew Publications, 1996 – 3r – 1 – $360.00 – uk Matthew [780]

EARLY MUSIC FROM LOW COUNTRIES LIBRARIES – (Pt 1: Concertos before 1820 259mf Dfl3,870 M371. Pt 2: Orchestral Music before 1820 427mf Dfl7,260 M374. Pt 3: Church Music, 1750-1820 541mf Dfl5,395 M377. Pt 4: Vocal and Instrumental Tutors 811mf Dfl8,110 M380. Pt 5: Historical Organ Collection 19 b/w mf Dfl1,195 M383 67 color mf M383C. Pt 6: Vocal Music 1650-1820 609mf Dfl6,100 M386. Pt 7: Keyboard Music, 1620-1820 326mf M387) – 9 – ne MMF Publ [780]

EARLY NARRATIVES OF BERKS COUNTY / Knowland, J B – Historical Society of Berks County, 1927. Pennsylvania Reel 12. (The Cox Library Collection) – 5 – us Americana [978]

THE EARLY NARRATIVES OF GENESIS: A BRIEF INTRODUCTION TO...GENESIS I-XI / Ryle, Herbert Edward – London: Macmillan, 1892.1 fiche – 9 – us A.T.L.A. [240]

EARLY NEW ENGLAND SCHOOLS / Small, Walter Herbert – Boston: Ginn and Company, 1914 – 1mf – us A.T.L.A. [370]

EARLY NEW HAMPSHIRE BAPTIST CHURCHES. NEW HAMPSHIRE : CHURCH RECORDS – (1. Hopkinton Baptist Church Society Records. 1794-1864. 2. Londonerry Baptist Church. 1799-1900 (2 vols.). 3. Main and New Hampshire Quarterly Meetings. 1783-1792. 4. Marlow Baptist Church. 1777-1807, 1859-1900 (2 vols.). 5. Mason Baptist Church. 1786-1836, original MS and typescripts. 6. Meridith Baptist Church. 1779-1829, Vol. 1) – Reel 2 – Items 1-6 – 1 – us Baptist [240]

EARLY NEW HAMPSHIRE BAPTIST CHURCHES. NEW HAMPSHIRE : CHURCH RECORDS – (1. Meredity Baptist Church. 1823-44 (2 vols.). 2. New Durham Quarterly Meeting. 1792-1801, Vol. 1; 1801-1807, Vol. 2; Record of Quarterly Meeting. Vol. 3, 1809; Vol. 4, 1832-1857) – Reel 3 – Items 1 and 2 – 1 – us Baptist [240]

EARLY NEW HAMPSHIRE BAPTIST CHURCHES. NEW HAMPSHIRE : CHURCH RECORDS – (1. New Durham Quarterly Meetings. 1857-1889; Treasurer's Report. 1868-1874. 2. New Durham Elders Conference Records. 1801-13, 1841-48 (2 vols.). 3. Ministers Conference Records. 1843-1865, 1870-1885 (2 vols.). 4. New Hampshire Ministers Conference of Yearly Meetings. 1884-1917. 5. Northwood Baptist Church. 1779-1829) – Reel 4 – Items 1-5 – 1 – us Baptist [240]

EARLY NEW HAMPSHIRE BAPTIST CHURCHES. NEW HAMPSHIRE : CHURCH RECORDS – (1. Sanbornton First Baptist Church. 1793-1848. 2. Sandwich Quarterly Meetings Minister's Meeting. 1845-1911. 3. Diary: Curtis, Silas. "A Tour Among Freedmen" (in VA, SC, NC, 1865). 4. White Mountain Quarterly Meetings. 1842-1871. 5. Seaman, Job. Papers. 1762-1820. 6. Diary No. 1, Original Journal of Elder Job Seamans. 1774 (breaks April 22, 1778-June 2, 1785; February 8, 1791-April 24, 1794; April 14, 1811-Dec. 8, 1814). 7. Diary No. 2. March 1802 – Jan. 9, 1810) – Reel 5 – Items 1-7 – 1 – us Baptist [240]

EARLY NEW HAMPSHIRE BAPTIST CHURCHES. NEW HAMPSHIRE : CHURCH RECORDS – 6 reels – 1 – 299.12 – us Baptist [240]

EARLY NEW ZEALAND / Sherrin & Wallace – (Earliest times to 1845. Lists early European settlers) – 6mf – 9 – NZ$24.00 – 0-908797-37-0 – NZNB S675 – nz BAB [980]

EARLY NINETEENTH CENTURY MANUSCRIPTS FROM KUMASI, GHANA / Kongelige Bibliotek. Copenhagen – Mss. Orientalisk Samling Cod. Arab. 302 – 1 – us Res Libr [090]

EARLY NONCONFORMITY, 1566-1800 : A CATALOGUE OF BOOKS IN DR. WILLIAMS'S LIBRARY. LONDON. 1968. SUBJECT CATALOGUE / Columbia University Libraries – (Available on microfilm by request) – 33,500 cards – 1 – $545.00 export $660.00 – 0-8161-0174-4 – uk Hall [240]

THE EARLY NORMAN CASTLES OF THE BRITISH ISLES / Armitage, E S – H-1222 2. 1912 – 8 – ne IDC [941]

EARLY OHIO POLITICAL LEADERS / Ohio Historical Society – (The Arthur St. Clair Collection 8r $680.00. The Winthrop Sargent Collection 5r $425.00. The Edward Tiffin Collection 1r $85.00. The Thomas Kirker Collection 1r $85.00. The Samuel Huntington Collection 3r $255.00. The Return Jonathan Meijs, Jr. Collection 5r $425.00. The Othniel Looker Collection 1r $85.00. The Thomas Worthington Collection 22r $1,870.00. The Ethan Allen Brown Collection 6r $510.00. The Allen Trimble Collection 2r $170.00. The Jeremiah Morrow Collection 1r $85.00. The Charles Hammond Collection 2r $170.00. The Micajah T. Williams Collection 9r $765.00. The Northwest Territory Transcripts 1r $85.00. Early Ohio Political Leaders Executive Letterbooks 1r $85.00) – With printed guide – 1 – D3179.P01-D3179.P15 – Dist. us Scholarly Res – us Ohio Hist [320]

THE EARLY PERSECUTIONS OF THE CHRISTIANS / Canfield, Leon Hardy – New York: Columbia University: Longmans, Green [distributor], 1913. (Studies in history, economics and public law; v55, no.2: whole no. 136) – 1mf – us A.T.L.A. [240]

EARLY PHOTOGRAPHS FROM EGYPT 1880-1910 / ed by Haarlem, W M van – (Book includes a printed guide) – 12mf – 9 – ne IDC [770]

EARLY PHOTOGRAPHY BOOKS – $1,135.00 – us UPA [770]

EARLY PIONEER FAMILIES OF VICTORIA AND RIVERINA / Henderson, Alexander – 1936 – 8mf – 9 – A$40.00 – at State Libr Vic [920]

EARLY PRESBYTERIANISM IN MARYLAND / McIlvain, J W – [Baltimore, Md.?: s.n., 1890?] – 1mf – us A.T.L.A. [240]

EARLY PRINTED AND MANUSCRIPT MUSIC / Westminster Abbey. Library – With printed index – 1 – £1,200.00 – uk World [780]

EARLY PRINTED BIBLES / ed by Buesser, F – (Includes a printed guide. All titles available separately) – 1994, 6 installments – 1,352mf – 9 (Dfl3,650.00 per installment) – ne IDC [220]

EARLY PRINTED BIBLES : PHILOLOGICAL TOOLS – (Individual titles available. Includes printed guide with detailed bibliographical information) – 325mf – 9 – ne IDC [220]

EARLY PRINTED BIBLES : PRINTED BIBLES AND BIBLE TRANSLATIONS IN THE 15TH AND 16TH CENTURIES / ed by Buesser, Fritz – (Major part of collection available in 1996) – 1989 – installments of 30-35 bibles ca 500mf – 9 – ne IDC [220]

EARLY PUPILS OF THE SPIRIT:...THE PROPHETS OF ISRAEL; AND, WHAT OF SAMUEL? / Whiton, James Morris – London: James Clarke, 1896. 1 fiche. 8370-5828-7 – 9 – us A.T.L.A. [240]

EARLY QUAKER WRITINGS, 1650-1750 / The Society of Friends. Library – (Second Series.-1. £425.00) – With printed index – 1 – £995.00 – uk World [240]

Early, R H *see* CAMPBELL CHRONICALS AND FAMILY SKETCHES

EARLY RARE BRITISH FILM MAKERS' CATALOGUES – (With printed index) – 1896-1913 – 1,14 – £375.00 – uk World [790]

EARLY RARE PHOTOGRAPHIC BOOKS COLLECTIONS / North Western Museum of Science and Industry – Printed Index – 1 – £440.00 – uk World [760]

EARLY RECORDS OF FURNIVAL'S INN / Bland, Desmond S – (Edited from a Middle Temple manuscript) – New Castle upon Tyne: King's College, 1957 – 1mf – 9 – $1.50 – LLMC 84-276 – us L.L.M.C. [340]

EARLY RECORDS OF GEORGIA / Davidson, Grace Gillan – 2v, 1932. Items E and F. Indexes. SW16-0032 – 5 – us A.G.L.L. [920]

THE EARLY RELATION AND SEPARATION OF BAPTISTS AND DISCIPLES / Gates, Errett – Chicago: Christian Century Co., 1904 – 1mf – us A.T.L.A. [240]

EARLY RELIGIOUS HISTORY OF / Barr, John – 1852 – 1 – $50.00 – us Presbyterian [920]

EARLY REMINISCENCES OF INDIANAPOLIS / Nowland, John H B – Indianapolis: Sentinel Book and Job Print House, 1870. Indiana Reel 20. (The Cox Library Collection) – 5 – us Americana [978]

THE EARLY ROMAN EPISCOPATE TO A.D. 384 / Beet, William Ernest – London: Charles H. Kelly, 1913 – 1mf – us A.T.L.A. [240]

EARLY SCIENCE FICTION NOVELS / ed by Clareson, Thomas D – 99 titles on 382 fiche. Printed guide by author, title, chronological and motif indexes – 9 – $1,255.00 – us UPA [830]

THE EARLY SCOTTISH CHURCH : THE ECCLESIASTICAL HISTORY OF SCOTLAND FROM THE FIRST TO THE TWELFTH CENTURY / Maclauchlan, Thomas – Edinburgh: T. & T. Clark, 1865 – 2mf – us A.T.L.A. [240]

EARLY SCOTTISH METRICAL TALES – 1889 – 1 – us I.U. Libraries [810]

EARLY SETTLERS OF ALABAMA / Saunders, James E – 1899. Item C. Includes biog. sketches of author's granddaughter, Elizabeth Stubbs. Index, 530p. SW16-0060 – 5 – us A.G.L.L. [978]

EARLY SETTLERS OF ALABAMA / Saunders & Stubbs – New Orleans: L. Graham and Son, Ltd., 1899. Alabama Reel 1. (The Cox Library Collection) – 5 – us Americana [978]

EARLY SLAVIC TEXTS / ed by Veder, William R – (1: The Scaliger Paterikon 16mf Dfl160.00; 3: The Izbornik of the 13 Century 15mf Dfl150.00) – 9 – ne IDC [460]

EARLY SOURCES OF ENGLISH UNITARIAN CHRISTIANITY / Bonet-Maury, Gaston – London: British & Foreign Unitarian Association, 1884 – 1mf – us A.T.L.A. [240]

EARLY TEXAS NEWSPAPERS / Institute of Texan Cultures. Library – Issues of The Weekly Telegraph (Houston), The Indianola Bulletin and The Texian Advocate (Victoria). Covers 1846-60. 3 rolls – 1 – $70.00 – us TX Culture [071]

EARLY TRADITIONS OF GENESIS / Gordon, Alexander R – Edinburgh: T.&T. Clark, 1907 – 9 – us A.T.L.A. [220]
EARLY TRUMBULL COUNTY STORE LEDGERS – Warren, Trumbull, OH. 1809; 1840-48 – 1r – 1 – us Western Res [978]
THE EARLY TUDORS : HENRY 7, HENRY 8 / Moberly, C E – New York: Scribner, 1887 (Epochs of modern history) – 1mf – us A.T.L.A. [240]
AN EARLY VICTORIAN RAILWAY STATION / Hutton, G H – 1953 – 7 – uk Microform Academic [941]
EARLY WELSH SCRIPT / Lindsay, Wallace Martin – Oxford: J. Parker, 1912.64p. illus – 1 – us U.W. Library [000]
EARLY WESTERN BOOKS 1500-1599 / School of Oriental and African Studies, London – (Includes "Catalogue of Printed Books 1500-1599 in the Library" compiled by L.E. Forbes 1968. Individual titles available, also listed separately) – 1,171mf – 9 – ne IDC [080]
THE EARLY WITNESSES, OR, PIETY AND PREACHING OF THE MIDDLE AGES / ed by Thompson, Joseph Parrish – New York: A.D.F. Randolph, 1857 – 1mf – us A.T.L.A. [240]
THE EARLY YEARS OF AN AFRICAN TRADER : BEING AN ACCOUNT OF JOHN HOLT WHO SAILED FOR WEST AFRICA ON 23RD JUN 1862 150=LONDON: PRIVATELY PUBL FOR JOHN HOLT & CO(LIVERPOOL) BY N NEAME, 1962 – us Res Libr [910]
THE EARLY YEARS OF CHRISTIANITY / Pressense, Edmond Dehault de – 4v. 1872-1879 – 1 – us A.T.L.A. [240]
THE EARLY YEARS OF JOHN CALVIN : A FRAGMENT, 1509-1536 / M'Crie, Thomas; ed by Ferguson, William – Edinburgh: D. Douglas, 1880 – 1mf – us A.T.L.A. [240]
THE EARLY YEARS OF THE LATE BISHOP HOBART / McVickar, John – New York: Protestant Episcopal Press, 1834 – 1mf – us A.T.L.A. [240]
AN EARNEST AND AFFECTIONATE ADDRESS TO THE PEOPLE CALLED METHODISTS / Stebbing, Henry – London, 1745 – 1mf – 9 – MP-327/1 – ne IDC [240]
AN EARNEST APPEAL TO THE PUBLICK ON OCCASION OF MR. WHITEFIELD'S EXTRAORDINARY ANSWER TO THE PASTORAL LETTER OF THE LORD BISHOP OF LONDON;... – London, 1739 – 1mf – 9 – MP-263/1 – ne IDC [240]
THE EARNEST CHRISTIAN – (Lacking: 1904-09) – v1-70. 1860-1909 – 5r – 1 – ATLA S0323 – us A.T.L.A. [073]
EARNEST CHRISTIANITY – Toronto: Published for the proprietors at the Wesleyan Book Room, [1873-1876] – 9 – cn C.I.H.M. [240]
EARNEST CHRISTIANITY *see* THE CANADIAN METHODIST MAGAZINE
Earnest, Edward K *see* SEASONAL CHANGES IN SELECTED PHYSIOLOGICAL VARIABLES OF FEMALE BASKETBALL PLAYERS
Earnest, Joseph B *see* THE RELIGIOUS DEVELOPMENT OF THE NEGRO IN VIRGINIA
EARNEST MEN : SKETCHES OF EMINENT PRIMITIVE METHODISTS, MINISTERS AND LAYMEN / Hurd, F H – London, 1872 – 3mf – 9 – ne IDC [240]
EARR (EUROPEAN APPLIED RESEARCH REPORTS) – (Environment and natural resources section) – 1,5,9 – us Harwood [500]
EARR (EUROPEAN APPLIED RESEARCH REPORTS) – (Nuclear science and technology section) – 1,5,9 – us Harwood [500]
EARTH – Wheaton, Illinois. v. 1-3 no. 6. Apr 1930-July 1932 – 1 – us NY Public [073]
EARTH AND EXTRATERRESTRIAL SCIENCES – 1970- – 1,5,9 – us Gordon [520]
EARTH AND PLANETARY SCIENCE LETTERS – v1-71. 1966-84 – 1,5,6,13 – sz Elsevier [073]
EARTH, MOON AND PLANETS – v30-. Feb 1984- – 1,5,6,9 – us UMI [073]
EARTH SCIENCE – 1976- – 1 – us UMI [073]
EARTH SCIENCE REVIEWS – v1-21. 1966-84 – 1,5,6,13 – sz Elsevier [550]
EARTH SPACE REVIEW / ed by Kleber, Peter et al – 9,5,1 – us Gordon [550]
EARTHLY SUFFERING AND HEAVENLY GLORY : WITH OTHER SERMONS / Boardman, Henry Augustus – Philadelphia: J.B. Lippincott, 1878 – 1mf – us A.T.L.A. [240]
EARTHQUAKE AND FIRE SCRAPBOOK OF SAN JOSE PUBLIC LIBRARY – San Francisco, 1906 – 2r – 1 – $100.00 – B40306 – us Library Micro [978]
EARTHQUAKE ENGINEERING AND STRUCTURAL DYNAMICS – v. 1-. 1972- – 1,5,6,9 – us UMI [550]
EARTHQUAKE PREDICTION : PROCEEDINGS OF THE INTERNATIONAL SYMPOSIUM ON EARTHQUAKE PREDICTION – 1984 – 995p – 9 – 92-3-101883-3 – Co-published with Terra Scientific Publishing Co. – fr UNESCO [550]
EARTH'S GRANDEST RIVER, THE ST LAWRENCE, AND THE THOUSAND ISLANDS: AN UNRIVALED SUMMER RESORT – Watertown, N.Y.: Hungerford & Coates, 1895. 04165. (Pre-1900 Canadiana) – 9 – cn C.I.H.M. [971]
EARTH'S MORNING, OR, THOUGHTS ON GENESIS / Bonar, Horatius – London: James Nisbet, 1875. 1 fiche – 9 – us A.T.L.A. [220]
EASCOM HISTORY, 1 OCTOBER 1944-1 APRIL 1945 / U.S. Army Air Forces. Eastern Command, Europe – 1945 – 1 – 19.00 – us L of C Photodup [947]
AN EASIE INTRODUCTION TO THE PHILOSOPHERS MAGICAL GOLD; TO WHICH IS ADDED, ZOROASTER'S CANE; AS ALSO JOHN PONTANUS EPISTLE UPON THE MINERAL FIRE / Thor, George, Astromagus – London, 1667 – 1 – us U.W. Library [150]
EASLEY FIRST BAPTIST CHURCH. EASLEY, SOUTH CAROLINA : CHURCH RECORDS – 1873-1972 – 1 – 50.40 – us Baptist [240]
EAST – Singapore, 25 Nov 17-31 Dec 1953 – 8ft – 1 – uk British Libr Newspaper [072]
EAST ABERDEENSHIRE OBSERVER, PETERHEAD, FRASERBURGH AND GENERAL ADVERTISER *see* BUCHAN OBSERVER, PETERHEAD, FRASERBURGH AND GENERAL ADVERTISER
EAST AFRICA AND ITS INVADERS FROM EARLIEST TIMES TO THE DEATH OF SEYYID SAID IN 1856 / Coupland, R – Oxford. 1938. BA-295 2 – 8 – ne IDC [900]
EAST AFRICA AND RHODESIA, 1924-1967 – 5 – uk Microform Academic [073]
East Africa High Commission *see* OFFICIAL GAZETTE
EAST AFRICAN PASTORALISM : ANTHROPOLOGICAL PERSPECTIVES AND DEVELOPMENT NEEDS / ed by Westley, S B – 1977 – 9 – $24.00 – 92-9053-132-0 – et ILRI [306]
East African Protectorate. Native Labour Commission, 1912-13 *see* EVIDENCE AND REPORT
EAST AFRICAN WILDLIFE JOURNAL *see* AFRICAN JOURNAL OF ECOLOGY
EAST AND WEST – Bombay, 1901-16. v.1-15 – 350mf – 8 – ne IDC [073]
EAST AND WEST: A SUMMER'S IDLENESS / Chapman, Edward John – Toronto: Trout and Todd, 1887. 00621. (Pre-1900 Canadiana) – 9 – cn C.I.H.M. [971]
EAST ANGELS, A NOVEL / Woolson, Constance Fenimore – New York, London: Harper & Brothers, 1886. 591p – 1 – us U.W. Library [830]
EAST ANGLIAN DAILY TIMES : EAST EDITION – Ipswich, England. 1984- – 208+ r – 1 – uk British Libr Newspaper [072]
EAST ANGLIAN DAILY TIMES : ESSEX EDITION – Ipswich, England. 1986- – 157+ r – 1 – uk British Libr Newspaper [072]
EAST ANGLIAN DAILY TIMES – Ipswich, England. 1984- – 208+ r – 1 – uk British Libr Newspaper [072]
EAST ANGLIAN DAILY TIMES – Ipswich, England. Oct 1874-84; Sep 1885-87; Oct-Dec 1889; 1896-Apr 1897; Sep 1897-Aug 1898; May-Aug 1899; Jan-Apr 1900; Jul-Sep 1907; Jul-Dec 1912; 1919-53; Jan-Mar 1960; Jun-Oct 1965; Jan-Apr 1966; 1971-75; 1977-83 – 372r – 1 – uk British Libr Newspaper [072]
EAST ANTRIM TIMES *see* LARNE TIMES
East Ardsley. Yorkshire *see*
- CONSTABLES' ACCOUNTS
- PARISH REGISTERS

EAST ASIA GENERAL CATALOGUE – (Sixth cumulative catalogue with 753 titles) – 753 titles – 9 – ne IDC [950]
EAST ASIA JOURNAL OF THEOLOGY – v1-. 1983- – 1,5,6,9 – us UMI [073]
EAST ASIA MILLIONS – (1985-. 5,6,9) – v69-. 1961- – 1 – us UMI [240]
EAST ASIAN HISTORICAL DOCUMENTS AND MANUSCRIPTS *see* HISTORICAL DOCUMENTS AND MANUSCRIPTS
EAST ASIATIC LIBRARY. AUTHOR-TITLE AND SUBJECT CATALOGS. 1968 : AUTHOR-TITLE CATALOG / University of California at Berkeley – 13r – 1 – $1,580.00 – 0-8161-1397-1 – uk Hall [950]
EAST ASIATIC LIBRARY. AUTHOR-TITLE AND SUBJECT CATALOGS. 1968 : FIRST SUPPLEMENT / University of California at Berkeley – 1973 – 2r – 1 – $290.00 – 0-8161-1359-9 – uk Hall [950]
EAST AVENUE BAPTIST CHURCH. SPRINGFIELD, MISSOURI : CHURCH RECORDS – 1890-1965 – 1 – 153.18 – us Baptist [240]
EAST BAY JEWISH OBSERVER – Oakland, CA. 1978-82 – 1 – us A.J.P.C. [071]
THE EAST BAY JOURNAL – Oakland, CA. 1992-1994 – 3r – 1 – $150.00 – B06042 – us Library Micro [071]
EAST BAY LABOR JOURNAL – Oakland, CA. 1945-74 – 11r – 1 – $550.00 – C02543 – us Library Micro [331]
EAST BAY MONITOR – San Ramon, CA. 1988-1992 – 1r – 1 – $50.00 – B03681 – us Library Micro [071]
EAST BAY TODAY – Oakland, CA. Nov 1979-Oct 1982 – 38r – 1 – $1,900.00 – B02544 – us Library Micro [071]
EAST BRIDGEWATER 1754-1900 – (Mf Town Records 1769-1825. Mf 3: Marriages 1759-1823; Vital Records 1754-1857. Mf 5-10: Town Records 1823-54. Mf 6: Marriage Banns 1823-50. Mf 7: Marriages: 1818-43. Mf 8: Births 1769-1849. Mf 9: Deaths 1822-44. Mf 11-18: Town Meetings 1823-46. Mf 19-27: Highways 1822-1920. Mf 28-35: Mortgages 1837-58. Mf 36-37: Intents Index 1849-84. Mf 38-41: Intentions 1849-82. Mf 42-45: Intentions 1883-1908. Mf 46-48: Birth Index 1769-1943. Mf 49-51: Marriages Index 1844-1943. Mf 52-54: Death Index 1844-1943. Mf 55: Births 1843-51. Mf 56: Marriages, Deaths 1844-51. Mf 57-60: Births 1852-90. Mf 61-63: Marriages 1852-90. Mf 64-67: Deaths 1852-90. Mf 68-69: Deaths 1891-1903. Mf 70: Marriages 1891-1903. Mf 71: Births 1891-99) – (mf ed 1995) – 71mf – 9 – 0-87623-378-7 – us Holbrook [920]
EAST BRIDGEWATER 1769-1849 – (Mf 1T-2T: Marriage Banns 1823-49. Mf 2T: Marriages 1811-43; Births 1769-1849. Mf 3T: Deaths 1822-44; Marriage Intentions 1849. Mf 3T-4T: Births 1844-49. Mf 5T: Marriages & Deaths 1844-49) – (mf ed 1996) – 5mf – 9 – 0-87623-246-2 – us Holbrook [920]
EAST CHARLTON TRIBUNE – 1921-1926. ECT1-5 – 5r – 1 – at Corangamite [072]
East China Christian Education Association *see*
- CCEA NEWSLETTER
- EAST CHINA CHRISTIAN EDUCATION ASSOCIATION BULLETIN

EAST CHINA CHRISTIAN EDUCATION ASSOCIATION BULLETIN / East China Christian Education Association – (Lacking: no 8) – no 1-30. 1925-32 – 1r – 1 – ATLA S0707F – us A.T.L.A. [073]
East China Regional Conference *see* FINDINGS ON FIVE YEAR MOVEMENT (CCC254)
East Cleveland. Ohio. First Presbyterian Church *see* CHURCH RECORDS, MS 1528
EAST COAST FEVER AND RELATED TICK-BORNE DISEASES – 1980 – 996p – it F.A.O. [616]
EAST COAST MAIL AND WAIROA GUARDIAN – New Zealand, 3 Jan-28 Dec 1908 (very imperfect) – 2r – 1 – uk British Libr Newspaper [072]
EAST CORNWALL TIMES – Launceston, England. 14 May 1859-1861; 1864-Jun 1866; 8, 29 Dec 1866. -w. 2 reels – 1 – uk British Libr Newspaper [072]
East, Edward H *see*
- DURNFORD AND EAST'S REPORTS
- EAST'S REPORTS

East, Edward Murray *see* INBREEDING AND OUTBREEDING; THEIR GENETIC AND SOCIOLOGICAL SIGNIFICANCE
EAST END ADVOCATE – Grand Rapids. Mich. -w. 1920-24 – 1 – us UMI [071]
EAST END NEWS – London, England. -w. 17 July 1869-26 April 1963. 87 reels – 1 – uk British Libr Newspaper [072]
EAST EUROPE – 1-24 1952-75 1; v20-24 5,6 – us UMI [943]
EAST EUROPEAN CULTURAL FOUNDATION – London. 20 docs. 1985-1991 – 24mf – 9 – ne IDC [947]
EAST EUROPEAN QUARTERLY – v1- 1967- 1; v8- 6; v10- 1976- 9 – us UMI [320]
EAST FIFE MAIL – (Available as a standing order) – 1975-1993 – 1. 197-234 – £42.00r – uk Scot News [072]
EAST FLORIDA PAPERS *see* RECORDS
EAST FLORIDA RECORDS – 175r – 1 – $6,125.00 – Dist. us Scholarly Res – us L of C Photodup [978]
EAST GALWAY DEMOCRAT – Ballinasloe. Ireland. -w. 11 Oct 1913-31 Dec 1921, 25 Apr 1936-27 Aug 1949. (9 reels) – 1 – uk British Libr Newspaper [072]
[EAST GERMAN CIVILIZATION AND CULTURE: PAMPHLET COLLECTION] – 1949-1984 – 1 – CSUXANS4733-B – us Hoover Inst Photo [306]
[EAST GERMAN FOREIGN RELATIONS: PAMPHLET COLLECTION] – 1947-1986 – 1 – CSUXANS3654-B – us Hoover Inst Photo [320]
[EAST GERMAN POLITICAL RELATIONS WITH AFRICA: PAMPHLET COLLECTION] – 1978 – 1 – CSUXANS3658-B – us Hoover Inst Photo [320]
[EAST GERMAN POLITICAL RELATIONS WITH CHILE: PAMPHLET COLLECTION] – 1973 – 1 – CSUXANS4675-B – us Hoover Inst Photo [320]
[EAST GERMAN POLITICAL RELATIONS WITH CZECHOSLOVAKIA: PAMPHLET COLLECTION] – 1968? – 1 – CSUXANS4677-B – us Hoover Inst Photo [320]
[EAST GERMAN POLITICAL RELATIONS WITH FINLAND: PAMPHLET COLLECTION] – 1972 – 1 – CSUXANS4680-B – us Hoover Inst Photo [320]
[EAST GERMAN POLITICAL RELATIONS WITH POLAND: PAMPHLET COLLECTION] – 1962-1981 – 1 – CSUXANS4698-B – us Hoover Inst Photo [320]
[EAST GERMAN POLITICAL RELATIONS WITH PORTUGAL: PAMPHLET COLLECTION] – 1975 – 1 – CSUXANS4705-B – us Hoover Inst Photo [320]
[EAST GERMAN POLITICAL RELATIONS WITH THE ARAB COUNTRIES: PAMPHLET COLLECTION] – 1977? – 1 – CSUXANS3660-B – us Hoover Inst Photo [320]
[EAST GERMAN POLITICAL RELATIONS WITH THE SOVIET UNION: PAMPHLET COLLECTION] – 1946-1985 – 1 – CSUXANS4710-B – us Hoover Inst Photo [320]
[EAST GERMAN POLITICAL RELATIONS WITH VIETNAM: PAMPHLET COLLECTION] – 1972? – 1 – CSUXANS4718-B – us Hoover Inst Photo [320]
[EAST GERMAN POLITICAL RELATIONS WITH WEST GERMANY: PAMPHLET COLLECTION] – 1952-1976 – 1 – CSUXANS4683-B – us Hoover Inst Photo [320]
[EAST GERMAN POLITICS AND GOVERNMENT: PAMPHLET COLLECTION] – 1949-1989 – 2r – 1 – CSUXANS3648-B – us Hoover Inst Photo [320]
[EAST GERMANY AND RELIGION PAMPHLET COLLECTION] – 19?? – 1 – CSUXAMJ5667-B – us Hoover Inst Photo [200]
[EAST GERMANY'S JUNE 1953 UPRISING: PAMPHLET COLLECTION] – 1953-1986 – 1 – CSUXANS4727-B – us Hoover Inst Photo [320]
EAST GRINSTEAD COURIER – 1983-96 – 38r – 1 – uk British Libr Newspaper [072]
EAST GRINSTEAD OBSERVER – England. 1977-81.-w. 9 reels – 1 – uk British Libr Newspaper [072]
THE EAST IN PRAYER / Dixon, Benjamin Homer – a true Catholic. Toronto: Copp, Clark, 1870. 02645. (Pre-1900 Canadiana) – 9 – cn C.I.H.M. [971]
East India Company *see* SELECTION OF PAPERS FROM THE RECORDS AT THE EAST-INDIA HOUSE RELATING TO THE REVENUE, POLICE, AND CIVIL AND CRIMINAL JUSTICE UNDER THE COMPANY'S GOVERNMENTS IN INDIA
EAST INDIA PARLIAMENTARY PAPERS – (Annual Lists and General Index to the Parlimentary Papers Relating to the East Indies Published During the Years 1801-1907 Inclusive) – London, Printed for H M Stationery Office by Eyre and Spottiswoode, 1909 – us Res Libr [324]

East Indonesia *see* KEMENTERIAN PENERANGAN
EAST JORDAN VALLEY: A SOCIAL AND ECONOMIC SURVEY, 1961 / Jordan. Ministry of National Economy – A. M. Watson. BNE-9821 1 – 9 – ne IDC [338]
EAST KENT TIMES AND DISTRICT ADVERTISER – Ramsgate, England. 6 Jan-15 Dec 1897. -w. 1 reel – 1 – uk British Libr Newspaper [072]
EAST KENT TIMES, ETC *see* KENT COAST TIMES ETC
THE EAST KENTUCKIAN – v1-2. 1965/66-1966/67. 4 fiches. F-1266 and F-1634 – 9 – us A.G.L.L. [920]
EAST LONDON DAILY DISPATCH – East London, South Africa: East London Daily Dispatch Ltd, oct 1922-24 – 1 – us Res Libr [960]
EAST LONDON DAILY DISPATCH – East London, South Africa: East London Daily Dispatch Ltd, [-1924]. oct 1922-1924 – us Res Libr [072]
EAST LONDON DAILY DISPTACH *see* THE DAILY DISPATCH
EAST LONDON DISPATCH *see* THE DAILY DISPATCH
EAST LONDON OBSERVER – London, England. City & East London Observer. -w. 19 Sept 1857-17 Nov 1944. 69 1 2 reels – 1 – uk British Libr Newspaper [072]
EAST LONDON STANDARD – East London, South Africa. 1 Oct 1891-30 Dec 1899. 9 reels. Continues: Frontier Standard and East London Gazette, 1890-91 – 1, 16 diazo available at reduced price – sa SA Libr [072]
EAST LONDON STANDARD *see* FRONTIER STANDARD AND EAST LONDON GAZETTE
EAST LONG BEACH ENTERPRISE – Long Beach, CA. 1959-1960 – 1r – 1 – $50.00 – H04022 – us Library Micro [071]
EAST LOTHIAN COURIER – 1 – £42.00r – uk Scot News [072]
EAST LOTHIAN NEWS – 1 – £42.00r – uk Scot News [072]
EAST LYNNE / Wood, Ellen – British Fiction Archive: Unit 1 – 9 – uk Bell [830]
EAST OAKLAND GAZETTE – Oakland, CA. 1911-1915 – 1r – 1 – $50.00 – C03362 – us Library Micro [071]
EAST OAKLAND NEWS – Oakland, CA. 1939-1977 – 18r – 1 – $900.00 – B03133 – us Library Micro [071]
EAST OF FIFE RECORD – Anstruther, Scotland, UK. 1870-26 Nov 1875; 1876-9 Aug 1917. -w. 29 reels – 1 – uk British Libr Newspaper [072]
EAST OF THE BARRIER : OR, SIDE LIGHTS ON THE MANCHURIA MISSION / Graham, J Miller – (Includes index) – New York: Fleming H Revell, 1902 – 1mf – 9 – 0-8370-6500-3 – 1986-0500 – us A.T.L.A. [240]
EAST OREGON HERALD – Burns, OR. -w. 23 Nov 1887-15 Jul 1896. 4 rolls – 1 – us U.O. Library [071]
EAST OREGON RANGER – John Day OR. Mar 7 1930-Feb 28 1931 – 1 – us U.O. Library [071]
EAST OREGONIAN – Pendleton. Or. 1905-1921; 1947-1963 – 1 – us UMI [071]
EAST OREGONIAN – Pendleton, OR. -d. 1 Mar 1888-28 Feb 1905, 9 rolls; 1 Oct 1921-27 Feb 1947, 55 rolls; 1 Jan 1892-9 Feb 1897; 1 Jan 1964-. – 1 – us U.O. Library [071]
EAST OREGONIAN – Pendleton, OR. -d. 1905-21, 1947-63 – 1 – 2129.00 – us Oregon Hist [071]
EAST OREGONIAN – Pendleton, OR. -sw. 2 May 1882-29 Dec 1885. 2 rolls – 1 – us U.O. Library [071]
EAST OREGONIAN – Pendleton, OR. -w. 6 Jan 1877-30 Dec 1904. 3 rolls – 1 – us U.O. Library [071]
EAST PARK BAPTIST CHURCH. GREENVILLE COUNTY, SOUTH CAROLINA : CHURCH RECORDS – 1913-1969 – 1r – 1 – $55.89 – us Baptist [240]
EAST PORTLAND CHRONICLE – Portland OR. Sep 18 Oct 2 1891 – 1 – us U.O. Library [071]
EAST PORTLAND VINDICATOR – Portland OR. Mar 31 Apr 14 1883 – 1 – us U.O. Library [071]
East, R M *see*
- A VERNACULAR BIBLIOGRAPHY FOR THE LANGUAGES OF NIGERIA
- A VERNACULAR BIBLIOGRAPHY FOR THE LANGUAGES OF NIGERIA

EAST RAND EXPRESS – Germiston, Benoni, Boksburg. South Africa. 1898-1936 – 1 – sa State Libr [072]
EAST RETFORD ADVERTISER – (Retford Advertiser-Retford, Newark, Worksop and Gainsbro' Advertiser). England. -w. 1 Jul 1854-31 Dec 1859. (3 reels) – 1 – uk British Libr Newspaper [072]
THE EAST SAINT LOUIS RACE RIOT OF 1917 – From National Archives and State of Illinois. Printed guide – 8r – 1 – $885.00 – 0-89093-742-7 – us UPA [360]
EAST SAN JOSE SUN – San Jose, CA. 1973-76 – 11r – 1 – $550.00 – B02877 – us Library Micro [071]
EAST SIDE BAPTIST CHURCH. FORT SMITH, ARKANSAS : CHURCH RECORDS – 1953-70 – 1 – 18.72 – us Baptist [240]
EAST SIDE BAPTIST CHURCH. PARAGOULD, ARKANSAS : CHURCH RECORDS – 1912-Jul 1986. Lacking Oct 1953-55. Formerly Second Baptist Church. 1884p – 1 – 84.78 – us Baptist [978]
EAST SIDE ENTERPRISE – Portland OR. July 19 1901, May 15 1930 – 1 – us U.O. Library [071]
EAST SIDE HERALD – Portland OR. May 15 1902 – 1 – us U.O. Library [071]
EAST SIDE POST – Portland OR. Aug 30 1935-Dec 29 1949 – 1 – us U.O. Library [071]
EAST SIDE SUN – Portland OR. Nov 5 1910 – 1 – us U.O. Library [071]
EAST SLAVIC ETHNOGRAPHY AND FOLKLORE / Strakhov, A B – 18 monographs and 47 serials and sets – 9 – ne IDC [390]
EAST STROUDSBURG PRESS – East Stroudsburg, PA. -w 1919-1923 – 13 – $25.00r – us I.M.R. [071]
EAST SUFFOLK MERCURY – 1864; Jan 1-Dec 29 1876; 1877-85; Jan 24-Dec 25 1896; 1897; 1993-95 – 19 1/4r – 1 – uk British Libr Newspaper [072]
East Tilton, New Hampshire. East Tilton Free Will Baptist Church *see* RECORDS
THE EAST TIMOR QUESTION, (C1900) 1975-1996 / Jolliffe, Jill – (With printed guide) – 1997 – 669mf – 9 – Dfl7,745.00 – ne MMF Publ [950]
East View PublicationsStatisticheskii komitet Sodruzhestva Nezavisimykh Gosudarstv *see* THE 1989 USSR CENSUS
EAST WEST DIGEST – v1- 1965- 1; v11-1975- 5,6,9 – us UMI [073]
EAST WEST JOURNAL – 1976- – 1 – us UMI [073]
EAST WEST JOURNAL – v.1-7. 1971-77. Superseded by yEastwest – 1 – us UMI [073]
EAST WEST JOURNAL – (v.9-. 1979- 5,6,9) – v8-. 1978- – 1 – us UMI [073]
East Winslow, Maine. East Winslow Baptist Church *see* RECORDS
EAST YOLO RECORD – West Sacramento, CA. 1952-71 – 16r – 1 – $800.00 – C03093 – us Library Micro [071]
EAST YOLO RECORD – West Sacramento. Calif. -w. 1952-67 – 1 – us UMI [071]
EASTBOURNE CHRONICLE – (Lacking: Aug-Dec 1896) – England, Oct 1865-Dec 1907; 1910-12; 1950 – 36r – 1 – uk British Libr Newspaper [072]
EASTBOURNE GAZETTE – (Lacking: 1897) – Eastbourne, England. Feb 1862-Sep 1912; 1913-27; 1950; 1986- – 80+ r – 1 – uk British Libr Newspaper [072]
EASTBOURNE HERALD – 1950; 1986-96 – 50r – 1 – uk British Libr Newspaper [072]
Eastcott, R *see* SKETCHES OF THE ORIGIN, PROGRESS AND EFFECTS OF MUSIC, WITH AN ACCOUNT OF THE ANCIENT BARDS AND MINSTRELS
EASTER GREETING – Aylmer, Ont.: The King's Daughters, [188- or 189–189- or 19–] – 9 – cn C.I.H.M. [073]
EASTER IN HEAVEN / Weninger, Francis Xavier – (Subsequently issued in German under title: Ostern im Himmel) – New York: D & J Sadlier, 1863 – 1mf – 9 – 0-8370-6857-6 – 1986-0857 – us A.T.L.A. [240]
THE EASTER SERMONS OF ST AUGUSTINE / Weller, PT – Washington, C.C. The Catholic University of America Studies in Sacred Theology: 1955 – 3mf – 9 – ne Slangenburg [240]
THE EASTER SONG; BEING THE FIRST EPIC OF CHRISTENDOM. / Sedulius, fifth century – Introd., verse-trans., and appendices by George Sigerson. Dublin: The Talbot Press, 1922. viii,269p – 1 – us U.W. Library [240]

EASTERN AFRICA HISTORY CONFERENCE ON LANGUAGE AND CULTURE IN EASTERN AFRICA PAPERS : SPONSORED BY THE MINISTRY OF CULTURE AND SOCIAL SERVICES AND GOETHE INSTITUT, NYERI, 17-20 SEP 1980 – Nairobi: University of Nairobi, Dept of History, 1980 – us Res Libr [470]
EASTERN ARGUS – London, England. 6 Jan 1877-14 Sept 1912 – 21r – 1 – uk British Libr Newspaper [072]
EASTERN ARGUS – Portland. Me. 1803-1820 – 1,3 – us Readex [071]
EASTERN ARGUS – Portland, ME: Day & Willis, sept 8 1803-dec 28 1824 – 7r – 1 – us Res Libr [071]
EASTERN BAPTIST CHURCH. EASTERN ASSOCIATION. NORTH CAROLINA : CHURCH RECORDS – 1869-86 – 1 – 5.68 – us Baptist [240]
Eastern Bengal and Assam *see* LEGISLATIVE COUNCIL DEBATES
Eastern Board of Cherokee Indians *see* CHEROKEE ONE FEATHER
EASTERN BUDDHIST : DEVOTED TO THE STUDY OF MAHAYANA BUDDHISM – (Filmed with: The Cultural East) – v1-8 no 4. May 1921-Aug 1958 (complete) – 2r – 1 – ATLA S00068A – us A.T.L.A. [073]
EASTERN BUDDHIST *see* THE CULTURAL EAST
[EASTERN CAMPAIGNS DURING WORLD WAR 1 PAMPHLET COLLECTION] – 1915-1929? – 1 – CSUXANL2894-B – us Hoover Inst Photo [355]
THE EASTERN CANAL OF FRANCE: FOR ESTABLISHING A LINE OF WATER COMMUNICATION FROM THE SAONE TO THE MEUSE / Dawson, William Bell – London?: s.n., 1879 (London: W. Clowes). 04213. (Pre-1900 Canadiana) – 9 – cn C.I.H.M. [971]
EASTERN CATHOLIC LIFE – Passaic, NJ: Eastern Catholic Press Assoc, nov 7 1965-1974 – 1 – us Res Libr [240]
EASTERN CHEROKEE APPLICATIONS OF THE U.S. COURT OF CLAIMS, 1906-09 / U.S. Court of Claims – RG 123. 348 rolls – 1 – M1104 – us Nat'l Archives [977]
EASTERN CHRONICLE – New Glasgow, Canada. 1866-73 – 3r – 1 – $204.00 – cn Library Assoc [971]
EASTERN CHURCHES BROADSTREET – complete – 1r – 1 – ATLA S0713A – us A.T.L.A. [073]
EASTERN CHURCHES REVIEW – v1- 1966- 1; v8- 5,6,9 – us UMI [240]
EASTERN CHURCHES REVIEW – 1(1966)-5(1973) – 43mf – 9 – Dfl151.00 – ne Slangenburg [073]
EASTERN CLACKAMAS JOURNAL – Sandy OR. Apr 17 1913 – 1 – us U.O. Library [071]
EASTERN COUNTIES DAILY PRESS – Norwich, England. 1870-74; 1924-30; 1935-37; 1979-81 – 123r – 1 – uk British Libr Newspaper [072]
EASTERN COURIER – George Town. Malaysia. -w. 6 Apr 1929-31 May 1930. (2 reels) – 1 – uk British Libr Newspaper [072]
EASTERN CUSTOMS IN BIBLE LANDS / Tristram, Henry Baker – (Includes indexes) – 2nd ed. London:Hodder and Stoughton, 1894 – 1mf – 9 – 0-8370-5575-X – 1985-3575 – us A.T.L.A. [220]
EASTERN DAILY PRESS *see* EASTERN COUNTIES DAILY PRESS
EASTERN DEMOCRAT – Eastport, ME: John Bent, may 1832-apr 1841 – 1r – 1 – us Res Libr [071]
THE EASTERN ERA – St. Thomas, Ont.: Wrigley & Grayson, v1 no 20 (May 17 1888)- – 9 – cn C.I.H.M. [971]
[EASTERN EUROPEAN PERSONAL NARRATIVES FROM WORLD WAR 2 PAMPHLET COLLECTION] – 1910-1967 – 1 – CSUXANL3716-B – us Hoover Inst Photo [800]
[EASTERN EUROPEAN POLITICS AND GOVERNMENT FROM 1945 TO 1989 PAMPHLET COLLECTION] – 1945?-1980 – 1 – CSUXANL7363-B – us Hoover Inst Photo [320]
EASTERN EUROPEAN POLITICS AND SOCIETIES – v1- . 1987- – 1,5,6,9 – us UMI [073]
EASTERN EUROPEAN REVIEW – London. -w. 10-31 May 1902. (20 ft) – 1 – uk British Libr Newspaper [073]
EASTERN FREEMAN – Ellsworth, ME: John Clark & Co, apr 22 1853-jul 28 1854 – 1 – us Res Libr [071]

EASTERN FRUIT ON WESTERN DISHES; THE MORALS OF ABOU BEN ADHEM / Locke, David Ross – Boston: Lee and Shepard; New York: Lee, Shepard and Dillingham, 1875 – 1 – us U.W. Library [830]
THE EASTERN HILLS CHRONICLE – Shillong, India: The Khasi-Jaintia Press, sep 9 1960-nov 8 1961 – 1r – 1 – us Res Libr [072]
EASTERN HORIZON – v. 1-. 1960- – 1. – v.13-6. v.15- 1976- 9 – us UMI [800]
EASTERN LAW REPORTER / Canada. General – v1-14. 1906-14 (all publ) – 95mf – 9 – $142.00 – LLMC 81-004 – us L.L.M.C. [340]
THE EASTERN LIBYANS: AN ESSAY / Bates, O – London. 1914. BA-676 2 – 8 – ne IDC [305]
EASTERN MANNERS ILLUSTRATIVE OF THE OLD TESTAMENT HISTORY / Jamieson, Robert – Philadelphia: Presbyterian Board of Publ, [1838?] – 1mf – 9 – 0-8370-9797-5 – 1986-3797 – us A.T.L.A. [956]
EASTERN MISSIONS FROM A SOLDIER'S STANDPOINT / Scott-Moncrieff, GK – London: Religious Tract Society, 1907 – 1mf – us A.T.L.A. [240]
EASTERN MONTANA CLARION – Ryegate. Mont. 1958-1959; 1966- – 1 – us UMI [071]
EASTERN MUHAFADAT INVENTORY / Libya. Ministry of Planning and Development. Doxiadis Associates – Document DOX-LIB-A65 (Dec 1965) prepared for the Government of the Kingdom of Libya. 8 v. BNE-1304 1 – 9 – ne IDC [338]
Eastern Navajo Council *see* RESOLUTIONS OF DISTRICT COUNCILS
EASTERN NEWS – Singapore. -d. 1 Jul 1940-31 Jul 1941. (12 reels) – 1 – uk British Libr Newspaper [072]
EASTERN NIGERIA DEVELOPMENT PLAN, 1962-68 / Nigeria. Eastern – Official Document No. 8 of 1962. Enugu. 1962. BD-375 1 – 9 – ne IDC [338]
EASTERN NIGERIA DEVELOPMENT PLAN, 1962-68 FIRST PROGRESS REPORT / Nigeria. Eastern. Ministry of Economic Planning – Official Document No. 15 of 1964. Enugu. 1964. BD-376 1 – 9 – ne IDC [338]
THE EASTERN NIGERIA GUARDIAN – Port Harcourt, Eastern Region, Nigeria. Jan 27, 29-31, Feb 1-2, 6, 8-10, 12, 15-17, 19, 21-24, 26-28, Mar 9, 11-12, 20-21, 26-29 1940 – 1 – us NY Public [960]
THE EASTERN OBSERVER – Homestead, PA: The Eastern Observer. v1 n1-v2 n22. jan 4 1942-nov 21 1943 – 1 – us Res Libr [073]
EASTERN OREGON DIRECTORY 1899-1900 / Portland Directory Co – Oregon reel 7. (Cox Library Collection) – 5 – us Americana [978]
EASTERN OREGON NEWS – Baker, OR. -w. 30 Jun 1933-1 Dec 1939. 2 rolls – 1 – us U.O. Library [071]
EASTERN OREGON OBSERVER – La Grande, OR. -w. 1903-05 – 1 – 24.00 – us Oregon Hist [071]
EASTERN OREGON OBSERVER – Lagrande, OR. -w. 28 Apr 1897-24 Oct 1902; 7 Feb 1902-24 Oct 1902; 9 Nov 1900; 1 Nov 1901. – 2r – 1 – us U.O. Library [071]
EASTERN OREGON OBSERVER – LaGranfr. Or. 1903-1905 – 1 – us UMI [071]
EASTERN OREGON OBSERVER – Ontario OR. Aug 11 1937-Aug 29 1947 – 1 – us U.O. Library [071]
EASTERN OREGON REPUBLICAN – Union OR. Aug 9 1888-Mar 13 1936, Mar 1 1890 (Railroad Edition) – 1 – us U.O. Library [071]
EASTERN OREGON REVIEW – LaGrande, OR. -w. 23 Mar 1934-17 Sep 1980. – 19r – 1 – us U.O. Library [071]
Eastern Orthodox Church. Russian Synod *see* VSEPODDANNISHII OTCHET OBER-PROKURORA
EASTERN OUTLOOK – Enugu, Nigeria. Nigerian Outlook. -d. 7 Jan 1954-15 Dec 1955; 3 Jan 1957-14 March 1966. Imperfect. 21 reels – 1 – uk British Libr Newspaper [072]
EASTERN POST – London. -w. Oct 1868-Oct 1938. (69 reels) – 1 – uk British Libr Newspaper [072]
EASTERN PROGRESS – Richmond. Ky. 1972- – 1 – us UMI [071]
EASTERN PROVINCE HERALD – Port Elizabeth, South Africa. 1845-1981 – 1 – sa State Libr [072]

THE EASTERN PROVINCE HERALD – (1 Jan 1982-31 Aug 1995 filmed currently) – Port Elizabeth, South Africa, 7 May-24 Dec 1845; 3 Jan 1982-29 Apr 1911 – 161+ r – 1,16 diazo available – sa SA Libr [072]
[EASTERN QUESTION PAMPHLET COLLECTION] – 1909-1924 – 1 – CSUXANL2868-B – us Hoover Inst Photo [947]
EASTERN REFLECTOR – Greenville. N.C. 1882-1912 – 1 – us UMI [071]
THE EASTERN REPORTER – (Covers ME, NH, VT, MA, RI, CT, NY and PA) – Albany: Wm Gould Jr & Co. v1-10. 1884-87 (all publ) – LLMC 95-116 – us L.L.M.C. [340]
THE EASTERN SEAS, ON VOYAGES AND ADVENTURES IN THE INDIAN ARCHIPELAGO, IN 1832-33-34 / Earl, G W – London, 1837 – 6mf – 9 – ne IDC [910]
EASTERN SHORE HERALD – Eastville. Va. -w. 1904-49 – 1 – us UMI [071]
EASTERN SHORE NEWS – Onancock. Va. -w. 1925-38, 1958- – 1 – us UMI [071]
EASTERN SHORE WHIG – Easton. Md. and Peoples advocate. 1819-25, 1828-41 – 1 – us UMI [071]
EASTERN SLOPE – Washoe City, NV. 1866-68 (scattered issues) – 1r – 1 – $50.00 – U04804 – us Library Micro [071]
EASTERN STAR – (Filmed with: Eastern Star & Washington Advertiser) – Machias, (East Falls), ME: J O Balch, dec 1823-nov 23 1824 – 1r – 1 – us Res Libr [071]
THE EASTERN STAR – Grahamstown 1871-87; Johannesburg 1887-89. 6 Jan 1871-29 Mar 1889. 17 reels. Continued by: The Star, Apr 1889 – 1, 16 diazo available at reduced price – sa SA Libr [072]
EASTERN STAR AND WASHINGTON ADVERTISER – (Filmed with: Eastern star (Machias, Me.)) – Machias East Falls, ME: Jeremiah O Balch, dec 2 1824-jul 21 1825 – 1r – us Res Libr [071]
EASTERN TELEGRAPH – Dungog, Apr 12 1912-Nov 22 1923 – 9 – at Pascoe [072]
EASTERN TIMES – Cuttack, India. 1962-Oct 1966 – 10r – 1 – us L of C Photodup [072]
EASTERN TIMES & TOWER HAMLETS GAZETTE – London, England. -w. 7 Dec 1859-13 Feb 1864. 2 reels – 1 – uk British Libr Newspaper [072]
THE EASTERN TOWNSHIPS ADVERTISER / ed by White, Peter G & Black, Conrad – (Cont: The Knowlton Advertiser and Eastern Townships Chronicle 27 jun 1957 1r Can$25.00) – Knowlton, 1 jun 1961 – 1r – 1 – Can$65.00 – cn Can Microfilming [072]
THE EASTERN TOWNSHIPS ADVERTISER *see* THE KNOWLTON ADVERTISER AND EASTERN TOWNSHIPS CHRONICLE
EASTERN TOWNSHIPS GAZETTE – Granby, Canada. v9 n22. 2 nov 1855-whole n542. 25 mai 1866 – 1r – 1 – Can$50.00 – cn Can Microfilming [072]
EASTERN UNITED STATES BUSINESS LAW REVIEW – v.7. 1974. Superseded by Business Law Review – 1 – us UMI [380]
EASTERN UNITED STATES BUSINESS LAW REVIEW *see* EASTERN UNITED STATES BUSINESS LAW REVIEW
EASTERN WORLD – 1947-1962 – 1 – uk Microform Academic [073]
EASTERN WORLD – Yokohama. Japan. -w. 4 Feb 1899-14 Nov 1908. (5 reels) – 1 – uk British Libr Newspaper [072]
EASTHAMPTON 1785-1892 – (Mf 1: Records 1785-1819 v1. Mf 2: Records 1822-45 v2. Mf 3-4: B,M,D 1844-64. Mf 5-6: Index to B,M,D 1787-1864. Mf 7-12: B,M,D 1785-1850. Mf 13-16: Births 1865-92 v2. Mf 17-19: Marriages 1858-92 v2. Mf 20-24: Deaths 1858-92 v2. Mf 25-27: Index to Births 1844-92. Mf 28-30: Index to Marriages 1789-1892. Mf 31-32: Index to Deaths 1845-92) – (mf ed 1987) – 32mf – 9 – 0-87623-013-3 – us Holbrook [920]
EAST-JERSEY REPUBLICAN – Bridgeton. N.J. 1816. and yWashington Whig. 1815-20. Sold as one unit – 1,3 – us Readex [071]
Eastlake, Charles L *see*
– A HISTORY OF THE GOTHIC REVIVAL
– MATERIALS FOR A HISTORY OF OIL PAINTING
EASTLAND BAPTIST CHURCH. NASHVILLE, TENNESSEE : CHURCH RECORDS – 1911-61 – 1 – 53.73 – us Baptist [240]
EASTLEIGH WEEKLY NEWS AND GAZETTE – England.1895-1900. -w. 6 reels – 1 – uk British Libr Newspaper [072]
EASTLEIGH WEEKLY NEWS AND HANTS GAZETTE – England, Oct 1895-96; 1897-1904; Feb 1905 – 80+ r – 1 – uk British Libr Newspaper [072]
Eastman, C R *see*
– A BIBLIOGRAPHY OF FISHES...
– A BIBLIOGRAPHY OF FISHES
Eastman Company *see* NEW HAMPSHIRE REGISTER AND BUSINESS DIRECTORY 1921/22
Eastman, E *see* MUSICAL EDUCATION AND MUSICAL ART
Eastman, George Herbert *see* PAPERS, 1913-1969
EASTON 1693-1900 – (Mf 1-8: Vital Records 1693-1889. Mf 9-13: Vital Records 1693-1813. Mf 14-16: Vital Records 1773-1854. Mf 17-19: Town Records 1732-74. Mf 20-28: Town Records 1766-1816. Mf 29-35: Town Records 1816-40. Mf 36-38: Intentions 1836-69. Mf 39-41: Birth Index 1843-1912. Mf 42-43: Marriage Index 1843-1913. Mf 44-45: Death Index 1843-1912. Mf 46-47: Births 1843-62. Mf 48: Marriages 1843-54. Mf 49: Deaths 1843-62. Mf 50-54: Births 1863-1900. Mf 55-58: Deaths 1863-1900. Mf 59-63: Marriages 1854-1900) – (mf ed 1992) – 63mf – 9 – 0-87623-131-8 – us Holbrook [920]
EASTON CENTINEL – Easton, PA., 1833-1836 – 13 – $25.00r – us I.M.R. [071]
Easton, George *see* TRAVELS IN AMERICA: WITH SPECIAL REFERENCE TO THE PROVINCE OF ONTARIO AS A HOME FOR WORKING MEN
Easton, Pennsylvania *see* MISCELLANEOUS EARLY NEWSPAPERS
Easton, Peter Zaccheus *see* DOES WOMAN REPRESENT GOD?
EASTPORT SENTINEL – Eastport, ME: B Folsom, [jul 26 1823?-aug 1 1832; 1853-68; dec 23 1869-jul 1953; jan-may 1954] – 1 – us Res Libr [071]
EASTPORT SENTINEL, AND PASSAMAQUODY ADVERTISER – Eastport, ME: Benjamin Folsom, [1819-jul 19 1823?] – us Res Libr [071]
EAST'S REPORTS : REPORTS OF CASES ARGUED AND DETERMINED IN THE COURT OF KING'S BENCH / East, Edward H – v1-16. 1800-12. London: J Butterworth & Son, 1805-18 (all publ) – 89mf – 9 – $133.00 – LLMC 95-293 – us L.L.M.C. [324]
EASTSIDE JOURNAL – Los Angeles, CA. 1935-1977 – 7r – 1 – $350.00 – R03290 – us Library Micro [073]
EASTSIDE JOURNAL – Los Angeles. Calif. -w. 1935-65 – 1 – us UMI [071]
EASTSIDE SUN – Los Angeles, CA. 1971 – 2r – 1 – $100.00 – R02379 – us Library Micro [071]
Eastward. Presbytery (Pres. Ch. in the U.S.A.) *see* MINUTES, 1771-92
EAST-WEST : THE CHINESE-AMERICAN JOURNAL – (English and Chinese edition) – San Francisco, CA. 1967-89 – 23r – 1 – $1,150.00 – B02812 – us Library Micro [071]
EASTWEST – v.7-8. 1977-78. Superseded by East West Journal – 1 – us UMI [073]
EAST-WEST TIES – Irvine, CA. 1983-1989 – 1r – 1 – $50.00 – R04033 – us Library Micro [071]
EAST-WEST WHITTIER REVIEW – Whittier, CA. 1983 – 18+ r – 1 – $900.00 ($90.00y) – R03577 – us Library Micro [071]
EASTWOOD AND KIMBERLEY ADVERTISER – (Lacking: 1898) – Eastwood, Kimberley, England. May 1895- – 62+ r – 1 – uk British Libr Newspaper [072]
EASTWOOD BAPTIST CHURCH. BOWLING GREEN, KENTUCKY : CHURCH RECORDS – 1953-79. 2060p – 1 – 92.70 – us Baptist [240]
Eastwood, R *see* WILLIAM MILNER OF HALIFAX – A PIONEER OF CHEAP LITERATURE
THE EASY INSTRUCTOR : OR, A NEW METHOD OF TEACHING SACRED HARMONY. / Little, William & Smith, William – 1798 – 1 – 5.00 – us Baptist [240]
EASY LESSONS IN CANADIAN HISTORY – Compiled by D. R. Coleman. s.l.: s.n., 1877 (Belleville, Ont.: "The Daily Ontario"). 03210. (Pre-1900 Canadiana) – 9 – cn C.I.H.M. [971]
EATING DISORDERS AMONG ATHLETES : PUBLIC POLICY TO PROMOTE SOCIAL AND INDIVIDUAL BEHAVIORAL CHANGE / Clary, J M – 1992 – 1mf – 9 – $4.00 – us Microform Publ [150]
Eaton, A *see* NORTH AMERICAN BOTANY
Eaton, Abbie Fiske *see* DAS SPIELMANNSKIND – DER STUMME RATSHERR
Eaton, Amasa M *see* ROGER WILLIAMS, THE FOUNDER OF PROVIDENCE THE PIONEER OF RELIGIOUS LIBERTY
Eaton, Arthur Wentworth *see* THE CHURCH OF ENGLAND IN NOVA SCOTIA AND THE TORY CLERGY OF THE REVOLUTION
Eaton, D C *see*
– BOTANY OF THE FORTIETH PARALLEL (U.S.A.)
– THE FERNS OF NORTH AMERICA
Eaton, E K *see*
– EATON'S SERIES OF NATIONAL AND POPULAR SONGS, FOR SMALL MILITARY BRASS BANDS, FROM FIVE TO TWELVE INSTRUMENTS. OP. 13
– TWELVE PIECES OF HARMONY FOR... MILITARY BRASS BANDS OF SEVENTEEN INSTRUMENTS
Eaton, John Richard Turner *see* PERMANENCE OF CHRISTIANITY:...EIGHT LECTURES
Eaton, John van *see* EXPOSITORY AND PRACTICAL LECTURES ON HAGGAI AND ZECHARIAH
Eaton, Samuel J M *see* HISTORY OF THE PRESBYTERY OF ERIE
Eaton, Sherburne Blake *see* A DISCUSSION OF THE CONSTITUTIONALITY OF THE ACT OF CONGRESS OF MARCH 2, 1867, AUTHORIZING THE SEIZURE OF BOOKS AND PAPERS FOR ALLEGED FRAUDS UPON THE REVENUE.
Eaton, Thomas Treadwell *see*
– THE BIBLE ON WOMEN'S PUBLIC SPEAKING
– BIOGRAPHICAL MATERIALS, CORRESPONDENCE, SERMONS
EATON'S BAPTIST CHURCH. SOUTH YADKIN ASSOCIATION. NORTH CAROLINA : CHURCH RECORDS – 1772-1902 – 1 – 36.72 – us Baptist [240]
EATON'S SERIES OF NATIONAL AND POPULAR SONGS, FOR SMALL MILITARY BRASS BANDS, FROM FIVE TO TWELVE INSTRUMENTS. OP. 13 / Eaton, E K – Boston: Henry Tolman, 1853. Includes: "Comin' thro' the Rye" and "Rule Britannia" in parts. MUSIC 1983, Item 1 – 1 – us L of C Photodup [780]
L'EAU EN ALGERIE / Algeria. Chambre de Commerce et d'Industrie d'Alger – 1967. BNE-8705 1 – 9 – ne IDC [333]
LES EAUX DU LAC LEMAN AU POINT DE VUE INTERNATIONAL / Crolard, A – Annecy, 1914 – 1mf – 1 – ILM-2275/1 – ne IDC [327]
Eayrs, G *see* OUR FOUNDERS AND THEIR STORY
Eban, Abba *see* ISRAEL'S POSITION ON THE JORDAN CANAL PROJECT
EBANO – Malabo, Equatorial Guinea. Aug 3 1980-Jne 22 1991 – 1r – 1 – us L of C Photodup [072]
EBAUCHE D'UNE DESCRIPTION ABREGEE DU DEPARTEMENT DE L'ARIEGE / Mercadier de Belesta, Jean-Baptiste – an IX – 9 – fr Hachette [944]
THE EBB TIDE : A TRIO AND QUARTETTE / Stevenson, Robert Louis & Osbourne, Lloyd – Chicago, Cambridge: Stone & Kimball, 1894, [c1893] – 1 roll – 1 – 1-55879-914-1 – uk Libr Preservation [830]
EBB UN FLOT : GLUECK UN NOT / Lau, Fritz – Hamburg: M Glogau, 1921 – 1r – 1 – us U.W. Library [830]
EBBE UND FLUT : EIN HANSISCHER ROMAN DEUTSCHER ZEITWENDE / Schupp, Johannes Martin – Muenchen: F Eher, 1942, c1938 – 1r – 1 – us U.W. Library [830]
EBBE UND FLUTH : GESAMMELTE LYRISCHE DICHTUNGEN: UND INGURTHA: TRAUERSPIEL IN FUENF AKTEN / Zuendt, Ernst Anton Joseph – Milwaukee, WI: Freidenker, 1894 – 1r – 1 – us U.W. Library [800]
Ebbecke, Dirk *see* ZUR BEDEUTUNG DER SOZIALPERSPEKTIVITAET IN DER MARKTPSYCHOLOGISCHEN IMAGEFORSCHUNG
Ebbinghaus, J *see* DIE PILZE UND SCHWAEMME DEUTSCHLANDS MIT BESONDERER RUECKSICHT AUF DIE ANWENDBARKEIT ALS NAHRUNGS-UND HEILMITTEL, SOWIE AUF DIE NACHTHEILE DERSELBEN
Ebeling, Erich *see*
– AUS DEM TAGEWERK EINES ASSYRISCHEN ZAUBERPRIESTERS
– DIE BABYLONISCHE FABEL UND IHRE BEDEUTUNG FUER DIE LITERATURGESCHICHTE
– LIEBESZAUBER IM ALTEN ORIENT
– NEUBABYLONISCHE BRIEFE AUS UKRUK.
Ebeling, Richard *see* IN DEFENCE OF FREE MIGRATION
Ebendorfer, Thomas *see*
– CHRONICA AUSTRIAE (MGH 6: 13.BD)
– EIN OESTERREICHISCHER GESCHICHTSSCHREIBER, THEOLOGE UND DIPLOMAT DES 15. JAHRHUNDERTS 1957 (MGH SCHRIFTEN..: 15.BD)
EBENEZER BAPTIST CHURCH. AURORA, INDIANA : CHURCH RECORDS – 1822-59 – 1 – 9.54 – us Baptist [240]
EBENEZER BAPTIST CHURCH. EDGEFIELD, SOUTH CAROLINA : CHURCH RECORDS – 1973-83.Incomplete, 126p – 1 – 5.67 – us Baptist [240]
EBENEZER BAPTIST CHURCH. LINCOLN COUNTY. MISSOURI : CHURCH RECORDS – Extinct.1915-23. 38p – 1 – 5.00 – us Baptist [240]
EBENEZER BAPTIST CHURCH. ORANGEBURG COUNTY. SOUTH CAROLINA : CHURCH RECORDS – (362p) – Nov 1882-July 1985 – 1 reel – 1 – $16.29 – us Baptist [240]
THE EBENEZER HAZARD COLLECTION – 8r – 1 – $280.00 – Dist. us Scholarly Res – us L of C Photodup [975]
Ebenezer United Methodist Church (Tiffin, Ohio) *see* RECORDS
THE EBENEZER-BOTE – Lincoln, NE. -m. Apr 1916; Mar-Apr 1917. In German – 1 – us NE Hist [071]
L'EBENISTE – Montreal. Canada. v1 n2. jun 1973; v2 n3. sep 1974 – 1r – 1 – Can$25.00 – cn Can Microfilming [072]
Eber, P *see*
– CATECHISMUSPREDIGTEN...
– PIA ET IN VERBO DEI FVNDATA ASSERTIO, DECLARATIO AND CONFESSIO D. PAVLI EBERI...DE SACRATISSIMA COENA...
– POSTILLA...
– VOM HEILIGEN SACRAMENT DES LEIBS VND BLUTS VNSERS HERREN IESV CHRISTI. UNTERRICHT VND BEKENTNIS...
EBERHARD VON GROOTE : EIN BEITRAG ZUR GESCHICHTE DER ROMANTIK AM RHEIN / Giesen, Adolf – Gladbach-Rheydt, 1929 – 148p – 9 – DM48.00 – 3-89349-019-1 – gw Hänsel [943]
Eberhard, W *see* DIE BEZIEHUNGEN DER STAATEN DER T'O-PA UND DER SHA-T' O ZUM AUSLAND
Eberhardt, Jacqueline *see* A SURVEY OF FAMILY CONDITIONS WITH SPECIAL REFERENCE TO HOUSING NEEDS, ORLANDO TOWNSHIP, JOHANNESBURG
Eberhart, Jean M *see* VALIDITY OF THE ASTRAND-RHYMING NOMOGRAM FOR MODERATELY ACTIVE ADULT FEMALES
Eberl, A *see* TROIS QUATUORS, OP. 13
Eberlein, Karl *see* GEDICHTE UND GEDANKEN
Eberlin, Johann E *see* 115 VERSETTEN UND CADENZEN FUER DIE ORGEL.
Ebermayer, Erich *see* EVIL GENIUS, THE STORY OF JOSEPH GOEBBELS
Ebers, Fritz *see* DAS GRABBE-BUCH
Ebersole, Ezra Christian *see* THE COURTS AND LEGAL PROFESSION OF IOWA.
Ebersole, Joseph L *see* DISCOVERY PROBLEMS IN CIVIL CASES
Ebert, Adolf *see* ALLGEMEINE GESCHICHTE DER LITERATUR DES MITTELALTERS IM ABENDLANDE
Ebert, Johannes *see* SEIN UND SOLLEN DES MENSCHEN BEI IMMANUEL HERMANN FICHTE
Ebhardt, Rolf *see* HEBBEL ALS NOVELLIST
EBONY – 1972- – 1 – us UMI [073]
EBONY – v. 1- 1945- – 1 – us UMI [073]
EBP 1 AND 2 *see* EARLY BRITISH PERIODICALS 1 AND 2, 1681-1921
EBP 3 *see* BRITISH PERIODICALS IN THE CREATIVE ARTS (EBP 3), 1770-1930
Ebrard, Johannes Heinrich August *see*
– APOLOGETICS: OR, THE SCIENTIFIC VINDICATION OF CHRISTIANITY
– HANDBUCH DER CHRISTLICHEN KIRCHEN- UND DOGMEN-GESCHICHTE
– WISSENSCHAFTLICHE KRITIK DER EVANGELISCHEN GESCHICHTE
Ebstein *see* DR. MARTIN LUTHERS KRANKHEITEN UND DEREN EINFLUSS AUF SEINEN KOERPERLICHEN UND GEISTIGEN ZUSTAND
Ebue-l'Kemal *see* DIVAN

EBURNEA – Abidjan: Agence ivoirienne de presse. n1-10. apr 1967-jan/feb 1968; n12-61. apr 1968-jul 1972; n63-77. sep 1972-feb 1974; n79-124. jul 1974-1978] – 5r – us Res Libr [072]

Eby, Ezra E *see* A BIOGRAPHICAL HISTORY OF THE EBY FAMILY: BEING A HISTORY OF THEIR MOVEMENTS IN EUROPE DURING THE REFORMATION: AND THEIR EARLY SETTLEMENT IN AMERICA: AS ALSO MUCH OTHER UNPUBLISHED HISTORICAL INFORMATION BELONGING TO THE FAMILY

Eby, Herbert Oscar *see* EXTRACT OF THE DISTRICT OF COLUMBIA CODE. 1935, REV. 1936

EC AND M – v80- 1981- – 1,5,6,9 – us UMI [073]

ECBASIS CUIUSDAM CAPTIVI PER TROPOLOGIAM (MGH 7: 24.BD) – 1935 – Dfl9.00 – ne Slangenburg [240]

ECCE ANCILLA DOMINI: MARY...STUDIES IN THE CHRISTIAN IDEAL OF WOMANHOOD / Charles, Elizabeth Rundle – London: S.P.C.K., 1894. 1 fiche – 9 – us A.T.L.A. [240]

ECCE DEUS : ESSAYS ON THE LIFE AND DOCTRINE OF JESUS CHRIST / Parker, Joseph – Boston: Roberts, 1867 – 1mf – 9 – 0-8370-4666-1 – 1985-2666 – us A.T.L.A. [240]

ECCE DEUS : STUDIES OF PRIMITIVE CHRISTIANITY / Smith, William Benjamin – London: Issued for the Rationalist Press Association [by] Watts, 1912 – 1mf – us A.T.L.A. [240]

ECCE FILIUS : OR, THE GOSPEL OF TRUTH AND GRACE BY POSITIVE MANIFESTATION / Swinney, James Oswald – Chicago: Fleming H Revell, 1894 – 1mf – 9 – 0-8370-2208-8 – 1985-0208 – us A.T.L.A. [240]

ECCE HOME / Gladstone, William Ewart – London: Strahan, 1868 – 9 – us A.T.L.A. [240]

ECCE HOMO / Saint Martin, Louis Claude de – Paris. Chez les Directeurs de l'Imprimerie du Cercle Social. 1791 – 9 – fr Hachette [321]

ECCE HOMO : A SURVEY OF THE LIFE AND WORK OF JESUS CHRIST / Seeley, John Robert – Boston: Roberts, 1890 – 1mf – 9 – 0-8370-5211-4 – 1985-3211 – us A.T.L.A. [240]

ECCE HOMO : A SURVEY OF THE LIFE AND WORK OF JESUS CHRIST / Seeley, John Robert – London, Cambridge: Macmillan and Co., 1866 – 1 roll – 1 – 1-55879-495-6 – uk Libr Preservation [240]

ECCE HOMO: A CRITIQUE ON BEHALF OF... FREE ENQUIRY AND FREE EXPRESSION / Presbyter Anglicanus – Ramsgate: Thomas Scott, 1866. 1 fiche – 9 – us A.T.L.A. [240]

ECCE HOMO: A SURVEY OF THE LIFE AND WORK OF JESUS CHRIST / Seeley, John Robert – London: J.M. Dent, 1907. 1 fiche – 9 – us A.T.L.A. [240]

ECCE REGNUM, OR, AN INQUIRY INTO THE... REVELATION OF THE GLORY OF THE KINGDOM OF GOD / Josslyn, William – New York: Wm. B. Mucklow, 1877. 1 fiche – 9 – us A.T.L.A. [240]

ECCE SPIRITUS : A STATEMENT OF THE SPIRITUAL PRINCIPLE OF JESUS AS THE LAW OF LIFE / Hayward, Edward Farwell – Boston: George H Ellis, 1881 – 1mf – 9 – 0-8370-4526-6 – 1985-2526 – us A.T.L.A. [230]

ECCENTRIC KINETIC CHAIN EXERCISE AS A CONSERVATIVE MEANS OF FUNCTIONALLY REHABILITATING CHRONIC ISOLATED POSTERIOR CRUCIATE LIGAMENT INSUFFICIENCY / MacLean, Christopher L – University of British Columbia, 1995 – 2mf – 9 – $8.00 – PE3608 – us Microform Publ [617]

ECCENTRIC PEAK TORQUE AND MAXIMAL REPETITION WORK PERCENTAGES OF THE DOMINANT EXTERNAL ROTATORS IN COLLEGE DIVISION 1 BASEBALL PLAYERS / Geisler, S A – 1991 – 1mf – 9 – $4.00 – us Microform Publ [790]

Eccles, Salomon *see* A MUSICK-LECTOR..

ECCLESIA THE CHURCH, BIBLE CLASS LECTURES / Carroll, BH – 1903 – 1 – 5.00 – us Baptist [240]

ECCLESIASTES : A STUDY / Erdman, William Jacob – Philadelphia:[s.n.], c1895 – 1mf – 9 – 0-8370-3068-4 – 1985-1068 – us A.T.L.A. [220]

ECCLESIASTES : WORDS OF KOHELETH SON OF DAVID, KING IN JERUSALEM, TRANSLATED ANEW, DIVIDED ACCORDING TO THEIR LOGICAL CLEAVAGE,... / Genung, John Franklin – Boston: Houghton, Mifflin, 1904 – 1mf – 9 – 0-8370-3253-9 – 1985-1253 – us A.T.L.A. [220]

ECCLESIASTES: A NEW TRANSLATION WITH NOTES / Coleman, John Noble – Edinburgh: Andrew Elliot, 1867. 1 fiche – 9 – us A.T.L.A. [240]

ECCLESIASTES, OR, KOHELETH / Zoeckler, Otto – New York: Charles Scribner, 1870. 199p.1 fiche – 9 – us A.T.L.A. [240]

ECCLESIASTICA : A TRIPLET OF OLD SERMONS / Henson, Hensley – [London?]: [s.n.], 1910 – 1mf – us A.T.L.A. [240]

THE ECCLESIASTICAL AND MISSIONARY RECORD FOR THE PRESBYTERIAN CHURCH OF – Hamilton [Ont.]: J. Webster, [1844-1861] – 9 – cn C.I.H.M. [240]

THE ECCLESIASTICAL AND MISSIONARY RECORD OF THE FREE CHURCH OF NOVA SCOTIA *see*
- THE MISSIONARY RECORD AND ECCLESIASTICAL INTELLIGENCER OF THE FREE CHURCH OF NOVA SCOTIA
- MISSIONARY REGISTER OF THE PRESBYTERIAN CHURCH OF NOVA-SCOTIA

ECCLESIASTICAL AUTHORITY IN ENGLAND: CHURCH COURT RECORDS C1400-C1660 – (Part 2: Office Act Books and Formularies, 1469-1639) – Series 1: The Church Court Records of Ely. Part 1. Instance act books and court papers, 1374-1640 – 1 – us Primary [240]

ECCLESIASTICAL AUTHORITY IN ENGLAND: CHURCH COURT RECORDS C1400-C1660 – (Part One: Instance Act Books, Deposition Books and Taxation Books, 1506-1696. Part Two: Detection Books, Excommunication Papers, Churchwarden's Presentments and other Papers, 1538-1700) – Series Two: Church Court Records of Chichester – 1 – us Primary [240]

AN ECCLESIASTICAL CATECHISM OF THE PRESBYTERIAN CHURCH : FOR THE USE OF FAMILIES, BIBLE-CLASSES, AND PRIVATE MEMBERS – (Includes bibliographical references) – 6th rev ed. Richmond: Presbyterian Committee of Publ, c1868 – 1mf – 9 – 0-8370-8779-1 – 1986-2779 – us A.T.L.A. [240]

THE ECCLESIASTICAL CLASS BOOK : OR, HISTORY OF THE CHURCH: FROM THE BIRTH OF CHRIST TO THE PRESENT TIME / Goodrich, Charles Augustus – [rev ed]. New York: F J Huntington, 1839, c1835 – 1mf – 9 – 0-8370-7146-1 – 1986-1146 – us A.T.L.A. [240]

THE ECCLESIASTICAL EXPANSION OF ENGLAND: IN THE GROWTH OF THE ANGLICAN COMMUNION : THE HULSEAN LECTURES FOR 1894-95 / Barry, Alfred – London, New York: Macmillan, 1895 – 1mf – us A.T.L.A. [240]

ECCLESIASTICAL GAZETTE – Kingston [Ont.]: Diocese of Ontario, v1 no 1 (Jan 1874)- – 9 – cn C.I.H.M. [240]

ECCLESIASTICAL HISTORY – 1 – uk Microform Academic [073]

AN ECCLESIASTICAL HISTORY FROM THE BIRTH OF CHRIST TO THE PRESENT TIME, WRITTEN ORIGINALLY IN FRENCH... / Formey, J H – London, 1766.-2v – 8mf – 9 – MP-439/1 – ne IDC [240]

AN ECCLESIASTICAL HISTORY OF IRELAND : FROM THE INTRODUCTION OF CHRISTIANITY INTO THAT COUNTRY TO THE YEAR 1829 / Brenan, Michael John – (Includes bibliographical references) – rev ed. Dublin: James Duffy, 1864 – 2mf – 9 – 0-8370-6025-7 – 1986-0025 – us A.T.L.A. [240]

THE ECCLESIASTICAL HISTORY OF IRELAND : FROM THE EARLIEST PERIOD TO THE PRESENT TIMES / Killen, W D – London: Macmillan, 1875 – 3mf – us A.T.L.A. [240]

THE ECCLESIASTICAL HISTORY OF NEW ENGLAND / Mather, Cotton – v. 1 and 2. 1620-98 – 1 – 46.20 – us Baptist [240]

ECCLESIASTICAL HISTORY OF NEWFOUNDLAND / Howley, Michael Francis – Boston: Doyle and Whittle, 1888, c1887 – 1mf – 9 – 0-8370-6984-X – 1986-0984 – us A.T.L.A. [240]

AN ECCLESIASTICAL HISTORY OF SCOTLAND : FROM THE INTRODUCTION OF CHRISTIANITY TO THE PRESENT TIME / Grub, George – Edinburgh: Edmonston and Douglas, 1861 – 4mf – us A.T.L.A. [240]

THE ECCLESIASTICAL HISTORY OF SOZOMEN : COMPRISING A HISTORY OF THE CHURCH FROM A.D. 324 TO A. D. 440 / Sozomen, Edward Walford – London: H.G. Bohn, 1855 – 1mf – us A.T.L.A. [240]

ECCLESIASTICAL JURISDICTION: A SKETCH OF ITS ORIGIN AND EARLY PROGRESS. / Edwards, Edwin – London, Benning, 1853. 176 p. LL-76 – 1 – us L of C Photodup [340]

ECCLESIASTICAL LAW IN THE STATE OF NEW YORK / Hoffman, Murray – New York: Pott and Amery, 1868. 346p. LL-1305 – 1 – us L of C Photodup [340]

ECCLESIASTICAL MANUAL / Lee, Luther – 1850 – 9 – us A.T.L.A. [240]

THE ECCLESIASTICAL PRINCIPLES AND POLITY OF THE WESLEYAN METHODISTS... / Peirce, W; ed by Jobson, F J – 3rd ed. London, 1873. xiii/812p – 9mf – 9 – ne IDC [240]

THE ECCLESIASTICAL PRINCIPLES AND POLITY OF THE WESLEYAN METHODISTS;... / Peirce, W – London, 1854. xv/668p – 15mf – 9 – ne IDC [240]

ECCLESIASTICAL RESEARCHES / Robinson, Robert – 1972 – 1 – 23.38 – us Baptist [240]

ECCLESIASTICAL REVIEW *see* AMERICAN ECCLESIASTICAL REVIEW

ECCLESIASTICAL VESTMENTS : THEIR DEVELOPMENT AND HISTORY / Macalister, R A S – London: E. Stock, 1896. (The Camden library) – 1mf – us A.T.L.A. [240]

O ECCLESIASTICO : PERIODICO DEDICADO AOS INTERESSES DA RELIGIAO – '(s.l.')-Sao Luis, Brazil. 1 Oct 1852-Sept 1857. Dec 1860. Jan-Sep, Dec 1861. Jan-30 Sept 1862 – 1,5,6 – bl Biblioteca [072]

ECCLESIASTICUS 39, 12-49, 16...IN FORMAM ORIGINALEM REDACTUS / Schloegl, Nivardus – Vienna: Mayer et Sociis, 1901. 1 fiche – 9 – us A.T.L.A. [240]

Ecclesiastiques du Seminaire de St-Sulpice de Montreal *see*
- REPONSE A UNE ADRESSE DE L'ASSEMBLEE LEGISLATIVE DU 20 SEPTEMBRE 1852...
- REPONSE A UNE ADRESSE DE L'ASSEMBLEE LEGISLATIVE DU VINGT SEPTEMBRE 1852...
- STATEMENT OF THE AFFAIRS OF THE CORPORATION OF THE ECCLESIASTICS OF THE SEMINARY OF ST SULPICE, MONTREAL

LES ECCLESIASTIQUES ET LES ROYALISTES FRANCAIS REFUGIES AU CANADA A L'EPOQUE DE LA REVOLUTION 1791-1802 / Dionne, Narcisse Eutrope – Quebec: s.n, 1905. SEM105P504 – 5mf – 9 – Can$11.25 – cn Bibl Nat [971]

Ecclesine, Joseph B *see* A COMPENDIUM OF THE LAWS AND DECISIONS RELATING TO MOBS, RIOTS, INVASION, CIVIL COMMOTION, INSURRECTION, &C., AS AFFECTING FIRE INSURANCE COMPANIES IN THE UNITED STATES

ECCLESIOLOGICAL NOTES ON THE ISLE OF MAN, ROSS, SUTHERLAND AND THE ORKNEYS, OR, A SUMMER PILGRIMAGE TO S. MAUGHOLD AND S. MAGNUS / Neale, John Mason – London: Joseph Masters, 1848 – 1mf – us A.T.L.A. [240]

ECCLESIOLOGY / Dargan, Edwin Charles – 1897 – 1 – 20.58 – us Baptist [240]

ECHANGE – (Publ delay at v16 1990) – Edmonton. v14- 1986/87- – 9 – Can$20.00y – cn Micromedia [020]

ECHANGE CANADA EXCHANGE – Ottawa. v1-16. 1972/73-1986/87 – 9 – Can$20.00y – cn Micromedia [073]

ECHANGE; REVUE LINEENNE – Lyon, 1885-1939/41. Nos 1-484 – 117mf – 1 – ne IDC [630]

ECHANGES ECONOMIQUES ET RELATIONS SOCIALES DANS DEUX COMMUNAUTES VILLAGEOISES DE COREE / Park, Song Yong – 2mf – 9 – 10417 – fr Atelier National [330]

ECHANGES, RESEAUX, MARCHES: L'IMPACT COLONIAL EN GUINEE / Goerg, O – Fin XIXe siecle-1913. 11 fiches – 9 – F160.00 – fr Ethnologie [306]

Echard, J *see*
- SCRIPTORES ORDINIS PRAEDICATORUM

Echard, N *see*
- BORI
- REPERTOIRE HISTORIQUE DE COMMUNAUTES RURALES DE LA PROVINCE DE TAWA

L'ECHEE DE LA SEDITION ESPAGNOLE – Madrid, 1936. Fiche W 850. (Blodgett Collection of Spanish Civil War Pamphlets) – 9 – us H.U. College Libr [946]

Echeverria, Frederico de *see* SPAIN IN FLAMES

ECHINOCOCCOSIS/HYDATIDOSIS : SURVEILLANCE, PREVENTION AND CONTROL – 1982 – 157p – it F.A.O. [616]

DE ECHO – (Ceased publication) – Amsterdam, 1885-1886. Nos 1-29 – 6mf – 9 – ne IDC [072]

L'ECHO – Castelnaudary. Journal scientifique, litteraire, industriel et agricole de la ville et de l'arrondissement de Castelnaudary. mai 1844-nov 1848, 23 juil 1850-10 mars 1852 – 1 – fr A.C.R.P.P. [073]

L'ECHO – Paris. Revue des theatres, de la litterature et des arts. Dir. M.-J. Bureau. 1839-11 nov 1844, 1er juil-27 dec 1846, 21 24 janv 1847, 1er janv-9 mai 1848, 31 janv, 25 sept 1851 – 1 – fr A.C.R.P.P. [410]

L'ECHO – Saint-Hyacinthe, Quebec: B. de LaBruere, v1 no 1 (19 mars 1891)- – 9 – cn C.I.H.M. [971]

DAS ECHO – v9-12. 1906-09 (complete) – 1r – 1 – ATLA 1994-S015 – us A.T.L.A. [073]

ECHO – Accrington, England. 16 Dec 1884-30 Aug 1887 – 1r – 1 – uk British Libr Newspaper [072]

ECHO – Beaver Crossing, NE. -w. Jan. 1913-Dec. 1913 – 1 – us NE Hist [071]

ECHO – Burlham. N.Y. -w. 1973- – 1 – us UMI [071]

ECHO – Cascade. Mont. 1913-1915 – 1 – us UMI [071]

ECHO – Earlham. Iowa. 1973- – 1 – us UMI [071]

ECHO – Green Springs, Ohio. 1972-77 – 2r – 1 – $32.50r – us Archival [071]

ECHO – Hysham. Mont. 1958-1959; 1966- – 1 – us UMI [071]

ECHO – Moundsville. West Virginia. -w. 1892-1929 – 1 – us UMI [071]

ECHO – Olympia. Wash. -w. 1868-77 – 1 – us UMI [071]

ECHO : PERIODICO LITTERARIO E NOTICIOSO – Maceio, Alagoas. 15-24 Jun 1894 – 1,5,6 – bl Biblioteca [072]

ECHO – Westerly. R.I. 1855-1856 – 1 – us UMI [071]

L'ECHO *see* L'ECHO DE SAINT-JUSTIN

O ECHO : JORNAL CRITICO E NOTICIOSO – '(s.l.')-Sao Luis, Brazil. 21 Mar-24 Apr 1886 – 1,5,6 – bl Biblioteca [072]

THE ECHO – Accra, Ghana. Oct 1937-Sep 1938; Jan-Feb 1939; Oct 1950-Dec 1951; Jul 1952-Dec 1953 (imperfect) – 11r – 1 – uk British Libr Newspaper [072]

THE ECHO – Haverhill, England. 3 issues 1888; 1890- – 57+ r – 1 – uk British Libr Newspaper [072]

THE ECHO – London, 8 Dec 1868-31 July 1905 – 76r – 1 – uk British Libr Newspaper [072]

THE ECHO – Montreal, Canada. 4 oct 1890; 25 dec 1892 – 1r – 1 – Can$25.00 – cn Can Microfilming [072]

THE ECHO – Montreal, Canada. v5 n12. 1 fev 1856-v16 n28. 10 jul 1867 – 1r – 1 – Can$25.00 – cn Can Microfilming [072]

THE ECHO / St. Francis College. Richmond, Canada – 14 fev 1880 – 1r – 1 – Can$25.00 – cn Can Microfilming [370]

THE ECHO – Sydney, Australia. 2 Jan 1885-22 Jul 1893 – 48r – 1 – uk British Libr Newspaper [072]

L'ECHO ABITIBIEN – Val d'Or, Canada. 18 jan 1950-30 dec 1992 – 107r – 1 – Can$85.00r – cn Can Microfilming [072]

O ECHO ALAGOANO – Maceio, Alagoas. 30 Abr 1837 – 1,5,6 – bl Biblioteca [072]

ECHO AMARGOENSE : PERIODICO IMPERIAL, LITTERARIO, NOTICIOSO E COMMERCIAL – Amargosa, BA. 22-30 Abr, Out 1886; Jun-1 Set 1890 – 1,5,6 – bl Biblioteca [072]

THE ECHO AND PROTESTANT EPISCOPAL RECORDER – (Includes: Toronto v5 n12 1 feb 1855-v9 n4 23 feb 1860; v16 n28 10 jul 1867) – Montreal, Canada. v5 n12. 1 fev 1856-v16 n28. 10 jul 1867 – 1r – 1 – Can$30.00 – cn Can Microfilming [072]

ECHO AND SPORTS ECHO – (Also known as: Sunderland Echo) – Jul-Dec 1993; Jan 1-15 1994; Jan 17-Apr 30 1994; May 2-Dec 1994; Jan 2-Apr 15 1995; Apr 18-29 1995; May-Dec 30 1995; 1996 – 82r – 1 – uk British Libr Newspaper [072]

ECHO AND SPORTS ECHO *see* SUNDERLAND ECHO

L'ECHO ANNAMITE – Organe de defense des interets francoannamites. Saigon. 1920-avr 1931 – 1 – fr A.C.R.P.P. [073]

L'ECHO BAZAAR – Montreal, Canada. v1 n3. 20 oct 1891 – 1r – 1 – Can$25.00 – cn Can Microfilming [072]

ECHO DA JUVENTUDE – San'Luiz, 11 Dec 1864-21 May 1865 – 1,5,6 – bl Biblioteca [072]

O ECHO DA MATTA – Pecanha, 20 Sep 1891-15 May 1892 – 1,5,6 – bl Biblioteca [072]

ECHO DA VERDADE – [s.l.]. Jan 1887 – 1,5,6 – bl Biblioteca [072]

O ECHO D'ALEM TUMULO : MONITOR D'O SPIRITISMO 'NO BRAZIL – '(s.l.')-BA, Brazil. Jul 1869-maio 1870 – 1,5,6 – bl Biblioteca [072]

L'ECHO D'ALGER – Alger, Algeria: s.n, 1956-apr 25 1961 – 26r – 1 – us Res Libr [072]

L'ECHO D'ALGER – Alger. Journal republicain du matin. Dir. E. Bailac. 1919-39 – 1 – fr A.C.R.P.P. [072]

L'ECHO D'ALMA – Alma, 12 avr 1941 – 1r – 1 – Can$25.00 – cn Can Microfilming [072]

L'ECHO DE BAZAR : HISTORIQUE DE VALLEYFIELD – Valleyfield, Canada. 14-19 avr 1913 – 1r – 1 – Can$25.00 – cn Can Microfilming [072]

L'ECHO DE BEAUHARNOIS *see* LE COURRIER DE BEAUHARNOIS

L'ECHO DE BEAUHARNOIS *see* LE COURRIER DE BEAUHARNOIS

ECHO DE BELGIQUE (DE STEM UIT BELGIE) – (Stem uit Belgie. 11 Feb 1916-21 Feb 1919) – London, UK. 25 Sept 1914-4 Feb 1916 – 1 – uk British Libr Newspaper [072]

L'ECHO DE BOURGET – Ville de Montreal-Est, Canada. v1 n2. 16 fev 1961 – 1r – 1 – Can$20.00 – cn Can Microfilming [072]

L'ECHO DE BULGARIE – Sofia, Bulgaria. 8 Aug 1916-30 Sep 1918; 2 Dec 1918-10 Jul 1919; 20 Jun 1922-30 Jan 1923 (imperfect) – 5r – 1 – uk British Libr Newspaper [072]

L'ECHO DE BULGARIE – Sofia, Bulgaria. Jun 1920-Feb 1921 – 1r – 1 – us L of C Photodup [949]

L'ECHO DE CHARLEVOIX – Baie St-Paul, Canada. 5 jan 1898-13 fev 1908 – 3r – 1 – Can$40.00r – cn Can Microfilming [072]

L'ECHO DE CHINE – Edition hebdomadaire. Journal des interets francais en Extreme-Orient. Chang-hai. 1903-sept 1919 – 1 – fr A.C.R.P.P. [073]

ECHO DE COMPTON NEWS – (Cont by and filmed with: Le Journal de Compton News 5 mai 1965-v17 n7 9oct 1974) – East Angus, Canada. v4 n28. 9 jan 1963-28 avr 1965 – 2r – 1 – Can$50.00r – cn Can Microfilming [072]

ECHO DE CUYABA – Cuiaba, 6 Mar-13 Jun 1884 – 1,5,6 – bl Biblioteca [072]

ECHO DE DRUMMONDVILLE *see* LE PRESENT

ECHO DE FRANCE – London, UK. 15 Aug-9 Dec 1914 – 1 – uk British Libr Newspaper [072]

ECHO DE FRANCE – London, UK. 20 Sept 1922-14 Jul 1926 – 1 – uk British Libr Newspaper [072]

L'ECHO DE FRASERVILLE – Riviere-du-Loup, Canada. 8 mai 1884; v1 n1. 31 mai 1884 – 1r – 1 – Can$25.00 – cn Can Microfilming [072]

L'ECHO DE FRONTENAC – Lac Megantic, Canada. v1 n38. 1 aut 1930-29 dec 1992 – 49r – 1 – Can$70.00r – cn Can Microfilming [072]

L'ECHO DE GRANBY – Granby, Canada. 1 mai 1909-13 jan 1912 – 1r – 1 – Can$35.00 – cn Can Microfilming [072]

O ECHO DE JARAGUA : PERIODICO COMMERCIAL, LITTERARIO E NOTICIOSO – Maceio, Alagoas. 14 Nov 1886 – 1,5,6 – bl Biblioteca [072]

L'ECHO DE LA FABRIQUE – Journal industriel de Lyon et du departement du Rhone. Lyon. oct 1831-janv 1834 – 1 – fr A.C.R.P.P. [331]

L'ECHO DE LA FRANCE – Montreal, Canada. nov 1865-jan 1870 – 3r – 1 – Can$50.00r – cn Can Microfilming [072]

L'ECHO DE LA GATINEAU / ed by Lusignan, Alphonse – Pointe Gatineau, Canada. 6 jul-7 sep 1889 – 1r – 1 – Can$25.00 – cn Can Microfilming [072]

ECHO DE LA GATINEAU = ECHO OF THE GATINEAU – Aylmer, Canada. dec 1952; v2 n1. jan 1954 – 1r – 1 – Can$30.00 – cn Can Microfilming [072]

L'ECHO DE LA LIEVRE – Mont-Laurier, Canada. v9 n22. 18 nov 1960-v11 n26. 28 dec 1962 – 1r – 1 – Can$50.00 – cn Can Microfilming [072]

ECHO DE LA LITTERATURE ET DES BEAUX-ARTS DANS LES DEUX MONDES – Paris. 1840-48 – 1 – fr A.C.R.P.P. [800]

L'ECHO DE LA MAYENNE : JOURNAL DE LAVAL (...) – (10 missing numbers) – Hebd. puis bi-hebd. puis quot., Laval (Mayenne), janv. 1842-juil. 1920 (10 n° manq.) – 53r – 1 – F28,890.01 – fr Armell [073]

L'ECHO DE LA PAROISSE JACQUES-CARTIER / ed by Duval, G – Quebec, Canada. 1 sep 1901 – 1r – 1 – Can$25.00 – cn Can Microfilming [072]

L'ECHO DE LA POINTE-AUX-TREMBLES – Pointe-aux-Trembles, Canada. jan 1960-v1 n7. jul 1960 – 1r – 1 – Can$35.00 – cn Can Microfilming [072]

L'ECHO DE LA PRESSE – Montmagny, Canada. 24 sep 1847-v1 n23. 17 mar 1848 – 1r – 1 – Can$25.00 – cn Can Microfilming [072]

L'ECHO DE LA RIVE SUD / ed by Blanchet, L J N – Chambly, Canada. 29 oct 1927 – 1r – 1 – Can$25.00 – cn Can Microfilming [072]

L'ECHO DE LA RUE SAINTE-CATHERINE – Montreal, Canada. mai 1877-15 dec 1878 – 1r – 1 – Can$25.00 – cn Can Microfilming [072]

L'ECHO DE LA SAINT-JEAN-BAPTISTE : HEBDO – Montreal, Canada. 4 dec 1884-1 jan 1885 – 1r – 1 – Can$25.00 – cn Can Microfilming [072]

ECHO DE LA SEMAINE – Boston, MA. v1 n45. 10 sep 1898 – 1r – 1 – Can$25.00 – cn Can Microfilming [071]

L'ECHO DE LA SESSION : JOURNAL DES DEBATS PARLEMENTAIRES – Quebec, Canada. 13 nov 1871; v1 n7. 26 dec 1871 – 1r – 1 – Can$30.00 – cn Can Microfilming [323]

ECHO DE LA TAMISE – London, UK. 6-13 May 1858 – 1 – uk British Libr Newspaper [072]

L'ECHO DE LA TUQUE *see* L'ECHO DE LA TUQUE ET DU HAUT SAINT-MAURICE

L'ECHO DE LA TUQUE ET DU HAUT SAINT-MAURICE – (Cont by and filmed with: L'Echo de la Tuque v19 n5 2 fev 1956-24 dec 1957; 2 jul 1959; 2 oct 1968-29 dec 1970) – La Tuque, Canada. 1938 – 4r – 1 – Can$75.00r – cn Can Microfilming [072]

L'ECHO DE LACHINE ET DU COMTE J.-CARTIER – Lachine, Canada. 12 fev 1898-v1 n5. 12 mar 1898 – 1r – 1 – Can$25.00 – cn Can Microfilming [072]

L'ECHO DE L'AMERIQUE DU SUD : JOURNAL POLITIQUE, COMMERCIAL ET LITTERAIRE – Rio de Janeiro, 30 Jun 1827-29 Mar 1828 – 1,5,6 – bl Biblioteca [072]

L'ECHO DE LAVAL – Quebec, Canada. 20 oct 1917; v1 n6. 24 nov 1917 – 1r – 1 – Can$25.00 – cn Can Microfilming [072]

L'ECHO DE LEVIS – Levis, Canada. 15 avr 1871-28 jul 1876 – 3r – 1 – Can$45.00r – cn Can Microfilming [072]

L'ECHO DE L'EXPOSITION – Montreal. n9. 22 sep 1882 – 1r – 1 – Can$25.00 – cn Can Microfilming [072]

ECHO DE LONDRES ET DE GRANDE-BRETAGNE – London, UK. 15 May 1933-28 May 1940 – 1 – uk British Libr Newspaper [072]

ECHO DE L'ORIENT – Journal de Smyrne. Smyrne. juil 1841-juin 1846. et Collection Dedeyan. A partir du 11 aout 1846 fusionne avec le Journal de Constantinople pour former: Journal de Constantinople. Echo de l'Orient – 1 – fr A.C.R.P.P. [073]

L'ECHO DE LOTBINIERE *see* LE LOTBINIERE

L'ECHO DE L'OUEST – Minneapolis, MN. 25 avr 1883-16 avr 1884; 11 jul 1891- 4 jan 1929 – 1r – 1 – Can$50.00 – cn Can Microfilming [071]

L'ECHO DE L'OUEST – San Francisco, CA. 28 Aug 1909-1915 – 7r – 1 – $350.00 – BO2835 – us Library Micro [071]

L'ECHO DE LOUISEVILLE – Louiseville, Canada. 27 avr 1894-31 aut 1897 – 1r – 1 – Can$40.00 – cn Can Microfilming [072]

L'ECHO DE LOUISEVILLE *see* L'ECHO DE SAINT-JUSTIN

L'ECHO DE LOUISEVILLE BERTHIER *see* L'ECHO DE SAINT-JUSTIN

L'ECHO DE MANITOBA : JOURNAL HEBDOMADAIRE – Winnipeg, Canada. 27 jan 1898-31 dec 1902 – 1r – 1 – Can$50.00 – cn Can Microfilming [072]

L'ECHO DE MONTMAGNY – Montmagny, Canada. 12 oct 1894-v7 n14. 4 jan 1901 – 1r – 1 – Can$45.00 – cn Can Microfilming [072]

L'ECHO DE NANCY – Sigmaringen. nov 1944-fevr 1945 – 1 – fr A.C.R.P.P. [073]

L'ECHO DE PARIS – Paris. 12 mars 1884-27 mars 1938. Le 28 mars 1938 fusionne avec: Le Jour – 1 – fr A.C.R.P.P. [073]

L'ECHO DE PARIS – Paris: Simond, jan-sep 14, 1934; apr 27-29, may 1-15, jun 24-dec 1935 – 8r – 1 – us Res Libr [072]

L'ECHO DE PARIS LITTERAIRE ILLUSTRE – Dir. Valentin Simond. no. 2-79. Paris. fevr 1892-aout 1893 – 1 – fr A.C.R.P.P. [800]

L'ECHO DE PORTNEUF-PRESSE – (Cont by: Portneuf-Presse 17 dec 1953-28 mai 1973. Cont by: L'Hebdo de Portneuf, Neuville 4 jun 1973-v2 n23 23 dec 1974) – Donnacona, Canada. v2 n23. 9 jun 1939-10 dec 1953 – 14r – 1 – Can$65.00r – cn Can Microfilming [072]

L'ECHO DE QUEBEC / ed by Duval, G – Quebec, Canada. 1 mai 1902-7 jan 1905 – 1r – 1 – Can$25.00 – cn Can Microfilming [072]

L'ECHO DE SAINTE-AGATHE : SPORTIF – (Bilingual) – Ste-Agathe, Canada. 1 dec 1934-2 avr 1935 – 1r – 1 – Can$45.00 – cn Can Microfilming [790]

L'ECHO DE SAINT-JUSTIN / ed by Gagne, W H – (Cont by and filmed with: L'Echo de Louiseville 30 avr 1948-26 oct 1977. Cont by: L'Echo de Louiseville Berthier 2 nov 1977-20 mar 1985. Cont by: L'Echo 27 mar 1985-29 dec 1992) – St-Justin, Canada. 2 nov 1921-23 avr 1948 – 64r – 1 – Can$70.00r – cn Can Microfilming [072]

ECHO DE SELESTAT – Selestat, France. 1919-23, 1925, 1928-8 mai 1940 – 1 – fr A.C.R.P.P. [072]

L'ECHO DE ST CESAIRE – St. Cesaire, v1-nos 1-5. mars-dec 1931. SEM35P196 – 1r – 1 – Can$15.00 – cn Bibl Nat [072]

L'ECHO DE STAN – (Issues filmed with: Bartlett, Robert E: Collection of African newspapers) – Stanleyville: [s.n.], jan 1959-feb 20 1960 – us Res Libr [072]

ECHO DE STAN, DE LA PROVINCE ORIENTALE – (Incomplete, 6 issues only) – 1960(April 9-July 9) – 1 reel – AF-121/3 – ne IDC [950]

L'ECHO DE TERREBONNE – Terrebonne, 1917-21. SEM35P19 – 1r – 1 – Can$15.00 – cn Bibl Nat [073]

L'ECHO DE TERREBONNE – Terrebonne, Canada. 27 jan 1917-v2 n1. 1 jul 1918 – 1r – 1 – Can$50.00 – cn Can Microfilming [072]

L'ECHO DE TOURCOING (ET DE SES CANTONS) – Quot. de Tourcoing (Nord), mars 1884-juin 1889 – 10r – 1 – F3,724.04 – fr Armell [073]

L'ECHO DE VAUDREUIL / ed by Boyer, Gustave – Rigaud, Canada. v2 n1. 9-10 jan 1908 – 1r – 1 – Can$25.00 – cn Can Microfilming [072]

L'ECHO DE VAUDREUIL ET DE JACQUES-CARTIER *see* L'ECHO DE VAUDREUIL-SOULANGES

L'ECHO DE VAUDREUIL-SOULANGES – (Cont: L'Echo de Vaudreuil et de Jacques-Cartier) – Dorion, Canada. 16 aut 1957-7 dec 1974 – 1r – 1 – Can$60.00 – cn Can Microfilming [072]

ECHO DER GEGENWART – (Cont: Aachener Anzeiger, -sep 8 1851) – Aachen, apr 9 1848-49, 1850-1935 – 1 – Dist. gw Mikrofilm – gw Misc Inst [943]

DAS ECHO DER WOCHE – Hamburg, Germany. 1932-33 – 1 – gw Mikrofilm [073]

L'ECHO DES BOIS-FRANCS – Arthabaska, Canada. 2 jun 1894-v18 n17. 3 dec 1910 – 3r – 1 – Can$50.00r – cn Can Microfilming [072]

L'ECHO DES CAMPAGNES – Berthier, Canada. 7 nov 1846-v6 n45. 15 mar 1856 – 1r – 1 – Can$40.00 – cn Can Microfilming [072]

L'ECHO DES COMORES *see* AL-WATWANY

L'ECHO DES DEUX MONTAGNES – (Filmed with: La Liberte v3 n5 1 dec 1892-v5 n52 24 nov 1895) – Ste-Scholastique, Canada. 6 nov 1890-v3 n4. 24 nov 1892 – 1r – 1 – Can$60.00 – cn Can Microfilming [072]

L'ECHO DES DEUX-MONDES – New York City, NY. 2 sep 1876-v1 n29. 17 mar 1877 – 1r – 1 – Can$35.00 – cn Can Microfilming [071]

L'ECHO DES DEUX-MONTAGNES – Ste-Cholastique. v1 n1. 27 sep 1866-v1 n25. 14 mar 1867 – 1r – 1 – $40.00 – cn Can Microfilming [072]

L'ECHO DES EGLISES WALLONNES – 1948-82 (complete) – 3r – 1 – ATLA S0475 – us A.T.L.A. [240]

L'ECHO DES IMBECILES – Beauport, Canada. 36 jul 1863 (numero unique) – 1r – 1 – Can$25.00 – cn Can Microfilming [072]

L'ECHO DES INSTITUTEURS – Organe de leurs sentiments et de leurs interets, ouvert a tous leurs voeux et a toutes leurs reclamations. Red. en chef Louis Arsene Meunier. Paris. 1845-juin 1850 – 1 – fr A.C.R.P.P. [330]

L'ECHO DES JEUNES : REVUE ECLECTIQUE – Ste-Cunegonde de Montreal. v1 no 1- (nov 1891)-. SEM16P327 – 1r – 5 – Can$9.00 – cn Bibl Nat [073]

L'ECHO DES LABORATOIRES – Bulletin de l'Association des chefs de travaux et preparateurs des Facultes des sciences. no. 6-19. Paris. juin 1910-oct 1913 – 1 – fr A.C.R.P.P. [500]

L'ECHO DES LAURENTIDES – La Malbaie, Canada. 13 jun 1884-v4 n20. 27 oct 1887 – 1r – 1 – Can$35.00 – cn Can Microfilming [072]

L'ECHO DES LAURENTIDES *see* L'ECHO DU NORD

L'ECHO DES MONTS – St-Bruno, Canada. v3 n3. 5 nov 1959; 3 jan 1961-v6 n11. 27 dec 1962 – 2r – 1 – Can$45.00r – cn Can Microfilming [072]

L'ECHO DES PRAIRIES – Duvernay, Canada. v1 n2. 17 nov 1960 – 1r – 1 – Can$25.00 – cn Can Microfilming [072]

L'ECHO DES SYNDICATS AGRICOLES – Lille. nov 1904-aout 1944 – 1 – fr A.C.R.P.P. [630]

L'ECHO DES THEATRES, DES ARTS, DE LA LITTERATURE – Paris. oct 1861-avr 1862 – 1 – fr A.C.R.P.P. [800]

L'ECHO DES TRIBUNAUX – Montreal, Canada. 10 sep 1898-v1 n12. 21 nov 1898 – 1r – 1 – Can$25.00 – cn Can Microfilming [072]

L'ECHO D'HAITI – Port-au-Prince: Imp Vve J Chenet, jul 3-31, aug 14-sep 11, sep 25-oct 2, oct 23-nov 20 1894; may 21-jul 9 1895; jan 7-jun 7, jun 30 1899 – 4r – 1 – us Res Libr [072]

L'ECHO D'IBERVILLE / ed by Menard, Joseph – Iberville, Canada. 19 sep 1919-2 avr 1920 – 1r – 1 – Can$30.00 – cn Can Microfilming [072]

L'ECHO D'IBERVILLE – St-Jean, Canada. 17 jan 1880-v3 n23. 30 jun 1882 – 1r – 1 – Can$25.00 – cn Can Microfilming [072]

ECHO DO MANGUABA : PERIODICO POLITICO – Maceio, Alagoas. 17 Mar 1860 – 1,5,6 – bl Biblioteca [072]

ECHO DO NORTE : ORGAO NOTICIOSO, LITTERARIO E CRITICO – Manaos, Amazonas. 11 Set-23 Out 1887 – 1,5,6 – bl Biblioteca [072]

ECHO DO NORTE – '(s.l.')-Sao Luis, Brazil. 3 Jul 1834-31 Oct 1836 – 1,5,6 – bl Biblioteca [072]

ECHO DO POVO – Corumba, Brazil. Mar-Apr 1893; Jan-Apr 1894 – 1 – bl Biblioteca [072]

ECHO DO POVO – Maceio, Alagoas. 30 Out 1887; Jan-Fev, Maio, Jul, Set-31 Out 1888 – 1,5,6 – bl Biblioteca [072]

O ECHO DO POVO – Cachoeira, BA. 21 Maio 1881 – 1,5,6 – bl Biblioteca [072]

O ECHO DO POVO – Hongkong: J J da Silva e Souza, may 15, jul 17, 31, sep 25, oct 30, 1859; apr 27 1862 – 1r – us Res Libr [072]

ECHO DO RIO S. FRANCISCO – Barra do Rio Grande, BA. 13 Maio-Jun, 5 Ago 1877 – 1,5,6 – bl Biblioteca [072]

O ECHO DO S. FRANCISCO : REVISTA QUINZENAL – SCIENCIAS, LETTRAS, ARTES, RELIGIAO – Penedo, Alagoas. 15 Ago-31 Set 1876 – 1,5,6 – bl Biblioteca [072]

ECHO DO SERTAO : PERIODICO POLITICO E COMMERCIAL – Uberaba, 6 Jun 1875 – 1,5,6 – bl Biblioteca [072]

L'ECHO D'ORAN – Oran. Journal quotidien du matin. 1907-juin 1940, mars-nov 1943, fevr 1946-56 – 1 – fr A.C.R.P.P. [072]

ECHO DOS ANDES *see* VOZ DO POVO

O ECHO DOS ANDES – Manaos, Amazonas. 16 Nov 1882 – 1,5,6 – bl Biblioteca [072]

L'ECHO D'OTTAWA – Ottawa, Ontariio. 6 jun 1896-24 jun 1896 – 1r – 1 – Can$45.00 – cn Can Microfilming [072]

L'ECHO DU BAS SAINT-LAURENT – (Cont by: Le Progres-Echo) – Rimouski, Canada. 3 mar 1933-29 avr 1970 – 44r – 1 – Can$80.00r – cn Can Microfilming [072]

L'ECHO DU BAZAAR – Riviere-du-Loup, Fraserville, Canada. 19 jul-28 jul 1905 – 1r – 1 – Can$25.00 – cn Can Microfilming [072]

L'ECHO DU BOUNDE – (In Russian) – Geneva, SZ. v1 no1 Mar 1909-no5 Feb 1911 – 1r – 1 – $30.00 – cn Can Microfilming [072]

L'ECHO DU CABINET DE LECTURE – Montreal, Canada. 1 jan 1859-dec 1873 – 5r – 1 – Can$40.00r – cn Can Microfilming [073]

L'ECHO DU CANADA – Boston, MA. v3 n76. 1875 – 1r – 1 – Can$20.00 – cn Can Microfilming [071]

L'ECHO DU CANADA – Fall River, MA. 19 jul 1873-v1 n52. 18 jul 1874 – 1r – 1 – Can$35.00 – cn Can Microfilming [071]

ECHO DU COLLEGE MONNOIR – Marieville, Canada. v1 n6. 24 dec 1872-v2 n14. 27 dec 1873 – 1r – 1 – Can$28.00 – cn Can Microfilming [370]

L'ECHO DU GOLFE – Rimouski, Canada. 2 jun 1885-18 nov 1886 – 1r – 1 – Can$30.00 – cn Can Microfilming [072]

L'ECHO DU KAMOURASKA – Riviere-du-Loup, Canada. v3 n3. 19 oct 1961 – 1r – 1 – Can$25.00 – cn Can Microfilming [072]

L'ECHO DU KIVU – (Issues filmed with: Bartlett, Robert E: Collection of African newspapers) – Bukavu, may 11-nov 6 1959 – us Res Libr [072]

L'ECHO DU LOIR : JOURNAL HEBDOMADAIRE DE LA FLECHE – (1 missing number) – Hebd., La Fleche (Sarthe), mai 1847-aout 1944 (1 no. manq.) – 20r – 1 – F10,322.94 – fr Armell [073]

L'ECHO DU MIDI – Journal politique, religieux et litteraire de la Haute-Garonne. Toulouse. 1821-janv 1829 – 1 – fr A.C.R.P.P. [073]

L'ECHO DU NORD – (Becomes: L'Echo des Laurentides v1 n9 19 jan 1945-29 aut 1964) – Ste-Agathe, Canada. v1 n1. 24 nov 1944-12 jan 1945 – 7r – 1 – Can$60.00r – cn Can Microfilming [072]

L'ECHO DU NORD – Politique, litteraire, industriel et commercial. Lille. 1902, 1937 – 1 – fr A.C.R.P.P. [073]

L'ECHO DU NORD – St-Jerome, Canada. 4 oct 1935-30 dec 1992 – 103r – 1 – Can$75.00r – cn Can Microfilming [072]

L'ECHO DU PARLEMENT – Brussels, Belgium. 1 Jan 1884-30 Sep 1885 – 4r – 1 – uk British Libr Newspaper [072]

L'ECHO DU PAYS : BULLETIN DE L'AIDE AUX CONSCRITS CANADIENS, SOCIETE S.V. DE PAUL – Montreal, aut 1918 – 1r – 1 – Can$25.00 – cn Can Microfilming [971]

L'ECHO DU PAYS / ed by Debartzch, P D – St-Charles, Canada. jan 1833; 28 fev 1833-26 mai 1836(?) – 1r – 1 – Can$35.00 – cn Can Microfilming [072]

L'ECHO DU PEUPLE – Montreal, Canada. 19 jan-v1 n6. 24 jan 1880; 2nd series: 29 jan-v1 n10. 16 dec 1880; 3rd series: Quebec, fev 1881; 4th series: Morissette, 15 avr-v1 n3. 29 avr 1882 – 1r – 1 – Can$40.00 – cn Can Microfilming [072]

L'ECHO DU PEUPLE – Quebec, Canada. 1 jun 1867-4 avr 1868 – 1r – 1 – Can$35.00 – cn Can Microfilming [072]

L'ECHO DU PEUPLE – Paris: Impr de Bureau et Comp, apr 9 1848 – us Res Libr [072]

L'ECHO DU PEUPLE – Paris: Maulde et Renou. [n1-2. undated-jun 8 1848] – us Res Libr [072]

L'ECHO DU RHIN – Journal des interets moraux et materiels des classes ouvrieres et agricoles. Red. en chef L.W. Ravenez. Strasbourg. janv-avr 1848 – 1 – fr A.C.R.P.P. [073]

L'ECHO DU RHIN – Mayence. Premier quotidien francais des pays Rhenans. 1920-21. mq no. 11-14, 24, 35-39, 210-240, 353, 363, 638 – 1 – fr A.C.R.P.P. [072]

L'ECHO DU RICHELIEU – Sorel. v1 n2. 19 nov 1869-v1 n48. 15 jun 1870 – 1 – 1 – Can$75.00 – cn Can Microfilming [072]

L'ECHO DU SAINT-MAURICE – (Becomes: L'Hebdo du Saint-Maurice 5 jan 1972-30 dec 1991) – Shawinigan, Canada. v2 n25. 4 jan 1917 – 58r – 1 – Can$70.00r – cn Can Microfilming [072]

L'ECHO DU SAINT-MAURICE – Trois-Rivieres, Canada. 29 jan 1858-21 jan 1859 – 1r – 1 – Can$35.00 – cn Can Microfilming [072]

L'ECHO DU SOIR – (Filmed as pt of: Commune de Paris newspapers) – Paris: Imp Serriere et Co, apr 27-28, 30, may 1 1871 – us Res Libr [072]

O ECHO ESTANCIANO : ORGAO DOS INTERESSES DO COMMERCIO, DA LAVOURA E DA INDUSTRIA – Estancia-SE, Brazil. 15 Jul 1877 – 1 – bl Biblioteca [072]

ECHO FEIRENSE : PERIODICO NOTICIOSO E LITTERARIO – Feira de Sant' Anna, BA. 2 Jul 1878 – 1,5,6 – bl Biblioteca [072]

L'ECHO FRANCAIS – Journal politique et litteraire, du commerce, des sciences, arts, tribunaux, theatres, modes. Paris. 10 janv 1829-6 fevr 1847 – 1 – fr A.C.R.P.P. [073]

ECHO FRANCAIS DE LONDRES – London, UK. 2 Dec 1837-20 Jan 1838 – 1 – uk British Libr Newspaper [072]

L'ECHO INDIGENE – Organe hebdomadaire de la defense des interets des Musulmans algeriens. no. 23-64. Constantine. 1934 – 1 – fr A.C.R.P.P. [073]

ECHO INDIGENE – 1934 – 1 – us Res Libr [073]

ECHO ITAPAGIPANO – Itapagipe, BA. 13 Jan 1889 – 1,5,6 – bl Biblioteca [072]

O ECHO JUVENIL : ORGAO LITTERARIO E ABOLICIONISTA – Aracaju, 8 Apr 1888 – 1,5,6 – bl Biblioteca [072]

ECHO KRAKOWSKIE – Krakow, Poland. May 1948-May 1949; 1953-Jan 1960. 12 reels – 1 – 23.00r – us L of C Photodup [943]

L'ECHO LAURENTIEN – Ste-Rose, Canada. v2 n14. 27 jul 1961 – 1r – 1 – Can$25.00 – cn Can Microfilming [072]

ECHO LAVAL – (Cont: L'Ombudsman, Cont by: L'Observateur) – Ville de Laval, Canada. 16 fev 1967-v3 n45. 19 dec 1968 – 1r – 1 – Can$40.00 – cn Can Microfilming [072]

ECHO LAVAL *see*
- L'OBSERVATEUR
- L'OMBUDSMAN

O ECHO LIBERAL : ORGAO DO PARTIDO DE SERGIPE – Aracaju, 11 Aug-Sep, Nov 1877; Jan-Feb 1878; Aug-Dec 1880; Jan-Jul, Sep-Nov 1881; Mar-Jul 1882; 19 Aug, 2 Sep 1883 – 1,5,6 – bl Biblioteca [072]

ECHO MACAENSE : PAO TSUNG HAI – Macau: Francisco H Fernandez, jul 18, oct 10 1893; may 8, 22 1898 – 1r – 1 – us Res Libr [072]

ECHO MACEIOENSE : PERIODICO ILLUSTRADO – Maceio, Alagoas. 11 Abr, Jun 1886 – 1,5,6 – bl Biblioteca [072]

ECHO MARAGOGIPANO : ORGAO NOTICIOSO, LITTERARIO, AGRICOLA E COMMERCIAL – Cidade de Maragogipe, BA. 10 Abr, Jul, Out 1884; 8 Set 1886 – 1,5,6 – bl Biblioteca [072]

ECHO MILITAR : PERIODICO CONSAGRADO AOS INTERESSES DA CLASSE MILITAR – Manaos, Amazonas. 1 Out, Dez 1878; 1 Jan 1879 – 1,5,6 – bl Biblioteca [072]

L'ECHO MUSICAL / ed by Filiatrault, AR & Hardy, Ed – Montreal, Canada. 1 jun 1888-v1 n8. jul/aut 1888 – 1r – 1 – Can$30.00 – cn Can Microfilming [780]

L'ECHO NATIONAL – Dir. A. Tardieu. Fond. Georges Clemenceau. Paris. 10 janv 1922-15 mai 1924 – 1 – fr A.C.R.P.P. [073]

L'ECHO NATIONAL – Paris: Imp Centrale de Napoleon Chaix et cie, sep 1848 – us Res Libr [072]

ECHO NEWS – Echo, OR. -w. 1917-42 – 1 – 144.00 – us Oregon Hist [071]

THE ECHO OF CLAIRVAUX – Tracadie, N.S.: A.T. McInnes, v1 no 1 (May 1880)- – 9 – cn C.I.H.M. [971]

THE ECHO OF NIAGARA – Toronto, Niagara, Ontario. 17 mai 1884 – 1r – 1 – Can$25.00 – cn Can Microfilming [072]

ECHO OF THE TEACHER – New York. N.Y. 1915 – 1 – us A.J.P.C. [071]

ECHO PILOT – Greencastle, PA. -w 1895-1912 – 13 – $25.00r – us I.M.R. [071]

ECHO POLSKIE – Toledo, Ohio. 1912-13 – 2r – 1 – $32.50r – us Archival [071]

ECHO POPULAR – Cachoeira, BA. 19 Maio-Jun 1877; 23 Jan 1878 – 1,5,6 – bl Biblioteca [072]

DAS ECHO, POST UND BEOBACHTER – Chicago: Beobachter Pub Co, 1918-apr 1920 – 2r – us Res Libr [071]

ECHO REGISTER – Echo, OR. -w. 28 May 1909-1 Oct 1909. 1 roll – 1 – us U.O. Library [071]

ECHO SANT' AMARENSE : JORNAL POLITICO, COMMERCIAL E AGRICOLA – Santo Amaro, BA. 8 Out 1881; 9 Out 1886 – 1,5,6 – bl Biblioteca [072]

ECHO SERGIPANO : JORNAL COMMERCIAL, NOTICIOSO, AGRICOLA E RECREATIVO – Aracaju, 12-20 Feb, 24 Apr 1881 – 1,5,6 – bl Biblioteca [072]

L'ECHO SIONISTE – Paris. v. 1-6 no. 9. Sept 1899-Sept 15 1905 – 1 – us NY Public [072]

L'ECHO SPORTIF : ORGANISATION ATHLETIQUE D'AMATEURS NATIONALE – Montreal, Canada. jan-v1 n5. mai 1926 – 1r – 1 – Can$25.00 – cn Can Microfilming [790]

ECHO SUD-AFRICAIN – London and Paris. 4 Oct 1894-10 Dec 1896 – 1 – uk British Libr Newspaper [072]

L'ECHO UNIVERSEL – Paris. Journal politique, litteraire, agricole et financier. Dir., Gustave Lazard. 10 dec 1868; 25 nov-9 dec 1869; 20 janv-4 aout 1870, 26 sept 1871-26 juil 1874; 2 fevr 1875-31 dec 1876; 1 juil-1 sept 1877 – 1 – fr A.C.R.P.P. [073]

DE ECHO VAN ISRAEL – Amsterdam, 1857. Pt 1 – 7mf – J-261-29/1 – ne IDC [956]

ECHO-DEUTSCHE WARTE IN BAYERN : ORGAN DER FDP – Nuernberg, West Germany. 1946-49 – 1 – gw Mikrofilm [072]

ECHOES / Imperial Order of the Daughters of the Empire – Canada. -irr. Jun 1909-Christmas 1938; Summer 1941-Christmas 1951. 11mqn reels – 1 – uk British Libr Newspaper [073]

ECHOES – (Lacking: 1892. 1896) – 1885-1982 – 21r – 1 – ATLA S0373 – us A.T.L.A. [240]

LES ECHOES – France. 1990- – 1 – us Primary [072]

ECHOES FROM EDINBURGH, 1910 : AN ACCOUNT AND INTERPRETATION OF THE WORLD MISSIONARY CONFERENCE / Gairdner, William Henry Temple – Author's ed. New York: Fleming H Revell, [1910?] – 1mf – 9 – 0-8370-6495-3 – 1986-0495 – us A.T.L.A. [240]

ECHOES FROM HELL : OR, LIGHT AFTER DARKNESS: ROME HOWLS WHILE ANGELS SHOUT VICTORY FROM THE BATTLEMENTS OF HEAVEN / Givens, Nick K – St Louis, MO: Columbia Book Concern, c1904 – 1mf – 9 – 0-8370-8509-8 – 1986-2509 – us A.T.L.A. [240]

ECHOES FROM PALESTINE / Mendenhall, James William – 1883 – 9 – us A.T.L.A. [240]

ECHOES FROM THE FLEETING YEARS / Gardner, George W – 1851-1923 – 1 – 5.53 – us Baptist [240]

ECHO-JOURNAL : BILINGUE – Montreal. v4 n13. 10 mai 1950; v4 n25. 13 sep 1950 – 1r – 1 – Can$25.00 – cn Can Microfilming [072]

ECHOLS COLLECTION : SELECTIONS ON THE VIETNAM WAR – (Over 30,000 volumes from the John M. Echols Collection at Corenell University. Unit 1 ca 400 titles 770mf $2885; Unit 2 over 400 pamphlets in English $1990; Unit 3 $2625) – 9 – $25,000.00 pre-paid for complete collection Units 1-10 – us UMI [977]

Echols Collection. Cornell University *see* SELECTIONS ON THE VIETNAM WAR

LES ECHOS – Bamako, Mali: Impr EDIM. [n6-may 26/jun 9 1989-] – us Res Libr [072]

ECHOS D'AMAZONIA – Manaos, Amazonas. 16 Set 1900 – 1,5,6 – bl Biblioteca [072]

ECHOS DE LA SEMAINE – Commune de Kinshasa: Ekatou MC, feb 1960 – us Res Libr [072]

LES ECHOS DE LA VALLEE DE MUNSTER – Munster.Juin 1865-mars 1869 – 1 – fr A.C.R.P.P. [073]

ECHOS D'ORIENT – Paris, 1897/98-1941/42 – 348mf – 9 – ne IDC [240]

ECHOS HEROI-COMIQUES DU NAUFRAGE DES ANGLAIS SUR L'ISLE-AUX-OEUFS EN 1711 / Hugolin, Pere – Quebec: [s.n.], 1910 ([Quebec]: [Imp. de l'Evenement]). SEM105P1473 – 1mf – 9 – Can$2.25 – cn Bibl Nat [780]

ECHOS (LES) – 6,1 – F2,445.00 – sz Infoprint [072]

ECHOS (LES) – 1988-1991 – 6 – F 3,929.00 – sz Infoprint [072]

ECHOS (LES) – 1990-1994 – 1 – F2,794.00 – sz Infoprint [072]

ECHOS VEDETTES – Montreal: Publications Quebecor. v1- 1963-. SEM35P101 – 99r – 1 – cn Bibl Nat [971]

DIE ECHTEN HEBRAEISCHEN MELODIEN / Heller, S – Ed. 3. Frankfurt a.M. 1908. BJ-421-32 1 – 9 – ne IDC [780]

DIE ECHTHEIT DER APOSTELGESCHICHTE DES HEILIGEN LUCAS: EIN WORT AN DEREN GEGNER / Koenig, Arthur – Breslau: G.P. Aderholz, 1867. 1 fiche – 9 – us A.T.L.A. [240]

DIE ECHTHEIT DER BILOAMSPRUECHE, NUM. 22-24 / Wobersin, Franz – Guetersloh: C Bertelsmann, 1900 – 1mf – 9 – 0-8370-9349-X – 1986-3349 – us A.T.L.A. [220]

DIE ECHTHEIT DER IGNATIANISCHEN BRIEFE : MIT EINER LITERARISCHEN BEILAGE, DIE ALTE LATEINISCHE UEBERSETZUNG DER USHER'SCHEN SAMMLUNG DER IGNATIUSBRIEFE UND DES POLYKARPBRIEFES / Funk, Franz Xaver – Tuebingen: H. Laupp, 1883 – 1mf – us A.T.L.A. [240]

DIE ECHTHEIT DES ZWEITEN THESSALONICHERBRIEFS (T.U.U. 2-24/2) / Wrede, William – Leipzig, 1903 – 2mf – 9 – ne Slangenburg [240]

Eck, Johann *see*
- APOLOGIA PRO PRINCIPIBUS CATHOLICIS ACALIJS ORDINIBUS IMPERIJ ADUERSUS MUCORES ET CALUMNIAS BUCERI, SUPER ACTIS COMICIORUM RATISPONAE
- REPLICA IOAN ECKII ADVERSVS SCRIPTA SECUNDA BUCERI APOSTATAE SUPER ACTIS RATISPONAE..

ECK SEGGE MAN BLOSS : SCHWAENKE UND GESCHICHTEN / Henze, Wilhelm – Hannover: F Gersbach, 1931 – 1r – 1 – us U.W. Library [830]

Eckardt, Ludwig *see*
- SCHILLER'S JUGENDDRAMEN
- WANDER-VORTRAEGE AUS KUNST UND GESCHICHTE

Eckdall, Ella *see*
- "1948"
- MAJOR GENERAL FREDERICK FUNSTON ("1948")

Ecke, Gustav *see*
- DIE EVANGELISCHEN LANDESKIRCHEN DEUTSCHLANDS IM NEUNZEHNTEN JAHRHUNDERT
- DIE THEOLOGISCHE SCHULE ALBRECHT RITCHLS
- UNVERRUECKBARE GRENZSTEINE: EIN OFFENES WORT AN HERRN D. RADE UND SEINE FREUNDE

Eckelmann, Ernst Otto *see* SCHILLERS EINFLUSS AUF DIE JUGENDDRAMEN HEBBELS

Eckenstein, Lina *see* WOMAN UNDER MONASTICISM

Ecker, Jakob *see* PORTA SION: LEXIKON ZUM LATEINISCHEN PSALTER

Ecker, KR *see* AEROBIC AND ANAEROBIC PERFORMANCE MEASURES IN ACTIVE AND INACTIVE YOUNG AND MIDDLE-AGED MALES

ECKERMANN : SCHAUSPIEL IN VIER AKTEN / Lissauer, Ernst – Berlin: Oesterheld, 1921 – 1r – 1 – us U.W. Library [820]

Eckermann, Johann Peter *see*
- CONVERSACIONES CON GOETHE EN LOS ULTIMOS ANOS DE SU VIDA
- GESPRAECHE MIT GOETHE IN DEN LETZTEN JAHREN SEINES LEBENS

Eckermann, Lee *see* THE STATE AND ECONOMIC PLANNING

ECKERNFOERDER ZEITUNG – Eckernfoerde, West Germany. 1 Mar 1980- – ca 5r per yr – 1 – gw Mikrofilm [072]

ECKERT AUF GROSSFAHRT : FAHRTENERLEBNISSE EINES HITLERJUNGEN / Jank, Martin – 3. Druck. Berlin: Junge Generation Verlag, [194-?] – 1r – 1 – us U.W. Library [430]

Eckert, Georg Heinrich *see* GOETHES URTEILE UEBER SHAKESPEARE AUS SEINER PERSOENLICHKEIT ERKLAERT

Eckford Luard, C *see* A BIBLIOGRAPHY OF THE LITERATURE...THE CENTRAL INDIA AGENCY

Eckhard, J G *see* MONATLICHER AUSZUG AUS ALLERHAND NEU HERAUSGEGEBENEN NUETZLICHEN UND ARTIGEN BUECHERN

Eckhardt, H von *see* FRIEDRICH VON GENTZ STAATSSCHRIFTEN UND BRIEFE

Eckhardt, J G von *see* DE ORIGINE GERMANORUM...

Eckhardt Monument Company. Tiffin, Ohio *see* MONUMENT ORDER RECORDS

Eckl, C *see* ATTITUDES TOWARDS PHYSICAL ACTIVITY AMONG AMERICAN AND GERMAN SENIOR CITIZENS

Eckley *see* HISTORY OF CARROLL AND HARRISON COUNTIES

Ecklon, C F *see* TOPOGRAPHISCHES VERZEICHNISS DER PFLANZENSAMMLUNG VON C. F. ECKLON
Ecklon, CF *see* ENUMERATIO PLANTARUM AFRICAE AUSTRALIS
L'ECLAIR : LIBERAL, POLITIQUE MUNICIPALE – Quebec, Canada. 16 jan-17 fev 1906 – 1r – 1 – Can$25.00 – cn Can Microfilming [305]
L'ECLAIR – Paris. 27 oct 1888, 15 mars 1889-28 janv 1926. Fait suite a: Le Peuple. 2 dec 1888-14 mars 1889. Le 29 janv 1926 absorbe par: L'Avenir de Paris – 1 – fr A.C.R.P.P. [072]
L'ECLAIR – Quebec, 7 nov 1940-13 dec 1940 et le 16 mai 1941 – 1r – 1 – Can$35.00 – cn Can Microfilming [072]
L'ECLAIR – Revue hebdomadaire de la litterature, des sciences et des arts paraissant tous les samedis. Paris. juin 1852-53 – 1 – fr A.C.R.P.P. [073]
L'ECLAIR : SUPPLEMENT ILLUSTRE – (Une soixantaine de figures contemporaines bien gravees) – 15e serie: Paris, nov 1910 – 1r – 1 – Can$25.00 – cn Can Microfilming [072]
L'ECLAIR – Waterloo, Canada. 20 fev 1974-v4 n11. 14 dec 1977 – 1r – 1 – Can$35.00 – cn Can Microfilming [072]
L'ECLAIR – Port-au-Prince: [s.n., 1889-]. [1ere annee, n1-2eme annee, n4. 8 fevr 1889-14 mars 1890] – 2r – 9 – us Res Libr [072]
ECLAIR SUR L'ASSOCIATION HUMAINE / Saint Martin, Louis Claude de – Paris. Au Cercle Social. 1797 – 9 – fr Hachette [321]
L'ECLAIRCISSEMENT DE LA LANGUE FRANCAISE / Palsgrave, John – 1852 – 9 – fr I.C.S. [440]
ECLAIRCISSEMENTS SUR LES PRINCIPES DE LA LANGUE FRANCAISE / Grimarest, J L le Gallois – 1712 – 9 – fr I.C.S. [440]
L'ECLAIREUR – (Filmed with: L'Eclaireur-Progres 15 nov 1960-27 dec 1992) – Beauceville, Canada. 1 oct 1908-8 nov 1960 – 101r – 1 – Can$70.00r – cn Can Microfilming [072]
L'ECLAIREUR – Journal democratique quotidien de Saint-Etienne. Saint-Etienne. 1869-28 janv 1872 – 1 – fr A.C.R.P.P. [073]
L'ECLAIREUR – Quebec, Canada. 13 aut 1877-30 mar 1880 – 2r – 1 – Can$40.00r – cn Can Microfilming [072]
L'ECLAIREUR D'ARGENTEUIL – Lachute, Canada. 6 mai 1961 – 1r – 1 – Can$25.00 – cn Can Microfilming [072]
L'ECLAIREUR DE L'AIN – Le sous-titre varie. Yonnax. 30 sept 1894-aout 1939; sept 1944-juin 1951 – 1 – fr A.C.R.P.P. [073]
L'ECLAIREUR DU PEUPLE – no. 1-19. Paris. aout 1797 – 1 – fr A.C.R.P.P. [073]
L'ECLAIREUR DU PEUPLE, OU, LE DEFENSEUR DE 24 MILLIONS D'OPPRIMES – no. 1-7. Paris. mars-avr 1796 – 1 – fr A.C.R.P.P. [073]
L'ECLAIREUR HAYTIEN : OU, LE PARFAIT PATRIOTE – Port-au-Prince: F Darfour, [n4-n5. 27 aout-8 sep 1818] – 1r – 1 – us Res Libr [072]
L'ECLAIREUR-PROGRES *see*
– BEAUCE NOUVELLE
– L'ECLAIREUR
– LE PROGRES DE SAINT-GEORGES
THE ECLECTIC ALMANAC FOR THE YEAR 1839 / Armstrong, John – 1 – us KS Hist [030]
ECLECTIC MAGAZINE OF FOREIGN LITERATURE – v. 1-148. 1844-1907. All pub – 1,5,6 – us Princeton Micro [410]
ECLECTIC MUSEUM OF FOREIGN LITERATURE, MUSIC AND ART *see* AMERICAN ECLECTIC
ECLESIASTICO...SANTA...SAN GABRIEL / Santano de Membrio, Juan – 1719 – 9 – 1.50f – sp Bibl Santa Ana [240]
L'ECLIPSE – Paris. 26 Jan 1868-30 Dec 1897 – 14r – 1 – uk British Libr Newspaper [072]
L'ECLIPSE – puis politique et financiere. puis Revue comique illustree. Paris. 1868-juin 1876 – 1 – fr A.C.R.P.P. [073]
ECLIPSE – Parsons. Kan. 1874-1880 – 1 – us UMI [071]
THE ECLIPSE : SATIRIQUE – Quebec, Canada. 24 nov 1877 – 1r – 1 – Can$25.00 – cn Can Microfilming [072]
ECLOGAE AMERICANAE / Vahl, M – B1582 2. 1796-1807 – 8 – ne IDC [574]
ECLOGAE HISTORICORUM DE REBUS BYZANTINIS (CDH 1,3) / od by Labbe, Ph – Parisiis,1648 – Dfl22.00 – ne Slangenburg [240]
ECLOGAE PLANTARUM RARIORUM AUT MINUS COGNITARUM / Jacquin, N J von – 2v. Vindobonae. 1811-44. B-5975 2 – 8 – ne IDC [580]
THE ECLOGUES OF MANTUAN, 1448-1516 / Mantuanus Spagnuoli, Baptista – 1567 – 9 – 10.00 – us Scholars' Facs [450]
L'ECLUSIER – Lachine (Canal Lachine), avr 1984-jul 1987f – 1r – 1 – Can$40.00 – cn Can Microfilming [072]
ECMA (EUROPEAN COMPUTER MANUFACTURERS ASSOCIATION) – Printed index. Updated every 60 days – 6,9 – us Info Handling [600]
ECO – London, UK. 23, 30 Nov 1895 – 1 – uk British Libr Newspaper [072]
O ECO : JORNAL E PROPAGANDA LTDA – Cruzeiro do Sul, Acre. 28 Set, 5 Nov 1972 – 1,5,6 – bl Biblioteca [072]
L'ECO COLONIALE DELLA NEW ENGLAND – Springfield, MA: Itala Print & Pub Co, dec 1917-oct 1919 – 1r – us Res Libr [071]
ECO DE AMBOS MUNDOS – London, UK. 17 May 1873-26 Mar 1874 – 1 – uk British Libr Newspaper [072]
ECO DE EXTREMADURA – Badajoz.1874-76 – 9 – 1.50f – sp Bibl Santa Ana [072]
ECO DE EXTREMADURA – Caceres.1860-61 – 9 – 1.50f – sp Bibl Santa Ana [072]
EL ECO DE EXTREMADURA – Caceres, 1860-1861 – 5 – sp Bibl Santa Ana [073]
EL ECO DE EXTREMADURA – La Habana, 1892 y 1 nº de 1894 – 5 – sp Bibl Santa Ana [073]
EL ECO DE FILIPINAS – Manila. Philippine Islands. -d. 1 Sep 1890-19 Oct 1891. (3 reels) – 1 – uk British Libr Newspaper [072]
ECO DE FREGENAL – Fregenal de la Sierra. 1880-81 – 9 – 1.50f – sp Bibl Santa Ana [072]
ECO DE FREGENAL.HOMENAJE A ARIAS MONTANOMY BRAVO MURILLO – 1881 – 9 – 1.50f – sp Bibl Santa Ana [946]
ECO DE LA MONTANA – Caceres.1898-99. No. sueltos – 9 – 1.50f – sp Bibl Santa Ana [072]
EL ECO DE LA MONTANA – Caceres, 1894 y 1899. 2 numeros – 5 – sp Bibl Santa Ana [073]
EL ECO DE LA MONTANA – Caceres, 1898-1899 – 5 – sp Bibl Santa Ana [073]
EL ECO DE LOS BARROS – Villafranca de los Barros, 1895. 1 numero – 5 – sp Bibl Santa Ana [073]
ECO DE PLASENCIA – Plasencia. 1895-96. No. sueltos – 9 – 1.50f – sp Bibl Santa Ana [072]
EL ECO DE TRUJILLO – Trujillo, 1908-1911 – 5 – sp Bibl Santa Ana [073]
EL ECO DEL PUEBLO – Zafra, 1918. 1 numero – 5 – sp Bibl Santa Ana [073]
L'ECO DEL RHODE ISLAND – Providence. R.I. 1897-1930 – 1 – us UMI [071]
L'ECO DELLE VALLI VALDESI – (Lacking some issues. Some original issues damaged) – 1969-79 – 3r – 1 – ATLA S0579 – us A.T.L.A. [073]
L'ECO D'ITALIA – New York, 1890-96 – 6r – 1 – us Ross [071]
L'ECO D'ITALIA – New York. Jan 1862-Nov 1894. Incomplete. Not collated – 1 – us NY Public [073]
ECO D'ITALIA *see* CRONACA
L'ECO D'ITALIA: RIVISTA ITALO-AMERICANA – New York. (Tri-Weekly.) Jan 9 1896-Dec 31 1896. Not collated – 1 – us NY Public [071]
EL ECO EXTREMENO – Plasencia, 1906. 1 numero – 5 – sp Bibl Santa Ana [073]
ECO-CLIMATIC CLASSIFICATION OF INTER-TROPICAL AFRICA – 1982 – 45p – it F.A.O. [550]
Ecolampadius, J *see*
– AIN GESPRECH ETLICHER PREDICANTEN ZU BASEL
– DER PROPHET MALEACHI, MIT AUSZLEGUNG. VERDEUETSCHT D. L. HAETZER
– UNDERRICHTUNG VON DEM WIDERTAUFF
– VOM SACRAMENT DER DANCKSAGUNG. VERTEUETSCHT D. L. HAETZER
L'ECOLE AUX APPARATIONS MYSTERIEUSES / Bourgeois, Phileas Frederic – Montreal: C. Beauchemin, 1896. 00208. (Pre-1900 Canadiana) – 9 – cn C.I.H.M. [370]
Ecole Biblique et Archeologique Francaise. Jerusalem *see*
– CATALOGUE
– CATALOGUE DE LA BIBLIOTHEQUE DE L'ECOLE BIBLIQUE ET ARCHEOLOGIQUE FRANCAISE
ECOLE DE L'HOMME ET DU CITOYEN – Journal hebdomadaire, paraissant le samedi. Red. en chef M. Gracieux-Faure. no. 1-2. Paris. 29 oct-26 nov 1870 – 1 – fr A.C.R.P.P. [073]
Ecole de service social affiliee a la Faculte des sciences sociales *see* SERVICE SOCIAL
L'ECOLE DES PEUPLES ET DES ROIS. OU ESSAI PHILOSOPHIQUE SUR LA LIBERTE LE POUVOIR ARBITRAIRE, LES JUIFS ET LES NOIRS / Sanchamau, J B – (Slave Trade and Abolitionism in France series). 1790 – 9 – fr Hachette [305]
L'ECOLE DU MONDE OU INSTRUCTION D'UN PERE A SON FILS / Noble, Eustache Le – Paris: Martin Jouvenel, 1700. SEM16P64 – 1r – 5 – Can$26.00 – cn Bibl Nat [830]
L'ECOLE EMANCIPEE – Revue pedagogique hebdomadaire. Paris. oct 1910-40 – 1 – fr A.C.R.P.P. [073]
Ecole Francaise d'Extreme-Orient *see*
– L'ART GRECO-BOUDDHIQUE DU GRANDHARA
– BULLETIN
– PUBLICATIONS
L'ECOLE GUINEENNE / Toure, Ahmed Sekou – Conakry: Imp Nationale "Patrice Lumumba", 1968 – us Res Libr [072]
L'ECOLE LIBERATRICE – Paris. France. 1929-1938 – 1 – us UMI [072]
ECOLE LITTERAIRE DE MONTREAL : PROCES-VERBAUX, ETC / BNQ – Montreal, 1896-1913 – 1r – 1 – cn Can Microfilming [090]
Ecole Normale Superieure. Paris *see* ANNALES SCIENTIFIQUES
ECOLE POLYTECHNIQUE DE MONTREAL: RAPPORT DU PRINCIPAL A L'HONORABLE SURINTENDANT DE L'INSTRUCTION PUBLIQUE / Archambault, Urgel Eugene – Montreal: Gazette, 1881.05214.(Pre-1900 Canadiana) – 9 – cn C.I.H.M. [370]
L'ECOLE POUR LA VIE / Toure, Ahmed Sekou – 2nd ed. Conakry, Republique de Guinee: Bureau de presse de la Presidence de la Republique, 1976 – us Res Libr [072]
L'ECOLE PRIMAIRE – Levis [Quebec]: Mercier & Cie, 1880 – 9 – cn C.I.H.M. [370]
L'ECOLE PUBLIQUE – Montreal. v1-7. 1969-76. SEM35P20 – 1r – 1 – Can$20.00 – cn Bibl Nat [073]
L'ECOLE RURALE – [Quebec?: s.n., 1904-19–?] – 9 – cn C.I.H.M. [370]
LES ECOLES EPISCOPALES ET MONASTIQUES EN OCCIDENT / Maitre, L – Avant les Universites (768-1180), 1924 – Dfl22.00 – ne Slangenburg [240]
LES ECOLES ET L'ENSEIGNEMENT DE LA THEOLOGIE PENDANT LA PREMIERE MOITIE DU 13E SIECLE / Robert, G – Paris: V. Lecoffre, 1909 – 1mf – us A.T.L.A. [240]
L'ECOLIER ANNAMITE – Organe qui defend les interets des Annamites et veille a l'avenir de leur pays. Saigon. nov 1924 – 1 – fr A.C.R.P.P. [073]
UN ECOLIER DU DIX-SEPTIEME SIECLE, OU, L'IDEAL DE L'EDUCATION JESUITIQUE / Reuss, Rodolph – (Includes bibliographical references) – Dole: L Bernin, 1901 – 1mf – 9 – 0-8370-8610-8 – 1986-2610 – us A.T.L.A. [370]
ECOLOGICAL EFFECTS OF EUCALYPTUS – 1985 3rd print 1988 – 93p – it F.A.O. [634]
ECOLOGICAL FRAMEWORK FOR MARINE FISHERY INVESTIGATIONS – 1986 – 162p – it F.A.O. [639]
ECOLOGICAL MODELLING – v1-26. 1975-84 – 1,5,6,13 – sz Elsevier [574]
ECOLOGICAL MONOGRAPHS – Durham, NC., 1931-41. v.1-11 – 114mf – 8 – ne IDC [580]
ECOLOGICAL MONOGRAPHS – v. 1-9. 1931-40 – 1,5,6 – us Princeton Micro [574]
ECOLOGICAL MONOGRAPHS – (v34- 1978-5,6,9) – 1- 1931- 1; v40- 5,6; v45- 9 – us UMI [574]
ECOLOGICAL RESEARCH ON DEVELOPMENT OF ARID ZONES (MEDITERRANEAN DESERTS) WITH WINTER PRECIPITATION / Israel. Ministry of Agriculture – Symposium Israel-France, Mar 11-14, 1974. Bet-Dagan, 1975. 193 p. Maps, diagr., illus – 9 – 6.00 – is I.T.T.I. [574]
ECOLOGIE ALIMENTAIRE DES MACROURIDAE (TELEOSTEENS GADIFORMES) / Geistdoerfer, Patrick – Alimentation, morphologie et histologie de l'appareil digestif. Place des Macrouridae dans la chaine alimentaire profonde Paris. 1975. 315p – 9 – F90.00 – fr Ethnologie [590]
ECOLOGIE DES POISSONS RECIFAUX DE POLYNESIE FRANCAISE. VARIATIONS SPATIO-TEMPORELLES DES PEUPLEMENTS. DYNAMIQUE DES POPULATIONS DE TROIS ESPECES DOMINANTES DES LAGONS NORD DE MOOREA. EVALUATION DE LA PRODUCTION ICHTYOLOGIQUE D'UN SECTEUR RECIFO-LAGONAIRE / Galzin, R – 9 – F70.00 – fr Ethnologie [590]
ECOLOGIST QUARTERLY – v.1-4. 1978 – 1 – us UMI [574]
ECOLOGY – v51- 1970- 1; v1- 5,6; v56- 9 – us UMI [574]
ECOLOGY – Lancaster, 1920-41. v.I-22 – 216mf – 8 – ne IDC [574]
ECOLOGY – v1-36. 1920-55 – 1,5,6 – us Princeton Micro [574]
ECOLOGY ABSTRACTS – 9 – us C.S.A. [574]
ECOLOGY AND CONTROL OF PERENNIAL WEEDS IN LATIN AMERICA – 1986 – 345p – it F.A.O. [631]
ECOLOGY AND EVOLUTION OF BOWERBIRD MATING SYSTEMS / Donaghey, Richard H – (PhD Thesis) – 1981 – microfiche – A$15.00 – at R.A.O.U. [590]
ECOLOGY AND MANAGEMENT OF AQUATIC-TERRESTRIAL ECOTONES / ed by Naiman, Robert J & Decamps, Henri – 1990 – xvi/316p – 9 – 92-3-102668-2 – Co-published with Parthenon Publishing – fr UNESCO [574]
ECOLOGY LAW QUARTERLY – (1985- . 5,6,9) – v1- . 1971- – 1 – us UMI [340]
ECOLOGY LAW QUARTERLY – (v1-12 1971-85 on reel $189.00. v13-22 1986-95 on mf $299.00. With index 1-10 1971-83) – University of California at Berkeley. v1-22. 1971-95 – 5,6,9 – $488.00 set – us Hein [340]
THE ECOLOGY OF CYCLOPS IN SOUTH-WEST NIGERIA AND THEIR RELATION TO THE OCCURRENCE OF DRACUNCULUS MEDINENSIS, THE GUINEA-WORM, IN THAT REGION / Onabamiro, Sanya Dojo – 1951 – us Res Libr [574]
ECOLOGY OF FOOD AND NUTRITION / ed by Kuhnlein, H et al – 1971- – 1,5,9 – us Gordon [630]
ECOLOGY OF THE BUDGERYGAH / Wyndham, Edmund – (PhD Thesis) – 1978 – microfiche – A$15.00 – at R.A.O.U. [590]
ECOLOGY TODAY – v1. 1971-72 – 6mf – 9 – $5.00f – us Ross [574]
ECONEWS – Arcata, CA. 1971-1990 – 3r – 1 – $150.00 – B03140 – us Library Micro [071]
ECONOMETRIC REVIEWS – v3-. 1984- – 1,5,6,9 – us UMI [073]
ECONOMETRICA – v1-23. 1933-55 – 1,5,6 – us Princeton Micro [330]
ECONOMETRICA – v.1-44. 1933-76 – 9 – 24370.00; 249.00v – uk Dawson [330]
ECONOMETRICA – (v.47. 1979 5,6,9) – v.1. 1933 – 1 – us UMI [073]
LA ECONOMIA ARGENTINA : LAS ETAPAS DE SU DESARROLLO Y PROBLEMAS ACTUALES / Ferrer, Aldo – Buenos Aires: Fondo de Cultura Economica, 2nd ed 1965 – 1 – CSUXADP8826-B – us Hoover Inst Photo [330]
LA ECONOMIA ARGENTINA, 1952-1963 : LIBRE IMPRESA CAPITALISMO POPULAR Y COLONIALISMO. LA DINAMICA DEL RETROCESO ECONOMICO. CONTESTACION A PLEBISCH / Bledel, Rodolfo – Buenos Aires: Ediciones Mensu, 1963 – 1 – CSUXADM9672-B – us Hoover Inst Photo [330]
LA ECONOMIA ARGENTINA (1952-1972) : APLICACION CONSTANTE DE LA POLITICA DE "LIBRE EMPRESA," LA CONFESION DE PREBISCH / Bledel, Rodolfo – Buenos Aires: Juarez Editor, [1972] – 1 – CSUXAJA7169-B – us Hoover Inst Photo [330]
ECONOMIA E AGRICULTURA *see* BRASIL ACUCAREIRO
ECONOMIA MUNDIAL – Madrid. Spain. -w. 9 Aug 1941-29 Dec 1945. (9 reels) – 1 – uk British Libr Newspaper [330]
ECONOMIC ACCOUNTS FOR AGRICULTURE (PRODUCTION AND CAPITAL FORMATION) : 2ND ISSUE – 1979 – 319p – it F.A.O. [338]
THE ECONOMIC ACTIVITIES OF THE JEWS OF AMSTERDAM IN THE SEVENTEENTH AND EIGHTEENTH CENTURIES / Bloom, H I – Williamsport. 1937. BJ-262-8 1 – 9 – ne IDC [949]
ECONOMIC ANALYSIS OF FORESTRY PROJECTS. SUPPLEMENT : READINGS – 1980 – 222p – it F.A.O. [338]

ECONOMIC ANALYSIS OF THE INLAND FISHERIES PROJECT IN EL SALVADOR / International Center for Aquaculture – Jan 1974 – 1, 5 – us Spaulding [639]
THE ECONOMIC ANALYST / Virginia. Polytechnic Institute. College of Agriculture – 1957-60 – 1,5,6 – us Spaulding [338]
ECONOMIC AND ENERGY INDICATORS / U.S. Central Intelligence Agency – 1981-86 – 149mf – 9 – $190.00 – us Updata [330]
ECONOMIC AND HUMAN RIGHTS ASPECTS IGNORED BY MODERN AUTHORS / Beckerath, Ulrich von – To Dr. Mann, an extract, 29 Sept 1957. 1p – 9 – 1.00f – at Libertarian Micro [335]
ECONOMIC AND POLITICAL WEEKLY – Bombay, Il. 1973-1992 – 36r – $1,800.00 – R63571 – us Library Micro [072]
ECONOMIC AND POLITICAL WEEKLY – Bombay: Sameeksha Trust, [v6-15. 1971-1980] – 20r – us Res Libr [300]
ECONOMIC AND SOCIAL COUNCIL OFFICIAL RECORDS : SUPPLEMENTS AND SPECIAL SUPPLEMENTS / United Nations – (1st Sess. 1946. No supplement issued. 2nd Sess. 9th Sess.: E/ 1946-1949. E/F.109; 10th Sess. – 15th Sess.: E/ 1950-1953. E/F.14 E.53 F.53; 16th Sess. – 63rd Sess.: Year 1978 Year 1989. E/Year/ 1953-1988. E.1425 F.1470 S.1232) – 9 – us U.N. Pubs [324]
ECONOMIC AND SOCIAL COUNCIL OFFICIAL RECORDS *see*
– ANNEXES
– RESOLUTIONS AND DECISIONS
– SUMMARY RECORDS OF PLENARY MEETINGS
ECONOMIC AND SOCIAL DEVELOPMENT PLAN 1967-1971 / Japan. Economic Planning Agency – D-1108 1. 1967 – 9 – ne IDC [338]
ECONOMIC AND SOCIAL INVESTIGATIONS IN ENGLAND SINCE 1833 / The Manchester Statistical Society. Transactions – (Part 2: Transactions 1876; 1877-1900; 1901) – Part 1: The Papers 1833-43 and the Transactions 1853 54-1875 76 – 9 – us Primary [941]
ECONOMIC AND SOCIAL INVESTIGATIONS IN IRELAND : THE TRANSACTIONS OF THE DUBLIN SOCIAL INQUIRY AND STATISTICAL SOCIETY, 1847-1919 – 1 – us Primary [360]
ECONOMIC AND SOCIAL SURVEY FOR ASIA AND THE PACIFIC / United Nations – 175 fiches – 9 – 320.00; 1.90f – uk UNIMICRO [950]
ECONOMIC AND SOCIAL SURVEY FOR ASIA AND THE PACIFIC / United Nations – (1974. E/CN.11/. E.4 F.4; 1975-1988. E/ESCAP/. E.53 F.39; 1985-87 is not yet available in French) – 9 – us U.N. Pubs [330]
ECONOMIC ANNALIST – (Cont by: Canadian Farm Economics, 1966) – Ottawa. v1-35. 1931-65 – 9 – Can$20.00y – cn Micromedia [330]
ECONOMIC ANNALIST *see* CANADIAN FARM ECONOMICS
ECONOMIC ASPECTS OF SPECIAL EDUCATION : CZECHOSLOVAKIA, NEW ZEALAND, UNITED STATES OF AMERICA – 1978 – 152p – 9 – 92-3-101514-1 – fr UNESCO [370]
THE ECONOMIC ASPECTS OF THE HISTORY OF THE CIVILIZATION OF JAPAN / Takekoshi, Yosaburo – New York: Macmillan, 1930. 3v – 1 – us U.W. Library [330]
[ECONOMIC ASPECTS OF WORLD WAR 2 PAMPHLET COLLECTION] – 1935-1947 – 3r – 1 – CSUXANM9865-B – us Hoover Inst Photo [330]
ECONOMIC ASSESSMENT OF FORESTRY PROJECT IMPACTS – 1992 – 145p – it F.A.O. [634]
AN ECONOMIC BILL OF RIGHTS / Anderson, Martin – 1984. 5 points – 9 – 1.00f – at Libertarian Micro [320]
ECONOMIC BILL OF RIGHTS / Economic Civil Liberties Association – 4 points – 9 – 1.00f – at Libertarian Micro [320]
ECONOMIC BOTANY – 1- 1947- 1; v25- 5,6; v13- 9 – us UMI [631]
ECONOMIC BOTANY – v. 1-21. 1947-1967 – 1,5,6 – us Princeton Micro [631]
ECONOMIC BULLETIN – Accra: Economic Society of Ghana. [v1 n10-v6 n4. oct 1957-62] – us Res Libr [330]
ECONOMIC BULLETIN FOR AFRICA / United Nations – Vols 1-12, 1961-1976 – E.45 F.48 – 9 (E/CN.14/) – us U.N. Pubs [330]
ECONOMIC BULLETIN FOR AFRICA – v. 1-12. 1960-76 – 1 – us UMI [330]
ECONOMIC BULLETIN FOR LATIN AMERICA – v. 1-19. 1956-74 – 1 – us UMI [330]
ECONOMIC BULLETIN FOR LATIN AMERICA *see* CEPAL REVIEW
ECONOMIC BULLETIN OF GHANA – Accra: Economic Society of Ghana. [v7 n1. 1963] – us Res Libr [330]
Economic Civil Liberties Association *see* ECONOMIC BILL OF RIGHTS
THE ECONOMIC CONDITION OF CANADA AND HER TRADE POLICY / Cartwright, Richard – The writer of this letter is the Hon. Sir Richard Cartwright, a member of the Dominion Parliament of Canada: and who was Minister of Finance in the Mackenzie Administration from 1873 to 1878. Kingston, Ont.: 1892? 02549. (Pre-1900 Canadiana) – 9 – cn C.I.H.M. [971]
[ECONOMIC CONDITIONS IN TURKEY PAMPHLET COLLECTION] – 1914-1919 – 1 – CSUXANQ7451-B – us Hoover Inst Photo [330]
[ECONOMIC CONDITIONS IN YUGOSLAVIA PAMPHLET COLLECTION] – 1947-1979 – 1 – CSUXANQ5310-B – us Hoover Inst Photo [330]
ECONOMIC CONTROLS AND COMMERCIAL POLICY IN ARGENTINA / U.S. Tariff Commission – Washington, 1948 – 1 – CSUXADQ3373-B – us Hoover Inst Photo [337]
ECONOMIC COOPERATION AMONG DEVELOPING COUNTRIES IN AGRICULTURAL TRADE – 1987 – 210p – it F.A.O. [338]
ECONOMIC COOPERATION FOR AGRICULTURAL DEVELOPMENT IN THE NEAR EAST REGION – 1992 – 57p – it F.A.O. [338]
ECONOMIC DEVELOPMENT 1966-68 REVIEW AND TRENDS / Ceylon. Ministry of Planning and Economic Affairs – Colombo. 1967. BD-440 1 – 9 – ne IDC [338]
ECONOMIC DEVELOPMENT AND CULTURAL CHANGE – v1- 1952- 1; v19- 5,6; v26- 9 – us UMI [330]
ECONOMIC DEVELOPMENT IN JORDAN: FRAMEWORK AND TARGETS, 1960/1969 / Jordan. Development Bank – L. J. Zimmerman. BNE-8822 1 – 9 – ne IDC [338]
ECONOMIC DEVELOPMENT IN THE LIBYAN ARAB REPUBLIC, 1968-1971 / Libya. Bank of Libya – Tripoli. 1971. BNE-530 1 – 9 – ne IDC [338]
ECONOMIC DEVELOPMENT OF AMERICAN INDIANS AND ESKIMOS, 1930-1967 : A BIBLIOGRAPHY / Snodgrass, Marjorie P – 1968 – 9 – $5.00f – us Ross [970]
THE ECONOMIC DEVELOPMENT OF JORDAN; REPORT OF A MISSION ORGANIZED BY THE IBRD AT THE REQUEST OF THE GOVERNMENT OF JORDAN / International Bank for Reconstruction and Development (World Bank) – 1957. BNE-9793 1 – 9 – ne IDC [338]
THE ECONOMIC DEVELOPMENT OF MALTA, A REPORT CONTAINING A REVISION OF THE 5 YEAR DEVELOPMENT PROGRAMME, 1956/57 TO 1960/61 / Bruce, Colin – Valletta. Oct 1957. BD-1691 1 – 9 – ne IDC [338]
THE ECONOMIC DEVELOPMENT OF MOROCCO: REPORT OF A MISSION ORGANIZED BY IBRD / International Bank for Reconstruction and Development (World Bank) – 1966. BNE-3059 1 – 9 – ne IDC [338]
ECONOMIC DEVELOPMENT OF PAPUA AND NEW GUINEA / Papua-New Guinea. (Territory) – Port Moresby. 1967. BD-634 1 – 9 – ne IDC [338]
ECONOMIC DEVELOPMENT OF PUERTO RICO, 1940-1950, 1951-1960 / Puerto Rico – San Juan. 1951. BD-778 1 – 9 – ne IDC [338]
THE ECONOMIC DEVELOPMENT OF SYRIA; REPORT, 1947 / Gibb, Alexander – BNE-9702 1 – 9 – ne IDC [956]
ECONOMIC DEVELOPMENT PLAN, 1958-1967 / Syria. Economic Development Organisation – (Text in Arabic). Damascus. 1958 – 9 – ne IDC [338]
ECONOMIC DEVELOPMENT PLAN, 1968-1972 / Greece. Ministry of Economic Coordination – D-1086 1. 1967 – 9 – ne IDC [338]
ECONOMIC DEVELOPMENT PLAN FOR GREECE, 1968-1972 / Greece. Ministry of Coordination – Athens. 1968. BD-592 1 – 9 – ne IDC [338]
ECONOMIC DEVELOPMENT PROGRAMME FOR THE REPUBLIC OF SOUTH AFRICA, 1964-69 / South Africa. Department of Planning – Pretoria. 1964. BD-225 1 – 9 – ne IDC [338]
ECONOMIC DEVELOPMENT PROGRAMME FOR THE REPUBLIC OF SOUTH AFRICA, 1965-1970 / South Africa. Department of Planning – D 1474 1. 1965 – 9 – ne IDC [338]
ECONOMIC DEVELOPMENT PROGRAMME FOR THE REPUBLIC OF SOUTH AFRICA, 1966-71 / South Africa. Department of Planning – Pretoria. 1966. BD-392 1 – 9 – ne IDC [338]
ECONOMIC DEVELOPMENT PROGRAMME FOR THE REPUBLIC OF SOUTH AFRICA, 1968-1973 / South Africa. Department of Planning – Pretoria. 1968 – 9 – ne IDC [338]
ECONOMIC DEVELOPMENT PROGRAMME FOR THE REPUBLIC OF SOUTH AFRICA, 1972-1977 / South Africa. Department of Planning – Pretoria. 1972. BD-2020 1 – 9 – ne IDC [338]
ECONOMIC DEVELOPMENT PROGRAMME FOR THE REPUBLIC OF SOUTH AFRICA, 1974-1979 / South Africa. The Office of the Economic Adviser to the Prime Minister – BD-1850 1 – 9 – ne IDC [338]
ECONOMIC DEVELOPMENT REVIEW – v1-. 1983- – 1,5,6,9 – us UMI [338]
THE ECONOMIC EFFECTS OF GOVERNMENT ASSISTANCE IN COMMERCIAL RESORT DEVELOPMENT : A CASE STUDY OF FRENCH LICK, INDIANA / Isogawa, Hiroaki & Theobald, William F – 1990 – 2mf – 9 – $8.00 – us Microform Publ [790]
ECONOMIC ESSAYS ON THE SOCIALIST(SIC) ECONOMY OF INDONESIA / Mears, Leon A – SE-4362 1 – 9 – ne IDC [335]
ECONOMIC FACTS – Nanking and Chengtu, China. Jun 1936-Apr 1946 – 1 – 25.00 – us Chinese Res [330]
ECONOMIC GEOGRAPHY – 1-56 1925-80 1; v45- 5,6; v51- 9 – us UMI [910]
ECONOMIC GEOGRAPHY – v. 1-20. 1925-1944 – 1 – us Princeton Micro [910]
ECONOMIC GEOGRAPHY OF THE TRANSVAAL / Williams, Owen – Aberystwyth, Wales, 1950 – us Res Libr [330]
ECONOMIC GEOLOGY – v1-50. 1905-55 – 1 – us Princeton Micro [550]
ECONOMIC GEOLOGY AND THE BULLETIN OF THE SOCIETY OF ECONOMIC GEOLOGISTS – v1- 1905- 1; v65- 5,6; v70- 9 – us UMI [550]
ECONOMIC GUIDELINES FOR CROP PEST CONTROL – 1984 – 102p – it F.A.O. [630]
ECONOMIC HISTORY LIBRARY / Economisch-Historische Bibliotheek, Amsterdam – 101mf – 9 – ne IDC [330]
THE ECONOMIC HISTORY OF LIBERIA / Brown, George W – Washington, DC, Associated Publishers [c1941] – us Res Libr [330]
THE ECONOMIC HISTORY REVIEW – London, 1927-40. v.1-10 – 61mf – 9 – ne IDC [330]
THE ECONOMIC HISTORY REVIEW – series 1: v1-18 + index; series 2: v1-23 + index. 1927-70 – 7r – 1 – us Ross [330]
THE ECONOMIC IMPACT OF DEAN E. SMITH ACTIVITIES CENTER EVENTS ON CHAPEL HILL, NORTH CAROLINA / Applegate, Michael T & Muellor, Frederick O – 1993 – 2mf – $8.00 – us Microform Publ [330]
ECONOMIC INFORMATION FOR WISCONSIN FARMERS / Wisconsin. Agricultural Extension Service – v.1-30. Feb. 1929-Jun 1964 – 1,5 – us Spaulding [338]
ECONOMIC INFORMATION REPORT / Minnesota. College of Agriculture. Dept. of Agricultural and Applied Economics – R67-1 thru R73-3. 1967-73 – 1,5,6 – us Spaulding [338]
ECONOMIC INQUIRY – v. 12-. 1974- – 1,5,6,9 – us UMI [330]
ECONOMIC INVESTIGATIONS : RECORDS OF THE FEDERAL TRADE COMMISSION, PART 2 / U.S. Federal Trade Commission – Series A: The Petroleum Industry. 34 reels with printed guide – 1 – $3,300.00 – 0-89093-885-7 – us UPA [324]
ECONOMIC ISSUES : STUDIES AND ISSUE BRIEFS OF THE CONGRESSIONAL RESEARCH SERVICE, 1976-1982 / U.S. Congressional Research Service – $965.00 – 0-89093-508-4 – us UPA [330]
ECONOMIC JOURNAL – v1- 1891- 1; v81- 5,6; v85- 9 – us UMI [330]
ECONOMIC JOURNAL / Royal Economic Society – v. 1-57. 1891-1947 – 1 – us Princeton Micro [330]
ECONOMIC JOURNAL – v1-3. 1968-70. Colombo, Sri Lanka. -w – 1 – us U.W. Library [330]
ECONOMIC JOURNAL – v1-57. 1891-1947 – 1 – us Princeton Micro [330]
ECONOMIC JOURNAL – (v.1-58 244.50v; 9. v.59-85, index. v.1-40. 245.00v; WDS; 9) – v.1-85. With index v.1-40. 1891-1975 – 9 – 24360.00 – uk Dawson [330]
ECONOMIC LEAFLET / South Carolina. Agricultural Experiment Station. Clemson – n.1A-19. 1952-56 – 1,5 – us Spaulding [330]
ECONOMIC LIBERTY / Cox, Harold & Williams, Ernest E – 1920. indexed, 262p – 9 – 1.00f – at Libertarian Micro [330]
ECONOMIC MONTHLY REVIEW / Libya. Bank of Libya – 1961. Monthly Economic Bulletin. 1962-66. Economic Bulletin. 1967-73. Statistical Supplement 1967. Lacking: v. 5 (7, 8) 1965; v. 10 (4) 1970; v. 12 (5, 6) 1972. BNE-626 1 – 9 – ne IDC [336]
ECONOMIC NOTES – Libertarian Alliance, London. Nos.1-5,9-10, 14p – 9 – 1.00f – at Libertarian Micro [335]
ECONOMIC OBSERVER – Karachi, Pakistan. -w. Jan 1951-Feb 1956. 2 reels – 1 – uk British Libr Newspaper [072]
THE ECONOMIC ORGANISATION OF AGRICULTURAL PRODUCTION IN WEST AFRICA / La-Anyane, Seth – London, 1951 – us Res Libr [338]
ECONOMIC ORGANISATION OF YAM MARKETING IN GHANA / Nyanteng, V K – Legon, 1969 – us Res Libr [650]
ECONOMIC ORIGINS OF JEFFERSONIAN DEMOCRACY / Beard, Charles A – New York: Macmillan, 1915 – 6mf – 9 – $9.00 – LLMC 95-074 – us L.L.M.C. [323]
ECONOMIC PAPERS PRESENTED AT SECOND NATIONAL SCIENTIFIC CONGRESS OF INDONESIA BY ECONOMIC FACULTY, UNIV. OF INDONESIA / Mears, Leon A – SE-3711 1. 1963 – 9 – ne IDC [330]
ECONOMIC PERSPECTIVES – v. 1- 1977- – 1,5,6,9 – us UMI [330]
ECONOMIC PLANS / Paraguay – (Departemento Nacional de Prensa y Propaganda. Plan Quinquennal 1943-1948 De Reconstruccion Nacional. D-1423; 1. 1944. SF 8.00; 9. Presidencia de la Republica. Plan Nacional De Desarrollo Economico Y Social Para El Bienio 1965-1966. D-1151; 1. 2 v. 1965. SF 31.00; IDC; 9. Secretaria Tecnica de Planificacion. Plan Nacional De Desarrollo Economico Y Social, Bieno 1967-1968. D-1424; 1. 1966. SF 41.00; IDC; 9. Secretaria Tecnica de Planificacion. Plan Nacional De Desarrollo Economico 1971-1975. D-1152; 1. 2 v. 1970. SF 14.00; IDC; 9) – ne IDC [338]
ECONOMIC PLANS / Portuguese Guinea. (Portugal) – (Plano Intecalar De Fomento Para 1965-1967. D 1443; 1. 1964. SF 8.00; 9. II Plano De Fomento Para 1959-1964. D 1163; 1. 1959. SF 8.00; IDC; 9. III Plano De Fomento Para 1968-1973. D-1164; 1. 1968. SF 10.00; IDC; 9) – ne IDC [338]
ECONOMIC PLANS / Surinam – (Aanvullend Opbouwplan Suriname, 1962-1966. D 1484; 1. 1961. SF 12,00; 9. Stichting Planbureau Suriname. Grondslagen Van Een Tienjarenplan Voor Suriname, 1953-1962. D 1482; 1. 1952. SF 12.00; IDC; 9. Stichting Planbureau Suriname. Raamwerk Integraal Opbouwplan Suriname, 1963-1972.m D 1485; 1. 1963. SF 16.00; IDC; 9. Stichting Planbureau. Tweede Vijfjarenplan 1972-1976. D 1524; 1. 1972. SF 14.00; IDC; 9. Surinam Planning Bureau. Ten year plan for surinam. Revised programme. D 1483; 1. 1955-1964. SF 10.00; IDC; 9) – ne IDC [338]
ECONOMIC PLANS / Tanzania – (Annual plan for 1971-1972. D 1540; 1. 1971. SF 10.00; 9. Economic survey and annual plan 1970-1971. D 1488; 1. 1970. SF 12.00; IDC; 9. Five year plan for economic and social development, 1st July, 1964-30 June, 1969. D 1214; 1. 2 v. 1964. SF 18.00; IDC; 9. Min. of Econ. Aff. and Dev. Plan. The people's plan for progr. – a popul. vers. of the 2nd five year plan for econ. and soc. dev., 1969-1974. D 890; 1. 1969. SF 8.00; IDC; 9. Proposals on the recommendation of the special presidential committee of enquiry into cooperative movement and marketing

boards. A 733; 2. 1966. SF 10.00; IDC; 8) – ne IDC [338]

ECONOMIC PLANS / Timor – (Ministerios da Economia e do Ultramar. Plano De Fomento 1953-1958. D 1216; 1. 1953. SF 8.00; 9. 2nd Plano De Fomento 1959-1964. D 1218; 1. 1959. SF 8.00; IDC; 9. Presidencia do Conselho. Plano Intercalar De Fomento Para 1965-1967. D 1493; 1. 1964. SF 8.00; IDC; 9. Presidencia do Conselho. 3rd Plano De Fomento Para 1968-1973. D 1219; 1. 1968. SF 8.00; IDC; 9) – ne IDC [338]

[ECONOMIC POLICY IN BULGARIA PAMPHLET COLLECTION] – 1916-1933 – 1 – CSUXANL7411-B – us Hoover Inst Photo [330]

ECONOMIC PREJUDICES / Guyot, Yves – 1910. 173p. Together with: Education, by Herbert Spencer. 187p. 1 fiche (24x) – 9 – 1.00f – at Libertarian Micro [320]

ECONOMIC PROBLEMS OF INDUSTRY AND MINING / Husein, Kartasasmita – SE-3445 1. 1960 – 9 – ne IDC [338]

ECONOMIC PROGRAM, 1963-1966 – Reykjavik. 1963. BD-404 1 – 9 – ne IDC [338]

ECONOMIC RECORD – v26- 1950- 1; v52- 5,6,9 – us UMI [330]

ECONOMIC RESEARCH SERVICE / U.S. Department of Agriculture – v1-679. 1961-83. 735 fiches – 9 – 770.00 – us Updata [324]

ECONOMIC RESEARCH SERVICE-FOREIGN / U.S. Department of Agriculture – v1-395. 1961-74. 440 fiches – 9 – 450.00 – us Updata [324]

ECONOMIC REVIEW – v1- 1948- 1; 1977- 5,6,9 – us UMI [330]

ECONOMIC REVIEW / Federal Reserve Bank of Richmond – 1976- – 1 – us UMI [073]

ECONOMIC REVIEW / Federal Reserve Bank of San Francisco – 1977- – 1 – us UMI [073]

ECONOMIC REVIEW / Israel. Bank of Israel. Research Department – Jerusalem. 1955-. Up to no. 33, Apr 1970 appeared as Bank of Israel Bulletin – 9 – 90.00; 4.00y – is I.T.T.I. [330]

ECONOMIC REVIEW / National Institute. London – no. 1-62. 1959-72 – 9 – 2480.00; 6.00v – uk Dawson [330]

ECONOMIC REVIEW OF INDONESIA – Djakarta, 1947-1953 – 30mf – 9 – ne IDC [330]

ECONOMIC REVIEW OF THE BANK NEGARA INDONESIA – (Monthly. Missing: 1967(8)) – Djakarta, 1966-1972 – 32mf – 9 – SE-1334/1 – ne IDC [332]

ECONOMIC REVIEW-FEDERAL RESERVE BANK OF DALLAS – (1986-. 1,5,6) – 1976- – 9 – us UMI [332]

ECONOMIC SELECTIONS: AN INTERNATIONAL BIBLIOGRAPHY – 1969- – 1,5,9 – us Gordon [330]

ECONOMIC SELF-SUPPORT 5-YEAR PLAN, DECIDED BY THE CABINET MEETING ON 23 DECEMBER 1955 / Japan. Economic Planning Board – 2v. Tokyo. 1955. BD-692 1 – 9 – ne IDC [338]

ECONOMIC SIGNIFICANCE OF TOBACCO – 1989 – 34p – it F.A.O. [338]

ECONOMIC SOCIETY BULLETIN – Accra: Economic Society of Ghana. [v1 n1-9. jan-sep 1957] – us Res Libr [330]

ECONOMIC SOPHISMS / Bastiat, Frederic – Trans. by P.J. Sterling, 1873, 240p – 9 – 1.00f – at Libertarian Micro [335]

ECONOMIC STABILIZATION AS AN ESSENTIAL CONDITION FOR EFFECTIVE ECONOMIC DEVELOPMENT / Sadli, Mohammad – In Indonesian. SE 4958 1. Inaugural speech Aug. 31, 1963 – 9 – ne IDC [338]

THE ECONOMIC STATUS OF BLACK WOMEN : AN EXPLORATORY INVESTIGATION / U.S. Commission on Civil Rights – Washington: GPO, 1990. LLMC 94-334 – 2mf – 9 – $3.00 – us L.L.M.C. [300]

ECONOMIC STRUCTURE AND DEVELOPMENT PROSPECTS OF THE WEST BANK AND THE GAZA STRIP / Ben-Shachar, C – (Rand Corporation). 1971 – 9 – ne IDC [338]

ECONOMIC STUDIES / Bagehot, Walter; ed by Holt Hutton, Richard – London: Longmans, Green, 1880 – 1 roll – 1 – 1-55879-821-8 – uk Libr Preservation [330]

ECONOMIC STUDY REPORT / Minnesota. College of Agriculture. Dep't. of Agricultural and Applied Economics – S68-1 thru S73-1. 1968-73 – 1,5,6 – us Spaulding [330]

ECONOMIC SURVEY / Gosudarstvennyi Bank. S.S.S.R. – v.1 7. Jul 1926-May 1932 9 reels – 1 – 22.00 – us L of C Photodup [330]

ECONOMIC SURVEY : STATE BANK OF THE U.S.S.R. – (Includes c.1: 1927:Sept.30-1932:May) – Moscow: The Bank, 1927-1932. 6v – 1 – CSUXAKZ1303-S – us Hoover Inst Photo [332]

ECONOMIC SURVEY AND DEVELOPMENT PLAN / Grenada – D-1314 1. 1960-1964 – 9 – ne IDC [338]

ECONOMIC SURVEY FOR ASIA AND THE FAR EAST / United Nations – 1948-1973 – E.141 F.161 – 9 (E/CN.11/) – us U.N. Pubs [330]

ECONOMIC SURVEY (MOSCOV, R.S.F.S.R.: 1927) *see* ECONOMIC SURVEY

ECONOMIC SURVEY OF LATIN AMERICA / United Nations – 184 fiches – 9 – 360.00; 1.90f – uk UNIMICRO [330]

ECONOMIC SURVEY OF LATIN AMERICA / United Nations – (1948-1958; 1963-1973. E/CN.12/. E.117 S.126; 1974-1979. E/CEPAL/. E.55 S.56; Not issued as sales publications for the years 1959-1962) – 9 – us U.N. Pubs [330]

ECONOMIC SURVEY OF LATIN AMERICA AND THE CARIBBEAN / United Nations – (1980-1981. E/CEPAL/. E.28 S.28; 1982-1988. LC/G. E.89 S.92; 1986 is not yet available in Spanish; 1988 is not yet available in English) – 9 – us U.N. Pubs [330]

ECONOMIC SURVEY OF SIERRA LEONE / Jack, D T – Freetown: Govt Printing Office, 1958 – us Res Libr [330]

AN ECONOMIC SURVEY OF THE COLONIAL TERRITORIES / Great Britain. Colonial Office – 7v. 1951-55 – 1r – 1 – us Ross [330]

ECONOMIC SURVEY-REFERENCE MATERIAL AND REPORTS-MIDDLE RIO GRANDE CONSERVANCY DISTRICT / New Mexico State University. Agricultural Extension Service – May 1936. 1 reel – 1,5 – us Spaulding [333]

ECONOMIC SYSTEMS RESEARCH – 1989- 5v – 9 – £205.00 – 0953-5314 – uk Carfax [330]

ECONOMIC TIMES – Bombay, India. 1962-Aug 1977; 1978 – 57r – 1 – us L of C Photodup [072]

ECONOMIC TRADE-OFFS BETWEEN MILK AND MEAT PRODUCTION UNDER VARIOUS SUPPLEMENTATION LEVELS IN BOTSWANA / Konandreas, P A et al – 1983 – 9 – $10.00 – 92-9053-114-2 – et ILRI [338]

ECONOMIC VALUE OF BREAST-FEEDING – 1979 – 97p – it F.A.O. [640]

ECONOMIC WEEK – v1- 1973- 1,5,6; v3- 1975- 9 – us UMI [330]

ECONOMIC WEEKLY – (Missing: 1949/1950, v1-2; 1965, v17(16-20, 24, 25, 38)) – Bombay, 1949-1965. v1-17 – 810mf – I-111/2 – ne IDC [330]

ECONOMIC WITNESS – Australian Institute for Public Policy. 22 May 1985, 8p – 9 – 1.00f – at Libertarian Micro [330]

ECONOMIC WORLD : A WEEKLY JOURNAL OF INSURANCE, INDUSTRY, COMMERCE AND FINANCE – New York. 1866-1926 – 27r – 1 – us Ross [330]

ECONOMIC X-RAY – Singapore. -w. 7 Jun 1937-30 Sep 1941. (3 reels) – 1 – uk British Libr Newspaper [073]

ECONOMICA – n.s. v. 1-40, no. 1-160. 1934-73. London – 9 – 24200.00; 5.00v – uk Dawson [330]

ECONOMICA – orig. s. v. 1-13, no. 1-42. 1921-33. London – 9 – 2465.00; 5.00v – uk Dawson [330]

ECONOMICA Y DESARROLLO – Havana, CU. 1968-1970 – 13r – $650.00 – R04200 – us Library Micro [072]

ECONOMICS : AN INTRODUCTORY ANALYSIS / Samuelson, Paul A – In Indonesian. SE 11,437/1. 1964? – 9 – ne IDC [330]

ECONOMICS AND FINANCE: INDEX TO PERIODICAL ARTICLES, 1947-71 / International Monetary Fund and World Bank. Library – 1972.-Approx. 101,000 entries 8 reels.-ISBN: 0-8161-1297-5 – 1 – $555.00 – uk Hall [332]

ECONOMICS COLLECTION / Bibliotheque Nationale – 14 diverse titles including 18th cent. essays on riches and resources of France; the poor tax; commerce with French colonies; rise and fall of the Bank of France; gold and silver rates in 1864; effect of population growth on economic scene, etc. 30 fiches. Titles available separately – 9 – 74.00 – fr Bibl Nationale [330]

ECONOMICS FOR HEALTH / Belloc, Hilaire – 1924. 246p. 1 fiche (24x) – 9 – 1.00f – at Libertarian Micro [320]

ECONOMICS INFORMATION REPORT / North Carolina. State University. Raleigh. Dept. of Economics – v.1-13. Jan 1967-Nov 19? – 1,5 – us Spaulding [630]

ECONOMICS INFORMATION REPORT / North Carolina State University.Department of Economics – No.13-68. 1969-82 – 1,5 – us Spaulding [330]

ECONOMICS INFORMATION REPORT / University of Florida. Agricultural Experiment Station.Food and Resource Economics Department – No.1-175. 1975-82. 75 fiches – 9 – us Spaulding [630]

ECONOMICS LETTERS – v1-16. 1978-84 – 1,5,6,13 – sz Elsevier [330]

ECONOMICS MADE EASY / Maxwell, Joclyn – 1fiche (29x) – 9 – 1.00f – at Libertarian Micro [320]

ECONOMICS OF ANIMAL BY-PRODUCTS UTILIZATION – 1989 – 74p – it F.A.O. [338]

ECONOMICS OF BOOK PUBLISHING IN DEVELOPING COUNTRIES / Smith, Datus C – 2nd impr 1982 – 9 – 92-3-101422-6 – fr UNESCO [070]

ECONOMICS OF EDUCATION REVIEW – v3- 1984- – 5,6,9 – us UMI [073]

THE ECONOMICS OF HERBERT SPENCER / Owen, W C – 1891. 256p. 1 fiche (24x) – 9 – $1.00f – at Libertarian Micro [330]

ECONOMICS OF INNOVATION AND NEW TECHNOLOGY / ed by Swann, Peter et al – 9,5,1 – us Harwood [330]

ECONOMICS OF JESUS, OR, WORK AND WAGES IN THE KINGDOM OF GOD / Griffith-Jones, Ebenezer – Cincinnati: Jennings & Graham, (1905). 1 fiche – 9 – us A.T.L.A. [240]

ECONOMICS OF NEW EDUCATIONAL MEDIA – 9 – fr UNESCO [370]

THE ECONOMICS OF RAPID GROWTH. MIDDLE EAST JOURNAL / Mallakh, R. El – v. 23 (3). Washington. Summer 1969. BNE-622 1 – 9 – ne IDC [330]

ECONOMICS REPORT / University of Florida. Agricultural Experiment Station.Food and Resource Economics Department – No.1-106. 1969-82. 62 fiches – 9 – us Spaulding [338]

ECONOMICS RESEARCH REPORT / North Carolina State University.Department of Economics – No.1-42.1967-82. 28 fiches – 9 – us Spaulding [338]

L'ECONOMIE DE GUERRE DANS LES ETATS DE SYRIE ET DU LIBAN / Leduc, G – Rapport presente a la Conference financiere du Moyen-Orient, Le Caire, 24-29 avril, 1944. 1944. BNE-9710 1 – 9 – ne IDC [350]

L'ECONOMIE DE L'ALGERIE : SOUS-DEVELOPPEMENT ET POLITIQUE DE CROISSANCE / Gendarme, R – F60.00 – fr Ethnologie [338]

ECONOMIE ET HUMANISME – Lyon. Red. en chef, R. Delprat.1942-85 – 1 – fr A.C.R.P.P. [073]

ECONOMIE ET PLAN DE DEVELOPPEMENT / Cameroon – 2e Ed. Paris, Ministere de la Cooperation. 1965. BD-614 1 – 9 – ne IDC [338]

ECONOMIE ET PLAN DE DEVELOPPEMENT / Central African Republic – Paris, Ministere de la Cooperation. 1963. BD-477 1 – 9 – ne IDC [338]

ECONOMIE ET PLAN DE DEVELOPPEMENT / Chad – Paris, Ministere de la Cooperation. 1963. BD-479 1 – 9 – ne IDC [338]

ECONOMIE ET PLAN DE DEVELOPPEMENT / Dahomey – Paris. (Ministere de la Cooperation). 1962. BD-607 1 – 9 – ne IDC [338]

ECONOMIE ET PLAN DE DEVELOPPEMENT / France. Ministere de la Cooperation – Paris. Ministere de la Cooperation. 1963 – 9 – ne IDC [330]

ECONOMIE ET PLAN DE DEVELOPPEMENT / Gabon – Paris, Ministere de la Cooperation. 1963. BD-474 1 – 9 – ne IDC [338]

ECONOMIE ET PLAN DE DEVELOPPEMENT / Malagasy Republic – Paris, Ministere de la Cooperation. 1963 – 9 – ne IDC [338]

ECONOMIE ET PLAN DE DEVELOPPEMENT / Mauritania – 2e Ed. Paris, Ministere de la Cooperation. 1963. BD-606 1 – 9 – ne IDC [338]

ECONOMIE ET PLAN DE DEVELOPPEMENT / Rwanda – Paris, Ministere de la Cooperation. 1963. BD-625 1 – 9 – ne IDC [338]

ECONOMIE ET PLAN DE DEVELOPPEMENT / Senegal – Paris, Ministere de la Cooperation. 1964 – 9 – ne IDC [338]

ECONOMIE ET PLAN DE DEVELOPPEMENT / Upper Volta – Paris, Ministere de la Cooperation. 1963 – 9 – ne IDC [338]

ECONOMIE ET PLAN DE DEVELOPPEMENT, 3EME ED / Congo. (Brazzaville) – Paris. Ministere de la Cooperation. 1965. BD-608 1 – 9 – ne IDC [338]

ECONOMIE ET PLAN DE DEVELOPPEMENT, REPUBLIQUE TOGOLAISE / Togo – 2e Ed. Paris, Ministere de la Cooperation. 1965. BD-582 1 – 9 – ne IDC [338]

ECONOMIE ET PLAN ET DEVELOPPEMENT / Mali – 2e ed Paris, Ministere de la Cooperation. 1965 – 9 – ne IDC [338]

ECONOMIE ET PREVISIONS – 1992-1995 – 12 times per yr – 9 – F1,920.00 – sz Infoprint [330]

L'ECONOMIE IVOIRIENNE / Ivory Coast – Ed. 1. 1970. BD-1562 1 – 9 – ne IDC [339]

L'ECONOMIE MARAICHERE ET FRUITIERE DANS LA REGION DU CAP-VERT, GRANDE BANLIEUE DE DAKAR / Arnaud, Jean-Claude – (Africa series). 1970 – 9 – fr Hachette [338]

L'ECONOMIE MAROCAINE EN 1968 / Morocco – Casablanca. 1969. BNE-3108 1 – 9 – ne IDC [339]

ECONOMIE POLITIQUE CHRETIENNE, OU RECHERCHES SUR LA NATURE ET LES CAUSES DU PAUPERISME EN FRANCE ET EN EUROPE, ET SUR LES MOYENS DE LE SOULAGER ET DE LE PREVENIR / Villeneuve-Bargemont, Alban de – (Condition of 19th C. French working class series). 1834 – 9 – fr Hachette [320]

ECONOMISCH EN SOCIAAL TIJDSCHRIFT – v. 30-. 1976- – 1,5,6,9 – us UMI [330]

ECONOMISCH EXPANSIEPROGRAMMA, 1961-1965 / Belgium. Ministere des Affaires Economiques – Brussel. 1961. BD-360 1 – 9 – ne IDC [338]

ECONOMISCH WEEKBLAD VOOR NEDERLANDSCH-INDIE – (Preceded by KORTE BERICHTEN VOOR LANDBOUW, NIJVERHEID EN HANDEL. Buitzenzorg, 1910-32. v.1-22) – Batavia, 1932-51. '(1943-45 have not been published)'. Lacking: 1951. v.17(11,20,21) – 1329mf – 9 – ne IDC [072]

ECONOMISCHE OPSTELLEN UIT DE INHEEMSCHE PERS – No. 1, Jan.-Dec., 1937. Batavia, (1938) – 3mf – 9 – ne IDC [333]

Economisch-Historische Bibliotheek *see* ALFABETISCHE CATALOGUS

Economisch-Historische Bibliotheek, Amsterdam *see* ECONOMIC HISTORY LIBRARY

ECONOMIST – A Periodical Paper Explanatory of the New System of Society Projected by Robert Owen. 1-2 (all publ). 1821-1822 – 10mf – 9 – $65.00 – us UPA [330]

ECONOMIST – Aurora. Ill. 1940-44; 1949-57 – 1 – us UMI [071]

ECONOMIST – (v. 246- 1973- 5,6. v. 238- 1971- 9) – v. 1- 1843- – 1 – us UMI [073]

THE ECONOMIST – Hawkesbury, Ontario. v1 n39. 23 dec 1858 – 1+ r – 1 – Can$25.00r – cn Can Microfilming [072]

THE ECONOMIST – London. -w. 1843-49. (12 reels) – 1 – uk British Libr Newspaper [330]

THE ECONOMIST – The case for free trade, 1929. Rev. for and issued by The North-Western Free-Trade Union, Manchester. 46p – 9 – 1.00f – at Libertarian Micro [330]

THE ECONOMIST – Toronto, Canada. Apr 1914-Dec 1921.-w. 2mqn reels – 1 – uk British Libr Newspaper [072]

THE ECONOMIST – Toronto: Economist Print and Pub Co, [1897?-19–] – 9 – cn C.I.H.M. [330]

ECONOMIST AND SUN – Markham, 1947-1977 – 34r – 1 – cn Preston [971]

ECONOMIST NEWSPAPERS: AUBURN COMMUNITY BOOSTER – Chicago. Ill. 1915-1921; 1922-1923. Englewood Economist. 1907-1924. Englewood Times. 1905-1924 – 1 – us UMI [071]

EL ECONOMISTA – (El Economista confidencial). Madrid. Spain. -w. 18 Oct 1958-31 Dec 1960. (Imperfect). (5 reels) – 1 – uk British Libr Newspaper [330]

L'ECONOMISTE CANADIEN-FRANCAIS – Montreal: [s.n., 1900?-19–?] – 9 – cn C.I.H.M. [330]

ECONOMISTE DE L'EST – Montreal. v2 n11. 29 nov 1962; v4 n5. 19 mai 1965 – 1r – 1 – Can$25.00 – cn Can Microfilming [072]

L'ECONOMISTE EUROPEEN – Paris. v1-3. 1892-Jun 1952 – 1 – us NY Public [330]
ECONOMISTE EUROPEEN – Paris. v1-111. 1892-1952 – 36r – 1 – us Ross [330]
L'ECONOMISTE HAITIEN – Port-au-Prince: Francois Dalencour. [v1 n2. jan/feb 1940] – 1r – 9 – us Res Libr [072]
ECONOMISTS' PAPERS : SERIES 1: THE PAPERS OF WILLIAM STANLEY JEVONS, 1835-1882 FROM THE JOHN RYLANDS UNIVERSITY LIBRARY OF MANCHESTER – (Guide included) – Marlborough: Adam Matthew Publications, 1991 – 25r – 1 – $2,950.00 – uk Matthew [330]
ECONOMISTS' PAPERS : SERIES 2: THE PAPERS OF JOHN NEVILLE KEYNES, 1864-1917 FROM CAMBRIDGE UNIVERSITY LIBRARY – (Guide included) – Marlborough: Adam Matthew Publications, 1991 – 12r – 1 – $1,450.00 – uk Matthew [330]
ECONOMISTS' PAPERS : SERIES 3: THE PAPERS OF CARL MENGER, 1840-1921 FROM THE WILLIAM R. PERKINS LIBRARY, DUKE UNIVERSITY – (A single guide accompanies Pts 1 and 2) – Marlborough: Adam Matthew Publications, 1996 – 2pts ca 42r – 1 – $2,500.00 ea – uk Matthew [330]
ECONOMISTS' PAPERS : SERIES 4: THE PAPERS OF NASSAU WILLIAM SENIOR, 1790-1864 – (Pt 1: Lectures on Political Economy, Correspondence and Papers 19r. Pt 2: The Complete Manuscript Journals 19r. A single guide accompanies Pts 1 and 2) – Marlborough: Adam Matthew Publications, 1997 – 2pts 38r – 1 – $2,300.00 – uk Matthew [330]
ECONOMY – (Ceased v14 no 1 1991) – Toronto. v7-14. 1984-1991 – 9 – Can$20.00y – cn Micromedia [330]
THE ECONOMY OF INDONESIA WITHIN THE LAST 150 YEARS, 1800-1950 / Sonda, Amir – In English. SE 10,973 1. 1963? – 9 – ne IDC [338]
ECONOMY OF SYRIA IN FACTS AND FIGURES / Syria. Directorate-General of Information – 1957. BNE-9698 1 – 9 – ne IDC [330]
THE ECONOMY OF THE CENTRAL BAROTSE PLAIN / Gluckman, M – 7 – uk Microform Academic [960]
ECONOSCOPE – Montreal. v1-17. 1977-1993/94 – 9 – Can$20.00y – cn Micromedia [330]
ECOS DE BAEPENDI – Baependi, 23 Dec 1961; May 1965; Jul, 5 Sep 1966 – 1,5,6 – bl Biblioteca [072]
ECOS DEL PARAISO / Sanchez-Arjona, Vicente – Sevilla: Imp. Alvarez, Tomo 1. 1955 – 1 – sp Bibl Santa Ana [810]
ECOS DEL PARAISO / Sanchez-Arjona, Vicente – Sevilla: Imp. Carlos Acuna, Tomo 3. 1955 – 1 – sp Bibl Santa Ana [810]
ECOS DEL PARAISO / Sanchez-Arjona, Vicente – Sevilla: Imprenta Alvarez, Tomo 2. 1955 – 1 – sp Bibl Santa Ana [810]
ECOS JUVENIS : ORGAO DAS ALUNAS DO COLEGIO N.S. AUXILIADORA – Campo Grande, 29 Nov 1936; Out 1939 – 1,5,6 – bl Biblioteca [072]
ECOS PERDIDOS / Diaz Perez, Nicolas – Poesias varias. 1881 – 9 – 1.50f – sp Bibl Santa Ana [810]
ECOSOC ECONOMIC AND SOCIAL COUNCIL / United Nations – (Official Records. 2800 fiches. 5400.00, 1.90f; 9. General distribution meeting documents. 10,000 fiches. 17,000.00; 1.90f; UNM; 9) – uk UNIMICRO [330]
ECOSOCIAL SYSTEMS AND ECOPOLITICS : A READER ON HUMAN AND SOCIAL IMPLICATIONS OF ENVIRONMENTAL MANAGEMENT IN DEVELOPING COUNTRIES / ed by Deutsch, Karl – 1977 – 368p – 9 – 92-3-101450-1 – fr UNESCO [360]
LES ECOSSAIS EN FRANCE – LES FRANCAIS EN ECOSSE / Francisque-Michel – Londres, 1862. 2v – 1r – 1 – Can$50.00 – cn Can Microfilming [940]
ECOTASS – 5,6,9 – us UMI [073]
L'ECOUTEUR AUX PORTES – no. 1-2. Paris. oct 1789 – 1 – fr A.C.R.P.P. [073]
ECRIN DE LA JEUNESSE – Montreal: Librairie St. Joseph; Cadieux Derome, 1885. SEM105P29 – 9 – Can$4.50 – cn Bibl Nat [240]
L'ECRIN LITTEA1RAIRE – Montreal, Canada. 27 nov 1892-22 jan 1893 – 1r – 1 – Can$25.00 – cn Can Microfilming [790]
LES ECRITS DE MONSEIGNEUR ARTHUR ROBERT, P.A., V.G. : BIBLIOGRAPHIE ANALYTIQUE / Trottier, Guy N – 1955. SEM105P4 – 3mf – 9 – cn Bibl Nat [240]
LES ECRITS DE SAINT PAUL – New trans. with introd. and notes by Henri Delafosse. Paris: F. Rieder, 1926-28. In French – 1 – us U.W. Library [240]
ECRITS DES CURES DE PARIS CONTRE LA POLITIQUE ET LA MORALE DES JESUITES (1656) AVEC UNE ETUDE SUR LA QUERELLE DU LAXISME / ed by Recalde, I de – 1921 – 1 – us A.T.L.A. [240]
LES ECRITS FRANCAIS – Dir. L. de Monti de Reze, M. Bresil, L. de Gonzague, Frick. no. spec. de nov 1913, no. 1-5. Paris. dec 1913-avr 1914 – 1 – fr A.C.R.P.P. [800]
LES ECRITS NOUVEAUX – Paris. nov 1917-22. devenu: La Revue europeenne voir a ce titre – 1 – fr A.C.R.P.P. [800]
ECRITS POUR L'ART – Fond. Gaston Dubedat. Paris. 1887-92, avr 1905 – 1 – fr A.C.R.P.P. [073]
ECRITS POUR L'ART – Paris, 1887 – 1r – 1 – £60.00 – uk Chadwyck [700]
ECRITS POUR L'ART: FLORICULTURE, ART DECORATIF, NOTICES D'EXPOSITION, 1884-1889 / Galle, Emile – Paris: H. Laurens, 1908 – 4mf, vi/382p – 9 – 10.00 – fr Bibl Nationale [740]
ECRITS SUR LA BIENHEUREUSE MARGUERITE BOURGEOIS, 1945-1962 : BIBLIOGRAPHIE ANALYTIQUE / Sainte-Zelia, Soeur – 1962 [i.e. 1963]. SEM105P4 – 3mf – 9 – cn Bibl Nat [240]
ECRITURE MAYA : LECTURE ET TRADUCTION DE KNOROZOV / Ermakoff, V – 6mf – 9 – F90.00 – fr Ethnologie [306]
LES ECRIVAINS FRANCO-RUSSES. BIBLIOGRAPHIE DES OUVRAGES FRANCAIS PUBLIES PAR DES RUSSES / Gennadi, G – (Russia-19th C. series). 1874 – 9 – fr Hachette [010]
LES ECRIVAINS JUIFS FRANCAIS DU 14 SIECLE / Renan, M E & Neubauer, A – Paris, 1893 – 13mf – ne IDC [470]
Ecroyd, William Farrer *see* THE POLICY OF SELF HELP: SUGGESTIONS TOWARDS THE CONSOLIDATION OF THE EMPIRE AND THE DEFENCE OF ITS INDUSTRIES AND COMMERCE: TWO LETTERS
ECSTASY : THE RELEASE OF THE SOUL FROM THE BODY / Crookall, Robert – 1st ed. Moradabad: Darshana International, 1973 – us Res Libr [140]
ECTJ : A JOURNAL OF THEORY, RESEARCH AND DEVELOPMENT – v26- 1978- – 1,5,6,9 – us UMI [380]
ECTJ – EDUCATIONAL AND TECHNOLOGY JOURNAL *see* AV COMMUNICATION REVIEW
ECUADOR : ANUARIO DE ESTADISTICA 1963/68-1966/71 / Ecuador. Instituto Nacional de Estadistica – (1966/77 not available. Coll title: Latin American and Caribbean Official Statistical Serials, 1821-1982) – 13mf – 9 – £7.00f (set £300.00 36mf) – uk Chadwyck [972]
ECUADOR : ECUADOR EN CIFRAS 1938-1942 / Ecuador. Direccion General de Estadistica – (Coll title: Latin American and Caribbean Official Statistical Serials, 1821-1982) – 6mf – 9 – £7.00f (set £300.00 36mf) – uk Chadwyck [972]
ECUADOR : SINTESIS ESTADISTICA DEL ECUADOR 1955/60-1955/62 / Ecuador. Direccion de Estadistica y Censos – (Coll title: Latin American and Caribbean Official Statistical Serials, 1821-1982) – 5mf – 9 – £7.00f (set £300.00 36mf) – uk Chadwyck [972]
Ecuador *see*
- GACETA DEL GOBIERNO DEL ECUADOR
- REGISTRO OFICIAL

Ecuador. Direccion de Estadistica y Censos *see* ECUADOR
Ecuador. Direccion General de Estadistica *see* ECUADOR
Ecuador. Instituto Nacional de Estadistica *see* ECUADOR
Ecuador. Junta Nacional de Planificacion y Coordinacion Economica *see*
- BASES Y DIRECTIVAS PARA PROGRAMMAR EL DESARROLLO ECONOMICO (1955-1965)
- LINEAMIENTOS FUNDAMENTALES DEL PLAN INTEGRAL DE TRANSFORMACION Y DESARROLLO 1973-1977
- PLAN GENERAL DE DESARROLLO ECONOMICO Y SOCIAL
- POLITICA PLANIFICADA PARA EL DESARROLLO RESUMEN DEL PLAN GENERAL DE DESARROLLO ECONOMICO Y SOCIAL
- RESUMEN DEL PLAN GENERAL DE DESARROLLO ECONOMICO Y SOCIAL DEL ECUADOR 1964-1973; VERSION PRELIMINAR

Ecuador. Ministerio de Economia *see* PLAN DE FOMENTO DE LA PRODUCCION
Ecuador. Ministerio de Gobierno *see* INFORME
EL ECUADOR Y EL PERU... / Cornejo, P – Quito, 1905 – 2mf – 1 – ILM-2111/1 – ne IDC [327]
ECUMENICAL COMMITTEE ON THE ANDES (ECO-ANDES) – New York. 95 docs. 1980-1990 – 14mf – 9 – ne IDC [320]
ECUMENICAL DOCUMENTATION AND INFORMATION CENTER FOR EASTERN AND SOUTHERN AFRICA – Harare. 42 docs. 1987-1991 – 14mf – 9 – ne IDC [320]
ECUMENICAL INFORMATION FROM CZECHOSLOVAKIA – v1-17. Jun 1954-1970 (complete) – 3r – 1 – ATLA S0152 – us A.T.L.A. [240]
ECUMENICAL MISSIONARY CONFERENCE, NEW YORK, 1900 : REPORT OF THE ECUMENICAL CONFERENCE ON FOREIGN MISSIONS, HELD IN CARNEGIE HALL AND NEIGHBORING CHURCHES, APRIL 21 TO MAY 1 – (Includes appendix and index) – New York: American Tract Society; London: Religious Tract Society, c1900 – 4mf – 9 – 0-8370-6112-1 – 1986-0112 – us A.T.L.A. [240]
ECUMENICAL MOVEMENT FOR JUSTICE AND PEACE – Quezon City. 27 docs. 1981-1991 – 25mf – 9 – ne IDC [320]
ECUMENICAL PRESS SERVICE : PAPERS / Ecumenical Press Service – (Some pgs missing) – 1946-76; 1984-91 – Inquire – 1 – ATLA S0581 – us A.T.L.A. [240]
Ecumenical Press Service *see* ECUMENICAL PRESS SERVICE
THE ECUMENICAL RECONSTRUCTION OF CHRISTIANITY: AN EXPOSITION AND EVALUATION OF THE CHRISTOLOGY OF JOHN HICK / Miles, S Daniel – 1982 – 1 – 5.00 – us Baptist [240]
ECUMENICAL REVIEW – 1- 1948- 1; v22- 5,6; v27- 9 – us UMI [240]
ECUMENICAL WOMEN'S CENTER – (Ceased publ: v16 no 8 Oct 1988) – v1-16. 1972-88 – 1r – 1 – ATLA S0862 – us A.T.L.A. [073]
ECUMENISM – v1-34. 1966-73 – 1 – us UMI [240]
ECUMENIST – 1977- – 1 – us UMI [073]
ED. L. HUNTLEY'S PANEGYRIC ON THE JEWS / Huntley, Edward L – Chicago: Ed. L. Huntley, 1891.1 fiche – 9 – us A.T.L.A. [270]
EDDA, DEUXIEME PARTIE: TRACTATUS PHILOGICUS ET ADDIMENTA EX LODICIBUS MANUSCRIPTIS / Sturleson, Snorre. (Sturlusen) – (Linguistic series). 1852 – 9 – fr Hachette [430]
EDDA SNORRA STURLUSONAR / ed by Jonssen, F – BH-364 2. 1931 – 8 – ne IDC [800]
Eddins, William C, Jr *see* A COMPARISON OF BONE MINERAL DENSITY BETWEEN ACTIVE AND NONACTIVE MEN WITH SPINAL CORD INJURIES
EDDOWES'S JOURNAL – Shrewsbury, England. 1849-52.-w. 2 reels – 1 – uk British Libr Newspaper [072]
Eddy, Daniel Clarke *see* HEROINES OF THE MISSIONARY ENTERPRISE
Eddy, Elizabeth Ann (Berryman) *see* PAPERS
Eddy, Richard *see* A HISTORY OF THE UNITARIANS AND THE UNIVERSALISTS IN THE UNITED STATES
EDDYSTONE / Jensen, Wilhelm – 2. Aufl. Berlin: Paetel, 1894 – 1r – 1 – us U.W. Library [830]
EDDYVILLE ENTERPRISE – Eddyville, NE. -w. Dec. 1911-Mar. 1920 – 1 – us NE Hist [071]
EDDYVILLE FIRST BAPTIST CHURCH. EDDYVILLE, KENTUCKY : CHURCH RECORDS – 1929-89. 1095p – 1 – 49.28 – us Baptist [240]
EDEB YAHU – Istanbul, 1908-1909; Sahib-i Imtiyaz: Mehmed Remzi, Mueduer-i Mes'ul: Taslizade Hasan Ruesdue, Osman Nuri, No 16. – 17 Kanunisani 1324 [1908] – 1mf – 9 – $12.00 – us MEDOC [949]
EDEBIYAT : THE JOURNAL OF MIDDLE EASTERN LITERATURES / ed by Meisami, Julie & Beard, Michael – 9,5,1 – us Harwood [470]
EDEBIYAT-I UMUMIYE MECMUASI – Istanbul: Kanaat Kuetuephanesi ve Matbaasi, 1916-1919; Mueduer-i Mes'ul: Mehmed Celaleddin, Mueduer: Giridi – 13mf – 9 – $250.00 – us MEDOC [949]
Edelmann, J F *see* SIX SONATAS POUR LE CLAVECIN AVEC ACCOMP. D'UN VIOLON AD LIB., OP. 1
Edelmann, Z H *see* GINZEI OXFORD
DER EDELSTEIN / Boner, Ulrich – 27p + 3 color mf – DM340.00 – 3-89219-004-6 – gw Lengenfelder [430]
DER EDELSTEIN / Boner, Ulrich – with a suppl: Des Teufels Netz – Sibyllenweissagung – 19p + 3 color mf – DM440.00 – 3-89219-007-0 – gw Lengenfelder [430]
EDEN / Hill, J – or A compleat body of gardening. London. 1757. B-7353 2 – 8 – ne IDC [630]
EDEN – (New York). 1924-25 – 1 – us A.J.P.C. [830]
Eden, Charles Henry *see*
- THE DOMINION OF CANADA
- THE FORTUNES OF THE FLETCHERS: A STORY OF LIFE IN CANADA AND AUSTRALIA
- THE HOME OF THE WOLVERENE AND BEAVER, OR, FUR-HUNTING IN THE WILDS OF CANADA

Eden, Emily *see* LETTERS FROM INDIA
EDEN LOST AND WON : STUDIES OF THE EARLY HISTORY AND FINAL DESTINY OF MAN AS TAUGHT IN NATURE AND REVELATION / Dawson, John William – New York:Fleming H. Revell, 1896 – 1mf – 9 – 0-8370-2850-7 – 1985-0850 – us A.T.L.A. [220]
EDEN TABLEAU, OR, BIBLE OBJECT-TEACHING / Beecher, Charles – Boston: Lee & Shepard, 1880. 1 fiche – 9 – us A.T.L.A. [240]
THE EDEN TABLEAU, OR, BIBLE OBJECT-TEACHING : A STUDY / Beecher, Charles – Boston: Lee and Shepard, 1880 – 1mf – 9 – 0-8370-2233-9 – 1985-0233 – us A.T.L.A. [220]
EDER HA-YEKAR / Horodezky, S A – Tel-Aviv. 1947. BJ-100-35 1 – 9 – ne IDC [180]
Eder, P J *see* FOREIGN AND HOME LAW
Ederberg, B *see* LAHKUSUD EESTIS
Edersheim, Alfred *see*
- PROPHECY AND HISTORY IN RELATION TO THE MESSIAH
- SKETCHES OF JEWISH SOCIAL LIFE IN THE DAYS OF CHRIST

Edersheim, Elisa Williamina *see* THE LAWS AND POLITY OF THE JEWS
DIE EDESSENISCHE ABGAR-SAGE / Lipsius, Richard Adelbert – Braunschweig: C.A. Schwetschke, 1880 – 1mf – us A.T.L.A. [240]
Edfeldt, Hans *see*
- OM BEVISEN FOER GUDS VERKLIGHET
- OM BEVISEN FOR GUDS VERKLIGHET

EDGAR. ACT 3, SCENE 4 / Puccini, G – (Holograph) – Manuscript, 1889 – 1 – us Sibley [780]
Edgar, Andrew *see*
- THE BIBLES OF ENGLAND
- BIBLES OF ENGLAND: A PLAIN ACCOUNT FOR PLAIN PEOPLE

EDGAR; DRAMMA LIRICO IN TRE ATTI... / Puccini, G – (Vocal score) – Milano: R. Stabilimento tito di Gio. Ricordi e francesco Lucca di G. Ricordi, & C., [1892, c1890] – 1 – us Sibley [780]
Edgar, Frank *see* LITAFI NA TATSUNIYOYI NA HAUSA
EDGAR INDEX – Edgar, NE. -w. Oct. 1898-Apr. 1899 – 1 – us NE Hist [071]
Edgar, James David *see*
- CANADA AND ITS CAPITAL: WITH SKETCHES OF POLITICAL AND SOCIAL LIFE AT OTTAWA
- THE CANADIAN TRADE QUESTION
- THE COMMERCIAL INDEPENDENCE OF CANADA: AN ADDRESS DELIVERED 26TH JANUARY, 1883 TO THE REFORM ASSOCIATIONS OF CENTRE TORONTO, ON "THE RIGHT OF CANADA TO MAKE HER OWN COMMERCIAL TREATIES"
- THE INSOLVENT ACT OF 1869: WITH TARIFF, NOTES, FORMS AND A FULL INDEX
- THE INSOLVENT ACT OF 1875: WITH AN INTRODUCTORY CHAPTER, NOTES, FORMS, TARRIFS OF ONTARIO, QUEBEC AND NEW BRUNSWICK, AND A FULL INDEX
- LOYALTY: AN ADDRESS DELIVERED TO THE TORONTO YOUNG MEN'S LIBERAL CLUB, JANUARY 19TH, 1885

- THE PPA IN ONTARIO: BEING EXTRACTS FROM SPEECHES AND TWO LETTERS OF MR. J. D. EDGAR, M.P
- SPEECH OF MR. J. D. EDGAR IN THE CANADIAN HOUSE OF COMMONS IN SUPPORT OF HIS MOTION FOR A COMMITTEE TO ENQUIRE INTO THE CHARGES AGAINST SIR ADOLPHE CARON, POSTMASTER GENERAL
- THIS CANADA OF OURS AND OTHER POEMS
- THE WHITE STONE CANOE: A LEGEND OF THE OTTAWAS
- THE WIMA-EDGAR LETTERS: A SERIES OF OPEN LETTERS BETWEEN MR. J. D. EDGAR, M.P., TORONTO AND MR. ERASTUS WIMAN, NEW YORK

Edgar, John Henry *see* A THEOLOGICAL UNDERSTANDING OF ANGER WITHIN GRIEF

Edgar, Lewis M *see* A HISTORY OF THE PRIMITIVE BAPTISTS IN THE WESTERN DISTRICTS OF TENNESSEE AND KENTUCKY

EDGAR. LIBRETTO. DRAMMA LIRICO IN QUATTRO ATTI / Puccini, G – (Libretto for the original production[1889] including additions and corrections by Puccini) – 1 – us Sibley [780]

EDGAR POST – Edgar, NE. -w. Oct. 1895-Apr. 1921 – 1 – us NE Hist [071]

EDGAR QUINET : HIS EARLY LIFE AND WRITINGS / Heath, Richard – London: Truebner, 1881 – 1mf – us A.T.L.A. [240]

Edgar, Ray *see* WORLD ART

Edgar, Robert McCheyne *see*
- THE GENIUS OF PROTESTANTISM
- GOSPEL OF A RISEN SAVIOUR

EDGAR SUN – Edgar, NE. -w. Mar. 1902; May 1902-Sep. 1902; Aug. 1909-Dec. 1956; Jan. 1958-Mar. 1974; Jan. 1975-Dec. 1976 – 1 – us NE Hist [071]

Edgarton, S C *see* THE FLORAL FORTUNE-TELLER

EDGARTOWN 1651-1900 – (Mf 1-7: Town & Vital 1651-1784. Mf 8-14: Town Records 1790-1832. Mf 8,11-14: Marriages 1782-1838. Mf 9-14: Intentions 1800-38. Mf 8,12-14: Vitals 1718-1840. Mf 15-20: Town Records 1832-51. Mf 21-28: Town Records 1839-70. Mf 21: Deaths 1839-66. Mf 21,24: Marriages 1837-43, 1851. Mf 21-28: Intentions 1838-71. Mf 23: Births 1841-44. Mf 25-28: Dog Records 1858-71. Mf 29-32: Birth Index 1663-1963. Mf 33-34: Marriage Index 1663-1843. Mf 35-39: Marriage Index 1699-1799; Marriage Index 1844-1979. Mf 40-43: Death Index 1663-1949. Mf 44-45: Births 1843-76. Mf 45-46: Marriages 1844-52. Mf 46: Deaths 1845-59. Mf 47: Births 1876-90. Mf 48-49: Marriages 1853-91. Mf 49: Out-of-Town Mariages 1699-1799. Mf 50-53: Deaths 1860-1907. Mf 54: Marriages 1891-1902. Mf 55: Births 1891-1901) – (mf ed 1994) – 55mf – 9 – 0-87623-191-1 – us Holbrook [920]

EDGARTOWN 1656-1849 – (Mf 1T: Vital Records 1656-1818. Mf 1T-3T: Births & Deaths 1718-1840. Mf 2T-3T: Marriages 1754-1831; Marriage Intentions 1810-29. Mf 4T-5T: Intentions & Marriages 1829-49; Deaths 1832-49; Vital Records 1782-1851. Mf 5T-6T: Births 1843-49 Mf 6T: Marriages & Deaths 1843-49) – (mf ed 1996) – 6mf – 9 – 0-87623-247-0 – us Holbrook [920]

EDGE – (Ceased v13 1985) – Vancouver. v1-13. 1973-1985 – 5 – Can$100.00 – cn Micromedia [073]

EDGEFIELD BAPTIST CHURCH. NASHVILLE, TENNESSEE : CHURCH RECORDS – 1903-79 – 1 – 179.46 – us Baptist [240]

EDGEFIELD FIRST BAPTIST CHURCH. EDGEFIELD, SOUTH CAROLINA : CHURCH RECORDS – 1854-1941. 872p – 1 – 39.24 – us Baptist [240]

Edgerton, W F *see* THE THUTMOSID SUCCESSION

EDGEWOOD BAPTIST CHURCH. COLLETON COUNTY. WALTERBORO, SOUTH CAROLINA : CHURCH RECORDS – 1959-72 – 1 – 14.00 – us Baptist [240]

EDGEWOOD BAPTIST CHURCH. HOPKINSVILLE, KENTUCKY : CHURCH RECORDS – 2Jul 1958-80 – 1 – 42.48 – us Baptist [240]

Edgeworth De Firmont, Henry E *see* RELATION DE LA MORT DE LOUIS 16, ROI DE FRANCE

Edgeworth, Maria *see*
- LETTRES INTIMES DE MARIA EDGEWORTH PENDANT SES VOYAGES
- THE PARENT'S ASSISTANT
- TALES AND NOVELS

Edghill, E A *see* FAITH AND FACT, A STUDY IN RITSCHLIANISM

EDGWARE AND MILL HILL TIMES – 1986-96 – 69r – 1 – uk British Libr Newspaper [072]

EDGWARE REPORTER – London. -w. 29 Mar 1890-31 Mar 1894. (3 reels) – 1 – uk British Libr Newspaper [072]

Edhem, I *see* LA CONDITION INTERNATIONALE DE L'EGYPTE

EDIB-I MUHTEREM MERHUM ZIYA PASA'NIN RUHYASI / Pasa, Ziya – Dersaadet: Kasbar Matbaasi, 1326 [1910] – $13.00 – us MEDOC [470]

THE EDIBLE MOLLUSCA OF GREAT BRITAIN AND IRELAND / Lovell, MS – Z-630 2. Ed. 2. 1884 – 8 – ne IDC [590]

EDIBLE PLANTS OF UGANDA : THE VALUE OF WILD AND CULTIVATED PLANTS AS FOOD – 1989 – 156p – it F.A.O. [580]

EDICION TRIDENTINA DEL MANUAL TOLEDANO Y SU INCORPORACION AL RITUAL ROMANO / Garcia, Alf. I – 2mf – 8 – Dfl9.00 – ne Slangenburg [240]

DAS EDICT DES ANTONIUS PIUS (T.U.U. 1-13/4A) / Harnack, Adolf von – Leipzig, 1895 – 1mf – 9 – ne Slangenburg [240]

EDICTS, ORDINANCES, DECLARATIONS AND DECREES RELATIVE TO THE SEIGNIORIAL TENURE, REQUIRED BY AN ADDRESS OF THE LEGISLATIVE ASSEMBLY, 1851 – Quebec: Printed by E R Frechette, 1852. SEM105P250 – 4mf – 9 – Can$9.00 – cn Bibl Nat [971]

EDICTUS CETERAEQUE LANGOBARDORUM LEGES (MGH LEGES 4: 2.BD) : CUM CONSTITUTIONIBUS ET PACTIS PRINCIPUM. PRINCIPUM BENEVENTANORM – 1869 – Dfl19.00 – ne Slangenburg [240]

LA EDIFICANTE AVENTURA DE GARIN / Oteyza, Luis de – Madrid: La Novela Mundial, 1927 – sp Bibl Santa Ana [940]

EDINA / Wood, Ellen – British Fiction Archive: Unit 1 – 9 – uk Bell [830]

EDINAIA ILI FEDERATIVNAIA ROSSIIA / Alekseev, Aleksandr Aleksandrovich – Rostov na Donu: [s.n.], 1919 – 1 – CSUX89-B3656 – us Hoover Inst Photo [320]

EDINBORO INDEPENDENT – Edinboro, PA. -w 1889-1912 – 13 – $25.00r – us I.M.R. [071]

EDINBURGH ADVERTISER – Scotland, UK. 1770-71. -w. 2 reels – 1 – uk British Libr Newspaper [072]

THE EDINBURGH ADVERTISER – (Includes index from 27 jun-30 dec 1777) – Edinburgh, Scotland. v28 n1418. 29 jul 1777-v28 n1459. 1 aug to 19-23 dec 1777 – 1r – 1 – Can$50.00 – cn Can Microfilming [072]

EDINBURGH CITIZEN – Scotland. -w. 1920. 1 reel – 1 – uk British Libr Newspaper [072]

EDINBURGH EVENING COURANT – Scotland. 1857-59.-d. 3 reels – 1 – uk British Libr Newspaper [072]

THE EDINBURGH EVENING COURANT – Edinburgh: James McEuen, 1727 – 1r – 1 – us Res Libr [072]

EDINBURGH EVENING DISPATCH – Scotland, UK. 1888; 1890. -w. 4 reels – 1 – uk British Libr Newspaper [072]

EDINBURGH GAZETTE – n18629-18839. 1968-69 – 2r – 1 – us Ross [072]

Edinburgh. Greyfriars Graveyard *see* REGISTER OF BURIALS

THE EDINBURGH JOURNAL OF SCIENCE – Edinburgh, 1824-1829. Edinburgh, new series, 1829-1832 – 3 – us Readex [500]

EDINBURGH LAW JOURNAL – v1-2. 1831-37 – 13mf – 9 – $19.50 – LLMC 84-460 – us L.L.M.C. [073]

THE EDINBURGH LITERARY ALMANAC *see* JANUS – THE EDINBURGH LITERARY ALMANAC

EDINBURGH MAGAZINE AND LITERARY MISCELLANY – v. 1-18. 1739-1826 – 1 – us UMI [073]

EDINBURGH MEDICAL MISSIONARY SOCIETY, [BY THE] CHINESE SUB-COMMITTEE – N.p., n.d. – 1mf – 9 – ne IDC [610]

THE EDINBURGH NEW PHILOSOPHICAL JOURNAL – v1-57; n.s. v1-19 1826-64 – 3 – us Readex [100]

EDINBURGH OBSERVER ETC – Scotland, UK. May-Dec 1832. -w. 1/2 reel – 1 – uk British Libr Newspaper [072]

THE EDINBURGH PHILOSOPHICAL JOURNAL : EXHIBITING A VIEW OF THE PROGRESS OF DISCOVERY IN NATURAL PHILOSOPHY, CHEMISTRY, NATURAL HISTORY, PRACTICAL MECHANICS, GEOGRAPHY, STATISTICS, AND THE FINE AND USEFUL ARTS – Edinburgh, 1819-26. v1-14 – 3 – us Readex [500]

EDINBURGH REVIEW : OR CRITICAL JOURNAL – Edinburgh. general index. v141-170. 1875-89 – 1r – 1 – us Ross [420]

EDINBURGH REVIEW – v. 1-250. 1802-1929 – 1 – us Princeton Micro [073]

EDINBURGH REVIEW – v1-250 1802-1929 – 1 – $1,016.00 – us L of C Photodup [420]

Edinburgh Royal Medical Society *see* DISSERTATIONS READ TO THE

EDINBURGH SATURDAY POST – Scotland. -w. 12 May 1827-3 May 1828. (36 ft) – 1 – uk British Libr Newspaper [072]

EDINBURGH SKETCHES AND MEMORIES / Masson, David – London, Edinburgh: Adam & Charles Black, 1892 – 1r – 1 – 1-55879-515-4 – uk Libr Preservation [880]

Edinburgh University *see* INDEX TO MANUSCRIPTS, EDINBURGH UNIVERSITY LIBRARY

Edinburgh University. Library *see* INDEX TO MANUSCRIPTS IN THE LIBRARY

EDINENIE : NOVOTORZHSKI I ORGAN SOVI ETA SOLDATSKIKH, RABOCHIKH, KRESTI ANSKIKH DEPUTATOV I TRUDOVO I INTELLIGENT SII – (Includes c.1: 1917:June 17) – Torzhok: Ispolnitelny i k-t sovi eta, 1917 – 1 – CSUXANR2808-S – us Hoover Inst Photo [947]

EDINENIE (TORZHOK, RUSSIA) *see* EDINENIE

EDING'S DIGEST OF HAWAII SUPREME COURT DEC / Edings, W S – (Covers v1-14 1847-1903) – Honolulu: Bulletin Publ. Co, 1903 – 6mf – 9 – $9.00 – LLMC 90-001 – us L.L.M.C. [340]

Edings, W S *see* EDING'S DIGEST OF HAWAII SUPREME COURT DEC

EDINOST – Chicago, 1919, 1921, 1923, 1924 – 3mf or 1 reel – 9,1 – us I.H.R.C. [975]

EDINOST – Chicago, 1920-1925 – 5r – 1 – us I.H.R.C. [975]

EDINOST – Pittsburgh, PA, 1911 – 1mf or 1 reel – 9,1 – us I.H.R.C. [975]

EDINOST – Toronto, Ontario, 1942 – 1mf or 1 reel – 9,1 – us I.H.R.C. [975]

EDINSTVO – (Includes c.1: no.2 1914:June 1-no.3 (1914:June 15)) – S.-Peterburg: A.O. Buri anov, 1914 – 1 – CSUXAKG9184-S – us Hoover Inst Photo [947]

EDINSTVO I NEZAVISIMOST = L'UNITE ET L'INDEPENDANCE – (Includes c.1: no.1 1935:Feb.19-no.3 (1935:Dec12)) – [Paris: Obshchestvo revnitele i kazachestva], 1935- – 1 – CSUXAKG4060-S – us Hoover Inst Photo [947]

EDINSTVO JEDINSTVO – (Includes c.1: 1932:Dec.30-1933:Sept.1, Oct.2-Dec.4; 1934:Jan.4) – Praha: Emanuel Lauseger, 193u – 1 – CSUXANR2743-S – us Hoover Inst Photo [947]

EDINSTVO (PRAGUE, CZECH REPUBLIC) *see* EDINSTVO JEDINSTVO

EDINSTVO (SAINT PETERSBURG, RUSSIA) *see* EDINSTVO

EDINY I FRONT! = LE FRONT UNIQUE! – (Includes c.1: no. 4 1930:Dec.-no.5 (1931:Jan.), no.8 (1933:Mar.3/16)) – Paris: [s.n], -1933 – 1 – CSUXAKB4809-S – us Hoover Inst Photo [947]

EDINY I FRONT!...NOVO I ROSSII = LE FRONT UNIQUE!... – (Includes c.1: no.9 1933:June 11/24-no.15 (1934:Aug.31/Sept.13)) – Paris: [s.n.], 1933- – 1 – CSUXAKB4840-S – us Hoover Inst Photo [947]

EDINY I (ORIENTIROVOCHNY I) GOSUDARSTVENNY I BI UDZHET SOI UZA SOT SIALISTICHESKIKH RESPUBLIK NA...BI UDZHETNY I GOD...ODOBRENNY I SOVETOM NARODNYKH KOMISSAROV SOI UZA SSR – (Includes c.1: 1924/1925) – Moskva: Finansovoe izd-vo NKF SSSR, 192u – 1 – CSUXAKZ2666-S – us Hoover Inst Photo [947]

EDINY I PARTI INY I BILET : INSTRUKTSII A ORGANIZATSII AM R.K.P. (BOLSHEVIKOV) O EDINOM PARTI INOM BILETE / T Sentralny i komitet Rossi isko i kommunistichesko i partii (bolshevikov) – Ekaterinburg: Uralskoe oblastnoe gos. izd-vo, 1920 – 1 – CSUX89-B6728 – us Hoover Inst Photo [320]

EDINYE KRATKOSROCHNYE KURSY POLITIKO-PROSVETITELNO I RABOTY : POLOZHENIE, INSTRUKTSII, PROGRAMMY, UCHEBNYE PLANY – [Moskva]: Glavpolitprosvet, Propagandicheski i otdel, 1921 – 1 – CSUX89-B3475 – us Hoover Inst Photo [320]

EDINYI SELSKOKHOZIAISTVENNY I NALOG 1924-25 G. : MATERIAL DLI A AGITATOROV – Moskva: "Krasnai a Nov", 1924 – 1 – CSUX89-B6380 – us Hoover Inst Photo [630]

EDINYI TARIFNO-KVALIFIKATSIONNYI SPRAVOCHNIK RABOTI PROFESSII RABOCHIKH / Gosudarstvenny i komitet Soveta Ministrov SSSR po voprosam truda i zarabotno i platy – Moskva: Mashinostroenie, 1969. 2v – 1 – CSUX90-B5688 – us Hoover Inst Photo [331]

Edip, Esref *see* SEBIL UER-RESAD

EDIRNE RAHNUEMASI : TARIHCE: 763-1337 HICRI SENELERI / Osman, Tosyali Rifat – Edirne: Vilayet Matbaasi, 1920 – $15.00 – us MEDOC [956]

EDISON ECHO – Edison, NE. -w. Jan. 1925-Nov. 1946 – 1 – us NE Hist [071]

EDISON KINETOGRAM – Berlin. jan 17, 1912 – 1 – gw Mikrofilm [790]

Edison Memorial Methodist Church (Milan, Ohio) *see* RECORDS

EDISON NEWS – Edison, NE. -w. Dec. 1911-Jul. 1915. Incomplete – 1 – us NE Hist [071]

Edison Phonograph Works *see* INSPECTOR'S HANDBOOK OF THE PHONOGRAPH

EDISON RECORD – Edison, NE. -w. Sep. 1915-Jan. 1917 – 1 – us NE Hist [071]

Edison, Thomas A *see* PAPERS OF THOMAS A. EDISON

EDISTO ISLAND CHURCH. SOUTH CAROLINA : CHURCH RECORDS – 1860 – 1 – 5.00 – us Baptist [240]

L'EDIT DE CALLISTE : ETUDE SUR LES ORIGINES DE LA PENITENCE CHRETIENNE / D'Ales, A – Paris, 1914 – 9mf – 8 – ne Slangenburg [240]

L'EDIT DE CALLISTE : ETUDE SUR LES ORIGINES DE LA PENITENCE CHRETIENNE / D'Ales, A – Paris: G Beauchesne, 1914 – 2mf – us A.T.L.A. [240]

EDITH DE FALSEN / Legouve, Ernest – L'Education d'un pere. Paris: L. Hachette, 1860. 325p.4 fiches. (Literature Collection) – 9 – 10.00 – fr Bibl Nationale [830]

EDITION CORVEY : LITERARY WORKS OF THE 18TH AND 19TH CENTURY – (English, German and French language editions available: silver halide microfiche on request) – Wildberg: BELSER WISS. DIENST, 1990-1992 – 2,8202mf – 9 – DM190,000.00 diazo – 3-628-90099-9 – gw Belser Wiss [410]

EDITION ST WALBURG, FRAUENKLOSTERBIBLIOTHEK 17.-19. JAHRHUNDERT – 1994 – 5800mf – 9 – DM74,400.00 – 3-628-77777-1 – gw Belser Wiss [240]

EDITOR AND PUBLISHER – v1- 1901- 1; v104- 5,6; v108- 9 – us UMI [070]

EDITOR AND PUBLISHER INTERNATIONAL YEAR BOOK – (1980-. 5,6,9) – 1959- – 1 – us UMI [070]

EDITOR AND PUBLISHER MARKET GUIDE – (1980-. 5,6,9) – 1943- – 1 – us UMI [380]

EDITOR OF BURLINGAME – Burlingame. Calif. 1948-49 – 1 – us UMI [071]

THE EDITOR OF BURLINGAME – Burlingame, CA. 1948-49 – 1r – 1 – $50.00 – C02084 – us Library Micro [071]

THE EDITOR-BISHOP, LINUS PARKER : HIS LIFE AND WRITINGS / Galloway, Charles B – Nashville, Tenn.: Southern Methodist Publishing House, 1886 – 1mf – us A.T.L.A. [240]

L'EDITORIAL – (Cont by: L'Editorial de Quebec Metropolitain, Quebec v5 n14 19 aut 1964-v7 n22 21 dec 1966) – Beauport, Canada. v1 n2. jan 1960-64 – 1r – 1 – Can$40.00 – cn Can Microfilming [072]

L'EDITORIAL DE QUEBEC METROPOLITAIN *see* L'EDITORIAL

EDITORIAL FROM THE DAILY MAIL OF TUESDAY, FEBRUARY 5TH, 1889 – Toronto?: Daily Mail, 1889. 02077. (Pre-1900 Canadiana) – 9 – cn C.I.H.M. [971]

EDITORIAL RESEARCH REPORTS – v1- 1955- 1; 1971- 5,6; 1977- 4 x 6 in. 9 – us UMI [300]

Editorial Sanchez Rodrigo *see* LECTURAS PARA LA JUVENTUD. COLECCION DE BIOGRAFIAS HIJOS ILUSTRES DE ESPANA

EDITORIALS FROM DJAKARTA PRESS / Jakarta - Djakarta, 1961(June 22)-1965(Jan 28). Lacking: 1963(Jan-May 9, June1-23, Sept 6-30, Nov 1-19); 1964(Jan 4-26, Jan 28-Feb 3, Feb 5-12, Feb 19-July 1, July 3-Aug 13, Aug 26-31, Sept 18-29, Nov-Dec 31); 1965(Jan 1-27) - 36mf - 9 - ne IDC [072]

EDITORIALS FROM DJAKARTA PRESS / Jakarta - Djakarta, 1961(June 27)-1965(Jan 19). Lacking: 1962(Aug-Sept); 1963(Jan-May 27, June-July), 1964(Oct, Nov 22-Dec) - 14mf - 9 - ne IDC [072]

EDITORIALS IN THE HEBREW PRESS / Israel. Prime Minister's Office. Information Services Administration. Government Press Office - (Ceased after 1974) - Jerusalem, 1948-74. Lacking: June, 1956, no. 2293. - 474mf - 9 - ne IDC [070]

EDITORIALS IN THE HEBREW PRESS / Israel. Prime Minister's Office. Information Services Administration. Government Press Office - Jerusalem, 1948-. Up to Aug 1959 appeared as cReview of the Hebrew Press.n - 9 - 200.00; 6.00y - is I.T.T.I. [956]

EDITORIALS ON FILE / ed by Trager, Oliver - (1970-80. $298.00; 1981-82. $99.00; 1983-84. $99.00; 1985-86. $99.00; 1987-88. $99.00; 1989-90. $99.00; 1991-92. $99.00) - 1970-92 - 9 - $700.00 - us Facts [070]

EDITS, ORDONNANCES, DECLARATIONS ET ARRETS RELATIFS A LA TENURE SEIGNEURIALE DEMANDES PAR UNE ADRESSE DE L'ASSEMBLEE LEGISLATIVE, 1851 - Quebec. Imprimerie de E R Frechette..., 1852. SEM105P248 - 4mf - 9 - Can$9.00 - cn Bibl Nat [323]

EDITS, ORDONNANCES ROYAUX / Nouvelle-France. Lois, etc. - Quebec, 1854-1856. SEM16P303 - 1r - 5 - Can$39.00 - cn Bibl Nat [324]

EDITS, ORDONNANCES ROYAUX - Quebec: De la Presse a vapeur de E R Frechette, 1854-1856. SEM105P83 - 22mf - 9 - Can$49.50 - cn Bibl Nat [324]

EDITS, ORDONNANCES ROYAUX, DECLARATIONS ET ARRET DE CONSEIL DU ROI, CONCERNANT LE CANADA. / Canada. New France. Laws, Statutes, etc - Quebec: Imprimes par P E Desbarats..., 1803-1806. SEM35P177 - 1r - 1 - Can$34.00 - cn Bibl Nat [324]

EDJAAN BAHASA INDONESIA DENGAN HURUF ARAB / Sastradiwirya, Umar - Title in Arabic: Latin orthography. SE-3935 c.1954 - 9 - ne IDC [950]

Edkins, C E *see* THE ABILITY OF UNDERGRADUATE PHYSICAL EDUCATION MAJORS TO VERBALLY IDENTIFY AND VISUALLY DISCRIMINATE CRITICAL ELEMENTS OF SELECT SPORT SKILLS

Edlund, Larry L *see* EFFECTS OF A SWIMMING PROGRAM ON CYSTIC FIBROSIS CHILDREN

Edmiston, Paula A *see* THE INFLUENCE OF PARTICIPATION IN A SPORTS TRAINING PROGRAM ON THE SELF-CONCEPTS OF THE EDUCABLE MENTALLY RETARDED ATTENDING A ONE-WEEK SPECIAL OLYMPICS SPORTS CAMP

EDMOND'S SELECT CASES : UNREPORTED APPEALS / New York. (State) - (A Pre-NRS title) - v1-2. 1831-50 (all publ) - 13mf - 9 - $19.50 - LLMC 80-003 - us L.L.M.C. [340]

Edmont, E *see* ATLAS LINGUISTIQUE DE LA FRANCE

EDMONTON BULLETIN - Canada. Sept 1906-March 1914. Lacking 1913, 1914. Imperfect - 9r - 1 - uk British Libr Newspaper [971]

EDMONTON BULLETIN - Edmonton, Alberta, CN. Jan 1907-Jan 1951 - 188r - 1 - cn Commonwealth Micro [073]

EDMONTON BULLETIN - Edmonton, Canada. 1880-1906 - 25r - 1 - $1,625.00 - cn Library Assoc [971]

EDMONTON CAPITAL - Edmonton, Alberta, CN. 1910-14 - 15r - 1 - cn Commonwealth Micro [072]

EDMONTON DAILY BULLETIN - Canada. March 1910-Nov 1915. Imperfect - 10r - 1 - uk British Libr Newspaper [971]

EDMONTON GAZETTE - London, UK. 1984-Jul 1986. -w.4 1/2 reels - 1 - uk British Libr Newspaper [072]

EDMONTON JOURNAL - Edmonton, Alberta, CN. Nov 1903- - 36r per yr - 1 - Can$53.00r - cn Commonwealth Micro [073]

EDMONTON MAGAZINE - (Ceased v10 no 8 1988) - Vancouver. v1-10. 1979/80-1988 - 9 - Can$28.00y - cn Micromedia [971]

EDMONTON NATIVE NEWS / Canadian Native Friendship Center - 1972-79. (American Indian Periodicals in the Princeton University Library). 4 fiches - 9 - $45.00 - us UPA [305]

EDMONTON PEOPLE'S WEEKLY - Edmonton, Alberta, CN. Sept 1944-Dec 1952 - 2r - 1 - cn Commonwealth Micro [072]

EDMONTON SATURDAY NEWS - Edmonton, Alberta, CN. Dec 1905-1912 - 3r - 1 - cn Commonwealth Micro [072]

EDMONTON SUN - (1978-1992.-389r) - Edmonton, 1993 - 36r - 1 - cn Preston [971]

EDMONTON UKRANIAN NEWS - (In Ukranian) - Edmonton, Alberta, CN. 1928-71 - 16r - 1 - cn Commonwealth Micro [072]

EDMUND BURKE: A LECTURE, DELIVERED IN DE LA SALLE INSTITUTE ON APRIL 30TH, 1880 / Dunne, John P - s.l.: s.n., 1880 (Toronto: Tribune). 05198. (Pre-1900 Canadiana) - 9 - cn C.I.H.M. [971]

Edmunds, A C *see* PEN SKETCHES OF NEBRASKANS

Edmundson, Henry *see* LINGUA LINGUARUM:THE NATURALL LANGUAGE OF LANGUAGES

EDN CAREER NEWS - 1984- - 1,5,6,9 - us UMI [073]

EDO BAKUFU KANKOBUTSU SHUSHEI = COLLECTION OF PUBLICATIONS UNDER THE EDO SHOGUNATE, 1599-1868 / ed by Kawase, Kazuma et al - 120r - 1 - Y1,284,000 - ja Yushodo [950]

EDO BUNGAKU SOKWAN = DAITOKYU COLLECTION OF EDO LITERATURE / Daitokyu Memorial Library. Tokyo; ed by Kawase, Kazuma - (Essential illustrated novelistic and dramatic works. Printed Guide) - 90r - 1 - Y858,000 - ja Yushodo [480]

EDOJIDAI RYUZU JIBIKI DAIHUSEI = COLLECTION OF POPULAR JAPANESE LANGUAGE DICTIONARIES IN THE EDO PERIOD / ed by Kawase, Kazuma - (Includes index) - 94r - 1 - Y1,135,000 - ja Yushodo [480]

EDON COMMERCIAL - Edon, Ohio. 1912- - 7r - 1 - $32.50r - us Archival [071]

Edouard, Emmanuel *see* LE PANTHEON HAITIEN

EDOUARD EN ECOSSE OU LA NUIT D'UN PROSCRIT / Duval - (French Theatre Series). Paris. Vente. 1814 - 9 - fr Hachette [820]

Edouard, Eugene *see* LES ANTILLES FRANCAISES, PARTICULIEREMENT LA GUADELOUPE, DEPUIS LEUR DECOUVERTE JUSQU'AU 1ER NOVEMBRE, 1825

EDP WEEKLY - (v.20 .1979. 5,6,9) - (Electronic Data Processing).v.1. 1960 - 1 - us UMI [073]

Edson, David Orr, M D *see* GETTING WHAT WE WANT; HOW TO APPLY PSYCHOANALYSIS TO YOUR OWN PROBLEMS

Edstone. Yorkshire *see* PARISH REGISTERS

EDUARD MOERIKE / Meyer, Herbert - (Includes bibliographical references) - Stuttgart: J F Steinkopf, 1950 - 1r - 1 - us U.W. Library [430]

EDUARD MOERIKE UND KLARA NEUFFER : NEUE UNTERSUCHUNGEN / Camerer, W - Marbach a.N.: A Rempps, 1908 - 1r - 1 - us U.W. Library [750]

EDUARD MOERIKES KUENSTLERISCHES SELBSTVERSTAENDNIS. IM SPIEGEL SEINER GEDICHTE "DIE ELEMENTE", "GOETTLICHE REMINISZENZ" UND "NEUE LIEBE" / Aley, Peter - Frankfurt a.M., 1970 - 3mf - 9 - DM76.00 - 3-89349-661-0 - gw Hänsel [430]

Eduardo de Noronha. Lisboa: Imprensa Nacional, 1895 *see* O DISTRICTO DE LOURENCO MARQUES E A AFRICA DO SUL

EDUARDO POSADA. SECRETAIRE PERPETUEL DE L'ACADEMIE NATIONALE...COLOMBIE / Bayle, Constantino - Madrid: Razon y Fe, 1926 - 1 - sp Bibl Santa Ana [946]

A EDUCACAO : ORGAO DO EXTERNATO PILARENSE - Pilar, Alagoas. 4 Dez 1891; 10 Mar 1892 - 1,5,6 - bl Biblioteca [072]

EDUCACAO POPULAR : ALFABETIZACAO E PRIMEIRAS CONTAS: EXPERIENCIAS NA ELABORACAO DE MATERIAL DIDACTICO PARA ADULTOS - Sao Paulo: Centro Ecumenico de Documentacao e Informacao, 1984 - us Res Libr [972]

EDUCACION DE LA MUJER EN AMERICA / Bayle, Constantino - Madrid: Razon y Fe, 1941 - 1 - sp Bibl Santa Ana [370]

EDUCACION EN VENEZUELA : PROBLEMAS Y SOLUCIONES: INFORME DE LA COMISION... / Venezuela. Comision Presidencial para el Estudio del Proyecto Educativo Nacional - Caracas, 1986 - 2mf - 9 - DE-647/1 - ne IDC [370]

LA EDUCACION INTEGRAL / Bejarano y Sanchez, Eloy - 1898 - 9 - 1.50f - sp Bibl Santa Ana [370]

LA EDUCACION MEDICA INTEGRAL / Bejarano y Sanchez, Eloy - Madrid: Establecimiento Tipografico de J.A. Garcia, 1902 - 1 - sp Bibl Santa Ana [370]

LA EDUCACION PERONISTA A TRAVES DEL PENSAMIENTO DE PERON / Argentina. Presidencia. Subsecretaria de Informaciones - Buenos Aires: [La Subsecretaria], 1952 - 1 - CSUXAJMO160-B - us Hoover Inst Photo [320]

EDUCACION SUPERIOR EN CIFRAS 1987-1988 / El Salvador. Direccion General de Educacion Superior - San Salvador, [1987] - 5mf - 9 - DE-628/1 - ne IDC [370]

EDUCACION SUPERIOR UNIVERSITARIA : UNIVERSIDADES, FACULTADES Y ESCUELAS SUPERIORES: UBICACION 1983 / Argentina. Ministerio de Educacion y Justicia. Departamento de Estadistica - Buenos Aires, 1984 - 1mf - 9 - DE-695/1 - ne IDC [370]

LA EDUCACIÓN Y LA JUSTICIA EN LOS ANOS : MEMORIA REMITIDA AL H CONGRESO DE LA NACION POR EL MINISTRO DE EDUCACION Y JUSTICIA - Asuncion: Impr Nacional, 1932/1933-1934 - 1r - us Res Libr [370]

EDUCATING AGAINST DRUG ABUSE - 1987 - 86p - 9 - 92-3-102479-5 - fr UNESCO [360]

EDUCATING FOR A BETTER WORLD : NOW! - (Series: United States Olympic Academy, 8) - Los Angeles Athletic Club, 1984 - 3mf - 9 - $12.00 - us Microform Publ [790]

EDUCATING HANDICAPPED YOUNG PEOPLE IN EASTERN AND SOUTHERN AFRICA / Ross, D H - 1988 - 153p - 9 - 92-3-102560-0 - fr UNESCO [370]

EDUCATING THROUGH DANCE : A MULTICULTURAL THEORETICAL FRAMEWORK / Staley, Kimberly T - Texas Woman's University, 1993 - 3mf - 9 - $12.00 - PE 3672 - us Microform Publ [790]

L'EDUCATION : INTELLECTUELLE ET MORALE / Compayre, Gabriel - (Includes bibliographies) - Paris: Librairie Classique Paul Delaplane, [1908?] - 2mf - 9 - 0-8370-7686-2 - 1986-1686 - us A.T.L.A. [370]

EDUCATION : A JOURNAL OF REPUTATION / Negro Needs Society - 1-2 2+4 (all publ). 1935-1936 - 2mf - 9 - $55.00 - us UPA [370]

EDUCATION - v. 1-66. 1880-1945 - 1 - us Princeton Micro [370]

EDUCATION - (v. 89- 1968- 5,6. v. 96- 1975-9) - v. 1- 1880- - 1 - us UMI [370]

EDUCATION, A FRAMEWORK FOR EXPANSION / Great Britain. Ministry of Education - 1972. Cmnd 5174 - 9 - uk Microform Academic [324]

EDUCATION ACT / Great Britain. Laws, Statutes, etc - 1944 - 9 - uk Microform Academic [324]

EDUCATION ACTS IN ENGLAND AND WALES / Great Britain. Laws, Statutes, etc - 1870-1918 - 1 - uk Microform Academic [324]

EDUCATION, ADJUSTMENT AND RECONSTRUCTION : OPTIONS FOR CHANGE / Reimers, Fernando & Tiburcio, Luis - 1995 - 121p - 9 - 92-3-102892-8 - fr UNESCO [370]

L'EDUCATION AFRICAINE - (Missing four issues) - Dakar, 1913-58 - 8r - 1 - $396.00 - us African Imprint [073]

EDUCATION AFRICAINE - v.24, no.88-n.s. no.48. 1935-58 - 1 - us Res Libr [370]

EDUCATION (AMENDMENT) ACT 1972 / Malaysia - Kuala Lumpur, 1972 - 1mf - 9 - DE-202/1 - ne IDC [370]

EDUCATION (AMENDMENT) REGULATIONS 1974 / Hong Kong. Governor in Council - Hong Kong Government Gazette, Legal Supplement 1974 (2, p. B415-B425) - 1mf - 9 - DE-152/1 - ne IDC [370]

EDUCATION AND BILINGUALISM / Siguan, Miguel & Mackey, William F - 1987 - 9 - 92-3-102340-3 - Co-published with Kogan Page, London, who has exclusive sales rights in the UK; Unesco has exclusive sales rights in the USA - fr UNESCO [370]

EDUCATION AND DEVELOPMENT 1980-1983 / Nepal. Tribhuvan University. Research Centre for Educational Innovation and Development - (Missing: 1981) - Kathmandu - 8mf - 9 - DE-565/1 - ne IDC [370]

EDUCATION AND ETHICS / Boutroux, Emile - New York: Macmillan, 1913 - 1mf - us A.T.L.A. [370]

EDUCATION AND INFORMATICS WORLDWIDE : THE STATE OF THE ART AND BEYOND - 1992 - 253p - 9 - 92-3-102798-0 - Co-published with Jessica Kingsley Publishers, London, who have exclusive sales rights in the UK - fr UNESCO [370]

EDUCATION AND THE HIGHER LIFE / Spalding, J L - Chicago: A.C. McClurg, 1897, c1890 - 1mf - us A.T.L.A. [240]

EDUCATION AND THE WORLD OF WORK / Carton, Michel - 1985 - 237p - 9 - 92-3-102220-2 - fr UNESCO [306]

EDUCATION AND TRAINING : PRELIMINARY OUTLINE OF THE SECOND FIVE YEAR PLAN / Pakistan. National Planning Board. Education Section - Karachi, 1958 - 1mf - 9 - DE-574/1 - ne IDC [370]

EDUCATION AND TRAINING OF ENGINEERS, TECHNICIANS CRAFTSMEN AND OPERATIVES IN SINGAPORE / Singapore. Ministry of Education - Singapore, 1971 - 1mf - 9 - DE-268/1 - ne IDC [370]

EDUCATION AND TRAINING OF THE MENTALLY RETARDED - (1980-. 5,6,9) - v.1-. 1966- - 1 - us UMI [370]

EDUCATION AND TRAINING OF USERS OF SCIENTIFIC AND TECHNICAL INFORMATION : UNISIST GUIDE FOR TEACHERS / Evans, A J & Rodes, R G & Keenan, S - 1982 - 143p - 9 - 92-3-101452-8 - fr UNESCO [370]

EDUCATION AND TRAINING STATISTICS 1986 / Tanzania. Bureau of Statistics - Dar es Salaam, 1988 - 2mf - 9 - DE-664/1 - ne IDC [370]

EDUCATION AND URBAN SOCIETY - v1-1968- 1; v8- 5,6,9 - us UMI [073]

[EDUCATION AND WORLD WAR 1 PAMPHLET COLLECTION] - 1914-1919 - 2r - 1 - CSUXANL5319-B - us Hoover Inst Photo [370]

[EDUCATION AND WORLD WAR 2 PAMPHLET COLLECTION] - 1937-1944 - 2r - 1 - CSUXANN2542-B - us Hoover Inst Photo [370]

EDUCATION ANNUAL REPORT 1977-1981 / Papua New Guinea. Department of Education - 5mf - 9 - DE-219/1 - ne IDC [370]

EDUCATION ASSOCIATION OF CHINA : MONTHLY BULLETIN / Education Association of China - no 16. 1908 (complete) - 1r - 1 - ATLA S0703B - us A.T.L.A. [073]

Education Association of China *see* EDUCATION ASSOCIATION OF CHINA

EDUCATION ASSOCIATION OF FUKIEN PROVINCE : JOURNAL / Education Association of Fukien Province - v1 noc 1-6. 1906-11 (complete) - 1r - 1 - ATLA S0701C - us A.T.L.A. [073]

Education Association of Fukien Province *see* EDUCATION ASSOCIATION OF FUKIEN PROVINCE

EDUCATION, BAS-CANADA / Canada. Bureau de l'Instruction Publique pour le Bas-Canada - Quebec: Imp. Louis Perrault, 1853. SEM105P324 - 6mf - 9 - Can$13.50 - cn Bibl Nat [324]

EDUCATION BEYOND APARTHEID : REPORT - Johannesburg, 1971 - us Res Libr [370]

EDUCATION BULLETINS 1974/75-1975/76(1) / Trinidad and Tobago. Central Statistical Office. Education Statistical Section - (Missing: 1974/75 (n1; 3)) - Port of Spain - 2mf - 9 - DE-526/1 - ne IDC [370]

EDUCATION CANADA - Toronto, v1- 1961- - 9 - Can$20.00y - cn Micromedia [073]

EDUCATION CANADA *see* CANADIAN EDUCATION AND RESEARCH DIGEST

THE EDUCATION CIRCULAR *see* SEMI-ANNUAL CIRCULAR

EDUCATION COLLECTION / Bibliotheque Nationale – Includes 7 18th cent. studies on public schools; critical study of French educational doctrines since 16th cent; 1892 guide to learning and teaching; review of estab. of municipal colleges (1790). 11 titles on 25 fiches. Available separately – 9 – 62.00 – fr Bibl Nationale [370]

L'EDUCATION DANS LA PROVINCE DE QUEBEC: DISCOURS DE L'HONORABLE M. FLYNN, PRONONCE A L'ASSEMBLEE LEGISLATIVE LE 7 JANVIER 1897 / Flynn, Edmund James – Quebec: s.n., 1897 (Quebec: Imprimerie generale). 02082. (Pre-1900 Canadiana) – 9 – cn C.I.H.M. [971]

EDUCATION DIGEST – (v. 34- 1968- 5,6. v. 36- 1970- 9) – 1- 1935- – 1 – us UMI [370]

L'EDUCATION DU CARACTERE / Gillet, Martin Stanislaus – new ed. Paris: Desclee, De Brouwer, 1910 – 1mf – 9 – 0-8370-8740-6 – 1986-2740 – us A.T.L.A. [240]

EDUCATION ECONOMICS – 1992- 1v – 9 – £153.00 – 0964-5292 – uk Carfax [330]

L'EDUCATION EN AFRIQUE A LA LUMIERE DE LA CONFERENCE DE HARARE (1982) / Cisse, S Y – (Etudes et documents d'education n50) – Paris, 1985 – 1mf – 9 – DE-134/1 – ne IDC [370]

EDUCATION ENQUIRY: ABSTRACT OF ANSWERS AND RETURNS / Great Britain – 1835 – 9 – uk Microform Academic [941]

EDUCATION ET DEVELOPPEMENT – no. 1-81. Paris. oct 1964-72 – 5 – fr A.C.R.P.P. [073]

EDUCATION ET SOCIOLOGIE / Durkheim, Emile – Paris. 1922. (La Condition Ouvriere. Part Two.) – 9 – 5.00 – fr Bibl Nationale [360]

EDUCATION FOR ALL / Haggis, Sheila M et al – 1994 – 3v 102p – 9 – fr UNESCO [370]

EDUCATION FOR DEVELOPMENT – (1981-. 5,6,9) – 1970- – 1 – us UMI [370]

EDUCATION FOR DEVELOPMENT : DRAFT STATEMENT ON EDUCATIONAL REFORM / Zambia. Ministry of Education – Lusaka, 1976 – 2mf – 9 – DE-496/1 – ne IDC [370]

EDUCATION FOR DEVELOPMENT OR UNDERDEVELOPMENT? : GUYANA'S EDUCATIONAL SYSTEM AND ITS IMPLICATIONS FOR THE THIRD WORLD / Bacchus, MK – 1980 – xviii/302p – $25.00 – 0-88920-145-5 – cn W.L.U. Press [370]

EDUCATION FOR GOVERNMENT ADMINISTRATION IN RURAL INDONESIA: SOME CONSIDERATIONS / Jones, Garth N – SE-11,063 1. 1961 – 9 – ne IDC [370]

EDUCATION FOR GOVERNMENT ADMINISTRATION IN RURAL INDONESIA: SOME CONSIDERATIONS / Jones, Garth N – SE-3573. 1960? – 9 – ne IDC [370]

EDUCATION FOR HEALTH *see* ANNALS OF COMMUNITY-ORIENTED EDUCATION

EDUCATION FOR HUMAN RIGHTS : AN INTERNATIONAL PERSPECTIVE / Ray, Douglas et al – 1995 – 304p – 9 – 92-3-103039-6 – fr UNESCO [320]

EDUCATION FOR INTERNATIONAL COOPERATION AND PEACE AT THE PRIMARY SCHOOL LEVEL – 1983 – 138p – 9 – 92-3-101964-3 – fr UNESCO [370]

EDUCATION FOR NATIONAL DEVELOPMENT; SOME DIRECTIONS : PRELIMINARY REPORT OF THE WORKING PARTY ON RURAL EDUCATION / Papua New Guinea. Manpower Planning Unit – Waigani, 1977 – 2mf – 9 – DE-249/1 – ne IDC [370]

EDUCATION FOR THE BLIND IN THAILAND / Thailand. Ministry of Education – Bangkok, 1981 – 1mf – 9 – DE-300/1 – ne IDC [370]

EDUCATION FOR THE DISADVANTAGED CHILD – v1-3 1973-78 1; v3- 5,6,9 – us UMI [370]

EDUCATION FORUM – (Cont: OSSTF Forum at v14 no 3 1988/89) – Don Mills. v15-20 1989/90-1994 – 9 – Can$20.00y – cn Micromedia [370]

EDUCATION IN A RURAL ENVIRONMENT – 2nd ed 1980 – 9 – 92-3-101764-0 – fr UNESCO [370]

EDUCATION IN AFRICA IN THE LIGHT OF THE HARARE CONFERENCE (1982) – 1986 – 35p – 9 – 92-3-102313-6 – fr UNESCO [370]

EDUCATION IN ASIA AND OCEANIA : A CHALLENGE FOR THE 1980S – 1979 – 64p – 9 – 92-3-101755-1 – fr UNESCO [370]

EDUCATION IN BANGLADESH / Bangladesh. Education Directorate – Dacca, 1974 – 1mf – 9 – DE-532/1 – ne IDC [370]

EDUCATION IN CHEMISTRY – Royal Society of Chemistry, Great Britain. 1964-84 (35mm only) – 1 – us UMI [073]

EDUCATION IN LATIN AMERICA AND THE CARIBBEAN : TRENDS AND PROSPECTS: 1970-2000 / Gimeno, Jose Blat – 1983 – 190p – 9 – 92-3-101908-2 – fr UNESCO [370]

EDUCATION IN MALAYSIA / Malaysia. Ministry of Education – New ed. Kuala Lumpur, 1970 – 2mf – 9 – DE-210/1 – ne IDC [370]

EDUCATION IN MALAYSIA 1974 / Malaysia. Ministry of Education – rev ed. Kuala Lumpur, 1975 – 2mf – 9 – DE-211/1 – ne IDC [370]

EDUCATION IN MALAYSIA 1980 / Malaysia. Ministry of Education. Educational Planning and Research Division – Kuala Lumpur, 1981 – 1mf – 9 – DE-212-1 – ne IDC [370]

EDUCATION IN RELATION TO THE CHRISTIANISATION OF NATIONAL LIFE : WITH SUPPLEMENT, PRESENTATION AND DISCUSSION OF THE REPORT IN THE CONFERENCE ON 17TH JUNE 1910 TOGETHER WITH THE DISCUSSION ON CHRISTIAN LITERATURE – (Includes indexes) – Edinburgh: Publ for the World Missionary Conference by Oliphant, Anderson & Ferrier; New York: Fleming H Revell, [1910?] – 2mf – 9 – 0-8370-6475-9 – 1986-0475 – us A.T.L.A. [230]

EDUCATION IN SCIENCE – 1966- 1; 1976- 5,6,9 – us UMI [370]

EDUCATION IN THE ARAB STATES IN THE LIGHT OF THE 1977 ABU DHABI CONFERENCE / Tazi, Abdelhadi – 1980 – 81p – 9 – 92-3-101630-X – fr UNESCO [370]

EDUCATION IN THE SOCIETY OF FRIENDS : PAST, PRESENT, AND PROSPECTIVE / Parrish, Edward – Philadelphia: J B Lippincott, 1865 – 1mf – 9 – 0-8370-8542-X – 1986-2542 – us A.T.L.A. [370]

EDUCATION JOURNAL – Toronto, 1887-97 – 3r – 1 – $204.00 – cn Library Assoc [971]

EDUCATION LAW BULLETIN – v1- 1975- 1; v8- 1977- 5,6,9 – us UMI [340]

EDUCATION LAW OF NORTHERN NIGERIA 1964 / Nigeria. Northern Region – Kaduna, 1964 – 1mf – 9 – DE-116/1 – ne IDC [370]

EDUCATION LIBRARIES – (1985-. 5,6,9) – v3-. 1977- – 1 – us UMI [020]

EDUCATION MANITOBA – (v14- 1986/87-.- 9.-v11 printed as v12) – Winnipeg, v1-13 1974/75-1985/86 – 5 – Can$20.00y – cn Micromedia [073]

EDUCATION MANITOBA *see* CURRICULUM BULLETIN

L'EDUCATION NATIONALE ET LE MOUVEMENT OUVRIER EN FRANCE / Zoretti, Ludovic – Paris. n.d. (La Condition Ouvriere. Part Two.) – 9 – 2.50 – fr Bibl Nationale [360]

EDUCATION NEW SOUTH WALES – Jun 1949-Dec 1978 – 9 – at Pascoe [073]

EDUCATION NEWSLETTER – 1972-86 (complete) – 1r – 1 – ATLA S0833 – us A.T.L.A. [073]

"THE EDUCATION OF A KANSAN" / Klingberg, Fran J – 1883-1911 – 1 – us KS Hist [978]

THE EDUCATION OF CHRIST : HILL-SIDE REVERIES / Ramsay, William Mitchell – New York: G P Putnam, 1902 – 1mf – 9 – 0-8370-4835-4 – 1985-2835 – us A.T.L.A. [240]

THE EDUCATION OF DEAF CHILDREN / Great Britain. Ministry of Education – 1968 – 9 – uk Microform Academic [324]

EDUCATION OF LIFE (CCC153) / Ho, Shih-ming – (In Chinese) – 1st ed. Hong Kong: Council on Christian Literature for Overseas Chinese, 1958 – 1r – 1 – 1984-B500 – us A.T.L.A. [240]

EDUCATION OF MIGRANT WORKERS AND THEIR FAMILIES – 1978 – 44p – 9 – 92-3-101536-2 – fr UNESCO [370]

EDUCATION OF THE ADOLESCENT: REPORT OF THE CONSULTATIVE COMMITTEE / Great Britain. Consultative Committee – 1927. Hadow Report – 9 – uk Microform Academic [324]

THE EDUCATION OF THE NEGRO PRIOR TO 1861 : A HISTORY OF THE EDUCATION OF THE COLORED PEOPLE OF THE UNITED STATES FROM THE BEGINNING OF SLAVERY TO THE CIVIL WAR / Woodson, Carter Godwin – New York: G.P. Putnam, 1915 – 2mf – us A.T.L.A. [305]

EDUCATION OF THE SPANISH SPEAKING CHILD IN THE FIVE SOUTHWESTERN STATES – 1933 – 1r – 1 – $50.00 – C63011 – us Library Micro [370]

THE EDUCATION OF THE WOMEN OF INDIA / Cowan, Minna G – Edinburgh: Olphant, Anderson & Ferrier, [1912?] – 1mf – us A.T.L.A. [370]

THE EDUCATION OF WOMEN IN CHINA / Burton, Margaret E – New York: Fleming H. Revell, c1911 – 1mf – us A.T.L.A. [306]

THE EDUCATION OF WOMEN IN JAPAN / Burton, Margaret E – New York: Fleming H. Revell, c1914 – 1mf – us A.T.L.A. [306]

EDUCATION ORDINANCE, CHAPTER 279, 1964 / Hong Kong – Rev ed. Hong Kong, 1964 – 2mf – 9 – DE-153/1 – ne IDC [370]

L'EDUCATION, OU, LA GRANDE QUESTION SOCIALE DU JOUR: RECUEIL DE DOCUMENTS PROPRES A ECLAIRER LES GENS DE BONNE FOI: MAI 1886 – Montreal?: s.n., 1886 (Montreal: "L'Etendard"). 02638. (Pre-1900 Canadiana) – 9 – cn C.I.H.M. [971]

DE L'EDUCATION PHYSIQUE ET MORALE DES ENFANTS DES DEUX SEXES / Ballier – Paris, Nyon. 1785. 6733 – 9 – fr Hachette [324]

EDUCATION PLAN 1976-1980 / Papua New Guinea. Department of Education – [Port Moresby], 1976 – 2mf – 9 – DE-226/1 – ne IDC [370]

EDUCATION PLAN OF MALAWI 1973-1980 : PRIMARY EDUCATION, PRIMARY TEACHER TRAINING, SECONDARY EDUCATION, INSTITUTE OF EDUCATION / Malawi. Ministry of Education – Zomba, 1973 – 4mf – 9 – DE-448/1 – ne IDC [370]

EDUCATION POLICY 1988-2003 / Gambia. Ministry of Education, Youth, Sports and Culture – Banjul, 1988 – 2mf – 9 – DE-645/1 – ne IDC [370]

EDUCATION POLICY APRIL 1965 / Hong Kong – Hong Kong, [1965] – 2mf – 9 – DE-148/1 – ne IDC [370]

EDUCATION PORTFOLIO: MINISTER'S BRIEF 1987 / Papua New Guinea. Department of Education – [Port Moresby]. 2v. 1987 – 2mf – 9 – DE-638/1 – ne IDC [370]

EDUCATION REGULATIONS 1971 / Hong Kong – Hong Kong Government Gazette, Legal Supplement 1971 (2, p. B310-B382) – 1mf – 9 – DE-154/1 – ne IDC [370]

EDUCATION RESEARCH BULLETIN / U.S. Bureau of Indian Affairs – 1973-76. (American Indian Periodicals in the Princeton University Library) – 6mf – 9 – $45.00 – us UPA [370]

THE EDUCATION SECTOR : A REVIEW OF FACT AND COMMENT REGARDING THE CURRENT STATUS OF EDUCATION IN INDONESIA / Indonesia. Office of Educational and Cultural Research and Development – Jakarta, 1976 – 12mf – 9 – DE-559/1 – ne IDC [370]

EDUCATION STAFFING AND ENROLMENT STATISTICS : NATIONAL EDUCATION SYSTEM 1975-1981 / Papua New Guinea. Department of Education – (Missing: 1976-1978) – 4mf – 9 – DE-220/1 – ne IDC [370]

EDUCATION STATISTICS 1968-1988 / Botswana. Educational Statistics Unit – (Missing: v12(1-2) 1978/79; v15(1-2) 1982/83) – Gaborone. v1-22 – 31mf – 9 – DE-419/1 – ne IDC [370]

EDUCATION STATISTICS 1968/69-1987 / Swaziland. Central Statistical Office – (Missing: 1970. 1980) – 25 mf – 9 – DE-478/1 – ne IDC [370]

EDUCATION STATISTICS 1974/75-1984/85 / Jamaica. Ministry of Education – (Missing: 1977/78; 1981/82-1983/84) – 26mf – 9 – DE-522/1 – ne IDC [370]

EDUCATION STATISTICS 1975-1976 / Farquharson, V M – Nassau – 2mf – 9 – DE-512/1 – ne IDC [370]

EDUCATION STATISTICS 1977-1986 / Lesotho. Bureau of Statistics – (Missing: 1983) – 23mf – 9 – DE-445/1 – ne IDC [370]

EDUCATION STATISTICS 1978/79-1981/82 / Sudan. Southern Region. Regional Ministry of Education and Guidance – (Missing: 1979/80-1980/81) – 11mf – 9 – DE-477/1 – ne IDC [370]

EDUCATION STATISTICS 1981-1989 / Malawi. Ministry of Education and Culture. Planning Unit – (Missing: 1983-1987) – Lilongwe – 7mf – 9 – DE-447/1 – ne IDC [370]

EDUCATION STATISTICS AND ANNUAL REPORT 1971/72-1984/85 / Gambia. Ministry of Economic Planning and Industrial Development. Education Department – (Missing: 1974/75-1983/84) – Banjul – 6mf – 9 – DE-427/1 – ne IDC [370]

EDUCATION STATISTICS FOR THE UNITED KINGDOM 1967-1975 – (Coll title: British Government Publications...1801-1977, Education) – 16mf – 9 (£970.00 education set of 152mf) – uk Chadwyck [370]

EDUCATION STATISTICS IN PUNJAB 1972/73-1983/84 / Pakistan. Punjab. Bureau of Education – (Missing: 1980/81; 1982/83) – Lahore – 26mf – 9 – DE-572/1 – ne IDC [370]

EDUCATION THREE-THIRTEEN – (v.7 .1979 5,6,9) – v.1. 1973 – 1 – us UMI [073]

THE EDUCATION THRUST OF THE 70'S / Jamaica. Ministry of Education – Kingston, 1973 – 1mf – 9 – DE-525/1 – ne IDC [370]

L'EDUCATION TRADITIONNELLE CHEZ LES VUTE, CAMEROUN CENTRAL / N'Goura, C – 9 – F30.00 – fr Ethnologie [370]

THE EDUCATION WE WANT, MILITARY GOVERNOR, MID-WESTERN NIGERIA / Ogbemudia, SO – 1968 – 1mf – 9 – DE-111/1 – ne IDC [370]

EDUCATION WEEK – v1-. 1981- – 1,5,6,9 – us UMI [073]

EDUCATION WHITE PAPER : GUIDELINES FOR A FOURTH DEVELOPMENT PLAN 1975-1985; PRESENTED TO THE CABINET BY THE MINISTER ... / Seychelles. Ministry of Education and Social Development – Victoria, 1975 – 1mf – 9 – DE-462/1 – ne IDC [370]

EDUCATIONAL ADMINISTRATION – v1- 1972- 1; v6- 1977- 5,6,9 – us UMI [370]

EDUCATIONAL ADMINISTRATION AND SUPERVISION – Baltimore. v. 1-45. 1915-59 – 1 – us Princeton Micro [370]

EDUCATIONAL ADMINISTRATION QUARTERLY – v7- 1971- 1; v1- 5,6; v11- 9 – us UMI [370]

EDUCATIONAL ADMINISTRATOR AND INSTRUCTIONAL MATERIALS – 1984 – 237p – 9 – 92-3-102202-4 – fr UNESCO [370]

EDUCATIONAL AND DRAMATIC SOCIETY OF YOUNG SLOVAKS – Ft. William, Ontario, 1924-1935 – 1 reel – 1 – us I.H.R.C. [370]

EDUCATIONAL AND PSYCHOLOGICAL MEASUREMENT – v1- 1941- 1,5,6; v35- 9 – us UMI [370]

EDUCATIONAL AND PSYCHOLOGICAL RESEARCH – v.1 .1981 – 1,5,6,9 – us UMI [073]

EDUCATIONAL BROADCASTING REVIEW – v1-7 1967-73 1; v5-7 5,6 – us UMI [370]

THE EDUCATIONAL CHART: BEING A COMPARATIVE ABSTRACT OF TWO ANTAGONISTIC SYSTEMS OF EDUCATION, THE MATHEMATICAL AND THE AESTHETIC / Dallas, Angus – Toronto: Hunter, Rose, 1881. 02255. (Pre-1900 Canadiana) – 9 – cn C.I.H.M. [971]

EDUCATIONAL CHARTERS AND DOCUMENTS A.D. 589-1909 / Leach, A F – H-1316 2. 1911 – 8 – ne IDC [025]

THE EDUCATIONAL CIRCULAR – [S.l. : s.n., 1876?-18–] – 9 – cn C.I.H.M. [370]

EDUCATIONAL COMMUNICATION AND TECHNOLOGY *see* ECTJ

EDUCATIONAL DEVELOPMENT : PROBLEMS AND PLANS / Swaziland. Ministry of Education – Mbabane, 1980 – 1mf – 9 – DE-484/1 – ne IDC [370]

EDUCATIONAL DEVELOPMENT IN THAILAND : REPORT OF THE MINISTRY TO THE ... INTERNATIONAL CONFERENCE ON EDUCATION, GENEVA 1973/75-1981/83 / Thailand. Ministry of Education – (Missing: v36 1975/76) – Bangkok. v35-39 – 4mf – 9 – DE-587/1 – ne IDC [370]

EDUCATIONAL DEVELOPMENT IN THE FOURTH PLAN 1969-1974 : REPORT OF THE STEERING COMMITTEE OF THE PLANNING GROUP ON EDUCATION / India. Planning Commission. Education Division – New Delhi, 1968 – 4mf – 9 – DE-546/1 – ne IDC [370]

EDUCATIONAL DEVELOPMENT IN THE SECOND NATIONAL DEVELOPMENT PLAN 1972-1976 / Zambia. Ministry of Education – 1972 – 1mf – 9 – DE-497/1 – ne IDC [370]

EDUCATIONAL DEVELOPMENTS IN INDIA 1971-1977 / India. Ministry of Education and Social Welfare – New Delhi, 1977 – 1mf – 9 – DE-543/1 – ne IDC [370]

EDUCATIONAL DIRECTORY AND BASIC EDUCATIONAL STATISTICS 1969/70-1978/79 / Grenada. Ministry of Education – (Mising: 1970/71; 1972/73; 1975/76-1977/78) – St. George's – 4mf – 9 – DE-517/1 – ne IDC [370]

EDUCATIONAL EVALUATION AND POLICY ANALYSIS – v. 1-. 1979- – 1,5,6,9 – us UMI [370]

EDUCATIONAL FILM LIBRARY ASSOCIATION (EFLA) EVALUATIONS *see* AFVA EVALUATIONS

EDUCATIONAL FORMATIONS OF THE JESUITS... / Jacobsen, Jerome V – Madrid: Razon y Fe, 1940 – sp Bibl Santa Ana [240]

EDUCATIONAL FORUM – v1- 1936- 1; v33- 5,6; v40- 9 – us UMI [370]

EDUCATIONAL FORUM *see* OSSTF FORUM

EDUCATIONAL GERONTOLOGY – v. 1-. 1976- – 1,5,6,9 – us UMI [370]

EDUCATIONAL GROWTH IN INDIA : DATA BASE / India. National Institute of Educational Planning and Administration – 1981 – 4mf – 9 – DE-619/1 – ne IDC [370]

EDUCATIONAL HISTORY OF ILLINOIS / Cook, John W – Chicago: Henry O. Sheppart Co., 1912. Illinois Reel 8. (The Cox Library Collection) – 5 – us Americana [978]

THE EDUCATIONAL IDEAL IN THE MINISTRY : THE LYMAN BEECHER LECTURES AT YALE UNIVERSITY IN THE YEAR 1908 / Faunce, William Herbert Perry – New York: Macmillan, 1908 – 1mf – us A.T.L.A. [240]

EDUCATIONAL INDICATORS IN KOREA 1988 / Korea. Korean Educational Development Institute – (In Korean and English) – Seoul, 1988 – 4mf – 9 – DE-629/1 – ne IDC [370]

EDUCATIONAL JOURNAL *see* THE CANADA SCHOOL JOURNAL

EDUCATIONAL JOURNAL OF WESTERN CANADA – Brandon [Man.: s.n., 1899-1903] – 9 – cn C.I.H.M. [370]

EDUCATIONAL LEADERSHIP – (v. 26- 1968- 5,6. v. 33- 1975- 9) – 1- 1943- – 1 – us UMI [370]

EDUCATIONAL METHOD – v. 1-22. 1921-1943 – 1 – us Princeton Micro [370]

EDUCATIONAL MISSIONS / Barton, James Levi – New York: Student Volunteer Movement for Foreign Missions, 1913 – 1mf – us A.T.L.A. [240]

EDUCATIONAL MISSIONS IN INDIA / Church of Scotland. General Assembly. Committee for the Propagation of the Gospel in Foreign Parts – 1890 – 1 – us A.T.L.A. [240]

THE EDUCATIONAL MONTHLY OF CANADA *see* THE CANADA EDUCATIONAL MONTHLY

THE EDUCATIONAL MUSEUM AND SCHOOL OF ART AND DESIGN FOR UPPER CANADA.. / Canada. Departement de l'Instruction Publique pour le Haut-Canada – Toronto: Printed for the Department of Public Instruction for Upper Canada by Lovell sic and Gibson, 1858. SEM105P334 – 1mf – 9 – Can$2.25 – cn Bibl Nat [370]

EDUCATIONAL NOTES – Libertarian Alliance, London, Nos.1,3. 6p – 9 – 1.00f – at Libertarian Micro [335]

EDUCATIONAL PHILOSOPHY AND THEORY – v1- 1969- 1; v9- 1977- 5,6,9 – us UMI [370]

THE EDUCATIONAL PHILOSOPHY OF NATIONAL SOCIALISM / Kneller, George Frederick – New Haven: Yale University Press, 1941. viii,299p. Bibliography – 1 – us U.W. Library [370]

EDUCATIONAL PLANNING AT THE LOCAL LEVEL / Thailand. National Economic Development Board – (In Thai and English) – Bangkok, c. 1968 – 2mf – 9 – DE-303/1 – ne IDC [370]

EDUCATIONAL PLANNING PRELIMINARY DRAFT OF THE LONG-RANGE EDUCATIONAL PLAN, 1964-1982 / China. Republic. Ministry of Education – Taipei. 1964. BD-345 1 – 9 – ne IDC [370]

THE EDUCATIONAL POLICY OF QATAR / Qatar. National Commission for Education, Culture and Science – [Doha], 1985 – 1mf – 9 – DE-634/1 – ne IDC [370]

THE EDUCATIONAL PROBLEMS OF SCHEDULED CASTE AND SCHEDULED TRIBE SCHOOL AND COLLEGE STUDENTS IN INDIA : A STATISTICAL PROFILE / Shah, V P – New Delhi, 1982 – 5mf – 9 – DE-542/1 – ne IDC [370]

EDUCATIONAL PROCESS AND HISTORIOGRAPHY IN AFRICA – 1985 – 152p – 9 – 92-3-102297-0 – fr UNESCO [960]

EDUCATIONAL PROGRAMMES IN THE FIFTH PLAN 1975-1980 / Nepal. Ministry of Education. Planning Division – Kathmandu, 1977 – 1mf – 9 – DE-561/1 – ne IDC [370]

EDUCATIONAL PROGRESS IN THE REPUBLIC OF INDONESIA / Indonesia – SE-10,477 1. 1954 – 9 – ne IDC [370]

EDUCATIONAL PSYCHOLOGIST – (v.14 .1979 5,6,9) – v.1. 1963 – 1 – us UMI [073]

EDUCATIONAL PSYCHOLOGY – 1981- 13v – 9 – £230.00 – 0144-3410 – uk Carfax [150]

EDUCATIONAL PSYCHOLOGY REVIEW – v1-6. 1989-94 – 1,5 – $65.00v – us UMI [150]

EDUCATIONAL RECONSTRUCTION / Great Britain. Ministry of Education – 1943. Cmnd 6548 – 9 – uk Microform Academic [324]

EDUCATIONAL RECORD – v. 1-25. 1920-1944 – 1 – us Princeton Micro [370]

EDUCATIONAL RECORD – (v. 50- 1969- 5,6. v. 56- 1975- 9) – 1- 1920- – 1 – us UMI [370]

THE EDUCATIONAL RECORD OF THE PROVINCE OF QUEBEC – Montreal: Protestant Committee of the Board of Education, v1 no 1 (Jan 1881)- – 9 – cn C.I.H.M. [370]

EDUCATIONAL REFORM : PROPOSALS AND RECOMMENDATIONS / Zambia. Ministry of Education – Lusaka, 1977 – 3mf – 9 – DE-498/1 – ne IDC [370]

EDUCATIONAL REFORM IN JAPAN, 1945-52 – (Guide only $90.00) – Part 1 – $2,635.00 – 0-88692-199-6 – us UPA [370]

EDUCATIONAL REFORMS : EXPERIENCES AND PROSPECTS – 1979 – 232p – 9 – 92-3-101669-5 – fr UNESCO [370]

EDUCATIONAL REPORT : INSTITUTIONS OF HIGHER EDUCATION 1975-1977 / Thailand. Office of University Affairs – (In Thai and English) – 25mf – 9 – DE-274/1 – ne IDC [370]

EDUCATIONAL RESEARCH – v1-21. 1958/59-78/79 – 5,9 – Dfl1,260.00;Dfl60.00 – ne Swets [370]

EDUCATIONAL RESEARCH – (v.24-. 1981-. 5,6,9) – v.1-. 1958- – 1 – us UMI [370]

EDUCATIONAL RESEARCH BULLETIN – v. 1-40. 1922-1961 – 1 – us Princeton Micro [370]

EDUCATIONAL RESEARCH QUARTERLY – v. 1- 1976- – 1,5,6,9 – us UMI [370]

EDUCATIONAL RESEARCHER – v15- 1964- 1; v6- 5,6,9 – us UMI [370]

EDUCATIONAL REVIEW – 1-76. 1891-1928. Superseded by yIntellect – 1 – us UMI [370]

EDUCATIONAL REVIEW – 1948- 45v – 9 – £225.50 – 0013-1911 – uk Carfax [370]

EDUCATIONAL REVIEW – (All published.) v. 1-76. 1892-1928 – 1,5,6 – us Princeton Micro [370]

EDUCATIONAL REVIEW – Birmingham. v1-21. 1948/49-68/69 – 5,9 – Dfl1,260.00; Dfl60.00v – ne Swets [370]

EDUCATIONAL REVIEW – New York, 1901-06 – 1r – 1 – us Ross [370]

EDUCATIONAL REVIEW – St. John and Fredericton, 1887-1931 – 8r – 1 – $520.00 – cn Library Assoc [370]

THE EDUCATIONAL REVIEW / China Christian Educational Association. Shanghai – v1-30, no. 4 (all publ). May 1907-Nov 1938 – 6r – 1 – $615.00 – us UPA [240]

EDUCATIONAL SCREEN *see* AV GUIDE

EDUCATIONAL SCREEN AND AUDIO-VISUAL GUIDE *see* AV GUIDE

EDUCATIONAL SIMULATION MODEL / Thailand. National Education Commission – (In Thai) – 1980 – 2mf – 9 – DE-304/1 – ne IDC [370]

EDUCATIONAL STATEMENT OF THE HON. ADAM CROOKS, MINISTER OF EDUCATION: ON MOVING THE ESTIMATES FOR 1880: IN COMMITTEE OF SUPPLY, HOUSE OF ASSEMBLY, PROVINCE OF ONTARIO / Crooks, Adam – Toronto?: s.n., 1880 (Toronto: C. B. Robinson). 04191. (Pre-1900 Canadiana) – 9 – cn C.I.H.M. [971]

EDUCATIONAL STATISTICS, 1965/66-1984/85 / Sudan. Ministry of Education – (1965/66-1979/80 in Arabic. 1980/81-1984/85 in Arabic and English. Missing: 1972/73-1975/76; 1977/78) – 37mf – 9 – DE-476/1 – ne IDC [370]

EDUCATIONAL STATISTICS 1972-1984 / Zambia. Ministry of Education and Culture. Development and Planning Unit – (Missing: 1975. 1981-1982) – Lusaka – 24mf – 9 – DE-495/1 – ne IDC [370]

EDUCATIONAL STATISTICS 1974/75-1976/77 / Antigua and Barbuda. Ministry of Education, Health and Culture. – St. John's – 5mf – 9 – DE-508/1 – ne IDC [370]

EDUCATIONAL STATISTICS 1975/76-1977/78 / Nigeria. Sokoto State. Ministry of Education. Statistics Section – 6mf – 9 – DE-123/1 – ne IDC [370]

EDUCATIONAL STATISTICS 1983-1985 / South Africa. Venda. Department of Education – Sibasa – 3mf – 9 – DE-475/1 – ne IDC [370]

EDUCATIONAL STATISTICS IN AFGHANISTAN 1969-1972 / Afghanistan. Ministry of Education Department of Planning – Kabul – 15mf – 9 – DE-706/1 – ne IDC [370]

EDUCATIONAL STATISTICS IN THE NORTH-WESTERN STATE, NIGERIA / Planning and Administrative Division, Ministry of Education and Community Development – Sokoto, North-Western State: The Division, 1968-72 – us Res Libr [370]

EDUCATIONAL STATISTICS OF MALAYSIA 1938 TO 1967 / Malaysia. Ministry of Education – Kuala Lumpur, 1968 – 2mf – 9 – DE-193/1 – ne IDC [370]

EDUCATIONAL STATISTICS OF MALAYSIA 1980 / Malaysia. Ministry of Education – Kuala Lumpur, 1980 – 4mf – 9 – DE-196/1 – ne IDC [370]

EDUCATIONAL STATISTICS OF MALAYSIA 1974/75 / Malaysia. Ministry of Education – Kuala Lumpur, 1978 – 3mf – 9 – DE-194/1 – ne IDC [370]

EDUCATIONAL STATISTICS OF MALAYSIA 1976-1979 / Malaysia. Ministry of Education – Kuala Lumpur, 1982 – 3mf – 9 – DE-195/1 – ne IDC [370]

EDUCATIONAL STATISTICS OF NEPAL AT A GLANCE 1976-1981 / Nepal. Ministry of Education and Culture. Planning Division – Kathmandu – 1mf – 9 – DE-560/1 – ne IDC [370]

EDUCATIONAL STRATEGIES FOR SMALL ISLAND STATES / Atchoarena, David – 1993 – 93p – 9 – 92-803-1147-6 – fr UNESCO [370]

EDUCATIONAL STUDIES – v1- 1970- 1; v7- 6; v6- 1975- 9 – us UMI [370]

EDUCATIONAL STUDIES – Oxford, England. 1975- 19v – 9 – £225.50 – 0305-5698 – uk Carfax [370]

EDUCATIONAL STUDIES IN MATHEMATICS – (v15-. 1984-. 5,6,9) – v1-. May 1968- – 1 – us UMI [073]

THE EDUCATIONAL SYSTEMS OF THE PURITANS AND JESUITS COMPARED : A PREMIUM ESSAY WRITTEN FOR "THE SOCIETY FOR THE PROMOTION OF COLLEGIATE AND THEOLOGICAL EDUCATION AT THE WEST" / Porter, Noah – (Includes bibliographical references) – New York: M W Wood, 1851 – 1mf – 9 – 0-8370-7657-9 – 1986-1657 – us A.T.L.A. [370]

EDUCATIONAL SYSTEMS REGULATION : A METHODOLOGICAL GUIDE / D'Hainaut, L – 1980 – 60p – 9 – 92-3-101606-7 – fr UNESCO [370]

EDUCATIONAL TECHNOLGOY – v4- 1964- 1; v8- 5,6; v15- 9 – us UMI [600]

EDUCATIONAL TECHNOLOGY ABSTRACTS – 1985- 9v – 9 – £244.50 – 0266-3368 – uk Carfax [370]

EDUCATIONAL THEATRE JOURNAL – (v. 21-30. 1969-78. 5,6. v. 27-30. 1975-78. 9) – 1-30. 1949-78. Superseded by theatre journal – 1 – us UMI [370]

EDUCATIONAL THEORY – v. 1-25. 1951-75 – 1 – us UMI [370]

EDUCATIONAL THOUGHTS FOR THE DIAMOND JUBILEE YEAR: INAUGURAL ADDRESS DELIVERED IN CONVOCATION HALL, MANITOBA COLLEGE, WINNIPEG, NOVEMBER 19TH, 1897 / Bryce, George – Winnipeg?, 1897? 02850. (Pre-1900 Canadiana) – 9 – cn C.I.H.M. [370]

EDUCATIONAL WEEKLY – v1-5. 1885-87 – 1 – cn Precision [370]

EDUCATIONAL WEEKLY *see* THE CANADA SCHOOL JOURNAL

THE EDUCATIONAL WEEKLY – (Merged with: Canada School Journal to become: The Educational Journal) – Toronto: Grip Print and Pub Co, [1884?-1887] – 9 – cn C.I.H.M. [370]

EDUCATIONAL WORD LESSONS / Baillairge, Charles – Quebec: C. Darveau, 18–?. 02496. (Pre-1900 Canadiana) – 9 – cn C.I.H.M. [370]

EDUCATIONALE TRENDS 1973-1977 / Kenya. Central Bureau of Statistics – 1978 – 2mf – 9 – DE-438/1 – ne IDC [370]

EDUCATIONALIST – Brighton, C.W. [Ont.]: H. Spencer, [1860-18– or 19–] – 9 – cn C.I.H.M. [370]

THE EDUCATOR – London [Ont.]: Jones & Co, [1868-18–?] – 9 – cn C.I.H.M. [370]

EDUCOM – v. 9-. 1974- – 1,5,6,9 – us UMI [370]

L'EDUEN [PUIS] LE NATIONAL DE SAONE-ET-LOIRE – Autun (Saone-et-Loire), March 1839 – Dec. 1851 – 3r – fr Armell [440]

EDULARIOS DE LA MONARQUIA ESPAÑOLA DE MARGARITA, NUEVA ANDALUCIA...TOMO 1 Y 2. CARACAS, 1967 / Otte, Enrique – Madrid: Graf. Calleja, 1968 – 1 – sp Bibl Santa Ana [946]

EDUQUEMOS A LAS MADRES / Rodriguez Pedreira, Jose – Plasencia: Imp. Gabriel y Galan, 1959 – 1 – sp Bibl Santa Ana [946]

EDUT BI-YEHOSEF / Sofer, J – Jerusalem. 1933. BJ-27-25 1 – 9 – ne IDC [900]

EDVARD GRIEGS BRIEFWECHSEL, BAND 1 : DIE BRIEFE MAX ABRAHAMS AN EDVARD GRIEG / ed by Oelmann, Klaus Henning – 1994 – 2mf – DM80.00 – 3-8267-2018-0 – gw Hänsel [780]

EDWARD 6 AND THE BOOK OF COMMON PRAYER : AN EXAMINATION INTO ITS ORIGIN AND EARLY HISTORY, WITH AN APPENDIX OF UNPUBLISHED DOCUMENTS / Gasquet, Francis Aidan & Bishop, Edmund – London: J. Hodges, 1890 – 2mf – us A.T.L.A. [240]

EDWARD 6TH AND THE BOOK OF COMMON PRAYER / Gasquet, Abbot & Bishop, E – London, 1948 – 4mf – 8 – Dfl19.00 – ne Slangenburg [240]

EDWARD AND PAMELA FITZGERALD. : BEING SOME ACCOUNT OF THEIR LIVES... / Campbell, Gerald Fitzgerald – London: Edward Arnold, 1904 – 1 roll – 1 – 1-55879-625-8 – uk Libr Preservation [920]

THE EDWARD BARNSLEY TRUST DRAWINGS COLLECTION – 7r – 14 – £350.00 – uk World [740]

EDWARD BULWER, FIRST BARON LYTTON OF KNEBWORTH : A SOCIAL, PERSONAL, AND POLITICAL MONOGRAPH / Escott, Thomas Hay Sweet – London: G. Routledge and Sons, Ltd; New York: E.P. Dutton and Co., 1910 – 1 roll – 1 – 1-55879-442-5 – uk Libr Preservation [320]

EDWARD DRUMGOOLE PAPERS / Drumgoole, Edward – 1770-1871. University of North Carolina Library. Guide – 1 – $90.00 – us U.N.C. Southern Hist [920]

EDWARD EVERETT PAPERS, 1675-1930 / Everett, Edward – Massachusetts Historical Society – 70r – 1 – $5325.00 – us UMI [920]

Edward, Henry *see* RELIGIO VIATORIS

Edward Hunt & Co. Bristol, England *see* CITY OF BRISTOL, NEWPORT AND WELCH TOWNS DIRECTORY

EDWARD IRVING : MAN, PREACHER, PROPHET / Root, Jean C – 1912 – 1 – $50.00 – us Presbyterian [240]

EDWARD IRVING AND HIS CIRCLE, INCLUDING SOME CONSIDERATION OF THE "TONGUES" MOVEMENT IN THE LIGHT OF MODERN PSYCHOLOGY / Drummond, A L – 9 – $12.00 – us I.R.C. [240]

EDWARD R. MURROW PAPERS, 1927-1965 / Murrow, Edward R – (Correspondence and personal and professional papers of 'founding father of broadcast journalism') – 50r – 1 – $3695.00 – us UMI [920]

Edward S Joynes *see* DER ZERBROCHENE KRUG

EDWARD WOODRUFF VS NORTH BLOOMFIELD GRAVEL MINING COMPANY : CONTROVERSIAL HYDRAULIC MINING CASE NEAR MARYSVILLE, CALIFORNIA – 10r – 5 – $500.00 – B50530 – us Library Micro [340]

Edwards, A M *see*
- DESCRIPTION DES CRUSTACES DE LA FAMILLE DES GALATHEIDES
- LES PORCELLANIDES ET DES BRACHYURES

EDWARDS ABSTRACTS FROM RECORDS – San Francisco, CA. 1984-88 – 6r – 1 – $300.00 – B02813 – us Library Micro [071]

Edwards, Alfred George *see* LANDMARKS IN THE HISTORY OF THE WELSH CHURCH

Edwards, BB *see* THE MISSIONARY GAZETTEER

Edwards, Bryan *see*
- THE HISTORY, CIVIL AND COMMERCIAL, OF THE BRITISH WEST INDIES WITH A CONTINUATION TO THE PRESENT TIME
- THE HISTORY OF THE BRITISH COLONIES IN THE WEST INDIES

EDWARD'S CHANCERY APPEALS REPORTS / New York. (State) – (A Pre-NRS title) – v1-4. 1831-50 (all publ) – 33mf – 9 – $49.50 – LLMC 80-021 – us L.L.M.C. [340]

Edwards, Charles *see* A PRACTICAL TREATISE ON PARTIES TO BILLS AND OTHER PLEADINGS IN CHANCERY: WITH PRECEDENTS

EDWARDS COUNTY LEADER – Kingsley. Kan. 1877-1880 – 1 – us UMI [071]

Edwards, David *see*
- NOTABILITIES OF TORONTO IN 1877
- PULPIT CRITICISM

Edwards, David, fl. 1882 *see* MEDICAL CRITICISM

Edwards, E *see* LIBER MONASTERII DE HYDA (RS45)

Edwards, Edward *see*
- THE MONTREAL GAZETTE
- MONTREAL GAZETTE

Edwards, Edwin *see* ECCLESIASTICAL JURISDICTION: A SKETCH OF ITS ORIGIN AND EARLY PROGRESS.

Edwards, FE *see* A MONOGRAPH OF THE EOCENE CEPHALOPODA AND UNIVALVES OF ENGLAND

Edwards, G W *see* ENERGY POLICY AND THE GAS AND FUEL CORPORATION OF VICTORIA

Edwards, Gus C *see* LEGAL LAUGHS

Edwards, J *see* THE HEMIPTERA-HOMOPTERA (CICADINA AND PSYLLINA) OF THE BRITISH ISLANDS...

Edwards, J Baker *see* ON THE WATER SUPPLY OF MONTREAL AND ITS SUBURBS

Edwards, Jonathan *see*
- AN ILLUSTRATED HISTORY OF SPOKANE COUNTY, STATE OF WASHINGTON
- ON THE TRINITY
- SERMONS

Edwards, Joseph Plimsoll *see* LOUISBOURG: AN HISTORICAL SKETCH: READ BEFORE THE NOVA SCOTIA HISTORICAL SOCIETY, 27TH NOVEMBER, 1894

Edwards, K A et al *see* THE WATER RESOURCE IN TROPICAL AFRICA AND ITS EXPLOITATION

Edwards, Morgan *see*
- THE CUSTOMS OF PRIMITIVE CHURCHES
- MANUSCRIPT SERMONS
- MATERIALS TOWARD A HISTORY OF BAPTISTS IN PROV. OF PENN., R.I., N.J., DEL., MD., VA., N.C., S.C., AND GEORGIA

Edwards, Oliver *see* ENGLISCHE DICHTUNG AUS GOETHES ZEITALTER IM LICHT DEUTSCHER KUNSTLEHRE

EDWARDS' PHILATELIC PRESS LIST [AND] ADVERTISER OF PHILATELISTS' SUPPLIES – Montreal: J. Edwards, [1896?-1898] – 9 – cn C.I.H.M. [760]

Edwards, S J Celestine *see* FROM SLAVERY TO A BISHOPRIC, OR, THE LIFE OF BISHOP WALTER HAWKINS OF THE BRITISH METHODIST EPISCOPAL CHURCH, CANADA

Edwards, S T *see* BOTANICAL REGISTER

Edwards, T *see* TWELVE FAVORITE NEW COUNTRY DANCES FOR THE VIOLIN, HARP OR PIANOFORTE

Edwards, Thomas Charles *see* EPISTLE TO THE HEBREWS

Edwards, Thomas, jr *see* QUIZ BOOK: QUESTIONS AND ANSWERS ON THE SUBJECT OF BAILMENTS AND CARRIERS.

Edwards, WE *see* A LETTER FROM THE...MINISTER OF WESTBURY-UPON-TRYM TO THE OCCASIONAL PREACHERS AT PORTLAND CHAPEL, LATELY OPENED IN THAT PARISH

Edwards, William Henry *see* SHAKSPER NOT SHAKESPEARE

EDWIN VON MANTEUFFEL ALS QUELLE ZUR GESCHICHTE FRIEDRICH WILHELMS 4TH / Schmitz, Elisabeth – Muenchen, Berlin, 1921 – 95p – 9 – DM48.00 – 3-89349-057-4 – gw Hänsel [943]

DIE EEDELE HOGHE ENDE TROOSTLIKE SENDEBRIEF, DEN DIE HEYLIGE APOSTEL PAULUS TO DEN ROMEREN GESCREUEN HEEFT, VERCLAERT ENDE. WTGELECHT / Hoffmann, M – 1533. BME-179 1 – 9 – ne IDC [240]

Eek, Dirk van *see* NAPOLEON IM SPIEGEL DER GOETHESCHEN UND DER HEINESCHEN DICHTUNG

THE EEL GROUND TIMES – Eel Ground [N.B.]: S.B.W. Francis, v1 no 1 (Apr 1869)- – 9 – cn C.I.H.M. [073]

EEL RIVER ECHO – Rio Dell, CA. 1971-1974 – 1r – 1 – $50.00 – B02700 – us Library Micro [071]

EEL VALLEY ADVANCE – Fortuna, CA. Mar 1970-Feb 1975 – 1r – 1 – $50.00 – B02245 – us Library Micro [071]

Eells, M *see* HISTORY OF THE CONGREGATIONAL ASSOCIATION OF OREGON AND WASHINGTON TERRITORY, THE HOME MISSIONARY SOCIETY OF OREGON AND ADJOINING TERRITORIES, AND THE NORTHWESTERN ASSOCIATION OF CONGREGATIONAL MINISTERS

Eells, Myron *see*
- FATHER EELLS, OR, THE RESULTS OF FIFTY-FIVE YEARS OF MISSIONARY LABORS IN WASHINGTON AND OREGON
- A HISTORY OF INDIAN MISSIONS OF THE PACIFIC COAST

EENDRACHT, DE – Aliwal North, South Africa. 31 Oct 1885-24 Dec 86. 1 reel – 1, 16 diazo available at reduced price – sa SA Libr [072]

EENIGE BYBELSE FIGUUREN GELYKENISSEN EN ZINNEBEELDEN : MET DE DAAR OP PASSENDE VERSSEN EN SCHRIFTUURPLAATSEN / Luyken, J – Sole ed. N.p., n.d. – 1mf – 9 – O-3112/1 – ne IDC [760]

EENIGE MEDEDEELINGEN OVER DE KERKELIJKE ARBEID EN DE GEESTELIJKE STROOMINGEN IN DE BURGER-INTERNEERINGSKAMPEN IN INDIE / Verkuyl, Johannes – SE 10,439 1. 1945 – 9 – ne IDC [360]

EENIGE OORZAKEN VAN DEN FINANTIEELEN NOOD DER NEDERLANDSCH-INDISCHE REGEERING, ENKELE BEZUINIGING-SUGGESTIES EN IETS OVER DE VERHOUDING INDIE-HOLLAND / Rinkes, J – 1932 – 2mf – 9 – ILM-995/1 – ne IDC [350]

EENIGE OPMERKINGEN OVER HET POLITIETOEZICHT OP ZEE, IN VERBAND MET DE ZEEVISCHERIJ-CONVENTIE VAN 6 MEI 1882 / Hacke, H C – Amsterdam, 1885 – 2mf – 1 – ILM-2321/1 – ne IDC [327]

EENIGE SCHETSEN VOOR EENE GESCHIEDENIS VAN DE TREKBOEREN, THANS BEKEND ANDER DE NAAM VAN DE GEREFORMEERDE GEMEENTE TE ST JANUARIO, HUMPATA, DISTRIKT MOSSAMEDES, PROVINCIE ANGOLA, OP DE WEST KUST VAN ZUID-AFRIKA – Amsterdam, Pretoria: Hoveker & Wormser, 1897 – 1 – us Res Libr [960]

EENVOUDIGE JAPANSCHE SPRAAKKUN EERSTE DEEL. EERSTE DRUK / Moosdijk, P van der – Batavia: N.V. Boekhandel Visser and Co., 2602. April, 1942. 112p – 112-113mf – 9 – ne IDC [480]

EENVULDIGHE VNDE CHRISTELIJCKE BERICHTINGHE OP VIJF VRAGHEN BY EENIGHE VAN MEN. SYM. GESINTHEYT VOORGHESTELT / Blesdijk, Nicolaas M van – Wtgegaen int Jaer 1547. 1607. BME-387 1 – 9 – ne IDC [240]

EEO (EQUAL EMPLOYMENT OPPORTUNITY) TODAY – v3- 1976- 1; v5- 1978- 5,6,9 – us UMI [330]

EEQ: EXCEPTIONAL EDUCATION QUARTERLY – v.1. 1980 – 1,5,6,9 – us UMI [073]

EERLYCKE TYTKORTING BESTAENDE IN VERSCHEYDE RYMEN / Krul, J H – (Contains: Minne-beelden: toe-gepast de lievende ionckheyt) – Amsterdam, 1635 [1640] – 1mf – 9 – O-3101/1 – ne IDC [760]

EERLYCKE TYTKORTING BESTAENDE IN VERSCHEYDE RYMEN GEMAECT / Krul, J H – Haarlem, 1634 – 9mf – 9 – O-3102/1 – ne IDC [760]

EERSTE BOEKJAAR DER INDISCHE PARTIJ 1912. SAMENGESTELD...ENZ / Ham, J G van – Bandoeng, 1913. – 3mf – 9 – ne IDC [950]

EERSTE NOTA OVER HET NATIONAAL WELVAARTSPLAN 1946 / Netherlands. Centraal Planbureau – (First Memorandum on the National Prosperity Plan 1946). 's-Gravenhage. 1946. BD-1698 1 – 9 – ne IDC [338]

EESTI AJALVO BIBLIOGRAFII, 1877-1917 – Bibliotheca Estoniae historica, 1877-1917. Comp. by E. Blumfeldt and N. Loone. 3 v. Tartu. 1933-37. BR-9821 1 – 9 – ne IDC [947]

EESTI BAPTISMI AJALUGU: I. ARKAMISE AEG / Tuttar, H & Dahl, H V – Estonian Baptist History: 1. Revival Time. Tallinn: Publishing House of the Estonian Baptist Churches, 1929. 134p – 1 – 5.36 – us Baptist [240]

EESTI BOLSHEVIK – (Cont as: Kommunist Estonii. Tallin, 1952-1970. Missing: 1946-1954; 1955(9-12)-1961) – Tallin, 1945-1951 – 168mf – 9 – ne IDC [320]

EESTI BOLSHEVIK – Tallin, 1945-51.Continued by: Kommunist Estonii, 1952-70. Lacking: 1946-54; 1955 (9-12)-1961. BR-10,400/1 – 9 – ne IDC [073]

EESTI HAAL – London, England. -m. Dec 1947-Dec 1952. 1 reel – 1 – uk British Libr Newspaper [072]

EESTI HAAL – London, UK. Jan 1953- – 1 – uk British Libr Newspaper [072]

EESTI NSV KRIMINAALPROTSESSI KOODEKS : KOMMENTEERITUD V ALJAANNE – Tallinn: Eesti raamat, 1965 – 1 – CSUX91-B2774 – us Hoover Inst Photo [360]

EESTI NSV KRIMINAALPROTSESSI KOODEKS. RUSSIAN UGOLOVNO-PROTSESSUALNY I KODEKS ESTONSKO I SSR – Moskva: Estonskoe gos. izd-vo, 1961 – 1 – CSUX91-B2782 – us Hoover Inst Photo [340]

EESTI NSV KRIMINAALPROTSESSI KOODEKS. RUSSIAN UGOLOVNO-PROTSESSUALNY I KODEKS ESTONSKO I SSR : OFITSIALNY I TEKST S IZMENENII AMI I DOPOLNENII AMI NA 29 MAI A 1970 GODA – Tallin: E esti raamat, 1971 – 1 – CSUX91-B2784 – us Hoover Inst Photo [340]

EESTI NSV UELMMNOUKOGU JA VALITSUSE TEATAJA – (Missing: 1985) – Tallin, 1967-1987 – 220mf – 9 – ne IDC [947]

EESTI PAEVALEHT – Stockholm, Sweden. 1979- – 1 – sw Kungliga [072]

EESTI POST – Geislingen and Neu-Ulm. Germany. -w. 1 Sep 1948-13 Aug 1952. (2 reels) – 1 – uk British Libr Newspaper [947]

EESTI RAAMATUTE ULDNIMESTIK – Tartu, Estonia. 1937-1939 – 1 – us NY Public [010]

EESTI RADA – Augsburg, nov 4 1947-aug 1952 – 3r – 1 – uk British Libr Newspaper [947]

EETBLADSTRYK DATERET GODTHAAB DEN 23 APRIL 1861. FOLGESKRIVELSE TIL ET PROVENUMMER AF "ATUAGAGDLIUTIT" HVIS UDGIVELSE JUST VAR PABEGYNDT / Rink, H J – BH-461 2 – 8 – ne IDC [910]

HET EEUWIGH LEVEN / Hertogenbosch, Ioannes Evangelista van 'S – Tot Loven, 1643 – 4mf – 8 – ne Slangenburg [240]

EFECTOS INTERNACIONALES DE LAS SENTENCIAS DE LOS TRIBUNALES... / Fiore, P – Madrid, 1888 – 1mf – 1 – ILM-3934/1 – ne IDC [327]

EFEMERIDES BURGALESCAS / Albarellos, Juan – Madrid: Archivo Ibero Americano, 1964 – 1 – sp Bibl Santa Ana [946]

Efendi, Ahmed Asim *see* ASIM TARIHI

Efendi, Ahmedi *see* VAHDETNAME

Efendi, Hayrullah *see* TARIH-I DEVLET-I ALIYYE-I 'OSMANIYYE

Efendi, Mustafa *see* TARIH-I NEFIS

Efendi, Rasit *see* TARIH-I RASIT

Efendi, Selaniki Mustafa *see* TARIH-I SELANIKI

EFES DAMIM / Levinsohn, I B – Vilna, 1837 – 2mf – 9 – ne IDC [947]

EFES DAMIM / Levinsohn, I B – Vilna. 1837 BJ-422-48 1 – 9 – ne IDC [947]

THE EFFECT OF A 12-WEEK RESISTIVE TRAINING PROGRAM IN THE HOME USING THE BODY BAR ON DYNAMIC AND ABSOLUTE STRENGTH IN MIDDLE-AGE WOMEN / Mortell, Rosemarie – 1992 – 1mf – $4.00 – us Microform Publ [612]

THE EFFECT OF A 60-MINUTE DURATION EXERCISE, AT THE INTENSITIES OF THE LACTATE AND THE INDIVIDUAL ANAEROBIC THRESHOLDS, ON THE CARDIOVASCULAR DRIFT / Buhre, U T – 1992 – 2mf – 9 – $8.00 – us Microform Publ [613]

THE EFFECT OF A CIRCUIT WEIGHT TRAINING PROGRAM FOLLOWED BY A DETRAINING PERIOD ON SALIVA CORTISOL AND TESTOSTERONE IN MALES / Mazzocca, Augustus D – 1989 – 164p 2mf – 9 – $8.00 – us Microform Publ [612]

THE EFFECT OF A LIFETIME OF PHYSICAL ACTIVITY ON THE QUANTITY OF BONE IN THE CANINE / Fedler, Joan M & Maynard, Jerry A – 1989 – 1mf – 9 – $4.00 – us Microform Publ [613]

EFFECT OF A PSYCHOLOGICAL SKILLS TRAINING PROGRAM ON COMPETITION ANXIETY AND PERFORMANCE OF SELECTED NATIONAL YOUTH SPORTS PROGRAM CAMPERS / Cox, Kimberley A – Temple University, 1995 – 2mf – 9 – $8.00 – PSY1842 – us Microform Publ [150]

EFFECT OF A SOFTSHELL PROPHYLACTIC ANKLE STABILIZER ON PERFORMANCE IN EVENTS INVOLVING SPEED, AGILITY, AND VERTICAL JUMP DURING LONG-TERM USE / Locke, Alison B – Temple University, 1996 – 1mf – 9 – PE 3662 – us Microform Publ [617]

THE EFFECT OF A STUDY OF THE BIBLICAL CONCEPT OF CHURCH ON ESTABLISHING LONG RANGE PLANNING GOALS / Duncan, Daniel Wendell – 1982 – 1 – 7.52 – us Baptist [240]

THE EFFECT OF A WEIGHT TRAINING PROGRAM ON THE BONE DENSITY OF WOMEN AGED 40-50 YEARS / Dornemann, Timothy M – 1994 – 1mf – $4.00 – us Microform Publ [612]

THE EFFECT OF A WILDERNESS THERAPY PROGRAM ON YOUTH-AT-RISK, AS MEASURED BY LOCUS OF CONTROL AND SELF-CONCEPT / Anderson, Amy – Brigham Young University, 1995 – 1mf – 9 – PSY 1879 – us Microform Publ [150]

EFFECT OF ACUPUNCTURE TENS ON SECOND DEGREE ANKLE SPRAINS / Javens, J A – 1988 – 1mf – 9 – $4.00 – us Microform Publ [790]

THE EFFECT OF ACUTE EXERCISE ON STATE ANXIETY AND ACOUSTIC STARTLE EYEBLINK RESPONSE IN PHYSICALLY ACTIVE AND INACTIVE MEN / Tieman, James G & Dishman, Rodney K – 1990 – 2mf – 9 – $8.00 – us Microform Publ [150]

THE EFFECT OF ADHESIVE ANKLE STRAPPING UPON ISOKINETIC STRENGTH AS MEASURED BY USE OF THE BIODEX DYNAMOMETER / Wennerberg, D K – 1989 – 2mf – 9 – $8.00 – us Microform Publ [613]

THE EFFECT OF AEROBIC EXERCISE ON THE RATE OF PROTEIN CATABOLISM DURING A SEVENTY-TWO HOUR FAST / Sourisseau, George E – 1981 – 1mf – 9 – $4.00 – us Microform Publ [790]

EFFECT OF AGE AND THIRTY MINUTES OF EXERCISE ON PROSTACYCLIN THROMBOXANE A2 RATIOS AND CIRCULATING CONCENTRATIONS OF PROSTACYCLIN AND THROMBOXANE A2 / Todd, M K – 1990 – 2mf – 9 – $8.00 – us Microform Publ [612]

EFFECT OF AGE ON REACTION AND MOVEMENT TIMES IN GIRLS AND WOMEN / Marranca, Harriett A & Gench, Barbara E – 1992 – 2mf – $8.00 – us Microform Publ [150]

THE EFFECT OF ALTERING SPEED OF BACKWARD MOVEMENT OF THE TRUNK ON ANTICIPATORY POSTURAL ADJUSTMENTS / Weissblueth, Eyal & Cole, Kelly J – 1991 – 2mf – 9 – $8.00 – us Microform Publ [612]

EFFECT OF AN ACTIVE ATTENTIONAL STRATEGY ON RUNNING ECONOMY OF LOW ECONOMICAL RUNNERS / Smith, Alan L & Gill, Diane L – 1993 – 2mf – 9 – $8.00 – us Microform Publ [150]

EFFECT OF AN INTERACTIVE MULTIMEDIA COMPUTER TUTORIAL ON STUDENTS' UNDERSTANDING OF BALLET ALLEGRO TERMINOLOGY / Fisher-Stitt, Norma S – Temple, University, 1996 – 2mf – 9 – $8.00 – PE 3640 – us Microform Publ [790]

THE EFFECT OF ANGLE, VELOCITY, AND ROTATION OF INCIDENCE ON THE ANGLE DEVIATION OF REBOUNDING TENNIS BALLS / Smith, James F – 1988 – 153p 2mf – 9 – $8.00 – us Microform Publ [790]

THE EFFECT OF ARM AND LEG VERSUS LEGS ALONE EXERCISE ON THE STAIRMASTER 4000PT IN FEMALES / Belford, Michele L – University of Wisconsin-La Crosse, 1995 – 1mf – 9 – PH 1486 – us Microform Publ [612]

THE EFFECT OF ARM MOVEMENT ON THE BIOMECHANICS OF STANDING UP / Carr, J H – 1991 – 2mf – 9 – $8.00 – us Microform Publ [790]

EFFECT OF BATTING STANCE ON GROUND REACTION FORCES, BAT VELOCITY, AND RESPONSE TIME / LaBranche, Matthew – 1994 – 1mf – $4.00 – us Microform Publ [612]

THE EFFECT OF BICYCLE CRANK ARM LENGTH ON OXYGEN CONSUMPTION AT A CONSTANT WORKLOAD AND CADENCE / Morris, D M – 1992 – 1mf – 9 – $4.00 – us Microform Publ [612]

THE EFFECT OF BODY POSITION ON SPINAL CORD INJURED SWIMMERS / Malone, KN – 1990 – 1mf – 9 – $4.00 – us Microform Publ [790]

THE EFFECT OF BREATHING TECHNIQUE ON BLOOD PRESSURE RESPONSE TO WEIGHT LIFTING / Linsenbardt, S – 1989 – 1mf – 9 – $4.00 – us Microform Publ [612]

THE EFFECT OF BROMELAIN ON RECOVERY FROM EXERCISE-INDUCED SKELETAL MUSCLE INJURY / Walker, J A – 1990 – 1mf – 9 – $4.00 – us Microform Publ [615]

THE EFFECT OF CADENCE ON AEROBIC AND ANAEROBIC CONTRIBUTIONS TO THE TOTAL ENERGY REQUIREMENTS OF CYCLING AT CONSTANT POWER OUTPUT / Reimer, Brad W & Sanderson, David – 1991 – 2mf – 9 – $8.00 – us Microform Publ [613]

THE EFFECT OF CALCIUM SUPPLEMENTATION ON BLOOD PRESSURE AND HEMODYNAMIC VARIABLES IN HYPERTENSIVE MALES / Shaeffer, Kristen L – Springfield College, 1994 – 2mf – 9 – $8.00 – PH1475 – us Microform Publ [612]

THE EFFECT OF CARBONATED SOLUTIONS ON GASTRIC EMPTYING DURING PROLONGED CYCLING / Beard, Glenn C – 1990 – 77p 1mf – 9 – $4.00 – us Microform Publ [612]

EFFECT OF CHRONIC COCAINE ON SELECTED PHYSIOLOGICAL RESPONSES DURING REST AND EXERCISE IN RATS / Kelly, K Patrick – 1993 – 2mf – $8.00 – us Microform Publ [619]

EFFECT OF CHRONIC ETHANOL CONSUMPTION AND MODERATE INTENSITY ENDURANCE TRAINING ON MURINE PLASMA CORTICOSTERONE CONCENTRATION / Sipp, T L – 1992 – 1mf – 9 – $4.00 – us Microform Publ [612]

THE EFFECT OF COCAINE ON MUSCLE CARBOHYDRATE METABOLISM AND ENDURANCE DURING HIGH INTENSITY EXERCISE IN RATS / Braiden, Russell W – 1993 – 1mf – $4.00 – us Microform Publ [619]

THE EFFECT OF COLD WATER BATHS ON POST TREATMENT LEG ELECTRICAL ACTIVITY AND ISOMETRIC STRENGTH / Schroeder, Christine – 1981 – 1mf – 9 – $4.00 – us Microform Publ [790]

THE EFFECT OF CRANKLENGTH ON OXYGEN CONSUMPTION WHEN CYCLING AT A CONSTANT WORK RATE / Carmichael, J Kevin – 1981 – 1mf – 9 – $4.00 – us Microform Publ [790]

THE EFFECT OF DAILY BEAN INGESTION ON THE LIPID PROFILES OF NORMOCHOLESTEROLEMIC COLLEGE STUDENTS / Damson, R L – 1991 – 1mf – 9 – $4.00 – us Microform Publ [612]

EFFECT OF DIETARY EDUCATION, EXERCISE, AND TWO DIETARY PROGRAMS ON WOMEN'S BODY COMPOSITION, CALORIC INTAKE, DIETARY COMPOSITION, AND SUBJECTIVE FEELINGS CONCERNING THE PROGRAMS / Peugnet, Jeffrey C – Brigham Young University, 1995 – 2mf – 9 – $8.00 – PH 1503 – us Microform Publ [612]

EFFECT OF EXERCISE INTENSITY AND DURATION ON POSTEXERCISE METABOLISM IN OBESE ADULTS / Creel, David B – Indiana University, 1995 – 2mf – 9 – $8.00 – PH1455 – us Microform Publ [612]

THE EFFECT OF EXERCISE INTENSITY ON THE EXTENT OF AND RECOVERY FROM FATIGUE OF LONG DURATION / Stefke, Elmar J & Lehman, Steven L – 1993 – 1mf – $4.00 – us Microform Publ [617]

THE EFFECT OF EXERCISE ON GLYCERALDEHYDE-3-PHOSPHATE DEHYDROGENASE AND SUPEROXIDE DISMUTASE ACTIVITIES IN THE POST-ISCHEMIC HEART / Gow, Andrew J – 1994 – 1mf – $4.00 – us Microform Publ [615]

EFFECT OF EXERCISE TRAINING ON THE FUNCTION OF THE RAT MYOCARDIUM DURING REPERFUSION FOLLOWING GLOBAL ISCHEMIA / Libonati, Joseph R & Paolone, Albert M – 1993 – 2mf – $8.00 – us Microform Publ [612]

THE EFFECT OF EXOGENOUS RECOMBINANT PORCINE SOMATOTROPIN ON PIG COMMON CALCANEAN TENDON BIOCHEMISTRY / Choy, Valerie E & Vailas, Arthur C – 1990 – 1mf – 9 – $4.00 – us Microform Publ [612]

THE EFFECT OF HALF-TIME WARM-UP PROCEDURES UPON INJURIES TO HIGH SCHOOL VARSITY FOOTBALL PLAYERS / Howat, Kenneth J – University of North Carolina at Chapel Hill, 1995 – 1mf – 9 – $4.00 – PE3600 – us Microform Publ [617]

EFFECT OF HEART RATE DECELERATION BIOFEEDBACK TRAINING ON GOLF PUTTING PERFORMANCE / Damarjian, Nicole M & Crews, Debra J – 1992 – 1mf – 9 – $4.00 – us Microform Publ [150]

THE EFFECT OF HEAT AND COLD ON ANKLE STABILITY / Keenan, Karen A – University of North Carolina at Chapel Hill, 1995 – 1mf – 9 – $4.00 – PE3604 – us Microform Publ [617]

THE EFFECT OF INTERMITTENT HYPERBARIC OXYGENATION ON SHORT TERM RECOVERY FROM GRADE 2 MEDIAL COLLATERAL LIGAMENT INJURIES / Soolsma, Serge J – University of British Columbia, 1996 – 2mf – 9 – $8.00 – PE 3671 – us Microform Publ [617]

THE EFFECT OF LACTIC ACID ON FAT MOBILIZATION AND UTILIZATION IN TRAINED SUBJECTS / Vega des Jesus, Ramon – 1988 – 84p 1mf – 9 – $4.00 – us Microform Publ [612]

THE EFFECT OF MASS ON THE KINEMATICS OF STEADY STATE WHEELCHAIR PROPULSION IN ADULTS AND CHILDREN WITH SPINAL CORD INJURY / Bednarczyk, Janet H & Sanderson, David – 1993 – 1mf – 9 – $4.00 – us Microform Publ [612]

THE EFFECT OF MODERATE EXERCISE ON LIPID PROFILES IN A HEALTHY COLLEGE AGE POPULATION / Calnin, R J – 1991 – 2mf – 9 – $8.00 – us Microform Publ [613]

THE EFFECT OF MUSCLE ISCHEMIA ON SARCOPLASMIC RETICULUM CA2+-ATPASE FUNCTION : AN IN SITU RAT MODEL / Stavrianeas, Stasinos – University of Oregon, 1995 – 1mf – 9 – $4.00 – PH1480 – us Microform Publ [612]

EFFECT OF MUSCLE LENGTH ON MOTOR UNIT FIRING BEHAVIOR IN HUMAN TIBIALIS ANTERIOR MUSCLE / Vander Linde, Darl W & Kukulka, Carl G – 1989 – 2mf – 9 – $8.00 – us Microform Publ [612]

THE EFFECT OF MUTUAL CHOICE PLACEMENT ON THE SATISFACTION OF STUDENT AND COOPERATING TEACHERS IN PHYSICAL EDUCATION / Johnson, Susan M – 1982 – 2mf – 9 – $8.00 – us Microform Publ [790]

THE EFFECT OF ORAL SMOKELESS TOBACCO ON THE CARDIOVASCULAR AND METABOLIC RESPONSES IN HUMANS DURING REST AND EXERCISE / Van Duser, Bruce L & Chevrette, John M – 1991 – 2mf – 9 – $8.00 – us Microform Publ [613]

EFFECT OF PEER GROUP PRESENCE ON THE GROSS MOTOR PERFORMANCE OF YOUNG CHILDREN / Bates, MK – 1990 – 2mf – 9 – $8.00 – us Microform Publ [150]

THE EFFECT OF PERCEPTION OF PERFORMANCE OUTCOMES ON MOOD FOLLOWING EXERCISE / Jennings, A – 1990 – 2mf – 9 – $8.00 – us Microform Publ [150]

THE EFFECT OF PLANNED EXERCISE AS A DISINHIBITOR OF DIETARY RESTRAINT : AN INVESTIGATION OF PERCEIVED CONTROL AND RESULTANT AFFECT / Hart, Elizabeth A – 1994 – 3mf – $12.00 – us Microform Publ [150]

EFFECT OF PRACTICE SCHEDULE VARIATION ON THE ACQUISITION, RETENTION, AND TRANSFER OF AN APPLIED MOTOR SKILL BY CHILDREN WITH AND WITHOUT MENTAL RETARDATION / Sutlive, Vinson H, 3rd – Indiana University, 1995 – 3mf – 9 – $12.00 – PSY1868 – us Microform Publ [611]

THE EFFECT OF PRE-COMPETITIVE PRACTICE ON THE ACTIVATION AND MOOD OF HIGH SCHOOL FOOTBALL PLAYERS / Thomas, PR – 1991 – 1mf – 9 – $4.00 – us Microform Publ [150]

THE EFFECT OF RAPID WEIGHT LOSS/ WEIGHT GAIN ON MUSCULAR POWER OF INTERCOLLEGIATE WRESTLERS / Vorhis, Phillip E – 1994 – 1mf – $4.00 – us Microform Publ [612]

THE EFFECT OF REFINEMENT AND TEACHER FEEDBACK ON FEMALE JUNIOR HIGH SCHOOL STUDENTS' VOLLEYBALL PRACTICE SUCCESS AND ACHIEVEMENT / Pellett, Tracy L – 1993 – 2mf – $8.00 – us Microform Publ [370]

THE EFFECT OF REGULARLY SCHEDULED DAILY SUPERVISOR VERBAL FEEDBACK ON USE OF PERSONAL PROTECTIVE EQUIPMENT / Vink, Marc P & Legos, Patricia M – 1993 – 2mf – $8.00 – us Microform Publ [613]

THE EFFECT OF RESISTANCE TRAINING ON RESTING BLOOD PRESSURE IN HYPERTENSIVE WOMEN / Lynes, Liliana K – 1994 – 3mf – $12.00 – us Microform Publ [612]

THE EFFECT OF SALBUTAMOL ON PERFORMANCE IN ELITE NON-ASTHMATIC ATHLETES / Meeuwisse, Willem H & McKenzie, Donald C – 1990 – 1mf – 9 – $4.00 – us Microform Publ [613]

THE EFFECT OF SEAT-TUBE ANGLE VARIATION ON CARDIORESPIRATORY RESPONSES DURING SUBMAXIMAL BICYCLING / Heil, DP – 1992 – 2mf – 9 – $8.00 – us Microform Publ [612]

THE EFFECT OF SELECTED BUFFERING AGENTS ON PERFORMANCE IN THE COMPETITIVE 1600 METER RUN / Avedisian, Lori-Ann – Oregon State University, 1995 – 1mf – 9 – PH 1484 – us Microform Publ [612]

THE EFFECT OF SEVEN WEEKS OF TRAINING ON THE DIETARY INTAKE AND SKINFOLDS OF A WOMAN 82 YEARS OF AGE / Shimidzu, Linda K – 1991 – 1mf – 9 – $4.00 – us Microform Publ [613]

THE EFFECT OF SHORT TERM EMG BIOFEEDBACK ON NECK MUSCLE RELAXATION FOR ROTARY PURSUIT PERFORMANCE / Li, J – 1990 – 2mf – 9 – $8.00 – us Microform Publ [612]

THE EFFECT OF SHORT-TERM SLIDE BOARD TRAINING ON LOWER EXTREMITY LATERAL MOVEMENT / Utsumi, Toshio – University of North Carolina at Chapel Hill, 1995 – 1mf – 9 – $4.00 – PH1482 – us Microform Publ [611]

EFFECT OF SLIDE BOARD TRAINING AS A COMPONENT OF PRE-SEASON CONDITIONING ON CONCENTRIC AND ECCENTRIC QUADRICEPS PEAK TORQUE, VERTICAL JUMP HEIGHT, AND AGILITY / Thomas, Tammy R – 1994 – 1mf – $4.00 – us Microform Publ [612]

EFFECT OF SODIUM AND WATER INTAKE ON PLASMA ALDOSTERONE DURING PROLONGED EXERCISE IN WARM ENVIRONMENT / Shi, Xiaocai & Costill, David L – 1990 – 1mf – 9 – $4.00 – us Microform Publ [612]

THE EFFECT OF SODIUM CITRATE INGESTION ON 1600 METER RUNNING PERFORMANCE / Guerra, Arthur – Oregon State University, 1995 – 1mf – 9 – PH 1494 – us Microform Publ [612]

EFFECT OF SPRINT TRAINING UPON SARCOPLASMIC RETICULUM CA2+ ATPASE AND NA+-CA2+ EXCHANGER MRNA EXPRESSION IN RAT MYOCARDIUM / Gow, Andrew J – Temple University, 1995 – 2mf – 9 – $8.00 – PH1460 – us Microform Publ [612]

THE EFFECT OF SUBMAXIMAL EXERCISE IN A NEUTRAL OR HOT-HUMID ENVIRONMENT ON RECOVERY HEMODYNAMICS IN MEN AND WOMEN / Fisher, Michele M – Springfield College, 1995 – 3mf – 9 – $12.00 – PH1458 – us Microform Publ [612]

THE EFFECT OF SUBSTRATE UTILIZATION, MANIPULATED BY NICOTINIC ACID, ON EXCESS POSTEXERCISE OXYGEN CONSUMPTION / Trost, Stewart G – Oregon State University, 1994 – 2mf – 9 – $8.00 – PH 1513 – us Microform Publ [612]

THE EFFECT OF SWIM TRAINING ON PLASMA SOMATOMEDIN-C LEVELS IN 8- TO 10-YEAR-OLD CHILDREN / Counts, Charlene L M & Ben-Ezra, Victor – 1991 – 1mf – 9 – $4.00 – us Microform Publ [612]

THE EFFECT OF TACTILE AND WHOLE/ PART DRILL ON THE ACQUISITION OF OPPOSITION IN A SUCCESSFUL BASKETBALL LAY-UP / Carlson, PD – 1991 – 2mf – 9 – $8.00 – us Microform Publ [150]

EFFECT OF THE ACHILLES TENDON ADHESIVE TAPING AND PRO M-P ACHILLES STRAP ON ECCENTRIC PLANTAR FLEXION PEAK TORQUE / Morales, Alan D – 1994 – 1mf – $4.00 – us Microform Publ [617]

EFFECT OF THE AIRCAST ON FUNCTIONAL MOVEMENTS USING THE BIOTRAN / Rockhill, Bryan H – 1994 – 1mf – $4.00 – us Microform Publ [617]

THE EFFECT OF THE AIRSTIRRUP AND A CONVENTIONAL METHOD OF STRAPPING THE ANKLE ON AGILITY AND VERTICAL JUMP PERFORMANCE / Brassard, Marc F – 1988 – 97p 1mf – 9 – $4.00 – us Microform Publ [617]

THE EFFECT OF THE EDUCATION OF THIRD WORLD WOMEN ON FAMILY HEALTH : A CHINESE EXAMPLE / Hallmann, Jayne E & Hill, J Stanley – 1992 – 2mf – $8.00 – us Microform Publ [613]

THE EFFECT OF THE LEAD LEG PLANT ON FACTORS AFFECTING DISTANCE ON KICKOFFS IN FOOTBALL / Snowden, Steven R & Dowell, Linus J – 1991 – 2mf – 9 – $8.00 – us Microform Publ [612]

THE EFFECT OF THE MENSTRUAL CYCLE ON BIOIMPEDANCE RELIABILITY / Larson, Lois A & Porcari, John P – 1993 – 1mf – $4.00 – us Microform Publ [612]

THE EFFECT OF THE PARADOXICAL INTERVENTION OF SYMPTOM PRESCRIPTION ON STATE ANXIETY LEVELS AND PERFORMANCE IN YOUNG COMPETITIVE SWIMMERS / Greenberg, Doreen L – 1994 – 2mf – $8.00 – us Microform Publ [150]

THE EFFECT OF THE PRESENCE OF THE COACH ON PAIN PERCEPTION AND PAIN TOLERANCE OF ATHLETES / Coutu, Debra L – Springfield College, 1995 – 2mf – 9 – $8.00 – PSY1841 – us Microform Publ [150]

THE EFFECT OF THREE TRAINING METHODS ON THE TEACHING PREPARATION OF COUNSELOR-TEACHERS IN A RESIDENT ENVIRONMENTAL EDUCATION PROGRAM / Johnson, Susan L – 1982 – 2mf – 9 – $8.00 – us Microform Publ [790]

THE EFFECT OF TIME OF SEASON ON THE ATHLETIC IDENTITY IN COLLEGIATE SWIMMERS / Antshel, Kevin M – 1994 – 2mf – $8.00 – us Microform Publ [150]

THE EFFECT OF TOE AND PLANTAR FLEXOR STRENGTH TRAINING ON VERTICAL JUMP PERFORMANCE OF FOLK DANCERS / Meiners, Earlet P – 1991 – 1mf – $4.00 – us Microform Publ [612]

THE EFFECT OF TRAINED HEARING PEER TUTORS ON THE PHYSICAL ACTIVITY LEVELS OF DEAF STUDENTS IN INCLUSIVE ELEMENTARY SCHOOL PHYSICAL EDUCATION CLASSES / Lieberman, Lauren J – Oregon State University, 1996 – 2mf – 9 – $8.00 – PE 3661 – us Microform Publ [370]

EFFECT OF TRAINING FREQUENCY ON CERVICAL ROTATION STRENGTH / DeFilippo, G J – 1991 – 2mf – 9 – $8.00 – us Microform Publ [612]

EFFECT OF TRAINING ON LACTATE UTILIZATION BY RAT MUSCLE MITOCHONDRIA / Murakami, Joan R – 1989 – 59p 1mf – 9 – $4.00 – us Microform Publ [612]

THE EFFECT OF TRANSVERSE PEDAL SPACING ON CYCLING EFFICIENCY / Carling, Jon & Fisher, A Garth – 1992 – 1mf – $4.00 – us Microform Publ [613]

THE EFFECT OF TWO TYPES OF PLYOMETRIC TRAINING IN IMPROVING VERTICAL JUMP ABILITY IN FEMALE COLLEGE SOCCER PLAYERS / Villarreal, Jose & Considine, William J – 1992 – 2mf – $8.00 – us Microform Publ [612]

THE EFFECT OF ULTRASOUND ON TEMPERATURE RISE IN THE PREHEATED TRICEPS SURAE MUSCLE GROUP / Harris, Shane T – Brigham Young University, 1994 – 1mf – 9 – PE 3650 – us Microform Publ [617]

THE EFFECT OF VARIOUS LIFTING INTENSITIES IN RELEASE OF HUMAN GROWTH HORMONE / Kang, H -Y – 1990 – 1mf – 9 – $4.00 – us Microform Publ [612]

EFFECT OF WAR... / Deane, J P – London, 1854 – 1mf – 1 – ILM-480/1 – ne IDC [327]

EFFECT OF WATER RUNNING AND CYCLING ON VO2MAX AND 2-MILE PERFORMANCE / Eyestone, Edward D & Fisher, A Garth – 1990 – 1mf – $4.00 – us Microform Publ [617]

THE EFFECT OF WRIST WEIGHT ON THE HEMODYNAMIC RESPONSE TO EXERCISE IN CORONARY ARTERY DISEASE / Kaplan, Linda & Paolone, Vincent J – 1993 – 2mf – $8.00 – us Microform Publ [612]

THE EFFECT OF YOGA AND RELAXATION TECHNIQUES ON OUTCOME VARIABLES ASSOCIATED WITH OSTEOARTHRITIS OF THE HANDS AND FINGER JOINTS / Garfinkel, Marian S & Levy, Marvin R – 1992 – 2mf – 9 – $8.00 – us Microform Publ [613]

EFFECTIVE MANAGER – (v.3 .1979 5,6,9) – v.1. 1977 – 1 – us UMI [650]

THE EFFECTIVENESS OF ACUPRESSURE IN THE TREATMENT OF PRIMARY DYSMENORRHEA / Fontenot, M E – 1989 – 1mf – 9 – $4.00 – us Microform Publ [612]

THE EFFECTIVENESS OF BEHAVIORAL CONTRACTS IN PROMOTING THE MAINTENANCE OF CANCER RISK REDUCTION BEHAVIOR WHILE UTILIZED IN A COLLEGE CANCER AVOIDANCE COURSE / Burkley, Renee L – 1990 – 69p 1mf – 9 – $4.00 – us Microform Publ [370]

EFFECTIVENESS OF EXERCISE VERSUS EXERCISE PLUS TAPE IN THE MANAGEMENT OF FEMALES WITH PATELLOFEMORAL PAIN / Froehling, Lori A – University of Wisconsin-La Crosse, 1996 – 1mf – 9 – PE 3642 – us Microform Publ [617]

THE EFFECTIVENESS OF JOB SPECIFIC TRAINING ON THE WORK PERFORMANCE OF FEMALE STUDENT NURSES / McCannon, Robin K & Miller, Marilyn K – 1993 – 2mf – $8.00 – us Microform Publ [370]

THE EFFECTIVENESS OF MICROCURENT ELECTRICAL NERVE STIMULATION (M.E.N.S.) IN THE TREATMENT OF POST ACUTE LYMPHEDEMA IN ANKLE INJURIES / Galley, Suzi-Lyn – 1994 – 1mf – $4.00 – us Microform Publ [617]

THE EFFECTIVENESS OF REPEATED SUBMAXIMAL CONCENTRIC EXERCISE AND HEATED WHIRLPOOL IN THE TREATMENT OF DELAYED ONSET MUSCULAR SORENESS / Miller, MK – 1991 – 1mf – 9 – $4.00 – us Microform Publ [613]

EFFECTIVENESS OF SELECTED COMPONENTS IN BEHAVIORAL WEIGHT-LOSS INTERVENTIONS : A META-ANALYSIS / Wood, Nadine MS & Donatelle, Rebecca J – 1992 – 2mf – 9 – $8.00 – us Microform Publ [150]

THE EFFECTIVENESS OF THE HINGED GOLF CLUB AS A TRAINING AID TO DEVELOP CONSISTENCY IN NOVICE GOLFERS / Dexter-Fogarty, Tracey – Springfield College, 1995 – 2mf – 9 – $8.00 – PE3589 – us Microform Publ [612]

THE EFFECTIVENESS OF THE STAGES OF CHANGE MODEL AND EXPERIMENTAL EXERCISE PRESCRIPTIONS IN INCREASING FEMALE ADULTS' PHYSICAL ACTIVITY AND EXERCISE BEHAVIOR / Cardinal, Bradloy J & Sachs, Michael L – 1993 – 3mf – 9 – $12.00 – us Microform Publ [150]

THE EFFECTS OF 6-WEEK AND 12-WEEK REHABILITATION PROGRAMS ON THE DEPRESSION LEVEL OF CARDIAC PATIENTS / Hazavehei, Seyyed M M – Texas Woman's University, 1993 – 2mf – 9 – $8.00 – PSY 1889 – us Microform Publ [150]

THE EFFECTS OF 90 DAYS OF KM SUPPLEMENTATION ON AEROBIC CAPACITY AND GENERAL WELL-BEING OF HEALTHY ADULTS / Pugliese, Ari – University of Wisconsin-La Crosse, 1996 – 1mf – 9 – $4.00 – PH1472 – us Microform Publ [613]

THE EFFECTS OF A CARBOHYDRATE-ELECTROLYTE REPLACEMENT DRINK TAKEN DURING HIGH INTENSITY EXERCISE ON SPRINT CAPACITY AT THE END OF EXERCISE / Ball, Thomas C – 1994 – 2mf – $8.00 – us Microform Publ [612]

EFFECTS OF A COMPETITIVE SEASON ON BODY COMPOSITION IN FEMALE INTERCOLLEGIATE ATHLETES / Williams, Salena – University of Wisconsin-La Crosse, 1995 – 1mf – 9 – PE 3679 – us Microform Publ [617]

EFFECTS OF A CREATIVE DANCE PROGRAM ON THE PERCEPTUAL MOTOR PERFORMANCE OF TRAINABLE MENTALLY RETARDED CHILDREN / Barnes, Carolyn M – 1978 – 1mf – 9 – $4.00 – us Microform Publ [790]

THE EFFECTS OF A DIFFERENT ARM SWING ON VERTICAL JUMP AND TOE-TOUCH JUMP PERFORMANCE / Munkasy, B A – 1990 – 2mf – 9 – $8.00 – us Microform Publ [790]

THE EFFECTS OF A FLEXIBILITY TRAINING PROGRAM ON FLEXIBILITY TEST SCORES IN ELEMENTARY SCHOOL CHILDREN / Dulaney, N M – 1991 – 1mf – 9 – $4.00 – us Microform Publ [790]

THE EFFECTS OF A GROUP-ORIENTED CONTINGENCY MANAGEMENT SYSTEM ON BEHAVIORALLY DISORDERED STUDENTS IN PHYSICAL EDUCATION / Vogler, E Williams – 1980 – 2mf – 9 – $8.00 – us Microform Publ [790]

THE EFFECTS OF A HEALTH RELATED PHYSICAL FITNESS CURRICULUM ON SELECTED FITNESS VARIABLES / Waite, Terence M – 1988 – 86p 1mf – 9 – $4.00 – us Microform Publ [613]

THE EFFECTS OF A LEISURE ACTIVITY VISITATION TRAINING PROGRAM ON THE VISITOR'S PERCEIVED SATISFACTION OF VISITS WITH INDIVIDUALS WITH DEMENTIA RELATED DISEASES INCLUDING ALZHEIMER'S DISEASE / Waskiewicz, Becky A – 1994 – 1mf – $4.00 – us Microform Publ [790]

EFFECTS OF A LOWER LIMB STRENGTH TRAINING PROGRAM ON BALANCE MEASURES IN MEN WITH MENTAL RETARDATION / Suomi, Rory & Surburg, Paul R – 1991 – 4mf – 9 – $16.00 – us Microform Publ [612]

THE EFFECTS OF A MINIUMUM IMPACT CAMPING SLIDE-TAPE PROGRAM ON WILDERNESS VISITORS' AWARENESS OF MINIMUM IMPACT CAMPING / Anderson, Lynn S – 1981 – 2mf – 9 – $8.00 – us Microform Publ [790]

EFFECTS OF A MULTIMEDIA PERFORMANCE PRINCIPLE TRAINING PROGRAM ON CORRECT ANALYSIS AND DIAGNOSIS OF THROWLIKE MOVEMENTS / Williams, Emyr W – Ohio State University, 1995 – 2mf – 9 – $12.00 – PE3623 – us Microform Publ [370]

THE EFFECTS OF A "PRESCRIPTIVE INDIVIDUALIZED PROGRAM" AND A "NONPRESCRIPTIVE GROUP TASK PROGRAM" ON FUNDAMENTAL MOTOR PATTERN AND ABILILTY ACQUISITION, SELF-CONCEPT, AND SOCIALIZATION SKILLS OF KINDERGARTEN CHILDREN / Moyer, Steve W – 1981 – 2mf – 9 – $8.00 – us Microform Publ [790]

THE EFFECTS OF A PROJECT LEARNING TREE WORKSHOP ON PRE-SERVICE TEACHERS' ATTITUDES TOWARD TEACHING ENVIRONMENTAL EDUCATION / Kunz, Dorothea E – 1989 – 114p 2mf – 9 – $8.00 – us Microform Publ [370]

EFFECTS OF A SEMIRIGID AND A SOFTSHELL PROPHYLACTIC ANKLE STABILIZER ON PERFORMANCE / Macpherson, Kevin – 1994 – 1mf – $4.00 – us Microform Publ [617]

THE EFFECTS OF A SIX-MONTH EXERCISE MAINTENANCE PROGRAM ON THE CARDIOVASCULAR FITNESS LEVELS OF PARTICIPANTS / Carney, Deborah A – 1981 – 2mf – 9 – $8.00 – us Microform Publ [790]

THE EFFECTS OF A STRENGTH TRAINING PROGRAM ON THE BODY IMAGE, SELF-CONCEPT, AND DYNAMIC STRENGTH OF SEVENTH GRADE GIRLS / Lucas, Jason – 1994 – 1mf – $4.00 – us Microform Publ [150]

EFFECTS OF A SWIMMING PROGRAM ON CYSTIC FIBROSIS CHILDREN / Edlund, Larry L – 1980 – 1mf – 9 – $4.00 – us Microform Publ [790]

THE EFFECTS OF A TEN-WEEK STEP AEROBIC TRAINING PROGRAM ON AEROBIC CAPACITY OF COLLEGE-AGED FEMALES / Chapek, Constance L & Porcari, John P – 1992 – 1mf – $4.00 – us Microform Publ [613]

THE EFFECTS OF A TEN-WEEK STEP AEROBIC TRAINING PROGRAM ON THE BODY COMPOSITION OF COLLEGE-AGED WOMEN / Huntley, Elizabeth A & Porcari, John P – 1992 – 1mf – $4.00 – us Microform Publ [612]

THE EFFECTS OF A TREATMENT PROGRAM FOR CHRONIC PAIN PATIENTS USING ENJOYABLE IMAGERY WITH BIOFEEDBACK INDUCED RELAXATION / Mckee, Patrick J – 1981 – 2mf – 9 – $8.00 – us Microform Publ [615]

THE EFFECTS OF A WEIGHT TRAINING COURSE ON STRESS LEVELS AND LOCUS OF CONTROL IN COLLEGE FEMALES / Fuller, Tamela G & Rhodes, Ronald L – 1992 – 1mf – $4.00 – us Microform Publ [150]

THE EFFECTS OF ACQUAINTANCE RAPE PREVENTION PROGRAMMING ON MALE ATHLETES' SEXUAL AND DATING ATTITUDES / Andersen, Steven J & Dosch, Margaret – 1992 – 1mf – $4.00 – us Microform Publ [150]

THE EFFECTS OF ACUTE EXERCISE OF VARYING INTENSITIES ON SUBJECTS WITH TYPE 1 DIABETES MELLITUS / Dauley, Patricia A – 1993 – 2mf – $8.00 – us Microform Publ [615]

EFFECTS OF ACUTE RESISTIVE EXERCISE ON THE RESTING METABOLIC RATE OF WOMEN / Brady, Christine P – Temple University, 1996 – 1mf – 9 – PH 1488 – us Microform Publ [612]

EFFECTS OF ADHESIVE SPRAY AND PREWRAP ON TAPED ANKLE INVERSION BEFORE AND AFTER EXERCISE / Keetch, Anita & Durrant, Earlene – 1992 – 1mf – $4.00 – us Microform Publ [617]

THE EFFECTS OF AEROBIC DANCE EXERCISE AND NUTRITION INTERVENTION IN CHOLESTEROL LEVELS / Vetro, VL – 1990 – 2mf – 9 – $8.00 – us Microform Publ [612]

EFFECTS OF AEROBIC EXERCISE ON THE LIPID PROFILE LEVELS OF PATIENTS WITH MODERATE TO SEVERE BURN INJURY / Bacon Hilda – 1994 – 1mf – $4.00 – us Microform Publ [615]

THE EFFECTS OF AGE AND ENDURANCE TRAINING ON RAT ADRENAL TISSUE : A MORPHOLOGICAL ANALYSIS AND DETERMINATION OF CATECHOLAMINE CONTENT / Schmidt, Kathryn & Stanley, William C – 1990 – 1mf – 9 – $4.00 – us Microform Publ [612]

EFFECTS OF AGE AND ETHANOL ON THERMOREGULATORY RESPONSES OF MEN TO A COLD AIR STRESS / Hopkins, Ruth A – Temple University, 1995 – 2mf – 9 – $8.00 – PH1464 – us Microform Publ [612]

EFFECTS OF AGE AND GENDER ON FUNCTIONAL ROTATION AND LATERAL FLEXION OF THE BACK AND THE NECK / Netzer, Ofra & Payne, V Gregory – 1992 – 1mf – 9 – $4.00 – us Microform Publ [612]

EFFECTS OF AGE, VELOCITY, AND ADDED MASS ON POSTURAL ADJUSTMENTS ASSOCIATED WITH A RAPID ARMRAISING MOVEMENT / Manchester, Diane L & Woollacott, Marjorie H – 1990 – 3mf – 9 – $12.00 – us Microform Publ [612]

THE EFFECTS OF ALCOHOL UPON THE HUMAN SYSTEM: AN ESSAY UPON THE CAUSE, NATURE AND TREATMENT OF ALCOHOLISM / Canniff, William – Toronto: Adam, Stevenson, 1872. 02069. (Pre-1900 Canadiana) – 9 – cn C.I.H.M. [360]

EFFECTS OF (ALPHA)-ADRENERGIC STIMULATION ON SR CA2+ ATPASE AND NA/CA MRNA EXPRESSION IN CULTURED NEONATAL RAT VENTRICULAR MYOCYTES / Toaldo, Gina-Lee – Temple University, 1995 – 1mf – 9 – $4.00 – PH1481 – us Microform Publ [612]

THE EFFECTS OF ALPHA-TOCOPHEROL ON METABOLIC DETERMINATIONS IN GRADED EXERCISE / Keroack, Christopher R & Paolone, Vincent J – 1992 – 1mf – $4.00 – us Microform Publ [612]

THE EFFECTS OF AMINO ACID SUPPLEMENTATION ON ENDURANCE PERFORMANCE / Laporte, Rebecca J & Paolone, Vincent J – 1993 – 2mf – $8.00 – us Microform Publ [612]

THE EFFECTS OF AN APPLICATION OF SUNSCREEN ON SELECTED PHYSIOLOGICAL VARIABLES DURING EXERCISE IN THE HEAT / Connolly, Declan A – Oregon State University, 1995 – 2mf – 9 – $8.00 – PH 1490 – us Microform Publ [612]

THE EFFECTS OF AN EVALUATIVE AUDIENCE UPON COLLEGE MALES' SELF-EFFICACY, PERCEIVED ABILITY, ANXIETY, AND LEARNING OF A NOVEL MOTOR TASK / Simensky, Steven G & Ewing, Martha E – 1991 – 2mf – 9 – $8.00 – us Microform Publ [150]

THE EFFECTS OF AN INDUCED INTERNAL AND EXTERNAL ATTENTIONAL FOCUS UPON UPPER BODY STRENGTH / Hein, Erica J & Pein, Richard L – 1993 – 1mf – $4.00 – us Microform Publ [150]

EFFECTS OF AN INTERVAL TRAINING DANCE CLASS ON SELECT CARDIOVASCULAR VARIABLES / Christensen, Kimberly M – University of Oregon, 1994 – 1mf – 9 – $4.00 – PE3585 – us Microform Publ [790]

THE EFFECTS OF ANKLE SPRAINS AND EXTERNAL SUPPORT ON MUSCLE ONSET LATENCIES / Van den Eikhof, Victoria E – University of Oregon, 1996 – 1mf – 9 – PE 3676 – us Microform Publ [617]

EFFECTS OF AQUATIC SIMULATED AND DRY LAND PLYOMETRICS ON VERTICAL JUMP HEIGHT / Stemm, John D – 1993 – 1mf – $4.00 – us Microform Publ [574]

THE EFFECTS OF ATHLETIC TRAINING ON BONE MINERAL DENSITY IN FEMALE COLLEGIATE GYMNASTS / Nichols, David L & Sanborn, Charlotte F – 1992 – 2mf – $8.00 – us Microform Publ [612]

THE EFFECTS OF AUDITORY BIOFEEDBACK ON THE ACCURACY OF THE TENNIS VOLLEY / Holcombe, Robert A & Lewis, Kathryn – 1991 – 2mf – $8.00 – us Microform Publ [150]

THE EFFECTS OF BODY SEGMENT LENGTH AND HEAD POSITION UPON SIT AND REACH FLEXIBILITY PERFORMANCE / Tardie, Gregory B & Pechar, Gary S – 1992 – 1mf – 9 – $4.00 – us Microform Publ [612]

EFFECTS OF CAFFEINE ON CENTRAL ON PERIPHERAL HEMODYNAMICS AT REST AND DURING EXERCISE / Baruch, Amy R – Springfield College, 1994 – 2mf – 9 – $8.00 – PH1452 – us Microform Publ [612]

EFFECTS OF CALORIC RESTRICTION AND RESISTIVE EXERCISE ON THE RESTING ENERGY EXPENDITURE OF WEIGHT-REDUCED OBESE WOMEN / Stopford, Jane L & Kendrick, Zebulon V – 1992 – 2mf – 9 – $8.00 – us Microform Publ [612]

THE EFFECTS OF CARDIAC REHABILITATION ON CORONARY HEART DISEASE RISK FACTORS IN POST MYOCARDIAL INFARCTION PATIENTS / Cobham, H W – 1991 – 2mf – 9 – $8.00 – us Microform Publ [612]

THE EFFECTS OF CHROMIUM SUPPLEMENTATION AND A LOW CARBOHYDRATE DIET ON HIGH-INTENSITY ENDURANCE PERFORMANCE / Kocher, Pamela L – 1994 – 1mf – $4.00 – us Microform Publ [612]

EFFECTS OF COCAINE ON GLUCAGON AND INSULIN IN EXERCISING RATS / Mitchell, James A – Brigham Young University, 1995 – 1mf – 9 – PH 1501 – us Microform Publ [615]

THE EFFECTS OF CONTEXTUAL INTERFERENCE AND THREE LEVELS OF DIFFICULTY ON THE ACQUISITION, RETENTION, AND TRANSFER OF HOCKEY STRIKING SKILLS BY SECOND GRADE CHILDREN / Halliday, Nancy & Goldberger, Michael – 1992 – 2mf – 9 – $8.00 – us Microform Publ [150]

EFFECTS OF CONTEXTUAL INTERFERENCE ON INITIAL LEARNING OF TENNIS GROUNDSTROKES / Smithee, Larry L – Brigham Young University, 1994 – 1mf – 9 – PSY 1901 – us Microform Publ [150]

THE EFFECTS OF CONTINUOUS AND INTERMITTENT EXERCISE BOUTS OF EQUAL WORK OUTPUT ON POST-EXERCISE ENERGY EXPENDITURE / Ziegenfuss, T N – 1991 – 1mf – 9 – $4.00 – us Microform Publ [612]

THE EFFECTS OF COOPERATIVE AND INDIVIDUALISTIC GOAL STRUCTURES ON THE LEARNING DOMAINS OF BEGINNING TENNIS STUDENTS / Brown, Joseph D – 1988 – 92p 1mf – 9 – $4.00 – us Microform Publ [150]

THE EFFECTS OF COPING SKILLS ON PHYSIOLOGICAL AND COGNITIVE ADAPTATION TO A HIGH RISK ACTIVITY / Lewis, Debra A – 1982 – 1mf – 9 – $4.00 – us Microform Publ [616]

THE EFFECTS OF COUPLE COMMUNICATION TRAINING ON MARITAL PERCEPTIONS / Griffith, William Herbert – 1981 – 1 – $5.20 – us Baptist [306]

THE EFFECTS OF CREATIVE DANCE ON MOVEMENT CREATIVITY IN THIRD GRADE CHILDREN / Funk, Wendy W – Brigham Young University, 1995 – 2mf – 9 – $8.00 – PE 3644 – us Microform Publ [790]

THE EFFECTS OF DEHYDRATION AND TEMPERATURE ON MOVEMENT AND REACTION TIME IN COLLEGE AGE MALES / Whittle, R C – 1991 – 1mf – 9 – $4.00 – us Microform Publ [613]

EFFECTS OF DEHYDRATION ON RATINGS OF PERCEIVED EXERTION AT THE LACTATE AND VENTILATORY THRESHOLDS / Dengel, DR – 1990 – 2mf – 9 – $8.00 – us Microform Publ [150]

THE EFFECTS OF DIET AND EXERCISE OF VARYING INTENSITIES ON THE BODY COMPOSITION OF ADULT WOMEN / Bradley, Carolyn G – 1980 – 2mf – 9 – $8.00 – us Microform Publ [790]

THE EFFECTS OF ENDURANCE EXERCISE ON METABOLIC WATER PRODUCTION AND PLASMA VOLUME CHANGES / Pivarnik, James M – 1982 – 1mf – 9 – $4.00 – us Microform Publ [790]

THE EFFECTS OF ENHANCED ECCENTRIC TRAINING ON IMPROVEMENT OF STRENGTH / Follenius, Christopher & Stopka, Christine – 1993 – 1mf – 9 – $4.00 – us Microform Publ [613]

EFFECTS OF ETHANOL ON THERMOREGULATORY RESPONSES DURING COLD AIR EXPOSURE IN MALE AND FEMALE SUBJECTS / Seo, Chungjin – Temple University, 1996 – 2mf – 9 – $8.00 – PH 1506 – us Microform Publ [612]

EFFECTS OF EXERCISE AND VITAMIN B12 SUPPLEMENTATION ON THE DEPRESSION SCALE SCORES OF A WHEELCHAIR CONFINED POPULATION / Dalton, Richard B – 1980 – 2mf – 9 – $8.00 – us Microform Publ [616]

EFFECTS OF EXERCISE INTENSITY ON GLUCOSE TOLERANCE AND INSULIN SENSITIVITY / Shriver, Timothy C – Iowa State University, 1993 – 1mf – 9 – $4.00 – PH1477 – us Microform Publ [612]

THE EFFECTS OF EXERCISE MODE ON POSTEXERCISE OXYGEN CONSUMPTION, URINARY NITROGEN, AND FAT UTILIZATION / Kolkhorst, FW – 1990 – 2mf – 9 – $8.00 – us Microform Publ [612]

THE EFFECTS OF EXERCISE ON LOW-DENSITY-LIPOROTEIN-RECEPTOR MEDIATED CLEARANCE AND ATHEROSCLEROTIC LESIONS IN DIETARY INDUCED HYPERLIPIDEMIC NZW RABBITS / Pujol, Thomas J & Westerfield, R Carl – 1991 – 1mf – 9 – $4.00 – us Microform Publ [612]

THE EFFECTS OF EXERCISE ON MYOCARDIAL CAPILLARY BED AND CONNECTIVE TISSUE IN SENESCENT RATS / Finch, Merry B – 1982 – 1mf – 9 – $4.00 – us Microform Publ [790]

THE EFFECTS OF EXERCISE ON STRESS AND FUNCTIONAL ABILITIES IN COMMUNITY DWELLING ELDERLY / Sergent, Evelyn H – Purdue University, 1995 – 1mf – 9 – $4.00 – PSY1863 – us Microform Publ [150]

THE EFFECTS OF EXERCISE ON THE STRENGTH OF THE LOW BACK / Knecht, John & Prentice, William E – 1992 – 1mf – 9 – $4.00 – us Microform Publ [617]

THE EFFECTS OF EXERCISE TRAINING AND SEVERE CALORIC RESTRICTION ON LEAN-BODY MASS IN THE OBESE / Leutholtz, Brian C & Heusner, William – 1991 – 1mf – $4.00 – us Microform Publ [612]

EFFECTS OF FATIGUE ON MECHANICAL AND MUSCULAR COMPONENTS OF PERFORMANCE DURING DROP LANDINGS / James, C Roger et al – 1991 – 2mf – 9 – $8.00 – us Microform Publ [612]

THE EFFECTS OF FIXED AND HINGED ANKLE FOOT ORTHOSES ON GAIT MYOELECTRIC ACTIVITY AND STANDING JOINT ALIGNMENT IN CHILDREN WITH CEREBRAL PALSY / Lough, Loretta K & Soderberg, Gary L – 1990 – 3mf – 9 – $12.00 – us Microform Publ [612]

THE EFFECTS OF FREEDOM OF CHOICE ON THE PARTICIPANTS IN A LEISURE EDUCATION PROGRAM / Richard, Anne B – 1989 – 151p 2mf – 9 – $8.00 – us Microform Publ [370]

THE EFFECTS OF FUNCTIONAL ISOMETRIC WEIGHT TRAINING IN CONJUNCTION WITH DYNAMIC WEIGHT TRAINING ON TWO BENCH PRESS MEASUREMENT TESTS / Johnston, David L – University of Wisconsin-La Crosse, 1995 – 2mf – 9 – $8.00 – PH 1498 – us Microform Publ [612]

THE EFFECTS OF GAME STRESS SITUATIONS ON THE HEART RATES OF SELECTED HIGH SCHOOL FOOTBALL COACHES / Delashmit, S J – 1991 – 1mf – 9 – $4.00 – us Microform Publ [150]

THE EFFECTS OF GENDER ON ALT-PE MOTOR IN JUNIOR HIGH PHYSICAL EDUCATION / Woerfel, Laurie A & Wurzer, David J – 1991 – 2mf – 9 – $8.00 – us Microform Publ [790]

THE EFFECTS OF GLASNOST AND PERESTROIKA ON THE SOVIET SPORT SYSTEM / Kim, Jong-Il. & DePauw, Karen P – 1993 – 2mf – 9 – $8.00 – us Microform Publ [790]

THE EFFECTS OF GOAL SETTING AND IMAGERY TRAINING PROGRAMS ON THE FREE-THROW PERFORMANCE OF FEMALE BASKETBALL PLAYERS / Lerner, Bart S – West Virginia University, 1995 – 2mf – 9 – $8.00 – PSY1850 – us Microform Publ [150]

THE EFFECTS OF GOAL SETTING ON PERFORMANCE ENHANCEMENT IN A COMPETITIVE ATHLETIC SETTING / Stitcher, Thomas P – 1989 – 85p 1mf – 9 – $4.00 – us Microform Publ [790]

THE EFFECTS OF HAND COOLING DURING STRENUOUS EXERCISE ON METABOLIC AND CARDIORESPIRATORY FUNCTION / Vanheest, Jaci L – 1988 – 87p 1mf – 9 – $4.00 – us Microform Publ [612]

THE EFFECTS OF HIGH AND LOW INTENSITY ECCENTRIC EXERCISE ON MUSCLE SORENESS AND STRENGTH / Scharnhorst, R L – 1991 – 2mf – 9 – $8.00 – us Microform Publ [790]

THE EFFECTS OF HIGH IMPACT EXERCISE VERSUS LOW IMPACT EXERCISE ON BONE DENSITY IN POSTMENOPAUSAL WOMEN / Grove, C A – 1990 – 4mf – 9 – $16.00 – us Microform Publ [613]

EFFECTS OF HIGH SCHOOL CONCEPTS-BASED PHYSICAL EDUCATION ON STUDENT BEHAVIOR, KNOWLEDGE, AND MOTIVATION / Mickelson, Connie L & Roundy, Elmo S – 1992 – 2mf – $8.00 – us Microform Publ [790]

THE EFFECTS OF HIGH SPATIAL CONSTRAINTS IN DETERMINING THE NATURE OF THE SPEED-ACCURACY TRADE-OFF IN AIMED HAND MOVEMENTS / Kim, Kyoung N – 1988 – 39p 1mf – 9 – $4.00 – us Microform Publ [790]

THE EFFECTS OF HIP POSITION AND ANGULAR VELOCITY ON QUADRICEPS AND HAMSTRING ECCENTRIC PEAK TORQUE / Hopkins, Joe R & Sitler, Michael R – 1992 – 1mf – 9 – $4.00 – us Microform Publ [612]

THE EFFECTS OF IMAGINARY MAXIMAL MUSCLE CONTRACTION TRAINING ON THE VOLUNTARY NEURAL DIRVE TO MUSCLE / Yue, Guang H & Cole, Kelly J – 1990 – 2mf – 9 – $8.00 – us Microform Publ [150]

EFFECTS OF IMITATIVE LEARNING ON THE ACQUISITION OF ROTARY PURSUIT SKILL BY EDUCABLE MENTALLY RETARDED BOYS / Nierengarten, Mark E – 1982 – 2mf – 9 – $8.00 – us Microform Publ [616]

EFFECTS OF INSTRUCTION ON THE ANALYTICAL PROFICIENCY OF PHYSICAL EDUCATION MAJORS IN FUNDAMENTAL SPORT SKILLS ANALYSIS / Gangstead, Sandra K – 1982 – 2mf – 9 – $8.00 – us Microform Publ [790]

THE EFFECTS OF INSTRUCTIONS AND MOVEMENT REVERSALS ON THE ACCURACY AND KINEMATICS OF A RAPID SEQUENTIAL TAPPING MOVEMENT / Song, S – 1992 – 1mf – 9 – $4.00 – us Microform Publ [150]

THE EFFECTS OF INTEGRATION IN PHYSICAL EDUCATION ON THE MOTOR PERFORMANCE AND PERCEIVED COMPETENCE CHARACTERISTICS OF EDUCABLE MENTALLY RETARDED AND NONHANDICAPPED CHILDREN / Smith, S D – 1989 – 3mf – 9 – $12.00 – us Microform Publ [150]

EFFECTS OF INTENSIVE FERTILIZER USE ON THE HUMAN ENVIRONMENT – 1978 – 368p – it F.A.O. [360]

THE EFFECTS OF INTERMITTENT COMPRESSION AND COLD ON EDEMA IN POSTACUTE ANKLE SPRAINS / Brewer, KD – 1990 – 1mf – 9 – $4.00 – us Microform Publ [616]

THE EFFECTS OF INTERMITTENT COMPRESSION ON EDEMA IN POST-ACUTE ANKLE SPRAINS / Rucinski, Terri J – 1989 – 47p 1mf – 9 – $4.00 – us Microform Publ [617]

THE EFFECTS OF INTERMITTENT HYPERBARIC OXYGEN ON PAIN PERCEPTION AN ECCENTRIC STRENGTH IN A HUMAN INJURY MODEL / Staples, James R – University of British Columbia, 1996 – 2mf – 9 – $8.00 – PE 3673 – us Microform Publ [617]

THE EFFECTS OF INTERNAL AND EXTERNAL IMAGERY ON MUSCULAR AND OCULAR CONCOMITANTS / Hale, Bruce D – 1981 – 2mf – 9 – $8.00 – us Microform Publ [616]

EFFECTS OF LEG EXERCISE AND INSULIN INJECTION SITES ON BLOOD GLUCOSE IN PERSONS WITH INSULIN DEPENDENT DIABETES MELLITUS (IDDM) / Gagalis, Zisis – 1992 – 1mf – $4.00 – us Microform Publ [616]

THE EFFECTS OF LEISURE EDUCATION ON LIFE SATISFACTION AND LEISURE SATISFACTION AMONG JAPANESE AMERICAN OLDER ADULTS / Shimura, Kenichi & Gushiken, Thomas – 1993 – 2mf – $8.00 – us Microform Publ [790]

EFFECTS OF LOW-INTENSITY, PAIN-FREE EXERCISE ON MUSCLE METABOLISM IN PATIENTS WITH PERIPHERAL VASCULAR DISEASE EVALUATED BY 31P-NMR SPECTROSCOPY / Marburger, Lorri K & Stopka, Christine – 1992 – 2mf – 9 – $8.00 – us Microform Publ [612]

THE EFFECTS OF MENSTRUAL CYCLE PHASE ON COMPETITIVE SWIMMING PERFORMANCE / Rogers, Mary Jane L – University of North Carolina at Chapel Hill, 1994 – 1mf – 9 – $4.00 – PSY1859 – us Microform Publ [150]

THE EFFECTS OF MUSIC ON PSYCHOPHYSIOLOGICAL STRESS RESPONSES TO GRADED EXERCISE / Bronwley, K A – 1991 – 1mf – 9 – $4.00 – us Microform Publ [790]

EFFECTS OF NUTRITIONAL INTERVENTION ON BLOOD GLUCOSE LEVELS IN WOMEN (AGE 73-85) / Warren, John R & Shier, Nathan W – 1992 – 3mf – 9 – $12.00 – us Microform Publ [613]

THE EFFECTS OF ORAL CONTRACEPTION AND HYPOXIA ON RESPIRATORY PARAMETERS DURING GRADED EXERCISE / Engelhard-Colton, Nancy – 1989 – 123p 2mf – 9 – $8.00 – us Microform Publ [612]

EFFECTS OF OVERUSE INJURY PRONENESS AND TASK DIFFICULTY ON JOINT KINETIC VARIABILITY DURING LANDING / James, Charles R – University of Oregon, 1996 – 3mf – 9 – $12.00 – PE 3654 – us Microform Publ [612]

THE EFFECTS OF PARTICIPATION IN A LEISURE EDUCATION PROGRAM UPON THE LESIURE BEHAVIOR OF MENTALLY RETARDED ADULTS / Marshall, Katharine R – 1982 – 1mf – 9 – $4.00 – us Microform Publ [616]

THE EFFECTS OF PERCEIVED DIRECTORS' LEADERSHIP BEHAVIORS AND SELECTED DEMOGRAPHIC VARIABLES ON PHYSICAL EDUCATION INSTRUCTORS' JOB SATISFACTION / Yang, Chih-hsien – 1994 – 2mf – $8.00 – us Microform Publ [150]

EFFECTS OF PERCEIVED QUALITY OF LIFE BETWEEN CORONARY ARTERY BYPASS GRAFT AND HEART TRANSPLANTATION PATIENTS WITH REGARD TO CARDIAC REHABILITATION / Hunt, L E – 1991 – 2mf – 9 – $8.00 – us Microform Publ [150]

THE EFFECTS OF PLYOMETRIC TRAINING ON SPRINTING PERFORMANCE OF COLLEGIATE MALES / Curley, Jeffrey J – University of North Carolina at Chapel Hill, 1995 – 1mf – 9 – $4.00 – PH1456 – us Microform Publ [611]

EFFECTS OF POSITIVE REINFORCEMENT ON INFLUENCING GRIP STRENGTH PERFORMANCE OF COLLEGE-AGED FEMALES / Putnam, Kelly – Texas Woman's University, 1994 – 2mf – 9 – $8.00 – PSY 1898 – us Microform Publ [150]

THE EFFECTS OF PROTOTYPIC EXAMPLES AND VIDEO REPLAY ON ADOLESCENT GIRLS' ACQUISITION OF BASIC FIELD HOCKEY SKILLS / Russell, Diane & Sinclair, Gary D – 1991 – 2mf – 9 – $8.00 – us Microform Publ [150]

EFFECTS OF RATIONAL BEHAVIOR TRAINING ON ATTITUDES OF REHABILITATION SUPPORT PERSONNEL / Hooge, N C – 1991 – 1mf – 9 – $4.00 – us Microform Publ [150]

THE EFFECTS OF RECOVERY TIME ON THROWING VELOCITY AND ACCURACY OF COLLEGE BASEBALL PITCHERS / Hendrickson, William R – 1993 – 1mf – $4.00 – us Microform Publ [150]

EFFECTS OF RELATIONSHIP STATUS, SETTING AND SEX OF PERPETRATOR ON COLLEGE STUDENT EVALUATIONS OF DATING VIOLENCE / Bethke, T – 1990 – 1mf – 9 – $4.00 – us Microform Publ [360]

THE EFFECTS OF RESISTANCE TRAINING ON FRACTURE RISK AND PSYCHOLOGICAL VARIABLES IN POSTMENOPAUSAL WOMEN / Shaw, Janet M – Oregon State University, 1995 – 2mf – 9 – $8.00 – PH 1507 – us Microform Publ [612]

THE EFFECTS OF RETROACTIVE INHIBITION AND CONTEXTUAL INTERFERENCE ON LEARNING A MOTOR TASK / Liu, X. – 1991 – 2mf – 9 – $8.00 – us Microform Publ [150]

THE EFFECTS OF REWARDS ON INTRINSIC MOTIVATIONS OF EXERCISERS AND NONEXERCISERS / Tally, Elizabeth – 1993 – 1mf – $4.00 – us Microform Publ [150]

THE EFFECTS OF ROAD SURFACE PITCH ON THE SUBTALAR JOINT WHILE RUNNING AT SELECTED VELOCITIES / Pankey, Robert B – 1988 – 107p 2mf – 9 – $8.00 – us Microform Publ [612]

THE EFFECTS OF RUNNING WITH A FUNCTIONAL KNEE BRACE ON LOWER EXTREMITY JOINT MOMENTS OF FORCE IN ANTERIOR CRUCIATE LIGAMENT INJURED SUBJECTS / Hunter, P B – 1990 – 2mf – 9 – $8.00 – us Microform Publ [790]

EFFECTS OF SAME-SEX AND COEDUCATIONAL PHYSICAL EDUCATION ON PERCEPTIONS OF SELF-CONFIDENCE AND CLASS ENVIRONMENT / Lirgg, Cathy D & Feltz, Deborah D – 1991 – 3mf – 9 – $12.00 – us Microform Publ [150]

EFFECTS OF SELECTED CURRICULUM MATERIALS AND TEACHING EXPERIENCE ON THE PREACTIVE PLANNING OF PHYSICAL EDUCATORS / Ballat, Paul C – Temple University, 1995 – 3mf – 9 – $12.00 – PE3582 – us Microform Publ [370]

THE EFFECTS OF SELF-TALK ON BATTING PERFORMANCE / Hamel, J M – 1991 – 2mf – 9 – $8.00 – us Microform Publ [150]

EFFECTS OF SENSORY BALANCE TRAINING IN OLDER ADULTS / Hu, M – 2mf – 9 – $8.00 – us Microform Publ [150]

THE EFFECTS OF SINGLE VERSUS MULTIPLE MEASURES OF BIOFEEDBACK ON BASKETBALL FREE THROW SHOOTING PERFORMANCE / Kavussanu, Maria et al – 1992 – 2mf – 9 – $8.00 – us Microform Publ [150]

THE EFFECTS OF SIZE AND WEIGHT ON BASKETBALL FREE THROW PERFORMANCE : A BIOMECHANICAL ANALYSIS OF UNSKILLED COLLEGE WOMEN / Wilkerson, Bethany A – 1989 – 48p 1mf – 9 – $4.00 – us Microform Publ [612]

THE EFFECTS OF SOCIAL PHYSIQUE ANXIETY, GENDER, AGE, AND DEPRESSION ON PERCEIVED EXERCISE BEHAVIOR / Lantz, C D – 1991 – 2mf – 9 – $8.00 – us Microform Publ [150]

THE EFFECTS OF SOLID AND LIQUID CARBOHYDRATE FEEDINGS ON HIGH INTENSITY INTERMITTENT EXERCISE PERFORMANCE / Walton, Peter T – University of British Columbia, 1996 – 1mf – 9 – $4.00 – PH1483 – us Microform Publ [612]

THE EFFECTS OF SPATTING AND ANKLE TAPING ON INVERSION BEFORE AND AFTER EXERCISE / Pederson, Troy S – Brigham Young University, 1995 – 1mf – 9 – PE 3665 – us Microform Publ [617]

EFFECTS OF STABILIZATION AND STRUCTURAL ADJUSTMENT PROGRAMMES ON FOOD SECURITY – 1989 – 59p – it F.A.O. [338]

EFFECTS OF STATICALLY PERFORMED TOE TOUCH STRETCHES ON TORQUE PRODUCTION OF THE HAMSTRING AND QUADRICEPS MUSCLE GROUPS / Thigpen, Lydia K – 1988 – 181p 2mf – 9 – $8.00 – us Microform Publ [617]

EFFECTS OF STEP HEIGHT VARIATION ON KNEE JOINT MOMENTS OF FORCE DURING LATERAL STEP-UP EXERCISES / Rauch, Mignone – Texas Woman's University, 1994 – 2mf – 9 – $8.00 – PE 3667 – us Microform Publ [612]

THE EFFECTS OF STICK LENGTH ON THE KINEMATICS OF MAXIMAL VELOCITY THROWING IN LACROSSE / Stevenson, John R – 1983 – 2mf – 9 – $8.00 – us Microform Publ [790]

EFFECTS OF STRENGTH TRAINING ON MUSCLE MASS AND MUSCULOSKELETAL INJURY IN MIDDLE AGED AND OLDER MEN / Redmond, R A – 1991 – 2mf – 9 – $8.00 – us Microform Publ [612]

EFFECTS OF SUBMAXIMAL EXERCISE ON THE MOOD OF FEMALE BULIMICS / Glazer, A R – 1991 – 1mf – 9 – $4.00 – us Microform Publ [150]

THE EFFECTS OF SUCCESS AND FAILURE ON CASUAL ATTRIBUTIONS AMONG SCHOLASTIC WRESTLERS / Scott, David – 1982 – 1mf – 9 – $4.00 – us Microform Publ [150]

THE EFFECTS OF SUPERVISED CARDIAC REHABILITATION ON SELECTED CORONARY ARTERY DISEASE RISK FACTORS FOLLOWING CORONARY ARTERY BYPASS GRAFT SURGERY / Goebel, BM – 1991 – 2mf – 9 – $8.00 – us Microform Publ [612]

EFFECTS OF SUPERVISORY PROFILING ON TARGETED FEEDBACK BEHAVIORS OF PRESERVICE PHYSICAL EDUCATORS / Smith, John O & Sinclair, Gary D – 1991 – 2mf – 9 – $8.00 – us Microform Publ [150]

THE EFFECTS OF SURFACE TYPE ON PLANTAR PRESSURE DISTRIBUTION AND RUNNING KINEMATICS / Killgore, Garry L – 1989 – 143p 2mf – 9 – $8.00 – us Microform Publ [612]

THE EFFECTS OF TELEVISION VIEWING ON THE SELF-REGULATION OF EXERCISE INTENSITY / Viteri, Jacqueline E – 1994 – 2mf – $8.00 – us Microform Publ [150]

THE EFFECTS OF THE CROSS WALK'S RESISTIVE ARM POLES ON THE METABOLIC COSTS OF TREADMILL WALKING / Foley, Thomas S – 1994 – 1mf – $4.00 – us Microform Publ [612]

THE EFFECTS OF THE KIDS' CONNECTION PROGRAM ON SIXTH GRADERS' DRUG KNOWLEDGE AND SELF-CONCEPT / Stumbaugh, T A – 1991 – 1mf – 9 – $4.00 – us Microform Publ [150]

EFFECTS OF THE MENSTRUAL CYCLE AND ORAL CONTRACEPTIVES ON ATHLETIC PERFORMANCE / Lebrun, Constance MT & McKenzie, Donald C – 1991 – 2mf – 9 – $8.00 – us Microform Publ [613]

THE EFFECTS OF THE MENSTRUAL CYCLE ON EXERCISE PERFORMANCE / McCracken, M A – 1990 – 1mf – 9 – $4.00 – us Microform Publ [612]

EFFECTS OF THE MENSTRUAL CYCLE PHASES ON THE ENERGY INTAKE AND EXPENDITURE IN PHYSICALLY ACTIVE AND INACTIVE WOMEN / Holliman, Susan C – 1993 – 3mf – $12.00 – us Microform Publ [612]

THE EFFECTS OF THE STRENGTH SHOE ON VERTICAL JUMP PERFORMANCE IN MALE COLLEGIATE BASKETBALL PLAYERS / Cody, SM – 1989 – 1mf – 9 – $4.00 – us Microform Publ [790]

EFFECTS OF THE USE OF TWO DIFFERENT TEACHING STYLES ON MOTOR SKILL ACQUISITION OF FIFTH-GRADE STUDENTS / Moore, Robert E – East Texas State University, 1996 – 1mf – 9 – PSY 1894 – us Microform Publ [150]

THE EFFECTS OF THREE SELECTED TRAINING PROGRAMS ON SHOULDER EXTERNAL ROTATION STRENGTH, FLEXIBILITY, AND THROWING VELOCITY IN COLLEGIATE BASEBALL PLAYERS / Ploeger, Robin – 1993 – 2mf – $8.00 – us Microform Publ [617]

EFFECTS OF THYMOPENTIN ON THE RESPONSES OF HYPOTHALAMIC-PITUITARY-ADRENAL AXIS TO A HIGH INTENSITY DYNAMIC EXERCISE PROTOCOL / Golan, Ron & Kendrick, Zebulon V – 1993 – 2mf – 9 – $8.00 – us Microform Publ [613]

EFFECTS OF TRADE AND EXCHANGE RATE POLICIES ON PRODUCTION INCENTIVES IN AGRICULTURE – 1990 – 97p – it F.A.O. [338]

THE EFFECTS OF TRAINING AND DETRAINING ON CORTICOSTERONE RHYTHMS AND DIETARY FAT SELECTION IN THE OSBORNE-MENDEL RAT / Schlabach, G A – 1991 – 2mf – 9 – $8.00 – us Microform Publ [590]

EFFECTS OF TRAINING IN STRENGTH SHOES(TM) ON SPEED, JUMPING ABILITY, AND CALF GIRTH / Pethan, Scott M – 1993 – 1mf – $4.00 – us Microform Publ [612]

EFFECTS OF TRAINING ON RESTING BLOOD PRESSURE IN MEN AT RISK FOR CORONARY HEART DISEASE : STRENGTH VS AEROBIC EXERCISE TRAINING / Dawson, PK – 1990 – 2mf – 9 – $8.00 – us Microform Publ [612]

THE EFFECTS OF TWELVE WEEKS OF WALKING OR EXERSTRIDING ON UPPER BODY MUSCULAR STRENGTH AND ENDURANCE / Karawan, Ariel & Porcari, John P – 1992 – 2mf – $8.00 – us Microform Publ [612]

THE EFFECTS OF TWO AEROBIC FITNESS LEVELS ON EXCESS POST-EXERCISE OXYGEN CONSUMPTION IN YOUNG ADULTS / Short, Kevin R – 1994 – 1mf – $4.00 – us Microform Publ [612]

THE EFFECTS OF TWO INSTRUCTIONAL CONDITIONS ON SPORT SKILL SPECIFIC ANALYTIC PROFICIENCY OF PHYSICAL EDUCATION MAJORS / Leis, Hans J & Gangstead, Sandra K – 1993 – 1mf – 9 – $4.00 – us Microform Publ [790]

THE EFFECTS OF VARIOUS EXERCISE MODALITIES ON SERUM CHOLESTEROL AND TRIGLYCERIDE CONCENTRATIONS / Crowder, Todd A & Roberts, John A – 1989 – 3mf – 9 – $12.00 – us Microform Publ [612]

EFFECTS OF VARYING LEVELS OF FATIGUE ON THE RATE OF FORCE DEVELOPMENT IN FEMALES / Ewing, John L, Jr – 1982 – 2mf – 9 – $8.00 – us Microform Publ [790]

THE EFFECTS OF VISUAL IMAGERY ABILITY COMBINED WITH VISUAL MENTAL PRACTICE TECHNIQUES UPON MOTOR PERFORMANCE / Hoffman, Diana M – 1980 – 1mf – 9 – $4.00 – us Microform Publ [612]

EFFECTS OF VISUAL TRAINING ON VISUAL PURSUIT, CATCHING, AND ATTENTIVENESS : A CASE STUDY / Shimakawa, Tsuguyo & Fisher, Janet M – 1992 – 2mf – 9 – $8.00 – us Microform Publ [150]

THE EFFECTS OF WEIGHT LOSS ON PLASMA CHOLESTEROL AND LIPOPROTEINS AMONG FEMALE PARTICIPANTS IN A RESIDENTIAL WELLNESS PROGRAM / Teague, S L – 1991 – 2mf – 9 – $8.00 – us Microform Publ [613]

EFFET DE LA FIXATION D'EMETTEURS CHEZ LE POISSON : UTILISATION DE LA METHODE DE TRACKING EN ECO-ETHOLOGIE / Zimmermann, Felix – Paris. 1977. 136p – 9 – F50.00 – fr Ethnologie [574]

LES EFFETS DE LA GUERRE EN BULGARIE / Danailov, G T – Paris. 1932. BR-3928 2 – 8 – ne IDC [950]

EFFETS DE L'AIR SUR LE CORPS HUMAIN. / Bethizy, J -L de – 1760 – 9 – us Sibley [780]

DES EFFETS DE L'OCCUPATION... / Depambour, J – Paris, 1900 – 2mf – 1 – ILM-504/1 – ne IDC [327]

EFFETTI INTERNAZIONALI DELLE SENTENZE E DEGLI ATTI / Fiore, P – Pisa, Roma. 2v. 1875 – 12mf – 1 – ILM-2020/1 – ne IDC [327]

EFFICACY COGNITIONS, INTRINSIC MOTIVATION, AND EXERCISE BEHAVIOR / Oman, R F – 1989 – 2mf – 9 – $8.00 – us Microform Publ [150]

THE EFFICACY OF TOPICAL IBUPROFEN IN AN INFLAMMATORY MODEL : DELAYED ONSET MUSCLE SORENESS / Mack, Rana L – University of British Columbia, 1995 – 1mf – 9 – $4.00 – PE3609 – us Microform Publ [617]

EFFICIENCY-BASED MANAGEMENT INFORMATION SYSTEM / McMahon, Walter W – 1994 – 84p – 9 – 92-803-1153-0 – fr UNESCO [000]

EFFICIENT FERTILIZER USE IN ACID UPLAND SOILS OF THE HUMID TROPICS – 1986 – 69p – it F.A.O. [631]

EFFICIENT FERTILIZER USE IN SUMMER RAINFED AREAS – 1988 – 45p – it F.A.O. [631]

Effingham County. Georgia *see* CEMETERY RECORDS

Effner, Ute Antonie *see* PHOTOELEKTRONENSPEKTROSKOPIE AN ALKALIMETALL/SI-GRENZFLAECHEN MIT SYNCHROTRONSTRAHLUNG

L'EFFORT – Lyon. aout 1940-aout 1944 – 1 – fr A.C.R.P.P. [073]

L'EFFORT – puis L'Effort libre. Dir. J.-R. Bloch. Poitiers puis Paris. juin 1910-juin 1914 – 1 – fr A.C.R.P.P. [073]

L'EFFORT – Revue federale de litterature, de sociologie et d'art. Dir. Robert de Miranda. no. 10-19. Paris. 1900 – 1 – fr A.C.R.P.P. [800]

L'EFFORT – Port-au-Prince, Haiti: [s.n., 1902-]. [1ere annee, n1-n28. 28 mars-22 juil 1902] – 2 sheets – 9 – us Res Libr [072]

L'EFFORT CULTUREL DU PEUPLE ESPAGNOL EN ARMES / Spain. Ministerio de Instruccion publica y bellas artes – n.p., 1937. Fiche W852. (Blodgett Collection of Spanish Civil War Pamphlets) – 9 – us H.U. College Libr [946]

Efimenko, R S *see* SBORNIK NARODNYKH IURIDICHESKIKH OBYCHAEV ARKHANGEL'SKOI GUBERNII

EFIMERIS TIS KUVERNISEOS : DAILY JOURNAL OF THE CABINET OF THE KINGDOM OF GREECE – Athens, 1948-54; 1959-67 – 110r – 1 – us Ross [949]

EFIOPSKIE RUKOPISI V ST PETERBURGE / Turaev, B – St. Petersburg, 1906. 136p. BR-10,778/1 – 9 – ne IDC [010]

Efremina, A *see* BEZ OTKAZU

Efremov, P A *see*
- MATERIALY DLIA ISTORII RUSSKOI LITERATURY
- SISTEMATICHESKAIA ROSPIS' KNIGAM PRODAIUSHCHIMSIA V KNIZHNOM MAGAZINE I. I. GLAZUNOVA

Efros, Il *see*
- MORE ABOUT ABRAHAM BAR HIYYA'S PHILOSOPHICAL TERMINOLOGY
- PHILOSOPHICAL TERMS IN THE MOREH NEBUKHIM
- THE PROBLEM OF SPACE IN JEWISH MEDIAEVAL PHILOSOPHY
- STUDIES IN PRE-TIBBONIAN PHILOSOPHICAL TERMINOLOGY

Efrusi, E *see* TERNISTYI PUT K SVOBODIE

EFSUS / Hanim, Nigar – Istanbul: Ahtar Matbaasi, 1308-9 [1891-2] – $50.00 – us MEDOC [470]

EFTA BULLETIN / European Free Trade Association – (1977- 5,6,9) – v1- 1960- – 1 – us UMI [337]

EFTERRETNINGER OM GEISTLIGE EMBEDER I NORGE / Boeck, Thorvald Olaf – Christiania: J. Dybwad, 187-. 660p – 1 – us U.W. Library [240]

EFTERRETNINGER OM GRONLAND; UDBRAGNE AF EN JOURNAL HOLDEN FRA 1721-1788 / Egede, P – Kjobenhavn. 1788. BN-198 2 – 8 – ne IDC [430]

E.G. KOLBENHEYERS PARACELSUS-TRILOGIE : EINE METAPHYSIK DES DEUTSCHEN MENSCHEN / Westhoff, Franz – (Includes bibliographical references) – Berlin: Junker und Duennhaupt, 1937 – 1 – us U.W. Library [430]

L'EGALITAIRE – Journal de l'organisation sociale. Red. en chef Dezami. no. 1-2. Paris. mai-juin 1840 – 1 – fr A.C.R.P.P. [073]

L'EGALITAIRE / Parti socialiste (SFIO) – Brest. mars 1907-sept 1908 – 1 – fr A.C.R.P.P. [335]

EGALITATEA – Bucharest, Romania. -w. 15 April 1890-25 Dec 1892. 1 reel – 1 – uk British Libr Newspaper [949]

L'EGALITE – (Filmed with: L'Egalite, St-Jerome 23 aut 1897-20 oct 1898) – Montreal, Canada. 7,28 jul 1897 – 1r – 1 – Can$35.00 – cn Can Microfilming [072]

L'EGALITE : JOURNAL DE L'ASSOCIATION INTERNATIONALE DES TRAVAILLEURS DE LA SUISSE ROMANDE / International Working Association – (See also series: Important Periodicals of Italian and International Socialism, 1868-1917) – Geneva. v1-4,no23. 1868-72. 1 reel – 1 – $65.00 – us UPA [335]

L'EGALITE – Journal republicain socialiste. Dir. Jules Roques. Paris. 8 fevr 1889-7 oct 1891 – 1 – fr A.C.R.P.P. [073]

L'EGALITE – Cap-Haitien: St-Cap Louis Blot, feb 15 1881-jun 12 1883 – 2 sheets – 9 – us Res Libr [072]

L'EGALITE – Paris: Dondey-Dupre, apr-may 1849 – us Res Libr [072]

EGALITE : JOURNAL REPUBLICAIN SOCIALISTE – Paris, 1877-82 – 1r – 1 – us Ross [320]

L'EGALITE DE ROUBAIX-TOURCOING – Roubaix. fevr 1896-juin 1914 – 1 – fr A.C.R.P.P. [073]

EGALITE DES HOMMES, DES PEUPLES, DES RACES – Alger. Dir, Ferhat Abbas. no.37-133. aout 1946-juil 1948 – 1 – fr A.C.R.P.P. [073]

L'EGALITE, ST-JEROME *see* L'EGALITE

EGALITERIANISM AS A REVOLT AGAINST NATURE AND OTHER ESSAYS / Rothbard, Murray N – 1fiche (29x) – 9 – 1.00f – at Libertarian Micro [320]

Egan, Thomas J *see* HISTORY OF THE HALIFAX VOLUNTEER BATTALION AND VOLUNTEER COMPANIES, 1859-1887

Egar, John Hodson *see* THE THREEFOLD GRACE OF THE HOLY TRINITY

EG-BINNENMARKT UND ENTWICKLUNG VON POLITIKFELDERN / Knaepper, Matthias – 1993 – 3mf – 9 – DM98.00 – 3-89349-686-6 – gw Hänsel [320]

Egede, H *see*
- DESCRIPTION ET HISTOIRE NATURELLE DU GROENLAND
- DET GAMLE GRONLANDS NEYE PERLUSTRATION
- RELATIONER FRA GRONLAND, 1721-36

Egede, N *see* CONTINUATION AF HANS EGEDES RELATIONER FRA GRONLAND; SAMT NIELS EGEDES BESKRIVELSE OVER GRONLAND; RE-ED. VED H. OSTERMANN

Egede, P *see*
- CONTINUATION AF HANS EGEDES RELATIONER FRA GRONLAND; SAMT NIELS EGEDES BESKRIVELSE OVER GRONLAND; RE-ED. VED H. OSTERMANN
- DICTIONARIUM GROENLANDICO-DANICO-LATINUM
- EFTERRETNINGER OM GRONLAND; UDBRAGNE AF EN JOURNAL HOLDEN FRA 1721-1788
- GRAMMATICA GROENLANDICA-DANICO-LATINA
- OMSTAENDELIG OG UDFORLIG RELATION ANGAAENDE DEN GRONLANDSKE MISSIONS BEGYNDELSE OG FORTSAETTELSE SAMT HVAD ELLERS MERE DER

Egelhaaf, Gottlob *see*
- GUSTAV ADOLF IN DEUTSCHLAND, 1630-1632
- LANDGRAF PHILIPP VON HESSEN

EGEMEN KAZAKHSTN = THE TRUTH OF KAZAKHTAN – (Comes in Kazakh) – 1919- – 1 – sz Infoprint [947]

EGERER TAGBLATT EGERER ZEITUNG – Cheb, Czechoslovakia. Jul-Aug 1938 – 1r – 1 – us L of C Photodup [072]

EGERER ZEITUNG – Eger (Cheb), Czechoslovakia. 3 Jan 1923-31 Dec 1938 – 33r – 1 – gw Mikrofilm [072]

EGERLAND – Eger (Cheb), Czechoslovakia. Nov 1928-Dec 1933 – 6r – 1 – gw Mikrofilm [072]
Egerton, Mrs. Fred *see* ADMIRAL OF THE FLEET, SIR GEOFFREY PHIPPS HORNBY G.C.B.: A BIOGRAPHY
Egerton, Hakluyt *see* LIBERAL THEOLOGY AND THE GROUND OF FAITH:...A CONSERVATIVE... APOLOGETIC
Egerton, Hugh Edward *see* A SHORT HISTORY OF BRITISH COLONIAL POLICY
EGERTON MANUSCRIPTS: PAPERS RELATING TO THE ENGLISH COLONIES IN AMERICA AND THE WEST INDIES, 1627-1699 / British Museum – Ms. 2395. BRRAM – 1 – uk Microform Academic [975]
Eggebrecht, Axel *see* GOETHE, SCHILLER: UEBER DAS THEATER; EINE AUSWAHL AUS IHREN SCHRIFTEN
Egger, Emile *see*
- ETUDES HISTORIQUES SUR LES TRAITES PUBLICS CHEZ LES GRECS ET CHEZ LES ROMAINS
- ISTORIIA KNIGI OT EIA POIAVLENIIA DO NASHIKH VREMEN
Egger, Franz *see* ABSOLUTE ODER RELATIVE WAHRHEIT DER HEILIGEN SCHRIFT
Egger, Victor *see* LA PAROLE INTERIEURE: ESSAI DE PSYCOLOGIE DESCRIPTIVE
Eggers Lan, Conrado *see*
- IZQUIERDA, PERONISMO Y SOCIALISMO NACIONAL
- PERONISMO Y LIBERACION NACIONAL
Eggert, Hermann *see* DIE CONCURRENZ FUER ENTWUERFE ZUM NEUEN REICHSTAGSGEBAEUDE
Eggert, KE *see* FIRST METATARSOPHALANGEAL JOINT RANGE OF MOTION AS A FACTOR IN TURF TOE INJURIES
Eggleston, Edward *see*
- THE BEGINNERS OF A NATION
- CHRIST IN LITERATURE: BEING A TREASURY OF CHOICE READINGS, IN PROSE AND VERSE
- THE CIRCUIT RIDER
- THE SCHOOLMASTER'S STORIES, FOR BOYS AND GIRLS
Eggleston, George Cary *see* DOROTHY SOUTH: A LOVE STORY OF VIRGINIA JUST BEFORE THE WAR
EGGS OF BRITISH BIRDS / Poynting, F – Z-1990. 1895-1896 – 9 – ne IDC [590]
EGGS OF THE BIRDS OF EUROPE / Dresser, H E – Z 1973. 1 v. text, 1 v. atlas. 1905-1910 – 9 – ne IDC [590]
Egharevba, Jacob U *see*
- BENIN GAMES AND SPORTS
- BENIN LAW AND CUSTOM
- THE CITY OF BENIN
- CONCISE LIVES OF FAMOUS IYASES OF BENIN
- THE ORIGIN OF BENIN
- SOME TRIBAL GODS OF SOUTHERN NIGERIA
Egiptio, A *see* AVISI PARTICULARI, ULTIMAMENTE MANDATI DAL MAGNIFICO M. ANTONIO EGIPTIO MAGGIOR DOMO DELL ILLUSTRISSIMO ET ECCELLENTISSIMO SIGNOR PAULO GIORDANO
Egle, William Henry *see* HISTORY OF DAUPHIN AND LEBANON COUNTIES
EGLENTIERS POETENS BORS / Rodenburg, Th – O 735. 1619 – 9 – ne IDC [760]
Egli, Emil *see* DIE ZUERICHER WIEDERTAEUFER ZUR REFORMATIONSZEIT
L'EGLISE A L'EPOQUE DU CONCILE DE TRENTE (17) – Paris, 1948 – Dfl46.00 – ne Slangenburg [240]
L'EGLISE AU BRESIL PENDANT L'EMPIRE ET PENDANT LA REPUBLIQUE / Badaro, F – Roma: Stabilimento Bontempelli, 1895 – 1mf – us A.T.L.A. [240]
L'EGLISE AU POUVOIR DES LAIQUES, 888-1057 (7) – Paris, 1940 – Dfl49.00 – ne Slangenburg [240]
L'EGLISE AU TEMPS DU GRAND SCHISME ET DE LA CRISE CONCILIAIRE, 1378-1449 (14) – Paris, 1962-1964 – Dfl112.00 – ne Slangenburg [240]
L'EGLISE CATHOLIQUE – Montreal, Canada. n2,5,7. 1901-05 – 1r – 1 – Can$25.00 – cn Can Microfilming [240]
L'EGLISE CATHOLIQUE ET LES PROTESTANTS / Romain, Georges – (Includes bibliographical references) – Paris: Librairie Bloud et Barral, 1900 – 1mf – 9 – 0-8370-8784-8 – 1986-2784 – us A.T.L.A. [230]
L'EGLISE CATHOLIQUE ET L'ETAT SOUS LA TROISIEME REPUBLIQUE (1870-1906) / Debidour, Antonin – Paris: F. Alcan, 1906-1909 – 3mf – us A.T.L.A. [240]
Eglise Catholique. Province de Quebec *see* LE CATECHISME DES PROVINCES ECCLESIASTIQUES DE QUEBEC, MONTREAL, OTTAWA
EGLISE DE MONTREAL *see* LA SEMAINE RELIGIEUSE DE MONTREAL
L'EGLISE DE PARIS PENDANT LA REVOLUTION FRANCAISE, 1789-1801 / Delarc, Odon – Paris: Desclee, de Brouwer, [1895-1897?] – 4mf – us A.T.L.A. [240]
L'EGLISE DE QUEBEC *see* LA SEMAINE RELIGIEUSE DE QUEBEC
L'EGLISE DE ROME / Chiniquy, Charles – Montreal: Impr. de l'Aurore, 1870. SEM105P45 – 1mf – 9 – Can$2.25 – cn Bibl Nat [240]
L'EGLISE ET LA REMISSION DES PECHES AUX PREMIERE SIECLES / Galtier, P – Paris, 1932 – 9mf – 8 – ne Slangenburg [240]
L'EGLISE ET LA RENAISSANCE, 1449-1517 (15) – Dfl35.00 – ne Slangenburg [240]
L'EGLISE ET LA SCIENCE : PRECIS HISTORIQUE / Francais, J – (Includes bibliographical references) – Paris: Librairie critique, 1908 – 1mf – 9 – 0-8370-8669-8 – 1986-2669 – us A.T.L.A. [210]
L'EGLISE ET LA SORCELLERIE : PRECIS HISTORIQUE, SUIVI DES DOCUMENTS OFFICIELS, DES TEXTES PRINCIPAUX, ET D'UN PROCES INEDIT / Francais, J – Paris: E. Nourry, 1910 – 1mf – us A.T.L.A. [240]
L'EGLISE ET LE PROGRES DU MONDE / Devas, Charles Stanton – (Includes bibliographical references) – Paris: Victor Lecoffre, 1909 – 1mf – 9 – 0-8370-7213-1 – 1986-1213 – us A.T.L.A. [240]
L'EGLISE ET L'ENSEIGNEMENT POPULAIRE : SOUS L'ANCIEN REGIME / Allain, Ernest – Paris: Bloud, [18–?] – 1mf – 9 – 0-8370-7521-1 – 1986-1521 – us A.T.L.A. [370]
L'EGLISE ET LES CAMPAGNES AU MOYEN AGE / Prevost, Gustave Amable – Paris: H. Champion, 1892 – 1mf – us A.T.L.A. [240]
L'EGLISE ET L'ETAT DANS LA SECONDE MOITIE DU 3E SIECLE (249-284) / Aube, Benjamin – Paris: E. Perrin, 1885 – 2mf – us A.T.L.A. [240]
L'EGLISE ET L'ETAT EN FRANCE / Desdevises du Dezert, Georges – Paris: Societe francaise d'imprimerie et de librairie, 1907-1908 – 2mf – us A.T.L.A. [320]
L'EGLISE GEORGIENNE : DES ORIGINES JUSQU'A NOS JOURS / Tamarati, Michel – (Includes index) – Rome: Societe typographico-editrice romaine, 1910 – 2mf – 9 – 0-8370-7512-2 – 1986-1512 – us A.T.L.A. [240]
L'EGLISE LATINE ET LE PROTESTANTISME AU POINT DE VUE DE L'EGLISE D'ORIENT / Khomiakov, Aleksei Stepanovich – Recueil d'articles sur des questions religieuses, ecrits a differentes epoques et a diverses occasions. 1872 – 1 – us A.T.L.A. [240]
EGLISE NATIONALE PROTESTANTE DE GENEVE : MEMORIAL DES SEANCES DU CONSISTOIRE / Eglise Nationale Protestante de Geneve – v1-119. 1873-1991 – Inquire – 1 – ATLA S0337 – us A.T.L.A. [240]
Eglise Nationale Protestante de Geneve *see* EGLISE NATIONALE PROTESTANTE DE GENEVE
L'EGLISE ORTHODOXE RUSSE; ORGANIZATION, DOGMES, HERESIES (DOUKHOBORSTES ET MOLOKANES) / Laflamme, Claire – SEM105P464 – 1mf – 9 – Can$2.25 – cn Bibl Nat [240]
L'EGLISE PRIMITIVE (1) – Paris, 1934 – Dfl42.00 – ne Slangenburg [240]
L'EGLISE REFORMEE DE PARIS SOUS HENRI 4 / Pannier, J – H-377 2. 1911 – 9 – ne IDC [944]
L'EGLISE REFORMEE DE PARIS SOUS LOUIS 13 (1610-1621) / Pannier, J – Paris. 1922. BH-378 2 – 8 – ne IDC [240]
L'EGLISE ROMAINE ET LES ORIGINES DE LA RENAISSANCE / Guiraud, Jean – Paris: V. Lecoffre, 1909 – 1mf – us A.T.L.A. [240]
L'EGLISE RUSSE ET L'EGLISE CATHOLIQUE : LETTRES DU R.P. ROZAVEN DE LA COMPAGNIE DE JESUS / Rozaven, R P – nouv ed. Paris: E Plon, 1876 – 1mf – 9 – 0-8370-7188-7 – 1986-1188 – us A.T.L.A. [230]
LES EGLISES DE JERUZALEM : LA DISCIPLINE ET LA LITURGIE AU 4TH SIECLE / Cabrol, F – Paris, 1895 – 4mf – 8 – Dfl19.00 – ne Slangenburg [240]
LES EGLISES DE LA REFORME ET LE PROBLEME DE LA PAIX AU COURS DU 19EME SIECLE / Allier, R – Paris, 1931 – 2mf – 9 – ILM-4057/1 – ne IDC [340]
LES EGLISES DU REFUGE EN ANGLETERRE / Schicler, Fernand de, Baron – Paris: Fischbacher, 1892 – 4mf – us A.T.L.A. [240]
EGLISES SEPAREES / Duchesne, Louis – (Includes bibliographical references) – 2e ed. Paris: Albert Fontemoing, 1905 – 1mf – 9 – 0-8370-7625-0 – 1986-1625 – us A.T.L.A. [240]
EGLISI = EGLISI: PRESS SERVICE OF THE CHURCH OF SILENCE : SERVICE DE PRESSE DE L'EGLISE DU SILENCE – Braine-Le-Comte. 223 docs. 1980-1991 – 40mf – 9 – ne IDC [320]
Eglitis, Anslavs *see* SVABU KAPRICO
EGLOGA A VELASCO Y GONZALEZ / Fernandez de Moratin, Nicolas – s.a. – 1mf – 9 – Pta1,000.00 – 84-7848-150-8 – sp Pentalfa [820]
EGLOGAS DEL PASTOR DE EXTREMADURA / Rocha, Manuel de la – 1821 – 9 – 1.50f – sp Bibl Santa Ana [810]
LAS EGLOGAS Y GEORGICAS...VIRGILIO / Mesa, Cristobal – 1793 – 9 – $1.50f – sp Bibl Santa Ana [450]
EGMONT STAR – Hawera. New Zealand. -d. 15 Jul 1899-26 Sep 1914. (Imperfect). (29 reels) – 1 – uk British Libr Newspaper [072]
Egnell, H *see* LA CHEQUE ET LA LOI DU LIEU DE PAIEMENT
Egner, Fritz *see* DER DICHTERISCHE ESSAY, DIE PROSAFORM DER ENGLISCHEN ROMANTIK
THE EGO AND HIS OWN / Stirner, Max – 1844. 383p. 1 fiche (29x) – 9 – 1.00f – at Libertarian Micro [320]
EGO DOCUMENTS FROM THE NETHERLANDS, 16TH CENTURY-1814 : PART 1: MANUSCRIPT TRAVEL JOURNALS IN LANGUAGES OTHER THEN DUTCH, 16TH CENTURY-1814 / ed by Dekker, R M – ca 200-250mf – 9 – Dfl2,950.00 – ne MMF Publ [910]
Ego, Michael M *see* LEISURE PREFERENCE PATTERNS OF SECOND-GENERATION JAPANESE-AMERICANS OF SELECTED CITIES IN THE UNITED STATES
EGO-FUTURISTY I KUBO-FUTURISTY AND OBRAZTSY FUTURISTICHESKIKH PROIZVEDENII / Chukovskii, K – Opyt khrestomatii. Shipovnik, XXII. v. 22. Spb. 1914. BR-3560 2 – 8 – ne IDC [460]
THE EGOIST: AN INDIVIDUAL REVIEW – v. 1-6, no. 5. 1914-19 – 1 – 17.00 – us L of C Photodup [410]
[EGON ERVIN KIRSCH PAMPHLET COLLECTION] – 19?? – 1 – CSUXANR9552-B – us Hoover Inst Photo [750]
Egorov, Iu. *see* VOPROSY ISTORII GOSUDARSTVA I PRAVA ESTONSKOI SSR DO OKTIABR'SKOI REVOLIUTSII
Egozcue, J *see* MEMORIAS DE LA COMISION DEL MAPA GEOLOGICO DE ESPANA. MEMORIA GEOLOGICA-MINERA DE LA PROVINCIA DE CACERES
LA EGREGIA FIGURA DE CARLOS DE YUSTE. (LAS POSTRIMERIAS DE SU VIDA Y SU MUERTE EJEMPLAR) / Gutierrez Macias, Valeriano – Badajoz: Dip. Provincial, 1958. Sep. REE – sp Bibl Santa Ana [920]
EGREMONT 1838-1897 – (Mf 1: Town & Vital Records 1834-43. Mf 2: Town & Vital Records 1841-44. Mf 3: Town & Vital Records 1844-48. Mf 4: Town & Vital Records 1847-53. Mf 5: Town & Vital Records 1852-53. Mf 6-7: Index to Births 1845-1987. Mf 8-9: Index to Marriages 1845-1987. Mf 10-11: Index to Deaths 1845-1987. Mf 12: Marriage Intentions 1846-83. Mf 13: Births 1844-61. Mf 14: Marriages & Deaths 1844-61. Mf 15: Births 1862-97; Marriages 1862-97. Mf 16: Marriages 1880-97; Deaths 1861-97) – (mf ed 1988) – 16mf – 9 – 0-87623-044-3 – us Holbrook [920]
EGRESADOS : EDUCACION PRIMARIA 1975-1976 / Argentina. Ministerio de Cultura y Educacion. Departamento de Estadistica – Buenos Aires, [1980] – 1mf – 9 – DE-632/1 – ne IDC [370]
Eguia, F *see* PAPEL O ESCRITO...SOBRE LAS BEBIDAS HELADAS...
Eguibar y Muniz, Juan Jose de *see* ZALAMEA DE LA SERENA (BADAJOZ) JAMAS FUE "ILIPA"
Egville, J d' *see*
- LE MARIAGE MEXICAIN, DIVERTISEMENT BALLET
- TELEMAQUE
EGYENLOSEG – Budapest. 1903-16 – 1 – 207.00 – us L of C Photodup [073]
EGYETEMES PHILOLOGIAI KOZLONY – Budapest. 1877. Available: 1877-1911. Lacking: 1877, v. 1. BR-5841 2 – 8 – ne IDC [400]
EGYPT – A monthly record of Egyptian and Near East news. London. -m. Mar 1911-Feb 1913. (22 ft) – 1 – uk British Libr Newspaper [960]
EGYPT : ANNUAIRE STATISTIQUE 1901-1959 / Egypt. Maslahat al-Ihsa wa-al-Ta'dad – (Coll title: African Official Statistical Serials, 1867-1982) – 317mf – 9 – £4.00f (set £1,670.00 318mf) – uk Chadwyck [960]
EGYPT : STATISTICAL RETURNS 1881-1897 / Egypt. Maslahat al-Ihsa wa-al-Ta'dad – (Coll title: African Official Statistical Serials, 1867-1982) – 1mf – 9 – £7.00f (set £1,670.00 318mf) – uk Chadwyck [960]
Egypt *see*
- AL-JARIDAH AL-RASMIYAH. (OFFICIAL GAZETTE)
- AL-WAQA'I' AL-MISRIYAH
- BUDGET FOR THE UNITED SERVICE IN THE REGIONS OF SYRIA AND EGYPT
- JOURNAL OFFICIEL DU GOUVERNEMENT EGYPTIEN
- NATIONAL INCOME OF EGYPT FOR 1953; OFFICIAL ESTIMATE, DEC 1954
Egypt. Agrarian Reform General Organization *see* REPLIES TO UNITED NATIONS QUESTIONNAIRE ON AGRARIAN REFORM IN THE EGYPTIAN REGION
EGYPT AND NUBIA, THE MOST INTERESTING SITES AND MONUMENTS / Teynard, Felix – 1851-52. 160 photographs (calotypes). (Collections of the Department of Prints and Photographs) – 1r – 1 – $50.00 – fr Bibl Nationale [930]
EGYPT AND SYRIA: THEIR PHYSICAL FEATURES IN RELATION TO BIBLE HISTORY / Dawson, John William – London: Religious Tract Society, 1885. 04209. (Pre-1900 Canadiana) – 9 – cn C.I.H.M. [956]
EGYPT AND THE CHRISTIAN CRUSADE / Watson, Charles Roger – (Includes index) – Philadelphia, PA: Board of Foreign Missions of the United Presbyterian Church of N A, c1907 – 1mf – 9 – 0-8370-6447-3 – 1986-0447 – us A.T.L.A. [240]
EGYPT AND THE PENTATEUCH: AN ADDRESS / Cooper, William Ricketts – London: Samuel Bagster, (1875). 1 fiche – 9 – us A.T.L.A. [240]
Egypt. Banque de Port Said *see* RAPPORT DU CONSEIL D'ADMINISTRATION. BILAN ET COMPTE DE PROFITS ET PERTES. 1946-1963
Egypt. Banque du Caire *see* BALANCE SHEET
Egypt. Banque Misr *see* RAPPORT DU CONSEIL D'ADMINISTRATION ET BILAN DU EXERCISE, 1947-1957
EGYPT BAPTIST CHURCH. MILLINGTON, TENNESSEE : CHURCH RECORDS – 1840-1961 – 1 – 51.12 – us Baptist [240]
Egypt. Central Agency for Public Mobilisation and Statistics *see* STATISTICAL HANDBOOK OF THE UNITED ARAB REPUBLIC
Egypt. Central Bank of Egypt *see*
- CREDIT AND BANKING DEVELOPMENTS, 1960-1969/70
- REPORTS ON THE BOARD OF DIRECTORS
Egypt. Commission Internationale du Canal de Suez *see* PROTOCOLES DE LA COMMISSION. PROCES VERBAUX DE LA SOUS-COMMISSION
Egypt. Compagnie Universelle du Canal Maritime de Suez *see*
- ASSEMBLEE GENERALE DES ACTIONNAIRES; REUNION: 1955-4 JUL 1958
- THE SUEZ CANAL COMPANY AND THE DECISION TAKEN BY THE EGYPTIAN GOVERNMENT ON 26 JUL 1956
- THE SUEZ CANAL; NOTES AND STATISTICS
Egypt. Compagnie Universelle du Canal Maritime du Suez *see* SURVEY OF THE FUTURE OF THE SUEZ CANAL
Egypt. Credit Agricole d'Egypte *see* RECUEIL
Egypt. Customs Dept *see* RAPPORT SUR LE COMMERCE EXTERIEUR
EGYPT, CYPRUS AND ASIATIC-TURKEY / Farley, James Lewis – London: Truebner & Co., 1878. xvi,270p – 1 – us U.W. Library [910]

Egypt. Dept. of Statistics and Census *see* CENSUS OF INDUSTRIAL PRODUCTION
Egypt Exploration Fund *see* ARCHAEOLOGICAL REPORT
Egypt. Federation Egyptienne de l'industrie *see* YEARBOOK
Egypt. General Desert Development Organisation *see* UAR DESERT DEVELOPMENT AND LAND RECLAMATION PROJECTS
Egypt. Hydro-Electric Power Commission *see* REPORT ON ECONOMIC UTILISATION OF ENERGY AVAILABLE FROM THE ASWAN DAM AND NILE BARRAGES HYDROELECTRIC SCHEMES
Egypt. Industrial Bank *see*
- THE DEVELOPMENT OF INDUSTRIAL CREDIT IN EGYPT
- THE INDUSTRIAL BANK, U.A.R
- REPORT OF THE ORDINARY GENERAL MEETING

Egypt. Insurance Department *see* EGYPTIAN INSURANCE YEARBOOK
Egypt. Laws, Statutes, etc *see* LA LEGISLATION EN MATIERE IMMOBILIERE EN EGYPTE; RECUEIL DES LOIS, REGLEMENTS ET INSTRUCTIONS ADMINISTRATIVES RELATIFS A LA PROPRIETE IMMOBILIERE
Egypt. Maslahat al-Ihsa wa-al-Ta'dad *see*
- ANNUAIRE STATISTIQUE
- EGYPT

Egypt. Maslahat al-Ihsa wa-al-Tadad *see* RECENSEMENT GENERAL DE L'EGYPTE
Egypt. Middle East Supply Centre *see* PRELIMINARY SURVEY OF EGYPT
Egypt. Ministry of Agrarian Reform *see* AGRARIAN REFORM AND LAND RECLAMATION IN TEN YEARS
Egypt. Ministry of Agriculture *see*
- AGRICULTURAL AND ECONOMIC STATISTICS
- AGRICULTURAL CENSUS OF EGYPT
- AGRICULTURAL ECONOMY
- COTTON IN EGYPT
- COTTON STATISTICS
- THE FIVE-YEAR AGRICULTURAL DEVELOPMENT PROGRAM, 1960-1965
- UAR AGRICULTURE

Egypt. Ministry of Commerce and Industry *see*
- REPORT OF THE INDUSTRIAL COMMITTEE
- REPORT ON EGYPT'S FOREIGN TRADE
- TIJARAT MISR AL KHARIJIA (FOREIGN TRADE OF EGYPT)

Egypt. Ministry of Communications *see* SEVEN YEARS OF TRANSPORT AND COMMUNICATIONS IN THE EGYPTIAN REGION OF THE UAR
Egypt. Ministry of Economy *see* A STATISTICAL PORTRAIT
Egypt. Ministry of Finance *see*
- FINAL ACCOUNTS
- FINANCIAL AND ECONOMIC LEGISLATION ISSUED DURING THE REVOLUTIONARY REGIME, 23 JUL 1952-23 JUL 1957
- POPULATION CENSUS OF EGYPT, 1937
- POPULATION CENSUS OF EGYPT, 1947: GENERAL TABLES
- STATISTIQUES DES SOCIETES ANONYMES TRAVAILLANT PRINCIPALEMENT EN EGYPTE

Egypt. Ministry of Foreign Affairs *see* WHITE PAPER ON THE NATIONALIZATION OF THE SUEZ MARITIME CANAL COMPANY
Egypt. Ministry of Industry *see* SECOND FIVE YEAR INDUSTRIAL PLAN
Egypt. Ministry of Treasury *see*
- BUDGET OF THE EGYPTIAN REGION
- DRAFT OF THE STATE BUDGET; STATEMENT BY THE MINISTER OF THE TREASURY

Egypt. National Bank *see*
- CREDIT AND BANKING DEVELOPMENTS
- REPORT OF THE BOARD OF DIRECTORS

EGYPT, NUBIA AND ETHIOPIA ILLUSTRATED BY ONE HUNDRED STEREOSCOPIC PHOTOGRAPHS TAKEN BY FRANCIS FRITH FOR MESSERS : NEGRETTI AND ZAMBRA; WITH DESCRIPTIONS AND NUMEROUS WOOD ENGRAVINGS BY JOSEPH BONOMI; AND NOTES BY SAMUEL SHARPE – (Filmed with: Christianity, Islam and the Negro Race/ E W Blyden) – London: Smith, Elder, 1862 – us Res Libr [960]
Egypt. Occupied Enemy Territory Administration (OETA) South *see* PROCLAMATIONS, ORDINANCES AND NOTICES
Egypt. Permanent Council for Social Services *see* THE SOCIAL SERVICES COUNCIL: SURVEY OF ITS ACTIVITIES SINCE ITS ESTABLISHMENT
Egypt. Permanent Council for the Development of National Production *see* REPORT
Egypt. Permanent Council of Public Service *see* THE POPULATION PROBLEM IN EGYPT
Egypt. Statistical Department *see*
- ANNUAIRE STATISTIQUE
- ANNUAL STATEMENT OF FOREIGN TRADE, 1919-1961
- STATISTICS OF WAGES AND WORKING HOURS IN EGYPT

Egypt. U.A.R. Central Agency for Public Mobilisation and Statistics *see*
- ANNUAL BULLETIN OF FOREIGN TRADE, 1964-1969
- STATISTICAL ABSTRACT OF THE UNITED ARAB REPUBLIC, 1967-1972
- UAR ECONOMIC INDICATORS, 1961-1970

Egypt. U.A.R. Suez Canal Authority *see* SUEZ CANAL REPORT
L'EGYPTE AVANT LES PYRAMIDES, 4E MILLENAIRE / Reunion des musees nationaux. Paris – 1973. 75 illus. 1 fiche – 9 – fr Réunion [700]
L'EGYPTE CONTEMPORAINE – Cairo. 1910-32. Missing no. 2 – 1 – 35.00r – us Hoover Inst Photo [073]
EGYPTIAN BIRDS / Whymper, C – Z 1960. 1909 – 9 – ne IDC [590]
THE EGYPTIAN CHURCH / Dowling, Theodore Edward – London: Cope & Fenwick, [1909?] – 1mf – us A.T.L.A. [240]
THE EGYPTIAN COFFIN TEXTS, VOL 2 : TEXTS OF SPELLS 76-163 / Buck, Adriaan de – 1938 – 9 – $12.00f – 0-226-07946-5 – us U.C. Orient [930]
THE EGYPTIAN COFFIN TEXTS, VOL 6 : TEXTS OF SPELLS 472-786 / Buck, Adriaan de – 1956 – 9 – $18.00f – 0-226-07944-9 – us U.C. Orient [930]
EGYPTIAN DAILY POST – Cairo. Egypt. -d. 29 Apr 1909-26 Nov 1910. (9 reels) – 1 – uk British Libr Newspaper [072]
EGYPTIAN GAZETTE – Alexandria, Cairo, Egypt. -d. 2 Jan 1893-31 Dec 1932. 147 reels – 1 – uk British Libr Newspaper [072]
THE EGYPTIAN GAZETTE – Alexandia: [s.n.], 1952-66 – 1 – us Res Libr [072]
EGYPTIAN INSCRIPTIONS FROM THE BRITISH MUSEUM AND OTHER SOURCES / Sharpe, S – 3v. London, 1837-55. BNE-455 1 – 9 – ne IDC [410]
EGYPTIAN INSURANCE YEARBOOK / Egypt. Insurance Department – 9v. 1949-61. (lacking 1950-51). BNE-4637 1 – 9 – ne IDC [650]
EGYPTIAN LETTERS TO THE DEAD. MAINLY FROM THE OLD AND MIDDLE KINGDOMS / Gardiner, A H & Sethe, K – London. 1928. BNE-463 1 – 9 – ne IDC [930]
EGYPTIAN MAIL – Cairo. Egypt. -w. 7 Mar 1916-30 Jun 1922. (Imperfect). (13 reels) – 1 – uk British Libr Newspaper [072]
EGYPTIAN MAIL – (Filmed consecutively with: Egyptian gazette) – Cairo: Societe oriental de publicite, 1952-55; 1955-66 – us Res Libr [380]
EGYPTIAN OPPOSITIONAL PERIODICALS – (Also available seperately) – 233mf – 9 – ne IDC [073]
EGYPTIAN ORGANIZATION FOR HUMAN RIGHTS – Giza. 54 docs. 1989-1991 – 5mf – 9 – ne IDC [320]
EGYPTIAN PLAIN DEALER – Harrisburg. Ill. 1934-35 – 1 – us UMI [071]
EGYPTIAN POETRY, FROM ITS RENAISSANCE TO THE PRESENT TIME / Megally, Shafik – Zug, 1974. BNE-385/1 – 9 – ne IDC [810]
EGYPTIAN PRESS EXTRACTS – [Cairo?]: [s.n.], feb 5, 1941-jan 1943; jan 19 1945-apr 19 1946 – us Res Libr [072]
EGYPTIAN REPUBLIC – Centralia. Ill. -w. 1859-61 – 1 – us UMI [071]
Egyptian Socialist Party *see* JARIDAT AL-SHAB
THE EGYPTIAN SUDAN : ITS HISTORY AND MONUMENTS / Budge, E A Wallis – Philadelphia: J.B. Lippincott, 1907 – 4mf – us A.T.L.A. [930]
EGYPTIAN TRADE JOURNAL AND SUDAN GAZETTE – London, UK. Oct 1906. -irr. 8 feet – 1 – uk British Libr Newspaper [072]
L'EGYPTIENNE : REVUE MENSUELLE POLITIQUE, FEMINISME, SOCIOLOGIE, ART (IN FRENCH) – (Missing issues: 12, 44, 58, 81, 96, 103, 110, 114, 148) – Cairo. v1-16 (nos1-164). Feb 1925-Apr 1940 – 1 – $950.00 – us MEDOC [073]
EGYPT'S PAST, PRESENT AND FUTURE / Howell, Joseph Morton – Dayton, OH: Service Publishing Company, 1929. xi,378p. plates, ports – 1 – us U.W. Library [956]
EGYPT'S PLACE IN UNIVERSAL HISTORY : AN HISTORICAL INVESTIGATION IN FIVE BOOKS / Bunsen, Christian Karl Josias, Freiherr von – London. 5v. 1848-67 – 2r – 1 – us Ross [960]
EGYSEGES MAGYARSAG = UNITED HUNGARIANS – Niagara Falls. v1-3. 1959-61 – 1 – $150.00 – cn McLaren [073]
DAS EHBUECHLIN... / Alber, E – N.p., [1539] – 2mf – 9 – ne IDC [240]
EHE DIE SPUR SICH VERLIERT / Langenbucher, Erich – Berlin: Junge Generation Verlag, [1942] – 1r – 1 – us U.W. Library [830]
DAS EHELICHE GUETERRECHT... / Hasler, K – Zuerich, 1897 – 2mf – 1 – ILM-3091/1 – ne IDC [327]
DAS EHELICHE UND UNVEREHELICHTE LEBEN DER ERSTEN CHRISTEN, NACH IHREN EIGENEN ZEUGNISSEN / Arnold, Gottfried – 1702 – 1 – us A.T.L.A. [240]
DIE EHELICHEN GUETERVERHAELTNISSE DER AUSLAENDER, ... / Behagel, W – Freiburg, 1873 – 1mf – 9 – ILM-3523/1 – ne IDC [327]
DAS EHERNE GESETZ : DIE DICHTUNGEN GEORG BUECHNERS / Buechner, Georg – 1. Aufl. Berlin: Verlag der Nation, 1950 – 1 – us U.W. Library [800]
EHESCHEIDUNG FRANZOESISCHER UND BELGISCHER STAATSANGEHOERIGER IN DEUTSCHLAND / Heinze, F K M – Berlin, 1916 – 1mf – 1 – ILM-3121/1 – ne IDC [327]
DIE EHESCHLIESSUNG, DIE TRENNUNG,... / Albisetti, E – Bern, 1937 – 2mf – 9 – ILM-3010/1 – ne IDC [340]
EHESPIEGEL MATHESIJ... / Mathesius, Johannes – Leipzig, 1591 – 7mf – ne IDC [240]
EHINGER TAGBLATT : BA DER SUEDWEST-PRESSE – Ehingen-Ulm, Germany. 2 Jan 1975- – 114r (1975-1990) – 1 – gw Mikrofilm [072]
EHITUS JA ARHITEKTUUR – Tallinn: [s.n.] n2. 1978 – us Res Libr [072]
Ehmke, Jochen *see* MEDIENFIGUREN IM ALLTAG VON KINDERN AM BEISPIEL DER TURTLES
EHNASYA / Petrie, William Matthew Flinders – 1905 – 9 – $10.00 – us I.R.C. [930]
EHNASYA (MEES VOL 26) / Flinders Petrie, W M – London, 1905 – 10mf – 8 – Dfl35.00 – ne Slangenburg [930]
EHP: ENVIRONMENTAL HEALTH PERSPECTIVES – (v.28 .1979 5,6,9) – v.1. 1972 – 1 – us UMI [616]
Ehrenberg, CG *see*
- DE MYCETOGENESI
- DIE INFUSIONSTHIERCHEN ALS VOLLKOMMENE ORGANISMEN
- MIKROGEOLOGIE

Ehrenbourg-Mannati, N *see* ASPECTS MECONNUS DE L'ART POPULAIRE RUSSE AU XIXEME SIECLE
Ehrenburg, Ilia Grigorevich *see*
- ESTAMPAS DE ESPANA
- NOT INTERVENTION...CONQUEST

Ehrenhaus, Martin *see* DIE OPERNDICHTUNG DER DEUTSCHEN ROMANTIK
Ehrenhauss, M *see* DIE NEUERE PHILOSOPHIE UND DER CHRISTLICHE GLAUBE IN IHREM VERHAELTNISSE
EHREN-RANGLISTE DES EHEMALIGEN DEUTSCHEN HEERES.. / Bund Deutscher Offizier – Berlin: E.S. Mittler, 1926. xvii,1275p – 1 – us U.W. Library [943]
Ehrensberger, H *see* LIBRI LITURGICI BIBLOTHECAE APOSTOLICAE VATICANAE MANU SCRIPTI
Ehrensvaerd, A *see* OM VERKAN AF UTLAENDSK STRAFFDOM
Ehrentheil, Adolf *see* MIT UNSERER JUGEND: NEUE CONFIRMATIONS-REDEN FUER DEN BARMIZWA
Ehret, G D *see* PLANTAE ET PAPILIONES RARIORES DEPICTAE ET AERI INCISAE
Ehret, Joseph *see* VOKIECIU LITERATUROS ISTORIJA
Ehrhard, A *see* STRASSBURGER THEOLOGISCHE STUDIEN
Ehrhard, Jean *see* COMMUNAUTE OU SECESSION?
Ehrhardt, Albert *see*
- DIE ALTCHRISTLICHE LITERATUR UND IHRE ERFORSCHUNG SEIT 1880
- DIE ALTCHRISTLICHE LITERATUR UND IHRE ERFORSCHUNG VON 1884-1900
- UEBERLIEFERUNG UND BESTAND DER HAGIOGRAPHISCHEN UND HOMILIETISCHEN LITERATUR DER GRIECHISCHEN KIRCHE VON DEN ANFAENGEN BIS ZUM ENDE DES 16. JAHRHUNDERTS

Ehrhardt, Traugott *see* DIE GESCHICHTE DER FESTUNG KOENIGSBERG/PR., 1257-1945
Ehrhart, B *see*
- OECONOMISCHE PFLANZENHISTORIE

Ehrhart, F *see* BEITRAEGE ZUR NATURKUNDE UND DEN DAMIT VERWANDTEN WISSENSCHAFTEN
Ehrle, F S J *see* HISTORIA BIBLIOTHECAE ROMANORUM PONTIFICUM
Ehrle, Franz *see*
- DER SENTENZENKOMMENTAR PETERS VON CANDIA

Ehrlich, Arnold B *see* DIE PSALMEN: NEU UEBERSETZT UND ERKLAERT
Ehrlich, Cyril *see* THE UGANDA COMPANY, LIMITED
Ehrlich, L *see* PRAWO NARODOW 1927
Ehrt, Carl *see* ABFASSUNGSZEIT UND ABSCHLUSS DES PSALTERS ZUR PRUEFUNG DER FRAGE NACH MAKKABAEERPSALMEN
Ehui, S *see* LIVESTOCK AND RESOURCE MANAGEMENT POLICY
Ehwald, R *see* ADHELMI OPERA (MGH 1: 15.BD)
EIA (ELECTRONICS INDUSTRIES ASSOCIATION) – Standards. Printed index. Updated every 60 days – 6,9 – us Info Handling [621]
Eibach, R., et al *see* VORTRAEGE DER THEOLOGISCHEN KONFERENZ ZU GIESSEN
Eichas, Tyler M *see* RELATIONSHIPS AMONG PERCEIVED LEADERSHIP STYLES, MEMBER SATISFACTION AND TEAM COHESION IN HIGH SCHOOL BASKETBALL TEAMS
Eichenbaum, J *see* KOL ZIMRAH
Eichenbaum, Martin S *see* A SHRED OF EVIDENCE ON PUBLIC ACCEPTANCE OF PRIVATELY ISSUED CURRENCY
EICHENDORFFS MENSCHENGESTALTUNG / Riepe, Christian – (Includes bibliographical references) – Berlin: Junker und Duennhaupt, 1941 – 1 – us U.W. Library [430]
Eichentopf, Hans *see* THEODOR STORMS ERZAEHLUNGSKUNST IN IHRER ENTWICKLUNG
Eichert, B S et al *see* METHODS OF HYDROLOGICAL COMPUTATIONS FOR WATER PROJECTS
Eichhoff, J J *see* PROJET DU REGLEMENT... NAVIGATION DU RHIN,...
Eichhorn, J G *see* EINLEITUNG IN DAS ALTE TESTAMENT
EICHHORNIA, GENUS NOVUM E FAMILIA PONTEDERIACEARUM / Kunth, C S – Berolini. 1842. B-5255 2 – 8 – ne IDC [580]
Eichler, A W *see* BLUETHENDIAGRAMME, CONSTRUIRT UND ERLAUETERT
Eichler, P A *see* DIE DSCHINN, TEUFEL UND ENGEL IM KORAN
Eichman, A *see* SAMMLUNG VERTRAEGE DER SCHWEIZ MIT...
Eichmann, Adolph *see* PAPERS
Eichmann, E *see* WEIHE UND KROENUNG DES PAPSTES IM MITTELALTER
Eichner, Ernst *see* SIX QUATUORS POUR UNE FLUTE, VIOLON, ALTO ET BASSE....OEUVRE 4
Eicholtz, W.H. and Sons *see* RECORDS
EICHSTAETTER KURIER : BA DES DONAU-KURIER – Ingolstadt, Germany. 1 Jun 1983- – ca 9r per yr – 1 – gw Mikrofilm [072]
Eichthal, Gustave d' *see*
- DEUX LETTRES A UN VIEIL AMI SUR LES DOMESTIQUES
- HISTOIRE ET ORIGINE DES FOULAHS OU FELLANS

Eichwald, C E von *see*
- LETHAEA ROSSICA, OU PALEONTOLOGIE DE LA RUSSIE
- PLANTARUM NOVARUM VEL MINUS COGNITARUM QUAS IN ITINERE CASPIO-CAUCASICO

Eickenroth, Manuela P *see* THEATERUNTERNEHMEN ZWISCHEN KUNST, KOMMERZ UND POLITIK
Eickstedt, Valentin von *see* EPITOME ANNALIUM POMERANIAE
DER EID IM ALTEN TESTAMENT : VOM STANDPUNKTE DER VERGLEICHENDEN RELIGIONSGESCHICHTE AUS / Happel, Julius – Leipzig: Wilhelm Friedrich, [1893] – 1mf – 9 – 0-8370-3467-1 – 1985-1467 – us A.T.L.A. [220]

DER EID WIDER DEN MODERNISMUS UND DIE THEOLOGISCHE WISSENSCHAFT / Mausbach, Joseph – (Includes bibliographical references) – Koeln: J P Bachem, 1911 – 1mf – 9 – 0-8370-8455-5 – 1986-2455 – us A.T.L.A. [240]

Eide, Asbjorn et al *see* FOOD AS A HUMAN RIGHT

EIDOS – London, 1950 – 1r – 1 – £60.00 – uk Chadwyck [760]

EIDYLIVM DE FOELICI ET CHRISTIANA PROFECTIONE ... CAROLI A LOTHARINGIA, ... AD SACRUM BELLUM IN TURCOS SUSCEPTUM 1572 – Parisiis, 1572 – 1mf – 9 – H-8192/1 – ne IDC [956]

DIE EIER DER EUROPAEISCHEN VOEGEL / Baedeker, F W J – 2691. 1855-1863 – 9 – ne IDC [590]

EIFAC *see*
- REPORT OF THE 15TH SESSION OF THE EUROPEAN INLAND FISHERIES ADVISORY COMMISSION
- REPORT OF THE 16TH SESSION OF THE EUROPEAN INLAND FISHERIES ADVISORY COMMISSION
- REPORT OF THE 17TH SESSION OF THE EUROPEAN INLAND FISHERIES ADVISORY COMMISSION

EIFAC EXPERIMENTS ON PELAGIC FISH STOCK ASSESSMENT BY ACOUSTIC METHODS IN LAKE CONSTANCE – 1985 – 19p – it F.A.O. [639]

EIFAC EXPERIMENTS ON PELAGIC FISH STOCK ASSESSMENT BY ACOUSTIC METHODS IN LAKE TEGEL – 1987 – 33p – it F.A.O. [639]

EIFAC EXPERIMENTS ON PELAGIC FISH STOCKS ASSESSMENT BY ACOUSTIC METHODS IN LAKE KONNEVESI, FINLAND – 1982 – 22p – it F.A.O. [636]

EIFAC WORKSHOP ON FISH-FARM EFFLUENTS (1981, SILKEBORG, DENMARK) – 1982 – 174p – it F.A.O. [639]

EIFELER NACHRICHTEN : BA DER AACHENER NACHRICHTEN – Monschau, West Germany. 1 Sept 1978-1991 – ca 7r per yr – 1 – gw Mikrofilm [072]

EIFELSAGEN, LIEDER UND GEDICHTE / Zirbes, Peter – 1891 – 1 – us I.U. Libraries [390]

Eig, A *see* OBSERVATIONS ON PALESTINE PLANTS/KNOWLEDGE OF THE FLORA OF PALESTINE

EIGENART DER BIBLISCHEN RELIGION = THE PECULIARITY OF THE RELIGION OF THE BIBLE / Orelli, Conrad v – (In English. Includes bibliographical references) – New York: Eaton & Mains; Cincinnati: Jennings & Graham, c1908 – 1mf – 9 – 0-8370-4631-9 – 1985-2631 – us A.T.L.A. [220]

DAS EIGENARTIGE DES CHRISTENTUMS ALS RELIGION / Noesgen, Karl Friedrich – Halle a.S.: Richard Muehlmann, 1902. 1 fiche – 9 – us A.T.L.A. [240]

Eigenbrodt, Wolrad *see* HAGEDORN UND DIE ERZAEHLUNG IN REIMVERSEN

DER EIGENE – Berlin, 1906-30/33 n9 – 4r – 1 – Dist. gw Mikrofilm – gw Misc Inst [072]

DAS EIGENE VERSCHULDEN EIN VERSCHULDEN GEGEN SICH SELBST ODER GEGEN DRITTE / Schumann, Wolfgang – Marburg, 1931 – 1mf – DM48.00 – 3-8267-3066-6 – gw Hänsel [340]

Eigenmann, C H *see*
- THE AMERICAN CHARACIDAE
- THE FRESHWATER FISHES OF BRITISH GUIANA

EIGHT ANTHEMS ON [SELECTED] PSALMS / Chappele, S – Ms – 1 – us Sibley [780]

EIGHT HOUR MILLER : 1903-1904, 1909-1910 / International Union of Flour and Cereal Mill Employees – (Coll title: Labor Union Periodicals, Pt 3) – 1r – 1 – $135.00 – 1-55655-609-8 – us UPA [331]

EIGHT LECTURES ON MIRACLES : PREACHED...IN THE YEAR 1865 ON THE FOUNDATION OF THE LATE REV. JOHN BAMPTON, M.A., CANON OF SALISBURY / Mozley, James Bowling – (Includes bibliographical references) – 2nd ed. London: Rivingtons, 1867 – 1mf – 9 – 0-8370-4517-7 – 1985-2517 – us A.T.L.A. [210]

EIGHT PAPERS, BOOKS AND STUDIES / Centre for Independent Studies:C. I. S – 2fiches (29x) – 9 – 1.00f – at Libertarian Micro [320]

EIGHT SERMONS PREACHED BEFORE THE UNIVERSITY OF OXFORD IN THE YEAR 1786... / Croft, G – Oxford, London, etc., 1786 – 3mf – 9 – MP-551/1 – ne IDC [240]

EIGHT SHORT MELODIOUS PIECES FOR PIANOFORTE DUET / Kiel, Friedrich – Op. 13. Book 2. 189-? – 9 – us Sibley [780]

EIGHT SILVER PATTERN BOOKS / Boulton, Mathew – 1 – uk Microform Academic [730]

EIGHTEEN CENTURIES OF THE ORTHODOX GREEK CHURCH / Hore, A H – London: James Parker, 1899 – 2mf – us A.T.L.A. [240]

EIGHTEEN MARCHES FOR 2 VIOLINS, [FLUTES OR HAUTBOYS], 2 FRENCH HORNS AD LIB AND A BASS / Key, J – (Violino primo part only, In Process) – London: Thompson, 177- – 1 – us Sibley [780]

EIGHTEEN MARCHES IN SEVEN PARTS FOR 2 HOBOYS, 2 HORNS, AND A BASS, BY AN EMINENT MASTER – (7 pts) – London: Thos. Cahusac & Sons, ca 1797 – 1 – us Sibley [780]

EIGHTEEN UNRATIFIED INDIAN TREATIES IN CALIFRONIA – 1851-53 – 1r – 1 – $50.00 – C63019 – us Library Micro [978]

EIGHTEEN YEARS IN UGANDA & EAST AFRICA / Tucker, Alfred Robert – London: E. Arnold, 1908 – 2mf – us A.T.L.A. [960]

EIGHTEEN YEARS ON LAKE BANGWEULU / Hughes, J E – London: Field House, [1933] – 1 – us Res Libr [960]

EIGHTEEN YEARS ON THE GOLD COAST / Cruikshank, B – 1853 – 7 – uk Microform Academic [900]

EIGHTEEN YEARS ON THE GOLD COAST OF AFRICA, INCLUDING AN ACCOUNT OF THE NATIVE TRIBES, AND THEIR INTERCOURSE WITH EUROPEANS / Cruikshank, B – 2v. London. 1853. BA-298 2 – 8 – ne IDC [960]

EIGHTEENTH CENTURY – (Ongoing project based upon The Eighteenth Century Short Title Catalogue (ESTC); currently 235 units. Subject breakouts available) – 1 – us Primary [410]

AN EIGHTEENTH CENTURY BIBLIOPHILE / Enelow, H G & Belinfante, I – A. S. Freidus Memorial Volume. New York. 1929. BJ-262-17 1 – 9 – ne IDC [070]

EIGHTEENTH CENTURY ENGLISH LITERATURE – 11r – 1 – $790.00 – us OmniSys [420]

EIGHTEENTH CENTURY ENGLISH PROVINCIAL NEWSPAPERS, SERIES 1 – (Unit 2: Bath Chronicle and other Papers) – Bath newspapers. Unit 1: The Bath Journal and other papers – 1 – us Primary [072]

EIGHTEENTH CENTURY ENGLISH PROVINCIAL NEWSPAPERS, SERIES 2 – Derby newspapers. Unit 3 – 1 – us Primary [072]

EIGHTEENTH CENTURY ENGLISH PROVINCIAL NEWSPAPERS, SERIES 3 – Ipswich newspapers. Units 4 and 5 – 1 – us Primary [072]

EIGHTEENTH CENTURY ENGLISH PROVINCIAL NEWSPAPERS, SERIES 4 – Newcastle upon Tyne. Units 6 and 7 – 1 – us Primary [941]

EIGHTEENTH CENTURY FRENCH FICTION – Based on S.P. Jones' a list of French prose fiction from 1700-1750. 1939, etc – 411mf – 9 – $1,240.00 – us OmniSys [440]

EIGHTEENTH CENTURY FRENCH LITERATURE: FICTION AND POETRY – 175r – 1 – $11,800.00 $2,180.00y – us OmniSys [830]

EIGHTEENTH CENTURY NONCONFORMITY / Colligan, J Hay – London; New York: Longmans, Green, 1915 – 1mf – us A.T.L.A. [900]

EIGHTEENTH CENTURY RUSSIAN PUBLICATIONS – 1964- – 837r – 1 – $51,000.00 $1,200.00y – us OmniSys [010]

EIGHTEENTH CENTURY RUSSIAN STUDIES / ed by Cross, A G – 9 – ne IDC [947]

EIGHTEENTH CENTURY SHORT TITLE CATALOGUE / British Library. Humanities and Social Sciences – 1990 Microfiche Edition – 220mf – 9 – £750.00 (+ VAT UK); £765.00 overseas – uk British Libr Humanities [010]

EIGHTEENTH-CENTURY LAW – Law titles selected from the Eighteenth Century Collection – 1 – us Primary [340]

EIGHTEENTH-CENTURY RELIGION AND PHILOSOPHY – Religion and philosophy titles selected from the Eighteenth Century Collection – 1 – us Primary [240]

EIGHTH ARMY NEWS – (Library has: Vol.3, no.20,22,29,31-33,35-39,41-46,48,50-56,58,73,81,90, 106,120,124,126,143-144,146-147 (Oct. 21, 1943-March 16, 1944)) – [England?: Eighth Army], 19uu – 1 – CSUX89-S124 – us Hoover Inst Photo [350]

EIGHTH CENSUS OF THE UNITED STATES / U.S. Bureau of the Census – 1860. 1438 rolls. M653 – 1 – us Nat'l Archives [324]

EIGHTH MEETING OF THE EAST AND SOUTHERN AFRICAN SUB-COMMITTEE FOR SOIL CORRELATION AND LAND EVALUATION : HARARE, 1989 – 1990 – 121p – it F.A.O. [631]

EIGHTH PLENUM OF THE CENTRAL COMMITTEE OF THE COMMUNIST PARTY OF INDONESIA; POLITICAL REPORT AND RESOLUTION / Communist Party. Indonesia. Comite Central – SE-2329 1. 1959 – 9 – ne IDC [950]

THE EIGHT-HOUR LAW. / National Eight-Hour Delegation – Washington: Darby, 1880. 32p. LL-2351 – 1 – us L of C Photodup [340]

EIGHTY MICROCOMPUTING – 1980 – 1,5,6,9 – us UMI [073]

EIGHTY YEARS OF ILLINOIS POLITICS AND POLITICIANS 1809-1889 / Lusk, D W – Springfield: H.W. Rokker, 1889. Illinois Reel 1. (The Cox Library Collection) – 5 – us Americana [978]

EIGNUNG VON UNTERSCHIEDLICH KONSERVIERTEN GEWEBEPROBEN VON MAJA CRISPATA UND CARCINUS MAENAS, ZUR UNTERSUCHUNG DES GENETISCHEN POLYMORPHISMUS IN POPULATIONEN MITTELS RAPD-FINGERPRINTING / Kaiser, Bernd – 1994 – 2mf – DM80.00 – 3-8267-2059-8 – gw Hänsel [574]

EIGYO HOKOKUSHO SHUSEI = COLLECTED ANNUAL REPORTS OF MAJOR COMPANIES IN JAPAN, 1872-1945 / ed by Yui, Tsunehiko – (1st series 917 companies 400r 88-page index Y3,576,000. 2nd series (supplement to 1st) 156 companies 2nd collected 304 companies 110r 40-page index Y1,093,000. 3rd series 831 companies 120r 48-page index Y1,109,000. 4th series 3057 companies 480r 136-page index Y4,400,000. 5th series 5733 companies 852r 200-page index Y10,224,000) – 1 – ja Yushodo [338]

Eikhe, Genrikh Khristoforovich *see* FORSIROVANIE REKI BELOI CHASTIAMI V ARMII VOSTOCHNOGO FRONTA VII UNE 1919 GODA

Eikhenbaum, B *see* ANNA AKHMATOVA

Eikhler, F *see* BIBLIOTEKOVEDENIE VYSSHAGO PORIADKA V EGO OTNOSHENIIA K METODAM NAUCHNAGO ISSLEDOVANIIA I PREPODAVANIIA

EILEEN HADDON COLLECTION OF SOUTHERN RHODESIA ARCHIVES, MANUSCRIPTS, AND DOCUMENTS – Chicago, University of Chicago, Photodup Dept, 1972 – 35r – us Res Libr [324]

EILFERTIGER ENTWURFF AUS DENEN SCHWEDIS. REICHS-GRUND-GESETZEN...1719 – N.p., n.d. – 1mf – 1 – ILM-1021/1 – ne IDC [327]

EIN DEM UNTERGANG NAHER ARAMAEER WAR MEIN VATER... DAS "KLEINE GESCHICHTLICHE CREDO" UND SEINE WIRKUNGSGESCHICHTE IM MIDRASCH DER PESSACH-HAGGADA / Homolka, Walter – 1993 – 1mf – 9 – DM75.00 – 3-89349-708-0 – gw Hänsel [270]

EINANDER : ODEN, LIEDER, GESTALTEN / Werfel, Franz – Muenchen: K Wolff, 1923 – 1r – 1 – us U.W. Library [800]

EINBLICKE IN DAS SPRACHLICHE DER SEMITISCHEN URZEIT BETREFFEND DIE ENTSTEHUNGSWEISE DER MEISTEN HEBRAEISCHEN WORTSTAEMME / Herzfeld, Levi – (Includes index) – Hannover: Hahn, 1883 – 1mf – 9 – 0-8370-9157-8 – 1986-3157 – us A.T.L.A. [470]

EINBLICKE IN DIE GESCHICHTE DER ENTSTEHUNG DER TALMUDISCHEN LITERATUR / Bloch, Joseph S – Wien: D. Loewy, 1884. 1 fiche – 9 – us A.T.L.A. [270]

EINDRESUME VAN HET GOEVERNEMENTSBESLUIT DD. 10/6/1867 NO. 2 BEVOLEN ONDERZOEK NAAR DE RECHTEN VAN DEN INLANDER OP DEN GROND OP JAVA EN MADOERA / Bergsma, W B – 3v. Batavia. 1876. BSE-20.111 1 – 9 – ne IDC [950]

EINE EINFACHE ELEKTRONENROEHRENANORD-NUNG / Schuleit, H H – Summary in English and Indonesian. SE 6902 1 – 9 – ne IDC [621]

DAS EINFACHE LEBEN : ROMAN / Wiechert, Ernst Emil – Muenchen: A Langen/G Mueller, 1939 – 1r – 1 – us U.W. Library [830]

EINFELTIGER BERICHT AUSZ GOTTES WORT VOM EIDSCHWEREN / Beszler, M – Nuernberg, G. Merckel. 1554. BME-136 1 – 9 – ne IDC [240]

DIE EINFLUESSE DER ANTIKE IN WIELANDS HERMANN : BEITRAG ZUR ENTWICKLUNGS-GESCHICHTE DER DEUTSCHEN LITERATUR IM 18. JAHRHUNDERT / Doell, M – (Includes bibliographical references) – Muenchen: M Schnidtmann, 1897 – 1r – 1 – us U.W. Library [430]

EINFLUESSE IMPLIZITER EIGNUNGSTHEORIEN AUF DIE BEOBACHTUNGSGENAUIGKEIT IN ASSESSMENT-CENTERN / Blankenburg, Roland, Gambla, Michael – 1994 – 2mf – DM80.00 – gw Hänsel [150]

DER EINFLUSS DER MAIMONIDISCHEN PHILOSOPHIE AUF DAS CHRISTLICHE ABENDLAND / Guttmann, J – Leipzig. 1908. BJ-33-38 1 – 9 – ne IDC [180]

DER EINFLUSS DER MYSTERIENRELIGIONEN AUF DAS AELTESTE CHRISTENTUM / Clemen, Carl – Giessen: A. Toepelmann, 1913. (Religionsgeschichtliche Versuche und Vorarbeiten; 13. Bd., 1. Heft) – 1mf – us A.T.L.A. [240]

DER EINFLUSS DER PHILOSOPHIE CHARLES BONNETS AUF FRIEDRICH HEINRICH JACOBI / Isenberg, Karl – (Includes bibliographical references) – Borna-Leipzig: R Noske, 1906 – 1r – 1 – us U.W. Library [430]

DER EINFLUSS DER PROTESTANTISCHEN SCHULPHILOSOPHIE AUF DIE ORTHODOX-LUTHERISCHE DOGMATIK / Weber, Emil – (Includes bibliographical references) – Leipzig: A Deichert, 1908 – 1mf – 9 – 0-8370-8798-8 – 1986-2798 – us A.T.L.A. [240]

DER EINFLUSS DES HUMANISMUS UND DER REFORMATION AUF DAS GLEICHZEITIGE ERZIEHUNGS- UND SCHULWESEN : BIS IN DIE ERSTEN JAHRZEHNTE NACH MELANCHTHONS TOD / Roth, Friedrich – Halle, Verein fuer Reformationsgeschichte, 1898. (Schriften des Vereins fuer Reformationsgeschichte; 15. Jahrg., Schrift 60) – 1mf – us A.T.L.A. [370]

DER EINFLUSS DES SUPREME COURT AUF DIE POLITIK DER U.S.A. VON 1789 BIS ZUM ENDE DES ZWEITEN WELTKRIEGS. / Jordan, Horst W – Mainz? 1952? LL-389 – 1 – us L of C Photodup [340]

DER EINFLUSS EINES NEUEN 30 MM BALLONKATHETERS AUF CORONARARTERIENDISSEKTIONEN BEI PERKUTANTER TRANSLUMINALER CORONARANGIOPLASTIE IM VERGLEICH ZUM KONVENTIONELLEN 20 MM BALLONKATHETER / Olschner, Gerhard Konrad – 1995 – 1mf – 9 – DM60.00 – 3-8267-2207-8 – gw Hänsel [617]

DER EINFLUSS VON GOETHES WILHELM MEISTER AUF DAS DRAMA DER ROMANTIKER / Wendriner, Karl Georg – Leipzig, 1909 – 2mf – 9 – DM62.00 – 3-89349-317-4 – gw Hänsel [430]

EINFLUSS VON WASSERDAMPF AUF DEN ABLAUF DER HETEROGEN KATALYSIERTEN OXIDATIVEN KUPPLUNG VON METHAN / Jankowski, Joachim – 1992 – 81p – DM75.00 – 3-89349-550-9 – gw Hänsel [540]

DIE EINFLUSSNAHME DER AMERIKANISCHEN BESATZUNGSMACHT AUF DIE BERLINER KULTURPOLITIK IN DEN NACHKRIEGSJAHREN, 1945-1947 / Kanzler, Melanie – 1992 – 9 – DM98.00 – 3-89349-508-8 – gw Hänsel [320]

EINFUEHRUNG DER REFORMATION IN DIE KURMARK BRANDENBURG DURCH JOACHIM / Steinmueller, Paul – Halle: Verein fuer Reformationsgeschichte, 1903. (Schriften des Vereins fuer Reformationsgeschichte; 20. Jahrg., Schrift 76) – 1mf – us A.T.L.A. [240]

DIE EINFUEHRUNG DER REFORMATION IN HAMBURG / Sillem, C H W – Halle: Verein fuer Reformationsgeschichte, 1886. ([Schriften des Vereins fuer Reformationsgeschichte; Bd. 16]) – 1mf – us A.T.L.A. [240]

DIE EINFUEHRUNG DER REFORMATION IN ROSTOCK / Vorberg, Axel – Halle: Verein fuer Reformationsgeschichte, 1897. (Schriften des Vereins fuer Reformationsgeschichte; 15. Jahrg., Schrift 58) – 1mf – us A.T.L.A. [240]

EINFUEHRUNG IN DAS ANGEWANDTE VOELKERRECHT / Bluehdorn, R – Wien, 1934 – 3mf – 9 – ILM-3127/1 – ne IDC [327]

EINFUEHRUNG IN DAS THEOLOGISCHE STUDIUM / Wernle, Paul – Tuebingen: J.C.B. Mohr, 1908 – 2mf – us A.T.L.A. [240]

EINFUEHRUNG IN DIE DEUTSCHE LITERATUR : DICHTUNGEN IN POESIE UND PROSA ERLAEUTERT FUER SCHULE UND HAUS, ZUGLEICH EINE GESCHICHTE DER DEUTSCHEN LITERATUR VON DEN AELTESTEN ZEITEN BIS ZUR GEGENWART / ed by Meyer, Johannes – (Includes bibliographical references and index) – Berlin: Gerdes & Hoedel, 1905-1913 – 1 – us U.W. Library [430]

EINFUEHRUNG IN DIE EVANGELISCHE MISSIONSKUNDE : IM ANSCHLUSS AN DIE BASLER MISSION / Bornemann, Wilhelm – Tuebingen: J.C.B. Mohr, 1902 – 1mf – us A.T.L.A. [240]

EINFUEHRUNG IN DIE GESCHICHTE DER THEOLOGISCHEN LITERATUR DER FRUEHSCHOLASTIK / Landgraf, Arthur M – Regensburg, 1948 – 3mf – 8 – ne Slangenburg [290]

EINFUEHRUNG IN RICHARD WAGNERS WERKE UND SCHRIFTEN / Pfordten, Hermann Ludwig, Freiherr von der – (Includes bibliographical references) – 2. Aufl. Bielefeld: Velhagen & Klasing, 1921 – 1r – 1 – us U.W. Library [780]

DER EINGANG DES JOHANNESEVANGELIUMS (KAPITEL 1, 6-18) : IN MEDITATIONEN / Philippi, Friedrich Adolph – Stuttgart: Samuel Gottlieb Liesching, 1866 – 1mf – 9 – 0-8370-4730-7 – 1985-2730 – us A.T.L.A. [220]

DIE EINGANGSBUECHER DES PARZIVAL UND DAS GESAMTWERK / Cucuel, Ernst – (Includes bibliographical references) – Frankfurt: Diesterweg, 1937 – 1r – 1 – us U.W. Library [390]

EINGANGSJOURNAL DAILY REGISTER OF LETTERS RECEIVED, 1895-1914 / New Guinea Compagnie, Landesverwaltung in Herbertshohe (New Guinea Company, Territorial Administration at Herbertshohe) – 10r – 1 – CRS G30 – at Archives [920]

EINGELAUFENE ORDINARI POSTZEITUNG – Braunschweig, 1682-85, 1689-1701, 1711 (incomplete), 1717 (many issues missing) – 1 – Inquire at Mikrofilmarchiv for details – gw Misc Inst [943]

EINGRIFFSQUALITAET UND RECHTLICHE REGELUNG POLIZEILICHER VIDEOAUFNAHMEN / Jendro, Frank – 1992 – 216p – 9 – DM98.00 – 3-89349-590-8 – gw Hänsel [340]

EINHARDI VITA KAROLI MAGNI (MGH 7: 25.BD) – 1911 – Dfl9.00 – ne Slangenburg [240]

DER EINHEIMISCHE KLERUS IN DEN HEIDENLAENDERN / Huonder, Anton – Freiburg i.B., St. Louis, Mo.: Herder, 1909 – 1mf – us A.T.L.A. [240]

DIE EINHEIT – Berlin, 1926-29 – 4r – 1 – Dist. gw Mikrofilm – gw Misc Inst [072]

EINHEIT – 1946-1989 – 1,412mf – 1 – DM8,048.40 – gw Mikro Press [900]

EINHEIT – v1-37. 1946-82. Incomplete. Zentralkomitee der Sozialistischen Einheitspartei Deutschlands. Berlin. -m – 1 – us U.W. Library [073]

DIE EINHEIT DER BIBLISCHEN URGESCHICHTE (1 MOS 1-3) : UND DIE UEBEREINSTIMMUNG DES SCHOEPFUNGSBERICHTES MIT DEN NATURVERHAELTNISSEN DER ERDE: NACHGEWIESEN MIT BEZIEHUNG AUF DIE ANSICHTEN DR. DELITZSCH'S, DR. HOELEMANN'S, UND DR. KEIL'S / Keerl, Philipp Friedrich – (Includes bibliographical references) – Basel: Bahnmaier (C Detloss), 1863 – 1mf – 9 – 0-8370-3861-8 – 1985-1861 – us A.T.L.A. [220]

EINHEIT DER WELTBEWEGUNG GEGEN IMPERIALISTISCHEN KRIEG UND FASCHISMUS : HALBMONATSORGAN DES WELTKOMITEES ZUM KAMPF GEGEN IMPERIALISTISCHEN KRIEG UND FASCHISMUS – Paris, FR. Feb-Jul 1935 – 1r – 1 – gw Mikrofilm [073]

EINHEIT FUER HILFE UND VERTEIDIGUNG : ZEITSCHRIFT DER INTERNATIONALEN SOLIDARITAETSBEWEGUNG – Paris, FR. Jan 1936-May 1938 – 1 – gw Mikrofilm [073]

DER EINHEITLICHE FESTELLUNGSBESCHEID / Stengel, Karl – Leipzig, 1940 – 1mf – DM48.00 – 3-8267-3001-1 – gw Hänsel [340]

DIE EINHEITLICHKEIT DER PAULINISCHEN BRIEFE / Clemen, Carl – Goettingen: Vandenhoeck & Rup., 1894. 1 fiche – 9 – us A.T.L.A. [240]

DIE EINHEITSFRONT – Berlin-Bohnsdorf, 1922-26 – 2r – 1 – Dist. gw Mikrofilm – gw Misc Inst [072]

DIE EINHEITSFRONT : KAMPFORGAN GEGEN DEN FASCHISMUS – (Only one issue) – New York, NY. Aug 1934 – 1 – gw Mikrofilm [071]

DIE EINHEITSLEHRE DER GOETTLICHEN TRINITAET NACH DER KIRCHLICHEN TRADITION BEWIESEN UND GEGEN DIE IRRLEHREN / Oischinger, Johann Nepomuk Paul – (Includes bibliographical references) – Muenchen: J J Lentner (G Stahl), 1862 – 1mf – 9 – 0-8370-3936-3 – 1985-1936 – us A.T.L.A. [240]

DIE EINHEITSLEHRE (MONISMUS) ALS RELIGION : EINE STUDIE / Bulova, J A – [S.l.: J. Bulova, 1897? (Stuttgart: Hoffmann) – 1mf – us A.T.L.A. [240]

Einhorn, David *see* AUSGEWAEHLTE PREDIGTEN UND REDEN

EINIGE BEMERKUNGEN ZU ADOLF HARNACK'S PRUEFUNG DER GESCHICHTE DES NEUTESTAMENTLICHEN KANONS (ERSTER BAND. ERSTE HAELFTE) / Zahn, Theodor – (Includes bibliographical references) – Erlangen: A Deichert, 1889 – 1mf – 9 – 0-8370-9354-6 – 1986-3354 – us A.T.L.A. [220]

EINIGE GEDANKEN ZUR AUSDIFFERENZIERUNG VON STAAT UND RECHT / Jansen, Brigitte E S – 1995 – 1mf – 9 – DM60.00 – 3-8267-2111-X – gw Hänsel [370]

EINIGE NOTIZEN UEBER BONNY AN DER KUSTE VON GUINEA : SEINE SPRACHE UND SEINE BEWOHNER – (With: Observations..by Richard Wharton) – Goettingen: In der Dieterichschen Univ.-Buchdruckerei, 1848 – 1 – us Res Libr [960]

EINIGE VON DER UN NICHT KODIFIZIERTE RECHTE DES MENSCHEN UND BUERGERS / Beckerath, Ulrich von – 26 May 1956. With translation – 9 – 1.00f – at Libertarian Micro [335]

EINIGE WORTE UEBER DIE INNUIT (ESKIMO) DES SMITH SUNDES NEBST BEMERKUNGEN UEBER INNUIT SCHAEDEL / Bessels, Emil – (Archiv fuer Anthropologie, v. 8). Braunschweig. 1875. BN-121 2 – 8 – ne IDC [305]

DIE EINIGKEIT – (Cont by: Mitteilungsblatt der Geschaeftskommission der Freien Vereinigung deutscher Gewerkschaften, 1914? Rundschreiben an die Vorstaende und Mitglieder aller der Freien Vereinigung deutscher Gewerkschaften angeschlossenen Vereine, 1915? Der Syndikalist, 1918? Beilagen: Der Frauenbund, 1921-25. Frei das Land, 1928, 1930. Jugendwille, 1928. Die junge Menschheit, 1920-23. All incomplete. These suppl are available at the same editor) – Berlin, 1910-may 1916, 1917 (very incomplete), dec 1918, 1919 (incomplete), 1920-32 – 1 – Dist. gw Mikrofilm – gw Misc Inst [072]

EINIGUNG – (Cont by: Initiative, nov 1 1960) – Bonn, nov 1958-jul 1960, nov 1960-66, 1971 n4 – 1r – 1 – Inquire at Mikrofilmarchiv for details – gw Misc Inst [072]

EINKEHR : NEUE GEDICHTE VON HEINRICH ANACKER / Anacker, Heinrich – Muenchen: F Eher, 1934 – 1r – 1 – us U.W. Library [810]

EINKEHR BEI JOSEF HOFMILLER / Hofmiller, Josef – (Includes bibliographical references) – Lindau: J Thorbecke, 1948 – 1 – us U.W. Library [430]

EINLADUNGSSCHRIFT DES GYMNASIUM BERNHARDINUM IN MEININGEN / Maercker, Friedrich – Meiningen: Keyszner, 1871. 1 fiche – 9 – us A.T.L.A. [240]

EINLASSUNGEN : AUFSAETZE ZU POLITIK UND LITERATUR / Boehner, Claus-Peter – 1992 – 204p – 9 – DM98.00 – 3-89349-490-1 – gw Hänsel [430]

EINLAYTTUNG (EIN GEMAYNE) IN DEN AYGENTLICHEN VERSTAND MOSI VND DER PROPHETEN – 1529. BME-66 1 – 9 – ne IDC [240]

EINLEITUNG IN DAS ALTE TESTAMENT / Eichhorn, J G – Leipzig Zweyter Band 1803 – 12mf – 8 – ne Slangenburg [220]

EINLEITUNG IN DAS ALTE TESTAMENT / Koenig, Eduard – Bonn: Eduard Weber, 1893. 2 fiches – 9 – us A.T.L.A. [220]

EINLEITUNG IN DAS ALTE TESTAMENT / Sellin, Ernst – 1920 – 1 – us A.T.L.A. [220]

EINLEITUNG IN DAS ALTE TESTAMENT:... APOKRYPHEN UND PSEUDEPIGRAPHEN / Strack, Hermann Leberecht – Muenchen: C.H. Beck, 1906. 1 fiche – 9 – us A.T.L.A. [240]

EINLEITUNG IN DAS NEUE TESTAMENT / Juelicher, Adolf – (Includes index) – 1. und 2. Aufl. Freiburg i.B: J C B Mohr (Paul Siebeck), 1894 – 1mf – 9 – 0-8370-3813-8 – 1985-1813 – us A.T.L.A. [220]

EINLEITUNG IN DEN CODEX NAPOLEON / Seidensticker, Johann Anton Ludwig – Tuebingen, 1908 – 6mf – 9 – DM198.00 – 3-8267-3072-0 – gw Hänsel [944]

EINLEITUNG IN DEN HEXATEUCH / Holzinger, H – 2191 2. 1893 – 8 – ne IDC [240]

EINLEITUNG IN DEN TALMUD / Strack, Hermann Leberecht – Leipzig: J.C. Hinrichs, 1908. 1 fiche – 9 – us A.T.L.A. [270]

EINLEITUNG IN DIE BUECHER DES ALTEN TESTAMENTES / Baudissin, Wolf Wilhelm, Graf – (Includes bibliographies and indexes) – Leipzig: S Hirzel, 1901 – 2mf – 9 – 0-8370-9442-9 – 1986-3442 – us A.T.L.A. [220]

EINLEITUNG IN DIE CONCHYLIENKENNTNISS NACH LINNE / Schroeter, J S – Z 781 2. 3 v. 1783-1786 – 8 – ne IDC [590]

EINLEITUNG IN DIE EVANGELISCHE DOGMATIK *see* COLLECTED WORKS

EINLEITUNG IN DIE HEILIGE SCHRIFT : ZWEITER THEIL: EINLEITUNG IN DAS NEUE TESTAMENT / Bleek, Friedrich – Berlin, 1862 – 14mf – 8 – ne Slangenburg [220]

EINLEITUNG IN DIE KANONISCHEN BUECHER DES ALTEN TESTAMENTS / Cornill, Carl Heinrich – (Includes appendix & indexes) – London: Williams & Norgate; New York: G P Putnam, 1907 – 1mf – 9 – 0-8370-2744-6 – 1985-0744 – us A.T.L.A. [220]

EINLEITUNG IN DIE KANONISCHEN BUECHER DES ALTEN TESTAMENTS / Cornill, Carl Heinrich – (Includes bibliographical references and index) – 6. neubearb Aufl. Tuebingen: J C B Mohr (Paul Siebeck), 1908 – 1mf – 9 – 0-8370-9692-8 – 1986-3692 – us A.T.L.A. [220]

EINLEITUNG ZUM KRIEGS-PROCESS : WORINNEN VON DER KRIEGS-JURISDICTION UND WEM DIESELBE ZUSTEHE / DENEN PERSONEN UND SACHEN / WELCHE UNTER DIE KRIEGS-JURISDICTION GEDHREN... / Ludovici, Jacob Friedrich – 8th ed. Halle: Wasenhaus, 1737 – 3mf – 9 – $4.50 – LLMC 89-020 – us L.L.M.C. [340]

EINSEITIGE ABHAENGIGKEITSVERHAELTNISSE ... / Bornhak, K – Leipzig, 1896 – 1mf – 9 – ILM-1927/1 – ne IDC [327]

EINSETZUNG EINES KOENIGS : ROMAN / Zweig, Arnold – (Completes the triptych, Trilogie des UEbergangs; Bks 1 and 2 of the series are respectively: Erziehung vor Verdun and Der Streit um dem Sergeanten Grischa) – Amsterdam: Querido, 1937 – 1r – 1 – us U.W. Library [830]

EINSIEDLER UND GENOSSE : SOZIALE GEDICHTE NEBST EINEM VORSPIEL VON BRUNO WILLE / Wille, Bruno – Berlin: Freie Verlags-Anstalt, [1890?] – 1r – 1 – us U.W. Library [810]

EINST AUF DER LORETTOHOEHE : AUFZEICHNUNGEN DES LEUTNANTS BRUCKNER / Goltz, Joachim, Freiherr von der – Muenchen: A Langen, G Mueller, c1934 – 1r – 1 – us U.W. Library [943]

Einstein, Albert *see* COMPLETE WORKS OF ALBERT EINSTEIN

EINTRACHT – Skokie, IL. 1972- – 1 – gw Mikrofilm [071]

DIE EINWIRKUNG DES CHRISTENTHUMS AUF DIE ALTHOCHDEUTSCHE SPRACHE : EIN BEITRAG ZUR GESCHICHTE DER DEUTSCHEN KIRCHE / Raumer, Rudolf von – Stuttgart: S.G. Liesching, 1845 – 1mf – us A.T.L.A. [430]

DIE EINWIRKUNGEN DER REFORMATION AUF DIE ORGANISATION UND BESETZUNG DES REICHSKAMMERGERICHTS / Broehmer, Heinrich – 1995 – 1mf – 9 – DM48.00 – gw Hänsel [340]

DER EINZIGE UND SEIN EIGENTUM / Stirner, Max – 1924. 1 fiche (24x) – 9 – 1.00f – at Libertarian Micro [320]

DER EINZIGE UND SEIN EIGENTUM / Stirner, Max – Berlin, 1924 – 5mf – 8 – ne Slangenburg [100]

DER EINZIGE UND SEINE LIEBE / Kroeger, Timm – Hamburg: A Janssen, 1905 – 1r – 1 – us U.W. Library [830]

EIRE-IRELAND – Ireland.26 Oct-4 Dec 1914 – 1 – ie Microforms [072]

AN EIRENIC ITINERARY : IMPRESSIONS OF OUR TOUR, WITH ADDRESSES AND PAPERS ON THE UNITY OF CHRISTIAN CHURCHES / McBee, Silas – New York: Longmans, Green, 1911 – 1mf – us A.T.L.A. [240]

EIRE-THE IRISH NATION – Ireland.20 Jan 1923-25 Oct 1924 – 1 – ie Microforms [072]

EIS DIGESTS OF ENVIRONMENTAL IMPACT STATEMENTS – (1993 subscription price $4,300.00y) – 1983-84.Continues: EIS: Key to Environmental Impact Statements – 9 – 200.00y – us C.S.A. [333]

EIS: MICROFICHES OF FULL ENVIRONMENTAL IMPACT STATEMENTS – (EIS. 1977-81. Cumulative. 9. EIS. 1982. Cumulative. 9. EIS. 1983. Cumulative. 9. EIS. 1984. Cumulative. 9) – 1970-76.Cumulative. 3v – 9 – us C.S.A. [333]

DER EISBAER – Berlin. 1918-19 (incomplete) – 1 – gw Mikrofilm [073]

Eisel, J P *see*
- MUSICUS AUTODIDACTOS. DER SICH SELBST INFORMIRENDE MUSICUS
- MUSICUS AUTODIDAKTOS

Eiselein, Joseph *see* SAEMTLICHE WERKE

Eiselen, F *see* GOETHE'S PAEDAGOGIK

Eiselen, Frederick Carl *see* THE WORKER AND HIS BIBLE

Eiselt, J N *see* GESCHICHTE, SYSTEMATIK UND LITERATUR DES INSEKTENKUNDE, VON DEN AELTESTEN ZEITEN BIS AUF DIE GEGENWART

Eisen, Gustavus A *see* ANCIENT ORIENTAL CYLINDER AND OTHER SEALS

Eisenacher Versammlung zur Besprechung der Socialen Frage, (1872) *see* VERHANDLUNGEN...AM 6 UND 7 OCTOBER 1872

EISENBAHN-JOURNAL UND NATIONAL-MAGAZIN FUER DIE FORTSCHRITTE IM HANDEL – Amberg, 1835-37 – 1 – Dist. gw Mikrofilm – gw Misc Inst [380]

EISENBAHN-ZEITUNG – (Cont by: Luebecker Nachrichten, aug 30 1900. Luebecker Vorstadt-Zeitung, apr 1 1919. Luebecker Neueste Nachrichten, apr 1 1921) – Luebeck, jun 6 1865-sep 15 1923 – 116r – 1 – gw Mikrofilm [072]

Eisenhofer, Ludwig *see* PROCOPIUS VON GAZA

Eisenhower, Dwight D *see*
- DIARIES, 1953-61
- MINUTES AND DOCUMENTS OF THE CABINET MEETINGS OF PRESIDENT EISENHOWER, 1953-61

Eisenlohr, August *see* EIN ALTBABYLONISCHER FELDERPLAN

Eisenmann, L *see* LE COMPROMIS AUSTROHONGROIS DE 1867 ETUDE SUR LE DUALISME

EISENMENGER DER ZWEITE / Ascher, S – Berlin. 1794. BJ-23-102 1 – 9 – ne IDC [190]

Eisentraut, Englehard *see* STUDIEN ZUR APOSTELGESCHICHTE: KRITISCHE UNTERSUCHUNGEN DER VON TH. V. ZAHN REKONSTRUIERTEN "URAUSGABE DER APOSTELGESCHICHTE DES LUCAS."

EISERNE BLAETTER – Berlin, jan 4 1931-39 – 6r – 1 – Dist. gw Mikrofilm – gw Misc Inst [072]

EISERNE BLAETTER : WOCHENSCHRIFT FUER DEUTSCHE POLITIK UND KULTUR – (Lacking: v12-13. v16 and some pgs) – v1-21. 1919-39 – 19r – 1 – ATLA S0047 – us A.T.L.A. [073]

EISERNE SONETTE / Winckler, Josef – (Subsequently publ as: Eiserne Welt) – Leipzig: Insel-Verlag, [191-?] – 1r – 1 – us U.W. Library [810]

EISERNE WELT *see* EISERNE SONETTE

Eisler, Leopold *see* BEITRAEGE ZUR RABBINISCHEN SPRACH- UND ALTERTHUMSKUNDE

Eisner, B *see* MEDJUNARODNO MEDJUPOKRAJINSKO (INTERLOKALNO) I MEDJUVJERSKO...

Eitelberger von Edelberg, R *see* ARETINO; ODER DIALOG UEBER MALEREI VON LODOVICO DOLCE. NACH DER AUSGABE VOM JAHRE 1557 AUS DEM ITALIENISCHEN UEBERSETZT VON CAJETAN CERRI

EITHER GREAT DESTRUCTION OF HUMAN LIFE AND FINAL MONARCHY... / Smolnikar, Andrew B – Columbus, [Ohio]: Ohio State Journal Co, 1856 – 1r – 1 – us Western Res [100]
Eitle, Hermann *see* DIE UNTERORDNUNG DER SAETZE BEI CHAUCER
Eitzen, P von *see*
- ADMONITIO DE PRAECIPVIS CAPITIBVS CONTROVERSIARVM DE COENA DOMINI,...
- RECHTE VND WARE MEINUNG VND VERSTAND GOETTLICHER SCHRIFFT VND DER AUGSPURGISCHEN BEKANDTNUS...

Eizalde, Bernardo *see* INTENDENCIA DE EXTREMADURA: CIRCULAR
EJECUCION DE LAS SENTENCIAS EXTRANJERAS / Fiore, P – Madrid, 1898 – 4mf – 1 – ILM-2498/1 – ne IDC [327]
LA EJECUCION DE SENTENCIAS EXTRANJERAS ES MATERIA FEDERAL O DE LEGISLACION DE LOS ESTADOS? / Garcia Carofalo, R – Mexico, 1895 – 1mf – 1 – ILM-3804/1 – ne IDC [327]
EJEMPLOS DE ORTOGRAFIA ESPANOLA... / Segura de la Garmilla, Ramon & Ganan Gonzalez, Felix – Madrid: Razon y Fe, 1927 – 1 – sp Bibl Santa Ana [440]
EJERCICIO DE 1931. PRESUPUESTO ORDINARIO FORMADO PARA EL REFERIDO EJERCICIO POR LA COMISION PERMANENTE Y APROBADO POR EL AYUNTAMIENTE PLENO Y E ILMO. SR.DELEGADO DE HACIENDA / Badajoz – Badajoz: Tipografia Espanola, S.A. – sp Bibl Santa Ana [946]
EJERCICIO SOCIAL DEL ANO 1912. MEMORIA Y BALANCE LEIDOS Y APROBADOS EN JUNTA GENERAL DE SOCIOS...1913 / Caja General Frexnense – Badajoz: Tip. Lib. y Enc.Uceda Hermanos, 1913 – sp Bibl Santa Ana [946]
EL EJERCITO : FACTOR PONDERABLE EN EL DESENVOLVIMIENTO ECONOMICO, SOCIAL Y POLITICO DE LA NACION. (EJERCITO, INDUSTRIA PRODUCTIVA DIRECTA) CONFERENCIA PRONUNCIADA EN EL CIRCULO MILITAR EL 20 DE MAYO DE 1949 / Anaya, Laureano Orencio – Buenos Aires, [1949] – 1 – CSUXADJ2515-B – us Hoover Inst Photo [300]
EL EJERCITO ALEMAN TAL COMO ES: DIARIOS DE OFICIALES Y SOLDADOS ALEMANES, HECHOS PRISIONEROS O CAIDOS EN EL FRENTE RUSO – Introduccion por Bodo Uhse. Mexico, Editorial "El Libro libre," 1944 – 1 – us U.W. Library [947]
EL EJERCITO ARGENTINO Y EL ARTE DE LO POSIBLE / Bortnik, Ruben – Buenos Aires: Ediciones Guemes, 1967 – 1 – CSUXADJ2503-B – us Hoover Inst Photo [355]
EJERCITO DE EXTREMADURA EN 1644. COMPETENCIAS DE JURISDICCION / Ruiz Garcia, Felix – Badajoz: Imprenta Diputacion Provincial, 1971 – sp Bibl Santa Ana [340]
EL EJERCITO DE LA MONARQUIA Y EL EJERCITO DE LA REPUBLICA / Vidal, Fabian – Barcelona, 1937? Fiche W1247. (Blodgett Collection of Spanish Civil War Pamphlets) – 9 – us H.U. College Libr [946]
EL EJERCITO EN LA SOCIODAD CONTEMPORANEA...CONFERENCIA PRONUNCIADA EN EL ISTITUTO BARBARA DE BRAGANZA DE BADAJOZ EL 11 DE ABRIL DE 1969 / Moro Cardenas, Ezequiel – Badajoz: Imprenta Doncel, 1969 – 1 – sp Bibl Santa Ana [946]
EJERCITO POPULAR UNIDO, EJERCITO DE LA VICTORIA / Ibarruri, Dolores – Madrid, 1938. Fiche W953. (Blodgett Collection of Spanish Civil War Pamphlets) – 9 – us H.U. College Libr [946]
UN EJERCITO POPULAR Y DEMOCRATICO AL SERVICIO DEL PUEBLO / Spain. Ministerio de Defensa Nacional – Barcelona, 19?? Fiche W855. (Blodgett Collection of Spanish Civil War Pamphlets) – 9 – us H.U. College Libr [946]
EJERCITO Y POLITICA NACIONALISTA : [1960-1970] / Ceresole, Norberto – Buenos Aires: Editorial Sudestada, 1968 – 1 – CSUXADJ9163-B – us Hoover Inst Photo [320]
Ekart, T P *see* SYNOPSIS JUGERMANNIARUM IN GERMANIA
Ekaterina 2 *see*
- SOCHINENIIA
- SOCHINENIIA IMPERATRITSY EKATERINY 2 NA OSNOVANII PODLINNYKH RUSKOPISEI S OB"IASNITEL'NIMI PRIMECHANIIAMI A. N. PYPINA

EKATERINA IVANOVA NELIDOVA, 1758-1839 / Shumigorskii, E S – Spb. 1902. BR-7905 2 – 8 – ne IDC [920]
Ekblaw, W E *see* THE MATERIAL RESPONSE OF THE POLAR ESKIMO TO THEIR FAR ARCTIC ENVIRONMENT
Ekendahl, D G von *see* NAPOLEONS ANSICHTEN VON DER GOTTHEIT JESU, SOWIE VON RELIGION, PRIESTERN UND KRICHENTHUM, PROTESTANTISMUS UND KATHOLICISMUS
EKHO – Ezhenedel'noe illiustrirovannoe izdanie. v. 1-4. Kiev. 1906. BR-3976 2 – 8 – ne IDC [073]
EKHO – (Includes c.1: 1925:Nov.7) – Kharbin: R. Litman, 1925 – 1 – CSUXAKF0337-S – us Hoover Inst Photo [947]
EKHO – Zhurnal Slovesnosti i Mov. St. Petersburg, 1831. v1-5.BR-3977-2 – 8 – ne IDC [073]
EKHO (HARBIN, CHINA) *see* EKHO
EKHO TVERSKOI KOOPERATSII *see* IZVESTIIA TVERSKOGO GUBSOIUZA
EKHO, WEEKLY – 1993 – 1 – sz Infoprint [947]
EKITABO KY'EKIKA KYA NSENENE = THE HISTORY OF THE GRASSHOPPER CLAN / Kagwa, Apolo – Mengo, Uganda: A K Press, [1905?] – 1 – us Res Libr [960]
Ekkard, Friedrich *see* ALLGEMEINES REGISTER UEBER DIE GOETTINGISCHEN GELEHRTEN ANZEIGEN VON 1753 BIS 1782
EKKEHARD : AUDIFAX UND HADUMOTH / Scheffel, Joseph Viktor von; ed by Handschin, Charles Hart & Luebke, William F – New York: American Book Company, c1911 – 1r – 1 – us U.W. Library [430]
EKKEHARD : EINE GESCHICHTE AUS DEM ZEHNTEN JAHRHUNDERT / Scheffel, Joseph Viktor von – 14., vom Verfasser durchgesehene Aufl., Stuttgart: J B Metzler, 1875 – 1r – 1 – us U.W. Library [830]
EKKEHARD : EINE GESCHICHTE AUS DEM ZEHNTEN JAHRHUNDERT / Scheffel, Joseph Viktor von – (Includes bibliographical references) – Stuttgart: Adolf Bonz, 1909 – 1r – 1 – us U.W. Library [830]
EKKEHARD : A TALE OF THE 10TH CENTURY / Scheffel, Joseph Viktor von – (Includes bibliographical references) – London: J M Dent; New York: E P Dutton, [1911] – 1 – us U.W. Library [430]
EKKEHARD : A TALE OF THE TENTH CENTURY / Scheffel, Joseph Viktor von – (Includes Biographical sketch of author, by Nathan Haskell Dole) – New York: T Y Crowell, 1895 – 1r – 1 – us U.W. Library [430]
EKKLESIA – Athens. Greece. -w. 25 Jul 1928-8 Mar 1941, 1 Jan 1947-15 Dec 1949. (Very imperfect). (4 reels) – 1 – uk British Libr Newspaper [072]
EKKLESIA UND POLIS IM NEUEN TESTAMENT UND IN DER ALTEN KIRCHE / Bieder, W – Zurich. 1941. BH-252 2 – 8 – ne IDC [240]
EKKLESIASTIKE ALETHEIA – Istanbul, Turkey. In Greek. -w. 15 May 1885-30 Dec 1897; 11 Jan 1920-29 Sept 1923. 9 reels – 1 – uk British Libr Newspaper [949]
EKONOM – Spb. 1841-53. Lacking: 1841-43; 1849 (52); 1850 (28, 52); 1851 (52); 1852 (51-52); 1853 (52). BR-3400 2 – 8 – ne IDC [330]
EKONOM – (1991 (oct, dec only) 1r. 1992-98 4r per y) – Czech Republic, 1999- – 4r per y standing order – 1 – us Ross [072]
EKONOMI – Djakarta. Incomplete. SE-282 1. 1959-1965 – 9 – ne IDC [330]
EKONOMI – (Scattered issues lacking) – Nicosia, Cyprus. Feb 20 1979-1991 – 7r – 1 – us L of C Photodup [072]
EKONOMI BUYUK GAZETE – Istanbul: Aydinlik Basimevi, jun 23 1949-mar 1952; aug 13 1953 – 9r – 1 – us Res Libr [330]
EKONOMI DAN INDUSTRI – Djakarta. Incomplete. SE-283 1. 1958-1964 – 9 – ne IDC [330]
EKONOMI GAZETESI – Istanbul: Aydinlik Basimevi, [-1949]. [nov 1948-jun 22 1949] – 1r – 1 – us Res Libr [330]
EKONOMI GAZETESI – Istanbul: Ekonomi Matbaasi, nov 5 1953-nov 29 1954 – 2r – us Res Libr [330]
EKONOMI KITA / Hatta, Mohammad – SE-2124 1. 1947 – 9 – ne IDC [330]
EKONOMI NASIONAL – South Vietnam. 1963-1966 – 1 – us UMI [072]
EKONOMI SELAJANG PANDANG / Tohir, Kaslan Abdullah – SE 4860 1. v. 2 only – 9 – ne IDC [330]
EKONOMICHESKAI A ZHIZN ASTRAKHANSKOGO KRAI A : EZHEMESI ACHNY I ORGAN GUBERNSKOGO EKONOMICHESKOGO SOVESHCHANII A OBLASTNOGO RYBNOGO UPRAVLENII A ASTRAKHANSKOGO RUPVODA., GUB. SOV. NAR. KHOZI A ISTVA, GUB. ZEMELNOGO OTDELA – (Library has: June, Aug./Sept. 1921) – Astrakhan: R.V.T S., 1921. 1v – 1 – CSUX89-S802 – us Hoover Inst Photo [330]
EKONOMICHESKAI A ZHIZN DALNEGO VOSTOKA : EZHEMESI ACHNOE IZD. DALNE-VOSTOCHNOGO EKONOMICHESKOGO SOVESHCHANII A – (Library has: Jan 1926 – March 1930; some issues missing) – Khabarovsk: Soveshchanie, 1922-1930 – 1 – CSUX90-S191 – us Hoover Inst Photo [330]
EKONOMICHESKAI A ZHIZN KAVKAZA – (Library has: Aug.-Oct./Nov. 1921, Jan. 1922) – Tiflis: Izd.T Sentropechati, 1921-1922. 2v – 1 – CSUX90-S121 – us Hoover Inst Photo [330]
EKONOMICHESKAIA GAZETA – Moscow. U.S.S.R. 1956- – 1 – us UMI [330]
EKONOMICHESKAIA ISTORIIA ROSSII, 1861-1917 GG / Paina, E S – Obzor publikatsii gosudarstvennykh Arkhivov SSSR (1918-63). Moscow, 1967. 90p. BR-10,732/1 – 9 – ne IDC [947]
EKONOMICHESKAIA PRIRODA KOOPERATIVOV I IKH KLASSIFIKATSIIA / Tugan-Baranovskii, M I – Ed 2. M., 1914 – 2mf – 9 – COR-127/1 – ne IDC [334]
EKONOMICHESKAIA ZHIZN' – 6Nov 1918-13 Jun 1941. 1920 wanting – 1 – 485.00 – us L of C Photodup [947]
EKONOMICHESKAIA ZHIZN' – Moscow, 1918-37 – 29r – 1 – us Ross [072]
EKONOMICHESKI I PUT : EZHEDNEVNAI A GAZETA SIMBIRSKOGO GUB EKONOMSOVESHCHANII A I GUBPROFSOVETA – (Includes c.1: 1922:Mar.12) – Simbirsk: Tip. No. 1 S.N.Kh., 1921 – 1 – CSUXANR2651-S – us Hoover Inst Photo [330]
Ekonomicheski i si ezd Moskovskogo promyshlennago ra iona (1st: 1917: Moscow (RSFSR) *see* TRUDY PERVAGO EKONOMICHESKAGO SIEZDA MOSKOVSKAGO PROMYSHLENNAGO RAIONA
EKONOMICHESKII BIULETEN (BERLIN, GERMANY) *see* EKONOMICHESKII BIULLETEN
EKONOMICHESKII BIULLETEN / Kon'iunkturnyi Institut. Moscow – 1922-28. Scattered issues missing – 1 – 41.00 – us L of C Photodup [330]
EKONOMICHESKII BIULLETEN : R.S.F.S.R., BERLINSKOE PREDSTAVITELSTVO – (Includes c1: n1 1920: Sep 2-n14 (1920: Dec 24)) – [Berlin: Predstavitelstvo, 1920-1921]. 27 no – 1 – CSUXAKZ1979-S – us Hoover Inst Photo [947]
EKONOMICHESKII BIULLETEN' KONIUNKTURNOGO INSTITUTA / Koniunkturnogo Instituta – M. 1925-28. BR-1752 2 – 61mf – 8 – R-1752/2 – ne IDC [330]
EKONOMICHESKII MAGAZIN, (SEL'SKO-KHOZIAISTVENNYI ZHURNAL IZDAVAVSHIISIA V 1780-1789 GG / Neustroev, A N – Bibliograficheskoe opisanie. Spb. 1874. BR-5656 2 – 8 – ne IDC [330]
EKONOMICHESKII ZHURNAL – St Petersburg, 1885-93 n11 – 142mf – 9 – COR-705/1 – ne IDC [334]
EKONOMICHESKOE OBOZRENIE : EZHEMESIACHNYI ZHURNAL (ORGAN SOVETA TRUDA I OBORONY) – M. v1-8. 1923-30 – 299mf – 9 – R-2441/1 – ne IDC [334]
EKONOMICHESKOE OBOZRENIE – Moscow. Jan. 1923-Dec. 1928 complete – 1 – 35.00r – us Hoover Inst Photo [330]
EKONOMICHESKOE OBOZRENIE – Zhurnal ekonomii, statistiki i sotsial'noi politiki. M. v. 1-2. 1916. BR-3978 2 – 8mf – 8 – R-3978/2 – ne IDC [330]
EKONOMICHESKOE OBOZRENIE KERCHENSKOGO OKRUGA : NEPERIODICHESKOE IZDANIE KERCHENSKOGO EKONOMSOVESHCHANII A – (Includes c.1: no.1 1923) – [Kerch: Soveshchanie], 1923- – 1 – CSUXAKZ2529-S – us Hoover Inst Photo [330]
EKONOMICHESKOE RA IONIROVANII ROSSII PRI GOSUDARSTVENNO I OBSHCHEPLANOVO I KOMISSII S.T.O. : MATERIALY PODKOMISSII PO RA IONIROVANII V / R.S.F.S.R. Gosplan – Moskva: [s.n.], 1921 – 1 – CSUX90-B9017 – us Hoover Inst Photo [330]
Ekonomicheskoe soveshchanie Tatarsko i ASSR *see* TRUD I KHOZIA ISTVO
EKONOMICHESKOE VOZROZHDENIE – Ezhemesiachnyi zhurnal. v. 1-2. Spb. 1922. BR-3401 2 – 4mf – 8 – R-3401/2 – ne IDC [330]
EKONOMICHESKOE VOZROZHDENIE ROSSII – v. 1-11. M. 1915. BR-3979 2 – 11mf – 8 – R-3979/2 – ne IDC [330]
EKONOMICHESKOYE OBOZRENIE – (Economic Review). Moscow. U.S.S.R. 1923-30 – 1 – us UMI [330]
EKONOMICHESKOYE OBOZRENIYE – Moscow. Jan. 1929-Mar. 1930 – 1 – us NY Public [947]
EKONOMIKA I KULTURA – (Includes c.1: no.1(1922:Mar.31)-no.3(1922:June 11) – Moskva: Izd-vo "Ekonomika i kultura", 1922 – 1 – CSUXANR2575-S – us Hoover Inst Photo [330]
EKONOMIKA I KULTURA ARMENII K 50-LETII U VELIKOGO OKTI ABRI A : STATISTICHESKI I SBORNIK / T SU SSSR, T Sentralnoe statisticheskoe upravlenie pri Sovete Ministrov Armi ansko i SSR – Erevan: [Statistika], 1967 – 1 – CSUX91-B2374 – us Hoover Inst Photo [330]
EKONOMIKA I POLITIKA VNESHNE I TORGOVLI : SBORNIK / ed by Soboleva, M N – Moskva: Izd-vo Narkomtorga SSSR i RSFSR, 1928 – 1 – CSUX89-B2950 – us Hoover Inst Photo [330]
EKONOMIKA I STATISTIKA KARELII = KARJALAN TALOUS JA TILASTO – (Library has: Oct.-Dec. 1925; Jan.-Apr. 1926) – Petrozavodsk: Izd. SNK AKSSR, 1925-1928. 4v – 1 – CSUX89-S940 – us Hoover Inst Photo [330]
EKONOMIKA I ZHIZN' – (Backfile through 1998 $85/r) – Russia, 1999- – 5r per y – 1 – $400.00 standing order – us Ross [072]
EKONOMIKA SELSKOGO KHOZI A ISTVA – (Includes c.1: 1957-1987//) – Moskva: Izd-vo MCX SSSR, 1957-1987. 37v – 1 – CSUXAKZ6169-S – us Hoover Inst Photo [330]
EKONOMIKA SEL'SKOGO KHOZIAISTVA – 1925-62. (Scattered issues lacking) – 1 – 480.00 – us L of C Photodup [630]
EKONOMISCHESKII BIULLETEN' / Moscow. Koniunkturnyi institut – 1922-1929. Missing: nos. 2, 4-5, 1922; nos. 1-2, 4-6, 1923; no. 6, 1924; nos. 2-4, 1928; nos. 10-12, 1929 not pub – 1 – 35.00r – us Hoover Inst Photo [324]
EKONOMISKT LANGTIDSPROGRAM, 1951-1955 / Sweden. Finansdepartementet. 1950 ars Langtidsutredning – (Long-Term Economic Program, 1951-1955). Stockholm. 1951. BD-1750 1 – 9 – ne IDC [338]
EKONOMIST ROSSII – 1909-12 – 46mf – 9 – $300.00 – us Ross [330]
EKONOMSKI DNEVNIK – Belgrade, Yugoslavia. Jan-Jul 1952 – 1r – 1 – us L of C Photodup [949]
EKPHRASIS TES HAGIAS SOPHIAS / Antoniades, M – Athen/Leipzig. Tom.1-3. 1907-1909 – Dfl207.00 – ne Slangenburg [240]
EKRAN – Moscow, 1921-22 – 15mf – 9 – $100.00 – us Ross [790]
Ekrem, Ali *see* LISAN-I OSMANI
Ekrem, Recaizade Mahmut *see* PEJMURDE
EKSKURSY V OBLAST' RUSSKOGO NARODNOGO EPOSA / Miller, V F – M., 1892 – 6mf – 9 – ne IDC [947]
EKSKURSY V OBLAST'RUSSKOGO NARODNOGO EPOSA / Miller, V F – M., 1892 – 6mf – 9 – 2225/2 – ne IDC [947]
Ekskuzovich, Nikolai, defendent *see* PROTSESS" EKSKUZOVICHA, FIKHGENDLERA I DAINA ZASIEDANIE UGOLOVNOGO DEPARTAMENTA ODESSKOI SUDEBNOI PALATY, S" UCHASTIEM" PRISIAZHNYKH" ZASIEDATELEI. STENOGRAFICHESKII OTCHET" I IZD. A. S. KARFUNKELIA
Ekspeditsii a Komzeta po obsledovanii u Birobidzhanskogo ra iona Dalnevostochnogo krai a (1927) *see* OTCHET EKSPEDITSII KOMZETA 1927 GODA PO OBSLEDOVANIIU BIROBIDZHANSKOGO RAIONA DALNEVOSTOCHNOGO KRAIA (BIROBIDZHANA)
EKSPOR = EXPORT – Djakarta, Biro Pusat Statistik. 1957, 1959-63. Incomplete. In Indonesian; tables of contents and explan. remarks also in English – 1 – us U.W. Library [073]

EKSPORT, IMPORT I KONTSESSII SOIUZA S.S.R: = EXPORTS, IMPORTS AND CONCESSIONS OF THE SOVIET UNION / ed by Troianovskogo, A et al – [Moskva]: Izd. Gos. kontory obi avleni i "Dvigatel", [1926] – 1 – CSUX88-B5061 – us Hoover Inst Photo [380]
EKSPORT PROMYSLOVOI KOOPERATSII / Zhabin, A I – M., 1929 – 1mf – 9 – COR-422/1 – ne IDC [334]
EKSPORTNAI A LI ESNAI A TORGOVLI A V PRIVISLINSKIKH GUBERNII AKH I EI A NUZHDY – S.-Peterburg: Tip. V.F. Kirshbauma, 1913 – 1 – CSUX89-B5918 – us Hoover Inst Photo [380]
EKSPRES = EXPRESS – Chicago, IL. 1936 – 1 – us A.J.P.C. [071]
Ekstroem, CV *see* A HISTORY OF SCANDINAVIAN FISHES
EKUMENISK ORIENTERING – 1972-87 (complete) – 2r – 1 – ATLA S0472 – us A.T.L.A. [073]
Ekwelie, Sylvanus Ajani *see* THE CONTENT OF BROADCASTING IN NIGERIA
Ekzempliarskii, A *see* VELIKIE I UDEL'NYE KNIAZI SEVERNOI RUSI V TATARSKOI PERIODE
EL CENTRO PROGRESS – El Centro, CA. 1913-1922 – 18r – 1 – $900.00 – C03206 – us Library Micro [071]
EL CENTRO STAR – El Centro, CA. 1908 – 1r – 1 – $50.00 – C03207 – us Library Micro [071]
EL CERRITO JOURNAL – El Cerrito, CA. 1950-51 – 2r – 1 – $100.00 – B02197 – us Library Micro [073]
EL COJO ILUSTRADO – 1892-1915 – 1 – 545.00 – us L of C Photodup [073]
EL DORADO CANYON MINER – El Dorado, NV. 1917 – 1r – 1 – $50.00 – U04492 – us Library Micro [622]
EL DORADO FANTASMA / Bayle, Constantino – Madrid: Razon y Fe, 1931 – 1 – sp Bibl Santa Ana [440]
EL DORADO REPUBLICAN – Auburn, CA, 1912; 1914 – 1 – us UMI [071]
EL DORADO REPUBLICAN – Placerville, CA, 1901-1923 – 12r – 1 – $600.00 – C03398 – us Library Micro [071]
EL DORADO REPUBLICAN – Placerville, CA, 1912-1914 – 1 – us UMI [071]
EL DORADO SECOND BAPTIST CHURCH. EL DORADO, ARKANSAS : CHURCH RECORDS – 1923-75 – 1 – $119.97 – us Baptist [240]
EL DORADO SPRINGS FIRST BAPTIST CHURCH. EL DORADO SPRINGS, MISSOURI : CHURCH RECORDS – 1882-Feb 1967 – 1 – $49.23 – us Baptist [240]
EL DORADO/AMADOR – 1928-38; 1992- – 13+ r – 1 – $650.00 – P00004 – us Library Micro [910]
El Maliki, Abderrahmane *see* L'EXODE RURAL AU MAROC. ETUDE SOCIOLOGIQUE DE L'EXODE DU TAFILALET VERS LA VILLE DE FES
El Masudi *see* MEADOWS OF GOLD AND MINES OF GEMS
EL MONTE HERALD AND PRESS – El Monte, CA. 1977-89 – 25r – 1 – $1,250.00 – R02198 – us Library Micro [071]
EL MONTE HERALD AND VALLEY HERALD – El Monte, CA. 1959-1960 – 2r – 1 – $100.00 – H04008 – us Library Micro [071]
EL SALVADOR : ANUARIO ESTADISTICO 1911-1965 / El Salvador. Direccion General de Estadistica – (1915, 1918, 1923-24 Estadistica Comercial. 1936, 1945 v1, 1963 v1 not available. Coll title: Latin American and Caribbean Official Statistical Serials, 1821-1982) – 288mf – 9 – £1,510.00 – uk Chadwyck [972]
EL SALVADOR : THE MAKING OF U.S. POLICY, 1977-1984 – (With 2-vol printed guide & index £630.00) – 870mf – 9 – £2,940.00 – uk Chadwyck [327]
EL SALVADOR 2 : HUMAN RIGHTS, DEATH SQUADS, CIVIL WAR AND U.S. POLICY, 1980-1993 – (With printed guide £630.00) – £2,940.00 – uk Chadwyck [327]
El Salvador. Direccion General de Estadistica *see* EL SALVADOR
El-Abbadi, Mostafa *see* LIFE AND FATE OF THE ANCIENT LIBRARY OF ALEXANDRIA
L'ELAN – no. 1-9. Paris. avr 1915-fevr 1916 – 1 – fr A.C.R.P.P. [073]
L'ELAN – Paris. v1-10. Apr 1915-1916 – 1 – us NY Public [073]
L'ELAN – St-Remi de Napierville, Canada. v5 n11. 11 aut 1960-v6 n26. 7 dec 1961 – 1r – 1 – Can$30.00 – cn Can Microfilming [072]
ELAN – Paris. n1-10. 1915-16 – 1r – 1 – us Ross [073]
L'ELAN DE LA RIVE SUD – Levis, Canada. v4 n1. jul 1965-v7 n5. sep 1968 – 1r – 1 – Can$35.00 – cn Can Microfilming [072]
L'ELAN SEPT-ILIEN – Sept-Iles, Canada. v1 n35. 10 nov 1966-20 dec 1972 – 1r – 1 – Can$50.00 – cn Can Microfilming [072]
Elanskaia, A I *see* KOPTSKIE RUKOPISI GOSUDARSTVENNOI PUBLICHNOI BIBLIOTEKI IMENI M.E. SALTYKOVA-SHCHEDRINA
ELASTOMERICS – (Formerly RUBBER AGE). v. 49-82. 1941-1958 – 1,5,6 – us Princeton Micro [600]
ELASTOMERICS – (See also: Rubber Age) – v109- 1977- – 1,5,6,9 – us UMI [600]
O ELBA : PERIODICO COMMERCIAL, LITTERARIO E NOTICIOSO – Maragogy, Alagoas. 3 Abr 1887 – 1,5,6 – bl Biblioteca [072]
El-Basri, Abdel-Gawad Daoud *see* ASPECTS OF IRAQI CULTURAL POLICY
Elbee, Sieur d' *see* JOURNAL DU VOYAGE DU SIEUR DELBEE, AUX ISLES, DANS LA COSTE DE GUYNEE EN L'ANNEE 1669 POUR L'ETABLISSEMENT DU COMMERCE EN CES PAYS, ET LA PRESENTE :
ELBE-JEETZEL-ZEITUNG – Luechow, West Germany. 1977- – ca 6r per yr – 1 – gw Mikrofilm [072]
ELBERFELDER ZEITUNG – Elberfeld (Wuppertal), Germany. 1848-49 – 4r – 1 – gw Mikrofilm [072]
ELBERON, IOWA: 1881-1981 – Comp. by Wilma Nielsen Parizek, 1981. Biog. and hist. sketches. Indexed. V30-0034 – 1 – us A.G.L.L. [920]
ELBETAL-ZEITUNG – Aussig, sep 1 1941-jun 30 1943, jan 3-jun 30 1944 – 1 – Dist. gw Mikrofilm – gw Misc Inst [943]
Elbing, Ulrich *see* AUTOAGGRESSION UND PATHOLOGISCHE INFORMATIONSVERARBEITUNG BEI GEISTIGBEHINDERTEN MIT AUTISTISCHEN ZUEGEN
Elbogen, I *see* STUDIEN ZUR GESCHICHTE DES JUEDISCHEN GOTTESDIENSTES
ELBOGENER ZEITUNG – Elbogen (Loket), Czechoslovakia. 27 Aug-31 Dez 1938 – 1r – 1 – gw Mikrofilm [072]
ELBRIDGE COMMUNITY BAPTIST CHURCH. ELBRIDGE, NEW YORK : CHURCH RECORDS – 1813-1966. (formerly First Baptist Church) – 1 – us Baptist [240]
ELBRIDGE GERRY PAPERS / Gerry, Elbridge – Massachusetts Historical Society – 7r – 1 – $525.00 – us UMI [920]
DIE ELBZOELLE : AKTENSTUECKE UND NACHWEISE 1814-1859 – Leipzig, 1860 – 5mf – 1 – ILM-2454/1 – ne IDC [327]
EL-CARMEL – 1920(Oct.)-1934(May) – 8r – 1 – J-91-205/3 – ne IDC [072]
EL-CHAMS – Paris. no1-35, fev-nov 1885 – 1 – fr A.C.R.P.P. [073]
El'chaninov, BE *see* SOCHINENIIA I PEREVODY
Elder Family *see* LETTERS AND SCRAPBOOK
ELDER LOTT CARY BIOGRAPHY / Taylor, J B – 1837 – 1 – $5.00 – us Baptist [240]
Elder, Marc *see* LE QUAI DE LA FOSSE A NANTES
Elder, William *see*
– IDEAS FROM NATURE: TALKS WITH STUDENTS
– MELIORA: AN ORATION BEFORE THE ALUMNI OF THE MOUNT ALLISON WESLEYAN COLLEGE, SACKVILLE, ON THE 1ST OF JUNE, 1880
ELDERBERRY TIMES – Old Town, ME. Jan-Oct 1974 – 1 – us Res Libr [071]
Eldering, Lotty *see* EARLY INTERVENTION AND CULTURE PREPARATION FOR LITERACY
ELDERS' JOURNAL – Kirtland, Ohio etc. v. 1 no. 1-4. Oct 1837-Aug 1838 – 1 – us NY Public [073]
ELDERS' JOURNAL OF THE CHURCH OF LATTER-DAY SAINTS – Kirtland, OH. v1. 1837-38 – 1r – 1 – us Ross [240]
ELDON – Santa Ana, CA. 1925 – 8+ r – 1 – $400.00 ($50.00y) – R04108 – us Library Micro [071]
THE ELDORADO OF THE ANCIENTS / Peters, Karl – London: C.A. Pearson, 1902. x,447p. illus. 2 fold. maps – 1 – us U.W. Library [930]
THE ELDRIDGE GAZETTE – Eldridge, CA. 1975 – 3+ r – 1 – $150.00 ($50.00y) – B06024 – us Library Micro [071]
Eldridge, William B *see*
– THE DISTRICT COURT EXECUTIVE PILOT PROGRAM
– THE SECOND CIRCUIT SENTENCING STUDY
ELEANOR / Ward, Mary Augusta – British Fiction Archive: Unit 2 – 9 – uk Bell [830]
ELEANOR LESLIE : A MEMOIR / Stone, Jean Mary – (Includes index) – London: Art and Book Co, 1898 – 1mf – 9 – 0-8370-7023-6 – 1986-1023 – us A.T.L.A. [920]
ELEANOR'S VICTORY / Braddon, Mary Elizabeth – British Fiction Archive: Unit 5 – 9 – uk Bell [830]
ELEAZAR WHEELOCK PAPERS – 16r – 1 – us UMI [240]
ELECCION AL MEJOR DEPORTISTA PROVINCIAL DE BADAJOZ-1970 / Junta Provincial de Educacion Fisica y Deportes – Badajoz: Graf. Nemesio Jimenez, 1971 – sp Bibl Santa Ana [946]
LAS ELECCIONES IN MERIDA – 1881 – 9 – $1.50f – sp Bibl Santa Ana [946]
ELECCIONES Y PARTIDOS EN ASTURIAS / Garcia Garcia, Carmen – 1854-1868 – 1mf – 9 – Pta1,000.00 – 84-85422-57-0 – sp Pentalfa [320]
ELECCIONES Y PARTIDOS POLITICOS EN CANTABRIA / Garrido Martin, Aurora – 1902-1923 – 1mf – 9 – Pta1,000.00 – 84-85422-71-6 – sp Pentalfa [320]
ELECCIONES Y PARTIDOS POLITICOS EN LA ARGENTINA : HISTORIA, INTERPRETACION Y BALANCE: 1910-1966 / Canton, Dario – [Buenos Aires]: Siglo Veintiuno Argentina Editores, [1st ed 1973] – 1 – CSUXADP3973-B – us Hoover Inst Photo [320]
ELECTED OR APPOINTED OFFICIALS?: A PAPER SUBMITTED TO THE AMERICAN ACADEMY OF POLITICAL AND SOCIAL SCIENCE / Bourinot, John George – Philadelphia: American Academy of Political and Social Science, 1895? 00228. (Pre-1900 Canadiana) – 9 – cn C.I.H.M. [971]
L'ELECTEUR – (Cont by: Le Soleil) – Quebec, Canada. 24 jun 1880-26 dec 1896 – 15r – 1 – Can$50.00r – cn Can Microfilming [072]
L'ELECTEUR – puis L' Electeur libre. Paris. 5 juin 1868-30 mars 1871 – 1 – fr A.C.R.P.P. [073]
L'ELECTEUR – Quebec, 1858-1896 – 7r – 1 – cn Preston [971]
L'ELECTEUR – Quebec, Canada. 19 mai 1866-11 mai 1867 – 1r – 1 – Can$40.00 – cn Can Microfilming [072]
L'ELECTEUR : REVUE PARTI LIBERAL DU QUEBEC – Montreal, Canada. 15 jul 1967-fev 1976 – 1r – 1 – Can$60.00 – cn Can Microfilming [072]
L'ELECTEUR CARNAVAL – (Numero special d'hiver de "L'Electeur") – Quebec, Canada. jan 1894; fev 1894 – 1r – 1 – Can$25.00 – cn Can Microfilming [073]
Electeur de Longueuil *see* ADRESSE AUX ELECTEURS MUNICIPAUX DE LA VILLE DE LONGUEUIL
L'ELECTEUR D'OUTREMONT – Outremont, Canada. 16 mar 1963-v1 n3. 30 mar 1963 – 1r – 1 – Can$25.00 – cn Can Microfilming [072]
ELECTEUR DU DEPARTEMENT DE PARIS, AUX VERITABLES AMIS DE LA LIBERTE / Bonneville, Nicolas de – Paris. Imp. du Cercle Social. s.d – 9 – fr Hachette [321]
L'ELECTEUR ILLUSTRE – (Numero special du quotidien "L'Electeur") – Quebec, Canada. jan 1889 – 1r – 1 – Can$25.00 – cn Can Microfilming [072]
ELECTEURS DE DORCHESTER, LISEZ CECI, S'IL VOUS PLAIT – Un conservateur.1897?.05225.(Pre-1900 Canadiana) – 9 – cn C.I.H.M. [971]
ELECTEURS DE LA PROVINCE DE QUEBEC – Quebec: s.n., 1878. 03183. (Pre-1900 Canadiana) – 9 – cn C.I.H.M. [971]
ELECTION BULLETIN – Ireland.17 Feb-15 Mar 1925 – 1 – ie Microforms [072]
ELECTION BY LOT: THE ONLY REMEDY FOR POLITICAL CORRUPTION – Montreal: Dawson, 1884. 05226. (Pre-1900 Canadiana) – 9 – cn C.I.H.M. [971]
THE ELECTION CAMPAIGN: A SUMMARY OF THE PUBLIC RECORDS OF THE PAST FIVE YEARS: FOR THE USE OF THE PEOPLE – Toronto?: s.n., 1878 (Toronto: "Daily Mail"). 05227. (Pre-1900 Canadiana) – 9 – cn C.I.H.M. [971]
ELECTION CASE LAW : A SUMMARY OF JUDICIAL PRECEDENT ON ELECTION ISSUES OTHER THAN CAMPAIGN FINANCING – 1989; 1993 – 7mf – 9 – $10.50 – LLMC 95-026 – us L.L.M.C. [340]
L'ELECTION DE NIERT AU XVIIIE SIECLE: NOTES ET DOCUMENTS / Desaivre, Leo – Saint-Maixene. 1886. lix, 386p. (Historical Studies Series) – 9 – 15.00 – fr Bibl Nationale [900]
THE ELECTION LAW. CONSTITUTIONALITY THEREOF MAINTAINED. AN OPINION OF ONE OF THE MOST EMINENT CONSTITUTIONAL LAWYERS IN THE UNITED STATES ON THE ELECTION LAW OF MISSISSIPPI – n.p., 1871? 10 p. LL-649 – 1 – us L of C Photodup [340]
ELECTION MANIFESTO – New Delhi: [s.n., 1967?] – us Res Libr [320]
ELECTION MANIFESTO : SAMYUKTA SOCIALIST PARTY – New Delhi: The Party, [1967?] – us Res Libr [320]
ELECTION MANIFESTO : SWATANTRA PARTY ELECTION MANIFESTO – [Bombay: Printed at Inland Printers, 1967?] – us Res Libr [320]
ELECTION MANIFESTO, 1967 / Indian National Congress – New Delhi: N Balakrishnan, [1967?] – us Res Libr [320]
ELECTION MANIFESTO, 1967 / Sangh, Bharatiya Jana – [s.l.]: The Sangh, [1967?] (Delhi: Arjun Press) – us Res Libr [320]
ELECTION MANIFESTO AND IMMEDIATE PROGRAMME : FOURTH GENERAL ELECTION, 1967 / Bangla Congress – New Delhi: [s.n.] 1967? – us Res Libr [320]
ELECTION MANIFESTO OF AKHIL BHARAT HINDU MAHASABHA – New Delhi: The Mahasabha, 1966 – us Res Libr [320]
ELECTION MANIFESTO OF THE COMMUNIST PARTY OF INDIA – New Delhi: D P Sinha, 1966 – us Res Libr [320]
ELECTION MANIFESTO OF THE COMMUNIST PARTY OF INDIA (MARXIST) – New Delhi: The Party, 1967 – us Res Libr [320]
ELECTION MANIFESTO OF THE REPUBLICAN PARTY OF INDIA, 1967 / ed by Khobragade, B D – Chanda, 1967 – us Res Libr [320]
ELECTION MANIFESTO OF THE TAMILNAD TOILERS WELFARE PARTY, MADRAS STATE : RELEASED OCT 9, 1966, AT THE CONFERENCE OF THE PARTY HELD IN MADRAS CITY – Madras: The Party, 1966 – us Res Libr [320]
THE ELECTION OF GRACE / Taylor, William MacKergo – London: Hodder & Stoughton, 1868 – 1mf – 9 – 0-8370-2198-7 – 1985-0198 – us A.T.L.A. [240]
ELECTION RETURNS, 1858-1962 / Minnesota. Secretary of State – 83r – 1 – $30.00r – us M.H.S. [324]
ELECTIONS DE 1881: SITUATION POLITIQUE ET ADMINISTRATIVE DE LA PROVINCE DE QUEBEC – Montreal: La Patrie, 1881. 04261. (Pre-1900 Canadiana) – 9 – cn C.I.H.M. [971]
ELECTIONS DE 1887: AUX ELECTEURS DU CANADA – Quebec?: s.n., 1887 (Quebec: C. Darveau). 05228. (Pre-1900 Canadiana) – 9 – cn C.I.H.M. [971]
ELECTIONS DE 1958 / France – D'apres la presse regionale. Dossiers de Presse – 1 – fr A.C.R.P.P. [944]
LES ELECTIONS DU 2 JANVIER, 1956 / Duverger, Maurice et al – 9 – F130.00 – fr Ethnologie [320]
LES ELECTIONS EPISCOPALES DANS L'EGLISE DE FRANCE DU IXE AU XIIE SIECLE : ETUDE SUR LA DECADENCE DU PRINCIPE ELECTIF, 814-1150 / Imbart de la Tour, Pierre – Paris: Hachette, 1891 – 2mf – us A.T.L.A. [240]
Elections, Loire-Inferieure *see* LISTE DE MESSIEURS LES ELECTEURS DES NEUF DISTRICTS DU DEPARTEMENT DE LA LOIRE-INFERIEURE...
ELECTIONS PRESIDENTIELLES ET LEGISLATIVES DU 27 DEC 1974 – Conakry: Impr national P Lumumba, 1975 – us Res Libr [320]
ELECTIONS PROVINCIALES : COMMITTEE CENTRAL LIBERAL – Montreal, Canada. nov 1935 – 1r – 1 – Can$25.00 – cn Can Microfilming [971]
ELECTIVE COURSE OF LECTURES IN SYSTEMATIC THEOLOGY / Curtis, Olin Alfred – Madison, NJ: Drew Theological Seminary, 1901 – 1mf – 9 – 0-8370-2792-6 – 1985-0792 – us A.T.L.A. [240]

ELECTORAL CAMPAIGN SPEECHES, OCT 26-NOV 5 1959 – Tunis: Secretariate of State for Information Publications, [1959?] – us Res Libr [320]

ELECTORAL ROLLS NEW SOUTH WALES : C. DIVISION – (Apply to publ for details) – 1903-28 – 9 – at Pascoe [320]

ELECTRA – Amsterdam, Netherlands. -w. May 1899-Nov 1902. 2 reels – 1 – uk British Libr Newspaper [949]

ELECTRA : ORGAM DA LIGA ANTICLERICAL PARANENSE – Curitiba, Aug 1901-Aug 1903 – 1,5,6 – bl Biblioteca [072]

ELECTRIC LIGHT AND POWER – (v.57 .1979 5,6,9) – v.1. 1923 – 1 – us UMI [073]

ELECTRIC MACHINES AND ELECTROMECHANICS – v. 1-. 1976- – 1,5,6,9 – us UMI [621]

ELECTRIC MACHINES AND POWER SYSTEMS – v8-. 1983- – 1,5,6,9 – us UMI [073]

ELECTRIC MESSAGES FROM JAPAN *see* OMS (ORIENTAL MISSIONARY STANDARD) OUTREACH

ELECTRIC PERSPECTIVES – (1981-. 5,6,9) – 1976- – 1 – us UMI [621]

ELECTRIC POWER COMMITTEE / UN Economic Commission for Europe (ECE) – 1947-89 – E/F.8 E.1041 F.1073 R.923 – 9 – us U.N. Pubs [340]

ELECTRIC POWER STATIONS – v. 1-. 1980- – 5,6,9 – us UMI [621]

ELECTRIC POWER SYSTEMS RESEARCH – v1-7. 1977-84 – 1,5,6,13 – sz Elsevier [073]

ELECTRIC REFRIGERATION NEWS *see* AIR CONDITIONING, HEATING AND REFRIGERATION NEWS

ELECTRIC TECHNOLOGY USSR *see* ELECTRICAL TECHNOLOGY

Electrica berlanguena S.A. Berlanga, Badajoz *see* MEMORIA Y BALANCE GENERAL EN 30 DE JUNIO DE 1938. 37 EJERCICIO SOCIAL. LEIDA Y APROBADA...1938

ELECTRICAL AND ELECTRONIC INSULATION – v1. 1955. Continued by: Insulation – 1 – us UMI [073]

ELECTRICAL AND ELECTRONIC TRADER – 1965- – 1 – us UMI [621]

ELECTRICAL AND ELECTRONICS ABSTRACTS – 1898-1995 – 1,5,6,9 – uk INSPEC [620]

ELECTRICAL AND ELECTRONICS ABSTRACTS : FOUR YEAR CUMULATIVE INDEXES – (With author-subject indexes) – 1957-1992 – 1,5,6,9 – uk INSPEC [620]

ELECTRICAL AND ELECTRONICS ABSTRACTS : SEMI-ANNUAL INDEXES – (Includes author-subject indexes) – 1898-1995 – 1,5,6,9 – uk INSPEC [620]

ELECTRICAL AND RADIO TRADING – (1976-. 5,6,9) – 1929- – 1 – us UMI [621]

ELECTRICAL BUSINESS – v.1. 1979 – 1,5,6,9 – us UMI [073]

ELECTRICAL BUSINESS – (v25 1989 Can$85.00y) – Mississauga. v25-30. 1989-94 – 1 – Can$60.00y – cn Micromedia [621]

ELECTRICAL COMMUNICATION – (1970-. 5,6. 1975-. 9) – 1- 1922- – 1 – us UMI [621]

ELECTRICAL CONSTRUCTION AND MAINTENANCE – (1970-80. 5,6. 1977-80. 9) – v. 20-79. 1920-80 – 1 – us UMI [621]

ELECTRICAL CONSTRUCTION AND MAINTENANCE *see* EC AND M

ELECTRICAL ENERGY MANAGEMENT – v43-45,no.6. 1979-Dec,Jan 1982 – 1,5,6,9 – us UMI [073]

ELECTRICAL ENGINEER – (1979 5,6,9) – 1976 – 1 – us UMI [073]

ELECTRICAL ENGINEERING – 1931-1963 – 1,5,6 – 900.00 – us I.E.E.E. [621]

ELECTRICAL ENGINEERING IN JAPAN – (v104-. 1984-. 5,6,9) – v83-. 1963- – 1 – us UMI [073]

THE ELECTRICAL EXPERIMENTER – New York: [s.n., -1920]. [v6, n1-5 may-sep 1918; n61-65; v6 n7-12 nov 1918-apr 1919; n67-72] – 1r – us Res Libr [071]

ELECTRICAL MANUFACTURING – v. 26-42. 1940-48 – 1,5,6 – us Princeton Micro [621]

ELECTRICAL NEWS – 1986- – 1 – us UMI [621]

ELECTRICAL POWER ENGINEER – v1- 1919-1; v58- 5,6,9 – us UMI [621]

ELECTRICAL POWER ENGINEER – 1920-59 – 1 – uk Microform Academic [073]

ELECTRICAL PROGRESS & MONTHLY REGISTER – London, UK. Nov-Dec 1906. -m. 8 feet – 1 – uk British Libr Newspaper [072]

ELECTRICAL REVIEW – London. v. 126-145. 1940-49 – 1,5,6 – us Princeton Micro [621]

ELECTRICAL REVIEW *see* FACTORY

ELECTRICAL REVIEW AND INDUSTRIAL ENGINEER *see* FACTORY

ELECTRICAL REVIEW AND WESTERN ELECTRICIAN *see* FACTORY

ELECTRICAL REVIEW INTERNATIONAL – v1-. Feb 1984- – 1,5,6,9 – us UMI [073]

ELECTRICAL TECHNOLOGY – (Formerly: Electric Technology USSR) – 1958- – 5,6,9 – us UMI [621]

ELECTRICAL TIMES E INGENIERO INDUSTRIAL – (Ingeniero Industrial Apr 1915-Aug 1917) – London, UK. 28 Jan 1915 – 1 – uk British Libr Newspaper [072]

ELECTRICAL WORLD – 1- 1883- 1; 163- 5,6; v183- 9 – us UMI [621]

ELECTRICAL WORLD – v1-144. 1883-1955 – 1,5,6 – us Princeton Micro [621]

ELECTRICIAN – v. 2-125. 1878-1940 – 1,5,6 – us Princeton Micro [621]

L'ELECTRICITE – Paris. 15 Jan 1876-9 Aug 1894 – 9r – 1 – uk British Libr Newspaper [073]

ELECTRICITY – v. 1-43. 1890-1929 – 1 – us UMI [621]

ELECTRIFIED INDUSTRY – v.1-42. 1937-78. Superseded by yElectrical Energy Management – 1 – us UMI [073]

ELECTRI-ONICS – v29-. 1983- – 1,5,6,9 – us UMI [073]

ELECTROCHEMICAL SOCIETY *see* AMERICAN ELECTRO-CHEMICAL SOCIETY MEETINGS

Electrochemical Society *see*
- JOURNAL
- JOURNAL AND TRANSACTIONS
- MEETINGS

ELECTROCHIMICA ACTA – v1- 1959- – 5,6,9 – us UMI [540]

ELECTROCOMPONENT SCIENCE AND TECHNOLOGY (INC. THIN FILMS) – 1974- – 1,5,9 – us Gordon [530]

ELECTROENCEPHALOGRAPHY AND CLINICAL NEUROPHYSIOLOGY – The EEG Journal.v1-59.1949-84 – 1,5,6,13 – sz Elsevier [073]

ELECTROMAGNETICS – (v3-. 1983-. 5,6,9) – v1-. 1981- – 1 – us UMI [073]

ELECTROMYOGRAPHIC CHANGES DURING INTENSE ISOKINETIC STRENGTH TRAINING / Lamack, Daniel D – Iowa State University, 1993 – 1mf – 9 – $4.00 – PH1467 – us Microform Publ [612]

ELECTRON – 1972- 1; 1976- 5,6,9 – us UMI [621]

ELECTRON MICROSCOPY REVIEWS *see* MICRON

ELECTRONIC BUSINESS – (1984-. 5,6,9) – 1975- – 1 – us UMI [380]

ELECTRONIC COMPOSITION AND IMAGING – Willowdale. v1-8. 1987-94 – 9 – Can$20.00y – cn Micromedia [621]

ELECTRONIC DESIGN – 1- 1953- 1; v13- 5,6; v23- 9 – us UMI [621]

ELECTRONIC ENGINEERING – v14- 1941- 1; v43- 5,6; v48- 9 – us UMI [621]

ELECTRONIC ENGINEERING – London. v. 12-20. 1939-48 – 1,5,6 – us Princeton Micro [621]

ELECTRONIC ENGINEERING INDEX – 1965. 5 sections. Updated 3 times per yr – 5 – uk Tech [621]

ELECTRONIC IMAGING – 1982- – 1,5,6,9 – us UMI [073]

ELECTRONIC INDUSTRIES – v. 1-5. 1942-1946 – 1,5,6 – us Princeton Micro [621]

ELECTRONIC LEARNING – (1983-. 1,5,6,9) – v1-. 1981- – 1 – us UMI [073]

ELECTRONIC MEDIA – 1982- – 1,5,6,9 – us UMI [073]

ELECTRONIC MEDIA – 1985-. -w – 1 – us UMI [073]

ELECTRONIC MODELLING – 1982- – 1,5,9 – us Gordon [621]

ELECTRONIC NEWS – New York, 1957- – 1 – $330.00y – us Fairchild Micro [621]

ELECTRONIC QUALITY ASSURANCE MICROFILE – 1979. Updated every 2 months. Specs. for BS9000 and CECC QA schemes – 9 – uk Tech [621]

ELECTRONIC SERVICING AND TECHNOLOGY – v.1-. 1981- – 1,5,6,9 – us UMI [073]

ELECTRONIC TECHNOLOGY – v. 1-33. 1923-56 – 1,5,6 – us Princeton Micro [621]

ELECTRONIC WARFARE/DEFENSE ELECTRONICS – (See also: Defense Electronics) – v9-11. 1977-1979 – 1,5,6,9 – us UMI [621]

ELECTRONICS – v. 1- 1930- – 1,5,6,9 – us UMI [621]

ELECTRONICS – v1-28. 1930-55 – 1,5,6 – us Princeton Micro [621]

ELECTRONICS AND COMMUNICATIONS IN JAPAN – (v67-. 1984-. 5,6,9) – v46-. 1963- – 1 – us UMI [073]

ELECTRONICS AND POWER – v1- 1955- 1; v21- 1975- 5,6 – us UMI [621]

ELECTRONICS AND TECHNOLOGY TODAY – (Cont: Electronics Today at v11 no 9 1987. Numbering erratic. Ceased v17 no 5 1987) – North York. v12-17. 1988-92 – 9 – Can$28.00y – cn Micromedia [621]

ELECTRONICS AND TECHNOLOGY TODAY *see* ELECTRONICS TODAY

ELECTRONICS LETTERS – v1- 1965- 1; v11-1975- 5,6 – us UMI [621]

ELECTRONICS LETTERS ON MICROFICHE – 1970- – uk INSPEC [621]

ELECTRONICS PURCHASING – 1986- – 1,5,6,9 – us UMI [380]

ELECTRONICS TEST – (1982-. 1,5,6,9) – v1-. 1978- – 1 – us UMI [073]

ELECTRONICS TODAY – (Cont by: Electronics and Technology Today at v11 no 9 1987) – North York. v1-11. 1977-87 – 9 – Can$28.00y – cn Micromedia [621]

ELECTRONICS TODAY *see* ELECTRONICS AND TECHNOLOGY TODAY

ELECTRONICS WORLD – (v. 73-86. 1965-71. 5,6. v. 83-86. 1970-71. 9) – 1-86. 1919-71 – 1 – us UMI [621]

ELECTROPHORESIS : AN INTERNATIONAL JOURNAL ON APPLICATIONS, METHODS AND THEORY – v1-17. 1980-96 – 1,5,6,13 – us V.C.H. [660]

ELECTROPLATING AND METAL FINISHING – 1954-59 – 1 – uk Microform Academic [670]

ELEFANTES BLANCOS, PAGINAS DORADAS. NUEVAS NOTICIAS DE INDOCHINA / Elias de Tejada Spinola, Francisco – Barcelona: Talleres Graficos Rafael Salva, 1957 – sp Bibl Santa Ana [590]

ELEFHEROTYPIA – (Yrly reel count varies) – 1990- – 1 – inquire – us Ross [072]

ELEGANCIAS – Revista mensual ilustrada artistica, literaria, modas y actualidades. no. 1-46. Paris. mai 1911-aout 1914. mq no. 2, 5. En 1913-14 contient des suppl., no. 1-13 – 1 – fr A.C.R.P.P. [073]

ELEGANT EXTRACTS FOR THE GERMAN FLUTE OR VIOLIN SELECTED FROM THE MOST FAVORITE SONGS &C. SUNG IN THE THEATRES AND PUBLIC PLACES – Baltimore: J. Carr 1794-1798. MUSIC 1467, Item 1 – 1 – us L of C Photodup [780]

DIE ELEGANTE WELT – Berlin, 1912-43 (incomplete) – 1 – Dist. gw Mikrofilm – gw Misc Inst [390]

ELEGANTISSIMORUM EMBLEMATUM CORPUSCULUM LATINIS BELGICISQUE VERSIBUS ELUCIDATUM – Leiden, 1696 – 1mf – 9 – ne IDC [700]

ELEGIAC SONNETS AND OTHER POEMS / Smith, Charlotte Turner – London: T. Cadell, Junior; W. Davies, 1797 – 1 roll – 1 – 1-55879-268-6 – uk Libr Preservation [810]

ELEH BENEI HA-NE'URIM / Luzzatto, E – Vienna. 1839. BJ-422-54 1 – 9 – ne IDC [270]

O ELEITOR – Passo, Alagoas. Nov 1884 – 1,5,6 – bl Biblioteca [072]

ELEKTRA : TRAGEDY IN ONE ACT / Strauss, Richard & Hofmannsthal, Hugo von – Berlin: A Fuerstner, c1910 – 1r – 1 – us U.W. Library [780]

ELEKTRA : TRAGOEDIE IN EINEM AUFZUGE / Strauss, Richard & Hofmannsthal, Hugo von – Berlin: A Fuerstner, c1908 – 1r – 1 – us U.W. Library [780]

ELEKTRIFIKAT SII A SELSKOGO KHOZI A ISTVA (LENINGRAD, R.S.F.S.R.: 1931 *see* ELEKTRIFIKAT SII A SELSKOGO KHOZI A ISTVA / ORGAN AGRARNOGO INSTITUTA KOMMUNISTICHESKO I AKADEMII I SOI UZSEL ELEKTRO NARKOMZEMA SSSR

ELEKTRIFIKAT SII A SELSKOGO KHOZI A ISTVA / ORGAN AGRARNOGO INSTITUTA KOMMUNISTICHESKO I AKADEMII I SOI UZSEL ELEKTRO NARKOMZEMA SSSR – (Library has: Apr. 1932) – Leningrad: Selkolkhozgiz, 1931-1937. 7v – 1 – CSUX89-S763 – us Hoover Inst Photo [947]

ELEKTRIFIKATSII A SSSR : SBORNIK DOKUMENTOV I MATERIALOV, 1926-1932 GG / ed by Gladkov, I A – Moskva: Ekonomika, 1966 – 1 – CSUX90-B2236 – us Hoover Inst Photo [333]

ELEKTRIFIKATSIIA / Gerasimov, Mikhail Prokopevich – Peterburg: Gos. izd-vo, 1922 – 1 – CSUX88-B8410 – us Hoover Inst Photo [333]

ELEKTRISCHE BAHNEN – v44-. 1973- – 1,5,6 – us UMI [073]

ELEKTRISCHE MESSUNGEN AN GESTAEUBTEN MOSI$_2$-SCHICHTEN / Lippert, Gunther – 1995 – 1mf – 9 – DM60.00 – 3-8267-2116-0 – gw Hänsel [621]

ELEKTRISCHE NACHRICHTEN-TECHNIK – v. 1-20. 1924-1943 – 1 – us Princeton Micro [621]

Elektrobank SSSR *see* OTCHET O DEI ATELNOSTI ZA...OPERAT SIONNY I GOD

ELEKTROCHEMISCHE THERMOSPRAY-MASSENSPEKTROMETRIE : ON-LINE-METHODE ZUR AUFKLAERUNG VON ELEKTROCHEMISCHEN REAKTIONEN IN SAUREN ELEKTROLYTLOESUNGEN SOWIE VON PROZESSEN IN MEMBRANEN / Stassen, Ingo – 1995 – 2mf – 9 – DM80.00 – 3-8267-2264-7 – gw Hänsel [540]

ELEKTROKINETISCHE UNTERSUCHUNGEN VON AEROSILOBERFLAECHEN UND AEROSIL-TRIARYLMETYLHALOGENID-ADSORBATEN IN ORGANISCHEN MEDIEN / Simon, Frank – 1993 – 1mf – 9 – DM60.00 – 3-89349-768-4 – gw Hänsel [540]

ELEKTRONENMIKROSKOPISCHE UNTERSUCHUNGEN ZUR STEREOSELEKTIVEN BILDUNG MIZELLARER LIPIDFASERN AUS N-ALKYLALDONAMIDEN / Boettcher, Christoph – 1992 – 130p – DM98.00 – 3-89349-458-8 – gw Hänsel [574]

ELEKTROPHYSIOLOGISCHE UNTERSUCHUNGEN ZUR VERARBEITUNG GRAMMATISCHER INFORMATION IN DER FINNISCHEN SPRACHE / Muente, Ava Sinikka – 1995 – 1mf – 9 – DM60.00 – 3-8267-2229-9 – gw Hänsel [616]

ELEKTROTEKHNICHESKOE DELO – Zhurnal. M. 1911-17. Available: 1911. BR-8139 2 – 8 – ne IDC [073]

ELEKTROTECHNISCHER ANZEIGER – Berlin, 1892-1909 – 25r – 1 – uk British Libr Newspaper [072]

ELEKTROTECHNISCHER ANZEIGER – Berlin, Germany. 1892-1909 (missing 1900-01).-w. 25 reels – 1 – uk British Libr Newspaper [073]

ELEKTROTECHNISCHES ECHO – Magdeburg, Germany. -w. 1890-93; 1896-1904. 6 reels – 1 – uk British Libr Newspaper [073]

ELEKTROZAVOD : EZHEDNEVNAI A GAZETA – ORGAN PARTKOMA I ZAVKOMA / Elektrozavod (Moscow, Russia) – (Includes c.1: v.5:no.57(1932:Mar.9)) – [Moskva]: Partkom i Zavkom Elektrozavoda, 192u – 1 – CSUXANR4017-S – us Hoover Inst Photo [947]

Elektrozavod (Moscow, Russia) *see* ELEKTROZAVOD

ELEMENS DE CHYMIE-PRATIQUE, CONTENANT LA DESCRIPTION DES OPERATIONS FONDAMENTALES DE LA CHYMIE, AVEC DES EXPLICATIONS ET DES REMARQUES SUR CHAQUE OPERATION / Macquer, Pierre Joseph – Paris: J. T. Herissant, 1751 – 1 – us U.W. Library [540]

ELEMENS DE LA GRAMMAIRE FRANCAISE / Lhomond, Charles F – 2e ed. Quebec: J Neilson, 1810. SEM16P58 – 1r – 5 – Can$9.00 – cn Bibl Nat [440]

ELEMENS DE LA GRAMMAIRE FRANCAISE / Lhomond, Charles F – 3e ed. Quebec: J Neilson, 1819. SEM16P59 – 1r – 5 – Can$9.00 – cn Bibl Nat [440]

ELEMENS DE LA GRAMMAIRE FRANCAISE / Lhomond, Charles F – Montreal: James Brown, 1820. SEM16P61 – 1r – 5 – Can$9.00 – cn Bibl Nat [440]

ELEMENS DE LA GRAMMAIRE FRANCAISE / Lhomond, Charles F – Montreal: Jh. Victor Delorme, 1817. SEM16P60 – 1r – 5 – Can$9.00 – cn Bibl Nat [440]

ELEMENS DE LA GRAMMAIRE FRANCAISE / Lhomond, Charles F – Quebec: J Neilson, 1800. SEM16P57 – 1r – 5 – Can$9.00 – cn Bibl Nat [440]

ELEMENS DE LA GRAMMAIRE LATINE / Lhomond, Charles F – Montreal: Roy & Bennett, 1797. SEM16P62 – 1r – 5 – Can$9.00 – cn Bibl Nat [450]

ELEMENS DE LA GRAMMAIRE LATINE, A L'USAGE DES COLLEGES / Lhomond, Charles F – Nouv. ed. Quebec: J Neilson, 1813. SEM16P174 – 1r – 5 – Can$9.00 – cn Bibl Nat [450]

ELEMENS DE LA GRAMMAIRE LATINE, A L'USAGE DES COLLEGES : METHODE / Lhomond, Charles F – Montreal: Louis Roy, 1796. SEM16P173 – 1r – 5 – Can$9.00 – cn Bibl Nat [450]

ELEMENS DE LA GRAMMAIRE LATINE, A L'USAGE DES COLLEGES : SYNTAXE / Lhomond, Charles F – Montreal: Louis Roy, 1796. SEM16P172 – 1r – 5 – Can$9.00 – cn Bibl Nat [450]

LES ELEMENS DE LA PHILOSOPHIE DE L'ART DU FEU OU CHEMIE / Davisson, William – Traduit du latin par Iean Hellot. Paris, 1651 – 1 – us U.W. Library [540]

ELEMENS DE L'ARCHITECTURE NAVALE OU TRAITE PRATIQUE DE LA CONSTRUCTION DES VAISSEAUX / Duhamel du Monceau, Henri Louis – Paris: Chez Charles Antoine Jombert, 1752. SEM105P291 – 7mf – 9 – Can$15.75 – cn Bibl Nat [623]

ELEMENS DE L'ART DE LA TEINTURE / Berthollet, Claude-Louis – Sec. ed., avec une description de l'art du blanchiment par l'acide muriatique. Paris: F. Didot, 1804. 2v. 7953-4 – 9 – fr Hachette [540]

ELEMENS DE STATISTIQUE: OU L'ON DEMONTRE... LES RESSOURCES DE CHAQUE ROYAUME, ETAT ET REPUBLIQUE DE L'EUROPE. / Playfair, William – Paris, Batillot jeune, Genets jeune, 1802. xxxii, 182 p. 3 fiches. (Statistics Series: Topography) – 9 – 8.00 – fr Bibl Nationale [944]

ELEMENS DU CALCUL DES PROBABILITES ET SON APPLICATION AUX JEUX DE HASARD, A LA LOTERIE ET AUX JUGEMENS DES HOMMES / Condorcet, Marie Jean Antoine Nicolas de – Paris: Royez, 1805. xii,210p. 3 fiches. (Science Collection) – 9 – 8.00 – fr Bibl Nationale [510]

LES ELEMENS PRIMITIFS DES LANGUES... / Bergier, [N S] – Besancon, 1837 – 4mf – 9 – ne IDC [400]

ELEMENTA : THE JOURNAL OF SLAVIC STUDIES AND COMPARATIVE CULTURAL SEMIOTICS / ed by Ivanov, Viacheslav – 9,5,1 – us Harwood [460]

ELEMENTA ANGLICANA / Fogg, Peter Walkden – 1796. 437p. (English Linguistics Series 1500-1800) – 9 – us UMI [420]

ELEMENTA BOTANICA / Necker, N J de – Neowedae ad Rhenum, 1790. 3 vols. B-244 prSF 84,00 IDC 8 – ne IDC [580]

ELEMENTA ENTOMOLOGICA / Schaeffer, J C – Regensburg, 1766. vip,135 pls. with descriptive letterpress. Z-1598/2 – 8 – ne IDC [590]

ELEMENTA IURIS NATURALIS INTERNATIONALIS / Cordovani, P M – Aretii, 1924 – 1mf – 1 – ILM-1721/1 – ne IDC [327]

ELEMENTA JURIS NATURAE / Fuchs, J S – Leutschoviae, 1803 – 2mf – 1 – ILM-1106/1 – ne IDC [327]

ELEMENTA MUSICA / Blankenburg, Q. van – Eerste-Tweede Deel. 1739 – 9 – us Sibley [780]

ELEMENTA MUSICA OF NIEUW LICHT TOT HET WELVERSTAAN VAN DE MUSIEC EN DE BASCONTINUO / Blankenburg, Q. van – 's-Gravenhage. 1739. BP-172 1 – 9 – ne IDC [780]

AN ELEMENTARY ACCOUNT... / Bate, J P – London, 1911 – 1mf – 9 – ILM-425/1 – ne IDC [340]

AN ELEMENTARY AND PRACTICAL GRAMMAR OF THE GALLA OR OROMO LANGUAGE / Hodson, Arnold Wienholt & Walker, Craven H – London: Society fro Promoting Christian Knowledge, 1922 – 1 – us Res Libr [490]

ELEMENTARY ENGLISH – (See now: Language Arts) – v1-52 1924-75 1; v46-52 1969-75 5,6; v52- 9 – us UMI [370]

THE ELEMENTARY FORMS OF THE RELIGIOUS LIFE : A STUDY IN RELIGIOUS SOCIOLOGY / Durkheim, Emile – London: G. Allen & Unwin; New York: Macmillan, [1915?] – 2mf – us A.T.L.A. [240]

AN ELEMENTARY GRAMMAR : WITH FULL SYLLABARY AND PROGRESSIVE READING BOOK OF THE ASSYRIAN LANGUAGE IN THE CUNEIFORM TYPE / Sayce, Archibald Henry – London: Samuel Bagster, [1875?] – 1mf – 9 – 0-8370-8470-9 – 1986-2470 – us A.T.L.A. [470]

AN ELEMENTARY HEBREW GRAMMAR : WITH READING AND WRITING LESSONS AND VOCABULARIES / Green, William Henry – (Contains Hebrew-English and English-Hebrew vocabularies) – new ed, thoroughly corr. New York: John Wiley; London: Chapman & Hall, 1898, c1871 – 1mf – 9 – 0-8370-9149-7 – 1986-3149 – us A.T.L.A. [470]

ELEMENTARY LAW / Robinson, William Callyhan – Boston: Little, Brown, 1882. 379p. LL-1246 – 1 – us L of C Photodup [340]

AN ELEMENTARY MANUAL OF NEW ZEALAND ENTOMOLOGY / Hudson, G V – London, 1892. 128p. Z/1360/2 – 9 – ne IDC [590]

ELEMENTARY MESSENGER – 1920-39 – 1 – 79.66 – us Baptist [240]

ELEMENTARY NATURAL HISTORY: AN INTRODUCTION TO THE STUDY OF MINERALS, PLANTS AND ANIMALS, WITH SPECIAL REFERENCE TO THOSE OF NEW BRUNSWICK / Bailey, Loring Woart – Prepared for the use of schools. Saint John, N.B.: J. McMillan, 1887. 02375. (Pre-1900 Canadiana) – 9 – cn C.I.H.M. [500]

ELEMENTARY SCHOOL GUIDANCE AND COUNSELING – 1- 1967- 1; v6- 5,6; v10- 9 – us UMI [370]

ELEMENTARY SCHOOL JOURNAL – v. 1-46. 1900-1946 – 1 – us Princeton Micro [370]

ELEMENTARY SCHOOL JOURNAL – (v. 67- 1966- 5,6. v. 78- 1977- 9) – v. 1- 1900- – 1 – us UMI [370]

ELEMENTARY TEXT BOOK OF ENTOMOLOGY / Kirby, W F – London, 1885. vii,240p.87 pls. Z-1395/2 – 8 – ne IDC [590]

AN ELEMENTARY TREATISE ON THE AMERICAN LAW OF REAL PROPERTY / Tiedeman, Christopher Gustavus – St. Louis, Thomas, 1885. 785 p. LL-1025 – 1 – us L of C Photodup [340]

ELEMENTE : DREI EINAKTER / Wolf, Friedrich – Ludwigsburg (Wuerttemberg): Chronos Verlag, 1922 – 1r – 1 – us U.W. Library [820]

ELEMENTE DER GESTEINSLEHRE / Rosenbuch, C H F – 2521 2. 1898 – 8 – ne IDC [550]

DIE ELEMENTE DES INTERNATIONALEN SEERECHTES UND SAMMLUNG VON VERTRAEGEN / Attlmayr, F von – Wien. 2v. 1872-73 – 14mf – 9 – ILM-317/1 – ne IDC [340]

ELEMENTE DESKRIPTIVER UND INFERENTIELLER STATISTIK UND IHRE VORLAEUFER / Kostrzewa, Frank – 1993 – 1mf – 9 – DM75.00 – 3-89349-696-3 – gw Hänsel [430]

ELEMENTI GRAMMATICALI DEL CALDEO BIBLICO E DEL DIALETTO TALMUDICO BABILONESE = GRAMMAR OF THE BIBLICAL CHALDAIC LANGUAGE AND THE TALMUD BABLI IDIOMS / Luzzatto, Samuel David – (In English) – New York: John Wiley, 1876 – 1mf – 9 – 0-8370-7083-X – 1986-1083 – us A.T.L.A. [470]

ELEMENTI GRAMMATICALI DEL CALDEO BIBLICO E DEL DIALETTO TALMUDICO BABILONESE / Luzzatto, Samuel David – Padova: A Bianchi, 1865 – 1mf – 9 – 0-8370-9167-5 – 1986-3167 – us A.T.L.A. [470]

ELEMENTI SCIENTIFICI DI ETICA CIVILE E DIRITTO. / Augias, Carlo – Ancona, Tip. del commercio, 1878. 275 p. LL-4027 – 1 – us L of C Photodup [340]

O ELEMENTO NEGRO: HISTORIA, FOLKLORE, LINGUISTICA / Ribeiro, Joao – Rio de Janeiro, 193-. 237p – 1 – us U.W. Library [305]

ELEMENTOS DE ARITMETICA / Garcia, Juan Justo – 1782 – 9 – 1.50f – sp Bibl Santa Ana [510]

ELEMENTOS DE ARITMETICA, ALGEBRA Y GEOMETRIA / Garcia, Juan Justo – Madrid: Joaquin Ibarra, 1782 – 1 – sp Bibl Santa Ana [510]

ELEMENTOS DE ARITMETICA.TOMO I / Garcia, Juan Justo – (Tomo I. 1801. 1.50f; 9. Tomo I. 1821. 1.50f; BSA; 9. Tomo II.1822. 1.50f; BSA; 9) – 1801 – 9 – 1.50f – sp Bibl Santa Ana [510]

ELEMENTOS DE DERECHO ELECTORAL; DESARROLLADOS CONFORME AL PROGRAMA Y EXPLICACIONES DEL PROFESOR TITULAR DE LA ASIGNATURA, EN LA UNIVERISDAD DE LA HABANA / Lancis y Sanchez, Antonio – Habana Publicaciones Universitarias 1954. 164 p. LL-8024 – 1 – us L of C Photodup [340]

ELEMENTOS DE FILOSOFIA / Prisco, Jose – Gabino Tejado, trans. 2v 1884 – 9 – $1.50f – sp Bibl Santa Ana [190]

ELEMENTOS DE FILOSOFIA MORAL.. / Romero de Castillay Perosso, Francisco – 1893 – 9 – 1.50f – sp Bibl Santa Ana [170]

ELEMENTOS DE GEOMETRIA Y FISICA EXPERIMENTAL... / Ameller, C – Cadiz, 1788 – 5mf – 9 – sp Cultura [510]

ELEMENTOS DE GRAMATICA / Servan, Juan – 1882 – 9 – 1.50f – sp Bibl Santa Ana [440]

ELEMENTOS DE GRAMMATICA TETENSE, LINGUA CHI-NYUNGUE; IDIOMA FALLADO NO DISTRICTO DE TETE EEM TODA A VASTA REGIAO DO ZAMBEZE INFERIOR / Courtois, Victor Joseph – New ed. 1899 – 1 – us A.T.L.A. [490]

ELEMENTOS DE HISTORIA UNIVERSAL / Villanueva y Canedo, Luis – (Tomo II.1846. 1.50f; 9) – 1845 – 9 – 1.50f – sp Bibl Santa Ana [900]

ELEMENTOS DE IDEOLOGIA Y GRAMATICA GENERAL-HISTORIA DE LA LOGICA / Ignacio Diaz, Melchor – 1841. Libros en Microficha no 9 – 1mf – 9 – Pta1,000.00 – 84-85422-34-1 – sp Pentalfa [160]

ELEMENTOS DE LOGICA / Romero de Castilla, Tomas – 1886 – 9 – $1.50f – sp Bibl Santa Ana [160]

ELEMENTOS DE MATEMATICAS O...INTRODUCCION A LA FISICA EXPERIMENTAL / Cibat, A – Barcelona, SA – 4mf – 9 – sp Cultura [510]

ELEMENTOS DE PSICOLOGIA / Romero de Castilla, Tomas – (1892 ed.1.50f; 9) – 1876 – 9 – 1.50f – sp Bibl Santa Ana [150]

ELEMENTOS DE RELIGION. LA DOCTRINA DE NUESTRO SENOR JESUCRISTO / Garcia Garcia, Casimiro – Caceres: Tip. Extremadura, 1940 – 1 – sp Bibl Santa Ana [240]

ELEMENTOS DE TRIGONOMETRIA RECTILINEA / Luna y Gomez, Sergio – Sevilla; Est. Tip. Angel Saavedra, 1908 – 1 – sp Bibl Santa Ana [510]

ELEMENTOS DEL DERECHO MERCANTIL DE ESPANA... / Carreras y Gonzalez, M & Revilla, L Gonzalez Revilla – Ed 6. Madrid, 1902 – 6mf – 1 – ILM 3975/1 – ne IDC [327]

ELEMENTOS DE...LOGICA / Garcia, Juan Justo – 1821 – 9 – $1.50f – sp Bibl Santa Ana [160]

ELEMENTOS GRIEGOS Y LATINOS QUE ENTRAN EN LA COMPOSICION DE NUMEROSOS TECNICISMOS ESPANOLES, FRANCESES E INGLESES. MADRID, 1929 / Bayle, Constantino & Ramos Yebes, Jose M – Madrid: Razon y Fe, 1930 – 1 – sp Bibl Santa Ana [400]

ELEMENTOS PRELIMINARES PARA PODER FORMAR UN SYSTEMA DE GOBIERNO DEL HOSPICIO GENERAL / Anzano, T – Madrid, 1778 – 4mf – 9 – sp Cultura [360]

ELEMENTOS...GRAMATICA CASTELLANA / Lemus y Rubio, Pedro – 1897 – 9 – 1.50f – sp Bibl Santa Ana [440]

ELEMENTS – (v. 6- 1979- 9) – v. 1-. 1974- – 1,5,6 – us UMI [500]

ELEMENTS – (v1-17 1969/70-1987/88. Ceased v19 no 2 1988) – Edmontion. v1-19. 1969/70-1987/88 – 5,9 – Price varies – cn Micromedia [073]

THE ELEMENTS AND PRACTICE OF NAVAL ARCHITECTURE : WITH A SERIES OF THIRTY-NINE DRAUGHTS / Steel, David – 3rd ed., with an appendix containing the principles and practice of constructing the Royal and mercantile Navies, as introduced by Sir R. Steppings. By F. Knowles. 1822 – 9 – uk Libr Preservation [623]

ELEMENTS DE BIBLIOGRAPHIE DES ETUDES ARABES / Aubert, Martin – 1975 – 9 – fr Orientalistes [010]

ELEMENTS DE BOTANIQUE ET DE PHYSIOLOGIE VEGETALE: SUIVIS D'UNE PETITE FLORE SIMPLE ET FACILE POUR AIDER A DECOUVRIR LES NOMS DES PLANTES LES PLUS COMMUNES DU CANADA / Brunet, Ovide – Quebec: P. Delisle, 1870. 00299. (Pre-1900 Canadiana) – 9 – cn C.I.H.M. [580]

ELEMENTS DE DROIT INTERNATIONAL PRIVE OU DU CONFLIT DES LOIS / Asser, T M C – Paris, 1884 – 4mf – 9 – ILM-417/1 – ne IDC [340]

ELEMENTS DE GRAMMAIRE GENERALE APPLIQUES A LA LANGUE FRANCAISE / Sicard, Roch A C – 3E ED. 1808 – 9 – fr I.C.S. [400]

ELEMENTS DE GRAMMAIRE NAGO / Bouche – Lyon. 1872 – 9 – $5.00 – fr Orientalistes [490]

ELEMENTS DE LA GRAMMAIRE JAPONAISE / Rodriguez – Traduction du Portugais. Paris, Dondey-Dupre. 1825 – 9 – $7.50 – fr Orientalistes [480]

ELEMENTS DE LA GRAMMAIRE MANCHOUE / Gabelentz, H. C. von der – Altenbourg. 1832. BU-476 2 – 8 – ne IDC [480]

ELEMENTS DE LA LANGUE FRANCAISE – 1810 – 9 – fr I.C.S. [440]

ELEMENTS DE LA MORALE UNIVERSELLE OU CATECHISME DE LA NATURE / Holbach, Paul-Thiry d' – (D'Holbach series). 1790 – 9 – fr Hachette [170]

ELEMENTS DE LA THEORIE DES FONCTIONS ELLIPTIQUES / Tannery, J & Molk, J – v. 1-4. Paris. 1893-1902. B-1488 2 – 8 – ne IDC [510]

ELEMENTS DE LANGUE PEULE DU NORD-CAMEROUN / Dauzats, Andre – 2e ed. Albi, France: Impr Albigeoise, 1944 – 1 – us Res Libr [490]

ELEMENTS DE MUSIQUE THEORIQUE ET PRATIQUE, SUIVANT LES PRINCIPES DE M RAMEAU / Alembert, Jean Le Rond d' – Nouvelle ed. 1762 – 9 – us Sibley [780]

ELEMENTS DE MUSIQUE THEORIQUE ET PRATIQUE, SUIVANT LES PRINCIPES DE M. RAMEAU / Alembert, Jean Le Rond d' – P-124. 1779 – 9 – ne IDC [780]

ELEMENTS DE POLITIQUE / Regnault-Warin, Jean-Joseph – Bar-le-Duc, Duval et Moucheron, l'an IV de la liberte. 1792 – 9 – fr Hachette [320]

ELEMENTS DE STATISTIQUE GENERALE DU DEPARTEMENT DE LA HAUTE-OIRE ET DICTIONNAIRE DES LIEUX HABITES / Malegue, H – Paris, 1872 – 2mf – 9 – F60.00 – fr F.F.G. [944]

ELEMENTS DE STATISTIQUE HUMAINE OU DEMOGRAPHIE COMPAREE. / Guillard, Achille – Paris, Guillaumin et Cie, 1855, xxxii, 376 p. 5 fiches. (Statistics Series: Demography) – 9 – 12.00 – fr Bibl Nationale [310]

ELEMENTS D'IDEOLOGIE / Destutt de Tracy, Antoine Louis Claude – 3e ed. 1817 – 9 – fr I.C.S. [190]

ELEMENTS D'INSTRUCTION MORALE ET CIVIQUE : DEGRES MOYEN ET SUPERIEUR: LA FAMILLE ET L'ECOLE, LA SOCIETE ET LA PATRIE, LA NATURE HUMAINE ET LA MORALE, LA SOCIETE POLITIQUE / Compayre, Gabriel – nouv ed. Paris: Librairie Classique Paul Delaplane, [ca 1882] – 1mf – 9 – 0-8370-7687-0 – 1986-1687 – us A.T.L.A. [370]

LES ELEMENTS DU REPUBLICANISME / Billaud-Varenne, Jacques N – Premiere partie (seule parue). Paris – 9 – fr Hachette [140]

ELEMENTS ET THEORIE DE L'ARCHITECTURE. / Guadet, Julien – Paris, Aulanier, 1901-04. 4v. in 8 fol., ill. (Architecture Series) – 9 – fr Hachette [720]

ELEMENTS IN BAPTIST DEVELOPMENT : A STUDY OF DENOMINATIONAL CONTRIBUTIONS TO NATIONAL LIFE, CHRISTIAN IDEALS AND WORLD MOVEMENTS / Boone, Ilsley – Boston: Backus Historical Society, 1913 – 1mf – us A.T.L.A. [240]

ELEMENTS IN LUVALE BELIEFS AND RITUALS / White, C M N – 7 – uk Microform Academic [960]

ELEMENTS OF BRITISH ENTOMOLOGY / ed by Shuckard, W E – London, 1839 – 240p – 8 – ne IDC [590]

THE ELEMENTS OF BUSINESS LAW / Huffcut, Wilson; ed by Bogert, George Gleason – Boston: Ginn & Co, 1917 – 4mf – 9 – $6.00 – LLMC 94-270 – us L.L.M.C. [340]

THE ELEMENTS OF CASE MANAGEMENT / Schwarzer, William – Washington: FJC, 1991 – 1mf – 9 – $1.50 – LLMC 95-384 – us L.L.M.C. [340]

ELEMENTS OF CONCHOLOGY / Burrow, E – Z-461 2. 1815 – 8 – ne IDC [590]

ELEMENTS OF CONCHOLOGY / Reeve, LA – Z 744 2. 2 v. 1846-1860 – 8 – ne IDC [590]

ELEMENTS OF DIVINE TRUTH : A SERIES OF LECTURES ON CHRISTIAN THEOLOGY TO SABBATH-SCHOOL TEACHERS / Symington, Andrew – (Includes indexes) – Edinburgh: Johnstone and Hunter, 1854 – 2mf – 9 – 0-8370-6527-5 – 1986-0527 – us A.T.L.A. [240]

ELEMENTS OF ELOCUTION / Walker, John – 1781 2v. 445p. (English Linguistics Series 1500-1800) – 9 – us UMI [400]
ELEMENTS OF ENGLISH / Sheridan, Thomas – 1786. 85p. (English Linguistics Series 1500-1800) – 9 – us UMI [420]
THE ELEMENTS OF ENGLISH GRAMMAR / Ussher, George Neville – 1785. 136p. (English Linguistics Series 1500-1800) – 9 – us UMI [400]
ELEMENTS OF ENTOMOLOGY / Dallas, W.S – London, 1857. vi,424p. Z-1172/2 – 8 – ne IDC [590]
ELEMENTS OF ETHICS / Davis, Noah Knowles – (Includes bibliographical reference & index) – New York: Silver, Burdett, c1907 – 1mf – 9 – 0-8370-6106-7 – 1986-0106 – us A.T.L.A. [170]
THE ELEMENTS OF ETHICS : AN INTRODUCTION TO MORAL PHILOSOPHY / Muirhead, John Henry – New York: Charles Scribner, 1892 – 1mf – 9 – 0-8370-6224-1 – 1986-0224 – us A.T.L.A. [170]
ELEMENTS OF GENERAL AND CHRISTIAN THEOLOGY / Townsend, Luther Tracy – New York: Nelson & Phillips; Cincinnatti: Hitchcock & Walden, 1879 – 1mf – 9 – 0-8370-5656-X – 1985-3656 – us A.T.L.A. [240]
ELEMENTS OF HEBREW SYNTAX BY AN INDUCTIVE METHOD / Harper, William Rainey – (Includes indexes of Hebrew words) – New York: Charles Scribner, 1888 – 1mf – 9 – 0-8370-9241-8 – 1986-3241 – us A.T.L.A. [470]
ELEMENTS OF HINDU ICONOGRAPHY / Gopinatha Rao, T A – 2v. Madras. 1914-16. BI-1135 1 – 9 – ne IDC [280]
ELEMENTS OF INTEGRATED CONTROL OF SORGHUM PESTS – 1979 – 167p – it F.A.O. [660]
THE ELEMENTS OF INTELLECTUAL PHILOSOPHY / De Concilio, Januarius – New York: Montreal: D & J. Sadlier, 1878. 04215. (Pre-1900 Canadiana) – 9 – cn C.I.H.M. [190]
THE ELEMENTS OF INTERNATIONAL LAW : WITH AN ACCOUNT OF ITS ORIGIN, SOURCES AND HISTORICAL DEVELOPMENT / Davis, George B – N.Y./London: Harper & Bros, 1900 – 7mf – 9 – $10.50 – LLMC 92-188 – us L.L.M.C. [340]
ELEMENTS OF JURISPRUDENCE – London: T Payne & Son, 1783 – 2mf – 9 – $3.00 – LLMC 95-170 – us L.L.M.C. [340]
THE ELEMENTS OF JURISPRUDENCE / Holland, Thomas E – 6th ed. Oxford: Clarendon Press, 1893 – 5mf – 9 – $7.50 – LLMC 95-177 – us L.L.M.C. [340]
THE ELEMENTS OF JURISPRUDENCE / Holland, Thomas E – 9th ed. N.Y./London: Oxford Univ Pr, Am.Branch/Henry Frowde, 1900 – 5mf – 9 – $7.50 – LLMC 95-176 – us L.L.M.C. [340]
THE ELEMENTS OF LAW: BEING A COMPREHENSIVE SUMMARY OF AMERICAN CIVIL JURISPRUDENCE / Hilliard, Francis – Boston: Hilliard, Gray, 1835. 345p. LL-1077 – 1 – us L of C Photodup [340]
ELEMENTS OF LIBERTARIAN LEADERSHIP / Read, Leonard E – 1962. 184p. Together with: Government – An Ideal Concept. 1954. 150p. 1 fiche (24x) – 9 – 1.00f – at Libertarian Micro [320]
ELEMENTS OF LIFE INSURANCE / Dawson, Miles M – 3rd ed. Chicago, New York: The Spectator Co, 1911 – 2mf – 9 – $3.00 – LLMC 92-177 – us L.L.M.C. [360]
THE ELEMENTS OF LOGICK / Duncan, William – 1748. 376p. (English Linguistics Series 1500-1800) – 9 – us UMI [160]
THE ELEMENTS OF MARITIME... / Burgh, W de – London, 1868 – 3mf – 1 – ILM-484/1 – ne IDC [327]
THE ELEMENTS OF MERCANTILE LAW / Parsons, Theophilus – 2d ed. Boston: Little, Brown, 1862. 684p. LL-1007 – 1 – us L of C Photodup [340]
ELEMENTS OF ORTHOEPY / Nares, Robert – 1784. 419p. (English Linguistics Series 1500-1800) – 9 – us UMI [420]
ELEMENTS OF PHYSIOPHILOSOPHY / Oken, L – Ray Society. 1847 – 1,7 – uk Microform Academic [100]
ELEMENTS OF POLITICAL ECONOMY / Mill, James – London: Baldwin, Cradock, and Joy, 3rd rev ed 1826 – 1 roll – 1 – 1-55879-351-8 – uk Libr Preservation [320]
ELEMENTS OF RELIGIOUS PEDAGOGY (CCC260) = TSUNG CHIAO CHIAO HSUEH FA TA KANG / P'eng, Ch'ang-lin – (In Chinese) – Shanghai: Christian Literature Society, 1925 – 1r – 1 – 1984-6599 – us A.T.L.A. [200]
THE ELEMENTS OF REMEMBRANCE AND CELEBRATION IN CHRISTIAN WORSHIP AND EDUCATION / Oswalt, Lynn T – 1981 – 1 – 8.56 – us Baptist [240]
ELEMENTS OF RHETORIC : COMPRISING THE SUBSTANCE OF THE ARTICLE IN THE ENCYCLOPAEDIA METROPOLITANA: WITH ADDITIONS, &C / Whately, Richard – London: John Murray; Oxford: J. Parker, 2nd ed 1828 – 1 roll – 1 – 1-55879-359-3 – uk Libr Preservation [420]
ELEMENTS OF RIGHT AND OF THE LAW : TO WHICH IS ADDED AN HISTORICAL AND CRITICAL ESSAY UPON THE SEVERAL THEORIES OF JURISPRUDENCE / Smith, George H – 2nd ed. Chicago: Callaghan, 1887 – 5mf – 9 – $7.50 – LLMC 95-210 – us L.L.M.C. [340]
ELEMENTS OF SPEECH / Holder, William – 1669. 180p. (English Linguistics Series 1500-1800) – 9 – us UMI [400]
THE ELEMENTS OF SPEECH / Herries, John – 1773. 279p. (English Linguistics Series 1500-1800) – 9 – us UMI [400]
[ELEMENTS OF TELUGU GRAMMAR] / Papayya Sastri, B – Anakapalle: SVRV Press, 1906 – 1 – us Res Libr [490]
THE ELEMENTS OF TEXAS PLEADING / Roberts, Oran Milo – Austin: Jones, 1890. 83 2p. LL-1397 – 1 – us L of C Photodup [340]
ELEMENTS OF THE CULTURE OF THE CIRCUMPOLAR ZONE / Bogoras, W G – BN 148 2. 1929 – 8 – ne IDC [306]
THE ELEMENTS OF THE HIGHER CRITICISM / Zenos, Andrew Constantinides – New York: Funk & Wagnalls, 1895.1 fiche – 9 – us A.T.L.A. [240]
THE ELEMENTS OF THE IRISH LANGUAGE / MacCurtin, Hugh – 1728. 168p. (English Linguistics Series 1500-1800) – 9 – us UMI [490]
ELEMENTS OF THE LAW OF BAILMENTS AND CARRIERS, INCLUDING PLEDGE AND PAWN AND INNKEEPERS / Van Zile, Philip Taylor – Chicago, Callaghan, 1908. 856 p. LL-1510 – 1 – us L of C Photodup [340]
ELEMENTS OF THE LAW OF DAMAGES. / Sedgwick, Arthur George – 2d ed. Boston: Little, Brown, 1909. 368p. LL-1017 – 1 – us L of C Photodup [340]
ELEMENTS OF THE LAW OF NEGOTIABLE CONTRACTS / Johnson, Elias Finley – Ann Arbor, Mich., Wahr, 1898. 707 p. LL-435 – 1 – us L of C Photodup [340]
ELEMENTS OF THE LAW OF PARTNERSHIP / Mechem, Floyd Russell – (2d ed. Chicago: Callaghan, 1920. 501p. LL-512) – 2d ed. Chicago: Callaghan, 1920. 501p. LL-645 – 1 – us L of C Photodup [340]
ELEMENTS OF THE STRUCTURE AND TERMINOLOGY OF AGRICULTURAL EDUCATION IN POLAND / Wieczorek, Tadeusz – 1984 – 181p – 9 – 92-3-102156-7 – fr UNESCO [630]
ELEMENTS OF THE STRUCTURE OF AGRICULTURAL EDUCATION IN THE PHILIPPINES / Mancebo, Samuel T – 1984 – 66p – 9 – 92-3-102162-1 – fr UNESCO [630]
ELEMENTS OF THE STRUCTURE OF AGRICULTURAL EDUCATION IN THE UNITED STATES OF AMERICA – 1983 – 72p – 9 – 92-3-102056-0 – fr UNESCO [630]
ELEMENTS OF THEOLOGY NATURAL AND REVEALED / Fairchild, James Harris – (Includes general index and index of biblical passages cited) – Oberlin, O[hio]: Edward J Goodrich, c1892 – 1mf – 9 – 0-8370-3793-X – 1985-1793 – us A.T.L.A. [210]
THE ELEMENTS OF TORTS / Cooley, Thomas McIntyre – Chicago, Callaghan, 1895. 335 p. LL-608 – 1 – us L of C Photodup [340]
ELEMENTS POUR UNE ETUDE DU SYSTEME ADVERBIAL DU FRANCAIS CONTEMPORAIN / Lenepveu, Veronique – 1mf – 9 – 10295 – fr Atelier National [440]
ELENCHUS FUNGORUM / Fries, E M – 2v. Gryphiswaldiae. 1828. B-5020 2 – 8 – ne IDC [580]
ELENCHUS FUNGORUM. CONTINUATIO 1 ET 2: 1786-1789 / Batsch, A J G C – Halae. 1783. B-2341 2 – 8 – ne IDC [580]
ELENCHUS PLANTARUM HORTI BOTANICI J. CAR. DINEGRO / Viviani, D – Genuae. 1802. B-5791 2 – 8 – ne IDC [580]
ELENCHUS PLANTARUM HORTI BOTANICI MONSPELIENSIS / Broussonet, P M A – Monspelii. 1805. B-5862 2 – 8 – ne IDC [580]
ELENCHUS PLANTARUM HORTI REGII BOTANICI MATRITENSIS / Cavanilles, A J – Madrid, 1803 – 1mf – 9 – ne IDC [580]
ELENCHUS PLANTARUM NOVARUM MINUSQUE COGNITARUM, QUAD IN ITINERE LEGIT / Boissier, E P – Geneve. 1838. B-5039 2 – 8 – ne IDC [580]
ELENCO DELLE PLANTE CRESCENTI NEL, CONTORNI DI TORINO / Balbis, G B – Torino. 1801. B-6452 – 8 – ne IDC [580]
Elenco, Generale Delle *see* PARROCCHIE D'ITALIA
ELEND UND GROESSE UNSERER TAGE : ANEKDOTEN, 1933-1947 / Weiskopf, Franz Carl – Berlin: Dietz, 1950 – 1r – 1 – us U.W. Library [880]
Eler, A *see*
– TROIS QUATUORS...OP. 11
– TROIS TRIOS (2 VLNS, VC)
Elert, W *see* JACOB BOEHMES DEUTSCHES CHRISTENTUM
Eles, G T *see* LE PRINCIPE DE L'UNANIMITE
ELET ES IRODALOM – Budapest, 1979-1982 – 4r – 1 – DM300.00 – gw Mikro Press [949]
ELETRORURAL : ORGAO OFICIAL DA CONFEDERACAO BRASILEIRA DAS COOPERATIVAS DE ELETRIFICACAO RURAL-CONBRACER – [s.l.], Maio 1978-Dez 1980; Jul 1981-Dez 1982 – 1 – bl Biblioteca [072]
Elets, I Ulii Lukianovich *see* NA KRESTNOM PUTI
L'ELETTRICISTA – Rome, 1902 – 28ft – 1 – uk British Libr Newspaper [073]
L'ELETTRICISTA – Rome, 1903-09 – 3r – 1 – uk British Libr Newspaper [073]
ELEUTHERIA – Athens. Greece. -d. 19 Nov 1944-Dec 1965. (1944-46 very imperfect). (76 reels) – 1 – uk British Libr Newspaper [949]
Eleutherobion, Saint *see* VOM WARHAFFTIGEN TAUFF JOANNIS, CHRISTI
ELEUTHERON BEMA – Athens, Greece. -d. 1 Jan-31 Dec 1928; 1 Jan 1938-22 April 1941. Lacking July 1939. 18 reels – 1 – uk British Libr Newspaper [949]
L'ELEVAGE DU CHEVAL EN CANADA / Duchene, John D – Quebec: Imp. Darveau, Jos. Beauchamp..., 1901. SEM105P471 – 2mf – 9 – Can$4.50 – cn Bibl Nat [636]
L'ELEVAGE INTENSIF DES LARVES ET DES JUVENILES DU BAR (DICENTRAXILIUS LABRAX (L.). DONNEES BIOLOGIQUES, ZOOTECHNIQUES ET PATHOLOGIQUES / Calleca Barahona Fernandes, MH – 9 – F70.00 – fr Ethnologie [590]
ELEVATIONS ET MOTETS A 2 ET 3 VOIX / Brossard, S de – 1699 – 9 – us Sibley [780]
ELEVATIONS POETIQUES / Burque, F-X. – Quebec: J.-P. Garneau de la Librairie Garneau: Imprimerie Ernest Tremblay, [1923?]. SEM105P1511 – 7mf – 9 – Can$15.75 – cn Bibl Nat [440]
ELEVEN LETTERS FROM THE LATE REV. MR. HERVEY TO THE REV. MR. JOHN WESLEY, CONTAINING AN ANSWER TO THAT GENTLEMAN'S 'REMARKS ON THERON AND ASPASIO'... / Hervey, James – London, 1765 – 4mf – 9 – MP-430/1 – ne IDC [240]
ELEVEN POINTS RIVER, SHANNON COUNTY / Baptist Associations. Missouri – 1973-87, 1981-87. 596p – 1 – 23.84 – us Baptist [240]
ELEVEN SELECTED PAPERS / Sampaio, G – 6445. 1917-1927 – 9 – ne IDC [025]
ELEVENTH CENSUS (1890): SPECIAL SCHEDULES ENUMERATING UNION VETERANS AND WIDOWS OF UNION VETERANS OF THE CIVIL WAR / U.S. Bureau of the Census – 118 rolls. M123 – 1 – us Nat'l Archives [324]
ELEVENTH CENSUS OF THE UNITED STATES / U.S. Bureau of the Census – 1890. 3 rolls. M407 – 1 – us Nat'l Archives [310]
ELEVENTH HOUR EMERGENCY BULLETIN – London, England. Eleventh Hour. March 1934-17 July 1935 – 1r – 1 – uk British Libr Newspaper [941]
ELF JAHRE GOUVERNEUR IN DEUTSCH-SUEDWESTAFRIKA / Leutwein, Theodor – 3. Aufl. Berlin: E S Mittler, 1908 – 1 – us Res Libr [920]
ELF PREUSSISCHE OFFIZIERE : NOVELLE / Paulus, Helmut – Dresden: W Heyne, 1941 – 1r – 1 – us U.W. Library [830]
Elfe, Thomas *see* ACCOUNT BOOK
ELFSBORGS LANS ALLEHANDA – Vanersborg, Sweden. 1984- – 1 – sw Kungliga [072]
ELFSBORGS LANS ANNONSBLAD – Skara, Vanersborg, Sweden. 1886-1984 – 1 – sw Kungliga [072]
ELFSBORGS LANS TIDNING *see* ALINGSAS TIDNING
Elger, W den *see*
– ZINNE-BEELDEN DER LIEFDE
ELGIN AND MORAYSHIRE COURIER – Scotland. -w. June 1849-Dec 1851; Jan 1855-Dec 1860; Jan 1869-June 1874. 8 reels – 1 – uk British Libr Newspaper [072]
ELGIN COURANT – Scotland. -w. 1845, 1866, 1869, 1873, 1875-79. 9 reels – 1 – uk British Libr Newspaper [072]
ELGIN COURIER – Scotland. -w. 13 July 1827-3 July 1829; April 1845-Dec 1847; Jan-May 1849. I 1 2 reels – 1 – uk British Libr Newspaper [072]
ELGIN RECORDER – Elgin, OR. -w 16 Aug 1895-17 Sep 1980. – 21r – 1 – us U.O. Library [071]
ELGIN REVIEW – Elgin, NE. -w. Jan. 1897-Apr. 1903. Incomplete; May 1903- – 1 – us NE Hist [071]
ELGINSHIRE, 1837 : BRITISH ISLES CENSUS DIRECTORIES PROJECT, SCOTLAND. VOL 37 – 1mf – 9 – A$9.00 – at Vine [941]
Elguero, Francisco *see* MUSEO INTELECTUAL. VANGUARDIA. MEXICO, 1928
ELH – (v38- Mar 1971- 5,6. v42- Spr 1975-9) – v1- 1934- – 1 – us UMI [420]
EL-HACK : JOURNAL POLITIQUE HEBDOMADAIRE. ORGANE DE DEFENSE DES INTERETS MUSULMANS – 2e. Oran. n1-46. 1911-12 – 1 – fr A.C.R.P.P. [073]
El-Hage Rahmat-Ullah Effendi de Dehli *see* IDH-HAR-HAQQ
ELI : AN ORATORIO / Costa, M – (Vocal score) – Boston: O Ditson, [1858?] – 1 – us Sibley [780]
ELI AND SYBIL JONES : THEIR LIFE AND WORK / Jones, Rufus M – Philadelphia: H.T. Coates, c1889 – 1mf – us A.T.L.A. [240]
Eliade, Mircea *see* IMAGES ET SYMBOLES: ESSAIS SUR LE SYMBOLISME MAGICO-RELIGIEUX
Elias de Tejada, F *see*
– EL HEGELISMO JURIDICO ESPANOL. MADRID, 1944
– EL RACISMO. BREVE HISTORIA DE SUS DOCTRINAS
ELIAS DE TEJADA, F. LAS DOCTRINAS POLITICAS DE LA EDAD MEDIA. MADRID, 1946 / Iturrios, J – Madrid: Razon y Fe, 1947 – 1 – sp Bibl Santa Ana [320]
Elias de Tejada, Francisco *see*
– LAS DOCTRINAS POLITICAS DE EUGENIO MARIA DE HOSTOS
– DIE GEBURTSSTUNDE...DE HEYELTE
– EL REINO DE GALICIA, TOMO 1. VIGO 1966
– SOCIOLOGIA DEL AFRICA NEGRA
Elias de Tejada Spinola, Francisco *see*
– LAS DOCTRINAS POLITICAS EN PORTUGAL (EDAD MEDIA)
– ELEFANTES BLANCOS, PAGINAS DORADAS. NUEVAS NOTICIAS DE INDOCHINA
– ENCRUCIJADA JURIDICA DE LA COSTA DE MARFIL
– LA FILOSOFIA JURIDICA DEL PROFESOR DE ASIS GARROTE
– LA FILOSOFIA JURIDICA EN LA ESPANA ACTUAL
– GERONIMO CASTILLO DE BOVADILLA
– EL HEGELISMO JURIDICO ESPANOL
– IDEAS POLITICAS DE ANGEL GANIVET
– LA MONARQUIA TRADICIONAL
ELIAS DE TEJADA SPINOLA, FRANCISCO. LA TRADICION GALLEGA. PROLOGO DE R. OTERO PEDRAYO. MADRID, 1944 / Marquez, Gabino – Madrid: Razon y Fe, 1945 – 1 – sp Bibl Santa Ana [946]
Elias Garcia, A *see* AS MOEDAS VISIGODAS DA LUSITANIA
Elias, H B *see* DIPALU ARUS REVOLUSI, KISSAH NJATA
ELIAS, JAHVE, UND BAAL / Gunkel, Hermann – Tuebingen: J.C.B. Mohr, 1906. 1 fiche – 9 – us A.T.L.A. [240]
Elias Perez, Alberto *see* EL DESPIDO DEL TRABAJADOR (COMENTARIOS DEL DECRETO DE 26 DE OCTUBRE DE 1956). MANUAL DE LA EMPRESA. 1
Eliasewich, H Z *see*
– DEVIR

Eliashevich, I Ya *see* S KRESTOM I EVANGELIEM PROTIV KOLKHOZOV
ELIE GOULET DE LA SOCIETE DES ECRIVAINS CANADIENS : BIO-BIBLIOGRAPHIE ANALYTIQUE / Allen, Marie-B – 1959. SEM105P4 – 3mf – 9 – cn Bibl Nat [400]
THE ELIGIBILITY OF WOMEN NOT A SCRIPTURAL QUESTION – Methodist Review, 75, 1891 – 9 – us A.T.L.A. [240]
EL-IHIA : REVUE ARABE LITTERAIRE, BIMENSUELLE – Alger. n1-7. fevr-mai 1907 – 1 – fr A.C.R.P.P. [073]
Elijah, Gaon of Vilna *see* HAGGAHOT YERUSHALMI
Elijah Wadsworth Family *see* PAPERS, MS 2729
ELIM BAPTIST CHURCH. MACON, GEORGIA : CHURCH RECORDS – 1843-68, 1926-63 – 1 – 26.91 – us Baptist [240]
ELIM: OR, HYMNS OF HOLY REFRESHMENT / Huntington, Frederic Dan – 1865 – 9 – us A.T.L.A. [240]
ELIMA – Kinshasa: Essolomwa-Nkoy Ea Linganga, [dec 31 1972/jan 1/2 1973-1977] – 30r – 1 – us Res Libr [072]
ELIMINATE ADMINISTRATIVE DISCHARGES IN LIEU OF COURT MARTIAL : GUIDANCE FOR PLEA AGREEMENTS IN MILITARY COURTS IS NEEDED; REPORT TO THE CONGRESS BY THE COMPTROLLER GENERAL OF THE U.S. – Washington: General Accounting Office, Apr 28 1978 (FPCD-77-47) – 1mf – 9 – $1.50 – LLMC 96-071 – us L.L.M.C. [340]
Eliodoro Valle, Rafael *see* EL CONVENTO DE TEPOTZOTLAN...1924
Eliot, Charles Norton Edgecumbe *see* TURKEY IN EUROPE, BY ODYSSEUS PSEUD
Eliot, George *see*
- DANIEL DERONDA
- IMPRESSIONS OF THEOPHRASTUS SUCH
- MIDDLEMARCH
- ROMOLA
- SILAS MARNER
- THE SPANISH GYPSY, A POEM

Eliot, John *see* THE ENGLISH SCHOOL
ELIOT NESS PAPERS *see* NESS, ELIOT, PAPERS, MS 3699
Eliot, Samuel *see* HISTORY OF LIBERTY
Eliot, Simon *see* PUBLISHERS' CIRCULAR 1837-1900
Eliot, William G *see*
- A DISCOURSE
- DISCOURSES ON THE UNITY OF GOD, AND OTHER SUBJECTS
- LECTURES TO YOUNG WOMEN

EL-IQTICAD EL-DJAZAIRI : L'ECONOMIE ALGERIENNE. ORGANE DE L'UNION GENERALE DU COMMERCE ALGERIEN – Alger. n1. oct 1956 – 1 – fr A.C.R.P.P. [073]
ELISA OU LE VOYAGE AU MONT BERNARD / Saint-Cyr, Reveroni & Cherubini – French Theatre Series. Paris. Huet, Denne et Charon. s.d – 9 – fr Hachette [820]
ELISABETH SETON / Conan, Laure – Montreal, 1903. SEM105P914 – 2mf – 9 – Can$4.50 – cn Bibl Nat [240]
ELISABETH VON ENGLAND : SCHAUSPIEL / Bruckner, Ferdinand – 8. und 9. Aufl. Berlin: S Fischer, 1932 – 1r – 1 – us U.W. Library [820]
Elisabeth-de-la-Trinite, Soeur *see* BIBLIOGRAPHIE ANALYTIQUE DE L'OEUVRE DE MONSEIGNEUR ALBERT TESSIER, P.D. DE LA SOCIETE ROYALE DU CANADA, DE LA SOCIETE DES DIX, VISITEUR EN CHEF DES INSTITUTS FAMILIAUX...
Elisaeus *see* HISTORY OF VARTAN
ELISCA OU L'AMOUR MATERNEL / Favieres & Gretry – French Theatre Series. Paris. Au Bureau General du Mercure de France, et Cailleau, an VII. 1799 – 9 – fr Hachette [820]
ELISE RUEDIGER GEB. VON HOHENHAUSEN : EIN BILD IHRES LEBENS UND SCHAFFENS / Esche, Annelinde – Emsdetten, 1939 – 71p – 9 – DM48.00 – 3-89349-004-3 – gw Hänsel [430]
ELISE VON HOHENHAUSEN : EINE WESTFAELISCHE DICHTERIN UND UEBERSETZERIN / Hackenberg, Fritz – (Enthaelt beide Teile von Hackenbergs Dissertation) – Muenster, 1913-1915 – 107p – 9 – DM48.00 – 3-89349-005-1 – gw Hänsel [430]
ELISE VON HOHENHAUSEN, GEB. VON OCHS (1789-1857) / Haensel-Hohenhausen, Markus – 1992 – 103p – 9 – DM98.00 – 3-89349-530-4 – gw Hänsel [430]
L'ELITE – Beauharnois, Canada. 14 jul 1965; v1 n14. 10 nov 1965 – 1r – 1 – Can$25.00 – cn Can Microfilming [072]
ELITE ATHLETES IN FLOW : THE PSYCHOLOGY OF OPTIMAL SPORT EXPERIENCE / Jackson, Susan A & Gould, Daniel – 1992 – 3mf – 9 – $12.00 – us Microform Publ [150]
THE ELITE DIRECTORY OF VANCOUVER – Vancouver: The Elite Directory, 1908 – 1r – 1 – cn U.B.C. Preserve [910]
ELITES Y DESARROLLO EN AMERICA LATINA / Lipset, SM & Solari, A E – Buenos Aires: Paidos, 2nd ed 1971 – 1 – CSUXAHZ3591-B – us Hoover Inst Photo [150]
ELIXIR SALUTIS / Daffy, A – M 340. 1673 – 9 – ne IDC [610]
ELIZABETH 1 AND THE ENGLISH PARLIAMENT / Walter, Beate – 1994 – 1mf – DM60.00 – 3-8267-2000-8 – gw Hänsel [941]
ELIZABETH BAPTIST CHURCH. SHELBY, NORTH CAROLINA : CHURCH RECORDS – 1910-54. Bulletins. 1955-63 – 1 – $47.79 – us Baptist [240]
ELIZABETH GASKELL AND VICTORIAN LITERATURE : MANUSCRIPTS FROM THE JOHN RYLANDS UNIVERSITY LIBRARY, MANCHESTER – 1 – us Primary [920]
ELIZABETH HERALD – Elizabeth, PA. -w 1889-1912 – 13 – $25.00r – us I.M.R. [071]
Elizabeth, New Jersey *see* MISCELLANEOUS EARLY NEWSPAPERS
THE ELIZABETHAN CLERGY AND THE SETTLEMENT OF RELIGION, 1558-1564 / Gee, Henry – Oxford: Clarendon Press, 1898 – 1mf – us A.T.L.A. [240]
ELIZABETHAN PART-SONG BOOKS / Carlisle Cathedral. Library – 1 – uk Microform Academic [780]
THE ELIZABETHAN PRAYER-BOOK AND ORNAMENTS : WITH AN APPENDIX OF DOCUMENTS / Gee, Henry – London; New York: Macmillan, 1902 – 1mf – us A.T.L.A. [240]
THE ELIZABETHAN RELIGIOUS SETTLEMENT : A STUDY OF CONTEMPORARY DOCUMENTS / Birt, Henry Norbert – London: G. Bell, 1907 – 2mf – us A.T.L.A. [240]
ELIZABETHTON FIRST BAPTIST CHURCH. ELIZABETHTON, TENNESSEE : CHURCH RECORDS – 1842-1943 – 1 – 93.51 – us Baptist [240]
ELIZABETHTOWN BAPTIST CHURCH. BLADEN ASSOCIATION. NORTH CAROLINA : CHURCH RECORDS – 1903-24 – 1 – 5.00 – us Baptist [240]
ELIZABETHTOWN CHRONICLE – Elizabethtown, PA. -w 1928-1983 – 13 – $25.00r – us I.M.R. [071]
ELK COUNTY GAZETTE – St. Marys. Pa. 1873-1915 – 1 – us UMI [071]
ELK CREEK BAPTIST CHURCH. STEWART COUNTY. CUMBERLAND CITY, TENNESSEE : CHURCH RECORDS – Feb 1961-Aug 1967 – 1 – 5.76 – us Baptist [240]
ELK CREEK BAPTIST CHURCH. STEWART COUNTY. CUMBERLAND CITY, TENNESSEE : CHURCH RECORDS – Feb 1961-Aug 1967 – 1 – 5.76 – us Baptist [240]
ELK CREEK HERALD – Elk Creek, NE. -w. Oct. 1895-Dec. 1898; Mar. 1899; Jul. 1900-Apr. 1906; Sep. 1906-Aug. 1910 – 1 – us NE Hist [071]
ELK DEMOCRAT – Ridgway, PA. -w 1869-1912 – 13 – $25.00r – us I.M.R. [071]
ELK GROVE CITIZEN – Elk Grove, CA. 1909-1912; 1947-1965; 1968 – 64+ r – 1 – $3,200.00 ($150.00y) – B05030 – us Library Micro [071]
ELK MOUNTAIN PILOT – Crested Butte. Col. -w. 1880-85 – 1 – us UMI [071]
Elkan, L *see*
- FLORA DER PROVINZ PREUSSEN
- TENTAMEN MONOGRAPHIAE GENERIS PAPAVER

ELKHORN EXCHANGE – Elkhorn, NE. -w. Nov. 1892; Jan. 1907; Jul. 1914-Jan. 1918 – 1 – us NE Hist [071]
ELKHORN VALLEY MIRROR – Norfolk, NE. -w. May 1926-May 1927 – 1 – us NE Hist [071]
Elkin, Aldophus Peter *see* LES ABORIGENES AUSTRALIENS
Elkina, D et al *see* DOLOI NEGRAMOTNOST
Elkins, Frank *see* THE COMPLETE SKI GUIDE.
ELKO BAPTIST CHURCH. ELKO, SOUTH CAROLINA : CHURCH RECORDS – 1896-1971 – 1 – 38.26 – us Baptist [240]
ELKO DAILY FREE PRESS – Elko, NV. 1876-77; 1883-90; 1892-1918; 1928- – 162+ r – 1 UN04494 – $8,100.00 ($300.00y) – us Library Micro [071]
ELKTON BAPTIST CHURCH. ELKTON, KENTUCKY : CHURCH RECORDS – 1825-1909 – 1 – 27.54 – us Baptist [240]
Ellbogen, Ismar *see* AUS DEM LEBEN DER JUDEN DEUTSCHLANDS IM MITTELALTER
ELLEH TOLEDOT KEREN MOSHEH MONTEFIORE / Meisl, J – Jerusalem. 1939. BJ-27-45 1 – 9 – ne IDC [320]
Ellenberger, J S *see* LEGISLATIVE HISTORY OF THE SECURITIES ACT OF 1933 AND SECURITIES EXCHANGE ACT OF 1934
THE ELLENDALE STAR – Ellendale, NV. 1909 – 1r – 1 – $50.00 – U04839 – us Library Micro [071]
Ellerd, Andria *see* VARIABLES RELATED TO KNOWLEDGE LEVELS OF AGING AND PLANNING FOR FUTURE AGING OF TEXAS HIGH SCHOOL GRADUATES
Ellerker, R *see* COLECCION DE LOS MAS PRECIOSOS ADELANTAMIENTOS DE LA MEDICINA...
Ellerman, J R *see* FAMILIES AND GENERA OF LIVING RODENTS
Elles, G L *see* A MONOGRAPH OF BRITISH GRAPTOLITES
ELLESMERE PORT PIONEER – 1945-46; 1950; 1986-96 – 34 1/2r – 1 – uk British Libr Newspaper [072]
Ellice, Edward *see* LES COMMUNICATIONS DE MERCATOR
Ellicott, Charles J *see*
- ADDRESSES ON THE REVISED VERSION OF HOLY SCRIPTURE
- CHRISTUS COMPROBATOR: THE TESTIMONY OF CHRIST TO THE OLD TESTAMENT: SEVEN ADDRESSES
- CRITICAL AND GRAMMATICAL COMMENTARY ON ST PAUL'S EPISTLE TO THE EPHESIANS
- FOUNDATIONS OF SACRED STUDY: SECOND SERIES
- HISTORICAL LECTURES ON THE LIFE OF OUR LORD JESUS CHRIST
- ST. PAUL'S EPISTLE TO THE GALATIANS: A CRITICAL AND GRAMMATICAL COMMENTARY
- ST. PAUL'S EPISTLE TO THE PHILLIPIANS, COLOSSIANS, AND PHILEMON
- ST. PAUL'S EPISTLES TO THE THESSALONIANS: CRITICAL AND GRAMMATICAL COMMENTARY

Ellicott, Charles John *see*
- THE GOSPEL ACCORDING TO ST. LUKE
- THE SECOND EPISTLE TO THE CORINTHIANS

ELLIL IN SUMER UND AKKAD / Noetscher, F – Hannover. 1927. BNE-408 1 – 9 – ne IDC [930]
Ellinger, Georg *see* PHILIPP MELANCHTHON
Ellingwood, Albert R *see* DEPARTMENTAL COOPERATION IN STATE GOVERNMENT
ELLINIKOS PHILOLOGIKOS SYLLOGOS – v6. 1871/1872; v8-33. 1873/1874-1910/1911; v34. 1912/1913. (Parartema) – 121mf – ne IDC [400]
ELLINOR; OR, THE WORLD AS IT IS : A NOVEL / Hanway, Mary Ann – London: Printed at the Minerva Press, for William Lane, 1798 – 2 rolls – 1 – 1-55879-250-3 – uk Libr Preservation [830]
Ellinwood, DeWitt *see*
- [PAPERS, 1913?-1924?]
- PAPERS, 1914-1919
- PAPERS, 1914-1920
- PAPERS, 1916-1925
- PAPERS, 1917?-1957
- SELECTIONS FROM THE HOME POLITICAL FILES, 1915-1919 OF THE NATIONAL ARCHIVES OF INDIA
- SELECTIONS FROM THE HOME POLITICAL FILES JULY 1914-1916, 1918, AND THE ARMY DEPARTMENT FILES 1914-MAY 1919

Ellinwood, Frank Field *see*
- THE GREAT CONQUEST
- QUESTIONS AND PHASES OF MODERN MISSIONS

Elliot, Charles Burke *see* AN OUTLINE OF THE LAW OF INSURANCE
Elliot, Daniel Giraud *see*
- A MONOGRAPH OF THE PARADISE IDAE...
- A MONOGRAPH OF THE PHASIANIDAE, OR FAMILY OF THE PHEASANTS
- THE NEW AND HERE TO FORE UNFIGURED SPECIES OF THE BIRDS OF NORTH AMERICA
- NORTH AMERICAN SHORE BIRDS...
- THE WILD FOWL OF THE UNITED STATES AND BRITISH POSSESSIONS, OR, THE SWAN, GEESE, DUCKS, AND MERGANSERS OF NORTH AMERICA: WITH ACCOUNTS OF THEIR HABITS, NESTING, MIGRATIONS, AND DISPERSIONS...

Elliot, Edward *see* BIOGRAPHICAL STORY OF THE CONSTITUTION
Elliot, George *see* GOD IS SPIRIT, GOD IS LOVE
Elliot, H W *see* AN ARCTIC PROVINCE
Elliot, Henry Miers *see* MEMOIRS ON THE HISTORY, FOLK-LORE, AND DISTRIBUTION OF THE RACES OF THE NORTH WESTERN PROVINCES OF INDIA..
Elliot, James Rupert *see* THE TRADE RELATIONS OF THE FARMERS OF NOVA SCOTIA
Elliot, Jonathan *see* THE DEBATES IN THE SEVERAL STATE CONVENTIONS ON THE ADOPTION OF THE FEDERAL CONSTITUTION, AS RECOMMENDED BY THE GENERAL CONVENTION AT PHILADELPHIA, IN 1787
Elliot, R H *see* SCLERO-CORNEAL TREPHINING IN THE OPERATIVE TREATMENT OF GLAUCOMA
Elliot, Robert Henry *see* THE EXPERIENCE OF A PLANTER IN THE JUNGLES OF MYSORE
Elliot, S R *see* MODERN SCIENCE AND THE ILLUSIONS OF PROFESSOR BERGSON
Elliot, W *see* FULL TEXT OF JUDGE ELLIOT'S JUDGEMENT IN THE LONDON ELECTION CASE, 1892
Elliot, William Fitzwilliam *see*
- FURTHER ESSAYS ON BORDER BALLADS
- THE TRUSTWORTHINESS OF BORDER BALLADS

Elliotson, J *see* NUMEROUS CASES OF SURGICAL OPERATIONS WITHOUT PAIN IN THE MESMERIC STATE
Elliott, Charles *see*
- THE BIBLE AND SLAVERY
- GENERAL INTRODUCTION TO THE PROPHETIC WRITINGS OF THE OLD TESTAMENT
- HISTORY OF THE GREAT SECESSION FROM THE METHODIST EPISCOPAL CHURCH IN THE YEARS 1845
- OLD TESTAMENT PROPHECY...AND NEW TESTAMENT FULFILMENT
- SOUTH-WESTERN METHODISM
- A TREATISE ON THE INSPIRATION OF THE HOLY SCRIPTURES
- TREATISE ON THE INSPIRATION OF THE HOLY SCRIPTURES
- A VINDICATION OF THE MOSAIC AUTHORSHIP OF THE PENTATEUCH
- VINDICATION OF THE MOSAIC AUTHORSHIP OF THE PENTATEUCH

Elliott, Edward Bishop *see* APOCALYPSIS ALFORDIANA, OR, FIVE LETTERS TO...H. ALFORD, DEAN OF CANTERBURY
Elliott, Ernest Eugene *see*
- MAKING GOOD IN THE LOCAL CHURCH
- THE PROBLEM OF LAY LEADERSHIP

Elliott, George Babington *see* OUT WEST-STOP THE EXODUS: BEING A BRIEF EXPOSE OF THE FRAUDS OF THE UNITED STATES IMMIGRATION AGENTS, AND PAMPHLETS
Elliott, Isaac H *see* RECORD OF THE SERVICES OF ILLINOIS SOLDIERS IN THE BLACK HAWK WAR, 1831-32 AND IN THE MEXICAN WAR, 1846-48
Elliott, Juliet Georgiana *see* ACCOUNT BOOK
Elliott, R G *see* LETTERS
Elliott, S *see* A SKETCH OF THE BOTANY OF SOUTH-CAROLINA AND GEORGIA
Elliott-Binns, L E *see* GALILEAN CHRISTIANITY
ELLIPSE – Sherbrooke. no 1-52. 1969- – 9 – Can$20.00y – cn Micromedia [073]
ELLIS : BATAVIA IN POST-WAR DAYS – Batavia, 1948. 48p – 1mf – 9 – ne IDC [950]
Ellis *see*
- HISTORY OF LANCASTER COUNTY
- THE PHILOSOPHICAL WORKS OF FRANCIS BACON, BARON OF VERULAM, VISCOUNT ST ALBANS.
- RUSSKIE SIMVOLISTY

Ellis, A D *see* AUSTRALIA AND THE LEAGUE OF NATIONS
Ellis, Alfred Burdon *see* HISTORY OF THE FIRST WEST INDIA REGIMENT
Ellis, Alfredo *see*
- FEIJO E A PRIMEIRA METADE DO SECULO 19
- POPULACOES PAULISTAS

Ellis, C A A *see* BUSINESS, GOVERNMENT AND ALL OF US
Ellis, Charles Mayo *see* AN ESSAY ON TRANSCENDENTALISM
Ellis County. Kansas *see* REGISTER OF MARRIAGES, BIRTHS AND DEATHS IN ELLIS COUNTY
Ellis County. Kansas. Big Creek Township. Justice of the Peace *see* CRIMINAL AND CIVIL DOCKETS
ELLIS COUNTY NEWS – Hays. Kan. 1899-1904; 1915-1955 – 1 – us UMI [071]
ELLIS COUNTY NEWS-REPUBLICAN – Hays. Kansas. -w. 1912-14 – 1 – us UMI [071]
ELLIS COUNTY STAR – Hays. Kan. 1876-1877; 1879-1881 – 1 – us UMI [071]
Ellis, Edward Sylvester *see* PONTIAC, CHIEF OF THE OTTAWAS: A TALE OF THE SIEGE OF DETROIT
Ellis, Franklin *see*
- HISTORY OF FAYETTE COUNTY
- HISTORY OF MONMOUTH COUNTY

Ellis, G *see* MEMOIR OF A MAP OF THE COUNTRIES COMPREHENDED BETWEEN THE BLACK SEA AND THE CASPIAN
Ellis, George E *see*
- AN ADDRESS DELIVERED IN THE FIRST CHURCH, SALEM, AT THE FUNERAL SERVICES OF CHARLES W. UPHAM, JUNE 18, 1875
- A HALF-CENTURY OF THE UNITARIAN CONTROVERSY
- HISTORY OF THE BATTLE OF BUNKER'S (BREED'S) HILL, ON JUNE 17, 1775: FROM AUTHENTIC SOURCES IN PRINT AND MANUSCRIPT
- THE PURITAN AGE AND RULE IN THE COLONY OF THE MASSACHUSETTS BAY, 1629-1685

Ellis, George W. et al *see* KING PHILIP'S WAR
Ellis, Griffith Ogden *see*
- BLACKSTONE QUIZZER B.
- QUIZZER NO. 2...BEING QUESTIONS AND ANSWERS ON CRIMINAL LAW.
- QUIZZER NO. 10...BEING QUESTIONS AND ANSWERS ON BILLS, NOTES, AND CHEQUES.

Ellis, H *see*
- CHRONICA (RS13)
- MONASTICON ANGLICANUM

Ellis, Harriet W *see* OUR EASTERN SISTERS AND THEIR MISSIONARY HELPERS
Ellis, Havelock *see*
- AFFIRMATIONS
- MAN AND WOMAN

Ellis, J *see* THE NATURAL HISTORY OF MANY CURIOUS AND UNCOMMON ZOOPHYTES
Ellis, J B *see* THE NORTH AMERICAN PYRENOMYCETES; A CONTRIBUTION TO MYCOLOGIC BOTANY
Ellis, J W *see* THE LEPIDOPTEROUS FAUNA OF LANCASHIRE AND CHESHIRE
Ellis, James W *see* HISTORY OF JACKSON COUNTY
Ellis, Lady *see* MEMOIRS AND SERVICES OF SIR SAMUEL BURDON ELLIS FROM HIS OWN MEMORANDA
Ellis, Marjorie K *see* COMPARISON OF BALANCE AND MAXIMAL OXYGEN CONSUMPTION AMONG HEARING, CONGENITAL NON-HEARING AND ACQUIRED NON-HEARING FEMALE INTERCOLLEGIATE ATHLETES
Ellis, PW *see* DISCOURS DE M. P.W. ELLIS... A LA CONVENTION ANNUELLE, TENUE A MONTREAL, MARDI ET MERCREDI 5-6 NOVEMBRE 1901
Ellis, Richard *see* THE REFUGEES IN CATALONIA
Ellis, Samuel Burdon *see* MEMOIRS AND SERVICES OF SIR SAMUEL BURDON ELLIS FROM HIS OWN MEMORANDA
Ellis, T Mullett *see* TALES OF THE KLONDYKE
Ellis, Thomas F *see*
- ADOLPHUS AND ELLIS' REPORTS
- ADOLPHUS AND ELLIS' REPORTS, NEW SERIES

Ellis, Tobias *see* THE ENGLISH SCHOOL
Ellis, Wade Hampton *see* LECTURES ON PRIVATE CORPORATIONS
Ellis, William *see*
- HISTORY OF MADAGASCAR...THE PROGRESS OF THE CHRISTIAN MISSION ESTABLISHED IN 1818, AND AN AUTHENTIC ACCOUNT OF THE...MARTYRDOM OF THE NATIVE CHRISTIANS
- THE MARTYR CHURCH
- THREE VISITS TO MADAGASCAR DURING THE YEARS 1853,1854-1856..

Ellis, William Patterson *see* LIBER ALBUS CIVITATIS OXONIENSIS
Ellis, William Smith *see* THE ANTIQUITIES OF HERALDRY...FROM LITERATURE, COINS, GEMS, VASES, AND OTHER MONUMENTS OF PRE-CHRISTIAN AND MEDIAEVAL TIMES.
Ellis, William Thomas *see* MEN AND MISSIONS
Ellison, Randall Erskine *see* AN ENGLISH-KANURI SENTENCE BOOK
Ellison, William Bruce *see*
- THE CANADIAN-AMERICAN FISHERIES
- THE POLITICAL UNIFICATION OF THE UNITED STATES AND CANADA: AN ADDRESS

Elliston. Ohio. Trinity United Church of Christ *see* RECORDS
ELLON ADVERTISER – 1 – £42.00r – uk Scot News [072]
ELLON TIMES AND EAST GORDON ADVERTISER – 1 – £42.00r – uk Scot News [072]
Ells, Robert Wheelock *see*
- A HISTORY OF NEW BRUNSWICK GEOLOGY
- ON THE GEOLOGY OF THE OTTAWA AND PARRY SOUND RAILWAY

Ellsworth, Abigal Wolcott *see* CEMETERY RECORDS IN WINDSOR, CT
ELLSWORTH AMERICAN – Ellsworth, ME: Wm H Chaney, 1855-1920 – 1 – us Res Libr [071]
Ellsworth County. Kansas. District Court *see*
- RECORDS

Ellsworth, Henry William *see* THE PAPERS OF HENRY WILLIAM ELLSWORTH, 1845-1849
ELLSWORTH HERALD – Ellsworth, ME: Couillard & Hilton, oct 17 1851-dec 1854 – 1r – 1 – us Res Libr [071]
Ellsworth. Kansas *see* RECORDS
Elly, Julia *see* 20 YEARS OF INDONESIAN FICTION 1940-1960
ELM GROVE BAPTIST CHURCH (FORMERLY: JONATHAN CREEK). MURRAY, KENTUCKY : CHURCH RECORDS – 1846-1977 – 1 – 82.17 – us Baptist [240]
ELM GROVE CEMETERY RECORD / Hancock County. Ohio. Marion Township. Board of Trustees – 1909-1913 – 1r – 1 – $32.50r – us Archival [324]
ELM SPRINGS METHODIST CHURCH: A PARTIAL HISTORY / Rothrock, Thomas – 1 fiche.F-0048 – 5 – us A.G.L.L. [978]
Elmaleh, A *see* LE-TOLEDOT ADAT HA-MAGRABIM BI-YRUSHALAYIM
EL'MAQSAD (VIES DES SAINTES DU RIF). / al-Badisi, "Abd al-Haqq ibn Ismail." – Traduction annotee de G.S. Colin. Paris, 1926 – 1 – us Res Libr [260]
ELMER FERN COPE PAPERS / Cope, Elmer Fern; ed by Higley, Mary – 1903-65. 54 reels – 1 – us Ohio Hist [977]
THE ELMER FERN COPE PAPERS / Cope, Elmer Fern – (With printed guide) – 1978 – 54r – 1 – $4,590.00 – D3197 – Dist. us Scholarly Res – us Ohio Hist [331]
ELMIRA INDEPENDENT – Ontario, CN. 1986- – 1r per yr – 1 – Can$57.00r – cn Commonwealth Micro [072]
Elmira, New York *see* MISCELLANEOUS EARLY NEWSPAPERS
ELMORE CEMETERY RECORDS – 1900-1988 – 19mf – 9 – at Corangamite [920]
Elmore. Ohio. St. John's United Church of Christ *see* RECORDS
Elmore, Wilber T *see* DRAVIDIAN GODS IN MODERN HINDUISM..
El-Morshidy, A M *see* PLANNING OF ECONOMIC DEVELOPMENT IN THE UNITED ARAB REPUBLIC
EL-MOUDJAHID / Front de Liberation Nationale Algerienne – Organe central. Reimpression. juin 1956-mars 1962 – 1 – fr A.C.R.P.P. [073]
EL-MOUTAKID : INDEPENDENT, POLITIQUE, CRITIQUE ET MORAL – (In Arabic) – Constantine, 1925 – 1 – fr A.C.R.P.P. [073]
ELMSHORNER NACHRICHTEN – Elmshorn, West Germany. 1 Sept 1978- – ca 5r per yr – 1 – gw Mikrofilm [072]
Elmslie, W A L *see* THE MISHNA ON IDOLATRY ABODA ZARA
Elmslie, Walter Angus *see* AMONG THE WILD NGONI
Elmslie, William Jackson *see* SEEDTIME IN KASHMIR:...WILLIAM JACKSON ELMSLIE... MEDICAL MISSIONARY
ELMWOOD ECHO – Elmwood, NE. -w. Nov. 1892-Jun. 1896. Incomplete – 1 – us NE Hist [071]
ELMWOOD LEADER-ECHO – Elmwood, NE. -w. Dec. 1892-Sep. 1899. Incomplete; Jan. 1900-Jan. 1901; Apr. 1901-Sep. 1953 – 1 – us NE Hist [071]
El-Nesawi *see* VIE DE DJELAL-EDDIN MANKOBIRTI
LA ELOCUENCIA MILITAR / Barado, Francisco – 1878 – 9 – 1.50f – sp Bibl Santa Ana [946]
Eloesser, Arthur *see* HEINRICH V. KLEIST
ELOGE DE J.J. ROUSSEAU / Bilhon, Jean F J – Geneve, Paris: Moureau, 1788 – 9 – fr Hachette [190]
ELOGE DE J.J. ROUSSEAU, CITOYEN DE GENEVE / Guillaume, J M – Montpellier, de l'imprimerie revolutionnaire, chez Bonnariq et Avignon, an II. 1793 – 9 – fr Hachette [321]
ELOGE DE J.J. ROUSSEAU MIS AU CONCOURS DE 1790 / Lorthe, Gabriel A de – Paris, l'auteur; Duplain. 1790 – 9 – fr Hachette [190]
ELOGE DE J.J. ROUSSEAU, QUI A CONCOURU POUR LE PRIX D'ELOQUENCE DE L'ACADEMIE FRANCAISE, EN L'ANNEE 1791 / Thiery, Avocat – L. Potier. 1791 – 9 – fr Hachette [190]
ELOGE DE M. DE VOLTAIRE / Palissot de Montenoy, Charles – Paris: J.F. Blastien, 1788 – 9 – fr Hachette [440]
ELOGE DE MARIE-FRANCOIS DE VOLTAIRE / Ruault, Nicolas – Suivi de notes instructives et edifiantes, par M. Ecrlinf. A l'Abbaye des Scellieres. 1788. VI – 9 – fr Hachette [810]
ELOGE DE VOLTAIRE / La Harpe, Jean Francois de – Geneve, Paris: Pissot, 1780 – 9 – fr Hachette [440]
ELOGE DE VOLTAIRE, PRONONCE DANS DANS LA L. MACONNIQUE DES NEUFS SOEURS / Bricaire de la Dixmerie, N – Geneve, Paris, Valleyre. 1779. VIII – 9 – fr Hachette [810]
ELOGE DU MARECHAL DE CATINAT / Guibert, J A H de – Edinburgh. 1775, 88p. ELOGE HISTORIQUE DE MICHEL DE L'HOSPITAL. 1777. 125p. ELOGE DU ROI DE PRUSSE. London 1787. 304p. (Strategy of War Series) – 9 – fr Hachette [355]
ELOGE HISTORIQUE DE M. A. THOUIN / Cuvier, Georges – (Mem. Mus. Hist. Nat.). v. 13. Paris. 1825. B-1022 2 – 8 – ne IDC [580]
ELOGE HISTORIQUE DE M. RAMEAU / Maret, H – 1766 – 9 – us Sibley [780]
ELOGE SUR LA VIE ET LES OEUVRES DE M. L'ABBE HYACINTHE MARTIAL: PRONONCE EVANT LES MEMBRES DE LA SOCIETE ST JEAN-BAPTISTE ET LES PAROISSIENS DE ST JOSEPHE GROSVENORDALE, CONN., LE 6 MAI, 1883 / Gagnon, Ferdinand – s.l.: s.n., 1883 (Worcester, Mass.: Le travailleur). 04324. (Pre-1900 Canadiana) – 9 – cn C.I.H.M. [971]
ELOGES DE PLUSIEURS PERSONNES O.S.B. / Blemur, R M J de – Paris, 1679 – Dfl63.00 – ne Slangenburg [240]
ELOGIO DE CARLOS 3 / Gomez Ortega, Casimiro – 1769 – 1mf – 9 – Pta1,000.00 – 84-7848-232-6 – sp Pentalfa [580]
ELOGIO DE CARLOS 3 / Jovellanos, Melchor Gaspar de – 1789 – 1mf – 9 – Pta1,000.00 – 84-7848-120-6 – sp Pentalfa [320]
ELOGIO DE EUGENIO HERMOSO : DISCURSO DEL ACADEMICO ELECTO Y CONTESTACION DEL EXCMO SR. ENRIQUE LAFUENTE FERRARI / Mosquera Gomez, Luis – Madrid: Blass S.A., 1964 – 1 – sp Bibl Santa Ana [946]
ELOGIO DE LOS PADRES Y HERMANOS DE LA COMPANIA DE JESUS, MUERTOS POR CRISTO EN ESPANA, 1936-39 / Lerida, Felipe – Buenos Aires, 1939. Fiche W995. (Blodgett Collection of Spanish Civil War Pamphlets) – 9 – us H.U. College Libr [946]
ELOGIO DE VENTURA RODRIGUEZ / Jovellanos, Melchor Gaspar de – 1790 – 1mf – 9 – Pta1,000.00 – 84-7848-119-2 – sp Pentalfa [946]
ELOGIO HISTORICO DEL...DOCTOR JOSEPH CERVI... / Ortega, J – Madrid, 1748 – 1mf – 9 – sp Cultura [610]
ELOGIO POETICO...A...PERSONAS...DE EXTREMADURA / Salas, Francisco Gregorio de – Madrid: Andres Ramirez, 1773 – 1 – sp Bibl Santa Ana [946]
ELOGIO...ANTONIO MENDES CORREIA / Castro, Jose de – Madrid: Archivo Ibero Americano, 1965 – 1 – sp Bibl Santa Ana [946]
ELOGIO...JOSE MORENO NIETO / Torres Aguilar-Amat, Salvador – 1882 – 9 – 1.50f – sp Bibl Santa Ana [810]
ELOGIOS DE LOS CINCO PRINCIPIOS / Mogroveio de Cerda, Ivan – 1636 – 9 – 1.50f – sp Bibl Santa Ana [810]
ELOGIOS EN LOOR...DON JAIME...DON FERNANDO CORTES / Lasso de la Vega Cotino, Garbriel – 1601 – 9 – $1.50f – sp Bibl Santa Ana [810]
ELOGIOS POETICOS / Salas, Francisco Gregorio de – 1773 – 9 – 1.50f – sp Bibl Santa Ana [810]
ELOHIM: EINE STUDIE ZUR ISRAELITISCHEN RELIGIONS- UND LITTERATURGESCHICHTE / Zimmermann, Hellmuth – Berlin: Mayer & Mueller, 1900. 1 fiche – 9 – us A.T.L.A. [270]
Elola, Jose *see* EL CREDO Y LA RAZON. 3RD ED. MADRID, 1928
L'ELOQUENCE DE LA CHAIRE ET DU BARREAU / Bretteville, Abbe de – 1689 – 9 – fr I.C.S. [240]
ELOQUENCIA FORENSE / Roxo de Flores, Felipe – 1793 – 9 – 1.50f – sp Bibl Santa Ana [340]
THE ELORA BACKWOODSMAN – 1852-58 – 1 – 75.00 – cn McLaren [073]
Elordury, E *see* GOMEZ MONSEGU C.P., BERNARDO Y ELIAS DE TEJADA, F. LA RIQUEZA ESPIRITUAL DE ESPANA
ELORE – New York: "Elore" Publishing Association, dec 10 1917-21 – 8r – 1 – us Res Libr [071]
EL-OUMA – Paris. n28, 58-59, 61-71. dec 1934-avr 1939 – 1 – fr A.C.R.P.P. [073]
Elovksii, I *see* GOLODNY I POKHOD ORENBURGSKO I ARMII
Eloy, F J Nicholas *see* DICTIONNAIRE HISTORIQUE DE LA MEDECINE ANCIENNE ET MODERNE (AEL, ABT 3; 19)
Elpat'evskii, S Ia *see*
- "BLIZKIE TENI."VOSPOMINANIIA. PT. 1. SPB. 1909; PT. 2. M. 1916. BR-9064/1
- VOSPOMINANIIA ZA 50 LET

Elpatevskii, Sergei I Akovlevich *see* ZEMLIA I SVOBODA
Elphinston, James *see*
- INGLISH ORTHOGGRAPHY EPITTOMIZED
- A MINNIATURE OV INGLISH ORTHOGGRAPHY

ELPS *see* ENGLISH LITERARY PERIODICALS (ELPS), 1681-1914
Els, Hans van *see* GRABBE ALS KRITIKER
DAS ELSASS UND DIE ERNEUERUNG DES KATHOLISCHEN LEBENS IN DEUTSCHLAND VON 1814 BIS 1848 / Schnuetgen, Alexander – Straßburg, 1913 – 164p – 9 – DM48.00 – 3-89349-157-0 – gw Hänsel [240]
Elsbach, A C *see* DER LEBENSGEHALT DER WISSENSCHAFTEN
Else, J *see* HISTOLOGY OF BRITISH MOSSES
ELSE VON DER TANNE : ODER, DAS GLUECK DOMINI FRIEDEMANN LEUTENBACHERS, ARMEN DIENERS AM WORT GOTTES ZU WALLRODE IM ELEND: ERZAEHLUNG / Raabe, Wilhelm Karl – Leipzig: P Reclam, 1943 – 1r – 1 – us U.W. Library [830]
Elsee, Charles *see* NEOPLATONISM IN RELATION TO CHRISTIANITY
Elsevier, Abraham *see* THE ELSEVIER REPUBLICS
Elsevier, Bonaventure *see* THE ELSEVIER REPUBLICS
THE ELSEVIER REPUBLICS / Elsevier, Bonaventure & Elsevier, Abraham – Complete text of all 35 original Republics published in Latin from 1625-50. Printed guide in English included – 106mf – 9 – $1,090.00 – us UPA [900]
ELSIE LEADER – Elsie, NE. -w. Oct. 1895-Aug. 1902 – 1 – us NE Hist [071]
Elsie, Robert *see* ELUSIVE EAGLE SOARS
EL-SIGLO – Santiago, juil 1970-sept 1973 – 1 – fr A.C.R.P.P. [073]
ELSINORE LEADER AND PRESS – Lake Elsinore, CA. 1890-1967 – 24r – 1 – $1,200.00 – R04044 – us Library Micro [071]
ELSINORE NEWS – Lake Elsinore, CA. 1885-1890 – 1r – 1 – $50.00 – R04043 – us Library Micro [071]
Elsmore Council. Kansas *see* LODGE RECORDS
Elsner, Richard *see* DIE DEUTSCHE DICHTUNG 1936-1937
Elson, Louis C *see* THE HISTORY OF AMERICAN MUSIC
Elster, Ernst *see* FRIEDRICH GOTTLIEB KLOPSTOCK
Elster, K H *see* OPTIMIZATION

ELSTER'S FOLLY / Wood, Ellen – British Fiction Archive: Unit 1 – 9 – uk Bell [830]

Elstgeest, Jos *see* UNESCO SOURCEBOOK FOR SCIENCE IN THE PRIMARY SCHOOL

Elstob, Elizabeth *see* THE RUDIMENTS OF GRAMMAR FOR THE ENGLISH-SAXON TONGUE

Elsum, J *see* EPIGRAMS UPON THE PAINTINGS OF THE MOST EMINENT MASTERS, ANCIENT AND MODERN

ELT JOURNAL – v36-. 1981- – 1,5,6,9 – us UMI [073]

ELTA INFORMATION SERVICE, SUPREME COMMITTEE FOR THE LIBERATION OF LIHUANIA – Washington DC. 141 docs. 1980-1991 – 38mf – 9 – ne IDC [320]

Elten, H *see* DIE GRUNDSAETZLICHE BEURTEILUNG DER RECHTE AN BEWEGLICHEN SACHEN...

ELTEN, LAND UND LEUTE : EINE CHRONIK VERGANGENER ZEITEN / Gies, L – Cleve, 1951 – Dfl19.00 – ne Slangenburg [240]

ELTERN TRIBUNE = PARENTS' TRIBUNE – (Yiddish monthly) – Warsaw, PL. v2 no2(9) Oct 1938-v3 no16-17 Jun 1939 – 1r – 1 – $25.00 – cn Can Microfilming [072]

ELTHAM AND DISTRICT TIMES – (Eltham and Kentish Times, 1928-45) – London, UK. 1905-Jun 1982; Jul 1985- – 204+ r – 1 – uk British Libr Newspaper [072]

ELTHAM AND GREENWICH TIMES *see* ELTHAM AND DISTRICT TIMES

ELTHAM AND KENTISH TIMES *see* ELTHAM AND DISTRICT TIMES

ELTHAM HOUSE / Ward, Mary Augusta – British Fiction Archive: Unit 2 – 9 – uk Bell [830]

ELTHETO HE BASILEIA SOU – nos 62-88. 1908-34 (complete) – 1r – 1 – ATLA S0720 – us A.T.L.A. [073]

ELTON FIRST BAPTIST CHURCH. ELTON, LOUISIANA : CHURCH RECORDS – 1910-Sept 1991 – 1 – $90.14 – us Baptist [240]

Elton, J *see* HISTORY OF CORN MILLING

Eltzbacher, Paul *see*
- ANARCHISM
- DER ANARCHISMUS

Eltz-Hoffmann, Lieselotte von *see* ADALBERT STIFTER UND WIEN

ELU JA SONAGE = WITH LIFE AND WORD / Marley, K L – Toronto: Estonian Free Church Publishing House. Publ. No. 6295 d. One item of four on a reel. Biographies of Evangelical Covenant religious workers. 71p – 1 – us Baptist [240]

ELUCIDATIO MUSICAE CHORALIS.. / Samber, Johann B – 1710 – 2 – us Sibley [780]

ELUCIDATIONES DE POTESTATE PAPAE / Caceres, Diego de – 1642 – 9 – 1.50f – sp Bibl Santa Ana [240]

ELUCIDATIONES IN OMNIA SANCTORUM APOSTOLORUM SCRIPTA / Arias Montano, Benito – 1588 – 9 – 1.50f – sp Bibl Santa Ana [240]

ELUCIDATIONES IN QUATOR EVANGELIA METTHAEI, MARCI, LUCAE, IOHANNIS... / Arias Montano, Benito – Antuerpiae: Officina christophori Plantini, 1575 – sp Bibl Santa Ana [240]

LAS "ELUCIDATIONESIN EVANGELIA" DE BENITO ARIAS MONTANO / Garcia Garcia, Rafael – Malaga: Revista Espanola de Estudios Biblicos, 1928 – 1 – sp Bibl Santa Ana [780]

ELUCIDATORIUM ECCLESIASTICUM AD OFFICIUM ECCLESIAE PERTINENTIA PLANIUS EXPONENS IN QUATTUOR LIBROS COMPLETENS / Clichtove, J – Basileae, 1517 – 9mf – 9 – CA-78/1 – ne IDC [240]

ELUCIDATORIUM ECCLESIASTICUM AD OFFICIUM ECCLESIAE PERTINENTIA PLANIUS EXPONENS IN QUATUOR LIBROS COMPLETENS / Clichtove, J – Ed 3. Parisiis, 1540 – 9mf – 9 – CA-77/1 – ne IDC [240]

ELUCUBRATIO DE DOGMATICA ROMANI PONTIFICIS INFALLIBILITATE EIUSQUE DEFINIBILITATE / Cardoni, Giuseppe – (Includes bibliographical references and index) – Romae: Typis Civilitatis Catholicae, 1870 – 1mf – 9 – 0-8370-8490-3 – 1986-2490 – us A.T.L.A. [240]

ELUSIVE EAGLE SOARS : ANTHOLOGY OF MODERN ALBANIAN POETRY / ed by Elsie, Robert – 1993 – 213p – 9 – 92-3-102847-2 – Co-published with Forest Books-which has exclusive sales rights in the UK – fr UNESCO [810]

ELUTTU – Madras: C S Chellappa. [n1-99. 1959-mar 1967] – 1r – us Res Libr [072]

Elvenich, Peter Joseph *see* DER UNFEHLBARE PAPST. ERSTER VORTRAG

Elviro Meseguer, Francisco *see*
- DISCURSOS
- PREGON DE LA SEMANA SANTA CACERENA
- TORRIJOS Y LA EUCARISTIA

Elwang, William Wilson *see*
- SOCIAL FUNCTION OF RELIGIOUS BELIEF
- THE SOCIAL FUNCTION OF RELIGIOUS BELIEF

Elwes, H J *see* A MONOGRAPH OF THE GENUS LILIUM

Elwin, Verrier *see* INDIA'S NORTH-EAST FRONTIER IN THE NINETEENTH CENTURY

Elwin, Warwick *see* THE MINISTER OF BAPTISM

ELWOOD BULLETIN – Elwood, NE. -w. Aug. 1896-Oct. 1902. Incomplete; Aug. 1908- – 1 – us NE Hist [071]

ELWOOD REPUBLICAN – Elwood, NE. -w. Oct. 1895-Jan. 1898. Incomplete – 1 – us NE Hist [071]

ELY DAILY TIMES – Ely, NV. 1920- – 164+ r – 1 UN04503 – $8,200.00 ($140.00y) – us Library Micro [071]

ELY LECTURES ON THE REVISED VERSION OF THE NEW TESTAMENT / Kennedy, Benjamin Hall – London: Richard Bentley, 1882. 1 fiche – 9 – us A.T.L.A. [240]

ELY RECORD *see* MINING RECORD

Ely, Richard Theodore *see*
- SOCIAL ASPECTS OF CHRISTIANITY
- SOCIAL ASPECTS OF CHRISTIANITY, AND OTHER ESSAYS
- THE SOCIAL LAW OF SERVICE

THE ELY VOLUME : OR, THE CONTRIBUTIONS OF OUR FOREIGN MISSIONS TO SCIENCE AND HUMAN WELL-BEING / Laurie, Thomas – (Includes index) – Boston: American Board of Commissioners for Foreign Missions, 1881 – 2mf – 9 – 0-8370-7229-8 – 1986-1229 – us A.T.L.A. [240]

Ely, William *see* THE BIG SANDY VALLEY: A HISTORY OF THE PEOPLE AND COUNTRY FROM EARLIEST SETTLEMENT TO PRESENT TIME

Ely, William D *see* KEYHOLE FOR ROGER WILLIAMS' KEY

Elyot, Thomas *see*
- BIBLIOTHECA ELIOTAE: ELIOTIS LIBRARIE
- THE BOKE NAMED THE GOVERNOUR
- THE CASTEL OF HELTH
- THE DICTIONARY

Elyria. Ohio. First Baptist Church, Women's Home Mission Society *see* CHURCH RECORDS, MS 788

Elyria. Ohio. Presbytery *see* CHURCH RECORDS, MS 418

Elyria-Lorain, Ohio *see* MISCELLANEOUS EARLY NEWSPAPERS

ELYSIUS JUCUNDARUM QUAESTIONUM CAMPUS, OMNIUM LITERARUM AMOENNISSIMA VARIETATE... / Reyes Franco, G – Francfurt, 1670 – 24mf – 9 – sp Cultura [450]

Elze, Karl *see* LORD BYRON

LA EMANCIPACION DE AMERICA Y SU REFLEJO EN LA CULTURA ESPANOLA. MADRID, 1944 / Fernandez Almagro, Melchor – Madrid: Razon y Fe, 1947 – 1 – sp Bibl Santa Ana [972]

O EMANCIPADOR : O GERMINAL / Marques, Lourenco – Special issues for jun 26, jul 15,12,19,26, aug 2,9,16,23,30, sep 13,20,27, oct 14 1926; oct 25, 1926-jul 1919/37 – 1r – us Res Libr [072]

L'EMANCIPATION – 32 no. Saint-Denis. mars 1902-1939 – 1 – fr A.C.R.P.P. [073]

L'EMANCIPATION – Lyon. No.1-18,22. oct-nov 1880 – 1 – fr A.C.R.P.P. [073]

L'EMANCIPATION – Organe central de l'unite totale des travailleurs. Dir. Jacques Doriot. 7 no. Saint-Denis. Ed. nationale. nov 1934-juin 1936. Elements repris par: L' Emancipation nationale – 1 – fr A.C.R.P.P. [073]

L'EMANCIPATION – Toulouse. aout 1838-mars 1839, 2 oct 1844, 1er mai 1845, 11 nov 1846, 10 oct 1847-52 – 1 – fr A.C.R.P.P. [073]

EMANCIPATION – Leopoldville: M A Nguvulu, apr 6-27 1960, jan 1 1961 – us Res Libr [072]

L'EMANCIPATION COLONIALE – Montreal, Canada. fev 1880 – 1r – 1 – Can$25.00 – cn Can Microfilming [072]

L'EMANCIPATION NATIONALE – Paris puis Marseille. juil 1936-aout 1944 – 1 – fr A.C.R.P.P. [073]

THE EMANCIPATION OF MASSACHUSETTS / Adams, Brooks – Boston: Houghton, Mifflin, 1899, c1886 – 1mf – us A.T.L.A. [240]

L'EMANCIPATION SEXUELLE DE LA FEMME / Pelletier, Madeleine – Paris: Giard et Briere, 1911. 85p. (Les Femmes Collection) – 1mf – 9 – $6.00 – fr Bibl Nationale [305]

THE EMANCIPATOR – Milwaukee, 1877 – 1r – 1 – us Ross [071]

EMANCIPATOR AND REPUBLICAN / American Anti-Slavery Society. Free Soil Party – New York. ns 2: n1-11; series 3: n1-4. 1835-40 – 1r – 1 – us Ross [073]

EMANCIPATOR AND REPUBLICAN – Boston. Mass. v. 8, no. 23-9, no. 35. 5 Oct 1843-25 Dec 1844 – 1 – us NY Public [071]

EMANU-EL – San Francisco. Calif. 1897-1949; 1958-67 – 1 – us A.J.P.C. [071]

EMANUEL SWEDENBORG / Fernald, Woodbury M – 1860 – 9 – us A.T.L.A. [240]

Emanuel, W V *see* THE NAVAL SIDE OF THE SPANISH WAR

Emard, M R *see* RELIGION AND LEISURE

EMASAR PHASE 2 : NOTES ON TREES AND SHRUBS IN ARID AND SEMI-ARID REGIONS (FAO/UNEP) – 1983 – 282p – it F.A.O. [634]

LA EMBAJADA DEL MARQUES DE COGOLLUDO A ROMA EN 1687 Y EL DUQUE DE MEDINACELI Y LA GIORGINA. MADRID, 1929 / Villaurrutia, W R – Madrid: Razon y Fe, 1930 – 1 – sp Bibl Santa Ana [946]

EMBAJADA DEL OBISPO DE CARTAGENA FR. ANTONIO TREJO PIDIENDO AL PAPA LA DEFINICION DE LA INMACULADA / Pou Marti, Jose – Archivo Ibero Americano, 1932 – 1 – sp Bibl Santa Ana [240]

LAS EMBAJADAS DE DON JUAN ANTONIO DE VERA Y ZUNIGA EN ITALIA : CONFERENCIA / Garcia Arias, Luis – Madrid: Graf. Valera, 1950 – 1 – sp Bibl Santa Ana [946]

THE EMBARGO / Bryant, William C – 1808-1809 – 9 – 5.00 – us Scholars' Facs [830]

Embden, Ludwig von *see* THE FAMILY LIFE OF HEINRICH HEINE

Emberson, Frederick C *see*
- THE ART OF TEACHING: A MANUAL FOR THE USE OF TEACHERS AND SCHOOL COMMISSIONERS
- GOLD AND SILVER: THE BEST TWENTY POEMS AND THOUGHTS EXTANT, SELECTED WITH SOME APPROACH TO ANALYTICAL CERTAINTY
- HOW TO READ CHARACTER

EMBLEM – Middletown. Ohio. -w. 1851-53 – 1 – us UMI [071]

EMBLEM BOOKS / ed by Dongen, Wim van – 995 titles – 9 – ne IDC [450]

EMBLEMAS MORALES / Horozco y Covarruvias, Juan de – O-638. 1604 – 9 – ne IDC [760]

EMBLEMATA / Alciati, Andrea – 16th Century – 1 – uk Microform Academic [760]

EMBLEMATA / Junius, H – O 812. 1575 – 9 – ne IDC [760]

EMBLEMATA / Mercier, Jean (Mercerius, Joannes) – O-691 1. 1592 – 9 – ne IDC [760]

EMBLEMATA, AD D. ARNOLDUM COBELIUM. EIUSDEM AENIGMATUM LIBELLUS, AD D. ARNOLDUM ROSENBERGUM / Junius, H – 1st ed. Antwerpen, 1565 – 2mf – 9 – O-3098/1 – ne IDC [760]

EMBLEMATA AMATORIA : AFBEELDINGHEN VAN MINNE. EMBLEMES D'AMOUR / Hooft, P C – Amsterdam, 1618 – 2mf – 9 – O-3085/1 – ne IDC [430]

EMBLEMATA AMATORIA / Ayres, P – Emblems of love.1683. In four languages. O-1230-1 – 9 – ne IDC [760]

EMBLEMATA AMATORIA : IAM DEMUM EMENDATA / Heinsius, D – Amsterdam, 1608 – 1mf – 9 – O-3176/1 – ne IDC [760]

EMBLEMATA AMATORIA : IAM DEMUM EMENDATA / Heinsius, D – Amsterdam, 1612 – 1mf – 9 – O-3177/1 – ne IDC [760]

EMBLEMATA AMATORIA : IAM DEMUM EMENDATA / Heinsius, D – (Combination of two defective copies) – Amsterdam, c1605 – 1mf – 9 – O-3178/1 – ne IDC [760]

EMBLEMATA AMATORIA : IAM DEMUM EMENDATA / Timmermans, I A – Amsterdam, c1608-1612 – 1mf – 9 – O-3181/1 – ne IDC [760]

EMBLEMATA ANNIVERSARIA ACADEMIAE ALTORFINAE STUDIORUM IUVENTUTIS / Altorfina – O-535 1. 1597 – 9 – ne IDC [370]

EMBLEMATA ANNIVERSARIA ACADEMIAE NORIBERGENSIS, QUAE EST ALTORFFII / Altorfina – O-536. 1617 – 9 – ne IDC [370]

EMBLEMATA CENTUM, REGIO POLITICA / Solorzano Pereira, Juan de – O 759. 1653 – 9 – ne IDC [320]

EMBLEMATA, CUM ALIQUOT NUMMIS ANTIQUI OPERIS / Sambucus, Joannes – O 743. 1564 – 9 – ne IDC [930]

EMBLEMATA: CUM ALIQUOT NUMMIS ANTIQUI OPERIS / Sambuscus, Joannes – Anvers: C. Plantin, 1564. 240p.3 fiches. (Miscellaneous selections) – 3mf – 9 – $8.00 – fr Bibl Nationale [740]

EMBLEMATA: CUM CLAUDII MINOIS DIVIONENSIS AD EADEM COMMENTARIIS / Alciati, Andrea – Editio quarta. Leiden, 1591 – 8mf – 9 – ne IDC [700]

EMBLEMATA CUM PRIVILEGIJS / Maccius, Paulus – O-681. 1628 – 9 – ne IDC [760]

EMBLEMATA. EMBLEMES CHRESTIENES ET MORALES / Heyns, Z – O 291. 1625 – 9 – ne IDC [240]

EMBLEMATA, ET ALIQUOT NUMMI ANTIQUI OPERIS / Sambucus, Joannes – O 1269 1. 1584 – 9 – ne IDC [930]

EMBLEMATA ETHICO-POLITICA CARMINE EXPLICATA / Kreihing, I – O 325. 1661 – 9 – ne IDC [760]

EMBLEMATA HEROICA, OF DE MEDALISCHE SINNEBEELDEN... / Smids, L – Amsterdam, 1712 – 2mf – 9 – ne IDC [700]

EMBLEMATA HORATIANA, IMAGINIBUS IN AES INCISIS ATQUE LATINO, GERMANICO, GALLICO ET BELGICO CARMINE ILLUSTRATA / Vaenius, O – Amsterdam, 1684 – 3mf – 9 – O-3188/1 – ne IDC [760]

EMBLEMATA I. SAMBUCI / Sambucus, Joannes – Antwerpen, 1566 – 3mf – 9 – ne IDC [700]

EMBLEMATA MORALIA NOVA / Cramer, Daniel – O-588. 1630 – 9 – ne IDC [760]

EMBLEMATA NICOLAI REUSNERI IC. PARTIM ETHICA, ET PHYSICA / Reusner, N – O 730 1. 1581 – 9 – ne IDC [760]

EMBLEMATA NOVA DAS IST NEW BILDERBUCH / Friedrichen, A – O-1245 1. 1617 – 9 – ne IDC [760]

EMBLEMATA OF ZINNEWERCK / Brune, J de – O 565. 1661 – 9 – ne IDC [760]

EMBLEMATA OFTE SINNE BEELDEN MET DICHTEN VERCIERT... / Zevecotius, J – Amsterdam, 1638 – 4mf – 9 – ne IDC [700]

EMBLEMATA POLITICA / Bruck, Iacobi a – O-178. 1618 – 9 – ne IDC [320]

EMBLEMATA POLITICA, AND ORATIONES / Boxhorn, MZ – 1st ed. Amsterdam, 1635 – 3mf – 9 – ne IDC [700]

EMBLEMATA SACRA : DAS IST GOTTLICHE ANDACHTEN, VOLLER FLAMMENDER BEGIERDEN EINER BUSZFERTIGEN, GEHEILIGTEN UND LIEBREICHEN SEELEN / Hoburg, Christiano – (Interleaved copy) – Amsterdam, Frankfurt, 1661 – 3mf – 9 – O-3226/1 – ne IDC [240]

EMBLEMATA SACRA DE FIDE, SPE, CHARITATE / Hesius, G – O 631. 1636 – 9 – ne IDC [240]

EMBLEMATA SACRA. S.L.1631 / Hulsius, B – O 312 – 9 – ne IDC [240]

EMBLEMATA SELECTIORA. TYPIS ELEGANTISSIMIS EXPRESSA, NEC – O 597. 1704 – 9 – ne IDC [760]

EMBLEMATA V. C. ANDREAE ALCIATI MEDIOLANENSIS IURISCONSULTI / Alciati, Andrea – Leiden, 1584 – 5mf – 9 – ne IDC [700]

DE EMBLEMATA VAN HADRIANUS JUNIUS : HERDRUK DER PLANTIJNSCHE UITGAVE VAN DE OORSPRONKELIJKE HOUTSNEDEN AFGEDRUKT MET EEN VOORWOORD VAN MAX ROOSES / Junius, H – Antwerpen, 1902 – 1mf – 9 – O-3234/1 – ne IDC [760]

EMBLEMATUM LIBELLUS / Alciati, Andrea – O-107 1. 1534 – 9 – ne IDC [760]

EMBLEMATUM LIBER / Boissard, J J – O-556 1. 1593 – 9 – ne IDC [760]

LES EMBLEMES DE L'AMOUR HUMAIN / Veen, O van – O 1273 1. 1667 – 9 – ne IDC [740]

EMBLEMES, OU DEVISES CHRESTIENNES / Montenay, G de – O-375 1. 1571 – 9 – ne IDC [240]

EMBLEMS OU DEVISES CHRETIENNES, OUVRAGE MELE DE PROSE ET DE VERS ET ENRICHI DE FIGURES EN TAILLE-DOUCE – O 603. 1697 – 9 – ne IDC [240]

EMBLESMES ROYALES A LOUIS LE GRAND / Martinet – O-364. 1673 – 9 – ne IDC [760]
Embury, Aymar *see* EARLY AMERICAN CHURCHES
EMDER VOLKSBLATT – Emden, Germany. 15 May 1848-30 Sept 1849 – 1r – 1 – gw Mikrofilm [072]
EMEL MECMUASI – Mesul Mueduerue: Muestecib H. Fazil, 1930-1935 – 16mf – 9 – $265.00 – us MEDOC [949]
Emel'ianova, M B *see* VOPROSY STANDARTIZATSII I KACHESTVA PRODUKTSII
THE EMERALD / ed by Brenan, P – Montreal, Canada. v1 n31. 20 fev 1841-v2 n3. 11 dec 1841 – 1r – 1 – Can$25.00 – cn Can Microfilming [072]
EMERALD EMPIRE NEWS – Eugene, OR. -w, -d. 12 May 1961-26 Mar 1962. 2 rolls – 1 – us U.O. Library [071]
L'EMERAUDE, MORCEAUX CHOISIS DE LITTERATURE MODERNE – Paris: Urbain Canel et Ad. Guyot, 1832. 219p. (Annales romantiques) – 1 – us U.W. Library [800]
EMERGENCY CARE QUARTERLY – 1985- – 1,5,6,9 – us UMI [617]
EMERGENCY LEAFLETS / Iowa State University. Cooperative Extension Service in Agriculture and Home Economics – 1917-20.No.1-54. 1 reel – 1,5 – us Spaulding [630]
EMERGENCY LEGISLATION OF THE U.S. 1775-1918 : DEALING WITH THE CONTROL AND TAKING OF PRIVATE PROPERTY FOR THE PUBLIC USE, BENEFIT, OR WELFARE; PRESIDENTIAL PROCLAMATIONS AND EXECUTIVE ORDERS THEREUNDER, TO AND INCLUDING JAN 31, 1918; TO WHICH IS ADDED A REPRINT OF ANALOGOUS LEGISLATION SINCE 1775 / ed by Clark, J Reuben Jr – Washington: GPO, 1918 (all publ) – 12mf – 9 – $18.00 – LLMC 94-357 – us L.L.M.C. [340]
EMERGENCY LIBRARIAN – (v.8-. 1980-. 5,6,9) – v.1-. 1973- – 1 – us UMI [020]
EMERGENCY LIBRARIAN – Vancouver. v16-21. 1988/89-1993/94 – 9 – Can$20.00y – cn Micromedia [020]
EMERGENCY MEDICINE CLINICS OF NORTH AMERICA – 1983- – 1,5,6,9 – us UMI [617]
EMERGENCY PLANNING DIGEST REVUE PLANS DES MESURES D'URGENCE – (v.6 .1979 5,6,9) – v.1. 1974 – 1 – us UMI [073]
EMERGENCY PRODUCT NEWS – 1975- – 1 – us UMI [617]
EMERGENCY RADIOLOGY : A JOURNAL OF PRACTICAL IMAGING – v1-3. 1994-1996 – 1 – $80.00r – us Williams [616]
EMERGENCY SERVICES N.Y – v1-3. 1982-84 – 9 – us UMI [617]
THE EMERGING NATIONS / Massachusetts Institute of Technology. Center for International Studies – In Indonesian. SE-10,498 1. 1963 – 9 – ne IDC [320]
EMERGING TRENDS – (1985-. 5,6,9) – v1-. 1979- – 1 – us UMI [073]
L'EMERILLON – 1930-65. SEM16P256 – 4r – 5 – Can$136.00 – cn Bibl Nat [073]
L'EMERILLON – Ottawa, Ontario. v13 n4. jul-aut 1942-jan 1965 – 5r – 1 – Can$50.00r – cn Can Microfilming [073]
L'EMERILLON – Quebec, jan 1936-nov/dec 1936 – 1r – 1 – Can$35.00 – cn Can Microfilming [072]
EMERITA AUGUSTA. APUNTES MONOGRAFICOS ACERCA DE LA CATEDRAL METROPOLITANA DE SANTA MARIA JERUSALEN / Gonzalez y Gomez de Soto, Juan Jose – Merida, 1903 – 1 – sp Bibl Santa Ana [240]
Emerson, Caleb *see*
- EMERSON FAMILY PAPERS, MS 830
- PAPERS

EMERSON CRESCENT – Emerson, NE. -w. Jun. 1904-Sep. 1905 – 1 – us NE Hist [071]
Emerson, Edgar C *see* OUR COUNTY AND ITS PEOPLE-JEFFERSON
Emerson, Ellen Russell *see* INDIAN MYTHS, OR, LEGENDS, TRADITIONS, AND SYMBOLS OF THE ABORIGINES OF AMERICA: COMPARED WITH THOSE OF OTHER COUNTRIES INCLUDING HINDOSTAN, EGYPT, PERSIA, ASSYRIA, AND CHINA
EMERSON ENTERPRISE – Emerson, NE. -w. Sep. 1896-May 1898; Mar. 1899-Dec. 1900; Apr. 1901-Jul. 1914 – 1 – us NE Hist [071]
EMERSON FAMILY PAPERS, MS 830 / Emerson, Caleb – (Correspondence, legal and financial papers) – 1795-1904 – 6r – 1 – us Western Res [920]
Emerson, Oliver Farrar *see* THE HISTORY OF THE ENGLISH LANGUAGE
Emerson, Phyllis S *see* INDEX OF ASTRANA MARINS' VIDA EJEMPLAR Y HEROICA DE MIGUEL DE CERVANTES SAAVEDRA
Emerson, Ralph Waldo *see*
- LETTERS AND SOCIAL AIMS
- NATURE

EMERSON TRI-COUNTY PRESS – Emerson, NE. -w. Mar. 1934- – 1 – us NE Hist [071]
Emerson, Wilimena H *see* THE DESCENDANTS OF JOHN ELIOT FROM 1598-1905
Emerton, Ephraim *see*
- DESIDERIUS ERASMUS OF ROTTERDAM
- AN INTRODUCTION TO THE STUDY OF THE MIDDLE AGES (375-814)
- MEDIAEVAL EUROPE (814-1300)
- UNITARIAN THOUGHT

Emerton, J H *see* THE STRUCTURE AND HABITS OF SPIDERS
Emery, Carlos Alberto *see* INTERPRETACION DE LA POLITICA AGRARIA JUSTICIALISTA
Emery, G F *see* LAWS RELATING TO FOREIGNERS AND FOREIGN CORPORATIONS
DER EMES – (Missing: Many numbers) – Moscow. v1-8. 1920-1938 – 8r – 1 – J-92-33/3 – ne IDC [072]
DER EMES – (New York). 1921 – 1 – us A.J.P.C. [073]
DER EMES = THE TRUTH – (In Yiddish) – Moscow, RU. v- no93. 10 Jan 1921 – 1r – 1 – $25.00 – cn Can Microfilming [072]
DER EMES = THE TRUTH – New York City, NY, 1921 – 1r – Can$25.00 – cn Can Microfilming [071]
EMES – Moscow. 1921-1935. Incomplete – 1 – us NY Public [073]
EMES – Moscow, 1921-35 – 7r – 1 – us Ross [072]
EMETH – London, UK. 7 Jun 1931 – 1 – uk British Libr Newspaper [072]
THE EMETH (TRUTH) – Boston. Die Wahrheit. 1895-96 – 1 – us A.J.P.C. [335]
LES EMEUTIERS : LES DEUX LUNDIS / Levy, Armand & Valleton, Henri – Paris: Impr Lacour et cie, [1849?] – us Res Libr [072]
AN EMG STUDY OF FOUR ELASTIC TUBING CLOSED KINETIC CHAIN EXERCISES : A PRELIMINARY STUDY / Bachler, Levi R – Brigham Young University, 1994 – 1mf – 9 – PE 3627 – us Microform Publ [617]
LA EMIGRACION EN BALEARES Y CANARIAS / Diaz Perez, Nicolas – 1882 – 9 – 1.50f – sp Bibl Santa Ana [946]
LA EMIGRACION EXTREMENA A INDIAS. SIGLO 16. FICHERO DOCUMENTAL / Rubio, Angel – Santiago de Chile: Imprenta Universitaria, 1948 – 1 – sp Bibl Santa Ana [946]
EMIGRACJA AMERYKANSKA A MACIERZYSLA GRUPA PARAFIALNA / Makarewicz, Tadeusz – Poznan-Warszawa, 1936 – 2r – 1 – us I.H.R.C. [304]
"EMIGRACJA JAKO ZJAWISKO SPOLECZNE" / Chalasinski, Jozef – Poznan-Warszawa – 2r – 1 – us I.H.R.C. [304]
EMIGRACYA I POLITYKA EMIGRACYJNA / Caro, Leopold – Poznan, 1914 – 1r – 1 – us I.H.R.C. [320]
THE EMIGRANT – Quebec, Canada. v1 n20. 8 jul 1848 – 1r – 1 – Can$25.00 – cn Can Microfilming [072]
THE EMIGRANT MECHANIC: AND OTHER TALES IN VERSE, TOGETHER WITH NUMEROUS SONGS UPON CANADIAN SUBJECTS / Cowherd, Thomas – Brantford, Ont.: T. Cowherd, 1884. 00267. (Pre-1900 Canadiana) – 9 – cn C.I.H.M. [810]
THE EMIGRANTS / Imlay, Gilbert & Wollstonecraft, Mary – 1793 – 9 – 20.00 – us Scholars' Facs [830]
EMIGRANTS: A SELECTION OF 17 GUIDES AND PAMPHLETS – BRRAM – 1 – uk Microform Academic [360]
EMIGRANTS FROM ENGLAND, 1773-1776 – 1913. Item E.Reprint from The New England Historical & Genealogical Register. v62-65. Indexed. 206p. SW16-0151 – 5 – us A.G.L.L. [978]
EMIGRANTS SAISONNIERS ESPAGNOLS EN FRANCE : ENQUETE PAR SONDAGE DANS LE DEPARTEMENT DE L'OISE EN 1959 / Hermet, G & Marquet, J – F50.00 – fr Ethnologie [320]
EMIGRATION. / Maconochie, Alexander – London. 1848 – 1 – us Res Libr [320]
L'EMIGRATION DANS LES BASSES-PYRENEES PENDANT SOIXANTE ANS / Etcheverry, Louis – Reprod. de l'extrait de la Revue des Pyrenees, v5, 1893, p509-20. 1 fiche.(Statistics Series: Demography). (Historical Studies Series) – 9 – 6.00 – fr Bibl Nationale [310]
EMIGRATION GAZETTE – London, 23 Oct 1841-13 May 1843 – 1r – 1 – uk British Libr Newspaper [072]
THE EMIGRATION OF GENTLEMEN'S SONS TO THE UNITED STATES AND CANADA / Bradley, Arthur Granville – Westminster England: Women's Printing Society, 18??. 00981. (Pre-1900 Canadiana) – 9 – cn C.I.H.M. [971]
EMIL GOETTS VERMAECHTNIS / Droop, Fritz – Konstanz a.B.: Reuss & Itta, 1917 – 1 – us U.W. Library [430]
THE EMIL J. GUMBEL COLLECTION : POLITICAL PAPERS OF AN ANTI-NAZI SCHOLAR IN WEIMAR AND EXILE, 1914-1966 – (Comes with printed guide) – 8r – 1 – $910.00 – 1-55655-212-2 – us UPA [320]
EMILE GALLE: DREAMS INTO GLASS / Warmus, William – 1984. 191p. 121 color illus. 4 fiches. Fiche no.8367 – 9 – $7.50 – us Corning Mus [730]
EMILE ZOLA / Xau, Fernand-Arthur-Pierre – Paris: C. Marpon, E. Flammarion, 1880 – fr Armell [440]
EMILIA GALOTTI / Lessing, Gotthold Ephraim; ed by Gast, E R – (Includes bibliographical references) – Goth [Germany]: F A Perthes, 1886 – 1r – 1 – us U.W. Library [820]
EMILY C. JUDSON: A MEMORIAL / Judson, Emily C – By Walter Newton Wyeth. 1890 – 9 – us A.T.L.A. [920]
EMILY HOLLAND PAPERS AT CORNELL UNIVERSITY / Holland, Emily – Patricia Harland Gaffney, ed. 15 reels. Printed guide only – 5.00 – 1 – us UMI [920]
EMILY HOWLAND PAPERS / Howland, Emily – 15r – 1 – $1105.00 – us UMI [920]
Emily, Jules *see* MISSION MARCHAND
EMILY N. BLAIR FAMILY PAPERS *see* BLAIR, EMILY N., FAMILY PAPERS, MS 4342
Emin, Resulzade Mehmet *see* AZERBAYCAN CUMHURIYET KEYFIYETI TESEKKUELUE VE SIMDIKI VAZIYETI
EMINENT AND SELF-MADE MEN / Western Biographical Publishing Co – Biographical history of the State of Indiana. Cincinnati, 1880. Vols. I and II. (Indiana Reel 2). (The Cox Library Collection) – 5 – us Americana [978]
EMINENT METHODIST WOMEN / Keeling, A E – London, 1889 – 3mf – 9 – ne IDC [240]
EMINENT MISSIONARY WOMEN / Gracey, Mrs J T – New York: Eaton & Mains; Cincinnati: Jennings & Graham, c1898 – 1mf – 9 – 0-8370-6056-7 – 1986-0056 – us A.T.L.A. [305]
EMI-Pathe Film Library *see* CARD CATALOGUE TO 75 YEARS OF NEWSREELS
L'EMIRAT DES TRARZAS / Marty, Paul – Paris: E Leroux, 1919 – 1 – us Res Libr [960]
EMISSION ET CIRCULATION DES TITRES DE SOCIETES ETRANGERES EN FRANCE / Dauphin, B P – Paris, 1907 – 2mf – 1 – ILM-3397/1 – ne IDC [327]
Emley. Yorkshire. St. Michael *see* PARISH REGISTERS
EMMA GOLDMAN PAPERS / University Berkeley. Institute for the Study of Social Change – (With guide £105.00) – 61r – 13 – £4,015.00 – uk Chadwyck [977]
EMMA LADY HAMILTON / Sichel, Walter Sydney – 3rd ed., rev. 1907 – 9 – uk Libr Preservation [920]
EMMANUEL BAPTIST CHURCH. CALINVILLE, ILLINOIS : CHURCH RECORDS – 1921-79 – 1 – 43.02 – us Baptist [240]
EMMANUEL BAPTIST CHURCH. JEFFERSON CITY, TENNESSEE : CHURCH RECORDS – 1924-65 – 1 – 22.86 – us Baptist [240]
Emmanuel Lutheran Church, Hoisington, KS *see* RECORDS
THE EMMANUEL MOVEMENT IN A NEW ENGLAND TOWN : A SYSTEMATIC ACCOUNT OF EXPERIMENTS AND REFLECTIONS DESIGNED TO DETERMINE THE PROPER RELATIONSHIP BETWEEN... / Powell, Lyman P – New York: G.P. Putnam, 1909 – 1mf – us A.T.L.A. [240]
EMMANUELE / Azevedo, Aluizio – 25 2. 1854 – 8 – ne IDC [440]
EMMETT COUNTY REPUBLICAN – Estherville. Iowa. 1887-1902 – 1 – us UMI [071]
Emmius, Ubbo *see* DE DAVID-JORISCHEN GHEEST IN LEVEN ENDE LEERE, S'-GRAVENHAGE
EL EMMO CARDENAL GOMA / Bayle, Constantino – Madrid: Razon y Fe, 1940 – sp Bibl Santa Ana [240]
Emmons, G T *see* THE THALTAN INDIANS
Emmott, Elizabeth B *see* LOVING SERVICE
EMMY – (1983-. 1,5,6,9) – v1-. 1979- – 1 – us UMI [073]
EMNIYET – Filibe, 1896-1897 – 9 – $95.00 – us MEDOC [956]
Emoan, Max *see* MONOGRAFIE DER REPRODUCTIVEN PHAENOMENE
EMORY INTERNATIONAL LAW REVIEW – (Title varies: v1-3 1986-89 as Emory Journal of International Dispute Resolution) – v1-8. 1986-94 – 9 – $125.00 set – us Hein [340]
Emory, John *see*
- A DEFENCE OF "OUR FATHERS" AND OF THE ORIGINAL ORGANIZATION OF THE METHODIST EPISCOPAL CHURCH AGAINST THE REV. ALEXANDER M'CAINE AND OTHERS
- THE EPISCOPAL CONTROVERSY REVIEWED

EMORY JOURNAL OF INTERNATIONAL DISPUTE RESOLUTION *see* EMORY INTERNATIONAL LAW REVIEW
EMORY LAW JOURNAL – (v1-33 1952-84 on reel or mf $440.00. v34-44 1985-95 on mf $294.00. Title varies: v1-22 1952-73 as Journal of Public Law) – v1-44. 1952-95 – 5,6,9 – $734.00 set – us Hein [340]
Emory, W H *see* REPORT ON THE UNITED STATES AND MEXICAN BOUNDARY SURVEY
THE EMOTIONS AND THE WILL / Bain, Alexander – London: Longmans, Green, 1899 – 2mf – us A.T.L.A. [240]
THE EMOTIONS AND THE WILL / Bain, Alexander – London: Longmans, Green, 3rd ed 1875 – 1 roll – 1 – 1-55879-791-2 – uk Libr Preservation [150]
EMPADRONAMIENTO DE MORISCOS DE GRANADA (ANNO 1573-1595, 1610, 1733) – Cordoba – 1r – 5,6 – sp Cultura [946]
EMPARONS-NOUS DE L'INDUSTRIE / Bouchette, Errol – Ottawa: Imprimerie generale, 1901. SEM105P466 – 1mf – 9 – Can$2.25 – cn Bibl Nat [971]
EMPATBELAS BOELAN PENDOEDOEKAN INGGERIS DI INDONESIA / Said, M – Medan, 1946 – 2mf – 9 – SE-813/1 – ne IDC [950]
EMPATHIC PARENTING – (Cont: Journal of the Canadian Society for the Prevention of Cruelty to Children v7 1984. v15 and 16 publ as a single vol) – Midland. v7-18. 1984-95 – 9 – Can$20.00y – cn Micromedia [306]
EMPATHIC PARENTING *see* JOURNAL OF THE CANADIAN SOCIETY FOR THE PREVENTION OF CRUELTY TO CHILDREN
EMPAT-K – (Buku anggauta). SE-5299 1 – 9 – ne IDC [950]
EMPATPULUH TAHUN REVOLUSI SOSIALIS OKTOBER BESAR / Khrushchev, Nikita Sergeevich – SE-5390 1. 1958 – 9 – ne IDC [335]
EMPEDOCLE; OU, LE PHILOSOPHE DE L'AMOUR ET DE LA HAIN / Brun, Jean – Presentation, choix de textes, traduction, bibliographie. Paris: Seghers, 1966 – 208p. Map, plates – 1 – us U.W. Library [180]
EMPEDOCLES ON ETNA AND OTHER POEMS / Arnold, Matthew – London: B. Fellowes, 1852 – 1 roll – 1 – 1-55879-499-9 – uk Libr Preservation [810]
EL EMPERADOR CARLOS V / Mignet, Mr – 1855 – 9 – $1.50f – sp Bibl Santa Ana [920]
EL EMPERADOR CARLOS V...YUSTE / Mignet; ed by Lobo, Miguel – 1855 – 9 – $1.50f – sp Bibl Santa Ana [946]
L'EMPEREUR ALMAMY SAMORI TOURE : GRAND ADMINISTRATEUR ET GRAND STRATEGE – Conakry: Imprimerie nationale, 1971 – us Res Libr [920]
THE EMPEROR AKBAR, A CONTRIBUTION TOWARDS THE HISTORY OF INDIA IN THE 16TH CENTURY / Noer, Graf Friedrich Christian Karl August von – Trans. and partly rev. by Annette S. Beveridge. Calcutta: Thacker, Spink & Co; London: Truebner, 1890. 2v – 1 – us U.W. Library [920]
THE EMPEROR HADRIAN : A PICTURE OF THE GRAECO-ROMAN WORLD IN HIS TIME / Gregorovius, Ferdinand – London; New York: Macmillan, 1898 – 1mf – us A.T.L.A. [240]

THE EMPEROR JULIAN AND HIS GENERATION: AN HISTORICAL PICTURE / Neander, Augustus – London: J.W. Parker, 1850 – 1mf – us A.T.L.A. [940]

EMPEROR OF ROME. ...IN QVO VIDETVR FINIS TVRCARUM IN PRAESENTI EORUM IMPERATORE / Septimus Severus – Brescia, 1596 – 2mf – 9 – H-8429/1 – ne IDC [956]

THE EMPEROR'S CLOTHES COST TWENTY DOLLARS / Darland, Lloyd – (A Critique of Marxism, by Sam Dolgoff, 24p. Protagoras, Nietzsche, Stirner: Platz dem Egoismus, by Benedict Lachmann. 71 S. Die Abschaffung des Krieges durch die Selbstbestimmung des Volkes, by Gustav Landauer. 24 S) – 2nd Ed. 1980. 39p. 1 fiche (24x). Together with: – 9 – 1.00f – at Libertarian Micro [320]

DIE EMPFINDSAMEN IN DARMSTADT : STUDIEN UEBER MAENNER UND FRAUEN AUS DER WERTHERZEIT / Tornius, Valerian – (Includes bibliographical references) – Leipzig: Klinkhardt & Biermann, [1910] – 1r – 1 – us U.W. Library [430]

EMPIRE – Concordia. Kansas. 1876-1919 – 1 – us UMI [071]

EMPIRE – Juneau. Alaska. 1970- – 1 – us UMI [071]

EMPIRE – Sydney, 1850-75 – 45r – 1 – A$1,395.00 silver A$1,215.00 vesicular – at Pascoe [072]

THE EMPIRE – London, England. Jan 1854-Jun 1856 – 3 1/2r – 1 – uk British Libr Newspaper [072]

THE EMPIRE : A SERIES OF LETTERS, PUBLISHED IN "THE DAILY NEWS", 1862, 1863 / Smith, Goldwin – Oxford, London: J.H. & J. Parker, 1863 – 1 roll – 1 – 1-55879-610-X – uk Libr Preservation [860]

THE EMPIRE – Toronto, Canada. -w, -d. 12 Jan 1888-6 Feb 1895. Lacking June-Nov 1890. 27 1 2 reels – 1 – uk British Libr Newspaper [072]

THE EMPIRE – Toronto. v. 1-8. 27 Dec 1887-6 Feb 1895 – 1 – 1285.00 – cn McLaren [971]

EMPIRE BUILDER – Coos Bay, OR. -w. 2 Feb 1966-8 Nov 1978. 8 rolls. – 1 – us U.O. Library [071]

EMPIRE COTTON GROWING REVIEW – 1924-58 – 1 – uk Microform Academic [630]

L'EMPIRE DE L'ALMENY-EMIZ LAMORY OU EMPIRE DU OUASSOULOU / Peroz, Etienne – Besancavon: Dodikers, 1888. 32p. 1 fiche. (Miscellaneous Selections) – 9 – 6.00 – fr Bibl Nationale [960]

L'EMPIRE DE ZAZIRIS SUR LES HUMAINS OU LA ZAZIROCRATIE / Tiphaigne de la Roche, Charles-Francois – (Utopias in the Enlightenment series). 1761 – 9 – fr Hachette [490]

L'EMPIRE JAPONAIS / Metchinikoff, Leon – Geneve, imprimerie de "l'Atsume Gusa". 1881 – 9 – 25.00 – fr Orientalistes [950]

THE EMPIRE OF CHRIST : BEING A STUDY OF THE MISSIONARY ENTERPRISE IN THE LIGHT OF MODERN RELIGIOUS THOUGHT / Lucas, Bernard – London: Macmillan, 1907 – 1mf – 9 – 0-8370-6208-X – 1986-0208 – us A.T.L.A. [240]

EMPIRE OF THE CZARS – 1995 – 9 – 92-3-102698-4 – fr UNESCO [947]

THE EMPIRE OF THE SOUTH SEAS / Coedes, G – 1944. SE-808-1 – 9 – ne IDC [980]

L'EMPIRE PEUL DU MACINA. / Ba, Amadou Hampate – 1955 – 1 – us Res Libr [960]

L'EMPIRE SOCIALISTE DES INKA / Baudin, L – 9 – F70.00 – fr Ethnologie [305]

EMPIRE STATE REPORT – v1- 1974- 1; v3- 5,6,9 – us UMI [320]

EMPIRES AND EMPERORS OF RUSSIA, CHINA, KOREA, AND JAPAN.NOTES AND RECOLLECTIONS / Vay, Peter – New York: Dutton, 1906. xxxii, 399p. illus – 1 – us U.W. Library [950]

EMPIRES OF THE VELD : BEING FRAGMENTS OF THE UNWRITTEN HISTORY OF THE TWO LATE BOER REPUBLICS, WITH OTHER PAPERS FOR THE MOST PART DESCRIPTIVE OF THE LIFE AND CHARACTER OF THE PEOPLE / Kok, K J de – Durban: J C Juta, 1904 – 1 – us Res Libr [960]

EMPIRE/VENTURE/THIRD WORLD – 1938-Jun 1975 – 9 – uk Microform Academic [073]

EMPIRICAL RESEARCH IN EDUCATION / Landsheere, G de – 1982 – 113p – 9 – 92-3-102023-4 – fr UNESCO [370]

AN EMPIRICAL STUDY OF RULE 11 SANCTIONS / Kassin, Saul M – Washington: FJC, 1985 – 1mf – 9 – $1.50 – LLMC 95-324 – us L.L.M.C. [340]

L'EMPLACEMENT DU FORT DE DOLLARD DES ORMEAUX: ETUDE REPRODUITE DE LA REVUE D'HISTOIRE DE L'AMERIQUE FRANCAISE / Morin, Victor – Montreal, 1952. SEM105P764 – 1mf – 9 – Can$2.25 – cn Bibl Nat [971]

L'EMPLOI DANS LE SECTEUR AUTOGERE AGRICOLE, CAMPAGNE 1967-1968 / Algeria. Ministere de l'Agriculture – 1970. BNE-8732 1 – 9 – ne IDC [630]

L'EMPLOI DU LOISIR / DuHays, Charles – Alencon. 1891. (La Condition Ouvriere. Part Two.) – 9 – 7.50 – fr Bibl Nationale [360]

L'EMPLOYE CEGETISTE DES MINES – nos 1-5, 10-12, 15-16, 18, 20, 22-24, 26. Lens. mai 1937-juin 1939 – 1 – fr A.C.R.P.P. [622]

EMPLOYEE ASSISTANCE QUARTERLY / ed by McClellan, Keith – v1- 1985- – 1, 9 ($250.00 in US $350.00 outside hardcopy subsc) – us Haworth [360]

EMPLOYEE BENEFITS JOURNAL – (1985-. 5,6,9) – v1-. 1975- – 1 – us UMI [331]

EMPLOYEE BENEFITS REPORT – v11, no.2-. Oct 1984- – 1,5,6,9 – us UMI [331]

EMPLOYEE HEALTH AND FITNESS – v.1. 1979 – 1,5,6,9 – us UMI [073]

EMPLOYEE RELATIONS LAW JOURNAL – v1- 1975- 1; v4- 1978- 5,6,9 – us UMI [331]

EMPLOYEE RELATIONS LAW JOURNAL – (v1-10 1976-85 on reel $223.00. v11-19 1985-94 on mf $375.00) – v1-19. 1976-94 – 5,6,9 – $598.00 set – us Hein [331]

EMPLOYEE RESPONSIBILITIES AND RIGHTS JOURNAL – v1-7. 1988-94 – 1,5 – $65.00v – us UMI [331]

EMPLOYEES' COMPENSATION APPEALS BOARD DECISIONS – (Index/Digest for v1-34) – v1-39. 1946-88 – 401mf – 9 – $601.00 – LLMC 81-219 – us L.L.M.C. [340]

EMPLOYERS' LIABILITY / Osgood, William Newton – Boston: Hodges, 1891. 30p. LL-1379 – 1 – us L of C Photodup [340]

THE EMPLOYERS' LIABILITY ACTS AND THE ASSUMPTION OF RISKS IN NEW YORK, MASSACHUSETTS, INDIANA, ALABAMA, COLORADO, AND ENGLAND / Dresser, Frank Farnum – St. Paul, Keefe-Davidson, 1902-08. 2 v. LL-258 – 1 – us L of C Photodup [340]

EMPLOYERS' LIABILITY, WORKMEN'S COMPENSATION AND LIABILITY INSURANCE. / Conner, Jeremiah Frederick – Chicago, Spectator 1916 262 p. LL-699 – 1 – us L of C Photodup [340]

EMPLOYMENT AND EARNINGS – 1- 1954- 1; v17- 5,6; v22- 9 – us UMI [331]

EMPLOYMENT AND INCOME POLICIES FOR IRAN / Hirsch, Etienne – Geneva, 1973 – 9 – Sfr40.00 – 92-2-107128-6 – sz I.L.O. [331]

EMPLOYMENT IN THE PETROLEUM MINING INDUSTRY IN LIBYA, 1964 / Libya. Ministry of Economy and Trade. Census and Statistical Department – 1965? BNE-912 1 – 9 – ne IDC [331]

EMPLOYMENT IN THE PETROLEUM MINING INDUSTRY IN LIBYA, 1964 / Libya. Ministry of Economy and Trade. Census and Statistical Department – Tripoli. BNE-1202 1 – 9 – ne IDC [331]

EMPLOYMENT MARKET REPORT / Libya. Ministry of Labour and Social Affairs – Issued by Manpower Section. Nr.3 Dec 1966. BNE-902 1 – 9 – ne IDC [360]

EMPLOYMENT OF DRAUGHT ANIMALS IN AGRICULTURE – 1972 2nd print 1978 – 261p – it F.A.O. [636]

THE EMPLOYMENT OF INDIANS IN THE WAR OF 1812 / Cruikshank, Ernest Alexander – Washington: G.P.O., 1896. 03635. (Pre-1900 Canadiana) – 9 – cn C.I.H.M. [971]

EMPLOYMENT SECURITY IN INDIANA / Indiana. Employment Security Board – n.1-42, 1936-77. 44 fiches. (Harvard Law School Library Collection.) – 9 – 1.50f – us H.U. Law [336]

EMPLOYMENT SECURITY REVIEW – (Began as: Employment Security Service) – v1-18. 1934-51 – 9 – LLMC 84-351 – us L.L.M.C. [331]

EMPLOYMENT SECURITY SERVICE *see* EMPLOYMENT SECURITY REVIEW

EMPLOYMENT-ORIENTED NATIONAL YOUTH PROGRAMMES IN AFRICA : SITUATIONS, PROBLEMS AND PROSPECTS – 1982 – 61p – 9 – 92-3-101777-2 – fr UNESCO [331]

Emporia Evangelical United Brethren Mission *see* RECORDS

Emporia. Kansas. St. Andrew's Episcopal Church *see* RECORDS

EMPORIO ITALIANO – London, UK. Mar-Jul 1857 – 1 – uk British Libr Newspaper [072]

EMPORIUM INDEPENDENT – Emporium, PA. -w 1904-1912 – 13 – $25.00r – us I.M.R. [071]

EMPORO ITALIANO – London, UK. 31 Mar-1 Jul 1857. -w. 18 feet – 1 – uk British Libr Newspaper [072]

EMPREINTES – Revue trimestrielle. Dir.-Fond. H. van den Driesche. no. 1-11. Bruxelles. 1946-52 – 1 – fr A.C.R.P.P. [073]

Empresa Ber-Maq *see* GUIA DE ESPECTACULOS. FERIA Y FIESTAS AGOSTO 1974

UNA EMPRESA EL SIGLO 18 : LOS NAVIOS DE LA ILUSTRACION... / Basterra, Ramon de – Madrid: Razon y Fe, 1926 – 1 – sp Bibl Santa Ana [355]

EMPRESAS MORALES / Boria, J de – O-569 1. 1680 – 9 – ne IDC [760]

EMPRESS EXPRESS – Alberta, CN. 1913-36 – 6r – 1 – cn Commonwealth Micro [072]

EMPROS – Athens, Greece. -d. 1 Oct 1917-3 Feb 1919. Imperfect. 3 reels – 1 – uk British Libr Newspaper [949]

EMPRUNT SAINT-SIMONIEN – Paris, Everat, 1832, 16 p. Les Saint-Simoniens, 1825-1834. 6880 – 9 – fr Hachette [335]

Emrah *see* DIVAN

Emrich, George *see* THOMAS JEFFERSON'S MARCH

Emrich, Hermann *see* GOETHES INTUITION

Emrich, Wilhelm *see* PAULUS IM DRAMA

Ems, Rudolf von *see*
– ALEXANDER
– WELTCHRONIK

EMT (EMERGENCY MEDICAL TECHNICIANS) JOURNAL – v. 1-. 1977- – 1,5,6,9 – us UMI [617]

EMU : A QUARTERLY MAGAZINE TO POPULARIZE THE STUDY AND PROTECTION OF NATIVE BIRDS... – Melbourne, 1901/1902-1941/1942. v1-41 – 297mf – Z-2018c/2 – ne IDC [590]

L'EMULATION / ed by Bilodeau, Ernest – Quebec, Canada. v1 n5. 15 jun 1897 – 1r – 1 – Can$25.00 – cn Can Microfilming [072]

EN 1900 / Veron, Pierre – Paris. 1878. 284p. (Historical Studies Series) – 9 – 12.00 – fr Bibl Nationale [900]

EN EL 4TH CENTENARIO DEL DOCTOR ARIAS MONTANO. LA VERSION METRICOLATINA DEL SALTERIO HEBRAICO / Diego, Sandalio – Madrid: REEB, 1928 – 1 – sp Bibl Santa Ana [780]

EN EL CUARTO DE MI MUJER / Hurtado, Antonio – 1866 – 9 – 1.50f – sp Bibl Santa Ana [830]

EN EL N° 2 CENTENARIO DEL NACIMIENTO DEL PRINCIPE DE LA PAZ (1767-1967). BADAJOZ Y SU HIJO GODOY, EL MAS ILUSTRE Y CALUMNIADO DE LOS 302 ILUSTRES BADAJOCENSES / Lopez, Benigno – Badajoz: Imp. INCA, s.a. – 1 – sp Bibl Santa Ana [946]

EN EL PAIS DE LOS ETERNOS HIELOS / Bayle, Constantino & Segundo, Llorente – Madrid: Razon y Fe, 1941 – sp Bibl Santa Ana [240]

EN EL PORTAL DE BELEN / Sanchez Loro, Domingo – Caceres: Publicaciones del Departamento de Seminarios de la Jefatura Provincial del Movimiento, 1953 – 1 – sp Bibl Santa Ana [946]

EN EL UMBRAL DEL MISTERIO / Roso de Luna, Mario – Madrid: Editorial Pueyo, 1921 – 1 – sp Bibl Santa Ana [240]

EN ELREMOTO CIGANGO. JORNADAS JAPONESAS / Oteyza, Luis de – Madrid: Editorial Pueyo, S.L. 1927 – sp Bibl Santa Ana [946]

EN GARDE CONTRE LES CONTREFACONS, LES MIRAGES ET LA FAUSSE MONNAIE DES REFORMES BOURGEOISES / Guesde, Jules – Paris. 1911. (La Condition Ouvriere. Part Two.) – 9 – 12.50 – fr Bibl Nationale [360]

EN LA CATEDRAL DE TOLEDO : HORAS DE LUZ...TOLEDO, 1928 / Segura Saenz, Pedro; ed by Bayle, Constantino – Madrid: Razon y Fe, 1928 – 9 – sp Bibl Santa Ana [720]

EN LA ESPANA LEAL HA NACIDO UN EJERCITO / Bates, Ralph – Mexico. 193? Fiche W 750. (Blodgett Collection of Spanish Civil War Pamphlets) – 9 – us H.U. College Libr [946]

EN LA SESION DEL 23 OCTUBRE...VACANTES...FUERON ELEGIDOS...ACADEMICOS DE NUMERO...DUQUE DE T'SERCLARES... / Fita, Fidel – Madrid: Est. Imp. Fortanet, 1908 – 1 – sp Bibl Santa Ana [946]

EN LAS TIERRAS DEL ORO DEL IMPERIO DEL SOL. MADRID, 1945 / Real, Cristobal – Madrid: Razon y Fe, 1947 – 1 – sp Bibl Santa Ana [946]

EN LOS ANDAMIOS / Trigo, Felipe – Madrid: Renacimiento, s.a. – sp Bibl Santa Ana [946]

EN LUTTE – (Filmed with: En Lutte – In Struggle 9/16 dec 1980-22 jun 1982. Index general du debut jusqu'au 21 aut 1973) – Montreal. prospectus mai 1973; 1 mai 1973-2/19 dec 1980 – 5r – 1 – Can$65.00r – cn Can Microfilming [072]

EN LUTTE – IN STRUGGLE *see* EN LUTTE

EN MARGE DE LA LEGENDE DOREE / Saintyves, Pierre – 1930 – 1 – us I.U. Libraries [390]

EN MEMORIA DE RAMON / Sociedad Economica de Amigos del Pais de Badajoz – Badajoz: Imprenta de la Diputacion Provincial, 1963 – sp Bibl Santa Ana [330]

EN NOTAS DE BIBLIOGRAFIA FRANCISCANA / Lopez, Atanasio & Moreno de Robles, Francisco – Archivo Ibero Americano, 1926 – 1 – sp Bibl Santa Ana [240]

EN PLEIN CONFICT / Dubruel, Marc; ed by Bayle, Constantino – Madrid: Razon y Fe, 1928 – 9 – sp Bibl Santa Ana [999]

EN PLEIN FAUBOURG (MOEURS OUVRIERES) / Leyret, Henry – Paris. 1895. (La Condition Ouvriere. Part Two.) – 9 – 7.50 – fr Bibl Nationale [360]

EN PLENA POLEMICA... / Delgado, P J OS A – Madrid: Razon y Fe, 1927 – 1 – sp Bibl Santa Ana [999]

EN PRO Y EN CONTRA (CRITICAS) / Gonzalez Serrano, Urbano – Madrid: Libreria de Victoriano Suarez, S.A. – 1 – sp Bibl Santa Ana [946]

EN ROUTE: SEPT JOURS DANS LES PROVINCES MARITIMES / Faucher de Saint-Maurice, Narcisse – Quebec: A. Cote, 1888. 03064. (Pre-1900 Canadiana) – 9 – cn C.I.H.M. [910]

EN VERITE / Taylor, Raynor – 179? – 9 – us Sibley [780]

EN VILLANUEVA DE LA SIERRA TUVO SU ORIGEN LA "FIESTA DEL ARBOL" / Gutierrez Macias, Valeriano – Badajoz: Imp. Dip. Provincial, 1968. Sep. REE – sp Bibl Santa Ana [390]

EN VILLE : BILINGUE / ed by Gutwillig, Mike – Montreal, 23 mar 1963-19 oct 1970 – 2r – 1 – Can$50.00 – cn Can Microfilming [072]

EN VILLE – Montreal, Canada. 23 mar 1963-12/19 oct 1970 – 2r – 1 – Can$50.00r – cn Can Microfilming [072]

ENAKOPRAVNOST – Cleveland, OH, 1919, 1940-1943, 1949, 1955, 1956 – 8mf or 1 reel – 9,1 – us I.H.R.C. [975]

ENAKOPRAVNOST : DAILY INDEPENDANT SLOVENIAN LANGUAGE NEWSPAPER – Cleveland, OH. 2 Jan-21 Dec 1925 – 2r – 1 – us Western Res [071]

ENARRATIO EPISTOLAE PAVLI, SCRIPTAE AD PHILIPPENSES / Major, G – [Wittenberg], 1559 – 4mf – ne IDC [240]

ENARRATIO PSALMI SEXAGESIMI OCTAVI,... / Major, G – Lipsiae, 1551 – 2mf – ne IDC [240]

ENARRATIONES IN QUINQUE PRIORA CAPITA LIBRI GENESEOS, ET ALII TRACTATUS / Politi, Ambr. Cathar. – Romae, 1552 – 14mf – 8 – ne Slangenburg [220]

ENARRATIONIS PSALMORUM DAVIDIS / Moller, Heinrich – 1610 – 1 – us A.T.L.A. [240]

Enault, E *see* DROIT ROMAIN

Enault, Louis *see* GOETHE OG WERTHER

Enbaev, A M *see* KUSTARNAIA PROMYSHLENNOST'I PROMYSLOVAIA KOOPERATSIIA V NATSIONAL'NYKH RESPUBLIKAKH I OBLASTIAKH SSSR

Encarnacion, Violeta V *see* AUSTRALIA AND ASEAN IN PERSPECTIVE

ENCEPHALE – v1- 1906- 1; n.3- 1977- 5,6,9 – us UMI [616]

L'ENCEPHALE DES CHONDROSTEENS : MORPHOLOGIE ET ANALYSE QUANTITATIVE / Diagne, M – Paris. 1979 – 38p – 9 – F30.00 – fr Ethnologie [590]
L'ENCHAINE / Comite Regional de l'Oranie du Parti Communiste – no. 1. Oran. aout 1932 – 1 – fr A.C.R.P.P. [073]
ENCHIRIDION BOTANICUM / Lipp, F J – Vindobonae. 1765. B-818 2 – 8 – ne IDC [580]
ENCHIRIDION CONTROVERSIARUM PRAECIPUARUM... / Coster, F – Coloniae Agrippinae, 1593 – 8mf – 9 – CA-47/1 – ne IDC [240]
ENCHIRIDION D. TIMOTHEI KIRCHNERI. JN WELCHEM DIE FUERNEMBSTEN HAUPTSTUCK DER CHRISTLICHEN LEHRE DURCH FRAG VND ANTWORT AUSS GOTTES WORT GRUENDTLICH ERKLAERET... / Kirchner, T – Heydelberg, 1584 – 10mf – ne IDC [240]
ENCHIRIDION MUSICAE MENSURALIS / Rhau, Georg – (Part 2 only, Enchiridion utriusque musicae practicae). 1531 – 2 – us Sibley [780]
ENCHIRIDION MUSICAE MENSURALIS / Rhau, Georg – (Part 2 only, Enchiridion utriusque musicae practicae). 1536 – 9 – us Sibley [780]
ENCHIRIDION MVSICAE MENSVRALIS, A GEORGIO RHAV CONGESTUM / Rhau, Georg – Home. lib. Odyss, 8. Vitebergae. 1538. BP-739 1 – 9 – ne IDC [780]
ENCHIRIDION O MANUAL INSTRUMENTO DE SALUD CONTRA EL MORBO ARTICULAR QUE LLAMAN GOTA... / Gomez Miedes, B – Zaragoza, 1589 – 4mf – 9 – sp Cultura [610]
ENCHIRIDION OFT HANDBOECXKEN VAN DE CHRISTELIJCKE LEERE ENDE RELIGION, IN CORTE SOMMA BEGREPEN / Philips, Dirk – 1578. BME-316 1 – 9 – ne IDC [240]
ENCHIRIDION OFT HANTBOECXKEN VAN DE CHRISTELIJCKE LEERE ENDE RELIGION, IN CORTE SOMMA BEGREPEN / Philips, Dirk – 1579. BME-317 1 – 9 – ne IDC [240]
ENCHIRIDION OFT HANTBOECXKEN VAN DE CHRISTELIJCKE LEERE ENDE RELIGION, IN CORTE SOMMA BEGREPEN / Philips, Dirk – 1600. BME-318 1 – 9 – ne IDC [240]
ENCHIRIDION OFT HANTBOECXKEN VAN DE CHRISTELIJCKE LEERE ENDE RELIGION, IN CORTE SOMMA BEGREPEN / Philips, Dirk – Emden? 1564. BME-315 1 – 9 – ne IDC [240]
ENCHIRIDION SIVE MANUALE CONFESSARIORUM ET POENITENTIUM / Martinus ab azpilcueta Navarrus – Antverpiae, 1575 – 18mf – 8 – ne Slangenburg [240]
ENCHIRIDION UTRIUSQUE MUSICAE PRACTICAE / Rhau, Georg – (Complete). 1546 – 2 – us Sibley [780]
ENCHIRIDION VTRIVSQVE MVSICAE PRACTICAE A GEORGIO RHAW EX UARIJS MUSICORUM LIBRIS / Rhau, Georg – Vitebergae. 1535. BP-750 1 – 9 – ne IDC [780]
ENCHIRIDION, OV, BRIEF RECVEIL DV DROICT ESCRIT: GARDE ET OBSERVE OV ABROGE EN FRANCE / Imbert, Jean – Revev, corrige, avgmente et additionne par M.P. Gvenois. Cologny: I. Arnavld, 1615 – 1 – us U.W. Library [944]
LAS ENCICLICAS : RERUM NOVARUM, QUADRAGESIMO ANNO, DIVINI REDEMPTORIS CONTRA EL COMUNISMO Y DIVINI ILLIUS MAGISTRI SOBRE LA EDUCACION CRISTIANA, AL ALCANCE DE TODOS / Marquez, Gabino – Madrid: Apostolado de la Prensa, S.A., 2nd ed 1941 – 1 – sp Bibl Santa Ana [946]
LAS ENCICLICAS : RERUM NOVARUM, QUADRAGESIMO ANNO Y DIVINI REDEMPTORIS CONTRA EL COMUNISMO, AL ALCANCE DE TODOS / Marquez, Gabino – Toledo: Ed. Catolica Toledana, 1938 – 1 – sp Bibl Santa Ana [946]
Encina y la Carrera, Juan Ignacio de la *see* POR LOS...MONASTERIOS DE...
ENCINITAS COAST DISPATCH – Encinitas, CA. 1925- – 138+ r – 1 HC02201 – $6,900.00 ($100.00y) – us Library Micro [071]
ENCINITAS COAST DISPATCH *see* THE PROGRESS
LAS ENCOMIENDAS DE INDIJENAS EN CHILE... : T. 1 AND 2 – SANTIAGO DE CHILE / Amunategui Solar, Domingo – Cervantes, 1909, 1910 – 1 – F518.99 – fr Armell [972]
ENCOMIENDAS. TOMO 1. CARACAS, 1927 / Davila, Vicente – Madrid: Razon y Fe, 1930 – 1 – sp Bibl Santa Ana [946]
ENCOMIUM MORIAE, STULTICIAE / Erasmus, Desiderius – O-247. 1515 – 9 – ne IDC [450]
ENCOMIUM MUSICAE VOCALIS ET INSTRUMENTALIS / Friedrich, Martin – 1610 – 9 – us Sibley [780]
ENCORE UN MOT SUR LA RELIGION SAINT-SIMONIENNE / Chavard – Paris, impr. de David, s.d., 4 p. Les Saint-Simoniens, 1825-1834. 6893 – 9 – fr Hachette [335]
ENCOUNTER – 1- 1940- 1; v30- 5,6; v36- 9 – us UMI [240]
ENCOUNTER – 1953-84 – 1 – uk Microform Academic [073]
A ENCRENCA : CRITICO, LITTERARIO E NOTICIOSO – Manaos, Amazonas. 14 Nov 1915-21 Jan 1917 – 1,5,6 – bl Biblioteca [072]
ENCRUCIJADA JURIDICA DE LA COSTA DE MARFIL / Elias de Tejada Spinola, Francisco – Sevilla: Publicaciones de la Universidad de Sevilla, 1974. Pub. en Estudios de Derechno. pp. 13-75 – 1 – sp Bibl Santa Ana [340]
ENCYCLOPAEDIA JUDAICA, DAS JUDENTUM IN GESCHICHTE UND GEGENWART – (Missing: v9 (p.1107-End); v10) – Berlin. v1-10. 1928-1934 – 62mf – ne IDC [270]
ENCYCLOPAEDIA OF EVIDENCE / ed by Camp, Edgar W et al – Los Angeles: L.D. Powell Co. v1-14 + 1st, 2nd suppl vols. 1902-09 (all publ) – 161mf – 9 – $241.00 – LLMC 82-510 – us L.L.M.C. [360]
ENCYCLOPAEDIA OF FORMS AND PRECEDENTS / ed by McConnel, W H & Mack, William – Northport, NY: Ed Thompson. v1-18. 1896-1904 (all publ) – 208mf – 9 – $312.00 – LLMC 82-511 – us L.L.M.C. [340]
ENCYCLOPAEDIA OF FORMS AND PRECEDENTS FOR PLEADING AND PRACTICE, AT COMMON LAW, IN EQUITY, AND UNDER THE VARIOUS CODES AND PRACTICE ACTS – Northport, N.Y., Cockcroft, 1896-1904. 18 v. LL-898 – 1 – us L of C Photodup [340]
ENCYCLOPAEDIA OF HEREDITY / Burke, J B & Burke, J B – 1 – uk Microform Academic [920]
ENCYCLOPAEDIA OF PLEADING AND PRACTICE / ed by McKinney, William M – Northport, NY: Ed Thompson. v1-23 + 1st, 2nd suppls. 1895-1909 (all publ) – 340mf – 9 – $510.00 – LLMC 82-512 – us L.L.M.C. [340]
THE ENCYCLOPAEDIA OF PLEADING AND PRACTICE, UNDER THE CODES AND PRACTICE ACTS, AT COMMON LAW, IN EQUITY AND IN CRIMINAL CASES – (Supplement. Northport, NY. 1903-09. 4 v. LL-638) – Northport, N.Y., Thompson, 1895-1902. 23 v – 1 – us L of C Photodup [340]
ENCYCLOPAEDIA POLITICA – SE-3000 1. 1960 – 9 – ne IDC [320]
ENCYCLOPAEDIE DER DEUTSCHEN NATIONAL-LITERATUR : ODER, BIOGRAPHISCH-KRITISCHES LEXIKON DER DEUTSCHEN DICHTER UND PROSAISTEN SEIT DEN FRUEHESTEN ZEITEN: NEBST PROBEN AUS IHREN WERKEN / Wolff, Oskar Ludwig Bernhard – Leipzig: C Wigand, 1835-42 – 1r – 1 – us U.W. Library [430]
ENCYCLOPAEDIE DER THEOLOGIE / Hofmann, Johann von – Noerdlingen: C.H. Beck, 1879. 1 fiche – 9 – us A.T.L.A. [240]
ENCYCLOPAEDIE FUER GAERTNER UND LIEBHABER DER GAERTNEREI / Roemer, J J – Tuebingen, 1797 – 5mf – ne IDC [580]
ENCYCLOPAEDIE VAN NEDERLANDSCH-INDIE – Ed. 2. 's-Gravenhage, Leiden, 1917-1939. v.1-8 – 84mf – 9 – ne IDC [950]
ENCYCLOPAEDISCHES WOERTERBUCH DER MEDICINISCHEN WISSENSCHAFTEN (AEL, ABT 3;13) / Graefe, CF v. & Hufeland, CW – Berlin. 37 bde. 1828-1849 (mf ed 1994) – 151mf – 9 – DM2,840.00 – 3-89131-181-8 – gw Fischer [610]
ENCYCLOPEDIA ARCTICA / ed by Stefansson, Vilhjalmur – 27r – 1 – $1945.00 – us UMI [910]
ENCYCLOPEDIA ARCTICA / ed by Stefansson, Vilhjalmur – 27r – 1 – $450.00 set – us Dartmouth [990]
ENCYCLOPEDIA BRITANNICA – Classical Encyclopedias collection – 30mf – 9 – us UMI [030]
ENCYCLOPEDIA JUDAICA : DAS JUDENTUM IN GESCHICHTE UND GEGENWART – Berlin. Band 1-10 (Aach-Lyra). 1928-34 – 168mf – 98 – Dfl588.00 – ne Slangenburg [270]
ENCYCLOPEDIA OF AMERICAN ASSOCIATIONS – 1 – uk Microform Academic [970]
AN ENCYCLOPEDIA OF ARCHITECTURE, HISTORICAL, THEORETICAL AND PRACTICAL... / Gwilt, Joseph – London, 1888 – 28mf – ne IDC [720]
ENCYCLOPEDIA OF CONNECTICUT BIOGRAPHY: GENEALOGICAL, MEMORIAL AND REPRESENTATIVE CITIZENS / American Historical Society – Boston, New York, Chicago, 1917. Connecticut Reel 2. (The Cox Library Collection) – 5 – us Americana [978]
ENCYCLOPEDIA OF GENEALOGY AND BIOGRAPHY OF LAKE COUNTY / Ball, T H – Chicago: Lewis Publ. Co., 1904. Indiana Reel 18. (The Cox Library Collection) – 5 – us Americana [978]
AN ENCYCLOPEDIA OF LAW AND FORMS / Spalding, Hugh Mortimer – Philadelphia, Ziegler, 1880. 676 p. LL-1004 – 1 – us L of C Photodup [340]
ENCYCLOPEDIA OF RELIGIOUS KNOWLEDGE / Brown, J Newton – v. 1 and 2. 1835 – 1 – 25.76 – us Baptist [240]
ENCYCLOPEDIA OF SOUTH DAKOTA / Robinson, Doane – Pierre, 1925. South Dakota Reel 4. (The Cox Library Collection) – 5 – us Americana [978]
ENCYCLOPEDIA OF SOUTHERN BAPTISTS – Original and edited ms. alphabetically arranged – 5 – 819.17 – us Baptist [240]
ENCYCLOPEDIA OF SOUTHERN BAPTISTS – v4 – 1 – 68.10 – us Baptist [240]
THE ENCYCLOPEDIA OF TEXAS / Davis & Grobes – Dallas: Texas Development Bureau. v1-2, Texas Reel 4. v3, Texas Reel 5. (The Cox Library Collection) – 5 – us Americana [978]
ENCYCLOPEDIA OF THE HISTORY OF MISSOURI / Conrad, Howard L – St. Louis: Southern History Co., 1901. v1-4, Missouri Reel 1. v5-6, Missouri Reel 2. (The Cox Library Collection) – 5 – us Americana [978]
ENCYCLOPEDIA OF THE HISTORY OF ST LOUIS / Hyde, William & Conrad, Howard L – St. Louis: Southern Historical Co., 1899. v1, Missouri Reel 29. v2-4, Missouri Reel 30. (The Cox Library Collection) – 5 – us Americana [978]
ENCYCLOPEDIA OF THE LAWS OF ENGLAND : BEING A NEW ABRIDGEMENT BY THE MOST EMINENT LEGAL AUTHORITIES – (Includes suppl and index vol) – London/Edinburgh: Sweet & Maxwell/ William Green & Sons. v1-12. 1897-1903 (all publ) – 84mf – 9 – $126.00 – LLMC 84-800 – us L.L.M.C. [340]
THE ENCYCLOPEDIA OF THE NEW WEST / ed by Speer & Brown – Marshall: United States Biographical Publ. Co., 1881. Texas Reel 7. (The Cox Library Collection) – 5 – us Americana [978]
ENCYCLOPEDIA OF THE U.S. SUPREME COURT REPORTS – (Covers the U.S. Reports v1-259) – Charlottesville, Michie. v1-13. 1908-23 (all publ) – 154mf – 9 – $231.00 – LLMC 90-021 – us L.L.M.C. [340]
ENCYCLOPEDIA OF VIRGINIA BIOGRAPHY / Tyler, Lyon G – New York, Lewis Publishing Co., 1915. Vols. 1-3. Virginia Reel 1; Vols. 4-5. Virginia Reel 2. (The Cox Library Collection) – 5 – us Americana [978]
(ENCYCLOPEDIE) / Diderot, Denis – VI Lutherie. P 237 – 9 – ne IDC [030]
(ENCYCLOPEDIE) / Diderot, Denis – VI Musique. P 238 – 9 – ne IDC [030]
ENCYCLOPEDIE / Diderot, Denis – 1751-1765 – 9 – fr I.C.S. [030]
ENCYCLOPEDIE : OU, DICTIONNAIRE RAISONNE – Classical Encyclopedias collection – 279mf – 9 – us UMI [030]
ENCYCLOPEDIE. 6 LUTHERIE / Diderot, D – N.P., n.d. Planches simples 33 – 2mf – ne IDC [780]
ENCYCLOPEDIE. 6 MUSIQUE / Diderot, D – N.p., n.d. Planches simples 28 – 2mf – ne IDC [780]
L'ENCYCLOPEDIE CANADIENNE / ed by Bibaud, Michel – Montreal, Canada. mar 1842-fev 1843 – 1r – 1 – Can$30.00 – cn Can Microfilming [072]
ENCYCLOPEDIE COLONIALE ET MARITIME – devenu: Encyclopedie mensuelle d'Outre-mer. Paris. sept 1950-avr 1957 – 1 – fr A.C.R.P.P. [944]
ENCYCLOPEDIE DER CHRISTELIJKE THEOLOGIE / Doedes, Jacobus Izaak – 2. vermeer. uit. Utrecht: Kemink & Zoon, 1883 – 1mf – 9 – 0-8370-2944-9 – 1985-0944 – us A.T.L.A. [240]
ENCYCLOPEDIE DER EVANGELISCHEN KIRCHENMUSIK / Kummerle, Salomon – 1885-95 – 1 – 30.00 – us L of C Photodup [780]
ENCYCLOPEDIE DES VOYAGES / Grasset de Saint-Saveur, J – Paris. 5v. 1796 – 47mf – 9 – A-309/2 – ne IDC [910]
ENCYCLOPEDIE GRAMMATICALE / Freville, AF J – 1810 – 9 – fr I.C.S. [400]
ENCYCLOPEDIE METHODIQUE : MEDECINE / d'Azyr, Felix Vicq – Paris/Liege. 13 bde. 1787-1830 (mf ed 1996) – 55mf – 9 – DM1,360.00 – 3-89131-180-X – gw Fischer [610]
ENCYCLOPEDIE METHODIQUE: ARCHITECTURE / Quatremere de Quincy, A C – Paris; Panckouke. Vve. Agasse, 1788-1825. 3v. in 4 fol, 738, 744, 664p. (Architecture Series) – 9 – fr Hachette [720]
ENCYCLOPEDIE METHODIQUE BOTANIQUE / ed by Lamarck, J B A P M de & Poiret, J L M – Paris. v1-8. 1783-1808. Suppl. v1-5. 1810-1817 – 221mf – ne IDC [580]
ENCYCLOPEDIE METHODIQUE MUSIQUE / Framery, Nicolas-Etienne & Ginguene, Pierre-Louis – 2 v. 1791-1818. – 9 – us Sibley [780]
ENCYCLOPEDIE METHODIQUE, OU PAR ORDRE DE MATIERES. 1782-86 – 9 – fr I.C.S. [030]
ENCYCLOPEDIE OECONOMIQUE, OU SYSTEME GENERAL : 1. D'OECONOMIE RUSTIQUE, 2. D'OECONOMIE DOMESTIQUE, 3. D'OECONOMIE POLITIQUE – Yverdon. 16 Bde. 1770-1771 (mf ed 1994) – 35mf – 9 – DM1,320.00 – 3-89131-205-9 – gw Fischer [030]
ENCYCLOPEDIE, OU DICTIONNAIRE RAISONNE DES SCIENCES... / ed by Diderot, M & d'Alembert M – Paris. v1-17. 1751-1780; 1751-1765; 1776-1777, Suppl 1-4; 1780, Suppl 1-2. Recueil des Planches, 1762-1777, 1-12 – 1318mf – 9 – 5437/2 – ne IDC [030]
ENCYCLOPEDIE OU DICTIONNAIRE RAISONNE DES SCIENCES, DES ARTS ET DES METIERS / Diderot, D & D'Alembert, J Le Rond – Paris. v1-17 + suppl 1-4 + planches 1-12. 1751-1777 – 9 – Dfl2,447.00 – ne Slangenburg [030]
ENCYCLOPEDIE, OU DICTIONNAIRE RAISONNE DES SCIENCES, DES ARTS, ET DES METIERS – 1770-75. 17v. 3rd ed – 9r – 1 – $650.00 – us OmniSys [500]
ENCYCLOPEDIE OU DICTIONNAIRE RAISONNE DES SCIENCES, DES ARTS ET DES METIERS (AEL, ABT 1;34) / ed by D'Alembert & Diderot – Paris. 35 bde. 1751-1780 (mf ed 1996) – 180mf – 9 – DM3,400.00 – 3-89131-224-5 – gw Fischer [030]
ENCYCLOPEDIE, OU DICTIONNAIRE UNIVERSEL RAISONNE DES CONNOISSANCES HUMAINE (AEL, ABT.1;7) / Fortune-Barthelemy de Felice – Yverdon, 1770-1780 (mf ed 1993) – 257mf – 9 – DM3,950.00 – 3-89131-069-2 – gw Fischer [030]
AN ENCYCLOPEDIST OF THE DARK AGES : ISIDORE OF SEVILLE / Brehaut, Ernest – New York: Columbia University, Longmans, Green, agents, 1912. (Studies in history, economics and public law; v48, no. 1: whole no. 120) – 1mf – us A.T.L.A. [900]
ENCYKLOPAEDIE DER THEOLOGISCHEN WISSENSCHAFTEN NEBST METHODENLEHRE : ZU AKADEMISCHEN VORLESUNGEN UND ZUM SELBSTSTUDIUM / Krieg, Cornelius – (Includes bibliographies and indexes) – Freiburg im Breisgau; St Louis, MO: Herder, 1899 – 1mf – 9 – 0-8370-4001-9 – 1985-2001 – us A.T.L.A. [240]
ENCYKLOPAEDIE NATURWISSENSCHAFTEN : ABT. 1. HANDBUCH DER BOTANIK – Breslau, 1879-1890. v1-4 – 39mf – 9 – 8606/1 – ne IDC [500]
ENCYKLOPAEDISCHES WOERTERBUCH DER WISSENSCHAFTEN, KUENSTE UND GEWERBE (AEL, ABT.1;6.1) – Altenburg, 1824-47 (mf ed 1992) – 197mf – 9 – DM2,100.00 – 3-89131-079-X – gw Fischer [943]

ENCYKLOPEDJA NAUK POMOCNICZYCH HISTORJI I LITERATURY POLSKIEJ / Ptaszycki, S – (Biblioteka Uniwersytetu Lubelskiego, Wydzial Nauk Humanistycznych, no. 2). Ed.2. Lublin, 1921-1922 – 4mf – 9 – R-14280/1 – ne IDC [460]
ENCYKLOPEDYA DO KRAJOZNAWSTWA GALICYI POD WZGLEDEM HISTORYCZNYM, STATYSTYCZYM, TOPOGRAFICZNYM, OROGRAFICZNYM, HYDROGRAFICZNYM, GEOGNOSTYCZNYM, ETNOGRAFICZNYM, HANDLOWYM, PRZEMYSLOWYM, SFRAGISTYCZNYM,... / Schneider, A – Lwow, 1868-1874. 2 vols – 11mf – 9 – R-17360/1 – ne IDC [947]
THE END OF THE IRISH PARLIAMENT / Fisher, Joseph Robert – London: E. Arnold, 1911.xii,315p. With: Lehrbuch der mechanischen naturlehre by E.G. Fisher. 1 reel. 1292 – 1 – us U.W. Library [941]
END POVERTY PAPER *see* UPTON SINCLAIR'S EPIC NEWS
Endacott, J Earl *see*
- D.D. EISENHOWER HOME AND FAMILY
- "DWIGHT D. EISENHOWER MATERIAL."
DAS ENDE DER EISERNEN SCHAR : MIT DEM "POLNISCHEN TAGEBUCH 1939" / Bodenreuth, Friedrich – Leipzig: Reclam, 1940 – 1r – 1 – us U.W. Library [430]
ENDE GUT, ALLES GUT : ERZAEHLUNG AUS DEM RIES / Meyr, Melchior – Bayreuth: Gauverlag Bayreuth, 1944 – 1r – 1 – us U.W. Library [430]
ENDE UND ANFANG : EIN LEBENSBUCH / Muehlen, Hermynia zur – Berlin: S Fischer, c1929 – 1r – 1 – us U.W. Library [880]
Endean, James Russell *see* DAME EUROPA'S REMOSTRANCE AND HER ULTIMATUM
THE ENDEAVOR HERALD – Toronto: Endeavor Herald Co, [1888?-189- or 19–] – 9 – cn C.I.H.M. [971]
ENDEAVOUR – (Back issues of journal available from UMI) – 4 issues/y. v17. 1993 – 9 – £70.00y – uk Elsevier Sci [910]
ENDEAVOUR – v1- 1977- – 5,6,9 – us UMI [073]
ENDECASILABO CON MOTIVO DEL BOMBARDEO DE ARGEL / Garcia de la Huerta, Vicente – 1783 – 1mf – 9 – Pta1,000.00 – 84-7848-202-4 – sp Pentalfa [946]
Enderbrock, D M *see* THE PARENTAL OBLIGATION TO CARE FOR THE RELIGIOUS EDUCATION OF CHILDREN
Enders, Carl *see* FESTSCHRIFT FUER BERTHOLD LITZMANN ZUM 60. GEBURTSTAG 18.4.1917
Enders, Carl Friedrich *see* GOTTFRIED KELLER
Endl, Elmar *see* DURCHFLUSSZYTOMETRISCHE UNTERSUCHUNGEN VON STOSSWELLENINDUZIERTEN ZELLSCHAEDEN
THE ENDLESS HUNT FOR A HAPPY SCHOOL / Coombs, Margaret – 1973. 1p – 9 – 1.00f – at Libertarian Micro [370]
Endlicher, S L *see*
- ATAKTA BOTANIKA
- CATALOGUS HORTI ACADEMICI VINDOBONENSIS
- ENUMERATIO PLANTARUM QUAS IN NOVAE HOLLANDIAE
- FLORA POSONIENSIS
- GENERA PLANTARUM
- ICONOGRAPHIA GENERUM PLANTARUM
- DIE MEDICINAL-PFLANZEN DER OESTERREICHISCHEN PHARMAKOPOEE
- MELETEMATA BOTANICA
- NOVA GENERA AC SPECIES PLANTARUM QUAS IN REGNO CHILENSI PERUVIANO
- NOVARUM STIRPIUM DECADES
- PRODROMUS FLORAE NORFOLKICAE
- SERTUM CABULICUM
- SYNOPSIS CONIFERARUM

DIE ENDLOSE STRASSE : EIN FRONTSTUECK IN VIER BILDERN / Graff, Sigmund & Hintze, Carl Ernst; ed by Matthaesius, Friedrich – Bielefeld: Velhagen & Klasing, 1936 – 1r – 1 – us U.W. Library [820]
DER ENDLOSE WALD : ROMAN AUS DEM BOEHMERWALD / Attenberger, Toni – 3. Aufl. Frankfurt am Main: Breidenstein, 1940 – 1r – 1 – us U.W. Library [830]
ENDOCRINE RESEARCH – v10-. 1984- – 1,5,6,9 – us UMI [073]
ENDOCRINE RESEARCH COMMUNICATIONS – v1-9. 1974-83 – 1 – us UMI [073]
Endocrine Society *see* ENDOCRINOLOGY
THE ENDOCRINOLOGIST – v1-6. 1991-96 – 1,5,6,9 – $95.00r – us Williams [616]
ENDOCRINOLOGY / Endocrine Society – (Endocrine Society: Association for the study of the internal secretions). v. 1-95. 1917-1974 – 1,5,6 – us Princeton Micro [610]
ENDOCRINOLOGY – (v. 80- 1967- 5,6. v. 86- 1970- 9) – v. 1- 1917- – 1 – us UMI [610]
ENDOCRINOLOGY INDEX – v. 3-4. 1970-1971 – 1,5,6 – us Princeton Micro [610]
Endore, S Guy *see* THE SLEEPY LAGOON MYSTERY
ENDOTHELIUM : JOURNAL OF ENDOTHELIAL CELL RESEARCH / ed by Rubanyi, Gabor M – 9,5,1 – us Harwood [574]
THE ENDOWMENTS AND ESTABLISHMENT OF THE CHURCH OF ENGLAND / Brewer, J S – London: John Murray, 1885 – 1mf – us A.T.L.A. [240]
ENDOWMENTS OF THE CHURCH OF SCOTLAND IN CANADA: EVIDENCE OF MR. DOUGLAS BRYMNER BEFORE THE SENATE COMMITTEE ON PRIVATE BILLS, IN OPPOSITION TO THE BILLS FOR TRANSFERRING THE SAID ENDOWMENTS TO THE PRESBYTERIAN CHURCH IN CANADA, 24TH AND 26TH APRIL, 1882 / Brymner, Douglas – Toronto: Hunter, Rose, 1883. 02847. (Pre-1900 Canadiana) – 9 – cn C.I.H.M. [240]
Endres, K *see* DIE VOELKERRECHTLICHEN GRUNDSAETZE DER KRIEGFUEHRUNG ZU LANDE UND ZUR SEE
Endress, Gerhard *see* DIE ARABISCHEN UEBERSETZUNGEN VON ARISTOTELES' SCHRIFT DE CAEOLO
Endroedi, A *see* HISTOIRE DE LA LITTERATURE HONGROISE
Enduran, Ludoix *see* LA TRAITE DES NEGRES; OU, DEUX MARINS AU SENEGAL
ENDYMION : A POETIC ROMANCE / Keats, John – London: Printed for Taylor and Hessey, 1818 – 1 roll – 1 – 1-55879-662-2 – uk Libr Preservation [810]
Endzelin, I *see* SLAVIANO-BALTIISKIE ETIUDY
Endzelin, J *see*
- ALTPREUSSISCHE GRAMMATIK
- BALTU VALODU SKANAS UN FORMAS
- IEVADS BALTU FILOLOG'IA
- LETTISCHE GRAMMATIK

ENEA SILVIO DE' PICCOLOMINI, ALS PAPST PIUS DER ZWEITE: UND SEIN ZEITALTER / Voigt, Georg – Berlin: G. Reimer, 1856-1863 – 4mf – us A.T.L.A. [240]
ENEAS ROMAN / Veldeke, Heinrich von – 27p + 6 color mf – DM620.00 – 3-89219-002-X – gw Lengenfelder [090]
LA ENEIDA DE... / Virgilio – Coria: Imp. de P. Evaristo Montero, 1873 – 1 – sp Bibl Santa Ana [946]
Enelow, H G *see* AN EIGHTEENTH CENTURY BIBLIOPHILE
THE ENEMY SIDE OF THE HILL / U.S. Army. Historical Division – The 1945 background on interrogation of German commanders. 1949 – 1 – 21.00 – us L of C Photodup [943]
DIE ENERGIE – Hannover, Germany. 1926-27 – 1 – gw Mikrofilm [072]
ENERGY : A CRISIS IN POWER / Holdren, John & Herrera, Philip – 1r – $50.00 – B70009 – us Library Micro [333]
ENERGY : THE INTERNATIONAL JOURNAL – v1- 1976- – 5,6,9 – us UMI [621]
ENERGY – (Merged with: Canada Stamp Sheet to become: Canada Stamp Sheet and Energy) – Berlin [Kitchener], Ont.: Energy Pub Co, [1899-] – 9 – cn C.I.H.M. [760]
ENERGY – v1- 1975- – 1,5,6,9 – us UMI [621]
ENERGY *see* THE CANADA STAMP SHEET
ENERGY ABSTRACTS 1994 – $700.00y $730.00y outside North America – us Ei [333]
ENERGY ABSTRACTS 1995 – $700y $730y outside North America – us Ei [333]
ENERGY ABSTRACTS 1996 – $1,075.00y $1,125.00y outside America – us Ei [333]
ENERGY AND AGRICULTURE – (Base collection 1816mf $5045; 1984 update 667mf $1865) – 2483mf complete collection – 9 – $6910.00 complete collection – us UMI [630]
ENERGY AND BUILDINGS – v1-7. 1977-84 – 1,5,6,13 – sz Elsevier [621]
ENERGY AND FUELS – v1- 1987- – 1,5,6,9 – us A.C.S. [621]
ENERGY AND PROTEIN REQUIREMENTS : REPORT OF A JOINT FAO/WHO AD HOC EXPERT COMMITTEE, ROME, 1971 – 3rd printing 1977 – 118p – it F.A.O. [612]
ENERGY BALANCE AND THE COMPONENTS OF TOTAL DAILY ENERGY EXPENDITURE IN ENDURANCE TRAINED AND UNTRAINED WOMEN / Beidleman, B A – 1991 – 3mf – 9 – $12.00 – us Microform Publ [613]
ENERGY BALANCES AND ELECTRICITY PROFILES / United Nations – E.34 – 9 (ST/ESA/STAT/Ser.W/1-4) – us U.N. Pubs [333]
ENERGY COMMITTEE / UN Economic Commission for Europe (ECE) – 1956-89 – E/F.249 E.135 F.87 R.84 – 9 – us U.N. Pubs [340]
ENERGY CONSERVATION IN THE MECHANICAL FOREST INDUSTRIES – 1990 – 130p – it F.A.O. [338]
ENERGY CONVERSION *see* ENERGY CONVERSION AND MANAGEMENT
ENERGY CONVERSION AND MANAGEMENT – (Formerly: Energy Conversion) – v1- 1961- – 5,6,9 – us UMI [621]
ENERGY COST OF WALKING WITH AND WITHOUT ARM ACTIVITY ON THE CROSS WALK DUAL MOTION CROSS TRAINER / Knox, Kelly M – 1993 – 1mf – $4.00 – us Microform Publ [612]
THE ENERGY COST OF WOMEN WALKING WITH AND WITHOUT HAND WEIGHTS WHILE PERFORMING RHYTHMIC ARM MOVEMENTS / Zywicki, Scott S & Butts, Nancy Kay – 1992 – 1mf – $4.00 – us Microform Publ [612]
ENERGY CROPPING VERSUS FOOD PRODUCTION – 1981 – 62p – it F.A.O. [338]
ENERGY EXPENDITURE OF STEP TRAINING VS. LOW IMPACT AEROBICS USING THREE COMMON MOVEMENT PATTERNS / Barry, Dawn M – Purdue University, 1995 – 1mf – 9 – PH 1485 – us Microform Publ [612]
THE ENERGY FLOW OF THE HUMAN BEING AND THE UNIVERSE : TAI JI PHILOSOPHY AS AN ARTISTIC AND PHILOSOPHICAL FOUNDATION FOR THE DEVELOPMENT OF CHINESE CONTEMPORARY DANCE / Yu, Jin-Wen – 1994 – 4mf – $16.00 – us Microform Publ [306]
ENERGY FOR WORLD AGRICULTURE / Stout, B A – 1979 repr 1981 – 286p – it F.A.O. [333]
ENERGY INFORMATION DATABASE – (Annual update. $22125.00y) – 1956-80. Ed. by R. Voight and G. Franklin – 9 – $22400.00; $225.00t – us I.R.E. [621]
ENERGY INFORMATION FICHE – Subscription service of current titles in energy information on microfiche. 2100 titles yearly taken from scholarly, scientific, industrial, technical and general periodicals and from U.S. Govt. documents and United Nations materials. All information cross-indexed. Issued monthly. Includes abstract journals, annual index and bound abstracts annual. Retrospective to 1971. Publ. ceased 1993 – 9 – $8,350.00 – us Bowker [621]
ENERGY JOURNAL – v1- 1980- – 1,5,6,9 – us UMI [621]
ENERGY LAW JOURNAL – v1- 1980- – 1,5,6,9 – us UMI [621]
ENERGY LAW JOURNAL – v1-16. 1980-1995 – 9 – $277.00 – us Hein [340]
ENERGY MANAGEMENT – v1-9 no 5. 1975-May 1983 – 1,5,6"9 – us UMI [621]
ENERGY MANAGEMENT TECHNOLOGY – 1984- – 1,5,6,9 – us UMI [621]
ENERGY POLICY – v1- 1973- – 1,5,6,9 – us UMI [621]
ENERGY POLICY AND THE GAS AND FUEL CORPORATION OF VICTORIA / Edwards, G W – CIS, 1983, 22p – 9 – 1.00f – at Libertarian Micro [333]
ENERGY PROCESSING CANADA – Calgary. v72-86. 1979/80-1993/94 – 9 – Can$20.00y – cn Micromedia [621]
ENERGY PROGRESS – v1- 1981- – 1,5,6,9 – us UMI [622]
ENERGY RESEARCH ABSTRACTS – v1-8. 1976-83. Continues: E.R.D.A. Abstracts – 1,5,6 – us Princeton Micro [530]
ENERGY RESEARCH ABSTRACTS: INDEX – v1-8. 1976-83 – 1,5,6 – us Princeton Micro [530]
ENERGY REVIEW – v1-5 1982-86 – 1,5,6 – us Princeton Micro [621]
ENERGY SENSE – 1984- – 1,5,6,9 – us UMI [621]
ENERGY SOURCES – (1975- 5,6,9) – v1-1973- – 1 – us UMI [621]
ENERGY STATISTICS YEARBOOK / United Nations – 1982-1988 – E/F.69 – 9 (ST/ESA/STAT/Ser.J/26-32) – us U.N. Pubs [333]
ENERGY SYSTEMS AND POLICY – v. 1-1974- – 1,5,6,9 – us UMI [530]
ENERGY USER NEWS – New York, 1976- – 1 – $175.00y – us Fairchild Micro [621]
ENERGYFICHE : RETROSPECTIVE 1976-1993 – (Access to key information identified by Energy Information Abstracts in Environment Abstracts database) – 9 – Apply for price – us CIS [020]
Enesco, G *see*
- SUITE POUR PIANO, OP. 10
- VARIATIONS POUR 2 PIANOS, OP. 5

Enestrom, G *see* JAHRESBERICHT DER DEUTSCHEN MATHEMATIKER-VEREINIGUNG
L'ENFANCE BAMBARA : APPROCHE PSYCHO-CULTURALE DE TROIS PHASES PRE-CIRCONCISIONELLES EN PAYS BAMBARA / Couloubaly, Pascal Baba F – Dakar: IFAN, 1986 – us Res Libr [300]
L'ENFANCE DE SUZETTE: LIVRE DE LECTURE COURANTE A L'USAGE DES JEUNES FILLES / Halt, Marie Malezieux – Paris: P. Delaplaine, 1892. 143p. gravures. (Literature Collection) – 2mf – 9 – $6.00 – fr Bibl Nationale [830]
L'ENFANCE DIFFICILE, VICIEUSE OU DELINQUANTE ET L'ASSISTANCE PUBLIQUE DEPARTEMENTALE / Lelievre, Julien – Rennes. 1921. (La Condition Ouvriere. Part Two.) – 9 – 5.00 – fr Bibl Nationale [360]
L'ENFANT TERRIBLE – Montreal, Canada. v1 n?. 3 aut 1872 – 1r – 1 – Can$25.00 – cn Can Microfilming [072]
Enfantin, BP *see*
- DE L'ALLEMAGNE
- LETTRE DU PERE A CHARLES DUVEYRIER SUR LA VIE ETERNELLE
- LETTRE DU PERE ENFANTIN A CHARLES DUVEYRIER. LETTRE DU PERE ENFANTIN A FRANCOIS ET A PEIFFER. LE PRETRE, L'HOMME ET LA FEMME

LES ENFANTS CELEBRES / Chaumette, E J M – Limoges: E. Ardant, 1888?. 191p. ill – 1 – us U.W. Library [920]
L'ENFER DETRUIT OU EXAMEN RAISONNE DU DOGME DE L'ETERNITE DES PEINES – (D'Holbach series). 1769 – 9 – fr Hachette [240]
ENFERMEDADES ROJAS DEL CERDO / Lopez Sanchez, Ernesto – Badajoz: La Alianza, 1934 – 1 – sp Bibl Santa Ana [946]
ENFIELD 1770-1890 – (Mf 1-3: B,M,Intents, Deaths 1783-1849. Mf 4-6: B,M,D 1844-54. Mf 7-9: B,M,D 1859-92. Mf 10-11: Marriage Intentions 1849-1905. Mf 12-28: Index to Births 1770-1938. Mf 29-45: Index to Marriage Intents 1816-1905. Mf 46-62: Index to Marriages 1816-1937. Mf 63-79: Index to Deaths 1802-1938. Mf 80: Index to Burials) – (mf ed 1984) – 80mf – 9 – 0-931248-73-6 – us Holbrook [920]
ENFIELD GAZETTE AND OBSERVER – London, UK. 1984. -w. 3 reels – 1 – uk British Libr Newspaper [072]
Enfield Waltham Sunday School *see* REPORTS
ENFORCEMENT JOURNAL – v. 1-. 1962- – 1 – us UMI [360]
THE ENFORCEMENT OF FOREIGN JUDGMENTS / Ball, WV – London, Liverpool, 1928 – 1mf – 9 – ILM-2247/1 – ne IDC [340]
ENFORCEMENT OF JUDGMENTS AND ORDERS / Obi-Okoye, A – Enugu, Nigeria: Reveille 1973. 58p. LL-12047 – 1 – us L of C Photodup [340]
ENGADIN EXPRESS AND ALPINE POST – Samaden, Switzerland. -w. 1 June 1901-24 Aug 1939. 56 reels – 1 – uk British Libr Newspaper [949]
Engberg *see* HISTORY OF THE SWEDES OF ILLINOIS
Engberg, Robert M *see* NOTES ON THE CHALCOLITHIC AND EARLY BRONZE AGE POTTERY AT MEGIDDO
Engdahl, Richard *see* BEITRAEGE ZUR KENNTNIS DER BYZANTINISCHEN LITURGIE
Engel, A *see*
- CALVINISCHER BETLERSMANTEL DARIN ANGEZEIGET WIRD MIT WAS KLEIDER SIE SICH BEKAPEN DEN SCHALCK VERBERGEN VND ZUDECKEN KOENNEN...
- THEWRUNGS SPIEGEL DARINNEN GEWIESEN WIRD WOHER THEWRUNG KOEME VND WARUMB...

Engel, Eduard *see* FREMDWOERTERBUCH
Engel, Johann Christian von *see* GESCHICHTE VON HALITSCH UND WLADIMIR BIS 1772..
Engel, S *see* ART. 5 UND ART. 14 SATZ 3 DER VOELKERBUNDSATZUNG

Engel, Samuel *see* ESSAI SUR CETTE QUESTION

Engelbach, Georg *see* RELIGIOESE FRAGEN

ENGELBERG : EINE DICHTUNG / Meyer, Conrad Ferdinand – 7. Aufl. Leipzig: H Haessel, 1900 – 1r – 1 – us U.W. Library [810]

Engelbrecht, I W *see* COMMENTATIO DE JURE PEREGRINANTIUM

Engel'gardt, A N *see* IZ DEREVNI

Engelgrave, H *see*
- COELUM EMPYREUM, NON VANIS ET FICTIS CONSTELLATIONUM MONSTRIS BELLUATUM, SED DIVUM DOMUS DOMINI JESU CHRISTI, EJUSQUE ILLIBATAE VIRGINIS MATRIS MARIAE, SANCTORUM APOSTOLORUM, MARTYRUM.....
- LUX EVANGELICA SUB VELUM SACRORUM EMBLEMATUM RECONDITA
- LUX EVANGELICA SUB VELUM SACRORUM EMBLEMATUM RECONDITA...

Engelhard, Karl *see* FRIEDRICH HEBBEL ALS LYRIKER

Engelhard-Colton, Nancy *see* THE EFFECTS OF ORAL CONTRACEPTION AND HYPOXIA ON RESPIRATORY PARAMETERS DURING GRADED EXERCISE

Engelhardt, D J *see* RICHARD VON ST VICTOR UND JOHANNES RUSBROEK

Engelhardt, E *see*
- DU REGIME CONVENTIONNEL DES FLEUVES INTERNATIONAUX
- HISTOIRE DU DROIT FLUVIAL CONVENTIONNEL
- LES PROTECTORATS ANCIENS ET MODERNES

Engelhardt, Zephyrin *see*
- THE FRANCISCANS IN ARIZONA
- THE FRANCISCANS IN CALIFORNIA
- THE MISSIONS AND MISSIONAIRES OF CALIFORNIA...SANTA BARBARA, 1929

ENGELHOLMS TIDNING – AEngelholm, 1867-1946 – 9 – sw Kungliga [072]

Engelkemper, W *see* DIE REL. PHIL. LEHRE SAADJA GAONS UEBER DIE HL. SCHRIFT

Engelkemper, Wilhelm *see*
- HEILIGTUM UND OPFERSTAETTEN IN DEN GESETZEN DES PENTATEUCH
- DIE REL. PHIL. LEHRE SAADJA GAONS UEBER DIE HL. SCHRIFT

Engelmann, CW *see* GENERA PLANTARUM ODER DIE PLFANZEN-GATTUNGEN DER IN DEN RUSSISCHEN OSTSEEPROVINZEN ESTH-, LIV- UND KURLAND WILDWACHSENDEN PFLANZEN

Engelmann, G *see*
- AMERICAN JUNIPERS-SECTION SABINA
- THE OAKS OF THE UNITED STATES
- SYNOPSIS OF THE AMERICAN FIRS
- SYNOPSIS OF THE CACTEAE OF THE UNITED STATES

Engelmann, J *see* DIE ZWANGSVOLLSTRECKUNG AUSWAERTIGER RICHTERLICHER URTHEILE IN RUSSLAND

Engel-Mitscherlich, Hilde *see* HEBBEL ALS DICHTER DER FRAU

Engels, Friedrich *see*
- DIE BAKUNISTEN AN DER ARBEIT
- DER DEUTSCHE BAUERKRIEG
- DIE ENTWICKLUNG DES SOZIALISMUS
- TENTANG OTORITET

Engelsmann, Walter *see* GOETHE UND BEETHOVEN

DER ENGELWIRT: EINE SCHWABENGESCHICHTE / Strauss, Emil – Berlin, c1921. 145p – 1 – us U.W. Library [830]

Engert, Horst *see* DIE TRAGIK DER DEM LEBEN NICHT GEWACHSENEN INNERLICHKEIT IN DEN WERKEN GERHART HAUPTMANNS

Engert, Thaddaeus *see* DER BETENDE GERECHTE DER PSALMEN

ENGINEER – v1- 1856- 1; v234- 5,6; v244- 9 – us UMI [620]

ENGINEER (LONDON) – v169-208 1940-59 – 1,5,6 – us Princeton Micro [620]

ENGINEERED SYSTEMS – v1- . 1984- – 1,5,6,9 – us UMI [073]

ENGINEERING – v1- 1866- 1; v199- 5,6; v216- 9 – us UMI [620]

ENGINEERING – London: Charles Robert Johnson, [v9. jan-jun 1895] – us Res Libr [620]

The Engineering and Allied Trades Shop Stewards' National Council *see* THE METAL WORKER

ENGINEERING AND CONSTRUCTION WORLD – 1965- 1; 1975- 5,6,9 – us UMI [620]

ENGINEERING AND MINING JOURNAL – 1-1866- 1; v171- 5,6; v176- 9 – us UMI [620]

ENGINEERING AND SERVICES, AIR FORCE ENGINEERING AND SERVICES QUARTERLY *see* AIR FORCE ENGINEERING AND SERVICES QUARTERLY

ENGINEERING APPLICATIONS, 2 : HAULING DEVICES FOR SMALL FISHING CRAFT – 1982 – 159p – it F.A.O. [623]

ENGINEERING APPLICATIONS, 3 : HYDRAULICS FOR SMALL FISHING VESSELS – 1989 – 190p – it F.A.O. [623]

ENGINEERING APPLICATIONS OF ARTIFICIAL INTELLIGENCE – 1,5,69 – us UMI [620]

ENGINEERING COSTS AND PRODUCTION ECONOMICS – v1-8 1976-84. Continues: Engineering and Process Economics – 1,5,6,13 – sz Elsevier [338]

ENGINEERING CYBERNETICS – (v22-. 1984-. 5,6,9) – v1-22. 1963-83 – 1 – us UMI [000]

ENGINEERING DESIGN AND MANUFACTURING INDEX – 1967. 1v. 6 sections. Updated 2 times per yr – 5 – uk Tech [621]

ENGINEERING DIGEST – (Suspended v38 no 5 1992) – Mississauga. v1-38. 1954/55-1992 – 5,9 – Price varies – cn Micromedia [620]

ENGINEERING FRACTURE MECHANICS – v1-1968- – 5,6,9 – us UMI [073]

ENGINEERING GEOLOGY – v. 1-20. 1965-82 – 1,5,6 – sz Elsevier [550]

ENGINEERING GEOLOGY – v1-20. 1965-82 – 1,5,6,13 – sz Elsevier [550]

ENGINEERING IN MEDICINE – v1- 1971- 1; v5- 5,6,9 – us UMI [610]

ENGINEERING INDEX – v1 1884-1891 – 1 – us NY Public [620]

THE ENGINEERING INDEX ANNUAL – (1884-1969 $400y, $425y overseas; 1970-1980 $500y, $540y overseas; 1981 $560y, $600y overseas; 1982 $630y, $670y overseas; 1983 $680y, $720y overseas; 1984 $720y, $760y overseas; 1985-86 $745y, $790y overseas; 1987 $840y, $890y overseas; 1988 $910y, $960y overseas; 1989 $940y, $990y overseas; 1990 $1,210y, $1,250y overseas; 1991 $1,460y $1,560y overseas; 1992 $1,540y $1,640y overseas, 1993 $1,820y $1,980y overseas; 1994 $2,100y $2,200y overseas) – 1,5,6,13 – us Ei [620]

THE ENGINEERING INDEX ANNUAL 1995 – (Abstracts of the worldwide engineering literature on annual basis, organized by subject) – v94. 1996 – 1,5,6,13 – $2,270.00; $2,375.00 outside North America – us Ei [620]

THE ENGINEERING INDEX COMBINATION – (1996 monthly. 1995 annual) – $3,490.00; $3,750.00 outside North America – us Ei [620]

THE ENGINEERING INDEX MONTHLY 1996 – 1,5,6,13 – $2,645.00y $2,970.00y outside North America – us Ei [620]

ENGINEERING INDUSTRIES COMMITTEE / UN Economic Commission for Europe (ECE) – 1963-89 – E/F.188 E.424 F.280 R.211 – 9 – us U.N. Pubs [340]

ENGINEERING JOURNAL – (5,6,9 1975-) – 1918- – 1 – us UMI [620]

ENGINEERING (LONDON) – v160-188 1945-59 – 1,5,6 – us Princeton Micro [620]

ENGINEERING MAGAZINE – v. 1-40. 1891-1911 – 1 – us UMI [620]

ENGINEERING MANPOWER : A COMPARATIVE STUDY ON THE EMPLOYMENT OF GRADUATE ENGINEERS IN THE WESTERN WORLD / Berghe, Wouter Van den – 1986 – 234p – 9 – 92-3-102382-9 – fr UNESCO [331]

ENGINEERING NEWS – No.1- . 1985- – 1,5,6,9 – us UMI [073]

ENGINEERING NEWS-RECORD – v1- 1874- – 1,5,6,9 – us UMI [620]

ENGINEERING OPTICS – v1-6. 1987-93. Publ. ceased – 1,5,6,9 – uk I.O.P. [621]

ENGINEERING OPTIMIZATION / ed by Templeman, A B – 1974- – 1,5,9 – us Gordon [620]

ENGINEERING SCHOOLS AND ENDOGENOUS TECHNOLOGY DEVELOPMENT – 1988 – 113p – 9 – 92-3-102528-7 – fr UNESCO [370]

ENGINEERING SCIENCES AND MECHANICS – (Suppl to v50, Advances) – 1983 – 2mf – 9 – $10.00 – 0-87703-215-7 – us Univelt [629]

ENGINEERING SERVICES AND PERSONNEL TRAINING FOR THE REPUBLIC OF INDONESIA, MINISTRY OF PUBLIC WORKS AND POWER : FINAL REPORT / Ralph M. Parsons Company – SE-10,705 1. 1963 – 9 – ne IDC [620]

ENGINEERING SIMULATION / ed by Pukhov, G E – 9,5,1 – us Gordon [620]

Engineering Societies. New York *see*
- CLASSED SUBJECT CATALOG OF THE ENGINEERING SOCIETIES LIBRARY AND INDEX TO THE CLASSED SUBJECT CATALOG
- CLASSIFIED SUBJECT CATALOG

ENGINEERING SOFTWARE DIRECTORY – 1985- – 1 – us UMI [073]

ENGINEERING TECHNICIANS : SOME PROBLEMS OF NOMENCLATURE AND CLASSIFICATION – 1981 – 144p – 9 – 92-3-101831-0 – fr UNESCO [600]

Engineers and Architects Association of Southern California *see* SOUTHWEST CONTRACTOR AND MANUFACTURER

ENGINEER'S DIGEST – 1984- – 1 – us UMI [620]

Englaender, Sigmund *see* GESCHICHTE DER FRANZOESISCHEN ARBEITER ASSOCIATIONEN

ENGLAND / Gairdner, James – London: S.P.C.K.; New York: Pott, Young, [1879?] – 1mf – us A.T.L.A. [941]

ENGLAND; A SHORT HISTORY / Smith, Goldwin Albert – New York: Scribner, (1971). xv,549p. geneal. tables, maps – 1 – us U.W. Library [941]

ENGLAND AND CANADA: A SUMMER TOUR BETWEEN OLD AND NEW WESTMINSTER: WITH HISTORICAL NOTES / Fleming, Sandford – Montreal: Dawson, 1884. 03129. (Pre-1900 Canadiana) – 9 – cn C.I.H.M. [910]

ENGLAND AND CHRISTENDOM / Manning, Henry Edward – London: Longmans, Green, 1867 – 1mf – us A.T.L.A. [240]

ENGLAND AND HER COLONIES – The five best essays on imperial federation submitted to the London Chamber of Commerce for their prize competition, and recommended for publication by the judges: J. Anthony Froude, Professor J. R. Seeley, and Sir Rawson W. Rawson. London: Sonnenschein, Lowrey, 1887. 02917. (Pre-1900 Canadiana) – 9 – cn C.I.H.M. [971]

THE ENGLAND AND HOLLAND OF THE PILGRIMS / Dexter, Henry Martyn & Dexter, Morton – Boston: Houghton, Mifflin, 1905 – 2mf – us A.T.L.A. [240]

ENGLAND AND IRELAND: A LECTURE / Bray, Alfred James – Montreal: A. Bray, 1880. 00254. (Pre-1900 Canadiana) – 9 – cn C.I.H.M. [941]

ENGLAND AND ROME : A HISTORY OF THE RELATIONS BETWEEN THE PAPACY AND THE ENGLISH STATE AND CHURCH FROM THE NORMAN CONQUEST TO THE REVOLUTION OF 1688 / Ingram, T Dunbar – London; New York: Longmans, Green,1892 – 2mf – us A.T.L.A. [240]

ENGLAND AND RUSSIA IN CENTRAL ASIA / Boulger, Demetrius Charles de Kavanagh – London: W.H. Allen, 1879. 2v. 2 maps and appendices – 1 – us U.W. Library [950]

ENGLAND AND THE HOLY SEE : AN ESSAY TOWARDS REUNION / Jones, Spencer – London; New York: Longmans, Green, 1902 – 2mf – us A.T.L.A. [240]

England. Exchequer Chamber *see* MEESON AND WELSBY'S REPORTS

England. Inns of Court *see*
- ACTS OF PARLIAMENT AND BENCH TABLE ORDERS OF THE INNER TEMPLE
- GESTA GREYORUM...

England, Joyce *see* A COMPARISON OF THE TENSILE STRENGTH OF THE UMBILICAL CORD OF BABIES OF SMOKING AND NON-SMOKING MOTHERS

England, Kathleen M *see* ANALYSIS OF THE INSTRUCTIONAL ECOLOGY IN TUTORIAL TENNIS SETTINGS

ENGLAND TWO HUNDRED YEARS AGO / Gillett, E H – Philadelphia: Presbyterian Board of Publication, c1866 – 1mf – us A.T.L.A. [941]

ENGLAND UNDER PROTECTOR SOMERSET : AN ESSAY / Pollard, AF – London: K. Paul, Trench, Truebner, 1900 – 1mf – us A.T.L.A. [941]

ENGLAND UNDER THE OLD RELIGION : AND OTHER ESSAYS / Gasquet, Francis Aidan – London: G. Bell; New Work: Macmillan [distributor], 1912 – 1mf – us A.T.L.A. [240]

ENGLAND VERSUS ROME : A BRIEF HAND-BOOK OF THE ROMAN CATHOLIC CONTROVERSY FOR THE USE OF MEMBERS OF THE ENGLISH CHURCH / Swete, Henry Barclay – London: Rivingtons, 1868 – 1mf – us A.T.L.A. [240]

ENGLAND'S DANGER / Horton, Robert Forman – London: James Clarke, 1899 – 1mf – 9 – 0-8370-8436-9 – 1986-2436 – us A.T.L.A. [240]

ENGLANDS EINFLUSS AUF DIE LEHRDICHTUNG HALLERS / Wyplel, Ludwig – Wien: Im Selbstverlage des Verfassers, 1888 – 1r – 1 – us U.W. Library [410]

ENGLANDS EINFLUSS AUF GEORG RUDOLF WECKHERLIN / Boehm, Wilhelm – (Includes bibliographical references) – Goettingen: Dieterich'sche Univ.-Buchdruckerei, 1893 – 1r – 1 – us U.W. Library [943]

Engler, A *see*
- AMTLICHER BERICHT UEBER DIE 50. VERSAMMLUNG DEUTSCHER NATURFORSCHER UND AERZTE
- BOTANISCHE JAEHRBUCHER FUER SYSTEMATIK, PFLANZENGESCHICHTE UND PFLANZENGEOGRAPHIC

Engler, Bruno *see* DIE VERWALTUNG DER STADT MUENSTER VON DEN LETZTEN ZEITEN DER FUERSTBISCHOEFLICHEN BIS ZUM AUSGANG DER FRANZOESISCHEN HERRSCHAFT 1802-1813

Engler, H G A *see*
- MONOGRAPHIEEN AFRIKANISCHER PFLANZEN-FAMILIEN UND GATTUNGEN
- DIE NATUERLICHEN PFLANZENFAMILIEN
- DIE NATURLICHEN PFLANZENFAMILLIEN
- SYLLABUS DER VORLESUNGEN UEBER SPECIELLE UND MEDICINISCH-PHARMACEUTISCHE BOTANIK. ED. 8

ENGLEWOOD TIMES – Chicago. Ill. 1905-1924 – 1 – us UMI [071]

Englich, Ulrich *see* ROENTGENOGRAPHISCHE UDN SPEKTROSKOPISCHE UNTERSUCHUNGEN AN ALKALI-MANGAN(3)-VERBINDUNGEN VOM KRYOLITH-TYP, SOWIE AN CR(H20)6MNF6

DAS ENGLISCHE CHRISTENVOLK UND WIR / Wurster, Paul – Tuebingen: Kloeres, 1915. 32p – 1 – us U.W. Library [940]

ENGLISCHE CORRESPONDENZ – London, UK. Aug 1850-Nov 1851; 1852-Aug 1856; Feb 1860-1861 – 1 – uk British Libr Newspaper [072]

ENGLISCHE DICHTUNG AUS GOETHES ZEITALTER IM LICHT DEUTSCHER KUNSTLEHRE / Edwards, Oliver – (Includes bibliographical references) – Bonn a. Rh.: L Roehrscheid, 1930 – 1r – 1 – us U.W. Library [420]

ENGLISCHE MOTTETEN UND MADRIGALE : AUS DER SAMMLUNG WAGENER, MARBURG – Karlsruhe: Abschrift von Carl Dreher, 19th century manuscript – 1 – us Sibley [780]

L'ENGLISE (SIC) DU CANADA / Gosselin, Auguste – Paris: Letouzey et Ane, 1895. 03473. (Pre-1900 Canadiana) – 9 – cn C.I.H.M. [240]

THE ENGLISH / Maclear, George Frederick – London: Society for Promoting Christian Knowledge; New York: E.& J.B. Young, [1878?] (Conversion of the West) – 1mf – us A.T.L.A. [240]

ENGLISH 19TH CENTURY CAMEO GLASS FROM THE COLLECTION OF MR. AND MRS. ALBERT CHRISTIAN REVI – 1963. 44p. 38 illus. 1 fiche. Fiche No.1034 – 9 – $2.50 – us Corning Mus [740]

THE ENGLISH ACCIDENCE – Anon. 1733. 117p. (English Linguistics Series 1500-1800) – 9 – us UMI [420]

THE ENGLISH ACCIDENCE: OR, A SHORT, PLAINE AND EASIE WAY FOR THE MORE SPEEDY ATTAINING TO THE LATINE TONGUE / Poole, Joshua – 1646. 57p. (English Linguistics Series 1500-1800) – 9 – us UMI [450]

THE ENGLISH ANCESTRY AND HOMES OF THE PILGRIM FATHERS – Passengers on the Mayflower (1620), Fortune (1621), and Anne (1623). By Charles Edward Banks 1929. Item D. 187p. Indexed. SW16-0079 – 5 – us A.G.L.L. [920]

THE ENGLISH AND AMERICAN REGISTER – Berlin, nov 5 1887-dec 28 1889 – 1r – 1 – Dist. gw Mikrofilm – gw Misc Inst [072]

ENGLISH AND CHINESE DICTIONARY OF THE AMOY DIALECT / MacGowan, John – Amoy, 1883 – 11mf – ne IDC [420]

ENGLISH AND CHINESE DICTIONARY OF THE AMOY DIALECT / MacGowan, John – Amoy. 1883. BCH-860 2 – 8 – ne IDC [480]

AN ENGLISH AND CHINESE VOCABULARY, IN THE COURT DIALECT / Williams, S W – Macao, 1844 – 6mf – ne IDC [420]

ENGLISH AND LATIN: A MANUAL OF PROSE COMPOSITION / Ogle, Marbury Bladen – New York, London: The Century Co., (c1926). viii,3+190p. (The Century College Latin Series).1 reel. 1263 – 1 – us U.W. Library [450]

ENGLISH AND SCOTTISH PSALM AND HYMN TUNES, 1543-1677 / Frost, Maurice – 1 – $25.90 – us Baptist [780]

AN ENGLISH AND SWEDISH DICTIONARY... / Serenius, J – (With large additions and amendments) – Harg, Stenbro. 1757 – 7mf – ne IDC [040]

ENGLISH AND TAMIL FIRST BOOK – Madras: Church of Scotland Missionary Press, 1857 – 1 – us Res Libr [490]

ENGLISH AND TELUGU DICTIONARY / Brown, Charles Philip – 2d ed. 1895 – 1 – us A.T.L.A. [420]

ENGLISH AND VICTORIAN PICTURES, DRAWINGS AND WATERCOLOURS – (13,000 images) – 117mf – 9 – $690.00 – 0-907006-97-3 – uk Mindata [700]

ENGLISH ARCHITECTURAL DRAWINGS / Victoria and Albert Museum. London – London – 1 – uk Microform Academic [720]

ENGLISH ART : SUBJECT COLLECTIONS – (Individual titles not listed separately) – 504 catalogues 613mf – 9 – £3,220.00 – uk Chadwyck [700]

THE ENGLISH AUGSBURG CONFESSION OF 1536 / ed by Jacobs, Henry Eyster – Philadelphia: Lutheran Publ Society: Publ for the Joint Committee, 1888 – 1mf – 9 – 0-8370-8623-X – 1986-2623 – us A.T.L.A. [240]

ENGLISH BAPTIST REFORMATION / Lofton, George A – 1899. 284p – 1 – 9.94 – us Baptist [240]

THE ENGLISH BAPTISTS : WHO THEY ARE, AND WHAT THEY HAVE DONE: BEING EIGHT LECTURES, HISTORICAL AND DESCRIPTIVE / ed by Clifford, John – London: E. Marlborough, 1881 – 1mf – us A.T.L.A. [240]

ENGLISH BENEDICTINE CALENDARS AFTER A.D. 1100 / Wormald, F – (Vol 1.-3mf; Vol 2.-2mf) – 1939, 1946 – 8 – ne Slangenburg [240]

THE ENGLISH BIBLE : A SKETCH OF ITS HISTORY / Milligan, George – New York: A D F Randolph, 1895 – 1mf – 9 – 0-8370-4435-9 – 1985-2435 – us A.T.L.A. [220]

THE ENGLISH BIBLE AND OUR DUTY WITH REGARD TO IT : A PLEA FOR REVISION / Abbott, Thomas Kingsmill – 2nd ed. Dublin: Hodges, Foster, 1871 – 1mf – 9 – 0-8370-2030-1 – 1985-0030 – us A.T.L.A. [220]

THE ENGLISH BOOKTRADE, 1660-1853 : 156 TITLES RELATING TO THE EARLY HISTORY OF ENGLISH PUBLISHING, BOOKSELLING AND THE STRUGGLE FOR COPYRIGHT AND THE FREEDOM OF THE PRESS / ed by Park, Stephen – New York: Garland Publ Inc, 1985? – 1mf – 9 – $1.50 – LLMC 91-078 – us L.L.M.C. [340]

ENGLISH CALENDARS BEFORE A.D. 1100 / Wormald, F – 1934 – 5mf – 8 – ne Slangenburg [240]

ENGLISH CARICATURISTS AND GRAPHIC HUMOURISTS OF THE NINETEETH CENTURY : HOW THEY ILLUSTRATED AND INTERPRETED THEIR TIMES / Everitt, Graham – London: Swan Sonnenschein, Le Bas & Lowrey, 1886 – 1 roll – 1 – 1-55879-766-1 – uk Libr Preservation [740]

ENGLISH CARTOONS AND SATIRICAL PRINTS, 1320-1832, IN THE BRITISH MUSEUM – (With catalogue. £2,065.00 excluding catalogue) – 32r – 1 – £2,700.00 – uk Chadwyck [740]

THE ENGLISH CHURCH AND ITS BISHOPS, 1700-1800 / Abbey, Charles J – London: Longmans, Green, 1887 – 2mf – us A.T.L.A. [240]

THE ENGLISH CHURCH FROM ITS FOUNDATION TO THE NORMAN CONQUEST (597-1066) / Hunt, William – London, New York: Macmillan, 1899 – 2mf – us A.T.L.A. [240]

THE ENGLISH CHURCH FROM THE ACCESSION OF CHARLES : TO THE DEATH OF ANNE (1625-1714) / Hutton, William Holden – London; New York: Macmillan, 1903. (A History of the English church; 6) – 1mf – us A.T.L.A. [240]

THE ENGLISH CHURCH FROM THE ACCESSION OF GEORGE 1 TO THE END OF THE EIGHTEENTH CENTURY (1714-1800) / Overton, John H & Relton, Frederic – London, New York: Macmillan, 1906 – 1mf – us A.T.L.A. [240]

THE ENGLISH CHURCH FROM THE NORMAN CONQUEST TO THE ACCESSION OF EDWARD 1 (1066-1272) / Stephens, William Richard Wood – London, New York: Macmillan, 1909 – 1mf – us A.T.L.A. [240]

ENGLISH CHURCH FURNITURE / Cox, Charles & Harvey, Alfred – New York: E.P. Dutton, 1907. (The Antiquary's books) – 2mf – us A.T.L.A. [740]

ENGLISH CHURCH HISTORY FROM THE DEATH OF ARCHBISHOP PARKER TO THE DEATH OF KING CHARLES I / Plummer, Alfred – Edinburgh: T. & T. Clark, 1904 – 1mf – us A.T.L.A. [240]

ENGLISH CHURCH HISTORY FROM THE DEATH OF CHARLES 1ST TO THE DEATH OF WILLIAM 3RD : FOUR LECTURES / Plummer, Alfred – Edinburgh: T. & T. Clark, 1907 – 1mf – us A.T.L.A. [240]

ENGLISH CHURCH HISTORY FROM THE DEATH OF KING HENRY 8TH TO THE DEATH OF ARCHBISHOP PARKER : FOUR LECTURES / Plummer, Alfred – Edingburgh: T & T Clark, 1905 – 1mf – us A.T.L.A. [240]

THE ENGLISH CHURCH IN THE EIGHTEENTH CENTURY / Abbey, Charles J & Overton, John H – London: Longmans, Green, 1878 – 3mf – us A.T.L.A. [240]

THE ENGLISH CHURCH IN THE EIGHTEENTH CENTURY / Carter, C Sydney – London; New York: Longmans, Green 1910. (Anglican church handbooks) – 1mf – us A.T.L.A. [240]

THE ENGLISH CHURCH IN THE FOURTEENTH AND FIFTEENTH CENTURIES / Capes, W W – London; New York: Macmillan, 1900. (A History of the English church; 3) – 1mf – us A.T.L.A. [240]

THE ENGLISH CHURCH IN THE MIDDLE AGES / Hunt, William – London: Longmans, Green, 1888. (Epochs of church history) – 1mf – us A.T.L.A. [240]

THE ENGLISH CHURCH IN THE NINETEENTH CENTURY / Cornish, Francis Warre – London: Macmillan, 1910 – 2mf – us A.T.L.A. [240]

THE ENGLISH CHURCH IN THE NINETEENTH CENTURY / Stock, Eugene – London, New York: Longmans, Green, 1910 – 1mf – us A.T.L.A. [240]

THE ENGLISH CHURCH IN THE NINETEENTH CENTURY (1800-1833) / Overton, John H – London, New York: Longmans, Green, 1894 – 1mf – us A.T.L.A. [240]

THE ENGLISH CHURCH IN THE REIGNS OF ELIZABETH AND JAMES I. (1558-1625) / Frere, Walter H – London; New York: Macmillan, c1904. (A History of the English church; 5) – 1mf – us A.T.L.A. [240]

THE ENGLISH CHURCH IN THE SEVENTEENTH CENTURY / Carter, Sydney – London; New York: Longmans, Green, 1909 (Anglican church handbooks) – 1mf – us A.T.L.A. [240]

ENGLISH CHURCH LIFE FROM THE RESTORATION TO THE TRACTARIAN MOVEMENT / Legg, J Wickham – London; New York: Longmans, Green,1914 – 2mf – us A.T.L.A. [240]

ENGLISH CHURCH WAYS : DESCRIBED TO RUSSIAN FRIENDS IN FOUR LECTURES / Frere, Walter H – Milwaukee: Young Churchman, 1914 – 1mf – us A.T.L.A. [240]

ENGLISH CIRCULAR – London, UK. 1841-44. -irr. 1/2 reel – 1 – uk British Libr Newspaper [072]

THE ENGLISH CLASSIFICATION TESTS / Orville, Glenn – Nebraska (ca 1930) – 2mf – DM62.00 – 3-8267-3089-5 – gw Hänsel [420]

AN ENGLISH CODE / Amos, Sheldon – London, 1873 – 3mf – 9 – ILM-841/1 – ne IDC [340]

ENGLISH DAILY BULLETIN – Aden: Aden News Agency, jul 20-30, aug 1-2, dec 22, 1987; mar 9-14, 16-26, apr 3-10 1988 – 1r – 1 – us Res Libr [072]

THE ENGLISH DICTIONARIE / Cockeram, Henry – 1623. 314p. (English Linguistics Series 1500-1800) – 9 – us UMI [420]

ENGLISH DICTIONARY; ENGLISH-INDONESIAN / Zain, Sutan M – SE 2352 1. 2nd ed 1958 – 9 – ne IDC [490]

AN ENGLISH DICTIONARY: EXPLAINING THE DIFFICULT TERMS. / Coles, Elisha – 1676. 330p. (English Linguistics Series 1500-1800) – 9 – us UMI [420]

ENGLISH DIOCESES : A HISTORY OF THEIR LIMITS FROM THE EARLIEST TIMES TO THE PRESENT DAY / Hill, Geoffry – London: E. Stock, 1900 – 1mf – us A.T.L.A. [240]

ENGLISH DRAMATISTS OF TO-DAY / Archer, William – London: S. Low, Marston, Searle, & Rivington, 1882 – 1 roll – 1 – 1-55879-809-9 – uk Libr Preservation [420]

ENGLISH EPISCOPAL PALACES : PROVINCE OF CANTERBURY / Morewood, Caroline C et al; ed by Rait, Robert Sangster – London: Constable, 1910 – 1mf – us A.T.L.A. [720]

ENGLISH EPISCOPAL PALACES : PROVINCE OF YORK / Niemeyer, N; ed by Rait, R S – London: Constable, 1911 – 1mf – us A.T.L.A. [720]

ENGLISH EVANGELICAL LUTHERAN SYNOD OF THE NORTHWEST : MINUTES / English Evangelical Lutheran Synod of the Northwest – 1891-1962 (complete) – 3R – 1 – ATLA S0053 – us A.T.L.A. [240]

English Evangelical Lutheran Synod of the Northwest *see* ENGLISH EVANGELICAL LUTHERAN SYNOD OF THE NORTHWEST

AN ENGLISH EXPOSITOR / Bullokar, John – 1616. 235p. (English Linguistics Series 1500-1800) – 9 – us UMI [420]

THE ENGLISH FACTORIES IN INDIA, 1618-1684 / ed by Foster, W & Fawsett, C – Oxford, 1906-1954. 17 vols – 130mf – 8 – ne IDC [338]

ENGLISH FOR SPECIFIC PURPOSES – 1,5,69 – us UMI [420]

ENGLISH GENTLEMAN *see*
- THE ARGUS
- BRITISH MONITOR

ENGLISH GIFT BOOKS AND LITERARY ANNUALS, 1823-1857 – (With index of contributors and "An Index to the Annuals 1820-1850" by Andrew Boyle 1967. Titles of coll also listed individually) – 1820s-1850s – 697mf coll – 9 – £2,585.00 coll – uk Chadwyck [800]

ENGLISH GIFT BOOKS AND LITERARY ANNUALS, 1823-1857 *see*
- ACKERMAN'S JUVENILE FORGET-ME-NOT
- AMETHYST
- AMULET
- ANNIVERSARY
- AURORA BOREALIS
- BIJOU
- CHRISTMAS BOX
- COMIC OFFERING
- FISHER'S JUVENILE SCRAPBOOK
- FORGET-ME-NOT
- FRIENDSHIP'S OFFERING
- GEM
- HEATH'S BOOK OF BEAUTY
- IRIS
- JANUS – THE EDINBURGH LITERARY ALMANAC
- JUVENILE FORGET-ME-NOT
- JUVENILE KEEPSAKE
- KEEPSAKE
- LITERARY SOUVENIR
- MARSHALL'S CHRISTMAS BOX
- NEW YEAR'S GIFT
- PLEDGE OF FRIENDSHIP
- WINTER'S WREATH

ENGLISH GRAMMAR / Murray, Lindley – 1795. 236p. (English Linguistics Series 1500-1800) – 9 – us UMI [420]

THE ENGLISH GRAMMAR / Aickin, Joseph – 1693. 122p. (English Linguistics Series 1500-1800) – 9 – us UMI [420]

THE ENGLISH GRAMMAR / Jonson, Ben – 1640. 64p. (English Linguistics Series 1500-1800) – 9 – us UMI [420]

THE ENGLISH GRAMMAR / Maittaire, Michael – 1712. 293p. (English Linguistics Series 1500-1800) – 9 – us UMI [420]

THE ENGLISH GRAMMAR / Miege, Guy – 1688. 203p. (English Linguistics Series 1500-1800) – 9 – us UMI [420]

ENGLISH GRAMMAR IN AMERICAN HIGH SCHOOLS SINCE 1900 / Gruen, Ferdinand Bernard – Washington D.C., 1934 – 4mf – DM90.00 – 3-8267-3088-7 – gw Hänsel [420]

AN ENGLISH GRAMMAR: OR, A PLAIN EXPOSITION OF LILIES GRAMMAR IN ENGLISH / R, R – 1641. 210p. (English Linguistics Series 1500-1800) – 9 – us UMI [420]

ENGLISH HISTORICAL REVIEW – v1- 1886- 1; v86- 5,6, v91- 9 – us UMI [941]

ENGLISH HISTORICAL REVIEW – London, 1886-1940. v.1-55 – 769mf – 8 – ne IDC [941]

ENGLISH HISTORICAL REVIEW – v. 1-62. 1886-1947 – 1 – us Princeton Micro [941]

THE ENGLISH HYMN : ITS DEVELOPMENT AND USE IN WORSHIP / Benson, Louis F – New York: Hodder & Stoughton, G.H. Doran, c1915 – 2mf – us A.T.L.A. [240]

ENGLISH HYMNS : THEIR AUTHORS AND HISTORY / Duffield, Samuel Willoughby – New York: Funk & Wagnalls, 1888 – 2mf – us A.T.L.A. [780]

ENGLISH HYMNS AND THEIR TUNES IN THE 16TH AND 17TH CENTURIES / Parks, Edna D – 1957 – 1 – 18.20 – us Baptist [240]

ENGLISH IDIOM FOR HIGH SCHOOLS / Van Delden, M – SE-3437 1. 1954 – 9 – ne IDC [420]

ENGLISH IN EDUCATION – v1- 1967- 1;v10- 5,6,9 – us UMI [370]

THE ENGLISH IN IRELAND IN THE EIGHTEENTH CENTURY / Froude, James Anthony – New York: Scribner, Armstrong, 1873-1874 – 4mf – us A.T.L.A. [240]

ENGLISH IN NEW ZEALAND – 1973- 1; 1976- 5,6,9 – us UMI [420]

THE ENGLISH IN THE WEST INDIES, OR, THE BOW OF ULYSSES / Froude, James Anthony – New York: Scribner, 1888 – 1mf – us A.T.L.A. [950]

THE ENGLISH INSTRUCTOR / Dixon, Henry – 1728. 149p. (English Linguistic Series 1500-1800) – 9 – us UMI [420]

ENGLISH INTERCOURSE WITH SIAM IN THE SEVENTEENTH CENTURY / Anderson, J – London, 1890 – 6mf – 9 – ne IDC [950]

ENGLISH JOURNAL – (v. 56- 1967- 5,6. v. 59- 1970- 9) – 1- 1912- – 1 – us UMI [370]

ENGLISH JOURNAL – v1-36 1912-1947 – 1 – us Princeton Micro [420]

ENGLISH LABOURER'S CHRONICLE – Leamington. England. -w. 1877-94. (6 reels) – 1 – uk British Libr Newspaper [072]

ENGLISH LANGUAGE NOVELS OF THE EDITION CORVEY : LITERARY WORKS OF THE 18TH AND 19TH CENTURY – (Silver halide microfiche on request) – Wildberg: BELSER WISS. DIENST, 1990-1992 – 6,885mf – 9 – DM49,500.00 diazo – 3-628-04009-4 – gw Belser Wiss [420]

ENGLISH LANGUAGE TEACHING – 1-27 1946-73 1; v25-27 1970-73 5,6 – us UMI [420]

ENGLISH LANGUAGE TEACHING JOURNAL – v28- 1973- 1,5,6; v31- 9 – us UMI [370]

ENGLISH LANGUAGE TITLES OF THE EDITION CORVEY : LITERARY WORKS OF THE 18TH AND 19TH CENTURY – (Silver halide microfiche on request) – Wildberg: BELSER WISS. DIENST, 1990-1992 – 9,993mf – 9 – DM70,400.00 diazo – 3-628-04008-6 – gw Belser Wiss [420]

ENGLISH LAW AND PRACTICE RELATING TO ESTATES OF PERSONS DYING DOMICILED ABROAD... / Thomson, K S – London, 1917 – 2mf – 9 – ILM-3372/1 – ne IDC [327]

ENGLISH LEADER – London, UK. 1866-67. -irr. 1 1/2 reels – 1 – uk British Libr Newspaper [072]

THE ENGLISH LEGAL MANUSCRIPTS PROJECT : STAGES 1-7 / ed by Baker, J H – (A coll of mss yr books, report cases, readings and moots from the Harvard Law School, Lincoln's Inn, Bodleian and Gray's Inn, the Yale Law School,and the Cambridge University Library. Also listed individually. With printed guide and bibliography) – 7247mf coll – 9 – ne IDC [340]

THE ENGLISH LEGAL MANUSCRIPTS PROJECT – (Stages listed and can be purchased separately. Includes a 90p printed guide with brief listing of the mss in each section. A bibliography "English Legal Manuscripts, Vols 1-2" by J.H. Baker is also available) – Stages 1-7 – 7247mf coll – 9 – ne IDC [340]

THE ENGLISH LEGAL MANUSCRIPTS PROJECT *see*
- BODLEIAN AND GRAY'S INN
- THE CAMBRIDGE UNIVERSITY LIBRARY
- THE HARVARD LAW SCHOOL
- THE HARVARD LAW SCHOOL ADDENDA
- LINCOLN'S INN
- YALE LAW SCHOOL

ENGLISH LEGAL SOURCES / ed by Baker, J H – (a: Abridgments of the Common Law; b: General works of reference; c: Pleadings and Procedure; d: Books of entries; e: Equity and court of Chancery; f: Criminal Law; g: Contract and Tort; h: Law of Property and Conveyancing; i: Printed Readings on Statutes) – 923mf – 9 – ne IDC [340]

THE ENGLISH LEPIDOPTERA: OR, THE AURELIAN'S POCKET COMPANION / Harris, M – London, 1775. Z/1330/2 – 8 – ne IDC [590]

ENGLISH LIFE AND MANNERS IN THE LATER MIDDLE AGES / Abram, A – London: G. Routledge; New York: E.P. Dutton,1913 – 1mf – us A.T.L.A. [306]

ENGLISH LIFE OF JESUS, PT 2 : COMPRISING AN ANALYSIS OF THE CAREER OF JOHN THE BAPTIST, AND OF THE BEGINNING OF THE PUBLIC MINISTRY OF JESUS / Scott, Thomas – Ramsgate:T. Scott, [ca. 1866] – 1mf – 9 – 0-8370-5193-2 – 1985-3193 – us A.T.L.A. [220]

ENGLISH LINGUISTICS, 1500-1800 / ed by Alston, R C – (365 titles essential to the study of English linguistics on a historical basis: textbooks of rhetoric and logic, early grammars, dictionaries, studies in the theory of language, studies on pronunciation and style. Individual titles available) – 1131mf, 365 titles – 9 – $3850.00 – us UMI [420]

ENGLISH LITERARY HISTORY *see* ELH

ENGLISH LITERARY PERIODICALS (ELPS), 1681-1914 – (233 significant early journals, magazines, and reviews reflecting British life and culture. Cataloging available) – 969r – 9 – $54,890.00 – us UMI [800]

ENGLISH LYRICS / Austin, Alfred; ed by Watson, William – London, New York: Macmillan, 2nd ed 1890 – 1 roll – 1 – 1-55879-457-3 – uk Libr Preservation [810]

THE ENGLISH MALADY / Cheyne, G – M 90. 1733 – 9 – ne IDC [610]

ENGLISH MEZZOTINT PORTRAITS / Burlington Fine Arts Club. London – 1902 – 9 – 4.90 – uk Chadwyck [700]

ENGLISH MINSTRELSIE / Baring-Gould, Sabine – Edinburgh. 1895. 8v – 1 – 23.00 – us L of C Photodup [780]

ENGLISH MIRACLE PLAYS, MORALITIES, AND INTERLUDES; SPECIMENS OF THE PRE-ELIZABETHAN DRAMA / ed by Pollard, Alfred William – 4th ed. rev. Oxford: Clarendon Press, 1904.ix,250p – 1 – us U.W. Library [820]

ENGLISH MONASTERIES / Hamilton Thompson, A – H-1288 2. 1913 – 8 – ne IDC [240]

ENGLISH MONASTIC LIFE / Gasquet, Abbot – London: Methuen, 1904 (The Antiquary's books) – 1mf – us A.T.L.A. [240]

ENGLISH MUSICAL GAZETTE – London. 1819. Drexel 279 no. 1-3. Jan.-Mar. 1819 – 1 – us NY Public [073]

ENGLISH NONCONFORMITY / Vaughan, Robert – London: Jackson, Walford and Hodder, 1862 – 2mf – us A.T.L.A. [240]

THE ENGLISH OPERA, OR THE VOCAL MUSICK IN PSYCHE...TO WHICH HAS BEEN ADJOYNED THE INSTRUMENTAL MUSICK IN THE TEMPEST / Locke, M – 1675 – 9 – us Sibley [780]

ENGLISH ORDERS FOR CONSECRATING CHURCHES IN THE 17TH CENTURY / Wickham Legg, J – 1911 – 7mf – 8 – ne Slangenburg [240]

ENGLISH ORTHOGRAPHIE / Price, Owen – 1668. 78p. (English Linguistics Series 1500-1800) – 9 – us UMI [420]

THE ENGLISH PARISH CHURCH : AN ACCOUNT OF THE CHIEF BUILDING TYPES & OF THEIR MATERIALS DURING NINE CENTURIES / Cox, John Charles – London: B.T. Batsford; New York: Scribner, [1914?] – 1mf – us A.T.L.A. [240]

THE ENGLISH PARNASSUS: OR, A HELP. TO ENGLISH POESIE / Poole, Joshua – 1657. 696p. (English Linguistics Series 1500-1800) – 9 – us UMI [420]

ENGLISH PARTIES AND POWER IN MODERN ARGENTINA (1930-1946) = PARTIDOS Y PODER EN LA ARGENTINA MODERNA / Ciria, Alberto – Albany: State University of New York Press, 1974 – 1 – CSUXADJ2642-B – us Hoover Inst Photo [320]

THE ENGLISH PHYSITIAN / Culpeper, N – London, 1656 – 6mf – 9 – ne IDC [170]

THE ENGLISH PHYSITIANS GUIDE OR A HOLYGUIDE; LEADING THE WAY TO KNOW ALL THINGS, PAST, PRESENT & TO COME / Heydon, John – London, 1662 – 1 – us U.W. Library [150]

ENGLISH PLACE-NAME SOCIETY – 1924-1938. v.1-15 – 126mf – 8 – ne IDC [941]

THE ENGLISH PRIMROSE / Hodges, Richard – 1644. 123p. (English Linguistics Series 1500-1800) – 9 – us UMI [420]

ENGLISH PSALTERS – 14th cent. Holkham mss. 23, 24.Holkham Hall, Norfolk, England – 1 – uk Microform Academic [025]

ENGLISH PSYCHOLOGY / Ribot, Theodule Armand – Trans. from the French. New York: D. Appleton and Co., 1891. viii,328p – 1 – us U.W. Library [150]

THE ENGLISH PURITANS / Brown, John – Cambridge: University Press; New York: Putnam, 1910. (The Cambridge manuals of science and literature) – 1mf – us A.T.L.A. [240]

ENGLISH QUARTERLY – (v1-9 Can$100.00. v10-19 Can$50.00y) – Montreal. v1-27. 1968-95 – 5,9 – Can$20.00y – cn Micromedia [420]

ENGLISH REPORTS (FULL REPRINT) – v1-176 + 2v table of cases – 1 – $2,475.00 – us Hein [340]

THE ENGLISH REPORTS (FULL REPRINT) – (Includes 2 index vols for which W Green & Sons is the sole publisher) – v1-176. 1378-1865. Repr. Edinburgh/London: Wm Green & Sons/Stevens & Sons, 1900-32 2456mf – 9 – $3,685.00 – us L.L.M.C. [340]

ENGLISH REPUBLIC – London, UK. 1851-55. -irr. 1 reel – 1 – uk British Libr Newspaper [072]

ENGLISH RETRACED, OR, REMARKS, CRITICAL AND PHILOLOGICAL : FOUNDED ON A COMPARISON OF THE BREECHES BIBLE WITH THE ENGLISH OF THE PRESENT DAY / Gurnhill, James – Cambridge [England]:H Wallis, 1862 – 1mf – 9 – 0-8370-3426-4 – 1985-1426 – us A.T.L.A. [420]

ENGLISH REVIEW – London. v. 1-64. Dec 1908-July 1937 – 1 – us NY Public [420]

ENGLISH REVIEW – London. v1-64. 1908-37 – 17r – 1 – us Ross [420]

ENGLISH REVIEW – (United with: National Review). v. 1-64. 1908-1937. All pub – 1,5,6 – us Princeton Micro [320]

ENGLISH REVIEW MAGAZINE – v. 1-64. 1908-37 – 1 – us UMI [420]

THE ENGLISH REVISERS' GREEK TEXT : SHOWN TO BE UNAUTHORIZED EXCEPT BY EGYPTIAN COPIES DISCARDED BY GREEKS AND TO BE OPPOSED TO THE HISTORIC TEXT OF ALL AGES AND CHURCHES / Samson, George Whitefield – Cambridge, MA: Moses King, c1882 – 1mf – 9 – 0-8370-5032-4 – 1985-3032 – us A.T.L.A. [220]

THE ENGLISH RUDIMENTS OF THE LATINE TONGUE / Dugard, William – 1656. 153p. (English Linguistics Series 1500-1800) – 9 – us UMI [450]

ENGLISH RULING CASES / Great Britain. Courts – 1307-1908 – 9r – 1 – $450.00 – us Trans-Media [340]

ENGLISH RULING CASES – (Publ as: Ruling Cases, Subscription Edition. Arranged, annotated and ed by Robert Campbell et al with American Notes by Irivng Browne) – v1-26. 1307-1894. Boston: Boston Book Co, 1902 (all publ) – 237mf – 9 – $355.00 – LLMC 81-406 – us L.L.M.C. [340]

THE ENGLISH SCHOLLAR'S ASSISTANT: OR, THE RUDIMENTS OF THE ENGLISH TONGUE / Saxon, Samuel – 1737. 119p. (English Linguistics Series 1500-1800) – 9 – us UMI [420]

THE ENGLISH SCHOOL / Eliot, John – 1680. 219p. (English Linguistics Series 1500-1800) – 9 – us UMI [420]

THE ENGLISH SCHOOL / Ellis, Tobias – 1680. 219p. (English Linguistics Series 1500-1800) – 9 – us UMI [420]

THE ENGLISH SCHOOLMASTER / Coote, Edmund – 1596. 114p. (English Linguistics Series 1500-1800) – 9 – us UMI [420]

ENGLISH SEAMEN : HOWARD, CLIFFORD, HAWKINS, DRAKE, CAVENDISH. EDITED WITH AN INTRODUCTION BY DAVID HANNAY / Southey, Robert – Chicago: Stone and Kimball; London: Methuen, 1895 – 1 roll – 1 – 1-55879-427-1 – uk Libr Preservation [380]

THE ENGLISH SECRETORIE / Day, Angel – 1586. 272p. (English Linguistics Series 1500-1800) – 9 – us UMI [650]

ENGLISH SECULARISM: A CONFESSION OF BELIEF / Holyoake, George Jacob – Chicago: Open Court, 1896. 1 fiche – 9 – us A.T.L.A. [240]

ENGLISH SOCIETY IN THE ELEVENTH CENTURY / Vinogradoff, Paul – Essays in English Medieval History. H 1163 2. 1908 – 8 – ne IDC [941]

ENGLISH SPEAKING WORLD – v1-38. 1919-56 – 1 – us Princeton Micro [073]

ENGLISH SPELLING AND SPELLING REFORM / Lounsbury, Thomas Raynesford – New York: Harper, 1909 – 1 roll – 1 – 1-55879-831-5 – uk Libr Preservation [420]

THE ENGLISH STAGE AFTER THE RESTORATION: ARCHIVES OF THE 18TH AND 19TH CENTURY BRITISH THEATRES ROYAL – (Part 2: Egerton Manuscripts) – Part 1: Concentrates on Covent Garden manuscripts from the British Library – 1 – us Primary [790]

ENGLISH STATE TRIALS, 1163-1858 / Great Britain; ed by Cobbett, William & Howell, T B & Howell, T J & MacDonnell, John & Wallis John E P – 14r – 1 – $1,190.00 – S1847 – us Scholarly Res [340]

ENGLISH STUDIES – (v1-39. Dfl80.00v; v40-71. Dfl140.00v; Suppl. to v45. Dfl30.00) – Lisse. v1-71 with general index v1-40 and suppl. to v45. 1919-1990 – 5,9 – Dfl7,630.00 – ne Swets [420]

ENGLISH SURNAMES 1602 – 1mf – 9 – A$5.00 – at State Libr Vic [941]

THE ENGLISH SYNOD NEWSLETTER – v1-55. 1976-87 (complete) – 1r – 1 – ATLA S0811 – us A.T.L.A. [073]

THE ENGLISH TEACHER / Cooper, Christopher – 1687. 134p. (English Linguistics Series 1500-1800) – 9 – us UMI [420]

ENGLISH TEXTS 17TH-19TH CENTURY – 40 titles – 9 – ne IDC [420]

ENGLISH TEXTS FOR THE USE OF STUDENTS AND PUPILS PREPARING FOR THE FINAL EXAMINATION OF HIGH SCHOOLS / Mulia, Todung gelar Sutan Gunung – SE-10,697 1. 1948 – 9 – ne IDC [370]

THE ENGLISH VERB / White, James – 1761. 325p. (English Linguistics Series 1500-1800) – 9 – us UMI [420]

ENGLISH WOMAN'S REVIEW AND DRAWING ROOM JOURNAL – London, UK. 21 Mar 1857-1859. -f. 1 1/2 reels – 1 – uk British Libr Newspaper [072]

THE ENGLISH WORKS OF SIR HENRY SPELMAN, KT. / Spelman, Henry – London, Browne, Mears, Clay etc. 1723. 42, xxvi, 38, li-lxv, 67-194, 168, 4, 256, 24 p. LL-979 – 1 – us L of C Photodup [340]

ENGLISH WORLD-WIDE – v.1. 1980 – 1,5,6,9 – us UMI [420]

ENGLISH-BEMBA PHRASE BOOK / Lewanika, Godwin A M – 3rd ed. London: Macmillan, 1955 – us Res Libr [040]

ENGLISH-BEMBA PHRASE BOOK – London, Macmillan, 1955 – us Res Libr [040]

ENGLISH-ESKIMO, ESKIMO-ENGLISH DICTIONARY / Thibert, A – Bn 424 2. 1954 – 8 – ne IDC [490]

ENGLISH-GERMAN LITERARY INFLUENCES : BIBLIOGRAPHY AND SURVEY / Price, Lawrence Marsden – (Includes bibliographical references and index) – Berkeley: University of California Press, 1919 – 1r – 1 – us U.W. Library [420]

THE ENGLISH-GRAMMAR / Wharton, Jeremiah – 1654. 128p. (English Linguistics Series 1500-1800) – 9 – us UMI [420]

ENGLISH-GRAMMAR UNTUK SEKOLAH LANDJUTAN PERTAMA / Suroso Purwamihardjo, R – SE 10,425 1. 1960 – 9 – ne IDC [420]

AN ENGLISH-HEBREW LEXICON : BEING A COMPLETE VERBAL INDEX TO GESENIUS' HEBREW LEXICON / Potter, Joseph Lewis – New York: Hurd and Houghton, 1877, c1872 – 1mf – 9 – 0-8370-9498-4 – 1986-3498 – us A.T.L.A. [470]

ENGLISH-INDONESIAN AND INDONESIAN-ENGLISH TERMS OF GEOLOGY AND RELATED SCIENCES / Indonesia. Direktorat Geologi – SE-6230 1. 1965 – 9 – ne IDC [550]

AN ENGLISH-KANURI SENTENCE BOOK / Ellison, Randall Erskine – London: Publ on behalf of the Govt of Nigeria by the Crown Agents for the Colonies, 1937 – 1 – us Res Libr [490]

ENGLISH-LANGUAGE NEWSPAPERS PUBLISHED IN CHINA – (The China News, Taipei: Apr-Sep 1952, Aug 1956-1961, 1963-1979, Sep 1982-Apr 1985 88r L9300123. China Post, Taipei, International Air Mail Edition: 1963, Oct 1964-Mar 1970, Oct 1970-Sep 1973, 1974-1980 55r L9300124. China Press, Shanghai: 1916-1924, Apr-May 1949 54r L9300125. North China Star, Tientsin: Nov 1929- 1941 75r L9300126. Peiping Chronicle, Peking: Jun 1932-1942 32r L9300127. Shanghai News, Shanghai: Jun 1950-1952 3r L9300128) – 307r – 1 – $40.00r – Dist. us Scholarly Res – us L of C Photodup [072]

ENGLISH-LOZI PHRASE BOOK / Lewanika, Godwin A M – London: Macmillan, 1949 – 1 – us Res Libr [040]

ENGLISHMAN *see* THE ATLAS

THE ENGLISHMAN – Calcutta, India. -d. 1834-1842; Jan 1857-Oct 1899; July-Dec 1906. 205 reels – 1 – uk British Libr Newspaper [072]

THE ENGLISHMAN – [London]: Printed for Staples Steare, jun 14, jul 13,23-30, aug 6-20 1768 – 1 – us Res Libr [073]

THE ENGLISHMAN – London. -w. 1874-86. (12 reels) – 1 – uk British Libr Newspaper [072]

THE ENGLISHMAN AT HOME, HIS RESPONSIBILITIES AND PRIVILEGES / Porritt, Edward – (While the title implies a civil liberties thrust, this work is really an extensive and detailed description of the English legal and governmental structure at the turn of the century) – New York: Thomas Y Crowell, 1893 – 5mf – 9 – $7.50 – LLMC 92-156 – us L.L.M.C. [340]

ENGLISHMAN'S OVERLAND MAIL – Calcutta, India. -w. 1864-1876. 16 reels – 1 – uk British Libr Newspaper [072]

ENGLISHMAN'S SATURDAY EVENING JOURNAL – Calcutta, India. -w. 1863-1875. Lacking Jan, Feb 1867. 24 reels – 1 – uk British Libr Newspaper [072]

THE ENGLISHMAN'S TREASURE / Vicary, T – M 416. 1596 – 9 – ne IDC [810]

THE ENGLISH-SCHOOL REFORMED / Browne, Richard – 1700. 127p. (English Linguistics Series 1500-1800) – 9 – us UMI [420]

ENGLISH-SPEAKING MISSIONS IN THE CONGO INDEPENDENT STATE (1878-1908) / Slade, Ruth M – Brussel, 1959 – 11mf – 8 – ne Slangenburg [240]

ENGLISH-TAGALOG VOCABULARY / Villa, Jose – Manila: University Publ Co, 1946 – us Res Libr [040]

AN ENGLISH-TELUGU SCIENTIFIC DICTIONARY / Holler, P – (Filmed with: A Small English-Telugu Dictionary) – Rajahmundry: Printed at Vivekavardhani Press, 1900 – 1 – us Res Libr [490]

ENGLISH-TONGA PHRASE BOOK... – London: Macmillan, 1950 – 1 – us Res Libr [490]

AN ENGLISH-TSWA DICTIONARY / Persson, J A – [Cleveland, Transvaal]: Inhambane Mission Press, 1928 – 1 – us Res Libr [040]

AN ENGLISHWOMAN'S TWENTY-FIVE YEARS IN TROPICAL AFRICA : BEING THE BIOGRAPHY OF GWEN ELEN LEWIS, MISSIONARY TO THE CAMEROONS AND THE CONGO / Hawker, George – London, New York: Hodder and Stoughton, [1911?] – 1mf – us A.T.L.A. [240]

ENGRAVINGS AND WOODCUTS BY OLD MASTERS (SEC 15-19) REPRODUCED IN FACSIMILE UNDER THE DIRECTION OF DR. FRIEDRICH LIPPMANN / Lippmann, F – 10 v. London. 1889-1900. BO-342 1 – 9 – ne IDC [760]

ENGRAVINGS FROM THE SMALL AND LARGE BOOKS OF DESIGNS / Blake, William – Copy A – 14 – uk Microform Academic [810]

ENGROSSED BILLS AND RESOLUTIONS OF THE U.S. SENATE, 1789-1817 / U.S. Senate – 5r – 1 – M1250 – us Nat'l Archives [324]

ENHANCING THE EFFECTIVENESS OF KIBBUTZ ULPANIM / Israel. Szold Institute – By. A. Silver and Shulamit W. Klaus. Jerusalem. 1975. 192, 8 p. (Research report no. 184; publication no. 537.) Summary also in Hebrew – 9 – 5.00 – is I.T.T.I. [324]

ENIGMAS OF LIFE, DEATH, AND THE FUTURE STATE / Dana, Alexander Hamilton – New York: Charles P. Somerset, 1882. 1 fiche – 9 – us A.T.L.A. [240]

L'ENIGME DU MACINA / Ouane, Ibrahima Manadou – Monte-Carlo: Regain, [1952] – 1 – us Res Libr [960]

Enis, Dede *see* DIVAN
ENISE ISKOE SLOVO – (Includes c.1: no.1 1906:Nov.10-no.14 (1906:Nov.26)) – Krasnoi arsk: F.I. Romanov, 1906- – 1 – CSUXAHZ7591-S – us Hoover Inst Photo [947]
ENISEISKII KOOPERATOR – (Missing: 1922 n1-11) – Krasnoiarsk, 1922-24 n5 – 19mf – 9 – COR-586/1 – ne IDC [334]
ENKELE OPMERKINGEN NAAR AANLEIDING VAN DE ENQUETE INZAKE : DE STEM VAN AMBON / Grondel, A H – Bussum, 1956. 20p – 1mf – 9 – ne IDC [950]
Enking, Ottomar *see* GERHART HAUPTMANNS "TILL EULENSPIEGEL"
ENKOEPINGS NYHETER – Enkoeping, Motala. 1925-31 – 9 – sw Kungliga [072]
ENKOPINGS WECKOBLAD – Enkoping, Sweden. 1856; 1863-79 – 5r – 1 – sw Kungliga [072]
ENKOPINGSPOSTEN – Enkoping, Sweden. 1879-1978 – 174r – 1 – sw Kungliga [072]
ENKOPINGSPOSTEN – Enkoping, Sweden. 1979- – 1 – sw Kungliga [072]
ENLIGHTENER – Carson City, NV. Aug-Sep 1914 – 1r – 1 – $50.00 – U04455 – us Library Micro [071]
Ennes, Antonio Jose *see* PROVIDENCIAS PUBLICADAS PELO COMMISSARIO REGIO NA PROVIDENCIA DE MOCAMBIQUE
Ennes, Ernesto *see* DOIS PAULISTAS INSIGNES
ENNIS CHRONICLE AND CLARE ADVERTISER – Ennis. Ireland. -sw. 5 Jan 1828-30 Nov 1831. (4 reels) – 1 – uk British Libr Newspaper [072]
ENNISCORTHY GUARDIAN – Enniscorthy, Ireland. -d. 1898-1903, 1986. 8 reels – 1 – PS27.50r – ie European Micro [072]
ENNISCORTHY GUARDIAN – Ireland.1889-96. -w. 5 reels – 1 – uk British Libr Newspaper [072]
ENNISCORTHY NEWS – Ireland.Mar 1861-1868; 1871-84; 1886-91; 1894-96. -w.11 reels – 1 – uk British Libr Newspaper [072]
ENNISCORTHY NEWS AND COUNTY OF WEXFORD ADVERTISER – Ireland.1881. -w. 1/4 reel – 1 – uk British Libr Newspaper [072]
ENNISCORTHY RECORDER – Gorey, Ireland. 1893-96. -w. 3 reels – 1 – uk British Libr Newspaper [072]
ENNISKILLEN ADVERTISER – Ireland.21 Jul 1864-28 Sept 1876. -w.4 1/2 reels. Missing: 1872, 1874 – 1 – uk British Libr Newspaper [072]
ENNISKILLEN CHRONICLE – Ireland. -w. 1 Jan 1824-31 May 1849. (10 reels) – 1 – uk British Libr Newspaper [072]
ENNISKILLEN WATCHMAN – Ireland. -w. 28 Sep-26 Oct 1848. (10 ft) – 1 – uk British Libr Newspaper [072]
THE ENNISKILLENER – Enniskillen. Ireland. -w. 13 Feb 1830-29 Dec 1836, 2 Jan-20 Feb 1840. (3 reels) – 1 – uk British Libr Newspaper [072]
L'ENNUI, ETUDE PSYCHOLOGIQUE / Tardieu, E – H 525 2. 1903 – 8 – ne IDC [150]
ENOCH ARDEN, ETC. / Tennyson, Alfred, Lord – London: Edward Moxon, 1864 – 1 roll – 1 – 1-55879-461-1 – uk Libr Preservation [810]
ENON BAPTIST CHURCH OF CHRIST (NOW FIRST BAPTIST CHURCH). HUNTSVILLE, ALABAMA : CHURCH RECORDS – Jun 1809-Apr 1861 – 1 – 9.18 – us Baptist [240]
ENON BAPTIST CHURCH. PICKENS COUNTY. EASLEY, SOUTH CAROLINA : CHURCH RECORDS – 1851-Aug 1942 – 1 – 52.20 – us Baptist [240]
Enon, Pennsylvania. Enon Baptist Church *see* MINUTES
EN-P'ING HSIEN-CHIH – 1825, v. 18. BCH-625 2 – 8 – ne IDC [950]
ENQUETE AGRICOLE – Ministere de l'agriculture. Documents recueillis a L'etranger. S.4. Paris, 1868. 2v – 55mf – 9 – 639/2 – ne IDC [630]
ENQUETE CINEMATOGRAPHIQUE SUR LES STEELBANDS DE TRINIDAD / Verba, Daniel – 1mf – 9 – 10453 – fr Atelier National [790]
ENQUETE COLONIALE DANS L'AFRIQUE FRANCAISE OCCIDENTALE ET EQUATORIALE SUR L'ORGANISATION DE LA FAMILLE INDIGENE, LES FINANCAILLES, LE MARIAGE = AVEC UNE ESQUISSE GENERALE DES LANGUES DE L'AFRIQUE / Delafosse, Maurice – (Et une esquisse ethnologique des principales populations de l'Afrlq. francalse equatorlale par le Dr Poutrin) – Paris: Societe d'Editions Geographiques, Maritimes et Coloniales, 1930 – 1 – us Res Libr [306]
ENQUETE DE LA COMMISSION EXTRA-PARLEMENTAIRE DES ASSOCIATIONS OUVRIERES, NOMMEE PAR M. LE MINISTRE DE L'INTERIEUR / France. Ministere de l'Interieur – (Condition of 19th C. French working class series). 1883 and 1888 – 9 – fr Hachette [944]
ENQUETE DEVANT LA CHAMBRE D'ASSEMBLEE DU BAS-CANADA SUR LES EVENEMENTS DU 21 MAI 1832 A MONTREAL / Bas-Canada. Parlement. Chambre d'assemblee – [s.l.]: Chambre d'assemble, [s.d.]. SEM105P110 – 6mf – 9 – Can$13.50 – cn Bibl Nat [323]
L'ENQUETE DEVANT LE COMITE DES COMPTES PUBLICS DE L'ASSEMBLEE LEGISLATIVE DANS L'AFFAIRE DE LA PEINTURE ET DE LA TAPISSERIE – Quebec, 1888? SEM105P565 – 1mf – 9 – Can$2.25 – cn Bibl Nat [971]
ENQUETE D'OPINION SUR LA PLANIFICATION FAMILIALE: MILIEU RURAL / Morocco. Ministere de la Sante Publique – Rabat. 1971. BNE-3120 1 – 9 – ne IDC [310]
ENQUETE D'OPINION SUR LA PLANIFICATION FAMILIALE: MILIEU URBAIN / Morocco. Ministere de la Sante Publique – Rabat. 1971 – 9 – ne IDC [310]
ENQUETE PARLEMENTAIRE SUR LES ACTES DU GOUVERNEMENT DE LA DEFENSE NATIONALE...DEPOSITIONS DES TEMOINS / France. Commission d'enquete sur les actes du gouvernement de la defense nationale – 6v. 1872-75 – 1 – 40.00 – us L of C Photodup [324]
ENQUETE SUR LA CONDITION DES CLASSES OUVRIERES ET SUR LE TRAVAIL DES ENFANTS / Belgium. Ministere de l'Interieur – (Condition of 19th C. French working class series). 1846-48 – 9 – fr Hachette [324]
ENQUETE SUR LA LOI DE LA CONVENTION COLLECTIVE ET SON APPLICATION: ANALYSE DES DECISIONS DES TRIBUNAUX / Lambert, Joseph A – Quebec: Comite d'Enquete sur la Loi de la Convention Collective..., fev 1965. SEM105P8 – 1mf – 9 – Can$2.25 – cn Bibl Nat [340]
ENQUETE SUR LA LOI DE LA CONVENTION COLLECTIVE ET SON EXPLICATION : ANALYSE DES DECISIONS DES TRIBUNAUX / Vaillancourt, Gerard – Quebec: Comite d'Enquete sur la Loi collective..., 1965 (i.e. 1964). SEM105P9 – 1mf – 9 – Can$2.25 – cn Bibl Nat [340]
ENQUETE SUR LE FRANCAIS DES ELEVES DE SIXIEME / Lamy, A – (Africa series). 1970 – 9 – fr Hachette [440]
UNE ENQUETE SUR LE PAUPERISME ET LA CRISE INDUSTRIELLE DANS LA REGION ROUENNAISE EN 1788 / Le Parquier, E – Rouen. 1935. (La Condition Ouvriere. Part Two.) – 9 – 2.50 – fr Bibl Nationale [360]
ENQUETE SUR L'ENSEIGNEMENT PROFESSIONNEL OU RECUEIL DE DEPOSITIONS FAITES EN 1863 ET 1864 DEVANT LA COMMISSION DE L'ENSEIGNEMENT PROFESSIONNEL – (Ministere de l'Agriculture, du Commerce et des Travaux Publics). (Condition of 19th C. French working class series). 1864 – 9 – fr Hachette [025]
ENQUETE SUR LES CONDITIONS DE L'HABITATION EN FRANCE – Paris. 1894-99. (La Condition Ouvriere. Part Two.) – 9 – 22.50 – fr Bibl Nationale [360]
ENQUETE SUR LES CONDITIONS DE TRAVAIL EN FRANCE PENDANT L'ANNEE 1872 / Chambre de Commerce de Paris – (Condition of 19th C. French working class series). 1875 – 9 – fr Hachette [025]
ENQUETE SUR LES CONSEILS DE PRUD'HOMMES ET LES LIVRETS D'OUVRIERS – (Condition of 19th C. French working class series). 1869 – 9 – fr Hachette [025]
ENQUETE SUR LES SERVICES DE SANTE (1948), PROVINCE DE QUEBEC – [Quebec: Ministere de la sante, 1951?]. SEM35P385 – 1r – 1 – Can$60.00 – cn Bibl Nat [360]
ENQUETE SUR LES SOCIETES DE COOPERATION / France. Ministere De l'Agriculture, Du Commerce Et Des Travaux Publics – (Condition of 19th C. French working class series). 1866 – 9 – fr Hachette [305]
LES ENQUETES DES PREFETS DE L'EMPIRE, 1795-1815 / Bibliotheque Nationale – 98 titles. 436 diazo fiches – 9 – fr Hachette [944]
ENQUETE...SUR LES EVENEMENTS DU 21 MAI 1832 A MONTREAL / Canada. Bas-Canada. Parlement. Chambre d'Assemblee – s.l: Chambre d'Assemblee, s.d. SEM105P110 – 6mf – 9 – Can$13.50 – cn Bibl Nat [324]
L'ENQUETEUR – Montreal, 16 sep 1973 – 1r – 1 – Can$25.00 – cn Can Microfilming [072]
ENQUIRER – Battle Creek. Mich. and News. 1918- – 1 – us UMI [071]
ENQUIRER – Cincinnati. Ohio. 1841- – 1 – us UMI [071]
ENQUIRER – Cincinnati. Ohio. (Ky. Edition). 1901- – 1 – us UMI [071]
ENQUIRER – Grand Rapids. Mich. -w. 1841-58, 1860-62 – 1 – us UMI [071]
ENQUIRER – Litchfield. Conn. -w. 1829- – 1 – us UMI [071]
ENQUIRER – Richmond. Va. 1804-1820 – 1,3 – us Readex [071]
ENQUIRER – Richmond. Va. 1861-62 – 1 – us UMI [071]
ENQUIRER – San Carlos, CA. 1949-56 – 10r – 1 – $500.00 – C02777 – us Library Micro [071]
ENQUIRER – San Carlos. Calif. -w. 1949-56 – 1 – us UMI [071]
ENQUIRER – St. Louis. Mo. 1819-1824 – 1 – us UMI [071]
ENQUIRER – York. S.C. -w. 1925-28 – 1 – us UMI [071]
ENQUIRER *see* OAKLAND POST ENQUIRER
THE ENQUIRER – Pleasant Hill, CA: Diablo Valley College, 1950-May 1983 – 7r – 1 – $350.00 – B02634 – us Library Micro [370]
THE ENQUIRER – Quebec: W.H. Shadgett, 1821-1822 – 9 – cn C.I.H.M. [971]
THE ENQUIRER : REFLECTIONS ON EDUCATION, MANNERS, AND LITERATURE. IN A SERIES OF ESSAYS / Godwin, William – London: G.G. and J. Robinson, 1797 – 1 roll – 1 – 1-55879-871-4 – uk Libr Preservation [390]
THE ENQUIRER – Toronto: T.J. Hamilton, [1880?-19–?] – 9 – cn C.I.H.M. [971]
THE ENQUIRER – Blantyre: Commercial Development Graphic Ltd, aug 2/8-sep 20/26; oct 5-dec 15, 31 1993; jan-dec 1994; jan-feb 3/9, 17/23-aug 3/8, 25/31-dec 19 1995; jan-jun 19/25; jul 5/11-19/25 1996 – 1r – 1 – us Res Libr [072]
ENQUIRER AND BELMONT NEWS ADVERTISER – San Carlos, CA. 1957-72 – 16r – 1 – $800.00 – B02778 – us Library Micro [071]
Enquirer Print *see* HISTORY OF NAPA COUNTY
ENQUIRER-BULLETIN – San Carlos, CA. 1986 – 9+ r – 1 – $450.00 ($90.00y) – B03658 – us Library Micro [071]
ENQUIRIDION CONTRA EL MORBO ARTICULAR / Gomez Miedes, B – Madrid, 1731 – 4mf – 9 – sp Cultura [610]
ENQUIRY – 1-2 2+3 (all publ). 1942-1945 – 5mf – 9 – $35.00 – us UPA [073]
AN ENQUIRY CONCERNING THE INTELLECTUAL AND MORAL FACULTIES AND LITERATURE OF NEGROES : FOLLOWED WITH AN ACCOUNT OF THE LIFE AND WORKS OF 15 NEGROES AND MULATTOES DISTINGUISHED IN SCIENCE, LITERATURE AND THE ARTS / Gregoire, H – (Filmed with: A tribute for the Negro/W Armistead) – Printed by T Kirk, 1810 – us Res Libr [305]
ENQUIRY INTO THE NATURE, CAUSE AND CURE OF THE CROUP / Home, F – M 104. 1765 – 9 – ne IDC [610]
AN ENQUIRY INTO THE PRESENT STATE OF THE MILITARY FORCE OF THE BRITISH EMPIRE, WITH A VIEW TO ITS REORGANIZATION / Wilson, Robert Thomas – 1804 – 9 – uk Libr Preservation [941]
AN ENQUIRY RESPECTING THE CAPTURE OF WASHINGTON BY THE BRITISH,...1814;... – Washington City, 1816 – 1mf – 1 – ILM-2857/1 – ne IDC [327]
ENREGISTREMENT DES PROJECTIONS, ENREGISTREMENT DES NEGATIFS : LABORATOIRE D'ANTHROPOLOGIE / Musee de l'Homme (Paris). Phototheque – (Catalogues des cliches photographiques conserves au laboratoire d' anthropologie; Registres d'inventaire des enregistrements photographiques. 12 vol. 1929-1938) – fr Armell [770]
ENRICO 4; TRAGEDIA IN TRE ATTI / Pirandello, Luigi – 3. ed. Firenze: R. Bemporad & Figlio, (c1923). 139p 1 reel. 1268 – 1 – us U.W. Library [820]
ENRICO ARNAUD : PASTORE E DUCE DE'VALDESI, 1641-1721 / Comba, Emilio – Firenze: Claudiana, 1889 – 1mf – us A.T.L.A. [920]
ENRICO HEINE NELLA LETTERATURA ITALIANA : AVANTI LA "RIVELAZIONE" DI T MASSARANI / Bonardi, Carlo – (Includes bibliographical references) – Livorno: R Guisti, 1907 – 1 – us U.W. Library [440]
Enriques, G *see*
– SUL..."OGGETTO DI NORME DI DIRITTO INTERNAZIONALE PRIVATO"
– UNIVERSALITA E TERRITORIALITA DEL FALLIMENTO...
Enriquez Anselmo, Juan *see* DOS MEDICOS EXTREMENOS DE AYER
Enriquez, Jose T *see* FILIPINO LANGUAGE LEXICON
ENROLLED ACTS AND RESOLUTIONS OF CONGRESS, 1893-1956 / U.S. Congress – 139r – 1 – M1326 – us Nat'l Archives [324]
ENROLLED CERTIFICATES OF NATURALIZATION AND MEMORIALS, 1859-1866 / General Registry Office – 1 reel – 1 – CRS A823 – at Archives [920]
ENROLLED ORIGINAL ACTS AND RESOLUTIONS OF THE CONGRESS OF THE UNITED STATES, 1789-1823 / U.S. Congress – 17r – 1 – M337 – us Nat'l Archives [324]
THE ENROLLMENT AND PERSISTENCE OF AFRICAN-AMERICAN DOCTORAL STUDENTS IN PHYSICAL EDUCATION AND RELATED DISCIPLINES / King, Susan E & Anderson, William G – 1992 – 3mf – 9 – $12.00 – us Microform Publ [790]
ENROLLMENT CARDS FOR THE FIVE CIVILIZED TRIBES, 1898-1914 / U.S. Bureau of Indian Affairs – RG 75. M1186. 93 rolls – 1 – us Nat'l Archives [975]
L'ENROLMENT DES GAMINS DE PARIS POUR L'ARMEE D'ITALIE – Paris, [1848?] – us Res Libr [944]
ENROLMENTS FORMS OF VICTORIAN CONTINGENTS, 1899-1900 / Department of Defence, Victoria – 5r – 1 – CRS B5177 – at Archives [920]
O ENSAIO : LITTERARIO, HUMORISTICO E SPORTIVO – Manoas, Amazonas. 26 Mar-2 Abr 1916 – 1,5,6 – bl Biblioteca [072]
O ENSAIO : ORGAO HUMORISTICO E NOTICIOSO – Queluz, 13 Aug-Nov 1910; Dec 1911; Feb-Apr, Jun, Sept-27 Oct 1912 – 1,5,6 – bl Biblioteca [072]
ENSAIO DE DICCIONARIO KIMBUNDU-PORTUGUEZ. / Cordeiro da Matta, J D – (Filmed with his: Jisabu, jiheng'ele, ifika ni jinongonongo, josoneke mu Kimbundu ni putu, kua mon'Angola Jakim Ria Matta) – Lisbon: A M Pereira, 1893 – 1 – us Res Libr [040]
ENSAIO JUVENIL : ORGAO DO CLUB JUVENIL – Campanha, 23 Aug-23 Sep 1889 – 1,5,6 – bl Biblioteca [072]
ENSAIOS POETICOS / Castro Sampaio, Manuel de – 1858 – 9 – 1.50f – sp Bibl Santa Ana [810]
ENSAYO BIBLIOGRAFICO SOBRE SAN PEDRO DE ALCANTARA / Recio Veganzones, Alejandro – Madrid, 1962 – 1 – sp Bibl Santa Ana [240]
ENSAYO BIOLOGICO SOBRE HERNANDO CORTES. TOMO 1. OAXACA, 1933 / Gutirrrez, Solano – Madrid: Razon y Fe, 1935 – 1 – sp Bibl Santa Ana [920]
ENSAYO DE CATALOGO DE LOS LUGARES DE SENORIO TEMPORAL, LOS OBISPOS DE ESPANA EN LA EDAD MEDIA / Perez-Villamil, Manuel – Madrid: Fortanet, 1916. B.R.A.H. 68, pp. 382-390 – sp Bibl Santa Ana [240]
ENSAYO DE MEDICINA GENERAL O SEA DE FILOSOFIA MEDICA... / Nieto y Serrano, M – Madrid, 1860 – 10mf – 9 – sp Cultura [610]
ENSAYO DE UN REGISTRO DEL CENSO ORGANIZADO...POR EL DISTRITO DE ROSMBLON EN 1895 – Manila, 1896 – 6mf – 9 – sp Cultura [946]
ENSAYO DE UNA BIBLIOTECA DE TRADUCTORES ESPANOLES / Pellicer Saforcada, Juan Antonio – 1778 – 1mf – 9 – Pta1,000.00 – 84-7848-356-X – sp Pentalfa [020]

ENSAYO DE UNA BIBLIOTECA DE TRADUCTORES ESPANOLES / Pellicer Saforcada, Juan Antonio – Madrid, 1778. 381p. 1mf. Libros en microficha no. 004 – 9 – Pta1,000.00 – 84-85422-28-7 – sp Pentalfa [020]
ENSAYO DE UNA BIBLIOTECA ESPANOLA DE LIBROS RAROS Y CURIOSOS / Gallardo, B J – Madrid, 1963-1966 – 50mf – 9 – sp Cultura [020]
ENSAYO HISTORICO DE OLIVENZA / Parra, Victoriano C – Badajoz: Tip. y Lib. Antonio Arqueros, 1909 – 1 – sp Bibl Santa Ana [946]
ENSAYO PARA UNA TEORIA DE EXTREMADURA / Becerro de Bengoa, Ricardo – Caceres: Imprenta Garcia Floriano, 1950 – sp Bibl Santa Ana [946]
ENSAYO POLITICO SOBRE EL REINO DE LA NUEVA ESPANA / Bayle, Constantino & Humboldt, Alejandro de – Madrid: Razon y Fe, 1944.-5v – 1 – sp Bibl Santa Ana [320]
ENSAYO SOBRE EL CATOLICISMO, EL LIBERALISMO Y EL SOCIALISMO / Donoso Cortes, Juan Francisco – Buenos Aires: Editorial Americalee, 1943 – 1 – sp Bibl Santa Ana [320]
ENSAYO SOBRE EL CATOLICISMO LIBERALISMO / Donoso Cortes, Juan Francisco – (1880 ed.1.50f; 9) – 1851 – 9 – 1.50f – sp Bibl Santa Ana [240]
ENSAYO SOBRE EL JUSTICIALISMO A LA LUZ DEL MATERIALISMO HISTORICO : DEL 4 DE JUNIO AL 2ND PLAN QUINQUENAL / Astesano, Eduardo – Rosario: Edici on del Autor, [1953] – 1 – CSUXAGP9549-B – us Hoover Inst Photo [360]
ENSAYO SOBRE EL RIO DE LA PLATA Y LA REVOLUCION FRANCESA / Cailler-Bois, Ricardo – Buenos Aires, 1929 – 1 – sp Bibl Santa Ana [946]
ENSAYO SOBRE EL TEATRO ESPANOL / Sebastian Latro, Tomas – 1773 – 1mf – 9 – Pta1,000.00 – 84-7848-279-2 – sp Pentalfa [790]
ENSAYO SOBRE VIRGILIO / Ricci, Clemente – Buenos Aires, 1931; Madrid: Razon y Fe, 1931 – 1 – sp Bibl Santa Ana [450]
ENSAYO TEORICO E HISTORICO SOBRE LA GENERACION DE LOS CONOCIMIENTOS HUMANOS : TRADUCCION DE A. GARCIA MORENO...TOMO 1 / Tiberghien, G – Madrid: Imp. de Federico Escamez Centeno, s.a. – 9 – sp Bibl Santa Ana [190]
ENSAYO...BIBLIOTECA...LIBROS RAROS / Gallardo, Bartolome Jose – (1888-89.1.50f; 9) – 1863-66.4v – 9 – 1.50f – sp Bibl Santa Ana [070]
ENSAYOS CRITICOS SOBRE FILOSOFIA, LITERATURA E INSTRUCCION PUBLICA / Laverde Ruiz, Gumersindo – 1868. Libros en Microficha no 7 – 2mf – 9 – Pta1,500.00 – 84-85422-32-5 – sp Pentalfa [190]
ENSAYOS DE ETICE. DUNS ESCOTO EN EXTREMADURA. 2 / Colegio San Antonio – Caceres: Imp. La Minerva, 2nd parte 1956 – 1 – sp Bibl Santa Ana [946]
ENSAYOS HISTORICOS. PUBLICACION DE HOMENAJE / Bayle, Constantino & Riverola, Rofolfo – Madrid: Razon y Fe, 1944 – 1 – sp Bibl Santa Ana [946]
ENSAYOS LITERARIOS / Arnes Luna, Alfredo – Madrid: Imp. Giralda, 1948 – 1 – sp Bibl Santa Ana [440]
ENSAYOS POETICOS / Sanchez Arjona y Sanchez Arjona, Jose – 1872 – 9 – 1.50f – sp Bibl Santa Ana [810]
ENSAYOS SOBRE ETNOLOGIA ARGENTINA / Cabrera, Pablo – Madrid: Razon y Fe, 1932 – 1 – sp Bibl Santa Ana [305]
ENSAYOS SOBRE LA HISTORIA ECONOMICA ARGENTINA / Diaz Alejandro, Carlos Federico – Buenos Aires: Amorrortu, 1975, c1970 – 1 – CSUXADQ4231-B – us Hoover Inst Photo [330]
ENSAYOS Y REVISTAS: 1888-1892 / Alas, Clarin – Madrid: Lasanta, 1892. 434p. 5 fiches.(Literature Collection) – 9 – 12.00 – fr Bibl Nationale [840]
Ense, K A Varnhagen von *see* TAGEBUECHER VON FRIEDRICH VON GENTZ
LES ENSEIGNANTS : LE TRAIT D'UNION ET L'APOSTROPHE DU MONDE ENSEIGNANT – Montreal. v1- 1970-. SEM35P21 – 3r – 1 – Can$166.00 – cn Bibl Nat [073]
L'ENSEIGNE : SON HISTOIRE, SA PHILOSOPHIE, SES PARTICULARITES, LES BOUTIQUES, LES MAISONS, LA RUE, LA RECLAME COMMERCIALE A LYON / Grand-Carteret, John – Grenoble: Librairie Dauphinoise; Moutiers: Librairie Savoyarde, 1902. SEM105P661 – 6mf – 9 – Can$13.50 – cn Bibl Nat [944]
L'ENSEIGNEMENT DE SAINT PAUL DANS LES EPITUS DE L'ANNEE LITURGIQUE, 1933 / Soubigon, P – Madrid: Razon y Fe, 1934 – 1 – sp Bibl Santa Ana [240]
L'ENSEIGNEMENT DES JESUITES AU CANADA: COLLEGE SAINTE-MARIE DE MONTREAL / Bellay, A – Montreal: Imprimerie de l'Etendard, 1891?. 03563. (Pre-1900 Canadiana) – 9 – cn C.I.H.M. [370]
L'ENSEIGNEMENT DES LETTRES CLASSIQUES D'AUSONE A ALCUIN : INTRODUCTION A L'HISTOIRE DES ECOLES CAROLINGIENNES / Roger, Maurice – (Includes index) – Paris: Alphonse Picard, 1905 – 2mf – 9 – 0-8370-8857-7 – 1986-2857 – us A.T.L.A. [370]
L'ENSEIGNEMENT ET L'EDUCATION EN REPUBLIQUE DE GUINEE / Toure, A S – Conakry: Impr nationale "Patrice Lumumba", 1972 – us Res Libr [370]
ENSEIGNEMENT MATHEMATIQUE – 1936-79 – 1,5,6 – us Princeton Micro [073]
ENSEIGNEMENT MEDICO-SOCIAL POUR COLONIAUX / Habig, Jean-Marie – Bruxelles: Edition Universelle, 1946-48 – 1 – us Res Libr [960]
L'ENSEIGNEMENT MENAGER AU CANADA FRANCAIS : BIBLIOGRAPHIE ANALYTIQUE, 1955-1963 / St-Claude-Marie, Soeur – 1964. SEM105P4 – 656mf – 9 – Can$1,476.00 – cn Bibl Nat [370]
L'ENSEIGNEMENT MENAGER DANS LA PROVINCE DE QUEBEC : REGLEMENTS ET PROGRAMMES – Quebec: [Departement de l'instruction publicque], 1943. SEM105P1827 – 2mf – 9 – Can$4.50 – cn Bibl Nat [350]
L'ENSEIGNEMENT PRIMAIRE – [Quebec: s.n., 1881-19-] – 9 – cn C.I.H.M. [370]
ENSEIGNEMENT PRIMAIRE ET APPRENTISSAGE / Salicis, Gustave A – Paris. 1875. (La Condition Ouvriere. Part Two.) – 9 – 5.00 – fr Bibl Nationale [360]
L'ENSEIGNEMENT QU'ON APPELLE AGRICOLE ET L'EVOLUTION DES ESPACES SOCIAUX A TRAVERS L'EXEMPLE DE LA BASSE-NORMANDIE / Lille, Jean – 2mf – 9 – fr Atelier National [307]
L'ENSEIGNEMENT: SITUATION, PROBLEMES PERSPECTIVES / Morocco. Ministere de l'Enseignement – 1970. BNE-3082 1 – 9 – ne IDC [370]
ENSEIGNEMENT TECHNIQUE ET FORMATION PROFESSIONNELLE : SITUATION COMPAREE DES RESULTATS AUX EXAMENS DE 1981 A 1983 / Ivory Coast. Office National de Formation Professionnelle – Abidjan, 1984 – 1mf – 9 – DE-617/1 – ne IDC [370]
ENSEMBLE : REVUE DE LA COOPERATION / ed by Legare, Jean-Paul – Quebec, Canada. 30 jan 1940-aut/sep 1943 – 1r – 1 – Can$40.00 – cn Can Microfilming [073]
ENSEMBLE DE PIECES MANUSCRITES CONCERNANT : J.-B.-L. CHOTARD, CONSEILLER-MAITRE A LA CHAMBRE DES COMPTES DE BRETAGNE / Chotard, Jean-Bapt. L – 18th cent – 1 – F84.45 – fr Armell [944]
ENSEMBLE DES MSS. CONSERVES A LA BIBL. MUN. DE NANTES / Rebell, Hugues – (1) oeuvres/works: – Contes de l'alcove et du champ de bataille – Defense d'Oscar Wilde – Stambouloff, du patriotisme et de l'intolerance – Sur une traduction collective des oeuvres de Nietzsche; 2) correspondance/letters: – 11 lettres a Etienne Desgranges, 189? – 9 lettres a Robert Sherard, 1893-1894) – 1 – F235.30 – fr Armell [944]
LA ENSENANZA DE LENGUAS CIVILIZADAS A LOS BARBAROS. UN CASO DE TEOLOGIA PASTORAL MISIONERA / Bayle, Constantino – Madrid: Razon y Fe, 1933 – 1 – sp Bibl Santa Ana [240]
LA ENSENANZA DEL DERECHO INTERNACIONAL PUBLICO / Arbelaiz, M – Montevideo, 1909 – 2mf – 9 – ILM-1600/1 – ne IDC [340]
ENSENANZA E INVESTIGACION EN PSICOLOGIA – (v.6 .1980 5,6,9) – v.1. 1975 – 1 – us UMI [073]
LA ENSENANZA EN BARCELONA A FINES DEL SIGLO 18 / Oriol Moncanut, Ana Maria – Madrid: Archivo Ibero Americano, 1960 – 1 – sp Bibl Santa Ana [946]
ENSENANZA...BADAJOZ / Saa Maldonado, Manuel – 1873 – 9 – 1.50f – sp Bibl Santa Ana [370]
Ensh, G A *see* DOKUMENTY PO ISTORII PRIBALTIKI SHVEDSKOGO PERIODA V ARKHIVAKH RIGI
ENSIGN – Fowler. Calif. -w. 1941-56 – 1 – us UMI [071]
THE ENSIGN – (Also: St-Lawrence News, Iroquois Falls v1 n26. 21 fev 1890) – Kingston, Ontario. v1 n1. 30 oct 1948 – 1r – 1 – Can$25.00 – cn Can Microfilming [072]
THE ENSIGN – (Quebec section (Montreal): 28 oct 1950-30 jun 1956 1r Can$65.00. Ontario section (Kingston): 1 jan 1949-30 jun 1956 1r Can$65.00. Maritimes section (Moncton): 2 jul 1949-17 dec 1949 1r Can$65.00. Western section (Winnipeg): 2 jul 1949-30 jun 1956 1r Can$65.00) – Montreal, (Kingston, Manitoba, Maritimes) Canada. 30 oct 1948-15 dec 1956 – 5r – 1 – Can$60.00r – cn Can Microfilming [072]
DEN ENSKILDE OCH KYRKAN : FOEREDRAG HALLET VID STUDENTMOETET I HUSKVARNA 1909 / Soederblom, Nathan – Uppsala: L. Norblad, [1909?] – 1mf – us A.T.L.A. [240]
ENSTEHUNG, FORTGANG UN IETZIGE BESCHAFFENHEIT DER RUSSISCHEN IAGDMUSIK / Hinrichs, I Ch – Spb. 1796. DP-099 1 – 9 – ne IDC [780]
ENT / University of Kentucky. Department of Entomology – No.1-42.1972-83. 14 fiches – 9 – us Spaulding [630]
ENTALPIIA PLAVLENIIA SOLEVYKH EVTEKTIK / Cherneeva, L I et al – Moskva: In-t vysokikh temperatur AN SSSR, 1980 – us Res Libr [947]
ENTALPIIA, TEPLOEMKOST, TEPLOTA I ENTROPIIA PLAVLENIIA NEKOTORYKH TUGOPLAVKIKH METALLOV / Chekhovskoi, V I A – Moskva: In-t vysokikh temperatur AN SSSR, 1979 – us Res Libr [947]
ENTARTUNG / Nordau, Max Simon – Berlin: C. Duncker, 1892-93. 2v – 1 – us U.W. Library [430]
DAS ENTDECKTE GEHEIMNISS DER NATUR IM BAU UND IN DER BEFRUCHTUNG DER BLUMEN / Sprengel, C K – Berlin, 1793. 444 pp., 25 pls. B-5747 2 – 8 – ne IDC [580]
ENTDECKTE VERDREHUNG DES WESTPHALISCHEN FRIEDENS-SCHLUSSES... – Franckfurt, Leipzig. 2pts. 1758-1759 – 2mf – 1 – ILM-2791/1 – ne IDC [327]
ENTDECKUNGEN UEBER DIE THEORIE DES KLANGES VON ERNST FLORENS FRIEDRICH CHLADNI / Chladni, E FF – 1787 – 9 – us Sibley [780]
DIE ENTDECKUNGSREISEN IN NORD- UND MITTEL-AFRIKA VON RICHARDSON, OVERWEG, BARTH UND VOGEL / ed by Arenz, Karl – Leipzig: C B Lorck, 1857 – 1 – us Res Libr [910]
ENTEN–ELLER : ET LIVS-FRAGMENT / Kierkegaard, Soren – Kjobenhavn: C.A. Reitzel, 1843 – 2mf – us A.T.L.A. [190]
L'ENTENTE – Ville St-Leonard, Canada. mai 1960-11 nov 1971 – 1r – 1 – Can$55.00 – cn Can Microfilming [072]
ENTENTE – London, UK. 14 Jul-9 Oct 1920 – 1 – uk British Libr Newspaper [072]
L'ENTENTE CORDIALE – Montreal, Canada. oct 1945-v1 n8. fev 1947 – 1r – 1 – Can$35.00 – cn Can Microfilming [072]
ENTENTE FRANCO-MUSULMANE – puis L'Entente. Organe hebdomadaire d'union et de defense des interets des Musulmans algeriens. Dir. Bendjelloul. Constantine. aout 1935-janv 1942 – 1 – fr A.C.R.P.P. [960]
ENTERPRISE – Albert Lea. Minn. 1872-75; 1879-1895; 1900-05 – 1 – us UMI [071]
ENTERPRISE – Bancroft. Neb. 1895-1896 – 1 – us UMI [071]
ENTERPRISE – Battle Creek. Neb. 1897-1898; 1908-1952 – 1 – us UMI [071]
ENTERPRISE – B.C. Canada. Aug 1903-Aug 1904 – 1 – cn Commonwealth Micro [072]
ENTERPRISE – Belmont Shore, CA. 1967 – 1r – 1 – $50.00 – H04003 – us Library Micro [071]
ENTERPRISE – Bennet, NE. -w. Oct. 1908-Dec. 1908. Incomplete; Feb. 1909-Oct. 1910 – 1 – us NE Hist [071]
ENTERPRISE – Berwick. Pa. 1954- – 1 – us UMI [071]
ENTERPRISE – Blair, NE. -w. Jan. 1897-Nov. 1897. Incomplete; Feb. 1898-Mar. 1899; Oct. 1902-Jan. 1903; Aug. 1908- – 1 – us NE Hist [071]
ENTERPRISE – Boron. Calif. 1954-1967 – 1 – us UMI [071]
ENTERPRISE – Burlingame. Kan. 1895-1920 – 1 – us UMI [071]
ENTERPRISE – Chico. Calif. -w., s.w. 1880-1907 – 1 – us UMI [071]
ENTERPRISE – Cleveland. Miss. 1902-1913; 1942-1945 – 1 – us UMI [071]
ENTERPRISE – Drain. Or. 1922-1953 – 1 – us UMI [071]
ENTERPRISE – East Greenwich. R.I. 1888-1889 – 1 – us UMI [071]
ENTERPRISE – Elk City. Kan. 1889-1905 – 1 – us UMI [071]
ENTERPRISE – Elko, NV. 1916-17 – 1r – 1 – $50.00 – U04497 – us Library Micro [071]
ENTERPRISE – Goldfield, NV. Feb-Nov 1958 – 1r – 1 – $50.00 – U04552 – us Library Micro [071]
ENTERPRISE – Greenville. S.C. 1871-80 – 1 – us UMI [071]
ENTERPRISE – Hickman. Neb. 1891-1952 – 1 – us UMI [071]
ENTERPRISE – High Point. N.C. 1915- – 1 – us UMI [071]
ENTERPRISE – Homestead. Fl. 1914-1921 – 1 – us UMI [071]
ENTERPRISE – Hubbard. Or. -w. 1917-35 – 1 – us UMI [071]
ENTERPRISE – Hudson. Ohio. 1877-1881 – 1 – us UMI [071]
ENTERPRISE – Indianola. Miss. 1902-1903; 1916-1927 – 1 – us UMI [071]
ENTERPRISE – Kansas City. (Western Journal Commerce). Mo. 1855-66 – 1 – us UMI [071]
ENTERPRISE – Katoomba, Sep 3 1913 – 9 – at Pascoe [072]
ENTERPRISE – Kennard. Neb. 1897-1962 – 1 – us UMI [071]
ENTERPRISE – Livingstone. Mont. 1924-1937 – 1 – us UMI [071]
ENTERPRISE – McComb. Miss. 1935-1940; 1941; 1942-1946 – 1 – us UMI [071]
ENTERPRISE – McComb. Miss. -w. 1931-35 – 1 – us UMI [071]
ENTERPRISE – Meshoppen. Pa. 1897-1907; 1926-1941 – 1 – us UMI [071]
ENTERPRISE – (Missing issues: 25 Jan, 27 Sept 1919; 28 Dec 1921) – Fairfield, CA. 1915-23 – 2r – 1 – $100.00 – B02229 – us Library Micro [071]
ENTERPRISE – Monument OR. July 15 Aug 12 Oct 7 1909 – 1 – us U.O. Library [071]
ENTERPRISE – Myrtle Point. Or. -w. 1907-17 – 1 – us UMI [071]
ENTERPRISE – New Concord. Ohio. 1880-1943; 1947-1966 – 1 – us UMI [071]
ENTERPRISE – Newport. R.I. 1886-1889; 1890-1897 – 1 – us UMI [071]
ENTERPRISE – Omaha, NE. -w. Aug 1895-Jul 1897; Aug-Oct 1908; Dec 1908-Feb 1911 – 1 – us NE Hist [071]
ENTERPRISE – Paris. Ky. 1958- – 1 – us UMI [071]
ENTERPRISE – Parkrose, OR. -w. 8 May 1957-18 June 1958; 22 Nov 1962-22 Sep 1964 – 1 – us U.O. Library [071]
ENTERPRISE – Patoka. Ill. -w. 1885-87 – 1 – us UMI [071]
ENTERPRISE – Pawnee City. Neb. 1878-1885 – 1 – us UMI [071]
ENTERPRISE – Pleasanton. Kan. 1899-1911 – 1 – us UMI [071]
ENTERPRISE – Porterville. Calif. -w. 1889-1901 – 1 – us UMI [071]
ENTERPRISE – Redmond OR. Dec 14 1912, Oct 25 1913 – 1 – us U.O. Library [071]
ENTERPRISE – Riverside. Calif. 1891-1893 – 1 – us UMI [071]
ENTERPRISE – Simi Valley, CA. 1951 – 516+ r – 1 – $25,800.00 ($600.00y) – H04065 – us Library Micro [071]
ENTERPRISE – South Hill. Va. -w. 1927- – 1 – us UMI [071]
ENTERPRISE – South San Francisco. Calif. -w. 1939-50 – 1 – us UMI [071]
ENTERPRISE – Stapleton. Neb. 1912-1957 – 1 – us UMI [071]
ENTERPRISE – Wesson. Miss. 1905-1910; 1936-1952 – 1 – us UMI [071]
ENTERPRISE – Westerly. R.I. 1867-1868 – 1 – us UMI [071]
ENTERPRISE – Willimantic. Conn. 1877-79 – 1 – us UMI [071]

ENTERPRISE – Yorkton, 1976-1990Se – 49r – 1 – cn Preston [971]
ENTERPRISE *see* PORTERVILLE PAPERS
THE ENTERPRISE – Albany, CA. Aug 1982-Dec 1983 – 6r – 1 – $300.00 – B02006 – us Library Micro [071]
THE ENTERPRISE – Arthur. Neb. 1911-1960 – 1 – us UMI [071]
THE ENTERPRISE – Big Spring. Tex. 1908-1911 – 1 – us UMI [071]
THE ENTERPRISE – Huntingdon, Canada. 1 mai 1890-v3 n49. 20 Apr 1893 – 1r – 1 – Can$40.00 – cn Can Microfilming [072]
THE ENTERPRISE – Noblesville. Ind. 1905-1909 – 1 – us UMI [071]
THE ENTERPRISE – Oakland, CA. 1982-1984 – 7r – 1 – 350.00 – RB03363 – us Library Micro [071]
THE ENTERPRISE : SOUTH SAN FRANCISCO – San Francisco, CA. 1907-38 – 15r – 1 – $750.00 – C03479 – us Library Micro [071]
THE ENTERPRISE – South San Francisco, CA. 1895-1950 – 22r – 1 BC03004 – $1,100.00 – us Library Micro [071]
THE ENTERPRISE – Stillwater. Mont. 1928-1933 – 1 – us UMI [071]
THE ENTERPRISE – Swellendam, South Africa. 1 Mar 1883-25 Aug 1886. 1 reel – 1, 16 diazo available at reduced price – sa SA Libr [072]
ENTERPRISE AND MESSENGER – Collingwood, 1882-1930 – 18r – 1 – cn Preston [971]
ENTERPRISE BULLETIN – (Ju1909-1992.-177r) – Collingwood, 1993 – 14r – 1 – cn Preston [971]
ENTERPRISE CHIEFTAIN – Enterprise, OR. -w. 1911-43. Inc. Enterprise Record-Chieftain – 1 – 264.00 – us Oregon Hist [071]
ENTERPRISE JOURNAL – McComb. Miss. 1946- – 1 – us UMI [071]
ENTERPRISE JOURNAL – South San Francisco. Calif. -w. 1953- – 1 – us UMI [071]
ENTERPRISE NEWS – Cambridge Springs. Pa. -w. 1900-69 – 1 – us UMI [071]
ENTERPRISE RECORD – Chico. Calif. 1896- – 1 – us UMI [071]
ENTERPRISE-COURIER – Oregon City, OR. -d. 1 Mar 1950-. – 1 – us U.O. Library [071]
ENTERPRISE-JOURNAL – (Cont. by: San Bruno Herald) – South San Francisco, CA. 1950-1979 – 53r – 1 – $2,650.00 – BC03005 – us Library Micro [073]
ENTERPRISE-MESSENGER – Merna, NE. -w. Feb 1905; Mar 1907-Oct 1944; Mar 1947-Oct 1952; Dec 1952-Jun 1953 – 1 – us NE Hist [071]
ENTERPRISE-RECORDER – Madison. Fl. -w. 1911- – 1 – us P.K. Yonge [071]
L'ENTERREMENT DU DICTIONNAIRE DE L'ACADEMIE / Chastein – 1697 – 9 – fr I.C.S. [440]
ENTERTAINMENT AND SPORTS LAW JOURNAL *see* UNIVERSITY OF MIAMI ENTERTAINMENT AND SPORTS LAW REVIEW
ENTERTAINMENT AND SPORTS LAWYER (ABA) – v1-12. 1982-95 – 9 – $98.00 set – us Hein [340]
THE ENTERTAINMENT OF HIS MOST EXCELLENT MAJESTIE CHARLES 2 / Ogilby, John – O-381 1. 1662 – 9 – ne IDC [941]
Entfelder, Chr *see*
– VON DEN MANIGFALTIGEN IM GLAUBENN ZERSPALTUNGENN
– VON GOTTES VNND CHRISTI JESU VNNSERS HERREN ERKANDTNUSZ, AIN BEDACHT
– VON WARER GOTSELIGKAYT, WIE DER MENSCH ALLHIE IN DISER ZEYT DARTZU KOMMEN MAG
DER ENTFESSELTE SAEUGLING : EINE KOMISCHE GESCHICHTE FUER ERWACHSENE / Vesper, Will – Muenchen: A Langen/G Mueller, 1935 – 1r – 1 – us U.W. Library [830]
Enthoven, R E *see* THE TRIBES AND CASTES OF BOMBAY
ENTHUSIASM DELINEATED : OR, THE ABSURD CONDUCT OF THE METHODISTS DISPLAYED,... / Blacksmith, A T – Bristol, [1764] – 1mf – 9 – MP-428/1 – ne IDC [240]
ENTHUSIASM DETECTED, DEFEATED, WITH PREVIOUS CONSIDERATIONS CONCERNING REGENERATION, THE OMNIPRESENCE OF GOD, AND DIVINE GRACE / Roe, S – Cambridge, 1768 – 4mf – 9 – MP-454/1 – ne IDC [240]
ENTHUSIASM EXPLAINED : OR, A DISCOURSE ON THE NATURE, KIND AND CAUSE OF ENTHUSIASM,... – London, 1739 – 1mf – 9 – MP-268/1 – ne IDC [240]
THE ENTHUSIASM OF METHODISTS AND PAPISTS COMPAR'D [PART 1] / Lavington, G – London, 1749 – 1mf – 9 – MP-336/1 – ne IDC [240]
THE ENTHUSIASM OF METHODISTS AND PAPISTS COMPARED, PART 2 / Lavington, G – London, 1749 – 3mf – 9 – MP-337/1 – ne IDC [240]
ENTHUSIASMUS UND BUSSGEWALT BEIM GRIECHISCHEN MOENCHTUM : EINE STUDIE ZU SYMEON DEM NEUEN THEOLOGEN / Holl, Karl – Leipzig, 1898 – 6mf – 8 – Dfl25.00 – ne Slangenburg [240]
ENTHUSIASMUS UND BUSSGEWALT BEIM GRIECHISCHEN MOENCHTUM : EINE STUDIE ZU SYMEON DEM NEUEN THEOLOGEN / Holl, Karl – Leipzig: J.C. Hinrichs, 1898 – 1mf – us A.T.L.A. [240]
THE ENTHUSIASTS OF PORT-ROYAL / Rea, Lilian – New York: Scribner, 1912 – 1mf – us A.T.L.A. [971]
GLI ENTI COLLETTIVI NEL DIRITTO INTERNAZIONALE PRIVATO... / Fedozzi, P – Verona, Padova, 1897 – 3mf – 1 – ILM-3319/1 – ne IDC [327]
Entick, John *see* SPECULUM LATINUM
ENTIDAD CONSTRUCTORA BENFICA NUESTRA SENORA DE LA SOLEDAD. OBISPADO DE BADAJOZ. ESTATUTOS SOCIALES Y DE LA COMUNIDAD DE VECINOS – Badajoz: Imprenta Espanola, 1968 – 1 – sp Bibl Santa Ana [946]
ENTIRE COMMENTARY UPON THE WHOLE EPISTLE OF ST PAUL TO THE EPHESIANS / Baynes, Paul – Edinburgh: James Nichol, 1866. 1 fiche – 9 – us A.T.L.A. [240]
AN ENTIRELY NEW AND ORIGINAL MILITARY OPERA IN THREE ACTS, ENTITLED: LEO, THE ROYAL CADET / Cameron, George Frederick – Libretto by George Frederic sic Cameron; music by Oscar F. Teigmann. 1889? 05123. (Pre-1900 Canadiana) – 9 – cn C.I.H.M. [780]
ENTOMOGRAPHIA IMPERII RUSSICCI / Fischer, G – 1820 – 1 – uk Microform Academic [590]
ENTOMOGRAPHIEN / Erichson, W F – Untersuchungen in dem Gebiete der Entomologie, mit besonderer Benutzung der Koenigl. Sammlung zu Berlin. Berlin, 1840, Pt.1. x,180p, 2pls. Z/1215/2 – 8 – ne IDC [590]
ENTOMOLOGIA BRITANNICA SISTENS INSECTA BRITANNIAE INDIGENA SECUNDUM METHODUM LINNAEANAM DISPOSITA – Londini, 1802. v1, Coleoptera, xxxi/547 [1]p – 8 – ne IDC [590]
ENTOMOLOGIAE NEAPOLITANAE SPECIMEN PRIMUM / Cirillo, D – Neapoli, 1787.8p. 12 pls. Z-1138/2 – 8 – ne IDC [590]
THE ENTOMOLOGICAL CABINET: BEING A NATURAL HISTORY OF BRITISH INSECTS / Samouelle, G – London, 1832-33.Z-1590/2 – 8 – ne IDC [590]
ENTOMOLOGICAL MAGAZINE / ed by Newman, E – London, etc., 1833-1838. v1-5 – 49mf – 9 – Z-937/2 – ne IDC [590]
ENTOMOLOGICAL NEWS AND PROCEEDINGS / Entomological Sect. Acad. Nat. Sci. Philadelphia – Philadelphia, 1890-1920. v.l-31 – 241mf – 8 – ne IDC [590]
ENTOMOLOGICAL REVIEW – (v63-. 1984-. 5,6,9) – v67-. 1958- – 1 – us UMI [073]
Entomological Sect. Acad. Nat. Sci. Philadelphia *see* ENTOMOLOGICAL NEWS AND PROCEEDINGS
Entomological Society of America *see*
– ANNALS
Entomological Society of London *see* TRANSACTIONS OF THE ENTOMOLOGICAL SOCIETY OF LONDON
ENTOMOLOGIE ANALYTIQUE / Dumeril, A M C – Paris, 1860. 1339p. (Mem. Acad. Sci. Paris, v31). Z/1206/2 – 8 – ne IDC [590]
ENTOMOLOGISCHE HEFTE – Frankfurt am Main, 1803. v1-2 – 5mf – 9 – Z-940/2 – ne IDC [590]
ENTOMOLOGISCHE MITTEILUNGEN / ed by Schenkling, S & Schaufuss, C – Berlin, 1912-1928. v1-17 – 109mf – 8 – ne IDC [590]
ENTOMOLOGISCHE MONATSBLAETTER / ed by Kraatz, G – Berlin, 1876-1880. v1-2 – 7mf – 9 – 2436/2 – ne IDC [590]
ENTOMOLOGISCHE NACHRICHTEN / ed by Katter, F & Karsch, F – Quedlinburg, 1875-1900. v1-26 – 169mf – 9 – Z-942/2 – ne IDC [590]
ENTOMOLOGISCHE VERSUCHE / Creutzer, C – Wien, 1799. 1428p. 3 pls. Z-1152/2 – 8 – ne IDC [590]
Entomologischer Verein in Stettin *see* LINNAEA ENTOMOLOGICA
ENTOMOLOGIST – London, 1840/42-1920. v.1-53 – 359mf – 8 – ne IDC [590]
L'ENTOMOLOGISTE GENEVOIS – Peney-Geneve, 1889-[1890]. Nos. 1-10 – 4mf – 9 – Z-950/2 – ne IDC [590]
ENTOMOLOGIST'S MONTHLY MAGAZINE – London, 1864/65-1920. v.1-56 2 – 353mf – 8 – ne IDC [590]
ENTOMOLOGIST'S RECORD AND JOURNAL OF VARIATION / ed by Tutt, J W – London, 1890-1908. v1-18 – 140mf – 9 – 2453/2 – ne IDC [590]
THE ENTOMOLOGIST'S USEFUL COMPENDIUM: OR, AN INTRODUCTION TO THE KNOWLEDGE OF BRITISH INSECTS / Samouelle, G – London, 1819. 496p. 12 pls. Z-1589/2 – 8 – ne IDC [590]
ENTOMOLOGIST'S WEEKLY INTELLIGENCER – London. 1856-61. v. 1-9 – 3 – us Readex [590]
ENTOMOLOGY / Auburn University. Agricultural Experiment Station – No.1. 1966-71. 1 reel – 1, 5 – us Spaulding [590]
ENTOMOLOGY / Duncan, J – Edinburgh, 1835-42. 6v.(Naturalist's Library, v10,14,18,29,33). Z/1207/2 – 8 – ne IDC [590]
ENTOMOLOGY ABSTRACTS – 9 – us C.S.A. [590]
THE ENTOMOLOGY OF AUSTRALIA / Gray, G R – Pt. 1 – Monograph of the genus phasma. 2471 2. 1838 – 8 – ne IDC [590]
ENTOMOLOGY PAMPHLET / South Dakota. State University. Agricultural Experiment Station – nos.1-16. 1940-52 – 1,5,6 – us Spaulding [630]
THE ENTOMOPHTHOREAE OF THE UNITED STATES / Thaxter, R – (Memoirs Boston Society of Nat. Hist.). Boston. 1886-93. BZ-2249 1 – 9 – ne IDC [590]
ENTOMOSTRACA SEU INSECTA TESTACEA.. / Mueller, Otto Frederik – Lipsiae: Havniae: Sumtibus J.G. Muelleriani, 1785. 134p. 21 leaves of plates. ill. Includes index – 1 – us U.W. Library [590]
ENTRACHT – Chicago. 1972/73-7 Sept 1985 – 1 – gw Mikrofilm [071]
L'ENTR'ACTE – Paris. Programme des spectacles. juil-dec 1832, 1850-53, 1855, 1858, janv-juin 1865, juin-dec 1871, janv-juin 1873 – 1 – fr A.C.R.P.P. [790]
THE ENTR'ACTE – London. 1870-1907. Journal of the musical and theatrical professions – 1 – uk World [790]
ENTR'ACTE AND LIMELIGHT – London. 1881-85 – 1 – 115.00 – us L of C Photodup [790]
ENTR'AIDE ET ACTION = HELP AND ACTION – Hericy. 41 docs. 1980-1990 – 35mf – 9 – ne IDC [320]
Entrambasaguas, Joaquin de *see* UNA FAMILIA DE INGENIOS, LOS RAMIREZ DE PRADO
ENTRAMBASAGUAS, JOAQUIN DE. LA BIBLIOTECA EN RAMIREZ DE PRADO. MADRID, 1943 / Hornedo, R M – Madrid: Razon y Fe, 1945 – 1 – sp Bibl Santa Ana [020]
Entrambasaguas Pena, Joaquin *see* POESIAS DE DONA CATALINA CLARA RAMIREZ DE GUZMAN
THE ENTRANCE – Essex, Ont.: [s.n., 1894-189- or 19–] – 9 – cn C.I.H.M. [971]
AN ENTRANCE TO THE SPANISH TONGUE / Sanford, John – 1611. 71p. (English Linguistics Series 1500-1800) – 9 – us UMI [440]
ENTRE DOS FILOS. MANAGUA, 1927 / Chamorro, Pedro Joaquin; ed by Bayle, Constantino – Madrid: Razon y Fe, 1929 – 9 – sp Bibl Santa Ana [999]
ENTRE DOS SIGLOS : EL URUGUAY ALREDEDOR DE 1800 / Falcao Espalter, Mario – Madrid: Razon y Fe, 1927 – 1 – sp Bibl Santa Ana [972]
ENTRE EL DEBER Y EL DERECHO / Hurtado, Antonio – 1873 – 9 – 1.50f – sp Bibl Santa Ana [830]
ENTRE LA LIBERTAD Y EL MIEDO / Arciniegas, German – [7. ed, rev y puesta al dia]. Buenos Aires: Editorial Sudamericana, [1956] – 1 – CSUXAJB8132-B – us Hoover Inst Photo [320]
ENTRE LE VICTORIA, L'ALBERT ET L'EDOUARD : ETHNOGRAPHIE DE LA PARTIE ANGLAISE DU VICARIAT DE L'UGANDA: ORIGINES, HISTOIRE, RELIGION, COUTUMES – Rennes, France: Impr Oberthur, 1920 – 1 – us Res Libr [305]
ENTRE MIS CUATRO PAREDES / Gonzalez Castell, Rafael – Montijo (Badajoz): Imp. Izquier do Hidalgo, 1934 – 1 – sp Bibl Santa Ana [946]
ENTRE NOUS / Beausoleil, Joseph Maxime – Montreal, 1897. 03530. (Pre-1900 Canadiana) – 9 – cn C.I.H.M. [971]
ENTRE NOUS – (Ceased v24 no 4 1991/92) – Ottawa. v14-24. 1981/82-1991/92 – 9 – Can$20.00y – cn Micromedia [073]
ENTRE NOUS CANADIENS-FRANCAIS : APPUIE LA CANDIDATURE DE CROTEAU A LA MAIRIE / ed by Fougieres, Luc de – Montreal, Canada. v1 n4. 28 avr 1961-30 mai 1961 – 1r – 1 – Can$25.00 – cn Can Microfilming [971]
Entrecolles, FX. *see*
– LETTRE DU P. D'ENTRECOLLES AU PERE DUHALDE. A PEKIN, CE 12 MAI 1726. PEKIN, 1726
– LETTRE...A PEKIN, LE 11 MAI 1726
L'ENTREE DANS LE MONDE / Picard – (French Theatre Series). Paris. Huet et Charon, an X. 1801 – 9 – fr Hachette [820]
ENTRENNES DE GUITARE. 4E ANNEE 1787. ENTIEREMENT COMPOSEES D'AIRS NOUVEAUX CHANSONS, ROMANCES .... / Porro, P J – Paris: L'auteur et Mme. Baillon. Versailles, Blaisot, 1787 – 1 – us Sibley [780]
ENTREPRENEUR – (v12-. 1984-. 5,6,9) – v6-. May 1978- – 1 – us UMI [073]
ENTREPRENEURSHIP, INNOVATION AND CHANGE – v1-2. 1992-93 – $65.00v – us UMI [650]
ENTREPRENEURSHIP THEORY AND PRACTICE *see* AMERICAN JOURNAL OF SMALL BUSINESS
LES ENTREPRISES – Montreal. v1 n12. 30 sep 1987-19-24 dec 1987f – 1r – 1 – Can$50.00 – cn Can Microfilming [072]
LES ENTREPRISES INDUSTRIELLES EN ALGERIE ET AU SAHARA / Algeria. Banque Nationale pour le Commerce et l'Industrie, Algiers – 1960. BNE-8606 1 – 9 – ne IDC [338]
LES ENTREPRISES PUBLIQUES AU MAROC; ESSAI D'ANALYSE DES FORMES D'ACTION MEDIATE DE LA PUISSANCE PUBLIQUE / Lahaye, R – These-Universite de Rabat. 1961. BNE-3062 1 – 9 – ne IDC [336]
O ENTRE-RIOS : ORGAO DEDICADO AOS INTERESSES DO POVO – Entrerios, 8 Dec 1898 – 1,5,6 – bl Biblioteca [072]
ENTRETENIMIENTOS POETICOS / Fernandez Garcia, Manuel – 1877 – 9 – 1.50f – sp Bibl Santa Ana [810]
ENTRETIEN DE JEAN PICHU AVEC SON SERGEANT AU SUJECT DU [...] – Paris: [s.n.]. [n1-3 1849] – us Res Libr [920]
ENTRETIEN DE SCIPION ET DE SEVERE SUR LA REPLIQUE FAITE POUR LE FACTUM DE MARIE BENOIST, DITE DE LA BUCAILLE – Rouen. 1699 – 9 – fr Hachette [360]
ENTRETIEN D'ORIGENE AVEC HERACLIDE ET LES EVEQUES SES COLLEGUES SUR LE PERE, LE FILS ET L'AME / Origenes; ed by Scherer, Jean – Le Caire, 1949 – 7mf – 9 – ne Slangenburg [240]
ENTRETIEN D'UN EUROPEEN AVEC UN INSULAIRE DU ROYAUME DE DUMOCALS. REPONSE A LA LETTRE D'UN AMI / Leczinski, Stanislas, roi de Pologne – (Utopias in the Enlightment series). 1752 – 9 – fr Hachette [830]
ENTRETIEN SUR LES SAINT-SIMONIENS ET LE SAINT-SIMONISME / Joua, Ferdinand – Rouen, impr. Delamare, 1831, 38 p. Les Saint-Simoniens, 1825-1834. 6983 – 9 – fr Hachette [335]
LES ENTRETIENS D'ARISTE ET D'EUGENE / Bouhours, D – 1671 – 9 – fr I.C.S. [190]
LES ENTRETIENS D'ARISTE ET D'EUGENE / Bouhours, D – Amsterdam, 1703 – 4mf – 9 – ne IDC [700]
ENTRETIENS DE ZERBES, ROI DE LYDIE ET DE SON MINISTRE SUR LA SITUATION DES AFFAIRES DE SON ROYAUME. QUESTIONS SOUMISES A L'EXAMEN DES CABINETS POLITIQUES / Andre de Ligneville, Jean-Francois – (Utopias in the Enlightenment series). 1788 – 9 – fr Hachette [320]

ENTRETIENS DES NON-COMBATTANTS DURANT LA GUERRE 1914-1918 – 2e s., no. 1; 4e s., no. 4 5. Paris. nov 1915-18 – 1 – fr A.C.R.P.P. [073]

ENTRETIENS D'ETE DE PONTIGNY – Versailles. aout sept 1910, 1926-27 (I, IX-X) – 1 – fr A.C.R.P.P. [073]

ENTRETIENS D'UN MOIS DE MARIE / ed by Speelman, R P – Tournai: J Casterman, 1856 – 1mf – 9 – 0-8370-9182-9 – 1986-3182 – us A.T.L.A. [240]

ENTRETIENS FAMILIERS POUR LES AMATEURS DE LA LANGUE FRANCOISE / Fenne, F de – 9 – fr I.C.S. [440]

LES ENTRETIENS IDEALISTES – Cahiers mensuels d'art et de philosophie. Paris. oct 1906-juil 1914 – 1 – fr A.C.R.P.P. [073]

ENTRETIENS POLITIQUES ET LITTERAIRES – no. 1-57. Paris. mars 1890-93 – 1 – fr A.C.R.P.P. [073]

ENTRETIENS SUR LE LOIS ECONOMIQUE ET DEFENCE DE LA PROPRIETE / Molinari, Gustave de – 1849. 4 fiches (24x) – 9 – 1.00f – at Libertarian Micro [320]

ENTRIES IN THE FAMILY BIBLE / Glen, John – 1 – uk Microform Academic [920]

ENTRY RECORD / Van Wert County. Ohio. Recorder – 1824-1864 – 1r – 1 – $32.50r – us Archival [324]

ENTRY RECORD / Wood County. Ohio. Recorder – 1817-1855 – 1r – 1 – $32.50r – us Archival [324]

DIE ENTSCHEIDUNG – Berlin. oct 9, 1932-mar 19, 1933 – 1r – 1 – gw Mikrofilm [073]

DIE ENTSCHEIDUNGEN AUSLAENDISCHER GERICHTE... / Francke, W – Berlin, 1884 – 2mf – 1 – ILM-2268/1 – ne IDC [327]

ENTSCHEIDUNGEN DER FILM-PRUEFSTELLE – Berlin. dec 30, 1929-sep 9, 1944 – 6r – 1 – gw Mikrofilm [073]

ENTSCHIENDENE SCHULREFORM – Berlin. Bd. 1-51; 1922-28. Title varies: Bd. 51, Sammlung entschiendene Schulreform. Film Mas C 620 – 1 – us H.U. Library [073]

ENTSIKLOPEDICHESKII GRANAT – Moscow. 1910-48 – 1 – us UMI [030]

ENTSIKLOPEDICHESKII SLOVAR – Moscow. 1890-1907 – 1 – us UMI [947]

ENTSIKLOPEDICHESKII SLOVAR' = THE ENCYCLOPEDIC DICTIONARY / ed by Andreev, I E et al – St Petersburg: Brockhaus & Efron Publishers. v1-43. 1890-1907 – 767mf – 9 – $4,500.00 – us Ross [947]

ENTSIKLOPEDICHESKII SLOVAR' – Izdateli: F.A. Brokgauz, (Leipsic). I.A. Efron. v1-82. Spb. 1890-1904. Index 1905-07. B-1583/2 – 826mf – 8 – ne IDC [947]

ENTSIKLOPEDICHESKII SLOVAR' GRANAT – (V.56 has not been published) – M., [1910]-1948. 58 vols – 368mf – 9 – R-18338/1 – ne IDC [947]

ENTSIKLOPEDICHESKII SLOVAR' SOSTAVLENNYI RUSSKIMI UCHENAMI I LITERATORAMI : A-ELIZABET – (Missing: V.1(p. 115-126; 343-346; 453-460; 469-476)) – Spb., 1861-1863 – 45mf – 9 – R-18339/1 – ne IDC [947]

ENTSIKLOPEDIIA GOSUDARSTVA I PRAVA / ed by Stuchka, Petr Ivanovich – M., 1925-1927. 3 vols – 59mf – 9 – 2380/2 – ne IDC [340]

ENTSIKLOPEDIIA PCHELOVODSTVA L / Khabachev, A E – Obzor periodicheskoi pchelovodnoi literatury za 5 let, 1909-1913 gg. Kazan. 1914. BR-7092 2 – 8 – ne IDC [460]

ENTSIKLOPEDIIA SOVETSKOGO EKSPORTA / ed by Belenkogo, B S et al – Izd. 2-e. Berlin: Izd. Torgovogo predstavitelstva SSSR v Germanii, T Sentrosoi uza i Gostorga, 1928- – 1 – CSUX89-B2351 – us Hoover Inst Photo [380]

DIE ENTSTEHUNG DER ALTKATHOLISCHEN KIRCHE / Ritschl, Albrecht Benjamin – 1857 – 1 – us A.T.L.A. [240]

DIE ENTSTEHUNG DER APOKALYPSE / Voelter, Daniel – (Includes bibliographical references) – 2., voellig neu gearbeitete Aufl. Freiburg i.B.: J C B Mohr (Paul Siebeck), 1885 – 1mf – 9 – 0-8370-9332-5 – 1986-3332 – us A.T.L.A. [220]

DIE ENTSTEHUNG DER APOSTELGESCHICHTE: EINE KRITISCHE STUDIE / Sorof, Martin – Berlin: Nicolai, 1890. 1 fiche – 9 – us A.T.L.A. [240]

DIE ENTSTEHUNG DER BIBEL / Zittel, Emil – (Includes bibliographical references) – 5. verb. Aufl. Leipzig: Philipp Reclam, [c1891] – 1mf – 9 – 0-8370-5967-4 – 1985-3967 – us A.T.L.A. [220]

DIE ENTSTEHUNG DER BISCHOEFLICHEN FUERSTENMACHT / Hauck, Albert – Leipzig: A. Edelmann, 1891 – 1mf – us A.T.L.A. [240]

DIE ENTSTEHUNG DER DRITTEN POLNISCHEN REPUBLIK, 1989-1991 / Mackow, Jerzy – 1992 – 9 – DM48.00 – 3-89349-514-2 – gw Hänsel [947]

DIE ENTSTEHUNG DER ECKERMANNSCHEN GESPRAECHE UND IHRE GLAUBWUERDIGKEIT : MIT EINEM FAKSIMILE UND EINEM ANHANG UNGEDRUCKTER BRIEFE VON UND AN ECKERMANN / Petersen, Julius – (Includes bibliographical references) – 2. verm. und verb. Aufl. Frankfurt am Main: M Diesterweg, 1925 – 1 – us U.W. Library [430]

DIE ENTSTEHUNG DER FAERBUNG DER VOGELEIER / Wickmann, H – Z 1998. 1893 – 9 – ne IDC [590]

DIE ENTSTEHUNG DER GOTTESLEHRE DES ARISTOTELES / Arnim, H von – Wien, 1931 – 2mf – 8 – ne Slangenburg [120]

DIE ENTSTEHUNG DER JOBSIADE / Dickerhoff, Hans – Muenster i.Westf.: Aschendorff, 1908 – 1r – 1 – us U.W. Library [430]

DIE ENTSTEHUNG DER KINDERTAUFE IM DRITTEN JAHRHUNDERT N.CHR. UND DIE WIEDEREINFUEHRUNG DER BIBLISCHEN TAUFE IM SIEBZEHNTEN JAHRHUNDERT N.CHR. : DER KIRCHEN- UND WELTGESCHICHTE GEMAESS / Rauschenbusch, August – Hamburg: J.G. Oncken, 1898 – 1mf – us A.T.L.A. [240]

DIE ENTSTEHUNG DER LUTHERISCHEN UND DER REFORMIERTEN KIRCHENLEHRE : SAMT IHREN INNERPROTESTANTISCHEN GEGENSAETZEN / Tschackert, Paul – (In German and Latin. Includes bibliographical references and index) – Goettingen: Vandenhoeck and Ruprecht, 1910 – 2mf – 9 – 0-8370-8717-1 – 1986-2717 – us A.T.L.A. [240]

DIE ENTSTEHUNG DER NEUTESTAMENTLICHEN HIRTENBRIEFE / Hesse, Friedrich Hermann – Halle a.S.: C.A. Kaemmerer, 1889. 1 fiche – 9 – us A.T.L.A. [240]

DIE ENTSTEHUNG DER PAULINISCHEN CHRISTOLOGIE / Bruecker, Martin – Strassburg: J.H.E. Heitz, 1903. 1 fiche – 9 – us A.T.L.A. [240]

ENTSTEHUNG DER PERIKOPEN DER ROEMISCHEN MESZBUECHER / Beissel, Stephan – Freiburg Brsg., 1907 – 4mf – 8 – Dfl19.00 – ne Slangenburg [240]

DIE ENTSTEHUNG DES ALTEN TESTAMENTES / Staerk, Willy – Leipzig: G.J. Goeschen 1905. 1 fiche – 9 – us A.T.L.A. [240]

DIE ENTSTEHUNG DES CHRISTENTUMS : NEUE BEITRAEGE ZUM CHRISTUSPROBLEM / Kalthoff, Albert – Leipzig: Eugen Diederichs, 1904 – 1mf – 9 – 0-8370-3839-1 – 1985-1839 – us A.T.L.A. [240]

DIE ENTSTEHUNG DES CHRISTENTUMS / Pfleiderer, Otto – Muenchen: J.F. Lehmann, 1907. 1 fiche – 9 – us A.T.L.A. [240]

DIE ENTSTEHUNG DES DEUTERONOMISCHEN GESETZES : KRITISCH UND BIBLISCH-THEOLOGISCH UNTERSUCHT / Steuernagel, Carl – Halle (Saale): J Krause, 1896 – 1mf – 9 – 0-8370-9310-4 – 1986-3310 – us A.T.L.A. [220]

DIE ENTSTEHUNG DES EMBRYO DER PHANEROGAMEN. EINE REIHE MIKROSKOPISCHER UNTERSUCHUNGEN / Hofmeister, W F B – Leipzig. 1849. B-7101 – 8 – ne IDC [580]

DIE ENTSTEHUNG DES NEUEN TESTAMENTS / Heinrich, Julius – Tuebingen: J.C.B. Mohr, 1906. 1 fiche – 9 – us A.T.L.A. [240]

DIE ENTSTEHUNG DES NEUEN TESTAMENTS UND DIE WICHTIGSTEN FOLGEN DER NEUEN SCHOEPFUNG / Harnack, Adolf von – Leipzig: J.C. Hinrichs, 1914 (Beitraege zur Einleitung in das Neue Testament / von Adolf von Harnack; 6) – 1mf – us A.T.L.A. [220]

ENTSTEHUNG UND AUFBAU VON GOTTFRIED KELLERS SELDWYLER NOVELLE "KLEIDER MACHEN LEUTE" / Wuest, Paul – (Includes bibliographical references) – Bonn: F Cohen, 1914 – 1r – 1 – us U.W. Library [430]

DIE ENTSTEHUNG UND FORTBILDUNG DES LUTHERTUMS UND DIE KIRCHLICHEN BEKENNTNISSCHRIFTEN DESSELBEN VON 1548-76 / Heppe, Heinrich – Cassel: J G Krieger, 1863 – 1mf – 9 – 0-8370-8747-3 – 1986-2747 – us A.T.L.A. [240]

ENTSTEHUNGSGESCHICHTE DER KIRCHENSLAVISCHEN SPRACHE / Jagic, V – Berlin: Weidmann, 1913 – 2mf – us A.T.L.A. [240]

DIE ENTSTEHUNGSGESCHICHTE VON HEBBELS MOLOCH / Saedler, Heinrich – (Includes bibliographical references) – Bonn: H Ludwig, 1914 – 1r – 1 – us U.W. Library [430]

DIE ENTSTEHUNGSZEIT VON LUTHER'S GEISTLICHEN LIEDERN / Achelis, Ernst Christian – Marburg: C.L. Pfeil, 1883 – 1mf – us A.T.L.A. [240]

ENTSYKLOPEDYCHNYI DOVIDNYK / ed by Kudryts'kyi, A V – Kyiv, 1981 – 8mf – 9 – R-14949/1 – ne IDC [947]

DIE ENTVOLKERUNG DES PLATTEN LANDES IN POMMERN VON 1890-1905 UND IHRE URSACHEN / Langerstein, Julius – Greifswald, 1912 – 1 – DM30.00 – gw Mikro Press [943]

DIE ENTWICKELUNG DES ALTISRAELITISCHEN PRIESTERTHUMS / Maybaum, Siegmund – Wroclaw: Wilhelm Koebner, 1880. 1 fiche. 8370-4330-1 – 9 – us A.T.L.A. [240]

DIE ENTWICKELUNG DES ISRAELITISCHEN PROPHETENTHUMS / Maybaum, Siegmund – Berlin: Ferd. Duemmlers, 1883. 1 fiche – 9 – us A.T.L.A. [240]

DIE ENTWICKELUNG UNSERER ORIENTPOLITIK / Rapp, Adolf – Tuebingen: Kloeres, 1916. 28p – 1 – us U.W. Library [943]

ENTWICKELUNGSGEDANKE UND GOTTESERFAHRUNG / Mueller, Adolf – Halle a.S.: Max Niemeyer, 1908. 1 fiche. 8370-4522-3 – 9 – us A.T.L.A. [240]

DIE ENTWICKLUNG DER AMTSHAFTUNG IN DEUTSCHLAND SEIT DEM 19. JAHRHUNDERT / Gehre, Horst – Bonn, 1958 – 1 – DM30.00 – gw Mikro Press [943]

DIE ENTWICKLUNG DER CHRISTLICHEN RELIGION: INNERHALB DES NEUEN TESTAMENTS / Clemen, Carl – Leipzig: G.J. Goeschen, 1908 – 9 – us A.T.L.A. [240]

DIE ENTWICKLUNG DER DERMATO-VENEROLOGIE AN DER FAKULTAET/DEM BEREICH MEDIZIN DER KARL-MARX-UNIVERSITAET VON 1945 BIS 1975 / Baumann, Simone – Leipzig, 1989 – 2mf – DM62.00 – 3-8267-2006-7 – gw Hänsel [616]

DER ENTWICKLUNG DER DEUTSCHEN KULTUR IM SPIEGEL DES DEUTSCHEN LEHNWORTS / Seiler, Friedrich – Halle (Saale), Buchhandlung des Waisenhauses, 1921-25. 8 v. in 6. Vol. I is 4 Aufl.; vol. 2 is 3 Aufl.; vol. 3 is 2 Aufl.; vol. 4 is 2 Aufl. Film Mas 8654 – 1 – us H.U. Library [430]

DIE ENTWICKLUNG DER EHE / Achelis, T – 1893 – 1 – us I.U. Libraries [390]

DIE ENTWICKLUNG DER EVANGELISCHEN MISSION : IM LETZTEN JAHRZEHNT (1878-1888) / Grundemann, R – Bielefeld: Velhagen & Klasing, 1890 – 1mf – us A.T.L.A. [240]

DIE ENTWICKLUNG DER FRAGE DER BUENDNISZUGEHOERIGKEIT EINES WIEDERVEREINIGTEN DEUTSCHLANDS VON DER MAUEROEFFNUNG BIS ZUM TREFFEN VON MICHAIL GORBATSCHOW UND HELMUT KOHL IN SCHELESNOWODSK UNTER BESONDERER BERUECKSICHTIGUNG DER SOWJETISCHEN POSITION / Brenner, Stefan – 1992 – 398p – 9 – DM125.00 – 3-89349-614-9 – gw Hänsel [943]

DIE ENTWICKLUNG DER HOHEREN SCHULBILDUNG IN INDONESIEN VON 1600-1941 / Oei-Tan Soey Nio – Bonn, 1965 – 1 – DM30.00 – gw Mikro Press [950]

DIE ENTWICKLUNG DER NOVELLISTISCHEN KOMPOSITIONSTECHNIK KLEISTS BIS ZUR MEISTERSCHAFT : DER FINDLING. DIE VERLOBUNG IN ST. DOMINGO. DAS ERDBEBEN IN CHILI. DIE MARQUISE VON O., UNTER AUSSCHLUSS DES KOHLHAAS-FRAGMENTES / Guenther, Kurt Martin – (Includes bibliographical references) – Altenburg: S Geibel, 1911 – 1r – 1 – us U.W. Library [430]

DIE ENTWICKLUNG DER PROTESTANTISCHEN THEOLOGIE IN DEUTSCHLAND SEIT KANT UND IN GROSSBRITANNIEN SEIT 1825 / Pfleiderer, Otto – (Includes bibliographical references) – Freiburg i.B.: J C B Mohr, 1891 – 2mf – 9 – 0-8370-8702-3 – 1986-2702 – us A.T.L.A. [240]

DIE ENTWICKLUNG DER WERKZEUGE / Kick, Friedrich – (Includes bibliographical references) – Prag: Verlag des deutschen Vereines zur Verbreitung gemeinnuetziger Kenntnisse, 187- – 1r – 1 – us U.W. Library [621]

DIE ENTWICKLUNG DES ARBEITSHAUSES UNTER BESONDERER BERUECKSICHTIGUNG DER REFORMATORISCHEN BESTREBUNGEN UND DER VEHAELTNISSE IN WESTFALEN / Kipper, Karl – 1995 – 1mf – 9 – DM48.00 – 3-8267-3164-6 – gw Hänsel [943]

DIE ENTWICKLUNG DES CHRISTENTUMS ZUR UNIVERSAL-RELIGION / Beth, Karl – Leipzig: Quelle & Meyer, 1913 – 1mf – us A.T.L.A. [240]

DIE ENTWICKLUNG DES LYRISCHEN STILS BEI DETLEV VON LILIENCRON / Assmann, Elisabeth – (Includes bibliographical references) – Koenigsberg: O Kuemmel, 1936 – 1r – 1 – us U.W. Library [430]

DIE ENTWICKLUNG DES SOZIALISMUS / Engels, Friedrich – Hottingen-Zuerich, 1883 – 1 – DM30.00 – gw Mikro Press [335]

ENTWICKLUNG EINES BIOSENSORS FUER GLUKARAT / Wunder, Uwe – 1995 – 1mf – 9 – DM60.00 – 3-8267-2267-1 – gw Hänsel [574]

ENTWICKLUNG EINES HPLC-SYSTEMS ZUR ANALYSE VON BENZO(A)PYREN-(DNA)-ADDUKTEN SOWIE UNTERSUCHUNGEN ZUR SYNTHESE VON BENZO(A)PYREN-DNA-ADDUKTEN / Schwertner, Heiko – 1993 – 2mf – 9 – DM98.00 – 3-89349-728-5 – gw Hänsel [621]

ENTWICKLUNG EINES IMMUNTESTS FUER DEN EINSATZ IN DER RUECKSTANDSANALYTIK / Klein, Peter – 1994 – 2mf – DM80.00 – 3-8267-2048-2 – gw Hänsel [540]

ENTWICKLUNG EINES KOMBINIERTEN LASER-ELEKTRODEN-KATHETERS ZUR AV-KNOTEN-KOAGULATION BEI TACHYKARDEN RHYTHMUSSTOERUNGEN / Hug, Bernhard – 1993 – 2mf – 9 – DM98.00 – 3-89349-690-4 – gw Hänsel [621]

DIE ENTWICKLUNG FRIEDRICH RUECKERTS BIS 1810 UND SEINE DICHTERISCHEN ANFAENGE : MIT BENUTZUNG SEINES HANDSCHRIFTLICHEN NACHLASSES DARGESTELLT / Magon, Leopold – 1995 – 1mf – 9 – DM48.00 – 3-8267-3116-6 – gw Hänsel [430]

ENTWICKLUNG IN EINER MONETAER GESTEUERTEN WELTWIRTSCHAFT : DIE VERSCHULDUNGSKRISE DER DRITTEN WELT AUS DER SICHT EINER KREDITORIENTIERTEN WIRTSCHAFTSTHEORIE / Strecker, Otto A – 1993 – 1mf – 9 – DM75.00 – 3-89349-638-6 – gw Hänsel [330]

DIE ENTWICKLUNG JESU: VORTRAG / Spaeth, H – Berlin: F. Henschel, 1872. 1 fiche – 9 – us A.T.L.A. [240]

ENTWICKLUNG UND ERPROBUNG EINES COMPUTERUNTERSTUETZTEN CURRICULUMS DES GRUNDLEGENDEN CHEMIEUNTERRICHTES FUER DIE SCHWERPUNKTTHEMEN "EINFUEHRUNG IN DIE CHEMIE" SOWIE "ATOMBAU UND CHEMISCHE BINDUNG" / Koehler, Georg – 1993 – 3mf – 9 – DM98.00 – 3-89349-726-9 – gw Hänsel [370]

DER ENTWICKLUNGSGEDANKE UND DAS CHRISTENTUM / Beth, Karl – (Includes index of names) – Berlin: Edwin Runge, 1909 – 1mf – 9 – 0-8370-2312-2 – 1985-0312 – us A.T.L.A. [210]

DIE ENTWICKLUNGSGESCHICHTE EINES DIE KLEEARTEN ZERSTOERENDEN PILZES / Rehm, E – (Peziza ciborioides, Fr.). Goettingen. 1872. B-6304 2 – 8 – ne IDC [580]

ENTWICKLUNGSGESCHICHTE UND MORPHOLOGIE DER POLYMORPHEN FLECHTENGATTUNG CLADONIA / Krabbe, G – Leipzig. 1891. B-6177 2 – 8 – ne IDC [580]

ENTWICKLUNGSGESCHICHTE UND SYSTEMATIK DER PFLANZEN – v.81, 1932; v.83-89, 1934-40; v.94-139, 1947-81. ISSN:0378-2697 – 1,5,9 – us UMI [580]

ENTWICKLUNGSGESCHICHTLICHE GOETHE-KRITIK / Wolff, Eugen – (Includes bibliographical references) – Oldenburg: Schulze (R Schwartz), 1925 – 1r – 1 – us U.W. Library [430]

ENTWICKLUNGSGESCHICHTLICHE UNTERSUCHUNGEN UEBER DIE DICTYOTACEEN UND DIE CUTLERIACEEN DES GOLFES VON NEAPEL / Reinke, J – (Nova Acta Leop.-Carol. Deutschen Akademie der Naturforscher. v. 40, v. 1-2). Dresden. 1878. B-669 2 – 8 – ne IDC [580]
ENTWICKLUNGSPOLITIK – (Lacking some issues) – 1970-91 – Inquire – 1 – ATLA S0430 – us A.T.L.A. [073]
DER ENTWICKLUNGSPOLITISCHE RUNDE TISCH IN DER DDR UND IM VEREINIGTEN DEUTSCHLAND : ZIELE, ARBEITSWEISE UND ERGEBNISSE EINER AUSSERGEWOEHNLICHEN INSTITUTION / Belle, Manfred – 1994 – 2mf – 9 – DM80.00 – 3-89349-854-0 – gw Hänsel [320]
ENTWICKLUNGSTENDENZEN IN DER LANDWIRTSCHAFTLICHEN PRODUKTION NACH DER EINFUEHRUNG MODERNER REISTECHNOLOGIE : EINE DARSTELLUNG AM BEISPIEL VON BANGLADESH / Hemrich, Guenter – 1993 – 2mf – 9 – DM80.00 – 3-89349-784-6 – gw Hänsel [338]
Entwisle, J *see* OUT-LETTERS, 1802-1841
ENTWURF, AUFBAU UND ERPROBUNG EINES RASTERTUNNEL-MESSKOPFES FUER DEN EINSATZ IN EINEM RASTERELEKTRONENMIKROSKOP / Foerster, Matthias – 1995 – 2mf – 9 – DM80.00 – 3-8267-2199-3 – gw Hänsel [530]
ENTWURF MASCHINE WODURCH ALLES WAS AUF DEM CLAVIER GESPIELET WIRD, SICH VON SELBER IN NOTEN SETZT / Unger, J F – Braunschweig. 1774. BP-767 1 – 9 – ne IDC [780]
ENTWURF UND ERPROBUNG EINES KONZEPTS FUER DIE ITG IN DER LEHRERBILDUNG AN PAEDAGOGISCHEN HOCHSCHULEN / Albrecht, Helmut – 1992 – 260p – 9 – DM98.00 – 3-89349-626-2 – gw Hänsel [370]
ENTWURF ZU EINER ARBEITSBESCHAFFUNGS-BANK / Beckerath, Ulrich von – 9 – 1.00f – at Libertarian Micro [335]
ENTWURZELT : SZENENFOLGE AUS DEM LEBEN EINER DEUTSCHEN KOLONIE IM KAUKASUS: ZEIT 1923-1935 / Walling, Hermine – Berlin: Volksbund fuer das Deutschtum im Ausland, 1938 – 1r – 1 – us U.W. Library [430]
Enukidze, Avel'Sofronovich *see* DOKLAD PO KONSTITUTSIONNYM VOPROSAM NA 7 S"EZD SOVETOV SOIUZA SSR. 5 FEVRALIA 1935 G
ENUMERATIC SEMINUM REGII HORTI BOTANICI TAURINENSIS / Moris, G G – 1831-32 – 1 – uk Microform Academic [580]
ENUMERATIO COLEOPTERORUM AGRI MONACENSIS / Gistl, J von N FX. – Augustae Vindelicorum, 1831. 38p. Z/1289/2 – 8 – ne IDC [590]
ENUMERATIO CRITICA LICHENUM EUROPAEORUM / Schaerer, L E – Bernae. 1850. B-6171 2 – 8 – ne IDC [580]
ENUMERATIO EUPHORBIARUM QUAE IN GERMANIA ET PANNONIA GIGUNTUR / Roeper, J A C – Gottingae. 1824. B-5687 2 – 8 – ne IDC [580]
ENUMERATIO FILICUM ET LYCOPODIACEARUM QUAS IN SURINAMO / Splitgerber, F L – Leiden, 1840. 56 pp. (Tijdschr. Nat. Geschied. en Physiol., v. 7). B-7264 1 – 9 – ne IDC [580]
ENUMERATIO FILICUM, QUAS IN ITENERE CIRCA TERRAM LEGIT / Kaulfuss, G F – Lipsiae. 1824. B-7206 1 – 9 – ne IDC [580]
ENUMERATIO GENERUM ET SPECIERUM FISSIDENTACEARUM / Jaeger, H – San Galli. 1869. B-6183 2 – 8 – ne IDC [580]
ENUMERATIO INSECTORUM ELYTRATORUM CIRCA ERLANGAM INDIGENARUM / Hoppe, DH – Erlangae, 1795. 70p, 1pl. Z/1354/2 – 8 – ne IDC [590]
ENUMERATIO INSECTORUM IN MUSEO G.J. BILLBERG / Billberg, G J – Stockholm, 1820.Z-1068/2 – 8 – ne IDC [590]
ENUMERATIO INSECTORUM NORVEGICORUM / ed by Siebke, J H S – Christiania, 1874-1880. Pt 1-5 – 8 – ne IDC [590]
ENUMERATIO LICHENUM FRETI BEHRINGII / Nylander, W – (Bull. Soc. Linn. Normandie, 1887). B-1553 2 – 8 – ne IDC [580]
ENUMERATIO LICHENUM ICONIBUS ET DESCRIPTIONIBUS ILLUSTRATA / Hoffmann, G F – Erlangae. 1784-86. B-579 2 – 8 – ne IDC [580]
ENUMERATIO LYCOPODINEARUM QUAS IN EJUSDEM PLANTARUM ORDINIS MONOGRAPHIA MOX EDENDA DESCRIPSIT / Spring, F A – (Bull. Acad. Roy. Sci. de Bruxelles, v. 8, 10). Bruxelles. 1841-43. B-7265 1 – 9 – ne IDC [580]
ENUMERATIO METHODICA PLANTARUM HORTI MEDICI HELMSTADIENSIS / Fabricius, P C – ed. 2. Helmstadii. 1763. B-632 2 – 8 – ne IDC [580]
ENUMERATIO METHODICA PLANTARUM HORTI MEDICI HELMSTADIENSIS / Fabricius, P C – ed. 3. Helmstadii. 1776. B-5332 2 – 8 – ne IDC [580]
ENUMERATIO METHODICA PLANTARUM HORTI MEDICI HELMSTADIENSIS / Fabricius, P C – Helmstadii. 1759. B-77 2 – 8 – ne IDC [580]
ENUMERATIO METHODICA STIRPIUM HELVETIAE INDIGENARUM / Haller, Albrecht von – 2v. Gottingae. 1742. B-5945 2 – 8 – ne IDC [580]
ENUMERATIO MOLLUSCORUM SICILIAE / Philippi, R A – Z 709 2. 2 v. 1836-1844 – 8 – ne IDC [590]
ENUMERATIO MUSCORUM FRONDOSORUM / Reinhardt, O – Berolini. 1863. B-5193 2 – 8 – ne IDC [580]
ENUMERATIO PLANTARUM / Vahl, M – 2v. Havniae. 1804-05. B-2290 2 – 8 – ne IDC [580]
ENUMERATIO PLANTARUM AFRICAE AUSTRALIS / Ecklon, CF & Zeyher, C LP – Hamburgi. 1834-37. B-5405 2 – 8 – ne IDC [580]
ENUMERATIO PLANTARUM HORTI BOTANICI REGIOMONTANI / Schweigger, A F – Regiomontani. 1812. B-6469 1 – 9 – ne IDC [580]
ENUMERATIO PLANTARUM HORTI REGII BOTANICI BEROLINENSIS / Willdenow, C L – Berolini. 1809; suppl. Berolini. 1813. B-356 2 – 8 – ne IDC [580]
ENUMERATIO PLANTARUM HORTI REGII BOTANICI BEROLINENSIS ALTERA / Link, J H F – 2v. Berolini. 1821-22. B-5508 2 – 8 – ne IDC [580]
ENUMERATIO PLANTARUM HORTI REGII ET AGRI GOTTINGENSIS AUCTA ET EMENDATA / Haller, Albrecht von – Gottingae. 1753. B-101 2 – 8 – ne IDC [580]
ENUMERATIO PLANTARUM IN DALMATIA LECTARUM / Portenschlag-Ledermayer, F von – Wien. 1824. B-679 2 – 8 – ne IDC [580]
ENUMERATIO PLANTARUM IN DESERTIS SONGORIAE ORIENTALIS / Karelin, GS & Kirilov, J – (Bull. Soc. Imp. Nat. Moscou, 1842). B-656 2 – 8 – ne IDC [580]
ENUMERATIO PLANTARUM IN JAPONICA SPONTE CRESCENTIUM / Franchet, A R & Savathier, P A L – 2v. Parisiis. 1873-, 1875-79. B-89 2 – 8 – ne IDC [580]
ENUMERATIO PLANTARUM JAVAE ET INSULARUM ADJACENTIUM / Blume, C L – 1826 – 7 – uk Microform Academic [580]
ENUMERATIO PLANTARUM JAVAE ET INSULARUM ADJACENTIUM / Blume, C L – Ed. novae. Hague, 1830. vi,x/274p. B-5290/2 – 5mf – 8 – ne IDC [580]
ENUMERATIO PLANTARUM JAVAE ET INSULARUM ADJACENTIUM / Blume, C L – Lugduni Batavorum, 1827-28. 2v. B-5234/2 – 6mf – 8 – ne IDC [580]
ENUMERATIO PLANTARUM NOVARUM A CL. SCHRENK LECTARUM / Fischer, FE L von & Meyer, C A von – Petropoli. 1841. Enumeratio altera. Petropoli. 1842. B-854 2 – 8 – ne IDC [580]
ENUMERATIO PLANTARUM OMNIUM HUCUSQUE COGNITARUM / Kunth, C S – 5v. Stuttgardiae, Tubingae. 1833-50. B-1537 2 – 8 – ne IDC [580]
ENUMERATIO PLANTARUM PHAENOGAMARUM / Roth, A W – 2v. Lipsiae. 1827. B-5398 2 – 8 – ne IDC [580]
ENUMERATIO PLANTARUM QUAE IN HORTO PROCOPII A DEMIDOF / Pallas, Peter Simon – Petropoli. 1781. B-843 2 – 8 – ne IDC [580]
ENUMERATIO PLANTARUM, QUAS IN CHINA BOREALI COLLEGIT / Bunge, A A von – St. Petersburg. 1833. B-5865 2 – 8 – ne IDC [580]
ENUMERATIO PLANTARUM QUAS IN INSULIS ARCHIPELAGI AUT LITTORIBUS PONTI-EUXINI, ANNIS 1819 ET 1820, COLLEGIT / Dumont d'Urville, J S C – Parisiis. 1822 – 8 – ne IDC [580]
ENUMERATIO PLANTARUM, QUAS IN INSULIS BALEARIBUS COLLEGIT / Cambessedes, J – Parisiis. 1827. B-5543 2 – 8 – ne IDC [580]
ENUMERATIO PLANTARUM QUAS IN ITINERE PER PROVINCIAM TALYSCH COLLEGIT / Hohenacker, R F – M. 1838. B-903 2 – 8 – ne IDC [580]
ENUMERATIO PLANTARUM QUAS IN NOVAE HOLLANDIAE / Endlicher, S L & Bentham, G & Fenzl, E & Schott, H W – Vindobonae. 1837. B-2297 2 – 8 – ne IDC [580]
ENUMERATIO PLANTARUM VASCULARIUM CRYPTOGAMICARUM CHILENSIUM. EIN BEITRAG ZUR FARN-FLORA CHILE'S / Sturm, J W – Nua5rnberg, 1858, 52 pp. (Abhandl. Naturh. Gesellsch. Nua5rnberg, v. 1). B-7268 1 – 9 – ne IDC [580]
ENUMERATIO PLANTARUM VASCULARIUM IN INSULA INARIME / Gussone, G – Neapoli. 1854. B-2397 2 – 8 – ne IDC [580]
ENUMERATIO PLANTARUM ZEYLANICAE. ASSISTED. J. D. HOOKER / Thwaites, G H K & Hooker, J D – London. 1858-64. B-5768 2 – 8 – ne IDC [580]
ENUMERATIO STIRPIUM IN AGRO PETROPOLITANO / Weinmann, J A – Petropoli. 1837. B-5175 2 – 8 – ne IDC [580]
ENUMERATIO STIRPIUM MAGNO TRANSSILVANIAE PRINCIPATUI / Baumgarten, J C G – 4v. Wien. 1816-46. Mantissa prima et indices autore Michael Fuss. Wien. 1846. B-696 2 – 8 – ne IDC [580]
ENUMERATIO STIRPIUM PLERARUMQUE QUAE SPONTE CRESCUNT IN AGRO VINDOBONENSI / Jacquin, N J von – Vindobonae. 1762. B-5343 2 – 8 – ne IDC [580]
ENUMERATIO STIRPIUM QUAE IN HELVETIA RARIORES PROVENIUNT / Haller, Albrecht von – n.p. 1760. B-102 2 – 8 – ne IDC [580]
ENUMERATIO SYSTEMATICA PLANTARUM, QUAS IN INSULIS CARIBAEIS / Jacquin, N J von – With an intro. by F. A. Stafleu. Lugduni Batavorum. 1760. B-775 2 – 8 – ne IDC [580]
ENUMERATION GENERALE DES LICHENS, AVEC L'INDICATION SOMMAIRE DE LEUR DISTRIBUTION GEOGRAPHIQUE / Nylander, W – Cherbourg. 1857. B-5388 2 – 8 – ne IDC [580]
ENUMERATION OF DEAF, DUMB, ETC / Ottawa County. Ohio. Auditor – 1870-1910 – 1r – 1 – $32.50r – us Archival [324]
AN ENUMERATION OF NORTH AMERICAN LICHENES / Tuckerman, E – 7113. 1845 – 9 – ne IDC [580]
AN ENUMERATION OF THE PLANTS OF GUAM / Merrill, E D – Manilla, 1914-1919. (Philippine Journ. Sci., 1914, v. 9, p. 17-155; 1919, v. 15, p. 539-544). B-794 2 – 8 – ne IDC [580]
ENUMERATION RECORDS / Defiance County, Ohio. Probate Court – 1847-1897 – 1r – 1 – $32.50r – us Archival [324]
ENUMERATION SAILORS AND SOLDIERS / Wood County. Ohio. Auditor – 1895-1908 – 1r – 1 – $32.50r – us Archival [324]
ENUMERATION SCHOOL AGE YOUTH / Sandusky County. Ohio. Woodville Township. Board of Education – 1887-1890 – 1r – 1 – $32.50r – us Archival [324]
ENUMERATION SCHOOL AGE YOUTH / Wood County. Ohio. Auditor – (Some issues missing) – 1927-1949 – 3r – 1 – $32.50r – us Archival [324]
ENUMERATION, SCHOOL AGE YOUTH / Lucas County, Ohio. Sylvania Township Township Clerk – 1857-1887 – 1r – 1 – $32.50r – us Archival [324]
ENUMERATION: SCHOOL, AGE, YOUTH / Sandusky County. Ohio. Woodville Township. Board of Education – 1887-1890 – 1r – 1 – $32.50r – us Archival [324]
ENUMERATION: SCHOOL, AGE, YOUTH / Wood County. Ohio. Perrysburg Township. Board of Education – 1884-1894 – 1r – 1 – $32.50r – us Archival [324]
ENUMERATIONS OF DEAF, DUMB... / Defiance County. Ohio. Auditor – 1874-1898 – 1r – 1 – $32.50r – us Archival [324]
ENUMERATIONS OF DEAF, DUMB, ETC / Henry County. Ohio. Auditor – 1910 – 1r – 1 – $32.50r – us Archival [324]
ENUMERATIONS OF SOLDIERS / Ottawa County. Ohio. Auditor – 1862-1907 – 1r – 1 – $32.50r – us Archival [324]
ENUMERATIONS OF SOLDIERS / Van Wert County. Ohio. Auditor – 1r – 1 – $32.50r – us Archival [324]
ENUMERATIONS OF YOUTH / Allen County. Ohio. Auditor – 1860-1881 – 1r – 1 – $32.50r – us Archival [324]
ENUMERATIONS OF YOUTH / Hancock County. Ohio. Biglick Township. Board of Education – 1867-1906 – 2r – 1 – $32.50r – us Archival [324]
ENUMERATIONS OF YOUTH / Hancock County. Ohio. Marion Township. Board of Trustees – 1883-1914 – 1r – 1 – $32.50r – us Archival [324]
ENUMERATIONS OF YOUTH / Ottawa County. Ohio. Auditor – 1835-1862 – 1r – 1 – $32.50r – us Archival [324]
ENUMERATIONS OF YOUTH / Williams County, Ohio. Auditor – 1914-1958 – 1r – 1 – $32.50r – us Archival [324]
ENUMERATIONS: SCHOOL, AGE, YOUTH / Ottawa County. Ohio. Put-in-Bay. Township Board of Education – (Incomplete) – 1878-1899 – 1r – 1 – $32.50r – us Archival [324]
ENUMERATO FILICUM AND OTHER ARTICLES / Kaulfuss, G F – 1828 – 7 – uk Microform Academic [580]
ENVAR UEL-'ASIKIN / Bican, Ahmed – Bulak, 1300 – 6mf – 9 – $36.00 – us MEDOC [949]
ENVAR-I VICDAN – Trabzon: Ikbal Matbaasi, S. Mirgovic Matbaasi, 1910-1912 – 9 – $20.00 – us MEDOC [956]
ENVAR-I ZEKA – (Sahib-i Imtiyaz ve Muharriri: Mustafa Resid. Nos. 13-24 (1299-1300[1883-1884])) – Istanbul: Mahmud bey Matbaasi, Matbaa-i Ebuezziya, 1883-1885 – 3mf – 9 – $75.00 – us MEDOC [949]
ENVELOPE AND PAPER CONVERTING INDUSTRY – 1933. Superseded by Journal for paper converters – 1 – us UMI [600]
ENVELOPE AND SPECIALTY PAPER INDUSTRY – 1931-33. Superseded by Envelope and Paper converting – 1 – us UMI [600]
ENVELOPE INDUSTRY – 1927-31. Superseded by Envelope and Specialty Paper Industry – 1 – us UMI [600]
L'ENVERS DU DECOR – Montreal: Theatre du Nouveau-Monde. v1 no 1- (nov 1968)-. SEM35P22 – 1r – 1 – Can$39.00 – cn Bibl Nat [073]
ENVIRONMENT – v1-24 1958-82 1; v12-24 5,6,9 – us UMI [333]
ENVIRONMENT ABSTRACTS AND ENVIROFICHE – (Microfiche and index coll available: Complete and Conferences Collection. Available on: monthly subsc, quarterly with CDRom index subsc, print index and CDRom and magnetic tape formats) – 1975- – Apply for prices – us CIS [020]
ENVIRONMENT AND BEHAVIOR – v1- 1969- 1; v7- 1975- 5,6,9 – us UMI [574]
Environment and Natural Resources Policy Division of the Library of Congress *see* TOXIC SUBSTANCES CONTROL ACT, 1976
ENVIRONMENT COMMITTEE / UN Economic Commission for Europe (ECE) – 1971-89 – E/F.17 E.703 F.540 R.368 – 9 – us U.N. Pubs [340]
ENVIRONMENT INTERNATIONAL. A JOURNAL OF SCIENCE TECHNOLOGY, HEALTH, MONITORING AND POLICY – v1- 1978- – 5,6,9 – us UMI [574]
ENVIRONMENT VIEWS – (v1 1978 Can$50.00 5. v2-4 1979/80-1981 Can$75.00 5) – Edmonton. v1-16. 1978-1993/94 – 5,9 – Can$20.00y – cn Micromedia [333]
ENVIRONMENTAL ACTION – (v.11 .1979 5,6,9) – v.1. 1970 – 1 – us UMI [360]
ENVIRONMENTAL AFFAIRS – (See also: Boston College. Environmental Affairs Law Review) – v1-6 1971-77 1; v4-6 1975-77 5,6,9 – us UMI [360]
ENVIRONMENTAL AFFAIRS LAW REVIEW / Boston College – 1978- – 1,5,6,9 – us UMI [333]
ENVIRONMENTAL ANALYST – v3-5, no.12. Mar 1982-84 – 1,5,6,9 – us UMI [360]
ENVIRONMENTAL AND EXPERIMENTAL BOTANY – (Formerly: Radiation Botany) – v1- 1961- – 5,6,9 – us UMI [580]
ENVIRONMENTAL BIOLOGY AND MEDICINE / ed by Mellanby, I – 1971- – 1,5,9 – us Gordon [574]
ENVIRONMENTAL CLAIMS JOURNAL – v1-6. 1988-94 – 9 – $206.00 set – us Hein [340]
ENVIRONMENTAL CONSERVATION – v1-11. 1974-84 – 1,5,6,13 – sz Elsevier [360]

ENVIRONMENTAL CONTROL AND AGRI-TECHNOLOGY – (v39 1976, Science and Technology) – 1976 – 9 – $20.00 – us Univelt [629]

ENVIRONMENTAL EDUCATION IN ISRAEL: ISRAEL NATIONAL REPORT TO THE UNITED NATIONS CONFERENCE ON ENVIRONMENTAL EDUCATION / Israel. Ministry of the Interior – By Devorah Ziv and Suzanne Friedman-Hochstein. Jerusalem. Oct. 1977. 54 p. (Publication no. 77-05). In cooperation with the Ministry of Education and Culture – 9 – $2.00 – is I.T.T.I. [370]

ENVIRONMENTAL EDUCATION IN THE LIGHT OF THE TBILISI CONFERENCE – 1980 – 100p – 9 – 92-3-101787-X – fr UNESCO [370]

ENVIRONMENTAL EDUCATION RESEARCH – 1995, Vol 1 – £127.00 – uk Carfax [370]

ENVIRONMENTAL EFFECTS OF ARID LAND IRRIGATION IN DEVELOPING COUNTRIES / ed by White, G F – 1978 – 9 – 92-3-101586-9 – fr UNESCO [360]

ENVIRONMENTAL ETHICS – (v.3-. 1981-. 5,6,9) – v.1-. 1979- – 1 – us UMI [170]

ENVIRONMENTAL FINANCE – v1-2. 1991-92 (all publ) – 9 – $36.00 set – us Hein [336]

ENVIRONMENTAL GEOLOGY – (v4-5, no.4. 1982-83,84. 5,6,9) – v1-5, no.4. 1975-83,84 – 1 – us UMI [550]

ENVIRONMENTAL GEOLOGY AND WATER SCIENCES – v6-. 1984- – 1,5,6,9 – us UMI [550]

ENVIRONMENTAL GUIDELINES FOR RESETTLEMENT PROJECTS IN THE HUMID TROPICS – 1988 – 74p – it F.A.O. [360]

ENVIRONMENTAL HEALTH PERSPECTIVES – No.1-7, v8-46. 1972-82 – 1,5,6 – us Princeton Micro [360]

ENVIRONMENTAL IMPACT OF ECONOMIC INCENTIVES FOR AGRICULTURAL PRODUCTION : A COMPARATIVE LAW STUDY – 1990 – 89p – it F.A.O. [340]

ENVIRONMENTAL IMPACT OF FORESTRY : GUIDELINES FOR ITS ASSESSMENT IN DEVELOPING COUNTRIES – it F.A.O. [634]

ENVIRONMENTAL IMPACT OF TSETSE CONTROL OPERATIONS – 1980 – 74p – it F.A.O. [360]

ENVIRONMENTAL IMPACT STATEMENT RELATIVE TO PROPOSED COMPACT OF FREE ASSOCIATION : SUMMARY OF THE ENVIRONMENTAL IMPACT STATEMENT SCOPING MEETING, AUGUST 28 1980, BETWEEN THE U.S. AND THE GOVERNMENTS OF PALAU, THE MARSHALL ISLANDS AND THE FEDERATED STATES OF MICRONESIA / Micronesia. (U.S.) – Washington: Office for Micronesian Status Negotiations, 5 Jan 1981 – 1mf – 9 – $1.50 – LLMC 82-100F Title 9 – us L.L.M.C. [324]

ENVIRONMENTAL LETTERS – v1-10. 1971-75 – 1 – us UMI [360]

ENVIRONMENTAL MANAGEMENT – v.1-5, 1977-81. ISSN: 0364-152X – 1,5,6,9,13 – $84.00v – us UMI [333]

ENVIRONMENTAL MANAGEMENT FOR VECTOR CONTROL IN RICE FIELDS – 1984 – 164p – it F.A.O. [630]

ENVIRONMENTAL MONITORING AND ASSESSMENT – (v4-. 1984-. 5,6,9) – v1-. Apr 1981- – 1 – us UMI [360]

ENVIRONMENTAL PATENT ABSTRACTS – (A selected compilation of Environmental Patents Categorized by subject with indexes which include Author and Corporation patent numbers and major and minor subjects.) Years: 1970-1972 – 1,5,6 – us Princeton Micro [360]

ENVIRONMENTAL PERIODICALS BIBLIOGRAPHY – v1-14. 1972-85 – 1,5,6 – us Princeton Micro [574]

ENVIRONMENTAL POLICY AND LAW – v1-11. 1974-84 – 1,5,6,13 – sz Elsevier [340]

ENVIRONMENTAL POLLUTION – (Series A: Ecological and Biological. v1-35. 1970-84. Series B: Chemical and Physical.v1-8. 1980-84) – Series B: Chemical and Physical. v1-4. 1980-82 – 1,5,6,13 – sz Elsevier [360]

ENVIRONMENTAL PRACTICE NEWS WILLIAM AND MARY JOURNAL OF ENVIRONMENTAL LAW *see* WILLIAM AND MARY ENVIRONMENTAL LAW AND POLICY REVIEW

ENVIRONMENTAL PROFESSIONAL – v. 1-. 1979- – 5,6,9 – us UMI [360]

ENVIRONMENTAL PROGRESS – v1-. 1982- – 1,5,6,9 – us UMI [360]

ENVIRONMENTAL REGULATION ANALYST – v.1. 1979 – 1,5,6,9 – us UMI [360]

ENVIRONMENTAL SCIENCE AND TECHNOLOGY – v1- 1967- – 1,5,6,9 – us A.C.S. [628]

ENVIRONMENTAL STUDIES SERVICE CENTER. SPECIAL REPORT / Auburn University. Agricultural Experiment Station – 1977. 1 reel – 1, 5 – us Spaulding [360]

ENVIRONMENTAL TOXICOLOGY AND CHEMISTRY – v1- 1982- – 5,6,9 – us UMI [615]

ENVIRONMENTS – v20- 1989/90- – 9 – Can$20.00y – cn Micromedia [333]

ENVOL – Leopoldville: Societe litteraire d'Afrique. [n26-49. 1957-1958] – us Res Libr [072]

ENVOY – 1949-51.5v. 20 pts. 21 fiches – 1 – ie Microforms [800]

DER ENZTAELER : BA DER SUEDWEST-PRESSE – Neuenbuerg-Ulm, Germany. 1980-30 Sep 1992 – 1 – gw Mikrofilm [072]

ENZYKLOPAEDISCHE INFORMATION IM 19. JAHRHUNDERT: DIE ERGAENZUNSWERKE ZUM BROCKHAUS KONSERVATIONSLEXIKON : "ZEITGENOSSEN" – "DIE GEGENWART" – "UNSERE ZEIT" MIT EINEM GESAMTREGISTER / ed by Seemann, Otmar – 1994/1995 – diazo DM8,200.00 (silver DM9,600.00 ISBN: 3-598-32295-X) – 3-598-32294-1 – gw Saur [943]

ENZYME AND MICROBIAL TECHNOLOGY – (1982-. 1,5,6,9) – v1-. 1979- – 1 – us UMI [073]

ENZYME AND PROTEIN – v19-. 1975- – 1,5,9 – us UMI [073]

ENZYMOLOGIA – v1-18. 1936-55 – 1,5,6 – us Princeton Micro [610]

Eoettevenyi, N O *see* A HAGAI KET BEKEKONFERENCIA CIMU ERTEKEZESE,...

Eom, Han J *see* COMPUTER-AIDED RECORDING AND MATHEMATICAL ANALYSIS OF TEAM PERFORMANCE IN VOLLEYBALL

EOS: TRANSACTIONS / American Geophysical Union – (1920-29 $50.00. 1930-34 $50.00. 1935-58 $25.00y. 1959-78 $25.00y. 1971-76 $20.00y. 1979 $35.00. 1982 $45.00. 1992 v73 $190.00. 1993 v74 $205.00y. 1994 v75 $230.00. 1995 v76 $260.00) – 1920-93. Published weekly – 1,5,6,13 – us A.G.U. [550]

EOTHEN, OR, TRACES OF TRAVEL BROUGHT HOME FROM THE EAST / Kinglake, Alexander William – London: John Ollivier, 1844 – 1 roll – 1 – 1-55879-454-9 – uk Libr Preservation [910]

EP AND P – v1-. 1986- – 1,5,6,9 – us UMI [073]

EP NEWS / European Parliament. Secretariat. Luxembourg – v1- 1979- – 1 – us U.W. Library [940]

EPA JOURNAL / U.S. Environmental Protection Agency – (v3- . 1977- . 5,6,9) – v. 1-. 1975- – 1 – us UMI [360]

EPA PESTICIDE LABEL FILE / U.S. National Technical Information Service – Quarterly. Information on registered pesticide labels – 9 – us N.T.I.S. [000]

Epalda Guerrero, Juan *see* RESUMEN DEL ESTADO...BADAJOZ

Epalza Guerrero, Juan *see* RESUMEN... INSTITUTO PROVINCIAL DE SEGUNDA ENSENANZA DE BADAJOZ...1874 A 1875... POR EL SECRETARIO ACCIDENTAL DON...

EPARGNE – (Nouvelle Epargne: 15 Oct-14 Dec 1871) – London, UK. 17 Dec 1870-8 Oct 1871 – 1 – uk British Libr Newspaper [072]

EPARKHIAL'NYE VEDOMOSTI, INDEXES TO – (Inquire for complete listing) – 23mf – 9 – $150.00 – us Ross [072]

EPD (EVANGELISCHE PRESSE). NACHRICHTENSPIEGEL – 1971-76.6 reels. Continued by: Evangelische Information – 1 – us A.T.L.A. [073]

EPD ZENTRALAUSGABE – 1970-86 – 1 – us A.T.L.A. [073]

EPHEMERA – Rio de Janeiro, BL. Misc. Publications – 1r – $50.00 – R04173 – us Library Micro [320]

EPHEMERI VITA / Swammerdam, Jan – M 410. 1681 – 9 – ne IDC [580]

EPHEMERIDES / Deutsche Akademie der Naturforscher – Noribergae etc., 1712-1722 – 3 – us Readex [580]

EPHEMERIDES DACES / Dapontes, C & Legrand, Emile L – 1880, 1881, 1888 – 9 – fr Orientalistes [800]

EPHEMERIDES DU CITOYEN – 1765-72. Also Nouvelles Ephemerides economiques, 1788. Complete collection of the most important journal of the 18th-century French economists. 116 fiches – 9 – $450.00 – us UPA [330]

EPHEMERIDES DU CITOYEN, OU CHRONIQUE DE L'ESPRIT NATIONAL – puis ou Bibliotheque raisonnee des sciences morales et politiques. devenu: Nouvelles ephemerides economiques ou Bibliotheque raisonnee de l'histoire, de la morale et de la politique. Paris. nov 1765-72, dec 1774-juin 1776, janv-mai 1788 – 1 – fr A.C.R.P.P. [073]

EPHEMERIDES ENTOMOLOGICAE / Dalman, J W – 1824 – 7 – uk Microform Academic [590]

EPHEMERIDES LITURGICAE – 1(1887)-82(1968) – 1,021mf – 9 – Dfl3,574.00 – ne Slangenburg [073]

EPHEMERIDES LITURGICAE – Rome. v1-82. 1887-1968 – 1021mf – 9 – ne IDC [240]

EPHEMERIS – Athens, Greece. -d. 5-11 May, 22 Oct 1874-12 March 1880; 1 Jan 1886-31 Dec 1891; 1 Jan-30 June 1897. 18 reels – 1 – uk British Libr Newspaper [949]

EPHERMERIDES ORDINIS CARTUSIENSIS / ed by Vasseur, Dom L Le – Monstrolii, v1-5. 1890-1893 – 8 – Dfl203.00 – ne Slangenburg [240]

DER EPHESERBRIEF DES APOSTELS PAULUS / Belser, Johannes Evangelist – Freiburg i.B.: Herder, 1908. 1 fiche – 9 – us A.T.L.A. [240]

EPHESIAN STUDIES: EXPOSITORY READINGS ON THE EPISTLE / Moule, Handley Carr Glynn – New York: A.C. Armstrong, 1900. 1 fiche – 9 – us A.T.L.A. [240]

EPHESIANS, COLOSSIANS, PHILEMON, AND PHILIPPIANS / Martin, George Currie – New York: Henry Frowde, (1902). 1 fiche – 9 – us A.T.L.A. [240]

EPHESUS BAPTIST CHURCH. BEULAH, NORTH CAROLINA : CHURCH RECORDS – 1835-1919 – 1 – 20.97 – us Baptist [240]

EPHESUS BAPTIST CHURCH. WINCHESTER, KENTUCKY : CHURCH RECORDS – 1848-1979 – 1 – 59.58 – us Baptist [240]

EPHIMERIDES ORDINIS CARTUSIENSIS / Le Vasseur, Dom L O Cart. – Monstrolii. v1-5. 1890-1893 – Dfl203.00 – ne Slangenburg [240]

Ephraem Syrus, Saint *see* S. EPHRAEMI SYRI, RABULAE EPISCOPI EDESSENI, BALAEI ALIORUMQUE OPERA SELECTA

Ephraemi Syri *see*
- HYMNI ET SERMONES
- OPERA OMNIA, GRAECE, SYRIACE ET LATINE
- RABULAE EPISCOPI EDESSENI, BALAEI ALIORUMQUE. OPERA SELECTA E CODICIBUS MSS. IN MUSEO BRITANNICO ET BIBLIOTHECA BODLEIANA ASSERVATIS

Ephraemius *see* CORPUS SCRIPTORUM HISTORIAE BYZANTINAE (CSHB 41)

EPHRAIM BROWN PAPERS *see* BROWN, EPHRAIM, PAPERS, MS 1872

Ephraim, Charlotte *see* WANDEL DES GRIECHENBILDES IM ACHTZEHNTEN JAHRHUNDERT

EPHRAIM GEORGE SQUIER – 15r – 1 – $525.00 – Dist. us Scholarly Res – us L of C Photodup [930]

EPHRAIM GEORGE SQUIER PAPERS, 1835-1872 / Squier, Ephraim George – (With printed guide) – 4r – 1 – $450.00 – us Ross [972]

EPHRAIM'S QUOTATIONS FROM THE GOSPEL / ed by Burkitt, F C – 1901 – 2mf – 9 – ne Slangenburg [220]

EPHRATA CODEX / Ephrata Community – Die bitter gute, oder das gesang der einsamen turtel-taube, der christlichen Kirche hier auf erden. Ephrata im jahr MDCCXLVI. Ms. MUSIC 404 – 1 – us L of C Photodup [780]

Ephrata Community *see*
- EPHRATA CODEX
- DAS LIED DER LIEDEREN, WELCHES IST SOLOMONS
- MUSIC BOOK OF THE EPHRATA CLOISTER
- MUSIC FOR THE HYMNS IN TURTEL-TAUBE
- MUSIC FOR THE ZIONITISCHER WEYRAUCHS HUEGEL
- NOTES WRITTEN IN 1749 BY THE SISTERS OF THE SISTERHOOD IN THE SISTERHOUSE OF THE SEVEN DAY BAPTISTS, AT EPHRATA IN LANCASTER COUNTY, PENNSYLVANIA
- PARADISCHES WUNDER-SPIEL WELCHES SICH IN DIESEN LETZTEN ZEITEN UND TAGEN IN DENEN ABENDLAENDISCHEN WELT-THEILEN ALS EIN VORSPIEL DER NEUEN WELT HERVORGETHAN

EPHREM LOUGPRE MYSTIQUE FRANCISCAIN / Barrado Manzano, Arcangel – Madrid: Graf. Calleja, 1969 – 1 – sp Bibl Santa Ana [240]

THE EPIC – (Los Angeles). 1934 – 1 – us A.J.P.C. [073]

THE EPIC FAST / Nair, Pyarelal – Ahmedabad: (M.M. Bhatt), 1932. xii,325p. On t-p, New York: Universal Publishing Co., 1934. Includes articles by Gandhi and others – 1 – us U.W. Library [950]

EPIC NEWS – Los Angeles. v1-13. 1933-47 – 5r – 1 – us Ross [073]

EPICEDIO EN LA MUERTE DE ISABEL DE FARNESIO / Lopez de Ayala, Ignacio – 1766 – 1mf – 9 – Pta1,000.00 – 84-7848-201-6 – sp Pentalfa [946]

EPICHARIS ET NERON OU CONSPIRATION POUR LA LIBERTE / Legouve – (French Theatre Series). Paris. Maradan, an II. 1794 – 9 – fr Hachette [820]

EPICRISIS SYSTEMATIS MYCOLOGICA / Fries, E M – 1836-38 – 1. 108.00; ; 7 – uk Microform Academic [580]

Epictetus *see* WORKS OF EPICTETUS

EPICUREA EDIDIT HERMANUS USENER – Lipsiae, 1887 – 14mf – 8 – ne Slangenburg [180]

THE EPICUREAN : A TALE / Moore, Thomas – London: Printed for Longman, Rees, Orme, Brown, and Green, 1827 – 1 roll – 1 – 1-55879-350-X – uk Libr Preservation [830]

EPICURO Y MARX / Gonzalez Escudero, Santiago – 5mf – 9 – Pta3,000.00 – 84-85422-61-9 – sp Pentalfa [335]

EPIDEMIA DE TERCIANAS...EN VARIOS PUEBLOS DE URGEL...EN 1785 / Balaguer, G – Barcelona, 1785 – 2mf – 9 – sp Cultura [614]

LA EPIDEMIA DE VIRUELA / Huertas y Barrero, Francisco – 1886 – 9 – 1.50f – sp Bibl Santa Ana [946]

L'EPIDEMIE DE CHOLERA AU GUILVINEC EN 1886 / Monod, Henri Charles – Reprod. d'un extrait de la Revue d'Hygiene..., 1886. p189-251. 1 fiche.(Statistics Series: Medical Studies) – 9 – 6.00 – fr Bibl Nationale [310]

EPIDEMIE NATURALISTE / Deraismes, Maria – Paris: E. Dentu, s.d. 93p. 1 fiche. (Literature Collection) – 9 – 6.00 – fr Bibl Nationale [300]

DES EPIDEMIES ET EN PARTICULIER DE LA GRANDE PESTE DU XVIIEME SIECLE EN LORRAINE / Deligny, Lucien – Nancy, Berger-Levrault, 1891. 1 fiche. (Statistics Series: Medical Studies) – 9 – 6.00 – fr Bibl Nationale [310]

DES EPIDEMIES SOUS LES RAPPORTS DE L'HYGIENE PUBLIQUE, DE LA STATISTIQUE MEDICALE ET DE L'ECONOMIE POLITIQUE / Villerme, Louis Rene – Reprod. d'un extrait des Annales d'Hygiene publique et de Medecine legale. v9, 1833. p1-58. 1 fiche. (Statistics Series: Medical Studies) – 9 – 6.00 – fr Bibl Nationale [310]

EPIDEMIOLOGIA ESPANOLA. TOMO 1 / Villalba, Joaquin – 1803 – 1mf – 9 – Pta1,000.00 – 84-7848-282-2 – sp Pentalfa [614]

EPIDEMIOLOGIA ESPANOLA. TOMO 2 / Villalba, Joaquin – 1803 – 1mf – 9 – Pta1,000.00 – 84-7848-283-0 – sp Pentalfa [614]

EPIDEMIOLOGIA, SIVE TRACTATUS DE PESTE AD REGNI SARDINIAE... / Angelerius, Q T – Madrid, 1598 – 4mf – 9 – sp Cultura [614]

AN EPIDEMIOLOGIC INVESTIGATION OF THE RELATIONSHIP BETWEEN RELIGIOSITY, SELECTED HEALTH BEHAVIORS, AND BLOOD PRESSURE / Hixson, Karen A – University of North Carolina at Greensboro, 1996 – 2mf – 9 – $8.00 – HE 565 – us Microform Publ [613]

EPIDEMIOLOGY – v3-5. 1992-1996 – 5r – 1,5,6,9 – $80.00r – us Williams [614]

EPIGRAFES HEBREOS DE BEJAR Y SALAMANCA / Fita, Fidel – Madrid: Tip. Fortanet, 1907. B.R.A.H. L, pp. 67-77 – sp Bibl Santa Ana [946]

EPIGRAFIA ROMANA / Blazquez, Vidal – Madrid: Fortanet, 1920. B.R.A.H. 77. pp. 539-540 – 1 – sp Bibl Santa Ana [946]

EPIGRAFIA ROMANA DE EXTREMADURA : MERIDA, GUARENA, TORREMEJIA, ALMENDRALEJO, VILLAFRANCA DE LOS BARROS / Monsalud, Marques de – Madrid: Est. Tip. Fortanet, 1897. B.R.A.H. 31, 1897, pp. 44-52 – sp Bibl Santa Ana [946]

EPIGRAFIA ROMANA DE EXTREMADURA. MARCAS DE ALFAREROS Y GRAFITOS (VILLAFRANCA DE LOS BARROS) / Monsalud, Marques de – Madrid: Est. Tip. Fortanet, 1907. B.R.A.H. Tomo 50, 1907, pp. 460-462 – 1 – sp Bibl Santa Ana [946]

EPIGRAFIA ROMANA DE MEDINA DE LAS TORRES Y FREGENAL DE LA SIERRA / Monsalud, Marques de – Madrid: Est. Tip. Fortanet, 1898. B.R.A.H. 32, 1898, pp. 471-475 – 1 – sp Bibl Santa Ana [946]

EPIGRAFIA ROMANA DE MERIDA / Fita, Fidel & Rodriguez Villa, Antonio – Madrid: Tip. Fortanet, 1896 – sp Bibl Santa Ana [946]

EPIGRAFIA ROMANA DE MONTANCHEZ, RENA, BANOS DE LA ENCINA. SANTISTEBAN DEL PUERTO, CARTAGENA Y CADIZ / Fita, Fidel – Madrid: Tip. de Fortanet, 1901 – sp Bibl Santa Ana [946]

EPIGRAFIA ROMANA DE ZARAGOZA Y EXTREMADURA. ZARAGOZA, TARAZONA, ALMENDRALEJO, VALLE DE SANTA ANA, JEREZ DE LOS CABALLEROS / Monsalud, Marques de – Madrid: Est. Tip. Fortanet, 1898. B.R.A.H. 33, 1898, pp. 401-413 – 1 – sp Bibl Santa Ana [946]

EPIGRAFIA ROMANA, GRIEGA Y VISIGOTICA DE EXTREMADURA (MERIDA, SOLANA DE LOS BARROS E ITALICA) / Monsalud, Marques de – Madrid: Est. Tip. Fortanet, 1907. B.R.A.H. Tomo 50, 1907, pp. 248-252 – 1 – sp Bibl Santa Ana [946]

EPIGRAFIA ROMANA Y GRIEGA DE LA PROVINCIA DE CACERES. NUEVAS ILUSTRACIONES : CACERES, PLASENZUELA, VALDELACASA / Fita, Fidel – Madrid: Fortanet, 1917. B.R.A.H. lxxii/pp. 431-437 – 1 – sp Bibl Santa Ana [946]

EPIGRAFIA ROMANA Y VISIGOTICA / Fita, Fidel – Madrid: Tip. Fortanet, 1896 – sp Bibl Santa Ana [946]

EPIGRAFIA ROMANA Y VISIGOTICA DE EXTREMADURA (MERIDA Y BARCARROTA) / Monsalud, Marques de – Madrid: Fortanet, 1904. B.R.A.H. 45, 1904 pp. 445-448 – sp Bibl Santa Ana [946]

EPIGRAFIA ROMANA Y VISIGOTICA DE EXTREMADURA Y ANDALUCIA / Monsalud, Marques de – Madrid: Establec Tipografico de Fortanet, 1908 – 1 – sp Bibl Santa Ana [946]

EPIGRAFIA ROMANA Y VISIGOTICA DE GARLITOS, CAPILLA, BELALCAZAR Y EL GUIJO / Fita, Fidel – Madrid: Fortanet, 1912. B.R.A.H. lxi/pp. 133-143 – 1 – sp Bibl Santa Ana [946]

EPIGRAFIA ROMANA Y VISIGOTICA DE MONTEMOLIN / Fita, Fidel & Hinojois, Marques de – Madrid: Tip. Fortanet, 1918. B.R.A.H. LXXII, pp. 152-155 – sp Bibl Santa Ana [946]

EPIGRAFIA ROMANA Y VISIGOTICA. POZA DE LA SAL. MERIDA. ALBURQUERQUE / Fita, Fidel – Madrid: Fortanet, 1915. B.R.A.H. lxvii/pp. 487-495 – 1 – sp Bibl Santa Ana [946]

EPIGRAFIA VISIGOTICA Y ROMANA DE BARCELONA, MERIDA, MORENTE Y BUJALANCE / Fita, Fidel – Madrid: Fortanet, 1909. B.R.A.H. 55, pp. 449-459 – sp Bibl Santa Ana [946]

EPIGRAM – Baker, OR. -w. 1900 – 1 – 17.00 – us Oregon Hist [071]

EPIGRAMAS AMERICANOS / Diez Canedo, Enrique – Mexico: Joaquin Martin. Editor, 1945 – 1 – sp Bibl Santa Ana [972]

EPIGRAMMATA / Porter, T – 1614. Holkham ms. 436. Holkham Hall, Norfolk, England – 1 – uk Microform Academic [025]

EPIGRAMME / Knortz, Karl – Lyck [Ostpreussen]: Emil Wiebe, 1878 – 1r – 1 – us U.W. Library [840]

EPIGRAMME : NEBST EINER AUSWAHL AUS SEINEN UEBRIGEN GEDICHTEN / Grob, Johann; ed by Lindqvist, Axel – (Includes bibliographical references and index) – Leipzig: K W Hiersemann, 1929 – 1 – us U.W. Library [810]

EPIGRAMME UND SPRUECHE / Morgenstern, Christian – Muenchen: R Piper, 1920 – 1r – 1 – us U.W. Library [880]

EPIGRAMS AND EXCERPTS SELECTED AND ARRANGED BY FRED C. MULLINIX. / Lamm, Henry – East Aurora, N.Y., Roycrofters 1922 354 p. LL-319 – 1 – us L of C Photodup [340]

EPIGRAMS OF ART, LIFE, AND NATURE / Watson, William – Liverpool: G.G. Walmsley, 1884 – 1 roll – 1 – 1-55879-487-5 – uk Libr Preservation [810]

EPIGRAMS UPON THE PAINTINGS OF THE MOST EMINENT MASTERS, ANCIENT AND MODERN / Elsum, J – O-1179 1. 1700 – 9 – ne IDC [810]

EPIGRAPHIA BIRMANICA: BEING LITHIC AND OTHER INSCRIPTIONS OF BURMA / ed by Mya, U. – v4. 2 pts. 'Mon Inscriptions' by C.O. Blagden. Rangoon, 1934-36. BI-703 2 – 8 – ne IDC [410]

EPIGRAPHIA CARNATICA / ed by Rice, B L – Bangalore. Mysore, 1886-1958; v.1-16; rev. ed. 1914-23. v.1-2 – 459mf – 8 – ne IDC [410]

EPIGRAPHIA INDICA – Calcutta, 1892-1966. v.1-36; Appendix, 1927-36. v.19-23. Lacking: 1965-66. v.36(3) – 525mf – 8 – ne IDC [410]

EPIGRAPHIA ZEYLANICA / Archaeological Survey of Ceylon; ed by Wickremasinghe, M de Zilva – London, 1904-28; 1934-43; 1955-65. v.1-5 – 8 – ne IDC [930]

EPIGRAPHISCHE DENKMAELER AUS CHINA / Franke, O & Laufer, B – v. 1. Berlin. 1914. Unfinished publication. BU-489 2 – 8 – ne IDC [930]

EPILOGO DELLA BRIOLOGIA ITALIANA / Notaris, G de – Genova, 1869. 781 pp. B-5456 2 – 8 – ne IDC [580]

EPILOGUS CHRONOLOGICUS EXPONENS SUCCINTE CONVENTUS ET FUNDATIONES SACRI ORDINIS PRAEDICATORUM IN REGNO HYBERNIAE = THE IRISH DOMINICANS OF THE SEVENTEENTH CENTURY / O'Heyne, John – (Text in Latin and English on opposite pages. Includes index) – Dundalk: William Tempest, 1902 – 2mf – 9 – 0-8370-7090-2 – 1986-1090 – us A.T.L.A. [240]

EPIMELIAE BOTANICAE / Presl, C B – 1851 – 1 – uk Microform Academic [580]

EPIMELIAE BOTANICAE / Presl, K B – Pragae. 1849. B-5335 2 – 8 – ne IDC [580]

Epinay, Adrien d' *see* RENSEIGNEMENTS POUR SERVIR A L'HISTOIRE DE L'ILE DE FRANCE JUSQU'A L'ANNEE 1810..

Epiney-Burgard, G *see* GERARD GROTE (1340-1384) ET LES DEBUTS DE LA DEVOTION MODERNE

EPIPHANIES OF THE RISEN LORD / Boardman, George Dana – New York: Appleton, 1879. 1 fiche – 9 – us A.T.L.A. [240]

Epiphanius, Saint, Bishop of Constantia in Cyprus *see*
– AD PHYSIOLOGUM
– DES HEILIGEN EPIPHANIUS VON SALAMIS.

EPIPSYCHIDION / Shelley, Percy Bysshe; ed by Potts, Robert Alfred – London: Pub. for the Shelley Society by Reeves and Turner, 1887 – 1 roll – 1 – 1-55879-846-3 – uk Libr Preservation [890]

DIE EPISCHE KUNST UND KUNSTTECHNIK ERNST VON WILDENBRUCHS / Morisse, Anne-Marie – Bonn: C Georgi, 1912 – 1r – 1 – us U.W. Library [430]

DIE EPISCHEN WERKE OTTO LUDWIGS UND IHR VERHAELTNIS ZU CHARLES DICKENS / Lueder, Fritz – Leipzig: A Hoffmann, 1910 – 1r – 1 – us U.W. Library [410]

EPISCOPACY AND UNITY : A HISTORICAL INQUIRY INTO THE RELATIONS BETWEEN THE CHURCH OF ENGLAND AND THE NON-EPISCOPAL CHURCHES AT HOME AND ABROAD, FROM THE ... / Wilson, H Austin – London, New York: Longmans, Green, 1912 – 1mf – us A.T.L.A. [240]

EPISCOPACY EXCLUSIVE / Beman, Nathan S S – 1856; Letters to Rev. John Hughes. 1851 – 1 – $50.00 – us Presbyterian [240]

THE EPISCOPAL CHURCH : ITS DOCTRINE, ITS MINISTRY, ITS DISCIPLINE, ITS WORSHIP, AND ITS SACRAMENTS / Hodges, George – New York: Thomas Whittaker, c1892 – 1mf – 9 – 0-8370-8678-7 – 1986-2678 – us A.T.L.A. [240]

THE EPISCOPAL CHURCH OF SCOTLAND : FROM THE REFORMATION TO THE REVOLUTION / Lawson, John Parker – Edinburgh: Gallie and Bayley, 1844 – 1mf – us A.T.L.A. [240]

THE EPISCOPAL CONTROVERSY REVIEWED / Emory, John – New York: T. Mason and G. Lane for the Methodist Episcopal Church, 1838 – 1mf – us A.T.L.A. [240]

THE EPISCOPAL INVITATION / Strong, Robert – Philadelphia: Presbyterian Publ Committee, c1866 – 1mf – 9 – 0-8370-8792-9 – 1986-2792 – us A.T.L.A. [230]

EPISCOPAL METHODISM AS IT WAS AND IS, OR, AN ACCOUNT OF THE ORIGIN, PROGRESS, DOCTRINES, CHURCH POLITY, USAGES, INSTITUTIONS, AND STATISTICS OF THE METHODIST EPISCOPAL CHURCH IN THE UNITED STATES : EMBRACING ALSO A SKETCH OF THE RISE OF METHODISM IN EUROPE, AND OF ITS ORIGIN AND PROGRESS IN CANADA / Gorrie, P Douglass – Auburn: Derby and Miller, 1852 – 1mf – us A.T.L.A. [240]

THE EPISCOPAL SUCCESSION IN ENGLAND, SCOTLAND AND IRELAND, A.D. 1400 TO 1875 : WITH APPOINTMENTS TO MONASTERIES AND EXTRACTS FROM CONSISTORIAL ACTS TAKEN FROM MSS. IN PUBLIC AND PRIVATE LIBRARIES IN ROME, FLORENCE, BOLOGNA, RAVENNA AND PARIS / Brady, W Maziere – Rome: Tipografia della Pace, 1876-1877 – 4mf – us A.T.L.A. [240]

EPISCOPAL TEACHER – 1986-88 – 1r – 1 – ATLA S0443 – us A.T.L.A. [073]

EPISCOPALIAN – v125, no.4-145. Apr 1960-1986 – 1 – us A.T.L.A. [073]

AN EPISCOPALIAN DEMAND FOR CHRISTIAN SCHOOLS / McMillan, Thomas – [S.l.: s.n., ca 1903] – 1mf – 9 – 0-8370-7565-3 – 1986-1565 – us A.T.L.A. [370]

L'EPISCOPAT NANTAIS A TRAVERS LES SIECLES ILLUSTRE DES BLASONS DES EVEQUES – Vannes: Lafolye, 1892 – fr Armell [240]

EPISCOPI CARPENTORACTI S.R.E.CARD. EPISTOLARUM LIBRI SEXDECIM / Sadoleti, Iac. – Col. Agrippinae, 1580 – 7mf – 8 – ne Slangenburg [240]

Episcopius, J *see* PARADIGMATA GRAPHICES VARIORUM ARTIFICIUM EX FORMIS NICOLAI VISSCHER

EPISCOPOLOGIO CAURIENSE / Orti Belmonte, Miguel Angel – Caceres: Dip. Prov. de Caceres, Servicios Culturales, 1958. Col. Estudios Extremenos – 1 – sp Bibl Santa Ana [240]

EPISEMOS EPHEMERIS TES KYPRIAKES DEMOKRATIAS – Cyprus. n621-701. 1968 – 1r – 1 – us Ross [320]

EPISKEPSIS – v3-22. 1972-91 (complete) – Inquire – 1 – ATLA S0424 – us A.T.L.A. [073]

UN EPISODE DE LA LUTTE FRATRICIDE: DEUX MOIS DE BOMBARDEMENT – Paris, 1938? Fiche W859. (Blodgett Collection of Spanish Civil War Pamphlets) – 9 – us H.U. College Libr [946]

UN EPISODE DE L'EPOPEE DU KAJOOR : LA BATTAILLE DE DEKHELE / Wade, Magatte – 1980 – us Res Libr [960]

EPISODIO DE LA GUERRA DE LA INDEPENDENCIA / Requesens, Francisco de – Madrid: Tip. Fortanet, 1889 – 1 – sp Bibl Santa Ana [946]

EPISODIO DE LA...INDEPENDENCIA / Requesens, Francisco de – 1889 – 9 – 1.50f – sp Bibl Santa Ana [946]

EPISTLE OF PAUL THE APOSTLE TO THE HEBREWS / Farrar, Frederic William – Cambridge: University Press, 1902. 1 fiche – 9 – us A.T.L.A. [240]

EPISTLE OF PAUL THE APOSTLE TO THE ROMANS / Abbott, Lyman – New York: A.S. Barnes, 1888. 1 fiche – 9 – us A.T.L.A. [240]

THE EPISTLE OF PAUL THE APOSTLE TO THE ROMANS : NOTES, COMMENTS, MAPS, AND ILLUSTRATIONS / Abbott, Lyman – (Series title on binding: Abbott's commentary) – New York: A S Barnes, [1888] – 1mf – 9 – 0-8370-2019-0 – 1985-0019 – us A.T.L.A. [220]

THE EPISTLE OF PAUL, THE APOSTLE, TO THE ROMANS / Summers, Thomas Osmond – Nashville: So. Methodist Pub., 1881. 1 fiche – 9 – us A.T.L.A. [240]

THE EPISTLE OF PAUL TO PHILEMON = BRIEF AN PHILEMON : A THEOLOGICAL AND HOMILETIC COMMENTARY / Oosterzee, Johannes Jacobus van – (In English) – New York: Charles Scribner, c1868 – 1mf – 9 – 0-8370-6766-9 – 1986-0766 – us A.T.L.A. [220]

THE EPISTLE OF PAUL TO THE CHURCHES OF GALATIA: WITH INTRODUCTION AND NOTES / Macgregor, James – Edinburgh: T. & T. Clark, 1879. 1 fiche – 9 – us A.T.L.A. [240]

EPISTLE OF PAUL TO THE EPHESIANS / Candlish, James S – Edinburgh: T. & T. Clark, 1895. 1 fiche – 9 – us A.T.L.A. [240]

THE EPISTLE OF PAUL TO THE EPHESIANS : WITH INTRODUCTION AND NOTES / Candlish, James S – Edinburgh:T & T Clark, 1895 – 1mf – 9 – 0-8370-2577-X – 1985-0577 – us A.T.L.A. [220]

THE EPISTLE OF PAUL TO THE GALATIANS / Duncan, George – Harper. 1934 – 9 – $10.00 – us I.R.C. [240]

THE EPISTLE OF PAUL TO THE GALATIANS / Schmoller, Otto – New York: Scribner, Armstrong, 1874. 1 fiche – 9 – us A.T.L.A. [240]

THE EPISTLE OF PAUL TO THE ROMANS / Dodd, C H – 1932 – 9 – $10.00 – us I.R.C. [240]

THE EPISTLE OF PAUL TO TITUS = PASTORALBRIEFE / Oosterzee, Johannes Jacobus van – (In English) – New York: Charles Scribner, c1868 – 1mf – 9 – 0-8370-6767-7 – 1986-0767 – us A.T.L.A. [220]

THE EPISTLE OF ST. JAMES : THE GREEK TEXT WITH INTRODUCTION, COMMENTARY AS FAR AS CHAPTER 4, VERSE 7, AND ADDITIONAL NOTES / Hort, Fenton John Anthony – (Includes indexes of Greek and Hebrew words and of subjects) – London: Macmillan, 1909 – 1mf – 9 – 0-8370-3661-5 – 1985-1661 – us A.T.L.A. [220]

THE EPISTLE OF ST. JAMES : THE GREEK TEXT WITH INTRODUCTION, NOTES AND COMMENTS / Mayor, Joseph Bickersteth – (Includes bibliographical references and indexes) – London; New York: Macmillan, 1892 – 2mf – 9 – 0-8370-9719-3 – 1986-3719 – us A.T.L.A. [220]

THE EPISTLE OF ST JAMES I 1-IV.7 / Hort, Fenton John Anthony – 1909 – 9 – $10.00 – us I.R.C. [240]

THE EPISTLE OF ST JAMES: WITH AN INTRODUCTION AND NOTES / Knowling, Richard John – London: Methuen, 1904. 1 fiche – 9 – us A.T.L.A. [240]

THE EPISTLE OF ST JUDE AND THE SECOND EPISTLE OF ST PETER / Mayor, Joseph Bickersteth – London: Macmillan, 1907.1 fiche. 8370-4333-6 – 9 – us A.T.L.A. [240]

EPISTLE OF ST PAUL TO THE ROMANS / Moule, Handley Carr Glynn – New York: A.C. Armstrong, 1901. 1 fiche – 9 – us A.T.L.A. [240]

THE EPISTLE OF THE APOSTLE PAUL TO ROMANS : A NEW TRANSLATION, WITH NOTES / Godwin, John Henry – London: Hodder & Stoughton, 1873 – 1mf – 9 – 0-8370-3325-X – 1985-1325 – us A.T.L.A. [220]

AN EPISTLE TO THE CLERGY OF THE SOUTHERN STATES / Grimke, Sarah – 1836 – 9 – us A.T.L.A. [240]

EPISTLE TO THE EPHESIANS / Bellett, John Gifford – London: R.L. Allan, 1871. 1 fiche – 9 – us A.T.L.A. [240]

EPISTLE TO THE EPHESIANS / Findlay, George G – New York: A.C. Armstrong, 1903. 1 fiche – 9 – us A.T.L.A. [240]

THE EPISTLE TO THE EPHESIANS : FROM NOTES OF READINGS / Bellett, John Gifford – London: Robert L Allan, 1871 – 1mf – 9 – 0-8370-2257-6 – 1985-0257 – us A.T.L.A. [220]

THE EPISTLE TO THE EPHESIANS / Parker, Joseph – New York: A C Armstrong, 1905 – 1mf – 9 – 0-8370-4668-8 – 1985-2668 – us A.T.L.A. [220]

THE EPISTLE TO THE GALATIANS / Findlay, George Gillanders – New York:A.C. Armstrong, [1889] – 2mf – 9 – 0-8370-2414-5 – 1985-0414 – us A.T.L.A. [220]

EPISTLE TO THE HEBREWS / Edwards, Thomas Charles – New York: A.C. Armstrong, (1888). 1 fiche – 9 – us A.T.L.A. [240]

EPISTLE TO THE HEBREWS : THE HARKLEAN VERSION, CHAPTERS 11, 28 – 13, 25 / ed by Bensly, Robert L – Cambridge, 1889 – Dfl6.00 – ne Slangenburg [220]

THE EPISTLE TO THE HEBREWS – Brooke Foss Westcott. 1903 – 9 – us A.T.L.A. [240]

THE EPISTLE TO THE HEBREWS / Goodspeed, Edgar Johnson – (Includes indexes) – New York: Macmillan, 1908 – 1mf – 9 – 0-8370-3338-1 – 1985-1338 – us A.T.L.A. [220]

THE EPISTLE TO THE HEBREWS : WITH INTRODUCTION AND NOTES / Davidson, Andrew Bruce – Edinburgh: T & T Clark, [1887?] – 1mf – 9 – 0-8370-2834-5 – 1985-0834 – us A.T.L.A. [220]

THE EPISTLE TO THE HEBREWS : WITH NOTES, CRITICAL, EXPLANATORY AND PRACTICAL / Cowles, Henry – New York:D Appleton, 1878 – 1mf – 9 – 0-8370-2752-7 – 1985-0752 – us A.T.L.A. [220]

EPISTLE TO THE PHILIPPIANS / Rainy, Robert – New York: A.C. Armstrong, 1903. 1 fiche – 9 – us A.T.L.A. [240]

THE EPISTLE TO THE ROMANS : A COMMENTARY, LOGICAL AND HISTORICAL / Stifler, James M – New York: Fleming H Revell, 1897 – 1mf – 9 – 0-8370-5419-2 – 1985-3419 – us A.T.L.A. [220]

THE EPISTLE TO THE ROMANS : WITH INTRODUCTION AND NOTES / Brown, David – Edinburgh: T & T Clark, [18–] – 1mf – 9 – 0-8370-2476-5 – 1985-0476 – us A.T.L.A. [220]

THE EPISTLE TO THE ROMANS : WITH NOTES CRITICAL AND PRACTICAL / Sadler, Michael Ferrebee – 2nd rev ed. London: George Bell, 1889 – 1mf – 9 – 0-8370-5020-0 – 1985-3020 – us A.T.L.A. [220]

THE EPISTLE TO THE THESSALONIANS / Denney, James – New York: A.C. Armstrong, 1892. 1 fiche – 9 – us A.T.L.A. [240]

THE EPISTLE TO TIMOTHY AND THE WOMAN QUESTION / Schmauk, Theodore Emanuel – (The Lutheran Church Review, v. 18, 1899, p. 525-536) – 9 – us A.T.L.A. [240]

THE EPISTLES AND GOSPELS OF THE SUNDAYS THROUGHOUT THE YEAR : WITH NOTES, CRITICAL AND EXPLANATORY / M'Carthy, Daniel – (Includes indexes) – Dublin: James Duffy; London: Burns, Lambert, and Oates, 1868 – 2mf – 9 – 0-8370-9402-X – 1986-3402 – us A.T.L.A. [220]

THE EPISTLES OF OUR LORD TO THE SEVEN CHURCHES OF ASIA / Dods, Marcus – Edinburgh: John Maclaren, 1867 – 1mf – 9 – 0-8370-2936-8 – 1985-0936 – us A.T.L.A. [220]

EPISTLES OF PAUL THE APOSTLE: A SKETCH OF THEIR ORIGIN AND CONTENTS / Findlay, George G – New York: Wilbur B. Ketcham, (1892). 1 fiche – 9 – us A.T.L.A. [240]

EPISTLES OF PAUL THE APOSTLE TO THE THESSALONIANS / Findlay, George G – Cambridge: The University Press, 1904. 1 fiche – 9 – us A.T.L.A. [240]

THE EPISTLES OF PAUL THE APOSTLE TO THE THESSALONIANS, CORINTHIANS, GALATIANS, ROMANS AND PHILIPPIANS / Drummond, James – New York: G P Putnam, 1899 – 1mf – 9 – 0-8370-2976-7 – 1985-0976 – us A.T.L.A. [220]

THE EPISTLES OF PAUL TO THE CORINTHIANS, GALATIANS, EPHESIANS, PHILIPPIANS, COLOSSIANS, THESSALONIANS, TIMOTHY, TITUS AND PHILEMON – With introd. and commentary by Abiel Abbot Livermore. Boston: Lockwood, Brooks, 1881. 308p – 1 – us U.W. Library [240]

EPISTLES OF PAUL WRITTEN AFTER HE BECAME A PRISONER / Boise, James R – New York: D. Appleton, 1887. 1 fiche – 9 – us A.T.L.A. [240]

EPISTLES OF SAINT IGNATIUS / Ignatius, Saint – The ancient Syriac version. 1845 – 1 – us A.T.L.A. [240]

THE EPISTLES OF ST. JOHN : TWENTY-ONE DISCOURSES : WITH GREEK TEXT, COMPARATIVE VERSIONS, AND NOTES CHIEFLY EXEGETICAL / Alexander, William – NY: A C Armstrong, 1899 – 1mf – 9 – 0-8370-2064-6 – 1985-0064 – us A.T.L.A. [220]

THE EPISTLES OF ST. JOHN / Westcott, Brooke Foss – 1883 – 9 – $15.00 – us I.R.C. [240]

THE EPISTLES OF ST. JOHN : WITH INTRODUCTION AND APPENDICES / Plummer, Alfred – (Includes general index) – Stereotyped ed. Cambridge:University Press, 1883 – 1mf – 9 – 0-8370-5396-X – 1985-3396 – us A.T.L.A. [220]

THE EPISTLES OF ST. PAUL TO THE COLOSSIANS, THESSALONIANS, AND TIMOTHY : WITH NOTES CRITICAL AND PRACTICAL / Sadler, Michael Ferrebee – 2nd ed. London, New York: George Bell, 1893 – 1mf – 9 – 0-8370-5021-9 – 1985-3021 – us A.T.L.A. [220]

THE EPISTLES OF ST PAUL TO THE GALATIANS, EPHESIANS, AND PHILIPPIANS : WITH NOTES CRITICAL AND PRACTICAL / Sadler, Michael Ferrebee – 2nd ed. London, New York: George Bell, 1892 – 1mf – 9 – 0-8370-5022-7 – 1985-3022 – us A.T.L.A. [220]

EPISTLES OF ST JOHN: 21 DISCOURSES: WITH GREEK TEXT, COMPARATIVE VERSIONS / Alexander, William – New York: A.C. Armstrong, 1899. 1 fiche – 9 – us A.T.L.A. [240]

THE EPISTLES OF ST JOHN: THE GREEK TEXT, WITH NOTES AND ESSAYS / Westcott, Brooke Foss – London: Macmillan, 1883.1 fiche – 9 – us A.T.L.A. [240]

THE EPISTLES OF ST PAUL TO THE COLOSSIANS AND PHILEMON / Maclaren, Alexander – New York: A.C. Armstrong, 1888 – 2mf – 9 – us A.T.L.A. [240]

THE EPISTLES OF ST PAUL TO THE COLOSSIANS AND PHILEMON / Maclaren, Alexander – New York: Armstrong, 1901. vii,493p – 1 – us U.W. Library [240]

EPISTLES OF ST PAUL TO THE EPHESIANS, COLOSSIANS, AND PHILEMON / Davies, John Llewelyn – London: Macmillan, 1866.1 fiche – 9 – us A.T.L.A. [240]

EPISTLES OF ST PAUL TO THE THESSALONIANS, GALATIANS AND ROMANS: WITH CRITICAL NOTES AND DISSERTATIONS / Jowett, Benjamin – 1859 – 9 – us A.T.L.A. [240]

THE EPISTLES OF ST PAUL TO TITUS, PHILEMON, AND THE HEBREWS : WITH NOTES CRITICAL AND PRACTICAL / Sadler, Michael Ferrebee – 2nd ed. London, New York: George Bell, 1893 – 1mf – 9 – 0-8370-5023-5 – 1985-3023 – us A.T.L.A. [220]

EPISTLES OF ST PETER / Jowett, John Henry – New York: A.C. Armstrong, 1906. 1 fiche – 9 – us A.T.L.A. [240]

EPISTLES OF ST PETER / Lumby, Joseph Rawson – New York: A.C. Armstrong, 1893 – 1mf – 9 – us A.T.L.A. [240]

EPISTLES ON WOMEN / Aikin, Lucy – London. 1810 – 1 – us Res Libr [840]

THE EPISTLES TO THE COLOSSIANS AND TO PHILEMON / Moule, Handly Carr Glynn – Cambridge: University Press, 1898. 1 fiche – 9 – us A.T.L.A. [240]

EPISTLES TO THE THESSALONIANS / Findlay, George G – Cambridge: University Press, 1904. 1 fiche – 9 – us A.T.L.A. [240]

THE EPISTLES TO THE THESSALONIANS / Denney, James – New York:A.C. Armstrong, 1892 – 1mf – 9 – 0-8370-2890-6 – 1985-0890 – us A.T.L.A. [220]

THE EPISTLES TO TIMOTHY AND TITUS : WITH INTRODUCTION AND NOTES / Humphreys, A E – (Includes appendix & index) – stereotyped ed. Cambridge: University Press, 1897 – 1mf – 9 – 0-8370-3692-5 – 1985-1692 – us A.T.L.A. [220]

EPISTOLA AD QUINTUM FRATREM, ETC / Cicero, Marcus Tullius – 15th cent. Holkham mss. 123, 379. Holkham Hall, Norfolk, England – 1 – uk Microform Academic [760]

EPISTOLA CONSTANTINOLOPI RECENS SCRIPTA. DE PRAESENTI TURCICI IMPERIJ STATU, ET GUBERNATORIBUS PRAECIPUIS, ET DE BELLO PERSICO / Billerberg, F de – N.p., 1582 – 1mf – 9 – H-8201/1 – ne IDC [956]

EPISTOLA D. PAVLI AD GALATAS...CVM COMMENTARIO... / Corner, C – Heidelbergae, 1583 – 5mf – 9 – ne IDC [240]

EPISTOLA DAN INDJIL HARI MINGGU DAN HARI RAYA / Wahjo, P – SE 4658 1. 1960 – 9 – ne IDC [950]

EPISTOLA DE LAUDIBUS PAETRIAE NOSTRAE / Carrillo Chumacero, Fernando – Majera, 1617 – 1 – sp Bibl Santa Ana [240]

EPISTOLA RELIGIOSA...CEFERINO GONZALEZ.. / Barrantes Moreno, Vicente – 1873 – 9 – 1.50f – sp Bibl Santa Ana [240]

EPISTOLAE / Gemblacensis, Guibertus – 1989 – 15mf – 9 – Bf2,995.00 – 2-503-63662-4 – be Brepols [240]

EPISTOLAE / Hieronymus, Saint – 15th cent. Holkham ms. 124. Holkham Hall, Norfolk, England – 1 – uk Microform Academic [240]

EPISTOLAE / Hieronymus, Saint – 15th cent. Holkham ms. 125. Holkham Hall, Norfolk, England – 1 – uk Microform Academic [240]

EPISTOLAE / Hieronymus, Saint – 15th cent. Holkham ms. 126. Holkham Hall, Norfolk, England – 1 – uk Microform Academic [240]

EPISTOLAE / Pliny – Libri IX and Livy, Orationes Hannibalis et Scipionis. Also, Plutarch, Epistola ad Trajanum ex Plutarcho. 15th cent.Holkham ms. 396. Holkham Hall, Norfolk, England – 1 – uk Microform Academic [760]

EPISTOLAE AND POEMATA / Boxhorn, MZ – Amsterdam, 1662 – 6mf – 9 – ne IDC [700]

EPISTOLAE DECRETALES : AC RESCRIPTA ROMANORUM PONTIFICUM – Matriti, 1821 – 7mf – 8 – ne Slangenburg [240]

EPISTOLAE FAMILIARES / Symmachus, Q.A – Argentoraci, 1510 – 2mf – 9 – H-8224/1 – ne IDC [956]

EPISTOLAE KAROLINI AEVI, TOM. 2 (MGH EPISTOLAE 1: 4.BD) – 1895 – Dfl60.00 – ne Slangenburg [240]

EPISTOLAE KAROLINI AEVI, TOM. 3 (MGH EPISTOLAE 1: 5.BD) – 1898-1899 – Dfl63.00 – ne Slangenburg [240]

EPISTOLAE KAROLINI AEVI, TOM. 4 (MGH EPISTOLAE 1: 6.BD) – 1902-1925 – Dfl74.00 – ne Slangenburg [240]

EPISTOLAE KAROLINI AEVI, TOM. 5 (MGH EPISTOLAE 1.7.BD) – 1912-1928 – Dfl46.00 – ne Slangenburg [240]

EPISTOLAE KAROLINI AEVI, TOM. 6 FASC. 1 (MGH EPISTOLAE 1: 8.BD) : HINCMARI ARCHIEPISCOPI REMENSIS EPISTOLARUM PARS 1 – 1939 – Dfl25.00 – ne Slangenburg [240]

EPISTOLAE MEROWINGICI ET KAROLINI AEVI, TOM. 1 (MGH EPISTOLAE 1: 3.BD) – 1892 – Dfl56.00 – ne Slangenburg [240]

EPISTOLAE OBSCURORUM VIRORUM : THE LATIN TEXT WITH AN ENGLISH RENDERING, NOTES, AND AN HISTORICAL INTRODUCTION / Stokes, Francis Griffin – Crotus Rubeanus, ca. 1480-ca. 1539. London: Chatto & Windus, 1909 – 2mf – us A.T.L.A. [220]

EPISTOLAE PRINCIPVM, RERVMPVBLICARVM, AC SAPIENTVM VIRORVM : EX ANTIQUIS ET RECENTIORIBUS, TAM GRAECIS, QUAM LATINIS, HISTORIJS ET ANNALIBUS COLLECTAE / Donzellini, G – Venetiis, 1574 – 5mf – 9 – H-8197/1 – ne IDC [450]

EPISTOLAE REVERENDI,...DANIELIS HOFFMANNI...DE LIBRO CONCORDIAE,... / Hoffmann, David – Ienae, 1597 – 1mf – ne IDC [240]

EPISTOLARIO DE MENENDEZ PELAYO CON JOSE LOPEZ PRUDENCIO (1902-1910) / Rodriguez Monino, Antonio – Badajoz: Imprenta de la Diputacion Provincial, 1958 – sp Bibl Santa Ana [946]

EPISTOLARIO DE NUEVA ESPANA... / Paso y Troncoso, Francisco del – Madrid: Razon y Fe, 1940 – sp Bibl Santa Ana [240]

EPISTOLARIO POETICO COMPLETO : NOTICIA PRELIMINAR POR A. RODRIGUEZ-MONINO / Aldana, Francisco de – Badajoz: Dip. Provincial, 1946 – 1 – sp Bibl Santa Ana [440]

EPISTOLAS FAMILIARES / Guevara, Antonio – 9 – 1.50f – sp Bibl Santa Ana [240]

EPISTOLE THURCI... – Lugduni, 1520 – 1mf – 9 – H-8136/1 – ne IDC [956]

EPISTOLICA QUAESTIO DE VITAE TERMINO..FATALI, AN MOBILI? / Beverovicius, Joh. – Ed. 2a. Lugd. Batavorum, 1636 – 11mf – 8 – ne Slangenburg [240]

EPITAPHES DE DEUX PRINCESSES TURQUES DE L'EPOQUE DES TANG / Chavannes, E – (Festschrift Thomsen). Leipzig. 1912. BU-595 2 – 8 – ne IDC [949]

EPITAPHS OF THE CATACOMBS, OR, CHRISTIAN INSCRIPTIONS IN ROME DURING THE FIRST FOUR CENTURIES / Northcote, James Spencer – London: Longmans, Green, 1878 – 1mf – us A.T.L.A. [240]

LES EPITHETES / Laporte, M – 1571 – 9 – fr I.C.S. [440]

EPITOMAE HISTORIARUM LIBRI 18 (CSHB 50) / Zonarad, Ioannes – Bonnae, 1897 – Dfl56.00 – ne Slangenburg [240]

EPITOME ANNALIUM POMERANIAE : KURTZER BERICHT VON BELEGENHEIT DES LANDES STETTIN POMMERN WIE DIESELBE VON ETZLICHEN JAHREN / Eickstedt, Valentin von – (Copy of/and/or translation of Epitome Annalium Pomeraniae, published eventually in 1728 in Greifswald) – 1600-1799 – 1r – 1 – us U.W. Library [943]

EPITOME BIBLIOTHECAE CONRADI GESNERI / Simler, J – Zuerich: Christoph Froschauer, 1555 – 5mf – 9 – ne IDC [240]

EPITOME COLLOQVII MONTISBELGARTENSIS INTER D. IACOBVM ANDREAE, ET D. THEODORUM BEZAM,... / Andreae d.A E, J – Tvbingae, 1588 – 1mf – 9 – ne IDC [240]

EPITOME DE LA VIDA Y HECHOS DEL INVICTO EMPERADOR CARLOS 5 / Vera y Figueroa, Juan Antonio – Madrid: Juan Sanchez, 1649 – 1 – sp Bibl Santa Ana [920]

EPITOME DE...MILAGROS...PEDRO DE ALCANTARA / Manzanares, Blas de – 1824 – 9 – 1.50f – sp Bibl Santa Ana [830]

EPITOME ENTOMOLOGIAE SYSTEMATICAE SECUNDUM FABRICIUM / Hentsch, G F – Lipsiae, 1804. Z/1340/2 – 8 – ne IDC [590]

EPITOME HISTORIAE SACRAE : AD USUM TYRONUM LINGUAE LATINAE / Lhomond, Charles F – Quebec: apud Joannem Neilson, 1803. SEM16P66 – 1r – 5 – Can$9.00 – cn Bibl Nat [450]

EPITOME HISTORIAL...JUAN DE LA PUEBLA / Tirado, Juan – 1724 – 9 – 1.50f – sp Bibl Santa Ana [946]

EPITOME HISTORICO DE MERIDA / Gonzalez y Gomez de Soto, Juan Jose – Merida: Tip.Juan F.Rivera Silva, 1906 – 1 – sp Bibl Santa Ana [946]

EPITOME HISTORICO...FREGENAL / Sanchez Cid, Antonio – 1843 – 9 – 1.50f – sp Bibl Santa Ana [946]

EPITOME OF GREEK GRAMMAR / Strong, James – [S.l.: s.n.], c1856 (New York: John F Trow) – 1mf – 9 – 0-8370-9188-8 – 1986-3188 – us A.T.L.A. [450]

AN EPITOME OF LEADING COMMON LAW CASES; WITH SOME SHORT NOTES THEREON...SMITH'S LEADING CASES / Indermaur, John – 5th ed. Boston, Soule and Bugbee, 1883. 107 p. LL-420 – 1 – us L of C Photodup [340]

EPITOME OF THE INSECTS OF ASIA / Donovan, E – 1805 – 7 – uk Microform Academic [590]

AN EPITOME OF THE NATURAL HISTORY OF THE INSECTS OF CHINA / Donovan, E – London, 1798. 50 pls. with descriptive letterpress. BZ-1192/2 – 8 – ne IDC [590]

AN EPITOME OF THE NATURAL HISTORY OF THE INSECTS OF INDIA / Donovan, E – Z-1193 2. 1800-04 – 8 – ne IDC [590]

AN EPITOME OF THE NATURAL HISTORY OF THE INSECTS OF NEW HOLLAND, NEW ZEALAND, NEW GUINEA / Donovan, E – London, 1805. 41 pls. with descriptive letterpress. Z-1194/2 – 8 – ne IDC [590]

EPITOME PASTORALIS AD USUM CLERI IN STATIBUS FOEDERATIS AMERICAE / Weninger, Francis Xavier – Buffalone: C Wieckmann & S Brandt, 1855 – 1mf – 9 – 0-8370-6789-8 – 1986-0789 – us A.T.L.A. [240]

EPITOME RERUM AB IOANNE ET ALEXIO COMNENIS GESTARUM (CSHB 26) : AD FIDEM COD. VAT. REC. AUG. MEINEKE. NICEPHORI BRYENNII COMMENTARII. REC. AUG. MEINEKE / Cinnami, Joannis – Bonnae, 1836 – Dfl46.00 – ne Slangenburg [240]

EPITOME THEOLOGIAE CHRISTIANAE / Abaelardus, Petrus – Berlijn, 1835 – 3mf – 8 – ne Slangenburg [240]

EPITOME THEOLOGIAE CHRISTIANAE / Abaelardus, Petrus; ed by Rheinwald, F H – Berlijn, 1835 – 3mf – 8 – ne Slangenburg [240]

EPITOME THESAVRI ANTIQVITATVM, HOC EST, IMPP. ROM. ORIENTALIUM ET OCCIDENTALIUM ICONUM EX ANTIQUIS NUMISMATIBUS QUAM FIDELISSIME DELINIATARUM / Strada, Jacobus de – Lugduni, 1553 – 1 – us U.W. Library [450]

EPITOME...CARLOS V / Vera y Figueroa, Juan Antonio – (1649 ed.1.50f; 9) – 1622 – 9 – 1.50f – sp Bibl Santa Ana [946]

EPITRE SUR LA MANIE DES JARDINS ANGLAIS / Chabanon, Michel Paul de – s.l., 1775. 8 fol., 16p. (Architecture Series) – 9 – fr Hachette [720]

L'EPOCA – Rome, 30 Dec 1917-9 July 1919 (imperfect) – 3r – 1 – uk British Libr Newspaper [072]
A EPOCA – Rio de Janeiro, 31 Jul 1912-30 Nov 1919 – 1,5,6 – bl Biblioteca [072]
EPOCA – 1973-1995 – 3r per y – 5,6 – Sfr615.00 – sz Infoprint [072]
EPOCA – London, UK. 4 Jan-15 Dec 1842 – 1 – uk British Libr Newspaper [072]
LA EPOCA – Madrid. Spain. -d. 2 Jan 1870-22 May 1874, 1 Jan 1875-11 Jul 1936. (223 reels) – 1 – uk British Libr Newspaper [072]
LA EPOCA – Santiago, Chile. Mar 1987-Feb 1990 – 39r – 1 – us L of C Photodup [072]
LA EPOCA – (Some issues lacking) – Madrid, Spain. Jul 1909-10 Jun 1936 – 54r – 1 – us L of C Photodup [072]
LA EPOCA – Tegucigalpa, Honduras: F Z Duron, 1956-jan 18 1958 – 5r – 1 – us Res Libr [072]
LA EPOCA – San Antonio, mar 1918-jun 7, 1931 – 14r – us Res Libr [072]
AN EPOCH IN PRINTING: BEING THE FIRST MATTER SET ON THE FIRST LINOTYPE MACHINE MANUFACTURED IN CANADA / Faustus – Montreal: Linotype Co., 1892. 03077. (Pre-1900 Canadiana) – 9 – cn C.I.H.M. [971]
EPOCH MAKERS OF MODERN MISSIONS / McLean, Archibald – New York: F.H. Revell, c1912 – 1mf – us A.T.L.A. [240]
A EPOCHA : ORGAM DO PARTIDO REPUBLICANO AMAZONENSE ITACO-ATIARA – Itacoatiara, Amazonas. 3 Jun 1917-23 Dez 1918 – 1,5,6 – bl Biblioteca [072]
A EPOCHA : ORGAM DOS INTERESSES DA REPUBLICA – Manaos, Amazonas. 5 Dez 1889 – 1,5,6 – bl Biblioteca [072]
DIE EPOCHEN DER KIRCHLICHEN GESCHICHTSCHREIBUNG / Baur, Ferdinand Christian – Tuebingen: Fues, 1852 – 1mf – us A.T.L.A. [240]
EPOCHS IN THE LIFE OF PAUL : A STUDY OF DEVELOPMENT IN PAUL'S CAREER / Robertson, A T – (Includes indexes) – New York: Charles Scribner, 1909 – 1mf – 9 – 0-8370-4920-2 – 1985-2920 – us A.T.L.A. [920]
EPOKHA – Ezhemesiachnyi literaturnyi zhurnal. M. 1886-88. Available: 1886, v. 1-12; 1887, v. 1; 1888, v. 1. B-1716 2 – 8 – ne IDC [073]
EPOKHA – Zhurnal literaturnyi i politicheskii. Ed. by M. Dostoevskii. Spb. 1864-65. Lacking: 1865 (3-12). B-5 2 – 8 – ne IDC [320]
EPOKHA BIELINSKAGO : OBSHCHII OCERK: IZ LEKTSII, CHITANNYKH V PETROGRADSKOM UNIVERSITETIE / Vengerov, S A – Izd. 2-e. [Petrograd]: Kn-vo "Prometei" N N Mikhailova, 1915 – 1 – us Res Libr [947]
EPOKHA TSENZURNYKH REFORM 1859-1865 GODOV / Lemke, M K – Spb. 1904. BR-10,515 1 – 9 – ne IDC [360]
EPOKHE = EPOCH – Montreal, CN, 1932 – 1r – 1 – Can$25.00 – cn Can Microfilming [072]
L'EPOPEE DE SAMBA GUELADIEGUI : ETUDE D'UNE VERSION INEDITE / Ly, Amadou – 1978 – us Res Libr [470]
L'EPOPEE D'EL HADJ OMAR : APPROCHE LITTERAIRE ET HISTORIQUE / Dieng, M Samba – 1984 – us Res Libr [470]
UNE EPOPEE ZARMA : WANGOUGNA ISSA KOROMBEIZE MODI, OU, ISSA KOYGOLO "MERE DE LA SCIENCE DE LA GUERRE" / Mahamane, Tandina Ousmane – 1984 – us Res Libr [470]
EPOPEIA – Literaturnyi ezhemesiachnik pod red. A. Belago. 1-4. Izd. Gelikom. M., Berlin. 1922-23. BR-1845 2 – 8 – ne IDC [460]
EPOPEIA – Moscow-Berlin. 1922-1923. no. 1-4 – 1 – us NY Public [073]
L'EPOQUE – Journal complet et universel. Paris. 1846 – 1 – fr A.C.R.P.P. [073]
L'EPOQUE – Journal politique et litteraire. Red. en chef E. Feydeau. Paris. 9 mars-21 sept 1865, 25 mai-1er dec 1868, 28 mars-25 juil 1869 – 1 – fr A.C.R.P.P. [944]
L'EPOQUE – no. 277-386. Paris. 12 mars-30 juin 1938 – 1 – fr A.C.R.P.P. [073]
L'EPOQUE CAROLINGIENNE (6) – Paris, 1937 – Dfl46.00 – ne Slangenburg [240]
EPOQUE MODERNE – London, UK. 2 Jun-1 Dec 1877 – 1 – uk British Libr Newspaper [072]
L'EPOUS REPUBLICAIN / Pompigny – (French Theatre Series). Paris. Cailleau, an II. 1794 – 9 – fr Hachette [820]
Epping, Joseph *see* ASTRONOMISCHES AUS BABYLON
EPPINGER ZEITUNG *see*
- HEILBRONNER STIMME
- NEUE EPPINGER ZEITUNG
Eppler, CF *see* GESCHICHTE DER GRUENDUNG DER ARMENISCH-EVANGELISCHEN GEMEINDE IN SCHAMACHI
Eppler, Christoph Friedrich *see* KARL RUDOLF HAGENBACH
L'EPREUVE – Revue d'art mensuelle. IV, n.s., no. 3-5; VI, n.s., no. 19-21. Paris. janv-mars 1903, sept-nov 1904 – 1 – fr A.C.R.P.P. [073]
Epshtein, D M *see* ISTORIIA ARKHEOGRAFII V DOREVOLIUTSIONNOI ROSSII
Epsilon Pi Tau *see* JOURNAL
Epstein, A L *see* JURIDICAL TECHNIQUES AND THE JUDICIAL PROCESS
Epstein, J N *see* DER GAONAEISCHE KOMMENTAR ZUR ORDNUNG TOHOROTH
THE EPWORTH SINGERS AND OTHER POETS OF METHODISM / Christophers, Samuel W – 1874 – 1 – us A.T.L.A. [240]
EPYTOMA JOHANNIS DE MURIS. IN MUSICAM BOECII. IN QUO OMNES COCLUSIONES MUSICE / Muris, J de – P 331. 1508 – 9 – ne IDC [780]
EQUADOR – Manaos, Amazonas. 1 Jan-20 Maio 1888 – 1,5,6 – bl Biblioteca [072]
O EQUADOR / Thome, S – jul 1926-sep 1927 – us Res Libr [072]
EQUAL JUSTICE / Communist Party. U.S.A. International Labor Defense – 1-16 no. 3 (all publ). 1926-42 – 37mf – 9 – $215.00 – us UPA [335]
EQUAL JUSTICE (LABOR DEFENDER) – USA. Jan. 1926-May 1940, Vol. 1, no. 1-Vol. 14, no. 2; Autumn 1940-Autumn 1941, Vol. 15, nos. 2-5; Winter 1941 42-Summer 1942, Vol. 16, nos. 1-3 – 1 – 35.00r – us Hoover Inst Photo [330]
EQUAL OPPORTUNITY FORUM – v1-9. no.6. 1976-Apr, May 1982 – 1,5,6,9 – us UMI [331]
EQUAL RIGHTS – v. 1-40. 1923-54 – 1 – 134.00 – us L of C Photodup [360]
Equal Rights Advocates and Anti-Monopolists of N.Y *see* DECLARATION OF RIGHTS
Equal Rights Association for the Province of Ontario *see* ADDRESS BY THE PROVINCIAL COUNCIL TO THE PEOPLE OF ONTARIO, DEALING MAINLY WITH SEPARATE SCHOOLS
EQUAL RIGHTS EXPOSITOR – Visalia, CA. Aug 1962-Mar 1863 – 1r – 1 CB03075 – $50.00 – us Library Micro [320]
EQUAL RIGHTS EXPOSITOR – Visalia. Calif. -w. 1862-65 – 1 – us UMI [071]
EQUAL RIGHTS: INDEPENDENT FEMINIST WEEKLY – Series 1 v1 nos 1-9; series 2 v1-2 no 43 (all publ). 1935-36 – 1r – 1 – $60.00 – us UPA [323]
EQUAL RIGHTS: MR. CHARLTON'S OPEN LETTER TO REV. PRINCIPAL CAVEN, D.D., DATED MAY 9TH, 1890 / Charlton, John – Ottawa?, 1890?. 02960. (Pre-1900 Canadiana) – 9 – cn C.I.H.M. [971]
EQUAL RIGHTS: THE LETTERS OF WILLIAM CAVEN / Caven, William – 1890? 00521. (Pre-1900 Canadiana) – 9 – cn C.I.H.M. [920]
EQUALITY – 1-2 2+10 (all publ). 1939-1940 – 7mf – 9 – $50.00 – us UPA [335]
EQUALITY – New York. N.Y. 1939-40 – 1 – us A.J.P.C. [071]
EQUALITY – The American Way: Equal Rights and Equal Opportunity for All. New York. v. 1-2 no. 10. May 1939-Oct Nov 1940 – 1 – us NY Public [977]
EQUALS – no.1-14; Apr May 1975-Jun Jul 1977. London, Race Relations Board. -bim. illus – 1 – us U.W. Library [073]
EL EQUILIBRIO UNIVERSAL PARA UN MUNDO DE PAZ / Baldassarre, Pedro B – Buenos Aires: El Ateneo, [1953] – 1 – CSUXADN3982-B – us Hoover Inst Photo [120]
EQUILIBRIOS POETICOS DE UN !DESEQUILIBRADO! / Sanchez-Arjona, Vicente – Sevilla: Imp. Alvarez, Tomo 3. 1956 – 1 – sp Bibl Santa Ana [810]
EQUILIBRIOS POETICOS, DE UN...! DESEQUILIBRADO! / Sanchez-Arjona, Vicente – Sevilla: Imp. Alvarez, Tomo 1. 1956 – 1 – sp Bibl Santa Ana [810]
EQUILIBRIOS POETICOS DE UN !DESEQUILIBRADO! / Sanchez-Arjona, Vicente – Sevilla: Imp. Alvarez, Tomo 2. 1956 – 1 – sp Bibl Santa Ana [810]
EQUILIBRIOS POETICOS DE UN !DESEQUILIBRADO! / Sanchez-Arjona, Vicente – Sevilla: Imp. Alvarez, Tomo 4. 1956 – 1 – sp Bibl Santa Ana [810]
Equiloecq, F V *see* ESSAI SUR LA LITTERATURE MERVEILLEUSE DES NOIRS, SUIVI DE CONTES INDIGENES DE L'OUEST-AFRICAIN FRANCAISE
EQUINE PRACTICE – v1. 1979 – 1,5,6,9 – us UMI [073]
EQUINOX – Camden East. v1-14. 1982-95 – 9 – Can$28.00y – cn Micromedia [073]
L'EQUIPE – 1946- – 3r per y – 5 – inquire – us Ross [072]
L'EQUIPE – 1946-1995 – 6r per y – 1,6 – F4,200.00y – sz Infoprint [944]
[EQUIPMENT AND SUPPLIES IN WORLD WAR 1 PAMPHLET COLLECTION] – 1916 – 1 – CSUXANM2794-B – us Hoover Inst Photo [355]
EQUIPMENT PLANNING GUIDES FOR VOCATIONAL AND TECHNICAL TRAINING AND EDUCATION PROGRAMMES / International Labour Organisation – 17 – Sfr255.00 – 92-2-105352-0 – sz I.L.O. [650]
[EQUIPMENT, SUPPLIES, AND INDUSTRY DURING WORLD WAR 2 PAMPHLET COLLECTION] – 1941-1944 – 2r – 1 – CSUXANN3565-B – us Hoover Inst Photo [338]
EQUIPPING THE LAITY AS WORSHIP LEADERS IN THE MINISTRY OF BIG BETHEL BAPTIST CHURCH / Dawson, Walter Robert – 1982 – 1 – 5.00 – us Baptist [240]
EQUITABLE COMMERCE / Warren, Josiah – (Meditations Upon Divine Justice and the Death of King Charles the First. Aeropagitica, a Speech for the Liberty of Unlicensed Printing. The Tenure of Kings and Magistrates. The Second Defence of the People of England... A Treatise of Civil Power in Ecclesiastical Causes.) – 1852. 1 fiche (24x). Together with the following works by John Milton: – 9 – 1.00f – at Libertarian Micro [320]
L'EQUITE – St-Bruno de Montarville, Canada. v2 n16. 14 jul 1966 – 1r – 1 – Can$20.00 – cn Can Microfilming [072]
EQUITY / Cook, Forrest – Los Angeles 1938 112 p. LL-360 – 1 – us L of C Photodup [340]
THE EQUITY – Bryson, Canada. 7 jun 1883-v3 n29. 31 dec 1885; Shawville. v6 n37. 21 fev 1889 – 1r – 1 – Can$30.00 – cn Can Microfilming [072]
THE EQUITY – Shawville (Quebec). v1- 1883-. SEM35P100 – 51r – 1 – cn Bibl Nat [073]
EQUITY AS APPLIED IN THE STATE AND FEDERAL COURTS IN TEXAS AND OTHER STATES / Simkins, William Stewart – 2d ed. Kansas City, Mo.: Vernon, 1911. 1002p. LL-1333 – 1 – us L of C Photodup [340]
EQUITY CASE FILES OF THE U.S. CIRCUIT COURT FOR THE SOUTHERN DISTRICT OF NEW YORK / U.S. Circuit and District Courts. New York – 1791-1846. 23 rolls – 1 – M884 – us Nat'l Archives [324]
EQUITY, ITS PRINCIPLES IN PROCEDURE, CODES AND PRACTICE ACTS. / Hughes, William Taylor – St. Louis: Central Law Journal Co., 1911. 383, 610p. LL-86 – 1 – us L of C Photodup [340]
EQUITY JURISDICTION, PLEADING AND PRACTICE IN MAINE / Whitehouse, Robert Treat – Portland, Loring, Short & Harmon, 1900. 949 p. LL-1647 – 1 – us L of C Photodup [340]
EQUITY JURISPRUDENCE. / Steele, Sherman – New York, Prentice-Hall, 1927. 897 p. LL-1071 – 1 – us L of C Photodup [340]
EQUITY PRACTICE IN THE UNITED STATES CIRCUIT COURTS / Shiras, Oliver Perry – 2d ed. Chicago: Callaghan, 1898. 226p. LL-1134 – 1 – us L of C Photodup [340]
EQUITY PRECEDENTS, 4TH ED / Curtis, Charles Ticknor – Boston, Little, Brown, 1869. 596 p. LL-555 – 1 – us L of C Photodup [340]
EQUITY PRECEDENTS; SUPPLEMENTARY TO MR. JUSTICE STORY'S TREATISE ON EQUITY PLEADINGS / Curtis, George Ticknor – Boston, Little, Brown, 1850. 562 p. LL-557 – 1 – us L of C Photodup [340]
EQUITY PROCEDURE, EMBODYING THE PRINCIPLES OF PLEADING AND PRACTICE APPLICABLE TO COURTS OF EQUITY...IN VIRGINIA AND WEST VIRGINIA.. / Hogg, Charles Edgar – Cincinnati: Anderson Co., 1921. 2v. LL-16206 – 1 – us L of C Photodup [340]
EQUITY RECORDS OF THE U.S. CIRCUIT COURT FOR THE EASTERN DISTRICT OF PENNSYLVANIA / U.S. Circuit and District Courts. Pennsylvania – 1790-1847. 23 rolls – 1 – M985 – us Nat'l Archives [324]
EQUUS – (v.15 .1979 5,6,9) – v.1. 1977 – 1 – us UMI [073]
E.R. Alderman and Sons *see* CENTENNIAL SOUVENIR OF MARIETTA, OHIO 1788-1888
ER: ENVIRONMENTAL REVIEW – (v.4 .1980 5,6,9) – v.1. 1976 – 1 – us UMI [360]
ERA : AURORA KING – Newmarket, 1977 – 1r – 1 – cn Preston [971]
ERA – Bradford. Pa. 1883- – 1 – us UMI [071]
ERA – Newmarket, 1930-1977 – 46r – 1 – cn Preston [971]
ERA : SOUTH SHORE – Newmarket, 1977 – 1r – 1 – cn Preston [971]
THE ERA : INCORPORATING THE CINEMATOGRAPHIC TIMES – London, 1851-1939 – 58r – 1 – us Ross [072]
THE ERA – London. -w. 1865-90. (68 reels) – 1 – uk British Libr Newspaper [072]
L'ERA NUOVA – Paterson, NJ, 1908-1919 – 3r – 1 – us I.H.R.C. [978]
THE ERA OF CONFRONTATION / Indonesia. Departemen Luar Negeri – Contents: I. Address by Pres. Soekarno to Second Conference of Non-Aligned Countries, Cairo, 6 Oct. 1964. II. Declaration adopted by Second Conference of Non-Aligned Countries, Cairo, 5th to 10th Oct. SE-10,673 1 – 9 – ne IDC [950]
L'ERABLE : TABLOID – Montreal. v1 n3. 14 sep 1928 – 1r – 1 – Can$25.00 – cn Can Microfilming [072]
ERADICATION OF TICKS – 1989 – 333p – it F.A.O. [660]
ERANSAHR NACH DER GEOGRAPHIE DES PS. MOSES XORENAC'I / Marquart, J – In: Abhandlungen der Koeniglichen Gesellschaft der Wissenschaften zu Goettingen, Philosophisch-Historischen Klasse, ns v3 no 2 Berlin 1901. BU-559 2 – 8 – ne IDC [900]
Eras, J F M *see* DE OVEREENKOMST IN HET INTERNATIONAAL PRIVAATRECHT
ERASMI BARTHOLINI DE NATURAE MIRABILIBUS QUAESTIONES ACADEMICAE / Bartholin, Rasmus – Hafniae Copenhagen, sumptibus P. Hauboldi, 1674. 3 fiches. (Science Collection) – 9 – $8.00 – fr Bibl Nationale [500]
ERASMUS : ONDERZOEK NAAR ZIJNE THEOLOGIE EN ZIJN GODSDIENSTIG GEMOEDSBESTAAN / Lindeboom, Johannes – Leiden: A.H. Adriani, 1909 – 1mf – us A.T.L.A. [190]
ERASMUS AND OTHER ESSAYS / Dods, Marcus – London: Hodder and Stoughton, 1891 – 1mf – us A.T.L.A. [190]
Erasmus, Desiderius *see*
- BRIEFWECHSEL DECEMBER 1522 BIS FRUELING 1523
- THE COMPLAINT OF PEACE
- ENCOMIUM MORIAE, STULTICIAE
- IN NOVUM TESTAMENTUM ANNOTATIONES
- OPERA OMNIA
- PROVERBS OR ADAGES, GATHERED OUT OF THE "CHILIADES" AND ENGLISHED BY RICHARD TAVERNER
- LA QUERELA PACIS
- SETENGAH LOESIN PERTJAKAPAN ERASMUS
ERASMUS IN ENGLISH – (Ceased no 15 1987/88) – Downsview, nos 1-15. 1970-1987/88 – 9 – Can$20.00 – cn Micromedia [450]
Erasmus of Rotterdam *see* QUERELA PACIS...
Erastus, Thomas *see* DISPVTATIONVM DE MEDICINA NOVA PHILIPPI PARACELSI PARS PRIMA: IN QVA, QVAE DE REMEDIIS..
Erbach, C *see* MODORUM SACRORUM SIVE CANTIONUM...
ERBACHER KREISBLATT *see* GRAEFLICH ERBACHISCHES WOCHEN-BLATT FUER DEN LANDKREIS ERBACH
DER ERBARZT – Berlin, 1934 n1-7, 1938 n8 – 1 – Dist. gw Mikrofilm – gw Misc Inst [575]
DAS ERBE DES OSTDEUTSCHEN VOLKSGESANGES / Salmen, Walter – 1956 – 1 – us I.U. Libraries [390]
DAS ERBE DES WUCHERERS : ORIGINAL-VOLKSSTUECK MIT GESANG IN FUENF ACTEN / Costa, Carl – [Wien?: s.n., 18–?] – 1 – us U.W. Library [820]
ERBE UND TRADITION IN DER LITERATUR / Dahnke, Hans-Dietrich – (Includes bibliographical references) – Leipzig: VEB Bibliographisches Institut, 1977 – 1r – 1 – us U.W. Library [430]

DAS ERBE WOLGASTS : EIN QUERSCHNITT DURCH DIE HEUTIGE JUGENDSCHRIFTENFRAGE / Fronemann, Wilhelm – Langensalza: J Beltz, 1927 – 1 – us Res Libr [890]

Erben, K J *see* PROSTONARODNI CESKE PISNE A RIKADLA. NAPEVY PROSTONARODNICH PISNI CESKYCH

Erberg, K *see* TSEL' TVORCHESTVA

Erbes, C *see* DIE TODESTAGE DER APOSTEL PAULUS UND PETRUS (T.U.U. 2-19/1A)

DIE ERBRECHTLICHEN VERHAELTNISSE DER SCHWEIZER IM AUSLAND / Anliker, P – Aarau, Leipzig, 1933 – 3mf – 9 – ILM-3116/1 – ne IDC [340]

DIE ERBSCHAFTSSTEUER IM INTERNATIONALEN RECHTE / Bartoszewicz, J von – Lemberg, 1899 – 1mf – 9 – ILM-3320/1 – ne IDC [340]

Erbt, Wilhelm *see*
- JEREMIA UND SEINE ZEIT: DIE GESCHICHTE DER LETZEN FUENFZIG JAHRE DES VOREXILISCHEN JUDA
- DIE SICHERSTELLUNG DES MONOTHEISMUS DURCH DIE GESETZGEBUNG IM VOREXILISCHEN JUDA

Ercegovicz, A *see* SUR LES CYSTOSEIRA ADRIATIQUES. LEUR MORPHOLOGIE, ECOLOGIE ET EVOLUTION

ERCILLA – Santiago, Chile: Prensas de la editorial Ercilla, SA. v3 n112-v10 n488 jul 1937-sep 5 1944 8r. v10 n489-v13 n632 sep 12 1944-jun 10 1947 4r – 12r – 1 – us Res Libr [072]

Erckmann, Emile *see* HISTOIRE D'UN PAYSAN, 1789

ERDA ENERGY RESEARCH ABSTRACTS / U.S. Energy Research and Development Administration – v1-2. 1976-77 – 1,5,6,9 – us UMI [324]

Erdant, Alexandre *see* LES REVOLUTIONNAIRES DE L'A.B.C

Erder, Cevat *see* OUR ARCHITECTURAL HERITAGE

ERDGEIST : TRAGOEDIE IN VIER AUFZUEGEN / Wedekind, Frank – 6. Aufl. Muenchen: A Langen, 1908 – 1r – 1 – us U.W. Library [820]

Erdman, B *see* PSYCHOLOGISCHE UNTERSUCHUNGEN UEBER DAS LESEN AUF EXPERIMENTELLER GRUNDLAGE

Erdman, C B *see* SIX SONATES A VIOLON, VIOLA, ET BASSE, OP. 1

Erdman, William Jacob *see* ECCLESIASTES

Erdmann, C *see* STUDIEN ZUR BRIEFLITERATUR DEUTSCHLANDS IM 11. JAHRHUNDERT (MGH SCHRIFTEN..: 1.BD)

Erdmann, D *see* LUTHER UND SEINE BEZIEHUNGEN ZUR SCHLESIEN, INSBESONDERE ZU BRESLAU

Erdmann, David *see* BUECHER SAMUELIS

Erdmann, H *see* ALASKA

Erdstein, D *see* LE STATUT JURIDIQUE DES MINORITES...

L'ERE NIGERIENNE : [ESSAI D'EPOPEE ANECTOTIQUE SUR L'HISTOIRE DE L'OUEST-AFRICAIN FRANCAIS] / Perron, Michel – Paris: Editions de la Pensee latine, 1926 – 1 – us Res Libr [960]

L'ERE NOUVELLE – Grand organe quotidien de l'entente des gauches. Paris. 27 dec 1919-juin 1940 – 1 – fr A.C.R.P.P. [073]

L'ERE NOUVELLE : JOURNAL DU DISTRICT DES TROIS-RIVIERES – Trois-Rivieres, Canada. 3 jul 1884; 4 nov 1884-v2 n8. 4 dec 1885 – 1r – 1 – Can$40.00 – cn Can Microfilming [072]

L'ERE NOUVELLE : LIGUE PROGRES ECONOMIQUE – Montreal, Canada. v1 n5. 16 jun 1925-v2 n41. 6 avr 1927 – 1r – 1 – Can$30.00 – cn Can Microfilming [072]

L'ERE NOUVELLE – Quebec, Canada. v2 n11. 25 jul 1936-v6 n87. 10 avr 1941 – 1r – 1 – Can$40.00 – cn Can Microfilming [072]

L'ERE NOUVELLE – Revue mensuelle de socialisme scientifique. Dir. G. Diamandy. Paris. juil 1893-nov 1894 – 1 – fr A.C.R.P.P. [073]

L'ERE NOUVELLE – Trois-Rivieres, Canada. 9 dec 1852-v14 n6. 28 dec 1865 – 4r – 1 – Can$50.00r – cn Can Microfilming [072]

O EREBO – Manaus, Amazonas. 5 Set 1895 – 1,5,6 – bl Biblioteca [072]

EREMA / Blackmore, Richard Doddridge – British Fiction Archive: Unit 3 – 9 – uk Bell [830]

Eremeev, K *see* SOTSIALISTICHESKAI A SOVETSKAI A RESPUBLIKA

L'EREMITA, LA CARCERE, E L' DIPORTO : OPERA NELLA QUALE SI CONTENGANO NOUELLE ET ALTRE COSE MORALI, ... / Granucci, N – Lucca, 1569 – 4mf – 9 – H-8309/1 – ne IDC [956]

EREMITENSCHULE IN ALTBAYERN / Heigenmooser, J – Berlin, 1903 – Dfl13.00 – ne Slangenburg [240]

EREMITES ET RECLUS : ETUDES SUR D'ANCIENNES FORMES DE VIE RELIGIEUSES / Gougaud, L – Liguge, 1928 – 3mf – 8 – ne Slangenburg [210]

Erenburg, I *see*
- IZ NEOPUBLIKOVANNAGO ILI ZABYTOGO
- LIUDI, GODY, ZHIZN'
- PORTRETY RUSSKIKH POETOV

ERETS ISRAEL – (Missing: 1938. v12(9)) – Padang, Bandoeng, 1926-1939. v1-14(1-3) – 54mf – 9 – J-261-30/1 – ne IDC [950]

EREVAN – Sofia, Bulgaria. Jul 1952-May 1958 (scattered issues) – 1r – 1 – us L of C Photodup [949]

DIE ERFAHRUNG IN PLATONS IDEENLEHRE : DIE IDEE ALS GESTALT DER ERFAHRUNG / Joannou, Petros-Perikles – Muenchen, 1936 – 93p – 9 – DM48.00 – 3-89349-056-6 – gw Hänsel [180]

DER ERFAHRUNGSBEWEIS FUER DIE WAHRHEIT DES CHRISTENTHUMS / Wendt, Hans Hinrich – Goettingen: Vandenhoeck & Ruprecht, 1897 – 1mf – 9 – 0-8370-5784-1 – 1985-3784 – us A.T.L.A. [230]

ERFASSUNG UND BEURTEILUNG GEOBOTANISCHER DATEN : KRITISCHE BETRACHTUNG AUSGEWAEHLTER METHODEN / Schleiter, Ingrid M – 1995 – 3mf – 9 – DM98.00 – 3-8267-2106-3 – gw Hänsel [574]

DIE ERFORSCHUNG AFRIKAS. / Hassert, Kurt – Leipzig: W. Goldmann, 1943. 259p. maps. Bibliog – 1 – us U.W. Library [960]

Erfurth, Fritz *see* DIE "DEUTSCHEN SAGEN" DER BRUEDER GRIMM

ERGAENZUNGS-CONVERSATIONSLEXIKON (AEL, ABT 1;19) / ed by Steger, Franz – Leipzig, spaeter Leipzig und Meißen, 1845-1859 (mf ed 1993) – 56mf – 9 – DM1,150.00 – 3-89131-107-9 – gw Fischer [030]

ERGANZUNGSHEFT ... : DER MITTEILUNGEN AUS DEN DEUTSCHEN SCHUTZGEBIETEN – Berlin: E S Mittler. [n1-13. 1908-1917] – 2r – us Res Libr [072]

ERGEBNISSE DER ENZYMFORSCHUNG – v. 1-11. 1932-50 – 1,5,6 – us Princeton Micro [610]

ERGEBNISSE DER RUNDTISCHGESPRACHES – [S.l.: s.n.], 1989-1990. 1v – 1 – CSUXAMF9479-B – us Hoover Inst Photo [943]

ERGEBNISSE EINER BEREISUNG DES GEBIETS ZWISCHEN OKAWANGO / Seiner, F – (Mitt. aus den Deutschen Schutzgebieten, Berlin, 1900, v. 22). B-6126 1 – 9 – ne IDC [580]

ERGENISSE DER ALLGEMEINEN PATHOLOGIE UND PATHOLOGISCHEN ANATOMIE (WIEBADEN) – v. 1-36. 1895-1943. Erganzungsband 1895-1943 – 1,5,6 – us Princeton Micro [616]

ERGONOMICS – Human factors in work, machine control and equipment design. v.1-18 with index v.1-10. 1958-75. London – 9 – 24240.00; 2413.00v – uk Dawson [620]

ERGONOMICS ABSTRACTS – v.1-7 with index for v.1-5. 1969-75. London – 9 – 24100.00; 2413.00v – uk Dawson [620]

Erhard, Chr *see*
- GRUENDLICHE KURTZ VERFASTE HISTORIA VON MUENSTERISCHEN WIDERTAUFFERN
- SALVS EX JNIMICIS. GOLIATHS SCHWERDT. AUGENSCHEINLICHE ERWEYSUNG, WAS WIR CATHOLISCHE VNND ALTE CHRISTEN FUER KLARE VND KRAEFFTIGE ARGUMENTA VNND ZEUGNUSSEN HABEN
- ZWELFF WICHTIGE VND STARCKE VRSACHEN HANSEN JEDELSHAUSERS VON VLM, WARUMB ER VON DEN WIDERTAUFFERN. SEY ABGETRETTEN

ERHARDI WEIGELII SACRAE CAESAR : PHILOSOPHIA MATHEMATICA: THEOLOGIA NATURALIS SOLIDA: PER SINGULAS SCIENTIAS CONTINUATA: UNIVERSAE ARTIS INVENIENDI PRIMA STAMINA COMPLECTENS / Weigel, Erhard – Jenae: Sumptibus Matth. Brickneri, bibliopolae Jen. & Helmstad., Typis Pauli Ehrichii, 1693 – 1 – us U.W. Library [100]

DIE ERHEBUNG PREUSSENS IM JAHRE 1813 UND DIE REKONSTRUKTION DES STAATES / Ranke, Leopold von; ed by Kaemmel, Otto – Leipzig, um 1900 – 210p – 9 – DM48.00 – 3-89349-115-5 – gw Hänsel [943]

ERHEBUNGSINSTRUMENTARIUM ZU AKZEPTANZPROBLEMEN BEIM EINSATZ INNOVATIVER INFORMATIONSTECHNOLOGIE IM BUERO- UND VERWALTUNGSBEREICH ANALYSIERT AM BEISPIEL EINES INDUSTRIEBETRIEBES / Wagner, Albert – Nuernberg, 1983 – 2mf – DM38.00 – 3-89349-904-0 – gw Hänsel [650]

ERHEITERUNGEN, 1811-1827 / ed by Kotzebue, August von – 1811-27 (mf ed 1997) – 102mf – 9 – DM2,320.00 – 3-89131-234-2 – gw Fischer [305]

ERIC CUMMULATIVE INDEXES TO RESOURCES IN EDUCATION, 1992 – (Includes six indexes: Title, Author, Subject, Sponsor, ERIC Descriptor and ERIC Identifer) – EDRS, 1993 – 500mf – 9 – $75.00 set – us EDRS [370]

ERICARUM ICONES ET DESCRIPTIONES / Wendland, J C – 27 pts. Hannover. 1798-1804-23. B-5805 2 – 8 – ne IDC [580]

[ERICH HONECKER: PAMPHLET COLLECTION] – 1967-1984 – 1 – CSUXANS5582-B – us Hoover Inst Photo [320]

Erich, R *see* PROBLEME DER INTERNATIONALEN ORGANISATION

Erichson, G F *see* DISSERTATIO DE FABRICA ET USU ANTENNARUM IN INSECTIS

Erichson, W F *see*
- ENTOMOGRAPHIEN
- GENERA ET SPECIES STAPHYLINORUM INSECTORUM COLEOPTERORUM FAMILAE
- NATURGESCHICHTE DER INSECTEN DEUTSCHLANDS

Erickson, Donald A *see* THE NEW PUBLIC SCHOOLS

ERICSON JOURNAL – Ericson, NE. -w. May 1914-Nov. 1915; Jan. 1916-Aug. 1939 – 1 – us NE Hist [071]

ERIE AND NIAGARA EXTENSION RAILWAY – No. 2: Statement of Wm. A. Thomson, President of the Provisional Board, Toronto, 14th December, 1869. Toronto: s.n., 1869? (Toronto: Hunter, Rose). 02030. (Pre-1900 Canadiana) – 9 – cn C.I.H.M. [971]

Erie County. Ohio. Auditor *see*
- LAND SALES, DELINQUENT TAXES
- REAL ESTATE APPRAISAL RECORDS
- TAX LISTS

Erie County. Ohio. Board of County Commissioners *see* COMMISSIONERS' JOURNALS

Erie County. Ohio. Common Pleas. Civil Division *see*
- CHANCERY RECORD NO. 5
- INDEX TO CHANCERY RECORD NO. 5

Erie County. Ohio. Huron, City City Council *see*
- MINUTES
- ORDINANCE RECORDS
- SCRAPBOOKS OF CITY AFFAIRS

Erie County. Ohio. Kelley's Island Twp Board of Trustees *see* MINUTES

Erie County. Ohio. Kelley's Island Twp Justice of the Peace *see* CIVIL DOCKET

Erie County. Ohio. Milan Township. Board of Education *see* COMMON SCHOOL RECORD BOOK

Erie County, Ohio. Milan Township. Board of Trustees *see* MINUTES

Erie County. Ohio. Milan Township. Board of Trustees *see* MINUTES

Erie County. Ohio. Milan Township. Justice of the Peace *see* DOCKETS

Erie County. Ohio. Milan, Village. Village Council *see*
- MINUTES
- ORDINANCE BOOK

Erie County, Ohio. Oxford Township. Board of Trustees *see*
- MINUTES
- ZONING COMMISSION MINUTES

Erie County. Ohio. Oxford Township. Board of Trustees *see* MINUTES

Erie County. Ohio. Probate Court *see* STATEMENTS OF BIRTH AND DEATHS

Erie County. Ohio. Sheriff *see* JAIL REGISTERS

Erie County. Ohio. Treasurer *see* TAX DUPLICATE

Erie County. Ohio. Vermilion. City Clerk *see* POLL BOOK AND TALLY SHEETS

Erie County. Ohio. Vermilion. City Council *see* MINUTES

Erie County. Ohio. Vermilion. Depository Commission *see* MINUTES

Erie County. Ohio. Vermilion. Mayor's Court *see* RECORD OF ARRESTS

Erie County. Ohio. Vermilion. Sinking Fund Trustees *see* MINUTES

Erie County. Ohio. Vermilion Township. Board of Education *see* MINUTES

Erie County. Ohio. Vermilion Township. Board of Health *see* MINUTES

Erie County, Ohio. Vermilion Township. Board of Trustees *see* MINUTES

Erie County. Ohio. Vermilion Township. Board of Trustees *see* ROAD RECORDS

Erie County. Ohio. Vermilion Township. Justice of the Peace *see* DOCKETS

Erie County. Ohio. Vermilion Township. Township Clerk *see*
- LIQUOR NOTICE RECORD
- LIST OF JUDGES OF ELECTION
- RECORD OF CHATTEL MORTGAGES

ERIE COUNTY REPORTER – Huron. Ohio. 1880- – 1 – us UMI [071]

ERIE COUNTY REPORTER – Huron, Ohio. 1973- – 21r – 1 – $32.50r – us Archival [071]

ERIE COUNTY REPORTER – Huron, Ohio, 1973-1994 – 21r – 1 – us Archival [978]

Erie. Presbytery (Pres. Ch. in the U.S.A.) *see* MINUTES, 1802-1924

Erie. Presbytery (Pres. Ch. in the U.S.A. New School) *see* MINUTES, 1838-1870

ERINNERUNGEN / Alexis, Willibald; ed by Ewerts, Max – Berlin, 1900 – xlii/388p – 9 – DM48.00 – 3-89349-105-8 – gw Hänsel [880]

ERINNERUNGEN / Thoma, Ludwig – Muenchen: R Piper, c1947 – 1r – 1 – us U.W. Library [943]

ERINNERUNGEN AN ANZENGRUBER / Rosner, L – Leipzig: J Klinkhardt, 1891 – 1r – 1 – us U.W. Library [943]

ERINNERUNGEN AN FRANZ GRILLPARZER : FRAGMENTE AUS TAGEBUCHBLAETTERN / Wartenegg, Wilhelm von – Wien: C Konegen, 1901 – 1r – 1 – us U.W. Library [920]

ERINNERUNGEN AN FRIEDRICH HEBBEL / Kulke, Eduard – Wien: C Konegen, 1878 – 1r – 1 – us U.W. Library [920]

ERINNERUNGEN AN FRIEDRICH NIETZSCHE / Deussen, Paul – (Includes index) – Leipzig: F A Brockhaus, 1901 – 1r – 1 – us U.W. Library [190]

ERINNERUNGEN AN GOTTFRIED KELLER / Frey, Adolf – 2., erw. Aufl. Leipzig: H Haessel, 1893 – 1r – 1 – us U.W. Library [920]

ERINNERUNGEN AUS DER SUEDAFRIKANISCHEN MISSION = REMINSCENCES OF THE SOUTH AFRICAN MISSION / Liefeld, Friedrich Wilhelm Albert – (In English) – Columbus, OH: Lutheran Book Concern, 1895, c1891 – 1mf – 9 – 0-8370-6491-0 – 1986-0491 – us A.T.L.A. [240]

ERINNERUNGEN. VOM JOURNALISTEN ZUM HISTORIKER DER DEUTSCHEN ARBEITERBEWEGUNG / Mayer, Gustav – Zurich, 1949 – 1 – DM30.00 – gw Mikro Press [331]

ERINNERUNGSBLAETTER DEUTSCHER REGIMENTER – Oldenburg. Heft 1-190; 1920-26 (Incomplete). Includes Artillerie, Heft 1-12; Infanterie, Heft 1-15; Kavallerie, Heft 2. Film Mas C 678 – 1 – us H.U. Library [073]

ERISA UPDATE / U.S. Department of Labor. Pension Benefit Guaranty Corporation – (Abstracts only. 580; 9) – 1974-84.Full text of opinion letters – 9 – 610.00 – us Washington [336]

ERISTISCHE DIALEKTIK / Schopenhauer, Arthur – With transl.: The Art of Controversy. 1896. 1 fiche (29x) – 9 – 1.00f – at Libertarian Micro [320]

ERITASSARD HAYASTAN – Boston: [s.n.], dec 12 1917-1921; jan 14-apr 29 1922; aug 7 1922-oct 13 1923; jan 6, feb 17 1934; sep 21 1948-aug 19 1949; aug 23 1949-may 16 1952 – 7r – 1 – us Res Libr [071]

"ERITIS SICUT DEUS", EIN BEITRAG ZUR GESCHICHTE DES RELIGIOESEN ROMANS / Dobbriner, Paul – Lucka, 1913 – 2mf – 9 – DM62.00 – 3-89349-345-X – gw Hänsel [410]

ERKENNTNIS – v1-7 1930-38 – 1 – us UMI [100]

ERKENNTNIS – (v20- 1984-. 5,6,9) – v9- May 1975- – 1 – us UMI [100]

DIE ERKENNTNISLEHRE DES WILHELM VON AUVERGNE / Baumgartner, M – Muenster, 1893 – 2mf – 8 – ne Slangenburg [100]

DIE ERKENNTNISS DES CHRISTENTHUMES VOM NATURWISSENSCHAFTLICHEN STANDPUNCTE : EIN BEITRAG ZUR DOGMATISCHEN REFORM DER PROTESTANTISCHEN KIRCHE / Bonorden, Hermann Friedrich – Leipzig: Siegismund & Volkening, 1876 – 1mf – 9 – 0-8370-2413-7 – 1985-0413 – us A.T.L.A. [210]

DIE ERKENNTNISTHEORETISCHE BEDEUTUNG DES GEFUEHLSMAESSIGEN ERFASSENS BEI SCHLEICHERMEIER / Hammer, Anton – Freiburg i.B., 1934 – 78p – 9 – DM48.00 – 3-89349-055-8 – gw Hänsel [100]

DIE ERKENNTNISTHEORETISCHEN UND METAPHYSISCHEN GRUNDLAGEN DER... BIEDERMANN & LIPSIUS / Fleisch, Urban – Berlin: C.A. Schwetschke, 1901. 1 fiche – 9 – us A.T.L.A. [190]

ERKLAERUNG DER BRIEFE PETRI / Beck, Johann Tobias; ed by Lindenmeyer, Julius – Guetersloh: C Bertelsmann, 1896 – 1mf – 9 – 0-8370-2226-6 – 1985-0226 – us A.T.L.A. [240]

ERKLAERUNG DER HISTORIE DES LEIDENS UND STERBENS UNSERS HERRN CHRISTI JESU : NACH DEN VIER EVANGELISTEN ALSO ANGESTELLET DASS WIR DADURCH ZUR ERKENNTNIS DER LIEBE CHRISTI ERWECKET WERDEN UND AM INNERLICHEN MENSCHEN SELIGLICH ZUNEHMEN MOEGEN / Gerhard, Johann – Berlin: Gustav Schlawitz, 1868 – 1mf – 9 – 0-8370-3254-7 – 1985-1254 – us A.T.L.A. [240]

ERKLAERUNG DER OFFENBARUNG JOHANNES, CAP. 1-12 / Beck, Johann Tobias; ed by Lindenmeyer, Julius – Guetersloh: C Bertelsmann, 1884 – 1mf – 9 – 0-8370-2227-4 – 1985-0227 – us A.T.L.A. [220]

ERKLAERUNG DER PROPHETEN MICHA UND JOEL : NEBST EINER EINLEITUNG IN DIE PROPHETIE / Beck, Johann Tobias; ed by Lindenmeyer, Julius – Guetersloh: C Bertelsmann, 1898 – 1mf – 9 – 0-8370-2228-2 – 1985-0228 – us A.T.L.A. [220]

ERKLAERUNG DER PROPHETEN NAHUM UND ZEPHANJA / Beck, Johann Tobias – Guetersloh: Bertelsmann, 1899. 1 fiche – 9 – us A.T.L.A. [240]

ERKLAERUNG DER ZWEI BRIEFE AN DIE THESSALONICHER UND DES BRIEFES AN DIE GALATER / Schaefer, Aloys – (Includes bibliographies) – Muenster i. W: Aschendorff, 1890 – 1mf – 9 – 0-8370-5065-0 – 1985-3065 – us A.T.L.A. [220]

ERKLAERUNG DES BRIEFES PAULI AN DIE GALATER / Philippi, Friedrich Adolph – Guetersloh: C. Bertelsmann, 1884. 1 fiche – 9 – us A.T.L.A. [240]

ERKLAERUNG UEBER DAS RECHT SICH ARBEIT ZU BESCHAFFEN / Beckerath, Ulrich von – Declaration about the rights of the unemployed to exhange, to supply themselves with job opportunities and to undertake all monetary and financial measures justified and required for this purpose. 1951 – 9 – 1.00f – at Libertarian Micro [335]

ERKLARUNG DER PROPHETEN NAHUM UND ZEPHANJA : NEBST EINEM PROPHETISCHEN TOTALBILD DER ZUKUNFT / Beck, Johann Tobias; ed by Gutscher, H & Lindenmeyer, Julius – Guetersloh: Bertelsmann, 1899 – 1mf – 9 – 0-8370-2229-0 – 1985-0229 – us A.T.L.A. [220]

ERKOW AP'E TSAP'E / Mankowni, N L – 1965 – 9 – $25.00 – us Scholars' Facs [490]

ERLAEUTERUNGEN ZU GOETHES WERKEN FUER SCHULGEBRAUCH UND SELBSTSTUDIUM ALS LITTERATURKUNDLICHES REPETITORIUM / Rothe, B – Breslau: G Sperber, 1897 – 1r – 1 – us U.W. Library [430]

ERLAEUTERUNGEN ZU LESSING'S HAMBURGISCHER DRAMATURGIE / Bischoff, Erich – Leipzig: H Beyer, [18–?] – 1r – 1 – us U.W. Library [430]

ERLAEUTERUNGEN ZU NIETZSCHES ZARATHUSTRA / Messer, August – Stuttgart: Strecker und Schroeder, 1922 – 1r – 1 – us U.W. Library [190]

ERLAEUTERUNGEN ZU WIELANDS OBERON *see* WIELANDS OBERON

ERLANGER NACHRICHTEN *see* ERLANGER TAGBLATT

ERLANGER REAL-ZEITUNG *see* CHRISTIAN-ERLANGISCHER ZEITUNGS-EXTRACT

ERLANGER TAGBLATT – (Title change: Erlanger Nachrichten, 2 Jan 1981) – Erlangen, West Germany. 1977- – ca 14r per yr – 1 – gw Mikrofilm [072]

ERLANGER ZEITUNG *see* CHRISTIAN-ERLANGISCHER ZEITUNGS-EXTRACT

ERLEBNISSE EINES SCHULDENBAUERS / Gotthelf, Jeremias; ed by Hunziker, Rudolf & Baehler, Eduard – (Includes bibliographical references) – Erlenbach, Zuerich: Eugen Rentsch Verlag, 1924 – 1 – us U.W. Library [830]

ERLEBTES, 1862-1901 / Meinecke, Friedrich – Leipzig: Koehler & Amelang, 1941. 224p – 1 – us U.W. Library [920]

DIE ERLEICHTERUNGEN DER SCHAMMAITEN UND DIE ERSCHWERUNGEN DER HILLELITEN : EIN BEITRAG ZUR ENTWICKLUNGSGESCHICHTE DER HALACHAH / Schwarz, Adolf – (Includes bibliographical references) – Wien: Isr-Theol Lehranstalt, 1893 – 1mf – 9 – 0-8370-5182-7 – 1985-3182 – us A.T.L.A. [270]

Erlenvein, A A *see* NARODNYE SKAZKI

Erler, Fritz *see*
- SOLL DEUTSCHLAND RUSTEN? DIE SPD ZUM WEHRBEITRAG
- WEHR- UND AUSSENPOLITIK IM GESPALTENEN DEUTSCHLAND. REFERAT AUF DEM SPD-PARTEITAG 1958 IN STUTTGART

Erler, Otto *see* DIE TRAGISCHEN PROBLEME DES STRUENSEE-STOFFES

ERLERNTE HILFLOSIGKEIT : EXPERIMENTELLE INDUKTION EMOTIONALER VERAENDERUNGEN UND KOGNITIVER INTERFERENZEN DURCH NICHT-KONTINGENTE LERNBEDINGUNGEN / Finzer, Michael – 1994 – 2mf – 9 – DM80.00 – 3-89349-855-9 – gw Hänsel [150]

ERM: EDUCATIONAL RESEARCH AND METHODS – (1976-. 5,6,9) – v. 1- 1968- – 1 – us UMI [370]

Ermakoff, V *see* ECRITURE MAYA

Erman, A *see*
- ARCHIV FUER WISSENSCHAFTLICHE KUNDE VON RUSSLAND
- ETHNOGRAFISCHE WAHRNEHMUNGEN UND ERFAHRUNGEN AN DEN KUESTEN DES BERINGS-MEERES
- HYMNEN AN DAS DIADEM DER PHARAONEN
- DIE MAERCHEN DES PAPYRUS WESTCAR
- ZAUBERSPRUECHE FUER MUTTER UND KIND

Erman, G *see*
- DEUTSCHLAND IM JAHRE 2000
- DIE MODERNE GESELLSCHAFT, IHRE GESELLIGKEIT UND IHRE MORAL

Erman, Wilhelm *see* BIBLIOGRAPHIE DER DEUTSCHEN UNIVERSITAETEN. SYSTEMATISCH GEORDNETES VERZEICHNIS DER BIS ENDE 1899 GEDRUCKTEN BUECHER UND AUFSAETZE UEBER DAS DEUTSCHE UNIVERSITAETSWESEN

Ermatinger, Charles Oakes *see* CANADIAN FRANCHISE AND ELECTION LAWS: A MANUAL FOR THE USE OF REVISING OFFICERS, MUNICIPAL OFFICERS, CANDIDATES, AGENTS, AND ELECTORS: WITH SUPPLEMENT CONTAINING THE AMENDING ACTS OF 1886

Ermatinger, Emil *see*
- DER GRUENE HEINRICH
- DIE WELTANSCHAUUNG DES JUNGEN WIELAND
- WIELAND UND DIE SCHWEIZ

Ermenc, Joseph J *see* ATOMIC BOMB SCIENTISTS

L'ERMITAGE – Revue mensuelle artistique et litteraire. Paris. avr 1890-juin 1906 – 1 – fr A.C.R.P.P. [073]

LAS ERMITAS DE CORDOBA / Aragon Fernandez, Antonio – Madrid: Razon y Fe, 1927 – 1 – sp Bibl Santa Ana [946]

ERMITAZH = HERMITAGE – (Cont: Vestnik Teatra) – Moscow. n1-15. may 1922-aug 1922 – 5mf – 9 – $50.00 – us Ross [790]

LES ERMITES DE LA BIGORRE / Laforgue, E – Lourdes, 1923 – Dfl6.00 – ne Slangenburg [240]

ERMITES ET RECLUS : ETUDES SUR D'ANCIENNES FORMES DE VIE RELIGIEUSE / Gougaud, L – Liguge, 1928 – 3mf – 8 – Dfl13.00 – ne Slangenburg [240]

ERMITTLUNG VON GRUNDLAGEN ZUR ULTRAFILTRATION / Driessen, Helmut – Manuskript 1977 – 1mf – 9 – DM48.00 – 3-89349-641-6 – gw Hänsel [621]

ERMLAENDISCHE ZEITUNG – Braunsberg, 1875-76, may 17-aug 30 1877, 1878-jun 30 1891, jan 1-jun 29 1892, 1893-jun 28 1907, 1908-09, jul 1 1910-jun 29 1913, 1914-20, 1927, may 1 1928-30, jul 1 1931-jun 30, aug 15-dec 30 1933, jan 11-jun 7 1934, jan 2-jun 30 1935, 1936, jul 1-dec 22 1937, jan 3-may 28 1939, mar 1-aug 20 1940 – 1 – Inquire at Mikrofilmarchiv for details – gw Misc Inst [947]

Ernest *see* MONSIEUR BOTTE OU LE NEGOCIANT ANGLAIS

ERNEST HEMINGWAY : CATALOG OF THE MANUSCRIPTS, CORRESPONDENCE AND OTHER MATERIAL IN THE JOHN F. KENNEDY LIBRARY / John F. Kennedy Library. Boston – 1982. 11,140 cards on 2 reels – 1 – $125.00 export $150.00 – 0-8161-1402-1 – uk Hall [420]

ERNEST HEMINGWAY: CATALOG OF THE MANUSCRIPTS, CORRESPONDENCE AND OTHER MATERIAL.. / John F. Kennedy Library. Boston – 1982.-11,140 cards 2 reels.-ISBN: 0-8161-1402-1 – 1 – $140.00 – uk Hall [420]

ERNEST HEMINGWAY'S "NOW I LAY ME" UND "SOLDIER'S HOME" : ANALYSE UND DIDAKTISCHE UMSETZUNG / Kostrzewa, Frank – 1993 – 1mf – 9 – DM75.00 – 3-89349-734-X – gw Hänsel [420]

ERNEST RENAN / Barry, William Francis – London: Hodder and Stoughton, 1905. (Literary lives) – 1mf – us A.T.L.A. [240]

Ernesti, Heinrich Friedrich Theodor Ludwig *see* DIE ETHIK DES APOSTELS PAULUS IN IHREN GRUNDZUEGEN

ERNESTO PINTO. EL SANTO DEL SIGLO / Bayle, Constantino – Madrid: Razon y Fe, 1941 – sp Bibl Santa Ana [240]

ERNEUERUNG DER HEILIGEN MISSION IN ZWEI ABTHEILUNGEN : VON DEN ZWEI FAHNEN, DIE FAHNE CHRISTI UND DIE DES LUZIFER, DIE MERKMALE DER KIRCHE REFLECTIRT IM CHARAKTER IHRER KINDER / Weninger, Francis Xavier – Cincinnati: [s.n.], 1885 – 2mf – 9 – 0-8370-6790-1 – 1986-0790 – us A.T.L.A. [240]

DIE ERNEUERUNG DES PAULINISCHEN CHRISTENTUMS DURCH LUTHER DEKANATSREDE GEHALTEN AM 31. OKTOBER 1902 IN WIEN / Feine, Paul – Leipzig: J C Hinrichs, 1903 – 1mf – 9 – 0-8370-5991-7 – 1985-3991 – us A.T.L.A. [220]

Ernle, Rowland Edmund Prothero *see* THE PSALMS IN HUMAN LIFE

Ernouf, Alfred Auguste *see* HISTOIRE DE TROIS OUVRIERS FRANCAIS: RICHARD LENOIR, ABRAHAM LOUIS BREGUET, MICHEL BREZIN

Ernshtedt, P V *see*
- KOPTSKIE TEKSTY GOSUDARSTVENNOGO ERMITAZHA
- KOPTSKIE TEKSTY GOSUDARSTVENNOGO MUZEIA IZOBRAZITEL'NYKH ISKUSSTV IMENI A.S. PUSHKINA

ERNST DER BEKENNER, HERZOG VON BRAUNSCHWEIG UND LUENEBURG / Wrede, Adolf – Halle: Verein fuer Reformationsgeschichte, 1888. ([Schriften des Vereins fuer Reformationsgeschichte; Bd. 25]) – 1mf – us A.T.L.A. [944]

ERNST FRIES (1801-1833) : STUDIEN ZU SEINEN LANDSCHAFTSZEICHNUNGEN / Bott, Elisabeth – Heidelberg, 1978 – 3mf – 9 – DM76.00 – 3-89349-761-7 – gw Hänsel [740]

ERNST HARDT UND DIE NEUROMANTIK : EIN MAHNRUF AN DIE GEGENWART / Schumann, Harry – Loetzen: P Kuehnel, 1913 – 1r – 1 – us U.W. Library [430]

ERNST HERZOG – Hrsg. von Karl Bartsch. Wien: W. Braunmueller, 1869. 172+308p.1 reel. 1297 – 1 – us U.W. Library [430]

Ernst, Johann *see*
- CYPRIAN UND DAS PAPSTTUM
- DIE KETZERTAUFANGELEGENHEIT IN DER ALTCHRISTLICHEN KIRCHE NACH CYPRIAN

ERNST JUENGER : EIN LEBEN IM UMBRUCH DER ZEIT / Mueller, Wulf Dieter – Berlin: Junker und Duennhaupt, 1934 – 1r – 1 – us U.W. Library [920]

ERNST JUENGER : MENSCH UND WERK / Becher, Hubert – (Includes bibliographical references) – Warendorf, Westfalen: J Schnell, 1949 – 1r – 1 – us U.W. Library [430]

ERNST JUENGER : DIE WANDLUNG EINES DEUTSCHEN DICHTERS UND PATRIOTEN / Paetel, Karl Otto – (Includes bibliographical references) – New York: F Krause, 1946 – 1r – 1 – us U.W. Library [430]

ERNST JUENGER UND DAS SCHICKSAL DES MENSCHEN / Nebel, Gerhard – Wuppertal: Marees-Verlag, 1948 – 1r – 1 – us U.W. Library [430]

ERNST KOCHS "PRINZ ROSA-STRAMIN" : EIN BEITRAG ZUR HESSISCHEN LITERATURGESCHICHTE / Froeb, Hermann – (Includes bibliographical references (4th prelim. leaf)) – Marburg a.L.: N G Elwert, 1925 – 1r – 1 – us U.W. Library [430]

ERNST MORITZ ARNDT : EIN LEBENSBILD / Muesebeck, Ernst – (Includes bibliographical references) – Gotha: F A Perthes, 1914- – 1r – 1 – us U.W. Library [943]

ERNST MORITZ ARNDT : SEIN POLITISCHES VERMAECHTNIS AN DIE DEUTSCHE GEGENWART; KERNSTELLEN AUS SEINEN SCHRIFTEN UND BRIEFEN / Arndt, Ernst Moritz; ed by Petersen, Carl & Ruth, Paul Hermann – Breslau: Hirt, [1934] – 1r – 1 – us U.W. Library [943]

ERNST MORITZ ARNDT : DER WEG EINES DEUTSCHEN MANNES / Heine, Gerhard – Leipzig: L Klotz, c1939 – 1r – 1 – us U.W. Library [943]

ERNST MORITZ ARNDT IN SCHWEDEN : NEUE BEITRAEGE ZUM VERSTAENDNIS SEINES LEBENS UND DICHTENS / Guelzow, Erich – Greifswald: L Bamberg, 1920 – 1r – 1 – us U.W. Library [943]

ERNST MORITZ ARNDTS BRIEFE AN EINE FREUNDIN / Arndt, Ernst Moritz; ed by Guelzow, Erich – (Letters to Charlotte von Kathen) – Stuttgart: J G Cotta, 1928 – 1r – 1 – us U.W. Library [920]

ERNST MORITZ ARNDTS FRAGMENTE UEBER MENSCHENBILDUNG IN IHRER PAEDAGOGISCHEN BEDEUTUNG / Koelle, Conrad – Langensalza: H Beyer, 1916 – 1r – 1 – us U.W. Library [943]

ERNST MORITZ ARNDT'S SAEMMTLICHE WERKE / Arndt, Ernst Moritz – Leipzig: K R Vogelsberg, 1892 – 1r – 1 – us U.W. Library [943]

Ernst, Otto *see*
- AUF SPUREN DES JUNGEN GOETHE
- NIETZSCHE DER FALSCHE PROPHET

Ernst, Paul *see* LEO TOLSTOI UND DER SLAVISCHE ROMAN

ERNST PENZOLDT UND DAS THEATER / Rahn, Konstanze – Frankfurt a.M., 1976 – 2mf – 9 – DM62.00 – 3-89349-647-5 – gw Hänsel [790]

[ERNST RUDIGER STARHEMBERG PAMPHLET COLLECTION] – 1934 – 1 – CSUXANQ2328-B – us Hoover Inst Photo [920]

ERNST SIMMELS PSYCHOANALYTISCHE KLINIK "SANATORIUM SCHLOß TEGEL GMBH" (1927-1983) : BEITRAG ZUR WISSENSCHAFTSGESCHICHTE EINER PSYCHOANALYTISCHEN PSYCHOSOMATIK / Schultz-Venrath, Ulrich – 1995 – 3mf – 9 – DM98.00 – 3-8267-2081-4 – gw Hänsel [616]

Ernst, Stacey L *see* PREDICTION OF INJURY IN HIGH SCHOOL VOLLEYBALL PLAYERS WITH PERCEIVED LEADERSHIP BEHAVIOR OF THE COACH

ERNST THEODOR AMADEUS HOFFMANN / Kroll, Erwin – (Includes bibliographical references) – Leipzig; Breitkopf & Haertel, 1923 – 1r – 1 – us U.W. Library [430]

ERNST THEODOR AMADEUS HOFFMANN : LEBENSSCHICKSAL EINES SELTSAMEN MANNES / Krieger, Erhard – (Includes bibliographical references) – Kitzingen/Main: Holzner-Verlag [1952] – 1 – us U.W. Library [430]

ERNST TOLLER : EINE STUDIE / Signer, Paul – Berlin: Verlag Landsberg, 1924 – 1r – 1 – us U.W. Library [430]

Ernst, Ulrich *see* GESCHICHTE DES ZUERCHERISCHEN SCHULWESENS

ERNST VON WILDENBRUCH : ERNSTES UND HEITERES AUS SEINEM LEBEN / Duncker, Dora – Berlin: H Paetel, 1909 – 1r – 1 – us U.W. Library [430]

ERNST VON WILDENBRUCH / Litzmann, Berthold – (Includes bibliographical references and index) – Berlin: G Grote. 2v. 1913-16 – 1 – us U.W. Library [430]

ERNST VON WILDENBRUCHS DRAMATISCHE TECHNIK / Mannes, Ulrich – (Includes bibliographical references) – Jena: [Universitaet Jena], 1934 – 1r – 1 – us U.W. Library [430]

ERNST ZAHN : DAS WERK UND DER DICHTER / Spiero, Heinrich – (Includes bibliographical references) – Stuttgart: Deutsche Verlags-Anstalt, 1927 – 1r – 1 – us U.W. Library [430]

ERNST ZAHNS GESAMMELTE WERKE : ERSTE SERIE / Zahn, Ernst – Stuttgart: Deutsche Verlags-Anstalt, [192-?] – 2r – 1 – us U.W. Library [943]

ERNSTE BLICKE IN DEN WAHN DER MODERNEN KRITIK DES ALTEN TESTAMENTES: NEUE FOLGE / Zahn, Adolph – Guetersloh: C. Bertelsmann, 1894. 1 fiche – 9 – us A.T.L.A. [240]

ERNSTELIJCK KLAGE, LEER VNDE ONDERWYSINGHE, OUER DEN NYDIGHEN BLOETDORSTIGHEN AARDT BELIALS YEMANDEN OM T'GELOOF OF DIE WETH HAERDER CONSCIENTIEN TE MOGEN VERVOLGEN ODER TE DOODEN 1544 / Joris, David – BME-364 1 – 9 – ne IDC [240]

ERNSTIGE OVERDENKINGEN OVER DE GEWAANDEN VOORUITGANG DER ISRAELIETEN / Pinto, J de A – 's-Gravenhage. 1851. BJ-262-46 1 – 9 – ne IDC [360]

Ernsting, Arthur Conrad *see* NUCLEUS TOTIUS MEDICINAE QUINQUE PARTITUS (AEL, ABT 3;11)

UN EROE DELL'ALA RIVOLUZIONARIA ITALIANA, GIORDANO VIEZZOLI – Paris, 1936? Fiche W 860. (Blodgett Collection of Spanish Civil War Pamphlets) – 9 – us H.U. College Libr [946]

EROES VAR – 1969-90 (complete) – 2r – 1 – ATLA S0617 – us A.T.L.A. [073]

Erokhin, N V *see* CHEREZ KOOPERATSIIU K ELEKTRIFIKATSII

Erondell, Peter *see* THE FRENCH GARDEN

EROS AND PSYCHE : A POEM IN TWELVE MEASURES / Bridges, Robert Seymour – London: George Bell, 1885 – 1 roll – 1 – 1-55879-779-3 – uk Libr Preservation [810]

EROSION OF THE RULE OF LAW IN ASIA : 1987 BANGKOK SEMINAR – 1988 – sz I.C.J. [320]

EROTEMATA MUSICAE PRACTICAE, EXPROBATISSIMIS QUIBUSQUE HUIUS DIUINAE ET DULCISSIMAE ARTIS SCRIPTORIBUS / Lossius, L – P 375. 1570 – 9 – ne IDC [780]

L'EROTISME AU CINEMA: PIN-UP / Duvillars, Pierre – Paris: Edition du xxe siecle, 1951. 77p. 1 fiche. (Les Femmes Collection) – 9 – 6.00 – fr Bibl Nationale [790]

Errandonea, Ignacio *see*
- DONOSO CORTES, JUAN. OBRAS COMPLETAS RECOPILADAS POR...2 VOL. MADRID, 1946
- ESTUDIOS CLASICOS. MORFOLOGIA GRIEGA. SINTAXIS GRIEGA DEL P. SANTIAGO MORILLOS J.
- NUEVO SALTERIO LATINO-ESPANOL. VERSION LATINA PROMULGADA POR S.S. PIO 12...
- POESIA CRISTIANA. ANTOLOGIA DE POESIA ROMANO-CRISTIANA Y LATINO MEDIEVAL (SIGLOS 4-15) TOLEDO, 1946
- SANTOS COCO, FRANCISCO. LA PRONUNCIACION DEL LATIN. BADAJOZ, 1929
- VIDA Y OBRAS DE DON JUAN PABLO FORNER Y SEGARRA, MADRID, 1944

Errard, Jean *see* LA FORTIFICATION DEMONSTREE ET REDUITE EN ART.

ERRATA DE L'ESSAI SUR LA MUSIQUE ANCIENNE ET MODERNE (DE J.B. DE LABORDE), OU LETTRE A L'AUTEUR DE CET ESSAI, PAR MADAME / Latour de Franqueville – Paris, 1780 – 2mf – 9 – us Sibley [780]

ERRATA DU DICTIONNAIRE DE L'ACADEMIE FRANCAISE / Pautex, B – 2E ED. 1862 – 9 – fr I.C.S. [440]

Errazuriz, Crescente *see* PEDRO DE VALDIVIA

DIE ERRETTUNG DES RUHRGEBIETS (1918-1920) – Darstellungen aus den nachkriegskampfen deutscher truppen und freikorps. 9. Bd. Berlin 1943 – 1 – DM40.00 – gw Mikro Press [943]

ERREURS OU SOPHISMES? / [Cremers, E] – La Haye, 1867 – 1mf – 1 – ILM-2873/1 – ne IDC [327]

ERREURS SUR LA MUSIQUE DANS L'ENCYCLOPEDIE / Rameau, Jean-Phillippe – Paris. 1755. BP-746 1 – 9 – ne IDC [780]

ERREURS SYSTEMATIQUES DE RECENSEMENT EN MILIEU RURAL TRADITIONNEL / Baillon, D – (Africa series). 1970 – 9 – fr Hachette [310]

ERRICHTUNG UND AUFHEBUNG LETZTWILLIGER VERFUEGUNGEN... / Dingel, F – Berlin, 1904 – 1mf – 1 – ILM-3110/1 – ne IDC [327]

ERROMANGA : THE MARTYR ISLE / Robertson, H A; ed by Fraser, John – New York: A C Armstrong; London: Hodder and Stoughton, 1902 – 2mf – 9 – 0-8370-6351-5 – 1986-0351 – us A.T.L.A. [240]

THE ERROR OF MODERN MISSOURI : ITS INCEPTION, DEVELOPMENT, AND REFUTATION / Stellhorn, F W; ed by Schodde, George – Columbus, Ohio: Lutheran Book Concern, 1897 – 2mf – us A.T.L.A. [240]

ERRORES ACTUALES QUE SE HALLAN EXTENDIDOS EN ESPANA CAUSANDO GRAVISIMOS ESTRAGOS EN EL PUEBLO CATOLICO... / Marquez, Gabino – Madrid: Razon y Fe, 1935 – 1 – sp Bibl Santa Ana [240]

LOS ERRORES DE NUESTRO TIEMPO / Donoso Cortes, Juan Francisco – Madrid: Feria Nacional del Libro, 1955 – sp Bibl Santa Ana [946]

ERRORES MODERNOS, EXPUESTOS Y REFUTADOS POR...CON UN APENDICE SOBRE LA NUEVA BULA DE LA SANTA CRUZADA / Marquez, Gabino – Jerez de la Frontera: Tipolitografia de Salido Hermanos, 1917 – 1 – sp Bibl Santa Ana [946]

ERRORES Y VICIOS DE NUESTRA DEMOCRACIA / Repetto, Nicolas – Buenos Aires: La Vanguardia, 1st ed 1953 – 1 – CSUXADJ7607-B – us Hoover Inst Photo [320]

ERRORS IN CRIMINAL PROCEEDINGS IN ALL STATES AND TERRITORIES AND FEDERAL COURTS WHERE JUDGMENTS HAVE BEEN AFFIRMED. / Walker, William Slee – Cincinnati, Anderson, 1916. 550p. LL-1551 – 1 – us L of C Photodup [340]

THE ERRORS OF HOPKINSIANISM / Bangs, Nathan – 1815 – 9 – us A.T.L.A. [240]

THE ERRORS OF THE PLYMOUTH BRETHREN: BEING THE SUBSTANCE OF THREE SERMONS PREACHED IN ST GEORGE'S CHURCH, MONTREAL / Carmichael, James – Montreal: Montreal Print. and Pub. Co., 1869. 00500. (Pre-1900 Canadiana) – 9 – cn C.I.H.M. [240]

DER ERSATZ DER RELIGION DURCH VOLLKOMMENERES UND DIE ABSTREIFUNG ALLES ASIATISMUS / Duehring, Eugen – Leipzig: Theod. Thomas, 1906. 1 fiche – 9 – us A.T.L.A. [240]

Ersch, J S *see*
- ALLGEMEINE ENCYCLOPAEDIE DER WISSENSCHAFTEN UND KUENSTE
- ALLGEMEINE ENCYCLOPAEDIE DER WISSENSCHAFTEN UND KUENSTE (AEL, ABT 1; 33)
- ALLGEMEINE LITERATUR-ZEITUNG

ERSHIWU SHI RENMING SUOYIN – Biographical Index to the Twenty-Five Histories. Comp. by Publication Committee of the Twenty-Five Histories. 6 fiches. F J22 – 9 – 4.00f – cc Microforms [950]

Ershov, A *see* KOMSOMOL I KOOPERATSIIA

ERSHTE SHRIT – (In Yiddish) – Lwow, PL. no1 Apr 1932 – 1r – 1 – $25.00 – cn Can Microfilming [072]

ERSITZUNG BEWEGLICHER SACHEN IM INTERNATIONALEN PRIVATRECHT / Ahrendts, C – Borna-Leipzig, 1911 – 2mf – 9 – ILM-414/1 – ne IDC [340]

ERSKINE CHURCH ECHOES – Hamilton, Ont.: The Church, [188- or 189–189- or 19–] – 9 – cn C.I.H.M. [240]

Erskine, J *see* MR. WESLEY'S PRINCIPLES DETECTED

Erskine, James St. Clair *see* REMARKS ON THE REPORT OF THE FACULTY OF ADVOCATES, APPOINTED TO CONSIDER THE PROVISIONS OF THE BILL FOR THE BETTER REGULATING OF THE PROCESS OF THE COURTS OF LAW IN SCOTLAND

ERSKINE OF LINLATHEN / Henderson, Henry F – 1899 – 9 – us A.T.L.A. [240]

Erskine, T *see* A VIEW OF THE CAUSES AND CONSEQUENCES OF THE PRESENT WAR WITH FRANCE

Erskine, Thomas *see*
- THE DOCTRINE OF ELECTION
- REMARKS ON THE INTERNAL EVIDENCE FOR THE TRUTH OF REVEALED RELIGION
- THE SUPERNATURAL GIFTS OF THE SPIRIT

THE ERSKINES / MacEwen, Alexander R – Edinburgh: Oliphant, Anderson & Ferrier, 1900. (Famous Scots series) – 1mf – us A.T.L.A. [240]

DAS ERSTE BUCH DER BIBEL: NACH SEINER INNEREN EINHEIT UND ECHTHEIT / Naumann, O – Guetersloh: C. Bertelsmann, 1890. 1 fiche – 9 – us A.T.L.A. [240]

DAS ERSTE BUCH DER TORA : GENESIS UEBERSETZT UND ERKLAERT / Jacob, B – Berlin, 1934 – Dfl154.00 – ne Slangenburg [220]

DER ERSTE CLEMENSBRIEF / Knopf, Rudolf – Leipzig: J.C. Hinrichs, 1899. (Texte und Untersuchungen zur Geschichte der altchristlichen Litratur; der ganzen Reihe Bd. 20, Heft 1. n.F., 5. Bd., Heft 1) – 1mf – us A.T.L.A. [240]

DER ERSTE CLEMENSBRIEF IN ALTKOPTISCHER UEBERSETZUNG (T.U.U. 3-32/1) / Schmidt, Carl – Leipzig, 1908 – 3mf – 9 – ne Slangenburg [240]

DER ERSTE CLEMENSBRIEF (T.U.U. 2-20/1) / Knopf, R – Leipzig, 1899 – 3mf – 9 – ne Slangenburg [240]

ERSTE INTERNATIONALE FILM-ZEITUNG : PARLAMENTSAUSGABE – Berlin. 1909-jul 3, 1915 (incomplete). aug 17, 1918-dec 11, 1920 – 7,5r – 1 – gw Mikrofilm [790]

ERSTE INTERNATIONALE FILM-ZEITUNG : PARLAMENTSAUSGABE – (Cont by: Die Film-Welt) – Berlin, 1912-20 – 1 – Dist. gw Mikrofilm – gw Mikrofilm [790]

ERSTE INTERNATIONALE KINEMATOGRAPHEN-ZEITUNG – Hamburg. mar 25, 1908 – 1 – gw Mikrofilm [790]

DER ERSTE KONGRESS DER KOMMUNISTISCHEN UND REVOLUTIONAEREN ORGANISATIONEN DES FERNEN OSTENS / Congress of the Toilers of the Far East. 1. Moscow and Leningrad. 1922 – Moscow and Hamburg, 1922 – 1 – $35.00r – us Hoover Inst Photo [335]

ERSTE LIEBE : ROMAN AUS DER JUGENDZEIT / Wehner, Josef Magnus – Hamburg: Hanseatische Verlagsanstalt, c1941 – 1r – 1 – us U.W. Library [830]

DER ERSTE PETRUSBRIEF : SEINE ENTSTEHUNG UND STELLUNG IN DER GESCHICHTE DES URCHRISTENTUMS / Voelter, Daniel – (Includes bibliographical references) – Strassburg: J H Ed Heitz, 1906 – 1mf – 9 – 0-8370-9333-3 – 1986-3333 – us A.T.L.A. [220]

DIE ERSTE SCHLACHT, VOM WERDEN UND VON DEN ERSTEN KAEMPFEN DES BATAILLONS EDGAR ANDRE / Uhse, Bodo – 2Auf. Strasbourg, 1938. Fiche W1235. (Blodgett Collection of Spanish Civil War Pamphlets) – 9 – us H.U. College Libr [946]

DIE ERSTE UND ZWEITE FASSUNG VON GOETHES "WANDERJAHREN" / Bimler, Kurt – (Includes bibliographical references) – Beuthen, O.-S.: M Immerwahr, 1907 – 1r – 1 – us U.W. Library [430]

DER ERSTE UND ZWEITE PETRUSBRIEF UND DER JUDASBRIEF / Wohlenberg, Gustav – 1. u 2. Aufl. Leipzig: A Deichert, 1915, c1914 – 1mf – 9 – 0-8370-9438-0 – 1986-3438 – us A.T.L.A. [220]

ERSTE UNTERSUCHUNGEN UEBER BIODISTRIBUTION UND THERAPEUTISCHE EFFEKTE NEUARTIGER ALBUMIN-CYTOSTATIKA-KONJUGATE : EINE TIEREXPERIMENTELLE STUDIE / Steinmann, Alexander – 1993 – 1mf – 9 – DM60.00 – 3-89349-816-8 – gw Hänsel [636]

DIE ERSTEN AUSGABEN VON GRIMMELSHAUSENS SIMPLICISSIMUS : EINE KRITISCHE UNTERSUCHUNG / Borcherdt, Hans Heinrich – (Includes bibliographical references) – Muenchen: H Stobbe, 1921 – 1r – 1 – us U.W. Library [430]

DIE ERSTEN BNOVELLEN OTTO LUDWIGS UND IHR VERHAELTNIS ZU LUDWIG TIECK / Greiner, Wilhelm – (Includes bibliographical references) – Poessneck i.Th.: B Feigenspan, 1903 – 1r – 1 – us U.W. Library [430]

DIE ERSTEN MAKAMEN AUS DEM TACHKEMONI ODER DIVAN DES CHARISI / Kaempf, Saul Isaac – Berlin. 1845. BJ-421-62 1 – 9 – ne IDC [470]

DIE ERSTEN POETISCHEN VERSUCHE HAMERLINGS : ZUR GESCHICHTE SEINES ZWETTLER AUFENTHALTS / Rabenlechner, Michael Maria – Hamburg: Verlagsanstalt und Druckerei A.-G. (vormals J F Richter), 1896 – 1r – 1 – us U.W. Library [430]

ERSTES ERLEBNIS : VIER GESCHICHTEN AUS KINDERLAND / Zweig, Stefan – Leipzig: Insel-Verlag, 1919 – 1r – 1 – us U.W. Library [830]

ERSTES TRIO, IN F DUR, PIANOFORTE, VIOLINE UND VIOLONCELLE. NEUE REV AUSG. / Bargiel, Woldemar – Leipzig: F.E.C. Leuckart, between 1870-1873 – 1 – us Sibley [780]

DIE ERSTLINGSNOVELLEN HEINRICH VON KLEIST / Davidts, Hermann – 1995 – 1mf – 9 – DM48.00 – 3-8267-3146-8 – gw Hänsel [430]

Erter, I *see* GESAMMELTE SCHRIFTEN

ERTUGRUL – Bursa. Mueduer-i Mes'ul: Ismail Hakki, Ahmed Refik; Sermuharriri: Hakki Baha, Ziya Sakir. Nos. 461 (27 Subat 1919), 463-464, 551 (6 Mayis 1920) – 9 – $20.00 – us MEDOC [956]

ERUDICION EVANGELICA...SANTA ORACION / Jimenez, Antonio – 1627 – 9 – 1.50f – sp Bibl Santa Ana [240]

LA ERUDICION EXTREMENA Y LA ACADEMIA DE LA HISTORIA / Rodriguez Monino, Antonio – Badajoz, 1946 – 1 – sp Bibl Santa Ana [946]

LOS ERUDITOS A LA VIOLETA Y SUPLEMENTO / Cadalso Vazquez, Jose – 1781 – 1mf – 9 – Pta1,000.00 – 84-7848-138-9 – sp Pentalfa [946]

Erusalimskii, Arkadii Samsonovich *see* GERMANIIA, ANTANTAI SSSR

ERVING 1844-1906 – (Mf 1: Index: B,M,D 1844-1906. Mf 2: Births 1844-80. Mf 3: Births 1881-1905. Mf 4: Marriages 1844-95. Mf 5: Marriages 1896-1906; Deaths 1845-67. Mf 6: Deaths 1868-1906) – (mf ed 1983) – 6mf – 9 – 0-931248-54-X – us Holbrook [920]

DAS ERWACHEN DES DEUTSCHEN NATIONALBEWUSSTSEINS IN DER PREUSSISCHEN JUDENHEIT (VON MOSES MENDELSSOHN BIS ZUM BEGINN DER REAKTION : EIN GEISTESGESCHICHTLICHER BEITRAG ZUR EMANZIPATIONSGESCHICHTE DER DEUTSCHEN JUDEN / Offenburg, Benno – 1996 – 1mf – 9 – DM48.00 – 3-8267-3189-1 – gw Hänsel [270]

DIE ERWAEHLUNG ISRAELS IN DER WUESTE / Bach, Robert – 1951 – 1 – us A.T.L.A. [240]

DIE ERWAEHLUNG ISRAELS NACH DER HEILSVERKUENDIGUNG DES APOSTELS PAULUS / Dalmer, Johannes – Guetersloh: C. Bertelsmann, 1894. 1 fiche – 9 – us A.T.L.A. [240]

...ERWEITERTE UND VERBESSERTE ORGEL-PROBE. / Werckmeister, A – 1698 – 2 – us Sibley [780]

ERWEITERTE UND VERBESSERTE ORGELPROBE / Werckmeister, A – P 512 2. 1698 – 8 – ne IDC [780]

ERWEITERUNGEN UND AENDERUNGEN IM VIERTEN EVANGELIUM / Wellhausen, Julius – (Includes bibliographical references) – Berlin: Georg Reimer, 1907 – 1mf – 9 – 0-8370-5770-1 – 1985-3770 – us A.T.L.A. [220]

ERWERB UND VERLUST DER STAATSANGEHOERIGKEIT IN HISPANO-AMERIKA / Glaeser, K – Leipzig, 1930 – 2mf – 1 – ILM-3214/1 – ne IDC [327]

ERWIN FIRST BAPTIST CHURCH (FORMERLY INDIAN CREEK). ERWIN, TENNESSEE : CHURCH RECORDS – 1822-1970 – 1 – 93.42 – us Baptist [240]

Erwin, Frank Alexander *see* A SUMMARY OF TORTS

Erwin, Milo *see* HISTORY OF WILLIAMSON COUNTY, ILLINOIS

Erwin, Theodor *see* TEMAS ALEMAES

Erxleben, Johann Christian Polykarp *see*
- ANFANGGRUNDE DER NATURLEHRE
- ANFANGSGRUENDE DER CHEMIE

ERYNGIORUM NEC NON GENERIS NOVI ASCLEPIDEAE HISTORIA / Delaroche, F – Parisiis. 1808. B-5890 2 – 8 – ne IDC [580]

ERYSIMORUM QUORUNDAM NOVORUM DIAGNOSES SIMULQUE ERYSIMI MURALIS DESCRIPTIONEM / Gay, J E – Parisiis. 1842. B-5550 2 – 8 – ne IDC [580]

THE ERYSIPHACEA-A MONOGRAPH / Salmon, E S A – 1900 – 9 – uk Microform Academic [580]

ERYTHEA : A JOURNAL OF BOTANY, WEST AMERICAN AND GENERAL – Berkeley, 1893-1899. v1-7 – 27mf – 9 – 1359/2 – ne IDC [580]

DER ERYTHROIDE ANIONENAUSTAUSCHER AE1 : STRUKTUELLE UNTERSUCHUNGEN DURCH MUTAGENESE DER MURINEN AEI-CDNA UND BESTIMMUNG DER KOPIENZAHL DER HUMANEN AE1-MRNA WAEHREND DER ERYTHROIDEN DIFFERENZIERUNG / Koenig,

Joerg Udo – 1995 – 2mf – 9 – DM80.00 – 3-8267-2094-6 – gw Hänsel [575]

ERZAEHLENDE SCHRIFTEN / Holtei, Karl von – Breslau, 1861-68. 37 v. Film Mas C 473 – 1 – us H.U. Library [830]

ERZAEHLUNGEN / Kleist, Heinrich von – Leipzig: Bibliographisches Institut, [1905?] – 1 – us U.W. Library [830]

ERZAEHLUNGEN / Stifter, Adalbert – Osnabrueck: Bernhard Wehberg, 1903 – 1 – us U.W. Library [830]

DIE ERZAEHLUNGEN EDUARD VON KEYSERLINGS : EIN BEITRAG ZUR DEUTSCHEN LITERATURGESCHICHTE / Knoop, Kaete – (Includes bibliographical references (3rd-4th prelim. leaves)) – Marburg a.L.: N G Elwert, 1929 – 1r – 1 – us U.W. Library [430]

ERZAEHLUNGEN UND NOVELLEN / Hebbel, Friedrich – Pesth: G Heckenast, 1855 – 1r – 1 – us U.W. Library [820]

ERZAEHLUNGSEINGAENGE IN DER DEUTSCHEN LITERATUR / Leib, Fritz – Gießen, 1913 – 2mf – 9 – DM62.00 – 3-8267-3109-3 – gw Hänsel [430]

DIE ERZAEHLUNGSTECHNIK VIKTOR SCHEFFELS / Grebe, Walter – (Includes bibliographical references) – Barmen-Wichlingh: Montanus & Ehrenstein, 1919 – 1r – 1 – us U.W. Library [430]

DER ERZBETER : UND DREI ANDERE LEGENDEN DER BOSHEIT / Kremer, Hannes – 5. Aufl. Muenchen: F Eher, 1943 – 1r – 1 – us U.W. Library [830]

ERZBISCHOF ALBRECHT 2. VON MAGDEBURG / Schmidt, Hermann – 1880 – 1mf – us A.T.L.A. [240]

ERZBISCHOF BRUNO VON TRIER. EIN BEITRAG ZUR GESCHICHTE DER GEISTIGEN STROEMUNGEN IM INVESTITURSTREIT / Schlechte, Horst – Leipzig, 1934 – 9 – DM48.00 – 3-89349-274-7 – gw Hänsel [240]

DER ERZBISCHOF VON KOELN JOHANNES CARDINAL VON GEISSEL UND SEINE ZEIT / Baudri – Koeln, 1881 – 2mf – 9 – DM62.00 – 3-89349-359-X – gw Hänsel [240]

DER ERZIEHERISCHE GEHALT IN J J BREITINGERS "CRITISCHER DICHTKUNST" / Braeker, Jakob – (Includes bibliographical references) – St Gallen: H Tschudy, 1950 – 1 – us U.W. Library [430]

DIE ERZIEHUNG DES MENSCHENGESCHLECHTS / Lessing, Gotthold Ephraim – 1780 – 8 – ne IDC [190]

DIE ERZIEHUNG ZUR EHE, EINE SATIRE / Hartleben, Otto Erich – Berlin: S. Fischer, 1893. 125p – 1 – us U.W. Library [830]

ERZIEHUNGS-BLATTER FUR SCHULE UND HAUS : ORGAN DES DEUTSCH-AMERIKANISCHEN LEHRERBUNDES – (Filmed with: Amerikanische Schulzeitung) – Milwaukee: Hailmann and Dorflinger, 1875-1899. [ns v2 n9-v9 n12 jun 1875-sep 1882] – us Res Libr [071]

DER ERZKETZER : EIN ROMAN VOM LEIDEN DES WAHRHAFTIGEN / Wolzogen, Ernst von – 2. Aufl. Berlin: F Fontane. 2v. 1910 – 1 – us U.W. Library [830]

ERZURUM – 1304H [1887], def'a 10 – $45.00 – us MEDOC [956]

ERZURUM – 1315H/1313M [1897], def' a 13 – 9 – $190.00 – us MEDOC [956]

ES ESPANA OTRA CHINA? / Linebarger, Paul Myron – Paris, 1931. Fiche W999. (Blodgett Collection of Spanish Civil War Pamphlets) – 9 – us H.U. College Libr [946]

ES KLINGT WIE EINE SAGE : ERZAEHLUNGEN AUS ALTEN CHRONIKEN / Storm, Theodor; ed by Langenbucher, Hellmuth – Bayreuth: Der Gauverlag, 1944 – 1r – 1 – us U.W. Library [390]

ES MUSS TAG WERDEN – Muenchen, DE. Dec 1848-Jan 1849 – 1r – 1 – gw Mikrofilm [072]

ES WAR : ROMAN / Sudermann, Hermann – 33. Aufl. Stuttgart: J G Cotta, 1902 – 1r – 1 – us U.W. Library [830]

ES WAR EINMAL : MODERN FAIRY TALES FOR BEGINNERS IN GERMAN / Baumbach, Rudolf – New York: American Book Co., c1893 – 1 – us U.W. Library [390]

ES WERDE LICHT : POESIEN / Jacoby, Leopold – 4. Aufl. Muenchen: M Ernst, 1893 – 1r – 1 – us U.W. Library [810]

ESA NOCHE DE PERON / Boizard, Ricardo – [Buenos Aires, Editorial De-Du], 3rd ed 1955 – 1 – CSUXADJ1908-B – us Hoover Inst Photo [972]

ESA NOCHE DE PERON / Boizard, Ricardo – Buenos Aires: H. del Valle, 4th ed 1955 – 1 – CSUXADJ3386-B – us Hoover Inst Photo [972]

Es'ad *see* DIVAN

Esad *see* BANET SUAD SERHI

Es'ad Pasa *see* DIVANCE

ESANZO, CHANTS POUR MON PAYS : POEMES / Bolamba, Antoine Roger – Paris: Presence africaine, [1955] – 1 – us Res Libr [960]

ES'AR / Memduh, Mehmed – Istanbul, 1332 – 4mf – 9 – $24.00 – us MEDOC [949]

Esarey, Logar *see* THE PIONEERS OF MORGAN COUNTY

ES'AR-I NEDIM – Istanbul, 1920 – 1mf – 9 – $6.00 – us MEDOC [949]

ESATIZ-I ELHAN / Yekta, Rauf – Istanbul: Mahmud Bey Matbaasi; Evkaf Islamiye, 1318-1341 [1903-1925] – $46.00 – us MEDOC [470]

ESAU : OU, LA ROYAUTE POPULAIRE – Paris 1848 – us Res Libr [072]

Esau *see* HERRIN UND SKLAVE NACH SACHER MASOCH

ESBATIMENT MORAL, DES ANIMAUX : LOUEZ LE SEIGNEUR VOUS QUI ESTES DE LA TERRE, DRAGONS ET TOUS ABSYMES. BESTES, ET TOUS TROUPEAUX, SERPENS, ET OYSEAUX QUI ONT AILES. PSAL. 148.7.10 / Heyns, P – (Combination of two defective copies) – Antwerpen, [1578] – 3mf – 9 – O-3082/1 – ne IDC [430]

ESBER / Hamid, Abduelhak – Istanbul, 1922 – $45.00 – us MEDOC [470]

Escagedo Salmon, Mateo *see* LA BIBLIOTECA DEL CAMARISTA DE CASTILLA D. FERNANDO JOSE DE VELASCO Y CEBALLOS

Escalante, B de *see* AN ACCOUNT OF THE EMPIRE OF CHINA...

Escalante, D *see* ABOGADO Y NOTORIO

Escalante de Mendoza, J *see* YTINERARIO DE NAVEGACION DE LOS MARES Y TIERRAS OCCIDENTALES...

Escalante, Gumersindo *see* MANUAL DE MISIONOLOGIA. VITORIA, 1933

L'ESCALE : COLLEGE MARIE-ANNE – (Includes: L'Escale C.M.A. (College Marie-Anne) v4 n5 sep 1959-jan 1962) – Montreal. v4 n5. sep/oct 1959-jun 1962 – 1r – 1 – Can$35.00 – cn Can Microfilming [072]

L'ESCALE C.M.A. *see* L'ESCALE

ESCALOFON DE CAPATACES Y CAMINEROS DE LA MISMA EN 31 DE DICIEMBRE DE 1959 / Jefatura de obras publicas de la provincia de Badajoz – Badajoz: Imp. Arqueros, 1960 – sp Bibl Santa Ana [946]

ESCALON TIMES – Escalon, CA. 1927-58; 1968- – 45+ r – 1 BC02202 – $2,250.00 ($90.00y) – us Library Micro [071]

Escalona, Romualdo *see* HISTORIA DEL REAL MONASTERIO DE SAHAGUN

Escamps, Henri d' *see* HISTOIRE ET GEOGRAPHIE DE MADAGASCAR

ESCARAMUZAS EN LA FRONTERA CACERENA, CON OCASION DE LAS GUERRAS POR LA INDEPENDENCIA DE PORTUGAL / Velo Nieto, Gervasio – Madrid: Imp. F. Martinez, 1952 – sp Bibl Santa Ana [946]

ESCARCEOS DE TOPONIMIA EXTREMENA / Garcia de Diego, Jose A – Badajoz: Dip. Provincial, 1975. Sep. REE – 1 – sp Bibl Santa Ana [946]

Escardo, Florencio *see* LA JUVENTUD Y LA HORA

L'ESCARMOUCHE – no. 1-3. Paris. 12 nov 1893-16 mars 1894 – 1 – fr A.C.R.P.P. [073]

L'ESCAUT... / Brigode, G and M Ducarne – Bruxelles, 1911 – 1mf – 1 – ILM-1887/1 – ne IDC [327]

L'ESCAUT... / Ducarne, M – Bruxelles, 1911 – 1 – ne IDC [327]

L'ESCAUT DEPUIS 1830 / Guillaume – Bruxelles, [1902] – 13mf – 1 – ILM-2455/1 – ne IDC [327]

L'ESCAUT ET LA NEUTRALITE PERMANENTE DE LA BELGIQUE... / Beer Poortugael, J C C den – La Haye, 1910 – 9 – 1mf – ILM-2283/1 – ne IDC [327]

L'ESCAUT FLEUVE INTERNATIONAL ... / Blondeau, A – Paris, Bordeaux, 1932 – 1mf – 9 – ILM-1838/1 – ne IDC [327]

Escayrac de Lauture, Pierre H S d' *see* MEMOIRE SUR LE SOUDAN

LA ESCENA ESPANOLA...TEATRO / Garcia de la Huerta, Vicente – 1786 – 9 – 1.50f – sp Bibl Santa Ana [440]

Eschallier, J C *see* ESSAI SUR L'HABITAT SEDENTAIRE TRADITIONNEL AU SAHARA ALGERIEN

ESCHANTILLON DES PRINCIPAUX PARADOXES DE LA PAPAUTE / Rivet, A – La Rochelle, 1603 – 3mf – 9 – CA-149/1 – ne IDC [240]

DIE ESCHATOLOGISCHEN AUSSAGEN JESU IN DEN SYNOPTISCHEN EVANGELIEN / Haupt, Erich – (Includes list of biblical texts cited) – Berlin: Reuther & Reichard, 1895 – 1mf – 9 – 0-8370-3525-2 – 1985-1525 – us A.T.L.A. [220]

THE ESCHATOLOGY OF JESUS, OR, THE KINGDOM COME AND COMING : A BRIEF STUDY OF OUR LORD'S APOCALYPTIC LANGUAGE IN THE SYNOPTIC GOSPELS.... / Muirhead, Lewis A – (Includes bibliographical references) – London:Andrew Melrose, 1904 – 1mf – 9 – 0-8370-4535-5 – 1985-2535 – us A.T.L.A. [220]

Eschbach, Alphons *see* DESPUTATIONES PHYSIOLOGICO-THEOLOGICAE

Eschbach, E R *see* HISTORICAL SKETCH OF EVANGELICAL REFORMED CHURCH, FREDERICK, MARYLAND

Esche, Annelinde *see* ELISE RUEDIGER GEB. VON HOHENHAUSEN

Eschelbacher, Joseph *see* DAS JUDENTHUM UND DAS WESEN DES CHRISTENTUMS

Eschenbach, A *see* DIE LEHREN DES BERGWERKSSTREIKES VOM MAI 1889

Eschenbach, Wolfram von *see* PARZIVAL

Eschenburg, Theodor *see* DAS KAISERREICH AM SCHEIDEWEG

Escher, Andreas *see* DIE RECHTSSTELLUNG DES VERWALTUNGSRATES NACH DEM AKTIENRECHT DER VEREINIGTEN STAATEN VON NORDAMERIKA

Escher, Karl *see* E.T.A. HOFFMANNS GESPENSTERSPIEL

Escherich, K L *see*
- DIE FORSTINSEKTEN MITTELEUROPAS
- TERMITENLEBEN AUF CEYLON

Escherny, Francois L d' *see* DE L'EGALITE OU PRINCIPES GENERAUX SUR LES INSTITUTIONS CIVILES, POLITIQUES ET RELIGIEUSES

Eschmann, Johann Carl (1826-82) *see* GUIDE DU JEUNE PIANISTE

Eschner, Max *see* DIE DEUTSCHEN SCHUTZGEBIETE IN AFRIKA

L'ESCHOLE FRANCOISE / Duval, J B – 1604 – 9 – fr I.C.S. [370]

L'ESCHOLIER *see* LE JOURNAL DES ETUDIANTS

Eschstruth, H AF von *see* MUSICALISCHE BIBLIOTHEK, HERAUSGEGEBEN VON H. A. FR. V. ESCHSTRUTH

Eschweiler, F G *see* SYSTEMA LICHENUM

Escipion *see* LA POLITICA EXTERIOR PERONISTA

L'ESCLARCISSEMENT DE LA LANGUE FRANCOYSE / Palsgrave, John – 1530. 1088p. (English Linguistics Series 1500-1800) – 9 – us UMI [440]

ESCLAVAGE : ISLAMISME ET CHRISTIANISME / Binger, Louis Gustave – Paris: Societe d'editions scientifiques, 1891 – fr Armell [260]

L'ESCLAVAGE AFRICAIN, DISCOURS PRONONCE / Lavigerie – Paris, A la procure des missions d'Afrique. 1888 – 9 – 5.00 – fr Orientalistes [305]

L'ESCLAVAGE AU SENEGAL EN 1880 / Schoelcher, Victor – Paris, Librairie centrale des publications populaires. 1880 – 9 – 5.00 – fr Orientalistes [305]

ESCLAVAGE DE LA RACE NOIRE AUX COLONIES FRANCAISES / Levavasseur, Charles – Imprimerie Cesar Bajat. 1840 – 9 – 5.00 – fr Orientalistes [305]

ESCLAVAGE ET TRAITE / Gasparin, Agenor de – (Slave Trade and Abolitionism in France Series). 1838 – 9 – fr Hachette [360]

LES ESCLAVES / Metral, Antoine – (Slave Trade and Abolitionism in France series). 1836 – 9 – fr Hachette [305]

LES ESCLAVES CHRETIENS : DEPUIS LES PREMIERS TEMPS DE L'EGLISE JUSQU'A LA FIN DE LA DOMINATION ROMAINE EN OCCIDENT / Allard, Paul – Paris: V. Lecoffre, 1914 – 2mf – us A.T.L.A. [240]

ESCLAVES, SERFS ET MAINMORTABLES / Allard, Paul – Bruxelles: A. Vromant; Paris: Sanard & Derangeon, 1894 – 1mf – us A.T.L.A. [240]

LA ESCLAVITUD EN ASIA MENOR HELENISTICA / Lozano Velilla, Arminda – 1mf – 9 – Pta1,000.00 – 84-85422-23-6 – sp Pentalfa [930]

LA ESCOBA – Valencia de Alcantara, 1911. 2 numeros – 5 – sp Bibl Santa Ana [073]

Escobar, Francisco *see* LA VISION DE SAN ALONSO RODRIGUEZ PINTADA POR FRANCISCO DE ZURBARAN EN 1630

Escobar, Justo *see* EXAMEN DE LA VIOLENCIA ARGENTINA

Escobar, L *see* LAS QUATROCIENTAS RESPUESTAS A OTRAS TANTAS PREGUNTAS

Escobar, M *see* TRATADO...DE LA ESENCIA, CAUSAS Y CURACIONES DE LOS BUBONES Y CARBUNCOS...

Escobar Prieto, Eugenio *see*
- ANTIGUEDAD Y LIMITES DEL OBISPADO DE CORIA. NUEVO ESTUDIO
- EL CASTILLO DE PIEDRABUENA
- ORACION FUNEBRE QUE EN EL 4TH CENTENARIO DE LA MUERTE DELA REINA CATOLICA PRONUNCIO EN LA IGLESIA CATOLICA DE SANTA MARIA DE CACERES...

Escofet, Jose *see*
- FRANCISCO DE PIZARRO O EL PAIS DEL ORO
- HERNANDO CORTES O LA CONQUISTA DE MEJICO

Escoiquiz, Juan de *see* TRATADO DE LAS OBLIGACIONES DEL HOMBRE

A ESCOLA : JOURNAL CRITICO E LITTERARIO – '(s.l.')-Sao Luis, Brazil. 29 Aug-Nov 1878; 10 Mar 1902 – 1,5,6 – bl Biblioteca [072]

A ESCOLA : LITTERARIO E RECREATIVO – Penedo, Alagoas. 15 Jun 1910 – 1,5,6 – bl Biblioteca [072]

A ESCOLA – Maceio, Alagoas. 8 Abr, Ago 1883; Abr, Jun 1884; 10 Maio 1885 – 1,5,6 – bl Biblioteca [072]

A ESCOLA : ORGAO DA ESCOLA NORMAL OFICIAL DE ITAUNA – Itauna, 21 Jun 1931; Feb 1932 – 1,5,6 – bl Biblioteca [072]

A ESCOLA : ORGAO DO EXTERNATO "15 DE NOVEMBRO" – Manaos, Amazonas. 23 Set, Nov 1900; Fev-23 Mar 1901 – 1,5,6 – bl Biblioteca [072]

A ESCOLA : REVISTA DO GREMIO DOS PROFESSORES PUBLICOS – Coritiba, Feb 1906-Dec 1908; Jun-Oct 1909; Jan-Dec 1910; May-Jun 1921 – 1,5,6 – bl Biblioteca [072]

A ESCOLA : REVISTA LITTERARIA E SCIENTIFICA – Maceio, Alagoas. 1 Fev 1892 – 1,5,6 – bl Biblioteca [072]

A ESCOLA NACIONAL DE MUSICA E AS PESQUISAS DE FOLCLORE MUSICAL DO BRASIL – 1944 – 1 – us I.U. Libraries [390]

O ESCOLAR : ORGAM DOS ALUMNOS DO GRUPO ESCOLAR "WENCESLAU BRAZ" – Itacoatiara, Amazonas. 1 Abr 1919 – 1,5,6 – bl Biblioteca [072]

EL ESCOLAR EXTREMENO – Badajoz, 1896 y 1897 – 5 – sp Bibl Santa Ana [073]

ESCONDIDO TIMES – Escondido, CA. 1893-94; 1907-08 – 4r – 1 RC02203 – $200.00 – us Library Micro [071]

Escontria, Alfredo *see* BREVE ESTUDIO DE LA OBRA Y PERSONALIDAD DEL ESCULTOR Y ARQUITECTO DON MANUEL TOLSA. MEXICO

Escott, Thomas Hay Sweet *see* EDWARD BULWER, FIRST BARON LYTTON OF KNEBWORTH

A ESCOVA : BISEMANARIO AMAZONENSE – Manaos, Amazonas. 30 Jun-28 Set 1913 – 1,5,6 – bl Biblioteca [072]

A ESCOVA : CRITICO E NOTICIOZO – Pilar, Alagoas. 13 Maio 1897 – 1,5,6 – bl Biblioteca [072]

A ESCOVA – [s.l.] 29 Abr-1 Maio 1907 – 1,5,6 – bl Biblioteca [072]

O ESCOVADO : ORGAO CRITICO E NOTICIOSO – Manaos, Amazonas. 25 Abr 1915 – 1,5,6 – bl Biblioteca [072]

ESCRIPTURA Y FUNDACION DEL CONVENTO DE JESUS DE MERIDA – 1 – sp Bibl Santa Ana [946]

ESCRITAS LITERARIOS DE RUFINO JOSE CUERVO / Bayony Posada, Nicolas – Madrid: Razon y Fe, 1940 – 1 – sp Bibl Santa Ana [440]

ESCRITO EN DERECHO...DUQUE DE VILLAHERMOSA – 1831 – 9 – 1.50f – sp Bibl Santa Ana [946]

ESCRITO EN VISTA DE PRUEBAS / Rodriguez Valdes, Manuel M – 1851 – 9 – 1.50f – sp Bibl Santa Ana [440]

LAS ESCRITORAS ESPANOLAS / Nelken, Margarita – Barcelona, 1930; Madrid: Razon y Fe, 1931 – 1 – sp Bibl Santa Ana [440]

ESCRITORES ESPANOLES: CAROLINA CORONADO / Ossorio, Bernard M – 1889 – 9 – 1.50f – sp Bibl Santa Ana [440]

ESCRITOS ANEJOS. SERIOS Y HUMURISTICOS / Doncel y Ordaz, Jose – Badajoz: Uceda Hermanos, 1906 – 1 – sp Bibl Santa Ana [800]
ESCRITOS LITERARIOS Y CIENTIFICOS / Cagigal, Juan Manuel – Caracas, 1930; Madrid: Razon y Fe, 1931 – 1 – sp Bibl Santa Ana [440]
LA ESCRITURA OGNEICA EN EXTREMADURA / Roso de Luna, Mario – Madrid: Fortanet, 1904. B.R.A.H. 44 y 45, 1904, pp. 357-359 y 352-353 – sp Bibl Santa Ana [946]
ESCRITURAS COMPLETAS. REVELACIONES DE ANTANO / Picon La Res, Eduardo – Madrid: Razon y Fe, 1940 – 1 – sp Bibl Santa Ana [946]
LAS ESCRITURAS...TAPIA / Tapia – v2-6, v8 1620-26 – 9 – $1.50f – sp Bibl Santa Ana [946]
ESCRUTINIO DE MARAVEDISES / Cantos Benitez, Pedro de – 1763 – 1mf – 9 – Pta1,000.00 – 84-7848-225-3 – sp Pentalfa [320]
ESCRUTINIO PHISICO MEDICO DE UN PEREGRINO ESPECIFICO DE LAS CALENTURAS INTERMITENTES / Munoz y Peralta, M – Sevilla, 1699 – 2mf – 9 – sp Cultura [610]
Escude, Carlos *see* GRAN BRETANA, ESTADOS UNIDOS Y LA DECLINACION ARGENTINA 1942-1949
Escudero Gonzalez, Jose *see*
- LA CATASTROFE DE BARCELONA
- LA TRAGEDIA DE RIBADELAGO
EL ESCUDO – 1952-57. 542p – 1 – 18.97 – us Baptist [240]
O ESCUDO – Manaos, Amazonas. Set 1927 – 1,5,6 – bl Biblioteca [072]
O ESCUDO DA CONSTITUICAO BRASILEIRA – '(s.l.')-BA, Brazil. 11 abr 1831 – 1,5,6 – bl Biblioteca [072]
ESCUDO DE LAS INDULGENCIAS DE LA RELIGION...DE S. FRANCISCO / Almendralejo, Pedro de – 1699 – 9 – 1.50f – sp Bibl Santa Ana [240]
EL ESCUDO DE MERIDA Y SU ORIGEN ROMANO / Alvarez Saenz de Buruaga, Jose – 1 – sp Bibl Santa Ana [946]
EL ESCUDO DE MERIDA Y SU ORIGEN ROMANO / Alvarez Saenz de Buruaga, Jose – Madrid: Revista de Archivos, Bibliotecas y Museos, 1954 – 1 – sp Bibl Santa Ana [946]
ESCUDO DEL ESTADO ESPANOL / Spain. Ministerio del Interior – n.p., 1938. Fiche W861. (Blodgett Collection of Spanish Civil War Pamphlets) – 9 – us H.U. College Libr [946]
LA ESCUELA DE LA AMISTAD O EL FILOSOFO ENAMORADO / Forner Segarra, Juan Pablo – 1796 – 9 – 1.50f – sp Bibl Santa Ana [830]
LA ESCUELA DE LOS MARIDOS / Fernandez de Moratin, Leandro – 1812 – 1mf – 9 – Pta1,000.00 – 84-7848-186-9 – sp Pentalfa [946]
LA ESCUELA DE MEDICINA DE GUADALUPE / Colegio Oficial de Medicos de la Provincia de Caceres – Caceres: Imprenta de la Viuda de Garcia Floriano, 1952 – sp Bibl Santa Ana [370]
Escuela Diocesana de Catequetica *see* MEMORIA DEL CURSO 1966
ESCUELA ELEMANTAL DE TRABAJO Y DE CAPATACES AGRICOLAS DE CACERES : MEMORIA RESUMEN DE LA ACTUACION... ENTRE LOS CURSOS 1935-36 Y 1943-44... / Galan Saval, Ricardo – Caceres: Imp. Garcia Floriano Cumbreno, 1945 – sp Bibl Santa Ana [360]
Escuela Graduada Jose Luis Cotallo *see* ESTATUTOS DE LA ASOCIACION DE PADRES DE FAMILIA Y AMIGOS DE LA ESCUELA
Escuela Oficial de Maestria *see* ESCUELA OFICIAL DE MAESTRIA INDUSTRIAL DE BADAJOZ
ESCUELA OFICIAL DE MAESTRIA INDUSTRIAL DE BADAJOZ / Escuela Oficial de Maestria – Badajoz: Tipgrafia Clasica, 1965 – sp Bibl Santa Ana [370]
Escuela Superior de Conducci on Politica del Movimiento Peronista *see* FUNDAMENTOS DE DOCTRINA NACIONAL JUSTICIALISTA
Escuelas de Maria Santisima *see* CONSTITUCIONES
ESCUELAS PARROQUIALES DEL SAGRADO CORAZON. OLIVENZA (BADAJOZ) 1969 – Olivenza (Badajoz): Tip. Martinez Rengifo, 1970 – 1 – sp Bibl Santa Ana [370]
ESCUELAS PARROQUIALES EL SAGRADO CORAZON / Olivenza – (Badajoz), 1969. (Olivenza). Tip. Martinez Reginfo, 1970 – 1 – sp Bibl Santa Ana [370]
EL ESCULTOR EXTREMENO JUAN DE AVALOS / Segura Otano, Enrique – Badajoz: Imp. Diputacion Provincial, 1958 – sp Bibl Santa Ana [946]
LA ESCULTURA EN EL ECUADOR, 1929 / Navarro, Jose Gabriel – Madrid: Razon y Fe, 1931 – 1 – sp Bibl Santa Ana [730]
ESCULTURAS PROTOHISTORICAS DE LA PENINSULA HISPANICA / Paredes Guillen, Vicente – Caceres: Tip. Enc. y Lib. Jimenez, 1902 – 1 – sp Bibl Santa Ana [930]
ESDALL'S NEWSLETTER – Dublin, Ireland.16 Feb 1746-24 Jun 1752. -irr. 11 feet – 1 – uk British Libr Newspaper [072]
L'ESECUTORIETA DELLE SENTENZE CIVILI STRANIERE IN ITALIA / Delfino, C – Rome, 1913 – 5mf – 1 – ILM-2254/1 – ne IDC [327]
LA ESECUTORIETA DELLE SENTENZE STRANIERE IN ITALIA / Garofalo, R – Napoli, 1914 – 1mf – 1 – ILM-2397/1 – ne IDC [327]
LA ESECUTORIETA, IN ITALIA, DELLE SENTENZE ESTERE... / Gatti, L – Roma, 1905 – 1mf – 1 – ILM-3658/1 – ne IDC [327]
L'ESECUZIONE DELLE SENTENZE STRANIERE... / Fusinato, G – Roma, 1884 – 2mf – 1 – ILM-2015/1 – ne IDC [327]
ESECUZIONE IN ITALIA DELLE SENTENZE ESTERE DI DIVORZIO / Esperson, P – Roma, 1903 – 1mf – 1 – ILM-2473/1 – ne IDC [327]
ESEMPLARE O SIA SAGGIO FONDAMENTALE PRATICO DI CONTRAPPUNTO SOPRA IL CANTO FERMO / Martini, G – 2v. Bologna. 1774-75. BP-395 1 – 9 – ne IDC [780]
LA ESENCIAL HETEROGENEIDAD DEL SER EN ANTONIO MACHADO / Frutos Cortes, Eugenio – Madrid, 1959. Sep. Rev. Filosofia, tomo XVIII, no 69-70 – sp Bibl Santa Ana [946]
Esenin, Sergei *see*
- ISUS MLADENETS
- IZBRANNOE
- IZBRANNYE PROIZVEDENIIA
- IZBRANNYIA STICHOTVORENIIA V ODNOM TOME
- MOI PUT'
- PUGACHOV
- SERGEI ESENIN
- SOBRANIE SOCHINENII V PIATI TOMAKH
- SOBRANIE STIKHOTVORENII
- SOBRANIE STIKHOV I POEM
- SOCHINENIIA V 2 TOMAKH
- STIKHI I POEMY
- STIKHOTVORENIIA
- STIKHOTVORENIIA 1910-1925
- STIKHOTVORENIIA I POEMY
- TRIPTIKH
- ZIZN', LICHNOST' TVORCHESTVO
ESER-I ESLAFTAN HEFT MECLIS : ALI MUSTAFA BIN AHMET, 1451-1599 – Dersaadet [Istanbul]: Ikdam Matbaasi, 1316 [1900] – 9 – $20.00 – us MEDOC [956]
LA ESFERA / Sender, Ramon Jose – Buenos Aires. 1947 – 1 – us Res Libr [830]
O ESFOLA : SEMANARIO CRITICO E HUMORISTICO – Manaos, Amazonas. 6 Dez 1913-15 Jan 1914 – 1,5,6 – bl Biblioteca [072]
O ESFOLA GATO – Curitiba, 7 Jun 1866 – 1,5,6 – bl Biblioteca [072]
ESG-NACHRICHTEN – 1968-81 (complete) – 4r – 1 – ATLA S0591 – us A.T.L.A. [073]
ESH LENINCHI – (Includes c.1: 1947:Apr. 10, 17) – Toshkent: Uzbekistan leninchi kommunist eshlar soi uzi, Markazii komiteti, 19uu – 1 – CSUXAKB2153-S – us Hoover Inst Photo [947]
ESHCHE SHAG GRIADUSHCHEGO KHAMA / Merezhkovskii, Dimitrii – Russkoe slovo. 29 Jun 1914. BR-3574 2 – 8 – ne IDC [460]
ESHCOL / Humphrey, Simon James – New York: Fleming H Revell, c1893 – 1mf – 9 – 0-8370-6667-0 – 1986-0667 – us A.T.L.A. [240]
Eshel, B *see* JERUSALEM. INVENTORY TO THE RECORDS OF THE CHIEF SECRETARY'S OFFICE, 1918-1925
ESHER NEWS – Surrey. 1936-65 – 1 – uk Microform Academic [072]
Eshete, Aleme *see* CULTURAL SITUATION IN SOCIALIST ETHIOPIA
Eshevskii, S V *see* SOCHINENIIA
ESHKOL HA-SOFER / Levinsohn, I B – Warsaw. 1893. BJ-422-51 1 – 9 – ne IDC [470]
ESIE, RITE DE GUERISON ET DE PURIFICATION BETI (CAMEROUN) / Onana, L – 9 – F50.00 – fr Ethnologie [960]
Esipov, G V *see*
- LIUDI STARAGO VEKA
- RASKOL'NICH'I DELA 18 STOLETIIA, IZVLECHENNYIA IZ DEL PREOBRAZHENSKOGO PRIKAZA I TAINOI ROZYSKNYKH DEL KANTSELIARII
- SAMOUCHITEL' CHTENIIA RUKOPISEI 17 STOLETIIA
ESKILSTUNA ALLEHANDA – Eskilstuna, Sweden. 1844-69 – 9r – 1 – sw Kungliga [072]
ESKILSTUNA TIDNING – Eskilstuna, Sweden. 1837-38. 1 reel; 1867-93. 15 reels – 1 – sw Kungliga [072]
ESKILSTUNA WECKOBLAD – Eskilstuna, Sweden. 1840-41 – 1 reel – 1 – sw Kungliga [072]
ESKILSTUNAKORRESPONDENTEN – Eskilstuna, 1865-66 – 9 – sw Kungliga [072]
ESKILSTUNAKURIREN – Eskilstuna, Sweden. 1979-. Strengnas Tidning – 1 – sw Kungliga [072]
ESKILSTUNAKURIREN – (Strengnas Tidning, 1964-78) – Eskilstuna, Sweden. 1890-1978 – 493r – 1 – sw Kungliga [072]
ESKILSTUNAPOSTEN – Eskilstuna, Sweden. 1883-1893 – 7r – 1 – sw Kungliga [072]
ESKILSTUNATIDNINGEN – Eskilstuna, Sweden. 1895-1898 – 3r – 1 – sw Kungliga [072]
THE ESKIMO ABOUT BERING STRAIT / Nelson, E W – BN 326 2. 1899 – 8 – ne IDC [306]
ESKIMO ARCHAEOLOGY AND ITS BEARING ON THE PROBLEM OF MAN'S ANTIQUITY IN AMERICA / Collins, H B – BN 170 2. 1943 – 8 – ne IDC [930]
ESKIMO EN OER-INDOGERMAANSCH / Uhlenbeck, C C – (Mededeelingen der Koninkl. Nederl. Akad. van Wetenschappen, Afd. Letterkunde. Deel 77. Serie A, no. 6). Amsterdam. 1935. BN-437 2 – 8 – ne IDC [490]
ESKIMO. HANDBOOK OF THE AMERICAN INDIAN LANGUAGES / Thalbitzer, W – BN 412 2. 1911 – 8 – ne IDC [490]
ESKIMO LANGUAGE / Bergsland, K – (Doc.Diss). BN 459 2. 1955 – 8 – ne IDC [490]
THE ESKIMO OF BAFFIN LAND AND HUDSON BAY / Boas, Franz – B-5510 2. 1907 – 8 – ne IDC [971]
THE ESKIMO OF SIBERIA / Bogoras, W G – BN-147 2. 1913 – 9 – ne IDC [970]
THE ESKIMO OF SMITH SOUND / Kroeber, A L – BN 286 2. 1900 – 8 – ne IDC [970]
THE ESKIMO RACE AND LANGUAGE / Chamberlain, Alexander Francis – BN 161 2. 1888 – 8 – ne IDC [305]
AN ESKIMO STRIKE-A-LIGHT FROM CAPE BATHURST / Hough, W – BN 256 2. 1888 – 8 – ne IDC [306]
ESKIMO STRING FIGURES / Jenness, D – Rep. Canad. Arct. Exp. 1913-18, v. 13: Eskimo Folklgre.m BNE 270 2. 1924 – 8 – ne IDC [390]
THE ESKIMO TRIBES 1-2 / Rink, H J – BN 374 2. MoG v. 2. 1891 – 8 – ne IDC [305]
ESKIMOERNE / Birket-Smith, K – BN 130 2. 1927 – 8 – ne IDC [306]
ESKIMOERNES INDVANDRING I GRONLAND / Schultz-Lorentzen, C W – MoG, v. 26). Kobenhavn. 1940. BN-383 2 – 8 – ne IDC [304]
ESKIMOISKE EVENTRY OG SAGN OVERSATTE EFTER DE INDODTE FORTAELLERES OPSKR. OG MEDDELELSER EVENTYR OG SAGN / Rink, H J – Suppl. Kjobenhavn. 1866-71. BH-498 2 – 8 – ne IDC [306]
DET ESKIMOISKE SLAEGTSKABSSYSTEM / Birket-Smith, K – (The Eskimo kinship system). N131. 1927 – 9 – ne IDC [306]
ESKIMOKUENSTLER / Himmelheber, H – BN 249 2. 1938 – 8 – ne IDC [306]
ESKIMOLAND SPEAKS / Van Valin, W B – BN 440 2. 1945 – 8 – ne IDC [306]
ESKIMOLIV / Nansen, Fridtjof – BN 325 2. 1891 – 8 – ne IDC [306]
THE ESKIMOS / Birket-Smith, K – Trans. by W. Calvert. BN-469 2. 1936 – 8 – ne IDC [970]
THE ESKIMOS; THEIR ENVIRONMENT AND FOLKWAYS / Weyer, E M – New Haven, 1932. 483 pp., maps, index. BN-457 2 – 8 – ne IDC [305]
ESKIMOSSKO RUSSKII SLOVAR' / Menovscikov, G A – BN 463 2. 1954 – 8 – ne IDC [305]
ESKIMOSSKO-RUSSKII SLOVAR' / Menovshchikov, G A – L., 1954 – 5mf – 9 – N-463/2 – ne IDC [460]
ESKUAL HERRIA – Los Angeles. 1893-98 – 1 – fr A.C.R.P.P. [073]
Eslava, DH *see* MUSEO ORGANICO ESPANOL
ESLOVS TIDNING *see* NORDVASTRA SKANES TIDNINGAR ENGELHOLMS TIDNING
Esmangart *see* ETAT PAR ORDRE ALPHABETIQUE DES VILLES, BOURGS, VILLAGES ET HAMEAUX DE LA GENERALITE DE FLANDRE-ARTOIS
Esmein, Adhemar *see* LES COLONS DU SALTUS BURUNITAKUS MOMMSEN
Esmenard, Joseph Alphonse *see* LA NAVIGATION: POEME
Esmenard, Lesueur *see* LE TRIOMPHE DE TRAJAN
Esmenard, Persuis *see* LE TRIOMPHE DE TRAJAN
ESMERALDA HERALD – Hawthorne, NV. 1883-84 – 1r – 1 – $50.00 – U04576 – us Library Micro [071]
ESMERALDA NEWS – Hawthorne, NV. 1887-89 – 1r – 1 – $50.00 – U04577 – us Library Micro [071]
ESMERALDA STAR – (Independent California newspaper) – Aurora, CA. v1 n1. May 20 1862 – 1r – 1 – us Western Res [071]
ESMERALDA STAR – (Suppl to 30 Dec 1863) – Aurora, NV. Jul 1862 – 1r – 1 – $50.00 – U04401 – us Library Micro [071]
Esmond, Henry *see* THE HISTORY OF HENRY ESMOND, ESQ.
L'ESOTERISME DE HEBBEL / Bastier, Paul – Paris: E Larose, 1910 – 1r – 1 – us U.W. Library [430]
ESPACE ET MOBILITE RURALE EN MILIEU SOUDANOSAHELIEN: LE CHANGEMENT DANS L'ISOLEMENT, GOURMA DU NORD, HAUTE-VOLTA / Senechal, J – 9 – F130.00 – fr Ethnologie [306]
ESPACE ET VIE *see* POINT DE MIRE
ESPACE GEOGRAPHIQUE – 1972- 1; 1977- 5,6,9 – us UMI [910]
ESPACES MELANESIENS / Zacot, F – 9 – F70.00 – fr Ethnologie [306]
A ESPADA : DEDICADA AOS INTERESSES DA ESCHOLA DOMINICAL – Lavras, May 1896 – 1,5,6 – bl Biblioteca [072]
Espagnat, Pierre d' *see* JOURS DE GUINEE
L'ESPAGNE ACCUSE / Alvarez del Vayo, Julio – Paris. 1936. Fiche W 1507. (Blodgett Collection of Spanish Civil War Pamphlets) – 9 – us H.U. College Libr [946]
L'ESPAGNE CHRETIENNE / Leclerq, H – Paris: V. Lecoffre, 1906 (Bibliotheque de l'enseignement de l'histoire ecclesiastique) – 1mf – us A.T.L.A. [240]
L'ESPAGNE DE FRANCO; SYNTHESE DE TROIS CONFERENCES DONNEES DU 17 JANVIER AU 10 FEVRIER 1938 / Joubert, Henri – Paris, 1938. Fiche W976. (Blodgett Collection of Spanish Civil War Pamphlets) – 9 – us H.U. College Libr [946]
L'ESPAGNE DU SUD : L'EXTREMADOURE / Sermet, Jean – Paris: B. Arthaud, 1953 – 1 – sp Bibl Santa Ana [946]
L'ESPAGNE ET LA PAIX – Paris, 1937? Fiche W 965. (Blodgett Collection of Spanish Civil War Pamphlets) – 9 – us H.U. College Libr [946]
ESPAKLARIA – (New York). 1907 – 1 – us A.J.P.C. [073]
ESPANA – Madrid, Spain. -w. 7 Sept 1916-31 July 1919. 2 reels – 1 – uk British Libr Newspaper [072]
ESPANA 1958. 1ST FESTIVAL HISPANOAMERICANO. CACERES / Festival de Folklore Hispanoamericano 1, 1958 – Madrid: Graf. Nilo, 1958 – 1 – sp Bibl Santa Ana [390]
ESPANA ANTE EL HEMISFERIO DE OCCIDENTE : TOMO 2. COLOMBIA, VENEZUELA, ECUADOR, PERU, BOLIVIA, CHILE, ARGENTINA / Lazurtegui, Julio de – Madrid: Razon y Fe, 1926 – 1 – sp Bibl Santa Ana [946]
ESPANA ANTE LA INDEPENDENCIA DE LOS ESTADOS UNIDOS POR EL DR. JUAN F... / ed by Bayle, Constantino – Madrid: Razon y Fe, 1926 – 1 – sp Bibl Santa Ana [946]
ESPANA ANTES Y DESPUES DE LA VENIDA DEL DIRECTORIO / Luna Rancel, Felipe – Jerez de los Caballeros, Competidora. 1924 – 1 – sp Bibl Santa Ana [946]

ESPANA ECONOMICA Y FINANCIERA – Madrid. Spain. -w. 3 Jan 1942-8 Sep 1945. (Imperfect). (4 reels) – 1 – uk British Libr Newspaper [336]

ESPANA EN AMERICA. DOS VELADAS LITERARIAS CELEBRADAS EN LA CIUDAD DE BURGOS 1892-1893, CON MOTIVO DEL CUARTO CENTENARIO DE COLON / Gomez Bravo, Vicente – Cadiz: Est. Ceron, 1943 – 1 – sp Bibl Santa Ana [440]

ESPANA EN EL CONGRESO DE VIENA SEGUN LA CORRESPONDENCIA OFICIAL DE D. PEDRO GOMEZ LABRADOR / Villaurrutia, W R – Madrid: Tip.Rev.Archiv., Bibliot.y Mus, 1907 – 1 – sp Bibl Santa Ana [946]

ESPANA EN EL SIGLO 20. GALERIA DE PERSONALIDADES ILUSTRES – Madrid: 1st part. s.i., s.a. – 1 – sp Bibl Santa Ana [946]

ESPANA EN INDIAS / Bayle, Constantino – Madrid: Editroa Nacional, 1942 – 1 – sp Bibl Santa Ana [950]

ESPANA EN INDIAS / Perez Bustamante, Ciriaco & Bayle, Constantino – Madrid: Revista de Indias, 1940 – 1 – sp Bibl Santa Ana [950]

ESPANA EN SUS GLORIOSAS JORNADAS DE JULIO Y AGOSTO DE 1936; REPRODUCCION DE 18 ARTICULOS Y DE 2 DISCURSOS DEL AUTOR / Saenz, Vicente – San Jose, Costa Rica, 1936. Fiche W1154. (Blodgett Collection of Spanish Civil War Pamphlets) – 9 – us H.U. College Libr [946]

ESPANA EN TRENTO. 2. EL CONCILIO DE TRENTO EN LAS INDIAS ESPANOLAS / Bayle, Constantino – Madrid: Razon y Fe, 1945 – 1 – sp Bibl Santa Ana [946]

ESPANA EVANGELICA – (Cont: Carts Circular) – 1984-89 (complete) – Inquire – 1 – ATLA S0365 – us A.T.L.A. [073]

ESPANA EVANGELICA *see* CARTA CIRCULAR

LA ESPANA FRANQUISTA, SATELITE DE HITLER / Ibarruri, Dolores – Toulouse? 194? Fiche W954. (Blodgett Collection of Spanish Civil War Pamphlets) – 9 – us H.U. College Libr [946]

ESPANA; IMPRESIONES Y REFLEJOS / Jerrold, Douglas – Salamanca, 1937. Fiche W969. (Blodgett Collection of Spanish Civil War Pamphlets) – 9 – us H.U. College Libr [946]

ESPANA. LA ABORTADA REPUBLICA / Bayle, Constantino – Madrid: Razon y Fe, 1931 – 1 – sp Bibl Santa Ana [946]

Espana, Leyes Decretos... *see* REGLAMENTO DE PASTOR HIERBAS Y RASTROJERAS

Espana, Leyes, Decretos... *see* LEY DE 15 DE JULIO DE 1952 SOBRE EXPLOTACIONES AGRARIAS

Espana. Leyes, decretos, etc *see* CODIGO DE LA CIRCULACION

ESPANA LIBRE – (Includes v.4, no.21,23,28,30-32,35-36,39,41-43,45-47,49-51; v.5, no.2,4-6,8,10,17-20,27,35-37,50-52; v.6-12) – Brooklyn, N.Y.: Spanish Confederated Societies of U.S.A., 1939- – 1 – CSUX85-S411 – us Hoover Inst Photo [978]

ESPANA LIBRO – Brooklyn. v.15-38. 1953-76 – 1 – 46.00 – us L of C Photodup [946]

ESPANA. LOS ANOS VITALES. PROLOGO DE SIR ARTHUR BRYANT. MADRID, 1967 / Bolin, Luis – Madrid: Graf. Calleja, 1967 – 1 – sp Bibl Santa Ana [946]

ESPANA MOSCOVITA Y SUS CONSECUENCIAS / Aristeguieta Silva, F – Bruselas? 1938? Fiche W 726. (Blodgett Collection of Spanish Civil War Pamphlets) – 9 – us H.U. College Libr [946]

LA ESPANA ORIENTAL – ((Edicion hispano-tagalog). 4 Jul-26 Dec 1889. (Imperfect). (33 ft)) – Manila. Philippine Islands. -w. 7 Apr 1889-30 Jun 1890. (Imperfect). (1 reel) – 1 – uk British Libr Newspaper [072]

ESPANA. PRIMERA ASAMBLEA DE ACCION CATOLICA / Bayle, Constantino – Madrid: Razon y Fe, 1930 – 1 – sp Bibl Santa Ana [240]

ESPANA ROJA – n.p., 193? Fiche W 1506. (Blodgett Collection of Spanish Civil War Pamphlets) – 9 – us H.U. College Libr [946]

ESPANA SACRADA – Madrid 1(1747)-52(1918) – 440mf – 8 – ne Slangenburg [946]

ESPANA SAGRADA – Madrid, 1784. v34; 1826. v44; 1832. v45 – 30mf – 9 – 1570/2 – ne IDC [946]

ESPANA SAGRADA : THEATRO GEOGR.-HIST. DE LA IGLESIA DE ESPANA / Florez, Henrique – Madrid. 1(1747)-52(1918) – 9 – Dfl1,565.00 – ne Slangenburg [440]

ESPANA SAGRADA. TOMO 1 / Florez Setien, Enrique – 1747 – 1mf – 9 – Pta1,000.00 – 84-7848-064-1 – sp Pentalfa [240]

ESPANA SAGRADA. TOMO 2 / Florez Setien, Enrique – 1754, 2nd ed – 1mf – 9 – Pta1,000.00 – 84-7848-065-X – sp Pentalfa [240]

ESPANA SAGRADA. TOMO 3 / Florez Setien, Enrique – 1754, 2nd ed – 2mf – 9 – Pta1,500.00 – 84-7848-066-8 – sp Pentalfa [240]

ESPANA SAGRADA. TOMO 4 / Florez Setien, Enrique – 1756, 2nd ed – 2 mf – 9 – Pta1,500.00 – 84-7848-067-6 – sp Pentalfa [240]

ESPANA SAGRADA. TOMO 5 / Florez Setien, Enrique – 1750 – 2mf – 9 – Pta1,500.00 – 84-7848-068-4 – sp Pentalfa [240]

ESPANA SAGRADA. TOMO 6 / Florez Setien, Enrique – 1751 – 2mf – 9 – Pta1,500.00 – 84-7848-069-2 – sp Pentalfa [240]

ESPANA SAGRADA. TOMO 7 / Florez Setien, Enrique – 1751 – 1mf – 9 – Pta1,000.00 – 84-7848-070-6 – sp Pentalfa [240]

ESPANA SAGRADA. TOMO 8 / Florez Setien, Enrique – 1752 – 1mf – 9 – Pta1,000.00 – 84-7848-071-4 – sp Pentalfa [240]

ESPANA SAGRADA. TOMO 9 / Florez Setien, Enrique – 1752 – 2mf – 9 – Pta1,500.00 – 84-7848-072-2 – sp Pentalfa [240]

ESPANA SAGRADA. TOMO 10 / Florez Setien, Enrique – 1753 – 2mf – 9 – Pta1,500.00 – 84-7848-073-0 – sp Pentalfa [240]

ESPANA SAGRADA. TOMO 11 / Florez Setien, Enrique – 1753 – 2mf – 9 – Pta1,500.00 – 84-7848-074-9 – sp Pentalfa [240]

ESPANA SAGRADA. TOMO 12 / Florez Setien, Enrique – 1754 – 2mf – 9 – Pta1,500.00 – 84-7848-075-7 – sp Pentalfa [240]

ESPANA SAGRADA. TOMO 13 / Florez Setien, Enrique – 1756 – 2mf – 9 – Pta1,500.00 – 84-7848-076-5 – sp Pentalfa [240]

ESPANA SAGRADA. TOMO 14 / Florez Setien, Enrique – 1758 – 2mf – 9 – Pta1,500.00 – 84-7848-077-3 – sp Pentalfa [240]

ESPANA SAGRADA. TOMO 15 / Florez Setien, Enrique – 1759 – 2mf – 9 – Pta1,500.00 – 84-7848-078-1 – sp Pentalfa [240]

ESPANA SAGRADA. TOMO 16 / Florez Setien, Enrique – 1762 – 2mf – 9 – Pta1,500.00 – 84-7848-079-X – sp Pentalfa [240]

ESPANA SAGRADA. TOMO 17 / Florez Setien, Enrique – 1763 – 1mf – 9 – Pta1,000.00 – 84-7848-080-3 – sp Pentalfa [240]

ESPANA SAGRADA. TOMO 18 / Florez Setien, Enrique – 1764 – 2mf – 9 – Pta1,500.00 – 84-7848-081-1 – sp Pentalfa [240]

ESPANA SAGRADA. TOMO 19 / Florez Setien, Enrique – 1765 – 2mf – 9 – Pta1,500.00 – 84-7848-082-X – sp Pentalfa [240]

ESPANA SAGRADA. TOMO 20 / Florez Setien, Enrique – 1765 – 2mf – 9 – Pta1,500.00 – 84-7848-083-8 – sp Pentalfa [240]

ESPANA SAGRADA. TOMO 21 / Florez Setien, Enrique – 1766 – 2mf – 9 – Pta1,500.00 – 84-7848-084-6 – sp Pentalfa [240]

ESPANA SAGRADA. TOMO 22 / Florez Setien, Enrique – 1767 – 1mf – 9 – Pta1,000.00 – 84-7848-085-4 – sp Pentalfa [240]

ESPANA SAGRADA. TOMO 23 / Florez Setien, Enrique – 1767 – 2mf – 9 – Pta1,500.00 – 84-7848-086-2 – sp Pentalfa [240]

ESPANA SAGRADA. TOMO 24, PARTE 1 / Florez Setien, Enrique – 1877, 3rd ed – 1mf – 9 – Pta1,000.00 – 84-7848-087-0 – sp Pentalfa [240]

ESPANA SAGRADA. TOMO 24, PARTE 2 / Florez Setien, Enrique – 1769 – 1mf – 9 – Pta1,000.00 – 84-7848-088-9 – sp Pentalfa [240]

ESPANA SAGRADA. TOMO 25 / Florez Setien, Enrique – 1770 – 1mf – 9 – Pta1,000.00 – 84-7848-089-7 – sp Pentalfa [240]

ESPANA SAGRADA. TOMO 26 / Florez Setien, Enrique – 1771 – 2mf – 9 – Pta1,500.00 – 84-7848-090-0 – sp Pentalfa [240]

ESPANA SAGRADA. TOMO 27 / Florez Setien, Enrique – 1772 – 3mf – 9 – Pta2,000.00 – 84-7848-091-9 – sp Pentalfa [240]

ESPANA SAGRADA. TOMO 28 / Florez Setien, Enrique – 1774 – 1mf – 9 – Pta1,000.00 – 84-7848-092-7 – sp Pentalfa [240]

ESPANA SAGRADA. TOMO 29 / Florez Setien, Enrique – 1775 – 2mf – 9 – Pta1,500.00 – 84-7848-093-5 – sp Pentalfa [240]

ESPANA SAGRADA. TOMO 30 / Risco, Manuel – 1775 – 2mf – 9 – Pta1,500.00 – 84-7848-095-1 – sp Pentalfa [240]

ESPANA SAGRADA. TOMO 31 / Risco, Manuel – 1776 – 2mf – 9 – Pta1,500.00 – 84-7848-096-X – sp Pentalfa [240]

ESPANA SAGRADA. TOMO 32 / Risco, Manuel – 1779 – 2mf – 9 – Pta1,500.00 – 84-7848-097-8 – sp Pentalfa [240]

ESPANA SAGRADA. TOMO 33 / Risco, Manuel – 1781 – 2mf – 9 – Pta1,500.00 – 84-7848-098-6 – sp Pentalfa [240]

ESPANA SAGRADA. TOMO 34 / Risco, Manuel – 1784 – 2mf – 9 – Pta1,500.00 – 84-7848-099-4 – sp Pentalfa [240]

ESPANA SAGRADA. TOMO 35 / Risco, Manuel – 1786 – 2mf – 9 – Pta1,500.00 – 84-7848-100-1 – sp Pentalfa [240]

ESPANA SAGRADA. TOMO 36 / Risco, Manuel – 1787 – 2mf – 9 – Pta1,500.00 – 84-7848-101-X – sp Pentalfa [240]

ESPANA SAGRADA. TOMO 37 / Risco, Manuel – 1789 – 1mf – 9 – Pta1,000.00 – 84-7848-102-8 – sp Pentalfa [240]

ESPANA SAGRADA. TOMO 38 / Risco, Manuel – 1793 – 2mf – 9 – Pta1,500.00 – 84-7848-103-6 – sp Pentalfa [240]

ESPANA SAGRADA. TOMO 39 / Risco, Manuel – 1795 – 1mf – 9 – Pta1,000.00 – 84-7848-104-4 – sp Pentalfa [240]

ESPANA SAGRADA. TOMO 40 / Risco, Manuel – 1796 – 2mf – 9 – Pta1,500.00 – 84-7848-105-2 – sp Pentalfa [240]

ESPANA SAGRADA. TOMO 41 / Risco, Manuel – 1798 – 2mf – 9 – Pta1,500.00 – 84-7848-106-0 – sp Pentalfa [240]

ESPANA SAGRADA. TOMO 42 / Risco, Manuel – 1801 – 1mf – 9 – Pta1,000.00 – 84-7848-107-9 – sp Pentalfa [240]

ESPANA SAGRADA..., TOMOS 01-51 / Florez, E et al – Madrid, 1745-1879 – 425mf – 9 – sp Cultura [946]

ESPANA VISTA OTRA VEZ / Noel, Martin S – Madrid: Edit. Espana, 1929 – 1 – sp Bibl Santa Ana [946]

ESPANA Y ALGUNOS ESPANOLES / Galvez, Manuel – Buenos Aires: Editorial Huarpes, 1945 – 1 – us U.W. Library [946]

ESPANA Y AMERICA – Revista Quincenal de Religion, Ciencia, Literatura y Arte. Madrid. Ano 1-25. 1903-27 – 1 – us NY Public [073]

ESPANA Y COLON. MADRID, 1935 / Real, Cristobal – Madrid: Razon y Fe, 1936 – 1 – sp Bibl Santa Ana [946]

ESPANA Y EL CLERO INDIGENA DE AMERICA / Bayle, Constantino – Madrid: Razon Fe, S.A. – sp Bibl Santa Ana [240]

ESPANA Y EL CLERO INDIGENA DE AMERICA / Bayle, Constantino – Madrid: Razon y Fe, 1931 – 1 – sp Bibl Santa Ana [946]

ESPANA Y FRANCISCO FRANCO. 25 ANIVERSARIO DE LA EXALTACION A LA JEFATURA DEL ESTADO / Delegacion Nacional de Prensa, Propaganda y Radio – Badajoz: Graf. Extremena, 1961 – sp Bibl Santa Ana [946]

ESPANA Y FRANCO / Gimenez Caballero, Ernesto – Cegama, 1938. Fiche W917. (Blodgett Collection of Spanish Civil War Pamphlets) – 9 – us H.U. College Libr [946]

ESPANA Y LA GUERRA IMPERIALISTA / Diaz, Jose – Mexico, 1939. Fiche W 833. (Blodgett Collection of Spanish Civil War Pamphlets) – 9 – us H.U. College Libr [946]

ESPANA Y SUS HOMBRES. RESENA HISTORICO-BIOGRAFICA DE SUS PRINCIPALES PERSONALIDADES – Madrid: Tip. Julian Frances, 1916 – 1 – sp Bibl Santa Ana [920]

ESPANA-PARIS – Organe du centre hispano-americain Espana-Paris. no. 1-14. Paris. 14 avr-21 juil 1900. mq no. 13 – 1 – fr A.C.R.P.P. [073]

EL ESPANOL : DEFENSOR DE LOS INTERESES ESPANOLES EN EL BRASIL – Manaus, Amazonas. 2 Maio 1903 – 1,5,6 – bl Biblioteca [072]

ESPANOL – Madrid. Spain. -w. 31 Oct 1942-29 Dec 1945. (Imperfect). (6 reels) – 1 – uk British Libr Newspaper [072]

UN ESPANOL AL SERVICIO DE LA SANTA SEDE. DON JUAN DE CARVAJAL, CARDENAL DE SANT'ANGELO, LUGADO EN ALEMANIA Y HUNGRIA (1.399-1.469) / Gomez Canedo, Luis – Madrid: C.S.I.C. Instituto Jeronimo Zurita, 1947 – 1 – sp Bibl Santa Ana [240]

ESPANOL – CASTELLANO : DIE NAMEN DES SPANISCHEN / Diederichs, Joern – 1993 – 3mf – 9 – DM98.00 – 3-89349-676-9 – gw Hänsel [440]

ESPANOL DE AMBOS MUNDOS – London, UK. 7 Aug 1860-10 Jan 1862 – 1 – uk British Libr Newspaper [072]

EL ESPANOL DE JALISCO. MADRID, 1967 / Cardenas, Daniel – Madrid: Graf. Calleja, 1968 – 1 – sp Bibl Santa Ana [946]

Espanol, Juan *see* QUIENES SON LOS RESPONSABLES? LIBERALES EL MUNDO

ESPANOLES E INGLESES EN AMERICA DURANTE EL SIGLO 17. EL CONDE DE GANDOMAR Y SU INTERVENCION EN EL PROCESO, PRISION Y MUERTE DE SIR WALTER RALEIGH. SANTIAGO DE COMPOSTELA, 1928 / Perez Bustamante, Ciriaco – Madrid: Razon y Fe, 1929 – 1 – sp Bibl Santa Ana [972]

ESPANOLES FUERA DE ESPANA / Figueroa y Melgar, Alfonso de – Badajoz: Imp. Dip. Provincial, 1973 – sp Bibl Santa Ana [946]

LOS ESPANOLES Y MAGALLANES EN LA EXPEDICION DEL ESTRECHO / Bayle, Constantino – Madrid: Razon y Fe, 1921 – 1 – sp Bibl Santa Ana [946]

ESPANOLISMO Y ANTIESPANOLISMO EN LA AMERICA HISPANA. LA POBLACION HISPANOAMERICANA A PARTIR DE LA INDEPENDENCIA. MADRID, 1945 / Baron Castro, Rodolfo – Madrid: Razon y Fe, 1947 – 1 – sp Bibl Santa Ana [320]

L'ESPANSIONE – 1985-1995 – 1r per y – 5,6 – Sfr401.00y – sz Infoprint [072]

ESPANSIONE – 1985-1995 – Annual – 6 – F1,500 – sz Infoprint [072]

Esparragalejo. Ayuntamiento *see* REVISTA DE LOS ESPARRENSES, NO 5 DEDICADA A LA 2ND SEMANA CULTURAL Y FIESTA DEL EMIGRANTE. AGOSTO 1980

ESPARTERO. HISTORIA / Florez, Jose Segundo – 1844-45.4v – 9 – 1.50f – sp Bibl Santa Ana [946]

ESPECTACULO DE LA NATURALEZA. TOMO 1 / Pluche, Manuel – s.a. – 1mf – 9 – Pta1,000.00 – 84-7848-298-9 – sp Pentalfa [550]

ESPECTACULO DE LA NATURALEZA. TOMO 2 / Pluche, Manuel – s.a. – 1mf – 9 – Pta1,000.00 – 84-7848-299-7 – sp Pentalfa [550]

ESPECTACULO DE LA NATURALEZA. TOMO 3 / Pluche, Manuel – s.a. – 1mf – 9 – Pta1,000.00 – 84-7848-300-4 – sp Pentalfa [550]

ESPECTACULO DE LA NATURALEZA. TOMO 4 / Pluche, Manuel – s.a. – 1mf – 9 – Pta1,000.00 – 84-7848-301-2 – sp Pentalfa [550]

ESPECTACULO DE LA NATURALEZA. TOMO 5 / Pluche, Manuel – s.a. – 1mf – 9 – Pta1,000.00 – 84-7848-302-0 – sp Pentalfa [550]

ESPECTACULO DE LA NATURALEZA. TOMO 6 / Pluche, Manuel – s.a. – 1mf – 9 – Pta1,000.00 – 84-7848-303-9 – sp Pentalfa [550]

ESPECTACULO DE LA NATURALEZA. TOMO 7 / Pluche, Manuel – s.a. – 1mf – 9 – Pta1,000.00 – 84-7848-304-7 – sp Pentalfa [550]

ESPECTACULO DE LA NATURALEZA. TOMO 8 / Pluche, Manuel – s.a. – 1mf – 9 – Pta1,000.00 – 84-7848-305-5 – sp Pentalfa [550]

ESPECTACULO DE LA NATURALEZA. TOMO 9 / Pluche, Manuel – s.a. – 1mf – 9 – Pta1,000.00 – 84-7848-306-3 – sp Pentalfa [550]

ESPECTACULO DE LA NATURALEZA. TOMO 10 / Pluche, Manuel – s.a. – 1mf – 9 – Pta1,000.00 – 84-7848-307-1 – sp Pentalfa [550]

ESPECTACULO DE LA NATURALEZA. TOMO 11 / Pluche, Manuel – s.a. – 1mf – 9 – Pta1,000.00 – 84-7848-308-X – sp Pentalfa [550]

ESPECTACULO DE LA NATURALEZA. TOMO 12 / Pluche, Manuel – s.a. – 1mf – 9 – Pta1,000.00 – 84-7848-309-8 – sp Pentalfa [550]

ESPECTACULO DE LA NATURALEZA. TOMO 13 / Pluche, Manuel – s.a. – 2mf – 9 – Pta1,500.00 – 84-7848-310-1 – sp Pentalfa [550]

ESPECTACULO DE LA NATURALEZA. TOMO 14 / Pluche, Manuel – s.a. – 1mf – 9 – Pta1,000.00 – 84-7848-311-X – sp Pentalfa [550]

ESPECTACULO DE LA NATURALEZA. TOMO 15 / Pluche, Manuel – s.a. – 2mf – 9 – Pta1,500.00 – 84-7848-312-8 – sp Pentalfa [550]

ESPECTACULO DE LA NATURALEZA. TOMO 16 / Pluche, Manuel – s.a. – 1mf – 9 – Pta1,000.00 – 84-7848-313-6 – sp Pentalfa [550]

EL ESPECTADOR – 1937-60.Incomplete. Bilingual weekly.6 reels – 1 – 108.00; 18.00r – us S.U. Libraries [071]

Espejo, Christobal *see* LAS ANTIGUAS FERIAS DE MEDINA DEL CAMPO

ESPEJO DE CONCIENCIA QUE TRATA DE TODOS LOS ESTADOS – 1525 – 9 – 1.50f – sp Bibl Santa Ana [946]

ESPELHO – London, UK. Sep 1914-15 Jun 1919 – 1 – uk British Libr Newspaper [072]

O ESPELHO – Maceio, Alagoas. 5 Abr, 6 Nov 1887 – 1,5,6 – bl Biblioteca [072]

O ESPELHO – Rio de Janeiro, 1 Oct 1821-27 Jun 1823 – 1,5,6 – bl Biblioteca [072]

O ESPELHO DA JUSTICA – Rio de Janeiro, 1 Dec 1830-3 Jun 1831 – 1,5,6 – bl Biblioteca [072]

O ESPELHO DIAMANTINO : PERIODICO DE POLITICA, LITTERATURA, BELLAS ARTES, THEATRO, E MODAS. DEDICADO AS SENHORAS BRASILEIRAS – Rio de Janeiro, 1 Oct 1827-28 Apr 1828 – 1,5,6 – bl Biblioteca [072]

Espenberger, J N *see* DIE PHILOSOPHIE DES PETRUS LOMBARDUS

Esper, E J C *see*
- ICONES FUCORUM
- ICONES FUCORUM. ABBILDUNGEN DER TANGE
- DIE PFLANZENTHIERE IN ABBILDUNGEN NACH DER NATUR

A ESPERANCA : FOLHA IMPARCIAL, NOTICIOSA E LITERARIA – Dores da Boa Esperanca, 13, 27 Nov 1927 – 1,5,6 – bl Biblioteca [072]

A ESPERANCA : ORGAM IMPARCIAL – Curvello, 12 Sep 1902 – 1,5,6 – bl Biblioteca [072]

ESPERANCA : PERIODICO LITTERARIO E CRITICO – Manaos, Amazonas. 21 Jan 1877 – 1,5,6 – bl Biblioteca [072]

L'ESPERANCE – 9e annee, no. 1-24. Paris. 7 janv-16 dec 1847 – 1 – fr A.C.R.P.P. [073]

L'ESPERANCE – Central Falls. R.I. 1891-1899 – 1 – us UMI [071]

L'ESPERANCE – Central Falls, RI. v1 n21. 5 jun 1891-v1 n27. 26 jun 1891 – 1r – 1 – Can$30.00 – cn Can Microfilming [071]

L'ESPERANCE – Quebec, Canada. v1 n3. 12 oct-30 nov 1872 – 1r – 1 – Can$25.00 – cn Can Microfilming [072]

LA ESPERANZA EN DIOS CARTA PATORAL / Perez Munoz, Adolfo – Badajoz: Tip. y Encuadern. de Uceda Hnos, 1917 – 1 – sp Bibl Santa Ana [240]

Esperson, P *see*
- CERTEZZA DEL DIRITTO INTERNAZIONALE...
- DIRITTO CAMBIARIO INTERNAZIONALE...
- IL DIVORZIO NEI RAPPORTI INTERNAZIONALI...
- ESECUZIONE IN ITALIA DELLE SENTENZE ESTERE DI DIVORZIO
- INEFFICACIO, DOPO LA CONVENZIONE DELL'AJA DEL 1902...
- LA LEGGE SULLA NATURALIZZAZIONE IN ITALIA
- IL PRINCIPIO DI NAZIONALITA...
- RIAQUISTO DELLA CITTADINANZA ITALIANA PERDUTA COLO SCOPO DI OTTENERE IL DIVORZIO

ESPHYNGE – Curitiba, Brazil. Jul 1899-Sept 1901; Nov 1902-Jun 1906 – 1 – bl Biblioteca [072]

O ESPIA : CRITICO E NOTICIOSO – Pilar, Alagoas. 22 Abr 1892 – 1,5,6 – bl Biblioteca [072]

O ESPIA – Maceio, Alagoas. 20 Out 1895 – 1,5,6 – bl Biblioteca [072]

O ESPIAO : CRITICO NOTICIOSO – Pao de Assucar, Alagoas. 16 Fev 1896 – 1,5,6 – bl Biblioteca [072]

O ESPIAO : JORNAL LITTERARIO, CRITICO E NOTICIOSO – Aracaju, 3 Dec 1882-15 Apr 1883 – 1,5,6 – bl Biblioteca [072]

Espias-Sanchez, Manuel *see* LA FAMILIA EN DIRECTO

ESPIGANDO EN !MI HEREDA! / Sanchez-Arjona, Vicente – Sevilla: Imp. Zambrano, Tomo 1. 1952 – 1 – sp Bibl Santa Ana [810]

ESPIGANDO EN !MI HEREDA! / Sanchez-Arjona, Vicente – Sevilla: Imp. Zambrano, Tomo 2. 1953 – 1 – sp Bibl Santa Ana [810]

ESPIGANDO EN !MI HEREDAD! / Sanchez-Arjona, Vicente – Sevilla: Imp. Alvarez, 1958 – 1 – sp Bibl Santa Ana [810]

ESPIGANDO EN !MI HEREDAD! / Sanchez-Arjona, Vicente – Sevilla: Imp. Zambrano, Tomo 3. 1955 – 1 – sp Bibl Santa Ana [810]

ESPIGANDO EN !MI HEREDAD! / Sanchez-Arjona, Vicente – Sevilla: Imp. Zambrano, Tomo 4. 1955 – 1 – sp Bibl Santa Ana [810]

Espinar, Jaime *see* NOVIEMBRE DE MADRID

Espine, Marc d' *see* ESSAI ANALYTIQUE ET CRITIQUE DE STATISTIQUE MORTUAIRE COMPAREE.

Espino de Caceres, Diego *see*
- SPECULUM TESTAMENTORUM...
- SPECULUM TESTAMENTORUM; SIVE..

Espinosa, Aurelio Macedonio *see* EL ROMANCERO ESPANOL

Espinosa, H E *see* ESTUDIO SOCIOJURIDICO DE LA NACIONALIDAD MEXICO Y LA NACION INDOIBERA

Espinosa, Isidro Felix *see* CRONICA DE LA PROVINCIA FRANCISCANA DE LOS APOSTOLES SAN PEDRO Y SAN PABLO DE MICHOACAN. 2ND ED. MEXICO, 1946

Espinosa, J Manuel *see* FIRST EXPEDITION OF VARGAS INTO NEW MEXICO, 1692

O ESPIRITA ALAGOANO : ORGAM DO GRUPO ESPIRITAS, VICENTE DE PAULA – Maceio, Alagoas. 21 Jun, Ago 1900; 15 Abr 1901 – 1,5,6 – bl Biblioteca [072]

EL ESPIRITU DE SANTA TERESA Y EL DE SAN IGNACIO / Bayle, Constantino – Madrid: Razon y Fe, 1922 y 1923 – 1 – sp Bibl Santa Ana [240]

EL ESPIRITU DEL SIGLO / Juras Reales, Baron de – 1833 – 9 – 1.50f – sp Bibl Santa Ana [946]

EL ESPIRITU GENUINO DE FALANGE ESPANOLA. ES CATOLICO? / Bayle, Constantino – Madrid: Razon y Fe, 1937 – 1 – sp Bibl Santa Ana [240]

EL ESPIRITU Y EL APOSTOLADO DE SOR MARIA JOSEFA ROSELLO... / Noberasco, Felipe – Madrid: Razon y Fe, 1926 – 1 – sp Bibl Santa Ana [240]

ESPISTOLARIO DE NUEVA ESPANA 1505-1812 RECOPILADO POR FRANCISCO DEL PASO Y TRONCOSO, TOMO 16, MEJICO, 1942 / Bayle, Constantino – Madrid: Razon y Fe, 1944 – 1 – sp Bibl Santa Ana [946]

THE ESPLANADE DIFFICULTY: THE REPLY OF THE CREDIT VALLEY RAILWAY COMPANY TO THE STATEMENTS OF THE GRAND TRUNK AND NORTHERN RAILWAY COMPANIES IN THE MATTER OF THE DISPUTED ENTRANCE TO TORONTO HARBOUR : LEGAL ARGUMENT IN THE FAVOUR OF THE CREDIT VALLEY'S CONTENTION: APPEAL TO PARLIAMENT / Credit Valley Railway Company – s.l.: s.n., 1880 (Toronto: Globe). 04187. (Pre-1900 Canadiana) – 9 – cn C.I.H.M. [971]

L'ESPLORAZIONE DEL GUIBA : VIAGGIO DI SCOPERTA NEL CUORE DELL'AFRICA, ESEGUITO SOTTO GLI AUSPICI DELLA SOCIETA GEOGRAFICA ITALIANA / Bottego, Vittorio – Roma: Societa editrice nazionale, [1900] – 1 – us Res Libr [910]

L'ESPOIR DE NICE ET DU SUD-EST – Nice. 1960-72 – 1 – fr A.C.R.P.P. [073]

O ESPORTIVO : ORGAO NOTICIOSO E PROPUGNADOR DOS ESPORTES ACREANOS – Rio Branco, Acre. 15 Fev-28 Maio 1953 – 1,5,6 – bl Biblioteca [072]

LA ESPOSA DE DONOSO CORTES / Munoz de San Pedro, Miguel – Badajoz, 1953. Sep. de la Revista de Rstudios Extremenos – sp Bibl Santa Ana [946]

ESPOSICION QUE PRESENTA AL CONGRESO CONSTITUCIONAL DE [...] / el Ministro Secretario de Estado en el Departamento del Interior y Relaciones Esteriores – Sucre: Impr de la Libertad, 1840 – 1r – 1 – us Res Libr [323]

ESPOSICION QUE PRESENTA EN BOLIVIA EL MINISTRO DE ESTADO EN EL DESPACHO DEL INTERIOR A LA CONVENCION NACIONAL EN [...] – Chuquisaca: Impr de Beeche y Cia, 1843 – 1r – 1 – us Res Libr [320]

ESPOSIZIONE DELLA DIVINA COMMEDIA DI DANTE-ALIGHIERI / Trucchi, Ernesto – Milano: A. Montaldi & C., (1943). 3v. plates – 1 – us U.W. Library [440]

ESPOSOCION(SIC) QUE DIRIGE A LAS CORTES CONSTINTUYENTES EN DEFENSA DE SU PADRE DON MANUEL GODOY... / Chinchon, Condesa de – Madrid: Imp. F. Andres y Comp., 1855 – 1 – sp Bibl Santa Ana [946]

L'ESPOUVANTABLE ET PRODIGIEUSE APPARITION ADVENUE EN LA PERNE DE IEAN HELIAS – Paris. 1623 – 9 – fr Hachette [360]

L'ESPRESSO – Rome, IT. 1968-1974 – 21r – $1,050.00 – R63618 – us Library Micro [072]

ESPRESSO – 1955-1974 – 1r per y – 5,6 – Sfr508.00 – sz Infoprint [945]

ESPRESSO – 1975-1987 – 2r per y – 5,6 – Sfr588.00 – sz Infoprint [072]

ESPRESSO – 1975-1987 – 2 times per yr – 6 – F2,200 – sz Infoprint [072]

ESPRESSO – 1984-1995 – 4 times per yr – 6 – F2,700 – sz Infoprint [072]

ESPRESSO – 1984-1995 – 4r per y – 5,6 – Sfr722.00 – sz Infoprint [072]

ESPRESSO – [Italy], 1955- – 4r per y – 5 – inquire – us Ross [072]

L'ESPRIT – Dir. Pierre Morhange. no. 1-2. Paris. mai 1926-janv 1927 – 1 – fr A.C.R.P.P. [073]

ESPRIT – Revue internationale. Fond. E. Mounier. Paris. oct 1932-juil 1941, dec 1944-1956 – 1 – fr A.C.R.P.P. [073]

L'ESPRIT DE L'ART MUSICAL / Blainville, Charles-H de – 1754 – 9 – us Sibley [780]

L'ESPRIT DES COURS DE L'EUROPE – La Haye puis Amsterdam. juin 1699-avr 1710 (I-XIX) – 1 – fr A.C.R.P.P. [073]

ESPRIT DES INSTITUTIONS MILITAIRES / Marmont, AF L de – Paris. J. Dumaine. 1845. xxii, 227p. (Strategy of War Series) – 9 – fr Hachette [355]

ESPRIT DES LIBRES DEFENDUS, OU ANTILOGIES PHILOSOPHIQUES / Bonafous, Louis-Abel de – (D'Holbach series). 1777 – 9 – fr Hachette [190]

L'ESPRIT DES USAGES ET DES COUTUMES DES DIFFERENTS PEUPLES OU OBSERVATIONS TIREES DES VOYAGEURS ET DES HISTORIENS / Demeunier, J N – 9 – F300.00 – fr Ethnologie [306]

Esprit du Bosroger, Le P *see* LA PIETE AFFLIGEE OU DISCOURS HISTORIQUE ET THEOLOGIQUE DE LA POSSESSION DES RELIGIEUSES DITTES DE SAINCTE ELIZABETH DE LOUVRIERS

L'ESPRIT DU CLERGE OU LE CHRISTIANISME PRIMITIF VENGE DES ENTERPRISES ET DES EXCES DE NOS PRETRES MODERNES – (D'Holbach series). 1767 – 9 – fr Hachette [240]

L'ESPRIT DU JUDAISME OU EXAMEN RAISONNE DE LA LOI DE MOISE, ET DE SON INFLUENCE SUR LA RELIGION CHRETIENNE – (D'Holbach series). 1770 – 9 – fr Hachette [270]

ESPRIT DU SYSTEME DE GUERRE MODERNE / Bulow, H D von – Paris. Bernard. 1801. viii, 225p. pl. (Strategy of War Series) – 9 – fr Hachette [355]

L'ESPRIT ET L'HISTOIRE : ESSAI SUR LA CONSCIENCE HISTORIQUE DANS LA LITTERATURE DU 20TH SIECLE / Simon, P H – F50.00 – fr Ethnologie [900]

L'ESPRIT FRANCAIS – puis Encyclopedie mensuelle vivante, ouverte et libre. no. 1-87. Paris. oct 1929-33 – apply; 1 – fr A.C.R.P.P. [073]

L'ESPRIT FRANCAIS / Renard, Jules – Paris: Societe de l'Edition et de Publications, 1911. 118p. 2 fiches. (Miscellaneous Selections) – 9 – 6.00 – fr Bibl Nationale [944]

L'ESPRIT NOUVEAU – Red. en chef A. de Gasperini. no. 1-23. Paris. janv-juin 1867 – 1 – fr A.C.R.P.P. [073]

L'ESPRIT NOUVEAU – Revue internationale illustree de l'activite contemporaine. Dir. Paul Dermee. no. 1-29. Paris. 1920-25 – 1 – fr A.C.R.P.P. [073]

ESPRIT NOUVEAU – Paris. n1-28. 1920-25 – 1r – 1 – us Ross [073]

L'ESPRIT PUBLIC – Paris. 16 fevr 1862-1er juil 1864 – 1 – fr A.C.R.P.P. [073]

ESPRONCEDA / Blanco Garcia, Francisco – Madrid: Saenz de Jubera, 1909 – sp Bibl Santa Ana [440]

ESPRONCEDA. ILUSTRACIONES BIOGRAFICAS Y CRITICAS / Alonso Cortes, Narciso – Valladolid: Libreria Santaren, 1942 – sp Bibl Santa Ana [920]

Espronceda, Jose de *see*
- A SALAMANCA DIAK
- BLANCA DE BORBON
- DE GIBRALTAR A LISBOA. VIAJE HISTORICO
- EL DIABLO MUNDO
- EL ESTUDIANTE DE SALAMANCA
- NI EL TIO NI EL SOBRINO
- OBRAS POETICAS
- OBRAS POETICAS COMPLETAS
- OBRAS POETICAS DE
- OBRAS POETICAS DE D..., ORDENADAS Y ANOTADAS POR J.E. HARTZENBUSCH A SABER
- OBRAS POETICAS DE.... PRECEDIDAS DE LA BIOGRAFIA DEL AUTOR
- OBRAS POETICAS Y ESCRITOS EN PROSA
- OBRAS POETICAS Y ESCRITOS EN PROSA. COLECCION COMPLETA...ORDENADA POR DON PATRICIO DE LA ESNOSURA
- PAGINAS OLVIDADAS
- PAGINAS OLVIDADAS DE...
- POESIAS
- POESIAS ELEGIDAS
- SANCHO SALDANA
- SANCHO SALDANA O EL CASTELLANO DE CUELLAR
- LAS TRES REINAS

ESPRONCEDA SU EPOCA SU VIDA Y SUS OBRAS / Cascales Munoz, Jose – Madrid: Biblioteca Hispania, 1914 – 1 – sp Bibl Santa Ana [946]

ESPRONCEDA...OBRAS / Rodriguez Solis, Enrique – 1884 – 9 – 1.50f – sp Bibl Santa Ana [890]

Esputa, J *see* THE TUNEER'S POLKA

O ESQUADRO : ORGAO DO LIVRE PENSAMENTO – [s.l.] Ago 1908 – 1,5,6 – bl Biblioteca [072]

Esquer, A *see* ESSAI SUR LES CASTES DANS L'INDE

LOS ESQUIMALES / Birket-Smith, K – Version espanola por F. Payarols. BN-465 2. 1953 – 8 – ne IDC [970]

LES ESQUIMAUX DU NORD DU LABRADOR / Waldmann, S – BN 444 2. 1910 – 8 – ne IDC [305]

ESQUIRE – (v. 71-78. 1969-78 5,6. v. 73-88 1970-78 9) – v. 1-89. 1933-78 – 1 – us UMI [073]

ESQUIRE – v92- 1979- – 1,5,6,9 – us UMI [073]

ESQUIRE FORTNIGHTLY – v.89-91. 1978-79 – 1,5,6,9 – us UMI [073]

Esquirol, Jean Etienne Dominique *see* DES MALADIES MENTALES CONSIDEREES SOUS LES RAPPORTS MEDICAL, HYGIENIQUE ET MEDICO-LEGAL

Esquiros, Alphonse *see* LES VIERGES FOLLES

ESQUISSE BIBLIOGRAPHIQUE RECENTE EN SCIENCES HUMAINES DU DEPARTEMENT DU CENTRE DE LA COTE D'IVOIRE / Bonnefond, Th – (Black Africa series). 1968 – 9 – fr Hachette [010]

ESQUISSE BIO-BIBLIOGRAPHIQUE DE MONSIEUR LE NOTAIRE LEONIDAS BACHAND, PRESIDENT DE L'ALLIANCE FRANCAISE DE SHERBROOKE / Desjardins, Soeur – 1962. SEM105P4 – 1mf – 9 – cn Bibl Nat [340]

ESQUISSE DE L'HISTOIRE DU KHANAT DE KHOKAND / Nalivkine – Traduit du russe par A. Dozon. 1889 – 9 – fr Orientalistes [950]

ESQUISSE DU COMMERCE DE PELLETERIES DES ANGLOIS, DANS L'AMERIQUE SEPTENTRIONALE / Selkirk, Thomas D – Montreal: James Brown, 1819. SEM16P82 – 1r – 5 – Can$9.00 – cn Bibl Nat [971]

ESQUISSE D'UNE ETUDE GENEALOGIQUE DES SARA KABA M'BANGA DU VILLAGE DE MIAMANE, REPUBLIQUE CENTRE-AFRICAINE / Chaventre, A & Jaeger, G – 9 – F60.00 – fr Ethnologie [920]

ESQUISSE D'UNE GRAMMAIRE COMPAREE DES DIALECTES CREE ET CHIPPEWAY / Adam, Lucien – Paris: Maisonneuve. 1876. 02391. (Pre-1900 Canadiana) – 9 – cn C.I.H.M. [490]

ESQUISSE D'UNE PHILOSOPHIE DE LA RELIGION D'APR ES LA PSYCHOLOGIE ET L'HISTOIRE = OUTLINES OF A PHILOSOPHY OF RELIGION BASED ON PSYCHOLOGY AND HISTORY / Sabatier, Auguste – (In English) – 1mf – 9 – 0-8370-5016-2 – 1985-3016 – us A.T.L.A. [200]

ESQUISSE D'UNE PHILOSOPHIE DE LA RELIGION D'APRES LA PSYCHOLOGIE ET L'HISTOIRE / Sabatier, Auguste – (Includes name index) – 7e ed. Paris: Fischbacher, 1903 – 1mf – 9 – 0-8370-5014-6 – 1985-3014 – us A.T.L.A. [100]

ESQUISSE GEOLOGIQUE DU CANADA POUR SERVIR A L'INTELLIGENCE DE LA CARTE GEOLOGIQUE ET DE LA COLLECTION DES MINERAUX ECONOMIQUES ENVOYEES A L'EXPOSITION UNIVERSELLE DE PARIS, 1855 / Logan, WE – Paris: Hector Bossange et fils, 1855. SEM105P227 – 2mf – 9 – Can$4.50 – cn Bibl Nat [550]

ESQUISSES ALLEMANDES / Jolivet, A et al – Paris: Aubier, [1942] – 1 – us U.W. Library [430]

ESQUISSES SENEGALAISES - PYSHIONOMIE DU PAYS - PEUPLADES - COMMERCE - RELIGIONS - PASSE ET AVENIR - RECITS ET LEGENDES / Boilat, PD – (African Library). Paris. P. Bertrand. 1853 – 9 – fr Hachette [960]

Esquivel, Antonio *see* ACUSADO A LA INQUISICION

Esquivel Obregon, Toribio *see*
- APUNTES PARA LA HISTORIA DEL DERECHO DE MEJICO
- HERNANDO CORTES Y EL DERECHOS INTERNACIONAL EN EL SIGLO 16

ESRA, NEHEMIA UND ESTHER / Siegfried, Carl – Goettingen: Vandenhoeck, 1901. 175p. 1 fiche – 9 – us A.T.L.A. [240]

Esrar Dede, Efendi *see* DIVAN

ESREF – (Missing issue No. 52, otherwise complete) – Istanbul: Birinci sene, aded 1-52, (25 Safer, 1327-21 Safer, 1328 [18 March, 1909-5 March, 1910]) – 7mf – 9 – $75.00 – us MEDOC [949]

Esref *see* ESREF UES-SU'ARA

ESREF UES-SU'ARA / Esref – Istanbul, 1278 – 4mf – 9 – $24.00 – us MEDOC [949]

Esrefoglu Abdulah, Al-Rumi *see* DIVAN

ESSA EINAY EL HE-HARIM – (Ha-Levanon, 29th Elul 5636). 1876. BJ-27-228 1 – 9 – ne IDC [630]

L'ESSAI – Montreal: [s.n., 1894-1895?] – 9 – cn C.I.H.M. [440]

ESSAI ANALYTIQUE ET CRITIQUE DE STATISTIQUE MORTUAIRE COMPAREE. / Espine, Marc d' – Geneve et Paris: J. Cherbuliez, 1858. xxii,466p. 6 fiches. (Statistics Series: Medical Studies) – 9 – 15.00 – fr Bibl Nationale [310]

ESSAI BIBLIOGRAPHIQUE : HISTOIRE ET GEOGRAPHIE, MANUELS POUR LES ELEVES DE LANGUE FRANCAISE... / Despins, Simonne – 1962. SEM105P4 – 1mf – 9 – cn Bibl Nat [900]

ESSAI BIBLIOGRAPHIQUE : LA RELIGION ET LE FRANCAIS: MANUELS POUR LES ELEVES DE LANGUE FRANCAISE, APPROUVES... / Robert, Fr – 1961. SEM105P4 – 2mf – 9 – cn Bibl Nat [240]

ESSAI COMPARATIF SUR LA FORMATION ET LA DISTRIBUTION DU REVENU DE LA FRANCE EN 1815 ET 1835 / Dutens, J M – (Condition of 19th C. French working class series). 1842 – 9 – fr Hachette [339]

ESSAI CONTRE LES SAINT-SIMONIENS – Metz, impr. de Collignon, 1831, 39 p. Les Saint-Simoniens, 1825-1834. 6988 – 9 – fr Hachette [335]

ESSAI CRITIQUE SUR L'ENSEIGNEMENT PRIMAIRE EN FRANCE DE 1800 A 1900 / Gossot, Emile – Paris. 1901. (La Condition Ouvriere. Part Two.) – 9 – 12.50 – fr Bibl Nationale [360]

ESSAI D'ANALYSE SUR LES JEUX DE HASARD / Montmort, Pierre-R de – Paris: Quillau, 1708 – 1 – F114.80 – fr Armell [306]

ESSAI D'APPRECIATION DES EFFETS DES OPERATIONS DE DEVELOPPEMENT A PARTIR DE L'ETUDE D'UN GROUPE DE BUDGETS FAMILIAUX / Michotte, J – (Africa series). 1967 – 9 – fr Hachette [330]

ESSAI DE BIBLIOGRAPHIE CHARITABLE / Granier, Camille – (Condition of 19th C. French working class series). 1891 – 9 – fr Hachette [360]

ESSAI DE BIBLIOGRAPHIE SUR LE REGIME MUNICIPAL DANS LA PROVINCE DE QUEBEC / Drapeau, Julien – 1955. SEM105P4 – 2mf – 9 – cn Bibl Nat [350]

ESSAI DE BIO-BIBLIOGRAPHIE ANNOTEE DU REVEREND FRERE MARC, S.C. / Marie-Clement, Frere – 1964. SEM105P4 – 2mf – 9 – cn Bibl Nat [240]

ESSAI DE BIO-BIBLIOGRAPHIE DE MONSIEUR LOUIS-GERARD "GERRY" GOSSELIN, AVOCAT, ECRIVAIN, JOURNALISTE / Sainte-Marie-de-l'Ange-Gardien, Soeur – 1962. SEM105P4 – 2mf – 9 – cn Bibl Nat [920]

ESSAI DE BIO-BIBLIOGRAPHIE SUR CECILE ROULEAU, EDUCATRICE / Roy-Tessier, Antoinette – 1964. SEM105P4 – 1mf – 9 – cn Bibl Nat [370]

ESSAI DE CLASSIFICATION DES LEPIDOPTERES PRODUCTEURS DE SOIE / Dusuzeau, J & Sonthonnax, L – Lyon, 1897-1911.7 fasc. Z/1210/2 – 8 – ne IDC [590]

ESSAI DE CRITIQUE MILITAIRE / Gilbert, Georges – Paris. Libr. de la "Nouvelle Revue". 1890, viii, 324p., iii, (Strategy of War Series) – 9 – fr Hachette [355]

ESSAI DE DEFINITION DE QUELQUES INDICATEURS DE STRUCTURE ET DE FONCTIONNEMENT DE L'ECONOMIE DES CENTRES SEMI-URBAINS / Chevassu, J – (Africa series). 1970 – 9 – fr Hachette [338]

ESSAI DE DICTIONNAIRE FRANCAIS-HAOUSSA ET HAOUSSA-FRANCAIS, PRECEDE D'UN ESSAI DE GRAMMAIRE DE LA LANGUE HAOUSSA, MAGNA N HAOUSSA, PALE PAR LES NEGRES DU SOUDAN / Leroux, J M – Alger, Adolphe Jourdan. 1886 – 9 – $10.00 – fr Orientalistes [470]

ESSAI DE DROIT INTERNATIONAL PRIVE,... / Durand, L – Paris, 1884 – 9mf – 1 – ILM-511/1 – ne IDC [327]

ESSAI DE GRAMMAIRE DE LA LANGUE TAMACHEK / Hanoteau, A – Alger, Adolphe Jourdan. 1896 – 9 – $10.00 – fr Orientalistes [470]

ESSAI DE GRAMMAIRE DOUMA (HAUT-OGOWE, CONGO FRANCAIS) / Reeb, Antoine – Paris. 1895 – 9 – $5.00 – fr Orientalistes [490]

ESSAI DE GRAMMAIRE MALGACHE / Montagne, Lucien – Paris: Societe d'editions, geographiques, maritimes et coloniales, 1931 – 1 – us Res Libr [490]

ESSAI DE GRAMMAIRE MALINKEE – 1896 – 9 – $5.00 – fr Orientalistes [490]

ESSAI DE GRAMMAIRE RUGANDA – Paris, Imprimerie F. Leve. 1885 – 9 – $5.00 – fr Orientalistes [490]

ESSAI DE MANUEL DE LA LANGUE AGNI, PARLEE DANS LA MOITIE ORIENTALE DE LA COTE D'IVOIRE – Paris: Libraire africaine et coloniale, 1900 – 1 – us Res Libr [490]

ESSAI DE MANUEL PRATIQUE DE LA LANGUE MANDE OU MANDINGUE / Delafosse, Maurice – 9 – fr Orientalistes [490]

ESSAI DE METHODOLOGIE DES SCIENCES THEOLOGIQUES / Vaucher, Edouard – Paris: Jules Claye, 1878 – 1mf – 9 – 0-8370-5621-7 – 1985-3621 – us A.T.L.A. [200]

ESSAI DE MISE EN RELATION DU SYSTEME DE PARENTE ET DE LA TENURE FONCIERE DANS LE VILLAGE DE ST-CYR-SUR-MORIN (SEINE ET MARNE) / Wajs, C – 9 – FF30.00 – fr Ethnologie [306]

ESSAI DE RECHERCHE EN LINGUISTIQUE CONSTRASTIVE SUR LE SYNTAGME NOMINAL EN AKAN ET EN FRANCAIS / Hammond, J A – 1983 – F100.00 – fr Ethnologie [410]

ESSAI DE RECHERCHE EN LINGUISTIQUE CONTRASTIVE: LE SYSTEME VERBAL CHICHEWA-FRANCAIS / Chilipaine, F A – 9 – F120.00 – fr Ethnologie [400]

ESSAI DE SEMANTIQUE / Breal, M – 1897 – 9 – fr I.C.S. [400]

ESSAI DE STATIQUE CHIMIQUE / Berthollet, Claude-Louis – Paris, Demonville, 1803, 2 v., 543 p., viii-555 p. Histoire des Sciences XVIIe-XIXe Siecles. 7951 2 – 9 – fr Hachette [540]

ESSAI DE STATISTIQUE / Mourgue, Jacques Antoine – Paris, Maradan, 1801. viii, 76 p. 2 fiches. (Statistics Series: Demography) – 9 – 6.00 – fr Bibl Nationale [310]

ESSAI DE VIVISION REGIONALE EN COTE D'IVOIRE / Trouchaud, J P – (Africa series). 1968 – 9 – fr Hachette [960]

ESSAI D'EDUCATION NATIONALE / Caradeuc de la Chalotais, Louis-Rene – ou PLAN D'ETUDES POUR LA JEUNESSE. s.l. de 1763. 6739 – 9 – fr Hachette [944]

ESSAI D'ETUDE D'UN NSAMBO / Vangroenweghe, D – (Tribu des E:ko:nda, Republique du Zaire) – 9 – F70.00 – fr Ethnologie [960]

ESSAI D'HYGROMETRIE OU SUR LA MESURE DE L'HUMIDITE / Lambert, Jean-Henri – HISTOIRE DE L'AC. R. DES SC. DE BERLIN POUR 1769, Berlin, 1771, p. 68-127, 3 pl. SUITE DE l'ESSAI D'HYGROMETRIE, NOUVEAUX MEMOIRES DE L'AC. DE BERLIN (1772), Berlin, 1774, p. 65-102. Histoire des Sciences XVIIe-XIXe Siecles. 7983 – 9 – fr Hachette [530]

ESSAI D'UN CODE PENAL INTERNATIONAL... / Cosentini, F – N.p., n.d. – 1mf – 1 – ILM-2804/1 – ne IDC [327]

ESSAI D'UN NOUVEAU COURS DE LANGUE ALLEMANDE OU CHOIX DES MEILLEURS POEMES DE ZACHARIE, KLEIST ET HALLER / Boulard, Antoine Marie Henri – Paris: Koenig, Fuchs et Honnert, 1798 – 2mf – 9 – 6.00 – fr Bibl Nationale [430]

ESSAI D'UNE BIBLIOGRAPHIE SUR LA QUESTION D'ORIENT : ORIENT EUROPEEN 1821-1897 / Bengesco, G – Bruxelles, Paris, 1897 – 4mf – 9 – ne IDC [956]

ESSAI D'UNE CLASSIFICATION NATURELLE DES CHAMPIGNONS, OU TABLEAU METHODIQUE DES GENRES RAPPORTES JUSQU'A PRESENT A CETTE FAMILLE / Brongniart, A T – Paris. 1825. B-6251 2 – 8 – ne IDC [580]

ESSAI D'UNE FAUNE ENTOMOLOGIQUE DE L'ARCHIPEL INDO-NEERLANDAIS / Vollenhoven, S C S van – La Haye, 1863-1868. 3 pts – 9mf – 9 – Z-1689/2 – ne IDC [580]

ESSAI D'UNE INTRODUCTION A LA DOGMATIQUE PROTESTANTE / Lobstein, Paul – Paris: Librairie Fischbacher, 1896. 1 fiche – 9 – us A.T.L.A. [240]

ESSAI D'UNE INTRODUCTION À LA DOGMATIQUE PROTESTANTE *see* COLLECTED WORKS

ESSAI D'UNE NOUVELLE AGROSTOGRAPHIE / Palisot de Beauvois, A M F J – Paris. 1812. B-7 2 – 8 – ne IDC [580]

ESSAI D'UNE STATISTIQUE GENERALE DE LA FRANCE / Peuchet, Jacques – (French Socialist Congresses Series). Paris. Testu, an IX – 9 – fr Hachette [310]

ESSAI D'UNE THEORIE... / Bailly, L – Paris, 1921 – 3mf – 9 – ILM-336/1 – ne IDC [340]

ESSAI HISTORIQUE ET MORAL SUR LA PAUVRETE DES NATIONS, LA POPULATION LA MENDICITE, LES HOPITAUX ET LES ENFANTS TROUVES / Fodere, FE – (Condition of 19th C. French working class series). 1825 – 9 – fr Hachette [360]

ESSAI HISTORIQUE SUR LA MUSIQUE ET LES MUSICIENS DANS LES PAYS-BAS / Gregoir, E – Bruxelles: Schott Freres, 1861 – 1 – us Sibley [780]

ESSAI HISTORIQUE SUR LE DROIT DES MARCHES ET DES FOIRES / Huvelin, Paul L – Paris. 1897. (La Condition Ouvriere. Part Two.) – 9 – 17.50 – fr Bibl Nationale [360]

ESSAI MONOGRAPHIQUE SUR LES CLERITES. INSECTES COLEOPTERES / ed by Spinola, M – Genes, 1844 – 2 vols – 8 – ne IDC [590]

ESSAI MONOGRAPHIQUE SUR LES GENRES SCROPHULARIA / Wydler, H – Geneve. 1828. B-5178 2 – 8 – ne IDC [580]

ESSAI OU PROJET D'EDUCATION NATIONALE POUR LES HOMMES / Fontaine de Saint-Freville, Louis – Paris. 1791. 6759 – 9 – fr Hachette [944]

ESSAI PHILOSOPHIQUE SUR LES PROBABILITES. / Laplace, Pierre Simon de – Paris: E. Chiron, 1920. xvi,264p. L'ed. ancienne faite partie de la Bibliotheque de Philosophie moderne. 3 fiches. (Philosophy Collection) – 9 – 8.00 – fr Bibl Nationale [190]

ESSAI SUR CETTE QUESTION : QUAND ET COMMENT L'AMERIQUE A-T-ELLE ETE PEUPLEE D'HOMMES ET D'ANIMAUX? / Engel, Samuel – Amsterdam. 5v. 1767 – 1r – 1 – us Ross [306]

ESSAI SUR LA CONDITION DE LA FEMME AU SIAM / Duplatre, Louis – Lyon: Rey, 1922. 112p. (Les Femmes Collection) – 2mf – 9 – $6.00 – fr Bibl Nationale [305]

ESSAI SUR LA CONFRERIE RELIGIEUSE DES AISSAOUA AU MAROC... / Brunel, Rene – Paris: Geuthner, 1926 – 1 – F133.78 – fr Armell [306]

ESSAI SUR LA DOCTRINE SOCINIENNE / Amphoux, Henri – Strasbourg: Imprimerie de Veuve Berger-Levrault, 1850 – 1mf – us A.T.L.A. [320]

ESSAI SUR LA FAMILLE DES CYPERACEES / Lestiboudois, T G – 1819. B-5084 2 – 8 – ne IDC [580]

ESSAI SUR LA GEOGRAPHIE DES PLANTES / Humboldt, Alexander von – Paris. 1805. B-5972 2 – 8 – ne IDC [580]

ESSAI SUR LA LANGUE CONGOLAISE / Cambier – Bruxelles, Imprimerie Polleunis et Ceuterick. 1891 – 9 – $5.00 – fr Orientalistes [490]

ESSAI SUR LA LANGUE DU BORNOU, SUIVI DES VOCABULAIRES DU BEGHARMI, DU MANDARA ET DE TIMPOUCTOU / Klaproth, Julius von – Paris, Imprimerie Decourchant. 1826 – 9 – $5.00 – fr Orientalistes [490]

ESSAI SUR LA LITTERATURE DES BERBERES / Basset, Henri – Alger: J. Carbonnel, 1920 – fr Armell [470]

ESSAI SUR LA LITTERATURE MERVEILLEUSE DES NOIRS, SUIVI DE CONTES INDIGENES DE L'OUEST-AFRICAIN FRANCAISE / Equiloecq, F V – Paris: E Leroux, 1913-16 – 1 – us Res Libr [490]

ESSAI SUR LA MEMOIRE COLLECTIVE DES HABITANTS DES MONTS DU LYONNAIS / Collin, P C – 9 – F60.00 – fr Ethnologie [305]

ESSAI SUR LA MORTALITE A STRASBOURG: PARTIE RETROSPECTIVE / Boersch, Charles – Strasbourg, G. Silbermann, 1836. 201 p. 3 fiches. (Statistics Series: Medical Studies) – 9 – 8.00 – fr Bibl Nationale [310]

ESSAI SUR LA MUSIQUE ANCIENNE ET MODERNE / Laborde, J-B de – 1780. 4v – 9 – us Sibley [780]

ESSAI SUR LA MUSIQUE ANCIENNE ET MODERNE / Laborde, J-B de – P 705. 4 v. 1780 – 9 – ne IDC [930]

ESSAI SUR LA NATALITE DANS LE CANTON DE BEAUMONT-HAGUE / Dumont, Arsene – Reprod. d'un extrait des Memoires de la Ste. d'Anthropologie de Paris, 1893-95. p1,49. 1 fiche. (Statistics Series: Medical Studies) – 9 – 6.00 – fr Bibl Nationale [310]

ESSAI SUR LA NATURE ET LA DESTINATION DE L'AME / Collins, Anthony – (D'Holbach series). 1769 – 9 – fr Hachette [120]

ESSAI SUR LA NATURE ET L'EXERCICE DE L'AUTORITE DU PEUPLE DANS UN ETAT / Morisse, Avocat – 1789 – 9 – fr Hachette [321]

ESSAI SUR LA NOTION DE REGLE DE DROIT... / Corbu, A C – Paris, 1935 – 2mf – 1 – ILM-1713/1 – ne IDC [327]

ESSAI SUR LA PEDAGOGIE DE LEIBNIZ / Vernay, Joseph – Heidelberg, 1914 – 2mf – 9 – DM62.00 – 3-89349-310-7 – gw Hänsel [430]

ESSAI SUR LA PHYSIONOMIE DES SERPENS / Schlegel, H – The Hague. 1837. BZ-2241 1 – 9 – ne IDC [590]

ESSAI SUR LA POESIE RYTHMIQUE / Bouchaud, M A – 1763 – 9 – fr I.C.S. [440]

ESSAI SUR LA POLICE GENERALE DES GRAINS, SUR LEURS PRIX ET SUR LES EFFETS DE L'AGRICULTURE / Herbert, Claude Jacques – Berlin: s.n., 1775. xviii,435p.5 fiches. (Economics Collection) – 9 – 12.00 – fr Bibl Nationale [338]

ESSAI SUR LA POLITIQUE DES SUBVENTIONS ADMINISTRATIVES / Boulouis, J – F60.00 – fr Ethnologie [350]

ESSAI SUR LA PREMIERE FROMATION DU LANGUES ET SUR LA DIFFERENCE DU GENIE / Smith, Adam – (Linguistic series). 1809 – 9 – fr Hachette [400]

ESSAI SUR LA SITUATION RUSSE / Ogarev, N P – (Russia – 19th C.) 1862 – 9 – fr Hachette [947]

ESSAI SUR LA STATISTIQUE DE LA POPULATION FRANCAISE, 1836 / Angeville, A d' – 1 – uk Microform Academic [944]

ESSAI SUR LA STATISTIQUE MORALE DE LA FRANCE PRECEDE D'UN RAPPORT A L'ACADEMIE DES SCIENCES PAR MM. LACROIX, SILVESTRE ET GIRARD / Guerry, Andre-Michel – (Condition of 19th C. French working class series). 1833 – 9 – fr Hachette [310]

ESSAI SUR LA VIE ET LES OUVRAGES DE NICOLE ORESME / Meunier, Francis – Paris: Lahure, 1857. 105p. 3mf. (Literature Collection) – 9 – $8.00 – fr Bibl Nationale [920]

ESSAI SUR L'ACCLIMATATION DE QUELQUES FOUGEA6RES ET LYCOPODES EXOTIQUES / Ternisien, T de – Cherbourg, 1860. 23 pp. B-7271 1 – 9 – ne IDC [580]

ESSAI SUR L'ACCOMPAGNEMENT DU CLAVECIN / Clement, Charles-F – 1758 – 9 – us Sibley [780]

ESSAI SUR L'ARCHITECTURE / Laugier, M A – Paris, Duchesne., 1753. 8 fol., xiv, 293, 18p. (Architecture Series) – 9 – fr Hachette [720]

ESSAI SUR L'ART DE RAMPER, A L'USAGE DES COURTISANS / Holbach, Paul-Thiry d' – (D'Holbach series) – 9 – fr Hachette [300]

ESSAI SUR LE CHAMEAU AU SAHARA OCCIDENTAL / Monteil, Vincent – Saint-Louis du Senegal, 1952 – 1 – us Res Libr [636]

ESSAI SUR LE DEPARTEMENT DE L'AUDE, ADRESSE AU MINISTRE DE L'INTERIEUR / Barante, Claude I B de – An XI – 9 – fr Hachette [944]

ESSAI SUR LE DEVELEOPPEMENT... / Deherpe, L – Paris, 1903 – 3mf – 1 – ILM-492/1 – ne IDC [327]

ESSAI SUR LE DROIT DES GENS – N.p., 1795 – 2mf – 1 – ILM-1032/1 – ne IDC [327]

ESSAI SUR LE DROIT DES GENS NAPOLEONIEN... / Chevalley, E – Paris, n.d. – 3mf – 1 – ILM-724/1 – ne IDC [327]

ESSAI SUR LE FONDEMENT METAPHYSIQUE DE LA MORALE / Rauh, Frederic – Paris: Felix Alcan, 1891 – 1mf – 9 – 0-8370-6340-X – 1986-0340 – us A.T.L.A. [170]

ESSAI SUR LE GOUT DE LA MUSIQUE, AVEC LE CARACTERE DES TROIS CELEBRES JOUERS DE VIOLON / Rangoni, J B de – Text in French and Italian. P 747. 1792 – 9 – ne IDC [780]

ESSAI SUR LE LIBRE ARBITRE : SA THEORIE ET SON HISTOIRE / Fonsegrive, George – (Includes bibliographical references) – 2e ed. Paris: Felix Alcan, 1896 – 2mf – 9 – 0-8370-6184-9 – 1986-0184 – us A.T.L.A. [210]

ESSAI SUR LE LIBRE ARBITRE / Schopenhauer, Arthur – 2e ed. Paris: Bailliere, 1880 – 1 – F114.80 – fr Armell [140]

ESSAI SUR LE PRINCIPE DES NATIONALITES – Paris, 1882 – 3mf – 1 – ILM-2374/1 – ne IDC [327]

ESSAI SUR LE STYLE / Thiebault, D – 1774 – 9 – fr I.C.S. [440]

ESSAI SUR LE SYSTEME ANGLAIS DE CONFLITS DE LOIS EN MATIERE DE SUCCESSIONS / Depitre, M – Paris, 1936 – 2mf – 1 – ILM-3684/1 – ne IDC [327]

ESSAI SUR LE SYSTEME ANGLAIS DE CONFLITS DE LOIS EN MATIERE DE SUCCESSIONS / Depitre, M – Paris, 1936 – 2mf – 1 – ILM-2961/1 – ne IDC [327]

ESSAI SUR L'ECCLESIOLOGIE DE ZWINGLE / Bachofen, Charles – Geneve: Rivera & Dubois, 1890 – 1mf – us A.T.L.A. [240]

ESSAI SUR L'EDUCATION NATIONALE / Bry, Jean A J de – Second partie. Laon. A. P. Courtois. 1790 – 9 – fr Hachette [370]

ESSAI SUR L'ENTOMOLOGIE DU DEPARTEMENT DU PUY-DE-DOME / Baudet-Lafarge, M J – Monographie des Carabiques. Clermont-Ferrand, 1835. Z-1050/2 – 8 – ne IDC [590]

ESSAI SUR L'ENTOMOLOGIE HORTICOLE, COMPRENANT L'HISTOIRE DES INSECTES NUISIBLES A L'HORTICULTURE / Boisduval, J B A D de – Paris, 1867. xvi,648p. Z-1079/2 – 8 – ne IDC [590]

ESSAI SUR LES CASTES DANS L'INDE / Esquer, A – Pondichery: A. Saligny, 1870. 500p. Bibliographic footnotes – 1 – us U.W. Library [950]

ESSAI SUR LES CRYPTOGAMES DES ECORCES EXOTIQUES OFFICINALES / Fee, A L A – Paris. 1824. Supplement a l'essai sur les cryptogames des ecorces exotiques officinales. Paris. 1835. B-573 2 – 8 – ne IDC [580]

ESSAI SUR LES DOCTRINES SOCIALES ET POLITIQUES DE TAKI-D-DIN-AHMAD B. TAIMIYA / Laoust, Henri – Le Caire, 1939 – 13mf – 8 – ne Slangenburg [260]

ESSAI SUR LES ERREURS ET LES SUPERSTITIONS / Castilhon, Jean-Louis – (D'Holbach series). 1765 – 9 – fr Hachette [130]

ESSAI SUR LES HALLUCINATIONS CONSCIENTES / Bessonnet, Rene – 1898 – 1 – us I.U. Libraries [390]

ESSAI SUR LES LANGUES EN GENERAL; SUR LA LANGUE FRANCOISE EN PARTICULIER... / Sablier, C – Paris, 1777 – 3mf – 9 – ne IDC [440]

ESSAI SUR LES LOIS DE LA POPULATION ET DE LA MORTALITE EN FRANCE / Demonferrand, Jean Baptiste Firmin – Reprod. d'un extrait de Journal de l'Ecole royale polytechnique, 1838. v26, 26e cahier, p249-309. 1 fiche. (Statistics Series: Demography). (Statistics Series: Medical Studies) – 9 – 6.00 – fr Bibl Nationale [310]

ESSAI SUR LES MOYENS DE REFORMER L'EDUCATION PARTICULIERE ET GENERALE / Fleury, Nicolas-Marie de – Paris: Guyllin and Duchesne, 1764. 6757 – 9 – fr Hachette [944]

ESSAI SUR LES MYODAIRES / Robineau-Desvoidy, J B – Z 2158 2. 1830 – 8 – ne IDC [590]

ESSAI SUR LES ORIGINES DES PARTIS SADUCEEN ET PHARISIEN... / Montet, Edouard Louis – (Includes bibliographical references) – Vienne: Adolphe Holzhausen, 1883 – 1mf – 9 – 0-8370-4472-3 – 1985-2472 – us A.T.L.A. [270]

ESSAI SUR LES ORIGINES DU ROMANCERO / Foulche-Delbosc, Raymond – 1912 – 1 – us I.U. Libraries [390]

ESSAI SUR LES PREJUGES, OU, DE L'INFLUENCE DES OPINION SUR LES MOEURS ET SUR LE BONHEUR DES HOMMES / Holbach, Paul-Thiry d' – (D'Holbach series). 1770 – 9 – fr Hachette [390]

ESSAI SUR LES PRINCIPES REGISSANT L'ADMINISTRATION DE LA JUSTICE AUX INDES ORIENTALES HOLLANDAISES SURTOUT DANS LES ILES DE JAVA ET DE MADOURA ET LEUR APPLICATION / Winckel, Christiaan Philip Karel – Samarang, van Dorp, 1880. 315 p. LL-10024 – 1 – us L of C Photodup [340]

ESSAI SUR LES PROTECTORATS / Despagnet, F – Paris, 1896 – 5mf – 1 – ILM-1957/1 – ne IDC [327]

ESSAI SUR LES RELATIONS DU TRAVAIL AVEC LE CAPITAL / Dupont-White, Charles – (Condition of 19th C. French working class series). 1846 – 9 – fr Hachette [331]

ESSAI SUR LES SOURCES DE L'ORDO-MISSAE PREMONTRE / Luykx, B – Postel, 1947 – 1mf – 8 – ne Slangenburg [240]

ESSAI SUR LES VICES DU LANGAGE / Sajus, B – 1821 – 9 – fr I.C.S. [400]

ESSAI SUR L'EVOLUTION INTELLECTUELLE DE L'ITALIE DE 1815-1930 / Luchaire, J – H-550 2. 1906 – 8 – ne IDC [945]

ESSAI SUR L'HABITAT SEDENTAIRE TRADITIONNEL AU SAHARA ALGERIEN / Eschallier, J C – Paris, Universite de Paris, Institut d'urbanisme, 1968 – us Res Libr [900]

ESSAI SUR L'HISTOIRE ANTIQUE D'ABYSSIENIE / Kammerer, A – 1926. BA-322 2 – 8 – ne IDC [930]

ESSAI SUR L'HISTOIRE DE LA BIBLE DANS LA FRANCE CHRETIENNE AU MOYEN AGE / Trochon, Charles – Paris: Alphonse Derenne, 1878. 1 fiche – 9 – us A.T.L.A. [240]

ESSAI SUR L'HISTOIRE DU CULTE REFORME PRINCIPALEMENT AU 16E ET AU 19E SI'ECLE / Doumergue, Emile – Paris: Fischbacher, 1890 – 1mf – us A.T.L.A. [240]

ESSAI SUR L'HISTOIRE DU PROTESTANTISME AU HAVRE ET DANS SES ENVIRONS / Amphoux, Henri – Havre: L. Dombre, 1894 – 2mf – us A.T.L.A. [240]

ESSAI SUR L'HISTOIRE LITTERAIRE DES PATOIS DU MIDI DE LA FRANCE AUX XVIEET XVIIESIECLES / Noulet, J B – 1859 – 9 – fr I.C.S. [440]

ESSAI SUR L'HISTOIRE NATURELLE DE LA FRANCE EQUINOXIALE / Barrere, P – Paris. 1741. B-5323 2 – 8 – ne IDC [574]

ESSAI SUR L'HISTOIRE NATURELLE DU CHILI / Molina, G J – Translated from Italian and extended by Gruvel. Paris, 1789. 351 pp. B-5451 2 – 8 – ne IDC [580]

ESSAI SUR L'ORIGINE DE LA NOBLESSE EN FRANCE AU MOYEN AGE / Guilhiermoz, P – H-211 2. 1902 – 8 – ne IDC [944]

ESSAI THEORIQUE ET PRATIQUE SUR LES BATAILLES / Grimoard, P H de – Paris. Vve. Desaint. 1775. xvi, 208p. (Strategy of War Series) – 9 – fr Hachette [355]

ESSAIES OR RATHER IMPERFECT OFFERS / Johnson, Robert – 1607 – 9 – 10.00 – us Scholars' Facs [840]

LES ESSAIS – Revue mensuelle. no. 1-9. Paris. avr 1904-avr 1906 – 1 – fr A.C.R.P.P. [073]

ESSAIS BIBLIQUES / Vernes, Maurice – (Includes bibliographical references) – Paris: Ernest Leroux, 1891 – 1mf – 9 – 0-8370-5672-1 – 1985-3672 – us A.T.L.A. [220]

ESSAIS D'ANALYSE / Condorcet, Marie Jean Antoine Nicolas de – Paris: Didot, 1768. li,93p. 2 fiches. (Science Collection) – 9 – 6.00 – fr Bibl Nationale [500]

ESSAIS D'ARITHMETIQUE POLITIQUE / Diannyere, Antoine – Paris: Goujon fils, Debray, Dupont, 1800. xvi,71p. 1 fiche. (Economics Collection) – 9 – 6.00 – fr Bibl Nationale [330]

ESSAIS D'ART LIBRE – Revue nouvelle. no. 1-33. Paris. fevr 1892-oct 1894 – 1 – fr A.C.R.P.P. [073]

ESSAIS DE PALEOCONCHOLOGIE / Cosmann, M – Paris. 1895. v.1-13. BZ-2240 1 – 9 – ne IDC [560]

ESSAIS DE PHILOSOPHIE RELIGIEUSE / Laberthonniere, Lucien – (Includes appendix) – Paris: P Lethielleux, c1903 – 1mf – 9 – 0-8370-4027-2 – 1985-2027 – us A.T.L.A. [200]

ESSAIS D'UN DICTIONNAIRE UNIVERSEL / Furetiere, Antoine – 1684 – 9 – fr I.C.S. [440]

ESSAIS SUR LE QUEBEC CONTEMPORAIN = ESSAYS ON CONTEMPORARY QUEBEC / Symposium sur les Repercussions Sociales de l'Industrialisation dans la Province de Quebec. – Quebec: Presses universitaires Laval, 1953. SEM16P209 – 1r – 5 – Can$9.00 – cn Bibl Nat [971]

ESSAIS SUR LES ISLES FORTUNEES ET L'ANTIQUE ATLANTIDE OU PRECIS DE L'HISTOIRE GENERALE DE L'ARCHIPEL DES CANARIES / Bory de Saint-Vincent, J B C M – Paris. 1803. B-5858 2 – 8 – ne IDC [910]

ESSAIS SUR LES PRINCIPES DE L'HARMONIE / Serre, J A – 1753 – 2 – us Sibley [780]

AN ESSAY CONCERNING HUMANE UNDERSTANDING / Locke, John – M-110. 1690 – 9 – ne IDC [190]

AN ESSAY CONCERNING THE MULTIPLICATION OF MANKIND : TOGETHER WITH ANOTHER ESSAY IN POLITICAL ARITHMETICK, CONCERNING THE GROWTH OF THE CITY OF LONDON... / Petty, W – London, 3rd ed 1698 – 4mf – 9 – ne IDC [304]

AN ESSAY CONTAINING EVIDENT PROOFS AGAINST THE METHODISTS, FROM CERTAIN OF THEIR SECRET ARTICLES AND PRACTICES,... – London, [1745] – 1mf – 9 – MP-325/1 – ne IDC [240]

ESSAY D'UN DICTIONNAIRE COMTOIS-FRANCOIS / Brun, Mme., nee Maisonforte – 1753 – 9 – fr I.C.S. [440]

ESSAY D'UN DICTIONNAIRE CONTENANT LA CONNAISSANCE DU MONDE, DES SCIENCES UNIVERSELLES... / Feuille, D de la – Amsterdam, 1700 – 5mf – 9 – O-659/1 – ne IDC [500]

ESSAY D'UN DICTIONNAIRE CONTENANT LA CONNAISSANCE DU MONDE, DES SCIENCES UNIVERSELLES... / Feuille, D de la – Wesel, 1700 – 2mf – 9 – O-1621/1 – ne IDC [500]

ESSAY D'UNE PARFAITE GRAMMAIRE DE LA LANGUE FRANCOISE / Chiflet, L – 6e ed. 1680 – 9 – fr I.C.S. [440]

AN ESSAY IN AID OF A GRAMMAR OF ASSENT / Newman, John Henry – London: Burns, Oates, 1870 – 1 roll – 1 – 1-55879-516-2 – uk Libr Preservation [240]

AN ESSAY IN REFUTATION OF ATHEISM / Brownson, Orestes A – Ed. by Henry F. Brownson. Detroit: T. Nourse, 1882. vii,100p – 1 – us U.W. Library [240]

AN ESSAY ON ASSYRIOLOGY / Evans, George – (In English and Akkadian) – London: Williams and Norgate, 1883 – 1mf – 9 – 0-8370-8421-0 – 1986-2421 – us A.T.L.A. [470]

ESSAY ON BEE KEEPING, OR, AN EASY METHOD OF MANAGING BEES IN THE MOST PROFITABLE MANNER TO THEIR OWNER: WITH INFALLIBLE RULES TO PREVENT THEIR DESTRUCTION BY THE MOTH, OR OTHERWISE / Bradt, Joseph – 1st ed. St. Catharines, Ont., 1869. 00238. (Pre-1900 Canadiana) – 9 – cn C.I.H.M. [630]

ESSAY ON CATHOLICISM, LIBERALISM AND SOCIALISM = ESSAYO SOBRE EL CATOLICISMO, EL LIBERALISMO Y EL SOCIALISMO : CONSIDERED IN THEIR FUNDAMENTAL PRINCIPLES / Donoso Cortes, Juan Francisco – Philadelphia: J B Lippincott, 1862 – 1mf – 9 – 0-8370-9228-0 – 1986-3228 – us A.T.L.A. [240]

AN ESSAY ON CHURCH POLITY : COMPREHENDING AN OUTLINE OF THE CONTROVERSY ON ECCLESIASTICAL GOVERNMENT, AND A VINDICATION OF THE ECCLESIASTICAL SYSTEM OF THE METHODIST EPISCOPAL CHURCH / Stevens, Abel – New York: Carlton & Porter, c1847 – 1mf – us A.T.L.A. [240]

ESSAY ON COLONIZATION / Wadstrom, Carl Bernhard – 1794 – 7 – uk Microform Academic [960]

AN ESSAY ON COLONIZATION, PARTICULARLY APPLIED TO THE WESTERN COAST OF AFRICA. / Wadstrom, Carl Bernhard – London. 1794-95 – 1 – us Res Libr [960]

AN ESSAY ON ELOCUTION / Mason, John – 1748. 45p. (English Linguistics Series 1500-1800) – 9 – us UMI [420]

AN ESSAY ON FEVERS / Huxham, J – 2nd ed 1750 – 6mf – 9 – ne IDC [610]

AN ESSAY ON GRAMMAR, AS IT MAY BE APPLIED TO THE ENGLISH LANGUAGE / Ward, William – 1765. 596p. (English Linguistics Series 1500-1800) – 9 – us UMI [420]

ESSAY ON HYDROCEPHALUS ACUTUS / Cheyne, J – M-91. 1808 – 9 – ne IDC [610]

ESSAY ON INDIFFERENCE IN MATTERS OF RELIGION = ESSAI SUR L'INDIFFERENCE EN MATI ERE DE RELIGION / Lamennais, Felicite Robert de – (In English. Includes bibliographical references) – London: John Macqueen, 1895 – 1mf – 9 – 0-8370-7401-0 – 1986-1401 – us A.T.L.A. [230]

AN ESSAY ON LAUGHTER; ITS FORMS, ITS CAUSES, ITS DEVELOPMENT AND ITS VALUE / Sully, James – London, New York, Bombay: Longmans, Green and Co., 1902.xvi,441p – 1 – us U.W. Library [150]

AN ESSAY ON LIBERTY AND SLAVERY / Bledsoe, Albert Taylor – Philadelphia: J.B. Lippincott, 1856 – 1mf – us A.T.L.A. [100]

AN ESSAY ON MILITARY LAW AND THE PRACTICE OF COURTS-MARTIAL / Tytler, Alexander F – 3rd ed. London: T Egerton, 1814 – 5mf – 9 – $7.50 – LLMC 88-118 – us L.L.M.C. [340]

ESSAY ON MR. W.H. LYNCH'S PAMPHLET ENTITLED SCIENTIFIC BUTTER MAKING / Barre, SM – Montreal, 1884. 02433. (Pre-1900 Canadiana) – 9 – cn C.I.H.M. [630]

AN ESSAY ON NAVAL TACTICS, SYSTEMATICAL AND HISTORICAL / Clerk, John – 3rd ed. 1827 – 9 – $20.00 – uk Libr Preservation [355]

AN ESSAY ON OBLIGATIONS: FOR LAWYERS, STUDENTS AND LAYMEN / Foran, Joseph Kearney – Toronto: Carswell, 1886. 03145. (Pre-1900 Canadiana) – 9 – cn C.I.H.M. [971]

AN ESSAY ON ORIGINAL GENIUS AND ITS VARIOUS MODES OF EXERTION IN PHILOSOPHY AND THE FINE ARTS, PARTICULARLY IN POETRY / Duff, William – 1767 – 9 – $20.00 – us Scholars' Facs [190]

AN ESSAY ON PAINTING / Algarotti, F – O-1188 1. 1764 – 9 – ne IDC [750]

AN ESSAY ON PANTHEISM / Hunt, John – rev ed. London: Gibbings, 1893 – 1mf – 9 – 0-8370-3693-3 – 1985-1693 – us A.T.L.A. [210]

AN ESSAY ON PUNCTUATION / Robertson, Joseph – 1785. 196p. (English Linguistics Series 1500-1800) – 9 – us UMI [420]

ESSAY ON SEPULCHRES : OR, A PROPOSAL FOR ERECTING SOME MEMORIAL OF THE ILLUSTRIOUS DEAD IN ALL AGES ON THE SPOT WHERE THEIR REMAINS HAVE BEEN INTERRED / Godwin, William – London: Printed for W. Miller, 1809 – 1 roll – 1 – 1-55879-305-4 – uk Libr Preservation [840]

AN ESSAY ON TASTE 1759, TOGETHER WITH / Gerard, Alexander – Observations concerning the imitative nature of poetry. 1780 – 9 – 20.00 – us Scholars' Facs [700]

AN ESSAY ON THE ADVANTAGES AND DISADVANTAGES WHICH RESPECTIVELY ATTEND FRANCE AND GREAT BRITAIN WITH REGARD TO TRADE... / Tucker, J – Glasgow, 1756 – 3mf – 9 – ne IDC [380]

AN ESSAY ON THE AGE AND ANTIQUITY OF THE BOOK OF NABATHAEAN AGRICULTURE : TO WHICH IS ADDED AN INAUGURAL LECTURE ON THE POSITION OF THE SHEMITIC NATIONS IN THE HISTORY OF CIVILIZATION / Renan, Ernest – (Includes bibliographical references) – London: Truebner, 1862 – 1mf – 9 – 0-8370-8855-0 – 1986-2855 – us A.T.L.A. [930]

AN ESSAY ON THE ANALYSIS OF MINERAL WATERS / Kirwan, Richard – London, 1799 – 1 – us U.W. Library [660]

ESSAY ON THE ARCHITECTURE OF THE HINDUS / Ram Raz – 1834. Royal Asiatic Society – 1 – uk Microform Academic [950]

AN ESSAY ON THE CAUSES OF THE VARIETY OF COMPLEXION AND FIGURE IN THE HUMAN SPECIES : TO WHICH ARE ADDED ANIMADVERSIONS ON CERTAIN REMARKS MADE ON THE 1ST ED OF THIS ESSAY BY MR CHARLES WHITE [...]: ALSO, STRICTURES ON LORD KAIMS' DISCOURSE ON THE ORIGINAL DIVERSITY OF MANKIND / Smith, Samuel Stanhope – (Includes appendix. Filmed with: La raza negra es la mas antigua de las razas humanas/G Fournier) – 2nd enl ed. New Brunswick, [NJ]: J Simpson, 1810 – us Res Libr [573]

AN ESSAY ON THE CHURCH PLAIN CHANT – 1782 – 9 – us Sibley [780]

ESSAY ON THE COMMON FEATURES WHICH APPEAR IN ALL FORMS OF RELIGIOUS BELIEF / Cust, Robert Needham – London: Luzac, 1895 – 1mf – us A.T.L.A. [200]

AN ESSAY ON THE DEVELOPMENT OF CHRISTIAN DOCTRINE / Newman, John Henry – London: J. Toovey, 1845 – 1 roll – 1 – 1-55879-378-X – uk Libr Preservation [240]

ESSAY ON THE ECONOMICS OF DETRIBALIZATION IN NORTHERN RHODESIA / Wilson, G – 7 – uk Microform Academic [960]

AN ESSAY ON THE EVILS OF POPULAR IGNORANCE / Foster, John – And A Discourse on the Communication of Christianity to the people of Hindoostan. New ed., rev. and enl. 1876 – 1 – us A.T.L.A. [240]

AN ESSAY ON THE HISTORY AND NATURE OF ORIGINAL TITLES TO LAND IN THE PROVINCE AND STATE OF PENNSYLVANIA / Huston, Charles – Philadelphia: Johnson, 1849. 484p. LL-650 – 1 – us L of C Photodup [340]

AN ESSAY ON THE IMPROVEMENT OF TIME, WITH NOTES OF SERMONS.. / Foster, John – 1886 – 1 – us A.T.L.A. [240]

ESSAY ON THE INDIGENOUS FOSSORIAL HYMENOPTERA / ed by Shuckard, W E – London, 1837 – XII, 259[8]p, 4pls – 8 – ne IDC [590]

AN ESSAY ON THE JURIDICAL HISTORY OF FRANCE, SO FAR AS IT RELATES TO THE LAW OF THE PROVINCE OF LOWER-CANADA / Sewell, Jonathan – Quebec: Thomas Cary and Co, 1824. SEM16P255 – 1r – 5 – Can$9.00 – cn Bibl Nat [971]

AN ESSAY ON THE LAW OF ART / Warden, Robert Bruce – Washington, D.C., The Ernest Institute, 1878. 300 p. LL-355 – 1 – us L of C Photodup [340]

AN ESSAY ON THE LAW OF PATENTS FOR NEW INVENTIONS / Fessenden, Thomas Green – Boston: Mallory etc. 1810. 229 1p. LL-1064 – 1 – us L of C Photodup [340]

AN ESSAY ON THE LEARNING OF PARTIAL, AND OF FUTURE INTERESTS IN CHATTELS PERSONAL / Keyes, Wade – Montgomery, Ala., Martin, 1853. 412 p. LL-297 – 1 – us L of C Photodup [340]

AN ESSAY ON THE MOST EFFECTUAL MEANS OF PRESERVING THE HEALTH OF SEAMEN IN THE ROYAL NAVY / Lind, J – M 234. 1757 – 9 – ne IDC [355]

AN ESSAY ON THE NATURE AND CONDUCT OF THE PASSIONS AND AFFECTIONS WITH ILLUSTRATIONS ON THE MORAL SENSE / Hutcheson, F – London, 4th ed 1756 – 4mf – 9 – ne IDC [170]

AN ESSAY ON THE ORIGIN AND FORMATION OF THE ROMANCE LANGUAGES / Lewis, George Cornewall – 2nd ed. London: Parker, son, and Bourn, 1862. xii,290p – 1 – us U.W. Library [440]

AN ESSAY ON THE PLACE OF ECCLESIASTICUS IN SEMITIC LITERATURE / Margoliouth, David Samuel – Oxford: Clarendon Press, 1890. 1 fiche – 9 – us A.T.L.A. [220]

ESSAY ON THE PLANTS COLLECTED BY MR. EUGENE FITZALAN / Mueller, Ferdinand Jakob Heinrich von – Melbourne, 1860. B-6463 1 – 9 – ne IDC [580]

AN ESSAY ON THE POWER AND HARMONY OF PROSAIC NUMBERS / Mason, John – 1749. 93p. (English Linguistics Series 1500-1800) – 9 – us UMI [400]

AN ESSAY ON THE POWER OF NUMBERS / Mason, John – 1749. 89p. (English Linguistics Series 1500-1800) – 9 – us UMI [400]

ESSAY ON THE PREVAILING METHODS OF THE EVANGELIZATION OF THE NON-CHRISTIAN WORLD / Cust, Robert Needham – London: Luzac, 1894. ix,296p. 1 fiche – 9 – us A.T.L.A. [240]

AN ESSAY ON THE PRINCIPLE OF POPULATION: OR, A VIEW OF ITS PAST AND PRESENT EFFECTS ON HUMAN HAPPINESS. / Malthus, Thomas Robert – 6th ed. London: J. Murray, 1826. 2v – 1 – us U.W. Library [310]

AN ESSAY ON THE PRINCIPLES OF CIRCUMSTANTIAL EVIDENCE, ILLUSTRATED BY NUMEROUS CASES...5TH ENGLISH ED. (1902) WITH AMERICAN NOTES BY GEORGE E. BEERS...AND ARTHUR L. CORBIN / Wills, William – Boston, Mass., Boston Book Co., 1905. 448 p. LL-1614 – 1 – us L of C Photodup [340]

ESSAY ON THE PROBABILITIES OF THE DURATION OF HUMAN LIFE / Deparcieux, M – 1746 – 1 – uk Microform Academic [120]

ESSAY ON THE QUESTION WHETHER ISLAM HAS BEEN BENEFICIAL OR INJURIOUS TO HUMAN SOCIETY IN GENERAL, AND TO THE MOSAIC AND CHRISTIAN DISPENSATIONS – Lahore: Mohammadan Tract & Book Depot, Punjab, 1891 – us Res Libr [230]

AN ESSAY ON THE REGISTRY LAWS OF LOWER CANADA / Bonner, John – Quebec: Printed by John Lovell, 1852 – 2mf – 9 – Can$4.50 – cn Bibl Nat [340]

ESSAY ON THE SHAKING PALSY / Parkinson, J – M-118. 1817 – 9 – ne IDC [610]

AN ESSAY ON THE SLAVERY... / Clarkson, T – London, 1786 – 3mf – 1 – ILM-619/1 – ne IDC [327]

ESSAY ON THE TIMES: CANADA / Armstrong, William Reginald – 1887. 00031. (Pre-1900 Canadiana) – 9 – cn C.I.H.M. [971]

AN ESSAY ON THE VITAL AND OTHER INVOLUNTARY MOTIONS OF ANIMALS / Whytt, R – M 280. 1751 – 9 – ne IDC [590]

AN ESSAY ON TRANSCENDENTALISM / Ellis, Charles Mayo – 1842 – 9 – $10.00 – us Scholars' Facs [190]

AN ESSAY ON UNIVERSAL ETYMOLOGY / Blacklock, Thomas – 1756. 33p. (English Linguistics Series 1500-1800) – 9 – us UMI [400]

AN ESSAY ON USES AND TRUSTS, AND ON THE NATURE AND OPERATION CONVEYANCES AT COMMON LAW. / Sanders, Francis Williams – 2d American ed., from the last London ed. Philadelphia: Small, 1855. 2v in 1. LL-1021 – 1 – us L of C Photodup [340]

AN ESSAY TOWARDS A CONTRAST BETWEEN QUAKERISM AND METHODISM,... / Rutty, John – Bristol, 1771 – 1mf – 9 – MP-473/1 – ne IDC [240]

ESSAY TOWARDS A DICTIONARY, TIBETAN AND ENGLISH / Csoma de Koeroes, A – Calcutta, 1834 – 4mf – ne IDC [480]

AN ESSAY TOWARDS A PRACTICAL ENGLISH GRAMMAR / Greenwood, James – 1711. 327p. (English Linguistics Series 1500-1800) – 9 – us UMI [420]

AN ESSAY TOWARDS A REAL CHARACTER, AND A PHILOSOPHICAL LANGUAGE / Wilkins, John – 1668. 624p. (English Linguistics Series 1500-1800) – 9 – us UMI [400]

ESSAY TOWARDS A REAL CHARACTER AND A PHILOSOPHICAL LANGUAGE / Wilkins, John – (Linguistic series). 1668 – 9 – fr Hachette [190]

AN ESSAY TOWARDS AN ENGLISH GRAMMAR / Fell, John – 1784. 213p. (English Linguistics Series 1500-1800) – 9 – us UMI [420]

AN ESSAY TOWARDS AN HISTORY OF THE ENGLISH TONGUE / Free, John – 1749. 93p. (English Linguistics Series 1500-1800) – 9 – us UMI [420]

AN ESSAY TOWARDS AN INDIAN BIBLIOGRAPHY: BEING A CATALOGUE OF BOOKS RELATING TO THE HISTORY, ANTIQUITIES, LANGUAGES, CUSTOMS, RELIGION, WARS, LITERATURE, AND ORIGIN OF THE AMERICAN INDIANS, IN THE LIBRARY OF THOMAS W. FIELD / Field, Thomas Warren – New York: Scribner, Armstrong, 1873. 03100. (Pre-1900 Canadiana) – 9 – cn C.I.H.M. [971]

AN ESSAY TOWARDS AN INVESTIGATION OF THE ORIGIN AND ELEMENTS OF LANGUAGE AND LETTERS / Nelme, LD – 1772. 172p. (English Linguistics Series 1500-1800) – 9 – us UMI [400]

AN ESSAY TOWARDS AN UNIVERSAL AND RATIONAL GRAMMAR / Shirley, James – 1726. 220p. (English Linguistics Series 1500-1800) – 9 – us UMI [400]

AN ESSAY TOWARDS ESTABLISHING THE MELODY AND MEASURE OF SPEECH TO BE EXPRESSED AND PERPETUATED BY PECULIAR SYMBOLS / Steele, Joshua – 1775. 223p. (English Linguistics Series 1500-1800) – 9 – us UMI [400]

AN ESSAY UPON PRINTS : CONTAINING REMARKS UPON THE PRINCIPLES OF PICTURESQUE BEAUTY; THE DIFFERENT KINDS OF PRINTS AND THE CHARACTERS OF THE MOST NOTED MASTERS / Gilpin, W – London, 2nd ed 1768 – 3mf – 9 – ne IDC [750]

ESSAY UPON THE INFLUENCE OF THE IMAGINATION ON THE NERVOUS SYSTEM CONTRIBUTING TO A FALSE HOPE IN RELIGION / Powers, Grant – Andover: Flagg and Gould, 1828, c1827 – 1mf – us A.T.L.A. [240]

DAS ESSAYISTISCHE WERK ZUR DEUTSCHEN LITERATUR IN 4 BAENDEN : SAEMTLICHE NACHTPROGRAMME UND AUFSAETZE / Schmidt, Arno – Zuerich: Arno-Schmidt-Stiftung im Haffmanns Verlag, 1988 – 1 – us U.W. Library [430]

ESSAYS / Benson, Arthur Christopher – London: William Heinemann, 1896 – 1 roll – 1 – 1-55879-456-5 – uk Libr Preservation [840]

ESSAYS / Praed, Winthrop Mackworth – London, New York: G. Routledge and Sons, 1887 – 1 roll – 1 – 1-55879-627-4 – uk Libr Preservation [840]

ESSAYS / Ryder, Henry Ignatius Dudley; ed by Bacchus, Francis – London, New York: Longmans, Green, 1911 – 1mf – us A.T.L.A. [240]

ESSAYS / Spencer, Herbert – 1891. Vol. III. 519p. 1 fiche (36x) – 9 – 1.00f – at Libertarian Micro [320]

ESSAYS : THEOLOGICAL AND LITERARY / Everett, Charles Carroll – Boston:Houghton, Mifflin, 1901 – 1mf – 9 – 0-8370-3717-4 – 1985-1717 – us A.T.L.A. [240]

ESSAYS / Wilberforce, Samuel – London: J. Murray, 1874 – 2mf – us A.T.L.A. [240]

ESSAYS AESTHETICAL AND PHILOSOPHICAL : INCLUDING THE DISSERTATION ON THE CONNEXION BETWEEN THE ANIMAL AND SPIRITUAL IN MAN / Schiller, Friedrich von – London: G. Bell and Sons, 1875 – 435p – 1 – us U.W. Library [840]

ESSAYS AND ADDRESSES / Dale, Robert William – New York: A.C. Armstrong, 1899. 1 fiche – 9 – us A.T.L.A. [240]

ESSAYS AND ADDRESSES CHIEFLY ON CHURCH SUBJECTS / Alford, Henry – London: Strahan, 1869 – 1mf – 9 – 0-8370-4725-0 – 1985-2725 – us A.T.L.A. [240]

ESSAYS AND ADDRESSES:...SOME RELIGIOUS QUESTIONS IN A SCIENTIFIC SPIRIT / Wilson, James Maurice – London: Macmillan, 1894.1 fiche – 9 – us A.T.L.A. [240]

ESSAYS AND CRITICISMS / Wainewright, Thomas Griffiths – London: Reeves & Turner, 1880 – 1 roll – 1 – 1-55879-480-8 – uk Libr Preservation [840]

ESSAYS AND CRITICISMS : WITH AN ACCOUNT OF THE AUTHOR. ... COLLECTED BY HIMSELF / Goldsmith, Oliver – London: Printed for J. Johnson, new ed 1798 – 1 roll – 1 – 1-55879-098-5 – uk Libr Preservation [420]

ESSAYS AND MONOGRAPHS / Allen, William Francis – Memorial volume.Boston: G.H. Ellis, 1890. vi,392p – 1 – us U.W. Library [900]

ESSAYS AND OBSERVATIONS, PHYSICAL AND LITERARY, READ BEFORE A SOCIETY IN EDINBURGH, AND PUBLISHED BY THEM / Philosophical Society of Edinburgh – Edinburgh, 1754-71 – 3 – us Readex [800]

ESSAYS AND REVIEWS / Church, R W – London: J. and C. Mozley, 1854 – 2mf – us A.T.L.A. [240]

ESSAYS AND SPEECHES / Dawe, Charles G – (Covers anti-trust law and policy, the Federal Reserve System and banking reform at the turn of the century) – Boston/NY: Houghton Mifflin, 1915 – 5mf – 9 – $7.50 – LLMC 96-055 – us L.L.M.C. [332]

ESSAYS AND SPEECHES / Lilly, William Samuel – (Includes index) – London: Chapman & Hall, 1897 – 1mf – 9 – 0-8370-6996-3 – 1986-0996 – us A.T.L.A. [080]

ESSAYS AND STUDIES – n.s. v. 1-25. London. 1948-72 – 9 – 375.00; 3.00v – uk Dawson [420]

ESSAYS AND STUDIES – orig. s. v. 1-32. London. 1910-47 – 9 – 2496.00; 3.00v – uk Dawson [420]

ESSAYS BIBLICAL AND ECCLESIASTICAL / Burgess, Henry – London: Longmans, Green, 1873. 1 fiche – 9 – us A.T.L.A. [240]

ESSAYS BY GERMAN OFFICERS AND OFFICIALS – (Includes printed guide) – 1991 – 7r – 1 – $595.00 – S3212 – Co-publ with the U.S. Naval Historical Center – us Scholarly Res [355]

ESSAYS BY THE LATE GEORGE BRIMLEY / Brimley, George; ed by Clark, William George – Cambridge: Macmillan, 1858 – 1 roll – 1 – 1-55879-943-5 – uk Libr Preservation [840]

ESSAYS CHIEFLY ON THE ORIGINAL TEXTS OF THE OLD AND NEW TESTAMENTS / Abbott, Thomas Kingsmill – (Includes index) – London: Longmans, Green, 1891 – 1mf – 9 – 0-8370-2031-X – 1985-0031 – us A.T.L.A. [220]

ESSAYS CRITICAL AND NARRATIVE / Forsyth, William – London: Longmans, Green, 1874 – 1 roll – 1 – 1-55879-529-4 – uk Libr Preservation [840]

ESSAYS DE MESSIRE MICHEL SEIGNEUR DE MONTAIGNE, ... / Montaigne, Michel de – Bordeaux: S. Millanges, 1580. 2v – fr Armell [840]

ESSAYS FOR SUNDAY READING / Caird, John – London: Pitman, 1906 – 1mf – us A.T.L.A. [240]

ESSAYS FOR THE DAY / Munger, Theodore Thornton – Boston: Houghton, Mifflin, 1904 – 1mf – 9 – 0-8370-4013-2 – 1985-2013 – us A.T.L.A. [240]

ESSAYS FOR THE TIMES: STUDIES OF EMINENT MEN AND IMPORTANT LIVING QUESTIONS / Dewart, Edward Hartley – Toronto: W. Briggs; Montreal: C. W. Coates; Halifax: S. F. Huestis, 1898. 02676. (Pre-1900 Canadiana) – 9 – cn C.I.H.M. [971]

ESSAYS FROM "ESSAYS ON LIBERTY" / Read, Leonard E – v. X-XII. Together with Die Maxime Laissez Faire Et Laissez Passer, Ihr Ursprung, Ihr Werden, by August Oncken, 1896; and Laissez Faire Definitions Etc., by John Zube,comp. 270p. 1 fiche (24x) – 9 – 1.00f – at Libertarian Micro [320]

ESSAYS FROM THE "GUARDIAN" / Pater, Walter – London: Printed for private circulation at the Chiswick Press, 1896 – 1 roll – 1 – 1-55879-717-3 – uk Libr Preservation [840]

ESSAYS HISTORICAL AND THEOLOGICAL / Mozley, James Bowling – London: Rivingtons, 1878 – 3mf – us A.T.L.A. [240]

ESSAYS IN HISTORY AND BIOGRAPHY / Skelton, John – Edinburgh, London: W. Blackwood, 1883 – 1 roll – 1 – 1-55879-416-6 – uk Libr Preservation [840]

ESSAYS IN JURISPRUDENCE AND ETHICS / Pollock, Frederick – London: Maxmillan & Co, 1882 – 5mf – 9 – $7.50 – LLMC 95-183 – us L.L.M.C. [340]

ESSAYS IN JURISPRUDENCE AND LEGAL HISTORY / Salmond, John W – London: Stevens & Haynes, 1891 – 3mf – 9 – $4.50 – LLMC 95-161 – us L.L.M.C. [340]

ESSAYS IN LEGAL HISTORY : READ BEFORE THE INTERNATIONAL CONGRESS OF HISTORICAL STUDIES HELD IN LONDON IN 1913 / Vinogradoff, Paul – London: Oxford Univ. Press, 1913 – 5mf – 9 – $7.50 – LLMC 95-146 – us L.L.M.C. [340]

ESSAYS IN LITTLE / Lang, Andrew – London: Henry, 1891 – 1 roll – 1 – 1-55879-715-7 – uk Libr Preservation [840]

ESSAYS IN PENTATEUCHAL CRITICISM / Wiener, Harold Marcus – (Includes indexes) – Oberlin, OH: Bibliotheca Sacra, 1909 – 1mf – 9 – 0-8370-5838-4 – 1985-3838 – us A.T.L.A. [220]

ESSAYS IN POLITICAL ARITHMETIC / Kerssebomn, W – 1748 – 1 – uk Microform Academic [900]

ESSAYS IN THE CONSTITUTIONAL HISTORY OF THE UNITED STATES IN THE FORMATIVE PERIOD, 1775-1789 : BY GRADUATES AND FORMER MEMBERS OF THE JOHNS HOPKINS UNIVERSITY / ed by Jameson, J Franklin – Boston/New York: Houghton, Mifflin & Co, 1889 – 4mf – 9 – $6.00 – LLMC 95-071 – us L.L.M.C. [323]

ESSAYS IN THE HISTORY OF RELIGIOUS THOUGHT IN THE WEST / Westcott, Brooke Foss – (Includes bibliographical references) – London, New York: Macmillan, 1891 – 1mf – 9 – 0-8370-5804-X – 1985-3804 – us A.T.L.A. [200]

ESSAYS IN THE STUDY OF FOLK-SONGS / Martinengo-Cesaresco, Evelyn Lilian Hazeldine – London: G. Redway, 1886.395p – 1 – us U.W. Library [390]

ESSAYS MEDICAL AND PHILOSOPHICAL / Martine, George – London, 1740 – 1 – us U.W. Library [610]

ESSAYS OF AN EX-LIBRARIAN / Garnett, Richard – London: W. Heinemann, 1901 – 1 roll – 1 – 1-55879-606-1 – uk Libr Preservation [840]

ESSAYS ON ARCHAEOLOGICAL SUBJECTS, AND ON VARIOUS QUESTIONS CONNECTED WITH THE HISTORY OF ART, SCIENCE AND LITERATURE IN THE MIDDLE AGES / Wright, Thomas – London: J.R. Smith, 1861. 2v. illus – 1 – us U.W. Library [930]

ESSAYS ON CANADIAN URBAN PROCESS AND FORM / ed by Russwurm, Lorne H et al – 1977 – 376p – 9 – $7.00 set – cn Geography [307]

ESSAYS ON CANADIAN URBAN PROCESS AND FORM 2 / ed by Preston, Richard E & Russwurm, Lorne H – 1980 – 505p – 9 – $8.00 set – cn Geography [307]

ESSAYS ON CANADIAN WRITING – (Index 1974-78 Can$20.00. v36 1988 Can$20.00y) – Toronto. nos 1-56. 1974-1994/95 – 9 – Can$28.00y – cn Micromedia [420]

ESSAYS ON CEREMONIAL BY VARIOUS AUTHORS / ed by Atchley, E G & Cuthbert F – (Includes bibliographical references and index) – London:De la More Press, 1904 – 1mf – 9 – 0-8370-5843-0 – 1985-3843 – us A.T.L.A. [240]

ESSAYS ON EDUCATION TOGETHER WITH THE TOWN REPORTS FOR 1859-1861 AND THE SCHOOL REPORTS FOR 1861-1862 OF CONCORD, MASSACHUSETTS / Alcott, Amos Bronson – 1830-1862 – 9 – 15.00 – us Scholars' Facs [370]

ESSAYS ON EDUCATIONAL REFORMERS / Quick, Robert Hebert – (Includes bibliographical references and index) – New York: D Appleton, 1897, c1890 – 2mf – 9 – 0-8370-7576-9 – 1986-1576 – us A.T.L.A. [370]

ESSAYS ON FICTION / Senior, Nassau William – London: Longman, Green, Longman, Roberts & Green, 1864 – 1 roll – 1 – uk Libr Preservation [420]

ESSAYS ON FREETHINKING AND PLAINSPEAKING / Stephen, Leslie – London: Longmans, Green and Co., 1873 – 1 roll – 1 – 1-55879-573-1 – uk Libr Preservation [190]

ESSAYS ON FREETHINKING AND PLAINSPEAKING / Stephen, Leslie – New York: G.P. Putnam, 1905. 2 fiches – 9 – us A.T.L.A. [240]

ESSAYS ON GERMAN LITERATURE / Boyesen, Hjalmar Hjorth – 4th rev ed. New York: C Scribner's Sons, 1898 – 1r – 1 – us U.W. Library [430]

ESSAYS ON GERMAN LITERATURE / Boyesen, Hjalmar Hjorth – New York: C Scribners, 1892 – 1r – 1 – us U.W. Library [430]

ESSAYS ON HIS OWN TIMES : FORMING A SECOND SERIES OF THE FRIEND / Coleridge, Samuel Taylor – London: William Pickering, 1850 – 2 rolls – 1 – 1-55879-059-4 – uk Libr Preservation [840]

ESSAYS ON HISTORY, PHILOSOPHY, AND THEOLOGY / Vaughan, Robert – London: Jackson and Walford, 1849 – 2mf – us A.T.L.A. [240]

ESSAYS ON LABOUR LAW IN THE PROVINCE OF QUEBEC / Spector, John Jacob – Montreal? 1952? 54 p. LL-2223 – 1 – us L of C Photodup [340]

ESSAYS ON LOZI LAND AND ROYAL PROPERTY / Gluckman, M – 7 – uk Microform Academic [960]

ESSAYS ON MILTON / Thompson, Elbert Nevius Sebring – New Haven: Yale University Press, 1914. 217p. The theme of Paradise Lost is reprinted from the publications of the Modern Language Association of America. 1 reel – 1 – us U.W. Library [420]

ESSAYS: ON POETRY AND MUSIC, AS THEY AFFECT THE MIND / Beattie, J – The 3rd ed., corrected. 1779 – 9 – us Sibley [410]

ESSAYS ON POETRY AND POETS / Noel, Roden Berkeley Wriothesley – London: K. Paul, Trench & Co., 1886 – 1 roll – 1 – 1-55879-180-9 – uk Libr Preservation [420]

ESSAYS ON POLITICAL ECONOMY / Bastiat, Frederic – Containing: Capital and Interest, 48p; That Which Is Seen and That Which Is Not Seen, 72p; Government, 19p; What Is Money?, 37p; The Law, 65p – 9 – 1.00f – at Libertarian Micro [335]

ESSAYS ON SOME BIBLICAL QUESTIONS OF THE DAY / ed by Swete, Henry Barclay – London; New York: Macmillan, 1909 – 2mf – 9 – 0-8370-5473-7 – 1985-3473 – us A.T.L.A. [220]

ESSAYS ON SOME OF THE DIFFICULTIES IN THE WRITINGS OF THE APOSTLE PAUL / Whately, Richard – Andover: Warren F. Draper, 1865.1 fiche – 9 – us A.T.L.A. [240]

ESSAYS ON SOME OF THE MODERN GUIDES OF ENGLISH THOUGHT IN MATTERS OF FAITH / Hutton, Richard Holt – London, New York: Macmillan, 1887 – 1 roll – 1 – 1-55879-879-X – uk Libr Preservation [210]

ESSAYS ON SUBJECTS CONNECTED WITH THE REFORMATION IN ENGLAND / Maitland, S R – London: F.& J. Rivington, 1849 – 2mf – us A.T.L.A. [240]

ESSAYS ON THE BIBLE BY THE AUTHOR OF "ESSAYS ON THE CHURCH" ETC / Seeley, Robert Benton – (Includes bibliographical references) – London:Seeley, Jackson, & Halliday, 1869 – 1mf – 9 – 0-8370-5213-0 – 1985-3213 – us A.T.L.A. [220]

ESSAYS ON THE CHARACTERISTICS / Brown, J – London, 1751 – 5mf – 9 – ne IDC [840]

ESSAYS ON THE CONSTITUTION OF THE UNITED STATES / Ford, Paul L – (Reprints of contemporary newspaper essays by 17 influential citizens) – Brooklyn: Historical Printing Club, 1892 – 5mf – 9 – $7.50 – LLMC 84-809 – us L.L.M.C. [340]

ESSAYS ON THE ENGLISH STATE CHURCH IN IRELAND / Brady, W Maziere – London: Strahan, 1869 – 1mf – us A.T.L.A. [240]

ESSAYS ON THE HISTORY OF MISSIONS IN THAILAND – By educational missionaries. 294p – 1 – us Baptist [240]

ESSAYS ON THE MONETARY HISTORY OF THE UNITED STATES / Bullock, Charles J – 1900. 3 fiches (29x) – 9 – 1.00f – at Libertarian Micro [320]

ESSAYS ON THE PREACHING REQUIRED BY THE TIMES: AND THE BEST METHODS OF OBTAINING IT : WITH REMINISCENCES AND ILLUSTRATIONS OF METHODIST PREACHING / Stevens, Abel – New York: Carlton and Phillips, 1856, c1855 – 1mf – us A.T.L.A. [240]

ESSAYS ON THE PRINCIPLES OF MORALITY : AND ON THE PRIVATE AND POLITICAL RIGHTS AND OBLIGATIONS OF MANKIND / Dymond, Jonathan – (Includes index) – Abridged, electrotyped ed. Philadelphia: Book Committee of the Philadelphia Yearly Meeting of Friends, 1896 – 2mf – 9 – 0-8370-6111-3 – 1986-0111 – us A.T.L.A. [170]

ESSAYS ON THE PUNISHMENT OF DEATH / Spear, Charles – 13th ed. Boston: self published, 1851 – 3mf – 9 – $4.50 – LLMC 91-077 – us L.L.M.C. [340]

ESSAYS ON THE SUPERNATURAL ORIGIN OF CHRISTIANITY / Fisher, George Park – 1890 – 9 – us A.T.L.A. [140]

ESSAYS ON TRUTH AND REALITY / Bradley, Francis Herbert – Oxford: Clarendon Press, 1914 – 2mf – us A.T.L.A. [120]

ESSAYS ON VARIOUS SUBJECTS / Wiseman, Nicholas Patrick – London: Charles Dolman. 3v. 1853 – 6mf – 9 – 0-8370-7354-5 – 1986-1354 – us A.T.L.A. [240]

ESSAYS PHILOSOPHICAL AND MORAL, HISTORICAL AND LITERARY / Belsham, William – London: Printed for G.G. and J. Robinson, 1799 – 2 rolls – 1 – 1-55879-263-5 – uk Libr Preservation [840]

ESSAYS SUBMITTED IN WRITING CONTEST / Native Sons and Daughters of Kansas – 1955 – 1 – us KS Hist [840]

ESSAYS UPON:... / Davenant, C – London, 1701 – 5mf – 1 – ILM-469/1 – ne IDC [327]

ESSAYS UPON PEACE AT HOME... / Avenant, C d' – London, 1704 – 5mf – 9 – ILM-788/1 – ne IDC [340]

Essen, L Van Der *see* ETUDE CRITIQUE ET LITTERAIRE SUR LES VITAE DES SAINTS MEROVINGIENS DE L'ANCIENNE BELGIQUE

ESSENCE – v1- 1970- 1; v3- 5,6; v6- 9 – us UMI [640]

L'ESSENCE D'UN CONTE / Houdeau. S – Analyse d'un conte rwanda des "deux filles." – 9 – F130.00 – fr Ethnologie [306]

ESSENCE: ISSUES IN THE STUDY OF AGEING, DYING AND DEATH – v. 1- 1976- – 1,5,6,9 – us UMI [360]

THE ESSENCE OF CHRISTIANITY / Feuerbach, Ludwig – London: J. Chapman, 1854 – 1mf – us A.T.L.A. [240]

THE ESSENCE OF CHRISTIANITY : A STUDY IN THE HISTORY OF DEFINITION / Brown, William Adams – New York: Scribner, 1902 – 1mf – us A.T.L.A. [240]

THE ESSENCE OF NATIONAL INDEPENDENCE AND THE REVOLUTION OF MANKIND / Subandrio – 3addresses. SE 6244 1. 1963 – 9 – ne IDC [335]

THE ESSENCE OF RELIGION / Bowne, Borden Parker – Boston: Houghton Mifflin, 1910 – 1mf – us A.T.L.A. [210]

THE ESSENCE OF THE FIFTH FIVE YEAR EDUCATIONAL DEVELOPMENT PLAN (1982-1986) / Thailand. National Education Commission. Macro Planning Section 1981 – 1mf – 9 – DE-589/1 – ne IDC [370]

ESSENER ARBEITER ZEITUNG *see* DIE ARBEITER-ZEITUNG

ESSENER ARBEITER-ZEITUNG – (Cont: Arbeiter-Zeitung) – Essen, Germany. Apr 1909-Apr 1926 – 24r – 1 – us L of C Photodup [072]

ESSENER VOLKS-HALLE – Essen, Germany. 15 Apr 1849-Jun 1850 – 1 – gw Mikrofilm [072]

ESSENER VOLKS-ZEITUNG – Essen, Germany. 1869-91 (incomplete) – 1 – gw Mikrofilm [072]

ESSENER ZEITUNG – Essen, Germany. 1865. No.151-307 (incomplete) – 1 – gw Mikrofilm [072]

ESSENER ZEITUNG *see* GLUECKAUF

THE ESSENES : THEIR HISTORY AND DOCTRINES / Ginsburg, Christian David – (Includes bibliographical references) – London: Longman, Green, Longman, Roberts, and Green, 1864 – 1mf – 9 – 0-8370-9386-4 – 1986-3386 – us A.T.L.A. [240]

DER ESSENISMUS IN SEINEM VERHAELTNISS ZUM JUDENTHUM / Lucius, Paul Ernst – Strassburg: C.F. Schmidt, 1881. 1 fiche – 9 – us A.T.L.A. [270]

THE ESSENTIAL NATURE OF LAW OR THE ETHICAL BASIS OF JURISPRUDENCE / Pattee, William Sullivan – Chicago: Callaghan, 1909 – 3mf – 9 – $4.50 – LLMC 95-197 – us L.L.M.C. [340]

THE ESSENTIALS OF AMERICAN CONSTITUTIONAL LAW / Thorpe, Francis Newton – New York, Putnam, 1917. 279 p. LL-1243 – 1 – us L of C Photodup [340]

THE ESSENTIALS OF CHRISTIAN BELIEF / Fyffe, David – New York: Hodder and Stoughton, [1912?] – 1mf – us A.T.L.A. [240]

ESSENTIALS OF EDUCATIONAL PSYCHOLOGY / Duric, Ladislav – 1990 – 163p – 9 – 92-3-102631-3 – fr UNESCO [150]

THE ESSENTIALS OF ELEMENTARY CHEMISTRY AND CHEMICAL PHYSICS – For the assistance of high school students and intermediate candidates. Compiled and collated by A. W. Aytoun Finlay. Toronto: W. Warwick, 1880. 03107. (Pre-1900 Canadiana) – 9 – cn C.I.H.M. [971]

THE ESSENTIALS OF LOGIC : BEING TEN LECTURES ON JUDGMENT AND INFERENCE / Bosanquet, Bernard – London, New York: Macmillan, 1895 – 1mf – us A.T.L.A. [160]

ESSENTIALS OF NEW TESTAMENT GREEK / Huddilston, John Homer – New York: Macmillan, 1896, c1895 – 1mf – 9 – 0-8370-9158-6 – 1986-3158 – us A.T.L.A. [450]

ESSENTIALS OF YMCA (CCC93) = CHI TU CHIAO CH'ING NIEN HUI SHIH YAO / Ch'en, Li-t'ing – (In Chinese) – Shanghai: Association Press of China, 1927 – 1r – 1 – 1984-B500 – us A.T.L.A. [360]

ESSENTIALS TO THE PRINCIPAL ACTIONS IN TORT AT COMMON LAW / Schermerhorn, Holden Bovee – Philadelphia: Rees, Welsh, 1913. 281p. LL-1127 – 1 – us L of C Photodup [340]

ESSEQUIE DEL SERENISSIMO DON FRANCESCO MEDICI GRAN DUCA DI TOSCANA 2 / Strozzi, G B – O 1110 1. 1587 – 9 – ne IDC [920]

ESSEX, 1823 : BRITISH ISLES CENSUS DIRECTORIES PROJECT, ENGLAND. VOL 213 – 2mf – 9 – A$15.00 – at Vine [941]

ESSEX, 1839 : BRITISH ISLES CENSUS DIRECTORIES PROJECT, ENGLAND – at Vine [941]

ESSEX, 1846 : BRITISH ISLES CENSUS DIRECTORIES PROJECT, ENGLAND. VOL 230 – 3mf – 9 – A$21.00 – at Vine [941]

ESSEX, 1848 : BRITISH ISLES CENSUS DIRECTORIES PROJECT, ENGLAND. VOL 139 – 4mf – 9 – A$27.00 – at Vine [941]

ESSEX, 1855 : BRITISH ISLES CENSUS DIRECTORIES PROJECT, ENGLAND. VOL 249 – 9mf – 9 – A$57.00 – at Vine [941]

ESSEX, 1863 : BRITISH ISLES CENSUS DIRECTORIES PROJECT, ENGLAND. VOL 38 – 5mf – 9 – A$33.00 – at Vine [941]

ESSEX, 1871 : BRITISH ISLES CENSUS DIRECTORIES PROJECT, ENGLAND – at Vine [941]

ESSEX, 1896 : BRITISH ISLES CENSUS DIRECTORIES PROJECT, ENGLAND – at Vine [941]

ESSEX, 1898 : BRITISH ISLES CENSUS DIRECTORIES PROJECT, ENGLAND. VOL 156 – 9mf – 9 – A$57.00 – at Vine [941]

ESSEX, 1908 : BRITISH ISLES CENSUS DIRECTORIES PROJECT, ENGLAND – at Vine [941]

ESSEX 1708-1849 – (Mf 1T: Deaths 1819-25; Births 1799-1825. Mf 1T-2T: Intents & Marriages 1819-49. Mf 2T-3T: Births 1819-43; Deaths 1829-43. Mf 3T: Out-of-Town Marriages 1708-99; Births 1843-49. Mf 4T: Marriages & Deaths 1843-49) – (mf ed 1996) – 4mf – 9 – 0-87623-248-9 – us Holbrook [920]

ESSEX 1819-1892 – (Mf 1-4: Record Book 1819-43. Mf 5-9: Town Records 1819-35. Mf 10-15: Town Records 1835-52. Mf 16: Births 1843-60. Mf 17: Births 1860-61; Marriages 1843-54; Deaths 1843-55. Mf 18-19: Deaths 1856-92. Mf 20-21: Marriages 1854-92. Mf 22-23: Births 1862-92) – (mf ed 1990) – 23mf – 9 – 0-87623-106-7 – us Holbrook [920]

Essex Bar Association. Salem, Massachusetts *see* MISUSE AND ABUSE OF THE RIGHT OF PETITION FOR THE REMOVAL OF JUDICIAL OFFICERS

ESSEX (COLCHESTER), 1805 : BRITISH ISLES CENSUS DIRECTORIES PROJECT, ENGLAND. VOL 175 – 1mf – 9 – A$9.00 – at Vine [941]

ESSEX COUNTY CHRONICLE – Chelmsford, England. Jun-Dec 1832; 1847; 1873; 1877; 1888-89; 1897-99; 1901-16; 1950; 1980- – 98+ r – 1 – uk British Libr Newspaper [072]

ESSEX COUNTY HERALD – Island Pond, VT. v43 n12. 15 oct 1915; v44 n38. 13 apr 1917 – 1r – 1 – Can$25.00 – cn Can Microfilming [071]

ESSEX COUNTY HISTORY AND DIRECTORY / Wood, C A & Wood, J F – Boston, 1870. Massachusetts Reel 3. (The Cox Library Collection) – 5 – us Americana [978]

Essex Field Club *see*
– JOURNAL OF PROCEEDINGS.V.1-. 1880-
– TRANSACTIONS

THE ESSEX GAZETTE – Salem. Mass. 1768-1775. Cambridge. yThe New England Chronicle. 1775-1776. Sold as one unit – 3 – us Readex [071]

Essex Institute *see* HISTORICAL COLLECTIONS

ESSEX INSTITUTE HISTORICAL COLLECTIONS *see* PEABODY ESSEX MUSEUM COLLECTIONS

Essex Institute. Salem, Mass *see* HISTORICAL COLLECTIONS

THE ESSEX JOURNAL – Newburyport. Mass. 1773-1777, 1784-1794 – 1,3 – us Readex [071]

ESSEX NATURALIST – (v.5-. 1980-. 5,6,9) – v.1-. 1887- – 1 – us UMI [574]

Essex Naturalists, Trust *see* BULLETIN

Essig, Montgomery F *see* THE CHURCHMEMBER'S GUIDE AND COMPLETE CHURCH MANUAL

[Esslaoui, Ahmed Ennasiri] *see* CHRONIQUE DE LA DYNASTIE ALAOUIE DU MAROC

ESSLINGER ALLGEMEINE – Esslingen, Germany. 16 Jul 1949-30 Apr 1955 – 12r – 1 – gw Mikrofilm [072]

ESSLINGER SCHNELLPOST – (Title changes: Esslinger Tagblatt, 1848; Esslinger Wochenblatt, Jan 1851) – Esslingen, Germany. 3 Jul 1847-57 – 1 – gw Mikrofilm [072]

ESSLINGER TAGBLATT *see* ESSLINGER SCHNELLPOST

ESSLINGER WOCHENBLATT *see* ESSLINGER SCHNELLPOST

ESSLINGER ZEITUNG – Esslingen, West Germany. 1976- – ca 8r per yr – 1 – gw Mikrofilm [072]

ESSO MAGAZINE – 1949- 1; 1975- 5,6,9 – us UMI [660]

L'ESSOR – St-Jean d'Iberville, Canada. v1 n45. 5 jun 1968-v3 n30. 25 fev 1970 – 1r – 1 – Can$50.00 – cn Can Microfilming [072]

ESSOR / Jeunesses National-Populaires – no. 27-37. Paris. mars-aout 1944. mq no. 35 – 1 – fr A.C.R.P.P. [073]

L'ESSOR DE LA LITTERATURE LATINE AU 12TH SIECLE / Ghellinck, J de – Tome 1, Bruxelles 5mf; Tome 2, Bruxelles 8mf – 8 – ne Slangenburg [240]

L'ESSOR DU CONGO – Elisabethville: [s.n.], feb 1960-may 1960 – us Res Libr [072]

L'ESSOR DU CONGO (KATANGA) – Elisabethville, 1960(Jan 4)-1967(Nov 27) – 25r – 1 – ne IDC [073]

L'ESSOR DU SALARIAT AU SENEGAL DANS L'ENTRE-DEUX-GUERRES, 1917-37 / Lakroum, M – 9 – F120.00 – fr Ethnologie [306]

L'ESSOR LITTERAIRE AND SCIENTIFIQUE – Port-au-Prince: Impr. Verrolot, [1912-]. [1ere annee, n1-3eme annee, n27; 3eme annee, 2s, n1-n8 (15 avr 1912-15 juin 1914; mars-oct 1916] – 17r – 1 – us Res Libr [072]

EST – Budapest. v7-11. 1916-20 (scattered issues) – 2r – 1 – us Ross [072]

EST *see* AZ EST

L'EST OUVRIER ET PAYSAN / Parti Communiste. Nancy – Nancy. mai 1933-sept 1935 – 1 – fr A.C.R.P.P. [073]

L'EST VAUDOIS – 1988-1993 – 3r per y – 5,6 – Sfr1,123.00y – sz Infoprint [944]

EST VAUDOIS – 1988-1993 – 3 times per yr – 6 – F4,200.00 – sz Infoprint [072]

ESTA ES PLASENCIA. 2ND CONGRESO DE ESTUDIOS EXTREMENOS. JAIME J. JIMENEZ GARCIA – Plasencia: Imp. La Victoria, 1970 – 1 – sp Bibl Santa Ana [946]

ESTABLECIMIENTO DE BANOS MINEROMEDICINALES DE ALANGE / Gaztelu, Teodoro – Madrid: Imp. La Editora, 1912 – 1 – sp Bibl Santa Ana [946]

ESTABLECIMIENTO...NUEVA ESPANA / Riva Palacio, Vicente – 1892 – 9 – 1.50f – sp Bibl Santa Ana [972]

ESTABLISHING PULP AND PAPER MILLS : A GUIDE FOR DEVELOPING COUNTRIES – 1983 – 99p – it F.A.O. [650]

THE ESTABLISHMENT AND CONSOLIDATION OF IMPERIAL GOVERNMENT IN SOUTHERN NIGERIA, 1891-1904 : THEORY AND PRACTICE IN A COLONIAL PROTECTORATE / Anene, J C O – 1952 – us Res Libr [960]

THE ESTABLISHMENT OF CHRISTIANITY AND THE PROSCRIPTION OF PAGANISM / Huttman, Maude Aline – New York: Columbia University: Longmans, Green [distributor], 1914. (Studies in history, economics and public law; v60, no. 2: whole no. 147) – 1mf – us A.T.L.A. [240]

ESTABLISHMENT OF DAIRY TRAINING CENTRES – 1979 – 64p – it F.A.O. [636]

THE ESTABLISHMENT OF PETROMIN / Saudi Arabia. General Petroleum and Mineral Organization – 1967 – 9 – ne IDC [338]

ESTABLISHMENT TECHNIQUES FOR FOREST PLANTATIONS – 1981 – 190p – it F.A.O. [634]

L'ESTABLISSEMENT D'ISSINY, 1682-1702 : VOYAGES DE DUCASSE, TIBIERGE ET D'AMON A LA COTE DE GUINEE – Paris: E Larose, 1935 – 1 – us Res Libr [960]

ESTABLISSEMENTS FRANCAIS DE L'OCEANIE : ARRETES DU GOUVERNEUR, COMMISSAIRE DU ROI, 1845-1855 – 1r – 1 – PMB Doc412 – at Pacific Mss [324]

Estabrook, Charles E *see*
- ANNUAL REPORT OF THE ADJUTANT GENERAL OF WISCONSIN, YEAR ENDING DECEMBER 30, 1865

ESTACADA CLACKAMAS COUNTY NEWS – Estacada, OR. -w. 31 Aug 1928-. – 1 – us U.O. Library [071]

ESTACADA NEWS – Estacada, OR. -w. 1 Dec 1904-20 Aug 1908. 1 roll – 1 – us U.O. Library [071]

ESTACADA PRESS – Estacada, OR. -w. 21 Apr 1955-20 Sep 1956. 1 roll – 1 – us U.O. Library [071]

ESTADISTICA COMERCIAL *see* EL SALVADOR

ESTADISTICA COMERCIAL DE LA REPUBLICA DE CHILE / Chile. Oficina Central de Estadistica – 1844-1915. Lacks 1890, 1907, 1909-10 – 1 – 190.00 – us L of C Photodup [310]

ESTADISTICA DE LA EMIGRACION E INMIGRACION DE ESPANA EN 1882-1895 / Instituto Geografico – Madrid, 1882-1895 – 22mf – 9 – sp Cultura [946]

Estadistica de la Navegacion *see* ESTADISTICA DE LA NAVEGACION EXTERIOR DE ESPANA EN 1924-1926

ESTADISTICA DE LA NAVEGACION EXTERIOR DE ESPANA EN 1924-1926 / Estadistica de la Navegacion – Madrid, 1927 – 22mf – 9 – sp Cultura [380]

ESTADISTICA DE LOS ALCANTARISTAS Y PASCUALISTAS HACIA 1567-1570. MEMORIA DE LAS CASAS DE LA PROVINCIA DE SANT JOSSEPH / Meseguer Fernandez, Juan – Madrid: Graf. Calleja, 1970 – 1 – sp Bibl Santa Ana [240]

ESTADISTICA DE LOS FERROCARRILES EN EXPLOITACION / Argentine Republic. Direccion general de ferrocarriles – v.1-15. 1892-1906. v.6 lacking – 1 – 60.00 – us L of C Photodup [324]

ESTADISTICA DE SANGRE Y DE GLORIA / Bayle, Constantino – Madrid: Razon y Fe, 1939 – 1 – sp Bibl Santa Ana [946]

ESTADISTICA DEL COMERCIO Y DE LA NAVEGACION DE LA REPUBLICA ARGENTINA...ANO 1885-1892 – Buenos Aires, 1886-1893 – 50mf – 9 – sp Cultura [380]

ESTADISTICA GENERAL DEL COMERCIO DE CABOTAJE ENTRE LOS PUERTOS DE LA PENINSULA E I. BALEARES – 1857-1920 – 594mf – 9 – sp Cultura [380]

ESTADISTICA GENERAL DEL COMERCIO EXTERIOR DE ESPANA CON SUS POSESIONES...EN 1857-1926 – Madrid, 1858-1927 – 939mf – 9 – sp Cultura [380]

ESTADISTICA GENERAL DEL COMERCIO EXTERIOR DE ESPANA. PROV. DE BARCELONA...EN 1922-1925 – Madrid, 1925 – 13mf – 9 – sp Cultura [380]

ESTADISTICA JUDICIAL DE LA ISLA DE PUERTO-RICO, 1877, 1879, 1880 – Puerto-Rico. 3v. 1878-81 – 3mf – 9 – $4.50 – LLMC 92-328 – us L.L.M.C. [340]

ESTADISTICA MORTUORIA DE LA CIUDAD DE BUENOS AIRES / Instituto Geografico – Buenos Aires, 1869-1877 – 2mf – 9 – sp Cultura [304]

ESTADISTICA MUNICIPAL / Barcelona. (City). Ayuntamiento – 1958-1968- – 1 – us NY Public [324]

ESTADISTICAS EDUCACIONALES 1988 : ESTADISTICA FINAL: CIFRAS PRELIMINARES / Guatemala. Unidad Sectorial de Investigacion y Planification Educativa. Division Documentacion y Estadistica – Guatemala, 1989 – 3mf – 9 – DE-627/1 – ne IDC [370]

ESTADISTICAS SANGRIENTAS : LAS VICTIMAS DEL CLERO SECULAR / Bayle, Constantino – Madrid: Razon y Fe, 1940 – sp Bibl Santa Ana [240]

EL ESTADO – Tegucigalpa. Honduras. 1 Jul 1904-21 Mar 1907 – 3r – 1 – uk British Libr Newspaper [072]

O ESTADO – Florianopolis, Brazil. 5 Nov 1892-1899; 1901-02; Mar-Dec 1915; 1916-41. Incomplete – 1 – bl Biblioteca [072]

O ESTADO : JORNAL SEMANAL NOTICIOSO – Rio Branco, Acre. 28 Ago 1958-Dez 1961; Jul 1962; Jun-Ago, Dez 1963; Jan, Jun-Jul, Set, Nov 1964; 16 Jan 1965 – 1,5,6 – bl Biblioteca [072]

O ESTADO : ORGAO DO PARTIDO AUTONOMISTA DO ALTO JURUA – Cruzeiro do Sul, Acre. 23 Ago-Out, Dez 1916; Mar-Out, Dez 1917; Jan, Mar, 18 Maio 1918 – 1,5,6 – bl Biblioteca [072]

O ESTADO : ORGAO DOS INTERESSES DO DEPARTAMENTO – Seabra, Acre. 29 Jan-20 Set 1914 – 1,5,6 – bl Biblioteca [072]

O ESTADO : ORGAO REPUBLICANO – Maceio, Alagoas. 15 Nov 1891; Jan-4 Fev 1892 – 1,5,6 – bl Biblioteca [072]

ESTADO DE ALAGOAS *see* O LIBERAL 1090 ORGAO DO PARTIDO LIBERAL DAS ALAGOAS

EL ESTADO DE COLIMA / Colima. Mexico. (State) – Periodico oficial del gobierno constitucional. Colima. On film: 1871-1949. LL-02019 – 1 – 230.00 – us L of C Photodup [340]

ESTADO DE EXTREMADURA...ISABEL LA CATOLICA / Barrantes Moreno, Vicente – 1872 – 9 – 1.50f – sp Bibl Santa Ana [946]

O ESTADO DE GOYAZ – Uberlandia, Brazil. Dec 1940-Aug 1945. Scattered issues except 1943-44 complete – 1 – bl Biblioteca [072]

EL ESTADO DE JALISCO / Jalisco. Mexico – Guadalajara. Aug. 1946-Nov. 1956- – applyNPL; 1 – us NY Public [972]

ESTADO DE LAS CUENTAS DE PARTICIPACION EN LOS FONDOS SOCIALES DE LOS SENORES MUTUALISTAS CON POLIZAS EN VIGOR EN 31 DE DICIEMBRE DE 1962 / Mutua Aseguradora de Transportistas – Caceres: Imp. Moderna, 1963 – 1 – sp Bibl Santa Ana [946]

ESTADO DE MINAS – (Cont as: Jornal Corrente) – Belo Horizonte, 1 Jan 1985 – 1,5,6 – bl Biblioteca [072]

O ESTADO DE MINAS GERAIS : ORGAO OFFICIAL – Ouro Preto, 20 Nov-Apr 1892; Nov 1893-Nov 1894; Jan-May 1895; Jan-Oct 1896; Apr-Aug, Oct-18 Nov 1897 – 1,5,6 – bl Biblioteca [072]

O ESTADO DE S. PAULO – (Suppl: Suplemento Literario do Estado de S. Paulo. Cont of: Jornal Corrente) – Sao Paulo, 4 Jan 1875- – 1,5,6 – bl Biblioteca [072]

O ESTADO DE SAO PAULO – Sao Paulo. Brazil. 4 Jan 1875-Aug 1956 – 353r – 1 – us L of C Photodup [072]

O ESTADO DE SAO PAULO – [Sao Paulo: s.n, sep 1956-] – 1 – us Res Libr [072]

O ESTADO DE SAO PAULO *see* SUPLEMENTO LITERARIO DO ESTADO DE S. PAULO

O ESTADO DE SAO PAULO.. / Amaral, Tancredo do – Rio de Janeiro: Alves, 1896. 189p. illus – 1 – us U.W. Library [972]

EL ESTADO DE SINALOA / Sinaloa. Mexico – Culiacan. Title varies. On film: 1902-22, 1925-60, 1963-69. LL-02034 – 1 – us L of C Photodup [340]

EL ESTADO DEL JALISCO: PERIODICO OFICIAL DEL GOBIERNO / Jalisco. Mexico – Guadalajara. On film: 1884-1924, 1926-69. LL-02024 – 1 – us L of C Photodup [340]

O ESTADO DO ACRE : JORNAL HEBDOMADARIO, NOTICIOSO, COMERCIAL E LITERARIO – Senna Madureira, Acre. 11 Mar 1909-12 Abr 1911 – 1,5,6 – bl Biblioteca [072]

O ESTADO DO ACRE – Rio Branco, Acre. 22 Abr 1965; Ago 1967; Ago, 28 Out 1978 – 1,5,6 – bl Biblioteca [072]

ESTADO DO AMAZONAS : JORNAL POLITICO, COMMERCIAL, NOTICIOSO E LITTERARIO – Manaos, Amazonas. 6 Jan-Fev, 25 Ago 1892 – 1,5,6 – bl Biblioteca [072]

ESTADO GENERAL DE LAS FUNDACIONES HECHAS POR DON JOSE ESCANDON... TOMOS 1, 2 Y 3 / Bayle, Constantino – Mexico, 1929-30; Madrid: Razon y Fe, 1932 – 1 – sp Bibl Santa Ana [972]

ESTADO Y RELACIONES OBRERO-PATRONALES EN LOS ORIGENES DE LA NEGOCIACION COLECTIVA EN ARGENTINA / Gaudio, Ricardo & Pilone, Jorge – Buenos Aires: Centro de Estudios de Estado y Sociedad, 1976 – 1 – CSUXADH7671-B – us Hoover Inst Photo [320]

ESTADOS UNIDOS CAMBIA LA CARA / Ferraris, Agustin – [Buenos Aires]: Editorial Periplo, [1954] – 1 – CSUXAHZ3579-B – us Hoover Inst Photo [380]

ESTADOS UNIDOS DE NORTEAMERICA CONTRA LA ARGENTINA *see* EU DE NORTEAMERICA CONTRA LA ARGENTINA

ESTADOS UNIDOS MEXICANOS... / ed by Bayle, Constantino – Madrid: Razon y Fe, 1927 – 1 – sp Bibl Santa Ana [972]

L'ESTAFETTE – Journal des journaux. Ed. du matin. 2 fevr-dec 1833-avr 1858 – 1 – fr A.C.R.P.P. [944]

L'ESTAFETTE – Paris. Dir., L. Detroyat. mai 1876-21 fevr 1883, 15 fevr 1884, 4 juin 1886-juill 1914 – 1 – fr A.C.R.P.P. [944]

L'ESTAFETTE – (Filmed as pt of: Commune de Paris newspapers) – Paris: Imp speciale de l'Estafette, apr 23, 26-27, may 2, 4, 6, 8-12, 15-23 1871. Ed du matin – us Res Libr [072]

L'ESTAFETTE DU KANSAS – Leavenworth, KA. v2 n16. 1 jan 1859 – 1r – 1 – Can$25.00 – cn Can Microfilming [071]

Estaing, Charles Henri *see* THE SIEGE OF SAVANNAH IN 1779 AS DESCRIBED IN TWO CONTEMPORANEOUS JOURNALS OF FRENCH OFFICERS IN THE FLEET OF COUNT D'ESTAING

ESTAMENTO ESPIRITUAL DEL DEVOTO JOSEFINO – Trujillo: Tip. Sobrina de B. Pena, s.a. – sp Bibl Santa Ana [240]

ESTAMPAS DE ESPANA / Ehrenburg, Ilia Grigorevich – n.p. 1937? Fiche W 853. (Blodgett Collection of Spanish Civil War Pamphlets) – 9 – us H.U. College Libr [946]

Estancelin, Louis *see* RECHERCHES SUR LES VOYAGES ET DECOUVERTES DES NAVIGATEURS NORMANDS, DANS LES INDES ORIENTALES ET EN AMERIQUE

ESTANCIA DE ISABEL LA CATOLICA EN TRUJILLO / Rubio Cercas, Manuel – 1951. Sep Rev. "Obras". no 77. Oct-Dic. 1951 – 1 – sp Bibl Santa Ana [946]

O ESTANDARTE : FOLHA POLITICA E INDUSTRIAL – '(s.l.')-Sao Luis, Brazil. 15 Jan-Dec 1849. Jan-Apr 1851. Oct 1853-4 Dec 1856 – 1,5,6 – bl Biblioteca [072]

O ESTANDARTE – Maceio, Alagoas. 22 Jun, Set, Nov 1883; Jul, Dez 1884; 22 Fev 1885 – 1,5,6 – bl Biblioteca [072]

L'ESTAT DE LA PERSE / Mans, P Raphael du – Ch. Schefer, 1890 – 9 – fr Orientalistes [950]

ESTAT PRESENT DE L'EGLISE ET DE LA COLONIE FRANCOISE DANS LA NOUVELLE FRANCE / Saint-Vallier, Jean B de la – Paris: R Pepie, 1688. SEM16P272 – 1r – 5 – Can$9.00 – cn Bibl Nat [971]

L'ESTAT PRESENTE DE L'ARCHIPEL / Des-Barres, Antoine – Paris, C. Barbin, 1678, 2 tomes en 1 v., 215 plus 206 p. French Voyagers in the Mediterranean 16th to 18th Centuries. 6007 – 9 – fr Hachette [944]

ESTATE AND TRUST PRACTICE IDEAS – (v.7-. 1979 5,6,9) – v.6-. 1978- – 1 – us UMI [073]

ESTATE PLANNERS QUARTERLY – 1952- 1; 1978- 5,6,9 – us UMI [332]

ESTATE PLANNING – v1- 1973- 1; v5- 1978- 5,6,9 – us UMI [332]

ESTATE PLANNING IDEAS – (v.24 .1979 5,6,9) – v.1. 1956 – 1 – us UMI [073]

ESTATE PRACTICE IDEA – 1-6. 1973, 1978. Superseded by Estate and Trust Practice Ideas – 1 – us UMI [073]

ESTATE RECEIPT BOOK / Vanderhorst, Elias – 1878-87.Charleston planter. 2 fiches – 9 – us South Carolina Historical [978]

ESTATE RECORDS OF THE EARLS OF LEICESTER / Leicester. (Earls) – Holkham Hall, Norfolk – 1 – uk Microform Academic [025]

ESTATE SETTLEMENTS / Wood County. Ohio. Common Pleas. Civil Division – 1828-1853 – 1r – 1 – $32.50r – us Archival [324]

ESTATES TIMES – 1968- – 1 – us UMI [336]

ESTATUROS DE LA VE...ANO 1977 / Manconumidad Internacional de la Vera – Caceres: Imp. de la Diputacion Provincial, 1977 – sp Bibl Santa Ana [060]

ESTATUTO DEL SINDICATO DE OBRAS AGRICOLAS Y OFICIOS VARIOS / Sindicato Amanecer, Hoyos – "Amanecer". Hoyos. Caceres: Tip. de Minerva, S.A., 1936 – 1 – sp Bibl Santa Ana [060]

ESTATUTOS / A.P.A. del Colegio "Santisima Trinidad" de Plasencia – Plasencia: Graf. Sandoval, 1976 – 1 – sp Bibl Santa Ana [060]

ESTATUTOS / Asociacion de Padres de Alumnos y Amigos de la Esuela de E.G.B. – Aldea Moret: Linez XXI, 1979 – 1 – sp Bibl Santa Ana [060]

ESTATUTOS / Asociacion Empresarial de panaderos de la Provincia de Caceres – Caceres: Tip. Extremadura, 1978 – sp Bibl Santa Ana [340]

ESTATUTOS / Asociacion familiar "Los Alamos" Casas de Don Antonio – Caceres: Tip. Extremadura, 1978 – sp Bibl Santa Ana [060]

ESTATUTOS / Asociacion Morala de Padres de Alumnos de Educ. General Basica. Navlamoral de la Mata – Plasencia: Graficas Sandoval, 1977 – sp Bibl Santa Ana [370]

ESTATUTOS / Banca Sanchez S.A. – Caceres: Tip. El Noticiero S.L., 1958 – 1 – sp Bibl Santa Ana [060]

ESTATUTOS / Caceres. Asociacion Cultural – Caceres: Imprenta Moderna, 1969 – 1 – sp Bibl Santa Ana [060]

ESTATUTOS / Caceres. Mutua Cerealistica – Caceres: Imp. La Minerva, 1970 – 1 – sp Bibl Santa Ana [060]

ESTATUTOS / Caja Rural de Ahorros y Prestamos de los Santos de Maimona – Badajoz: Tip. Lit. y Encuad. de Uceda Hermanos, 1911 – sp Bibl Santa Ana [370]

ESTATUTOS / Central Obrera Nacional Sindicalista – Caceres: Imp. y Enc. Garcia Floriano, 1936 – 1 – sp Bibl Santa Ana [060]

ESTATUTOS / Central Obrera Nacional Sindicalista – Caceres: Imprenta Moderna, 1936 – sp Bibl Santa Ana [340]

ESTATUTOS / Club Alfaya – Plasencia: Imp. Sanchez Rodrigo, S.A. 1976 – 1 – sp Bibl Santa Ana [060]

ESTATUTOS / Cooperativa Local del Campo y Ganaderos "San Isidro". Miajadas – Caceres: Imprenta Moderna, 1971 – 1 – sp Bibl Santa Ana [060]

ESTATUTOS / Plasencia. Aula Medica – Plasencia: Graficas Sandoval, 1970 – 1 – sp Bibl Santa Ana [060]

ESTATUTOS / Sindicato Independiente de trabajadores del Credito (S.I. T.C.). Caceres – Caceres: Imp. La Minerva, 1977 – sp Bibl Santa Ana [331]

ESTATUTOS / Sociedad Economica Amigos del Pais – 1847 – 9 – $1.50f – sp Bibl Santa Ana [060]

ESTATUTOS... / Caceres. Pena. Amigos del Flamenco de Extremadura – Caceres: Editorial Extremadura, 1981 – 1 – sp Bibl Santa Ana [946]

ESTATUTOS... / Cooperativa del Campo – Plasencia: Imprenta La Victoria, 1961 – 1 – sp Bibl Santa Ana [060]

ESTATUTOS APROBADOS POR ORDEN MINISTERIAL HACIENDA DE 1960 / Caceres. Mutua Aseguradora de Transportistas de la Provincia de Caceres – Caceres: Imp. La Minerva, 1960 – sp Bibl Santa Ana [240]

ESTATUTOS DE... / Terpresa – Caceres: Imp. La Minerva, 1969 – 1 – sp Bibl Santa Ana [350]

ESTATUTOS DE LA... / Asociacion Empresarial Harino-Panadera de la provincia de Caceres – Caceres: Tip. Extremadura, 1977 – 1 – sp Bibl Santa Ana [350]

ESTATUTOS DE LA... / Asociacion Provincial de amas de casa – Caceres: Imp. Extremadura, 1971 – 1 – sp Bibl Santa Ana [060]

ESTATUTOS DE LA... / Cooperativa de Suministros y Consumo de Nuestra Senora de Guadalupe de Caceres – Caceres: Tip. El Noticiero, s.a., 1945? – 1 – sp Bibl Santa Ana [060]

ESTATUTOS DE LA... / Cooperativa del Campo Union de Cultivadores de tabaco de Jaraiz de la Vera – Caceres: Tip. El Noticiero, s.a. (1948) – sp Bibl Santa Ana [360]

ESTATUTOS DE LA... / Cooperativa Farmaceutica Extremena "Cofex" – Caceres: Tip. El Noticiero, S.L. 1958 – 1 – sp Bibl Santa Ana [610]

ESTATUTOS DE LA ASOCIACION DE PADRES DE FAMILIA Y AMIGOS DE LA ESCUELA / Escuela Graduada Jose Luis Cotallo – Caceres: Edit. Extremadura, 1972 – 1 – sp Bibl Santa Ana [060]

ESTATUTOS DE LA COFRADIA DE LA VIRGEN DE LA MONTANA – 1899 – 9 – 1.50f – sp Bibl Santa Ana [240]

ESTATUTOS DE LA COFRADIA DE LOS RAMOS, CRISTO DE LA BUENA MUERTE Y VIRGEN DE LA ESPERANZA / Cofradia de los Ramos, Cristo de la Buena Muerte y Virgen de la Esperanza – Caceres: Imp. Sanguino, 1962 – 1 – sp Bibl Santa Ana [360]

ESTATUTOS DE LA COFRADIA DEL SANTISIMO SACRAMENTO / Almendralejo. Spain – 1885 – 9 – 1.50f – sp Bibl Santa Ana [946]

ESTATUTOS DE LA COOPERATIVA AGRICOLA DE LOS COLONOS DE VALDELACALZADA – Badajoz: Imp. Arqueros, 1967 – 1 – sp Bibl Santa Ana [630]

ESTATUTOS DE LA COOPERATIVA AGRICOLA OLIVARERA NUESTRA SENORA DE SANTA MARTA DE SALVALEON (BADAJOZ) – Badajoz: Tip. Graf. Extremena, 1961 – sp Bibl Santa Ana [240]

ESTATUTOS DE LA COOPERATIVA AGROPECUARIA DE GRANJA DE TORREHERMOSA (BADAJOZ) – Baajoz: Imprenta Inca, 1965 – sp Bibl Santa Ana [946]

ESTATUTOS DE LA COOPERATIVA DE CASAS BARATAS NUESTRA SENORA DE LA ASUNCION DE CACERES / Cooperativa se Casas Baratas – Caceres: Editor. Extremadura, 1974 – 1 – sp Bibl Santa Ana [060]

ESTATUTOS DE LA COOPERATIVA DE VIVIENDAS DE PROTECCION OFICIAL "SAN CARLOS BARROMERO" DEL SINDICATO PROVINCIAL DE BANCA, BOLSA Y AHORRO DE CACERES / Delegacion Provincial de Sindicatos – Caceres: El Noticiero S.L., 1966 – 1 – sp Bibl Santa Ana [350]

ESTATUTOS DE LA COOPERATIVA DEL CAMPO "ARRAGO" / Cooperativa del campo "Arrago" – Caceres: Imp. Moderna, 1976 – 1 – sp Bibl Santa Ana [060]

ESTATUTOS DE LA COOPERATIVA DEL CAMPO "LA BENFICA" DE OLIVA DE LA FRONTERA (BADAJOZ) – Jerez de los Caballeros: Tip. Horizonte, 1960 – sp Bibl Santa Ana [946]

ESTATUTOS DE LA COOPERATIVA DEL CAMPO NUESTRA SENORA DE LA ESTRELLA DE AGRADO (CIUDAD REAL) – Villanueva de la Serena: Imp. Parejo, 1970 – sp Bibl Santa Ana [946]

ESTATUTOS DE LA COOPERATIVA DROGUERA EXTREMENA. CODEX, DETALLISTA DE DROGUERIAS – Merida: Imp. Rodriguez, 1965 – sp Bibl Santa Ana [946]

ESTATUTOS DE LA COOPERATIVA GANADERA. "ALTA EXTREMADURA" – Caceres: Caceres Tip. El Noticiero, s.a., 1947 – 1 – sp Bibl Santa Ana [334]

ESTATUTOS DE LA COOPERATIVA PROVINCIAL DE AUTOMOBILES DE ALQUILER DE BADAJOZ – Badajoz: Graf. Jimenez, 1960 – sp Bibl Santa Ana [946]

ESTATUTOS DE LA COOPERATIVA Y CAJA RURAL DE... – Caceres: Tip. El Noticiero – sp Bibl Santa Ana [340]

ESTATUTOS DE LA FEDERACION DE SINDICATOS DE PROPIETARIOS DE FINCAS RUSTICAS DE LA PROVINCIA DE BADAJOZ – Badajoz: Tip. de Arqueros, 1931 – 1 – sp Bibl Santa Ana [340]

ESTATUTOS DE LA REAL...DE CACERES / Cofradia de Nuestra Senora de la Soledad y del Santo Entierro – Caceres: Imp. y Enc. de Vda. de Garcia Floriano, 1953 – 1 – sp Bibl Santa Ana [060]

ESTATUTOS DE LA SOCIEDAD DE PREVISION SOCIAL DE MERIDA – Merida: A. Rodriguez, 1932 – 1 – sp Bibl Santa Ana [060]

ESTATUTOS DE LA SOCIEDAD OBRERA DENOMINADA LA UNION DE FUENTE DE CANTOS (PROVINCIA DE BADAJOZ) – Badajoz: Tip. Y Enc. La Minerva Extremena, 1906 – 1 – sp Bibl Santa Ana [946]

ESTATUTOS DE LA...CACERES / Caceres. Asociacion de Padres de Alumnos del Colegio San Antonio de Padua – Edit. Extremadura, 1977 – 1 – sp Bibl Santa Ana [360]

ESTATUTOS DE LA...DENOMINADA DE SANTIAGO Y SANTA MARGARITA / Cooperativa Local de Consumo – Zorita: Imp. Carrasco, 1975 – 1 – sp Bibl Santa Ana [350]

ESTATUTOS DE LA...EN LA IGLESIA PARROQUIAL DE ALMENDRALEJO / Cofradia Santisimo Sacramento – 1885 – 9 – 1.50f – sp Bibl Santa Ana [240]

ESTATUTOS DE LOS CAPELLANES (ANNO 1607) – Avila – 1r – 5,6 – sp Cultura [240]

ESTATUTOS DE SOCIEDAD DE SOCORROS MUTUOS Y CAJA DE AHORROS, CONSTITUIDA EN VILLAFRANCA DE LOS BARROS EN 7 DE MAYO DE 1905, S.L.,S.I.,S.A. / Villafranca de los BarrosEl Credito Extremeno – 1 – sp Bibl Santa Ana [332]

ESTATUTOS DE...CACERES / Marco, S A – Tip. La Minerva, 1962 – 1 – sp Bibl Santa Ana [060]

ESTATUTOS DEL CENTRO JUVENIL NUESTRA SENORA DEL ROSARIO DE HUERTA DE ANIMAS / Huerta de Animas – Trujillo: Imp. Gexme, 1972 – 1 – sp Bibl Santa Ana [060]

ESTATUTOS DEL HOGAR EXTREMENO DE MADRID APROBADOS EN LA JUNTA GENERAL CELEBRADA AL EFECTO EL DIA 1ST DE JULIO DE 1934 – Madrid: Imprenta Cava Baja 17, s.a. – 1 – sp Bibl Santa Ana [340]

ESTATUTOS DEL PATRONATO DE VIVIENDAS SOCIALES DE ALCANTARA. 1971 / Alcantara. Ayuntamiento – Caceres: Imp. La Minerva, 1971 – 1 – sp Bibl Santa Ana [060]

ESTATUTOS DEL SINDICATO AGRICOLA DE ZARZA-CAPILLA (BADAJOZ) – Toledo: Imp. de Viuda e hijos de J. Pelaez, 1905 – sp Bibl Santa Ana [630]

ESTATUTOS DEL...Y EL GENERAL DE PROCURADORES DE LOS TRIBUNALES DE ESPANA / Colegio Provincial de Procuradores de Badajoz – Badajoz: Tip. Clasica, 1960 – sp Bibl Santa Ana [340]

ESTATUTOS GENERALES / Caja Ahorros y Monte de Piedad de Caceres. – Caceres: Tip. Extremadura, 1978 – sp Bibl Santa Ana [060]

ESTATUTOS GENERALES / Caja de Ahorros y Monte de Piedad. Caceres – Caceres: Edit. Extremadura, 1976 – 1 – sp Bibl Santa Ana [350]

ESTATUTOS O CONSTITUCIONES...DE LA PIEDAD...ALMENDRALEJO – 1879 – 9 – 1.50f – sp Bibl Santa Ana [240]

ESTATUTOS PARA EL REGIMEN Y ADMINISTRACION DE LA... / Cofradia de la Santisima Virgen del Pilar de Casas de Don Antonio – Caceres: Tip. El Noticiero – 1 – sp Bibl Santa Ana [060]

ESTATUTOS PARA EL REGIMEN Y ADMINISTRACION DE LA HERMANDAD DE CABALLEROS DE LA SANTISIMA VIRGEN DE LA VICTORIA – Trujillo: Tip. Sobrino de B. Pena, 1944 – sp Bibl Santa Ana [340]

ESTATUTOS POR LOS QUE HA DE REGIRSELA... / Cooperativa Industrial Cacerena – Caceres: Imp. Moderna, 1971 – 1 – sp Bibl Santa Ana [350]

ESTATUTOS POR LOS QUE SE RIGE LA PENA "LOS CAMBORIOS" / Los Camborios – Plasencia: Imp. Gercilasso, 1974 – 1 – sp Bibl Santa Ana [350]

ESTATUTOS PROVISIONALES. OCTUBRE, 1946 / Asociacion de Amigos de Guadalupe – Caceres: Imp. Garcia Floriano, s.a. – sp Bibl Santa Ana [060]

ESTATUTOS QUE HAN DE REGULAR EL FUNCIONAMIENT TO DE LA ASOCIACION CULTURAL CENTRO DE ESTUDIOS HISTORICOS DE CACERES / Caceres. Centro de Estudios Historicos – Trujillo: Imp. Sobrino de B. Pena, 1960 – 1 – sp Bibl Santa Ana [946]

ESTATUTOS QUE HAN DE REGULAR EL FUNCIONAMIENTO DE LA ASOCIACION CULTURAL CENTRO DE ESTUDIOS HISTORICOS DE CACERES – Trujillo: Sobrino de B. Pena, 1960 – sp Bibl Santa Ana [946]

ESTATUTOS SOCIALES DEL... / Caceres. Club de tenis "Cabeza Rubia" – Caceres: Imp. Sergio Dorado, 1971 – 1 – sp Bibl Santa Ana [360]

ESTATUTOS. SOCIEDAD LA FORTUNA EMERITENSE – Merida, 1924 – 1 – sp Bibl Santa Ana [946]

ESTATUTOS Y ORDENACIONES DESTA PROVINCIA DE SAN GABRIEL...BROZAS...1615... – S.l., s.i., s.a. – 1 – sp Bibl Santa Ana [946]

ESTATUTOS Y ORDENACIONES...SAN GABRIEL – 1602 – 9 – 1.50f – sp Bibl Santa Ana [946]

ESTATUTOS Y ORDENACIONES...SAN JOSE – 1802 – 9 – 1.50f – sp Bibl Santa Ana [946]

ESTATUTOS Y REGLAMENTO / Asociacion de Medicina Extremena – Badajoz: Tip. Clasica, 1965 – sp Bibl Santa Ana [610]

ESTATUTOS Y REGLAMENTO DE LA... / Cooperativa de Viviendas "San Antonio" – Caceres: Imp. Rodriguez, 1979 – 1 – sp Bibl Santa Ana [060]

ESTATUTOS Y REGLAMENTO DEL CASINO DE ALMENDRALEJO – Almendralejo: Imp. y Enc. de Juan Bote Gonzalez, 1910 – 1 – sp Bibl Santa Ana [340]

ESTATUTOS Y REGLAMENTO DEL CENTRO AGRICOLA-MERCANTIL DE CACERES – Caceres: Imp. La Minerva de Serafin Rodas, 1903 – 1 – sp Bibl Santa Ana [630]

ESTATUTOS Y REGLAMENTOS / Caja Rural de Ahorros y Prestamos de Almendralejo – Almendralejo: Imprenta Macarro, 1950 – sp Bibl Santa Ana [340]

ESTATUTOS Y REGLAMENTOS / Federacion Provincial de Empresarios de la Construccion – Caceres: Ed. Extremadura, 1979 – 1 – sp Bibl Santa Ana [350]

ESTATUTOS Y REGLAMENTOS DE LA... / Mutua Extremena de Vehiculos – Caceres: Imp. Rodriguez, 1971 – 1 – sp Bibl Santa Ana [060]

ESTATUTOS Y REGLAMENTOS DE LA CAJA RURAL DE AHORROS Y PRESTAMOS DE ALMENDRALEJO. ANO DE 1906 – Sevilla: Imp. L. Vilches, 1915 – 1 – sp Bibl Santa Ana [340]

ESTATUTOS Y REGLAMENTOS DE LA CAJA RURAL DE AHORROS Y PRESTAMOS DE MONESTERIO. ANO DE 1906 – Badajoz: Tip. Antonio Arqueros, 1906 – sp Bibl Santa Ana [240]

ESTATUTOS...CATEDRAL DE PLASENCIO / Norona, Andres – 1704 – 9 – 1.50f – sp Bibl Santa Ana [946]

ESTAUTOS DE LA... / Obra de Ayuda Nacional-Sindicalista – Caceres: Imp. Garcia Floriano, 1944 – 1 – sp Bibl Santa Ana [060]

Estave Barba, Francisco *see* DESCUBRIMIENTO Y CONQUISTA DE CHILE. BARCELONA, 1946

EST-CE LEGALEMENT QUE LE GOUVERNMENT A FAIT SUSPENDRE L'EXERCISE DU CULTE SAINT-SIMONIEN? / Decourdemanche, A – Paris, Everat, 1832, 18 p. Les Saint-Simoniens, 1825-1834. 6957 – 9 – fr Hachette [335]

ESTE E O LIVRO DAS CHYMERAS / Pimenta, Alfredo – ue para consolacao das proprias saudades, e para perpetuacao de instantes transcondentais, Alfredo Pimenta escrevoo, quando, tendo descido da torre do seo orgulho, entrava na cathedral magnifica da sua humildade. Lisboa: Portugalia, 1922 – 1 – us U.W. Library [240]

ESTE ES EL CORTEJO...SALAMANCA 1938 / Castro Albarran, A de – Burgos: Razon y Fe, 1938 – 1 – sp Bibl Santa Ana [946]

Este, T *see* METHODISM DISPLAY'D

Esteban, Juan Carlos *see* IMPERIALISMO Y DESARROLLO ECONOMICO

L'EST-ECLAIR – Troyes. Quotidien republicain d'information. janv-oct 1966 – 1 – fr A.C.R.P.P. [944]

ESTECO Y CONCEPCION DEL BERMEJO. DOS CIUDADES DESAPARECIDAS. BUENOS AIRES, 1943 / Torre Revello, Jose – Madrid: Razon y Fe, 1946 – 1 – sp Bibl Santa Ana [946]

LA ESTELA DE UN CAMPESINO / ed by Bayle, Constantino – Madrid: Razon y Fe, 1926 – 1 – sp Bibl Santa Ana [920]

LA ESTELA DE UN CAMPESINO. MUESTRARIO DE ACCION, IDEAS Y SENTIMIENTOS / Masides Rosado, Severiano – Plasencia: Tip. de Mariano San Jose, 1926 – 1 – sp Bibl Santa Ana [946]

Estella *see* TRA GLI EROI I MARTIRI DELLA LIBERTA

Estelrique, I *see* TRATADO BREVE Y PARECER ACERCA DEL METHODO DE CURAR CON SANGRIAS...

O ESTENTOR : ORGAO DE ALUMNOS DO GYMNASIO AMAZONENSE – Manaos, Amazonas. 8 Jul 1909 – 1,5,6 – bl Biblioteca [072]

Estere-Forriol, Jose *see* DIE TRAUER- UND TROSTGEDICHTE IN DER ROMISCHEN LITERATUR

Esterno, FC P d' *see* DE LA MISERE, DE SES CAUSES, DE SES REMEDES

Estes, David Foster *see*
– AN OUTLINE OF NEW TESTAMENT THEOLOGY
– OUTLINE OF NEW TESTAMENT THEOLOGY

Estes, Henry B 2 *see* GOD IS IN HEAVEN

ESTESTVENNOE DVIZHENIE NASELENII A RSFSR ZA 1926 GOD = MOUVEMENT NATUREL DE LA POPULATION DE RSFSR EN 1926 / T Sentralnoe statisticheskoe upravlenie RSFSR, Sektor sotsialno i statistiki – Moskva: Izd. T SSR RSFSR, 1928 – 1 – CSUX91-B15 – us Hoover Inst Photo [304]

ESTETICA SIEMPREVIVAS Y ENSAYOS / Gomez-Bravo, Vicente – Madrid: La difusora del libro, 1959 – sp Bibl Santa Ana [946]

Esteva Ruiz, R A *see* EL DERECHO PUBLICO...

Esteve, P *see* NOUVELLE DECOUVERTE DU PRINCIPE DE L'HARMONIE

Estevez Verdejo, Ramiro *see* MONOGRAFIA DE S. VICENTE DE ALCANTARA

ESTHER / Adams, Henry – A novel. 1884 – 9 – 20.00 – us Scholars' Facs [830]

ESTHER : A DRAMA OF JEWISH HISTORY: BEING THE STORY OF THE BOOK OF ESTHER / Gill, William Hugh – Philadelphia: George W Jacobs, c1899 – 1mf – 9 – 0-8370-3284-9 – 1985-1284 – us A.T.L.A. [220]

ESTHER / Sirkis, I – Warsaw. 1887. BJ-422-86 1 – 9 – ne IDC [470]

ESTI BAPTISTI...25 JUUBELI AASTA MALESTUSETS / Feisberg, J & Tetermann, A – Historical Album of the Estonian Baptist Churches: 25th Jubilee Year of Reminiscences. Tallinn, 1911. 178p – 1 – 7.12 – us Baptist [240]

ESTI BUDAPEST – Hungary, Apr 1952-Dec 1954; Feb 1955-Oct 1956 – 15r – 1 – uk British Libr Newspaper [072]

ESTI HIRLAP – Budapest, Hungary. 1962-1990 – 53r – 1 – us L of C Photodup [072]

ESTI MAGYARORSZAG – Budapest, Hungary. Jun 1942; Sept 1943 (scattered issues) – 2r – 1 – us L of C Photodup [072]

ESTIA *see* HESTIA

Estienne, Emiland *see* STATISTIQUE DE LA BATAVIE

Estienne, Henri *see*
- THE ART OF MAKING DEVISES. TREATING OF HIEROGLYPHICKS, SYMBOLES, EMBLEMES
- CONFORMITE DU LANGAGE FRANCOIS AVEC LE GREC
- DE CRITICIS VET. GR. ET LATINIS
- DE LA PRECELLENCE DU LANGAGE FRANCOIS
- DEUX DIALOGUES DU NOUVEAU LANGAGE FRANCOIS
- DICTIONARIUM MEDICUM, VEL EXPOSITIONES VOCUM MEDICINALIUM AD VERVUM EXCERPTAE ES HIPPOCRATE, ARETEO ETC. (AEL, ABT 3;21)
- ORATIONES 2. 1. ADUERSUS LIB. VBERTI FOLIETAE DE MAGNITUDINE ET PERPETUA IN BELLIS FELICITATE IMPERII TURCICI. 2. AD EXPENDITIONEM IN TURCAS FORTITER ET CONSTANTER PERSEQUENDAM EXHORTATORIA
- LE PREMIER LIVRE DES PROVERBES EPIGRAMMATIZEZ
- THESAVRVS GRAECAE LINGVAE,...
- TRAITE DE LA CONFIRMITE DU FRANCAIS AVEC LE GREC

Estienne, R *see* DICTIONNAIRE FRANCOIS-LATIN

Estienne, Robert *see*
- LES CENSURES DES THEOLOGIENS DE PARIS
- CONCORDANTIAE BIBLIORUM VTRIUSQUE TESTAMENTI,...
- DICTIONNAIRE FRANCOIS-LATIN
- LES MOTS FRANCOIS SELON L'ORDRE DES LETTRES
- TRAICTE DE LA GRAMAIRE FRANCOISE

EST-IL BON? EST-IL MECHANT? / Diderot, Denis; ed by Undank, J – (Studies on Voltaire and the eighteenth century, v16) – Oxford. 1961 – 9 – $45.00 – 0-7294-0070-0 – uk Voltaire [830]

LOS ESTILOS POLITICOS EN LA ARGENTINA 1853-1955 / Agozino, Adalberto C – [Buenos Aires]: Editorial El Templario, [1985] – 1 – CSUXAHZ6098-B – us Hoover Inst Photo [320]

ESTIMATE OF CERTAIN EXPENSES OF THE CIVIL GOVERNMENT OF THE PROVINCE OF CANADA,... – Toronto: Rollo Campbell, [1857]. SEM105P1757 – 1mf – 9 – Can$2.25 – cn Bibl Nat [336]

AN ESTIMATE OF FERTILITY LEVEL OF THE POPULATION OF DJAKARTA BY POLYNOMIAL FUNCTION / Bhatta, Jitandra Nath – English & Indonesian. SE-6322 1. 1966 – 9 – ne IDC [310]

AN ESTIMATE OF THE MANNERS AND PRINCIPLES OF THE TIMES / Brown, J – London, 6th ed 1757-1758. 2v – 6mf – 9 – ne IDC [390]

ESTIMATES / Canada. Department of Finance – 1924/25-1974/75 – 9 – cn Micromedia [324]

ESTIMATES OF PRIVATE FINAL CONSUMPTION EXPENDITURE OF THE LIBYAN ARAB REPUBLIC, 1962-1969 / Libya. Directorate General of Economic and Social Planning – 1971. BNE-715 1 – 9 – ne IDC [338]

ESTIMATES OF REVENUE AND EXPENDITURE – 8v. 1956-65. (lacking 1960 61). BNE-9604 1 – 9 – ne IDC [339]

ESTIMATES OF REVENUE AND EXPENDITURE / Arabian Gulf Emirates. Abu-Dhabi – 3v. in 1. 1967-69. BNE-10,001 1 – 9 – ne IDC [336]

ESTIMATES OF REVENUE AND EXPENDITURE FOR CURRENT AND DEVELOPMENT BUDGET FOR THE FISCAL YEAR / Sudan. Ministry of Treasury – 15 v. 1956-74. (lacking 1957 58, 1959 60, 1962 63, 1963 64, 1971 72, 1972 73). BNE-7678 1 – 9 – ne IDC [336]

ESTIMATES OF SOME ENGLISHMEN AND SCOTCHMEN : A SERIES OF ARTICLES REPRINTED BY PERMISSION PRINCIPALLY FROM THE NATIONAL REVIEW / Bagehot, Walter – London: Chapman and Hall, 1858 – 1 roll – 1 – 1-55879-822-6 – uk Libr Preservation [920]

ESTIMATING SOVIET AND EAST EUROPEAN HARD CURRENCY DEBT: A RESEARCH PAPER – National Foreign Assessment Center. Washington, DC, (1980). v,32p. Incl. bibliog. references. 1 fiche. 4351 – 9 – us U.W. Library [330]

ESTIMATION OF CROP AREAS AND YIELDS IN AGRICULTURAL STATISTICS – 1982 – 193p – it F.A.O. [338]

ESTIMATION OF IRRIGABLE AREAS IN THE SUDAN, 1951-1953 : REPORT / Gibb, Sir Alexander and Partners, Consulting Engineers, London – Feb 1954 – 9 – BNE-7644 1 – ne IDC [624]

ESTIMATION OF VO(2MAX) FROM A SUBMAXIMAL 1-MILE TRACK JOG FOR RELATIVELY FIT TEENAGE INDIVIDUALS / Hunt, Brian R – 1993 – 1mf – $4.00 – us Microform Publ [612]

O ESTIMULO : ORGAO CRITICO E LITTERARIO – Penedo, Alagoas. 16 Jul 1893 – 1,5,6 – bl Biblioteca [072]

Estius, G *see*
- IN LIBROS SENTENTIARUM COMMENTARIA
- IN OMNES BEATI PAULI ET SEPTEM CATHOLICAS APOSTOLORUM EPISTOLAS COMMENTARIA

Estius, Guilielmus *see* IN OMNES D. PAULI EPISTOLAS

ESTLIN PAPERS – 1840-44.From Dr. William's Library, London. BRRAM – 1 – uk Microform Academic [305]

L'ESTOC : COLLEGE SAINT-ALEXANDRE – Limbour, Canada. mar 1961-v3 n2. dec 1962 – 1r – 1 – Can$25.00 – cn Can Microfilming [370]

Estonia. Riigikogu *see* PROTOKOLLID

ESTONIAN AMERICAN NATIONAL COUNCIL – New York. 20 docs. 1980-1990 – 5mf – 9 – ne IDC [320]

Estonian Baptist Union *see* ARUANNE

ESTONIAN NEWSPAPERS 1918-1940 – Helsinki: Helsinki University Library, 1994 – ca 525r – 1 – fi H.U. Libr [072]

ESTONIAN PERIODICALS AND BOOKS IN FINNISH LIBRARIES / Aav, Yrjo – Zug. 1970. 2v. – 5mf – 9 – ne IDC [947]

ESTONIAN PERIODICALS AND BOOKS IN FINNISH LIBRARIES / Aav, Yrjo – Zug. 2v. 1970 – 5mf – 9 – ne IDC [073]

Estoppey, A *see* LA LOI FEDERALE DU 3 JUILLET 1876 SUR LA NATURALISATION...

Estournelles de Constant, Paul Henri Benjamin Baron d' *see* AMERICA AND HER PROBLEMS

Estrada, Antonio *see* VIDA EJEMPLAR FR. PEDRO DE LA PURIFICACION

ESTRANGER A LONDRES (THE FOREIGNER) – London, UK. 1, 15-29 Oct 1904 – 1 – uk British Libr Newspaper [072]

LES ESTRANGES ET ESPOUVANTABLES AMOURS D'UN DIABLE, EN FORME D'UN GENTILLOME ET D'UNE DEMOISELLE, DE BRETAGNE – Rennes. 1620 – 9 – fr Hachette [360]

ESTRATEGIA PARA EL DESARROLLO NACIONAL, 1970-80 / Panama. Direccion General de Planificacion y Administracion, Departamento de Planificacion – (Strategy for National Development 1970-80). 1970. BD-1727 1 – 9 – ne IDC [338]

ESTRATEGIA SOCIO-ECONOMICA DEL DESARROLLO NACIONAL 1971-1991 / Bolivia. Ministerio de Planificacion y Coordinacion – (Socio-Economic Strategy for National Development 1971-1991). La Paz. 1970. BD-1623 1 – 9 – ne IDC [338]

L'ESTRATERRITORIALITA DELLE PERSONE GIURIDICHE / Battaglia, A G – Palermo, 1903 – 1mf – 9 – ILM-3354/1 – ne IDC [340]

A ESTREA : SEMANARIO DE LITTERATURA, SCIENCIAS E ARTES – Maceio, Alagoas. 5 Ago 1878-24 Mar 1879 – 1,5,6 – bl Biblioteca [072]

EL ESTRECHO DE MAGALLANES. LO QUE ERA Y LO QUE ES / Bayle, Constantino – Madrid: Razon y Fe, 1921 – 1 – sp Bibl Santa Ana [946]

A ESTRELA BRASILEIRA – Rio de Janeiro, 17 Nov-Dec 1823; 31 May, 12 Jul 1824 – 1,5,6 – bl Biblioteca [072]

A ESTRELA POLAR : ORGAM CATHOLICO DA DIOCESE DE DIAMANTINA – Diamantina, 2 Nov 1913; Mar 1914; Dec 1922; Mar 1923; Dec 1941; Jan-Feb, May-Jul 1942; Jan 1943-Dec 1944; Jan 1945-Nov 1947; Mar-May, Oct-Dec 1948; Jul-Oct, Dec 1954; Mar-Apr, Dec 1955; Aug-Sep 1956; Feb, Apr, Nov 1957; Jan, Apr, Jun-Jul, Sep 1958; Jan, May-Jun, Nov 1959; Nov 1960; 29 Oct 1961 – 1,5,6 – bl Biblioteca [072]

LA ESTRELLA – 1961. 842p – 1 – 29.47 – us Baptist [240]

A ESTRELLA DA OESTE : ORGAM DOS PODERES MUNICIPAES – Divinopolis, 16 Mar, May, Jul, Sept 1924; 18-25 Jan 1925 – 1,5,6 – bl Biblioteca [072]

A ESTRELLA DA TARDE : PERIODICO RECREATIVO – '(s.l.')-Sao Luiz, Brazil. 7 Jun-27 Sept 1857 – 1,5,6 – bl Biblioteca [072]

ESTRELLA DE PANAMA – Panama, Apr 1904-Dec 1914; Sept 1951-May 1955; Jul 1978; Sept 1978-1985 – 161r – 1 – us L of C Photodup [072]

LA ESTRELLA DE PANAMA – Panama City, Panama. 3 Jan-8 Mar 1920 – 6r – 1 – us L of C Photodup [072]

LA ESTRELLA DE PANAMA – Panama: The Star & Herald Co, 1956-oct 1970; han-feb 1971; [oct 1971-jun 1972] – 1 – us Res Libr [072]

LA ESTRELLA DE PANAMA : STEAMER EDITION – Jan 9 1864-Oct 10 1864 – 1r – 1 – us L of C Photodup [072]

ESTRELLA DO AMAZONAS – Barra do Rio Negro, Amazonas. 4 Jan-Dez 1854; Jan-Out, Dez 1855; Jan-Set, Nov 1856; Jan-Maio 1857; Jan-Dez 1862; Jul 1863 – 1,5,6 – bl Biblioteca [072]

A ESTRELLA DO NORTE DO BRASIL – '(s.l.')-Sao Luiz, Brazil. 11 Jul 1829-15 May 1830 – 1,5,6 – bl Biblioteca [072]

ESTRELLA DO SUL : ORGAM OFFICIAL DO P.R.M. DO MUNICIPIO – Estrella do Sul, 16, 30 Jan-27 Mar 1927 – 1,5,6 – bl Biblioteca [072]

Estrella Estralla, Jose Emilio *see*
- DIALOGOS PARA EL FUTURO
- JUAN DE BORBONY BATTEMBERG
- LA LIBERTAD
- VERDAD DE POLITICA

A ESTRELLA MARANHENSE : JORNAL INSTRUCTIVO, MORAL E RECREATIVO – San' Luiz, Brazil. 1-18 Sept 1859 – 1,5,6 – bl Biblioteca [072]

ESTRELLA MINEIRA – Tres Pontas, 4 Feb 1906; 27 May 1917 – 1,5,6 – bl Biblioteca [072]

Estridge, H W *see* SIX YEARS IN SEYCHELLES

L'ESTRIEN *see* LE JOURNAL DES ETUDIANTS DE L'UNIVERSITE DE SHERBROOKE

L'ESTRIEN REGIONAL – (Includes super Hebdo de l'Estrie 10 sep 1989-7 jan 1990) – Magog, 12/18 fev 1989-3 sep 1989 – 2r – 1 – Can$70.00 – cn Can Microfilming [072]

ESTRINDENCIAS POESIAS / Ducasse, Angel Braulio – Badajoz: Tip. Vda. de A. Arqueros, 1936 – 1 – sp Bibl Santa Ana [810]

[ESTRO ARMONICO, N 3] VIVALDI'S 3D CONCERTO, CON VIOLINO SOLO OBLIGATO / ed by Vivaldi, A – (Solo violin part only) – London: Longman, [17–] – 1 – us Sibley [780]

[ESTRO ARMONICO, N 12] VIVALDI'S 5TH CONCERTO / Vivaldi, Antonio – London: Longman & Co, [17–] – 1 – us Sibley [780]

L'ESTRO ARMONICO, OP. 3, NO. 5 / Vivaldi, Antonio – (Solo violin part only) – London: Longman & Co, mid 1700s – 1 – us Sibley [780]

ESTRUCTURA DE LA EPICA FRANCESA Y LOS PERSONAJES FEMENINOS / Donaire Fernandez, Maria Luisa – 2mf – 9 – Pta1,500.00 – 84-85422-08-2 – sp Pentalfa [440]

LA ESTRUCTURA ECONOMICA Y EL DESARROLLO INDUSTRIAL DE LA REPUBLICA ARGENTINA / Hopkins, John Abel – Buenos Aires, 1944 – 1 – CSUXAHZ5770-B – us Hoover Inst Photo [330]

ESTRUCTURAS SOCIALES Y ECONOMICAS EN LUSITANIA DURANTE EL ALTO IMPERIO / Francisco Martin, Julian – 2mf – 9 – Pta1,500.00 – 84-85422-46-5 – sp Pentalfa [306]

Estuardo, Nunez *see* AUTORES GERMANOS EN EL PERU

ESTUARIES – v. 1-. 1978- – 1,5,6,9 – us UMI [574]

ESTUDANTE : FOLHA LITTERARIA DE EDUCACAO E RECREIO, DEDICADA A MOCIDADE MACEIOENSE – Maceio, Alagoas. 10 Ago-Set, 10 Nov 1888 – 1,5,6 – bl Biblioteca [072]

O ESTUDANTE – Manaos, Amazonas. 15 Dez 1907 – 1,5,6 – bl Biblioteca [072]

O ESTUDANTE : ORGAM DE ESTUDANTES – Manaus, Amazonas. 9 Maio 1911-15 Mar 1912 – 1,5,6 – bl Biblioteca [072]

O ESTUDANTE : ORGAM DE UMA SOCIEDADE DE ALUMNOS DO GYMNASIO – Manaos, Amazonas. 10 Jul-12 Out 1915 – 1,5,6 – bl Biblioteca [072]

O ESTUDANTE – Rio Branco, Acre. 23 Maio 1965 – 1,5,6 – bl Biblioteca [072]

L'ESTUDIANT / ed by Corbeil, Wilfrid – Joliette, Canada. v1 n1. dec 1936-v10 n4-5. mai/jun 1946 – 1r – 1 – Can$50.00 – cn Can Microfilming [072]

EL ESTUDIANTE DE SALAMANCA / Espronceda, Jose de – Madrid: Est. Tipografico A Marzo, 1903 – sp Bibl Santa Ana [946]

ESTUDIO AGROECOLOGICO : MAIZ-TRIGO DEL POLIGONO DE RIEGO DE LA VIOLADA / Campillo Ruiz, Ana – 1mf – 9 – Pta1,000.00 – 84-85422-70-8 – sp Pentalfa [630]

ESTUDIO BIBLIOGRAFICO DE DON MANUEL EDUARDO DE GOROSTIZA. MEXICO, 1932 / Agular, M Maria Esperanza – Madrid: Razon y Fe, 1935 – 1 – sp Bibl Santa Ana [920]

ESTUDIO BIOGRAFICO HERNANDO DE SOTO / Villanueva y Canedo, Luis – Badajoz: Tip.Lit.y Enc.La Industria, de Uceda Hermanos, 1892 – 1 – sp Bibl Santa Ana [910]

ESTUDIO COMPARATIVO DE LA HIPOTECA MINERA Y LA HIPOTECA COMUN. / Barrientos Lavin, Oscar – Santiago, Talleres graficos "Simiente." 1944. 45 p. LL-8002 – 1 – us L of C Photodup [340]

ESTUDIO DE GUITARRA, EM QUE SE EXPOEM O MEIO MAIS FACIL PARA APRENDER A TOCAR ESTE INSTRUMENTO: DIVIDIDO EM DUAS PARTES / Silva Leite, A da – Porto. 1796. BP-669 1 – 9 – ne IDC [780]

ESTUDIO DE LA ATMOSFERA DE UN NUCLEO URBANO EMPLEANDO EL RADON / Gonzalez Fernandez, Carlos – 1mf – 9 – Pta1,000.00 – 84-85422-15-5 – sp Pentalfa [550]

ESTUDIO DE LA FUENTE DE IONES GRANDES POSITIVOS EN OVIEDO / Perez Iglesias, Jose Manuel – 1mf – 9 – Pta1,000.00 – 84-85422-16-3 – sp Pentalfa [450]

ESTUDIO DE LAS TIERRAS DE LOS NUEVOS REGADIOS DE LA PROVINCIA DE BADAJOZ / Remon Camacho, Juan – Madrid, 1955 – 1 – sp Bibl Santa Ana [550]

ESTUDIO DE MATERIALES ARQUEOLOGICOS DEL YACIMIENTO DE CELADA MARLANTES / Marcos-Garcia, Miguel Angel – 2mf – 9 – Pta1,500.00 – 84-85422-66-X – sp Pentalfa [930]

ESTUDIO DE UN METODO ANALITICO PARA VALORACION CUANTITATIVA CONJUNTA DE LOS ACIDOS ORGANICOS EN VINOS DE TIERRA DE BARROS / Henao Davila, Fernando – Badajoz: Universidad de Extremadura, 1980 – 1 – sp Bibl Santa Ana [946]

ESTUDIO DEMOGRAFICO COMPARATIVO DE ESPANA Y LA PROVINCIA DE CACERES (DECENIO 1921-1930) / Campo Cardona, Antonio del – Caceres: Imprenta La Minerva, 1939 – sp Bibl Santa Ana [304]

ESTUDIO ELEMENTAL DE GRAMATICA HISTORICA DE LA LENGUA CASTELLANA / Alemany Bolufer, Jose – 3rd ed. Madrid, 1911. 367p. Includes bibliographical references – 1 – us U.W. Library [440]

ESTUDIO FILOSOFICO...A. LOPEZ DE AYALA / Lopez de Ayala, Adelardo – 1882 – 9 – 1.50f – sp Bibl Santa Ana [190]

ESTUDIO HISTORICO SOBRE EL DESCUBRIMIENTO Y CONQUISTA DE LA PATAGONIA Y DE LA TIERRA DE FUEGO / Morla Vicuna, Carlos – Leipzig: F.A. Brockans, 1903 – 1 – sp Bibl Santa Ana [946]

ESTUDIO JURIDICO Y LEGAL... / Aguilera, M – Bogota, 1931 – 1mf – 9 – ILM-3855/1 – ne IDC [340]

ESTUDIO PETROGRAFICO DEL METEORITO DE GUARENA / Calderon, S & Quiroga, F – 1892 – 9 – 1.50f – sp Bibl Santa Ana [550]

ESTUDIO SINTETICO SOBRE LA IGLESIA EN LA CONSTITUCION / Tejero Garcia, Angel – Caceres: Tip. Extremadura, 1972 – 1 – sp Bibl Santa Ana [240]

ESTUDIO SOBRE EL FUERO DE BAYLIO / Mahillo Santos, Juan – Badajoz: Imp. Dip. Provincial, 1958. Sep. REE – sp Bibl Santa Ana [946]

ESTUDIO SOBRE LOS CONFLICTOS DE LAS LEGISLACIONES EN MATERIA DE DERECHO PENAL / Brocher, C – N.p., n.d. – 3mf – 1 – ILM-2265/1 – ne IDC [327]

ESTUDIO SOBRE UNE LEGISLACION UNIFORME EN MATERIA DE LETRAS DE CAMBIO... / Alta Comision Internacional – Washington, 1918 – 4mf – 9 – ILM-3824/1 – ne IDC [340]

ESTUDIO SOCIO-ECONOMICO DE UN MUNICIPIO RURAL : MALPARTIDA DE CACERES / Lancho Moreno, Juan Jose – Caceres: Tip. El Noticiero, 1969 – 1 – sp Bibl Santa Ana [330]

ESTUDIO SOCIOJURIDICO DE LA NACIONALIDAD MEXICO Y LA NACION INDOIBERA / Espinosa, H E – Mexico, 1934 – 2mf – 1 – ILM-3852/1 – ne IDC [327]

ESTUDIO TECNICO ACERCA DE LA APLICACION DE LAS REGLAS PARA LA DEMARCACION DE LIMITES...EN LA CORDILLERA DE LOS ANDES... / Bertrand, Alejandro – Santiago de Chile: Cervantes, 1895 – 1 – F234.35 – fr Armell [910]

ESTUDIOS – Montevideo. nos. 1-66. 1956-73 – 1 – 35.00r – us Hoover Inst Photo [073]

ESTUDIOS / Recinos, Adrian et al – Guatemala: Edit. Universitaria, 1958 – sp Bibl Santa Ana [946]

ESTUDIOS BIBLIOGRAFICOS SOBRE RAFAEL LANDIVAR. GUATEMALA, 1931 / Villacorta, J Antonio – Madrid: Razon y Fe, 1934 – 1 – sp Bibl Santa Ana [920]

ESTUDIOS CLASICOS. MORFOLOGIA GRIEGA. SINTAXIS GRIEGA DEL P. SANTIAGO MORILLOS J. / Errandonea, Ignacio – Madrid: Razon y Fe, 1943 – 1 – sp Bibl Santa Ana [574]

ESTUDIOS CRITICOS / Gonzalez Serrano, Urbano – 1892 – 9 – 1.50f – sp Bibl Santa Ana [300]

ESTUDIOS CRITICOS ACERCA DE LA DOMINACION ESPANOLA EN AMERICA / Cappa, Ricardo S J – (1889 ed. 1890 ed) – 1887 – 9 – 1.50f – sp Bibl Santa Ana [946]

ESTUDIOS DE DERECHO INTERNACIONAL PUBLICO / Diaz Cisneros, S – La Plata, 1926 – 2mf – 1 – ILM-3366/1 – ne IDC [327]

ESTUDIOS DE DERECHO INTERNACIONAL PUBLICO Y PRIVADO / Fernandez Prida, J – Madrid, 1901 – 4mf – 1 – ILM-3575/1 – ne IDC [327]

ESTUDIOS DEL CENTRO DE DOCUMENTACION – Havana, CU. 1965-1969 – 1r – $50.00 – R04201 – us Library Micro [072]

ESTUDIOS ECUMENICOS – Mexico: Centro de Estudios Ecumenicos. [n2 apr/may 1969 [2nd ed only]; n8-41 sep 1970-1980; ns n1-32 dec 1984-1992] – 4r – 1 – us Res Libr [072]

LOS ESTUDIOS EN LA ORDEN CAPUCHINA EN EL PRIMER SIGLO DE SU EXISTENCIA / Felder, Hilario – Madrid: Archivo Ibero Americano, 1960 – 1 – sp Bibl Santa Ana [240]

ESTUDIOS FILOSOFICOS Y RELIGIOSOS / Giner de los Rios, Francisco – 1876. Libros en Microficha no 15 – 1mf – 9 – Pta1,000.00 – 84-85422-42-2 – sp Pentalfa [190]

ESTUDIOS GEOGRAFICOS, INSTITUTO JUAN SEBASTIAN EL CANO (CSIC) – Madrid, Ano 1940-1961 – 325mf – 9 – sp Cultura [910]

ESTUDIOS HISPANOAMERICANOS. HOMENAJE A HERNAN CORTES / Cortes, Hernando – Badajoz: Imp. Dip. Provincial, 1948. Por Constantino Bayle – 1 – sp Bibl Santa Ana [972]

ESTUDIOS HISTORICOS. CARACAS, 1927 / Rojas, Aristides – Madrid: Razon y Fe, 1930 – 1 – sp Bibl Santa Ana [946]

ESTUDIOS PARA LA HISTORIA DEL ARTE COLONIAL. VOL 1. ARQUITECTURA VIRREINAL SEGUIDA DE UNA ADICION DOCUMENTAL POR JOSE TORRE...BUENOS AIRES, 1934 / Noel, Martin – Madrid: Razon y Fe, 1936 – 1 – sp Bibl Santa Ana [720]

ESTUDIOS PRELIMINARES PARALA HORA DE LA PROVINCIA DE CACERES / Rivas Mateos, Marcelo – Caceres: S.L., s.i., 1898 – 1 – sp Bibl Santa Ana [946]

ESTUDIOS SOBRE EL PERONISMO : HISTORIA, METODO, PROYECTO / Feinmann, Jose Pablo – Buenos Aires: Editorial Legasa, 2nd ed 1984 – 1 – CSUXADJ8041-B – us Hoover Inst Photo [320]

ESTUDIOS SOBRE EL PRISCILIANISMO EN LA GALICIA ANTIGUA / Cabrera Moreno, Juliana – 1mf – 9 – Pta1,000.00 – 84-85422-21-X – sp Pentalfa [946]

ESTUDIOS SOBRE EL VOCABULARIO POLITICO ESPANOL (1931-1971). TESIS DOCTORAL / Rebollo Torio, Miguel Angel – Caceres: La Minerva Cacerena, 1976 – 1 – sp Bibl Santa Ana [320]

ESTUDIOS SOBRE JESUS Y SU INFLUENCIA / Nin Frias, Alberto – Montevideo, c1906. 1 fiche – 9 – us A.T.L.A. [240]

ESTUDIOS SOBRE LA FLORA DE LAS ISLAS DE JUAN FERNANDEZ...CON UNA INTODUCCION...POR DON ROBERTO POEHLMANN / Johow, Frederico – Santiago de Chile: Cervantes, 1896 – 1 – F176.48 – fr Armell [580]

ESTUDIOS SOBRE LOS RESTOS DE CERAMICA ROMANA / Barrantes Moreno, Vicente – Madrid, 1877 – 1 – sp Bibl Santa Ana [730]

ESTUDIOS SOBRE SAN PEDRO DE ALCANTARA / Pedro de Alcantara, Saint – Madrid: Archivo Ibero Americano, 1924 – 1 – sp Bibl Santa Ana [240]

ESTUDIOS SOCIALES / Moya, Francisco J – 1855 – 9 – 1.50f – sp Bibl Santa Ana [300]

ESTUDIOS SOCIALES CENTROAMERICANOS – San Jose, CR. 1974-1978 – 2r – $100.00 – R63600 – us Library Micro [300]

ESTUDIO...VIRGEN MARIA...ALMOHARIN (CACERES) / Gonzalez y Grez, Juan J – 1898 – 9 – 1.50f – sp Bibl Santa Ana [240]

ESTUDOS DE RELIGIAO – Sao Bernardo do Campo, Brasil: Impr Metodista. [v1-3 n5 mar 1985-jun 1988] – 1r – 1 – us Res Libr [072]

ESTUDOS SOCIAIS – Rio de Janeiro, BL. 1958-1964 – 1r – $50.00 – R04174 – us Library Micro [320]

ESTUDOS TEOLOGICOS : ORGAO DA FACULDADE DE TEOLOGIA – Sao Leopoldo, RGS [Rio Grande do Sul]: Federacao Sinodal, Igreja Evangelica de Confissao Luterana no Brasil, [v1-31 (1961-1991] – 4r – 1 – us Res Libr [072]

Eswein, F L *see* DAS RECHT DER LUFTSCHIFFAHRT

ESZAKMAGYARORSZAG – Miskolc, Hungary. 1962-1990 – 54r – 1 – us L of C Photodup [072]

ET CETERA – v. 34-. 1977- – 1,5,6,9 – us UMI [073]

ET LE-DABBER – Havazzelet. Jerusalem. 5632. 1872. BJ-27-202 1 – 9 – ne IDC [630]

ET MANUSKRIPT AF RASMUS RASK OM ALEUTERNES SPROG. SAMMENLIGNET MED GRONLAENDERNES / Thalbitzer, W – (Oversigt. Vidensk. selskabs forhandlinger, no. 3). Kobenhavn. 1916-17. BN-417 2 – 8 – ne IDC [910]

E.T.A. HOFFMANN / Bergengruen, Werner – Stuttgart: J G Cotta, 1944, c1939 – 1r – 1 – us U.W. Library [430]

E.T.A. HOFFMANN : DIE DREI REICHE SEINER GESTALTENWELT / Willimczik, Kurt – Berlin: Junker und Duennhaupt, 1939 – 1 – us U.W. Library [430]

E.T.A. HOFFMANN : LICHNOST I TVORCHESTVO / Ignatov, S S – (Includes bibliographical references) – Moskva: Tipografiia O L Somovoi, 1914 – 1 – us U.W. Library [430]

E.T.A. HOFFMANN / Schaukal, Richard von – (Includes bibliographical references (p.[99])) – Berlin: Schuster & Loeffler, [1904] – 1r – 1 – us U.W. Library [920]

E.T.A. HOFFMANNS GESPENSTERSPIEL / Escher, Karl – 2. Aufl. Berlin-Lichterfelde: E Runge, [19–?] – 1r – 1 – us U.W. Library [430]

E.T.A. HOFFMANNS LEBEN UND WERKE : VOM STANDPUNKTE EINES IRRENARZTES / Klinke, Otto – (Includes bibliographical references) – Braunschweig: R Sattler, [1902?] – 1 – us U.W. Library [430]

E.T.A. HOFFMANNS PERSOENLICHKEIT : ANEKDOTEN, SCHWAENKE UND CHARAKTERZUEGE AUS DEM LEBEN DES KAMMERGERICHTSRATS, DICHTERS UND KAPELLMEISTERS ERNST THEODOR AMADEUS HOFFMANN, NACH MITTEILUNGEN SEINER ZEITGENOSSEN AUS DEN QUELLEN ZUSAMMENGETRAGEN / Schollenheber, Wilhelm Heinrich – (Includes bibliographical references) – Muenchen: Verlag Parcus, 1922 – 1 – us U.W. Library [920]

E.T.A. HOFFMANNS WELTANSCHAUUNG / Dahmen, Hans – (Includes bibliographical references) – Marburg a.L.: N G Elwert, 1929 – 1r – 1 – us U.W. Library [430]

ETABLISSEMENTS BALLANDE : AGENDAS (BUSINESS DIARIES) – Port Vila, Santo, New Hebrides, 1933-42; 1950-54 – 2r – 1 – PMB 1130 – at Pacific Mss [380]

LES ETABLISSEMENTS FRANCAIS DU GOLFE DU BENIN... / Albeca, Alexandre-L d' – Paris: Baudouin, 1889 – 1 – F131.88 – fr Armell [944]

ETAH AND BEYOND / MacMillan, DB – BN-307 2. 1928 – 8 – ne IDC [910]

ETAPA EXTREMENA EN LA BIOGRAFIA DEL MINISTRO FERNANDEZ NEGRETE / Mota Arevalo, Horacio – Badajoz: (Imprenta de la Diputacion Provincial), 1964. Sep. Rev. Est. Extr. – 1 – sp Bibl Santa Ana [350]

ETAPES ET PERSPECTIVES DE L'UNION FRANCAISE / Gueye, Lamine – Paris: Editions de l'Union francaise, [1955] – 1 – us Res Libr [960]

ETAPY ZHIZNENNOGO TSIKLA I BYT RABOTAIUSHCHEI ZHENSHCHINY / Gordon, L et al – (Filmed with: Dinamika izmeneniia polozheniia dagestanskoi zhenshchiny i semia/S Gadzhieva) – Moskva: In-t konkretnykh sotsialnykh issledovanii AN SSSR, 1972 – us Res Libr [072]

L'ETAT ACTUEL DU PROBLEME TOTEMIQUE / Van Gennep, Arnold – Paris: Leroux, 1920 – 1 – F184.07 – fr Armell [944]

L'ETAT CHRETIEN CALVINISTE A GENEVE : AU TEMPS DE THEODORE DE BEZE / Choisy, Eugene – Geneve: Ch. Eggimann; Paris: Fischbacher, [1902?] – 2mf – us A.T.L.A. [320]

ETAT CRITIQUE DU TEXTE D'AGEE : QUATRE TABLEAUX COMPARATIFS / Andre, Louis Edward Tony – Paris: Fischbacher, 1895 – 1mf – 9 – 0-8370-2099-9 – 1985-0099 – us A.T.L.A. [220]

L'ETAT DE GUERRE... / Dupuy, M – Paris, 1912 – 2mf – 1 – ILM-1095/1 – ne IDC [327]

ETAT DE L'INSTRUCTION PRIMAIRE EN 1864, D'APRES LES RAPPORTS OFFICIELS DES INSPECTEURS D'ACADEMIE / France. Ministere de l'Instruction Publique – Paris. 1866 – 1 – fr A.C.R.P.P. [324]

ETAT DE POITOU SOUS LOUIS XIV / Colbert de Croissy, Charles – 1865. (Historical Studies Series) – 9 – 18.00 – fr Bibl Nationale [900]

ETAT DES SOMMES DEPENSEES A MEME L'OCTROI DE 30,000 VOTE DANS LE BUT D'AIDER A L'ETABLISSEMENT DES TERRES VACANTES DE LA COURONNE DANS LE BAS-CANADA / Canada. Ministere des Terres de la Couronne – s.l., s.n, 1855. SEM105P239 – 1mf – 9 – Can$2.25 – cn Bibl Nat [336]

ETAT DES SOMMES PAYEES PAR LE GOUVERNEMENT, ET CORRESPONDANCE ECHANGEE ENTRE LES INGENIEURS ET AUTRES OFFICIERS, RELATIVEMENT A CERTAINS CHEMINS DE FER – Quebec: John Lovell, 1853. SEM105P1461 – 1mf – 9 – Can$2.25 – cn Bibl Nat [336]

ETAT DES STATISTIQUES MINIERES / Morocco. Direction des Mines et de la Geologie – 1962-72 (lacking 1962-67, 1969). BNE-3036 1 – 9 – ne IDC [622]

ETAT DES TRAVAUX LEGISLATIFS.. / France. Assemblee nationale. Chambre des Deputes – Paris. 1886-Sept 1939. 12 reels – 1 – 23.00r – us L of C Photodup [944]

ETAT DETAILLE DES DEPENSES FAITES PENDANT LE VOYAGE EN EUROPE DES HONORABLES MM. MERCIER, PREMIER MINISTRE, ET SHEHYN, TRESORIER PROVINCIAL. – 1891. SEM105P613 – 1mf – 9 – Can$2.25 – cn Bibl Nat [971]

L'ETAT ET LES COMPAGNIES ... / Boullay, B – Lyon, 1942 – 2mf – 9 – ILM-610/1 – ne IDC [327]

ETAT FEDERAL ET... / Fur, L le – Paris, 1896 – 10mf – 1 – ILM-1686/1 – ne IDC [327]

L'ETAT MAHDISTE DU SOUDAN / Dujarric, Gaston – Paris: J Maisonneuve, 1901 – 1 – us Res Libr [960]

ETAT PAR ORDRE ALPHABETIQUE DES VILLES, BOURGS, VILLAGES ET HAMEAUX DE LA GENERALITE DE FLANDRE-ARTOIS / Esmangart – Lille, 1787 – 2mf – 9 – F90.00 – fr F.F.G. [944]

L'ETAT PONTIFICAL APRES LE GRAND SCHISME : ETUDE DE GEOGRAPHIE POLITIQUE / Guiraud, Jean – Paris: A. Fontemoing, 1896 – 1mf – us A.T.L.A. [320]

ETAT PRESENT DE LA NOBLESSE FRANCAISE CONTENANT LE DICTIONNAIRE DE LA NOBLESSE CONTEMPORAINE. – 2nd ed. Paris: Librairie Bachelin-Deflorenne, 1868. SEM105P84 – 10mf – 9 – Can$22.50 – cn Bibl Nat [360]

L'ETAT PRIMITIF DE L'HOMME DANS LA TRADITION DE L'EGLISE AVANT SAINT AUGUSTIN / Slomkowski, A – Paris, 1928 – 3mf – 9 – ne Slangenburg [240]

L'ETAT RELIGIEUX ET POLITIQUE DE LA FRANCE CONTEMPORAINE / Alexis, R P – Quebec: Impr. de l'Evenement, 1912. SEM105P686 – 1mf – 9 – Can$2.25 – cn Bibl Nat [240]

L'ETATISME INDUSTRIEL / Carnot, R – Paris. 1920. (La Condition Ouvriere. Part Two.) – 9 – 7.50 – fr Bibl Nationale [360]

LES ETATS DE BLOIS / Raynouard – (French Theatre Series). Paris. Mame Freres. 1814 – 9 – fr Hachette [820]

ETATS FINANCIERS PRESENTES A L'ASSEMBLEE LEGISLATIVE LE 17 OCTOBRE 1843 – [S.l.: s.n., 1843 ?]. SEM105P1758 – 1mf – 9 – Can$2.25 – cn Bibl Nat [350]

Etats Generaux de 1789 *see* DOCUMENTS RELATIFS AUX ETATS – GENERAUX DE 1789

LES ETATS UNIS: ORIGINE, INSTITUTIONS, DEVELOPPEMENT / DeCelles, Alfred Duclos – Ottawa: (s.n.), 1896. 02693. (Pre-1900 Canadiana) – 9 – cn C.I.H.M. [975]

LES ETATS-UNIS : ORIGINE, INSTITUTIONS, DEVELOPPEMENT / DeCelles, Alfred Duclos – 1913 (i.e. 1924). SEM105P510 – 4mf – 9 – Can$9.00 – cn Bibl Nat [975]

LES ETATS-UNIS : ORIGINE, INSTITUTIONS, DEVELOPPEMENT / DeCelles, Alfred Duclos – 1925. SEM105P511 – 4mf – 9 – Can$9.00 – cn Bibl Nat [975]

LES ETATS-UNIS D'EUROPE ONT COMMENCE; LA COMMUNAUTE EUROPEENE DU CHARBON ET DE L'ACIER, DISCOURS ET ALLOCUTIONS, 1952-54 / Monnet, Jean – Paris: R. Laffont, 1955. 171p – 1 – us U.W. Library [940]

LES ETATS-UNIS DEVANT L'OPINION FRANCAISE 1815-1852 / Remond, R – 1962 – F250.00 – fr Ethnologie [975]

ETC – A Review of General Semantics.Superseded by et cetera – 1. ; 5,6. ; 9 – apply; v.27-; v.33- – us UMI [400]

Etcheverry, Louis *see*
- LES BASQUES ET LEUR EMIGRATION EN AMERIQUE
- L'EMIGRATION DANS LES BASSES-PYRENEES PENDANT SOIXANTE ANS

Etchie, Michael P *see* A SUBMAXIMAL ONE-MILE TRACK JOG TO ESTIMATE VO2MAX IN FIT MEN AND WOMEN, AGES 30-39 YEARS

THE ETCHINGS OF HOLLAR IN THE ROYAL LIBRARY / Windsor Castle. Royal Library – (The most complete collection of Hollar's etchings. Filming follows sequence of the 1853 Parthey catalogue. Captions by permission of Cambridge University Press. Descriptive catalogue by Richard Pennington (printed) available from Cambridge University Press (1982)) – 71mf – 9 – $450.00 – 0-907006-23-X – uk Mindata [760]

ETEENPAIN – New York, 1921-Aug. 1950 – 36r – 1 – us I.H.R.C. [975]

Etelae-Pohjanmaa *see* AMERICA LETTERS

L'ETENDARD – Administrateur-gerant Jules Pic. Paris. 27 juin 1866-25 avr 1869 – 1 – fr A.C.R.P.P. [073]

L'ETENDARD / ed by Trudel, F-X – Montreal, Canada. 23 jan 1883-20 mar 1893 – 9r – 1 – Can$45.00r – cn Can Microfilming [072]

L'ETENDARD DE BELLECHASSE : HEBDO, TABLOID – (Cont by: Le Courrier de Bellechasse) – Montmagny, Canada. v1 n2. 11 avr 1931-7 avr 1933 – 1r – 1 – Can$45.00 – cn Can Microfilming [072]

L'ETENDARD DE BELLECHASSE *see* LE COURRIER DE BELLECHASSE

L'ETENDARD NATIONAL – Worcester, MA. 3 nov 1869-v1 n76. 18 oct 1870; 12 sep 1872-v3 n46. 14 nov 1872 – 1r – 1 – Can$40.00 – cn Can Microfilming [071]

L'ETENDARD REVOLUTIONNAIRE – Organe anarchiste hebdomadaire. no. 1-12. juil-oct 1882. Remplace: Le Droit social – 1 – fr A.C.R.P.P. [073]

ETEOCLE / Legouve – (French Theatre Series). Paris. Surosne. 1800 – 9 – fr Hachette [820]

THE ETERNAL IN MAN / Vance, James Isaac – (Includes bibliographical references) – New York: Fleming H Revell, c1907 – 1mf – 9 – 0-8370-5647-0 – 1985-3647 – us A.T.L.A. [240]

THE ETERNAL PRIESTHOOD / Manning, Henry Edward – New York: Catholic Publ Society, [between 1875-1892] – 1mf – 9 – 0-8370-7407-X – 1986-1407 – us A.T.L.A. [240]

THE ETERNAL PURPOSE OF GOD IN CHRIST JESUS OUR LORD : BEING THE FOURTH SERIES OF LECTURES / Kelly, James – 4th rev enl ed. London: James Nisbet, 1860 – 1mf – 9 – 0-8370-4361-1 – 1985-2361 – us A.T.L.A. [240]

ETERNALISM: A THEORY OF INFINITE JUSTICE / Smith, Orlando Jay – Boston: Houghton, Mifflin, 1902 – 1mf – 9 – us A.T.L.A. [210]

ETERNITY *see* OUR HOPE

ETERNITY, WHAT DOES THE BIBLE SAY OF IT – London: Samuel Bagster, (188?). 1 fiche – 9 – us A.T.L.A. [240]

Ethelwold, Saint *see* THE BENEDICTIONAL

Etherington, A G *see* A SHORT SURVEY OF THE MAIN FACTORS AND PRINCIPLES BEARING UPON THE DEVELOPMENT OF EFFICIENT NATIONAL SHIPPING SERVICES

THE ETHIC OF FREETHOUGHT AND OTHER ADDRESSES AND ESSAYS / Pearson, Karl – London: Adam & Charles Black, 1901. 1 fiche – 9 – us A.T.L.A. [240]

ETHICA GENERALIS / Signoriello, Nuntio – (Includes bibliographical references) – 4 ed. Neapoli: Bibliothecae Catholicae Scriptorum, 1889 – 1mf – 9 – 0-8370-7428-2 – 1986-1428 – us A.T.L.A. [230]

ETHICA NATURALIS / Weigel, Chr – O 826 – 9 – ne IDC [170]

ETHICA, POLITICA, OECONOMICA / Aristotle – 15th century. Holkham ms. 444. Holkham Hall, Norfolk, England – 1 – uk Microform Academic [170]

ETHICA SPECIALIS / Signoriello, Nuntio – (Includes bibliographical references) – 4 ed. Neapoli: Bibliothecae Catholicae Scriptorum, 1889 – 1mf – 9 – 0-8370-7429-0 – 1986-1429 – us A.T.L.A. [230]

ETHICA SYMBOLICA E FABULARUM UMBRIS IN VERITATIS LUCEM VARIA ERUDITIONE, NOVITER EVOLUTA / Pexenfelder, M – O-398. 1675 – 9 – ne IDC [760]

ETHICAL AND MORAL INSTRUCTION IN SCHOOLS / Palmer, George Herbert – Boston: Houghton, Mifflin, c1909 – 1mf – 9 – 0-8370-8541-1 – 1986-2541 – us A.T.L.A. [230]

THE ETHICAL APPROACH TO THEISM / Barbour, G F – Edinburgh: W. Blackwood, 1913 – 1mf – us A.T.L.A. [240]

AN ETHICAL MOVEMENT : A VOLUME OF LECTURES / Sheldon, W L – New York: Macmillan, 1896 – 1mf – us A.T.L.A. [240]

ETHICAL REVIEW – London. 1906 – 1 – uk Microform Academic [073]

ETHICAL STUDIES / Bradley, Francis Herbert – London: H.S. King, 1876 – 1mf – us A.T.L.A. [170]

ETHICAL STUDIES / Bradley, Francis Herbert – Oxford: Clarendon Press, 2nd ed rev [1935] – 1 roll – 1 – 1-55879-901-X – uk Libr Preservation [170]

ETHICAL TEACHINGS FOR THE YOUNG (CCC111) = CHU TZE HSIAO HSUEH / Chu, Hsi – (In Chinese) – Shanghai: Publication Dept., National Committee, YMCAs of China, 1926 – 1r – 1 – 1984-B500 – us A.T.L.A. [240]

ETHICAL TEACHINGS OF JESUS / Briggs, Charles Augustus – New York: Scribner's, 1904. 1 fiche – 9 – us A.T.L.A. [240]

THE ETHICAL THOUGHT OF CARLYLE MARNEY / Blackwell, Michael C – 1982 – 1 – $5.00 – us Baptist [170]

ETHICAL WORLD – London. 1898-1900 – 1 – uk Microform Academic [073]

ETHICAL WORLD (NEW SERIES) – London. 1907-16 – 1 – uk Microform Academic [073]

THE ETHICAL WORLD SERIES – 1898-1916 – 1 – uk Microform Academic [170]

ETHICS – v1- 1890- 1; v78- 5,6; v88- 1977- 9 – us UMI [170]

ETHICS / Dewey John & Tufts James H – New York/London: Henry Holt & Co; George Bell & Sons, 1909 – 7mf – 9 – $10.50 – LLMC 92-239 – us L.L.M.C. [170]

ETHICS : AN INTERNATIONAL JOURNAL OF SOCIAL, POLITICAL AND LEGAL PHILOSOPHY – v1-59. Oct 1890-Jul 1949 (complete) – 1 – ATLA S0009 – us A.T.L.A. [170]

ETHICS – London. 1901-06 – 1 – uk Microform Academic [073]

ETHICS : OR, SCIENCE OF DUTY / Bascom, John – (Includes index) – New York: G P Putnam, 1879 – 1mf – 9 – 0-8370-6010-9 – 1986-0010 – us A.T.L.A. [170]

ETHICS – v1-97 1890-1987 – 1 – us Princeton Micro [170]

ETHICS AND ATONEMENT / Lofthouse, William Frederick – London: Methuen, 1906. xi,302p.1 fiche – 9 – us A.T.L.A. [240]

ETHICS AND THE "NEW EDUCATION" / Bryant, Wm M – Chicago: S C Griggs, 1894 – 1mf – 9 – 0-8370-7448-7 – 1986-1448 – us A.T.L.A. [370]

ETHICS: DESCRIPTIVE AND EXPLANATORY / Mezes, Sidney Edward – New York: Macmillan, 1910 – xxi/435p 2mf – 9 – us A.T.L.A. [170]

ETHICS FOR YOUNG PEOPLE / Everett, Charles Carroll – Boston: Ginn, 1892, c1891 – 1mf – 9 – 0-8370-8736-8 – 1986-2736 – us A.T.L.A. [170]

ETHICS IN SCIENCE AND MEDICINE – v.1-7. 1973-80 – 5,6,9 – us UMI [170]

THE ETHICS OF ARISTOTLE / Burnet, John – London: Methuen, 1900 – 2mf – us A.T.L.A. [170]

THE ETHICS OF GEORGE ELIOT'S WORKS / Brown, John Crombie – Edinburgh, London: William Blackwood, 1879 – 1 roll – 1 – 1-55879-600-2 – uk Libr Preservation [420]

THE ETHICS OF LITERARY ART : THE CAREW LECTURES FOR 1893, HARTFORD THEOLOGICAL SEMINARY / Thompson, Maurice – Hartford, CT: Hartford Seminary Press, 1893 – 1mf – 9 – 0-8370-9190-X – 1986-3190 – us A.T.L.A. [170]

THE ETHICS OF THE DUST : TEN LECTURES TO LITTLE HOUSEWIVES ON THE ELEMENTS OF CRYSTALLISATION / Ruskin, John – London: Smith, Elder, 1866 – 1 roll – 1 – 1-55879-491-3 – uk Libr Preservation [840]

ETHICS OF THE GREAT RELIGIONS / Gorham, Charles Turner – (Includes bibliographical references) – London: Watts, 1898 – 1mf – 9 – 0-8370-6055-9 – 1986-0055 – us A.T.L.A. [170]

THE ETHICS OF THE OLD TESTAMENT / Bruce, William Straton – (Includes index) – 2nd enl ed. Edinburgh: T & T Clark, 1909 – 1mf – 9 – 0-8370-2489-7 – 1985-0489 – us A.T.L.A. [220]

DE ETHIEK VAN ULRICH ZWINGLI / Bavinck, Herman – Kampen: G.Ph. Zalsman, 1880 – 1mf – us A.T.L.A. [170]

DIE ETHIK DES APOSTELS PAULUS IN IHREN GRUNDZUEGEN / Ernesti, Heinrich Friedrich Theodor Ludwig – Goettingen: Vandenhoeck & Rup, 1880. 1 fiche – 9 – us A.T.L.A. [240]

DIE ETHIK DES CLEMENS VON ALEXANDRIEN / Winter, Julius – Leipzig: Doerffling und Franke, 1882 – 1mf – us A.T.L.A. [170]

DIE ETHIK DES MAIMONIDES / Rosin, David – Wroclau: H. Skutsch, 1876. 1 fiche – 9 – us A.T.L.A. [170]

DIE ETHIK HULDREICH ZWINGLIS / Kuegelgen, Constantin von – Leipzig: R. Woepke, 1902 – 1mf – us A.T.L.A. [240]

ETHIK IN IHREN GRUNDZUEGEN ENTWORFEN: EIN BEITRAG ZUR GESCHICHTE DER CHRISTLICHEN ETHIK *see* COLLECTED WORKS

DIE ETHIK PASCALS / Bornhausen, Karl – Giessen: Alfred Toepelmann, 1907. (Studien zur Geschichte des neueren Protestantismus; 2. Heft) – 1mf – us A.T.L.A. [170]

ETHIK UND MATERIALISTISCHE GESCHICHTSAUFFASSUNG = ETHICS AND THE MATERIALIST CONCEPTION OF HISTORY / Kautsky, Karl – (In English) – Chicago: Charles H Kerr, 1907 – 1mf – 9 – 0-8370-7161-5 – 1986-1161 – us A.T.L.A. [170]

ETHIK UND MYSTIK IN HEBBELS WELTANSCHAUUNG / Lahnstein, Ernst – (Includes bibliographical references) – Berlin: B Behr, 1913 – 1r – 1 – us U.W. Library [430]

ETHIOPIA : STATISTICAL ABSTRACT 1963-1976 / Ethiopia. Central Statistical Office – (1973, 1974 not publ. Coll title: African Official Statistical Serials, 1867-1982) – 32mf – 9 – £270.00 – uk Chadwyck [960]

Ethiopia *see*
- FIVE YEAR DEVELOPMENT PLAN, 1957-1961
- SECOND FIVE YEAR DEVELOPMENT PLAN, 1955-1959
- SECOND FIVE YEAR DEVELOPMENT PLAN, 1963-1967
- SECOND FIVE YEAR DEVELOPMENT PLAN OF ETHIOPIA, 1955-1959 E.C. 1963-1967 G.C. OUTLINE
- THIRD FIVE YEAR DEVELOPMENT PLAN, 1961-1965

Ethiopia. Central Statistical Office *see* ETHIOPIA

Ethiopia. Ministry of Education *see* BASIC EDUCATION STATISTICS

Ethiopia. Ministry of Education. Planning and External Relations Service *see* BASIC EDUCATION STATISTICS 1980 EC

ETHIOPIA OBSERVER – 1956-74. Formerly: New Times and Ethiopian News. 1936-56 – 1 – uk World [960]

ETHIOPIA OBSERVER : JOURNAL OF INDEPENDENT OPINION, ECONOMICS, HISTORY AND THE ARTS – Ethiopia and Britain, 1956-68. v.1-12 – 155mf – 8 – ne IDC [073]

Ethiopia. Planning Board *see* IMPLEMENTATION OF FIVE YEAR PLAN-EVALUATION REPORT FOR 1949-1951

ETHIOPIAN ECONOMIC REVIEW – Addis Ababa. [n1-10. dec 1959-jun 1968] – us Res Libr [072]

ETHIOPIAN HERALD – Addis Ababa, Ethiopia. Apr. 21, 1956-May 3, 1958 – 1 – us NY Public [072]

ETHIOPIAN HERALD – Addis Ababa: Ethiopian Press & Information Off, jun 23 1956- – 1 – us Res Libr [072]

THE ETHIOPIC LITURGY / Mercer, Samuel A B – London, 1915 – 9mf – 8 – Dfl32.00 – ne Slangenburg [240]

THE ETHIOPIC VERSION OF THE BBOK OF ENOCH / ed by Charles, R H – Oxford v1-pt 11 1906 – 9mf – 8 – ne Slangenburg [220]

THE ETHIOPIC VERSION OF THE HEBREW BOOK OF JUBILEES / Charles, R H – Oxford. 1895. BJ-411-2 1 – 9 – ne IDC [220]

THE ETHIOPIC VERSION OF THE HEBREW BOOK OF JUBILEES / ed by Charles, R H – Oxford v1-pt 8 1895 – 7mf – 8 – ne Slangenburg [270]

ETHIOPICA – (Individual titles available) – 1428mf – 9 – ne IDC [960]

DIE ETHISCHE ERSCHEINUNG DES CHRISTLICHEN LEBENS / Beck, Johann Tobias; ed by Lindenmeyer, Julius – Guetersloh: Bertelsmann, 1883 – 1mf – us A.T.L.A. [240]

DER ETHISCHE GEHALT IN GRILLPARZERS WERKEN / Freybe, Albert – Guetersloh: C Bertelsmann, 1893 – 1r – 1 – us U.W. Library [170]

DIE ETHISCHEN GRUNDFRAGEN : ZEHN VORTRAEGE / Lipps, Theodor – (Includes bibliographical references) – 2. teilweise umgearb. Aufl. Hamburg: Leopold Voss, 1905 – 1mf – 9 – 0-8370-6142-3 – 1986-0142 – us A.T.L.A. [170]

DIE ETHISCH-RELIGIOESE BEDEUTUNG DER ALTTESTAMENTLICHEN NAMEN: NACH TALMUD / Sarsowsky, Abraham – Kirchhain N.L.: Max Schmersow, 1904. 1 fiche – 9 – us A.T.L.A. [220]

[ETHNIC AND RACE RELATIONS IN BRITAIN PAMPHLET COLLECTION] – 1971-1974 – 1 – CSUXANP3015-B – us Hoover Inst Photo [305]

ETHNIC AND SOCIAL RELATIONS IN INDONESIA / Jaspan, Mervyn Aubrey – SE-2249 21. 1959 – 9 – ne IDC [305]

ETHNIC CONFLICT AND VIOLENCE IN SRI LANKA – 1983 – sz I.C.J. [360]

ETHNIC GROUPS (INC. AFRO-AMERICAN STUDIES) – 1970- – 1,5,9 – us Gordon [305]

ETHNIC NEWS FROM THE BALCH INSTITUTE FOR ETHNIC STUDIES *see*
- BANNER VON BERKS, UND WOCHENBLATT DER READING POST
- CHRISTLICHER BUNDES-BOTE
- GAZETTE DEMOCRAT
- HELLENIC NEWS
- ITALIAN-AMERICAN HERALD
- JEDNOSC
- THE JEWISH RECORD
- JEWISH VOICE
- KATHOLISCHE VOLKSZEITUNG
- LIBERA PAROLA
- MOMENTO
- NOWINY POLSKIE
- L'OPINIONE
- PATRYOTA
- PHILADELPHIA GAZETTE-DEMOCRAT
- PHILADELPHIA HEROLD
- PHILADELPHIA TAGEBLATT
- PHILADELPHIA-I FUGGETLENSEIG
- DER PILGER
- RABOCHY GOLOS
- READINGER POSTBOTHE UND BERKS, SCHUYLKILL UND MONTGOMERY COUNTIES ADVERTISER
- READINGER ZEITUNG
- REPUBLIKANER VON BERKS
- SLOVENSKY OBCAN

ETHNIC NEWSPAPERS FROM THE BALCH INSTITUTE FOR ETHNIC STUDIES *see* THE AMERICAN CITIZEN

THE ETHNIC QUESTION : CONFLICTS, DEVELOPMENT, AND HUMAN RIGHTS / Stavenhagen, Rodolfo – 9 – $12.00 – 92-808-0752-8 – ja U.N. Univ [320]

ETHNIKOS KERUX = THE NATIONAL HERALD – New York: Enossis Publ Co, [1915- ; jul 1922-29; may 1938-apr 1940; 1949-mar 1967; jul 1967-72 (daily ed only). jan 2 1949-dec 25 1955; jan 6-dec 29 1957; jul 7-dec 28 1958 (Sunday issues only) – 1 – us Res Libr [071]

ETHNIKOS KERUX – New York. (The National Herald In Greek). 12 Sep 1929-28 Jun 1939; 12 Feb 1940-18 May 1946 (imperfect).-w. 140 reels – 1 – uk British Libr Newspaper [071]

ETHNIKOS KERYX = THE NATIONAL HERALD – New York: Enossis Publ Co, [1915-]. [jul 1922-1929; may 1938-apr 1940; 1949-mar 1967; jul 1967-1972; Daily ed only; jan 2, 1949-dec 25, 1955; jan 6-dec 29 1957; jul 7-dec 28 1958; Sunday issues only] – us Res Libr [071]

ETHNO-ESTHETIQUE DU GOLFE DE PAPOUASIE / Drouilleau, A – 9 – F60.00 – fr Ethnologie [980]

THE ETHNO-GEOGRAPHY OF THE POMO AND NEIGHBORING INDIANS / Barrett, S A – UCB: 1908 – 1r – 1 – $50.00 – B63015 – us Library Micro [305]

ETHNOGRAFISCHE WAHRNEHMUNGEN UND ERFAHRUNGEN AN DEN KUESTEN DES BERINGS-MEERES / Erman, A – (Zeitschrift fuer Ethnologie, v. 2, 1870; v. 3, 1871). Berlin. Lacking: v. 3. BN-205 2 – 8 – ne IDC [305]

ETHNOGRAPHIA – Budapest, 1890-1904. v1-15. Lacking, 1893, v4; 1894, v5p. 155-222 – 8 – ne IDC [305]

ETHNOGRAPHIE BORORO, OBJETS PROVENANT DU VILLAGE DE KEJARA (BRESIL) / Dreyfus, D.Levi-Strauss, C. – 9 – F240.00 – fr Ethnologie [305]

L'ETHNOGRAPHIE DE MADAGASCAR / Faublee, Jacques – n.s. Paris. 1946. BA-363 2 – 8 – ne IDC [305]

ETHNOGRAPHIE DE MADAGASCAR / ed by Grandidier, Alfred & Grandidier, Guillaume – Paris, 1908-28. 4 vols – 78mf – 8 – ne IDC [305]

ETHNOGRAPHISCHE BEOBACHTUNGEN UEBER DIE VOELKER DES BERINGSMEERES 1789-91 / Merck, C H – BN 317 2. 1936 – 8 – ne IDC [305]

ETHNOGRAPHISCHE SKIZZEN UEBER DIE VOELKER DES RUSSISCHEN AMERIKA / Holmberg, H J – BN 255 2. 1856 – 8 – ne IDC [305]

DIE ETHNOGRAPHISCHE STELLUNG DER TOCHARER / Charpentier, J – (In ZDMG). v. 71. Leipzig. 1917. BU-560 2 – 8 – ne IDC [305]

DER ETHNOGRAPHISCHE ZUSAMMENHANG DER ESKIMO GROENLWNDS MIT DENEN DER HUDSONBAI / Thalbitzer, W – BN 413 2. 1912 – 8 – ne IDC [971]

[**ETHNOGRAPHY IN TURKEY PAMPHLET COLLECTION]** – 1913?-1919 – 1 – CSUXANQ7467-B – us Hoover Inst Photo [305]
[ETHNOGRAPHY OF BULGARIA PAMPHLET COLLECTION] – 1858?-1917 – 1 – CSUXANL7397-B – us Hoover Inst Photo [305]
[ETHNOGRAPHY OF POLAND PAMPHLET COLLECTION] – 1915-1932 – 1 – CSUXANL6625-B – us Hoover Inst Photo [305]
[ETHNOGRAPHY OF THE BALKANS PAMPHLET COLLECTION] – 1858?-1946 – 1 – CSUXANL7324-B – us Hoover Inst Photo [305]
ETHNOGRAPHY OF THE EGEDESMINDE DISTRICT / Birket-Smith, K – BH-162 2. 1924 – 8 – ne IDC [970]
THE ETHNOGRAPHY OF THE TANAINA. NEW HAVEN / Osgood, C – BN 331 2. 1937 – 8 – ne IDC [305]
ETHNOHISTORY – (1985- . 5,6,9) – v1- . 1954- – 1 – us UMI [306]
ETHNOHRAFICHNYI ZBIRNYK : VYDAE NAUKOVE TOVARYSTVO IM. SHEVCHENKA – (Missing: v20) – L'viv. v1-38. 1895-1916 – 199mf – 9 – ne IDC [947]
ETHNOLOGICAL PROBLEMS IN CANADA / Boas, Franz – BM 143 2 1910 – 8 – ne IDC [971]
ETHNOLOGICAL RESULTS OF THE POINT BARROW EXPEDITION / Murdoch, John – BN 323 2. 1892 – 8 – ne IDC [306]
ETHNOLOGIE UND GEOGRAPHIE DES ALTEN ORIENTS / Hommel, F – Ed. by I. von Mueller and W. Otto. (Handbuch der Altertumswissenschaft. Dritte Abteilung. Erster Teil. Erster Band). Muenchen. 1926. BNE-417 1 – 9 – ne IDC [306]
ETHNOLOGISCHE MITTEILUNGEN AUS UNGARN : ZEITSCHRIFT FUER DIE VOLKSKUNDE DER BEWOHNER UNGARNS AND SEINER NEBENLAENDER – Budapest, 1887-1905. v.1-9 – 56mf – 8 – ne IDC [306]
ETHNOLOGISCHE VORLESUNGEN UEBER DIE ALTAISCHEN VOELKER / Castren, M A – St. Petersburg, 1857. 257p. BU-510/2 – 8 – ne IDC [306]
DIE ETHNOLOGISCHEN UND ANTHROPOGEOGRAPHISCHEN ANSCHAUUNGEN BEI J KANT UND J REINHARD FORSTER / Unold, Joh. – Leipzig: [s.n.], 1886 – us Res Libr [190]
ETHNOLOGISK SKIZZE AF ANGMAGSALIKERNE / Holm, G – BN 252 2. 1888 – 8 – ne IDC [999]
ETHNOLOGY – v1- 1962- 1; v10- 5,6; v15- 9 – us UMI [306]
[ETHNOLOGY AND CULTURE PAMPHLET COLLECTION] – 193?-19?? – 1 – CSUXANQ7844-B – us Hoover Inst Photo [305]
ETHNOLOGY OF THE KWAKIUTL / Boas, Franz – BN 146 2. 1921 – 8 – ne IDC [306]
ETHNOLOGY OF THE NORTH CALIFORNIA COAST INDIAN TRIBES HUPA WYOT POMO MIWAK / Goddard, Pliny E – 3v. 1903-1927 – 3r – 1 – $150.00 – B63016 – us Library Micro [306]
ETHNOLOGY OF THE UNGAVA DISTRICT, HUDSON BAY TERRITORY / Turner, L M – BN 427 2. 1894 – 8 – ne IDC [971]
L'ETHNOMINERALOGIE ET LA VIE RELIGIEUSE DES BAHNAR JOLONG, PROVINCE DE KONTUM, VIETNAM / Leger, D – 9 – F130.00 – fr Ethnologie [290]
ETHNOPOETICS *see* ALCHERINGA – ETHNOPOETICS
ETHNOPSYCHOLOGIE – Le Havre. v1-37. 1946-1982. v1-25 as Revue de Psychologie des Peuples – 5,9 – Dfl2,220.00; Dfl60.00 – ne Swets [150]
ETHNOS – Athens, Greece. -d. 13 June 1917-31 Aug 1918. Imperfect. 2 reels – 1 – uk British Libr Newspaper [949]
ETHOCRATIE OU LE GOUVERNEMENT FONDE SUR LA MORALE / Holbach, Paul-Thiry d' – (D'Holbach series). 1776 – 9 – fr Hachette [321]
ETHOLOGY AND SOCIOBIOLOGY – v1-5. 1980-84 – 1,5,6,13 – sz Elsevier [306]
ETHOS – (v.7 .1979 5,6,9) – v.1. 1973 – 1 – us UMI [306]
Etia, Abel Moume *see* LE FOULBE DU NORD-CAMEROUN
ETICA / Marquez, Gabino – Madrid: Editorial Razon y Fe, 1928 – sp Bibl Santa Ana [946]
ETICA ELEMENTAL / Frutos Cortes, Eugenio – Caceres: Imp. Moderna, 1935 – 1 – sp Bibl Santa Ana [540]
ETICA ELEMENTAL / Nunez Gonzalez, Salvador – Badajoz: Libreria La Alianza, 1931 – 1 – sp Bibl Santa Ana [170]
ETICA GENERAL / Conde, Prudencio – Barcelona: Luis Gili, 1917.-v1 – 1 – sp Bibl Santa Ana [170]
LA ETICA O ESTETICA POLITICA DE MAQUIAVELO / Santos Neila, Francisco – Badajoz: Imp. Diput. Provincial, 1974 – sp Bibl Santa Ana [320]
Etienne *see*
– L'INTRIGANTE OU L'ECOLE DES FAMILLES
– LA PETITE ECOLE DES PERES
ETIENNE UND LUISE : NOVELLE / Penzoldt, Ernst – Leipzig: P Reclam, c1929 – 1 – us U.W. Library [830]
Etienne-Nugue, J *see* ARTISANATS TRADITIONNELS EN COTE D'IVOIRE
Etiennez, Hippolyte *see* GUIDE DU VOYAGEUR A NANTES ET AUX ENVIRONS...
Etievant, George *see* REWARD AND PUNISHMENT
ETIKA SEKSUIL / Verkuyl, Johannes – SE 5163 1963 – 9 – ne IDC [950]
L'ETINCELLE – (Becomes: La Petite France v1 n9 5 mai 1883-v1 n10 12 mai 1883) – Montreal, Canada. 20 jan-24 fev 1883 – 1r – 1 – Can$30.00 – cn Can Microfilming [072]
L'ETINCELLE – devenu: Le Rassemblement. Paris. 26 avr 1947-24 30 juin 1954 – 1 – fr A.C.R.P.P. [944]
L'ETINCELLE – French West Indies. 1944-1961 – 1 – us UMI [072]
L'ETINCELLE : JOURNAL DES OUVRIERS – Quebec, Canada. 4 sep 1909 – 1r – 1 – Can$25.00 – cn Can Microfilming [072]
L'ETINCELLE : JOURNAL HEBDOMADAIRE, POLITIQUE, LITTERAIRE, ARTISTIQUE – 1902-03. SEM16P269 – 1r – 5 – Can$9.00 – cn Bibl Nat [073]
L'ETINCELLE – Le sous-titre varie. no. 1-1538. Pau. 1933-janv 1952 – 1 – fr A.C.R.P.P. [073]
L'ETINCELLE – Windsor. v8 n13. 4 jan 1978-v9 n11. 20 dec 1978 – 1r – 1 – Can$35.00 – cn Can Microfilming [072]
L'ETINCELLE DU SACRE-COEUR – Quebec (St-Sauveur), Canada. 3 nov 1916-v2 n49. 15 avr 1922 – 1r – 1 – Can$40.00 – cn Can Microfilming [072]
L'ETINCELLE SOCIALISTE – Paris. 4 sept 1925-19 mars 1927, 1er mai 1932 – 1 – fr A.C.R.P.P. [073]
ETIOPI IN PALESTINA : STORIA DELLA COMUNITA ETIOPICA DI GERUSALEMME – Roma: Libreria dello Stato, 1943-47 – 1 – us Res Libr [960]
ETIOPIA OCCIDENTALE (DALLO SCIOA ALLA FRONTIERA DEL SUDAN) : NOTE DEL VIAGGIO, 1927-1928 – Roma: Sindicato Italiano arti grafiche, [1930] – 1 – us Res Libr [960]
ETIUDY / Korsh, V F – Tom pervyi. Spb. 1885. BR-10.588 2 – 8 – ne IDC [460]
Etkin, Nina L *see* REVIEWS IN ANTHROPOLOGY
ETLICH SCHLUSRED VOM GNADEN BUNDT CHRISTI DAS IST VOM TAUFF VND VOM KINDER GLAUBEN / Huberinus, Caspar – Wittenberg: [Joseph Klug], 1528. [G.F.: 9.1] – 1mf – 9 – HUB-27/1 – ne IDC [240]
ETLICHE FRAGSTUECK VON DER BEICHT, ABSOLUTION, VND VOM HOCHWIRDIGEN SACRAMENTS DES ALTARS, FUER DIE CHRISTLICHE JUGENT... / Mathesius, Johannes – Nuernberg, 1568 – 1mf – ne IDC [240]
ETLICHE PROPOSITIONES WIDER DIE LEHR DER WIDERTEUFFER / Melanchthon, Philip – 1535. BME-103 1 – 9 – ne IDC [240]
ETLICHE TROSTSPRUECH FUER DIE BLOEDEN SCHWACHEN GEWISSEN... / Huberinus, Caspar – [Augsburg: Philipp Ulhart], 1528. [G.F.: 7.7] – 2mf – 9 – HUB-25/1 – ne IDC [240]
ETLICHE TROSTSPRUECHE FUER DIE BLOEDEN VND SCHWACHEN GEWISSEN... / Huberinus, Caspar – Nuernberg: Johann Daubmann, 1550. [G.F.: 7.14a] – 2mf – 9 – HUB-74/1 – ne IDC [240]
ETLICHE UNDERRICHT / Duerer, Albrecht – O 999. 1527 – 9 – ne IDC [760]
ETLICHER WIDERTEUFFERISCHER SCHWERMEREYEN, WELCHE SICH JETZT WIDER REGEN, WIDERLEGUNG / Wigandus, J – Koenigszperg, G. Osterberger. 1576. BME-236 1 – 9 – ne IDC [240]
ETNA STANDARD – Etna Mills, CA. Mar-Aug 1898 – 1r – 1 – $50.00 – B02205 – us Library Micro [071]
ETNICHESKIE PROTSESSY I SEMIA / Terenteva, L – Moskva: In-t konkretnykh sotsialnykh issledovanii AN SSSR, 1972 – us Res Libr [072]
ETNOGRAFICHESKII SBORNIK, IZDAVAEMYI IMPERATORSKIM RUSSKIM GEOGRAFICHESKIM OBSHCHESTVOM – Spb. v1-6. 1853-1864 – 52mf – 9 – ne IDC [947]
ETNOGRAFICHESKOE OBOZRENIE – M. v1-28(1-112). 1889-1916 – 378mf – 9 – 1429/2 – ne IDC [947]
ETNOGRAFICHNII VISNIK / Akademiia Nauk. URSR. Kiev. Etnografichna Komisiia – v1-9. 1921-30 – 1r – 1 – us Ross [305]
ETNOGRAFICHNYI VISNYK – Kiev. v. 1-9. 1925-1930 – 1 – us NY Public [305]
ETNOGRAFICHNYI VISNYK – v. 1-9. Kyiv. 1925-30. BR-3406 2 – 8 – ne IDC [305]
ETNOGRAFISKE OF ANTROPO-GEOGRAFISKE REJSETUDIER I NORD-GRONLAND / Steensby, H P – (MoG., v. 50). Kobenhavn. 1912. BN-401 2 – 8 – ne IDC [910]
ETNOGRAF-ISSLEDOVATEL' : ZHURNAL NAUCHNO-ISSLEDOVATEL' NOGO KRUZHKA ETNOOTDELENIIA GZOFAKA LENINGRADSKOGO GOSUDARSTVENNOGO UNIVERSITETA – L. v1-3. 1927-1928 – 3mf – 9 – ne IDC [947]
ETNOHRAFICHNYI VISNYK : VSEUKRAIN'SKA AKADEMIIA NAUK, ETNOHRAFICHNA KOMISIIA – Kyiv. v1-9. 1925-1930 – 39mf – 9 – ne IDC [947]
ETNOLOGY (ILMU BANGSA-BANGSA) / Lubis, Harun – SE-5395 1. v. 1 only. 1953- – 9 – ne IDC [306]
ETOBICOKE GAZETTE – Etobicoke, 1971-1981 – 27r – 1 – cn Preston [971]
ETOBICOKE GUARDIAN – (1952-1992.-91r) – Etobicoke, 1993 – 6r – 1 – cn Preston [971]
ETOBICOKE PRESS – Etobicoke, 1946-1969 – 11r – 1 – cn Preston [971]
L'ETOILE – (Filmed as pt of: Commune de Paris newspapers) – Paris: Imp Serriere ct co, may 5-10 1871 – us Res Libr [072]
L'ETOILE – Lowell, MA. v5 n244. 4 jun 1891-v62 n18. 24 oct 1947 – 1r – 1 – Can$35.00 – cn Can Microfilming [071]
L'ETOILE = NYOTA – (Issues filmed as pt of: Herbert J Weiss collection on the Belgian Congo) – Elisabethville: Service de l'information de la Province, apr 17-may 1 1958; feb 19-dec 31 1959 – us Res Libr [072]
L'ETOILE – Paris. Journal du soir. 1er nov 1820-1er juil 1827 – 1 – fr A.C.R.P.P. [944]
L'ETOILE – Trois-Rivieres, Canada. v1 n2. 11 mai 1900; v1 n35. 12 sep 1900 – 1r – 1 – Can$25.00 – cn Can Microfilming [072]
L'ETOILE ALGERIENNE – Mouvement pour le triomphe des libertes democratiques. n.s., no. 1-3. Alger. juil-aout 1952 – 1 – fr A.C.R.P.P. [073]
L'ETOILE DE BEDFORD – Bedford, Canada. n8. 20 jan 1956-n10. mar 1956 – 1r – 1 – Can$25.00 – cn Can Microfilming [072]
L'ETOILE DE GRAVELBOURG – Gravelbourg, Saskatchewan. v13 n52. 27 dec 1934 (numero souvenir +) – 1r – 1 – Can$30.00 – cn Can Microfilming [072]
L'ETOILE DE LA FRANCE – Paris: Impr de Sapia, sep 1848 – us Res Libr [072]
L'ETOILE DE L'EST – (2nd series: 23 sep 1927-22 jun 1950 3r Can$50.00) – Coaticook, Canada. v1 n5. 5 nov 1887-7 dec 1897 – 1r – 1 – Can$50.00 – cn Can Microfilming [072]
L'ETOILE DE L'OUTAOUAIS-SAINT LAURENT – Dorion, Canada. v2 n40. 15 oct 1969-23 dec 1970, v6 n47. 5 dec 1974 – 1r – 1 – Can$65.00 – cn Can Microfilming [072]
ETOILE DU CONGO – Kinshasa, 1963(Aug 1)-1968(Jan 1) – 9r – 1 – ne IDC [073]
L'ETOILE DU LAC – (Cont: Le Colon) – Roberval, Canada. 26 sep 1946-29 dec 1991 – 56r – 1 – Can$70.00r – cn Can Microfilming [072]
L'ETOILE DU LAC *see* LE COLON
L'ETOILE DU NORD – Joliette, Canada. 5 jun 1884-16 avr 1965 – 32r – 1 – Can$75.00r – cn Can Microfilming [072]
L'ETOILE DU ROUSSILLON – no. 1-213. Perpignan. 7 sept 1849-14 dec 1851 – 1 – fr A.C.R.P.P. [073]
L'ETOILE FRANCAISE – puis L' Etoile de France. Red. en chef E. Taine. Paris. 14 dec 1880-9 dec 1899, 14 fevr-21 nov 1903 – 1 – fr A.C.R.P.P. [073]
ETOILES DE KEBEC – (Kebec: 18 dec 1966) – Quebec, Canada. v1 n14. 4 dec 1966 – 1r – 1 – Can$25.00 – cn Can Microfilming [072]
Eton, William *see* TABLEAU HISTORIQUE, POLITIQUE, ET MODERNE DE L'EMPIRE OTTOMAN
L'ETONNANTE AVENTURE DE LA MISSION BARSAC / Verne, Jules – Paris: Hachette, 1920. 2v. 8 fiches. (Literature Collection) – 9 – 20.00 – fr Bibl Nationale [830]
ETOWAH BAPTIST CHURCH. ETOWAH, NORTH CAROLINA : CHURCH RECORDS – 9 Feb 1917-Mar 1984. 2779p – 1 – 125.06 – us Baptist [240]
ETOWAH BAPTIST CHURCH. HENDERSONVILLE, NORTH CAROLINA : CHURCH RECORDS – 9 Feb 1917-Mar 1984 – 1 – 125.06 – us Baptist [240]
UN ETRANGER PEUT-IL PRATIQUER UNE SAISIE-ARRET EN FRANCE SUR UN FRANCAIS? / Clunet, E – Paris, 1882 – 1mf – 1 – ILM-2412/1 – ne IDC [327]
LES ETRANGERS EN FRANCE / Brunet, G – Paris, 1898 – 3mf – 1 – ILM-2413/1 – ne IDC [327]
LES ETRANGES EVENEMENTS DU VOYAGE DE SON ALTESSE LE PRINCE ZAGA-CHRIST D'ETHIOPIE DU GRAND EMPIRE DES ABYSSINE / Sainte-Marie, Jean de – (African Library series). 1635 – 9 – fr Hachette [830]
LES ETRENNES / ed by Duquet, J-N – Quebec, Canada. dec 1880 – 1r – 1 – Can$25.00 – cn Can Microfilming [072]
ETRENNES DE L'EMPEREUR DE LA CHINE... 1782 – Constantinople, 1782 – 1mf – 1 – ILM-1229/1 – ne IDC [327]
L'ETRILLE : ILLUSTRE DE CARICATURES: ANTI-HOUDE – Montreal, Canada. 28 oct 1934-v2 n1. 15 out 1936 – 1r – 1 – Can$30.00 – cn Can Microfilming [072]
LES ETRIVIERES – Par C. Martel. no. 1-2. Londres. janv-fevr 1872 – 1 – fr A.C.R.P.P. [073]
'ETS HA-DA'ATH – New York. v. 1 no. 1-2. Feb-Mar 1896 – 1 – us NY Public [071]
Etscheid, Lisel *see* DAS GOTTERLEBNIS DES GERMANISCHEN MENSCHEN
ETSIJA – 1967-86 (complete) – 2r – 1 – ATLA S0834 – us A.T.L.A. [073]
Ette, A van *see* LES CHANOINES REGULIERS DE SAINT AUGUSTIN. APERCU HISTORIQUE
ETTELA'AT *see* ITTILLAAT
ETTELMIDH – Bulletin mensuel des etudiants musulmans algeriens. Dir. Ferhat Abbas. Alger. nov 1931-avr 1933 – 1 – fr A.C.R.P.P. [073]
Ettinger-Hengstebeck, Irmlind *see*
– DIE THEMATIK "ILLUSION UND WIRKLICHKEIT" IN TENNESSEE WILLIAMS' DRAMEN "THE GLASS MENAGERIE" UND "A STREETCAR NAMED DESIRE"
– VOM UEBEN UND SPIELEN ZUMN GESTALTEN MIT DEM BALL
Ettingshausen, C von *see*
– DIE FARNKRAEUTER DER JETZTWELT
– A MONOGRAPH OF THE BRITISH EOCENE FLORA
Ettlinger, Josef *see* CHRISTIAN HOFMANN VON HOFMANNSWALDAU
Ettmueller, Michael *see*
– METHODE DE CONSULTER ET DE PRESCRIRE LES FORMULES DE MEDICINE
– NOUVELLE CHYMIE RAISONNEE
THE ETUDE – Philadelphia. v2-10, 11-18. 1883-1929 – r2-19 – 1 – £980.00 – uk Chadwyck [780]
THE ETUDE – v1-58. Oct 1883-1899 – 1 – 700.00 – us Opus [073]
ETUDE ANTHROPO-BIOLOGIQUE DES GROUPES HMONG DE GUYANE, ENQUETE PRELIMINAIRE. RAPPORT DE MISSION CNRS / Ducros, A & Ducros, J & Lefevre-Witier, P – 9 – F20.00 – fr Ethnologie [573]
ETUDE ANTHROPOLOGIQUE DE L'ILE DE SILBA / Rudan, P & Chaventre, A – 9 – F30.00 – fr Ethnologie [301]
ETUDE ANTHROPOLOGIQUE DE L'ILE D'OLIB. GEOMORPHOLOGIE, ETHNO-HISTOIRE, DEMOGRAPHIE / Sujoldzic, A et al – 9 – F20.00 – fr Ethnologie [306]
ETUDE BIOGRAPHIQUE SUR M. JEAN RAIMBAULT: ARCHIPRETRE, CURE DE NICOLET, ETC / Bois, Louis Edouard – Quebec: A. Cote, 1869. 00165. (Pre-1900 Canadiana) – 9 – cn C.I.H.M. [920]

ETUDE COMPARATIVE DE CINQ STRATES D'EXPLOITATIONS DE LA ZONE RURALE DE BROBO. EVALUATION 1961-1967 / Ancey, G – (Africa series). 1968 – 9 – fr Hachette [960]

ETUDE COMPAREE DES FETES DE LA MOISSON ET DES COUTUMES DU PREMIER MAI / Baticle, Y – 9 – F60.00 – fr Ethnologie [390]

ETUDE CRITIQUE ET LITTERAIRE SUR LES VITAE DES SAINTS MEROVINGIENS DE L'ANCIENNE BELGIQUE / Essen, L Van Der – Louvain, 1907 – Dfl30.00 – ne Slangenburg [240]

ETUDE CRITIQUE SUR L'ETAT DU TEXTE DU LIVRE DES PROVERBES / Baumgartner, Antoine Jean – Leipzig: Imp. Or. Drugulin, 1890 – 1mf – 9 – us A.T.L.A. [240]

ETUDE DE DEVELOPMENT. PLAN INTERIMAIRE D'URGENCE / Rwanda – D 1464 1. 4 v. 1965-1969 – 9 – ne IDC [338]

ETUDE DE DEVELOPPEMENT. PLAN INTERIMAIRE D'URGENCE / Rwanda – (Development study. Interim emergency plan). Paris. Sep 1970. BD-1742 1 – 9 – ne IDC [338]

ETUDE DE GROUPES D'HABITATIONS DU CENTRE CEREMONIAL MAYA DU MUNDO PERDIDO, TIKAL, GUATEMALA / Valdes Gomez, J A – 9 – F100.00 – fr Ethnologie [306]

ETUDE DE LA CONVENTION DE BARCELONE... / Corthesy, F – Paris, 1827 – 3mf – 1 – ILM-2352/1 – ne IDC [327]

ETUDE DE LA MISE EN VALEUR DE LA REGION DU CHELIF / Algeria. Institut pour l'Etude et le Developpement de l'Industrie en Algerie – 1961. BNE-8647 1 – 9 – ne IDC [338]

ETUDE DE LA VEGETATION ADVENTICE DES PALMERAIES / Tchoume, Mezan – (Africa series). 1968 – 9 – fr Hachette [580]

ETUDE DE LA ZONE RURALE DE BROBO / Ancey, G – (Africa series). 1967 – 9 – fr Hachette [960]

ETUDE DE L'ORGANOGENESE DE L'ACTINIE ACOUTIAIRE CEREUS PEDUNCULATUS PENNANT / Doumenc, D A – 9 – F70.00 – fr Ethnologie [590]

ETUDE DE QUELQUES CENTRES SEMI-URBAINS / Chevassu, J – (Africa series). 1968 – 9 – fr Hachette [338]

ETUDE DEMOGRAPHIQUE DE LA DIMINUTION OU DE L'ACCROISSEMENT DES FAMILLES / Lagneau, Gustave – Reprod. d'un extrait du Bulletin de l'Academie de Medecine, v20, 1888. p498-514. 1 fiche. (Statistics Series: Demography) – 9 – 6.00 – fr Bibl Nationale [310]

ETUDE DES ACTES INTERNATIONAUX... / Garipuy, G – Toulouse, 1900 – 4mf – 1 – ILM-1069/1 – ne IDC [327]

ETUDE DES PLANTES DES COLONIES FRANCAISES / Bocquillon-Limousin, H – Paris, 1891 – 1mf – 9 – ne IDC [615]

ETUDE DES POTENTIALITES D'ELEVAGE INTENSIF DU GOUJON, GOBIO GOBIO, L. REPRODUCTION ET CROISSANCE LARVAIRE / Kestemont, P – 9 – F80.00 – fr Ethnologie [590]

ETUDE D'HYGIENE ET D'ECONOMIE SOCIALE. ENQUETE SUR LES LOGEMENTS, PROFESSIONS, SALAIRES ET BUDGETS / Du Mesnil et Mangenot – (Condition of 19th C. French working class series). 1899 – 9 – fr Hachette [360]

ETUDE DU CONTEXTE SOCIAL ET HISTORIQUE DE LA REVOLTE DES IWELLEMMEDDAN DE 1916 / Chaventre, A – Firhun, heros malien d'une guerre d'independance – 9 – F50.00 – fr Ethnologie [360]

ETUDE DU DEVELOPPEMENT ECONOMIQUE DE L'EST ALGERIEN / Algeria. Institut pour l'Etude et le Developpement de l'Industrie en Algerie – 1959. BNE-8648 1 – 9 – ne IDC [338]

ETUDE DU DEVELOPPEMENT ECONOMIQUE DE L'OUEST ALGERIEN / Algeria. Institut pour l'Etude et le Developpement de l'Industrie en Algerie – 1969. BNE-8651 1 – 9 – ne IDC [338]

ETUDE DU PEUPLEMENT PISCICOLE DE PLANS D'EAU NON VIDANGEABLES / Boujard, T – Methodologie d'echantillonnage, dynamique de population des principales especes – 9 – F40.00 – fr Ethnologie [580]

ETUDE D'UN MARCHE URBAIN AFRICAIN / Donnenfeld, J – (Africa series) – 9 – fr Hachette [960]

ETUDE D'UNE EXPERIENCE D'ANIMATION RURALE EN COTE D'IVOIRE / Michotte, J – (Africa series). 1967 – 9 – fr Hachette [360]

ETUDE ECONOMIQUE SUR LE MATE OU THE DU PARAGUAY / Demersay, Alfred – Reprod. d'un tire a part de Memoires d'Agriculture, d'Economie rurale et domestique.Ste. Royale d'Agriculture de Paris, 1865. Paris: Vve. Bouchard-Huzard, 1867.45p. 1 fiche.(Economics Collection) – 9 – 6.00 – fr Bibl Nationale [338]

ETUDE EN COULEUR DES SUPERPOSITIONS DE LA TOCA DO BOQUEIRAO DO SITIO DA PEDRA FURADA, SUD-EST DU PIAUI, BRESIL / Pessis, A M – 9 – F240.00 – fr Ethnologie [306]

ETUDE ETHNIQUES AU CANADA *see* CANADIAN ETHNIC STUDIES

ETUDE ETHNOLINGUISTIQUE D'UN CORPUS DE CONTES DIOULA (HAUTE VOLTA) / Nebie, M A – 9 – F220.00 – fr Ethnologie [306]

ETUDE GENERALE DU GROUPE DES EUPHORBIACEES / Baillon, H E – Paris. 1858. B-638 2 – 8 – ne IDC [580]

ETUDE HISTORIQUE ET BIBLIOGRAPHIQUE SUR LA DISCIPLINE ECCLESIASTIQUE DES EGLISES REFORMEES DE FRANCE / Frossard, C L – Paris: Grassart, 1887 – 1mf – us A.T.L.A. [240]

ETUDE HISTORIQUE ET PRATIQUE SUR LA PROPHYLAXIE ET LE TRAITEMENT DU CHOLERA, BASEE SUR LES OBSERVATIONS FOURNIES PAR L'EPIDEMIE DE MARSEILLE (1884) / Mireur, Hippolyte – Paris, G. Masson, 1884, 193 p. 3 fiches. (Statistics Series: Medical Studies) – 9 – 8.00 – fr Bibl Nationale [310]

ETUDE HISTORIQUE SUR L'EXTRATERRITORIALITE DE LA LOI PENALE... / Derumaux, M – Paris, 1915 – 2mf – 1 – ILM-2068/1 – ne IDC [327]

ETUDE LEGALE, OU, REPONSE A CERTAINES QUESTIONS CONCERNANT LES SUCCURSALES DE L'UNIVERSITE LAVAL, A MONTREAL / Archambault, Joseph Louis – Montreal?: 1880. 02478. (Pre-1900 Canadiana) – 9 – cn C.I.H.M. [340]

ETUDE MEDICO-LEGALE SUR L'INFANTICIDE / Tardieu, Ambroise – Paris: J.B. Bailliere et fils, 1868. viii,342p.4 fiches. (Statistics Series: Medical Studies) – 9 – 10.00 – fr Bibl Nationale [310]

ETUDE MENSUELLE SUR L'ECONOMIE ET LES FINANCES DES PAYS ARABES / Libya. Centre d'Etudes et de Documentation Economiques. Financieres et Sociales S.A.L. Beyrouth-Damas – v. 12(12). Douzieme Annee-no. 144. Dec 1969. BNE-621 1 – 9 – ne IDC [330]

ETUDE MONOGRAPHIQUE DE LA COMMUNE DE BAUBIGNY (COTE D'OR) / Varoqui, J F – 9 – F60.00 – fr Ethnologie [305]

ETUDE MONOGRAPHIQUE DE LA COMMUNE DE CHERISY (EURE-ET-LOIR) / Guimier, J M – 9 – F60.00 – fr Ethnologie [305]

ETUDE MONOGRAPHIQUE DE LA COMMUNE DE DRY (LOIRET) / Moquet, A – 9 – F70.00 – fr Ethnologie [305]

ETUDE MORPHOLOGIQUE DE LA PIROGUE A BALANCIER AUX COMORES ET DANS L'OUEST DE L'OCEAN INDIEN / Boulinier-Giraud, G – 9 – F50.00 – fr Ethnologie [306]

ETUDE PHONETIQUE ET SYNTAXIQUE DU FRANCAIS D'ELEVES DE COURS PRPARATOIRE DE LA REGION D'ABIDJAN / Herault, G – (Africa series). 2 v – 9 – fr Hachette [440]

ETUDE POLITIQUE: LUE DEVANT L'ASSOCIATION CONSERVATRICE DE MONTREAL EN FEVRIER 1887 / Archambault, Joseph Louis – Montreal?: 1887. 02477. (Pre-1900 Canadiana) – 9 – cn C.I.H.M. [971]

ETUDE PRATIQUE DE LA LEGISLATION CIVILE ANNAMITE / Denjoy, Paul – Paris, Challamel 1894. 271 p. LL-10002 – 1 – us L of C Photodup [340]

ETUDE PROSPECTIVE "SENEGAL 2015" / Senegal. Ministere du Plan et de la Cooperation – Dakar, 1989 – 5mf – 9 – ne IDC [338]

ETUDE SCIENTIFIQUE SUR LE SOMNAMBULISME, SUR LES PHENOMENES QU'IL PRESENTE ET SUR SON ACTION THERAPEUTIQUE DANS CERTAINES MALADIES NERVEUSES / Despine, Prosper – (French Precursors of Psychiatry Series). Paris. F. Savy. 1880 – 9 – fr Hachette [616]

ETUDE SEMIOLOGIQUE DE LA REPRESENTATION DU PERSONNAGE DE L'ENSEIGNANT DANS LES OEUVRES DE FICTION AU CINEMA ET A LA TELEVISION / Baticle, Y – 9 – F90.00 – fr Ethnologie [410]

ETUDE STATISTIQUE NATIONALE DE LA POPULATION: PRESENTATION GENERALE DE L'ENQUETE / Algeria. Commissariat National au Recensement de la Population – 1971. BNE-8710 – 9 – ne IDC [310]

ETUDE STATISTIQUE NATIONALE DE LA POPULATION: PRESENTATION GENERALE DE L'ENQUETE FECONDITE / Algeria. Commissariat National au Recensement de la Population – 1971. BNE-8709 1 – 9 – ne IDC [310]

ETUDE STATISTIQUE PAR PRODUIT 1959-1967 / Morocco. Ministere de l'Agriculture – 1969. BNE-3070 1 – 9 – ne IDC [630]

ETUDE STATISTIQUE PAR PRODUIT, 1967-1968 / Morocco. Ministere de l'Agriculture – 1969. BNE-3068 1 – 9 – ne IDC [630]

ETUDE SUR ALEXANDRE VINET : CRITIQUE DE PASCAL / Nazelle, L J – Alencon: Impr. typ. Veuve F. Guy, 1901 – 1mf – us A.T.L.A. [190]

ETUDE SUR CATULLE. / Couat, Auguste Henri – Paris: E. Thorin, 1875. xviii,19-295p – 1 – us U.W. Library [450]

ETUDE SUR LA BARONNIE ET L'ABBAYE D'AUNAY-SUR-ODON / Hardy, MG Le – Caen, 1897 – 8mf – 8 – Dfl30.00 – ne Slangenburg [240]

ETUDE SUR LA CLASSIFICATION NATURELLE ET LA MORPHOLOGIE DES LICHENS DU BRESIL / Wainio, E A – (Acta Soc. Fauna et Flora Fennica, v. 7, 1890). 2 pts. Helsingfors. 1890. B-622 2 – 8 – ne IDC [580]

ETUDE SUR LA DEMOGRAPHIE ET LA DEPOPULATION DE LA SARTHE / Mordret, Ambroise Eusebe – Reprod. de l'article extrait du Bulletin de la Societe d' Agriculture, Sciences et Arts de la Sarthe, 1891-92. 2eme serie, v25. p161-248. 2 fiches. (Statistics Series: Demography) – 9 – 6.00 – fr Bibl Nationale [310]

ETUDE SUR LA DONATION ET LE TESTAMENT... / Champcommunal, J – Paris, 1869 – 1mf – 1 – ILM-3316/1 – ne IDC [327]

ETUDE SUR LA LANGUE DE MONTAIGNE / Voizard, E – 1885 – 9 – fr I.C.S. [440]

ETUDE SUR LA LETTRE DE CHANGE / Chretien, A – Nancy, 1881 – 3mf – 1 – ILM-3412/1 – ne IDC [327]

ETUDE SUR LA LETTRE DE CHANGE... / Champcommunal, J – Paris, 1894 – 1mf – 1 – ILM-3383/1 – ne IDC [327]

ETUDE SUR LA LOI CRIMINELLE DU CANADA EN RAPPORT AVEC LES LOIS PENALES DE LA PROVINCE DE QUEBEC / Chagnon, Joseph Antoine – St. Hyacinthe: des Presses a vapeur de l'Union, 1891. couv. 1892. SEM105P40 – 1mf – 9 – Can$2.25 – cn Bibl Nat [360]

ETUDE SUR LA MASCULINITE / Maurel, E – Paris, 1903. p353-60, 424-31. (Les Femmes Collection) – 1mf – 9 – $6.00 – fr Bibl Nationale [150]

ETUDE SUR LA MORTALITE ET LA MORBIDITE DANS LA CLASSE OUVRIERE A PARIS / Lorcin, Louis – Paris. 1897. (La Condition Ouvriere. Part Two.) – 9 – 2.50 – fr Bibl Nationale [360]

ETUDE SUR LA NATIONALITE DE LA FEMME ETRANGERE QUI EPOUSE UN SUJET OTTOMAN / Tawil, A – Le Caire, 1912 – 1mf – 9 – ILM-3433/1 – ne IDC [327]

ETUDE SUR LA PROTECTION DU SALAIRE A L'EGARD DU PATRON / Lambert, Maurice – Montpellier. 1896. (La Condition Ouvriere. Part Two.) – 9 – 7.50 – fr Bibl Nationale [360]

ETUDE SUR LA REPUBLIQUE DES ETAS-UNIS D'AMERIQUE / Dino, Charles Maurice Camille de Talleyrand-Perigord – par le marquis de Talleyrand-Perigord. New York: Hurd & Houghton, 1876. 02710. (Pre-1900 Canadiana) – 9 – cn C.I.H.M. [971]

ETUDE SUR LA RESERVE DES ENFANTS LEGITIMES / Latour, Rene – Toulouse, Imprimerie Lagarde et Sebille, 1899. 132 p. LL-4039 – 1 – us L of C Photodup [340]

ETUDE SUR LA SUCCESSION AB INTESTAT... / Champcommunal, J – Paris, 1892 – 8mf – 1 – ILM-3317/1 – ne IDC [327]

ETUDE SUR LA THEORIE DU DROIT MUSULMAN / Savvas, Pasha – Paris: Marchal et Billard, 1892-98. 2v. LL-12031 – 1 – us L of C Photodup [340]

ETUDE SUR LA VIE ET LES OEUVRES DE JEAN PAUL FREDERIC RICHTER / Firmery, Joseph Leon – (Includes bibliographical references) – Rennes: Typographie Oberthur, 1886 – 1r – 1 – us U.W. Library [430]

ETUDE SUR L'ACQUISITION DU DROIT DE CITE A ROME ... / Bickart, E – Paris, 1890 – 2mf – 9 – ILM-3154/1 – ne IDC [327]

ETUDE SUR L'ADULTERE AU POINT DE VUE PENAL EN DROIT ROMAN ET EN DROIT FRANCAIS / Loustaunau, Joseph – Aire-sur-l'Adour: Dehez, 1889. viii,269p. (Les Femmes Collection) – 3mf – 9 – $8.00 – fr Bibl Nationale [306]

ETUDE SUR L'AGE DE LA PIERRE EN NOUVELLE-CALEDONIE. DECOUVERTE DE MONUMENTS GRAVES / Glaumont, G – 9 – FF60.00 – fr Ethnologie [980]

ETUDE SUR LE COMMERCE INTERIEUR / Morocco. Division du Plan et des Statistiques – 3v. 1966? BNE-3047 1 – 9 – ne IDC [310]

ETUDE SUR LE COMMERCE INTERIEUR / Morocco. Haut Commissariat au Plan et a la Promotion Nationale. Division du Plan et des Statistiques – v. 1. 1965. BNE-3207 1 – 9 – ne IDC [380]

ETUDE SUR LE CONTRAT DE MARIAGE... / Deglin, H – Paris, 1883 – 3mf – 1 – ILM-3066/1 – ne IDC [327]

ETUDE SUR LE DEVELOPPEMENT ECONOMIQUE DU CENTRE D'ARZEW / Algeria. Institut pour l'Etude et le Developpement de l'Industrie en Algerie – Ruty, Antoine, Barthes a.o. 1961. BNE-8649 1 – 9 – ne IDC [338]

ETUDE SUR LE DROIT DE LA GUERRE DE GROTIUS / Hely, V – Paris, 1875 – 3mf – 1 – ILM-1149/1 – ne IDC [327]

ETUDE SUR LE GREC DU NOUVEAU TESTAMENT : LE VERBE, SYNTAXE DES PROPOSITIONS / Viteau, Joseph – (Includes errata) – Paris: Emile Bouillon, 1893 – 1mf – 9 – 0-8370-9195-0 – 1986-3195 – us A.T.L.A. [450]

ETUDE SUR LE GREC DU NOUVEAU TESTAMENT COMPARE AVEC CELUI DES SEPTANTE : SUJET, COMPLEMENT ET ATTRIBUT / Viteau, Joseph – (Includes bibliographical references and indexes) – Paris: Emile Bouillon, 1896 – 1mf – 9 – 0-8370-9196-9 – 1986-3196 – us A.T.L.A. [450]

ETUDE SUR LE LANGAGE POPULAIRE / Nisard, Ch – 1872 – 9 – fr I.C.S. [440]

ETUDE SUR LE MAL REVOLUTIONNAIRE EN CANADA – Humble recours au Saint-Siege.Paris?: s.n., 1881 (Paris: E. Pion). 02078. (Pre-1900 Canadiana) – 9 – cn C.I.H.M. [971]

ETUDE SUR LE MONOTHEISME DES HEBREUX: SON CARACTERE, SES ORIGINES / Vuilleumier, Henri – Lausanne: Georges Bridel, 1864. 1 fiche – 9 – us A.T.L.A. [240]

ETUDE SUR LE MOUVEMENT DE LA POPULATION EN FRANCE DEPUIS LE COMMENCEMENT DUE XIXE SIECLE / Bausset-Roquefort, J BG F – Marseille, Typographie Roux, 1862. 93 p. 1 fiche. (Statistics Series: Demography) – 9 – 6.00 – fr Bibl Nationale [310]

ETUDE SUR LE PRINCIPE DU PROTESTANTISME D'APRES LA THEOLOGIE ALLEMANDE CONTEMPORAINE / Lichtenberger, Frederic – Strassbourg: Treuttel et Wuertz, 1857 – 1mf – us A.T.L.A. [240]

ETUDE SUR LE PURGATOIRE DE SAINT PATRICE / Zanden, C M van der – Amsterdam, 1927 – 5mf – 8 – Dfl22.00 – ne Slangenburg [240]

ETUDE SUR LE SENEGAL. : PRODUCTIONS AGRICULTURE, COMMERCE, GEOLOGIE, ETHNOGRAPHIE...EVENEMENTS DEPUIS 1884 / Courtet, M – Paris: A Challamel, 1903 – 1 – us Res Libr [960]

ETUDE SUR LE STYLE POLEMIQUE DE VOLTAIRE : LE DICTIONNAIRE PHILOSOPHIQUE / Monty, Jeanne R – (Studies on Voltaire and the eighteenth century, v44) – Oxford. 1966 – 9 – $27.00 – 0-7294-0024-7 – uk Voltaire [440]

ETUDE SUR LES CHRONIQUES DES COMTES D'ANJOU ET DES SEIGNEURS D'AMBOIS / Halphen, Louis – Paris. 1906 – 1 – us Res Libr [944]

ETUDE SUR LES CONDITIONS DE VALIDITE DU TESTAMENT... / Goirand, H – Paris, 1901 – 2mf – 1 – ILM-3280/1 – ne IDC [327]

ETUDE SUR LES COUTUMES DES CABRAIS (TOGO) / Puig, Francois – Toulouse: Imp. Toulousaine – Lion et fils, 1934. 204p. LL-12070 – 1 – us L of C Photodup [340]

ETUDE SUR LES ISRAELITES DE MONTPELLIER AU MOYEN AGE / Azemard, E – Nimes, 1924. BJ-22-174 1 – 9 – ne IDC [270]

ETUDE SUR LES MANUSCRITS DES QUODLIBETS / Hoffmans, J & Pelzer, A – 1937 – 11mf – 8 – ne Slangenburg [100]

ETUDE SUR LES PRIVILEGES D'EXEMPTION ET DE JURISDICTION ECCLESIASTIQUES DES ABBAYES NORMANDES / Lemarignier, J -F – 1937 – Dfl32.00 – ne Slangenburg [240]

ETUDE SUR LES RAPPORTS DE L'AMERIQUE ET DE L'ANCIEN CONTINENT AVANT CHRISTOPHE COLOMB / Gaffarel, Paul – Paris: E. Thorin, 1869. 03274. (Pre-1900 Canadiana) – 9 – cn C.I.H.M. [971]

ETUDE SUR LES STATISTIQUES / Khouri-Saint-Pierre, Anastassia – Montreal: Bibliotheque Nationale du Quebec, 1976. (Document de Travail: no. 1). SEM16P262 – 1r – 5 – Can$9.00 – cn Bibl Nat [310]

ETUDE SUR LES TUMULI DU KILLI / Desplagnes, Louis – Paris, Masson et Cie – 9 – 5.00 – fr Orientalistes [960]

ETUDE SUR L'EVOLUTION DE LA NATIONALITE DES SOCIETES EN FRANCE / Gain, R – Paris, 1924 – 3mf – 1 – ILM-3407/1 – ne IDC [327]

ETUDE SUR L'INSURRECTION DU DHARA (1845-1846) / Richard, Charles Louis Florentin – Alger: A Besancenes, 1846 – 1 – us Res Libr [960]

ETUDE SUR VOLTAIRE GRAMMAIRIEN / Vernier, L – 1888 – 9 – fr I.C.S. [440]

ETUDE SYNTAXIQUE ET SEMANTIQUE DU COUPLE QUESTION-REPONSE EN FRANCAIS ORAL / Rukapan, W – 9 – F90.00 – fr Ethnologie [440]

ETUDES – v.2-289. July 1878-June 1956 – 1 – 1656.00 – us L of C Photodup [073]

ETUDES ANGLAISES – (v1-27. Dfl70.00v; v28-30. Dfl100.00v) – Paris. v1-30. 1937-77 – 5,9 – Dfl2,190.00 – ne Swets [420]

ETUDES ARCHEOLOGIQUES : CORBILON. SAMNITES, VENETES... / Sioc'han de Kersabiec, Edouard – Nantes: Forest, 1868 – 1 – F92.03 – fr Armell [930]

ETUDES ASIATIQUES DE GEOGRAPHIE ET D'HISTOIRE / Rosny, Leon de – Paris: Challamel aine. 1864 – 9 – 12.50 – fr Orientalistes [910]

ETUDES BAKONGO : HISTOIRE ET SOCIOLOGIE / Wing, R P van – Bruxelles: Goemaere, [1921] – 1 – us Res Libr [960]

ETUDES BAKONGO : NOTES DE SOCIOLOGIE COLONIALE / Calonne-Beaufaict, Adolphe de – Liege: M Thone, 1912 – 1 – us Res Libr [300]

ETUDES BIBLIQUES / Loisy, Alfred Firmin – (Includes bibliographical references) – 3e rev et augm. ed. Paris: Alphonse Picard, 1903 – 1mf – 9 – 0-8370-9401-1 – 1986-3401 – us A.T.L.A. [220]

ETUDES BIBLIQUES = STUDIES ON THE OLD TESTAMENT : PREMIERE SERIE: ANCIEN TESTAMENT / Godet, Frederic Louis – (In English. Includes bibliographical references) – 6th ed. New York: E P Dutton, 1897 – 1mf – 9 – 0-8370-3319-5 – 1985-1319 – us A.T.L.A. [220]

ETUDES BIBLIQUES. DEUXIEME SERIE: NOUVEAU TESTAMENT / Godet, Frederic Louis – Neuchatel: Delachaux & Niestle, 1889. 1 fiche – 9 – us A.T.L.A. [240]

ETUDES BIOLOGIQUES, ENERGETIQUES ET BIOCHIMIQUES DU KRILL ANTARCTIQUE EUPHAUSIA SUPERBA ET THYSANOESSA MACRURA, RECOLTE AU COURS DE LA CAMPAGNE FIBEX / Farber Lorda, J – 9 – F60.00 – fr Ethnologie [570]

ETUDES BYZANTINES – 1(1943)-4(1946) – 26mf – 9 – ne Slangenburg [073]

ETUDES CAMBODGIENNES – Phnom Penh, 1965-1966. Nos. 1-6 – 9mf – 9 – ne IDC [073]

ETUDES CAMEROUNAISES – 1935-1958; nos. 1-56 complete. Not published 1938-1942 – 1 – 35.00r – us Hoover Inst Photo [960]

ETUDES CAMEROUNAISES – Duala: Institut francais d'Afrique noire. n21/22-52, 56 jun/sep 1948-1958 – us Res Libr [072]

ETUDES CONGOLAISES : REVUE DE L'INSTITUT POLITIQUE CONGOLAIS / Congo – Leopoldville, 1961-64. v1-7 – 72mf – 9 – ne IDC [960]

ETUDES CUNEIFORMES / Lenormant, Frandcois – (Commentary in French; some texts in Sumerian, Akkadian and French) – Paris: Imprimerie nationale. 5v. 1878-80 – 5mf – 9 – 0-8370-8587-X – 1986-2587 – us A.T.L.A. [470]

ETUDES DE DROIT INTERNATIONAL PRIVE / Bartin, E – Paris, 1899 – 4mf – 9 – ILM-422/1 – ne IDC [340]

ETUDES DE GEOGRAPHIE LINGUISTIQUE D'APRES L'ATLAS LINGUISTIQUE DE LA FRANCE / Gillieron, J & Roques, M – Paris, 1912 – 5mf – ne IDC [400]

ETUDES DE GUERRE / Lewal, Jules Louis – Paris. J. Dunmaine. 1873-79. 4v. Fig., pl. (Strategy of War Series) – 9 – fr Hachette [355]

ETUDES DE LA LANGUE FRANCAISE SUR RACINE / Fontanier, P – 1818 – 9 – fr I.C.S. [440]

ETUDES DE LANGUE FRANCAISE (XVIE ET XVIIE SIECLES) / Marty-Laveaux, Charles Joseph – 1901 – 9 – fr I.C.S. [440]

ETUDES DE LEPIDOPTEROLOGIE COMPAREE / ed by Oberthur, C – Rennes, 1904-1925. v1-23. Index – 231mf – 9 – 2480/2 – ne IDC [590]

ETUDES DE MYTHOLOGIE ET DE FOLKLORE GERMANIQUE / Krappe, Alexander Haggerty – 1928 – 1 – us I.U. Libraries [390]

ETUDES DE PLANIFICATION EN COTE D'IVOIRE, L'OFFICE DE LA RECHERCHE SCIENTIFIQUE ET TECHNIQUE OUTRE-MER. (ORSTROM) – Regional analyses, demographic studies, urban economics – 9 – fr Hachette [300]

ETUDES DE SOCIOLOGIE ELECTORALE / Moraze, Charles et al – F20.00 – fr Ethnologie [303]

ETUDES DE SOCIOLOGIE: LES ANARCHISTES / Lombroso, Cesare – Paris: E. Flammarion, 1896. xx,258p. 3 fiches. (Political Science Collection) – 9 – 8.00 – fr Bibl Nationale [335]

ETUDES DE SOCIOLOGIE RURALE : NOVIS ET VIRGIN / Mendras, H – F30.00 – fr Ethnologie [307]

ETUDES DE THEOLOGIE MODERNE / Frommel, Gaston – (Includes bibliographical references) – Saint-Blaise: Foyer Solidariste, 1909 – 1mf – 9 – 0-8370-4768-4 – 1985-2768 – us A.T.L.A. [240]

ETUDES D'ECONOMIE POLITIQUE ET DE STATISTIQUE / Wolowski, Louis Francois M R – Paris: Guillaumin, 1848.lxviii,423p. 6 fiches. (Political Science Collection) – 9 – 15.00 – fr Bibl Nationale [310]

ETUDES D'ENTREPRISES INDUSTRIELLES RECOMMANDEES AUX CAPITAUX NATIONAUX / Morocco. Direction de l'Industrie – BNE-3035 1 – 9 – ne IDC [338]

ETUDES DES ENTREPRISES ET DES INDUSTRIES DU BATIMENT EN ALGERIE / Algeria. Institut pour l'Etude et le Developpement de l'Industrie en Algerie – 1960. BNE-8650 1 – 9 – ne IDC [338]

ETUDES EBURNEENNES – Macon, France: Institut francais d'Afrique noire, Centre de Cote d'Ivoire, 1950-1968. [n1-8 1950-1960] – us Res Libr [072]

ETUDES ENTOMOLOGIQUES / ed by Moschulsky, V de – Helsingfors, Dresden, [1852]1853-1862. v1-11 – 18mf – 9 – Z-954/2 – ne IDC [590]

ETUDES ENTOMOLOGIQUES, OU DESCRIPTION D'INSECTES NOUVEAUX ET OBSERVATIONS SUR LEUR SYNONYMIE / Castelnau, K L de – Paris, 1834-35. 159p. 4 pls. Z-1126/2 – 8 – ne IDC [590]

ETUDES ET DOCUMENTS / France. Conseil d'Etat – Paris. 1947-51 – 1 – fr A.C.R.P.P. [073]

ETUDES ET DOCUMENTS POUR L'HISTOIRE MISSIONAIRE DE L'ESPAGNE ET DU PORTUGAL / Robert, Ricard – Louvain, 1931; Madrid: Razon y Fe, 1932 – 1 – sp Bibl Santa Ana [240]

ETUDES ET GLANURES / Littre, E – 1880 – 9 – fr I.C.S. [440]

ETUDES ET RECITS / Bedard, P J – Montreal: G. Dumont, 1890?. 03309. (Pre-1900 Canadiana) – 9 – cn C.I.H.M. [830]

ETUDES ET TRAVAUX. LES HALLES CENTRALES DE PARIS / France. Conseil Economique – Paris: Presses universitaires de France.1949. (La Condition Ouvriere. Part Two) – 9 – 5.00 – fr Bibl Nationale [360]

ETUDES FOLKLORIQUES / Cosquin, Emmanuel – 1922 – 1 – us I.U. Libraries [390]

ETUDES GUINEENNES – Institut Francais d'Afrique Noire. Centre de Guinee. Conakry, 1947-1955. v1-13 – 26mf – 9 – A-378/2 – ne IDC [073]

ETUDES HISTORIQUES SUR LES TRAITES PUBLICS CHEZ LES GRECS ET CHEZ LES ROMAINS / Egger, Emile – Paris, 1866. xviii, 320p. (Historical Studies Series) – 9 – 12.00 – fr Bibl Nationale [900]

ETUDES HISTORIQUES SUR L'INFLUENCE DE LA CHARITE DURANT LES PREMIERS SIECLES CHRETIENS : ET CONSIDERATIONS SUR SON ROLE DANS LES SOCIETES MODERNES / Chastel, Etienne Louis – Paris: Capelle, 1853 – 1mf – us A.T.L.A. [240]

ETUDES LES QUESTION D'ETAT ET DE CAPACITE... / Gentet, F – Geneve, 1883 – 2mf – 1 – ILM-3418/1 – ne IDC [327]

ETUDES LITTERAIRES – v1- 1968- 1; v9-5,6,9 – us UMI [410]

ETUDES LITTERAIRES – Quebec: Presses de l'Universite Laval. v1 no 1- 1968-. SEM16P309 – 5r – 5 – Can$157.00 – cn Bibl Nat [073]

ETUDES MEDICO-PSYCHOLOGIQUES SUR L'ALIENATION MENTALE / Renaudin, Louis Francois Emile – (French Precursors of Psychiatry Series). Paris. J. B. Bailliere. 1854 – 9 – fr Hachette [150]

ETUDES MEROVINGIENNES : ACTES DES JOURNEES DE POITIERS – Paris, 1953 – Dfl35.00 – ne Slangenburg [240]

ETUDES MORALES SUR LE TEMPS PRESENT / Caro, Elme – Paris: L Hachette, 1855 – 1mf – 9 – 0-8370-7205-0 – 1986-1205 – us A.T.L.A. [170]

ETUDES PHYCOLOGIQUES / Bornet, J BE & Thuret, G – Paris. 1878. B-1506 2 – 8 – ne IDC [580]

ETUDES RELIGIEUSES ET SOCIALES / Frommel, Gaston – (Includes bibliographical references) – Saint-Blaise: Solidariste, 1907 – 1mf – 9 – 0-8370-4952-0 – 1985-2952 – us A.T.L.A. [230]

ETUDES ROUTIERES – Dir. Victor Azam. Geneve. 1962-69 – 5 – fr A.C.R.P.P. [073]

ETUDES SENEGALAISES, 1785-1826 – Paris: Societe de l'histoire des colonies francaises, Editions Leroux, [19–?] – 1 – us Res Libr [960]

ETUDES SOCIALES – Paris, 1881-1940 – 22r – 1 – us Ross [073]

LES ETUDES SOCIALES – Paris. v. 1-60 ser 1-10. Jan 1881-Feb 1940 – 1 – us NY Public [300]

ETUDES SOCIALES ET ECONOMIQUES SUR LE CANADA / Bouchette, Errol – Montreal: La Compagnie de Publication de la Revue canadienne, 1905. Sem105P519 – 3mf – 9 – Can$6.75 – cn Bibl Nat [330]

ETUDES SOCIALISTES – Dir. G. Jacques. no. 1-6. Paris. 1903 – 1 – fr A.C.R.P.P. [073]

ETUDES STATISTIQUES : LES PROJECTIONS DE POPULATION SCOLAIRE A L'AN 2000 / Reunion. Academie de la Reunion. Service Statistique Rectoral – [Saint-Denis], 1986 – 2mf – 9 – DE-624/1 – ne IDC [370]

ETUDES STATISTIQUES SUR LA MORTALITE ET LA DUREE DE LA VIE DANS LA VILLE ET L'ARRONDISSEMENT DE DIJON DEPUIS LE 17EME SIECLE JUSQU'A NOS JOURS / Noirot, Louis – Paris: J.B. Bailliere, 1850. 88p. 1 fiche. (Statistics Series: Medical Studies) – 9 – 6.00 – fr Bibl Nationale [310]

ETUDES SUR DANIEL ET L'APOCALYPSE / Bruston, Charles – Paris: Librairie Fischbacher, 1896 – 1mf – 9 – 0-8370-2498-6 – 1985-0498 – us A.T.L.A. [220]

ETUDES SUR DENIS DIDEROT / Johansson, J V – Recherches sur un volume Manuscrit conserve a la Bibliotheque Publique de l'Etat a Leningrad. Goeteborg, Paris, 1927. 209p. BR-10,870/1 – 9 – ne IDC [440]

ETUDES SUR LA LANGUE SECHUANA / Casalis, Eugene – Paris, Imprimerie Royale. 1841 – 9 – $5.00 – fr Orientalistes [490]

ETUDES SUR LA MÉTHODE DE LA DOGMATIQUE PROTESTANTE: LA NOTION DE LA PRÉEXISTENCE DU FILS DE DIEU: FRAGMENT DE CHRISTOLOGIE *see* COLLECTED WORKS

ETUDES SUR LA MORALISATION ET LE BIEN-ETRE DES CLASSES OUVRIERES / Lefort, Joseph – (Condition of 19th C. French working class series). 1875 – 9 – fr Hachette [360]

ETUDES SUR LA NOUVELLE TACTIQUE DE L'INFANTERIE / Scherff, W von – Paris. Firman, Didot Freres. 1874. 197, 194p. (Strategy of War Series) – 9 – fr Hachette [355]

ETUDES SUR LA QUESTION DE L'ABOLITION DE SERVAGE EN RUSSIE, PAR UN CONTEMPORAIN / Thoerner, Th. de – (Russia 19th C. series).n 1859 – 9 – fr Hachette [360]

ETUDES SUR LA REFORME FRANCAISE / Hauser, Henri – Paris: Alphonse Picard, 1909. (Bibliotheque d'histoire religieuse) – 1mf – us A.T.L.A. [240]

ETUDES SUR LA REVOCATION DE L'EDIT DE NANTES / Puaux, F & Sabatier, A – Paris: Grassart, 1886 – 1mf – us A.T.L.A. [240]

ETUDES SUR LA SIGNIFICATION DES CHOSES LITURGIQUES / Desloge, T – Paris, 1906 – 10mf – 8 – Dfl35.00 – ne Slangenburg [240]

ETUDES SUR LA SITUATION INTERIEURE, LA VIE NATIONALE ET LES INSTITUTIONS DE LA RUSSIE / Haxthausen, August von – (Russia-19th C. series). 1847-53 – 9 – fr Hachette [947]

ETUDES SUR LA TERREUR : LES NOYADES DE NANTES / Lallie, Alfred – (Microf. avec Les Noyades de Nantes: deuxieme edition.... Nantes: Libaros, 1879) – Nantes: Forest et Grimaud, 1878 – 1 – F153.71 – fr Armell [944]

ETUDES SUR L'ADMINISTRATION DE ROME AU MOYEN AGE (751-1252) / Halphen, Louis – Paris: H. Champion, 1907 – 1mf – us A.T.L.A. [350]

ETUDES SUR L'ANCIEN POEME FRANCAIS DU VOYAGE DE CHARLEMAGNE EN ORIENT / Coulet, Jules – Montpellier: Coulet, 1907. 466p – 1 – us U.W. Library [440]

ETUDES SUR LE COMBAT / Ardant du Picq, Colonel Charles – Paris. Hachette. 1880. vii, 296p. (Strategy of War Series) – 9 – fr Hachette [355]

ETUDES SUR LE LIBER PONTIFICALIS / Duchesne, Louis – Paris: Ernest Thorin, 1877 – 1mf – us A.T.L.A. [240]

ETUDES SUR LE MONACHISME EN ESPAGNE...PARIS, 1966 / Cocheril, Maurice – Madrid: Graf. Calleja, 1966 – 1 – sp Bibl Santa Ana [240]

ETUDES SUR LE RECENSEMENT DE LA POPULATION DE DIJON EN 1872 / Noirot, Louis – Dijon, E. Jobard, 1872. 32 p. 1 fiche. (Statistics Series: Demography) – 9 – 6.00 – fr Bibl Nationale [310]

ETUDES SUR LE REGIME DES MANUFACTURES. CONDITIONS DES OUVRIERS EN SOIE / Reybaud, Louis – (Condition of 19th C. French working class series). 1859 – 9 – fr Hachette [360]

ETUDES SUR LE SYMBOLISME DE LA NATURE / La Bouillerie, Francois Alexandre Roullet de – Estudios sobre el simbolismo de la naturaleza. 1877 – 1 – us I.U. Libraries [390]

ETUDES SUR LE THEATRE CONTEMPORAIN EN ALLEMAGNE : GERHART HAUPTMANN / Besson, Paul – Paris: A Laisney, 1900 – 1r – 1 – us U.W. Library [430]

ETUDES SUR L'EMPIRE DES TSARS. HISTOIRE INTIME DE LA RUSSIE SOUS LES EMPEREURS ALEXANDRE ET NICOLAS ET PARTICULIEREMENT PENDANT LA CRISE DE 1825 / Schnitzler, Jean Henri – (Russia 19th C. series). 1847 – 9 – fr Hachette [947]

ETUDES SUR LES CAUSES DE LA MISERE TANT MORALE QUE PHYSIQUE ET SUR LES MOYENS D'Y PORTER REMEDE / Cherbuliez, A E – (Condition of 19th C. French working class series). 1853 – 9 – fr Hachette [360]

ETUDES SUR LES EFFETS INTERNATIONAUX DES JUGEMENTS / Bartin, E – Paris, 1907 – 3mf – 9 – ILM-2238/1 – ne IDC [340]

ETUDES SUR LES LANGUES DU HAUT-ZAMBEZE / Jacottet, E; ed by Leroux, Ernest – Paris. 1896 – 9 – $5.00 – fr Orientalistes [490]

ETUDES SUR LES MOINES D'EGYPTE / Cauwenbergh, P Van – Paris, 1914 – 4mf – 8 – Dfl19.00 – ne Slangenburg [240]

ETUDES SUR LES PRODUITS DE LA FAMILLE DES SAPOTEES / Planchon, L – Montpellier. 1888. B-7135 1 – 9 – ne IDC [580]
ETUDES SUR LES RELIGIONS SEMITIQUES / Lagrange, Marie Joseph – Paris, 1903 – 8mf – 8 – ne Slangenburg [270]
ETUDES SUR L'ETAT INTERIEUR DES ABBAYES CISTERCIENNES ET PRINCIPALEMENT DE CLAIRVAUX AU 12TH ET AU 13TH SIECLE / D'Arbois de Jubainville, MH – Paris, 1858 – 7mf – 8 – Dfl28.00 – ne Slangenburg [240]
ETUDES SUR L'INDUSTRIE ET LA CLASSE INDUSTRIELLE A PARIS AU XIIIE ET AU XIVE SIECLE / Fagniez, Gustave Charles – Paris: F. Vieweg, 1877. With: An Account of the Danes and the Norwegians in England, Scotland, and Ireland by J.J.A. Worsaae. 1 reel. 1272 – 1 – us U.W. Library [380]
ETUDES SUR L'ISLAM AU DAHOMEY : LE BAS DAHOMEY, LE HAUT DAHOMEY – Paris: E Leroux, 1926 – 1 – us Res Libr [260]
ETUDES SUR L'ISLAM AU SENEGAL – Paris: E Leroux, 1917 – 1 – us Res Libr [960]
ETUDES SUR L'ISLAM EN COTE D'IVOIRE – Paris: E Leroux, 1922 – 1 – us Res Libr [960]
ETUDES SUR L'ISLAM ET LES TRIBUS DU SOUDAN... – Paris: E Leroux, 1920-21 [v3] – 1 – us Res Libr [960]
ETUDES SUR L'ISLAM ET LES TRIBUS MAURES : LES BRAKNA / Marty, Paul-N – Paris: Leroux, 1921 – fr Armell [260]
ETUDES SUR L'ISLAM ET LES TRIBUS MAURES : LES BRAKNA – Paris: E Leroux, 1921 – 1 – us Res Libr [960]
ETUDES SUR SCHILLER – (Includes bibliographical references) – Paris: F Alcan, 1905 – 1 – us U.W. Library [430]
ETUDES VOLTAIQUES : MEMOIRES – Ouagadougou, Centre IFAN. ns: n1-5. 1960-1965 – us Res Libr [072]
L'ETUDIANT – Montreal, 1897-9? SEM35P97 – 1r – 1 – Can$15.00 – cn Bibl Nat [073]
L'ETUDIANT : ORGANE DE LA JEUNESSE – Montreal, Canada. 30 mar 1901-v1 n5. 27 avr 1901 – 1r – 1 – Can$25.00 – cn Can Microfilming [072]
L'ETUDIANT : REVUE – Joliette, Canada. jan 1885-15 dec 1892 – 1r – 1 – Can$30.00 – cn Can Microfilming [073]
L'ETUDIANT *see* LE JOURNAL DES ETUDIANTS
ETUDIANT EN MEDECINE – Aux Etats-Unis et dans Ontario. par un etudiant en medecine. Montreal: s.n., 1892 (Montreal: A. T. Lepine). 02449. (Pre-1900 Canadiana) – 9 – cn C.I.H.M. [971]
L'ETUDIANT NOIR : JOURNAL DE L'ASSOCIATION DES ETUDIANTS MARTINIQUAIS EN FRANCE – (Filmed with les continents and 11 other titles L'Europe democratique. Paris: Boule, Dec 1849) – Paris: Sauphanor, [v1 n1 mar 1935] – us Res Libr [072]
L'ETUDIANT SOCIALISTE / L' Association Generale des Etudiants Socialistes. Flenu, Jupille, Liege, etc – 1926-dec 1936 janv 1937. devenu: Essais et combats. fevr 1937; Paris. fevr 1928-janv 1939 – 1 – fr A.C.R.P.P. [073]
ETUMBA – Brazzaville: [Parti congolais du travail, dec 27 1969-1972 – 3r – 1 – us Res Libr [072]
ETWAS FUER ALLE : DAS IST, EINE KURZE BESCHREIBUNG ALLERLEY STAND-, AMTS- UND GEWERKPERSONEN... / Abraham a Sancta Clara – Halle: Hendel, [18–?] – 1r – 1 – us U.W. Library [943]
ETWAS FUR HERZ! = SOMETHING FOR THE SPIRIT! – (Sermons written by the leader of the Separatist colony at Zoar, in German) – Zoar, Tuscarawas, OH – 1r – 1 – us Western Res [240]
ETWAS VON IND XUBER MUSIK FUERS JAHR 1777 / Kraus, Joseph Martin – Frankfurt am Mayn: bey den Eichenbergschen Erben, 1778 – 1 – us Sibley [780]
ETWAS ZU CHARAKTERISTICK DER JUDEN / Bendavid, L – Leipzig. 1793. BJ-23-106 – 9 – ne IDC [270]
ETYMOLOGICON LINGUA ANGLICANAE... / Skinner, S – Londini, 1671 – 14mf – 9 – ne IDC [420]
ETYMOLOGICUM LINGUAE GRAECAE, SIVE OBSERVATIONES AD SINGULAS VERBORUM NOMINUMQUE STIRPES / Lennep, J D van – In French. (Linguistic series). 2 v. 1790 – 9 – fr Hachette [450]
ETYMOLOGICUM TEUTONICAE LINGUAE SIVE DICTIONARIUM TEUTONICO-LATINUM / Kilianus, C – (Tomus 1 22mf; Tomus 2 32mf) – Traecti Batavorum, 1777 – 8 – ne Slangenburg [430]
ETYMOLOGISCHE STUDIEN ZUM SEMITISCHEN / Barth, Jakob – Leipzig. 1893. BNE-464 1 – 9 – ne IDC [470]
ETYMOLOGISCHES WOERTERBUCH DER GRIECHISCHEN SPRACHE : MIT BESONDERER BERUECKSICHTIGUNG DES NEUHOCHDEUTSCHEN UND EINEM DEUTSCHEN WOERTERVERZEICHNIS / Prellwitz, Walther – (Includes index) – Goettingen: Vandenhoeck und Ruprecht, 1892 – 1mf – 9 – 0-8370-9264-7 – 1986-3264 – us A.T.L.A. [450]
ETYMOLOGISCHES WOERTERBUCH DER ROMANISCHEN SPRACHEN / Diez, F – Bonn, 1853 – 15mf – ne IDC [440]
ETYMOLOGISCHES WOERTERBUCH DER TURKO-TATARISCHEN SPRACHEN / Vambery, H – Leipzig, 1878 – 5mf – 9 – U-373/2 – ne IDC [490]
ETZ HADATH – New York. Tree of knowledge. 1896 – 1 – us A.J.P.C. [073]
EU DE NORTEAMERICA CONTRA LA ARGENTINA / Brignole, Dardo – Ed. econ omica. Buenos Aires: Editorial "Defensa Patria", 1945 – 1 – CSUXADQ7979-B – us Hoover Inst Photo [330]
EUCALYPTOGRAPHIA. A DESCRIPTIVE ATLAS OF THE EUCALYPTS OF AUSTRALIA AND THE AJOINING ISALNDS. DECAS I-X / Mueller, Ferdinand Jakob Heinrich von – Melbourne, etc. 1879-84. B-8053 1 – 9 – ne IDC [580]
EUCALYPTS FOR PLANTING – 1981 – 677p – it F.A.O. [634]
LA EUCARISTIA Y LA VIDA CRISTIANA. 2ND ED. 2 TOMOS. BARCELONA, 1934 / Goma, Isidoro – Madrid: Razon y Fe, 1934 – 1 – sp Bibl Santa Ana [240]
EUCARISTICAS. ANTOLOGIA / Corredor Garcia, Antonio – Caceres: Tip. Vda. Floriano, 1955 – 1 – sp Bibl Santa Ana [240]
EUCHARIST AND PENANCE IN THE FIRST SIX CENTURIES OF THE CHURCH / Rauschen, Gerhard – St. Louis, Mo.: B. Herder, 1913 – 1mf – us A.T.L.A. [240]
THE EUCHARISTIC LIFE OF JESUS CHRIST = VIE DE JESUS CHRIST DANS LE ST. SACREMENT DE L'ABTEL : PREACHED DURING THE OCTAVE OF THE HOLY SACRAMENT, IN THE CHURCH OF S. ANDRE DES ARCS, IN THE YEAR 1657 / Biroat, Jacques – London: Swan Sonnenschein, Lowrey, [1886?] – 1mf – 9 – 0-8370-9683-9 – 1986-3683 – us A.T.L.A. [240]
EUCHARISTIC PRESENCE, EUCHARISTIC SACRIFICE, AND EUCHARISTIC ADORATION : BEING AN EXAMINATION OF "A THEOLOGICAL DEFENCE FOR THE REV. JAMES DE KOVEN, D.D., WARDEN OF RACINE COLLEGE, FEBRUARY 12, 1874" / Buel, Samuel – New York: T. Whittaker, c1874 – 1mf – us A.T.L.A. [240]
L'EUCHARISTIE : DES ORIGINES A JUSTIN MARTYR / Goguel, Maurice – Paris: Fischbacher, 1910 – 1mf – us A.T.L.A. [240]
THE EUCHARISTIE DOCTRINE AND LITURGY OF THE MYSTAGOGICAL CATECHESE OF THEODORE OF MOPSUESTIA / Reine, J – 1942 – 4mf – 9 – ne Slangenburg [240]
EUCHOLOGION TO MEGA – Roma, 1873 – 15mf – 8 – Dfl53.00 – ne Slangenburg [240]
Eucken, Rudolf *see*
- CAN WE STILL BE CHRISTIANS?
- CHRISTIANITY AND THE NEW IDEALISM
- DIE LEBENSANSCHAUUNGEN DER GROSSEN DENKER
- THE LIFE OF THE SPIRIT
- LIFE'S BASIS AND LIFE'S IDEAL
- MAIN CURRENTS OF MODERN THOUGHT
- NATURALISM OR IDEALISM?

Euclid *see* TAHRIR USUL LI UQLIDAS
THE EUCLID ERA – Toronto: [s.n., 1897?-189- or 19–] – 9 – cn C.I.H.M. [240]
EUCLID TOWNSHIP BOARD OF TRUSTEES MINUTES – Euclid Township, Cuyahoga, OH. 29 Aug 1908-22 Sept 19? – 1r – 1 – us Western Res [978]
Euclides *see*
- EVCLIDE MEGARENSE PHILOSOPHO: SOLO INTRODVTTORE DELLE SCIENTIE MATHEMATICE
- LA PERSPECTIVA Y ESPECULARIA DE EUCLIDES

EUDAMONIA ODER DEUTSCHES VOLKSGLUK, EIN JOURNAL FUER FREUNDE VON WAHRHEIT UND RECHT – Leipzig, 1795-1798. v1-6 – 39mf – 9 – VR-14.3/1 – ne IDC [340]
Eudel, Paul *see*
- ASSOCIATION PARISIENNE DES ANCIENS ELEVES DU LYCEE DE NANTES [AVEC DES NOTES MANUSCR. DE P. EUDEL DANS LES MARGES/ WITH HANDWR. NOTES BY P.E. IN THE MARGINS]
- FIGURES NANTAISES...
- LES LOCUTIONS NANTAISES

EUDEMISCHE ETHIK UND METAPHYSIK / Arnim, H von – Wien, 1928 – 1mf – 8 – ne Slangenburg [110]
[EUGEN GERSTENMAIER PAMPHLET COLLECTION] – 1941-1966 – 1 – CSUXANS2500-B – us Hoover Inst Photo [943]
EUGENE CITY REGISTER – Eugene OR. Oct 7 1885-Mar 27 1889 – 1 – us U.O. Library [071]
EUGENE CITY REVIEW – Eugene OR. Mar 5 1864-Sep 9 1865 – 1 – us U.O. Library [071]
EUGENE DAILY GUARD – Eugene, OR. 8 Dec 1891-17 Nov 1930; 16 May 1874. – 76r – 1 – us U.O. Library [071]
EUGENE DISTRICT NEWS – Eugene OR. Mar 5-Oct 29 1931 – 1 – us U.O. Library [071]
EUGENE HERALD – Eugene OR. Mar 26 1906 – 1 – us U.O. Library [071]
EUGENE MAGAZINE – Eugene OR. Winter 1971 – 1 – us U.O. Library [071]
EUGENE MAXIMILIEN HAITIAN COLLECTION, 1847-1933 : FROM THE HOLDINGS OF THE SCHOMBURG CENTER FOR RESEARCH IN BLACK CULTURE, MANUSCRIPTS, ARCHIVES AND RARE BOOKS DIVISION: THE NEW YORK PUBLIC LIBRARY, ASTOR, LENOX AND TILDEN FOUNDATIONS – (Guide which covers all coll under "International Affairs" sold separately for $20.00 D3305.G5) – 1995 – 5r – 1 – $425.00 – D3305P17 – Dist. us Scholarly Res – us L of C Photodup [972]
EUGENE MORNING REGISTER – Eugene, OR. -d. 15 Sep 1895-17 Nov 1930. – 76r – 1 – us U.O. Library [071]
EUGENE NEWS – (Set incl. Eugene Shopping News; Eugene District News) – Eugene, OR. -d. 6 Nov 1931-8 May 1942. – 29r – 1 – us U.O. Library [071]
EUGENE PICTURE PRESS – Eugene OR. July 23 Aug 2 21 29 1947, Sep 5-27 Oct 4 1947, Nov Dec 1947, Jan-May July 1948 – 1 – us U.O. Library [071]
EUGENE RECORD – Eugene OR. Apr 3 Sep 22 Oct 20 Nov 10 1931 – 1 – us U.O. Library [071]
EUGENE REGISTER – Eugene OR. Apr 3-Dec 7 1899 – 1 – us U.O. Library [071]
EUGENE REGISTER-GUARD – Eugene, OR. -d. 18 Nov 1930-31 Oct 1977; Dec 1977. – 397r – 1 – us U.O. Library [071]
EUGENE SHOPPING NEWS – Eugene OR. Feb 6-26 1931 – 1 – us U.O. Library [071]
EUGENE TWICE A WEEK REGISTER – Eugene OR. Mar 8-Dec 23 1904 – 1 – us U.O. Library [071]
EUGENE WEEKLY GUARD – Eugene, OR. 11 Feb 1899-29 Sep 1910. – 1 – us U.O. Library [071]
EUGENE WEEKLY REGISTER – Eugene, OR. 14 Dec 1899-3 Mar 1904 – 1 – us U.O. Library [071]
EUGENIO NOEL : NOVELA DE LA VIDA DE UN HOMBRE INTENSO / Caba, Pedro – Valencia: Editorial America, s.a. – sp Bibl Santa Ana [830]
EUGENIO SARRALBO AQUARELES, ANTONIO CORREA Y ARTURO ALVAREZ. (OFM). INVENTARIO... / Borges, Pedro – Madrid: Archivo Ibero-Americano, 1959 – 1 – sp Bibl Santa Ana [020]
EUGIPPII VITA SANCTI SEVERINI (MGH1: 1.BD. 2.TEIL) / ed by Sauppe, H – 1877 – Dfl25.00 – ne Slangenburg [240]
EUGIPPII VITA SEVERINI (MGH 7: 26.BD) – 1898 – Dfl9.00 – ne Slangenburg [240]
Eukleidos (Euclides) *see* EUKLEIDOU EISAGOGE HARMONIKE. EUCLIDIS RUDIMENTA MUSICES
EUKLEIDOU EISAGOGE HARMONIKE. EUCLIDIS RUDIMENTA MUSICES / Eukleidos (Euclides); ed by Pena, J – P-255. 1557 – 9 – ne IDC [780]
Eulenberg, A *see* ZEITSCHRIFT FUER SEXUALWISSENSCHAFT (HQ 8)
Eulenburg, Albert *see* REAL-ENCYCLOPAEDIE DER GESAMMTEN HEILKUNDE (AEL, ABT.3;8)
DER EULENSPIEGEL *see*
- ROTER PFEFFER

EULENSPIEGEL, ODER, SCHABERNACK UEBER SCHABERNACK : POSSE IN VIER AUFZUEGEN / Nestroy, Johann – Wien: Theodor Daberkow, [1895?] – 1r – 1 – us U.W. Library [790]
Euler *see* RECHERCHES GENERALES SUR LA MORTALITE ET LA MULTIPLICATION DU GENRE HUMAIN
Euler, L *see* LEONARD EULER. PEREPISKA. ANNOTIROVANNYI UKAZATEL
Euler, Leonhard *see* TENTAMEN NOVAE THEORIAE MUSICAE EX CERTISSIMIS HARMONIAE PRINCIPIIS DILUCIDE EXPOSITAE
EULOGIUM (HISTORIARUM SIVE TEMPORIS) (RS9) : CHRONICON AB ORBE CONDITO USQUE AD ANNUM DOMINI 1366 A MONACHO QUODAM MALMESBUERIENSI EXARATUM. ACCEDUNT CONTINUATIONES DUAE, QUARUM UNA AD ANNUM 1413, ALTERA AD ANNUM 1490 PERDUCTA EST / ed by Haydon, F S – (v1 1858 Dfl32.00. v2 1860 Dfl32.00. v3 1863 Dfl42.00) – ne Slangenburg [240]
EULOGY ON CHIEF-JUSTICE CHASE, DELIVERED BY WILLIAM M. EVARTS, BEFORE THE ALUMNI OF DARTMOUTH COLLEGE, AT HANOVER, JUNE 24, 1874 / Evarts, William Maxwell – New York, Appleton, 1874. 30 p. LL-167 – 1 – us L of C Photodup [340]
EULOGY ON WILLIAM HENRY BARTLETT, LATE ASSOCIATE JUSTICE OF THE SUPREME COURT OF NEW HAMPSHIRE. / Smith, Isaac William – Before the Alumni of Dartmouth College, at commencement, June 23, 1880. Concord, N.H.: Republican, 1881. 16p. LL-1078 – 1 – us L of C Photodup [340]
EULOGY UPON LIFE AND CHARACTER OF GEORGE EUSTIS, FORMERLY CHIEF JUSTICE OF THE SUPREME COURT OF LA....AT LYCEUM HALL, ON THE 31ST MAR., 1859, BY HON. PIERRE A. ROST, AT THE REQUEST OF NEW ORLEANS LAW ASSOC / Rost, Pierre Adolphe – New Orleans: Daily Delta, 1859. 13p. LL-468 – 1 – us L of C Photodup [340]
Eummelen, H *see* SICK ROOM ALTER MANUAL: WITH PRAYERS, FORMULAS, INSTRUCTIONS IN ADMINISTERING THE SACRAMENTS: AND A COMPLETE COURSE OF INSTRUCTIONS TO NURSES IN ATTENDING THE SICK
EUPENER NACHRICHTEN – Eupen, Belgium. 1 Apr 1927-14 Jun 1940 – 1 – gw Mikrofilm [949]
EUPENER ZEITUNG – Eupen, Belgium. 4 Jan-30 Dez 1899; Sept-17 Dez 1921; 1922-21 Jun 1941; 23 Jun 1941-31 Mar 1944 (incomplete) – 1 – gw Mikrofilm [949]
EUPHEMISTIC LITURGICAL APPENDIXES IN THE OLD TESTAMENT / Grimm, Karl Josef – Baltimore:[s.n.], 1901 (Leipzig:August Pries) – 1mf – 9 – 0-8370-3399-3 – 1985-1399 – us A.T.L.A. [220]
EUPHONOLOGIA LINGUAE ANGLICANAE, ET MIRUM SONORUM ARTIFICIUM / Adams, James – 1794. 246p. (English Linguistics Series 1500-1800) – 9 – us UMI [400]
EUPHORION : ZEITSCHRIFT FUER LITERATURGESCHICHTE – (Missing: 1936. v37) – Hamburg, etc., 1894-1941. v1-41 – 555mf – 9 – H-408c/2 – ne IDC [430]
EUPHYTICA. NETHERLANDS JOURNAL OF PLANT BREEDING – 7712. V. 1-18. 1952-1969 – 9 – ne IDC [580]
EUREKA AND ARCATA CITY DIRECTORIES – Humboldt Co, CA. 1946-1950 – 3r – 1 – $150.00 – D041 – us Library Micro [910]
EUREKA BAPTIST CHURCH. ANDERSON COUNTY. SOUTH CAROLINA : CHURCH RECORDS – 1889-1972 – 1 – 19.49 – us Baptist [240]
EUREKA CENSUS OF THE INDIANS OF CALIFORNIA – Humboldt Co, CA. 1936-1938; 1941-1942 – 3r – 1 – $150.00 – D040 – us Library Micro [978]
EUREKA CENTRAL BAPTIST CHURCH. EUREKA, MISSOURI : CHURCH RECORDS – Oct 1931-Jun 1942; Aug-Sept 1954. Formerly Allenton Baptist Church – 1 – 13.05 – us Baptist [240]
EUREKA GOLD MINING COMPANY – Prospectus, reports and statistics of the Eureka Gold Mining Company of Nova Scotia: with a plan of the Wine Harbour Gold District: limited liability, capital stock, $100,000 in 100,000 shares of $1 each:

to be organized under a special charter from the legislature of Nova Scotia, head office, Toronto. Toronto: The Company, 1868 (Toronto: Globe Print Co.). 02922. (Pre-1900 Canadiana) – 9 – cn C.I.H.M. [971]
THE EUREKA INDEPENDENT – Eureka, CA. 1952-1958 – 3r – 1 – $150.00 – B02217 – us Library Micro [071]
EUREKA SENTINEL – Eureka, NV. 31 Oct 1872; 1875- – 59+ r – 1 UN04516 – $2,950.00 ($50.00y) – us Library Micro [071]
EUREKA SENTINEL – Tonopah, NV. 1993 – 2+ r – 1 – $100.00 ($90.00y) – B06069 – us Library Micro [071]
L'EURIDICE D'OTTAVIO RINUCCINI / Rinuccini, Ottavio – Composed by Jacopo Peri. (Libretto.) 1600 – 9 – us Sibley [780]
Euringer, Sebastian *see*
- DIE AUFFASSUNG DES HOHENLIEDES BEI DEN ABESSINIERN
- DER MASORAHTEXT DES KOHELETH: KRITISCH UNTERSUCHT

Euripides *see*
- THE BACCHAE.
- DIE TROERINNEN

EURIPIDES MEDEA UND DAS GOLDENE VLIESS VON GRILLPARZER / Grillparzer, Franz – Blankenburg, Ger.: O Kircher, 1896 – 1r – 1 – us U.W. Library [820]
EUROCAE (EUROPEAN ORGANIZATION FOR CIVIL AVIATION ELECTRONICS) – Printed index. Updated every 60 days – 6,9 – us Info Handling [621]
Euroepan Parliament *see* DEBATES OF THE EUROPEAN PARLIAMENT
EUROPA : WOCHENSCHRIFT FUER KULTUR UND POLITIK – Berlin, jan-jun 1905 – 1 – Dist. gw Mikrofilm – gw Misc Inst [073]
EUROPA – Wochenzeitung fuer Tat und Freiheit. no. 1-19. Paris. dec 1935-mai 1936 – 1 – fr A.C.R.P.P. [073]
EUROPA EN 1949 : COMENTARIO A DOS DISCURSOS DE DONOSO CORTES / Calvo Serer, Rafael – Madrid: Arbor, 1949 – 1 – sp Bibl Santa Ana [320]
EUROPA LIBRE – Bogota, Colombia. Sept 1942 – 1r – 1 – gw Mikrofilm [072]
EUROPA LIBRE – Bogota, sep 1942 – 1r – 1 – Inquire at Mikrofilmarchiv for details – gw Misc Inst [072]
EUROPA MEDIO PHYSICA – 1965- 1; 1975- 5,6,9 – us UMI [615]
EUROPA ODER EUROPA AG? / Schumacher, Kurt – Hannover 1949 – 1 – DM30.00 – gw Mikro Press [940]
EUROPA UND DIE REVOLUTION / Goerres, Joseph – Stuttgart, 1821 – 356p – 9 – DM48.00 – 3-89349-245-3 – gw Hänsel [320]
EUROPA UND DIE REVOLUTION / Goerres, Joseph von – Stuttgart, 1821. 356p – DM60.00 – 3-89349-171-6 – gw Hänsel [940]
EUROPA UNION : EUROPAEISCHE ZEITUNG FUER POLITIK, WIRTSCHAFT UND KULTUR – Bonn, DE. 1963-77 – 2r – 1 – gw Mikro Press [072]
EUROPA UNION – v1-28 1950 – May 1977. Europa Union Verlag. ill. -m. Continued by: Europaeische Zeitung – 1 – us U.W. Library [320]
EUROPA Y AMERICA. BIOGRAFIAS Y SEMBLANZAS UNIVERSALES POR VARIOS DISTINGUIDOS ESCRITORES – Madrid: Tip. Julian Frances, s.a. – 1 – sp Bibl Santa Ana [920]
EUROPAEISCHE HEFTE : WOCHENSCHRIFT FUER POLITIK, KULTUR, WIRTSCHAFT – (Title change: Europaeische Hefte vereinigt mit Aufruf, 1934, no.25-) – Prag (Praha), Czechoslovakia. 24 Dec 1934-30 Nov 1935 – 1 – gw Mikrofilm [073]
EUROPAEISCHE HEFTE VEREINIGT MIT AUFRUF *see* EUROPAEISCHE HEFTE
EUROPAEISCHE KIRCHENFREIE RUNDSCHAU – 1971-82 (complete) – 1r – 1 – ATLA S0598 – us A.T.L.A. [073]
DIE EUROPAEISCHE MUSIK : OESTERREICHISCHE NATIONALBIBLIOTHEK, MUSIKSAMMLUNG; DEUTSCHE STAATSBIBLIOTHEK BERLIN, MUSIKSAMMLUNG; KATALOG DER MUSIKSAMMLUNG DER NATIONALBIBLIOTHEK PRAG – (See individual titles: Katalog, alphabetischer, der Musiksammlung der Staatsbibliothek zu Berlin Preussischer Kulturbesitz. Katalog der Musiksammlung der Nationalbibliothek Prag. Katalog der Libretti. Katalog der Musikhandschriften. Katalog, alter, der Musikdrucke der oesterreichischen Nationalbibliothek. Die Haydn-Drucke der Hoboken-Sammlung. Die Bach-Drucke der Hoboken-Sammlung. Die Drucke der Bachsoehne der Hoboken- Sammlung) – 2606mf – 9 – DM26,950.00 diazo DM30,800.00 silver – gw Olms [780]
DIE EUROPAEISCHE MUSIK *see*
- DIE HAYDN-DRUCKE DER HOBOKEN-SAMMLUNG MUSIKALISCHER ERST- UND FRUEHDRUCKE
- KATALOG, ALPHABETISCHER, DER MUSIKSAMMLUNG DER STAATSBIBLIOTHEK BERLIN PREUSSISCHER KULTURBESITZ
- KATALOG, ALTER, DER MUSIKDRUCKE DER OESTERREICHISCHEN NATIONALBIBLIOTHEK
- KATALOG DER LIBRETTI
- KATALOG DER MUSIKDRUCKE DER NATIONALBIBLIOTHEK ZU PRAG-NARODNI KNIHORNA
- KATALOG DER MUSIKHANDSCHRIFTEN

EUROPAEISCHE PARLAMENTS-CHRONIK – Leipzig, Germany. 8 Apr-30 Jun 1848 – 1 – gw Mikrofilm [940]
DIE EUROPAEISCHE RELATION – Hamburg, Germany. 1701-02, 1703 – 11r – 1 – gw Mikrofilm [072]
EUROPAEISCHE SENDERPROGRAMME *see* BAYERISCHE RADIO-ZEITUNG UND BAYERNFUNK
DAS EUROPAEISCHE VOELKERRECHT... / Heffter, H W – Berlin, 1844 – 5mf – 1 – ILM-107/1 – ne IDC [327]
EUROPAEISCHE ZEITUNG – (Neue Europaeische Zeitung, 26 Sep 1774; Hanauer Neue Europaeische Zeitung, 1784; Hanauer Neue Zeitung, 1814; Hanauer Zeitung, 1 Jan 1826) – Hanau, Germany. 1701; 1703-14; 1717-19; 1721-65; 1767-95; 1797-1810 – 83r – 1 – gw Mikrofilm [072]
EUROPAEISCHE ZEITUNG – v28- . Jun 1977- . Europa Union Verlag. ill. -m. Continues: Europa Union – 1 – us U.W. Library [320]
EUROPAEISCHE ZEITUNG *see* EUROPA-UNION
EUROPAFAEHIGKEIT DER SCHWEIZERISCHEN ALTERS- UND HINTERLASSENENVERSICHERUNG (AHV) MIT BLICK AUF EINEN BEITRITT ZUR EUROPAEISCHEN UNION / Grießhaber, Christoph – 1995 – 2mf – 9 – DM80.00 – 3-8267-2083-0 – gw Hänsel [360]
EUROPAS OCH NORD AMERIKAS HVITMOSSOR (SPHAGNA) / Lindberg, S O – 7578 2. 1882 – 9 – ne IDC [580]
EUROPA-UNION – (Cont: Europa-Union Deutschland, -1950. Cont by: Europaeische Zeitung, jun 1977) – Bonn, 1963-77, 1987-96 – 1 – Inquire at Mikrofilmarchiv for details – gw Misc Inst [940]
EUROPA-UNION DEUTSCHLAND *see* EUROPA-UNION
Europe *see* NATIONAL DEVELOPMENT PLANS
EUROPE, 1946-76 / U.S. Central Intelligence Agency – 1982. Series: CIA Research Reports – 1 – $415.00 – 0-89093-452-5 – us UPA [940]
EUROPE, 1950-61 : SUPPLEMENT / U.S. Office of Strategic Services – 1980. Series: US State Department Intelligence and Research Reports, Pt 10 – $1,060.00 – 0-89093-294-8 – us UPA [940]
EUROPE, A PROPHECY / Blake, William – (Copy K). Linnell-Riches – 14 – uk Microform Academic [810]
Europe, Agence Internationale d'Information pour la Presse *see* EUROPE DOCUMENTS LUXEMBOURG: EUROPE
EUROPE AND NATO, 1970-94 : SPECIAL STUDIES SERIES / ed by Kesaris, Paul – (1970-80: 11r $1,210.00 ISBN 0-89093-393-6; Supplements, 1980-85: 12r $1,320.00 ISBN 0-89093-681-1; 1985-88: 8r $880.00 ISBN 1-55655-113-4; 1989-91: 10r $1,105.00 ISBN 1-55655-429-X; 1992-94: 14r $1,670.00 ISBN 1-55655-536-9) – 1 – us UPA [320]
EUROPE AND THE NEW SEA LAW;... / Dembski, V – London, [1912] – 3mf – 1 – ILM-500/1 – ne IDC [327]
EUROPE BRIEF NOTES – 1988- – 1 – us U.W. Library [073]
L'EUROPE DIPLOMATIQUE : GAZETTE INTERNATIONALE – Continued as: La Gazette diplomatique. Paris. Feb 1876-1887 – 1 – fr A.C.R.P.P. [940]
EUROPE DOCUMENTS LUXEMBOURG: EUROPE / Europe, Agence Internationale d'Information pour la Presse – Bulletins quotidiens et supplements. -w(-irr). 1988- – 1 – us U.W. Library [940]
EUROPE ET JUPITER, CONCERT FRANCOIS A DEUX VOIX / Alexandre, P – Paris: Author, 1715 – 1 – us Sibley [780]
EUROPE FINANCIERE – London, UK. 26 Nov-10 Dec 1870 – 1 – uk British Libr Newspaper [072]
EUROPE IN THE SEVENTEENTH CENTURY / Ogg, David – London: A. & C. Black, 1925. xi,579p. maps. Bibliog – 1 – us U.W. Library [940]
EUROPE LEFT – 1963-1972 – 9 – us Primary [073]
L'EUROPE LITTERAIRE – Journal de la litterature nationale et etrangere. Paris. mars 1833-janv 1834 – 1 – fr A.C.R.P.P. [410]
L'EUROPE NOUVELLE – Revue hebdomadaire des questions exterieures, economiques et litteraires. Dir. Madeleine Le Verrier. Paris. 1918-juin 1940 – 1 – fr A.C.R.P.P. [400]
LA EUROPEADA / Serrano Serrano, Ildefonso – Fuente de Cantos: Imp. Libr. San Jose, 1915 – 1 – sp Bibl Santa Ana [946]
DIE EUROPEAISCHE MUSIK *see* DIE DRUCKE DER BACHSOEHNE DER HOBOKEN-SAMMLUNG MUSIKALISCHER ERST- UND FRUEHDRUCKE
THE EUROPEAN – 1991-1994 – 1 – F3,231.00 – sz Infoprint [072]
THE EUROPEAN – May 1990- – us Primary [072]
THE EUROPEAN – May 1990-Dec – 1 – F2,532.00 – sz Infoprint [072]
THE EUROPEAN – Subscription – 1 – F2,532.00 – sz Infoprint [072]
EUROPEAN AND NORTH AMERICAN BRYINEAE / Kindberg, N C – Linkoeping. 1897. B-5454 2 – 8 – ne IDC [580]
EUROPEAN BAPTIST PRESS SERVICE – 1961-89. 9111p – 1 – $371.34 – us Baptist [240]
EUROPEAN BAPTIST PRESS SERVICE – Rueschlikon. European Baptist Federation Press releases. 1961-81. Single reels available – 1 – 170.35 – us A.B.H.S. [240]
EUROPEAN BEGINNINGS IN WEST AFRICA 1454-1578: A SURVEY OF THE FIRST CENTURY OF WHITE ENTERPRISE IN WEST AFRICA / Blake, John William – London. 1937. BA-528 2 – 8 – ne IDC [900]
EUROPEAN BEGINNINGS IN WEST AFRICA, 1454-1578; A SURVEY OF THE FIRST CENTURY OF WHITE ENTERPRISE IN WEST AFRICA. / Blake, John William – London: Pub. for the Royal Empire Society by Longmans, Green and Co., 1937. 212p.fold. maps. Bibliography – 1 – us U.W. Library [960]
EUROPEAN BOARD MARKETS – London. v5-6. 1970 – 5mf – 9 – $5.00f – us Ross [380]
EUROPEAN BUSINESS LAW REVIEW – v1-6. 1950-95 – 5,6,9 – $220.00 set – us Hein [340]
EUROPEAN BUSINESS REVIEW – 1964- 1; 1975- 5,6,9 – us UMI [650]
EUROPEAN BUTTERFLIES AND MOTHS / Kirby, W F – London, 1882. lvi,427p.62 pls. Z-1394/2 – 8 – ne IDC [590]
European Centre for Higher Education *see* INTERNATIONAL DIRECTORY OF RESEARCH INSTITUTIONS ON HIGHER EDUCATION
EUROPEAN CIVILIZATION = PROTESTANTISMO COMPARADO CON EL CATOLICISMO : PROTESTANTISM AND CATHOLICITY COMPARED IN THEIR EFFECTS ON THE CIVILIZATION OF EUROPE / Balmes, Jaime Luciano – (In English. Includes index) – 10th ed. Baltimore: John Murphy, 1868, c1850 – 2mf – 9 – 0-8370-7363-4 – 1986-1363 – us A.T.L.A. [240]
European Coal and Steel Community. Common Assembly *see*
- DEBATS
- DOCUMENT

European Consortium for Political Research Manifestos Group *see* POLITICAL MANIFESTOS IN THE POST-WAR ERA 1945-1981
[EUROPEAN CULTURAL CENTRE PAMPHLET COLLECTION] – 19??-1959 – 1 – CSUXANP1994-B – us Hoover Inst Photo [306]
[EUROPEAN CULTURAL FOUNDATION PAMPHLET COLLECTION] – 1959?-1961? – 1 – CSUXANP1998-B – us Hoover Inst Photo [306]
[EUROPEAN CULTURE PAMPHLET COLLECTION] – 1953-1979 – 1 – CSUXAMK5700-B – us Hoover Inst Photo [306]
EUROPEAN ECONOMIC REVIEW – v1-26. 1970-84 – 1,5,6,13 – sz Elsevier [330]
EUROPEAN EXPRESS – Brussels, Belgium. Belgian Times & News Continental Review. -w. 9 Nov 1901-21 Oct 1909. 7 reels – 1 – uk British Libr Newspaper [949]
EUROPEAN FERNS / Britten, J – Coloured illustrations from nature by D. Blair. London. 1879-81. B-7166 1 – 9 – ne IDC [580]
European Free Trade Association *see* EFTA BULLETIN
EUROPEAN GUIDE TO GOLD – 1985, 59p – 9 – 1.00f – at Libertarian Micro [332]
EUROPEAN HERALD – London, England. -w. 2 Nov 1933-21 Nov 1936. 2 reels – 1 – uk British Libr Newspaper [072]
EUROPEAN JOURNAL OF APPLIED MICROBIOLOGY – v1-4. 1975-77 – 1,5,6,9 – us UMI [073]
EUROPEAN JOURNAL OF APPLIED MICROBIOLOGY AND BIOTECHNOLOGY – v5-18. 1978-83 – 1,5,9 – 765.00 – us UMI [073]
EUROPEAN JOURNAL OF APPLIED PHYSIOLOGY AND OCCUPATIONAL PHYSIOLOGY – v. 14-45. 1949-80 – 1,5,9 – 4560.00 – us UMI [073]
EUROPEAN JOURNAL OF BIOCHEMISTRY – v.1-121, 1967-81. Pub. on behalf of the Federation of European Biochemical Societies (FEBS). ISSN: 0014-2956 – 1,5,6,9,13 – 113.00v – us UMI [073]
EUROPEAN JOURNAL OF CANCER : PARTS A AND B – (Part B, Oral Oncology, is also available separately.) – v1- 1965- – 5,6,9 us UMI [610]
EUROPEAN JOURNAL OF CANCER AND CLINICAL ONCOLOGY *see* EUROPEAN JOURNAL OF CANCER
EUROPEAN JOURNAL OF CARDIOLOGY – v1-12. 1973-80 – 1,5,6,13 – sz Elsevier [073]
EUROPEAN JOURNAL OF CLINICAL INVESTIGATION – v. 1-6. 1970-76 – 1,5,9 – us UMI [616]
EUROPEAN JOURNAL OF CLINICAL PHARMACOLOGY – v. 1-18. 1968-80 – 1,5,9 – 1755.00 – us UMI [073]
EUROPEAN JOURNAL OF EDUCATION – 1966- 28v – 9 – £246.50 – 0141-8211 – uk Carfax [370]
EUROPEAN JOURNAL OF EDUCATION *see* PAEDAGOGICA EUROPAEA
EUROPEAN JOURNAL OF ENDOCRINOLOGY *see* ACTA ENDOCRINOLOGICA
EUROPEAN JOURNAL OF ENGINEERING EDUCATION – 1976- 18v – 9 – £246.50 – 0304-3797 – uk Carfax [370]
EUROPEAN JOURNAL OF ENGINEERING EDUCATION – v1-8 1975-83 – 1,5,6,13 – sz Elsevier [620]
EUROPEAN JOURNAL OF HUMAN GENETICS – v1-. 1993- – us UMI [573]
EUROPEAN JOURNAL OF IMMUNOLOGY : ASSOCIATED WITH THE EUROPEAN FEDERATION OF IMMUNOLOGICAL SOCIETIES – v1-26. 1971-96 – 1,5,6,13 – us V.C.H. [576]
EUROPEAN JOURNAL OF INTENSIVE CARE MEDICINE – v. 1-2. 1974-76 – 1,5,9 – 74.00 – us UMI [073]
EUROPEAN JOURNAL OF NUCLEAR MEDICINE – v.1-6, 1976-81. ISSN: 0340-6997 – 1,5,6,9,13 – 129.00v – us UMI [600]
EUROPEAN JOURNAL OF OBSTETRICS, GYNECOLOGY AND REPRODUCTIVE BIOLOGY – v1-18. 1971-84 – 1,5,6,13 – sz Elsevier [618]
EUROPEAN JOURNAL OF OPERATIONAL RESEARCH – v1-18. 1977-84 – 1,5,6,13 – sz Elsevier [000]
EUROPEAN JOURNAL OF ORTHODONTICS – (1982-. 1,5,6,9) – v1-. 1979- – 1 – us UMI [073]
EUROPEAN JOURNAL OF PEDIATRICS – v. 65-134. 1947-80 – 1,5,9 – 12,075.00 – us UMI [618]
EUROPEAN JOURNAL OF PEDIATRICS *see* ZEITSCHRIFT FUER KINDERHEILKUNDE
EUROPEAN JOURNAL OF PHARMACEUTICAL SCIENCES *see* ACTA PHARMACEUTICA NORDICA
EUROPEAN JOURNAL OF PHARMACOLOGY – v. 1-85. 1967-82 – 1,5,6 – sz Elsevier [073]
EUROPEAN JOURNAL OF PHYSICS – v1-. 1980- – 1,5,6,9 – £168.00 – uk I.O.P. [530]
EUROPEAN JOURNAL OF POLITICAL RESEARCH – v. 1-10. 1973-82 – 1,5,6 – sz Elsevier [073]

EUROPEAN JOURNAL OF SEXUALLY TRANSMITTED DISEASES – v1-. 1982- – 1,5,6,9 – us UMI [616]

EUROPEAN JOURNAL OF SOCIAL PSYCHOLOGY – v. 1- 1971- – 1,5,6,9 – us UMI [300]

EUROPEAN JOURNAL OF SPECTROSCOPY – (1982-. 1,5,6,9) – 1975- – 1 – us UMI [073]

EUROPEAN JOURNAL OF SURGERY *see* ACTA CHIRURGICA SCANDINAVICA

EUROPEAN JOURNAL OF TEACHER EDUCATION – 1978- 16v – 9 – £214.50 – 0261-9768 – uk Carfax [370]

EUROPEAN JUDAISM – v1- 1966- – v1- 1; v11- 5,6,9 – us UMI [270]

EUROPEAN LABOUR BULLETIN – 1959-1962 – 9 – us Primary [073]

EUROPEAN MANAGEMENT JOURNAL – 1,5,69 – us UMI [650]

[EUROPEAN MOVEMENT PAMPHLET COLLECTION] – 1949-1978 – 1 – CSUXANP2012-B – us Hoover Inst Photo [304]

EUROPEAN MUSICAL INSTRUMENTS ON PRINTS AND DRAWINGS / ed by Hul, Dick van den – (Book includes a printed guide) – 44mf – 9 – ne IDC [780]

EUROPEAN MUSICAL INSTRUMENTS ON PRINTS AND DRAWINGS / ed by Hul, Dick van den – (Includes printed guide) – 44mf – 9 – P-781/1 – ne IDC [780]

EUROPEAN NEUROLOGY – v13-. 1975- – 1,5,9 – us UMI [073]

THE EUROPEAN NEWS – no. 86-93, 96-117. Paris. juin 1870-71 – 1 – fr A.C.R.P.P. [073]

EUROPEAN OFFICIAL STATISTICAL SERIALS, 1841-1984 – (Individual titles also listed and may be purchased separately) – 7,214mf – 9 – £33,075.00 coll – uk Chadwyck [940]

EUROPEAN OFFICIAL STATISTICAL SERIALS, 1841-1984 *see*
- AUSTRIA
- BELGIUM
- BULGARIA
- BULGARIA. STATISTICHESKI GODISHNIK NA BULGARSKOTO TSARSTVO
- CZECHOSLOVAKIA
- DENMARK
- FINLAND
- FRANCE
- GERMANY (FORMERLY DEMOCRATIC REPUBLIK)
- GERMANY (FORMERLY FEDERAL REPUBLIC)
- GERMANY (FORMERLY FEDERAL REPUBLIK)
- GREECE
- HUNGARY
- ITALY
- NETHERLANDS
- NORWAY
- POLAND
- PORTUGAL. ANUARIO ESTATISTICO DE PORTUGAL
- ROMANIA
- RUSSIA
- SPAIN
- SWEDEN
- SWITZERLAND
- USSR
- YUGOSLAVIA

European Parliament *see* COMMITTEE REPORTS OF THE EUROPEAN PARLIAMENT

European Parliament. Secretariat. Luxembourg *see* EP NEWS

European Parliamentary Assembly *see* L'ACTIVITEA1 DE L'ASSEMBLEA1E PARLEMENTAIRE EUROPEA1ENE

EUROPEAN PLANNING STUDIES – 1992- 1v – 9 – £139.00 – 0965-4313 – uk Carfax [350]

EUROPEAN PLASTICS NEWS – 1929- 1; 1976- 5,6,9 – us UMI [660]

EUROPEAN POLYMER JOURNAL – v1- 1965- – 5,6,9 – us UMI [073]

EUROPEAN PRESS – Bremen, 1921 – 1r – 1 – Inquire at Mikrofilmarchiv for details – gw Misc Inst [072]

EUROPEAN PRESSE – Bremen, Germany. 1921 – 1r – 1 – gw Mikrofilm [072]

EUROPEAN REVIEW OF HISTORY = REVUE EUROPEENNE D'HISTOIRE – 1995, Vol 2 – £68.00 – uk Carfax [940]

THE EUROPEAN ROMANTIC TRADITION : THE SIR WALTER SCOTT MSS – (Pt 1: Literary and Historical MSS. from the National Library of Scotland. Pt 2: The Scott Correspondence, Section A from the National Library of Scotland. Pt 3: The Scott Correspondence, Section B from the National Library of Scotland) – 1 – us Primary [430]

European Society of Parenteral and Enteral Nutrition *see* CLINICAL NUTRITION

EUROPEAN SURGICAL RESEARCH – v7-. 1975- – 1,5,9 – us UMI [073]

THE EUROPEAN TOUR / Allen, Grant – New York: Dodd, Mead, 1899. 05031. (Pre-1900 Canadiana) – 9 – cn C.I.H.M. [910]

EUROPEAN TWENTIETH CENTURY ART : SUBJECT COLLECTIONS – (Individual titles not listed separately) – 187 catalogues on 206mf – 9 – £1,300.00 – uk Chadwyck [700]

EUROPEAN UROLOGY – v1-. 1975- – 1,5,9 – us UMI [073]

EUROPEAN WOMEN'S PERIODICALS – (Unit 1: Austrian and Belgian Journals; Unit 2: French Periodicals; Unit 3: German Periodicals; Unit 4: Dutch Periodicals) – IISG and IIAV, Amsterdam – 1 – us Primary [305]

EUROPE-ASIA STUDIES – 1992- 45v. Formerly: Soviet Studies – 9 – £163.00 – 0966-8136 – uk Carfax [910]

L'EUROPEEN – Hebdomadaire economique, artistique et litteraire. Fond. F.-H. Turot. no. 1-239. Paris. avr 1929-33. mq no. 104-132, 134-137, 139, 141-158, 164, 168, 173, 185, 190, 195, 211 – 1 – fr A.C.R.P.P. [073]

L'EUROPEEN – Journal des sciences morales et economiques. suite de: Journal des sciences morales et politiques. no. 1-4. 3-24 dec 1831. Paris. dec 1831-oct 1832, oct 1835-oct 1838. devenu: Revue nationale voir a ce titre – 1 – fr A.C.R.P.P. [073]

EUROPEO – 1980-1995 – 2 times per yr – 6 – F2,250 – sz Infoprint [072]

EUROPEO – 1980-1995 – 2r per y – 5,6 – Sfr601.00 – sz Infoprint [072]

EUROPLASTICS MONTHLY – v. 1-31. 1929-58 – 1,5,6 – us Princeton Micro [660]

EURYDICE AHOY: A SHORT ACCOUNT OF A YACHT CRUISE ON LAKE CHAMPLAIN IN THE SUMMER OF 1880 – Montreal: J. Lovell, 1881. 05492. (Pre-1900 Canadiana) – 9 – cn C.I.H.M. [910]

EUSEBIA COSME PAPERS : FROM THE HOLDINGS OF THE SCHOMBURG CENTER FOR RESEARCH IN BLACK CULTURE, MANUSCRIPTS, ARCHIVES AND RARE BOOKS DIVISION: THE NEW YORK PUBLIC LIBRARY, ASTOR, LENOX AND TILDEN FOUNDATIONS – (Guide which covers all coll under "Literature and the Arts" sold separately for $20.00 D3305.G6) – 5r – 1 – $425.00 – D3305P21 – Dist. us Scholarly Res – us L of C Photodup [790]

EUSEBIO (NOVELA). TOMO 1 / Montengon, Pedro – 1786 – 1mf – 9 – Pta1,000.00 – 84-7848-357-8 – sp Pentalfa [830]

EUSEBIO (NOVELA). TOMO 2 / Montengon, Pedro – 1786 – 1mf – 9 – Pta1,000.00 – 84-7848-358-6 – sp Pentalfa [830]

EUSEBIO (NOVELA). TOMO 3 / Montengon, Pedro – 1787 – 1mf – 9 – Pta1,000.00 – 84-7848-359-4 – sp Pentalfa [830]

EUSEBIO (NOVELA). TOMO 4 / Montengon, Pedro – 1788 – 1mf – 9 – Pta1,000.00 – 84-7848-360-8 – sp Pentalfa [830]

Eusebius *see* HISTORY OF THE CHURCH FROM OUR LORD'S INCARNATION

EUSEBIUS KIRCHENGESCHICHTE BUCH 6 UND 7 AUS DEM ARMENISCHEN UEBERSETZT (T.U.U. 2-22/3) / Preuschen, Erwin – Leipzig, 1902 – 2mf – 9 – ne Slangenburg [240]

EUSEBIUS SCHRIFT PERI TOON TOPIKOON ONOMATOON (T.U.U. 2-23/2B) / Klostermann, Erich – Leipzig, 1902 – 1mf – 9 – ne Slangenburg [240]

Eustacchi, B *see*
- SANCTO SEVERINATIS MEDICA AC PHILOSOPHI OPUSCULA ANATOMICA
- TABULAE ANATOMICAE

EUSTATHIUS : ANCIENNE VERSION LATINE DES NEUF HOMELIES SUR L'HEXAEMERON DE BASILE DE CESAREE (T.U.U. 5-66) / Mendieta, E A & Rudberg, SY – Berlin, 1958 – 4mf – 9 – ne Slangenburg [240]

EUSTATHIUS VON SEBASTE UND DIE CHRONOLOGIE DER BASILIUS-BRIEFE : EINE PATRISTISCHE STUDIE / Loofs, Friedrich – Halle a.S.: M. Niemeyer, 1898 – 1mf – us A.T.L.A. [240]

EUSTIS NEWS – Eustis, NE. -w. Jun. 1904- – 1 – us NE Hist [071]

EUTANVILLE BAPTIST CHURCH. ORANGEBURG COUNTY. SOUTH CAROLINA : CHURCH RECORDS – 1859-1972. (Incomplete) – 1 – 5.00 – us Baptist [240]

Eutawville. South Carolina. Epiphany Episcopal Church *see* REGISTERS

EUTERPE. EINE MUSIK-ZEITSCHRIFT FUR LEHRER, KANTOREN, ORGANISTEN UND FREUNDE DER TONKUNST UBERHAUPT – v. 1-43. 1841-84 – 1 – 67.00 – us L of C Photodup [780]

EUTHANALIA : STUDIES OF EUTHALIUS, CODEX H OF THE PAULINE EPISTLES AND THE ARMENION VERSION / Robinson, J A – 1895 – 3mf – 9 – ne Slangenburg [240]

EUTHANASIA REVIEW – v1-. 1986- – 1,5,6,9 – us UMI [610]

EUTHANASY, OR, HAPPY TALK TOWARDS THE END OF LIFE / Mountford, William – 2nd ed. London: Edward T. Whitfield, 1850 – 2mf – 9 – 0-8370-5979-8 – 1985-3979 – us A.T.L.A. [230]

Euting, Julius *see* NABATAEISCHE INSCHRIFTEN AUS ARABIEN

EUTROPI BREVIARIUM AB URBE CONDITA CUM VERSIONIBUS GRAECIS ET PAULI LANDOLFIQUE ADDITAMENTIS (MGH 1: 2. BD) / ed by Droysen, H – 1879 – Dfl46.00 – ne Slangenburg [240]

EUTROPIA : OR, HOW TO FIND A WAY OUT OF DARKNESS AND DOUBT INTO LIGHT AND CERTAINTY / Devine, Pius – London: Burns and Oates, 1880 – 2mf – 9 – 0-8370-7056-2 – 1986-1056 – us A.T.L.A. [230]

Euvrard, Paul *see* VERRERIES ET VERRIERS DANS LE DEPARTEMENT DE LA HAUTE-MARNE 1500 A 1830

EV. LUTH. KIRK. *see* LUTHERANEREN

[EVA BRAUN PAMPHLET COLLECTION] – 1978-1980 – 1 – CSUXANR9491-B – us Hoover Inst Photo [943]

EVA PERON : UNA APROXIMACION PSICOANALITICA / Deutsch, Mario et al – Montevideo, Uruguay: Imago, [1983] – 1 – CSUXAJB7817-B – us Hoover Inst Photo [320]

EVA PERON / Borroni, Otelo & Vacca, Roberto – Buenos Aires: Centro Editor de America Latina, 1970 – 1 – CSUXAJA8004-B – us Hoover Inst Photo [320]

EVA PERON – Buenos Aires: Editorial del Noroeste: Distribuidor en Capital, Troisi v Vaccaro, [1974] – 1 – CSUXAJB8042-B – us Hoover Inst Photo [320]

EVA PERON / Demitropulos, Libertad – Buenos Aires: Centro Editor de America Latina, c1984 – 1 – CSUXADJ7669-B – us Hoover Inst Photo [320]

EVA PERON / Fraser, Nicholas & Navarro, Marysa – London: A. Deutsch, 1980 – 1 – CSUXADH8442-B – us Hoover Inst Photo [320]

EVA PERON : LOS QUE SUPIERON DE SU BONDAD Y SU TERNURA – [Buenos Aires]: Servicio Internacional Publicaciones Argentinas, [1952?] – 1 – CSUXAHZ2200-B – us Hoover Inst Photo [320]

EVA PERON / Reiner, Silvain – Paris: Flammarion, [1960] – 1 – CSUXADP1500-B – us Hoover Inst Photo [320]

EVA PERON : DER ROMAN EINER UNGEWOEHNLICHEN FRAU / Wolter, Udo – Stuttgart: Wappen Verlag, [1953?] – 1 – CSUXAHZ7044-B – us Hoover Inst Photo [972]

EVA PERON / S.I.P.A., International Service Argentine Publications – [Buenos Aires]: S.I.P.A., [1952?] – 1 – CSUXAGN1108-B – us Hoover Inst Photo [320]

EVA PERON : T EMOIGNAGES DE SA BONT E ET DE SA TENDRESSE – [Buenos Aires?: S.I.P.A. Service international argentin publications, 1952?] – 1 – CSUXAHZ2196-B – us Hoover Inst Photo [320]

EVA PERON : VIVA O MUERTA / Crespo, Alfonso – Lima: Librerias-Editorial Studium, 1978 – 1 – CSUXADQ0967-B – us Hoover Inst Photo [320]

EVA PERON EN EL BRONCE – [Buenos Aires]: Presidencia de la Nacion, Subsecretaria de Informaciones, [1952] – 1 – CSUXADQ5195-B – us Hoover Inst Photo [320]

EVA PERON EN LA PLEGARIA DE SU PUEBLO – Buenos Aires: Presidencia de la Nacion, Subsecretaria de Informaciones, 1952 – 1 – CSUXAJA7525-B – us Hoover Inst Photo [320]

EVA PERON, INMORTAL / Servicio Internacional Radiofonico Argentino – [Argentina?]:[Servicio Internacional Publicaciones Argentinas, 1953?] – 1 – CSUXAHZ5817-B – us Hoover Inst Photo [320]

EVA PERON Y SU OBRA SOCIAL : 2A. EXPOSICION, SAL ON "17 DE OCTUBRE" – [Buenos Aires]: Presidencia de la Nacion, Subsecretaria de Informaciones, [1951 or 1952] – 1 – CSUXAGN1532-B – us Hoover Inst Photo [320]

EVA Y PERON – Buenos Aires: [Editorial Publicencia], 1971 – 1 – CSUXAHZ5002-B – us Hoover Inst Photo [320]

EVAEQUES ET DIOCESES. DEUXI EME SERIE / Houtin, Albert – (Includes bibliographical references and index) – Paris: A Houtin, 1909 – 1mf – 9 – 0-8370-8829-1 – 1986-2829 – us A.T.L.A. [240]

EVAGATORIUM IN TERRAE SANCTAE, ARABIAE ET EGYPTI PEREGRINATIONEM / Fabri, Fratris Felicis; ed by Hassler, C D – Stuttgardiae. v1-3. 1843-1849 – 29mf – 8 – Dfl102.00 – ne Slangenburg [240]

EVAGRIUS PONTICUS / ed by Frankenberg, W – 1912 – 13mf – 8 – ne Slangenburg [240]

EVALUACION DEL PLAN. DE GUATEMALA, 1965-1969 / Guatemala. Inter-American Economic and Social Council – Washington. 1966 – 9 – ne IDC [338]

EVALUACION DEL PLAN DE LA NACION 1963-1966 DE VENEZUELA / Venezuela. Inter-American Economic and Social Council – Washington. 1963 – 9 – ne IDC [338]

EVALUACION DEL PLAN NAC. DE INV. PUB. 1963-1964 DE HONDURAS / Honduras. Inter-American Economic and Social Council – Washington. 1963. BD-234 1 – 9 – ne IDC [338]

EVALUACION DEL PLAN NACIONAL. DE NICARAGUA, 1965-1969 / Nicaragua. Inter-American Economic and Social Council – Washington. 1966. BD-238 1 – 9 – ne IDC [338]

EVALUACION DEL PROGRAMA GENERAL DE DESARROLLO ECONOMICO Y SOCIAL DE COLOMBIA / Colombia – Washington, Alliance for Progress. 1962 – 9 – ne IDC [338]

EVALUACION DEL PROGRAMA NAC. DE DES. EC. Y SOCIAL DE CHILE / Chile. Inter-American Economic and Social Council – Washington. 1962. BD-235 1 – 9 – ne IDC [330]

EVALUATING AND RESHAPING A MODEL OF CHURCH RENEWAL AT THE FIRST BAPTIST CHURCH OF LONGWOOD, FLORIDA / Hammock, James W – 1981 – 1 – 6.96 – us Baptist [240]

EVALUATING THE BOATER EXPERIENCE : THE INTERRELATIONSHIP OF RECREATIONAL USE, USER CONTACTS, EXPERIENTIAL IMPACTS, SATISFACTION AND DISPLACEMENT / Drogin, E B – 1991 – 2mf – 9 – $8.00 – us Microform Publ [790]

EVALUATION AND MAPPING OF TROPICAL AFRICAN RANGELANDS = INVENTAIRE ET CARTOGRAPHIE DES PATURAGES TROPICAUX AFRICAINS : PROCEEDINGS OF THE ILCA CONFERENCE AND WORKSHOP, BAMAKO, MALI, 3-8 MARCH 1975 – 1981 – xvi/399p – 9 – $15.00 – 92-9053-131-2 – et ILRI [574]

EVALUATION AND PROGRAM PLANNING. AN INTERNATIONAL JOURNAL – v1- 1978- – 5,6,9 – us UMI [300]

EVALUATION AND THE HEALTH PROFESSIONS – (1983-. 1,5,6,9) – v1-. 1978- – 1 – us UMI [073]

EVALUATION DES PRODUCTIVITES DES RACES BOVINES MAURE ET PEUL A LA STATION DU SAHEL, NIONO, MALI / CIPEA – 1978 – 9 – $7.00 – 92-9053-190-8 – et ILRI [636]

EVALUATION FOR ACREAGE, LIVESTOCK AND CROPS, 1870 / Illinois. Census – Macoupin-Woodford Counties. V123-0014 – 1 – us A.G.L.L. [310]

EVALUATION IN EDUCATION. INTERNATIONAL PROGRESS *see* INTERNATIONAL JOURNAL OF EDUCATIONAL RESEARCH

EVALUATION IN LATIN AMERICA AND THE CARIBBEAN : SELECTED EXPERIENCES – 1986 – 181p – 9 – 92-3-102327-6 – fr UNESCO [350]

EVALUATION MANUAL / Grabe, Sven – 1983 – 84p – 9 – 92-3-102099-4 – fr UNESCO [999]

AN EVALUATION OF A HOME-BASED EXERCISE PROGRAM INVOLVING NON-EXERTIONAL HYPOXEMIC AND EXERTIONAL HYPOXEMIC CHRONIC OBSTRUCTIVE PULMONARY DISEASED PATIENTS / Kotarski, Mark & Berger, Richard A – 1991 – 1mf – 9 – $4.00 – us Microform Publ [612]

EVALUATION OF ACREAGE, 1870 / Illinois. Census – Adams-MaCoupin Counties. V123-0013 – 1 – us A.G.L.L. [310]

EVALUATION OF CERTAIN FOOD ADDITIVES : 19TH REPORT OF THE JOINT FAO/WHO EXPERT COMMITTEE ON FOOD ADDITIVES, GENEVA, 1975 – 1975 – 23p – it F.A.O. [640]

EVALUATION OF CERTAIN FOOD ADDITIVES : 20TH REPORT OF THE JOINT FAO/WHO EXPERT COMMITTEE ON FOOD ADDITIVES, ROME, 1976 – 1976 – 32p – it F.A.O. [640]

EVALUATION OF COURT-ANNEXED ARBITRATION IN THREE FEDERAL DISTRICT COURTS / Lind, E Allan & Shapard, John E – Washington: FJC, Mar 1981 – 2mf – 9 – $3.00 – LLMC 95-800 – us L.L.M.C. [340]

EVALUATION OF COURT-ANNEXED ARBITRATION IN THREE FEDERAL DISTRICT COURTS : SEPTEMBER 1983 REVISION / Lind, E Allan & Shapard, John E – Washington: FJC, 1983 – 2mf – 9 – $3.00 – LLMC 95-313 – us L.L.M.C. [340]

EVALUATION OF METABOTRIM(TM) SUPPLEMENTATION OF BODY COMPOSITION, STRENGTH AND VO2MAX IN TRAINING FEMALE ATHLETES / Murray, Teena – University of North Carolina at Greensboro, 1996 – 1mf – 9 – PH 1502 – us Microform Publ [612]

AN EVALUATION OF NATURE CENTER MANAGERS'PERCEPTIONS OF THEIR JOB RESPONSIBILITIES WITH REGARD TO EDUCATIONAL BACKGROUND, SERVICES/RESOURCES OFFERED, NUMBER OF YEARS AS ADMINISTRATOR, AND BUDGET OF THE NATURE CENTER / Wilson, D B – 1991 – 2mf – 9 – $8.00 – us Microform Publ [150]

EVALUATION OF NUTRITION INTERVENTIONS : AN ANNOTATED BIBLIOGRAPHY AND REVIEW OF METHODOLOGIES AND RESULTS – 2nd ed 1982 – 198p – it F.A.O. [640]

EVALUATION OF SHUGOR, DUBASI AND WATISH SUBTYPES OF SUDAN DESERT SHEEP AT THE EL-HUDA NATIONAL SHEEP RESEARCH STATION, GEZIRA PROVINCE, SUDAN = EVALUATION DES SOUSESPECES SHUGOR, DUBASI ET WATISH DU MOUTON SUDAN DESERT A LA STATION NATIONALE DE RECHERCHE OVINE DE EL-HUDA, PROVINCE DE GEZIREH (SOUDAN) / Suleiman, A H et al – 1990 – 9 – $10.00 – 92-9053-223-8 – et ILRI [630]

EVALUATION OF STRETCH LOAD CAPACITY AND UTILIZATION OF STORED ELASTIC ENERGY IN LEG EXTENSOR MUSCLES DURING VERTICAL JUMPS / He, Qin – 1989 – 69p 1mf – 9 – $4.00 – us Microform Publ [612]

AN EVALUATION OF STUDENT ATTITUDES, INTENTIONS, AND PERSONAL HEALTH BEHAVIORS AS A RESULT OF HAVING COMPLETED HEALTH EDUCATION 214 AT THE OHIO STATE UNIVERSITY DURING THE SPRING QUARTER OF 1990 / Michael, J F – 1991 – 2mf – 9 – $8.00 – us Microform Publ [613]

EVALUATION OF THE ACHIEVEMENTS OF THE 2ND / Syria. Syrian Documentation Papers – five-year plan, 1966-1970: economic and social development. Analytical study and figures. 1971. BNE-9740 1 – 9 – ne IDC [338]

AN EVALUATION OF THE CHARACTERISTICS OF SUCCESSFUL STUDENTS AT THE BRINKMAN-FROEMMING UMPIRE SCHOOL / Robertson, Stuart A – 1993 – 1mf – $4.00 – us Microform Publ [370]

AN EVALUATION OF THE EFFECTIVENESS OF THE 1981 HEALTH WORKSHOPS FOR LANE COUNTY CETA EMPLOYEES / Paddon, Kathleen S – 1981 – 2mf – 9 – $8.00 – us Microform Publ [610]

AN EVALUATION OF THE EFFECTS OF A SMOKING PREVENTION PROGRAM ON MIDDLE SCHOOL STUDENTS' KNOWLEDGE AND ATTITUDES CONCERNING CIGARETTE SMOKING / Tennent, Sylvia R & Baker, Judith A – 1991 – 1mf – 9 – $4.00 – us Microform Publ [613]

EVALUATION OF THE GENERAL ECONOMIC AND SOCIAL DEVELOPMENT PROGRAM OF COLOMBIA / Colombia. Inter-American Economic and Social Council – Washington. 1962. BD-232 1 – 9 – ne IDC [338]

EVALUATION OF THE NATIONAL ECONOMIC AND SOCIAL DEVELOPMENT PLAN OF NICARAGUA, 1965-1969 / Nicaragua – Washington, Alliance for Progress. 1966 – 9 – ne IDC [338]

AN EVALUATION OF THE NATIONAL LITERACY PROGRAMME / Botswana. University of Botswana. Institute of Adult Education – Gaborone, 1987 – 3mf – 9 – DE-422/1 – ne IDC [370]

AN EVALUATION OF THE PHYSICAL FITNESS EFFECTS OF A HIGH SCHOOL AEROBIC DANCE CURRICULUM / Baldwin, Susan & Pechar, Gary S – 1991 – 1mf – 9 – $4.00 – us Microform Publ [612]

AN EVALUATION OF THE PROBABLE IMPACT OF SELECTED PROPOSALS FOR IMPOSING MANDATORY MINIMUM SENTENCES IN THE FEDERAL COURTS / Eaglin, James B – Washington: FJC, July 1977 – 1mf – 9 – $1.50 – LLMC 95-814 – us L.L.M.C. [340]

EVALUATION OF THE PRODUCTIVITIES OF DJALLONKE SHEEP AND N'DAMA CATTLE AT THE CENTRE DE RECHERCHES ZOOTECHNIQUES, KOLDA, SENEGAL = EVALUATION DES PRODUCTIVITES DES OVINS DJALLONKE ET DES TAURINS N'DAMA AU CENTRE DE RECHERCHES ZOOTECHNIQUES DE KOLDA, SENEGAL / Fall, A et al – 1982 – 9 – $10.00 – 92-9053-108-8 – et ILRI [636]

EVALUATION OF THE PRODUCTIVITIES OF MAURE AND PEUL CATTLE BREEDS AT THE SAHELIAN STATION, NIONO, MALI / ILCAInstitut d'Economie Rurale du Mali – 1978 – 9 – $7.00 – 92-9053-124-X – et ILRI [636]

EVALUATION OF THE PRODUCTIVITY OF CROSSBRED DAIRY CATTLE ON SMALLHOLDER AND GOVERNMENT FARMS IN THE REPUBLIC OF MALAWI / Agyemang, K & Nkhonjera, LP – 1986 – 9 – $8.00 – 92-9053-116-9 – et ILRI [636]

EVALUATION OF THE SET-POINT AND PROPORTIONAL CONTROL MODELS OF HUMAN THERMOREGULATION DURING EXERCISE / Ward, Jeffrey J & Quigley, Brian – 1990 – 3mf – 9 – $12.00 – us Microform Publ [612]

EVALUATION OF THE WASHINGTON STATE UNIVERSITY INTRAMURAL SPORTS PROGRAM / Rinaldi, Nancy E – 1989 – 97p 1mf – 9 – $4.00 – us Microform Publ [370]

EVALUATION QUARTERLY – v1-3. 1977-79 – 1 – us UMI [073]

EVALUATION REPORT : AREA VOCATIONAL CENTERS PROJECT. MID-TERM EVALUATION (1980-1982) / Thailand. National Education Commission. Educational Planning Division – Bangkok, 1983 – 2mf – 9 – DE-602/1 – ne IDC [370]

EVALUATION REPORT : COMMUNITY SCHOOL PROJECT. MID-TERM EVALUATION (1980-1982) / Thailand. National Education Commission. Educational Planning Division – Bangkok, 1983 – 3mf – 9 – DE-596/1 – ne IDC [370]

EVALUATION RESEARCH AND SOCIAL CHANGE / Weilenmann, Alexander – 1980 – 104p – 9 – 92-3-101699-7 – fr UNESCO [303]

EVALUATION REVIEW – (1983-. 1,5,6,9) – v4-. 1980- – 1 – us UMI [073]

AN EVALUATIVE STUDY OF PRIMARY SCHOOL EFFICIENCY IN THAILAND : THE DETERMINANT OF PRIMARY SCHOOL EFFICIENCY / Thailand. National Education Commission – Bangkok, 1982 – 6mf – 9 – DE-595/1 – ne IDC [370]

EVANGEELIUMI KRISTLASTE VABAKOGUDUSE AJALOOLINE ULEVAADE, 1905-1930 = HISTORICAL SURVEY OF THE EVANGELICAL CHRISTIAN FREE CHURCH / Laks, Johannes – Tallinn: Evangelical Christian Free Church Publ. House, 1930. Publ. No. 6295 a. One of four items on a reel. 162p – 1 – us Baptist [240]

EVANGEL – San Francisco. Calif. 1867-Jun 1869 – 1 – 22.33 – us Baptist [240]

THE EVANGEL – v7-20. 1914-26 (complete) – 1r – 1 – ATLA S0701D – us A.T.L.A. [073]

THE EVANGEL *see* THE BALTIMORE BAPTIST

EVANGELARIUM – 24p + 5 color mf – DM690.00 – 3-89219-005-4 – gw Lengenfelder [220]

EVANGELIA DE COMMUNI SANCTORUM : EXPLICATIONIBUS AD MENTEM SANCTORUM PATRUM ALIORUMQUE INTERPRETUM DILUCIDATA, UT NON MINUS POPULI INSTRUCTIONI QUAM SACERDOTUM DEVOTIONI SERVIANT: ADJUNCTIS NONNULLIS EX EVANGELIIS FERIALIBUS QUADRAGESIMAE / Schouppe, Francois Xavier – Bruxellis: H Goemaere, 1869 – 2mf – 9 – 0-8370-7505-X – 1986-1505 – us A.T.L.A. [240]

EVANGELIA (SIECLE 14) – Avila – 1r – 5,6 – sp Cultura [240]

EVANGELIARIUM EPTERNACENSE (UNIVERSITAETSBIBLIOTHEK AUGSBURG, COD.I.2.4°2) – (Includes: Evangelistarium (Erzbischoefliches Priesterseminar Sankt Peter, Cod.ms.25)) – 1988 – 45p + 5 color mf – DM620.00 – 3-89219-009-7 – gw Lengenfelder [090]

THE EVANGELICAL – v1-35. 14 Nov 1887-1922 (complete) – 35r – 1 – ATLA S0080 – us A.T.L.A. [073]

Evangelical Alliance *see* PROCEEDINGS OF THE GENEVA CONFERENCE..

Evangelical Alliance for the U.S. *see* DOCUMENTS

Evangelical and Reformed Church, Hoisington, KS *see* CHURCH BOOK

EVANGELICAL BEGINNINGS IN THE ARIZONA TERRITORY / Bell, Earl S – 70p – 1 – 5.00 – us Baptist [240]

EVANGELICAL FRIEND – v16-26. 1982-93 – Inquire – 1 – ATLA S0877 – us A.T.L.A. [073]

EVANGELICAL INQUIRER – Virginia. Oct 1826-Sep 1827 – 1 – 13.65 – us Baptist [240]

EVANGELICAL INTELLIGENCER, (1805-1809) – Philadelphia, Pa. – 1 reel – 1 – $50.00 – us Presbyterian [240]

THE EVANGELICAL INVASION OF BRAZIL : OR, A HALF CENTURY OF EVANGELICAL MISSIONS IN THE LAND OF THE SOUTHERN CROSS / Gammon, Samuel R – (Includes appendixes) – Richmond, VA: Presbyterian Committee of Publ, c1910 – 1mf – 9 – 0-8370-6050-8 – 1986-0050 – us A.T.L.A. [240]

Evangelical Lutheran Church *see* LUTHERAN HERALD

EVANGELICAL LUTHERAN CHURCH IN AMERICA : YEARBOOK – 1988-91 (complete) – Inquire – 1 – ATLA S0880 – us A.T.L.A. [030]

EVANGELICAL LUTHERAN CHURCH IN AMERICA NORTHEASTERN PENNSYLVANIA SYNOD : MINUTES – 1988-92 (complete) – Inquire – 1 – ATLA S0885 – us A.T.L.A. [240]

Evangelical Lutheran Church in the United States of America. General Synod. Liturgy and ritual *see*
- BOOK OF WORSHIP
- THE LITURGY OF THE EVANGELICAL LUTHERAN CHURCH

EVANGELICAL LUTHERAN CHURCH OF FINLAND : NEWS / Evangelical Lutheran Church of Finland – 1968-91 (complete) – Inquire – 1 – ATLA S0636 – us A.T.L.A. [073]

Evangelical Lutheran Church of Finland *see* EVANGELICAL LUTHERAN CHURCH OF FINLAND

EVANGELICAL LUTHERAN INTELLIGENCER – v1-5. 1826-31 (complete) – 1r – 1 – ATLA S0524A – us A.T.L.A. [073]

EVANGELICAL LUTHERAN SYNOD IN THE CENTRAL STATES : MINUTES OF THE ANNUAL CONVENTION / Evangelical Lutheran Synod in the Central States – v87-95. 1955-61 (complete) – 1r – 1 – ATLA S0077 – us A.T.L.A. [240]

Evangelical Lutheran Synod in the Central States *see* EVANGELICAL LUTHERAN SYNOD IN THE CENTRAL STATES

EVANGELICAL LUTHERAN SYNOD OF MISSOURI, OHIO, AND OTHER STATES : PROCEEDINGS – 1847-1975 (complete) – Inquire – 1 – ATLA S0937 – us A.T.L.A. [240]

EVANGELICAL MAGAZINE AND MISSIONARY CHRONICLE – London. v. 27. 1819 – 1 – 20.02 – us Baptist [240]

THE EVANGELICAL MESSENGER – (Several titles) – v1-99. 1848-1946 (complete) – 76r – 1 – ATLA S0079 – us A.T.L.A. [073]

EVANGELICAL MISSIONS QUARTERLY – (1985-. 5,6,9) – v1-. 1964- – 1 – us UMI [240]

EVANGELICAL MISSIONS QUARTERLY – v1-8. Fall 1967-Summer 1972 (complete) – 1r – 1 – ATLA T0004 – us A.T.L.A. [073]

EVANGELICAL NEWSLETTER; A WORLD-WATCH OF TRENDS AND ANALYSIS FOR ALERT CHRISTIANS – v1-13,no.5. 1973-14 Feb 1986. Ceased publication – 1 – us UMI [073]

EVANGELICAL NONCONFORMISTS AND HIGHER CRITICISM IN THE NINETEENTH CENTURY / Glover, W B – London, 1954 – 6mf – 8 – ne Slangenburg [240]

THE EVANGELICAL QUARTERLY – London. v1-44. 1929-1972 – 264mf – 9 – ne IDC [240]

Evangelical Reformirten Schonfeld Gemeinde Kirchenbuch, Barton County, KS *see* RECORDS

EVANGELICAL REVIEW – v1-21. 1849-70 (complete) – 7r – 1 – ATLA S0017 – us A.T.L.A. [073]

THE EVANGELICAL REVIVAL IN THE EIGHTEENTH CENTURY / Overton, John H – New York: A.D.F. Randolph, [1886?] – 1mf – us A.T.L.A. [240]

Evangelical Theological Society *see*
- BULLETIN
- JOURNAL

EVANGELICAL THEOLOGICAL SOCIETY BULLETIN/JOURNAL – v1-11. 1958-81 (complete) – 5r – 1 – ATLA S0568 – us A.T.L.A. [073]

EVANGELICAL VISITOR – v22-65. 1908-52 (complete) – Inquire – 1 – ATLA 1994-S022 – us A.T.L.A. [073]

THE EVANGELICAN QUARTERLY – 1(1929)-44(1972) – 264mf – 9 – Dfl924.00 – ne Slangenburg [073]

LOS EVANGELICOS EN EL TIEMPO DE PERON : MEMORIAS DE UN PASTOR BAUTISTA SOBRE LA LIBERTAD RELIGIOSA EN LA ARGENTINA / Canclini, Santiago – [Buenos Aires]: Editorial Mundo Hispano, [1972] – 1 – CSUXADQ8007-B – us Hoover Inst Photo [320]

HET EVANGELIE IN SPANJE – Mar 1869-Nov 1937 (incomplete) – 2r – 1 – ATLA B0139 – us A.T.L.A. [073]

DIE EVANGELIEN DES MATTHAEUS UND DES MARCUS (T.U.U. 1-1/4A) / Gebhardt, Oscar von – Leipzig, 1883 – 3mf – 9 – ne Slangenburg [240]

DIE EVANGELIENCITATE JUSTIN DES MAERTYRERS IN IHREM WERT FUER DIE EVANGELIENKRITIK VON NEUEM UNTERSUCHT / Bousset, Wilhelm – Goettingen:Vandenhoeck und Ruprecht, 1891 – 1mf – 9 – 0-8370-2419-6 – 1985-0419 – us A.T.L.A. [220]

DAS EVANGELIENFRAGMENT VON FAJJUM (T.U.U. 1-5/4B) / Harnack, Adolf von – 1mf – 9 – ne Slangenburg [240]

EVANGELIKUS ELET; ORSZAGOS EVANGELIKUS HETILAP – (Lacking: v41 1976) – v32-54. 1967-89 – Inquire – 1 – ATLA S0165 – us A.T.L.A. [073]

L'EVANGELINE – (Cont by: Moncton 1 jun 1905-31 jan 1980 138r Can$60.00r) – Weymouth, Nova Scotia. 23 nov 1887-25 mai 1905 – 3r – 1 – Can$60.00r – cn Can Microfilming [072]

L'EVANGELINE : JOURNAL HEBDOMADAIRE – Moncton, New Brunswick. 23 nov 1887-27 sep 1982 – 158r – 1 – Can$60.00r – cn Can Microfilming [072]

L'EVANGELINE – Moncton, Canada. 1887-1910 – 8r – 1 – $520.00 – cn Library Assoc [971]

EVANGELINE / Longfellow, Henry Wadsworth – Limoges: Eugene Ardant, 1894. SEM105P531. – 2mf – 9 – Can$4.50 – cn Bibl Nat [810]

EL EVANGELIO COMENTADO CONFERENCIAS POR RADIO / Bayle, Constantino & Peiro, Francisco – Madrid: Razon y Fe, 1943 – 1 – sp Bibl Santa Ana [240]

EL EVANGELIO EXPLICADO, VOL 1, BARCELONA, 1930 / Goma y Tomas, Isidro – Madrid: Razon y Fe, 1930 – 1 – sp Bibl Santa Ana [240]

EVANGELION DA-MEPHARRESHE : THE CURETONIAN VERSION OF THE FOUR GOSPELS, WITH THE READINGS OF THE SINAE PALIMPSEST AND THE EARLY SYRIAC PATRISTIC EVIDENCE / ed by Burkitt, F Crawford – Cambridge. v1-2. 1904 – Dfl56.00 – ne Slangenburg [220]

EVANGELION DA-MEPHARRESHE – The Curetonian version of the four Gospels. 2 v. 1904 – 1 – us A.T.L.A. [240]

EVANGELISADOR : ORGAO BAPTISTA – Manaos, Amazonas. 18 Jan 1905-6 Out 1907 – 1,5,6 – bl Biblioteca [072]

L'EVANGELISATION DES INDIGENES PAR LES INDIGENES DANS LES ILES CENTRALES DU PACIFIQUE (DE TAHITI A LA NOUVELLE CALEDONIE) / Marchand, Leon – 1911 – 1 – us A.T.L.A. [240]

L'EVANGELISATION EN PAYS DE LANGUE FRANCAISE AU 19ME SIECLE : ET NOTAMMENT PENDANT LES 30 DERNIERES ANNEES / Olivet, A – Geneve: P. Richter, 1902 – 1mf – us A.T.L.A. [240]

EVANGELISATION OF PAGAN AFRICA : A HISTORY OF CHRISTIAN MISSIONS TO THE PAGAN TRIBES OF CENTRAL AFRICA / Du Plessis, Johannes – Cape Town: J C Juta, [1930] – 1 – us Res Libr [240]

THE EVANGELISATION OF PAGAN AFRICA: HISTORY OF CHRISTIAN MISSIONS TO THE PAGAN TRIBES OF CENTRAL AFRICA / Du Plessis, Johannes – Cape Town and Johannesburg: J.C. Juta, (1930). xii,408p. Fold. map – 1 – us U.W. Library [240]

THE EVANGELISATION OF THE WORLD : A MISSIONARY BAND: A RECORD OF CONSECRATION, AND AN APPEAL / ed by Broomhall, B – (Includes index) – [3rd ed]. London: Morgan & Scott, [1889?] – 1mf – 9 – 0-8370-7129-1 – 1986-1129 – us A.T.L.A. [240]

DER EVANGELISATIONS-BOTE – v1-29. 1918-39 (gaps) – Inquire – 1 – ATLA 1994-S034 – us A.T.L.A. [073]

EVANGELISATIONSBOTE AND GOSPEL TIDINGS – v29-31. 1939-41 (complete) – Inquire – 1 – ALTA 1994-S035 – us A.T.L.A. [073]

EVANGELISCH COMMENTAR – 1982-91 – Inquire – 1 – ATLA S0849 – us A.T.L.A. [073]

DAS EVANGELISCHE DEUTSCHLAND – Berlin, sep 22 1935-aug 20 1939 – 2r – 1 – uk British Libr Newspaper [072]

EVANGELISCHE INFORMATION – 1977-87.Continues: EPD Nachrichtenspiegel. 10 reels – 1 – us A.T.L.A. [073]

EVANGELISCHE JAHRESBRIEFE – 6(1937)-17(1953) – 46mf – 9 – Dfl161.00 – ne Slangenburg [073]

EVANGELISCHE KIRCHE IM RHEINLAND : KIRCHLICHES AMTSBLATT – (Lacking some pgs) – v112-130. 1971-89 – 7r – 1 – ATLA S0363 – us A.T.L.A. [073]

EVANGELISCHE KIRCHE IN DEUTSCHLAND : AMTSBLATT – (Inchudes index 1971-80) – v23-43. 1969-91 (complete) – Inquire – 1 – ATLA S0371 – us A.T.L.A. [240]

EVANGELISCHE KIRCHE IN DEUTSCHLAND. KIRCHENKANZLEI : BERICHTE – (lacks: 1953, 1959, 1962, 1964, 1969) – 1948-91 – Inquire – 1 – ATLA S0574 – us A.T.L.A. [240]

Evangelische Kirche in Deutschland. Kirchenkanzlei *see* BERICHT

EVANGELISCHE KIRCHE IN HESSEN UND NASSAU : AMTSBLATT – 1968-92 (complete) – Inquire – 1 – ATLA S0777 – us A.T.L.A. [073]

DIE EVANGELISCHE KIRCHE IN RUSSLAND / Dalton, Hermann – Leipzig: Duncker & Humblot, 1890 – 1mf – us A.T.L.A. [240]

EVANGELISCHE KIRCHE VON WESTFALEN : KIRCHLICHES AMTSBLATT – 1977-89 (complete) – 2r – 1 – ATLA S0801 – us A.T.L.A. [073]

EVANGELISCHE KIRCHE VON WESTFALEN : VERHANDLUNGEN – (Lacking some pgs) – 1946-78 – 8r – 1 – ATLA S0402 – us A.T.L.A. [073]

Evangelische Kirche von Westfalen *see* VERHANDLUNGEN

EVANGELISCHE KIRCHENZEITUNG – 1(1827)-63(1858) – 381mf – 9 – Dfl336.00 – ne Slangenburg [073]

EVANGELISCHE KIRCHENZEITUNG – Berlin. v1-63. 1827-1858 – 381mf – 9 – ne IDC [240]

Evangelische Landeskirche in Baden *see*
– GESETZES-UND VERORDUNGSBLATT
– VERHANDLUNGEN DER LANDESSYNODE DER EVANGELISCHEN LANDESKIRCHE IN BADEN

EVANGELISCHE LANDESKIRCHE IN GREIFWALD : AMTSBLATT – 1970-89 (complete) – 3r – 1 – ATLA S0680 – us A.T.L.A. [073]

EVANGELISCHE LANDESKIRCHE VON WURTEMBURG : BEIBLATT ZUM AMTSBLATT – nos 46-50 – 1r – 1 – ATLA S0796 – us A.T.L.A. [073]

DIE EVANGELISCHE LEHRE : AUF DEM GRUNDE DER HEILIGEN SCHRIFT UND NACH IHREM INNERN ZUSAMMENHANGE FUER FREUNDE DES GOETTLICHEN WORTES / Kritz, Wilhelm – 2. Aufl. Leipzig: J C Hinrichs, 1858 – 1mf – 9 – 0-8370-4418-9 – 1985-2418 – us A.T.L.A. [240]

DIE EVANGELISCHE MISSION : IHRE LAENDER, VOELKER UND ARBEITEN / Gundert, Hermann – (Includes bibliographical references and index) – 4. durchaus verm. Aufl. Calw: Verlag der Vereinsbuchh, 1903 – 2mf – 9 – 0-8370-6259-4 – 1986-0259 – us A.T.L.A. [240]

DER EVANGELISCHE OBER-KIRCHENRATH IN BERLIN UND DAS CONCIL – (Includes bibliographical references) – Freiburg i.B.: Herder, 1869 – 1mf – 9 – 0-8370-8890-9 – 1986-2890 – us A.T.L.A. [240]

EVANGELISCHE POLEMIK GEGEN DIE ROEMISCHE KIRCHE / Tschackert, Paul – (Includes index) – 2., verb Aufl. Gotha: Friedrich Andreas Perthes, 1888 – 2mf – 9 – 0-8370-8625-6 – 1986-2625 – us A.T.L.A. [240]

EVANGELISCHE SCHULORDNUNGEN / ed by Vormbaum, R – (Bd 1: Die Ev. Schulordnungen Des 16en Jhts. Guetersloh 1860 Dfl46.00. Bd 2: Die Ev. Schulordnungen Des 17en Jhts. Guetersloh 1863 Dfl49.00. Bd 3: Die Ev. Schulordnungen Des 18en Jhts. Guetersloh 1864 Dfl42.00) – ne Slangenburg [240]

EVANGELISCHE STROEMUNGEN IN DER RUSSISCHEN KIRCHE DER GEGENWART / Dalton, Hermann – Heilbronn: Henninger, 1881 – 1mf – us A.T.L.A. [240]

EVANGELISCHE THEOLOGIE – 25(1965)-34(1974) – 118mf – 9 – Dfl413.00 – ne Slangenburg [073]

EVANGELISCHE VERANTWORTUNG – 1958-93 (complete) – Inquire – 1 – ATLA S0639 – us A.T.L.A. [073]

EVANGELISCHE VOLKSSCHULE – Berlin, 1900-05 – 1 – Dist. gw Mikrofilm – gw Misc Inst [370]

EVANGELISCHE WOCHE – 1970-92 (complete) – 8r – 1 – ATLA S0444 – us A.T.L.A. [073]

EVANGELISCHE-LUTHERISCHE KIRCHE IN THUERINGEN : AMTSBLATT – 1963-88 (complete) – 6r – 1 – ATLA S0733 – us A.T.L.A. [073]

EVANGELISCHEN KIRCHE DER PFALZ : AMTSBLATT – (Title varies) – v1. 1921; v7-65. 1927-85 (complete) – 10r – 1 – ATLA S0799 – us A.T.L.A. [073]

DIE EVANGELISCHEN KIRCHENORDNUNGEN DES 16. JAHRHUNDERTS / ed by Richter, Ae.L – Weimar. Bd 1-2. 1846 – v1 22mf; v2 30mf – 8 – Dfl182.00 – ne Slangenburg [240]

DIE EVANGELISCHEN KIRCHENORDNUNGEN DES 16. JAHRHUNDERTS / ed by Sehling, Emil – (Band 1: Sachsen und Thueringen 1, 1902. 25mf. Dfl88.00; Band 2: Sachsen und Thueringen 2, 1904. 20mf. Dfl70.00; Band 3: Die Mark Brandenburg, 1909. 17mf. Dfl60.00; Band 4: Herzogthum Preussen, 1911. 19mf. Dfl67.00; Band 5: Livland-Estland, 1913. 19mf. Dfl67.00) – Thuebingen, 1902-13 – 8 – ne Slangenburg [240]

DIE EVANGELISCHEN LANDESKIRCHEN DEUTSCHLANDS IM NEUNZEHNTEN JAHRHUNDERT : BLICKE IN IHR INNERES LEBEN / Ecke, Gustav – Berlin: Reuther & Reichard, 1904. (Die theologische Schule Albrecht Ritschls und die evangelische Kirche der Gegenwart / von Gustav Ecke; 2. Bd.) – 2mf – us A.T.L.A. [240]

EVANGELISCHER ARBEITERBOTE – Hattingen, 1896-1922 – 4r – 1 – DM400.00 – gw Mikro Press [240]

EVANGELISCHER ARBEITERBOTE – Hattingen, Germany. 1917-1920 – 1r – 1 – gw Mikrofilm [072]

EVANGELISCHER PRESSEDIENST FUER OESTERREICH : EPD – (Lacking some pgs) – 10 Oct 1958-1991 – 23r – 1 – ATLA S0398 – us A.T.L.A. [073]

EVANGELISCHE-REFORMIERTE KIRCHE IN NORDWEST DEUTSCHLAND : GESETZ- UND VERORDNUNGSBLATT – (Includes index 1961-71) – v13-16. 1971-92 (complete) – Inquire – 1 – ATLA S0836 – us A.T.L.A. [073]

EVANGELISCHE-REFORMIERTE LANDESKIRCHE DES KANTONS ZUERICH : JAHRESBERICHT – (Earlier issues filmed as S0439) – 1974-91 (complete) – Inquire – 1 – ATLA S0502 – us A.T.L.A. [073]

EVANGELISCHE-REFORMIERTES KIRCHENBLATT FUER BAYERN – (Some pgs lacking) – 1971-90 – Inquire – 1 – ATLA S0470 – us A.T.L.A. [073]

EVANGELISCHES CHRISTENTUM IN DER GEGENWART : DREI VORTRAEGE / Wernle, Paul – Tuebingen: J.C.B. Mohr, 1914 – 1mf – us A.T.L.A. [240]

DAS EVANGELISCHES MAGAZIN – 1811-17 (complete) – 1r – 1 – ATLA B0524F – us A.T.L.A. [073]

DAS EVANGELISCHES MAGAZIN – 1829-33 (complete) – 1r – 1 – ATLA S0524G – us A.T.L.A. [073]

EVANGELISCHES MONATSBLATT – (Cont: Kirche und Mann) – v30-36. 1977-86 (complete) – 2r – 1 – ATLA S0202A – us A.T.L.A. [073]

EVANGELISCHES MONATSBLATT *see* KIRCHE UND MANN

EVANGELISCHES PFARRERBLATT – (Lacking: indexes for 1955, 1964, 1966) – 1955-72 – 5r – 1 – ATLA S0640B – us A.T.L.A. [073]

Evangelisches Zentralarchiv Berlin *see* KIRCHLICHER ZENTRALKATALOG BEIM EVANGELISCHEN ZENTRALARCHIV IN BERLIN

EVANGELISCH-LUTERISCHES VOLKSBLATT – Dresden, Germany. 1921-22 – 1r – 1 – gw Mikrofilm [073]

EVANGELISCH-LUTHERISCHE KIRCHE IN BAYERN : AMTSBLATT – 1969-91 (complete) – Inquire – 1 – ATLA S0414 – us A.T.L.A. [073]

EVANGELISCH-LUTHERISCHE KIRCHE IN BAYERN : NACHRICHTEN – v16-48. 1961-93 (complete) – Inquire – 1 – ATLA S0338 – us A.T.L.A. [073]

EVANGELISCH-LUTHERISCHE KIRCHE IN BAYERN. LANDESSYNODE : VERHANDLUNGEN DER LANDESSYNODE – 1924-93 (complete) – Inquire – 1 – ATLA S0919 – us A.T.L.A. [240]

EVANGELISCH-LUTHERISCHE LANDESKIRCHE MECKLENBURGS : KIRCHLICHES AMTSBLATT – 1969-77 (complete) – Inquire – 1 – ATLA S0881 – us A.T.L.A. [073]

DIE EVANGELISCH-LUTHERISCHE LANDESKIRCHE SCHAUMBURG-LIPPE : KIRCHLICHE AMTSBLATT – 1970-85 (complete) – 1r – 1 – ATLA S0838 – us A.T.L.A. [073]

EVANGELISCH-LUTHERISCHE LANDESKIRCHE SCHLESWIG-HOLSTEINS : LANDESSYNODE BERICHTE – 1947-76 (complete) – 4r – 1 – ATLA S0512 – us A.T.L.A. [073]

EVANGELISCH-REFORMIERTE LANDESKIRCHE BEIDER APPENZELL : AMTSBERICHT – v102-117. 1979-92 (complete) – Inquire – 1 – ATLA S0907 – us A.T.L.A. [240]

EVANGELISCH-REFORMIERTE LANDESKIRCHE DES KANTONS ARGAU : JAHRESBERICHT – 1958-64 (complete) – 2r – 1 – ATLA S0683 – us A.T.L.A. [073]

EVANGELISCH-REFORMIERTE LANDESKIRCHE DES KANTONS ZUERICH : JAHRESBERICHT – (Lacking some pgs) – 1929-73 – 3r – 1 – ATLA S0439 – us A.T.L.A. [240]

EVANGELISCH-REFORMIERTE LANDESKIRCHE DES KANTONS ZUERICH : KIRCHLICHES AMTSBLATT – v1-27. 1956-85 – 1r – 1 – ATLA S0804 – us A.T.L.A. [073]

EVANGELISCH-REFORMIERTE LANDESKIRCHE VON APPENZELL AM RHEIN : AMTSBERICHT – 1968-79 (complete) – 1r – 1 – ATLA S0401 – us A.T.L.A. [240]

EVANGELISK LUTHERSK KIRKETIDENDE – (Lacking some pgs. Some original pgs damaged. Several titles merged) – v1-44. 1874-1917 – 18r – 1 – ATLA S0188 – us A.T.L.A. [073]

EVANGELISKE FOSTERLANDS STIFTELSEN, ARSBOG – 1968-83 (complete) – 3r – 1 – ATLA S0604 – us A.T.L.A. [073]

EVANGELISKET VITTNESBORG – 1927-41 (complete) – 1r – 1 – ATLA S0690 – us A.T.L.A. [073]

EVANGELISM OLD AND NEW : GOD'S SEARCH FOR MAN IN ALL AGES / Dixon, Amzi Clarence – New York: American Tract Society, c1905 – 1mf – 9 – 0-8370-6178-4 – 1986-0178 – us A.T.L.A. [240]

THE EVANGELIST – 1868-69 – 1 – uk Microform Academic [240]

O EVANGELISTA : ORGAM DEDICADO AOS INTERESSES DO EVANGELHO – Macelo, Alagoas. 1 Ago 1902 – 1,5,6 – bl Biblioteca [072]

O EVANGELISTA : ORGAM DO PURO EVANGELHO – Manaos, Amazonas. 1 Fev-Dez 1903; Fev 1904 – 1,5,6 – bl Biblioteca [072]

O EVANGELISTA : ORGAO DA PROPAGANDA EVANGELICA NESTA CIDADE – Maceio, Alagoas. 2 Maio 1885; Fev 1886 – 1,5,6 – bl Biblioteca [072]

EVANGELISTEN – (Lacking some pgs and issues) – v2-67. 1891-1955 – 18r – 1 – ATLA S0879 – us A.T.L.A. [073]

THE EVANGELISTIC RECORD *see* THE RECORD OF CHRISTIAN WORK

THE EVANGELISTS : PAPERS ON THE FOUR GOSPELS / Bellett, John Gifford – New York: Loizeaux Bros, [18–] – 2mf – 9 – 0-8370-6244-6 – 1986-0244 – us A.T.L.A. [220]

EVANGELISTS AND LAY-EXHORTERS / Otts, John Martin Philip – (The Presbyterian Quarterly and Princeton Review, new series, v. 6, April 1877, p. 291-309) – 9 – us A.T.L.A. [240]

EVANGELISTS IN THE CHURCH : FROM PHILIP, A.D. 35, TO MOODY AND SANKEY, A.D. 1875 / Headley, P C – Boston: H. Hoyt, 1875 – 2mf – us A.T.L.A. [240]

DAS EVANGELIUM JOHANNIS / Wellhausen, Julius – (Includes bibliographical references) – Berlin: Georg Reimer, 1908 – 1mf – 9 – 0-8370-5771-X – 1985-3771 – us A.T.L.A. [220]

DAS EVANGELIUM LUCAE / Wellhausen, Julius – Berlin: Georg Reimer, 1904. 1 fiche – 9 – us A.T.L.A. [240]

DAS EVANGELIUM MARCI / Wellhausen, Julius – 2. Ausg. Berlin: Georg Reimer, 1909 – 1mf – 9 – 0-8370-5773-6 – 1985-3773 – us A.T.L.A. [220]

DAS EVANGELIUM MARCIONS IN SEINER URSPRUENGLICHEN GESTALT : NEBST DEM VOLLSTAENDIGSTEN BEWEISE DARGESTELLT, DASS ES NICHT SELBSTAENDIG, SONDERN EIN VERSTUEMMELTES UND VERFAELSCHTES LUKAS-EVANGELIUM WAR ... / Hahn, August – Koenigsberg: Universitaets-Buchh., 1823 – 1mf – us A.T.L.A. [240]

DAS EVANGELIUM MATTHAEI / Wellhausen, Julius – Berlin: Georg Reimer, 1904 – 1mf – 9 – 0-8370-5774-4 – 1985-3774 – us A.T.L.A. [220]

DAS EVANGELIUM MATTHAEI VOR DEM FORUM DER BIBEL UND DES TALMUD / Lippe, Karpel – Jassy: Jsidor Schorr, 1889. 1 fiche – 9 – us A.T.L.A. [220]

DAS EVANGELIUM NACH JOHANNES / Lange, Johann Peter – Bielefeld: Velhagen & Klasing, 1868. 1 fiche – 9 – us A.T.L.A. [240]

EVANGELIUM NACH JOHANNES = THE GOSPEL ACCORDING TO JOHN / Lange, Johann Peter – (In English) – New York: Charles Scribner, 1871 – 2mf – 9 – 0-8370-5977-1 – 1985-3977 – us A.T.L.A. [220]

DAS EVANGELIUM NACH THOMAS (T.U.U. 5-101) / Leipoldt, Johannes – Berlin, 1967 – 2mf – 9 – ne Slangenburg [240]

EVANGELIUM SECUNDUM LUCAM, SIVE, LUCAE AD THEOPHILUM LIBER PRIOR / Blass, Fridericus – Lipsiae: B.G. Teubner, 1897. 1 fiche – 9 – us A.T.L.A. [240]

EVANGELIUMS PANIER – 1879 (complete) – 1r – 1 – ATLA 1994-S005 – us A.T.L.A. [073]

DER EVANGELIUMS-BOTE – (Cont by: The Canadian Evangel) – Berlin [Kitchener]; Ont: [s.n., 1888-1917?] – 9 – cn C.I.H.M. [240]

THE EVANGELIZATION OF A GREAT CITY : OR, THE CHURCHES' ANSWER TO THE BITTER CRY OF OUTCAST LONDON / Smiley, Francis Edward – Philadelphia: Sunshine Pub, 1890 – 1mf – 9 – 0-8370-6380-9 – 1986-0380 – us A.T.L.A. [240]

THE EVANGELIZATION OF THE WORLD IN THIS GENERATION / Mott, John Raleigh – (Includes index) – New York: Student Volunteer Movement for Foreign Missions, 1905, c1900 – 1mf – 9 – 0-8370-6588-7 – 1986-0588 – us A.T.L.A. [240]

EVANGELSICHE LANDESKIRCHE VON WURTEMBURG : AMTSBLATT – 1968-91 (complete) – Inquire – 1 – ATLA S0795 – us A.T.L.A. [073]

EVANGEL'SKII VESTNIK VOLS 1-199 (INCOMPLETE) = GOSPEL MESSENGER – (Lacking vols 2,3,6,52,60,71,167) – Chicago, Wheaton, Illinois: Slavic Gospel Association (Formerly: Russian Gospel Association), 1936-1984 – 2r. 4,452p – 1 – $178.08 – us Baptist [240]

L'EVANGILE DE JESUS-CHRIST / Lagrange, Marie Joseph – 1932 – 12mf – 8 – ne Slangenburg [240]
EVANGILE DE LA RAISON – Ouvrage Posthume De M.D.M. y (sic) (D'Holbach series). 1764 – 9 – fr Hachette [140]
L'EVANGILE DE MARC ET SES RAPPORTS AVEC CEUX DE MATHIEU ET DE LUC / Goguel, Maurice – Paris: Ernest Leroux, 1909 – 9 – us A.T.L.A. [240]
L'EVANGILE DE PARIS – Paris: [s.n.], dec 1848 – us Res Libr [072]
L'EVANGILE DE PIERRE / Vaganay, L – Paris, 1900 – 7mf – 8 – ne Slangenburg [240]
L'EVANGILE DU JOUR / Voltaire, Francois-Marie Arouet de – Londres: (s.n.). Description based on v10 (1773). Consists of writings by Voltaire and articles – 1 – us U.W. Library [880]
EVANGILE SELON SAINT JEAN / Lavigne, A – Paris: Henri Plon, 1867 – 2mf – 9 – 0-8370-6994-7 – 1986-0994 – us A.T.L.A. [220]
DIE EVANGLIENZITATE DES ORIGENES (T.U.U. 3-34/2A) / Hautsch, E – Leipzig, 1909 – 3mf – 9 – ne Slangenburg [240]
DIE EVANGLISCHE KIRCHE : IHRE ORGANISATION UND IHRE ARBEIT IN DER GROSSSTADT / Gruenberg, Paul – Goettingen: Vandenhoeck & Ruprecht, 1910 – 1mf – us A.T.L.A. [240]
EVANGLISCHE LANDESKIRCHE IN BADEN : GESETZES- UND VERORDNUNGSBLATT DER EVANGELISCHEN LANDESKIRCHE IN BADEN – 1969-91 (incomplete) – Inquire – 1 – ATLA S0389A – us A.T.L.A. [240]
EVANGLISCH-LUTHERISCHE KIRCHE IN BAYERN. LANDESSYNODE : VERHANDLUNGEN DER ORDENT... – 1922 (complete) – Inquire – 1 – ATLA S0918 – us A.T.L.A. [240]
Evans *see*
– CYCLOPEDIA OF GEORGIA
– HISTORY OF ADAMS COUNTY
– HISTORY OF LANCASTER COUNTY
Evans, A J *see* EDUCATION AND TRAINING OF USERS OF SCIENTIFIC AND TECHNICAL INFORMATION
Evans, Albert S *see* SKETCHES OF LIFE IN THE GOLDEN STATE
EVANS AND RUFFY'S FARMER'S JOURNAL – London. -w. Dec 1809-Jul 1832. (11 reels) – 1 – uk British Libr Newspaper [630]
EVANS AVENUE BAPTIST CHURCH. FORT WORTH, TEXAS : CHURCH RECORDS – 1904-Mar 1963 – 1 – 10.53 – us Baptist [240]
Evans, C *see*
– ADVICE TO STUDENTS HAVING IN VIEW THE CHRISTIAN MINISTRY ADDRESSED TO THEM AT THE ACADEMY AT BRITSOL
– POLITICAL SOPHISTRY DETECTED
– A REPLY TO THE REV. MR. FLETCHER'S VINDICATION OF MR. WESLEY'S 'CALM ADDRESS TO OUR AMERICAN COLONIES'
Evans, Charles *see* AMERICAN BIBLIOGRAPHY
Evans, D H *see* PHYSIOLOGICAL MEASUREMENT
Evans, David *see* BREVISSIMA RHETORICES INSTITUTIO
Evans, David, J *see* PARALLEL ALGORITHMS AND APPLICATIONS
Evans, E P *see*
– ANIMAL SYMBOLISM IN ECCLESIASTICAL ARCHITECTURE
– FIRST HISTORICAL TRANSFORMATIONS OF CHRISTIANITY
Evans, Edward Waterman *see* WALTER SAVAGE LANDOR
Evans, Elaine Shemoney *see* THE MARGARET CROSS NORTON WORKING PAPERS, 1924-1958
Evans, Eliza (Pruitt) *see* DIARY
Evans, Elizabeth Edison *see*
– THE CHRIST MYTH
– CHRIST MYTH: A STUDY
Evans, F W *see*
– AUTOBIOGRAPHY OF A SHAKER
– SHAKER MUSIC
– SHAKERS
Evans, Frank B *see*
– HISTORY OF ARCHIVES ADMINISTRATION
– MADRAS DISTRICT GAZETTEER
Evans, Gail G *see* THE KINEMATIC VARIABLES RELATED TO THE EFFICIENCY OF THROWING
Evans, George *see* AN ESSAY ON ASSYRIOLOGY
Evans, Howard Heber *see* ST. JOHN
Evans, Hugh *see*
– THE ABLE MINISTER
– MARYLAND PRACTICE
Evans, J *see* MONASTIC LIFE AT CLUNY, 910-1157
Evans, J E *see* INTERNATIONAL JOURNAL OF COMPUTER MATHEMATICS
Evans, John *see*
– ADDRESSES
– THE PALACE OF PROFITABLE PLEASURE
Evans, John Swanton *see*
– BAPTIZING AND TEACHING: EVANS' NEW EXPOSITION OF RITUAL BAPTISM AND OF BAPTISM WITH THE HOLY SPIRIT, AS SEEN WHEN SET BACK IN THEIR RIGHT PLACES IN THE GREAT SYSTEM OF REVEALED TRUTH..
– THE ONE MEDIATOR: SELECTIONS AND THOUGHTS ON THE PROPITIATORY SACRIFICE AND INTERCESSION PRESENTED BY THE LORD JESUS CHRIST AS OUR GREAT HIGH PRIEST: WITH APPENDED CHAPTERS ON THE CONDITIONS OF SALVATION: ALSO APPENDED EXPOSITION OF ROMANS V. 11-21..
Evans, Len *see* BIOFOULING
Evans, Maurice S *see*
– BLACK AND WHITE IN SOUTH EAST AFRICA
– BLACK AND WHITE IN THE SOUTHERN STATES
Evans, Milton G *see* NEW TESTAMENT THEOLOGY, PT I
Evans, Morgan O *see* THEORIES AND CRITICISMS OF SIR HENRY MAINE
Evans, Nelson W *see* A HISTORY OF SCIOTO COUNTY AND SOUTHERN OHIO PIONEER RECORD
Evans, R *see* EARLY CHILD DEVELOPMENT AND CARE
Evans, Robert *see* TABOR MELODIES
Evans, Sebastian *see* BROTHER FABIAN'S MANUSCRIPT
Evans, T *see* THE HISTORY OF MODERN ENTHUSIASM FROM THE REFORMATION TO THE PRESENT TIMES
Evans, Thomas *see* A CONCISE ACCOUNT OF THE RELIGIOUS SOCIETY OF FRIENDS, COMMONLY CALLED QUAKERS
EVANS VALLEY NEWS – Wimer, OR. -w. 3 Mar 1966-29 Sept 1966. 1 roll – 1 – us U.O. Library [071]
Evans, Walter Norton *see*
– CARTIER AND HOCHELAGA: MAISONNEUVE AND VILLE-MARIE: TWO HISTORIC POEMS OF MONTREAL
– MOUNT ROYAL
Evans, William *see*
– HOW TO PREPARE SERMONS AND GOSPEL ADDRESSES
– A LETTER TO THE REV. MR. M–RE B–K-R CONCERNING THE METHODIST
Evans, William David *see* A LETTER TO SIR SAMUEL ROMILLY,KNT. ON THE REVISION OF THE BANKRUPT LAW
Evans, Willis F *see* HISTORY OF BERKLEY COUNTY
EVANSIA – v1-. 1984- – 1,5,6,9 – us UMI [580]
EVANSTON SPEAKS (CCC90) : REPORTS FROM THE 2ND ASSEMBLY OF THE WORLD COUNCIL OF CHURCHES, AUGUST 15-31 1954 – (In Chinese) – 1st ed. Hong Kong: Council on Christian Literature for Overseas Chinese, 1956 – 1r – 1 – 1984-B500 – us A.T.L.A. [240]
EVANSVILLE AND ITS MEN OF MARK / ed by White, Edward – Evansville: Historical Publishing Company, 1873.Indiana Reel 28. (The Cox Library Collection) – 5 – us Americana [920]
THE EVANSVILLE ARGUS – Evansville. Ind. Sept. 13, 1940; Dec. 27, 1941 – 1 – us NY Public [071]
Evanturel, Eudore *see* PREMIERES POESIES
Evanturel, Francois *see* LES DEUX COCHERS DE QUEBEC: SOUVENIRS HISTORIQUES
Evarts, William Maxwell *see* EULOGY ON CHIEF-JUSTICE CHASE, DELIVERED BY WILLIAM M. EVARTS, BEFORE THE ALUMNI OF DARTMOUTH COLLEGE, AT HANOVER, JUNE 24, 1874
LAS EVAS DEL PARAISO / Trigo, Felipe – Madrid: Renacimiento, 5th ed 1923 – sp Bibl Santa Ana [946]
Evatt, H V *see* THE BRITISH DOMINIONS AS MANDATORIES
Evatt, Herbert Vere *see* INJUSTICE WITHIN THE LAW; A STUDY OF THE CASE OF THE DORSETSHIRE LABOURERS
EVCLIDE MEGARENSE PHILOSOPHO: SOLO INTRODVTTORE DELLE SCIENTIE MATHEMATICE / Euclides – Diligentemente reassettato et alla integrita ridotto per...Nicolo Tartalea, brisciano, secondo le due Tradottioni, e per commvne commodo et vtilita di latino in volgar Tradotto, con vna ampla espositione dello istesso tradottore di novo aggionta. Vinegia: Venturino Hoffinelli, 1543 – 1 – us U.W. Library [510]
Evdokimov, A A *see* NARODNYI TEATR I KOOPERATSIIA
Evdokimov, Andrei Aandreevich *see*
– K TEORII KOOPERATIZMA
– KOOPERATIVNYI SBYT PRODUKTOV SEL'SKOGO KHOZIAISTVA V ROSSII
– KREST'IANSKAIA KOOPERATSIIA V SVOBODNOI ROSSII
– SELO I GOROD V ROSSIISKOI KOOPERATSII
– SEL'SKOKHOZIASTVENNYE TOVARISHCHESTVA, KAK IKH USTRAIVAT'I VESTI
– VOZROZHDENIE SELA I KOOPERATSIIA
Evdokimov, Andrei Andreevich *see* VNI ESHKOLNIKI I NAROD
Evdokimov, L V *see* ZHURNAL DEZHURNYKH GENERAL A.D. IUDANTOV
Eve *see* MADAME ANGOT OU LA POSSARDE PARVENUE
EVE AND HER DAUGHTERS; HEROINES OF HOME / McConnell, T M – 1900 – 9 – us A.T.L.A. [240]
EVE DANS L'HUMANITE / Deraismes, Maria – Paris: L. Sauvaitre, 1891. 223p. 3 fiches. (Literature Collection) – 9 – 8.00 – fr Bibl Nationale [300]
THE EVE OF CATHOLIC EMANCIPATION : BEING THE HISTORY OF THE ENGLISH CATHOLICS DURING THE FIRST THIRTY YEARS OF THE NINETEENTH CENTURY / Ward, Bernard – London, New York: Longmans, Green, 1911-1912 – 3mf – us A.T.L.A. [240]
EVEFIALA : OR, EWE-ENGLISH DICTIONARY / Westermann, Diedrich – Berlin: D Reimer, [1928] – 1 – us Res Libr [490]
L'EVEIL – Laprairie, Canada. v11 n19. 4 avr 1963-v15 n21. 27 dec 1967; v15 n22. 3 jan 1968-v19 n26. 5 jul 1972 – 2r – 1 – Can$55.00r – cn Can Microfilming [072]
L'EVEIL – Longueuil, Canada. v1 n2. 20 sep 1938 – 1r – 1 – Can$25.00 – cn Can Microfilming [072]
L'EVEIL : MENSUEL – Trois-Rivieres, Canada. jan 1918-v2 n12. dec 1919 – 1r – 1 – Can$25.00 – cn Can Microfilming [072]
L'EVEIL – Montreal, Canada. 25 oct 1934 – 1r – 1 – Can$25.00 – cn Can Microfilming [072]
L'EVEIL – Sorel: La Cie generale d'imprimerie de Sorel. v1-6. 1911-17. SEM35P333 – 1r – 1 – Can$33.00 – cn Bibl Nat [072]
L'EVEIL DU PEUPLE / Mouvement Republicain Populaire – 3no. speciaux. Lille. mai 1947-51, 1953 – 1 – fr A.C.R.P.P. [073]
Eveleth, Stanford *see* MISS DEXIE: A ROMANCE OF THE PROVINCES
EVELINA. A FAVOURITE MARCH... / Sacchini, A M – London: Rt. Birchall – 1 – us Sibley [780]
Even, Louis *see* VERS DEMAIN
DE EVENAAR. CHATTULISTIWA – (Missing: 1948, v1; 1949, v2(11-12); 1951, v4(11-12)-1951, v5(1, 5, 8-12)-1952, v6(1-2, 4, 8-12); 1954, v7(Aug.-Sept.); 1957, v10(4)-1960(Jan.-Nov.)) – Amsterdam, 1947-1960 – 25mf – 9 – SE-748/1 – ne IDC [073]
Evenbeck, Elizabeth J *see* RATING STANDARDS AND RELATED FACTORS IN HIGH LEVEL AMATEUR SPORTS OFFICIATING
EVENEMENS INTERESSANS – Bayreuth, 1757, 1762-66, 1768-70 (all incomplete) – 1 – Dist. gw Mikrofilm – gw Misc Inst [072]
L'EVENEMENT – (Cont by: L'Evenement-Journal 29 oct 1938-3 mar 1967) – Quebec, Canada. 13 mai 1867-28 oct 1938 – 248r – 1 – Can$60.00r – cn Can Microfilming [072]
L'EVENEMENT – Paris. Fond., Victor Hugo. Red. en chef, Edmond Magnier. Quot., mens. en 1915. 7 avr 1872-6 juin 1940, 2 fevr 1946-1949, 1951- – 1 – fr A.C.R.P.P. [800]
L'EVENEMENT – Paris. illustre. Journal litteraire quotidien. Dir. gerant Edouard Bauer. no. 1-284. 11 avr 1868-29 janv 1869 – 1 – fr A.C.R.P.P. [800]
L'EVENEMENT : SEMI-QUOTIDIEN – Quebec, Canada. 20 mai 1867-30 dec 1872 – 3r – 1 – Can$60.00r – cn Can Microfilming [072]
L'EVENEMENT DU JEUDI – 1984- – 3r per y – 5 – inquire – us Ross [072]
L'EVENEMENT DU JEUDI – 1984-1995 – 3r per y – 5,6 – FF2,750.00y – sz Infoprint [944]
EVENEMENT DU JEUDI – 1984-1995 – 3 times per yr – 6 – F2,750.00 – sz Infoprint [072]
L'EVENEMENT, LE SOLEIL, L'ACTION – Quebec, 1868-1937 – 135r – 1 – cn Preston [971]
L'EVENEMENT-CHAMBLY – Chambly, Canada. 30 avr 1975 – 1r – 1 – Can$25.00 – cn Can Microfilming [072]
L'EVENEMENT-JOURNAL *see* L'EVENEMENT
LES EVENEMENTS DE MAI-JUIN 1968 / France – (Les Quotidiens du 2 mai-3 juillet: sept journaux de Paris et vingt journaux de province classes par ordre chronologique. 54 bobines. 1. Les Hebdomadaires: Aspects de la France; l'Express; Le Figaro-selection hebdomadaire; L'Humanite-Dimanche; Minute; Le Monde-selection hebdomadaire; Le Nouvel Observateur; Reforme; Temoignage chretien; La Tribune socialiste. 4 bobines. 1) – fr A.C.R.P.P. [072]
LES EVENEMENTS DE PARIS – Red. en chef H. de Villemessant. devenu: La Chronique de Paris. Paris. 28 mai-30 sept 1867 – 1 – fr A.C.R.P.P. [073]
EVENING ADVERTISER – Swindon, England. 1899-1909; Sep-Dec 1910; 1913-25; 1950- – 396+ r – 1 – uk British Libr Newspaper [941]
EVENING AMUSEMENT – Containing fifty air's, song's, duett's, hornpipe's, reel's, marches, minuett's, &c, &c for 1 and 2 German flutes or violins. Philadelphia: B. Carr 1796 MUSIC 123, Item 7; MUSIC 1467, Item 3 – 1 – us L of C Photodup [780]
EVENING AMUSEMENT CONTAINING AIRS...FOR THE GERMAN FLUTE OR VIOLIN – Second edition. ca.1797 – 9 – us Sibley [780]
EVENING AND MORNING STAR – Independence. Mo. 1832-1834 – 1 – us UMI [071]
EVENING AND MORNING STAR – Kirtland, OH. v1-2. 1832-34 – 1r – 1 – us Ross [071]
EVENING AND MORNING STAR – Kirtland, Ohio. v. 1-2 no. 24. June 1832-Sept 1834 – 1 – us NY Public [073]
EVENING AT HOME – v1-2. 1874-1975 (complete) – 1r – 1 – ATLA 1993-S019 – us A.T.L.A. [073]
EVENING AT HOME – v2-5. 1875-78 (complete) – 1r – 1 – ATLA 1993-S021 – us A.T.L.A. [073]
EVENING BANNER – Bluffton. Ind. 1914-1929 – 1 – us UMI [071]
EVENING BANNER – Greenville. Tex. 1915-1954 – 1 – us UMI [071]
EVENING BEE – Toledo. Ohio. 1884-1901 – 1 – us UMI [071]
THE EVENING BLADE – Santa Ana, CA. 1897-1905; 1913-18 – 32r – 1 CR02934 – $1,600.00 – us Library Micro [071]
THE EVENING BOOK: OR, FIRESIDE TALK ON MORALS AND MANNERS, WITH SKETCHES OF WESTERN LIFE / Kirkland, Caroline Matilda Stansbury – New York: C. Scribner, 1852 – 1 – us U.W. Library [390]
EVENING BULLETIN – Decatur. Ill. 1895-96 – 1 – us UMI [071]
EVENING BULLETIN – Edmonton, Canada. Nov 1915-Dec 1917 (imperfect) – 2r – 1 – uk British Libr Newspaper [971]
EVENING BULLETIN – Providence. Rhode Island. 1863- – 1 – us UMI [071]
EVENING BULLETIN – Virginia City, NV. 1863-64 – 3r – 1 – $150.00 – U04788 – us Library Micro [071]
EVENING CHRONICLE – Allentown. Pa. 1875-1939; 1960- – 1 – us UMI [071]
EVENING CHRONICLE – London, 31 Jan-30 Dec 1835 – 1r – 1 – uk British Libr Newspaper [072]
EVENING CHRONICLE – Oldham, England. 17 Mar 1880-Dec 1885 – 12r – 1 – uk British Libr Newspaper [072]
EVENING CHRONICLE – Uhrichsville. Ohio. 1958-1959 – 1 – us UMI [071]
EVENING CHRONICLE – Vallejo, CA. 1868-1904; 1907; 1910-22 – 83r – 1 – $4,150.00 – B03060 – us Library Micro [071]
EVENING CHRONICLE – Vallejo. Calif. 1910-1922 – 1 – us UMI [071]
EVENING CITIZEN – Cairo. Ill. 1899-1902; 1903- – 1 – us UMI [071]
EVENING CITIZEN – Glasgow, Scotland, UK. 1882-84; 1887-88; 1890-91. -d. 14 reels – 1 – uk British Libr Newspaper [072]

EVENING COMMERCIAL – Portland OR. July 2 1869, Apr 11 May 13 Aug 3 1870 – 1 – us U.O. Library [071]
AN EVENING CONVERSATION BETWEEN FOUR VERY GOOD OLD LADIES OVER A COMFORTABLE GAME AT QUADRILLE / Hill, Richard – (Missing: Title-page) – Bath, [?1769] – 1mf – 9 – MP-462/1 – ne IDC [240]
EVENING COURIER – Camden. N.J. 1947-49 – 1 – us UMI [071]
EVENING COURIER – Champaign Urbana. Ill. 1910-1927; 1935- – 1 – us UMI [071]
EVENING COURIER – Lansford. Pa. 1932-1933 – 1 – us UMI [071]
EVENING COURIER – Tamaqua. Pa. 1874-1971 – 1 – us UMI [071]
EVENING DAILY PRESS – Pawnee City, NE. Aug 1895-Feb 1896 – 1 – us NE Hist [071]
EVENING DAY BOOK – v3-12. 1852-61 – 6r – 1 – us Ross [976]
EVENING DEMOCRAT – (Also known as: Daily Democrat; Marysville Democrat) – Marysville, CA. 1884-86; 1888-1927 – 88r – 1 – $4,400.00 – B02431 – us Library Micro [071]
EVENING DEMOCRAT – Fort Madison. Iowa. -w. 1897- – 1 – us UMI [071]
EVENING DEMOCRAT – Hamilton. Ohio. 1897-1907 – 1 – us UMI [071]
EVENING DEMOCRAT – Moberly. Mo. 1896; 1899-1925 – 1 – us UMI [071]
EVENING DEMOCRAT – Portland OR. Oct 7 1886 – 1 – us U.O. Library [071]
EVENING DEMOCRAT – Sedalia. Mo. 1891-1906 – 1 – us UMI [071]
EVENING DISPATCH – Auburn. Ind. 1898-1899 – 1 – us UMI [071]
EVENING DISPATCH – Columbus. Ohio. 1871- – 1 – us UMI [071]
EVENING DISPATCH – Michigan City. Ind. 1881-1907; 1909-1910; 1926-1932; 1937-1942 – 1 – us UMI [071]
EVENING DISPATCH – New Martinsville. West Virginia. 1901-1906 – 1 – us UMI [071]
EVENING DISPATCH – Omaha. Neb. 1883-85 – 1 – us UMI [071]
EVENING DISPATCH – Richmond. Va. and Journal. 1905-23 – 1 – us UMI [071]
EVENING DISPATCH – Seattle. Wash. 1872-1878 – 1 – us UMI [071]
EVENING DRUM (CCC144) : OR, BED-TIME STORIES / ed by Happy Childhood Staff – (In Chinese) – 4th ed. Shanghai: Christian Literature Society, 1938 – 1r – 1 – 1984-B500 – us A.T.L.A. [240]
EVENING EAGLE – Wichita. Kan. 1927-1963 – 1 – us UMI [071]
EVENING ECHO – Bournemouth, England. -d. 1976. 12 reels – 1 – uk British Libr Newspaper [072]
THE EVENING ECHO – Cork, Ireland. 1930-80.290 reels – 1 – ie Microforms [072]
EVENING EXPOSITOR – Adrian. Mich. -w. 1858-59 – 1 – us UMI [071]
EVENING EXPRESS – East Saginaw. Mich. 1881-1884 – 1 – us UMI [071]
EVENING EXPRESS – Halifax, Canada. 1858-74 – 17r – 1 – $1,105.00 – cn Library Assoc [971]
EVENING EXPRESS – Liverpool, England. Jan-Jun 1899. 1 reel – 1 – uk British Libr Newspaper [072]
EVENING EXPRESS – Portland. Maine. 1886- – 1 – us UMI [071]
EVENING EXPRESS – Rochester. N.Y. 1859-82 – 1 – us UMI [071]
EVENING EXPRESS AND STAR *see* MIDLAND COUNTIES EVENING EXPRESS
EVENING FREE LANCE – Hollister. Calif. 1944- – 1 – us UMI [071]
EVENING FREE LANCE *see* FREE LANCE
EVENING FREE PRESS – Easton. Pa. 1869-1872 – 1 – us UMI [071]
EVENING FREE PRESS – Oklahoma City. Okl. 1910-1911 – 1 – us UMI [071]
EVENING FREEMAN – (Evening Telegraph, Sept 1871-96) – Dublin, Ireland. 1851-72; Jan-5 Nov 1874; 30 Aug 1875-1896 – 140r – 1 – uk British Libr Newspaper [072]
EVENING GAZETTE – Aberdeen, Scotland, UK. 1890. -d. 2 reels – 1 – uk British Libr Newspaper [072]
EVENING GAZETTE – Burlington. Iowa. 1893-1933 – 1 – us UMI [071]
EVENING GAZETTE – (Cont by: Reno Gazette Journal) – Reno, NV. 1876-1983 – 792r – 1 – $39,600.00 – R04669 – us Library Micro [071]
EVENING GAZETTE – Indiana. Pa. 1904- – 1 – us UMI [071]
EVENING GAZETTE – (Reading Gazette: Jan-18 Oct 1939) – England, 28 Aug-Dec 1935; 1936-39 – 24r – 1 – uk British Libr Newspaper [072]
EVENING GAZETTE – Shanghai. China. -d. 15 Jan-31 Dec 1874. (2 reels) – 1 – uk British Libr Newspaper [072]
EVENING HERALD – 1960-1980 – 250r – 1 – ie Microforms [941]
EVENING HERALD – Dayton. Ohio. 1869-74 – 1 – us UMI [071]
EVENING HERALD – Decatur. Ill. 1927-31 – 1 – us UMI [071]
EVENING HERALD – Dublin, Ireland. 1897-1907 (missing 1 Jan-23 Mar 1900).-d. 33 reels – 1 – uk British Libr Newspaper [072]
EVENING HERALD – Dublin. Ireland. -sw. 17 May 1786-31 Dec 1787. (1 reel) – 1 – uk British Libr Newspaper [072]
EVENING HERALD – Huntington. Ind. 1903-1911 – 1 – us UMI [071]
EVENING HERALD – Ireland.-d. 1960- – 1 – PS27.50r – ie European Micro [072]
EVENING HERALD – Joliet. Ill. 1906-12; 1915 – 1 – us UMI [071]
EVENING HERALD – Klamath Falls, OR. -d. 1 Feb 1908-30 May 1942. 63 rolls – 1 – us U.O. Library [071]
EVENING HERALD – Manchester. Conn. 1934- – 1 – us UMI [071]
EVENING HERALD – Norwalk. Ohio. 1902-13 – 1 – us UMI [071]
EVENING HERALD – Rock Hill. S.C. 1880- – 1 – us UMI [071]
EVENING HERALD – Shenandoah, PA. 1969-80 – 13 – $25.00r – us I.M.R. [071]
EVENING HERALD – St. John's, Canada. -d. May 1890-Feb 1892; July 1898-Dec 1920. 1913, 1919 imperfect. 88 1 2 reels – 1 – uk British Libr Newspaper [072]
EVENING HERALD – St. Joseph. Mich. 1902-1916 – 1 – us UMI [071]
EVENING HERALD AND ASHLAND DAILY – Shenandoah, PA., 1967-1969 – 13 – $25.00r – us I.M.R. [071]
EVENING HERALD AND EXPRESS – Los Angeles. Calif. 1960-1961 – 1 – us UMI [071]
EVENING HERALD NEWS – Joliet. Ill. 1915; 1917-19; 1924; 1936 – 1 – us UMI [071]
EVENING INDEPENDENT – Massillon. Ohio. 1900-1932; 1956- – 1 – us UMI [071]
EVENING INDEPENDENT – St. Petersburg. Fl. 1907-1945; 1947-1950; 1958- – 1 – us UMI [071]
EVENING INDEX – San Bernardino, CA. 1906-18 – 13r – 1 – $650.00 – R02763 – us Library Micro [071]
EVENING IRISH TIMES – Dublin, Ireland.1880-96. -d. 65 reels – 1 – uk British Libr Newspaper [072]
EVENING JOURNAL – Albany. N.Y. 1830-1873 – 1 – us UMI [071]
EVENING JOURNAL – Billings. Mont. 1906-1911 – 1 – us UMI [071]
EVENING JOURNAL – Corry. Pa. 1954- – 1 – us UMI [071]
EVENING JOURNAL – Dallas. Tex. 1914-1939 – 1 – us UMI [071]
EVENING JOURNAL – Hamilton. Ohio. 1908-1937 – 1 – us UMI [071]
EVENING JOURNAL – Huntingdon, PA. -d 1917-1918 – 13 – $25.00r – us I.M.R. [071]
EVENING JOURNAL – Jamestown. N.Y. 1870-1941 – 1 – us UMI [071]
EVENING JOURNAL – Lewiston. Maine. 1873-1926; 1953- – 1 – us UMI [071]
EVENING JOURNAL – Lincoln. Neb. and pred. 1881- – 1 – us UMI [071]
EVENING JOURNAL – Nevada. Iowa. 1941-1942; 1947; 1951-1964 – 1 – us UMI [071]
EVENING JOURNAL – St. Catherines, Canada. -d. March 1919-May 1920. 3 reels – 1 – uk British Libr Newspaper [072]
EVENING JOURNAL – Washington. Iowa. 1893- – 1 – us UMI [071]
EVENING JOURNAL – Wilmington. Del. 1888-1932; 1961- – 1 – us UMI [071]
EVENING JOURNAL EVERY EVENING – Wilmington. Del. 1932-1960 – 1 – us UMI [071]
EVENING LEADER – Corning. N.Y. 1903- – 1 – us UMI [071]
EVENING LEADER – Eureka, NV. 1878 (scattered issues) – 1r – 1 – $50.00 – U04511 – us Library Micro [071]
EVENING LEADER – Grand Rapids. Mich. 1879-1892 – 1 – us UMI [071]
EVENING LEADER – Richmond. Va. 1896-1903 – 1 – us UMI [071]
EVENING MAIL – Halifax, Canada. -d. May 1911-Dec 1917. 17 reels – 1 – uk British Libr Newspaper [072]
EVENING MERCURY – St. John's, Canada. -d. Dec 1883-Nov 1887. 6 reels – 1 – uk British Libr Newspaper [072]
EVENING MESSENGER – Valparaiso. Ind. 1907-1916; 1918-1926 – 1 – us UMI [071]
EVENING MIRROR – New York. (Contains several Poe contributions.) Oct 7 1844-Dec 1847 – 1 – us NY Public [071]
EVENING NEWS – (1976-1992.-151r) – New Glasgow, 1993 – 12r – 1 – cn Preston [971]
EVENING NEWS – Battle Creek. Mich. 1911-1918 – 1 – us UMI [071]
EVENING NEWS – Bayonne. N.J. and Review. 1913-30 – 1 – us UMI [071]
EVENING NEWS – Beacon. N.Y. 1925- – 1 – us UMI [071]
EVENING NEWS – Benton Harbor. Mich. 1896-1903 – 1 – us UMI [071]
EVENING NEWS – Birmingham. Ala. 1888-1889 – 1 – us UMI [071]
EVENING NEWS – Buffalo. N.Y. 1932- – 1 – us UMI [071]
EVENING NEWS – Cleveland, Cuyahoga, OH. 1 Mar 1869-30 Dec 1880 – 9r – 1 – us Western Res [071]
EVENING NEWS – Daytona Beach. Fl. 1937- – 1 – us UMI [071]
EVENING NEWS – Dublin, Ireland.1859-64. -d. 18 reels – 1 – uk British Libr Newspaper [072]
EVENING NEWS – Edinburgh: Scotsman Publ Ltd, 1978-81 – 48r – 1 – us Res Libr [072]
EVENING NEWS – Great Bend. Kan. 1890-1897 – 1 – us UMI [071]
EVENING NEWS – Harrisburg, PA. 1917-49. 220 rolls – 13 – $25.00r – us I.M.R. [071]
EVENING NEWS – Harrisburg. Pa. 1949- – 1 – us UMI [071]
EVENING NEWS – Jackson. Mich. 1919-1920 – 1 – us UMI [071]
EVENING NEWS – Kenosha. Wis. 1901- – 1 – us UMI [071]
EVENING NEWS – Lincoln. Neb. 1881-1917 – 1 – us UMI [071]
EVENING NEWS – London, England. -d. 1881-1945. 299 reels – 1 – uk British Libr Newspaper [072]
EVENING NEWS – Michigan City. Ind. 1887-1922 – 1 – us UMI [071]
EVENING NEWS – Monroe. Mich. 1951- – 1 – us UMI [071]
EVENING NEWS – Newburgh. N.Y. 1886- – 1 – us UMI [071]
EVENING NEWS – Omaha. Neb. 1878-1880 – 1 – us UMI [071]
EVENING NEWS – Plattsmouth, NE. -d. Mar-Oct 1892; Dec 1892-Jan 1893; Mar 1893; May 1893-Nov 1908 – 1 – us NE Hist [071]
EVENING NEWS – Port Angeles. Wash. 1916-1955 – 1 – us UMI [071]
EVENING NEWS – Providence. R.I. 1909-18 – 1 – us UMI [071]
EVENING NEWS – Roanoke. Va. 1903-13 – 1 – us UMI [071]
EVENING NEWS – Roseburg, OR. 1 Nov 1909-30 Mar 1920. 15 rolls – 1 – us U.O. Library [071]
EVENING NEWS – Saginaw. Mich. 1881-1918 – 1 – us UMI [071]
EVENING NEWS – Santa Cruz, CA. 1907-41 – 109r – 1 – $5,450.00 – B02954 – us Library Micro [071]
EVENING NEWS – Sault Ste. Marie. Mich. 1903- – 1 – us UMI [071]
EVENING NEWS – St. Joseph. Mo. 1879-85 – 1 – us UMI [071]
EVENING NEWS – Sydney, Australia. Feb 1875-Dec 1888.-d. 42 reels – 1 – uk British Libr Newspaper [072]
EVENING NEWS – Tonawanda. N.Y. 1880-1885; 1893-1895; 1896-1898; 1800-1940; 1941- – 1 – us UMI [071]
EVENING NEWS – Tuscarora, NV. Sep-Dec 1907 (scats) – 1r – 1 – $50.00 – U04773 – us Library Micro [071]
EVENING NEWS – Vallejo, CA. 1910-22; 1923-42 – 103r – 1 BC03062 – $5,150.00 – us Library Micro [071]
EVENING NEWS – Vallejo. Calif. 1910-1922 – 1 – us UMI [071]
EVENING NEWS – Youngstown. Ohio. 1877-1879 – 1 – us UMI [071]
EVENING NEWS – Accra: Star Pub Co, [-1968]. [aug 21 1958-jul 9 1964] – us Res Libr [072]
THE EVENING NEWS – Los Angeles, CA. 1905-1907 – 9r – 1 – $450.00 – R03292 – us Library Micro [071]
THE EVENING NEWS – Quebec, Canada. 25 sep 1869-v1 n46. 19 fev 1870 – 1r – 1 – Can$30.00 – cn Can Microfilming [072]
THE EVENING NEWS – Sayre, PA., 1899-1986 – 13 – $25.00r – us I.M.R. [071]
THE EVENING NEWS – Williamsport, PA., 1895-1907 – 13 – $25.00r – us I.M.R. [071]
EVENING NEWS AND PINK PAPER – 1 – £42.00r – uk Scot News [072]
EVENING OBSERVER – Dunkirk. N.Y. 1883- – 1 – us UMI [071]
EVENING OUTLOOK – Santa Monica, CA. 1875- – 957+ r – 1 – $47,850.00 ($680.00y) – R02968 – us Library Micro [071]
EVENING PACKET AND CORRESPONDENT – Dublin, Ireland.1848; 1-12 Jul 1850; 1851-61; Jan-15 Mar 1862.-w. 15 1/4 reels – 1 – uk British Libr Newspaper [072]
EVENING PAJARONIAN – Watsonville. Calif. 1903-37 – 1 – us UMI [071]
THE EVENING PAJARONIAN – Watsonville, CA. 1903-1930 – 62r – 1 – $3,100.00 – C03569 – us Library Micro [071]
EVENING PATRIOT – (1993.-12r; 1889-1900.-24r) – Charlottetown, 1901-1992 – 413r – 1 – cn Preston [971]
EVENING POST – (Also known as: Reading Post) – 14 Sep-Dec 1965; 1966-75; 1977-30 Jun 1997 – 378 1/2r – 1 – uk British Libr Newspaper [072]
EVENING POST – Baltimore. Md. 1805-1811 – 1 – us UMI [071]
EVENING POST – Bridgeport. Conn. 1893-1908; 1911-1947 – 1 – us UMI [071]
EVENING POST – Charleston. S.C. 1894- – 1 – us UMI [071]
EVENING POST – Columbia City. Ind. 1917-20; 1922-27 – 1 – us UMI [071]
EVENING POST – Gary. Ind. 1909-21 – 1 – us UMI [071]
EVENING POST – New York, 1802-1901 – 25r – 1 – us Ross [071]
EVENING POST – New York. Weekly. Oct 28 1852-Dec 28 1854. Incomplete. Not collated – 1 – us NY Public [073]
EVENING POST – Reading, England. 14 Sept 1965-1970. -d. 63 reels – 1 – uk British Libr Newspaper [072]
EVENING POST – Vicksburg. Miss. 1936- – 1 – us UMI [071]
EVENING POST – Wellington, 1991- – 12r per y – 1 – us Ross [072]
EVENING POST *see* THE PORT ELIZABETH ADVERTISER
THE EVENING POST – (Cont by: The Post 9 Dec 1880-20 May 1884. Cont by: The Montreal Daily Post 21 May 1884-17 Dec 1888) – Montreal, Canada. v1 n6. 15 Jun 1878-22 May 1880 – 10r – 1 – Can$50.00r – cn Can Microfilming [072]
THE EVENING POST – Wellington, NZ: Blundell Bros Ltd, jul 1938-1981 – 1 – us Res Libr [072]
EVENING POST ANNUAL, 1884 / Evening Post Association – Biographical sketches of state officers, Reps. in Congress, Governor's Staff, Senators and Members of the Conn. General Assembly. Hartford, 1884. Connecticut Reel 2. (The Cox Library Collection) – 5 – us Americana [978]
Evening Post Association *see* EVENING POST ANNUAL, 1884
EVENING POST ECHO – Watford, England. Post Echo – Watford edition. -d. Hemel Hempstead Jan 1980-Dec 1981. 23 1 2 reels – 1 – uk British Libr Newspaper [072]
EVENING POST ESSAYS IN REVIEW OF "THE BIBLE FOR LEARNERS" / Schaff, Philip et al – New York:Evening Post, 1880 – 1mf – 9 – 0-8370-3082-X – 1985-1082 – us A.T.L.A. [220]
EVENING POST, SUN, DAILY DEMOCRAT, NEWS, TIMES – Aurora. Ill. and Misc. early Aurora newspapers. 1884-1920 – 1 – us UMI [071]
EVENING PRESS – 1978-1980 – 48r – 1 – ie Microforms [941]
EVENING PRESS – Asbury Park. N.J. 1905- – 1 – us UMI [071]
EVENING PRESS – Bay City. Mich. 1880-1891 – 1 – us UMI [071]

EVENING PRESS – Belfast, Ireland. 15 May 1873-21 May 1874. -d.1 1/2 reels – 1 – uk British Libr Newspaper [072]
EVENING PRESS – Carthage. Mo. 1963- – 1 – us UMI [071]
EVENING PRESS – Ireland.-d. 1978- – 1 – PS27.50r – ie European Micro [072]
EVENING PRESS – Muncie. Ind. 1905- – 1 – us UMI [071]
EVENING PRESS – Princeton. West Virginia. 1917-23 – 1 – us UMI [071]
EVENING PRESS – Providence. R.I. 1859-1884 – 1 – us UMI [071]
EVENING PRESS – Savannah. Ga. 1931-1950; 1961- – 1 – us UMI [071]
EVENING RECORD – Allegheny. Pa. 1896-1899 – 1 – us UMI [071]
EVENING RECORD – Greenville. Pa. 1899-1923 – 1 – us UMI [071]
EVENING RECORD – Lansford. Pa. 1920- – 1 – us UMI [071]
EVENING RECORD – Marshfield OR. July 8 1916-Mar 31 1920, Jan 23 1915 – 1 – us U.O. Library [071]
EVENING RECORD – St. Augustine. Fl. 1899-1935 – 1 – us UMI [071]
EVENING RECORDER – Albion. Mich. 1904- – 1 – us UMI [071]
EVENING RECORDER – Amsterdam. N.Y. 1879- – 1 – us UMI [071]
EVENING RECORDER – Brockville, 1873-1918 – 58r – 1 – cn Preston [971]
EVENING RECORDER – Tamaqua. Pa. 1896-99 – 1 – us UMI [071]
EVENING RECORDER *see* PORTERVILLE PAPERS
EVENING REGISTER – Torrington. Conn. 1898-1914 – 1 – us UMI [071]
EVENING REPORT – Lebanon, PA. -d 1898-1937. (Missing dates) – 13 – $25.00r – us I.M.R. [071]
EVENING REPORT – Virginia City, NV. 1887-1903 – 9r – 1 – $450.00 – U04789 – us Library Micro [071]
EVENING REPORTER – Woonsocket. R.I. 1873-1908 – 1 – us UMI [071]
EVENING REPORTER STAR – Orlando. Fl. 1928-1933; 1937 – 1 – us UMI [071]
EVENING REPUBLICAN – Columbus. Ind. -w. (Filmed with Herald). 1878-1967 – 1 – us UMI [071]
EVENING REPUBLICAN – Meadville. Pa. 1951-55 – 1 – us UMI [071]
EVENING REPUBLICAN – Pendleton OR. Feb 28 1888 – 1 – us U.O. Library [071]
EVENING REPUBLICAN – Rushville. Ind. 1904- – 1 – us UMI [071]
EVENING REVIEW – Elkhart. Ind. 1872-79 – 1 – us UMI [071]
EVENING REVIEW JOURNAL – Las Vegas, NV. 1932-1941 – 1r – 1 – $50.00 – U04599 – us Library Micro [073]
EVENING ROSEBURG REVIEW – Roseburg OR. Jan 3 1902-Dec 20 1905 – 1 – us U.O. Library [071]
EVENING SEARCHLIGHT – Bremerton. Wash. 1920-22 – 1 – us UMI [071]
EVENING SENTINEL – Ansonia. Conn. 1896- – 1 – us UMI [071]
EVENING SENTINEL – Carlisle. Pa. 1881- – 1 – us UMI [071]
EVENING SENTINEL – Holland. Mich. 1948-1949; 1952- – 1 – us UMI [071]
EVENING SENTINEL – Red Bluff, CA. 1901; 1904-05; 1909-20 – 34r – 1 – $1,700.00 – B02658 – us Library Micro [071]
EVENING SENTINEL – Santa Cruz, CA. 1896-1907 – 15r – 1 – $750.00 – B02955 – us Library Micro [071]
EVENING SENTINEL – Sedalia. Mo. 1898-1906 – 1 – us UMI [071]
EVENING SONG TO THE VIRGIN / Browne, H – Ms, publ Baltimore; New York: J Cole, Mesier, 183- – 1 – us Sibley [780]
EVENING STANDARD – London, 1860-1968 – 514r – 1 – uk British Libr Newspaper [072]
EVENING STANDARD – London, England. 1962-1981 – 112r – 1 – us L of C Photodup [072]
EVENING STANDARD – Milton. Pa. 1934-1944 – 1 – us UMI [071]
EVENING STANDARD – Uniontown. Pa. 1889-1893; 1941- – 1 – us UMI [071]
EVENING STANDARD – Wheeling. West Virginia. 1877-1878 – 1 – us UMI [071]
EVENING STANDARD AND ST JAMES'S GAZETTE – London: W E Hobbs, [1905-]. [mar 14 1905-sep 1909] – us Res Libr [072]
EVENING STAR – Eureka, CA. 1876-78 – 1r – 1 – $50.00 – B02210 – us Library Micro [071]
EVENING STAR – Ipswich, England. Feb 1885-1975; 1978- – 578+ r – 1 – uk British Libr Newspaper [072]
EVENING STAR – London, 17 Mar 1856-Dec 1859; Jan 1861-Dec 1862 – 17r – 1 – uk British Libr Newspaper [072]
EVENING STAR – London, 25 Jul 1842-28 Feb 1843 – 2r – 1 – uk British Libr Newspaper [072]
EVENING STAR – Orlando. Fl. 1950- – 1 – us UMI [071]
EVENING STAR – Pasadena. Calif. 1889-1910 – 1 – us UMI [071]
EVENING STAR – Peekskill. N.Y. 1959- – 1 – us UMI [071]
EVENING STAR – Winchester. Va. 1905- – 1 – us UMI [071]
THE EVENING STAR – Cincinnati. Jan. 4-Jun. 29, 1872 – 1 – us NY Public [071]
THE EVENING STAR *see* THE MORNING STAR
EVENING STAR NEWS – Culver City, CA. 1945-56 – 53r – 1 – $2,650.00 – C02153 – us Library Micro [071]
EVENING STAR NEWS – Culver City. Calif. 1945-56 – 1 – us UMI [071]
EVENING STATESMAN – Walla Walla. Wash. 1891-1910 – 1 – us UMI [071]
EVENING SUN – Baltimore. Md. 1910- – 1 – us UMI [071]
EVENING SUN – Hamilton. Ohio. 1902-1906 – 1 – us UMI [071]
EVENING SUN – Hanover. Pa. 1915- – 1 – us UMI [071]
EVENING SUN – Merced, CA. 1907-25 – 32r – 1 – $1,600.00 – B02447 – us Library Micro [071]
EVENING SUN – New York, 1897-99; 1916-17 – 24r – 1 – us Ross [071]
EVENING TELEGRAM – (1910-1992.-741r) – St. John's, 1993 – 24r – 1 – cn Preston [971]
EVENING TELEGRAM – New York, 1867-1926 – 223r – 1 – us Ross [071]
EVENING TELEGRAM – Omaha, NE. -d. May 1881-Jan 1882 – 1 – us NE Hist [071]
EVENING TELEGRAM – Portland. Or. 1891-1897 – 1 – us UMI [071]
EVENING TELEGRAM – Portland, OR. -d. May 1891-20 Aug 1897 – 1 – $240.00 – us Oregon Hist [071]
EVENING TELEGRAM – Portland OR. May 25 1885-Nov 16 1897, July 15 1886-Nov 30 1918, Feb 2 1878-June 5 1978 + – 1 – us U.O. Library [071]
EVENING TELEGRAM – Providence. R.I. 1880-1906 – 1 – us UMI [071]
EVENING TELEGRAM – Reno, NV. Apr-Jun 1903 – 1r – 1 – $50.00 – U04670 – us Library Micro [071]
EVENING TELEGRAM – San Bernardino, CA. 1921-74 – 683r – 1 – $34,150.00 – C02762 – us Library Micro [071]
EVENING TELEGRAM – San Bernardino. Calif. 1946- – 1 – us UMI [071]
EVENING TELEGRAM – St. John's, Newfoundland, Canada. 1879-1909 – 58r – 1 – $3,770.00 – cn Library Assoc [971]
EVENING TELEGRAM – Victoria, British Columbia, CN. Jul-Nov 1866 – 1r – 1 – cn Commonwealth Micro [072]
EVENING TELEGRAPH – (Also known as: Northamptonshire Evening Telegraph; Kettering Evening Telegraph) – 1986-Aug 1987; 1988-Aug 15 1992; Aug 17 1992-Jun 30 1997 – 163 1/2r – 1 – uk British Libr Newspaper [072]
EVENING TELEGRAPH – Alton. Ill. 1836- – 1 – us UMI [071]
EVENING TELEGRAPH – Brownsville. Pa. 1927-49 – 1 – us UMI [071]
EVENING TELEGRAPH – Dixon. Ill. 1885- – 1 – us UMI [071]
EVENING TELEGRAPH – Dundee, Scotland. 1890 – 2r – 1 – uk British Libr Newspaper [072]
EVENING TELEGRAPH – Ireland.-d. 1916-19. 10 reels – 1 – PS27.50r – ie European Micro [072]
EVENING TELEGRAPH – Lancashire – 1 – uk Microform Academic [072]
EVENING TELEGRAPH – Montreal, Canada. 9 fev 1891 – 1r – 1 – Can$25.00 – cn Can Microfilming [072]
EVENING TELEGRAPH – North Platte, NE. -d. Apr 1896-Jul 1898; Jan 1899-Jan 1901; Apr 1901-Oct 1902; May-Dec 1908; Jan-Dec 1914; Mar 1915-Sept 1941 – 1 – us NE Hist [071]
EVENING TELEGRAPH – North Platte. Neb. 1896-1936 – 1 – us UMI [071]
EVENING TELEGRAPH – Pittsburgh. Pa. 1873-1883 – 1 – us UMI [071]
EVENING TELEGRAPH *see*
- EVENING FREEMAN
- FOOTHILL WEEKLY TIDINGS

EVENING TELEGRAPH AND DAILY COMMERCIAL ADVERTISER – Montreal, Canada. v1 n34. 12 dec 1863-17 dec 1868; v7 n1. 3 jan 1870-v7 n183. 8 aut 1870 – 1r – 1 – Can$50.00 – cn Can Microfilming [072]
EVENING TELEGRAPH AND STAR. (YORKSHIRE TELEGRAPH & STAR) – Sheffield, England. 1890-1920 (missing Jan-Apr 1898, 1911).-d. 76mqn reels – 1 – uk British Libr Newspaper [072]
EVENING TIMES – (1951-1990. 389r £10,500 set. £33.00r) – ca 18r per annum – 1 – £495.00y – uk Herald [072]
EVENING TIMES – Akron. Ohio. 1921-1925 – 1 – us UMI [071]
EVENING TIMES – Ames. Iowa. 1892-1919 – 1 – us UMI [071]
EVENING TIMES – Cumberland. Md. 1872-97; 1898- – 1 – us UMI [071]
EVENING TIMES – Galena. Kan. 1896-1918 – 1 – us UMI [071]
EVENING TIMES – Glasgow, Scotland, UK. 1882. -d. 2 reels – 1 – uk British Libr Newspaper [072]
EVENING TIMES – Grand Island, NE. -w. Nov 1893-Aug 1894 – 1 – us NE Hist [071]
EVENING TIMES – Grand Island. Neb. 1893-1894 – 1 – us UMI [071]
EVENING TIMES – Little Falls. N.Y. 1973- – 1 – us UMI [071]
EVENING TIMES – Monroe. Wis. 1945- – 1 – us UMI [071]
EVENING TIMES – Newport News. Va. 1900-01 – 1 – us UMI [071]
EVENING TIMES – Olean. N.Y. 1907-1931 – 1 – us UMI [071]
EVENING TIMES – Pawtucket. R.I. 1886-1919 – 1 – us UMI [071]
EVENING TIMES – Trenton. N.J. 1883- – 1 – us UMI [071]
EVENING TIMES – West Memphis. Ark. 1957-1967 – 1 – us UMI [071]
THE EVENING TIMES – New York. N.Y. Die abend zeitung. 1906 – 1 – us A.J.P.C. [071]
THE EVENING TIMES – Sayre, PA., 1891-1985 – 13 – $25.00r – us I.M.R. [071]
THE EVENING TIMES – Sayre. Pa. 1921-1970 – 1 – us UMI [071]
EVENING TIMES STAR *see* ALAMEDA TIMES STAR
THE EVENING TIMES-GLOBE – St John, New Brunswick, CN. 1970- – 12r per yr – 1 – Can$55.00r – cn Commonwealth Micro [072]
EVENING TRANSCRIPT – Boston. Mass. 1848-1915 – 1 – us UMI [071]
EVENING TRANSCRIPT – San Bernardino. Calif. 1899-1902 – 1 – us UMI [071]
THE EVENING TRANSCRIPT – San Bernardino, CA. 1898-1902 – 6r – 1 – $300.00 – R03453 – us Library Micro [071]
EVENING TRIBUNE – (1993.-12r; 1926-1974.-154r) – Welland, 1976-1992 – 212r – 1 – cn Preston [971]
EVENING TRIBUNE – Albert Lea. Minn. 1897- – 1 – us UMI [071]
EVENING TRIBUNE – Beaver Falls. Pa. 1904-07; 1912-1922 – 1 – us UMI [071]
EVENING TRIBUNE – Bowling Green, Ohio. 1893-1906 – 12r – 1 – $32.50r – us Archival [071]
EVENING TRIBUNE – Hornell. N.Y. 1900-1905; 1961- – 1 – us UMI [071]
EVENING TRIBUNE – Lawrence. Kan. and pred. 1884-90 – 1 – us UMI [071]
EVENING TRIBUNE – Pawtucket. R.I. 1888-1900 – 1 – us UMI [071]
EVENING TRIBUNE – Pendleton. Or. 1914-1918 – 1 – us UMI [071]
EVENING TRIBUNE – Providence. R.I. 1906-29 – 1 – us UMI [071]
EVENING TRIBUNE – San Diego. Calif. 1895- – 1 – us UMI [071]
THE EVENING TRIBUNE – San Diego, CA. Apr-Dec 1896 (broken series) – 1r – 1 – $50.00 – C02781 – us Library Micro [071]
EVENING TRIBUNE NUNEATON *see* MIDLAND DAILY TRIBUNE
EVENING UNION – Newburgh. N.Y. 1908-12 – 1 – us UMI [071]
EVENING VANGUARD – Venice. Calif. 1944- – 1 – us UMI [071]
EVENING VOLUNTEER – Carlisle, PA., 1901-1903 – 13 – $25.00r – us I.M.R. [071]
EVENING WISCONSIN – Milwaukee. Wis. 1847-1918 – 1 – us UMI [071]
EVENING WISCONSIN – Milwaukee. Wis. and Daily News. 1918 – 1 – us UMI [071]
EVENING WORLD – Chicago, 1906-12 – 9r – 1 – us Ross [071]
EVENING WORLD – Roanoke. Va. 1911-1912 – 1 – us UMI [071]
EVENINGS WITH THE SKEPTICS, OR, FREE DISCUSSION ON FREE THINKERS / Owen, John – New York: J.W. Bouton, 1881 – 3mf – us A.T.L.A. [240]
L'EVENMENT – Paris. Journal quotidien. Red. en chef H. de Villemessant. 1er nov 1865-15 nov 1866 avec un no. spec. du 2 oct 1865 – 1 – fr A.C.R.P.P. [944]
L'EVENMENT – Paris. Quot. 1re ed. 2 janv-30 juin 1851 – 1 – fr A.C.R.P.P. [944]
L'EVENMENT – Paris. Quot. 30 juil 1848-18 sept 1851. suivi de: L' Avenement du peuple voir a ce titre – 1 – fr A.C.R.P.P. [944]
L'EVENMENT – Paris. Quot. Ed. du soir. 1er sept-30 nov 1850 – 1 – fr A.C.R.P.P. [072]
Evens, E P *see* ANIMAL SYMBOLISM IN ECCLESIASTICAL ARCHITECTURE
EVENT – New Westminster. v1-23. 1971-94 – 9 – Can$20.00y – cn Micromedia [971]
L'EVENTAIL – Revue de litterature et d'art. Dir. Francois Laya. Geneve. 1918-oct 1919 – 1 – fr A.C.R.P.P. [800]
EVENTS – Ottawa: "Events" Pub. Co, [1898-19–] – 9 – cn C.I.H.M. [072]
EVENTS AND EPOCHS IN RELIGIOUS HISTORY : BEING THE SUBSTANCE OF A COURSE OF TWELVE LECTURES DELIVERED IN THE LOWELL INSTITUTE, BOSTON, IN 1880 / Clarke, James Freeman – Boston: J.R. Osgood, 1881 – 1mf – us A.T.L.A. [240]
EVENTS AND EPOCHS IN RELIGIOUS HISTORY; BEING THE SUBSTANCE OF A COURSE OF TWELVE LECTURES...LOWELL INSTITUTE, BOSTON, IN 1880 / Clarke, James Freeman – Boston: J.R. Osgood, 1881. xx,402p – 1 – us U.W. Library [240]
EVENTS AT THE COURT OF RANJIT SINGH, 1810-1817: TRANSLATED FROM THE PAPERS IN THE ALIENATION OFFICE, POONA / Garrett, Herbert Leonard Offley – 1935. 288p. Punjab Govt. Record Office publications – 1 – us U.W. Library [950]
EVER FORWARD TO STORM IMPERIALISM AND FEUDALISM BY D.N. AIDIT. DOCUMENTS OF THE SECOND PLENUM, END DECEMBER, 1960 / Communist Party. Indonesia. Comite Central – SE-2679 1. 1961 – 9 – ne IDC [335]
EVER UPWARD, NEVER GO DOWN / Sukarno, Pres. Indonesia – SE 10,845 1. 1965 – 9 – ne IDC [025]
Everett, Charles Carroll *see*
- ESSAYS
- ETHICS FOR YOUNG PEOPLE
- GOSPEL OF PAUL
- THE GOSPEL OF PAUL
- IMMORTALITY, AND OTHER ESSAYS
- THE PSYCHOLOGICAL ELEMENTS OF RELIGIOUS FAITH
- THEISM AND THE CHRISTIAN FAITH

Everett, Craig A *see* JOURNAL OF DIVORCE AND REMARRIAGE
Everett, Edward *see*
- DEFENSE OF CHRISTIANITY AGAINST THE WORK OF GEORGE B. ENGLISH
- EDWARD EVERETT PAPERS, 1675-1930

Everett, Franklin *see* MEMORIALS OF THE GRAND RIVER VALLEY
Everett, J *see*
- IN- AND OUT-LETTERS, 1820-1849
- NOTES AND MEMORANDA, 1784-1868

[Everett, J] *see* WESLEYAN TAKINGS; OR, CENTENARY SKETCHES OF MINISTERIAL CHARACTER, AS EXHIBITED IN THE WESLEYAN CONNEXION DURING THE FIRST HUNDRED YEARS OF ITS EXISTENCE
EVERETT PRESS – Everett, PA., 1881-1983 – 13 – $25.00r – us I.M.R. [071]
EVERETT PRESS AND LEDGER – Everett, PA., 1892-1893 – 13 – $25.00r – us I.M.R. [071]
EVERETT PRESS/LEADER – Pennsylvania. -w 1892-1893 – 13 – $25.00r – us I.M.R. [071]
EVERGLADES NEWS – Canal Point, Pahokee. Fl. -w. 1929-1967. Everglades Observer. -W. 1967- – 1 – us P.K. Yonge [071]
EVERGLADES OBSERVER – Pahokee. Fla. Oct 1967-1979 – 1 – us P.K. Yonge [071]

EVERGREEN BAPTIST CHURCH. FLORENCE, SOUTH CAROLINA : CHURCH RECORDS – 1891-1912, 1941-72 – 1 – 16.61 – us Baptist [240]
EVERGREEN BAPTIST CHURCH. FRANKFORT, KENTUCKY : CHURCH RECORDS – 1884-1977 – 1 – 72.72 – us Baptist [240]
EVERGREEN REVIEW – v1-17 1957-73 1; v15-16 5,6 – us UMI [800]
EVERGREEN REVIEW – 1973 – 1 – us UMI [073]
Everhart, BM *see* THE NORTH AMERICAN PYRENOMYCETES; A CONTRIBUTION TO MYCOLOGIC BOTANY
Everitt, Graham *see* ENGLISH CARICATURISTS AND GRAPHIC HUMOURISTS OF THE NINETEETH CENTURY
THE EVERLASTING RIGHTEOUSNESS, OR, HOW SHALL MEN BE JUST WITH GOD / Bonar, Horatius – New York: Robert Carter, 1873. 1 fiche – 9 – us A.T.L.A. [240]
Everling, Otto *see* DIE PAULINISCHE ANGELOLOGIE UND DAEMONOLOGIE
Evermann, B W *see*
- THE FISHES OF NORTH AND MIDDLE AMERICA
- THE FISHES OF PORTO RICO

Evers, Ernst August *see* UEBER DIE SCHULBILDUNG ZUR BESTIALITAET
Evers, Tilman Tonnies *see* MILITARREGIERUNG IN ARGENTINIEN
Eversmann, E *see* FAUNA LEPIDOPTEROLOGICA VOLGO-URALENSIS
Everts *see*
- HISTORY OF BRANCH COUNTY
- HISTORY OF CUMBERLAND COUNTY, MAINE
- HISTORY OF LIVINGSTON COUNTY. BIOGRAPHICAL SKETCHES
- HISTORY OF ONEIDA COUNTY
- HISTORY OF SUSQUEHANNA AND JUNIATA VALLEYS

Everts, E J G *see*
- COLEOPTERA NEERLANDICA
- NIEUWE NAAMLIJST VAN NEDERLANDSCHE SCHILDVLEUGELIGE INSECTEN (INSECTA COLEOPTERA)

Everts, Louis H *see* HISTORY OF THE CONNECTICUT VALLEY IN MASSACHUSETTS
Everwijn, D *see* ABRAHAM VAN WICQUEFORT...
THE EVERY DAY OF LIFE / Miller, James Russell – New York: Thomas Y Crowell, c1892 – 1mf – 9 – 0-8370-7180-1 – 1986-1180 – us A.T.L.A. [240]
EVERY DAY WITH BEGINNERS – 1956-61 – 1 – 26.95 – us Baptist [240]
EVERY DAY WITH PRIMARIES – 1956-61 – 1 – 27.02 – us Baptist [240]
Every, E F *see* THE ANGLICAN CHURCH IN SOUTH AMERICA
EVERY EVENING – Wilmington. Del. 1871-1932 – 1 – us UMI [071]
EVERY FRIDAY – Cincinnati. Ohio. 1958-65 – 1 – us A.J.P.C. [071]
EVERY LANDLORD OR TENANT HIS OWN LAWYER. / Paul, John – London: Strahan and Woodfall, 1775. 144p. LL-717 – 1 – us L of C Photodup [340]
EVERY MAN'S MINE OF USEFUL KNOWLEDGE, OR, A BOOK FOR ALL / Borthwick, John Douglas – Montreal: G. & W. Clarke, 1869? 04231. (Pre-1900 Canadiana) – 9 – cn C.I.H.M. [030]
EVERY ONE HAS HIS FAULT : A COMEDY, IN FIVE ACTS: AS PERFORMED AT THE THEATRE ROYAL, COVENT-GARDEN / Inchbald, Mrs. – London: Printed for G.G. and. J. Robinson, 1793 – 1 roll – 1 – 1-55879-293-7 – uk Libr Preservation [840]
EVERY SATURDAY : A JOURNAL OF CHOICE READING – Boston. ns: v1-3. 1870-71 – 3r – 1 – us Ross [073]
EVERY SATURDAY – Ottawa: [Mason and Reynolds, 1886] – 9 – cn C.I.H.M. [072]
EVERY WEEK – 1904-1946 – 18mf – 9 – at Corangamite [980]
EVERYBODY'S LAW BOOK / Shirley, John L – New York?: Lupton,? 1886. 124,ivp. LL-214 – 1 – us L of C Photodup [340]
EVERYBODY'S LAW BOOK; LEGAL RIGHTS AND LEGAL REMEDIES. / Koones, John Alexander – (1905 ed. 808 p. LL-800. 1) – New York, Hitchcock, 1893. 768 p. LL-358 – 1 – us L of C Photodup [340]
EVERYBODY'S LAWYER AND COUNSELOR IN BUSINESS... / Crosby, Frank – Philadelphia: John E Potter, 1860 – 4mf – 9 – $6.00 – LLMC 91-083 – us L.L.M.C. [340]
EVERY-DAY EVANGELISM : PERSONAL, TRAINED, CO-OPERATIVE / Leete, Frederick Deland – Cincinnati: Jennings and Graham; New York: Eaton and Mains, c1909 – 1mf – us A.T.L.A. [240]
EVERY-DAY LIFE IN SOUTH AFRICA / Lowndes, E E K – London: S W Patridge, 1900 – 1 – us Res Libr [300]
EVERYDAY LIFE IN THE OLD STONE AGE / Quennell, Marjorie (Courtney) – New York, London: G.P. Putnam's Sons, 1922. xxii,201p. incl. plates. col. front., fold. tab. (The Everyday Life Series) – 1 – us U.W. Library [573]
EVERYDAY SOLDIER LIFE : OR A HISTORY OF THE 113TH OHIO VOLUNTEER INFANTRY / McAdams, F M – Columbus, OH: Chas M Cott & Co, 1884 – 1r – 1 – us Western Res [976]
EVERYMAN'S LAWYER...BEING A NEW EDITION...OF THE HOME LIBRARY OF LAW / Bolles, Albert Sidney – New York, Doubleday, Page, 1908. 3 v. LL-1069 – 1 – us L of C Photodup [340]
EVERYWOMAN'S FAMILY CIRCLE *see* FAMILY CIRCLE
EVERYWOMAN'S WORLD – 1914-21 – 1 – $145.00 – cn McLaren [640]
Evetts, B T A *see* THE CHURCHES AND MONASTERIES OF EGYPT AND SOME NEIGHBOURING COUNTRIES, ATTRIBUTED TO ABU SALIH, THE ARMENIAN
Evgen'ev-Maksimov, V *see*
- IZ PROSHLOGO RUSSKOI ZHURANLISTIKI
- IZ PROSHLOGO RUSSKOI ZHURNALISTIKI

Evgenev-Maksimov, Vladislav Evgenevich *see* OCHERK ISTORII NOVE ISHE I RUSSKO I LITERATURY
Evgenii, Mitropolit *see*
- SLOVAR' ISTORICHESKII O BYVSHIKH V ROSSII PISATELIAKH, DUKHOVNAGO CHINA, GREKOROSSIISKIIA TSERKVI
- SLOVAR' ISTORICHESKII O BYVSHIKH V ROSSII PISATELIAKH DUKHOVNOGO CHINA GREKOROSSIISKIIA TSERKVI
- SLOVAR' RUSSKIKH SVETSKIKH PISATELEI, SOOTECHESTVENNIKOV I CHUZHESTRANTSEV, PISAVSHIKH V ROSSII

EVIAN CONFERENCE / Jewish Agency for Palestine. Jerusalem – Statistical tables on the distribution, migration and natural increase of the Jews in the world, with special reference to Jewish activities in Palestine. Jul 1938. BJ-28-138 1 – 9 – ne IDC [956]
EVIDENCE / Natal Colony. Native Affairs Commission – Pietermaritzburg: P Davis & Sons, Govt Printers, 1907 – 1 – us Res Libr [960]
EVIDENCE AND CROSS EXAMINATION OF WILLIAM D. HAYWOOD IN THE CASE OF THE U.S.A. VS. WM. D. HAYWOOD, ET. AL / Haywood, William Dudley – Chicago: General Defense Committee, 1918?. 312p. LL-308 – 1 – us L of C Photodup [340]
EVIDENCE AND OPINIONS ON THE HOUSE OF LAYMEN IN ALLIANCE WITH THE SYNOD OF TORONTO SUBMITTED TO THE LAITY OF THE CHURCH OF ENGLAND / Association of the Laity of the Church of England. Toronto – Toronto: Williamson Book Co., 1893. 00846. (Pre-1900 Canadiana) – 9 – cn C.I.H.M. [240]
EVIDENCE AND REPORT / East African Protectorate. Native Labour Commission, 1912-13 – Nairobi: [s.n.], 1913 – 1 – us Res Libr [960]
THE EVIDENCE IN THE CASE : AN ANALYSIS OF THE DIPLOMATIC RECORDS SUBMITTED BY ENGLAND, GERMANY, RUSSIA AND BELGIUM IN THE SUPREME COURT OF CIVILIZATION, AND THE CONCLUSIONS DEDUCIBLE AS TO THE MORAL RESPONSIBILITY FOR THE WAR / Beck, James M – N.Y. & London: G P Putnam's Sons, 1914 – 3mf – 9 – $4.50 – LLMC 92-118 – us L.L.M.C. [340]
EVIDENCE OF BIOMECHANICAL FUNCTIONAL SYMMETRY IN THE PRESENCE OF LOWER EXTREMITY STRUCTURAL ASYMMETRY DURING RUNNING / McBride, Margaret E & Sanderson, David – 1989 – 2mf – 9 – $8.00 – us Microform Publ [612]
EVIDENCE OF GEORGE WASHINGTON'S RELIGION / Gano, John – 1874-91. 398p – 1 – 13.93 – us Baptist [240]
THE EVIDENCE OF SALVATION : OR, THE DIRECT WITNESS OF THE SPIRIT / Stackpole, Everett Schermerhorn – (Includes bibliographical references) – New York: Thomas Y Crowell, c1894 – 1mf – 9 – 0-8370-5512-1 – 1985-3512 – us A.T.L.A. [210]
THE EVIDENCE OF THE MOTIVES AND OBJECTS OF THE BUSHMAN WARS, 1769-77. / Moodie, Donald – Cape Town. 1841 – 1 – us Res Libr [960]
EVIDENCE TAKEN AT AN INQUIRY INSTITUTED BY THE SHIPPING INTEREST AND THE MARINE UNDERWRITERS INTO THE NEEDS OF THE ST LAWRENCE ROUTE FROM MONTREAL TO THE SEA – Montreal?: s.n., 1900?. 05493. (Pre-1900 Canadiana) – 9 – cn C.I.H.M. [971]
EVIDENCE TAKEN BY THE COMMISSION... / Rhodesia. Northern. Commission Appointed to Enquire into the Disturbances in the Copperbelt – Lusaka: Govt Printer, 1935 – 1 – us Res Libr [960]
EVIDENCE TAKEN BY THE COMMISSION APPOINTED TO ENQUIRE INTO THE DISTURBANCES IN THE COPPERBELT, NORTHERN RHODESIA, JUL-SEP 1935 – [Salisbury?: s.n., 193-?]. v1 – us Res Libr [960]
THE EVIDENCES AND DOCTRINES OF THE CATHOLIC CHURCH : SHOWING THAT THE FORMER ARE NO LESS CONVINCING THAN THE LATTER ARE PROPITIOUS TO THE HAPPINESS OF SOCIETY / MacHale, John – (Includes bibliographical references) – 3rd ed. Dublin: M H Gill, 1885 – 2mf – 9 – 0-8370-6999-8 – 1986-0999 – us A.T.L.A. [230]
EVIDENCES OF ANCIENT CIVILIZATION IN AMERICA: CONSTITUTING A LECTURE DELIVERED ON BEHALF OF THE MECHANICS' INSTITUTE ON TUESDAY, 1ST OF MARCH, 1870 / Bessey, W E – Guelph: Mechanics' Institute of Guelph, 1870. 00093. (Pre-1900 Canadiana) – 9 – cn C.I.H.M. [970]
EVIDENCES OF CHRISTIANITY / Bergen, John Tallmadge – (Includes index) – Holland, MI. Wm. H. Bingham, 1902 – 1mf – 9 – 0-8370-2285-1 – 1985-0285 – us A.T.L.A. [210]
EVIDENCES OF CHRISTIANITY / Ragg, Lonsdale – New York: Edwin S. Gorham, 1909.1 fiche. 8370-4825-7 – 9 – us A.T.L.A. [240]
THE EVIDENCES OF CHRISTIANITY : IN THEIR EXTERNAL DIVISON / McIlvaine, Charles Pettit; ed by Gregory, Olinthus – (Includes bibliographical references) – London: James Blackwood, 1871 – 2mf – 9 – 0-8370-4355-7 – 1985-2355 – us A.T.L.A. [230]
EVIDENCES OF CHRISTIANITY: LECTURES BEFORE THE LOWELL INSTITUTE / Hopkins, Mark – Boston: T.R. Marvin, 1909. 1 fiche – 9 – us A.T.L.A. [240]
EVIDENCES OF DIVINE REVELATION: IN A LETTER TO A JUDGE / Spencer, Ichabod Smith – Boston: American Tract Society, 1865. 1 fiche – 9 – us A.T.L.A. [240]
EVIDENCES OF REVEALED RELIGION / Thomson, Edward A – Cincinnati: Hitchcock & Walden, 1872. 1 fiche – 9 – us A.T.L.A. [240]
EVIDENCES OF THE AUTHENTICITY, INSPIRATION, AND CANONICAL AUTHORITY OF THE HOLY SCRIPTURES / Alexander, Archibald – (Expanded version of a work which appeared under the title: A Brief Outline of the Evidences of the Christian Religion) – 5th ed. Philadelphia: Presbyterian Bd of Publ, c1836 – 1mf – 9 – 0-8370-2060-3 – 1985-0060 – us A.T.L.A. [220]
THE EVIDENCES OF THE GENUINENESS OF THE GOSPELS / Norton, Andrews – 2nd ed. 3 v. 1846-48 – 9 – us A.T.L.A. [240]
THE EVIDENTIAL VALUE OF THE ACTS OF THE APOSTLES / Howson, John Saul – New York: E P Dutton, 1880 – 1mf – 9 – 0-8370-3681-X – 1985-1681 – us A.T.L.A. [220]
EVIL AND EVOLUTION : AN ATTEMPT TO TURN THE LIGHT OF MODERN SCIENCE ON TO THE ANCIENT MYSTERY OF EVIL / Millin, George Francis – 3rd ed. London, New York: Macmillan, 1899 – 1mf – 9 – 0-8370-6149-0 – 1986-0149 – us A.T.L.A. [210]
EVIL GENIUS, THE STORY OF JOSEPH GOEBBELS / Ebermayer, Erich – Trans. and freely adapted by Louis Hagen. London: A. Wingate, (1953). 245p. illus – 1 – us U.W. Library [920]
EVITA : LIBRO DE LECTURA PARA PRIMER GRADO INFERIOR / Albornoz de Videla, Graciela – Buenos Aires: Editorial Luis Lasserre, 1953 – 1 – CSUXADJ8874-B – us Hoover Inst Photo [440]
EVITA, FIRST LADY : A BIOGRAPHY OF EVA PERON / Barnes, John – New York: Grove Press: distibuted by Random House, 1978 – 1 – CSUXADL7563-B – us Hoover Inst Photo [320]
EVITA FUERA DEL BALC ON / Jamandreu, Paco – [Buenos Aires]: Ediciones del Libro Abierto, [1981] – 9 – us Hoover Inst Photo [972]
EVITA MONTONERA – (Includes c.1: v.1:no.6 1975:Aug.-v.2:no.11 (1976:Jan.); v.2:no.14 1976:Oct.; v.3:no.17 1977:Apr) – [Cordoba, Argentina?: s.n., 1975- – 1 – CSUXADH9680-S – us Hoover Inst Photo [972]
Evliya, Chelebi *see* TRAVELS IN EUROPE, ASIA AND AFRICA
EVOCACION DE ORTIZ GUERRERO / Recalde, Facundo – Asuncion: [El Arte, 1952] – 1 – CSUXAJA7313-B – us Hoover Inst Photo [920]
EVOLIUTSIIA OSNOVNYKH ELEMENTOV SELSKOGO KHOZIA ISTVA ODESSKOI GUBERNII / Chernenkov, BN – Odessa: [s.n.], 1925. 1v. (various pagings) – 1 – CSUX91-B1215 – us Hoover Inst Photo [630]
EVOLUCAO – Manaos, Amazonas. 8 Maio-10 Jun 1906 – 1,5,6 – bl Biblioteca [072]
EVOLUCAO : ORGAO REPUBLICANO – Manaos, Amazonas. 15 Abr-28 Jun 1888 – 1,5,6 – bl Biblioteca [072]
EVOLUCAO – Penedo, Alagoas. 25 Maio-8 Jun 1890 – 1,5,6 – bl Biblioteca [072]
EVOLUCION DE LA ENERGIA ELECTRICA EN LA PROVINCIA DE BADAJOZ / Juarez Sanchez-Rubio, Cipriano – Badajoz: Dip. Provincial, 1974. Sep. REE – 1 – sp Bibl Santa Ana [333]
EVOLUCION DE LA MORFOLOGIA URBANA DE PONTEVEDRA HASTA 1900 / Mendez Martinez, Gonzalo – 1mf – 9 – Pta1,000.00 – 84-85422-79-1 – sp Pentalfa [910]
EVOLUCION DEL MOVIMIENTO OBRERO / Borlenghi, Angel G – Buenos Aires: [s.n.], 1950 – 1 – CSUXAHZ3406-B – us Hoover Inst Photo [320]
LA EVOLUCION ECONOMICA 2 : LA PRODUCCION / Munoz Casillas, Juan – Madrid: Ed. Iberoam, 1952 – 1 – sp Bibl Santa Ana [330]
LA EVOLUCION ECONOMICA 3 : LA EMPRESA / Munoz Casillas, Juan – Barcelona: Tip.Vda. de Golo Saenz, 1952 – 1 – sp Bibl Santa Ana [330]
LA EVOLUCION ECONOMICA 4 : LOS MEDIOS DE ACCION DEL ESTADO Y LA COLABORACION DE LA SOCIEDAD / Munoz Casillas, Juan – Madrid: Tip.Vda.Galo Saenz, 1952 – 1 – sp Bibl Santa Ana [330]
EVOLUCION SOLAIRE ET SERIES ASTRO-CHIMIQUES PAR... / Roso de Luna, Mario – Paris: Imprimerie Bussiere, 1909 – 1 – sp Bibl Santa Ana [440]
EVOLUCIONISTA – Maceio, Alagoas. 8 Set 1902; Mar, Maio-16 Jun 1903 – 1,5,6 – bl Biblioteca [072]
O EVOLUCIONISTA : JORNAL DA TARDE – Maceio, Alagoas. 2 Jan-Dez 1905; Jan-30 Nov 1906 – 1,5,6 – bl Biblioteca [072]
O EVOLUCIONISTA : ORGAM DA SOCIEDADE ACTIVIDADE CHRISTA DA EGREJA PRESBYTERIANA EM MANAOS – Manaos, Amazonas. 18 Set-2 Out 1904 – 1,5,6 – bl Biblioteca [072]
EVOLUSI MASJARAKAT / Brown, James Alexander Campbell – SE-11,639 1. 1949 – 9 – ne IDC [950]
DE EVOLUTIELEER EN HET GODSDIENSTIG GELOOF / Groenewegen, H Ij – Baarn: Hollandia-Drukkerij, 1909. 1 fiche – 9 – us A.T.L.A. [240]
L'EVOLUTION – Port-au-Prince, Haiti: Imp. de l'Abeille, [v1 n2-v2 n90] (1916-1917) – 5 sheets – 9 – us Res Libr [072]
EVOLUTION – 1- 1947- 1; v19- 5,6; v30- 9 – us UMI [575]
EVOLUTION: A LECTURE DELIVERED IN MONTREAL, MARCH 1883. / Adams, Robert Chamblet – New York: Putnam, 1883. 04005. (Pre-1900 Canadiana) – 9 – cn C.I.H.M. [575]
EVOLUTION AND CHRISTIAN FAITH / Lane, Henry Higgins – Princeton: Princeton University Press, 1923. xi,214p – 1 – us U.W. Library [240]
EVOLUTION AND CHRISTIANITY / Iverach, James – London: Hodder & Stoughton, 1894. 1 fiche – 9 – us A.T.L.A. [240]

EVOLUTION AND CHRISTIANITY : A STUDY / Grumbine, Jesse Charles Fremont – Chicago: Charles H Kerr, 1887 – 1mf – 9 – 0-8370-4789-7 – 1985-2789 – us A.T.L.A. [210]
EVOLUTION AND RELIGION / Beecher, Henry Ward – New York: Fords, Howard, & Hulbert, 1885 – 1mf – 9 – 0-8370-6161-X – 1986-0161 – us A.T.L.A. [210]
EVOLUTION AND RELIGION / Osborn, Henry Fairfield – New York: C. Scribner's sons, 1923. vii,21p. Reprinted from the New York Times, 5 Mar 1922 – 1 – us U.W. Library [240]
EVOLUTION AND RELIGION : A PARENT'S TALKS WITH HIS CHILDREN CONCERNING THE MORAL SIDE OF EVOLUTION / Trumbull, William – (Includes bibliographical references) – New York:Grafton Press, 1907 – 1mf – 9 – 0-8370-5582-2 – 1985-3582 – us A.T.L.A. [170]
EVOLUTION AND RELIGION: FROM THE STANDPOINT OF ONE WHO BELIEVES IN BOTH / Savage, Minot Judson – Philadelphia: Geo. H. Buchanan, 1886. 1 fiche – 9 – us A.T.L.A. [240]
EVOLUTION AND RELIGION, OR, FAITH AS A PART OF A COMPLETE COSMIC SYSTEM / Bascom, John – New York: G.P. Putnam, 1897. 1 fiche – 9 – us A.T.L.A. [240]
EVOLUTION, AS TAUGHT IN THE BIBLE / Hasskarl, Gottlieb Christopher Henry – Philadelphia: Lutheran Publications Society, 1887. 1 fiche – 9 – us A.T.L.A. [240]
L'EVOLUTION DE LA FOI CATHOLIQUE / Hebert, Marcel – (Includes bibliographical references) – Paris:Felix Alcan, 1905 – 1mf – 9 – 0-8370-4488-X – 1985-2488 – us A.T.L.A. [240]
L'EVOLUTION DE L'ENSEIGNEMENT DU PREMIER ET DU SECOND DEGRE DANS L'ANCIEN CAMEROUN ORIENTAL DEPUIS L'INDEPENDANCE / Batjeck, A – 9 – F120.00 – fr Ethnologie [306]
EVOLUTION DE L'INDUSTRIE MANUFACTURIERE EN ALGERIE, 1962/1968 / Algeria – BNE-8602 1 – 9 – ne IDC [324]
EVOLUTION DES COUTUMES LIEES AUX FETES DE PAQUES EN CONFLENS / Gouaux, M – 9 – F30.00 – fr Ethnologie [306]
L'EVOLUTION DES DOGMES / Guignebert, Charles – (Includes bibliographical references) – Paris: Ernest Flammarion, 1910 – 1mf – 9 – 0-8370-8821-6 – 1986-2821 – us A.T.L.A. [240]
EVOLUTION DES SYSTEMES DE CHARGES EN MESO-AMERIQUE AU XXE SIECLE / Figuerolas, H – 9 – F60.00 – fr Ethnologie [306]
EVOLUTION DU DROIT FLUVIAL INTERNATIONAL... / Eysinga, W J M van – Leyde, n.d. – 1mf – 1 – ILM-2347/1 – ne IDC [327]
L'EVOLUTION DU "JUS SOLI"... / Baumann, C – Macon, 1931 – 3mf – 9 – LLM-3411/1 – ne IDC [340]
L'EVOLUTION DU ROMAN EN ALLEMAGNE AU XIE SIECLE / Pineau, L – H 557 2. 1908 – 9 – ne IDC [430]
L'EVOLUTION DU ROYAUME RWANDA DES ORIGINES A 1900 / Vansina, Jan – Bruxelles, 1962 – us Res Libr [960]
EVOLUTION D'UNE EXPLOITATION AGRICOLE DANOISE DE 1924 A 1972 / Morisset-Andersen, C – 9 – F50.00 – fr Ethnologie [305]
EVOLUTION EXPLAINED AND COMPARED WITH THE BIBLE / Smyth, William Woods – London: Elliot Stock, 1883. 1 fiche – 9 – us A.T.L.A. [240]
L'EVOLUTION FEMININE: LA FEMME AU FOYER ET DANS LA CITE / Goyau, Lucie Faure – Paris: Perrin, 1917. xvi,366p. (Les Femmes Collection) – 4mf – 9 – $10.00 – fr Bibl Nationale [305]
EVOLUTION IN MY MISSION VIEWS OR GROWTH OF GOSPEL MISSION PRINCIPLES IN MY OWN MIND / Crawford, Tarleton P – 1852-1902, 1903 – 1 – 5.88 – us Baptist [240]
EVOLUTION IN SCIENCE AND REVOLUTION IN RELIGION: WITH OTHER ADDRESSES / Ball, Wayland Dalrymple – Philadelphia: Porter & Coates, 1893. 1 fiche – 9 – us A.T.L.A. [240]
EVOLUTION: ITS NATURE, ITS EVIDENCES, AND ITS RELATION TO RELIGIOUS THOUGHT / LeConte, Joseph – New York: D. Appleton, 1897. 1 fiche – 9 – us A.T.L.A. [240]
THE EVOLUTION OF CHRISTIANITY / Abbott, Lyman – Boston: Houghton, Mifflin, 1892.1 fiche – 9 – us A.T.L.A. [240]
THE EVOLUTION OF GLOBAL STRATEGEY / Kittredge, Tracy B – 1 roll. T1174 – 1 – us Nat'l Archives [355]
THE EVOLUTION OF LAW : A HISTORICAL REVIEW / Scott, Henry W – New York: Borden Press, 1908 – 2mf – 9 – $3.00 – LLMC 95-156 – us L.L.M.C. [340]
THE EVOLUTION OF MAN AND CHRISTIANITY / MacQueary, Howard – (Includes bibliographical references and index) – rev enl ed. New York: D Appleton, 1891 – 1mf – 9 – 0-8370-4251-8 – 1985-2251 – us A.T.L.A. [210]
THE EVOLUTION OF NEW CHINA / Brewster, William Nesbitt – (Includes bibliographical references) – Cincinnati: Jennings & Graham; New York: Eaton & Mains, c1907 – 1mf – 9 – 0-8370-6026-5 – 1986-0026 – us A.T.L.A. [240]
THE EVOLUTION OF OLD TESTAMENT RELIGION / Orchard, William Edwin – London: James Clarke, 1908. 1 fiche – 9 – us A.T.L.A. [240]
THE EVOLUTION OF PLANNING IN LIBYA / Libya. Ministry of Planning and Development – Commentary nr. 14. Background paper for discussion. Tripoli. Farley, R. Senior Economist. BNE-703 1 – 9 – ne IDC [338]
THE EVOLUTION OF RELIGION : AN ANTHROPOLOGICAL STUDY / Farnell, LR – New York: Putnam, 1905 – 1mf – us A.T.L.A. [200]
THE EVOLUTION OF SPIRITUAL MAN / Lisle, William McIntire – Boston: Silver, Burdett, 1894. 1 fiche – 9 – us A.T.L.A. [240]
EVOLUTION OF TECHNOLOGY IN ITALIAN FISHERIES – 1987 – 86p – it F.A.O. [639]
EVOLUTION OF THE AMERICAN MAGAZINE – 1741-1891 – 3r – 1 – us Ross [073]
THE EVOLUTION OF THE ATMOSPHERE...: A...SCIENTIFIC REPLY TO MODERN MATERIALISTIC ATHEISM / Phin, John – New York: Industrial Pub. Co., 1908. 1 fiche. 8370-4736-6 – 9 – us A.T.L.A. [240]
EVOLUTION OF THE BLACK UNIVERSITY – 1 – us Ross [370]
EVOLUTION OF THE MESSIANIC IDEA: A STUDY IN COMPARATIVE RELIGION / Oesterley, William Oscar Emil – London: Isaac Pitman, 1908. 1 fiche – 9 – us A.T.L.A. [230]
THE EVOLUTION OF THE MONASTIC IDEAL : FROM THE EARLIEST TIMES DOWN TO THE COMING OF THE FRIARS / Workman, Herbert Brook – London: C.H. Kelly, 1913 – 1mf – us A.T.L.A. [240]
THE EVOLUTION OF THE SUNDAY SCHOOL / Cope, Henry Frederick – Boston: Pilgrim Press, c1911. (Modern Sunday-School manuals) – 1mf – us A.T.L.A. [240]
EVOLUTION OR CREATION:...SCIENTIFIC AND SCRIPTURAL THEORIES OF CREATION / Townsend, Luther Tracy – New York: Fleming H. Revell, 1896. 1 fiche – 9 – us A.T.L.A. [240]
EVOLUTION, OR, THE DIVINE METHOD OF CREATION AND PRESERVING THE UNIVERSE / Frost, AF – Philadelphia: Wm. A. Alden, 1892. 1 fiche – 9 – us A.T.L.A. [240]
EVOLUTIONAERE ETHIK / Funken, Michael – 1991 – 129p – 9 – DM98.00 – 3-89349-430-8 – gw Hänsel [170]
EVOLUTIONARY STUDIES ON SOME AUSTRALIAN HONEYEATERS / Martindale, John – (MSc Thesis) – 1980 – 9 – A$15.00 – at R.A.O.U. [590]
EVRAZIYA – Paris, France. Eurasie Hebdomadaire russe. -w. 24 Nov 1928-7 Sept 1929. 28 ft – 1 – uk British Libr Newspaper [072]
EVREI V ROSSII V TSARSTVOVANIE NIKOLAI A 2 *see* EVREI V TSARSTVOVANIE NIKOLAIA 2, 1894-1914
EVREI V SSSR / ed by Mindlinu, Z L – Moskva: Pravlenie Vserossi iskogo ORT, 1929 – 1 – CSUX91-B3380 – us Hoover Inst Photo [305]
EVREI V TSARSTVOVANIE NIKOLAIA 2, 1894-1914 / Dubnow, Simon – Peterburg: Evre iski i izdatelski i kooperativ "Kadima", 1922 – 1 – CSUX89-B5346 – us Hoover Inst Photo [305]
O EVREIAKH / Gorky, Maksim – [Petrograd]: Izd. Petrogradskago sovieta rabochikh i krasn. deputatov, 1919 – 1 – CSUX89-B6754 – us Hoover Inst Photo [947]
Evreinov, Grigorii Aleksandrovich *see* NATSIONALNYE VOPROSY NA INORODCHESKIKH OKRAINAKH ROSSII
EVREISKAIA BIBLIOTEKA – Istoriko-literaturnyi sbornik. v. 1-4, 6-8. Spb. 1871-80; Ed. 2. v. 1-4, 9-10. Spb. 1881-1903. BR-1587 2 – 8 – ne IDC [460]
EVREISKAIA BIBLIOTEKA – St Petersburg. v. 1-10. 1871-1903 – 1 – us NY Public [460]
EVREISKAIA ENTSIKLOPEDIIA : SVOD ZNANII O EVREISTVE I EGO KUL'TURE V PROSHLOM I NASTOIASHCHEM – Spb., 1906-1913 – 175mf – 9 – R-10512/1 – ne IDC [290]
EVREISKAIA NEDELIA – v. 1-11. Spb. 1910. BR-4164 2 – 8 – ne IDC [073]
EVREISKAIA NIVA – Ezhemesiachnyi zhurnal posviashchennyi voprosam emigratsii i kolonizatsii. v. 1-6. Spb. 1913. BR-4165 2 – 8 – ne IDC [947]
EVREISKAIA SHKOLA – Ezhemesiachnyi zhurnal, posviashchennyi vospitaniiu i obrazovaniia evreev. Spb. 1904-05. Lacking: 1904 (3, 6, 7); 1905 (2, 6, 7, 9, 10). BR-3407 2 – 8 – ne IDC [947]
EVREISKAIA STARINA – Spb. 1909-16. BR-3408 2 – 8 – ne IDC [947]
EVREISKAIA ZHIZN = JEWISH LIFE – (In Russian) – St-Petersburg, RU. no5,6,7 1904 – 1r – 1 – $25.00 – cn Can Microfilming [072]
EVREISKI VESTI – Sofia, Bulgaria. Apr 1945-1955 – 1r – 1 – us L of C Photodup [949]
EVREISKIIA ZAPISKI : EZHEMESIACHNOE ISTORIKO-LITERATURNOE IZDANIE – Riga. v1-12. 1881 – 14mf – 9 – ne IDC [947]
EVREISKIIA ZAPISKI – Ezhemesiachnoe istoriko-literaturnoe izdanie. v. 1-12. Riga. 1881. BR-3410 2 – 8 – ne IDC [947]
EVREISKOE BEZPRAVIE I EGO PLODY / Ancharova, Mariia – Moskva: Zadruga, 1917 – 1 – CSUX89-B5906 – us Hoover Inst Photo [947]
EVREISKOE MESTECHKO V REVOLIUTSII : OCHERKI / ed by Tana-Bogoraza, V G – Moskva: Gos. izd-vo, 1926 – 1 – CSUX89-B5932 – us Hoover Inst Photo [947]
EVREISKOE OBOZRIENIE – St Petersburg, 1884 – 1r – 1 – us Ross [270]
EVREISKOE OBOZRIENIE – St Petersburg. Jan-July 1884 – 1 – us NY Public [073]
EVREISKOE ZEMLEUSTROENIE V SOVETSKOM SOIUZE / Finkel, K A – 2-e ispr. i dop. izd. Kharkov: Izd. Ukrozeta i kharkovskogo otdnie OZET, 1927 – 1 – CSUX89-B6389 – us Hoover Inst Photo [947]
EVROPEETS – Zhurnal nauki i slovesnosti. v. 1-3. M. 1832. Lacking: v. 3. BR-3411 2 – 8 – ne IDC [460]
EV'RY MONTH AND PIANO MUSIC MAGAZINE – 1895-1903. Incomplete – 1 – us Sibley [780]
EVSEBIANA : ESSAYS ON THE ECCLESIASTICAL HISTORY OF EUSEBIUS, BISHOP OF CAESAREA / Lawlor, Hugh Jackson – Oxford: Clarendon Press, 1912 – 1mf – us A.T.L.A. [240]
Evseev, I *see* KNIGA PROROKA DANIILA, V DREVNESLAVIANSKOM PEREVODE
Evtushenko, Yu. G *see* OPTIMIZATION METHODS AND SOFTWARE
Evzlin, Z P *see* ORGANIZATSIIA I TEKHNIKA KREDITNYKH KOOPERATIVOV
Ewald, Alexander Charles *see*
– THE LIFE AND TIMES OF THE HON. ALGERNON SYDNEY, 1622-1683
– OUR PUBLIC RECORDS: A BRIEF HANDBOOK TO THE NATIONAL ARCHIVES
Ewald, Heinrich *see*
– ABHANDLUNG UEBER DES ATHIOPISCHEN BUCHES HENOKH
– COMMENTARY ON THE BOOK OF JOB
– DIE DICHTER DES ALTEN BUNDES
– EWALD'S INTRODUCTORY HEBREW GRAMMAR
– GESCHICHTE DES APOSTOLISCHEN ZEITALTERS ZUR ZERSTOERUNG JERUSALEM'S
– GESCHICHTE DES VOLKES ISRAEL
– JESAJA MIT DEN UEBRIGEN AELTEREN PROPHETEN
– THE LIFE OF JESUS CHRIST
– OLD AND NEW TESTAMENT THEOLOGY
– DIE PROPHETEN DES ALTEN BUNDES
Ewald, Paul *see* DAS HAUPTPROBLEM DER EVANGELIENFRAGE UND DER WEG ZU SEINER LOESUNG
EWALD'S INTRODUCTORY HEBREW GRAMMAR = HEBRAEISCHE SPRACHLEHRE FUER ANFAENGER / Ewald, Heinrich – (Includes indexes) – London: Asher, 1870 – 1mf – 9 – 0-8370-9230-2 – 1986-3230 – us A.T.L.A. [470]
EWANGEELIUMI KRISLANE = THE EVANGELICAL CHRISTIAN – 1930-1933. Estonian. 776p – 1 – $31.04 – us Baptist [240]
EWANGELISTS = THE EVANGELIST – Riga, 1883, Nos. 1-24, 27. 208p – 1 – $8.32 – us Baptist [240]
Ewart, Felicie *see* GOETHES VATER
Ewart, J *see* ANIMAL REMAINS
Ewart, John Skirving *see* EWART'S INDEX OF THE STATUTES, BEING AN ALPHABETICAL INDEX OF ALL THE PUBLIC STATUTES PASSED BY THE LEGISLATURES OF THE LATE PROVINCE OF CANADA.
EWART'S INDEX OF THE STATUTES, BEING AN ALPHABETICAL INDEX OF ALL THE PUBLIC STATUTES PASSED BY THE LEGISLATURES OF THE LATE PROVINCE OF CANADA. / Ewart, John Skirving – 2nd ed. Toronto: Carswell, 1874. 191p.LL-2329 – 1 – us L of C Photodup [340]
THE EWE PEOPLE AND THE COMING OF EUROPEAN RULE, 1850-1914 / Amenumey, Divine Edem Kobla – London, 1964 – us Res Libr [960]
Ewell, D Jesse *see* COLLECTION OF AIRS FOR ONE AND TWO FLUTES, OR OTHER TREBLE INSTRUMENTS
Ewell, John D *see* LIFE OF REV. WILLIAM KEELE
Ewen, Robert *see* THROUGH CANADA IN 1878
Ewen, T E *see* HOW TO DOUBLE THE WEALTH OF CANADA: IMPERIAL FEDERATION, CONTINENTAL UNION
Ewers, Hanns Heinz *see*
– ALRAUNE
– DER ZAUBERLEHRLING, ODER, DIE TEUFELSJAEGER
Ewerts, Max *see* ERINNERUNGEN
EWIG EDICT UND GEBODT... – Bruessel, 1577 – 1mf – 1 – ILM-1217/1 – ne IDC [327]
EWIG WIEDERKEHRT DIE FREUDE : GEDICHTE / Goltz, Joachim, Freiherr von der – Muenchen: A Langen, G Mueller, 1944, c1942 – 1r – 1 – us U.W. Library [810]
DER EWIGE JAN : ROMAN / Uphoff, Carl Emil – Braunschweig: G Westermann, c1937 – 1r – 1 – us U.W. Library [830]
DIE EWIGE ORDNUNG : GERMANENLEBEN IN DER BRONZEZEIT / Auerswald, Annmarie von – Berlin: Junge Generation Verlag, [1941?] – 1r – 1 – us U.W. Library [830]
DER EWIGE TAG / Heym, Georg – Leipzig: E Rowohlt, 1911 – 1r – 1 – us U.W. Library [810]
DIE EWIGE VNND EINIGE GRUNDFESTE AUFF WELCHEM DER SELIGMACHENDE GLAUBE STEHEN VND VERHARREN MUSS / Huber, S – Vrsel, 1599 – 1mf – ne IDC [240]
EWIGES ARKADIEN! : ROMAN / Bartsch, Rudolf Hans – Leipzig: L Staackmann, 1920 – 1r – 1 – us U.W. Library [830]
EWING ADVOCATE – Ewing, NE. -w. Nov. 1892-May 1907. Incomplete; Aug. 1908-Apr. 1911; Jan. 1921-Sep. 1954 – 1 – us NE Hist [071]
Ewing, Clymer and Co. Westport, Mo *see* ACCOUNT BOOK
EWING DEMOCRAT – Ewing, NE. -w. Jun. 1888-Jul. 1892. Incomplete – 1 – us NE Hist [071]
Ewing, John *see* SERMONS, 1755-1801
Ewing, John L, Jr *see* EFFECTS OF VARYING LEVELS OF FATIGUE ON THE RATE OF FORCE DEVELOPMENT IN FEMALES
Ewing, Joseph L *see* SKETCHES OF THE FAMILIES OF THOMAS EWING
Ewing, Juliana Horatia *see*
– BROTHERS OF PITY
– THE BROWNIES
– A FLAT IRON FOR A FARTHING
– A GREAT EMERGENCY
– JACKANAPES
– JAN OF THE WINDMILL
– JULIANA HORATIA EWING AND HER BOOKS
– LOB LIE-BY-THE-FIRE
– MARY'S MEADOW
– MELCHIOR'S DREAM
– MISCELLANEA
– MRS. OVERTHEWAYS REMEMBRANCES
– OLD-FASHIONED FAIRY TALES
– THE PEACE EGG

- SIX TO SIXTEEN
- VERSES FOR CHILDREN
- WE AND THE WORLD

Ewing, Martha *see* THE RELATIONSHIP OF MALE IDENTITY, THE MESOMORPHIC IMAGE, AND ANABOLIC STEROID USE IN BODYBUILDING

Ewing, Martha E *see* THE EFFECTS OF AN EVALUATIVE AUDIENCE UPON COLLEGE MALES' SELF-EFFICACY, PERCEIVED ABILITY, ANXIETY, AND LEARNING OF A NOVEL MOTOR TASK

EWING NEWS – Ewing, NE. -w. Sep. 1958-Jun. 1967 – 1 – us NE Hist [071]

Ewing, Thomas, Jr *see* THOMAS EWING JR. PAPERS

Ewing, Thomas, Sr *see* PAPERS

ewish National and University Library. Jerusalem *see* ARABIC MANUSCRIPTS IN THE JNUL, JERUSALEM

EWTONVILLE BAPTIST CHURCH. DUNLAP, TENNESSEE : CHURCH RECORDS – 1836-1952 – 1 – 35.10 – us Baptist [240]

EX BELLARMINO EPITOME CONTROVERSIARUM OMNIUM HUIUS AEVI LUTHERO-CALVINISTICARUM / Coppenstein, Ioan – Moguntiae. v1-3. 1624-1626 – 37mf – 8 – ne Slangenburg [240]

EL EX CONVENTO E SAN BENITO DE ALCANTARA EN LA PROVINCIA DE CACERES / Melida, Jose Ramon – Madrid: Tip. Fortanet. B.R.A.H. LIV, pp. 436-439 – sp Bibl Santa Ana [240]

EX HIPPOCRATIS ET GALENI MONUMENTIS ISAGOGE... / Collado, L – Valencia, 1561 – 6mf – 9 – sp Cultura [610]

EX RERUM ANGLICARUM SCRIPTORIBUS SAEC. 12 ET 13 (MGH 5: 27.BD) – 1885 – Dfl53.00 – ne Slangenburg [240]

EX RERUM ANGLICARUM SCRIPTORIBUS SAEC. 13 (MGH 5: 28.BD) – 1888 – Dfl63.00 – ne Slangenburg [240]

EX RERUM DANICARUM SCRIPTORIBUS SAEC. 12 ET 13 (MGH 5: 29.BD) : EX HISTORIIS ISLANDICIS – 1892 – Dfl60.00 – ne Slangenburg [240]

EX RERUM FRANCOGALLICARUM SCRIPTORIBUS (MGH 5: 26.BD) : EX HISTORIIS AUCTORUM FLANDRENSIUM FRANCOGALLICA LINGUA SCRIPTIS (SUPPL. TOMI 24) – 1882 – Dfl81.00 – ne Slangenburg [240]

EX SITU CRYOCONSERVATION OF GENOMES AND GENES OF ENDANGERED CATTLE BREEDS BY MEANS OF MODERN BIOTECHNOLOGICAL METHODS – 1989 – 127p – it F.A.O. [575]

EX SUMMA PHILIPPI CANCELLARII QUESTIONES DE ANIMA / Keeler, L W – (Opusc. et Textus ser. Schol. Fasc. 22) – 3mf – 8 – ne Slangenburg [290]

EX SUMMA PHILIPPI CANCELLARII QUESTIONES DE ANIMA. OPUSC. ET TEXTUS SER. SCHOL. FASC. 20 / Keeler, L W – 3mf – 8 – ne Slangenburg [290]

EXALTACION DE EVA PERON EN EL DIA DE LA LEALTAD : 17 DE OCTUBRE DE 1951 [DISCURSOS DE JUAN PERON Y EVA PERON] – Buenos Aires: [Presidencia de la Nacion, Subsecretaria de Informaciones, 1951?] – 1 – CSUXAJA7281-B – us Hoover Inst Photo [320]

EXAMEN CHIMICO-MEDICO...DE LAS AGUAS TERMALES Y BANO DE FITERO / Ramirez, A – Pamplona, SA – 3mf – 9 – sp Cultura [610]

EXAMEN CRITIQUE DE LA DOCTRINE DITE RELIGION SAINT-SIMONIENNE / Vagner, Nicolas – Nancy, Vincenot, 1832, 44 p. Les Saint-Simoniens, 1825-1834. 6994 – 9 – fr Hachette [335]

EXAMEN CRITIQUE DE LA VIE DE JESUS DE M. RENAN / Freppel, l'Abbe – Paris: A. Bray, 1864. 1 fiche. .PR.-apply; ATL; 9 – us A.T.L.A. [240]

EXAMEN CRITIQUE DE LA VIE ET DES OUVRAGES DE SAINT PAUL. AVEC UNE DISSERTATION SUR SAINT PIERRE – (D'Holbach series). 1770 – 9 – fr Hachette [240]

EXAMEN CRITIQUE DE L'HISTOIRE DU SANCTUAIRE DE L'ARCHE : TOME PREMIER / Poels, Henricus Andreas – (Includes indexes) – Louvain: J. van Linthout, 1897 – 1mf – 9 – 0-8370-4773-0 – 1985-2773 – us A.T.L.A. [270]

EXAMEN CRITIQUE DES APOLOGISTES DE LA RELIGION CHRETIENNE / Burigny, Jean-Levesque de – (D'Holbach series) – 9 – fr Hachette [240]

EXAMEN CRITIQUE DES DICTIONNAIRES DE LA LANGUE FRANCOISE / Nodier, Charles – 2e ed. 1829 – 9 – fr I.C.S. [440]

EXAMEN CRITIQUE DU "DICTIONNAIRE DE L'ACADEMIE FRANCAISE."1873 / Gary, J M – 9 – fr I.C.S. [440]

EXAMEN DE BOTICARIOS / Villa, E de – Burgos, 1632 – 9mf – 9 – sp Cultura [615]

EXAMEN DE INGENIOS: THE EXAMINATION OF MENS WITS / Huarte de San Juan, Juan – 1594 – 9 – 20.00 – us Scholars' Facs [150]

EXAMEN DE LA POSSESSION DES RELIGIEUSES DE LOUVIERS / Yvelin, Pierre – Paris. 1643 – 9 – fr Hachette [360]

EXAMEN DE LA SITUACION ECONOMICA DE MEXICO / Banco Nacional de Mexico – Nos. 1-529, 1925-69 – 1 – 184.00 – us L of C Photodup [339]

EXAMEN DE LA VIOLENCIA ARGENTINA / Escobar, Justo & Velazquez, Sebastian – Mexico: Fondo de Cultura Economica, 1st ed 1973 – 1 – CSUXADH4097-B – us Hoover Inst Photo [360]

EXAMEN DE PLUSIEURS PREJUGES ET USAGES ABUSIFS CONCERNANT LES FEMMES ENCEINTES / Saucerotte, Louis Sebastien – Strasbourg, 1777. 99p. (Les Femmes Collection) – 2mf – 9 – $6.00 – fr Bibl Nationale [305]

EXAMEN DES OUVRAGES DE M. DE VOLTAIRE / Linguet, Simon N H – Considere comme poete, comme prosateur, comme philosophe. Bruxelles, Lemaire. 1788 – 9 – fr Hachette [190]

EXAMEN DES PROPHETIES QUI SERVENT DE FONDEMENT A LA RELIGION CHRETIENNE. AVEC UN ESSAI DE CRITIQUE SUR LES PROPHETES ET LES PROPHETIES EN GENERAL / Collins, Anthony – (D'Holbach series). 1768 – 9 – fr Hachette [240]

EXAMEN DU BUDGET DE 1832. REFORMES FINANCIERES. EXAMEN THEORIQUE ET PRATIQUE DE L'AMORTISSEMENT / Pereire, Emile – Paris, Revue encyclopedique, 1831, 55 p. Les Saint-Simoniens, 1825-1834. 6884 – 9 – fr Hachette [336]

EXAMEN D'UN ESSAI SUR L'ARCHITECTURE, AVEC QUELQUES REMARQUES SUR CETTE SCIENCE TRAITEE DANS L'ESPIRIT DES BEAUX-ARTS / La Font de Saint-Yenne – Paris, M. Lambert, 1753. 8 fol. xvi, 206p. (Architecture Series) – 9 – fr Hachette [720]

EXAMEN IMPARTIAL DES PRINCIPALES RELIGIONS DU MONDE – (D'Holbach series) – 9 – fr Hachette [230]

EXAMEN IMPARTIAL DES TRAITES CONCLUS ENTRE LA GRANDE-BRETAGNE... – The Hague, 1779 – 1mf – 1 – ILM-381/1 – ne IDC [327]

EXAMEN IURIS GENTIUM... / Busse, CF de – Hallae Salicae, 1754 – 1mf – 1 – ILM-1224/1 – ne IDC [327]

AN EXAMEN OF THE WAY OF TEACHING THE LATIN TONGUE TO LITTLE CHILDREN BY USE ALONE – Anon. 1669. 95p. (English Linguistics Series 1500-1800) – 9 – us UMI [450]

EXAMEN OMNIUM CATAPOTIORUM UEL PILULARUM. CONRADI GESNERI ENVMERATIO MEDICAMETORUM PURGANTIUM.. / Brasavola, Antonio Musa – Basileae, 1543 – 1 – us U.W. Library [610]

EXAMEN SUCINTO SOBRE LOS ANTIQUOS LIMITES...[1757] – N.p., n.d. – 1mf – 1 – ILM-1235/1 – ne IDC [327]

EXAMEN THEOLOGICVM, COMPLECTENS PRAECIPVA CAPITA DOCTRINAE CHRISTIANAE, DE QVIBVS INTERROGATI... / Hesshusen, T – [Ienae], 1571 – 4mf – ne IDC [240]

EXAMEN VARIANTIUM LECTIONUM JOHANNIS MILLII / Whitby, Daniel – 1724 – 1 – us A.T.L.A. [240]

EXAMEN...DE LA ALEGACION APOLOGETICA MEDICO-PHYSECA / Melero Ximenez, M – Cordoba, SA: 1699 – 4mf – 9 – sp Cultura [612]

THE EXAMINATION AND TRYAL OF OLD FATHER CHRISTMAS / King, Josiah – London: Charles Brome, 1686 – 1mf – 9 – $1.50 – LLMC 91-094 – us L.L.M.C. [870]

EXAMINATION BEFORE ADMISSION TO A BENEFICE BY THE BISHOP OF EXETER : FOLLOWED BY A REFUSAL TO INSTITUTE, ON THE ALLEGATION OF UNSOUND DOCTRINE RESPECTING THE EFFICACY OF BAPTISM / Gorham, George Cornelius – London: Hatchard, 1848 – 1mf – us A.T.L.A. [240]

AN EXAMINATION OF A MODEL OF BURNOUT IN DUAL-ROLE TEACHER-COACHES / Kelley, B C – 1990 – 3mf – 9 – $12.00 – us Microform Publ [150]

AN EXAMINATION OF ENVIRONMENTAL ATTITUDES AMONG COLLEGE STUDENTS / McGuire, John R & Graefe, Alan R – 1992 – 2mf – 9 – $8.00 – us Microform Publ [790]

AN EXAMINATION OF EPINEPHRINE AND ATHLETIC PERFORMANCE: PSYCHOPHYSIOLOGICAL, COGNITIVE, AND BEHAVIORAL INDICES OF AROUSAL / Wilkinson, Michael O – 1982 – 2mf – 9 – $8.00 – us Microform Publ [790]

EXAMINATION OF GILLESPIE : BEING AN ANALYTICAL CRITICISM OF THE ARGUMENT A PRIORI FOR THE EXISTENCE OF A GREAT FIRST CAUSE... / Barrett, Thomas Squire – (Includes appendixes) – 2nd ed. London: Provost, 1871 – 1mf – 9 – 0-8370-2186-3 – 1985-0186 – us A.T.L.A. [230]

EXAMINATION OF MR. ISAAC MARLOW'S TWO PAPERS, ONE CALLED A DISCOURSE AGAINST SINGING, ETC., THE OTHER, AN APPENDIX / Keach, Benjamin – London. 1691 – 1 – 5.00 – us Baptist [240]

AN EXAMINATION OF PROFESSOR BERGSON'S PHILOSOPHY / Balsillie, David – London: Williams & Norgate, 1912 – 1mf – us A.T.L.A. [140]

AN EXAMINATION OF RIDER AROUSAL IN THE THREE PHASES OF AN EQUESTRIAN COMBINED TRAINING EVENT / Berno, K A – 1990 – 1mf – 9 – $4.00 – us Microform Publ [150]

AN EXAMINATION OF THE ACADEMIC PERFORMANCE OF STUDENT-ATHLETE ADMISSION EXCEPTIONS AT A DIVISON 1-A INSTITUTION / Gilmore, Carole A – University of North Carolina at Chapel Hill, 1995 – 1mf – 9 – $4.00 – PE3591 – us Microform Publ [370]

AN EXAMINATION OF THE BRITISH DOCTRINE,... – London, 1806 – 3mf – 1 – ILM-672/1 – ne IDC [327]

AN EXAMINATION OF THE DOCTRINE OF PREDESTINATION / Bangs, Nathan – 1817 – 9 – us A.T.L.A. [240]

AN EXAMINATION OF THE MOTIVATIONAL DIFFERENCES BETWEEN ADULTS IN STRUCTURED AND UNSTRUCTURED EXERCISE PROGRAMS / Piepkorn, M B – 1990 – 2mf – 9 – $8.00 – us Microform Publ [150]

AN EXAMINATION OF THE RELATIONSHIP AMONG TARGET STRUCTURES, TEAM MOTIVATIONAL CLIMATE, AND ACHIEVEMENT GOAL ORIENTATION / Becker, Susan L – Oregon State University, 1995 – 2mf – 9 – $8.00 – PSY 1880 – us Microform Publ [150]

AN EXAMINATION OF THE RELATIONSHIP BETWEEN ANGLER SPECIALIZATION AND CONSTRAINTS TO TROUT FISHING / Lloyd, Gregory S – 1993 – 2mf – $8.00 – us Microform Publ [790]

AN EXAMINATION OF THE RELATIONSHIP BETWEEN TEACHER ENTHUSIASM AND ALT-PE / Griffin, Lisa M – West Virginia University, 1995 – 2mf – 9 – $8.00 – PE3594 – us Microform Publ [370]

AN EXAMINATION OF THE REV. MR. JOHN WESLEY'S 'PRIMITIVE PHYSIC', SHEWING THAT A GREAT NUMBER OF THE PRESCRIPTIONS THEREIN CONTAINED ARE FOUNDED ON IGNORANCE OF THE MEDICAL ART AND OF THE POWER AND OPERATION OF MEDICINES,... / Hawes, W – London, 1776 – 1mf – 9 – MP-513/1 – ne IDC [240]

AN EXAMINATION OF THE SOURCES AND LEVELS OF PERCEIVED COMPETENCE IN MALE AND FEMALE INTERSCHOLASTIC COACHES / Barber, Heather & Weiss, Maureen R – 1992 – 2mf – 9 – $8.00 – us Microform Publ [150]

AN EXAMINATION OF THE TEST CHARACTERISTICS OF THE 12 MINUTE AEROBIC SWIM TEST / Fried, Constance R – 1983 – 2mf – 9 – $8.00 – us Microform Publ [790]

AN EXAMINATION OF THE UNDERSTANDING OF THE HUMAN PERSON IN THE PHILOSOPHY OF JOHN MACMURRAY / Reinecker, Virginia M. – 1982 – 1 – $5.00 – us Baptist [190]

AN EXAMINATION OF THE VALIDITY OF THE PROFILE OF MOOD STATES (POMS) IN THE ASSESSMENT OF MENTAL HEALTH IN ATHLETES / Sullivan, John P, Jr – Springfield College, 1995 – 1mf – 9 – $4.00 – PSY1867 – us Microform Publ [150]

AN EXAMINATION OF TWO THEORETICAL DISTRIBUTIONS USING THREE METHODS OF SCORING CRITERION-REFERENCED MEASURES OF MOTOR PERFORMANCE / Douglass, Jacqueline A – 1981 – 2mf – 9 – $8.00 – us Microform Publ [790]

EXAMINATION QUESTIONS GIVEN IN THE LAW SCHOOL OF COLUMBIAN UNIVERSITY / George Washington University. Department of Law – Washington, D.C., 1898. 27p. LL-414 – 1 – us L of C Photodup [340]

THE EXAMINATIONS AND WRITINGS / Philpot, J – H-431 2. 1842 – 8 – ne IDC [025]

EXAMINER – (1993.-12r; 1930-1940.-11r) – Barrie, 1976-1992 – 205r – 1 – cn Preston [971]

EXAMINER – Aberdeen. Miss. -w. 1881- – 1 – us UMI [071]

EXAMINER – Albert Lea. Minn. 1920-22 – 1 – us UMI [071]

EXAMINER – Charlottetown, Canada. 1847-1900 – 58r – 1 – $3,770.00 – cn Library Assoc [971]

EXAMINER – Dillon. Mont. 1951-1954; 1956-1957 – 1 – us UMI [071]

EXAMINER – Franklin. Ind. 1845-1852 – 1 – us UMI [071]

EXAMINER – Independence. Mo. -d. 1967- – 1 – us UMI [071]

EXAMINER – Lancaster. Pa. and Herald. 1834-52, 1855-76 – 1 – us UMI [071]

EXAMINER – Lancaster. Pa. -sw. 1891-1920 – 1 – us UMI [071]

EXAMINER – Los Angeles. Calif. 1950-1961 – 1 – us UMI [071]

EXAMINER – Moorefield. West Virginia. -w. 1903-68 – 1 – us UMI [071]

EXAMINER – Omaha, NE. -w. Sept 1901-Jun 1924 – 1 – us NE Hist [071]

EXAMINER – Omaha. Neb. 1900-1924 – 1 – us UMI [071]

EXAMINER – Owensboro. Ky. 1875-1878 – 1 – us UMI [071]

EXAMINER – Portland OR. May 1930 – 1 – us U.O. Library [071]

EXAMINER – Richmond. Va. 1802-1803 – 1 – us UMI [071]

EXAMINER – San Francisco, CA. 1876; 1885; Oct 1989-Loma Prieta earthquake-1mf – 5r – 1 – $225.00 – C02816 – us Library Micro [071]

EXAMINER – San Francisco. Calif. 1865- – 1 – us UMI [071]

EXAMINER – Toronto, Canada. 1840-55 – 3r – 1 – $204.00 – cn Library Assoc [971]

EXAMINER – Yonkers. N.Y. 1857-63 – 1 – us UMI [071]

EXAMINER – Yuma. Ariz. 1909-14 – 1 – us UMI [071]

THE EXAMINER – (Absorbed by: Toronto Globe) – Toronto. v1 n6. 8 aut 1838-v14 n11. 3 sep 1851 – 1r – 1 – Can$50.00 – cn Can Microfilming [072]

THE EXAMINER – Frederick. Md. 1849-1913 – 1 – us UMI [071]

THE EXAMINER – London. 1852-54.-w. 3 reels – 1 – uk British Libr Newspaper [072]

THE EXAMINER = L'OBSERVATEUR – Quebec: Printed for the proprietors by J Lovell, [1861] – 9 – cn C.I.H.M. [340]

THE EXAMINER – v1-72. 28 Jun 1855-11 Oct 1894 (complete) – 18r – 1 – ATLA R0106 – us A.T.L.A. [073]

THE EXAMINER *see* LAUNCESTON EXAMINER

EXAMINER. A WEEKLY PAPER ON POLITICS, LITERATURE, MUSIC AND THE FINE ARTS – 1-3813. 1808-1881 – 1 – us UMI [073]

EXAMINER AND CHRONICLE – New York. 1876 – 1 – us A.B.H.S. [071]

EXAMINER AND CHRONICLE – New York. Feb 1865-74. (Complete); The Examiner. 1912 – 1 – 182.31 – us Baptist [240]

EXAMINER AND MELBOURNE WEEKLY NEWS – Melbourne, Australia. 11 Jul 1857-17 Oct 1863 (very imperfect).-w. 6mqn reels – 1 – uk British Libr Newspaper [072]

EXAMINER LAUNCESTON – Launceston, 1880-1969 – 250r – 1 – at Pascoe [072]

EXAMINER (ROMSEY) – 1883-1884. EX1 – 1r – 1 – at Corangamite [072]

EXAMINER-COURIER *see* THE WEEKLY EXAMINER

EXAMINER-INDEX – Colville. Wash. 1908-1920 – 1 – us UMI [071]
EXAMPLE (CCC287) / Surdam, T Janet – (In Chinese) – 1st ed. Hong Kong: Council on Christian Literature for Overseas Chinese, 1958 – 1r – 1 – 1984-6626 – us A.T.L.A. [240]
THE EXAMPLE OF FRANCE, A WARNING TO BRITAIN / Young, A – 2nd ed 1793 – 2mf – 9 – ne IDC [320]
EXAMPLES OF ASTRONOMIC AND GEODETIC CALCULATIONS FOR THE USE OF LAND SURVEYORS / Deville, Edouard – Quebec: P.G. Delisle, 1878. 02672. (Pre-1900 Canadiana) – 9 – cn C.I.H.M. [971]
EXAMPLES OF RECORDS IN THE NATIONAL ARCHIVES FREQUENTLY USED IN GENEALOGICAL RESEARCH / U.S. National Archives and Records Service – 1r – 1 – T325 – us Nat'l Archives [324]
EXCALIBUR – Cape Town, South Africa. 21 May 1886-22 Aug 1890 – 2r – 1, 16 diazo available – sa SA Libr [960]
EXCAVACIONES ARQUEOLOGICAS EN LA CIUDAD DE MERIDA / Melida, Jose Ramon – Madrid: Tip. Fortanet, 1911. B.R.A.H. LVIII pp. 62-63 – sp Bibl Santa Ana [930]
EXCAVACIONES ARQUEOLOGICAS EN LA ZONA DE MERIDA : LA CASA DEL ANFITEATRO / Garcia Sandoval, Eugenio – Sevilla-Malaga, 1963. Sep. Actas 8 Congreso Arqueologico Nacional de Sevilla-Malaga de 1963 – sp Bibl Santa Ana [930]
EXCAVACIONES DE AMERICA / Carmona, Miguel – Badajoz: Dip. Provincial, 1963. Sep. REE – sp Bibl Santa Ana [930]
LAS EXCAVACIONES DE MERIDA / Melida, Jose Ramon – Madrid: Brah, abril 1911 – 1 – sp Bibl Santa Ana [930]
EXCAVACIONES DE MERIDA. LAS. ULTIMOS HALLAZGOS / Melida, Jose Ramon – Madrid: Fortanet, 1913. B.R.A.H. 62. pp. 158-163 – 1 – sp Bibl Santa Ana [930]
EXCAVACIONES DE MERIDA. MEMORIA DE LOS TRABAJOS PRACTICADOS EN 1926 Y 1927 / Melida, Jose Ramon & Macias, Maximiliano – Madrid: Rev. Arch. Bibl. Mus, 1929 – 1 – sp Bibl Santa Ana [930]
EXCAVACIONES DE RUINAS DE EPOCA VISIGODA EN LA ALDEA DE SAN PEDRO DE MERIDA / Almagro Basch, Martin & Marco Pons, Alejandro – Badajoz: Dip. Provincial, 1958. Sep. REE – 1 – sp Bibl Santa Ana [930]
EXCAVACIONES EN LA ANTIGUA CAPPARA (CAPARRA.CACERES) / Floriano Cumbreno, Antonio C – sp Bibl Santa Ana [930]
EXCAVACIONES EN LA SIERRA DE SANTA CRUZ / Roso de Luna, Mario – Caceres: Tip. Enc. y Lib. Jimenez, 1902 – 1 – sp Bibl Santa Ana [930]
EXCAVACIONES EN MERIDA / Floriano Cumbreno, Antonio C – Madrid, 1944 – 1 – sp Bibl Santa Ana [930]
EXCAVACIONES EN MERIDA. MEMORIA / Melida, Jose Ramon – Madrid: Tip. Archivos, 1916 – 1 – sp Bibl Santa Ana [930]
THE EXCAVATION OF ARMAGEDDON / Fisher, Clarence S – 1929 – 9 – $10.00 – us I.R.C. [930]
THE EXCAVATION OF GEZER / Macalister, R A S – 3v. 1912 – 9 – $42.00 – us I.R.C. [930]
EXCAVATIONS AT AIN SHEMS / Mackenzie, Duncan – 2v. 1911-1913 – 9 – $15.00 – us I.R.C. [930]
THE EXCAVATIONS AT BABYLON / Koldewey, Robert – Macmillan. 1914 – 9 – $12.00 – us I.R.C. [930]
EXCAVATIONS AT THE KESSLERLOCH NEAR THAYNGEN, SWITZERLAND. A CAVE OF THE REINDEER PERIOD / Merk, Conrad – Trans. by John Edward Lee. London: Longmans, Green, 1876. viii,68p. illus – 1 – us U.W. Library [930]
EXCAVATIONS AT UR: A RECORD OF TWELVE YEARS WORK / Woolley, Leonard – Benn Ltd., 1954 – 9 – $12.00 – us I.R.C. [930]
EXCAVATIONS OF THE HILL OF OPHEL / Macalister, R A S – 1926 – 9 – $12.00 – us I.R.C. [930]
LAS EXCELENCIAS...Y...PROPIEDADES DEL TABACO... / Ayo, C – Salamanca, 1645 – 1mf – 9 – sp Cultura [630]
Excell, Edwin O *see* TRIUMPHANT SONGS
THE EXCELLENT AND PLEASANT WORK COLLECTANEA RERUM MEMORABILIUM / Solinus, Caius Julius – 9 – 15.00 – us Scholars' Facs [450]
EXCELLENT COMPENDIUM OF MUSICK / Descartes, Rene – P670. 1653 – 9 – ne IDC [780]
EXCELLENT ENCOURAGEMENTS AGAINST AFFLICTIONS / Pierson, Thomas – Edinburgh: James Nichol, 1868. 1 fiche – 9 – us A.T.L.A. [240]
AN EXCELLENT TREATISE OF WOUNDS MADE WITH GONNESHOT / Gale, T – M-231 2. 1563 – 8 – ne IDC [617]
L'EXCELSIOR – Paris. Journal illustre quot. 16 nov 1910-avr 1935, 11 juin 1940, 16 juin 1942, 16 juin 1943 – 1 – fr A.C.R.P.P. [944]
EXCELSIOR – Bucharest, Romania. -w. 2 March 1935-8 June 1940. Imperfect. 4 reels – 1 – uk British Libr Newspaper [949]
EXCELSIOR – Mexico: DF: Excelsior, mar 18 1917-1918 – 1 – us Res Libr [072]
EXCELSIOR – Omaha. Neb. 1884-1921 – 1 – us UMI [071]
EXCELSIOR DEL CONDADO DE ORANGE – Orange Co, CA. 1992 – 2+ r – 1 – $100.00 ($50.00y) – R04079 – us Library Micro [071]
EXCELSIOR JOURNAL – Port-au-Prince: Imp Les Presses Libres. [v1 n1-13 feb-may 4 1952] – 2 sheets – 9 – us Res Libr [072]
Excelsior Publishing Co *see* PORTRAIT AND BIOGRAPHICAL RECORD OF SHEYBOYGAN COUNTY
LES EXCENTRICITES DE LA LANGUE FRANCAISE EN 1860 / Larchey, L – 1861 – 9 – fr I.C.S. [440]
LES EXCENTRICITES DU LANGAGE / Larchey, L – 4e ed. 1862 – 9 – fr I.C.S. [440]
LES EXCENTRICITES DU LANGAGE / Larchey, L – 5e ed. 1865 – 9 – fr I.C.S. [440]
EXCEPTIONAL CHILD – Brisbane. v1-29. 1954-82 – 5r – 1 – us Ross [305]
EXCEPTIONALITY EDUCATION CANADA – Calgary. v1-4. 1991-94 – 9 – Can$20.00y – cn Micromedia [370]
EXCERPTA CYPRIA : MATERIALS FOR A HISTORY OF CYPRUS / Cobham, Claude Delaval – Cambridge: University Press; New York: Putnam [distributor], 1908 – 2mf – us A.T.L.A. [956]
EXCERPTA DE ANTIQUITATIBUS CONSTANTINOPOLITANI (CSHB 46) / Codini, Georgii; ed by Bekkeri, Imm – Bonnae, 1843 – Dfl25.00 – ne Slangenburg [930]
EXCERPTA DE ANTIQUITATIBUS CONSTANTINOPOLITANIS (CBH 12,2) / Codini, Georgii et al; ed by Medonius, B – Parisiis, 1655 – Dfl49.00 – ne Slangenburg [930]
EXCERPTA DE LEGATIONIBUS (CBH 1,2) / ed by Cantoclarus, CaR & Valesii, Notae H – Parisiis, 1648 – Dfl39.00 – ne Slangenburg [240]
EXCERPTA INDONESICA – (Special issue: Current Studies. Leiden, 1978-1979) – Leiden, 1970-1985. Nos. 1-32 – 60mf – 9 – SE-600/1 – ne IDC [950]
EXCERPTS FROM HER DIARIES RELATING TO HER SERVICE WITH THE METHODIST OVERSEAS MISSION IN THE SOLOMON ISLANDS / Harkness, Effie – 15 jul 1941-7 may 1957 – r1-3 – 1 – PMB1096 – at Pacific Mss [920]
EXCERPTS OF IMPORTANCE TO THE OIL INDUSTRY FROM THE DRAFT BASIC LAWS FOR THE OVERALL NATIONAL DEVELOPMENT; EIGHT YEAR PLAN: 1961-1969 / Indonesia. Dewan Perantjang Nasional – SE-5361 1. 1959? – 9 – ne IDC [338]
EXCESS POSTEXERCISE OXYGEN CONSUMPTION AND ENERGY EXPENDITURE OF ENDURANCE TRAINED AND UNTRAINED WOMEN / Marshall, Kristin R & Maniscalco, Ignatius A – 1993 – 2mf – $8.00 – us Microform Publ [612]
EXCHANGE – Hot Springs. Mont. 1951-1954; 1956-1957 – 1 – us UMI [071]
THE EXCHANGE AND MART – Toronto: [s.n., 1884-18– or 19–] – 9 – cn C.I.H.M. [072]
EXCHANGE BIBLIOGRAPHIES. NUMERICAL LIST / Committee of University Industrial Relations Librarians – no. 1-1266 – 1 – us NY Public [330]
EXCHANGE BIBLIOGRAPHIES. SUBJECT INDEX / Committee of University Industrial Relations Librarians – no. 1-1300 – 1 – us NY Public [330]
Exchange National Bank. Atchison, Kansas *see* RECORDS
THE EXCHANGE NEWS – (Cont by: The Exchange News and Commerical Advertiser) – Montreal: M M Sabiston, [1898-1899] – 9 – cn C.I.H.M. [332]
THE EXCHANGE NEWS *see* THE EXCHANGE NEWS AND COMMERICAL ADVERTISER
THE EXCHANGE NEWS AND COMMERICAL ADVERTISER – (Cont: The Exchange News) – Montreal: M M Sabiston, [1899-1900] – 9 – cn C.I.H.M. [332]
THE EXCHANGE NEWS AND COMMERICAL ADVERTISER *see* THE EXCHANGE NEWS
THE EXCHANGE OF MINORITIES: BULGARIA, GREECE AND TURKEY / Ladas, S P – New York. 1932. Illus. BR-3887 2 – 8 – ne IDC [949]
EXCHANGE OF PATENT RIGHTS AND TECHNICAL INFORMATION UNDER MUTUAL AID PROGRAMS / Cardozo, Michael H – Washington: GPO, 1958. 51p. LL-2303 – 1 – us L of C Photodup [340]
EXCHEQUER REPORTS OF CANADA / Canada. Exchequer Court – (Cont by: Canada Law Reports, Exchequer Court. Not offered by LLMC) – v1-21. 1877-1922 (all publ) – 123mf – 9 – $184.00 – LLMC 81-002 – us L.L.M.C. [324]
THE EXCISE AND HOTEL LAWS OF THE STATE OF NEW YORK. / Becker, Frank Silvester – Rochester, Williamson, 1895. 159 p. LL-672 – 1 – us L of C Photodup [340]
EXCISION OF THE KNEEJOINT: WITH REPORT OF TWENTY-EIGHT CASES / Fenwick, George Edgeworth – Montreal: Dawson Bros., 1883. 03085. (Pre-1900 Canadiana) – 9 – cn C.I.H.M. [971]
LA EXCLUSIVA DADA POR ESPANA CONTRA EL CARDENAL CIUSTINIANI EN EL CONCLAVE DE 1830-1831, SEGUN LOS DESPACHOS DIPLOMATICOS / March, Jose – Madrid: Razon y Fe, 1932 – 1 – sp Bibl Santa Ana [320]
EL EXCMO. SR. D. XAVIER MARIA DE MUNIBE, CONDE DE PENAFLORIDA / Altube, Gregorio de – San Sebastian, 1932; Madrid: Razon y Fe, 1933 – 1 – sp Bibl Santa Ana [920]
THE EXCURSION : BEING A PORTION OF THE RECLUSE, A POEM / Wordsworth, William – London: Printed for Longman, Hurst, Rees, Orme, and Brown, 1814 – 1 roll – 1 – 1-55879-872-2 – uk Libr Preservation [810]
EXCURSION A FREGENAL DE LA SIERRA Y LOS JARALES... / Barras de Aragon, Francisco de las – Caceres: Tip. Enc. y Lib. Jimenez, 1905 – 1 – sp Bibl Santa Ana [946]
EXCURSION A LA COTE DU NORD, AU DESSOUS DE QUEBEC / Faribault, Georges Bartelemy – Quebec: Atelier typographique du "Canadien." SEM105P413 – 1mf – 9 – Can$2.25 – cn Bibl Nat [910]
UNE EXCURSION A L'ILE AUX COUDRES / Casgrain, Henri-Raymond – Montreal: Librairie Beauchemin, limitee, 1925. SEM105P1596 – 2mf – 9 – Can$4.50 – cn Bibl Nat [910]
UNE EXCURSION A L'ILE AUX COUDRES: LEGENDE CANADIENNE / Casgrain, Henri-Raymond – Montreal: Beauchemin, 1885. 00645. (Pre-1900 Canadiana) – 9 – cn C.I.H.M. [830]
UNA EXCURSION AL REAL MONASTERIO DE GUADALUPE. MADRID, 1927 / Zurbitu, D – Madrid: Razon y Fe, 1928 – 9 – sp Bibl Santa Ana [240]
UNE EXCURSION AUX RUINES DE CARTHAGE – Auch. 1863. 25p. (Travel series) – 9 – 3.00 – fr Bibl Nationale [910]
EXCURSION ENTOMOLOGIQUE AUX DUNES DE BASCARROSSE ET D'ARCACHON / Dufour, L – Bordeaux, 1854. 40p (Actes Soc. Linn. Bordeaux, v19). Z/1204/2 – 8 – ne IDC [590]
EXCURSION ENTOMOLOGIQUE DANS LES MONTAGNES DE LA VALLEE D'OSSAU / Dufour, L – Pau, 1843. 118p. (Bull. Soc. Sci. Lett. et Arts). Z/1203/2 – 8 – ne IDC [590]
EXCURSION EPIGRAFICA POR VILLAR DEL REY, ALHAMBRA, VENTA DE LOS SANTOS, CARTAGENA, LOGRONO Y ORENSE / Fita, Fidel – Madrid: Fortanet, 1903. B.R.A.H. 41. pp. 281-310 – 1 – sp Bibl Santa Ana [946]
EXCURSION POR EL CAMPO TEOSOFICO / Bayle, Constantino – Razon y Fe, 1929 – 1 – sp Bibl Santa Ana [240]
EXCURSION POR EL CAMPO TEOSOFICO. 2 / Bayle, Constantino – Madrid: Razon y Fe, 1929 – 1 – sp Bibl Santa Ana [290]
EXCURSIONES BRIOLOGICAS POR, LA PROVINCIA DE BADAJOZ / Fructucso y Tristancho, Gonzalo – Madrid: Imprenta de Fortanet, 1914 – 1 – sp Bibl Santa Ana [946]
EXCURSIONES EPIGRAFICAS. DE MONESTERIO A MERIDA / Fita, Fidel – Madrid: Tip. Fortanet, 1894 – 1 – sp Bibl Santa Ana [240]
EXCURSIONS IN AFRICA / Bowditch, Thomas Edward – 1825 – 7 – uk Microform Academic [910]
EXCURSIONS IN CRITICISM : BEING SOME PROSE RECREATIONS OF A RHYMER / Watson, William – London: E. Mathews & J. Lane; New York: Macmillan & Co., 1893 – 1 roll – 1 – 1-55879-753-X – uk Libr Preservation [420]
EXECUTAREA HOTARIRILOR STRAINE... / Banu, CG – Bucuresci, 1900 – 2mf – 9 – ILM-2931/1 – ne IDC [340]
L'EXECUTION D'UN MANDAT / Ducros, A – Lyon, 1928 – 3mf – 1 – ILM-1935/1 – ne IDC [327]
EXECUTION EN SUISSE DES... / Dupraz, E – Fribourg, 1913 – 2mf – 1 – ILM-2250/1 – ne IDC [327]
THE EXECUTION OF JUSTICE IN ENGLAND / Burghley, William Cecil – 1583 – 9 – 5.00 – us Scholars' Facs [941]
EXECUTIVE – (Cont by: Successful Executive 1986) – Don Mills. v9-27. 1967-85 – 9 – Can$28.00y – cn Micromedia [650]
EXECUTIVE – (v.6 .1979 5,6,9) – v.1 1974 – 1 – us UMI [650]
EXECUTIVE *see*
– ACADEMY OF MANAGEMENT EXECUTIVE
– SUCCESSFUL EXECUTIVE
THE EXECUTIVE AGREEMENT SERIES / U.S. Department of State – (Cont: The Treaty Series. Cont by: Treaties and Other International Acts of the United States) – nos 1-506. 1929-45 (all publ) – 74mf – 9 – $111.00 – LLMC 80-906 – us L.L.M.C. [324]
THE EXECUTIVE AGREEMENT SERIES *see* TREATIES AND OTHER INTERNATIONAL ACTS OF THE UNITED STATES
EXECUTIVE ALERT NEWSLETTER – 1982- – 1,5,6,9 – us UMI [650]
EXECUTIVE BOARD MINUTES / Indiana. State Convention of Baptists – 16 Jan 1975-10 Jan 1980. 184p – 1 – us Baptist [240]
EXECUTIVE BOARD MINUTES, 1883-86 / South Carolina. Orangeburg Association. First Union Division – Treasurer's Report, 1883-89; Financial Report, 1889-1918. 92p – 1 – us Baptist [240]
EXECUTIVE COMMITTEE MINUTES / Typographical Union No 6. New York City – New York. 1870-1884; Apr 1893-Nov 1899 – 1 – us NY Public [070]
EXECUTIVE COMMITTEE MINUTES, 21 APR 1921-5 MAR 1925, AND FINANCE BOARD MINUTES, 25 MAR 1925-31 JUL 1934 / Melanesian Mission – 2r – 1 – PMB1092 – at Pacific Mss [350]
EXECUTIVE COMPENSATION AND EMPLOYEE BENEFITS REPORT – v7, no.3-v11, no.1. Nov 1980-Sept 1984 – 1,5,6,9 – us UMI [331]
EXECUTIVE COMPENSATION REPORT – v1-7,no.2. 1974-Oct 1980 – 1,5,6,9 – us UMI [331]
EXECUTIVE CONTROL OF RULEMAKING : THE OFFICE OF ADMINISTRATIVE LAW IN CALIFORNIA / Price, Monroe E – Washington: GPO, Apr 1981 (all publ) – 2mf – 9 – $3.00 – LLMC 94-347 – us L.L.M.C. [340]
EXECUTIVE DIRECTORY PACKAGE – (Package includes the Federal Executive Directory Annual, State Executive Directory Annual, and the Municipal/County Executive Directory Annual; Set updated annually in July) – 30mf – 9 – $150.00 – us UMI [350]
EXECUTIVE EDUCATOR – v.1 .1979 – 1,5,6,9 – us UMI [073]
EXECUTIVE ORDER / U. S. President – Washington, DC. On film: no1-7403; 1845-1936. LL-033 – 1 – us L of C Photodup [340]
EXECUTIVE ORDERS / U. S. President – Nos. 1-7521, 1862-1936. RG11. 17 rolls – 1 – M1118 – us Nat'l Archives [975]

EXECUTIVE ORDERS IN TIMES OF WAR AND NATIONAL EMERGENCY: REPORT OF THE SPECIAL COMMITTEE ON NATIONAL EMERGENCIES AND DELEGATED EMERGENCY POWERS, UNITED STATES SENATE / U.S. Congress. Senate. Special Committee on National Emergencies and Delegated Emergency Powers – June 1974. Washington, Govt. Print. Off., 1974. 283 p. LL-2364 – 1 – us L of C Photodup [340]

EXECUTIVE RECORD, 1818-60 / Illinois. Office of the Governor – Actions of the Governor's Office. Indexed in Name Index to Early Illinois Records. V147-0001 to 0004 – 1 – us A.G.L.L. [978]

EXECUTIVE REGISTER / Illinois Territory – 25 Apr 1809-9 Sept 1818. V148-0001 – 1 – us A.G.L.L. [978]

EXECUTIVE REGISTER, 2ND SERIES / Illinois. Office of the Governor – 1 Jan 1855-Sept 1857. Actions of the Governor's office. Indexed in Name Index to Early Illinois Records – 1 – us A.G.L.L. [920]

EXECUTIVE SESSIONS / U.S. Congress. Senate. Foreign Relations Committee – v1-11. 1947-59 – 9 – $260.00 set – 0-89941-270-X – us Hein [324]

EXECUTIVE'S MAGAZINE – St. Louis. v1-20. 1917-37. Continues: West at Work (1917-19); America at Work (1919-24) – 1,5,6 – us Princeton Micro [073]

EXECUTOR'S BONDS AND APPOINTMENTS / Hancock County. Ohio. Probate Court – 1897-1920 – 2r – 1 – $32.50r – us Archival [324]

EXECUTOR'S BONDS AND LETTERS / Hancock County. Ohio. Probate Court – 1866-1892 – 1r – 1 – $32.50r – us Archival [324]

DIE EXEGESE BEI DEN FRANZOESISCHEN ISRAELITEN VOM 10. BIS 14. JAHRHUNDERT / Levy, Antoine – (In German and Hebrew) – Leipzig: Oskar Leiner, 1873 – 1mf – 9 – 0-8370-4093-0 – 1985-2093 – us A.T.L.A. [220]

DIE EXEGESE DER SIEBZIG WOCHEN DANIELS IN DER ALTEN UND MITTLEREN ZEIT / Fraidl, Franz – Graz: Leuschner & Lubensky, (1883). 1 fiche – 9 – us A.T.L.A. [220]

EXEGESIS OF I CORINTHIANS XIV: 34,35; AND I TIMOTHY XI: 11-12 / Brown, Antoinette L – From the Oberlin quarterly review, v.4, 1849, pp 358-75 – 9 – us A.T.L.A. [240]

EXEGESIS PERSPICVA ET FERME INTEGRA CONTRAVERSIAE DE SACRA COENA,... / Curaeus, J – Heidelbergae, 1575 – 5mf – 9 – ne IDC [240]

THE EXEGETICAL METHOD OF THE AUTHOR OF HEBREWS / Martin, Raymond A – Princeton. 1952 – 1 – us A.T.L.A. [240]

DIE EXEGETISCHE TERMINOLOGIE DER JUEDISCHEN TRADITIONSLITERATUR / Bacher, Wilhelm – 2pts. Pt. 1: Die bibelexegetische Terminologie der Tannaiten. Leipzig. 1899. Pt. 2: Die bibel- und traditionsexegetische Terminologie der Amoraeer. Leipzig. 1905. BJ-32-24 1 – 9 – ne IDC [270]

DIE EXEGETISCHE TERMINOLOGIE DER JUEDISCHEN TRADITIONSLITERATUR : ERSTER TEIL: DIE BIBELEXEGETISCHE TERMINOLOGIE DER TANNAITEN / Bacher, Wilhelm – (Zweiter Teil: Die Bibel-und Traditionsexegetische Terminologie der Amoraeer Leipzig, 1905 Dfl22.00) – Leipzig, 1899 – Dfl19.00 – ne Slangenburg [220]

EXEMPEL NEBST ACHTZEHN PROBE-STUECKEN IN SECHS SONATEN ZU CARL PHILIPP EMANUEL BACHS VERSUCHE UEBER DIE WAHRE ART DAS CLAVIER ZU SPIELEN / Bach, C P E – Auf XXVI Kupfer Tafeln. S. 1. BP-140 1 – 9 – ne IDC [780]

DIE EXEMPLA DES JACOB VON VITRY : EIN BEITRAG ZUR GESCHICHTE DER ERZAEHLUNGSLITERATUR DES MITTELALTERS. TEIL 1. / Frenken, Goswin – Muenchen, 1914 – 1mf – DM48.00 – 3-8267-3083-6 – gw Hänsel [430]

EXEMPLAR...ANTONIO DE LA VISITACION / Santa Ana, Juan de – 1758 – 9 – 1.50f – sp Bibl Santa Ana [240]

EXEMPLARISCHE ORGANISTEN-PROBE IM ARTIKEL VOM GENERAL-BASS.. / Mattheson, J – 1719 – 9 – us Sibley [780]

UN EXEMPLE D'ECONOMIE COLONIALE, LE SINE-SALOUM, SENEGAL, DE 1887 A 1940 : CULTURES ARACHIDIERES ET MUTATIONS SOCIALES / Mbodj, M – 9 – F190.00 – fr Ethnologie [306]

EXEMPTIONS FROM MILITARY SERVICE / Ottawa County. Ohio. Auditor – 1864-1865 – 1r – 1 – $32.50r – us Archival [324]

EXERCICE TRES DEVOT ENVERS S. ANTOINE DE PADOUE LE THAUMATURGE / Du Monceaux, Alexis – Quebec: Nouvelle Imprimerie, 1804. SEM16P25 – 1r – 5 – Can$9.00 – cn Bibl Nat [240]

EXERCICE TRES DEVOT ENVERS S. ANTOINE DE PADOUE LE THAUMATURGE, DE L'ORDRE SERAPHIQUE DE S. FRANCOIS, AVEC UN PETIT RECUEIL DE QUELQUES PRINCIPAUX MIRACLES / Du Monceaux, Alexis – Quebec: Nouvelle Imprimerie, 1804. SEM16P25 – 1r – 6 – Can$9.00 – cn Bibl Nat [240]

EXERCICE TRES DEVOT ENVERS ST-ANTOINE DE PADOUE LE THAUMATURGE / Du Monceaux, Alexis – Montreal: James Brown, 1813. SEM16P26 – 1r – 5 – Can$9.00 – cn Bibl Nat [240]

EXERCICES ET EVOLUTIONS D'INFANTERIE TELS QUE REVISES PAR ORDRE DE SA MAJESTE, 1862 – Quebec: G Desbarats, 1863. SEM105P1286 – 4mf – 9 – Can$9.00 – cn Bibl Nat [355]

EXERCICES ORTHOGRAPHIQUES : COURS DE PREMIERE ANNEE MIS EN RAPPORT AVEC L'EXTRAIT DE LA GRAMMAIRE DES FRERES DES ECOLES CHRETIENNES / F.P.B. – Montreal: [freres de ecoles chretiennes, entre 1895 et 1927]. SEM105P1677 – 4mf – 9 – Can$9.00 – cn Bibl Nat [440]

EXERCICES ORTHOGRAPHIQUES : COURS DE PREMIERE ANNEE MIS EN RAPPORT AVEC L'EXTRAIT DE LA GRAMMAIRE DES FRERES DES ECOLES CHRETIENNES / F.P.B. – Montreal: freres des ecoles chretiennes, 1875 (Montreal: Eusebe Senecal, imprimeur). SEM105P1655 – 4mf – 9 – Can$9.00 – cn Bibl Nat [440]

EXERCICES POUR LES NOVICES (DE L'ABBAYE DE BEAUMONT-LES-TOURS) / Bethune, Anne B de – 1 – F123.50 – fr Armell [240]

EXERCICES POUR LES NOVICES [DE L'ABBAYE DE BEAUMONT-LES-TOURS] / Bethune, Anne B de – 18th c. – fr Armell [240]

EXERCICES STRUCTURAUX : QUATRE LECONS RADIODIFFUSEES / Lamy, A & Duponchel, L – (Africa series). 1971 – 9 – fr Hachette [380]

EXERCICIO DE LAS VELAS...DIVINO MAESTRO – 1815 – 9 – 1.50f – sp Bibl Santa Ana [240]

EXERCISE / Algeria. Compagnie de Recherches et d'Exploitation de Petrole au Sahara – 1958-69.12v in 6. BNE-8626-1 – 9 – ne IDC [324]

EXERCISE / Morocco. Compagnie Marocaine de Credit et de Banque – 6v. 1959-74. BNE-3023 1 – 9 – ne IDC [330]

EXERCISE ADHERENCE : EFFECTIVENESS OF A BROAD-BASED ADULT FITNESS PROGRAM / Culligan, C T – 1991 – 1mf – 9 – $4.00 – us Microform Publ [150]

EXERCISE ADOPTION AND ADHERENCE OF COLLEGE WOMEN / Merrill, Joanne & Mann, Betty J – 1992 – 2mf – $8.00 – us Microform Publ [150]

EXERCISE: BILAN, COMPTES D'EXPLOITATION GENERALE, COMPTES DE PERTES ET PROFITS / Algeria. Caisse Algerienne de Developpement – 4v. in 2. 1966-69. BNE-8609 1 – 9 – ne IDC [338]

EXERCISE EXCHANGE – (1975-. 5,6,9) – v. 1-. 1953- – 1 – us UMI [790]

EXERCISE OXYGEN UPTAKE IN 3- THROUGH 6-YEAR-OLD CHILDREN / Shuleva, K M – 1989 – 1mf – 9 – $4.00 – us Microform Publ [612]

EXERCISES ET EVOLUTIONS D'INFANTERIE TELS QUE REVISES PAR ORDRE DE SA MAJESTE, 1862 – Quebec: imprime par Geo. Desbarats, 1863. SEM105P1286 – 4mf – 9 – Can$9.00 – cn Bibl Nat [355]

EXERCISES ORTHOGRAPHIQUES, SUIVIS D'UN LEXIQUE ET DE DEVOIRS DE STYLE / Robert, E – 1886. SEM16P80 – 1r – 5 – Can$9.00 – cn Bibl Nat [440]

EXERCISIS, HUIT, AVEC LEUR DOIGTE POUR LE PIANOFORTE TIREES DE LA METHODE DE PIANO...2ND EDITION / Steibelt, Daniel – Offenbach: Jean Andre, [1810-12] – 1 – us Sibley [780]

EXERCITATIO ANATOMICA DE MOTU CORDIS ET SANGUINIS IN ANIMALIBUS / Harvey, W – Francofurti, 1628 – 2mf – 9 – ne IDC [611]

EXERCITATIO DE ORIGINE ET VIRIBUS GEMMARUM / Boyle, R – London, 1673 – 3mf – 9 – ne IDC [610]

EXERCITATIO HISTORICA DE ORIGINE LINGVAE ITALICAE EX BARBARORUM INCVRSIONIBUS NATAE / Cellarius, C & Klein-Nicolai, G – Halae, 1703 – 1mf – 9 – ne IDC [440]

EXERCITATION 36...EL LETARGO... / Luna Vega, J – Sevilla, 1617 – 1mf – 9 – sp Cultura [610]

EXERCITATION 37. CENSURA AL DISCURSO... / Luna Vega, J – SL, 1617 – 1mf – 9 – sp Cultura [610]

EXERCITATION MEDICA PHYLOSOPHICA SOBRE LA ESSENCIA DEL MORBO GALLICO / Bonilla Samaniego, A – Cordoba, 1664 – 1mf – 9 – sp Cultura [610]

EXERCITATIONES DE GENERATIONE ANIMALIUM / Harvey, W – M-58. 1651 – 9 – ne IDC [590]

EXERCITATIONES HYMENOPTEROLOGICAE / Dahlbom, A G – London. 1831-33. 79p. 6pts. Z-1165 2 – 8 – ne IDC [590]

EXERCITATIONES MUSICAE THEORETICO-PRACTICAE CURIOSAE DE CONCORDANTIIS SINGULIS / Printz, Wolfgang C – (Contains a "Prodomus" and 8 dissertations, each part having a separate title page). 1687-89 – 9 – us Sibley [780]

EXERCITIA PHYTOLOGICA / Gilibert, Jean Emmanuel – 2v. Lugduni Gallorum. 1792. B-5930 2 – 8 – ne IDC [580]

EXERCITIA SPIRITUALIA : MEDITATIONIBUS ILLUSTRATA AD USUM PP. AC FF. SOCIETATIS JESU / Ignatius of Loyola, Saint – Cincinnati: Typis Hermanni Lehmann, 1849 – 1mf – 9 – 0-8370-9250-7 – 1986-3250 – us A.T.L.A. [240]

EXERCITITIA SPIRITUALIA / Loyola, Ignatius, Saint – Die geistlichen Uebungen des Ignatius von Loyola – 1 – us A.T.L.A. [240]

EXERCUTATIO 31...VERSATUR IUSTA...GALENI DOCTRINAM... / Luna Vega, J – SL, 1613 – 1mf – 9 – sp Cultura [610]

EXETER ENTERPRISE – Exeter, NE. -w. Sep. 1877-Oct. 1880; Jan. 1881-Aug. 1882; Nov. 1884-Mar. 1891; Sep. 1891-Aug. 1898. Incomplete; Oct. 1898-Jan. 1905; Jan. 1906-Nov. 1906. Incomplete; Jan. 1907-Jun. 1909 – 1 – us NE Hist [071]

EXETER MERCURY OR WEEKLY INTELLIGENCE OF NEWS – England.24 Sept 1714-30 Sept 1715; 11 Oct 1715. 1/2 reel – 1 – uk British Libr Newspaper [072]

Exeter, New Hampshire. Exeter Baptist Church *see* RECORDS

EXETER SUN – Exeter, CA. 1982 – 13+ r – 1 – $650.00 ($90.00y) – B03217 – us Library Micro [071]

EXETER TIMES ADVOCATE – Exeter, Ontario, Canada.1980-1979 sic – 1 – cn Commonwealth Micro [072]

EXHALACIONES DEL ALMA / Moreno Torrado, Luis – 1885 – 9 – 1.50f – sp Bibl Santa Ana [810]

EXHALACIONES DEL ALMA / Moreno Torrado, Luis – Badajoz: Tip La Minerva Extremena, 1885 – 1 – sp Bibl Santa Ana [440]

EXHIBIT – v1-16. 1954-61. Continued by: Newsletter. American Library Association, Exhibits Round Table – 1 – us UMI [020]

EXHIBIT MATERIAL / McKay, Claude – 1 – us Ross [975]

AN EXHIBIT OF GERMAN MILITARY DOCUMENTS..., 1679-1935 / Heeresarchiv. Potsdam – 2r – 1 – M129. (World War II Collection of Seized Enemy Records) – us Nat'l Archives [943]

EXHIBITION BY THE ITALIAN FUTURIST PAINTERS / Sackville Gallery. London – 1912 – 9 – $4.90 – uk Chadwyck [750]

EXHIBITION CATALOGUES / National Gallery of Canada – (With printed guide) – 1919-59 – 9 – $550.00 – cn McLaren [700]

EXHIBITION CRITIC ILLUSTRATED – Montreal: J L Wiseman, [1880] – 9 – cn C.I.H.M. [380]

EXHIBITION CRITIC ILLUSTRATED – Montreal. v- n-. 16 sep 1880 – 1r – 1 – Can$25.00 – cn Can Microfilming [072]

EXHIBITION EXPOSITE AND ADVERTISER – Dublin, Ireland.1853. -w. 1/4 reel – 1 – uk British Libr Newspaper [072]

EXHIBITION HERALD *see* COURRIER DES EXPOSITIONS

EXHIBITION OF PAINTINGS,15-24 JAN., 1960, BANGKOK. SE-2195/1. 1960 / Basuki Abdullah – 9 – ne IDC [760]

EXHIBITOR'S TRADE REVIEW; OF, FOR, AND BY THE MOTION PICTURE EXHIBITOR – New York. 9 Dec 1916-27 Feb 1926 – 1 – 1200.00 – us L of C Photodup [770]

EXHIBITS – (1979- 5,6,9) – v.20-. 1975- – 1 – us UMI [020]

EXHIBITS / International Military Tribunal for the Far East – Tokyo. In Japanese. On film: Documents 238-277, 286-473, 476-838, 845-1045, 1107-1225, 1227-1245, 1249-1764, 1766-1820; 1946-48. LL-026 – 1 – us L of C Photodup [340]

EXHORTACION PASTORAL...CON MOTIVO DE LA EPIDEMIA REINANTE / Perez Munoz, Adolfo – Badajoz: Tip. Uceda Hermanos, 1918 – 1 – sp Bibl Santa Ana [240]

EXHORTATION ET REMONSTRANCE, FAITE D'UN COMMUN...1586 – N.p., n.d. – 1mf – 1 – ILM-1240/1 – ne IDC [327]

EXHORTATIONES AD MONACHOS / Trithemius, J – Parisiis, 1549 – 7mf – 8 – Dfl28.00 – ne Slangenburg [240]

EXILE – (Suspended publ temporarily 1983-84) – Toronto. v1-18. 1972-1993/94 – 9 – Can$28.00y – cn Micromedia [073]

THE EXILE – Chicago. no. 1-3. Spring 1927-Autumn 1928 – 1 – us NY Public [073]

THE EXILES' BOOK OF CONSOLATION CONTAINED IN ISAIAH 40-66 : A CRITICAL AND EXEGETICAL STUDY / Koenig, Eduard – (Includes bibliographical references and index) – Edinburgh: T & T Clark, 1899 – 1mf – 9 – 0-8370-3966-5 – 1985-1966 – us A.T.L.A. [220]

Eximeno, Antonio *see*
- DELL' ORIGINE E DELLE REGOLE DELLA MUSICA COLLA STORIA DEL SUO PROGRESSO, DECADENZA, E RINNOVAZIONE
- DELL'ORGINE E DELLE REGOLE DELLA MUSICA
- DUBBIO DI DON ANTONIO EXIMENO SOPRA IL SAGGIO FONDAMENTALE PRATICO DI CONTRAPPUNTO

L'EXISTENCE A L'ETRANGER DES SOCIETES RUSSES / Goeldlin de Tiefenau, E – Paris, 1928 – 2mf – 1 – ILM-3297/1 – ne IDC [327]

THE EXISTENCE OF GOD / Moyes, James – London: Sands; St Louis, MO: Herder, 1906 – 1mf – 9 – 0-8370-7251-4 – 1986-1251 – us A.T.L.A. [210]

EXKURSIONSFLORA VON JAVA... / Koorders, SH – Jena, 1911-1937. 4v – 30mf – 9 – ne IDC [580]

EXLEX – Kristiania, Norway; Kobenhavn, Denmark. 1919-20 – 1 – sw Kungliga [073]

EXMOUTH JOURNAL *see* FREEMAN'S EXMOUTH JOURNAL

L'EXODE DES CLASSES DIRIGEANTES A LA CESSION DU CANADA / Baby, Georges – Montreal, 1899. 02211. (Pre-1900 Canadiana) – 9 – cn C.I.H.M. [971]

L'EXODE RURAL AU MAROC. ETUDE SOCIOLOGIQUE DE L'EXODE DU TAFILALET VERS LA VILLE DE FES / El Maliki, Abderrahmane – 2mf – 9 – 10089 – fr Atelier National [307]

EXODUS – San Francisco, CA. 1970-78 – 1 – us A.J.P.C. [071]

EXODUS ERKLAERT / Holzinger, Heinrich – (Includes bibliographical references & subject index) – Tuebingen: J C B Mohr, 1900 – 1mf – 9 – 0-8370-3646-1 – 1985-1646 – us A.T.L.A. [220]

EXODUS-LEVITICUS-NUMERI / Baentsch, Bruno – (Includes index) – Goettingen: Vandenhoeck und Ruprecht, 1903 – 2mf – 9 – 0-8370-9441-0 – 1986-3441 – us A.T.L.A. [220]

EXORTACION PASTORAL / Varela, Cipriano – 1827 – 9 – 1.50f – sp Bibl Santa Ana [240]

DER EXOTE : ROMAN / Wiechert, Ernst Emil – Muenchen: K Desch, 1951, c1945 – 1r – 1 – us U.W. Library [830]

EXOTIC BOTANY: CONSISTING OF COLOURED FIGURES AND SCIENTIFIC DESCRIPTIONS / Smith, J E – London, 1804-1805. 2 vols. B-5397b 2 – 8 – ne IDC [580]

EXOTIC CONCHOLOGY / Swainson, W – 2506 2. Ed. 2. 1841 – 8 – ne IDC [590]

EXOTIC FLORA, CONTAINING FIGURES AND DESCRIPTIONS OF EXOTIC PLANTS / Hooker, W J – 3v. Edinburgh. 1822-, 1823-27. B-5962 2 – 8 – ne IDC [580]

EXOTIC MICROLEPIDOPTERA / Meyrick, E – 2417 2. 2 v. 1912-1921 – 8 – ne IDC [590]

EXOTIC ORNITHOLOGY / Sclater, P L & Salvin, O – Z 1921. 1866-1869 – 9 – ne IDC [590]

EXOTISCHE SCHMTTERLINGE / ed by Staudinger, O & Schatz, E – Fuerth, (1884)-1888-1892 – 2 vols – 8 – ne IDC [590]

L'EXOTISME : LA LITTERATURE COLONIALE / Cario, Louis & Regismanset, Charles – Paris: Mercure de France, 1911 – 1 – us Res Libr [910]

EXPANDING AGRICULTURAL COMMODITY TRADE AMONG DEVELOPING COUNTRIES – 1983 – 121p – it F.A.O. [380]

EXPANDING OLYMPIC HORIZONS – (Series: United States Olympic Academy, 5) – Olympic Training Center at Colorado Springs, 1981 – 4mf – 9 – $16.00 – us Microform Publ [790]

EXPANSAO GEOGRAPHICA DO BRASIL COLONIAL / Macalhaes, Basilio de – Sao Paulo, 2nd ed 1935 – 7mf – 8 – ne Slangenburg [972]

EXPANSION – 1967- – 1; 1975- 5,6,9 – us UMI [331]

EXPANSION – 1967-1995 – 2r per y – 5,6 – Sfr815.00 – sz Infoprint [944]

EXPANSION – 1967-1995 – 2 times per yr – 6 – F3,150.00 – sz Infoprint [072]

LA EXPANSION CULTURAL DE ESPANA EN EL EXTRANJERO... / Sangroniz, Jose Antonio de – Madrid: Razon y Fe, 1927 – 1 – sp Bibl Santa Ana [946]

L'EXPANSION FRANCAISE EN AFRIQUE OCCIDENTALE – Paris: Societe de l'histoire des colonies francaises [194-?] – us Res Libr [960]

THE EXPANSION OF THE CHRISTIAN LIFE / Lang, John Marshall – (Includes bibliographical references & index) – Edinburgh: William Blackwood, 1897 – 1mf – 9 – 0-8370-6202-0 – 1986-0202 – us A.T.L.A. [240]

EXPATRIATION ACADIENNE, NOTES FOURNIES...LE 24 MAI, 1885. BANISHMENT AND REMOVAL OF THE ACADIANS / Morel de la Durantaye, A – 1885?. 02183. (Pre-1900 Canadiana) – 9 – cn C.I.H.M. [971]

O EXPECTADOR : ORGAM DOS INTERESSES SOCIAES – Cuiaba, 17 Jan-Aug 1884; Feb-Jul, Sep, Nov-Dec 1885; Mar, Jun 1886; Feb-22 Mar 1888 – 1,5,6 – bl Biblioteca [072]

EXPECTATIONS OF LUTHERAN MILITARY PERSONNEL AS FACTORS IN SHAPING CHAPLAIN MINISTRY / Baldwin, Charles Stealey – 1982 – 1 – 5.36 – us Baptist [240]

EXPECTING – 1967- – 1 1975- 5,6,9 – us UMI [618]

EXPECTING – 1975- – 1 – us UMI [073]

EXPEDICAO AS REGIOES CENTRAIS DA AMERICA DO SUL. T. 1 / Castelnau – Sao Paulo, 1949 – 7mf – 8 – ne Slangenburg [910]

EXPEDICAO AS REGIOES CENTRAIS DA AMERICA DO SUL. T. 2 / Castelnau – Sao Paulo, 1949 – 7mf – 8 – ne Slangenburg [910]

EXPEDICION CORTESIANA A LAS MOLUCAS 1527 / Romero, Luis – Mexico: Editorial Jus, 1950 – 1 – sp Bibl Santa Ana [910]

LA EXPEDICION DE HERNANDO DE SOTO A LA FLORIDA / Serrano Sanz, Manuel – Madrid: Tip. de Archivos, 1933. B.R.A.Historia – 1 – sp Bibl Santa Ana [910]

EXPEDICION DEL ADELANTADO HERNANDO DE SOTO A LA FLORIDA : NOTAS Y DOCUMENTOS... / Hernandez Diaz, Jose – Burgos: Razon y Fe, 1939 – 1 – sp Bibl Santa Ana [910]

EXPEDICION DEL MAESTRE DE CAMPO BERNARDO DE ALDANA A HUNGRIA / Villela de Aldana, Fr. Juan – 1879 – 9 – 1.50f – sp Bibl Santa Ana [910]

EXPEDIENTE SOBRE LA REBELION DE LARES, 1868-69 (CASE FILE ON THE REBELLION OF LARES) / Puerto Rico. Spanish Governors – 6rolls. T1120 – 1 – us Nat'l Archives [324]

EXPEDITING PATENT OFFICE PROCEDURE; LEGISLATIVE HISTORY / U.S. Library of Congress. Legislative Reference Service – Washington, Govt. Print. Off., 1960. 105 p. LL-2310 – 1 – us L of C Photodup [340]

EXPEDITING SETTLEMENT OF EMPLOYEE GRIEVANCES IN THE FEDERAL SECTOR : AN EVALUATION OF THE MSPB'S APPEALS PROCESS / Adams, Arvil V & Figueroa, Jose R – Washington: GPO, 1985 (all publ) – 2mf – 9 – $3.00 – LLMC 94-349 – us L.L.M.C. [340]

"THE EXPEDITION AT BEISAN" / Rowe, Alan – University of Pennsylvania Museum Journal: Dec 1927 – 9 – $10.00 – us I.R.C. [930]

EXPEDITION C. A. VERMINCK / Zweifel, J & Moustier, M – Voyage aux sources de Niger. Paris, Challamel Aine. 1879 – 9 – $5.00 – fr Orientalistes [910]

Expedition de Cochinchine. Puis, de la Cochinchine francaise *see* BULLETIN OFFICIEL

L'EXPEDITION DE MADAGASCAR : RAPPORT D'ENSEMBLE FAIT AU MINISTRE DE LA GUERRE LE 25 AVRIL 1896 / Duchesne, J – Paris: H C Lavauzelle, 1896 – 1 – us Res Libr [910]

L'EXPEDITION DU DAHOMEY / Nicolas, Victor – Paris, Limoges, Imprimerie et Librairie militaires, Henri Charles-Lavauzelle. 1893 – 9 – 5.00 – fr Orientalistes [910]

EXPEDITION IN NORTH RUSSIA, 1918-1919 / U.S. Army. A. E. F., 1917-1920 – 1918-19? – 1 – 21.00 – us L of C Photodup [947]

EXPEDITION REPORTS OF THE OFFICE OF FOREIGN SEED AND PLANT INTRODUCTION OF THE DEPARTMENT OF AGRICULTURE / U.S. Department of Agriculture – 1900-38. 38 rolls. M840 – 1 – us Nat'l Archives [630]

EXPEDITION SCIENTIFIQUE DE MOREE / Bory de Saint-Vincent, J B C M – Section des sciences physiques. v. 3, pt. 2. Botanique. Paris 1832-33. B-5860 2 – 8 – ne IDC [910]

EXPEDITION SCIENTIFIQUE DE MOREE / Chaubard, LA & Bory de Saint-Vincent, J BG M – Paris. 1832 – 8 – ne IDC [910]

EXPEDITION SCIENTIFIQUE DU CAP HORN : EXPOSITION DES INSTRUMENTS ET COLLECTIONS / Riviere, Emile – Paris: Bureau des revues, 1884 – fr Armell [910]

AN EXPEDITION THROUGH THE BARREN LANDS OF NORTHERN CANADA / Tyrrell, J B – (Geograph. Journal, v. 4). London. 1894. BN-429 2 – 8 – ne IDC [910]

EXPEDITION TO DISCOVER THE SOURCES OF THE WHITE NILE, IN THE YEARS 1840, 1841 / Werne, Ferdinand – From the German by Charles William O'Reilly. London: R. Bentley, 1849. 2v. illus – 1 – us U.W. Library [910]

THE EXPEDITION TO THE RIVER ZAIRE / Tuckey, James Kingston – 1818 – 7 – uk Microform Academic [910]

EXPEDITIONS AUTOUR DE MA TENTE: BOUTADES MILITAIRES / Des Ecorres, Charles – Paris: E. Pion, 1887. 00583. (Pre-1900 Canadiana) – 9 – cn C.I.H.M. [971]

EXPEDITIONS SCIENTIFIQUES DU "TRAVAILLEUR" ET DU "TALISMAN" PENDANT LES ANNEES 1880, 1881, 1882, 1883 / ed by Vaillant, M L & Milne-Edwards, M et al – Paris. 1888-1927. BZ-2250 1 – 9 – ne IDC [910]

EXPEDITIONUM SPIRITUALIUM SOCIETATIS IESU, LIBRI QUINQUE / San Roman, M de – Lugduni, 1644 – 8mf – 9 – CA-24/1 – ne IDC [240]

EXPENDITURE ON EDUCATION AS SHOWN IN CENTRAL AND STATE ANNUAL BUDGETS 1977/78-1979/80 / India. Department of Education – New Delhi – 4mf – 9 – DE-539/1 – ne IDC [370]

EXPENSES UNDER CANADIAN INCOME TAX ACT / Commerce Clearing House Canadian Limited – 6th ed. Don Mills, Ont. 1968 156 p. LL-2380 – 1 – us L of C Photodup [340]

EXPERIENCE IN THE SUPREME COURT OF THE UNITED STATES, WITH SOME REFLECTIONS AND SUGGESTIONS AS TO THAT TRIBUNAL / Garland, Augustus Hill – Washington, D.C.: Byrne, 1898. 100p. LL-491 – 1 – us L of C Photodup [340]

THE EXPERIENCE OF A PLANTER IN THE JUNGLES OF MYSORE / Elliot, Robert Henry – London: Chapman and Hall, 1871. 2v. illus – 1 – us U.W. Library [630]

EXPERIENCE, THE CROWNING EVIDENCE OF THE CHRISTIAN RELIGION / Granbery, John C – Nashville, Tenn.: Publishing House of the M.E. Church, South, 1901 – 1mf – us A.T.L.A. [240]

EXPERIENCED BUSINESS MAN – A tract on the situation. By an experienced business man. Toronto?: s.n., 1890 (Toronto: Budget). 05569. (Pre-1900 Canadiana) – 9 – cn C.I.H.M. [971]

EXPERIENCES AND RELATIONS IN THE WORK OF WOMEN TEACHER/COACHES : A CRITICAL INQUIRY / Jeffreys, Arcelia T – 1989 – 216p 3mf – 9 – $12.00 – us Microform Publ [305]

THE EXPERIENCES OF A BARRISTER / Warner, Warren – New York: Cornish, Lamport & Co, 1852 – 3mf – 9 – $4.50 – LLMC 92-144 – us L.L.M.C. [340]

THE EXPERIENCES OF A BARRISTER AND CONFESSIONS OF AN ATTORNEY / Warren, Samuel – Boston: Wentworth & Co. 2v in one. 1857 – 4mf – 9 – $6.00 – LLMC 92-146 – us L.L.M.C. [340]

EXPERIENCES OF A DIPLOMATIST, BEING RECOLLECTIONS OF GERMANY, FOUNDED ON DIARIES KEPT DURING THE YEARS 1840-1870 / Ward, John – London: Macmillan, 1872.viii,279p – 1 – us U.W. Library [941]

EXPERIENCES POUR SERVIR A L'HISTOIRE DE LA GENERATION DES ANIMAUX ET DES PLANTES AVEC UNE EBAUCHE DE L'HISTOIRE DES ETRES ORGANISES AVANT LEUR FECONDATION, PAR SENEBIER / Spallanzani, Lazzaro – Geneve, 1785, xlvi-413 p. Histoire des Sciences XVIIe-XIXe Siecles. 7937 – 9 – fr Hachette [590]

EXPERIENCIAS SOBRE EL PODER ATRAYENTE, PARA LA MOSCA DEL OLIVO, DEL FOSFATO AMONICO A DIVERSAS CONCENTRACIONES / Moreno Marquez, Victor – Madrid: Direccion Gral. de Agricultura. Seccion de plagas del campo y fitopatologia. Servicio de defensa sanitaria del olivo, 1941. Sep. del Boletin de Patologia Vegetal – 1 – sp Bibl Santa Ana [630]

EXPERIMENT – Norwalk, Ohio. 1835-74 – 11r – 1 – $32.50r – us Archival [071]

EXPERIMENT STATION NOTES / Wisconsin. Agricultural Experiment Station – Feb 1954-Apr 1966 – 1,5 – us Spaulding [630]

EXPERIMENT STATION RECORD / U.S. Department of Agriculture. Office of Experiment Stations – v. 1-95. 1889-1946 – 1,5,6 – us Princeton Micro [630]

EXPERIMENT STATION RECORD. U.S. DEPARTMENT OF AGRICULTURE – Washington, 1889-1893. v1-4; 1904-1908. v16-19. Index 1889-1919 – 137mf – 9 – 8001/1 – ne IDC [630]

EXPERIMENTA NOVA ANATOMICA, QUIBUS / Pecquet, J – M-220. 1651 – 9 – ne IDC [611]

EXPERIMENTAL AGING RESEARCH – (v.6 .1980 5,6,9) – v.1. 1975 – 1 – us UMI [073]

EXPERIMENTAL AND CLINICAL GASTROENTEROLOGY – v1- 1991- – 5,6,9 – us UMI [616]

EXPERIMENTAL AND CLINICAL IMMUNOGENETICS – v1-. 1984- – 1,5,9 – us UMI [073]

EXPERIMENTAL BRAIN RESEARCH – v. 1-40. 1965-80 – 1,5,9 – 5040.00 – us UMI [073]

EXPERIMENTAL CINEMA : A MONTHLY PROJECTING IMPORTANT INTERNATIONAL FILM MANIFESTATIONS – Philadelphia. v1. 1930-31 – 1r – 1 – us Ross [790]

EXPERIMENTAL CINEMA – Philadelphia, Penn. v. 1 no. 1-3. 1930-31 – 1 – us NY Public [790]

EXPERIMENTAL FACILITIES IN WATER RESOURCES EDUCATION – 1983 – 83p – 9 – 92-3-102107-9 – fr UNESCO [333]

EXPERIMENTAL GERONTOLOGY – v1- 1965- – 5,6,9 – us UMI [073]

EXPERIMENTAL INQUIRIES / Hewson, W – M-181. 1774 – 9 – ne IDC [500]

EXPERIMENTAL LUNG RESEARCH – (v6-. 1984-. 5,6,9) – v1-. Mar 1980- – 1 – us UMI [073]

EXPERIMENTAL MEDICINE AND SURGERY – v. 1-27. 1943-1969 – 1,5,6 – us Princeton Micro [619]

EXPERIMENTAL NEPHROLOGY – v1-. 1993- – us UMI [616]

AN EXPERIMENTAL RURAL CHURCH (CCC109) / Chu, Ching-i – (In Chinese) – [s.l: s.n, 1954] – 1r – 1 – 1984-B500 – us A.T.L.A. [240]

EXPERIMENTAL STRESS ANALYSIS: PROCEEDINGS.. / Society for Experimental Stress Analysis – v1-v2,no.2. 1943-44 – 1 – us UMI [073]

EXPERIMENTAL TECHNIQUES – (1983-. 1,5,6,9) – v1-. 1976- – 1 – us UMI [073]

EXPERIMENTATION IN THE LAW : REPORT OF THE FJC ADVISORY COMMITTEE ON EXPERIMENTATION IN THE LAW – Washington: GPO, 1981 – 2mf – 9 – $3.00 – LLMC 95-308 – us L.L.M.C. [340]

EXPERIMENTELLE UND KLINISCHE UNTERSUCHUNGEN ZUR THERAPIE VON NEUROGENEN BLASENFUNKTIONSSTOERUNGEN / Hohenfellner, R Markus – 1995 – 2mf – 9 – DM80.00 – 3-8267-2128-4 – gw Hänsel [616]

EXPERIMENTELLE UNTERSUCHUNG DER ANTIBIOTIKAPRODUKTION SOWIE DES WACHSTUMS VON PILZEN BEI FERMENTATIONEN IM HUBSTRAHL-BIOREAKTOR / Wudtke, Alexander – 1994 – 2mf – DM80.00 – 3-8267-2073-3 – gw Hänsel [574]

EXPERIMENTELLE UNTERSUCHUNG ZUM PROBLEM DES ZUSAMMENHANGS ZWISCHEN ERFRAGTEM UND BEOBACHTETEM VERHALTEN / Hueneke, Heinrich – Heidelberg, 1972 – 2mf – 9 – DM62.00 – 3-89349-797-8 – gw Hänsel [150]

EXPERIMENTELL-PSYCHOLOGISCHE UNTERSUCHUNGEN UEBER DAS URTEILH-526/2. 1901 / Marbe, K – 8 – ne IDC [150]

EXPERIMENTS / Grew, N – M 362. 1678 – 9 – ne IDC [580]

EXPERIMENTS AND DEMONSTRATIONS IN PSYCHOLOGY : STUDENTS' MANUAL / Shaffer, Laurence Frederic & Haller Gillmer, Beverly von & Porter, James M – New York, London: Harper & Bros., 1942. xi,230p. illus., plates, forms, diagrs – 1 – us U.W. Library [150]

EXPERIMENTS AND OBSERVATIONS IN THE GASTRIC JUICES / Beaumont, W – M-186. 1833 – 9 – ne IDC [610]

EXPERIMENTS IN AMBER CANE AND THE ENSILAGE OF FODDERS / Wisconsin. Agricultural Experiment Station – 1st and 2nd reports. 1882-83 – 1,5 – us Spaulding [580]

EXPERIMENTS IN GOVERNMENT AND THE ESSENTIALS OF THE CONSTITUTION / Root, Elihu – Princeton/London/Oxford: Princeton UP/Henry Frowde/Oxford UP, 1913 – 1mf – 9 – $1.50 – LLMC 92-202 – us L.L.M.C. [323]

EXPERIMENTS IN PERSONAL RELIGION (CCC297) / ed by Tseng, Pao-sun – (In Chinese) – 1st ed. Shanghai: Association Press of China, 1934 – 1r – 1 – 1984-6636 – us A.T.L.A. [240]

EXPERIMENTS IN POPULAR EDUCATION IN PORTUGAL 1974-1976 / Melo, Alberto & Benavente, Ana – 1978 – 45p – 9 – 92-3-101556-7 – fr UNESCO [370]

THE EXPERT MIDWIFE / Rueff, J – M 400. 1637 – 9 – ne IDC [618]

EXPERT SYSTEMS WITH APPLICATIONS – 1,5,69 – us UMI [000]

EXPERT TESTIMONY BEFORE THE COMMISSION / U.S. Indian Claims Commission – (Suppl. 1. 48 titles. 125 fiches. $420.00; Suppl. 2. 97 titles. 209 fiches. $705.00) – Contains nearly 100,000 pages in 400 vol. of anthropological, historical, geographical and economic reports previously unpublished. Includes printed index. 1270 fiches – 9 – $4,160.00 – us UPA [305]

EXPERTENSYSTEM-WARTUNG / Fischer, Stefan – 1993 – 2mf – 9 – DM98.00 – 3-89349-682-3 – gw Hänsel [000]

THE EXPLANATIO SYMBOLI AD INITIANDOS : A WORK OF ST. AMBROSE. A PROVISIONALLY CONSTRUCTED TEXT, WITH INTRODUCTION, NOTES AND A TRANSLATION / ed by Connolly, R H – 1952 – 1mf – 9 – Dfl6.00 – ne Slangenburg [240]

EXPLANATION OF GOVERNMENT OF REPUBLIC OF INDONESIA'S STATEMENT OF 4 AUG. 1956; INDONESIA'S DEBTS TO THE DUTCH / Indonesia. Kementerian Luar Negeri – SE-3346 1. 1956 – 9 – ne IDC [336]

AN EXPLANATION OF THE ELEMENTARY CHARACTERS OF THE CHINESE / Hager, Joseph – 1801. 126p. (English Linguistics Series 1500-1800) – 9 – us UMI [410]

AN EXPLANATION OF THE ELEVENTH CHAPTER OF THE BOOK OF DANIEL / Collins, George – (Ottawa: J. Loveday), 1870. 00713. (Pre-1900 Canadiana) – 9 – cn C.I.H.M. [240]

EXPLANATION OF THE HOLY SACRAMENTS : A COMPLETE EXPOSITION OF THE SACRAMENTS AND THE SACRAMENTALS OF THE CHURCH / Rolfus, Hermann – (Also issued under title: Illustrated explanation of the holy sacraments) – New York: Benziger, c1898 – 1mf – 9 – 0-8370-7187-9 – 1986-1187 – us A.T.L.A. [240]

AN EXPLANATION OF THE THIRTY-NINE ARTICLES : WITH AN EPISTLE DEDICATORY TO THE LATE REV. E.B. PUSEY / Forbes, Alexander Penrose – (Includes bibliographical references) – 5th ed. New York: E P Dutton; Oxford: Parker, [ca 1875] – 3mf – 9 – 0-8370-8668-X – 1986-2668 – us A.T.L.A. [240]

AN EXPLANATION OF THE VISIONS OF THE FOUR BEASTS. DANIEL 7 / Collins, George – Ottawa?, 1870?. 00714. (Pre-1900 Canadiana) – 9 – cn C.I.H.M. [240]

EXPLANATIONS AND ILLUSTRATIONS OF THE SACRED EDICT, VOL 1 (CCC122) – (In Chinese) – [s.l: s.n, 1856] – 1r – 1 – 1984-B500 – us A.T.L.A. [220]

EXPLANATORY ANALYSIS OF ST PAUL'S EPISTLE TO THE ROMANS / Liddon, Henry Parry – London: Longmans, Green, 1897. 1 fiche – 9 – us A.T.L.A. [240]

EXPLANATORY LECTURE ON VISIBLE SPEECH, THE SCIENCE OF UNIVERSAL ALPHABETICS...FEB. 9, 1870 / Bell, Alexander Melville – London: Simpkin, Marshall, 1870.07075.(Pre-1900 Canadiana) – 9 – cn C.I.H.M. [410]

EXPLANATORY MEMOIR OF THE METALLOGENIC MAP OF EUROPE AND NEIGHBOURING COUNTRIES – 1984 – 660p – 9 – 92-3-002251-9 – fr UNESCO [550]

EXPLANATORY MEMORANDUM, BASUTO NATIONAL TREASURY – [S.l: s.n., 1944?] – us Res Libr [324]

EXPLANATORY MEMORANDUM ON DEVELOPMENT BUDGETS / Sudan – 4v. 1964-68. BNE-7688 1 – 9 – ne IDC [332]

EXPLANATORY NOTES UPON THE OLD TESTAMENT / Wesley, John – 3v. 1765 – 1 – us A.T.L.A. [240]

EXPLICACION DE LA SAGRADA PASION DE NUESTRO SENOR JESUCRISTO.. – 196? – 1 – us I.U. Libraries [390]

EXPLICACION DE LOS ESTADOS QUE FORMAN LA BALANZA DEL COMERCIO RECIPROCO QUE HIZO ESPANA...EN 1795 / Archivo Ministerio de Hacienda MS. – 5mf – 9 – sp Cultura [380]

EXPLICACION LITERAL DEL CATECISMO DEL PADRE ASTETE CON UNA EXPOSICION Y REFUTACION DE LOS ERORES MODERNOS Y LA EXPLICACION DE LA BULA DE LA SANTA CRUZADA / Marquez, Gabino – Madrid: Razon y Fe 1929 – 1 – sp Bibl Santa Ana [240]

EXPLICACION...CONFESORES.. / Blazquez del Barco, Juan – 1721 – 9 – 1.50f – sp Bibl Santa Ana [240]

EXPLICACION...REGLA DE SAN AGUSTIN / Logrosan, Juan de – 1716 – 9 – 1.50f – sp Bibl Santa Ana [240]

EXPLICATIO EPISTOLAE PAVLI AD GALATAS / Hesshusen, T – [Helmstedt], 1579 – 8mf – ne IDC [240]

EXPLICATIO EPISTOLAE PAVLI AD ROMANOS / Hesshusen, T – Ienae, 1571 – 10mf – ne IDC [240]

EXPLICATIO MALACHIAE PROPHETAE,... / Chytraeus, D – Rostochii, 1568 – 2mf – 9 – ne IDC [240]

EXPLICATIO PRIORIS EPISTOLAE PAVLI AD CORINTHIOS / Hesshusen, T – Ienae, 1573 – 8mf – ne IDC [240]

EXPLICATIO PSALMI CX. IN QVA DOCTRINA DE SPIRITUALI REGNO... / Hesshusen, T – Helmstadii, 1580 – 2mf – ne IDC [240]

EXPLICATIO SECVNDAE EPISTOLAE PAVLI AD CORINTHIOS / Hesshusen, T – Helmstadii, 1580 – 7mf – ne IDC [240]

EXPLICATION DE LA DOCTRINE SAINT-SIMONIENNE – Premier et Deuxieme bulletin. Toulon, impr. de L. Laurent, s.d., 8 plus 8 p. Le Pere aux capitaines Hoart et Bruneau, a Roge et Massol. Toulon, impr. de Canquoin, 1833, 7 p. Les Saint-Simoniens, 1825-1834. 6942 – 9 – fr Hachette [335]

EXPLICATION DE L'APPEL D'UN PROTESTANT AU PAPE – (Includes bibliographical references) – Geneve: Vve Auguste Garin, 1869 – 1mf – 9 – 0-8370-6940-8 – 1986-0940 – us A.T.L.A. [327]

EXPLICATION DE L'EDICT DE NANTES PAR LES AUTRES EDICTS DE PACIFICATION, DECLARATIONS ET ARRESTS DE REGLEMENT / Bernard, P – Paris, 1666 – 12mf – 9 – CA-109/1 – ne IDC [240]

L'EXPLICATION DE L'EDIT DE NANTES DE M. BERNARD, AVEC DE NOUVELLES OBSERVATIONS... / Soulier, P – Paris, 1683 – 7mf – 9 – CA-107/1 – ne IDC [240]

EXPLICATION DU SYSTEME DE L'HARMONIE / Lirou, J -F E de – 1785 – 9 – us Sibley [780]

EXPLICATION FACILE ET BREVE DES CINQ ORDRES D'ARCHITECTURE. / Cotte, Fremin de – Paris, 1644. 10 ff., illus – 9 – fr Hachette [720]

EXPLICATION HISTORIQUE DES FABLES / Banier, Antoine – 1742 – 1 – us I.U. Libraries [390]

EXPLICATOR – (v. 27-41. 1968-83. 5,6. v. 34-41. 1975-83. 9) – v. 1-41. 1942-83 – 1 – us UMI [420]

THE EXPLICATOR – Fredericksburg. West Virginia. 1943-1944 – 1 – us UMI [071]

THE EXPLOITATION OF EAST AFRICA, 1854-1890: THE SLAVE TRADE AND THE SCRAMBLE / Coupland, R – London. 1939. BA-296 2 – 8 – ne IDC [960]

EXPLOITATIONS AGRICOLES EN PAYS DIAMALA-DJIMINI / Ancey, G – (Africa series). 1969 – 9 – fr Hachette [630]

L'EXPLOITE – Organe socialiste revolutionnaire de la region Nord. Douai. aout-nov 1884 – 1 – fr A.C.R.P.P. [073]

EXPLOITING THE TROPICAL RAIN FOREST : AN ACCOUNT OF PULPWOOD LOGGING IN PAPUA NEW GUINEA / Lamb, D – 1990 – 9 – 92-3-102646-1 – Co-published with Parthenon Publishing – fr UNESCO [634]

LES EXPLOITS DE MASIRE ISSE DIEYE : UN EPISODE DE L'EPOPEE DU KAYOR / Dioum, Abdoulaye – 1978 – us Res Libr [960]

LES EXPLOITS POLICIERS DU DOMINO NOIR – 888 nos. 1948-1965. SEM16P325 – 10r – 5 – Can$312.00 – cn Bibl Nat [073]

EXPLORACIONES PRACTICADAS EN EL ALTO PARAGUAY... / Bolland, Henry – [S.l.]: Compania americana de billetes de banco, 1901 – 1 – F92.03 – fr Armell [910]

EXPLORACOES BOTANICAS EM TIMOR / Gomes, Ruy Cinatti Vaz Monteiro – Lisbon, 1950 – 1 – us Res Libr [580]

EXPLORADORES Y CONQUISTADORES EXTREMENOS EN AMERICA : ESTUDIO BIOGRAFICO: HERNANDO DE SOTO / Villanueva y Canedo, Luis – 2nd ed. Badajoz: Tip., Lib. y Enc. de A. Arqueros, 1929 – 1 – sp Bibl Santa Ana [972]

L'EXPLORATEUR – Journal geographique et commercial. Paris. 1875-aout 1876 (I-IV) – 1 – fr A.C.R.P.P. [910]

UN EXPLORATEUR DE LA LOUISIANE : JEAN BAPTISTE ET BERNARD DE LA HARPE, 1683-1765 / Villiers du Terrage, Marc de – Rennes: Imp. Oberthur, 1934. SEM105P943 – 1mf – 9 – Can$2.25 – cn Bibl Nat [910]

THE EXPLORATION AND COLONIZATION OF AFRICA, 1794-1844 : BRITISH COLONIAL OFFICE FILES 2 AND 392 – (With printed guide) – 1979 – 14r – 1 – $1,190.00 – D3256 – us Scholarly Res [960]

EXPLORATION AND MINING GEOLOGY – 1,5,69 – us UMI [550]

EXPLORATION BOTANIQUE DE L'AFRIQUE OCCIDENTALE FRANCAISE / Chevalier, Auguste – Paris. 1920. B-5230 2 – 8 – ne IDC [910]

EXPLORATION DE LA COTE ORIENTALE D'AFRIQUE / Guillain, Charles – 9 – 10.00 – fr Orientalistes [910]

EXPLORATION DE L'ILE D'ANTICOSTI. / Combes, Paul – Paris: J. Andre, 1896. 00721. (Pre-1900 Canadiana) – 9 – cn C.I.H.M. [910]

L'EXPLORATION DU SAHARA : ETUDE HISTORIQUE ET GEOGRAPHIQUE / Vuillot, Paul – Paris: A Challamel, 1895 – 1 – us Res Libr [960]

AN EXPLORATION OF THE LONG-TERM PROSPECTS FOR THE FURTHER DEVELOPMENT OF THE NILEWATERS IN THE SUDAN FOR IRRIGATION AND HYDROELECTRIC POWER / Wynn, R F – 1968. BNE-7699 1 – 9 – ne IDC [338]

EXPLORATION OF THE NILE TRIBUTARIES OF ABYSSINIA. THE SOURCES, SUPPLY, AND OVERFLOW OF THE NILE.. / Baker, Samuel White – Hartford: O.D. Case & Co., 1868.xx,1 leaf, (23)-624p. maps – 1 – us U.W. Library [910]

AN EXPLORATION OF THE OPINIONS OF RECREATION AND PARKS/LEISURE STUDIES FACULTY AND PUBLIC SECTOR PRACTITIONERS CONCERNING THE COMPUTER COMPETENCY SKILLS OF RECREATION AND PARKS/LEISURE STUDIES BACCA-LAUREATE STUDENTS / Case, Alan J & Christiansen, Monty L – 1991 – 3mf – 9 – $12.00 – us Microform Publ [790]

EXPLORATION SCIENTIFIQUE DE L'ALGERIE / Cosson, E S C – Botanique II. Phanerogamie. Groupe des Glumacees. Paris. 1854-68 – 8 – ne IDC [910]

EXPLORATIONS AMONG THE WATERSHED ROCKIES OF CANADA / Allen, Samuel E S – 1894?. 06576. (Pre-1900 Canadiana) – 9 – cn C.I.H.M. [910]

EXPLORATIONS AND ADVENTURES IN EQUATORIAL AFRICA / Du Chaillu, Paul Belloni – A 158. 1861 – 9 – ne IDC [910]

EXPLORATIONS AND ADVENTURES IN EQUATORIAL AFRICA / Du Chaillu, Paul Belloni – London. 1861. BA-158 2 – 8 – ne IDC [910]

LES EXPLORATIONS AU SENEGAL ET DANS LES CONTREES VOISINES DEPUIS L'ANTIQUITE JUSQU'A NOS JOURS / Ancelle, J – (Filmed with: Les francais au Niger par Pietri Camille) – Paris: Maisonneuve & C Leclerc, 1886 – 1 – us Res Libr [550]

EXPLORATIONS DU ZAMBESE ET DE SES AFFLUENTS ET DECOUVERTE DES LACS CHIROUA ET NYASSA. 1858-1864 / Livingstone, David & Livingstone, Charles – Paris, L. Hachette et Cie. 1866 – 9 – $17.50 – fr Orientalistes [910]

EXPLORATIONS IN ECONOMIC RESEARCH – v1-4 1974-78 1; v4- 5,6,9 – us UMI [330]

EXPLORATIONS IN HITTITE ASIA MINOR / Von der Osten, Hans Henning – 1929 – 9 – $10.00 – us I.R.C. [930]

EXPLORATIONS IN THE TYROPOEON VALLEY / Crowfoot, J W – 1929 – 9 – $10.00 – us I.R.C. [910]

AN EXPLORATORY STUDY OF QUALITY ASSURANCE METHODOLOGY IN THERAPEUTIC RECREATION USING THE DELPHI TECHNIQUE / Riley, Robert G – 1989 – 332p 4mf – 9 – $16.00 – us Microform Publ [790]

EXPLORATORY SURVEY: REPORTS, RECOMMENDATIONS AND ORDERS IN COUNCIL IN REFERENCE TO THE LOSS OF LIFE OF OFFICERS AND MEN, IN CONNECTION WITH THE SURVEY IN THE YEAR 1873 / Canadian Pacific Railway Company – (Ottawa: MacLean, Roger), 1874. 00444. (Pre-1900 Canadiana) – 9 – cn C.I.H.M. [971]

EXPLORE – Calgary. v1-70. 1981-1994/95 – 9 – Can$20.00y – cn Micromedia [073]

EXPLORERS JOURNAL – v1- 1921- 1; v56- 1978- 5,6,9 – us UMI [910]

EXPLORING THE KARATE WAY OF LIFE : COPING, COMMITMENT, AND PSYCHOLOGICAL WELL-BEING AMONG TRADITIONAL KARATE PARTICIPANTS / Wingate, Catherine F & Sachs, Michael L – 1993 – 4mf – 9 – $16.00 – us Microform Publ [150]

EXPLOSIONES DEL SENTIMIENTO / Moreno Torrado, Luis – 1884 – 9 – 1.50f – sp Bibl Santa Ana [810]

EXPLOTACION RACIONAL DEL SERDO / Moreno de Arteaga, Antonio – Madrid: MAG, 1954 – 1 – sp Bibl Santa Ana [946]

EXPO JOURNAL TERRE DES HOMMES – Montreal, Canada. v1 n2. 1 oct 1964-v2 n11. dec 1965 – 1r – 1 – $30.00 – cn Can Microfilming [900]

EXPOMAT ACTUALITES : MAGAZINE TECHNIQUE DES TRAVAUX PUBLICS ET DE LA CONSTRUCTION – Nos 25-42. Paris. Feb 1971-73 – 5 – fr A.C.R.P.P. [624]

EXPONENT – Bozeman. Mont. 1902-1922; 1924-1926 – 1 – us UMI [071]

EXPONENT – Chagrin Falls. Ohio. 1874- – 1 – us UMI [071]

EXPONENT – Clarksburg. West Virginia. 1932-1961 – 1 – us UMI [071]

EXPONENT – Reedley. Calif. -w. 1957-67 – 1 – us UMI [071]

EXPONENTIAL OUTLINE WITH DEFINITIONS OF BLACKSTONE'S COMMENTARIES. / Bates, W C – Columbus, Ohio, London, 1893. 94 p. LL-209 – 1 – us L of C Photodup [340]

EXPORT – 1937-70 – 1 – uk Microform Academic [380]

EXPORT *see* AMERICAN EXPORTER

EXPORT BY COMMODITY SPECIFIED BY THE MOST IMPORTANT COUNTRIES AND PORTS OF EXPORT / Indonesia. Biro Pusat Statistik – In Indonesian. SE-85 1. 1957-1960 – 9 – ne IDC [324]

THE EXPORT OF SAW LOGS: A BRIEF STATEMENT OF THE ONTARIO GOVERNMENT'S POSITION IN THIS MATTER – Toronto?: s.n., 1899?. 05495. (Pre-1900 Canadiana) – 9 – cn C.I.H.M. [971]

LA EXPORTACION DEL URUGUAY – Montevideo. 1948-55 – 1 – $46.00 – us L of C Photodup [972]

EXPOSE BUDGETAIRE: CHAMBRE DES COMMUNES, MARDI, 5 MARS 1889 / Foster, George Eulas – Ottawa?: s.n., 1889 (Ottawa: A. Senecal). 04341. (Pre-1900 Canadiana) – 9 – cn C.I.H.M. [971]

EXPOSE BUDGETAIRE: CHAMBRE DES COMMUNES, MARDI, 22 MARS 1892 / Foster, George Eulas – Ottawa?: s.n., 1892 (Ottawa: S. E. Dawson). 04337. (Pre-1900 Canadiana) – 9 – cn C.I.H.M. [971]

EXPOSE BUDGETAIRE: CHAMBRE DES COMMUNES, MARDI 23 JUIN 1891 / Foster, George Eulas – Ottawa: s.n., 1891 (Ottawa: B. Chamberlin). 04336. (Pre-1900 Canadiana) – 9 – cn C.I.H.M. [971]

EXPOSE BUDGETAIRE: CHAMBRE DES COMMUNES, MARDI, 27 MARS 1894 / Foster, George Eulas – Ottawa?: s.n., 1894 (Ottawa: S. E. Dawson). 04339. (Pre-1900 Canadiana) – 9 – cn C.I.H.M. [971]

EXPOSE BUDGETAIRE: CHAMBRE DES COMMUNES, VENDREDI, 31 JANVIER 1896 / Foster, George Eulas – Ottawa?: s.n., 1896 (Ottawa: S. E. Dawson). 04333. (Pre-1900 Canadiana) – 9 – cn C.I.H.M. [971]

EXPOSE BUDGETAIRE: DANS LA CHAMBRE DES COMMUNES, VENDREDI, 3 MAI 1895 / Foster, George Eulas – Ottawa?: s.n., 1895 (Ottawa: S. E. Dawson). 04340. (Pre-1900 Canadiana) – 9 – cn C.I.H.M. [971]

EXPOSE DE LA SITUATION DE L'EMPIRE PRESENTE AU CORPS LEGISLATIF. LE 12 DEC 1809 / Montalivet, J -P Bachasson – Paris: Imp. imperiale, 1809 – 9 – fr Hachette [944]

EXPOSE DE LA SITUATION DE L'EMPIRE PRESENTE AU CORPS LEGISLATIF. LE 25 FEV 1813 / Montalivet, J -P Bachasson – Paris: Imp. imperiale, 1813 – 9 – fr Hachette [944]

EXPOSE DE LA SITUATION GENERALE DE L'ALGERIE / Algeria. Gouvernement General – 4v. 1951-55. (lacking 1953). BNE-8643 1 – 9 – ne IDC [324]

EXPOSE GENERAL DES RESULTATS DU PATRONAGE DES ESCLAVES DANS LES COLONIES FRANCAISES – (Slave Trade and Abolitionism in France Series). 1844 – 9 – fr Hachette [360]

EXPOSE HISTORIQUE ET PHILOSOPHIQUE PLACE EN REGARD DE LA DOCTRINE SAINT-SIMONIENNE / Gordon, Alex – Paris, A. Desanges, 1831, 46 p. Les Saint-Simoniens, 1825-1834. 6981 – 9 – fr Hachette [335]

EXPOSE PRELIMINAIRE DES DROITS DE LA COURONNE DE HONGRIE SUR LA RUSSIE ROUGE ET SUR LA PODOLIE;... – Vienne, 1772 – 2mf – 1 – ILM-2842/1 – ne IDC [327]

EXPOSE SOMMAIRE DES AFFAIRES RELATIVES A L'INTERPRETATION DES DECRETS DE FEVRIER 1876 ET 1883 / Desjardins, Ls. E – s.l.: s.n., 1883? (Rome: Edition Romana). 02162. (Pre-1900 Canadiana) – 9 – cn C.I.H.M. [971]

EXPOSE...NOTAMMENT DU DROIT INTERNATIONAL COMMERCIAL... / Bartoche, M – Paris, 1927 – 4mf – 9 – ILM-3771/1 – ne IDC [340]

EXPOSICAO EVANGELISTA – '(s.l.')-Sao Luiz, Brazil. 16 Apr 1865-25 Mar 1866 – 1,5,6 – bl Biblioteca [072]

EXPOSICION A LA REAL ACADEMIA DE LA HISTORIA EN FAVOR DE LA APARICION DE LA VIRGEN DE GUADALUPE EN MEXICO... / Fabie, Antonio Maria – Madrid: Ed. Reus, 1922. B.R.A.H. 81. pp. 229-255 – 1 – sp Bibl Santa Ana [240]

EXPOSICION AL NUNCIO / Caceres, Diego de – S.l., s.i., s.a. 1642? – 1 – sp Bibl Santa Ana [946]

EXPOSICION DE LA OBRA GRAFICA ORIGINAL MIRO EN EXTREMADURA / Malpartida de Caceres. Ayuntamiento – Caceres: Edit. Extremadura, 1981 – 1 – sp Bibl Santa Ana [700]

EXPOSICION DE LIBROS DEL SIGLO 15TH AL 20TH ANO 1944 – S.E.U. Tip. El Noticiero, s.a. – 1 – sp Bibl Santa Ana [020]
EXPOSICION DE REPRODUCCIONES EN COLOR DE LA UNESCO 90 ANOS DE PINTURA UNIVERSAL. CATALOGO / Diputacion Provincial – Badajoz: Dip. Provincial, 1954 – sp Bibl Santa Ana [946]
EXPOSICION DEL PLAN SECRETO PARA ESTABLECER UN SOVIET EN ESPANA – Bilbao, 1939? Fiche W 865. (Blodgett Collection of Spanish Civil War Pamphlets) – 9 – us H.U. College Libr [946]
EXPOSICION DEL...AYUNTAMIENTO...BADAJOZ / Gavino Rodriguez, Martin – 1840 – 9 – 1.50f – sp Bibl Santa Ana [946]
EXPOSICION HISTORIA DE LA FERIA DE MAYO EN CACERES (DOCUMENTACION DEL ARCHIVO MUNICIPAL) CATALOGO 1973 / Caceres. Ayuntamiento – Caceres: Tip. Extremadura, 1973 – 1 – sp Bibl Santa Ana [390]
EXPOSICION HISTORICO CRITICA DE LOS SISTEMAS FILOSOFICOS MODERNOS Y PRINCIPIOS DE LA CIENCA / Azcarate y Corral, Patricio de – 1861. 4v. Libros en Microficha no 1 – 4mf – 9 – Pta2,500.00 – 84-85422-10-4 – sp Pentalfa [190]
LA EXPOSICION INTERNACIONAL DE BARCELONA / Bayle, Constantino – Madrid: Razon y Fe, 1929 – 1 – sp Bibl Santa Ana [946]
EXPOSICION JUEZ / Juez, Antonio – Badajoz, 1917 – 1 – sp Bibl Santa Ana [946]
LA EXPOSICION MISIONAL DEL VATICANO / Bayle, Constantino – Madrid: Razon y Fe, 1925 – 1 – sp Bibl Santa Ana [240]
EXPOSICION PROVINCIAL DE ARTE / Obra Sindical Educacion y Descanso. Caceres – Caceres, s.i. 1949 – sp Bibl Santa Ana [700]
EXPOSICION QUE A LA LEGISLATURA NACIONAL PRESENTA EL MINISTRO DE HACIENDA... – Caracas: Imprenta del Teatro de Legislacion de Pedro P. del Castillo e Hijos, 1866-67 – us Res Libr [972]
EXPOSICION QUE DIRIGE AL CONGRESO DE VENEZUELA EN [...] EL SECRETARIO DE HACIENDA SOBRE LOS NEGOCIOS DE SU CARGO – Caracas: Imprenta de Valentin Espinal, 1833-61 – us Res Libr [972]
EXPOSICION QUE DIRIGE AL CONGRESO NACIONAL DE LOS ESTADOS UNIDOS DE VENEZUELA EL MINISTRO DE HACIENDA EN [...] – Caracas: Impr de "La concordia," de Evaristo Fombona, 1874-77 – us Res Libr [972]
EXPOSICION QUE DIRIJE AL CONGRESO NACIONAL DE LOS ESTADOS UNIDOS DE VENEZUELA EL MINISTRO DE HACIENDA EN [...] – Caracas: Impr Bolivar, 1892, 1894-1909 – us Res Libr [972]
EXPOSICION QUE DIRIJE AL CONGRESO NACIONAL DE LOS ESTADOS UNIDOS DE VENEZUELA EL MINISTRO DE HACIENDA Y CREDITO PUBLICO EN [...] – Caracas: Empresa El Cojo, 1910-12 – us Res Libr [972]
EXPOSICION QUE DIRIJE AL PRESIDENTE DE LOS ESTADOS UNIDOS DE VENEZUELA EL MINISTRO DE HACIENDA EN [...] – Caracas: Impr de "La concordia," de Evaristo Fombona, 1873 – us Res Libr [972]
EXPOSICION QUE EL MINISTRO DE OBRAS PUBLICAS PRESENTA AL JEFE DEL PODER EJECUTIVO NACIONAL DE LOS ASUNTOS DE SU DEPARTAMENTO... – Caracas: Imprenta Bolivar, 1893 – us Res Libr [972]
EXPOSICION QUE PRESENTA EL MINISTERIO DE HACIENDA DE LOS ESTADOS UNIDOS DE VENEZUELA AL CONGRESO NACIONAL EN [...] – Caracas: Impr de Pedro Coll Otero, [1878-] – us Res Libr [972]
EXPOSICION REGIONAL EXTREMENA – 1892 – 9 – 1.50f – sp Bibl Santa Ana [946]
EXPOSITE IN TERENTIUM, ETC / De Cass, Anthonius de P – 14th and 15th cents. Holkham mss. 301, 426, 427, 489, 496, 511. Holkham Hall, Norfolk, England – 1 – uk Microform Academic [760]
EXPOSITIO ACTUUM APOSTOLORUM – RETRACTATIO IN ACTUS APOSTOLORUM – NOMINA REGIONUM ATQUE LOCORUM DE ACTIBUS APOSTOLORUM – IN EPISTULAS 7 CATHOLICAS / Beda Venerabilis – 1983 – 9mf – 9 – Bf975.00 – 2-503-61212-1 – be Brepols [240]
EXPOSITIO ALEXANDRI...ORDINIS...SAN JACOBI / Ramirez, Juan – 1599 – 9 – $1.50f – sp Bibl Santa Ana [946]
EXPOSITIO DECALOGI, SYMBOLI, APOSTOLICI, SACRAMENTORU, AND DOMINICAE PRAECATIONIS,... / Corvinus, A – [Lipsiae], 1540 – 2mf – 9 – ne IDC [240]
EXPOSITIO DOCTRINAE AUGUSTINI DE CREATIONE MUNDI, PECCATO, GRATIA / Ritschl, Albertus – Halis: Formis expressum Hendelianis, [1843?] – 1mf – us A.T.L.A. [240]
EXPOSITIO IM EPISTOLAM AD ROMANOS / Theodorico, Guillelmus a S – 1990 – 6mf – 9 – Bf1,395.00 – 2-503-63862-7 – be Brepols [240]
EXPOSITIO IN LAMENTATIONES HIEREMIAE / Radbertus, Pascasius – 1989 – 8mf – 9 – Bf1,650.00 – 2-503-63852-X – be Brepols [240]
EXPOSITIO IN OCTO LIBROS PHISICORUM ARISTOTELIS... / Celaya, J de – Paris, 1517 – 7mf – 9 – sp Cultura [600]
EXPOSITIO IN PSALMUM 44 / Radbertus, Pascasius – 1991 – 3mf – 9 – Bf1,250.00 – 2-503-63942-9 – be Brepols [240]
EXPOSITIO SUPER DANIELEM / Victore, Andreas de Sancto – 1991 – 3mf – 9 – Bf1,150.00 – 2-503-50051-X – be Brepols [240]
EXPOSITION AGRICOLE ET INDUSTRIELLE DE LA PROVINCE DE QUEBEC (1881: MONTREAL, QUEBEC) – Liste des prix de...ouvert a l'universe: qui aura lieu sur le terrain de l'Exposition, Mile-End, dans la cite de Montreal...Montreal: s.n., 1881?. 04266. (Pre-1900 Canadiana) – 9 – cn C.I.H.M. [338]
EXPOSITION AND DEFENSE OF THE WESTMINSTER ASSEMBLY'S CONFESSION / Annan, Robert – 1855 – 1 – $50.00 – us Presbyterian [240]
EXPOSITION DAILY – Portland OR. Sep 30 Oct 1 2 1889 – 1 – us U.O. Library [071]
EXPOSITION DE LA DOCTRINE DE L'EGLISE CATHOLIQUE ORTHODOXE : ACCOMPAGNEE DES DIFFERENCES QUI SE RENCONTRENT DANS LES AUTRES EGLISES CHRETIENNES / Guettee, Wladimir – Paris: Fischbacher, 1884 – 2mf – us A.T.L.A. [240]
EXPOSITION DE LA DOCTRINE DE L'EGLISE CATHOLIQUE SUR LES MATIERES DE CONTROVERSE / Bossuet, J -B – Paris, 1679 – 5mf – 9 – CA-117/1 – ne IDC [240]
EXPOSITION DE LA DOCTRINE DE L'EGLISE CATHOLIQUE SUR LES MATIERES DE CONTROVERSE / Bossuet, Jacques B – Paris, 1671 – 3mf – 9 – CA-98/1 – ne IDC [240]
EXPOSITION DE LA RELIGION SAINT-SIMONIENNE / Curie, P – Mulhouse, J. Risler, 1832, 23 p. Les Saint-Simoniens, 1825-1834. 6934 – 9 – fr Hachette [335]
EXPOSITION DE LA THEORIE ET DE LA PRATIQUE DE LA MUSIQUE SUIVANT LES NOUVELLES DECOUVERTES / Bethizy, J -L de – Paris. Michel Lambert. 1754. BP-166 1 – 9 – ne IDC [780]
EXPOSITION DE LA THEORIE ET DE LA PRATIQUE DE LA MUSIQUE, SUIVANT LES NOUVELLES DECOUVERTES / Bethizy, J -L de – 1754 – 9 – us Sibley [780]
L'EXPOSITION DE PARIS (1889) – Paris: Librairie illustree, 1889. n1-80 oct 1888-feb 1890 – us Res Libr [900]
L'EXPOSITION DE PARIS (1900) – Paris: Montgredien et Cie. v1-120. 1898-1900 – us Res Libr [900]
EXPOSITION DES FAITS ET DE LA SITUATION ACTUELLE DE LA SOCIETE DE COLONISATION DU TEMISCAMINGUE VIS-A-VIS DES ACTIONNAIRES FRANCAIS / Bodard, Auguste – Montreal?, 1892. 00854. (Pre-1900 Canadiana) – 9 – cn C.I.H.M. [971]
EXPOSITION DES FAMILLES NATURELLES / Jaume Saint-Hilaire, J H – 2v. Paris. 1805. B-5979 2 – 8 – ne IDC [580]
EXPOSITION EN HOMMAGE A PAUL RIVET / Rivet, Paul – Commissaire: Georgette Soustelle – 9 – F50.00 – fr Ethnologie [306]
EXPOSITION ET EXAMEN DE LA DOCTRINE SAINT-SIMONIENNE – Neuchatel, impr. C.-H. Wolfrath, 1831, 2-48 p. Les Saint-Simoniens, 1825-1834. 6989 – 9 – fr Hachette [335]
THE "EXPOSITION" EXPOUNDED, DEFENDED AND SUPPLEMENTED / Carroll, John – Toronto: Methodist Book and Publishing House, 1881. 02552. (Pre-1900 Canadiana) – 9 – cn C.I.H.M. [240]
AN EXPOSITION OF THE APOCALYPSE OF ST. JOHN THE APOSTLE / Putnam, Edward – Boston: Patrick Donahoe, 1858 – 1mf – 9 – 0-8370-7425-8 – 1986-1425 – us A.T.L.A. [220]
AN EXPOSITION OF THE BOOK OF ECCLESIASTES / Bridges, Charles – (Includes index) – New York: Robert Carter, 1860 – 1mf – 9 – 0-8370-2445-5 – 1985-0445 – us A.T.L.A. [220]
AN EXPOSITION OF THE CONDUCT OF FRANCE TOWARDS AMERICA : ILLUSTRATED BY CASES DECIDED IN THE COUNCIL OF PRIZES IN PARIS / Goldsmith, L – Ed 3. London, 1810 – 2mf – 1 – ILM-691/1 – ne IDC [327]
AN EXPOSITION OF THE CONFESSION OF FAITH OF THE WESTMINSTER ASSEMBLY OF DIVINES / Shaw, Robert – (Includes bibliographical references and index) – 9th ed. London: Blackie, 1861 – 1mf – 9 – 0-8370-8787-2 – 1986-2787 – us A.T.L.A. [240]
EXPOSITION OF THE CREED / Pearson, K B – 1710 – 1 – uk Microform Academic [240]
EXPOSITION OF THE EPISTLE OF JAMES / Adam, John – Edinburgh: T. & T. Clark, 1867. 1 fiche – 9 – us A.T.L.A. [240]
EXPOSITION OF THE EPISTLE OF SAINT PAUL TO THE COLOSSIANS / Daille, Jean – Edinburgh: James Nichol, 1863. 1 fiche – 9 – us A.T.L.A. [240]
EXPOSITION OF THE EPISTLE OF SAINT PAUL TO THE PHILIPPIANS / Daille, Jean – Edinburgh: James Nichol, 1865. 1 fiche – 9 – us A.T.L.A. [240]
AN EXPOSITION OF THE FAITH OF THE RELIGIOUS SOCIETY OF FRIENDS, COMMONLY CALLED QUAKERS, IN THE FUNDAMENTAL DOCTRINES OF THE CHRISTIAN RELIGION : PRINCIPALLY SELECTED FROM THEIR EARLY WRITINGS – (Includes index) – 5th American ed. Philadelphia: For sale at Friends' Book Store, 1878 – 1mf – 9 – 0-8370-8897-6 – 1986-2897 – us A.T.L.A. [240]
AN EXPOSITION OF THE FIRST EPISTLE TO THE CORINTHIANS / Hodge, Charles – NY: Robert Carter, 1860, c1857 – 1mf – 9 – 0-8370-3607-0 – 1985-1607 – us A.T.L.A. [220]
EXPOSITION OF THE FIRST EPISTLE TO THE CORINTHIANS / Hodge, Charles – New York: Robert Carter, 1860. 1 fiche – 9 – us A.T.L.A. [240]
AN EXPOSITION OF THE GOSPEL OF MARK / Kelly, William; ed by Whitfield, E E – (Includes indexes) – London: Elliot Stock, 1907 – 1mf – 9 – 0-8370-3875-8 – 1985-1875 – us A.T.L.A. [220]
EXPOSITION OF THE MOTIVES... – London, [1752] – 2mf – 1 – ILM-514/1 – ne IDC [327]
EXPOSITION OF THE NINTH CHAPTER OF THE EPISTLE TO THE ROMANS / Morison, James C – London: Hodder & Stoughton, 1888. 1 fiche – 9 – us A.T.L.A. [240]
AN EXPOSITION OF THE PRINCIPLES OF CODE PLEADING / Phillips, George Lemon – 2nd ed. Chicago: Callaghan, 1932. 775p. LL-1178 – 1 – us L of C Photodup [340]
AN EXPOSITION OF THE PRINCIPLES OF PARTNERSHIP / Parsons, James – Boston: Little, Brown, 1889. 709p. LL-1405 – 1 – us L of C Photodup [340]
AN EXPOSITION OF THE PRINCIPLES OF PLEADING UNDER THE CODES OF CIVIL PROCEDURE / Phillips, George Lemon – Chicago: Callaghan, 1896. 604p. LL-1338 – 1 – us L of C Photodup [340]
AN EXPOSITION OF THE SECOND EPISTLE TO THE CORINTHIANS / Hodge, Charles – New York:Robert Carter, 1866, c1859 – 1mf – 9 – 0-8370-3608-9 – 1985-1608 – us A.T.L.A. [220]
EXPOSITION OF THE SECOND EPISTLE TO THE CORINTHIANS / Hodge, Charles – New York: Robert Carter, 1866. 1 fiche – 9 – us A.T.L.A. [240]
AN EXPOSITION OF THE THIRTY-NINE ARTICLES : HISTORICAL AND DOCTRINAL / Browne, Edward Harold – (Includes bibliographical references and indexes) – 14th ed. London; New York: Longmans, Green, 1894 – 2mf – 9 – 0-8370-8654-X – 1986-2654 – us A.T.L.A. [240]
EXPOSITION RAISONNEE DES PRINCIPES DE L'UNIVERSITE, RELATIVEMENT A L'EDUCATION / Gosse, Abbe – Paris. Buisson. 1788. 6760 – 9 – fr Hachette [370]
Exposition Universelle 1900. Paris *see* BULLETIN DES LOIS, DEA1CRETS ET DOCUMENTS OFFICIELS
Exposition universelle internationale de 1878, a Paris. Commissariat General *see* CATALOGUE OFFICIEL
Exposition Universelle. Paris, 1878 *see* CATALOGUE OFFICIEL
EXPOSITION UPON THE EPISTLE OF JUDE / Jenkyn, William – Edinburgh: James Nichol, 1865. 1 fiche – 9 – us A.T.L.A. [240]
AN EXPOSITION WITH NOTES : UNFOLDED AND APPLIED ON JOHN 17 / Newton, George – (Includes index) – Edinburgh: James Nichol, 1867 – 1mf – 9 – 0-8370-4578-9 – 1985-2578 – us A.T.L.A. [220]
EXPOSITIONES HISTORICAE IN LIBROS SALOMONIS / Victore, Andreas de Sancto – 1991 – 5mf – 9 – Bf1,300.00 – 2-503-63536-9 – be Brepols [240]
EXPOSITOR – 1875-1925 – 1 – 429.00 – us L of C Photodup [240]
EL EXPOSITOR BAUTISTA – 1909-13. Paper of the Argentine Baptist Convention. 960p – 1 – 33.60 – us Baptist [240]
EL EXPOSITOR BIBLICO – 1890, 1916-17, 1929. 1212p – 1 – 42.42 – us Baptist [240]
THE EXPOSITOR OF HOLINESS – Toronto: Published under the auspices of the Canada Holiness Association, [1882-189- or 19–] – 9 – cn C.I.H.M. [240]
THE EXPOSITOR'S BIBLE *see*
- THE BOOK OF ISAIAH
- THE BOOK OF JOSHUA
- THE BOOK OF THE TWELVE PROPHETS
- THE BOOKS OF CHRONICLES
- EZRA, NEHEMIAH, AND ESTHER
- THE FIRST BOOK OF KINGS
- THE FIRST EPISTLE TO THE CORINTHIANS
- THE SECOND BOOK OF SAMUEL
- THE SECOND EPISTLE TO THE CORINTHIANS

EXPOSITORY AND PRACTICAL LECTURES ON HAGGAI AND ZECHARIAH / Eaton, John van; ed by Robinson, W J – Pittsburgh: United Presbyterian Bd of Publ, [1882?] – 1mf – 9 – 0-8370-5617-9 – 1985-3617 – us A.T.L.A. [220]
EXPOSITORY LECTURES ON ST. PAUL'S EPISTLES TO THE CORINTHIANS / Robertson, Frederick William – new ed. London: Kegan Paul, Trench, 1883 – 2mf – 9 – 0-8370-4921-0 – 1985-2921 – us A.T.L.A. [220]
EXPOSITORY LIFE OF CHRIST (CCC146) / Hayes, W M – (In Chinese) – [s.l: s.n, 1911] – 1r – 1 – 1984-B500 – us A.T.L.A. [240]
EXPOSITORY NOTES ON THE BOOK OF JOSHUA / Crosby, Howard – (Includes appendix) – New York: Robert Carter, 1875 – 1mf – 9 – 0-8370-2781-0 – 1985-0781 – us A.T.L.A. [220]
EXPOSITORY THOUGHTS ON THE GOSPELS : ST. MATTHEW FOR FAMILY AND PRIVATE USE: WITH THE TEXT COMPLETE / Ryle, John Charles – New York: Robert Carter, 1857 – 1mf – 9 – 0-8370-9815-7 – 1986-3815 – us A.T.L.A. [220]
THE EXPOSITORY TIMES – 1889-1993. Continued annually – 1 – £1,600.00 – uk World [073]
THE EXPOSITORY TIMES – (Yrly reel count varies) – 1889- – 1 – inquire – us Ross [072]
EXPOSSITIO LATINITATIS – 1992 – 5mf – 9 – Bf1,300.00 – 2-503-50281-4 – be Brepols [240]
AN EXPOSTULATORY LETTER TO THE REVEREND MR. WHITEFIELD, AND THE REST OF HIS BRETHREN, THE METHODISTS OF THE CHURCH OF ENGLAND,... – London, 1739 – 1mf – 9 – MP-248/1 – ne IDC [240]
EXPOSURE OF INFANTS AND CHILDREN TO LEAD : WORKING DOCUMENT FOR THE 30TH MEETING OF JECFA, ROME 1986 – 1989 – 58p – it F.A.O. [360]
EXPOSURE OF POPERY = POPIYAT KA AHWAL : BEING A FREE TRANSLATION, WITH SOME ADDITIONS, OF POPIYAT KA AHWAL, A WORK WRITTEN IN HINDUSTANI / Ullmann, Julius Frederick – (In English) – Bombay: A W Prautch, [1892?] – 1mf – 9 – 0-8370-8394-X – 1986-2394 – us A.T.L.A. [240]

AN EXPOSURE OF THE MISCHIEVIOUS PERVERSIONS OF HOLY SCRIPTURE IN THE NATIONAL TEMPERANCE SOCIETY'S PUBLICATIONS: ADDRESSED TO MEN OF SENSE AND CANDOR / Carry, John – Toronto: Rowsell and Hutchison, 1885. 00493. (Pre-1900 Canadiana) – 9 – cn C.I.H.M. [240]
L'EXPRESS – Paris. Journal quotidien republicain independant. 14 janv 1881-4 fevr 1883 – 1 – fr A.C.R.P.P. [944]
L'EXPRESS – (Yrly reel count varies. Also available with suppl on 16 mm) – 1954- – 6r in 1996 – 1 – inquire – us Ross [072]
EXPRESS – 1954-1976 – 1 – F2,400.00 – sz Infoprint [072]
EXPRESS – 1977-1990 – 1 – F2,600.00 – sz Infoprint [072]
EXPRESS – 1977-1992 – 1 – F2,400.00 – sz Infoprint [072]
EXPRESS – 1992-1995 – 6 times per yr – 1 – F2,800.00 – sz Infoprint [072]
EXPRESS – Aurora. Ill. 1882-1901 – 1 – us UMI [071]
EXPRESS – Beatrice. Neb. 1868-1924 – 1 – us UMI [071]
EXPRESS – Beatrice. Neb. -w and sw. 1871-1912 – 1 – us UMI [071]
EXPRESS – Big Timber. Mont. 1896-1900 – 1 – us UMI [071]
EXPRESS – Chicago.18 Dec 1936. English & Yiddish. Ceased publ – 1 – us A.J.P.C. [071]
EXPRESS – Columbus. Ohio. 1858-64 – 1 – us UMI [071]
EXPRESS – Dallas. Tex. 1930- – 1 – us UMI [071]
EXPRESS – Displaced persons newspaper. (Polish ed.). Munich. Germany. -w. 11 Jan-25 Sep 1948. (1 reel) – 1 – uk British Libr Newspaper [947]
EXPRESS – Dubuque. Iowa. and Herald. -w, -d. 1854-57 – 1 – us UMI [071]
EXPRESS – Easton. Pa. 1856- – 1 – us UMI [071]
EXPRESS – Ellinwood. Kan. 1878-88 – 1 – us UMI [071]
EXPRESS – Holton. Kan. -w. 1872-75 – 1 – us UMI [071]
EXPRESS – Koeln, Germany. 1976-1991 – ca 5r per yr – 1 – gw Mikrofilm [072]
EXPRESS – Lock Haven. Pa. 1889- – 1 – us UMI [071]
EXPRESS – Lodge Pole. Neb. 1892-1949 – 1 – us UMI [071]
EXPRESS – Maumee, Ohio. 1837-40 – 1r – 1 – $32.50r – us Archival [071]
EXPRESS – Merced, CA. 1875-81; 1890-1972 – 28r – 1 BC02448 – $1,400.00 – us Library Micro [071]
EXPRESS – Merced. Calif. -w. 1943-58 – 1 – us UMI [071]
EXPRESS – Monticello. Iowa. -w. 1951-56 – 1 – us UMI [071]
EXPRESS – Pasco. Wash. -w. 1905-18 – 1 – us UMI [071]
EXPRESS – Spartanburg. S.C. 1857 – 1 – us UMI [071]
EXPRESS : SUPPLEMENTS – (Also available on CD-ROM) – 1988-1992 – 2r per y – 5,6 – Sfr214.00 – sz Infoprint [072]
EXPRESS – Winters. Calif. -w. 1945-58 – 1 – us UMI [071]
EXPRESS – Zanesville. Ohio. 1812-20 – 1 – us UMI [071]
EXPRESS *see* THE UITENHAGE TIMES
THE EXPRESS – Berkeley, CA. 1979- – 34+ r – 1 – $1,700.00 ($120.00y) – B05027 – us Library Micro [071]
THE EXPRESS – Dublin. Ireland. -d. 8 Oct 1832-2 Feb 1833. (1 reel) – 1 – uk British Libr Newspaper [072]
THE EXPRESS – Freemantle, Australia. 5 Jan-31 Mar, 1 Jul-31 Dec 1870 (imperfect).-w. 1mqn reels – 1 – uk British Libr Newspaper [072]
THE EXPRESS – Sydney, Australia. -w. 17 Jan 1880-29 Dec 1883. 4 reels – 1 – uk British Libr Newspaper [072]
THE EXPRESS – Dar es Salaam: Media Holdings Ltd, [feb 1992-] – us Res Libr [072]
EXPRESS AND ORANGE FREE STATE ADVERTISER – Bloemfontein, South Africa. Express en Oranjevrijstaatsch advertentieblad. -w. March 1875-99. 1880, 1881 imperfect. 14 1 2 reels – 1 – uk British Libr Newspaper [072]
EXPRESS AND STANDARD – Newport, VT. v42 n92. 20 Nov 1896-v67 n37. 14 sep 1916 – 1r – 1 – Can$25.00 – cn Can Microfilming [071]
EXPRESS CAHIERS – 1991-1995 – 1 times per yr – 6 – F800.00 – sz Infoprint [072]
L'EXPRESS DU MIDI – Toulouse. 1924, 1929 – 1 – fr A.C.R.P.P. [944]
EXPRESS EN ORANJEVRIJSTAATSCH ADVERTENTIEBLAD – Bloemfontein. South Africa. 1875-1900 – 1 – sa State Libr [072]
EXPRESS ILUSTROWANY – Lodz, Poland. Dec 1952-Aug 1953; 8 Jun 1959 – 1r – 1 – us L of C Photodup [947]
THE EXPRESS LINE : THE FRESNO BEE – Fresno, CA. 1993 – 4+ r – 1 – $200.00 ($90.00y) – R04025 – us Library Micro [071]
EXPRESS POZNANSKI – (Some issues missing) – Poznan, Poland. Jul 1952-1959 – 11r – 1 – us L of C Photodup [947]
EXPRESS SUPPLEMENTS – 1988-1992 – 2 times per yr – 6 – F800.00 – sz Infoprint [072]
L'EXPRESS VERSION INTERNATIONAL – (Also available on 35mm and CD-ROM) – 1970-1995 – 2r per y – 5,6 – FF1,900.00y – sz Infoprint [072]
EXPRESS VERSION NATIONALE – 1988-1995 – 3 times per yr – 6 – F2,800.00 – sz Infoprint [072]
EXPRESS WIECZORNY – (Some missing issues) – Warsaw, Poland. Jul 1946-Aug 1948; Mar 1950-Jun 1970 – 43r – 1 – us L of C Photodup [947]
EXPRESSEN – (Newsbills, 1944-63. 34 reels) – Stockholm, Sweden. 1944-78. 473 reels – 1 – sw Kungliga [072]
EXPRESSEN – Stockholm, Sweden. 1979- – 1 – sw Kungliga [072]
EXPRESSING UNIVERSAL THEMES THROUGH STORYDANCE CHOREOGRAPHY : THE CREATION AND PRODUCTION OF TWO NARRATIVES / Cambridge, Lark A – 1993 – 2mf – $8.00 – us Microform Publ [790]
L'EXPRESSION DU TEMPS / Lamy, A & Berthet, P – (Africa series). 1970 – 9 – fr Hachette [073]
EXPRESSION OF THE EMOTIONS IN MAN AND ANIMALS / Darwin, Charles – M-94. 1872 – 9 – ne IDC [150]
THE EXPRESSION OF THE EMOTIONS IN MAN AND ANIMALS / Darwin, Charles – London: John Murray, 1872 – 1 roll – 1 – 1-55879-713-0 – uk Libr Preservation [150]
EXPRESSIONISM : SUBJECT COLLECTIONS – (Individual titles not listed separately) – 80 catalogues on 109mf – 9 – £685.00 – uk Chadwyck [700]
EXPRESSIONIST THEATER – (Lists 15 productions) – 16mf – 9 – £110.00 – uk Chadwyck [790]
EXPRESSIONS FIGUREES DE LA LANGUE MALGACHE / Grandidier, Guillaume – Paris: C Lamy, 1902 – 1 – us Res Libr [490]
EXPRESSIONS OF LAW AND FACT CONSTRUED BY THE COURTS OF GEORGIA / Dutcher, Salem – Atlanta, Franklin, 1899. 172 p. LL-605 – 1 – us L of C Photodup [340]
EXPRESSIONS OF OPINION ON IMPERIAL FEDERATION: BY PUBLIC MEN AT HOME IN THE COLONIES / Imperial Federation League – 18–?. 05479. (Pre-1900 Canadiana) – 9 – cn C.I.H.M. [971]
L'EXPRESSIVITE CHEZ SALVIEN DE MARSEILLE, 1 : LAT. CHRIST. PRIMAEVA: 7 / Janssen, O – 1937 – 5mf – 8 – ne Slangenburg [240]
EXPRESSO – Lisbon. Nos.1-380, 6 Jan 1973-9 Feb 1980. Incomplete. (Portuguese Revolution of 1974. Newspapers from Portugal publ. from 21 Feb 1971 to 15 Feb 1980, collected and filmed by University of Wisconsin-Madison libraries.) – 1 – us U.W. Library [072]
EXPRIT DE LA REVOLUTION ET DE LA CONSTITUTION DE FRANCE / Saint Just, Antoine Louis Leon de – Paris: Beuvin, 1791. viii,174p.2 fiches. (Political Science Collection) – 9 – 6.00 – fr Bibl Nationale [323]
EXPULSION DE LOS MORISCOS DE DENIA (ANNO 1596-1621) – Barcelona – 1r – 5,6 – sp Cultura [946]
EXPUNEREA SITUATIUNEI FINANCIARE A TESAURULUI PUBLIC / Romania.Ministerul Finantelor – Bucharest. 31v.1880-1911 – 1 – 69.00 – us L of C Photodup [336]
THE EXTEL RECORDS. ARCHIVES OF THE EXCHANGES TELEGRAPH CO. LTD. / Guildhall Library, London – 1872-1966. 122 reels with printed guide – £7,800.00 – uk World [380]
EXTENSION BULLETIN / Clemson University. Agricultural Extension Division – No.124-128. 1970-82. 1 reel – 1,5 – us Spaulding [630]
EXTENSION BULLETIN / Iowa State University. Cooperative Extension Service in Agriculture and Home Economics – No.1-198. 1907-34 – 1,5 – us Spaulding [630]
EXTENSION BULLETIN / Kansas. State University of Agriculture and Applied Science. Division of College Extension – nos.1-94. 1915-62 – 1,5,6 – us Spaulding [630]
EXTENSION BULLETIN / Minnesota. Agricultural Extension Service – nos.1-360. 1915-69 – 1,5,6 – us Spaulding [630]
EXTENSION BULLETIN / Minnesota. Agricultural Extension Service. Agricultural Extension Division. Minnesota Farmers' Library – nos.1-65. 1910-19 – 1,5,6 – us Spaulding [630]
EXTENSION BULLETIN / Nebraska. College of Agriculture. Extension Service – n.1-66. 1911-21 – 1, 5 – us Spaulding [630]
EXTENSION BULLETIN / New Hampshire. Cooperative Extension Service – v. 1-178. 1913-70 – 1,5,6 – us Spaulding [630]
EXTENSION BULLETIN – New York. v. 6, no. 1-5, 7 no. 1-4, 6; 14-17. Jan-May 1903, Jan-Apr, Jun 1904; Sep 1910-Jun 1914 – 1 – us NY Public [780]
EXTENSION BULLETIN / Purdue University. Cooperative Extension Service – No.1-415. 1910-56 – 1,5 – us Spaulding [630]
EXTENSION BULLETIN / Washington. Agricultural Extension Service – nos.1-600. 1913-69 – 1,5,6 – us Spaulding [630]
EXTENSION BULLETIN / Wisconsin. Agricultural Extension Service – Sep 1952 only – 1,5 – us Spaulding [630]
EXTENSION CIRCULAR / Iowa State University. Cooperative Extension Service in Agriculture and Home Economics – No.1-263. 1934-39. 1 reel – 1,5 – us Spaulding [630]
EXTENSION CIRCULAR / Kansas. State University of Agriculture and Applied Science. Extension Service – nos.1-599. 1913-79 – 1,5,6 – us Spaulding [630]
EXTENSION CIRCULAR / Mississippi. State College. Agricultural Extension Service – v. 1-156. 1916-50 – 1,5,6 – us Spaulding [630]
EXTENSION CIRCULAR / Nebraska. College of Agriculture. Extension Service – n.1-9999 and 54-100-69-2216 – 1, 5 – us Spaulding [630]
EXTENSION CIRCULAR / New Hampshire. Cooperative Extension Service – v. 1-404. 1911-71 – 1,5,6 – us Spaulding [630]
EXTENSION CIRCULAR / North Carolina. State University. Raleigh. Agricultural Extension Service – n.1-508. Jun 1915-Jan 1974 – 1,5 – us Spaulding [630]
EXTENSION CIRCULAR / North Carolina State University.Agricultural Extension Service – No.509-608. 1970-76 – 1,5 – us Spaulding [630]
EXTENSION CIRCULAR / Purdue University. Cooperative Extension Service – No.420-539. 1956-69 – 1,5 – us Spaulding [630]
EXTENSION CIRCULAR / University of Missouri. Agricultural Extension Service – No.1-946. 1915-82 – 1,5 – us Spaulding [630]
EXTENSION CIRCULAR / Washington. Agricultural Extension Service – nos.1-398. 1916-75 – 1,5,6 – us Spaulding [630]
EXTENSION CIRCULARS / Illinois. College of Agriculture – n.1-45. 1916-21 – 1,5 – us Spaulding [630]
L'EXTENSION DES PRINCIPES DE LA CONVENTION DE GENEVE AUX GUERRES MARITIMES / Cauwes, G – Paris, 1899 – 3mf – 1 – ILM-373/1 – ne IDC [327]
EXTENSION DIVISION NEWS / Virginia. Polytechnic Institute. Extension Division – v.1-27. Nov 1918-Dec1945 – 1,5 – us Spaulding [630]
L'EXTENSION ET L'UTILISATION DES TERRAINS CONQUIS SUR LA MER AU JAPON / Cordes, Marie-Dominique – 1975 – 9 – fr Orientalistes [910]
EXTENSION FOLDER / New Hampshire. Cooperative Extension Service – v. 1-70. 1943-70 – 1,5,6 – us Spaulding [630]
EXTENSION LEAFLET / Mississippi. State College. Agricultural Extension Service – v. 1-109. 1934-50 – 1,5,6 – us Spaulding [630]
EXTENSION LEAFLET / South Dakota. Agricultural Extension Service. State College of Agriculture and Mechanic Arts – nos.1-208. 1921-65 – 1,5,6 – us Spaulding [630]
EXTENSION MANUALS / University of Missouri. Agricultural Extension Service – No.1-126. 1938-83 – 1,5 – us Spaulding [630]
EXTENSION MIMEO / Washington. Agricultural Extension Service – nos.1000-3199 – 1,5,6 – us Spaulding [630]
EXTENSION NEWS / North Carolina. State University. Raleigh. Agricultural Extension Service – v.1-56, n.4. Feb. 1915-69 – 1,5 – us Spaulding [630]
EXTENSION NEWS / North Carolina State University.Agricultural Extension Service – No.56-69. 1969-82. 1 reel – 1,5 – us Spaulding [630]
EXTENSION NEWSLETTER / Wisconsin. Agricultural Extension Service – n.1-55 to 9-66. 1942-66 – 1,5 – us Spaulding [630]
EXTENSION OF THE RECONSTRUCTION AND DEVELOPMENT PROGRAMME. 1960-1966 / Mauritius – Port Louis. 1964. BD-358 1 – 9 – ne IDC [338]
EXTENSION OFFSET CIRCULAR / South Dakota. Agricultural Extension Service. State College of Agriculture and Mechanic Arts – nos.1-16. 1946-48 – 1,5,6 – us Spaulding [630]
EXTENSION REVIEW / Rhode Island. Agricultural Extension Service – v. 1-8. 1918-20 – 1,5,6 – us Spaulding [630]
EXTENSION SELF-SUPPORTING RICE PROGRAM / Hasmosuwignjo – In Indonesian. Summary in English. SE-5355 1. 1962 – 9 – ne IDC [630]
EXTENSION SERVICE NEWS / Virginia. Polytechnic Institute. Extension Division – v.1-24. 1946-69 – 1,5 – us Spaulding [630]
EXTENSION URBANA DE LA MERIDA ROMANA / Gil Farres, Octavio – 1 – sp Bibl Santa Ana [946]
THE EXTENT OF THE MARGINAL SEA / Crocker, H G – Washington, 1919 – 8mf – 1 – ILM-1832/1 – ne IDC [327]
THE EXTENT TO WHICH THE TITLE OF A PURCHASER TO LAND, BOUGHT AT A SHERIFF'S SALE, IS AFFECTED BY ERROR IN THE PROCEEDINGS, IN PENNSYLVANIA / Lancaster, Joseph Campbell, 1861-1916 – Philadelphia, Welsh, 1884. 92 p. LL-324 – 1 – us L of C Photodup [340]
EXTERNAL AFFAIRS – (Cont by International Perspectives, 1972) – Toronto. v1-23. 1949-71 – 9 – Can$20.00y – cn Micromedia [900]
EXTERNAL AFFAIRS – v1-16. 1959-Oct 1964 – 1 – cn Precision [327]
EXTERNAL AFFAIRS *see* INTERNATIONAL PERSPECTIVES
EXTERNAL RADIO BROADCASTING AND INTERNATIONAL UNDERSTANDING : BROADCASTING TO YUGOSLAVIA – 1977 – 51p – 9 – 92-3-101523-0 – fr UNESCO [380]
EXTERNAL TRADE INDICES, 1962-1966 / Libya. Ministry of Planning and Development. Census and Statistical Department – Tripoli. BNE-611 1 – 9 – ne IDC [380]
EXTERNAL TRADE STATISTICS / Jordan. Department of Statistics – 8v. (in 5). 1965-77. BNE-9768 1 – 9 – ne IDC [310]
EXTERNAL TRADE STATISTICS / Libya. Ministry of Economy and Trade. Census and Statistical Department – Tripoli. 1955-75. BNE-612 1 – 9 – ne IDC [380]
EXTERNAL TRADE STATISTICS OF GHANA / Ghana. Central Bureau of Statistics – v. 11-17. 1961-1967 – 1,5,6 – us Princeton Micro [960]
THE EXTERRITORIALITY OF AMBASSADORS... / Adair, E R – London, New York, 1929 – 4mf – 9 – ILM-934/1 – ne IDC [340]
EXTINCT AND DORMANT BARONETCIES OF ENGLAND / Burke, J B & Burke, J B – 1 – uk Microform Academic [920]
EXTINCT BIRDS / Rothschild, L W – Z 1894. 1907 – 9 – ne IDC [590]
EXTINCTION DU PAUPERISME / Bonaparte, Louis-Napoleon – (Condition of 19th C. French working class series). 1848 – 9 – fr Hachette [360]
THE EXTINCTION IN PERPETUITY... / Anderson, A W – London, 1908 – 3mf – 9 – ILM-805/1 – ne IDC [340]
THE EXTINCTION OF THE CHRISTIAN CHURCHES IN NORTH AFRICA : HULSEAN PRIZE ESSAY, 1895 / Holme, LR – London: C.J. Clay, 1898 – 1mf – us A.T.L.A. [240]

LA EXTIRPACION DE LA IDOLATRA EN EL PERU...POR HORACIO H. URTEAGA : BIOGRAFIA DEL PADRE ARRIAGA POR CARLOS A. ROMERO / Arriaga, Pablo Jose de – Lima: Sanmarti, 1920 – 1 – F113.86 – fr Armell [972]

EXTIRPACION DE LA IDOLATRIA DEL PIRU / Arriaga, Pablo Jose de – 1621. Libros en Microficha no. 11 – 9 – Pta1,000.00 – 84-85422-36-8 – sp Pentalfa [972]

LA EXTIRPACION DE LA IDOLATRIA EN EL PERU DEL P. PABLO JOSEPH DE ARRIAGA / Bayle, Constantino – Madrid: Razon y Fe, 1922 – 1 – sp Bibl Santa Ana [240]

EXTIRPACION TOTAL DE LA LARINGE POR CACINOMA / Gisneros y Sevillano, Juan – Madrid: Establecimiento Tipografico de Fortanet, 1961 – 1 – sp Bibl Santa Ana [946]

THE EXTRA EXAMINED : A REPLY TO MR. A. CAMPBELL'S M. HARBINGER / Broaddus, Andrew – 1836 – 1 – $50.00 – us Presbyterian [240]

EXTRA SERIES / Hakluyt Society – v1-12 – 7 – uk Microform Academic [910]

THE EXTRA SUN – (Prospectus of: New York Weekly Sun) – New York City, NY. 1849 – 1r – 1 – Can$25.00 – cn Can Microfilming [071]

THE EXTRA-CANONICAL LIFE OF CHRIST / Pick, Bernhard – New York: Funk & Wagnalls, 1903.1 fiche – 9 – us A.T.L.A. [240]

EXTRACELLULAR CALCIUM AND THE INOTROPIC EFFECT OF EPINEPHRINE ON ISOLATED SKELETAL MUSCLE / Williams, Jay H – 1988 – 125p 2mf – 9 – $8.00 – us Microform Publ [612]

EXTRACT FROM A RETURN DATED THE 2ND OF DECEMBER, 1854.. / Canada. Parliament. Legislative Council – Quebec: Rollo Campbell, 1855. SEM105P277 – 1mf – 9 – Can$2.25 – cn Bibl Nat [323]

EXTRACT FROM A RETURN DATED THE 2ND OF DECEMBER, 1854, TO ADDRESSES PRESENTED BY THE LEGISLATIVE COUNCIL TO HIS EXCELLENCY THE GOVERNOR GENERAL, ON THE SUBJECT OF THE SEIGNIORIAL TENURE / Canada. Parlement. Conseil legislatif – Quebec: Rollo Cambell..., 1855. SEM105P277 – 1mf – 9 – Can$2.25 – cn Bibl Nat [333]

EXTRACT FROM PRES. AZANA'S SPEECH AT VALENCIA UNIVERSITY, JULY 18, 1937 / Azana, Manuel – Washington, DC. 1937. Fiche W 739. (Blodgett Collection of Spanish Civil War Pamphlets) – 9 – us H.U. College Libr [946]

EXTRACT FROM THE JOURNALS OF THE LEGISLATIVE COUNCIL OF THE 2ND OF MARCH 1814 / Canada. Bas-Canada. Parlement. Conseil legislatif – Quebec: John Neilson, 1814. SEM105P809 – 1mf – 9 – Can$2.25 – cn Bibl Nat [324]

EXTRACT OF A DESPATCH FROM LORD GLENELG TO THE EARL OF DURHAM, G.C.B., DATED DOWNING-STREET, 20TH JANUARY 1838 / Grant, Charles Baron Glenelg – [London, England: s.n., 1838]. SEM105P1390 – 1mf – 9 – Can$2.25 – cn Bibl Nat [971]

AN EXTRACT OF SUNDRY PASSAGES TAKEN OUT OF MR. WHITEFIELD'S PRINTED SERMONS, JOURNALS AND LETTERS,... – (Originally published in Philadelphia in 1740 under the title of The querists) – London, 1741 – 1mf – 9 – MP-286/1 – ne IDC [240]

EXTRACT OF THE DISTRICT OF COLUMBIA CODE. 1935, REV. 1936 / Eby, Herbert Oscar – Washington, D.C., Students Law Book Corp., 1936. Various pagings. LL-870 – 1 – us L of C Photodup [340]

EXTRACT UIT HET REGISTER DER RESOLUTIEN VAN DE HOOG MOGENDE HEEREN STAATEN GENERAAL DER VEREENIGDE NEDERLANDEN, VENERIS DEN 21 OCTOBER 1785 – ['s-Gravenhage: s.n, 1785?) – 1 – us Res Libr [949]

L'EXTRACTION DU SILEX EN EUROPE OCCIDENTALE / Soulier, P – (Allemagne, Angleterre, Belgique, France) – 9 – F60.00 – fr Ethnologie [622]

EXTRACTO DE LA TESIS DE SOBRE LA ACCION CULTURAL DE ESPANA EN MARRUECOS / Garcia Carrasco, Francisco Andres – Caceres: Tip. Extremadura, 1977 – 1 – sp Bibl Santa Ana [306]

EXTRACTO DE LAS ORDENANZAS DE LOS DISTINTOS ARBITRIOS VOTADOS PARA EL PRESUPUESTO MUNICIPAL PARA 1924-25 – Almendralejo: Imprenta Bote, 1924 – 1 – sp Bibl Santa Ana [350]

EXTRACTO DE LAS SIETE PARTIDAS: FORMADO PARA FACILITAR LA LECTURA, INTELIGENCIA Y MEMORIA DE SUS DISPOSICIONES / Castile. Laws, Statutes, etc – Por Juan de la Reguera Valdelomar. Madrid: Impr. de la viuda e hijo de Marin, 1799 – 1 – us U.W. Library [946]

EXTRACTO PUNTUAL DE TODAS LAS PRAGMATICAS, CEDULAS, PROVISIONES PUBLICADAS EN EL REINADO DE CARLOS III. 2 VOL / Sanchez, S – Madrid, 1794 – 14mf – 9 – sp Cultura [946]

EXTRACTS / Hieronymus, Saint – 1455. Illum. by Philippus de Diversis de Quartigianis of Lucca at Venice. Holkham ms. 131. Holkham Hall, Norfolk, England – 1 – uk Microform Academic [240]

EXTRACTS FROM A SPEECH DELIVERED BY THE PRES. OF THE SPANISH REPUBLIC, JANUARY 21, 1937 / Azana, Manuel – Washington, DC. 193? Fiche W 740. (Blodgett Collection of Spanish Civil War Pamphlets) – 9 – us H.U. College Libr [946]

EXTRACTS FROM CHINA MAINLAND PUBLICATIONS / U.S. Consulate General. Hong Kong – 1 Apr 1962-31 Aug 1964 (ceased publication) – 1 – $52.00 – us L of C Photodup [950]

EXTRACTS FROM HON. EDWARD BLAKE'S FAMOUS SPEECH DELIVERED IN THE CANADIAN HOUSE OF COMMONS, APRIL 16TH, 1880 / Blake, Edward – 1880? 02283. (Pre-1900 Canadiana) – 9 – cn C.I.H.M. [971]

EXTRACTS FROM MY SOUTH-AFRICAN JOURNAL DURING FIVE YEARS' SERVICE IN THE 2ND BATT., 10TH FOOT, FROM JANUARY 1860 TO DECEMBER 1864 / Bulger, George Ernest – Bangalore: Regimental Press, 1867. 00856. (Pre-1900 Canadiana) – 9 – cn C.I.H.M. [960]

EXTRACTS FROM REPORT ON ENGLISH LANGUAGE MATERIALS DEVELOPMENT PROJECT CONFERENCES / Indonesia. English Language Materials Development Project (1962) – SE-10,268 1 – 9 – ne IDC [420]

EXTRACTS FROM THE ANGLO-SAXON LAWS / Cook, Albert Stanburrough – New York, Holt, 1880. 19 p. LL-109 – 1 – us L of C Photodup [340]

EXTRACTS FROM THE CHIEF SUPERINTENDENT'S REPORT ON EDUCATION IN UPPER CANADA FOR THE YEAR 1857 / Canada Province. Chief Superintendent of Education for Upper Canada – Toronto: printed by Lovell & Gibson, 1859. SEM105P1683 – 2mf – 9 – Can$4.50 – cn Bibl Nat [370]

EXTRACTS FROM THE DIARY AND CORRESPONDENCE...WITH A BRIEF ACCOUNT OF SOME INCIDENTS IN HIS LIFE / Lawrence, Amos – Ed. by William R. Lawrence. Boston: Gould and Lincoln, 1855. viii,369p. illus – 1 – us U.W. Library [920]

EXTRACTS FROM THE JOURNALS OF THE LEGISLATIVE COUNCIL OF THE PROVINCE OF LOWER-CANADA FROM THE YEAR 1795 TO 1813 INCLUSIVE,... / Canada. Legislative Council – Quebec: P E Desbarats, 1821. SEM35P280 – 1r – 1 – Can$15.00 – cn Bibl Nat [323]

EXTRACTS FROM THE JOURNALS OF THE LEGISLATIVE COUNCIL OF THE PROVINCE OF LOWER-CANADA FROM THE YEAR 1795-1813 INCLUSIVE.. / Canada. Bas-Canada. Parlement. Conseil legislatif – Quebec: P E Desbarats, 1821. SEM35P280 – 1r – 1 – Can$15.00 – cn Bibl Nat [324]

EXTRACTS FROM THE MINUTES...AND OTHER DOCUMENTS WITH REFERENCE TO HYDRAULIC LOTS ON MILL STREET / Harbour Commissioners of Montreal – Montreal: Montreal Herald Printing and Publishing Co., 1877. 02088. (Pre-1900 Canadiana) – 9 – cn C.I.H.M. [971]

EXTRACTS FROM THE MUNICIPAL RECORDS OF THE CITY OF YORK, DURING THE REIGNS OF EDWARD 4, EDWARD 5 AND RICHARD 3, WITH NOTES. / Davies, Robert – London: J.B. Nichols, 1843. Includes appendix. vii/304p – 1 – us U.W. Library [941]

EXTRACTS, FROM THE SEVERAL TREATIES... GREAT BRITAIN AND OTHER KINGDOMS... – London, 1758 – 4mf – 1 – ILM-732/1 – ne IDC [327]

EXTRACTS FROM THE TREATIES BETWEEN GREAT BRITAIN AND OTHER KINGDOMS AND STATES OF SUCH ARTICLES AS RELATE TO THE DUTY AND CONDUCT OF THE COMMANDERS OF HIS MAJESTY'S SHIPS OF WAR / ed by Gostling, George – 1792 – 9 – uk Libr Preservation [941]

EXTRACTS FROM WOMAN'S SERVICE ON THE LORD'S DAY / Bickersteth, Emily – 1865 – 9 – us A.T.L.A. [240]

EXTRACTS OF LETTERS RELATING TO METHODISTS AND MORAVIANS / Thorold, John – London, 1745 – 1mf – 9 – MP-326/1 – ne IDC [240]

EXTRAICT DES LETTRES D'VN GENTIL HOMME DE LA SUITTE DE MONSIEUR DE RAMBOUILLET, AMBASSADEUR DUR ROY AU ROYAUME DE POLOGNE, A VN SEIGNEUR DE LA COURT – Paris, 1574 – 1mf – 9 – H-8198/1 – ne IDC [943]

EXTRAICT DES REGISTRES DE COMMISSION ORDONNEE PAR LA ROY POUR LE JUGEMENT DU PROCEZ CRIMINEL FAIT A L'ENCONTRE DE MAISTRE URBAIN GRANDIER ET SES COMPLICES – Poictiers. 1634 – 9 – fr Hachette [360]

EXTRAIT DE TROIS MEMOIRES. DES PLANTES ORCHIDEES DES ISLES AUSTRALES D'AFRIQUE / Du Petit-Thouars, L M A A – (Nouveaux Bull. Sc. par la Soc. Philomatique de Paris. v. 1. 1809). B-5913 2 – 8 – ne IDC [580]

EXTRAIT DES OEUVRES DU PDG – Conakry: Le Bureau de Presse de la Presidence de la Republique, 1978 – us Res Libr [324]

EXTRAIT DES PROCES VERBAUX DE L'ASSEMBLEE LEGISLATIVE DE 1892 A 1897 – Montreal: Cultivateur, 1897?. 02936. (Pre-1900 Canadiana) – 9 – cn C.I.H.M. [971]

EXTRAIT DU PROJET DE PAIX PERPETUELLE DE M. L'ABBE DE SAINT PIERRE / Rousseau, Jean-Jacques – s.l., s.n. 1761. xiv, 114p. (Strategy of War Series) – 9 – fr Hachette [355]

EXTRAIT D'UNE REPONSE DE M. RAMEAU A M. EULER, SUR L'IDENTITE DES OCTAVES / Rameau, Jean-Phillippe – 1753 – 9 – us Sibley [780]

EXTRAITS DES ANNALES MANUSCRITES DE L'HOTEL-DIEU DU PRECIEUX-SANG, QUEBEC – [Quebec: s.n., 1923]. SEM105P1538 – 1mf – 9 – Can$2.25 – cn Bibl Nat [240]

EXTRAITS DES COMPTES-RENDUS DES SEANCES DE LA SOCIETE LINNEENNE DE BORDEAUX – Bordeaux, 1876/1877-1939/1940. v31-91 – 178mf – 9 – 7333c/2 – ne IDC [944]

EXTRAITS DES PROCES-VERBAUX / Bordeaux. France. Chambre de Commerce – v. 1-89. 1850-1938 – 1 – us NY Public [073]

EXTRAITS DES TITRES DES ANCIENNES CONCESSIONS DE TERRE EN FIEF ET SEIGNEURIE / Vondenvelden, William – Quebec: P E Desbarats, 1803. SEM16P92 – 1r – 5 – Can$9.00 – cn Bibl Nat [971]

EXTRAITS ET COPIES PAR BIZEUL DE CHARTES RELATIVES A DIVERS MONASTERES DU DIOCESE DE NANTES... / Bizeul, Louis-Jacques-Marie – 19th c. – fr Armell [240]

EXTRAITS HISTORIQUES SUR L'ANJOU ET LE DEPARTEMENT DE MAINE-ET-LOIRE / Berthe, J -A – 1846. 2v – 1 – F427.50 – fr Armell [944]

EXTRAITS OU PRECEDENTS, TIRES DES REGISTRES DE LA PREVOSTE DE QUEBEC 1726-1756, ET DEDIES AUX HONORABLES JUGES, AUX GENS DU ROI, AUX AVOCATS, PROCUREURS, ET PRATICIENS DE LA PROVINCE DU BAS-CANADA / Perrault, Joseph Francois – Quebec: Cary, 1824. 88p. LL-2221 – 1 – us L of C Photodup [340]

EL EXTRAORDINARIO PODER DE LAS PLANTAS / Fernandez Casco, Juan – Plasencia: Imp. Garcilasso, 1973 – 1 – sp Bibl Santa Ana [946]

EXTRAORDINARY CASES / Clinton, Henry Lauren – New York: Harper, 1896. 403p. LL-453 – 1 – us L of C Photodup [340]

EXTRAORDINARY GEOMETRICAL DISCOVERY: TRISECTION OF ANY RECTILINEAL ANGLE BY ELEMENTARY GEOMETRY: AND SOLUTIONS OF OTHER PROBLEMS CONSIDERED IMPOSSIBLE EXCEPT BY AID OF THE HIGHER GEOMETRY / Doyle, Andrew – Ottawa: s.n., 1880 (Ottawa: A. Bureau). 02754. (Pre-1900 Canadiana) – 9 – cn C.I.H.M. [971]

EXTRAPOLATION – v. 20-. 1979- – 1,5,6,9 – us UMI [073]

EXTRAPOLATION – v1-15. Dec 1959-May 1974. Wooster, Ohio: MLA Seminar on Science Fiction. (Science Fiction Periodicals, Series 1) – 2r – 1 – $100.00 – us UPA [830]

EXTRAPOLATION – v16-19. Dec 1974-May 1978. Wooster, Ohio: MLA Seminar on Science Fiction. (Science Fiction Periodicals, Series 2) – 1 reel – 1 – $50.00 – us UPA [830]

EXTRATERRITORIAL CASES : THE U.S. COURT FOR CHINA, 1844-1924 / Lobinger, CS – Manila: Bureau of Printing. 2v. 1920-1928 (all publ) – 9mf – 9 – $13.50 – LLMC 81-483 – us L.L.M.C. [340]

EXTREMADURA – Caceres, 1923-1930 y 1934-1936 – 5 – sp Bibl Santa Ana [073]

EXTREMADURA / Diaz Perez, Nicolas – 1887 – 9 – 1.50f – sp Bibl Santa Ana [946]

EXTREMADURA – Periodico Regionalista. Badajoz, 1900 2 numeros – 5 – sp Bibl Santa Ana [073]

EXTREMADURA ARTISTICA E INDUSTRIAL (1930-1931) – Sevilla: Imp. Bergali, s.a. – sp Bibl Santa Ana [700]

EXTREMADURA. CONFERENCIA DADA EN EL ATENEO ESPANOL DE MEXICO, EL 2 DE MAYO DE 1950 / Castillo, Manuel – Mexico D.F. s.i, 1950 – 1 – sp Bibl Santa Ana [972]

LA EXTREMADURA DEL S.15 EN TRES DE SUS PALADINES / Munoz de San Pedro, Miguel – Madrid: Tall. Asilo del Corazon de Jesus, 1964 – 1 – sp Bibl Santa Ana [946]

EXTREMADURA EN 1829 (DATOS DE SUS PARTIDOS Y LOCALIDADES) / Munoz de San Pedro, Miguel – Badajoz: Imp. de la Diputacion Provincial, 1963 – sp Bibl Santa Ana [946]

EXTREMADURA EN LA GUERRA DE LA INDEPENDENCIA ESPANOLA / Gomez Villafranca, Ramon – Badajoz: Tip.Lit.y Enc. de Uceda Hnos., 1908 – 1 – sp Bibl Santa Ana [320]

EXTREMADURA EN LA GUERRA DE LA INDEPENDENCIA (INFORME DE GOMEZ VILLAFRANCA) / Blazquez, Antonio – Madrid: Fortanet, 1911. B.R.A.H. lix, pp. 417-419 – sp Bibl Santa Ana [946]

EXTREMADURA EN LAS OBRAS DE CERVANTES / Berjano Escobar, Daniel – Caceres: Revista de Extremadura, 1905 – 1 – sp Bibl Santa Ana [946]

EXTREMADURA EN TOLEDO. IMPRESIONES DE TURISTA / Hurtado de Mendoza, Publio – Caceres: Tip. Enc. y Lib. de Luciano Jimenez Merino, 1920 – sp Bibl Santa Ana [946]

EXTREMADURA, FOTOGRAFIAS DE JOSIP CIGANOVIC, ENSAYO PRELIMINAR DE PEDRO DE LORENZO : TEXTOS DE JOAQUIN FERNANDEZ, DIRECCION DE FERMIN H. GARBAYO – Madrid: Hauser y Menet, 1968 – 1 – sp Bibl Santa Ana [770]

EXTREMADURA, LA FANTASIA HEROICA / Lorenzo, Pedro de – Madrid: Edit. Nacional, 1961 – 1 – sp Bibl Santa Ana [946]

Extremadura. Spain (Province.) *see*
- CALENDARIO DE EXTREMADURA PARA EL ANO 1863...Y AUMENTADO CON EL CALENDARIO PORTUGUES DE BARDA D'AGUA
- CALENDARIO PARA LA PROVINCIA DE EXTREMADURA..

EXTREMADURA Y AMERICA. SEVILLA, 1929 / Rubio y munoz-Bocanegra, A – Madrid: Razon y Fe, 1930 – 1 – sp Bibl Santa Ana [972]

EXTREMADURA Y EL MAR / Asociacion Amigos de Guadalupe – Caceres: Imp. Sanguino, 1952 – sp Bibl Santa Ana [946]

EXTREMADURA Y ESPANA. CONFERENCIAS FAMILIARES SOBRE LA RAZA DE LOS CONQUISTADORES / Lopez Prudencio, Jose – Badajoz: Ed. Arqueros, 1929 – 1 – sp Bibl Santa Ana [946]

EXTREMADURA Y LOS EXTREMENOS / Hernandez Pacheco, Eduardo – Madrid, 1931 – 1 – sp Bibl Santa Ana [946]

EXTREMADURA Y SUS HOMBRES. LAS ESCUELAS PARROQUIALES DE LOS SANTOS / Suarez Murillo, Marcos – Los Santos: Tip.Sanchez Hnos., 1914 – 1 – sp Bibl Santa Ana [370]

EXTREMADURA...INSCRIPCIONES Y DOCUMENTOS / Viu, Jose de – v1 1852 – 9 – $1.50f – sp Bibl Santa Ana [946]
LOS EXTREMANOS EN LAS CORTES DE CADIZ / Gomez Villafranca, Ramon – Badajoz: Top. y Libreria de A. Arqueros, 1912 – 1 – sp Bibl Santa Ana [946]
EXTREME-ASIE – Revue indochinoise. Saigon. juil 1926-mars 1935 – 1 – fr A.C.R.P.P. [073]
Extremena de Seguros *see* MEMORIA EJERCICIO 1978
EL EXTREMENO – (Es continuacion del siguiente(72)en su primera epoca que empezo en 1869) – Plasencia, 1879-1884 – 5 – sp Bibl Santa Ana [073]
EL EXTREMENO; ALMANAQUE SATIRICO-LITERARIO – 1868 – 9 – 1.50f – sp Bibl Santa Ana [800]
UN EXTREMENO EN LA CORTE DE LOS AUSTRIAS / Munoz de San Pedro, Miguel – Badajoz: Dip. Provincial, 1947 – 1 – sp Bibl Santa Ana [946]
EXTREMO NORTE : JORNAL DE PROPAGANDA – Santo Antonio do Madeira, Amazonas. 1 Jan 1913-1 Nov 1914 – 1,5,6 – bl Biblioteca [072]
EXTREMO NORTE – Manaos, Amazonas. 20 Out 1907 – 1,5,6 – bl Biblioteca [072]
EXZITONENTRANSFER IN SEMIMAGNETISCHEN CDTE/CDMNTE-DOPPEL-QUANTENGRABENSTRUKTUREN / Hiecke, Katharina – 1995 – 2mf – 9 – DM80.00 – 3-8267-2260-4 – gw Hänsel [530]
Ey, Adolf *see* SCHILLERS BALLADEN
THE EYAK INDIANS OF THE COPPER RIVER DELTA / Birket-Smith, K – N 137. 1938 – 9 – ne IDC [970]
Eydoux, J F T *see* VOYAGE AUTOUR DU MONDE. LES ANNEES 1830, 1831, 1832
EYE – Burwell, NE. -w. Jul. 1892; Jan. 1895-Aug. 1896; Oct. 1896-May 1898 – 1 – us NE Hist [071]
EYE – Needles. Calif. 1891-1894 – 1 – us UMI [071]
EYE – Oberlin. Kan. 1883-1910 – 1 – us UMI [071]
EYE – Snohomish. Wash. -w, tw. 1882-97 – 1 – us UMI [071]
EYE : STUDENT NEWSPAPER OF ST IGNATIUS HIGH SCHOOL – Cleveland, OH. 3 Feb 1927-28 May 1992 – 4r – 1 – us Western Res [071]
EYE, EAR, NOSE AND THROAT MONTHLY – v. 1-55. 1922-76. Superseded by ear, nose and throat journal – 1 – us UMI [617]
AN EYE FOR AN EYE / Darrow, Clarence S – Girard, Kansas: Haldeman-Julius Co, 1905? – 1mf – 9 – $1.50 – LLMC 91-061 – us L.L.M.C. [340]
THE EYE GLASS – Stratford, Ont: H C Brown, [19–] – 9 – cn C.I.H.M. [680]
EYE OPENER – Ireland.19 Feb-18 Mar 1916 – 1 – ie Microforms [072]
EYE-OPENER – (Ceased 1993. 1989-90 Can$60.00) – Ottawa, 1989-93 – 1 – Can$60.00y – cn Micromedia [999]
EYE-OPENER / Witty, Frank – (Cont. as: Awakener. W.T. Stead's memorial; Available: Eye-Opener: 1912, v1(1-10). Awakener: 1912, v1(1-2, 4, 6); 1913, v1(7-37, 39-41, 48), v2(53, 66-81)) – London, 1912-1914 – 15mf – 9 – W-18/1 – ne IDC [073]
"EYES ALONE" CORRESPONDENCE OF GENERAL JOSEPH W. STILWELL, JANUARY 1942-OCTOBER 1944 – 5r – 1 – M1419 – us Nat'l Archives [355]
Eyestone, Edward D *see* EFFECT OF WATER RUNNING AND CYCLING ON VO2MAX AND 2-MILE PERFORMANCE
Eyguieres, Joseph E d' *see* STATISTIQUE DU DEPARTEMENT DES BOUCHES DU RHONE
EYN SCHOENE UND GOTSELIGE KURTZWEIL EINES CHRISTLICHEN LOSSBUCHS, NACH ORDNUNG EINES ALPHABETS / Vogtherr, H – Strassburg, 1539. BO-1012 1 – 9 – ne IDC [240]
Eynard, J *see* LA LOI DU PAVILLON
Eynard, Samuel *see* MADAGASCAR ILLUSTRE: GEOGRAPHIE, CLIMATOLOGIE, FAUNE ET FLORE, POPULATION, CHRISTIANISME MALGACHE
EYNIKAYT = UNITY – (In Yiddish) – Moscow, RU. no21-22(no42-43) 31 Aug 1943; no140 no701 20 Nov 1948 – 2r – 1 – $30.00 – cn Can Microfilming [072]
Eyrard, Francois *see* OBSERVATIONS SUR L'EDUCATION PUBLIQUE POUR SERVIR DE REPONSE AUX QUESTIONS POSEES PAR MM. LES AGENTS GENERAUX DU CLERGE DE FRANCE
EYROPE = EUROPE – (In Yiddish) – London, GB. 1943 (?) – 1r – 1 – $25.00 – cn Can Microfilming [072]
Eysinga, W J M van *see*
– LA COMMISSION CENTRALE POUR LA NAVIGATION DU RHIN
– EVOLUTION DU DROIT FLUVIAL INTERNATIONAL...
– LEER EN LEVEN DER STATENVERVORMINGEN
– DE STUDIE VAN HET INTERNATIONALE RECHT
EYSSENHARDT ITERUM RECOGNOVIT / Macrobius – Lipsiae, 1893 – 12mf – 8 – ne Slangenburg [999]
EZECHIEL-STUDIEN / Mueller, David Heinrich – Berlin: Reuther and Reichard, 1895. 1 fiche – 9 – us A.T.L.A. [240]
EZEKIEL : INTRODUCTION, REVISED VERSION WITH NOTES AND INDEX / Lofthouse, William Frederick – (Includes bibliographical references and index) – New York:Henry Frowde; Edinburgh:T C & E C Jack, [1907] – 1mf – 9 – 0-8370-4168-6 – 1985-2168 – us A.T.L.A. [220]
EZEKIEL PRICE PAPERS, 1754-1785 / Price, Ezekiel – Massachusetts Historical Society – 1r – 1 – $85.00 – us UMI [920]
EZEKIELS VISION UND DIE SALOMONISCHEN WASSERBECKEN / Venetianer, Ludwig – (Includes bibliographical references) – Budapest: Friedrich Kilian Nachfolger, 1906 – 1mf – 9 – 0-8370-9326-0 – 1986-3326 – us A.T.L.A. [220]
EZEL MOVEMENT ARCHIVES, 1936-1948 / Jabotinski Institute, Tel Aviv – (Includes a printed guide and plastic binder) – 191mf – 9 – ne IDC [320]
Ezerskii, Nikolai Fedorovich *see* GOSUDARSTVENNAIA DUMA PERVAGO SOZYVA
EZHEGODNIK – Opyt obzora knig dlia narodnago chteniia. 1892-94. M. 1893-95. BR-4311 2 – 8 – ne IDC [460]
EZHEGODNIK EKSPERIMENTAL'NOI PEDAGOGIKI – v. 1-8. Spb. 1908-14. Lacking: 1908 (1), 1914 (8). BR-3797 2 – 8 – ne IDC [370]
EZHEGODNIK GLUKHOVSKAGO UCHITEL'SKAGO INSTITUTA – v. 1-2. Kiev. 1912. BR-3413 2 – 8 – ne IDC [370]
EZHEGODNIK IMPERATORSKOGO RUSSKOGO GEOGRAFICHESKOGO OBSHCHESTVA – v. 1-4. Spb. 1890-94. B-1719 2 – 8 – ne IDC [910]
EZHEGODNIK LITERATIRY I ISKUSSTVA NA 1929 GOD – v. 1. M. 1929. BR-3414 2 – 8 – ne IDC [460]
EZHEGODNIK NARODNOI SHKOLY – v. 1. M. 1908. BR-3415 2 – 8 – ne IDC [460]
EZHEGODNIK PETROGRADSKIKH GOSUDARSTVENNYKH TEATROV – Sezon. 1918-19; Petrograd. 1920. BR-3416 2 – 8 – ne IDC [460]
EZHEGODNIK PROIZVODSTVENNOI KOOPERATSII 1925 G – Moscow, Leningrad. pt1-3. 1925 – 7mf – 9 – COR-585/1 – ne IDC [334]
EZHEGODNIK RUKOPISNOGO OTDELA PUSHKINSKOGO DOMA NA 1969-NA 1973 GOD – 5v. L. 1971-75. BR-11,091 1 – 9 – ne IDC [460]
EZHEGODNIK RUSSKOI MEDITSINSKOI PECHATI – I obzor 1911 g. 2 Obzor 1912 g. M. 1912-14. BR-7098 – 8 – ne IDC [073]
EZHEGODNIK SOVETSKOGO STROITEL' STVA I PRAVA – Moskva, Gosudarstvennoe sotsial' neokonomicheskoe izdatel'stvo, 1931. 1 v. 559 p.. LL-4212 – 1 – us L of C Photodup [340]
EZHEGODNIK TOBOL'SKOGO GUBERNSKOGO MUZEIA, SOSTOIASHCHEGO POD AVGUSTEISHIM EGO IMP. VELICHESTVA POKROVITEL'STVOM – (Missing: Pt6. 1897) – Tobol'sk. pt1-29. 1893-1918 – 92mf – 9 – RET-1/1 – ne IDC [947]
EZHEGODNIK VLADIMIRSKOGO GUBERNSKOGO STATISTICHESKOGO KOMITETA – Vladimir. v1-5. [1875-1885] – 21mf – 9 – RET-2/1 – ne IDC [947]
EZHEMESI ACHNY I STATITICHESKI I BI ULLETEN = BULLETIN STATISTIQUE MENSUEL / VYSSHI I SOVET NARODNOGO KHOZI A ISTVA, T SENTRALNY I OTDEL STATISTIKI – (Includes c.1: v8:no.1 1930:Jan.-v8:no.10 (1930:July)) – Moskva: Gos. tekhnicheskoe izd-vo, 1923 – 1 – CSUXAKY5593-S – us Hoover Inst Photo [947]
EZHEMESIACHNYE SOCHINENIIA – Literaturnyi zhurnal. Spb. 1900-03. B-1721 2 – 8 – ne IDC [073]
EZHEMESIACHNYE SOCHINENIIA K POL'ZE UVESELENIIU SLUZHASHCHIE – Spb. 1755-64. B-1412 2 – 8 – ne IDC [460]
EZHEMESIACHNYI ZHURNAL LITERATURY NAUKI I OBSHCHESTVENNOI ZHIZNI – Spb. 1914-17. Lacking: 1916 (1), 1917 (1-4, 7-12). B-1723 2 – 8 – ne IDC [073]
EZHEMESIACHNYIA SOCHINENIIA I IZVESTIIA O UCHENYKH DELAKH – Spb. 1763-64. BR-3418 2 – 8 – ne IDC [460]
EZHEMIESIACHNYI BIULLETEN POVGODU MOSKVIE / Moscow. Gorodskaia Uprava. Statisticheskii Otdiel – 1888-1915, 1925-29 – 1 – 92.00 – us L of C Photodup [310]
EZHEMIESIACHNYI LITERATURNYI ZHURNAL – 1885-1902. (1892-95, 1900-01, and 3 scattered issues wanting) – 1 – 240.00 – us L of C Photodup [073]
EZHENEDEL'NIK CHREZVCHAINYKH KOMISSII PO BOR"BE S KONTR-REVOLIUTSIEI I SPEKULIATSIEI – Moscow, 1918. Available: No.1. BR-9284/1 – 9 – ne IDC [335]
EZHENEDELNIK NARODNOGO KOMISSARIATA PO PROSVESHCHENII U – (Library has: Nov. 5, 14 1918) – [Moskva]: Komissariat, 1918-1929. 12v – 1 – CSUX89-S618 – us Hoover Inst Photo [947]
EZHENEDEL'NIK PETROGRADSKIKH GOSUDARSTVENNYKH AKADEMICHESKIKH TEATROV – Petrograd, 1922-23 – 31mf – 9 – us Ross [780]
EZHENEDELNIK PRAVDA : ORGAN T SENTRALNOGO KOMITETA, MOSKOVSKOGO KOMITETA I MOSKOVSKOGO OKRUZHNOGO KOMITETA ROSSI ISKO I KOMMUNISTICHESKO I PARTII (BOLSHEVIKOV) – (Library has: 1919, nos. 5-13; 1920, no. 14) – Moskva: T SK RKP, 1919-1920. 2v – 1 – CSUX89-S817 – us Hoover Inst Photo [947]
EZHENEDEL'NIK SOVETSKOI IUSTITSII – (47 issues in 1922. Weekly 1923-1929. 36 yrly from 1930-1932, 1935-1936. Semi-monthly in 1933, 1937-1940, and 1961 to date. 33 issues in 1934. 25 in 1941. 10 in 1957. Monthly in 1958-1959. 18 in 1960. Missing: 1922(12-13, 28, 31-32, 35). 1924(50). 1930(12). 1941(15, p3-4, 29-30, 20). Supplemented: 1988-1990(24). Cont as: Sovetskaia iustitsiia 1930-41, 1957-90) – M., 1922-1929 – 46mf – 9 – R-8282/1 – ne IDC [340]
EZHENEDEL'NOE NOVOE VREMIA – Literaturno-nachnyi zhurnal. v. 1-7. Spb. 1879-80. BR-4862 2 – 8 – ne IDC [073]
Ezhov, I S *see* RUSSKAIA POEZIIA 20 VEKA
Ezhov, V *see*
– PUTI RABOCHEI KOOPERATSII NA ZAPADE I U NAS
– RABOCHAIA KOOPERATSIIA I EE ZADACHI
Ezobi, J *see* KA'ARAT HA-KESEL
EZOP – (Continued as Karakus Ezop) – Istanbul, 1908 – 9 – $25.00 – us MEDOC [956]
EZRA AND NEHEMIAH : THEIR LIVES AND TIMES / Rawlinson, George – (Includes bibliographical references) – New York: Anson D F Randolph, [1890?] – 1mf – 9 – 0-8370-4846-X – 1985-2846 – us A.T.L.A. [220]
EZRA, NEHEMIAH AND ESTHER : INTRODUCTION, REVISED VERSION WITH NOTES, MAPS AND INDEX / ed by Davies, Thomas Witton – (Includes index) – New York:Henry Frowde, [ca. 1908] – 1mf – 9 – 0-8370-2846-9 – 1985-0846 – us A.T.L.A. [220]
EZRA, NEHEMIAH, AND ESTHER / Adeney, Walter Frederic – New York: A C Armstrong, 1893 – 1mf – 9 – 0-8370-2050-6 – 1985-0050 – us A.T.L.A. [220]
F D P *see* MITTEILUNGEN DER FDP IN BAYERN
F. NORDY HOFFMANN, SENATE SERVICE 1975-1981 : SERGEANT-AT-ARMS FOR THE SENATE – 3mf – 9 – $15.00 – us Scholarly Res [320]
F O *see* THE LAW-FRENCH DICTIONARY. ALPHABETICALLY DIGESTED... TO WHICH IS ADDED THE LAW-LATIN DICTIONARY
A F S M JOURNAL – (Association of Field Service Managers). v1-2. 1975-77. Continued as: Field Service Manager – 1 – us UMI [073]
F.A. Battey and Co *see*
– BIOGRAPHICAL SOUVENIR OF THE COUNTIES OF BUFFALO, KEARNEY AND PHELPS
– BIOGRAPHICAL SOUVENIR OF THE COUNTIES OF BUFFALO, KEARNEY, PHELPS, HARLAN AND FRANKLIN
– BIOGRAPHICAL SOUVENIR OF THE STATE OF TEXAS
– COUNTIES OF LAGRANGE AND NOBLE
– COUNTIES OF WARREN, BENTON, JASPER AND NEWTON
– COUNTIES OF WHITE AND PULASKI
FA YIN – The Dharmoghosa Bimonthly. In Chinese. F p31 – 9 – $4.50f – cc Microforms [073]
FAA AVIATION NEWS – (Cont by: FAA General Aviation News, a DOT/FAA Flight Standards Safety Publication) – Washington. v1-14. may 1962-jan 1976 1; v10-14. may 1971-jan 1976 5 – 1,5 – D1572 – us UMI [629]
FAA AVIATION NEWS – (Cont: FAA General Aviation News, a DOT/FAA Flight Standards Safety Publication) – Washington. v26-36. mar 1987-97+ – 1,5,9 – D1572.02 – us UMI [629]
FAA AVIATION NEWS *see* FAA GENERAL AVIATION NEWS
FAA GENERAL AVIATION NEWS : A DOT/FAA FLIGHT STANDARDS SAFETY PUBLICATION – (Cont: FAA Aviation News. Cont by: FAA Aviation News) – Washington. v14-26. feb 1976-feb 1987 1,5; v16-26. may 1977-feb 1987 9 – 1,5,9 – D1572.01 – us UMI [629]
FAA GENERAL AVIATION NEWS – A DOT/FAA FLIGHT STANDARDS SAFETY PUBLICATION *see*
– FAA AVIATION NEWS
Faas, V V *see* UKAZATEL' LITERATURY PO LESNOI TORGOVLE I PROMYSHLENNOSTI
Fabbrizi, Pietro *see* REGOLE GENERALI DI CANTO FERMO ECCLESIASTICO
Fabel, Karel *see* UMENI A REMESLA
FABELN / Pestalozzi, Johann Heinrich – Bern: H Feuz, [1940] – 1r – 1 – us U.W. Library [390]
FABER – Stockville, NE. -w. May 1887; Jul 1892; Sept 1892; Jun 1895; Aug 1895-Nov 1904 – 1 – us NE Hist [071]
FABER – Stockville, NE. -w. Nov 1892; Oct 1895-Dec 1900; Apr-Dec 1901; Feb 1902-Aug 1906; Aug 1908-Jan 1928 – 1 – us NE Hist [071]
THE FABER BIRREN COLLECTION OF BOOKS ON COLOR – Based on collections at Yale University's Art and Architecture Library and the Royal College of Art in London – 1,14 – us Primary [700]
Faber, F *see* PRODROMUS DES ISLANDISCHEN ORNITHOLOGIE, ODER GESCHICHTE DER VOEGEL ISLANDS
Faber, F C von *see* BEITRAG ZUR VERGLEICHENDEN ANATOMIE DER CYPRIPEDILINAE
Faber, G H von *see* OUD SOERABAIA. DE GESCHIEDENIS VAN INDIE'S EERSTE KOOPSTAD VAN DE OUDSTE TIJDEN TOT DE INSTELLING VAN DE GEMEENTERAAD
Faber, J *see*
– MUSICA LIBRIS QUATOR DEMONSTRATA
– SERMONES. ADVERSVS ANABAPTISTAS
Faber, Nicolaus *see* MUSICAE RUDIMENTA
FABER, ODER, DIE VERLORENEN JAHRE : ROMAN / Wassermann, Jakob – Berlin: S Fischer, 1925, c1924 – 1r – 1 – us U.W. Library [830]
Faber Stapulensis, J *see* JACOBI FABRI STAPULENSIS ELEMENTA MUSICALIA AD CLARISSIMU VIRU NICOLAUM DE HAQUEUILLE INQUISITORIUM PRESIDETEM
Fabian, Bernhard *see* KATALOGE DER FRANKFURTER UND LEIPZIGER BUCHMESSEN 1594-1860
FABIAN ECONOMIC AND SOCIAL THOUGHT : SERIES ONE: THE PAPERS OF EDWARD CARPENTER, 1844-1929, FROM SHEFFIELD CITY LIBRARIES: PART 1 CORRESPONDENCE AND MANUSCRIPTS – (Part 2: Manuscripts, Cuttings, Pamphlets and Selected Publications. 26r.$3,050.00) – Marlborough: Adam Matthew Publications, 1993 – 22r – 1 – $2,650.00 – uk Matthew [335]
FABIAN NEWS – v. 1-67. Mar 1891-Dec 1956. Apr 1938-Aug 1941 and scattered issues wanting – 1 – 52.00 – us L of C Photodup [335]
Fabian Society *see*
– ARCHIVES OF THE FABIAN SOCIETY
– RESEARCH PAMPHLETS
– YOUNG FABIAN PAMPHLETS
FABIAN TRACTS – nos. 1-472. 1884-1980 – 1,9 – uk Microform Academic [335]
FABIANELO / Diaz Maciaz, Jose – 1896 – 9 – 1.50f – sp Bibl Santa Ana [830]

Fabie, Antonio Maria *see* EXPOSICION A LA REAL ACADEMIA DE LA HISTORIA EN FAVOR DE LA APARICION DE LA VIRGEN DE GUADALUPE EN MEXICO...

Fabito, Cornelia D *see* PHILIPPINE LIBERATION THEOLOGY

Fabius, D P D *see* VOLKENRECHT

A FABLE – Concordance to the novel – 14mf – 9 – us UMI [420]

UNE FABLE DE FLORIAN / Ristelhuber, Paul – 1881 – 1 – us I.U. Libraries [390]

FABLES ALLEMANDES ET CONTES FRANCAIS EN VERS, AVEC UN ESSAI SUR LA FABLE / Lessing, Gotthold Ephraim & Coudray, Alexandre J C du – Paris: S. Jorry, 1770. xlix, 116p. (Literature Collection) – 2mf – 9 – $6.00 – fr Bibl Nationale [390]

FABLES ANCIENT AND MODERN : ADAPTED FOR THE USE OF CHILDREN / Godwin, William – London: Printed for M.J. Godwin and Co., 9th ed 1821 – 1 roll – 1 – 1-55879-733-5 – uk Libr Preservation [830]

FABLES LITTERAIRES... / Yriarte, Tomas de – Paris: Bailleul, 1804 – 1 – F83.49 – fr Armell [390]

FABLES SENEGALAISES RECUEILLIES DE L'OUOLOF ET MISES EN VERS FRANCAIS AVEC DES NOTES / Roger, Jacques F – Paris, Nepveu, Firmin Didot, Ponthieu. 1828 – 9 – 7.50 – fr Orientalistes [390]

FABLIAUX OR TALES / Le Grand d'Aussy, Pierre Jean Baptiste – 1815 – 1 – us I.U. Libraries [390]

Fabo de Maria *see* SAN AGUSTIN DE JOVEN

Fabre de Parrel, R *see* OBSERVATIONS SUR LES LOIS DE NATURALISATION DES ETRANGERS EN ALGERIE

Fabre d'Olivet, Antoine *see* LA MUSIQUE

Fabre, F *see* LE COLLEGE ANGLAIS DE DOUAI

Fabre, Hector *see*
- CHRONIQUES
- L'ORDRE

Fabre, J H *see* SOUVENIRS ENTOMOLOGIQUES

Fabre, Paul *see* NOTES DE VOYAGE

Fabre, Philippe d'Eglantine *see*
- LE PHILINTE DE MOLIERE OU LA SUITE DU "MISANTHROPE."(FRENCH THEATRE SERIES). PARIS. PRAULT. 1791
- LES PRECEPTEURS

Fabregas, Juan P *see* LOS FACTORES ECONOMICOS DE LA REVOLUCION ESPANOLA

Fabregon, Louis *see* A LETTER TO LA DEPECHE

Fabres y Fernandez, Jose Clement *see* OBRAS COMPLETAS DE DON JOSE CLEMENTE FABRES, RECOPILADAS Y PUBLICADAS POR LA UNIVERSIDAD CATOLICA DE SANTIAGO DE CHILE

Fabri *see* GRANT ET VRAY ART DE PLEINE RHETORIQUE

Fabri, Fratris Felicis *see* EVAGATORIUM IN TERRAE SANCTAE, ARABIAE ET EGYPTI PEREGRINATIONEM

Fabri, J *see* SERMONES. ADVERSVS ANABAPTISTAS

Fabri, Joseph *see* LES BELGES AU GUATEMALA, 1840-1845

Fabri von Hailbrunn, J *see*
- CHRISTENLICHE VNDTERWEISUNG AN DIE WIDERTAUFFER VON DEM TAUFF DER JUNGEN KINDLEIN. VND VON DER GAISTLICHEN VNND WELTLICHEN OBERKAIT, AN DIE WIDERTAUFFER
- VON DEM AYD SCHWOEREN

FABRICA DE CORPORIS HUMANI, LIBRI SEPTEM / Vesalius, A – Brasilea, 1555 – 15mf – 9 – sp Cultura [611]

FABRICHNO-ZAVODSKAI A PROMYSHLENNOST R.S.F.S.R. ZA... : T SENTRALNOE STATISTICHESKOE UPRAVLENIE R.S.F.S.R., SEKTOR STATISTIKI PROMYSHLENNOSTI – (Includes c.1: v.1:no.1 1926/1927) – Moskva: Upravlenie, 1927- – 1 – CSUXAKZ3043-S – us Hoover Inst Photo [947]

FABRICHNO-ZAVODSKAI A PROMYSHLENNOST SOI UZA SSR : T SENTRALNOE STATISTICHESKOE UPRAVLENIE, SEKTOR STATISTIKI PROMYSHLENNOSTI – (Includes c.1: 1924/1927) – Moskva: Statizdat T SSU SSSR, 1929- – 1 – CSUXAKZ3031-S – us Hoover Inst Photo [947]

FABRICHNO-ZAVODSKAI A PROMYSHLENNOST SOI UZA SSR (MOSCOW, R.S.F.S.R.: 1929 *see* FABRICHNO-ZAVODSKAI A PROMYSHLENNOST SOI UZA SSR

FABRICHNO-ZAVODSKAIA PROMYSHLENNOST SSSR V 1925/26 GODU : ITOGI RAZRABOTKI MATERIALOV SROCHNOI EZHEMESIACHNOI OTCHETNOSTI PROMYSHLENNYKH ZAVEDENII ZA 1925/26 GOD / T Sentralnoe statisticheskoe upravlenie SSSR, Sektor statistiki promyshlennosti – Moskva: Upravlenie, 1927 – 1 – CSUX91-B99 – us Hoover Inst Photo [947]

Fabricius, J A *see*
- BIBLIOTHECA GRAECA
- BIBLIOTHECA LATINA MEDIAE ET INFIMAE AETATIS
- SEXTI EMPIRICI
- SEXTI EMPIRICI OPERA GRAECE ET LATINE...

Fabricius, J C *see*
- PHILOSOPHIA ENTOMOLOGICA
- SYSTEMA RHYNGOTORUM SECUNDUM ORDINES, GENERA, SPECIES

Fabricius, O *see*
- FAUNA GROENLANDICA
- FORSOG TIL EN FROBEDRET GRONLANDSK GRAMMATICA; ANDET OPLAG
- GRONLANDSK GRAMMATICA
- DEN GRØNLANDSKE ORDBOG.
- UDFORLIG BESKRIVELSE OVER DE GRONLANDSKE SAELE 1/2

Fabricius, P C *see*
- ENUMERATIO METHODICA PLANTARUM HORTI MEDICI HELMSTADIENSIS

Fabricius, Sara *see* BARE ALBERTE, ROMAN CORA SANDEL

Fabricus, Cajus *see* A CONCORDANCE TO GREGORY OF NYSSA

Fabricus, Johann P *see* A GRAMMAR FOR LEARNING THE PRINCIPLES OF THE MALABAR LANGUAGE

Fabrig, Peter *see* FESTSCHRIFT ANLAESSLICH DER EMERITIERUNG VON PROF. DR.-ING. WALTER RAAB

DIE FABRIK ZU NIEDERBRONN : SCHAUSPIEL IN 5 AUFZUEGEN / Wichert, Ernst – Leipzig: P Reclam, [1874?] – 1r – 1 – us U.W. Library [820]

FABRIKI I ZAVODY MOSKOVSKOI OBLASTI NA 1928-29 GOD – Moskva: Moskovski i oblastno i statisticheski i otdel, 1929 – 1 – CSUX91-B2696 – us Hoover Inst Photo [330]

Fabrique, Andrew Hinsdale *see* MEDICAL RECORDS

Fabritsius, M *see* KREML' V MOSKVE, OCHERKI I KARTINY PROSHLOGO I NASTOIASHCHEGO

Fabrotus, C *see* BREVIARIUM HISTORICUM (CBH 12,1)

Fabrotus, C A *see*
- DE VITA ET HONESTATE CLERICORUM
- HISTORIA (CBH 13)
- HISTORIA DE VITIS ROMANORUM PONTIFICUM (CBH 19,2)
- HISTORIA ECCLESIASTICA SIVE CHRONOGRAPHIA TRIPERTITA (CBH 19,1)

FABULAS DE SALON Y POESIAS / Sanchez Arjona y Sanchez Arjona, Francisco – 1880 – 9 – 1.50f – sp Bibl Santa Ana [830]

FABULAS MORALES SATIRICAS Y.. / Doncel y Ordaz, Jose – 1895 – 9 – 1.50f – sp Bibl Santa Ana [830]

FABULOUS MONSTER / Chamier, Jacques Daniel – New York: Longmans, Green and Co., 1934.viii,357p. Printed in Great Britain – 1 – us U.W. Library [943]

FACE A FACE, OU, LUTTES MENTALES D'UN CATHOLIQUE ROMAN / Beaudry, Louis Napoleon – Montreal: L.E. Rivard, 1882. 03521. (Pre-1900 Canadiana) – 9 – cn C.I.H.M. [240]

THE FACE AND THE MASK / Barr, Robert – New York: F. Stokes, c1895. 03345. (Pre-1900 Canadiana) – 9 – cn C.I.H.M. [830]

FACE AUX REALITES, LA DIRECTION DES FINANCES FRANCAISES SOUS L'OCCUPATION / Cathala, Pierre Adolphe Juste – Paris, Editions du Triolet 1948 – 1 – us U.W. Library [944]

LA FACE DE L'EGLISE PRIMITIVE / Martin, G – Ed 2. Paris, 1656 – 6mf – 9 – CA-139/1 – ne IDC [240]

THE FACE OF THE DEEP : A DEVOTIONAL COMMENTARY ON THE APOCALYPSE / Rossetti, Christina – London: Society for Promoting Christian Knowledge; New York: E. & J.B. Young, 3rd ed 1895 – 1 roll – 1 – 1-55879-419-0 – uk Libr Preservation [240]

EL FACEDOR DE UN ENTUERTO...AGRAVIOS / Hurtado, Antonio – 1869 – 9 – 1.50f – sp Bibl Santa Ana [830]

FACETIAE AND MISCELLANIES / Hone, William – London: Publ for W Hone by Hunt and Clarke, 1827 – 1r – 1 – 1-55879-746-7 – uk Libr Preservation [880]

FACETIEN DREI BUECHER : HISTORISCH-KRITISCHE AUSGABE / Bebel, Heinrich; ed by Bebermeyer, Gustav – (Latin text with an introduction in German. Includes bibliographical references and index) – Leipzig: K W Hiersemann, 1931 – 1 – us U.W. Library [890]

Fachbereich Politische Wissenschaft der Freien Universitaet Berlin, Pressearchiv des Bibliotheks- und Informationssystem *see* PRESSEARCHIV ZUR GESCHICHTE DEUTSCHLANDS SOWIE ZUR INTERNATIONALEN POLITIK VON 1949-60

Fachenetti, Cesar *see*
- AUTO DEL NUNCIO CONTRA UNA ASSERTA SENTENCIA IMPRESSA...
- PUNTOS DE LA SENTENCIA QUE DIO EL SENOR NUNCIO DE SU SANTIDAD CONTRA LOS TRES DIPUTADOS DEL CAPITULO PRIVADO DE LA ORDEN DE SAN JERONIMO EN TRES DE ABRIL DE 1642
- LE SAINT DU PEUPLE ANTONIE DE PADOUE
- SENTENCIA DADA POR...NUNCIO...EN EL PLEYTO QUE HA TRATADO EL...PADRE GENERAL DE LA ORDEN DE SAN GERONIMO Y OTROS RELIGIOSOS DEL MONASTERIO DE YUSTE CON EL PRIOR DE...
- SENTENCIA TRADUCIDO DEL LATIN EN ROMANCE QUE DIO EL NUNCIO EN LAS CONTROVERSIAS QUE HAN PASADO ENTRE EL CAPITULO DIFINITORIO DE LA ORDEN DE SAN GERONIMO Y EL PADRE GENERAL CACERES DELLA
- SENTENTIA...NUNTII APSTOLICI...
- TRES DIPUTADOS DEL CAPITULO PRIVADO DE LA SAN GERONIMO

Fachinger, Josef *see* DAS STAATLICHE AUFSICHTSRECHT UEBER GEMEINDEN UND GEMEINDEVERBAENDE IN RECHTSVERGLEICHENDER DARSTELLUNG UNTER BERUECKSICHTIGUNG DER PREUSSISCHEN ENTWUERFE

FACH-ZEITUNG DES BUNDES DEUTSCHER KOCHE IN GROSSBRITTANNIEN UND IRLAND – 1 Sept 1902-1 Oct 1903 – 1 – uk British Libr Newspaper [072]

FACHZEITUNG FUER DEN COLPORTAGE-BUCHHANDEL – Berlin, 1890-1910 – 2r – 1 – Dist. gw Mikrofilm – gw Misc Inst [072]

FACHZEITUNG FUER SCHNEIDER – Verband der Schneider.... v11, no.52-53; v20, no.24. 1898-1907. (Serial publications of German trade unions in the Memorial Library, University of Wisconsin-Madison.) – 1 – us U.W. Library [330]

FACIAL PAINTINGS OF THE INDIANS OF NORTHERN BRITISH COLUMBIA / Boas, Franz – 1889? 02417. (Pre-1900 Canadiana) – 9 – cn C.I.H.M. [306]

FACILITIES DESIGN AND MANAGEMENT – v1-. 1982- – 1,5,6,9 – us UMI [720]

FACING THE FUTURE : YOUNG PEOPLE AND UNEMPLOYMENT AROUND THE WORLD – 1991 – 250p – 9 – 92-3-102492-2 – Co-published with Orient Longman Ltd, India – fr UNESCO [331]

LE FACISTE CANADIEN / ed by Arcand, Adrien – (Cont by: Le Combat National, Montreal jul 1938-aut 1939) – Montreal, jun 1935-38 – 1r – 1 – Can$50.00 – cn Can Microfilming [072]

DIE FACKEL – Berlin, 1909, 1913, jan-jul 1914, feb-nov 1916, jan-nov 1917 – 1 – Dist. gw Mikrofilm – gw Misc Inst [072]

DIE FACKEL – Chicago, IL: Socialist Pub Society, apr 8 1883-jan 11 1891 – 1 – us Res Libr [071]

DIE FACKEL – (Cont by: Das Kampfsignal, 1932) – Berlin, sep 1931-feb 8 1933 – 1 – Dist. gw Mikrofilm – gw Misc Inst [072]

Fackert, Juergen *see* HUGO VON HOFMANNSTHALS NACHGELASSENES LUSTSPIELFRAGMENT "DIE RHETORENSCHULE" ODER "TIMON DER REDNER"

FACKLAN – Chicago: Scandinavian Socialist Federation, 1921-22. jul 22 1921 – us Res Libr [072]

FACLIA – Cluj, Romania. 1962-70; Jan 1971-75; 1976-89 – 34r – 1 – us L of C Photodup [949]

FACONS DE PARLER PROVERBIALES, TRIVIALES, FIGUREES DES CANADIENS AU XVIIIE / Potier, Le P – Siecle. 1904-06 – 9 – fr I.C.S. [440]

FACSIMILES OF EGYPTIAN HIERATIC PAPYRI IN THE BRITISH MUSEUM / Budge, E A W – London, 1910. BNE-458 1 – 9 – ne IDC [470]

FACSIMILES OF HORAE DE B.M.V. 11TH CENTURY / Dewick, E S – 1902 – 4mf – 8 – Dfl19.00 – ne Slangenburg [240]

FACSIMILES OF THE CREEDS FROM EARLY MANUSCRIPTS / Burn, AU – 1909 – 4mf – 8 – ne Slangenburg [220]

FACT – New York. v1-4. 1964-aug 1967 – 1 – D1808 – us UMI [073]

THE FACT DIVINE : AN HISTORICAL STUDY OF THE CHRISTIAN REVELATION AND OF THE CATHOLIC CHURCH / Broeckaert, Joseph – (Includes bibliographical references) – Portland, ME: McGowan & Young, 1885 – 1mf – 9 – 0-8370-7203-4 – 1986-1203 – us A.T.L.A. [230]

THE FACT OF CHRIST : A SERIES OF LECTURES / Simpson, Patrick Carnegie – (Includes bibliographical references) – [2nd ed]. NY: Fleming H Revell, [1901?] – 1mf – 9 – 0-8370-5386-2 – 1985-3386 – us A.T.L.A. [240]

FACT SHEET / South Dakota. Agricultural Extension Service. Cooperative Extension Service – nos.1-616. 1959-74 – 1,5,6 – us Spaulding [630]

FACT SHEET / Wisconsin. Agricultural Extension Service – n.1-41. 1968-69 – 1,5 – us Spaulding [630]

FACT SHEETS ON MAJOR U.S. A.I.D. AND OTHER U.S. ASSISTED PROJECTS IN INDONESIA / U.S. Agency for International Development – SE 4928 1. 1964? – 9 – ne IDC [324]

LE FACTEUR – Port-au-Prince: [s.n.], 1902. [1ere annee, n1-n43. 6 aout-18 nov 1902] – 3 sheets – 9 – us Res Libr [072]

THE FACTIONIST – Ireland.1 Jan-6 Sept 1917 – 1 – ie Microforms [072]

A FACTOR ANALYSIS OF SELECTED BADMINTON SKILLS TESTS FOR COLLEGE STUDENTS / Louie, L H – 1990 – 2mf – 9 – $8.00 – us Microform Publ [790]

LOS FACTORES ECONOMICOS DE LA REVOLUCION ESPANOLA / Fabregas, Juan P – Barcelona, 1937. Fiche W 866. (Blodgett Collection of Spanish Civil War Pamphlets) – 9 – us H.U. College Libr [946]

FACTORIAL VALIDITY OF A TEACHER EFFECTIVENESS SCALE FOR THE TEACHER PREPARATION PROGRAM IN HONG KONG / Ho, Winnie WY – Springfield College, 1995 – 2mf – 9 – $8.00 – PE3597 – us Microform Publ [370]

FACTORS AFFECTING THE PERFORMANCE OF INTRAMURAL OFFICIALS IN COMPETITIVE SITUATIONS / Blumenthal, Harvey – 1989 – 105p 2mf – 9 – $8.00 – us Microform Publ [790]

FACTORS ASSOCIATED WITH THE RECALL OF PHYSICAL ACTIVITY / Cunningham, Lynda F & Ainsworth, Barbara E – 1992 – 2mf – $8.00 – us Microform Publ [150]

FACTORS INFLUENCING AFRICAN-AMERICAN STUDENTS AT HISTORICALLY BLACK COLLEGES AND UNIVERSITIES TO ENTER THE ADAPTED PHYSICAL EDUCATION PROFESSION / Webb, Daniel – University of Wisconsin-La Crosse, 1995 – 1mf – 9 – $4.00 – PSY1870 – us Microform Publ [150]

FACTORS INFLUENCING FAMILY USE OF HEALTH CARE SERVICES IN TAMIL NADU (INDIA) VILLAGES / Harding, AKW – 1990 – 3mf – 9 – $12.00 – us Microform Publ [613]

FACTORS INFLUENCING INVESTMENT IN EGYPT / Little, A.D., Inc. – 1954. BNE-4643 1 – 9 – ne IDC [332]

FACTORS RELATED TO FASTING BEHAVIOR AMONG AMERICAN ADULTS / Cho, Ho S – Temple University, 1995 – 1mf – 9 – $4.00 – PSY1840 – us Microform Publ [150]

FACTORS WHICH INFLUENCE PATIENT SATISFACTION WITH SEXUALITY EDUCATION / Young, Elaine W – 1982 – 3mf – 9 – $12.00 – us Microform Publ [613]

FACTORY – (Cont by: Factory Management. Supersedes: Factory. Absorbed: Plant Operating Management, dec 1973. Former title: Modern Manufacturing, jun 1968-apr 1971) – New York. v1-9. jun 1968-dec 1976 1; v3-9. 1970-76 5 – 1,5 – D5330 – us UMI [650]

FACTORY – (Cont by: Modern Manufacturing. former titles: New York Review of the Telegraph and Telephone, feb 15, 1882-jun 1, 1882. Review of the Telegraph and Telephone, jun 15, 1882-mar 1, 1883. Electrical Review, mar 22, 1883-feb 18, 1893. Illustrated Electrical Review, feb 25, 1893-dec 29, 1897. Electrical Review, jan 5, 1898-oct 31, 1908. Electrical Review and Western Electrician, nov 7, 1908-jun 30, 1917. Electrical Review, jul 7, 1917-dec 31, 1921. Electrical Review and Industrial Engineer, jan 1922-jun 1922. Industrial Engineer, jul 1922-aug 1927. Industrial Engineering, sep 1927-mar 1931. Maintenance Engineering in Plants, Mills and Factories, apr 1931-feb 1933. Factory Management and Maintenance, mar 1933-dec 1958) – New York. v1-126. 1882-may 1968 – 1 – D24 – us UMI [620]

FACTORY *see*
- FACTORY
- FACTORY MANAGEMENT

FACTORY MANAGEMENT – (Cont: Factory) – New York. v10. jan-jul 1977 – 1,5,9 – D5330.01 – us UMI [650]

FACTORY MANAGEMENT *see* FACTORY

FACTORY MANAGEMENT AND MAINTENANCE *see* FACTORY

THE FACTS – Redlands. Calif. 1891-1893 – 1 – us UMI [071]

FACTS ABOUT BANKRUPTCY YOU OUGHT TO KNOW / Isaac, Max – New York, American Bankruptcy Review, 1927. 347 p. LL-538 – 1 – us L of C Photodup [340]

FACTS ABOUT IRELAND; A CURVE-HISTORY OF RECENT YEARS / MacDowell, Alexander B – London: E. Stanford, 1888. 32p.illus – 1 – us U.W. Library [941]

FACTS ABOUT ISRAEL (1951-1979) – (Ceased after 1979; 1960, 1974, 1976, 1977 have not been published) – Israel Information Centre. N.p., n.d. – 44mf – 9 – J-81-26/1 – ne IDC [950]

FACTS ABOUT SPAIN TO BE USED BY SPEAKERS / North American Committee to Aid Spanish Democracy – N.Y., 193? Fiche W1082. (Blodgett Collection of Spanish Civil War Pamphlets) – 9 – us H.U. College Libr [946]

FACTS AND COMMENTS / Spencer, Herbert – 1902. 209p. 1 fiche (24x) – 9 – 1.00f – at Libertarian Micro [320]

FACTS AND FANCIES ABOUT JAVA / Wit, Augusta de – 2nd ed. rev. and enl. The Hague: W.P. van Stockum, 1900. 266p.ill – 1 – us U.W. Library [950]

FACTS AND FANCIES IN MODERN SCIENCE : STUDIES OF THE RELATIONS OF SCIENCE TO PREVALENT SPECULATIONS AND RELIGIOUS BELIEF BEING THE LECTURES... / Dawson, John William – Philadelphia:American Baptist Publication Society, c1882 – 1mf – 9 – 0-8370-2851-5 – 1985-0851 – us A.T.L.A. [210]

FACTS AND FIGURES : LAND DISTRIBUTION AND SETTLEMENT / Saudi Arabia. Ministry of Information. The Kingdom of Saudi Arabia – February, 1971 – 9 – ne IDC [333]

FACTS AND FIGURES, 5709 (OCT 1948-SEP 1949) / Jewish National Fund (Keren Kayemeth Leisrael) – Jerusalem. 1949. BJ-28-36 1 – 9 – ne IDC [956]

FACTS AND FIGURES REGARDING THE LIQUOR TRAFFIC – Toronto?: s.n., 1897?. 05481. (Pre-1900 Canadiana) – 9 – cn C.I.H.M. [971]

FACTS AND REFLECTIONS BEARING ON ANNEXATION, INDEPENDENCE AND IMPERIAL FEDERATION / Douglas, James – Ottawa: Mortimer, 18??. 02745. (Pre-1900 Canadiana) – 9 – cn C.I.H.M. [971]

FACTS AND REPORTS – Amsterdam: Angola Comite, [1979-]. [v1-5 n25 nov 1970-dec 13 1975] – us Res Libr [072]

THE FACTS AND THE FAITH : A STUDY IN THE RATIONALISM OF THE APOSTLES' CREED / Warner, Beverley Ellison – (Includes bibliographical references and index) – New York: Thomas Whittaker, c1897 – 1mf – 9 – 0-8370-5697-7 – 1985-3697 – us A.T.L.A. [210]

FACTS AND TRENDS – 1955-72. (Education Division Newsletter. 1955-56; SSB Newsletter. 1957-65; Facts and Trends. 1966-71) – 1 – 55.09 – us Baptist [240]

FACTS DISCLOSED IN SOME UNREPORTED CASES: PUBLISHED FOR THE PUBLIC GOOD/BY A VICTIM / Gugy, Augustus – 1870?. 05124. (Pre-1900 Canadiana) – 9 – cn C.I.H.M. [971]

FACTS FOR BAPTIST CHURCHES / Foss, A T & Mathews, E – 1850 – 1 – 14.63 – us Baptist [240]

FACTS FOR MEGANTIC: EVERY ELECTOR SHOULD VOTE AND VOTE ACCORDING TO HIS OWN INTERESTS – Quebec?, 1889? 04267. (Pre-1900 Canadiana) – 9 – cn C.I.H.M. [971]

FACTS NEWS – Seattle. Wash. 1966-68; 1970- – 1 – us UMI [071]

FACTS ON FILE 5-YEAR INDEXES – (1986-90. $90.00) – 1946-90 – 9 – $230.00 – us Facts [020]

FACTS ON FILE YEARBOOKS – (1941-49. $338.00; 1950-59. $375.00; 1960-69. $375.00; 1970-79. $375.00; 1980-89. $375.00; 1990-91. $90.00; 1992-93. $90.00) – 1941-91. Annual. – 9 – $1,595.00 – us Facts [030]

FACTUM POUR CATHERINE BEDEL DITE LA RIGOLETTE QUI DOIT SERVIR DE REPONSE A CELUI DE MARIE BENOIST DITE DE LA BUCAILLE – Rouen. 1699 – 9 – fr Hachette [360]

FACTUM POUR MAISTRE URBAIN GRANDIER, PRESTRE CURE DE L'EGLISE S. PIERRE DU MARCHE DE LOUDUN – S. 1. 1634 – 9 – fr Hachette [360]

FACTUM POUR MARIE BENOIST DITE DE LA BUCAILLE – Rouen – 9 – fr Hachette [360]

FACULA VERITATIS / Pennotto, Gabr. – Colonia Agrippina, 1644 – 32mf – 8 – Dfl112.00 – ne Slangenburg [240]

FACULTAD DE FILOSOFIA Y LETRAS. UNIVERSIDAD DE BUENOS AIRES. PUBLICACIONES HISTORICAS / Bayle, Constantino – Madrid: Razon y Fe, 1925 – 1 – sp Bibl Santa Ana [100]

THE FACULTY OF LAWS, AND THE IDEA OF LAW / Hopkinson, Alfred – Manchester: Cornish, 1875. 20p. LL-374 – 1 – us L of C Photodup [340]

Fadairo, D *see* PROVERBES ET CRITIQUE SOCIALE CHEZ LES FON DU BENIN: UNE APPROCHE ANTHROPOLOGIQUE

Fadda, C *see* LA NAZIONALITA DELLE PERSONE GIURIDICHE

Faden, W *see* A SHORT TOPOGRAPHICAL DESCRIPTION OF HIS MAJESTY'S PROVINCE OF UPPER CANADA, IN NORTH AMERICA

Fader, Daniel *see* TWO CENTURIES OF BRITISH PERIODICALS, 1732-1914

FADERNESLANDET – Stockholm, Sweden. 1830-1954 – 89r – 1 – sw Kungliga [072]

FADIMATA, LA PRINCESSE DU DESERT : SUIVI DU DRAME DE DEGUEMBERE / Ouane, Ibrahim Manadou – [Avignon]: Presses universelles, [1955] – 1 – us Res Libr [820]

Fadli, M *see* L'OPERATION-LABOUR

Fadon Sanchez, Antonio *see*
- LIGERAS E INSIGNIFICANTES OBSERVACIONES SOBRE ALGUNOS PUNTOS CUESTIONABLES Y DUDOSOS EN LA HISTORIA DE MERIDA
- SUCINTA...MANICOMIO DEL CARMEN DE MERIDA

FAEDRELANDET – Copenhagen, Denmark. -d. 1875-81. 14 1 2 reels – 1 – uk British Libr Newspaper [072]

DAS FAEHNLEIN DER SIEBEN AUFRECHTEN : ERZAEHLUNG / Keller, Gottfried – Wiesbaden: Verlag des Volksbildungsvereins zu Wiesbaden, 1913 – 1r – 1 – us U.W. Library [830]

DER FAEHRMANN AN DER WEICHSEL : ZWEI ERZAEHLUNGEN / Planner-Petelin, Rose – Berlin: Furche-Verlag, 1941 – 1r – 1 – us U.W. Library [830]

DIE FAELSCHUNGEN ERZBISCHOF LANFRANKS VON CANTERBURY / Boehmer, Heinrich – Leipzig: Dieterich, 1902 – 1mf – us A.T.L.A. [240]

Faerber, Wilhelm *see* KATECHISMUS FUER DIE KATHOLISCHEN PFARRSCHULEN DER VEREINIGTEN STAATEN

FAERBER-ZEITUNG – Berlin, 1902-09 – 4r – 1 – uk British Libr Newspaper [072]

Faesi, J K *see* ABHANDLUNGEN UEBER DIE GESCHICHTE DES FRIEDENSSCHLUSSES ZU UTRECHT

Faesi, Robert *see* GERHART HAUPTMANNS "EMANUEL QUINT"

Faesser, Johann Chr *see* GESCHICHTE DER WIEDERTAEUFER ZU MUENSTER

Faeulhammer, Adalbert *see* FRANZ GRILLPARZER

FAG RAG – Boston, MA. 1983. OCLC 9353865 – 1 – us U.W. Library [360]

Fagen, Richard *see* CUBA: THE POLITICAL CONTENT OF ADULT EDUCATION

Fager, Karl E *see* A SURVEY OF DIVISION 1 ATHLETIC ADMINISTRATOR'S COMPETENCY DIMENSIONS FOR ADMINISTRATION AND MENTORING

FAGERSTAPOSTEN – Hedemora, Sweden. 1963-78 – 57r – 1 – sw Kungliga [072]

FAGERSTAPOSTEN – Sala, Sweden. 1979- – 1 – sw Kungliga [072]

Fagnani, Charles Prospero *see* A PRIMER OF HEBREW

Fagniez, Gustave Charles *see* ETUDES SUR L'INDUSTRIE ET LA CLASSE INDUSTRIELLE A PARIS AU XIIIE ET AU XIVE SIECLE

FAH REVIEW – (Cont by: Investor-owned Hospital Review) – Little Rock. v1-6. 1967-jun 1973* – 1 – D12216 – us UMI [610]

FAHNDUNGSVERZEICHNIS ZU DEM ZENTRALPOLIZEIBLATTE, DEM WIENER, GRAZER UND INNSBRUCKER TAEGLICHEN FAHNDUNGSBLATTE / Austria. Bundespolizeidirektion, Vienna – 28 Feb 1947-15 Nov 1953. Scattered issues wanting – 1 – 367.00 – us L of C Photodup [360]

DIE FAHNE : KAMPFBLATT DEUTSCHER JUGEND IN POLEN – Posen (Poznan), Poland. 5 Jan-20 Sept 1936 – 1r – 1 – gw Mikrofilm [072]

DIE FAHNE DES KOMMUNISMUS – Berlin, 1927-30 – 1 – Dist. gw Mikrofilm – gw Mikrofilm [072]

DIE FAHNE DES KOMMUNISMUS – Berlin. v. 1-4. 1927-30 – 1 – us NY Public [335]

DER FAHRENDE SCHUELER : EINE DICHTUNG / Wolff, Julius – Berlin: G Grote, 1900 – 1 – us U.W. Library [810]

Fahrner, Rudolf *see*
- HOELDERLINS BEGEGNUNG MIT GOETHE UND SCHILLER
- K. PH. MORITZ' GOETTERLEHRE
- WORTSINN UND WORTSCHOEPFUNG BEI MEISTER ECKEHART

FAHRT FREI : DIE WOCHENZEITUNG DER DEUTSCHEN EISENBAHNER – Berlin, 1951-89 – 17r – 1 – Dist. gw Mikrofilm – gw Misc Inst [072]

DIE FAHRT NACH LETZTESAND / Luserke, Martin – Wien: W Frick, 1943 – 1r – 1 – us U.W. Library [830]

FAHRTGENOSS : MONATSSCHRIFT FUER PROLETARISCHES WANDERN – Berlin, 1922 n1-1929 n6 – 1r – 1 – Dist. gw Mikrofilm – gw Misc Inst [790]

Fahs, Charles Harvey et al *see* THE OPEN DOOR

FAHZI RIBAO = THE LEGAL DAILY – (Yrly reel count varies) – 1981- – 1 – inquire – us Ross [072]

Faidherbe, Louis Leon Cesar *see*
- GRAMMAIRE ET VOCABULAIRE DE LA LANGUE POUL
- NOTICE SUR LA COLONIE DU SENEGAL ET SUR LES PAYS QUI SONT EN RELATIONS AVEC ELLE
- VOCABULAIRE D'ENVIRON 1500 MOTS FRANCAIS AVEC LEURS CORRESPONDANTS EN OUOLOF DE SAINT-LOUIS, EN POULAR (TOUCOULEUR) DU FOUTA, EN SONINKE (SARAKHOLLE) DE BAKEL

FAIENCES ROUEN, LILLE, ETC., A DECOR DE "LAMBREQUINS." / Reunion des musees nationaux. Paris – 1952. 13 illus. 1 fiche – 9 – fr Réunion [730]

Faiershtein, M *see* SOVETSKAIA KOOPERATSIIA

Faik, Mehmet *see* SUEVARILERE MAHSUS MALUMAT VE TERBIYE-I ASKERIYE

THE FAILURE OF LIBERAL CHRISTIANITY, AND, SOME THOUGHTS ON THE ATHANASIAN CREED : TWO ADDRESSES / Burkitt, FC – Cambridge: Bowes & Bowes, 1910 – 1mf – us A.T.L.A. [240]

THE FAILURE OF MODERN LINGUISTICS IN THE FACE OF LINGUISTIC PROBLEMS OF THE 20TH CENTURY / Alisjahbana, Sutan Takdir – (lecture Dec. 22, 1964). SE-5173 1. 1965 – 9 – ne IDC [400]

FAILURE OF REVENUE TARIFF AND OTHER SUBJECTS / Carey, Henry C – A letter to President Grant. 11p – 9 – 1.00f – at Libertarian Micro [335]

FAILURE OF THE CHURCHES / Churchman – London: Eveleigh Nash, 1903. 1 fiche – 9 – us A.T.L.A. [240]

THE FAILURE OF THE "HIGHER CRITICISM" OF THE BIBLE / Reich, Emil – (Includes bibliographical references) – Cincinnati: Jennings & Graham; New York: Eaton & Malns, c1905 – 1mf – 9 – 0-8370-5442-7 – 1985-3442 – us A.T.L.A. [220]

THE FAILURE OF THE REBEL POLICY – Valencia, 193? Fiche W 868. (Blodgett Collection of Spanish Civil War Pamphlets) – 9 – us H.U. College Libr [946]

Fainblit, S *see* REVOLIUTSIONNAIA ZAKONNOST' I NASHA KARATEL'NAIA POLITIKA

Fair Employment Practice Committee *see* RECORDS

THE FAIR HAVEN : A WORK IN DEFENCE OF THE MIRACULOUS ELEMENT IN OUR LORD'S MINISTRY UPON EARTH, BOTH AS AGAINST RATIONALISTIC IMPUGNERS AND CERTAIN ORTHODOX DEFENDERS / Butler, Samuel – London: Trbner, 1873 – 1 roll – 1 – 1-55879-944-3 – uk Libr Preservation [240]

FAIR HOUSING – FAIR LENDING – Englewood Cliffs. 1985-94* 1; 1995-97+ 1,5,9 – 1,5,9 – D24938 – us UMI [640]

THE FAIR JOURNAL – Cincinnati. Ohio. 1881 – 1 – us A.J.P.C. [071]

THE FAIR OAKS POST – Fair Oaks, CA. 1984-1989 – 2r – 1 – $100.00 – B05035 – us Library Micro [071]

FAIR OAKS PROGRESS – Fair Oaks, CA. 1918-1931 – 2r – 1 – $100.00 – C03218 – us Library Micro [071]

FAIR OAKS/FOLSOM – 1992- – 5+ r – 1 – $250.00 – P00026 – us Library Micro [910]

FAIR PLAY – Sioux City, IA. v1-3. 1888-91 + suppl 1906-08 – 1r – 1 – us Ross [071]

A FAIR STATEMENT OF THE REAL GRIEVANCES EXPERIENCED BY THE OFFICERS AND SAILORS IN THE NAVY OF GREAT BRITAIN WITH A PLAN OF REFORM... IN A LETTER TO H[ENRY] D[UNDAS]. BY A NAVAL OFFICER / Dundas, Henry – London, 1797 – 1mf – 1 – 1-55879-051-9 – uk Libr Preservation [355]

Fairbairn, Andrew Martin *see*
- CATHOLICISM, ROMAN AND ANGLICAN
- THE PLACE OF CHRIST IN MODERN THEOLOGY
- STUDIES IN THE LIFE OF CHRIST
- STUDIES IN THE PHILOSOPHY OF RELIGION AND HISTORY

Fairbairn, J *see* BOOK OF CRESTS

Fairbairn, Patrick *see* THE TYPOLOGY OF SCRIPTURE VIEWED IN CONNECTION WITH THE WHOLE SERIES OF THE DIVINE DISPENSATIONS

Fairbairn, Patrick et al *see* DIVINE REVELATION EXPLAINED AND VINDICATED

Fairbairn, Robert B *see* OF THE DOCTRINE OF MORALITY IN ITS RELATION TO THE GRACE OF REDEMPTION

Fairbanks, J *see* PAST AND PRESENT OF GREENE COUNTY

Fairbrother, William Henry *see*
- THE PHILOSOPHY OF THOMAS HILL GREEN

FAIRBURY DAILY NEWS – Fairbury, NE. -w., sw., d. Sep. 1870-Dec. 1916; May 1919-Aug. 1965 – 1 – us NE Hist [071]

FAIRBURY ENTERPRISE – Fairbury, NE. -w. Aug. 1895-Aug. 1902 – 1 – us NE Hist [071]

FAIRBURY JOURNAL-NEWS – Fairbury, NE. -sw., w., tw. Apr. 1892-Dec. 1964; Jan. 1968- – 1 – us NE Hist [071]

FAIRBURY NEWS – Fairbury, NE. -w. Mar. 1898-Jun. 1899. Incomplete; Mar. 1908-Sep. 1911 – 1 – us NE Hist [071]

Fairchild, George Moore *see* ROD AND CANOE, RIFLE AND SNOWSHOE IN QUEBEC'S ADIRONDACKS

Fairchild, J H *see* LECTURES ON SYSTEMATIC THEOLOGY

Fairchild, James H *see*
- OBERLIN
- WOMAN'S RIGHTS AND DUTIES

Fairchild, James Harris *see* ELEMENTS OF THEOLOGY NATURAL AND REVEALED

FAIRFAX COUNTY, VIRGINIA COURT RECORDS ABSTRACTS OF CHANCERY PAPERS 1748-1870 INCLUDING SURNAME AND SUBJECT INDEXES / Virginia. Fairfax County – 9 – $475.00 – us Bloch [340]

FAIRFAX COUNTY, VIRGNIA RECORD OF ROADS / Virginia. Fairfax County – 9 – $75.00 – us Bloch [380]

FAIRFAX FIRST BAPTIST CHURCH (FORMERLY BETHLEHEM). FAIRFAX, SOUTH CAROLINA : CHURCH RECORDS – 1917-75 – 1 – 42.30 – us Baptist [240]

FAIRFAX GAZETTE – Fairfax, CA. 1927-47 – 7r – 1 – $350.00 – B02227 – us Library Micro [071]

Fairfield, Asa Merrill *see* FAIRFIELD'S PIONEER HISTORY OF LASSEN COUNTY

FAIRFIELD AUXILIARY – Fairfield, NE. -w. Jul. 1914-Feb. 1922; May 1922-Feb. 1923. Incomplete; Feb. 1925-Oct. 1965 – 1 – us NE Hist [071]
FAIRFIELD BAPTIST CHURCH. FAIRFIELD COUNTY. SOUTH CAROLINA : CHURCH RECORDS – (204p) – 1881-1905, 1950-1984 – 1 reel – 1 – $9.18 – us Baptist [240]
FAIRFIELD COUNTY BUSINESS JOURNAL – (Cont: Southern Connecticut Business Journal) – Stamford. v19-22 apr 1988-jan 1991*. v31-33 1992-94*. v34-36 1995-97+ – 1 – D17865.04 – us UMI [650]
Fairfield County. Connecticut *see*
- NORWALK AFTER TWO HUNDRED AND FIFTY YEARS
- WILTON PARISH, 1726-1800

FAIRFIELD FIRST BAPTIST CHURCH. FREESTONE COUNTY. FAIRFIELD, TEXAS : CHURCH RECORDS – Oct 1871-Feb 1961 – 1 – 40.50 – us Baptist [240]
FAIRFIELD HERALD – Fairfield, NE. -w. Oct. 1895-May 1898; Jan. 1899-Jan. 1901; Apr. 1901-Dec. 1904; Feb. 1905-Jun. 1905. Incomplete; Jul. 1905-Oct. 1906; Mar. 1907-Dec. 1907 – 1 – us NE Hist [071]
FAIRFIELD INDEPENDENT – Fairfield, NE. -w. Jan. 1908-Feb. 1917 – 1 – us NE Hist [071]
FAIRFIELD MESSENGER – Fairfield, NE. -w. Oct. 1895-Mar. 1896; Aug. 1898-Feb. 1899; Feb. 1900-Dec. 1901 – 1 – us NE Hist [071]
FAIRFIELD'S PIONEER HISTORY OF LASSEN COUNTY / Fairfield, Asa Merrill – San Francisco: H.S. Crocker Co., 1916. California Reel 14. (The Cox Library Collection) – 5 – us Americana [978]
FAIRFIELD/VACAVILLE – 1992- – 3+ r – 1 – $150.00 – P00027 – us Library Micro [910]
FAIRFOREST BAPTIST CHURCH. SPARTANBURG, SOUTH CAROLINA : CHURCH RECORDS – (701p) – 1885-1980 – 1 reel – 1 – $31.55 – us Baptist [240]
Fairholt, FW *see*
- A DICTIONARY OF TERMS IN ART
- A DICTIONARY OF TERMS IN ART... WITH 500 ENGRAVINGS ON WOOD

FAIRLEIGH DICKINSON UNIVERSITY BUSINESS REVIEW – (Former titles: Fairleigh Dickinson University, College of Business Administration: Fairleigh Dickinson University Business Review, win 1961-spr 1968) – Madison. v1-17. win 1961-spr 1977 1; v14-17. spr 1974-spr 1977 5; v15-17. spr 1975-spr 1977 9 – 1,5,9 – D9624 – us UMI [650]
FAIRLEIGH DICKINSON UNIVERSITY, COLLEGE OF BUSINESS ADMINISTRATION – FAIRLEIGH DICKINSON UNIVERSITY BUSINESS REVIEW *see* FAIRLEIGH DICKINSON UNIVERSITY BUSINESS REVIEW
Fairlie, Robert Francis *see* PAPER ON RAILWAY GAUGES
Fairman, Charles E *see* ART AND ARTISTS OF THE CAPITOL OF THE UNITED STATES OF AMERICA
Fairmont. North Carolina. First Baptist Church *see* THE BAPTIST INFORMER, BULLETIN
FAIRMONT TRIBUNE – Fairmont, NE. -w. Jan. 1897-Jul. 1899 – 1 – us NE Hist [071]
FAIRPLAY – Alzada. Mont. 1924-1931 – 1 – us UMI [071]
FAIRPLAY – London, England. A journal for the consideration of financial, shipping & commercial subjects. 18 May 1883-Dec 1918. 96 reels – 1 – uk British Libr Newspaper [073]
FAIRSHARE – Clifton. 1981-94*. 1995-97+ – 1,5,9 – D24939 – us UMI [073]
FAIR-TRADE – A weekly journal devoted to industry and commerce. London. -w. 16 Oct 1885-25 Dec 1891. (5 reels) – 1 – uk British Libr Newspaper [380]
FAIRVIEW BAPTIST CHURCH. GREENVILLE COUNTY. SOUTH CAROLINA : CHURCH RECORDS – (1,265p) – 1886-1985 – 1 reel – 1 – $56.93 – us Baptist [240]
FAIRVIEW BAPTIST CHURCH. MOHAWK, TENNESSEE : CHURCH RECORDS – 1912-Jul 1924 – 1 – 7.56 – us Baptist [240]
FAIRVIEW BAPTIST CHURCH. SPARTANBURG COUNTY. SOUTH CAROLINA : CHURCH RECORDS – 1852-1982 – 1 – 33.13 – us Baptist [240]
FAIRVIEW BAPTIST CHURCH. STEWART COUNTY. FAIRVIEW, TENNESSEE : CHURCH RECORDS – 1935-40, 1948, 1965-Jan 1968 – 1 – 5.94 – us Baptist [240]
FAIRVIEW BAPTIST CHURCH. UNION COUNTY. SOUTH CAROLINA : CHURCH RECORDS – (690p) – 1843-1910, 1951-1980 – 1 reel – 1 – $31.05 – us Baptist [240]
FAIRVIEW HERALD : WEEKLY NEWSPAPER PUBLISHED IN A WESTERN CLEVELAND SUBURB – Fairview Park, OH. Feb 27 1947-Feb 5 1959 – 10r – 1 – us Western Res [071]
Fairweather, George Edwin *see* THE STONE CHURCH BELL AND OTHER POEMS
Fairweather, Jean *see* ROSE WOOD, OR, THE OCTOROON'S BRIDE
Fairweather, William *see* JESUS AND THE GREEKS: OR, EARLY CHRISTIANITY IN THE TIDEWAY OF HELLENISM
FAIRY LEGENDS AND TRADITIONS OF THE SOUTH OF IRELAND / Croker, Thomas Crofton – London: J. Murray, 1834 – 1 roll – 1 – 1-55879-730-0 – uk Libr Preservation [390]
A FAISCA – Perdoes de Lavras, 11 Aug-1 Sep 1895 – 1,5,6 – bl Biblioteca [072]
A FAISCA : PERIODICO LIVRE – Maceio, Alagoas. 30 Out 1886 – 1,5,6 – bl Biblioteca [072]
LE FAIT COLONIAL ET L'IMPERIALISME EN AFRIQUE : PARTI DEMOCRATIQUE DE GUINEE – Conakry: l'Imprimerie Nationale "Patrice Lumumba", [1968?] – us Res Libr [960]
FAITH AND FACT, A STUDY IN RITSCHLIANISM / Edghill, E A – 1910 – 1 – us A.T.L.A. [240]
FAITH AND FORM – 1968-86 (complete) – 1r – 1 – ATLA S0826 – us A.T.L.A. [073]
FAITH AND FORM : AN ATTEMPT AT A PLAIN RE-STATEMENT OF CHRISTIAN BELIEF IN THE LIGHT OF TO-DAY / Varley, Henry – London: James Clarke, 1908 – 1mf – 9 – 0-8370-5667-5 – 1985-3667 – us A.T.L.A. [240]
FAITH AND FREE PRESS – High Point. N.C. v. 13-16. May 1957-Aug 1960 – 1 – 7.49 – us Baptist [240]
FAITH AND FREEDOM – Oxford. v1-41 1947-88*. v42-50 1989-97+ 1; v42-47 1989-94*. v48-50 1995-97+ 5; v42-50 1989-97+ 9 – 1,5,9 – D15264 – us UMI [240]
FAITH AND ITS EFFECTS, OR, FRAGMENTS FROM MY PORTFOLIO / Palmer, Phoebe Worrell – 1867 – 9 – us A.T.L.A. [240]
FAITH AND MISSION – Wake Forest. v1-2 fal 1983-spr 1984*. v3-10 fal 1985-spr 1993. v11 fal 1993-spr 1994*. v12-15 fal 1994-spr 1998+ 1; v3-12 fal 1985-spr 1995*. v13-15 fal 1995-spr 1998+ 5; v3-10 fal 1985-spr 1993. v11 fal 1993-spr 1994*. v12-15 fal 1994-spr 1998+ 9 – 1,5,9 – D15288 – us UMI [240]
FAITH AND MODERN THOUGHT / Welch, Ransom Bethune – (Includes bibliographical references) – New York: G P Putnam, 1876 – 1mf – 9 – 0-8370-5775-2 – 1985-3775 – us A.T.L.A. [210]
Faith and Order Commission *see* MINUTES
FAITH AND ORDER: MEETINGS – A'dam-Baarn, 1948 – 2mf – 8 – ne Slangenburg [240]
FAITH AND ORDER: MEETINGS – Bievres, 1950 – 1mf – 8 – ne Slangenburg [240]
FAITH AND ORDER: MEETINGS – Chichester, 1949 – 1mf – 8 – ne Slangenburg [240]
FAITH AND ORDER: MEETINGS – Clarens, 1951 – 2mf – 8 – ne Slangenburg [240]
FAITH AND ORDER: MEETINGS – Geneve, 1946 – 1mf – 8 – ne Slangenburg [240]
FAITH AND ORDER: MEETINGS – Larens, 1947 – 2mf – 8 – ne Slangenburg [240]
FAITH AND ORDER: MEETINGS – London, 1952 – 1mf – 8 – ne Slangenburg [240]
FAITH AND ORDER: REPORTS – 1951 (paper 10) Churchdivision – 1mf – 8 – ne Slangenburg [240]
FAITH AND ORDER: REPORTS – 1951 (paper 10) Division des Eglises – 1mf – 8 – ne Slangenburg [240]
FAITH AND ORDER: REPORTS – 1951 (paper 10) Kirchenspaltung – 1mf – 8 – ne Slangenburg [240]
FAITH AND ORDER: REPORTS – Lund, 1952 (paper 5) Intercommunion – 1mf – 8 – ne Slangenburg [240]
FAITH AND ORDER: REPORTS – Lund, 1952 (paper 6) Formen des Gottesdienstes – 1mf – 8 – ne Slangenburg [240]
FAITH AND ORDER: REPORTS – Lund, 1952 (paper 6) Ways of Worship – 1mf – 8 – ne Slangenburg [240]
FAITH AND ORDER: REPORTS – Lund, 1952 (paper 7) Die Kirche – 2mf – 8 – ne Slangenburg [240]
FAITH AND ORDER: REPORTS – Lund, 1952 (paper 7) The Church – 2mf – 8 – ne Slangenburg [240]
FAITH AND PHILOSOPHY : JOURNAL OF THE SOCIETY OF CHRISTIAN PHILOSOPHERS – Wilmore. v1-14. 1984-97+ 1,9; v1-6 1984-89. v7 1990*. v8 1991. v9-11 1992-94*. v12-14 1995-97+ 5 – 1,5,9 – D15246 – us UMI [240]
FAITH AND RATIONALISM : WITH SHORT SUPPLEMENTARY ESSAYS ON RELATED TOPICS / Fisher, George Park – New York: Charles Scribner, 1885 – 1mf – 9 – 0-8370-4978-4 – 1985-2978 – us A.T.L.A. [230]
FAITH AND SOUTHERN BAPTISTS – Mayfield. Ky. v. 1-13. Apr 1945-Mar 1957 – 1 – 57.12 – us Baptist [240]
THE FAITH AND THE WAR : A SERIES OF ESSAYS / ed by Foakes-Jackson, F J – London; New York: Macmillan, 1916, c1915 – 1mf – us A.T.L.A. [240]
FAITH AND VERIFICATION, WITH OTHER STUDIES IN CHRISTIAN THOUGHT AND LIFE / Griffith-Jones, E – London: J. Clarke, 1907 – 1mf – us A.T.L.A. [240]
FAITH AND WORKS – Providence. R.I. 1897-1899 – 1 – us UMI [071]
FAITH BAPTIST CHURCH. KINGS MOUNTAIN, NORTH CAROLINA : CHURCH RECORDS – 1953-63 – 1 – 6.12 – us Baptist [240]
FAITH BAPTIST CHURCH. SASKATOON, SASKATCHEWAN. CANADA : CHURCH RECORDS – Nov 1955-4 Apr 1973 – 1 – 11.04 – us Baptist [240]
FAITH, DOUBT, AND EVIDENCE: GOD'S VOUCHERS FOR HIS WRITTEN WORD / Cheever, George Barrell – New York: Anson D.F. Randolph, 1881. 1 fiche – 9 – us A.T.L.A. [240]
A FAITH FOR A NEW AGE (CCC170) = HSIN SHIH-TAI TI HSIN-YANG / Hsieh, Fu-ya – (In Chinese) – Shanghai: Publication Dept., National Committee, YMCAs of China, 1925 – 1r – 1 – 1984-B500 – us A.T.L.A. [240]
A FAITH FOR TO-DAY : SUGGESTIONS TOWARDS A SYSTEM OF CHRISTIAN BELIEF / Campbell, Reginald John – London:James Clarke, 1900 – 1mf – 9 – 0-8370-3154-0 – 1985-1154 – us A.T.L.A. [240]
FAITH, FREEDOM, AND THE FUTURE / Forsyth, Peter Taylor – New York: Hodder and Stoughton, [1912?] – 1mf – us A.T.L.A. [240]
FAITH IN PRACTICE (CCC155) = SHIH CHIEN TI HSIN YANG / Ho, Shih-ming – (In Chinese) – 1st ed. Hong Kong: Chinese Christian Literature Council, 1966 – 1r – 1 – 1984-B500 – us A.T.L.A. [240]
FAITH IN UNITY / Gowon, Yakubu – Lagos, Printed by Academy Press, [n.d.] – us Res Libr [320]
FAITH MISSIONARY – Oberlin, OH. 1882-88 – 1r – 1 – us Western Res [071]
THE FAITH OF A MODERN PROTESTANT / Bousset, Wilhelm – New York: Scribners, 1909. 1 fiche – 9 – us A.T.L.A. [240]
THE FAITH OF FRANCE; STUDIES IN SPIRITUAL DIFFERENCES & UNITY / Barres, Maurice – Transl. by Elisabeth Marbury, foreward by Henry van Dyke. Boston & New York: Houghton Mifflin Company, (1918). xxiv, 294p – 1 – us U.W. Library [240]
THE FAITH OF ISLAM / Sell, Edward – 3rd ed. rev. and enl. London: Society for Promoting Christian Knowledge; New York: E.S. Gorham, 1907. xvi,427p – 1 – us U.W. Library [260]
THE FAITH OF OUR FATHERS : BEING AN EXPOSITION AND VINDICATION OF THE CHURCH FOUNDED BY OUR LORD JESUS CHRIST / Gibbons, James – (Includes bibliographical references and index) – 76th rev ed. Baltimore, MD: John Murphy, c1904 – 1mf – 9 – 0-8370-8344-3 – 1986-2344 – us A.T.L.A. [230]
THE FAITH OF REASON : A SERIES OF DISCOURSES ON THE LEADING TOPICS OF RELIGION / Chadwick, John White – Boston: Roberts Bros, 1879 – 1mf – 9 – 0-8370-2621-0 – 1985-0621 – us A.T.L.A. [200]
FAITH OF REASON: A SERIES OF DISCOURSES ON THE LEADING TOPICS OF RELIGION / Chadwick, John White – Boston: Roberts Bros., 1879. 1 fiche – 9 – us A.T.L.A. [240]
THE FAITH OF THE EASTERN CHURCH : A CATECHISM / Platon, Metropolitan of Moscow – [New York]: G P Putnam, 1867 – 1mf – 9 – 0-8370-7497-5 – 1986-1497 – us A.T.L.A. [240]
THE FAITH ONCE DELIVERED TO THE SAINTS: A SERMON, DELIVERED AT WORCESTER, MASS., 15 OCT. 1823 / Beecher, Lyman – Second ed., 1824 – 9 – us A.T.L.A. [240]
FAITH OR FACT / Taber, Henry Moorehouse – New York: Peter Eckler, 1897 – 1mf – 9 – 0-8370-5475-3 – 1985-3475 – us A.T.L.A. [240]
FAITH VS. KNOWLEDGE / Badgley, Erastus Irvine – And CHRIST, THE LIGHT OF THE WORLD by J. Cooper Antliff. Being the ninth annual lecture and sermon, delivered before the Theological Union of Victoria University in 1887. Toronto: W. Briggs, 1887. 02379. (Pre-1900 Canadiana) – 9 – cn C.I.H.M. [240]
FAITHFUL MEN / Swaine, S A – 402p – 1 – 14.07 – us Baptist [240]
FAITHFUL UNTO DEATH : AN ACCOUNT OF THE SUFFERINGS OF THE ENGLISH FRANCISCANS DURING THE 16TH AND 17TH CENTURIES: FROM CONTEMPORARY RECORDS / Stone, J M – London: Kegan Paul, Trench, Truebner, 1892 – 1mf – us A.T.L.A. [941]
A FAITHFUL WARNING TO THE FOLLOWERS OF THE REV. MR. JOHN WESLEY, SHEWING THE FALSHOOD, CALUMNY AND ART MADE USE OF IN THAT GENTLEMAN'S SOCIETIES TO DECEIVE THE IGNORANT AND UNWARY IN THE THINGS OF GOD;... – London, 1774 – 1mf – 9 – MP-496/1 – ne IDC [240]
FAITHFUL WORD – (Lacks some pgs. v15 nos 3-4 not publ) – v1-23. 1961-86 – 2r – 1 – ATLA S0837 – us A.T.L.A. [073]
FAITH-HEALING, CHRISTIAN SCIENCE AND KINDRED PHENOMENA / Buckley, James Monroe – New York: Century, 1892 – 1mf – us A.T.L.A. [290]
FAITH-LIFE – (Lacking some pgs) – v1-65. 1928-92 – 9r – 1 – ATLA S0369 – us A.T.L.A. [073]
FAITHS OF FAMOUS MEN IN THEIR OWN WORDS : COMPRISING RELIGIOUS VIEWS OF THE MOST DISTINGUISHED SCIENTISTS, STATESMEN,... / Kilbourn, John Kenyon – (Includes index) – Philadelphia: Henry T Coates, 1900 – 1mf – 9 – 0-8370-3896-0 – 1985-1896 – us A.T.L.A. [210]
Faitlovitch, J *see* PROVERBES ABYSSINS, TRADUITS, EXPLIQUES ET ANNOTES
LES FAITS RELATIFS A L'ADMINISTRATION DES AFFAIRES DES SAUVAGES AU NORD-OUEST – s.l.: s.n., 1886?. 03739. (Pre-1900 Canadiana) – 9 – cn C.I.H.M. [971]
Fajardo, Eliecer L *see* LA ROSA DEL GUAYAS
Fak-Ao Tinapua Mata, Dick *see* TWO TEXTS IN THE LANGUAGE OF TONGOA ISLAND IN THE SHEPHERD ISLANDS GROUP, VANUATU
FAKKEL – Batavia, Antwerpen, 1940-1942 – 13mf – 9 – ne IDC [999]
FAKLYA – Oradea, Romania. 1967; 1975-80 – 6r – 1 – us L of C Photodup [949]
FAKS – (Cont: Mladez and Narodna Mladez) – 1976- – 1r per y – 1 – us Ross [072]
FAKS *see* NARODNA MLADEZ
FAKTY I TSIFRY PROTIV DEMAGOGII I IZMYSHLENII OPPOZITSII / Agitprop T SK i MK VKP (b) – Moskva: Moskovski i rabochi i, 1927 – 1 – CSUX89-B6528 – us Hoover Inst Photo [947]
Falaise, Rayliane de la *see* CARAJA...KOU TROIS ANS CHEZ LES INDIENS DU BRASIL
FALANGE DESDE FEBRERO DE 1936 AL GOBIERNO NACIONAL / Garceran, Rafael – n.p. 1936? Fiche W 906. (Blodgett Collection of Spanish Civil War Pamphlets) – 9 – us H.U. College Libr [946]
Falange Espanola de las Jons *see* REGLAMENTO DE PRIMERA LINEA
Falange Espanola Tradicionalista y de la Jons *see*
- ORDENANZA
- QUE ES EL SERVICIO DE ADMINISTRACION LOCAL (LA FALANGE Y EL AYUNTAMIENTO RURAL)

Falange Espanola Tradicionalista y de las Juntas Ofensivas Nacional-Sindicalistas *see*
- ARGUMENTO DE LA NUEVA ESPANA

- CONTESTACIONES OFICIALES DE DOCTRINA DEL MOVIMENTO, PARA OPOSICIONES EN LAS QUE SE EXIGE TITULO ELEMENTAL
- LA FALANGE Y EL COMBATIENTE
- NACIONALSINDICALISMO
- PRIMER DISCURSO DE LA FALANGE A CATALUNA
- UNIDAD DE DESTINO

Falange Espanola Tradicionalista y de las Juntas Ofensivas nacional-Sindicalistas *see* EL FUTURO DE LA AGRICULTURA NACIONAL-SINDICALISTA

Falange Espanola Tradicionalista y de las Juntas Ofensivas Nacional-Sindicalistas. Seccion Femenina *see* CONCENTRACION NACIONAL DE LA FALANGES FEMENINAS EN HONOR DEL CAUDILLO Y DEL EJERCITO ESPANOL

FALANGE EXTERIOR – Boletin decenal informativo de la delegacion nacional del servicio exterior de Falange espanola tradicionalista y de las J.O.N.S. n.p., 1938. Fiche W 873. (Blodgett Collection of Spanish Civil War Pamphlets) – 9 – us H.U. College Libr [946]

LA FALANGE: REVISTA DE CULTURA LATINA – Mexico. Dec 1922-Feb 1923, July-Oct 1923 – 1 – us NY Public [073]

LA FALANGE Y EL COMBATIENTE / Falange Espanola Tradicionalista y de las Juntas Ofensivas Nacional-Sindicalistas – Bilbao, 1938. Fiche W 874. (Blodgett Collection of Spanish Civil War Pamphlets) – 9 – us H.U. College Libr [946]

Falardeau, Edith *see* L'ARTISANAT AU CANADA FRANCAIS (1900-1950)

Falcao Espalter, Mario *see* ENTRE DOS SIGLOS

Falck, Anton Reinhard *see* AMBTS-BRIEVEN: 1802-1842

Falck, P T *see* DER DICHTER J.M.R. LENZ IN LIVLAND

Falcke, H P *see* LE BLOCUS PACIFIQUE,...

FALCON – Mansfield. v1-10. 1970-80 1; v1-4 1970-73. v5-10 1974-80* 5; v5-10 1974-80* 9 – 1,5,9 – D6395 – us UMI [073]

Falcon, Cesar *see* SIMILAR FATES: TOWNS OF ENGLAND, TOWNS OF FRANCE YOU WILL ALSO BE RAIDED

Falconer, John *see* THE ROYAL COMMONWEALTH SOCIETY, LONDON

Falconer, William *see* AN UNIVERSAL DICTIONARY OF THE MARINE: OR, A COPIOUS EXPLANATION OF THE TECHNICAL TERMS EMPLOYED IN THE CONSTRUCTION OF A SHIP. TO WHICH IS ANNEXED A TRANSLATION OF FRENCH SEA-TERMS

Faldbakken, Knut *see*
- SWEETWATER
- TWILIGHT COUNTRY

Faleroni, Alberto Daniel *see* LA CONQUISTA DEL ESTADO POR LA REVOLUCION NACIONAL

Fales, William E S *see* BROOKLYN'S GUARDIANS-RECORD OF POLICE FORCE IN CITY OF HOMES

Falgairolle, Edmond *see* MONTCALM DEVANT LA POSTERITE: ETUDE HISTORIQUE

Falise, Jean Baptiste *see* LITURGIAE PRACTICAE COMPENDIUM

Falk, Brigitte *see* KREATIVE PROZESSE IM UNTERRICHT

FALK UND GOETHE : IHRE BEZIEHUNGEN ZU EINANDER NACH NEUEN HANDSCHRIFTLICHEN QUELLEN / Schultze-Gallera, Siegmar Baron von – Halle a.S.: C A Kaemmerer, 1900 – 1r – 1 – us U.W. Library [920]

Falk, Victor von *see* DIE TODTENFELDER VON SIBIRIEN, ODER DAS GEHEIMNISS DES RUSSISCHEN KAISERSCHLOSSES

Falke, Gustav *see* TIMM KROEGER

DER FALKE VOM MONS REGIUS : GESCHICHTE EINER JAGD- UND LIEBESLEIDENSCHAFT / Bartsch, Rudolf Hans – Berlin: Deutsche Buch-Gemeinschaft, c1930 – 1r – 1 – us U.W. Library [830]

Falkenberg, Heinrich *see* WIR KATHOLIKEN UND DIE DEUTSCHE LITERATUR

Falkenberg, P *see*
- DIE RHODOMELACEEN DES GOLFES VON NEAPEL

FALKENBERGSPOSTEN – Falkenberg, Sweden. 1905-07; 1909-19 – 13r – 1 – sw Kungliga [072]

Falkenmark, Malin *see* COMPARATIVE HYDROLOGY

Falkenstein, A *see* ARCHAISCHE TEXTE AUS URUK

Falkenstein, George N *see* HISTORY OF THE GERMAN BAPTIST BRETHREN CHURCH

Falkland, A *see* HYDROLOGY AND WATER RESOURCES OF SMALL ISLANDS

Falkland Islands *see* FALKLAND ISLANDS GAZETTE

FALKLAND ISLANDS GAZETTE / Falkland Islands – Stanley. 1958-Dec. 7, 1967 – 1 – us NY Public [972]

FALKLAND ISLANDS GAZETTE – v77-79 + indexes & suppls. 1968-70 – 1r – 1 – us Ross [072]

FALKLAND / MALVINAS : DER UMSTRITTENE ARCHIPEL IM SUEDATLANTIK / Mann, Gerald H – 1995 – 1mf – 9 – DM60.00 – 3-8267-2158-6 – gw Hänsel [320]

Falkner, Semen Anisimovich *see* PERELOM V RAZVITII MIROVOGO PROMYSHLENNOGO KRIZISA

FALKOPINGS TIDNING – (Tidning fran Falkopings stad och Falbygden, 1857-79) – Falkoping, Sweden. 1879-1978 – 176r – 1 – sw Kungliga [072]

FALKOPINGS TIDNING – (Vastgotabladet, 1981) – Falkoping, Sweden. 1979- – 1 – sw Kungliga [072]

FALKSADVOKAT = THE VOLKS ADVOCATE – New York, NY. 1888-89 – 1 – us A.J.P.C. [071]

DER FALL : ERZAEHLUNG / Mueller, Wolfgang – Stuttgart: E Klett, 1948 – 1r – 1 – us U.W. Library [830]

Fall, A et al *see* EVALUATION OF THE PRODUCTIVITIES OF DJALLONKE SHEEP AND N'DAMA CATTLE AT THE CENTRE DE RECHERCHES ZOOTECHNIQUES, KOLDA, SENEGAL

Fall, George Howard *see* THE LAW OF THE APOTHECARY: A COMPENDIUM OF BOTH THE COMMON AND STATUTORY LAW GOVERNING DRUGGISTS AND CHEMISTS IN MASSACHUSETTS, MAINE, NEW HAMPSHIRE, VERMONT, RHODE ISLAND AND CONNECTICUT

Fall, H C *see* LIST OF THE COLEOPTERA OF SOUTHERN CALIFORNIA, WITH NOTES ON HABITS AND DISTRIBUTION AND DESCRIPTIONS OF NEW SPECIES

DER FALL HEBBEL : EIN KUENSTLER-PROBLEM / Friedrich, Paul – Leipzig: Xenien-Verlag, 1908 – 1r – 1 – us U.W. Library [430]

DER FALL MAURIZIUS : ROMAN / Wassermann, Jakob – Berlin: S Fischer, 1928 – 1r – 1 – us U.W. Library [830]

THE FALL OF CHICAGO *see*
- HARDSCRABBLE, OR, THE FALL OF CHICAGO.
- HARDSCRABBLE OR THE FALL OF CHICAGO

THE FALL OF JERUSALEM : A DRAMATIC POEM / Milman, Henry Hart – London: J. Murray, 1820 – 1 roll – 1 – 1-55879-317-8 – uk Libr Preservation [810]

THE FALL OF NINEVEH – No. 21,901 in the British Museum. Edited, with transliteration, translation, notes, etc. by C.J. Gadd.1923 – 1 – us U.W. Library [900]

FALL RIVER 1803-1889 – (Mf 1-18: Vital Records 1724-1856. Mf 19-26: Vitals Index 1724-1856. Mf 27-33: Vital Records 1843-49. Mf 34-36: Vitals Index 1843-49. Mf 37-38: Vital Records 1857-62. Mf 39-40: Vitals Index 1857-62. Mf 41-57: Births 1843-64. Mf 58-87: Births 1865-78. Mf 88-113: Births 1879-86. Mf 114-128: Births 1887-90. Mf 129-200: Intentions 1843-90. Mf 201-213: Ints Index 1843-92. Mf 214-220: Marriages 1850-64. Mf 221-226: Marriages 1865-70. Mf 227-233: Marriages 1871-74. Mf 234-239: Marriages 1875-78. Mf 240-246: Marriages 1879-82. Mf 247-255: Marriages 1883-86. Mf 256-262: Marriages 1887-89. Mf 263-271: Deaths 1850-64. Mf 272-278: Deaths 1865-70. Mf 279-287: Deaths 1871-74. Mf 288-296: Deaths 1875-78. Mf 297-304: Deaths 1879-82. Mf 305-312: Deaths 1883-86. Mf 313-318: Deaths 1887-89) – (mf ed 1985) – 318mf – 9 – 0-931248-71-X – us Holbrook [920]

THE FALLACIES OF PROTECTION / Craigie, E J – 1fiche (29x) – 9 – 1.00f – at Libertarian Micro [320]

FALLACIES OF RACE THEORIES AS APPLIED TO NATIONAL CHARACTERISTICS / Babington, William Dalton – London and New York: Longmans, Green and Co., 1895. 277p – 1 – us U.W. Library [572]

FALLACY DETECTED IN A LETTER TO THE REV. MR. JOHN WESLEY, MASTER OF ARTS, WHEREIN HIS 'FREE THOUGHTS ON THE STATE OF PUBLIC AFFAIRS' AND HIS 'CALM ADDRESS TO THE AMERICANS' ARE CONSIDERED AND COMPARED / Juniolus – [?London], 1775 – 1mf – 9 – MP-507/1 – ne IDC [240]

THE FALLACY OF CENTRAL BANKING / Cobb, Joe – NOMOS, Autumn 1983. 4p – 9 – 1.00f – at Libertarian Micro [332]

FALLBROOK ENTERPRISE – Fallbrook, CA. 1911-1959; 1978 – 48+ r – 1 – $2,400.00 ($50.00y) – H03219 – us Library Micro [071]

FALLBROOK REVIEW – West Fallbrook, CA. Sep 1885-91 – 1r – 1 – $50.00 – C03092 – us Library Micro [071]

FALLECIMIENTO / Castalleda, Vicente & Perez Jimenez, Nicolas – Madrid: Rev. Arch. Bibl. y mus, 1927. B.R.A.H. 90, p. 242 – sp Bibl Santa Ana [946]

FALLECIMIENTO / Perez de Guzman, Juan & Sanguino y Michel, Juan – Madrid: Editorial Reus, 1921. B.R.A.H 78, p. 786 – sp Bibl Santa Ana [946]

FALLECIMIENTO DE D. FRANCISCO JARRIN, OBISPO DE PLASENCIA / Fita, Fidel – Madrid: Fortanet, 1912. B.R.A.H. 61. p. 533 – 1 – sp Bibl Santa Ana [240]

FALLECIMIENTO DE DON VICENTE PAREDES GUILLEN / Perez de Guzman, Juan – Madrid: Fortanet, 1916. B.R.A.H. 68, pp. 327 – sp Bibl Santa Ana [920]

FALLECIMIENTO DEL MARQUES DE MONSALUD / Fita, Fidel – Madrid: Fortanet, 1910. B.R.A.H. 56, 1910, p. 160 – sp Bibl Santa Ana [946]

FALLECIMIENTO EN CACERES / Acedo, Federico – Madrid: Ed. Reus, 1922. B.R.A.H. 80. p. 494 – 1 – sp Bibl Santa Ana [946]

FALLECIMIENTO EN PLASENCIA DE DON JOSE BENAVIDES CHECA / Fita, Fidel – B.R.A.H. 61. pp. 458-459. 1912 – 1 – sp Bibl Santa Ana [946]

Fallen, C F *see*
- DIPTERA SVECIAE
- HEMIPTERA SVECIAE

Fallersleben, Hoffmann von *see*
- GESCHICHTE DES DEUTSCHEN KIRCHENLIEDES BIS AUF LUTHERS ZEIT
- IN DULCI IUBILO, NUN SINGET UND SEID FROH

FALLING IN LOVE: WITH OTHER ESSAYS ON MORE EXACT BRANCHES OF SCIENCE / Allen, Grant – New York: D. Appleton, 1890. 05034. (Pre-1900 Canadiana) – 9 – cn C.I.H.M. [830]

FALLON COUNTY TIMES – Baker. Mont. -w. 1919-49, 1966-68 – 1 – us UMI [071]

FALLON EAGLE *see* CHURCHILL COUNTY EAGLE

FALLOS...: CON LA RELACION DE SUS RESPECTIVAS CAUSAS / Argentine Republic. Corte Suprema de Justicia de la Nacion – 1864-. Annual – 1 – us U.W. Library [324]

Fallouard, P *see* LES MUSICIENS NORMANDS, ESQUISSE BIOGRAPHIQUES; COMPRENANT LES NORMS DES ARTISTES MUSICIENS LES PLUS CELEBRES NEE EN NORMANDIE DU 11E AU 19E SIECLE

Falls Church. Virginia. Columbia Baptist Church *see* INDEX OF MATERIALS AT BEGINNING, ASSOCIATIONAL CHURCH LETTERS AT END

FALLS CITY – Oregon City OR. Sep 26 1881 (extra) – 1 – us U.O. Library [071]

FALLS CITY DAILY NEWS – Falls City, NE. -w., sw., d. Feb. 1875-Mar. 1884; Jan. 1885-Sep. 1890; Jan. 1891-Feb. 1904; May 1904-Apr. 1934 – 1 – us NE Hist [071]

FALLS CITY ENTERPRISE – Falls City OR. Apr 15 1926 – 1 – us U.O. Library [071]

FALLS CITY JOURNAL – Falls City, NE. -w., d. Jan. 1869-Jul 1875; Jul 1877-Dec. 1883; Jan. 1885-Jan. 1886; Mar. 1886-May 1909; Jan. 1910- – 1 – us NE Hist [071]

FALLS CITY NEWS – (Set incl. Falls City Enterprise for Apr 15, 1926) – Falls City, OR. -w. 4 Mar 1909-27 Jul 1918. – 1r – 1 – us U.O. Library [071]

FALLS CITY TIMES – Falls City, NE. -w. Aug. 1928-Nov. 1929 – 1 – us NE Hist [071]

FALLS CITY TRIBUNE – Falls City, NE. -w. Jan. 1904-Jul. 1911 – 1 – us NE Hist [071]

FALLS CREEK BAPTIST ASSEMBLY. OKLAHOMA : CHURCH RECORDS – 1917. 58p – 1 – us Baptist [240]

THE FALLS OF NIAGARA / Dewart, Edward Hartley – Toronto? s.n., 18??. 02648. (Pre-1900 Canadiana) – 9 – cn C.I.H.M. [971]

FALLSTON BAPTIST CHURCH. KINGS MOUNTAIN ASSOCIATION. NORTH CAROLINA : CHURCH RECORDS – 1902-56 – 1 – 37.62 – us Baptist [240]

FALMOUTH 1688-1892 – (Mf 1-2: B,M,D 1668-1753. Mf 3-7: Vital Records 1681-1757. Mf 8-13: Vital Records 1750-1831. Mf 14-20: Vital Records Index 1756-1831. Mf 21-26: B,M,D 1780-1858. Mf 27-29: Index to Records 1780-1858. Mf 30-32: B,M,D 1855-92. Mf 33-38: B,M,D 1855-1892. Mf 39-41: Vital Records Index 1843-92. Mf 42-46: Congregational Church Records 1731) – (mf ed 1987) – 46mf – 9 – 0-931248-92-2 – us Holbrook [920]

FALMOUTH AND PENRYN WEEKLY TIMES – (Lacking: 1897) – Falmouth, Penryn, England. Jun 1861-Oct 1952 – 73r – 1 – uk British Libr Newspaper [072]

FALMOUTH GAZETTE AND JAMAICA GENERAL ADVERTISER – Jamaica, 3 Jan 1879-29 Dec 1888 – 5r – 1 – uk British Libr Newspaper [072]

FALMOUTH PACKET – Falmouth, England. Apr 1829-48; 1858-1971; 1988- – 113+ r – 1 – uk British Libr Newspaper [072]

FALMOUTH PENRYN LEADER – (Discontinued) – Jun 4-Dec 24 1988; 1989-Jun 1990; Jul 7-Dec 22 1990; 1991-92; Jan 9-Jun 26 1993; Jul-Dec 1993; Jan 8-Jun 25 1994; Jul 2-Dec 24 1994; Jan-Dec 16 1995 – 13 1/2r – 1 – uk British Libr Newspaper [072]

Falret, Jean Pierre *see* DES MALADIES MENTALES ET DES ASILES D'ALIENES. LECONS CLINIQUES ET CONSIDERATIONS GENERALES

FALSAFAH PERDJUANG ISLAM / Anshary, Muhammed Isa – Tjet. 1. Bandung. Pasifik. 1951 ed. 287p. SEM-14329 14332 1 – 9 – ne IDC [260]

FALSAFAH PERDUANGAN ISLAM / Anshary, Muhammed Isa – Tjet. 1. Bandung, Pasifik, 1949. 240p. SEM-844 846 1 – 9 – ne IDC [260]

DER FALSCHE DEMETRIUS IN DER DICHTUNG / Popek, A (Anton) – Linz: Verlag des k.k. Staats-Gymnasiums, 1893, 1895 – 1r – 1 – us U.W. Library [430]

FALSCHER ZUSCHAUER *see* DEUTSCHER ZUSCHAUER

FALSE CONSONANCE DELLA MUSICA PER TOCCAR LA CHITARRA SOPRA ALL PARTIE IN BREVE... – Autograph, MS. – 1 – us Sibley [780]

LE FALSE CONSONANSE DELLA MUSICA.. / Matteis, N – Autograph manuscript. c.1680 – 9 – us Sibley [780]

FALSE WITNESSES ANSWERED / Clarke, James Freeman – Boston. 1835. With which is filmed: HIS, A look at the life of Theodore Parker. Boston. 1910 – 9 – us A.T.L.A. [240]

FALSIFIKATORY ISTORII : ISTORICHESKAI A SPRAVKA – [Moskva]: Gos. izd-vo polit. lit-ry, 1948 – 1 – CSUX90-B8880 – us Hoover Inst Photo [947]

FALUKURIREN – Falun, Sweden. 1894-1978 – 393r – 1 – sw Kungliga [072]

FALUKURIREN – Falun, Sweden. 1979- – 1 – sw Kungliga [072]

Falvo, Lisa A *see* MECHANICAL AND PHYSIOLOGICAL DIFFERENCES BETWEEN RUNNING AND WALKING AT VARIOUS VELOCITIES

FAMA, ECLIPSE Y RESURRECCION DE DONOSO / Armas, Gabriel – Madrid: Imp. Aguirre, 1969. En Verbo, ano VIII, no 74, pp. 321-333 – sp Bibl Santa Ana [946]

A FAMILIA : JORNAL DEDICADO A EDUCACAO DA MAE DE FAMILIA – Sao Paulo/Rio de Janeiro, 18 Nov-Dec 1888; Jan-Aug, Oct-Dec 1889; Jan-Dec 1890; Feb-Dec 1891; Jan-Feb, Jul, Sep 1892; Jan-Dec 1893; Jan-Jun, 20 Oct 1894 – 1,5,6 – bl Biblioteca [072]

A FAMILIA – Theophilo Ottoni, 27 Dec 1913; Feb-May, Jul-Nov 1927; Jun-Dec 1928; Jan-Feb, Apr-Jul, Sep-Oct 1929; Jan-26 Apr 1930 – 1,5,6 – bl Biblioteca [072]

EN FAMILIA : POESIAS / Sanchez-Arjona, Vicente – Sevilla: Establecimiento Tipografico Juan Mejias, 1930 – 1 – sp Bibl Santa Ana [810]

LA FAMILIA CRISTIANA / Perez Munoz, Adolfo – Cordoba: Imprenta El defensor, 1921 – 1 – sp Bibl Santa Ana [240]

LA FAMILIA DE DON PEDRO DE VALDIVIA / Roa y Ursua, Luis – Sevilla: Imprenta de la Gavidra, 1935 – 1 – sp Bibl Santa Ana [920]

UNA FAMILIA DE INGENIOS, LOS RAMIREZ DE PRADO / Hornedo, A M & Entrambasaguas, Joaquin de – Madrid: Razon y Fe, 1944 – 1 – sp Bibl Santa Ana [920]

LA FAMILIA EN DIRECTO / Aradillas Agudo, Antonio & Espias-Sanchez, Manuel – Madrid: Doncel, 1973 – 1 – sp Bibl Santa Ana [306]
LA FAMILIA PREOCUPACION FUNDAMENTAL DEL ESTADO ESPANOL / Leal Ramos, Leon – Caceres: Tip. El noticiero, s.a. 1950 – sp Bibl Santa Ana [946]
LA FAMILIA RURAL HACIA LA CONQUISTA DE UN MEJOR NIVEL DE CULTURA. ENCUESTA CAMPANA EXPERIMENTAL 1963-1964 / Comision Diocesana de Apostolada Rural – Plasencia: Imp. Padilla, 1963 – 1 – sp Bibl Santa Ana [240]
LA FAMILIA, SEGUN EL DERECHO NATURAL Y CRISTIANO... / Goma, Isidoro – Madrid: Razon y Fe, 1927 – 1 – sp Bibl Santa Ana [360]
LA FAMILIA SOBRE TODO / Mendoza, Luis de – 1879 – 9 – 1.50f – sp Bibl Santa Ana [830]
EN FAMILIA. VERSOS VIEJOS / Gomez-Bravo, Vicente – Badajoz: Arqueros, 1952 – sp Bibl Santa Ana [946]
FAMILIAL PATTERNS OF VO(2MAX) AND PHYSICAL ACTIVITY LEVELS / Guion, Willie K – 1994 – 2mf – $8.00 – us Microform Publ [612]
FAMILIAR ARCHITECTURE / Rawlins, Thomas – Printed for the Author, 1768. SEM35P78 – 1r – 1 – Can$15.00 – cn Bibl Nat [720]
FAMILIAR ARCHITECTURE, CONSISTING OF ORIGINAL DESIGNS OF HOUSES FOR GENTLEMEN AND TRADESMEN... / Rawlins, Thomas – [S.l.]: printed for the Author, 1768. SEM35P78 – 1r – 1 – Can$15.00 – cn Bibl Nat [720]
FAMILIAR DIALOGUES / Bellot, James – 1586. 109p. (English Linguistics Series 1500-1800) – 9 – us UMI [400]
FAMILIAR STUDIES OF MEN AND BOOKS / Stevenson, Robert Louis – London: Chatto and Windus, 1882 – 1 roll – 1 – 1-55879-528-6 – uk Libr Preservation [420]
FAMILIARUM NATURALIUM REGNI VEGETABILIS SYNOPSES MONOGRAPHICAE / Roemer, J J – 4v. Vimariae. 1846-47. B-5686 2 – 8 – ne IDC [580]
DIE FAMILIE DER HELICINIDAE / Wagner, A – Z 162 2. 1911 – 8 – ne IDC [590]
DIE FAMILIE MENDELSSOHN 1729-1847 / Hensel, Sebastian – Berlin. 1879. 3 v – 1 – 23.00 – us L of C Photodup [780]
FAMILIEN-JOURNAL – New York. N.Y. 1911-12 – 1 – us A.J.P.C. [306]
FAMILIEN-KALENDER – 1871-1940 (complete) – 4r – 1 – ATLA 1994-S004 – us A.T.L.A. [073]
FAMILIES : CELEBRATION AND HOPE IN A WORLD OF CHANGE / Boyden, Jo – 1993 – 176p – 9 – 92-3-102873-1 – Co-published with Gaia Books Ltd – fr UNESCO [306]
THE FAMILIES AND GENERA OF BATS / Miller, G S – 2429 2. 1907 – 8 – ne IDC [590]
FAMILIES AND GENERA OF LIVING RODENTS / Ellerman, J R – 2395 2. 3 v. 1940-1949 – 8 – ne IDC [590]
FAMILIES IN SOCIETY – (Cont: Social Casework) – Milwaukee. v71-78. 1990-97+ – 1,5,9 – D984.01 – us UMI [360]
FAMILIES OF THE PILGRIMS / Warren, Richard – Item B. 11p. SW16-0130 – 5 – us A.G.L.L. [920]
FAMILIES OF THE WYOMING VALLEY / Kulp, George B – Sketches of the Bench and Bar. Wilkes-Barre, 1885. Vols. 1-3, Pennsylvania Reel 5. (The Cox Library Collection) – 5 – us Americana [978]
FAMILJETIDNINGEN SMALAENNINGEN – Stockholm, Sweden. 1925 – 1 – sw Kungliga [072]
LA FAMILLE : REVUE – Joliette, Canada. 1 jan 1891-10 jan 1892; no unique 1893 – 1r – 1 – Can$35.00 – cn Can Microfilming [640]
LA FAMILLE – Paris: N Chaix, may 6-jun 17 1848 – us Res Libr [072]
FAMILLE ALEXIS REAU : PETITES NOTES BIOGRAPHIQUES ET GENEALOGIQUES / Marguerite-Marie, Soeur OSU – Les Trois-Rivieres: Imp. le Bien public, 1923. SEM105P1830 – 1mf – 9 – Can$2.25 – cn Bibl Nat [920]
LA FAMILLE BONAPARTE DEVANT LE TRIBUNAL DU PEUPLE – Paris, 1848 – us Res Libr [944]
LA FAMILLE CHRETIENNE – Masson [Quebec]: Jeanne d'Arc, [1898-1902] – 9 – cn C.I.H.M. [240]
LA FAMILLE COUSINEAU / Girouard, Desire – s.l., s.n., 1884?. 03438. (Pre-1900 Canadiana) – 9 – cn C.I.H.M. [971]
LA FAMILLE DE SALABERRY – 18–. SEM105P654 – 1mf – 9 – Can$2.25 – cn Bibl Nat [920]
LA FAMILLE ET SES TRADITIONS / Brunet, Louis Alexandre – Montreal: Senecal, 1881. 00297. (Pre-1900 Canadiana) – 9 – cn C.I.H.M. [306]
LA FAMILLE GIROUARD / Girouard, Desire – (s.l.: s.n., 1884?. 03439. (Pre-1900 Canadiana) – 9 – cn C.I.H.M. [920]
LA FAMILLE JANELLE : HISTOIRE ET GENEALOGIE / Janelle, Joseph-Emile – Drummondville: "La Parole", limite, imprimeurs-editeurs, 1928. SEM105P1838 – 5mf – 9 – Can$11.25 – cn Bibl Nat [920]
Famille Joseph *see* DOCUMENTS GRATZ AND JOSEPH
LA FAMILLE KERDALEC AU SOUDAN : ESSAI DE VULGARISATION COLONIALE / Decourt, Fernand – Paris: Vuibert, [1910] – 1 – us Res Libr [306]
Famille Miller *see* DOCUMENTS DE SOLA
FAMILLE QUEBEC – Montreal, Canada. v1 n4. jan 1973 – 1r – 1 – $20.00 – cn Can Microfilming [640]
FAMILLE SANS NOM / Verne, Jules – Paris: J. Hetzel, 1889. 2v. 8 fiches. (Literature Collection) – 9 – 20.00 – fr Bibl Nationale [830]
LA FAMILLE SIRVEN / Dupetit-Mere, Frederic – ou Voltaire a Castres. Melodrame. Paris. Quoy. 1820 – 9 – fr Hachette [410]
FAMILLES DES PLANTES / Adanson, Michel – 1763 – 5 – uk Microform Academic [580]
FAMILLES DES PLANTES / Adanson, Michel – 2v. Paris. 1763. B-4 2 – 8 – ne IDC [580]
LES FAMILLES ROYALES ACTUELLES EN EUROPE : COMPLEMENT AU PROGRAMME D'HISTOIRE DU COURS SECONDAIRE / St-Nom-de-Jesus, Soeur – 1962. SEM105P4 – 1mf – 9 – cn Bibl Nat [920]
FAMILY ADVOCATE – Chicago. v1-12. 1978-89* 1; v13-20 1990-98+ 1,5,9 – 1,5,9 – D17376 – us UMI [360]
FAMILY ADVOCATE – v1-18. 1978-96 – 9 – $238.00 set – us Hein [640]
FAMILY ALMANAC – 1871-1955 (complete) – 3r – 1 – ATLA 1993-S002 – us A.T.L.A. [073]
FAMILY AND CHILD MENTAL HEALTH JOURNAL : JOURNAL OF THE JEWISH BOARD OF FAMILY AND CHILDREN'S SERVICES – (Cont: Issues in Child Mental Health) – New York. v6-7. spr 1980-win 1981 1,5,9; v7 spr-win 1981* 5 – 1,5,9 – D11188.02 – us UMI [613]
FAMILY AND COMMUNITY HEALTH – Gaithersburg. v1-20. apr 1978-jan 1998+ – 1,5,9 – D12730 – us UMI [073]
FAMILY AND CONCILIATION COURTS REVIEW – (Cont: Conciliation Courts Review) – Los Angeles. v27-31. 1989-93* 1; v32 1994*. v33-35 1995-97+ 1,5,9 – 1,5,9 – D21524.02 – us UMI [360]
FAMILY AND CONSUMER SCIENCES RESEARCH JOURNAL – (Cont: Home Economics Research Journal) – Thousand Oaks. v23-26. sep 1994-jun 1998+ – 1,5,9 – D10308.01 – us UMI [640]
THE FAMILY AND HEIRS OF SIR FRANCIS DRAKE / Fuller-Eliott-Drake, Elizabeth Douglas – London: Smith, Elder 1911. 2v. Illus. Plates, maps, geneal. table. With: Antiquities from San Tome and Mylapore by H. Hosten. 1 reel. 1263 – 1 – us U.W. Library [920]
FAMILY AND HOME OFFICE COMPUTING – (Cont: Family Computing. Cont by: Home Office Computing) – New York. v5-6. oct 1987-aug 1988 – 1,5,9 – D13402.01 – us UMI [000]
FAMILY AND HOME OFFICE COMPUTING *see* FAMILY COMPUTING
FAMILY BUDGET SURVEY IN TRIPOLI TOWN / Libya. Ministry of National Economy – S. W. Dajani. 1962. BNE-615 1 – 9 – ne IDC [339]
FAMILY BUSINESS REVIEW – San Francisco. v1-10. 1988-97+ 1,5,9; v1-7. 1988-94* 5 – 1,5,9 – D17615 – us UMI [073]
FAMILY CIRCLE – (Former titles: Family Circle, 1932-may 1958. Everywoman's Family Circle, jun 1958-dec 1962) – New York. 1932-73* 1; v84-110. 1974-97+ 1,5,9; v92-96. 1979-83* 5 – 1,5,9 – D60014 – us UMI [073]
THE FAMILY CIRCLE – London, Ont: J T Latimer, [187-?-188- or 19–] – 9 – cn C.I.H.M. [640]
FAMILY COMPUTING – (Cont by: Family and Home Office Computing) – New York. v1-5. 1983-87 – 1,5,9 – D13402 – us UMI [000]
FAMILY COMPUTING *see* FAMILY AND HOME OFFICE COMPUTING
FAMILY COOK AND HOME JOURNAL – London, UK. Dec 1906 – 9ft – 1 – uk British Libr Newspaper [640]
FAMILY COORDINATOR – (Cont by: Family Relations. Former titles: Coordinator, 1952-jun 1959. Family Life Coordinator, 1959-67) – Minneapolis. v1-28. 1952-79 1; v17-28. 1968-79 5; v25-28. 1976-79 9 – 1,5,9 – D3492 – us UMI [640]
FAMILY COORDINATOR *see* FAMILY RELATIONS
FAMILY CORRESPONDENCE / Ward, Allen T – 1828-1964, Letters of a Methodist Indian missionary in Kansas, 1828-1928, 1928-1964 (2 copies) – 1 – us KS Hist [920]
FAMILY DIGEST – v1-30. oct 1945-jun 1975 1; v26-28. oct 1970-sep 1973 5 – 1,5 – D2446 – us UMI [073]
FAMILY ECONOMICS AND NUTRITION REVIEW – (Cont: Family Economics Review) – Washington. v8-10. 1995-97+ – 1,5,9 – D6947.01 – us UMI [640]
FAMILY ECONOMICS AND NUTRITION REVIEW *see* FAMILY ECONOMICS REVIEW
FAMILY ECONOMICS REVIEW – (Cont by: Family Economics and Nutrition Review) – Washington. 1957-95 1; 1976-1995 5,9 – 1,5,9 – D6947 – us UMI [640]
FAMILY ECONOMICS REVIEW *see* FAMILY ECONOMICS AND NUTRITION REVIEW
FAMILY EXPENDITURE SURVEY 1957/59-1977 – (Coll title: British Government Publications... 1801-1977, Health and Public Welfare) – 31mf – 9 (£1,080.00 health and public welfare set of 171mf) – uk Chadwyck [339]
FAMILY FAVORITE AND TEMPERANCE JOURNAL – Adrian. v1. dec 1849-sep 1850 – 1 – D3981 – us UMI [073]
A FAMILY FLIGHT OVER EGYPT AND SYRIA / Hale, Edward Everett – Boston: D. Lothrop and company, c1882.387p. front., plates – 1 – us U.W. Library [910]
FAMILY GUIDE = GUIDE DE LA FAMILLE – Sherbrooke, Canada. v1 n13. mar 1961 – 1r – 1 – Can$20.00 – cn Can Microfilming [072]
FAMILY HANDYMAN – (Absorbed: Home Garden's Natural Gardening Magazine) – Minneapolis. v1-25 1951-75*. v26-47 1976-97+ 1,5; v26-48 1976-98+ 9 – 1,5,9 – D10998 – us UMI [640]
FAMILY HEALTH – (Cont by: Health. Absorbed: Today's Health, apr 1976) – New York. v1-13. 1969-81 1; v7-13. 1975-81 5; v3-13. 1971-81 9 – 1,5,9 – D10761 – us UMI [613]
FAMILY HEALTH *see* HEALTH
FAMILY HERALD – London. v1-67. May 1843-Oct 1891. Incomplete – 1 – us NY Public [640]
FAMILY HERALD – Montreal, 1859-1968 – 224r – 1 – cn Preston [971]
THE FAMILY HERALD – London. v1-67. 1843-90 – 17r – 1 – us Ross [072]
THE FAMILY HERALD – New York. v1-6. 1858-62 – 17r – 1 – us Ross [071]
THE FAMILY HERALD – New York. Weekly. Jan 6 1858-Nov 20 1862. Incomplete. Not collated – 1 – us NY Public [640]
FAMILY HERALD AND WEEKLY STAR : AMERICAN EDITION – Montreal. v11 n44. 28 oct 1880; v- n-. 7 jan 1885 – 1r – 1 – Can$25.00 – cn Can Microfilming [072]
FAMILY HERALD & WEEKLY STAR – Montreal, Canada. -w. Nov 1903-March 1915. 5 1 2 reels – 1 – uk British Libr Newspaper [072]
FAMILY HISTORY – Canterbury. v1-7 1962-73*. v8-20 aug 1973-1997+ 1; v8 aug 1973-dec 1974*. v10 jul 1977-nov 1979. v11-17 1980-jul 1995*. v18-20 1995-97+ 5; v8 aug 1973-dec 1974. v10-20 jul 1977-97+ 9 – 1,5,9 – D3378 – us UMI [920]
FAMILY, HOUSEHOLD AND GENDER RELATIONS IN LATIN AMERICA / ed by Jelin, Elizabeth – 1991 – 9 – 92-3-102657-7 – Co-published with Kegan Paul International Ltd, London – fr UNESCO [301]
FAMILY LAW NEWSLETTER (ABA) – v1-18. 1960-78 (all publ) – 9 – us Hein [340]
FAMILY LAW QUARTERLY (ABA) – (v1-18 1967-85 on reel $229.00. v19-29 1985-96 on mf $297.00. Supersedes: American Bar Association. Section of Family Law) – v1-29. 1967-96 – 5,6,9 – $526.00 set – us Hein [340]
FAMILY LIFE – v1- 1968- 1; v7- 5,6; v9- 9 – us UMI [306]
FAMILY LIFE COORDINATOR *see* FAMILY COORDINATOR
THE FAMILY LIFE OF HEINRICH HEINE : ILLUSTRATED BY ONE HUNDRED AND TWENTY-TWO HITHERTO UNPUBLISHED LETTERS ADDRESSED BY HIM TO DIFFERENT MEMBERS OF HIS FAMILY / ed by Embden, Ludwig von – London: W Heinemann, 1896 – 1 – us U.W. Library [920]
THE FAMILY MINSTREL – v. 1. no. 1, 5-9. 1835 – 9 – us Sibley [780]
FAMILY MIRROR – Dar es Salaam: General Publications Ltd, feb 1 1991; feb 15-sep 1 1992; nov-dec 1992; jan-oct 1 1993; nov-dec 1993; jan-dec 1994; jan-nov 21/30 1995; dec 21/31 1995 – 2r – us Res Libr [072]
FAMILY NAMES OF HUGUENOT REFUGEES TO AMERICA – By Mrs. James M. Lawton.Item Q. 20p. SW16-0080 – 5 – us A.G.L.L. [920]
FAMILY PAPERS – 1906-1962 – 1 – us Res Libr [920]
FAMILY PAPERS / Ball, Elias, 14th – 1631-1920. 52 fiches – 9 – us South Carolina Historical [920]
FAMILY PAPERS / Banvard, John – 1752-1985. 2 rolls including filmed inventory – 1 – $30.00r – us M.H.S. [920]
FAMILY PAPERS / Bartlett, Josiah – 1713-1931 – 1 – 362.00 – us L of C Photodup [920]
FAMILY PAPERS / Reid, Whitelaw – (in part). 1829-1912 – 1 – 4,965.00 – us L of C Photodup [920]
FAMILY PAPERS / Rivers, Elias – 1827-1913. 3 fiches – 9 – us South Carolina Historical [025]
THE FAMILY PAPERS OF JAMES G. BLAINE – 21r – 1 – $735.00 – Dist. us Scholarly Res – us L of C Photodup [975]
FAMILY PHYSICIAN *see* AMERICAN FAMILY PHYSICIAN
THE FAMILY PHYSICIAN, OR, EVERY MAN HIS OWN DOCTOR – An encyclopedia of medicine, containing knowledge that will promote health, cure disease and prolong life, describing all diseases...Compiled by leading Canadian medical men. Toronto: Rose, 1889. 02946. (Pre-1900 Canadiana) – 9 – cn C.I.H.M. [971]
FAMILY PLANNING PERSPECTIVES – (With cum index for v1-2 1) – New York. v1-29. 1969-97+ 1; v4-29. 1972-97+ 5; v7-29. 1975-97+ 9 – 1,5,9 – D6785 – us UMI [360]
FAMILY PLANNING/POPULATION REPORTER – New York. v1-10. dec 1972-jun 81* – 1 – D12678 – us UMI [360]
FAMILY PRACTICE – Oxford. v1-5. 1984-88* 1; v6-14. 1989-97+ 1,5,9 – 1,5,9 – D14050 – us UMI [073]
FAMILY PRACTICE MANAGEMENT – Kansas City. 1994*. 1995-97+ – 1,5,9 – D21792 – us UMI [073]
FAMILY PRACTICE NEWS – New York. v1-11 1971-81. v12-24 1982-94*. v25-27 1995-97+ – 1 – D6868 – us UMI [073]
THE FAMILY PRACTICE OF PHYSIC / Hill, John – London, 1769 – 1 – us U.W. Library [610]
FAMILY PRACTICE RESEARCH JOURNAL – New York. v1-2. fal 1981-sum 1983* 1; v3-14. fal 1983-dec 1994 1,5,9 – 1,5,9 – D14130 – us UMI [073]
FAMILY PROCESS – (With cum indexes for v1-10 1) – New York. v1-11. 1962-72 1; v12-36 1973-97+ 1,5,9 – 1,5,9 – D9860 – us UMI [073]
FAMILY RECORDS: EARLY LYON COUNTY SETTLERS / Kansas State Historical Society – ca1911 – 1 – us KS Hist [978]
FAMILY RELATIONS – (Cont: Family Coordinator) – Minneapolis. v29-46. 1980-97+ – 1,5,9 – D3492.01 – us UMI [306]
FAMILY RELATIONS *see* FAMILY COORDINATOR
FAMILY REUNION MINUTE BOOKS / Koehler Family – 1916-1992 – 1r – 1 – $32.50r – us Archival [920]
FAMILY REUNION MINUTES / Bucher Family – 1928-1976 – 1r – 1 – $32.50r – us Archival [978]

FAMILY SAFETY – (Cont by: Family Safety and Health. Former title: Home Safety Review) – Chicago. v1-42. dec 1942-win 1984 1; v34-42. spr 1975-win 1984 5; v35 spr 1976-win 1977*. v36-42 spr 1977-win 1984 9 – 1,5,9 – D10610 – us UMI [613]
FAMILY SAFETY *see* FAMILY SAFETY AND HEALTH
FAMILY SAFETY AND HEALTH – (Cont: Family Safety) – Chicago. v43-56. spr 1984-win 1998+ 1,5,9; v46-53. spr 1987-win 1995* 5 – 1,5,9 – D10610.01 – us UMI [613]
FAMILY SAFETY AND HEALTH *see* FAMILY SAFETY
FAMILY STRUCTURE IN 17TH-CENTURY WINDSOR, CONNECTICUT / Holbrook, Jay Mack – (An argument illustrating the possibility of a modified-extended family structure in a pre-industrial community through an analysis of mortality, migration and fertility data) – (mf ed 1990) – 1mf – 9 – 0-87623-121-0 – us Holbrook [978]
A FAMILY SYSTEMS ANALYSIS OF ANXIETY, DEPRESSION, AND SOMATIZATION IN GRADUATE NURSING STUDENTS / Kleeman, Karen M – 1983 – 3mf – 9 – $12.00 – us Microform Publ [150]
FAMILY SYSTEMS MEDICINE – New York. v1-15. 1983-97+ 1,5,9; v10-12. 1992-94* 5 – 1,5,9 – D13361 – us UMI [616]
FAMILY THERAPY – San Diego. v1-24. 1972-97+ 1,5,9; v11-21. 1984-94* 5 – 1,5,9 – D10972 – us UMI [150]
FAMILY VIOLENCE SLIM / U.S. National Institute of Justice – 1985. 151 documents – 9 – $120.00 – us N.C.J.R.S. [360]
THE FAMILY VISITOR – Hudson. Ohio. -w. 1850-53 – 1 – us UMI [640]
FAMILY WEEKLY – (Cont by: USA Weekend) – sep 1953-dec 1980. jan 1981-sep 1985* – 1 – D6494 – us UMI [073]
Famin, N P *see* CARMEN PACIS
THE FAMINE IN SOVIET RUSSIA / Fisher, Harold H – 1919-23. The operations of the American Relief Administration. 1935. 609p – 1 – 35.00r – us Hoover Inst Photo [947]
Famintsyn, A S *see* SKOMOROKHI NA RUSI
FAMIRA-KIFARED. VAKKHICHESKAIA DRAMA / Annenskii, I F – Posthumous ed. M. 1913. BR-501 2 – 8 – ne IDC [460]
FAMIRA-KIFARED. VAKKHICHESKAIA DRAMA / Annenskii, I F – Spb. 1919. BR-502 2 – 8 – ne IDC [460]
O FAMOSO BOTAO DE ANCORA (1600-1895) / Marques Esparteiro, Antonio – Madrid: Archivo Ibero Americano, 1960 – 1 – sp Bibl Santa Ana [946]
FAMOSSISIMOS ROMANCES / Cepeda, Joaquin – S.L. s.i..s.a. – 1 – sp Bibl Santa Ana [946]
A FAMOUS DUTCH WRITER DENOUNCES REBEL ATROCITIES / Brouwer, Johannes – n.p. 193? Fiche W 766. (Blodgett Collection of Spanish Civil War Pamphlets) – 9 – us H.U. College Libr [946]
FAMOUS FANTASTIC MYSTERIES – New York. mar 1943-jun 1953* – 1 – D8288 – us UMI [073]
FAMOUS FIRESIDES OF FRENCH CANADA / Alloway, Mary Wilson – s.l., s.n. 1899. 00040. (Pre-1900 Canadiana) – 9 – cn C.I.H.M. [971]
FAMOUS INDIANS : A COLLECTION OF SHORT BIOGRAPHIES / U.S. Bureau of Indian Affairs – 1966 – 9 – $5.00f – us Ross [970]
FAMOUS LUTE AND GUITAR BOOKS BETWEEN 1500 AND 1800 – 70mf – 9 – MS-a – ne IDC [780]
FAMOUS MEN OF THE OLD TESTAMENT / Wharton, Morton Bryan – Chicago: W.P. Blessing, 1903. 1 fiche – 9 – us A.T.L.A. [240]
FAMOUS MISSIONARIES OF THE REFORMED CHURCH / Good, James I – [S.l.]: Sunday-School Board of the Reformed Church in the United States, 1903 – 1mf – us A.T.L.A. [240]
FAMOUS MODERN BATTLES / Atteridge, Andrew Hilliard – With maps and plans drawn by the author.Boston: Small, Maynard and Co., c1913. viii, 401p – 1 – us U.W. Library [940]
FAMOUS PLACES OF THE REFORMED CHURCHES : A RELIGIOUS GUIDEBOOK TO EUROPE / Good, James Isaac – Philadelphia: Heidelborg Press, 1910 – 2mf – 9 – 0-8370-8673-6 – 1986-2673 – us A.T.L.A. [240]
FAMOUS WOMEN OF HISTORY: CONTAINING NEARLY THREE THOUSAND BRIEF BIOGRAPHIES AND OVER ONE THOUSAND FEMALE PSEUDONYMS / Browne, William Hardcastle – 1895 – 9 – us A.T.L.A. [920]
FAMOUS WOMEN OF THE NEW TESTAMENT: A SERIES OF POPULAR LECTURES / Wharton, Morton Bryan – New York: E.B. Treat, 1890. 1 fiche – 9 – us A.T.L.A. [240]
Fan, I *see* CHINA'S DIAMONDS IN THE ROUGH (CCC123)
FANAL : ANARCHISTISCHE MONATSSCHRIFT – Berlin. v1-5. 1926-31 – 1 – us Ross [320]
FANAL – Berlin. oct 1926-jul 1931 – 1r – 1 – gw Mikrofilm [073]
FANAL – Berlin. v. 1-5. 1926-1931 – 1 – us NY Public [073]
FANAL – Cidade do Pomba, 18 Aug 1895 – 1,5,6 – bl Biblioteca [072]
FANAL – Curitiba, 14 May 1911-Dec 1913 – 1,5,6 – bl Biblioteca [072]
LE FANAL : HUMORISTIQUE – Montreal, Canada. 24 mai-7 jun 1879 – 1r – 1 – Can$25.00 – cn Can Microfilming [072]
O FANAL – Maceio, Alagoas. 17 Dez 1900 – 1,5,6 – bl Biblioteca [072]
FANATICAL CONVERSION : OR, METHODISM DISPLAYED: A SATIRE ILLUSTRATED AND VERIFIED BY NOTES FROM J. WESLEY'S FANATICAL JOURNALS AND BY THE AUTHOR,... / Combe, W – London, 1779 – 1mf – 9 – MP-535/1 – ne IDC [870]
FANATICISM. BY THE AUTHOR OF NATURAL HISTORY OF ENTHUSIASM / Taylor, Isaac – Boston: Crocker & Brewster, 1834 – 1 – us U.W. Library [240]
LE FANATISME, OU MAHOMET LE PROPHETE : TRAGEDIE... / Voltaire, Francois-Marie Arouet de – (Microf. avec Mahomet: tragedie... Nouv. ed. Bruxelles:[s.n.], 1778) – Nouv. ed. Paris: Cie des Libraires associes, 1771 – 1 – F59.77 – fr Armell [820]
FAN-CARDINAL / Otterbein College – Westerville. Ohio. 1918-69 – 1 – us UMI [370]
Fancher, Issac A *see* PAST AND PRESENT OF ISABELLA COUNTY
FANCHON LA VIELLEUSE / Bouilly, Jean Nicolas – French Theatre Series. Paris. Barba, an XI. 1803 – 9 – fr Hachette [820]
FANCISCI IUNII BITURIGIS : OPERA THEOLOGICA TOMUS 1 EN 2 – 1608 – 93mf – 8 – ne Slangenburg [290]
Fancourt, Charles Saint John *see* THE HISTORY OF YUCATAN, FROM ITS DISCOVERY TO THE CLOSE OF THE SEVENTEENTH CENTURY
FANDROSOAM BAOVAO *see* NY FANDROSOAM-BAOVAO
Fane, Cecil *see* NEWFOUNDLAND
Fane, Violet *see* DENZIL PLACE
FANEUIL PAPERS – 1979 – 1r – 1 – $30.00 – us New England [920]
DIE FANFARE – Berlin, 1924-25 n42 – 1r – 1 – Dist. gw Mikrofilm – gw Misc Inst [072]
DIE FANFARE – Berlin, 1932-jan 1933 – 1r – 1 – Dist. gw Mikrofilm – gw Misc Inst [072]
DIE FANFARE : GEDICHTE DER DEUTSCHEN ERHEBUNG / Anacker, Heinrich – Muenchen: Zentralverlag der NSDAP, F Eher, 1936 – 1r – 1 – us U.W. Library [810]
FANFARE – Goettingen. nov 1, 1931-mar 23, 1933 (incomplete) – 1r – 1 – gw Mikrofilm [072]
DIE FANFARE IM PARISER EINZUGSMARSCH : EINE PREUSSISCHE NOVELLE / Welk, Ehm – Berlin: Im Deutschen Verlag, c1942 – 1r – 1 – us U.W. Library [830]
FANFULLA – Sao Paulo, Brazil. 1893-95; 1911; 1914-15; 1921-30 – 1 – bl Biblioteca [072]
Fang, J *see* PREDICTION OF THE WORLD MEN'S BEST PERFORMANCES IN HIGH JUMP AND LONG JUMB BY THE TOP AVERAGE PERFORMANCE
FANGST, JAKT OCH FISKE – 1955 – 1 – us I.U. Libraries [390]
FANGYAN – (Dialect). In Chinese but Table of Contents in English in each issue. F p23 – 9 – $4.50f – cc Microforms [800]
FANGZHI XUEBAO – Journal of China Textile Engineering Association. In Chinese, with English abstracts of the main articles. p141 – 9 – $4.50f – cc Microforms [740]
FANNIE LOU HAMER PAPERS, 1917-77 / Hamer, Fannie Lou – 1 – $435.00 – us Amistad [920]
FANNY KELLEY V. SARAH L. LARIMER, ET AL / Kelley, Fanny – 1869-77 – 1 – us KS Hist [978]
Fanshawe, Anne Harrison *see* MEMOIRS.
Fanshawe, Evelyn Leighton *see* LIQUOR LEGISLATION IN THE UNITED STATES AND CANADA: REPORT OF A NON-PARTISAN INQUIRY ON THE SPOT INTO THE LAWS AND THEIR OPERATION
FANTAISIE POUR FLUTE ET PIANO SUR L'AIR / Farrenc, A – Paris; Frey, 182? – 1 – us Sibley [780]
LA FANTASIA EN !SONETOS! / Sanchez-Arjona, Vicente – Sevilla: Imp. Alvarez, Tomo 1. 1955 – 1 – sp Bibl Santa Ana [810]
LA FANTASIA EN...!SONETOS! / Sanchez-Arjona, Vicente – Sevilla: Imp. Alvarez, Tomo 2. 1955 – 1 – sp Bibl Santa Ana [810]
LA FANTASIA EN...!SONETOS! / Sanchez-Arjona, Vicente – Sevilla: Imp. Alvarez, Tomo 3. 1955 – 1 – sp Bibl Santa Ana [810]
LA FANTASIA EN...!SONETOS! / Sanchez-Arjona, Vicente – Sevilla: Imp. Alvarez, Tomo 4. 1955 – 1 – sp Bibl Santa Ana [810]
FANTASIA, PIANO, OP. 16, E MAJOR / Mendelssohn, Felix – (Holograph) – Vienna: C A Spira – 1 – us Sibley [780]
FANTASIE AND FUGE, HARPSICHORD, S. 906 IN C MINOR / Bach, Johann Sebastian – Leipsic, Bureau de musique: Vienne, Hoffmeister et Kuhnel, 1802 – 1 – us Sibley [780]
FANTASIE AVEC NEUF VARIATIONS SUR UN AIR DES MISTERES D'ISIS:POUR LE PIANOFORTE... / Steibelt, Daniel – Paris: Erard, [181-?] – 1 – us Sibley [780]
FANTASIE, DEUXIEME, POUR PIANO ET COR OU VIOLON / Duvernoy, F – (Score and violin part) – Paris: J J de Momigney, 182- – 1 – us Sibley [780]
FANTASIE POUR FLUTE AVEC ACCOMPAGNEMENT DE PIANO... OP. 29... / Tulou, J L – Paris: I Pleyel & Fils aine, [182-] – 1 – us Sibley [780]
FANTASIE, QUATRIEME, POUR LE PIANO, COR OU VIOLON / Duvernoy, F – (Score and Violin part) – Paris: Erard, 182- – 1 – us Sibley [780]
FANTASIE, TROISIEME, POUR PIANO, COR OU VIOLON / Duvernoy, F – (Score and violin part) – Paris: Erard, 182- – 1 – us Sibley [780]
FANTASIES OF 3 PARTES- – (Collection of unrecorded instrumental fantasies by Orlando Gibbons, Jenkins, Facio, John Wythie) – 17th C English ms – us Sibley [780]
LE FANTASQUE / ed by Aubin, Napoleon – Quebec, Canada. 1 aut 1837-24 fev 1849 – 2r – 1 – Can$40.00r – cn Can Microfilming [072]
LE FANTASQUE – Ottawa, Ontario. 23 oct 1879-22 nov 1879 – 1r – 1 – Can$30.00 – cn Can Microfilming [072]
LE FANTASQUE – Quebec: O Cote, Proulx, 1857-1858 – 9 – cn C.I.H.M. [971]
FANTASTIC ADVENTURES – v1-7. 1939-45 – 7r – 1 – $545.00 – us UPA [830]
FANTASTIC NOVELS – New York. mar 1948-jun 1951* – 1 – D8291 – us UMI [830]
FANTASTIC STORIES – Series 1, v8-15. Feb 1946-Mar 1953. Series 2, v2, no. 3-v24. May-Jun 1953-Oct 1975. (Science Fiction Periodicals, Series 2) – 25r – 1 – $2,310.00 – us UPA [830]
FANTASY AND SCIENCE FICTION – (Cum index available from the New England Science Fiction Association. Cont: Magazine of Fantasy and Science Fiction) – West Cornwall. v73-93. oct 1987-dec 1997+ – 1,5,9 – D6119.01 – us UMI [830]
FANTI CONFEDERATION / A RECONSIDERATION / Brown, James W – Brighton, 1967 – us Res Libr [320]
FANTI LAW REPORT OF DECIDED CASES ON FANTI CUSTOMARY LAWS : SECOND SELECTION / Sarbah, John Mensah – London: W Clowes, 1904 – us Res Libr [340]
Fanua, Tupou Posesi *see* PAPERS, 1959-1992
F.A.O. *see*
– DICTIONARIES AND VOCABULARIES 1966-1981 IN THE TERMINOLOGY AND REFERENCE LIBRARY
– DICTIONARIES AND VOCABULARIES 1982-1985 IN THE TERMINOLOGY AND REFERENCE LIBRARY
– PUBLICATIONS CATALOGUE
FAO AGRICULTURAL COMMODITY PROJECTIONS TO 1990 – 1989 – 215p – it F.A.O. [338]
FAO AGRICULTURAL PRODUCTION INDEX – 1986 – 72p – it F.A.O. [338]
FAO COMMODITY REVIEW AND OUTLOOK – it F.A.O. [338]
FAO CONFERENCE REPORTS – it F.A.O. [060]
FAO PLANT PROTECTION BULLETIN – (The publisher has requested that only 1954-57, 1960-61, 1963 and 1965-67 be filmed and sold. Former title: Plant Protection Bulletin, oct 1952) – Rome. v2-15. 1954-67 – 1 – D8758 – us UMI [631]
FAO PRINCIPLES OF SURPLUS DISPOSAL AND CONSULTATIVE OBLIGATIONS OF MEMBER NATIONS – 1972 2nd ed 1980 – 83p – it F.A.O. [350]
FAO PROCESSED STATISTICS SERIES – it F.A.O. [310]
FAO PRODUCTION YEARBOOK – it F.A.O. [338]
FAO REGIONAL CONFERENCE FOR AFRICA : REPORT OF THE 16TH SESSION; MARRAKECH, MOROCCO, 1990 – 1990 – 57p – it F.A.O. [630]
FAO REGIONAL CONFERENCE FOR AFRICA : REPORT OF THE 17TH SESSION; ACCRA, 1992 – 1992 – 63p – it F.A.O. [630]
FAO REGIONAL CONFERENCE FOR ASIA AND THE PACIFIC : REPORT OF THE 21ST SESSION; NEW DELHI, 1992 – 1992 – 65p – it F.A.O. [630]
FAO REGIONAL CONFERENCE FOR EUROPE : REPORT OF THE 18TH SESSION; PRAGUE, 1992 – 1992 – 59p – it F.A.O. [630]
FAO REGIONAL CONFERENCE FOR LATIN AMERICA AND THE CARIBBEAN : REPORT OF THE 22ND SESSION; MONTEVIDEO, 1992 – 1992 – 55p – it F.A.O. [630]
FAO REGIONAL CONFERENCE FOR THE NEAR EAST : REPORT OF THE 21ST SESSION; TEHERAN, 1992 – 1992 – 63p – it F.A.O. [630]
FAO REGIONAL CONFERENCE FOR THE NEAR EAST (1981, ROME) – 1981 – 54p – it F.A.O. [630]
FAO RICE REPORT – it F.A.O. [631]
FAO RURAL ORGANIZATIONS ACTION PROGRAMME (ROAP) : RESEARCH GUIDELINES FOR FIELD ACTION PROJECTS TO PROMOTE PARTICIPATION OF THE POOR IN RURAL ORGANIZATIONS – 1979 – 63p – it F.A.O. [060]
FAO SEED REVIEW 1979-1980. AGP/SIDP/81/7, 1981 – 1981 – 225p – it F.A.O. [631]
FAO SPECIES CATALOGUE – it F.A.O. [590]
FAO SPECIES IDENTIFICATION SHEETS FOR FISHERY PURPOSES : FIELD GUIDE TO THE COMMERCIAL MARINE RESOURCES OF THE GULF OF GUINEA – 1990 – 280p – it F.A.O. [333]
FAO SPECIES IDENTIFICATION SHEETS FOR FISHERY PURPOSES : FIELD GUIDE TO THE FRESHWATER FISHES OF TANZANIA – 1992 – 150p – it F.A.O. [590]
FAO SPECIES INDENTIFICATION SHEETS FOR FISHERY PURPOSES : SOUTHERN OCEAN. CCAMLR CONVENTION AREA. FISHING AREAS 48, 58, AND 88 / Fischer, W & Hureau, J C – 1985 – it F.A.O. [639]
FAO STATISTICAL DEVELOPMENT SERIES – it F.A.O. [310]
FAO STUDIES IN AGRICULTURAL ECONOMICS AND STATISTICS 1952-1977 – 1978 – 442p – it F.A.O. [330]
FAO STUDIES IN FOOD AND POPULATION – 1976 – 227p – it F.A.O. [338]
FAO TRADE YEARBOOK – it F.A.O. [380]
FAO WATERSHED MANAGEMENT FIELD MANUA : GULLY CONTROL – 1986 – 63p – it F.A.O. [631]
FAO WATERSHED MANAGEMENT FIELD MANUAL : VEGETATIVE AND SOIL TREATMENT MEASURES – 1985 – 70p – it F.A.O. [631]
FAO/ISRIC SOIL DATABASE (SDB) – 1990 – 94p – it F.A.O. [631]
FAO/UNESCO : SOIL MAP OF THE WORLD: REVISED LEGEND – 1990 – 123p – it F.A.O. [631]
FAO/WHO FOOD ADDITIVES DATA SYSTEM : EVALUATIONS BY THE JOINT F.A.O./WHO EXPERT COMMITTEE ON FOOD ADDITIVES 1956-1984 – 1985 – 152p – it F.A.O. [660]
FAO/WHO FOOD ADDITIVES DATA SYSTEM : EVALUATIONS BY THE JOINT F.A.O./WHO EXPERT COMMITTEE ON FOOD ADDITIVES, 1985 – 1986 – 23p – it F.A.O. [660]

FAO/WHO FOOD ADDITIVES DATA SYSTEM : EVALUATIONS BY THE JOINT F.A.O./WHO EXPERTS COMMITTEE ON FOOD ADDITIVES, 1986, 1987, 1988 – 25p – it F.A.O. [660]
FAR : THE FRENCH-AMERICAN REVIEW – Fort Worth. v1-7. win 1976-fal 1983* – 1 – D12006 – us UMI [073]
FAR ABOVE RUBIES (CCC257) / On, Lan – (In Chinese) – 1st ed. Hong Kong: Council on Christian Literature for Overseas Chinese, 1959 – 1r – 1 – 1984-6596 – us A.T.L.A. [240]
THE FAR EAST : INTERNAL AND FOREIGN AFFAIRS, 1945-59 – (1945-49: 21r $2,505.00 ISBN 1-55655-314-5; 1950-54: 26r $3,100.00 ISBN 1-55655-315-3; 1955-59: 30r $3,570.00 ISBN 1-55655-316-1) – Series: Confidential US State Department Central Files. With printed guides – 1 – $8,710.00 set – us UPA [950]
FAR EAST REPORTER – Houston. 1977-79 1; mar-sep 1977*. feb-dec 1978. 1979* 5; 1977-79* 9 – 1,5,9 – D9294 – us UMI [950]
FAR EAST TRADE DEVELOPMENT – 1945-87.Continued annually – 1 – uk World [380]
FAR EAST VIEWS / U.S. Library of Congress. Prints and Photographs Division – six albums of travel views by major commercial studios active in the Orient in the 1870's and 1880's. 1 reel. P&P6615-6620 – 1 – 23.00r – us L of C Photodup [080]
FAR EASTERN ECONOMIC REVIEW – (Backfiles 1) – Hong Kong. 1946 – 1,5 – us Primary [330]
FAR EASTERN ECONOMIC REVIEW – Hong Kong. v71-160. 1971-97+ 1; 1946-60*. v31-78 1961-72. v79-82 1973*. v83-98 1974-77. v99-102 1978*. v103-160 1979-97+ 5; v95-160. 1977-97+ 9 – 1,5,9 – D6396 – us UMI [330]
FAR EASTERN ECONOMIC REVIEW, 1947-1956 – 12r – 1 – $420.00 in US $40.00r outside – L9000001 – Dist. us Scholarly Res – us L of C Photodup [320]
FAR EASTERN ECONOMIC REVIEW INDEX ON MICROFICHE / BISA – Sydney: BISA, 1981-1984 – 9 – A$15.00y – at BISA [330]
FAR EASTERN ECONOMIC REVIEW INDEX ON MICROFICHE / Ismail, A Hamid – (Jan 1-Mar 31, 1981 (Vol 111)) – 1982 – A$10.00 – 0-86758-073-9 – at BISA [330]
FAR EASTERN LANGUAGES CATALOG / U.S. Library of Congress – 1972.-339,000 cards 22 reels.-ISBN: 0-8161-1480-3 – 1 – $2490.00 – uk Hall [480]
FAR EASTERN LAW REVIEW – (Former title: FEU Law Quarterly, jan 1953-jan 1956) – Manila. v23-24 jul 1977-mar 1979*. v25 sep 1979-mar 1980 1,5; v23-25. jul 1977-mar 1980 9 – 1,5,9 – D7993 – us UMI [340]
FAR EASTERN REVIEW – Shanghai. China. -m. Jun 1907, Mar 1919-Oct 1941. (35 reels) – 1 – uk British Libr Newspaper [072]
FAR EASTERN REVIEW – Shanghai. v1-38. jun 1904-oct 1941* – 1 – D5656 – us UMI [950]
FAR EASTERN REVIEW : ENGINEERING, COMMERCE, FINANCE – Manila: GB Rea, 1904-41. [v6, n9 feb 1910] – us Res Libr [073]
THE FAR EASTERN REVIEW, 1904-1933 – (Vol 23 no 7 is missing from this collection) – 19r – 1 – $665.00 in US $40.00r outside – L9000002 – Dist. us Scholarly Res – us L of C Photodup [330]
FAR EASTERN REVIEW. (ENGINEERING, COMMERCE AND FINANCE) – Manila, 1904-1925. v1-21 – 443mf – 9 – CH-120/2 – ne IDC [620]
FAR EASTERN SURVEY – (Cont by: Asian Survey. Former title: Institute of Pacific Relations. American Council: Memorandum, mar 3, 1932-dec 21, 1934) – New York. v19-30. 1950-feb 1961 – 1 – D300 – us UMI [950]
FAR FROM THE MADDING CROWD / Hardy, Thomas – London: Smith, Elder, 1874 – 1 roll – 1 – 1-55879-223-6 – uk Libr Preservation [830]
FAR NORTH IN INDIA : A SURVEY OF THE MISSION FIELD AND WORK OF THE UNITED PRESBYTERIAN CHURCH IN THE PUNJAB / Anderson, William B & Watson, Charles Roger – (Includes index) – Philadelphia, PA: Board of Foreign Missions of the United Presbyterian Church of North America, c1909 – 1mf – 9 – 0-8370-6002-8 – 1986-0002 – us A.T.L.A. [240]
FAR OUT: ROVINGS RETOLD / Butler, William Francis – London: W. Isbister, 1880. 00367. (Pre-1900 Canadiana) – 9 – cn C.I.H.M. [910]
FAR POINT – (Cont by: Northern Light, 1974) – Antigonish. v1-8. 1968-73 – 9 – Can$100.00 – cn Micromedia [073]
FAR POINT *see* NORTHERN LIGHT
FAR WESTERN ECONOMIE REVIEW – 1 – F1,135.00 – sz Infoprint [073]
FAR WESTERN ECONOMIE REVIEW – 1946-1947 – 1 – F1,091.00 – sz Infoprint [073]
FAR WESTERN ECONOMIE REVIEW – 1948-1960 – 1 – F1,091.00 – sz Infoprint [073]
FAR WESTERN ECONOMIE REVIEW – 1961-1993 – 1 – F1,615.00 – sz Infoprint [073]
[FAR WESTERN SLAVIC CONFERENCE AT STANFORD UNIVERSITY PAMPHLET COLLECTION] – 1963 – 1 – CSUXANR3579-B – us Hoover Inst Photo [460]
Farabeuf, Louis Hubert *see* PRECIS DE MANUEL OPERATOIRE.
FARADAY AS A DISCOVERER / Tyndall, John – London: Longmans, Green, 1868 – 1 roll – 1 – 1-55879-387-9 – uk Libr Preservation [530]
FARADAY DISCUSSIONS – (Cont: Faraday Discussions of the Chemical Society) – London. v92-104. 1991-97+ 1,5,9; v99-100. 1994-95* 5 – 1,5,9 – D7188.01 – us UMI [540]
FARADAY DISCUSSIONS *see* FARADAY DISCUSSIONS OF THE CHEMICAL SOCIETY
FARADAY DISCUSSIONS OF THE CHEMICAL SOCIETY – (Cont in pt: Journal of the Chemical Society. Cont by: Faraday Discussions. Former title: Faraday Society: Discussions of the Faraday Society, 1947-71) – London. v53-91. 1972-91 1,5; v61-91. 1976-91 9 – 1,5,9 – D7188 – us UMI [540]
FARADAY DISCUSSIONS OF THE CHEMICAL SOCIETY *see* FARADAY DISCUSSIONS
Faraday, Michael *see* A COURSE OF SIX LECTURES ON THE CHEMICAL HISTORY OF A CANDLE
FARADAY SOCIETY - DISCUSSIONS OF THE FARADAY SOCIETY *see* FARADAY DISCUSSIONS OF THE CHEMICAL SOCIETY
Faraday Society. London *see*
- DISCUSSIONS
- GENERAL DISCUSSIONS. DISCUSSIONS ON DIELECTRICS AND ON SWELLING AND SHRINKING
- SYMPOSIA
- TRANSACTIONS

FARBE UND LACK – Hannover. 1893-1969*. v76-103 1970-97+ 1; v78-80 1972-74. v82-103 1976-97+ 5; v80 1974*. v82-103 1976-97+ 9 – 1,5,9 – D5813 – us UMI [660]
Farber Lorda, J *see* ETUDES BIOLOGIQUES, ENERGETIQUES ET BIOCHIMIQUES DU KRILL ANTARCTIQUE EUPHAUSIA SUPERBA ET THYSANOESSA MACRURA, RECOLTE AU COURS DE LA CAMPAGNE FIBEX
LE FARCEUR : HUMORISTIQUE / ed by Beaugrand, Honore – Montreal, Canada. 26 oct 1878-29 mar 1884 – 1r – 1 – Can$25.00 – cn Can Microfilming [072]
Fardoulis-Vitart, A *see* LE CABINET DU ROI ET LES ANCIENS CABINETS DE CURIOSITES DANS LES COLLECTIONS DU MUSEE DE L'HOMME
FAREHAM STANDARD – Gosport, England. 28 Sept 1978-20 Dec 1979; Jan-24 Dec 1980; 8 Jan 1981-22 Jul 1982. -w.3 reels – 1 – uk British Libr Newspaper [072]
Fares, Raimundo *see* EL LLAMADO DE LAS ARMAS, 17 DE OCTUBRE DE 1945
FAREWELL TO PARADISE / Thiess, Frank – New York: A A Knopf, 1929 – 1r – 1 – us U.W. Library [430]
FARFALLA. POUR VIOLIN ET PIANO [PAR] MILE AURET / Sauret, E – [Berlin, 1907], Manuscript – 1 – us Sibley [780]
Farfan de los Godos, Antonio *see* DISCURSOS EN DEFENSA DE LA RELIGION CATHOLICA
FARFOROVYI PAVIL'ON / Gumilev, Nikolai Sepanovich – Ed. 2. Izd., dopoln. Petrograd. 1922. BR-3617 2 – 8 – ne IDC [460]
FARFOROVYI PAVIL'ON / Gumilev, Nikolai Sepanovich – Kitaiskie stikhi. Spb. 1918. BR-1138 2 – 8 – ne IDC [460]
FARGO FORUM – N.D. and preds. 1892- – 1 – us UMI [071]
FARHANG – (Sal-i 1, shumarah-i 1-7 (Burj-i Jadi 1298-Burj-i Saratan 1299[November 1919-May 1920]). Sal-i 2, shumarah-i 1-11 (Burj-i Hamal 1304-Bahman 1304[March 1925-January 1926]). Sal-i 3, shumarah-i 1-12 (Farvardin 1305-Isfand 1305[March 1926-February 1927]). Sal-i 4, shumarah-i 1-7 (Farvardin 1307-Shahrivar va Mihr 1307[March 1928-August and September 1928])) – Rasht – 1 reel – 1 – $350.00 – us MEDOC [950]
FARHANG-I KHURASAN – (Sal-i 2, shumarah-i 1-12 (Farvardin 1337-Bahman 1338[March 1958-January 1960])) – Khurasan. Sal-i 1, shumarah-i 1-6 (Farvardin 1336-Shahrivar 1336 [March 1957-August 1957]) – 1 reel – 1 – $225.00 – us MEDOC [950]
FARHANGISTAN-I IRAN (LUGHAT'HA-YI NAW) – Tehran. Shumarah-i 4-7 (Farvardin 1317-Isfand 1319 [Mar 1937-23 Mar 1941]) – 9 – $175.00 – us MEDOC [956]
Farhi, I *see* TUV YERUSHALAYIM
Faria, Julio Cezar de *see* JOSE BONIFACIO O MOCO
Faria, OA *see* DICCIONARIO GEOGRAPHICO, HISTORICO E ESTATISTICO
Farias Galindo, Jose *see* EL SIMBOLISMO MEDICO INDIGENA
Faribault, Eugene Rodolphe *see* THE GOLD MEASURES OF NOVA SCOTIA AND DEEP MINING: PAPER READ BEFORE THE CANADIAN MINING INSTITUTE, MARCH, 1899
Faribault, Georges Bartelemy *see*
- EXCURSION A LA COTE DU NORD, AU DESSOUS DE QUEBEC
- NOTICE SUR LA DESTRUCTION DES ARCHIVES ET BIBLIOTHEQUES DES DEUX CHAMBRES LEGISLATIVES DU CANADA, LORS DE L'EMEUTE QUI A EU LIEU A MONTREAL LE 25 AVRIL 1849

Farid, S M *see* TOP MANAGEMENT IN EGYPT: ITS STRUCTURE, QUALITY AND PROBLEMS
Faridi, Abid Hasan *see* AN OUTLINE HISTORY OF PERSIAN LITERATURE, A.D. 822-1926
Farina, P Jose Agustin *see* VIDA DE LA SIERVA DE DIOS SOR ASUNCION GALAN DE SAN CAYETANO
Farinelli, Arturo *see*
- GOETHE
- PAUL HEYSE

Farington, Joseph *see* THE DIARY. 1788-1821
Farish, Thomas Edwin *see* HISTORY OF ARIZONA
Fariss *see* HISTORY OF ONEIDA COUNTY
Farizov, Ivan Omarovich *see* SOVETSKI-INDONEZIISKOE EKONOMICHESKOE SOTRUDNICHESTVO
Farland, Merle *see* DIARY AND INDEX
Farley, James Lewis *see* EGYPT, CYPRUS AND ASIATIC-TURKEY
Farley, Robert *see* KALENDARIUM HUMANAE VITAE
Farlow, WG *see* MARINE ALGAE OF NEW ENGLAND AND ADJACENT COAST
FARM AND DAIRY *see*
- FARM AND DAIRY AND RURAL HOME
- WALLACES FARMER

FARM AND DAIRY AND RURAL HOME – (Cont: Canadian Dairyman and Farming World. Cont by: Farm and Dairy) – Peterboro [Peterborough], Ont: Rural Pub. Co, [1909-1918] – 9 – cn C.I.H.M. [630]
THE FARM AND FIRESIDE – Toronto: [s.n., 18–?] – 9 – cn C.I.H.M. [630]
FARM AND GARDEN INDEX – Ann Arbor. 1978-86 – D15638 – us UMI [631]
FARM AND GARDEN PERIODICALS INDEX – Quarterly – 1 – $65.00y – us Gabriel Micro [630]
FARM AND HOME – Montreal: Phelps Pub. Co, [1880?-1925] – 9 – cn C.I.H.M. [630]
FARM AND INPUT PRICES : COLLECTION AND COMPILATION – 1980 – 55p – it F.A.O. [338]
FARM AND RANCH – (Former titles: Southern Agriculturist, apr 1869-1949. Farm and Ranch. Southern Agriculturist, 1950-jun 1959) – Nashville. v81-93. 1951-63 – 1 – D334 – us UMI [630]
FARM AND RANCH ECONOMIC REVIEW / South Dakota. Agricultural Extension Service. State College of Agriculture and Mechanic Arts – v.1-7. 1947-53 – 1,5,6 – us Spaulding [636]
FARM AND RANCH LIVING – 1984- – 1,5,6,9 – us UMI [630]
FARM AND RANCH (SOUTHERN AGRICULTURIST) – 1904-05 – 1r – 1 – us Ross [630]
FARM AND RANCH - SOUTHERN AGRICULTURIST *see* FARM AND RANCH
FARM BALLADS / Carleton, Will – New York: Harper & Bros, 1875 – 2mf – 9 – $3.00 – LLMC 91-008 – us L.L.M.C. [810]
FARM BUSINESS ANALYSIS BY FARMING AREAS / Auburn University. Extension Service – 1960. 1 fiche – 9 – us Spaulding [630]
FARM BUSINESS ANALYSIS BY TYPES OF FARMS / Auburn University. Extension Service – v. 1-8. 1960-62 – 1,5,6 – us Spaulding [630]
FARM BUSINESS ANALYSIS OF 36 HOLDINGS IN EL USETA AREA OF JEBEL AL AKHDAR IN THE EASTERN REGION OF LIBYA / United Nations. Food and Agriculture Organization. The Development of Tribal Lands and Settlement Project – Benghazi, Libya. Jun 1966. H. Singh, FAO Technical Officer (Farm Management). BNE-1010 1 – 9 – ne IDC [630]
FARM BUSINESS SUMMARY / Wisconsin. College of Agricultural and Life Sciences. Dept. of Agricultural Economics – 1966-69 – 1,5 – us Spaulding [650]
A FARM BUSINESS SURVEY OF THE EARLY POTATO SEASON OF VIRGINIA / Virginia. Agricultural Experiment Station. Blacksburg – Jan & Nov 1930. 1 fiche – 9 – us Spaulding [630]
FARM CHEMICALS – (Formed by the union of: Farm Chemicals and Crop Life; and: Ag Chem and Commercial Fertilizer) – Willoughby. v136-160. 1973-97+ 1,5; v139-160. 1976-97+ 9 – 1,5,9 – D1414.01 – us UMI [631]
FARM CHEMICALS *see*
- FARM CHEMICALS AND CROP LIFE
- AG CHEM AND COMMERCIAL FERTILIZER

FARM CHEMICALS AND CROP LIFE – (Merged with: Ag Chem and Commercial Fertilizer; to form: Farm Chemicals. Former titles: American Fertilizer, 1894-sep 1950. American Fertilizer and Allied Chemicals, sep 16, 1950-jul 1951. Farm Chemicals, aug 1951-aug 1970) – Willoughby. v92-136. 1940-apr 1973 1; v134-136. 1971-apr 1973 5 – 1,5 – D1414 – us UMI [631]
FARM CHEMICALS AND CROP LIFE *see*
- FARM CHEMICALS
- AG CHEM AND COMMERCIAL FERTILIZER

FARM EC.-MISC / Kentucky. Agricultural Experiment Station – v. 101-142. 1941-45 – 1,5,6 – us Spaulding [630]
FARM ECONOMIC BRIEFS / Georgia. University. Agricultural Extension Service – 1957-65 – 1,5,6 – us Spaulding [630]
FARM ECONOMICS CIRCULAR / Tennessee. University. Agricultural Experiment Station and Extension Service – n.1-6, Jul 1954-Jan 1956 – 1,5 – us Spaulding [330]
FARM FACTS / Iowa State University. Cooperative Extension Service in Agriculture and Home Economics – 1934-38.1 reel – 1,5 – us Spaulding [630]
FARM HOLIDAY NEWS – St Paul etc. v. 1-3, no. 15. Feb 20 1933-Aug 14 1936 – 1 – us NY Public [630]
FARM IMPLEMENTS FOR ARID AND TROPICAL REGIONS / Hopfen, H J – 2nd rev ed 1981 – 159p – it F.A.O. [332]
FARM INDEX / U.S. Department of Agriculture – v1-18. 1962-79.205 fiches – 9 – 200.00 – us Updata [630]
FARM INDEX *see*
- FARMLINE
- AGRICULTURAL SITUATION

FARM INDUSTRY NEWS MIDWEST – (1986-. 1,5,6) – 1982- – 9 – us UMI [630]
FARM INSECTS, BEING THE NATURAL HISTORY AND ECONOMY OF THE INSECTS / Curtis, J – London. 1883. 528p., 16pls. Z-1163 2 – 8 – ne IDC [630]
FARM JOURNAL – Ottawa, 1887-1955 – 114r – 1 – cn Preston [971]
FARM JOURNAL – (v. 92- 1968- 5,6. v. 94- 1970- 9) – v. 1- 1877- – 1 – us UMI [630]
FARM JOURNAL *see*
- FARMER'S WIFE
- THE RURAL CANADIAN

FARM JOURNAL, MIDWESTERN EDITION – (v.92- 1968- 5,6. v.94- 1970- 9) – v.1- 1877- – 1 – us UMI [630]
FARM JOURNALS / Burroughs, Joseph Washington – undated, Business dealings, life, and activities of a Cloud county, KS, family – 1 – us KS Hist [920]

FARM LABOR CAMP DESIGN IN RURAL MARION COUNTY / Gossman, Stephen J – 1989 – 56p 1mf – 9 – $4.00 – us Microform Publ [790]
FARM LABOR NEWS *see* SHARECROPPER'S VOICE, 1935-1937 : SOUTHERN FARM LEADER, 1936 : STFU NEWS, 1938-1939 : TENANT FARMER, 1941-1942 : FARM WORKER, 1943-1944 : FARM LABOR NEWS, 1946-1951 : THE UNION FARMER, 1952-1953 : AGRICULTURAL UNIONIST, 1952-1954
FARM LEAFLET: REDUCTION OF ACREAGE COTTON IN 1915 / Auburn University. Extension Service – 1fiche – 9 – us Spaulding [630]
FARM MANAGEMENT DATA COLLECTION AND ANALYSIS – 1977 repr 1980 – 163p – it F.A.O. [650]
FARM MANAGEMENT GLOSSARY – 1985 – 227p – it F.A.O. [650]
FARM MANAGEMENT INPUT TO RURAL FINANCIAL SYSTEMS DEVELOPMENT – 1985 – 69p – it F.A.O. [650]
FARM MANAGEMENT RESEARCH FOR SMALL FARMER DEVELOPMENT – 1981 repr 1984 – 155p – it F.A.O. [650]
FARM NEWS – Bakersfield. Calif. 1954-1967 – 1 – us UMI [630]
FARM OBSERVER – Woodland. Calif. 1973- – 1 – us UMI [630]
FARM OUTLOOK / Iowa State University. Cooperative Extension Service in Agriculture and Home Economics – 1925-39.1 reel – 1,5 – us Spaulding [630]
FARM PLAN FOR A 4-HECTARE FARM IN GWARSHA PROJECT AREA (BENGHAZI) / Singh, H – Benghazi, Libya. Nov 1965. BNE-1008 1 – 9 – ne IDC [630]
FARM PLAN FOR THE BU TRABA SETTLEMENT IN THE EASTERN REGION OF LIBYA / United Nations. Food and Agriculture Organization. The Development of Tribal Lands and Settlements Team Project – Benghazi, Libya. 4 Dec 1965. H. Singh, Technical Officer (Farm Management). BNE-1009 1 – 9 – ne IDC [630]
FARM PLANNING IN THE EARLY STAGES OF DEVELOPMENT – 1968 repr 1983 – 106p – it F.A.O. [338]
FARM RECORD SUMMARIES: REPORT / Wisconsin. College of Agricultural and Life Sciences. Dept. of Agricultural Economics – 1955-70 – 1,5 – us Spaulding [630]
FARM SAFETY REVIEW – (1976-. 5,6,9) – v. 1-. 1943- – 1 – us UMI [630]
FARM SCIENCE REPORTER / Iowa State University. Cooperative Extension Service in Agriculture and Home Economics – No.1-7. 1940-46. 1 reel – 1,5 – us Spaulding [630]
FARM SECURITY ADMINISTRATION-OFFICE OF WAR INFORMATION COLLECTION / U.S. Library of Congress. Prints and Photographs Division – The most famous pictorial record of American life in the 1930's and early 1940's. 109 reels. P&P3 – 1 – 23.00r – us L of C Photodup [080]
FARM STORE MERCHANDISING *see* FARM SUPPLIER
FARM SUPPLIER – (Absorbed by: Farm Store Merchandising, 1988. Former titles: Tiny Poultry Tribune, feb-sep 1927. Hatchery Tribune, oct 1927-oct 1945. Hatchery Tribune and Feed Retailer, nov 1945-jun 1948. Hatchery and Feed, jul 1948-jan 1961. Feed and Farm Supplier, feb 1961-may 1967) – Mount Morris. v1-62. 1927-88* – 1 – D11513 – us UMI [630]
FARM TECHNOLOGY *see* FARM TECHNOLOGY AND AGRI-FIELDMAN
FARM TECHNOLOGY AND AGRI-FIELDMAN – (Cont by: Agri-fieldman. Former titles: National County agent and Extension Review, sep 1945-aug 1947. National County Agent and Vo-ag Teacher, sep 1947-sep 1951. County Agent and Vo-ag Teacher, mar 1951-feb 1963. Farm Technology, mar 1963-sum 1972) – Willoughby. v17-29. 1961-mar 1973 1; v28-29. 1972-mar 1973 5 – 1,5 – D1415 – us UMI [630]
FARM TECHNOLOGY AND AGRI-FIELDMAN *see* AGRI-FIELDMAN
THE FARM TRIBUNE – Porterville, CA. 1949-59; 1961 – 1r – 1 – $50.00 – B02642 – us Library Micro [071]
FARM WAR NEWS / Washington. Agricultural Extension Service – nos.1-33. Mar 1944-Oct 1944 – 1,5,6 – us Spaulding [630]
FARM WIFE NEWS – v1-14. 1971-84 – 1 – us UMI [630]
FARM WOMEN NEWS – Canadian ed. 1984- – 1,5,6,9 – us UMI [630]
FARM WOMEN NEWS – U.S. ed.v15-.1985- – 1,5,6,9 – us UMI [630]
FARM WORKER *see* SHARECROPPER'S VOICE, 1935-1937 : SOUTHERN FARM LEADER, 1936 : STFU NEWS, 1938-1939 : TENANT FARMER, 1941-1942 : FARM WORKER, 1943-1944 : FARM LABOR NEWS, 1946-1951 : THE UNION FARMER, 1952-1953 : AGRICULTURAL UNIONIST, 1952-1954
FARMACO – v20-35. 1965-80 – 1,5,6 – us Princeton Micro [073]
FARMACOPEA TRADICIONAL INDIGENA Y PRACTICAS RITUALES – Lima. 1946 – 1 – us Res Libr [615]
FARMAP: THE F.A.O. FARM ANALYSIS PACKAGE : A GENERAL INTRODUCTION – 1983 – 25p – it F.A.O. [630]
FARMER – (Cont by: USAgriculture. Former titles: Farmer, 1886-may 1925. Farmer and Farm, Stock and Home, jun 1929-dec 1934. Farmer, North and South Dakota Edition, 1935-79. Dakota Farmer, 1980) – Minneapolis. v1-103 1886-1985*. v104 1986. v105 1987*. v106-107 1988-89. v108-110 1990-jul 1992* 1; v104-110. 1986-jul 1992* 5; v100-103 1982-85*. v104-107 1986-89. v108-110 1990-jul 1992* 9 – 1,5,9 – D15037 – us UMI [630]
FARMER – Dunkirk. N.Y. 1870-1899 – 1 – us UMI [630]
THE FARMER – (Missing: 1887, v1, v2(27-52); 1888-1894, v3-14; 1896, v14(2-24); 1897, v15(1-16); 1898, v16(9,22)) – St. Paul, Minn., 1887-1936. v1-54 – 944mf – 9 – 13258c/1 – ne IDC [630]
Farmer, A H *see* DEEP THINGS OF THE BIBLE...EXPOSITION OF THE FUNDAMENTAL DOCTRINES
FARMER AND *see* AMERICAN FARMER
FARMER AND FARM, STOCK AND HOME *see* FARMER
THE FARMER AND MECHANIC – Toronto, CW [Ont]: Eastwood, [1848-18–] – 9 – cn C.I.H.M. [630]
FARMER AND MINER – Fort Jones, CA. 1902-16 – 6r – 1 – $300.00 – B02240 – us Library Micro [071]
FARMER AND SETTLER – Sydney, Australia. -w. 3 May 1912-7 Aug 1914. Imperfect. 3 reels – 1 – uk British Libr Newspaper [072]
Farmer, James Eugene *see* VERSAILLES AND THE COURT UNDER LOUIS XIV
Farmer, John Stephen *see* AMERICANISMS, OLD AND NEW: A DICTIONARY OF WORDS, PHRASES AND COLLOQUIALISMS PECULAIR TO THE UNITED STATES, BRITISH AMERICA, THE WEST INDIES, ETC., ETC., THEIR DERIVATION, MEANING AND APPLICATION
Farmer, Larry *see* THE IMPACT OF WORD PROCESSING AND ELECTRONIC MAIL ON U.S. COURTS OF APPEALS
Farmer, Larry C *see*
– APPEALS EXPEDITING SYSTEMS
– OBSERVATION AND STUDY
FARMER – NORTH AND SOUTH DAKOTA EDITION *see* FARMER
Farmer, Silas *see* CHAMPIONS OF CHRISTIANITY
FARMER STOCKMAN – Oklahoma City. Okl. 1911- – 1 – us UMI [071]
FARMER TOMKINS AND HIS BIBLES / Beecher, Willis Judson – Philadelphia: Presbyterian Bd of Publ, 1874 – 1mf – 9 – 0-8370-2240-1 – 1985-0240 – us A.T.L.A. [830]
FARMER'S ADVOCATE – Canada. Eastern Edition. 1867-1920 – 41r – 1 – $2,665.00 – cn Library Assoc [630]
FARMER'S ADVOCATE – Canada. Western Edition. 1890-1910 – 12r – 1 – $780.00 – cn Library Assoc [630]
FARMER'S ADVOCATE – Canada. Western Edition. 2 trailer reels. (Issues that were missing for 1901-10) – 2r – 1 – $136.00 – cn Library Assoc [630]
FARMERS ADVOCATE – Charles Town. West Virginia. 1897-1947 – 1 – us UMI [071]
FARMERS ADVOCATE – Ithaca. N.Y. and Advertiser. 1823-35 – 1 – us UMI [071]
FARMERS ADVOCATE – Topeka. Kan. 1899-1908 – 1 – us UMI [071]
THE FARMER'S ADVOCATE – Huntingdon, Canada. 8 mar 1883-19 jun 1884 – 1r – 1 – Can$50.00 – cn Can Microfilming [072]
FARMERS' ADVOCATE AND TOWNSHIPS GAZETTE – Sherbrooke, Canada. v1 n2. 30 jun 1834-v2 n98. 3 mai 1836 – 1r – 1 – Can$25.00 – cn Can Microfilming [072]
Farmers Alliance of Burt County.Nebraska *see* THE ALLIANCE SUN
FARMER'S AND MECHANIC'S JOURNAL AND SAINT-FRANCIS GAZETTE – Sherbrooke, Canada. v1 n8. 16 feb 1839-v3 n49. 25 nov 1841 – 1r – 1 – Can$30.00 – cn Can Microfilming [630]
FARMERS AND MINERS JOURNAL – Lykens, PA., 1856-1857 – 13 – $25.00r – us I.M.R. [071]
FARMERS' AND PLANTERS' FRIEND – Philadelphia. v1-7. 1821 – 1 – D3802 – us UMI [978]
FARMERS' BULLETIN – (With cum indexes) – Washington. n1-1650. 1889-1930 – 1 – D5657 – us UMI [630]
FARMERS' BULLETINS / U.S. Department of Agriculture – Nos. 1-2278. 838 fiches – 9 – $1100.00 – us Updata [630]
FARMER'S CABINET – Amherst. N.H. 1802-20 – 1,3 – us Readex [630]
FARMERS' CABINET *see* FARMERS' CABINET AND AMERICAN HERD-BOOK
FARMERS' CABINET AND AMERICAN HERD-BOOK : DEVOTED TO AGRICULTURE, HORTICULTURE, AND RURAL AND DOMESTIC AFFAIRS – (Absorbed by: American Agriculturist. Former title: Farmers' Cabinet, 1836-jul 1840) – Philadelphia. v1-12. 1836-48 – 1 – D3983 – us UMI [630]
FARMERS' CABINET AND AMERICAN HERD-BOOK *see* AMERICAN AGRICULTURIST AND THE RURAL NEW YORKER
FARMERS CO-OPERATIVE MERCANTILE ASSOCIATION – Kettle River, Minnesota. 1913-1931 – us I.H.R.C. [630]
FARMER'S DIGEST – Brookfield. v1-61. may 1937-apr 1998+ 1; v35-37 may 1971-apr 1974. v41-44 may 1977-apr 1981*. v45-61 may 1981-apr 1998+ 5; v41-61 may 1977-apr 1998+ 9 – 1,5,9 – D1809 – us UMI [630]
FARMERS' EXCHANGE – Bayard, NE. -w. Mar. 1919-Sep. 1923 – 1 – us NE Hist [071]
FARMERS' EXCHANGE – Bayard. Neb. 1919-23 – 1 – us UMI [630]
FARMERS' FEDERATION NEWS – Asheville. v30-38. sep 1949-aug 1958 – 1 – D423 – us UMI [630]
FARMERS FREE PRESS – Fairmont. West Virginia. 1913-1924 – 1 – us UMI [071]
FARMER'S FRIEND – Mechanicsburg, PA. -w 1891-1912. 8 rolls – 13 – $25.00r – us I.M.R. [071]
FARMERS GAZETTE – Barre, MA. 1824-35 – 1 – us Readex [071]
FARMERS GAZETTE *see* IRISH FARMERS GAZETTE ETC
FARMERS' GAZETTE AND MIDLAND COUNTIES ADVERTISER – Oxford, England. -w. 7 Nov 1843-2 July 1844. 20 ft – 1 – uk British Libr Newspaper [072]
FARMER'S JOURNAL – St-Hyacinthe, Canada. v71 n9. 7 nov 1941 – 1r – 1 – Can$25.00 – cn Can Microfilming [630]
FARMERS JOURNAL – Turlock. Calif. -d. 1921-23 – 1 – us UMI [630]
THE FARMER'S JOURNAL – Montreal, Canada. v2 n2. jun 1854-v4 n2. jun 1856 – 1r – 1 – Can$34.50 – cn Can Microfilming [630]
FARMER'S MAGAZINE – Edinburgh. v1-26. 1800-25 – 1 – D5344 – us UMI [941]
THE FARMER'S MANUAL – Fredericton [NB]: Print. and pub. by P A Phillips, [1844-1845?] – 9 – cn C.I.H.M. [630]
THE FARMER'S MANUAL – Kentville, NS: G W Woodworth, [1880-1881?] – 9 – cn C.I.H.M. [630]
FARMERS NATIONAL WEEKLY – Minneapolis. n.s. v. 1-3 no. 25. Jan 15 1934-Aug 21 1936 – 1 – us NY Public [630]
FARMER'S REGISTER : A MONTHLY PUBLICATION – Shelbanks. v1-10/1. jun 1833-mar 1843 – 1 – D4372 – us UMI [976]
FARMERS REGISTER – Greensburg. Pa. 1799-1802 – 1 – us UMI [071]
FARMERS REGISTER – Greensburg, PA., 1808-1811 – 13 – $25.00r – us I.M.R. [071]
FARMER'S REPOSITORY – Charlestown. W. Va. 1808-20 – 1,3 – us Readex [071]
FARMER'S UNION NEWS – Eugene OR. Mar May 1929 – 1 – us U.O. Library [071]
FARMER'S UNION NEWS – Independence OR. Jan-July 1906, June 1925, May Nov Dec 1927 – 1 – us U.O. Library [071]
FARMERS UNION NEWS – Helena. Mont. 1940-1959; 1968-1969 – 1 – us UMI [071]
FARMERS VINDICATOR – Valley Falls. Kan. 1890-1925 – 1 – us UMI [071]
FARMERS WEEKLY – Wallington. v1-87 1934-77*. v88-93 1978-80. v94-121 1981-94*. v122-127 1995-97+ – 1 – D11286 – us UMI [630]
THE FARMER'S WEEKLY MUSEUM – Walpole. N.H. 1797-1810. with The New Hampshire Journal. 1793-1797. and The New Hampshire Mercury. 1784-1788. Sold as one unit – 3 – us Readex [071]
FARMER'S WIFE – (Merged into: Farm Journal) – St Paul. 1897-1939* – 1 – D5345 – us UMI [640]
THE FARMER'S WIFE – St Paul: Webb Publ Co [-1935]. [v15-16, n8 may 1910-11; v14, n9-11 jan-mar 1912; v15-18 may 1912-may 1916; v19, n8-v21, n7 1917-1918; v26, n8-v38 1924-nov 1935] – us Res Libr [071]
THE FARMER'S WIFE MAGAZINE – St Paul: Webb Pub Co. [v38 n12 dec 1935; v39-42 n4 1939-apr 1939] – us Res Libr [071]
FARM-HOME NEWS / South Dakota. Agricultural Extension Service. State College of Agriculture and Mechanic Arts – v.1-9. 1934-42 – 1,5,6 – us Spaulding [630]
FARMING – (Cont: Canadian Live-Stock and Farm Journal. Cont by: The Farming World) – Toronto: Bryant Press, [1895?-1900?] – 9 – cn C.I.H.M. [630]
FARMING *see*
– THE CANADIAN LIVE-STOCK AND FARM JOURNAL
– THE FARMING WORLD
THE FARMING AND ACCOUNTS BOOKS OF 1641 / Best, Henry – 7 – uk Microform Academic [650]
FARMING SYSTEMS DEVELOPMENT : GUIDELINES FOR THE CONDUCT OF A TRAINING COURSE IN FARMING SYSTEMS DEVELOPMENT – 1991 – 267p – it F.A.O. [630]
FARMING TODAY – St. Thomas, 1989-1992 – 3r – 1 – cn Preston [971]
FARMING WORLD – Toronto, Canada. -w. Nov 1903-Feb 1908. 4 reels – 1 – uk British Libr Newspaper [630]
THE FARMING WORLD – (Cont: Farming. Merged with: Canadian Farm and Home; Merged to become: The Farming World and Canadian Farm and Home) – Toronto: D T McAinsh, [1900-1902] – 9 – cn C.I.H.M. [630]
THE FARMING WORLD – (Cont: The Farming World and Canadian Farm and Home. Merged with: The Canadian Dairyman. Merged to become: Canadian Dairyman and Farming World) – Toronto: Farming World, [1907-1908?] – 9 – cn C.I.H.M. [630]
THE FARMING WORLD *see*
– FARMING
– THE FARMING WORLD AND CANADIAN FARM AND HOME
THE FARMING WORLD AND CANADIAN FARM AND HOME – (Merger of: The Farming World. Merger of: Canadian Farm and Home. Cont by: The Farming World) – Toronto: Dominion Phelps, [1903-1907] – 9 – cn C.I.H.M. [630]
THE FARMING WORLD AND CANADIAN FARM AND HOME *see*
– THE FARMING WORLD
Farmingdale, South Dakota. Farmingdale Baptist Church *see* RECORDS
Farmington. Ohio. United Presbyterian and Congregational Church *see* CHURCH RECORDS, MS 2125
FARMLAND NEWS – Archbold, Ohio. 1981-1995 – 25r – 1 – $32.50r – us Archival [071]
FARMLINE – (Formed by the union of: Agricultural Situation; and: Farm Index) – Washington. v1-14. apr 1980-mar 1993 1,5,9; v8 dec 1986-nov 1987*. v14 dec 1992-mar 1993* 5 – 1,5,9 – D12429 – us UMI [630]
FARMLINE / U.S. Department of Agriculture – v1-7. 1980-86. 34 fiches – 9 – 50.00 – us Updata [630]
FARMLINE *see* AGRICULTURAL SITUATION
FARMS, HOW AND WHERE TO OBTAIN THEM: MANITOBA, ASSINIBOIA, ALBERTA, SASKATCHEWAN: THE FOUR GREAT FERTILE PROVINCES OF THE CANADIAN NORTHWEST DESCRIBED AND ILLUSTRATED – s.l.: s.n., 1891. 05649. (Pre-1900 Canadiana) – 9 – cn C.I.H.M. [333]
THE FARM'S LITTLE PEOPLE: A SEQUEL TO "ON GRANDFATHER'S FARM" / Frechette, Annie Thomas – Philadelphia: American Baptist Publication Society, c1897. 02901. (Pre-1900 Canadiana) – 9 – cn C.I.H.M. [830]

FAR'N FOLK – London, UK. 7 Mar-2 May 1916 – 1 – uk British Libr Newspaper [072]
FARN FOLK = FOR THE PEOPLE – (A Bi-Weekly) – Mexico, MX. v3 no 2/3. 1936 – 1r – 1 – Can$25.00 – cn Can Microfilming [072]
Farnaby, Thomas *see*
– INDEX RHETORICUS
– SYSTEMA GRAMMATICUM
FARNAM ECHO – Farnam, NE. -w. Dec. 1903-Jun. 1905; May 1914-Feb. 1940 – 1 – us NE Hist [071]
FARNAM PRESS – Farnam, NE. -w. Sep. 1940-Jun. 1965 – 1 – us NE Hist [071]
Farnaud, Pierre A *see* DESCRIPTION ABREGEE DU DEPARTEMENT DES HAUTES-ALPES
Farnell, Lewis R *see* GREECE AND BABYLON
Farnell, LR *see* THE EVOLUTION OF RELIGION
Farnese, L *see* PROPOSTA DI UN CODICE DI...
Farney, Roger *see* LA RELIGION DE L'EMPEREUR JULIEN ET LE MYSTICISME DE SON TEMPS
FARNFLORA DER GEGEND VON HANNOVER / Holle, G von – Hannover. 1862. B-7195 2 – 8 – ne IDC [580]
DIE FARNGATTUNG NIPHOBOLUS / Giesenhagen, K F G – Eine Monographie. Jena. 1901. B-7189 2 – 8 – ne IDC [580]
DIE FARNKRAEUTER DER ERDE / Christ, H – Jena, 1897. xll,388p. B-7172/1 – 9 – ne IDC [580]
DIE FARNKRAEUTER DER JETZTWELT / Ettingshausen, C von – Wien. 1865. B-6521 2 – 8 – ne IDC [580]
FARNWORTH CHRONICLE – England. 8 Sep 1906-21 Dec 1917.-w. 15 reels – 1 – uk British Libr Newspaper [072]
FARNWORTH EXPRESS – Farnworth, England. -w. 10 April 1890-4 June 1891. 14 ft – 1 – uk British Libr Newspaper [072]
FARNWORTH MESSENGER – Farnworth, England. -m. July 1874-Aug 1876. 19 ft – 1 – uk British Libr Newspaper [072]
FARNWORTH OBSERVER – England. 7 Nov 1868-25 Sep 1869; 8 Jan 1870-23 Aug 1873.-w. 4 reels – 1 – uk British Libr Newspaper [072]
FARNWORTH WEEKLY – Farnworth, England. -w. 4 Dec 1952-12 Aug 1954. 25 ft – 1 – uk British Libr Newspaper [072]
EL FARO DOMINICAL – 1927. 260p – 1 – 9.10 – us Baptist [240]
Faro Vasconcelos, D *see* INDICE DEL TEATRO CRITICO DE FEIJOO
O FAROL – Bahia, Brazil. Feb 19, Sept-Oct 1828; Aug, Oct 1832 – 1 – bl Biblioteca [072]
O FAROL – Nanuque, Brazil. Nov 1968 – 1 – bl Biblioteca [072]
O FAROL – Sao Paulo, Brazil. Jan-Mar 1916 – 1 – bl Biblioteca [072]
FAROL MARANHENSE – '(s.l.')-Sao Luis, Brazil. 26 Dec 1827-Aug 1828. Jan-Dec 1829. Jan, Jun-Jul, Dec 1830. Jan-Nov 1831. Jan-29 Oct 1833 – 1,5,6 – bl Biblioteca [072]
EL FAROUK – Revue musulmane litteraire, economique et d'education sociale. Dir. Omar Ben Kaddour el Djazairi. Alger. 1913-15, 1920-21. (I-III, VIII-IX) – 1 – fr A.C.R.P.P. [073]
A FARPA – Manaos, Amazonas. 9 Out-1 Nov 1909 – 1,5,6 – bl Biblioteca [072]
Farquhar, J N *see* MODERN RELIGIOUS MOVEMENTS IN INDIA
Farquhar, JN *see* THE APPROACH OF CHRIST TO MODERN INDIA
Farquharson, V M *see* EDUCATION STATISTICS 1975-1976
Farr, FC *see* HISTORY OF IMPERIAL COUNTY
Farrand, Max *see*
– THE FRAMING OF THE CONSTITUTION OF THE UNITED STATES
– RECORD OF THE FEDERAL CONVENTION OF 1789
– THE RECORDS OF THE FEDERAL CONVENTION OF 1787
Farrar, Adam Storey *see*
– A CRITICAL HISTORY OF FREE THOUGHT IN REFERENCE TO THE CHRISTIAN RELIGION
– SCIENCE IN THEOLOGY
Farrar, Archdeacon, et al *see* INSPIRATION: A CLERICAL SYMPOSIUM
Farrar, Estelle Sinclaire *see* THE CUT AND ENGRAVED GLASS OF CORNING, 1868-1940
Farrar, Frederic William *see*
– BIBLE: ITS MEANING AND SUPREMACY
– BOOK OF DANIEL
– THE EARLY DAYS OF CHRISTIANITY
– EPISTLE OF PAUL THE APOSTLE TO THE HEBREWS
– THE FIRST BOOK OF KINGS
– THE GOSPEL ACCORDING TO ST LUKE
– THE HERODS
– THE LIFE AND WORK OF ST. PAUL
– LIVES OF THE FATHERS
– MEN I HAVE KNOWN
– THE SECOND BOOK OF KINGS
– SOLOMON
– TEXTS EXPLAINED, OR, HELPS TO UNDERSTAND THE NEW TESTAMENT
– WITNESS OF HISTORY TO CHRIST: FIVE SERMONS
Farrell, John P *see* AN OUTLINE OF THE LAWS OF THE TTPI RELATING TO REAL PROPERTY
Farrenc, A *see* FANTAISIE POUR FLUTE ET PIANO SUR L'AIR
Farrer, James Anson *see* ZULULAND AND THE ZULUS
Farrer, Thomas Henry *see*
– RETALIATION AND COMMERCIAL FEDERATION: LORD SALISBURY AND SIR CHARLES TUPPER: WITH NOTES ON THE RECENT TARIFF DOCTRINES OF PROTECTIONISTS, FAIR TRADERS, AND COMMERCIAL FEDERATIONISTS
– THE SUGAR CONVENTION
FARRIER'S MAGAZINE – Philadelphia. v1-2. 1818 – 1 – D3803 – us UMI [073]
Farries, Francis Wallace *see*
– ANNIVERSARY SERMON PREACHED IN KNOX CHURCH, NOVEMBER 30TH, 1890
– SERMON DELIVERED BEFORE ST ANDREW'S SOCIETY IN KNOX CHURCH, OTTAWA, ON SUNDAY EVENING, NOVEMBER 25TH, 1888
– THE TRANSCENDENT VALUE OF MAN: A SERMON DELIVERED BEFORE ST ANDREW'S SOCIETY IN KNOX CHURCH, OTTAWA ON SUNDAY EVENING, NOVEMBER 29TH, 1891
Farringdon, Michael G *see*
– A CONCORDANCE AND WORD-LISTS TO DYLAN THOMAS' UNDER MILK WOOD
– A CONCORDANCE AND WORD-LISTS TO HENRY FIELDING'S JOSEPH ANDREWS
– A CONCORDANCE AND WORD-LISTS TO HENRY FIELDING'S SHAMELA
Farrington, Anthony *see* BRITISH POLICY IN ASIA: INDIA OFFICE MEMORANDA
Farrington, Joseph R *see* THE AMERICAN SAMOAN COMMISSION'S VISIT TO SAMOA, SEPTEMBER-OCTOBER 1931
DIE FARRNKRAEUTER IN KOLORIRTEN ABBILDUNGEN NATURGETREU ERLAEUTERT UND BESCHRIEBEN / Kunze, G – Leipzig. 1840-51. B-5995 2 – 8 – ne IDC [580]
LA FARSA MEDIEVAL EN FRANCIA : TEMAS Y SITUACIONES DRAMATICAS / Muela Ezquerra, Julian – 3mf – 9 – Pta2,000.00 – 84-85422-39-2 – sp Pentalfa [440]
FARUK – Athens. Idare Mueduerue: Ivanaki Pasfidi; Muharriri: Mevlanazade Rifat. No. 1 (25 Tesrinisani 1327 [1911]) – 9 – $25.00 – us MEDOC [956]
Farwell, Beatrice *see*
– FRENCH POPULAR LITHOGRAPHIC IMAGERY 1815-1870, VOL 3
– FRENCH POPULAR LITHOGRAPHIC IMAGERY, VOL 4
– FRENCH POPULAR LITHOGRAPHIC IMAGERY, VOL 5
– FRENCH POPULAR LITHOGRAPHIC IMAGERY, VOL 6
– FRENCH POPULAR LITHOGRAPHIC IMAGERY, VOL 7
– FRENCH POPULAR LITHOGRAPHIC IMAGERY, VOL 8
– FRENCH POPULAR LITHOGRAPHIC IMAGERY, VOL 9
– FRENCH POPULAR LITHOGRAPHIC IMAGERY, VOL 10
– FRENCH POPULAR LITHOGRAPHIC IMAGERY, VOL 11
– FRENCH POPULAR LITHOGRAPHIC IMAGERY, VOL 12
Farwell, Mary E *see* THE LIFE OF WILLIAM CAREY
Farwell, William Washington *see*
– QUESTIONS FOR LAW STUDENTS ON COOLEY'S CONSTITUTIONAL LIMITATIONS
– QUESTIONS FOR LAW STUDENTS ON STORY'S EQUITY PLEADINGS
FARYAD-I GAWD'NISHINAN – (Missing issues: 51-54, 56-57) – Tehran: [Sazman-i Mujahidin-i Khalq-i Iran], 1979. Shumarah-'i 1-66 (21 July 1979-29 Oct 1979) – 1 reel – 1 – $25.00 – us MEDOC [950]
Fasano, Frank Paul *see* THE ITALIAN-AMERICAN HOME AS INFLUENCED BY FACTORS OF FAMILY DISORGANIZATION
FASCHISMUS – Amsterdam, 1939-45 (incomplete) – 1 – Dist. gw Mikrofilm – gw Misc Inst [949]
FASCIAL PLASTIC SURGERY: FPS – (1985-. 5,6,9) – v1-. 1983- – 1 – us UMI [617]
FASCICULI ZIZANIORUM MAGISTRI WYCLIF CUM TRITICO (RS5) / Netter, Thomas; ed by Schirley, W W – 1858 – Dfl39.00 – ne Slangenburg [240]
FASCICULUS IOANNI WILLIS CLARK DICATUS / Clark, J W – H-1256 2. 1909 – 9 – ne IDC [025]
FASCICULUS OBSERVATIONUM BOTANICARUM / Retzius, A J – Lundini. 1774. B-5668 2 – 8 – ne IDC [580]
FASCICULUS PLANTARUM CIRCA CANTABRIGIAM NASCENTIUM / Lyons, I – Londini, 1763. 56 pp. B-5138 2 – 8 – ne IDC [580]
FASCICULUS PLANTARUM CUM NOVIS GENERIBUS ET SPECIEBUS / Vandelli, D – Olisipone (Lisboa). 1771. B-5787 1 – 9 – ne IDC [580]
FASCICULUS SANCTORUM ORDINIS CISTERCIENSIS / Henriquez, Chrysostomus – Bruxellae, 1623 – 19mf – 8 – Dfl67.00 – ne Slangenburg [240]
FASCISM, 1933-1945 – 22mf – 9 – uk Microform Academic [320]
EL FASCISMO AL DESNUDO – Madrid, 1937. Fiche W 876. (Blodgett Collection of Spanish Civil War Pamphlets) – 9 – us H.U. College Libr [946]
EL FASCISMO INTENTA DESTRUIR EL MUSEO DEL PRADO – Madrid, 1936? Fiche W 877. (Blodgett Collection of Spanish Civil War Pamphlets) – 9 – us H.U. College Libr [946]
EL FASCISMO INTERNACIONAL Y LA GUERRA ANTIFASCISTA ESPANOLA / Garcia Oliver, Juan – Barcelona? 1937? Fiche W 908. (Blodgett Collection of Spanish Civil War Pamphlets) – 9 – us H.U. College Libr [946]
EL FASCISMO PRETENDE ENCARCELAR ESPANA / Catalonia. Comissariat de Propaganda – n.p. 193? Fiche W 878. (Blodgett Collection of Spanish Civil War Pamphlets) – 9 – us H.U. College Libr [946]
EL FASCISMO Y LAS ARMAS Y LAS LETRAS ESPANOLAS / Albornoz, Alvaro de – Madrid, 1938. Fiche W 707. (Blodgett Collection of Spanish Civil War Pamphlets) – 9 – us H.U. College Libr [946]
FASCIST SPAIN, MENACE TO WORLD PEACE / Wolff, Milton – New York: New Century, 1947. 16p – 1 – us U.W. Library [946]
FASCIST SPAIN, MENACE TO WORLD PEACE / Wolff, Milton – N.Y., 1947. Fiche W1255. (Blodgett Collection of Spanish Civil War Pamphlets) – 9 – us H.U. College Libr [946]
THE FASCIST THREAT TO CULTURE; A SPEECH DELIVERED ON MARCH 8, 1937, IN THE NEW LECTURE HALL, HARVARD UNIVERSITY / Malraux, Andre – Under the auspices of the Cambridge Union of University Teachers and the Harvard Student Union. Cambridge, 1937. Fiche W1017. (Blodgett Collection of Spanish Civil War Pamphlets) – 9 – us H.U. College Libr [946]
LE FASCISTE CANADIEN – Montreal, 8 jun 1935-jun 1938f – 1r – 1 – Can$50.00 – cn Can Microfilming [072]
FASEB JOURNAL – (Cont: Federation of American Societies for Experimental Biology, Federation Proceedings) – Bethesda. v1-11. jul 1987-dec 1997+ – 1,5,9 – D16278 – us UMI [574]
DIE FASERPFLANZE HANF : MATERIALIEN ZUR GESCHICHTE IHRES ANBAUS, IHRER VERARBEITUNG UND HANDELS / Heubach, Helga – 1995 – 2mf – 9 – DM80.00 – 3-8267-2104-7 – gw Hänsel [631]
FASHION ADVERTISING COLLECTION, 1942-1982 – 7 sections. 1r per y – 1 – $8,850.00 diazo; $9,990.00 silver – us Alper [740]
FASHION FOR AMERICA! / Fashion Institute of Technology. New York – (Charts the devt of American fashion industry. Includes sketches of European designs to innovative originals. With printed index) – 56 colour mf – 15 – $1,360.00 – 1-869934-41-5 – uk Emmett [740]
Fashion Institute of Technology. New York *see* FASHION FOR AMERICA!
FASHION UPDATE 1981-1996 – (A quartely review of world's fashion reproduced over 1,300 photographs each year of fashion shows in Paris, London, Milan and New York. Back issues v1-13 are still available. With printed index) – 15 – $302.00v – ISSN 0625-1084 – uk Emmett [740]
THE FASHIONABLE LADY; OR HARLEQUIN'S OPERA.. / Ralph, James – Libretto. 1730 – 9 – us Sibley [780]
Fassel, Hort *see* BEITRAEGE ZUR LITERATURGESCHICHTE UND – METHODOLOGIE
FAST FERRY INTERNATIONAL – (Cont: High-speed Surface Craft) – Kingston-Upon-Thames. v28-36. 1989-97+ 1,5,9; v31-33. 1992-94* 5 – 1,5,9 – D2997.02 – us UMI [623]
FAST FOOD – (Cont by: Restaurant Business. Former titles: Soda Fountain, 1902-32. Soda Fountain Magazine, 1933-40. Soda Fountain and Quick Food-service, 1941-43. Soda Fountain Service, 1944-aug 1945. Fountain Service, sep 1945-sep 1951. Fountain and Fast Food service, oct 1951-jun 1952. Fountain and Fast Food, jul 1952-jul 1956) – New York. v1-72 1902-73*. v73 1974 – 1 – D2967 – us UMI [660]
FAST LANE – 1984- – 1,5,6,9 – us UMI [073]
FAST SERMONS TO PARLIAMENT: REPRODUCTIONS IN FACSIMILE WITH NOTES / ed by Jeffs, Robin – London: Cornmarket Press, 1970-1971 – 1 – us U.W. Library [240]
FASTES CHRONOLOGIQUES DE LA VILLE DE SFAKS / DuPaty de Clam, Antoine Amedee – Paris: A. Challamel, 1890. 32p.1 fiche. (Miscellaneous selections) – 9 – 6.00 – fr Bibl Nationale [520]
FASTES EPISCOPAUX DE L'ANCIENNE GAULE, TOME 1 : PROVINCES DU SUD-EST / Duchesne, Louis – Paris, 1894 – Dfl28.00 – ne Slangenburg [240]
FASTES EPISCOPAUX DE L'ANCIENNE GAULE, TOME 2 : L'AQUITAINE ET LES LYONNAISES / Duchesne, Louis – Paris, 1900 – Dfl32.00 – ne Slangenburg [240]
FASTES EPISCOPAUX DE L'ANCIENNE GAULE, TOME 3 : LES PROVINCES DU NORD ET DE L'EST / Duchesne, Louis – Paris, 1915 – Dfl22.00 – ne Slangenburg [240]
LES FASTES HISTORIQUES DU VIEUX MONTREAL = THE HISTORICAL RECORDS OF OLD MONTREAL / Morin, Victor – Montreal, 1944. SEM105P745 – 2mf – 9 – Can$4.50 – cn Bibl Nat [910]
FASTI – Toronto: University College, [1884-18– or 19–] – 9 – cn C.I.H.M. [370]
FASTI APOSTOLICI : A CHRONOLOGY OF THE YEARS BETWEEN THE ASCENSION OF OUR LORD AND THE MARTYRDOM OF SS. PETER AND PAUL / Anderdon, William Henry – London: Kegan Paul, Trench, 1882 – 1mf – 9 – 0-8370-2090-5 – 1985-0090 – us A.T.L.A. [220]
FASTI MONASTICI AEVI SAXONICI, OR, AN ALPHABETICAL LIST OF THE HEADS OF RELIGIOUS HOUSES IN ENGLAND PREVIOUS TO THE NORMAN CONQUEST : TO WHICH IS PREFIXED A CHRONOLOGICAL CATALOGUE OF CONTEMPORARY FOUNDATIONS / Birch, Walter de Gray – London: Truebner, 1873 – 1mf – us A.T.L.A. [240]
FASTI OF THE IRISH PRESBYTERIAN CHURCH, 1613-1840 / McConnell, James – Pts. 5-12 – 1 – $50.00 – us Presbyterian [240]
FASTI SACRI : OR, A KEY TO THE CHRONOLOGY OF THE NEW TESTAMENT / Lewin, Thomas – (Includes bibliographical references and index) – London: Longmans, Green, 1865 – 2mf – 9 – 0-8370-4098-1 – 1985-2098 – us A.T.L.A. [220]
THE FATAL THREE / Braddon, Mary Elizabeth – British Fiction Archive: Unit 5 – 9 – uk Bell [830]
FATALISME ET LIBERTE DANS L'ANTIQUITE GRECQUE / Amand, D – Louvain, 1945 – 11mf – 8 – ne Slangenburg [180]
FATAT BOSTON – Boston: Publ by W E Shakir, [dec 28 1917-may 8 1919] – us Res Libr [071]
FATAWA AL-'ALAMGIRIYAH *see* AL-FATAWA AL-'ALAMGIRIYAH. FUTAWA ALEMGIRI
FATE – St Paul. v23-50. 1970-97+ 1; v1-22 1948-69. v24-50 1971-97+ 5; v29-50. 1976-97+ 9 – 1,5,9 – D5876 – us UMI [240]

FATE RIDES A TORTOISE; A BIOGRAPHY OF ELLEN SPENCER MUSSEY / Hathaway, Grace – Philadelphia: Winston Co., 1937. 204p. LL-206 – 1 – us L of C Photodup [340]
FATH : NEWSLETTER – [S.l: Fath, jun 1969-mar 1970] – 1r – us Res Libr [071]
FATHER CLARK, OR, THE PIONEER PREACHER : SKETCHES AND INCIDENTS OF REV. JOHN CLARK / Peck, John Mason – New York: Sheldon, Lamport & Blakeman, 1855 – 1mf – us A.T.L.A. [240]
"FATHER CORSON", OR, THE OLD STYLE CANADIAN ITINERANT: / ed by Carroll, John – Embracing the life and gospel labours of the Rev. Robert Corson, fifty-six years a minister in connection with the central Methodism of Upper Canada. Toronto: Published by Samuel Rose at the Methodist Book Room – 9 – cn C.I.H.M. [971]
FATHER EELLS, OR, THE RESULTS OF FIFTY-FIVE YEARS OF MISSIONARY LABORS IN WASHINGTON AND OREGON : A BIOGRAPHY OF REV. CUSHING EELLS, D.D. / Eells, Myron – Boston: Congregational Sunday-School and Publishing Society, c1894 – 1mf – us A.T.L.A. [240]
FATHER MARQUETTE / Thwaites, Reuben Gold – New York: D. Appleton, 1902 – 1mf – us A.T.L.A. [240]
THE FATHERHOOD OF GOD / Adams, John Coleman – Boston: Universalist Pub. House, 1890. 1 fiche – 9 – us A.T.L.A. [240]
THE FATHERHOOD OF GOD : AND ITS RELATION TO THE PERSON AND WORK OF CHRIST AND THE OPERATIONS OF THE HOLY SPIRIT / Wright, Charles Henry Hamilton – (Includes bibliographical references and indexes) – Edinburgh: T & T Clark, 1867 – 1mf – 9 – 0-8370-6551-8 – 1986-0551 – us A.T.L.A. [210]
THE FATHERLAND. (VIERECK'S THE AMERICAN WEEKLY.-VIRECK'S THE AMERICAN MONTHLY.-AMERICAN MONTHLY) – New York. 24 Aug 1914-Jan 1933.-w,m. 10 reels – 1 – uk British Libr Newspaper [071]
A FATHER'S CURSE / Bray, Anna Eliza – British Fiction Archive: Unit 2 – 9 – uk Bell [830]
THE FATHERS OF THE DESERT; OR, AN ACCOUNT OF THE ORIGIN AND PRACTICE OF MONKERY AMONG HEATHEN NATIONS; ITS PASSAGE INTO THE CHURCH...AND STORIES. / Ruffner, Henry – New York: Baker and Scribner, 1850. 2v – 1 – us U.W. Library [240]
THE FATHERS OF THE GERMAN REFORMED CHURCH IN EUROPE AND AMERICA / Harbaugh, Henry – 12 v. 1881-88 – 1 – us A.T.L.A. [240]
FATHOM – Washington. v5-29. sum 1973-dec 1997+ 1; v6-21 sum 1974-jan 1990. v22-26 feb 1990-feb 1995*. v27-29 mar 1995-dec 1997+ 5; v7-27. sum 1975-dec 1997+ 9 – 1,5,9 – D7353 – us UMI [073]
FATIGUE / Mosso, Angelo – 1972 – 5mf – 9 – $15.00 – us Microform Publ [612]
FATIGUE AND FRACTURE OF ENGINEERING MATERIALS AND STRUCTURES – (Former title: Fatigue of Engineering Materials and Structures, 1979-84) – Oxford. v1-15 1979-92. v16-17 1993-94*. v18-20 1995-97+ – 1,5,9 – D49301 – us UMI [620]
FATIGUE OF ENGINEERING MATERIALS AND STRUCTURES : THE INTERNATIONAL JOURNAL – v1- 1979- – 5,6,9 – us UMI [620]
FATIGUE OF ENGINEERING MATERIALS AND STRUCTURES *see* FATIGUE AND FRACTURE OF ENGINEERING MATERIALS AND STRUCTURES
Fatin *see* DIVAN
Fatio, V *see* FAUNE DES VERTEGRES DE LA SUISSE. V.2
Faublee, Jacques *see*
- L'ETHNOGRAPHIE DE MADAGASCAR
- INTRODUCTION AU MALGACHE

LE FAUBOURG – (Filmed as pt of: Commune de Paris newspapers) – Paris: Assoc generale typogr, mar 26 1871 – us Res Libr [072]
Faucet, Henry *see* PROTECTION AND FREE TRADE
FAUCETT BAPTIST CHURCH. FAUCETT, MISSOURI : CHURCH RECORDS – 1895-1972 – 1 – 41.21 – us Baptist [240]
Faucher de Saint-Maurice, Narcisse *see*
- A LA BRUNANTE: CONTES ET RECITS
- A LA VEILLEE: CONTES ET RECITS
- L'ABBE C. H. LAVERDIERE
- LE CANADA ET LES CANADIENS-FRANCAIS PENDANT LA QUERRE FRANCO-PRUSSIENNE
- DE TRIBORD A BABORD: TROIS CROISIERES DANS LE GOLFE SAINT LAURENT: NORD ET SUD
- EN ROUTE: SEPT JOURS DANS LES PROVINCES MARITIMES
- LA GASPESIE, PROMENADES DANS LE GOLFE SAINT-LAURENT NOUVELLE ECOSSE, ILE DU PRINCE EDOUARD, NOUVEAU BRUNSWICK, LA BAIE DES CHALEURS, LA GASPESIE
- NOTES POUR SERVIR A L'HISTOIRE DE L'EMPEREUR MAXIMILIEN: D'APRES SES OEUVRES, LES RECITS DU CAPITAINE D'ARTILLERIE ALBERT HANS, DU MEDECIN PARTICULIER DE S. M. LE DOCTEUR BASCH ET DES TEMOINS OCULAIRES DE L'EXECUTION
- NOTES POUR SERVIR A L'HISTOIRE DES OFFICIERS DE LA MARINE ET DE L'ARMEE FRANCAISE QUI ONT FAIT LA QUERRE DE L'INDEPENDANCE AMERICAINE
- NOTES SUR LA FORMATION DU FRANCO-NORMAND ET DE L'ANGLO-SAXON
- NOTICE SUR JEAN VAUQUELAIN DE DIEPPE: LIEUTENANT DE VAISSEAU (1727-1764): D'APRES M. FAUCHER DE SAINT-MAURICE
- LA QUESTION DU JOUR, RESTERONS-NOUS FRANCAIS

Fauchet, C *see* RECUEIL DE L'ORIGINE DE LA LANGUE ET POESIE FRANCOISE
Fauchet, Claude *see*
- MANDEMENT DE CLAUDE FAUCHET, EVEQUE DU CALVADOS, DEPUTE A L'ASSEMBLEE NATIONALE
- DE LA RELIGION NATIONALE
- SERMON SUR L'ACCORD DE LA RELIGION ET DE LA LIBERTE

Fauchet, Joseph *see* LE DESPOTISME DECRETE PAR L'ASSEMBLEE NATIONALE
Fauchet, Joseph H A *see* DESCRIPTION ABREGEE DU DEPARTEMENT DU VAR
Fauchille, P *see*
- DU BLOCUS MARITIME
- LOUIS RENAULT. SA VIE – SON OEUVRE
- TRAITE DE DROIT INTERNATIONAL PUBLIC

Fauconberg, Thomas *see* TERROR OF THE ESTATE OF LORD THOMAS FAUCONBERG
THE FAUCONBERGE MEMORIAL: AN ACCOUNT OF HENRY FAUCONBERGE, LL.D. OF BECCLES AND OF THE ENDOWMENT...TO ENCOURAGE LEARNING AND THE INSTRUCTION OF YOUTH / Rix, Samuel Wilton – Ipswich: J.M. Burton, 1849. iv,84p. illus – 1 – us U.W. Library [370]
Fauconnier, G *see* MASS MEDIA
Faughnan, Thomas *see* STIRRING INCIDENTS IN THE LIFE OF A BRITISH SOLDIER
Fauleau *see* PLAN D'UN EDUCATOIRE NATIONAL
Faulhaber, Johann *see*
- ARITHMETISCHER TAUSENDKUNSTLER
- NEWE GEOMETRISCHE UND PERSPECTIUISCHE INUENTIONES ETLICHER SONDERBAHRER INSTRUMENT

FAULKNER AND GRAY'S BANKRUPTCY LAW REVIEW – New York. v1-4. spr 1989-spr 1992* – 1,5,9 – D18369 – us UMI [340]
FAULKNER AND GRAY'S CARD FAX – Chicago. 1990-94*. 1995-97+ – 1 – D18389 – us UMI [073]
FAULKNER AND GRAY'S MEDICINE AND HEALTH – (Former titles: Washington Report on the Medical Sciences, jun 9, 1947-sep 9, 1968. Mc-Graw-Hill's Washington Report on Medicine and Health, sep 16, 1968-jul 21, 1986. McGraw-Hill's Medicine and Health, jul 28, 1986-oct 9, 1989) – Washington. 1989-93* 1; 1994*. 1995-97+ 1,5,9 – 1,5,9 – D17751 – us UMI [610]
Faulkner Concordance Advisory Board *see* CONCORDANCES TO THE WORKS OF WILLIAM FAULKNER
FAULKNER JOURNAL – Akron. v1-13. fal 1985-spr 1998+ 1,5,9; v7-10. fal 1991-spr 1995* 5 – 1,5,9 – D17768 – us UMI [420]
Faulkner, William *see* CONCORDANCES TO THE WORKS OF WILLIAM FAULKNER
FAULKNER'S DUBLIN JOURNAL – Dublin, Ireland.1726-1805. 27 reels – 1 – ie Microforms [072]
FAULTES FAULTS, AND NOTHING ELSE BUT FAULTES / Rich, Barnaby – 1606 – 9 – 15.00 – us Scholars' Facs [840]
FAULTS AND FAILURES OF THE LATE PRESBYTERIAN UNION IN CANADA / Brymner, Douglas – London, Ont.: London Free Press Print Co., 1879. 00313. (Pre-1900 Canadiana) – 9 – cn C.I.H.M. [240]
FAUN – Berlin, dec 23 1918-jun 9 1919 – 1r – 1 – Dist. gw Mikrofilm – gw Misc Inst [072]
THE FAUNA AND GEOGRAPHY OF THE MALDIVE AND LACCADIVE ARCHIPELAGOES / ed by Gardiner, J S – Being the account of the Work carried on and of the Collections made by an Expedition during the years 1899 and 1900. 2 v. Cambridge. 1903-06. Illus. BZ-2248 1 – 9 – ne IDC [910]
FAUNA AUSTRIACA. DIE FLIEGEN (DIPTERA) / Schiner, J R – 2469 2. 2 v. 1862-1864 – 8 – ne IDC [590]
FAUNA BRASILIENSIS, QUAM. PRAESIDE C. P. THUNBERG / Thunberg, C P – Z 148 2. 1823 – 8 – ne IDC [590]
FAUNA CAYANENSIS / Thunberg, C P – 2400 2. 1823 – 8 – ne IDC [590]
FAUNA CHINENSIS / Thunberg, C P – 2410 2. 1823 – 8 – ne IDC [590]
FAUNA COLEOPTERORUM HELVETICA / Heer, Oswald – Turici, 1838-41.Z/1136/2 – 8 – ne IDC [590]
FAUNA DER IN DER PALAEARCTISCHEN REGION. LEBENDEN BINNENCONCHYLIEN / Westerlund, C A – 2v. Lund. 1844-, 1886-90; suppl. Berlin. 1890. BZ-861 2 – 8 – ne IDC [590]
FAUNA E FLORA DEL GOLFO DI NAPOLI: MONOGRAFIE/FAUNA UND FLORA DES GOLFES VON NEAPEL UND DER ANGRENZENDEN MEERES-ABSCHNITTE : MONOGRAPHIEN – v1-38. 1880-1956 – 9 – Dfl3,500.00 – ne Schierenberg [580]
FAUNA EUROPAEA MOLLUSCORUM EXTRAMARINORUM / Westerlund, C A – Z 858 2. 1876-1878 – 8 – ne IDC [590]
FAUNA GERMANICA / Reitter, E – 2781 2. 5 v. 1908-1916 – 8 – ne IDC [580]
FAUNA GROENLANDICA / Fabricius, O – BN 208 2. 1929 – 8 – ne IDC [590]
FAUNA INSECTORUM EUROPAE / Ahrens, A & Germar, E F – 24 pts. 2144 2. 1812-1847 – 8 – ne IDC [590]
FAUNA INSECTORUM LAPPONICA / Zetterstedt, J W – pt. 1. Hammone. 1828. BZ-1738 2 – 8 – ne IDC [590]
FAUNA JAPONICA CONTINUATIO / Thunberg, C P – 2411 2. 1823 – 8 – ne IDC [590]
FAUNA JAPONICA, SIVE DESCRIPTIO ANIMALIUM, QUAE IN ITINERE PER JAPONIAM / Siebold, P F von – 2054 2. 6 v. 1833-1850 – 8 – ne IDC [590]
FAUNA LEPIDOPTEROLOGICA VOLGO-URALENSIS / Eversmann, E – Casani, 1844. xiv,633p.Z/1221/2 – 8 – ne IDC [590]
FAUNA ORNITHOLOGIQUE DE LA SICILE / Malherbe, A – (Mem. Acad. Roy.). Metz. 1843. Z-1847 2 – 8 – ne IDC [590]
FAUNA SVECICA / Linnaeus, Carl – ed. 2. Stockholmiae. 1761. B-2657 2 – 8 – ne IDC [590]
FAUNA SVECICA: INSECTA / Paykull, G von – Upsaliae, 1798- 1800. 3v. Z/1533/2 – 8 – ne IDC [590]
FAUNAE INSECTORUM AMERICES BOREALIS PRODROMUS / Panzer, G W F – Norimbergae, 1794. 8p., 1 pl. Z-1527/2 – 8 – ne IDC [590]
FAUNAE INSECTORUM GERMANICAE INITIA / ed by Panzer, G W F – Nuernberg, Regensburg, 1792-1844. Pt.1-190 – 172mf – 9 – 2455/2 – ne IDC [590]
Faunce, Daniel Webster *see*
- ADVENT AND ASCENSION
- THE CHRISTIAN IN THE WORLD
- HOURS WITH A SCEPTIC
- INSPIRATION CONSIDERED AS A TREND
- PRAYER AS A THEORY AND A FACT
- YOUNG MAN'S DIFFICULTIES WITH HIS BIBLE

Faunce, Daniel Worcester *see* SHALL WE BELIEVE IN A DIVINE PROVIDENCE?
Faunce, William Herbert Perry *see*
- THE EDUCATIONAL IDEAL IN THE MINISTRY
- THE SOCIAL ASPECTS OF FOREIGN MISSIONS
- WHAT DOES CHRISTIANITY MEAN?

Faundes Rivera, H *see* LA SUCESION ANTE EL DERECHO INTERNACIONAL PRIVADO
FAUNE DES VERTEGRES DE LA SUISSE. V.2 : HISTOIRE NATURELLE DES OISEAUX / Fatio, V & Studer, T – Geneve, Bale, 1899-1904 – 2pts – 8 – ne IDC [590]
FAUNE ENTOMOLOGIQUE DE MADAGASCAR, BOURBON ET MAURICE / Boisduval, J B A D de – Paris, 1833. 122p. 16 plts. Z-1077/2 – 8 – ne IDC [590]
FAUNE ENTOMOLOGIQUE DES ENVIRONS DE PARIS / Boisduval, J B A D de & Lacordaire, J T – Paris, 1835. v1. 3pls. Z-1082/2 – 8 – ne IDC [590]
FAUNE ORNITHOLOGIQUE DE LA SIBERIE ORIENTALE / Taczanowski, W – Z 1945. 1893 – 9 – ne IDC [590]
FAUNULA COLEOPTERORUM BIRMANIAE / Schmidt-Goebel, H M – Prag, 1846. viii,94p, 3 pls. Z-1611/2 – 8 – ne IDC [590]
FAUNULA MOLLUSCORUM HISPALENSIS / Westerlund, C A – Z 863 2. 1892 – 8 – ne IDC [590]
FAUNULE COLEOPTEROLOGIQUE DU MONT-ALIRIC (AUDE) / Gavoy, L – Carcassone, 1893 – 47p – 8 – ne IDC [590]
FAUQUIER DEMOCRAT – Warrenton. Va. 1940-45; 1950- – 1 – us UMI [071]
Faure, Edgar et al *see* LEARNING TO BE
Faure, Gabriel *see*
- LA BONNE CHANSON
- LA DERNIERE JOURNEE DE SAPPHO

Faure, J B *see*
- 20 MELODIES, DEUXIEME RECUEIL
- 20 MELODIES, QUATRIEME RECUEIL

Faure, Pierre-Joseph *see* REFLEXIONS D'UN CITOYEN SUR LA MARINE
Fausset, A R *see* STUDIES IN THE CL PSALMS...COINCIDENCES WITH THE INDEPENDENT SCRIPTURE HISTORIES
LA FAUSSETE DES MIRACLES DES DEUX TESTAMENTS – (D'Holbach series) – 9 – fr Hachette [240]
FAUST : A DRAMATIC POEM / Goethe, Johann Wolfgang von – 7th ed. Edinburgh, London: W Blackwood, 1879 – 1r – 1 – us U.W. Library [820]
FAUST : A DRAMATIC POEM / Goethe, Johann Wolfgang von – Edinburgh: W Blackwood, 1887 – 1r – 1 – us U.W. Library [820]
FAUST : EIN DRAMATISCHES GEDICHT IN DREI ABSCHNITTEN / Wolfram, Ludwig Hermann; ed by Neurath, Otto – (Includes bibliographical references and indexes) – Berlin: Frensdorff, [1906] – 1 – us U.W. Library [810]
FAUST / Spohr, Ludwig – For voice and pianoforte. With English and German words. (instrumentation indicated). 187-? – 9 – us Sibley [780]
FAUST : EINE TRAGOEDIE / Goethe, Johann Wolfgang von – Muenchen: T Stroefer, [1887?] – 1r – 1 – us U.W. Library [820]
FAUST, A TRAGEDY / Goethe, Johann Wolfgang von – Transl. into English verse, with notes and preliminary remarks by John Stuart Blackie. 2nd ed., carefully rev. and largely rewritten. London: Macmillan, 1880. ixxvii, 296p – 1 – us U.W. Library [820]
Faust, Albert Bernhardt *see*
- CHARLES SEALSFIELD (CARL POSTL)
- THE GERMAN ELEMENT IN THE UNITED STATES

FAUST ALS TRAGOEDIE / Wiese, Benno von – (Includes bibliographical references) – Stuttgart: W Kohlhammer, [1946] – 1r – 1 – us U.W. Library [430]
FAUST, FIRST PART / Goethe, Johann Wolfgang von; ed by Salm, Peter – (German and English parallel texts on facing pages with an introduction in English. Includes bibliographical references) – New York: Bantam Books, 1967 – 1 – us U.W. Library [820]
Faust, Johanna *see* THE SOUL OF WOMAN UNDER SOCIALISM
FAUST UND DER WEG ZUM LEBEN : FAUSTS HEIMKEHR / Wizemann, Karl – 9. Aufl. Stuttgart: Wege-Verlag Wilhelm Kaz, 1932 – 1r – 1 – us U.W. Library [410]
FAUSTS LEBEN, TATEN UND HOELLENFAHRT / Klinger, Friedrich Maximilian – (Includes bibliographical references) – Berlin: Aufbau-Verlag, 1958 – 1 – us U.W. Library [830]
EIN FAUSTSCHLAG : SCHAUSPIEL IN DREI AKTEN / Anzengruber, Ludwig – Wien: L Rosner, 1878 – 1r – 1 – us U.W. Library [820]
Faustus *see* AN EPOCH IN PRINTING: BEING THE FIRST MATTER SET ON THE FIRST LINOTYPE MACHINE MANUFACTURED IN CANADA
FAUSTUS, HIS LIFE, DEATH, AND DOOM : A ROMANCE IN PROSE / Klinger, Friedrich Maximilian – London: W Kent, 1864 – 1 – us U.W. Library [830]
Faut, S *see* DIE CHRISTOLOGIE SEIT SCHLEIERMACHER

IL FAUT UN ETAT OU LA REVUE DE L'AN 6 / Leger, Chazet et Buhan – (French Theatre Series). Paris. Chez le Libraire "Au theatre du Vaudeville." an 7. 1798 – 9 – fr Hachette [820]

Fauteux, Aegidius *see*
- LES CARNETS D'UN CURIEUX COLLABORATION SPECIALE A "LA PATRIE"
- L'INTRODUCTION DE L'IMPRIMERIE AU CANADA UNE BREVE HISTOIRE
- LE RAPPEL

Fauth, Gertrud *see* JOERG WICKRAMS ROMANTECHNIK

Fauvel, A J *see* QUATUOR, TROIS, OP. 6, LIV. 2

Fauvel, P *see* POLYCHETES ERRANTES. FAUNE DE FRANCE

Fauvet, J *see* LES PAYSANS ET LA POLITIQUE DANS LA FRANCE CONTEMPORAINE

LES FAUX BRILLANTS COMEDIE EN CINQ ACTES ET EN VERS / Marchand, Felix-Gabriel – Montreal: Prendergast, 1885. SEM16P265 – 1r – 5 – Can$9.00 – cn Bibl Nat [820]

LES FAUX LIBERAUX DE L'EGLISE ROMAINE : REPONSE AU P. PERRAUD ET A SES ADHERENTS / Michaud, Eugene – (Includes bibliographical references) – Paris: Sandoz et Fischbacher, 1872 – 1mf – 9 – 0-8370-8534-9 – 1986-2534 – us A.T.L.A. [240]

Favart, CS *see* MEMOIRES ET CORRESPONDANCE. ET PRECEDES D'UNE NOTICE HISTORIQUE, REDIGEES SUR PIECES AUTHENTIQUES ET ORIGINALES

Favero, Terence G *see* THE ABILITY OF SARCOPLASMIC RETICULUM TO REGULATE INTRACELLULAR CALCIUM FOLLOWING A FATIGUING BOUT OF EXERCISE

Faverot de Kerbrech, Francois Nicholas Guy Napoleon *see* MEMOIRE SUR LES CHEVAUX DE L'AMERIQUE DU NORD, ETATS-UNIS ET CANADA

Faverot, I *see* REVEILLE-MATIN A DOUBLE MONTRE

FAVERSHAM MERCURY ETC – England.1862; 1897; 1900. -w.2 1/2 reels – 1 – uk British Libr Newspaper [072]

FAVERSHAM NEWS AND EAST KENT JOURNAL – (North East Kent News, 1894-96) – Faversham, England. 24 Feb-Dec 1883; 1884-96; 1898-1906; 1908-11; 1913-35. -w – 48r – 1 – uk British Libr Newspaper [072]

Favieres *see* ELISCA OU L'AMOUR MATERNEL

THE FAVORITE / Desbarats Co – Montreal, 28 dec 1872-16 mai 1874 – 1r – 1 – Can$60.00 – cn Can Microfilming [072]

THE FAVORITE – Montreal: G E Desbarats, [1873-1874] – 9 – cn C.I.H.M. [971]

THE FAVORITE BALLET MUSIC IN THE ENTERTAINMENT OF RAYMOND AND AGNES... / Reeves, W – (Arranged for pianoforte by Mr. Reeves) – London: Preston & Son [1797?] – 1 – us Sibley [780]

THE FAVORITE BALLET OF LA FILLE SAUVAGE, OU LE POUVOIR DE LA MUSIQUE, PERFORMED AT THE KING'S THEATRE HAYMARKET / Mortelli, M – London: Rt Birchall, [1805?] – 1 – us Sibley [780]

A FAVORITE QUINETETTO FOR 2 VIOLINS, TWO TENORS, AND A BASS / Haydn, Joseph – London: G Gardom, [179-?] – 1 – us Sibley [780]

A FAVORITE SOLO FOR THE VIOLIN AND HARPSICHORD... / Bach, C P E – London: C & S Thompson, [c. 1775] – 1 – us Sibley [780]

FAVORITE SOLO[S] FOR THE VIOLIN AND HARPSICHORD BKS 1-2 / Angelini, C A – London: C & S Thompson, 1770? – 1 – us Sibley [780]

A FAVORITE SONATA FOR THE PIANO FORTE WITH AN ACCOMPANIMENT FOR THE VIOLIN / Willson, Joseph – New Brunswick: Printed for the Author 1801-1804. MUSIC 123, Item 7 – 1 – us L of C Photodup [780]

FAVOUR AND FORTUNE: A NOVEL – Toronto: W. Bryce, 1889. 03079. (Pre-1900 Canadiana) – 9 – cn C.I.H.M. [830]

Favre de Vaugelas, Cl *see*
- NOUVELLES REMARQUES SUR LA LANGUE FRANCAISE
- REMARQUES SUR LA LANGUE FRANCAISE

Favre, Jules *see* PLAIDOYERS ET DISCOURS DU BATONNAT

THE FAWCETT AND LISTER PAPERS / Halifax Central Library. Archives – 1733-75. BRRAM – 1 – uk Microform Academic [025]

FAWCETT LIBRARY ON WOMEN'S STUDIES / City of London Polytechnic – (The autograph letter collection of the Fawcett library including indexes 333mf Dfl2,905.00; The Josephine Butler letter collection including indexes 273mf Gld2,315.00) – 9 – ne IDC [305]

Fawcett, Trevor *see*
- NINETEENTH CENTURY BOOKS ON ART AND ARCHITECTURE
- VISUAL ARTS AND ARCHITECTURE SPECIALIST COLLECTION

Fawkes, Alfred *see* STUDIES IN MODERNISM

FAWQ AL-'ADAH-'I KHABARI-I KAR – [S.l.]: Sazman-i Chirik'ha-yi fada-i-i khalq, 1981. Sal-i 3, shumarah-'i 1-4 (28 Khurdad 1360-8 Tir 1360 [18 Jun 1981-29 Jun 1981]) – 1 reel – 1 – $25.00 – us MEDOC [950]

Fawsett, C *see* THE ENGLISH FACTORIES IN INDIA, 1618-1684

FAX – Portland OR. Feb 7 Mar 17 Apr 14 May 8 16 1934, Dec 7 1934, Jan 15 June 22 1935, July 27 Sep 11 Oct 4 Nov 30 1935, May 13 Oct 12 26 Nov 2 1936 + – 1 – us U.O. Library [071]

FAX – Portland OR. May 14 Nov 2 1942, Nov 2 1944 + – 1 – us U.O. Library [071]

FAX/NET ELECTRONIC-MAIL SOURCE DIRECTORY – Elmsford. v1-11 1984-94*. v12-14 1995-97+ – 1,5,9 – D49546 – us UMI [380]

FAXON, F.W. CO BOSTON *see* CUMULATED MAGAZINE SUBJECT INDEX, 1907-1949

FAXUE YANJIU – Studies in Law. In Chinese but Table of Contents in English in each issue. F p8 – 9 – $4.50f – cc Microforms [073]

FAXUE ZAZHI – Journal of Jurisprudence. 1982-. F P259 – 9 – $4.50f – cc Microforms [073]

Fay, F R *see* BOOK OF JOSHUA

Fay, H A *see* COLLECTION OF THE OFFICIAL ACCOUNTS IN DETAIL OF ALL THE BATTLES FOUGHT BY SEA AND LAND, BETWEEN THE NAVY AND ARMY OF THE UNITED STATES, AND THE NAVY AND THE ARMY OF GREAT BRITAIN DURING THE YEARS 1812-15

Fay, Thomas F *see* THE SPIRO T. AGNEW CASE

Faye, Eugene de *see*
- CLEMENT D'ALEXANDRIE
- GNOSTIQUES ET GNOSTICISME

FAYETTE TRIBUNE – Fayetteville. West Virginia. 1911-1913; 1915-1940 – 1 – us UMI [071]

FAYETTE TRIBUNE – Oak Hill. West Virginia. 1912-1940; 1958-1966 – 1 – us UMI [071]

FAYETTEVILLE TIMES – N.C. 1973- – 1 – us UMI [071]

Fayle, C Ernest *see* A HISTORY OF LLOYD'S FROM THE FOUNDING OF LLOYD'S COFFEE HOUSE TO THE PRESENT DAY

Faypoult de Maisoncelle, Guillaume C *see* MEMOIRE STATISTIQUE DU DEPARTEMENT DE L'ESCAUT

Fayrer, J *see* THE THANATOPHIDIA OF INDIA

Fayrer, Joseph *see* INSPECTOR-GENERAL SIR JAMES RANALD MARTIN

Fayt, Carlos S *see* NATURALEZA DEL PERONISMO

FAZ MAGAZIN – 1980-1994 – 4 times per yr – 1 – DM200.00 – sz Infoprint [073]

Fazal, Cyril P K *see* A GUIDE TO PUNJAB GOVERNMENT REPORTS AND STATISTICS

Fazey, C *see* AETIOLOGY OF PSYCHOACTIVE SUBSTANCE USE

FAZHI RIBAO = THE LEGAL DAILY – (1981-87. $34.00r; 1988- . $55.00r) – In Chinese. Current subscription. Annual delivery. As Zhongguo Fazhi Bao (China's Legislation Gazette) until 1988. M D8 – 1 – cc Microforms [072]

Fazil *see* DIVANCE

FAZ-MAGAZIN – (Subsc 1995 DM180.00) – 1980-1994 – 47r – 1 – DM3,525.00 – gw Mikro Press [943]

FBI AMERICAN LEGION CONTACT PROGRAM / U.S. Federal Bureau of Investigation; ed by Theoharis, Athan – (Documents from 1940s-1960s) – 1985 – 1r – 1 – $85.00 – S1751 – us Scholarly Res [360]

FBI DETECTIVE – New York. feb 1949-may 1951* – 1 – D8276 – us UMI [360]

FBI FILE : ROBERT F. KENNEDY – (With printed guide) – 1991 – 1r – 1 – $85.00 – S3242 – us Scholarly Res [360]

FBI FILE: MIBURN (MISSISSIPPI BURNING) : THE INVESTIGATION OF THE MURDERS OF HENRY SCHWERNER, ANDREW GOODMAN, AND JAMES EARL CHANEY, JUNE 21 1964 / U.S. Federal Bureau of Investigation – (With printed guide) – 1990 – 1r – 1 – $85.00 – S3244 – us Scholarly Res [360]

FBI FILE ON A. PHILIP RANDOLPH / U.S. Federal Bureau of Investigation – (With printed guide) – 1990 – 1r – 1 – $85.00 – S3202 – us Scholarly Res [331]

FBI FILE ON ALBERT EINSTEIN / U.S. Federal Bureau of Investigation – 1986 – 1r – 1 – $85.00 – S1764 – us Scholarly Res [323]

FBI FILE ON CESAR CHAVEZ AND UNITED FARM WORKERS – (Guide can also be purchased separately S3354.G $10.00) – 1996 – 2r – 1 – $170.00 – S3354 – us Scholarly Res [331]

FBI FILE ON ELEANOR ROOSEVELT – (Guide also sold separately $10.00) – 3r – 1 – $255.00 – S3355 – us Scholarly Res [360]

FBI FILE ON ELIJAH MUHAMMED – (With Guide which is also sold separately S3342.G $10.00) – 3r – $255.00 – S3342 – us Scholarly Res [360]

FBI FILE ON JOSEPH MCCARTHY – (Guide also sold separately $10.00 S3353.G) – 1996 – 4r – 1 – $340.00 – S3353 – us Scholarly Res [360]

FBI FILE ON MALCOLM X / U.S. Federal Bureau of Investigation – (Supersedes: Malcolm X FBI Surveillance File) – 1996 – 10r – 1 – $850.00 – S3341 – us Scholarly Res [320]

FBI FILE ON MUSLIM MOSQUE, INC. – (With Guide which is also sold separately S3343.G $10.00) – 3r – $255.00 – S3343 – us Scholarly Res [360]

FBI FILE ON OSAGE INDIAN MURDERS / U.S. Federal Bureau of Investigation – (With guide) – 1986 – 3r – 1 – $255.00 – S3022 – us Scholarly Res [360]

FBI FILE ON PAUL ROBESON / U.S. Federal Bureau of Investigation – (Printed guide sold separately $10.00 S3040.G) – 1986 – 2r – 1 – $170.00 – S3040 – us Scholarly Res [780]

FBI FILE ON ROY WILKINS / U.S. Federal Bureau of Investigation – (With printed guide) – 1990 – 1r – 1 – $85.00 – S3201 – us Scholarly Res [320]

FBI FILE ON THE AMERICAN CHURCHWOMEN KILLED IN EL SALVADOR, DECEMBER 1980 / U.S. Federal Bureau of Investigation – (With printed guide) – 1990 – 2r – 1 – $170.00 – S3204 – us Scholarly Res [360]

FBI FILE ON THE ATLANTA CHILD MURDERS (ATKID) / U.S. Federal Bureau of Investigation – (With printed guide) – 1990 – 3r – 1 – $255.00 – S3200 – us Scholarly Res [360]

FBI FILE ON THE BLACK PANTHER PARTY, NORTH CAROLINA / U.S. Federal Bureau of Investigation – (With printed guide) – 1986 – 2r – 1 – $170.00 – S3039 – us Scholarly Res [320]

FBI FILE ON THE COMMITTEE FOR PUBLIC JUSTICE / U.S. Federal Bureau of Investigation; ed by Theoharis, Athan – 1r – 1 – $85.00 – S1752 – us Scholarly Res [360]

FBI FILE ON THE FIRE BOMBING AND SHOOTING AT KENT STATE UNIVERSITY / U.S. Federal Bureau of Investigation – 1986 – 7r – 1 – $595.00 – S1763 – us Scholarly Res [360]

FBI FILE ON THE HIGHLANDER FOLK SCHOOL / U.S. Federal Bureau of Investigation – (With guide) – 1990 – 1r – 1 – $85.00 – S3241 – us Scholarly Res [331]

FBI FILE ON THE HOUSE COMMITTEE ON UN-AMERICAN ACTIVITIES (HUAC) / U.S. Federal Bureau of Investigation – (With printed guide) – 1986 – 9r – 1 – $765.00 – S1765 – us Scholarly Res [360]

FBI FILE ON THE KU KLUX KLAN MURDER OF VIOLA LIUZZO / U.S. Federal Bureau of Investigation – (With printed guide) – 1990 – 1r – 1 – $85.00 – S3243 – us Scholarly Res [360]

FBI FILE ON THE MOORISH SCIENCE TEMPLE OF AMERICA (NOBLE DREW ALI) – (With Guide which is also sold separately S3352.G $10.00) – 1990 – 3r – $255.00 – S3245 – us Scholarly Res [360]

FBI FILE ON THE NATIONAL ASSOCIATION FOR THE ADVANCEMENT OF COLORED PEOPLE (NAACP) / U.S. Federal Bureau of Investigation – (With printed guide) – 1990 – 4r – 1 – $340.00 – S3203 – us Scholarly Res [320]

FBI FILE ON THE NATIONAL NEGRO CONGRESS / U.S. Federal Bureau of Investigation – (With printed guide) – 1986 – 2r – 1 – $170.00 – S3045 – us Scholarly Res [320]

FBI FILE ON THE ORGANIZATION OF AFRO-AMERICAN UNITY (OAAU) – (With Guide which is also sold separately S3344.G $10.00) – 1r – $85.00 – S3344 – us Scholarly Res [360]

FBI FILE ON THE STUDENT NONVIOLENT COORDINATING COMMITTEE (SNCC) / U.S. Federal Bureau of Investigation – (With guide) – 1990 – 2r – 1 – $170.00 – S3245 – us Scholarly Res [320]

FBI FILE ON THE STUDENTS FOR A DEMOCRATIC SOCIETY AND THE WEATHERMAN UNDERGROUND ORGANIZATION / U.S. Federal Bureau of Investigation – (With printed guide) – 1990 – 8r – 1 – $680.00 – S3246 – us Scholarly Res [320]

FBI FILE ON W.E.B. DU BOIS – (With Guide which is also sold separately S3345.G $10.00) – 1r – $85.00 – S3345 – us Scholarly Res [360]

THE FBI FILES ON THE AMERICAN INDIAN MOVEMENT AND WOUNDED KNEE – 26r with printed guide – 1 – $2,510.00 – 0-89093-989-6 – us UPA [360]

FBI FILES ON THE ASSASSINATION OF PRESIDENT KENNEDY, 1963-1973 – 31r – 1 – $2250.00 – us UMI [977]

FBI FILES ON THE REVEREND JESSE JACKSON / U.S. Federal Bureau of Investigation – (With printed guide) – 1988 – 1r – 1 – $85.00 – S3158 – us Scholarly Res [320]

FBI FILING AND RECORDS PROCEDURES / U.S. Federal Bureau of Investigation; ed by Theoharis, Athan & O'Reilly, Kenneth – 1984 – 1r – 1 – $85.00 – S1755 – us Scholarly Res [360]

FBI LAW ENFORCEMENT BULLETIN – (Former title: Fugitives Wanted by Police, sep 1932-sep 1935) – Washington. v1-46. sep 1932-sep 1977* 1; v47-66. 1978-97+ 1,5,9 – 1,5,9 – D11747 – us UMI [360]

FBI MANUALS OF INSTRUCTION, INVESTIGATIVE PROCEDURES, AND GUIDELINES, 1927-1978 / U.S. Federal Bureau of Investigation; ed by Theoharis, Athan & O'Reilly, Kenneth – (Four manuals dated 1927, 1936, 1941 and 1978. Printed guide) – 1984 – 2r – 1 – $170.00 – S1759 – us Scholarly Res [360]

FBI WIRETAPS, BUGS, AND BREAK-INS : THE NATIONAL SECURITY ELECTRONIC SURVEILLANCE CARD FILE AND THE SURREPTITIOUS ENTRIES FILE / ed by Theoharis, Athan – 4r – 1 – $550.00 – 1-55655-088-X – us UPA [327]

FCC RECORD : A COMPREHENSIVE COMPILATION OF DOCUMENTS, REPORTS, PUBLIC NOTICES, AND OTHER DOCUMENTS OF THE FCC / U.S. Federal Communications Commission – (With a cumulative index for v1-2. Updates planned) – Washington: GPO. v1-9 no 20. 1986-94 – 804mf – 9 – $1,206.00 – LLMC 88-006 – us L.L.M.C. [324]

FCC TELEPHONE EQUIPMENT REGISTRATION LIST / U.S. National Technical Information Service – Quarterly. Listed in order of equipment type – 9 – us N.T.I.S. [000]

FDA CONSUMER – (Former title: FDA Papers, feb 1967-jun 1972) – Rockville. v1-31. 1967-97+ 1; v4-31. 1970-97+ 5; v9-31. 1975-97+ 9 – 1,5,9 – D2979 – us UMI [640]

FDA HANDBOOK OF TOTAL DRUG QUALITY / U.S. Food and Drug Administration – Washington, 1970 92 p. LL-2238 – 1 – us L of C Photodup [340]

FDA PAPERS *see* FDA CONSUMER

FDA-HEW *see* RADIATION CONTROL FOR HEALTH AND SAFETY ACT, 1968

FDM : FURNITURE DESIGN AND MANUFACTURING – (v1-28 & issues for jan-mar 1958 & may 1959 were not available for filming. Former title: Furniture News, 19??-58) – Newton. v29-65 1957-93. v66 1994*. v67-69 1995-97+ 1; v43-45 1971-73. v47-54 1975-82. v55-59 1983-87*. v60-63 1988-91. v64-66 1992-94+. v67-69 1995-97+ 5; v47-65 1975-93. v66 1994*. v67-69

1995-97+ 9 – 1,5,9 – D1798 – us UMI [680]
FE – (Cont: Financial Executive. Cont by: Financial Executive) – Morristown. v1-2. 1985-86 – 1,5,9 – D14465 – us UMI [650]
A FE CHRISTA : HEBDOMADARIO DEDICADO AOS INTERESSES DA RELIGIAO CATHOLICA – Penedo, Alagoas. 11 Jan 1902-13 Jul 1907 – 1,5,6 – bl Biblioteca [072]
F.E. DZERZHINSKII PAMPHLET COLLECTION – 1945-1976 – 1 – CSUXANS0754-B – us Hoover Inst Photo [331]
FE NEWS : 1943-1949 / United Farm Equipment and Metal Workers of America – (Coll title: Labor Union Periodicals, Pt 1) – 1r – 1 – $135.00 – 1-55655-236-X – us UPA [331]
LA FE TRIUNFANTE DEL AMOR / Garcia de la Huerta, Vicente – Madrid: Pantaleon Aznar, 1748 – 1 – sp Bibl Santa Ana [946]
F.E. Weakley and Co *see* HISTORY OF DEARBORN AND OHIO COUNTIES
FE Y COMPROMISO HUMANO / Perez Lozano, Jose Maria & Ruiz Ginenez, Joaquin y Jose Maria Perez Lozano – Salamanca: Ediciones Secratariado Trinitario, 1969 – 1 – sp Bibl Santa Ana [946]
FEAR / Mosso, Angelo – Trans. from the 5th ed. of the Italian by E. Lough and F. Kiesow. London, New York: Longmans, Green and Co., 1896. 278p. illus., plates – 1 – us U.W. Library [150]
FEAR OF FALLING AMONG COMMUNITY ELDERS / Ferrari, Anne – Temple University, 1996 – 2mf – 9 – $8.00 – PSY 1885 – us Microform Publ [150]
FEAR OR FREEDOM – Johannesburg: SPRO-CAS 2, [n.d.] – us Res Libr [072]
Fearnley, Thomas *see* THE HARMONY OF SCRIPTURE
THE FEAST OF BACCHVS / Bridges, Robert Seymour – Oxford: Priv. print. by H. Daniel, 1889 – 1 roll – 1 – 1-55879-201-5 – uk Libr Preservation [810]
THE FEAST OF SAINT ANNE AND OTHER POEMS / Hamilton, Pierce Stevens – Halifax: J. Burgoyne, 1878. 05350. (Pre-1900 Canadiana) – 9 – cn C.I.H.M. [810]
Feather, J *see* LAST OF THE PROPHETS:...A STUDY OF...JOHN THE BAPTIST
FEATHER RIVER BULLETIN – Quincy, CA. 1931-47; 1954-59; 1972; 1977- – 35+ r – 1 – $1,750.00 ($90.00y) – B02650 – us Library Micro [071]
FEATHER RIVER BULLETIN – Quincy. Calif. -w. and pred. 1885- – 1 – us UMI [071]
Featherston, Howell Colston *see* FEATHERSTON'S INDEX TO THE VIRGINIA CORPORATION LAW, ACTS 1902-3, PAGE 437 ET SEQ. SUPPLEMENT TO THE VIRGINIA LAW REGISTER, SEPTEMBER 1903
Featherstonhaugh, George W *see* PAPERS
FEATHERSTON'S INDEX TO THE VIRGINIA CORPORATION LAW, ACTS 1902-3, PAGE 437 ET SEQ. SUPPLEMENT TO THE VIRGINIA LAW REGISTER, SEPTEMBER 1903 / Featherston, Howell Colston – Lynchburg, Bell, 1903. 16 p. LL-865 – 1 – us L of C Photodup [340]
Feaux, M *see* CATALOGUE MANUSCRIT DE SA COLLECTION
Febres Cordero, Julio *see*
- ARCHIVO DE HISTORIA Y VARIEDADES
- COLECCION DE CUENTOS
- DON QUIJOTE EN AMERICA

FEBRIOLOGIAE LECTIONES PINCIANAE, APRENDIX AD FEBRILOGIAM, DOLORIS DIAGNOSIM... / Gutierrez, J L – Lyon, 1668 – 7mf – 9 – sp Cultura [610]
FEBS LETTERS – v1-178. 1968-84 – 1,5,6,13 – sz Elsevier [073]
LA FECHA EN LA CONQUISTA DE CACERES ANTE LOS DOCUMENTOS (LA CARTA POPULATIONIS) / Floriano Cumbreno, Antonio C – Gran Canaria: Caja Insular de Ahorros, 1975 – 1 – sp Bibl Santa Ana [946]
Fechner, Gustav Theodor *see* DIE DREI MOTIVE UND GRUENDE DES GLAUBENS
Fechner, Helmuth *see* DEUTSCHLAND UND POLEN, 1772-1945
Fecht, Friedrich *see* LESSING-GALERIE
FECHTBUCH / ed by Hils, Hans-Peter – 1990 – 30p + 3 color mf – ca DM530.00 – 3-89219-301-0 – gw Lengenfelder [790]
Fechter, Paul *see*
- GESCHICHTE DER DEUTSCHEN LITERATUR

DER FECHTER VON RAVENNA : TRAUERSPIEL IN FUENF AKTEN / Halm, Friedrich – 6. Aufl. Wien: C Gerold, 1894 – 1r – 1 – us U.W. Library [820]
Fechter, Werner *see* DAS PUBLIKUM DER MITTELHOCHDEUTSCHEN DICHTUNG
FECHTER-ZEITUNG – Hanau a.M. 1931-1938 – 1 – us NY Public [073]
Fedde, F *see*
- BEIHEFTE
- REPERTORIUM SPECIERUM NOVARUM REGNI VEGETABILIS

Feder, Alfred Leonhard *see* JUSTINS DES MAERTYRERS LEHRE VON JESUS CHRISTUS
Feder, Donald A *see* GUN CONTROL, A LIBERTARIAN PARTY POSITION PAPER
A FEDERACAO : ORGAM DO PARTIDO REPUBLICANO FEDERAL – Manaos, Amazonas. 11-29 Dez 1895; Jan-Maio, Set 1896; Out 1898-Dez 1899; Maio, Jul-30 Dez 1900 – 1,5,6 – bl Biblioteca [072]
A FEDERACAO – Porto Alegre, Brazil. Jan 1907-Jun 1912 – 1 – bl Biblioteca [072]
A FEDERACAO – Sao Paulo, Brazil. Nov-Dec 1891; Jan-Jul 1892 – 1 – bl Biblioteca [072]
LA FEDERACION / Castillo, Marciano – San Salvador 1906. 91p. LL-8004 – 1 – us L of C Photodup [340]
LA FEDERACION / Correa y Zafrilla, P – Madrid, 1880 – 3mf – 1 – ILM-1678/1 – ne IDC [327]
Federacion Argentina de Periodistas *see* DIEZ ANOS DE ORGANIZACION SINDICAL
Federacion Empresarial Cacerena *see* PRESENTACION DE LA FEDERACION EMPRESARIAL CACERENA. BORRADOR PARA EXAMEN
Federacion Espanola de Trabajadores de la Ensenanza *see*
- BOLETIN DE INFORMACION
- LES PROFESSIONNELS DE L'ENSEIGNEMENT LUTTENT POUR LA LIBERATION DU PEUPLE ESPAGNOLE

Federacion Estudiantil Universitaria *see* CRIMINALES DE GUERRA
Federacion Extremena de Futbol *see* CALENDARIO DEL CAMPEONATO 1972-73
LA FEDERACION INTERAMERICANA DE ABOGADOS; MEMORIA DE PRUEBA PARA OPTAR AL GRADO DE LICENCIADO EN LA FACULTAD DE CIENCIAS JURIDICAS Y SOCIALES DE LA UNIVERSIDAD DE CHILE / Gutierrez Carrasco, Octavio – Santiago? Imprenta Sanchez 1946. 66 2 p. LL-8010 – 1 – us L of C Photodup [340]
FEDERACION LATINOAMERICANA DE ASOCIACIONES DE FAMILIARES DE DETENIDOS-DESAPARECIDOS (FEDEFAM) = LATIN AMERICAN FEDERATION OF ASSOCIATIONS OF RELATIVES OF THE DETAINED-DISAPPEARED – Caracas. 20 docs. 1982-1991 – 11mf – 9 – ne IDC [360]
Federacion Ornitologica Espanola *see* 15TH CAMPEONATO NACIONAL FEDERAL DE CANARICULTURA Y PAJAROS EXOTICOS E INDIGENAS Y 7TH CONCURSO EXPOSICION DE LA U.C.E...
Federacion Provincial de Empresarios de la Construccion *see* ESTATUTOS Y REGLAMENTOS
LE FEDERAL – Ottawa, Ontario. 4 mai 1878-14 sep 1878 – 1r – 1 – Can$45.00 – cn Can Microfilming [072]
FEDERAL ACCOUNTANT – (See also: Government Accountants Journal) – v6-24 1956-1975 1; v24 1975 5,6 – us UMI [650]
FEDERAL ADMINISTRATIVE LAW JUDGE HEARINGS, STATISTICAL REPORTS : REPORTS FOR 1975 AND 1976-1978 / Administrative Conference of the U.S. (ACUS) – Washington: GPO, 1977 and 1980 (all publ) – 7mf – 9 – $10.50 – LLMC 94-339 – us L.L.M.C. [340]
FEDERAL ADMINISTRATIVE REGULATORY AGENCIES AND THE DOCTRINE OF THE SEPARATION OF POWERS / Lattin, Ward Elgin – Washington, D.C., 1938. 95 p. LL-283 – 1 – us L of C Photodup [340]
FEDERAL AGRICULTURAL CENSUS, 1850 / Illinois. Census – Alphabetical by county. V123-0003/V123-0004 – 1 – us A.G.L.L. [310]
FEDERAL AGRICULTURAL CENSUS, 1860 / Illinois. Census – Alphabetical by county. V123-0005/V123-0010 – 1 – us A.G.L.L. [310]
FEDERAL AGRICULTURAL CENSUS, 1865 / Illinois. Census – MaCoupin-Ogle County. V123-0012 – 1 – us A.G.L.L. [310]
FEDERAL AGRICULTURAL CENSUS, 1870 / Illinois. Census – Alphabetical by county. V123-0012/V123-0022 – 1 – us A.G.L.L. [310]
FEDERAL AGRICULTURAL CENSUS, 1880 / Illinois. Census – Alphabetical by county. V123-0023/V123-0046 – 1 – us A.G.L.L. [310]
FEDERAL AND STATE CONSTITUTIONS : COLONIAL CHARTERS AND OTHER ORGANIC ACTS OF THE STATES, TERRITORIES AND COLONIES OF THE UNITED STATES / Thorpe, Francis N – Washington: GPO. v1-7. 1909 – 49mf – 9 – $73.00 – LLMC 82-713 – us L.L.M.C. [323]
THE FEDERAL AND STATE CONSTITUTIONS, COLONIAL CHARTERS, AND OTHER ORGANIC LAWS OF THE STATE, TERRITORIES, AND COLONIES. / Thorpe, Francis Newton – Washington, Govt. Print. Off., 1909. 7 v. LL-466 – 1 – us L of C Photodup [340]
FEDERAL AND STATE CRIMINAL REPORTER / ed by Silvernail, WM H – Albany: W C Little & Co. v1-3. 1896-97 (all publ) – 21mf – 9 – $31.50 – LLMC 84-264 – us L.L.M.C. [360]
FEDERAL ANTITRUST DECISIONS, 1890-1931 / U. S. Courts – (Add vol entitled: Decrees and Judgements in Antitrust Cases) – Washington: GPO. v1-12 + add vol. 1890-1931 – 141mf – 9 – $211.00 – LLMC 79-430A/B – us L.L.M.C. [340]
THE FEDERAL APPELLATE JUDICIARY IN THE 21ST CENTURY / ed by Harrison, Cynthia & Wheeler, Russel R – Washington: FJC, 1989 – 3mf – 9 – $4.50 – LLMC 95-367 – us L.L.M.C. [340]
FEDERAL BAR ASSOCIATION JOURNAL *see*
- FEDERAL BAR JOURNAL
- FEDERAL LAWYER

FEDERAL BAR JOURNAL – (Title varies: v1-5 1931-58 as Federal Bar Association Journal) – v1-39. 193-80 – 9 – $466.00set – us Hein [340]
FEDERAL BAR NEWS AND JOURNAL *see* FEDERAL LAWYER
FEDERAL BILL OF LADING ACT, TO TAKE EFFECT JANUARY 1, 1917. / U. S. Laws, Statutes, etc – New York National City Bank of New York 1916 32 p. LL-388 – 1 – us L of C Photodup [340]
FEDERAL CASES – (With digest) – Law Library Microform Consortium. v1-30. 1788-1879 – 9 – $657.00 set – us Hein [340]
THE FEDERAL CASES : COMPRISING CASES ARGUED AND DETERMINED IN THE CIRCUIT AND DISTRICT COURTS OF THE U.S. FROM THE EARLIEST TIMES TO THE BEGINNING OF THE FEDERAL REPORTER / U. S. – (West's major retrospective repr of all lower federal case reports prior to coverage provided by "Federal reporter") – St Paul: West Pub Co. v1-30. 1894-98 (all publ) – 438mf – 9 – $657.00 – LLMC 78-054 – us L.L.M.C. [340]
FEDERAL CASES 1789-1879 / U.S. Federal Court – 16r – 1 – $550.00 – us Trans-Media [340]
THE FEDERAL CASES: COMPRISING CASES ARGUED AND DETERMINED IN THE CIRCUIT AND DISTRICT COURTS OF THE UNITED STATES FROM THE EARLIEST TIMES TO THE BEGINNING OF THE FEDERAL REPORTER, 1789-1880. / U.S. Circuit and District Courts – (Table. St. Paul, 1894. 365 p. Suppl. Digest. St. Paul, 1898. 83, 259 p. Suppl. 2) – St. Paul, West, 1894-97. 30 v. LL-1712 – 1 – us L of C Photodup [340]
FEDERAL CENSUS OF THE DEAF, DUMB, BLIND AND INSANE, 1855 / Illinois. Census – Alphabetical by county. V123-0058 – 1 – us A.G.L.L. [310]
FEDERAL COMMUNICATIONS BAR JOURNAL *see* FEDERAL COMMUNICATIONS LAW JOURNAL
FEDERAL COMMUNICATIONS COMMISSION REPORTS / U.S. Federal Communications Commission – 1st series: v1-45. 1934-65. 2nd series: v1-104 no 4 + index/ digests 1965-86 (all publ) – 2054mf – 9 – $3,082.00 – LLMC 78-216 – us L.L.M.C. [324]
FEDERAL COMMUNICATIONS LAW JOURNAL – (v1-36 1937-84 on reel $330.00. v37-47 1985-95 on mf $222.00. Title varies: v1-29 1937-76 as Federal Communications Bar Journal) – University of California at Los Angeles. v1-47. 1937-95 – 5,6,9 – $552.00 set – us Hein [340]
FEDERAL COUNCIL BULLETIN – v1-33. 1918-50 (complete) – Inquire – 1 – ATLA 1993-S509 – us A.T.L.A. [240]
Federal Council of the Churches of Christ in America *see* THE KOREAN SITUATION; THE KOREAN SITUATION NO. 2
Federal Council of the Churches of Christ in America. Commission on Christian Education *see* SELECTED QUOTATIONS ON PEACE AND WAR
Federal Council of the Churches of Christ in America. Committee on Financial and Fiduciary Matters *see* WILLS, WHY MAKE THEM, HOW MAKE THEM; AN EFFORT TO BE OF SERVICE.
THE FEDERAL COURTS / Simonton, Charles Henry – (The federal courts. 2d ed. Richmond, Va.: Johnson, 1898. 248 (i.e.249), xxixp. LL-1689) – Richmond, Va.: Johnson, 1896. 120p. LL-1357 – 1 – us L of C Photodup [340]
FEDERAL COURTS AND PRACTICE: ALL SHERMAN LAW TRUST PROSECUTIONS AND SYLLABUS OF EQUITY, JURISDICTION, PLEADING AND PRACTICE / Shields, John A – New York: Banks, 1912. 874p. LL-1139 – 1 – us L of C Photodup [340]
THE FEDERAL COURTS AND THE ORDERS OF THE INTERSTATE COMMERCE COMMISSION / Newcomb, Harry Turner – Washington, D.C.: Gibson, 1905. 206p. LL-1045 – 1 – us L of C Photodup [340]
FEDERAL COURTS AND WHAT THEY DO – Washington: FJC, n.d. (1987?) – 1mf – 9 – $1.50 – LLMC 95-840 – us L.L.M.C. [340]
FEDERAL CRIMINAL PROCEDURE, WITH FORMS FOR THE DEFENSE. / Byrne, John Elliott – Chicago: Callaghan, 1916. 446p. LL-1274 – 1 – us L of C Photodup [340]
FEDERAL DECISIONS : CASES IN THE SUPREME, CIRCUIT AND DISTRICT COURTS OF THE UNITED STATES / U. S. Supreme Court; ed by Myer, William G – St Louis: Gilbert Book Co. v1-30. 1790-1884 (all publ) – 306mf – 9 – $459.00 – LLMC 81-426 – us L.L.M.C. [340]
FEDERAL ELECTION CAMPAIGN LAWS – (Oct 1990 ed. Washington: GPO, 1990, 2mf LLMC 95-024 $3.00) – June 1986 ed. Washington: GPO, 1986 – 2mf – 9 – $3.00 – LLMC 95-024 – us L.L.M.C. [340]
Federal Election Commission *see* CAMPAIGN FINANCE LAW
FEDERAL ELECTION COMMISSION RECORD – v1-20 – 9 – LLMC 90-008 – us L.L.M.C. [340]
FEDERAL ENVIRONMENTAL PESTICIDES CONTROL ACT: HEARING...MAY 1, 1975 / U.S. Congress. Senate. Committee on Commerce. Subcommittee on the Environment – Washington, Govt. Print. Off., 1975. 41 p. LL-2391 – 1 – us L of C Photodup [340]
FEDERAL FACILITIES ENVIRONMENTAL JOURNAL – v1-4. 1990-94 – 9 – $95.00 set – us Hein [333]
FEDERAL FOOD AND DRUG ACT DECISIONS : DECISIONS OF THE COURTS IN CASES UNDER THE FEDERAL FOOD AND DRUG ACTS / Gates, Otis H – Washington, GPO, 1934 (all publ) – 16mf – 9 – $24.00 – LLMC 84-111 – us L.L.M.C. [340]
FEDERAL GAZETTE – Philadelphia. Pa. 1788-1793 – 3 – us Readex [071]
FEDERAL GAZETTE, 1788-1802 / Philadelphia, Pennsylvania – 1972 – 28r – 1 – $2,380.00 – S1711 – us Scholarly Res [071]
FEDERAL GLASS COMPANY, CATALOGS AND PRICE LISTS / Federal Glass Company. Columbus, Ohio – 1910-79 – 4r – 1 – us Ohio Hist [660]
Federal Glass Company. Columbus, Ohio *see* FEDERAL GLASS COMPANY, CATALOGS AND PRICE LISTS
FEDERAL GOVERNMENT DEVELOPMENT PROGRAMME, 1962-68 FIRST PROGRESS REPORT / Nigeria. Federal Ministry of Economic Development – (Sessional Paper No. 3 of 1964). Lagos. 1964. BD-616 1 – 9 – ne IDC [338]
FEDERAL GOVERNMENT GAZETTE / Federation of Rhodesia and Nyasaland – Salisbury. 1956-1963 – 1 – us NY Public [960]
FEDERAL GOVERNMENT IN CANADA / Bourinot, John George – Baltimore: Johns Hopkins University, 1889. 02140. (Pre-1900 Canadiana) – 9 – cn C.I.H.M. [971]
FEDERAL GUARDIAN AND COMMERCIAL ADVERTISER – Kuala Lumpur. Malaysia. -w. 4 Sep 1915-28 Oct 1916. (40 ft) – 1 – uk British Libr Newspaper [072]

FEDERAL HABEAS CORPUS REVIEW OF STATE JUDGEMENTS, 27 MAY 1988 – Washington: GPO, 1988 – 2mf – 9 – $3.00 – LLMC 94-365 – us L.L.M.C. [340]

FEDERAL HOME LOAN BANK BOARD ANNUAL REPORTS – (Includes 1989 financial report. Lacking: 1972) – 1960-75 – 26mf – 9 – $39.00 – LLMC 90-378 – us L.L.M.C. [336]

FEDERAL HOME LOAN BANK BOARD JOURNAL – v1-17 no3. 1968-Apr 1984 – 9 – LLMC 90-379 – us L.L.M.C. [336]

FEDERAL HOME LOAN BANK BOARD JOURNAL – v17, no.4-. May 1984- – 1,5,6,9 – us UMI [073]

FEDERAL HOME LOAN BANK REVIEW – v1-13. 1934-47 (all publ) – 41mf – 9 – $106.00 – LLMC 84-461 – us L.L.M.C. [073]

FEDERAL HOUSING AND HOME FINANCE AGENCY ANNUAL REPORTS – (Lacking: 1947-52. 1956. 1960) – 1947-64 – 9 – LLMC 90-376 – us L.L.M.C. [340]

FEDERAL INCOME TAX RECORD FOR INDIVIDUALS / D.B. Lewis & Co – (An early example of a compliance manual for the newly enacted income tax) – Boston: Thomas Groom & Co, 1914? – 1mf – 9 – $1.50 – LLMC 94-269 – us L.L.M.C. [336]

FEDERAL INDUSTRIAL AND SOCIAL STATISTICS, 1850 / Illinois. Census – Alphabetical by county. V123-0048 – 1 – us A.G.L.L. [310]

FEDERAL INDUSTRIAL AND SOCIAL STATISTICS, 1870 / Illinois. Census – Alphabetical by county. V123-0051; V123-0058; V123-0050 – 1 – us A.G.L.L. [310]

FEDERAL INDUSTRIAL CENSUS, 1860 / Illinois. Census – Alphabetical by county. V123-0049 – 1 – us A.G.L.L. [310]

FEDERAL JUDICIAL WORKLOAD STATISTICS – Admin Office of the US Courts, 1978-85 (all publ) – 21mf – 9 – $31.50 – LLMC 95-005 – us L.L.M.C. [340]

THE FEDERAL JUDICIARY ACTS OF 1875 AND 1887 / Foster, Roger – New York: Strouse, 1887. 109p. LL-1290 – 1 – us L of C Photodup [340]

FEDERAL JUROR – (Title may have add vols) – Grand Jury Association, Southern District of New York. v1-31. 1929-61 – 11mf – 9 – $16.50 – LLMC 84-462 – us L.L.M.C. [073]

FEDERAL LABOR RELATIONS AUTHORITY DECISIONS AND ORDERS – (Cont: Federal Labor Relations Council and Interpretations) – v1-17. 1979-85 – 185mf – 9 – $277.00 – LLMC 82-603 – us L.L.M.C. [340]

FEDERAL LABOR RELATIONS AUTHORITY DECISIONS AND ORDERS *see* FEDERAL LABOR RELATIONS COUNCIL DECISIONS AND INTERPRETATIONS

FEDERAL LABOR RELATIONS AUTHORITY/ FEDERAL SERVICE IMPASSE PANEL ANNUAL REPORTS – 1st-6th. 1979-84 – 8mf – 9 – $12.00 – LLMC 95-003 – us L.L.M.C. [340]

FEDERAL LABOR RELATIONS COUNCIL AND INTERPRETATIONS *see* FEDERAL LABOR RELATIONS AUTHORITY DECISIONS AND ORDERS

FEDERAL LABOR RELATIONS COUNCIL DECISIONS AND INTERPRETATIONS – (Cont by: Federal Labor Relations Authority Decisions and Orders: v1-17 1979-1985. Cite als FLRA. 185mf LLMC 82-603 $277.00) – v1-6. 1970-78 (all publ) – 57mf – 9 – $85.00 – LLMC 80-507 – us L.L.M.C. [340]

FEDERAL LAND RECORDS FOR IDAHO, 1860-1934 – 23r – 1 – M1620 – us Nat'l Archives [324]

FEDERAL LAW OF SCIENCE AND TECHNOLOGY / ed by Reams, Bernard D Jr – 1945-1984 – 9 – $2,595.00 set – us Hein [340]

FEDERAL LAWS GOVERNING LICENSED DEALERS / Capers, John G – Chicago: Criterion, 1910. 187p. LL-920 – 1 – us L of C Photodup [340]

FEDERAL LAWYER – (Title varies: v1-28 1953-81 as Federal Bar Association Journal. v28 no 10-41 1981-94 as Federal Bar News and Journal) – v1-42. 1953-95 – 9 – $581.00 set – us Hein [340]

FEDERAL MANUFACTURERS CENSUS, 1880 / Illinois. Census – Alphabetical by county. V123-0052/V123-0057 – 1 – us A.G.L.L. [310]

FEDERAL MARITIME ADMINISTRATION AND MARITIME SUBSIDY BOARD ANNUAL REPORTS / U. S. Dept of Commerce – 1962-1979 – 28mf – 9 – $42.00 – LLMC 81-227B – us L.L.M.C. [380]

FEDERAL MARITIME BOARD AND MARITIME ADMINISTRATION ANNUAL REPORTS / U. S. Dept of Commerce – 1950-61 (all publ) – 13mf – 9 – $19.50 – LLMC 81-227A – us L.L.M.C. [324]

FEDERAL MARITIME COMMISSION ANNUAL REPORTS – 1st 1962; 15th 1976; 17th 1978 – 18mf – 9 – $27.00 – LLMC 94-355 – us L.L.M.C. [340]

FEDERAL MARITIME COMMISSION DECISIONS – (Lacking: v21-22) – v1-20, 23-24. 1919-82 – 176mf – 9 – $264.00 – LLMC 78-024 – us L.L.M.C. [340]

FEDERAL MARITIME COMMISSION DECISIONS *see* FEDERAL MARITIME COMMISSION ANNUAL REPORTS

FEDERAL MEDIATION AND CONCILIATION SERVICE ANNUAL REPORTS – 1st-32nd. 1948-79 – 37mf – 9 – $55.00 – LLMC 81-223 – us L.L.M.C. [324]

FEDERAL MINE SAFETY AND HEALTH REVIEW COMMISSION DECISIONS AND ORDERS / U.S. Federal Mine Safety and Health Review Commission – (Includes indexes for 1978-92. Updates planned) – v1-16 no 10. 1979-94 – 512mf – 9 – $768.00 – LLMC 82-601 – us L.L.M.C. [340]

FEDERAL MORTALITY CENSUS SCHEDULES, 1850-80, AND RELATED INDEXES IN THE CUSTODY OF THE DAUGHTERS OF THE AMERICAN REVOLUTION / U.S. Bureau of the Census – 30 rolls. T655 – 1 – us Nat'l Archives [324]

FEDERAL NEWS – London. 1944-1955 – 9 – us Primary [072]

FEDERAL NONPOPULATION CENSUS SCHEDULES IN THE CUSTODY OF THE PENNSYLVANIA STATE LIBRARY, 1850-80 / U.S. Bureau of the Census – 23 rolls. M597 – 1 – us Nat'l Archives [324]

FEDERAL NONPOPULATION DECENNIAL CENSUS SCHEDULES FOR NEBRASKA, 1860-80 / U.S. Bureau of the Census – 16 rolls. T1128 – 1 – us Nat'l Archives [324]

FEDERAL OFFENDERS IN THE UNITED STATES DISTRICT COURTS *see* FEDERAL OFFENDERS IN THE U.S. COURTS

FEDERAL OFFENDERS IN THE U.S. COURTS – (1980-1983 are titled "Federal offenders in the United States District Courts". Coverage for the years 1986-1990 is combined into one report) – Admin Office of the US Courts, 1980-90 (all publ) – 25mf – 9 – $37.50 – LLMC 95-004 – us L.L.M.C. [340]

FEDERAL POWER COMMISSION ANNUAL REPORTS / U.S. Federal Power Commission – (No report publ for 1940-45, 1977. Lacking: 1928-34) – 1921-76 – 106mf – 9 – $159.00 – LLMC 81-224 – us L.L.M.C. [340]

FEDERAL POWER COMMISSION OPINIONS AND DECISIONS / U.S. Federal Power Commission – (Includes index/digest) – v1-58. 1931-77 (all publ) – 981mf – 9 – $1,471.00 – LLMC 78-060 – us L.L.M.C. [324]

THE FEDERAL POWER OVER COMMERCE AND ITS EFFECT ON STATE ACTION / Lewis, William Draper – Philadelphia, University of Pennsylvania, 1892. 145 p. LL-185 – 1 – us L of C Photodup [340]

FEDERAL PROBATION – v1- 1937- 1; v35- 5,6; v39- 9 – us UMI [324]

FEDERAL PROBATION / U.S. Department of Justice. Bureau of Prisons – (v1-4 entitled: Federal Probation Newsletter. v5-13: Federal Probation – A Quarterly Journal of Correctional Philosophy and Practice. v14-53: Federal Probation – A Journal of Correctional..... Updates planned) – v1-58 no 3. Apr 1937-94 – 253mf – 9 – $379.00 – LLMC 80-504 – us L.L.M.C. [340]

FEDERAL PROBATION NEWSLETTER *see* FEDERAL PROBATION

FEDERAL PROCEDURE AT LAW. / Bates, Chrisenberry Lee – Chicago, Flood, 1908. 2 v. LL-536 – 1 – us L of C Photodup [340]

FEDERAL PUBLIC POLICY: PERSONAL ACCOUNTS OF TEN SENIOR FEDERAL CIVIL SERVICE EXECUTIVES / ed by Taylor, Theodore W – 1984. 327p. Index. ISBN: 0-912338-48-2 – 9 – 13.50 – us Lomond [320]

Federal Publishing Co *see* MEMOIRS OF THE LOWER OHIO VALLEY

FEDERAL REGISTER / National Archives and Records Administration, Office of the Federal Register – (Issued daily) – 9 – $433.00y in US $541.25 outside – 0-16-012696-7 – 769-003-00000-2 – us Gov't Printing [324]

FEDERAL REGISTER / U. S. – 1956-. With indexes – 3 – us Readex [324]

FEDERAL REGISTER / U. S. – (Includes presidential documents and annual cumulation index. Updated as released by GPO) – Washington: US GPO, backfile 1936-95 – 9 – $15,995.00 set (1996 subsc $560.00) – 0-89941-214-9 – us Hein [340]

FEDERAL REGISTER / U. S. – v1-49. 1936-84 – 1,5,6 – us Princeton Micro [324]

FEDERAL REGISTER / U. S. – v1-51. 1936-86 – 1,5 – us Princeton Micro [324]

FEDERAL REGISTER / U.S. – (v. 34- 1969- 5,6. v. 36- 1971- 9) – v. 1- 1936- – 1 – us UMI [324]

THE FEDERAL REGISTER / U.S. National Archives and Records Service – 1936-81. 388 rolls. M190 – 1 – us Nat'l Archives [025]

FEDERAL REGISTER: INDEXES / U. S. – v. 1-40. 1936-75 – 1,5,6 – us Princeton Micro [324]

FEDERAL REGISTER ON MICROFICHE / U. S. – (Printed index available separately) – v1- 1936- – 9 – Apply for price – us CIS [324]

FEDERAL REGULATORY LIBRARIES – (All required FAA publications including all FAR's (except airspace), AD's (v1-2), Type Certificate Data Sheets. Summary of Supplemental Type Certificates, Advisory Circulars, FAA Handbooks, Manufacturer Service Bulletins and Appliances for aircraft, engines, propellers. Canadian and Australian Regulatory Libraries also available. Updated biweekly) – 9 – $785.00. Annual revision ca $470.00 – us Aircraft Tech [629]

FEDERAL REPORTER *see* THE FEDERAL CASES

THE FEDERAL REPORTER – (Title part of: National Reporter System publ by West Pub Co. Updates planned) – 1st series: v1-258. 1880-1919 – 2782mf – 9 – $4,173.00 – LLMC 79-404B – us L.L.M.C. [340]

FEDERAL REPUBLIC OF GERMANY : FOREIGN AFFAIRS, 1950-1954 / U.S. Department of State – (Series: Confidential US State Department Central Files: Germany) – 9r – 1 – $1,070.00 – 0-89093-910-1 – us UPA [320]

FEDERAL REPUBLIC OF GERMANY : FOREIGN AFFAIRS, 1955-1959 / U. S. State Department – (Series: Confidential US State Department Central Files. With printed guides) – 5r – 1 – $595.00 – 1-55655-446-X – us UPA [320]

FEDERAL REPUBLIC OF GERMANY : INTERNAL AFFAIRS, 1955-1959 / U. S. State Department – (Pt 1: Political Governmental and National Defense Affairs 29r $3,455.00 ISBN 1-55655-447-8. Pt 2: Social, Economic and Industrial Affairs 40r $4,760.00 ISBN 1-55655-448-6. Series: Confidential US State Department Central Files: Germany) – 1 – us UPA [320]

FEDERAL REPUBLIC OF GERMANY: INTERNAL AFFAIRS, 1950-1954 : PART 1: POLITICAL, GOVERNMENTAL AND NATIONAL DEFENSE AFFAIRS / U.S. Department of State – (Series: Confidential US State Department Central Files: Germany) – 56r – 1 – $6,675.00 – 0-89093-911-X – us UPA [320]

Federal Reserve Bank of Minneapolis. Ninth District *see* QUARTERLY

Federal Reserve Bank of New York *see*
- MONTHLY REVIEW
- QUARTERLY REVIEW

Federal Reserve Bank of Richmond *see* ECONOMIC REVIEW

Federal Reserve Bank of San Francisco *see* ECONOMIC REVIEW

Federal Reserve Bank of St. Louis *see* NATIONAL ECONOMIC TRENDS

FEDERAL RESERVE BULLETIN / U.S. Board of Governors of the Federal Reserve System – v1- 1915- 1; v54- 5,6; v61- 9 – us UMI [336]

FEDERAL RESERVE BULLETIN / U.S. Federal Reserve Board – v1-70. 1915-Apr 1984 – 1168mf – 9 – $1,752.00 – LLMC 81-225 – us L.L.M.C. [073]

FEDERAL RESERVE BULLETIN / U.S. Board of Governors of the Federal Reserve System – v. 1-58. 1915-1972 – 1,5,6 – us Princeton Micro [324]

FEDERAL RULEMAKING : PROBLEMS AND POSSIBILITIES / Brown, Winifred R – Washington: FJC, June 1981 – 2mf – 9 – $3.00 – LLMC 95-309 – us L.L.M.C. [340]

FEDERAL RULES OF EVIDENCE : LEGISLATIVE HISTORIES AND RELATED DOCUMENTS / ed by Bailey, James F & Trelles, Oscar M – (Covers the major publications considered by Congress prior to the effective date, July 1, 1975) – 4v. 1980 – 9 – $115.00 set – 0-89941-235-1 – us Hein [323]

FEDERAL SERVICES IMPASSES PANEL RELEASES – no1-174. 1970-80 – 9 – LLMC 84-115 – us L.L.M.C. [340]

THE FEDERAL STATUTES ANNOTATED...1789-1903 / McKinney, William M & Moore, Charles C – New York: Thompson. 10v + suppls. 1903-25 (all publ) – 252mf – 9 – $378.00 – LLMC 80-032 – us L.L.M.C. [324]

FEDERAL SUPPLEMENT – (For copyright reasons, filming of vols not expected before year 2007) – 1932- – 9 – us L.L.M.C. [340]

FEDERAL SURVEILLANCE OF AFRO-AMERICANS (1917-25) / U.S. Federal Bureau of Investigation – The First World War, the Red Scare, and the Garvey Movement. 25 reels with printed guide – 1 – $2,750.00 – 0-89093-741-9 – us UPA [360]

FEDERAL TAX POLICY FOR ECONOMIC GROWTH AND STABILITY / U.S. Congress. Joint Committee on the Economic Report – Washington: GPO. 1v. 1955 – 10mf – 9 – $15.00 – LLMC 82-702 – us L.L.M.C. [336]

FEDERAL TAX REGULATIONS – v3 1954-v3 1979 – 9 – $1,575.00 set – us Hein [336]

THE FEDERAL TAX SYSTEM : FACTS AND PROBLEMS / U.S. Congress. Joint Economic Committee – Washington: GPO. 1v. 1964 – 4mf – 9 – $6.00 – LLMC 82-704 – us L.L.M.C. [336]

FEDERAL TELEPHONE DIRECTORIES – (Treasury. Federal Energy Administration. Department of State (selected agencies). NASA. HEW. U.S. Senate. Department of Labor. U.S. House of Representatives. State government energy-related agencies. Department of Defense. Federal Telecommunications. Department of Agriculture. Office of the Secretary of Transportation. Department of Commerce) – 14 categories – 1 – us UMI [380]

FEDERAL TRADE COMMISSION : ADVISORY OPINION DIGESTS, NO 1-313. 1 JUN 1962-31 DEC 1968 / ed by McMahill, Richard B – Washington: GPO, 1969? (all publ) – 4mf – 9 – $6.00 – LLMC 94-320 – us L.L.M.C. [340]

FEDERAL TRADE COMMISSION ANNUAL REPORTS / U.S. Federal Trade Commission – (Lacking: 1972. Updates planned) – 1915-79 – 125mf – 9 – $187.00 – LLMC 80-509 – us L.L.M.C. [380]

FEDERAL TRADE COMMISSION DECISIONS, FINDINGS, ORDERS AND STIPULATIONS / U.S. Federal Trade Commission – (Updates planned) – v1-114. 1915-91 – 1502mf – 9 – $2,253.00 – LLMC 78-028 – us L.L.M.C. [324]

FEDERAL TRADE COMMISSION, STATUTES AND COURT DECISIONS / U.S. Federal Trade Commission – (Add vols will be added if any) – v1-16. 1914-82 (all publ?) – 203mf – 9 – $304.00 – LLMC 81-226 – us L.L.M.C. [324]

FEDERAL UNION NEWS – London. 1939-1944 – 9 – us Primary [072]

FEDERAL USER FEES : PROCEEDINGS OF A SYMPOSIUM WASHINGTON, DC 1988 / Administrative Conference of the U.S. (ACUS); ed by Hopkins, Thomas D – Acus: n.p., 1988? (all publ) – 2mf – 9 – $3.00 – LLMC 94-350 – us L.L.M.C. [340]

FEDERAL WRITERS' PROJECT – (Over 12,000 pages of oral history from holdings of Southern Historical Collection at University of North Carolina, Chapel Hill) – 220mf – 9 – $985.00 – us UMI [975]

THE FEDERALIST : A COMMENTARY ON THE CONSTITUION OF THE UNITED STATES / ed by Lodge, Henry Cabot – (With index) – New York/London: G P Putnam's Sons, 1888 – 7mf – 9 – $10.50 – LLMC 90-362 – us L.L.M.C. [323]

THE FEDERALIST : A COMMENTARY ON THE CONSTITUTION OF THE UNITED STATES, A COLLECTION OF ESSAYS / Hamilton, Alexander et al – Philadelphia: J B Lippincott, 1864 – 9mf – 9 – $13.50 – LLMC 95-062 – us L.L.M.C. [323]
THE FEDERALIST – St. George's, Grenada. -w. 11 March 1896-23 Jan 1901; 2 March 1901-17 April 1907; 30 Oct 1907-25 June 1908; 29 Dec 1909-25 Dec 1920. Very imperfect. 6 reels – 1 – uk British Libr Newspaper [072]
THE FEDERALIST AND OTHER CONSTITUTIONAL PAPERS / Hamilton, Alexander; ed by Scott, E H – Chicago: Scott, Foresman & Co, 1902 – 10mf – 9 – $15.00 – LLMC 90-363 – us L.L.M.C. [323]
O FEDERALISTA : PERIODICO REPUBLICANO – S. Paulo, 5 Apr-5 Sep 1880 – 1,5,6 – bl Biblioteca [072]
O FEDERALISTA ALAGOENSE : JORNAL POLITICO, LITERARIO E MORAL – Maceio, Alagoas. 3 Out 1832 – 1 – bl Biblioteca [320]
LE FEDERALISTE – (Filmed as pt of: Commune de Paris newspapers) – Paris: Imp Schiller, may 1871 – us Res Libr [072]
Federated Association of Letter Carriers of the Dominion of Canada *see* CONSTITUTION AND BY-LAWS OF THE FEDERATED ASSOCIATION OF LETTER CARRIERS OF THE DOMINION OF CANADA, ADOPTED SEPTEMBER 28 AND 29, 1892
FEDERATED LABOR PRESS – Sacramento, CA. 1927-1929 – 1r – 1 – $50.00 – C03645 – us Library Micro [071]
Federated States of Micronesia *see*
- CHUUK – TRUK DISTRICT CHARTER, 1977
- COMPACT OF FREE ASSOCIATION AND RELATED AGREEMENTS BETWEEN THE FEDERATED STATES OF MICRONESIA AND THE UNITED STATES, 1 OCTOBER 1982
- CONSTITUTION OF THE STATE OF YAP, 1982
- THE FEDERATED STATES OF MICRONESIA
- FINAL REPORT OF THE PLEBISCITE COMMISSION ON THE PUBLIC INFORMATION PROGRAM AND PLEBISCITE ON THE FUTURE POLITICAL STATUS OF THE FEDERATED STATES OF MICRONESIA
- FOREIGN INVESTMENT LAW 2-5 AND REGULATIONS, 1981-1986
- KOSRAE DISTRICT CHARTER, 1978
- LAWS AND RESOLUTIONS OF THE FEDERATED STATES OF MICRONESIA, 1979-1986
- LAWS AND RESOLUTIONS OF THE STATE OF YAP, 1983-1984
- POHNPEI – PONAPE DISTRICT CODE, 1978
- THE POHPEI CONSTITUTION AND THE LEGISLATURE RULES OF ORDER, 1984
- REPORT OF THE COMMISSION ON FUTURE POLITICAL STATUS AND TRANSITION
- YAP DISTRICT CHARTER, 1978
- YAP STATE CODE

THE FEDERATED STATES OF MICRONESIA : REPORT ISSUED BY THE FSM REPRESENTATIVE OFFICE / Federated States of Micronesia – Washington, 1 Dec 1983 – 1mf – 9 – $1.50 – LLMC 82-100H Title 9 – us L.L.M.C. [324]
FEDERATION – London, UK. 24 Aug-28 Sept 1872; 15 Mar 1875 – 1 – uk British Libr Newspaper [072]
FEDERATION – Miami, FL. Mar 1973-Jun 1979. Some issues missing. Continued by: Federation (1979) – 1 – us A.J.P.C. [071]
FEDERATION – Miami, FL. Oct 1979-1986 – 1 – us A.J.P.C. [071]
LA FEDERATION – no. 1-7. Londres. aout 1872-janv 1873 – 1 – fr A.C.R.P.P. [073]
LA FEDERATION – Revue de l'ordre vivant. no. 48-141. Paris. 1949-oct 1956 – 1 – fr A.C.R.P.P. [073]
LA FEDERATION BALCANIQUE – Vienna. Text in all Balkan languages. July 15, 1924-Apr. 5, 1931. Missing: issues 4, 5, 11-13 – 1 – 35.00r – us Hoover Inst Photo [460]
LA FEDERATION BALKANIQUE – I-VI, no. 1-123. Wien. juil 1924-nov 1929. Texte multilingue suivi de: La Federation balkanique. Organe des peuples opprimes et minorites nationales des Balkans. Edition francaise-allemande puis europeenne. Wien puis Frankfurt am Main. VI-VIII, no. 124-147. dec 1929-fevr 1932 – 1 – fr A.C.R.P.P. [949]
FEDERATION BULLETIN – (v.66-. 1979-5,6,9) – Federation of State Medical Boards of the United States. v7-. 1921-. Continues Monthly Bulletin – 1 – us UMI [073]
La Federation Communiste des Soviets *see* LE SOVIET
LA FEDERATION CONGOLAISE – (Issues filmed as pt of: Herbert J Weiss collection on the Belgian Congo) – Leopoldville: E Nzeza-Nlandu, jun 11, jul 9, sep 5 1961 – us Res Libr [960]
La Federation de Syndicats Chretiens de Mineurs *see* LE MINEUR
La Federation des Comites d'Alliance Ouvriere *see* INFORMATIONS OUVRIERES
Federation des Mineurs du Nord et du Pas-de-Calais *see* LA VOIX DU MINEUR 1907-1914
La Federation des Ouvriers des Metaux et Similaires de France *see* L'UNION DES METAUX
Federation des Ouvriers des Metaux et Similaires de France. 4e-6e Congres National *see* DOCUMENTS
La Federation des Syndicats de Cultivateurs de la Region de Moulins *see* LE TRAVAILLEUR RURAL
La Federation des travailleurs de la metallurgie *see* L'UNION DES METALLURGISTES
La Federation des Travailleurs Socialistes de France *see* LA FRANCE SOCIALISTE
Federation des Travailleurs Socialistes de France. Parti Ouvrier Socialiste Revolutionnaire. IXe Congres Regional de l'Union Federative du Centre. Paris du 17 au 26 juin 1888 *see* COMPTE RENDU
La Federation des Travailleurs Socialistes des Ardennes *see* LE SOCIALISTE ARDENNAIS
Federation du Nord du Parti Socialiste *see* LA BATAILLE
La Federation du Nord. (S.F.I.O.) *see* LE TRAVAILLEUR
La Federation Generale des Functionnaires *see* LA TRIBUNE DES FONCTIONNAIRES ET DES RETRAITES
Federation International des Hot Clubs Francais *see* JAZZ HOT
FEDERATION INTERNATIONALE DES DROITS DE L'HOMME = INTERNATIONAL FEDERATION OF HUMAN RIGHTS – Paris. 531 docs. 1980-1991 – 183mf – 9 – ne IDC [320]
Federation Nationale des Ouvriers Metallurgistes de France *see* BULLETIN OFFICIEL
Federation Nationale des Syndicats du Cuivre et Similaires *see* LE CUIVRE
La Federation Nationale des Travailleurs des Chemins de Fer. C.G.T. *see* LA TRIBUNE DES CHEMINOTS
Federation nationale des Travailleurs du Sous-Sol *see* DOCUMENTS DU CONGRES
La Federation Nationale des Travailleurs du Sous-sol et Parties Similaires (Mineurs, Miniers et Ardoisiens) *see* LE TRAVAILLEUR DU SOUS-SOL
FEDERATION OF AMERICAN SOCIETIES FOR EXPERIMENTAL BIOLOGY – FEDERATION PROCEEDINGS *see* FASEB JOURNAL
FEDERATION OF MINING UNIONS PAPERS – ((Case history)) – 3r – 1 – sa Microfile [331]
FEDERATION OF NIGERIA OFFICIAL GAZETTE – Lagos. v45-57. 1958-70 – 14r – 1 – us Ross [960]
Federation of Rhodesia and Nyasaland *see*
- DEVELOPMENT PLANS, 1954-1957
- DEVELOPMENT PLANS, 1957-1961
- DEVELOPMENT PLANS, 1962-1965
- FEDERAL GOVERNMENT GAZETTE

Federation of Saskatchewan Indians *see* THE SASKATCHEWAN INDIAN
FEDERATION OF SOUTH AFRICA WOMEN PAPERS – 4r – 1 – sa Microfile [960]
Federation ouvriere de l'industrie textile de France *see* L'OUVRIER TEXTILE
FEDERATION PROCEEDINGS / American Society for Experimental Biology – (1965-5,6. 1970-. 9) – v. 1- 1942- – 1 – us UMI [580]
Federation radicale et radicale-socialiste de Guyane. Comite Executif *see* BULLETIN
La Federation Republicaine de France *see* LA NATION
La Federation Revolutionnaire de la Region du Nord *see* LE VENGEUR
FEDERATION SUN – Portland OR. Aug 25 1933 – 1 – us U.O. Library [071]
La Federation unitaire des Travailleurs du Sous-Sol et similaires *see* LE MINEUR UNITAIRE
FEDERATION WORLD – (Vol. 23, no. 7 (July 1983)-v. 26, no. 1 (Jan. 1986); Continues JWF Report) – Indianapolis, Indiana – 1 – us A.J.P.C. [978]
FEDERATSIIA – 1 – sz Infoprint [947]
FEDERATSIIA – (Backfile through 1998 $85/r) – Russia, 1999- – 2r per y – 1 – $160.00 standing order – us Ross [320]
Federici, F *see* PIGMALIONE. OPERA IN UN ATTO... MANUSCRIPT
Federici, G *see* CLINICAL CHEMISTRY AND ENZYMOLOGY COMMUNICATIONS
Federici, V *see* AFFANI CRUDELI
Federmann, Arnold *see* GOETHE ALS BILDENDER KUENSTLER
Fedin, Konstantin *see* GORODA I GODY
Fedler, Joan M *see* THE EFFECT OF A LIFETIME OF PHYSICAL ACTIVITY ON THE QUANTITY OF BONE IN THE CANINE
O FEDORE SOLOGUBE – Kritika. Stat'i i zametki Sostavl. A. Chebotarevskoi. Spb. 1911. BR-1466 2 – 8 – ne IDC [920]
FEDOROVSKIE CHTENIIA – Moskva: [Gos. biblioteka SSSR im V I Lenina], 1976- (publ 1978) – 1 – us Res Libr [460]
FEDOSEEV, NIKOLAI EVGRAFOVICH, ODIN IZ PIONEROV REVOLIUTSIONNOGO MARKSIZMA V ROSSII : SBORNIK VOSPOMINANI I – Moskva: Gos. izd.-vo, 1923 – 1 – CSUX89-B6310 – us Hoover Inst Photo [947]
Fedoseyev, Anatoly *see* THE MODERN GENGHIS KHAN
Fedozzi, P *see*
- LE COLONIE STRANIERE...
- DELLE POSSIBILI CONSEQUENZE DEL POSITIVISMO PENALE...
- GLI ENTI COLLETTIVI NEL DIRITTO INTERNAZIONALE PRIVATO...
- SAGGIO SUL PROTETTORATO

Fee, A L A *see*
- ESSAI SUR LES CRYPTOGAMES DES ECORCES EXOTIQUES OFFICINALES
- FLORE DE VIRGILE
- MATERIAUX POUR UNE FLORE LICHENOLOGIQUE DU BRESIL
- MEMOIRES SUR LA FAMILLE DES FOUGERES
- MEMOIRES SUR LA FAMILLE DES FOUGERES. 5. GENERA FILICUM
- MONOGRAPHIE DU GENRE CHIODECTON
- MONOGRAPHIE DU GENRE TRYPETHELIUM

FEED AND FARM SUPPLIER *see* FARM SUPPLIER
FEED AND FEEDING OF FISH AND SHRIMP : A MANUAL ON THE PREPARATION AND PRESENTATION OF COMPOUND FEED FOR SHRIMP AND FISH IN AQUACULTURE – 1987 – 284p – it F.A.O. [636]
FEED EVALUATION / Osuji, PO et al – 1993 – 9 – $6.50 – 92-9053-503-2 – et ILRI [636]
FEED FROM ANIMAL WASTES : FEEDING MANUAL – 1982 – 224p – it F.A.O. [636]
FEED FROM ANIMAL WASTES : STATE OF KNOWLEDGE – 1980 – 201p – it F.A.O. [636]
FEED INDUSTRY – v56-. 1980- – 1 – us UMI [073]
FEED INDUSTRY REVIEW – v1-55. 1925-79 – 1 – us UMI [073]
FEEDING DAIRY COWS IN THE TROPICS – 1991 – 254p – it F.A.O. [636]
FEEDING TOMORROW'S WORLD / Sassong, Albert – 1990 – 9 – 92-3-102083-8 – Co-published with the Technical Centre for Agricultural and Rural Cooperation (CTA), Netherlands – fr UNESCO [320]
FEEDSTUFFS – v. 1- 1929- – 1 – us UMI [636]
FEELOSOFIA PRAVA / Chicherin, Boris N – Moskva: Kushnerev, 1900. 336p. LL-4054 – 1 – us L of C Photodup [340]
Feely, J A *see*
- INDEX TO THE ARGUS 1855 – APRIL 1859
- INDEX TO THE ARGUS 1846-1854

Feeman, Harlan L *see* THE KINGDOM AND THE FARM
Feeney, Bernard *see* HOW TO GET ON
Feeney, Robert E *see* COMMENTS ON AGRICULTURAL AND FOOD CHEMISTRY
FEES AND TAXES CHARGED INSURANCE COMPANIES UNDER THE LAWS OF NEW YORK TOGETHER WITH ABSTRACTS OF FEES, TAXES AND OTHER REQUIREMENTS OF OTHER STATES / New York. Insurance Dept – 1909-78. 85 fiches. (Harvard Law School Library Collection.) – 9 – 1.50f – us H.U. Law [336]
FEHDE UM BRANDENBURG : GESCHICHTE EINES REBELLEN / Helke, Fritz – Stuttgart: Union Deutsche Verlagsgesellschaft, 1943 – 1r – 1 – us U.W. Library [830]
Fehim, Sueleyman *see* DIVANCE
FEHLER BEI DER MESSUNG UND AUSWERTUNG VON FESTKOERPER-MAS-NMR-SPEKTREN / Jeschke, Gunnar – 1992 – 1mf – 9 – DM75.00 – 3-89349-582-7 – gw Hänsel [540]
FEHLHALTUNG BEIM INSTRUMENTALSPIEL UND IHRE VERMEIDUNG / Wunsch, Hildrun – 1994 – 2mf – DM80.00 – 3-8267-2074-1 – gw Hänsel [780]
FEHMARNSCHES TAGEBLATT – Burg auf Fehmarn, Germany. 1 Jun 1983- – 4r per yr – 1 – gw Mikrofilm [072]
FEHMARNSCHES TAGEBLATT – Burg auf Fehmarn, jun 1 1983- – 4r per yr – 1 – Inquire at Mikrofilmarchiv for details – gw Misc Inst [072]
Fehme, Hermann *see* UEBER DAS VERHAELTNIS HEINRICH VON KLEISTS ZU C.M. WIELAND
Fehn, Andreas *see* DIE GESCHICHTSPHILOSOPHIE IN DEN HISTORISCHEN DRAMEN JULIUS MOSENS
Fehr, J G *see* ALPHABETISCHES VERZEICHNIS ALLER IN BOISDUVAL'S SYSTEM DER EUROPAEISCHEN SCHMETTERLINGE
Fehrle, Eugen *see* DEUTSCHE FESTE UND VOLKSBRAUCHE
Fehse, Wilhelm *see* RAABE UND JENSEN
FEIA EIOLE. POEZY 1920-1921 GG / Severianin, I – Berlin. 1922. BR-1025 2 – 8 – ne IDC [460]
Feichtinger de B Nadasd, A *see* DIRITTO MARITTIMO...
Feierfell, Georg *see* OTTO LUDWIGS LEHRE VON DER TRAGISCHEN SCHULD
DAS FEIERLICHE GELUEBDE ALS EHEHINDERNIS : IN SEINER GESCHICHTLICHEN ENTWICKLUNG / Scharnagl, Anton – Freiburg im Breisgau, St. Louis, Mo.: Herder, 1908 – 1mf – us A.T.L.A. [240]
Feifer, E *see* LA DOMAINE RESERVE
Feige, L *see* MARCELLA: EPISODE DRAMATIQUE
Feigin, V *see* KUSTARNO-REMESLENNAIA PROMYSHLENNOST' SSSR
Feigina, S A *see* ALANDSKII KONGRESS
FEIJINSHUKUANG – Nonmetallic Minerals. 1981-. F P235 – 9 – $4.50f – cc Microforms [622]
FEIJO E A PRIMEIRA METADE DO SECULO 19 / Ellis, Alfredo – Sao Paulo, 1940 – 10mf – 8 – ne Slangenburg [972]
Feijoo Montenegro, Benito J *see*
- ADICIONES
- CARTAS ERUDITAS. TOMO 1
- CARTAS ERUDITAS. TOMO 2
- CARTAS ERUDITAS. TOMO 3
- CARTAS ERUDITAS. TOMO 4
- CARTAS ERUDITAS. TOMO 5
- ILUSTRACION APOLOGETICA
- JUSTA REPULSA
- TEATRO CRITICO UNIVERSAL. TOMO 1
- TEATRO CRITICO UNIVERSAL. TOMO 2
- TEATRO CRITICO UNIVERSAL. TOMO 3
- TEATRO CRITICO UNIVERSAL. TOMO 4
- TEATRO CRITICO UNIVERSAL. TOMO 5
- TEATRO CRITICO UNIVERSAL. TOMO 6
- TEATRO CRITICO UNIVERSAL. TOMO 7
- TEATRO CRITICO UNIVERSAL. TOMO 8

Feilchenfeld, E H *see* PUBLIC DEBTS AND STATE SUCCESSION
[Feilchenfeld, E H] *see* VOELKERRECHTSPOLITIK ALS WISSENSCHAFT
Feilchenfeld, Wolf *see* DAS HOHELIED: INHALTLICH UND SPACHLICH ERLAEUTERT
Feinberg, N *see* SOME PROBLEMS OF THE PALESTINE MANDATE
FEINDE DES VOLKES : EINE ERZAEHLUNG IM RAHMEN DER GESCHICHTLICHEN EREIGNISSE IM ERZSTIFT BREMEN FRUEHJAHR 1557 / Holscher, Kurt Heimart – Berlin: Nordland Verlag, c1939 – 1r – 1 – us U.W. Library [830]
Feine, Paul *see*
- DIE ERNEUERUNG DES PAULINISCHEN CHRISTENTUMS DURCH LUTHER DEKANATSREDE GEHALTEN AM 31. OKTOBER 1902 IN WIEN
- DAS GESETZESFREIE EVANGELIUM DES PAULUS: NACH SEINEM WERDEGANG
- DER JAKOBUSBRIEF: NACH LEHRANSCHAUUNGEN UND ENTSTEHUNGSVERHAELTNISSEN
- JESUS CHRISTUS UND PAULUS
- DER ROEMERBRIEF: EINE EXEGETISCHE STUDIE

- EINE VORKANONISCHE UEBERLIEFERUNG DES LUKAS IN EVANGELIUM UND APOSTELGESCHICHTE
Feinmann, Jose Pablo *see*
- ESTUDIOS SOBRE EL PERONISMO
- EL PERONISMO Y LA PRIMACIA DE LA POLITICA
Feinstein, A L *see* IR TEHILLAH
Feinstone, Sol *see* THE SOL FEINSTONE COLLECTION OF THE AMERICAN REVOLUTION
Feisberg, J *see* ESTI BAPTISTI...25 JUUBELI AASTA MALESTUSETS
Feise, Ernst *see* DER KNITTELVERS DES JUNGEN GOETHE
Feistmantel, O *see* FOSSIL FLORA OF THE GONDWANA SYSTEM
Feistritzer, W P *see* CEREAL SEED TECHNOLOGY
Feit, Marvin D *see*
- JOURNAL OF HEALTH AND SOCIAL POLICY
- JOURNAL OF HUMAN BEHAVIOR IN THE SOCIAL ENVIRONMENT
Feiveson, Harold A *see* SCIENCE AND GLOBAL SECURITY
FEJER MEGYEI HIRLAP – Szekesfehervar, Hungary. 1962-79 – 34r – 1 – us L of C Photodup [072]
Fel', S E *see* KARTOGRAFIIA ROSSII XVIII VEKA
Felbermann, Lajos *see* HUNGARY AND ITS PEOPLE.
FELDBLATT POSEN : NACHRICHTENBLATT DES WEHRKREISES XXI – Posen (Poznan), Poland. 23 Sept 1939-26 Dec 1941 – 1r – 1 – gw Mikrofilm [072]
FELDBLUMEN AUS DEM HEILIGEN LAND *see* FLEURS DE LA PALESTINE
Felder, Hilario *see* LOS ESTUDIOS EN LA ORDEN CAPUCHINA EN EL PRIMER SIGLO DE SU EXISTENCIA
Felder, Vada P *see* A MIGHTY ARMY
FELDGEISTLICHER BEI LEGION CONDOR: SPANISCHES KRIEGSTAGEBUCH EINES EVANGELISCHEN LEGIONSPFARRERS / Keding, Karl – Berlin, 1939. Fiche W978. (Blodgett Collection of Spanish Civil War Pamphlets) – 9 – us H.U. College Libr [946]
Feldkeller, Paul *see* UNTERSUCHUNGEN UEBER NORMATIVES UND NICHT-NORMATIVES DENKEN
Feldman, W *see* GESCHICHTE DER POLITISCHEN IDEEN IN POLEN SEIT DESSEN TEILUNGEN
FEL'DMARSHAL RUMIANTSEV V PERIOD RUSSKO-TURETSKOI VOINY 1768-1774. G.G / Klokman, Iu. R – M. 1951. BR-6207 2 – 8 – ne IDC [920]
FELDMUENSTER : ROMAN AUS EINEM JESUITENINTERNAT / Zedtwitz, Franz Xaver, Graf – Berlin: Nordland-Verlag, 1943 – 1r – 1 – us U.W. Library [830]
FELDMUENSTER : ROMAN AUS EINEM JESUITENINTERNAT / Zedtwitz, Franz Xaver, Graf – Berlin: Nordland-Verlag, 1943 – 1 – us U.W. Library [830]
FELDZUGSERINNERUNGEN AUS DEM KRIEGSJAHRE 1908 / ed by Kircheisen, F M – Hamburg, 1909 – 5mf – 9 – ne IDC [943]
Felgner, Harald *see* KONSENS UND DISSENS IM BILDUNGSSYSTEM VON BADEN-WUERTTEMBERG
Felibien, A *see* DES PRINCIPES DE L'ARCHITECTURE
Felibien, Andre *see* DES PRINCIPES DE L'ARCHITECTURE, DE LA SCULPTURE, DE LA PEINTURE.
Felibien, Dom M OSB *see* HISTOIRE DE L'ABBAYE ROYALE DE SAINT-DENYS EN FRANCE
O FELICANO – Curitiba, Brazil. 1 Oct-3 Nov 1897 – 1 – bl Biblioteca [072]
Felice, Algernon A D *see* PERCEIVED EXERTION OF PARAPLEGICS DURING SUBMAXIMAL ARM CRANK ERGOMETRY
Felice, G de *see*
- HISTOIRE DES SYNODES NATIONAUX DES EGLISES REFORMEES DE FRANCE
- HISTORY OF THE PROTESTANTS OF FRANCE
FELICE. SI J'ADORAI LISETTE; ARR / Catrufo, G – Ms pts – 1 – us Sibley [780]
Felici, Osea *see* IL BRASILE COM'E
Feliciano, Gloria D *see* RESEARCH IN POPULATION COMMUNICATION
FELICIDAD DE MEXICO...GUADALUPE EXTREMUROS / Bezerra Tanco, Luis – 1685 – 9 – 1.50f – sp Bibl Santa Ana [946]
FELICITER – 1956-90 – 13r – 1 – $845.00 – cn Library Assoc [073]
FELIKS DZERZHINSKI I : AVTOBIOGRAFIIA I STATI N. BUKHARINA I I A. GANET SKOGO: VOZZVANII A T SK VKP (B), KOMINTERNA I DR. – [Moscow R.S.F.S.R.]: Gos. izd-vo, 1926 – 1 – CSUX89-B6781 – us Hoover Inst Photo [920]
Feline, Marie Charles *see* L'ARTILLERIE AU MAROC
Felinger, Martina *see* HERZTAETIGKEIT UND EEG-NEGATIVIERUNG IN ERWARTUNG BEDROHLICHER INFORMATIONEN
FELIPE 2ND Y LA EVANGELIZACION DE AMERICA / Bayle, Constantino – Madrid: Imprenta del Ministerio de Asuntos Exteriores, 1947 – 1 – sp Bibl Santa Ana [240]
FELIPE 3 EN MERIDA DE PASO PARA PORTUGAL / Lopez Martinez, Antonio – Badajoz: Dip. Provincial, 1970. Sep. REE – 1 – sp Bibl Santa Ana [946]
FELIPE 5 EN MORALEJA, ANO DE 1704 / Doncel, Fernando – Madrid: Tip. de Fortanet, 1895 – 1 – sp Bibl Santa Ana [946]
FELIPE 5 Y PORTUGAL. MATRIMONIOS REALES EN CAYA (1729) / Rodriguez Amaya, Esteban – Badajoz: Diputacion Provincial, 1945 – sp Bibl Santa Ana [320]
Felipe, Dionisio de *see* EL PADRE CRISTOBAL, OTRO GIGANTE. VIDA DEL VENERABLE PADRE CRISTOBAL DE SANTA CATALINA
FELIPE TRIGO. EXPOSICION Y GLOSA DE SU VIDA, SU FILOSOFIA, SU MORAL, SU ARTE, SU ESTILO / Abril, Manuel – Madrid: Renacimiento, 1917 – sp Bibl Santa Ana [170]
FELIX DAHN'S SAEMTLICHE WERKE POETISCHEN INHALTS / Dahn, Felix – Leipzig: Breitkopf & Haertel. 21v. 1898-1911 – 1 – us U.W. Library [800]
FELIX FARLEY'S BRISTOL JOURNAL – Bristol.1752-1800 – 1 – uk Microform Academic [072]
FELIX FARLEY'S BRISTOL JOURNAL – England. 1813. 1 reel – 1 – uk British Libr Newspaper [072]
THE FELIX FRANKFURTER PAPERS / Frankfurter, Felix – (Pt 1, Supreme Court...Case Files of Opinions and Memoranda, October Terms, 1938-52: 74r ISBN 0-89093-809-1 $8,145.00; Pt 2, 1953-61: 92r ISBN 0-89093-810-5 $10,115.00; Pt 3, Correspondence and Related Material: 43r ISBN 0-89093-811-6 $4,735.00; Guide only to all three parts $220.00) – 1 – us UPA [920]
FELIX KERSTEN PAMPHLET COLLECTION – 1956 – 1 – CSUXANR9550-B – us Hoover Inst Photo [080]
FELIX PANORAMAS INTIMOS / Valverde Grimaldi, Felix – Merida: Tipografia Rodriguez, 1958 – sp Bibl Santa Ana [946]
FELIX RAVENNA – Ravenna, 1911-1917. Pt.1-28; 1919, Pt.1 – 28mf – 9 – O-500/1 – ne IDC [073]
FELIXSTOW TIMES – Felixstow, England. Felixstowe Times & Mercury. -w. April 1925-Dec 1981. Lacking 1977. 54 1 2 reels – 1 – uk British Libr Newspaper [072]
FELL AND LANGLEY'S BRITISH COLUMBIA SPEAKER'S DECISIONS / British Columbia. Canada – v1-3. 1877-1943 (all publ) – 5mf – 9 – $7.50 – LLMC 81-021 – us L.L.M.C. [340]
Fell, John *see* AN ESSAY TOWARDS AN ENGLISH GRAMMAR
FELLING GAZETTE – England. -f. 20 Feb 1880-22 Nov 1889. (Wanting Jan-Apr 1886). (4 reels) – 1 – uk British Libr Newspaper [072]
Fellner, H *see* PUBLISHING, THE BOOKTRADE AND THE DIFFUSION OF KNOWLEDGE SPECIALIST COLLECTION
Fellows, Charles *see* TRAVELS AND RESEARCHES IN ASIA MINOR: MORE PARTICULARLY IN THE PROVINCE OF LYCIA
FELLOWSHIP – v1 no6-v16 no11. 1935-50 (complete) – Inquire – 1 – ATLA 1993-S514 – us A.T.L.A. [073]
FELLOWSHIP BAPTIST CHURCH. DUBBERLY, LOUISIANA : CHURCH RECORDS – 1848-64 – 1 – 5.94 – us Baptist [240]
FELLOWSHIP BAPTIST CHURCH. MERIDIAN, MISSISSIPPI : CHURCH RECORDS – 1838-98, Aug 1906 – 1 – 12.24 – us Baptist [240]
FELLOWSHIP BAPTIST CHURCH. MOUNT MORIAH, ALABAMA : CHURCH RECORDS – 1828-1909 – 1 – 16.32 – us Baptist [240]
THE FELLOWSHIP FORUM – (Library has: v.10, no.15,21; v.15, no.3,5,12,15 (Sept. 27, 1930-May 1, 1936)) – Washington, D.C.: The Independent Pub. Co., 1921-1937 – 1 – CSUX89-S87 – us Hoover Inst Photo [978]
FELLOWSHIP IN THE LIFE ETERNAL: AN EXPOSITION OF THE EPISTLES OF ST JOHN / Findlay, George G – London: Hodder & Stoughton, (1900). 1 fiche – 9 – us A.T.L.A. [240]
THE FELLOWSHIP NEWS BULLETIN – (Lacking: v6 no 7) – v1-23. 1943-66 – 2r – 1 – ATLA S0132 – us A.T.L.A. [073]
THE FELLOWSHIP OF THE MYSTERY : BEING THE BISHOP PADDOCK LECTURES / Figgis, John Neville – London; New York: Longmans, Green, 1914 – 1mf – us A.T.L.A. [240]
Y FELLTEN – Merthyr Tydfil, Wales. Oct 1868-Sep 1876 – 2 1/2r – 1 – uk British Libr Newspaper [072]
THE FELON SETTER – Ireland.1916 – 1 – ie Microforms [072]
Fels, I *see* DE CONFOEDERATIONIBUS LIBERARUM...
Fels, Jacqueline de *see* SOMDET PHRA CHAO TAK SIN MAHARAT
DER FELS VON ERZ / Brachvogel, Albert Emil – Philadelphia: Hoffman & Morwitz. 2v. [189-?] – 1 – us U.W. Library [830]
FELSEFE VE ICTIMAIYYAT MECMUASI – (Yayimliyan: Tuerk Felsefe Cemiyeti. Mueessisi: Agah Sirri[Levend], Mueduerue: Mehmed Servet. Nos. 3 (Temmuz 1927), 7 (Tesrinievvel 1928)) – Istanbul: Matbaa-i Ebuezziya, 1927-? – 3mf – 9 – $75.00 – us MEDOC [949]
Felsenthal, Bernhard *see* WANDERING JEW: A STATEMENT...OF THE JEWISH VIEW OF JUDAISM
FELSOBIROSAGAINK ELVI HATAROZATAI / Hungary. Kuria – Budapest. On film: v1-20; 1891-1910. LL-0276 – 1 – us L of C Photodup [340]
Felt, Joseph B *see*
- DID THE FIRST CHURCH OF SALEM ORIGINALLY HAVE A CONFESSION OF FAITH DISTINCT FROM THEIR COVENANT?
- A MEMOIR OR DEFENCE OF HUGH PETERS
Felten, J *see* DIE APOSTELGESCHICHTE UEBERSETZT UND ERKLAERT
Felton, Cornelius Conway *see* GREECE, ANCIENT AND MODERN
FELTRINELLI ARCHIVES *see* COMMUNIST INTERNATIONAL PERIODICALS FROM THE FELTRINELLI ARCHIVES
Feltz, Deborah D *see* EFFECTS OF SAME-SEX AND COEDUCATIONAL PHYSICAL EDUCATION ON PERCEPTIONS OF SELF-CONFIDENCE AND CLASS ENVIRONMENT
FEMALE CHARACTERS OF HOLY SCRIPTURE : IN A SERIES OF SERMONS / Williams, Isaac – London: Rivingtons, 1873 – 1mf – 9 – 0-8370-5857-0 – 1985-3857 – us A.T.L.A. [220]
Female Charitable Association. Charleston *see* MINUTES
FEMALE EDUCATION FROM A MEDICAL POINT OF VIEW / Clouston, T S – Edinburgh: Macniven & Wallace, 1882 – us Res Libr [618]
FEMALE PATIENT – (v.5 .1980 5,6,9) – v.1. 1976 – 1 – us UMI [073]
FEMALE SCRIPTURE BIOGRAPHY: INCLUDING AN ESSAY ON WHAT CHRISTIANITY HAS DONE FOR WOMEN / Cox, F A – 1831 – 9 – us A.T.L.A. [240]
THE FEMININ 'MONARCHI', OR THE HISTORI OF THE BEE'S / Butler, Charles – 17th Century – 1 – uk Microform Academic [400]
THE FEMININE SOUL / Strutt, Elizabeth – 1870 – 9 – us A.T.L.A. [240]
FEMININITY AND MASCULINITY : SPORT AND SOCIAL CHANGE / Karwas, Marcia R & DePauw, Karen P – 1993 – 2mf – 9 – $8.00 – us Microform Publ [150]
LE FEMINISME / Avril de Saint-Croix, Mme. Ghenia – Paris: Giard et Briere, 1907. vii,219p. (Les Femmes Collection) – 3mf – 9 – $8.00 – fr Bibl Nationale [305]
LE FEMINISME DANS LE SOCIALISME FRANCAIS, DE 1830 A 1850 / Thibert, Marguerite – Paris: Giard, 1926. vii,377p. (Les Femmes Collection) – 4mf – 9 – $10.00 – fr Bibl Nationale [305]
FEMINIST ISSUES – 1980 – 1,5,6,9 – us UMI [305]
FEMINIST ISSUES – 1985- – 1 – us UMI [305]
O FEMINISTA : ORGAO DE PROPAGANDA DA EMANCIPACAO DA MULHER – Maceio, Alagoas. 9 Fev 1902 – 1,5,6 – bl Biblioteca [072]
LA FEMME – Montreal, Canada. avr 1908-v2 n50. jul 1912 – 1r – 1 – Can$40.00 – cn Can Microfilming [640]
LA FEMME AMOUREUSE DANS LA VIE ET DANS LA LITTERATURE / Almeras, Henri d' – Paris: Albin-Michel, n.d. 6v. (Les Femmes Collection) – 21mf – 9 – $52.00 – fr Bibl Nationale [410]
LA FEMME AU DIX-HUITIEME SIECLE / Goncourt, Edmond et Jules – Paris: Flammarion, 1939. 158p. (Les Femmes Collection) – 2mf – 9 – $6.00 – fr Bibl Nationale [305]
LA FEMME AUPRES DU MALADE A NOTRE EPOQUE: CONFERENCE.. / Benoit, Emmanuel P – Montreal: E. Senecal, 1895. 00136. (Pre-1900 Canadiana) – 9 – cn C.I.H.M. [610]
LA FEMME BIBLIQUE : SA VIE MORALE ET SOCIALE / Bader, Clarisse – Paris: Didier, 1866. 1 fiche – 1mf – 9 – us A.T.L.A. [240]
LA FEMME DANS LA SOCIETE / Toure, Ahmed Sekou – Conakry: Bureau de presse de la Presidence de la Republique populaire revolutionnaire de Guinee, [197-?] – us Res Libr [960]
LA FEMME DANS LE DROIT PENAL DU PROCHE-ORIENT ANCIEN / Demare, Sophie – 3mf – 9 – 10513 – fr Atelier National [340]
LA FEMME EN CULOTTE / Grand-Carteret, John – Paris: Flammarion, 1899. viii,393p. (Les Femmes Collection) – 5mf – 9 – $12.00 – fr Bibl Nationale [305]
LA FEMME EN LUTTE POUR SES DROITS / Pelletier, Madeleine – Paris: Giard et Briere, 1908. 79p. (Les Femmes Collection) – 1mf – 9 – $6.00 – fr Bibl Nationale [305]
LA FEMME ESCLAVE / Chaughi, Rene – Conflans-Ste.-Honorine: L'Idee Libre, 1920. 8p. (Les Femmes Collection) – 1mf – 9 – $6.00 – fr Bibl Nationale [305]
LA FEMME ET LA DEMOCRATIE DE NOTRE TEMPS / Allart de Meritens, Hortense – Paris: de Launay, 1836. 124p. (Les Femmes Collection) – 2mf – 9 – $6.00 – fr Bibl Nationale [323]
LA FEMME ET LA DEMOCRATIE DE NOTRE TEMPS / Allart de Meritens, Hortense – Paris, Delaunay. 1836, 124 p. Les Saint-Simoniens, 1825-1834. 6911 – 9 – fr Hachette [305]
LA FEMME ET LA FAMILLE / Casaubon, E A – Paris, Gautier, 1834, 24 p. Les Saint-Simoniens, 1825-1834. 7005 – 9 – fr Hachette [305]
LA FEMME ET LE FEMINISME. COLLECTION DE LIVRES, PERIODIQUES, ETC.. / Jacobs, Aletta Henriette – Faisant partie de la bibliotheque de M. et Mme. C.V. Gerritsen a Amsterdam. Paris: V. Giard & E. Briere, 1900.xvi,240p. Comp. by H.J. Mehler – 1 – us U.W. Library [305]
LA FEMME ET LE SOCIALISME / Bebel, Auguste – Nouvelle traduction francaise d'apres l'ed. allemande par Avanti. Reprod. de l'ed. de Grand. Imp. Volksdruckerei 1911. 749p. (Political Science Collection) – 8mf – 9 – $20.00 – fr Bibl Nationale [335]
LA FEMME FUTURE / Desmarest, Henri – Paris: Victor-Harvard, 1890. ix,229p. (Les Femmes Collection) – 3mf – 9 – $8.00 – fr Bibl Nationale [305]
LA FEMME MARIEE ANGLAISE EN ANGLETERRE ET EN FRANCE / Cheron, A – Paris, 1906 – 4mf – 1 – ILM-3094/1 – ne IDC [327]
LA FEMME MARIEE ET LES CHARGES DU MENAGE / Brunel, J – Montpellier: Firmin, 1910. 203p. (Les Femmes Collection) – 3mf – 9 – $8.00 – fr Bibl Nationale [640]
LA FEMME NOUVELLE – Apostolat des femmes. Les premiers numeros ont paru sous le titre: La femme libre. A partir du 4 (14), tome 1er, le sous-titre devient: Tribune des femmes. Parait a Paris, a partir du 15 aout 1832, Derniere livraison: avril 1834. Au total: 44 livraisons a pag. continue, 280 et 184 p. Les Saint-Simoniens, 1825-1834. 6904 – 9 – fr Hachette [305]
LA FEMME NOUVELLE ET LA CLASSE OUVRIERE / Kollontai, Alexandra – Paris: L'Eglantine, 1932. 107p. (Les Femmes Collection) – 2mf – 9 – $6.00 – fr Bibl Nationale [305]

LA FEMME PAUVRE AU XIXE SIECLE / Daube, Julie – 3v. 1899. (Condition of 19th century French working class series) – 9 – fr Hachette [305]
LA FEMME SANS PECHE / Lemonnier, Leon – Paris: Flammarion, 1927. 246p. (Les Femmes Collection) – 3mf – 9 – $8.00 – fr Bibl Nationale [410]
LA FEMME SEULE / Brieux, Eugene – Paris: Stock, 1913. 240p. (Les Femmes Collection) – 3mf – 9 – $8.00 – fr Bibl Nationale [305]
LA FEMME SOCIALISTE – Organe feministe socialiste. Dir. Louise Saumoneau. Paris. mai 1901-sept 1902, mars 1912- fevr mars 1940, oct 1947-juil sept 1949 – 1 – fr A.C.R.P.P. [335]
FEMMES / Prevost, Marcel – Paris: Lemerre, 1907. iii,321p. (Les Femmes Collection) – 4mf – 9 – $10.00 – fr Bibl Nationale [305]
LES FEMMES / Bibliotheque Nationale – Rare works from France on microfiche. 17th to 20th cent. 129 titles on 480mf. Individual titles available – 9 – $1188.00 – fr Bibl Nationale [305]
FEMMES AFRICAINES ET COMMERCE : LES REVENDENSES DE TISSU DE LA VILLE DE LOME, TOGO / Cordonnier, R – 9 – F120.00 – fr Ethnologie [306]
LES FEMMES COLLECTION *see* LES CARRIERES FEMININES INTELLECTUELLES
FEMMES CRIMINELLES / Mace, G – Paris: Bibliotheque-Charpentier, 1904 – us Res Libr [360]
FEMMES D'ALGERIE / L'Union des Femmes d'Algerie – Revue mensuelle. Alger. sept 1944-avr 1946 – 1 – fr A.C.R.P.P. [073]
LES FEMMES DANS L'HISTOIRE: LES AMAZONES / Lacour, Paul – Paris: Perrin, 1901. 306p. (Les Femmes Collection) – 4mf – 9 – $10.00 – fr Bibl Nationale [305]
LES FEMMES ET LE MARIAGE DANS L'ILE DE LAMU (KENYA) / Le Guennec-Coppens, F – 9 – F30.00 – fr Ethnologie [306]
FEMMES GALANTES DU XVIIE SIECLE: MME. DE VILLEDIEU (1632-1692) / Magne, Emile – Paris: Mercure de France. 434p. (Les Femmes Collection) – 5mf – 9 – $12.00 – fr Bibl Nationale [920]
FEMMES HEROIQUES! : LES SOEURS GRISES DANS L'EXTREME-NORD / Duchaussois, P – 8emille. Lyon [etc.]: Oeuvre apostolique de Marie Immaculee; [Montreal]: [Librairie Beauchemin Itee], [1920 ?]. SEM105P669 – 3mf – 9 – Can$6.75 – cn Bibl Nat [240]
LES FEMMES MILITAIRES, RELATION HISTORIQUE D'UNE ILE NOUVELLEMENT DECOUVERTE PAR LE C. D / Rustaing de Saint-Jory, Louis – (Utopias in the Enlightenment series). 1735 – 9 – fr Hachette [830]
LES FEMMES POETES DANS L'INDE / Tassy, M Garcin de – Paris: J Rouvier, 1854 – us Res Libr [305]
LES FEMMES VENGEES / Sedaine, Jean Michel – Opea1ra comique. 1775. (Libretto) – 1 – us Sibley [780]
FEMS IMMUNOLOGY AND MEDICAL MICROBIOLOGY – (Cont: FEMS Microbiology Immunology) – Amsterdam. v6-10 1993-feb 1995*. v11-19 1995-97+ – 1,5,9 – D42685.01 – us UMI [574]
FEMS MICROBIOLOGY IMMUNOLOGY *see* FEMS IMMUNOLOGY AND MEDICAL MICROBIOLOGY
FEMS-MICROBIOLOGY LETTERS – v1-25. 1977-84 – 1,5,6,13 – sz Elsevier [576]
Fenaroli, Fedele *see* PARTIMENTI OSSIA BASSO NUMERATO OPERA COMPLETA
FENCE INDUSTRY ACCESS CONTROL *see* ACCESS CONTROL, FENCE INDUSTRY
FENCHOW / American Board of Commissioners for Foreign Missions. North China Mission. Fenchow Station – v1-19, no. 1 (?) (all publ ?). Aug 1919-Dec 1936 (?) – 1 reel – 1 – $135.00 – us UPA [240]
Fendt, Leonhard *see* DIE DAUER DER OEFFENTLICHEN WIRKSAMKEIT JESU
Fenelon *see*
- LETTRES A L'ACADEMIE
- LETTRES SUR LES OCCUPATIONS DE L'ACADEMIE

FENELON, ARCHBISHOP OF CAMBRAI : A BIOGRAPHICAL SKETCH / Lear, H L Sidney – London: Rivingstons, 1877 – 2mf – us A.T.L.A. [240]
Fenelon, Francois de Salignac de La Mothe *see* LES AVENTURES DE TELEMAQUE, FILS D'ULYSSE
Fenelon, Francois de Salignac de la Mothe *see* LETTRES SPIRITUELLES
FENELON OU LES RELIGIEUSES DE CAMBRAI / Chenier, Marie-Joseph – (French Theatre Series). Paris. Moutard. 1793 – 9 – fr Hachette [820]
Fenety, George Edward *see*
- IMPERIAL FEDERATION
- LIFE AND TIMES OF THE HON. JOSEPH HOWE, THE GREAT NOVA SCOTIAN AND EX-LIEUT. GOVERNOR: WITH BRIEF REFERENCES TO SOME OF HIS PROMINENT CONTEMPORARIES

Feng, Chih *see* DIE ANALOGIE VON NATUR UND GEIST ALS STILPRINZIP IN NOVALIS' DICHTUNG
Feng, Shang-li *see* THINGS NEW AND OLD (CCC125)
Feng, Yu-hsiang *see*
- K'ANG CHAN SHIH KO CHI, VOL 5 (CCC126)
- WEI LIAO HSIEN CH'IH CHIU KUO KEI AI KUO P'ENG YU TI (CCC127)

Fenger, J Ferd *see* HISTORY OF THE TRANQUEBAR MISSION
FENG-HUO – (Beacon Fire). v1-2. 1937 – 8 – BCH-972 2 – ne IDC [920]
FENG-SHUN HSIEN-CHIH – 1746, 8. BCH-619 2 – 8 – ne IDC [950]
FENG-SHUN HSIEN-CHIH – 1884, 8, 1. BCH-620 2 – 8 – ne IDC [950]
THE FENIAN – Ireland.19 Jul-3 Oct 1922 – 1 – ie Microforms [072]
A FENIX – Sao Paulo, Brazil. Feb 1838-Oct 1841 – 1 – bl Biblioteca [072]
Fenix, Victoria *see* VEINTI UN DIAS EN EL ASILO SAN MIGUEL
Fenn, Courtenay Hughes *see*
- DIARY
- OVER AGAINST THE TREASURY

Fenn, MG *see* MARKETING LIVESTOCK AND MEAT
Fenn, P T *see* THE ORIGIN OF THE RIGHT OF FISHERY IN TERRITORIAL WATERS
Fenn, William Wallace *see* TEACHING OF JESUS: READINGS ON THE GOOD LIFE
Fenne, F de *see* ENTRETIENS FAMILIERS POUR LES AMATEURS DE LA LANGUE FRANCOISE
Fennell, D A *see* A PROVILE OF ECOTOURISTS AND THE BENEFITS DERIVED FROM THEIR EXPERIENCE
Fenner, Charles Erasmus *see* THE CIVIL CODE OF LOUISIANA AS A DEMOCRATIC INSTITUTION
Fenning, Daniel *see* A NEW GRAMMAR OF THE ENGLISH LANGUAGE
FENNY STRATFORD TIMES *see* FENNY STRATFORD WEEKLY TIMES
FENNY STRATFORD WEEKLY TIMES – (Fenny Stratford Times. 1882-86. North Bucks Times etc. 1887-) – Fenny, Stratford, England. 21 Aug 1879-1918; 1942. -w – 38r – 1 – uk British Libr Newspaper [072]
IL FENOMENO STORICO DI GINEVRA / Alonzo, S – Cireale, 1935 – 1mf – 9 – ILM-4018/1 – ne IDC [340]
Fenouillot, Falbaire De *see* L'HONNETE CRIMINEL OU L'INNOCENCE RECONNUE
Fenster, Samuel Benjamin *see* FENSTER'S GEORGIA LAW PROBLEMS AND ANSWERS.
FENSTER'S GEORGIA LAW PROBLEMS AND ANSWERS. / Fenster, Samuel Benjamin – Atlanta, 1941. LL-606 – 1 – us L of C Photodup [340]
Fenton, Jennifer M *see* LINKING GIRLS' EXPERIENCES IN PHYSICAL ACTIVITY TO SCHOOL CULTURE AND SOCIAL AND POLITICAL CONTEXTS
Fenton, John *see* EARLY HEBREW LIFE: A STUDY IN SOCIOLOGY
Fenton, W J *see* THE RIDDLE OF EXISTENCE SOLVED
FENTON'S QUEST / Braddon, Mary Elizabeth – British Fiction Archive: Unit 5 – 9 – uk Bell [830]
Fenwick, C G *see* WARDSHIP IN INTERNATIONAL LAW
Fenwick, George Edgeworth *see* EXCISION OF THE KNEEJOINT: WITH REPORT OF TWENTY-EIGHT CASES
FENWICK'S CAREER / Ward, Mary Augusta – British Fiction Archive: Unit 2 – 9 – uk Bell [830]
FENXI HUAXUE – (1982 $3.50f; 1977-1987, 1983, 1986- $4.50f) – Analytical Chemistry. In Chinese but English abstracts to the main articles. F p88 – 9 – cc Microforms [073]
FENXI YIQI WENZHAI – Analytical Instruments Digest. 1981-. F P245 – 9 – $4.50f – cc Microforms [073]
Fenzl, E *see*
- ENUMERATIO PLANTARUM QUAS IN NOVAE HOLLANDIAE
- GENERA PLANTARUM
- ILLUSTRATIONES ET DESCRIPTIONES PLANTARUM NOVARUM SYRIAE ET TAURI OCCIDENTALIS
- PUGILLUS PLANTARUM NOVARUM SYRIAE ET TAURI OCCIDENTALIS
- SERTUM CABULICUM

FEODOSII FEDOROVICH SHCHEDRIN 1751-1825 / Kaganovich, A – M. 1953. BR-6195 2 – 8 – ne IDC [460]
FEOFAN PROKOPOVICH I EGO VREMIA / Chistovich, I A – Spb. 1868. BR-6011 2 – 8 – ne IDC [947]
FEOFAN PROKOPOVICH KAK PISATEL' / Morozov, P O – Spb. 1880. B-1545 2 – 8 – ne IDC [460]
LE FER ET LA HOUILLE, SUIVI DU CANON KRUPP ET DU FAMILISTERE DE GUISE. DERNIERE SERIE DES ETUDES SUR LE REGIME DES MANUFACTURES / Reybaud, Louis – (Condition of 19th C. French working class series). 1874 – 9 – fr Hachette [380]
Feral, J P *see*
- NUTRITION CHEZ UN INVERTEBRE MARIN DETRITIVORE: LEPTOSYNAPTA GALLIENNEI (HOLOTHURIOIDEA: ECHINODERMATA)
- LA REGENERATION DES BRAS DE SEPIA OFFICINALIS L. (MOLLUSQUE, CEPHALOPODE, COLEOIDE)

Feraud, Abbe *see*
- DICTIONNAIRE CRITIQUE DE LA LANGUE FRANCAISE
- DICTIONNAIRE GRAMMATICAL DE LA LANGUE FRANCOISE

Feraud-Giraud, L J D *see*
- DE LA JURIDICTION FRANCAISE...
- FRANCE ET SARDAIGNE

Ferber, D *see* RECHTSVERHAELTNISSE DER KRIEGS- UND HANDELSSCHIFFE...
FER-DE-LANCE BRIEFING: SOVIET SCALAR ELECTROMAGNETIC WEAPONS / Bearden, Thomas E – 3p. From: Bulletin, Committee to Restore the Constitution, No.291, Sept 1986 – 9 – 1.00f – at Libertarian Micro [335]
FERDINAND CHRISTIAN BAUR / Weizsaecker, Karl Heinrich von – Rede zur akademischen Feier seines 100. Geburtstages, 21 Juni 1892 in der Aula in Tuebeingen. 1892 – 1 – us A.T.L.A. [240]
FERDINAND GAGNON, SA VIE ET SES OEUVRES: NOTICE BIOGRAPHIQUE ET OEUVRES DE FERDINAND GAGNON...PAR M. LE CHANOINE J.-R. OUELLETTE, SUPERIEUR DU SEMINAIRE DE ST HYACINTHE, PROVINCE DE QUEBEC / Gagnon, Ferdinand – Worcester, Mass.: O. Lawrence, 1886. 03086. (Pre-1900 Canadiana) – 9 – cn C.I.H.M. [971]
FERDINAND GREGOROVIUS ALS DICHTER / Hoenig, Johannes – (Includes bibliographical references) – Stuttgart: Metzler, 1914 – 1r – 1 – us U.W. Library [430]
FERDINAND RAIMUND : LEBENSWERK UND WIRKUNGSRAUM EINES DEUTSCHEN VOLKSDRAMATIKERS / Kindermann, Heinz – (Includes indexes) – Wien: Adolf Luser, 1940 – 1r – 1 – us U.W. Library [430]
FERDINAND RAIMUNDS SAEMTLICHE WERKE IN DREI TEILEN = WORKS / Raimund, Ferdinand; ed by Castle, Eduard – (Includes bibliographical references) – Leipzig: Hesse & Becker, [1923?] – 1 – us U.W. Library [800]
FERDINAND V. HAYDEN PAPERS *see* HAYDEN, FERDINAND V., PAPERS, MS 3154
Ferenc, F *see* MAGYAR ALLAMPOLGARSAGI JOG
Ferenczi, Z *see* DEAK ELETE
Fergus, Dyjan *see* TISAB TING, OR, THE ELECTRIC KISS
Ferguson, Archibald *see* THE NEW MONTREAL GAZETTE
Ferguson, Donald *see*
- AGRICULTURAL EDUCATION: A LECTURE DELIVERED BEFORE THE YOUNG MEN'S CHRISTIAN ASSOCIATION, CHARLOTTETOWN, P. E. ISLAND, ON THURSDAY EVENING, JANUARY 17, 1884
- LOVE OF COUNTRY: A LECTURE DELIVERED BEFORE THE BENEVOLENT IRISH SOCIETY, CHARLOTTETOWN, PRINCE EDWARD ISLAND, ON MONDAY EVENING, FEBRUARY 23, 1885

Ferguson, J A *see* BIBLIOGRAPHY OF THE NEW HEBRIDES ISLANDS
Ferguson, J F *see* THE INTERNATIONAL CONFERENCE OF THE HAGUE
Ferguson, J H *see* MANUAL OF INTERNATIONAL LAW...
Ferguson, John R *see* PROPOSAL FOR ADVOCATING TAXATION METHODS.
FERGUSON LODE – Helene, NV. 1892-93 – 1r – 1 – $50.00 – U04586 – us Library Micro [071]
Ferguson, Mary Catharine Guinness *see* THE STORY OF THE IRISH BEFORE THE CONQUE FROM THE MYTHICAL PERIOD TO THE INVASION UNDER STRONGBOW
Ferguson, Phyllis *see* CATALOGUE OF ARABIC MANUSCRIPTS FROM GHANA AND ADJACENT TERRITORIES FROM INSTITUTE OF AFRICAN STUDIES
Ferguson, Thomas James *see* 1734-1884: SESQUI-CENTENNIAL...SILVER SPRINGS PRESBYTERIAN CHURCH
Ferguson, William *see* THE EARLY YEARS OF JOHN CALVIN
Fergusson, James *see* TEMPLES OF THE JEWS AND OTHER BUILDINGS IN THE HARAM AREA OF JERUSALEM
FERIA DE AGOSTO, 1927 / Almendralejo – Almendralejo: Imp. de J. Bote, 1927 – 1 – sp Bibl Santa Ana [946]
FERIA DE LAS MERCEDES EN ALMENDRALEJO / Almendralejo. Ayuntamiento – Badajoz: Imp. V. Rodriguez, 1913 – 1 – sp Bibl Santa Ana [946]
FERIA DE LAS MERCEDES EN ALMENDRALEJO DE 1913. CONCURSO DE GANADERIA / Almendralejo. Ayuntamiento – Badajoz: La Minerva Extremana – 1 – sp Bibl Santa Ana [946]
FERIA DE SAN MIGUEL – Caceres: Caceres, Imp. Sanguino, s.a. – 1 – sp Bibl Santa Ana [240]
FERIA DE SAN MIGUEL, 1954 / Caceres. Ayuntamiento – Caceres: Tip. El Noticiero – sp Bibl Santa Ana [390]
FERIA DE SANTIAGO DE TODA CLASE DE GANADO. DURANTE...JULIO, 1961 / Casatejada. Ayuntamiento – Caceres: La Minerva, 1961 – 1 – sp Bibl Santa Ana [390]
FERIA DE SANTIAGO DE TODA CLASE DE GANADOS. DURANTE...JULIO, 1962 / Casatejada. Ayuntamiento – Caceres: Tip. La Minerva, 1962 – 1 – sp Bibl Santa Ana [390]
FERIA DE SANTIAGO. PARA TODA CLASE DE GANADOS. JULIO 1973 – Caceres: Imp. La Minerva, 1973 – 1 – sp Bibl Santa Ana [390]
FERIA DE SEPTIEMBRE, 1947. ARROYO DE LA LUZ – Imp. Moderna. Caceres. 1947, 1948, 1954, 1963, 1972 – 1 – sp Bibl Santa Ana [946]
Feria. Spain. Ayuntamiento *see* ORDENANZAS MUNICIPALES
FERIA Y FEISTAS DE...AGOSTO 1970 / Olivenza – (Olivenza Tip. Martinez – Reginfo, 1970) – 1 – sp Bibl Santa Ana [946]
FERIA Y FIESTAS – Valencia de Alcantara: Tip. Avila, 1959 – 1 – sp Bibl Santa Ana [390]
FERIA Y FIESTAS 1945 / San Vicente de Alcantara – Olivenza: Imprenta Marquez, 1945 – sp Bibl Santa Ana [390]
FERIA Y FIESTAS, 1945 / Jerez de los Caballeros. Badajoz – Jerez de los Caballeros: Tip. Horizonte, 1945 – sp Bibl Santa Ana [390]
FERIA Y FIESTAS, 1947. CABEZA DEL BUEY / Cabeza del Buey. Ayuntamiento – Imprenta Juan F. Lozano, 1947 – 1 – sp Bibl Santa Ana [390]
FERIA Y FIESTAS 1958 – Plasencia: Imp. La Victoria, 1958 – 1 – sp Bibl Santa Ana [390]
FERIA Y FIESTAS. 1967 / Don Benito – Don Benito: Tip. Trejo – sp Bibl Santa Ana [390]
FERIA Y FIESTAS 1975 – Jaraiz de la Vera: Imp. La Verata, 1975 – 1 – sp Bibl Santa Ana [390]
FERIA Y FIESTAS 1977 / Valencia de Alcantara. Ayuntamiento – Valencia de Alcantara: Tip. Avila, 1977 – sp Bibl Santa Ana [390]
FERIA Y FIESTAS DE 1945 / Zarza de Alange – Olivenza: Tip. M. Reginfo, 1945 – sp Bibl Santa Ana [390]
FERIA Y FIESTAS DE 1946 / Llerena – Badajoz: Tip. Clasica, 1946 – sp Bibl Santa Ana [390]
FERIA Y FIESTAS DE JARAIZ DE LA VERA 1974 / Jaraiz de la Vera. Ayuntamiento – Jaraiz de la Vera: Imp. La Verata, 1974 – 1 – sp Bibl Santa Ana [390]

FERIA Y FIESTAS DE JUNIO 1975 – Plasencia: Imp. Padilla, 1975. Tambien Ano 1976 – 1 – sp Bibl Santa Ana [390]

FERIA Y FIESTAS DE PRIMAVERA 1974 / Canaveral. Ayuntamiento – Plasencia: Talleres Sanguino, 1973 – 1 – sp Bibl Santa Ana [390]

FERIA Y FIESTAS DE PRIMAVERA 1975 / Canaveral. Ayuntamiento – Plasencia: Sandoval, 1975 – 1 – sp Bibl Santa Ana [390]

FERIA Y FIESTAS DE SAN BARTOLOME, 1973 – Caceres: Imp. M. Sergio Dorado, 1973 – 1 – sp Bibl Santa Ana [390]

FERIA Y FIESTAS EN HONOR DE NUESTRO EXCELSO PATRON EL SANTISIMO CRISTO DE LA EXPIRACION... – Jerez de los Caballeros: Imp. Horizonte, 1970 – 1 – sp Bibl Santa Ana [240]

FERIA Y FIESTAS EN HONOR DE SAN AGUSTIN...1970 – Fregenal de la Sierra: Imp. Angel Verde, 1970 – 1 – sp Bibl Santa Ana [240]

FERIA Y FIESTAS EN LA CIUDAD DE ALFONSO 8, 1965 / Plasencia. Ayuntamiento – Caceres, 1965 – 1 – sp Bibl Santa Ana [390]

FERIA Y FIESTAS. JUNIO, 1965 / Plasencia. Ayuntamiento – Plasencia: Imprenta Padilla, 1965 – 1 – sp Bibl Santa Ana [390]

FERIA Y FIESTAS MAYO 1970 / Canaveral. Ayuntamiento – Plasencia: Imp. La Victoria, 1970 – 1 – sp Bibl Santa Ana [390]

FERIA Y FIESTAS MAYO DE 1952. GUIA COMERCIAL / Caceres. Ayuntamiento – Caceres: Imp. Sanguino – sp Bibl Santa Ana [390]

FERIA Y FIESTAS MAYO-JUNIO, 1953 / Caceres, Ayuntamiento, Trujillo. Ayuntamiento – sp Bibl Santa Ana [390]

FERIA Y FIESTAS. MERIDA – Badajoz: Argreus, 1933 – 1 – sp Bibl Santa Ana [946]

FERIA Y FIESTAS MERIDA. 1932 – 1 – sp Bibl Santa Ana [946]

FERIA Y FIESTAS. PROGRAMA OFICIAL 1972 / Valencia de Alcantara. Ayuntamiento – Valencia de Alcantara: Tip. Avila, 1972 – 1 – sp Bibl Santa Ana [390]

FERIA Y FIESTAS SEPTIEMBRE 1970 / Monterrubio de la Serena, Ayuntamiento – (Castuera: Imprenta de Eladio Fernandez, 1970) – 1 – sp Bibl Santa Ana [946]

FERIA Y FIESTAS...1960 / Malagon (Ciudad Real). Ayuntamiento – Plasencia: Tip. La Victoria, 1960 – 1 – sp Bibl Santa Ana [390]

FERIAS DE GANADOS DURANTE...SEPTIEMBRE 1962 / Malpartida de Plasencia. Ayuntamiento – Caceres: Tip. La Minerva, 1962 – 1 – sp Bibl Santa Ana [390]

FERIAS DE SAN JUAN. JUNIO 1956 / Coria. Ayuntamiento – Plasencia: Imp. La Victoria, 1956 – 1 – sp Bibl Santa Ana [390]

FERIAS DE SANTIAGO DE TODA CLASE DE GANADOS – Caceres: Tip. La Minerva, 1963 – 1 – sp Bibl Santa Ana [390]

FERIAS Y FIESTA EN HONOR DE NUESTRA SENORA DEL SALOR, PATRONA DE... SEPTIEMBRE 1975 – Caceres: La Minerva, 1975 – 1 – sp Bibl Santa Ana [240]

FERIAS Y FIESTAS / Oliva de la Frontera – Jerez de los Caballeros. I. Horizontes, 1970 – 1 – sp Bibl Santa Ana [946]

FERIAS Y FIESTAS 1928. MERIDA – 1 – sp Bibl Santa Ana [946]

FERIAS Y FIESTAS 1944. NUESTRA SENORA DE LA PIEDAD – 1 – sp Bibl Santa Ana [946]

FERIAS Y FIESTAS, 1945 / Don Benito – Badajoz: Arqueros, 1945 – sp Bibl Santa Ana [390]

FERIAS Y FIESTAS 1952 / Caceres. Ayuntamiento. Caceres – Caceres: Imp. Sanguino, y 1953 – sp Bibl Santa Ana [390]

FERIAS Y FIESTAS 1954 – (Tambien Anos 1955, 1956, 1957, 1958, 1959, 1960, 1961, 1962, 1965, 1968) – Badajoz: Imp. Arqueros, 1954 – 1 – sp Bibl Santa Ana [390]

FERIAS Y FIESTAS, 1954 / Hervas. Ayuntamiento – Valencia: Viuda de Climent, 1954 – sp Bibl Santa Ana [390]

FERIAS Y FIESTAS 1961 / Hervas. Ayuntamiento – Plasencia: La Victoria, 1961 – 1 – sp Bibl Santa Ana [390]

FERIAS Y FIESTAS 1964 / Hervas. Ayuntamiento – Plasencia: El autor, 1964 – 1 – sp Bibl Santa Ana [390]

FERIAS Y FIESTAS. 1970 – Fregenal de la Sierra: Imp. Angel Verde, 1970 – 1 – sp Bibl Santa Ana [390]

FERIAS Y FIESTAS 1971 – Caceres: Imp. La Minerva, 1971 – 1 – sp Bibl Santa Ana [390]

FERIAS Y FIESTAS 1971 / Cilleros. Ayuntamiento – Coria: Imp. Fernandez, 1971 – 1 – sp Bibl Santa Ana [390]

FERIAS Y FIESTAS 1972 / Sotillo de la Andrada. Ayuntamiento – Jaraiz de la Vera: Imp. La Verata, 1972 – 1 – sp Bibl Santa Ana [390]

FERIAS Y FIESTAS 1973 / Asociacion Cultural "Pedro de Trejo" – Plasencia, Caceres: A.C.P. Pedro de Trejo, 1973 – 1 – sp Bibl Santa Ana [390]

FERIAS Y FIESTAS 1973 / Malpartida de Caceres. Ayuntamiento – Caceres: Imp. Tomas Rodriguez Santano, 1973 – 1 – sp Bibl Santa Ana [390]

FERIAS Y FIESTAS. 1973. GUIA OFICIAL / Caceres. Ayuntamiento – Caceres: Ed. Extremadura, 1973 – 1 – sp Bibl Santa Ana [390]

FERIAS Y FIESTAS 1974 – Caceres: Tip. La Minerva, 1974 – 1 – sp Bibl Santa Ana [390]

FERIAS Y FIESTAS 1974 / Navas del Madrono. Ayuntamiento – Caceres: Tip. Extremadura, 1974 – 1 – sp Bibl Santa Ana [390]

FERIAS Y FIESTAS 1975 – Caceres: Imp. La Minerva, 1975 – 1 – sp Bibl Santa Ana [390]

FERIAS Y FIESTAS 1977 – Caceres: Edit. Extremadura, s.a. 1977 – 1 – sp Bibl Santa Ana [390]

FERIAS Y FIESTAS. AGOSTO, 1973 – Caceres: Imp. La Minerva, 1973 – 1 – sp Bibl Santa Ana [390]

FERIAS Y FIESTAS AGOSTO 1976 – Caceres: Tip. Extremadura, 1976 – 1 – sp Bibl Santa Ana [390]

FERIAS Y FIESTAS. AGOSTO DE 1945 / Almendralejo – Almendralejo: Imp. Macarro, 1945 – 1 – sp Bibl Santa Ana [390]

FERIAS Y FIESTAS. CACERES, MAYO 1958 / Odarial Publicidad – Caceres: Odarial Publicidad, 1958 – 1 – sp Bibl Santa Ana [390]

FERIAS Y FIESTAS. CACERES, TRUJILLO, LOGROSAN / Publicidad Fefa – Caceres: Publicidad "Fefa", 1954 – 1 – sp Bibl Santa Ana [390]

FERIAS Y FIESTAS DE 1974 / Malpartida de Plasencia. Ayuntamiento – Plasencia: Imp. Padilla, 1974 – 1 – sp Bibl Santa Ana [390]

FERIAS Y FIESTAS DE AGOSTO. 1975 / Olivenza. Ayuntamiento – (Tambien 1980) – Zafra: Ind. Tip. Extremenas, 1975 – 1 – sp Bibl Santa Ana [390]

FERIAS Y FIESTAS DE CACERES, 1947 – Caceres: Tip. Garcia Floriano, 1947 – 1 – sp Bibl Santa Ana [390]

FERIAS Y FIESTAS DE JUNIO, 1960 / Trujillo. Ayuntamiento – s.l. s.i., 1960 – sp Bibl Santa Ana [390]

FERIAS Y FIESTAS DE JUNIO. 1963 / Malpartida de Plasencia. Ayuntamiento – Caceres: Tip. La Minerva, 1963 – 1 – sp Bibl Santa Ana [390]

FERIAS Y FIESTAS DE LA VELADA, 1945 / Zorita. Ayuntamiento – Caceres: Tip. El Noticiero, s.a. 1945 – sp Bibl Santa Ana [390]

FERIAS Y FIESTAS DE MAYO 1954 / Caceres. Ayuntamiento – Caceres: Imp. Sanguino – sp Bibl Santa Ana [390]

FERIAS Y FIESTAS DE MAYO DE 1950 GUIA COMERCIAL / Caceres. Ayuntamiento – Caceres: Imp. Moderna – sp Bibl Santa Ana [390]

FERIAS Y FIESTAS DE MIAJADAS 1972 / Miajadas. Ayuntamiento – Caceres: Tip. Extremadura, 1972 – 1 – sp Bibl Santa Ana [390]

FERIAS Y FIESTAS DE NUESTRA SENORA DE LA ASUNCION 1974 – Plasencia: J. Luis Heras, 1974 – 1 – sp Bibl Santa Ana [240]

FERIAS Y FIESTAS DE NUESTRA SENORA DE LA ASUNCION, 1975 – Plasencia: Imp. Las Heras, 1975 – 1 – sp Bibl Santa Ana [240]

FERIAS Y FIESTAS DE NUESTRA SENORA DE LA ASUNCION 1976 – Plasencia: Imp. Luis Heras, 1976 – 1 – sp Bibl Santa Ana [240]

FERIAS Y FIESTAS DE NUESTRA SENORA DE LA ASUNCION DURANTE...AGOSTO 1962 / Galisteo. Ayuntamiento – Plasencia: Imp. Luis Heras, 1962 – 1 – sp Bibl Santa Ana [390]

FERIAS Y FIESTAS DE NUESTRA SENORA DE LA ASUNCION. GALISTEO 1973. AGOSTO – Plasencia: Imp. Luis Heras, 1973 – 1 – sp Bibl Santa Ana [240]

FERIAS Y FIESTAS DE NUESTRA SENORA DE LA ASUNCION LOS DIAS...AGOSTO 1960 / Galisteo. Ayuntamiento – Plasencia: Imp. Luis Heras, 1960 – 1 – sp Bibl Santa Ana [390]

FERIAS Y FIESTAS DE NUESTRA SENORA DE LA PIEDAD – Almendralejo, 1947 – 1 – sp Bibl Santa Ana [946]

FERIAS Y FIESTAS DE PLASENCIA 1973 – Plasencia: Imp. Sanguino, 1973 – 1 – sp Bibl Santa Ana [390]

FERIAS Y FIESTAS DE PLASENCIA 1975 / Asociacion Cultural Placentina Pedro de Trejo – Plasencia: Imp. Padilla, 1975 – 1 – sp Bibl Santa Ana [390]

FERIAS Y FIESTAS DE PLASENCIA. JUNIO, 1959 / Plasencia. Ayuntamiento – Plasencia: Imp. Gabriel y Galan, 1959 – 1 – sp Bibl Santa Ana [390]

FERIAS Y FIESTAS DE PRIMAVERA 1972 / Aleantara. Ayuntamiento – Caceres: Imp. La Minerva, 1972 – 1 – sp Bibl Santa Ana [390]

FERIAS Y FIESTAS DE SAN AGUSTIN – Villanueva de la Serena: Hijo de Pedro Parejo, 1971 – 1 – sp Bibl Santa Ana [240]

FERIAS Y FIESTAS DE SAN GIL ABAD, SEPTIEMBRE, 1953 / Jerte, Ayuntamiento de – Caceres: Tip. El Noticiero – sp Bibl Santa Ana [390]

FERIAS Y FIESTAS DE SAN GIL ABAD, SEPTIEMBRE DE 1952 / Jerte, Ayuntamiento de – Caceres: Tip. El Noticiero – sp Bibl Santa Ana [390]

FERIAS Y FIESTAS DE SAN JUAN. 1946 / Badajoz – Badajoz: A. Arqueros, 1946 – sp Bibl Santa Ana [390]

FERIAS Y FIESTAS DE SAN JUAN. GUIA DE ESPECTACULOS 1953 / Badajoz – Badajoz: Casa Arqueros, 1953 – sp Bibl Santa Ana [390]

FERIAS Y FIESTAS DE SEPTIEMBRE 1970 / Barcarrota – Fregenal de la Sierra: Imp. Angel Verde, 1970 – sp Bibl Santa Ana [390]

FERIAS Y FIESTAS DURANTE LOS DIAS 28, 29 Y 30...1960 / Navalmoral de La Mata. Ayuntamiento – Caceres: Imp. Rivero, 1960 – 1 – sp Bibl Santa Ana [390]

FERIAS Y FIESTAS DURANTE...8, 9 Y 10 DE JUNIO, 1960 / Plasencia. Ayuntamiento – Plasencia: Imp. Luis Heras, 1960 – 1 – sp Bibl Santa Ana [390]

FERIAS Y FIESTAS EN 1974 / Plasencia. Asociacion Cultural Placentina Pedro de Trejo – S.l., s.i, s.a. – 1 – sp Bibl Santa Ana [390]

FERIAS Y FIESTAS EN BARCARROTA. SEPTIEMBRE DE 1946 / Barcarrota – Jerez de los Caballeros: Tip. Horizonte, 1946 – sp Bibl Santa Ana [390]

FERIAS Y FIESTAS EN HONOR A SAN MIGUEL. 1979 / Cabeza del Buey. Ayuntamiento – (Tambien 1980) – Cabeza del Buey: Imp. Lorenzo Gonzalez, 1979 – 1 – sp Bibl Santa Ana [390]

FERIAS Y FIESTAS EN HONOR DE LA SANTISIMA VIRGEN DE CARRION, PATRONA DE ALBURQUERQUE / Alburquerque. Ayuntamiento – Valencia de Alcantara: Tip. Avila, 1972 – 1 – sp Bibl Santa Ana [390]

FERIAS Y FIESTAS EN HONOR DE NTRA. SRA. DE GRACIA. 1974 / Membrio. Ayuntamiento – Valencia de Alcantara: Imp. Avila, 1974 – 1 – sp Bibl Santa Ana [390]

FERIAS Y FIESTAS EN HONOR DE NTRA. SRA. DE LA ASUNCION. 1971 / Galisteo. Ayuntamiento – Plasencia: Imp. Luis Heras, 1971 – 1 – sp Bibl Santa Ana [390]

FERIAS Y FIESTAS EN HONOR DE NUESTRA SENORA DE GRACIA. AGOSTO 1975 – Caceres: La Minerva, 1975 – 1 – sp Bibl Santa Ana [240]

FERIAS Y FIESTAS EN HONOR DE SAN ISIDRO LABRADOR. MAYO DE 1951 / Aldea de Trujillo. Ayuntamiento – Caceres: Imp. El Noticiero – sp Bibl Santa Ana [390]

FERIAS Y FIESTAS EN MALPARTIDA DE CACERES. SEPTIEMBRE 1972 – Caceres: Edit. Extremadura, 1972 – 1 – sp Bibl Santa Ana [390]

FERIAS Y FIESTAS EN MEDELLIN (BADAJOZ) DURANTE LOS DIAS 20, 21, 22 DE FEBRERO – Villanueva de la Serena: Imp. Julian Gil y Cia, 1957 – 1 – sp Bibl Santa Ana [390]

FERIAS Y FIESTAS EN PLASENCIA, 1958 / Plasencia. Ayuntamiento – Plasencia: Tip. La Victoria – sp Bibl Santa Ana [390]

FERIAS Y FIESTAS. HERVAS, 1962 / Hervas. Ayuntamiento – Plasencia: Imp. Victoria, 1962 – 1 – sp Bibl Santa Ana [390]

FERIAS Y FIESTAS HERVAS 1971 / Hervas. Ayuntamiento – Plasencia: Imp. Garcilasso, 1971 – 1 – sp Bibl Santa Ana [390]

FERIAS Y FIESTAS JUNIO, 1961 – Plasencia: Imprenta Gabriel y Galan, 1961 – 1 – sp Bibl Santa Ana [390]

FERIAS Y FIESTAS LOS DIAS...1960 / Malpartida de Plasencia. Ayuntamiento – Caceres: Imprenta La Minerva, 1960 – sp Bibl Santa Ana [390]

FERIAS Y FIESTAS, MALAGON 1961 / Malagon. Ayuntamiento – Plasencia: La Victoria, 1961 – 1 – sp Bibl Santa Ana [390]

FERIAS Y FIESTAS MAYO 1947 / Caceres. Ayuntamiento – Caceres: Tip. El Noticiero – sp Bibl Santa Ana [390]

FERIAS Y FIESTAS MAYO 1963 / Caceres. Ayuntamiento – Caceres: Tip. El Noticiero, 1963 – 1 – sp Bibl Santa Ana [390]

FERIAS Y FIESTAS PATRONALES EN HONOR DE LA VIRGEN DEL SOTERRANO. 1980 / Barcarrota – (Tambien ano 1979) – Fregenal de la Sierra: Imp. Angel Verde, 1980 – 1 – sp Bibl Santa Ana [390]

FERIAS Y FIESTAS PATRONALES. SAN JORGE, 1960 / Caceres. Ayuntamiento – Caceres: Imprenta La Minerva, 1960 – 1 – sp Bibl Santa Ana [390]

FERIAS Y FIESTAS S. GIL ABAD, 1973 – Plasencia: Graf. Sandoval, 1973 – 1 – sp Bibl Santa Ana [390]

FERIAS Y FIESTAS. SEPTIEMBRE, 1961 / Torrecillas de la Tiesa. Ayuntamiento – Caceres: Imp. Sanguino, 1961 – 1 – sp Bibl Santa Ana [390]

FERIAS Y FIESTAS. SEPTIEMBRE 1973 – Caceres: Imp. La Minerva, 1973 – 1 – sp Bibl Santa Ana [390]

FERIAS Y FIESTAS...1972 / Santiago de Alcantara. Ayuntamiento – Caceres: Imp. La Minerva, 1972 – 1 – sp Bibl Santa Ana [390]

FERIAS Y FIESTAS...MAYO 1959...FERIA DE GANADOS DE TODAS CLASES / Navas del Madrono. Ayuntamiento – Caceres: Imprenta La Minerva, 1959 – 1 – sp Bibl Santa Ana [390]

FERIAS Y FIESTAS...SEPTIEMBRE, 1960 EN HONOR DE LA SANTISIMA VIRGEN DE CARRION / Alburquerque. Ayuntamiento – Valencia de Alcantara: Tip. Avila, 1960 – 1 – sp Bibl Santa Ana [390]

FERIAS Y FIETAS 1963 / Hervas. Ayuntamiento – Jaraiz de la Vera: Imp. Los Veratos, 1963 – 1 – sp Bibl Santa Ana [390]

FERIENREISE EINES EVANGELISCHEN PREDIGERS : ZEITGESCHICHTLICHE STUDIEN / Dalton, Hermann – Bremen: C.Ed. Mueller, 1886 – 1mf – us A.T.L.A. [240]

Feriet, R de *see* L'APPLICATION D'UN MANDAT

FERISHTAH'S FANCIES / Browning, Robert – London: Smith, Elder, 1884 – 1 roll – 1 – 1-55879-167-1 – uk Libr Preservation [810]

Ferla, Salvador *see*
- DOCTRINA DEL NACIONALISMO
- MARTIRES Y VERDUGOS
- "LA TERCERA POSICION IDEOLOGICA" Y APRECIACIONES SOBRE EL RETORNO DE PERON

Ferland, Albert *see* MELODIES POETIQUES

Ferland, Jean Baptise Antoine *see* MGR. JOSEPH OCTAVE PLESIS: EVEQUE DE QUEBEC

Ferlus, Francois *see* PROJET D'EDUCATION NATIONALE PRESENTE A L'ASSEMBLEE NATIONALE

FERMANAGH HERALD – Mar 14-Dec 16 1903; Jan 2-Mar 12 1904; Apr 30-Dec 1904; 1905-50; Jan-Jun 1986; Jul 5 1986-89; Jan 13-Jun 30 1990; Jul 7 1990-Jan 5 1991; Jan 12-Dec 1991; Jan 11-Mar 28 1992; Apr 1992-Jun 1995; Jul 5 1995-Jan 3 1996; Jul-Dec 1996 – 65 1/2r – 1 – uk British Libr Newspaper [072]
FERMANAGH MAIL ETC – Enniskillen, Ireland. 23 Aug 1849-4 Nov 1850; 20 Mar-25 Dec 1851; 1852-89; 2 Mar-Dec 1890. -w. 32 3/4 reels. Missing: 1860, 1883 – 1 – uk British Libr Newspaper [072]
FERMANAGH SENTINEL AND NORTH WEST ADVERTISER – Enniskillen, Ireland. 7 Mar-26 Dec 1854; 2 Jan 1855. -w. 1/2 reel – 1 – uk British Libr Newspaper [072]
FERMENTA COGNITIONIS / Baader, Franz von – Berlin, 1822-1824 – 350p – 9 – DM48.00 – 3-89349-075-2 – gw Hänsel [100]
FERMENTED FISH IN AFRICA : A STUDY ON PROCESSING, MARKETING AND CONSUMPTION – 1992 – 87p – it F.A.O. [338]
Fermoso Palmeco, Aristides *see* NORMAS DE TRABAJO VIGENTES EN LAS INDUSTRIAS DE LA CONSTRUCCION YUNOBRAS PUBLICAS Y TABLAS DE LIQUIDACION DE SALARIOS
THE FERN ALLIES; A SUPPLEMENT TO THE FERNS OF GREAT BRITAIN / Johnson, C – London. 1856. B-7204 1 – 9 – ne IDC [580]
A FERN BOOK FOR EVERYBODY / Cooke, M C – Containing all the British ferns, with the foreign species suitable for a fernery. London. 1867. B-7176 1 – 9 – ne IDC [580]
FERN GROWING. FIFTY YEARS' EXPERIENCE IN CROSSING AND CULTIVATION / Lowe, E J – London, 1895. 1, 196 pp. B-7217 1 – 9 – ne IDC [580]
Fernald, Woodbury M *see*
- EMANUEL SWEDENBORG
- GOD IN HIS PROVIDENCE
- THE TRUE CHRISTIAN LIFE AND HOW TO ATTAIN IT

Fernand Braudel Center for the Study of Economies, Historical Systems, and Civilizations *see* REVIEW
FERNAND CORTEZ OU LA CONQUETE DU MEXIQUE / Jouy, Esmerard & Spontini – French Theatre Series. Paris. Roullet. 1809 – 9 – fr Hachette [820]
Fernandes, Benjamin Dias *see* A SERIES OF LETTERS ON THE EVIDENCES OF CHRISTIANITY
Fernandes Gaytan, J *see* MARINOS EXTREMENOS
Fernandex Mato, Romas *see* EL GENERALISIMO TRUJILLO.
Fernandez Abelehira, Maria Isabel *see* COMO ES LA VIDA
Fernandez Almagro, Melchor *see* LA EMANCIPACION DE AMERICA Y SU REFLEJO EN LA CULTURA ESPANOLA. MADRID, 1944
Fernandez Almuzara, E *see* CARTAS LITERARIAS...SOBRE GREGORIO SILVESTRE
Fernandez Barea, M *see* JUICIO PRACTICO SOBRE LAS VIRTUDES MEDICINALES...
Fernandez, Benjamin Dias *see* LETTERS OF BENJAMIN DIAS FERNANDEZ ON THE EVIDENCES OF CHRISTIANITY
Fernandez, C *see* NOCIONES DE DERECHO INTERNACIONAL MARITIMO,...
Fernandez Cardo, Jose Maria *see* FUNCIONAMIENTO DE LOS PERSONAJES EN LAS NOVELAS DE ROBBE GRILLET
Fernandez Casco, Juan *see* EL EXTRAORDINARIO PODER DE LAS PLANTAS
Fernandez Caton, Jose Maria *see* CATALOGO DE LOS MATERIALES CODIGOLOGICOS....DE AUSPACH 1966...
Fernandez Cortes, Gil *see* MEMORIAL...D. ISIDRO DE CARVAJAL
Fernandez D, Cesareo *see*
- COLON ESTREMENA
- COLON EXTREMENO? DE VICENTE PAREDES
- NOTICIAS

Fernandez de Bethencourt, Francisco *see*
- CARLOS 4 Y MARIA LUISA, DE JUAN PEREZ DE GUZMAN Y GALLO
- EL MARQUES DE MONSALUD ES SUSTITUIDO POR D. ADOLFO BONILLA

Fernandez de Castro, Eduardo Felipe *see*
- DOS PALABRAS SOBRE EL PRESENTE NUMERO-HOMENAJE. BENITO ARIAS MONTANO
- ICONOGRAFIA DE BENITO ARIAS MONTANO POR CARLOS DOETSCH

Fernandez de Enciso, M *see* SUMA DE GEOGRAPHIA QUE TRATA DE TODOS LOS PARTIDOS E PROVINCIAS DEL MUNDO...
Fernandez de los Rios, Angel *see* MUNOZ TORRERO
Fernandez de Molina Menitez Donoso, Antonio *see* CORDOBESAS
Fernandez de Moratin, Leandro *see*
- EL BARON
- LA COMEDIA NUEVA
- LA DERROTA DE LOS PEDANTES
- LA ESCUELA DE LOS MARIDOS
- EL MEDICO A PALOS
- LA MOGIGATA
- EL SI DE LAS NINAS
- LA SOMBRA DE NELSON
- EL VIEJO Y LA NINA

Fernandez de Moratin, Nicolas *see*
- DESENGANO AL TEATRO ESPANOL
- LA DIANA O ARTE DE LA CAZA
- EGLOGA A VELASCO Y GONZALEZ
- LA HORMESINDA. TRAGEDIA
- LUCRECIA
- LAS NAVES DE CORTES DESTRUIDAS
- LA PETIMETRA
- EL POETA

Fernandez de Oviedo Valdes, Gonzalo *see*
- DE LA NATURAL HISTORIA DE LAS INDIAS
- DE LA NATURAL HISTORIA DE LAS INDIAS. SUMARIO DE HISTORIA NATURAL DE LAS INDIAS. CON UN ESTUDIO PRELIMINAR Y NOTAS POR ENRIQUE ALVAREZ LOPEZ
- GENERAL Y NATURAL HISTORIA DE LAS INDIAS
- HISTORIA...INDIAS...MAR OCEANO
- SUMARIO DE LA NATURAL Y GENERAL HISTORIA DE LAS INDIAS

Fernandez de Quesada, Juan Antonio *see* MEMORIAL AJUSTADO...CONVENTO DEL AMPARO DE ALMENDRALEJO...DONA MARIANA GOLFIN...DUQUE DE VILLAHERMOSA Y D. GARCIA GOLFIN...VINCULO DE DONA JUANA...
Fernandez de Ribera, Rodrigo *see* LAGRIMAS DE SAN PEDRO
Fernandez de S Corde, J *see* BULLARIUM ORDINIS RECOLLECTORUM SANCTI AUGUSTINI
Fernandez de Soria, Rafael *see* DISCURSO... CIENCIAS MORALES
Fernandez de Soria y Villanueva, Fernando *see* ARRENDAMIENTOS RUSTICOS PROTEGIDOS (COMENTARIOS A LA LEY DE 15 DE JULIO DE 1954)
Fernandez del Castillo, Francisco *see* DON PEDRO DE ALVARADO. OBRA POSTUMA REVISADA POR ANTONIO FERNANDEZ DEL CASTILLO
Fernandez del Valle, J *see*
- TRATADO COMPLETO DE LA FLEBOTOMIA U OPERACIONES DE LA SANGRIA
- TRATADO TEORICO Y PRACTICO DE LAS HERNIAS EN GENERAL Y DE LAS ESTRANGULADAS

Fernandez Duro, Cesareo *see*
- D. FRANCISCO FERNANDEZ DE LA CUEVA
- JUAN DE LA TORRE (DE J.A. LAVALLE. INFORME)
- UN SOLDADO DE LA CONQUISTA DE CHILE

Fernandez, E *see* ADONDE VA EL PERONISMO
Fernandez, F *see*
- DE FACULTATIBUS NATURALIBUS DISPUTATIONES MEDICAE ET PHYLOSOPHICAE
- DISERTACION FISICO-LEGAL DE LOS SITIOS...PARA SEPULTURAS
- INSTRUCCIONES PARA...LA CONSERVACION Y AUMENTO DE LAS POBLACIONES
- EL JUICIO DE PARIS VERDADERO DESENGANO DEL AGUA

Fernandez Fernandez, Juan *see*
- AMOR ALOS ENEMIGOS EN EL ANTIGUO TESTAMENTO
- LA CARIDAD CRISTIANA

Fernandez, Francisco *see* PRONTUARIO DE ORTOGRAFIA
Fernandez Garcia, Manuel *see* ENTRETENIMIENTOS POETICOS
Fernandez Golfin, Luis *see* BREVES...ISLA DE CUBA
Fernandez Gonzalez, Francisco *see* PLAN DE UNA BIBLIOTECA DE AUTORES ARABES ESPANOLES
Fernandez Guardia, Ricardo *see* COSAS Y GENTES DE ANTANO...
Fernandez Guerra, Aureliano *see* LAPIDAS ROMANAS DE BURGUILLOS
Fernandez Jilberto, Alex E *see* COLLECCION DE DOCUMENTOS PARA LA HISTORIA DE LA OPOSICION POLITICA AL ESTADO AUTORITARIO EN CHILE (1973-1981)
Fernandez, Juan *see* UN MANUSCRITO DE PEDRO DE VALENCIA QUE LLEVA POR TITULO EN SU PORTADA
Fernandez, Juan Antonio *see* MADRID. ARCHIVO HISTORICO NACIONAL. SECCION DE ORDENES MILITARES. INVENTARIO DEL ARCHIVO DE UCLES, TOMO 1-3
Fernandez, Luis *see* TRATADO SOBRE EL ARTE DE LA TINTURA
Fernandez Molina, Antonio *see* BIOGRAFIA DE ROBERTO G.
Fernandez Morejon, Antonio *see* HISTORIA BIBLIOGRAFICA DE LA MEDICINA ESPANOLA
Fernandez Moreno, Ramon *see* RESTAURACION DE LA PATRONA DE LOS SANTOS DE MAIMONA. NUESTRA SENORA DE LA ESTRELLA
Fernandez Navarette, D *see*
- AN ACCOUNT OF THE EMPIRE OF CHINA
- TRATADOS, HISTORICOS POLITICOS, ETHICOS, Y RELIGIOSOS DE LA MONARCHIA DE CHINA

Fernandez Navarro, Lucas *see* EL METEORITO DE OLIVENZA (BADAJOZ)
Fernandez, Pardo *see* SOCIALISMO NACIONAL
Fernandez Pascual, Alfonso *see* MADRE, YA TENEMOS BANDERA
Fernandez Pesquero, J *see* AMERICA, SU GEOGRAFIA, SU HISTORIA
Fernandez, Placido Jose *see*
- EL SEMINARISTA
- TEATRO NACIONAL...

Fernandez Prida, J *see* ESTUDIOS DE DERECHO INTERNACIONAL PUBLICO Y PRIVADO
Fernandez, Salvador Diego *see* LOS PACTOS DE BUCASELI Y EL TRATADO DE LA MESILLA...
Fernandez Sanchez, Ma Carmen *see* HUMOR E IRONIA EN LA OBRA DE THEOPHILE GAUTIER
Fernandez Sanchez, Teodoro *see*
- GRAN MATEMATICO Y FECUNDO POETA. ARSENIO GALLEGO HERNANDEZ
- HISTORIA DE LA IMAGEN DE NUESTRA SENORA DE LA FUENTE SANTA EXCELSA PATRONA DE ZORITA
- JUAN MACIAS, INCLITA GLORIA DE EXTREMADURA Y DE LA IGLESIA

Fernandez Santana, Ezequiel *see*
- APUNTES DE PEDAGOGIA DEPORTIVA
- CATECISMO SOCIAL
- CONFERENCIA
- LA CUESTION SOCIAL EN EXTREMADURA A LA LUZ DE LAS ENCICLICAS RERUM NOVARUM Y QUADREGESIMO ANNO
- HOMENAJE DE GRATITUD A DR. EZEQUIEL FERNANDEZ SANTANA
- ORGANIZACION Y PROCEDIMIENTO PEDAGOGICOS DE LAS ESOUELAS PARROQUIALES DE LOS SANTOS

Fernandez Serrano, Francisco *see* DE RE BIBLIOGRAPHICA
Fernandez, T *see* DEFENSA DE LA CHINA Y VERDADERA RESPUESTA A LAS FALSAS RAZONES OVE PARA SU REPROBACION TRAE EL DOCTOR DON JOSE COLMENERO
Fernandez Valbuena, Ramiro *see*
- CATOLICO O KRAUSISTA?
- DE SANTO TOMAS A KRAUSE?
- DISCURSOS LEIDOS...SAN BENITO DE VILLANUEVA
- EL TESTIMONIO DE LAS PIEDRAS-DISCURSO

Fernandez y Fernandez, J *see* LA CARIDAD MISIONAL Y LA EPISTOLA DE SAN PABLO A LOS FILIPENSES. BADAJOZ
Fernandez y Fernandez, Juan *see* EL MISTERIO DEL CRISTO MISTICO (LECCIONES DIVULGADORAS DE LA EPISTOLA DE SAN PABLO A LOS EFESIOS) BADAJOZ, 1944
Fernandez y Perez, Gregorio *see* HISTORIAS...MERIDA
Fernandez-Davila, Guillermo *see*
- EL ASESINATO DE DON FRANCISCO PIZARRO
- EL ASESINATO DEL CONQUISTADOR DEL PERU

Fernandez-Ouesta, Raimundo *see* DISCURSOS
Fernando 1 *see* COMMUNE SIGILLI SECRET (ANNO 1412-1416)
Fernando 2 *see*
- CURIAE SIGILLI SECRETI (ANNO 1479-1516)
- DIVERSORUM (ANNO 1479-1516)

FERNANDO DE GABRIEL / Blanco Garcia, Francisco – Madrid: Saenz de Jubera, 1909 – sp Bibl Santa Ana [440]
EL FERNANDO DO SEVILLA RESTAURADA / Vera y Figueroa, Juan Antonio – 1632 – 9 – 1.50f – sp Bibl Santa Ana [946]
Fernando, Henry *see* SINHALESE DIARY, 1893
Fernando, Hugo *see* POCHITO VERSUS ALBERTO BATILANA (EX VICE) CAIGA QUIEN CAIGA
Fernando, J S A *see*
- CENTENARY SOUVENIR, 1851-1951
- JUBILEE MEMORIALS, 1860-1910

Fernando, R *see* TRADITIONAL AND NON-TRADITIONAL FOODS
FERNDALE CEMETERY REGISTER – Ferndale, CA. 1876-1982 – 1r – 1 – $50.00 – B40223 – us Library Micro [920]
THE FERNDALE ENTERPRISE – Ferndale, CA. 1878- – 78+ r – 1 – $3,900.00 ($50.00y) – B02234 – us Library Micro [071]
DER FERNE SOHN : ERZAEHLUNG / Vring, Georg von der – Muenchen: R Piper, 1942 – 1r – 1 – us U.W. Library [830]
FERNE STIMMEN : ERZAEHLUNGEN / Raabe, Wilhelm Karl – Berlin: Otto Janke, 1865 – 1 – us U.W. Library [830]
DER FERNEMPFANG *see* FUNKSCHAU
Fernig, L *see* PLACE OF INFORMATION IN EDUCATIONAL DEVELOPMENT
FERNLEY LEADER-DAYTON COURIER – Yerington, NV. 1985 – 10+ r – 1 – $500.00 ($120.00y) – U04905 – us Library Micro [071]
Fernos-Isern, A *see* TEXT OF THE CONSTITUTION OF THE COMMONWEALTH OF PUERTO RICO
Fernow, Bertold *see* THE OHIO VALLEY IN COLONIAL DAYS
THE FERNS AND FERN ALLIES OF NEW ZEALAND / Thomson, G M – 5170. 1882 – 9 – ne IDC [580]
FERNS, BRITISH AND EXOTIC / Lowe, E J – London, 1864. 8 vols. B-7214 1 – 9 – ne IDC [580]
FERNS: BRITISH AND FOREIGN. HISTORY, ORGANOGRAPHY, CLASSIFICATION AND ENUMERATION / Smith, J – 7263. 1866 – 9 – ne IDC [580]
Ferns, H S *see* THE DISEASE OF GOVERNMENT
Ferns, Henry Stanley *see* LA ARGENTINA
THE FERNS OF GREAT BRITAIN / Johnson, C – London. 1855. B-7203 1 – 9 – ne IDC [580]
THE FERNS OF GREAT BRITAIN AND IRELAND / Moore, T – Lindley, J. ed. London, 1855. 51 pls. with descriptive text. B-7235 prSF 31,00 IDC 9 – ne IDC [580]
FERNS OF KENTUCKY / Williamson, J – 7324. 1878 – 9 – ne IDC [580]
THE FERNS OF NEW ZEALAND AND ITS IMMEDIATE DEPENDENCIES / Field, H C – London, etc. 1890. B-7185 2 – 8 – ne IDC [580]
THE FERNS OF NORTH AMERICA / Eaton, D C – London, Boston. 1877, 1879-80. B-5916 2 – 8 – ne IDC [580]
THE FERNS OF SOUTH AFRICA / Sim, T R – 5163. 1892 – 9 – ne IDC [580]
THE FERNS OF SOUTHERN INDIA / Beddome, R H – Being descriptions and plates of the ferns of the Madras Presidency. Madras. 1863. B-7158 2 – 8 – ne IDC [580]
THE FERNS OF SURINAM AND OF FRENCH AND BRITISH GUIANA / Posthumus, O – Malang. 1928. B-7246 2 – 8 – ne IDC [580]
THE FERNS OF WALES / Young, E – 7285. 1856 – 9 – ne IDC [580]
THE FERNS OF YORK / Ibbotson, H – York. 1884. B-7201 2 – 8 – ne IDC [580]
FERNSEH-INFORMATIONEN – Muenchen, 1950-96 – 20r – 1 – gw Mikrofilm [790]
Fernsworth, Lawrence A *see*
- BACK OF THE SPANISH REBELLION

FERNWOOD BAPTIST CHURCH. SPARTANBURG, SOUTH CAROLINA : CHURCH RECORDS – (7,825p) – 1959-1988 – 6r – 1 – $352.13 – us Baptist [240]
FERNY COMBES. A RAMBLE AFTER FERNS IN THE GLENS AND VALLEYS OF DEVONSHIRE / Chanter, C – London, 1857. 3rd ed. B-7171/1 – 9 – ne IDC [580]
Ferotin, M *see*
- LE LIBER MOZARABICUS SACRAMENTORUM ET LES MANUSCRITS MOZARABES
- LE LIBER ORDINUM DANS L'EGLISE WISIGOTH. ET MOZAR. D'ESPAGNE, DU 5E-19THS
- LA VERITABLE AUTEUR DE LA PEREGRINATIO SOLVIAE, LA VIERGE ESPAGNOLE ETHERIA

Feroux, Christophe-Leon *see* NOUVELLE INSTITUTION NATIONALE PAR L'AUTEUR DES VUES D'UN SOLITAIRE PATRIOTE

Ferrand, G *see* LES POIDS MESURES ET MONNAIES DES MERS DU SUD AUX XVI ET XVIIE SIECLES
Ferrand, Gabriel *see* LES COMALIS
Ferrandi, Ugo *see* LUGH
Ferrandis Torres, Manuel *see* EL MITO DEL ORO EN LA CONQUISTA DE AMERICA. VALLADOLID, 1933
Ferrante, S *see* IL DIRITTO DELLA NATURA...
THE FERRAR PAPERS, 1590-1790 / Ransome, David – 1992 – 14r – 1 – £30.00 – 1-85117-016-2 – uk Microform Academic [941]
Ferrari, Anne *see* FEAR OF FALLING AMONG COMMUNITY ELDERS
Ferrari, Antoine *see* ATIEKWA. UN VILLAGE DE COTE D'IVOIRE
Ferrari, G G *see* TROIS GRANDES SONATES POUR HARPE AVEC VIOLON ET VIOLONCELLE, OP. 18
Ferrari, Gustavo *see* POLITICA EXTERIOR ARGENTINA, 1930-1962
Ferrari, Joseph R *see* JOURNAL OF PREVENTION AND INTERVENTION IN THE COMMUNITY
Ferrari, O *see* ORIGINES LINGVAE ITALICAE
Ferraris, Agustin *see*
- EL DEMAGOGO
- ESTADOS UNIDOS CAMBIA LA CARA
- PIDO LA PALABRA

Ferrars, B *see* BURMA
Ferrars, M *see* BURMA
LA FERRASSIE [SUIVIE DE] LES CUIRASSES HALLSTATIENNES DE ELLINGES... / Peyrony, Denis – Paris. Leroux, 1934 – I – F83.49 – fr Armell [306]
Ferraz Alvim, O *see* SUCCESSAO DO ESTRANGEIRO NO BRASIL
Ferreira da Silva, Francisco, BP *see* APONTAMENTOS PARA A HISTORIA DA ADMINISTRACAO DA DIOCESE E DA ORGANISCAO DO SEMINARIO LYCEU..
Ferreiros Espinosa, A *see* LES KON CAU DE LA DA'NYING
Ferrell, M D *see* AN ANALYSIS OF THE BERNOULLI LIFT EFFECT AS A PROPULSIVE COMPONENT OF SWIMMING STROKES
Ferrer, Aldo *see*
- LA ECONOMIA ARGENTINA
- LA POSGUERRA

Ferrer de Esparza, T *see* TRATADO...DE LA FACULTAD MEDICAMENTOSA QUE SE HALLA EN EL AGUA DE LOS BANOS...
Ferrer, Gustavo *see* LOS PARTIDOS POLITICOS
Ferrer, Morales A *see* BIBLIOGRAFIA PUERTORRIQUENA, ESCRITA EN 1892-1894
Ferrere, F *see* LA SITUATION RELIGIEUSE DE L'AFRIQUE ROMAINE DEPUIS LA FIN DU IVE SIECLE JUSQU'A L'INVASION DES VANDALES (429)
Ferrero, Roberto A *see* DEL FRAUDE A LA SOBERANIA POPULAR
Ferresheim, Fritz *see* SCHILLER ALS HERAUSGEBER DER RHEINISCHEN THALIA, THALIA, UND NEUEN THALIA, UND SEIN MITARBEITER
Ferret, Pierre Victoire *see* VOYAGE EN ABYSSINIE DANS LES PROVINCES DU TIGRE
FerretGalinier *see* VOYAGE EN ABYSSINIE, DANS LES PROVINCES DU TIGRE, DU SAMEN ET DE L'AMHARA
Ferretti, Augustus *see* INSTITUTIONES PHILOSOPHIAE MORALIS
Ferri *see* SCULTORI PEREGRINI A EMERITA
Ferri, C E *see* LE TEORICA DEI MANDATI INTERNAZIONALI
Ferri, Silvia *see* LA TESTA DI MERIDA CENNI SULLA CRITICA ICONOGRAFICA
Ferrier, Simon *see* STATUS OF THE RUFOUS SCRUB-BIRD
Ferriere, Philippe La *see* LE COMMIS DE BANQUE
O FERRINHO : ORGAO CRITICO E NOTICIOSO – Jaragua, Alagoas. 17 Out 1901; 13 Fev 1902 – 1,5,6 – bl Biblioteca [072]
Ferris, George Hooper *see* FORMATION OF THE NEW TESTAMENT
Ferris, Isaac *see* JUBILEE MEMORIAL OF THE AMERICAN BIBLE SOCIETY
Ferro, G *see* TEATRO D'IMPRESE
FERROELECTRICS / ed by Taylor, G W – 1970- – 1,5,9 – us Gordon [530]
FERROELECTRICS LETTERS SECTION / ed by Taylor, George W – 9,5,1 – us Gordon [530]
Ferroli, Domenico *see* THE JESUITS IN MALABAR
Ferron, Jacques *see* LE BICORNE
Ferrua, Pietro *see*
- ANARCHISTS IN FILMS
- ANARCHISTS SEEN BY PAINTERS
- PAPERS
- SURREALISME ET ANARCHISME

Ferrus, Guillaume Marie Andre *see* DES PRISONNIERS, DE L'EMPRISONNEMENT ET DES PRISONS
Ferry, M P *see* LES DITS DE LA NUIT. CONTES TENDA, SENEGAL ORIENTAL
DER FERTIG ORGELSPIELER, ODER CASUALMAGAZIN FUER ALLE VORKOMMENDE FAELLE IM ORGELSPIELE / Guentersberg, Christian Carl – P 305 – 9 – ne IDC [780]
FERTILIZER AND PLANT NUTRITION GUIDE – 1984 – 190p – it F.A.O. [631]
FERTILIZER DISTRIBUTION AND CREDIT SCHEMES FOR SMALL-SCALE FARMERS – 1979 – 47p – it F.A.O. [631]
FERTILIZER MARKETING / Wierer, K & Abbott, J C – 1978 – 156p – it F.A.O. [380]
FERTILIZER PROCUREMENT – 1981 – 65p – it F.A.O. [631]
FERTILIZER STRATEGIES – 1987 – 148p – it F.A.O. [631]
FERTILIZER TECHNOLOGY – v1-. 1985- – 1,5,6,9 – us UMI [073]
FERTILIZER USE UNDER MULTIPLE CROPPING SYSTEMS : REPORT OF AN EXPERT CONSULTATION. NEW DELHI, 1982 – 1983 – 215p – it F.A.O. [631]
FERTILIZERS AND THEIR USE : A POCKET GUIDE FOR EXTENSION OFFICERS – 3rd printing 1976 – 54p – it F.A.O. [631]
Ferus, Ioan. *see*
- IN SACROSANCTUM IESU CHRISTI..EVANGELIUM SECUNDUM IOANNEM ENARRATIONES
- IN SACROSANCTUM IESU CHRISTI..EVANGELIUM SECUNDUM MATHEUM..ENARRATIONES

FERYAD – Nigde. Cumhuriyetci ve Birlikci siyasi haftalik halk gazete. Sahibi: Cemil Sakir. Mueduerue: Riza Ratib. No. 8 (4 Eyluel 1340 [1924]) – 9 – $20.00 – us MEDOC [956]
Fesch, W de *see* 10 SONATAS FOR 2 GERMAN FLUTES OR 2 VIOLINS WITH A THOROUGH BASS...
FESPACO '97 : FESTIVAL PANAFRICAIN DU CINEMA ET DE LA TELEVISION DE OUAGADOUGOU – Bethlehem, PA, 1997 – us Res Libr [770]
Fessenden, Clementine *see* OUR UNION JACK
Fessenden, Elisha Joseph *see* A CENTENARY STUDY, UPPER CANADA: A PAPER READ BEFORE THE LUNDY'S LANE HISTORICAL SOCIETY
Fessenden, Thomas Green *see* AN ESSAY ON THE LAW OF PATENTS FOR NEW INVENTIONS
Fessenden, William P *see* PAPERS
Fessler, I A *see*
- REVISION DES MAURERISCHEN TASCHENBUCHES AUF DAS JAHR 5802 BIS 5803...
- RUECKBLICKE AUF DIE LETZTEN SECHS JAHRE SEINER LOGENTHAETIGKEIT
- SAEMMTLICHE SCHRIFTEN UEBER FREYMAUREREY

Fessler, Joseph *see*
- DAS LETZTE UND DAS NAECHSTE ALLGEMEINE CONCIL
- SAMMLUNG VERMISCHTER SCHRIFTEN UEBER KIRCHENGESCHICHTE UND KIRCHENRECHT
- THE TRUE AND THE FALSE INFALLIBILITY OF THE POPES

FESTAS E TRADICOES POPULARES DO BRASIL / Morais Filho, Melo – 3a. ed. Rio de Janeiro. 1946 – 1 – us Res Libr [390]
FESTBREVIER UND KIRCHENJAHR DER SYRISCHEN JAKOBITEN / Baumstark, Anton – Paderborn, 1910 – 6mf – 8 – Dfl25.00 – ne Slangenburg [280]
FESTCHRIFT FUER FRIEDRICH HIRTH ZU SEINEM 75 GEBURTSTAG 16 APRIL 1920 / Hirth, Friedrich – Berlin. 1920. Illus. Index. BU-292 2 – 8 – ne IDC [920]
Festeau, Paul *see* A NEW AND EASIE FRENCH GRAMMAR
FESTEJOS EN HONOR DE LA SANTISIMA VIRGEN DE CARRION 1975 – Valencia de Alcantara: Tip. Avila, 1975 – 1 – sp Bibl Santa Ana [240]
FESTEJOS EN HONOR DE LA SANTISIMA VIRGEN DE CARRION, 1977 / Alburquerque. Ayuntamiento – Valencia de Alcantara: Imp. Avila, 1977 – sp Bibl Santa Ana [390]
FESTEJOS EN HONOR DE LA SANTISIMA VIRGEN DE CARRION. ALBURQUERQUE, 1980 – Valencia de Alcantara: Tip. Avila, 1980 – 1 – sp Bibl Santa Ana [240]
FESTEJOS EN HONOR DE NUESTRA MADRE LA SANTISIMA VIRGEN DE CARRION. ALBURQUERQUE, 1979 – Valencia de Alcantara: Tip. Avila, 1979 – 1 – sp Bibl Santa Ana [240]
FESTEJOS EN HONOR DEL PRINCIPE DE LA PAZ HABIDOS EN BADAJOZ EN 1807 / Guerra Guerra, Arcadio – Badajoz: Dip. Provincial, 1967 – sp Bibl Santa Ana [946]
FESTEJOS TAURINOS TRADICIONALES EN GUADALUPE (CACERES). 1971 – S.l., s.i., s.a. – 1 – sp Bibl Santa Ana [390]
FESTEJOS Y ROMERIA EN HONOR DEL SANTO PATRON DE LAS HERMANDADES. "SAN ISIDRO LABRADOR" / Villar del Rey – Badajoz: Imp. Inca, 1970 – sp Bibl Santa Ana [390]
FESTGABE FUER EDUARD BEREND, ZUM 75. GEBURTSTAG, AM 5. DEZEMBER 1958 / ed by Seiffert, Hans Werner & Zeller, Bernhard – (Includes bibliographical references) – Weimar: H Boehlaus Nachfolger, 1959 – 1 – us U.W. Library [430]
FESTGABE HERRN DR. RUDOLPH VON JHERING ZUM DOKTORJUBILAUM AM 6, AUGUST 1892 / Tubingen. Universitat. Juristische Facultat – Tubingen, Laupp, 1892 185 p. LL-4117 – 1 – us L of C Photodup [340]
FESTGABE PHILIPP STRAUCH ZUM 80. GEBURTSTAGE AM 23. SEPTEMBER 1932 DARGEBRACHT VON FACHKOLLEGEN UND SCHUELERN / ed by Baesecke, Georg & Schneider, Ferdinand Joseph – (Includes bibliographical references) – Halle (Saale): M. Niemeyer, 1932 – 1r – 1 – us U.W. Library [430]
FESTGABE VON FACHGENOSSEN UND FREUNDEN A. VON HARNACK ZUM SIEBZIGSTEN GEBURTSDAG DARGEBRACHT – Tuebingen, 1921 – 8mf – 8 – ne Slangenburg [290]
FESTGABE ZUM NEUNZIGSTEN GEBURTSTAG LEOPOLDS VON RANKE : MARBURG AM 21. DECEMBER 1885 / Ranke, Ernst Constantin – (Caption title: Zur Beurtheilung Wielands: ein kritischer Versuch) – Marburg: Universitaets-Buchdruckerei, 1885 – 1r – 1 – us U.W. Library [943]
FESTGRUSS BERNHARD STADE : ZUR FEIER SEINER 25. JAEHRIGEN WIRKSAMKEIT / Diehl, W et al – Giessen: J. Ricker, 1900 – 1mf – 9 – us A.T.L.A. [240]
LE FESTIN D'ESOPE – Revue des belles-lettres. Red. en chef Guillaume Apollinaire. no. 1-9. Paris. nov 1903-aout 1904 – 1 – fr A.C.R.P.P. [800]
LE FESTIVAL ARTISTIQUE ET CULTUREL ET LE PANAFRICANISME – Conakry: Impr National "Patrice Lumumba", 1975 – us Res Libr [700]
Festival de Folklore Hispanoamericano 1, 1958 *see* ESPANA 1958. 1ST FESTIVAL HISPANOAMERICANO. CACERES
Festivales de Espana N. Plasencia, 1972 *see* 4 FESTIVALES DE ESPANA. PLASENCIA 23-29 JUNIO 1972
THE FESTIVAL-HALLOF CSORKON 2 IN THE GREAT TEMPLE OF BUBASTIS (MEES VOL 10) / Naville, E – London, 1892 – 6mf – 8 – Dfl25.00 – ne Slangenburg [720]
FESTIVIDAD DE SAN FERNANDO 30 DE MAYO 1959, VALENCIA DE ALCANTARA / Valencia de Alcantara. Estacion de Renfe – Avila, 1959 – 1 – sp Bibl Santa Ana [390]
Festoni, A *see* SONATE, TWO VIOLINS AND BASS
FESTSCHRIFT / Berliner, Abraham – 3v. Frankfurt a.M. 1903. BJ-100-16 1 – 9 – ne IDC [920]
FESTSCHRIFT / Carlebach, S – Berlin. 1910. BJ-100-17 1 – 9 – ne IDC [920]
FESTSCHRIFT / Freimann, J – Berlin. 1935. (Soncino Blaetter v. 5). Berlin. 1931. BJ-100-19 1 – 9 – ne IDC [900]
FESTSCHRIFT / Guttmann, J – Leipzig. 1915. BJ-100-30 1 – 9 – ne IDC [100]
FESTSCHRIFT / Heller, B – Budapest. 1941. BJ-100-22 1 – 9 – ne IDC [900]
FESTSCHRIFT / Kroner, T – Breslau. 1917. BJ-100-25 1 – 9 – ne IDC [920]
FESTSCHRIFT / Maybaum, S – Berlin. 1914. BJ-100-31 1 – 9 – ne IDC [920]
FESTSCHRIFT / Philippson, M – Leipzig. 1916. BJ-100-28 1 – 9 – ne IDC [920]
FESTSCHRIFT / Schwartz, A – Berlin. Vienna. 1917. BJ-100-29 1 – 9 – ne IDC [920]
FESTSCHRIFT / Simonsens, D – Kobenhavn. 1923. BJ-100-20 1 – 9 – ne IDC [920]
FESTSCHRIFT ANLAESSLICH DER EMERITIERUNG VON PROF. DR.-ING. WALTER RAAB / ed by Fabrig, Peter – 1994 – 2mf – DM80.00 – 3-8267-2023-7 – gw Hänsel [620]
FESTSCHRIFT DER 56. VERSAMMLUNG DEUTSCHER NATURFORSCHER UND AERTZE GEWIDMET VON DER NATURFORSCHENDEN GESELLSCHAFT ZU FREIBURG I.B. – Freiburg i.B, 1883 – 2mf – ne IDC [610]
FESTSCHRIFT. EMET LE-YA'AKOV / Freimann, J – Berlin. 1937. BJ-100-36 1 – 9 – ne IDC [920]
FESTSCHRIFT FOR RALPH FARRELL / ed by Stephens, Anthony et al – (Contributions in English or German. Includes bibliographical references) – Bern: P. Lang, 1977 – 1r – 1 – us U.W. Library [430]
FESTSCHRIFT FRIEDRICH GIESE AUS ANLASS DES SIEBZIGSTEN GEBURTSTAGS UEBERREICHT VON FREUNDEN UND SCHUELERN / Giese, F – Ed. by G. Jaeschke. (Welt des Islams, Sonderband). Berlin, Leipzig. 1941. BU-291 2 – 8 – ne IDC [956]
FESTSCHRIFT FUER BERTHOLD LITZMANN ZUM 60. GEBURTSTAG 18.4.1917 : IM AUFTRAGE DER LITERARHISTORISCHEN GESELLSCHAFT BONN / ed by Enders, Carl – (Includes bibliographical references and index) – Bonn: F Cohen, 1920 – 1 – us U.W. Library [430]
FESTSCHRIFT FUER EDUARD CASTLE ZUM ACHTZIGSTEN GEBURTSTAG : GEWIDMET VON SEINEN FREUNDEN UND SCHUELERN / ed by Gesellschaft fuer Wiener Theaterforschung; Wiener Goethe-Verein – (Includes bibliographical references) – Wien: Notring der Wissenschaftlichen Verbaende OEsterreichs, 1955 – 1 – us U.W. Library [790]
FESTSCHRIFT FUER FRIEDRICH KEINECKER ZUM 60. GEBURTSTAG : GEWIDMET VON SEINEN KOLLEGEN, SCHUELERN UND MITARBEITERN / ed by Michels, Gerd – (Includes bibliographical references) – Heidelberg: J Groos, c1980 – 1r – 1 – us U.W. Library [430]
FESTSCHRIFT FUER WOLFGANG STAMMLER ZU SEINEM 65. GEBURTSTAG – (Includes bibliographical references) – Berlin: E Schmidt, c1953 – 1r – 1 – us U.W. Library [943]
FESTSCHRIFT MEINHOF – Hamburg: Kommissionsverlag von L Friederichsen, 1927 – 1 – us Res Libr [920]
FESTSCHRIFT MEINHOF. SPRACHWISSENSCHAFTLICHE UND ANDERE STUDIEN – (Gluckstadt und J.J. Augustin, 1927). xii,514p.Illus. (inc. music, map). With: Midrash Hasirot ve-Yiterot. 1 reel. 1251 – 1 – us U.W. Library [400]
FESTSCHRIFT, OR A COLLECTION OF BOTANICAL PAPERS PRESENTED TO PROF. KINGO MIYABE ON THE OCCASION OF THE TWENTY-FIFTH ANNIVERSARY OF HIS ACADEMIC SERVICE BY HIS FRIENDS AND PUPILS / Miyabe, K – Tokyo, 1911. Text in English and Japanese. B-7446 1 – 9 – ne IDC [580]
FESTSCHRIFT ZUM 50 JAEHRIGEN BESTEHEN DER FRANZ-JOSEF LANDESRABBINERSCHULE IN BUDAPEST / Franz Josef Landesrabbinerschule. Budapest – Ed. by L. Blau. Budapest. 1927. BJ-100-34 1 – 9 – ne IDC [270]
FESTSCHRIFT ZUR FEIER DES HUNDERTJAEHRIGEN BESTEHENS DER WETTERAUISCHEN GESELLSCHAFT FUER DIE GESAMMTE NATURKUNDE – Hanau, 1908 – 2mf – 9 – ne IDC [500]
DIE FESTSTELLUNG DER RUMAENISCHEN STAATSANGEHOERIGKEIT / Dutczak, B – Cernauti, 1924 – 1mf – 1 – ILM-3334/1 – ne IDC [327]
Festugiere, A *see* L'IDEAL RELIGIEUX DES GRECS ET L'EVANGILE
Festugiere, A J *see*
- ANTIOCHE PAIENNE ET CHRETIENNE
- L'IDEAL RELIGIEUX DES GRECS ET L'EVANGILE

DER FESTUNGS-BOTE – Rastatt, Germany. 1849 – 1 – gw Mikrofilm [072]
DER FESTUNGSBOTE – Nachrichtenblatt fuer den Festungsbereich. La Rochelle. sept 1944-mai 1945 – 1 – fr A.C.R.P.P. [073]
FESTUS : A POEM / Bailey, Philip James – London: William Pickering, 1839 – 1 roll – 1 – 1-55879-366-6 – uk Libr Preservation [810]

FEST-ZEITUNG / Saengerbund des Nordwestens Saengerfest. 18th. Davenport, Iowa, 1898 – Davenport, Iowa. Aug 1898. nr. (13) – 1 – us NY Public [780]

FEST-ZEITUNG / Saengerbund des Nordwestens Saengerfest. 24th. Omaha. 1910 – 10 Feb-5 Jul 1910. (Nr. 1-6) – 1 – us NY Public [780]

FETAL DIAGNOSIS AND THERAPY – v1-. 1986- – 1,5,9 – us UMI [618]

UNE FETE A L'IMPRIMERIE DU CANADIEN / Duquet, Joseph Norbet – Quebec?: s.n., 1878?. 02806. (Pre-1900 Canadiana) – 9 – cn C.I.H.M. [971]

FETE CHAMPETRE CELEBREE A MONTMORENCY EN L'HONNEUR DE J.-J. ROUSSEAU / Thiery, Avocat – Paris, Denne; Montmorency, Cheron et Neyris. 1791 – 9 – fr Hachette [190]

LA FETE DE LA RAISON / Marechal, Sylvain et Gretry – (French Theatre Series). Paris. Impr. C. F. Patris, an II. 1793 – 9 – fr Hachette [820]

FETE DE L'INVESTITURE DU PALLIUM A SA GRACE MGR JOSEPH THOMAS DUHAMEL, ARCHEVEQUE D'OTTAWA, JEUDI 29 JUILLET 1886 – Notices biographiques et potraits de Mgr l'archeveque Duhamel et de Son Eminence le cardinal Taschereau: programme des fetes du 28 et 29 juillet. Ottawa: s.n., 1886? (Ottawa: Typ. du Canada). 03094 (Pre-1900 Canadiana) – 9 – cn C.I.H.M. [971]

FETE DE ST GREGOIRE 7 – Souvenir du Franc-Parleur a l'Union-Allet. Montreal: Franc-Parleur, 1873. 04270. (Pre-1900 Canadiana) – 9 – cn C.I.H.M. [971]

FETE DU TRAVAIL – Quebec, Canada. 1929; 1930 – programmes souvenir – 1r – 1 – Can$25.00 – cn Can Microfilming [072]

FETE DU TRAVAIL – Quebec, Canada. 4 sep 1911 – 1r – 1 – Can$25.00 – cn Can Microfilming [072]

FETE MACONNIQUE... AU GENERAL LAFAYETTE – Paris, 1830 – 1mf – ne IDC [944]

FETE NATIONALE DES CANADIENS-FRANCAIS CELEBREE A WINDSOR, ONTARIO LE 25 JUIN 1883 / Dionne, Narcisse Eutrope – Quebec: Imp. Leger Brousseau, 1883. SEM105P33 – 2mf – 9 – Can$4.50 – cn Bibl Nat [971]

FETES A L'OCCASION DU MARIAGE DE S.M. NAPOLEON AVEC MARIE-LOUISE / Goulet, M – O-1107 1. 1810 – 9 – ne IDC [944]

LES FETES ANNUELLEMENT CELEBREES A EMOUI (AMOY). ETUDE CONCERNANT LA RELIGION POPULAIRE DES CHINOIS / Groot, J J M de – (Ann. Mus. Guimet. Transl. by C. G. Chavannes, v. 11, 12). 2 v. Paris, Ernest Leroux. 1886. BCH-891 2 – 8 – ne IDC [290]

FETES CHRETIENNES: HISTORIQUE, CONSIDERATIONS ET TRAITS EDIFIANTS: LRE SERIE / Constans, S – s.l.: s.n., 1893 (Montreal: Impr. de l'Institution des sourds-muets). 00101. (Pre-1900 Canadiana) – 9 – cn C.I.H.M. [971]

LES FETES COLOMBIENNES A QUEBEC – compte-rendu et discours. s.l.: s.n., 1893 (Quebec: L. Brousseau). 03095. (Pre-1900 Canadiana) – 9 – cn C.I.H.M. [971]

LES FETES DE CHAMPLAIN A QUEBEC, SEPTEMBRE 1898 – s.l.: s.n., 1898 (Quebec?: Courrier du livre). 03096. (Pre-1900 Canadiana) – 9 – cn C.I.H.M. [971]

FETES DE SAMUEL CHAMPLAIN – ler et 2 juillet. s.l.: s.n., 1893?. 04271. (Pre-1900 Canadiana) – 9 – cn C.I.H.M. [971]

LES FETES DU TROISIEME CENTENAIRE DE L'HOTEL-DIEU DE QUEBEC, 1639-1939 : BIBLIOGRAPHIE ANALYTIQUE / Saint-Clement, Soeur – 1964. SEM105P4 – 7mf – 9 – cn Bibl Nat [360]

FETES JUBILAIRES CELEBREES A OTTAWA LES 25 ET 26 OCTOBRE 1899 – s.l.: s.n., 1899 (Ottawa: C. Boudreault). 03097. (Pre-1900 Canadiana) – 9 – cn C.I.H.M. [971]

FETES JUBILAIRES CELEBREES AUX TROIS-RIVIERES LES 24 & 25 FEVRIER 1892 – Trois-Rivieres Quebec: P. Ayotte, 1892?. 03098. (Pre-1900 Canadiana) – 9 – cn C.I.H.M. [971]

IL "FETHA NAGAST," O "LEGISLAZIONE DEI RE" : CODICE ECCLESIASTICO E CIVILE DI ABISSINIA, PUBBLICATO DA IGNAZIO GUIDI A SPESE DEL R ISTITUTO ORIENTALE IN NAPOLI – Roma, Tip della Casa editrice italiana, 1897-99 – us Res Libr [072]

FETICH IN THEOLOGY, OR, DOCTRINALISM TWIN TO RITUALISM / Miller, John – New York:Dodd & Mead, 1874 – 1mf – 9 – 0-8370-4434-0 – 1985-2434 – us A.T.L.A. [240]

FETICHISM AND FETICH WORSHIPERS / Baudin, P – New York, Cincinnati [etc]: Benziger Bros, 1885 – 1 – us Res Libr [290]

Fetis, Francois J *see*
- RESUME PHILOSOPHIQUE DE L'HISTOIRE DE LAS MUSIQUE...
- TRAITE DU CONTREPOINT ET DE LA FUGUE, CONTENANT L'EXPOSE ANALYTIQUE DES REGLES...

Fetler, Robert *see* BLAGOVESTNIK

Fetler, V A *see*
- PORKORNEISHEE KHODATAISTVO
- THE STUNDIST IN SIBERIAN EXILE AND OTHER POEMS

Fetler, William *see* KA ES ATKLAHJU MODERNISUMU (WILTIGU MAHZIBU) STARP AMERIKANU BAPTISTEEM UN KAPEHZ ES NODIBINAJU ANGLU-AMERIKANU MISSIONES BEEDRIBU

FETTE, SEIFEN, ANSTRICHMITTAL – v. 1-. 1894- – 1 – us UMI [540]

Fetter, Frank Whitson *see*
- LEGAL TENDER DURING THE ENGLISH AND IRISH BANK RESTRICTIONS
- SOME NEGLECTED ASPECTS OF GRESHAM'S LAW

Fettweis-Vienot, M *see* LES PEINTURES MURALES POSTCLASSIQUES DU QUINTANA ROO, MEXIQUE

FEU LAW QUARTERLY *see* FAR EASTERN LAW REVIEW

FEUDAL ENGLAND. HISTORICAL STUDIES ON THE 11TH AND 12TH CENTURIES / Round, J H – H 1153 2. 1895 – 8 – ne IDC [941]

FEUDAL GOVERNMENTAL GAZETTE / ed by Minami, Kazuo – (Senyorui-shu 202r. Jisha-Bugyo Shorui 293r. Shisei-Kankei-Sho 269r. Keizai-Kankei-Sho (economics), Chishi-Kankei-Sho (geography), & Gaikoku Jikein-Sho (foreign affairs) 160r) – inquire – us Ross [324]

FEUDATORY AND ZEMINDARI INDIA – v. 1 (1-10). Madras. 1921-22. – 11mf – 8 – ne IDC [950]

DIE FEUER SIND ENTGLOMMEN : ROMAN AUS DEM GROSSEN KAMPF GEGEN DIE ZWINGHERREN DER ERDE, DER IM JAHRE 1914 BEGANN / Schworm, Karl – 4. Aufl. Muenchen: F Eher, 1944 – 1r – 1 – us U.W. Library [830]

Feuer, Willie *see* THE RELATIONSHIP BETWEEN THE TIMING OF ARM MOVEMENT AND THE FORCE OF LANDING

Feuerbach, Henriette *see* UZ UND CRONEGK

Feuerbach, Ludwig *see* THE ESSENCE OF CHRISTIANITY

LE FEU-FOLLET : HUMORISTIQUE / ed by Morissette, J-F – Montreal, Canada. 23 avr; 11 jun 1892 – 1r – 1 – Can$25.00 – cn Can Microfilming [072]

LA FEUILLE – Socialiste, syndicaliste, revolutionnaire. no.1-61. Paris. 3 aout 1916-10 janv 1918 – 1 – fr A.C.R.P.P. [073]

FEUILLE BIMENSUELLE D'INFORMATIONS SYNDICALES / Centre Syndical d'Action Contre la Guerre – no. 1-24. Paris. 14 juil 1938-28 aout 1939. mq no. 18-23 – 1 – fr A.C.R.P.P. [073]

Feuille, D de la *see*
- ESSAY D'UN DICTIONNAIRE CONTENANT LA CONNAISSANCE DU MONDE, DES SCIENCES UNIVERSELLES...
- METHODE NOUVELLE POUR APPRENDRE L'ART DU BLASON

LA FEUILLE D'ERABLE – Berthier, Canada. v1 n4. mar 1849 – 1r – 1 – Can$25.00 – cn Can Microfilming [072]

LA FEUILLE D'ERABLE : HEBDO DU COURRIER DE MONTREAL – Montreal, Canada. 1 mai 1880-20 mai 1882 – 1r – 1 – Can$40.00 – cn Can Microfilming [072]

LA FEUILLE D'ERABLE – Montreal, Canada. serie 2: n1-4. oct-25 dec 1909 – 1r – 1 – Can$25.00 – cn Can Microfilming [072]

LA FEUILLE D'ERABLE – New York City, NY. 1 jan 1887-v2 n13. 29 mar 1888 – 1r – 1 – Can$30.00 – cn Can Microfilming [071]

LA FEUILLE D'ERABLE – Plessisville, Canada. 29 mar 1945-25 aut 1992 – 35r – 1 – Can$75.00r – cn Can Microfilming [072]

FEUILLE DES JEUNES NATURALISTES – Rennes, 1870-1914. Nos. 1-528 – 96mf – 9 – 8601/1 – ne IDC [073]

FEUILLE DU COMMERCE – Port-au-Prince: Jh Courtois, may 1843-dec 1861 – 46 sheets – 9 – us Res Libr [072]

LA FEUILLE DU JOUR – Par Parisot. Paris. dec 1790-aout 1792 – 1 – fr A.C.R.P.P. [073]

LA FEUILLE NANTAISE – suite de: La Feuille maritime de Nantes. Nantes. nov 1793-1810. BM. Nantes 60580 81 – 1 – fr A.C.R.P.P. [073]

LA FEUILLE NECESSAIRE – Contenant divers details sur les sciences, les lettres et les arts. no. 1-47. Paris. 1759. devenu: L' Avant-coureur voir a ce titre – 1 – fr A.C.R.P.P. [073]

FEUILLE OFFICIELLE – Neuchatel, Switzerland, 1957-68 – 8r – 1 – us Ross [324]

LA FEUILLE VILLAGEOISE ADRESSEE CHAQUE SEMAINE A TOUS LES VILLAGES DE LA FRANCE – Par Cerutti, Rabaud Saint-Etienne, Grouvelle et Guinguene. Paris. avr 1793-aout 1795 – 1 – fr A.C.R.P.P. [073]

FEUILLES D'AFFICHES ANNONCES ET AVIS DIVERS(ES) DE BONN/BONNER NACHRICHTS- UND ANZEIGEBLATT (ZWEISPRACHIG) *see* BONNER WOCHENBLATT

FEUILLES DEMOCRATIQUES / ed by Bouchard, T D – Montreal, Canada. jun 1945-jan 1947 – 1r – 1 – Can$30.00 – cn Can Microfilming [072]

LES FEUILLES D'ERABLE / Chapman, William – Montreal: Gebhardt-Berthiaume, 1890. 00573. (Pre-1900 Canadiana) – 9 – cn C.I.H.M. [971]

LES FEUILLES LIBRES – Lettres et arts. Revue mensuelle. Dir. M. Raval. no. 1-48. Paris. dec 1918-juin 1928 – 1 – fr A.C.R.P.P. [800]

FEUILLES LIBRES (JOURNAL D'ALAIN) – ns 9, no.10-12. 1 Dec 1935-. Running title: Propos d'Alain – 1 – us U.W. Library [073]

FEUILLES VOLANTES / Frechette, Louis-Honore – Quebec: C. Draveau, 1890. 03232. (Pre-1900 Canadiana) – 9 – cn C.I.H.M. [971]

LE FEUILLETON – Montreal, Canada. v2 n1. 1 oct 1866; v2 n3. 2 nov 1866; v2 n4. 15 nov 1866 – 1r – 1 – Can$25.00 – cn Can Microfilming [072]

FEUILLETON AUS DER NIEDERSCHLESISCHEN ZEITUNG – Goerlitz, Okt 1850-Juni 1851 – 1r – 1 – DM75.00 – gw Mikro Press [943]

FEUILLETON ILLUSTRE – Montreal: Houle, [1880-188-?] – 9 – cn C.I.H.M. [971]

LE FEUILLETON, OU, SUPPLEMENT DU FANTASQUE – Quebec: N Aubin, [1838] – 9 – cn C.I.H.M. [320]

Feuquieres, Antoine de Pas *see* MEMOIRES SUR LA GUERRE OU L'ON A RASSEMBLE LES MAXIMES LES PLUS NECESSAIRES DANS LES OPERATIONS DE L'ART MILITAIRE

FEVAID – Bursa: Matbaa-i Emri, 1896-? – 9 – $20.00 – us MEDOC [956]

Feval, Paul *see* JESUITS!

FEVRALSKAI A REVOLIUTSII A – Izd. 2-e. Moskva: Gos. izd-vo, 1926 – 1 – CSUX88-B5540 – us Hoover Inst Photo [320]

FEVRAL'SKAIA REVOLIUTSIIA / Alekseev, S A – M., L., 1925. 509p – 6mf – 9 – ne IDC [320]

Fevral'skii, A *see* MAIAKOVSKII-DRAMATURG

Fevre, Justin Louis Pierre *see* HISTOIRE CRITIQUE DU CATHOLICISME LIBERAL EN FRANCE

A FEW HINTS FOR THE CONSIDERATION OF THE METHODISTS AND OTHER DISSENTERS,... / Russel, W – Worcester, 1793 – 1mf – 9 – MP-582/1 – ne IDC [240]

A FEW PRACTICAL HINTS TO THE OFFICERS, N.C. OFFICERS AND MEN OF THE 26TH BATTALION: RELATIVE TO THEIR DUTIES IN CAMP / Attwood, P H – London, Ont.: Free Press Print. and Pub. Co., 1875. 00844. (Pre-1900 Canadiana) – 9 – cn C.I.H.M. [355]

Fewster, Jonathan B *see* THE ROLE OF MUSCULOSKELETAL FORCES IN THE HUMAN WALK-RUN TRANSITION

Feydel, Gabriel *see*
- UN CAHIER D'HISTOIRE LITTERAIRE
- REMARQUES MORALES

Feyerabend, M *see* SAEMTLICHE BRIEFE

Feyjoo, B Geronimo *see* JUSTA REPULSA... TEATRO CRITICO...FRANCISCO SOTO Y MARNE

Feyrol, Jacques *see* LES FRANCAIS EN AMERIQUE: CANADA, ACADIE, LOUISIANE

Feyzi, Emin *see* ICMAL-I NETAYIC YAHUT MUTIRA-I FUNUN-I IDADIYE

FEZKEKE-I TARIH / Celebi, Katib – [Istanbul]: Ceride-i Havadis Matbaasi, 1287 [1870] – 9 – $200.00 – us MEDOC [956]

FEZZAN INVENTORY REPORT / Libya. Ministry of Planning and Development. Kingdom of Libya. Fezzan – 7v. BNE-1305 1 – 9 – ne IDC [330]

FF FUNK UND FERNSEHEN DER DDR *see* DER RUNDFUNK

FF-DABEI *see* DER RUNDFUNK

FFF-COURIER *see*
- TV-CONTACT

FFF-PRESS – (Incl suppl) – Hamburg. jul 1952-dec 22, 1966 – 25r – 1 – gw Mikrofilm [072]

Ffoulkes, Edmund S *see*
- THE ATHANASIAN CREED
- CHRISTENDOM'S DIVISIONS
- GREEKS AND LATINS

LA FIACCOLA – Buffalo, NY, Aug. 7, 1909-Dec. 1, 1912 – 1r – 1 – us I.H.R.C. [978]

LA FIACCOLA – New York. v14-23. 1912-21 – 1r – 1 – us Ross [071]

LA FIACCOLA – New York. Weekly, Italian. Sept 5 1912-Feb 10 1921. Not collated. Incomplete – 1 – us NY Public [073]

LES FIANCES DE 1812 : ESSAI DE LITTERATURE CANADIENNE / Doutre, Joseph – Montreal: L Perreault, 1844. SEM16P23 – 1r – 5 – Can$9.00 – cn Bibl Nat [420]

FIANNA – Ireland.Feb 1915-Jan 1916 – 1 – ie Microforms [072]

FIANNA – Buenos Aires: [s.n.], [1910-]. [v1 n1-v2 n7 mar 17 1910-jul 1913] – 1r – 1 – us Res Libr [072]

FIANNA FAIL BULLETIN – Ireland.Mar 1935-Jul 1939 – 1 – ie Microforms [072]

FIANSOVAI A GAZETA – (Library has no. 1-252 (Jan. 1-Oct. 31, 1926)[missing no. 2, 103]) – Moskva: Narkomfin SSSR, 1924-1926. 3v – 1 – CSUX88-S506 – us Hoover Inst Photo [947]

FIAT LUX / Solar y Taboada, Antonio – Badajoz: La Minerva Extremena, 1913 – 1 – sp Bibl Santa Ana [946]

FIBER AND INTEGRATED OPTICS – v. 1-. 1977- – 1,5,6,9 – us UMI [073]

FIBER PRODUCER – v1-11. Jul 1973-1983 – 1,5,6,9 – us UMI [670]

FIBER PRODUCER INTERNATIONAL – v12, no.1-6. Feb-Dec 1984 – 1,5,6,9 – us UMI [670]

FIBER/LASER NEWS – 1981 – 1,5,6,9 – us UMI [073]

FIBONACCI MATHEMATICAL QUANTITY – San Francisco, CA. 1963-69 – 7r – 1 – $350.00 – B02817 – us Library Micro [510]

FIBRE CHEMISTRY – v1-25. 1969-93 – 1,5 – $65.00v – us UMI [540]

FIBRE CONTAINERS *see* PAPERBOARD PACKAGING

FIBRE CONTAINERS AND PAPERBOARD MILLS *see* PAPERBOARD PACKAGING

THE FIBROUS PLANTS OF INDIA / Royle, J F – 5156. 1855 – 9 – ne IDC [580]

Ficheleff, S *see* LE STATUT INTERNATIONAL DE LA PALESTINE ORIENTALE

FICHIER AUGUSTINIEN-AUGUSTINE BIBLIOGRAPHY / Institut des Etudes Augustiniennes. Paris – 1972.-63,000 cards 8 reels.-0-8161-1327-0 – 1 – $390.00 – uk Hall [240]

FICHIER D'AUTORITE DES ORGANISMES GOUVERNEMENTAUX DU QUEBEC / Bibliotheque Nationale. Quebec. Service de catalogage – 1981. SEM16P307 – 4r – 5 – Can$80.00 – cn Bibl Nat [020]

FICHIERS D'AUTORITE AUTEURS (PERSONNES PHYSIQUES, COLLECTIVITES ET TITRE UNIFORMES) ET MATIERES : EDITIONS SEMESTRIELLES CUMULATIVES – (Collectivites:- subsc 2 ed per y. F750.00y; per ed F450.00; Personnes physiques; Titres uniformes:- subsc 2 ed per y. F1,100.00y; per ed F650.00; Matieres) – 9 – fr Bibl Nationale [020]

FICHTE ALS RELIGIOESER DENKER / Gogarten, F – Jena, 1914 – 2mf – 8 – ne Slangenburg [290]

Fichte, J G *see* PHILOSOPHISCHES JOURNAL EINER GESELLSCHAFT TEUTSCHER GELEHRTEN

Fichte, Johann Gottlieb *see*
- ANTHOLOGIE AUS DEN WERKEN VON JOHANN GOTTLIEB FICHTE
- NACHGELASSENE SCHRIFTEN

Ficino, M *see* LIBRO...PARA CURAR...DE PESTILENCIA...

Ficino, Marsilio *see* PLATONIS OPERA OMNIA...

Ficinus, H D A *see* FLORA DER GEGEND UM DRESDEN
Ficinus, Marsilius *see* PLATONIS OPERA OMNIA...
Ficker, J *see* THESAURUS BAUMIANUS. VERZEICHNIS DER BRIEFE UND AKTENSTUECKE. KAISERLICHE UNIVERSITAETS- UND LANDESBIBLIOTHEK STRASSBURG
Ficker, Johannes *see* DIE KONFUTATION DES AUGSBURGISCHEN BEKENNTNISSES
Fickert, Karl Rudolph *see* ALMAE OPTIMORUM STUDIORUM MATRI VIADRINAE ACADEMIAE ILLUSTRISSIMAE
FICTION – (v. 7- 1979- 5,6,9) – v. 1-. 1972- – 1 – us UMI [830]
FICTION ON FICHE / British Library. National Bibliographic Service – Adult Fiction. Bibliographic records from 1950 to present, updated annually. First available 1992 – £175.00 – uk British Libr [830]
Fictuld, Hermann *see* DES LANGST GEWUNSCHTEN UND VERSPROCHENEN CHYMISCH-PHILOSOPHISCHEN PROBIER-STEINS, ERSTE CLASSE, IN WELCHER DER WAHREN UND ACHTEN ADEPTORUM UND ANDERER WURDIG ERFUNDENEN SCHRIFFTEN...
Fidalgo Carasa, Pilar *see* UNE JEUNE MERE DANS LES PRISONS DE FRANCO
Fidalgo Hijano, Concepcion *see* ANALISIS DE PAISAJE VEGETAL
FIDDLEHEAD – Frederiction. n1-182. 1945-1994/95 – 5,9 – Price varies – cn Micromedia [073]
FIDES ET HISTORIA – (1985-. 5,6,9) – v1-. 1968- – 1 – us UMI [000]
Fides. Service de bibliographie et de documentation *see* LECTURES
FIDUCIARY REPORTER – (Lacking: 1956) – First National City Bank: New York, 1940-62 – 7mf – 9 – $31.50 – LLMC 84-463 – us L.L.M.C. [073]
Fiebig, Paul *see*
- DIE AUFGABEN DER NEUTESTAMENTLICHEN FORSCHUNG IN DER GEGENWART
- JESU BLUT, EIN GEHEIMNIS

Fiebig, Wilfried *see* ABSTRAKTE ARBEIT UND ABSTRAKTWERDEN DER KUNST
Fiedler, H *see* DIE KOLLISIONSNORMEN DES INTERNATIONALEN WECHSELRECHTES
Fiedler, K F B *see* SYNOPSIS DER LAUBMOOSE MECKLENBURGS
Fiedler Leonhard *see* DEUTSCHE LITERATURGESCHICHTE
LES FIEFS DU BOURBONNAIS, LA PALISSE / La Faige & La Boutresse – Paris/Mouline, 1895 – 2mf – 9 – F60.00 – fr F.F.G. [944]
THE FIELD – 1957-60 – 1 – uk Microform Academic [072]
THE FIELD – London. 1-82. 1853-1893 – 1 – us NY Public [073]
Field, A D *see* WORTHIES AND WORKERS OF THE ROCK RIVER CONFERENCE
FIELD AND FOREST RAMBLES: WITH NOTES AND OBSERVATIONS ON THE NATURAL HISTORY OF EASTERN CANADA / Adams, Andrew Leith – London: S. King. 1873. 00012. (Pre-1900 Canadiana) – 9 – cn C.I.H.M. [574]
FIELD AND HEDGEROW : BEING THE LAST ESSAYS OF RICHARD JEFFERIES. COLLECTED BY HIS WIDOW / Jefferies, Richard – London, New York: Longmans, Green, 1889 – 1 roll – 1 – 1-55879-894-3 – uk Libr Preservation [840]
FIELD AND STREAM – (v. 79- 1974- 5,6. v. 80- 1975- 9) – v. 1- 1896- – 1 – us UMI [639]
FIELD ARTILLERY JOURNAL – 1911-50 – 1 – 579.00 – us L of C Photodup [355]
FIELD ARTILLERYMAN – n. 43-50. 1969-1972 – 1 – us UMI [355]
FIELD BOOKS / Lucas County. Ohio. Engineer – 9r – 1 – $32.50r – us Archival [324]
Field, Clive *see*
- THE PEOPLE CALLED METHODISTS. A DOCUMENTARY HISTORY OF THE METHODIST CHURCH IN GREAT BRITAIN AND IRELAND, PHASE 1
- THE PEOPLE CALLED METHODISTS. A DOCUMENTARY HISTORY OF THE METHODIST CHURCH IN GREAT BRITAIN AND IRELAND, PHASE 2
- THE PEOPLE CALLED METHODISTS. A DOCUMENTARY HISTORY OF THE METHODIST CHURCH IN GREAT BRITAIN AND IRELAND, PHASE 3

FIELD CROP PRODUCTION AND IMPROVEMENT / Libya – F.A.O. Report of the Government of Libya. Rome. 1966. BNE-1015 1 – 9 – ne IDC [630]
FIELD CROPS RESEARCH – v1-9. 1978-84 – 1,5,6,13 – sz Elsevier [073]
FIELD CROPS VARIETY TRIALS / Georgia. Agricultural Experiment Station. Athens – 1951-68 – 1,5,6 – us Spaulding [630]
Field, D D *see*
- GREATER SAFETY AT SEA...
- OUTLINES OF AN INTERNATIONAL CODE

Field, David Dudley *see* THE CIVIL CODE
FIELD DIARY / Andrews, Caesar – 1835 – 3 fiche – 9 – sa SA Libr [960]
FIELD GUIDE TO THE TYPES OF INSECTS AND MITES INFESTING CURED FISH – 1989 – 39p – it F.A.O. [590]
Field, H C *see* THE FERNS OF NEW ZEALAND AND ITS IMMEDIATE DEPENDENCIES
Field, Harry Hubert *see* AFTER MOTHER INDIA
Field, Henry Martyn *see* OUR WESTERN ARCHIPELAGO
Field, Homer H *see* HISTORY OF POTTAWATAMIE COUNTY
Field, John Edward *see* SAINT BERIN, THE APOSTLE OF WESSEX: THE HISTORY, LEGENDS AND TRADITIONS OF THE BEGINNING OF THE WEST-SAXON CHURCH
Field, M J *see* ADA FIELD NOTES
FIELD MANUAL ON COST ESTIMATION IN SAWMILLING INDUSTRIES – 1985 – 54p – it F.A.O. [338]
Field, Maunsell Bradhurst *see* MEMORIES OF MANY MEN AND OF SOME WOMEN: BEING PERSONAL RECOLLECTIONS OF EMPERORS, KINGS, QUEENS, PRINCES, PRESIDENTS, STATESMEN, AUTHORS.
Field, Moses Whelock *see* FINANCE-CURRENCY: SPEECH OF HON. MOSES W. FIELD, OF MICHIGAN, IN THE HOUSE OF REPRESENTATIVES, APRIL 8, 1874
FIELD NOTEBOOKS / Brower, Jacob V – Archaeological notebooks (1897-1905) of maps of ancient midwestern Indian mounds.Sketches and drawings of mounds, sites, Indian implements and other artifacts. 3 reels including filmed inventory – 1 – $90.00; $30.00r – us M.H.S. [930]
FIELD NOTES / Shawnee County. Kansas. Surveyor – 1861-64 – 1 – us KS Hist [978]
FIELD NOTES AND CORRESPONDENCE REGARDING INDIAN AND MILITARY RESERVATIONS – 1839-83 – 1 – us KS Hist [978]
FIELD NOTES FROM SELECTED...TOWNSHIP SURVEYS / U.S. General Land Office – 281 rolls. T1240 – 1 – us Nat'l Archives [310]
FIELD NOTES OF THE SURVEY OF THE CHEROKEE LANDS / McCoy, John Calvin – 1836-37 – 1 – us KS Hist [978]
THE FIELD OF ETHICS : BEING THE WILLIAM BELDEN NOBLE LECTURES FOR 1899 / Palmer, George Herbert – Boston: Houghton Mifflin, 1901 – v/213p 1mf – 9 – us A.T.L.A. [170]
THE FIELD OF ETHICS / Palmer, George Herbert – Boston/New York: Houghton, Mifflin & Co, 1901 – 3mf – 9 – $4.50 – LLMC 92-174 – us L.L.M.C. [170]
Field, Richard H *see* THE RICHARD H. FIELD PAPERS
Field, Samuel *see* IN MEMORIAM...AND OTHER GENEALOGICAL DATA ON THE FIELD FAMILY
FIELD SERVICE MANAGER – (v.4-. 1979- 5,6,9) – v.2-. 1977-. Continues: A F S M Journal – 1 – us UMI [073]
A FIELD SYSTEMS ANALYSIS OF DUAL LEARNING ENVIRONMENTS / Neel, Wallace B – West Virginia University, 1995 – 2mf – 9 – $8.00 – PSY 1896 – us Microform Publ [150]
Field, Thomas Warren *see* AN ESSAY TOWARDS AN INDIAN BIBLIOGRAPHY: BEING A CATALOGUE OF BOOKS RELATING TO THE HISTORY, ANTIQUITIES, LANGUAGES, CUSTOMS, RELIGION, WARS, LITERATURE, AND ORIGIN OF THE AMERICAN INDIANS, IN THE LIBRARY OF THOMAS W. FIELD
FIELD TRIP TO WEST BORNEO, FEB. 20 MAR. 7, 1959 / Beery, Lawrence A – SE-10,646 1 – 9 – ne IDC [980]
Fielding, Henry *see* A DIALOGUE BETWEEN A GENTLEMAN OF LONDON...AND AN HONEST ALDERMAN OF THE COUNTRY PARTY

Fielding, John *see* A PLAN FOR PREVENTING ROBBERIES WITHIN TWENTY MILES OF LONDON: WITH AN ACCOUNT OF THE RISE AND ESTABLISHMENT OF THE REAL THIEFTAKERS; TO WHICH IS ADDED, ADVICE TO PAWNBROKERS, STABLEKEEPERS, AND PUBLICANS
Fielding, John W L *see* GI CANCER
Fielding, William Stevens *see*
- THE COAL MINES OF NOVA SCOTIA: THE GOVERNMENT'S SCHEME OF EXTENDING THE COAL TRADE
- DISCOURS DE L'HON. W. S. FIELDING, M.P., MINISTRE DES FINANCES. SIR RICHARD CARTWRIGHT, M.P., MINISTRE DU COMMERCE ET L'HON. WILLIAM PATERSON, M.P., MINISTRE DES DOUANES, CHAMBRE DES COMMUNES, OTTAWA, 5, 12 & 13 AVRIL 1898

Fielding-Hall, Harold *see* HEARTS OF MEN
Fields, Annie Adams *see* ANNIE ADAMS FIELD PAPERS, 1852-1912
A FIELDWORK STUDY OF HOW YOUNG CHILDREN LEARN FUNDAMENTAL MOTOR SKILLS AND HOW THEY PROGRESS IN THE DEVELOPMENT OF STRIKING / Garcia, Clersida & Branta, Crystal – 1991 – 3mf – 9 – $12.00 – us Microform Publ [150]
Fierle, Karen M *see* DEVELOPMENT AND EVALUATION OF A LEISURE EDUCATION MODULE FOR USE IN A COLLEGE RESOURCE CENTER
THE FIERY CROSS – Atlanta: Knights of the Ku Klux Klan. [v1-4 n6 jul 1939-sep/oct 1942] – 1r – 1 – us Hes Libr [071]
FIESTA DE LA HISPANIDAD. 1972 / Plasencia. Ayuntamiento – Plasencia: Talleres Graficos Sanguino, 1972 – 1 – sp Bibl Santa Ana [390]
FIESTA DE NUESTRA SENORA, DE LA VICTORIA / Trujillo – Trujillo: Imp. Sobrino de B. Pena, 1966 – sp Bibl Santa Ana [240]
FIESTA DE SAN JORGE, 1953 / Caceres. Ayuntamiento – Caceres: Tip. Jomarin – sp Bibl Santa Ana [390]
FIESTAS 1976 – Caceres: Edit. Extremadura, 1976 – 1 – sp Bibl Santa Ana [390]
FIESTAS 1977 / Torrejoncillo. El Pechin – Caceres: Imp. Extremadura, 1977 – 1 – sp Bibl Santa Ana [390]
FIESTAS. AGOSTO 1954 – Madrid: Graf. Garcia, 1954? – 1 – sp Bibl Santa Ana [390]
FIESTAS BARRIADA MARIA AUXILIADORA – Merida: Imp. Vadillo, 1971 – 1 – sp Bibl Santa Ana [390]
FIESTAS COMARCALES A SANTA RITA 1973 – Caceres: Imp. Tomas Rodriguez Santano, 1973 – 1 – sp Bibl Santa Ana [240]
FIESTAS COMARCALES DE SANTA CRUZ DE LA SIERRA...MAYO 1981 EN HONOR DE SANTA RITA... / Pastor Serrano, Juan Jose – Santa Cruz de la Sierra: Cofradia de Santa Rita, 1981 – 1 – sp Bibl Santa Ana [390]
FIESTAS DE AGOSTO, 1979 EN LOGROSAN. NUESTRA SENORA DEL CONSUELO – Zorita: Imp. Carrasco, 1979 – 1 – sp Bibl Santa Ana [390]
FIESTAS DE AGOSTO DE 1971 EN HONOR DE NTRA. SRA. DE LA ASUNCION / Valverde del Fresno – Coria: Imp. Fernandez, 1971 – 1 – sp Bibl Santa Ana [390]
FIESTAS DE LA JUVENTUD. 1974 / Madronera. Ayuntamiento – Trujillo: Imp. Gexme, 1974 – 1 – sp Bibl Santa Ana [390]
FIESTAS DE LA JUVENTUD. CACERES 26 ABRIL 30 MAYO 1973 / Delegacion Provincial de la Juventud – Caceres: N. Sergio Dorado, 1973 – 1 – sp Bibl Santa Ana [390]
FIESTAS DE LA SANTISIMA VIRGEN DE LA VENDIMIA / Trujillo – Trujillo: Tip. Sobrino de B. Pena, 1968 – sp Bibl Santa Ana [240]
FIESTAS DE LA SOLEDAD, 1961 / Casatejada. Ayuntamiento – Plasencia: Imprenta La Victoria, 1961 – 1 – sp Bibl Santa Ana [390]
FIESTAS DE LA SOLEDAD...1960 / Casatejada. Ayuntamiento – Plasencia: Imp. La Victoria, 1960 – 1 – sp Bibl Santa Ana [390]
FIESTAS DE LA VELA EN ZORITA...EN HONOR...LA VIRGEN DE FUENTE SANTA 1979 / Zorita. Ayuntamiento – Imp. Carrasco, 1979 – 1 – sp Bibl Santa Ana [390]
FIESTAS DE NTRA. SRA. DE LOS REMEDIOS. ABRIL 1964 – Fragenal de la Sierra: Angel Verde, 1964 – 1 – sp Bibl Santa Ana [946]

FIESTAS DE NUESTRA SENORA DE LA PIEDAD. 1975 – Caceres: Imp. Padilla, 1975 – 1 – sp Bibl Santa Ana [240]
FIESTAS DE SAN AGUSTIN. 1980 – Caceres: Imp. Offset Rodriguez, 1980 – 1 – sp Bibl Santa Ana [390]
FIESTAS DE SAN ANTON. 1977 – Caceres, 1977 – 1 – sp Bibl Santa Ana [390]
FIESTAS DE SAN BUENAVENTURA. JUNIO 1969 – Coria: Imp. Fernandez, 1969 – 1 – sp Bibl Santa Ana [390]
FIESTAS DE SAN CRISTOBAL 1974 / Cofradia de San Cristobal – Coria: Imp. Fernandez, 1974 – 1 – sp Bibl Santa Ana [390]
FIESTAS DE SAN CRISTOBAL 1976 / Cofradia de San Cristobal – Coria: Imp. Fernandez, 1976 – 1 – sp Bibl Santa Ana [390]
FIESTAS DE SAN CRISTOBAL 1976 / Cofradia de San Cristobal – Coria: Imp. Fernandez, 1976 – 1 – sp Bibl Santa Ana [390]
FIESTAS DE SAN CRISTOBAL. PATRONO DE LOS AUTOMOVILISTAS – Caceres: Imp. Fernandez, 1973 – 1 – sp Bibl Santa Ana [240]
FIESTAS DE SAN JOSE. 1971 / Badajoz – Badajoz: Graf. Tejado, 1971 – sp Bibl Santa Ana [390]
FIESTAS DE SAN JUAN 1971 / Badajoz – Badajoz: La Minerva Extremena, 1971 – sp Bibl Santa Ana [390]
FIESTAS DE SAN JUAN 1972 / Badajoz – Badajoz: Imp. Manuel Barrena, 1972 – 1 – sp Bibl Santa Ana [390]
FIESTAS DE SAN JUAN 1975 / Badajoz – Zafra: Ind Tip. Extremenas, 1974 – 1 – sp Bibl Santa Ana [390]
FIESTAS DE SAN JUAN 1976 / Pena Viva la Gente – Plasencia: Imp. Sanchez Rodrigo, 1976 – 1 – sp Bibl Santa Ana [390]
FIESTAS DE SAN JUAN 1977 / Pena Viva la Gente – Plasencia: Imp. Sanchez Rodrigo, 1977 – 1 – sp Bibl Santa Ana [390]
FIESTAS DE SAN MARCOS. DESDE EL CERRO DE LA SALVE / Oliva de la Frontera – (Badajoz): Imprenta Espanola, 1970 – 1 – sp Bibl Santa Ana [946]
FIESTAS DE SAN PEDRO 1973 – Caceres: Imp. La Minerva, 1973 – 1 – sp Bibl Santa Ana [390]
FIESTAS DE SAN PEDRO 1974 – Caceres: Imp. La Minerva, 1974 – 1 – sp Bibl Santa Ana [240]
FIESTAS DE SAN PEDRO 1976 – Caceres: Imp. La Minerva, 1976 – 1 – sp Bibl Santa Ana [390]
FIESTAS DE SAN ROQUE EN ALMARAZ 1980 / Almaraz. Ayuntamiento – Navalmoral de la Mata: Imp. Rivero, 1980 – 1 – sp Bibl Santa Ana [390]
FIESTAS DE SANTO DOMINGO DE GUZMAN. 1971 – s.l, s.i, s.a. – 1 – sp Bibl Santa Ana [390]
FIESTAS DE SEPTIEMBRE DE 1970 / Zarza de Alange – Olivenza: Tip. M. Reginfo, 1970 – sp Bibl Santa Ana [390]
FIESTAS DE SU PATRONA LA VIRGEN DE LA VICTORIA / Trujillo – Plasencia: Imp. La Victoria, 1970 – sp Bibl Santa Ana [240]
FIESTAS DE SU PATRONA LA VIRGEN DE LA VICTORIA / Trujillo – Plasencia: Imp. La Victoria, 1972 – sp Bibl Santa Ana [240]
FIESTAS DE SU SANTO PATRON SAN BUENAVENTURA DURANTE...JULIO 1958 / Moraleja. Ayuntamiento – Caceres: Tip. El Noticiero, 1958 – 1 – sp Bibl Santa Ana [390]
FIESTAS DE SU SANTO PATRON. SAN BUENAVENTURA. DURANTE...JULIO 1962 / Moraleja. Ayuntamiento – Caceres: Tip. El Noticiero, 1962 – 1 – sp Bibl Santa Ana [390]
FIESTAS DE SU SANTO PATRON SAN BUENAVENTURA JULIO, 1959 – Caceres: Tip. El Noticiero, S.L., 1959 – 1 – sp Bibl Santa Ana [240]
FIESTAS DE TENTUDIA, 1969 / Calera de Leon – Fregenal de la Sierra: Imprenta Angel Verde, 1969 – sp Bibl Santa Ana [390]
FIESTAS DE TENTUDIA, 1970 / Calera de Leon – Fregenal de la Sierra: Imp. Angel Verde, 1970 – sp Bibl Santa Ana [390]
FIESTAS DEL CARMEN / Villafranca de los Barros – Villafranca de los Barros: Imp. Machuca, 1967 – 1 – sp Bibl Santa Ana [390]
FIESTAS DEL CARMEN / Villafranca de los Barros – Villafranca de los Barros: Imp. Machuca, 1968 – 1 – sp Bibl Santa Ana [390]

FIESTAS DEL CARMEN, 1964 / Villafranca de los Barros – Villafranca de los B. Graficas Gisver e Imprenta Machuca, 1964 – 1 – sp Bibl Santa Ana [390]
FIESTAS DEL CARMEN 1976 / Villafranca de los Barros – Villafranca: Imp. Machuca, 1976 – 1 – sp Bibl Santa Ana [390]
FIESTAS DEL CARMEN, JULIO 1963 / Vilia Franca de Los Barros. Ayuntamiento – Villafranca: Graf. Grisferv, 1963 – 1 – sp Bibl Santa Ana [390]
FIESTAS DEL CRISTO DE PARDALERAS – Badajoz: Graficas Tejado, 1970 – 1 – sp Bibl Santa Ana [240]
FIESTAS DEL RISCO 1979 / Asociacion Cultural Chambra – Caceres: Imp. Marosa, 1979 – 1 – sp Bibl Santa Ana [390]
FIESTAS DEL SANTISIMO CRISTO DEL RISCO – Sierra de Fuentes, Caceres: Imp. Oftset T. Rodriguez, 1980 – 1 – sp Bibl Santa Ana [240]
FIESTAS DEL TABACO Y DEL PIMIENTO 1980 / Jaraiz de la Vera. Ayuntamiento – Navalmoral de la Mata: Imp. Rivero, 1980 – 1 – sp Bibl Santa Ana [390]
FIESTAS EN BELEN DE TRUJILLO 1974 / Parroquia de Nuestra Senora de Belen – Trujillo: Imp. Gexme, 1974 – 1 – sp Bibl Santa Ana [240]
FIESTAS EN GARGANTA LA OLLA 1974 / Garganta la Olla. Ayuntamiento – (Tambien ano 1973) – Jaraiz de la Vera: Imp. La Verata, 1974 – 1 – sp Bibl Santa Ana [390]
FIESTAS EN GARGANTA LA OLLA DEL...JULIO DE 1972 – Jaraiz de la Vera: Imp. La Verata, 1972 – 1 – sp Bibl Santa Ana [390]
FIESTAS EN HONOR DE LA SANTISIMA VIRGEN DEL PILAR – Coria: Imp. Fernandez, 1972 – 1 – sp Bibl Santa Ana [240]
FIESTAS EN HONOR DE LA SANTISIMA VIRGEN DEL ROSARIO, 1971 / Alcuescar. Ayuntamiento – Caceres: Imp. La Minerva, 1971 – sp Bibl Santa Ana [390]
FIESTAS EN HONOR DE LA VIRGEN DE FUENSANTA. 1975 – Zorita: Imp. Carrasco, 1975 – 1 – sp Bibl Santa Ana [240]
FIESTAS EN HONOR DE LA VIRGEN DE LA SOTERRANA. 1975 – Trujillo: Imp. Gexme, 1975 – 1 – sp Bibl Santa Ana [240]
FIESTAS EN HONOR DE LA VIRGEN DE LA SOTERRANA (NUESTRA SENORA DE LAS NIEVAS) AGOSTO 1973 – Trujillo: Imp. Gex, 1973 – 1 – sp Bibl Santa Ana [240]
FIESTAS EN HONOR DE LOS EMIGRANTES. ALCOLLARIN, 7 Y 8 AGOSTO 1971 / Alcollarin. Ayuntamiento – Zorita: Imp. Carrasco, 1971 – 1 – sp Bibl Santa Ana [390]
FIESTAS EN HONOR DE NTRA. SRA. DE SOTERRANA (VIRGEN DE LAS NIEVES). 1971 / Madronera. Ayuntamiento – Trujillo: Imp. Gexme, 1971 – 1 – sp Bibl Santa Ana [390]
FIESTAS EN HONOR DE NUESTRA EXCELSA PATRONA LA SANTISIMA VIRGEN DE FUENTE SANTA. 1974 / La Velada – Tambien 1976 – 1 – sp Bibl Santa Ana [240]
FIESTAS EN HONOR DE SAN ISIDRO LABRADOR – Badajoz: Imp. Vicente Campini, 1970 – 1 – sp Bibl Santa Ana [240]
FIESTAS EN HONOR DE SAN JOSE OBRERO 1971 / Rincon del Obispo-Coria. Ayuntamiento – Coria: Imp. Fernandez, 1971 – 1 – sp Bibl Santa Ana [390]
FIESTAS EN HONOR DE SAN ROQUE 1945 / Badajoz – Badajoz: Graf. Iberia, 1945 – sp Bibl Santa Ana [390]
FIESTAS EN HONOR DE SUS EMIGRANTES. AGOSTO DE 1972 – Zorita: Imp. Carrasco, 1972 – 1 – sp Bibl Santa Ana [390]
FIESTAS EN HONOR DEL EMIGRANTE. 1971 / Torrejoncillo. Ayuntamiento – Caceres: Tip. La Minerva, 1971 – 1 – sp Bibl Santa Ana [390]
FIESTAS EN HONOR DEL SANTISIMO CRISTO 1974 – Caceres: Tip. La Minerva, 1974 – 1 – sp Bibl Santa Ana [240]
FIESTAS EN MONROY DURANTE...SEPTIEMBRE 1962 / Monroy. Ayuntamiento – Caceres: Tip. La Minerva, 1962 – 1 – sp Bibl Santa Ana [390]
FIESTAS EN RINCON DEL OBISPO EN HONOR DE SAN JOSE OBRERO. MAYO 1973 / Rincon del Obispo – Caceres: Imp. Fernandez, 1973 – 1 – sp Bibl Santa Ana [240]
FIESTAS EN SOTILLO DE ANDRADA ANO 1973 – Jaraiz de la Vera: Imp. La Verata, 1973 – 1 – sp Bibl Santa Ana [390]
FIESTAS JUBILARES DE LA ADORACION NOCTURNA. TRUJILLO 1971 – Plasencia: Imp. La Victoria, 1971 – 1 – sp Bibl Santa Ana [390]
FIESTAS LOCALES Y FERIA DEGANADOS...LOS DIAS 1,2,3 Y 4 DE MAYO DE 1981 / Zarza de Alange – Trujillo: Imprenta Gezme, 1981 – 1 – sp Bibl Santa Ana [390]
FIESTAS PATRONALES 1971 / Talavan. Ayuntamiento – Caceres: Imp. La Minerva, 1971 – 1 – sp Bibl Santa Ana [390]
FIESTAS PATRONALES AGOSTO 1974 – Caceres: Tip. La Minerva, 1974 – 1 – sp Bibl Santa Ana [240]
FIESTAS PATRONALES AGOSTO DE 1973 – Caceres: Imp. La Minerva, 1973 – 1 – sp Bibl Santa Ana [390]
FIESTAS PATRONALES DE NTRA. SRA. DE LA ESTRELLA. 1975 / Santos de Maimona, Los. Ayuntamiento – Zafra: Ind Tip. Extremenas, 1975 – 1 – sp Bibl Santa Ana [946]
FIESTAS PATRONALES DE NUESTRA SENORA LA SANTISIMA VIRGEN DE LA SOLEDAD / Aceuchal – Almendralejo: V. Rodriguez, 1970 – 1 – sp Bibl Santa Ana [240]
FIESTAS PATRONALES DE SANTA ANA Y SANTIAGO LOS DIAS 25-26 DE JULIO 1973 – Zorita: Imp. Carrasco, 1973 – 1 – sp Bibl Santa Ana [240]
FIESTAS PATRONALES EN HONOR DE LA SANTISIMA VIRGEN DEL ROSARIO / Huerta de Animas – Trujillo: Imp. Gexme, 1972 – 1 – sp Bibl Santa Ana [240]
FIESTAS PATRONALES EN HONOR DE LA VIRGEN DEL ROSARIO. 1973 / Huerta de Animas – Trujillo: Imp. Gexme, 1973. Tambien ano 1974 – 1 – sp Bibl Santa Ana [240]
FIESTAS PATRONALES EN HONOR DE NTRA. SRA. DE LOS MILAGROS. 1979 / Bienvenida. Ayuntamiento – Los Santos de Maimona: Grafisur, 1979 – 1 – sp Bibl Santa Ana [390]
FIESTAS PATRONALES EN HONOR DE NTRA. SRA. DEL CONSUELO 1971 / Logrosan. Ayuntamiento – Caceres: Imp. La Minerva, 1971 – sp Bibl Santa Ana [390]
FIESTAS PATRONALES EN HONOR DE NUESTRA SENORA DE LOS MILAGROS. SEPTIEMBRE 1970 / Bienvenida. Ayuntamiento – Fregenal de la Sierra: Imp. Angel Verde, 1970 – sp Bibl Santa Ana [240]
FIESTAS PATRONALES EN HONOR DE SAN BARTOLOME / Herguijuela. Ayuntamiento – Trujillo: Imp. Gexme, 1976 – 1 – sp Bibl Santa Ana [390]
FIESTAS PATRONALES EN LA BARRIADA DEL SAGRADO CORAZON... / Olivenza, Teleclub no 23 – Olivenza: Tip. Martinez Reginfo, 1970 – 1 – sp Bibl Santa Ana [946]
FIESTAS PATRONALES SAN JORGE, 1955 / Caceres. Ayuntamiento – Caceres: Imp. Jomarin – sp Bibl Santa Ana [390]
FIESTAS PATRONALES SAN JORGE 1959 / Caceres. Ayuntamiento – Caceres: Comision de Festejos Patronales, 1959 – 1 – sp Bibl Santa Ana [650]
FIESTAS PATRONALES. SANTISIMO CRISTO DE LA AGONIA – Caceres: Edit. Extremadura, 1974 – 1 – sp Bibl Santa Ana [240]
FIESTAS PATRONALES. SEPTIEMBRE 1975 / Fuente del Maestre – Zafra: Ind. Tip. Extremenas, 1974 – 1 – sp Bibl Santa Ana [390]
FIESTAS PATRONALES SEPTIEMBRE-OCTUBRE, 1977 / Hogar Extremeno de Zaragoza – sp Bibl Santa Ana [390]
FIESTAS POPULARES. AGOSTO 1980 / Orellana la Vieja. Ayuntamiento – Villanueva de la Serena: Graf. Samat, 1980 – 1 – sp Bibl Santa Ana [390]
FIESTAS POPULARES EN HONOR DE LA VIRGEN DE ARGEME, PATRONA DE... / Puebla de Argeme. Ayuntamiento – Plasencia: Imp. La Victoria, 1972 – 1 – sp Bibl Santa Ana [390]
FIESTAS Y DANZAS EN EL CUZCO Y EN LOS ANDES / Verger, Pierre – Madrid: Missionalia Hispanica, 1948 – 1 – sp Bibl Santa Ana [390]
FIESTAS Y FERIA DE LA BARRIADA DE SAN ROQUE...1971 / Badajoz – Badajoz: Graf. Tejado, 1971 – sp Bibl Santa Ana [390]
FIESTAS Y FESTEJOS EN HONOR DE SU PATRONA LA SANTISIMA VIRGEN DEL ROSARIO 1977 / Valdemorales. Ayuntamiento – Caceres: Tip. Extremadura, 1977 sp Bibl Santa Ana [390]
FIESTAS...SEPTIEMBRE 1960 / Tornavascas. Ayuntamiento – Plasencia: Imp. La Victoria, 1960 – 1 – sp Bibl Santa Ana [350]
FIEVRES D'AFRIQUE / Carbonneau, Louis – Paris: J Ferenczi, [1926] – 1 – us Res Libr [960]
Fiey, J M *see* COMMUNAUTES SYRIAQUES EN IRAN ET IRAK DES ORIGINES A 1552
FIFE AND KINROSS EXTRA – 1 – £42.00r – uk Scot News [072]
FIFE FREE PRESS – Kirkcaldy, Scotland. -w. 1871-99. 24 reels – 1 – uk British Libr Newspaper [072]
FIFE HERALD – Cupar, Scotland, UK. 18 Mar 1824-9 Mar 1826; 11 Mar 1830-27 Dec 1832; 3 Jan-28 Feb 1833; 5 Mar 1835-28 Dec 1837; 1838-43. -w. 5 reels – 1 – uk British Libr Newspaper [072]
FIFE HERALD – Kirkaldy, Scotland. -w. 1880. 1 reel – 1 – uk British Libr Newspaper [072]
Fife, LK *see* THE RELIABILITY OF THE DYNAVEC (TM) LVD
FIFE SENTINEL – Scotland, UK. 12 Jan 1843-30 Jan 1845. -w. 1 reel – 1 – uk British Libr Newspaper [072]
FIFESHIRE, 1837 : BRITISH ISLES CENSUS DIRECTORIES PROJECT, SCOTLAND. VOL 38 – 1mf – 9 – A$9.00 – at Vine [941]
FIFESHIRE ADVERTISER – Kirkcaldy, Scotland. -w. 1849-99. 31 reels – 1 – uk British Libr Newspaper [072]
FIFESHIRE EXPRESS – Cupar, Scotland, UK. 4 Aug-23 Jan 1856.-w. 24 feet – 1 – uk British Libr Newspaper [072]
FIFESHIRE JOURNAL – Cupar, Scotland, UK. 7 Jan-Dec 1836; 1839-43; 1844-49; 26 Nov 1850; 3 Dec 1850-28 Jan 1851; 4 Feb-Dec 1851; 1852-92; Jan-31 Aug 1893. -w. 48 reels – 1 – uk British Libr Newspaper [072]
FIFESHIRE JOURNAL – Kirkaldy, Scotland, UK. 26 Jan 1833-7 Jan 1835.-w. 1 reel – 1 – uk British Libr Newspaper [072]
FIFESHIRE NEWS *see* THE NEWS
FIFINE AT THE FAIR / Browning, Robert – London: Smith, Elder, 1872 – 1 roll – 1 – 1-55879-168-X – uk Libr Preservation [810]
FIFINE, THE FISHER MAID, OR, THE MAGIC SHRIMPS / Dixon, Frederick Augustus – Ottawa: A. Woodburn, 1877. 02721. (Pre-1900 Canadiana) – 9 – cn C.I.H.M. [971]
FIFTEEN SERMONS PREACHED BEFORE THE UNIVERSITY OF OXFORD BETWEEN A.D. 1826 AND 1843 / Newman, John Henry – 3d ed. 1872 – 1 – us A.T.L.A. [240]
FIFTEEN YEARS AGO: OR THE PATRIOTISM OF WILL COUNTY / Woodruff, George E – Joliet: Goodspeed Publ. Co., 1876. Illinois Reel 61. (The Cox Library Collection) – 5 – us Americana [978]
FIFTEEN YEARS AMONG THE TOP-KNOTS, OR, LIFE IN KOREA / Underwood, Lillias Horton – Boston: American Tract Society, c1908 – 1mf – us A.T.L.A. [950]
FIFTEEN YEARS OF PRAYER IN THE FULTON STREET MEETING / Prime, Samuel Irenaeus – New York: Scribner, Armstrong, 1872 – 1mf – us A.T.L.A. [240]
FIFTEENTH CENTURY HOLKHAM MANUSCRIPT / Holkham Hall. Norfolk. England – Nos. 521, 523, 524 and 543 – 1 – uk Microform Academic [025]
FIFTH ANNUAL REPORT FOR THE PERIOD ENDING 30 JUN 1961 / Council on Library Resources – Washington, 1961. 66p. H-133/2 – 8 – ne IDC [020]
THE FIFTH ARMY HISTORY, 1943-1945 / U.S. Army. Fifth Army – 2r – 1 – $170.00 – S1684 – us Scholarly Res [355]
FIFTH AVENUE JOURNAL : A MIRROR OF ART, LITERATURE AND SOCIETY – v1-2. 1871-73 – 1r – 1 – us Ross [420]
FIFTH CENSUS OF THE UNITED STATES / U.S. Bureau of the Census – 1830. 201 rolls. M19 – 1 – us Nat'l Archives [324]
FIFTH DEVELOPMENT PLAN / Solomon Islands. British. Protectorate – (1 Apr 1968 to 31 Mar 1970). Honiara. 1968. BD-1197 1 – 9 – ne IDC [338]
FIFTH DEVELOPMENT PLAN, 1968-1970 / British Solomon Islands – D-973 1 – 9 – ne IDC [338]
FIFTH FOUR-YEAR ECONOMIC DEVELOPMENT PLAN, 1969-1972 / China. Republic. Council for International Economic Cooperation and Development – D-1022 1 – 9 – ne IDC [338]
THE FIFTH FREEDOM IS OUR WEAPON / Sukarno, Pres. Indonesia – Address 10 Apr 1964 at Meeting of Ministers in Prjparation of Second Asian-African Conference. SE 10,374 1. 1964 – 9 – ne IDC [950]
THE FIFTH GOSPEL: THE LAND WHERE JESUS LIVED / Otts, John Martin Philip – New York: Fleming H. Revell, 1892. 1 fiche – 9 – us A.T.L.A. [240]
FIFTH MEETING OF THE EAST AFRICAN SUB-COMMITTEE FOR SOIL CORRELATION AND LAND EVALUATION. WAD MEDANI, SUDAN, 1985 – 1985 – 210p – it F.A.O. [631]
FIFTH PROGRESS REPORT ON THE RECONSTRUCTION AND DEVELOPMENT PROGRAMME 1960-66, FOR THE YEAR 1964-65 / Mauritius – Sessional Paper No. 7 of 1966. Port Louis. 1966. BD-669 1 – 9 – ne IDC [338]
FIFTH SIX-YEAR FINANCIAL PROGRAM, 1948-49 TO 1953-54 / Puerto Rico. Junta de Planificacion, Urbanizacion y Zonificacion – Santurce. 1948 – 9 – ne IDC [338]
FIFTH WORLD FOOD SURVEY (1985) – 1987 – 75p – it F.A.O. [360]
THE FIFTIETH ANNIVERSARY OF THE FORMATION OF THE CARLETON BAPTIST CHURCH IN CARLETON, SAINT JOHN, MAY 16, 1841, SUNDAY MAY 17, 1891 – Saint John, N. B.: s.n., 1891 (Saint John, N. B.: G. Day). 05581. (Pre-1900 Canadiana) – 9 – cn C.I.H.M. [971]
THE FIFTIETH ANNIVERSARY OF THE INTHRONIZATION OF THE RIGHT REVEREND JOHN MEDLEY, FIRST BISHOP OF FREDERICTON – Papers read at Fredericton, June 10, 1895. Saint John, N. B.: Ellis, Robertson, 1895. 05460. (Pre-1900 Canadiana) – 9 – cn C.I.H.M. [971]
FIFTY "BAB" BALLADS : MUCH SOUND AND LITTLE SENSE / Gilbert, W S – London: George Routledge, 1881 – 1 roll – 1 – uk Libr Preservation [810]
FIFTY PLUS – v. 18- 1978- – 1,5,6,9 – us UMI [300]
FIFTY YEARS AMONG THE BAPTISTS / Benedict, David – New York and Boston. 1860 – 1 – $15.96 – us Baptist [240]
FIFTY YEARS AMONG THE BAPTISTS / Benedict, David – New York: Sheldon, 1860, c1859 – 1mf -- us A.T.L.A. [240]
FIFTY YEARS AND OVER, AKRON AND SUMMIT COUNTY / Lane, Samuel A – Akron: Beacon Job Department, 1892. Ohio Reel 61. (The Cox Library Collection) – 5 – us Americana [978]
FIFTY YEARS AS A PRESIDING ELDER / Cartwright, Peter – Cincinnati: Hitchcock and Walden; New York: Nelson and Phillips, c1871 – 1mf – us A.T.L.A. [240]
FIFTY YEARS AT EAST BRENT : THE LETTERS OF GEORGE ANTHONY DENISON, 1845-1896, ARCHDEACON OF TAUNTON / Denison, George Anthony; ed by Denison, Louisa Evelyn – New York: E.P. Dutton; London: John Murray, 1902 – 1mf – us A.T.L.A. [240]
FIFTY YEARS' DOCUMENTS OF THE FOUNDATION OF THE REPUBLIC OF CHINA *see* 50 YEARS' DOCUMENTS OF THE FOUNDATION OF THE REPUBLIC OF CHINA
FIFTY YEARS OF CONCESSIONS TO IRELAND, 1831-1881 / O'Brien, Richard Barry – London: S. Low, Marston, Searle & Rivington, 1883-85. 2v. illus – 1 – us U.W. Library [941]
FIFTY YEARS OF MASONRY IN CALIFORNIA / Sherman, Edwin A – San Francisco: George Spaulding & Co., 1898. 2v. California Reel 1. (The Cox Library Collection) – 5 – us Americana [360]
FIFTY YEARS WITH THE BAPTIST MINISTERS AND CHURCHES OF THE MARITIME PROVINCES OF CANADA / Bill, IE – Saint John, N.B.: Printed by Barnes, 1880 – 2mf – us A.T.L.A. [240]
FIFTY-TWO LETTERS TO DR. JOHN RYLAND / Carey, William – 1781-1825 – 1 – 21.00 – us Baptist [240]
FIGARO – 1879-1963 – 1 – sz Infoprint [944]
FIGARO – 1970-1995 – 12 times per y – 1 – F6,200.00 – sz Infoprint [944]
FIGARO – 1988-1995 – 6 times per yr – 6 – F4,700.00 – sz Infoprint [072]
FIGARO – San Francisco, 1870-1904 – 1r – 1 – us Ross [071]
FIGARO – Stockholm, Sweden. 1878-1925 – 20r – 1 – sw Kungliga [790]
FIGARO – v1-5. 1868-72 – 1 – 200.00 – us Opus [073]

LE FIGARO – (Also available on 35mm and CD-ROM) – 1988-1995 – 6r per y – 5,6 – Sfr1,230.00 – sz Infoprint [072]
LE FIGARO – Biddeford, ME. dec 1895 – 1r – 1 – Can$25.00 – cn Can Microfilming [071]
LE FIGARO / ed by Buies, Arthur & Achintre, A – Montreal, Canada. 2 mar-13 avr 1883 – 1r – 1 – Can$25.00 – cn Can Microfilming [072]
LE FIGARO – Edition hebdomadaire internationale. no. 1-60. Paris. 1974-1er mars 1975 – 1 – fr A.C.R.P.P. [072]
LE FIGARO – Journal non politique. Paris. 1 avr 1854-24 nov 1942, 23 aout 1944-1990 – 1 – fr A.C.R.P.P. [072]
LE FIGARO – (Le titre de Figaro a ete repris successivement par:. Figaro. Electeur, jure, contribuable, artiste, financier puis Nouvelliste du soir; Journal quotidien, politique et litteraire; Journalivre. Revue quotidienne; Journal quotidien, politique et litteraire. 15 fevr-20 aout 1835 no. 1-180, 16 mai-10 juil 1836 n.s., no. 1-56, 1er oct-24 dec 1836 no. 1-86, 26-27 dec 1836, 1er janv-13 juin 1837, 16 juin-15 aout 1837, 15 oct 1837-6 sept 1838 no. 1-322. Figaro. 30 dec 1838-28 fevr 1839. Le Figaro. Journal litteraire et d'arts puis de litterature et d'arts. no. 1-188. 3 mars 1839-27 dec 1840. Le Nouveau Figaro. 19 dec 1841-mai 1842. Absorbe par: Les Coulisses. Le Figaro. Journal de l'apres-midi. 25 dec 1847-8 mars 1848. Figaro. no. 1, 15. mai 1848. Nouveau Figaro. Programme des theatres, journal quotidien du soir, politique, litteraire et satirique. no. 1-6. 8-15 juin 1848. Figaro. Journal non politique. no. 1-3. 18-20 aout 1852) – Journal non politique. Dir. Lepoitevin-Saint-Alme et M. Alhoy. Paris. 1826-34 – 1 – fr A.C.R.P.P. [072]
LE FIGARO : LITTERAIRE – Montreal, Canada. 4 dec 1879 – 1r – 1 – Can$25.00 – cn Can Microfilming [072]
LE FIGARO / ed by Morissette, J-F – Montreal, Canada. 15 aut 1885 – 1r – 1 – Can$25.00 – cn Can Microfilming [072]
LE FIGARO – Paris, 16 nov 1966 (numero du centenaire) – 1r – 1 – cn Can Microfilming [072]
LE FIGARO – Paris. France. 1964- – 1 – us UMI [072]
LE FIGARO – Paris. France. Aug. 1914-June 1919 (gaps) – 1 – 35.00r – us Hoover Inst Photo [072]
LE FIGARO – Quebec, Canada. 10 mar-14 avr 1876 – 1r – 1 – Can$25.00 – cn Can Microfilming [072]
LE FIGARO – Supplement litteraire. Paris. 1876-1895, dec 1905-aout 1914 – 1 – fr A.C.R.P.P. [072]
LE FIGARO – (Yrly reel count varies) – 1854 – 1 – inquire – us Ross [072]
LE FIGARO. – Paris: Figaro, 1953-54 – us Res Libr [072]
O FIGARO : FOLHA ILLUSTRADA – Rio de Janeiro, 1 Jan 1876-13 Apr 1878 – 1,5,6 – bl Biblioteca [072]
FIGARO LITTERAIRE – 1946-1978 – 1 – sz Infoprint [072]
LE FIGARO LITTERAIRE – Paris. France. -w. 1963-70 – 1 – us UMI [072]
LE FIGARO LITTERAIRE – Paris. mars 1946-1978 – 1 – fr A.C.R.P.P. [073]
FIGARO MADAME – 1989-1993 – 2 times per yr – 6 – F2,800.00 – sz Infoprint [072]
FIGARO MADAME – 1994-1995 – 6 times per yr – 1 – F3,200.00 – sz Infoprint [072]
FIGARO MAGAZINE – 1989-1993 – 3 times per yr – 6 – F2,800.00 – sz Infoprint [072]
FIGARO MAGAZINE – 1994-1995 – 6 times per yr – 1 – F3,200.00 – sz Infoprint [072]
FIGARO-REVUE – Quebec, Canada. 26 mai 1863 – 1r – 1 – Can$25.00 – cn Can Microfilming [072]
FIGARO'S CHRONIK *see* LANDSTREICHER
FIGAROSCOPE – 1991-1993 – 2 times per yr – 6 – F2,400.00 – sz Infoprint [072]
FIG-ECO – 1991-1995 – 2 times per yr – 6 – F2,400.00 – sz Infoprint [072]
Figgis, John Neville *see*
- ANTICHRIST AND OTHER SERMONS
- CHRISTIANITY AND HISTORY
- CHURCHES IN THE MODERN STATE
- CIVILISATION AT THE CROSS ROADS
- THE DIVINE RIGHT OF KINGS
- THE FELLOWSHIP OF THE MYSTERY
- THE GOSPEL AND HUMAN NEEDS
- LECTURES ON MODERN HISTORY
- LECTURES ON THE FRENCH REVOLUTION
- RELIGION AND ENGLISH SOCIETY

FIGHT CRIME, HELP THE DELINQUENTS AND LOVE HUMANITY / Gunzburg, Nico – In Indonesian. SE-3506 1. 1956.m – 9 – ne IDC [360]
THE FIGHT IN THE BEECHWOODS: A STUDY IN CANADIAN HISTORY / Cruikshank, Ernest Alexander – Welland Ont.: W. Sawle, 1889. 02228. (Pre-1900 Canadiana) – 9 – cn C.I.H.M. [971]
A FIGHT WITH DISTANCES: THE STATES, THE HAWAIIAN ISLANDS, CANADA, BRITISH COLUMBIA, CUBA, THE BAHAMAS / Aubertin, John James – London: Kegan Paul, Trench, 1888. 00052. (Pre-1900 Canadiana) – 9 – cn C.I.H.M. [970]
FIGHTER : OFFICIAL PUBLICATION OF THE REVOLUTIONARY COUNCIL OF THE HUNGARIA FREEDOM FIGHTER MOVEMENT – Cleveland: The Council, v5-8 n1/2 feb 1979-mar 1982 – 1r – 1 – us Res Libr [071]
FIGHTING APARTHEID : A CARTOON HISTORY – 1988 – 9 – 92-3-102503-1 – Co-publication: International Defence and Aid Fund for Southern Africa (IDAF)/Unesco. IDAF have exclusive sales rights in the UK – fr UNESCO [320]
FIGHTING CHINA'S FAMINES / Baker, John Earl – 1943. Typed manuscript. 1 reel – 1 – us U.W. Library [956]
"THE FIGHTING CUSTERS" / Sibrava, Frank – 1 – us KS Hist [978]
THE FIGHTING MECHANIC – Reno, NV. Aug-Nov 1918 – 1r – 1 – $50.00 – U04671 – us Library Micro [071]
FIGHTING MEN OF ILLINOIS – Chicago, 1918. (Illinois Reel 20). (The Cox Library Collection) – 5 – us Americana [978]
FIGHTING TALK – 1954-62 – 1 – uk Microform Academic [960]
FIGHTING TALK – Johannesburg. Republic of South Africa. v. 10, no. 1-v. 17, no. 2. Jan. 1954-Feb. 1963 (gaps) – 1 – 35.00r – us Hoover Inst Photo [072]
FIGHTING THE MILL CREEKS / Anderson, Robert – 1909 – 1r – 1 – $50.00 – B63017 – us Library Micro [978]
FIGHTING WORKER: REVOLUTIONARY WORKERS LEAGUE OF THE U.S – v1-12. no. 11 (all publ). 1936-1947 – 1 reel – 1 – $115.00 – us UPA [335]
Figlio, D *see* SIX TRIOS FOR TWO GERMAN FLUTES OR 2 VIOLINS WITH A VIOLONCELLO OBLIGATO, OP. 4
FIGUEIREDO DE ESTUDIOS DE HISTORIA AMERICANA / Bayle, Constantino – S. Paulo, 1929; Madrid: Razon y Fe, 1931 – 1 – sp Bibl Santa Ana [370]
FIGUELO – (Backfile 3r per y $85r) – Hungary, 1999- – 3r per y standing order – 1 – us Ross [072]
Figueres *see* LES NOMS REVOLUTIONNAIRES DES COMMUNES DE FRANCE, PAR DEPARTEMENT ET ORDRE ALPHABETIQUE... L'HISTOIRE DE LA REVOLUTION FRANCAISE
Figueroa, F *see*
- DE UNA ESPECIE DE GARROTILLO O ESQUILENCIA MORTAL
- LIBRO DE LAS CALIDADES Y EFFECTOS DE LA ALOXA

Figueroa, Jose R *see* EXPEDITING SETTLEMENT OF EMPLOYEE GRIEVANCES IN THE FEDERAL SECTOR
Figueroa y Melgar, Alfonso de *see*
- ESPANOLES FUERA DE ESPANA
- LITERATOS CACERENSES
- PREGON DE LAS FIESTAS PATRONALES DE TRUJILLO, PRONUNCIADO EN SEPTIEMBRE DE 1970, POR EL EXCMO. SR. D. ALFONSO DE FIGUEROA Y MELGAR, DUQUE DE TOVAR
- LOS SUAREZ DE FIGUEROA, DE FERIA Y ZAFRA

Figueroa-Cruz, Blas E *see* A HISTORICAL DOCUMENTATION, AN INSTRUCTIONAL MANUAL AND AN ANNOTATED BIBLIOGRAPHY OF SELECTED FOLK DANCES OF PUERTO RICO
Figuerola, Francisco Jose *see* EL HUMANISMO JUSTICIALISTA EN LA ERA TECNOTRONICA
Figuerolas, H *see* EVOLUTION DES SYSTEMES DE CHARGES EN MESO-AMERIQUE AU XXE SIECLE
FIGURAS CONTEMPORANEAS – Madrid: Imp. Plaza de los Montenses 7, 1913 – 1 – sp Bibl Santa Ana [946]
FIGURAS ILUSTRES / Gutierrez Macias, Valeriano – Badajos: Imp. Diputacion Provincial, 1965. Sep. REE – sp Bibl Santa Ana [920]
FIGURAS Y FIGURONES, BIOGRAFIAS DE LOS HOMBRES QUE MAS FIGURAN ACTUALMENTE EN ESPANA. 2 VOL / Segovia, A – Madrid, 1877-78 – 52mf – 9 – sp Cultura [946]
LA FIGURE DE LA TERRE DETERMINEE PAR LES OBSERVATIONS FAITES PAR ORDRE DU ROY AU CERCLE POLAIRE / Maupertuis, Pierre-Louis M de – Paris, 1738, 184 p., 10 pl. Histoire des Sciences XVIIe-XIXe Siecles. 7970 – 9 – fr Hachette [520]
FIGUREN- UND KONFLIKTDARSTELLUNG BEI FRIEDRICH SPIELHAGEN, THEODOR FONTANE, FERDINAND VON SAAR, EDUARD VON KEYSERLING : EINE VERGLEICHENDE UNTERSUCHUNG DER ERZAEHLUNGEN "ZUM ZEITVERTREIB", "EFFIE BRIEST", "SCHLOSS KOSTENITZ" UND "AM SUEDHANG" / Manko, Mandane – 1995 – 3mf – 9 – DM98.00 – 3-8267-2105-5 – gw Hänsel [430]
FIGUREN-ATLAS ZU DEN ORCHIDACEEN VON DEUTSCH-NEU-GUINEA / Schlechter, R – Berlin. v22. 1923-1928 – 11mf – ne IDC [580]
FIGUREN-ATLAS ZU DEN ORCHIDEEN FLOREN DER SUEDAMERIKANISCHEN KORDILLERENSTAATEN / Schlechter, R – Dahlem bei Berlin. v57. 1929 – 4mf – ne IDC [580]
FIGURES DE COROT / Reunion des musees nationaux. Paris – 1962. 83 illus. 3 fiches – 9 – fr Réunion [700]
FIGURES DE LA FLORE DES PYRENEES / Lapeyrouse, P P de – Paris. 1795. B-5561 2 – 8 – ne IDC [580]
FIGURES NANTAISES... / Eudel, Paul – (Vol. 1 – Rennes: Impr. de l'"Ouest-Eclair", 1909; Vol.2. – Nantes: Impr. du Commerce, 1911) – 1 – F248.59 – fr Armell [910]
FIGURES OF THE MOST BEAUTIFUL, USEFUL AND UNCOMMON PLANTS DESCRIBED IN THE GARDENERS DICTIONARY / Miller, P – London, 1755-1760. 2 vols. B-243 2 – 8 – ne IDC [580]
FIGURES PEINTES DES CHAMPIGNONS DE LA FRANCE. 1881-1893. SUITES A L'ICONOGRAPHIE DE BULLIARD. B-5101/1 / Lucand, J L – 9 – ne IDC [580]
FIGURONES Y ESTAMPAS. CARACAS, 1937 / Zaraza, Lorenzo A – Madrid: Razon y Fe, 1940 – 1 – sp Bibl Santa Ana [700]
FIGYELO – Budapest, 1976-1993ff – 22r – 1 – DM1,650.00 – gw Mikro Press [949]
FIGYELO – (Yrly reel count varies) – 1976- – 1 – us Ross [072]
FIGYELOT – 1976-1995 – 4 times per yr – 1 – F519.00 – sz Infoprint [072]
FIHRIST AL-KUTUB (AL-MAKHTUTAT) AL-'ARABIYAH AL-MAHFUZAH BI-AL-KUTUBKHANAH AL-KHIDIWIYAH – Cairo, Egypt: Al-Kutubkhanah al-Khidiwiyah, 1308-1310 H. (1890-1892). 2d Impression. v1-7 – $200.00 – us MEDOC [470]
Fiji *see*
- DEVELOPMENT PLAN, 1948-1960 ESTIMATES, 1957
- DEVELOPMENT PLAN, 1961-65
- DEVELOPMENT PLAN, 1964-1968 (DEVELOPMENT PLAN 4)
- DEVELOPMENT-PROGRESS REPORT
- REPORT OF THE DEVELOPMENT REVISION COMMITTEE, REVISED TEN-YEAR DEVELOPMENT PLAN, 1949-1958

Fiji. Central Planning Office *see*
- DEVELOPMENT PLAN, 1966-1970 DEVELOPMENT PLANNING REVIEW
- DEVELOPMENT PLAN, 1966-1970 OUTLINE AND PUBLIC EXP
- DEVELOPMENT PLAN, 1971-1975

FIJI COURT OF APPEAL : JUDGEMENTS, 1949-1996; TOGETHER WITH PRIVY COUNCIL JUDGEMENTS RELATING TO FIJI CASES, 1936-1986 – r1-12 – 1 – PMB 1137 – at Pacific Mss [340]
Fiji Independent News Service *see* ARCHIVES, 1987-1992
Fiji. Methodist Church *see* CIRCUIT REPORTS, 1835-1898, AND THE SWANSTON COLLECTION ON THE RA AND BA MILITARY CAMPAIGNS, 1873
Fiji. Ministry of Education *see* REPORT FOR THE YEAR 1977-1986
FIJI ROYAL GAZETTE – Suva, 1944-68 – 9r – 1 – us Ross [324]
Fiji. Teacher Education Planning Committee *see* FIRST REPORT 1970
Fiji Trades Union Congress *see* ARCHIVES, 1962-1994
Fikenscher, Georg Wolfgang Augustin *see* GELEHRTES FUERSTENTHUM BAIREUT
FILANTROPIA SOSPECHOSA / Bayle, Constantino – Madrid: Razon y Fe, 1925 – 1 – sp Bibl Santa Ana [946]
EL FILANTROPO – Progresso humano, y classificacaion general de los Partidos Politicos. Paris, 20 de mayo 1832, Lachevardiere, 4 p. Les Saint-Simoniens, 1825-1834. 6901 – 9 – fr Hachette [320]
Filaret, Mitropolit M *see*
- PIS'MA K ARKHIMANDRITU ANTONIIU, 1831-1867
- PIS'MA K VYSOCHAISHIM OSOBAM I RAZNYM DRUGIM LITSAM

FILASTIN – (Missing: 1948(May-Dec.); 1949(Jan., Sept.-Dec.); 1951(July-Dec.); 1952(Sept.-Dec.); 1953-1955(Jan.)) – Jaffa, Jerusalem, 1911-1914, 1921-1967(March) – 99r – 1 – J-93-7/3 – ne IDC [072]
FILASTIN – Jaffa: I D Elissa, 1956-mar 21 1967 – 31r – us Res Libr [072]
Filatov, VB *see*
- NOVYI ZAKON O PROMYSLOVOI KOOPERATSII 11 MAIA 1927 G. S POSTATEINYMI RAZ"IASNENIIAMI
- PROMYSLOVOE KOOPERATIVNOE TOVARISHCHESTVO (ARTEL')

LA FILATURE DE COTON DANS LE NORD DE LA FRANCE / Houdoy, Jules – Paris. 1903. (La Condition Ouvriere. Part Two.) – 9 – 12.50 – fr Bibl Nationale [360]
FILE – (Microfilm available to v6 1984/85 only. v1-3 1972-77 Can$115.00) – Toronto. v1-6. 1972-1984/85 – 1 – Can$60.00y – cn Micromedia [073]
FILE NOTE : MANPOWER ASSESSMENT / Swaziland Labour Department – [S.l: s.n., 196-?] – us Res Libr [331]
FILE OF CORRESPONDENCE RELATING TO EMIN PASHA EXTRACTED FROM THE ZANZIBAR ARCHIVES / ed by Gray, John – [s.l: s.n.], 1971 – 1 – us Res Libr [960]
Filelfe, Francois *see* CENT-DIX LETTRES GRECQUES
Fileppeli, Ronald L *see* THE SOCIALIST PARTY OF THE UNITED STATES
FILES / Baptist Faith and Message Committee – 1962-63. 728p – 1 – 25.48 – us Baptist [240]
FILES CONCERNING BENGAL, 1927-1947 / Indian National Congress. All-India Congress Committee – Chicago, IL: Uni of Chicago Photodup Dept, 1973 (mf ed) – 1 – us Res Libr [950]
FILES ON THE JOHN FRUM MOVEMENT / New Hebrides British Service. Southern District Administration – Tanna, 1947-56 – 1r – 1 – PMB 1133 – at Pacific Mss [350]
O FILHOTE : ORGAO DE APREDIZAGEM DA MOCIDADE – Cuiaba, 5 Mar 1899 – 1,5,6 – bl Biblioteca [072]
Filiarchi, C *see* TRATTATO DELLA GVERRA, ET DELL' VNIONE DE' PRINCIPI CHRISTIANI CONTRA I TURCHI, ET GLI ALTRI INFEDELI
Filiatrault, AR *see* L'ECHO MUSICAL
Filiatrault, Aristide *see* CANADA ARTISTIQUE
FILICES AFRICANAE / Kuhn, M – Lipsiae. 1868. B-5210 2 – 8 – ne IDC [580]
FILICES AFRICANEA / Kuhn, M – 1868 – 7 – uk Microform Academic [580]
FILICES BRITANNICAE / Bolton, J – 2pts. Leeds, London etc. 1785-90. With descriptive letterpress. B-7162 1 – 9 – ne IDC [580]
FILICES DECKENIANAE / Kuhn, M – Lipsiae. 1867. B-7208 1 – 9 – ne IDC [580]
FILICES EUROPAE ET ATLANTIDIS, ASIAE MINORIS ET SIBIRIAE / Milde, J – Lipsiae, 1867, 311 pp. B-7231 1 – 9 – ne IDC [580]
FILICES EXOTICAE; OR COLOURED FIGURES AND DESCRIPTIONS OF EXOTIC FERNS, CHIEFLY OF SUCH AS ARE CULTIVATED IN THE ROYAL GARDENS OF KEW / Hooker, W J – London. 1859. B-7196 2 – 8 – ne IDC [580]
FILICES HORTI BOTANICI LIPSIENSIS / Mettenius, G H – 1856 – 1 – uk Microform Academic [580]
FILICES HORTI BOTANICI LIPSIENSIS / Mettenius, G H – Leipzig, 1856. 135 pp., 30 pls. B-1252 2 – 8 – ne IDC [580]
FILICES IN CHARLES WILKES' U.S. EXPLORING EXPEDITION / Brackenridge, W D – v16. 1854 – 1 – uk Microform Academic [580]
FILICES JAVANICAE SEU OBSERVATIONES BOTANICAE,... / Hasskarl, J K – Bataviae, 1856 – 1mf – 9 – ne IDC [580]

FILICES LECHLERIANAE, CHILENSES AC PERUANAE, CURA R. F. HOHENACKERI EDITAE / Mettenius, G H – Lipsiae, 1856-1859. 2 Fasc. 30, 38 pp., 2 pls. B-7227 1 – 9 – ne IDC [580]
FILICES SAXONICAE / Wuensche, F O – 7281. Ed. 2. 1878 – 9 – ne IDC [580]
FILICETUM AMERICANUM SEU FILICUM / Plumier, C – 1703 – 1 – uk Microform Academic [580]
FILICUM BEROLINENSIUM SYNOPSIS / Strempel, J C F – Berolini, 1822. 48 pp., 1 pl. B-7267 1 – 9 – ne IDC [580]
FILICUM GENERA ET SPECIES / Hedwig, J – Lipsiae. 1799-1803. B-442 2 – 8 – ne IDC [580]
FILICUM SPECIES IN HORTO REGIO BOTANICO BEROLINENSI CULTAE / Link, J H F – Berolini. 1841. B-6034 2 – 8 – ne IDC [580]
LES FILIGRAINES: A HISTORICAL DICTIONARY OF WATERMARKS, 1923 / Briquet, C M – 1 – uk Microform Academic [010]
Filion, Gerard *see* LA TERRE DE CHEZ-NOUS
FILIPINO LANGUAGE LEXICON / Enriquez, Jose T & Abasolo-Enriquez, Lorenza; ed by Balmaceda, Julian C – Manila: Jose C Velo, c1958 – us Res Libr [040]
EL FILIPINO LIBRE – Manila: M Xerez y Burgos, feb 13 1900 – us Res Libr [072]
THE FILIPINO NATIONAL LANGUAGE / Panganiban, Cirio H – Bruxelles: International Institute of Differing Civilizations, 1952 – us Res Libr [490]
FILIPINO-ENGLISH VOCABULARY, WITH PRACTICAL EXAMPLES OF FILIPINO AND ENGLISH GRAMMARS / Daluz, Eusebio T – First ed. Manila, 1915 – 1 – us U.W. Library [490]
Filipoov, N G *see* CHTO CHITAT' PO ISTORII KOMMUNISTICHESKOI PARTII SOVETS-KOGO SOIUZA
Filipov, I Urii Dmitrievich *see* OCHERK USLOVI I RAZVITII A OTECHESTVENNAGO TORGOVAGO MOREPLAVANIIA
Filipowicz, Tytus *see* POLSKA I AUTONOMIA
Filippo, Virgilio *see*
- CONFABULACION CONTRA LA ARGENTINA
- EL PLAN QUINQUENAL DE PERON Y LOS COMUNISTAS

Filippov, L P et al *see* DISSIPATIVNYE SVOISTVA METALLOV I METALLICHESKIKH SPLAVOV
Filippov, M S *see* ISTORIIA BIBLIOTEKI AKADEMII NAUK SSSR, 1714-1964
Filippov, PO *see* PERVOE MINISTERSTVO SVOBODNOI ROSSII
Filippov, ST *see* BOEVYE DEISTVIIA NA ZAKASPIISKOM FRONTE, 1918-1920 G.G.
Filippov, T *see* SBORNIK
Filippov, V V *see* GELMINTOZY CHELOVEKA, ZHIVOTNYKH, RASTENII I MERY BORBY S NIMI
Filippova, L P *see* DISSIPATIVNYE SVOISTVA METALLOV I METALLICHESKIKH SPLAVOV
Filips, Teri L *see* MEANING AND SURVIVAL
FILIPSTADS STADS OCH BERGSLAGS TIDNING – Filipstad, Sweden. 1850-1958 – 1 – sw Kungliga [072]
FILIPSTADS TIDNING – (Varmlandsberg, 1963-74) – Filipstad, Sweden. 1959- – 1 – sw Kungliga [072]
FILIPSTADSPOSTEN – Filipstad, 1991-92 – 9 – sw Kungliga [072]
LA FILLE DE MO-TCH'O QAGHAN ET SES RAPPORTS AVEC KUL-TEGIN / Pelliot, P – T'oung Pao, v. 13. 1912. BU-596 2 – 8 – ne IDC [305]
LA FILLE DU PEUPLE / Michel, Louise – Paris: Librairie Nationale, 1883. 796p. (Les Femmes Collection) – 9mf – 9 – $22.00 – fr Bibl Nationale [830]
Fillebrown, C B *see* THE A B C OF TAXATION
LA FILLEUL DE L'EVOQUE / Chervet, Eugenie-Caroline Saffray – Paris: P. Lethielleux, 1866. 301p. 4 fiches. (Literature Collection) – 9 – 10.00 – fr Bibl Nationale [830]
FILLEY REPUBLICAN – Filley, NE. -w. Oct. 1895-Oct. 1896; Mar. 1897-Jan. 1898; Mar. 1898-May 1900, incomplete – 1 – us NE Hist [071]
FILLEY REVIEW – Filley, NE. -w. Feb. 1890-Nov. 1890; Nov. 1892 – 1 – us NE Hist [071]
FILLEY SPOTLIGHT – Filley, NE. -w. Nov. 1915-Oct. 1917; Aug. 1918-Dec. 1926 – 1 – us NE Hist [071]
FILLMORE CHRONICLE – Fairmont, NE. -w. May 1872-Sept 1884 (scattered issues missing); May 1895-Apr 1957 – 1 – us NE Hist [071]
FILLMORE COUNTY NEWS – Exeter, NE. -w. Jan. 1893-Dec. 1894. Incomplete; Jul. 1895- – 1 – us NE Hist [071]
THE FILLMORE SUN – Fillmore, CA. 1917-1918 – 1r – 1 – $50.00 – C03595 – us Library Micro [071]
DER FILM – 1916-1943 – Cumul – 1 – DM2,500.00 – sz Infoprint [072]
DER FILM – Berlin, 1916-apr 23 1943 – 26r – 1 – DM2,470.00 set DM95.00r – gw Mikro Press [073]
DER FILM – Berlin. nov 15, 1927-dec 24, 1931 – 1 – gw Mikrofilm [790]
FILM / The British Federation of Film Societies – 1954-93. Continued annually – 1 – £550.00 – uk World [790]
LE FILM – Hebdomadaire illustre. Cinematographe theatre, concert, music-hall. Paris. fevr-juil 1914, avr 1916-18, dec 1919-20 – 1 – fr A.C.R.P.P. [790]
FILM AND TELEVISION CATEGORY / The NewsBank Review of the Arts – 1975-. Monthly index with cumulations – 9 – us NewsBank [790]
FILM AND TELEVISION DAILY – New York. v1-80. 1915-41 – 30r – 1 – us Ross [071]
FILM AND VIDEO LENDING COLLECTION 1/2 INCH VHS CATALOGUE / National Library of Australia – 1990- – A$12.50y – at Nat'l Libr [790]
FILM AND VIDEO LENDING COLLECTION CATALOGUE / National Library of Australia – 1990- – 9 – A$24.95y – at Nat'l Libr [790]
FILM AND VIDEO REVIEW INDEX – v. 1-. 1978- – 1,5,6,9 – us UMI [790]
FILM ANIMATION : A SIMPLIFIED APPROACH – 2nd ed 1979 – 92p – 9 – 92-3-101367-X – fr UNESCO [770]
FILM ART : AN INDEPENDENT QUARTERLY DEVOTED TO THE SERIOUS FILM – v1-3. 1934-36 – 1r – 1 – us Ross [073]
FILM ART – London. v. 1 no. 3-v. 3 no. 8. Spring 1934-1936 – 1 – us NY Public [790]
FILM CANADIANA – (Cont by: Film/Video Canadiana 1985-86) – Montreal, 1969-1984 – 9 – Can$20.00y – cn Micromedia [790]
FILM CANADIANA *see* FILM/VIDEO CANADIANA
THE FILM CATALOG: A LIST OF FILM HOLDINGS / Museum of Modern Art. New York – 1985.-1 reel.-ISBN: 0-8161-1562-1 – 1 – $65.00 – uk Hall [790]
FILM COMMENT – 1- 1962- 1; v7- 5,6; v12- 9 – us UMI [790]
FILM DAILY *see* MAJOR FILM PERIODICALS FOR MEDIA RESEARCH, SERIES 1
FILM FUER ALLE – Berlin. 1928-feb 1935 (incomplete) – 1r – 1 – gw Mikrofilm [790]
FILM FUER ALLE – Berlin, 1929-36 – 1 – Dist. gw Mikrofilm – gw Mikrofilm [790]
FILM JOURNALS FROM GREAT BRITAIN AND AUSTRALIA – (Afterimage, 1970-85; The Australian Journal of Screen Theory, 1976-85; Framework, 1975-85; Historical Journal of Film, Radio and Television, 1981-85; Primetime, 1981-85; Undercut, 1981-85) – 1 – $530.00 set; $95.00 ea – us UPA [790]
FILM JOURNALS FROM THE UNITED STATES AND CANADA – (Camera Obscura. No.1-12, Fall 1976-Summer 1984. 1 reel; Cine-Tracts. No.1-17, Spring 1977-Fall 1982. 1 reel; Dreamworks. v1,no.1-v3,no.4. Spring 1980-84. 1 reel; Film Criticism. v1,no.1-v9,no.1. Spring 1976-Fall 1984. 1 reel; Film Reader. No.1-5. 1975-82. 1 reel; Millennium Film Journal. No.1-13. Winter 1977/78-Fall/Winter 1983/84. 1 reel) – 1 – $530.00 set; $95.00 ea – us UPA [790]
FILM QUARTERLY – (v. 24- 1970- 5,6,9) – 1-1945- – 1 – us UMI [790]
FILM, TELEVISION AND MASS COMMUNICATION 1949-1977 (PVB 1895-1977, PT 2) – (With printed bibliography & subject index) – 488mf – 9 – £1,955.00 – uk Chadwyck [790]
FILM UND BRETTL – Berlin. apr 1919-aug 1923 – 1 – gw Mikrofilm [790]
FILM UND KINO – Berlin/Muenchen. 1918-jan 26, 1919 – 1 – gw Mikrofilm [790]
FILM UND PRESSE – Berlin. jul 1920-21 – 1r – 1 – gw Mikrofilm [790]
FILM WEEKLY, 1928-1939 – oct 1928-sep 1939 – 235mf – 9 – £830.00 – uk Chadwyck [790]
FILMA – Revue photo-phonocinematographique puis Revue cinematographique. Dir. A. Millo. Paris. juin-dec 1908, fevr 1917-mai 1921, 1924-juil 1928, 1930-sept 1936 – 1 – fr A.C.R.P.P. [490]
FILM-ALMANACH – Berlin. 1917.1920 – 1 – gw Mikrofilm [790]
FILM-ATELIER : DIE ZEITUNG FUER DEN PRODUKTIONS-FACHMANN – Berlin. apr 10, 1929-mar 15, 1936 – 1 – gw Mikrofilm [790]
FILM-EXPRESS / ed by Redaktion der "Lichtbild-Buehne" – Berlin. oct-dec 1920 – 1 – gw Mikrofilm [790]
DER FILMHANDEL – Berlin. jul 6, 1919-jan 21, 1921 (incomplete) – 1 – gw Mikrofilm [380]
FILM-HOELLE – Berlin, 1920-23 (incomplete) – 1 – Dist. gw Mikrofilm – gw Misc Inst [790]
FILM-HOELLE – Berlin. jan, jun-jul, dec 1922. apr-mai 1923 – 1 – gw Mikrofilm [790]
FILMJOURNALEN – Stockholm, 1919-53 – 28r – 1 – sw Kungliga [790]
FILMKUNST – Berlin. may 30-aug 1, 1913 (incomplete) – 1 – gw Mikrofilm [790]
FILM-KURIER – Berlin, apr 30 1919-sep 29 1944 – 1 – Dist. gw Mikrofilm – gw Mikrofilm [790]
FILM-KURIER – Berlin. apr 30, 1919-sep 29, 1944 (incomplete) – 37r – 1 – gw Mikrofilm [790]
FILM-NACHRICHTEN – Berlin. oct 7, 1944-mar 24, 1945 – 1r – 1 – gw Mikrofilm [790]
FILMS IN REVIEW – New York NY. Feb 1950-Dec 1960 – 1 – us U.O. Library [071]
FILMS IN REVIEW – (v.30 .1979 5,6,9) – v.1. 1950 – 1 – us UMI [790]
FILMSCHAU – Berlin. oct 25, 1919. dec 20, 1919. n4 1920 – 1 – gw Mikrofilm [790]
DER FILM-SPIEGEL – Berlin, DE. 4 Oct 1925-Jul 1933 – 1 – gw Mikrofilm [790]
FILMSPIEGEL – 1970-1974, 1976-1983 – 437mf – 1 – DM2,490.90 – gw Mikro Press [790]
FILMTECHNIK – Berlin. 1929-44. oct 1947-jun 1948 – 5r – 1 – gw Mikrofilm [790]
FILM-TRIBUENE – Berlin. jun 30, 1919-jan 23, 1920 (incomplete). nov 14, 1920-nov 22, 1921 (incomplete) – 1 – gw Mikrofilm [790]
FILM/VIDEO CANADIANA – (Cont: Film Canadiana, 1985/86. Ceased 1987/88) – Montreal, 1985-1987/88 – 9 – Can$28.00y – cn Micromedia [790]
FILM/VIDEO CANADIANA *see* FILM CANADIANA
FILMWISSENSCHAFTLICHE BEITRAGE – 1969-1; 1974- 5,6; 1975- 9 – us UMI [770]
DIE FILMWOCHE – Wien, mar 16 1913-sep 21 1918 – 7r – 1 – gw Mikrofilm [790]
FILOLOGICHESKIIA ZAPISKI – Voronezh. 1860-1916. Lacking: 1861 (1), 1864 (6), 1865 (4-6), 1866 (6), 1868 (4-6), 1897 (5-6). B-1727 2 – 8 – ne IDC [400]
FILOSOFIA CRISTIANA. TOMO 2: PROLEGOMENOS / Torre Isunza de Hita, Ramon – Madrid: Imp. y Lit. de Felipe Gonzalez Rojas, 1901. Tambien Tomo 3 – 9 – sp Bibl Santa Ana [240]
LA FILOSOFIA DE CALDERON EN SUS AUTOS SACRAMENTALES / Frutos Cortes, Eugenio – Zaragoza: Institucion Fernando el Catolico de la Dip. Prov., 1952 – sp Bibl Santa Ana [440]
FILOSOFIA DE LA ELOCUENCIA / Capmany Montpalau, Antonio – 1777 – 1mf – 9 – Pta1,000.00 – 84-7848-036-6 – sp Pentalfa [100]
FILOSOFIA DE LA NATURALEZA / Nieto y Serrano, M – Madrid, 1884 – 6mf – 9 – sp Cultura [100]
LA FILOSOFIA DE LA NATURALEZA Y LA PSICOLOGIA SEGUN IBN HAZM / Gomez Nogales, Salvador – Milano: Societa Editrice Vita e Pensiero, 1964 – 9 – sp Bibl Santa Ana [180]
FILOSOFIA DE LA PRESENCIA HUMANA / Caba, Pedro – Mexico: Editorial Herrero, 1961 – sp Bibl Santa Ana [100]
FILOSOFIA DE LO MARAVILLOSO POSITIVO / Sanchez Calvo, Estanislao – 1889. Libros en Microficha no 13 – 1mf – 9 – Pta1,000.00 – 84-85422-40-6 – sp Pentalfa [190]
LA FILOSOFIA DEL CONOCIMIENTO DE SAN AGUSTIN / Caba, Pedro – Madrid – sp Bibl Santa Ana [240]
LA FILOSOFIA DEL NO-SER EN EL PENSAMIENTO GRIEGO (ANAXIMANDRO-PLATON) / Caba, Pedro – Madrid, 1957. Revista Crisis, Ano 4, no 13. Enero-Marzo 1957 – sp Blbl Santa Ana [100]
LA FILOSOFIA EN LA CIENCIA. ENSAYO SOBRE EL CONCEPTO Y CONDICIONES DE AMBAS... / Moreno Izquierdo, Juan – Madrid: Enrique Teodoro, 1882 – 1 – sp Bibl Santa Ana [100]
LA FILOSOFIA ESPANOLA : INDICACIONES BIBLIOGRAFICAS / Vidart Schuch, Luis – 1866. Libros en Microficha no 6 – 2mf – 9 – Pta1,500.00 – 84-85422-31-7 – sp Pentalfa [190]
LA FILOSOFIA JURIDICA DEL PROFESOR DE ASIS GARROTE / Elias de Tejada Spinola, Francisco – Sevilla: Imp. Gonzalez-Cabanas, 1970 – 1 – sp Bibl Santa Ana [190]
LA FILOSOFIA JURIDICA EN LA ESPANA ACTUAL / Elias de Tejada Spinola, Francisco – Madrid: Instituto Editorial Reus, 1949 – 1 – sp Bibl Santa Ana [190]
FILOSOFIA MORAL / Aristoteles – 1692. Derivada de Aristoteles de Manuel Thesauro, traducela Don Gomez de la Roca y Figueroa – 9 – 1.50f – sp Bibl Santa Ana [170]
FILOSOFIA MORAL / Aristotle – 1715. Derivada de Aristoteles de Manuel Thesauro, traducela Don Gomez de la Roca y Figueroa – 9 – $1.50f – sp Bibl Santa Ana [170]
FILOSOFIA MORAL / Marquez, Gabino – Madrid: Prensa Nueva, 4th ed 1927 – 1 – sp Bibl Santa Ana [170]
FILOSOFIA MORAL / Rocha y Figueroa, Gomez – Lisboa: Antonio de Creesbeck de Mello, 1682 – 1 – sp Bibl Santa Ana [170]
FILOSOFIA MORAL DERIVADA DE ARISTOTELES / Tesauro, Emanuel – 1770, 1750, 1723 – 9 – $1.50f – sp Bibl Santa Ana [170]
FILOSOFIA MORAL, DERIVADA DE LA ALTA FUENTE DEL GRANDE ARISTOTELES / Tesauro, Emanuel – Madrid: Juan de Zuniga, 1733 – 1 – sp Bibl Santa Ana [170]
FILOSOFIA MORAL DERIVADA DE LA ALTA... DEL GRANDE ARISTOTELES. TRADUCIDA EN ESPANOL D. IUAN LUIS DE ORLEANS... / Thesauro, Manuel – Lisboa: Imp. de Antonio Craesbeeck Mello, 1682 – 1 – sp Bibl Santa Ana [170]
FILOSOFIA MORAL PARA LA JUVENTUD ESPANOLA / Piquer, Andres – Madrid, 1775 – 12mf – 9 – sp Cultura [170]
FILOSOFIA MORAL. TOMO 2. LA MORALIDAD EN PARTICULAR, O SEA, EL DERECHO NATURAL / Marquez, Gabino – Madrid: Escelicer, S.A. 5th ed 1942 – 1 – sp Bibl Santa Ana [170]
FILOSOFIA Y FISIOLOGIA COMPARADAS EN SU HISTORIA CON EL CRITERIO DE LA CIENCIA VIVIENTE... 3 VOL / Nieto y Serrano, M – Madrid, 1889-1890 – 17mf – 9 – sp Cultura [612]
FILOSOFIKIE NAUKI – (Philosophy of Science). Moscow. U.S.S.R. 1966- – 1 – us UMI [100]
FILOSOFISCHE UND PATRIOTISCHE TRAEUME EINES MENSCHENFREUNDES / Iselin, Isaak – Freiburg: s.n., 1755. 192p – 1 – us U.W. Library [320]
FILOSOFSKIE OCHERKI / Vvedenskii, A I – Spb. 1901. BR-5805 – 8 – ne IDC [190]
FILOSOFSKII EZHEGODNIK – Ed. by Ia. Kolubovskii. God pervyi 1893. (Voprosy filosofii i psikhologii, v 1894). M. 1894. BR-3412 – 8 – ne IDC [100]
FILOSOFSKII EZHEGODNIK / Kolubovskii, Ia – Obzor knig, statei i zametok, preimushchestvenno na russkom iazyke, imeiushchikh otnoshenie k filosofskim znaniiam. God pervyi i vtoroi, 1893 i 1894. M. 1894-96. BR-5953 2 – 8 – ne IDC [100]
FILOSOFSKOE ZNACHENIE PSIKHOLOGICHESKIKH VOZZRENII DZHEMSA / Lapshin, I I – Spb. 1896. BR-5809 2 – 8 – ne IDC [100]
Filov, B D *see*
- GESCHICHTE DER ALTBULGARISCHEN KUNST BIS ZUR EROBERUNG DES BULGARISCHEN REICHES DURCH DIE TUERKEN
- GESCHICHTE DER BULGARISCHEN KUNST UNTER DER TUERKISCHEN HERRSCHAFT UND IN DER NEUEREN ZEIT

FILS DU SOLEIL – 9 – F20.00 – fr Ethnologie [306]
THE FILSON CLUB HISTORICAL QUARTERLY – v2, 1928-v19, 1945. Some vols. missing.Indexed. F-0510 to F-0523 – 9 – us A.G.L.L. [978]

THE FILSON CLUB & ITS ACTIVITIES – 1884-1922. By Otto A. Rothert. 1922. Indexed.1 fiche. F-0509 – 9 – us A.G.L.L. [920]
Filson, FV *see* THE NEW TESTAMENT AGAINST ITS ENVIRONMENT
Filteau, Louis Honore *see*
- GENEALOGIE DE LA FAMILLE FILTEAU
- GENEALOGY OF THE FAMILY NORMANDEAU, DIT DESLAURIERS
Filtsch, Eugen *see* GOETHE'S STELLUNG ZUR RELIGION
FIMIAMY / Sologub, F – Petrograd. 1921. BR-860 2 – 8 – ne IDC [460]
FIN DE LA ECONOMIA PERONISTA? / Concatti, Rolando – Buenos Aires: Accion Popular Ecumenica, 1976 – 1 – CSUXADH9660-B – us Hoover Inst Photo [330]
LA FIN DE L'EMPIRE ESPAGNOL D'AMERIQUE PAR MARINS ANDRE / Bayle, Constantino – Madrid: Razon y Fe, 1922 – 1 – sp Bibl Santa Ana [972]
FIN DE L'INDEPENDENCE BOHEME / Denis, E – 2v. Paris. 1890. BR-5087 2 – 8 – ne IDC [940]
FIN DE SIECLE / Bahr, Hermann – Berlin: A Zoberbier, 1891 – 1 – us U.W. Library [830]
FIN DE SIECLE – Le sous-titre varie. Paris. 27 dec 1890-1910. A partir du 21 nov 1909 a paru sous le titre de: Le Nouveau siecle. Ex Fin de siecle – 1 – fr A.C.R.P.P. [073]
EL FIN DE UN CICLO HISTORICO EN ARGENTINA / Reissig, Luis – Buenos Aires: S.E.P.A., 1956 – 1 – CSUXADH0581-B – us Hoover Inst Photo [972]
LA FIN DU CHOMAGE PAR LE PARTAGE DU TRAVAIL / Pacault, Emile – Paris. 1902. (La Condition Ouvriere. Part Two.) – 9 – 2.50 – fr Bibl Nationale [360]
LA FIN DU MONDE EN 1911 D'APRES UNE PROPHETIE CELEBRE – St. Hyacinthe Quebec: M. Keroack, 1867. 04319. (Pre-1900 Canadiana) – 9 – cn C.I.H.M. [971]
LA FIN DU PAGANISME : ETUDE SUR LES DERNIERES LUTTES RELIGIEUSES EN OCCIDENT AU QUATRIEME SIECLE / Boissier, Gaston – Paris: Hachette, 1891 – 3mf – us A.T.L.A. [940]
LA FIN D'UN CHRISTIANISME : TROIS CONFERENCES / Monod, Wilfred – Paris: Fischbacher, 1903 – 1mf – 9 – 0-8370-3825-1 – 1985-1825 – us A.T.L.A. [240]
FIN, FUR AND FEATHER – Amherst, NS: C de L Black, [1893-1894?] – 9 – cn C.I.H.M. [630]
FINAL ACCOUNTS / Egypt. Ministry of Finance – 1953-54. BNE-4663 1 – 9 – ne IDC [336]
FINAL ACCOUNTS, 1963-1974 / Lebanon. Ministere des Finances – 12 v. Lacking: 1962 63; 1966 67; 1969 72; 1974. BNE-9673 1 – 9 – ne IDC [336]
FINAL RECORD BOOKS OF THE U.S. CIRCUIT COURT FOR WEST MIDDLE DISTRICT OF TENNESSEE / U.S. Circuit and District Courts. Tennessee – 1839-65. 10 rolls – 1 – M1212 – us Nat'l Archives [324]
FINAL RECORD BOOKS OF THE U.S. DISTRICT COURT FOR WEST TENNESSEE / U.S. Circuit and District Courts. Tennessee – 1803-39. U.S. District Court for the middle district of Tennessee, 1839-50. Land Claims records for West Tennessee, 1807-20. 1 roll – 1 – M1215 – us Nat'l Archives [324]
FINAL REPORT / Singapore. Commission of Inquiry into Education – Singapore, [1964] – 2mf – 9 – DE-260/1 – ne IDC [370]
FINAL REPORT ... JULY 1971 / Hong Kong. Polytechnic Planning Committee – Hong Kong, 1972 – 2mf – 9 – DE-179/1 – ne IDC [370]
FINAL REPORT ... MARCH 1971 / Hong Kong. Industrial Training Advisory Committee – Hong Kong, 1971 – 2mf – 9 – DE-177/1 – ne IDC [370]
FINAL REPORT OF THE DROUGHT INVESTIGATION COMMISSION : OCTOBER 1923 – (Filmed with: Transvaal (Province) Local Government Commission Report) – Cape Town: Cape Times Govt Printers, 1923 – 1 – us Res Libr [960]
FINAL REPORT OF THE PLEBISCITE COMMISSION ON THE PUBLIC INFORMATION PROGRAM AND PLEBISCITE ON THE FUTURE POLITICAL STATUS OF THE FEDERATED STATES OF MICRONESIA / Federated States of Micronesia – Kolonia, Ponape: the Commission, 15 Jul 1983 – 6mf – 9 – $9.00 – LLMC 82-100H Title 8 – us L.L.M.C. [324]
FINAL REPORT ON EDUCATION STATISTICS 1972-1980 / Thailand. Ministry of Education. National Statistical Office and Educational Planning Office – (In Thai and English. Missing: 1973-1977) – Bangkok – 20mf – 9 – DE-272/1 – ne IDC [370]
FINAL REPORT ON NUERNBERG WAR CRIMES TRIALS : FINAL REPORT TO THE SECRETARY OF THE ARMY ON THE NUERNBERG WAR CRIMES TRIALS UNDER CONTROL COUNCIL LAW NO. 10 / Taylor, Telford – 4mf – 9 – $6.00 – LLMC 97-007 – us L.L.M.C. [327]
FINAL REPORT, TOGETHER WITH...MINUTES OF PROCEEDINGS / Papua-New Guinea. House of Assembly. Select Committee on Constitutional Development – Port Moresby, 1971. 32p. LL-2338 – 1 – us L of C Photodup [340]
FINAL REPORTS OF THE U.S. STRATEGIC BOMBING SURVEY / U.S. Army – 1945-47. 25 rolls. M1013 – 1 – us Nat'l Archives [324]
FINAL REVIEW AND WINDING UP OF THE CAPITAL EXPENDITURE PROGRAMME, 1957-62 / Mauritius – (Sessional Paper No. 9 of 1960). Port Louis. 1960. BD-668 1 – 9 – ne IDC [338]
FINAL ROLLS OF CITIZENS AND FREEDMEN OF THE FIVE CIVILIZED TRIBES IN INDIAN TERRITORY (AS APPROVED BY THE SECTY. OF THE INT. ON OR BEFORE MAR. 4, 1907, WITH SUPPLEMENTS DATED SEPT. 25, 1914) / U.S. Department of the Interior. Office of the Secretary – 3rolls. T529 – 1 – us Nat'l Archives [324]
THE FINAL SCIENCE, OR, SPIRITUAL MATERIALISM / Stuckenberg, John Henry Wilburn – New York: Funk & Wagnalls, 1885.1 fiche – 9 – us A.T.L.A. [270]
FINAL STATEMENT TO THE INDIAN PENETRATION COMMISSION APPOINTED BY THE UNION GOVERNMENT OF SOUTH AFRICA, 1940-1941 / Natal Indian Association – [Durban: The Association, 1941] – 1 – us Res Libr [960]
FINALE VERSLAG VAN DIE KOMMISSIE VAN ONDERSOEK NA SEKERE ORGANISASIES 109=CHRISTELIKE INSTITUUT VAN SUIDELIKE AFRIKA = FINAL REPORT OF THE COMMISSION OF INQUIRY INTO CERTAIN ORGANISATIONS. CHRISTIAN INSTITUTE OF SOUTHERN AFRICA – Pretoria: Staatsdrukker, 1975 – us Res Libr [360]
THE FINALITY OF THE CHRISTIAN RELIGION / Foster, George Burman – Chicago: University of Chicago Press, 1906 – 2mf – us A.T.L.A. [240]
FINANCE – Montreal, 1 oct 1979-14 oct 1990f – 17r – 1 – Can$75.00 – cn Can Microfilming [072]
FINANCE ACCOUNTS OF GREAT BRITAIN FOR THE YEAR ENDED 5TH JANUARY... 1801-1817 – (Coll title: British Government Publications...1801-1977, Finance) – 2r – 1 (£2,260.00 finance set of 93mf + 30r) – uk Chadwyck [336]
FINANCE ACCOUNTS OF IRELAND FOR THE YEAR ENDED 5TH JANUARY 1801-1817 – (Coll title: British Government Publications... 1801-1977, Finance) – 1r – 1 (£2,260.00 finance set of 93mf + 30r) – uk Chadwyck [336]
FINANCE ACCOUNTS OF THE UNITED KINGDOM OF GREAT BRITAIN AND IRELAND FOR THE FINANCIAL YEAR ENDED 31ST MARCH...1818-1966 – (Coll title: British Government Publications...1801-1977, Finance) – 9r – 1 (£2,260.00 finance set of 93mf + 30r) – uk Chadwyck [336]
FINANCE AND COMMERCE – Shanghai. China. -w. Jan 1934-May 1941. (13 reels) – 1 – uk British Libr Newspaper [073]
FINANCE AND DEVELOPMENT – (v. 8- 1971- 5,6,9) – v. 1- 1964- – 1 – us UMI [336]
FINANCE AND INDUSTRY – Cleveland, 1900-34 – 32r – 1 – us Ross [071]
[FINANCE AND WORLD WAR 1 PAMPHLET COLLECTION] – 1914-1932 – 2r – 1 – CSUXANL3569-B – us Hoover Inst Photo [332]
FINANCE ANGLAISE – London, UK. 11 Jul 1891 – 1 – uk British Libr Newspaper [072]
LA FINANCE INTERNATIONALE ET LA GUERRE D'ESPAGNE / Bougouin, E – Paris, 1938. Fiche W 761. (Blodgett Collection of Spanish Civil War Pamphlets) – 9 – us H.U. College Libr [946]
FINANCE MANAGEMENT AND ORGANIZATION OF SECOND LEVEL AUTONOMOUS GOVERNMENTS *see* STATE FINANCE ADMINISTRATION; FINANCE MANAGEMENT; ORGANIZATION OF SECOND-LEVEL AUTONOMOUS GOVERNMENT (BY SOEPARDI)
FINANCE PLANS: / Sao Tome and Principe Islands. (Portugal) – (Plano De Fomento (1953-1958). D 1467; 1. 1953. SF 8.00; 9. II Plano De Fomento (1959-1964). D 1183; 1. 1959. SF 8.00; IDC; 9. Plano Intercalar De Fomento Para 1965-1967. D 1468; 1. 1964. SF 8.00; IDC; 9) – ne IDC [336]
FINANCE, SEPTEMBER 1974-JANUARY 1975 : REPORT / Ghana. National Consultative Committee on Education – Accra, 1975 – 1mf – 9 – DE-436/1 – ne IDC [370]
FINANCE-CURRENCY: SPEECH OF HON. MOSES W. FIELD, OF MICHIGAN, IN THE HOUSE OF REPRESENTATIVES, APRIL 8, 1874 / Field, Moses Whelock – Washington D.C.: Govt. Print. Off., 1874. 05466. (Pre-1900 Canadiana) – 9 – cn C.I.H.M. [971]
LE FINANCEMENT DU PLAN, 1953-1957 / French West Africa. Direction Generale des Services Economiques et du Plan – Paris, Diloutremer. 1957. BD-484 1 – 9 – ne IDC [332]
FINANCES PUBLIQUES DU MAROC / Morocco. Ministere de l'Economie Nationale – (Champion, M.) 1961. BNE-3073 1 – 9 – ne IDC [336]
FINANCIAL ACCOUNTS / Legare, James – 1840-64.South Carolina planter. Plantation and personal accounts. 3 fiches – 9 – us South Carolina Historical [978]
FINANCIAL AGE : DEVOTED TO THE INTEREST OF THE MEMBERS OF THE AMERICAN BANKERS ASSOCIATION AND STATE ASSOCIATIONS – New York. v5-82. 1902-40 – 53r – 1 – us Ross [332]
FINANCIAL AID COLLECTION / Career Guidance Foundation – Over 200,000 sources of financial aid are indexed by 10 selection criteria. Includes information on grants, scholarships, loans, fellowships, and work-study programs – 150mf – 9 (cache system) – $299.00 – us Career [370]
FINANCIAL ANALYSIS IN AGRICULTURAL PROJECT PREPARATION – 1991 – 228p – it F.A.O. [332]
FINANCIAL ANALYST JOURNAL – (v1-. 1945-. 5,6. v31-. 1975-. 9) – v. 27- 1971- – 1 – us UMI [336]
FINANCIAL AND COMMERCIAL STATISTICS OF BRITISH INDIA – v. 11-13. Calcutta. 1904-07. Cont. as: Statistics of British India. BI-484 2 – 8 – ne IDC [310]
FINANCIAL AND ECONOMIC AGREEMENT (BETWEEN KINGDOM OF THE NETHERLANDS AND THE GOVERNMENT OF THE REPUBLIK INDONESIA SERIKAT) / Netherlands. Treaties, etc., 1948- – SE-12,022 1. 1949 – 9 – ne IDC [950]
FINANCIAL AND ECONOMIC ANNUAL OF JAPAN, 1901-1929 – (In English) – 3r – 1 – $105.00 in US $40.00r outside – L9400080 – Dist. us Scholarly Res – us L of C Photodup [332]
FINANCIAL AND ECONOMIC LEGISLATION ISSUED BY THE CENTRAL MINISTRIES OF ECONOMY AND TREASURY / Syria. Ministry of Economy and Treasury – 2v. 1957-61. BNE-9713 1 – 9 – ne IDC [330]
FINANCIAL AND ECONOMIC LEGISLATION ISSUED DURING THE REVOLUTIONARY REGIME, 23 JUL 1952-23 JUL 1957 / Egypt. Ministry of Finance – 1960. BNE-4666 1 – 9 – ne IDC [336]
FINANCIAL AND ECONOMIC REVIEW; SPECIAL SUPPLEMENT: 1966/1967 BUDGET / Sudan. Ministry of Finance and Economics – 1967. BNE-7668 1 – 9 – ne IDC [336]
FINANCIAL AND ECONOMIC STATEMENT / Kuwait. Ministry of Finance and Industry – 1v. 1964 65. BNE-9027 1 – 9 – ne IDC [338]
FINANCIAL AND PRODUCT SPONSORSHIP WITHIN ATHLETIC TRAINING PROGRAMS / Sanderson, Natalie – Ball State University, 1996 – 1mf – 9 – PE 3669 – us Microform Publ [790]
A FINANCIAL AND STATISTICAL ANALYSIS OF SWAZILAND'S EDUCATIONAL SYSTEM, WITH PROJECTIONS TO 1986 / Swaziland. Ministry of Education. Education Planning Section – Mbabane, 1978 – 3mf – 9 – DE-480/1 – ne IDC [370]
FINANCIAL CONTROL AND COMPLIANCE MANUAL FOR PRESIDENTIAL PRIMARY CANDIDATES RECEIVING PUBLIC FINANCING – Washington: The Commission, July 1979 (rev 1983, 1987 and 1992) – 3mf – 9 – $4.50 – LLMC 95-025 – us L.L.M.C. [340]
FINANCIAL DATA / Israel. Prime Minister's Office. Ministry of the Interior. Local authorities in Israel 1973 74 – Jerusalem, 1975. 33, 221, 17 p. (Special Series no. 493). Text also in Hebrew – 9 – 6.00 – is I.T.T.I. [336]
FINANCIAL EXECUTIVE – v1-. 1985- – 1,5,6,9 – us UMI [073]
FINANCIAL EXECUTIVE – (v39-. 1971-. 5,6. v45-. 1975-. 9) – v1-52. 1932-84 – 1 – us UMI [380]
FINANCIAL EXECUTIVE *see* FE
FINANCIAL EXPRESS – Bombay, India. 1962-1993 – 125r – 1 – us L of C Photodup [072]
FINANCIAL HISTORY OF THE UNITED STATES / Dewey, Davis R – 7th ed. New York: Longmans, Green & Co, 1920 – 7mf – 9 – $10.50 – LLMC 92-148 – us L.L.M.C. [340]
FINANCIAL MAIL – (From 9th Oct 1987 surveys filmed together with Financial Mail) – Johannesburg, South Africa. 6 Mar 1959- – 168r – 1 – sa Microfile [960]
FINANCIAL MAIL : SURVEYS – Johannesburg, South Africa. 28 Mar 1969-2 Oct 1987 end – 23 rolls – sa Microfile [960]
FINANCIAL MANAGEMENT – (v6-. 1977-. 5,6,9) – v. 1-. 1972- – 1 – us UMI [650]
FINANCIAL NEWS – London. -d. Jan 1885-Dec 1887. (6 reels) – 1 – uk British Libr Newspaper [073]
FINANCIAL PLANNER – (1982-. 1,5,6,9) – v1-. 1972- – 1 – us UMI [073]
FINANCIAL POLICY IN JORDAN / Jordan. Central Bank – 1970. BNE-9756 1 – 9 – ne IDC [336]
FINANCIAL POST – Toronto, 1 apr 1927 – 1r – 1 – Can$25.00 – cn Can Microfilming [072]
FINANCIAL POST – Toronto, 1907-95 – 1,9 – Price varies – cn Micromedia [332]
FINANCIAL POST MAGAZINE – (Publ as Financial Post Moneywise Magazine, 1988-1989) – Toronto, 1981-95 – 9 – Can$40.00y – cn Micromedia [332]
FINANCIAL POST MAGAZINE *see* FINANCIAL POST MONEYWISE MAGAZINE
FINANCIAL POST MONEYWISE MAGAZINE – (Cont by: Financial Post Magazine 1990) – Toronto, 1988-89 – 9 – Can$40.00y – cn Micromedia [332]
FINANCIAL POST MONEYWISE MAGAZINE *see* FINANCIAL POST MAGAZINE
FINANCIAL POST OF CANADA – Toronto, Canada. Financial Post. -w. June 1909-May 1925; June 1967-July 1968. 25 1 2 reels – 1 – uk British Libr Newspaper [072]
FINANCIAL RECORDS / Pratt, Hilton – undated, Records of Cottonwood Ranch, Sheridan County, KS – 1 – us KS Hist [630]
FINANCIAL RECORDS AND JOURNALS / Ridgecrest. North Carolina. Ridgecrest Baptist Assembly – 1909-12, 1911-12; hotel building fund, 1918-20; blue prints; guide map for Blue Mont (now Ridgecrest). 390p – 1 – 13.65 – us Baptist [240]
FINANCIAL REFORMER – Liverpool, England. -w. 1 July-Dec 1878. 4 reels – 1 – uk British Libr Newspaper [072]
FINANCIAL REPORT / Mississippi State University. Cooperative Extension Service – 1957-69 – 1,5,6 – us Spaulding [630]
FINANCIAL REPORT / Mississippi State University. Cooperative Extension Service – 1969-79.1 reel – 1,5 – us Spaulding [630]
FINANCIAL REPORTS / Hancock County. Ohio. Biglick Township. Township Clerk – 1939-1988 gaps in holdings – 1r – 1 – $32.50r – us Archival [324]
FINANCIAL REPORTS / Massachusetts. Comptroller's Division – 1922-77. 154 fiches. (Harvard Law School Library Collection.) – 9 – 1.50f – us H.U. Law [324]
FINANCIAL TIMES – 1888-1959 – 1 – F1,703.00 – sz Infoprint [072]
FINANCIAL TIMES – 1960-1974 – 1 – F4,191.00 – sz Infoprint [072]
FINANCIAL TIMES – 1975-1989 – 1 – F7,465.00 – sz Infoprint [072]
FINANCIAL TIMES – 1990-1994 – 1 – F9,517.00 – sz Infoprint [072]

FINANCIAL TIMES – Frankfurt/Main, DE. Jan 1979- – ca 10r per yr – 1 – gw Mikrofilm [072]
FINANCIAL TIMES – London, England.1888-. Index available, 1981- – 1 – us Primary [072]
FINANCIAL TIMES – Subscription – 1 – F5,937.00 – sz Infoprint [072]
FINANCIAL TIMES – Toronto, 1990-1992 – 6r – 1 – cn Preston [971]
THE FINANCIAL TIMES – Montreal. v1 n24. 30 nov 1912 – 1r – 1 – Can$20.00 – cn Can Microfilming [072]
FINANCIAL TIMES: FOR THE DECISION-MAKER – v70-. 1981- – 1,5,6,9 – us UMI [073]
FINANCIAL TIMES OF CANADA – 1 – $125.00y Positive, 35mm Vesicular Film (Current Year) $150.00y Negative or Positive Silver $100.00y High School Rate Positive Vesicular – cn Globe Info [332]
FINANCIAL TREND – v1-16, no.3. Apr 1970-14-20 Jan 1985 – 1,5,6,9 – us UMI [073]
FINANCIAL TREND *see* AMERICAN LAW REVIEW
FINANCIER FRANCO-ANGLAIS – London, UK. 14 Sept 1899-14 Jun 1900 – 1 – uk British Libr Newspaper [072]
EL FINANCIERO – Mexico City, Mexico. 1990-June 1991 – 18r – 1 – us L of C Photodup [072]
FINANCING OF DEVELOPMENT PROGRAMMES: A REPORT ON DEVELOPMENT EXPENDITURES PLANNED AND MADE, 1952/1953-1957/1958 / Libya – BNE-712 1 – 9 – ne IDC [338]
FINANSI I KREDIT – Sofia. May 1956-Dec. 1962 – 1 – us NY Public [073]
FINANSIROVANIE VNESHNE I TORGOVLI SSSR (1920-1924 G.) / Gorkov, Mikhail – Moskva: RIO NKVT, 1925 – 1 – CSUX89-B1846 – us Hoover Inst Photo [380]
FINANSOVAI A GAZETA – Petrograd: I.O. Abelson, 191u – 1 – CSUXAKB2444-S – us Hoover Inst Photo [947]
FINANSOVAI A GAZETA (MOSKOW, R.S.F.S.R. : 1924) *see* FIANSOVAI A GAZETA
FINANSOVAI A GAZETA (PETROGRAD, R.S.F.S.R.) *see* FINANSOVAI A GAZETA
FINANSOVAIA GAZETA – Moscow. no.1-25. Nov. 16 1937-June 13 1941 – 1 – 94.00 – us L of C Photodup [947]
FINANSOVOE I KHOZI A ISTVENNOE ZAKONODATELSTVO – Moskva: Gosfinizdat, 1936-1938. 2v – 1 – CSUX89-S561 – us Hoover Inst Photo [332]
FINANSOVOE POLOZHENIE DOMOVOGO KHOZI A ISTVA GOR. MOSKVY PO KATEGORII AM DOMOVLADENI I V 1926/1927 GODU : MATERIALY SPLOSHNOGO ANKETNOGO OBSLEDOVANII A, PROIZVEDENNOGO V MAE–II UNE 1928 GODA – Moskva: Izd. Mosstatotdela, 1929 – 1 – CSUX91-B7 – us Hoover Inst Photo [332]
FINANSOVYE PERSPEKTIVY RAZVITII A PROMYSHLENNOSTI / Abramovich, S D – Moskva: Promizdat, 1927 – 1 – CSUX89-B2343 – us Hoover Inst Photo [332]
FINANSOVYE PROBLEMY – Moscow. U.S.S.R. 1922-31 – 1 – us UMI [380]
FINANSOVYE PROBLEMY = PROBLEMS OF FINANCE – Moscow. 1922-31 – 3 – us Readex [336]
FINANSOVYE PROBLEMY PLANOVOGO KHOZIAISTVA – 1922-31 – 1 – 209.00 – us L of C Photodup [947]
FINANSTIDNINGEN – Stockholm, Sweden. 1989- – 1 – sw Kungliga [072]
FINANSY I NARODNOE KHOZI A ISTVO : EZHENDELNAI A GAZETA KOMISSARIAT FINANSOV I SOVETA NARODNOGO KHOZI A ISTVA SEVERNO I OBLASTI – (Includes c.1: 1918:Nov.22, 24-26) – Petrograd: Komissariat i Sovet, 19uu – 1 – CSUXADQ1027-S – us Hoover Inst Photo [947]
FINANSY I PROMYSHLENNOST – (Includes c.1: 1923:Apr) – Moskva, Petrograd: [s.n.], 1922 – 1 – CSUXAKZ6817-S – us Hoover Inst Photo [947]
FINANSY SSSR – (Soviet Finance). Moscow. U.S.S.R. 1966- – 1 – us UMI [380]
FINANSY SSSR MEZHDU 6 I 7 SEZDAMI SOVETOV (1931-1934) : DELEGATY 7 VSESOI UZNOGO SEZDA SOVETOV – Moskva: Gosfinizdat, 1935 – 1 – CSUX90-B7489 – us Hoover Inst Photo [332]
LA FINANZA INTERNACIONAL Y LA GUERRA DE ESPANA / Bougouin, E – Paris, 1938. Fiche W 762. (Blodgett Collection of Spanish Civil War Pamphlets) – 9 – us H.U. College Libr [946]
LA FINANZA ITALIANA – Rome, Italy. -w. 22 Nov 1924-14 June 1930. Imperfect. 2 reels – 1 – uk British Libr Newspaper [072]
FINANZ-CHRONIK *see* REUTER'S FINANZ-CHRONIK
DER FINANZER : ERZAEHLUNG VOM BODENSEE / Achleitner, Arthur – Leipzig: M Hesse, [19–] – 1r – 1 – us U.W. Library [830]
DIE FINANZSKANDALE DES KAISERREICHS / Heinig, Kurt – Berlin: Verlag fuer Sozialwissenschaft, 1925. 80p. bibliog. index – 1 – us U.W. Library [943]
FIN-BACK – Seattle. Wash. -w, tw. 1879-81 – 1 – us UMI [071]
Finch, Laura M *see* AN ASSESSMENT OF THE FACTOR VALIDITY OF THE PRECOMPETITIVE STRESS INVENTORY
Finch, Merry B *see* THE EFFECTS OF EXERCISE ON MYOCARDIAL CAPILLARY BED AND CONNECTIVE TISSUE IN SENESCENT RATS
Finch, R *see* A CONGRATULATORY LETTER TO THE REVD. DR. TRAPP, OCCASIONED BY HIS FOUR SERMONS AGAINST ENTHUSIASM,...
Fincham, Jack E *see* JOURNAL OF PHARMACOEPIDEMIOLOGY
FINCHLEY FREE PRESS – London. (Free Press-Finchley Press) -w. Nov 1895-1960; 1970-78; 1980-81. (88 reels) – 1 – uk British Libr Newspaper [072]
FINCHLEY PRESS – London, UK. Jan-Jul 1986. -w. 2 1/2 reels – 1 – uk British Libr Newspaper [072]
FINCHLEY TIMES AND GUARDIAN. (FINCHLEY TIMES) – London. 20 Jan 1962-25 Dec 1964.-w. 8 reels – 1 – uk British Libr Newspaper [072]
Finck, FN *see*
- KATALOG DER ARMENISCHEN HANDSCHRIFTEN DES HERRN ABGAR JOANNISSIANY ZU TIFLIS
- VERZEICHNIS DER ARMENISCHEN HANDSCHRIFTEN DER KOENIGLICHEN UNIVERSITAETSBIBLIOTHEK ZU TUEBINGEN

Finck, H *see* PRACTICA MUSICA
Finck, N F *see* DIE GRUNDBEDEUTUNG DES GROENLAENDISCHEN SUBJECTIVS
Finck, William J *see* LUTHERAN LANDMARKS AND PIONEERS IN AMERICA
FIN-DE-SIECLE SYMBOLIST AND AVANT-GARDE PERIODICALS – Based on "A Chronological List of the Most Important Periodicals in the Symbolist Movement, 1881-99". Comp. by Kenneth Cornell in his book, The Symbolist Movement. New Haven, 1951 – 1 – us Primary [800]
FINDING AIDS / Yale University Divinity School, New Haven, CT. – (Inventories of historical, archival and mss colls, personal and organizational papers, printed pamphlets and ephemera related to various aspects of American religious history) – 35mf – 9 – H-3062/1 – ne IDC [020]
FINDING AIDS TO MANUSCRIPT AND ARCHIVE COLLECTIONS (ALL UNPUBLISHED) / Jewish National and University Library. Jerusalem – (With printed detailed list of contents) – 130mf – 9 – J-10-3-J-10-15/1 – ne IDC [020]
FINDING AIDS TO NATIONAL ARCHIVES PHOTOGRAPHS RELATING TO THE THIRD GERMAN REICH / U.S. National Archives and Records Service – 47 rolls. M1137 – 1 – us Nat'l Archives [324]
FINDING FISH WITH ECHO-SOUNDERS / Burczynski, J & Ben-Yami, M – 1985 – 96p – it F.A.O. [639]
FINDING THE WAY / Miller, James Russell – New York: Thomas Y Crowell, c1904 – 1mf – 9 – 0-8370-7311-1 – 1986-1311 – us A.T.L.A. [240]
FINDINGS ON FIVE YEAR MOVEMENT (CCC254) / East China Regional Conference – (In Chinese) – Shanghai: National Christian Council of China, 1929 – 1r – 1 – 1984-6593 – us A.T.L.A. [240]
FINDLAY DAILY COURIER – Findlay, Ohio. 1887-1913 – 48r – 1 – $32.50r – us Archival [071]
Findlay, George G *see*
- CHRISTIAN DOCTRINE AND MORALS VIEWED IN THEIR CONNEXION
- EPISTLE TO THE EPHESIANS
- EPISTLES OF PAUL THE APOSTLE: A SKETCH OF THEIR ORIGIN AND CONTENTS
- EPISTLES OF PAUL THE APOSTLE TO THE THESSALONIANS
- EPISTLES TO THE THESSALONIANS
- FELLOWSHIP IN THE LIFE ETERNAL: AN EXPOSITION OF THE EPISTLES OF ST JOHN
- WESLEY'S WORLD PARISH

Findlay, George Gillanders *see* THE EPISTLE TO THE GALATIANS
FINDLAY JEFFERSONIAN – Findlay, Ohio. 1871-81 – 5r – 1 – $32.50r – us Archival [071]
Findlay, Mary Grace *see* WESLEY'S WORLD PARISH
Findlay. Ohio. Howard Methodist Church *see* RECORDS
FINDLAY REPUBLICAN – Findlay, Ohio. 1883-91 – 3r – 1 – $32.50r – us Archival [071]
FINDLAY WEEKLY JEFFERSONIAN – Findlay, Ohio. 1881-1904 – 8r – 1 – $32.50r – us Archival [071]
Findlay.Ohio. St. Andrew's United Methodist Church *see* RECORDS
Findlay.Ohio. St. Paul's United Methodist Church *see* CHURCH RECORDS
FINE – Edmonton, 1988/89-1994 – 9 – Can$20.00y – cn Micromedia [073]
FINE AND DECORATIVE ART IN FRANCE – (Extensive coverage, illustrating over 70,000 items from over 200 museums and galleries. Publ in nine sections. Individual titles also listed separately) – 1021mf – 9 – $4,875.00 complete coll – 0-907006-01-9 – uk Mindata [700]
FINE AND DECORATIVE ARTS IN FRANCE *see*
- ANTIQUITIES
- DECORATIVE ART
- DRAWINGS IN PROVINCIAL AND OTHER MUSEUMS
- DRAWINGS IN THE LOUVRE AND NATIONAL MUSEUMS
- INDEXES
- MANUSCRIPTS
- PAINTINGS IN PROVINCIAL AND OTHER MUSEUMS
- PAINTINGS IN THE LOUVRE
- SCULPTURE

FINE ART / Victoria and Albert Museum. London – (9,000 captioned illustrations. Paintings, watercolours, drawings. Arranged alphabetical order by artist. Printed index of artists) – 152mf – 9 – $850.00 – 0-907006-35-3 – uk Mindata [700]
FINE ART AND ARCHAEOLOGY – 123mf – $610.00 – 1-900853-05-1 – uk Mindata [740]
FINE ART AND DESIGN IN THE VICTORIA AND ALBERT MUSEUM / Victoria and Albert Museum. London – (A pictorial record of fine and graphic art and design in 3 sections. Titles also listed individually) – 489mf – 9 – $2,500.00 set – 0-907006-50-7 – uk Mindata [700]
FINE ART AND DESIGN IN THE VICTORIA AND ALBERT MUSEUM *see*
- DESIGN
- FINE ART
- GRAPHIC ART

FINE ART SOCIETY CATALOGUE – (Individual titles not listed separately) – London, 1878-1976 – 85 catalogues on 91mf – 9 – £670.00 – uk Chadwyck [700]
Fine Art Trade Guild *see* LIST OF MEMBERS
FINE ARTS AND ARCHITECTURE CATEGORY / The NewsBank Review of the Arts – 1975-. Monthly index with cumulations – 9 – us NewsBank [720]
THE FINE ARTS IN ITALY IN THEIR RELIGIOUS ASPECT : LETTERS FROM ROME, NAPLES, PISA, AND C. : WITH AN APPENDIX ON THE ICONOGRAPHY OF THE IMMACULATE CONCEPTION / Coquerel, Athanase – London: Edward T. Whitfield, 1859 – 1mf – us A.T.L.A. [700]
FINE ARTS QUARTERLY REVIEW – London. v. 1-3, n.s. v. 1-2. May 1863-June 1867 – 1 – us NY Public [073]
FINE ARTS QUARTERLY REVIEW – London. v1-3; ns: v1-2. 1863-67 – 1r – 1 – us Ross [700]
Fine, Deborah L *see* THE INFLUENCE OF FITNESS-ORIENTED PHYSICAL ACTIVITY ON THE PHYSICAL SELF-PERCEPTION AND GLOBAL SELF-WORTH OF BOYS AND GIRLS
FINE DINING – 1985- – 1,5,6,9 – us UMI [640]
Fine, Sidney *see* FRANK MURPHY IN WORLD WAR I
Finegan, Mark T *see* THE STATUS OF CONTINUOUS ECG MONITORING IN PHASE 2 CARDIAC REHABILITATION PROGRAMS
Fineman, Helene H *see* THE PAPERS OF ALBERT GALLATIN
FINES Y UTILIDAD DE LA SINDICACION GANADERA POR... / Villamor Angulo, Hilario – Caceres: Tip. Garcia Floriano, 1938 – 1 – sp Bibl Santa Ana [946]
Finestres de Monsalvo, Jose *see* SYLLOGE INSCRIPTIONUM ROMANARUM
Finetti, G F *see* DE PRINCIPIIS JURIS NATURAE,...
Finettus, I F *see* DE PRINCIPIIS JURIS NATURAE,...
FINGAL, AN ANCIENT EPIC POEM : IN SIX BOOKS, TOGETHER WITH SEVERAL OTHER POEMS / Macpherson, James – London: Printed for T. Becket and P.A. De Hondt, 2nd ed 1762 – 1 roll – 1 – 1-55879-339-9 – uk Libr Preservation [810]
Finger, Charles Joseph *see* HISTORIC CRIMES AND CRIMINALS
Finger, Richard *see* HEINRICH VON KLEISTS GEHEIMNIS
Fingerhuth, K A *see* MONOGRAPHIA GENERIS CAPSICI
FINISHING – (v8-. 1984-. 5,6,9) – v6-. Jun 1982- – 1 – us UMI [073]
FINISHING INDUSTRIES – v1-6. 1977-May 1982 – 1 – us UMI [073]
THE FINISHING STROKE, CONTAINING SOME STRICTURES ON THE REV. MR. FLETCHER'S PAMPHLET ENTITLED 'LOGICA GENEVENSIS : OR, A FOURTH CHECK TO ANTINOMIANISM' / Hill, Richard – London, 1773 – 1mf – 9 – MP-486/1 – ne IDC [240]
THE FINISHING STROKE TO MR. WESLEY'S 'CALM ADDRESS' TO THE PEOPLE OF ENGLAND / Murray, J – Newcastle upon Tyne, 1778 – 1mf – 9 – MP-523/1 – ne IDC [240]
Fink, R A *see* WOMEN IN THE CHURCH
Finke, G *see* WER HAT DIE FUENF BUECHER MOSES VERFAS EINE HISTORISCH-KRITISCHE STUDIE
Finke, Heinrich *see*
- KONZILIENSTUDIEN ZUR GESCHICHTE DES 13. JAHRHUNDERTS
- DER MADONNENMALER FRANZ ITTENBACH (1813-1879)
- UEBER FRIEDRICH UND DOROTHEA SCHLEGEL

Finkel, IM *see* KAK NADO USTROIT UPRAVLENIE SVOBODNOI ROSSIEI
Finkel, K A *see* EVREISKOE ZEMLEUSTROENIE V SOVETSKOM SOIUZE
Finkel, L *see* BIBLIOGRAFIA HISTORII POLSKIEJ
Finkel, Robert J *see* A REVISION OF THE HEART DISEASE LOCUS OF CONTROL SCALE
Finkelstein, L *see* CORPUS TANNAITICUM
FINLAND : BIDRAG TILL FINLANDS OFFICIELA STATISTIK 1885-1914 / Finland. Statisticka Centralbyran – (Coll title: European Official Statistical Serials, 1841-1984) – 39mf – 9 – £7.00f (set £2,360.00 450mf) – uk Chadwyck [948]
FINLAND = STATISTICAL YEARBOOK OF FINLAND 1879-1970 : SUOMEN TILASTOLLINEN VUOSIKIRJA ARSBOK FOR FINLAND 1879-1970 / Finland. Tilastollinen Paatoimisto – (Coll title: European Official Statistical Serials, 1841-1984) – 411mf – 9 – £4.00f (set £2,360.00 450mf) – uk Chadwyck [948]
Finland *see* SUOMEN VIRALLINEN LEHTI
Finland. Economic Planning Centre *see* GROWTH PROSPECTS FOR THE FINNISH ECONOMY UP TO 1980
Finland. Statisticka Centralbyran *see* FINLAND
Finland. Talouspoliitiinen Suunnitteluneuvosto *see* TALOUSPOLITIIKAN PERUSOHJELMA
Finland. Tilastollinen Paatoimisto *see* FINLAND
LA FINLANDE, COMME PARTIE INTEGRANTE DE L'EMPIRE RUSSE / Borodkine, M – 2345 2. 1910 – 8 – ne IDC [947]
FINLANDS BOTANISKA LITERATUR TILL OCH MED AR 1900 / Saelan, A T – Helsinki. v43 (1). 1916 – 7mf – ne IDC [580]
FINLANDS FISKAR / Sundman, G et al – Z 2127 2. 1883-1893 – 8 – ne IDC [948]
FINLANDS FOGLAR, HUFVUDSAKLIGEN TILL DERAS DRAGTER BESKRIFNA / Wright, M von – Ed. by J. A. Palmen. Helsingfors. 1873. Bidrag till kannedom of Finalnds Naturoch Folk. Z-1876 2 – 8 – ne IDC [590]

Finlason, W F *see* REPORT OF THE TRIAL AND PRELIMINARY PROCEEDINGS IN THE CASE OF THE QUEEN ON THE PROSECUTION OF G. ACHILLI V. DR. NEWMAN
Finlay, Ernest L *see* HISTORY OF SONOMA COUNTY
FINLAY'S AMERICAN NAVAL AND COMMERCIAL REGISTER – Philadelphia. Pennsylvania. 1795-1798 – 3 – us Readex [071]
Finlayson, Thomas Campbell *see* MEDITATIONS AND MAXIMS OF KOHOLETH
FINLEY FREE PRESS – Jan 22 1897-Feb 7 1908 – 9 – at Pascoe [072]
Finley, James B *see*
- AUTOBIOGRAPHY OF REV. JAMES B. FINLEY, OR, PIONEER LIFE IN THE WEST
- MEMORIALS OF PRISON LIFE
- SKETCHES OF WESTERN METHODISM

FINLEY MAIL – Mar 21 1912-Dec 21 1920 – 9 – at Pascoe [072]
FINLIANDIIA TA FINLIANDSKE PYTANNIE / Bochkovskyi, Olgerd Ippolit – 2-e vyd. Viden: Nakladom "Soi uza vyzvolenni a Ukrainy", 1916 – 1 – CSUX88-B9215 – us Hoover Inst Photo [947]
FINLIANDSKAIA OKRAINA ROSSII / Petrovskii, S A – Sbornik statei, ocherkov, pisem, dokumentov i inykh materialov dlia izucheniia tak nazyvaemago "Finliandskago Voprosa". v. 1. 1891; v. 2. 1894; v. 3. 1897. BR-10,607 1 – 9 – ne IDC [948]
Finn, George *see* DATUS
FINN SANOMAT – Goteborg, Sweden. 1979-85 – 1 – sw Kungliga [072]
Finnan, Alan Pierson *see* VARIANT USES OF ALEPH IN IQISA
Finnegan, Dana *see* JOURNAL OF CHEMICAL DEPENDENCY TREATMENT
Finnell, Reuben A *see* STUDY OF THE BOOK OF REVELATION
Finnelly, W *see*
- CLARK AND FINNELLY'S REPORTS
- HOUSE OF LORDS CASES (CLARK AND FINNELLY)

Finney, Charles G *see*
- THE CHARACTER, CLAIMS AND PRACTICAL WORKINGS OF FREEMASONRY
- LECTURES ON REVIVALS OF RELIGION
- LECTURES ON SYSTEMATIC THEOLOGY
- MEMOIRS
- MEMOIRS OF REV. CHARLES G. FINNEY
- SERMONS ON IMPORTANT SUBJECTS
- SERMONS ON VARIOUS SUBJECTS
- VIEWS OF SANCTIFICATION

Finney, Charles Grandison *see* LETTERS ON REVIVALS OF RELIGION
Finney County Historical Society *see* HISTORY OF FINNEY COUNTY
FINNEY PAPERS – 1792-1875 – 1 – us UMI [240]
Finney, Ross Lee *see* THE AMERICAN PUBLIC SCHOOL: A GENETIC STUDY OF PRINCIPLES, PRACTICES AND AND PRESENT PROBLEMS
FINNISCHE NOVELLE / Kurzbach, Herbert – Muenchen: Deutscher Volks-Verlag, 1943 – 1r – 1 – us U.W. Library [830]
FINNISH CHEMICAL LETTERS – (1976-. 5,6,9) – 1974- – 1 – us UMI [540]
FINNISH EVANGELICAL LUTHERAN CHURCH – Republic, Michigan – 6r – 1 – us I.H.R.C. [240]
FINNISH NEWSPAPERS – (The collection increases annually with ca 900r) – ca 30,000r – 1 – fi H.U. Libr [072]
Finnish Organization of Canada *see* FINNISH-CANADIAN PLAY AND OPERETTA MANUSCRIPT COLLECTION
FINNISH PERIODICALS ON MICROFILM – Helsinki: Helsinki University Library, 1994 – ca 215r 10,000mf – 1,9 – fi H.U. Libr [073]
FINNISH SOCIALIST FEDERATION : MINUTES – 1913-1925 – 2r – 1 – us I.H.R.C. [335]
FINNISH-CANADIAN PLAY AND OPERETTA MANUSCRIPT COLLECTION / Finnish Organization of Canada – (Microfilm original) – 9 – $325.00 – cn McLaren [490]
FINNVEDEN – Jonkoping, Sweden. 1981-89 – 1 – sw Kungliga [072]
FINNVEDEN FREDAG – Vaernamo, 1992- – 9 – sw Kungliga [072]
FINNVEDEN ONSDAG – Vaernamo, 1992- – 9 – sw Kungliga [072]
Finot, Ed *see* PORT-ROYAL ET MAGNY
Finot, P A P *see* LES ORTHOPTERES DE LA FRANCE
FINSBURY – London, England. Published by the Finsbury Independent Labour Party. -m. Jan-May 1900. 10 ft – 1 – uk British Libr Newspaper [072]
Finsch, F H O *see* ZUR ORNITHOLOGIE DER SUEDSEE-INSELN: I: DIE VOEGEL DER PALAU-GRUPPE
Finster, Reinhard et al *see* LEIBNIZ-LEXICON, A DUAL CONCORDANCE TO LEIBNIZ'S PHILOSOPHISCHE SCHRIFTEN
Finzer, Michael *see* ERLERNTE HILFLOSIGKEIT
Fiolka, Marion *see* STADTENTWICKLUNGSPOLITIK IN DRESDEN
FIOR ANGELICO DI MUSICA NOUAMENTE DAS R.P. FRATE ANGELO DA PICITONO, CONUENTUALE, DELL' ORDINE MINORE, ORGANISTA PRECLARISSIMO, COMPOSTO;... / Picitone, Angelo da – In Vinegia: Per Agostino Bindoni, 1557 – 1 – us Sibley [780]
Fioravanti, L *see*
- A COMPENDIUM OF THE RATIONAL SECRETES OF THE WORTHY KNIGHT AND MOST EXCELLENT DOCTOR OF PHYSICKS – L. PHIERANAM
- A SHORT DISCOURS...UPON CHIRURGERIE

Fiore, P *see*
- CONTROVERSIA TRA LA GRECIA E LA ROMANIA
- DELLA GIURISDIZIONE PENALE...AL REATI COMMESSI ALL'ESTERO
- DELLA PERSONALITA GIURIDICA DEI CORPI MORALI...
- DELLE AGGREGAZIONI LEGITTIME...
- LE DROIT INTERNATIONAL
- LE DROIT INTERNATIONAL PRIVE;...
- EFECTOS INTERNACIONALES DE LAS SENTENCIAS DE LOS TRIBUNALES...
- EFFETTI INTERNAZIONALI DELLE SENTENZE E DEGLI ATTI
- EJECUCION DE LAS SENTENCIAS EXTRANJERAS
- I NUOVI ORIZZONTI DELLA SCIENZA...
- INTERNATIONAL LAW CODIFIED...
- MATRIMONIO CELEBRATO DAVANTI L'AGENTE DIPLOMATICO DA CITTADINI ITALIANI RESIDENTI ALL'ESTERO:...
- NUOVO DRITTO INTERNAZIONALE...
- LA PERSONALIDAD JURIDICA DE LOS ENTES MORALES Y DEL ESTADO...
- SE IL GIUDIZIO DI DELIBAZIONE...
- SE UN R. AGENTE DIPLOMATICO POSSA ESERCITARE LE FUNZIONI DI UFFICIALE DI STATO CIVILE...
- SUL QUESTIONARIO PROPOSTO DAL SOCIO PROF. GIANTURCO...
- SULLA CONTROVERSIA DEL DIVORZIO IN ITALIA
- SULL'ARTICOLO 8 DELLE DISPOSIZIONI GENERALI DEL CODICE CIVILE ITALIANO
- TRAITE DE DROIT PENAL INTERNATIONAL...
- TRATADO DE DERECHO PENAL INTERNACIONAL Y DE LA EXTRADICION

THE FIORELLO LA GUARDIA PAPERS – (With guide) – Rare Books and Manuscripts Division: The New York Public Library, Astor, Lenox and Tilden Foundations 1995 – ca 54r – 1 – ca $4,590.00 – D3340 – us Scholarly Res [320]
FIORETTI VESCOVILI, OU, EXTRAITS DES MANDEMENTS, LETTRES PASTORALES ET CIRCULAIRES DE MSG. IGNACE BOURGET SECOND EVEQUE DE MONTREAL / Bourget, Ignace – Par trois anciens camarades du regiment des Zouaves pontificaux. Montreal: Le Franc-Parleur, 1872. 02899. (Pre-1900 Canadiana) – 9 – cn C.I.H.M. [240]
Fiorillo, F *see*
- FIVE PIECES SELECTED FROM THE OPERA [LA CLEMENZA DI TITO]...ADAPTED FOR THE PIANOFORTE WITH AN ACCOMPAGNEME FOR THE FLUTE BY F. FIORILLO
- SIX QUATUORS CONCERTANTS POUR FLUTE, VIOLON, ALTO ET BASSE
- SIX QUATUORS CONCERTANTS POUR FLUTE, VIOLON, ALTO ET BASSE...OEUVRE 4

FIORINO – 1991-1995 – 1r per y – 5,6 – Sfr748.00 – sz Infoprint [944]
Fiorvanti, Leonardo *see* THREE EXACT PIECES..
Firbank, Mr. *see*
- LA CYBELLINE
- MR. CAVERLEY'S SLOW MINUET

THE FIR..CONFERENCE HELD IN SHAFTESBURY HALL, TORONTO, FROM MONDAY OCT. 21ST UNTIL FRIDAY, OCT. 25TH, 1878 / Canadian Christian Conference. First. 1878. Toronto, Ontario – Toronto: Willard 1878?. 00426. (Pre-1900 Canadiana) – 9 – cn C.I.H.M. [240]
Firdausi *see* SHAH NAMEH
Firdawsi *see* ROSTEM UND SUHRAB
FIRE!! : DEVOTED TO YOUNGER NEGRO ARTISTS – v1 2+1 (all publ). 1926 – 1mf – 9 – $55.00 – us UPA [305]
FIRE AND FROST: STORIES, DIALOGUES, SATIRES, ESSAYS, POEMS, ETC / Cross, Ethelbert F H – Toronto?: s.n., 1898 (Toronto: Bryant). 02133. (Pre-1900 Canadiana) – 9 – cn C.I.H.M. [971]
FIRE AND FUEL MANAGEMENT IN MEDITERRANEAN-CLIMATE ECOSYSTEMS : RESEARCH PRIORITIES AND PROGRAMMES / ed by Agee, James K – 1979 – 9 – 92-3-101688-1 – fr UNESCO [574]
FIRE AND MATERIALS – (1982-. 1,5,6,9) – v1-. 1976- – 1 – us UMI [073]
FIRE AND SWORD IN THE CAUCASUS / Villari, Luigi – London: T.F. Unwin, 1906. 347p.64 pl – 1 – us U.W. Library [947]
FIRE CONSIDERED AS THE SEAMAN'S SCOURGE / Matthews, Alfred – n.d – 9 – $20.00 – uk Libr Preservation [623]
FIRE INSURANCE MAPS FROM THE SANBORN MAP COMPANY ARCHIVES : LATE 19TH CENTURY TO 1990 (A-O) – (Alabama 1945-81 6r $995.00 ISBN 1-55655-343-9. Alaska ca 1r $125.00 ISBN 1-55655-353-6. Arizona ca 1r $125.00 ISBN 1-55655-354-4. Arkansas 1944-70 3r $500.00 ISBN 1-55655-351-X. California 88r $14,610.00 ISBN 1-55655-348-X. Colorado ca 4r $500.00 ISBN 1-55655-355-2. Connecticut 1945-90 7r $1,160.00 ISBN 1-55655-330-7. Delaware 1951-88 1r $165.00 ISBN 1-55655-321-8. District of Columbia 1984-85 2r $330.00 ISBN 1-55655-318-8. Florida 1945-87 9r $1,495.00 ISBN 1-55655-332-3. Georgia 1940-78 6r $995.00 ISBN 1-55655-333-1. Hawaii ca 1r $125.00 ISBN 1-55655-356-0. Idaho ca 2r $250.00 ISBN 1-55655-357-9. Illinois 1938-89 36r $5,975.00 ISBN 1-55655-337-4. Indiana 1933-80 13r $2,160.00 ISBN 1-55655-340-4. Iowa 1946-80 6r $995.00 ISBN 1-55655-346-3. Kansas ca 5r $625.00 ISBN 1-55655-358-7. Kentucky 1946-92 7r $1,160.00 ISBN 1-55655-341-2. Louisiana 1940-94 9r $1,495.00 ISBN 1-55655-352-8. Maine 1943-88 3r $500.00 ISBN 1-55655-329-3. Maryland 1946-82 9r $1,495.00 ISBN 1-55655-317-X. Massachusetts Michigan 1946-92 24r $3,985.00 ISBN 1-55655-339-0. Minnesota 1946-69 8r $1,330.00 ISBN 1-55655-345-5. Mississippi 1945-70 2r $330.00 ISBN 1-55655-344-7. Missouri 1933-92 13r $2,160.00 ISBN 1-55655-347-1. Montana ca 3r $375.00 ISBN 1-55655-359-5. Nebraska ca 3r $375.00 ISBN 1-55655-360-9. Nevada ca 1r $125.00 ISBN 1-55655-362-5. New Hampshire 1937-89 3r $500.00 ISBN 1-55655-326-9. New Jersey 1945-91 24r $3,985.00 ISBN 1-55655-331-5. New Mexico ca 2r $250.00 ISBN 1-55655- 361-7. New York 1909-90 32r $5,310.00 ISBN 1-55655-324-2. North Carolina 1945-79 7r $1,160.00 ISBN 1-55655-322-6. North Dakota ca 1r $125.00 ISBN 1-55655-363-3. Ohio 1946-89 26r $4,315.00 ISBN 1-55655-336-6. Oklahoma ca 5r $625.00 ISBN 1-55655-364-1. Oregon 1912-78 8r $1,330.00 ISBN 1-55655-349-8) – 1 – us UPA [978]
FIRE INSURANCE MAPS FROM THE SANBORN MAP COMPANY ARCHIVES : LATE NINETEENTH CENTURY TO 1900 (P-W) – (Pennsylvania 1935-90 40r $6,640.00 ISBN 1-55655-323-4. Rhode Island 1941-90 4r $665.00 ISBN 1-55655-328-5. South Carolina 1946-74 3r $500.00 ISBN 1-55655-334-X. South Dakota ca 1r $125.00 ISBN 1-55655-365-X. Tennessee 1947-69 7r $1,160.00 ISBN 1-55655-342-0. Texas 1940-86 18r $2,990.00 ISBN 1-55655-335-8. Utah ca 1r $125.00 ISBN 1-55655-366-8. Vermont 1946-89 1r $165.00 ISBN 1-55655-327-7. Virginia 1946-89 11r $1,825.00 ISBN 1-55655-319-6. Washington 1912-89 13r $2,160.00 ISBN 1-55655-350-1. West Virginia 1946-89 5r $830.00 ISBN 1-55655-320-X. Wisconsin 1945-86 9r $1,495.00 ISBN 1-55655-338-2. Wyoming ca 1r $165.00 ISBN 1-55655-367-6) – 1 – us UPA [978]
FIRE JOURNAL – (5,6 v66- 1972- ; 9 v67-1973-) – v1- 1907- – 1 – us UMI [360]
THE FIRE JOURNAL – Toronto: Toronto Pub. Co, [1879-18-?] – 9 – cn C.I.H.M. [360]
FIRE NEWS – v744- Feb 1985- – 1,5,6,9 – us UMI [620]
FIRE RETARDANT CHEMISTRY – (v. 2. 1975. 9) – v. 1-2. 1974-1975 – 1,5,6 – us UMI [670]
FIRE SAFETY JOURNAL – v1-7 1977-84. Continues: Fire Research – 1,5,6,13 – sz Elsevier [629]
FIREBAUGH-MENDOTA JOURNAL – Firebaugh, CA. 1991- – 8+ r – 1 – $400.00 ($50.00y) – B02235 – us Library Micro [073]
FIRELANDS FARMER – Berlin Heights, Ohio. 1952-57 – 2r – 1 – $32.50r – us Archival [071]
FIREMANS JOURNAL AND MILITARY GAZETTE – San Francisco, CA. 1855-1859 – 1r – 1 – $50.00 – C03669 – us Library Micro [073]
FIRENZE CITTA NOBILISSIMA ILLUSTRATA / Migliore, F L del – O-958 1. 1684 – 9 – ne IDC [945]
FIRESIDE STUDIES / Kingsley, Henry – British Fiction Archive: Unit 2 – 9 – uk Bell [830]
FIRING LINE – New York. n1-240 + index to programs 1-240. 1966-71 – 241mf – 9 – $5.00f – us Ross [320]
Firishta, Abdulmacid ibn *see* ISHQ-NAME
THE FIRM FOUNDATION OF THE CHRISTIAN FAITH / Beet, Joseph Agar – 1891 – 9 – us A.T.L.A. [240]
Firman Muntaco *see* GAMBANG DJAKARTE; KUMPULAN
Firman, Philippe *see* DISSERTATION SUR LA QUESTION: S'IL EST PERMIS D'AVOIR EN SA POSSESSION DES ESCLAVES ET DE S'EN SERVIR COMME TELS, DANS LES COLONIES DE L'AMERIQUE
Firmery, Joseph Leon *see* ETUDE SUR LA VIE ET LES OEUVRES DE JEAN PAUL FREDERIC RICHTER
FIRMES / Aradillas Agudo, Antonio & Castaneda, P – Madrid: Editorial Atenas, 1964 – 1 – sp Bibl Santa Ana [338]
Firmicus Maternus, Julius *see* AD MAVORTIUM LOLLIANUM ASTRONOMICON, LIB. VIII
FIRMILIAN: OR, THE STUDENT OF BADAJOZ : A SPASMODIC TRAGEDY / Jones, T Percy; ed by Aytoun, William Edmondstoune – Edinburgh, London: William Blackwood and Sons, 1854 – 1 roll – 1 – 1-55879-357-7 – uk Libr Preservation [820]
Firmin-Didot, A *see* OBSERVATIONS SUR L'ORTHOGRAPHE
Firminger, Walter Kelly *see* RELIGION
Firpo, M Eduardo *see* PERON Y LOS PERONISTAS
Firsov, N N *see* PRAVITEL'STVO I OBSHCHESTVO V IKH OTNOSHENIIAKH
THE FIRST 100 YEARS OF THE FIRST BAPTIST CHURCH, DENTON, TEXAS / Floyd, LP – 1858-1958. 470p – 1 – 16.45 – us Baptist [240]
A FIRST ACCOUNT OF LABOUR ORGANISATION IN SOUTH AFRICA / Gitsham, Ernest & Trembath, James F – Durban: Printed by E P & Commercial Printing Co, 1926 – 1 – us Res Libr [331]
THE FIRST AGE OF CHRISTIANITY AND THE CHURCH / Doellinger, Ignaz von – London: Gibbings, 1906 – 2mf – us A.T.L.A. [240]
THE FIRST AND SECOND DEMOGRAPHIC SURVEYS IN INDONESIA / Indonesia. Biro Pusat Statistik – Kozo Ueda. 1965. SE-6318-1 – 9 – ne IDC [310]
FIRST AND SECOND INTERIM REPORTS OF THE COMMISSION OF INQUIRY INTO CERTAIN ORGANISATIONS : SOUTH AFRICA COMMISSION OF INQUIRY INTO CERTAIN ORGANISATIONS. – [s.l: s.n., 197-] – us Res Libr [360]
FIRST AND SECOND REPORTS / Great Britain. Royal Commission on Technical Instruction – 9 – uk Microform Academic [324]
FIRST AND SECOND REPORTS OF GOVERNOR SHOUP'S COMMITTEE ON CHILD WELFARE LEGISLATION FOR COLORADO / Colorado. Committee on Child Welfare Legislation – Denver, Eastwood 1923? 160 p. LL-600 – 1 – us L of C Photodup [305]
FIRST AND SECOND REPORTS OF THE SELECT COMMITTEE...APPOINTED TO ENQUIRE INTO THE PUBLIC INCOME AND EXPENDITURE OF THE PROVINCE / Canada. Parliament. Legislative Assembly. Select Committee – Toronto: Printed by Lovell and Gibson, 1850. SEM105P140 – 3mf – 9 – Can$6.75 – cn Bibl Nat [324]
THE FIRST AND SECONDE PARTES OF THE HERBAL OF WILLIAM TURNER... / Turner, William – Collen, 1568 – 22mf – 9 – ne IDC [615]
FIRST ANNUAL CATALOG, 1901-02 / Theodore Harris Institute. Pineville, Kentucky – 24p – 1 – 5.00 – us Baptist [240]
THE FIRST ANNUAL REPORT 1395/1396 H / Saudi Arabia. Islamic Development Bank – 1975-76. BNE-6643 1 – 9 – ne IDC [336]

FIRST ANNUAL REPORT 1974-1975 / Abu Dhabi. Abu Dhabi Fund for Arab Economic Development – BD-1866 1 – 9 – ne IDC [330]

FIRST ANNUAL REVIEW OF THE COPPER MINING INDUSTRY OF LAKE SUPERIOR: CONTAINING A CAREFULLY AND CONCISELY WRITTEN ACCOUNT OF EARLY EXPLORATIONS AND DISCOVERIES IN THE LAKE SUPERIOR COPPER REGION / Russell, James – Marquette, Mich.: Mining Journal Co., 1899 – 1 – us U.W. Library [622]

FIRST BAPTIST CHURCH. ABBEVILLE, SOUTH CAROLINA : CHURCH RECORDS – 1910-1946 – 5r – 1 – $305.28 – us Baptist [240]

FIRST BAPTIST CHURCH. DOVER, FLORIDA : CHURCH RECORDS – 1904-1991 – 2r – 1 – $88.79 – us Baptist [240]

FIRST BAPTIST CHURCH. ELDON, MISSOURI : CHURCH RECORDS – 1895-July 1907 – 1r – 1 – $8.19 – us Baptist [240]

FIRST BAPTIST CHURCH, FARMERSVILLE, TEXAS CENTENNIAL STORY / Rike, Charles Jesse – 1865-1965. 1961 – 1 – 5.00 – us Baptist [240]

First Baptist Church, Ottawa, KS *see* RECORDS

FIRST BAPTIST CHURCH PULPIT – Yarmouth, NS: [s.n., 1889?-18–?] – 9 – cn C.I.H.M. [240]

FIRST BAPTIST CHURCH. SHAWNEE, OKLAHOMA : CHURCH RECORDS – 1904-Aug. 1916 – 1r – 1 – $24.93 – us Baptist [240]

THE FIRST BATTLE OF LAKE CHAMPLAIN / Bixby, George F – Albany, NY: Weed, Parsons, 1893. 00144. (Pre-1900 Canadiana) – 9 – cn C.I.H.M. [971]

FIRST BIANNUAL REVIEW OF THE CAPITAL EXPENDITURE PROGRAMME, 1957-62 / Mauritius – (Sessional Paper no. 11 of 1958). Port Louis. 1958 – 9 – ne IDC [338]

THE FIRST BOOK OF KINGS / Farrar, Frederic William – New York: A C Armstrong, 1893 – 2mf – 9 – 0-8370-2404-8 – 1985-0404 – us A.T.L.A. [220]

THE FIRST BOOK OF KINGS: WITH MAPS, INTRODUCTION AND NOTES / Lumby, Joseph Rawson – Cambridge: University Press, 1890 – 1mf – 9 – us A.T.L.A. [240]

FIRST BOOK OF SAMUEL / Blaikie, William Garden – New York: A.C. Armstrong, 1896. 2 fiches – 9 – us A.T.L.A. [220]

FIRST BOOK OF SAMUEL / Kirkpatrick, Alexander F – Cambridge: University Press, 1886. 1 fiche – 9 – us A.T.L.A. [220]

THE FIRST BOOK OF SAMUEL : WITH MAP, NOTES AND INTRODUCTION / Kirkpatrick, Alexander Francis – (Includes appendix on special interpretations of 1st Samuel. Includes index) – Cambridge: University Press, 1886 – 1mf – 9 – 0-8370-3906-1 – 1985-1906 – us A.T.L.A. [220]

FIRST CALVARY BAPTIST CHURCH (FORMERLY: PLEASANT HILL BAPTIST CHURCH). LEXINGTON COUNTY. SOUTH CAROLINA : CHURCH RECORDS – 1886-88, 1922-48, 1959-71 – 1 – 22.64 – us Baptist [240]

FIRST CATALOGUES AND CIRCULARS OF THE BOTANICAL GARDEN OF TRANSYLVANIA UNIVERSITY AT LEXINGTON IN KENTUCKY, FOR THE YEAR 1824 / Rafinesque-Schmaltz, Constantine S – Lexington, 1824 – 1mf – ne IDC [580]

FIRST CATALOGUES AND CIRCULARS OF THE BOTANICAL GARDEN OF TRANSYLVANIA UNIVERSITY AT LEXINGTON KENTUCKY, FOR THE YEAR 1824 / Rafinesque-Schmaltz, Constantine S – Lexington. 1824 – 9 – ne IDC [580]

FIRST CEDAR CREEK BAPTIST CHURCH. BARDSTOWN, KENTUCKY : CHURCH RECORDS – 1849-85. 1938-1974 – 1 – 34.92 – us Baptist [240]

FIRST CENSUS OF KENTUCKY, 1790 / Kentucky – Comp. by Charles B. Heinman, 1940. Item N. A list of taxpayers, privately compiled to be used in lieu of lost 1790 census records. 118p. SW16-0014 – 5 – us A.G.L.L. [920]

FIRST CENSUS OF POPULATION AND HOUSING, 18 NOV 1961 / Jordan. Department of Statistics – 4v. 1964-65. BNE-9767 1 – 9 – ne IDC [310]

FIRST CENSUS OF THE UNITED STATES / U.S. Bureau of the Census – 1790. 12 rolls. M637 – 1 – us Nat'l Archives [324]

FIRST CENTURY MESSAGE TO 20TH CENTURY CHRISTIANS / Morgan, George Campbell – New York: F.H. Revell, 1902. 1 fiche – 9 – us A.T.L.A. [240]

FIRST CHURCH ENDEAVORER – Hamilton, Ont: Young People's Society of Christian Endeavor, [1890-189- or 19–] – 9 – cn C.I.H.M. [240]

THE FIRST CODE OF LAWS.. / Russia. (1917-R.S.F.S.R.). Laws, Statutes, etc – Petrograd: Peoples Commissariat of Justice, 1919 – 1 – us U.W. Library [340]

THE FIRST COMEDY OF PUB. TERENTIUS, CALLED ANDRIA / Webbe, Joseph – 1629. 213p. (English Linguistics Series 1500-1800) – 9 – us UMI [820]

FIRST COMPTROLLER, DEPARTMENT OF THE TREASURY, DECISIONS : 1880-1894 / U.S. Treasury Department. Comptroller – (None publ 1886-93. The office was abolished in 1894. Cont by: Comptroller of the Treasury Decisions) – v1-7 (all publ) – 50mf – 9 – $75.00 – LLMC 80-505 – us L.L.M.C. [336]

First Congregational and Presbyterian Society (Peru, Ohio) *see* RECORDS

First Congregational Church, Emporia KS *see* THE EARLY CHURCH

First Congregational Church, Emporia, KS *see* RECORD

FIRST CONGREGATIONAL CHURCH, STONINGTON, CONNECTICUT HISTORY / New London County. Connecticut – 1674-1874. By Richard Wheeler, 1875. Item B. Includes T.O.C. 300p. SW16-0139 – 5 – us A.G.L.L. [920]

FIRST CREEK BAPTIST CHURCH. ANDERSON COUNTY. SOUTH CAROLINA : CHURCH RECORDS – 1824-1911, 1919-82. Deacons' Minutes: 1824-1923, misc. material. 1802p – 1 – 81.09 – us Baptist [240]

THE FIRST CZECHOSLOVAK ECONOMIC FIVE-YEAR PLAN ACT / Czechoslovakia – Prague. 1948. BD-518 1 – 9 – ne IDC [338]

THE FIRST CZECHOSLOVAK ECONOMIC FIVE-YEAR PLAN, ACT AND GOVERNMENT MEMORANDUM / Czechoslovakia – Prague. 1949. BD-147 1 – 9 – ne IDC [338]

THE FIRST CZECHOSLOVAK ECONOMIC PLAN / Czechoslovakia – The Explanatory Memo. On the Bill and the Text of the 2 Year Econ. Plan Act. (Orbis). Prague. 1947. BD-554 1 – 9 – ne IDC [338]

THE FIRST DECADE OF THE CIRCUIT COURT EXECUTIVE : AN EVALUATION / Macy, John W Jr. – Washington: FJC, 1985 – 1mf – 9 – $1.50 – LLMC 95-361 – us L.L.M.C. [340]

FIRST DECADE OF THE WOMAN'S FOREIGN MISSIONARY SOCIETY OF THE METHODIST EPISCOPAL CHURCH, WITH SKETCHES ON ITS MISSIONARIES / Wheeler, Mary Sparkes – 1881 – 9 – us A.T.L.A. [240]

FIRST DEVELOPMENT PLAN, 1951-1956 / Iraq. Development Board – 9 – ne IDC [338]

FIRST DEVELOPMENT PLAN, 1961-1964 REVIEW OF PROGRESS FOR THE THREE YEARS ENDING 31 DEC 1963 / Singapore. Prime Ministers Office. Economic Planning Unit – 1964 – 9 – ne IDC [338]

FIRST DEVELOPMENT PLAN 1970-1974 / Nigeria. North Eastern State of Nigeria, Ministry of Economic Planning – Maiduguri. 1970. BD-1717 1 – 9 – ne IDC [338]

FIRST DEVELOPMENT PLAN, 1970-1974 / Nigeria. Kwara State, Ministry of Finance, Economic Planning Division – Kwara. BD-1718 1 – 9 – ne IDC [338]

FIRST DEVELOPMENT PLAN 1970-74 / Nigeria. East Central State of Nigeria, Ministry of Economic Development and Reconstruction – Enugu. 1971. BD-1712 1 – 9 – ne IDC [338]

FIRST DEVELOPMENT PLAN 1970-74 / Nigeria. North Central State of Nigeria, Economic Planning Division – Kaduna. 1970. BD-1709 1 – 9 – ne IDC [338]

THE FIRST DIVORCE OF HENRY 8 : AS TOLD IN THE STATE PAPERS / ed by Hope, Anne Fulton – London: K. Paul, Trench, Truebner, 1894 – 1mf – us A.T.L.A. [941]

THE FIRST EASTER DAWN : AN INQUIRY INTO THE EVIDENCE FOR THE RESURRECTION OF JESUS / Gorham, Charles Turner – (Includes bibliography and index) – London: Watts, 1908 – 1mf – 9 – 0-8370-3347-0 – 1985-1347 – us A.T.L.A. [240]

FIRST EASTER DAWN: AN INQUIRY INTO THE EVIDENCE FOR THE RESURRECTION OF JESUS / Gorham, Charles Turner – London: Watts, 1908. 1 fiche – 9 – us A.T.L.A. [240]

THE FIRST ENGLISH LIFE OF KING HENRY THE FIFTH, WRITTEN IN 1513 BY AN ANONYMOUS AUTHOR KNOWN COMMONLY AS THE TRANSLATOR OF LIVIUS / ed by Kingsford, C L – H-1314 2. 1911 – 8 – ne IDC [941]

THE FIRST EPISTLE OF PAUL THE APOSTLE TO THE CORINTHIANS : IN THE REVISED VERSION: WITH INTRODUCTION AND NOTES / Parry, Reginald St John – (Includes index) – Cambridge: University Press; New York: G P Putnam, 1916 – 1mf – 9 – 0-8370-6830-4 – 1986-0830 – us A.T.L.A. [220]

THE FIRST EPISTLE OF PAUL TO THE CORINTHIANS = ERSTE BRIEF PAULI AN DIE KORINTHER / Kling, Christian Friedrich – 2nd rev ed. New York: Charles Scribner, 1886, c1868 – 1mf – 9 – 0-8370-6200-4 – 1986-0200 – us A.T.L.A. [220]

THE FIRST EPISTLE OF PAUL TO THE CORINTHIANS / Moffatt, J – 1938 – 9 – $12.00 – us I.R.C. [240]

FIRST EPISTLE OF PETER: REVISED TEXT, WITH INTRODUCTION AND COMMENTARY / Johnstone, Robert – Edinburgh: T. & T. Clark, 1888. 1 fiche – 9 – us A.T.L.A. [240]

FIRST EPISTLE OF ST JOHN / Haupt, Erich – Edinburgh: T.&T. Clark, 1893. 1 fiche – 9 – us A.T.L.A. [240]

THE FIRST EPISTLE OF ST PETER / Selwyn, E G – 1946 – 9 – $18.00 – us I.R.C. [240]

THE FIRST EPISTLE OF ST PETER 1. 1-2. 17 : THE GREEK TEXT WITH INTRODUCTORY LECTURE, COMMENTRAY, AND ADDITIONAL NOTES / Hort, Fenton John Anthony – (Text in Greek. Introduction & notes in English. Includes bibliographial references & index) – London, New York: Macmillan, 1898 – 1mf – 9 – 0-8370-3662-3 – 1985-1662 – us A.T.L.A. [220]

THE FIRST EPISTLE OF ST PETER, I.1-II.17 / Hort, Fenton John Anthony – 1898 – 9 – $10.00 – us I.R.C. [240]

FIRST EPISTLE TO THE CORINTHIANS / Goudge, Henry Leighton – London: Methuen, 1903. 1 fiche – 9 – us A.T.L.A. [240]

THE FIRST EPISTLE TO THE CORINTHIANS / Dods, Marcus – New York: A C Armstrong, 1890 – 1mf – 9 – 0-8370-2937-6 – 1985-0937 – us A.T.L.A. [220]

THE FIRST EPISTLE TO THE CORINTHIANS / Shore, Thomas Teignmouth – London: Cassell Petter & Galpin, 1879.1 fiche – 9 – us A.T.L.A. [240]

THE FIRST EPISTLE TO THE CORINTHIANS: WITH NOTES, MAP AND INTRODUCTION / Lias, John James – Cambridge: University Press, 1892. 1 fiche – 9 – us A.T.L.A. [240]

FIRST EVANGELICAL SLOVAK SOCIETY OF THE HOLY TRINITY – Cleveland, OH, 1892-1943 – 1 reel – 1 – us I.H.R.C. [240]

FIRST EXHIBITION OF WORKS OF ART IN BLACK & WHITE, FEBRUARY, 1881: THE CATALOGUE / Art Association of Montreal – 1881?. 02465. (Pre-1900 Canadiana) – 9 – cn C.I.H.M. [700]

FIRST EXPEDITION OF VARGAS INTO NEW MEXICO, 1692 / Bayle, Constantino & Espinosa, J Manuel – Alburquerque, 1940; Madrid: Missionalia Hispanica, 1945 – 1 – sp Bibl Santa Ana [910]

FIRST EXPLORATIONS OF KENTUCKY – By J. Stoddard Johnston, 1898. Contains Dr. Thomas Walker's & Col. Christopher Gist's journals. 5 fiches. F-0491 – 9 – us A.G.L.L. [920]

FIRST FAMILIES OF OHIO / Ohio Genealogical Society – 17??-1994 – 77r – 5 – $32.50r – us Archival [920]

FIRST FAMILIES OF OTTAWA COUNTY, OHIO / Ohio Genealogical Society. Ottawa County Chapter – 1984-1991 – 6r – 5 – $32.50r – us Archival [978]

FIRST FAMILIES OF WOOD COUNTY, OHIO / Ohio Genealogical Society. Wood County Chapter – 1820-1995 – 6r – 5 – $32.50r – us Archival [920]

FIRST FIVE HUNDRED YEARS / Temple, Sarah – Short history of Cobb County. Atlanta, Walter W. Brown Publ. Co., 1935. Georgia Reel 3. (The Cox Library Collection) – 5 – us Americana [978]

FIRST FIVE YEAR DEVELOPMENT PLAN, 1963-1967 / Turkey. Devlet Planlama Teskilati – Ankara. 1963. BD-121 1 – 9 – ne IDC [338]

THE FIRST FIVE YEAR DEVELOPMENT PLAN, 1967/68-1971/72 / Kuwait – D-866 1 – 9 – ne IDC [338]

THE FIRST FIVE YEAR PLAN / India. Planning Commission – New Delhi. 1952. BD-110 1 – 9 – ne IDC [338]

FIRST FIVE YEAR PLAN, 1963-1967 / Somali Republic. Planning and Coordination Committee – Mogadiscio. 1963. BD-333 1 – 9 – ne IDC [338]

THE FIRST FIVE YEAR PLAN, 1973-1978 / Bangladesh. Planning Commission – Nov 1973. BD-1854 1 – 9 – ne IDC [338]

THE FIRST FIVE-YEAR DEVELOPMENT PLAN 1961/62-1965/66 / Uganda – Entebbe. 1964. BD-181 1 – 9 – ne IDC [338]

FIRST FIVE-YEAR DEVELOPMENT PLAN (1969/70-1973/74) / Indonesia. Departemen Penerangan – D-894 1. 4 pts. in 6 v. 1969 – 9 – ne IDC [338]

FIRST FIVE-YEAR DEVELOPMENT PLAN, 1970/71-1974/75 / Lesotho. Central Planning and Development Office – Maseru. Dec 1970 – 9 – ne IDC [338]

FIRST FIVE-YEAR ECONOMIC DEVELOPMENT PLAN (1962-1966), ADJUSTED VERSION / Korea. South. Economic Planning Board – Seoul. 1964. BD-135 1 – 9 – ne IDC [338]

THE FIRST FIVE-YEAR PLAN, 1955-1960 / Pakistan. National Planning Board – Karachi. 1958 – 9 – ne IDC [338]

THE FIRST FIVE-YEAR PLAN A DRAFT OUTLINE / India. Planning Commission – Delhi. 1951 – 9 – ne IDC [338]

FIRST FIVE-YEAR PLAN FOR DEVELOPMENT OF THE NATIONAL ECONOMY IN 1953-1957 / China. People's Republic – Peking, Foreign Languages Press. 1956. BD-281 1 – 9 – ne IDC [338]

FIRST FIVE-YEAR PLAN FOR TECHNICAL DEVELOPMENT SUPPLEMENT TO FIRST FIVE-YEAR ECONOMIC PLAN / Korea. South. Economic Planning Board – Seoul. 1962. BD-428 1 – 9 – ne IDC [338]

FIRST (FOURTH) CONTRIBUTION TO THE SOUTH-AFRICAN COLEOPTEROUS FAUNA. 1884-92). BZ-1538/2 / Peringuey, L – 8 – ne IDC [590]

FIRST GENERAL ASSEMBLY, 1ST SESSION, 1812, LEGISLATIVE COUNCIL JOURNAL / Illinois. General Assembly – V148-0008 – 1 – us A.G.L.L. [978]

FIRST GENERAL ASSEMBLY, 2ND SESSION, 1813 / Illinois. General Assembly – V148-0008 – 1 – us A.G.L.L. [978]

FIRST GENERAL EPISTLE OF ST JOHN THE APOSTLE / Hardy, Nathaniel – Edinburgh: James Nichol, 1865. 1 fiche – 9 – us A.T.L.A. [240]

FIRST GENERAL REPORT OF THE GOVERNMENT BOTANIST ON THE VEGETATION OF THE BOTANY OF VICTORIA / Mueller, Ferdinand Jakob Heinrich von – Melbourne, 1853. B-6464 1 – 9 – ne IDC [580]

FIRST HISTORICAL TRANSFORMATIONS OF CHRISTIANITY : FROM THE FRENCH OF ATHANASE COQUEREL THE YOUNGER / Evans, E P – Boston: W.V. Spencer, 1867 – 1mf – us A.T.L.A. [240]

THE FIRST INTERPRETERS OF JESUS / Gilbert, George Holley – (Includes bibliographical references and index) – New York: Macmillan, 1901 – 1mf – 9 – 0-8370-3278-4 – 1985-1278 – us A.T.L.A. [220]

THE FIRST LESSONS FOR THE HARPSICHORD OR SPINNET / Colizzi, J AK – London: Longman, Lukey & Co, 18– – 1 – us Sibley [780]

FIRST LESSONS IN ENGLISH AND TAMUL. : DESIGNED TO ASSIST TAMUL YOUTH IN THE STUDY OF THE ENGLISH LANGUAGE – Manepy: Press of the American Mission, 1835-36 – 1 – us Res Libr [490]

FIRST LINE INDEX OF MANUSCRIPT POETRY IN THE FOLGER SHAKESPEARE LIBRARY – (Guide included) – 1996 – 3r – 1 – $375.00 – uk Matthew [090]

FIRST LINE INDEX OF MANUSCRIPT POETRY IN THE HUNTINGTON LIBRARY – Marlborough: Adam Matthew Publications, 1991 – 15mf – 9 – $140.00 – uk Matthew [020]

FIRST MALAYSIA PLAN, 1966-1970 / Malaysia – Kuala Lumpur. 1965 – 9 – ne IDC [338]

FIRST MEMORANDUM ON THE CENTRAL ECONOMIC PLAN, 1946 / Netherlands. Centraal Planbureau – and National Budget, 1947. The Hague. 1946. BD-533 1 – 9 – ne IDC [338]

THE FIRST MEN IN THE MOON / Wells, H G – London: G. Newnes, 1901 – 1 roll – 1 – 1-55879-773-4 – uk Libr Preservation [830]

FIRST METATARSOPHALANGEAL JOINT RANGE OF MOTION AS A FACTOR IN TURF TOE INJURIES / Eggert, KE – 1990 – 1mf – 9 – $4.00 – us Microform Publ [790]

FIRST METHODIST EPISCOPAL CHURCH RECORDS – Van Wert. Ohio. 1897-1942 – 1 reel – 1 – us Archival [920]

First Methodist Episcopal Church (Van Wert, Ohio) *see* RECORDS

First National City Bank of New York. Morocco *see* MOROCCO

FIRST NATIONAL DEVELOPMENT PLAN, 1966-1970 / Zambia. Office of National Development and Planning – Lusaka. 1966 – 9 – ne IDC [338]

FIRST NATIONAL DEVELOPMENT PLAN 1972-74 / Brazil – In English. D-1546 1 – 9 – ne IDC [338]

FIRST NATIONAL DEVELOPMENT PLAN 1972/74 / Brazil – Feb 1972. BD-1603 1 – 9 – ne IDC [338]

A FIRST OF MAY IN THE MIDST OF TRAGEDY / Prieto, Indalecio – Washington, DC. 1937. Fiche W1177. (Blodgett Collection of Spanish Civil War Pamphlets) – 9 – us H.U. College Libr [946]

THE FIRST PART OF THE ELEMENTARIE / Mulcaster, Richard – 1582. 292p. (English Linguistics Series 1500-1800) – 9 – us UMI [420]

(FIRST PART OF THE) MUSICIAN'S COMPANION / Howe, Elias – containing 18 setts of cotillions arranged with figures, and a large number of popular marches, quick-steps, waltzes, hornpipes, contra dances, songs, &c. &c. several of which are in three parts–first, second & bass, for the flute, violin, clarionett, bass-viol, &c. Also, several new and popular pieces in 6 and 8 parts, for a brass band, containing in all over 300 pieces, more than 100 of which are original. Compiled by Elias Howe, Jr. and arranged by Messrs. A. F. Knight and J. H. Seipp, of the Boston Brigade Band. Boston: Elias Howe, Jr., 1844. MUSIC 1979 – 1 – us L of C Photodup [780]

FIRST PLATFORM... / Creasy, E S – London, 1876 – 8mf – 1 – ILM-157/1 – ne IDC [327]

FIRST POPULATION CENSUS OF SUDAN, 1955/1956 / Sudan. Dept. of Statistics – Methods report. 2 v. 1958-60. BNE-7619 1 – 9 – ne IDC [310]

FIRST POPULATION CENSUS OF SUDAN. 1955/1956. FINAL REPORT / Sudan. Dept. of Statistics – 3v. Suppl.-Town planners suppl. 2 v. 1960. 1961-62. BNE-7613 1 – 9 – ne IDC [310]

FIRST POPULATION CENSUS OF SUDAN, 1955/1956 INTERIM REPORT / Sudan. Ministry of Social Affairs – 9v. (in 10). 1956 58. BNE-7677 1 – 9 – ne IDC [360]

First Presbyterian Church, Topeka, KS *see*
- CHURCH RECORDS
- RECORDS

FIRST PROGRESS REPORT ON THE ECONOMIC PROGRAMME, 1955-60 / Nigeria – (Sessional Paper No. 2 of 1957). Lagos. 1957. BD-659 1 – 9 – ne IDC [338]

FIRST PROGRESS REPORT ON THE RECONSTRUCTION AND DEVELOPMENT PROGRAMME 1960-65 FOR THE PERIOD 1960-61 / Mauritius – (Sessional Paper No. 4 of 1962). Port Louis. 1962. BD-445 1 – 9 – ne IDC [338]

THE FIRST PUBLISHERS OF TRUTH : BEING EARLY RECORDS (NOW FIRST PRINTED) OF THE INTRODUCTION OF QUAKERISM INTO THE COUNTIES OF ENGLAND AND WALES / ed by Penney – London: Headley; Philadelphia: H. Newman, 1907 – 1mf – us A.T.L.A. [240]

A FIRST READER IN NEW TESTAMENT GREEK / Moulton, James Hope – London: Charles H Kelly, 1896 – 1mf – 9 – 0-8370-9297-3 – 1986-3297 – us A.T.L.A. [450]

FIRST REPORT / Great Britain. Committee on Modern Languages Research and Development – 1968 – 9 – uk Microform Academic [324]

FIRST REPORT / Great Britain. Public Schools Commission – 1968 – 9 – uk Microform Academic [324]

THE FIRST REPORT... : MEETINGS OF THE LEGISLATIVE COUNCIL, URBAN COUNCIL, GOVERNMENT BOARDS AND COMMITTEES FEBRUARY 1971 / Hong Kong. Chinese Language Committee – Hong Kong, 1971 – 1mf – 9 – DE-159/1 – ne IDC [370]

FIRST REPORT 1970 / Fiji. Teacher Education Planning Committee – 1mf – 9 – DE-605/1 – ne IDC [370]

FIRST REPORT FROM THE SELECT COMMITTEE ON EMIGRATION, SCOTLAND, TOGETHER WITH THE MINUTES OF EVIDENCE AND APPENDIX – s.l: House of Commons, 1841. SEM105P157 – 3mf – 9 – Can$6.75 – cn Bibl Nat [324]

FIRST REPORT OF THE COMMITTEE OF THE HOUSE OF ASSEMBLY... / Bas-Canada. Parlement. Chambre d'assemblee. Comite sur Cette Partie... – Quebec: J Neilson, 1821. SEM105P1281 – 3mf – 9 – Can$6.75 – cn Bibl Nat [333]

FIRST REPORT OF THE COMMITTEE OF THE HOUSE OF ASSEMBLY ON THAT PART OF THE SPEECH OF HIS EXCELLENCY... / Bas-Canada. Parlement. Chambre d'Assemblee. Comite sur Cette Partie... – Quebec: J Neilson, 1821 – 3mf – 9 – Can$6.75 – cn Bibl Nat [971]

FIRST REPORT OF THE GLASGOW ASSOCIATION IN AID OF CHINESE MEDICAL MISSIONS – [Hackney], 1846 – 1mf – 9 – ne IDC [610]

THE FIRST REPORT OF THE MEDICAL MISSIONARY SOCIETY'S HOSPITAL AT MACAO – Canton, 1838 – 1mf – 9 – ne IDC [610]

THE FIRST RESULTS OF THE GENERAL POPULATION CENSUS 1964 / Libya. Ministry of National Economy – BNE-510 1 – 9 – ne IDC [304]

FIRST, SECOND AND THIRD CONFERENCES / United Nations. Conferences on the Law of the Sea – 22v. 81-906 – 9 – $40.00 – us L.L.M.C. [340]

THE FIRST SIX-YEAR PLAN OF NIGERIA / Nigeria. General Agreement on Tariffs and Trade – Geneva. 1966. BD-241 1 – 9$6.00 – ne IDC [380]

THE FIRST SOCIAL EXPERIMENTS IN AMERICA. A STUDY IN THE DEVELOPMENT OF SPANISH INDIAN POLICY...CAMBRIDGE (USA), 1935 / Hanke, Lewis – Madrid: Razon y Fe, 1936 – 1 – sp Bibl Santa Ana [320]

FIRST SOUTHERN BAPTIST CHURCH. OMAHA, NEBRASKA : CHURCH RECORDS – 1956-61 – 1 – 6.75 – us Baptist [240]

FIRST STATE DEVELOPMENT PLAN 1970-74 / Nigeria. South-Eastern State of Nigeria, Ministry of Economic Development and Reconstruction – Calabar. BD-1711 1 – 9 – ne IDC [338]

FIRST STEPS IN ASSYRIAN : A BOOK FOR BEGINNERS: BEING A SERIES OF HISTORICAL, MYTHOLOGICAL, RELIGIOUS, MAGICAL, EPISTOLARY AND OTHER TEXTS PRINTED IN CUNEIFORM CHARACTERS WITH INTERLINEAR TRANSLITERATION AND TRANSLATION: AND A SKETCH OF ASSYRIAN GRAMMAR, SIGN-LIST AND VOCABULARY / King, Leonard William – (Includes glossary) – London: Kegan Paul, Trench, Truebner, 1898 – 2mf – 9 – 0-8370-8915-8 – 1986-2915 – us A.T.L.A. [470]

FIRST STEPS IN NEW TESTAMENT GREEK / Clapperton, John Alexander – London: Charles H Kelly, 1901 – 1mf – 9 – 0-8370-9134-9 – 1986-3134 – us A.T.L.A. [450]

FIRST STEPS TOWARD CHURCH UNITY / Parkhurst, Charles H – New York: F.H. Revell, c1891 – 1mf – us A.T.L.A. [240]

THE FIRST THREE CENTURIES OF APPALACHIAN TRAVEL – 9 – us Primary [910]

FIRST THREE GOSPELS: THEIR ORIGIN AND RELATIONS / Carpenter, Joseph Estlin – London: Br. & For. Unitarian Assoc., 1909. 1 fiche – 9 – us A.T.L.A. [240]

FIRST TRUE GENTLEMAN: A STUDY OF THE HUMAN NATURE OF OUR LORD – Boston: John W. Luce, 1907. 1 fiche – 9 – us A.T.L.A. [240]

FIRST TWELVE MILE BAPTIST CHURCH. CAMPBELL COUNTY. KENTUCKY : CHURCH RECORDS – 1818-1957. Lacks 1885-1926 – 640p – 1 – $28.80 – us Baptist [240]

THE FIRST TWO YEARS DEVELOPMENT OF THE VENEREAL DISEASE RESEARCH INSTITUTE / Indonesia. Venereal Disease Research Institute – SE-3195 1. 1953 – 9 – ne IDC [616]

First United Methodist Church (New Lexington, Ohio) *see* RECORDS

First United Methodist Church (Oberlin, Ohio) *see* RECORDS

FIRST UNITED METHODIST CHURCH RECORDS – Oberlin. Ohio. 1860-1990 – 2r – 1 – us Archival [920]

First United Methodist Church, Wellington, KS *see* MEMBERSHIP REGISTER

FIRST U.S. ARMY REPORT OF OPERATIONS, 1943-1945 / U.S. Army. First Army – 2r – 1 – $170.00 – S1682 – us Scholarly Res [355]

FIRST VICTORIA DIRECTORY – West Coast. 1860 – 1r – 1 – $50.00 – D118 – us Library Micro [978]

FIRST WOMEN PHYSICIANS TO THE ORIENT / Baker, Frances J – 1904 – 9 – us A.T.L.A. [240]

FIRST WORLD – v. 1-. 1977- – 1,5,6,9 – us UMI [305]

FIRST WORLD WAR: A DOCUMENTARY RECORD / ed by Winter, J M – (Series One: European War 1914-1919, The War Reserve Collection (WRA-WRE) from Cambridge University Library. Part 1: The Card Catalogue Index and Manuscript Listings. Part 2: Trench Journals, Personal Narratives & Reminiscences. 20r. 1993. $2,300.00. Part 3: Allied Propaganda of the First World War. 20r. 1993. $2,300.00. Part 4: German Propaganda of the First World War. 20r. 1994. $2,300.00. Part 5: The Royal Army Medical Corps, Red Cross and Other Auxiliary Services. 20r.$2,300.00) – Marlborough: Adam Matthew Publications, 1991 – 7r – 1 – $800 00 – uk Matthew [940]

THE FIRST WORLD WAR: POLITICAL, SOCIAL AND MILITARY MANUSCRIPT SOURCES – (Part One: Haig's autograph Great War diary (NLS Acc. 3155, Nos. 96, 97 and 141-153)) – Series One: The Haig Papers from the National Library of Scotland – 1 – us Primary [920]

FIRST YEAR PROGRESS REPORT ON THE FIVE YEAR DEVELOPMENT PLAN (PUBLIC SECTOR) 1 JUL 1964 TO 30 JUN 1965 / Tanzania. Ministry of Economic Affairs and Dev. Planning – Dar es Salaam. 1965 – 9 – ne IDC [338]

THE FIRST YEARS OF EMERITA AUGUSTA. (LOS PRIMEROS ANOS DE EMERITA AUGUSTA) / Richmond, I A – London: Imp. Instituto Lancaster House, 1931. Reimp. Archaeological Journal. vol 86. 1930. Original y traduccion – 1 – sp Bibl Santa Ana [946]

Firstov, I I *see* MORDOVIIA V GODY PERVOI RUSSKOI REVOLIUTSII

Firth, Charles Harding *see* THE LAST YEARS OF THE PROTECTORATE, 1656-1658

FIRTH GRAPHIC – Firth, NE. -w. Oct. 1895-Jan. 1896; Mar. 1896-Aug. 1896; Oct. 1896-Jul. 1897; Sep. 1897-Jun. 1899; Mar. 1908-Nov. 1910 – 1 – us NE Hist [071]

Firth, John B *see*
- AUGUSTUS CAESAR AND THE ORGANIZATION OF THE EMPIRE OF ROME
- CONSTANTINE THE GREAT

FIS *see* FIZKULTURA I SPORT

FISCAL POLICY FORUM – v1-. 1983- – 1,5,6,9 – us UMI [073]

FISCAL STUDIES – (1982-. 1,5,6,9) – 1979- – 1 – us UMI [073]

THE FISCAL SUPERSTITION (H. OPPOSES PROTECTIONISM) / Hirsch, Max – 1895. With: The Liberation by Heinrich Heine and The Scab by Jack London. 1905. 1 fiche (24x) – 9 – 1.00f – at Libertarian Micro [320]

Fisch, Richard *see* GENERALMAJOR V. STILLE UND FRIEDRICH DER GROSSE CONTRA LESSING

Fischart, J *see* BEWAERUNG VND ERKLAERUNG DES VRALTEN GEMEYNEN SPRUECHWORTS: DIE GELEHRTEN DIE VERKEHRTEN

Fischel, A *see* DER PANSLAWISMUS BIS ZUM WELTKRIEG

Fischer *see* PLANTES RECUILLIES PENDANT LE VOYAGE DES RUSSES AUTOUR DU MONDE

Fischer, A *see* UNTERSUCHUNGEN UEBER DEN BAU DER CYANOPHYCEEN UND BAKTERIEN

Fischer, Bernhard *see* OTTO LUDWIGS TRAUERSPIELPLAN "DER SANDWIRT VON PASSEIER"

Fischer, C E C *see* FLORA OF THE PRESIDENCY OF MADRAS

Fischer, Chr. A *see* ANTWORT AUFF DIE WIDERLEGUNG SO CLAUSZ BREUETEL. HAT GETHAN AUFF DAS BUCH, VON DER WIDERTAUFFER VERFLUCHTEN VRSPRUNG

Fischer, Desmond *see* RIGHT TO COMMUNICATE

Fischer, Engelbert Lorenz *see* DER TRIUMPH DER CHRISTLICHEN PHILOSOPHIE

Fischer, Ernst *see* GOETHE DER GROSSE HUMANIST

Fischer, Ernst Gottfried *see* LEHRBUCH DER MECHANISCHEN NATURLEHRE

Fischer, F *see* DIE FORMELLE NATUR DER VOELKERRECHTLICHEN MANDATE...

Fischer, FE L von *see*
- CATALOGUE DU JARDIN DES PLANTES DE... A. DE RAZOUMOFFSKY... A GORENSKI PRES DE MOSCOU
- CATALOGUE DU JARDIN DES PLANTES DE A. DE RAZOUMOFFSKY A GORENSKI PRES DE MOSCOU
- CATALOGUE DU JARDIN DES PLANTES DE... A. DE RAZOUMOFFSKY... A GORENSKI PRES DE MOSCOU
- CATALOGUS HORTI IMPERIALIS PETROPOLITANI
- ENUMERATIO PLANTARUM NOVARUM A CL. SCHRENK LECTARUM
- INDEX SEMINUM, QUAE HORTUS BOTANICUS IMPERIALIS PETROPOLITANUS PRO MUTUA COMMUTATIONE OFFERT...
- SERTUM PETROPOLITANUM SEU ICONES ET DESCRIPTIONES PLANTARUM QUAE IN HORTO BOTANICO

Fischer, Fritz *see* LUDWIG NICOLOVIUS

Fischer, G *see* ENTOMOGRAPHIA IMPERII RUSSICCI

Fischer, Gerhard *see* GESAMTVERANT-WORTUNG UND SPEZIFIK: DIE CDU-PRESSE IN DER ENTWICKLUNG DES DDR-JOURNALISMUS 1957 BIS 1961

Fischer, Gottlob Nathanael *see* DEUTSCHE MONATSSCHRIFT/NEUE DEUTSCHE MONATSSCHRIFT

Fischer, H *see* DIE SACHMAENGELHAFTUNG BEIM KAUF BEWEGLICHER SACHEN...

Fischer, Hanns *see* ABERGLAUBE ODER VOLKSWEISHEIT?

Fischer, Hermann *see* HERMANN KURZ' SAEMTLICHE WERKE

Fischer, J *see* THE DISCOVERIES OF THE NORSEMEN IN AMERICA

Fischer, J B *see*
- FLORA JAVAE NEC NON INSULARUM ADJACENTIUM
- J.B. FISCHERS ZUSAETZE (SIC) ZU EINEM VERSUCH EINER NATURGESCHICHTE VON LIVLAND,...

Fischer, J E *see* SIBIRISCHE GESCHICHTE VON DER ENTDECKUNG SIBIRIENS BIS AUF DIE EROBERUNG DIESES LANDES DURCH DIE RUSSISCHE WAFFEN

Fischer, J G *see*
- SCHILLERS WERKE
- SCHILLER'S WORKS

Fischer, J P A *see*
- KORT EN GRONDIG ONDERWYS VAN DE TRANSPOSITIE BENEFFENS EENIGE KORTE AENMERKINGEN OVER DE MUSIEK DER OUDEN
- KORTE EN NOODIGSTE GRONDREGELEN VAN DE BASSUS-CONTINUUS

Fischer, Johann Carl *see* PHYSIKALISCHES WOERTERBUCH ODER ERKLAERUNG DER VORNEHMSTEN ZUR PHYSIK GEHOERENDEN BEGRIFFE UND KUNSTWOERTER

Fischer, Joseph *see* DIE CHRONOLOGISCHEN FRAGEN IN DEN BUECHERN ESRA-NEHEMIA

Fischer, Joseph C *see* THE CONSTRUCT VALIDITY OF A SCALE TO MEASURE TEACHER ENTHUSIASM IN SECONDARY PHYSICAL EDUCATION

Fischer, Kuno *see*
- BRIEFWECHSEL ZWISCHEN GOETHE UND K. GOETTLING IN DEN JAHREN 1824-1831
- A CRITIQUE OF KANT

Fischer, L *see* DIE KIRCHLICHEN QUATERTEMBER

Fischer, L H *see* ORTHOPTERA EUROPAEA

Fischer, Louis *see*
- THE WAR IN SPAIN
- WHY SPAIN FIGHTS ON

Fischer, Manfred et al *see* GEOGRAPHICAL SYSTEMS

Fischer, Max *see* HEINRICH VON KLEIST

Fischer, Paul *see* GOTT-NATUR

Fischer, Peter W *see* EL CAPITAL EXTERNO EN EL DESARROLLO ECONOMICO DE ARGENTINA
Fischer, Richard *see* CONRAD FERDINAND MEYER
Fischer, Stefan *see* EXPERTENSYSTEM-WARTUNG
Fischer, Tim *see* ABGASUNTERSUCHUNGEN AN EINEM PFLANZENOELBETRIEBENEN VORKAMMER-DIESELMOTOR
Fischer, Uwe *see* LIBERALISMUS UND STAATSUMFANG
Fischer von Waldheim, G *see* ORYCTOGRAPHIE DU GOUVERNEMENT DE MOSCOU
Fischer, W *see* FAO SPECIES INDENTIFICATION SHEETS FOR FISHERY PURPOSES
Fischer-Ooster, C von *see* DIE FOSSILEN FUCOIDEN DER SCHWEIZERALPHEN
Fischer-Piette, Edouard *see*
- REVISION DES CULTELLIDAE ET SOLECURTIDAE (MOLLUSQUES LAMELLIBRANCHES)
- REVISION DES PSAMMOBIIDAE
- SYNOPSIS PROVISOIRE DES SOLEN (MOLLUSQUES LAMELLIBRANCHES)

Fischmann, N I *see* SISERA
Fiscus, Douglas L *see* COMPARISON OF THE MID-AMERIACN CONFERENCE ATHLETIC DEPARTMENT REGARDING COMPLIANCE WITH TITLE 9
Fiser Funeral Home (Clyde, Ohio) *see* FUNERAL RECORD AND LEDGER
Fish and Game Club. Montreal. *see* CONSTITUTION AND RULES OF THE FISH AND GAME CLUB...IN CONNECTION WITH THE FISH AND GAME PROTECTION CLUB OF THE PROVINCE OF QUEBEC: ADOPTED MAY 12TH, 1882.
FISH AND GAME PROTECTION CLUB OF THE PROVINCE OF QUEBEC : CONSTITUTION AND BY-LAWS OF THE FISH – Montreal? s.n., 1879 (Montreal: Gazette). 04351. (Pre-1900 Canadiana) – 9 – cn C.I.H.M. [971]
FISH CULTURE – 1992 – 204p – it F.A.O. [639]
FISH CULTURE IN CENTRAL EAST AFRICA / Maar, A et al – 1966 3rd print 1983 – 160p – it F.A.O. [639]
FISH CULTURE IN UNDRAINABLE PONDS : A MANUAL FOR EXTENSION – 1992 – 247p – it F.A.O. [639]
FISH FEED TECHNOLOGY : LECTURES PRESENTED AT THE F.A.O./UNEP TRAINING COURSE IN FISH FEED TECHNOLOGY, HELD AT THE COLLEGE OF FISHERIES, UNIVERSITY OF WASHINGTON, WASHINGTON, 1978 – 1980 2nd print 1985 – 400p – it F.A.O. [636]
FISH FEEDS AND FEEDING IN DEVELOPING COUNTRIES : AN INTERIM REPORT ON THE ADCP FEED DEVELOPMENT PROGRAMME – 1983 – 103p – it F.A.O. [636]
Fish, Henry Clay *see*
- HANDBOOK OF REVIVALS
- HISTORY AND REPOSITORY OF PULPIT ELOQUENCE, DECEASED DIVINES
- PRIMITIVE PIETY REVIVED, OR, THE AGGRESSIVE POWER OF THE CHRISTIAN CHURCH
- PULPIT ELOQUENCE OF THE NINETEENTH CENTURY

FISH PRODUCTION IN IRRIGATION CANALS : A REVIEW – 1991 – 116p – it F.A.O. [338]
FISH RESOURCES OF THE NORTHWEST PACIFIC – 1985 – 203p – it F.A.O. [333]
Fishback, James *see* A DEFENCE OF THE ELKHORN ASSOCIATION IN SIXTEEN LETTERS, ADDRESSED TO ELDER HENRY TOLER, ENTITLED UNION-NO UNION
Fishburne, Benjamin Postell *see* THE PATENT APPLICATION, PREPARATION AND PROSECUTION
Fisher *see* COMPENDIUM OF HISTORY AND BIOGRAPHY OF KALAMAZOO COUNTY
Fisher, A Garth *see*
- A COMPARISON OF BODY COMPOSITION CHANGES IN MODERATELY OBESE AND EXTREMELY OBESE WOMEN WHO EXPERIENCE THE SAME CALORIC DEFICIT
- THE EFFECT OF TRANSVERSE PEDAL SPACING ON CYCLING EFFICIENCY
- EFFECT OF WATER RUNNING AND CYCLING ON VO2MAX AND 2-MILE PERFORMANCE
- A SUBMAXIMAL ONE-MILE TRACK JOG TO ESTIMATE VO2MAX IN FIT MEN AND WOMEN, AGES 30-39 YEARS

Fisher, Ann *see* A NEW GRAMMAR
Fisher, Carl Melchior *see* THE RELATIONSHIPS OF FINANCIAL SUBSIDY TO THE GROWTH AND DEVELOPMENT OF THE LUTHERAN CHURCH IN MALAYSIA
Fisher, CG *see* GENERAL LAND OFFICE CIRCULARS AND GENERAL REGULATIONS
Fisher, Charles A *see* A STUDY OF THE GUIDANCE CONSIDERED ESSENTIAL FOR TEACHER'S INTELLIGENT SELF-DIRECTION IN THE PROCESS OF SECURING EMPLOYMENT IN THE MIDDLE ATLANTIC STATES
Fisher, Clarence S *see*
- "BETHSHEAN"
- THE EXCAVATION OF ARMAGEDDON
- THE THRONE ROOM OF MERENPTAH

Fisher, Edward *see* THE MARROW OF MODERN DIVINITY
Fisher, Elliot D *see* THE TEMPLE...IN THE TIME OF OUR SAVIOUR
Fisher, Ernest B *see* HISTORY OF GRAND RAPIDS AND KENT COUNTY. FROM THE FIRST SETTLEMENT TO THE PRESENT TIME
Fisher, George Park *see*
- THE BEGINNINGS OF CHRISTIANITY: WITH A VIEW OF THE STATE OF THE ROMAN WORLD AT THE BIRTH OF CHRIST
- THE CHRISTIAN RELIGION
- THE COLONIAL ERA
- A DISCOURSE: COMMEMORATIVE OF THE HISTORY OF THE CHURCH OF CHRIST IN YALE COLLEGE
- DISCUSSIONS IN HISTORY AND THEOLOGY
- ESSAYS ON THE SUPERNATURAL ORIGIN OF CHRISTIANITY
- FAITH AND RATIONALISM
- THE GROUNDS OF THEISTIC AND CHRISTIAN BELIEF
- HISTORY OF CHRISTIAN DOCTRINE
- HISTORY OF THE CHRISTIAN CHURCH
- MANUAL OF CHRISTIAN EVIDENCES
- MANUAL OF NATURAL THEOLOGY
- NATURE AND METHOD OF REVELATION
- THE REFORMATION

Fisher, Harold H *see*
- THE FAMINE IN SOVIET RUSSIA
- PUBLIC RELATIONS OF THE COMMISSION FOR RELIEF IN BELGIUM: DOCUMENTS

Fisher, Herbert *see* THE MEDIEVAL EMPIRE
Fisher, Herbert Albert Laurens *see* FREDERIC WILLIAM MAITLAND, DOWNING PROFESSOR OF THE LAWS OF ENGLAND; A BIOGRAPHICAL SKETCH
Fisher, Hugh Dunn *see* PAPERS OF HUGH DUNN FISHER
Fisher, Jacob Carney *see* A SELECTED LIST OF PROBATE ATTORNEYS WITH GENERAL PRACTICE, AS COMPILED FOR FISHER'S PROBATE LAW DIRECTORY...1935-36
Fisher, James *see*
- LIFE AND TRAVELS OF JAMES FISHER: AN AUTOBIOGRAPHY
- OUR HIGHWAYS TO THE SEA BY RAIL AND WATER: THE ENLARGEMENT OF THE CANALS AN INTERNATIONAL WORK

Fisher, Janet M *see*
- EFFECTS OF VISUAL TRAINING ON VISUAL PURSUIT, CATCHING, AND ATTENTIVENESS
- FUNCTIONAL MOTOR SKILLS AND THE DEVELOPMENTALLY DISABLED

Fisher, Joseph Robert *see* THE END OF THE IRISH PARLIAMENT
Fisher, M K *see* LUNDA FOR BEGINNERS
Fisher, Michele M *see* THE EFFECT OF SUBMAXIMAL EXERCISE IN A NEUTRAL OR HOT-HUMID ENVIRONMENT ON RECOVERY HEMODYNAMICS IN MEN AND WOMEN
Fisher, N M *see* MUSCLE REHABILITATION OF PATIENTS WITH OSTEOARTHRITIS OF THE KNEES
Fisher, R *see* FISHER'S PRIZE CASES IN PENNSYLVANIA
Fisher, S B *see*
- PROBLEMS AND QUIZ. BILLS AND NOTES
- PROBLEMS AND QUIZ ON COMMON-LAW PLEADING
- QUIZ ON INTERNATIONAL LAW

Fisher, S J *see* A STUDY OF THE AMERICAN NEGRO
Fisher, S S *see* FISHER'S PATENT REPORTS IN THE U.S. SUPREME AND CIRCUIT COURTS
Fisher, Sidney G *see* THE TRIAL OF THE CONSTITUTION
Fisher, William A *see* NOTES ON MUSIC IN OLD BOSTON
Fisher, William H *see* FISHER'S PATENT CASES IN THE U.S. CIRCUIT COURTS
FISHERIES ACOUSTICS : A PRACTICAL MANUAL FOR AQUATIC BIOMASS ESTIMATION – 1983 – 257p – it F.A.O. [639]
FISHERIES CREDIT PROGRAMMES AND REVOLVING LOAN FUNDS : CASE STUDIES – 1989 – 134p – it F.A.O. [332]
FISHERIES FORECASTING SYSTEM IN JAPAN FOR COASTAL PELAGIC FISH – 1988 – 80p – it F.A.O. [639]
FISHERIES IN THE FOOD ECONOMY – 1968 – 79p – it F.A.O. [338]
FISHERIES OF TURKEY / International Center for Aquaculture – 1972. 1 reel – 1, 5 – us Spaulding [639]
FISHERIES REGULATIONS UNDER EXTENDED JURISDICTION AND INTERNATIONAL LAW – 1992 – 28p – it F.A.O. [340]
FISHERIES RESOURCES OF THE MEDITERRANEAN. PART 2 : BLACK SEA – 1985 – 149p – it F.A.O. [333]
FISHER'S JUVENILE SCRAPBOOK – 1836-50 – 30mf – 9 – £250.00 – uk Chadwyck [800]
FISHER'S PATENT CASES IN THE U.S. CIRCUIT COURTS / Fisher, William H – Cincinnati: Clarke & Co. v1-6. 1840-73 (all publ) – 48mf – 9 – $72.00 – LLMC 81-449 – us L.L.M.C. [340]
FISHER'S PATENT REPORTS IN THE U.S. SUPREME AND CIRCUIT COURTS / Fisher, S S – Cincinnati: Clarke & Co. 1v. 1821-50 (all publ) – 9mf – 9 – $13.50 – LLMC 84-325 – us L.L.M.C. [340]
FISHER'S PRIZE CASES IN PENNSYLVANIA / Fisher, R – Philadelphia: Redwood Fisher. 1v. 1813 (all publ) – 1mf – 9 – $1.50 – LLMC 81-450 – us L.L.M.C. [340]
FISHER'S PROBATE LAW DIRECTORY, 1914-1918 – (Digests the probate laws for the US states and territories of the period) – St Louis: The Legal Directory Publ Co, 1918 – 4mf – 9 – $6.00 – LLMC 96-053 – us L.L.M.C. [340]
FISHER'S RAILWAY ADVERTISER – Dublin, Ireland.Sept 1846-1849. -w. 1/4 reel – 1 – uk British Libr Newspaper [072]
Fisher-Stitt, Norma S *see* EFFECT OF AN INTERACTIVE MULTIMEDIA COMPUTER TUTORIAL ON STUDENTS' UNDERSTANDING OF BALLET ALLEGRO TERMINOLOGY
FISHERY BULLETINS / U.S. Fish and Wildlife Service – v1-84:4.1881-1986. 804 fiches – 9 – $1200.00 – us Updata [639]
FISHERY FLEET STATISTICS : 1970, 1975, 1977-1986 – 1988 – 327p – it F.A.O. [639]
FISHERY FLEET STATISTICS 1970, 1975, 1977-81 – 1985 – 237p – it F.A.O. [310]
FISHERY FLEET STATISTICS 1970, 1975, 1980-89 – 1992 – 354p – it F.A.O. [338]
FISHERY LEAFLETS / U.S. National Marine Fisheries Service (NOAA) – Nos. 1-638. 1948-71. 680 fiches – 9 – 1400.00 – us Updata [324]
FISHERY MANAGEMENT IN JAPAN – 1983 – 32p – it F.A.O. [338]
FISHERY MANAGEMENT OPTIONS FOR LESSER ANTILLES COUNTRIES – 1990 – 136p – it F.A.O. [650]
THE FISHERY QUESTION – s.l.: s.n., 1890?. 05461. (Pre-1900 Canadiana) – 9 – cn C.I.H.M. [971]
THE FISHERY QUESTION: ITS IMPERIAL IMPORTANCE / Bourinot, John George – Ottawa: J. Durie, 1886. 00189. (Pre-1900 Canadiana) – 9 – cn C.I.H.M. [971]
FISHERY RESOURCES OF PACIFIC ISLAND COUNTRIES : HOLOTHURIANS – 1990 – 152p – it F.A.O. [333]
FISHERY RESOURCES OF PACIFIC ISLAND COUNTRIES : TROCHUS – 1990 – 95p – it F.A.O. [333]
FISHERY RESOURCES OF PACIFIC ISLAND COUNTRIES. PART 1 : DEEP-WATER SHRIMPS – 1985 – 50p – it F.A.O. [333]
FISHERY STATISTICS OF THE UNITED STATES / U.S. National Marine Fisheries Service (NOAA) – 1919-77.263 fiches. Formerly: Fishery Industries of U.S., 1919-38. Current title, 1939- , with subtitle, Statistical Digest, Nos. 1-71, to 1977 – 9 – 360.00 – us Updata [324]
FISHERY WORKER : 1948-1954 / Cannery Workers' Union of the Pacific, Los Angeles County Harbor District – (Coll title: Labor Union Periodicals, Pt 3) – 1996 – 1r – 1 – $135.00 – 1-55655-629-2 – us UPA [331]
FISHES, LIVING AND FOSSIL / Dean, B – Z-2098 2. 1895 – 8 – ne IDC [590]
FISHES OF AUSTRALIA / Stead, D G – Z 2131 2. 1906 – 8 – ne IDC [590]
THE FISHES OF GREAT BRITAIN AND IRELAND / Day, F – Z-2097 2. 2 v. 1880-1884 – 8 – ne IDC [590]
THE FISHES OF INDIA. BURMA AND CEYLON / Day, F – Supp. 1888. 2123 2. 1876-1878 – 8 – ne IDC [590]
THE FISHES OF MALABAR / Day, F – London. 1865. B-2612 2 – 8 – ne IDC [590]
FISHES OF NEW ZEALAND / Hutton, FW & Hector, J – Z-2115 2. 1872 – 8 – ne IDC [590]
THE FISHES OF NORTH AND MIDDLE AMERICA / Jordan, D S & Evermann, B W – 2133 2. 4v 1896-1900 – 8 – ne IDC [590]
THE FISHES OF OCEANIA / Fowler, H W – 2629 2. 1928 – 8 – ne IDC [590]
THE FISHES OF PORTO RICO / Evermann, B W & Marsh, M C – 2628 2. 1900 – 8 – ne IDC [590]
THE FISHES OF SAMOA / Jordan, D S & Seale, A – Z-2119 2 – 8 – ne IDC [590]
FISHES OF THE NORTH-EASTERN ATLANTIC AND THE MEDITERRANEAN / ed by Whitehead, P J P et al – 3v – 9 – fr UNESCO [590]
THE FISHES OF ZANZIBAR / Playfair, R L & Guenther, A C L – Z-2125 2. 1866 – 8 – ne IDC [590]
Fishgendler, A M *see* USPEKHI POTREBITEL'SKOI KOOPERATSII
Fishgendler, Abram Markovich *see*
- DVA PUTI
- KOOPERATSIIA V ZAPADNOI EVROPE I ROSSII
- OSNOVNYE VOPROSY SOVETSKOI KOOPERATSII
- SOLDATY FRONTA I VOPROSY VO INY I MIRA

FISHING BOAT CONSTRUCTION 1 : BUILDING A SAWN-FRAME FISCHING BOAT – 1988 – 61p – it F.A.O. [623]
FISHING BOAT DESIGNS, 3 : SMALL TRAWLERS – 1990 – 60p – it F.A.O. [623]
FISHING BOAT DESIGNS-4 : SMALL STEEL FISHING BOATS – 1984 – 59p – it F.A.O. [623]
FISHING CREEK BAPTIST CHURCH. SOMERSET, KENTUCKY : CHURCH RECORDS – 1813-1949 – 1 – 17.10 – us Baptist [240]
FISHING NEWS – 1966-73 – 1 – uk World [073]
FISHING RESORTS ALONG THE CANADIAN PACIFIC RAILWAY, EASTERN DIVISION – Where to go for trout, bass and maskinonge, and what it costs to get there: from special explorations by commissioners of the Canadian Sportsman. Montreal: Canadian Pacific Railway, 1887. 00431. (Pre-1900 Canadiana) – 9 – cn C.I.H.M. [971]
FISHING WITH BOTTOM GILLNETS – 1980 – 39p – it F.A.O. [639]
FISHKILL DAILY HERALD – Newburgh. N.Y. 1903-1913 – 1 – us UMI [071]
FISHRAPPER – Wheeler OR. July 8 1976-Sep 26 1985 – 1 – us U.O. Library [071]
Fishwick, Wilfred *see*
- STRENGTHENING COOPERATION BETWEEN ENGINEERING SCHOOLS AND INDUSTRY
- STRUCTURES OF TECHNOLOGICAL EDUCATION AND CONTRIBUTING SOCIAL FACTORS

FISICA MODERNA RACIONAL Y EXPERIMENTAL. 1ER T. / Piquer, Andres – Valencia, 1745 – 8mf – 9 – sp Cultura [610]
FISIOGRAFIA DEL GUADIANA / Hernandez Pacheco, Eduardo – Badajoz: Imprenta del Hospicio Provincial, 1929 – 1 – sp Bibl Santa Ana [550]
Fisk, Amos Kidder *see* JEWISH SCRIPTURES...IN THE LIGHT OF THEIR ORIGIN AND HISTORY
FISK EXPOSITOR AND FISK HERALD – Ed. by W. E. B. DuBois. v. 1-5. 1878-88. Nov 1885-Jun 1888. No. 77-3. One reel – 1 – 20.00 – us Partington [305]
Fisk, James L *see* IDAHO, HER GOLD FIELDS AND THE ROUTE TO THEM: A HANDBOOK FOR EMIGRANTS
Fisk University Libary. Nashville *see* DICTIONARY CATALOG OF THE NEGRO COLLECTION OF THE FISK UNIVERSITY LIBRARY
Fiske, Amos Kidder *see* MYTHS OF ISRAEL: THE ANCIENT BOOK OF GENESIS
Fiske, Asa Severance *see* REASON AND FAITH
Fiske, John *see*
- A CENTURY OF SCIENCE AND OTHER ESSAYS
- CIVIL GOVERNMENT IN THE UNITED STATES
- THE DESTINY OF MAN VIEWED IN THE LIGHT OF HIS ORIGIN

- MYTHS AND MYTH-MAKERS
- THROUGH NATURE TO GOD

Fison, Lorimer *see*
- ARTICLES, LETTERS AND MISCELLANEOUS PAPERS, 1873-1907
- CORRESPONDENCE, 16 OCTOBER 1873-15 OCTOBER 1878
- CORRESPONDENCE, 1870-1881
- LETTERBOOKS
- LINGUISTIC MATERIAL AND CORRESPONDENCE ON LOCAL CUSTOMS, 1880-1894
- VARIOUS MANUSCRIPTS AND PAPERS, 188?-19-?; AND PRESS COPY BOOK

FISONOMIA MORAL DE A. MONTANO / Roldan, Federico – Malaga: Revista Espanola de Estudios Biblicos, 1928 – 1 – sp Bibl Santa Ana [170]

Fita, Fidel *see*
- ALFAR MORUNO DE BADAJOZ
- ANTIGUAS EPIGRAFES DE TANGER, JEREZ Y ARCOS DE LA FRONTERA (MERIDA)
- ARA ROMANA DE BARCARROTA
- CARTAS DE BAROLOME JOSE GALLARDO. NOTICIA
- EL CASTRO ROMANO DE CACERES EL VIEJO. NUEVAS INSCRIPCIONES
- COLON ESTREMENA
- COLON EXTREMENO? DE VICENTE PAREDES
- CORIA COMPOSTELANA Y TEMPLARIA
- DISQUISICIONES AMERICANAS 2. DON MARTIN CORTES Y DON DIEGO COLON, CABALLEROS DE SANTIAGO
- DUQUE DE T'SERCLAES TOMA POSESION ACADEMICO NUMERO REAL DE LA HISTORIA. NOTICIAS
- DURANTE EL SEMESTRE PASADO FALLECIERON...TAMBIEN D. PEDRO MARIA PLANO, EN MERIDA...
- EN LA SESION DEL 23 OCTUBRE...VACANTES...FUERON ELEGIDOS...ACADEMICOS DE NUMERO...DUQUE DE T'SERCLARES...
- EPIGRAFES HEBREOS DE BEJAR Y SALAMANCA
- EPIGRAFIA ROMANA DE MERIDA
- EPIGRAFIA ROMANA DE MONTANCHEZ, RENA, BANOS DE LA ENCINA. SANTISTEBAN DEL PUERTO, CARTAGENA Y CADIZ
- EPIGRAFIA ROMANA Y GRIEGA DE LA PROVINCIA DE CACERES. NUEVAS ILUSTRACIONES
- EPIGRAFIA ROMANA Y VISIGOTICA
- EPIGRAFIA ROMANA Y VISIGOTICA DE GARLITOS, CAPILLA, BELALCAZAR Y EL GUIJO
- EPIGRAFIA ROMANA Y VISIGOTICA DE MONTEMOLIN
- EPIGRAFIA ROMANA Y VISIGOTICA. POZA DE LA SAL. MERIDA. ALBURQUERQUE
- EPIGRAFIA VISIGOTICA Y ROMANA DE BARCELONA, MERIDA, MORENTE Y BUJALANCE
- EXCURSION EPIGRAFICA POR VILLAR DEL REY, ALHAMBRA, VENTA DE LOS SANTOS, CARTAGENA, LOGRONO Y ORENSE
- EXCURSIONES EPIGRAFICAS. DE MONESTERIO A MERIDA
- FALLECIMIENTO DE D. FRANCISCO JARRIN, OBISPO DE PLASENCIA
- FALLECIMIENTO DEL MARQUES DE MONSALUD
- FALLECIMIENTO EN PLASENCIA DE DON JOSE BENAVIDES CHECA
- EL GUIJO, BELALCAZAR Y CAPILLA. NUEVAS INSCRIPCIONES ROMANAS
- HAN SIDO NOMBRADOS...EN PLASENCIA D. VICENTE PAREDES...
- LA INQUISICION EN GUADALUPE
- INSCRIPCION HEMISFERICA DE SANTA CRUZ Y LAPIDA DE SOLANS DE CABANAS. NOTAS A UNA CARTA DE ROSO DE LUNA
- INSCRIPCION ROMANA DE LA PARRA Y DE ALMENDRALEJO
- INSCRIPCION ROMANA DE MERIDA
- INSCRIPCION ROMANA DE RIOLOBOS
- INSCRIPCION ROMANA DE VALERA LA VIEJA, JUNTO A FREGENAL
- INSCRIPCIONES CONSTANTINIANAS DE MERIDA
- INSCRIPCIONES INEDITAS DE MERIDA, BADAJOZ, ALANJE, CANETE DE LAS TORRES Y VILCHES
- INSCRIPCIONES ROMANAS DE CACERES, UBEDA Y ALCALA DE HENARES
- INSCRIPCIONES ROMANAS DE MERIDA Y NAVA DE RICO MALILLO
- INSCRIPCIONES ROMANAS INEDITAS DE CACERES, BRANDOMIL, NARANCO Y LERIDA
- INSCRIPCIONES ROMANAS INEDITAS DE TRUJILLO
- INSCRIPCIONES VISIGOTICAS
- LAPIDA ROMANA INEDITA DE ALMENDRALEJO
- LAPIDA ROMANA INEDITA, MERIDA
- LAPIDAS INEDITAS DE MARCHAMALO, CACERES, PALENCIA Y LUGO
- LAPIDAS ROMANAS DE GARLITOS, ARROYO DEL PUERCO Y ARAYA, EN EXTREMADURA
- LAPIDAS ROMANAS DE JEREZ DE LOS CABALLEROS Y MORON DE LA FRONTERA
- LAPIDAS ROMANAS INEDITAS
- EL MARQUES DE MONSALUD ES SUSTITUIDO POR D. ADOLFO BONILLA
- EL MARQUES DE MONSALUD MIEMBRO DEL INSTITUTO ARQUEOLOGICO DE BERLIN
- MONTANCHEZ. NUEVA INSCRIPCION ROMANA
- MONUMENTOS HEBREOS (SALAMANCA, BEJAR, PLASENCIA, BEMIBRE)
- NECROLOGIA DEL MARQUES DE MONSALUD
- NERTOBRIGA BETURICA
- NOTICIA SOBRE REVISTA DE EXTREMADURA Y LAPIDAS
- NOTICIAS
- NOTICIAS DE...
- NOTICIAS SOBRE EL ESTADO DE LA BASILICA DE SANTA EULALIA Y NUEVOS HALLAZGOS EN MERIDA
- NUEVA INSCRIPCION ROMANA DE SANTA AMALIA
- NUEVA LAPIDA ROMANA DEL ESCURIAL (TRUJILLO)
- NUEVA LAPIDA ROMANA EN SERRADILLA (CACERES)
- NUEVAS INSCRIPCIONES DE MERIDA Y SEVILLA
- NUEVAS INSCRIPCIONES ROMANAS (CORIA, GIJON)
- NUEVAS INSCRIPCIONES ROMANAS DE IBAHERNANDO
- NUEVAS INSCRIPCIONES ROMANAS DE MERIDA
- NUEVAS INSCRIPCIONES ROMANAS Y VISIGOTICAS
- NUEVAS INSCRIPCIONES ROMANAS Y VISIGOTICAS DE TALAVAN Y MERIDA
- NUEVAS LAPIDAS ROMANAS DE NOYA, CANDO, CEREZO Y JUMILLA
- NUEVAS LAPIDAS ROMANAS DE SANTISTEBAN DEL PUERTO, BERLANGA (BADAJOZ), AVILA Y RETORTILLO (SALAMANCA)
- NUEVAS LAPIDAS ROMANAS DE TARRAGONA, PALENCIA, SALVARIERRA DE LOS BARROS BAEZA Y NAVA DE MENA
- NUNEZ DE BALBOA. CONGRESO DE HISTORIA Y GEOGRAFIA HISPANOAMERICANA, CELEBRADO EN SEVILLA
- PASA A LA COMISION DE RECOMPENSAR DE LA REAL ACADEMIA DE LA HISTORIA
- PRESENTO...NUEVAS INSCRIPCIONES ROMANAS QUE ACABAN DE HACER EN PLASENICA...EXTENSION DE LA PENINSULA
- RESENA EPIGRAFICA. SAN MARTIN E TREBEJO, MESTANZA, MAZARRON, TOBARRA, ORETO, PERALES DE MILLA, LIRIA RUBI, AMPURIAS Y OLLEROS DE PISUERGA
- UN SARCOFAGO ROMANO DE MERIDA
- SELLO LEGIONARIO (DE AZUAGA)
- SILVA Y FIGUEROA, GARCIA DE. COMENTARIOS A LA EMBAJADA DE PERSIA
- TALAVERA LA VIEJA. LAPIDA
- TESERA ROMANA DE PLOMO EXTREMENA, QUE POSEE DON ANTONIO VIVES
- TRES LAPIDAS VISIGODAS DE MERIDA

Fitch, E R *see* THE BAPTISTS OF CANADA

Fitch, John *see* PAPERS

FITCHBURG 1751-1895 – (Mf 1-3: Index: B,M,D 1751-1872. Mf 4: Marriages & Intentions 1754-96. Mf 5-14: Town & Vital Records 1776-1842. Mf 15-17: Town & Vital Records 1814-50. Mf 18-23: Births & Deaths by Family 1797-1843. Mf 24-37: Index to Births 1844-1915. Mf 38-39: B,M,D 1843-59. Mf 40-58: Births 1860-95. Mf 59-63: Marriages 1851-72. Mf 64-70: Index to Marriages 1873-1916. Mf 71-81: Marriages 1873-1900. Mf 82-90: Index to Deaths 1844-1916. Mf 91-112: Deaths 1856-1907) – (mf ed 1987) – 112mf – 9 – 0-87623-041-9 – us Holbrook [920]

Fitchett, William Henry *see*
- THE BELIEFS OF UNBELIEF
- BELIEFS OF UNBELIEF
- NELSON AND HIS CAPTAINS: SKETCHES OF FAMOUS SEAMEN

Fite, Warner *see* AN INTRODUCTORY STUDY OF ETHICS

Fitger, E *see* DIE RUECKWIRKUNG DES OSTASIATISCHEN KRIEGES...

FITNAH SEBAGAI SUATU SISTIM "PEREBUTAN KEKUASAAN."SE 5914/1. 1966? / Simandjuntak, L – 9 – ne IDC [950]

Fitnam, John Christopher *see* A PRACTICAL TREATISE ON THE CODE SUMMONS AND THE MODE OF SERVING IT AS PRESCRIBED BY THE CIVIL CODES OF COLORADO, WYOMING, KANSAS, NEVADA, NEBRASKA AND OTHER STATES.

FITNESS LEVELS OF CHILDREN IN NORTH CAROLINA / Baines, KC – 1991 – 1mf – 9 – $4.00 – us Microform Publ [613]

THE FITNESS OF CHRISTIANITY TO MAN / Huntington, Frederic Dan – New York: Thomas Whittaker, 1878 – 1mf – 9 – 0-8370-3698-4 – 1985-1698 – us A.T.L.A. [240]

THE FITNESS OF HOLY SCRIPTURE FOR UNFOLDING THE SPIRITUAL LIFE OF MEN; 2 / Trench, Richard Chenevix – Philadelphia: H. Hooker, 1860. 1mf – 9 – us A.T.L.A. [240]

FITOTERAPIA : REVISTA DI STUDI ED APPLICAZIONI DELLE PIANTE MEDICINALI – Milano: Inverni and Della Beffa SpA, [v51-52. 1980-81] – 1r – 1 – us Res Libr [072]

FITTING HUMAN PERFORMANCE DATA: A COMPARISON OF THREE METHODS OF DATA SMOOTHING WITH MLAB / York, Sherril L – 1981 – 2mf – 9 – $8.00 – us Microform Publ [790]

Fittz, Hervey *see* THE FRIENDS OF CHRIST KEEP HIS COMMANDMENTS OR OBEDIENCE THE TEST OF DISCIPLESHIP

FITZ OF FITZ-FORD / Bray, Anna Eliza – British Fiction Archive: Unit 2 – 9 – uk Bell [830]

Fitzgerald, Charles Cooper Penrose *see* LIFE OF VICE-ADMIRAL SIR GEORGE TRYON, K.C.B

Fitzgerald, Edward *see* MISCELLANIES

Fitzgerald, Percy Hetherington *see*
- CHARLES LAMB
- CROKER'S BOSWELL AND BOSWELL. STUDIES IN THE LIFE OF JOHNSON
- THE HISTORY OF PICKWICK
- LIFE AND WORK OF HENRY IRVING
- PRINCIPLES OF COMEDY AND DRAMATIC EFFECT

Fitzgerald, Robert Allan *see* WICKETS IN THE WEST, OR, THE TWELVE IN AMERICA

Fitzgerald, W J *see* REPORT ON THE LOCAL ADMINISTRATION OF JERUSALEM

FitzGibbon, Mary Agnes *see* A VETERAN OF 1812: THE LIFE OF JAMES FITZGIBBON

Fitzherbert, K *see* ROLE OF ENERGETIC FACTORS IN THE EVOLUTION OF THE BREEDING BIOLOGY OF THE SHORT-TAILED SHEARWATER (PUFFINUS TENUIROSTRIS TEMMENIK)

Fitzinger, L J F J *see*
- UEBER DAS SYSTEM UND DIE CHARAKTERISTIK DER NATUERLICHEN FAMILIEN DER VOEGEL
- WISSENSCHAFTLICH-POPULAERE NATURGESCHICHTE DER VOEGEL

Fitzpatrick, Liam *see* LE VIEUX MONTREALAIS

Fitzpatrick, T J *see*
- RAFINESQUE
- RAFINESQUE, A SKETCH OF HIS LIFE WITH BIBLIOGRAPHY

Fitzpatrick, William John *see*
- THE LIFE, TIMES AND CORRESPONDENCE OF THE RIGHT REV. DR. DOYLE, BISHOP OF KILDARE AND LEIGHLIN
- THE LIFE, TIMES, AND CORRESPONDENCE OF THE RIGHT REV. DR. DOYLE, BISHOP OF KILDARE AND LEIGHLIN

Fitzsimmons, Mabel Trott *see* HOT WORDS AND HAIR TRIGGERS

Fitzwilliam Museum. Cambridge *see* SELECTED ILLUMINATIONS FROM MANUSCRIPTS

FIVE ARTICLES ON INSECTS / Kerrich, G J – 1932-43 – 1 – uk Microform Academic [590]

THE FIVE BOOKS OF MOSES / Allis, O T – 2nd ed. Presbyterian and Reformed, 1949 – 9 – $12.00 – us I.R.C. [220]

FIVE CITIES TIMES PRESS RECORDER – Grover City, CA. 1970-79 – 36r – 1 – $1,800.00 – B02282 – us Library Micro [071]

FIVE CITIES TIMES PRESS RECORDER – Los Angeles, CA. 1986-1988 – 18r – 1 – $900.00 – R04058 – us Library Micro [071]

FIVE CITIES TIMES PRESS RECORDER – Nipomo, CA. 1970-76 – 36r – 1 – $1,800.00 – B02528 – us Library Micro [071]

FIVE CITIES TIMES PRESS RECORDER – Oceano, CA. 1972-1978 – 28r – 1 – $1,400.00 – B02554 – us Library Micro [071]

FIVE CITIES TIMES PRESS RECORDER – Pismo Beach, CA. 1970-1979 – 36r – 1 – $1,800.00 – B02626 – us Library Micro [071]

FIVE CITIES TIMES PRESS RECORDER – Port San Luis, CA. 1970-1979 – 36r – 1 – $1,800.00 – B02647 – us Library Micro [071]

FIVE FEATHER NEWS – 1971-n.d. (American Indian Periodicals in the Princeton University Library). 9 fiches – 9 – $50.00 – us UPA [305]

FIVE HUNDRED ESKIMO WORDS : A COMPARATIVE VOCUBULARY FROM GREENLAND AND CENTRAL ESKIMO DIALECTS / Birket-Smith, K – Copenhagen, 1928 – 2mf – ne IDC [490]

FIVE HUNDRED FIRST FAMILIES OF AMERICA – Comp. and ed. by Alexander DuBin, 1967-68. Item J. Indexed, 346p. SW16-0068 – 5 – us A.G.L.L. [978]

FIVE JATAKAS – 1861 – 1 – us I.U. Libraries [390]

FIVE LETTERS TO THE REVEREND MR. F——R RELATIVE TO HIS 'VINDICATION' OF THE MINUTES OF THE REVEREND MR. JOHN WESLEY,... / Hill, Richard – London, 1771 – 1mf – 9 – MP-471/1 – ne IDC [240]

FIVE MONTHS' FINE WEATHER IN CANADA, WESTERN U. S. AND MEXICO / Carbutt, E H – London: Sampson Low, Marston, Searle & Rivington, 1889. 03839. (Pre-1900 Canadiana) – 9 – cn C.I.H.M. [971]

FIVE OLD FRIENDS / Thackeray, Anne – British Fiction Archive: Unit 3 – 9 – uk Bell [830]

FIVE PIECES SELECTED FROM THE OPERA [LA CLEMENZA DI TITO]...ADAPTED FOR THE PIANOFORTE WITH AN ACCOMPAGNEME FOR THE FLUTE BY F. FIORILLO / Mozart, Wolfgang Amadeus & Fiorillo, F – London: R Birchall, 179- – 1 – us Sibley [780]

FIVE POINTS NEWS – El Monte, CA. 1945-1946 – 1r – 1 – $50.00 – H04009 – us Library Micro [071]

FIVE PROBLEMS OF STATE AND RELIGION / Wood, Will C – Boston: H. Hoyt, 1877 – 1mf – us A.T.L.A. [240]

FIVE THEMES *see* 5 THEMES

FIVE TOMES AGAINST NESTORIUS / Cyrillus, Patriarch of Alexandria – 1881 – 1 – us A.T.L.A. [240]

FIVE YEAR DEVELOPMENT, 1966-1970 / St. Lucia. Premier's Office – Castries. 1966 – 9 – ne IDC [338]

FIVE YEAR DEVELOPMENT PLAN, 1957-1961 / Ethiopia – Addis Ababa. 1959 – 9 – ne IDC [338]

FIVE YEAR DEVELOPMENT PLAN, 1960-1964 / Barbados – D-947 1 – 9 – ne IDC [338]

FIVE YEAR DEVELOPMENT PLAN 1967-1972 / Lesotho – D-1114 1 – 9 – ne IDC [338]

FIVE YEAR DEVELOPMENT PLAN, 1968-1972 / Abu Dhabi. Directorate General of Planning and Coordination – Summary and index. Dubai. 1968 – 9 – ne IDC [330]

FIVE YEAR DEVELOPMENT PLAN 1970/71 TO 1974/75 / Sudan – D 1204 1. 1971 – 9 – ne IDC [338]

FIVE YEAR DEVELOPMENT PROGRAM (1952-1957) / Nicaragua – D-1386 1. 1953 – 9 – ne IDC [338]

FIVE YEAR DEVELOPMENT PROGRAMME, 1958-1962 / Trinidad and Tobago – Port of Spain. 1958. BD-601 1 – 9 – ne IDC [338]

FIVE YEAR DEVELOPMENT PROGRAMME, 1958-1962 PROJECTS FOR 1959 / Trinidad and Tobago. Economic Planning and Developpement Dept – Port of Spain. 1959 – 9 – ne IDC [338]

FIVE YEAR DEVELOPMENT PROGRAMME, 1974-1978 / Somali Republic. Planning and Coordination Committee – Mogadishu. 1974. BD-1823 1 – 9 – ne IDC [338]

FIVE YEAR DRAFT PLAN, 1966-1970 / Antigua – St. Johns. 1965 – 9 – ne IDC [338]

FIVE YEAR ECONOMIC DEVELOPMENT PLAN / Afghanistan. Ministry of National Economy – B-922 1. Sept. 1956-Aug. 1961 – 9 – ne IDC [338]

A FIVE YEAR ECONOMIC DEVELOPMENT PROGRAM FOR THE MINDANO REGION FY 70-71 TO FY 74-75 / Philippines. Mindano Development Authority – Davao City. 1970. BD-1831 1 – 9 – ne IDC [338]
FIVE YEAR ECONOMIC PROGRAMME 1950-1955 / Trinidad and Tobago – D 1495 1. 2 v. 1950 – 9 – ne IDC [338]
FIVE YEAR EDUCATION PLAN 1978-1983 / Jamaica. Ministry of Education. Planning Division – [Kingston], Draft 2 – 4mf – 9 – DE-524/1 – ne IDC [370]
FIVE YEAR INDEPENDENCE PLAN, 1963-1968 / Jamaica – Kingston. 1964. BD-124 1 – 9 – ne IDC [338]
FIVE YEAR PLAN 1968-1972 / Morocco. Ministry of Economic Affairs, Planning and Training Div – D-1127 1. 2v. 1968 – 9 – ne IDC [338]
FIVE YEAR PLAN, 1968-1972 / Morocco. Ministere des Affaires Economiques – 2v. 1968. BNE-3071 1 – 9 – ne IDC [338]
FIVE YEAR PLAN FOR ECONOMIC AND SOCIAL DEVELOPMENT, JULY 1975-JUNE 1980 / Gambia. Government Printer – Banjul. 1976. BD-1870 1 – 9 – ne IDC [338]
THE FIVE YEAR PLAN OF ECONOMIC AND SOCIAL DEVELOPMENT FOR THE PERIOD 1970/1971-1974/1975 / Sudan. Ministry of Planning – 1970. BNE-7674 1 – 9 – ne IDC [338]
FIVE YEAR PLAN OF JAIPUR STATE / Jaipur. India (State). Development and Planning Department – Jaipur City. 1948. BD-495 1 – 9 – ne IDC [338]
FIVE YEAR PLAN PROGRESS REPORT FOR 1951-52 AND 1952-53 / India. Planning Commission – New Delhi. 1953. BD-441 1 – 9 – ne IDC [338]
FIVE YEAR PLAN PROGRESS REPORT FOR 1953-54 / India. Planning Commission – Delhi. 1954 – 9 – ne IDC [338]
THE FIVE YEARS DETAILED ECONOMIC PLAN FOR 1961/62-1965/66 / Iraq. Ministry of Guidance – (Weekly Gazette. 15 Aug 1962). Baghdad. 1962. BD-150 1 – 9 – ne IDC [338]
THE FIVE YEARS' DEVELOPMENT PLAN / Yugoslavia – Beograd. 1947. BD-399 1 – 9 – ne IDC [324]
THE FIVE YEARS ECONOMIC PLAN, 1965/1969, (LAW NO. 87 OF 1965) / Iraq – (Weekly Gazette. 1 Dec 1965). Baghdad. 1965 – 9 – ne IDC [338]
FIVE YEARS IN A SAILOR'S LIFE / Bech, Birger – Toronto: Queen's City Pub. Co., 1886. 03533. (Pre-1900 Canadiana) – 9 – cn C.I.H.M. [920]
FIVE YEARS IN CHINA; FROM 1842 TO 1847. WITH AN ACCOUNT OF THE OCCUPATION OF LABUAN AND BORNEO BY HER MAJESTY'S FORCES / Forbes, Frederick E – 1848 – 9 – 20.00 – uk Libr Preservation [941]
FIVE YEARS IN KAFFIRLAND : WITH SKETCHES OF THE LATE WAR IN THAT COUNTRY, TO THE CONCLUSION OF PEACE / Ward, Harriet – London: H Colbourn, 1848 – 1 – us Res Libr [960]
FIVE YEARS IN SIAM, FROM 1891 TO 1896 / Smyth, Herbert Warington – Maps and illus. by author. London: J. Murray, 1898. illus. 9 maps. 2 v – 1 – us U.W. Library [950]
FIVE YEARS OF PRAYER, WITH THE ANSWERS / Prime, Samuel Irenaeus – New York: Harper, 1864, c1863 – 1mf – us A.T.L.A. [240]
A FIVE-MILE MOUNTAIN BICYCLE TEST TO PREDICT VO2MAX / Veldhuis, Robert J & Butts, Nancy Kay – 1993 – 2mf – $8.00 – us Microform Publ [612]
THE FIVE-YEAR AGRICULTURAL DEVELOPMENT PROGRAM, 1960-1965 / Egypt. Ministry of Agriculture – 1962. BNE-4653 1 – 9 – ne IDC [630]
A FIVE-YEAR CAPITAL DEVELOPMENT PLAN, 1955-1960 / Uganda – Sessional Paper No. 13 of 1956/57. Entebbe. 1957 – 9 – ne IDC [338]
FIVE-YEAR DEVELOPMENT PLAN / Grenada – 1964-1968. D-884 1. 1965 – 9 – ne IDC [338]
FIVE-YEAR DEVELOPMENT PLAN 1967-1971 / Grenada – D-1087 1. 1966 – 9 – ne IDC [338]
FIVE-YEAR DEVELOPMENT PLAN, SUMMARY OF PROPOSALS 1954-1958 / Brunei – D-1249 1 – 9 – ne IDC [338]
FIVE-YEAR DEVELOPMENT PROGRAMME, 1955/56-1959/60 / Jamaica – D-1346 1. 1954 – 9 – ne IDC [338]
FIVE-YEAR DEVELOPMENT PROGRAMME, 1958-1962 1958 REPORT / Trinidad and Tobago – Port-of-Spain. 1960. BD-679 1 – 9 – ne IDC [338]
FIVE-YEAR DEVELOPMENT PROGRAMME 1958-1962 REPORT OF THE PREMIER ON DEVELOPMENT PROJECTS FOR THE YEAR 1960 / Trinidad and Tobago. Economic Planning Division – Port of Spain. 1962 – 9 – ne IDC [338]
FIVE-YEAR ECONOMIC AND SOCIAL DEVELOPMENT PLAN, 1963-1968 / Libya. Ministry of Planning and Development – BNE-701 1 – 9 – ne IDC [338]
THE FIVE-YEAR ECONOMIC DEVELOPMENT PLAN OF AFGHANISTAN / Afghanistan – Kabul. 1956. BD-149 1 – 9 – ne IDC [338]
THE FIVE-YEAR FISCAL PLAN, 1961-1965 : BUDGET FOR THE FISCAL YEAR 1962 / Philippines. Budget Commission – Manila, 1961 – 9 – BD-1435 1 – ne IDC [350]
FIVE-YEAR INTEGRATED SOCIO-ECONOMIC PROGRAM FOR THE PHILIPPINES / Philippines. President – Manila. 1962. BD-224 1 – 9 – ne IDC [338]
FIVE-YEAR PHASED PROGRAMME OF ECONOMIC DEVELOPMENT / Jordan. Development Board – D-1349 1. (Rev. Oct. 1954). 1953 54-1957 58 – 9 – ne IDC [338]
FIVE-YEAR PLAN / Ceylon. Ministry of Planning and Employment – D-1548 1. 1972 76 – 9 – ne IDC [338]
FIVE-YEAR PLAN OF DEVELOPMENT AND TAXATION / Barbados – 1952/53-1956/57. BD-1614 1 – 9 – ne IDC [338]
FIVE-YEAR PLAN OF ECONOMIC DEVELOPMENT OF YUGOSLAVIA, 1961-1965 / Yugoslavia – Beograd. 1961. BD-1784 1 – 9 – ne IDC [338]
A FIVE-YEAR PLAN OF MINISTRY FOR THE FIRST BAPTIST CHURCH, MADISON, ILLINOIS / Lindsey, Wilford Daniel – 1982 – 1 – 5.04 – us Baptist [240]
THE FIVE-YEAR PLAN OF THE HUNGARIAN PEOPLE'S REPUBLIC / Hungary – Budapest. 1950. BD-648 1 – 9 – ne IDC [943]
FIVE-YEAR PROGRAM FOR AGRICULTURAL DEVELOPMENT / Virginia. Polytechnic Institute. Extension Division – 3fiches – 9 – us Spaulding [630]
FIVE-YEAR PROGRAM FOR THE DEVELOPMENT OF VIRGINIA AGRICULTURE / Virginia. Polytechnic Institute. Extension Division – 2fiches – 9 – us Spaulding [630]
FIVE-YEAR PROGRAMME FOR THE ECONOMIC DEVELOPMENT OF GREECE, 1960-1964 / Greece. Ministry of Coordination – Athens. 1960 – 9 – ne IDC [338]
FIVE-YEAR PROGRAMME OF ECONOMIC DEVELOPMENT AN ADDRESS OF THE PRESIDENT, 21 AUG 1961 / Cyprus. President – Nicosia. 1961. BD-148 1 – 9 – ne IDC [338]
Fix, Theodore *see*
- OBSERVATIONS SUR L'ETAT DES CLASSES OUVRIERES
- SITUATION DES CLASSES OUVRIERES. EXTRAIT DU JOURNAL DES ECONOMISTES, CAHIER DE DECEMBRE 1844

FIZKULTURA I SPORT : FIS – (Library has: May/June 1946) – Moskva: Gos. izd-vo "Fizkultura i sport", 1922- – 1 – CSUX89-S926 – us Hoover Inst Photo [790]
FJALLKONAN – Reykjavik, Iceland. -w. 29 Feb 1884-7 April 1911. 6 reels – 1 – uk British Libr Newspaper [072]
FJC Prisoner Civil Rights Committee *see* RECOMMENDED PROCEDURES FOR HANDLING PRISONER CIVIL RIGHTS CASES IN THE FEDERAL COURTS
FL. MEROBAUDIS RELIQUIAE (MGH 1: 14.BD) : BLOSII AEMILII DRACONTII CARMINA - EUGENII TOLETANI EPISCIPI CARMINA ET EPISTULAE / ed by Vollmer, F – 1905 – Dfl46.00 – ne Slangenburg [240]
FLACARA IASULUI – Iasi, Romania. 1962-Jun 1980; Apr-Oct 1981; 1982-88 – 26r – 1 – us L of C Photodup [949]
FLACARA SIBIULUI – Sibiu, Romania. 4 Jan 1956-1957; 4 Jan 1959-1962 – 3r – 1 – us L of C Photodup [949]
Flacius Illyricus d.A E, M *see*
- ANTILOGIA PAPAE: HOC EST, DE CORRUPTO ECCLESIAE STATU, AND TOTIUS CLERI PAPISTICI PERUERSITATE,...
- ANTWORT MATTHIAE FLACII ILLIRICI, AUFF DAS STENCKFELDISCHE BUECHLEIN IUDICIUM UND C. GENANT
- APOLOGIA MATTHIAE FLACIJ ILLYRICI AD SCHOLAM VITEBERGENSEM IN ADIAPHORORUM CAUSA
- DAS DIE BUSS REWE ODER ERKENTNIS DES ZORNS VND DER SUENDEN EIGENTLICH ALLEIN AUS DEM GESETZ...
- CATALOGUS TESTIVM VERITATIS, QVI ANTE NOSTRAM AETATEM RECLAMARUNT PAPAE
- EINE CHRISTLICHE PREDIGT VBER DER LEICHE DES...HERRN M
- COMPENDIARIA EXPOSITIO DOCTRINAE DE ESSENTIA ORIG: PECCATI
- ...DE ESSENTIA ORIGINALIS IVSTITIAE ET INIVSTITIAE SEU IMAGINIS DEI ET CONTRARIAE,...
- DE TRANSLATIONE IMPERII ROMANI AD GERMANOS...
- DE VOCABVLO FIDEI ET ALIIS QVIBVSDAM VOCABVLIS, EXPLICATIO UERA ET UTILIS, SUMTA EX FONTIBUS EBRAICIS
- DEFENSIO CONFESSIONIS MINISTRORVM IESV CHRISTI, ECCLESIAE ANTUERPIENSIS, QUAE AUGUSTANAE CONFESSIONI ADSENTITUR, CONTRA IVDOCI TILETANI UARIA SOPHISMATA
- DEFENSIO SANAE DOCTRINAE DE ORIGINALI IVSTITIA AC INIUSTITIA, AUT PECCATO,...
- DEMONSTRATIONES EVIDENTISSIMAE DOCTRINAE DE ESSENTIA IMAGINIS DEI AND DIABOLI,...
- LIBER DE VERIS ET FALSIS ADIAPHORIS, IN QUO INTEGRE PROPEMODUM ADIAPHORICA CONTROUERSIA EXPLICATUR
- MATTHIAE FLACIJ ILLYRICI, DE VOCE AND RE FIDEI, QUODQUE SOLA FIDE IUSTIFICEMUR, CONTRA PHARISAICUM HIPOCRITARUM FERMENTUM...
- OMNIA LATINA SCRIPTA...
- PIA ET NECESSARIA ADMONITIO DE DECRETIS ET CANONIBVS CONCILII TRIDENTINI, SUB PIO QUARTO ROM. PONTIFICE, ANNO AND C. 62. AND 63. CELEBRATI...
- REFVTATIO INVECTIVAE BRVNI CONTRA CENTURIAS HISTORIAE ECCLESIASTICAE:...

Flacius, M *see* CATALOGUS TESTIUM VERITATIS, QUI ANTE NOSTRAM AETATEM RECLAMARUNT PAPAE
Flackton, W *see* THE CHACE. SELECTED FROM THE...POEMS OF WILLIAM SAMMERVILLE...
Flagellan, C *see* A FUNERAL DISCOURSE OCCASIONED BY THE MUCH LAMENTED DEATH OF MR. YORICK, PREBENDARY OF Y–K AND AUTHOR OF THE MUCH ADMIRED 'LIFE AND OPINIONS OF TRISTRAM SHANDY',...
FLAGELLATION AND THE FLAGELLANTS : A HISTORY OF THE ROD / Cooper, William M – (Includes index) – London: John Camden Hotten, 1869? – 7mf – 9 – $10.50 – LLMC 91-082 – us L.L.M.C. [340]
Flagg, Wilson *see* STUDIES IN THE FIELD AND FOREST
FLAGLER PALM COAST NEWS-TRIBUNE – Bunnell, Florida. -biw. Jul 1982- – 1 – us P.K. Yonge [071]
FLAGLER TRIBUNE – Bunnell. Fl. -w. Jun 1955-3 Sep 1981 – 1 – us P.K. Yonge [071]
Flaherty, R J *see* THE BELCHER ISLANDS OF HUDSON BAY
Flaherty, Robert F *see* RUNNING ECONOMY AND KINEMATIC DIFFERENCES AMONG RUNNING WITH THE FOOT SHOD, WITH THE FOOT BARE, AND WITH THE BARE FOOT EQUATED FOR WEIGHT
Flaischlen, G G *see* DE L'INITIATIVE CONSULAIRE EN FAIT DE TUTTELLE ET DE CURATELLE...
Flajshans, V *see* CESKA PRISLOVI
FLAKA E VELLAZERIMIT – (Some issues missing) – Skopje, Yugoslavia. Apr 1945-1955; Apr 1957-1960 – 4r – 1 – us L of C Photodup [949]
FLAKA E VLLAZNIMIT – Skoplje, Yugoslavia. -w. 4 April-7 May 1945; Jan 1960-Dec 1970. 16 reels – 1 – uk British Libr Newspaper [949]
LE FLAMBEAU : AU SERVICE DES MEILLEURS INTERETS DE LABELLE ET DE PAPINEAU – Mont-Laurier. v11 n1. 6 jan 1951-v11 n52. 29 dec 1951 – 1r – 1 – Can$50.00 – cn Can Microfilming [072]
LE FLAMBEAU : MENSUEL - ARTS, SCIENCES, LETTRES – Trois Rivieres, Canada. jan 1935-jan/fev/mar 1936 – 1r – 1 – Can$25.00 – cn Can Microfilming [073]
LE FLAMBEAU – Quebec, jun 1956 – 1r – 1 – Can$25.00 – cn Can Microfilming [072]
FLAMBEAU DE L'EST – Ville d'Anjou. v47 n1. 2 jan 1990-29 dec 1991 – 4r – 1 – Can$60.00 – cn Can Microfilming [072]
LE FLAMBEAU DEMOCRATIQUE – Port-au-Prince. Haiti. mar. 8, 20, 1948 – 1 – us NY Public [072]
LE FLAMBEAU DES ANCIENS COMBATTANTS DE L'AVANT / Mouvement Croix de Feu – Paris. nov 1929-aout 1937, mars 1941-juil 1942 – 1 – fr A.C.R.P.P. [073]
LE FLAMBEAU DU NORD – (Missing Years: 1939-1947) – Tourcoing (Nord), 1924-1948 – 2r – fr Armell [073]
LE FLAMBEAU; REVUE BELGE DES QUESTIONS POLITIQUES ET LITERAIRES – v. 1-23. 1918-40. N.S. v. 31-32. 1948-49. Jan-Apr 1936 wanting – 1 – $277.00 – us L of C Photodup [949]
FLAMBEAU SAGUENEEN, MONSIEUR L'ABBE CHARLES-ELZEAR TREMBLAY / Tremblay-Boily, Germaine – [1964?]. SEM105P4 – 4mf – 9 – cn Bibl Nat [240]
THE FLAME OF HISPANICISM / Gonzalez, Palencia Angel – New York, 1938. Fiche W928. (Blodgett Collection of Spanish Civil War Pamphlets) – 9 – us H.U. College Libr [946]
FLAMEN = FLAMES – (Yiddish magazine) – Lodz, PL. no2. 28 Feb 1948 – 1r – 1 – $25.00 – cn Can Microfilming [073]
Flamen, Albert *see* DEVISES ET EMBLESMES D'AMOUR
FLAMETTI, ODER, VOM DANDYSMUS DER ARMEN / Ball, Hugo – Berlin: E. Reiss, 1918. 224p – 1 – us U.W. Library [800]
FLAMMEN UND WINDE : NEUE GEDICHTE UND GESAENGE / Lissauer, Ernst – Stuttgart: Deutsche Verlags-Anstalt, 1923 – 1r – 1 – us U.W. Library [810]
FLAMMENZEICHEN : AUSGEWAEHLTE ZEITGEDICHTE / Juengst, Hugo C – 2. Aufl. Dresden-Blasewitz: Verlag der "Deutschen Litteratur- und Kunstzeitung", [194-?] – 1r – 1 – us U.W. Library [810]
Flammermont, J *see* CORRESPONDANCE SECRETE DU COMTE DE MERCY-ARGENTEAU AVEC L'EMPEREUR JOSEPH 2
FLAMMPUNKTSBERECHNUNG VON KOHLENWASSERSTOFFGEMISCHEN / Baumann, Frank – 1994 – 1mf – DM60.00 – 3-8267-2039-3 – gw Hänsel [540]
A FLAMMULA – Queluz de Minas, 30 Jul, Sep-Dec 1914; Jan-Apr, Jun, Aug-Dec 1915; Jan-Feb, Jul-17 Aug 1916 – 1,5,6 – bl Biblioteca [072]
Flamsteed, John *see*
- CORRESPONDENCE
- HISTORIAE COELESTIS BRITANNICAE..

FLAMURA PRAHOVEI – Ploiesti, Romania. 1962-81 – 23r – 1 – us L of C Photodup [949]
FLAMURI – Rome. Italy. -m. Jan 1950-Apr 1968. (Imperfect). (1 reel) – 1 – uk British Libr Newspaper [072]
Flanagan, Brigid *see* HENRY CLOETE IN NATAL, 1843-1855
Flanagan, Lance *see* THE HISTORY OF VOLLEYBALL IN THE UNITED STATES
Flanders, George E *see* CIVIL WAR LETTERS
Flanders, Steven *see*
- THE 1979 FEDERAL DISTRICT COURT TIME STUDY
- CASE MANAGEMENT AND COURT MANAGEMENT IN U.S. DISTRICT COURTS
- OPERATION OF THE FEDERAL JUDICIAL COUNCILS

FLANDRIA ILLUSTRATA / Sanderus, A – 's-Gravenhage. Tom 1-3. 1735 – Dfl368.00 – ne Slangenburg [240]
FLANDRICISMES, WALLONISMES / Poyart, AF – 1806 – 9 – fr I.C.S. [440]
LE FLANEUR – Paris: H V de Surcy et Cie, may 1848 – us Res Libr [072]
LE FLANEUR DES DEUX RIVES – Bulletin d'etudes apollinariennes. no. 1-7 8. Paris. mars 1954-sept dec 1955 – 1 – fr A.C.R.P.P. [073]
Flanigan, J C *see*
- GWINNETT CHURCHES; A COMPLETE HISTORY OF EVERY CHURCH IN GWINNETT COUNTY, GEORGIA, WITH SHORT BIOGRAPHICAL SKETCHES OF ITS MINISTERS
- HISTORY OF GWINNETT COUNTY 1818-1943

FLARE – (Numbering started with v3 1981) – Toronto, 1973-95 – 9 – Can$55.00y – cn Micromedia [073]
Flaschner, G B *see* ZWANZIG LIEDER VERMISCHTEN INHALTS

FLASH – Issue Nos. 11-15 Nov 1940-Mar 1941 – 5mf – 15 – $31.95 – us Comics [760]
FLASH – Issue Nos. 1-5 Jan 1940-May 1940 – 5mf – 15 – $31.95 – us Comics [760]
FLASH – Issue Nos. 16-20 Apr 1941-Aug 1941 – 5mf – 15 – $31.95 – us Comics [760]
FLASH – Issue Nos. 21-25 Sept 1941-Jan 1942 – 5mf – 15 – $31.95 – us Comics [760]
FLASH – Issue Nos. 6-10 Jun 1940-Oct 1940 – 5mf – 15 – $31.95 – us Comics [760]
THE FLASH – Carson City, NV. 1969-1970 – 1r – 1 – $50.00 – N04456 – us Library Micro [071]
THE FLASH LIGHT – Mansfield, PA. 1916-88. 7 rolls – 13 – $25.00r – us I.M.R. [071]
FLASH ON ANGOLA – Lusaka: Dept of Information and Propagande [sic] of the M P L A, nov 1971; apr-may 1972 – us Res Libr [960]
FLASHBACK – Biog. and hist. sketches. v1-10, 1951-60. F-0058 to F-0067 – 9 – us A.G.L.L. [978]
FLASHLIGHTS ON EVANGELICAL HISTORY : A VOLUME OF ENTERTAINING NARRATIVES, ANECDOTES AND INCIDENTS, ILLUSTRATIVE OF THE EVANGELICAL WORK FOUNDED BY REV. JACOB ALBRIGHT IN A.D. 1800 / Stapleton, A – York, Penna.: A. Stapleton, 1908 – 1mf – us A.T.L.A. [240]
FLASHLIGHTS ON NATURE / Allen, Grant – Toronto: W. Briggs, 1899. 05035. (Pre-1900 Canadiana) – 9 – cn C.I.H.M. [574]
FLAT CREEK BAPTIST CHURCH. PETIS COUNTY. MISSOURI : CHURCH RECORDS – 1846-81 – 1 – 12.87 – us Baptist [240]
FLAT CREEK BAPTIST CHURCH. WEAVERVILLE, NORTH CAROLINA : CHURCH RECORDS – 1833-1931. WMU Minutes. 1915-21 – 1 – 44.69 – us Baptist [240]
FLAT GAP BAPTIST CHURCH. ENTERPRISE ASSOCIATION. KENTUCKY : CHURCH RECORDS – Apr 1869-Sep 1914 – 1 – 8.82 – us Baptist [240]
A FLAT IRON FOR A FARTHING / Ewing, Juliana Horatia – British Fiction Archive: Unit 1 – 9 – uk Bell [830]
Flat River Association. North Carolina *see* MANUSCRIPT MINUTES
FLAT ROCK BAPTIST CHURCH. ANDERSON COUNTY. SOUTH CAROLINA : CHURCH RECORDS – 1871-1911, 1913-54. Deacons' Minutes. 1970-72 – 1 – 18.77 – us Baptist [240]
Flatbush, Adda M *see* METHODS AND RESULTS OF RESCUE WORK
FLATHEAD COUNTY NEWS – Polson. Mont. 1908-1915 – 1 – us UMI [071]
FLATHEAD COURIER – Polson. Mont. 1958-1959; 1966- – 1 – us UMI [071]
FLATHEAD MONITOR AND TIMES MONITOR – Kalispell. Mont. 1948-1954 – 1 – us UMI [071]
Flaubert, Gustave *see*
- MADAME BOVARY
- LE THEATRE DE VOLTAIRE

Flaviana, Metropolitan of Kiev *see* SISTEMATICHESKII KATALOG KNIG BIBLIOTEKI VYSOKOPREOSVIASHCHENNAGO FLAVIANA, MITROPOLITA KIEVSKAGO I GALITSKAGO
FLAVII IOSEPHI ANTIQUITATUM IUDAICARUM EPITOME / Josephus, Flavius; ed by Niese, Benedictus – 1896 – 1 – us A.T.L.A. [270]
Flavio Josefo *see* LOS SIETE LIBROS...DE LA GUERRA QUE TUVIERON LOS JUDIOS CON LOS ROMANOS...
Flavius, Josephus *see* VOM JUEDISCHEN KRIEGE
DIE FLAVIUS JOSEPHUS BEIGELEGTE SCHRIFT UEBER DIE HERRSCHAFT DER VERNUNFT (4 MAKKABAEERBUCH) : EINE PREDIGT AUS DEM ERSTEN NACHCHRISTLICHEN JAHRHUNDERT / Freudenthal, Jacob – (Includes bibliographical references) – Breslau [Wroclaw]: Schletter, 1869 – 1mf – 9 – 0-8370-3194-X – 1985-1194 – us A.T.L.A. [270]
FLAYING AND CURING OF HIDES AND SKINS AS A RURAL INDUSTRY / Aten, A & Innes, R F & Knew, E – 1958 3rd printing 1978 – 136p – it F.A.O. [670]
LE FLEAU DES DEMONS ET SORCIERS / Bodin, Jean – Niort. 1616 – 9 – fr Hachette [360]
A FLECHA – '(s.l.')-Sao Luiz, Brazil. 15 Mar 1879-9 Oct 1880 – 1,5,6 – bl Biblioteca [072]
LA FLECHE / Frontisme – de Paris. Dir. politique G. Bergery. Paris. aout 1934-aout 1939 – 1 – fr A.C.R.P.P. [073]
Flechier *see*
- HISTORIA DE TEODOSIO EL GRANDE. TOMO 1
- HISTORIA DE TEODOSIO EL GRANDE. TOMO 2

DIE FLECHTENSTOFFE / Hesse, O – Abderhalden's biochemisches Handlexikon. v. 7. Berlin. 1912. B-6173 2 – 8 – ne IDC [580]
DIE FLECHTENSTOFFE IN CHEMISCHER BOTANISCHER, PHARMAKOLOGISCHER UND TECHNISCHER BEZIEHUNG / Zopf, W – Jena. 1907. B-6174 2 – 8 – ne IDC [580]
Fleckenstein, J *see* DIE HOFKAPELLE DER DEUTSCHEN KOENIGE (MGH SCHRIFTEN..: 16.BD. 1.TEIL)
Fleer, Matvei Gustavovich *see*
- PETERBURGSKII KOMITET BOLSHEVIKOV V GODY VOINY, 1914-1917
- RABOCHEE DVIZHENIE V ROSSII V GODY IMPERIALISTICHESKOI VOINY

THE FLEET OF THE FUTURE: IRON OR WOOD? CONTAINING A REPLY TO SOME CONCLUSIONS OF GENERAL SIR HOWARD DOUGLAS IN FAVOUR OF WOODEN WALLS / Russell, John Scott – 1861 – 9 – $20.00 – uk Libr Preservation [623]
FLEET OWNER – Small Fleet Edition. 1978 – 1,5,6,9 – us UMI [073]
FLEET OWNER – (v62-. 1967-. 5. v71-. 1976-. 9) – 1- 1928- – 1 – us UMI [629]
FLEET PAPERS : BEING LETTERS FROM RICHARD OASTLER WITH OCCASIONAL COMMUNICATIONS FROM FRIENDS – 1-4 (all publ). 1841-1844 – 20mf – 9 – $70.00 – us UPA [330]
FLEET SPECIALIST – (v7-. 1978-. 5,6,9) – v. 7-. 1978- – 1 – us UMI [380]
FLEETWOOD CHRONICLE – Fleetwood, England. -w. 12 April 1845-26 Oct 1849; 9 May 1851-Dec 1876; Jan 1888-Dec 1894; Jan 1897-Dec 1898. Lacking 1874. 22 reels – 1 – uk British Libr Newspaper [072]
FLEETWOOD CHRONICLE – Lancashire – 1 – uk Microform Academic [072]
FLEETWOOD EXPRESS – Blackpool, England. 1896-1920. -w. 35 reels – 1 – uk British Libr Newspaper [072]
Fleetwood, W *see* THE PERFECTIONISTS EXAMIN'D
FLEETWOOD WEEKLY NEWS – 1988; Jul 1989-96 – 17r – 1 – uk British Libr Newspaper [072]
Flegel, Eduard *see* VOM NIGER-BENUE
Flegmatov, Andrei *see* BESEDY PO RUSSKOMU RASKOLU I SEKTANTSTVU
Fleisch, Urban *see* DIE ERKENNTNISTHEORETISCHEN UND METAPHYSISCHEN GRUNDLAGEN DER... BIEDERMANN & LIPSIUS
Fleischauer, C *see* L'ANTI-MACHIAVEL
Fleischer, George W *see* CIVIL WAR LETTERS
Fleischer, Johannes *see* DE IRIDIBUS DOCTRINA ARISTOTELIS ET VITELLIONIS..
Fleischer, M *see* DIE MUSCI DER FLORA VON BUITENZORG...
Fleischhack, Marianne *see* SEIN BAUERNMAEDCHEN
Fleischlin, B *see* STUDIEN UND BEITRAEGE ZUR SCHWEIZERISCHEN KIRCHENGESCHICHTE
Fleischmann, M *see* GRUNDGEDANKEN EINES LUFTRECHTS
Fleming, Caleb *see* A LETTER TO THE REVD. MR. JOHN WESLEY, OCCASIONED BY HIS 'ADDRESS TO THE CLERGY', FEBRUARY 6, 1756
Fleming, David Hay *see*
- MARY QUEEN OF SCOTS
- THE REFORMATION IN SCOTLAND
- THE SCOTTISH REFORMATION
- THE STORY OF THE SCOTTISH COVENANTS IN OUTLINE

Fleming, Hay *see* SIX SAINTS OF THE CONVENANT
Fleming, Henry *see* PAPERS OF HENRY FLEMING
Fleming, Rachel M *see* STORIES FROM THE EARLY WORLD
Fleming, Robert *see*
- APOCALYPTICAL KEY
- THE RISE AND FALL OF PAPACY
- SKETCH OF THE LIFE OF ELDER HUMPHREY POSEY

Fleming, Sandford *see*
- ADDRESS DELIVERED IN CONVOCATION HALL, QUEEN'S COLLEGE, KINGSTON, APRIL 28TH, 1885
- AN APPEAL TO THE CANADIAN INSTITUTE ON THE RECITATION OF PARLIAMENT
- CANADIAN PACIFIC RAILWAY, OTTAWA, 1ST JULY, 1880
- CANADIAN PACIFIC RAILWAY: REPORTS IN REFERENCE TO LOCATION OF SECOND SECTION WEST OF RED RIVER
- ENGLAND AND CANADA: A SUMMER TOUR BETWEEN OLD AND NEW WESTMINSTER: WITH HISTORICAL NOTES
- LETTER TO THE PRESIDENT OF THE AMERICA SIC SOCIETY FOR THE ADVANCEMENT OF SCIENCE: ON THE SUBJECT OF STANDARD TIME FOR THE UNITED STATES OF AMERICA, CANADA AND MEXICO
- RAPPORT SUR L'EXPLORATION PRELIMINAIRE DU CHEMIN DE FER INTERCOLONIAL, FAITE EN VERTU D'INSTRUCTIONS DU GOUVERNEMENT CANADIEN EN L'ANNEE 1864

Fleming, W K *see* MYSTICISM IN CHRISTIANITY
Fleming, Walter L *see* DOCUMENTARY HISTORY OF RECONSTRUCTION
Flemming, J *see*
- DAS BUCH HENOCH
- DIE SYRISCHE DIDASKALIA
- DIE SYRISCHE DIDASKALIA (T.U.U. 2-25/2)

Flemming, N C *see* SCIENTIFIC DIVING
Flemming-Benz, Hasso Graf von *see* DER KREIS CAMMIN
FLENSBURG AVIS : ZWEISPRACHIGE TAGESZEITUNG – Flensburg, Germany. 1 Mai 1976- – ca 6r per yr – 1 – gw Mikrofilm [072]
FLENSBURGER TAGEBLATT – Flensburg, West Germany. 1969- – ca 7r per yr – 1 – gw Mikrofilm [072]
Flerov, A E *see*
- UKAZATEL' KNIG DLIA DETSKAGO CHTENIIA
- UKAZATEL' KNIG PO VOPROSAM VOSPITANIIA I OBUCHENIIA

Flerov, V S *see*
- DALSOVNARKOM, 1917-1918 GG
- REVOLIUTSIONNOE DVIZHENIE V SIBIRI I NA DAL'NEM VOSTOKE

Flerovskii, N *see* SOVREMENNAIA ZAPADNOEVROPEISKAIA TSIVILIZATSIIA
Flesch, Fritz, collector *see* FRITZ FLESCH COLLECTION ON JEWS IN SOUTH AFRICA
Fletcher, Edward Taylor *see* NESTORIOUS: A PHANTASY
Fletcher, Edwin W *see* HELLENISM IN ENGLAND
FLETCHER FORUM *see* FLETCHER FORUM OF WORLD AFFAIRS
FLETCHER FORUM OF WORLD AFFAIRS – (Title varies: v1-12 1976-88 as Fletcher Forum) – v1-19. 1976-95 – 9 – $220.00 set – us Hein [337]
Fletcher, Henry Charles *see* REPORT ON THE MILITARY ACADEMY AT WEST POINT, U.S
Fletcher, J S *see* A SHORT LIFE OF CARDINAL NEWMAN
Fletcher, J W *see*
- OUT-LETTERS, 1752-1784
- OUT-LETTERS, 1752-1785

Fletcher, John Joseph Kilpin *see* THE SIGN OF THE CROSS IN MADAGASCAR
Fletcher, John W *see* WORKS
Fletcher, N *see*
- A METHODIST DISSECTED
- A VINDICATION OF THE 'METHODIST DISSECTED'

Fletcher, Russell H *see* WHO'S WHO IN CALIFORNIA, 1942-1943
Fletcher, T B *see* SOME SOUTH INDIAN INSECTS
FLEUR DE LYS – Quebec, Canada. v1 n2. nov 1966; v1 n3. dec 1966 – 1r – 1 – Can$25.00 – cn Can Microfilming [072]
UNE FLEUR DU CARMEL: LA PREMIERE CARMELITE CANADIENNE, MARIE-LUCIE-HERMINE FREMONT: EN RELIGION SOEUR THERESE DE JESUS / Braun, Antoine – Montreal: Cie. d'Imp. Canadienne, 1875. 00250. (Pre-1900 Canadiana) – 9 – cn C.I.H.M. [240]
Fleuret, Fernand *see* DE GILLES DE RAIS A GUILLAUME APOLLINAIRE
Fleuriau d'Armenonville, T *see* NOUVEAUX MEMOIRES DES MISSIONS DE LA COMPAGNIE DE JESUS DANS LE LEVANT
LES FLEURS BOREALES, LES OISEAUX DE NEIGE: POESIES CONADIENNES / Frechette, Louis-Honore – Quebec?: s.n., 1879 (Quebec: C. Darveau). 03233. (Pre-1900 Canadiana) – 9 – cn C.I.H.M. [580]
FLEURS CHAMPETRES / Francoise – s.l.: s.n., 1895 (Montreal: Cie d'impr. DeSaulniers). 03172. (Pre-1900 Canadiana) – 9 – cn C.I.H.M. [580]
LES FLEURS DE LA CHARITE – [S.l.: s.n., 1897?-19–] – 9 – cn C.I.H.M. [360]
FLEURS DE LA PALESTINE = WILD FLOWERS OF THE HOLY LAND : 54 FEUILLES EN CHROMOLITHOGRAPHIE / Zeller, Hannah – (Also publ in German under title: Feldblumen aus dem heiligen Land) – Bale: C F Spittler, [1876?] – 1mf – 9 – 0-8370-5955-0 – 1985-3955 – us A.T.L.A. [580]
FLEURS DES ALPES : EPISODE DE LA VIE DU ROI LOUIS II DE BAVIOERE / Baltz, Johanna – (Translation of: Alpenrosen und Gentianen) – Lausanne: Bureau de la Bibliothoeque Universelle, 1888 – 1 – us U.W. Library [830]
LES FLEURS DES HISTOIRES DE LA TERRE D'ORIENT : DIVISEES EN CINQ PARTIES – (Pt 1: Traicte de la situation ds Royaumes d'Orient. Pt 2: Des seigneurs qui ont regne en Orient despuis l'Incarnation de nostre Seigneur. Pt 3: Des Tartarins. Pt 4: Des Sarrazins & des Turcz, depuis le premier, iusques aux presents qui ont conqueste Rhodes, Hongrie, & dernierement assailly Austriche. Pt 5: Du Sophy de Perse, & du prince Tamburlan) – Lion, 1585 – 3mf – 9 – H-8421/1 – ne IDC [956]
Fleury, C *see* TROIS DUOS CONCERTANS POUR DEUX VIOLONS
Fleury, Claude *see* CATECHISME HISTORIQUE, CONTENANT EN ABREGE L'HISTOIRE SAINTE ET LA DOCTRINE CHRETIENNE
FLEURY MESPLET (1734-1794); THE FIRST FRENCH PRINTER IN THE DOMINION OF CANADA / Greig, Peter E – 1 – 45.00 – cn McLaren [971]
FLEURY MESPLETS, PIONNIER DE L'IMPRIMERIE A MONTREAL : ...DINER ANNUEL DES MAITRES IMPRIMEURS DE MONTREAL...19 AVRIL 1939 / Morin, Victor – Montreal, 1939. SEM105P763 – 1mf – 9 – Can$2.25 – cn Bibl Nat [920]
Fleury, Nicolas-Marie de *see*
- ESSAI SUR LES MOYENS DE REFORMER L'EDUCATION PARTICULIERE ET GENERALE
- PROJET D'UNE ECOLE GRATUITE DES SCIENCES POUR TOUTES LES PROVINCES DU ROYAUME OU TOUS LES CITOYENS, DE QUELQUE ORDRE QU'ILS SOIENT, TROUVERAIENT LES SECOURS DE L'EDUCATION

Flew, Anthony *see*
- INTENDED ACTIONS AND UNINTENDED CONSEQUENCES
- THE PROFIT MOTIVE

Flewelling, Ralph Tyler *see*
- CHRIST AND THE DRAMAS OF DOUBT
- PERSONALISM AND THE PROBLEMS OF PHILOSOPHY

Flewellyn, Julia Colliton *see* HILL CREST
FLEXIBLE ARBEITSZEIT : BEDINGUNGEN UND ZIELE DER DURCHFUEHRUNG FLEXIBLER ARBEITSZEITEN UNTER BESONDERER BERUECKSICHTIGUNG IHRER ANWENDUNG BEI MECHANISCHER TECHNOLOGIE / Utsch, Juergen – 1994 – 2mf – 9 – DM98.00 – 3-89349-864-8 – gw Hänsel [331]
Fliche, A *see* HISTOIRE DE L'EGLISE DEPUIS LES ORIGINES JUSQUA NOS JOURS
Flick, Alexander Clarence *see* THE RISE OF THE MEDIAEVAL CHURCH
Flickinger, Daniel Kumler *see* HISTORY OF THE ORIGIN AND DEVELOPMENT AND CONDITION OF MISSIONS AMONG THE SHERBRO AND MENDI TRIBES IN WESTERN AFRICA
Flickinger, Robert E *see* PIONEER HISTORY OF POCAHONTAS COUNTY
Fliedner, Wilhelm *see* GOETHE UND CHRISTENTUM
FLIEG, ROTER ADLER VON TIROL! : VOLKSSTUECK IN DREI AKTEN / Angermayer, Fred A – Stuttgart: J G Cotta, 1930 – 1r – 1 – us U.W. Library [820]
FLIEGENDE BLAETTER FUER MUSIK : WAHRHEIT UEBER TONKUNST UND TONKUENSTLER / ed by Lobe, J C – Leipzig, 1855-1857. v1-3 – 16mf – 9 – P-578/1 – ne IDC [780]

DER FLIEGENDE HOLLAENDER : ROMANTISCHE OPER IN 3 AUFZUEGEN / Wagner, Richard – (With: Tannhaeuser) – Berlin: C F Meser, [18–?] – 1r – 1 – us U.W. Library [790]

FLIEGENDE MISSIONS BLAETTER – nos 23-43. Feb 1924-Nov 1942 (complete) – 2r – 1 – ATLA S0685A – us A.T.L.A. [073]

DIE FLIEGENDE TAUBE – Aubel, nov 19 1918-22, 1924-apr 24 1940 (incomplete) – 1 – Dist. gw Mikrofilm – gw Misc Inst [072]

FLIEGENDE VOLKSBLAETTER [...] – Bayreuth, jul-nov 1797, 1798 – 1r – 1 – Dist. gw Mikrofilm – gw Misc Inst [943]

Flieger, Heinrich *see* DIE OEFFENTLICHE MEINUNG IN DER STAATSPHILOSOPHIE VON THOMAS HOBBES

FLIGHT AIRCRAFT ENGINEER – 1909-58 – 1 – 2,461.00 – us L of C Photodup [629]

FLIGHT FROM INFLATION – THE MONETARY ALTERNATIVE / Riegel, E C – 2fiches (24x) – 9 – 1.00f – at Libertarian Micro [320]

FLIGHT INTERNATIONAL *see* AEROPLANE

FLIGHT MAGAZINE – 1934-63 – 1 – 458.00 – us L of C Photodup [073]

FLIGHT OF CHARLES A. LINDBERGH – 1 – us Ross [910]

Flinders Petrie, W M *see*
- ABYDOS (MEES VOL 22)
- ABYDOS (MEES VOL 24)
- DENDEREH (MEES VOL 17)
- DESHASHEH (MEES VOL 15)
- DIOSPOLIS PARVA (MEES VOL 20)
- EHNASYA (MEES VOL 26)
- NAUKRATIS (MEES VOL 3)
- THE ROYAL TOMBS OF THE EARLIEST DYNASTIES (MEES VOL 21)
- THE ROYAL TOMBS OF THE FIRST DYNASTY (MEES VOL 18)
- TANIS (MEES NO 2)
- TANIS (MEES VOL 5)

Flinders Petrie, W M et al *see* TANIS

Flinn, John J *see* HAND BOOK OF CHICAGO BIOGRAPHY

FLINT CENTRAL BAPTIST CHURCH. FLINT, MICHIGAN : CHURCH RECORDS – 1953-Feb 1969 – 1 – 29.97 – us Baptist [240]

FLINT CHIPS. A GUIDE TO PRE-HISTORIC ARCHAEOLOGY, AS ILLUSTRATED BY THE COLLECTION IN THE BLACKMORE MUSEUM, SALISBURY / Stevens, Edward Thomas – London: Bell and Daldy, 1870. illus – 1 – us U.W. Library [930]

FLINT HILL BAPTIST CHURCH. SHELBY, NORTH CAROLINA : CHURCH RECORDS – 1909-63 – 1 – 30.33 – us Baptist [240]

Flint, James Henry *see* THE LAW OF TRUSTS AND TRUSTEES AS DETERMINED BY THE DECISIONS OF THE PRINCIPAL ENGLISH AND AMERICAN COURTS

FLINT JOURNAL – Flint. Michigan. 1898- – 1 – us UMI [071]

Flint, Matthew O *see* THE INFLUENCE OF HEALTH BEHAVIOR CONTRACTING ON INTERNAL LOCUS OF CONTROL

FLINT RIDGE BAPTIST CHURCH. LANCASTER COUNTY. SOUTH CAROLINA : CHURCH RECORDS – 1942-45; 1949-60; 1965-83. Deacons' Minutes, 1963-65 – 1 – 37.63 – us Baptist [240]

FLINT RIVER BAPTIST CHURCH. HUNTSVILLE, ALABAMA : CHURCH RECORDS – Oct 1808-Oct 1868 – 1 – 6.93 – us Baptist [240]

Flint, Robert *see*
- CHRIST'S KINGDOM UPON EARTH
- PHILOSOPHY AS SCIENTIA SCIENTIARUM
- SERMONS AND ADDRESSES

Flinter, G D *see* CONSIDERACIONES SOBRE LA ESPANA Y SUS COLONIAS,...

FLINTSHIRE OBSERVER – Mold, Colwyn Bay & Holywell, Wales. Flintshire Observer & News. -w. Jan 1857-Feb 1916; April 1919-Dec 1932. Lacking Jan-Dec 1896; Jan-Feb 1899. 50 reels – 1 – uk British Libr Newspaper [072]

Flippen, W S *see* FLIPPEN'S REPORTS OF CASES IN THE SIXTH CIRCUIT, 1859-1881

FLIPPEN'S REPORTS OF CASES IN THE SIXTH CIRCUIT, 1859-1881 / Flippen, W S – Chicago: Callaghan. v1-2. 1881-89 (all publ) – 17mf – 9 – $25.50 – LLMC 81-451 – us L.L.M.C. [340]

Flitner, J *see* NEBULO NEBULONUM HOC EST

FLOATING ECOSYSTEMS – Pattee, University Park, PA, 1990 – 4p 101 cards – 9 – us Lawrence Pub [720]

THE FLOATING ISLAND. / Strode, William – Libretto. 1655 – 2 – us Sibley [780]

Floeck, Oswald *see* DIE TAGEBUECHER DES DICHTERS ZACHARIAS WERNER

Floericke, C E *see*
- NATURGESCHICHTE DER DEUTSCHEN SUMPE- UND STRANDVOGEL
- VERSUCH EINER AVIFAUNA VON PREUSSISCH-SCHLESIEN

Floerke, H G *see* DEUTSCHE LICHENEN GESAMMELT UND MIT ANMERKUNGEN HERAUSGEGEBEN

Floigl, Victor *see* GESCHICHTE DES SEMITISCHEN ALTERTUMS IN TABELLEN

FLOOD CONTROL SERIES / United Nations – Nos. 1-22 – E.69 – 9 (ST/ECAFE/Ser.F/1-22) – us U.N. Pubs [360]

Flood, John Charles Henry *see* A TRACTATE ON THE RULE OF PRACTICE IN ENGLISH LAW, EMBODYING WHAT IS KNOWN AS THE EQUITABLE DOCTRINE OF ELECTION.

"THE FLOOD-1903" / Imes, Merle Graybill – 1 – us KS Hist [978]

FLOOR COVERING NEWS – (Ceased v16 no 10 1991) – Toronto. v15-16. 1990-91 – 1 – Can$60.00y – cn Micromedia [740]

A FLOR : ORGAM DEDICADO AO BELLO SEXO – Penedo, Alagoas. 11 Ago-20 Out 1909 – 1,5,6 – bl Biblioteca [072]

Flor, F *see* ZUR FRAGE DES RENTIERNOMADISMUS

Flor, Karen K *see* THE RELATIONSHIP BETWEEN PERSONALITY HARDINESS, STRESS AND BURNOUT IN SELECTED COLLEGIATE ATHLETES

Flor O'Squarr, Charles M *see* LA BOHEME BOURGEOISE

FLORA ABREDONENSIS / Dickie, G – Comprehending a list of the flowering plants and ferns found in the neighbourhood of Aberdeen. Aberdeen. 1838 – 9 – ne IDC [580]

FLORA AEGYPTIACO-ARABICA / Forsskal, P – Havniae. 1775. B-5045 2 – 8 – ne IDC [580]

FLORA ALTAICA / Ledebour, C F von – 4v. Berolini. 1829-1833-34. B-5296 2 – 8 – ne IDC [580]

FLORA AMERICAE SEPTENTRIONALIS / Pursh, F T – 2v. London. 1814. B-263 2 – 8 – ne IDC [580]

FLORA ANGELICA / Hudson, W – 1798 – 7 – uk Microform Academic [580]

FLORA ANGLICA / Hudson, W – London. 1762. B-5970 2 – 8 – ne IDC [580]

FLORA ATLANTICA / Desfontaines, R L – 1800 – 5 – uk Microform Academic [580]

FLORA ATLANTICA / Desfontaines, R L – Parisiis. 1798-1800 – 8 – ne IDC [580]

FLORA AUSTRALASICA / Sweet, R – or A selection of handsome, or curious plants, natives of New Holland, and the South Sea Islands. London. 1827-28. B-8324 1 – 9 – ne IDC [580]

FLORA AUSTRALIENSIS / Bentham, G – 7v. London. 1863-78. B-734 2 – 8 – ne IDC [580]

FLORA AUSTRIACA / Host, N T – 2v. Viennae. 1827-31. B-8322 1 – 9 – ne IDC [580]

FLORA BAICALENSI-DAHURICA / Turczaninov, N S – v. 1-2. appendix. Mosquae. 1842-56. B-5266 2 – 8 – ne IDC [580]

FLORA BARBEDENSIS. 1830 / Maycock – 5 – uk Microform Academic [580]

FLORA BEROLINENSIS SIVE ENUMERATIO VEGETABILIUM CIRCA BEROLINUM SPONTE CRESCENTIUM / Kunth, C S – Borolini. 1813. B-5989 2 – 8 – ne IDC [580]

FLORA BOEEMICA INCHOATA / Schmidt, F W – Centuria 1-4. Pragae. 1793-94. B-5484 2 – 8 – ne IDC [580]

FLORA BOREALI AMERICAN / Michaux, A – 1803 – 1 – uk Microform Academic [580]

FLORA BOREALI-AMERICANA / Hooker, W J – 2v. London. 1833-40. B-5368 2 – 8 – ne IDC [580]

FLORA BOREALI-AMERICANA / Michaux, A – ed. 2. Paris, 1820. 2 vols. B-1061 2 – 8 – ne IDC [580]

FLORA BOREALI-AMERICANA / Michaux, A – Parisiis et Argentorati, 1803. v. 1, x, 330 pp., v. 2, 340 pp. B-6130 1 – 9 – ne IDC [580]

FLORA BRASILIAE MERIDIONALIS / Saint-Hilaire, A F C P de – 3v. Parisis. 1825-32. B-309 2 – 8 – ne IDC [580]

FLORA BRASILIENSIS / Martius, Karl Friedrich Philipp von – 1833 – 1 – uk Microform Academic [580]

FLORA BRASILIENSIS, SEU ENUMERATIO PLANTARUM IN BRASILIA / ed by Martius, Karl Friedrich Philipp von – Monachii, Lipsiae. 1840-1906. 15v – 636mf – 8 – ne IDC [580]

FLORA BRITANNICA / Smith, J E – 917. 3 V. 1800-1804 – 9 – ne IDC [580]

FLORA BRUXELLENSIS / Kickx, J – Bruxelles. 1812. B-5984 2 – 8 – ne IDC [580]

FLORA CALPENSIS / Kelaart, E F – London. 1846. B-5136 2 – 8 – ne IDC [580]

FLORA CANTABRIGIENSIS / Relhan, R – Cantabrigae. 1785. B-5667 2 – 8 – ne IDC [580]

FLORA CAPENSIS / Thunberg, C P – Edidit et praefatus est J. A. Schultes. Stuttgardtiae. 1823. B-338 2 – 8 – ne IDC [580]

FLORA CAPENSIS / Thunberg, C P – Upsaliae. 1807-13. B-337 2 – 8 – ne IDC [580]

FLORA CAPENSIS, SISTENS PLANTAS / Thunberg, C P – 2v. Hafniae. 1818-20. B-7426 1 – 9 – ne IDC [580]

FLORA CARNIOLICA / Scopoli, Giovanni Antonio – Ed. 2. 2 v. Vindobonensis. 1772. B-332 2 – 8 – ne IDC [580]

FLORA CARNIOLICA / Scopoli, Giovanni Antonio – Viennae. 1760. B-5736 2 – 8 – ne IDC [580]

FLORA CAROLINIANA / Walter, T – Londini. 1788. B-5420 2 – 8 – ne IDC [580]

FLORA CARPATORUM PRINCIPALIUM / Wahlenberg, G – Goettingae. 1814. B-5798 2 – 8 – ne IDC [580]

FLORA CECHICA / Presl, J S & Presl, K B – Pragae. 1819. B-5051 2 – 8 – ne IDC [580]

FLORA CESTRICA / Darlington, W – 7529 2. 1837 – 8 – ne IDC [580]

FLORA COCHINCHINENSIS / Loureiro, J de – 1790 – 5 – uk Microform Academic [580]

FLORA COCHINCHINENSIS / Loureiro, J de – ed. 2. Berolini, 1793. 882 pp. B-566 2 – 8 – ne IDC [580]

FLORA COCHINCHINENSIS / Loureiro, J de – Ulyssipone, 1790. 2 vols. B-6525 2 – 8 – ne IDC [580]

FLORA CRETACAE BOHEMIAE NEUE BEITRAEGE / Velenovski, J – 2v. Praze. 1926-27. B-5352 2 – 8 – ne IDC [580]

FLORA CRYPTOGAMICA ERLANGENSIS / Martius, Karl Friedrich Philipp von – Norimbergae, 1817. 508 pp., 6 pls. B-6050 2 – 8 – ne IDC [580]

FLORA CRYPTOGAMICA GERMANIAE / Wallroth, C F W – 2v. Norimbergae. 1831-33. Bluff, M. J. and K. A. Fingerhuth. Compendium florae germanicae. Sectio 2. v. 3-4. B-5800 2 – 8 – ne IDC [580]

FLORA CUBANA / Sauvalle, F A – 1581. 1868-1873 – 9 – ne IDC [580]

FLORA DALMATICA / Visiani, R de – 3v. Lipsiae. 1842-52. B-343 2 – 8 – ne IDC [580]

FLORA DANICAE : ICONES PLANTARUM SPONTE NASCENTIUM IN REGNIS DANICAE ET NORVEGIAE / ed by Oeder, G C – Hauniae. 17v. [1761-]1764-1883 – 177mf – 9 – 692/2 – ne IDC [073]

FLORA D'AUVERGNE / Delarbre, A – Clermont-Ferrand. 1795. B-5889 2 – 8 – ne IDC [580]

FLORA DE CHILE / Reiche, C F – 6v. Santiago de Chile. 1894-1896-1911. B-1187 2 – 8 – ne IDC [580]

FLORA DE FILIPINAS / Blanco, F M – Ed. 2. Manila. 1845. B-36 2 – 8 – ne IDC [580]

FLORA DE FILIPINAS / Blanco, F M – Grand Edicion. 4 v. Manila. 1877-80. B-5850 2 – 8 – ne IDC [580]

FLORA DE FILIPINAS / Blanco, F M – Manila. 1837. B-6122 2 – 8 – ne IDC [580]

FLORA DE GOA E SAVANTVADI / Dalgado, D G – Lisboa. 1898. B-995 2 – 8 – ne IDC [580]

DIE FLORA DER DEUTSCHEN SCHUTZGEBIETE IN DER SUEDSEE / Schumann, K & Lauterbach, K – Leipzig, 1901-1905. v1-2 – 9 – ne IDC [580]

FLORA DER GEFUERSTETEN GRAFSCHAFT TIROL, DES LANDES VORARLBERG, UND DES FUERSTENTHUMES LIECHTENSTEIN / Dalla Torre, K W von – v. 4:Die Flechten. Innsbrueck. 1902 – 8 – ne IDC [580]

FLORA DER GEGEND UM DRESDEN / Ficinus, H D A – ed. 2. Dresden. 1821-23. B-5243 2 – 8 – ne IDC [580]

FLORA DER GEGEND UM FRANKFURT AM MAIN / Becker, J – 2v. Frankfurt a. M. 1828. B-913 2 – 8 – ne IDC [580]

FLORA DER PROVINZ BRANDENBURG, DER ALTMARK / Ascherson, P F A – Berlin. 1864. B-5535 2 – 8 – ne IDC [580]

FLORA DER PROVINZ PREUSSEN / Patze, C & Meyer, E H F & Elkan, L – Koenigsberg. 1850. B-5633 2 – 8 – ne IDC [580]

FLORA DER VORWELT / Sternberg, G K – 1825 – 1 – uk Microform Academic [560]

FLORA DES GROSSHERZOGTHUMS BADEN / Doell, J C – 3v. Karlsruhe. 1857-62. B-5391 2 – 8 – ne IDC [580]

FLORA DES OESTERREICHISCHEN KAISERTHUMES / Trattinick, L – 2v. Wien. 1814-, 1816-20. B-5773 1 – 9 – ne IDC [580]

FLORA DESCRIPTIVA E ILLUSTRADA DE GALICIE / Merino, R P B – Santiago, 1905. v. 1, 620 pp.; Santiago, 1906. v. 2, 634 pp.; Santiago, 1909, v. 3, 692 pp. B-905 2 – 9 – ne IDC [580]

FLORA D'OWARE SET DE BENIN EN AFRIQUE / Palisot de Beauvois, A M F J – 1804 and 1821 – 5 – uk Microform Academic [580]

FLORA EDIENSIS / Greville, R K – Edinburgh. 1824. B-5286 2 – 8 – ne IDC [580]

FLORA EDINENSIS / Greville, R K – 1824 – 7 – uk Microform Academic [580]

FLORA ESPANOLA / Quer y Martinez, J – 6v. Madrid. 1762-84. B-861 2 – 8 – ne IDC [580]

FLORA EUROPAEA ALGARUM AQUAE DULCIS ET SUBMARINAE / Rabenhorst, G L – Lipsiae. 1864-68. B-6399 2 – 8 – ne IDC [580]

FLORA EUROPAEA INCHOATA / Roemer, J J – Norimbergae. 1797-1811. B-5682 2 – 8 – ne IDC [580]

FLORA FANEROGAMICA DE LA PENINSULA IBERICA / Amo y Mora, M del – Granada. 1871-73. B-5534 2 – 8 – ne IDC [580]

FLORA FARMACEUTICA... / Nocca, D – Pavia, 1826. 2v – 7mf – 9 – ne IDC [615]

FLORA FOSSILIS ARCTICA / Heer, Oswald – 7v. Zuerich. 1868-83. B-2310 2 – 8 – ne IDC [560]

FLORA FOSSILIS HELVETIAE / Heer, Oswald – 1877 – 1 – uk Microform Academic [560]

FLORA FOSSILIS HELVETIAE / Heer, Oswald – 2311 2. 1876-1877 – 9 – ne IDC [560]

FLORA FRANCAIS / Lamarck, J B A P M de & Candolle, A P de – Paris. 1915 – 7 – uk Microform Academic [580]

FLORA FRIDRICHSDALINA / Mueller, Otto Frederik – Argentorati, 1767. 238 pp., 2 pls. B-5481 2 – 8 – ne IDC [580]

FLORA GALLO-PROVINCIALIS / Gerard, L – Parisiis. 1761. B-5406 – 8 – ne IDC [580]

FLORA GRAECA, SIVE PLANTARUM RARIORUM HISTORIA, QUAS IN PROVINCIIS AUT INSULIS GRAECIAE / Sibthorp, J – 10 v. London. 1806-40. B-323 2 – 8 – ne IDC [580]

FLORA HALENSIS / Leysser, F W von – Halae Salicae. 1761. B-1210 2 – 8 – ne IDC [580]

FLORA HELVETICA / Gaudin, J F A G P – 7v. Turici. 1828-33. B-5549 2 – 8 – ne IDC [580]

FLORA HERBORNENSIS / Leers, J D – ed. 2. Berolini. 1789. B-6010 2 – 8 – ne IDC [580]

FLORA HIBERNICA / MacKay, J T – Dublin, 1836. 2 vols. B-907 2 – 8 – ne IDC [580]

FLORA INDIAE BATAVAE / Miquel, F A W – Amstelaedami, 1855-1859. 3v – 68mf – 9 – ne IDC [580]

FLORA INDIAE BATAVAE...SUPPLEMENTUM PRIMUM. PRODROMUS FLORAE SUMATRANAE / Miquel, F A W – Amstelaedami, 1860[-1861] – 12mf – 9 – ne IDC [580]

FLORA INDIAE OCCIDENTALIS / Swartz, O P – 487. 3 V. 1797-1806 – 9 – ne IDC [580]

FLORA INDICA / Hooker, J D & Thomson, T – A systematic account of the plants of British India. London. 1855. B-5958 2 – 8 – ne IDC [580]

FLORA INDICA / Roxburgh, W – 2v. Serampore. 1820-24. B-300 2 – 8 – ne IDC [580]

FLORA INDICA / Roxburgh, W – Ed. by W. Carey. 5679. 3 v. 1832 – 9 – ne IDC [580]

FLORA INDICA. LUGDUNI BATAVORUM, 1768 / Burman, N L B – B-5194 2 – 8 – ne IDC [580]

FLORA INGRICA SIVE HISTORIA PLANTARUM GUBERNII PETROPOLITANI / Ruprecht, F J – Spb., Riga, Leipzig, 1860 – 8mf – 9 – ne IDC [580]

FLORA ITALIANA / Parlatore, F – 10 v. and index. Firenze. 1848-94. B-5059 2 – 8 – ne IDC [580]

FLORA ITALICA / Bertoloni, A – 10 v. Bononiae. 1833-54. B-5370 2 – 8 – ne IDC [580]

FLORA ITALICA CRYPTOGAMA / Bertoloni, A – 2v. Bononiae. 1858-67. B-5281 2 – 8 – ne IDC [580]

FLORA ITALICAE PRODROMUS / Turra, A – Vicetiae. 1780. B-847 2 – 8 – ne IDC [580]

FLORA JAPONICA / Siebold, P F von & Zuccarini, J G – 5741. 2 V. 1835-1870 – 9 – ne IDC [580]

FLORA JAPONICA / Thunberg, C P – 1784 – 7 – uk Microform Academic [580]

FLORA JAPONICA / Thunberg, C P – 339. 1784 – 9 – ne IDC [580]

FLORA JAPONICA / Thunberg, C P – 7393. 1812 – 9 – ne IDC [580]

FLORA JAVAE ET INSULARUM ADJACENTIUM / Blume, C L – Nova series. v1 (Orchidaceae). Lugduni, 1858-59. 162p. 66 pls. B-5853/2 – 30mf – 8 – ne IDC [580]

FLORA JAVAE NEC NON INSULARUM ADJACENTIUM / Blume, C L & Fischer, J B – Bruxellis, 1828-51. x/548p. 238 pls. B-5212/2 – 50mf – 8 – ne IDC [580]

FLORA JOURNAL – Flora, OR. -w. 20 Jun 1902-21 Aug 1903. 1 roll – 1 – us U.O. Library [071]

FLORA JURASSIENNE / Babey, C M P – 4v. Paris. 1845. B-5111 2 – 8 – ne IDC [580]

FLORA LAPPONICA / Linnaeus, Carl – Amstelaedami. 1737. B-163 2 – 8 – ne IDC [580]

FLORA LAPPONICA / Linnaeus, Carl – editio altera. Londini. 1792. B-8318 1 – 9 – ne IDC [580]

FLORA LAPPONICA, EXHIBENS PLANTAS GEOGRAPHICE / Wahlenberg, G – Berolini. 1812. B-5797 2 – 8 – ne IDC [580]

FLORA LIPSIENSIS / Baumgarten, J C G – Lipsiae. 1790. B-5468 2 – 8 – ne IDC [580]

FLORA LIPSIENSIS PHARMACEUTICA... / Reichenbach, Heinrich G L – Leipzig, 1817 – 3mf – 9 – ne IDC [615]

FLORA LONDINENSIS / Curtis, W – 2v. Suppl. London. 1777-98 – 8 – ne IDC [580]

FLORA LONDINENSIS / Curtis, W – 5v. London. 1817-28. B-877 2 – 8 – ne IDC [580]

FLORA LUSITANICA, SEU PLANTARUM / Brotero, F di Avelar – 2v. Olissipone. 1804. B-5041 2 – 8 – ne IDC [580]

FLORA MALABARICA / Burman, J – Amsterdam. 1759. B-8306 1 – 9 – ne IDC [580]

FLORA MALABARICA / Commelin, C – Lugduni Batavorum. 1696. B-8305 1 – 9 – ne IDC [580]

FLORA MALESIANA / ed by Steenis, C G G J van – S.l. Spermatophyta. Groningen (The Netherlands), 1948-1954. v1, 4; 1960-1972. v6 – 29mf – 9 – 8159/1 – ne IDC [580]

FLORA MEDICA DELLA PROVINCIA DI NAPOLI / Pasquale, G A – Napoli, 1841 – 3mf – 9 – ne IDC [615]

FLORA MELITENSIS / Grech Delicata, G C – Melitae. 1853. B-5131 2 – 8 – ne IDC [580]

FLORA MEXICANA : COLLECTION DES PLANTES RARES OU PEU CONNUES OBSERVEES AU MEXIQUE ET DANS LA NOUVELLE ESPAGNE / Sesse y Lacasta, Martin de & Mocino, Jose Mariano – 2nd ed 1894 – 71mf – 9 – ne IDC [580]

FLORA MEXICANA : JARDIN BOTANICO 4-11 / Sesse y Lacasta, Martin de & Mocino, Jose Mariano – 1,305mf – 9 – sp Cultura [580]

FLORA MICRONESICA / Kanehira, R – Tokyo. 1933. B-966 2 – 8 – ne IDC [580]

FLORA MOENO-FRANCOFURTANA. FRANCOFURTI AD MOENUM, 1772-1778 / Reichard, J J – 2v. B-5659 1 – 9 – ne IDC [580]

FLORA MONSPELIACA, SISTENS PLANTAS NO. 1850 / Gouan, A – Lugduni. 1765. B-5935 2 – 8 – ne IDC [580]

FLORA MONSPELIENSIS / Nathhorst, T E – Uppsala, 1756. B-5344 2 – 8 – ne IDC [580]

FLORA NAPOLITANA / Tenore, M – Napoli, 1811-1838. 5 vols. B-721 2 – 8 – ne IDC [580]

FLORA NORVEGICA / Gunnerus, J E – 2v. Nidrosiae, Hafniae. 1766-72. B-497 2 – 8 – ne IDC [580]

FLORA ODER ALLGEMEINE BOTANISCHE ZEITUNG / ed by Hoppe, D H – (Preceded by BOTANISCHE ZEITUNG) – Regensburg. 1818-1939/40. v 1-134 – 1533mf – 9 – ne IDC [580]

FLORA OF AFGHANISTAN / Kitamura, S – (Results of the Kyoto University Scientific Expedition to the Karakoram and Hindukush, v. 2, 1955). Kyoto. 1960. B-990 2 – 8 – ne IDC [580]

FLORA OF BRITISH INDIA / Hooker, J D – 7v. London. 1875-97. B-119 2 – 8 – ne IDC [580]

A FLORA OF CALIFORNIA / Jepson, W L – 7565 2. v. 1. 1909-1921 – 8 – ne IDC [580]

THE FLORA OF CANADA / Ross, A M – 7614 2. 1875 – 8 – ne IDC [580]

THE FLORA OF ESSEX COUNTY, MASSACHUSETTS / Robinson, J – 7613 2. 1880 – 8 – ne IDC [580]

THE FLORA OF JAMAICA / MacFadyen, J – London, 1837. 351 pp. B-6048 2 – 8 – ne IDC [580]

FLORA OF KWANTUNG AND HONGKONG (CHINA) / Dunn, ST & Tutcher, W J – (Bulletin of Miscellaneous Information, Kew, Additional Series 10). London. 1912. B-5308 2 – 8 – ne IDC [580]

FLORA OF NEW MEXICO / Wooton, E O & Standley, P C – B7641 2. 1915 – 8 – ne IDC [580]

A FLORA OF NORTH AMERICA / Barton, W P C – 3v. Philadelphia. 1821-23. B-803 2 – 8 – ne IDC [580]

A FLORA OF NORTH AMERICA / Torrey, J & Gray, A – 5771. V. 1. 1838-1840. V. 2. 1841-1843 – 9 – ne IDC [580]

FLORA OF PENNSYLVANIA / Porter, T C – 7605 2. 1903 – 8 – ne IDC [580]

FLORA OF SAGHALIN / Miyabe, K & Miyake, T – Publ. by the Gvt. of Saghalin, 1915. 648 pp., 13 pls. B-7445 1 – 9$6.00 – ne IDC [580]

THE FLORA OF SINGAPORE / Ridley, H N – 5085. 1900 – 9 – ne IDC [580]

FLORA OF SOUTH AUSTRALIA / Black, J M – Adelaide. 1922-29. B-6523 2 – 8 – ne IDC [580]

FLORA OF THE BRITISH WEST INDIAN ISLANDS / Grisebach, A – London. 1864. B-230 2 – 8 – ne IDC [580]

FLORA OF THE BRITISH WEST INDIES / Grisebach, A – 1859-1864 – 5 – uk Microform Academic [580]

FLORA OF THE NORTHERN AND MIDDLE SECTIONS OF THE UNITED STATES / Torrey, J – 5769. 1824 – 9 – ne IDC [580]

FLORA OF THE PRESIDENCY OF MADRAS / Gamble, J S & Fischer, C E C – 3v. London. 1915-36. B-7313 2 – 8 – ne IDC [580]

FLORA OF THE VICINITY OF NEW YORK / Taylor, N – 7627 2. 1915 – 8 – ne IDC [580]

FLORA OF TROPICAL AFRICA / Oliver, D et al; ed by Thiselton-Dyer, W T – London, 1868-1937. v1-10 – 143mf – 9 – 272/2 – ne IDC [580]

THE FLORA OF WALLS IN ISRAEL / Israel. Ministry of Agriculture – By A. Weinstein and R. Karschon. Bet-Dagan. Feb 1977. lop. (leaflet no. 60) – 9 – 2.00 – is I.T.T.I. [580]

FLORA ORIENTALIS / Boissier, E P – 14th cent. Holkham ms. 402. Holkham Hall, Norfolk, England – 1 – uk Microform Academic [580]

FLORA ORIENTALIS / Boissier, E P – 5v. Basileae. 1867-88. B-2250 2 – 8 – ne IDC [580]

FLORA ORIENTALIS SIVE RECENSIO PLANTARUM QUAS BOTANICORUM CORYPHAEUS LEONHARDUS RAUWOLFFUS / Gronovius, J F – Lugduni Batavorum. 1755. B-774 2 – 8 – ne IDC [580]

FLORA OXONIENSIS / Sibthorp, J – Oxonii. 1794. B-6471 1 – 9 – ne IDC [580]

FLORA PEDEMONTANA, SIVE ENUMERATIO METHODICA STIRPIUM INDIGENARUM PEDEMONTII / Allioni, C – 3v. Turin. 1785. B-1128 2 – 8 – ne IDC [580]

FLORA PERUANA..., 1778-1783 : JARDIN BOTANICO 4-1-1 / Ruiz Lopez, Hipolito – 1,304mf – 9 – sp Cultura [580]

FLORA PERUVIANA ET CHILENSIS... / Ruiz Lopez, Hipolito & Pavon y Jimenez, Jose Antonio – Madrid. 3v. 1798-1802 – 70mf – 9 – ne IDC [580]

FLORA PISANA / Savi, G – 2v. Pisa. 1798. B-864 2 – 8 – ne IDC [580]

FLORA POSONIENSIS / Endlicher, S L – Posonii. 1830. B-808 2 – 8 – ne IDC [580]

FLORA REGNI BORUSSICI / Dietrich, A G – 12 v. Berlin. 1832-33-1844. B-5899 2 – 8 – ne IDC [580]

FLORA REIPUBLICAE POPULARIS ROMANICAE – Ed. by T. Savulescu. Bucuresti, 1952-53. v1-2.1094- – 8 – ne IDC [580]

FLORA ROMANA / Maratti, G F – Romae, 1822. 2 vols. B-914 2 – 8 – ne IDC [580]

FLORA ROSSICA / Pallas, Peter Simon – 5089. 1 V. 1784-1788 – 9 – ne IDC [580]

FLORA SARAEPONTANA FOSSILS / Goldenberg, C F – 2571 2. 1855-1862 – 8 – ne IDC [560]

FLORA SARDOA / Moris, G G – Taurini, 1837-1859. 3 vols. B-6166 2 – 8 – ne IDC [580]

FLORA SCOTICA / Hooker, W J – Edinburgh, London. 1821. B-5093 2 – 8 – ne IDC [580]

FLORA SCOTICA / Lightfoot, J – 1777 – 1 – uk Microform Academic [580]

FLORA SCOTICA / Lightfoot, J – 2v. London. 1777. B-6020 2 – 8 – ne IDC [580]

FLORA SIBIRICA SIVE HISTORIA PLANTARUM SIBIRIAE / Gmelin, J G – 4v. Petropoli. 1747-69. B-5423 2 – 8 – ne IDC [580]

FLORA SICULA, EXHIBENS PLANTAS VASCULOSAS / Presl, K B – Pragae. 1826. B-282 2 – 8 – ne IDC [580]

FLORA SICULA, O DESCRIZIONE DELLE PIANTE IN SICILIA / Lojacono, M – Palermo, 1889-1908. B-5568 2 – 8 – ne IDC [580]

FLORA SILESIACA RENOVATA / Krocker, A J – 4v. Vratislavae. 1787-1823. B-5988 2 – 8 – ne IDC [580]

FLORA SIMLENSIS / Collett, H – Calcutta. 1902 – 9 – ne IDC [580]

FLORA SOMALA / Chiovenda, E – 3v. Roma. 1929-36 – 8 – ne IDC [580]

FLORA SVECICA / Linnaeus, Carl – Editio secunda aucta et emendata. Stockholmiae. 1755. B-180 2 – 8 – ne IDC [580]

FLORA SVECICA / Linnaeus, Carl – Lugduni Batavorum. 1745. B-179 2 – 8 – ne IDC [580]

FLORA TAURICO-CAUCASICA / Bieberstein, Friedrich August Marschall von – Charkoviae, 1808-1819. 3 vols. B-197 2 – 8 – ne IDC [580]

FLORA TAURICO-CAUCASICA EXHIBENO STIRPES PHANOGAMAS, IN CHERSONESO TAURICA ET REGIONIBUS CAUCASICIS SPONTE CRESCENTES... / Bieberstein, Friedrich August Marschall von – Charkouiae. 3v. 1808-1819 – 29mf – 9 – ne IDC [580]

FLORA TELLURIANA / Rafinesque-Schmaltz, Constantine S – Philadelphia. 1836. B-6158 1 – 9 – ne IDC [580]

FLORA TEMISCOUATENSIS / Ami, Henry Marc – 1888? 02410. (Pre-1900 Canadiana) – 9 – cn C.I.H.M. [560]

FLORA TURKESTANICA ELABORATA EX PLANTIS / Regel, E A von – St. Petersburgh. 1876. B-6194 1 – 9 – ne IDC [580]

FLORA URSS / ed by Komarov, V L – Leningrad, 1934-1963. v1-30. Index – 280mf – 9 – 8037/1 – ne IDC [580]

FLORA VAN BATAVIA / Backer, C A – Batavia, 1907. Pt.1 – 6mf – 9 – ne IDC [580]

FLORA VENETA / Naccari, F L – Venezia, 1826-1828. 6 vols. B-889 2 – 8 – ne IDC [580]

FLORA VIRGINICA / Gronovius, J F – Lugduni Batavorum. 1762. B-559 2 – 8 – ne IDC [580]

FLORA VITIENSIS: A DESCRIPTION OF THE PLANTS OF THE VITI OR FIJI ISLANDS / Seemann, Berthold Carl – 329. 1865-1873 – 9 – ne IDC [580]

FLORA VON DEUTSCHLAND, OESTERREICH UND DER SCHWEIZ / Thome, S – 992. V. 5-11. 1901-1931 – 9 – ne IDC [580]

FLORA VON TJIBODAS... / Koorders, SH – Batavia, 1918-1923. 3v – 12mf – 9 – ne IDC [580]

FLORA WIRCEBURGENSIS / Heller, F X. – 2v. Wirceburgi. 1810-11. B-916 2 – 8 – ne IDC [580]

FLORA ZEYLANICA / Linnaeus, Carl – Holmiae. 1747. B-2335 2 – 8 – ne IDC [580]

FLORAE AFRICAE AUSTRALIORIS / Nees von Esenbeck, C G D – Glogaviae, 1841. 490 pp. B-246 2 – 8 – ne IDC [580]

FLORAE AUSTRIACAE SIVE PLANTARUM SELECTARUM IN AUSTRIAE ARCHIDUCATA / Jacquin, N J von – 5v. Viennae. 1773-78. B-653 2 – 8 – ne IDC [580]

FLORAE BEROLINENSIS PRODROMUS / Willdenow, C L – Berolini. 1787. B-496 2 – 8 – ne IDC [580]

FLORAE COLUMBIAE TERRARUMQUE ADJACENTIUM SPECIMINA SELECTA / Karsten, GKW H – 2v. Berolini. 1858-69. B-1356 2 – 8 – ne IDC [580]

FLORAE COMITATUS PESTIENSIS / Sadler, J – 2v. Pestini. 1825-26. B-5336 2 – 8 – ne IDC [580]

FLORAE DANICAE. ICONES PLANTARUM SPONTE NASCENTIUM IN REGNIS DANICAE ET NORVEGIAE / Oeder, G C – v. 1-17. Hauniae. 1766-1883. B-692 2 – 8 – ne IDC [580]

FLORAE FIBERGENSIS SPECIMEN / Humboldt, Alexander von – Berolini. 1793. B-6185 2 – 8 – ne IDC [580]

FLORAE FLUMINENSIS / Vellozo, J M da Conceicao – 11 vols. Rio de Janeiro. 1825; Paris. 1825-35. B-5174 2 – 8 – ne IDC [580]

FLORAE FLUMINENSIS, SEU DESCRIPTIONUM PLANTARUM PRAEFECTURA FLUMINENSI SPONTE NASCENTIUM / Vellozo, J M da Conceicao – Reprint. Rio de Janeiro. 1881. B-5788 2 – 8 – ne IDC [580]

FLORAE GOETTINGENSIS SPECIMEN / Link, J H F – Goettingen. 1789. B-6032 2 – 8 – ne IDC [580]

FLORAE GRAECAE PRODROMUS / Sibthorp, J & Smith, J E – London, 1806-1813. 2 vols. B-560 2 – 8 – ne IDC [580]

FLORAE HALENSIS TENTAMEN NOVUM / Sprengel, K P J – Halae Saxonum, 1806. 420 pp., 12 pls. Mantissa prima. Halae, 1807. 58 pp. B-5749 2 – 8 – ne IDC [580]

FLORAE LEYDENSIS PRODOMUS / Royen, A van – Lugduni Batavorum. 1740. B-299 2 – 8 – ne IDC [580]

FLORAE LIBYCAE SPECIMEN / Viviani, D – Genuae. 1824. B-6482 2 – 8 – ne IDC [580]

FLORAE LUSITANICAE ET BRASILIENSIS SPECIMEN / Vandelli, D – Conimbricae. 1788. B-868 2 – 8 – ne IDC [580]

FLORAE PERUVIANAE ET CHILENSIS PRODROMUS...... / Ruiz Lopez, Hipolito & Pavon y Jimenez, Jose Antonio – Madrid, 1794 – 14mf – 9 – ne IDC [580]

FLORAE ROMANAE PRODROMUS / Sebastiani, A & Mauri, E – Romae. 1818. Lacking: 1818, v. 1. B-6470 2 – 8 – ne IDC [580]

FLORAE SCANDINAVIAE PRODROMUS / Retzius, A J – Holmiae. 1779. B-5669 2 – 8 – ne IDC [580]

FLORAE SENEGAMBIAE TENTAMEN / Guillemin, J B A et al – Paris. 1830-33. B-5942 2 – 8 – ne IDC [580]

FLORAE SICULAE PRODROMUS / Gussone, G – 2. v. Neapoli. 1827-28. Suppl. 1832-43. B-98 2 – 8 – ne IDC [580]

FLORAE SICULAE SYNOPSIS / Gussone, G – 2v. Neapoli. 1842-1844-45. B-122 2 – 8 – ne IDC [580]

LES FLORAISONS MATUTINALES / Beauchemin, Neree – Trois Rivieres: V. Ayotte, 1897.03518.(Pre-1900 Canadiana) – 9 – cn C.I.H.M. [631]

THE FLORAL CABINET, AND MAGAZINE OF EXOTIC BOTANY – London, 1837-1840 – 3 – us Readex [580]

THE FLORAL FORTUNE-TELLER : A GAME FOR THE SEASON OF FLOWERS / Edgarton, S C – Boston: A Tompkins, c1846 – us Res Libr [790]

FLORAS LAKE BANNER – Lakeport OR. Oct 7 1911 – 1 – us U.O. Library [071]

FLORE AGENAISE / Saint Amand, Jean F B de – ou Description methodique des plantes. Agen. 1821. B-5082 2 – 8 – ne IDC [580]

FLORE ANALYTIQUE ET DICHOTOMIQUE DES LICHENS DE L'ORNE DEPARTMENT CIRCONVOISINS / Olivier, H – Autheuil (Orne). 1882-84. B-1574 2 – 8 – ne IDC [580]

LA FLORE DE INSECTOPHILES PRECEDEE D'UN DISCOURS SUR L'UTILITE DES INSECTES ET DE L'ETUDE DE L'INSECTOLOGIE / Brez, J – Utrecht, 1791 – XXVI, 324p – 8 – ne IDC [590]

FLORE DE L'ALGEA1RIE / Munby, G – Paris, 1847. 120 pp., 7 pls. B-6197 1 – 9 – ne IDC [580]
FLORE DE VIRGILE / Fee, A L A – Paris. 1822. B-5124 2 – 8 – ne IDC [580]
FLORE DES ALGUES DE BELGIQUE / Wildeman, E de – Bruxelles, Paris. 1896. B-6422 2 – 8 – ne IDC [580]
FLORE DES ANTILLES / Tussac, F R de – 4v. Paris. 1808-1827-28. B-5783 1 – 9 – ne IDC [580]
LA FLORE DES ENVIRONS DE PARIS / Thuillier, J L – Paris. 1790. B-6476 1 – 9 – ne IDC [580]
FLORE DES PLANTES QUI CROISSENT DANS LES DEA1PARTEMENTS DU HAUT- ET BAS-RHIN / Stolz, J C – Strasbourg, 1802. 62 pp. B-5754 2 – 8 – ne IDC [580]
FLORE DES SERRES ET DES JARDINS D'EUROPE – 23 v. Gand. 1845-80. – 208mf – 8 – ne IDC [580]
FLORE D'EUROPE / Boissieu, C V de – 3v. Lyon. 1805-07. Lacking: 1806 07, v. 3. B-5855 2 – 8 – ne IDC [580]
FLORE D'OWARE ET DE BENIN EN AFRIQUE / Palisot de Beauvois, A M F J – 2v. Paris. 1804-07, 1805-20. B-5277 2 – 8 – ne IDC [580]
FLORE DU CALVADOS ET DES TERREINS ADJACENS, COMPOSEE SUIVANT LA METHODE DE M. JUSSIEU COMPAREE AVEC CELLE DE TOURNEFORT ET DE LINNE / Roussel, H F A – Ed. 2. Caen. 1806. B-5346 2 – 8 – ne IDC [580]
FLORE DU DEPARTEMENT DES HAUTES-PYRENEES / Dulac, J – Paris. 1867 – 8 – ne IDC [580]
FLORE DU KOUY-TCHEOU / Leveille, H – Le Mans. 1914-15. B-904 2 – 8 – ne IDC [580]
FLORE DU NORD DE LA FRANCE / Roucel, F A – 2v. Paris. 1803. B-5695 2 – 8 – ne IDC [580]
FLORE FORESTIERE DE LA COCHINCHINE / Pierre, J B L – 5v. Paris. 1879-1907. B-5638 2 – 8 – ne IDC [580]
FLORE FRANCAISE / Lamarck, J B A P M de – ou Description succinctes de toutes les plantes. 3 v. Paris. 1778. B-6002 2 – 8 – ne IDC [580]
FLORE FRANCIASE / Lamarck, J B A P M de & Candolle, A P de – ou Descriptions succinctes de toutes les plantes. ed. 3. 6 v. Paris. 1805-15. B-48 1 – 9 – ne IDC [580]
FLORE LYONNAISE OU DESCRIPTION DES PLANTES QUI CROISSENT DANS LES ENVIRONS DE LYON ET SUR LE MONT-PILAT / Balbis, G B – 2v. Lyon. 1827-28. B-5245 2 – 8 – ne IDC [580]
FLORE MEDICALE / Chaumeton, F P – 7v. Paris. 1814-20. B-6219 2 – 8 – ne IDC [580]
FLORE MYCOLOGIQUE DE GENTINNES / Limminghe, A de – Namur. 1875. B-6287 2 – 8 – ne IDC [580]
FLORE MYCOLOGIQUE DU DEPARTEMENT DE TARN-ET-GARONNE / Roumeguere, C – Montauban. 1879. B-6308 2 – 8 – ne IDC [580]
FLORE PARISIENNE / Poiteau, P A & Turpin, P J F – Paris, 1808-13. B-5644 1 – 9 – ne IDC [580]
FLORE PHANEROGAMIQUE DES ANTILLES FRANCAISES / Duss, Le R P – (Annales de l'Institut Colonial Marseille. v. 3). Macon. 1897. B-1144 2 – 8 – ne IDC [580]
FLORE [PITTORESQUE ET] MEDICALE DES ANTILLES / ed by Descourtilz, M E – Paris, 1821-1829. 8v – 83mf – 9 – 5893/2 – ne IDC [580]
FLORE PLANEROGAMIQUE DES ANTILLES FRANCAISES / Duss, Le R P – Martinique et Guadeloupe. 1897 – 1 – us UMI [580]
FLORE PORTUGAISE / Hoffmannsegg, J C von & Link, J H F – 2v. Berlin. 1809-40. B-5049 2 – 8 – ne IDC [580]
FLORE ROSSICA; SIVE, ENUMERATIO PLANTARUM / Ledebour, C F von – 4v. Stuttgart. 1841-1842-53. B-6009 2 – 8 – ne IDC [580]
FLORECILLAS DE SAN FRANCISCO DE SAN FRANCISCO CONTADAS A LOS NINOS / Sobral, Maria da Luz – Barcelona, 1931; Madrid: Razon y Fe, 1931 – 1 – sp Bibl Santa Ana [580]
Florence *see* LIBRI STATUTORUM COMMUNITATIS FLORENTIAE
Florence, A T *see* JOURNAL OF DRUG TARGETING
FLORENCE BAPTIST CHURCH. KENTUCKY : CHURCH RECORDS – Oct 1893-Nov 1894, May 1902-Jun 1962 – 1 – 55.98 – us Baptist [240]
FLORENCE BAPTIST CHURCH. LEXINGTON COUNTY. SOUTH CAROLINA : CHURCH RECORDS – 1938-1973 – 1 – 5.00 – us Baptist [240]
FLORENCE BAPTIST CHURCH. TEXAS : CHURCH RECORDS – 1856-1942 – 1 – 44.82 – us Baptist [240]
FLORENCE FIRST BAPTIST CHURCH. FLORENCE, ALABAMA : CHURCH RECORDS – 1907-59 – 1 – 72.24 – us Baptist [240]
FLORENCE FIRST BAPTIST CHURCH. FLORENCE, SOUTH CAROLINA : CHURCH RECORDS – 1866-1946 – 1 – 40.86 – us Baptist [240]
FLORENCE FONTENELLE AND MINNE LUSA REVIEW – Florence, NE. -w. Aug. 1919-Feb. 1933 – 1 – us NE Hist [071]
FLORENCE GAZETTE – Florence, Italy. Italian Gazette. -m. Sept 1890-12 May 1894; 3 Nov 1894-3 Nov 1903; 1 Nov 1904-4 June 1907. 6 reels – 1 – uk British Libr Newspaper [072]
FLORENCE GAZETTE – Florence, NE. -w. Jun. 1903-Jul. 1903; Sep. 1903-Jan. 1904; Jun. 1906-Dec. 1908 – 1 – us NE Hist [071]
FLORENCE; ITS HISTORY, THE MEDICI, THE HUMANISTS, LETTERS, ARTS / Yriarte, Charles – New ed. rev...by Maria Hornor Lansdale. Philadelphia: H.T. Coates, 1897. viii,478p. plates, maps, geneal. tab – 1 – us U.W. Library [945]
Florence of Worcester *see* FLORENTII WIGORNIENSIS MONACHI
FLORENCE TRIBUNE – Florence, NE. -w. Jun. 1909-Dec. 1916 – 1 – us NE Hist [071]
Florence, William James *see* THE GENTLEMEN'S HANDBOOK ON POKER
FLORENTII WIGORNIENSIS MONACHI / Florence of Worcester – English Historical Society, Publications, 1848-49. 1 reel. 1247 – 1 – us U.W. Library [941]
FLORENTINE HISTORY, FROM THE EARLIEST AUTHENTIC RECORDS TO THE ACCESSION OF FERDINAND THE THIRD, GRAND DUKE OF TUSCANY / Napier, Henry Edward – London: E. Moxon, 1846-47. 6v. plates, maps – 1 – us U.W. Library [945]
FLORENTINISCHE NAECHTE = FLORENTINE NIGHTS / Heine, Heinrich – (In English) – London: Methuen, 1927 – 1 – us U.W. Library [830]
Flores, A *see* LA NATURALIZACON EN LOS ESTADOS UNIDOS
Flores, Antonio *see* SERMON...CATEDRAL DE BADAJOZ
Flores Barrera, Jose Miguel *see*
- CRONICA DE DON ALVARO DE LUNA
- CRONICA DE ENRIQUE EL QUARTO

FLORES DE HEROISMO. SEVILLA, 1939 / Garcia Alonso, Francisco – Madrid: Razon y Fe, 1940 – 1 – sp Bibl Santa Ana [946]
FLORES DE SAN BERNARDO. DE LA LAMENTACION DE LA VIRGEN MARIA / Bravo Riesco, Agustin – S.l., s.i, s.a. – 1 – sp Bibl Santa Ana [240]
FLORES DEL VALLE / Garcia Miranda, Vicenta – 1855 – 9 – 1.50f – sp Bibl Santa Ana [810]
LAS FLORES EN LA TRADICION EXTREMENA / Gil Garcia, Bonifacio – Badajoz: Dip. Provincial, 1962 – sp Bibl Santa Ana [946]
Flores, Hector Alberto *see* LA RESPUESTA PERONISTA
FLORES HISTORIARUM (RS95) : PER MATTHAEUM WEST-MONASTERIENSEM COLLECTI / Matthew Of Westminster; ed by Luard, H R – (v1 1890 Dfl39.00. v2 1890 Dfl32.00. v3 1890 Dfl42.00) – ne Slangenburg [240]
Flores, Jose *see* OPERACION "ROSA NEGRA"
Flores, L L *see* REGIMEN DE RECIPROCIDADE...
FLORES MUSICAE / Spechtshart, Hugo of Reutlingen – [Strasburg?, 1495?] – 1 – us Sibley [780]
FLORES OMNIUM DOCTORUM ILLUSTRIUM... / Hibernicus, Thomas – Lugduni. Tome 1 + 2. 1678 – 14mf – 9 – ne Slangenburg [240]
Flores, R *see* SUCESION DE EXTRANJEROS...
Flores, S L de *see* DESEMPENO AL METODO RACIONAL EN LA CURACION DE LAS CALENTURAS TERCIANAS
FLORES SIN AROMA / Sanchez-Arjona, Vicente – Sevilla: Imp. Carlos Acuna, Tomo 1-4. 1956 – 1 – sp Bibl Santa Ana [810]
FLORES Y ABROJOS / Vargas, Adolfo de – 1883 – 9 – 1.50f – sp Bibl Santa Ana [810]
FLORES Y ESPINAS : COLECCION DE POESIAS PARA EL OFRECIMIENTO DE LAS FLORES DE MAYO / Castro Bajo, Julian – Barcelona: Eugenio Subirana, 1912 – 1 – sp Bibl Santa Ana [580]
FLORES Y FRUTOS DE MI CORAZON DEDICACDOS A TI / Cruz Marin, Eugenio de la – Badajoz: Tip. Espanola, 1947 – 1 – sp Bibl Santa Ana [810]
FLORESTA DE DISERTACIONES HISTORICO-MEDICAS... / Baguer y Oliver, J – Valencia, 1741 – 22mf – 9 – sp Cultura [610]
Floret, C *see* CASE STUDIES ON DESERTIFICATION
Florez Canseco, Casimiro *see*
- OBRAS DE JENOFONTE. TOMO 1
- OBRAS DE JENOFONTE. TOMO 2
- LA POETICA DE ARISTOTELES
- EL SUENO DE LUCIANO Y LA TABLA DE CEBES

Florez de Ocariz, Juan *see* GENEALOGIAS DEL NUEVO REYNO DE GRANADA. 2 VOL. BOGOTA, 1943
Florez, E et al *see* ESPANA SAGRADA..., TOMOS 01-51
Florez, Enrique *see* RELACION DEL VIAGE QUE AMBROSIO DE MORALES...HIZO POR SU MANDADO AL ANO DE 1572 EN GALICIA Y ASTURIAS
Florez, F *see* REGIMIENTO DE SANIDAD DE TODAS LAS COSAS QUE SE COMEN Y BEVEN, CON MUCHOS CONSEJOS
Florez, Henrique *see* ESPANA SAGRADA
Florez, Jose Segundo *see*
- ESPARTERO. HISTORIA
- PRIMERAS NOCIONES DE CRONOLOGIA

Florez, L A *see* RIOS INTERNACIONALES SU LIBRE NAVEGACION
Florez Setien, Enrique *see*
- CLAVE HISTORIAL
- ESPANA SAGRADA. TOMO 1
- ESPANA SAGRADA. TOMO 2
- ESPANA SAGRADA. TOMO 3
- ESPANA SAGRADA. TOMO 4
- ESPANA SAGRADA. TOMO 5
- ESPANA SAGRADA. TOMO 6
- ESPANA SAGRADA. TOMO 7
- ESPANA SAGRADA. TOMO 8
- ESPANA SAGRADA. TOMO 9
- ESPANA SAGRADA. TOMO 10
- ESPANA SAGRADA. TOMO 11
- ESPANA SAGRADA. TOMO 12
- ESPANA SAGRADA. TOMO 13
- ESPANA SAGRADA. TOMO 14
- ESPANA SAGRADA. TOMO 15
- ESPANA SAGRADA. TOMO 16
- ESPANA SAGRADA. TOMO 17
- ESPANA SAGRADA. TOMO 18
- ESPANA SAGRADA. TOMO 19
- ESPANA SAGRADA. TOMO 20
- ESPANA SAGRADA. TOMO 21
- ESPANA SAGRADA. TOMO 22
- ESPANA SAGRADA. TOMO 23
- ESPANA SAGRADA. TOMO 24, PARTE 1
- ESPANA SAGRADA. TOMO 24, PARTE 2
- ESPANA SAGRADA. TOMO 25
- ESPANA SAGRADA. TOMO 26
- ESPANA SAGRADA. TOMO 27
- ESPANA SAGRADA. TOMO 28
- ESPANA SAGRADA. TOMO 29
- MEDALLAS DE LAS COLONIAS. TOMO 1
- MEDALLAS DE LAS COLONIAS. TOMO 2
- MEDALLAS DE LAS COLONIAS. TOMO 3
- MEMORIAS DE LAS REINAS CATOLICAS. TOMO 1
- MEMORIAS DE LAS REINAS CATOLICAS. TOMO 2

Floria, Carlos Alberto et al *see* EL PERONISMO
Floriano, Antonio *see* FLORIANO, ANTONIO. LA IGLESIA DE SANTIAGO DE LOS CABALLEROS EN CACERES
FLORIANO, ANTONIO. LA IGLESIA DE SANTIAGO DE LOS CABALLEROS EN CACERES / Ortega, Angel & Floriano, Antonio – Madrid: Archivo Ibero-Americano, 1916 – 1 – sp Bibl Santa Ana [240]
Floriano Cumbreno, Antonio C *see*
- CACERES ANTE LA HISTORIA. LA CUESTION CRITICA DE LA FUNDACION Y EL NOMBRE DE CACERES
- CATALOGO DEL ARCHIVO DE LA DIPUTACION PROVINCIAL DE TERUEL
- CURSO GENERAL DE DIDACTICA (METODOLOGIA Y ORGANIZACION ESCOLAR)
- CURSO GENERAL DE PALEOGRAFIA Y DIPLOMATICA ESPANOLES. SELECCION DIPLOMATICA
- EXCAVACIONES EN LA ANTIGUA CAPPARA (CAPARRA.CACERES)
- EXCAVACIONES EN MERIDA
- LA FECHA EN LA CONQUISTA DE CACERES ANTE LOS DOCUMENTOS (LA CARTA POPULATIONIS)
- LAS FUENTES PARA LA HISTORIA DE LA PEDAGOGIA ESPANOLA
- HALLAZGO DE LA NECROPOLIS JUDAICA DE LA CIUDAD DE TERUEL
- LA IGLESIA DE SANTIAGO DE LOS CABALLEROS DE CACERES Y EL ESCULTOR ALONSO BERRUGUETE
- LA IGLESIA DE SANTIAGO DE LOS CABALLEROS. DESCRIPCION HISTORICO-ARTISTICA
- INFORME SOBRE LA CATALOGACION DE LA COLECCION NUMISMATICA DEL MUSEO DE CACERES
- ORIGENES HISTORICOS DE LA AGRICULTURA Y DE LA GANADERIA EN CACERES
- PREGON DE LA SEMANA SANTA CACERENA
- LOS PROBLEMAS DE SU RECONQUISTA Y DE SU NOMBRE
- EL RETABLO DE SANTIAGO DE LOS CABALLEROS DE CACERES Y EL ESCULTOR ALONSO BERRUGUETE
- TERUEL EN EL SIGLO 15. LA VIDA ECONOMICA Y LA CUESTION MONETARIA
- TRANSCRIPCION PALEOGRAFICA Y VERSION CASTELLANA DE LA CARTA DE POBLACION O FUERO LATINO DE CACERES
- EL TRIBUNAL DEL SANTO OFICIO EN ARAGON
- EL TRIBUNAL DEL SANTO OFICIO EN ARAGON ESTABLECIMIENTO DE LA INQUISICION EN TERUEL
- LA VILLA DE CACERES Y LA REINA CATOLICA: 2. ORDENANZAS SOBRE LAS LABRANZAS Y PASTOS DE ZAFRA Y ZAFRILLA, DE LA "PENAS DE GANADOS" Y ADMINISTRACION DE LOS BIENES PROPIOS DEL CONCEJO DE CACERES...LOS JURAMENTOS DE LOS REYES CATOLICOS

FLORICULTURAL CABINET AND FLORIST'S MAGAZINE – v. 1-27. London. 1833-59. – 271mf – 8 – ne IDC [580]
FLORIDA – 6r – 1 – $480.00 – us Scholarly Res [370]
FLORIDA : SESSION LAWS OF AMERICAN STATES AND TERRITORIES – 1822-1995 – 9 – $3,329.00 set – us Hein [340]
FLORIDA : WEST'S FLORIDA STATUTES ANNOTATED – St Paul: West Pub Co, 1943-Feb 1996 update – 9 – $2,966.00 set – us Hein [340]
Florida *see*
- LETTERS SENT, REGISTERS OF LETTERS RECEIVED, AND LETTERS RECEIVED BY HEADQUARTERS, TROOPS IN FLORIDA, AND HEADQUARTERS, DEPARTMENT OF FLORIDA
- REPORTS AND OPINIONS (A-G)
- REPORTS, POST-NRS
- REPORTS, PRE-NRS

FLORIDA 1781-1900 – (Mf 1: Births 1781-1859. Mf 2: Births 1826-63; Marriages 1810-60; Deaths 1806-60. Mf 3: Births 1861-96. Mf 4: Births 1896-1900. Mf 5: Marriages 1861-1901. Mf 6: Deaths 1860-1914) – (mf ed 1990) – 6mf – 9 – 0-87623-114-8 – us Holbrook [920]
FLORIDA ADVOCATE – Wauchula. Fl. -w. 1945-55 – 1 – us P.K. Yonge [071]
Florida. Agricultural Experiment Station *see*
- AGRONOMY MIMEO REPORT
- ANNUAL REPORT
- BULLETIN
- CIRCULAR
- PUBLICATION
- SUNSHINE STATE AGRICULTURAL RESEARCH REPORT

Florida. Agricultural Experiment Station. Southern Cooperative Series *see* BULLETIN
Florida. Agricultural Extension Service *see*
- ANNUAL REPORT
- BULLETIN
- CIRCULAR

FLORIDA ALLIGATOR – Gainesville. Fla. 1976- – 1 – us P.K. Yonge [071]
FLORIDA ATTORNEY GENERAL REPORTS AND OPINIONS – (6 1845-1978 $455.00. 9 1979-1994 $182.00) – 1845-1994 – 6,9 – $637.00set – us Hein [340]
Florida. Baptist Associations *see* ANNUALS
FLORIDA BAPTIST WITNESS – Jacksonville, Florida: Florida Baptist Convention, 1885-1991 – 1 – $2,914.96 – us Baptist [240]
FLORIDA BAPTIST WITNESS: INDEX – 1908-56 – 1,5 – 80.32 – us Baptist [240]

FLORIDA BAR JOURNAL – (v1-58 1927-84 on reel or mf $625.00. v59-69 1985-95 on mf $238.00. Title varies: v1-8 1927-34 as Florida State Bar Association Law Journal. v8-27 1934-53 as Florida Law Journal) – 5,6,9 – $863.00 set – us Hein [340]
FLORIDA BAR NEWS – (1979 5,6,9) – 1974 – 1 – us UMI [073]
FLORIDA CATHOLIC – Orlando. Dec 1939-Nov 1941, May 1949-1967 – 1 – us P.K. Yonge [240]
THE FLORIDA CATHOLIC – Orlando. Fl. 1939- – 1 – us UMI [071]
FLORIDA: CENSUS – (Baker, Bradford, Brevard, Calhoun & Dade Counties. M845-0001. Duval County. M845-0002. Escambia, Franklin & Gadsden Counties. M845-0003. Hamilton, Hernando, Hillsborough & Holmes Counties.M845-0004. Jackson County. M845-0005. Jefferson & Lafayette Counties. M845-0006. Leon, Levy & Liberty Counties. M845-0007. Madison & Manatee Counties.M845-0008. Marion & Monroe Counties. M845-0009. Orange & Polk Counties. M845-0010. Putnam, St. Johns & Santa Rosa Counties. M845-0011. Sumter, Suwannee & Taylor Counties.M845-0012. Volusia, Wakulla, Walton & Washington Counties. M845-0013) – 1885 – 1 – us A.G.L.L. [920]
FLORIDA CHEMICAL WORKER – 1-2. 1948-1949 – 1 – us P.K. Yonge [660]
Florida. Constitution Revision Commission *see* COMMISSION MINUTES, COMMITTEE MINUTES AND PROPOSALS, JANUARY 1966-JUNE 1966
LA FLORIDA DEL INCA : HISTORIA DEL ADELANTADO HERNANDO DE SOTO... / Laso de la Vega, Garcia – Mexico: Fondo de Cultura Economica, 1956 – 1 – sp Bibl Santa Ana [972]
LA FLORIDA DEL INCA. HISTORIA DEL ADELANTADO HERNANDO DE SOTO. TOMO 1 / Laso de la Vega, Garcia – Cuzco (Peru): Imp. H.G. Rozas, 1958 – sp Bibl Santa Ana [350]
FLORIDA, DISCOVERY AND CONQUEST / Rye, W B – Hakluyt Society – 7 – uk Microform Academic [910]
FLORIDA DISPATCH – Jacksonville. Fla. 1882-1888 – 1 – us UMI [071]
FLORIDA EXPLORER – Tampa. Fla. 1960- – 1 – us P.K. Yonge [071]
FLORIDA FACTS – 1890-1908 – 1 – us P.K. Yonge [380]
FLORIDA FARMER AND FRUIT GROWER – Jacksonville. Fl. n.s. 5-9. ser. 3, 1-11. 1889-99 – 1 – us P.K. Yonge [631]
FLORIDA FARMER AND FRUIT GROWER – Jacksonville. Fla. 1888-1898 – 1 – us UMI [071]
FLORIDA FIREMAN – v1-3. 1932-1936 – 1 – us P.K. Yonge [360]
FLORIDA FOOD AND GROCERY NEWS – 1952-to date – 1 – us P.K. Yonge [380]
FLORIDA INTERNATIONAL LAW JOURNAL *see* FLORIDA JOURNAL OF INTERNATIONAL LAW
FLORIDA JOURNAL OF INTERNATIONAL LAW – (Title varies: v1-5 1984-90 as Florida International Law Journal) – v1-8. 1984-93 – 9 – $115.00 set – us Hein [340]
FLORIDA LABOR NEWS – Tallahassee. Fla. 1948-49, 1967-69, 1971-74 – 1 – us P.K. Yonge [071]
FLORIDA LAW JOURNAL *see* FLORIDA BAR JOURNAL
FLORIDA LAW REVIEW – (v1-36 1948-84 on reel $492.00. v37-46 1985-94 on mf $232.00. Title varies: v1-40 1948-88 as University of Florida Law Review) – v1-46. 1948-94 – 5,6,9 – $733.00 set – us Hein [340]
Florida Memorial College *see* CATALOGS
FLORIDA MOTORIST – Miami. Fla. 1966-72 – 1 – us P.K. Yonge [071]
FLORIDA OCCIDENTAL – Sevilla – 11r – 5,6 – sp Cultura [977]
FLORIDA OCCIDENTAL Y LUISIANA. CAJA REAL (ANNO 1783-1821) – Sevilla – 23r – 5,6 – sp Cultura [977]
FLORIDA OCCIDENTAL Y LUISIANA. CORRESPONDENCIA (ANNO 1775-1814) – Sevilla – 112r – 5,6 – sp Cultura [977]
FLORIDA OCCIDENTAL Y LUISIANA. CORRESPONDENCIA GOBERNADORES (ANNO 1764-) – Sevilla – 122r – 5,6 – sp Cultura [977]
FLORIDA OCCIDENTAL Y LUISIANA. CORRESPONDENCIA GOBERNADORES (ANNO 1766-) – Sevilla – 73r – 5,6 – sp Cultura [977]
FLORIDA ORIENTAL – Sevilla – 8r – 5,6 – sp Cultura [977]
FLORIDA ORIENTAL. CAJA REAL (ANNO 1783-1821) – Sevilla – 93r – 5,6 – sp Cultura [977]
FLORIDA RADIO NEWS – 1. 1933 – 1 – us P.K. Yonge [380]
FLORIDA SENTINEL – Tallahassee. Fl. 1854-55, 1862-63, 1866-76 – 1 – us P.K. Yonge [071]
FLORIDA STAR – Jacksonville. Fl. -w. 1956- – 1 – us P.K. Yonge [071]
Florida. State Bar Association *see* PROCEEDINGS
FLORIDA STATE BAR ASSOCIATION LAW JOURNAL *see* FLORIDA BAR JOURNAL
FLORIDA STATE BAR ASSOCIATION PROCEEDINGS – (Lacking: v4-11) – v1-20. 1907-27 (all publ) – 22mf – 9 – $33.00 – LLMC 84-464 – us L.L.M.C. [340]
FLORIDA STATE UNIVERSITY LAW REVIEW – (v1-12 1973-85 on reel $215.00. v13-22 1985-95 on mf $232.00) – v1-22. 1973-95 – 5,6,9 – $447.00 set – us Hein [340]
Florida. Supreme Court *see* FLORIDA SUPREME COURT REPORTS
FLORIDA SUPREME COURT REPORTS / Florida. Supreme Court – (Pre-NRS: v1-22 1846-86 168mf $252.00. Updates not poss until year 2006) – v1-103. 1846-1931 – 938mf – 9 – $1,407.00 – LLMC 80-821 – us L.L.M.C. [340]
THE FLORIDA TATTLER – Jacksonville. Fla. oct. 4, 11, 1941 – 1 – us NY Public [071]
FLORIDA TIMES-UNION – Jacksonville. Fla. 1882- – 1 – us UMI [071]
FLORIDA TIMES-UNION – Jacksonville. Fla. (Star Ed.). 1950-1966 – 1 – us UMI [071]
FLORIDA TIMES-UNION – Jacksonville. Fla. (State News). 1963- – 1 – us UMI [071]
FLORIDA UNION – Jacksonville. FL. Aug 18 1866 – 1 – us Western Res [071]
FLORIDA UNITED METHODIST – Lakeland. Fla. Sep 1972- – 1 – us P.K. Yonge [071]
Florida. University. Gainesville. Libraries *see* CATALOG OF THE LATIN AMERICAN COLLECTION
Florida. University. Gainesville. P.K. Yonge Library of Florida History *see* CATALOG..
FLORIDA VOCATIONAL JOURNAL – (v.6-. 1980-. 5,6,9) – v.1-. 1976- – 1 – us UMI [370]
FLORIDA VOICE OF SAFETY – 1951-1954 – 1 – us P.K. Yonge [600]
Floridablanca, Conde de *see*
– CENSO ESPANOL
– CENSO ESPANOL EXECUTADO POR ORDEN DEL REY EN EL ANO 1787
LA FLORIDE FRANCAISE – Miami, FL. 15 fev 1955-v6 n1. jan/fev 1959 – 1r – 1 – Can$50.00 – cn Can Microfilming [071]
LE FLORIDEE ITALICHE / Ardissone, F – 6339 2. 1869 and 1874-1878 – 8 – ne IDC [580]
FLORIDIAN – St. Petersburg. Fl. -w. 1944, 1948, 1950-59 – 1 – us UMI [071]
FLORIDIAN AND JOURNAL – (Weekly Confederate newspaper) – Tallahassee, FL. Mar 5 1864 – 1r – 1 – us Western Res [071]
FLORIDSDORF : THE VIENNA WORKERS IN REVOLT: A PLAY / Wolf, Friedrich – 1st American ed. New York: Universum Publishers and Distributors, c1935 – 1r – 1 – us U.W. Library [820]
FLORILEGIA : FLORILEGIUM FRISINGENSE. TESTIMONIA DIVINAE SCRIPTURAE ET PATRUM – 1987 – 3mf – 9 – Bf975.00 – 2-503-61082-X – be Brepols [240]
FLORILEGIO...IGLESIA...DIVIDIDO EN DISCURSOS / Soto y Marne, Francisco de – 1738 – 9 – 1.50f – sp Bibl Santa Ana [240]
FLORILEGIUM HISTORICO-CRITICUM LIBRORUM RARIORUM / Gerdes, Dan – Editio 3 Croningae Bremae, 1763 – 9mf – 8 – ne Slangenburg [090]
FLORILEGIUM NOVUM / Bry, J T de – Oppenheim. 1612. B-7411 1 – 9 – ne IDC [580]
FLORILEGIUM PATRISTICUM TAM VETERIS QUAM MEDII AEVI AUCTORES COMPLECTENS 1-45 – Bonn, 1911-1938 – 112mf – 9 – Dfl392.00 – ne Slangenburg [580]
FLORILOGIUM PHRASICON / Hewes, John – 1633. 504p. (English Linguistics Series 1500-1800) – 9 – us UMI [400]
Florio, John *see*
– QUEEN ANNA'S NEW WORLD OF WORDS
– SECOND FRUTES
FLORISSANT VALLEY BAPTIST CHURCH. MISSOURI : CHURCH RECORDS – 1955-60. and Bulletins (Voice). 1956-59 – 1 – 48.60 – us Baptist [240]
FLORIST, FRUITIST AND GARDEN MISCELLANY – London, 1848-1861. v1-14 – 72mf – 9 – 7350/2 – ne IDC [580]
FLORIST'S EXCHANGE – (Missing: 1918. v45(p. 49-77)) – New York, 1912-1920. v33-49 – 767mf – 9 – 7349/1 – ne IDC [580]
Florit, Carlos A *see* LAS FUERZAS ARMADAS Y LA GUERRA PSICOLOGICA
FLORULA BELGICA / Dumortier, B C J – Tornaci Nerviorum. 1827. B-5221 2 – 8 – ne IDC [580]
FLORULA BOSTONIENSIS / Bigelow, J – Boston. 1814. B-919 2 – 8 – ne IDC [580]
FLORULA JUVENALIS / Godron, D A – ou Enumeration des plantes etrangeres. Ed. 2. Nancy. 1854. B-7291 1 – 9 – ne IDC [580]
FLORULA LUDOVICIANA / Rafinesque-Schmaltz, Constantine S – or A Flora of the state of Louisiana. New York. 1817. B-5054 2 – 8 – ne IDC [580]
FLORULAE INSULARUM AUSTRALIUM PRODROMUS / Forster, J G A – Gottingae. 1786. B-7698 2 – 8 – ne IDC [580]
FLORULE DU FINISTERE / Crouan, PL & Crouan, H M – Paris. 1867 – 8 – ne IDC [580]
DIE FLOTTE : MONATSBLATT DES DEUTSCHEN FLOTTEN-VEREINS UND DES HAUPTVERBANDES DEUTSCHER FLOTTEN-VEREIN IM AUSLAND – Berlin. v13 no 1-v22 no 12, Jun 1910-Dec 1919. Missing Nov 1911, May 1918, and Jul 1919 – 1 – $35.00r – us Hoover Inst Photo [355]
Flottes, J BM *see* INTRODUCTION AUX OUVRAGES DE VOLTAIRE
Flou, Karel de *see* DIE BEDUDINGHE NADEN SINNE VAN SUNTE AUGUSTIJNS REGULE
Flourens, M *see* DE LA NOTION DE CONTREBANDE...
FLOURES FOR LATINE SPEKYNAE SELECTED AND GATHERED OUTE OF TERENCE, AND THE SAME TRANSLATED IN TO ENGLYSSHE / Udall, Nicholas – 1533. 428p. (English Linguistics Series 1500-1800) – 9 – us UMI [450]
Flournoy, Parke P *see* NEW LIGHT ON THE NEW TESTAMENT
FLOW OF GOODS IN THE JORDAN ECONOMY / Jordan. Department of Statistics – 1970. BNE-9770 1 – 9 – ne IDC [310]
FLOW QUARTERLY *see* HANDLING AND SHIPPING
FLOWER AND GARDEN – (1980-. 1,5,6,9) – Northern ed. v1-. 1957- – 1 – us UMI [073]
FLOWER AND WEED; AND OTHER TALES / Braddon, Mary Elizabeth – British Fiction Archive: Unit 5 – 9 – uk Bell [830]
Flower, George *see* HISTORY OF THE ENGLISH SETTLERS IN EDWARDS COUNTY
Flower, H F *see* RECENT MEMOIRS ON THE CETACEA
FLOWERING PLANT INDEX OF ILLUSTRATION AND INFORMATION / The Garden Center of Greater Cleveland – 1979.-50,556 cards 2 reels – 1 – $210.00 export $255.00 – 0-8161-1459-5 – uk Hall [580]
THE FLOWERING PLANTS AND FERNS OF NEW SOUTH WALES / Maiden, J H & Campbell, W S – Sydney, 1895-1898. 80 pp., 28 pls. B-7221 1 – 9 – ne IDC [580]
FLOWERING PLANTS AND FERNS OF THE RIVIERA AND NEIGHBOURING MOUNTAINS / Bicknell, C – London, 1885 – VIII, 82, IVp, 82pls – 8 – ne IDC [580]
FLOWERING PLANTS OF TRAVANCORE / Rao, R – Trivandrum. 1914. B-6468 1 – 9 – ne IDC [580]
FLOWERS AND FRUITS IN THE WILDERNESS / Morrell, Z N – 1886 – 1 – 17.57 – us Baptist [240]
FLOWERS AND THEIR PEDIGREES / Allen, Grant – New York: D. Appleton, 1884. 05036. (Pre-1900 Canadiana) – 9 – cn C.I.H.M. [580]
FLOWERS OF PASSION / Moore, George – London: Provost, 1878 – 1 roll – 1 – 1-55879-394-1 – uk Libr Preservation [830]
FLOW-THROUGH AND RECIRCULATION SYTEMS : REPORT OF THE WORKING GROUP ON TERMINOLOGY FORMAT AND UNITS OF MEASUREMENT – 1986 – 111p – it F.A.O. [639]
Floyd, J. L. and Co *see* GENEALOGICAL AND BIOGRAPHICAL ANNALS OF NORTHUMBERLAND COUNTY
Floyd, John *see* LETTERS
Floyd, LP *see* THE FIRST 100 YEARS OF THE FIRST BAPTIST CHURCH, DENTON, TEXAS
FLOYD M. RIDDICK, SENATE SERVICE 1947-1974 : SENATE PARLIAMENTARIAN – 6mf – 9 – $30.00 – us Scholarly Res [320]
Floyd, Thomas *see* A NEW COLLECTION OF INSTRUMENTAL MUSIC, IN THREE PARTS, ARRANGED FOR THE VIOLIN, CLARIONETT, BASS-VIOL, ETC
Floyd, William *see*
– A COMPARISON OF BODY DENSITY AND PERCENT BODY FAT USING FUNCTIONAL RESIDUAL CAPACITY AND RESIDUAL VOLUME AND DEVELOPMENT OF IMMERSED FUNCTIONAL RESIDUAL CAPACITY AND RESIDUAL VOLUME PREDICTION FORMULAS
– A COMPARISON OF SELECTED CORONARY HEART DISEASE RISK FACTORS IN WEIGHT TRAINED MALES
Floyer, J *see*
– PHARMAKO-BASANOS
– A TREATISE OF THE ASTHMA
FLQ, FILM LIBRARY QUARTERLY – (v4-17, no.2-4. Winter 1970-84. 5,6. v8-17, no.2-4. 1975-84. 9) – v1-17, no.2-4. Winter 1967-84 – 1 – us UMI [790]
DER FLUCH DER SCHOENHEIT : NOVELLE / Riehl, Wilhelm Heinrich; ed by Leonard, Arthur N – (German text with introd etc in English) – Boston: Ginn, c1908 – 1r – 1 – us U.W. Library [830]
DIE FLUCHT : NOVELLEN / Alverdes, Paul – Potsdam: L Voggenreiter, c1935 – 1r – 1 – us U.W. Library [830]
DIE FLUCHT : ROMAN / Wiechert, Ernst Emil – Berlin: G Grote, 1936 – 1r – 1 – us U.W. Library [830]
"FLUCHT AUS DER ZEIT?" ANARCHISMUS, KULTURKRITIK UND CHRISTLICHE MYSTIK – HUGO BALLS KONVERSIONEN / Steinbrenner, Manfred – Frankfurt a.M., 1983 – 2mf – DM62.00 – 3-89349-879-6 – gw Hänsel [430]
FLUCHT- UND WERBUNGSSAGEN IN DER LEGENDE / Schmeing, Karl – Muenster: Aschendorff, 1911. 50p – 1 – us U.W. Library [390]
FLUCTUAT NEC MERGITUR. LA PREVOTE DES MARCHANDS ET L'URBANISME PARISIEN AU 15 SIECLE D'APRES LA JURISPRUDENCE DU PARLEMENT (1380-1500) / Auzary, Bernadette – 2mf – 9 – 10299 – fr Atelier National [320]
Flud, R *see* ULTRIUSQUE COSMI MALORIS SCILICET ET MINORIS METAPHYSICA ATQUE TECHNICA HISTORIA
Fludd, Robert *see* TRACTATVS APOLOGETICVS INTEGRITATEM SOCIETATIS DE ROSEA CRVCE DEFENDENS
FLUECHTLINGS-KURIER – Bremen, 1948 – 1 – Inquire at Mikrofilmarchiv for details – gw Misc Inst [943]
Flueckiger, F A *see* HISTOIRE DES DROGUES D'ORIGINE VEGETALE
"FLUEGEL AUF!" : NOVELLEN / Frapan, Ilse – Berlin: Gebrueder Paetel, 1895 – 1r – 1 – us U.W. Library [830]
Fluegel, G *see* KITAB-AL-FIHRIST MIT ANMERKUNGEN
Fluegel, Gustav *see*
– AL-KINDAI
– DIE GRAMMATISCHEN SCHULEN DER ARABER
Fluegel, Maurice *see* THE HUMANITY, BENEVOLENCE AND CHARITY LEGISLATION OF THE PENTATEUCH AND THE TALMUD
Fluegel, Otto *see* DAS WUNDER UND DIE ERKENNBARKEIT GOTTES
Fluegge, D J *see* GRAMINUM MONOGRAPHIAE
FLUGSCHRIFTEN *see* PAMPHLETS
FLUGSCHRIFTENSAMMLUNG GUSTAV FREYTAG = PAMPHLET COLLECTION OF GUSTAV FREYTAG : VOLLSTAENDIGE WIEDERGABE DER 6265 FLUGSCHRIFTEN AUS DEM 15.-17. JAHRHUNDERT SOWIE DES KATALOGS VON PAUL HOHENEMSER AUF MICROFICHE / Frankfurt. Stadt- und Universitaetsbibliothek. Flugschriftensammlung Gustav Freytag – 1980-81 – 746mf (1:42) – 9 – silver DM13,800.00 – 3-598-21189-9 – gw Saur [240]

FLUID DYNAMICS – v1-29. 1966-94 – 1,5 – $80.00v – us UMI [530]
FLUID MECHANICS.SOVIET RESEARCH – (v13-. 1984-. 5,6,9) – v1-. 1972- – 1 – us UMI [073]
FLUID PHASE EQUILIBRIA – v1-18. 1978-84 – 1,5,6,13 – sz Elsevier [073]
FLUID POWER HANDBOOK & DIRECTORY – 1984- – 1,5,6,9 – us UMI [600]
FLURNAMENSTUDIEN ANHAND EINER SAMMLUNG DER ALTEN NAMEN VON OFFENBACH/M.-BIEBER / Schwarz, Werner – Frankfurt a.M., 1967 – 2mf – 9 – DM62.00 – 3-89349-707-2 – gw Hänsel [943]
FLUSSSLAGGENRECHT UND STROMINTERNATIONALISIERUNG / Andrae, W – Magdeburg, n.d. – 1mf – 9 – ILM-2456/1 – ne IDC [340]
FLUTE BOOK / Beck, Henry – Manuscript book of 280 tunes for treble instrument copied by Beck in 1786. Pages 1-3 missing. Includes: Drink to Me Only; God Save the King; and College Hornpipe. Music-838 – 1 – us L of C Photodup [780]
FLUTE BOOK, MS. NO. 1 – Manuscript book of tunes for a treble instrument, ca. 1791. Solos and duets, one song with melody and text. Composers mentioned are Arne, Frederick Granger, and Reinagle. MUSIC 3079 – 1 – us L of C Photodup [780]
FLUTE DUETS OF THE 18TH CENTURY – 51mf – 9 – MS-i – ne IDC [780]
THE FLUTIST – Asheville. 1-10, no. 2. January 1920-February 1929 – 1 – us NY Public [073]
DIE FLUTSAGEN / Andree, Richard – Braunschweig: Friedrich Vieweg, 1891 – 1mf – 9 – 0-8370-2101-4 – 1985-0101 – us A.T.L.A. [230]
F.L.W. MEYER : SEIN LEBEN UND SEINE SCHRIFTSTELLERISCHE WIRKSAMKEIT; EIN BEITRAG ZUR LITTERATURGESCHICHTE DES 18. UND 19. JAHRHUNDERTS / Zimmermann, Curt – (Includes bibliographical references) – [S.l.: s.n.] (Halle a.S.: Druck von E Karras), 1890 – 1 – us U.W. Library [430]
FLY FISHERMAN – v1- 1969- 1; v10- 1978- 5,6,9 – us UMI [790]
FLY ON, RADJAWALI / Sukarno, Pres. Indonesia – SE 6195 1. Speech on 17th August 1955 – 9 – ne IDC [324]
FLY, OR JUVENILE MISCELLANY – v1 1805-1806 – 1 – us UMI [073]
FLYER – Reno, NV. 1943-45 – 1r – 1 – $50.00 – U04672 – us Library Micro [071]
FLYGPOSTEN – Malmoe, 1876-78 – 9 – sw Kungliga [072]
FLYING – 1927-63 – 1 – 840.00 – us L of C Photodup [629]
FLYING – (v. 82- 1968- 5,6. v. 86- 1970- 9) – 1- 1927- – 1 – us UMI [629]
FLYING CHIPS – v28-32; v37-39. 1959-63; 1968-70 – 16mf – 9 – $5.00f – us Ross [740]
FLYING MODELS – Canton, OH. v1-62. 1928-55 – 1 – 345.00 – us L of C Photodup [600]
FLYING POST: OR, THE POSTMASTER – Dublin, Ireland. 6 Jan, 3 Jun, 2, 24 Aug, 4, 23, 29, 30 Sep, 29 Nov, 2 Dec 1708; 17, 26 Mar, 25, 27 Apr, 2 May, 29 Jun, 4, 14, 28 Jul, 8 Aug 1709; 10 May, 7 Jun, 4, 10 Jul, 24 Aug 1710.-d. 14 ft – 1 – uk British Libr Newspaper [072]
FLYING SAFETY *see* AEROSPACE SAFETY
FLYING SAFETY JOURNAL *see* AEROSPACE SAFETY
Flynn, Edmund James *see*
- CHEMINS DE FER DANS LA PROVINCE DE QUEBEC: DISCOURS PRONONCE A L'ASSEMBLEE LEGISLATIVE LE 29E JOUR DE DECEMBRE 1896, SUR LES RESOLUTIONS TOUCHANT LES SUBSIDES AUX CHEMINS DE FER
- DISCOURS DE L'HONORABLE E. J. FLYNN, DEPUTE DE GASPE, PRONONCE A LA SEANCE DE L'ASSEMBLEE LEGISLATIVE DU 22 JANVIER 1883
- DISCOURS DE L'HONORABLE E. J. FLYNN, DEPUTE DE GASPE, SUR LES RESOLUTIONS DE LA CONFERENCE INTERPROVINCIALE, PRONONCE DEVANT L'ASSEMBLEE LEGISLATIVE A SA SEANCE DU LUNDI LE 21 MAI 1888
- L'EDUCATION DANS LA PROVINCE DE QUEBEC: DISCOURS DE L'HONORABLE M. FLYNN, PRONONCE A L'ASSEMBLEE LEGISLATIVE LE 7 JANVIER 1897
- HOME RULE FOR IRELAND: EXTRACT OF A SPEECH MADE BEFORE THE LEGISLATIVE ASSEMBLY OF THE PROVINCE OF QUEBEC, ON THE 16TH OF APRIL, 1886
- THE LEADER OF THE OPPOSITON, TO THE ELECTORS OF THE PROVINCE OF QUEBEC
- QUEBEC ISSUES DISCUSSED AT NICOLET BY THE MINISTERS: HON. MR. FLYNN ON FINANCES, TELLS WHAT HAS BEEN DONE TO RESTORE RIGHT CONDITIONS: WORK ON AGRICULTURE, HON. MR. BEAUBIEN DELIVERS A MOST INTERESTING ADDRESS ON AN INTERESTING SUBJECT
- RESUME DU DISCOURS PRONONCE PAR L'HONORABLE M. FLYNN: LORS DE LA DEUXIEME LECTURE DU PROJET DE LOI CONCERNANT LES MINES
- LA SITUATION PROVINCIALE: POURQUOI LES ELECTEURS DOIVENT VOTER CONTRE LE GOUVERNMENT MERCIER: DISCOURS DE L'HON. M. FLYNN, PRONONCE A MONTREAL LE 30 OCTOBRE 1889

Flynn, Thomas et al *see* GEOTHERMAL SCIENCE AND TECHNOLOGY
FM ENGINEERING DATA BASE IN ORDER BY CHANNEL AND LOCATION / U.S. National Technical Information Service – Monthly.Sorted by frequency, and secondarily by state.Includes call letters, city, state, frequency, licensee's name, power, height, etc – 9 – us N.T.I.S. [000]
FM ENGINEERING DATA BASE IN ORDER BY LOCATION / U.S. National Technical Information Service – Monthly.Sorted by state and secondarily by city – 9 – us N.T.I.S. [000]
LE F.N.Q. – Montreal, Canada. v3 n1. sep 1965-v3 n7. avr 1966 – 1r – 1 – Can$25.00 – cn Can Microfilming [072]
FO HEBDO : ORGANE OFFICIEL DE LA CGTFO – Paris: s.n., [1966-]. [n1068-1203 nov 23 1966-69] – us Res Libr [072]
FO MAGAZINE – Paris: Imp Chaix-Desfosses, Neogravure. [n1-39. nov 1965-69] – us Res Libr [072]
FO VECKOTIDNINGEN – Norrkoping, Sweden. 1980-83 – 1 – sw Kungliga [072]
Foa, Edouard *see*
- A TRAVERS L'AFRIQUE CENTRALE DU CAP AU LAC NYASSA
- LE DAHOMEY
- LE DAHOMEY, HISTOIRE, GEOGRAPHIE, MOEURS, COUTUMES, COMMERCE, INDUSTRIE, EXPEDITIONS FRANCAISES
- MES GRANDES CHASSES DANS L'AFRIQUE CENTRALE

Foakes-Jackson, F J *see* THE FAITH AND THE WAR
Foch, Ferdinand *see* DES PRINCIPES DE LA GUERRE
Focherini, A *see* PAGINE DI STORA DEL DIRITTO INTERNAZIONALE
Fock, Gorch *see* SCHULLENGRIEPER UND TUNGENKNIEPER
Fock, Otto *see* DER SOCINIANISMUS
Foclin, A *see* LA RHETORIQUE FRANCOISE
O FOCO – Manaos, Amazonas. 31 Mar 1918 – 1,5,6 – bl Biblioteca [072]
FOCUS – (Cont: Weekly Focus) – Kampala, Uganda. June 12 1984-Dec 27 1987; Jan 5 1988-Sept 28 1990 – 2r – 1 – us L of C Photodup [072]
FOCUS – Fredericton. v19-24. 1988/89-1993/94 – 9 – Can$20.00y – cn Micromedia [073]
FOCUS – Montreal, CN. v1 no 10. 1947-1948 – 1r – 1 – Can$30.00 – cn Can Microfilming [072]
FOCUS – (v. 19- 1968- 5,6,9) – 1- 1950- – 1 – us UMI [073]
THE FOCUS – Blantyre: Blantyre Print and Packaging, dec 1994-apr/may 1996 – 1r – 1 – us Res Libr [072]
FOCUS: METROPOLITAN PHILADELPHIA'S BUSINESS NEWSWEEKLY – 1978- – 9 – us UMI [380]
FOCUS ON CRITICAL CARE – v10-. Feb 1983- – 1,5,6,9 – us UMI [617]
FOCUS ON ENGLISH LITERATURE, 1708-1907 – (40 British literary periodicals of 18th and 19th centuries selected from larger UMI collections English Literary Periodicals and Early British Periodicals. Cataloging available) – 139r – 1 – $8850.00 – us UMI [420]
FOCUS ON EXCEPTIONAL CHILDREN – v1-1969- 1; v7- 1975- 5,6,9 – us UMI [370]
FOCUS ON GUIDANCE – (v8-9. 1975-77. 5,6,9) – v1-9. 1968-77. Continued by: Counseling and Human Development – 1 – us UMI [370]
FOCUS ON THE FUTURE : WHITE PAPER ON EDUCATION / Bahamas. Ministry of Education and Culture – Nassau – 1mf – 9 – DE-513/1 – ne IDC [370]
FODDERS FOR THE NEAR EAST : ALFALFA – 1989 – 215p – it F.A.O. [636]
FODDERS FOR THE NEAR EAST : ANNUAL MEDIC PASTURES – 1989 – 125p – it F.A.O. [636]
Fodere, FE *see* ESSAI HISTORIQUE ET MORAL SUR LA PAUVRETE DES NATIONS, LA POPULATION LA MENDICITE, LES HOPITAUX ET LES ENFANTS TROUVES
Fodor, A *see* QUATUOR POUR LE PIANOFORTE ACCOMPAGNE D'UN VIOLON, VIOLA ET VIOLONCELLE, OP 7
Fodor, J *see*
- SIX QUATUORS CONCERTANS POUR DEUX VIOLONS, ALTO ET BASSE
- TROIS DUOS POUR DEUX VIOLONS

FOEBADIUS, VICTRICIUS, LEPORIUS, VINCENTIUS, EVAGRIUS, RURICIUS – 1985 – 7mf – 9 – Bf1,650.00 – be Brepols [240]
FOEDERA, CONVENTIONES, LITERAE, ET CUJUSCUNQUE GENERIS ACTA PUBLICA – Accurante Thomas Rymer. 17v. 1727-29 – 697mf – 9 – Dfl4,191.00 – H-893/2 – ne IDC [320]
FOEDERA, CONVENTIONES, LITERAE ET CUJUSCUNQUE GENERIS ACTA PUBLICA, INTER REGES ANGLIAE, ET ALIOS QUOSVIS IMPERATORES, REGES PONTIFICES, PRINCIPES, VEL COMMUNITATES / Rymer, Thomas – Ed. 2a. Londini. Tome 1-20. 1727-35 – 9 – Dfl2,615.00 – ne Slangenburg [240]
FOEDERA, CONVENTIONES, LITERAE, ET CUJUSCUNQUE GENERIS ACTA PUBLICA, INTER REGES ANGLIAE, ET ALIOS QUOSVIS IMPERATORES, REGES, PONTIFICES, PRINCIPES, VEL COMMUNITATES / Rymer, Thomas – Londini, 1727-1735. 2nd ed. 20v – 9 – Bf60,500.00 set – 1-799-00502-X – be Brepols [240]
Foederation der kommunistischen Anarchisten Deutschlands *see* DER FREIE ARBEITER
FOEDERIS LVDOVICI GERMANIAE, ET KAROLI GALLIAE REGUM, PII FILIOR... / Freher, M – [Heidelberg], 1611 – 1mf – 9 – ne IDC [430]
FOEGL D'ENGIADINA – Zuoz, Switzerland. 23 Dec 1857-28 Dec 1878. 5 reels – 1 – uk British Libr Newspaper [949]
Foelix, J J G *see* TRAITE DU DROIT INTERNATIONAL...
FOERSOEK TILL EN MONOGRAPHI OEFVER ALGSLAEGTET MONOSTROMA / Wittrock, V B – Stockholm. 1866. B-6426 2 – 8 – ne IDC [580]
Foerster, A *see* HYMENOPTEROLOGISCHES STUDIEN
Foerster, F *see* ALBRECHT VON WALLENSTEIN,...
Foerster, Gerhard *see* DAS MOSAISCHE STRAFRECHT IN SEINER GESCHICHTLICHEN ENTWICKELUNG
Foerster, Matthias *see* ENTWURF, AUFBAU UND ERPROBUNG EINES RASTERTUNNEL-MESSKOPFES FUER DEN EINSATZ IN EINEM RASTERELEKTRONENMIKROSKOP
Foerster, Wilhelm Julius *see* LEBENSERINNERUNGEN UND LEBENSHOFFNUNGEN: 1832 BIS 1910
FOES IN LAW / Broughton, Rhoda – British Fiction Archive: Unit 4 – 9 – uk Bell [830]
FOG BELLS : A SEQUEL TO NAZARETH / Dall, Caroline Wells Healey – Boston:To be found at Little, Brown, 1905 (S.l:Thomas Todd) – 1mf – 9 – 0-8370-2807-8 – 1985-0807 – us A.T.L.A. [240]
Fogazzaro, Antonio *see* THE SAINT
Fogdall, S J M P *see* DANISH-AMERICAN DIPLOMACY 1776-1920
Fogelevich, LG *see* DEISTVUIUSHCHEE ZAKONODATELSTVO O PECHATI
Fogg, Alonzo J *see* STATISTICS AND GAZETTEER OF NEW HAMPSHIRE
Fogg, Peter Walkden *see* ELEMENTA ANGLICANA
Foggini, N *see* IL MUSEO CAPITOLINO...
Fogginius, P *see* NOVA APPENDIX
Foght, H W *see* THE TRAIL OF THE LOUP
Fogliano, L *see* MUSICA THEORICA
Foglietta, U *see*
- DE CAUSIS MAGNITUDINIS IMPERII TVRCICI, ET VIRTVTIS AC FELICITATIS TVRCARUM IN BELLIS PERPETUAE:...
- DE SACRO FOEDERE IN SELIMVM. LIBRI QUATTOR
- HISTORIAE GENUENSIUM LIBRI 12
- ISTORIA...DELLA SACRA LEGA CONTRA SELIM,...

Foguet, Juan *see* EL TAUMATURGO CATALAN BEATO SALVADOR DE HORTA
O FOGUETAO – Rio Branco, Acre. 3 Out 1917 – 1,5,6 – bl Biblioteca [072]
O FOGUETE – Manaos, Amazonas. 11-16 Dez 1900 – 1,5,6 – bl Biblioteca [072]
Fohlen, C *see* UNE AFFAIRE DE FAMILLE AU XIXE SIECLE: MEQUILLET-NOBLOT
FOHNE (THE HEBREW STANDARD) – London, UK. 5 Sept-5 Nov 1897 – 1 – uk British Libr Newspaper [072]
FOI EDUCATION – France, 1947-92 (complete) – Inquire – 1 – ATLA S0571 – us A.T.L.A. [073]
FOI ET GNOSE. INTRODUCTION A L'ETUDE DE LA CONNAISSANCE MYSTIQUE CHEZ CLEMENT D'ALEXANDRIE / Camelot, PT – Paris, 1945 – 3mf – 8 – ne Slangenburg [240]
FOI NOUVELLE – Omnibus Saint-Simonien. Bordeaux, Bertu, 1833, 16 p. Terson, Jean. Dialogues Saint-Simoniens ou reponse aux accusations portees contre la religion Saint-Simonienne et ses apotres. Bordeaux, impr. P. Coudert, 1833, 12 p. Les Saint-Simoniens, 1825-1834. 6919 – 9 – fr Hachette [335]
FOI NOUVELLE, LIVRE DES ACTES – Publie par les femmes. Tome premier (seul paru). Paris, Alexandre Johanneau, 1833, 270 p. Les Saint-Simoniens, 1825-1834. 6905 – 9 – fr Hachette [335]
Foignet *see* HELENA OU LES MIQUELETS
Foigny, Gabriel de *see* LES AVENTURES DE JACQUES SADEUR DANS LA DECOUVERTE ET LE VOYAGE DE LA TERRE AUSTRALE CONTENANT LES COUTUMES ET LES MOEURS DES AUSTRALIENS, LEUR RELIGION, LEURS EXERCICES, LEURS ETUDES, LEURS GUERRES
Foillet, J *see* NEW MODELBUCH. MUEMPELGARTEN
[Fokker, G A] *see* LE BARRAGE DE L'ESCAUT ORIENTAL
Fokker, T H *see* BIJDRAGE TOT...REGELING DER SCHEEPSVOORRECHTEN
LE FOKONOLONA ET LE POUVOIR : MEMOIRE POUR LE DIPLOME D'ETUDES SUPERIEURES DE SCIENCE POLITIQUE / Lejamble, Georges – Tananarive: Publication du Centre de droit publique et de sciences politique, 1963 – us Res Libr [072]
Folard, Jean Charles de *see* NOUVELLES DECOUVERTES SUR LA GUERRE DANS UNE DISSERTATION SUR POLYBE
Folarin, Abedesin *see*
- THE LAWS AND CUSTOMS OF EGBA-LAND
- A SHORT HISTORICAL REVIEW OF THE LIFE OF THE EGBAS FROM 1829 TO 1930

FOLDER / Montana. Agricultural Extension Service – nos.1-106. 1949-69 – 1,5,6 – us Spaulding [630]
FOLDER A / Canadian Pacific Railway Company – 1892. 00454. (Pre-1900 Canadiana) – 9 – cn C.I.H.M. [380]
FOLESHILL AND BEDWORTH EXPRESS – Foleshill, Bedworth, England. 2 May 1874-8 April 1876. 59 ft – 1 – uk British Libr Newspaper [072]
Foley, Deodatus Francis *see* SKETCH OF THE PARISH OF ST MARY, ALMONTE, ONTARIO, 1823 TO 1885
Foley, M S et al *see* JOURNAL OF COMMERCE
Foley, S *see* THE CANADIAN COLONIST
Foley, Thomas S *see* THE EFFECTS OF THE CROSS WALK'S RESISTIVE ARM POLES ON THE METABOLIC COSTS OF TREADMILL WALKING
DIE FOLGEN DER REFORMATION / Ball, Hugo – Munchen, Duncker & Humblot, 1924 – 1 – us U.W. Library [190]
FOLGEN DER TECHNIK – VERANTWORTUNG DER INGENIEURE : ZU EINEM ETHISCHEN PROBLEM UND SEINER BEDEUTUNG FUER DIE PAEDAGOGIK / Schlotter, Herbert – 1994 – 3mf – DM98.00 – 3-8267-2007-5 – gw Hänsel [170]
Folger Shakespeare Library. Washington, D.C. *see* CATALOG OF PRINTED BOOKS OF THE FOLGER SHAKESPEARE LIBRARY
Folger Shakespeare Library. Washington, DC *see*
- CATALOG OF MANUSCRIPTS OF THE FOLGER SHAKESPEARE LIBRARY
- CATALOG OF PRINTED BOOKS
- CATALOG OF PRINTED BOOKS OF THE FOLGER SHAKESPEARE LIBRARY

A FOLHA – Barbacena, 15 Jan 1893-30 Jun 1894 – 1,5,6 – bl Biblioteca [072]

FOLHA : JORNAL INTEGRACAO – Vicosa, 19 Mar 1978-27 May 1979 – 1,5,6 – bl Biblioteca [072]
FOLHA ACADEMICA : ORGAO DE DIVULGACAO DO DIRETORIO ACADEMICO DA FACULDADE DE DIREITO DO ACRE – Rio Branco, Acre. 19 Mar 1967; 8 Set 1968 – 1 – bl Biblioteca [370]
FOLHA DA MATA : ORGAO DEMOCRATICO INDEPENDENTE – Carangola, 26 May 1960 – 1,5,6 – bl Biblioteca [072]
FOLHA DE ANNUNCIOS – S Tome: Ezeguiel Pires dos Santos Ramos, jul 10-20 1911 – us Res Libr [072]
FOLHA DE GUANHAES : ORGAM DOS INTERESSES DO POVO – S. Miguel de Guanhaes, 20 Feb-10 Apr 1898 – 1,5,6 – bl Biblioteca [072]
FOLHA DE ITUIUTABA : BI-SEMANARIO DEDICADO AOS INTERESSES DA REGIAO – Ituiutaba, 22 Sep 1951-Dec 1953; Jan-Apr, Jul-Oct, Dec 1954; Mar-Apr, Jul, Dec 1955; Feb, Aug, Nov 1956; Feb, Apr, Nov 1957; Jan, May-Jul 1958; Jan, Jun, Oct-Nov 1959; Oct 1960; Oct 1961; Jan-21 Feb 1962 – 1,5,6 – bl Biblioteca [072]
FOLHA DE JAGUARY : ORGAM REPUBLICANO – Jaguary, 1 Aug 1897 – 1,5,6 – bl Biblioteca [072]
FOLHA DE NANUQUE – Nanuque, Brazil. Feb 1962-Dec 1977. Very scattered issues – 1 – bl Biblioteca [072]
FOLHA DE POCOS – Pocos de Caldas, 1 Dec 1958 – 1,5,6 – bl Biblioteca [072]
FOLHA DE SAO PAOLO – (Yrly reel count varies) – Brazil, 1971-98 – 1 – inquire – us Ross [072]
FOLHA DE SAO PAULO – 1921-1995 – 1 – sz Infoprint [072]
FOLHA DE VICOSA : UM JORNAL A SERVICO DO POVO – Vicosa, 22 Sep-17 Nov 1968 – 1,5,6 – bl Biblioteca [072]
FOLHA DO ACRE – Cidade da Empreza, Acre. 14 Ago 1910-Jun 1915; Out 1917-Ago 1918; Jan 1920-Maio 1923; Jan 1926-Dez 1927; Fev-24 Mar 1946 – 1,5,6 – bl Biblioteca [072]
FOLHA DO AMAZONAS : JORNAL DOS MUNICIPIOS – Parintins, Amazonas. Set-Out 1973; Out 1974 – 1,5,6 – bl Biblioteca [072]
FOLHA DO AMAZONAS : ORGAO DO PARTIDO REPUBLICANO FEDERAL – [s.l.] Ago-Dez 1910; Jan-Abr, Ago-Dez 1911; Jan 1912-Dez 1915 – 1,5,6 – bl Biblioteca [072]
FOLHA DO DOMINGO – Rio de Janeiro, 10 Apr-22 May 1887 – 1,5,6 – bl Biblioteca [072]
FOLHA DO POVO : ORGAM COMMERCIAL, INDUSTRIAL E AGRICOLA – Cidade de Uba, 11 Apr, Jun, Aug, Nov 1908; Aug 1909; Feb, May-Jun 1910; May 1911; Dec 1912; Jan 1914; May 1927; Jan 1942; Oct 1943; Jul 1944; Jan 1945; Jan 1949; May 1950; Aug, Dec 1953; Jun 1963; Apr 1964; Nov 1965; Jun 1967; Jan 1968; Jun-Nov 1969; Jan, Mar-Nov 1970; May 1971; Feb, Apr, Dec 1973; Mar, Dec 1974; Mar 1977; Aug, Nov-Dec 1978; Jan, Aug-Dec 1979; Jan-27 Dec 1980 – 1,5,6 – bl Biblioteca [072]
FOLHA DO POVO – Paracatu, 7 Apr 1910-Oct 1911; Oct 1913; Apr 1914; Apr 1915; Jun, Dec 1917; Jun-Jul 1918; 20 Apr 1919 – 1,5,6 – bl Biblioteca [072]
FOLHA DO TRIANGULO – Uberlandia, Brazil. Jun 1960 – 1 – bl Biblioteca [072]
FOLHA ESTUDANTIL : ORGAO DE PUBLICIDADE DO GREMIO 1. DE JUNHO – Rio Branco, Acre. Jun 1963 – 1,5,6 – bl Biblioteca [072]
FOLHA ISRAELITA – Rio de Janeiro, Brazil, v1, no. 0 (Dec. 1984); v2, no. 2 (1985); v3, no. 10 (June 1986) – us A.J.P.C. [270]
FOLHA MARITIMA : ORGAM DA FEDERACAO MARITIMA – Manaos, Amazonas. 16 Abr-13 Maio 1916 – 1,5,6 – bl Biblioteca [072]
FOLHA MERCANTIL – Rio de Janeiro, 4 Jun-Oct 1824; 13-29 Sep 1825 – 1,5,6 – bl Biblioteca [072]
FOLHA MINEIRA – Juiz de Fora, 26 Mar 1953; Set-Oct 1959; Jan-Jun, Aug, Dec 1960; Jan, 31 May 1961 – 1,5,6 – bl Biblioteca [072]
FOLHA NOVA : ORGAM DOS INTERESSES DO POVO – Juiz de Fora, 14 Feb 1898 – 1,5,6 – bl Biblioteca [072]
FOLHA OFFICIAL – Xapury, Acre. 1 Ago-Set, Dez 1908; Jan-Nov 1909; Jan-24 Jun 1910 – 1,5,6 – bl Biblioteca [072]
FOLHA REPUBLICANA – Divinopolis, 16 Apr-1 May 1949 – 1,5,6 – bl Biblioteca [072]
FOLHA RURAL : PUBLICACAO OFFICIAL DA ESCOLA SUPERIOR DE AGRICULTURA E VETERINARIA DO ESTADO DE MINAS GERAIS – Vicosa, 1 Jan-20 Dec 1935 – 1,5,6 – bl Biblioteca [072]
FOLHA SOCIALISTA / Partido Socialista Brasileiro – Sao Paulo, 1 (1947) no 1 – 1 – us Hoover Inst Photo [335]
FOLIA ORCHIDACEA / Lindley, J – An enumeration of the known species of orchids. London. 1852-55-59. B-6031 2 – 8 – ne IDC [580]
FOLIA PHONIATRICA ET LOGOPAEDICA – v27-. 1975- – 1,5,9 – us UMI [574]
FOLIA PRIMATOLOGICA – v. 4-20. 1966-1973 – 1,5,6 – us Princeton Micro [590]
FOLIA PRIMATOLOGICA – v23-. 1975- – 1,5,9 – us UMI [590]
DE LA FOLIE CONSIDEREE DANS SES RAPPORTS AVEC LES QUESTIONS MEDICO-JUDICIARIES / Marc, Charles Chretien Henri – (French Precursors of Psychiatry Series). Paris. J. B. Bailliere. 1840 – 9 – fr Hachette [150]
DE LA FOLIE CONSIDEREE SOUS LE POINT DE VUE PATHOLOGIQUE, PHILOSOPHIQUE, HISTORIQUE ET JUDICIAIRE / Calmeil, Louis Florentin – (French Precursors of Psychiatry Series). Paris. J. B. Bailliere. 1845 – 9 – fr Hachette [150]
THE FOLIO – Boston. v1-42. 1869-95 – 12r – 1 – £655.00 – uk Chadwyck [780]
THE FOLIO : F.C.C. (FORMAN CHRISTIAN COLLEGE) MAGAZINE – v26-34. 1934-43 (complete) – 1r – 1 – ATLA S0540 – us A.T.L.A. [073]
THE FOLIO – v1-42. Sept 1869-Oct 1895 – 1 – 850.00 – us Opus [073]
FOLK – v1, no.1-2. 1937 – 1 – us I.U. Libraries [390]
FOLK ARTS, ARTS AND CRAFTS : ARCHITECTURE, APPLIED ARTS, STUDIO ARTS – (Individual titles not listed separately) – 43 catalogues on 52mf – 9 – £380.00 – uk Chadwyck [740]
FOLK MASS AND MODERN LITURGY MAGAZINE – v1-3. 1973-76. Continued by: Modern Liturgy – 1 – us UMI [240]
FOLK MUSIC IN AMERICA / Barry, Phillips – 1939 – 1 – us I.U. Libraries [390]
FOLK MUSIC PERIODICALS, 1946-87 – 3 titles: Broadside, People's Songs, New City Songster. See indiv. listings for prices – 9 – $225.00 set – us UPA [780]
FOLK OG KIRKE I MIDDELALDEREN : STUDIER TIL NORGES HISTORIE / Bull, Edvard – Kristiania: Gyldendal, 1912 – 1mf – us A.T.L.A. [948]
FOLK OG KIRKE PAA MADAGASKAR / Jorgensen, Simon Emanuel – 1887 – 1 – us A.T.L.A. [240]
FOLK SONGS FROM SOMERSET / Sharp, Cecil James – 1904-06 – 1 – us I.U. Libraries [390]
FOLK TALES OF ANGOLA / Chatelain, H – Memoirs of American Folk-Lore Society. v1. Boston, 1894. BA-359-2 – 8 – ne IDC [390]
FOLK UN VELT – New York. N.Y. 1952-57 – 1 – us A.J.P.C. [071]
FOLK WANDERINGS AND CULTURE DRIFTS IN NORTHERN NORTH AMERICA / Birket-Smith, K – BN 135 2. 1930 – 8 – ne IDC [304]
Folkard, Henry Coleman *see* FOLKARD'S STARKIE ON SLANDER AND LIBEL.
FOLKARD'S STARKIE ON SLANDER AND LIBEL. / Folkard, Henry Coleman – 4th Eng. ed. New York: Banks, 1877. 992p. LL-591 – 1 – us L of C Photodup [340]
FOLKBLADET – Norrkoping, Sweden. 1981- – 1 – sw Kungliga [072]
FOLKBLADET – Stockholm, Sweden. 1894-1907. 5 reels. 1930-35. 4 reels – 1 – sw Kungliga [072]
FOLKBLADET FOR VASTMANLAND *see* VASTMANLANDS FOLKBLAD
FOLKBLADET JOENKOEPING – Joenkoeping, 1992- – 9 – sw Kungliga [072]
FOLKBLADET OSTGOTEN – Norrkoping, Sweden. 1979-81 – 1 – sw Kungliga [072]
FOLKBLADET OSTGOTEN – (Ostergotlands Folkblad 1905-66. Folkbladet Ostgoten 1966-78) – Norrkoping, Sweden – 377r – 1 – sw Kungliga [072]
Folkerth, Jean E *see* PARENTS' ATTITUDES REGARDING THE LEISURE BEHAVIOR OF THEIR HANDICAPPED CHILD
FOLKESTONE CHRONICLE – Folkestone, England. -w. 1886-1906. 20 reels – 1 – uk British Libr Newspaper [072]
FOLKESTONE EXPRESS – Folkestone, England. -w. 14 March 1868-Dec 1902. Lacking 1898, 1901. 36 reels – 1 – uk British Libr Newspaper [072]
FOLKESTONE OBSERVER – Folkestone, England. -w. 8 Dec 1860-29 Sept 1870. 5 reels – 1 – uk British Libr Newspaper [072]
FOLKET – Eskilstuna, Sweden. 1979-82 – 1 – sw Kungliga [072]
FOLKET – Eskilstuna, Sweden. 1989- – 1 – sw Kungliga [072]
FOLKET – (Sormlandskuriren, 1975) – Eskilstuna, Sweden. 1906-78 – 438r – 1 – sw Kungliga [072]
FOLKET *see* VASTMANLANDS FOLKBLAD
FOLKET I BILD – Stockholm, Sweden. 1934-63:4 – 1 – sw Kungliga [073]
FOLKET NORD – Eskilstuna, Sweden. 1982-89 – 1 – sw Kungliga [072]
FOLKET SYD – Eskilstuna, Sweden. 1982-89 – 1 – sw Kungliga [072]
FOLKETRU – 1935 – 1 – us I.U. Libraries [390]
FOLKETS DAGBLAD – (Politiken, 1916-17. Folkets Dagblad, 1917-45) – Stockholm, Sweden – 153r – 1 – sw Kungliga [072]
FOLKETS DEGBLAD POLITIKEN – Stockholm, Sweden. -d. 1 July 1918-8 Aug 1919. 5 reels – 1 – uk British Libr Newspaper [072]
FOLKETS ROEST – Stockholm, 1891-92 – 9 – sw Kungliga [072]
FOLKETS ROST – Goteborg, Sweden. 1887-90 – 1 – sw Kungliga [072]
FOLKETS TIDNING – Omaha, NE. -w. 5 Jul 1877-31 Jan 1878. In Swedish – 1 – us NE Hist [071]
FOLKETS VAN – Stromsburg, NE. -w. Dec 1885-May 1886; Oct 1886-Jun 1887; Sept 1887 – 1 – us NE Hist [071]
FOLKEVISOR – 1931 – 1 – us I.U. Libraries [390]
FOLKLIV – v1, 1937; v2-34, 1938-70 – 1 – us I.U. Libraries [390]
FOL'KLOR CHKALOVSKOI OBLASTI / Bardin, A V – 1940. Russian folk literature – 1 – us I.U. Libraries [390]
FOLKLORE / Folklore Society. London – v. 1-68. 1890-1957 – 1 – us Princeton Micro [390]
LE FOLK-LORE / Sebillot, Paul – 1913 – 1 – us I.U. Libraries [390]
LE FOLKLORE / Gennep, Arnold van – 1924 – 1 – us I.U. Libraries [390]
LE FOLKLORE BRABANCON – (16e annee n91-96(1936-1937). 11mf) – 9e Annee: n40-50(1929-1930) – 7mf – 9 – Dfl28.00 – ne Slangenburg [073]
EL FOLKLORE DE MADRID / Olavarrieta y Huarte, Eugenio – 1884 – 1 – sp Bibl Santa Ana [390]
FOLKLORE EXTREMENO. EXTREMADURA Y LA POSIBLE REGIONALIZACION DE SU MUSICA POPULAR. LA TRADICION EN LA CANCION EXTREMENA Y SU EVOLUCION / Gil Garcia, Bonifacio – Badajoz: Dip. Provincial, 1938. Comunic. 3 Congreso Internacional de Musicologia. Barcelona. 1936 – 1 – sp Bibl Santa Ana [780]
LE FOLKLORE FLAMMAND – 1895 – 1 – us I.U. Libraries [390]
Folklore Society. London *see* FOLKLORE
FOLKLORE STUDIES – (Cont. as: Asian Folklore Studies. Tokyo, 1963-1966. v22-25) – Peking, 1942-1962. v1-21 – 201mf – 9 – CH-123/2 – ne IDC [380]
FOLKMIMEN OCH FOLKTANKAR – v1-15. 1914-28 – 1 – us I.U. Libraries [390]
FOLKRAKNINGEN DEN 1 NOV 1960 / Sweden. Statistika centralbyran – Stockholm, 1961-65. 11v. illus., map – 1 – us U.W. Library [310]
FOLKS TSAYTUNG – Los Angeles. 1936-37 – 1 – us A.J.P.C. [071]
FOLKSBLAT – (Missing: Several numbers) – Kovno. v1-11. 1930-1940 – 20r – 1 – J-92-51/3 – ne IDC [947]
FOLKSBLAT = PEOPLE'S NEWSPAPER – (In Yiddish) – Kaunas, LT. no258. 13 Nov 1935 – 1r – 1 – $25.00 – cn Can Microfilming [072]
FOLKSCAJTUNG – Warsaw. Poland. -m. Aug 1946-Jan 1949. (1 reel) – 1 – uk British Libr Newspaper [947]
FOLKSFRAINT – Pittsburgh. Jan. 15, 1892-Dec. 13, 1901, Dec. 27, 1901-1923 – 1 – us NY Public [071]
FOLKSFRAYND – (In Yiddish) – Przemysl, PL. v3 no2 25 Jan 1929 – 1 – 1 – $25.00 – cn Can Microfilming [072]
FOLKSGEZUNT = PEOPLE'S HEALTH – (In Yiddish) – Vilnius, LT. no2. 20 Feb 1935 – 1r – 1 – $25.00 – cn Can Microfilming [072]
FOLKSHILF = PEOPLE'S HELP – (Yiddish monthly) – Warsaw, PL. v9 no1(97) Jan 1939-v9 no3(99) Mar 1939 [A triple number: v9 no1/2/3]; Map: Cities of Poland – 1 – $25.00 – cn Can Microfilming [072]
FOLK-SONGS OF AMERICA / Gordon, Robert Winslow – 1938 – 1 – us I.U. Libraries [390]
FOLKS-SHTIME = PEOPLE'S VOICE – (In Yiddish) – Lodz, PL. no39 1 Nov 1947-no653 30 Dec 1952 – 2r – 1 – $55.00 – cn Can Microfilming [072]
FOLKSSHTIME – Wilna. v. 1-16. Dec. 1, 1906-Aug. 17, 1907. and supplement Di Shtime. 1907 – 1 – us NY Public [073]
FOLKS-SZTVME – Warsaw, Poland. In Yiddish. -d. Feb 1952-Dec 1955. 12 reels – 1 – uk British Libr Newspaper [947]
FOLKS-SZTYME – (Nasz Glos (Suppl) 1957-Jun 1968 2r) – Warsaw, Poland. 1952-1991 – 48r – 1 – us L of C Photodup [947]
FOLKS-TSAYTUNG 1080 PEOPLES' NEWSPAPER – (In Yiddish) – Warsaw, PL. v4 no12,13 1 Jun 1948 no40-41 – 1r – 1 – $25.00 – cn Can Microfilming [072]
FOLKTRO OCH TROLLDOM – v1-5. 1919-55 – 1 – us I.U. Libraries [390]
FOLKVILJAN – (Folkviljan 1906. Nya Folkviljan 1906-20) – Malmo, Sweden – 5r – 1 – sw Kungliga [072]
FOLKVILJAN – Lulea, Sweden. 1980-89 – 1 – sw Kungliga [072]
FOLKVILJAN – Malmo, Sweden. 1882-85 – 1 reel – 1 – sw Kungliga [072]
FOLKVILJAN – Stockholm, Sweden. 1891-92 – 1 – sw Kungliga [072]
FOLKVISOR – v1,3. 1934-67 – 1 – us I.U. Libraries [390]
FOLLE-FARINE / Ouida – British Fiction Archive: Unit 3 – 9 – uk Bell [830]
Follenius, Christopher *see* THE EFFECTS OF ENHANCED ECCENTRIC TRAINING ON IMPROVEMENT OF STRENGTH
FOLLET – London, UK. Oct 1846-Jul 1900 – 1 – uk British Libr Newspaper [072]
FOLLETO DE LAS CONFERENCIAS DADAS DURANTE LA SEMANA AGRICOLA DE BADAJOZ DEL 12-18 NOV. 1912 / Conseso Provincial de Fomento – Badajoz: C.P.F., 1913 – 1 – sp Bibl Santa Ana [630]
FOLLETO DEL COMBATIENTE – Salamanca, 1938. Fiche W 887. (Blodgett Collection of Spanish Civil War Pamphlets) – 9 – us H.U. College Libr [946]
FOLLETO INFORMATIVO SOBRE EL SERVICIO MUNICIPAL DE LIMPIEZA / Caceres – Caceres: Imp. T. Rodriguez, s.a. 1965? – sp Bibl Santa Ana [350]
FOLLETO PRIMERO DON BENITO... / Don Benito – Plasencia: Imprenta La Victoria, s.a. – sp Bibl Santa Ana [946]
FOLLETO REFUTADO DE INJURIAS...A PAREDES – 1888 – 9 – 1.50f – sp Bibl Santa Ana [946]
FOLLETOS / Repetto, Nicolas – [s.l.: s.n., 19–]. 2v – 1 – CSUXADP7842-B – us Hoover Inst Photo [972]
Follett, M P *see* THE SPEAKER OF THE HOUSE OF REPRESENTATIVES
Folleville, D de *see* TRAITE THEORIQUE ET PRATIQUE DE LA NATURALISATION
LA FOLLIA DI NEW YORK – New York, NY. -w. 6 Jan 1907-1911; 4 Jan 1914-21 Dec 1924; 1926-30 Dec 1928; 26 Aug 1934-15 Dec 1946.32 reels – 1 – us I.H.R.C. [071]
Follie, M *see* VOYAGES DANS LES DESERTS DU SAHARA PAR M. FOLLIE, OFFICIER D'ADMINISTRATION DANS LES COLONIES. CONTENANT: 1)LA RELATION DE SON NAUFRAGE ET DE SES AVENTURES PENDANT SON ESCLAVAGE. 2)UN PRECIS EXACT DES MOEURS DES UAGES ET DES OPINIONS DES HABITANTS
Folliot, George *see* DIARY
FOLLOWING THE SUNRISE : A CENTURY OF BAPTIST MISSIONS, 1813-1913 / Montgomery, Helen Barrett – Philadelphia: American Baptist Publication Society, c1913 – 1mf – us A.T.L.A. [240]
FOLLOW-UP STUDY OF WORD PROCESSING AND ELECTRONIC MAIL IN THE 3RD CIRCUIT COURT OF APPEALS / Greenwood, J Michael – Washington: FJC, June 1980 – 1mf – 9 – $1.50 – LLMC 95-816 – us L.L.M.C. [340]

THE FOLSOM TELEGRAPH – Folsom, CA. 1873-88; 1889-1982 (irregular) – 53r – 1 – $2,650.00 – C02236 – us Library Micro [071]

Fombona, E *see* CUESTION INTERNACIONAL

Fomenko, Kliment *see* RAZBOR DESYATI PRAVIL VEROCHENIYA SHTUNDISTOV

EL FOMENTO – Caceres, 1901. 1 numero – 5 – sp Bibl Santa Ana [073]

Fomento de Caceres *see*
- COMISION ORGANIZADORA DE FESTEJOS. MEMORIA DE 1920
- REGLAMENTO DE LA SOCIEDAD...1921 Y 1923

Fomin, A *see* MATERIALY DLIA FLORY KAVKAZA. FLORA CAUCASICA CRITICA

Fomina, V *see* BOR'BA PLEKHANOVA PROTIV MODERNIZMA V ISKUSSTVE

FONAR – (Includes c.1: 1917:Nov.20) – Moskva: Izd-vo "Fonar", 19uu – 1 – CSUXANR3349-S – us Hoover Inst Photo [947]

FONAR (MOSCOW, RUSSIA) *see* FONAR

LA FONCTION DE LA FEMME DANS L'EVOLUTION SOCIALE / Lind af Hageby, Louise – Conflans-Ste.-Honorine, Edition de l'Idee Libre, 1922. 16p. (Les Femmes Collection) – 1mf – 9 – $6.00 – fr Bibl Nationale [305]

LA FONCTION GONADOTROPE DE L'HYPOPHYSE AU COURS DU CYCLE SEXUEL DE DEUX POISSONS TELEOSTEENS, LA CARPE (CYPRINUS CARPIO) ET LA TRUITE (SALMO GAIRDNERI) SON CONTROLE PAR L'HYPOTHALAMUS, LES GONADES ET LES FACTEURS EXTERNES / Weil, C – 9 – F85.00 – fr Ethnologie [590]

LA FONCTION PUBLIQUE AUX ETATS-UNIS : ESSAI SUR LE REGIME DU CIVIL SERVICE FEDERAL / Conac, G – F50.00 – fr Ethnologie [350]

LE FONCTIONNAIRE – (Filmed with: Le Fonctionnaire Provincial ns: v4 n5 jun 1964) – Quebec, Canada. mai 1922-mar 1924 – 1r – 1 – Can$25.00 – cn Can Microfilming [072]

LE FONCTIONNAIRE PROVINCIAL *see* LE FONCTIONNAIRE

LE FONCTIONNEMENT DU MARCHE DU LOGEMENT ET LE PEUPLEMENT RESIDENTIEL / Vervaeke, Monique – 1mf – 9 – 10361 – fr Atelier National [307]

FONCTIONNEMENT DU POUVOIR REVOLUTIONNAIRE LOCAL (PRL) – Conakry: Impr nationale "Patrice Lumumba", 1974 – us Res Libr [072]

LE FONCTIONNEMENT SOCIOLOGIQUE DE LA LITTERATURE ORALE : L'EXEMPLE DES DIOULA DE KONG (COTE D'IVOIRE) / Derive, J – (Tome II. Recueil de textes. F300.00) – Analyse. Tome I – 9 – F250.00 – fr Ethnologie [306]

FOND BERTHIAUME-DU TREMBLAY / Archives Nationales. Ministere des Affaires culturelles – Montreal, sommaire – 6r – 1 – cn Can Microfilming [090]

FONDAMENTUM. EEN FONDAMENT / Simons, Menno – 1567. BME-295 1 – 9 – ne IDC [240]

LES FONDATEURS DE L'U.N. – Montreal, jul(?) 1936 – 1r – 1 – Can$25.00 – cn Can Microfilming [073]

LES FONDATEURS DE L'UNION NATIONALE / [LIBERATOR] / Liberator – [Quebec (Province): s.n., 1936 ?]. SEM105P1755 – 2mf – 9 – Can$4.50 – cn Bibl Nat [320]

LES FONDATEURS D'EMPIRE : CEREMONIES EN HOMMAGE A LA MISSION SAHARIENNE FOUREAU-BLIDE (AVRIL 30) / Lehuraux, Leon Joseph – Alger: Ancienne Maison Bastide Jourdan J Carbonel, 1931 – 1 – us Res Libr [960]

FONDATEURS, SUPERIEURS, PROFESSEURS ET ELEVES DU COLLEGE DE L'ASSOMPTION – Montreal: Beauchemin, 1883. 03042. (Pre-1900 Canadiana) – 9 – cn C.I.H.M. [971]

Fondation nationale des Sciences politiques. Paris *see* BIBLIOGRAPHIE COURANTE D'ARTICLES DE PERIODIQUES POSTERIEURS A 1944 SUR LES PROBLEMES POLITIQUES, ECONOMIQUES ET SOCIAUX

FONDATION TEYLER : CATALOGUE DE LA BIBLIOTHEQUE. TOME 2 / Foundation Teyler – 6mf – 8 – ne Slangenburg [012]

FONDS ANCIEN / Bibliotheque Municipale. Dole – 29 fiches. (Rare Books Catalogs) – 9 – 72.00 – fr Bibl Nationale [020]

LE FONDS ANCIEN / Bibliotheque Municipale. Beaune – Incunables, livres de la Reserve, livres du XVIe siecle.25 fiches. (Rare Books Catalogs) – 9 – 62.00 – fr Bibl Nationale [020]

FONDS BOUCHER / Seminaire des Trois Rivieres (Canada). Archives – Trois-Rivieres, Canada – 3r – 1 – cn Can Microfilming [240]

FONDS BRAININ / Archives de la Bibliotheque Juive – 5r – 1 – cn Can Microfilming [920]

FONDS CONTRECOEUR ET PARTIE DU FONDS VERREAU / Seminaire de Quebec. Archives – Montreal, Canada – 4r – 1 – cn Can Microfilming [240]

FONDS COUILLARD-DUPUIS – Montreal, 1681-1947 – 2r – 1 – cn Can Microfilming [090]

THE FONDS CURTIN, I F A N, UNIVERSITE DE DAKAR, SENEGAL : ARABIC DOCUMENTS PHOTOGRAPHED IN THE DEPT DE BAKEL, MAR AND APR 1966 – (Includes index) – Bloomington, 1966 – us Res Libr [470]

FONDS DES LIVRES DU XVIE SIECLE / Institut Catholique. Paris. Bibliotheque – 17 fiches. (Rare Books Catalogs) – 9 – 51.00 – fr Bibl Nationale [010]

FONDS DU SEMINAIRE ET DE L'EVECHE / Bibliotheque Municipale. Autun – 29 fiches. (Rare Books Catalogs) – 9 – 72.00 – fr Bibl Nationale [020]

FONDS FAILLON / Seminaire Saint Sulpice de Montreal. Archives – Montreal, Canada – 8r – 1 – cn Can Microfilming [025]

FONDS FLEURY-LAMOTHE – Montreal, 1925-60 – 2r – 1 – cn Can Microfilming [090]

FONDS GENERAL : BROME COUNTY HISTORICAL SOCIETY (1754-1945) / Brome County Historical Society. Knowlton, Canada – Knowlton, Canada – 6r – 1 – cn Can Microfilming [971]

FONDS HART / Seminaire des Trois Rivieres (Canada). Archives – Trois-Rivieres, Canada – 15r – 1 – cn Can Microfilming [025]

FONDS HERZL / Archives de la Bibliotheque Juive – 3r – 1 – cn Can Microfilming [920]

FONDS HUSID / Archives de la Bibliotheque Juive – 2r – 1 – cn Can Microfilming [920]

FONDS MADAME SALLUSTE LAVERY / Archives Nationales. Ministere des Affaires culturelles – Montreal, 1920-40 – 2r – 1 – cn Can Microfilming [090]

FONDS MANUSCRITS OU EN EDITION RESTREINTE CONCERNANT LA NOUVELLE-CALEDONIE / Centre Documentaire pour L'Oceanie – 9 – F90.00 – fr Ethnologie [980]

FONDS MASSON: CATALOGUE DES IMPRESSIONS DU XVE AU XVIIIE SIECLE / Bibliotheque Municipale. Amiens – Par Albert Labarre. 4 fiches. (Rare Books Catalogs) – 9 – 10.00 – fr Bibl Nationale [010]

FONDS ROSAIRE ARMAND – Montreal, 1930-70 – 1r – 1 – cn Can Microfilming [090]

FONDS RUBENSTEIN : WORLD CHAMPION SKATER, 1890 / Archives de la Bibliotheque Juive – 1r – 1 – cn Can Microfilming [920]

FONDS SEGAL / Bibliotheque Juive. Montreal. Archives – 15r – 1 – cn Can Microfilming [920]

FONDS TIFERETH JERUSALEM CONGREGATION (JOURNAL) / Archives de la Bibliotheque Juive – Montreal, 1908-55 – 1 – cn Can Microfilming [470]

FONDS ZIPPER / Archives de la Bibliotheque Juive – 3r – 1 – cn Can Microfilming [920]

FONDY I DEIATEL'NOST' OTDELA RUKOPISEI GOSUDARSTVENNOI BIBLIOTEKI SSSR IMENI V.I. LENINA / Safronova, G F – Bibliografiia 1836-1962. Basic bibliography of published finding aids for MS division of Lenin Library (GBL). BR-11,000/1 – 9 – ne IDC [010]

THE FONETIC HERALD – (Cont by: The Herald) – Port Hope [Ont: s.n. 1885?-1886] – 9 – cn C.I.H.M. [971]

THE FONETIC HERALD *see* THE HERALD

FONETIKA TEATRA / Kruchenykh, A – Izd. "MAF". M. 1923. BR-954 2 – 8 – ne IDC [460]

O FON-FON : ORGAM LITTERO-HUMORISTICO – Natal, 22 Mar 1896 – 1,5,6 – bl Biblioteca [072]

Fong, H D *see* COTTON INDUSTRY AND TRADE IN CHINA

Fonk, Friedrich Hermann *see* DAS STAATLICHE MISCHEHENRECHT IN PREUSSEN VOM ALLGEMEINEN LANDRECHT AN

FONOGRAPH (THE PHONOGRAPH) – London, UK. 22 Nov 1907-7 Aug 1914 – 1 – uk British Libr Newspaper [072]

FONS VITAE / Baeumker, C Avencebrolis – Muenster, 1892/95 – 10mf – 8 – ne Slangenburg [100]

Fonseca Hermes, J S da *see* EL PROBLEMA DE LA DOBLE NACIONALIDAD

Fonseca, Jaime M *see* COMMUNICATION POLICIES IN COSTA RICA

Fonseca, P *see* INSTITUTIONUM DIALECTICARUM...LIBRO OCTO

Fonsegrive, George *see* ESSAI SUR LE LIBRE ARBITRE

Fonssagrives, E *see* MARIE DE BRETAGNE

Fonssagrives, J B *see* HYGIENE ET ASSAINEMENT DES VILLES

Font Obrador, Bartolome *see* EL PADRE BOSCANA, HISTORIADOR DE CALIFORNIA. PALMA DE MALLORCA, 1965

FONTAINE – Revue mensuelle de la poesie et des lettres francaises. Dir. Max-Pol Fouchet. no. 1-63. Alger puis Paris. nov 1938-1947. Les no. 1-2 ont paru sous le titre de: Mithra – 1 – fr A.C.R.P.P. [800]

LE FONTAINE – Montreal, avr 1917-dec 1917 – 1r – 1 – Can$30.00 – cn Can Microfilming [072]

Fontaine, A *see* AIR ALLEMAND VARIE POUR LE VIOLON AVEC ACCOMP. DE PIANO

Fontaine de Saint-Freville, Louis *see* ESSAI OU PROJET D'EDUCATION NATIONALE POUR LES HOMMES

Fontaine, FP *see* RECUEIL DE DECORATIONS INTERIEURES.

Fontaine, Jacques *see* DISCOURS DES MARQUES DES SORCIERS ET DE LA REELLE POSSESSION QUE LE DIABLE PREND SUR LE CORPS DES HOMMES

Fontaine, L Urgele *see* CENT TRENTE-CINQ ANS APRES, OU, LA RENAISSANCE ACADIENNE: SUIVI DE NOTU LES HISTORIQUES ET ANECDOTIQUES, ET D'UN PETIT DISCOURS PRONONCE PAR L'AUTEUR LE 15 AOUT 1890 A ANNAPOLIS, NOUVELLE-ECOSSE (ANCIENNE ACADIE)

Fontaine, P *see* ASPECTS LINGUISTIQUES DE L'ACCULTURATION DES ACADIENS (PROVINCES MARITIMES DU CANADA)

Fontaine, Pamela *see* WHEELCHAIR BASKETBALL

Fontaine, Pierre *see* MARCHE DES BRAVES

Fontaine, Raphael Ernest *see*
- UN DUEL A POUDRE: COMEDIE EN TROIS ACTES
- FRICOTS POLITIQUES: PEINTEURS DE MOEURS AMERICAINES

LES FONTAINES EN BRETAGNE / Denefle, S – Fichier documentaire – 8mf – 9 – F120.00 – fr Ethnologie [306]

Fontan Lobe, J *see*
- BIBLIOGRAFA COLONIAL, CONTRIBUCION A UN INDICE DE PUBLICATIONES AFRICANAS
- BIBLIOGRAFIA COLONIAL, CONTRIBUCION A UN INDICE DE PUBLICACIONES AFRICANAS

FONTANA NEWS HERALD – Fontana, CA. 1989-1990 – 5r – 1 – $250.00 – R04024 – us Library Micro [071]

Fontane, Theodor *see* CHRISTIAN FRIEDRICH SCHERENBERG UND DAS LITERARISCHE BERLIN VON 1840 BIS 1860

Fontanes, Ernest *see* LE CHRISTIANISME MODERNE

Fontanes, Louis J-P de *see* UNIVERSITE IMPERIALE

Fontanier, P *see* ETUDES DE LA LANGUE FRANCAISE SUR RACINE

Fontanus, J *see*
- DE BELLO RHODIO, LIBRI TRES, CLEMENTI 7. PONT. MAX. DEDICATI...
- DELLA GVERRA DI RHODI LIBRI 3. AGGIUNTA LA DISCRITTIONE DELL' ISOLA DI MALTA CONCESSA A CAUALIERI, DOPO CHE RHODI FU PRESO

FONTENELLA. HISTORIA DE LOS ORACULOS – 1868 – 9 – 1.50f – sp Bibl Santa Ana [946]

Fontenelle *see* HISTORIA DE LOS ORACULOS

Fontenot, M E *see* THE EFFECTIVENESS OF ACUPRESSURE IN THE TREATMENT OF PRIMARY DYSMENORRHEA

FONTES DA HISTORIA DA IGREJA NO BRASIL : SEPARATA DA REVISTA DO INSTITUTO HISTORICO E GEOGRAFICO BRASILEIRO / Soares, J C de Macedo – Rio de Janeiro, Julho-Setembro. v220. 1953 – 4mf – 9 – ne IDC [972]

Fontoynont, Antoine Maurice *see* LA GRANDE COMORE

Fonvizin, D I *see* SOBRANIE SOCHINENII

FOOCHOW MESSENGER / American Board of Commissioners for Foreign Missions. Foochow – v1- Nov 1903-Oct 1917 (?). n.s. (all publ ?). Apr 1922-Spring 1940 (?) – 1 reel – 1 – $180.00 – us UPA [240]

FOOD – v45 no 4- Apr 1985- . Continues: Food in Canada – 1,5,6,9 – us UMI [640]

FOOD AID AND FOOD SECURITY : PAST PERFORMANCE AND FUTURE POTENTIAL – 1985 – 60p – it F.A.O. [337]

FOOD AID FOR DEVELOPMENT : THREE STUDIES / Blau, Gerda et al – 1985 – 343p – it F.A.O. [337]

FOOD AID IN FIGURES, 1985, NO 3 – 1986 – 118p – it F.A.O. [337]

FOOD AID IN FIGURES-1986, NO 4 – 1986 – 123p – it F.A.O. [337]

FOOD AID IN FIGURES-1987, NO 5 – 1988 – 137p – it F.A.O. [338]

FOOD AID PROJECTS – 1987 – 273p – it F.A.O. [337]

FOOD AND AGRICULTURAL IMMUNOLOGY – 1989- 5v – 9 – £227.00 – 0954-0105 – uk Carfax [580]

Food and Agriculture Organization of the United Nations *see* PUBLICATIONS CATALOGUE

FOOD AND CHEMICAL TOXICOLOGY – (Formerly: Food and Cosmetics Toxicology) – v1- 1963- – 5,6,9 – us UMI [660]

FOOD AND COSMETICS TOXICOLOGY *see* FOOD AND CHEMICAL TOXICOLOGY

FOOD AND DRUG PACKAGING – v22-23. 1970 – 17mf – 9 – $5.00f – us Ross [680]

FOOD AND DRUG REVIEW / U.S. Food and Drug Administration – Washington, DC. v1-50. 1917-66 – 1 – 276.00 – us L of C Photodup [615]

FOOD AND ENERGY : STRATEGIES FOR SUSTAINABLE DEVELOPMENT / Sachs, Ignacy & Silk, Dana – 9 – $10.00 – 92-808-0757-9 – ja U.N. Univ [333]

FOOD AND FOODWAYS / ed by Aymard, M et al – 1,5,9 – us Harwood [640]

FOOD AND FRUIT-BEARING FOREST SPECIES – it F.A.O. [634]

FOOD AND NUTRITION – (Base collection $3995; 1983 update $3815. Cataloging available) – 1507mf base collection; 1244mf 1983 update – 9 – $7810.00 complete collection – us UMI [612]

FOOD AND NUTRITION IN THE AFRICAN RAIN FOREST : SELECTED DATA FROM THE RESEARCH TEAM IN FOOD ANTHROPOLOGY "ANTHROPOLOGIE ALIMENTAIRE DIFFERENTIELLE" / ed by Hladik, C M et al – 1990 – 9 – 92-3-102626-7 – fr UNESCO [574]

FOOD AND NUTRITION PLANNING – 1981 – 109p – it F.A.O. [640]

FOOD AND NUTRITION STRATEGIES IN NATIONAL DIVELOPMENT : 9TH REPORT OF THE JOINT FAO/WHO EXPERT COMMITTEE ON NUTRITION, ROME, 1974 – 2nd printing 1977 – 64p – it F.A.O. [640]

FOOD AS A HUMAN RIGHT / ed by Eide, Asbjorn et al – 1984 – $5.00 – 92-808-0503-7 – ja U.N. Univ [340]

FOOD BALANCE SHEET FOR LIBYA 1959 / Libya. Ministry of National Economy – Aug 1960. E. H. Koreller, FAO Statistics Expert. BNE-1021 1 – 9 – ne IDC [339]

FOOD BALANCE SHEETS – it F.A.O. [640]

FOOD BALANCE SHEETS, 1979-1981 AVERAGE – 1984 – 290p – it F.A.O. [339]

FOOD CHEMISTRY – v1-15 1976-84 – 1,5,6,13 – sz Elsevier [660]

FOOD CONSUMPTION TABLES FOR THE NEAR EAST – 1982 – 275p – it F.A.O. [339]

FOOD, COOKERY, AND CATERING MICROFICHE LIBRARY / ed by O'Connor, John – (18th-20th centuries. Titles from John Fuller collection at Oxford Polytechnic) – 211mf – 9 – $690.00 – us UMI [640]

FOOD ECONOMY LEAFLET / South Dakota. Agricultural Extension Service. State College of Agriculture and Mechanic Arts – Nos 1-24 1931-34 – 1,5,6 – us Spaulding [630]

FOOD ENGINEERING – (v43- 1971- 5,6 v48- 1976- 9) – 1- 1928- – 1 – us UMI [660]

FOOD FOR THOUGHT *see* ADULT LEARNING

FOOD GRAIN CONSUMPTION TRENDS AND THEIR EFFECTS ON FOOD GRAIN MARKETING IN INDONESIA / Mears, Leon A – SE-10,947 1. 1962 – 9 – ne IDC [630]

FOOD IN CANADA – (1985- 5,6,9) – v1-45 no 3 Nov 1941-Mar 1985 – 1 – us UMI [640]

FOOD IN CANADA – (v1-29 1941-69 Can$415.00 5) – Toronto. v1-54. 1941-94 – 5,9 – Can$28.00y – cn Micromedia [640]

FOOD LEGUMES : DISTRIBUTION, ADAPTABILITY AND BIOLOGY OF YIELD – 1978 – 131p – it F.A.O. [634]

FOOD LOSS PREVENTION IN PERISHABLE CROPS – 1981 repr 1988 – 91p – it F.A.O. [630]

FOOD MANAGEMENT – v19- Dec 1984- – 1,5,6,9 – us UMI [640]

FOOD MANUFACTURE – (v47- 1972- 5,6 v49- 1974- 9) – 1- 1927- – 1 – us UMI [660]

FOOD MARKET COMMENTARY – (Ceased v13 no 2 1991) – Ottawa. v813. 1986-91 – 9 – Can$20.00y – cn Micromedia [640]

FOOD MONITOR – n1- 1977- – 1,5,6,9 – us UMI [660]

THE FOOD OF THE GODS : AND HOW IT CAME TO EARTH / Wells, H G – London: Macmillan and Co., 1904 – 1 roll – 1 – 1-55879-774-2 – uk Libr Preservation [830]

FOOD PROCESSING – Chicago: Putman Pub Co. [v47 n7-13 jul-dec 1986] – 1r – 1 – us Res Libr [660]

FOOD REVIEWS INTERNATIONAL – v1- 1985- – 1,5,6,9 – us UMI [640]

FOOD SCIENCE AND TECHNOLOGY ABSTRACTS – v. 1-6. 1969-74 – 1,5,6 – us Princeton Micro [630]

FOOD SECURITY POLICY ISSUES IN WEST AFRICA : PAST LESSONS AND FUTURE PROSPECTS; A CRITICAL REVIEW – 1990 – 90p – it F.A.O. [338]

[FOOD SUPPLY DURING WORLD WAR 1 PAMPHLET COLLECTION] – 1915? – 1 – CSUXANM2724-B – us Hoover Inst Photo [630]

[FOOD SUPPLY DURING WORLD WAR 2 PAMPHLET COLLECTION] – 1940-1944 – 1 – CSUXANN2551-B – us Hoover Inst Photo [630]

FOOD TECHNOLOGY – (v19- 1965- 5,6 v24- 1970- 9) – v1- 1947- – 1 – us UMI [660]

Food, Tobacco and Agricultural and Allied Workers *see* FTA NEWS

FOOD TRADE REVIEW – 1955-60 – 1 – uk Microform Academic [640]

FOODSERVICE EQUIPMENT DEALER – v20-29 1967-77 – 1 – us UMI [660]

FOODSERVICE EQUIPMENT SPECIALIST – (1984- 5,6,9) – v30- 1977- – 1 – us UMI [660]

A FOOL IN HER FOLLY / Broughton, Rhoda – British Fiction Archive: Unit 4 – 9 – uk Bell [830]

FOOLS OF FORTUNE : OR, GAMBLING AND GAMBLERS / Quinn, John Philip – (Comprehending a history of the vice in ancient and modern times, and in both hemispheres, an exposition of its alarming prevalence and destructive effects, with an unreserved and exhaustive disclosure of such frauds, tricks and devices as are practiced by "professional" gamblers, "confidence men" and "bunko steerers") – Chicago: The Anti-Gambling Association, 1892 – us Res Libr [360]

FOON TSITE TSOO TSITE – New York. N.Y. 1925 – 1 – us A.J.P.C. [071]

FOOT AND ANKLE INTERNATIONAL – v1-17. 1980-96 – 1,5,6,9 – $80.00r – us Williams [617]

Foot, Jesse *see*
- THE LIFE OF ARTHUR MURPHY, ESQ.
- THE LIFE OF JOHN HUNTER F.R.S. (1728-93) AND JOHN HUNTER'S 'DIRECTIONS FOR PRESERVING ANIMALS AND PARTS OF ANIMALS FOR EXAMINATION.'

Foot, Lionel R *see* THE GOLD COAST AND THE FANTIS

FOOTBALL GAZETTE AND TELEGRAPH – South Shields, England. Sports Gazette. -w. March 1910-April 1915, Aug 1919-Sept 1939, Sept 1946-Dec 1959. 12 reels – 1 – uk British Libr Newspaper [072]

Foote, C C *see* WOMAN'S RIGHTS AND DUTIES

Foote, H S *see* GARDEN OF THE WORLD OR SANTA CLARA COUNTY

Foote, LeRoy *see*
- CHRISTIAN LIBERTY AND ITS ENEMIES: A BOOK FOR YOUTH
- GOD'S TRUTH AND MAN'S INFIDELITY, OR, FAITH AND SIGHT CONTRASTED: A BOOK FOR "THOSE LAST DAYS"

Foote, S *see* A LETTER...TO THE REVEREND AUTHOR OF THE 'REMARKS, CRITICAL AND CHRISTIAN, ON "THE MINOR"'

Foote, William H *see* SKETCHES OF VIRGINIA

Foote, William Henry *see* THE HUGUENOTS; OR, REFORMED FRENCH CHURCH

FOOTHILL WEEKLY TIDINGS – (Also known as: Evening Telegraph, Weekly Telegraph, Weekly Tidings, Foothill Weekly Tidings-Telegraph) – Grass Valley, CA. 1877-1904 – 8r – 1 – $400.00 – C03601 – us Library Micro [071]

FOOTHILL WEEKLY TIDINGS-TELEGRAPH *see* FOOTHILL WEEKLY TIDINGS

THE FOOTLIGHT – Virginia City, NV. 10 Sep 1871; 1875-84; 1886-87 – 13r – 1 – $650.00 – U04790 – us Library Micro [071]

Footman, Henry *see* REASONABLE APPREHENSIONS AND REASSURING HINTS

A FOOTNOTE TO HISTORY : EIGHT YEARS OF TROUBLE IN SAMOA / Stevenson, Robert Louis – NY: Chas Scribner's Sons, 1892 – 4mf – 9 – $6.00 – LLMC 82-100C Title 22 – us L.L.M.C. [980]

FOOTPRINTS OF ITALIAN REFORMERS / Stoughton, John – [London]: Religious Tract Society, [1881?] – 1mf – us A.T.L.A. [900]

FOOTPRINTS OF SORROW / Reid, John – 1869 – 9 – us A.T.L.A. [240]

THE FOOTPRINTS OF THE PIONEERS / Pioneer Publishing Co – Genealogical record. Freeport, 1900. (Illinois Reel 56). (The Cox Library Collection) – 5 – us Americana [920]

THE FOOTPRINTS OF TIME : A COMPLETE ANALYSIS OF OUR AMERICAN SYSTEM OF GOVERNMENT / Bancroft, Charles – Burlington, IA: T T Root, 1879 – 8mf – 9 – $12.00 – LLMC 95-057 – us L.L.M.C. [323]

FOOTSCRAY ADVERTISER – 1923-1966. FA1-36 – 36r – 1 – at Corangamite [072]

THE FOOTSTEPS OF ST PAUL / Macduff, John Ross – New York: Robert Carter, 1861. 1 fiche – 9 – us A.T.L.A. [240]

FOOTSTEPS OF ST PAUL IN ROME...FROM...PUTEOLI TO HIS DEATH / Forbes, S Russell – London: Thomas Nelson, 1891. 1 fiche – 9 – us A.T.L.A. [240]

FOOTSTEPS OF THE FLOCK : ORIGINS OF LOUISIANA BAPTISTS / Wise, Ivan M – (Vol 2, part 1. 134p) – 1910 – 1 reel – 1 – $5.36 – us Baptist [240]

FOOTSTEPS OF THE FLOCK : ORIGINS OF LOUISIANA BAPTISTS / Wise, Ivan M – (Vol 2, Part 1. 2nd edition) – 1 reel – 1 – $7.84 – us Baptist [240]

FOOTSTEPS OF THE MASTER / Stowe, Harriet Beecher – New York: J.B. Ford, 1877. 1 fiche – 9 – us A.T.L.A. [240]

FOOTWEAR NEWS – New York, 1946- – 1 – $175.00y – us Fairchild Micro [680]

Foppens, J F *see*
- DIPLOMATUM BELGICORUM NOVA COLLECTIO
- OPERA DIPLOMATICA ET HISTORICA

FOR / University of Kentucky. Department of Forestry – No.1-13.1972-83. 4 fiches – 9 – us Spaulding [630]

FOR A LASTING PEACE, FOR A PEOPLE'S DEMOCRACY – Bucharest, Romania. [s.n.], nov 10 1947-apr 17 1956 – 7r – 1 – us Res Libr [949]

FOR A LASTING PEACE, FOR A PEOPLE'S DEMOCRACY – Bucharest, [s.n.]. nov 10, 1947-apr 17, 1956 – 7r – 1 – us Res Libr [320]

FOR BETTER RELATIONS WITH OUR LATIN AMERICAN NEIGHBORS : A JOURNEY TO SOUTH AMERICA / Bacon, R – Washington, D.C. 1916 – 3mf – 9 – ILM-4066/1 – ne IDC [340]

FOR CANADA, TRANSPORTATION THE PROBLEM / Campbell, James B – By a grain dealer. Montreal: W. Brown, 1893. 02274. (Pre-1900 Canadiana) – 9 – cn C.I.H.M. [971]

FOR CHRIST IN FUH-KIEN / McClelland, Thomas Calvin – London: Church Missionary Society, 1904 – 1mf – us A.T.L.A. [240]

FOR CLOSER UNION: SOME SLIGHT OFFERINGS TO A GREAT CAUSE / Crofton, Francis Blake – Halifax: A. & W. Mackinlay, 1897. 02127. (Pre-1900 Canadiana) – 9 – cn C.I.H.M. [971]

FOR INDIA'S UPLIFT; A COLLECTION OF SPEECHES AND WRITINGS ON INDIAN QUESTIONS / Besant, Anne Wood – Madras: G.A. Natesan, 1913?. 283p – 1 – us U.W. Library [950]

FOR KAEMPEVISERNE – 1847 – 1 – us I.U. Libraries [390]

FOR LIBERTY (LIBERTY LUMINANTS) / Carlyle, S & Bool, Henry – An anthology of Revolt, indexed, 104p – 9 – 1.00f – at Libertarian Micro [335]

FOR THE BEST THINGS / Miller, James Russell – New York: Thomas Y Crowell, c1907 – 1mf – 9 – 0-8370-7312-X – 1986-1312 – us A.T.L.A. [240]

FOR THE ELECTION OF MEMBERS OF THE CONSTITUENT ASSEMBLY AND OF THE HOUSE OF REPRESENTATIVES / Indonesia. Kementerian Penerangan – SE-5236 1. 1953 – 9 – ne IDC [324]

FOR THE ELECTION OF MEMBERS OF THE CONSTITUENT ASSEMBLY AND OF THE HOUSE OF REPRESENTATIVES / Indonesia. Laws, Statutes, etc – SE-2176 1. 1953 – 9 – ne IDC [323]

FOR THE FREEDOM OF THE SEA: A ROMANCE OF THE WAR OF 1812 / Brady, Cyrus Townsend – New York: Scribner's, 1899. 00870. (Pre-1900 Canadiana) – 9 – cn C.I.H.M. [830]

FOR THE INDEPENDENCE OF SPAIN, FOR LIBERTY, FOR THE REPUBLIC, UNION OF ALL SPANIARDS / Ibarruri, Dolores – Complete text of the report to the plenary session of the Central Committee of the Communist Party of Spain. Madrid, 1938. Fiche W1757. (Blodgett Collection of Spanish Civil War Pamphlets) – 9 – us H.U. College Libr [946]

FOR THE RIGHT – v1 nos 2-13; v2 nos 2-6 (complete) – 1r – 1 – ATLA BS0032 – us A.T.L.A. [073]

FOR THE WORK OF THE MINISTRY : A MANUAL OF HOMILETICAL AND PASTORAL THEOLOGY / Blaikie, William Garden – (Includes index) – 6th rev ed. London: J Nisbet, 1896 – 1mf – 9 – 0-8370-6023-0 – 1986-0023 – us A.T.L.A. [240]

THE FORAGE PLANTS OF AUSTRALIA / Turner, D – 6478 1891 – 9 – ne IDC [580]

Foran, Joseph F *see* PREDICTING MUSCLE FIBER TYPE THROUGH SELF-REPORTING

Foran, Joseph Kearney *see* AN ESSAY ON OBLIGATIONS: FOR LAWYERS, STUDENTS AND LAYMEN

Foran, Thomas Patrick *see*
- DIGEST OF REPORTED CASES TOUCHING THE CRIMINAL LAW OF CANADA.
- DIGEST OF REPORTED CASES TOUCHING THE CRIMINAL LAW OF CANADA: WITH REFERENCES TO THE STATUTES AND AN INDEX

Foran, William Robert *see* A CUCKOO IN KENYA

FORBEREDENDE UNDERSOGELSER TIL EN ALMINDELIG LIKENOKOLOGI / Galloe, O – (Dansk Botanisk Arkiv, v. 1, nr. 3). Kobenhavn. 1913. B-185 2 – 8 – ne IDC [580]

FORBES – (v. 103- 1969- 5,6. v. 105- 1970- 9) – 1- 1917- – 1 – us UMI [380]

FORBES ADVOCATE – Dec 8 1911-Dec 24 1919 – 9 – at Pascoe [072]

Forbes, Alexander Penrose *see*
- AN EXPLANATION OF THE THIRTY-NINE ARTICLES
- LIVES OF S. NINIAN AND S. KENTIGERN

Forbes, Archibald *see* WILLIAM OF GERMANY: A SUCCINCT BIOGRAPHY OF WILLIAM 1, GERMAN EMPEROR AND KING OF PRUSSIA

Forbes, Duncan *see* A GRAMMAR OF THE HINDUSTANI LANGUAGE IN THE ORIENTAL AND ROMAN CHARACTER..

Forbes, E A *see*
- A HISTORY OF BRITISH MOLLUSCA AND THEIR SHELLS
- MALACOLOGIA MONENSIS
- MONOGRAPH OF THE BRITISH NAKED-EYE MEDUSAE
- TRAVELS IN LYCIA, MILYAS AND CIBYRATIS

Forbes, F E *see* DAHOMEY AND THE DAHOMANS

Forbes, Frances Alice *see* A SCOTTISH KNIGHT-ERRANT

Forbes, Francis et al *see* PATENT AND TRADEMARK LAWS COMMISSION

Forbes, Frederick E *see* FIVE YEARS IN CHINA; FROM 1842 TO 1847. WITH AN ACCOUNT OF THE OCCUPATION OF LABUAN AND BORNEO BY HER MAJESTY'S FORCES

Forbes, Henry Prentiss *see*
- JOHANNINE LITERATURE AND THE ACTS OF THE APOSTLES
- THE JOHANNINE LITERATURE AND THE ACTS OF THE APOSTLES

Forbes, John *see*
- PREDESTINATION AND FREEWILL AND THE WESTMINSTER CONFESSION OF FAITH
- THE SERVANT OF THE LORD IN ISAIAH 40-66
- SERVANT OF THE LORD IN ISAIAH 40-66 RECLAIMED TO ISAIAH AS THE AUTHOR
- STUDIES ON THE BOOK OF PSALMS: THE STRUCTURAL CONNECTION OF THE BOOK OF PSALMS

FORBES PAPERS, 1723-1931 – Massachusetts Historical Society – 57r – 1 – $4295.00 – us UMI [920]

Forbes, S Russell *see* FOOTSTEPS OF ST PAUL IN ROME...FROM...PUTEOLI TO HIS DEATH

Forbes, S T *see* MANUAL OF METHODS FOR FISHERIES RESOURCE SURVEY AND APPRAISAL, PART 2

FORBES TIMES – Jan 7 1899-Mar 31 1920 – 9 – at Pascoe [072]

FORBES' TOURIST'S DIRECTORY – Rome, Italy. Rome Directory Roman News. -m. 1874-15 April 1898. 6 reels – 1 – uk British Libr Newspaper [910]

Forbes, Viv *see*
- THE FREEDOM TO SELL
- SHOULD AUSTRALIA HAVE FOREIGN AFFAIRS?

Forbes, William Cameron *see* PRESENT CONDITIONS IN SPAIN, JANUARY 1938

Forbes-Leith, William *see* NARRATIVES OF SCOTTISH CATHOLICS UNDER QUEEN MARY STUART AND KING JAMES 6TH

FORBIDDEN BOOKS FROM THE LIBRARY OF A.I. OSTROGLAZOV : FROM THE STATE HISTORICAL LIBRARY IN MOSCOW – 694mf – 1 – $3,500.00 coll – us Ross [020]

Forbiger, Albert *see* HELLAS UND ROM

Forbus, W R *see* THE SUITABILITY AND RELIABILITY OF THE PHYSICAL BEST FITNESS TEST WITH SELECTED SPECIAL POPULATIONS

LE FORCAT – Organe socialiste de la region Nord. Lille. juil 1882-juil 1883 – 1 – fr A.C.R.P.P. [073]

LES FORCATS POUR LA FOI : ETUDE HISTORIQUE (1684-1775) / Coquerel, Athanase – Paris: Michel Levy, 1866 – 1mf – us A.T.L.A. [240]

FORCE ET MISERE DU SOCIALISME / Viance, Georges – Paris. 1932. (La Condition Ouvriere. Part Two.) – 9 – 7.50 – fr Bibl Nationale [360]

Force, Fred P *see* THE LIFE STORY OF L. R. MILLICAN

Force, Manning F *see* MANNING F. FORCE PAPERS

FORCE OUVRIERE / C G T -F O – Puis hebdomadaire de la Confederation Force ouvriere. Dir., Andre Bergeron. Paris. 1950-1993 – 1 – fr A.C.R.P.P. [073]

FORCE OUVRIERE – Paris: Imp cent de la presse, [1945-66]. 1953-nov 23 1966 – us Res Libr [071]

Force, Peter *see* COLLECTION

Forcellini, Aeq *see* TOTIUS LATINITATIS LEXICON

FORCES : REVUE TRIMESTRIELLE DE PRESTIGE – Montreal. v1 n1. 1967-n99. aut 1992 – 6r – 1 – Can$70.00 – cn Can Microfilming [072]

FORCES NOUVELLES / Mouvement Republicain Populaire – Hebdomadaire. no. 1-106. Paris. 10 fevr 1945-14 fevr 1947. mq no. 99 – 1 – fr A.C.R.P.P. [073]

DES FORCES PRODUCTIVES, DESTRUCTIVES ET IMPRODUCTIVES DE LA RUSSIE / Jourdier, Auguste – (Russia – 19th C.). 1860 – 9 – fr Hachette [360]

DES FORCES PRODUCTIVES ET COMMERCIALES DE LA FRANCE / Dupin, Charles – (Condition of the 19th C. French working class series). 1827 – 9 – fr Hachette [339]

LES FORCES RELIGIEUSES ET LA VIE POLITIQUE : LE CATHOLICISME ET LE PROTESTANTISME / Latreille, A & Siegfried, A – F60.00 – fr Ethnologie [320]

Forchhammer, Ejnar *see* OM RICHARD WAGNER OG HANS TANNHAEUSER

FORD COUNTY GLOBE – Dodge City. Kan. 1878-84 – 1 – us UMI [071]

Ford County. Kansas. Board of Commissioners *see* JOURNALS

Ford County. Kansas. District Court *see*
- RECORDS
- SELECTED CASE RECORDS

Ford County. Kansas. Register of Deeds *see* RECORDS

FORD COUNTY RECORD – Spearville. Kan. -w. 1885-86 – 1 – us UMI [071]

FORD COUNTY REPUBLICAN – Dodge City. Kan. 1887-89 – 1 – us UMI [071]

Ford, David B *see* NEW ENGLAND'S STRUGGLES FOR RELIGIOUS LIBERTY

Ford Foundation *see* LETTER

FORD FOUNDATION ANNUAL REPORTS – 1950-70 – 20mf – 9 – $90.00 – LLMC 84-465 – us L.L.M.C. [360]

Ford Foundation. Indonesia *see*
- A BRIEF REVIEW OF FOREIGN ASSISTANCE IN INDONESIA'S ENGLISH LANGUAGE PROGRAM
- SOME DESCRIPTIVE NOTES ON FOREIGN ASSISTANCE IN INDONESIAN TECHNICAL EDUCATION

Ford, H A *see*
- HISTORY OF CINCINNATI, OHIO
- HISTORY OF HAMILTON COUNTY

Ford, Henry Jones *see*
- THE RISE AND GROWTH OF AMERICAN POLITICS
- THE SCOTCH-IRISH IN AMERICA

Ford, James E *see* HISTORY OF GRUNDY COUNTY

Ford, K B *see*
- HISTORY OF CINCINNATI, OHIO
- HISTORY OF HAMILTON COUNTY

Ford, Melbourne Haddock *see* THE STUDENT'S LEGAL ANALYSIS

Ford, Paul L *see*
- BIBLIOGRAPHY AND REFERENCE LIST OF THE HISTORY AND LITERATURE
- ESSAYS ON THE CONSTITUTION OF THE UNITED STATES
- PAMPHLETS ON THE CONSTITUTION OF THE UNITED STATES

Ford, Thomas *see* HISTORY OF ILLINOIS 1814-1847

Forda, Balduinus de *see* SERMONES

Forder, Archibald *see* WITH THE ARABS IN TENT AND TOWN

Forder, Winter Rand *see* THE FORMATION OF A MINISTRY TO THE PARENTS OF INFANTS. 1981

FORDHAM ENTERTAINMENT MEDIA AND INTELLECTUAL PROPERTY LAW FORUM *see* FORDHAM INTELLECTUAL PROPERTY, MEDIA AND ENTERTAINMENT LAW JOURNAL

FORDHAM ENVIRONMENTAL LAW JOURNAL – (Title varies: v1-4 1989-93 as Fordham Environmental Law Report) – v1-6. 1989-95 – 9 – $81.00 set – us Hein [340]

FORDHAM ENVIRONMENTAL LAW REPORT *see* FORDHAM ENVIRONMENTAL LAW JOURNAL

FORDHAM FRANCE – Fordham, NY. v11 n5. 6 jan 1941-v13 n4. 4 mar 1943 – 1r – 1 – Can$25.00 – cn Can Microfilming [071]

Fordham, Frieda *see* AN INTRODUCTION TO JUNG'S PSYCHOLOGY

FORDHAM INTELLECTUAL PROPERTY, MEDIA AND ENTERTAINMENT LAW JOURNAL – (Title varies: v1-3 1990-93 as Fordham Entertainment Media and Intellectual Property Law Forum) – v1-5. 1990-95 – 9 – $67.00 set – us Hein [340]

FORDHAM INTERNATIONAL LAW FORUM *see* FORDHAM INTERNATIONAL LAW JOURNAL

FORDHAM INTERNATIONAL LAW JOURNAL – (Title varies: v1-3 1977-80 as Fordham International Law Forum) – v1-17. 1977-94 – 9 – $303.00 set – us Hein [340]

FORDHAM LAW REVIEW – (This journal ceased publication after v3, but was revived in 1935 with a v4 to date. For copyright reasons only v1-3 can be offered at this time) – v1-3. 1914-1917 (all offered) – 5mf – $7.50 – LLMC 95-106 – us L.L.M.C. [073]

FORDHAM LAW REVIEW – (v1-53 1914-85 on reel or mf $712.00. v54-64 1985-96 on mf $326.00. Suspended 1917-34) – v1-65. 1914-96 – 5,6,9 – $1,038.00 set – us Hein [340]

Fordham, Reginald Sydney Walter *see* INCOME TAX APPEAL BOARD PRACTICE; A PRACTICAL TREATISE ON PROCEDURE BEFORE THE BOARD

FORD'S CHRISTIAN REPOSITORY – 1852-Sep 1905 – 1 – 1445.22 – us Baptist [240]

Fordyce, Alexander Dingwall *see*
- THE AULD KIRKYARD, FERGUS: IN IT, AND ABOUT IT
- GLEANINGS FROM THE CHURCH-YARD: A SELECTION OF OLD INSCRIPTIONS
- THE MONUMENTAL INSCRIPTIONS IN THE CEMETARY AT BELLESIDE, FERGUS (ONTARIO)

Fordyce, James *see* SERMONS TO YOUNG WOMEN

Fordyce, John *see* ASPECTS OF SCEPTICISM: WITH SPECIAL REFERENCE TO THE PRESENT TIME

FORDYCE PRESS – Fordyce, NE. -w. Jan. 1914-Mar. 1915 – 1 – us NE Hist [071]

FORECAST FOR HOME ECONOMICS – (v14-1968- 5,6 v21- 1975- 9) – v1- 1956- Continues: Practical Forecast for Home Economics – 1 – us UMI [640]

FOREIGN AFFAIRS – v1- 1922- 1; v47- 5,6,9 – us UMI [977]

FOREIGN AFFAIRS – v1-73. 1922-94 – 9 – $1,339.00 set – us Hein [977]

FOREIGN AGRICULTURAL ECONOMIC REPORTS / U.S. Department of Agriculture – v1-223. 1961-86. 294 fiches – 9 – 330.00 – us Updata [324]

FOREIGN AGRICULTURAL TRADE. U.S. / U.S. Department of Agriculture – 1962-86. 353 fiches – 9 – $380.00 – us Updata [330]

FOREIGN AGRICULTURE / U.S. Department of Agriculture – 1937-86.Two distinct titles: Title 1, v1-26, 1937-62; Title 2, 1963-86. 232 fiches – 9 – 320.00 – us Updata [630]

FOREIGN AGRICULTURE *see* AGEXPORTER

FOREIGN AND HOME LAW / Eder, P J – New York, 1916 – 2mf – 9 – ILM-2951/1 – ne IDC [327]

FOREIGN CAPITAL INVESTMENT REGULATIONS / Indonesia. Laws, Statutes, etc – SE-6485 1. 1968 – 9 – ne IDC [324]

FOREIGN CLAIMS SETTLEMENT COMMISSION DECISIONS – (Bk 1: Settlement of Claims by the Foreign Claims Settlement Commission of the US and its Predecessors from 14 Sept 1949-31 Mar 1955. Bk 2: Decisions and Annotations, 1950-1967. Index/digest of Decisions, 1949-1977) – Washington: GPO. bk1 1955; bk2 1968; 2 pamphlets 1964, 1967 – 20mf – 9 – $30.00 – LLMC 94-356B – us L.L.M.C. [340]

FOREIGN COLONIAL ADMINISTRATION IN THE FAR EAST / Bell, Heaketh – Reel 4002. 1928 – 1 – ja CEACS [950]

FOREIGN COMMERCE.. / Philippines. Department of Finance and Justice. Bureau of Customs – Manila: Bureau of Printing, 1913 14 – 1 – us U.W. Library [324]

FOREIGN CONSPIRACY AGAINST THE LIBERTIES OF THE UNITED STATES : THE NUMBERS UNDER THE SIGNATURE OF BRUTUS, ORIGINALLY PUBLISHED IN THE NEW YORK OBSERVER / Morse, Samuel Finley Breese – 7th ed. New York: American and Foreign Christian Union, 1855, c1835 – 1mf – 9 – 0-8370-8363-X – 1986-2363 – us A.T.L.A. [240]

THE FOREIGN FIELD OF THE WESLEYAN METHODIST CHURCH *see* WORK AND WORKERS IN THE MISSION FIELD

FOREIGN GAZETTEERS OF THE U.S. BOARD ON GEOGRAPHIC NAMES ON MICROFICHE / U.S. Defense Mapping Agency – (Printed guide included) – 2 grps. 1987-90 – 168mf – 9 – $4,555.00 set – us CIS [910]

The foreign General Representation of the USSR Finance-Commissariat *see* THE BUDGET OF THE SOVIET-UNION FOR THE FINANCIAL YEAR 1924/25 AND THE ESTIMATE FOR THE CURRENT FINANCIAL YEAR 1925/26

[FOREIGN INFLUENCES ON RUSSIA'S CIVILIZATION AND CULTURE PAMPHLET COLLECTION] – 1917 – 1 – CSUXANS1197-B – us Hoover Inst Photo [306]

FOREIGN INVESTMENT ATMOSPHERE IN SAUDI ARABIA / Saudi Arabia. General Petroleum and Mineral Organization – Dallas, Texas. June 22, 1966 – 9 – ne IDC [332]

FOREIGN INVESTMENT LAW 2-5 AND REGULATIONS, 1981-1986 / Federated States of Micronesia – n.p., n.d. – 1mf – 9 – $1.50 – LLMC 82-100H Title 10 – us L.L.M.C. [324]

FOREIGN INVESTMENT LAWS AND REGULATIONS / Trust Territory of the Pacific – Saipan: Foreign Investment Branch, Dep of the Attorney General, sep 1976 – 1mf – 9 – $1.50 – LLMC 82-100F Title 99 – us L.L.M.C. [332]

FOREIGN INVESTMENT REVIEW – (Ceased v6 no 1 1982/83) – Ottawa. v1-6. 1977/78-1982/83 – 9 – Can$20.00y – cn Micromedia [332]

FOREIGN JOURNALISTS UNDER FRANCO'S TERROR – London, 1937. Fiche W 889. (Blodgett Collection of Civil War Pamphlets) – 9 – us H.U. College Libr [946]

FOREIGN LANGUAGE ANNALS – v1 1967- 1; v8- 1975- 5,6,9 – us UMI [400]

FOREIGN LETTERS OF THE CONTINENTAL CONGRESS AND THE DEPARTMENT OF STATE, 1785-1790 / U. S. Department of State – 1r – 1 – M61 – us Nat'l Archives [977]

FOREIGN LETTERS...1785-90 / U.S. Continental Congress and the Department of State – M61 – 1r – 1 – us Nat'l Archives [976]

FOREIGN MISSION EXECUTIVE MINUTE BOOKS / New Zealand. Methodist Church. Overseas Mission – 8 jan 1925-15 dec 1931 – 1r – 1 – PMB1097 – at Pacific Mss [240]

THE FOREIGN MISSION JOURNAL *see* PERIODICALS

FOREIGN MISSIONARY – v1-83. 1880-1963 (complete) – 18r – 1 – ATLA S0181 – us A.T.L.A. [073]

THE FOREIGN MISSIONARY; AN INCARNATION OF A WORLD MOVEMENT / Brown, Arthur Judson – New York, Chicago: Fleming H. Revell, c1907. 412p – 1 – us U.W. Library [240]

FOREIGN MISSIONARY CHRONICLE – v. 1-7. 1833-39 – 1 – $50.00 – us Presbyterian [240]

THE FOREIGN MISSIONARY CHRONICLE – Pittsburgh, Pa. v1-9. 1833-1841 – 3r – 1 – $150.00 – us Presbyterian [240]

FOREIGN MISSIONARY TIDINGS / Presbyterian Church in Canada. Woman's Foreign Missionary Society. Western Divison – (Cont: Presbyterian Church in Canada. Woman's Foreign Missionary Society) – (S.l.: s.n. 1897-1914) : Arbuthnot Bros) – 9 – cn C.I.H.M. [240]

FOREIGN MISSIONARY TIDINGS *see* MONTHLY LETTER LEAFLET

FOREIGN MISSIONS : BEING A STUDY OF SOME PRINCIPLES AND METHODS IN THE EXPANSION OF THE CHRISTIAN CHURCH / Malden, Richard Henry – (Includes index) – London, New York: Longmans, Green, 1910 – 1mf – 9 – 0-8370-6215-2 – 1986-0215 – us A.T.L.A. [240]

FOREIGN MISSIONS / Martin, George Currie – (Includes index) – London: National Council of Evangelical Free Churches, 1905 – 1mf – 9 – 0-8370-6757-X – 1986-0757 – us A.T.L.A. [240]

FOREIGN MISSIONS : THEIR PLACE IN THE PASTORATE, IN PRAYER, IN CONFERENCES: TEN LECTURES / Thompson, Augustus Charles – (Includes index) – New York: Charles Scribner, 1889 – 2mf – 9 – 0-8370-6422-8 – 1986-0422 – us A.T.L.A. [240]

FOREIGN MISSIONS : THEIR RELATIONS AND CLAIMS / Anderson, Rufus – (Includes bibliographical references & index) – New York: Charles Scribner, 1869 – 1mf – 9 – 0-8370-6083-4 – 1986-0083 – us A.T.L.A. [240]

FOREIGN MISSIONS AFTER A CENTURY / Dennis, James Shepard – (Includes index) – New York: Fleming H Revell, c1893 – 1mf – 9 – 0-8370-6253-5 – 1986-0253 – us A.T.L.A. [240]

FOREIGN MISSIONS OF THE PROTESTANT CHURCHES / Baldwin, Stephen Livingstone – (Includes table & index) – New York: Eaton & Mains; Cincinnati: Jennings & Pye, c1900 – 1mf – 9 – 0-8370-6005-2 – 1986-0005 – us A.T.L.A. [240]

FOREIGN MISSIONS OF THE PROTESTANT CHURCHES : THEIR STATE AND PROSPECTS / Mitchell, John Murray – (Includes index) – Toronto, Canada: Toronto Willard Tract Depot, 1888 – 1mf – 9 – 0-8370-6761-8 – 1986-0761 – us A.T.L.A. [240]

FOREIGN NATIONALITIES BRANCH FILES, 1942-45 / U.S. Office of Strategic Services – (Europe (general and misc.) $840.00; Eastern Europe $2,615.00; Central Europe $3,000.00; Southeastern Europe $3,460.00; Western Europe $1,460.00; Jewish groups $475.00; Index only $745.00) – Covers governments in exile, exiled leaders, resistance movements, internal political activities, disputes within ethnic communities and activities of U.S. foreign language press. Includes printed index – 1,900mf – 9 – $8,050.00 set – us UPA [324]

FOREIGN NEWS IN THE MEDIA : INTERNATIONAL REPORTING IN 29 COUNTRIES – 1985 – 96p – 9 – 92-3-102265-2 – fr UNESCO [070]

FOREIGN OFFICE CONFIDENTIAL PRINT : AFRICA – 71r – 1 – $2,790.00 – us Trans-Media [960]

FOREIGN OFFICE CONFIDENTIAL PRINT: AMERICA – 26r – 1 – $980.00 – us Trans-Media [970]

FOREIGN OFFICE FILES FOR JAPAN AND THE FAR EAST – (Series One: Embassy & Consular Archives – Japan (Public Record Office Class FO 262); Part 1: Correspondence to and from Japan, 1905-1920 (PRO Class FO 262/1466-1511, 2033-34); Part 2: Detailed Correspondence for 1921-1923 (PRO Class FO 262/1512-1601) 44r. $5,400.00; Part 3: Detailed Correspondence for 1924-26 (PRO Class FO 262/1602-72) 44r. $5,400.00; Part 4: Detailed Correspondence for 1927-29 (PRO Class FO 262/1673-1741) 42r. $5,150.00; Part 5: Detailed Correspondence for 1930-31 (PRO Class FO 262/1742-96, 1989-91, 2035) ca 38r. $4,650.00; Part 6: Detailed Correspondence for 1932-1933 (PRO Class FO 262/1797-1860 1992-2003) 45r.$5,500.0 0; Part 7: Detailed Correspondence for 1934-1935 (PRO Class FO 262/1861-1926, 20004-8) 45r.$5,500.00; Part 8: Detailed Correspondence for 1936-1940 (PRO Class FO 262/1927-88, 2009-32, 2036-39) 45r.$5,500.00; Part 9: Detailed Correspondence for 1945-1952 (PRO Class FO 262/2040-2083) 25r.$3,075.00; Part 10: Detailed Correspondence for 1953-1957 (PRO Class FO 262/2084-2132) 27r.$3,300.00; Series Two: British Foreign Office Files for Post-War Japan, 1952-1962 (Public Record Office Class FO 371) $2,450.00) – Marlborough: Adam Matthew Publications, 1994 – 18r – 1 – $2,000.00 – uk Matthew [950]

FOREIGN OFFICE FILES FOR POST-WAR EUROPE, SERIES ONE : THE SCHUMAN PLAN AND THE EUROPEAN COAL AND STEEL COMMUNITY – (Public Record Office Class FO371. 1950-1955. 3 Parts) – Marlborough: Adam Matthew Publicaton, Part 1, March 1995 – 25r – 1 – $2,950.00 – uk Matthew [940]

FOREIGN OFFICE REGISTERS AND INDEXES OF CORRESPONDENCE, 1793-1919 : ASIA AND THE PACIFIC / Great Britain. Foreign Office. Public Record Office; ed by Palmer, Greg – 94v on 1078mf – 9 – £4,070.00 – uk Chadwyck [941]

FOREIGN OFFICE REGISTERS AND INDEXES OF CORRESPONDENCE, 1793-1919 : RUSSIA, PERSIA AND CENTRAL ASIA / Great Britain. Foreign Office. Public Record Office; ed by Palmer, Greg – 96v on 1211mf – 9 – £4,300.00 – uk Chadwyck [940]

FOREIGN OFFICE REGISTERS AND INDEXES OF CORRESPONDENCE, 1793-1919 : UNITED STATES OF AMERICA / Great Britain. Foreign Office. Public Record Office; ed by Palmer, Greg – 55v on 660mf – 9 – £2,520.00 – uk Chadwyck [941]

FOREIGN POLICY – v1- 1970- 1,5,6; v21- 9 – us UMI [977]

THE FOREIGN POLICY OF TANZANIA, 1961-68 / Shaw, T M – Kampala, 1969 – us Res Libr [327]

FOREIGN POST WORLD WAR 2 NEWSPAPERS – Collection of Newspapers for Various Countries during 1945-1954 – 1 – us NY Public [072]

FOREIGN PRESS REPORT ON WEST IRAN : PERMANENT MISSION TO THE UNITED NATIONS – (Missing: 1961. v1-9; in Dutch) – New York, 1961-1962. v1-17 – 38mf – 9 – SE-1686/1 – ne IDC [073]

FOREIGN PROTESTANTISM WITHIN THE CHURCH OF ENGLAND : THE STORY OF AN ALIEN THEOLOGY AND ITS PRESENT OUTCOME / Wirgman, A Theodore – London: Catholic Literary Association, 1911 – 1mf – us A.T.L.A. [240]

[FOREIGN RELATIONS BETWEEN CZECHOSLOVAKIA AND GREAT BRITAIN PAMPHLET COLLECTION – 1938-1947 – 1 – CSUXANL4395-B – us Hoover Inst Photo [320]

[FOREIGN RELATIONS BETWEEN FRANCE AND SERBIA PAMPHLET COLLECTION] – 1970 – 1 – CSUXANL5807-B – us Hoover Inst Photo [320]

[FOREIGN RELATIONS BETWEEN GREAT BRITAIN AND GREECE PAMPHLET COLLECTION] – 1947?-1951 – 1 – CSUXANL4399-B – us Hoover Inst Photo [320]

[FOREIGN RELATIONS BETWEEN GREAT BRITAIN AND THE SOVIET UNION PAMPHLET COLLECTION] – 1920-1946 – 1 – CSUXANL4405-B – us Hoover Inst Photo [320]

[FOREIGN RELATIONS BETWEEN GREECE AND TURKEY PAMPHLET COLLECTION] – 1974-1982? – 1 – CSUXANL6467-B – us Hoover Inst Photo [320]

[FOREIGN RELATIONS BETWEEN RUSSIA AND FRANCE PAMPHLET COLLECTION] – 1896-1931? – 1 – CSUXANR5992-B – us Hoover Inst Photo [320]

[FOREIGN RELATIONS BETWEEN RUSSIA AND THE FAR EAST PAMPHLET COLLECTION] – 1899-1916 – 1 – CSUXANR4830-B – us Hoover Inst Photo [320]

[FOREIGN RELATIONS BETWEEN THE SOVIET UNION AND AFGHANISTAN PAMPHLET COLLECTION] – c1978?-1988 – 1 – CSUXANR4865-B – us Hoover Inst Photo [320]

[FOREIGN RELATIONS BETWEEN THE SOVIET UNION AND CHINA PAMPHLET COLLECTION] – 1950-1983 – 1 – CSUXANR4889-B – us Hoover Inst Photo [320]

[FOREIGN RELATIONS BETWEEN THE SOVIET UNION AND EASTERN EUROPE PAMPHLET COLLECTION] – 1985 – 1 – CSUXANR3197-B – us Hoover Inst Photo [320]

[FOREIGN RELATIONS BETWEEN THE SOVIET UNION AND FINLAND PAMPHLET COLLECTION] – 1939-1968 – 1 – CSUXANR5960-B – us Hoover Inst Photo [320]

[FOREIGN RELATIONS BETWEEN THE SOVIET UNION AND FRANCE PAMPHLET COLLECTION] – 1931-1954 – 1 – CSUXANR4720-B – us Hoover Inst Photo [320]

[FOREIGN RELATIONS BETWEEN THE SOVIET UNION AND GERMANY PAMPHLET COLLECTION] – 1939-1959 – 1 – CSUXANR4728-B – us Hoover Inst Photo [320]

[FOREIGN RELATIONS BETWEEN THE SOVIET UNION AND PERU PAMPHLET COLLECTION] – 1973 – 1 – CSUXANR4765-B – us Hoover Inst Photo [320]

[FOREIGN RELATIONS BETWEEN THE SOVIET UNION AND POLAND PAMPHLET COLLECTION] – 1944-1982 – 1 – CSUXANR4777-B – us Hoover Inst Photo [320]

[FOREIGN RELATIONS BETWEEN THE SOVIET UNION AND THE FAR EAST PAMPHLET COLLECTION] – 1934-1974 – 1 – CSUXANR4843-B – us Hoover Inst Photo [320]

[FOREIGN RELATIONS BETWEEN THE SOVIET UNION AND THE UNITED STATES PAMPHLET COLLECTION] – 1950-1973 – 1 – CSUXANR4789-B – us Hoover Inst Photo [320]

[FOREIGN RELATIONS BETWEEN THE SOVIET UNION AND TURKEY PAMPHLET COLLECTION] – 1926 – 1 – CSUXANR4895-B – us Hoover Inst Photo [320]

[FOREIGN RELATIONS BETWEEN THE SOVIET UNION AND WEST GERMANY] – 1958-1968 – 1 – CSUXANR4735-B – us Hoover Inst Photo [320]

[FOREIGN RELATIONS BETWEEN THE SOVIET UNION AND YUGOSLAVIA] – 1958?-1976 – 1 – CSUXANR4814-B – us Hoover Inst Photo [320]

[FOREIGN RELATIONS BETWEEN TURKEY AND CYPRUS] – 1977 – 1 – CSUXANQ7680-B – us Hoover Inst Photo [320]

[FOREIGN RELATIONS BETWEEN TURKEY AND GREECE PAMPHLET COLLECTION] – 1976? – 1 – CSUXANQ7690-B – us Hoover Inst Photo [320]

[FOREIGN RELATIONS BETWEEN YUGOSLAVIA AND GHANA PAMPHLET COLLECTION] – 1961 – 1 – CSUXANQ5745-B – us Hoover Inst Photo [320]

[FOREIGN RELATIONS BETWEEN YUGOSLAVIA AND ROMANIA PAMPHLET COLLECTION] – 1953 – 1 – CSUXANQ5752-B – us Hoover Inst Photo [320]

[FOREIGN RELATIONS BETWEEN YUGOSLAVIA AND THE SOVIET UNION PAMPHLET COLLECTION] – 1949-1987 – 1 – CSUXANQ5761-B – us Hoover Inst Photo [320]

[FOREIGN RELATIONS OF GREECE PAMPHLET COLLECTION] – 1907-1949 – 1 – CSUXANL6458-B – us Hoover Inst Photo [320]

FOREIGN RELATIONS PAPERS OF THE UNITED STATES – 354bks. 1861-1963 – 9 – $6,611.00 set – us Hein [327]

FOREIGN RELATIONS PAPERS OF THE UNITED STATES / U.S. Department of State – (The official State Dept compilation of letters and documents generated in the course of diplomatic relations between US and other countries) – 375bks. 1861-1964/68 v1. The official State Dept. compilation – 4407mf – 9 – $6,611.00 – LLMC 79 444 us L.L.M.C. [977]

FOREIGN SCOUTING SERVICE MICROFICHES OF HISTORICAL FOREIGN SCOUTING REPORTS – Geneva, 1959- – 9 – Sfr75,000.00 set, 1993 update Sfr17,000.00 – sz Petro [622]

FOREIGN SERVICE LISTS / U.S. Department of State – 1929-75 – 1,5,6 – us Princeton Micro [977]

FOREIGN STUDENTS IN INDIAN UNIVERSITIES, INSTITUTIONS 1982-1983 / India. Department of Education – New Delhi, 1987 – 2mf – 9 – DE-641/1 – ne IDC [370]

FOREIGN STUDENTS: THE SOVIET EDUCATIONAL WEAPON / Raymond, E A – Stanford, Calif. 1973 – 1 – 35.00r – us Hoover Inst Photo [370]

FOREIGN TRADE – (Cont by: Canada Commerce, 1973) – Ottawa. v1-136. 1947-72 – 5 – Can$100.00 – cn Micromedia [380]

FOREIGN TRADE : STANDARD TABLES ON MICROFICHE – 9 – at Statistics [337]

FOREIGN TRADE *see* CANADA COMMERCE

FOREIGN TRADE AND INTERNAL STATISTICS / Sudan. Dept. of Statistics – 1948-61. (lacking 1956 (Jun-Jul)). BNE-7629 1 – 9 – ne IDC [310]

FOREIGN TRADE OF NIGERIA / Ihaza, Daniel E – 1954 – us Res Libr [380]

FOREIGN TRADE REPORT. (WITH SOME INTERNAL STATISTICS), 1946-1954 / Sudan. Dept. of Statistics – 9v in 5. BNE-7628 1 – 9 – ne IDC [310]

FOREIGN TRADE STATISTICAL DIGEST / Sudan. Bank of Sudan – 4v. in 2. 1968-76. BNE-7601 1 – 9 – ne IDC [310]

FOREIGN TRADE STATISTICS / Israel. Prime Minister's Office. Central Bureau of Statistics – v. 1-8. 1969-76. BJ-81-5 1 – 9 – ne IDC [380]

FOREIGN TRADE STATISTICS / Sudan. Dept. of Statistics – 16 v. in 10. 1955 72. (lacking 1955, 1970). BNE-7615 1 – 9 – ne IDC [310]

FOREIGN TRADE STATISTICS / Syria. Dept. of Statistics – 1951-52 – 9 – ne IDC [310]

FOREIGN TRADE STATISTICS, 1969, 1972 / Saudi Arabia. Central Department of Statistics – 9 – ne IDC [380]

FOREIGN TRADE STATISTICS FOR THE YEMEN ARAB REPUBLIC FOR THE FISCAL YEAR / Yemen. Central Bank of Yemen, Sana'a – 4v. 1969 70-1972. BNE-9610 1 – 9 – ne IDC [337]

FOREIGN TRADE STATISTICS OF ASIA AND THE FAR EA SERIES A / United Nations – Vols 1-7; 8, No. 1; 9, No. 1 – E.351 – 9 (E/CN.11/) – us U.N. Pubs [380]

FOREIGN TRADE STATISTICS OF ASIA AND THE FAR EA SERIES B / United Nations – Vols 4-6 – E.38 – 9 (E/CN.11/) – us U.N. Pubs [380]

FOREIGN TRADE STATISTICS OF ASIA AND THE PACIFIC / United Nations – 1981-1986 – E.12 – 9 (ST/ESCAP) – us U.N. Pubs [380]

FOREIGN TRADE STATISTICS OF ASIA AND THE PACIFIC / United Nations – 208 fiches – 9 – 390.00; 1.90f – uk UNIMICRO [380]

FOREIGN TRADE STATISTICS OF ASIA AND THE PACIFIC. SERIES A / United Nations – (Vols 9, No.2; 10, No. 1. E/CN.11/. E.26; Vols 8, No. 2; 9, No.3; 10, No.2; 11-22. E/ESCAP/. E.108) – 9 – us U.N. Pubs [380]

FOREIGN TRADE STATISTICS OF ASIA AND THE PACIFIC. SERIES B / United Nations – (Vol 7. E/CN.11/. E.7; Vols 8-17. E/ESCAP/. E.46) – 9 – us U.N. Pubs [380]

THE FOREIGN VOCABULARY OF THE QUR'AN / Jeffery, Arthur – Oriental Institute Baroda, 1938 – 6mf – 8 – ne Slangenburg [260]

FOREIGNERS IN TURKEY;... / Brown, P M – Princeton, 1914 – 2mf – 1 – ILM-656/1 – ne IDC [327]

Forelli, A J *see* OBRAS COMPLETAS Y CORRESPONDENCIA CIENTIFICA

FORELOBIGT BIDRAG TIL KAP FARVEL-DISTRIKTERNES KULTURHISTORIE / Birket-Smith, K – (MoG., v. 53). Kobenhavn. 1917. BN-125 2 – 8 – ne IDC [306]

FORENSIC SCIENCE INTERNATIONAL – (v.7-18. 1976-80. 1,5,6,9) – v1-26. 1972-84 – 1,5,6,13 – sz Elsevier [614]

FORERUNNER – v1-7 (all publ). 1909-1916 – 29mf – 9 – $170.00 – us UPA [640]

FORERUNNERS AND RIVALS OF CHRISTIANITY : BEING STUDIES IN RELIGIOUS HISTORY FROM 330 B.C. TO 330 A.D. / Legge, F – Cambridge: University Press; New York: Putnam [distributor], 1915 – 2mf – us A.T.L.A. [230]

FORESHADOWS : LECTURES ON OUR LORD'S PARABLES / Cumming, John – Philadelphia: Lindsay & Blakiston, 1863 – 1mf – 9 – 0-8370-2787-X – 1985-0787 – us A.T.L.A. [240]

FOREST ADVERTISER – Forest, Ohio. 1907-12 – 1r – 1 – $32.50r – us Archival [071]

FOREST AND STREAM : A JOURNAL OF OUTDOOE LIFE, TRAVEL, NATURE STUDY. SHOOTING, FISHING, YACHTING – New York: [Forest and Stream Publ Co,] v1-77. aug 14 1873-dec 30 1911 – 1 – us Res Libr [790]

FOREST AND STREAM – v25-26. 1885-86 – 1r – 1 – us Ross [639]

Forest, Charles *see*
- THE SACRAMENT OF REGENERATION: THE DOCTRINE OF HOLY BAPTISM
- TWO LETTERS TO THE LORD BISHOP OF ONTARIO ON THE QUESTION, IS LAY BAPTISM VALID?

FOREST CLUB ANNUAL / Nebraska. College of Agriculture – n.1-6. 1909-15 – 1,5 – us Spaulding [634]

FOREST ECOLOGY AND MANAGEMENT – v1-9. 1978-84 – 1,5,6,13 – sz Elsevier [634]

Forest, Edmund William *see* VELLENAUX: A NOVEL

FOREST ENTOMOLOGY / Gillanders, A T – Edinburgh, London, 1908.xxii,422p. Z/1285/2 – 8 – ne IDC [590]

FOREST ESTIMATION AND YIELD PREDICTION – 1980 – it F.A.O. [634]

FOREST FIRE CONTROL / Clarke, B & Show, SB – 2nd printing 1978 – 110p – it F.A.O. [634]

FOREST FIRES IN NORTHERN CANADA / Bell, Robert – Washington, DC: Gibson, 1889. 03552. (Pre-1900 Canadiana) – 9 – cn C.I.H.M. [971]

THE FOREST FLORA OF NORTH-WEST AND CENTRAL INDIA / Stewart, J L & Brandis, D – 7319. 1874 – 9 – ne IDC [580]

A FOREST FLORA OF THE PUNJAB WITH HAZARA AND DELHI / Parker, R N – Lahore. 1918. B-5345 2 – 8 – ne IDC [580]

FOREST GROVE EXPRESS – Forest Grove, OR. -w. 12 Jan 1916-19 Sept 1918. 1 roll – 1 – us U.O. Library [071]

FOREST GROVE INDEPENDENT – Forest Grove OR. Apr 5 12 19, May 3 24 1873, Aug 23 Nov 1 1873, Apr 2 23 July 2 9 Oct 1 1874 + – 1 – us U.O. Library [071]

FOREST GROVE MONTHLY – Forest Grove OR., Sep 1869 – 1 – us U.O. Library [071]

FOREST GROVE PRESS – Forest Grove, OR. -w. 20 Jan 1910-19 Mar 1914. 1 roll – 1 – us U.O. Library [071]

FOREST GROVE TIMES – Forest Grove OR. Feb 13 1891-June 22 1899 + – 1 – us U.O. Library [071]

FOREST GROVE TIMES – Forest Grove, OR. -w. 1891-94, 1899-1909 – 1 – 113.00 – us Oregon Hist [071]

FOREST HEIGHTS BAPTIST CHURCH. ATHENS, GEORGIA : CHURCH RECORDS – 1984-87 – 1 – 5.00 – us Baptist [240]

FOREST HILL AND SYDENHAM EXAMINER – (South London Advertiser). London. -w. 1895-1960. (42 reels) – 1 – uk British Libr Newspaper [072]

FOREST HILL BAPTIST CHURCH. FOREST HILL, LOUISIANA : CHURCH RECORDS – 1899-1985 – 1 – 60.03 – us Baptist [240]

FOREST IMPROVEMENTS BY THE CCC – Washington, DC: US GPO, 1939 – us Res Libr [634]

FOREST INDUSTRIES – v1- 1889- 1; v98- 5,6; v102- 9 – us UMI [634]

FOREST INFLUENCES : AN INTRODUCTION TO ECOLOGICAL FORESTRY – 1978 – 307p – it F.A.O. [634]

Forest, J H de *see* SUNRISE IN THE SUNRISE KINGDOM

FOREST JOURNAL – Forest, Ohio. 1920-23 – 2r – 1 – $32.50r – us Archival [071]

FOREST LEGISLATION IN SELECTED AFRICAN COUNTRIES – 1986 – 462p – it F.A.O. [340]

FOREST LIEU SELECTION DOCKET REGISTERS / U.S. General Land Office – 6 rolls. T1169 – 1 – us Nat'l Archives [310]

FOREST NEWS – Forest, Ohio. 1877-78 – 1r – 1 – $32.50r – us Archival [071]

FOREST OF DEAN EXAMINER – Cinderford and Blakeney. England. -w. 2 Aug 1873-5 Oct 1877. (3 reels) – 1 – uk British Libr Newspaper [072]

THE FOREST OF HERMANSTADT. A MELODRAMA, IN TWO ACTS / Jouve, J – (Translated from French by Thomas Dibdin. Arranged for pianoforte) – London: Clementi, Banger, Hyde, Collard & Davis, [180-?] – 1 – us Sibley [780]

FOREST PARK BAPTIST CHURCH. GAINESVILLE, FLORIDA : CHURCH RECORDS – 1947-74. Formerly Immanuel Baptist Church, 1947-54. Disbanded in 1974. 1126p – 1 – 50.67 – us Baptist [240]

FOREST PRESERVATION IN CANADA / Drummond, Andrew Thomas – Montreal: s.n., 1885 (Montreal: "Witness"). 02768. (Pre-1900 Canadiana) – 9 – cn C.I.H.M. [971]

FOREST PRESS – Tionesta, PA., 1962-1973 – 13 – $25.00r – us I.M.R. [071]

FOREST PRODUCT NEWS – Portland, OR. 15 Feb 1944-29 Nov 1947. 1 roll – 1 – us U.O. Library [071]

FOREST PRODUCT NEWS – Portland OR. Feb 15 1944-Nov 29 1947 – 1 – us U.O. Library [071]

FOREST PRODUCTS – it F.A.O. [634]

FOREST PRODUCTS : WORLD OUTLOOK PROJECTIONS 1985-2000 – 1986 – 101p – it F.A.O. [338]

FOREST PRODUCTS JOURNAL – Proceedings v1-13 1947-1963 – 1,5,6 – us Princeton Micro [670]

FOREST PRODUCTS PRICES 1961-1980 – 1981 – 113p – it F.A.O. [338]

FOREST PRODUCTS PRICES 1962-1981 – 1982 – 115p – it F.A.O. [339]

FOREST PRODUCTS PRICES 1963-1982 – 1983 – 125p – it F.A.O. [339]

FOREST PRODUCTS PRICES 1965-1984 – 1985 – 120p – it F.A.O. [339]

FOREST PRODUCTS PRICES, 1969-1988 – 1990 – 238p – it F.A.O. [338]

FOREST PRODUCTS PRICES, 1971-1990 – 1992 – 254p – it F.A.O. [650]

FOREST PRODUCTS: WORLD OUTLOOK PROJECTIONS : PRODUCT AND COUNTRY TABLES 1987-2000 – 1988 – 357p – it F.A.O. [338]

FOREST PROTECTION AND THE TARIFF ON LUMBER: SPIRIT OF THE PRESS – New York: s.n., 1883. 03150. (Pre-1900 Canadiana) – 9 – cn C.I.H.M. [971]

FOREST REPUBLICAN – Tionesta, PA. -w 1889-1894; 1895-1921; 1924-1932 – 13 – $25.00r – us I.M.R. [071]

FOREST RESEARCH SERIES / Clemson University. Department of Forestry – No.19-35. 1970-82. 1 reel – 1,5 – us Spaulding [630]

FOREST RESOURCES IN THE ASIA AND FAR EAST REGION – 1976 – 104p – it F.A.O. [634]

FOREST RESOURCES IN THE EUROPEAN REGION – 1976 – 35p – it F.A.O. [634]

FOREST RESOURCES OF TROPICAL AFRICA, PART 1 : REGIONAL SYNTHESIS. TECHNICAL REPORT NO. 2 – 1981 – 115p – it F.A.O. [634]
FOREST RESOURCES OF TROPICAL AFRICA, PART 2 : COUNTRY BRIEFS. TECHNICAL REPORT NO. 2 – 1981 – 590p – it F.A.O. [634]
FOREST RESOURCES OF TROPICAL ASIA (F.A.O./U.N.E.P.) : TECHNICAL REPORT NO. 3 – 1981 – 484p – it F.A.O. [634]
FOREST REVENUE SYSTEMS IN DEVELOPING COUNTRIES : THEIR ROLE IN INCOME GENERATION AND FOREST MANAGEMENT STRATEGIES – 1983 – 283p – it F.A.O. [330]
FOREST REVIEW – Forest, Ohio. 1879-1960 – 11r – 1 – $32.50r – us Archival [071]
FOREST SCIENCE RESEARCH NOTES / Texas A & M University. Department of Forest Science – No.1-3. 1972-76. 1 fiche – 9 – us Spaulding [634]
FOREST TREE IMPROVEMENT : REPORT ON THE FAO/DANIDA TRAINING COURSE ON FOREST TREE IMPROVEMENT. MERIDA, VENEZUELA, 1980 – 1985 – 278p – it F.A.O. [634]
FOREST TREE SEED DIRECTORY 1975 – 1975 – 283p – it F.A.O. [634]
FOREST TREES OF THE PACIFIC SLOPE / Sudworth, G B – 7623 2. 1908 – 8 – ne IDC [634]
FOREST UTILIZATION CONTRACTS ON PUBLIC LAND – 1977 – 209p – it F.A.O. [634]
FOREST WILDLIFE INVESTIGATIONS / Minnesota. College of Agriculture. Cloquet Forest Research Center – 1956-62 – 1,5,6 – us Spaulding [639]
FORESTER *see* AMERICAN FORESTS
THE FORESTERS : ROBIN HOOD AND MAID MARIAN / Tennyson, Alfred, Lord – London, New York: Macmillan, 1892 – 1 roll – 1 – 1-55879-503-0 – uk Libr Preservation [810]
FORESTER'S GUIDE FOR COMMUNITY INVOLVEMENT IN UPLAND CONSERVATION : WITH SPECIAL REFERENCE TO THE ASIA AND PACIFIC REGION – 1986 – 130p – it F.A.O. [333]
FOREST-GARDEN FARMS OF KANDY, SRI LANKA – 1992 – 126p – it F.A.O. [630]
Forestie, Emerand *see*
– HISTOIRE DE L'IMPRIMERIE ET DE LA LIBRAIRIE A MONTAUBAN: BIBLIOGRAPHIE MONTALBANAISE
– RECUEIL DE TEXTES
LE FORESTIER = THE FORESTER – Ste-Cunegonde a Montreal, Canada. v1 n2. fev 1895 – 1r – 1 – Can$25.00 – cn Can Microfilming [073]
FORESTRY ABSTRACTS – v1-17. 1939-56 – 1,5,6 – us Princeton Micro [634]
FORESTRY AND FOOD SECURITY – 1989 – 136p – it F.A.O. [634]
FORESTRY AND IRRIGATION *see* AMERICAN FORESTS
FORESTRY AND RURAL DEVELOPMENT – 1981 – 38p – it F.A.O. [634]
FORESTRY BULLETIN / Clemson University. Department of Forestry – No.4-35.1970-82. 1 reel – 1,5 – us Spaulding [634]
FORESTRY DEPARTMENT SERIES / Alabama. Agricultural Experiment Station – no.1-2. 1 fiche – 9 – us Spaulding [634]
FORESTRY DEPARTMENTAL SERIES / Auburn University. Agricultural Experiment Station – No.1-11.1964-79. 1 reel – 1, 5 – us Spaulding [634]
FORESTRY EXTENSION METHODS – 1987 – 164p – it F.A.O. [634]
FORESTRY EXTENSION ORGANIZATION – 1986 2nd print 1987 – 177p – it F.A.O. [634]
FORESTRY FOR LOCAL COMMUNITY DEVELOPMENT – 1978 – 116p – it F.A.O. [634]
FORESTRY IN CHINA – 1982 – 322p – it F.A.O. [634]
FORESTRY MIMEOGRAPH / New Hampshire. Department of Forest Resources (also called Department of Forestry) – v1-6. 1954-57 – 1,5,6 – us Spaulding [634]
FORESTRY NOTE / Illinois. Department of Forestry – n.1-126. 1948-69 – 1, 5 – us Spaulding [634]
FORESTRY NOTES / Clemson University. Agricultural Extension Division – No.16-25. 1970-82. 1 reel – 1,5 – us Spaulding [634]
FORESTRY POLICIES IN EUROPE – 1988 – 289p – it F.A.O. [634]
FORESTRY POLICIES IN EUROPE : AN ANALYSIS – 1989 – 126p – it F.A.O. [634]
FORESTRY PUBLICATIONS / Clemson University. Department of Forestry – 1,5 – us Spaulding [634]
FORESTRY RESEARCH NOTES / Wisconsin. College of Agricultural and Life Sciences. Dept. of Forestry – n.1-147, 152-Apr 1969 – 1,5 – us Spaulding [634]
FORESTRY TECHNICAL NOTE / New Hampshire. Department of Forest Resources (also called Department of Forestry) – v1-14. 1965-68 – 1,5,6 – us Spaulding [634]
THE FORESTS AND GARDENS OF SOUTH INDIA / Cleghorn, H F C – London. 1861. B-7308 1 – 9 – ne IDC [580]
THE FORESTS OF CANADA / Bell, Robert – Montreal: Gazette Print. Co., 1886. 00102. (Pre-1900 Canadiana) – 9 – cn C.I.H.M. [971]
FORESTS PROTECTED BY THE CCC – Washington, DC: US GPO, 1938 – us Res Libr [634]
FORESTS, WATERS, SOILS AND MINERALS *see* AMERICAN FORESTS
LA FORET DU HAUT-NIGER / Cousturier, Lucie – Bruges: Les Cahiers d'Aujourd'hui, 1923 – 1 – us Res Libr [910]
LA FORET MAROCAINE / Morocco. Ministere de l'Agriculture – 1960. BNE-3065 1 – 9 – ne IDC [630]
LA FORET PERILLEUSE OU LES BRIGANDS DE LA CALABRE / Loaisel-Treogate – (French Theatre Series). Paris. Fages. 1812 – 9 – fr Hachette [820]
FORETAGS EKONOMI – v1- 1921- 1; v55- 5,6,9 – us UMI [330]
FOREWARNED AGAINST FASCISM – London: Anti-fascist Democratic Action. v2-9. 1978-81 – 1 – us U.W. Library [073]
FORFAR DISPATCH – 1 – £42.00r – uk Scot News [072]
FORFAR HERALD – (Angus Herald). Forfar. Scotland. -w. 4 Apr 1884-29 Sep 1933. (50 reels) – 1 – uk British Libr Newspaper [072]
FORFAR REFORMER – Forfar. Scotland. -w. 24 Feb 1883-5 Jan 1885. (27 ft) – 1 – uk British Libr Newspaper [072]
FORFAR REVIEW – Forfar. Scotland. -w. 5 Jan 1912-16 Apr 1926. (5 reels) – 1 – uk British Libr Newspaper [072]
FORFARSHIRE, 1837 : BRITISH ISLES CENSUS DIRECTORIES PROJECT, SCOTLAND. VOL 39 – 1mf – 9 – A$9.00 – at Vine [941]
FORFARSHIRE (DUNDEE AND MONTROSE), 1820 : BRITISH ISLES CENSUS DIRECTORIES PROJECT, SCOTLAND. VOL 66 – 1mf – 9 – A$9.00 – at Vine [941]
LA FORGE = THE FORGE – (Index to end of jun 1982. English version entitled: The Forge nov 1975- dec 1982 with index to end of dec 1981 3r Can$75.00) – Montreal, nov 1975-avr 1983 – 3r – 1 – Can$75.00r – cn Can Microfilming [072]
Forgeron, Jean Baptiste *see* LE PROTECTORAT EN AFRIQUE OCCIDENTALE FRANCAISE ET LES CHEFS INDIGENES
Forget, J *see* DE VITA ET SCRIPTIS APHRAATIS, SAPIENTIS PERSAE
Forget, L-J *see* LE JOURNAL
FORGET-ME-NOT – 1823-47 – 112mf – 9 – £705.00 – uk Chadwyck [800]
FORGING HIS CHAINS : THE AUTOBIOGRAPHY OF GEORGE BIDWELL... / Bidwell, George – Hartford: S S Scranton & Co, 1888 – 7mf – 9 – $10.50 – LLMC 92-172 – us L.L.M.C. [340]
FORGIVENESS AND LAW : GROUNDED IN PRINCIPLES, INTERPRETED BY HUMAN ANALOGIES / Bushnell, Horace – New York:Scribner, Armstrong, 1874 – 1mf – 9 – 0-8370-3066-8 – 1985-1066 – us A.T.L.A. [230]
THE FORGIVENESS OF SINS AND OTHER SERMONS / Smith, George Adam – New York: A C Armstrong, 1904 – 1mf – 9 – 0-8370-9745-2 – 1986-3745 – us A.T.L.A. [240]
FORGOTTEN HEROES OF DELAWARE / Pub, Emerson W – Cambridge, Deltos Publ. Co., 1969. Delaware Reel 2. (The Cox Library Collection) – 5 – us Americana [978]
THE FORGOTTEN MAN AND OTHER ESSAYS / Sumner, William Graham – 1918. 561p. 2 fiches (24x) – 9 – 1.00f – at Libertarian Micro [320]
FORGOTTEN PEOPLE – Canada, 1972-74 – 1 – cn Commonwealth Micro [072]
FORK SHOALS BAPTIST CHURCH (CALLED HORSE CREEK, 1789-1799). GREENVILLE COUNTY. SOUTH CAROLINA : CHURCH RECORDS – 1814-1990, incomplete. WMU Minutes 1978-1986. History 1777 – 1 – $92.07 – us Baptist [240]
FORK SHOALS CHURCH. FORK SHOALS, SOUTH CAROLINA : CHURCH RECORDS – 1857-99 – 1 – 19.20 – us Baptist [240]
Forkel, J N *see*
– ALLGEMEINE GESCHICHTE DER MUSIK
– ALLGEMEINE LITERATUR DER MUSIK
– ALLGEMEINE LITERATUR DER MUSIK...
– ALLGEMEINE LITERATUR DER MUSIK. SYSTEMATISCH GEORDNET. ERSTER UND ZWEYTER THEIL
– MUSIKALISCHER ALMANACH FUER DEUTSCHLAND AUF DAS JAHR 1782-1784, 1789
– MUSIKALISCH-KRITISCHE BIBLIOTHEK
Forkel, JN *see*
– UEBER DIE THEORIE DER MUSIK
– UEBER DIE THEORIE DER MUSIK, INSOFERN SIE LIEBHABERN UND KENNERN NOTHWENDIG UND NUESSLICH IST
Forkner *see* HISTORICAL SKETCHES AND REMINISCENCES OF MADISON COUNTY
FORKS OF ELKHORN CHURCH / Darnell, Ermina Jett – 340p – 1 – 11.90 – us Baptist [240]
FORKS OF OTTER CREEK BAPTIST CHURCH. HARDIN COUNTY. KENTUCKY : CHURCH RECORDS – July 1827-1904 – 1 – $14.04 – us Baptist [240]
Forlong, James George Roche *see* SHORT STUDIES IN THE SCIENCE OF COMPARATIVE RELIGIONS, EMBRACING ALL THE RELIGIONS OF ASIA
FORM – London, 1921-22 – 1r – 1 – £60.00 – uk Chadwyck [760]
FORM UND GESCHICHTE : STUDIE ZU EINIGEN METHODISCH ZENTRALEN ELEMENTEN DER KRITIK DER POLITISCHEN OEKONOMIE VON KARL MARX / Mueller, Ulrich – Heidelberg, 1977 – 3mf – 9 – DM76.00 – 3-89349-387-5 – gw Hänsel [320]
FORM UND UEBERLIEFERUNG DER LUKAS-HOMILIEN DES ORIGENES (T.U.U. 4-47/3) / Rauer, M – Leipzig, 1932 – 2mf – 9 – ne Slangenburg [240]
FORMA TESTAMENTELOR IN DREPTUL INTERNATIONAL PRIVAT / Busdugan, C N – Buccuresti, 1900 – 1mf – 1 – ILM-3322/1 – ne IDC [327]
FORMA Y SENTIDO DE LA RESISTENCIA UNIVERSITARIA DE OCTUBRE 1945 / Durelli, Augusto J – Buenos Aires, 1945 – 1 – CSUXADH2546-B – us Hoover Inst Photo [320]
FORMACAO TERRITORIAL DO BRASIL; ORIGEM E EVOLUCAO / Dias, Demosthenes de Oliveira – Rio de Janeiro: No Loja Carlos Ribeiro, 1956. 137p. illus. With: Para e Amazonas by J. Mattos; Los Capitales Yanquis en la Argentina by L.V. Sommi; Passos dos Lusiadas Estuados by G. Vasconcel los Abreu.Incl. bibliog. 1 reel. 1273 – 1 – us U.W. Library [972]
FORMACION DE LA NACIONALIDADCCHILENA. SANTIAGO DE CHILE, 1943 / Amunategui Solar, Domingo – Madrid: Razon y Fe, 1944 – 1 – sp Bibl Santa Ana [972]
FORMACION DE LAS FALANGES JUVENILES DE FRANCO / Montes, Jose – Caceres: Tip. El Noticiero – sp Bibl Santa Ana [946]
LA FORMACION PROFESIONAL DEL JURISTA / Cuellar Grajera, Antonio – Badajoz: Imp. Dip. Provincial, 1965. Sep. REE – sp Bibl Santa Ana [340]
FORMACION RELIGIOSA DE JOVENES. 2ND ED. TRAD. DE ANTONIO SANCHO NEBOT / Toth, Tihamez – Madrid: Razon y Fe, 2v. 1944 – 1 – sp Bibl Santa Ana [240]
FORMAL OPINIONS (A-G) / Pennsylvania – 1889-1950; 1931-42. 7 reels – 1 – $35.00r – us Trans-Media [340]
DAS FORMALPRINZIP DES PROTESTANTISMUS : NEUE PROLEGOMENA ZU EINER EVANGELISCHEN DOGMATIK / Resch, Alfred – Berlin: F Berggold, 1876 – 1mf – 9 – 0-8370-8782-1 – 1986-2782 – us A.T.L.A. [240]
FORMAN CHRISTIAN COLLEGE MONTHLY – (Many issues missing. Title varies) – 1908-34 – 2r – 1 – ATLA S0692 – us A.T.L.A. [073]
Forman, H Buxton *see* LETTERS OF EDWARD JOHN TRELAWNY. EDITED WITH A BRIEF INTRODUCTION AND NOTES BY H. BUXTON FORMAN, C.B.
Forman, Maurice Buxton *see* GEORGE MEREDITH
THE FORMATION OF A MINISTRY TO THE PARENTS OF INFANTS. 1981 / Forder, Winter Rand – 1 – $5.28 – us Baptist [240]
THE FORMATION OF CHRISTIAN CHARACTER : A CONTRIBUTION TO CHRISTIAN ETHICS / Bruce, William S – (Includes bibliographical references & index) – Edinburgh: T & T Clark, 1908 – 1mf – 9 – 0-8370-6090-7 – 1986-0090 – us A.T.L.A. [240]
THE FORMATION OF THE GOSPEL TRADITION / Taylor, Vincent – 1935 – 9 – $10.00 – us I.R.C. [240]
FORMATION OF THE NEW TESTAMENT / Ferris, George Hooper – Philadelphia: Griffith & Row., 1907. 1 fiche – 9 – us A.T.L.A. [240]
THE FORMATION OF VEGETABLE MOULD : TROUGH THE ACTION OF WORMS, WITH OBSERVATIONS ON THEIR HABITS / Darwin, Charles – London: John Murray, 1881 – 1 roll – 1 – 1-55879-793-9 – uk Libr Preservation [580]
LA FORMATION PROFESSIONELLE PAR SES PROPRES MOYENS DANS LES PAYS EN VOIE DE DEVELOPPEMENT / Hauet, D – Rabat. 1961. BNE-3055 1 – 9 – ne IDC [303]
LA FORMATION PROFESSIONNELLE EN ALGERIE / Algeria. Ministere de l'Information et de la Culture – 1968. BNE-8735 1 – 9 – ne IDC [303]
FORMATION PROFESSIONNELLE: PROJET DE PROGRAMME POUR LA PERIODE QUADRIENNALE 1970-1978 / Algeria. Ministere du Travail – 1969. BNE-8736 1 – 9 – ne IDC [338]
FORMATIONS – 1984- – 1,5,6,9 – us UMI [500]
FORMATIVE INFLUENCES OF LEGAL DEVELOPMENT / Kocourek, Albert & Wigmore, John H – Boston: Little-Brown, 1918 – 8mf – 9 – $12.00 – LLMC 95-171 – us L.L.M.C. [340]
LA FORME DES PRIERES ET CHANTS ECCLESIASTIQUES / Calvin, Johannes – (Facsimile de l'edition originale d'apres l'exemplare de la Bibliotheque de Stuttgart: Kassel-Bale, 1959) – Geneve, 1542 – 3mf – 8 – Dfl13.00 – ne Slangenburg [240]
FORME DI LEPIDOTTERI ESCLUSIVAMENTE ITALIANE / Perlini, R – Bergamo, 1905. 77p, 6 pls. Z-1539/2 – 8 – ne IDC [590]
FORME GENERALE ET PARTICULIERE DE LA CONVOCATION ET DE LA TENUE DES ASSEMBLEES NATIONALES OU ETATS GENERAUX DE FRANCE, JUSTIFIEE PAR PIECES AUTHENTIQUES / Lalource & Duval – Recueilli par Lalource et Duval. Paris (1-3). 1789 – 1 – fr A.C.R.P.P. [324]
DIE FORMELLE NATUR DER VOELKERRECHTLICHEN MANDATE... / Fischer, F – Tuebingen, 1935 – 2mf – 1 – ILM-1968/1 – ne IDC [327]
FORMEN DER REGIONALEN ZUSAMMENARBEIT AM SCHWARZEN MEER UND IN ZENTRALASIEN VOR DEM HINTERGRUND EUROPAEISCHER INTEGRATIONSERFAHRUNGEN : GEOSTRATEGISCHE IMPLIKATIONEN FUER DIE AUSSENPOLITIK DER TUERKEI / Waltmann, Frank – 1995 – 3mf – 9 – DM98.00 – 3-8267-2276-0 – gw Hänsel [320]
FORMEN UND MOTIVE IN DEN APOKRYPHEN APOSTELGESCHICHTEN (T.U.U. 4-48/1) / Blumenthal, M – Leipzig, 1933 – 3mf – 9 – ne Slangenburg [240]
DIE FORMENLEHRE BEI JOHN LYLY / Kneile, Karl – Tuebingen, 1914 – 2mf – DM62.00 – 3-8267-3038-0 – gw Hänsel [400]
THE FORMER ESKIMO SETTLEMENTS ON THE EAST COAST OF GREENLAND BETWEEN SCORESBYSUND AND THE ANGMAGSSALIK DISTRICT / Amdrup, G – BN-103 2. 1909 – 8 – ne IDC [305]
FORMERLY PHYSICS OF FLUIDS B *see* PHYSICS OF PLASMAS
LES FORMES ANIMALES DANS L'ORNEMENTATION POPULAIRE EN BULGARIE AU 19E ET AU DEBUT DU 20E SIECLE / Ribeyrol, M – 9 – F60.00 – fr Ethnologie [949]
Formey *see*
– HISTOIRE DE L'ACADEMIE
– PRINCIPES DU DROIT DE LA NATURE ET DES GENS

Formey, J H *see* AN ECCLESIASTICAL HISTORY FROM THE BIRTH OF CHRIST TO THE PRESENT TIME, WRITTEN ORIGINALLY IN FRENCH...
FORMIROVANIE BURZHUAZII V POLITICHESKUIU SILU V SIBIRI / Mosina, IG – Tomsk, 1978. 170p – 2mf – 9 – ne IDC [320]
FORMOSAN TREES INDIGENOUS TO THE ISLAND / Kanehira, R – Formosa. 1936. B-147 2 – 8 – ne IDC [580]
FORMS FOR MISSOURI PLEADING / Pattison, Everett Wilson – St. Louis, Mo.: Gilbert, 1891. 383p. LL-1310 – 1 – us L of C Photodup [340]
FORMS FOR VIRGINIA AND WEST VIRGINIA ANNOTATED, INCLUDING STATUTORY, COMMON LAW AND EQUITY, COMMERCIAL, CORPORATION, AND CRIMINAL FORMS / Gregory, George Craghead – 2d ed. Charlottesville, VA: Michie, 1925. 1390p. LL-697 – 1 – us L of C Photodup [340]
FORMS IN CIVIL ACTIONS AND PROCEEDINGS IN THE COURTS OF RECORD OF WISCONSIN / Bryant, Edwin Eustace – 2d ed. Madison, Democrat, 1892. 408 p. LL-819 – 1 – us L of C Photodup [340]
FORMS IN CONVEYANCING, COMPRISING PRECEDENTS FOR ORDINARY USE, AND CLAUSES ADAPTED TO SPECIAL AND UNUSUAL CASES / Jones, Leonard Augustus – Boston, Houghton, Mifflin, 1886. 826 p. LL-89 – 1 – us L of C Photodup [340]
FORMS OF ACKNOWLEDGMENTS FOR DEEDS AND OTHER INSTRUMENTS USED IN THE STATES AND TERRITORIES OF THE UNITED STATES. / Reardon, George Evett – Baltimore, Cox, 1882. 140 p. LL-1328 – 1 – us L of C Photodup [340]
FORMS OF CIVIL PROCEDURE ADAPTED TO PRACTICE AND PLEADING UNDER THE CODE OF CIVIL PROCEDURE OF THE STATE OF NEW YORK / Lansing, William – Albany, Banks, 1885-88. 3v LL-501 – 1 – us L of C Photodup [340]
FORMS OF CODE PLEADING FOR NEBRASKA, KANSAS AND OKLAHOMA, FULLY ANNOTATED / Campbell, William S – St. Louis: Thomas, 1912-27. 3v. LL-1278 – 1 – us L of C Photodup [340]
THE FORMS OF HEBREW POETRY / Gray, George Buchanan – 1915 – 9 – $12.00 – us I.R.C. [470]
FORMS OF OATHS FOR USE IN THE U.S. DISTRICT COURTS / Crawford, Kenneth C – Washington: FJC, 1976 – 1mf – 9 – $1.50 – LLMC 95-387 – us L.L.M.C. [340]
FORMS OF PLEADINGS IN CIVIL AND CRIMINAL CASES. / Matthews, William Baynham – Richmond, Va.: Randolph & English, 1873. 395p. LL-700 – 1 – us L of C Photodup [340]
FORMS OF PROCEDURE IN THE COURTS OF ADMIRALTY OF THE UNITED STATES OF AMERICA / Pugh, Edward Fox – 2nd, rev. ed. Philadelphia: Johnson, 1903. 376p. LL-1417 – 1 – us L of C Photodup [340]
FORMULAE MEDICAE / Llorens y Masdevall, F – Madrid, 1789 – 1mf – 9 – sp Cultura [610]
FORMULAIRE DE LA PRIERE EN FAMILLE – Ed. Sans Renvois, 32e Mille. Quebec: Editions de l'Action Sociale Catholique, 1924 – 2mf – 9 – Can$4.50 – cn Bibl Nat [240]
FORMULAIRE DE PRIERES A L'USAGE DES ELEVES DES URSULINES – s.l.: s.n., 1875 (Quebec: C. Darveau). 03151. (Pre-1900 Canadiana) – 9 – cn C.I.H.M. [971]
FORMULAIRE DES CONSULATS / Borel, F – Spb, 1808 – 2mf – 9 – ILM-138/1 – ne IDC [327]
FORMULAIRE DU CODE MUNICIPAL DE LA PROVINCE DE QUEBEC: SUIVI D'UNE TABLE ALPHABETIQUE ET DE TOUTES LES FORMULES NECESSAIRES POUR L'ORGANISATION ET LE FONCTIONNEMENT DANS UNE PAROISSE, D'UNE COMPAGNIE D'ASSURANCE MUTUELLE CONTRE LE FEU / Coupal, Maximilien – Montreal: Institution des sourds-muets, 1897. 00310. (Pre-1900 Canadiana) – 9 – cn C.I.H.M. [971]
FORMULARIOS PARA LOS FISCALES MUNICIPALES Y COMARCALES / Agundez, Antonio – Caceres: Tip. Extremadura, s.a. – sp Bibl Santa Ana [330]
A FORMULARY OF THE PAPAL PENITENTIARY IN THE THIRTEENTH CENTURY / ed by Lea, Henry Charles – Philadelphia: Lea Brothers, 1892 – 1mf – us A.T.L.A. [240]
THE FORMULATION AND USE OF A STAFF POLICY MANUAL WITHIN THE GREENE COUNTY BAPTIST ASSOCIATION / Joslin, James Elliott – 1981 – 1 – 5.04 – us Baptist [240]
FORMY EKONOMICHESKOI SAMOPOMOSHCHI V OBLASTI REMESLENNOGO TRUDA / Zak, L S – Spb., 1912 – 2mf – 9 – COR-29/1 – ne IDC [334]
FORMY I METODY KOLLEKTIVNOGO INSTRUKTIROVANIIA V KOOPERATSII : METOD. RUKOVODSTVO PO ORG. I PROVEDENIIU KOLLEKTIV. INSTRUKTIROVANIIA / ed by Toranskii, M G – Khar'kov, 1929 – 2mf – 9 – COR-276/1 – ne IDC [334]
FORMY KOLONIAL'NOI ZAVISIMOSTI / Chernogolovkin, N V – Moscow, 1956. 214p. BR-8549/1 – 9 – ne IDC [340]
Forner Segarra, Juan Pablo *see*
- AMOR DE LA PATRIA
- EL ASNO ERUDITO
- CARTA DE BARTOLO SOBRINO DE DON FERNANDO PEREZ
- CONVERSACIONES FAMILIARES ENTRE EL CENSOR
- COTEJO DE LAS EGLOGAS QUE HA PREMIADO LA REAL ACADEMIA DE LA LENGUA
- DEFENSA DE DON FERNANDO PEREZ... PARACUELLOS
- DISCURSO ANTISOFISTICO EXTRACTADO DEL HOMBRE
- DISCURSOS FILOSOFICOS SOBRE EL HOMBRE
- LA ESCUELA DE LA AMISTAD O EL FILOSOFO ENAMORADO
- INTRODUCCION...QUE SE RECITO...SEVILLA
- OBRAS
- ORACION APOLOGERICA POR LA ESPANA Y SU MERITO LITERARIO
- ORACION APOLOGETICA POR LA ESPANA Y SU MERITO LITERARIO
- ORACION APOLOGETICA POR LA ESPANA... LITERARIO
- PASATIEMPO DE...RESPUESTA A SU ORACION APOLOGETICA
- PASATIEMPO EN RESPUESTA A LAS OBJECIONES A SU ORACION
- LA PAZ. CANTO HEROICO
- REFLEXIONES...ESCRIBIR LA HISTORIA DE ESPANA

Forner y Segarra, Agustin F *see* ANTIGUEDADES DE MERIDA
Forneri, R S *see* THE UNITED EMPIRE LOYALISTS: AND THE MEMORIAL CHURCH, ADOLPNUSTOWN, ONTARIO: A SKETCH
Forney, Eugene *see* TAILLE ET CULTURE DU ROSIER: SUIVIES DE LA TAILLE DES ARBUTES D'AGREMENT
Foronda, Valentin de *see* MISCELANEA O COLECCION DE VARIOS DISCURSOS
FORORD : MORSKABSLAESNING FOR ENKELTE STAENDER EFTER TID OG LEILIGHED / Notabene, Nicolaus – Kjobenhavn: C.A. Reitzel, 1844 – 1mf – us A.T.L.A. [190]
FORORT VAST – Lerum, Sweden. 1979-80 – 1 – sw Kungliga [072]
FOROYS = AVANT-GARDE – (Monthly) – Mexico, MX. no 1. 1941; no 13/14. 1943 – 1r – 1 – Can$25.00 – cn Can Microfilming [072]
FORPOSTEN – Goteborg, Sweden. 1865-1919 – 20r – 1 – sw Kungliga [072]
Forrer, E *see* DIE PROVINZEINTEILUNG DES ASSYRISCHEN REICHES
FORRES, ELGIN AND NAIRN GAZETTE – 1 – £42.00r – uk Scot News [072]
FORRES, ELGIN & NAIRN GAZETTE – Scotland. -w. 5 Jan 1844-Dec 1883. 11 reels – 1 – uk British Libr Newspaper [072]
Forrest, David W *see* THE AUTHORITY OF CHRIST
Forrest, Edmund William *see* NED FORTESCUE, OR, ROUGHING IT THROUGH LIFE: A STORY FOUNDED ON FACT
Forrest, James *see* RAILWAY CONSTRUCTION AND WORKING...: WITH AN ABSTRACT OF THE DISCUSSION UPON THE PAPERS
Forrest, T *see* A VOYAGE TO NEW GUINEA, AND THE MOLUCCAS, FROM BALAMBANGAN
Forrester, Alexander *see* THE TEACHER'S TEXT BOOK
Forrester, George *see* HISTORICAL AND BIOGRAPHICAL ALBUM OF THE CHIPPEWA VALLEY
Forrester, Henry *see* CHRISTIAN UNITY AND THE HISTORIC EPISCOPATE
FORS CLAVIGERA : LETTERS TO THE WORKMEN AND LABOURERS OF GREAT BRITAIN / Ruskin, John – Orpington, Kent: G. Allen, 1871-1884 – 4 rolls – 1 – 1-55879-796-3 – uk Libr Preservation [860]
DAS FORSCHENDE ORCHESTRE, ODER DESSELBEN DRITTE EROEFFNUNG / Mattheson, J – 1721 – 9 – us Sibley [780]
FORSCHUNGEN ZUR GESCHICHTE DES NEUTESTAMENTLICHEN KANONS UND DER ALTKIRCHLICHEN LITERATUR / Zahn, Theodor – Teil I-X. Erlangen, etc., 1881-1929. No more published. Film Mas C 480 – 1 – us H.U. Library [240]
FORSCHUNGEN ZUR KULTUR- UND LITTERATURGESCHICHTE BAYERNS – Muenchen, Z. Franzscher Verlag. 1.-5. Buch; 1893-97. Film Mas C 272 – 1 – us H.U. Library [000]
DIE FORSCHUNGSREISE S.M.S. "GAZELLE" 1874 BIS 1876 / Schleinitz, GE G von – v3. Zoologie Und Geologie. 2829 2. 1889 – 8 – ne IDC [910]
DIE FORSCHUNGSREISE S.M.S. " PLANET" 1906-1907 / Planet. (Ship) – Pt. 3 contains: Brennecke, W. Ozeanographie. 2826 2 – 8 – ne IDC [910]
Forsell, K B J *see* BEITRAEGE ZUR KENNTNISS DER ANATOMIE UND SYSTEMATIK DER GLOEOLICHENEN
Forsey, G *see* UNIVERALISM AND ORTHODOXY: A COURSE OF EIGHT SERMONS
FORSIROVANIE REKI BELOI CHASTIAMI V ARMII VOSTOCHNOGO FRONTA VII UNE 1919 GODA / Eikhe, Genrikh Khristoforovich – Moskva: Gos. izd-vo, otdel voen. lit-ry, 1928 – 1 – CSUX88-B7668 – us Hoover Inst Photo [355]
FORSOG TIL DANSK OKONOMISK PLANTELAERE / Hornemann, J W – ed. 3. 2 V. Kjobenhavn. 1821-37. B-6517 2 – 8 – ne IDC [580]
FORSOG TIL EN AFHANDLING OM GRONLAENDERNES SKIKKE VED HVALFISKERIET / Glahn, H C – Kjoabenhavn, 1784. (Nye Saml. Kgl. Norske Vidnsk, Selsk. Skr. Bd. I, p. 275-296). BN-222 2 – 8 – ne IDC [910]
FORSOG TIL EN FROBEDRET GRONLANDSK GRAMMATICA; ANDET OPLAG / Fabricius, O – Kjobenhavn. 1801. BH-475 2 – 8 – ne IDC [430]
FORSOG TIL EN OVERSAETTELSE AF FORSTE BOG AF DAVIDS PSALMER = BIBLE. O.T. PSALMS NORWEGIAN PARAPHRASES 1854 : I EN VERSEFORM, HVORVED DE KUNNE SYNGES EFTER BEKJENDTE PSALMEMELODIER, A SOREN DAHL – Christiania: B C Fabritius, 1854 – 1r – 1 – us U.W. Library [240]
Forsskal, P *see*
- FLORA AEGYPTIACO-ARABICA
- HERBARIUM
- ICONES RERUM NATURALIUM QUAS IN ITINERE ORIENTALI DEPINGI CURAVIT P. FOSKAL

Forssman, Julius *see* J.K. LAVATER UND DIE RELIGIOESEN STROEMUNGEN DES ACHTZEHNTEN JAHRHUNDERTS
Forst de Battaglia *see* DER KAMPF MIT DEM DRACHEN
FORSTER AND DYCE COLLECTIONS FROM THE NATIONAL ART LIBRARY, VICTORIA AND ALBERT MUSEUM, LONDON – (Part Two: 18th Cent. MSS. Part Three: 19th Cent. MSS., Section A. Part Four: 19th Cent. MSS., Section B. Part Five: Charles Dickens MSS) – Part One: 16th and 17th Cent. MSS – 1 – us Primary [090]
Forster, Brix *see* DEUTSCH-OSTAFRIKA
Forster, Charles *see* THE LIFE OF JOHN JEBB, D.D., F.R.S., BISHOP OF LIMERICK, ARDFERT, AND AGHADOE
FORSTER FIRST (SOUTH FORSTER; SCITUATE) BAPTIST CHURCH. RHODE ISLAND : CHURCH RECORDS; 1769-1837 – Merged with Johnston First (Graniteville) General Six Principle in 1837. 24p – 1 – us Baptist [240]
Forster, G *see* HERVARIUM AUSTRALE GOTTINGAE
Forster, Henry L *see* BIBLICAL PSYCHOLOGY
Forster J G A *see* DICTIONARIVM HEBRAICVM NOVVM,...
Forster, J G A *see*
- CHARACTERES GENERUM PLANTARUM
- FLORULAE INSULARUM AUSTRALIUM PRODROMUS
- HERBARIUM AUSTRALE SEU CATALOGUS PLANTARUM EXSICCATARUM

Forster, J R *see*
- A CATALOGUE OF THE ANIMALS OF NORTH AMERICA, CONTAINING AN ENUMERATION OF KNOWN QUADRUPEDS, FISH
- CHARACTERES GENERUM PLANTARUM

Forster, Jonathan Langstaff *see* BIBLICAL PSYCHOLOGY
Forster, T I M *see* A SYNOPTICAL CATALOGUE OF BRITISH BIRDS
Forster, William Edward *see* IMPERIAL FEDERATION
DAS FORSTHAUS / Lorm, Hieronymus – Wien: Selbstverlag des Verfassers, 1864 – 1 – us U.W. Library [820]
DIE FORSTINSEKTEN MITTELEUROPAS / Escherich, K L – 2793 2. v. 1-5. Lacking v. 3-4. 1914-1942 – 8 – ne IDC [590]
Forstmann, Max Dieter *see* DER RECHTSSCHUTZ IM SCHWEDISCHEN VERWALTUNGSVERFAHREN
FORSTWISSENSCHAFTLICHES SCHRIFTSTELLER-LEXIKON / Ratzeburg, J T C – Berlin, 1872 – 10mf – ne IDC [574]
Forsyth Grant, Minnie *see* SCENES IN HAWAII, OR, LIFE IN THE SANDWICH ISLANDS
Forsyth, John R *see* JOURNAL
Forsyth, Peter Taylor *see*
- THE CHARTER OF THE CHURCH
- CHRIST ON PARNASSUS
- THE CRUCIALITY OF THE CROSS
- FAITH, FREEDOM, AND THE FUTURE
- THE PRINCIPLE OF AUTHORITY
- ROME, REFORM AND REACTION

Forsyth, William *see*
- ESSAYS CRITICAL AND NARRATIVE
- HISTORY OF TRIAL BY JURY
- HORTENSIUS THE ADVOCATE

Fort Adams, Mississippi *see* MISCELLANEOUS EARLY NEWSPAPERS
THE FORT BEAUFORT ADVOCATE AND GENERAL ADVERTISER – Fort Beaufort, South Africa. 23 Jul 1859-31 Dec 1874. 8 reels – 1, 16 diazo available at reduced price – sa SA Libr [072]
FORT CALHOUN CHRONICLE – Fort Calhoun, NE. -w. Jul. 1915-Nov. 1946 – 1 – us NE Hist [071]
Fort Dodge, KS *see* REPORTS AND JOURNALS OF SCOUTS AND MARCHES
FORT ERIE TIMES REVIEW – Ontario, CN. 1930-44 – 15r – 1 – cn Commonwealth Micro [072]
LE FORT ET LE CHATEAU SAINT-LOUIS (QUEBEC): ETUDE ARCHEOLOGIQUE ET HISTORIQUE / Gagnon, Ernest – Quebec: s.n., 1895 (Quebec: L. Brousseau). 03278. (Pre-1900 Canadiana) – 9 – cn C.I.H.M. [971]
FORT FREEDOM / Beckmann, Petr – 2p leaflet on his computer bulletin board – 9 – 1.00f – at Libertarian Micro [335]
FORT GEORGE HERALD – Fort George, British Columbia, CN. Aug 1910-Jan 1913 – 1r – 1 – cn Commonwealth Micro [072]
FORT GEORGE TRIBUNE – Fort George, British Columbia, CN. Nov 1909-May 1915 – 1r – 1 – cn Commonwealth Micro [072]
Fort, Gertrude von *see* LE PAPE DU GHETO. PARIS
FORT HARE PAPERS – (1985- . 5,6,9) – v1- . 1945- – 1 – us UMI [370]
Fort Harker. Kansas *see* JOURNAL OF POST SUTLER
Fort Larned. Kansas *see* RECORDS
Fort Leavenworth. Kansas *see* RECORDS
FORT MCLEOD COLLECTION – Alberta, CN. 1897-19 – 1r – 1 – cn Commonwealth Micro [072]
FORT MCMURRAY TODAY – Fort McMurray, Alberta, CN. Oct 1974- – 6r per yr – 1 – Can$55.00r – cn Commonwealth Micro [072]
FORT MEIGS: A CONDENSED HISTORY OF THE MOST IMPORTANT MILITARY POINT IN THE NORTHWEST, TOGETHER WITH SCENES AND INCIDENTS CONNECTED WITH THE SIEGES OF 1813 AND MINUTE DESCRIPTION OF THE OLD FORT AND ITS SURROUNDINGS, AS THEY NOW APPEAR / Averill, James P – Toledo, Ohio: Blade Print, 1886. 02206. (Pre-1900 Canadiana) – 9 – cn C.I.H.M. [971]
FORT MEIGS REVEILLE – Perrysburg, Ohio. 1848-51 – 1r – 1 – $32.50r – us Archival [071]
FORT MEYERS NEWS PRESS – Fort Meyers. Fl. 1932-51 – 1 – us P.K. Yonge [071]

FORT MILL FIRST BAPTIST CHURCH. YORK BAPTIST ASSOCIATION. FORT MILL, SOUTH CAROLINA : CHURCH RECORDS – 1966-73 – 1 – $79.83 – us Baptist [240]

FORT MITCHELL BAPTIST CHURCH. KENTUCKY : CHURCH RECORDS – 1924-67 – 1 – 114.39 – us Baptist [240]

Fort Motte. South Carolina. St. Matthew's (Episcopal) Church *see* VESTRY MINUTES

FORT SHAWNEE INCORPORATION SCRAPBOOK – 1958-1995 – 1r – 1 – $32.50r – us Archival [978]

FORT ST GEORGE GAZETTE / Madras. Presidency – 1962-1966 – 1 – us NY Public [324]

FORT WILLIAM DAILY-TIMES JOURNAL – Thunder Bay, 1893-1972 – 347r – 1 – cn Preston [971]

FORT WILLIAM JOURNAL AND THUNDER BAY MIN. NEWS – Thunder Bay, 1887-1907 – 6r – 1 – cn Preston [971]

FORT WORTH AND THE TEXAS NORTHWEST / Paddock, BB – Chicago: Lewis Publ. Co., 1922. 4v. Texas Reel 8. (The Cox Library Collection) – 5 – us Americana [978]

FORTAELLINGER AF DANMARKS KIRKEHISTORIE FRA 1517 TIL 1848 / Koch, L & Rordam, H F – Kobenhavn: G.E.C. Gad, 1889 – 1mf – us A.T.L.A. [240]

FORTECKNING OVER TALARE OCH MATERIAL TILL DE LOKALA SPANIENKOMMITTEERNA, AUGUSTI 1937 / Svenska Hjaelpkommitten for Spanien – Stockholm, 1937. Fiche W1218. (Blodgett Collection of Spanish Civil War Pamphlets) – 9 – us H.U. College Libr [946]

Forter, E Emma *see* HISTORY OF MARSHALL COUNTY

Fortescue, Adrian *see*
- THE LESSER EASTERN CHURCHES
- THE ORTHODOX EASTERN CHURCH

Fortescue, John William *see*
- THE GOVERNANCE OF ENGLAND
- STATE SOCIALISM AND THE COLLAPSE IN AUSTRALIA
- THE WRITING OF HISTORY

FORTGESETZTE BEITRAEGE ZUR NATURKUNDE – Berlin, 1765 – 3 – us Readex [500]

FORTGESETZTE NACHRICHTEN VON DEM ZUSTANDE DER WISSENSCHAFTEN UND KUENSTE IN DER KOENIGL DAENISCHEN REICHEN UND LAENDERN – Copenhagen & Leipzig. 1758-68 – 3 – us Readex [500]

FORTH – v105-125,no.3. 1940-Mar 1960 – 1 – us A.T.L.A. [073]

THE FORTH BRIDGE / Baker, Benjamin – Read at the British Association, Montreal, 1884. London, 1884. 00842. (Pre-1900 Canadiana) – 9 – cn C.I.H.M. [624]

Forti, A *see* ALGHI DI AUSTRALIA, TASMANIA E NUOVA ZELANDA RACCOLTE DAL G. CAPRA NEL 1908-1909

Forti, Augusto *see* SCIENTIFIC FORECASTING AND HUMAN NEEDS

Fortier, Alcee *see* LOUISIANA STUDIES: LITERATURE, CUSTOMS AND DIALECTS, HISTORY AND EDUCATION

Fortier, J H et al *see* LE NOUVELLISTE

Fortier, Marie-Marthe *see* BIBLIOGRAPHIE ANALYTIQUE DE L'OEUVRE DE I.-W. JONES, GEOLOGUE, DIRECTEUR DES SERVICES GEOLOGIQUES, MINISTERE DES RICHESSES NATURELLES

Fortier, Onesime Laurent *see* LE R. PERE VINCENT ROUTIER DE L'ORDRE DES FRERES PRECHEURS

Fortier, Suzanne *see* BIBLIOGRAPHIE DE LA POESIE CANADIENNE-FRANCAISE 1935-1958

LA FORTIFICATION DEMONSTREE ET REDUITE EN ART. / Errard, Jean – 1622. 70 ff., illus. (Architecture Series) – 9 – fr Hachette [720]

LES FORTIFICATIONS. / Ville, Antoine de – Lyon, P. Borde, 1640. 441p., illus. (Architecture Series) – 9 – fr Hachette [720]

FORTIFICATIONS AND GARRISON FORCES IN THE MANDATES BEFORE PEARL HARBOR, 1934-1941 / U.S. Army. Office of Military History – 1952 – 1 – 19.00 – us L of C Photodup [950]

DES FORTIFICATIONS ET ARTIFICES, ARCHITECTURE ET PERSPECTIVES. / Perret, Jacques – Paris, 1601, 60 ff., pl. (Architecture Series) – 9 – fr Hachette [720]

Fortin, Edouard *see* MON MAGAZIN

Fortin, Isabelle *see* BIBLIOGRAPHIE ANALYTIQUE DES TRAVAUX DE PAUL-EDOUARD GAGNON...

Fortin, J-A *see* LA RIPOSTE

Fortin, Pierre *see*
- LETTERS FROM HONORABLE P. FORTIN, M.P. ON THE TELEGRAPH AND SIGNAL SERVICE SYSTEM IN THE GULF OF ST LAWRENCE, ON THE UNITED STATES SIGNAL SERVICE AND ON THE NORWEGIAN TELEGRAPH SYSTEM
- REPORTS OF PIERRE FORTIN AND THEOPHILE TETU...IN COMMAND OF THE EXPEDITION FOR THE PROTECTION OF THE FISHERIES IN THE GULF OF ST LAWRENCE... 1867
- SYSTEME DE TELEGRAPHES ET DE SEMAPHORES A L'USAGE DE LA MARINE, DANS LE GOLFE ST LAURENT: LETTERS DE L'HONORABLE PIERRE FORTIN

DAS FORTLEBEN DES HEIDENTUMS IN DER ALTCHRISTLICHEN KIRCHE / Soltau, Wilhelm – Berlin: G. Reimer, 1906 – 1mf – us A.T.L.A. [240]

FORTNIGHTLY – (Formerly: Fortnightly Review). Old series. v. 1-182. 1865-1954 – 1,5,6 – us Princeton Micro [073]

Fortnightly Club. Topeka, Kansas *see* RECORDS

FORTNIGHTLY TELEPHONE ENGINEER – Pontiac. v1-10 1940-49 – 1,5,6 – us Princeton Micro [629]

Fortov, V E *see* THERMAL PHYSICS REVIEWS

FORTRESS GWALIOR / Keith, J B – Calcutta, 1883. 79 pp., figs. BI-691 2 – 8 – ne IDC [720]

THE FORTRESS OF QUEBEC 1608-1903 / Doughty, Arthur G – Quebec: Dussault & Proulx, 1904. SEM105P81 – 3mf – 9 – Can$6.75 – cn Bibl Nat [720]

FORTRESSES ET VILLAGES DESERTES DU TOUAT-GOUARA (SAHARA ALGERIEN) : ESSAI D'APPLICATION DE L'ANALYSE PHOTOGRAPHIQUE AERIENNE A LA RECHERCHE ARCHELOLGIQUE EN REGIONS DESERTIQUES – Paris, Ecole pratique des hautes etudes, 1970 – us Res Libr [930]

FORTSCHRIFT UND VOLLENDUNG BEI PHILO VON ALEXANDRIEN (T.U.U. 4-49/1) / Voelker, W – Leipzig, 1938 – 6mf – 9 – ne Slangenburg [240]

DER FORTSCHRITT – New York. N.Y. Progress. 1915-32 – 1 – us A.J.P.C. [071]

DER FORTSCHRITT = THE PROGRESS – New York, NY. 1865-66 – 1 – us A.J.P.C. [071]

FORTSCHRITTE DER BOTANIK – Berlin. v1-11. 1931-41. – 69mf – 8 – ne IDC [580]

FORTSCHRITTE DER ELEKTROTECHNIK – v. 1-20. 1887-1906. Superseded by: Jahrbuch der Elektrotechnik – 1,5,6 – us Princeton Micro [621]

DER FORTSHRITT – (See also: Progress. New York. N.Y) – us A.J.P.C. [071]

Fortt, J M *see* THE DISTRIBUTION OF AFRICAN POPULATION, NATIVE AND IMMIGRANT, IN BUGANDA

FORTUNAT : DRAMATISCHES MAERCHEN IN FUENF ACTEN / Bauernfeld, Eduard von – [Wien?: s.n., 1871?] – 1 – us U.W. Library [820]

FORTUNAT. ETUDE SUR UN DERNIER REPRESENTANT DE LA POESIE LATINE DANS LA GAULE MEROVINGIENNE / Tardi, D – Paris, 1927 – 6m – 8 – ne Slangenburg [240]

Fortunatianus, Severianus, Julius, etc *see* VARIA RHETORICA

Fortunatov, AF *see* OB IZUCHENII KOOPERATSII

Fortunatus, A *see* ISTORICA DESCRIZIONE DE TRE REGNI CONGO, MATAMBA ET ANGOLA SITUATI. CAPUCCINI. CACAZZI DA MONTECUCCOLO

FORTUNE – (v73- 1966- 5,6. v81- 1970- 9) – v1- 1930- – 1 – us UMI [330]

LA FORTUNE : LITTERAIRE – Montreal, Canada. mai 1892-v1 n30. 7 jan 1893 – 1r – 1 – Can$25.00 – cn Can Microfilming [073]

LA FORTUNE POUR TOUS – Montreal, Canada. 25 jun 1910-v1 n5. 20 oct 1910 – 1r – 1 – Can$25.00 – cn Can Microfilming [072]

Fortune, Robert *see* TWO VISITS TO THE TEA COUNTRIES OF CHINA AND THE BRITISH TEA PLANTATIONS IN THE HIMALAYA; WITH A NARRATIVE OF ADVENTURES, AND...DESCRIPTION OF THE TEA PLANT.

FORTUNE. THE STRUGGLE IN SPAIN – NY, 1937. Fiche W 1215. (Blodgett Collection of Spanish Civil War Pamphlets) – 9 – us H.U. College Libr [946]

Fortune-Barthelemy de Felice *see* ENCYCLOPEDIE, OU DICTIONNAIRE UNIVERSEL RAISONNE DES CONNOISSANCES HUMAINE (AEL, ABT.1;7)

THE FORTUNES OF THE FLETCHERS: A STORY OF LIFE IN CANADA AND AUSTRALIA / Eden, Charles Henry – London: Society for Promoting Christian Knowledge, 1873. 02657. (Pre-1900 Canadiana) – 9 – cn C.I.H.M. [971]

LES FORTUNES SCANDALEUSES. LES CHEFS DE LA CLIQUE DE PAUVRES QU'ILS ETAIENT DEVIENNENT SUBITEMENT RICHES, ROULENT CARROSSES ET ACHETENT DES CHATEAUX ET DES TERRES – s.l.: s.n., 189?. 03192. (Pre-1900 Canadiana) – 9 – cn C.I.H.M. [971]

FORTY DAYS AFTER OUR LORD'S RESURRECTION / Hanna, William – New York: Robert Carter, 1864. 1 fiche – 9 – us A.T.L.A. [240]

THE FORTY MARTYRS OF THE SINAI DESERT : AND THE STORY OF EULOGIOS: FROM A PALESTINIAN SYRIAC AND ARABIC PALIMPSEST / ed by Lewis, Agnes Smith – (Text in Syriac and Arabic; introduction in English) – Cambridge: University Press, 1912 – 1mf – 9 – 0-8370-7402-9 – 1986-1402 – us A.T.L.A. [240]

FORTY YEARS AT RARITAN : EIGHT MEMORIAL SERMONS, WITH NOTES FOR A HISTORY OF THE REFORMED DUTCH CHURCHES IN SOMERSET COUNTY, N.J. / Messler, Abraham – New York: A. Lloyd, 1873 – 1mf – us A.T.L.A. [240]

FORTY YEARS' FAMILIAR LETTERS OF JAMES W. ALEXANDER, D.D. : CONSTITUTING, WITH THE NOTES, A MEMOIR OF HIS LIFE / Alexander, James W; ed by Hall, John – New York: Scribner; London: Sampson Low, 1860 – 2mf – us A.T.L.A. [240]

FORTY YEARS IN NEW ZEALAND.. / Buller, James – 1878 – 1 – us A.T.L.A. [240]

FORTY YEARS IN THE TURKISH EMPIRE, OR, MEMOIRS OF REV. WILLIAM GOODELL / Prime, Edward Dorr Griffin – New York: Robert Carter, 1876. xii,489p. 2 fiches – 9 – us A.T.L.A. [240]

FORTY YEARS OF AMERICAN LIFE / Nichols, Thomas Low – London. 2v. 1864 – 1r – 1 – us Ross [920]

FORTY YEARS OF OFFICIAL AND UNOFFICIAL LIFE IN AN ORIENTAL CROWN COLONY : BEING THE LIFE OF SIR RICHARD F MORGAN, KT., QUEEN'S ADVOCATE AND ACTING CHIEF JUSTICE OF CEYLON – Madras: Higginbotham, 1879 – 1 – us Res Libr [920]

FORTY-ONE RED HEARTS ARE WITH CHAIRMAN MAO FOR EVER / Peking, Foreign Languages Press – SE-6369 1. 1967 – 9 – ne IDC [335]

FORTY-SEVEN IDENTIFICATIONS OF THE LOST BRITISH NATION AND THE U.W. WITH THE TEN LOST TRIBES / Hine, Edward – London: W.E. Guest; Utica: S.E. Lawrence, 1879. 82p – 1 – us U.W. Library [300]

FORTY-SEVEN ISSUE PAPERS: THE LIBERTARIAN SOLUTION TO CRUCIAL SOCIAL ISSUES / Society for Individual Liberty (SIL) – 133p. 1 fiche (29x) – 9 – 1.00f – at Libertarian Micro [320]

FORTY-TWO YEARS AMONGST THE INDIANS AND ESKIMO: PICTURES FROM THE LIFE OF THE RIGHT REVEREND JOHN HORDEN, FIRST BISHOP OF MOOSONEE / Batty, Beatrice – London: Religious Tract Society, 1893. 02998. (Pre-1900 Canadiana) – 9 – cn C.I.H.M. [971]

THE FORUM *see* DICKINSON LAW REVIEW

FORUM – (1985-. 1,5,6) – 1978- – 9 – us UMI [073]

FORUM / American Bar Association. Section of Insurance, Negligence and Compensation – v1-5 1966-81 – 1,6,9 – us UMI [999]

FORUM – (Continues: NYU forum) – (New York, N.Y.) v2, no. 1 (Dec.1980)-v9, no. 6 (Apr. 1987) – us A.J.P.C. [073]

FORUM – Dutch Flat, CA. 1875-78 – 2r – 1 – $100.00 – B02191 – us Library Micro [071]

FORUM – Maryville. Mo. 1910- – 1 – us UMI [071]

FORUM – Stockton. Calif. -w. 1941-59 – 1 – us UMI [071]

FORUM : ZEITUNG FUER GEISTIGE PROBLEME DER JUGEND – Berlin, 1950-mar 31 1983 – 23r – 1 – Dist. gw Mikrofilm – gw Misc Inst [072]

LE FORUM – Montreal, Canada. v1 n2. 12 aut 1911-v2 n10. 5 oct 1912 – 1r – 1 – Can$25.00 – cn Can Microfilming [072]

LE FORUM – Quebec, v- n-. 9 fev 1938-19 fev 1938 – 1r – 1 – Can$25.00 – cn Can Microfilming [072]

THE FORUM – Dickenson Law School. v1-12. 1897-1908 (all publ) – 75mf – 9 – $112.00 – LLMC 84-466 – us L.L.M.C. [073]

THE FORUM – Providence. R.I. 1946-1950 – 1 – us UMI [071]

THE FORUM – Sherbrooke, Canada. v1 n79. 19 nov 1926; v1 n250. 6 mar 1930; v1. 12 nov 1931 – 1r – 1 – Can$25.00 – cn Can Microfilming [072]

THE FORUM – Stockton, CA. 1921-66 – 11r – 1 – $550.00 – C03013 – us Library Micro [071]

THE FORUM *see*
- DICKINSON LAW REVIEW
- NEVADA FORUM

THE FORUM (ABA) *see* TORT AND INSURANCE LAW JOURNAL (ABA)

FORUM AND CENTURY – 1-103. 1886-1940 – 1 – us UMI [073]

FORUM AND CENTURY – 1886-1950 – 1 – us Princeton Micro [073]

THE FORUM, BENCH AND BAR REVIEW – nos 1-8. 1874-75 (all publ) – 19mf – 9 – $28.50 – LLMC 82-923 – us L.L.M.C. [073]

FORUM FOR PROTECTION OF HUMAN RIGHTS – Kathmandu. 40 docs. 1989-1990 – 9mf – 9 – ne IDC [320]

FORUM ITALICUM – v.1-. 1967- – 1. – apply; v.11- 1977- 5,6,9 – us UMI [440]

FORUM ON TAXING AND SPENDING – v.1-3. 1978-80. Superseded by Journal of Contemporary Studies – 1,5,6,9 – us UMI [073]

FORUM ON THE JEWISH PEOPLE, ZIONISM AND ISRAEL – (1979- 5,6,9) – 1975- – 1 – us UMI [270]

FORUM UND TRIBUNE – (Library has: v1 n2-v4 n9, 11-v7 n2; Jl 1942-Jl 1948) – New York: Austro American Tribune, 1942- – 1 – CSUX86-S168 – us Hoover Inst Photo [943]

FORUMEER – San Jose, CA. 1966-72 – 2r – 1 – $100.00 – R02878 – us Library Micro [071]

FORVERTS = FORWARD – New York City, NY, 1937 (40th Ann. Issue) – 1r – Can$25.00 – cn Can Microfilming [071]

FORVERTS = FORWARD – New York City, NY. v52 no 18,403. 1948 (Rise of Israel Issue) – 1r – Can$25.00 – cn Can Microfilming [071]

FORVERTS = JEWISH DAILY FORWARD – Chicago: Forward Association, mar 1919-jun 1951 – us Res Libr [071]

FORVERTS – New York: Jewish Socialist Press Federation, jul 5-dec 1951 – us Res Libr [071]

FORWARD – Glasgow. Scotland. -w. 13 Oct 1906-Dec 1921; 1923. (10 reels) – 1 – uk British Libr Newspaper [072]

FORWARD – Johannesburg. South Africa. -w. Dec 1924-Dec 1926. (1 reel) – 1 – uk British Libr Newspaper [072]

FORWARD – (Lacking: v14 no 2 1927) – v1-16. 1914-Jul 1929 – 2r – 1 – ATLA S0262 – us A.T.L.A. [073]

FORWARD – Philadelphia. Pa. Vorwarts. 1903-67 – 1 – us A.J.P.C. [071]

FORWARD – Yorkshire. 1904-08. and West Bradford Gazette. 1905-06 – 1 – uk Microform Academic [072]

FORWARD – (Issues filmed as pt of: St Clair Drake collection of Africana) – Johannesburg: Commercial Print Co Ltd, 1924-oct 17-dec 5 1952; jan 2-9 1953 – us Res Libr [071]

THE FORWARD *see* THE JEWISH FORWARD

FORWARD BLOC – Calcutta, India. Aug 1939-Jul 1940 – 1r – 1 – us L of C Photodup [072]

FORWARD TIMES – Houston. Tex. 1960- – 1 – us UMI [071]

FORWARD TO FREEDOM : CONSTITUTIONAL PROPOSALS FOR A UNITED NIGERIA – (Filmed with: United Labour Congress, Nigeria. A program for the future and Trades Union Congress of Nigeria. Social Security Committee. Report to the first annual conference.) – Lagos, 1957 – us Res Libr [321]

Forwerg, Walter *see* DARSTELLUNG UND EIGENSCHAFTEN DER METAGERMANATE DES MANGANS, EISENS UND KOBALTS

Forzanini, G P *see* CANZONE NELLA NATIVITA DI NOSTRO SIGNOR GIESV CHRISTO. NELLA ALLEGREZZA DELLA VITTORIA HAUUTA CONTRA TURCHI

Fosdick, Harry Emerson *see*
- THE ASSURANCE OF IMMORTALITY
- THE MEANING OF PRAYER

FO-SHAN CHUNG-I-HSIANG CHIH – 1923, 19, 2. Lacking: v. 2, 1923. BCH-590 2 – 8 – ne IDC [950]

THE FO-SHO-HING-TSAN-KING : A LIFE OF BUDDHA / Bodhisattva, Asvaghosha; ed by Mueller, Friedrich Max – (Translated from Sanskrit into Chinese by Dharmaraksha, A.D. 420, and from Chinese into English by Samuel Beal) – 1883 – 8mf – 8 – ne Slangenburg [280]

Foslie, M *see*
- CONTRIBUTION TO KNOWLEDGE OF THE MARINE ALGAE OF NORWAY. PTS.1-2
- NEW OR CRITICAL NORWEGIAN ALGAE
- THE NORWEGIAN FORMS OF CERAMIUM
- THE NORWEGIAN FORMS OF LITHOTHAMNION

Foss, A T *see* FACTS FOR BAPTIST CHURCHES

Fossatis, D *see* CURRUS TRIUMPHALES ADVENTUM CLARISSIMORUM MOSCHOVIAE PRINCIPUM PAUL PETROVITZ ET MARIAE THEODOROWNAE CONJUGIS...IN DIVI MARCI VENETIARUM FORO DIE 22. JANUARII ANNO MDCCLXXXII

Fossatis, G *see* CURRUS TRIUMPHALES ADVENTUM CLARISSIMORUM MOSCHOVIAE PRINCIPUM PAUL PETROVITZ ET MARIAE THEODOROWNAE CONJUGIS...IN DIVI MARCI VENETIARUM FORO DIE 22. JANUARII ANNO MDCCLXXXII

Fosse, J C de la *see* NOUVELLE ICONOLOGIE HISTORIQUE, OU ATTRIBUTS HIEROGLYPHIQUES

THE FOSSIL FISHES OF THE ENGLISH CHALK / Woodward, A S – 2564 2. 7 pts. 1902-1912 – 8 – ne IDC [560]

FOSSIL FLORA OF THE GONDWANA SYSTEM / Foictmantel, O – 1867-86 – 7 – uk Microform Academic [560]

THE FOSSIL INSECTS OF NORTH AMERICA, WITH NOTES ON SOME EUROPEAN SPECIES / ed by Scudder, S H – New York, 1890 – 2 vols – 9 – ne IDC [560]

FOSSIL JOURNAL – Fossil, OR. -w. 15 Oct 1886-26 Sept 1975; 8 Jan 1952-25 Dec 1952. – 15r – 1 – us U.O. Library [071]

FOSSIL MEN AND THEIR MODERN REPRESENTATIVES: AN ATTEMPT TO ILLUSTRATE THE CHARACTERS AND CONDITIONS OF PRE-HISTORIC MEN IN EUROPE, BY THOSE OF THE AMERICAN RACES / Dawson, John William – Montreal: Dawson, 1880. 02621. (Pre-1900 Canadiana) – 9 – cn C.I.H.M. [560]

FOSSILE FLORA DER GRENZSCHICHTEN DES KEUPERS UND LIAS FRANKENS / Schenk, A – Wiesbaden. 1865 – 1. 8.00; ; 7 – uk Microform Academic [560]

DIE FOSSILEN FUCOIDEN DER SCHWEIZERALPHEN / Fischer-Ooster, C von – 79 2. 1858 – 8 – ne IDC [560]

Foster, Arnold *see* CHRISTIAN PROGRESS IN CHINA

FOSTER CITY PROGRESS – Foster City, CA. 1966-1977 (incomplete); 1978- – 23+ r – 1 – $1,150.00 ($90.00y) – B02247 – us Library Micro [071]

Foster, Frank Hugh *see*
- A GENETIC HISTORY OF THE NEW ENGLAND THEOLOGY
- OUTLINE OF LECTURES IN SYSTEMATIC THEOLOGY
- THE SEMINARY METHOD OF ORIGINAL STUDY IN THE HISTORICAL SCIENCES

Foster, George Burman *see*
- THE FINALITY OF THE CHRISTIAN RELIGION
- THE FUNCTION OF RELIGION IN MAN'S STRUGGLE FOR EXISTENCE
- FUNCTION OF RELIGION IN MAN'S STRUGGLE FOR EXISTENCE

Foster, George Eulas *see*
- THE BROKEN PLEDGES OF LIBERALS: SPEECH IN REPLY TO SIR WILFRID LAURIER. BY HON. GEORGE E. FOSTER, HOUSE OF COMMONS, OTTAWA, MARCH 21ST, 1899
- THE CANADA TEMPERANCE MANUAL AND PROHIBITIONIST'S HANDBOOK
- EXPOSE BUDGETAIRE: CHAMBRE DES COMMUNES, MARDI, 5 MARS 1889
- EXPOSE BUDGETAIRE: CHAMBRE DES COMMUNES, MARDI, 22 MARS 1892
- EXPOSE BUDGETAIRE: CHAMBRE DES COMMUNES, MARDI 23 JUIN 1891
- EXPOSE BUDGETAIRE: CHAMBRE DES COMMUNES, MARDI, 27 MARS 1894
- EXPOSE BUDGETAIRE: CHAMBRE DES COMMUNES, VENDREDI, 31 JANVIER 1896
- EXPOSE BUDGETAIRE: DANS LA CHAMBRE DES COMMUNES, VENDREDI, 3 MAI 1895
- THE POLITICAL SITUATION: SPEECH DELIVERED BY THE HON. GEO. E. FOSTER, MINISTER OF FINANCE, IN THE MECHANICS INSTITUTE, ST JOHN, N.B., ON DECEMBER 15TH, 1891
- A SPEECH ON THE BUDGET, IN THE CANADIAN HOUSE OF COMMONS, ON THURSDAY, APRIL 5TH, 1883

Foster, Harry La Tourette *see* A BEACHCOMBER IN THE ORIENT

Foster, J E *see* CHURCHWARDENS' ACCOUNTS OF ST. MARY THE GREAT

Foster, John *see*
- AUX DIRECTEURS DE LA COMPAGNIE DU CHEMIN DE FER DE PHILLIPSBURG, FARNHAM ET YAMASKA
- AN ESSAY ON THE EVILS OF POPULAR IGNORANCE
- AN ESSAY ON THE IMPROVEMENT OF TIME, WITH NOTES OF SERMONS..
- NEW SYSTEM OF WOODEN RAIL

Foster, John W *see* A CENTURY OF AMERICAN DIPLOMACY

Foster, Joseph *see*
- A PEDIGREE OF THE FORSTERS AND FOSTERS, OF THE NORTH OF ENGLAND, AND OF SOME OF THE FAMILIES CONNECTED WITH THEM
- PEDIGREES OF THE COUNTY FAMILIES OF YORKSHIRE...AND AUTHENTICATED BY THE MEMBERS OF EACH FAMILY
- THE VISITATION OF YORKSHIRE, MADE IN THE YEARS 1584-85, BY ROBERT GLOVER, SOMERSET HERALD..

Foster, Phyllis M *see* ACTIVITIES, ADAPTATION AND AGING

Foster, R *see* INDIA OFFICE RECORDS: GUIDE, 1600-1858

Foster, R S *see* UNION OF EPISCOPAL METHODISMS

Foster, Randolph Sinks *see*
- CREATION
- PHILOSOPHY OF CHRISTIAN EXPERIENCE: EIGHT LECTURES
- SIN

Foster, Robert V *see*
- BRIEF INTRODUCTION TO THE STUDY OF THEOLOGY
- COMMENTARY ON THE EPISTLE TO THE ROMANS

Foster, Robert Verrell *see*
- A BRIEF INTRODUCTION TO THE STUDY OF THEOLOGY
- A COMMENTARY ON THE EPISTLE TO THE ROMANS
- OLD TESTAMENT STUDIES
- SYSTEMATIC THEOLOGY

Foster, Roger *see*
- THE FEDERAL JUDICIARY ACTS OF 1875 AND 1887
- A TREATISE ON PLEADING AND PRACTICE IN EQUITY IN THE COURTS OF THE UNITED STATES.

Foster, W *see*
- THE ENGLISH FACTORIES IN INDIA, 1618-1684
- LETTERS RECEIVED BY THE EAST INDIA COMPANY, FROM ITS SERVANTS IN THE EAST, 1602-1617

FOSTER'S MUSICAL JOURNAL – v1-5. Feb 1879-Jan 1884 – 1 – 375.00 – us Opus [073]

Fostoria. Ohio. Bethel United Methodist Church *see* RECORDS

Fothergill, J *see* AN ACCOUNT OF THE SORE THROAT ATTENDED WITH ULCERS

Fotheringham, L Monteith *see* ADVENTURES IN NYASALAND.

Fotheringham, Thomas Francis *see* THE JOHN KNOX LITURGY, OR, SCOTTISH "BOOK OF COMMON ORDER": A LECTURE DELIVERED BEFORE THE ST STEPHEN'S CHURCH GUILD, ST JOHN, N.B., AND PUBLISHED AT THE REQUEST OF THE GUILD

FOTO-FOTO DAM REPORTASE TENTANG PERDJALANAN PRESIDEN SOEKARNO DI AMERIKA SERIKAT / U.S. Information Service, Djakarta – SE 3764 1. 1956? – 9 – ne IDC [950]

FOTO-NOVOSTI – (Includes c.1: no.35 1939:Sept.13-no. 39 (1939:Oct.11); no.42 1939:Nov.1-no.44 (1939:Nov.15); no.46 1939:Nov.29-no.47 (1939:Dec.6); no.49 1939:Dec.2; no.51 194) – [S.l.: s.n.], – 1 – CSUXAKH2069-S – us Hoover Inst Photo [947]

Fotsch, K A *see* DIE BEGONIEN. IHRE BESCHREIBUNG, KULTUR, ZUCHTUNG UND GESCHICHTE

Fouard, Constant *see*
- LAST YEARS OF ST PAUL
- SAINT PAUL AND HIS MISSIONS
- SAINT PAUL, SES MISSIONS

Foubert, Auguste *see* LA VIE D'EMIGRANT EN AMERIQUE (REPUBLIQUE ARGENTINE, ETATS-UNIS ET CANADA)

Foucart, A *see* CATALOGUE METHODIQUE ET RAISONNE DES LEPIDOPTERES DES ENVIRONS DE DOUAI

Foucaux, Marie Filon *see* CONTES ET LEGENDES DE L'INDE ANCIENNE

Fouche, Joseph *see*
- MEMOIRS OF JOSEPH FOUCHE...MINISTER OF THE GENERAL POLICE OF FRANCE
- MEMOIRS RELATING TO FOUCHE, MINISTER OF POLICE UNDER NAPOLEON 1

Foucher, A *see*
- L'ART GRECO-BOUDDHIQUE DU GANDHARA
- THE MONUMENTS OF SANCHI

Foucher de Careil, Louis A *see* LES HABITATIONS OUVRIERES ET LES CONSTRUCTIONS CIVILES

LE FOUET : OPPOSE A CAMILIEN HOUDE, MAIRE DE MONTREAL, CHEF DE L'OPPOSITION A QUEBEC – Quebec, Canada. 17 oct 1930-10 avr 1931 – 1r – 1 – Can$25.00 – cn Can Microfilming [072]

LE FOUET NATIONAL – Puis Tableau de l'Europe et de la France corrigee. 20 no. Paris. sept 1789-mai 1790 – 1 – fr A.C.R.P.P. [073]

LE FOUET THEATRAL ET LITTERAIRE – puis Le Fouet. Art, theatre, litterature. Paris. mars 1868-avr 1869. suivi de: Le Heraut d'armes voir a ce titre – 1 – fr A.C.R.P.P. [790]

LES FOUGERES DE FRANCE / Rey-Pailhade, C de – Paris. 1893. B-7250 2 – 8 – ne IDC [580]

Fougleres, Luc de *see* ENTRE NOUS CANADIENS-FRANCAIS

FOUILLES DANS TROIS SITES BRESILIENS DU HAUT PARANAPANEMA: METHODE ET RESULTATS / Pallestrini, L – 9 – F70.00 – fr Ethnologie [972]

LES FOUILLES DE MERIDA / Melida, Jose Ramon – Archaeciogischen Instituts – 1 – sp Bibl Santa Ana [930]

FOUL PLAY / Reade, Charles L – British Fiction Archive: Unit 2 – 9 – uk Bell [830]

LE FOULBE DU NORD-CAMEROUN / Etia, Abel Moume – Bergerac: H Trillaud, 1948 – 1 – us Res Libr [960]

Foulche Delbosc, Isabel *see* BIBLIOGRAFIA DE R. FOULCHE-DELBOSC NEW YORK

Foulche-Delbosc, Raymond *see* ESSAI SUR LES ORIGINES DU ROMANCERO

Foulkes, Edmund Salisbury *see* THE CHURCH'S CREED, OR THE CROWN'S CREED?

THE FOUNDACION OF RHETORIKE / Reynolds, Richard – 1563 – 9 – 10.00 – us Scholars' Facs [420]

FOUNDATION CHARACTERS, BK 1 (CCC128) = P'ING MIN TS'IEN TZU K'O / Yen, Y C James & Fu, Daniel C – (In Chinese. Complete in 4 bks) – 40th rev ed. Shanghai: Association Press of China, 1922 – 1r – 1 – 1984-B500 – us A.T.L.A. [240]

FOUNDATION FOR ECONOMIC EDUCATION (FEE): CLICHES OF SOCIALISM – Toward an encyclopaedia of libertarian refutations. 1 fiche (24x) – 9 – 1.00f – at Libertarian Micro [320]

FOUNDATION FOR REFORMATION RESEARCH : BULLETIN OF THE LIBRARY – 1966-73 (complete) – 1r – 1 – ATLA S0599 – us A.T.L.A. [073]

FOUNDATION FOR REFORMATION RESEARCH : MONTHLY NEWSLETTER – 1967-88 (complete) – 2r – 1 – ATLA S0600 – us A.T.L.A. [073]

FOUNDATION FOR RESEARCH ON THE NATURE OF MAN – FRNM BULLETIN *see* PARAPSYCHOLOGY BULLETIN

Foundation for Study of Treaty Law *see* TREATY LAW MANUAL

FOUNDATION OF MONTREAL, 250TH ANNIVERSARY CELEBRATION 1892: ORGANIZING COMMITTEES, LIST OF MEMBERS – s.l.: s.n., 1892? (Montreal: Gazette Printing Co.). 03159. (Pre-1900 Canadiana) – 9 – cn C.I.H.M. [971]

THE FOUNDATION OF PROFESSIONAL SUCCESS / Pryor, Roger Atkinson – Chicago: La Salle, Extension University 1911. 18p. LL-1193 – 1 – us L of C Photodup [340]

Foundation Teyler *see* FONDATION TEYLER

FOUNDATIONS *see* AMERICAN BAPTIST QUARTERLY

THE FOUNDATIONS : A SERIES OF LECTURES ON THE EVIDENCES OF CHRISTIANITY / Gibson, John Monro – 2nd ed. Chicago: Jansen, McClurg, 1880 – 1mf – 9 – 0-8370-3265-2 – 1985-1265 – us A.T.L.A. [230]

FOUNDATIONS: A SERIES OF LECTURES ON THE EVIDENCES OF CHRISTIANITY / Gibson, John Monro – Chicago: Jansen, McClurg, 1880. 1 fiche – 9 – us A.T.L.A. [240]

FOUNDATIONS: A SURVEY OF 25 YEARS OF ACTIVITY OF THE PALESTINE FOUNDATION FUND-KEREN HAYESOD, FACTS AND FIGURES, 1921-1946 / Palestine Foundation Fund (Keren Hayesod) – Jerusalem. 1947. BJ-28-41 1 – 9 – ne IDC [956]

FOUNDATIONS OF BELIEF / Balfour, Arthur James – New York: Longmans, Green, 1895.1 fiche – 9 – us A.T.L.A. [240]

THE FOUNDATIONS OF HISTORY : A SERIES OF FIRST THINGS / Schieffelin, Samuel Bradhurst – 3rd ed. New York: Anson D F Randolph, 1864, c1863 – 1mf – 9 – 0-8370-5089-8 – 1985-3089 – us A.T.L.A. [900]

THE FOUNDATIONS OF LEGAL LIABILITY. / Street, Thomas Atkins – Northport, N.Y., Thompson, 1906. 3 v. LL-1502 – 1 – us L of C Photodup [340]

THE FOUNDATIONS OF OUR FAITH : PAPERS READ BEFORE A MIXED AUDIENCE OF MEN / Auberlen, Carl August et al – London:Alexander Strahan, 1867 – 1mf – 9 – 0-8370-2459-5 – 1985-0459 – us A.T.L.A. [240]

FOUNDATIONS OF PHOTOGRAPHY – Tutorial series by Derek Keeling, ex science editor of British Journal of Photography. Printed text – 9 – £60.00 – uk World [770]

FOUNDATIONS OF PHYSICS – (v12-24 1982-94 $125.00v) – v1-11. 1970-81 – 1,5 – $70.00v – us UMI [530]

FOUNDATIONS OF PHYSICS LETTERS – v1-7. 1988-94 – 1,5 – $80.00v – us UMI [530]

THE FOUNDATIONS OF RELIGION: A STUDY OF FIRST PRINCIPLES / Slicer, Thomas Roberts – New York: T.R. Slicer, 1902. 1 fiche – 9 – us A.T.L.A. [200]

THE FOUNDATIONS OF RELIGIOUS BELIEF... NATURAL THEOLOGY VINDICATED / Wilson, William Dexter – New York: D. Appleton, 1883. 1 fiche – 9 – us A.T.L.A. [240]

FOUNDATIONS OF SACRED STUDY: SECOND SERIES / Ellicott, Charles J – New York: E. & J.B. Young, 1895.1 fiche – 9 – us A.T.L.A. [240]

FOUNDATIONS OF SUCCESS AND LAWS OF TRADE: BOOK DEVOTED TO BUSINESS AND ITS SUCCESSFUL PROSECUTION.. – By a Barrister-at-law. London, Ont.: S. Smith, 1877. 03160. (Pre-1900 Canadiana) – 9 – cn C.I.H.M. [380]

THE FOUNDATIONS OF THE BIBLE : STUDIES IN OLD TESTAMENT CRITICISM / Girdlestone, Robert Baker – (Includes appendix & indexes) – 4th rev ed. London: Eyre & Spottiswoode, 1892 – 1mf – 9 – 0-8370-2533-8 – 1985-0533 – us A.T.L.A. [220]

THE FOUNDATIONS OF THE ENGLISH CHURCH / Maude, J H – London: Methuen, 1909. (Handbooks of English church history; 1) – 1mf – us A.T.L.A. [240]

THE FOUNDATIONS OF THE ORIGIN OF SPECIES : TWO ESSAYS WRITTEN IN 1842 AND 1844 / Darwin, Charles; ed by Darwin, Francis – Cambridge: University Press, 1909 – 1 roll – 1 – 1-55879-881-1 – uk Libr Preservation [590]

THE FOUNDER OF CHRISTENDOM / Smith, Goldwin – Boston: Am. Unitarian Assoc., 1903. 1 fiche – 9 – us A.T.L.A. [240]

Founder of Divine Science Organization *see* HARMONY

THE FOUNDER OF MORMONISM : A PSYCHOLOGICAL STUDY OF JOSEPH SMITH, JR. / Riley, I Woodbridge – New York: Dodd, Mead, 1903, c1902 – 2mf – us A.T.L.A. [150]

THE FOUNDERS AND FIRST THREE PRESIDENTS OF THE BIBLE SOCIETY / Morris, Henry – London: Religious Tract Society, [1890?] – 1mf – 9 – 0-8370-6587-9 – 1986-0587 – us A.T.L.A. [920]

FOUNDERS OF NEW ENGLAND / Drake, Samuel G – Item L. From research among the British Archives, 1858-60. 131p. Indexed. SW16-0076 – 5 – us A.G.L.L. [978]
FOUNDERS OF OLD TESTAMENT CRITICISM : BIOGRAPHICAL, DESCRIPTIVE AND CRITICAL STUDIES / Cheyne, Thomas Kelly – New York: Scribner's, 1893 – 1mf – 9 – 0-8370-2645-8 – 1985-0645 – us A.T.L.A. [220]
FOUNDING FATHERS / ed by Rutsch, E – 8000p of letters and other documents from the Morristown Historical Park, NJ, and the Dawes Library, Marietta College, OH. Printed guide and cassette tape introduction – 143mf – 1 – $415.00 – us UMI [976]
FOUNDRY – Superseded by Foundry Management and Technology – v1-102 1892-1974 1; v93-102 1965-74 5,6 – us UMI [670]
THE FOUNDRY BUDGET OPENED : OR, THE ARCANUM OF WESLEYANISM DISCLOSED / MacGowan, John – London, 1780 – 1mf – 9 – MP-539/1 – ne IDC [240]
FOUNDRY MANAGEMENT AND TECHNOLOGY – v102- 1974- 1,5,6; 1977- 9 – us UMI [622]
FOUNDRY TRADE JOURNAL – v22- 1920- 1; v130- 5,6; v140- 9 – us UMI [670]
FOUNTAIN AND FAST FOOD *see* FAST FOOD
FOUNTAIN AND FAST FOOD SERVICE *see* FAST FOOD
FOUNTAIN CITY ARGUS – Bryan, Ohio. 1876-79 – 2r – 1 – $32.50r – us Archival [071]
FOUNTAIN LEDGER – Attica. Ind. 1864-1866 – 1 – us UMI [071]
FOUNTAIN SERVICE *see* FAST FOOD
FOUNTAIN VALLEY DAILY PILOT – Fountain Valley, CA. 1966 (Scats) – 8r – 1 – $400.00 – H04011 – us Library Micro [071]
FOUNTAIN WARREN DEMOCRAT – Attica. Ind. 1898-1920; 1927-1929; 1931 – 1 – us UMI [071]
FOUNTAINS ABBEY *see* VYNER MANUSCRIPTS
Fouques Duparc, J *see* LA PROTECTION DES MINORITES...
Fouquet, Karl *see* JAKOB AYRERS "SIDEA", SHAKESPEARES "TEMPEST" UND DAS MAERCHEN
Fouquet, Leon *see*
– LUCIFERIANISM OR SATANISM IN ENGLISH FREEMASONRY, AN ESSAY. PART 1
– LUCIFERIANISM OR SATANISM IN ENGLISH FREMASONRY, AN ESSAY. PART 2
Fouquet, Leon Charles *see* DIARY
FOUR BIBLE STUDIES: SHAMELESSNESS, REVENGE, PRAYER, FIDELITY / Osborne, John H – New York: A.C. Armstrong, 1896. 1 fiche – 9 – us A.T.L.A. [240]
FOUR CENTURIES OF ENGLISH AND AMERICAN PLAYS – (1516-1641. Elizabethan, Shakespeare, Jacobean. 3. 1642-1700. Restoration Drama. 3. 1701-50. Early 18th Century. 3. 1751-1800. Late 18th Century. 3. 1737-1800. Larpent MS. plays. 3. 1714-1830. American. 3) – Three centuries: 1500-1830 – 3 – us Readex [820]
FOUR CENTURIES OF ENGLISH AND AMERICAN PLAYS – (American: 1831-1900. 3596 plays. 3) – 19th century. English: 1801-1900. 7360 plays – 3 – us Readex [820]
FOUR CENTURIES OF SCOTTISH PSALMODY / Patrick, M – London, 1949 – 4mf – 8 – Dfl19.00 – ne Slangenburg [240]
FOUR CENTURIES OF SILENCE, OR, FROM MALACHI TO CHRIST / Redford, Robert Ainslie – Chicago: A.C. McClurg, 1887. 1 fiche – 9 – us A.T.L.A. [240]
FOUR CHARGES TO THE CLERGY OF THE ARCHDEACONRY OF ESSEX:... / Rutherford, T – Cambridge, 1763 – 2mf – 9 – MP-420/1 – ne IDC [240]
FOUR CONQUEST OF ENGLAND / St John, James Augustive – London: Smith Elder & Co., 1862. 448p – 1 – us U.W. Library [941]
FOUR CORNERS NEWS – Salem OR. Dec 18 1953-Dec 17 1954 – 1 – us U.O. Library [071]
FOUR EARLY PAMPHLETS, 1783-84 / Godwin, William – Reprint Gainesville, 1966; Delmar, 1977.Introd. by Burton R. Pollin. Essays on politics, education and literature – 9 – 20.00 – us Scholars' Facs [320]
FOUR ESSAYS UPON THE ENGLISH LANGUAGE / Ward, John – 1758. 251p. (English Linguistics Series 1500-1800) – 9 – us UMI [420]
LE FOUR ET LA PANIFICATION DU SUD-EST DE LA GRANDE POLOGNE / Gorecki, P – 9 – F30.00 – fr Ethnologie [306]
THE FOUR EVANGELISTS : WITH THE DISTINCTIVE CHARACTERISTICS OF THEIR GOSPELS / Thomson, Edward A – Edinburgh: T & T Clark, 1868 – 1mf – 9 – 0-8370-9316-3 – 1986-3316 – us A.T.L.A. [220]
FOUR GOSPELS FROM A LAWYER'S STANDPOINT / Bennett, Edmund Hatch – Boston: Houghton, Mifflin, 1899.1 fiche – 9 – us A.T.L.A. [240]
THE FOUR GOSPELS FROM A LAWYER'S STANDPOINT / Bennett, Edmund Hatch – Boston: Houghton, Mifflin, 1899 – 1mf – 9 – 0-8370-2265-7 – 1985-0265 – us A.T.L.A. [220]
THE FOUR GOSPELS IN THE EARLIEST CHURCH HISTORY / Nicol, Thomas – Edinburgh: William Blackwood, 1908. 1 fiche – 9 – us A.T.L.A. [240]
FOUR HOLES BAPTIST CHURCH. ORANGEBURG COUNTY. SOUTH CAROLINA : CHURCH RECORDS – 1849-1964, 1867-1903 – 1 – 25.65 – us Baptist [240]
FOUR HUNDRED YEARS OF FREETHOUGHT / Putnam, Samuel Porter – New York: The Truth Seeker Company, 1894 – 874p – 1 – us U.W. Library [210]
FOUR HUNDRED YEARS OF WORLD PRESBYTERIANISM / Drury, Clifford Merril – 1961 – 1 – us A.T.L.A. [240]
FOUR L LUMBER NEWS – Portland OR. Nov 10 1929 – 1 – us U.O. Library [071]
FOUR LAW DRAFTS TO FIGHT DEFLATION, PREVENT INFLATION AND LOWER THE INTEREST RATE / Rittershausen, Beckerath, Zander et al – 1fiche. (24x) – 9 – 1.00f – at Libertarian Micro [320]
FOUR LECTURES : DELIVERED IN THE CHURCH OF THE HOLY TRINITY, PHILADELPHIA, IN THE YEAR 1877... / Vinton, Alexander Hamilton – Boston: Alfred Mudge, 1877 – 1mf – 9 – 0-8370-5674-8 – 1985-3674 – us A.T.L.A. [240]
FOUR LECTURES ON THE EARLY HISTORY OF THE GOSPELS DELIVERED AT MILBORNE PORT, SOMERSET, ADVENT, 1897 / Wilkinson, J H – London; New York:Macmillan, 1898 – 1mf – 9 – 0-8370-5851-1 – 1985-3851 – us A.T.L.A. [220]
FOUR MIDDLE SCHOOL PHYSICAL EDUCATION TEACHERS' EXPERIENCES DURING A COLLABORATIVE ACTION RESEARCH STAFF DEVELOPMENT PROJECT / Butt, K L – 1989 – 2mf – 9 – $8.00 – us Microform Publ [613]
FOUR MILE BAPTIST CHURCH. CAMPBELL COUNTY. KENTUCKY : CHURCH RECORDS – 1819-74 – 336p – 1 – $15.12 – us Baptist [240]
FOUR MONTHS IN NORTH AMERICA / Charlton, William Henry – Hexham, England: J. Catherall, 1873? 05715. (Pre-1900 Canadiana) – 9 – cn C.I.H.M. [971]
FOUR NEGRO POETS / ed by Locke, Alain LeRoy – New York, 1927 – 1r – 1 – us Ross [420]
FOUR PHASES OF MORALS: SOCRATES, ARISTOTLE, CHRISTIANITY, UTILITARIANISM / Blackie, John Stuart – New York: Scribner, Armstrong, 1872. vii,354p. 1 fiche – 9 – us A.T.L.A. [170]
FOUR SHORT LECTURES ON THE BOOK OF REVELATION / Douglass, Benjamin – Chicago: [s.n], 1866 – 1mf – 9 – 0-8370-2958-9 – 1985-0958 – us A.T.L.A. [220]
FOUR SONATAS FOR THE PIANO / Reinagle, Alexander – Composer's manuscript, not dated. MUSIC 136, Item 1 – 1 – us L of C Photodup [780]
FOUR SONATAS OR DUETS / Burney, Charles – A second set of four sonatas for two performers on one pianoforte or harpsichord composed by C. Burney. 1778 – 9 – us Sibley [780]
FOUR SONATAS OR DUETS FOR TWO PERFORMERS ON ONE PIANO FORTE OR HARPSICHORD / Burney, Charles – 1777 – 9 – us Sibley [780]
FOUR SPEECHES DELIVERED IN GUILD-HALL, 1643 / Calamy, Edmund – 1646 – 1 – $50.00 – us Presbyterian [941]
FOUR STAR MORNING CITY HOME EDITION *see* 4 STAR MORNING CITY HOME EDITION
THE FOUR STREAMS : NEWSLETTER OF THE DIOCESAN ASSOCIATION FOR WESTERN CHINA / Diocesan Association for Western China – v1-178. n.s. no. 1. (?)-Jan 1951. n.s. July 1951 – 1 reel – 1 – $125.00 – us UPA [240]
FOUR TALKS ON THEOLOGY (CCC78) = SHEN HSUEH SZU CHIANG / Chao, Tzu-ch'en – (In Chinese) – 1st ed. Hong Kong: Council on Christian Literature for Overseas Chinese, 1955 – 1r – 1 – 1984-B500 – us A.T.L.A. [240]
THE FOUR THEORIES OF VISIBLE CHURCH UNITY : AN ADDRESS / Huntington, William Reed – [S.l.: s.n., 1909?] – 1mf – us A.T.L.A. [240]
FOUR TUDOR BOOKS ON EDUCATION / ed by Pepper, Robert D – 1533-1588 – 9 – 15.00 – us Scholars' Facs [370]
FOUR WING NEWS – Holden. West Virginia. 1943-1949 – 1 – us UMI [071]
FOUR WISCONSIN COUNTIES / Schafer, Joseph – Madison: State Historical Society of Wisconsin, 1927. Wisconsin Reel 13. (The Cox Library Collection) – 5 – us Americana [978]
FOUR YEAR DEVELOPMENT PLAN 1970-1974 (IN BRIEF) / Nigeria. North Western State of Nigeria – Sokoto. 1971. BD-2004 1 – 9 – ne IDC [338]
FOUR YEAR DEVELOPMENT PLAN OF ISRAEL, 1950-53 SUMMARY / Israel. Prime Minister's Office – Gruenbaum, Al. Jerusalem. 1951. BD-337 1 – 9 – ne IDC [338]
THE FOUR YEAR ECONOMIC AND SOCIAL DEVELOPMENT PLAN OF PUERTO RICO, 1969-1972 / Puerto Rico. Junta de Planificacion – D 878 1. 1968 – 9 – ne IDC [338]
FOUR YEAR PLAN FOR ECONOMIC AND SOCIAL DEVELOPMENT, 1967-1970 / Liberia. National Planning Council – Monrovia. 1967 – 9 – ne IDC [338]
FOUR YEARS' CAMPAIGN IN INDIA / Taylor, William MacKergo – New York: Nelson & Phillips, 1875 – 1mf – us A.T.L.A. [240]
FOUR YEARS IN ASHANTEE / Ramseyer, Friedrich August – New York: R. Carter, 1875 – 1mf – us A.T.L.A. [240]
FOUR YEARS IN ASHANTEE BY THE MISSIONARIES RAMSEYER AND KUEHNE. / Ramseyer, Friedrich August & Kuhne; ed by Weitbrecht, Mrs – New York: R Carter, 1875 – 1 – us Res Libr [960]
FOUR YEARS IN THE OLD WORLD: COMPRISING THE TRAVELS, INCIDENTS, AND EVANGELISTIC LABORS OF DR. AND MRS. PALMER IN ENGLAND, IRELAND, SCOTLAND AND WALES / Palmer, Phoebe Worrell – 1866 – 9 – us A.T.L.A. [240]
FOUR YEARS IN HER MAJESTY'S SHIP COLLINGWOOD, FROM 1844 TO 1848 / Walpole, Frederick – 2nd ed. 2v. 1850 – 9 – uk Libr Preservation [941]
FOUR YEARS IN THE WHITE NORTH / MacMillan, DB – BN-306 2. 1925 – 8 – ne IDC [910]
FOUR YEARS OF IRISH HISTORY, 1845-1849 / Duffy, Charles Gavan – London, New York: Cassell, Petter, Galpin, (1883). xv,780p. With: Dawn Ginsbergh's Revenge by S.J. Perelman. 1 reel. 1285 – 1 – us U.W. Library [941]
FOUR YEARS ON THE GEORGIAN BAY: LIFE AMONG THE ROCKS, INFORMATION FOR TOUISTS, CAMPERS, AND PROSPECTIVE SETTLERS: PORTRAYING THE FISHING AND HUNTING GROUNDS, ISLAND AND SUMMER RESORTS, TO FRENCH RIVER, WITH SCENIC VIEWS & DESCRIPTIONS – s.l.: s.n., 18–? (s.l.: Copp, Clark). 05600. (Pre-1900 Canadiana) – 9 – cn C.I.H.M. [910]
Fourchault, C *see* DE LA MEDIATION...
THE FOUR-FOLD GOSPEL / Simpson, Albert B – New York: Alliance Press, c1890 – 1mf – 9 – 0-8370-7337-5 – 1986-1337 – us A.T.L.A. [240]
THE FOURFOLD STORY : A STUDY OF THE GOSPELS / Genung, George Frederick – Boston: Congregational Sunday-School & Publ Society, c1891 – 1mf – 9 – 0-8370-3251-2 – 1985-1251 – us A.T.L.A. [220]
FOURFOLD STORY: A STUDY OF THE GOSPELS / Genung, George F – Boston: Congregational Sunday School Pub. Society, 1891.1 fiche – 9 – us A.T.L.A. [240]
Fourier, Charles *see* PIEGES ET CHARLATANISME DES DEUX SECTES SAINT-SIMON ET OWEN QUI PROMETTENT L'ASSOCIATION ET LE PROGRES
LA FOURMI – Port-au-Prince: Impr de L'Oeuvre. 1ere annee: n2-n8. 3 mai-22 mai 1902 – 1 sheet – 9 – us Res Libr [072]
Fournel, Henri *see*
– ARTICLES SUR L'HEREDITE DE LA PROPRIETE
– AU ROI
– BIBLIOGRAPHIE SAINT-SIMONIENNE
Fournel, Marc *see* LA TRIPOLITAINE
Fournier *see* PENSEES RELIGIEUSES PAR UN SAINT-SIMONIEN
Fournier, A *see*
– DIE GEHEIMPOLIZEI AUF DEM WIENER KONGRESS
– TAGEBUECHER VON FRIEDRICH VON GENTZ (1829-1831)
Fournier, Georges *see* HYDROGRAPHIE, CONTENANT LA THEORIE ET LA PRATIQUE DE TOUTES LES PARTIES DE LA NAVIGATION
Fournier, Jules *see*
– L'ACTION
– SIR LOMER GOUIN OU LE PREMIERMINISTRE DES "CONTRACTEURS"
Fournier, Pierre-Simon *see* TRAITE HISTORIQUE ET CRITIQUE SUR L'ORIGINE ET LES PROGRES DES CARACTERES DE FONTE POUR L'IMPRESSION DE LA MUSIQUE..
Fourreau, P J *see*
– BREVIARIUM PLANTARUM NOVARUM
– ICONES AD FLORAM EUROPAE NOVO FUNDAMENTO INSTAURANDAM SPECTANTES
FOURTEEN QUESTIONS : ARTICLE LISTING AND RESPONDING TO THE FOURTEEN MOST OFTEN ASKED QUESTIONS ENCOUNTERED BY THE JOINT COMMITTEE ON FUTURE STATUS SUBCOMMITTEES IN THEIR DISTRICT HEARINGS / Joint Committee on Future Status Subcommittees [TTPI (U.S.)] – n.a, n.p, n.d. – 1mf – 9 – $1.50 – LLMC 82-100F, Title 53 – us L.L.M.C. [323]
FOURTEEN YEARS IN BASUTOLAND / Widdicombe, John – asketch of African mission life. 1891 – 1 – us A.T.L.A. [960]
FOURTEEN YEARS IN BASUTOLAND; A SKETCH OF AFRICAN MISSION LIFE / Widdicombe, John – London. 1891 – 1 – us Res Libr [960]
THE FOURTH (AND FINAL) REPORT... : GOVERNMENT TRANSLATION AND INTERPRETATION SERVICES, HONG KONG'S EDUCATIONAL SYSTEM, CHINESE AS AN OFFICIAL LANGUAGE / Hong Kong. Chinese Language Committee – Hong Kong, 1971 – 1mf – 9 – DE-162/1 – ne IDC [370]
FOURTH ANNUAL PLAN, 1972 / China. Republic. Council for International Economic Cooperation and Development – Taipei, 1973. BD-1634/1 – 9 – ne IDC [338]
THE FOURTH ASIAN GAMES – SE-538 1. 1962 – 9 – ne IDC [950]
THE FOURTH BOOK OF EZRA, THE LATIN VERSION FROM THE MSS : WITH AN INTRODUCTION BY M.R. JAMES / ed by Bensly, Robert L – 1895 – 4mf – 9 – ne Slangenburg [220]
FOURTH CENSUS OF THE UNITED STATES / U.S. Bureau of the Census – 1820. 142 rolls M33 – 1 – us Nat'l Archives [324]
FOURTH CENSUS OF THE U.S. – 1820 – 1r – 1 – $50.00 – B50001 – us Library Micro [975]
FOURTH FIVE YEAR PLAN / India. Planning Commission – Revised Outlay 1969-1974. Mar 1970. BD-1096 1 – 9 – ne IDC [330]
FOURTH FIVE YEAR PLAN 1969-1974 / India. Planning Commission – D-1095 1 – 9 – ne IDC [338]
FOURTH FIVE YEAR PLAN, 1969-74-DRAFT / India. Planning Commission – New Delhi. 1969. BD-897 1 – 9 – ne IDC [338]
FOURTH FIVE YEAR PLAN A DRAFT OUTLINE / India. Planning Commission – New Delhi. 1966. BD-469 1 – 9 – ne IDC [338]
FOURTH FIVE YEAR PLAN IN EDUCATION 1969/70-1973/74 / India. Gujarat. Directorate of Education – Ahmedabad, [1969] – 2mf – 9 – DE-550/1 – ne IDC [370]
FOURTH FIVE YEAR PLAN ON GENERAL EDUCATION 1969-1974 : REPORT OF THE WORKING GROUP / India. Bihar. Education Department – Patna, 1968 – 1mf – 9 – DE-549/1 – ne IDC [370]

FOURTH FOUR-YEAR PLAN FOR ECONOMIC DEVELOPMENT OF THE PROVINCE OF TAIWAN, 1965-1968 / China. Republic. Council for International Economic Cooperation and Development – Taipei. 1965. BD-138 1 – 9 – ne IDC [338]

THE FOURTH GOSPEL : EVIDENCES EXTERNAL AND INTERNAL OF ITS JOHANNEAN AUTHORSHIP / Abbot, Ezra et al – (Includes indexes) – New York: Scribner's, 1891 – 1mf – 9 – 0-8370-2006-9 – 1985-0006 – us A.T.L.A. [220]

THE FOURTH GOSPEL / Hoskyns, Ed – 1947 – 9 – $21.00 – us I.R.C. [240]

THE FOURTH GOSPEL : THE QUESTION OF ITS ORIGIN STATED AND DISCUSSED / Clarke, James Freeman – Boston: Geo H Ellis, 1886 – 1mf – 9 – 0-8370-2671-7 – 1985-0671 – us A.T.L.A. [220]

THE FOURTH GOSPEL AND SOME RECENT GERMAN CRITICISM / Jackson, Henry Latimer – (Includes bibliographical references) – Cambridge: University Press, 1906 – 1mf – 9 – 0-8370-3741-7 – 1985-1741 – us A.T.L.A. [220]

THE FOURTH GOSPEL AND THE SYNOPTISTS:...THE JOHANNINE PROBLEM / Worsley, Frederick William – Edinburgh: T. & T. Clark, 1909. 1 fiche – 9 – us A.T.L.A. [240]

FOURTH INTERNATIONAL – New York. v. 1-17 no. 1-135. May 1940-Spring 1956 – 1 – us NY Public [073]

FOURTH INTERNATIONAL CONFERENCE ON ADULT EDUCATION, PARIS, 19-29 MARCH 1985 : THE DEVELOPMENT OF ADULT EDUCATION, ASPECTS AND TRENDS / UNESCO – Paris, 1985 – 2mf – 9 – DE-135/1 – ne IDC [370]

FOURTH INTERNATIONAL CONFERENCE ON ADULT EDUCATION, PARIS, 19-29 MARCH 1985 : DRAFT FINAL REPORT / UNESCO – Paris, 1985 – 3mf – 9 – DE-138/1 – ne IDC [370]

Fourth International. International Executive Committee *see* QUATRI'EME INTERNATIONALE

FOURTH MEETING OF THE EAST AFRICAN SUB-COMMITTEE FOR SOIL CORRELATION AND LAND EVALUATION. ARUSHA, 1980 – 1982 – 210p – it F.A.O. [631]

FOURTH NATIONAL DEVELOPMENT PLAN, 1968-1972 / Iran. Plan Organization – Tehran. 1968. BD-682 1 – 9 – ne IDC [338]

FOURTH OF JULY MESSAGE / Galbraith, Francis J – SE-11,032 1. 1965 – 9 – ne IDC [300]

FOURTH PLAN 1970-1975 / National Planning Commission – English trans. D-1556 1. 1972 – 9 – ne IDC [338]

FOURTH PLAN 1970-75 / Nepal. Economic plans – (Ministry of Economic Planning. Economic Affairs Report – special five year plan issue 1965-1970. D-1383; 1. 1965. SF 8.00; 9) – D-1131 1. 1970 – 9 – ne IDC [338]

THE FOURTH POPULATION CENSUS OF BAHRAIN: A BRIEF ANALYTICAL AND COMPARATIVE STUDY / Bahrain. Statistical Bureau – 1969. BNE-10.013 – 9 – ne IDC [310]

FOURTH PROGRESS REPORT ON THE RECONSTRUCTION AND DEVELOPMENT PROGRAMME 1960-66 FOR THE PERIOD 1963-64 / Mauritius – (Sessional Paper no. 7 of 1964). Port Louis. 1964 – 9 – ne IDC [338]

FOURTH REPORT OF THE STANDING COMMITTEE OF GRIEVANCES / Bas-Canada. Parlement. Chambre d'Assemblee. Comite Permanent des Griefs – [S.l.]: [s.n.], [1836?]. SEM105P1225 – 7mf – 9 – Can$15.75 – cn Bibl Nat [971]

FOUR-YEAR DEVELOPMENT PLAN FY 1972-1975 / Philippines. National Economic Council – Manila. Jul 1971. BD-1732 1 – 9 – ne IDC [338]

FOUR-YEAR DEVELOPMENT PLAN FY 1974-1977 / Philippines. National Economic and Development Authority – Manila. 1973. BD-2017 1 – 9 – ne IDC [338]

FOUR-YEAR NATIONAL ECONOMIC DEVELOPMENT PLAN. 1972-1975 / Vietnam. Directorate General of Planning – 1972. BD-1812 1 – 9 – ne IDC [950]

THE FOUR-YEAR PLAN (1970-73) / Algeria. Ministere de l'Information et de la Culture – Alger. Dec. 1970. BD-1794 1 – 9 – ne IDC [960]

FOUR-YEAR PLAN OF CAPITAL EXPENDITURES 1956/57-1959/60 / Burma. Ministry of National Planning – D-1260 1 – 9 – ne IDC [332]

Fowkes, Henry L *see* HISTORICAL ENCYCLOPEDIA OF ILLINOIS AND HISTORY OF CHRISTIAN COUNTY

Fowle, Thomas Welbank *see*
- THE RECONCILIATION OF RELIGION AND SCIENCE
- RECONCILIATION OF RELIGION AND SCIENCE

Fowler *see*
- THE COLEOPTERA OF THE BRITISH ISLANDS
- HISTORY OF PEMBROKE, NEW HAMPSHIRE 1730-1895

FOWLER COLLECTION OF EARLY ARCHITECTURAL BOOKS – Based on the Fowler Architectural Collection of the Johns Hopkins University – 1 – us Primary [720]

FOWLER COURIER – (Also known as: Fowler Ensign) – Fowler, CA. 1894-1897 – 1r – 1 – $50.00 – B06026 – us Library Micro [071]

Fowler, D D et al *see* JOHN WESLEY POWELL AND THE ANTHROPOLOGY OF THE CANYON COUNTRY

FOWLER ENSIGN – Fowler, CA. 1898-1956; 1976-82 – 28r – 1 BC02248 – $1,400.00 – us Library Micro [071]

FOWLER ENSIGN *see* FOWLER COURIER

Fowler, H W *see*
- THE FISHES OF OCEANIA
- A SYNOPSIS OF THE FISHES OF CHINA

Fowler, Henry T *see*
- THE AMERICAN PULPIT
- THE AMERICAN PULPIT: SKETCHES, BIOGRAPHICAL
- PROPHETS AS STATESMEN AND PREACHERS

Fowler, Henry Thatcher *see* THE PROPHETS AS STATESMEN AND PREACHERS

Fowler, John A *see* THE PENNSYLVANIA INSURANCE DIGEST

Fowler, LN *see* NEW ILLUSTRATED SELF-INSTRUCTOR IN PHRENOLOGY AND PHYSIOLOGY

Fowler, Montague *see*
- CHRISTIAN EGYPT
- CHURCH HISTORY IN QUEEN VICTORIA'S REIGN

Fowler, OS *see* NEW ILLUSTRATED SELF-INSTRUCTOR IN PHRENOLOGY AND PHYSIOLOGY

Fowler, Philemon H *see*
- HISTORICAL SKETCH OF PRESBYTERIANISM WITHIN THE BOUNDS OF THE SYNOD OF CENTRAL NEW YORK
- HISTORICAL SKETCH... SYNOD OF CENTRAL NEW YORK

Fowler, Robert Ludlow *see*
- THE PERSONAL PROPERTY LAW OF THE STATE OF NEW YORK BEING CHAPTER FORTY-SEVEN OF THE GENERAL LAWS.
- THE REAL PROPERTY LAW OF THE STATE OF NEW YORK: BEING CHAPTER FORTY-SIX OF THE GENERAL LAWS.

Fowler, W W *see* THE COLEOPTERA OF THE BRITISH ISLANDS

Fowler, William Warde *see*
- THE CITY-STATE OF THE GREEKS AND ROMANS
- THE RELIGIOUS EXPERIENCE OF THE ROMAN PEOPLE
- THE ROMAN FESTIVALS OF THE PERIOD OF THE REPUBLIC
- ROMAN IDEAS OF DEITY IN THE LAST CENTURY BEFORE THE CHRISTIAN ERA
- SOCIAL LIFE AT ROME IN THE AGE OF CICERO

Fowles, J H *see* THE NECESSITY OF PERSONAL COMMUNION WITH CHRIST

Fox, Cyndy M *see* PSYCHOSOCIAL FACTORS IN THE DEVELOPMENT OF BREAST CANCER

Fox, George *see*
- INSTRUCTIONS FOR RIGHT SPELLING
- THE JOURNAL OF GEORGE FOX
- PASSAGES FROM THE LIFE AND WRITINGS OF GEORGE FOX, TAKEN FROM HIS JOURNAL

Fox, George et al *see* A BATTLE-DOOR FOR TEACHERS AND PROFESSORS TO LEARN SINGULAR AND PLURAL

Fox, George T *see* AMERICAN JOURNALS

Fox, Harry Halton *see*
- GENERAL REPORT ON THE COMMERCIAL, INDUSTRIAL, & ECONOMIC SITUATION OF CHINA IN JUNE, 1921
- REPORT ON THE COMMERCIAL, INDUSTRIAL AND ECONOMIC SITUATION OF CHINA IN JULY 1922

Fox, J S *see* HA-ESHKOL

Fox, James Joseph *see* RELIGION AND MORALITY

Fox, Lawrence K *see* FOX'S WHO'S WHO AMONG SOUTH DAKOTANS 1924-25

Fox, M A S Columba *see* THE LIFE OF... JOHN BAPTI..NEW YORK, 1925

Fox Novel, M *see* VEASE FORNER Y SEGARRA, JUAN PABLO

FOX RIVER LEADER – Aurora. Ill. -w. 1909-22 – 1 – us UMI [071]

FOXBOROUGH 1720-1849 – (Mf 1T-2T: Births 1753-1818. Mf 2T-3T: Marriages & Intents 1773-1819. Mf 3T: Deaths1775-1819. Mf 3T-6T: Vital Records 1720-1849. Mf 5T: Transient Births 1785-1834; Deaths 1819-44. Mf 6T-7T: Marriage Intentions 1819-49. Mf 7T-8T: Marriages 1842-49; Births 1843-49. Mf 8T-9T: Deaths 1843-49. Mf 9T: Out-of-Town Marriages 1779-98) – (mf ed 1996) – 9mf – 9 – 0-87623-249-7 – us Holbrook [920]

FOXBOROUGH 1720-1897 – (Mf 1-7: Vital Records 1720-1860. Mf 8-10: Town Records 1778-92. Mf 10-16: Town Records 1792-1816. Mf 17-25: Town Records 1817-49. Mf 26-35: Town Records 1849-69. Mf 36-37: Boundaries 1834-1927. Mf 38-40: Voters 1884-1915. Mf 41-42: Vital Records 1843-54. Mf 43-44: Birth Index 1849-97. Mf 44-45: Marriage Index 1848-97. Mf 454-46: Death Index 1848-97. Mf 47-50: Births 1855-97. Mf 50-53: Marriages 1851-98. Mf 54-56: Deaths 1852-97) – (mf ed 1996) – 56mf – 9 – 0-87623-383-3 – us Holbrook [920]

Foxcroft, Edmund John Buchanan *see* AUSTRALIAN NATIVE POLICY, ITS HISTORY ESPECIALLY IN VICTORIA

THE FOXES OF THE DESERT / Carell, Paul – Trans. from the German by Mervyn Savill.New York: Dutton, 1961. 370p. illus – 1 – us U.W. Library [940]

FOXPORT BAPTIST CHURCH. WALLINGFORD, KENTUCKY : CHURCH RECORDS – 1873-Oct. 1988 (incomplete) – 1r – 1 – $61.02 – us Baptist [240]

FOX'S DECISIONS *see* HASKELL'S JUDGEMENTS OF THE HONORABLE EDWARD FOX FOR THE MAINE DISTRICT AND FIRST CIRCUIT, 1866-1881

FOX'S WEEKLY – Bradford, England. -w. 11 Jan-8 Nov 1883. 30 ft – 1 – uk British Libr Newspaper [072]

FOX'S WHO'S WHO AMONG SOUTH DAKOTANS 1924-25 / ed by Fox, Lawrence K – Pierre: Statewide Service Co., 1924. 2v. South Dakota Reel 5. (The Cox Library Collection) – 5 – us Americana [978]

Foy *see* BENCH AND BAR OF ILLINOIS – 1920

LA FOY DEVOILEE PAR LA RAISON, DANS LA CONNAISSANCE DE DIEU, DE SES MYSTERES, ET DE LA NATURE / Parisot, Jean Patrocle – 1. ed. Paris: Parisot, 1681 – 1 – us U.W. Library [240]

FO-YAL : FORT-DE-FRANCE, 1835-1935 / Nay-Reine, Lucien – Imp. Bezaudin, 1935 – 1 – F82.55 – fr Armell [944]

Foye, Edward M *see* HOW TO MAKE ABSTRACTS OF TITLE AND SEARCHES

LE FOYER : MENSUEL – Montreal, 1 mai 1892 – 1r – 1 – Can$25.00 – cn Can Microfilming [073]

LE FOYER CANADIEN – (Index included) – Montreal, 1863-1866 – 1r – 1 – Can$70.00 – cn Can Microfilming [073]

LE FOYER CANADIEN – Worcester, MA. v4 n1. 18 mar 1873-v5 n78. 22 sep 1874 – 1r – 1 – Can$50.00 – cn Can Microfilming [071]

LE FOYER DE L'INDUSTRIE / ed by Belair, Louis – Joliette, Canada. 10 aut 1880 – 1r – Can$25.00 – cn Can Microfilming [338]

LE FOYER DES FAMILLES ILLUSTRE – Montreal: C.A. Marchand, v1 no 1(23 Oct 1896)- – 9 – cn C.I.H.M. [440]

LE FOYER DOMESTIQUE – Ottawa: Foyer domestique. 1986?-1879? – 9 – cn C.I.H.M. [440]

LE FOYER DOMESTIQUE / L'ALBUM DES FAMILLES – Ottawa, Ontario. 1 mar 1876-1 jun 1881 – 2r – 1 – Can$50.00r – cn Can Microfilming [640]

Foy-Vaillant, Jo. *see* NUSIMATA AEREA IMPERATORUM, AUGUSTARUM ET CAESARUM, IN COLONIIS, MUNICIPIIS, ET URBIBUS JURE LATIO DONATUS, EX OMNI MODULO PERCUSSA

F.P.B. *see*
- EXERCICES ORTHOGRAPHIQUES

FR. ALONSO DE LA CRUZ (ALONSO DE SOTOMAYOR) DOTA A SU HIJA FELIPA / Meseguer Fernandez, Juan – Madrid: Graf. Calleja, 1970 – 1 – sp Bibl Santa Ana [946]

FR. ALONSO GUERRO EN LA INMACULADA EN LA LITERATURA FRANCISCANO-ESPANOLA / Uribe, Angel – Archivo Ibero Americano, 1955 – 1 – sp Bibl Santa Ana [440]

FR. HEBBELS VERHAELTNIS ZU DEN POLITISCHEN UND SOZIALEN FRAGEN / Steves, Heinrich – (Includes bibliographical references) – Greifswald: F W Kunike, 1909 – 1r – 1 – us U.W. Library [430]

FR. HERNANDO DE SANTIAGO. SANTANDER, 1929 / Perez, Luintin – Madrid: Razon y Fe, 1930 – 1 – sp Bibl Santa Ana [240]

FR. JUAN DE CARTAGENA / Vazquez, Isaac – Madrid: Archivo Ibero Americano, 1965 – 1 – sp Bibl Santa Ana [240]

DAS F.R. KREUTZWALD-LITERATURMUSEUM / Kahu, M – Tartu, 1970 – 1mf – ne IDC [400]

FR. LUIS DE GRANADA, VERDADERO Y UNICO AUTOR DEL LIBRO DE LA ORACION / Cuervo, Justo OP – Madrid: Imprenta Revista Archivos, Bibliotecas y Museos, 1918 – 1 – sp Bibl Santa Ana [240]

FR. PEDRO DE JEREZ EN LOS CUSTODIOS Y PROVINCIALES DE LA PROVINCIA DE SAN JOSE / Perez, Lorenzo – (Tambien Fr. Jose de Santa Maria en...; Fr. Baltasar de los Angeles...; Fr. Francisco de Montemayor...; Fr. Fco. de la Oliva...) – Madrid: Archivo Ibero Americano, 1924 – 1 – sp Bibl Santa Ana [240]

FRA ARABIEN – v35-40. 1935-40 (complete) – 1r – 1 – ATLA S0527 – us A.T.L.A. [073]

FRA DIAVOLO, ODER GASTHAUS VON TERRACINO... VOLLSTANDISH AUSZUG FUR DAS PIANOFORTE AUF 4 HANDS / Auber, D F E – Ms score – 1 – us Sibley [780]

FRA FORST TIL SIDST: GAMLE OG NY FORTAELLINGER / Nielsen, Anton – Odense: Hans Jensens Forlag, 1883. 361p – 1 – us U.W. Library [430]

FRA GRONLAND TIL STILLEHAVET / Rasmussen, Knud – BN 361 2.2 v. 1925-26 – 8 – ne IDC [910]

FRA GRONLANDSFORSKNINGENS FORSTE DAGE / Thalbitzer, W – Kobenhavn. 1932. Illus. BN-421 2 – 8 – ne IDC [910]

FRA GRUNDTVIGIANISMENS OG DEN INDRE MISSIONS TID 1848-1898 / Koch, L – Kobenhavn: G.E.C. Gad, 1898 – 1mf – us A.T.L.A. [240]

FRA LAALAND: NY FORTAELLINGER / Henningsen, Emanuel – Kjobenhavn: N.C. Rom, 1880. 295p – 1 – us U.W. Library [390]

FRA LUCA PACIOLI DIVINA PROPORTIONE (DIE LEHRE VON GOLDENEN SCHMITT) / Winterberg, Constantin – O 517q. 1889 – 9 – ne IDC [700]

FRA PAOLO SARPI : THE GREATEST OF THE VENETIANS / Robertson, Alexander – London: G. Allen, 1911 – 1mf – us A.T.L.A. [240]

FRA POL TIL POL;. / Bauditz, Sophus Gustav – Kjobenhavn, 1897. 2v in 1. illus – 1 – us U.W. Library [430]

EL FRACASO DE FRONDIZI : LA REDACCION DE ESTE LIBRO HASIDO PREPARADA POR LA SECCION PRENSA POLITICA DE EDICIONES COLON, DIRECTOR: A.E. BOTANA / Botana Santamarina, A E – Buenos Aires: Ediciones Colon, [1959] – 1 – CSUXADQ4971-B – us Hoover Inst Photo [320]

Fracastoro, G *see* SYPHILIS SIVE MORBUS GALLICUS

Frachetta, G *see*
- IL PRIMO LIBRO ORATIONI NEL GENERE DELIBERATIVO...
- IL RAGGVAGLIO DELLE MARAUIGLIOSE POMPE CON LE QUALI MEHEMET SETTERGI GENERALE DI MEHEMET 3. IMPERATOR DE' TURCHI E VSCITO FUORI DI CONSTATINOPOLI

Frachon, A *see* LES OPINIONS ALLEMANDES SUR LA RECONSTRUCTION DU DROIT INTERNATIONAL

FRACTIONS AND SECTIONS IN THE HOUSE OF REPRESENTATIVES OF THE REPUBLIC OF INDONESIA, AND A SHORT BIOGRAPHY OF THE CHAIRMAN, VICE CHAIRMAN AND MEMBERS OF HOUSE OF REPRESENTATIVES OF REPUBLIC OF INDONESIA ON AUGUST 1, 1954 / Indonesia.

Dewan Perwakilan Rakjat – SE-10,674 1. 1954 – 9 – ne IDC [323]
Fraenkel, Jonas *see*
- GOETHE'S BRIEFE AN CHARLOTTE VON STEIN
- MARGINALIEN ZU GOETHES BRIEFEN AN CHARLOTTE VON STEIN
- ZACHARIAS WERNERS WEIHE DER KRAFT

Fraenkel, O K *see* A DIGEST OF CASES...RELATING TO RECOGNITION OF GOVERNMENT
FRAENKISCHE LANDESZEITUNG : ANSBACHER TAGEBLATT – Ansbach, 1977- – ca 15r per yr – 1 – Dist. gw Mikrofilm – gw Misc Inst [072]
DER FRAENKISCHE MERKUR – Bamberg, 1794-95 – 1 – Dist. gw Mikrofilm – gw Misc Inst [943]
FRAENKISCHE NACHRICHTEN – Tauberbischofsheim, West Germany. 1977- – ca 8r per yr – 1 – gw Mikrofilm [072]
FRAENKISCHE TAGESZEITUNG – Nuernberg, 1933-1945 – 4r – 1 – DM3,300.00 – gw Mikro Press [943]
FRAENKISCHE TAGESZEITUNG – Nuernberg, Germany. 1 Jun 1933-15 Apr 1945 (incomplete) – 42r – 1 – gw Mikrofilm [072]
FRAENKISCHER KURIER – Nuernberg, jul 1 1913-aug 31 1944 – 128r – 1 – gw Mikrofilm [072]
FRAENKISCHER MERKUR – (Cont: Bamberger Zeitung, -1801; Kurpfalzbaierische Bamberger Zeitung, -feb1803; Bamberger Zeitung, -1809) – Bamberg, 1796-98, 1800-01, 1803 (incomplete), 1804-05, 1806 (almost complete) , 1807-aug 6 1848 – 1 – Dist. gw Mikrofilm – gw Misc Inst [943]
FRAENKISCHER MERKUR – Schweinfurt, 1794-95 – 1r – 1 – gw Mikrofilm [943]
FRAENKISCHER TAG – Bamberg, 1968- – ca 9r per yr – 1 – Dist. gw Mikrofilm – gw Misc Inst [072]
FRAENKISCHER TAGESPOST – Nuremberg, Germany. -d. 1 Sept 1916-6 Aug 1919. Imperfect. 8 reels – 1 – uk British Libr Newspaper [072]
FRAENKISCHES VOLK – (Cont by: Bayerische Ostwacht, jun 23 1934; Bayerische Ostmark, oct 1 1934) – Bayreuth, oct 1 1932-34 – 8r – 1 – gw Mikro Press [943]
FRAENKISCHES VOLK – (Cont by: Bayerische Ostwacht, jun 23 1934; Bayerische Ostmark, oct 1 1934) – Bayreuth, oct 1 1932-34 – 8r – 1 – Dist. gw Mikrofilm – gw Misc Inst [943]
FRAENKISCHES VOLK : NATIONALSOZIALISTISCHE TAGESZEITUNG – (Cont as: Bayerische Ostmark 1934) – Bayreuth, 1932-1934 – 8r – 1 – DM80.00r DM640.00set – gw Mikro Press [943]
FRAENKISCHES VOLK *see* BAMBERGER TAGBLATT
FRAENKISCHES VOLKSBLATT – Wuerzburg, West Germany. 1 Sept 1978- – ca 10r per yr – 1 – gw Mikrofilm [072]
FRAENZCHENS LIEDER / Hoffmann von Fallersleben, August Heinrich – Luebeck: Dittmer, 1859 – 1 – us U.W. Library [810]
DAS FRAEULEIN VON SCUDERI : ERZAEHLUNG AUS DEM ZEITALTER LUDWIGS 14 / Hoffmann, Ernst Theordor Amadeus – Heidelberg: H Meister, 1945 – 1r – 1 – us U.W. Library [830]
DAS FRAEULEIN VON SCUDERI : ERZAEHLUNG AUS DEM ZEITALTER LUDWIGS XIV / Hoffmann, Ernst Theordor Amadeus – Leipzig: H Seemann Nachfolger, [1900?] – 1 – us U.W. Library [830]
DIE FRAGE NACH DEM WESEN DER RELIGION / Reischle, Max – Freiburg i.B.: J.C.B. Mohr, 1889. 124p.1 fiche – 9 – us A.T.L.A. [240]
DIE FRAGE UEBER DIE NIEDERLANDE UND DIE RHEINLANDE / Arndt, Ernst Moritz – Leipzig, 1831 – 1mf – 9 – ILM-2546/1 – ne IDC [340]
FRAGEN DER ARBEITSOEKONOMIK – Berlin: Die Wirtschaft, 1954-60.Ceased with v19 (1960?). Each no. has distinctive title – 1 – us U.W. Library [330]
FRAGEN FUER LEBEN – 1911 – 1r – 1 – us Ross [270]
FRAGMENS D'UN VOYAGE EN AFRIQUE / Golbery, Sylvain M X. de – Paris, Treuttel et Wuertz. 1802 – 9 – 30.00 – fr Orientalistes [910]
DAS FRAGMENT DES DEMETRIUS / Schiller, Friedrich von – (Includes bibliographical references) – Wien: K Graeser, [1893?] – 1r – 1 – us U.W. Library [820]
FRAGMENT EINER SCHRIFT DES MAERTYRER-BISCHOFS PETRUS VON ALEXANDRIEN (T.U.U. 2-20/4B) / Schmidt, Carl – Leipzig, 1901 – 1mf – 9 – ne Slangenburg [240]
A FRAGMENT OF THE BABYLONIAN "DIBBARRA" EPIC / Jastrow, Morris – (Text in English and Akkadian; commentary in English. Includes bibliographical references) – New York: N D C Hodges, agent; Philadelphia: University of Pennsylvania Press, 1891 – 1mf – 9 – 0-8370-7223-9 – 1986-1223 – us A.T.L.A. [470]
A FRAGMENT OF THE OLIVER HART DIARY, AUG. 4, 1754-OCT. 27, 1754 / Hart, Oliver – Typed. 25p – 1 – 5.00 – us Baptist [920]
A FRAGMENT OF THE TRUE RELIGION, BEING THE SUBSTANCE OF TWO LETTERS FROM A METHODIST PREACHER IN CAMBRIDGESHIRE TO A CLERGYMAN IN NOTTINGHAMSHIRE / Berridge, J – London, 1760 – 1mf – 9 – MP-393/1 – ne IDC [240]
FRAGMENTA APOLOGETIKA; KRITIK DAN DJAWAB / Verkuyl, Johannes – SE 5164 1. 1963 – 9 – ne IDC [950]
FRAGMENTA BOTANICA / Jacquin, N J von – Vienna. 1800-09. B-5977 2 – 8 – ne IDC [580]
FRAGMENTA FLORULAE AETHIOPICOAEGYPTIACAE EX PLANTIS PRAECIPUE / Webb, P B – Paris. 1854. B-1050 2 – 8 – ne IDC [580]
FRAGMENTA HISTORICORUM GRAECORUM / ed by Didot, Ambr – Appolodori Bibliotheca cum fragmentis. Auxerunt, notis et prolegomenis illustrarunt indice plenissimo instruxerunt Car. et Theod. Muelleri. Accedunt marmora Parium et Rosettanum, hoc cum Letronnii, illud cum C. Muelleri commentariis. Parisiis. 1848-53. BHP-6289 6292 2 – 8 – ne IDC [900]
FRAGMENTA HISTORICORUM GRAECORUM / Muelleri, C – H-114 2. v. 1-5. 1841-1870 – 8 – ne IDC [930]
FRAGMENTA LITURGICA / Hall, Peter – 7v. 1848 – 1 – us A.T.L.A. [240]
FRAGMENTA PHYTOGRAPHIAE AUSTRALIAE / Mueller, Ferdinand Jakob Heinrich von – Melbourne, 1858-1882. v. 1-12. B-6085 1 – 9 – ne IDC [580]
FRAGMENTA SOCIALIA / Sumantri Praptokusumo – SE 1162 1. 1956 – 9 – ne IDC [300]
FRAGMENTARY RECORDS OF MISCELLANEOUS REICH MINISTRIES AND OFFICES, 1919-45 – 28r – 1 – T178 – us Nat'l Archives [324]
FRAGMENTE DER HOMILIEN DES CYRILL VON ALEXANDRIEN ZUM LUKASEVANGELIUM (T.U.U. 3-34/1B) / Sickenberger, J – Leipzig, 1909 – 1mf – 9 – ne Slangenburg [240]
FRAGMENTE EINER LEDERHANDSCHRIFT ENTHALTEND MOSE'S LETZTE REDE AN DIE KINDER ISRAEL MITGETHEILT UND GEPRUEFT / Guthe, Hermann – Leipzig:Breitkopf & Haertel, 1883 – 1mf – 9 – 0-8370-3428-0 – 1985-1428 – us A.T.L.A. [220]
FRAGMENTE EINER MONOGRAPHIE DER CHARACEEN / Braun, A C H – (Abhandl. Koenigl. Akad. der Wiss.). Berlin. 1882. B-989 2 – 8 – ne IDC [580]
FRAGMENTE EINIGER GEDANKEN DES MUSIKALISCHEN ZUSCHAUERS DIE BESSERE AUFNAME DER MUSIK IN DEUTSCHLAND BETREFFEND / Dressler, E C – Gotha. 1767. BP-671 1 – 9 – ne IDC [780]
FRAGMENTE UEBER MENSCHENBILDUNG / Arndt, Ernst Moritz – Altona: J F Hammerich, 1805 – 1r – 1 – us U.W. Library [943]
FRAGMENTE VORNICAENISCHER KIRCHENVAETER AUS DEN SACRA PARALLELA / John, of Damascus, Saint – Leipzig: J.C. Hinrichs, 1899. (Texte und Untersuchungen zur Geschichte altchristlicher Literatur; der ganzen Reihe Bd 20 Heft 2. n.F, 5. Bd Heft 2) – 1mf – us A.T.L.A. [240]
FRAGMENTE VORNICAENISCHER KIRCHENVAETER AUS DEN SACRA PARALLELA (T.U.U. 2-20/2) / Holl, Karl – Leipzig, 1899 – 5mf – 9 – ne Slangenburg [240]
FRAGMENTOS MUSICOS, REPARTIDOS EN QUATRO TRATADOS / Nassarre, P – 1700 – 9 – us Sibley [780]
FRAGMENTS DE TACTIQUE / Mesnil-Durand – Paris. C. A. Jombert pere. 1774. lxviii, 421p. pl.; viii, 144p. pl. (Strategy of War Series) – 9 – fr Hachette [355]
FRAGMENTS D'UN VOYAGE EN AFRIQUE FAIT PENDANT LES ANNEES 1785, 1786, ET 1787 DANS LES CONTREES OCCIDENTALES DE CE CONTINENT, COMPRISES ENTRE LE CAP BLANC DE BARBARIE ET LE CAP DES PALMES / Golbery, Sylvain M X. de – (African Library series). 2 v. 1802 – 9 – fr Hachette [910]
FRAGMENTS D'UNE FLORE DE L'ARABIE PETREE / Delile, A R – Paris. 1833 – 8 – ne IDC [580]
FRAGMENTS FROM GRAECO-JEWISH WRITERS / ed by Stearns, Wallace Nelson – Chicago: Uni of Chicago Press, 1908 – 1mf – 9 – 0-8370-5380-3 – 1985-3380 – us A.T.L.A. [450]
FRAGMENTS IN PHILOSOPHY AND SCIENCE : BEING COLLECTED ESSAYS AND ADDRESSES / Baldwin, James Mark – New York: Scribner, 1902 – 1mf – us A.T.L.A. [100]
THE FRAGMENTS OF HERACLEON / ed by Brooke, Alan E – 1891 – 3mf – 9 – ne Slangenburg [240]
FRAGMENTS OF THE BOOKS OF KINGS ACCORDING TO THE TRANSLATION OF AQUILA / Burkitt, F Crawford – Cambridge, 1987 – 2mf – 8 – ne Slangenburg [220]
FRAGMENTS OF THE NEGRO ECONOMICS DIVISION FILES, 1919-21 – Washington, DC, National Archives and Records Service [19–] – us Res Libr [330]
FRAGMENTS POLITIQUES ET LITTERAIRES / Boerne, Ludwig – [Paris]: Pagnerre, 1842 – 1 – us U.W. Library [840]
Fragonard, J H *see* LA CONDITION DES PERSONNES DANS LA CITE DU VATICAN
Fragoso, J *see* DISCURSO DE COSAS AROMATICAS...DE LAS INDIAS...PARA USO DE MEDICINAS
FRAGRANT MEMORIES OF THE TUESDAY MEETING: AND THE GUIDE TO HOLINESS,AND THEIR FIFTY YEARS' WORK FOR JESUS / Hughes, George – 1886 – 9 – us A.T.L.A. [240]
Frahm, Ronald et al *see* SYNCHROTRON RADIATION NEWS
Fraidl, Franz *see* DIE EXEGESE DER SIEBZIG WOCHEN DANIELS IN DER ALTEN UND MITTLEREN ZEIT
FRAIE ARBAITER VELT – London, UK. Heroisgegeben fun Anarchistishen Press Farein. 10 Nov 1905-28 Jun 1906 – 1 – uk British Libr Newspaper [072]
FRAIE PRESSE – London, UK. 30 Sept 1937 – 1 – uk British Libr Newspaper [072]
FRAIE VELT (THE FREE WORLD) – London, UK. May-Jul 1891 – 1 – uk British Libr Newspaper [072]
FRAIE VORT – London, UK. 15 Sept 1933-26 Jul 1935 – 1 – uk British Libr Newspaper [072]
FRAIE VORT – London, UK. Aroisgegeben fun Anarchistishen Propaganda Komitet.Sept 1925 – 1 – uk British Libr Newspaper [072]
FRAIE YIDISHE TRIBUNE (FREE JEWISH TRIBUNE) – London, UK. Jun/Jul 1946-Jan/Mar 1948 – 1 – uk British Libr Newspaper [072]
Frailas, A *see* CONOCIMIENTO, CURACION Y PRESERVACION DE LA PESTE
UN FRAILE EXTREMENO EN FILIPINAS / Munoz de San Pedro, Miguel – Badajoz: Dip.Prov., 1952 – 1 – sp Bibl Santa Ana [950]
Frain du Tremblay, J *see*
- DISCOURS SUR L'ORIGINE DE LA POESIE
- TRAITE DES LANGUES
- TRAITE DES LANGUES OU L'ON DONNE DES PRINCIPES ET DES REGLES POUR JUGER DU MERITE ET DE L'EXCELLENCE DE CHAQUE LANGUE ET EN PARTICULIER DE LA LANGUE FRANCAISE

DER FRAIND – (Missing: 1903 v1(several nos); 1904, v2(1-148 daily issues); 1905, v3(several nos); 1906 v4(72,105)) – Spb., Warsaw. v1-12. 1903-1913 – 11r – 1 – J-92-8/3 – ne IDC [072]
DER FRAIND – St Petersburg, 1903-13 – 16r – 1 – us Ross [072]
DER FRAIND – St Petersburg, Warsaw. Jan 1903-Dec 1908; Jan 1910-Oct 1913 – 1 – us NY Public [072]
FRAIND (THE FAMILY FRIEND WEEKLY) – London, UK. 6 Jan 1922-27 Jun 1924; 13 Feb 1925-20 Apr 1926 – 1 – uk British Libr Newspaper [072]
Fraknoi, V *see* MAGYARORSZAG EGYHAZI ES POLITIKAI OESSEKOETTETESEI A ROMAI SZENTSZEKKEL
FRAKTSIIA PROGRESSISTOV V 4-I GOSUDARSTVENNOI DUMIE – S-Peterburg: Tip. V F Kirshbauma, 1913- – 1 – CSUXA89-B4262 – us Hoover Inst Photo [947]
FRAM – London, UK. 5 Dec 1942; 20 Feb, 20 Mar-30 Oct 1943; 8, 22 Jan, 4 Mar-23 Dec 1944; 6 Jan-23 Apr, 12 May 1945 – 1 – uk British Libr Newspaper [072]
FRAMAT – Malmo, Sweden. 1871-83 – 7r – 1 – sw Kungliga [072]
Frame, Elizabeth *see*
- A LIST OF MICMAC NAMES OF PLACES, RIVERS, ETC., IN NOVA SCOTIA
- THE TWILIGHT OF FAITH

FRAME SAW MANUAL : FAO/SIDA SAWMILL MANUALS – 1982 – 107p – it F.A.O. [621]
Framery, Nicolas-Etienne *see* ENCYCLOPEDIE METHODIQUE MUSIQUE
FRAMES OF MIND / Walkley, Arthur Bingham – London: G. Richards, 1899 – 1 roll – 1 – 1-55879-579-0 – uk Libr Preservation [790]
FRAMEWORK FOR LAND EVALUATION – 1981 – 79p – it F.A.O. [333]
THE FRAMEWORK OF THE CHURCH : A TREATISE ON CHURCH GOVERNMENT / Killen, W D – Edinburgh: T.& T. Clark, 1890 – 1mf – us A.T.L.A. [240]
THE FRAMEWORK OF THE ECONOMIC AND FINANCIAL POLICIES OF THE GOVERNMENT OF BASUTOLAND, 1967-72 – Mazenod: Mazenod Institute, [197-?] – us Res Libr [330]
FRAMFARI – (In Icelandic. Some issues missing) – Canada, Sept 1877-1880 – 1r – 1 – cn Commonwealth Micro [072]
THE FRAMING OF THE CONSTITUTION OF THE UNITED STATES / Farrand, Max – New Haven, London: Yale University Press, 1913 – 4mf – 9 – $6.00 – LLMC 95-077 – us L.L.M.C. [323]
FRAMING THE CONSTITUTION OF JAPAN, 1944-49 – (Guide only $380.00) – Primary sources in English – $3,145.00 – 0-88692-155-4 – us UPA [323]
FRAMINGHAM 1687-1849 – (Mf 1T-2T: Births & Deaths 1687-1734. Mf 1T-4T: Marriages 1700-55. Mf 3T: Vital Records 1708-49. Mf 4T: Births 1738-65. Mf 5T-7T: Vital Records 1738-1808. Mf 7T-10T: Births & Deaths 1761-1849+. Mf 10T-12T: Marriage Intentions 1807-49. Mf 12T-14T: Marriages 1806-44. Mf 14T-15T: Births 1844-49. Mf 15T-16T: Marriages & Deaths 1844-49. Mf 16T: Out-of-Town Marriages 1695-1799) – (mf ed 1996) – 16mf – 9 – 0-87623-250-0 – us Holbrook [920]
Framingham, Massachusetts. First Baptist Church and Society *see* RECORDS
FRAMLINGTON & EYE MERCURY – England. 1978-81. -w. 8 reels – 1 – uk British Libr Newspaper [072]
FRAN DE SVARTAS VAERLDSDEL / Kolmodin, Adolf – Taresadd i Uganda. 1891 – 1 – us A.T.L.A. [240]
FRAN TRA TILL STAL – 1953 – 1 – us I.U. Libraries [390]
FRANC JEU – Amos, Canada. 19 dec 1958; v4 n8. 19 dec 1962 – 1r – 1 – Can$25.00 – cn Can Microfilming [072]
LE FRANC PARLER – Quebec, Canada. 5 oct 1913-v1 n5. 1 nov 1913 – 1r – 1 – Can$30.00 – cn Can Microfilming [072]
LE FRANC PARLER : REVUE HEBDOMADAIRE – St-Jean, Canada. v1 n36. 20 nov 1909 – 1r – 1 – Can$25.00 – cn Can Microfilming [072]
Franca Cannizzo, S la *see* DELLE CONDIZIONI IMPOSTE ALLO STRANIERO IN ITALIA...
LE FRANCAIS – Ed. du soir du journal: Le Matin. paris. 3 dec 1900-juin 1901, 1902-13 sept 1903 – 1 – fr A.C.R.P.P. [072]
LE FRANCAIS – Paris. Journal du soir.2 aout 1868-1 nov 1887, 12 oct 1890, 10 oct 1892, 30 mars 1895, 5 juin 1897, 16 mars 1898.Contient egalement l'ed. de Bordeaux, 9-13 mars 1871 – 1 – fr A.C.R.P.P. [072]
LE FRANCAIS – (Filmed as pt of: Commune de Paris newspapers) – Paris: Impr centrale du Chemins du fer, mar 24, apr 19 1871 – us Res Libr [072]
LE FRANCAIS ALSACIEN / Dhauteville, J – 1852 – 9 – fr I.C.S. [440]
LES FRANCAIS AU CANADA ET EN ACADIE / Gourmont, Remy de – Paris: Firmin-Didot, 1888. 03492. (Pre-1900 Canadiana) – 9 – cn C.I.H.M. [971]

LES FRANCAIS AU CANADA ET EN ACADIE : OUVRAGE ILLUSTRE DE 50 GRAVURES / Gourmont, Remy de – Paris: Firmin-Didot et cie, 1888. SEM16P266 – 1r – 5 – Can$9.00 – cn Bibl Nat [971]

LES FRANCAIS AU NIGER : VOYAGE ET COMBATS... / Pietri, Camille – (Filmed with: Les explorations au Senegal et dans les contrees voisines par J Ancelle) – Paris: Hatchette, 1885 – 1 – us Res Libr [960]

LES FRANCAIS DANS L'AMERIQUE DE NORD, OU, HISTOIRE DES PRINCIPALES FAMILLES DU CANADA. SUPPLEMENT / Daniel, Francois – Montreal: E. Senecal, 1868. 04202. (Pre-1900 Canadiana) – 9 – cn C.I.H.M. [971]

LES FRANCAIS DANS L'INDE / Vinson, J – 9 – fr Orientalistes [944]

LES FRANCAIS EN AMERIQUE: CANADA, ACADIE, LOUISIANE / Feyrol, Jacques – Paris: H. Lecene et H. Oudin, 1886?. 05463. (Pre-1900 Canadiana) – 9 – cn C.I.H.M. [305]

FRANCAIS ET ALLEMANDS, HISTOIRE DE LEURS RELATIONS INTELLECTUELLES ET SENTIMENTALES / Reynaud, Louis – Paris: A. Fayard et Cie., 1930. 386p – 1 – us U.W. Library [944]

Francais, J *see*
- L'EGLISE ET LA SCIENCE
- L'EGLISE ET LA SORCELLERIE

FRANCAIS, MALGACHES, BANTOUS, ARABES, TURCS, CHINOIS, CANAQUES...PARLONS-NOUS UNE MEME LANGUE? : ESSAI DE SEMANTIQUE COMPAREE, LES GRANDS THEMES UNIVERSELS DU LANGAGE / Auber, Jacques – Tananarive: Impr officielle, 1958 – us Res Libr [410]

LE FRANCAIS MODERNE – Revue de linguistique francaise. Paris. 1933-72 – 1 – fr A.C.R.P.P. [073]

UNE FRANCAISE AU SOUDAN SUR LA ROUTE DE TOMBOUCTOU, DU SENEGAL AU NIGER / Bonnetain, Paul (Madame) – 2. ed. Paris: Librairies-Impr Reunies, 1894 – us Res Libr [910]

UNE FRANCAISE AU SOUDAN SUR LA ROUTE DE TOMBOUCTOU, DU SENEGAL AU NIGER / Bonnetain, Madame Paul – 2nd ed. Paris, Librairies-Imprimeries Reunies, 1894 – us Res Libr [960]

LES FRANCAISES FACE A LA POLITIQUE. COMPORTEMENT POLITIQUE ET CONDITION SOCIALE / Dogan, M & Narbonne, J – 4mf – 9 – F60.00 – fr Ethnologie [320]

LE FRANCARIO – Bourget, Ontario. 10 dec 1959-v1 n23. 18 mai 1960 – 1r – 1 – Can$25.00 – cn Can Microfilming [072]

FRANCE : ANNUAIRE STATISTIQUE DE LA FRANCE 1878-1965 / France. Institut National de la Statistique et des Etudes Economiques – (Coll title: European Official Statistical Serials, 1841-1984) – 499mf – 9 – £2,620.00 – uk Chadwyck [944]

FRANCE : CHRISTIANISME ET CIVILISATION / Bonet-Maury, Gaston – Paris: Hachette, 1907 – 1mf – us A.T.L.A. [944]

FRANCE – (Library wants: no 846 (May 19, 1943) and no 40 (July 27, 1945); some issues slightly mutilated) – London: [s.n.], 1940-1946. 1377 no – 1 – CSUX85-S374 – us Hoover Inst Photo [944]

FRANCE – London, UK. 6 Oct 1921-9 Jul 1969 – 1 – uk British Libr Newspaper [072]

France *see*
- 3E PLAN DE MODERNISATION ET D'EQUIPEMENT 1958-1961 (DECRET NO. 59-443 DU 19 MAR 1959)
- 5E PLAN DE DEVELOPPEMENT ECONOMIQUE ET SOCIAL (1966-1970)
- ANNUAIRE METEOROLOGIQUE DE LA FRANCE POUR 1849-52
- BULLETIN ANNEXE AU JOURNAL OFFICIEL
- BULLETIN DES ANNONCES LEGALES OBLIGATOIRES (B.A.L.O.)
- BULLETIN OFFICIEL DE LA CONCURRENCE ET DE LA CONSOMMATION DEPUIS 1941
- BULLETIN OFFICIEL DES AFFAIRES SOCIALES ET DE LA SOLIDARITE
- BULLETIN OFFICIEL DES ANNONCES COMMERCIALES
- BULLETIN OFFICIEL DES FORCES FRANCAISES LIBRES
- CONSEIL ECONOMIQUE ET SOCIAL
- DEMANDES A FAIRE A CHAQUE ADMINISTRATION DE DEPARTEMENT
- DEUXIEME PLAN DE MODERNISATION ET D'EQUIPEMENT (1954-1957)
- DEUXIEME PLAN DE MODERNISATION ET D'EQUIPEMENT 1954-1957 (LOI NO. 56-342 DU 27 MAR 1956)
- DOCUMENTS ADMINISTRATIFS
- DOCUMENTS DIPLOMATIQUES FRANCAIS
- ELECTIONS DE 1958
- LES EVENEMENTS DE MAI-JUIN 1968
- FRENCH ROYAL AND ADMINISTRATIVE ACTS, 1256-1794
- LE JOURNAL OFFICIEL
- JOURNAL OFFICIEL DE LA REPUBLIQUE FRANCAISE
- JOURNAL OFFICIEL DE L'AFRIQUE OCCIDENTALE FRANCAISE
- JOURNAL OFFICIEL DE L'EMPIRE FRANCAIS
- LOIS ET DECRETS
- LOIS ET DECRETS ASSOCIATIONS
- MEMOIRES DES COMMISSAIRES DU ROI ET DE CEUX DE SA MAJESTE BRITANIQUE SUR LES POSSESSIONS ET LES DROITS RESPECTIFS DES DEUX COURONNES EN AMERIQUE, AVEC LES ACTES PUBLICS ET PIECES JUSTIFICATIVES
- PERIODIQUES CLANDESTINS 1939-1945
- PLAN INTERMEDIAIRE, 1960-61
- QUATRIEME PLAN DE DEVELOPPEMENT ECONOMIQUE ET SOCIAL (1962-1965)
- QUESTIONS SUR LESQUELLES LES COMMUNES DE LA REPUBLIQUE SONT PRIEES DE FOURNIR DES SOLUTIONS AU MINISTRE DE L'INTERIEUR
- RAPPORT GENERAL SUR LES OBJECTIFS GENERAUX ET LES ACTIONS PRIORITAIRES DU VIE PLAN
- RAPPORT GENERAL SUR LES OBJECTIFS GENERAUX ET LES ACTIONS PRIORITAIRES DU VIE PLAN, 1971-1975
- RECUEIL DE CIRCULAIRES PREFECTORALES ET DE MODELES DE TABLEAUX CONCERNANT LA STATISTIQUE DES DEPARTEMENTS
- RECUEIL DES ACTES ADMINISTRATIFS EN ALGERIE
- SELECTION DE JOURNAUX DE LA PERIODE DE LA COMMUNE MARS A MAI 1871
- SELECTION DE JOURNAUX EPHEMERES 1848-1849
- SELECTION DE JOURNAUX EPHEMERES 1848-1849, 1
- SELECTION DE JOURNAUX EPHEMERES 1869-1871
- SELECTION DE JOURNAUX EPHEMERES 1869-1871, 1
- SELECTION DE JOURNAUX EPHEMERES 1869-1871, 3
- SELECTION DE JOURNAUX EPHEMERES DE LA PERIODE DE LA REVOLUTION
- SELECTION DE JOURNAUX EPHEMERES DE LA PERIODE DE LA REVOLUTION, 1
- SELECTION DE JOURNAUX EPHEMERES DE LA PERIODE DE LA REVOLUTION, BOBINE 6
- SELECTION DE JOURNAUX EPHEMERES DE LA PERIODE DE LA REVOLUTION, BOBINES 1-7
- TABLES ANNUELLES
- TEXTES D'INTERET GENERAL
- TEXTES D'INTERET GENERAL. PREPARATIONS DU VIEPLAN

LA FRANCE : ACTIVITES DE L'UNION NATIONALE FRANCAISE / ed by Dallemand, Henry – Montreal, Canada. 6 dec 1908; 13 dec 1908 – 1r – 1 – Can$25.00 – cn Can Microfilming [072]

LA FRANCE – Dir. Jacques Menard, Henry Mercadier. Sigmaringen. oct 1944-mars 1945 – 1 – fr A.C.R.P.P. [073]

LA FRANCE – Journal des interets monarchiques et religieux de l'Europe. Dir. A.M. De Lisle. Paris. janv-15 mars 1837 – 1 – fr A.C.R.P.P. [073]

LA FRANCE : JOURNAL QUOTIEN DU MATIN – (Herausgegeben von der Vichy-Regierung (Marschall Pe£1tain) waehrend der letzten Kriegsmonate) – Sigmaringen, Wuerttemberg – 1r – 1 – DM80.00 – gw Mikro Press [072]

LA FRANCE – Politique, scientifique et litteraire puis Organe du Parti republicain progressiste. Paris. janv-avr 1863, janv-juin 1870, janv-juin 1871, 1881-82, 1884, juil-dec 1885, janv-juin 1890 – 1 – fr A.C.R.P.P. [073]

FRANCE, 1919-41 : REPORTS / U.S. Military Intelligence – 12 reels with printed guide – 1 – $1,240.00 – us UPA [355]

FRANCE AFRICAINE, SAHARA ET SOUDAN : ESSAI SUR LA MISE EN VALEUR DU SAHARA ET SUR LES COMMUNICATIONS DU CENTRE AFRICAINE AVEC L'EUROPE / Pavard, C – Paris: F Leve, 1905 – 1 – us Res Libr [960]

France. Agence Generale des Colonies *see* BULLETIN

France. Ancien Regime *see*
- ARRETS DE LA CHAMBRE DES COMPTES DE PARIS
- ARRETS DE LA COUR DES AIDES
- ARRETS DE LA COUR DES MONNAIES
- ARRETS DE LA COUR DU PARLEMENT
- ARRETS DU CONSEIL D'ETAT DU ROI
- ARRETS DU GRAND CONSEIL DU ROI
- ARRETS ROYAUX

[FRANCE AND THE CAUSES AND ORIGINS OF WORLD WAR 1 PAMPHLET COLLECTION] – 1892-1918 – 1 – CSUXAML2958-B – us Hoover Inst Photo [320]

France. Annam *see* MONITEUR DU PROTECTORAT DE L'ANNAM ET DU TONKIN

France. Assemblee consultative provisoire *see*
- DEBATS
- DOCUMENTS

France. Assemblee de l'Union francaise *see*
- DEBATS
- DOCUMENTS

France. Assemblee Nationale *see*
- ANNALES
- DEBATS DE L'ASSEMBLEE NATIONALE
- DEBATS PARLEMENTAIRES
- DOCUMENTS DE L'ASSEMBLEE NATIONALE
- DOCUMENTS PARLEMENTAIRES

France. Assemblee nationale *see* IMPRESSIONS

France. Assemblee nationale. Chambre des Deputes *see* ETAT DES TRAVAUX LEGISLATIFS..

France. Assemblee nationale. Senat *see* (IMPRESSIONS)

France. Assemblee puis Nationale Constituante *see* DEBATS

LA FRANCE AU DAHOMEY / Albeca, Alexandre L d' – Paris, Hachette. 1895 – 9 – 7.50 – fr Orientalistes [960]

FRANCE BEFORE EUROPE / Michelet, Jules – Tr. from the French. Boston: Roberts Brothers, 1871. xxiv,111p – 1 – us U.W. Library [944]

France. Bibliotheques publiques *see* LES BREVIAIRES MANUSCRITS DES BIBLIOTHEQUES PUBLIQUES DE FRANCE

LA FRANCE CATHOLIQUE – L'hebdomadaire d'information et de culture chretiennes. 1957 – 1 – fr A.C.R.P.P. [073]

France. Centre national du commmerce exterieur *see* LE MARCHE MAROCAIN

France. Chambre des Deputes *see*
- DEBATS PARLEMENTAIRES
- DOCUMENTS PARLEMENTAIRES
- IMPRESSIONS
- NOTICES ET PORTRAITS

France. Chambres francaises *see* ARCHIVES PARLEMENTAIRES DE 1787-1860

France. Commissariat General du Plan *see*
- 2E PLAN DE MODERNISATION ET D'EQUIPEMENT RAPPORT GENERAL DE LA COMMISSION D'ETUDE. DES TERRITORIES D'OUTRE-MER
- 2E PLAN FRANCE, RAPPORT GENERAL DE LA COMMISSION D'ETUDE. ALGERIE
- 2E PLAN RAPPORT GENERAL DE LA COMMISSION D'ETUDE ET DE COORDINATION DES PLANS. DES DEPARTEMENTS D'OUTRE-MER
- 3E PLAN, 1958-1961 RAPPORT GENERAL DE LA COMMISSION DE MODERNISATION ET D'EQUIPEMENT DES DEP. D'OUTRE-MER
- 4E PLAN, 1962-1965 LA RECHERCHE SCIENTIFIQUE ET TECHNIQUE
- 4E PLAN, 1962-1965 RAPPORT DE LA COMMISSION DE L'ARTISANAT
- 4E PLAN, 1962-1965 RAPPORT DE LA COMMISSION DES PECHES MARITIMES
- 4E PLAN, 1962-1965 RAPPORT GENERAL DE LA COMMISSION DE LA CHIMIE
- 4E PLAN, 1962-1965 RAPPORT GENERAL DE LA COMMISSION DE LA RADIODIFFUSION ET DE LA TELEVISION
- 4E PLAN, 1962-1965 RAPPORT GENERAL DE LA COMMISSION DE L'AGRICULTURE
- 4E PLAN, 1962-1965 RAPPORT GENERAL DE LA COMMISSION DE L'ECONOMIE GENERALE ET DU FINANCEMENT
- 4E PLAN, 1962-1965 RAPPORT GENERAL DE LA COMMISSION DE L'ENERGIE
- 4E PLAN, 1962-1965 RAPPORT GENERAL DE LA COMMISSION DE L'EQUIPEMENT SCOLAIRE, UNIVERSITAIRE ET SPORTIF
- 4E PLAN 1962-1965 RAPPORT GENERAL DE LA COMMISSION DE L'EQUIPEMENT URBAIN
- 4E PLAN, 1962-1965 RAPPORT GENERAL DE LA COMMISSION DES CARBURANTS
- 4E PLAN, 1962-1965 RAPPORT GENERAL DE LA COMMISSION DES INDUSTRIES AGRICOLES ET ALIMENTAIRES
- 4E PLAN, 1962-1965 RAPPORT GENERAL DE LA COMMISSION DES POSTES ET TELECOMMUNICATIONS
- 4E PLAN, 1962-1965 RAPPORT GENERAL DE LA COMMISSION DU TOURISME
- 4E PLAN DE DEVELOPPEMENT ECONOMIQUE ET SOCIAL (1962-1965) RAPPORT GENERAL DE LA COMMISSION DE LA MAIN-D'OEUVRE
- 5E PLAN, 1966-1970 COMMISSION DE L'HABITATION
- 5E PLAN, 1966-1970 ECONOMIC AND SOCIAL DEVELOPMENT PLAN
- 5E PLAN, 1966-1970 ENFANCE INADAPTEE, RAPPORT DE L'INTERGROUPE
- 5E PLAN, 1966-1970 ORIENTATION ET FINANCEMENT DE LA POLITIQUE FONCIERE
- 5E PLAN, 1966-1970 ORIENTATIONS DE LA POLITIQUE D'URBANISME
- 5E PLAN, 1966-1970 RAPPORT GENERAL DE LA COMMISSION CENTRALE DES DEPARTEMENTS D'ONTRE-MER
- 5E PLAN, 1966-1970 RAPPORT GENERAL DE LA COMMISSION DE LA CHIMIE
- 5E PLAN, 1966-1970 RAPPORT GENERAL DE LA COMMISSION DE LA MAIN-D'OEUVRE
- 5E PLAN, 1966-1970. RAPPORT GENERAL DE LA COMMISSION DE LA PRODUCTIVITE
- 5E PLAN, 1966-1970 RAPPORT GENERAL DE LA COMMISSION DE L'EAU
- 5E PLAN, 1966-1970 RAPPORT GENERAL DE LA COMMISSION DE L'ENERGIE
- 5E PLAN, 1966-1970 RAPPORT GENERAL DE LA COMMISSION DE L'EQUIPEMENT SCOLAIRE, UNIVERSITAIRE ET SPORTIF
- 5E PLAN, 1966-1970 RAPPORT GENERAL DE LA COMMISSION DE L'EQUIPEMENT URBAIN
- 5E PLAN, 1966-1970 RAPPORT GENERAL DE LA COMMISSION DES CARBURANTS
- 5E PLAN, 1966-1970 RAPPORT GENERAL DE LA COMMISSION DES INDUSTRIES AGRICOLES ET ALIMENTAIRES
- 5E PLAN, 1966-1970 RAPPORT GENERAL DE LA COMMISSION DES INDUSTRIES DE TRANSFORMATION
- 5E PLAN, 1966-1970 RAPPORT GENERAL DE LA COMMISSION DES PECHES MARITIMES
- 5E PLAN, 1966-1970 RAPPORT GENERAL DE LA COMMISSION DES POSTES ET TELECOMMUNICATIONS
- 5E PLAN. 1966-1970 RAPPORT GENERAL DE LA COMMISSION DU COMMERCE
- 5E PLAN, 1966-1970 RAPPORT GENERAL DE LA COMMISSION DU SECTEUR DES METIERS ET DE L'ARTISANAT
- 5E PLAN, 1966-1970 RAPPORT GENERAL DE L'EQUIPEMENT SANITAIRE ET SOCIAL
- 5E PLAN DE DEVELOPPEMENT ECONOMIQUE ET SOCIAL LA RECHERCHE SCIENTIFIQUE ET TECHNIQUE
- CINQUIEME PLAN, 1966-1970 RAPPORT GENERAL DE LA COMMISSION DE L'EQUIPEMENT CULTUREL ET DU PATRIMOINE ARTISTIQUE
- CINQUIEME PLAN, 1966-1970 RAPPORT GENERAL DE LA COMMISSION DES BUREAUX ET ORGANISMES D'ETUDES TECHNIQUES
- CINQUIEME PLAN, 1966-1970 RAPPORT GENERAL DE LA COMMISSION DES PRESTATIONS SOCIALES
- PREMIER RAPPORT DE LA COMMISSION DE MODERNISATION DES TERRITOIRES D'OUTRE-MER
- RAPPORT ANNUEL SUR L'EXECUTION DU PLAN DE MODERNISATION ET D'EQUIPEMENT
- RAPPORT SUR LE REALISATION DU PLAN DE MODERNISATION ET D'EQUIPEMENT DE L'UNION FRANCAISE ANNEE 1952
- RAPPORT SUR L'EXECUTION DU PROGRAMME D'EQUIPMENT DE L'ALGERIE EN 1961

France. Commissariat General du Plan. Banque Industrielle de Financement et de Credit, Paris *see* RAPPORTS ET RESOLUTIONS

France. Commissariat general du plan de modernisation et d'equipement *see*
- CINQ ANS D'EXECUTION DU PLAN DE MODERNISATION ET D'EQUIPEMENT DE L'UNION FRANCAISE REALISATIONS 1947-1951 ET PROGRAMME 1952
- QUATRE ANS D'EXECUTION DU PLAN DE MODERNISATION ET D'EQ1906-1920/21
- RAPPORT GENERAL SUR LE PREMIER PLAN DE MODERNISATION ET D'EQUIPEMENT (1947-1950)

France. Commission d'enquete sur les actes du gouvernement de la defense nationale *see*
- ENQUETE PARLEMENTAIRE SUR LES ACTES DU GOUVERNEMENT DE LA DEFENSE NATIONALE...DEPOSITIONS DES TEMOINS
- RAPPORTS FAITS AU NOM DE LA COMMISSION D'ENQUETE

France. Commission des Annales des Ponts et Chaussees *see*
- LOIS, DECRETS, ARRETES
- MEMOIRES ET DOCUMENTS

France. Commission des Colonies *see* RAPPORT SUR LES TROUBLES DE SAINT-DOMINGUE..

France. Commission d'Etude Tunisie *see* 2E PLAN FRANCE, RAPPORT GENERAL DE LA COMMISSION D'ETUDE. TUNISIE

LA FRANCE CONNUE SOUS SES PLUS UTILES RAPPORTS OU NOUVEAU DICTIONNAIRE UNIVERSEL DE LA FRANCE DRESSE D'APRES LA CARTE EN 180 FEUILLES DE CARSIGNY / Dupain-Triel, Jean Louis – Paris: Le Cellot, 1786. 115p. 2 fiches. (Statistics Series: Topography) – 9 – 6.00 – fr Bibl Nationale [944]

France. Conseil de la Republique *see*
- DEBATS PARLEMENTAIRES
- DOCUMENTS PARLEMENTAIRES

France. Conseil d'Etat *see*
- ETUDES ET DOCUMENTS
- RECUEIL DES ARRETS

France. Conseil Economique *see*
- AVIS ET RAPPORTS
- BULLETIN
- ETUDES ET TRAVAUX. LES HALLES CENTRALES DE PARIS

France. Convention Nationale *see* BULLETIN

France. Cour de Cassation. Chambre criminelle *see* BULLETIN DES ARRETS

France. Cour de Cassation. Chambres civiles *see* BULLETIN DES ARRETS

FRANCE, CURRENT RESEARCH – (History, sociology and political science. Theses and dissertations selected for excellence by the Association Universitaire pour la Diffusion internationale de la Recherche. 209 titles (available separately) in French. Printed guide and index) – 9 – $3,209.00 – us Ross [944]

LA FRANCE DANS L'AFRIQUE DU NORD : ALGERIE ET TUNISIE / Vignon, Louis Valery – 2e. ed. Paris: Guillaumin, 1887 – 1 – us Res Libr [960]

LA FRANCE D'ASIE – Saigon. 5 nov 1901-30 juin 1906 – 1 – fr A.C.R.P.P. [073]

LA FRANCE DE DEMAIN – Paris, France. -d. 30 Sept 1914-10 Jan 1916. 2 reels – 1 – uk British Libr Newspaper [072]

LA FRANCE DE DEMAIN – Paris. -m June 1898-Jul 1914. 18 reels – 1 – uk British Libr Newspaper [072]

LA FRANCE DEMANDANT SES COLONIES, OU RECLAMATIONS DE L'AGRICULTURE, DU COMMERCE, DES MANUFACTURES, DES ARTISTES ET DES OUVRIERS DE TOUS LES DEPARTEMENTS ADRESSEES AU CORPS LEGISLATIF... / Limochel, F – (Slave Trade and Abolitionism in France series). 1797 – 9 – fr Hachette [380]

France. Direction de la Documentation *see* ACCORDS PASSES ENTRE LA FRANCE ET L'ALGERIE DE JUILLET 1962 AU 31 DEC 1963

LA FRANCE EN TUNISIE – Tunis, Impr Rapide, 1920-33. v1-2, 5-6 – us Res Libr [072]

FRANCE ET ANGLETERRE... / Darcy, J – Paris, 1904 – 6mf – 9 – ILM-461/1 – ne IDC [327]

FRANCE ET CANADA / Artois, Hugues d' – Arras, France: Sueur-Charruey, 1887. 02462. (Pre-1900 Canadiana) – 9 – cn C.I.H.M. [971]

LA FRANCE ET L'ABOLITION DE LA TRAITE DES NOIRS DE 1814 A 1831 / Daget, S – Introduction a l'etude de la repression francaise de la traite des noirs au XIXe siecle francoise – 9 – F100.00 – fr Ethnologie [306]

LA FRANCE ET LE CANADA: RAPPORT AU SYNDICAT MARITIME ET FLUVIAL DE FRANCE / Agostini, Edouard – Paris: s.n., 1886. 00016. (Pre-1900 Canadiana) – 9 – cn C.I.H.M. [971]

LA FRANCE ET L'ETRANGER: ETUDES DE STATISTIQUE COMPAREE / Legoyt, Alfred – Paris et Strasbourg: Vve. Berger-Levrault, 1864-70. 2v.15 fiches. (Statistics Series: Topography) – 9 – 37.00 – fr Bibl Nationale [944]

FRANCE ET SARDAIGNE / Feraud-Giraud, L J D – Paris, 1859 – 6mf – 1 – ILM-1757/1 – ne IDC [327]

LA FRANCE EXTERIEURE ET COLONIALE – Paris, France. -f. 3 Dec 1937-31 May 1940. 1 reel – 1 – uk British Libr Newspaper [072]

FRANCE INDEPENDANTE – L'hebdomadaire des Independants et des paysans. Paris. 1950-nov 1962 – 1 – fr A.C.R.P.P. [073]

FRANCE INDEPENDANTE – Paris: Imp parisiennes reunies, mar 19-apr 2, may 7-21 1962 – us Res Libr [072]

France. Institut National de la Statistique et des Etudes Economiques *see*
- FRANCE
- GUADELOUPE
- GUYANE
- MARTINIQUE

France. Journal officiel *see* LISTE DE BENEFICIAIRES DE CITATIONS

France. L'Assemblee nationale *see* BULLETIN

France. Laws, Statutes, etc *see*
- RECUEIL DES DECISIONS DES TRIBUNAUX ARBITRAUX MIXTES INSTITUES PAR LES TRAITES DE PAIX
- RECUEIL DES TEXTES REGLEMENTANT L'ENSEIGNEMENT PRIVE EN COCHINCHINE.

LA FRANCE LIBRE – Journal socialiste. Paris. 2 juil 1918-14 15 mars 1931 – 1 – fr A.C.R.P.P. [073]

LA FRANCE LIBRE – Paris, France. -w. 1 Sept 1918-11 Aug 1919. Imperfect. 2 reels – 1 – uk British Libr Newspaper [072]

LA FRANCE LITTERAIRE – Annales universelles des lettres, des arts et des sciences. Paris. 1832-5 aout 1843 – 5 – fr A.C.R.P.P. [073]

LA FRANCE LITTERAIRE – Contenant les auteurs francais de 1771 a 1796. Ersche, J. S. Hambourg (I-IV). 1797-1802 – 1 – fr A.C.R.P.P. [440]

FRANCE (LONDON: 1940) *see* FRANCE

LA FRANCE MILITAIRE – Journal non politique des armees de terre et de mer. Dir. Ch. Lavauzelle. Limoges. 1893, 1911-13, 1919 – 1 – fr A.C.R.P.P. [073]

France. Ministere de la Cooperation *see* ECONOMIE ET PLAN DE DEVELOPPEMENT

France. Ministere de la Marine et des Colonies *see*
- COMMISSION INSTITUTEE PAR DECISION ROYALE DU 26 MAI 1840 POUR L'EXAMEN DES QUESTIONS RELATIVES A L'ESCLAVAGE ET A LA CONSTITUTION POLITIQUE DES COLONIES
- COMPTE-RENDU AU ROI DE L'EXECUTION DES LOIS DES 18 ET 19 JUILLET 1845 SUR LE REGIME DES ESCLAVES, LA CREATION D'ETABLISSEMENTS AGRICOLES PAR LE TRAVAIL LIBRE, ETC
- SENEGAL ET NIGER

France. Ministere De l'Agriculture, Du Commerce Et Des Travaux Publics *see* ENQUETE SUR LES SOCIETES DE COOPERATION

France. Ministere de l'Education nationale *see* VERDUN, ARGONNE-METZ (1914-1918)

France. Ministere de l'Instruction Publique *see* ETAT DE L'INSTRUCTION PRIMAIRE EN 1864, D'APRES LES RAPPORTS OFFICIELS DES INSPECTEURS D'ACADEMIE

France. Ministere De l'Instruction Publique Et Des Beaux-Arts *see* COMMISSION D'ENQUETE SUR LA SITUATION DES OUVRIERS ET DES INDUSTRIES D'ART

France. Ministere de l'Instruction Publique et des Beaux-Arts *see*
- DIRECTION DE L'ENSEIGNEMENT PRIMAIRE. RAPPORT SUR L'ORGANISATION ET LA SITUATION DE L'ENSEIGNEMENT PRIMAIRE PUBLIC EN FRANCE
- RECUEIL DES MONOGRAPHIES PEDAGOGIQUES PUBLIEES A L'OCCASION DE L'EXPOSITION UNIVERSELLE DE 1889

France. Ministere de l'Interieur *see*
- ENQUETE DE LA COMMISSION EXTRA-PARLEMENTAIRE DES ASSOCIATIONS OUVRIERES, NOMMEE PAR M. LE MINISTRE DE L'INTERIEUR
- NOTE SUR LES TABLEAUX STATISTIQUES

France. Ministere des Affaires Etrangeres *see*
- DOCUMENTS DIPLOMATIQUES: AFFAIRES DE TERRE-NEUVE
- DOCUMENTS DIPLOMATIQUES. CONFERENCE INTERNATIONALE DE LA HAYE (1910)...
- DOCUMENTS DIPLOMATIQUES FRANCAIS 1871-1914
- LES ORIGINES DIPLOMATIQUES DE LA GUERRE DE 1870-71. RECUEIL DE DOCUMENTS PAR LE MINISTERE DES AFFAIRES ETRANGERES

France. Ministere des Affairs Etrangeres *see* RECUEIL DES TRAITES DE LA FRANCE

France. Ministere des Colonies *see* BULLETIN OFFICIEL

France. Ministere des Finances et des Affaires Economiques *see* PLAN REGIONAL DE DEV. ECON. ET SOCIAL ET D'AMENAGEMENT DU TERRITOIRE POUR LA CIRCONSCR. DE PROVENCE-COTE D'AZUR

France. Ministere du Commerce, de l'Industrie, des Postes et des Telegraphes. Office du Travail *see* LES ASSOCIATIONS PROFESSIONNELLES OUVRIERES

France. Ministere du Commerce, de l'Industrie, des Postes et des Telegraphes. Statistique generale *see* RESULTATS STATISTIQUES DU DENOMBREMENT DE 1896

France. Ministere du Commerce, de l'Industrie, des Postes et Telegraphes. Office du Travail *see* SALAIRES ET DUREE DU TRAVAIL DANS L'INDUSTRIE FRANCAISE

France. Ministere du Commerce et de l'Industrie. Office du travail *see* LE PLACEMENT DES EMPLOYES, OUVRIERS ET DOMESTIQUES EN FRANCE. SON HISTOIRE. SON ETAT ACTUEL. AVEC UN APPENDICE RELATIF AU PLACEMENT DANS LES PAYS ETRANGERS

France. Ministere du Travail et de la Prevoyance sociale *see* STATISTIQUE GENERALE DE LA FRANCE. SALAIRES ET COUT DE L'EXISTENCE A DIVERSES EPOQUES JUSQU'EN 1910

France. Ministry of Foreign Affairs, Paris *see* INVENTORIES AND GUIDES TO DIPLOMATIC ARCHIVES

LA FRANCE MUSICALE – Paris, 1837-1869. v. 1-33. Lacking v. 10 (p1-9).1847; v. 11-14. P 579. 1848-1850 – 407mf – 9 – ne IDC [780]

LA FRANCE NOUVELLE – Lavalle (Argentine). Contient un suppl. en castillano. 1943 – 1 – fr A.C.R.P.P. [073]

LA FRANCE NOUVELLE – Quotidien, independant, politique, litteraire et financier. Paris. 22 mai-23 dec 1911 – 1 – fr A.C.R.P.P. [073]

LA FRANCE NOUVELLE – Red. en chef Alphonse Pages. no. 1-115. Paris. 7 dec 1870-1er avr 1871. mq no. 63, 89 – 1 – fr A.C.R.P.P. [073]

France. Office Colonial *see* LES PRODUCTIONS DE L'AFRIQUE OCCIDENTALE FRANCAISE

France. Organization for European Economic Cooperation *see* REPORT TO THE ECONOMIC COOPERATION ADMINISTRATION ON THE 1949/50 PROGRAMME

LA FRANCE ORIENTALE – Organe independant. Journal politico-satirique. no. 2, 5, 7, 35, 37, 40-46, 50; 2e s., no. 7-11 12. Tamatave. avr 1891-juil 1892 – 1 – fr A.C.R.P.P. [073]

France. Parlement. Assemblee Constituante *see* TABLE DES MATIERES DES NOMS DE LIEUX ET DES NOMS DE PERSONNES CONTENUS DAUS LES PROCES-VERBAUX DES SEANCES DEPUIS LE 5 MAI 1789 JUSQU'AU 30 SEPTEMBRE 1791

France. Parlement. Assemblee des Etats generaux *see* PROCES-VERBAL HISTORIQUE DES ACTES DU CLERGE DISPUTE A L'ASSEMBLEE DES ETATS GENERAUX DES ANNEES 1789 ET 1790

France. Parlement. Assemblee Nationale *see*
- PROCES-VERBAL
- TABLE GENERALE DES MATIERES DU PROCES-VERBAL

France. Parlement. Assemblee nationale constituante *see* RECUEIL DES RAPPORTS, DISCOURS ET AUTRES PIECES

France. Parlement. Chambre de l'Ordre de la noblesse aux Etats Generaux a Versailles *see* PROCES-VERBAL DES SEANCES

France. Parlement. Convention Nationale *see*
- PIECES IMPRIMEES PAR ORDRE DE LA CONVENTION
- PROCES-VERBAL

FRANCE PARLIMENT – Paris, FR. 1975-1976 – 12r – $600.00 – R63610 – us Library Micro [072]

LA FRANCE PROTESTANTE / Haag, EugeneHaag, Emile – 2nd ed. 6v, A – Gasparin. Paris, 1877-88 – 9mf – 9 – F270.00 – fr F.F.G. [920]

LA FRANCE PROTESTANTE / Haag, Eugene & Haag Emile – Paris, 1st ed 1846-1858. A a Z. 10v – 13mf – 9 – F390.00 – fr F.F.G. [240]

LA FRANCE REPUBLICAINE – Paris: E Marc-Aurel, 1848. apr ?-29 1848 – us Res Libr [072]

France. Senat *see*
- DEBATS DU SENAT
- DEBATS PARLEMENTAIRES
- DOCUMENTS DU SENAT
- DOCUMENTS PARLEMENTAIRES
- IMPRESSIONS
- NOTICES ET PORTRAITS

FRANCE: SOCIAL STRUCTURES UNDER THE OLD REGIME – Recent research using contemporary statistical sources on urban society in the environs of Paris under the Old Regime. Papers prepared under Prof. Roland Mousnier. 18 titles – 9 – fr Hachette [944]

LA FRANCE SOCIALISTE / La Federation des Travailleurs Socialistes de France – Bulletin officiel. no. 2-57. Paris. 8 sept 1894-9 nov 1895 – 1 – fr A.C.R.P.P. [073]

FRANCE SOIR – 1988- – 3r per y – 5 – inquuire – us Ross [072]

FRANCE SOIR – 1988-1995 – 3r per y – 5,6 – Sfr1,176.00 – sz Infoprint [944]

France. Sovereigns, etc., 1715-1774. Louis XV *see* MEMOIRES DES COMMISAIRES DU ROI ET DE SA MAJESTE BRITANNIQUE. PARIS IMPR. ROYALE

FRANCE: STATISTICAL SOURCES ON THE HISTORY OF FRANCE DURING THE REVOLUTION AND THE EMPIRE / ed by Perrot, Jean-Claude – 98 titles – 9 – fr Hachette [944]

France. Supplement au Journal officiel *see* LISTE OFFICIELLE D'ENNEMIS

France, Thaddeus J *see* THE IMPACT OF PROJECT ADVENTURE ACTIVITIES ON SELF-PERCEPTION

FRANCE TO-DAY : ITS RELIGIOUS ORIENTATION / Sabatier, Paul – London: J.M. Dent; New York: E.P. Dutton, 1913 – 1mf – us A.T.L.A. [200]

LA FRANCE TRANSATLANTIQUE: LE CANADA / Clapin, Sylvia – Paris: E. Plon, Nourrit, 1885. 00655. (Pre-1900 Canadiana) – 9 – cn C.I.H.M. [360]

France. Treaties, etc *see*
- TRAITE DE NEUTRALITE CONCLU A LONDRES LE SEIZIEME NOVEMBRE 1686, ENTRE LES ROYS DE FRANCE ET D'ANGLETERRE, TOUCHANT LES PAYS DES DEUX ROYS EN AMERIQUE
- TRAITEZ DE PAIX CONCLUS ENTRE S. M. LE ROY DE FRANCE ET LES INDIENS DU CANADA

FRANCE-AMERIQUE : LE COURRIER DES ETATS-UNIS – New Rochelle, NY. v11 n553. 16 avr 1944-28 sep 1977 – 12r – 1 – Can$55.00r – cn Can Microfilming [071]

FRANCE-AMERIQUE – Hebdomadaire d'information pour les Francais aux Etats-Unis. New York. juil 1943-avr 1947 – 1 – fr A.C.R.P.P. [073]

FRANCE-AMERIQUE – New York, NY. -w. 23 May 1943-12 Aug 1945; 19 May 1946-28 Dec 1947; 12 Sept-26 Dec 1948; 13 Feb 1949-13 Dec 1953. 7 reels – 1 – uk British Libr Newspaper [071]

FRANCE-AMERIQUE MAGAZINE – (Comprenant: France Canada jan 1911-aut 1914) – Paris, jan 1910-dec 1969 – 11r – 1 – Can$60.00 – cn Can Microfilming [073]

FRANCE-EQUATEUR – Brazzaville. sept 1952-oct 1959 – 1 – fr A.C.R.P.P. [073]

FRANCE-EQUATEUR L'AVENIR – Brazzaville: R Mahe & F Senez, jan 3 1956-mar 3 1960 – 7r – 1 – us Res Libr [072]

FRANCE-LUXEMBOURG – Revue politique economique et litteraire. no. 1-2, 5-7, 10. Paris. mars 1919-mai 1921 – 1 – fr A.C.R.P.P. [073]

FRANCE-NOUVELLE / Communist Party. France – Hebdomadaire. Dir. politique, Francois Billoux.Paris.24 nov 1945-1980 – 1 – fr A.C.R.P.P. [073]

FRANCE-OUTRE-MER – Paris, France. Europe France outremer. -m. 1948-76. 28 reels – 1 – uk British Libr Newspaper [073]

[FRANCE'S DIPLOMATIC RELATIONS WITH CZECHOSLOVAKIA PAMPHLET COLLECTION] – 1938 – 1 – CSUXANQ3175-B – us Hoover Inst Photo [320]

[FRANCE'S DIPLOMATIC RELATIONS WITH DENMARK PAMPHLET COLLECTION] – 1935 – 1 – CSUXANQ3179-B – us Hoover Inst Photo [320]

[FRANCE'S DIPLOMATIC RELATIONS WITH GERMANY PAMPHLET COLLECTION] – 1911-1935 – 1 – CSUXANQ4833-B – us Hoover Inst Photo [320]

[FRANCE'S DIPLOMATIC RELATIONS WITH GREAT BRITAIN PAMPHLET COLLECTION] – 1941-1947 – 1 – CSUXANQ4836-B – us Hoover Inst Photo [320]

[FRANCE'S DIPLOMATIC RELATIONS WITH GREECE PAMPHLET COLLECTION] – 1913 – 1 – CSUXANQ4838-B – us Hoover Inst Photo [320]

[FRANCE'S DIPLOMATIC RELATIONS WITH HUNGARY PAMPHLET COLLECTION] – 1935 – 1 – CSUXANQ4843-B – us Hoover Inst Photo [320]

[FRANCE'S DIPLOMATIC RELATIONS WITH ITALY PAMPHLET COLLECTION] – 1918 – 1 – CSUXANQ4844-B – us Hoover Inst Photo [320]

[FRANCE'S DIPLOMATIC RELATIONS WITH POLAND PAMPHLET COLLECTION] – 1921 – 1 – CSUXANQ4848-B – us Hoover Inst Photo [320]

[FRANCE'S DIPLOMATIC RELATIONS WITH ROMANIA PAMPHLET COLLECTION] – 1917 – 1 – CSUXANQ4854-B – us Hoover Inst Photo [320]

[FRANCE'S DIPLOMATIC RELATIONS WITH RUSSIA PAMPHLET COLLECTION] – 1919-1920 – 1 – CSUXANQ4860-B – us Hoover Inst Photo [320]

[FRANCE'S DIPLOMATIC RELATIONS WITH SUB-SAHARAN AFRICA PAMPHLET COLLECTION] – 1981 – 1 – CSUXANQ3172-B – us Hoover Inst Photo [320]

[FRANCE'S DIPLOMATIC RELATIONS WITH THE UNITED STATES PAMPHLET COLLECTION] – 1915-1960 – 1 – CSUXANQ4869-B – us Hoover Inst Photo [320]

Frances, Madeleine *see* SPIONZA DANS LES PAYS NEERLANDAIS DANS LE SECONDE MOITIE DU 17E SIECLE

Franceschi, Gustavo Juan *see* EL MOVIMIENTO ESPANOL Y EL CRITERIO CATOLICO

Franceschini, Gaetano *see* SIX SONATAS FOR TWO VIOLINS AND VIOLONCELLO WITH A THOROUGH BASS FOR THE HARPSICHORD...OPERA 2

FRANCESCO CRISPI, DER ADVOKAT ITALIENS : HISTORISCHER ROMAN / Zeidler, Paul Gerhard – Berlin-Schoeneberg: P J Oestergaard, c1939 – 1r – 1 – us U.W. Library [830]

Francesco d'Assisi, Saint *see* OPUSCULA SANCTI PATRIS FRANCISCI ASSISIENSIS

Francesco, P *see* LA CONVENZIONE INTERNAZIONALE E LA LEGGE UNIFORME CAMBIARIA...

FRANCE-SOIR – (Toute derniere ed. 1969-Oct 1992. suite de: Defense de la France. 1) – Paris. Toutes eds. sept 1944-86 – 1 – fr A.C.R.P.P. [072]

FRANCE-SOIR – Paris: France Editions et Publications, 1953-69 – us Res Libr [072]

Franch, Hiram *see* HISTORY OF IDAHO

Franchassin, L *see* DES CONFLITS DE LOIS EN MATIERE DE MARIAGE AU MAROC

Franchere, Gabriel *see*
- RELATION D'UN VOYAGE A LA COTE DU NORD OUEST DE L'AMERIQUE SEPTENTRIONALE EN 1810, 1811, 1812, 1813 ET 1814
- RELATION D'UN VOYAGE A LA COTE DU NORD-OUEST DE L'AMERIQUE SEPTENTRIONALE, DANS LES ANNEES 1810, 11, 12, 13 ET 14

Franchet, A R *see*
- ENUMERATIO PLANTARUM IN JAPONICA SPONTE CRESCENTIUM
- PLANTAE DAVIDIANAE

Franchi, Antonino *see* IL CONCILIO 2 DI LEONE...

Franchi, G *see* LA CETRA SONARA. SONATE A TRE...OP. 1

FRANCHINI GAFURII LAUDENSIS REGII MUSICI PUBLICE PROFITENSIS / Gaffurius, F – Mediolani. 1518. BP-678 1 – 9 – ne IDC [780]

FRANCHISE LAW JOURNAL (ABA) – (Title varies: v1-3 1980-84 as Journal of the Forum Committee on Franchising) – v1-15. 1980-96 – 9 – $121.00 set – us Hein [340]

LA FRANCIA Y LA MONARQUIA EN EL PLATA (1818-1820). LA POLITICA DEL DUQUE DE RICHELIEU. MISIONES...BUENOS AIRES, 1933 / Belgrano, Mario – Madrid: Razon y Fe, 1935 – 1 – sp Bibl Santa Ana [972]

Francillon-Vieillot, H *see* LA CROISSANCE DES OS LONGS CHEZ LES AMPHIBIENS. SON UTILISATION COMME CRITERE D'AGE

Francis A. Countway Library of Medicine *see* AUTHOR TITLE CATALOG OF THE FRANCIS A. COUNTWAY LIBRARY OF MEDICINE FOR IMPRINTS THROUGH 1959

FRANCIS AND DOMINIC AND THE MENDICANT ORDERS / Herkless, John – 1mf 1500 New York: Scribner, 1901. (The World's epoch-makers) – us A.T.L.A. [240]

Francis, Edmund *see* PAPERS

Francis, G W *see* AN ANALYSIS OF THE BRITISH FERNS AND THEIR ALLIES

FRANCIS HOPKINSON: HIS BOOK / Hopkinson, Francis – Autograph songbook. Contains songs and part-songs with keyboard accomp., some with figured bass by Hopkinson and others. Pages 151-152 and 177-178 missing. music 626, music 1045 – 1 – us L of C Photodup [780]

FRANCIS J. ATTIG, SENATE SERVICE 1952-1974 : REPORTER OF SENATE DEBATES – 1mf – 9 – $5.00 – us Scholarly Res [320]

FRANCIS LONGE COLLECTION OF THEATRICAL WORKS / U.S. Library of Congress. Rare Book and Special Collections Division – 2269 English plays, satires, musical dramas, pastorals, masques, etc. 1607-1812. 326v – 56r – 1 – $1,131.00 – us L of C Photodup [820]

Francis, Mark E *see* COVERAGE OF AFRICAN AMERICAN BASKETBALL ATHLETES IN SPORTS ILLUSTRATED (1954 TO 1986)

Francis, Nicholas C *see* COLLEGIATE SOCCER PLAYERS' PERCEPTIONS OF SPORT PSYCHOLOGY, SPORT PSYCHOLOGISTS AND SPORT PSYCHOLOGICAL SERVICES

FRANCIS O. WILCOX, SENATE SERVICE 1947-1955 : FIRST CHIEF OF STAFF, SENATE FOREIGN RELATIONS COMMITTEE – 3mf – 9 – $15.00 – us Scholarly Res [320]

Francis of Assisi, Saint *see* LEGEND. SPECULUM PERFECTIONIS. S. FRANCIS OF ASSISI: THE MIRROR OF PERFECTION

Francis, P *see* LAND AND THEE TENURE IN HUMID WEST AFRIA

FRANCIS PARKMAN – Boston: Little, Brown and Co., 1896. 04332. (Pre-1900 Canadiana) – 9 – cn C.I.H.M. [971]

FRANCIS PARKMAN / Casgrain, Henri-Raymond – Quebec: C. Darveau, 1872. 00520. (Pre-1900 Canadiana) – 9 – cn C.I.H.M. [920]

FRANCIS PATRICK KENRICK'S OPINION ON SLAVERY / Brokhage, J D – Washington, D.C., 1955 – 7mf – 8 – ne Slangenburg [290]

Francis, Phil *see* BEAUTIFUL SANTA CRUZ COUNTY

FRANCIS THE FIRST AND HIS TIMES / Coignet, Clarisse Gauthier – From the French by Fanny Twemlow. London: R. Bentley and Son, 1888. iv,371p – 1 – us U.W. Library [944]

Francis, W *see* SOUTH ARCOT DISTRICT GAZETTEER

Francis, W D *see* AUSTRALIAN RAIN-FOREST TREES

Francis-Boeuf, Jean *see* LA SOUDANAISE ET SON AMANT; ROMAN

Franciscain de Montreal *see* MEDITATIONS SERAPHIQUES SUR LA PASSION DE JESUS: EN FORME DE CHEMIN DE CROIX

FRANCISCAINS, SAINT-MARTIN-DE TEILLE : MODUS VIVENDI FRATRUM MINORUM CONVENTUUM ROBINERIARUM, AC SANCTI MARTINI A TELLEIO – Nantes, vers 1700 – 1 – F50.00 – fr Armell [240]

FRANCISCAN LEGENDS IN ITALIAN ART: PICTURES IN ITALIAN CHURCHES AND GALLERIES / Gurney-Salter, Emma – London: J.M. Dent, 1905.20 illus. Bibliography p214-216 – 1 – us U.W. Library [240]

FRANCISCAN MARTYRS IN ENGLAND / Hope, Anne Fulton – (Includes bibliographical references) – London: Burns and Oates, 1878 – 1mf – 9 – 0-8370-6983-1 – 1986-0983 – us A.T.L.A. [920]

FRANCISCAN STUDIES – New York. NS v1-30. 1941-1970 – 231mf – 9 – ne IDC [240]

FRANCISCAN STUDIES – ns: 1(1941)-30(1970) – 231mf – 9 – Dfl809.00 – ne Slangenburg [073]

FRANCISCANISMO DE CORTES Y CORTESANISMO DE LOS FRANCISCANOS / Lejarza, Fidel de – Madrid: Missionalia Hispanica, 1948 – 1 – sp Bibl Santa Ana [240]

(FRANCISCANO DE LA PROVINCIA DE SAN MIGUEL) EN NOTAS DE BIBLIOGRAFIA FRANCISCANA / Lopez, Atanasio & Blazquez del Barco, Juan – Archivo Ibero Americano, 1926 – 1 – sp Bibl Santa Ana [240]

LOS FRANCISCANOS CAPUCHINOS EN VENEZUELA / Lodores, Baltasar de – Caracas, 1929-1931; Madrid: Razon y Fe, 1933. 3v – 1 – sp Bibl Santa Ana [240]

LOS FRANCISCANOS Y LA IMPRENTA EN MEXICO / Zulaica Garate, Roman – Madrid: Razon y Fe, 1940 – sp Bibl Santa Ana [946]

LOS FRANCISCANOS Y LA IMPRENTA EN MEXICO EN EL SIGLO 16 : ESTUDIO BIO-BIBLIOGRAFICO / Zulaica Garate, Roman – Mexico: Pedro Robredo, 1939 – 4mf – 9 – ne IDC [972]

THE FRANCISCANS IN ARIZONA / Engelhardt, Zephyrin – Harbor Springs, Mich.: Holy Childhood Indian School, 1899 – 1mf – us A.T.L.A. [305]

THE FRANCISCANS IN CALIFORNIA / Engelhardt, Zephyrin – Harbor Springs, Mich.: Holy Childhood Indian School, 1897 – 2mf – us A.T.L.A. [305]

FRANCISCI IUNII BITURIGIS : OPERA THEOLOGICA TOMUS 1 EN 2 – 1608 – 93mf – 8 – ne Slangenburg [290]

FRANCISCI SALINAE. DE MUSICA LIBRI SEPTEM, IN QUIBUS EIUS DOCTRINAE VERITAS TAM QUAE AD HARMONIAM, QUAM QUAE AD RHYTHMUM PERTINET / Salinas, F – 1577 – 9 – us Sibley [780]

FRANCISCI...ALCIATI...ILUSTRATA / Sanchez de las Brozas, Francisco – 1573 – 9 – 1.50f – sp Bibl Santa Ana [440]

FRANCISCII SANCTII BROCENSIS...COMENT. IN AND. ALCIATI EMBLEMATA...FIGURIS ILUSTRATA / Sanchez de las Brozas, Francisco – Lugduni: Guliel Ruvillum, 1573 – 1 – sp Bibl Santa Ana [946]

FRANCISCO BENEGAS GALVAN. OBISPO DE QUERETARO... – Madrid: Razon y Fe, 1939 – 1 – sp Bibl Santa Ana [240]

FRANCISCO DE ALDANA. EL DIVINO CAPITAN / Rivers, Elias L – Badajoz: Institucion de – Servicios Culturales de la Excma. Diputacion Provincial, 1955 – 1 – sp Bibl Santa Ana [946]

FRANCISCO DE ASIS BUSCA AL HOMBRE... / Anasagasti, Pedro de – Madrid: Arch. Ibero Americano, 1965 – 1 – sp Bibl Santa Ana [240]

FRANCISCO DE HINOJOSA. EL PERSONAJE INEDITO DE UN DRAMA HISTORICO / Munoz de San Pedro, Miguel – Badajoz: Diput. prov. de Badajoz, 1946. Sep. Rev. Est. Ex. – 1 – sp Bibl Santa Ana [946]

Francisco de la Encarnacion *see* LA MUJER FUERTE

FRANCISCO DE LIZAUR (1477-1535) / Munoz de San Pedro, Miguel – Madrid: Juan Bravo, 1962 – 1 – sp Bibl Santa Ana [920]

FRANCISCO DE LIZAUR. HIDALGO INDIANO DE PRINCIPIOS DE SIGLO 16 / Munoz de San Pedro, Miguel – Madrid: Imp. y Ed Maestre, 1948 – 1 – sp Bibl Santa Ana [946]

FRANCISCO DE PIZARRO O EL PAIS DEL ORO / Escofet, Jose – Barcelona: S.A. IG.S.Barral Herms, 1929. Col. Los grandes exploradores espanoles. vol 5 – sp Bibl Santa Ana [350]

FRANCISCO DE ZURBARAN / Pantorba, Bernardino de – Barcelona: Iberia. Joaquin Gil Editores, S.A., 1946 – 1 – sp Bibl Santa Ana [946]

FRANCISCO DE ZURBARAN. SU EPOCA, SU VIDA Y SUS OBRAS / Cascales Munoz, Jose – Madrid: C.I.A.P. (S.A.), 1931 – sp Bibl Santa Ana [920]

Francisco Martin, Julian *see* ESTRUCTURAS SOCIALES Y ECONOMICAS EN LUSITANIA DURANTE EL ALTO IMPERIO

FRANCISCO PIZARRO / Orellana-Pizarro Perez-Aloe, Antonio. Vizconde de Amaya – Madrid: Editorial Saturnino Calleja, S.A., 1928 – 1 – sp Bibl Santa Ana [920]

FRANCISCO PIZARRO / Quintana, Manuel Jose – Budapest, 1962 – sp Bibl Santa Ana [350]

FRANCISCO PIZARRO 2° EDICION / Tena Fernandez, Juan – Plasencia: Editorial Sanchez Rodrigo, 1955 – 1 – sp Bibl Santa Ana [946]

FRANCISCO PIZARRO. BIOGRAFIA DEL CONQUISTADOR DEL PERU / Arciniega, Rosa – Santiago de Chile: Editorial Nascimento, 2nd ed 1941 – sp Bibl Santa Ana [350]

FRANCISCO PIZARRO DEBIO LLAMARSE DIAZ O HINOJOSA / Munoz de San Pedro, Miguel – Badajoz: Imprenta Diputacion Provincial, 1951. Sep. Revista de Estudios Extremenos – sp Bibl Santa Ana [946]

FRANCISCO PIZARRO, LARGO EN VIDA Y EN HAZANAS / Marquerie, Alfredo – Madrid: Boris. Barrena, Ediciones, 1954 – sp Bibl Santa Ana [910]

FRANCISCO PIZARRO Y EL TESORO DE ATAHUALPA / Pereyra, Carlos – Madrid: Editorial America, s.a. – sp Bibl Santa Ana [920]

FRANCISCO PIZARROSO, OFM, EN NOTASDE BIBLIOGRAFIA FRANCISCANA... / Castro, Manuel – Madrid: Graf. Calleja, 1968 – 1 – sp Bibl Santa Ana [240]

FRANCISCO SANCHEZ EL BROCENSE / Bell, Aubrey FG – Oxford University Press, 1925 – 1 – sp Bibl Santa Ana [920]

Francisco, Tonolo *see* MANUAL DEL CATEQUISTA. TRAD. DEL ITALIANO POR D. FELIX MERINO REVUELTA. BARCELONA, 1943

Franciscus, J *see* ORATIO AD PIUM QUINTUM PONT. MAX. QUA PRINCIPES AD BELLUM CONTRA SELINUM EXCITANTUR POST VICTAM CLASSEM TURCICAM

FRANCISCUS JUNIUS : EEN LEVENSBEELD UIT DEN EERSTEN TIJD DER KERKHERVORMING / Reitsma, Johannes – Groningen: J.B. Huber, 1864 – 1mf – us A.T.L.A. [240]

Francisque-Michel *see* LES ECOSSAIS EN FRANCE – LES FRANCAIS EN ECOSSE

LE FRANCISTE / Franzismus – Auflage fuer Elsass und Lothringen. Fond. Marcel Bucard. No.1-3. Metz. aout 1934-1937, juin 1941-aout 1944 – 1 – fr A.C.R.P.P. [073]

LE FRANCISTE / Revolution Socialiste Francais – (Ed. de Marseille. dec 1941-29 juin 1944. 1) – Hebdomadaire. Dir. Marcel Bucard. 1934-37, juin 1941-aout 1944 – 1 – fr A.C.R.P.P. [073]

LE FRANCISTE D'ALSACE ET DE LORRAINE – Faszistisches Kampfblatt. Fond. Marcel Bucard. Strasbourg. 1er juil-1er aout 1937, avr 1938 – 1 – fr A.C.R.P.P. [073]

Francistown, New Hampshire. Francistown Baptist Church *see* RECORDS

Franck, Hans *see* EIN STUECK ERDE

Franck, Harry Alverson *see* WORKING NORTH FROM PATAGONIA: BEING THE NARRATIVE OF A JOURNEY, EARNED ON THE WAY, THROUGH SOUTHERN AND EASTERN SOUTH AMERICA

Franck, J R *see* CATALOGUE DES LEPIDOPTERES QUI COMPOSENT LA COLLECTION DE FEU MR. FRANCK

Franck, L *see* LA RESPONSABILITE DES ARMATEURS...

Franck, Ludwig *see* STATISTISCHE UNTERSUCHUNGEN UEBER DIE VERWENDUNG DER FARBEN IN DEN DICHTUNGEN GOETHE'S

Franck von Woerd, S *see*
- CHRONICA. ZEITBUCH VNND GESCHICHTBIBELL VON ANBEGYN BISZ IN DISS GEGENWERTIG M.D.XXXVI. JAR VERLENGT
- DIE GULDIN ARCH DAREIN DER KERN VNND DIE BESTEN HAUPTSPRUECH DER HEYLIGEN SCHRIFFT
- PARADOXA DVCENTA OCTOGINTA, DAS IST: ZWEYHUNDERT VNND ACHTZIG WUNDERRED
- WELTBUCH: SPIEGEL VND BILDTNISZ DES GANTZEN ERDTBODENS

Francke, August Hermann *see* A HISTORY OF WESTERN TIBET, ONE OF THE UNKNOWN EMPIRES

Francke, Kuno *see*
- GOETHES VERMAECHTNIS AN AMERIKA
- DIE KULTURWERTE DER DEUTSCHEN LITERATUR DES MITTELALTERS
- DIE KULTURWERTE DER DEUTSCHEN LITERATUR IN IHRER GESCHICHTLICHEN ENTWICKLUNG
- DIE KULTURWERTE DER DEUTSCHEN LITERATUR VON DER REFORMATION BIS ZUR AUFKLAERUNG
- WELTBUERGERTUM IN DER DEUTSCHEN LITERATUR VON HERDER BIS NIETZSCHE

Francke, W *see* DIE ENTSCHEIDUNGEN AUSLAENDISCHER GERICHTE...

Francken, Aegidius *see* HEILIG GEBRUIK DES ORGELS..

Franc-Maconnerie *see* 8 DOCUMENTS MAN. INTERESSANT LA FRANC-MACONNERIE, DONNES PAR A. LE BEAU A LA BIBL. MUNIC. DE NANTES

LA FRANCMASONERIA ESPANOLA / Diaz Perez, Nicolas – Madrid. 1894. 637p. (Historical Studies Series) – 9 – $21.00 – fr Bibl Nationale [360]
LE FRANCO *see* LE FRANCO-ALBERTAIN
Franco, Alberto *see*
- LA MISTICA SOCIAL DE EVA PERON
- SENTIDO Y FORMA DE LA LEALTAD

FRANCO AMI DE LA FRANCE? – Paris, 1938. Fiche W 893. (Blodgett Collection of Spanish Civil War Pamphlets) – 9 – us H.U. College Libr [946]
Franco Arias, Froilan *see* LE VOCABULAIRE ET LA SOCIETE DE ROBERT BRASILLACH ET P. LA ROCHELLE
Franco, Francisco *see* HABLA EL CAUDILLO
FRANCO IN BARCELONA – London, 1939. Fiche W 894. (Blodgett Collection of Spanish Civil War Pamphlets) – 9 – us H.U. College Libr [946]
Franco, Juan Pablo *see* EL PERONISMO, ANTECEDENTES Y GOBIERNO
Franco, Luis *see* BIOGRAFIA PATRIA
Franco, M *see* DISCURSO MEDICINAL...EN EL QUE SE DECLARA LA HORDEN...PARA PRESERVARSE DE LA PESTE
Franco, Secondo *see* DIRECTION DE CONSCIENCE: LETTRE A UNE SUPERIEUR RELIGIEUSE AU SUJECT D'UN RECENT DECRET PONTIFICAL
FRANCO SPAIN...AMERICA'S ENEMY / White, David McKelvy – N.Y., 1945. Fiche W1012. (Blodgett Collection of Spanish Civil War Pamphlets) – 9 – us H.U. College Libr [946]
FRANCO: WHO IS HE, WHAT DOES HE FIGHT FOR? / Curran, Edward Lodge – NY, 1937. Fiche W 822. (Blodgett Collection of Spanish Civil War Pamphlets) – 9 – us H.U. College Libr [946]
Franco y Lozano, Francisco *see*
- ANTOLOGIA LATINA
- DIALOGOS DE LOS MUERTOS DE LUCIANO
- GEOGRAFIA DE...BADAJOZ
- HOMILIA A...SAN JUAN CRISOSTOMO

Franco y Lozano, Francisco et al *see* TROZOS SELECTOS...CLASICOS LATINOS
LE FRANCO-ALBERTAIN – (Cont by: Le Franco 2 mar 1979-3 jul 1992) – Edmonton, Alberta. 15 nov 1967-16 fev 1979 – 18r – 1 – Can$75.00r – cn Can Microfilming [072]
LE FRANCO-ALBERTAIN *see* LA SURVIVANCE
LE FRANCO-CALIFORNIEN – San Francisco, CA. 1907-21 – 18r – 1 – $900.00 – B02836 – us Library Micro [071]
LE FRANCO-CALIFORNIEN – San Francisco: Le Franco-Californien Pub Co, dec 7 1917-26] – 18r – us Res Libr [071]
LE FRANCO-CANADIEN / ed by Marchand, Felix-Gabriel – St-Jean, Canada. 1 jun 1860-28 dec 1893 – 7r – 1 – Can$75.00r – cn Can Microfilming [072]
Francoeur, Jacques *see* DIMANCHE-MATIN
Francoeur, Louis et al *see* LE JOURNAL
[FRANCO-GERMAN WAR–1870 TO 1871–PAMPHLET COLLECTION] – 1871?-1913? – 1 – CSUXANQ4882-B – us Hoover Inst Photo [355]
FRANCOIS DE FOIX. OPERA EN TROIS ACTES / Berton, H – Paris: Duhan et Co, 1809? – 1 – us Sibley [780]
Francois de Neufchateau, Nicolas-Louis *see* VOYAGE AGRONOMIQUE DANS LE SENATORERIE DE DIJON
Francois de Sales *see* COMMENT IL FAUT PLEURER NOS CHERS D'EFUNTS
Francois, Georges Alphonse Florent Octave *see* L'AFRIQUE OCCIDENTALE FRANCAISE
FRANCOIS (J.E.C.) : SECTION DES JEUNES – Montreal. v13 n1. jan 1948- 1 mai 1956 – 1r – 1 – Can$50.00 – cn Can Microfilming [072]
FRANCOIS PIERREFEU, CATHOLIC WRITER AND SCIENTIST AND FORMER REBEL SYMPATHISER SPEAKS OF THE FASCIST REPRESSION – n.p. 193? Fiche W 895. (Blodgett Collection of Spanish Civil War Pamphlets) – 9 – us H.U. College Libr [946]
Francoise *see*
- CHRONIQUES DE LUNDI DE FRANCOISE
- FLEURS CHAMPETRES

Francois-Poncet, Andre *see* LES AFFINITES ELECTIVES DE GOETHE
FRANCOIS-XAVIER GARNEAU: SA VIE ET SES OEUVRES / Chauveau, Pierre J O – Montreal: Beauchemin & Valois, 1883. 00592. (Pre-1900 Canadiana) – 9 – cn C.I.H.M. [920]
Franco-Mendes, D *see* GEMUL ATALIAH
FRANCO'S MEIN KAMPF; THE FASCIST STATE IN REBEL SPAIN / Spanish Information Bureau. New York – N.Y., 1939. Fiche W896. (Blodgett Collection of Spanish Civil War Pamphlets) – 9 – us H.U. College Libr [946]
LE FRANC-PARLER : HEBDO – Quebec, Canada. 22 nov 1930-16 mai 1931 – 1r – 1 – Can$30.00 – cn Can Microfilming [072]
LE FRANC-PARLEUR – Montreal, Canada. 1870-78 – 4r – 1 – $260.00 – cn Library Assoc [971]
LE FRANC-PARLEUR – Montreal, Canada. 28 jul 1870-30 avr 1878 – 3r – 1 – Can$55.00r – cn Can Microfilming [072]
LE FRANC-PARLEUR / ed by Renault, Raoul – Quebec, Canada. 10 jul 1915-21 jun 1940 – 3r – 1 – Can$45.00r – cn Can Microfilming [072]
Francq, G *see* LE CHAT BOTTE
Francs-Macons. Grande loge de Quebec *see* THE BOOK OF CONSTITUTION OF THE GRAND LODGE OF QUEBEC, ANCIENT FREE AND ACCEPTED MASONS
LE FRANC-TIREUR – Montreal, 10 dec 1938 – 1r – 1 – Can$25.00 – cn Can Microfilming [072]
LE FRANC-TIREUR – Paris. Aug. 21, 1944-Oct. 14, 1947 – 1 – 35.00r – us Hoover Inst Photo [072]
Francus, D *see* GLI ILLVSTRI ET GLORIOSI GESTI, ET VITTORIOSE IMPRESSE, FATTE CONTRA TURCHI,...
Francus, I *see* HISTORICAE RELATIONIS CONTINVATIO
Frangepan, W *see* ORATIO AD SERENISSIMVM CAROLVM V. SACRI ROMANI IMPERIJ CAESAREM INCLYTUM
FRANGES D'INTERFERENCE ET LEURS APPLICATIONS METROLOGIQUES / Mace de Lepinay, Jules Charles Antoine – Chartres: Durand, 1901. 101p. 2 fiches. (Science Collection) – 9 – $9.00 – fr Bibl Nationale [380]
FRANGULA, ODER, DIE HIMMLISCHEN WEIBER IM WALD / Jahn, Moritz – Leipzig: P Reclam, 1943, c1933 – 1r – 1 – us U.W. Library [830]
Frank, A *see* GESCHIEDENIS DER JODEN IN NEDERLAND
FRANK B. GILBRETH PAPERS / Gilbreth, Frank B – (1910-1924) – 4r – 1 – $295.00 – us UMI [920]
THE FRANK BAKER COLLECTION OF MANUSCRIPTS, MANUSCRIPT DEPARTMENT, PERKINS LIBRARY, DUKE UNIVERSITY [HANDLISTED BY JOHN ASHLEY VICKERS] / Durham, North Carolina. -Duke University: Perkins Library – 1987 – 1mf – 9 – ne IDC [090]
Frank, C *see* LAMASTU, PAZUZU UND ANDERE DAEMONEN. EIN BEITRAG ZUR BABYL-ASSYR. DAEMONOLOGIE
Frank, Dirk *see* DAS PARADOX DER METAFIKATION
Frank E *see* THE REPRESENTATIVE MEN OF THE PHILIPPINES
Frank, Eli *see* TITLE TO REAL AND LEASEHOLD ESTATES AND LIENS
Frank, F *see* LEXIQUE DE LA LANGUE DE BONAVENTURE DES PERIERS
Frank, Felix *see* MARGUERITE D'ANGOULEME, QUEEN OF NAVARRE, 1492-1549
Frank, Franz H R *see*
- SYSTEM DER CHRISTLICHEN WAHRHEIT
- UEBER DIE KIRCHLICHE BEDEUTUNG DER THEOLOGIE R. RITSCHL: CONFERENZVORTRAG
- VADEMECUM FUER ANGEHENDE THEOLOGEN

Frank, Franz Hermann Reinhold *see* DOGMATISCHE STUDIEN
Frank, Friedrich *see*
- DER RITUALMORD VOR DEN GERICHTSHOEFEN DER WAHRHEIT UND DER GERECHTIGKEIT

Frank, Gary *see* JUAN PERON VS. SPRUILLE BRADEN
Frank, Gustav *see* GESCHICHTE DER PROTESTANTISCHEN THEOLOGIE
Frank, H *see*
- INTERNATIONAL PENAL POLICY
- ZWISCHENSTAATLICHE STRAFRECHTSPOLITIK

Frank, H R *see* ZUR THEOLOGIE A. RITSCHL'S
Frank, Henry *see*
- DOOM OF DOGMA AND DAWN OF TRUTH
- THE DOOM OF DOGMA AND THE DAWN OF TRUTH

Frank, Julius F *soo* NETWORKING IN BRUCELLOSIS RESEARCH
Frank, K *see*
- BABYLONISCHE BESCHWOERUNGRELIEFS. EIN BEITRAG ZUR ERKLAERUNG DER SOG. HADESRELIEFS
- BILDER UND SYMBOLE BABYLONISCH-ASSYRISCHER GOETTER

Frank, Laura B *see* THE "HEART AT WORK" PROGRAM
FRANK LESLIE'S BOY'S AND GIRL'S WEEKLY – An illustrated record of outdoor and home amusements. v. 1-36. 13 Oct 1866-9 Feb 1884. 4 nos. wanting – 1 – $260.00 – us L of C Photodup [790]
FRANK LESLIE'S BUDGET OF HUMOROUS AND SPARKLING STORIES, TALES OF HEROISM, ADVENTURE AND SATIRE – 1878-1896. (May-Jun 1891; Mar 1892, and Dec 1894 wanting) – 1 – 273.00 – us L of C Photodup [073]
FRANK LESLIE'S CHIMNEY CORNER – v. 1-39, no. 1-1018. 3 Jun 1865-29 Nov 1884. 2 nos. wanting – 1 – 276.00 – us L of C Photodup [073]
FRANK LESLIE'S FACT AND FICTION FOR THE CHIMNEY CORNER – v. 1-2, no. 1-28. 6 Dec 1884-6 Jun 1885 – 1 – 19.00 – us L of C Photodup [073]
FRANK LESLIE'S LADY'S JOURNAL – Devoted to fashion and choice literature. v. 1-20, no. 1-517. 18 Nov 1871-8 Oct 1881. no. 517 wanting – 1 – 162.00 – us L of C Photodup [073]
FRANK LESLIE'S LADY'S MAGAZINE – v. 1-51. Sep 1857-Dec 1882. 5 nos. wanting – 1 – 308.00 – us L of C Photodup [073]
FRANK LESLIE'S NEW MONTHLY – 1881 – 1 – 19.00 – us L of C Photodup [073]
FRANK LESLIE'S NEW MONTHLY – Devoted to light and entertaining literature. v. 1-6. Aug 1863-Jul 1866 – 1 – 26.00 – us L of C Photodup [073]
FRANK LESLIE'S PLEASANT HOURS – Devoted to light and entertaining literature. v. 1-60, no. 3. Aug 1866-Apr 1896. Scattered issues wanting – 1 – 260.00 – us L of C Photodup [073]
FRANK LESLIE'S POPULAR MONTHLY *see* AMERICAN MAGAZINE
FRANK LESLIE'S SUNDAY MAGAZINE – v. 1-25. Jan 1877-Jun 1889 – 1 – 254.00 – us L of C Photodup [073]
FRANK MURPHY IN WORLD WAR I / Fine, Sidney – Ann Arbor: Michigan Historical Collections 1968. 44p. LL-2279 – 1 – us L of C Photodup [340]
Frank, R *see* DIE RECHTS- UND GESCHAEFTSFAEHIGKEIT...
Frank, Robyn *see* JOURNAL OF AGRICULTURAL AND FOOD INFORMATION
Frank, Ulrich *see* SIMON EICHELKATZ; THE PATRIARCH
Frank, Uwe *see*
- DIE PHOTOAKUSTISCHE BESTIMMUNG ABSOLUTER OPTISCHER EXTINKTIONSKOEFFIZIENTEN VON ADSORBIERTEN FARBSTOFFEN
- PHOTOAKUSTISCHE UNTERSUCHUNG DES ENERGIETRANSFERS AUF FRAKTALEN OBERFLAECHEN

Frank, Viktor *see* RUSSISCHES CHRISTENTHUM
FRANK WEDEKIND / Friedrich, Paul – Berlin: W Borngraeber Verlag Neues Leben, [1913] – 1r – 1 – us U.W. Library [430]
FRANK WEDEKIND / Pissin, Raimund – Berlin: Gose und Tetzlaff, [1905?] – 1r – 1 – us U.W. Library [430]
Franke, D *see* PHOTOGRAPHS OF EGYPTIAN ART AND OF EGYPT
Franke, Eberhard *see* DAS RUHRGEBIET UND OSTPREUSSEN
Franke, Martin *see* JOHANN FRIEDRICH AUGUST TISCHBEIN
Franke, O *see*
- EINE CHINESISCHE TEMPELINSCHRIFT AUS INDIKUSAHRI BEI TURFAN
- EPIGRAPHISCHE DENKMAELER AUS CHINA

Franke, W *see* CHINESISCHE FELDZUEGE DURCH DIE MONGOLEI IM FRUEHEN 15. JAHRHUNDERT
Frankel, Zacharias *see*
- DARKHEI HA-MISHNAH
- MEVO HA-YERUSHALMI
- UEBER DEN EINFLUSS DER PALAESTINISCHEN EXEGESE AUF. DIE ALEXANDRINISCHE HERMENEUTIK
- ZEITSCHRIFT FUER DIE RELIGIOESEN INTERESSEN DES JUDENTHUMS

Frankel, Zacharias et al *see* MONATSSCHRIFT FUER GESCHICHTE UND WISSENSCHAFT DES JUDENTHUMS
Frankenberg, W *see*
- EVAGRIUS PONTICUS
- DIE SYRISCHEN CLEMENTINEN (T.U.U. 4-48/3)

Frankenberg, Wilhelm *see* DIE DATIERUNG DER PSALMEN SALOMOS: EIN BEITRAG ZUR JUEDISCHEN GESCHICHTE
FRANKENPOST – Hof, Germany. 2 Oct 1945-78. Vg – 1 – DM6440.00 – gw Mikro Press [072]
FRANKENPOST – Hof. oct 12, 1945-aug 3, 1967 – 1 – gw Mikrofilm [072]
FRANKENTHALER WOCHENBLATT – Frankenthal-Pfalz, Germany. 1848 – 1r – 1 – gw Mikrofilm [072]
Frankfort, Henri *see*
- PRELIMINARY REPORTS OF THE IRAQ EXPEDITIONS, 1-5
- THE PROBLEM OF SIMILARITY IN ANCIENT NEAR EASTERN RELIGIONS

[FRANKFURT AM MAIN: PAMPHLET COLLECTION] – 1912 – 1 – CSUXANS9180-B – us Hoover Inst Photo [943]
Frankfurt. Stadt- und Universitaetsbibliothek. Flugschriftensammlung Gustav Freytag *see* FLUGSCHRIFTENSAMMLUNG GUSTAV FREYTAG
FRANKFURTER ALLGEMEINE – Frankfurt: Frankfurter Allgemeine Zeitung, [1949-jun 1 1953-] – 1 – us Res Libr [072]
FRANKFURTER ALLGEMEINE SONNTAGSZEIT. – 1990-1994 – 2 times per yr – 1 – DM180.00 – sz Infoprint [072]
FRANKFURTER ALLGEMEINE SONNTAGSZEITUNG – 1990-1993 – 7r – 1 – DM525.00 – gw Mikro Press [943]
FRANKFURTER ALLGEMEINE ZEITUNG – 1949- – 12-14r per y in recent yrs – 1 – us Ross [072]
FRANKFURTER ALLGEMEINE ZEITUNG – 1949-1994 – 16 times per yr – 1 – DM1,170.00 – sz Infoprint [072]
FRANKFURTER ALLGEMEINE ZEITUNG – (1965-80 153r DM11,475.00. 1981-91 141r DM10,575.00. 1992-94 43r DM3,225.00.) – Frankfurt Main, DE. 1949-64 – 65r – 1 – DM4,875.00 (DM840.00 subsc 1995) – gw Mikro Press [072]
FRANKFURTER ALLGEMEINE ZEITUNG : AUSGABE FRANKFURT: STADTAUSGABE – (1965-93 415r DM31,125.00) – Frankfurt Main, DE. 1949-1964 – 90r – 1 – DM6,750.00 (DM840.00 subsc 1995) – gw Mikro Press [072]
FRANKFURTER ALLGEMEINE ZEITUNG – Frankfurt/Main. jun 2, 1975-may 22, 1978. jul 21, 1978-79 – 1 – gw Mikrofilm [072]
FRANKFURTER ALLGEMEINE ZEITUNG, MAGAZIN – Frankfurt/Main, DE. 1980- – 1 – gw Mikrofilm [072]
FRANKFURTER ALLGEMEINE ZEITUNG MAGAZINE – 1980- – ca 3r per y – 1 – us Ross [072]
DIE FRANKFURTER BERICHTE GUSTAVS V. MEYERN-HOHENBERG : MIT EINEM LEBENSBILD UND EINER WUERDIGUNG SEINES LITERARISCHEN SCHAFFENS / Kummer, Rolf – (Includes bibliographical references) – [S.l.: s.n.] (Leipzig: Druck von Gerhardt), 1934 – 1 – us U.W. Library [943]
FRANKFURTER BUECHERFREUND 1.1900-11.1913, NEUE FOLGE 1. (12) 1914-19 BIS 4. (15) 1922 : MITTHEILUNGEN AUS DEM ANTIQUARIATE / Baer, Joseph – Frankfurt, 1900-1922 (mf ed 1994) – 50mf – 9 – DM420.00 – 3-89131-170-2 – gw Fischer [090]
Frankfurter, Felix *see*
- THE BUSINESS OF THE SUPREME COURT: A STUDY IN THE FEDERAL JUDICIAL SYSTEM
- THE FELIX FRANKFURTER PAPERS
- PAPERS
- A SELECTION OF CASES UNDER THE INTERSTATE COMMERCE ACT

FRANKFURTER GELEHRTE ANZEIGEN / ed by Merck, Johann Heinrich – Frankfurt am Main, 1772-90. Hildesheim, 1980 – 226mf – 9 – DM1,550.00 diazo DM1,750.00 silver – gw Olms [430]
FRANKFURTER GESCHAEFTSBERICHT : AUSGABE: STADTBLATT – (Cont by: Frankfurter Handelszeitung, aug 27, 1856. Neue Frankfurter Zeitung, sep 1, 1859. Neue Deutsche Zeitung, nov 2, 1866. Frankfurter Zeitung, nov 16, 1866) – Frankfurt/Main. jan 3, 1923-33 – 16r – 1 – gw Mikrofilm [072]

FRANKFURTER GESCHAEFTSBERICHT : STADTAUSGABE – (Cont by: Frankfurter Handelszeitung, aug 27, 1856. Neue Frankfurter Zeitung, sep 1, 1859. Neue Deutsche Zeitung, nov 2, 1866. Frankfurter Zeitung, nov 16, 1866) – Frankfurt/Main. jan-jun 1936. nov 1936-apr 1937. sep 1937-jun 30, 1939 – 12r – 1 – gw Mikrofilm [072]
DER FRANKFURTER GOETHE / Mentzel, Elisabeth Schippel – Frankfurt a.M.: Ruetten & Loening, 1900 – 1r – 1 – us U.W. Library [430]
FRANKFURTER HANDELSZEITUNG *see* – FRANKFURTER GESCHAEFTSBERICHT
FRANKFURTER JOURNAL – (1840-60 62r DM4,650.00) – Frankfurt Main, 1 Jan-30 Jun 1832 – 1 – DM150.00 – gw Mikro Press [072]
FRANKFURTER JOURNAL *see* JOURNAL
FRANKFURTER NACHRICHTEN UND INTELLIGENZ-BLATT *see* INTELLIGENZ-BLATT DER FREIEN STADT FRANKFURT
FRANKFURTER NEUE PRESSE – Frankfurt Main, DE. Jan 1951; 1976- – ca 7r per yr – 1 – gw Mikrofilm [072]
FRANKFURTER OBER-POST-AMTS-ZEITUNG – (Various title changes. Known as: Frankfurter Postzeitung from Apr 1852) – Frankfurt-Main, DE. 1814-Jul 1866 – 103r – 1 – gw Mikrofilm [072]
FRANKFURTER POSTZEITUNG *see* FRANKFURTER OBER-POST-AMTS-ZEITUNG
FRANKFURTER PRESSE : DER AMERIKANISCHEN 12. HEERESGRUPPE FUER DIE DEUTSCHE ZIVILBEVOELKERUNG – 21 Apr-26 Jul 1945 – 1r – 1 – DM75.00 – gw Mikro Press [072]
FRANKFURTER PRESSE / ed by Der Amerikanischen 12. Heeresgruppe fuer die deutsche Zivilbevoelkerung – Frankfurt-Main, DE. 21 Apr-26 Jul 1945 – 1r – 1 – gw Mikrofilm [072]
FRANKFURTER RUNDSCHAU – 1945-1994 – 12 times per yr – 1 – DM1,080.00 – sz Infoprint [072]
FRANKFURTER RUNDSCHAU – (1957-69 75r DM5,625.00. 1970-79 87r DM6,525.00. 1980-91 112r DM8,400.00. 1992-94 36r DM2,700.00.) – Frankfurt Main, DE. 1945-57 – 30r – 1 – DM2,250.00 (DM660.00 subsc 1995) – gw Mikro Press [072]
FRANKFURTER RUNDSCHAU – (1979- inquire for price) – 1945- – 10-12r per y – 1 – inquire – us Ross [072]
FRANKFURTER RUNDSCHAU : ABENDAUSGABE – Frankfurt/Main. feb 25, 1962-nov 17, 1975 – 1 – gw Mikrofilm [072]
FRANKFURTER RUNDSCHAU : AUSGABE LAND 12 – Frankfurt/Main. aug 3, 1970-74 – 1 – gw Mikrofilm [072]
FRANKFURTER RUNDSCHAU : AUSGABE LAND 13 – Frankfurt/Main. nov 2, 1970-74 – 1 – gw Mikrofilm [072]
FRANKFURTER RUNDSCHAU : AUSGABE LAND 2 – Frankfurt/Main. nov 28, 1972-74 – 1 – gw Mikrofilm [072]
FRANKFURTER RUNDSCHAU : AUSGABE LAND 6 – Frankfurt/Main. oct 8, 1968-74. 1982-95 – 1 – gw Mikrofilm [072]
FRANKFURTER RUNDSCHAU : AUSGABE LAND 7 – Frankfurt/Main. oct 28, 1968-74. jan 19, 1988-95 – 1 – gw Mikrofilm [072]
FRANKFURTER RUNDSCHAU : AUSGABEN LAND 3 – 5 – Frankfurt/Main. oct 8, 1968-95 – 1 – gw Mikrofilm [072]
FRANKFURTER RUNDSCHAU : AUSGABEN LAND 8 – 11 – Frankfurt/Main. oct 8, 1968-74 – 1 – gw Mikrofilm [072]
FRANKFURTER RUNDSCHAU : BEILAGE: ZEIT UND BILD – Frankfurt/Main. jan 9, 1949-sep 28, 1955 – 1 – gw Mikrofilm [072]
FRANKFURTER RUNDSCHAU : DEUTSCHLAND-AUSGABE – Frankfurt/Main. aug 2, 1947-79 – 1 – gw Mikrofilm [072]
FRANKFURTER RUNDSCHAU – Frankfurt: Frankfurter Rundschau, 1945 (Deutschland Ausg) 1953-1981 – 1 – us Res Libr [072]
FRANKFURTER RUNDSCHAU – Frankfurt Main, DE. 1979- – ca 460mf per yr – 9 – gw Alpha Com [072]
FRANKFURTER RUNDSCHAU : STADTAUSGABE – Frankfurt/Main. aug 1, 1945-75. 1982-96 – 1 – gw Mikrofilm [072]
FRANKFURTER SCHULZEITUNG – Frankfurt/Main, DE. 1884 – 1r – 1 – gw Mikrofilm [072]
FRANKFURTER STAATS-RISTRETTO – Frankfurt, 1783-1800 – 8r – 1 – DM800.00 DM100.00r – gw Mikro Press [072]
FRANKFURTER STAATS-RISTRETTO – Frankfurt-Main, DE. 1783-1800 – 8r – 1 – gw Mikro Press [072]
Frankfurter Verein fuer Geschichte und Landeskunde *see* MITTHEILUNGEN AN DIE MITGLIEDER
FRANKFURTER VOLKSBLATT – Frankfurt Main, DE. 1851-Jun 1852 – 1 – gw Mikrofilm [072]
FRANKFURTER VOLKSBOTE – Frankfurt Main, DE. Apr 1849-Dec 1856 – 1 – gw Mikrofilm [072]
FRANKFURTER ZEITUNG – 1864-1889 – Cumul – 1 – DM5,500.00 – sz Infoprint [072]
FRANKFURTER ZEITUNG – 1918-1943 – Cumul – 1 – DM7,500.00 – sz Infoprint [072]
FRANKFURTER ZEITUNG – (1918-43 100r DM7,500.00) – Frankfurt, 1864-1889 – 76r – 1 – DM5,700.00 – gw Mikro Press [072]
FRANKFURTER ZEITUNG – 1924-29 – 1 – us UMI [072]
FRANKFURTER ZEITUNG – Frankfurt. Germany. 24 Jul 1914-14 Aug 1920. Missing scattered issues – 1 – 35.00r – us Hoover Inst Photo [072]
FRANKFURTER ZEITUNG – Frankfurt Main, DE. 2 Feb-30 Sep 1849 – 1 – gw Mikrofilm [072]
FRANKFURTER ZEITUNG *see* – FRANKFURTER GESCHAEFTSBERICHT
FRANKFURTER ZEITUNG UND HANDELSBLATT – Frankfurt am Main, Germany. 1900-Jul 1914; Aug 1920-1923 – 116r – 1 – us L of C Photodup [072]
FRANKFURTER ZEITUNG UND HANDELSBLATT – (Various eds bound together. Eds filmed consecutively, except for sep 1938-aug 1943, Reichsausgabe only) – Frankfurt, [1870-98; jan-jul 1914; 1930-aug 1943] – 1 – us Res Libr [072]
FRANKFURTER ZEITUNG UND HANDELSBLATT – Frankfurt am Main: Frankfurter Societats-Druckerei, 1866-1943. jan 4, 1870-98; jan-jul 1914; 1930-38 – us Res Libr [072]
FRANKFURTER ZEITUNG UND HANDELSBLATT – Frankfurt am Main: Frankfurter Societats-Druckerei, Reichsausg. sep 1938-jun 1941; nov 1941-aug 1943 – 33r – 1 – us Res Libr [072]
[FRANKISCHE SCHWEIZ: PAMPHLET COLLECTION] – 192? – 1 – CSUXANS6077-B – us Hoover Inst Photo [943]
Frankl, Ludwig August *see*
– ANASTASIUS GRUEN'S GESAMMELTE WERKE
– NACH JERUSALEM
– ZUR BIOGRAPHIE FERDINAND RAIMUNDS
– ZUR BIOGRAPHIE FRANZ GRILLPARZER'S
Frankland, B *see* RECOLLECTIONS OF MY OWN LIFE AND TIMES
FRANKLIN ADVOCATE – Meadville. Miss. 1902-1907; 1936-1960 – 1 – us UMI [071]
Franklin, Benjamin *see*
– BENJAMIN FRANKLIN'S ACCOUNT BOOKS
– PAPERS OF BENJAMIN FRANKLIN
– THE PENNSYLVANIA GAZETTE, 1728-1815
– QUATUOR POUR TROIS VIOLONS ET VIOLONCELLE
FRANKLIN CLUB RECORDS, MS 445 – 1895-1901 – 1r – 1 – us Western Res [320]
FRANKLIN COUNTRY CHRONICLE – Benton. Ill. 1881-83 – 1 – us UMI [071]
Franklin County and Douglas County, KS *see* FUNERAL REGISTERS
FRANKLIN COUNTY AT THE BEGINNING OF THE 20TH CENTURY / Historical Publishing Co – Biographical sketches. Columbus, 1901. Ohio Reel 32. (The Cox Library Collection) – 5 – us Americana [978]
FRANKLIN COUNTY NEWS – Franklin, NE. -w. except -sw. 1910-16. Mar. 1910-May 1929 – 1 – us NE Hist [071]
FRANKLIN COUNTY SENTINEL – Franklin, NE. -w. Oct. 1895-Sep. 1896; Dec. 1896-Sep. 1899; May 1901-Jul. 1901; Sep. 1901-Dec. 1917; Aug. 1918-Jul. 1918; Jan. 1919- – 1 – us NE Hist [071]
FRANKLIN COUNTY TRIBUNE – Bloomington, NE. -w. Dec. 1917-Oct. 1922 – 1 – us NE Hist [071]
FRANKLIN D. ROOSEVELT : DIARY AND ITINERARIES/USHER BOOKS – 78mf – 9 – $375.00 – us UPA [320]
FRANKLIN D. ROOSEVELT AND FOREIGN AFFAIRS / ed by Scheve, Donald – (Guide only $110.00) – Second series, 1937-39, v4-16 and printed index vol. 1979. 1981. 66 fiches – 9 – $420.00 – us UPA [920]
FRANKLIN DEMOCRAT – Brookville. Ind. 1852-1895 – 1 – us UMI [071]
FRANKLIN EVENING NEWS – Franklin, PA., 1886-1920 – 13 – $25.00r – us I.M.R. [071]
FRANKLIN FREE PRESS – Franklin, NE. -w. Jul. 1900-May 1906 – 1 – us NE Hist [071]
FRANKLIN GAZETTE – Rocky Mount. Va. 1958-1959; 1963-1967 – 1 – us UMI [071]
THE FRANKLIN INSTITUTE AND THE MAKING OF INDUSTRIAL AMERICA – Reports on research at the Institute, minutes of meetings, lantern slides of lectures, membership books, exhibition catalogs, etc. With printed guide – 536 fiches – 9 – $2,355.00 – us UPA [975]
Franklin Institute. Philadelphia *see* JOURNAL
Franklin, John *see*
– NARRATIVE OF A JOURNEY TO THE SHORES OF THE POLAR SEA
– NARRATIVE OF A SECOND EXPEDITION TO THE SHORES OF THE POLAR SEA. INCLUDING AN ACCOUNT. BY J. RICHARDSON
THE FRANKLIN KENTUCKY BAPTIST – May 17, 1866 – Jun 22, 1867 – 1 – 6.72 – us Baptist [240]
Franklin, New Hampshire.East Franklin Baptist Church *see* RECORDS
FRANKLIN NEWS HERALD – Franklin, PA. -d 1970 – 13 – $25.00r – us I.M.R. [071]
FRANKLIN NEWS POST – Rocky Mount. Va. -w. 1940- – 1 – us UMI [071]
Franklin. Ohio. First Congregational Church *see* CHURCH RECORDS, MS 421
FRANKLIN, OHIO, TAXES, MS V.F.O. – (List of the land given in by residents) – 1804 – 1r – 1 – us Western Res [978]
FRANKLIN PIERCE PAPERS – (With guide) – 7r – 1 – $245.00 – Dist. us Scholarly Res – us L of C Photodup [975]
Franklin. Presbytery (Pres. Ch. in the U.S.A. New School) *see* MINUTES, 1846-1870
Franklin Publishing Co *see* HISTORY OF SHEBOYGAN COUNTY
FRANKLIN REPOSITORY – Chamberburg. Pa. 1884-1901 – 1 – us UMI [071]
FRANKLIN REPOSITORY – Chambersburg, PA. 1808-15, 1863-65, 1884-1901 – 1 – us UMI [071]
FRANKLIN'S ROLE IN THE DEVELOPMENT OF BOOK-PUBLISHING IN INDONESIA / Shadily, Hassan – SE 10,772 1. 1964 – 9 – ne IDC [070]
FRANKLINTON BAPTIST CHURCH. PLEASUREVILLE, KENTUCKY : CHURCH RECORDS – 1848-1940; 1956-66. Formerly Drennons Ridge – 1 – 43.65 – us Baptist [240]
Franko, I *see* APOKRIFY I LEHENDY Z UKRAINS'KYKH RUKOPISIV/ZIBRAV, UPORIADKOVAV I POIASNYV
FRANKREICHS SICHERHEITS- UND DEUTSCHLANDPOLITIK 1931-1935 IM WIDERSTREIT DER FRANZOESISCHEN OEFFENTLICHEN DISKUSSION / Schumacher, Alois – Frankfurt a.M., 1970 – 4mf – 9 – DM90.00 – 3-89349-693-9 – gw Hänsel [327]
Franks, Cyril M *see* CHILD AND FAMILY BEHAVIOR THERAPY
Franks, Dorothy W *see* SELF-ESTEEM AND ADOLESCENT PREGNANCY
Franks, Ian *see* PREPROGRAMMING VS. ON-LINE PREPARATION IN SIMPLE MOVEMENT SEQUENCES
Franks, James *see* MEMOIRS OF PRETENDED PROPHETS WHO HAVE APPEARED IN DIFFERENT AGES OF THE WORLD, AND ESPECIALLY IN MODERN TIMES, POINTING OUT, FROM AUTHENTIC SOURCES, THEIR BLUNDERS AND THE PERNICIOUS CONSEQUENCES OF THEIR PRETENSIONS;...
Franquet, Louis *see* VOYAGES ET MEMOIRES SUR LE CANADA
LA FRANSCATANA. OPERA BUFFA IN TRE ATTI / Paisiello, G – Partition: MS copy, 1774 – 1 – us Sibley [780]
Franssen, M *see* LES PERSPECTIVES DE L'UNIFICATION DU DROIT DE CHANGE DEPUIS 1910
Fransz, A L *see* DR. JOHN R. MOTT; PELOPOR PEKABARAM INDJIL DAN KESATUAN KRISTEN
[IL FRANTICO BURLATO] OVERTURE, ARRANGED PIANO WITH AD LIB VIOLIN / Paisiello, G – (Piano part only) – Paris: Boyer, 179- – 1 – us Sibley [780]
Frantsev, V A *see* ALEXANDER SERGEVICH PUSHKIN V CHESHSKOI LITERATURE
FRANTSISK ASSIZSKII / Merezhkovskh, D – Berlin. 1938. BR-762 2 – 8 – ne IDC [240]
FRANTSUZSKAIA INTERVENTSIIA NA IUGE 1918-1919 / Akushkin, Evgenii Evgenevich – Moskva: Gos. izdvo, 1919 – 1 – CSUX88-B8394 – us Hoover Inst Photo [355]
FRANTSUZSKIE RUKOPISI GOSUDARSTVENNOI PUBLICHNOI BIBLIOTEKI / Shishmarev, V F – 1965. Description and texts of French manuscripts in Saltykov-Shchedrin Library. BR-10,861/1 – 9 – ne IDC [090]
FRANTSUZSKIE SREDNEVEKOVYE RUKOPISNYE KNIGI V SOBRANII GOSUDARSTVENNOI PUBLICHNOI BIBLIOTEKI IM. M.E. SALTYKOVA-SHCHEDRINA / Voronova, T P – BR-10,862/1 – 9 – ne IDC [010]
FRANTSUZY V ODESSE : IZ BELYKH MEMUAROV / Denikin, Anton Ivanovich et al; ed by Shchegoleva, P E – Leningrad: "Krasnai a gazeta", 1928 – 1 – CSUX88-B4735 – us Hoover Inst Photo [305]
Frantz, Clamor *see* VERSUCH EINER GESCHICHTE DES MARIEN- UND ANNEN-CULTUS IN DER KATHOLISCHEN KIRCHE
Frantz, Susanne K *see*
– CONTEMPORARY GLASS
– THIRTY YEARS OF NEW GLASS, 1957-1987
Franz, Albert *see*
– DIE KIRCHLICHEN BENEDIKTIONEN IM MITTELALTER
– DIE MESSE IM DEUTSCHEN MITTELALTER
– DAS RITUALE VON ST FLORIAN AUS DEM 12 JHT
– DER SOZIALE KATHOLIZISMUS IN DEUTSCHLAND BIS ZUM TODE KETTELERS
Franz, Albin *see* JOHANN KLAJ
Franz, G *see* WORKS BY CASPAR HUBERINUS
FRANZ GRILLPARZER : EINE BIOGRAPHISCHE STUDIE / Faeulhammer, Adalbert – (Includes bibliographical references) – Graz: Leuschner & Lubensky, 1884 – 1r – 1 – us U.W. Library [920]
FRANZ GRILLPARZER : EINE CHARAKTERISTIK / Koch, Max – Frankfurt am Main: Knauer, 1891 – 1r – 1 – us U.W. Library [430]
FRANZ GRILLPARZER : SEIN LEBEN, DICHTEN UND DENKEN / Lange, E – (Includes bibliographical references) – Guetersloh: C Bertelsmann, 1894 – 1r – 1 – us U.W. Library [920]
FRANZ GRILLPARZER : SEIN LEBEN UND SCHAFFEN: IM HINBLICK AUF DEN 100. GEBURTSTAG / Mahrenholtz, Richard – Leipzig: Renger, 1890 – 1r – 1 – us U.W. Library [920]
FRANZ GRILLPARZER : EINE STUDIE / Vancsa, Kurt – 1r – 1 – us U.W. Library [430]
FRANZ GRILLPARZERS LEBENSGESCHICHTE / Laube, Heinrich – Stuttgart: J G Cotta, 1884 – 1r – 1 – us U.W. Library [920]
FRANZ GRILLPRARZER : EIN KAMPF UM LEBEN UND KUNST / Alker, Ernst – (Includes bibliographical references) – Marburg a.L.: N G Elwert, 1930 – 1 – us U.W. Library [430]
Franz Josef Landesrabbinerschule. Budapest *see* FESTSCHRIFT ZUM 50 JAEHRIGEN BESTEHEN DER FRANZ-JOSEF LANDESRABBINERSCHULE IN BUDAPEST
[FRANZ JOSEF STRAUSS: PAMPHLET COLLECTION] – 1971-1987 – 1 – CSUXANS3226-B – us Hoover Inst Photo [943]
FRANZ KAFKA – DIE INSZENIERUNG UNMOEGLICHER UEBERSCHREITUNG IN "DER PROCESS" UND ANDEREN SCHRIFTEN / Wuelfingen, Klaus Bock von – 1995 – 2mf – 9 – DM80.00 – 3-8267-2135-7 – gw Hänsel [430]
FRANZ LAMBERT VON AVIGNON : NACH SEINEN SCHRIFTEN UND DEN GLEICHZEITIGEN QUELLEN / Baum, Johann Wilhelm – Strassburg: Treuttel und Wuertz, 1840 – 1mf – us A.T.L.A. [240]
FRANZ LISZT'S BRIEFE / Liszt, Franz – Leipzig: Breitkopf & Haertel, 1893 – 1 – us Sibley [780]
Franz, M *see* PERSONAL- UND REALUNION
Franz, Martin *see* POSTNATALE ENTWICKLUNG DES MITTELOHRS BEI PACHYUROMYS DUPRASI
Franz Schubert's copy *see* KURZGEFASSTES MUSICALISCHES LEXICON...
FRANZ VON ASSISI UND DIE NACHAHMUNG CHRISTI / Walter, Johannes von – Lichterfelde-Berlin: E. Runge, 1910 – 1mf – us A.T.L.A. [240]

FRANZ VON KOBELL : SEIN LEBEN UND SEINE WERKE: 1. TEIL, LEBENS- UND ENTWICKLUNGSGANG: 1. PERIODE (1803-1845) / Dreyer, Aloys; ed by Dreyer, Aloys – Freising: F P Datterer, 1903 – 1r – 1 – us U.W. Library [920]
FRANZ VON SICKINGEN / Maenss, Johannes – Berlin: C Habel, 1877 – 1r – 1 – us U.W. Library [943]
FRANZ VON SICKINGEN : NACH MEISTENS UNGEDRUCKTEN QUELLEN / Ulmann, Heinrich – (Includes bibliographical references) – Leipzig: S Hirzel, 1872 (Grimme & Troemel) – 1r – 1 – us U.W. Library [430]
FRANZ VON SICKINGENS FEHDE GEGEN TRIER : UND EIN GUTACHTEN CLAUDIUS CANTIUNCULAS UEBER DIE RECHTSANSPRUECHE DER SICKINGENSCHEN ERBEN / Bremer, Franz Peter – (Includes bibliographical references) – Strassburg: J H E Heitz, 1885 – 1r – 1 – us U.W. Library [943]
Franz, Wilhelm *see* BRITANNIEN UND DER KRIEG
Franzelin, Bernhard *see* DIE NEUESTE LEHRE GEYSERS UEBER DAS KAUSALITAETSPRINZIP
Franzen, Raymond H *see*
- THE ACH INDEX OF NUTRITIONAL STATUS
- PHYSICAL DEFECTS: THE PATHWAY TO CORRECTION
- PHYSICAL MEASURES OF GROWTH AND NUTRITION

Franzen, Stefan *see* GADOLINIUM-DTPA- UND TEMPERATURSTUDIEN ZUR INTERSTITIELLEN TUMORTHERAPIE FUER DIE INTERVENTIONELLE KERNSPINTOMOGRAPHIE
Franzero, Charles Marie *see* THE LIFE AND TIMES OF CLEOPATRA
Franzinger, D *see* GRUNDZUEGE EINER JURISTISCHEN CONSTRUCTION...
FRANZISCA HERNANDEZ UND FRAI FRANZISCO ORTIZ : ANFAENGE REFORMATORISCHER BEWEGUNGEN IN SPANIEN UNTER KAISER KARL V / Boehmer, Eduard – Leipzig: H. Haessel, 1865 – 1mf – us A.T.L.A. [946]
Franzismus *see* LE FRANCISTE
Franzius, Enno *see*
- BRIAND: STATESMAN OF PEACE
- CAILLAUX: STATESMAN OF PEACE

Franzke, Joachim *see* PSEUDOSCHALLWELLEN-LASERSPEKTROSKOPIE AN NIEDERDRUCKPLASMEN
FRANZOESISCHE EINFLUESSE BEI SCHILLER / Schanzenbach, Otto – Stuttgart: C Liebich, 1885 – 1r – 1 – us U.W. Library [430]
DER FRANZOESISCHE EINFLUSS IM ZWEITEN TEIL VON GOTTSCHEDS CRITISCHER DICHTKUNST / Blanck, Karl – (Includes bibliographical references) – Goettingen: W F Kaestner, 1910 – 1r – 1 – us U.W. Library [410]
DIE FRANZOESISCHE REVOLUTION IM DEUTSCHEN DRAMA UND EPOS NACH 1815 / Hirschstein, Hans – (Includes bibliographical references and index) – Stuttgart: J B Metzler, 1912 – 1 – us U.W. Library [430]
DIE FRANZOESISCHE TRAGOEDIE DER ERSTEN HAELFTE DES 17. JAHRHUNDERTS IM URTEILE IHRER ZEITGENOSSEN / Pizzo, Piero – Zuerich, 1914 – 2mf – DM62.00 – 3-8267-3042-9 – gw Hänsel [440]
DIE FRANZOESISCHEN MANDATSGEBIETE KAMERUN UND TOGO / Bergfeld, E – Greifswald, 1935 – 2mf – 9 – ILM-1934/1 – ne IDC [327]
DER FRANZOESISCH-RUSSISCHE ENTSCHAEDIGUNGS-PLAN... – Regensburg, 1802 – 3mf – 1 – ILM-2773/1 – ne IDC [327]
Franzos, Karl Emil *see*
- HEINES GEBURTSTAG
- DIE JUDEN VON BARNOW
- DER KLEINE MARTIN
- MOSCHKO VON PARMA
- NEUE NOVELLEN
- DER POJAZ
- SAEMMTLICHE WERKE UND HANDSCHRIFTLICHER NACHLASS

DER FRANZOSE IM DEUTSCHEN DRAMA / Schilling, Helmut – Heidelberg, 1930 – 2mf – 9 – DM62.00 – 3-89349-775-7 – gw Hänsel [430]
Frapan, Ilse *see* "FLUEGEL AUF!"
Frapie, Leon *see* L'INSTITUTRICE DE PROVINCE
FRARY, GEORGE S., DIARY, MS 3079 – 1864 – 1r – 1 – us Western Res [976]
FRASEOLOGIA DE CERVANTES / Sune Benagages, Juan – Barcelona. 1929 – 1 – us Res Libr [440]
Fraser, Alexander Campbell *see*
- BERKELEY AND SPIRITUAL REALISM
- PHILOSOPHY OF THEISM
- THE WORKS

Fraser, Christine *see* DER AUSTRITT DEUTSCHLANDS AUS DEM VOLKERBUND, SEINE VORGESCHICHTE UND SEINE NACHWIRKUNGEN
Fraser, Christopher Findlay *see* A SPEECH DELIVERED BY HON. C. F. FRASER, COMMISSIONER OF PUBLIC WORKS IN THE LEGISLATIVE ASSEMBLY, MARCH 25TH, 1890, ON SEPARATE SCHOOLS AND THE POSITION OF THE ROMAN CATHOLIC ELECTORS WITH THE TWO POLITICAL PARTIES
Fraser, Donald *see*
- AUTOBIOGRAPHY OF THE LATE DONALD FRASER, D.D.: AND A SELECTION FROM HIS SERMONS
- THE FUTURE OF AFRICA
- THE SPEECHES OF THE HOLY APOSTLES
- SPEECHES OF THE HOLY APOSTLES
- WINNING A PRIMITIVE PEOPLE

FRASER FAMILY PAPERS : WRITINGS ON THE NEW HEBRIDES BY VARIOUS MEMBERS OF THE FRASER FAMILY, 1881-1921 – 1r – 1 – at Pacific Mss [920]
Fraser, George A *see* HOW WE ARE GOVERNED
FRASER HERALD – Warren. Mich. 1926-31 – 1 – us UMI [071]
Fraser, J *see* THE LAWFULNESS AND DUTY OR SEPARATION FROM CORRUPT MINISTERS AND CHURCHES EXPLAINED AND VINDICATED;...
Fraser, J Alban *see* SPAIN AND THE WEST COUNTRY. LONDON, 1935
Fraser, J P Munro *see* HISTORY OF CONTRA COSTA COUNTY
Fraser, James *see* A TREATISE OF JUSTIFYING FAITH
Fraser, John *see*
- CANADIAN PEN AND INK SKETCHES
- ERROMANGA
- HISTORIC CANADIAN GROUND: THE LA SALLE HOMESTEAD OF 1666 AND OTHER OLD LANDMARKS OF FRENCH CANADA ON THE LOWER LACHINE ROAD

Fraser, L *see* ZOOLOGIA TYPICA, OR FIGURES OF NEW AND RARE MAMMALS AND BIRDS, IN THE ZOOLOGICAL SOCIETY OF LONDON
Fraser, N C et al *see* MODERN GEOLOGY
Fraser, Nicholas *see* EVA PERON
Fraser, P *see* THE CONFLICT OF LAWS IN CASES OF DIVORCE
Fraser, P N *see* BRITISH FERNS AND THEIR VARIETIES
Fraser, T T *see* NOTES ON THE PHYSIOLOGICAL ACTION OF THE CALABAR POISON BEAN
Fraser, Thomas *see* SERMONS BY THE REV. THOMAS FRASER: FORMERLY OF LANARK AND OTHER PLACES, AND LEFT BY HIM AS A MEMENTO OF HIS PRESENCE AND LABOURS AMONG THEM
Fraser, William *see* BLENDING LIGHTS
FRASERBURGH HERALD – 1 – £42.00r – uk Scot News [072]
THE FRASERIAN PAPERS OF THE LATE WILLIAM MAGINN, LL.D. : ANNOTATED, WITH A LIFE OF THE AUTHOR BY R. SHELTON MACKENZIE / Maginn, William – New York: Redfield, 1857 – 1r – 1 – 1-55879-426-3 – uk Libr Preservation [920]
FRASER'S MAGAZINE – London. v1-80 1830-69; n.s. v1-26 1870-82 – 1,5,6 – us Princeton Micro [800]
Fraser-Winthrop *see* PAPERS OF FRASER-WINTHROP
FRASES HISTORICAS. VULGANIZACIONES / Oteyza, Luis de – Madrid: Renacimiento, 2th ed 1930 – sp Bibl Santa Ana [946]
Frassen, C *see* PHILOSOPHIA ACADEMICA...
FRATE ANGELO DA CHIARINO...OSIMO 1964 / Berardini, Lorenzo – Madrid: Graf. Calleja, 1966 – 1 – sp Bibl Santa Ana [946]
FRATER THOMERL : ORIGINAL-ZEITBILD AUS TYROL MIT GESANG, IN EINEM ACTE / Berla, Alois – Wien: J Schoenwetter, 1874 – 1 – us U.W. Library [820]
DIE FRATERHERREN IM LUECHTENHOFE ZU HILDESHEIM / Bruggeboes, W – Hildesheim, 1939 – 2mf – 8 – Dfl9.00 – ne Slangenburg [240]
FRATERNAL SOCIETY LAW ASSOCIATION PROCEEDINGS – 1920-41 (all publ) – 48mf – 9 – $72.00 – LLMC 84-467 – us L.L.M.C. [073]
A FRATERNIDADE : JORNAL MACONICO – Aracaju, 5 Oct-27 Apr 1876 – 1,5,6 – bl Biblioteca [072]
FRATERNITA – (L'Incontro). Turin. Italy. -m. Mar 1949-Dec 1969. (2 reels) – 1 – uk British Libr Newspaper [072]
FRATERNITE – Treichville, Ivory Coast. Apr. 24, 1959-Dec. 28, 1962 – 1 – 35.00r – us Hoover Inst Photo [072]
LA FRATERNITE – Journal de l'Aude. no. 1-113. Carcassonne. 6 sept 1848-5 juil 1850. mq no. 111 – 1 – fr A.C.R.P.P. [073]
LA FRATERNITE – Journal moral et politique. Red. en chef Richard Lahautiere. no. 1-23. Paris. mai 1841-mars 1843 – 1 – fr A.C.R.P.P. [073]
LA FRATERNITE – Philosophie, sciences, beaux-arts, inventions, musique, theatres. Dir. Stanislas Champein. Paris. 20 nov 1869-8 janv 1870 – 1 – fr A.C.R.P.P. [073]
LA FRATERNITE DE 1845 – Organe des interets du peuple. Journal de reorganisation sociale et de politique generale. Paris. 1845-janv 1848 – 1 – fr A.C.R.P.P. [073]
FRATERNITE FRANCAISE – (Library has: May 12, 1956-Dec. 28, 1962; Jan. 26, 1957 and Jan. 30, 1959 wanting) – Paris, St. Cere: Fraternite francaise, 195u – 1 – CSUX89-S45 – us Hoover Inst Photo [944]
LA FRATERNITE UNIVERSELLE – Paris: Pommeret et Moreau. v1 n1. dec 1848 – us Res Libr [072]
FRATERNITE-REVUE – Revue laique et chretienne de questions sociales, morales, economiques, politiques, artistiques et litteraires. Alencon puis Chartres. oct 1904-janv 1906 – 1 – fr A.C.R.P.P. [073]
DIE FRAU – Berlin, 1893/94-1940/41, 1942/43 – 1 – Dist. gw Mikrofilm – gw Misc Inst [072]
FRAU AVENTIURE : LIEDER AUS HEINRICH VON OFTERDINGENS ZEIT / Scheffel, Joseph Viktor von – (Includes bibliographical references) – 19. Aufl. Stuttgart: A Bonz, 1902 – 1r – 1 – us U.W. Library [780]
FRAU GESKE AUF TRUBERNES : EINE SAGA / Tuegel, Ludwig – Muenchen: A Langen, G Mueller, 1936 – 1r – 1 – us U.W. Library [390]
DIE FRAU (HQ 1) : MONATSSCHRIFT FUER DAS GESAMTE FRAUENLEBEN UNSERER ZEIT / Lange, Helene & Baeumer, Gertrud – Berlin. v1-51. 1893/94-1943/44 (mf ed 1991) – 368mf – 9 – DM2,650.00 DM59.00y – 3-89131-042-0 – gw Fischer [305]
DIE FRAU IM ROEMISCHEN CHRISTENPROCESS (T.U.U. 2-28/4C) / Augar, F – Leipzig, 1905 – 2mf – 9 – ne Slangenburg [240]
DIE FRAU IM STAAT (HQ 9) – 1919-1933 (mf ed 1993) – 34mf – 9 – DM390.00 – 3-89131-121-4 – gw Fischer [305]
DIE FRAU IN DER DICHTUNG CONRAD FERDINAND MEYERS / Clauss, Gertrud – (Includes bibliographical references (p.[v-vi])) – Stuttgart: J B Metzler, 1934 – 1r – 1 – us U.W. Library [430]
FRAU MESECK : EINE DORFGESCHICHTE / Halbe, Max – Berlin: G Bondi, 1897 – 1r – 1 – us U.W. Library [830]
FRAU RAT : ELISABETH GOETHE, GEB. TEXTOR / Hoeffner, Johannes – 4. Aufl. Bielefeld: Velhagen & Klasing, 1926 – 1r – 1 – us U.W. Library [920]
FRAU RAT GOETHE UND IHRE WELT : EINE FARBENSKIZZE / Paquet, Alfons – Frankfurt am Main: Kommissionsverlag von Englert und Schlosser, 1931 – 1r – 1 – us U.W. Library [920]
FRAU SORGE : ROMAN / Sudermann, Hermann – Stuttgart: Cotta, 1923 – 1r – 1 – us U.W. Library [830]
FRAU VON STEIN : GOETHES FREUNDIN UND FEINDIN / Nobel, Alphons – [Muenchen]: Muenchner Verlag, c1939 – 1r – 1 – us U.W. Library [920]
"FRAUD" AND CIVIL LIABILITY UNDER THE FEDERAL SECURITIES LAWS / Loss, Louis – Washington: FJC, Aug 1983 – 1mf – 9 – $1.50 – LLMC 95-805 – us L.L.M.C. [340]
A FRAUD UNMASKED: THE CAREER OF MRS. MARGARET L. SHEPERD, "EX-ROMANIST", "EX-NUN", "EX-PENITENT" AND BIGAMIST: HER OWN CONFESSIONS ATTESTED BY THE MOST RELIABLE WITNESSES / Brady, M J – Woodstock, Ont., 1893. 00240. (Pre-1900 Canadiana) – 9 – cn C.I.H.M. [360]
FRAUDE NOS TRIBUNAIS ECLESIASTICOS / Aradillas Agudo, Antonio – Lisboa: Liber, 1975 – 1 – sp Bibl Santa Ana [240]
FRAUDULENT MORTGAGES OF MERCHANDISE / Jones, Leonard Augustus – St. Louis, Jones, 1879. 46 p. LL-434 – 1 – us L of C Photodup [340]
FRAUDULENT MORTGAGES OF MERCHANDISE / Pierce, James Oscar – St. Louis: Thomas, 1884. 310p. LL-1060 – 1 – us L of C Photodup [340]
FRAUEN IM MANAGEMENT : FORSCHUNGSBERICHT UND ANALYSE AUSGEWAEHLTER AMERIKANISCHER PUBLIKATIONEN (1977-1993) / Bauer, Ina – 1995 – 2mf – 9 – DM80.00 – 3-8267-2249-3 – gw Hänsel [650]
FRAUEN UND FILM – Berlin, 1974-93 – 3r – 1 – DM270.00 – gw Mikro Press [305]
FRAUENANWALT, 1. 1870/71 – 6. 1875/76; DEUTSCHER FRAUENANWALT, 1878-81 (HQ 29) : ORGAN DES VERBANDES DEUTSCHER FRAUENBILDUNGS- UND ERWERBVEREINE – Berlin, 1870-81 (mf ed 1997) – 46mf – 9 – DM460.00 – 3-89131-141-9 – gw Fischer [305]
FRAUENBERUF (HQ, 18) : ZEITSCHRIFT FUER DIE INTERESSEN DER GEBILDETEN FRAUENWELT. 1.1887-6.1892 – mf ed 1996 – 29mf – 9 – DM420.00 – 3-89131-130-3 – gw Fischer [305]
DIE FRAUENBEWEGUNG (HQ 10) – 1895-1919 (mf ed 1994) – 94mf – 9 – DM820.00 – 3-89131-122-2 – gw Fischer [305]
FRAUENBILDER AUS GOETHE'S JUGENDZEIT : STUDIEN ZUM LEBEN DES DICHTERS / Duentzer, Heinrich – (Includes bibliographical references) – Stuttgart: J G Cotta, 1852 – 1r – 1 – us U.W. Library [430]
FRAUENBILDUNG, 1. 1902-22. 1923 (HQ 23) : ZEITSCHRIFT FUER DIE GESAMTEN INTERESSEN DES WEIBLICHEN UNTERRICHTSWESENS / Wychgram, J – Leipzig/Berlin, 1902-23 (mf ed 1996) – 136mf – 9 – DM1,280.00 – 3-89131-135-4 – gw Fischer [305]
Frauenfeld, G von *see* DIE ALGEN DER DALMATISCHEN KUESTE
Frauenfels, G Ritter von *see* NEU AUFGEFUNDENE ABBILDUNG DES DRONTE UND EINES ZWEITEN KURZFLUEGELIGEN VOGELS
DIE FRAUENFRAGE / Cathrein, Victor – (Includes bibliographical references and index of names) – 3., umgearb u verm Aufl. Freiburg i.B.; St Louis, MO: Herder, 1909 – 1mf – 9 – 0-8370-6890-8 – 1986-0890 – us A.T.L.A. [305]
DAS FRAUENHAUS VON BRESCIA / Strobl, Karl Hans – Leipzig: L Staackmann, c1911 – 1r – 1 – us U.W. Library [830]
FRAUENLIEBE : WOCHENSCHRIFT FUER FREUNDSCHAFT, LIEBE UND SEXUELLE AUFKLAERUNG – Berlin, 1926-31 n48 – 2r – 1 – Dist. gw Mikrofilm – gw Misc Inst [072]
FRAUENLOBS STREITGEDICHT ZWISCHEN MINNE UND WELT : TEXT UND UNTERSUCHUNGEN / Hildebrand, Alexander – Frankfurt a.M., 1970 – 2mf – 9 – DM62.00 – 3-89349-691-2 – gw Hänsel [430]
FRAUENLOS UND FRAUENARBEIT IN DER GESCHICHTE DES CHRISTENTUMS : VORTRAEGE GEHALTEN AUF DEM "VIERTEN APOLOGETISCHEN INSTRUKTIONSKURSUS" ZU BERLIN AM 17. – 21. OKTOBER 1910..." / Walter, Johannes von – Berlin: Trowitzsch, 1911 – 1mf – us A.T.L.A. [240]
FRAUENTASCHENBUCH (HQ, 22) / ed by de la Motte Fouque, Georg Doering – Nuernberg, 1.1817-17.1831 – 40mf – 9 – DM820.00 – 3-89131-134-6 – gw Fischer [305]
FRAUEN-ZEITUNG – Koeln, Germany. No.1, 1848 – 1 – gw Mikrofilm [072]
FRAUEN-ZUKUNFT, 1.1910-3.1913 (HQ, 21) / ed by Lieber, Gabriele v. & Hammerschlag, Meta – Muenchen, Leipzig, 1910-1913 (mf ed 1995) – 18mf – 9 – DM310.00 – 3-89131-133-8 – gw Fischer [305]
Fraunce, Abraham *see*
- THE ARCADIAN RHETORIKE
- THE LAWIERS LOGIKE

LES FRAVASHIS : ETUDE SUR LES TRACES DANS LE MAZDEISME / Soederblom, Nathan – Paris: Ernest Leroux, 1899 – 1mf – us A.T.L.A. [240]

FRAY BARTOLOME DE LAS CASAS, SUS TIEMPOS Y SU APOSISLADO / Gutierres, Carlos – Madrid, 1878. xxxix, 460p – 1 – us U.W. Library [240]

FRAY D. ALONSO DE VALENCIA Y BRAVO, DEL ORDEN Y CABALLERIA DE ALCANTARA (1723-1778) / Velo Nieto, Gervasio – Badajoz: Imprenta de la Diputacion Provincial, 1952 – sp Bibl Santa Ana [240]

FRAY LUIS BOLANOS, APOSTOL DEL PARAGUAY Y DEL RIO DE LA PLATA. CORDOBA (TUCUMAN). 1934 / Oro, Buenaventura – Madrid: Razon y Fe, 1935 – 1 – sp Bibl Santa Ana [240]

FRAY LUIS DE LEON : EINE BIOGRAPHIE AUS DER GESCHICHTE DER SPANISCHEN INQUISITION UND KIRCHE IM SECHZEHNTEN JAHRHUNDERT / Wilkens, C A – Halle: C.E.M. Pfeffer, 1866 – 1mf – us A.T.L.A. [240]

FRAY LUIS DE LEON Y BENITO ARIAS MONTANO / Lopez de Toro, Jose – Madrid: Rev. Arch. Bibl. y Mus., 1955. pp. 531-548 – 1 – sp Bibl Santa Ana [946]

FRAY PEDRO NUNEZ MACHADO (ZAFRA 1550-BURGOS 1609) / Guede, Lisardo – Badajoz: Dip. Provincial, 1969. Sep. Ree – 1 – sp Bibl Santa Ana [240]

FRAYE ARBEITER STIMME = FREE WORKERS' VOICE – (In Yiddish) – Philadelphia & New York. v41 no1 5 Jan 1940-v50 no29 23 Dec 1950 – 2r – 1 – $50.00 – cn Can Microfilming [071]

FRAYE ARBETER SHTIME = FREE WORKER'S VOICE – New York City, NY. v41 no 1, v50 no 29. 1940-1950 – 1r – Can$50.00 – cn Can Microfilming [071]

DI FRAYE SHTUNDE = FREE TIME – New York City, NY. v1 no 3. 1904 – 1r – Can$25.00 – cn Can Microfilming [071]

DI FRAYE SHTUNDE – (New York). 1904 – 1 – us A.J.P.C. [071]

DOS FRAYE VORT = THE FREE WORD – (In Yiddish) – Buenos Aires, AG. v1 no6 Jul 1936-v27 no- Jun 1963 – 1r – 1 – $45.00 – cn Can Microfilming [072]

DOS FRAYE VORT = THE FREE WORD – (In Yiddish. Bi-monthly) – Berlin, DE. v1 no1 Mar 1923-v1 no5 Aug 1923 – 1r – 1 – $25.00 – cn Can Microfilming [072]

DOS FRAYE VORT = THE FREE WORD – New York City, NY. v1 no 1. 1911 – 1r – Can$25.00 – cn Can Microfilming [071]

FRAYE WELT – London. v. 1-3. 1891-1893 – 1 – us NY Public [073]

FRAYE YIDISHE TRIBUNE = FREE JEWISH TRIBUNE – (In Yiddish) – London, GB. v-Dec 1943; v- Jan/Mar 1948 – 1r – 1 – $25.00 – cn Can Microfilming [072]

FRAYE YUGNT ["JUVENTUD LIBRE"] = LIBERATED YOUTH – (In Yiddish) – Buenos Aires, AG. no3. Jun 1947 – 1r – 1 – $25.00 – cn Can Microfilming [072]

DER FRAYER GEDANK = FREE THOUGHT – New York City, NY. v1 no 1. 1910 – 1r – Can$25.00 – cn Can Microfilming [071]

DER FRAYND – (In Yiddish) – St-Petersburg, RU. v1 no45 [1 Feb 1903-14 Aug 1905] v3 no166 – 1r – 1 – $25.00 – cn Can Microfilming [072]

Fraysse, C B *see* QUELQUES OBSERVATIONS A PROPOS DE L'ORGANIZATION DU TRAVAIL

Frazer, James George *see*
- ADONIS, ATTIS, OSIRIS
- THE GOLDEN BOUGH, A STUDY IN MAGIC AND RELIGION
- LE TOTEMISME

Frazier, Edwin Ray *see* LEADING TEACHERS OF ADULTS AND YOUTH TO STUDY THE HISTORICAL CONTEXTS OF SCRIPTURE

FRAZIER-LEMKE FARM DEBT MORATORIUM ACT. / Skeels, William O – (1938 supplement. Oklahoma City, 1938. 46p. LL-1098) – Oklahoma City: Leader, 1937. 100p. LL-1098 – 1 – us L of C Photodup [340]

FREARSON'S MONTHLY ILLUSTRATED ADELAIDE NEWS – Adelaide, Australia. Pictorial Australian. -m. 1881-95. 5 reels – 1 – uk British Libr Newspaper [072]

Freart, Roland *see*
- AN IDEA OF THE PERFECTION OF PAINTING
- PARALLELE DE L'ARCHITECTURE ANTIQUE ET DE LA MODERNE.

Frechette, Annie Thomas *see*
- THE FARM'S LITTLE PEOPLE: A SEQUEL TO "ON GRANDFATHER'S FARM"
- ON GRANDFATHER'S FARM

Frechette, Louis H *see* LA DECOUVERTE DU MISSISSIPI: POEME

Frechette, Louis-Honore *see*
- A PROPOS D'EDUCATION
- CHENIER: EPISODE DE L'INSURRECTION CANADIENNE DE 1837
- LE DERNIER DES MARTYRS
- FEUILLES VOLANTES
- LES FLEURS BOREALES, LES OISEAUX DE NEIGE: POESIES CONADIENNES
- LA LEGENDE D'UN PEUPLE
- LETTRES A BASILE: A PROPOS DES CAUSERIES DU DIMANCHE DE M. A. B. ROUTHIER
- LOURDES: CONFERENCE PAR LOUIS FRECHETTE LE 12 DECEMBRE 1895, A L'INSTITUT CANADIEN DE QUEBEC
- MES LOISIRS
- ORIGINAUX ET DETRAQUES: DOUZE TYPES QUEBECQUOIS, ONEILLE, GRELOT, DRAPEAU
- PAPINEAU: DRAME HISTORIQUE CANADIEN EN QUATRE ACTES ET NEUF TABLEAUX
- POESIES CHOISIES
- LES RENEGATS DU 29 OCTOBRE: PAQUET, CHAUVEAU, FLYNN, RACICOT ET FORTIN
- LE RETOUR DE L'EXILE: DRAME EN CINQ ACTES ET HUIT TABLEAUX
- LA VOIX D'UN EXILE

Frechette, O *see* LE TRESOR DES FAMILLES

Fred Bryers *see* THE CYCLISTS' ROAD GUIDE OF CANADA

FRED BURRY'S JOURNAL – (Cont: Fred Burry's Journal of New Thought) – Toronto: F.W. Burry, [1899 or 1900-19–] – 9 – cn C.I.H.M. [100]

FRED BURRY'S JOURNAL *see* FRED BURRY'S JOURNAL OF NEW THOUHT

FRED BURRY'S JOURNAL OF NEW THOUGHT *see* FRED BURRY'S JOURNAL

FRED BURRY'S JOURNAL OF NEW THOUHT – (Cont by: Fred Burry's Journal) – Toronto: F.W. Burry, [1898-1899 or 1900] – 9 – cn C.I.H.M. [100]

FREDEGARII ET ALIORUM CHRONICA (MGH 2: 2.BD) : VITAE SANCTORUM / ed by Krusch, B – 1888 – Dfl56.00 – ne Slangenburg [240]

FREDERIC 2. LA PEINTURE FRANCAISE DU 18E SIECLE A LA COUR DE FREDERIC 2 / Reunion des musees nationaux. Paris – 1963. 53 illus. 2 fiches – 9 – fr Réunion [750]

FREDERIC GODET (1812-1900): D'APRES SA CORRESPONDANCE ET D'AUTRES DOCUMENTS INEDITS / Godet, Frederic Louis – 1913 – 9 – us A.T.L.A. [240]

FREDERIC WILLIAM MAITLAND, DOWNING PROFESSOR OF THE LAWS OF ENGLAND; A BIOGRAPHICAL SKETCH / Fisher, Herbert Albert Laurens – Cambridge: University Press, 1910. 179p – 1 – us U.W. Library [920]

Frederichs, Julius *see* DE SECTE DER LOISTEN, OF, ANTWERPSCHE LIBERTIJNEN (1525-1545)

Frederici, Daniel *see* MUSICA FIGURALIS ODER NEUE KLAERICHE RICHTIGE UND VERSTAENDLICHE UNTERWEISUNG DER SINGE KUNST MIT GEWISSEN REGULEN KLAREN UND VERSTAENDLICHEN EXEMPELN NEBEN VOLLKOMMENER ERKLAERUNG DER MODORUM MUSICORUM

Frederick 2nd, King of Prussia *see*
- L'ANTI-MACHIAVEL
- REFLEXIONS SUR LES PROJETS DE CAMPAGNE.

Frederick, Archbishop of Canterbury *see* THE RELATIONS BETWEEN RELIGION AND SCIENCE: EIGHT LECTURES

FREDERICK CARDER: A PORTRAIT OF A GLASSMAKER / Gardner, Paul V – 1985. 120p. 3 fiches. Fiche No.8545 – 9 – $6.25 – us Corning Mus [920]

FREDERICK CARDER: HIS LIFE AND WORK / Buechner, Thomas S – 1985-1952. 23p. 5 illus. 1 fiche. Fiche no. 1033 – 9 – $2.50 – us Corning Mus [700]

FREDERICK CHASE CORRESPONDENCE, 1861-1874 – Dartmouth College Library collection – 3r – 1 – us UMI [920]

FREDERICK DENISON MAURICE / Masterman, Charles FG – London: A.R. Mowbray, 1907. (Leaders of the church, 1800-1900) – 1mf – us A.T.L.A. [240]

Frederick, John Hutchinson *see* THE DEVELOPMENT OF AMERICAN COMMERCE

FREDERICK L. OLMSTED PAPERS / Olmsted, Frederick Law – 1777-1952 – 1 – $1,362.00 – us L of C Photodup [920]

Frederick, Maryland *see* MISCELLANEOUS EARLY NEWSPAPERS

THE FREDERICKSBURG NEWS – (Issues for feb 4-Jun 1848 filmed with: Semi-Weekly News) – 1r – 1 – us Res Libr [072]

Fredericq, P *see* CORPUS DOCUMENTORUM INQUISITIONIS HAERETICAE

FREDERICTON TELEGRAPH – Fredericton, Canada. 1806-07 – 1 reel – 1 – $68.00 – cn Library Assoc [971]

FREDI WASHINGTON PAPERS – 1925-79 – 1 – $72.00 – us Amistad [920]

FREDIGUNDIS : HISTORISCHER ROMAN AUS DER VOELKERWANDERUNG / Dahn, Felix – Leipzig: Breitkopf & Haertel, 1899 – 1 – us U.W. Library [830]

FREDMANS EPISTIAR / Bellman, C – Stockholm: tryckt hos Anders Zetterberg, 1790 – 1 – us Sibley [780]

FREDONIAN – (Scattered issues of this weekly National Republican newspaper) – Chillicothe, OH. mar 30, 1808-july 20, 1815 – 1r – 1 – us Western Res [071]

THE FREE AMERICAN AND DEUTSCHER WECKRUF UND BEOBACHTER – 5 Jul 1935-11 Dec 1941 – 2r – 1 – $70.00 – us L of C Photodup [073]

THE FREE AND LIBERAL VENTILATION OF SEWERS IN ITS RELATION TO THE SANITATION OF OUR BUILDINGS / Baillairge, Charles – 1892?. 00051. (Pre-1900 Canadiana) – 9 – cn C.I.H.M. [628]

FREE ANGOLA – New York, Angola Office. n1. 1965; n3 1965 – us Res Libr [071]

FREE BANKING IN CANADA / Breckenridge, Roeliff Morton – 1894? 05690. (Pre-1900 Canadiana) – 9 – cn C.I.H.M. [971]

FREE BAPTIST – 1882-1904 (complete) – 2r – 1 – ATLA R0133 – us A.T.L.A. [073]

FREE BAPTIST CYCLOPAEDIA / Burgess, G A – 1889 – 1 – $25.55 – us Baptist [240]

THE FREE CHINA JOURNAL. TZU CHUNG-KUO CHI SHIH PAO – v1-. 1984- – 1,5,6,9 – us UMI [073]

FREE CHINA WEEKLY – Taipei, Taiwan. -w. 19 July 1964-29 Dec 1974. 3 reels – 1 – uk British Libr Newspaper [072]

FREE CHINA WEEKLY – Taipil, CH. 1968-1985 – 5r – $250.00 – R63583 – us Library Micro [072]

FREE CHURCH CHRONICLE – (Lacking some issues) – v7-45. ns: v1-21. 1937-90 – 7r – 1 – ATLA S0388 – us A.T.L.A. [073]

FREE CHURCH OF SCOTLAND : MONTHLY RECORD – (Lacking: 1892 p2-3. Title varies) – 1886-1900; 1959-89 – 13r – 1 – ATLA S0366 – us A.T.L.A. [073]

THE FREE CHURCH OF SCOTLAND : HER ANCESTRY, HER CLAIMS, AND HER CONFLICTS / McCrie, CG – Edinburgh: T. & T. Clark, [1896?] – mf – us A.T.L.A. [240]

THE FREE CHURCH OF SCOTLAND : HER ORIGIN, FOUNDERS AND TESTIMONY / Bayne, Peter – Edinburgh: T.& T. Clark; New York: Scribner, (distributor), 1893 – 1mf – us A.T.L.A. [240]

THE FREE CHURCH PRINCIPLE : ITS CHARACTER AND HISTORY: THE FIRST SERIES OF THE CHALMERS LECTURES / Moncreiff, Henry Wellwood – Edinburgh: Macniven & Wallace, 1883 – 1mf – us A.T.L.A. [240]

THE FREE CHURCHES *see* CONGREGATIONALIST

FREE DEMOCRAT : WEEKLY FREE SOIL NEWSPAPER – Chardon, OH. 22 Dec 1849-15 Oct 1850 – 1r – 1 – us Western Res [071]

FREE DEMOCRAT : WEEKLY FREE SOIL NEWSPAPER – Chardon, OH. 30 Mar 1852-20 Dec 1853 – 1r – 1 – us Western Res [071]

FREE ENQUIRER – (Series 1: v1-3 (all publ). 1825-1828. Series 2: v1-5 (all publ). 1828-1833. Series 3: v1-2 (all publ). 1833-35) – 48mf – 9 – $130.00 – us UPA [335]

FREE ENQUIRER – v. 1-5. 1829-1833 – 1 – us Princeton Micro [335]

FREE ENTERPRISE MARKETING / Nixon, Robert – Pamphlet. 3 fiches (29x) – 9 – 1.00f – at Libertarian Micro [320]

FREE ENTERPRISE MONEY / Riegel, E C – With Inflation Newsletter. 1942. 3 fiches (24x) – 9 – 1.00f – at Libertarian Micro [320]

FREE ENTERPRISE, MYTHS AND TRUTHS / Coast Federal Savings – 3fiches (29x) – 9 – 1.00f – at Libertarian Micro [320]

FREE GRACE INDEED : A LETTER TO THE REVEREND MR. JOHN WESLEY RELATING TO HIS SERMON AGAINST ABSOLUTE ELECTION, PUBLISHED UNDER THE TITLE OF 'FREE GRACE' – London, 1740 – 1mf – 9 – MP-276/1 – ne IDC [240]

FREE GRACE INDEED : SET FORTH IN A SCRIPTURAL VIEW OF THE PRINCIPLE OF GRACE WROUGHT IN THE HEART BY THE SPIRIT,... / Pike, S – London, 1760 – 1mf – 9 – MP-389/1 – ne IDC [240]

FREE INDONESIA – (Lacking: 1946 (Aug.-Sept.)) – Brisbane: Central Committee of Indonesian Independence, 1946 – 3mf – 9 – ne IDC [320]

FREE INQUIRY – 1972-78 – 1 – us UMI [073]

FREE INQUIRY – v.1. 1980 – 1,5,6,9 – us UMI [073]

Free, J *see*
- A CONTROVERSY WITH THE PEOPLE CALLED METHODISTS CONCERNING THE TRUE NATURE OF THE CHRISTIAN RELIGION,...
- A DISPLAY OF THE BAD PRINCIPLES OF THE METHODISTS, IN CERTAIN ARTICLES PROPOSED TO THE SERIOUS CONSIDERATION OF THE WORSHIPFUL COMPANY OF SALTERS IN LONDON
- DR. FREE'S EDITION OF THE REV. MR. JOHN WESLEY'S FIRST PENNY-LETTER,...
- DR. FREE'S EDITION OF THE REV. MR. JOHN WESLEY'S SECOND LETTER, WITH PROLEGOMENA FOR THE BETTER INFORMATION OF THE STUDIOUS ENGLISH READER AND A PERPETUAL COMMENT UPON THE ORIGINAL TEXT;...
- DR. FREE'S REMARKS UPON MR. JONES'S LETTER AND THE AFFIDAVITS RELATIVE TO THE COMPOSING,...
- RULES FOR THE DISCOVERY OF FALSE PROPHETS
- THE WHOLE SPEECH WHICH WAS DELIVERED TO THE REVEREND CLERGY OF THE GREAT CITY OF LONDON ON TUESDAY THE 8TH OF MAY 1759,...

Free, John *see* AN ESSAY TOWARDS AN HISTORY OF THE ENGLISH TONGUE

FREE LABOUR GAZETTE – Nov 1894-Apr 1896 – 1 – uk Microform Academic [072]

FREE LABOUR PRESS AND INDUSTRIAL REVIEW – England. 1899-1907 – 1 – uk Microform Academic [338]

FREE LANCE – (Also known as: Evening Free Lance) – Hollister, CA. 1886-1923; 1926- – 225+ r – 1 BC02297 – $11,250.00 ($150.00y) – us Library Micro [071]

FREE LANCE – Fredericksburg. Va. 1885-1926 – 1 – us UMI [071]

FREE LANCE : A MAGAZINE OF POETRY AND PROSE – Cleveland. v1-13. 1953-69 – 30mf – 9 – $5.00f – us Ross [073]

FREE LANCE – Schuyler, NE. -w. May 1903-May 1904 – 1 – us NE Hist [071]

THE FREE LANCE – Montreal, Canada. v1 n1. 28 aut 1867-ns: v1 n5. 13 dec 1873 – 1r – 1 – Can$40.00 – cn Can Microfilming [072]

THE FREE LANCE – Ottawa: Free Lance Print Co, [1893-1896] – 9 – cn C.I.H.M. [072]

THE FREE LANCE – Reno, NV. 1889 – 1r – 1 – $50.00 – U03710 – us Library Micro [071]

FREE LANCE POLITICAL CARICATURE IN CANADA = CARICATURE POLITIQUE AU CANADA / Ryan, Alonzo – Montreal: Dominion Pub. Co. A T Chapman, 1904. SEM105P57 – 2mf – 9 – Can$4.50 – cn Bibl Nat [760]

FREE LANCE STAR – Fredericksburg. Va. 1927- – 1 – us UMI [071]

Free Library of Philadelphia. Hampton L. Carson Collection *see* CATALOG OF THE HAMPTON L. CARSON COLLECTION ILLUSTRATIVE OF THE GROWTH OF THE COMMON LAW

FREE LIFE – London. 8 Aug 1890-Aug 1901.-w,-m. 1mqnreels – 1 – uk British Libr Newspaper [072]

FREE LOVE NEWSPAPERS *see* AGE OF FREEDOM

THE FREE MAN'S ALMANACH / Read, Leonard E – 1974. 383p. 1 fiche (24x) – 9 – 1.00f – at Libertarian Micro [320]

A FREE MARKET IN HUMAN ORGANS / Burrage, Robert – 1986, LA Economic Note, No.10, 2p – 9 – 1.00f – at Libertarian Micro [335]

FREE MARKET YELLOW PAGES / Dagny Enterprises – (1986, 60p. 1987/88, 108p) – 1984 ed., 24p – 9 – 1.00f – at Libertarian Micro [380]

THE FREE METHODIST – 1868-1970. Winona Lake. Ind. Superseded by Light and Life – 1 – us A.T.L.A. [240]
THE FREE METHODIST *see* LIGHT AND LIFE
FREE OPINIONS / Corelli, Marie – British Fiction Archive: Unit 1 – 9 – uk Bell [830]
THE FREE PEOPLE : OFFICIAL ORGAN OF THE FARMERS' AND WORKERS' PARTY – Johannesburg: Farmers' and Workers' Party, [-1951]. v2 n2 aug 1938; v2 n12 jun 1939; v3 n7-v4 n2 jan 1940-jan 1941; v4 n39-v13 n79 apr 1941-apr 1951 – 1r – 1 – us Res Libr [360]
FREE PRESBYTERIAN – Yellow Springs, OH. 10 Aug 1853-30 Sept 1857 – 2r – 1 – us Western Res [240]
FREE PRESS – (1976-1992.-89r) – Midland, 1993 – 12r – 1 – cn Preston [971]
FREE PRESS – Bristol. Fl. -w. 1932- – 1 – us P.K. Yonge [071]
FREE PRESS – Burlington. Vt. 1848- – 1 – us UMI [071]
FREE PRESS – Caldwell. Kan. -w. 1885-86 – 1 – us UMI [071]
FREE PRESS – Canadian. Tex. 1887-90 – 1 – us UMI [071]
FREE PRESS – DeWitt, NE -w. Feb. 1878-Dec. 1878. Incomplete; Feb. 1879-Dec. 1879 – 1 – us NE Hist [071]
FREE PRESS – Easton. Pa. -w. 1859-1913 – 1 – us UMI [071]
FREE PRESS – Eau Claire. Wis. 1873-1900 – 1 – us UMI [071]
FREE PRESS – Eau Claire. Wis. -w. 1858-88 – 1 – us UMI [071]
FREE PRESS – Elwood. Ind. -w. 1893-1909 – 1 – us UMI [071]
FREE PRESS – Gouveneur. N.Y. 1882-1929 – 1 – us UMI [071]
FREE PRESS – Grand Island, NE. -w. Aug 1895-Aug 1898; Nov 1901; Aug-Dec 1902; Feb 1908-Jan 1913; Jan-Apr 1915 – 1 – us NE Hist [071]
FREE PRESS – Hays. Kan. 1887-1924 – 1 – us UMI [071]
FREE PRESS – Hope Valley. R.I. 1900-1904 – 1 – us UMI [071]
FREE PRESS – Kinston. N.C. -w. 1888-1902 – 1 – us UMI [071]
FREE PRESS – Lafayette. Ind. 1833-1839 – 1 – us UMI [071]
FREE PRESS – Las Vegas, NV. 1950 – 1r – 1 – $50.00 – U04855 – us Library Micro [071]
FREE PRESS – Leipsic, Ohio. 1878-1979 – 45r – 1 – $32.50r – us Archival [071]
FREE PRESS – (Library has: v.5, no.1-2, 4-5, 7-18, 20-32; Feb. 15-Dec. 20, 1985) – Accra, Ghana: Tommy Thompson, 19uu – 1 – CSUX88-S367 – us Hoover Inst Photo [960]
FREE PRESS – Mayo. Fl. -w. 1940-44, 46-47, 55- – 1 – us P.K. Yonge [071]
FREE PRESS – Milwaukee. Wis. -d. 1901-18 – 1 – us UMI [071]
FREE PRESS – Moline. Kan. 1883-1885 – 1 – us UMI [071]
FREE PRESS – Mt. Pleasant. Iowa. -w. 1951-60 – 1 – us UMI [071]
FREE PRESS – Oakland, CA. 1924-42 – 5r – 1 – $250.00 – C02546 – us Library Micro [071]
FREE PRESS – Osage City. Kan. 1875-1916 – 1 – us UMI [071]
FREE PRESS – Poplarville. Miss. 1902-1923 – 1 – us UMI [071]
FREE PRESS – Redding, CA. 1901-1906 – 4r – 1 BC02672 – $200.00 – us Library Micro [071]
FREE PRESS – Redding. Calif. 1891-1926 – 1 – us UMI [071]
FREE PRESS – Redding. Calif. -d. 1896-1905 – 1 – us UMI [071]
FREE PRESS – Redmond OR. Oct 29 Nov 12 Dec 10 1948 – 1 – us U.O. Library [071]
FREE PRESS – San Bernardino. Calif. 1897-1905 – 1 – us UMI [071]
FREE PRESS – (Set incl. Deschutes County Advertiser (Bend, OR); Free Press. (Bend)) – Burns, OR. -w. 23 Apr 1931-12 Jul 1940. – 2r – 1 – us U.O. Library [071]
FREE PRESS – St. John's, Canada. -w. March 1904-Dec 1921. 18 reels – 1 – uk British Libr Newspaper [072]
FREE PRESS – Streator. Ill. -w. 1873-88, 1890-1910 – 1 – us UMI [071]
FREE PRESS – Taft. Calif. 1940-1941 – 1 – us UMI [071]
FREE PRESS – Urbana. Ohio. 1858-1860 – 1 – us UMI [071]
FREE PRESS – Wellsville. N.Y. 1867-1870 – 1 – us UMI [071]
FREE PRESS – Wilber, NE. -w. Dec 1879-Dec 1880 – 1 – us NE Hist [071]
FREE PRESS – Wisner. Neb. 1898-1916 – 1 – us UMI [071]
FREE PRESS – San Bernardino, CA. 1897-1905 – 8r – 1 – $400.00 – R03451 – us Library Micro [071]
THE FREE PRESS / ed by MacCulloch, Lewis Luke – (A partir du 14 ieme no: Burlington, Vermont) – Montreal, 10 oct 1822-24 jun 1824 – 1r – 1 – Can$40.00 – cn Can Microfilming [072]
THE FREE PRESS – Ottawa, Ontario. v3 n785. 1 aut 1872-v16 n5098. 21 aut 1886 – 1r – 1 – Can$35.00 – cn Can Microfilming [072]
THE FREE PRESS – Quakertown, PA. -d 1972. 4 rolls – 13 – $25.00r – us I.M.R. [071]
THE FREE PRESS – Riverdale, CA. Sept 1975-78 – 2r – 1 – $100.00 – B02712 – us Library Micro [071]
FREE PRESS (ACCRA, GHANA) *see* FREE PRESS
FREE PRESS AND ADVERTISER – South Shields, England. -w. Jan 1895-Jan 1904. 6 reels – 1 – uk British Libr Newspaper [072]
FREE PRESS AND EAST BAY LABOR JOURNAL – Oakland. Calif. -w. 1940-45 – 1 – us UMI [071]
FREE PRESS EVENING BULLETIN – Manitoba, CN. Oct 1894-Apr 1935 – 256r – 1 – cn Commonwealth Micro [072]
FREE PRESS JOURNAL AND BHARAT IYOTI – Bombay, India. Apr 1944-1993 – 182r – 1 – us L of C Photodup [072]
FREE PRESS NEWS BULLETIN – Winnipeg. v5 n43. 23 nov 1899-v5 n116. 21 feb 1900 – 1r – 1 – Can$30.00 – cn Can Microfilming [072]
Free Press Printing Co *see* MANKATO: ITS FIRST FIFTY YEARS 1852-1902
FREE PRESS REPORT ON FARMING – Winnipeg, CN. 1872-1983 – 237r – 1 – cn Commonwealth Micro [073]
FREE PRESS. (WEST SUFFOLK & NORTH ESSEX FREE PRESS.-SUFFOLK & ESSEX PRESS.-SUFFOLK FREE PRESS) – England. Jul 1855-Dec 1869; Apr 1884-Dec 1886; Apr 1888-1975; 1978-80.-w. 109 reels – 1 – uk British Libr Newspaper [072]
Free Public Library, Ottawa, KS *see* BOARD OF DIRECTORS MINUTE BOOKS
FREE RADICAL BIOLOGY AND MEDICINE – v1- 1986- – 5,6,9 – us UMI [574]
FREE RADICAL BIOLOGY AND MEDICINE *see* ADVANCES IN FREE RADICAL BIOLOGY AND MEDICINE
FREE RADICAL RESEARCH / ed by Halliwell, Barry – 1,5,9 – us Gordon [574]
THE FREE RELIGIOUS ASSOCIATION...AN ADDRESS / Potter, William J – Boston: Free Religious Association of America, 1892. 1 fiche – 9 – us A.T.L.A. [240]
FREE REVIEW – London. 1893-97 – 1 – uk Microform Academic [073]
FREE RUSSIA / Society of Friends of Russian Freedom – New York. v1-4. 1890-94 – 1r – 1 – us Ross [320]
FREE RUSSIA – The organ of the English Society of Friends of Russian Freedom. London. -m. Jun 1890-Oct 1914 Jan 1915. (2 reels) – 1 – uk British Libr Newspaper [073]
Free Southern Theater *see* RECORDS, 1963-78
FREE SPAGHETTI – (Includes index) – Santa Cruz, CA. Oct 1969-Nov 1970 – 2r – 1 – $100.00 – B02956 – us Library Micro [071]
FREE SPEECH AND FREE THOUGHT IN AMERICA / Haldeman-Julius, Emanuel – Girard, KS: Haldeman-Julius Publications, 1927. 128p. (Big Blue Book No. B-37) – 1 – us U.W. Library [323]
THE FREE STATE – Ireland.25 Feb-11 Nov 1922 – 1 – ie Microforms [072]
FREE SUNDAY ADVOCATE AND NATIONAL SUNDAY LEAGUE RECORD – London. -w. 3 Jul 1869-1 Dec 1890. (2 reels) – 1 – uk British Libr Newspaper [072]
FREE THINKERS MAGAZINE – London, UK. 1850-51. -irr. 16 feet – 1 – uk British Libr Newspaper [073]
FREE THOUGHTS CONCERNING A SEPARATION OF THE PEOPLE CALLED METHODISTS FROM THE CHURCH OF ENGLAND,... – London, 1785 – 1mf – 9 – MP-548/1 – ne IDC [240]
FREE TRADE / Avebury, Lord – 1904. 164p – 9 – 1.00f – at Libertarian Micro [335]
FREE TRADE / Carlisle, John G – 7p – 9 – 1.00f – at Libertarian Micro [335]
FREE TRADE / Cobden, Richard – 13p – 9 – 1.00f – at Libertarian Micro [380]
THE FREE TRADE ADVOCATE AND JOURNAL OF POLITICAL ECONOMY – Philadelphia. v. 1-2. 3 Jan-28 Nov 1829 – 1 – us NY Public [380]
FREE TRADE FOR SHIPPING / Blaine, James G – 3p – 9 – 1.00f – at Libertarian Micro [335]
FREE TRADE IN LAND / Kay, Joseph – 1880. 1 fiche (24x) – 9 – 1.00f – at Libertarian Micro [320]
THE FREE TRADE MOVEMENT AND ITS RESULTS / Armitage-Smith, G – 1898 – 9 – 1.00f – at Libertarian Micro [335]
FREE TRADE VS PROTECTION / Cox, Harold & Williams, Ernest E – A debate, 1903. 99p – 9 – 1.00f – at Libertarian Micro [380]
FREE TRADER – London. -w. and m. 31 Jul 1903-Dec 1905. (1 reel) – 1 – uk British Libr Newspaper [380]
FREE TRADER – Natchez. Miss. 1858-1860 – 1 – us UMI [071]
FREE TRADER – Natchez. Miss. -w. 1843-60 – 1 – us UMI [071]
FREE TRADER – Ottawa. Ill. -w. 1843-1914 – 1 – us UMI [071]
FREE TRADER – Pontiac. Ill. and Observer. 1884-1906 – 1 – us UMI [071]
FREE TRADER JOURNAL – Ottawa. Ill. 1917-1927 – 1 – us UMI [071]
FREE TURNPIKE RECORD / Huron County. Ohio. Engineer – 1884 – 1r – 1 – $32.50r – us Archival [324]
FREE TURNPIKE RECORDS / Allen County. Ohio. Engineer – 1903-1921 – 2r – 1 – $32.50r – us Archival [324]
FREE VOICE OF THE AMALGAMATED FOOD WORKERS : 1920-1935 / Amalgamated Food Workers of America – (Coll title: Labor Union Periodicals, Pt 3) – 1996 – 3r – $270.00 – 1-55655-619-5 – us UPA [331]
FREE WEST INDIAN – St. George, GO. 1980-1983 – 4r – $200.00 – R63659 – us Library Micro [072]
FREE WILL AND HUMAN RESPONSIBILITY : A PHILOSOPHICAL ARGUMENT / Horne, Herman Harrell – New York: The Macmillan Company, 1912 – xvi/197p – 1 – us U.W. Library [120]
FREE WILL AND PREDESTINATION IN EARLY ISLAM / Montgomery Watt, W – London. 1948. BNE-496 1 – 9 – ne IDC [260]
FREE WILL BAPTIST – Abstract of the former Articles of Faith confessed by the original Baptist Church, an. 1912. 25p – 1 – 5.00 – us Baptist [240]
Free Will Baptist Foreign Mission Society *see* RECORDS
FREE WORLD – v.1-12. 1941-46 – 1 – 2266.00 – us Princeton Micro [073]
FREEBORN COUNTY STANDARD – Albert Lea. Minn. 1870-1924 – 1 – us UMI [071]
FREEBORN COUNTY TIMES – Albert Lea. Minn. 1896-1906 – 1 – us UMI [071]
FREEBORN PATRIOT – Albert Lea. Minn. 1934-37 – 1 – us UMI [071]
Freedley, Angelo Tillinghast *see*
– THE CORPORATION LAWS OF 1883; BEING A SUPPLEMENT TO THE GENERAL CORPORATION LAWS OF PENNSYLVANIA
– THE GENERAL CORPORATION LAW OF PENNSYLVANIA, APPROVED 29 APRIL, 1874.
FREEDMAN / American Tract Society – v1-6, no. 3 (all publ). 1864-69 – 1 reel – 1 – $55.00 – us UPA [976]
FREEDMAN'S ADVOCATE / National Freedmen's Relief Association – v1-2, no. 1 (all publ). 1864-65 – 1 – $55.00 – us UPA [976]
FREEDMAN'S JOURNAL / American Tract Society – v1-2 (all publ). 1865-66 – 1 reel – 1 – $55.00 – us UPA [976]
FREEDMEN'S BULLETIN *see* AMERICAN FREEDMEN'S BULLETIN
FREEDOM – A journal of anarchist socialism (Communism). London. -m. Oct 1866-Nov Dec 1927, May 1930-Jul Sep 1936. (3 reels) – 1 – uk British Libr Newspaper [072]
FREEDOM – Ed. by L. E. Burnham. v. 1, no. 1-v. 5, no. 6. New York. v. 4 incomplete. No. 77-7. One reel – 1 – 15.00 – us Partington [071]
FREEDOM – Ireland.29 Aug-12 Nov 1922 – 1 – ie Microforms [072]
FREEDOM : A JOURNAL OF ANARCHIST COMMUNISM – London: Freedom Publ Comm. v20-30. 1906-jun 1916 – 1 – us Res Libr [073]
FREEDOM – New York. N.Y. 1913 – 1 – us A.J.P.C. [071]
FREEDOM / Smuts, Jan C – London: Alexander Maclehouse & Co, 1934 – 1mf – 9 – $1.50 – LLMC 92-203 – us L.L.M.C. [320]
FREEDOM! : AN ANARCHIST MONTHLY – 1-2 2+4 (all publ). 1933-1934 – 3mf – 9 – $35.00 – us UPA [335]
FREEDOM – London: J Turner, v20-30 n203-326. 1906-jun 1916 – 1r – 1 – us Res Libr [072]
FREEDOM AND FELLOWSHIP IN RELIGION : A COLLECTION OF ESSAYS AND ADDRESSES – Boston:Roberts, 1875 – 1mf – 9 – 0-8370-3186-9 – 1985-1186 – us A.T.L.A. [240]
FREEDOM AND THE CHURCHES : THE CONTRIBUTIONS OF AMERICAN CHURCHES TO RELIGIOUS AND CIVIL LIBERTY / Wendte, Charles William – Boston: American Unitarian Association, 1913 – 1mf – us A.T.L.A. [323]
FREEDOM AT ISSUE – v1- 1969- 1; v29-1975- 5,6,9 – us UMI [320]
THE FREEDOM AVALANCHE OF 1980 / Brookes, Patrick – AIR paper, c1972 – 9 – 1.00f – at Libertarian Micro [335]
FREEDOM FOR SPAIN – London, 1945. Fiche W 897. (Blodgett Collection of Spanish Civil War Pamphlets) – 9 – us H.U. College Libr [946]
THE FREEDOM FREEWAY / Read, Leonard E – 1979. 135p. Together with: Who's Listening. 1973. 221p. 1 fiche (24x) – 9 – 1.00f – at Libertarian Micro [320]
FREEDOM HOUSE – New York. 250 docs. 1980-1991 – 123mf – 9 – ne IDC [320]
FREEDOM IN THE CHURCH OF ENGLAND : SIX SERMONS SUGGESTED BY THE VOYSEY JUDGMENT / Brooke, Stopford Augustus – London: Henry S. King, 1871 – 1mf – us A.T.L.A. [240]
FREEDOM NEWS – (Library has: v.7, no.1; v.11, no.1-3, 6 (April 1, 1946-May 29, 1947)) – San Antonio, Tex.: William Walker, 1940 – 1 – CSUX89-S76 – us Hoover Inst Photo [978]
FREEDOM NEWS (SAN ANTONIO, TEX.: 1940) *see* FREEDOM NEWS
THE FREEDOM OF AUTHORITY : ESSAYS IN APOLOGETICS / Sterrett, James Macbride – (Includes index) – New York: Macmillan, 1905 – 1mf – 9 – 0-8370-5402-8 – 1985-3402 – us A.T.L.A. [230]
THE FREEDOM OF FAITH / Munger, Theodore Thornton – Boston: Houghton, Mifflin 1891. 1 fiche – 9 – us A.T.L.A. [240]
FREEDOM OF INFORMATION CASELIST / Department of Justice, Office of Information & Privacy – (Add vols planned) – 1985-94 – 59mf – 9 – $88.00 – LLMC 94-358 – us L.L.M.C. [340]
FREEDOM OF MIND IN WILLING : OR, EVERY BEING THAT WILLS A CREATIVE FIRST CAUSE / Hazard, Rowland Gibson – New York, London: D. Appleton and Co., 1864 – xviii/465p – 1 – us U.W. Library [190]
[FREEDOM OF RELIGION IN ESTONIA PAMPHLET COLLECTION] – 1979? – 1 – CSUXANL2142-B – us Hoover Inst Photo [320]
[FREEDOM OF RELIGION IN THE SOVIET UNION PAMPHLET COLLECTION] – 1976 – 1 – CSUXANR1053-B – us Hoover Inst Photo [320]
FREEDOM OF THE INDIVIDUAL IN THE USSR / Babin, N & Anashkin, G – 92p – 9 – 1.00f – at Libertarian Micro [335]
FREEDOM OF THE PRESS : THE STRUGGLE FOR COPYRIGHT AND THE LAWS OF LIBEL, 1660-1821; A CATALOG / ed by Parks, Stephen – NY: Garland Publishing Inc, 1974? – 1mf – 9 – $1.50 – LLMC 91-079 – us L.L.M.C. [340]
THE FREEDOM OF THE SEAS / Brown, L F – New York, 1919 – 3mf – 1 – ILM-1813/1 – ne IDC [327]
THE FREEDOM OF THE SEAS / Davison, C S – New York, 1918 – 2mf – 1 – ILM-478/1 – ne IDC [327]
THE FREEDOM OF THE SEAS... / Grotius, H – New York, 1916 – 2mf – 1 – ILM-3897/1 – ne IDC [327]
THE FREEDOM OF THE SEAS:... / Cababe, M – London, 1918 – 2mf – 1 – ILM-348/1 – ne IDC [327]

THE FREEDOM OF THE WILL : AS A BASIS OF HUMAN RESPONSIBILITY AND A DIVINE GOVERNMENT / Whedon, Daniel Denison - (Includes index of authors cited) - New York: Carlton & Lanahan, c1864 - 1mf - 9 - 0-8370-6538-0 - 1986-0538 - us A.T.L.A. [120]

THE FREEDOM TO SELL / Forbes, Viv - 1fiche (29x) - 9 - 1.00f - at Libertarian Micro [320]

FREEDOM'S JOURNAL : DEVOTED TO THE IMPROVEMENT OF THE COLOURED POPULATION - New York. v1-2. 1827-29 - 1r - 1 - us Ross [073]

FREEDOMWAYS: A QUARTERLY REVIEW OF THE FREEDOM MOVEMENT - v1- 1961- 1; v9- 5,6; v15- 9 - us UMI [305]

FREEHOLD LAND TIMES BUILDING NEWS - (Building News. 1862- ; Land and Building News. 1855) - London, UK. 1 Apr 1854-1855; Jul-Dec 1862; Jul 1869-1892. -w - 67r - 1 - uk British Libr Newspaper [072]

FREEHOLDER - Cornwall, 1883-1932 - 24r - 1 - cn Preston [971]

THE FREEHOLDER - Cornwall, Ontario. v17 n36. 2 avr 1863-v45 n52. 28 dec 1916 - 1r - 1 - Can$35.00 - cn Can Microfilming [072]

FREEHOLDER'S JOURNAL - London. no. 1-76. Jan 31 1721-May 18 1723 - 1 - us NY Public [073]

FREEHOLDERS' JOURNAL - London. n1-76. 1721-23 - 1r - 1 - us Ross [073]

FREELAND - New York. v. 1-8. Dec 1944-Dec 1955. Incomplete - 1 - us NY Public [073]

FREELAND A SOCIAL ANTICIPATION / Hertzka, Theodor - 5fiches (24x) - 9 - 1.00f - at Libertarian Micro [320]

FREEMAN - v1- 1950- 1; v18- 5,6; v27- 9 - us UMI [073]

FREEMAN - Indianapolis. Ind. 1888-1916 - 1 - us UMI [071]

FREEMAN - Kingston. N.Y. -d. 1915- - 1 - us UMI [071]

FREEMAN - McPherson. Kansas. 1878-1919 - 1 - us UMI [071]

FREEMAN - Persia. N.Y. and Messenger. 1839-40 - 1 - us UMI [071]

FREEMAN - Waukesha. Wis. 1859- - 1 - us UMI [071]

THE FREEMAN - Ireland.? -13 Oct 1928 - 1 - ie Microforms [072]

THE FREEMAN - Cebu: Freeman Pub Co, jul 10 1925-nov 9 1928 - us Res Libr [072]

Freeman, Abraham Clark *see* A TREATISE ON THE LAW OF EXECUTIONS IN CIVIL CASES, AND OF PROCEEDINGS IN AID AND RESTRAINT THEREOF

Freeman, Edward A *see*
- THE CHIEF PERIODS OF EUROPEAN HISTORY
- WESTERN EUROPE IN THE FIFTH CENTURY: AN AFTERMATH

Freeman, Harrup A *see* PALAU'S CONSTITUTIONAL CONVENTION. AN INFORMAL REPORT

Freeman, J J *see* A DICTIONARY OF THE MALAGASY LANGUAGE IN TWO PARTS

Freeman, James Edward *see* THE MAN AND THE MASTER

Freeman, James M *see* SHORT HISTORY OF THE ENGLISH BIBLE: WITH BRIEF NOTICES OF THE TRANSLATORS

Freeman, Joan *see* QUALITY BASIC EDUCATION

Freeman, John *see* THE TYRANNY OF POLITICS

Freeman, John Haskell *see* AN ORIENTAL LAND OF THE FREE, OR, LIFE AND MISSION WORK AMONG THE LAOS

Freeman, Jonathan *see* SERMONS, 1798-1821

FREEMAN JOURNAL - Webster City. Iowa. -w. 1857-1919 - 1 - us UMI [071]

Freeman, Z *see* MANUAL OF AMERICAN COLLEGES AND THEOLOGICAL SEMINARIES

FREEMAN'S CHANCERY CASES / Mississippi. Supreme Court - (Not a Pre-NRS title) - 1v. 1839-1843 (all publ) - 24mf - 9 - $6.00 - LLMC 95-100 - us L.L.M.C. [340]

FREEMAN'S EXMOUTH JOURNAL - (Exmouth Journal, 27 Apr 1907-) - England, 24 Jul 1869-1933 - 57r - 1 - uk British Libr Newspaper [072]

FREEMAN'S JOURNAL - Dublin, Ireland. -w. May-June 1892. 1 2 reel - 1 - uk British Libr Newspaper [072]

FREEMAN'S JOURNAL - New York City, NY. v3 n19. 5 nov 1842-v72 n3707. 20 aug 1904 - 1r - 1 - Can$30.00 - cn Can Microfilming [071]

FREEMAN'S JOURNAL - Sydney, 1850-75; 1897-1911 - 24r - 1 - at Pascoe [073]

FREEMANS JOURNAL - Ireland.1763-1924. 386 reels - 1 - PS27.50r - ie European Micro [072]

THE FREEMAN'S JOURNAL - Philadelphia. Pa. 1781-1792 - 3 - us Readex [071]

THE FREEMAN'S JOURNAL, 1763-1924 - (A 5 reel index for the period 1763-71 is included) - 380r - 1 - Ir£5,800.00 - ie Microforms [072]

THE FREEMAN'S JOURNAL AND COMMERCIAL ADVERTISER - Quebec, Canada. v1 n58. 24 dec 1844-v3 n59. 29 dec 1846 - 1r - 1 - Can$45.00 - cn Can Microfilming [073]

FREEMAN'S JOURNAL & CHILLICOTHE ADVERTISER - (Second newspaper to be publ in Ohio, weekly, National Republican) - Chillicothe, OH. july 11-sept 26, 1800 - 1r - 1 - us Western Res [071]

FREEMANS JOURNAL INDEX - Ireland.1763-1771. 5 reels - 1 - PS27.50r - ie European Micro [072]

FREEMARKET - an Australian free enterprise magazine, continuing with: U.S.Dept. of the Interior: Fees and Charges Handbook for Parks. 4 fiches. (24x) - 9 - 1.00f - at Libertarian Micro [073]

THE FREEMASON - Toronto: Cowan, [1881?]- - 9 - cn C.I.H.M. [360]

FREEMASONRY / ed by Jacob, Margaret C - 651 titles - 9 - ne IDC [360]

FREEMASONS AND SPAIN; STRUGGLE OF MASONIC LIBERALISM AGAINST REACTIONISM IN SPAIN - NY, 1938? Fiche W 898. (Blodgett Collection of Spanish Civil War Pamphlets) - 9 - us H.U. College Libr [946]

FREEMASONS' CALENDAR AND POCKET-BOOK - London, 1828, 1834, 1837, 1841, 1845 - 10mf - 9 - VR-2.2/1 - ne IDC [360]

Freemasons. Grand Lodge (Canada) *see* THE BOOK OF CONSTITUTION OF THE GRAND LODGE OF ANCIENT, FREE AND ACCEPTED MASONS OF CANADA

THE FREEMASON'S JOURNAL - Montreal, 15 jan 1870-v1 n9. 15 sep 1870 - 1r - 1 - Can$28.00 - cn Can Microfilming [073]

FREE-MASONS' MAGAZINE - London, 1793-1798. 9v - 50mf - 9 - VR-32.2/1 - ne IDC [360]

THE FREEMASONS' QUARTERLY REVIEW - London, 1834-1842; S.2, 1843-1849. 16v - 106mf - 9 - VR-32.3/1 - ne IDC [360]

FREENETWORK ECONOMIC SYSTEM / Dagny, Sharon - 1p draft, with letter by John Zube, 4 Mar 1986 - 9 - 1.00f - at Libertarian Micro [338]

FREEPORT JOURNAL - Freeport, PA. -w 1885-1932 - 13 - $25.00r - us I.M.R. [071]

Freer, A J *see* JACQUES LE FATALISTE ET LA RELIGIEUSE

Freer Gallery of Art, Smithsonian Institution *see* DICTIONARY CATALOG OF THE LIBRARY OF THE FREER GALLERY OF ART; SMITHSONIAN INSTITUTION 2ND ENLARGED EDITION

DAS FREER-LOGION / Gregory, Caspar Rene - Leipzig: J C Hinrichs, 1908 - 1mf - 9 - 0-8370-3385-3 - 1985-1385 - us A.T.L.A. [240]

THE FREETHINKER - London. 1881-1959 - 1 - uk Microform Academic [120]

THE FREETHINKER'S CATECHISM / Monteil, Edgar - Translated by Frederic W. Mitchell. New York: The Truth Seeker Company, 1880? - 1 - us U.W. Library [210]

FREETHOUGHT JOURNAL - Toronto: Ontario Free Thought Print and Pub. Co, v1 no 1(Sept 14 1877)- - 9 - cn C.I.H.M. [200]

FREETHOUGHT TODAY - Freedom from Religion Foundation. Jan 1984- - 1 - us U.W. Library [073]

FREETHOUGHT VINDICATED, OR, INFIDEL CHRISTIANITY V. HONEST UNBELIEF : A LECTURE DELIVERED IN THE TEMPERANCE HALL, SYDNEY, JUNE 25, 1880, IN REPLY TO THE REVS. A.C. GILLIES, J.A. DOWIE, THE CATHOLIC EXPRESS, AND THE PRESBYTERIAN WITNESS BY J. TYERMAN / Tyerman, J - (With an appendix containing correspondence between the Rev. A.C. Gillies and J. Tyerman) - Sydney: R.W. Skinner, 1880 - 1mf - 9 - 0-8370-5590-3 - 1985-3590 - us A.T.L.A. [210]

FREETOWN 1686-1890 - (Mf 1-4: Records 1686-1764 Bk 1. Mf 5-10: Records 1759-95 Bk 2. Mf 11-13: Records 1795-1847 Bk 3. Mf 14-15: Records 1836-71 Bk 5. Mf 16-18: Records 1822-92 Bk 6. Mf 19-20: B,M,D 1843-55. Mf 21-22: Birth Records 1856-90 Bk 12. Mf 23-24: Marriages 1854-90 Bk 11. Mf 25-26: Deaths 1852-90 Bk 10. Mf 27-28: Birth Index to Bks 1,2,3,5,6,9,12. Mf 29-30: Marriage Index to Bks 1,2,3,5,9,11. Mf 31-32: Marriage Intention Index to Bks 1,2,3,5,6. Mf 33-34: Death Index to Bks 1,2,3,5,6,9,10. Mf 35-37: B,M,D Index 1686-1844) - (mf ed 1985) - 37mf - 9 - 0-931248-91-4 - us Holbrook [920]

FREETOWN EXPRESS AND CHRISTIAN OBSERVER - Freetown. Sierra Leone. - m. Jul 1882-Nov 1884. (33 ft) - 1 - uk British Libr Newspaper [072]

FREEWATER COOPERATIVE NEWS - Freewater, OR. -w. 21 Feb 1939-17 Dec 1940. 1 roll - 1 - us U.O. Library [071]

FREEWATER TIMES - Freewater, OR. -w. 16 Jan 1903-Dec 1904; Jan 1928-26 Jan 1951. - 1 - us U.O. Library [071]

FREE-WILL AND MERIT FAIRLY EXAMINED : OR, MEN NOT THEIR OWN SAVIOURS,... / Toplady, Augustus Montague - Manchester, 5th ed n.d. - 1mf - 9 - MP-501/1 - ne IDC [240]

Freewill Baptist Associations. Yearly Conference. Maine. 1799-1814 *see* PAPERS

Freewill Baptist Church (Ridgefield, Ohio) *see* RECORDS

FREEWILL BAPTIST MAGAZINE - Providence, RI. May 1826-May 1830 - 1 - us A.B.H.S. [073]

FREEWILL BAPTIST MISSIONARY - Mar 1843-Jul 1845 (complete) - 1r - 1 - ATLA R0100A - us A.T.L.A. [073]

FREEWILL BAPTIST QUARTERLY - (Some pgs missing) - v1-17. 1853-69 - 5r - 1 - ATLA S0824 - us A.T.L.A. [073]

FREEWILL BAPTIST QUARTERLY MAGAZINE - Jun 1039-Mar 1041 - 1r - 1 - ATLA R0100B - us A.T.L.A. [073]

FREEWILL BAPTIST REGISTER - 1831-55, 1863-69 - 1 - 954.45 - us Baptist [240]

THE FREEWOMAN - A weekly feminist review. London. -w. 23 Nov 1911-10 Oct 1912. (1 reel) - 1 - uk British Libr Newspaper [305]

Frege, W H *see* THE LEOFRIC COLLECTAR, VOL. 2

Fregenal de la Sierra. Spain *see*
- ALGUNAS PAGINAS DEL EXPEDIENTE... CONSTRUCCION DE UN CEMENTERIO
- PROYECTO DE ORDENANZAS MUNICIPALES

Fregeville, Antoine de *see* PALINODIE CHIMIQUE: OV LES ERREVRS DE CEST ART

Fregier, H A *see* DES CLASSES DANGEREUSES DE LA SOCIETE DANS LES GRANDES VILLES ET DES MOYENS DE LES RENDRE MEILLEURES

Freher, M *see* FOEDERIS LVDOVICI GERMANIAE, ET KAROLI GALLIAE REGUM, PII FILIOR...

FREI UND GEWISS IM GLAUBEN: BEITRAEGE ZUR VERTIEFUNG IN...DER CHRISTLICHE RELIGION / Koehler, Franz - Berlin: Arthur Glaue, 1909. 1 fiche - 9 - us A.T.L.A. [240]

Freiburger Geschichtsverein *see* ZEITSCHRIFT

FREIBURGER ZEITUNG - (Title changes: Allgemeines Intelligenzblatt, 1802-1808; Grossherzoglich Badisches privilegirtes Freyburger Wochenblatt, 1810-1820; Neue Freiburger Zeitung, 1848-1851) - Freiburg, Germany. 1848-1849 - 3r - 1 - gw Mikrofilm [072]

DER FREIDENKER - Milwaukee, WI. 1872-1942 - 1 - gw Mikrofilm [071]

FREIDENKER - Berlin, 1925-33 (incomplete) - 1r - 1 - Dist. gw Mikrofilm - gw Misc Inst [072]

FREIDENKER : ORGAN DER FREIGEISTIGEN VEREINIGUNG DER SCHWEIZ - (Lacking: v42-44) - v39-41 1956-58. v45-74 1962-91 - 4r - 1 - ATLA S0438 - us A.T.L.A. [073]

EINE FREIDIGE VERMANUNG, ZU KLAREM VND OEFFENTLICHEM BEKENTNIS JHESU CHRISTI, SEHR NUETZLICH ZU LESEN / Civilus - Magdeburgk, M. Lother. 1550. BME-269 1 - 9 - ne IDC [240]

Freidrich, Paul *see* DAS GRABBE-BUCH

Freidus, A S *see* YAD VA SHEM... STUDIES IN JEWISH BIBLIOGRAPHY... IN MEMORY OF A.S. FREIDUS

DER FREIE ANGESTELLTE - Zeitschrift des Zentralverbandes der Angestellten. v25, 28-29, 31-36. -1932. -biw. (Serial publications of German trade unions in the Memorial Library, University of Wisconsin-Madison.) - 1 - us U.W. Library [331]

DER FREIE ARBEITER - Berlin, 1904-feb 1933 - 1 - Dist. gw Mikrofilm - gw Misc Inst [072]

DER FREIE ARBEITER - Berlin. v1-6. 1904-09 - 1 - us Res Libr [072]

DER FREIE ARBEITER / Foederation der kommunistischen Anarchisten Deutschlands - Berlin. 1919-1924. Gaps - 1 - $35.00r - us Hoover Inst Photo [320]

FREIE ARBEITER STIMME - New York, NY. In Yiddish. -w. 6 Jan 1950-15 Dec 1961. 2 reels - 1 - uk British Libr Newspaper [071]

FREIE ARBEITER STIMME - New York.Free voice of labor. 1943-45 - 1 - us A.J.P.C. [331]

DER FREIE BAUER - (Cont by: Neue Deutsche Bauernzeitung) - Berlin, nov 1 1945-oct 1960 - 10r - 1 - Dist. gw Mikrofilm - gw Misc Inst [072]

DER FREIE BAUER *see* NEUE DEUTSCHE BAUERNZEITUNG

FREIE BLAETTER / ed by Glassbrenner, Adolf - Berlin. may 6-dec 1848 - 1 - gw Mikrofilm [073]

FREIE BLAETTER *see* FREIE VOLKSBLAETTER

FREIE BUEHNE FUER DEN ENTWICKLUNGSKAMPF DER ZEIT *see*
- DIE NEUE RUNDSCHAU

FREIE BUEHNE FUER MODERNES LEBEN - (Cont. as: Freie Buehne fuer Entwicklungskampf der Zeit. v.3-4-.Berlin. 1892- 93. Cont. as: Neue Deutsche Rundschau. v. 5-14. Berlin. 1894-1903.) - v. 1-2. Berlin. 1890-91. - 323mf - 8 - ne IDC [430]

FREIE BUEHNE FUER MODERNES LEBEN *see*
- DIE NEUE RUNDSCHAU

DER FREIE DEMOKRAT - Hannover, West Germany. 16 May-24 Sept 1946; 1 Jan-15 Apr, 26 Jun-30 Dec 1947; 16 Jan-6 Aug 1948 - 1 - gw Mikrofilm [072]

FREIE DEMOKRATISCHE KORRESPONDENZ - Bonn, 1950-1957 - 5r - 1 - DM375.00 - gw Mikro Press [072]

FREIE DEMOKRATISCHE KORRESPONDENZ (FDK) - Bonn, 1950-mar 9 1957 - 1 - Inquire at Mikrofilmarchiv for details - gw Misc Inst [320]

FREIE DEMOKRATISCHE KORRESPONDENZ (FDK) - Bonn, West Germany. 17 Jan 1950-9 Mar 1957 - 5r - 1 - gw Mikrofilm [072]

FREIE DEUTSCHE JUGEND - Paris, FR. 1937-1939 - 1 - gw Mikrofilm [072]

FREIE DEUTSCHE PRESSE - (Ausgabe Nordfranken) - Coburg, DE. 24 Dec 1948-May 1960 - 1 - gw Mikrofilm [072]

FREIE DEUTSCHE PRESSE *see*
- FREISINNIGE ZEITUNG
- MITTEILUNGEN DER FDP IN BAYERN

FREIE DEUTSCHE SCHULZEITUNG - Leipzig, DE. 1881 - 1r - 1 - gw Mikrofilm [072]

DAS FREIE DEUTSCHLAND/MITTEILUNGEN DER... *see* MITTEILUNGEN DER DEUTSCHEN FREIHEITSBIBLIOTHEK

FREIE ERDE - (Nordkurier, 2 Apr 1990) - Neubrandenburg, Germany. 1992- - 6r per yr - 1 - gw Mikrofilm [072]

DIE FREIE GENERATION - Berlin. v. 1-2. July 1906-June 1908 - 1 - us NY Public [073]

DIE FREIE GENERATION - v.2 3 & 9-12, 1907 08. Incomplete. Includes Jahrbuch der Freien generation, 1910 - 9 - 1.00f - at Libertarian Micro [320]

Freie Generation *see* JAHRBUCH DER FREIEN GENERATION

DIE FREIE GEWERKSCHAFT - Berlin, 1947-Oct 1949 - 9r - 1 - uk British Libr Newspaper [072]

DIE FREIE GEWERKSCHAFT - Berlin, Oct 1945-46 - 2r - 1 - DM150.00 - gw Mikro Press [072]

DIE FREIE GEWERKSCHAFT : ORGAN DES FDGB - (Cont by: Tribuene, 1947) - Berlin, oct 9 1945-80 - 88r - 1 - Dist. gw Mikrofilm - gw Mikrofilm [072]

DIE FREIE GEWERKSCHAFT *see* TRIBUENE

FREIE GEWERKSCHAFT - Hamburg, DE. 1922-1930 (incomplete) - 1 - gw Mikrofilm [072]

DER FREIE HANSEAT - Bremen, Germany. 5 Sept-23 Dez 1947; Jan-Sept 1948 - 1r - 1 - gw Mikrofilm [072]

DER FREIE HANSEAT – Bremen, sep 5-dec 23 1947, jan-sep 1948 – 1r – 1 – Inquire at Mikrofilmarchiv for details – gw Misc Inst [072]

FREIE JUEDISCHE LEHRERSTIMME : MONATSSCHRIFT FUER DIE PFLEGE DER INTERESSEN DES JUDENTHUMS IN SCHULE UND HAUS – Vienna. v1-9, 1912-20. Complete. 1 reel. B77 (Leo Baeck Institute. German-Jewish Periodicals, Pt 2) – 1 – $75.00 – us UPA [270]

FREIE JUGEND – Berlin, 1919 n4-1920 n18 – 1 – Dist. gw Mikrofilm – gw Misc Inst [072]

FREIE KUNST UND LITERATUR – Paris. Sept 1938-Jul 1939, no9 – 1r – 1 – gw Mikrofilm [072]

FREIE MEINUNG – Bremen, 1919 n1-2 – 1r – 1 – Inquire at Mikrofilmarchiv for details – gw Misc Inst [072]

DIE FREIE PRESSE – Chicago: Free Press Print Co, feb 5-may 26 1872 – 1r – 1 – us Res Libr [072]

FREIE PRESSE – Bielefeld, 1946-50 – 6r – 1 – DM450.00 – gw Mikro Press [072]

FREIE PRESSE – Bielefeld, West Germany. 3 Apr 1946-1950 – 6r – 1 – gw Mikrofilm [072]

FREIE PRESSE – (Cont by: Freie Presse, Karl-Marx-Stadt) – Zwickau, East Germany. Apr 1952-1 Dec 1966 (incomplete); 13 Jan 1968-1974 (incomplete); 12 Jul 1983-1984; 1986; 1989-1990 – 1 – gw Mikrofilm [072]

FREIE PRESSE – Elberfeld Barmen, 1918; 1925-28 – 14r – 1 – DM1,050.00 – gw Mikro Press [072]

FREIE PRESSE – (In the beginning Hauptausgabe, since 1963 Bereichsausgabe der Freien Presse, Karl-Marx-Stadt/ Chemnitz) – Zwickau, jan 2-mar 31 1984, jul 2 1984-88, jun 1 1992-96 – 48r – 1 – gw Mikrofilm [072]

FREIE PRESSE – Lodz, Poland. 28 Nov 1928; 10-23 Sept 1939 – 1r – 1 – us L of C Photodup [947]

FREIE PRESSE – (Publ started as Bereichsausgabe of Freie Presse, Zwickau, and became main edition in 1963, while the Zwickau-edition became Bereichsausgabe. Today the main edition is called FREIE PRESSE: CHEMNITZER ZEITUNG. Also Bereichsausgaben available (nur Kreisseiten): ANNABERG, apr 26 1958-oct 31 1961; AUE, apr 1 1958-oct 30 1961; AUERBACH, apr 1 1958-oct 27 1961, sep 19 1985-90; BRAND-ERBISDORF, mar 29 1958-oct 30 1961; FLOEHA, apr 1 1948-oct 31 1961, jan 3-nov 21 1963; FREIBERG, mar 31 1958-oct 30 1961, mar 22 1962-nov 26 1963, may 6 1965-dec 22 1966 (incomplete); GLAUCHAU, jan 5 1958-oct 31 1961; HAINICHEN, apr 1 1958-nov 29 1963 (incomplete); HETTSTEDT, apr 2 1958-nov 25 1966 (incomplete); HOHENSTEIN-ERNSTTHAL, apr 1 1958-64 (incomplete); KARL-MARX-STADT-LAND, apr 22 1958-oct 11 1961, jul 15 1963-dec 2 1964 (incomplete), jun 2 1988-dec 17 1990; KLINGENTHAL, apr 1 1958-aug 31 1963 (incomplete), sep 19 1985-89; MARIENBERG, apr 3 1958-oct 4 1961, may 17-oct 16 1965; OELSNITZ, apr 1 1958-oct 31 1961, jan 5 1963-jul 29 1966 (incomplete), may 7 1968-oct 21 1969 (incomplete), jul 19 1983-90; PLAUEN, apr 1 1958-sep 14 1963, feb 25 1965-dec 15 1966 (all incomplete); PLAUEN-LAND, apr 3 1958-oct 30 1961, 1964 (incomplete), jan 27 1967-apr 4 1970 (incomplete), jul 19 1983-90; REICHENBACH, 1958-dec 4 1969, jan 5 1971-sep 20 1979, sep 20 1985-90 (all incomplete); ROCHLITZ, apr 1 1958-oct 31 1961 (incomplete), jan 15-jun 6 1963, feb 6 1968-aug 30 1969; SCHWARZENBERG, apr 1 1958-oct 31 1961, jul 23-dec 10 1966; STOLLBERG, apr 1 1958-oct 31 1961; WERDAU, apr 1 1958-nov 19 1966 (incomplete); ZSCHOPAU, apr 1 1958-oct 31 1961, jun 16-nov 15 1966, jul 3 1984-90; ZWICKAU, apr 1952-dec 1 1966 (incomplete), jan 13 1968-74 (incomplete), jul 12 1983-84, 1986, 1989-90; ZWICKAU-LAND, apr 1 1958-oct 31 1961, jun 30-jul 17 1965, jul 5-dec 23 1966, 1986-88) – Karl-Marx-Stadt/Chemnitz, apr 1 1952- – 1 – Inquire at Mikrofilmarchiv for details – gw Misc Inst [072]

FREIE PRESSE : TAGESZEITUNG – Buenos Aires, 1972-76/77 – 15r – 1 – Inquire at Mikrofilmarchiv for details – gw Misc Inst [072]

FREIE PRESSE : TAGESZEITUNG – Buenos Aires, Argentina. 1972-76/77 – 15r – 1 – gw Mikrofilm [072]

FREIE PRESSE – (United with Westfaelische Zeitung to form Neue Westfaelische, Bielefeld) – Bielefeld, apr 3 1946-jul 1 1967 – 1 – Inquire at Mikrofilmarchiv for details – gw Misc Inst [072]

FREIE PRESSE : WOCHENBLATT FUER GEISTIGE UND POLITISCHE FREIHEIT – Amsterdam, jul 15 1933-jan 27 1934 – 1r – 1 – Dist. gw Mikrofilm – gw Misc Inst [949]

FREIE PRESSE – Wuppertal, Germany. 1918; 1925-28 – 14r – 1 – gw Mikrofilm [072]

FREIE PRESSE *see* LODZER FREIE PRESSE

FREIE PRESSE – Council Bluffs: [s.n.],jul 27 1917-19 – 2r – 1 – us Res Libr [072]

FREIE PRESSE AND WOCHENLICHTE TRIBUNE – Omaha, NE. -d. Mar-Dec 1892; Sept-Oct 1894; Jan-Dec 1903; May 1908-Dec 1921; Jan 1924-Aug 1926 – 1 – us NE Hist [071]

FREIE PRESSE: CHEMNITZER ZEITUNG – Chemnitz, Germany. 1992- – 8r per yr – 1 – gw Mikrofilm [072]

FREIE PRESSE: CHEMNITZER ZEITUNG *see* FREIE PRESSE

FREIE PRESSE FUER ELSASS LOTHRINGEN – Strasbourg, France. 1898-1916, janv-22 aout 1939 – 1 – fr A.C.R.P.P. [072]

FREIE PRESSE FUR TEXAS – San Antonio: H Pollmar, [1865-]. aug 1917-jul 1918 – 1r – 1 – us Res Libr [072]

FREIE PRESSE UND WOCHENTLICHE TRIBUNE – Omaha. mar 29 1923-24 – us Res Libr [072]

FREIE PRESSE, ZWICKAU *see* FREIE PRESSE

FREIE SHRIFTN – Vilna. n1-17.1926-35 – 1r – 1 – us Ross [072]

FREIE SHRIFTN – Wilna. no. 1-17. Sept 1926-Oct 1935 – 1 – us NY Public [073]

DER FREIE STAATSBUERGER – Nuernberg, DE. 1 Jul 1848-11 Apr 1850 – 1 – gw Mikrofilm [072]

FREIE TRIBUENE – London. Jan 1944-27 Jun 1946 – 1r – 1 – gw Mikrofilm [072]

FREIE VEREINIGUNG DEUTSCHER GEWERKSCHAFTEN – Berlin, 1914-15 – 1 – Dist. gw Mikrofilm – gw Misc Inst [072]

Freie Vereinigung Deutscher Gewerkschaften *see* PROTOKOLL UEBER DIE VERHANDLUNGEN VOM KONGRESS..

DAS FREIE VOLK / ed by Breitscheid, Rudolf – Berlin, Aug 1910-14 – 2r – 1 – DM220.00 – gw Mikro Press [072]

DAS FREIE VOLK : DEMOKRATISCHES WOCHENBLATT – Berlin, 1909- aug 8 1914 – 2r – 1 – Dist. gw Mikrofilm – gw Misc Inst [072]

FREIE VOLKSBLAETTER – (Cont by: Freie Blaetter, oct 29 1848) – Koeln, apr 12 1848-jan 7 1849 – 1r – 1 – gw Mikrofilm [943]

FREIE VOLKSTIMME – Zabreh, Czechoslovakia. Aug 1906-1908 – 1r – 1 – us L of C Photodup [072]

DIE FREIE WELT : ILLUSTRIERTE WOCHENSCHRIFT DER USPD – Berlin, 1919-20 – 1r – 1 – Dist. gw Mikrofilm – gw Misc Inst [072]

FREIE WELT – 1970-1983 – 1,134mf – 1 – DM6,463.80 – gw Mikro Press [320]

DAS FREIE WORT – Bern, 1917-18 (incomplete) – 1r – 1 – Inquire at Mikrofilmarchiv for details – gw Misc Inst [072]

DAS FREIE WORT – Bern, Switzerland. 1917-18 – 1r – 1 – gw Mikrofilm [949]

DAS FREIE WORT – Bielitz-Biala (Bielsko-Biala), Poland. Jan-Jul 1927 – 1r – 1 – gw Mikrofilm [943]

DAS FREIE WORT – Bielitz-Biala, jan-jul 1927 – 1r – 1 – Inquire at Mikrofilmarchiv for details – gw Misc Inst [072]

DAS FREIE WORT – Bonn, oct 1 1960-jun 27 1964 – 1 – Inquire at Mikrofilmarchiv for details – gw Misc Inst [072]

DAS FREIE WORT – Essen. jan 8, 1919-22 (incomplete). jan 4, 1925-aug 7, 1927 (very incomplete) – 2r – 1 – gw Mikrofilm [073]

DAS FREIE WORT : ZEITUNG DER DEUTSCHEN KRIEGSGEFANGENEN IN DER SOWJETUNION – (Cont by: Freies Deutschland. Organ des Nationalkomitees "Freies Deutschland") – Moscow, U.S.S.R. Nov 1941-3 Nov 1945 – 2r – 1 – gw Mikrofilm [943]

DAS FREIE WORT *see* FREIES WORT

DIE FREIE ZEITUNG – Bern, 1917-20 – 1r – 1 – Inquire at Mikrofilmarchiv for details – gw Misc Inst [072]

DIE FREIE ZEITUNG – Bern, Switzerland. 1917-20 – 1r – 1 – gw Mikrofilm [949]

DIE FREIEN BAUERN : ERZAEHLUNG AUS DEM NORWEGISCHEN VOLKSLEBEN / Muegge, Theodor – Berlin: C Flemming und C T Wiskott, [1924?] – 1r – 1 – us U.W. Library [390]

Freier Deutscher Gewerkschaftsbund. Berlin *see* GESCHAEFTSBERICHT

FREIER DEUTSCHER KULTURBUND IN SCHWEDEN : MITTEILUNGSBLATT DES FDKB – Stockholm, Sweden. Feb 1945-Apr 1946 – 1 – gw Mikrofilm [072]

FREIER GOLDMARKT VERSUS EINLOESUNG / Beckerath, Ulrich von – Mit Anm. von H. Ritterhausen – 9 – 1.00f – at Libertarian Micro [335]

FREIES BLATT : ORGAN ZUR ABWEHR DES ANTISEMITISMUS – Vienna. v1-5? 1892-96? Complete. 1 reel. B80 (Leo Baeck Institute. German-Jewish Periodicals, Pt 1) – 1 – $75.00 – us UPA [270]

FREIES DEUTSCHLAND – Moscow. USSR. -w. 3 Jan 1943-14 May, 16 Aug-27 Sep 1945. (1 reel) – 1 – uk British Libr Newspaper [072]

FREIES DEUTSCHLAND : ORGAN DER DEUTSCHEN OPPOSITION – Antwerpen und Creil (Oise), jan 14 1937-aug 24 1939 – 1r – 1 – Dist. gw Mikrofilm – gw Misc Inst [949]

FREIES DEUTSCHLAND : ORGAN IM SINNE DES NATIONALKOMITEES "FREIES DEUTSCHLAND" – Zurich, Switzerland. 3 Sept 1943-Jan 1946 – 1r – 1 – gw Mikrofilm [949]

FREIES DEUTSCHLAND : REVISTA ANTINAZI/ ANTINAZI MONTHLY – (Title change: Deutschland (Nueva Alemania), Jan 1946) – Mexico City. Nov 1941-Jun 1946 – 2r – 1 – gw Mikrofilm [072]

FREIES DEUTSCHLAND – Stockholm, Sweden. May 1944 – 1 – gw Mikrofilm [072]

FREIES DEUTSCHLAND. ORGAN DES NATIONALKOMITEES "FREIES DEUTSCHLAND" *see* DAS FREIE WORT

FREIES HEIM – Zagreb, Yugoslavia. Oct 1923-1924 – 1r – 1 – us L of C Photodup [949]

FREIES HESSISCHES VOLKSBLATT – Darmstadt, Germany. 12 Mar 1848-22 Sept 1849 – 1r – 1 – gw Mikrofilm [072]

FREIES VOLK – Duesseldorf. Germany. -d. 21 Nov 1949-2 Jan 1952. (7 reels) – 1 – uk British Libr Newspaper [072]

FREIES VOLK : ZENTRALORGAN DER KPD – Duesseldorf, 1949-56 – 17r – 1 – DM1,275.00 – gw Mikro Press [072]

FREIES WORT – (Title change: Das Freie Wort, 8 Mar 1956) – Suhl, East Germany. 2 Aug 1954-Jun 1990 – 70r – 1 – gw Mikrofilm [072]

DIE FREIFRAUEN : EIN POSSENSPIEL IN DREI AUFZUEGEN / Hoellrigl, Franz – Leipzig: August Schulze, 1896 – 1 – us U.W. Library [820]

FREIGEIST – Liberec, Czechoslovakia. Sept 1921-1924; Oct 1929-Sept 1938 – 9r – 1 – us L of C Photodup [072]

DIE FREIHEIT – Berlin, DE. Nov 1918-Sep 1922 – 11r – 1 – DM825.00 – gw Mikro Press [072]

DIE FREIHEIT – Braunschweig, Germany. Oct 1919-Oct 1922 – 4r – 1 – gw Mikrofilm [072]

DIE FREIHEIT – Braunschweig, oct 1 1919-oct 31 1922 – 4r – 1 – Inquire at Mikrofilmarchiv for details – gw Misc Inst [943]

DIE FREIHEIT – Braunschweig, Oct 1919-Oct 1922 – 4r – 1 – DM300.00 – gw Mikro Press [072]

DIE FREIHEIT – (Cont by: Freiheit, since mar 1 1919) – Berlin, nov 15 1918-sep 30 1922 – 10r – 1 – Dist. gw Mikrofilm – gw Misc Inst [072]

FREIHEIT – Breslau, jan 10-feb 7 1929 – 1r – 1 – Inquire at Mikrofilmarchiv for details – gw Misc Inst [072]

FREIHEIT – (Cont: Mitteldeutsche Tageszeitung "Freiheit", -jul 15 1958. Cont by: Mitteldeutsche Zeitung, mar 17 1990. Also Bereichsausgaben available (nur Kreisseiten): ARTERN, apr 1 1958-oct 31 1961, may 17 1967-nov 12 1969 (incomplete); ASCHERSLEBEN, apr 2 1958-oct 31 1961, mar 4-dec 2 1967, 1969 (incomplete), sep 20 1985-90; BERNBURG, apr 2 1958-61, 1967, 1969 (incomplete); BITTERFELD, apr 1 1958-oct 31 1961, feb 27 1967-dec 5 1970 (incomplete), jul 19 1983-90; DESSAU, apr 12 1958-jun 9 1972, jul 19 1983-90 (all incomplete); EISLEBEN, apr 1 1958-oct 31 1961, may 19 1988-dec 14 1990; GRAEFENHAINICHEN, apr 1 1958-oct 31 1961; HOHENMOELSEN, apr 1 1958-oct 31 1961; KOETHEN, mar 31 1958-nov 20 1964 (incomplete); MERSEBURG, apr 3 1958-apr 10 1970 (incomplete), jul 3 1984-90; NAUMBURG, apr 1 1958-oct 31 1961, may 25 1964-sep 17 1966 (incomplete), may 19 1988-dec 17 1990; NEBRA, apr 1 1958-61, apr 11 1964-jun 30 1965 (inccomplete); QUEDLINBURG, apr 1 1958-jul 3 1965 (incomplete), jan 30 1967-68 (incomplete), sep 19 1985-90; QUERFURT, apr 2 1958-oct 31 1961; ROSSLAU, apr 2 1958-oct 31 1961, jan 7-nov 20 1963; SAALKREIS, apr 2 1958-66 (incomplete); WEISSENFELS, apr 1 1958-dec 18 1969 (incomplete); WITTENBERG, apr 8 1958-apr 7 1970 (incomplete); ZEITZ, apr 1 1958-dec 4 1965 (incomplete)) – Halle/Saale, jul 5 1946-47, mar 2 1953- – 1 – Inquire at Mikrofilmarchiv for details – gw Misc Inst [072]

FREIHEIT – Halle. 17 Apr 1946-Dec 1949 – 1 – 35.00r – us Hoover Inst Photo [072]

FREIHEIT – Halle, 1946-47 – 2r – 1 – DM150.00 – gw Mikro Press [072]

FREIHEIT – Halle, Germany. 1950-Feb 1953; 1962-Apr 1976 – 47r – 1 – us L of C Photodup [072]

FREIHEIT / Independent Socialist Party. Germany – (Missing: Sep 17 1920) – Berlin, 1918-1922 – 1 – $35.00r – us Hoover Inst Photo [072]

FREIHEIT – London, Exeter & New York. 4 Jan 1879-29 Dec 1883 – 1 – uk British Libr Newspaper [072]

FREIHEIT – New York (etc.). Jahrg. 5-31. 1883-1909 – 1 – us NY Public [073]

FREIHEIT : NIEDERRHEINISCHE TAGESZEITUNG DER KPD – Duesseldorf, 1921-1933 – 27r – 1 – DM2,025.00 – gw Mikro Press [072]

FREIHEIT – Teplice-Sanov, Czechoslovakia. 1937 – 1r – 1 – us L of C Photodup [072]

FREIHEIT – (Title change: Mitteldeutsche Zeitung, 17 Mar 1990) – Halle, East Germany. 1992- – 7r per yr – 1 – gw Mikrofilm [072]

FREIHEIT *see* DIE FREIHEIT

DER FREIHEIT EINE GASSE : AUS DEM LEBEN UND WERK GEORG HERWEGHS / ed by Kaiser, Bruno – (Includes bibliographical references) – Berlin: Verlag Volk und Welt, 1948 – 1 – us U.W. Library [430]

FREIHEIT FUER OSTERREICH *see* FORUM UND TRIBUNE

FREIHEIT UND BROT – Muenchen, DE. Jan-Dec 1933 – 1 – gw Mikro Press [072]

FREIHEIT UND RECHT : EINE AUSWAHL AUS SEINEN WERKEN MIT EINER BIOGRAPHIE / Seume, Johann Gottfried – (Includes bibliographical references) – Hildesheim: Verlag Jugend und Volk, [1947?] – 1 – us U.W. Library [943]

FREIHEIT-KORRESPONDENZ – Muehlhausen/ Elsaß, 1933-1940 – 3r – 1 – DM225.00 – gw Mikro Press [072]

DER FREIHEITLICHE SOZIALISMUS, IM GEGENSATZ ZUM STAATSKNECHTSTUM DER MARXISTEN / Friedlaender, Benedict – 1892. 123 S. Together with: L'anarchisme aux Etats-Unis, by Paul Ghio. 212p. 1 fiche (24x) – 9 – 1.00f – at Libertarian Micro [320]

FREIHEITS FREUND – Pittsburgh. Pa. 1853-1900 – 1 – us UMI [071]

FREIHEITSBUND DEUTSCHER SOZIALISTEN – London, 1942-1947 – 1r – 1 – gw Mikrofilm [072]

DER FREIHEITSKAMPF *see* BAUTZENER NACHRICHTEN

DER FREIHEITSSUCHER / MacKay, John Henry – 1920. 260p. 1 fiche (24x) – 9 – 1.00f – at Libertarian Micro [320]

FREIKUGELN : SATIRISCHE ZEITSCHRIFT – Leipzig, DE. 1842; 1846 – 2r – 1 – gw Mikrofilm [072]

Freimann, J *see*
- FESTSCHRIFT
- FESTSCHRIFT. EMET LE-YA'AKOV

FREIMAURERZEITUNG – Berlin, 1783. 6 nos – 1mf – 9 – VR-32.4/1 – ne IDC [360]

DER FREIMUETHIGE : ODER BERLINISCHES UNTERHALTUNGSBLATT FUER GEBILDETE, UNBEFANGENE LESER – Berlin, feb 15-jun 27 1808 (incomplete) – 1 – Dist. gw Mikrofilm – gw Misc Inst [072]

DER FREIMUETHIGE, 1804-1811 / ed by Kotzebue, August von – 1803-11 (mf ed 1997) – 50mf – 9 – DM1,210.00 – 3-89131-231-8 – gw Fischer [305]

Freire, Jose Maria *see* POR LOS CAMINOS DEL JUSTICIALISMO

Freise, Otto *see*
- DIE DREI FASSUNGEN VON WIELANDS AGATHON

Freisen, J *see* LIBER AGENDARUM ECCLESIE ET DIOCESIS SLESZWICENSIS

FREISINGER TAGBLATT – Freising, West Germany. 1981- – 15r per yr – 1 – gw Mikrofilm [072]

FREISINNIGE ZEITUNG – (Also known as: Freie Deutsche Presse) – Berlin, 1899-1906 – 19r – 1 – Dist. gw Mikrofilm – gw Misc Inst [072]

FREISINNIGE ZEITUNG – Berlin, 1899-1906 – 19r – 1 – DM1,425.00 – gw Mikro Press [072]

DIE FREISTATT – Alljuedische Revue. Monatsschrift fuer juedische Kultur und Politik. Berlin. 1913-14. Lacking: 1914, v. 2 (1-3); 1915. – 15mf – 9 – ne IDC [290]

FREITAG – Berlin, nov 9 1990- – 1 – Dist. gw Mikrofilm – gw Misc Inst [072]

FREITAG *see* DEUTSCHE VOLKSZEITUNG/ FREITAG

Freitag, Britta *see* TOURISMUSENTWICKLUNG IN NIZZA

Freitas, S de *see*
- DE IUSTO IMPERIO...
- JUSTIFICATION DE LA DOMINATION PORTUGAISE EN ASIE

FREIWIRTSCHAFT-FUEHRT DIE GELDREFORM AUS DER KRISE / Cramer von Clausbruch, Juliane – Diplomarbeit, Berlin, 1985 – 9 – 1.00f – at Libertarian Micro [335]

Frejus, Roland *see* RELATION D'UN VOYAGE FAIT DANS LA MAURITANIE, EN AFRIQUE, DE MARSEILLE EN 1666

FRELIMO INFORMATION – Alger: Representation en Algerie du Front de liberation du Mozambique, jul 1968?; jun 1970/may 1971 – us Res Libr [072]

Fremantle, Edmund Robert *see* THE NAVY AS I HAVE KNOWN IT, 1849-1899

Fremantle, John Morton *see* GAZETTEER OF MURI PROVINCE, UP TO DECEMBER 1919

Fremantle, S J *see* THE STATE OF MORALS AND OF SOCIETY IN THE EASTERN CHURCH IN THE TIME OF S. CHRYSOSTOM

Fremantle, W H *see* THE GOSPEL OF THE SECULAR LIFE

Fremaux, Paul *see* DER STERBENDE NAPOLEON. UNVEROEFFENTLICHTES TAGEBUCH

DIE FREMDEN : EIN ROMAN AUS DER GEGENWART / Domanig, Karl – 3., verb. Aufl. Klagenfurt: Verlag der St Josefbuecherbruderschaft, 1911 – 1 – us U.W. Library [830]

FREMDEN-BLATT – Vienna, Austria. -d. June 1915-March 1919. Imperfect. 22 reels – 1 – uk British Libr Newspaper [072]

FREMDWOERTER IM GRIECHISCHEN UND LATEINISCHEN / Vanicek, Alois – Leipzig: B G Teubner, 1878 – 1mf – 9 – 0-8370-9325-2 – 1986-3325 – us A.T.L.A. [450]

FREMDWOERTERBUCH : EIN HANDWEISER ZUR ENTWELSCHUNG FUER AMT, SCHULE, HAUS, LEBEN / Engel, Eduard – Leipzig, 1922 – 2mf – 9 – DM62.00 – 3-89349-781-1 – gw Hänsel [040]

DAS FREMDWORT BEI GRIMMELSHAUSEN : EIN BEITRAG ZUR FREMDWORTERFRAGE DES 17. JAHRHUNDERTS / Hechtenberg, Klara – (Includes bibliographical references) – [S.l.: s.n.], 1901 (Heidelberg: Universitaets-Buchdruckerei von J. Hoerning) – 1r – 1 – us U.W. Library [430]

Fremin *see* MEMOIRES CRITIQUES D'ARCHITECTURE.

Fremont d'Ablancourt, Nicolas *see* SUITE DU NEPTUNE FRANCOIS OU ATLAS NOUVEAU DES CARTES MARINES.

FREMONT DAILY NEWS – Fremont, Ohio. 1912-38 – 65r – 1 – $32.50r – us Archival [071]

FREMONT HERALD – Fremont, NE. -d. Jan. 1877-Dec. 1878; Mar. 1879-May 1904. Incomplete; Jan. 1905-Oct. 1928 – 1 – us NE Hist [071]

Fremont, Joseph *see*
- COMPENDIUM OF DOMINION LAWS OF CANADA, 1867-1883, IN FORCE ON THE FIRST DAY OF JANUARY, 1884, INDICATING AMENDMENTS, REPEALS, & C., WITH INDEX
- LE DIVORCE ET LA SEPARATION DE CORPS: THESE

FREMONT MORNING GUIDE – Fremont, NE. -d. Jan. 1939-Jul. 1942 – 1 – us NE Hist [071]

Fremont. Ohio. Memorial United Methodist Church *see* RECORDS

FREMONT TRIBUNE – Fremont, NE. -d. Mar. 1887; Jun. 1890; Jul. 1891-Apr. 1899; Jun. 1899-Jan. 1910; Jul. 1918- – 1 – us NE Hist [071]

FREMONT TRI-WEEKLY HERALD – Fremont, NE. -w. sw., triw. Jan. 1872; Feb. 1876-Dec. 1882. Incomplete; Mar. 1883-Jun. 1888; Dec. 1888-Mar. 1890; Jun. 1890-Dec. 1900; Jul. 1901-Apr. 1905 – 1 – us NE Hist [071]

FREMONT TRI-WEEKLY TRIBUNE – Fremont, NE. -w., sw., triw. Jul. 1868-Jul. 1876; Jan. 1877-Sep. 1878. Incomplete; Jul. 1879-Aug. 1917 – 1 – us NE Hist [071]

FREMONT/HAYWARD – 1992- – 6+ r – 1 – $300.00 – P00028 – us Library Micro [910]

Fremont.Ohio. First United Presbyterian Church *see* RECORDS

Fremont.Ohio. St. John's Evangelical Lutheran Church *see* RECORDS

Fremont.Ohio. St. Paul's Episcopal Church *see* RECORDS

Fremy, P *see*
- CYANOPHYCEES DES COTES D'EUROPE
- LES MYXOPHYCEES DE L'AFRIQUE EQUATORIALE FRANCAISE

[FRENCH ALMANACS PAMPHLET COLLECTION] – 1850-1919 – 1 – CSUXAMJ3164-B – us Hoover Inst Photo [030]

French, Alvah P *see* HISTORY OF WESTCHESTER COUNTY

FRENCH ARCHITECTURAL WRITINGS: 16TH-19TH CENTURIES / ed by Mignot, Claude – In French. 105 titles. Available by title – 624mf – 9 – fr Hachette [720]

FRENCH BIBLE – 13th and 14th cents. Holkham mss. 10, 13. Holkham Hall, Norfolk, England – 14 – uk Microform Academic [240]

FRENCH BIBLE – French. 13th cent. Holkham ms. 10. Holkham Hall, Norfolk, England – 1 – uk Microform Academic [240]

FRENCH BOOKS 1601-1700 – 225r – 1 – $14,000.00 $1,200.00y – us OmniSys [010]

FRENCH BOOKS BEFORE 1601 – 1965- – 493r – 1 – $30,800.00 $1,200.00y – us OmniSys [010]

French Cameroons *see*
- PLAN DE DEVELOPPEMENT ECONOMIQUE ET SOCIAL, 1947-1952
- PLAN DE DEVELOPPEMENT ECONOMIQUE ET SOCIAL DU TERRITOIRE, 1947-1952
- SECOND PLAN GENERAL DE DEVELOPPEMENT ECONOMIQUE ET SOCIAL, 1953-1957

[FRENCH CAMPAIGNS DURING WORLD WAR 2 PAMPHLET COLLECTION] – 1942-1944 – 1 – CSUXANM9116-B – us Hoover Inst Photo [355]

THE FRENCH CANADIAN, IMPERIUM IN IMPERIO: A LECTURE ON OUR CREED AND RACE PROBLEM / Burton, John – Toronto: Copp, Clark, 1887. 00357. (Pre-1900 Canadiana) – 9 – cn C.I.H.M. [971]

FRENCH CANADIAN LIFE AND CHARACTER: WITH HISTORICAL AND DESCRIPTIVE SKETCHES OF THE SCENERY AND LIFE IN QUEBEC, MONTREAL, OTTAWA, AND SURROUNDING COUNTRY / ed by George Munro Grant – 9 – cn C.I.H.M. [306]

French, Charles *see* BIOGRAPHICAL HISTORY OF THE AMERICAN IRISH IN CHICAGO

THE FRENCH CHIRURGERYE / Guillemeau, J – Trans. by A. M. Dort. M 365. 1597 – 9 – ne IDC [617]

[FRENCH CIVILIZATION, CULTURE, SOCIAL LIFE, AND CUSTOMS PAMPHLET COLLECTION] – 1851-1987 – 1 – CSUXANQ3150-B – us Hoover Inst Photo [306]

French, D S *see* ANATOLIA AND THE AEGEAN IN THE THIRD MILLENNIUM B.C.

FRENCH DIOCESAN CATECHISMS, 1615-1900 – (Includes printed guide) – 1,134mf – 9 – ne IDC [240]

FRENCH DRAMA – 30,025mf – 9 – $81,000.00 $1,280.00y – us OmniSys [440]

FRENCH DRAWINGS AND SKETCHBOOKS OF THE NINETEENTH CENTURY, VOL 1 / Olsen, Sandra Haller – (122p accompanying text) – 1978 – 5 color mf – 15 – $90.00f – 0-226-68796-1 – us Chicago [740]

FRENCH DRAWINGS AND SKETCHBOOKS OF THE NINETEENTH CENTURY, VOL 2 / Olsen, Sandra Haller – (140p accompanying text) – 1978 – 7 color mf – 15 – $120.00f – 0-226-68798-8 – us Chicago [740]

FRENCH DRAWINGS OF THE SIXTEENTH AND SEVENTEENTH CENTURIES / Olsen, Sandra Haller – (32p accompanying text) – 1977 – 1 color mf – 15 – $28.50f – us Chicago [740]

FRENCH EQUATORIAL AFRICA : ANNUAIRE STATISTIQUE DE L'AFRIQUE EQUATORIALE FRANCAISE 1936-1955 / French Equatorial Africa. Service de la Statistique Generale – (Coll title: African Official Statistical Serials, 1867-1982) – 8mf – 9 – £67.00 – uk Chadwyck [960]

French Equatorial Africa *see*
- BILAN DES DEUX PREMIERS PLANS SITUATION ECONOMIQUE, SOCIALE ET FINANCIERE (EVOLUTION DEPUIS 1946)
- JOURNAL OFFICIEL
- MEMOIRE SUR L'EXECUTION DU PLAN D'EQUIPEMENT EN AFRIQUE EQUATORIALE FRANCAISE. 1947-48 ET 48-49
- TROISIEME PLAN QUADRIENNAL

French Equatorial Africa. Service de la Statistique Generale *see* FRENCH EQUATORIAL AFRICA

A FRENCH ETON, OR, MIDDLE CLASS EDUCATION AND THE STATE / Arnold, Matthew – London, Cambridge: Macmillan, 1864 – 1 roll – 1 – 1-55879-164-7 – uk Libr Preservation [370]

THE FRENCH FORCES OF THE INTERIOR; THEIR ORGANIZATION AND PARTICIPATION IN THE LIBERATION OF FRANCE, 1944 / U.S. Army. European Theater of Operations – 1945 – 1 – $67.00 – us L of C Photodup [355]

[FRENCH FOREIGN RELATIONS AND DIPLOMATIC HISTORY PAMPHLET COLLECTION] – 1915-1961 – 1 – CSUXANQ3168-B – us Hoover Inst Photo [320]

THE FRENCH GARDEN / Erondell, Peter – 1605. 244p. (English Linguistics Series 1500-1800) – 9 – us UMI [440]

French, George, 1853-1935 *see* ADVERTISING: THE SOCIAL AND ECONOMIC PROBLEM

FRENCH GRAMMAR, WITH ADDITIONS / Mauger, Cl – 9 – fr I.C.S. [440]

French Guiana *see*
- ANNUAIRE
- BULLETIN DES ACTS ET ADMINISTRATIFS
- BULLETIN OFFICIEL DE LA GUYANE FRANCAISE

French Guiana. Comite departmental d'action economique de la Guyane *see* PLAN DE DEVELOPPEMENT ECONOMIQUE

French Guinea *see* JOURNAL OFFICIEL

FRENCH HISTORY – 1808-1924. Supplements-1761-1839. Tables- 1559-1839 – 1 – us UMI [944]

[FRENCH HISTORY DURING THE GERMAN OCCUPATION OF 1940 TO 1945 PAMPHLET COLLECTION] – 1940?-1978 – 2r – 1 – CSUXANQ5581-B – us Hoover Inst Photo [944]

[FRENCH HISTORY DURING THE GERMAN OCCUPATION OF 1914-1918 PAMPHLET COLLECTION] – 1914-1919 – 1 – CSUXANQ5574-B – us Hoover Inst Photo [944]

[FRENCH HISTORY–1914 TO 1940–PAMPHLET COLLECTION] – 1918?-1948 – 1 – CSUXANQ5576-B – us Hoover Inst Photo [944]

THE FRENCH IMAGE OF CHINA BEFORE AND AFTER VOLTAIRE / Guy, Basil – (Studies on Voltaire and the eighteenth century, v21) – Oxford. 1963 – 9 – $72.00 – 0-7294-0073-5 – uk Voltaire [944]

FRENCH, ITALIAN AND ENGLISH KEYBOARD MUSIC OF THE BAROQUE – 108mf – 9 – MS-f – ne IDC [780]

French, J H *see* GAZETTEER OF THE STATE OF NEW YORK

FRENCH JANSENISTS / Tollemache, Marguerite – (Includes bibliographical references) – London: Kegan Paul, Trench, Truebner, 1893 – 1mf – 9 – 0-8370-8553-5 – 1986-2553 – us A.T.L.A. [920]

FRENCH LANGUAGE NOVELS AND SHORT STORIES OF THE EDITION CORVEY : LITERARY WORKS OF THE 18TH AND 19TH CENTURY – (Silver halide microfiche on request) – Wildberg: BELSER WISS. DIENST, 1990-1992 – 5,930mf – 9 – DM44,800.00 diazo – 3-628-04016-7 – gw Belser Wiss [440]

FRENCH LANGUAGE TITLES OF THE EDITION CORVEY : LITERARY WORKS OF THE 18TH AND 19TH CENTURY – (Silver halide microfiche on request) – Wildberg: BELSER WISS. DIENST, 1990-1992 – 11,347mf – 9 – DM78,780.00 diazo – 3-628-04015-9 – gw Belser Wiss [440]

THE FRENCH LAW OF MARRIAGE... / Kelly, E – New York, 1885 – 2mf – 9 – ILM-3069/1 – ne IDC [327]

THE FRENCH LAW OF MARRIAGE, MARRIAGE CONTRACTS AND DIVORCE ... / Bodington, O E – 2nd ed. London, 1895 – 4mf – 9 – ILM-3881/1 – ne IDC [327]

THE FRENCH LITTELTON / Desainliens, Claude – 1576. 254p. (English Linguistices Series 1500-1800) – 9 – us UMI [440]

French, MH *see* OBSERVATIONS ON THE GOAT

[FRENCH NAVAL OPERATIONS DURING WORLD WAR 2 PAMPHLET COLLECTION] – 194? – 1 – CSUXANM9215-B – us Hoover Inst Photo [355]

FRENCH NINETEENTH CENTURY ART (INCLUDING SALON CATALOGUES) : SUBJECT COLLECTIONS – (Individual titles not listed separately) – 172 catalogues on 269mf – 9 – £1,410.00 – uk Chadwyck [700]

FRENCH OPERA SCORES / ed by Hul, Dick van den – (Includes a printed guide) – 2649mf – 9 – TF – ne IDC [780]

French Overseas Departments. Departement de la Martinique *see* CINQUIEME PLAN DE DEVELOPPEMENT ECONOMIQUE ET SOCIAL 1966-1970

French Overseas Territories. Commissariat general au plan de modernisation et d'equipement *see* RAPPORT GENERAL DE LA COMMISSION D'ETUDE ET DE COORDINATION DES PLANS DE MODERNISATION ET D'EQUIPEMENT DES TERRITOIRES D'OUTRE-MER

FRENCH PHILOLOGY / ed by Osborn, Charles B – (Individual titles available) – 9,801mf – 9 – ne IDC [440]

FRENCH POLITICAL PAMPHLETS – Based on the bibliography French Political Pamphlets, 1547-1648 by Lindsay and Neu – 1 – us Primary [944]

FRENCH POLITICAL PAMPHLETS, 1560-1653 – Newberry Library Collections – 28r – 1 – $2075.00 – us UMI [944]

[FRENCH POLITICS AND GOVERNMENT IN THE 20TH CENTURY PAMPHLET COLLECTION] – 1912-1941 – 1 – CSUXANQ4912-B – us Hoover Inst Photo [320]

[FRENCH POLITICS AND GOVERNMENT–1945 TO 1958–PAMPHLET COLLECTION] – 1946-1954 – 1 – CSUXANQ5586-B – us Hoover Inst Photo [320]

[FRENCH POLITICS AND GOVERNMENT–1958 TO THE PRESENT–PAMPHLET COLLECTION] – 1961-1984 – 1 – CSUXANQ5604-B – us Hoover Inst Photo [320]

French Polynesia *see* JOURNAL OFFICIEL

FRENCH POPULAR LITHOGRAPHIC IMAGERY 1815-1870, VOL 3 : URBAN AND MILITARY / Farwell, Beatrice – (90p accompanying text) – 1983 – 6mf – 9 – $90.00f – 0-226-69014-8 – us Chicago [760]

FRENCH POPULAR LITHOGRAPHIC IMAGERY, VOL 4 : THE CITY / Farwell, Beatrice – (122p accompanying text) – 1986 – 6mf – 9 – $90.00f – 0-226-69015-6 – us Chicago [760]

FRENCH POPULAR LITHOGRAPHIC IMAGERY, VOL 5 : THE COUNTRY / Farwell, Beatrice – (88p accompanying text) – 1986 – 4mf – 9 – $90.00f – 0-226-69016-4 – us Chicago [760]

FRENCH POPULAR LITHOGRAPHIC IMAGERY, VOL 6 : PIETY AND THE FAMILY / Farwell, Beatrice – (112p accompanying text) – 1987 – 5mf – 9 – $90.00f – 0-226-69017-2 – us Chicago [760]

FRENCH POPULAR LITHOGRAPHIC IMAGERY, VOL 7 : LOVE AND COURTSHIP / Farwell, Beatrice – (79p accompanying text) – 1988 – 5mf – 9 – $90.00f – 0-226-69018-0 – us Chicago [760]

FRENCH POPULAR LITHOGRAPHIC IMAGERY, VOL 8 : CONTEMPORARY EVENTS AND CARICATURE / Farwell, Beatrice – (102p accompanying text) – 1988 – 6mf – 9 – $90.00f – 0-226-69019-9 – us Chicago [760]
FRENCH POPULAR LITHOGRAPHIC IMAGERY, VOL 9 : HISTORICISM AND EXOTICISM / Farwell, Beatrice – (112p accompanying text) – 1990 – 6mf – 9 – $90.00f – 0-226-69020-2 – us Chicago [760]
FRENCH POPULAR LITHOGRAPHIC IMAGERY, VOL 10 : TOURISM AND TRAVEL / Farwell, Beatrice – (110p accompanying text) – 1992 – 6mf – 9 – $93.50f – 0-226-69021-0 – us Chicago [760]
FRENCH POPULAR LITHOGRAPHIC IMAGERY, VOL 11 : PINUPS AND EROTICA / Farwell, Beatrice – (72p accompanying text) – 1995 – 4mf – 9 – $90.00f – 0-226-69022-9 – us Chicago [760]
FRENCH POPULAR LITHOGRAPHIC IMAGERY, VOL 12 : LITHOGRAPHY IN ART AND COMMERCE / Farwell, Beatrice – (136p accompanying text) – 1997 – 9 – $100.00f – 0-226-23902-0 – us Chicago [760]
FRENCH PRAIRIE GAZETTE – Gervais OR. Dec 1 1888 – 1 – us U.O. Library [071]
FRENCH PRECURSORS OF PSYCHIATRY AND PSYCHOANALYSIS – Ed. by Dr. Serge Wasersztrum. 31 titles – 9 – fr Hachette [616]
FRENCH PRECURSORS OF PSYCHIATRY AND PSYCHOANALYSIS, 1750-1900 / ed by Wasersztrum, Serge – 9 – fr Hachette [150]
[FRENCH PROPAGANDA DURING WORLD WAR 1 PAMPHLET COLLECTION] – 1915-1921 – 2r – 1 – CSUXANL5389-B – us Hoover Inst Photo [320]
FRENCH PROPHETS OF YESTERDAY : A STUDY OF RELIGIOUS THOUGHT UNDER THE SECOND EMPIRE / Guerard, Albert Leon – London: T.F. Unwin, 1913 – 1mf – us A.T.L.A. [240]
FRENCH PROPHETS OF YESTERDAY; A STUDY OF RELIGIOUS THOUGHT UNDER THE SECOND EMPIRE / Guerard, Albert Leon – New York: D. Appleton, 1913. 288p – 1 – us U.W. Library [240]
FRENCH PROTESTANT CHURCH ARCHIVES : ARCHIVES OF THE HUGUENOT COMMUNITY IN LONDON – 1560-1889. 37 reels with printed guide – £1,850.00 – uk World [240]
FRENCH RENAISSANCE MUSICAL MANUSCRIPT – (8 parchment leaves, all with illuminated floridated borders of 15th century Burgundian origin) – 9 – us Sibley [780]
FRENCH REVIEW – v45- 1971- 1; v1- 5,6; v50- 9 – us UMI [440]
FRENCH REVIEW / American Association of Teachers of French – v. 1-28. 1927-1954 – 1 – us Princeton Micro [440]
FRENCH REVIEW – v1-28. 1927-54 – 1 – us Princeton Micro [073]
FRENCH REVOLUTION – (Collection de Documents inedits sur l'Histoire economique de la Revolution francaise Paris 1906-1952 1,129mf Dfl6,783.00; Collection de Documents relatifs a l'Histoire de Paris 1883-1923 706mf Dfl4,245.00) – 9 – ne IDC [944]
FRENCH REVOLUTION : CRITICAL AND HISTORICAL SOURCES – 217r – 1 – $14,000.00 – us OmniSys [944]
THE FRENCH REVOLUTION : A SKETCH / Mathews, Shailer – New York: Longmans, Green, 1906, c1901 – 1mf – us A.T.L.A. [944]
THE FRENCH REVOLUTION AND RELIGIOUS REFORM : AN ACCOUNT OF ECCLESIASTICAL LEGISLATION AND ITS INFLUENCE ON AFFAIRS IN FRANCE FROM 1789 TO 1804 / Sloane, William Milligan – New York: Scribner, 1901 – 1mf – us A.T.L.A. [944]
[FRENCH REVOLUTION PAMPHLET COLLECTION] – 19?? – 1 – CSUXANQ4874-B – us Hoover Inst Photo [320]
FRENCH REVOLUTION RESEARCH COLLECTION / ed by Lucas, Colin – (Sections: 1: Newspapers £3,750. 2: Memoirs & Autobiographies £3,750. 3: Basic Colls £5,565. 4: Bibliographical Tools £830. 5: Pre-Revolution Debate £1,200. 6: Political Themes £5,945. 7: Resistances £3,750. 8: Religion: £3,750. 9: Reorganisation of Society £4,675. 10: Economy: £3,750. 11: War and the Colonies £2,475. 12: Culture £3,560. Videodisc is available free of charge with an order for one or more sections) – Oxford: Micro Grafix Ltd, 1989 – 22,000mf – 9 – £43,000.00 – uk Micro Graphix [944]
THE FRENCH REVOLUTION RESEARCH COLLECTION AND VIDEODISK = LES ARCHIVES DE LA REVOLUTION FRANCAISE / ed by Lucas, Colin – (Videodisk (Images of the French Revolution), catalog and software only – $1,460.00) – Four Common Core sections, eight Thematic sections. Publ. in cooperation with the Bibliotheque Nationale, Paris – 9 – $65,000.00 – uk Hall [944]
FRENCH REVOLUTIONARY PAMPHLETS – 17,521mf – 9 – $41,500.00 $925.00y – us OmniSys [944]
FRENCH REVOLUTIONARY PERIODICALS – Publ. by private individuals. Various titles. See also: Maclure Collection, Bulletin de la Convention, Courier Republicain, Devaux, Gorsas, Lagrange, Prudhomme, Revolutions de France, Saultchev Reuil – 1 – us Primary [944]
FRENCH ROCOCO MUSIC FOR MUSETTE OR VIELLE – 36mf – 9 – MS-b – ne IDC [780]
FRENCH ROYAL AND ADMINISTRATIVE ACTS, 1256-1794 / France – 1 – us Primary [944]
THE FRENCH SCHOOLE-MAISTER / Desainliens, Claude – 1573. 334p. (English Linguistics Series 1500-1800) – 9 – us UMI [440]
FRENCH SOCIALIST CONGRESSES / ed by Haupt, Georges – 1876-1914. 70 titles reproducing official reports, newspaper articles, government reports, comprising the most complete collection possible on the multitude of congresses – 9 – fr Hachette [944]
FRENCH SOCIALIST CONGRESSES, 1876-1914 – (Collection of minutes, resolutions, newspaper articles and documents. 70 titles. Printed guide. Titles available individually) – 9 – fr Hachette [944]
French Sudan *see*
- JOURNAL OFFICIEL

THE FRENCH THEATER: 1789-1813 – Plays of the revolution and the empire. (Series). 132 extremely rare scripts. Ed. by Marc Regaldo – 9 – fr Hachette [790]
FRENCH TRANSLATIONS OF VIETNAMESE LEGAL ARTICLES AND ENACTMENTS... – 2mf – 9 SEL-121/1 – ne IDC [340]
THE FRENCH TUTOUR / Sherwood, Robert – 1634. 244p. (English Linguistics Series 1500-1800) – 9 – us UMI [440]
FRENCH VOYAGERS IN THE MEDITERRANEAN AND THE NEAR EAST, 16TH-19TH CENTURIES – 37 titles on 260 fiches – 9 – fr Hachette [910]
FRENCH WEST AFRICA : ANNUAIRE STATISTIQUE DE L'AFRIQUE OCCIDENTALE FRANCAISE 1949-1954 / French West Africa. Direction des Services de la Statistique Generale et de la Mecanographie – (Coll title: African Official Statistical Serials, 1867-1982) – 22mf – 9 – £185.00 – uk Chadwyck [960]
French West Africa *see*
- JOURNAL OFFICIEL
- LA MAURITANIE

French West Africa. Direction des Services de la Statistique Generale et de la Mecanographie *see* FRENCH WEST AFRICA
French West Africa. Direction Generale des Services Economiques et du Plan *see* LE FINANCEMENT DU PLAN, 1953-1957
THE FRENCH WRITER, ANDRE VIOLLIS, SPEAKS IN PARIS ABOUT THE ADMIRABLE DEFENSE OF THE SPANISH CAPITAL / Ardenne de Tizac, Andree Francoise Cardine d' – n.p. 193? Fiche W 724. (Blodgett Collection of Spanish Civil War Pamphlets) – 9 – us H.U. College Libr [946]
FRENCH-AMERICAN MILITARY RELATIONS IN THE CARIBBEAN THEATRE IN WORLD WAR 2 / U.S. Army. Caribbean Defense Command – 1 – $26.00 – us L of C Photodup [977]
THE FRENCHE METHODE / Bellot, James – 1588. 233p. (English Linguistics Series 1500-1800) – 9 – us UMI [440]
FRENCH-ENGLISH, ENGLISH-FRENCH LAW DICTIONARY / Langstaff, Annie Macdonald – Montreal Wilson and Lafleur, 1937. 141p. LL-2320 – 1 – us L of C Photodup [340]
A FRENCHMAN IN AMERICA: THE ANGLO-SAXON RACE REVISITED / O'Rell, Max – Toronto: W. Bryce, 1891.00149.(Pre-1900 Canadiana) – 9 – cn C.I.H.M. [971]
FRENCHMAN VALLEY TIMES – Palisade, NE. -w. Oct 1895-Nov 1896 – 1 – us NE Hist [071]
THE FRENCH-WAR PAPERS OF THE MARECHAL DE LEVIS / Casgrain, Henri-Raymond – ...with comments by francis parkman and justin winsor. Cambridge Mass: J. Wilson, 1888. 02545. (Pre-1900 Canadiana) – 9 – cn C.I.H.M. [971]
Freneau, Philip *see* LETTERS ON VARIOUS INTERESTING AND IMPORTANT SUBJECTS
Frenette, Alf. *see* LE CANADIEN
Frenkel, Leopoldo *see* EL JUSTICIALISMO
Frenkel, Zakharii Grigorevich *see*
- SOTSIALNAIA GIGIENA

Frenken, Goswin *see* DIE EXEMPLA DES JACOB VON VITRY
Frensdorf, F *see* MUENCHHAUSENS BERICHTE UEBER SEINE MISSION NACH BERLIN IN JUNI 1740
FRENSENIUS' ZEITSCHRIFT FUER ANALYTISCHE CHEMIE – v1-148. 1862-1955 – 1,5,6 – us Princeton Micro [540]
Frenssen, Gustav *see* DAS LEBEN DES HEILANDS DARGESTELLT
FRENTE POPULAR, BOLETIN DE LAS ORGANIZACIONES ANTIFASCISTAS HISPANAS DE LOS E. U. DE NORTE AMERICA – Brooklyn, 1937. Fiche W 899. (Blodgett Collection of Spanish Civil War Pamphlets) – 9 – us H.U. College Libr [946]
Frente Sandinista de Liberacion Nacional. Nicaragua *see* BARRICADA
Frenzel, A *see* DE ORIGINIBUS LINGUAE SORABICAE
Frenzel, Herbert Alfred *see* DATEN DEUTSCHER DICHTUNG
Freppel, l'Abbe *see* EXAMEN CRITIQUE DE LA VIE DE JESUS DE M. RENAN
Freppel, Monseigneur *see* CLEMENT D'ALEXANDRIE
Frere, Alexandre *see* TRANSPOSITIONS DE MUSIQUE..
FRERE ROBERT SYLVAIN, E.C., DOCTEUR ES LETTRES : BIBLIOGRAPHIE ANALYTIQUE / Vigneault-Page, Celine – 1964. SEM105P4 – 1mf – 9 – cn Bibl Nat [400]
Frere, S *see* UNE VILLE FRANCAISE MODERNE
Frere, Walter H *see*
- THE ANAPHORA OR GREAT EUCHARISTIC PRAYER
- THE ENGLISH CHURCH IN THE REIGNS OF ELIZABETH AND JAMES I. (1558-1625)
- ENGLISH CHURCH WAYS
- THE HEREFORD BREVIARY, VOL. 1
- THE HEREFORD BREVIARY, VOL. 2
- THE HEREFORD BREVIARY, VOL. 3
- THE MARIAN REACTION IN ITS RELATION TO THE ENGLISH CLERGY
- A NEW HISTORY OF THE BOOK OF COMMON PRAYER
- PURITAN MANIFESTOES
- SOME PRINCIPLES OF LITURGICAL REFORM
- STUDIES IN EARLY ROMAN LITURGY
- THE USE OF SARUM
- THE WINCHESTER TROPER, FROM MANUSCRIPTS OF THE 10TH AND 11TH CENTURIES...
- THE WINCHESTER TROPER, FROM MSS OF THE 10TH AND 11TH CENTURIES, WITH OTHER DOC. ILL. THE HISTORY OF TROPES IN ENGLAND AND FRANCE

Freres du Sacre-Coeur *see*
- DICTEES GRADUEES ET ANALYSES
- LIVRE DE LECTURE COURANTE
- MES PREMIERES LECONS DE REDACTION
- MES PREMIERES LECONS DE REDATION
- METHODE DE LECTURE

FRERES ET AMIS – Le Directoire du Cercle Social. Paris. Impr. du Cercle Social, in-folio plano – 9 – fr Hachette [321]
LES FRERES GRIMM / Tonnelat, Ernest – 1912 – 1 – us I.U. Libraries [390]
Freret, Nicolas *see*
- LETTRE DE THRASIBULE A LEUCIPPE
- OEUVRES COMPLETES DE FRERET...MISES DANS UN NOUVEL ORDRE, AUGMENTEES... PAR M. CHAMPOLLION-FIGEAC...

FRESCOES / Ouida – British Fiction Archive: Unit 3 – 9 – uk Bell [830]
Fresemann, Vietor, J *see* DE KRACHT VAN BUITENLANDSCHE VONNISSEN
Fresenius, J BG W *see*
- BEITRAEGE ZUR FLORA VON ABYSSINIEN
- BEITRAEGE ZUR FLORA VON AEGYPTEN UND ARABIEN
- BEITRAEGE ZUR MYKOLOGIE

FRESENIUS' ZEITSCHRIFT FUER ANALYTISCHE CHEMIE *see* ZEITSCHRIFT FUER ANALYTISCHE CHEMIE
FRESENIUS' ZEITSCHRIFT FUR ANALYTISCHE CHEMIE – v. 128-304. 1947-80 – 1,5,9 – 16,594.00 – us UMI [073]
A FRESH APPROACH TO THE NEW TESTAMENT / Dibelius, Martin – 1936 – 9 – $10.00 – us I.R.C. [240]
FRESH FISH : QUALITY AND QUALITY CHANGES – 1988 – 132p – it F.A.O. [360]
FRESH LAURELS FOR THE SUNDAY SCHOOL / Bradbury, William Batchelder – 1867 – 1 – 5.95 – us Baptist [240]
FRESH TRACKS IN THE BELGIAN CONGO FROM THE UGANDA BORDER TO THE MOUTH OF THE CONGO / Norden, Hermann – 57 photographs and two maps. London: H.F. & G. Witherby, 1924. 303p – 1 – us U.W. Library [960]
Freshman, Charles *see*
- THE AUTOBIOGRAPHY OF THE REV. CHARLES FRESHMAN, LATE RABBI OF THE JEWISH SYNAGOGUE AT QUEBEC, AND GRADUATE OF THE JEWISH THEOLOGICAL SEMINARY AT PRAGUE, AT PRESENT GERMAN WESLEYAN MINISTER AT PRESTON, ONTARIO
- THE JEWS AND THE ISRAELITES: THEIR RELIGION, PHILOSOPHY, TRADITIONS AND LITERATURE, IN CONNECTION WITH THEIR PAST AND PRESENT CONDITION, AND THEIR FUTURE PROSPECTS

FRESHMAN ELIGIBILITY IN INTERCOLLEGIATE ATHLETICS / Hick, Barbara A & Parkhouse, Bonnie L – 1992 – 1mf – 9 – $4.00 – us Microform Publ [370]
FRESHMAN ENGLISH NEWS – v. 1-. 1972- – 1. – apply; v.6- 1977- 5,6,9 – us UMI [370]
FRESHMEN ATHLETES' PERCEPTIONS OF ADJUSTMENT TO INTERCOLLEGIATE ATHLETICS / Armenth-Brothers, Francine R – Ball State University, 1995 – 2mf – 9 – $8.00 – PSY1837 – us Microform Publ [150]
FRESHWATER ALGAE OF SIERRA LEONE / Woodhead, N & Tweed, R D – 1959 – 1 – uk Microform Academic [580]
FRESH-WATER ALGAE OF THE UNITED STATES EXCL. OF THE DIATOMACEAE / Wolle, F – 504. 2 V. 1887 – 9 – ne IDC [580]
Freshwater Biological Association *see* THE FRITSCH COLLECTION OF ALGAL ILLUSTRATIONS
FRESHWATER FISHES OF ALABAMA / Auburn University. Agricultural Experiment Station – 1 reel – 1, 5 – us Spaulding [639]
THE FRESHWATER FISHES OF BRITISH GUIANA / Eigenmann, C H – Z-2100 1912 – 8 – ne IDC [590]
THE FRESH-WATER FISHES OF EUROPE / Seeley, H G – 2140 2. 1886 – 8 – ne IDC [590]
FRESHWATER PRAWN FARMING : A MANUAL FOR THE CULTURE OF MACROBRACHIUM ROSENBERGII – 1989 – 125p – it F.A.O. [639]
FRESH-WATER SHELL MOUNDS OF THE ST JOHN'S RIVER, FLORIDA / Wyman, J – Z 888 2. 1875 – 8 – ne IDC [590]
FRESHWATER-MARITIME INTERFACE : LEGAL AND INSTITUTIONAL ASPECTS – 1990 – 105p – it F.A.O. [340]
FRESKEN : NEUE DICHTUNGEN / Vierordt, Heinrich – Heidelberg: C Winter, 1901 – 1r – 1 – us U.W. Library [810]
Freslon, A *see* NECESSITE D'UN NOUVEAU PARTI POLITIQUE
FRESNO ASBAREZ – Fresno, CA. 1908-12; 1952-73 – 10r – 1 – $500.00 – C02254 – us Library Micro [071]
FRESNO ASSEMBLY CENTER DIRECTORY – Fresno Co, CA. 1942 – 1r – 1 – $50.00 – D025 – us Library Micro [978]
THE FRESNO BEE – Fresno, CA. 1922- – 1497+ r – 1 – $74,850.00 ($1,440.00y) – B02255 – us Library Micro [071]
FRESNO BEE AND GUIDE INDEX – Fresno, CA. 1870-1974 – 5r; 1mf set – 1,9 – $300.00 1 $500.00 set 9 – B06001 – us Library Micro [071]
FRESNO BUSINESS – Fresno, CA. 1967-1988 – 3r – 1 – $150.00 – B03599 – us Library Micro [071]
FRESNO BUSINESS *see* FRESNO COUNTY AND CITY CHAMBER OF COMMERCE BUSINESS
FRESNO CITY DIRECTORIES – Fresno Co, CA. 1871-1873; 1881-1882; 1886-1990 – 120r – 1 – $6,000.00 – D019 – us Library Micro [910]

FRESNO COUNTY – 1881-82; 1891; 1900-19; 1955-56 – 22r – 1 – $1,100.00 – D017 – us Library Micro [978]

FRESNO COUNTY AND CITY CHAMBER OF COMMERCE BUSINESS – (Cont. by: Fresno Business) – Fresno, CA. 1955-1967 – 1r – 1 – $50.00 – B03598 – us Library Micro [071]

FRESNO COUNTY AND CITY CHAMBER OF COMMERCE BUSINESS *see* FRESNO TOPICS

FRESNO COUNTY ASSESSOR'S ROLLS – Fresno Co, CA. 1860; 1862 – 2r – 1 – $100.00 – D018 – us Library Micro [978]

FRESNO COUNTY "BLUE BOOK" / Walker, Ben – Fresno Co, CA. 1941 – 1r – 1 – $50.00 – B40215 – us Library Micro [978]

FRESNO COUNTY, CALIFORNIA AND THE EVOLUTION OF THE FRUIT VALE, 1930 – Fresno Co, CA. 1930 – 1r – 1 – $50.00 – B40216 – us Library Micro [978]

FRESNO COUNTY ENTERPRISE – (Cont by: Selma Enterprise) – Selma, CA. 1891-1912 – 12r – 1 – $600.00 – B02992 – us Library Micro [071]

FRESNO DAILY MORNING REPUBLICAN – Fresno, CA. 1887-99 – 16r – 1 – $800.00 – R04026 – us Library Micro [071]

FRESNO, INYO, KERN, MERCED, SAN BERNARDINO, STANISLAUS AND TULARE COUNTIES – Fresno Co, CA. 1884-1885 – 2r – 1 – $100.00 – D020 – us Library Micro [978]

FRESNO, INYO, KERN, MERCED, SAN BERNARDINO, STANISLAUS AND TULARE COUNTIES – Inyo Co, CA. 1884-1885 – 2r – 1 – $100.00 – D020 – us Library Micro [978]

FRESNO, INYO, KERN, MERCED, SAN BERNARDINO, STANISLAUS AND TULARE COUNTIES – Kern Co, CA. 1884-1885 – 2r – 1 – $100.00 – D020 – us Library Micro [978]

FRESNO, INYO, KERN, MERCED, SAN BERNARDINO, STANISLAUS AND TULARE COUNTIES – Merced Co, CA. 1884-1885 – 2r – 1 – $100.00 – D020 – us Library Micro [978]

FRESNO, INYO, KERN, MERCED, SAN BERNARDINO, STANISLAUS AND TULARE COUNTIES – San Bernardino Co, CA. 1884-1885 – 2r – 1 – $100.00 – D020 – us Library Micro [978]

FRESNO, KERN, INYO, MERCED, SAN BERNARDINO, STANISLAUS AND TULARE COUNTIES – Stanislaus Co, CA. 1884-1885 – 2r – 1 – $100.00 – D020 – us Library Micro [978]

FRESNO, KERN, INYO, MERCED, SAN BERNARDINO, STANISLAUS AND TULARE COUNTIES – Tulare Co, CA. 1884-1885 – 2r – 1 – $100.00 – D020 – us Library Micro [978]

FRESNO NEGRO DIRECTORY – Fresno Co, CA. 1936 – 1r – 1 – $50.00 – D024 – us Library Micro [978]

THE FRESNO NEWS – Fresno, CA. 1936-1939 – 1r – 1 – $50.00 – B07454 – us Library Micro [370]

FRESNO POLICE ANNUALS – Fresno Co, CA. 1951-1990 – 6r – 1 – $300.00 – D026 – us Library Micro [350]

FRESNO SANBORN MAPS – Fresno Co, CA. 1888-1919 – 11r – 1 – $550.00 – D021 – us Library Micro [978]

FRESNO SHERIFF'S REVIEW – Fresno Co, CA. 1958-1990 – 6r – 1 – $300.00 – D027 – us Library Micro [350]

FRESNO TOPICS – (Cont. by: Fresno County and City Chamber of Commerce Business) – Fresno, CA. 1946-1955 – 1r – 1 – $50.00 – B03597 – us Library Micro [071]

FRESNO TRIBUNE – Fresno, CA. 1932-1933 – 6 – 1 – $300.00 – C03223 – us Library Micro [071]

FRESNO WEEKLY REPUBLICAN – Fresno, CA. 1876-1899 – 11r – 1 – $550.00 – R04027 – us Library Micro [071]

FRESNO/CLOVIS – 1966-67; 1980; 1989- – 15+ r – 1 – $750.00 – P00029 – us Library Micro [910]

FRESNO/MADERA – 1965-66; 1980; 1989- – 9+ r – 1 – $450.00 – P00030 – us Library Micro [910]

FREUD OR JUNG / Glover, Edward – New York: W.W. Norton, 1950. 207p. Includes index – 1 – us U.W. Library [616]

Freud, Sigmund *see*
- BEYOND THE PLEASURE PRINCIPLE
- GESAMMELTE SCHRIFTEN
- LE MOT D'ESPRIT ET SES RAPPORTS AVEC L'INCONSCIENT
- THE PROBLEM OF LAY-ANALYSES
- DIE TRAUMDEUTUNG

FREUDE DER KINDERJAHRE. GRABLIED AUF EINEN SOLDATEN / Schubert, Franz – Manuscript – 1 – us Sibley [780]

DIE FREUDE IN DEN SCHRIFTEN DES ALTEN BUNDES / Wuensche, August – Weimar: Emil Felber, 1896. 1 fiche – 9 – us A.T.L.A. [240]

FREUDE UND ARBEIT – Berlin, 1936-42 (incomplete) – 1 – Dist. gw Mikrofilm – gw Misc Inst [072]

FREUDENSTAEDTER KREISBOTE : BA DES SCHWARZWAELDER BOTEN – (Title change: Freudenstaedter Kreiszeitung, 30 Sep 1950) – Freudenstadt-Oberndorf, Germany. 1977- – ca 8r per yr – 1 – gw Mikrofilm [072]

FREUDENSTAEDTER KREISZEITUNG *see* FREUDENSTAEDTER KREISBOTE

Freudenthal, Jacob *see* DIE FLAVIUS JOSEPHUS BEIGELEGTE SCHRIFT UEBER DIE HERRSCHAFT DER VERNUNFT (4 MAKKABAEERBUCH)

FREUDENTHALER ZEITUNG – Freudenthal (Bruntal), Germany. 29 Mai 1920-5 Feb 1921 – 1r – 1 – gw Mikrofilm [072]

DER FREUND DER WAHRHEIT UND DES VOLKES – Bamberg, aug 18 1848-jan 29 1849 – 1r – 1 – Dist. gw Mikrofilm – gw Misc Inst [943]

DER FREUND DES LANDMANNES – Breslau, 1791, 1793 – 9 – Inquire at Mikrofilmarchiv for details – gw Misc Inst [072]

Freund, H A *see* RUSSIA FROM A TO Z

FREUND HEIN : EINE LEIDENSGESCHICHTE / Strauss, Emil – Berlin: S Fischer, 1921 – 1r – 1 – us U.W. Library [830]

Freund, W *see* ZUR JUDENFRAGE IN DEUTSCHLAND

Freund, Wilhelm *see* TRIENNIUM PHILOLOGICUM ODER GRUNDZUEGE DER PHILOLOGISCHEN WISSENSCHAFTEN FUER JUENGER DER PHILOLOGIE ZUR WIEDERHOLUNG UND SELBSTPRUEFUNG BEARB. VON WILHELM FREUND

DIE FREUNDE MACHEN DEN PHILOSOPHEN, DER ENGLAENDER, DER WALDBRUDER / Kaiser, Ilse – (Includes bibliographical references) – Erlangen: E T Jacob, 1917 – 1r – 1 – us U.W. Library [430]

FREUNDESBILDER AUS GOETHES LEBEN : STUDIEN ZUM LEBEN DES DICHTERS / Duentzer, Heinrich – (Includes bibliographical references) – 2., wohlfeile Ausg. Leipzig: Dyk, [1853] – 1r – 1 – us U.W. Library [430]

DIE FREUNDIN : ROMAN / Hoppe, Ingeborg Marei – Berlin: E Schmidt, 1944 – 1r – 1 – us U.W. Library [830]

FREUNDIN – Berlin, 1924-33 n10 – 2r – 1 – Dist. gw Mikrofilm – gw Misc Inst [072]

FREUND'S DAILY MUSIC AND DRAMA – New York City, 1882-83 – 1 – £60.00 – uk Chadwyck [780]

J C FREUND'S WEEKLY – New York City, 1883-92 – 6r – 1 – £330.00 – uk Chadwyck [780]

H E FREUND'S WEEKLY / MUSICAL AGE – New York City – 9 – £820.00 – uk Chadwyck [780]

DIE FREUNDSCHAFT / Tuegel, Ludwig – Hamburg: Hanseatische Verlagsanstalt, c1939 – 1r – 1 – us U.W. Library [830]

FREUNDSCHAFT – Berlin, 1919-33 n3 – 5r – 1 – Dist. gw Mikrofilm – gw Misc Inst [072]

FREUNDSCHAFT – (German Language) – Alma Ata (Kazakhstan), USSR. 1970-1981 – 12r – $600.00 – B63584 – us Library Micro [072]

FREUNDSCHAFT : MITTEILUNGEN DER TREUGEMEINSCHAFT SUDETENDEUTSCHER SOZIALDEMOKRATEN IN ENGLAND – London. Jan-Nov 1941 – 1r – 1 – gw Mikrofilm [072]

FREUNDSCHAFT : TAGESZEITUNG DER SOWJETDEUTSCHEN BEVEOLKERUNG KASACHSTANS – (Title change: Deutsche Allgemeine Zeitung der Russlanddeutschen, Alma-Ata) – Tselinograd (Celinograd), U.S.S.R. 1967-1967; 1972-1990; 1 Feb 1991- – 1 – gw Mikrofilm [943]

O FREUNDSCHAFT! : ZEITGEMAELDE IN DREI ABTHEILUNGEN / Tremler, Wenzel – Wien: U Klopf Senior und Alex Eurich, [18–?] – 1r – 1 – us U.W. Library [820]

FREUNDSCHAFT UND FREIHEIT : EIN BLATT FUER MAENNERRECHTE GEGEN SPIESSBUERGERMORAL, PFAFFENHERRSCHAFT UND WEIBERWIRTSCHAFT – Berlin, 1921 n1-11 – 1r – 1 – Dist. gw Mikrofilm – gw Misc Inst [072]

DAS FREUNDSCHAFTSBLATT *see* DIE INSEL DER EINSAMEN

Freville, AF J *see* ENCYCLOPEDIE GRAMMATICALE

Frey, Adolf *see*
- ERINNERUNGEN AN GOTTFRIED KELLER
- J. GAUDENZ VON SALIS-SEEWIS

Frey, Axel *see* BIBLIOTHEK DER DEUTSCHEN LITERATUR

Frey, Bernd *see* COMPARISON OF BODY COMPOSITION BETWEEN GERMAN AND AMERICAN ADULTS WITH MENTAL RETARDATION

Frey, F A *see* AN DIE SOUVERAINE DER RHEINISCHEN KONFOEDERATION

Frey, H *see* DIE LEPIDOPTEREN DER SCHWEIZ

Frey, Henri Nicolas *see*
- L'ANNAMITE, MERE DES LANGUES: COMMUNAUTE D'ORIGINE DES RACES CELTIQUES, SEMITIQUES, SOUDANAISES ET DE L'INDO-CHINE;..
- CAMPAGNE DANS LE HAUT SENEGAL ET DANS LE HAUT NIGER, 1885-1886

Frey, J *see* DIE GEBIETSHOHEIT IM SCHWEIZERISCHEN STAATSRECHT...

Frey, J A *see* BALTIJAS BAPTISTI UN BUNDE, JEB BALTIJAS BAPTISTU TAGADEJS STAHSOKLIS

Frey, Johannes *see* TOD, SEELENGLAUBE UND SEELENKULT IM ALTEN ISRAEL

Frey, Joseph Samuel Christian Frederick *see* THE SCRIPTURE TYPES

Frey, Lucius J *see* PHILOSOPHIE SOCIALE DEDIEE AU PEUPLE FRANCAIS

Frey, Peter *see* DIE PHILOSOPHIE DER KUNST DENKT SICH ZU ENDE

FREY TIDSKRIFT FOR VETENSKAP OCH KONST – Upsala, 1841-1850 – 3 – us Readex [073]

Frey, Winfried *see* TEXTKRITISCHE UNTERSUCHUNGEN ZU OTTES "ERACLIUS"

FREYA – Stuttgart, 1861-1867 (mf ed 1993) – 38mf – 9 – DM320.00 – 3-89131-127-3 – gw Fischer [305]

Freybe, Albert *see* DER ETHISCHE GEHALT IN GRILLPARZERS WERKEN

Freycinet, Louis de *see*
- VOYAGE AUTOUR DU MONDE EXECUTE SUR LES CORVETTES DE S.M. L'URANIE ET LA PHYSICIENNE, 1817-1820
- VOYAGE DE DECOUVERTE AUX TERRES AUSTRALES

DER FREYDENKER – Danzig (Gdansk), Poland. 1741-43 (incomplete) – 2r – 1 – gw Mikrofilm [943]

Freyer, CF *see* NEUERE BEITRAEGE ZUR SCHMETTERLINGSKUNDE

"FREYGEISTER, NATURALISTEN, ATHEISTEN" : EIN AUFSATZ LESSINGS IM WAHRSAGER / Consentius, Ernst – (Includes bibliographical references) – Leipzig: E Avenarius, 1899 – 1r – 1 – us U.W. Library [430]

Freymond, Jacques *see* LA PREMIERE INTERNATIONALE, RECUEIL DE DOCUMENTS

FREYMUETHIGE NACHRICHTEN VON NEUEN BUECHERN UND ANDERN ZUR GELEHRTHEIT GEHOERIGEN SACHEN 1.1744-20.1763 = WOECHENTLICHE ANZEIGEN ZUM VORTHEIL DER LIEBHABER DER WISSENSCHAFTEN UND KUENSTE 1.1764-3.1766 – Zuerich, 1744-1766 (mf ed 1995) – 90mf – 9 – DM1,400.00 – 3-89131-209-1 – gw Fischer [943]

Freytag, Gustav *see*
- DEBIT AND CREDIT
- GESAMMELTE WERKE
- MARTIN LUTHER

Frezier, AF *see* LA THEORIE ET LA PRATIQUE DE COUPE DES PIERRES ET DES BOIS.

DET FRI AKTUELT – (Yrly reel count varies) – 1992 – 1 – inquire – us Ross [072]

DET FRI AKTUELT *see* SOCIAL-DEMOKRATEN; AKTUELT; DET FRI AKTUELT

Frick, Alfons *see* UEBER POPES EINFLUSS AUF HAGEDORN

Frick Art Reference Library, New York *see* FRICK ART REFERENCE LIBRARY SALES CATALOGUE INDEX

Frick Art Reference Library. New York *see* THE FRICK ART REFERENCE LIBRARY ORIGINAL INDEX TO ART PERIODICALS

THE FRICK ART REFERENCE LIBRARY ORIGINAL INDEX TO ART PERIODICALS / Frick Art Reference Library. New York – 1983 – 12r – 1 – $1,715.00 export $2,080.00 – 0-8161-1584-2 – uk Hall [700]

FRICK ART REFERENCE LIBRARY SALES CATALOGUE INDEX / Frick Art Reference Library, New York – Boston: G.K. Hall & Co., 1992 – 180,000 cards on 230mf – 9 – $995.00 export $1,095.00 – 0-8161-1794-2 – uk Hall [017]

Frick, William K *see* HENRY MELCHIOR MUHLENBERG

Fricke, A *see* DAS VOELKERRECHTLICHE MANDAT

Fricke, G *see* METAPHYSIK UND DOGMATIK... UNTER BESONDERER BEZIEHUNG AUF DIE RITSCHL'SCHE THEOLOGIE

Fricke, Gustav Adolf *see* IST GOTT PERSOENLICH?

Fricke, Gustav Adolfus *see* DE MENTE DOGMATICA LOCI PAULINI AD ROM. 5, 12 SQ

Fricke, Heiko *see* UNTERSUCHUNG DES BEI DER VERFORMUNG VON METALLTRAEGERN ENTSTEHENDEN KOERPERSCHALL

Fricker, Karl Viktor *see* GEBIET UND GEBIETSHOHEIT

DIE FRICKES : A TRILOGY / Wilhelm, Hans Hermann – Berlin: Brunnen-Verlag. 3v. 1918-41 – 1 – us U.W. Library [830]

FRICOTS POLITIQUES: PEINTEURS DE MOEURS AMERICAINES / Fontaine, Raphael Ernest – Par Pekin. s.l.: s.n., 1878 (St. Hyacinthe Quebec: l'Union). 03142. (Pre-1900 Canadiana) – 9 – cn C.I.H.M. [971]

FRIDAY CALLER – Plainfield. Ind. -w. 1904-13, 1915 – 1 – us UMI [071]

FRIDAY FLYER – Canyon Lake, CA. 1990- – 1+ r – 1 – $50.00 ($50.00y) – R04013 – us Library Micro [071]

Friday, James R *see*
- ARCHIVES OF BRITISH MEN OF SCIENCE
- JOHN TYNDALL, NATURAL PHILOSOPHER, 1820-1893: CATALOGUE OF CORRESPONDENCE, JOURNALS AND COLLECTED PAPERS

Fridberger, B *see*
- 26 SCHLUSZREDEN DIE BALTHAZAR FRIDBERGER DEM J. ECKIO
- ACHT U. DREYSSIG SCHLUSZREDE
- ACHTZEHEN SCHLUSZREDE
- AIN SUMME AINS GANTZEN CHRISTLICHEN LEBENS
- VON KETZERN UND IREN VERBRENNEN ETC

Fridell, Egon *see* NOVALIS ALS PHILOSOPH

Fridenberg, A *see* RUKOPISNYE MATERIALY, KHRANIASHCHIESIA V GTSTM

Friderich, C G *see* NATURGESCHICHTE ALLER DEUTSCHEN ZIMMER-, HAUS- UND JAGDVOEGEL, NEBST EINEM ANHANGE UEBER DIE AUSLAENDISCHEN VOEGEL, WELCHE IN DEUTSCHLAND IM HANDEL VORKOMMEN

Fridlender, P *see* POLOVOI VOPROS, GOSUDARSTVO, KULTURA

Fridman, Saadii Lazarevich *see* KAPITALY GOSUDARSTVENNO I TORGOVLI SSSR

Fridolin, S P *see* MOLOCHNYE TOVARICHESTVA MOSKOVSKOI GUB. V 1914 GODU

Friebe, Freimut *see* DAS RISORGIMENTO IM ROMAN BEI GEORGE MEREDITH UND ANTONIO FOGAZZARO

Friebe, Karl *see*
- CHRISTIAN HOFMANN VON HOFMANNSWALDAUS GRABSCHRIFTEN
- UEBER C. HOFMANN VON HOFMANNSWALDAU UND DIE UMARBEITUNG SEINES GETREUEN SCHAEFERS

Friebe, Michael Horst *see* ORTSAUFLOESENDE TEMPERATURMESSUNG IM NIEDRIGFELD- UND HOCHFELD KERNSPINTOMOGRAPHEN UND UNTERSUCHUNG DER MOEGLICHKEIT ZUR ANWENDUNG IN DER INTRA-TUMORALEN LASERTHERAPIE

Fried, Constance R *see* AN EXAMINATION OF THE TEST CHARACTERISTICS OF THE 12 MINUTE AEROBIC SWIM TEST

Friedberg, A *see* CORPUS IURIS CANONICI 1-2

Friedberg, A S *see* SEFER HA-ZIKHRONOT

Friedberg, Emil *see*
- AUS DEUTSCHEN BUSSBUECHERN
- LEHRBUCH DES KATHOLISCHEN UND EVANGELISCHEN KIRCHENRECHTS
- DER STAAT UND DIE KATHOLISCHE KIRCHE IM GROSSHERZOGTHUM BADEN

FRIEDBERGER ANZEIGENBLATT – Friedberg. may 6-jul 23, 1949 – 1 – gw Mikrofilm [072]

FRIEDBERGER INTELLIGENZBLATT *see* INTELLIGENZBLATT FUER DIE PROVINZ OBERHESSEN

FRIEDBERGER WOCHENBLATT ZU DEN WETTERAUER ANZEIGEN *see* ALLGEMEINES FRIEDBERGER WOCHENBLATT FUER STADT- UND LANDLEUTE

FRIEDE AUF ERDEN! : ODER DIE AUSWEISUNG AM WEIHNACHTSABEND; SOZIALES BILD IN ZWEI AUFZUEGEN / Lipinski, Richard – 8. Aufl. Berlin: A Hoffmann, 1921 – 1r – 1 – us U.W. Library [820]

DER FRIEDENSBOTE : AMTLICHE ZEITSCHRIFT DER EVANGELISCHEN UND REFORMIERTEN KIRCHE – v1-96 nos 1-13. 1850-1958 (complete) – 32r – 1 – ATLA S0091 – us A.T.L.A. [073]

Friedensburg, Walter et al *see* JUBILAEUMSSCHRIFT (HEFT 100)

DIE FRIEDENSFAHRT DEUTSCHER KIRCHENMAENNER NACH ENGLAND / Bornemann, D W – Giessen, 1908 – 2mf – 9 – ILM-4073/1 – ne IDC [327]

DIE FRIEDENSFRONT – Heide, Germany. 1929-33 – 1 – gw Mikrofilm [072]

FRIEDENSTIMME – Halbstadt, Russia. (German Mennonites.) 1906-Nov. 1914 – 1 – 225.29 – us Baptist [240]

Friederich, G WE *see* ORCHESTRAL JOURNAL

Friederici, C *see* BIBLIOTHECA ORIENTALIS

FRIEDERIKE BRION : EIN BEITRAG ZU GOETHES ELSAESSISCHER SCHULD UND ZUR PSYCHOLOGIE SEINER LIEBE / List, Friedrich – Giessen: Ferber, 1923 – 1r – 1 – us U.W. Library [430]

FRIEDERIKE VON SESENHEIM IM LICHTE DER WAHRHEIT / Duentzer, Heinrich – Stuttgart: J G Cotta, 1893 – 1r – 1 – us U.W. Library [430]

Friedlaender, Benedict *see* DER FREIHEITLICHE SOZIALISMUS, IM GEGENSATZ ZUM STAATSKNECHTSTUM DER MARXISTEN

Friedlaender, D *see* AKTEN-STUECKE DIE REFORM DER JUEDISCHEN KOLONIEN IN DEN PREUSSISCHEN STAATEN BETREFFEND

Friedlaender, F J *see* MAGNETIC AND ELECTRICAL SEPARATION

Friedlaender, I *see* ARABISCH-DEUTSCHES LEXIKON ZUM SPRACHGEBRAUCH DES MAIMONIDES

Friedlaender, Ludwig *see* ROMAN LIFE AND MANNERS UNDER THE EARLY EMPIRE

Friedlaender, Moriz *see*
- DER ANTICHRIST IN DEN VORCHRISTLICHEN JUEDISCHEN QUELLEN
- ZUR ENTSTEHUNGSGESCHICHTE DES CHRISTENTHUMS...SEPTUAGINTA ZUM EVANGELIUM

FRIEDLAENDER ZEITUNG – Friedland (Frydlandt), Czechoslovakia. 5 Jan-31 Dez 1938 – 1r – 1 – gw Mikrofilm [072]

Friedman, M et al *see* TAXATION, INFLATION AND THE ROLE OF GOVERNMENT

Friedman, S *see* LE PROBLEME DES MINORITES ETHNIQUES ET SA SOLUTION PAR L'AUTONOMIE ET LA PERSONNIFICATION

Friedmann, Sigismund *see* LUDWIG ANZENGRUBER

Friedrich 2nd *see* DIE MORGEN STUNDEN EINES KOENIGES AN SEINEN BRUDER SOHN 1766

Friedrich, C *see* KOENNEN DEUTSCHE GERICHTE BEI AUSLAENDERN...

FRIEDRICH DE LA MOTTE FOUQUE ALS ERZAEHLER / Jeuthe, Lothar – (Includes bibliographical references) – Breslau: F Hirt, 1910 – 1 – us U.W. Library [430]

FRIEDRICH DER WEISE UND DIE SCHLOSSKIRCHE ZU WITTENBERG : FESTSCHRIFT ZUR EINWEIHUNG DER WITTENBERGER SCHLOSSKIRCHE, AM TAGE DES REFORMATIONSFESTES, DEN 31. OKTOBER 1892 / Koestlin, Julius – Wittenberg: R. Herrose, 1892 – 1mf – us A.T.L.A. [240]

FRIEDRICH ENGELS / Lenin, Vladimir Ilyich – SE-5394 1. 1963 – 9 – ne IDC [335]

Friedrich, Erich *see* DIE SIEGFRIED-TRAGOEDIE IM NIBELUNGENRING

FRIEDRICH GOTTLIEB KLOPSTOCK / ed by Luetcke, Heinrich – Bielefeld: Velhagen & Klasing, 1931 – 1 – us U.W. Library [810]

FRIEDRICH GOTTLIEB KLOPSTOCK : REDE GEHALTEN ZUR KLOPSTOCKFEIER DER UNIVERSITAET MARBURG AM 6. JULI 1924 / Elster, Ernst – Marburg a.L.: N G Elwert, 1924 – 1r – 1 – us U.W. Library [850]

FRIEDRICH GRIESE / Melcher, Kurt – (Includes bibliographical references) – Berlin: Junker und Duennhaupt, 1936 – 1 – us U.W. Library [430]

FRIEDRICH HAUGS EPIGRAMME UND IHRE QUELLEN / Steiner, Emil – (Includes bibliographical references) – [S.l.: s.n.], 1907 (Borna-Leipzig: Buchdruckerei R Noske) – 1r – 1 – us U.W. Library [430]

FRIEDRICH HEBBEL : DENKER, DICHTER, MENSCH / Schuder, Kurt – Leipzig: O Weber, [1909?] – 1r – 1 – us U.W. Library [430]

FRIEDRICH HEBBEL ALS DENKER / Muenz, Bernhard – (Includes bibliographical references) – 2. Aufl. Wien: W Braumueller, 1907 – 1r – 1 – us U.W. Library [430]

FRIEDRICH HEBBEL ALS LYRIKER / Engelhard, Karl – Leipzig: Verlag fuer Literature, Kunst und Musik, 1907 – 1r – 1 – us U.W. Library [430]

FRIEDRICH HEBBEL UND DIE GEGENWART : DIE TRAGISCHE SITUATION DES NORDISCHEN MENSCHEN / Tideman, Wilhelm – [Heidelberg]: Kampmann & Schnabel, 1922 – 1r – 1 – us U.W. Library [430]

FRIEDRICH HEBBEL UND OTTO LUDWIG / Bartels, Adolf – [S.l.: s.n.], 1895 – 1r – 1 – us U.W. Library [430]

FRIEDRICH HEBBEL UND SEINE DRAMEN : EIN VERSUCH / Walzel, Oskar Franz – Leipzig: B G Teubner, 1913 – 1r – 1 – us U.W. Library [430]

FRIEDRICH HEBBELS DEMETRIUS / Hebbel, Friedrich – Stuttgart: J G Cotta, [1910] – 1r – 1 – us U.W. Library [820]

FRIEDRICH HEBBELS DRAMATISCHER STIL / Wagner, Albert Malte – (Includes bibliographical references) – Hamburg: L Voss, 1910 – 1r – 1 – us U.W. Library [430]

FRIEDRICH HEBBELS UND RICHARD WAGNERS NIBELUNGEN-TRILOGIEN : EIN KRITISCHER BEITRAG ZUR GESCHICHTE DER NEUEREN NIBELUNGENDICHTUNG / Meinck, Ernst – Leipzig: M Hesse, 1905 – 1r – 1 – us U.W. Library [790]

FRIEDRICH HEINRICH JACOBI : A STUDY IN THE ORIGIN OF GERMAN REALISM / Wilde, Norman – (Includes bibliographical references) – New York: Columbia College, 1894 – 1r – 1 – us U.W. Library [430]

FRIEDRICH HEINRICH JACOBI IM VERHAELTNIS ZU SEINEN ZEITGENOSSEN, BESONDERS ZU GOETHE : EIN BEITRAG ZUR ENTWICKLUNGSGESCHICHTE DER NEUEN DEUTSCHEN LITERATUR / Deycks, Ferdinand – (Includes bibliographical references) – Frankfurt a.M.: Verlag der Joh. Christ. Hermann'schen Buchhandlung, F E Suchsland, 1848 – 1r – 1 – us U.W. Library [430]

FRIEDRICH HEINRICH JACOBI UND DIE FRUEHROMANTIK / Bossert, Theodor Adolf – (Includes bibliographical references) – Giessen: [s.n.], 1926 – 1r – 1 – us U.W. Library [430]

FRIEDRICH HOELDERLIN : LEBEN UND VERMAECHTNIS / Thiele, Herbert – Metz: H Pfleger, 1943 – 1r – 1 – us U.W. Library [920]

FRIEDRICH HOELDERLIN / Michel, Wilhelm – Weimar: E Lichtenstein, c1925 – 1r – 1 – us U.W. Library [430]

FRIEDRICH HOELDERLIN / Unruh, Friedrich Franz von – Stuttgart: G Truckenmueller, 1942 – 1r – 1 – us U.W. Library [920]

FRIEDRICH HOELDERLIN – FRITZ REUTER : ZWEI BIOGRAPHIEN / Wilbrandt, Adolf von – Berlin: E Hoffmann, 1894 – 1r – 1 – us U.W. Library [920]

FRIEDRICH HOELDERLIN UND JOHN KEATS ALS GEISTESVERWANDTE DICHTER / Wenzel, Guido – (Includes bibliographical references) – Magdeburg: E Baensch, 1896 – 1r – 1 – us U.W. Library [410]

Friedrich, Johann *see*
- BEITRAEGE ZUR GESCHICHTE DES JESUITEN-ORDENS
- DIE CONSTANTINISCHE SCHENKUNG
- IGNAZ VON DOELLINGER
- JOHANN ADAM MOEHLER, DER SYMBOLIKER
- JOHANN ADAM MOEHLER DER SYMBOLIKER
- JOHANN WESSEL
- JOHANNES HUS
- DAS LUKASEVANGELIUM UND DIE APOSTELGESCHICHTE
- DER MECHANISMUS DER VATIKANISCHEN RELIGION
- DIE MEROVINGERZEIT
- DIE ROEMERZEIT
- UEBER WAHRHEIT UND GERECHTIGKEIT
- ZUR AELTESTEN GESCHICHTE DES PRIMATES IN DER KIRCHE

Friedrich, Karl Josef *see* DAS HANS THOMA-BUCH

FRIEDRICH LEOPOLD STOLBERGS JUGENDPOESIE / Keiper, Wilhelm – (Includes bibliographical references) – Berlin: Mayer & Mueller, 1893 – 1r – 1 – us U.W. Library [430]

FRIEDRICH LEOPOLDS GRAFEN ZU STOLBERG ERSTE GATTIN AGNES GEB. VON WITZLEBEN : EIN LEBENSBILD AUS DER ZEIT DER EMPFINDLICHKEIT / Hellinghaus, Otto – Koeln, 1919 – 9 – DM48.00 – 3-89349-120-1 – gw Hänsel [943]

FRIEDRICH LUDWIG SCHROEDER : EIN BEITRAG ZUR DEUTSCHEN LITTERATUR- UND THEATERGESCHICHTE / Litzmann, Berthold – (Includes bibliographical references) – Hamburg: L Voss, 1890-94 – 1r – 1 – us U.W. Library [430]

Friedrich, Martin *see* ENCOMIUM MUSICAE VOCALIS ET INSTRUMENTALIS

FRIEDRICH MELCHIOR GRIMM ALS KRITIKER DER ZEITGENOESSISCHEN LITERATUR IN SEINER "CORRESPONDANCE LITTERAIRE" (1753-1770) : EINE LITERARHISTORISCHE STUDIE / Georges, Karl August – (Includes bibliographical references) – 1r – 1 – us U.W. Library [430]

[FRIEDRICH NAUMANN PAMPHLET COLLECTION] – 1897?-1969? – 1 – CSUXANR3401-B – us Hoover Inst Photo [943]

[FRIEDRICH NAUMANN STIFTUNG PAMPHLET COLLECTION] – 1974 – 1 – CSUXAMJ3140-B – us Hoover Inst Photo [943]

FRIEDRICH NIETZSCHES KULTURPHILOSOPHIE UND UMWERTUNGSLEHRE / Bubnov, Nikolai Mikhailovich – (Includes bibliographical references) – Leipzig: A Kroener, 1924 – 1r – 1 – us U.W. Library [190]

Friedrich, Paul *see*
- DER FALL HEBBEL
- FRANK WEDEKIND

FRIEDRICH RUECKERT : EIN LEBENS- UND CHARAKTERBILD FUER HAUS UND SCHULE / Beyer, Konrad – (Includes bibliographical references) – Frankfurt a. M: J D Sauerlaender, 1888 – 1r – 1 – us U.W. Library [920]

FRIEDRICH SCHILLER : LEBEN, WERK UND WIRKUNG / Kleinschmidt, Karl – Berlin: Kongress-Verlag, 1955 – 1r – 1 – us U.W. Library [920]

FRIEDRICH SCHILLER : STUERMENDE JUGEND. LEBENSWERK / Scholz, Wilhelm – Muenchen: Deutsches Verlagshaus Bong, c1956 – 1r – 1 – us U.W. Library [920]

FRIEDRICH SCHILLER, SEIN LEBEN UND SEINE DICHTUNGEN : MIT 701 ABBILDUNGEN NACH ZEITGENOESSISCHEN BILDERN UND ILLUSTRATIONEN / Guentter, Otto – Leipzig: J J Weber, c1925 – 1r – 1 – us U.W. Library [920]

FRIEDRICH SCHLEGEL 1794-1802 : SEINE PROSAISCHEN JUGENDSCHRIFTEN / ed by Minor, J – Wien: C Konegen, 1882 – 1r – 1 – us U.W. Library [430]

FRIEDRICH SCHLEIERMACHER : EINE AKADEMISCHE REDE, AM 21. NOVEMBER 1868 / Schenkel, Daniel – Heidelberg: J.C.B. Mohr, 1868 – 1mf – us A.T.L.A. [240]

FRIEDRICH SCHLEIERMACHER'S REDEN UEBER DIE RELIGION : KRITISCHE AUSGABE MIT ZUGRUNDELEGUNG DES TEXTES DER ERSTEN AUFLAGE / Schleiermacher, Friedrich; ed by Puenjer, G C Bernhard – Braunschweig: C.A. Schwetschke, 1879 – 1mf – us A.T.L.A. [240]

FRIEDRICH UND CAROLINE PERTHES / Adler, Ottilie – Leipzig, 1900 – 339p – 9 – DM48.00 – 3-89349-076-0 – gw Hänsel [930]

FRIEDRICH VON GENTZ STAATSSCHRIFTEN UND BRIEFE / ed by Eckhardt, H von – Muenchen. 2v. 1921 – 10mf – 9 – ne IDC [943]

FRIEDRICH VON HAGEDORNS JUGENDGEDICHTE : EINE LITERARHISTORISCHE SKIZZE / Badstueber, Hubert – (Includes bibliographical references) – Wien: A Pichler, 1904 – 1r – 1 – us U.W. Library [430]

FRIEDRICH VON HARDENBERGS "CHRISTENHEIT ODER EUROPA" / Hederer, Edgar – (Includes bibliographical references) – Zeulenroda: B Sporn, 1936 – 1r – 1 – us U.W. Library [430]

FRIEDRICH WILHELM WEBERS JUGENDLYRIK : AUF IHRE LITERARISCHEN QUELLEN UND VORBILDER UNTERSUCHT UND KRITISCH GEWUERDIGT MIT BENUTZUNG SEINES UNGEDRUCKTEN NACHLASSES / Peters, Maria – (Includes bibliographical references) – [S.l: s.n, 1916?] – 1 – us U.W. Library [810]

FRIEDRICH WILHELM ZACHARIAE IN BRAUNSCHWEIG / Zimmermann, Paul – (Includes bibliographical references and index) – Wolfenbuettel: J Zwissler, 1896 – 1r – 1 – us U.W. Library [430]

FRIEDRICH WILHELME / Rosenberg, Alfred – Muenchen: Zentralverlag der NSDAP, F Eher, 1944 – 1r – 1 – us U.W. Library [190]

Friedrichen, A *see* EMBLEMATA NOVA DAS IST NEW BILDERBUCH

Friedrichs, Heinz Michael *see* VALIDIERUNG FLUOROMETRISCHER BESTIMMUNGEN VON ENZYMAKTIVITAETEN UND BIOMASSEPARAMETERN UNTER BESONDERER BERUECKSICHTIGUNG MINIATURISIERTER TESTANSAETZE

THE FRIEND – Bloemfontein South Africa. 1891-1950 – 1 – sa State Libr [072]

THE FRIEND / The Society of Friends – 1843-1993. Continued annually – 1 – £4,350.00 – uk World [240]

A FRIEND AT COURT – v1-2. 1896-98 – 4mf – 9 – $6.00 – LLMC 82-924 – us L.L.M.C. [073]

FRIEND FREE PRESS – Friend, NE. -w. Apr. 1890-Oct. 1890 – 1 – us NE Hist [071]

THE FRIEND OF CHINA – Canton: William Tarrant, oct 6 1860-dec 21 1861; feb 18 1863 – us Res Libr [072]

THE FRIEND OF CHINA – Hong Kong: Richard Oswald, mar 17 1842 – us Res Libr [072]

THE FRIEND OF CHINA AND HONG KONG GAZETTE – Victoria, HK: [Richard Oswald], mar 24 1842-1858 – 10r – 1 – us Res Libr [072]

FRIEND OF INDIA – Serampore, India. 1852.-w. 1 reel – 1 – uk British Libr Newspaper [072]

FRIEND OF INDIA AND STATESMAN – Calcutta. 1878-89. – 32reels – 1 – ne IDC [072]

FRIEND OF PEACE – 1816-28 – 21mf – 9 – $85.00 – us UPA [320]

THE FRIEND OF RUSSIANS – (Cont: Russian Millions) – Chicago, IL. nos 12-44. 1942-48 (complete) – 1r – 1 – ATLA S0713B – us A.T.L.A. [073]

FRIEND OF THE FREE STATE AND BLOEMFONTEIN GAZETTE – Bloemfontein, South Africa. 1857-90 – 1 – sa State Libr [072]

A FRIEND OF THE QUEEN (MARIE ANTOINETTE-COUNT DE FERSEN) / Gaulot, Paul – Trans. by Mrs. Cashel Hoey, authorized ed. New York: Appleton, 1893. xii,371p. port – 1 – us U.W. Library [920]

FRIEND OF THE SOVEREIGNTY AND BLOEMFONTEIN GAZETTE – Bloemfontein, South Africa. 1850-57 – 1 – sa State Libr [960]

FRIEND SENTINEL – Friend, NE. -w. Jan. 1895-Aug. 1907. Incomplete; Dec. 1911; Mar. 1912; Jul. 1912- – 1 – us NE Hist [071]

FRIEND TELEGRAPH – Friend, NE. -w. Feb. 1878-Mar. 1879; Sep. 1879-Jan. 1888; Mar. 1888-Feb. 1891. Incomplete; Jan. 1892-Apr. 1895; Jul. 1895-Aug. 1942 – 1 – us NE Hist [071]

A FRIENDLY ADDRESS TO THE METHODISTS / Hall, R – Nottingham, 1796 – 1mf – 9 – MP-593/1 – ne IDC [240]

FRIENDLY AND COMPASSIONATE ADDRESS TO ALL SERIOUS AND WELL DISPOSED METHODISTS,... / Jephson, A – London, 1760 – 1mf – 9 – MP-397/1 – ne IDC [240]

THE FRIENDLY ARCTIC / Stefansson, Vilhjalmur – BN 406 2. 1922 – 8 – ne IDC [910]

A FRIENDLY EXCHANGE OF VIEWS BETWEEN QUEBEC AND ONTARIO – Quebec: the Telegraph Printing Co, 1917. SEM105P1438 – 1mf – 9 – Can$2.25 – cn Bibl Nat [971]

A FRIENDLY LETTER – 1981-90 (complete) – 2r – 1 – ATLA S0772 – us A.T.L.A. [073]

FRIENDLY RELATIONS AND CULTURAL EXCHANGE BETWEEN THE CHINESE AND INDONESIAN PEOPLES / Chu, Hsieh – In Chinese. SE-10,080 1. 1956 – 9 – ne IDC [950]

FRIENDLY REMARKS OCCASIONED BY THE SPIRIT AND DOCTRINES CONTAINED IN THE REV. MR FLETCHER'S 'VINDICATION', AND MORE PARTICULARLY IN HIS 'SECOND CHECK TO ANTINOMIANISM';... / Hill, Richard – London, 1772 – 1mf – 9 – MP-481/1 – ne IDC [240]

THE FRIENDLY RETRIEVERS : A CALM ADDRESS,... – [N.p.], 1780 – 1mf – 9 – MP-541/1 – ne IDC [240]

A FRIENDLY TALK ABOUT REVISION / Morris, Edward D – 1891 – 9 – $50.00 – us Presbyterian [240]

FRIENDS AND FOES IN THE TRANSKEI : AN ENGLISHWOMAN'S EXPERIENCE DURING THE CAPE FRONTIER WAR OF 1877-78 / Pritchard, Helen M – London: Low, Marston, Searle & Rivington, 1880 – 1 – us Res Libr [960]

FRIENDS ASSOCIATION FOR ABOLISHING STATE REGULATION OF VICE (1873-1910) AND FRIENDS ASSOCIATION FOR THE PROMOTION OF SOCIAL PURITY (1910-1926) / Religious Society of Friends (Quakers) – 4r – 1 – £180.00 – 1-897955-29-4 – uk Academic [360]

FRIENDS (CCC288) / Surdam, T Janet – (In Chinese) – 1st ed. Hong Kong: Council on Christian Literature for Overseas Chinese, 1958 – 1r – 1 – 1984-6627 – us A.T.L.A. [240]

FRIENDS FOR JAMAICA – New York. 103 docs. 1980-1991 – 18mf – 9 – ne IDC [320]

FRIENDS GENERAL CONFERENCE / Society of Friends – 1968-90 (complete) – Inquire – 1 – ATLA S0592 – us A.T.L.A. [073]

FRIENDS IN COUNCIL : A SERIES OF READINGS AND DISCOURSES THEREON / Helps, Arthur – London. 2v. 1872 – 1r – 1 – us Ross [975]

THE FRIENDS OF CHRIST KEEP HIS COMMANDMENTS OR OBEDIENCE THE TEST OF DISCIPLESHIP / Fittz, Hervey – (A sermon). 1834 – 1 – 5.00 – us Baptist [240]

Friends of Democracy and Independence in Spain *see* ITALIANS IN SPAIN

FRIENDS OF MOSLEMS – v1 no 2-v25 no 3. 1927-51 (complete) – 1r – 1 – ATLA S0276 – us A.T.L.A. [260]

FRIENDS OF RUSSIA *see* GOSPEL IN RUSSIA

THE FRIENDS OF RUSSIANS *see* RUSSIAN MILLIONS

FRIENDS OF RUSSIANS – (Filmed with: Gospel in Russia) – London. nos 12-44. 1937-41 (complete) – 1r – 1 – ATLA S0702A – us A.T.L.A. [073]

Friends of Spain *see* THE SPANISH PEOPLE ARE FIGHTING OUR BATTLE

Friends of Spanish Democracy *see* SPAIN

FRIENDS OF THE FILIPINO PEOPLE (FFP) – Durham. Doc 1-43; 45-47. 1980-1989 – 9mf – 9 – ne IDC [320]

FRIENDS OF WINE – (v17- 1980- 5,6,9) – v12- 1975- Continues: Amis du Vin – 1 – us UMI [640]

FRIENDS ORIENTAL NEWS – v25-51. Jun 1934-May 1962 (complete) – 1r – 1 – ATLA S0495 – us A.T.L.A. [073]

FRIENDS' QUARTERLY / The Society of Friends – 1867-1993. Continued annually – 1 – £1,095.00 – uk World [240]

FRIENDS WORLD COMMITTEE FOR CONSULTATION : QUAKER UNITED NATIONS OFFICE (GENEVA) – Geneva. 44 docs. 1988-1991 – 6mf – 9 – ne IDC [320]

FRIENDS WORLD NEWS – v1-27. 1939-86 (complete) – 2r – 1 – ATLA S0821 – us A.T.L.A. [073]

FRIENDSHIP / Black, Hugh – Chicago: Fleming H Revell, c1903 – 1mf – 9 – 0-8370-6021-4 – 1986-0021 – us A.T.L.A. [240]

FRIENDSHIP / Ouida – British Fiction Archive: Unit 3 – 9 – uk Bell [830]

FRIENDSHIP BAPTIST CHURCH. JEFFERSON COUNTY. TENNESSEE : CHURCH RECORDS – 12 Mar 1819-97 – 1 – 12.78 – us Baptist [240]

FRIENDSHIP BAPTIST CHURCH. JEFFERSON COUNTY. TENNESSEE : CHURCH RECORDS – 1858-1902 – 1 – 8.28 – us Baptist [240]

FRIENDSHIP BAPTIST CHURCH. SPARTANBURG COUNTY. SOUTH CAROLINA : CHURCH RECORDS – 1801-1933, 1919-74 – 1 – 72.68 – us Baptist [240]

THE FRIENDSHIP OF BOOKS AND OTHER LECTURES / Maurice, Frederick Denison; ed by Hughes, T – London: Macmillan, 2nd ed 1874 – 1r – 1 – 1-55879-362-3 – uk Libr Preservation [070]

FRIENDSHIP'S GARLAN : BEING THE CONVERSATIONS, LETTERS AND OPINIONS OF THE LATE ARMINIUS, BARON VON THUNDER-TEN-TRONCKH... / Arnold, Matthew – London: Smith, Elder, 1871 – 1 roll – 1 – 1-55879-520-0 – uk Libr Preservation [860]

FRIENDSHIP'S OFFERING – 1824-44 – 98mf – 9 – £720.00 – uk Chadwyck [800]

Fries, Adelaide L *see*
- THE MORAVIANS IN GEORGIA, 1735-1740

Fries, BF *see* A HISTORY OF SCANDINAVIAN FISHES

Fries, E M *see*
- ELENCHUS FUNGORUM
- EPICRISIS SYSTEMATIS MYCOLOGICA
- HYMENOMYCETES EUROPAEI
- LICHENOGRAPHIA EUROPAEA REFORMATA
- LICHENUM DIANOME NOVA
- NAGRE TROPISKE LAFVAR
- OBSERVATIONES MYCOLOGICAE
- SCHEDULAE CRITICAE DE LICHENIBUS EXSICCATIS SUECIAE
- SUMMA VEGETABILIUM SCANDINAVIAE
- SYMBOLAE GASTEROMYCORUM AD ILLUSTRANDAM FLORAM SVECICAM
- SYSTEMA MYCOLOGICUM
- SYSTEMA ORBIS VEGETABILIS

Fries, J *see*
- DICTIONARIOLUM PUERORUM TRIBUS LINGUIS LATINA, GALLICA ET GERMANICA CONSCRIPTUM...
- DICTIONARIUM LATINO-GERMANICUM...

Fries, Samuel Andreas *see* DIE GESETZESSCHRIFT DES KOENIGS JOSIA

Fries, T M *see*
- EN BOTANISK RESA I FINMARKEN
- LICHENES ARCTOI EUROPAE GROENLANDIAEQUE
- LICHENOGRAPHIA SCANDINAVICA
- MONOGRAPHIA STEREOCAULORUM ET PHILPHORUM
- NYA SKANDINAVISKA LAFARTER

FRIESEN-COURIER – Bredstedt, apr 11 1903-42 – 1 – Inquire at Mikrofilmarchiv for details – gw Misc Inst [072]

Frigerio, Reinaldo A *see* INTRODUCCION AL ESTUDIO DEL PROBLEMA AGRARIO ARGENTINO

Frigerio, Rogelio *see*
- LAS CONDICIONES DE LA VICTORIA
- CONDICIONES Y METODOS PARA LA RECONSTITUCION DEL FRENTE DEL 23 DE FEBRERO
- DESARROLLO Y BIENESTAR, O CONTRACCION, MISERIA Y DICTADURA
- DIEZ ANOS DE LA CRISIS ARGENTINA
- UNIDAD NACIONAL O LUCHA DE FACCIONES

FRIHETSVAENNEN – Stockholm, 1860-64 – 9 – sw Kungliga [072]

Friis, A *see* DANMARK EKSPEDITIONEN TIL GRONLANDS NORDOSTKYST

Frikkers, C *see* STRAFRECHTELIJKE ONTZETTING VAN RECHTEN...

Frimigacci, D *see* LA PREHISTOIRE NEO-CALEDONIENNE

Frimmel, Theodor *see* DER ANONIMO MORELLIANO

FRIMORGEN – Riga. 2 Jan-13 May 1934. Incomplete. KJ-92-52-3 – 1 – ne IDC [947]

FRIMORGN – (Missing: nos 1,8,76,78-81) – Riga, Jan 2-May 13 1934 – 1r – 1 – J-92-52/3 – ne IDC [947]

FRIMORGN – Riga, 1926-34 – 7r – 1 – us Ross [072]

FRIMORGN – Riga. Apr 16 1926-May 13 1934. Incomplete – 1 – us NY Public [072]

Fripp, Edgar Innes *see* COMPOSITION OF THE BOOK OF GENESIS: WITH ENGLISH TEXT AND ANALYSIS

Frisch, J L *see* BESCHREIBUNGEN VON ALLERLEY INSECTEN IN DEUTSCHLAND

FRISCHE CLAVIER FRUECHTE.. / Kuhnau, J – 1700 – 9 – us Sibley [780]

Frischmann, D *see*
- RESHAFIM
- SIFRUT

Frischmuth, L *see* GEDAGTEN OVER DE BEGINSELEN EN ONDERWYZINGEN DES CLAVECIMBAALS

DAS FRISIERTE TESTAMENT : EINE KOMOEDIE IN PROSA / Pfannenschmidt, Heinz – Berlin: P Neff, c1940 – 1r – 1 – us U.W. Library [430]

Fristoe, William *see* A CONCISE HISTORY OF THE KETOCTON BAPTIST ASSOCIATION

FRIT DANMARK – London, UK. 16 Dec 1940-29 Jun 1945 – 1 – uk British Libr Newspaper [072]

Frith, Francis *see* THE QUAKER IDEAL

Fritsch, A *see* MILES TRANSIENS INNOXIUS,...

Fritsch, A J *see* NATURGESCHICHTE DER VOEGEL EUROPAS

THE FRITSCH COLLECTION OF ALGAL ILLUSTRATIONS / ed by Freshwater Biological Association – (A Fuji REP2 microfiche read (value Dfl 500.00) comes free with the complete collection) – 2,785mf – 9 – ne IDC [580]

Fritsch, Erdmann *see* ISLAM UND CHRISTENTUM IM MITTELALTER

Fritsch, F E *see*
- A COLLECTION OF 500,000 ALGAL ILLUSTRATIONS, WITH INDEX AND FOREWORD BY DR. J.W.G. LUND
- A TREATISE ON THE BRITISH FRESHWATER ALGAE

Fritsch, FE *see* THE COLLECTION OF ALGAE ILLUSTRATIONS

Fritsch, Otto *see* MARTIN OPITZEN'S BUCH VON DER DEUTSCHEN POETEREI

Fritts, Charles Edgar *see* THE WATCH ADJUSTER'S MANUAL: BEING A PRACTICAL GUIDE FOR THE WATCH AND CHRONOMETER ADJUSTER FOR ISOCHRONISM, POSITIONS AND TEMPERATURES

Fritts, Suzanne M *see* PSYCHOLOGICAL FACTORS THAT PREDISPOSE ATHLETES TO INJURY

Fritz, B *see* ONDERWYS OM OP EENE TUIGWERKELYKE WYZE CLAVIEREN, CLAVECIMBELS EN ORGELS IN ALLE 24 TOONEN EVEN ZUIVER TE STEMMEN

Fritz, Dr. *see* DER JUNGE MYSTIKER, ODER, DIE DREI LETZTEN FESTZEITEN AUS SEINEM LEBEN

FRITZ FLESCH COLLECTION ON JEWS IN SOUTH AFRICA / Flesch, Fritz, collector – 1946-72 – 1 – us Res Libr [270]

Fritz, J F *see* NEU EROEFFNETES IN HUNDERT SPRACHEN BESTEHENDES A.B.C. BUCH,...

FRITZ MAUTHNERS AUSGEWAEHLT SCHRIFTEN / Mauthner, Fritz – Stuttgart und Berlin, Deutsche Verlags-anstalt, c 1910. 6 v. Film Mas 8595 – 1 – us H.U. Library [080]

FRITZ REUTER / Griese, Friedrich – Stuttgart: J G Cotta, 1938 – 1r – 1 – us U.W. Library [430]

FRITZ REUTER, HEINRICH SEIDEL UND DER HUMOR IN DER NEUEREN DEUTSCHEN DICHTUNG / Biese, Alfred – Kiel: Lipsius und Tischer, 1891 – 1r – 1 – us U.W. Library [430]

FRITZ STAVENHAGENS "MUDDER MEWS" / Stolle, Carl – (Includes bibliographical references) – Marburg a.L.: N G Elwert, 1926 – 1r – 1 – us U.W. Library [430]

FRITZ UND DIE SOLDATENSTIEFEL : GESCHICHTEN VOM KRIEGE / Wiemer, Rudolf Otto – Muenchen: Deutscher Volksverlag, 1943 – 1r – 1 – us U.W. Library [943]

Fritzhans, J *see* WIE MANN DAS KLAR HELL GOTS WORT PREDIGEN SOLL

FRITZLAR-HOMBERGER ALLGEMEINE *see* HESSISCHE ALLGEMEINE (HNA)

Fritzsch, Robert *see* UEBER WOLFRAMS VON ESCHENBACH RELIGIOSITAET

Fritzsche, Volkmar *see* DAS BERUFSBEWUSSTSEIN JESU MIT BERUECKSICHTIGUNG GESCHICHTLICHER ANALOGIEN UNTERSUCHT

Frivaldszky von Frivald, I *see* PLANTAE NOVAE TURCICAE EX BALCANO

Frizen, F *see* POD GNETOM RELIGII

FRNM BULLETIN *see* PARAPSYCHOLOGY BULLETIN

Frobisher, M *see* THE THREE VOYAGES..

Froeb, Hermann *see* ERNST KOCHS "PRINZ ROSA-STRAMIN"

FROEBEL JOURNAL – 1965-74 – 9 – uk Microform Academic [073]

EIN FROEHLICH HERZ / Kinau, Rudolf – Hamburg: Quickborn-Verlag, 1941 – 1r – 1 – us U.W. Library [430]

DER FROEHLICHE BOTSCHAFTER – (Title varies) – 1841-1901 (complete) – 17r – 1 – ATLA S0115 – us A.T.L.A. [240]

DER FROEHLICHE WEINBERG : LUSTSPIEL IN DREI AKTEN / Zuckmayer, Carl – Berlin: Propylaeen-Verlag, c1925 – 1r – 1 – us U.W. Library [820]

DIE FROEHLICHE WEINREISE *see* DIE WEINHEILIGEN

Froehling, Lori A *see* EFFECTIVENESS OF EXERCISE VERSUS EXERCISE PLUS TAPE IN THE MANAGEMENT OF FEMALES WITH PATELLOFEMORAL PAIN

Froelich, J *see* MUSCI BORNMULLERIANA; BRYOPHTEN AUS IRAN

Froelich, Jean Claude *see* LA TRIBU KONKOMBA DU NORD TOGO

DIE FROEMMIGKEIT DES GRAFEN LUDWIG VON ZINZENDORF : EIN PSYCHOANALYTISCHER BEITRAG ZUR KENNTNIS DER RELIGIOESEN SUBLIMIERUNGSPROZESSE UND ZUR ERKLAERUNG DES PIETISMUS / Pfister, Oskar – Leipzig: F. Deuticke, 1910 – 1mf – us A.T.L.A. [150]

Froger, Dom J *see* LES ORIGINES DE LA PRIME

Froger, Francois *see* RELATION D'UN VOYAGE FAIT EN 1695, 1696 ET 1697 AUX COTES D'AFRIQUE DETROIT DE MAGELLAN, BREZIL, CAYENNE ET ANTILLES PAR UNE ESCADRE DES VAISSEAUX DU ROI COMMANDEE PAR M. DE GENNES

Froger, L *see* LES CHANTS DE LA MESSE AUX 8TH ET 9TH SIECLE

FROHES LEBEN : GESCHICHTEN / Steguweit, Heinz – Muenchen: A Langen, G Mueller, 1943, c1934 – 1r – 1 – us U.W. Library [830]

Frohlich, Louis D *see* THE LAW OF MOTION PICTURES, INCLUDING THE LAW OF THE THEATRE TREATING OF THE VARIOUS RIGHTS OF THE AUTHOR, ACTOR.

Frohman, Daniel *see* MEMORIES OF A MANAGER; REMINISCENCES OF THE OLD LYCEUM AND OF SOME PLAYERS OF THE LAST QUARTER CENTURY

Frohnmeyer, Ludwig Johannes *see* A PROGRESSIVE GRAMMAR OF THE MALAYALAM LANGUAGE FOR EUROPEANS

Frohschammer, J *see*
- ATHENAEUM
- ATHENAEUM. PHILISOPHISCHE ZEITSCHRIFT
- DAS NEUE WISSEN UND DER NEUE GLAUBE

Froidmont, Libert *see* LABYRINTHVS SIVE DE COMPOSITIONE CONTINVI LIBER VNVS

Froitzheim, Johann *see*
- GOETHE UND HEINRICH LEOPOLD WAGNER
- LENZ UND GOETHE

FROM AKBAR TO AUSINGZEB / Moreland, W H – 1923 – 1 – uk Microform Academic [330]

FROM ANTICIPATION TO ACTION : A HANDBOOK OF STRATEGIC PROSPECTIVE / Godet, Michel – 1994 – 284p – 9 – 92-3-102832-4 – fr UNESCO [650]

FROM APOLLYONVILLE TO THE HOLY CITY: A POEM / Allen, John Slater – 1880. 05825. (Pre-1900 Canadiana) – 9 – cn C.I.H.M. [810]

FROM ATHEISM TO CHRISTIANITY / Porter, George P – New York: Nelson & Phillips, 1873. 1 fiche. 8370-4781-1 – 9 – us A.T.L.A. [240]

FROM BACA TO BEULAH: SEQUEL TO VALLEY OF BACA / Smith, Jennie – 1880 – 9 – us A.T.L.A. [240]

FROM BOMBAY TO BUSHIRE, AND BUSSORA; INCLUDING AN ACCOUNT OF THE PRESENT STATE OF PERSIA, AND NOTES ON THE PERSIAN WAR / Shepherd, William Ashton – London: R. Bentley, 1857. xi,236p – 1 – us U.W. Library [950]

FROM BOSTON TO BAREILLY AND BACK / Butler, William – New York: Phillips & Hunt; Cincinnati: Cranston & Stowe, 1885. 512p – 1 – us U.W. Library [240]

FROM BUDDHISM TO CHRISTIANITY (CCC207) = SENG LU HSIN CHU CHI / Kung, Tien-min – (In Chinese) – 1st ed. Hong Kong: Council on Christian Literature for Overseas Chinese, 1958 – 1r – 1 – 1984-B500 – us A.T.L.A. [230]

FROM 'COOLIE LOCATION' TO GROUP AREA : A BRIEF ACCOUNT OF JOHANNESBURG'S INDIAN COMMUNITY / Randall, Peter & Desai, Yunus – Johannesburg, South African Institute of Race Relations, 1967 – us Res Libr [960]

FROM DARKNESS TO LIGHT: THE STORY OF A TELUGU CONVERT / Clough, John Everett – 3rd ed. Boston: W.G. Corthell, 1882. 288p. illus – 1 – us U.W. Library [240]

FROM DATA TO ACTION : INFORMATION SYSTEMS IN EDUCATIONAL PLANNING / ed by Chapman, David W & Mahlck, Lars O – 1993 – 259p – 9 – 92-803-1148-4 – Co-Published with Pergamon Press – fr UNESCO [000]
FROM EQUIVALENCE OF DEGREES TO EVALUATION OF COMPETENCE : PRESENT PROCEDURES AND PRACTICE. NEW AVENUES / Guiton, Jean – 1977 – 138p – 9 – 92-3-101419-6 – fr UNESCO [331]
FROM FAR FORMOSA : THE ISLAND, ITS PEOPLE AND MISSIONS / Mackay, George Leslie; ed by Macdonald, J A – New York: F.H. Revell, c1895 – 1mf – us A.T.L.A. [950]
FROM FUNDAMENTAL TO ACCESSORY IN THE DEVELOPMENT OF THE NERVOUS SYSTEM AND OF MOVEMENTS / Burk, Frederic – 1898? 00872. (Pre-1900 Canadiana) – 9 – cn C.I.H.M. [610]
FROM HIS BIRTH, 9 SEPT 1826 UNTIL AUG 1876 / Spencer, John Henderson – Incomplete transcription by Mrs. J. Henry Simpson, 1947. 230p – 1 – 8.05 – us Baptist [240]
FROM JEWISH MESSIANISM TO THE CHRISTIAN CHURCH / Alfaric, Prosper – 9 – 1.00f – at Libertarian Micro [320]
FROM JOSEPH TO JOSHUA / Rowley, H H – Oxford, 1948 – 9 – $10.00 – us I.R.C. [220]
FROM MALACHI TO MATTHEW : OUTLINES OF THE HISTORY OF JUDEA FROM 440 TO 4 B.C. / Moss, Richard Waddy – (Includes index) – London: Charles H Kelly, 1899 – 1mf – 9 – 0-8370-9406-2 – 1986-3406 – us A.T.L.A. [270]
FROM MANET TO TOULOUSE-LAUTREC / British Museum – (395 lithographs including works by Mnat, Redon, Pissaro, Millet, Gaugin, Degas, Renoir, Cezanne and Toulouse-Lautrec) – 1983 – 6mf – 15 – $144.00 – 0-907696-12-0 – uk Emmett [760]
FROM NAPTOWN TO SPORTSTOWN : GROWTH POLITICS, URBAN DEVELOPMENT, AND ECONOMIC CHANGE IN INDIANAPOLIS / Schimmel, Kimberly S – 1994 – 3mf – $12.00 – us Microform Publ [303]
FROM NOWHERE TO BEULAHLAND : A PERSONAL NARRATIVE / Brown, Elijah P – 2nd ed. Chicago: Winona, 1904 – 1mf – 9 – 0-8370-7368-5 – 1986-1368 – us A.T.L.A. [920]
FROM OLIVET TO PATMOS: THE FIRST CHRISTIAN CENTURY IN PICTURE AND STORY / Houghton, Louise – New York: American Tract Society, 1893. 1 fiche – 9 – us A.T.L.A. [240]
FROM PRINTED CATALOGUE TO DATA BASE / Karni, R S – Paper for the Asian Librarianship Panel,. at the 30th International Congress. Mexico City, 3-8 Aug 1976. Leiden. 1976. BSE-20,109 1 – 9 – ne IDC [510]
FROM PUSHKIN TO MAYAKOVSKY / Lavrin, J – A Study in the Evolution of a Literature. Sylvan Press. London. 1948. BR-1357 2 – 8 – ne IDC [460]
FROM SLAVERY TO A BISHOPRIC, OR, THE LIFE OF BISHOP WALTER HAWKINS OF THE BRITISH METHODIST EPISCOPAL CHURCH, CANADA / Edwards, S J Celestine – London: J. Kensit, 1891. 02887. (Pre-1900 Canadiana) – 9 – cn C.I.H.M. [971]
FROM SPACE LAB TO SPACE STATION – (v56 1984, Advances) – 1984 – 9 – $30.00 – us Univelt [629]
FROM ST FRANCIS TO DANTE : TRANSLATIONS FORM THE CHRONICLE OF THE FRANCISCAN SALIMBENE, 1221-1288 : WITH NOTES AND ILLUSTRATIONS FROM OTHER MEDIEVAL SOURCES / Coulton, G G – London: David Nutt, 1907 – 2mf – us A.T.L.A. [240]
FROM TALK TO TEXT : OR, A LIKELY STORY!–LIKELY ENOUGH / Ballard, Addison – New York:Longmans, Green, 1904 – 1mf – 9 – 0-8370-2172-3 – 1985-0172 – us A.T.L.A. [240]
FROM THE CRADLE TO THE GRAVE (INDEX) : REMINISCENCES OF WM. BULL MEEK CAMPTONVILLE, CALIFORNIA – 1r – 5,9 – $50.00 – B40150 – us Library Micro [920]
FROM THE HILLS OF DREAM : MOUNTAIN SONGS AND ISLAND RUNES / Sharp, William – Edinburgh: P. Geddes, [1897] – 1 roll – 1 – 1-55879-177-9 – uk Libr Preservation [810]
FROM THE PORCH / Thackeray, Anne – British Fiction Archive: Unit 3 – 9 – uk Bell [830]
FROM THE REFORMATION TO THE PURITAN REVOLUTION / Great Britain. York Court of High Commission – Papers of the York Court, c1560-1641, from the Borthwick Institute for Historical Research, University of York – 1 – us Primary [941]
FROM THE RESTORATION OF 1660 TO THE REVOLUTION OF 1688 / Brown, John – London: National Council of Evangelical Free Churches, 1904. (Eras of nonconformity; 7) – 1mf – us A.T.L.A. [240]
FROM THE TABLETS OF SUMER / Kramer, SN – Falcons Wing Press, 1956 – 9 – $12.00 – us I.R.C. [930]
[FROM] THE TEMPEST[:] WHERE THE BEE SUCKS... / Arne, T A – London: ca 1770 – 1 – us Sibley [780]
FROM TRUSTEESHIP TO ... ? : MICRONESIA AND ITS FUTURE / Micronesia Support Committee and the Pacific Concerns Research Center – 2nd ed. Honolulu: Maka'ainana Media, aug 1982 – 1mf – 9 – $1.50 – LLMC 82-100F, Title 102 – us L.L.M.C. [323]
FROM VISION TO REALITY / Yaari, M – Tel Aviv. 1963. BJ-28-25 1 – 9 – ne IDC [956]
FROM WALRAS TO MENGER: GENERAL EQUILIBRIUM AND ITS MICRO FOUNDATIONS. / Shenoy, Sudha – 1fiche (29x) – 9 – 1.00f – at Libertarian Micro [320]
FROM WHOSE BOURNE, ETC / Barr, Robert – London: Chatto & Windus, 1893. 03346. (Pre-1900 Canadiana) – 9 – cn C.I.H.M. [830]
Fromant, Abbe *see* GRAMMAIRE GENERALE ET RAISONNEE
FROMINO, DIALOGO DI VINCENTIO GALILEI..... / Galilei, Vincenzo – Vineggia: Appresso l'herede di G Scotto, 1584 – 1 – us Sibley [780]
Frommel, Gaston *see*
- ETUDES DE THEOLOGIE MODERNE
- ETUDES RELIGIEUSES ET SOCIALES

Frommel, Otto *see* DIE POESIE DES EVANGELIUMS JESU: EIN VERSUCH
Frommel, Wilhelm *see* SAMMLUNG VON VORTRAEGEN FUER DAS DEUTSCHE VOLK, ERSTER BAND
Frommett, B R *see*
- DESIAT' LET SOVETSKOI PROMYSLOVOI KOOPERATSII, 1917-27
- KOOPERATIVNOE VOSPITANIE DETEI I VOZROZHDENIE CHELOVECHESTVA
- RUSSKII SOTSIALIZM I KOOPERATSIIA

LA FRONDE – Journal feministe. Dir. Marguerite Durand. Paris. Quot. jusqu'en 1903 et a partir de 1926. 9 dec 1897-1er mars 1905, 3-24 juil 1914, 26 mai-dec 1926, 26 avr, 4 mai 1929 – 1 – fr A.C.R.P.P. [073]
LE FRONDEUR – Liege, Belgium. -w. 24 April 1880-30 Sept 1888. 3 reels – 1 – uk British Libr Newspaper [949]
Frondizi, Arturo *see*
- DIALOGOS CON FRONDIZI
- NI ODIO NI MIEDO
- PETROLEO Y POLITICA
- LA POLITICA EXTERIOR ARGENTINA

Frondizi, Silvio *see*
- LA CRISIS POLITICA ARGENTINA
- DOCE ANOS DE POLITICA

Fronemann, Wilhelm *see*
- DAS ERBE WOLGASTS
- HAMMERSCHLAEGE

Fronmueller, G F C *see*
- BRIEF JUDAE
- DIE BRIEFE PETRI UND DER BRIEF JUDAE

Fronsac, Frederic Gregory Forsyth *see*
- A GENEALOGICAL RECORD: FORSYTH OF NYDIE
- MEMORIAL OF THE DE FORSYTHS DE FRONSAC

FRONT – The Hague. v. 1 no. 1-4. Dec. 1930-June 1931 – 1 – us NY Public [073]
LE FRONT – Paris. nov 1935-38 – 1 – fr A.C.R.P.P. [073]
FRONT 1918-1919 / Reisner, L – M. 1924. BR-1228 2 – 8 – ne IDC [947]
FRONT COMMUN / Mouvement Frontiste – Bulletin bimensuel. no. 1-5. Paris. dec 1933-mai juin 1934 – 1 – fr A.C.R.P.P. [073]
Front de liberation du Quebec *see* VICTOIRE
Front de Liberation Nationale Algerienne *see* EL-MOUDJAHID
FRONT DER HERZEN : ROMAN / Hohlbaum, Robert – Berlin: K H Bischoff, 1944 – 1r – 1 – us U.W. Library [830]
Front der Sozialistischen Demokratie und Einheit *see* NEUER WEG
FRONT MOLODYKH : VI ESTNIK NAT SIONALNO I REVOLI UT SII – (Library has: no. 1 (23 noi abri a 1930 g.)) – Paris: Front molodykh, 1930- – 1 – CSUX89-S47 – us Hoover Inst Photo [947]
FRONT MONDIAL – (Weltfront-Worldfront). no. 1-9. janv-sept 1933. devenu: Front mondial. Contre la guerre et le fascisme. n.s., no. 1-52. oct 1933-nov 1935. Fond. Henri Barbusse. Paris. devenu: Paix et liberte voir a ce titre – 1 – fr A.C.R.P.P. [073]
FRONT NASIONAL – (Tjetakan 2. i.e. 3?). Bandung; Dua-R (1961?) SE-4794 1 – 9 – ne IDC [335]
Front national-syndicaliste *see* L'ASSAULT
FRONT NAUKI I TEKHNIKI – Moscow. Jan 15 1930-July 1938 – 1 – us NY Public [500]
LE FRONT OUVRIER : CENTRE SOCIAL OUVRIER CATHOLIQUE – Montreal, Canada. 2 dec 1944-20 mar 1954 – 6r – 1 – Can$55.00r – cn Can Microfilming [072]
LE FRONT POPULAIRE ET LE SENEGAL / Bernard-Duquenet, N – 9 – F90.00 – fr Ethnologie [306]
LE FRONT POPULAIRE ET LES SELECTIONS DE 1936 / Dupeux, G – F30.00 – fr Ethnologie [320]
FRONT SOCIAL – Bulletin mensuel de la troisieme force. Ni fascisme, ni bolchevisme, contre le capitalisme. no. 7, 13-15. Paris. 1933-Oct 1934 – 1 – fr A.C.R.P.P. [073]
FRONT UNIQUE! *see* EDINY I FRONT!
FRONT UNIQUE!... *see* EDINY I FRONT!... NOVO I ROSSII
FRONT UNIQUE DE LA NOUVELLE RUSSIE *see* EDINY I FRONT!...NOVO I ROSSII
FRONTENAC LEAD MINE – s.l.: s.n., 1869?. 03262. (Pre-1900 Canadiana) – 9 – cn C.I.H.M. [971]
EL FRONTERIZIO – Juarez, MX. 1967-1973 – 53r – $2,650.00 – R04214 – us Library Micro [072]
FRONTIER – O'Neill, NE. -w. Sep 1880-Oct 1881, scattered issues missing; Dec 1881-Feb 1884; Aug 1884-May 1965 – 1 – us NE Hist [071]
THE FRONTIER – Missoula, Montana. v. 1-19. May 1920-Summer 1939. Incomplete – 1 – us NY Public [073]
THE FRONTIER – O'Neill. Neb. 1880-1960 – 1 – us UMI [071]
THE FRONTIER / Platt, Ward – New York: Presbyterian Home Missions, 1908. 291p. 1 fiche – 9 – us A.T.L.A. [240]
FRONTIER AND HOLT COUNTY INDEPENDENT – O'Neill, NE. -w. Dec 1892; Jun 1897-Jul 1903; Jan 1905 to date – 1 – us NE Hist [071]
FRONTIER AND MIDLAND – Missoula, MT. v1-19. 1920-39 – 2r – 1 – us Ross [073]
FRONTIER GAZETTE – Covelo, CA. 1963-1964 – 1r – 1 – $50.00 – B06017 – us Library Micro [071]
FRONTIER HUMOR: SOME RATHER LUDICROUS EXPERIENCES THAT BEFELL MYSELF AND MY ACQUAINTANCES AMONG FRONTIER CHARACTERS BEFORE I MADE THE ACQUAINTANCE OF MY ESTEEMED FRIENDS "THE BROWNIES" / Cox, Palmer – s.l.: s.n., 18??. 05407. (Pre-1900 Canadiana) – 9 – cn C.I.H.M. [971]
FRONTIER SENTINEL – (Lacking: Dec 1930) – Newry, Ireland. 15 Oct 1904-26 Aug 1972 – 58 1/2r – 1 – uk British Libr Newspaper [072]
FRONTIER SENTINEL – Stanstead, Canada. v1 n3. 10 mar 1859-v3 n19. 4 jul 1861 – 1r – 1 – Can$45.00 – cn Can Microfilming [072]
FRONTIER STANDARD AND EAST LONDON GAZETTE – (Cont by: East London Standard) – East London, South Africa. 11 Feb 1890-29 Jun 1891 – 1r – 1, 16 diazo available at reduced price – sa SA Libr [072]
LA FRONTIERE / ed by Bonneville, Jean-Pierre – Rouyn, Canada. 24 jun 1937-29 dec 1992 – 102r – 1 – Can$75.00r – cn Can Microfilming [072]
LA FRONTIERE NORD DE LA PROVINCE DE QUEBEC / Cazes, Paul de – Quebec: A. Cote, 1886. 02119. (Pre-1900 Canadiana) – 9 – cn C.I.H.M. [971]
LA FRONTIERE SINO-ANNAMITE / Deveria, G – 1886 – 9 – fr Orientalistes [950]
LES FRONTIERES DE LA COTE D'IVOIRE, DE LA COTE D'OR ET DU SOUDAN / Delafosse, Maurice – Paris: Masson, 1908 – 1 – us Res Libr [960]
FRONTIERS – (1983-. 1,5,6,9) – v1- 1975- – 1 – us UMI [073]
FRONTIERS OF HEALTH SERVICES MANAGEMENT – v1-. Sept 1984- – 1,5,6,9 – us UMI [073]
FRONTIERS OF PLANT SCIENCE / Connecticut. Agricultural Experiment Station. New Haven – v. 1-22. 1948-69 – 1,5,6 – us Spaulding [631]
Frontisme *see* LA FLECHE
FRONTLINE – v1-6,no.3. 1975-80 – 1 – us UMI [073]
FRONTY KRASNOI ARMII I FLOTA : SBORNIK STATE I K SEZDU SOVETOV / ed by Kameneva, S S – Moskva: Gos. izd-vo, 1920 – 1 – CSUX88-B9681 – us Hoover Inst Photo [355]
DER FROSCH : FAMILIENDRAMA IN EINEM ACT NACH HENRIK IPSEN / Hartleben, Otto Erich – 3. Aufl. Berlin: S Fischer, 1901 – 1 – us U.W. Library [820]
Frosch, J *see* RERUM MUSICORUM OPUSCULUM RARUM AC SIGNE.
Frossard, C L *see*
- ETUDE HISTORIQUE ET BIBLIOGRAPHIQUE SUR LA DISCIPLINE ECCLESIASTIQUE DES EGLISES REFORMEES DE FRANCE
- LES ORIGINES DE LA FACULTE DE THEOLOGIE PROTESTANTE DE MONTAUBAN

Frossard, John D *see* THE NICKEL ORES OF SUDBURY (CANADA)
Frossard, LO *see*
- MON JOURNAL DE VOYAGE EN RUSSIE
- RAPPORT SUR LES NEGOCIATIONS CONDUITES A MOSCOU, SUIVI DES THESES PRESENTEES AU 2EME CONGRES DE L'INTERNATIONALE COMMUNISTE

Frossart, Benjamin-Sigismond *see* LA CAUSE DES ESCLAVES NEGRES ET DES HABITANTS DE LA GUINEE, PORTEE AU TRIBUNAL DE LA JUSTICE, DE LA RELIGION, DE LA POLITIQUE; OU HISTOIRE DE LA TRAITE ET DE L'ESCLAVAGE DES NEGRES, PREUVES DE LEUR ILLEGITIMITE, MOYEN DE LES ABOLIR SANS NUIRE AUX COLONIES
Frost, AF *see* EVOLUTION, OR, THE DIVINE METHOD OF CREATION AND PRESERVING THE UNIVERSE
FROST GENEALOGY / Frost, Josephine C – 1r – 1 – us Western Res [920]
Frost, George E *see* THE PATENT SYSTEM AND THE MODERN ECONOMY.
Frost, Gilman Dubois *see*
- DR. GILMAN FROST'S GENEALOGICAL RECORDS OF HANOVER, NEW HAMPSHIRE
- GENEALOGICAL RECORDS OF HANOVER, NEW HAMPSHIRE

Frost, J M *see* CORRESPONDENCE FILES OF CORRESPONDING SECRETARIES, BAPTIST SUNDAY SCHOOL BOARD
Frost, J M et al *see* BAPTISTS' WHY AND WHY NOT
Frost, Josephine C *see* FROST GENEALOGY
Frost, Maurice *see* ENGLISH AND SCOTTISH PSALM AND HYMN TUNES, 1543-1677
Frost, Thomas *see* THE OLD SHOWMAN AND THE OLD LONDON FAIRS
Frost, Thomas Gold *see* A TREATISE ON THE FEDERAL CORPORATION TAX LAW.
Frothingham, A L *see* STEPHEN BAR SUDALI, THE SYRIAN MYSTIK
Frothingham, Arthur L *see* CHRISTIAN PHILOSOPHY
Frothingham, Ephraim L *see* CHRISTIAN PHILOSOPHY
Frothingham, Octavius Brooks *see*
- BOSTON UNITARIANISM, 1820-1850
- GEORGE RIPLEY
- GERRIT SMITH
- TRANSCENDENTALISM IN NEW ENGLAND

Frothingham, Washington *see* HISTORY OF FULTON COUNTY
Frothington, Washington *see* HISTORY OF MONTGOMERY COUNTY
FROTOLA...PER LA VITTUORIA DE I NUOSTRI SEGNORE CONTRA I TURCHI / Magagno, G B – N.p., [1571] – 1mf – 9 – H-8320/1 – ne IDC [956]
D'FROU KAETHELI UND IHRI BUEBE : DES "STAERN VO BUEBEBAERG" ZWEITER TEIL: BERNDEUTSCHE ERZAEHLUNG / Tavel, Rudolf von – 2. Aufl. Bern: A Francke, 1910 – 1r – 1 – us U.W. Library [430]

Froude, James Anthony *see*
- BUNYAN
- THE DIVORCE OF CATHERINE OF ARAGON
- THE ENGLISH IN IRELAND IN THE EIGHTEENTH CENTURY
- THE ENGLISH IN THE WEST INDIES, OR, THE BOW OF ULYSSES
- LECTURES ON THE COUNCIL OF TRENT
- LIFE AND LETTERS OF ERASMUS
- LUTHER
- THE NEMESIS OF FAITH
- OCEANA, OR, ENGLAND AND HER COLONIES
- THEOLOGICAL UNREST: DISCUSSIONS IN SCIENCE AND RELIGION

Froude, Richard Hurrell *see* REMAINS OF THE LATE REVEREND RICHARD HURRELL FROUDE

FROU-FROU – Hull [Quebec: s.n. 1896] – 9 – cn C.I.H.M. [440]

FRUCHT VOM BAUM DES LEBENS – Ozar Perot ez Chajim. (Trans. and ed. by M. M. Hirsch). Berlin. Antwerp. 1936. BJ-262-20 1 – 9 – ne IDC [999]

Fructucso y Tristancho, Gonzalo *see* EXCURSIONES BRIOLOGICAS POR, LA PROVINCIA DE BADAJOZ

Fructuoso, Gonzalo *see* INDUSTRIAS RURALES

DAS FRUEHCHRISTLICHE UND MEROWINGISCHE MAINS NACH DEN BODENFUNDEN DARGESTELLT / Behrens, G – Mainz, 1950 – Dfl9.00 – ne Slangenburg [240]

DIE FRUEHE DEUTSCHSPRACHIGE OSCAR-WILDE-REZEPTION (1893-1906) / Haensel-Hohenhausen, Markus – Egelsbach, 1990 – 9 – DM48.00 – 3-89349-247-X – gw Hänsel [430]

DIE FRUEHEN KRAENZE / Zweig, Stefan – Leipzig: Insel-Verlag, 1917 – 1r – 1 – us U.W. Library [810]

DIE FRUEHEREN UND GEGENWAERTIGEN VERHAELTNISSE DER JUDEN IN DE SAEMMTLICHEN LANDESTHEILEN DES PREUSSISCHEN STAATES / ed by Roenne, L & Simon, H – Breslau. 1843. BJ-23-117 1 – 9 – ne IDC [943]

EIN FRUEHLING / Raabe, Wilhelm Karl – Berlin: Otto Janke, 1872 – 1r – 1 – us U.W. Library [830]

FRUEHLING EINES DEUTSCHEN MENSCHEN : DIE GESCHICHTE DES JUNGEN GOETHE / Hofer, Klara – (Includes bibliographical references) – Leipzig: Hesse & Becker, [1932] – 1r – 1 – us U.W. Library [920]

DER FRUEHLINGSWALZER : A SHORT NOVEL / Hohlbaum, Robert – Reichenberg: Stiepel, c1925 – 1r – 1 – us U.W. Library [830]

DAS FRUEHROEMISCHE LAGER BEI HOFHEIM IM TAUNUS / Ritterling, E – Wiesbaden, 1913 – Dfl46.00 – ne Slangenburg [240]

FRUEHROT : EIN BUCH VON HEIMAT UND JUGEND / Winnig, August – Stuttgart: J G Cotta, 1926 – 1r – 1 – us U.W. Library [920]

Fruehsorge, Gotthard *see* FUERSTEN POSTKARTEN

Fruges, G-M, de *see* J.-J. OLIER, 1608-1657, CURE DE SAINT-SULPICE ET FONDATEUR DES SEMINAIRES

DIE FRUHSCHRIFTEN / Marx, Karl – Stuttgart, 1953. 588p – 1 – us U.W. Library [335]

FRUIT JUICE PROCESSING – 1973 repr 1986 – 108p – it F.A.O. [338]

FRUIT-BEARING FOREST TREES : TECHNICAL NOTES – 1982 2nd print 1985 – 182p – it F.A.O. [634]

A FRUITFUL LIFE / Drury, B Paxson – A narrative of the experiences and missionary labors of Stephen Paxson. 1882 – 1 – 8.26 – us Baptist [240]

FRUITS AND VEGETABLES IN WEST AFRICA / Tindall, H D & Sai, F A – 4th printing 1976 – 259p – it F.A.O. [634]

FRUITVALE SHOPPING NEWS – Fruitvale, CA. 1934-1939 – 1r – 1 – $50.00 – B03132 – us Library Micro [071]

Frumkin, A L *see* TOLEDOT HAKHMEI YERUSHALAYIM

Frumkin, I D *see* SHELOM YERUSHALAYIM

Frumkin, Moiseilich *see* NARODNOE KHOZIAISTVO I VNESHNI AIA TORGOVLIA SSSR

Frutaz, A P *see* CONTRIBUTO ALLA STORIA DELLA RIFORMA DEL MESSALE PROMULGATO DA SAN PIO 5TH NEL 1570

Frutos Cortes, Eugenio *see*
- ANTROPOLOGIA FILOSOFICA 1. PRELIMINARES Y CUESTIONES BASICAS
- ANTROPOLOGIA FILOSOFICA 2. DIMENSIONES ENTITATIVAS DEL HOMBRE
- BALMES EN LA ENCRUCIJADA FILOSOFICA
- CALDERON DE LA BARCA
- CALDERON DE LA BARCA. AUTOS SACRAMENTALES. ANTOLOGIA
- CONTRIBUCION A UNA ANTOLOGIA DE LA REALIDAD HISTORICA
- CREACION FILOSOFICA Y CREACION POETICA
- CREACION POETICA (J. GUILLEN, SALINAS, A. MACHADO, D. ALONSO, S.J. DE LA CRUZ, M. PINILLOS)
- DE LA CARACTEROLOGIA INDIVIDUAL A LA COLECTIVA
- LA ESENCIAL HETEROGENEIDAD DEL SER EN ANTONIO MACHADO
- ETICA ELEMENTAL
- LA FILOSOFIA DE CALDERON EN SUS AUTOS SACRAMENTALES
- HISTORIA DE LA FILOSOFIA Y DE LAS CIENCIAS
- EL HUMANISMO Y LA MORAL DE JUAN PABLO SARTRE (CRITICA)
- IDEA DEL TEATRO DE ORTEGA Y GASSET
- IMMANENCIA Y TRASCENDENCIA DEL SER Y DEL CONOCER EN HEIDEGGER
- INTRODUCCION A LA FILOSOFIA 1. INTRODUCCION Y LOGICA
- INTRODUCCION A LA FILOSOFIA 2. PSICOLOGIA Y ETICA
- EL NUEVO HUMANISMO
- ORIGEN, NATURALEZA Y DESTINO DEL HOMBRE EN LOS AUTOS SACRAMENTALES DE CALDERON
- LA PERSONA HUMANA
- EL PRIMER BERGSON EN ANTONIO MACHADO
- TEORIA DEL CONOCIMINETO Y ONTOLOGIA
- LA VINA DESTRUIDE. A HUNGRIA, EN SU MARTIRIO
- LA VOLUNTAD Y EL LIBRE ALBEDRIO EN LOS AUTOS SACRAMENTALES DE CALDERON

Fry, Benjamin St. James *see* WOMAN'S WORK IN THE CHURCH

Fry, Benjamin St. James *see*
- THE LIFE OF REV. WILLIAM M'KENDREE
- THE LIFE OF REVEREND ENOCH GEORGE

Fry, Elizabeth *see* DIARIES

Fry, Francis *see* THE BIBLE BY COVERDALE 1805

Fry, Henry *see* A BIOGRAPHICAL SKETCH OF SIR N. F. BELLEAU

Fry, J *see* SOME REMARKS ON A PAMPHLET INTITULED A LETTER TO A PERSON LATELY JOIN'D WITH THE PEOPLE CALL'D QUAKERS,...

Fry, Joan Mary *see* THE COMMUNION OF LIFE

AIN FRYDSAMS VNND CHRISTLICHS GESPRECH, AINS EUANGELISCHEN. VND AINS WIDERTEUFFERS / Meuszlin, W – Augspurg. 1533. BME-125 1 – 9 – ne IDC [240]

Frye, E M *see* QBS HANDY GUIDE TO HALIFAX AND ENVIRONS: WITH MAPS AND ILLUSTRATIONS

Frye, T C *see* A MORPHOLOGICAL STUDY OF CERTAIN ASCLEPIADEA

FRYKSDALSBYGDEN – (Nordvarmland, 1979) – Sunne, Sweden. 1979- – 1 – sw Kungliga [072]

FRYSK EN FRIJ – Leeuwarden, Netherlands. 25 May 1945-28 Oct 1966 – 9r – 1 – uk British Libr Newspaper [949]

FSJ NOVENA...VIRGEN DE LA CORONADA... VCA DE LOS BARROS – 1878 – 9 – $1.50f – sp Bibl Santa Ana [240]

FTA NEWS : 1939-1950 / Food, Tobacco and Agricultural and Allied Workers – (Coll title: Labour Union Periodicals, Part 3) – 1996 – 1r – 1 – $135.00 – 1-55655-618-7 – us UPA [331]

FTA NEWS *see* CANNERY AND FIELD UNION NEWS, 1937 : CIO NEWS CANNERY WORKERS EDITION, 1938-1939 : UCAPAWA NEWS, 1939-1944 : FTA NEWS, 1945-1950

FTD MISAL BREVE... – Madrid: Razon y Fe, 1927 – 1 – sp Bibl Santa Ana [946]

FTO VIDA Y VIRTUDES DEL VENERABLE SIERVO DE DIOS MARCELINO CHAMPAGNAT. BARCELONA, FTO. 1929 / Bayle, Constantino – Madrid: Razon y Fe, 1929 – 1 – sp Bibl Santa Ana [240]

Fu, Daniel C *see* FOUNDATION CHARACTERS, BK 1 (CCC128)

IL FU MATTIA PASCAL, ROMANZO / Pirandello, Luigi – Firenze: R. Bemporad & Figlio, 1921. 1 reel. 1268 – 1 – us U.W. Library [820]

FU YIN HSIN PAO *see* GOSPEL NEWS REPORT

Fuad, Koeprueluezade Mehmed *see* YENI OSMANLI TARIH EDEBIYATI

FU-CHIEN HSIANG-SHIH LU – List of successful candidates in the imperial examination in Fukien province: 1751, 1752, 1875, 1876, 1879, 1882, 1885, 1888, 1889, 1891, 1893, 1897. 1 reel – 1 – 14.00 – us Chinese Res [950]

FU-CHIEN JIH-PAO – Foochow, Fukien. March 1961-Dec 11, 1963. Scattered issues missing. 6 reels – 1 – 105.00 – us Chinese Res [072]

FU-CHOU FU-CHIH – 1754. 76, 1. BCH-555 2 – 8 – ne IDC [950]

Fuchs, Albert *see* GOETHE, UN HOMME FACE A LA VIE

Fuchs, Georg *see* DES BURSCHEN HEIMKEHR

Fuchs, J S *see* ELEMENTA JURIS NATURAE

Fuchs, Jaime *see*
- ARGENTINA
- LOS TRUSTS YANQUIS CONTRA LA ARGENTINA

Fuchs, Karl *see* JOHANN GABRIEL SEIDL

Fuchs, Meik *see* DREIGUDS UN NOSCHENS

Fuchs, W *see*
- BEITRAEGE ZUR MANDJURISCHEN BIBLIOGRAPHIE UND LITERATUR
- DIE SOGENANNTEN SIEBENBUERGISCHEN EHEN...
- DAS TURFANGEBIET

Fuchsperger, O *see* KURTZE SCHLOSZREDE WIDER DEN IRSALL DER NEUEGEROTTENN TAUFFER; DARIN DER KINDERTAUFF BESTETTIGT. WIRD

FUCI, SIVE PLANTARUM FUCORUM GENERI A BOTANICIS / Turner, D – 4v. Londini. 1808-19. B-6438 1 – 9 – ne IDC [580]

FUCI SIVE PLANTARUM FUCORUM GENERI A BOTANIIS ASCRIPTARUM IEONES DESCRIPTIONES ET HISTORIA / Dawson Turner, A M & Dillwyn, L W – 1808-19 – 7 – uk Microform Academic [580]

Fuckel, KWG L *see* SYMBOLAE MYCOLOGICAE. BEITRAEGE ZUR KENNTNISS DER RHEINISCHEN PILZE

FUDAN XUEBAO – Shehui Kexue Ban. Journal of Fudan University, Social Science. In Chinese but Table of Contents in English in each issue. F p203 – 9 – $4.50f – cc Microforms [073]

FUDAN XUEBAO – Ziran Kexue Ban. Journal of Fudan University, Natural Science. In Chinese but English abstracts to the main articles. F p183 – 9 – 4.00f – cc Microforms [073]

DER FUEHRER – 1927-1945 – Cumul – 1 – DM4,900.00 – sz Infoprint [072]

DER FUEHRER – (Also available: Ausgabe KRAICHGAU, jan-apr 1943; Ausgabe MERKUR-RUNDSCHAU, sep 6-dec 1942; Ausgabe ORTENAU, oct 7-dec 4 1944. Also Bereichsausgaben available: BRUCHSAL, may 1 1943-44 (incomplete); BUEHL, may 1943-44 (incomplete); RASTATT, may 1 1943-jun 30 1944, oct 7-dec 4 1944) – Karlsruhe, nov 5 1927-dec 29 1928, jan 4 1930-mar 30 1945 – 69r – 1 – Inquire at Mikrofilmarchiv for details – gw Misc Inst [943]

DER FUEHRER – Berlin, 1921-23 – 1r – 1 – Dist. gw Mikrofilm – gw Misc Inst [072]

DER FUEHRER : WECKRUFE NATIONALSOZIALISTISCHEN GLAUBENS UND WOLLENS – Karlsruhe, 1927-1945 – 69r – 1 – DM5,175.00 – gw Mikro Press [072]

DER FUEHRER : WECKRUFE NATIONALSOZIALISTISCHEN GLAUBENS UND WOLLENS – Karlsruhe, DE. 1930-Mar 1945 – 69r – 1 – gw Mikrofilm [072]

Fuehrer, A *see* LISTS OF CHRISTIAN TOMBS AND MONUMENTS OF ARCHAEOLOGICAL AND HISTORICAL INTEREST AND THEIR INSCRIPTIONS IN THE N.W. PROV. AND OUDH

FUEHRER CONFERENCES ON MATTERS DEALING WITH THE GERMAN NAVY, 1939-1945 / Germany. Kriegsmarine Oberkommando – 1983. Translated into English by the U.S. Office of Naval Intelligence – 1 – $95.00 – 0-89093-198-4 – us UPA [943]

FUEHRER CONFERENCES ON MATTERS DEALING WITH THE GERMAN NAVY, SEPT 1939-APRIL 1945 – 1984 – 1r – 1 – $85.00 – S1654 – Co-publ with the U.S. Naval Historical Center – us Scholarly Res [355]

FUEHRER DURCH DIE SAMMLUNGEN DES MUSEUMS FUER VOELKERKUNDE / Berlin. Staatliche Museen. Museum fuer Voelkerkunde – 3. 9., 11. 16. Aufl. Berlin, 1887-1929. Film Mas 9263 – 1 – us H.U. Library [390]

Fuehrer, J *see* DIE ADOPTION, LEGITIMATION UND DIE KINDESANERKENNUNG...

FUEL OIL AND OIL HEAT – v1- 1942- 1; v30-5,6; v36- 9 – us UMI [660]

FUEL PROCESSING TECHNOLOGY – v1-9. 1978-84 – 1,5,6,13 – sz Elsevier [660]

[FUEL SUPPLIES DURING WORLD WAR 2 PAMPHLET COLLECTION] – 19??-1942 – 1 – CSUXANN2554-B – us Hoover Inst Photo [338]

Fueller, Franziska *see* DAS PSYCHOLOGISCHE PROBLEM DER FRAU IN KLEISTS DRAMEN UND NOVELLEN

Fuellkrug, Gerhard *see* GOTTESKNECHT DES DEUTEROJESAJA: EIN KRITISCH-EXEGETISCHE UND BIB.-THEOL. STUDIE

Fueloep-Miller, Rene *see* THE MIND AND FACE OF BOLSHEVISM: AN EXAMINATION OF CULTURAL LIFE IN SOVIET RUSSIA

FUELWOOD SUPPLIES IN THE DEVELOPING COUNTRIES – 1983 – 134p – it F.A.O. [333]

FUENFF PREDIGEN: VON DEM WERCKE DER CONCORDIEN,... / Andreae d.A E, J – Dreszden, etc., n.d. – 3mf – 9 – ne IDC [240]

DER FUENFFUESSIGE JAMBUS BEI CHRISTIAN DIETRICH GRABBE : EIN BEITRAG ZUR METRIK / Kessler, Hugo – (Includes bibliographical references) – Muenster: Westfaelische Vereinsdruckerei, 1913 – 1r – 1 – us U.W. Library [430]

DER FUENFFUESSIGE JAMBUS BEI HEBBEL : EIN BEITRAG ZUR GESCHICHTE DES METRUMS / Rube, Wolrad – (Includes bibliographical references) – [S.l.: s.n.], 1910 (Heidelberg: Buchdruckerei C Pfeffer) – 1r – 1 – us U.W. Library [430]

DER FUENFFUESSIGE JAMBUS IN DEN DRAMEN FRIEDRICHS HALMS : EINE METRISCHE UNTERSUCHUNG / Lambertz, Paul – Muenster, 1914 – 1mf – DM48.00 – 3-8267-3108-5 – gw Hänsel [430]

FUENFZIG FELDPOSTBRIEFE EINES FRANKFURTERS : AUS DEN JAHREN 1870 UND 1871 / Wuelker, Richard Paul – 2. Aufl. Halle (Saale): M Niemeyer, 1876 – 1 – us U.W. Library [860]

FUENFZIG FEUILLETONS : MIT EINEM PRAELUDIUM IN VERSEN / Kuernberger, Ferdinand – Wien: T Daberkow, [1905?] – 1 – us U.W. Library [840]

Fuenn, S J *see*
- HA-OZAR
- KIRYAH NE'EMANAH

Fuente de Cantos. Ayuntamiento *see* ORDENANZAS MUNICIPALES

Fuente del Maestre *see*
- FIESTAS PATRONALES. SEPTIEMBRE 1975
- REGLAMENTO Y ORDENANZAS DE LA COMUNIDAD DE LABRADORES DE FUENTE DEL MAESTRE
- REVISTA DE LAS FIESTAS QUE SE CELEBRAN EN FUENTE DEL MAESTRE EN HONOR DEL SANTISIMO CRISTO DE LAS MISERICORDIAS

FUENTES HISTORICAS SOBRE COLON Y AMERICA / Angleria, Pedro Martir – 1892. v. 1-4 – 9 – 1.50f – sp Bibl Santa Ana [970]

FUENTES PARA LA HISTORIA DE LA FILOSOFIA EL EN PERU / Mejia Valera, M – Univ. San Marcos, Fac. de Letras, 1963 – 3mf – 9 – ne IDC [100]

LAS FUENTES PARA LA HISTORIA DE LA PEDAGOGIA ESPANOLA / Floriano Cumbreno, Antonio C – Madrid, 1943 – 1 – sp Bibl Santa Ana [370]

Fuentes y Guzman, Francisco A *see* HISTORIA DE GUATEMALA

Fuentes y Guzman, Francisco Antonio de *see* RECORDACION FLORIDA. DISCURSO HISTORIAL Y DE DEMOSTRACION NATURAL, MATERIAL, MILITAR Y POLITICA DEL REYNO DE GUATEMALA

FUER BANKFREIHEIT, 1870 / Benndorf, Alex – 38p with note by J. Zube on the title, which is misleading regarding the contents – 9 – 1.00f – at Libertarian Micro [335]

FUER DAS VOELKERRECHT / Mueller, Max Ludwig – Tuebingen: Kloeres, 1916. 32p – 1 – us U.W. Library [340]
FUER EINE OFFENE KIRCHE *see* OFFENE KIRCHE
FUER FREUNDE DER TONKUNST / Rochlitz, Johann Friedrich – Leipzig, C. Cnobloch, 1830-45. 4 v. Film Mas 9112 – 1 – us H.U. Library [780]
FUER GEIST UND HERZ, 1786 / ed by Kotzebue, August von – 1786 (mf ed 1997) – 13mf – 9 – DM220.00 – 3-89131-237-7 – gw Fischer [305]
FUER HEILIGE GUETER: APHORISMEN ZUR GESCHICHTLICHEN RECHTFERTIGUNG DES ALTEN TESTAMENTS / Stosch, Georg – Stuttgart: Max Kielmann, 1905. 1 fiche – 9 – us A.T.L.A. [240]
Fuerbringer, Hermann *see* DIE KUENSTLERISCHEN VORAUSSETZUNGEN DES GENTER ALTARS DER BRUEDER VAN EYCK
Fuerer-Haimendorf, Christoph von *see* THE ABORIGINAL TRIBES OF HYDERABAD..
DIE FUERNEMSTEN HEUPSTUECK DER CHRISTLICHEN LEHRE / Chemnitz, Martin – Wulffenbuettel, 1569 – 4mf – 9 – ne IDC [240]
FUERO DE ALBARRACIN (SIECLE 13) – Albarracin – 1r – 5,6 – sp Cultura [340]
FUERO DE CACERES (ANNO 1229-1231) – Caceres – 1r – 5,6 – sp Cultura [340]
FUERO DE CORDOBA. EXPEDIENTES SOBRE EL FUERO (ANNO 1241-SIECLO 1900) – Cordoba – 1r – 5,6 – sp Cultura [340]
EL FUERO DE PLASENCIA / Benavides Checa, Jose – 1896 – 9 – 1.50f – sp Bibl Santa Ana [946]
FUERO DE POBLACION OTORGADO POR... DON CARLOS 3 A LAS LOCALIDADES FORMADAS EN LA SIERRA MORENA POR LA LLAMADA "COLONIZACION INTERIOR"... / Cotta y Marquez de Prado, Ventura de – s.1, s.i, s.a. Sep. a Mancha. pp. 1-30 – 1 – sp Bibl Santa Ana [946]
FUERO DE POBLACION OTORGADO...CARLOS 3 A LAS LOCALIDADES FORMADAS EN LA SIERRA MORENA POR LA LLAMADA "COLONIZACION INTERIOR" DE ESPANA, QUE AFECTO A PARTE DE LA PROVINCIA DE CIUDAD REAL – Badajoz, 1961. Sep.Rev. de Est. Regionales. La Mancha – sp Bibl Santa Ana [946]
FUERO DE USAGRE (SIGLO 18) / Urena y Semenjaud, Rafael & Bonilla y San Martin, Adolfo; ed by Hijos de Reus – Madrid, 1907 – 1 – sp Bibl Santa Ana [946]
EL FUERO REAL DE ESPANA HECHO POR ALFONSO 9 / Diaz de Montalvo, A – Burgos, 1533 – 11mf – 9 – sp Cultura [320]
FUERST BISMARCK: SEIN POLITISCHES LEBEN UND WIRKEN / ed by Hahn, Ludwig Ernst – Berlin, W. Hertz. 1878-91. 5 v. Vol. 5 is a continuation by Karl Wipperman. Film Mas C 701 – 1 – us H.U. Library [320]
FUERST BISMARCK UND DIE KAISERIN AUGUSTA / Bosbach, Heinz – Koeln, 1936 – 1mf – 9 – DM48.00 – 3-89349-335-2 – gw Hänsel [943]
Fuerst, Julius *see*
- DER KANON DES ALTEN TESTAMENTS
- DER ORIENT

Fuerst, Max *see* BIOGRAPHISCHES LEXIKON FUER DAS GEBIET ZWISCHEN INN UND SALZACH
Fuerst, Rudolf *see* STUDIEN
FUERSTEN POSTKARTEN = ROYAL POSTCARDS: THE FRUEHSORGE COLLECTION : SAMMLUNG FRUEHSORGE / ed by Fruehsorge, Gotthard – (Printed guide included) – 1988 – 86mf (1:24) – 9,15 – silver DM2,400.00 – 3-598-32532-0 – gw Saur [900]
DIE FUERSTENSPIEGEL DES HOHEN UND SPAETEN MITTELALTERS (MGH SCHRIFTEN..: 2.BD) / Berges, W – 1938 – Dfl35.00 – ne Slangenburg [240]
Fuerstenthal, Johann August Ludwig *see* REPERTORIUM UEBER SAEMMTLICHE, DURCH DIE GESETZ-SAMMLUNG UND DIE AMTS-BLAETTER DER KOENIGLICHEN REGIERUNGEN
DAS FUERSTENTHUM BULGARIEN / Jirecek, C J – Seine Bodengestaltung, Natur, Bevoelkerung, wirtschaftliche Zustaende, geistige Kultur, Staatsverfassung, Staatsverwaltung und neueste Geschichte. Vienna. 1891. BR-3877 2 – 8 – ne IDC [940]
DIE FUERSTIN : ERZAEHLUNGEN / Heuschele, Otto – Stuttgart: J F Steinkopf, 1945 – 1r – 1 – us U.W. Library [830]
DIE FUERSTIN AMALIE VON GALITZIN UND FRIEDRICH LEOPOLD GRAF ZU STOLBERG-STOLBERG : EIN BEITRAG ZUR STELLUNG DES GALLITZIN-KREISES IN DER DEUTSCHEN LITERATUR- UND GEISTESGESCHICHTE / Wolf, Otmar – Wuerzburg, 1952 – 224p – 9 – DM98.00 – 3-89349-243-7 – gw Hänsel [430]
FUERSTLICH LIPPISCHES INTELLIGENZBLATT *see* LIPPISCHE INTELLIGENZBLAETTER
FUERSTLICH LIPPISCHES REGIERUNGS- UND ANZEIGEBLATT – Detmold, Germany. 1848-49 – 2r – 1 – gw Mikrofilm [072]
FUERSTLICH LIPPISCHES REGIERUNGS- UND ANZEIGEBLATT *see* LIPPISCHE INTELLIGENZBLAETTER
Fuertes Acevedo, Maximo *see*
- EL ANO METEOROLOGICO 1879
- EL ANO METEOROLOGICO 1881
- BOSQUEJO...LITERATURA DE ASTURIAS..
- BOSQUEJOS CIENTIFICOS
- DISCURSO...PEDRO CALDERON
- MINERALOGIA ASTURIANA

Fuertes, Damaso *see* CRONICA DE LA PRIMERA ASAMBLEA MISIONAL DIOCESANA DE BADAJOZ CELEBRADA EN ZAFRA...
Fuertes, Jose V *see* LECCIONES DE RITOS ROMANOS
FUERTHER NACHRICHTEN – (Bereichsausgabe der Nuernberger Nachrichten) – Fuerth. jun 1, 1978-96 – 1 – gw Mikrofilm [072]
FUERTHER TAGBLATT – Fuerth, Germany. 1848-49 – 1r – 1 – gw Mikrofilm [072]
FUERZA EXTRATERRITORIAL DE LAS LEYES SUCESORIAS / Biedma, C M – Buenos Aires, 1899 – 2mf – 9 – ILM-3584/1 – ne IDC [327]
LA FUERZA MAYOR EN EL DERECHO MERCANTIL. / Hewstone Burotto, Luis – Santiago de Chile: Cultura 1945. 109p. LL-4073 – 1 – us L of C Photodup [340]
LAS FUERZAS ARMADAS RESTITUYEN EL IMPERIO DE LA SOBERANIA POPULAR : LAS ELECCIONES GENERALES DE 1946 / Agentina. Ministerio del Interior – Buenos Aires: Imprenta de la Camara de diputados, 1946. 2v – 1 – CSUXAHZ2499-B – us Hoover Inst Photo [320]
LAS FUERZAS ARMADAS Y LA GUERRA PSICOLOGICA / Florit, Carlos A – Buenos Aires: Ediciones Aray u [1963] – 1 – CSUXADQ0045-B – us Hoover Inst Photo [320]
FUERZAS ESPIRITUALES DEL PERONISMO – [Buenos Aires?: Presidencia de la Nacion, Subsecretaria de Informaciones, 195-?] – 1 – CSUXADP5158-B – us Hoover Inst Photo [320]
FUERZAS ESPIRITUALES DEL PERONISTA – [s.l.: s.n.], 1950 – 1 – CSUXADP5188-B – us Hoover Inst Photo [320]
Fuessly, J C *see* MAGAZIN FUER DIE LIEBHABER DER ENTOMOLOGIE
Fueter, Eduard *see* RELIGION UND KIRCHE IN ENGLAND IM FUENFZEHNTEN JAHRHUNDERT
FUEYUZAT – Selanik: Yeni Asir Matbaasi. Sahib-i Imtiyaz: Ali Riza; Mueduer ve Sermuharriri: Hakki Baha, 1908-1909 – 9 – $25.00 – us MEDOC [956]
FUGHE E CAPRICCJ : PER CLAVICEMBALO O PER L'ORGANO: OPERA PRIMA... / Marpurg, Friedrich Wilhelm – Berlin: J J Hummel, [1777] – 1 – us Sibley [780]
THE FUGITIVE – Nashville. v. 1-4. Apr 1922-Dec 1925 – 1 – us NY Public [073]
THE FUGITIVE BLACKSMITH : OR, EVENTS IN THE HISTORY OF JAMES W C PENNINGTON FORMERLY A SLAVE IN THE STATE OF MARYLAND, UNITED STATES – London, 1850 – 1r – 1 – us Ross [976]
A FUGITIVE FROM SPAIN / Sassone, Felipe – San Francisco, 1937. Fiche W1156. (Blodgett Collection of Spanish Civil War Pamphlets) – 9 – us H.U. College Libr [946]
FUGITIVE PIECES AND REMINISCENCES OF LORD BYRON... / Byron, George Gordon Byron – London: Printed for Whittaker, Treacher, and Co., 1829 – 1 roll – 1 – 1-55879-641-X – uk Libr Preservation [810]
FUGITIVES WANTED BY POLICE *see* FBI LAW ENFORCEMENT BULLETIN
Fuhn, S J *see* HA-KARMEL
FUHRER ZUR EROFFNUNGSFEIER DES NORD-OSTSEE-KANALS: MIT LAGENPLAN DER KRIEGSSCHIFFE, STADTPLAN UND-ANSICHTEN; EISENBAHN-UND DAMPFSCHIFFS-FAHRPLANEN; PROGRAMM DER KIELER WOCHO.. – Kiel: Verlag der "Nord-Ostsee-Zeitung", 1895 – 1 – us U.W. Library [949]
Fuhrmann, J *see* IRISH MEDIEVAL MONASTERIES ON THE CONTINENT
Fuhrmann, MH *see* MUSICALISCHER-TRICHTER, DADURCH EIN...
FUJIAN QIAOXIANG BAO – Fujian Overseas Chinese Journal. -w. 1983-. M D45 – 1 reel/y – 1 – $28.00r – cc Microforms [072]
FUJIAN RIBAO – Fujian Daily. China. In Chinese. Current subscription. Annual delivery. 1981-, 1 reel/y. M D21 – 1 – $55.00r – cc Microforms [072]
Fujii, Joji *see* NIHONSI KANKEI SHIRYO
Fujii, Sadafumi *see* SHAJI TORISHIRABE RUISAN
Fujimoto-Kanatani, Koichiro *see* DETERMINING THE ESSENTIAL ELEMENTS OF GOLF SWINGS USED BY ELITE GOLFERS
FUKIEN CHINES WEEKLY – San Francisco, CA. 1986-1987 – 1r – 1 – $50.00 – B03670 – us Library Micro [071]
Fukien Mission *see* FUKIEN MISSION. GENERAL REPORT. WOMEN'S AUXILIARY
FUKIEN MISSION. GENERAL REPORT. WOMEN'S AUXILIARY : CHINA'S CHILDREN'S HELPING BAND / Fukien Mission – (Lacking: 1924. 1928-29) – 1919-35 – 1r – 1 – ATLA S0724A – us A.T.L.A. [073]
FUKUZAWA KANKEI MONJO = RECORDS CONCERNING YUKICHI FUKUZAWA AND KEIO GIJUKI – Basic materials of Yukichi Fukuzawa (1834-1901), who laid the foundation for Keio University and modern Japan – 94r – Y1,034,000.00 – ja Yushodo [950]
A FULANI GRAMMAR / Leith-Ross, Sylvia – [Lagos: Govt Printing Office, 1919?] – 1 – us Res Libr [490]
THE FULANI OF NORTHERN NIGERIA / St Croix, F W de – Lagos. 1944. BA-399 2 – 8 – ne IDC [960]
THE FULANI OF NORTHERN NIGERIA : SOME GENERAL NOTES / St Croix, F W de – [Lagos: Govt Printer, 1944; 1945] – 1 – us Res Libr [305]
Fulda, Hermann *see* DAS KREUZ UND DIE KREUZIGUNG
Fulda, U *see* DAS WESEN DES VOELKERRECHTLICHEN MANDATS...
FULDAER ZEITUNG – Fulda. mar 17, 1951-68 – 57r – 1 – gw Mikrofilm [072]
FULHAM CHRONICLE – London, 1888-1989; 1992- – 126+ r – 1 – uk British Libr Newspaper [072]
THE FULHAM PAPERS / Lambeth Palace. Library – (Second ed. includes additional reel). With printed index – 1 – £875.00 – uk World [025]
A FULL AND CIRCUMSTANTIAL ACCOUNT OF THE TRIAL OF THE REV. DOCTOR DODD, AT THE SESSIONS HOUSE IN THE OLD BAILEY, ON SATURDAY THE 22ND OF FEBRUARY, 1777. / Dodd, William – London, Richardson and Urquhart 1777? 55 p. LL-2249 – 1 – us L of C Photodup [340]
A FULL AND CORRECT ACCOUNT OF THE CHIEF NAVAL OCCURRENCES OF THE LATE WAR BETWEEN GREAT BRITAIN AND THE UNITED STATES OF AMERICA, PRECEDED BY... AMERICAN ACCOUNTS OF THEIR NAVAL ACTIONS FOUGHT PREVIOUS TO THAT PERIOD / James, William – 1817 – 9 – $20.00 – uk Libr Preservation [941]
A FULL AND IMPARTIAL EXAMINATION OF THE REV. MR. JOHN WESLEY'S ADDRESS TO THE AMERICANS,... – St. Helen's, 1776 – 1mf – 9 – MP-511/1 – ne IDC [240]
A FULL, CLEAR, AND SUCCINCT DISCUSSION OF THE PRELIMINARY ARTICLES OF PEACE, AS PUBLISHED BY AUTHORITY – London, [1762] – 1mf – 1 – ILM-2738/1 – ne IDC [327]
A FULL CONFUTATION OF THE REV. JOHN FLETCHER'S APPEAL,... / Manners, N – Hull, 1789 – 2mf – 9 – MP-563/1 – ne IDC [240]
A FULL CONFUTATION OF THE REV. MR. JOHN FLETCHER'S APPEAL TO MATTER OF FACT AND COMMON SENSE / Manners, N – London, 1787 – 1mf – 9 – MP-553/1 – ne IDC [240]
A FULL DESCRIPTION OF THE SOIL, WATER, TIMBER, AND PRAIRIES OF EACH LOT, OR QUARTER SECTION OF THE MILITARY LAND BETWEEN THE MISSISSIPPI AND ILLINOIS RIVERS / Van Zandt, Nicholas B – 1818. 127p. 1r – 1 – $8.00 – us M.H.S. [355]
A FULL DESCRIPTION OF THE TWO HISTORICAL PAINTINGS OF THE FUNERAL OF THE LATE SIR JOHN S.D. THOMPSON, K.M.G., M.P., ETC / Bell-Smith, Frederick Marlett – Toronto: Apted Bros., 1895?. 02323. (Pre-1900 Canadiana) – 9 – cn C.I.H.M. [750]
THE "FULL FAITH AND CREDIT CLAUSE" OF THE UNITED STATES CONSTITUTION; AN INSTRUMENT OF FEDERALISM / Virginia. Commission on Constitutional Government – Richmond, 1966 25 p. LL-4 – 1 – us L of C Photodup [340]
FULL SERVICE CA (MICROFORM) – All abstracts in CA. -w. 1907-. Printed volume indexes – 6,9 – us Chemical [540]
FULL TEXT OF JUDGE ELLIOT'S JUDGEMENT IN THE LONDON ELECTION CASE, 1892 / Elliot, W – s.l.: s.n., 1892?. 02904. (Pre-1900 Canadiana) – 9 – cn C.I.H.M. [971]
Fuller, Andrew *see*
- THE CARE OF THE SOUL
- THE COMPLETE WORKS OF THE REV. ANDREW FULLER, WITH A MEMOIR OF HIS LIFE BY ANDREW GUNTON FULLER

Fuller, B A G *see* THE PROBLEM OF EVIL IN PLOTINUS
Fuller, Francis *see* MEDICINA GYMNASTICA
Fuller, John Frederick Charles *see* THE CONQUEST OF RED SPAIN
Fuller, Tamela G *see* THE EFFECTS OF A WEIGHT TRAINING COURSE ON STRESS LEVELS AND LOCUS OF CONTROL IN COLLEGE FEMALES
Fuller, Thomas *see* A COMMENT ON RUTH
Fuller, Thomas Brock *see* THE SCRIPTURAL WAY OF SUPPORTING SERVICES OF RELIGION
Fuller, William Henry *see* THE UNSPECIFIC SCANDAL: AN ORIGINAL, POLITICAL, CRITICAL AND GRITTICAL EXTRAVAGANZA, PERFORMED AT THE GREAT DOMINION THEATRE, OTTAWA, IN THE YEAR OF GRACE, 1873
Fuller-Eliott-Drake, Elizabeth Douglas *see* THE FAMILY AND HEIRS OF SIR FRANCIS DRAKE
FULLER'S PRACTICE REPORTS / Michigan. Supreme Court – 1v. 1896 – 1mf – 9 – $4.50 – LLMC 84-161 – us L.L.M.C. [340]
FULLERTON CITY DIRECTORIES – Orange Co, CA. 1913-1914; 1936 – 2r – 1 – $100.00 – D069 – us Library Micro [071]
Fullerton, George Stuart *see* A PLAIN ARGUMENT FOR GOD
Fullerton, Georgiana *see* THE LIFE OF LUISA DE CARVAJAL
FULLERTON NEWS – Fullerton, NE. -w. Aug. 1895-Dec. 1896 – 1 – us NE Hist [071]
FULLERTON NEWS TRIBUNE – Fullerton, CA. 1895- – 425+ r – 1 – $21,400.00 ($440.00y) – R02262 – us Library Micro [071]
FULLERTON POST – Fullerton, NE. -w. Nov. 1892; Mar. 1895-Sep. 1928 – 1 – us NE Hist [071]
Fullerton, Robert Stewart *see* MEMOIR
Fullerton, William Young *see* C.H. SPURGEON
Fullwood, R H *see* ACCOUNTS
Fulmore, Z T *see* HISTORY AND GEOGRAPHY OF TEXAS AS TOLD IN COUNTY NAMES
THE FULNESS OF BLESSING : OR, THE GOSPEL OF CHRIST: AS ILLUSTRATED FROM THE BOOK OF JOSHUA / Smiley, Sarah Frances – (Includes index) – London: Hodder & Stoughton, 1876 – 1mf – 9 – 0-8370-5276-9 – 1985-3276 – us A.T.L.A. [220]
FULTON COUNTY EXPOSITOR – Wauseon, Ohio. 1932- – 31r – 1 – $32.50r – us Archival [071]
Fulton County. Ohio. Archbold. Village. Board of Public Affairs *see* MINUTES
Fulton County. Ohio. Archbold. Village. Fire Department *see* MINUTES
Fulton County. Ohio. Archbold. Village. Village Council *see*
- MINUTES
- ORDINANCE RECORDS

Fulton County. Ohio. Auditor *see*
- JOURNAL OF WARRANTS ISSUED
- MILITIA ROLLS
- RECORDS OF RELIEF DISBURSEMENT
- SCHOOL FUND SETTLEMENTS
- SCHOOL LAND RECORDS

- TRANSFER RECORDS
Fulton County. Ohio. Board of County Commissioners *see*
- BLIND RELIEF APPLICATIONS
- BLIND RELIEF RECORDS AND MINUTES
- COMMISSIONERS' JOURNALS
- INDEX TO JOURNALS
- INDIGENT SOLDIERS' BURIAL RECS
- JOURNALS, COUNTY HOME
Fulton County. Ohio. Board of Education *see*
- ANNUAL FINANCIAL REPORTS
- BOARD OF EXAMINERS' MINUTES
- NORMAL SCHOOL APPLICATIONS
- SCHOOL ATTENDANCE REPORTS
- SCHOOL EXAMINERS' REPORTS
- STATE AUDIT REPORTS
Fulton County. Ohio. Board of Railroad Appraisers *see* RAILROAD APPRAISEMENT RECORDS
Fulton County. Ohio. Board of Revision *see* MINUTES
Fulton County. Ohio. Budget Commission *see* MINUTES
Fulton County, Ohio. Common Pleas. Civil Division *see* QUADRENNIAL ENUMERATIONS
Fulton County. Ohio. Common Pleas. Civil Division *see*
- CHANCERY RECORD
- COMPLETE RECORDS
- JOURNALS
- NATURALIZATION RECORDS
- NATURALIZATIONS, DECLARATIONS
Fulton County. Ohio. Common Pleas. Criminal Div *see* CORONERS' INQUESTS
Fulton County. Ohio. Common Pleas. Juvenile Division *see* MOTHERS' PENSION DOCKETS
Fulton County. Ohio. County Home *see*
- ANNUAL FINANCIAL REPORTS
- ANNUAL REPORTS
- APPLICATIONS FOR RELIEF
- MINUTES
- PAUPERISM STATISTICS
- REGISTERS
- SEMI-ANNUAL REPORTS
Fulton County. Ohio. Engineer *see* DITCH RECORDS
Fulton County, Ohio. Franklin Township. Board of Education. SubDist.2 *see* MINUTES
Fulton County. Ohio. Probate Court *see*
- COMPLETE RECORDS
- CRIMINAL RECORDS
- JOURNALS
- LAND SALES RECORDS
- REGISTER OF PATENTS
- WILL RECORDS
Fulton County. Ohio. Recorder *see* DEED RECORD
Fulton County. Ohio. Sheriff *see* JAIL REGISTERS
Fulton County. Ohio. Swan Creek Township. Board of Trustees *see*
- DITCH ASSESSMENT RECORDS
- MISCELLANEOUS RECORDS
Fulton County. Ohio. Swan Creek Township. Justice of the Peace *see*
- CIVIL DOCKETS
- CRIMINAL DOCKETS
Fulton County. Ohio. Swanton, Village. Mayor's Court *see* CRIMINAL DOCKETS
Fulton County. Ohio. Treasurer *see* CASH JOURNALS
Fulton County, Ohio. York Township. Board of Education *see* SUPERINTENDENT VISITATION REC.
FULTON COUNTY SUN – Rochester. Ind. 1913-1921 – 1 – us UMI [071]
FULTON COUNTY TRIBUNE – Wauseon, Co. 1883-1924 – 23r – 1 – $32.50r – us Archival [071]
FULTON DEMOCRAT – McConnellsburg, PA. -w 1889-1981 – 13 – $25.00r – us I.M.R. [071]
FULTON DEMOCRAT – McConnellsburg. Pa. -w. 1955- – 1 – us UMI [071]
FULTON FIRST BAPTIST CHURCH. FULTON, KENTUCKY : CHURCH RECORDS – 1891-1971. Includes minutes of Buckingham United Baptist Church, Fulton, Kentucky, Dec 1865-75.1734p – 1 – 78.03 – us Baptist [978]
Fulton, John *see*
- THE CHALCEDONIAN DECREE, OR, HISTORICAL CHRISTIANITY, MISREPRESENTED BY MODERN THEOLOGY, CONFIRMED BY MODERN SCIENCE, AND UNTOUCHED BY MODERN CRITICISM
- INDEX CANONUM
Fulton, Justin Dewey *see*
- IS IT MARY OR THE LADY OF THE JESUITS?
- THE TRUE WOMAN
Fulton, Maurice G *see* BRYCE ON AMERICAN DEMOCRACY
Fulton, T W *see* THE SOVEREIGNTY OF THE SEA
FULTON'S FOLLY – 1 – $60.00r – us Ross [975]
Fulwider, Addison L *see* HISTORY OF STEPHENSON COUNTY
Fumagalli, Camillo *see* IL DIRITTO DI FRATERNA NELLA GIURISPRUDENZA DA ACCURSIO ALLA CODIFICAZIONE
Fumagalli, Guiseppe *see* BIBLIOGRAFIA ETIOPICA
Fumet, Stanislas *see* LE BIENHEREUX MARTIN DE PORRES...PARIS
FUMEURS D'OPIUM / Boissiere, Jules – Paris: E. Flammarion, 1896. 381p. 4 fiches. (Literature Collection) – 9 – 10.00 – fr Bibl Nationale [830]
Fumimaro, Konoe, Prince *see* COLLECTION
FU-MIN HSIEN-CHIH – 1731, 1. BCH-662 2 – 8 – ne IDC [950]
FUN ON THE ROAD / Gair, John R – By an old-timed drummer. Toronto: Grip, 1886. 03282. (Pre-1900 Canadiana) – 9 – cn C.I.H.M. [910]
Funaioli, G B *see* DELLA REPARAZIONE...
Funakubo, Hiroyasu *see* PRECISION MACHINERY INCORPORATING LIFE SUPPORT TECHNOLOGY
Funchal, Agostinho de Sousa Coutinho *see* O CONDE DE LINHARES
LA FUNCION DEL CAPITAL EN EL JUSTICIALISMO / Argentina. Direccion General de Relaciones Culturales y Difusion – [Buenos Aires?, 1953?] – 1 – CSUXADQ7494-B – us Hoover Inst Photo [360]
LA FUNCION SOCIAL [CONFERENCIAS] / Amadeo, Tomas – Buenos Aires: Libreria El Ateneo, [2nd ed 1949] – 1 – CSUXADN3482-B – us Hoover Inst Photo [335]
FUNCIONAMIENTO DE LOS PERSONAJES EN LAS NOVELAS DE ROBBE GRILLET / Fernandez Cardo, Jose Maria – 2mf – 9 – Pta1,500.00 – 84-85422-07-4 – sp Pentalfa [440]
Funck, Heinrich *see* BEITRAEGE ZUR WIELAND-BIOGRAPHIE
Funck, J *see* AUSZUG VND KURTZER BERICHT: VON DER GERECHTIGKEIT DER CHRISTEN FUR GOTT AUS EINER PREDIG VBER DIE WORT JOHANNIS
Funck, J N *see* DE ORIGINE ET PVERITIA LATINAE LINGVAE, LIBRI DVO... ACCEDIT SPICILEGIVM LITERARIVM, ET INDEX...
Funck-Brentano, Th *see* PRECIS DU DROIT DES GENS...
FUNCTION AND ORGANIZATION OF A NATIONAL DOCUMENTATION CENTRE IN A DEVELOPING COUNTRY – 1985 – 218p – 9 – 92-3-101240-1 – fr UNESCO [020]
FUNCTION OF RELIGION IN MAN'S STRUGGLE FOR EXISTENCE / Foster, George Burman – Chicago: University of Chicago, 1909. 1 fiche – 9 – us A.T.L.A. [200]
THE FUNCTION OF RELIGION IN MAN'S STRUGGLE FOR EXISTENCE / Foster, George Burman – Chicago:University of Chicago Press, 1909 – 1mf – 9 – 0-8370-3166-4 – 1985-1166 – us A.T.L.A. [210]
THE FUNCTION OF THE DEPARTMENT OF RELIGIOUS AFFAIRS IN THE REPUBLIC OF INDONESIA / Indonesia. Departemen Agama – SE-6210 1. 1963? – 9 – ne IDC [360]
THE FUNCTION OF UNIVERSITIES IN RELIGION : AN ADDRESS AT THE DINNER OF THE UNITARIAN CLUB IN SAN FRANCISCO, APRIL 26, 1897 / Howison, George H – San Francisco: C.A. Murdock, 1897 – 1mf – us A.T.L.A. [240]
FUNCTIONAL ANALYSIS AND ITS APPLICATIONS – v1-28. 1967-94 – 1,5 – $80.00v – us UMI [510]
FUNCTIONAL ECOLOGY – v1- . 1987- – 1,5,6,9 – us UMI [574]
FUNCTIONAL LITERACY PROGRAM FOR HILL TRIBE GROUPS / Thailand. Ministry of Education – c. 1977 – 1mf – 9 – DE-294/1 – ne IDC [370]
FUNCTIONAL LITERACY TEACHER TRAINING HANDBOOK / Thailand. Ministry of Education. Adult Education Division – 1977 – 1mf – 9 – DE-309/1 – ne IDC [370]
FUNCTIONAL MOTOR SKILLS AND THE DEVELOPMENTALLY DISABLED / Young, Marnie J & Fisher, Janet M – 1991 – 2mf – 9 – $8.00 – us Microform Publ [150]
FUNCTIONS – Fredericton. v18-22. 1988-93 – 9 – Can$20.00y – cn Micromedia [073]
THE FUNCTIONS OF A GREAT UNIVERSITY: INAUGURAL ADDRESS DELIVERED ON NOVEMBER 16TH, 1894 / Clark, John Murray – (Toronto: Bryant), 1895. 00664. (Pre-1900 Canadiana) – 9 – cn C.I.H.M. [370]
THE FUNCTIONS OF DANCE IN SOCIAL GATHERINGS IN SEATTLE'S ARAB-AMERICAN COMMUNITY / Wartluft, Elizabeth M – 1994 – 2mf – $8.00 – us Microform Publ [790]
Fundacion Ayuda Social Maria Eva Duarte de Peron *see*
- EL HOGAR DE LA EMPLEADA
- HOGARES DE TRANSITO
LA FUNDACION DE MERIDA / Alvarez Saenz de Buruaga, Jose – Sep. de "Emerita Augusta" – 1 – sp Bibl Santa Ana [946]
FUNDACION DEL COLEGIO DE COYOACAN HERNAN Y MARTIN CORTES / Mateos, S F – Madrid: Missionalia Hispanica, 1947 – 1 – sp Bibl Santa Ana [060]
FUNDACION ESPANOLA...POR EL VIRREY DEL PERU, DON FRANCISCO DE TOLEDO. LIMA, 1926 / Urteaga, H H & Romero, Carlos A – Madrid: Razon y Fe, 1929 – 1 – sp Bibl Santa Ana [946]
FUNDACION FERNANDO VALHONDO CALAFF / Fundacion "Fernando Valhondo Calaff" – Caceres: Tip. La Minerva, 1960 – 1 – sp Bibl Santa Ana [060]
Fundacion "Fernando Valhondo Calaff" *see* FUNDACION FERNANDO VALHONDO CALAFF
FUNDACION Y FABRICA DEL CONVENTO DE SAN ANTONIO DE PADUA DE ALMENDRALEJO EN LA PROVINCIA FRANCISCANA DE SAN GABRIEL / Barrado Manzano, Arcangel – Madrid: Archivo Ibero-Americano, 1960 – 1 – sp Bibl Santa Ana [240]
FUNDACIONES BENFICAS DE LA PROVINCIA DE CACERES ANTERIORES A 1850 / Orti Belmonte, Miguel Angel – Caceres: Imp. Sanguino, 1949 – 1 – sp Bibl Santa Ana [946]
FUNDACIONES TESTAMENTARIAS DE FR. MIGUEL DE MEDINA, JERONIMO DE GUADALUPE EN EL CONVENTO DE SAN FRANCISCO DE MEDINA DE POMAR, BURGOS, 1915 / Gracia Villacampa, Carlos – Madrid: Archivo Ibero Americano, 1916 – 1 – sp Bibl Santa Ana [240]
EL FUNDADOR DE MONTEVIDEO. MONTEVIDEO, 1928 / Sallaberry, Juan Faustino – Madrid: Razon y Fe, 1929 – 1 – sp Bibl Santa Ana [946]
LOS FUNDADORES DE BOGOTA / Bayle, Constantino – Madrid: Razon y Fe, 1924 – 1 – sp Bibl Santa Ana [946]
EEN FUNDAMENT / Simons, Menno – 1579. BME-296 1 – 9 – ne IDC [240]
EEN FUNDAMENT / Simons, Menno – 1583. BME-297 1 – 9 – ne IDC [240]
DAT FUNDAMENT DES CHRISTELYCKEN LEERS OP DAT ALDER CORSTE GESCHREUEN. ANNO 1939 / Simons, Menno – BME-271 1 – 9 – ne IDC [240]
EIN FUNDAMENT VND KLARE ANWISINGE, VAN DE HEYLSAME VND GODTSELLYGHE LEERE JESU CHRISTI / Simons, Menno – BME-276 1 – 9 – ne IDC [240]
FUNDAMENTA AGROSTOGRAPHIAE SIVE THEORIA CONSTRUCTIONIS FLORIS GRAMINEI..... / Trinius, Carl Bernhard – Viennae, 1820 – 5mf – 9 – ne IDC [580]
FUNDAMENTA BOTANICA / Linnaeus, Carl – Amstelodami. 1736. B-164 2 – 8 – ne IDC [580]
FUNDAMENTA MUSICA CANTUS ARTIFIALIS / Schmelz, S – 1752 – 9 – us Sibley [780]
FUNDAMENTA PARTITURAE IN COMPENDIO DATA. DAS 1ST: KURTZER UND GRUENDLICHER UNTERRICHT, DEN GENERAL-BASS, ODER PARTITUR, NACH DENEN REGLEN RECHT UND WOHL SCHLAGEN ZU LEHRNEN.. / Gugl, Matthaeus – 1757 – 2 – us Sibley [780]
FUNDAMENTA SCIENTIAE – v. 1-. 1980- – 5,6,9 – us UMI [500]
FUNDAMENTAL AND APPLIED RESEARCH ON THE BRINE SHRIMP ARTEMIA SALINA (L.) IN BELGIUM / ed by Jaspers, E – 1977 – vi/110p – 9 – Bf300.00 – be E.A.S. [590]
FUNDAMENTAL AND APPLIED TOXICOLOGY – v.1-. 1981- – 1,5,6,9 – us UMI [615]
Fundamental Baptist Fellowship *see* INFORMATION BULLETIN
THE FUNDAMENTAL CHRISTIAN FAITH : THE ORIGIN, HISTORY AND INTERPRETATION OF THE APOSTLES' AND NICENE CREEDS / Briggs, Charles Augustus – New York: Charles Scribner, 1913 – 1mf – us A.T.L.A. [240]
FUNDAMENTAL CONSTITUTION / Carolina – 1669. 3 fiches – 9 – us South Carolina Historical [323]
THE FUNDAMENTAL FALLACY OF SOCIALISM : AN EXPOSITION OF THE QUESTION OF LANDOWNERSHIP: COMPRISING AN AUTHENTIC ACCOUNT OF THE FAMOUS MCGLYNN CASE / ed by Preuss, Arthur – (Includes bibliographical references) – St Louis, MO: B Herder, 1908 – 1mf – 9 – 0-8370-7010-4 – 1986-1010 – us A.T.L.A. [333]
FUNDAMENTAL GYMNASTICS / Bukh, Niels E – 1938 – 3mf – 9 – $9.00 – us Microform Publ [790]
THE FUNDAMENTAL IDEAS OF CHRISTIANITY / Caird, John – Glasgow: J. MacLehose; New York: Macmillan, 1899 – 2mf – us A.T.L.A. [240]
THE FUNDAMENTAL PRINCIPLES OF CHRISTIAN ETHICS : FIVE LECTURES / Conway, James Joseph – Chicago: D H McBride, 1896 – 1mf – 9 – 0-8370-6728-6 – 1986-0728 – us A.T.L.A. [230]
FUNDAMENTAL PRINCIPLES OF THE METAPHYSIC OF ETHICS / Kant, Immanuel – Trans. by Thomas Kingsmill Abbott. 10th ed. London, New York: Longmans, Green and Co., 1926.102p – 1 – us U.W. Library [190]
FUNDAMENTAL QUESTIONS : CHIEFLY RELATING TO THE BOOK OF GENESIS AND THE HEBREW SCRIPTURES / Clark, Edson Lyman – New York: G P Putnam, 1882 – 1mf – 9 – 0-8370-2665-2 – 1985-0665 – us A.T.L.A. [220]
THE FUNDAMENTAL TRUTHS OF THE CHRISTIAN RELIGION = GRUNDWAHRHEITEN DER CHRISTLICHEN RELIGION : SIXTEEN LECTURES DELIVERED IN THE UNIVERSITY OF BERLIN DURING THE WINTER TERM 1901-02 / Seeberg, Reinhold; ed by Morrison, W D – New York: G P Putnam; London: Williams & Norgate, 1908 – 1mf – 9 – 0-8370-7426-6 – 1986-1426 – us A.T.L.A. [240]
DIE FUNDAMENTALE GLAUBENSLEHRE DER KATHOLISCHEN KIRCHE : VORGELEGT UND GEGEN DIE MODERNEN SOZIALEN IRRTUEMER VERTEIDIGT VON PAPST LEO 13. – (Includes index) – Paderborn: Ferdinand Schoeningh, 1903 – 2mf – 9 – 0-8370-8492-X – 1986-2492 – us A.T.L.A. [240]
FUNDAMENTALIST – 1917-53. (Name change: The Searchlight, 1917-27) – 1 – 525.73 – us Baptist [240]
THE FUNDAMENTALS – A Testimony to the Truth. Chicago: Testimony Publishing Co., n.d. v1-12.1660p – 1 – 66.40 – us Baptist [240]
FUNDAMENTALS AND THEIR CONTRASTS / Buckley, James Monroe – Nashville: Methodist Episcopal Ch. So., 1906. 1 fiche – 9 – us A.T.L.A. [240]
FUNDAMENTALS OF CIVIL LEGISLATION OF THE U.S.S.R. AND THE UNION REPUBLICS. FUNDAMENTALS OF CIVIL PROCEDURE OF THE U.S.S.R. AND THE UNION REPUBLICS / Russia. (1923-U.S.S.R.). Laws, Statutes, etc – Official texts. Translated from the Russian. Moscow: Progress Publishers 1968. 130p. LL-4211 – 1 – us L of C Photodup [340]
FUNDAMENTALS OF COSMIC PHYSICS / ed by Canuto, V et al – 1974- – 1,5,9 – us Gordon [530]
FUNDAMENTALS, OR, BASES OF BELIEF CONCERNING MAN, GOD, AND THE CORRELATION OF GOD AND MEN : A HANDBOOK OF MENTAL, MORAL, AND RELIGIOUS PHILOSOPHY / Griffith, Thomas – (Includes appendix) – London:Longmans, Green, 1871 – 1mf – 9 – 0-8370-3395-0 – 1985-1395 – us A.T.L.A. [170]
FUNDAMENTORUM BOTANICORUM / Linnaeus, Carl – 3v. Coloniae Allobrogum. 1786-87. B-5418 2 – 8 – ne IDC [580]
FUNDAMENTOS DE DOCTRINA NACIONAL JUSTICIALISTA : TEXTO OFICIAL / Escuela Superior de Conducci on Politica del Movimiento Peronista – Buenos Aires: La Escuela, 1966 – 1 – CSUXAJB7923-B – us Hoover Inst Photo [320]

FUNDAMENTOS DE RELIGION / Marquez, Gabino – Madrid: Apostolado de la Prensa, 2nd ed 1915 – 1 – sp Bibl Santa Ana [200]
FUNDAMENTOS DE RELIGION / Marquez, Gabino – Madrid: Apostolado de la Prensa, 3rd ed 1920 – 1 – sp Bibl Santa Ana [240]
FUNDAMENTOS DE SOCIOLOGIA / Colorado, Vicente – 1883. Prologo por Urbano Gonzalez Serrano – 9 – 1.50f – sp Bibl Santa Ana [300]
FUNDAMENTOS DE UNA LOGICA SIMBOLICA DE LA CONTRADICCION / Lopez Medina, Emilio – 1mf – 9 – Pta1,000.00 – 84-85422-12-0 – sp Pentalfa [170]
LOS FUNDAMENTOS DEL BATTLISMO / Giudici, Roberto B – Montevideo: (Prometeo), 1946. 142p – 1 – us U.W. Library [972]
FUNDAMENTUM HISTORIAE NATURALIS MUSCORUM FRONDOSORUM / Hedwig, J – 2pts. Lipsaie. 1782. B-6203 2 – 8 – ne IDC [580]
FUNDE UND FORSCHUNGEN : EINE FESTGABE FUER JULIUS WAHLE ZUM 15. FEBRUAR 1921 / Deetjen, Werner et al – Leipzig: Insel Verlag, 1921 – 1r – 1 – us U.W. Library [430]
FUNDGRUBEN DES ORIENTS / ed by Hammer-Purgstall, Josef von – Wien, 1810-19. Hildesheim, 1994 – 34mf – 9 – DM290.00 diazo DM350.00 silver – gw Olms [950]
DIE FUNDLANDSCHAFT GUSPINI, PROVINZ CAGLIARI, SARDINIEN : ARCHAEOLOGISCHE STUDIEN IN SUEDWESTSARDINIEN MIT EINER EINFUEHRUNG ZUR SARDISCHEN VORGESCHICHTE / Koberstein, Astrid Beate – 1993 – 4mf – 9 – DM98.00 – 3-89349-704-8 – gw Hänsel [930]
FUNERAL AGENDA / Stolz, Joseph – 1897. 1 fiche – 9 – us A.T.L.A. [240]
THE FUNERAL DIRECTOR – Montreal: D.R. Nelson, [1887?-18–] – 9 – cn C.I.H.M. [390]
A FUNERAL DISCOURSE OCCASIONED BY THE MUCH LAMENTED DEATH OF MR. YORICK, PREBENDARY OF Y–K AND AUTHOR OF THE MUCH ADMIRED 'LIFE AND OPINIONS OF TRISTRAM SHANDY',... / Flagellan, C – London, 1761 – 1mf – 9 – MP-409/1 – ne IDC [240]
Funeral Home, Havana, KS *see* RECORDS
FUNERAL HOME RECORDS / Taylor Funeral Home (Oakwood, Ohio) – 1950-92 – 5r – 1 – $32.50r – us Archival [920]
THE FUNERAL OF ARMINIANISM, DELIVERED IN SUBSTANCE AT PROVIDENCE CHAPEL ON SUNDAY MORNING, MARCH 13, 1791 / Huntington, W – London, 1791 – 1mf – 9 – MP-570/1 – ne IDC [240]
FUNERAL RECORD AND LEDGER / Fiser Funeral Home (Clyde, Ohio) – 1914-1971 – 3r – 1 – $32.50r – us Archival [978]
FUNERAL RECORDS / Gibbons Mortuary (GSU), Coffey County, KS – undated – 1 – us KS Hist [920]
FUNERAL RECORDS / Ochs Funeral Home (Ottawa, Ohio) – 1891-1948 – 1r – 1 – $32.50r – us Archival [978]
FUNERAL RECORDS / Port Clinton. Ohio. Neidecker and Crosser Funeral Home – 1907-1986 – 4r – 1 – $32.50r – us Archival [920]
FUNERAL REGISTERS / Franklin County and Douglas County, KS – undated – 1 – us KS Hist [920]
FUNERAL REGISTERS / Labette County, KS – 1889-1926 – 1 – us KS Hist [920]
FUNERAL REGISTERS / Newill-Planson Company (Delta, Ohio) – 1910-46 – 1r – 1 – $32.50r – us Archival [920]
FUNERAL REGISTERS / Nieman-Beckman Funeral Home (Pemberville, Ohio) – 1893-1986 – 2r – 1 – $32.50r – us Archival [978]
FUNERAL SERMON OF THE LATE JOHN MELVILLE: LOCOMOTIVE DEPARTMENT OF G.T.R.: FOR MANY YEARS A MEMBER OF ST MATTHEWS'S CHURCH, POINT ST CHARLES: PREACHED IN ST MATTHEW'S CHURCH, ON SUNDAY, 24TH JUNE, 1874 / Doudiet, Charles A – Montreal?: s.n., 1874 (Montreal: "Witness" Print). 02741. (Pre-1900 Canadiana) – 9 – cn C.I.H.M. [971]
Funes, Jorge Ernesto *see* CABALLEROS DE ESPUELA DORADA (DESCUBRIMIENTO Y CONQUISTA DEL PERU)
Funes, Rafael *see* REFLEXIONES POLITICAS PARA MILITARES
Fung, Ch'eng-chun *see* NOTES ON THE NESTORIAN INSCRIPTION OF SI-AN (CCC129)
FUNGHI SICILIANI STUDII / Inzenga, G – 2v. Palermo. 1865-69. B-6277 2 – 8 – ne IDC [580]
FUNGI AND DISEASE IN PLANTS / Butler, E J – 7450 2. 1918 – 8 – ne IDC [580]
FUNGI HYPOGAEI. HISTOIRE ET MONOGRAPHIE DES CHAMPIGNONS HYPOGES / Tulasne, LR – Parisiis. 1851. B-6332 1 – 9 – ne IDC [580]
FUNGI ITALICI AUTOGRAPHICE DELINEATI / Saccardo, P A – Patavii. 1877-86. B-5704 2 – 8 – ne IDC [580]
FUNGI POMICOLI / Thuemen, F K A von – Monographische Beschreibung der auf den Obstfruechten der gemaessigten Climate vorkommenden Pilze. Wien. 1879. B-6323 1 – 9 – ne IDC [580]
FUNGI QUI IN BAVARIA ET PALATINATU / Schaeffer, J C – 4v. Ratisbonae. 1762-64. B-5304 2 – 8 – ne IDC [580]
FUNGORUM AGRI ARIMINENSIS HISTORIA / Battarra, G A – Faventiae. 1755. B-2342 2 – 8 – ne IDC [580]
FUNK : BEILAGE: DIE FUNK-BASTLER – Berlin. 1924-33 – 3r – 1 – gw Mikrofilm [380]
FUNK – Berlin. 1924-jun 1944 – 5r – 1 – gw Mikrofilm [380]
FUNK *see* FUNKSCHAU
Funk, Alfred *see* KLEINE BEITRAEGE ZU AKTUELLEN FRAGESTELLUNGEN IN DER MODERNEN KRIMINOLOGIE
FUNK ALLE TAGE *see* DIE MIRAG
FUNK ENTERPRISE – Funk, NE. -w. Sept 1898-Mar 1899. Scattered issues missing – 1 – us NE Hist [071]
Funk, Franz Xaver *see*
- DIE APOSTOLISCHEN KONSTITUTIONEN
- DIE ECHTHEIT DER IGNATIANISCHEN BRIEFE
- KIRCHENGESCHICHTLICHE ABHANDLUNGEN UND UNTERSUCHUNGEN
- A MANUAL OF CHURCH HISTORY
- DAS TESTAMENT UNSERES HERRN UND DIE VERWANDTEN SCHRIFTEN

Funk, Isaac Kaufman *see* THE NEXT STEP IN EVOLUTION
FUNK UND BEWEGUNG – Berlin, 1933-37 – 1 – Dist. gw Mikrofilm – gw Mikrofilm [790]
FUNK UND SCHALL – Frankfurt/Main. oct 15, 1929-aug 28, 1935 (incomplete) – 2r – 1 – gw Mikrofilm [073]
Funk, Wendy W *see* THE EFFECTS OF CREATIVE DANCE ON MOVEMENT CREATIVITY IN THIRD GRADE CHILDREN
Funk, W-P *see* DIE ZWEITE APOKALYPSE DES JACOBUS AUS NAG-MAMMADI-CODEX 5 (T.U.U. 5-119)
FUNK-BASTLER *see* FUNK
DER FUNKE – Berlin? n.d. – 1 – Dist. gw Mikrofilm – gw Misc Inst [072]
Funken, Michael *see* EVOLUTIONAERE ETHIK
FUNK-KORRESPONDENZ – Koeln, dec 2 1953- – 40r until 1995 – 1 – gw Mikrofilm [790]
FUNKSCHAU – (New from: Funk / Der Bastler / Der Fernempfang) – Muenchen, jan 1-dec 24 1929 – 1r – 1 – gw Mikrofilm [380]
FUNKSCHAU *see* BAYERISCHE RADIO-ZEITUNG UND BAYERNFUNK
FUNKSTUNDE – Berlin. nov 16, 1924-dec 26, 1937 – 16r – 1 – gw Mikrofilm [380]
DIE FUNKTION DER NEBENFIGUREN IN FONTANES ROMANEN / Buscher, Heide – Bonn, 1969 – 1 – DM30.00 – gw Mikro Press [440]
DER FUNKTIONALE ASPEKT DER TRAEUME IM WERK WILHELM RAABES / Schottelius-Winter, Lotti – 1993 – 5mf – 9 – DM125.00 – 3-89349-660-2 – gw Hänsel [430]
FUNKTIONELLE CHARAKTERISIERUNG VON DOMAENEN DES ELONGATIONSFAKTORS G / Borowski, Christian – 1995 – 1mf – 9 – DM60.00 – 3-8267-2192-6 – gw Hänsel [574]
FUNKTIONELLE MORPHOLOGIE UND CYTOCHEMIE OSTEOBLASTAERER RATTENOSTEOSARKOMZELLEN UNTER EINWIRKUNG VON CALCIUM; PARATHORMON ODER ALUMINIUM / Meyer, Gernot – 1995 – 2mf – 9 – DM80.00 – 3-8267-2269-8 – gw Hänsel [616]
FUNK-WACHT – Hamburg. dec 31, 1933-may 31, 1941 – 13r – 1 – gw Mikrofilm [790]
Funston, Frederick *see* PAPERS
FUNTSEIT TSU TSEIT = FROM TIME TO TIME – (In Yiddish) – Tel-Aviv, IS. (-) Nov 1946 – 1r – 1 – $25.00 – cn Can Microfilming [072]
FU-NU TSA-CHIH – The ladies' journal. v. 1-17. Shanghai. 1915-31. Lacking: v. 1 (8-9) 1915. BCH-252 2 – 8 – ne IDC [073]
FUR, FIN, AND FEATHER : A COMPILATION OF THE GAME LAWS OF THE PRINCIPAL STATES AND PROVINCES OF THE UNITED STATES AND CANADA: TOGETHER WITH A LIST OF HUNTING AND FISHING LOCALITIES AND OTHER USEFUL INFORMATION FOR GUNNERS AND ANGLERS – New York: Charles Suydam, Publisher, 1875 – us Res Libr [340]
Fur, L le *see* ETAT FEDERAL ET...
FUR WORKER / International Fur and Leather Workers' Union of the United States and Canada – New York. v1-14. 1916-31 – 1r – 1 – us Ross [331]
THE FUR WORKER – Long Island City, N.Y. v. 1-14 no. 7. Oct 3 1916-Apr 1931 – 1 – us NY Public [331]
DIE FURCHE – Wien. 19 Jan 1946-27 Dec 1975 – 1 – gw Mikrofilm [072]
DAS FURCHTMOTIV IN DER KATHOLISCHEN BUSSLEHRE VON AUGUSTIN BIS PETRUS LOMBARDUS / Hunzinger, A W – Naumburg, 1906 – 1mf – 9 – DM48.00 – 3-89349-340-9 – gw Hänsel [240]
DAS FURCHTPROBLEM IN DER KATHOLISCHEN LEHRE VON AUGUSTIN BIS LUTHER / Hunzinger, A W – Leipzig: A. Deichert, 1906 – 1mf – us A.T.L.A. [240]
LE FURET : SATIRIQUE – Quebec, Canada. 9 avr 1885 – 1r – 1 – Can$25.00 – cn Can Microfilming [072]
Furet, Auguste T *see* LETTRES A M. LEON DE ROSNY SUR L'ARCHIPEL JAPONAIS ET LA TARTARIE ORIENTALE
FURET DE LONDRES – London, UK. 8-19 Jan 1942 – 1 – uk British Libr Newspaper [072]
LE FURET DU VESINET – Journal illustre des concerts et fetes. Saint-Germain. 1862-63 – 1 – fr A.C.R.P.P. [073]
Furetiere, Antoine *see*
- DICTIONAIRE UNIVERSEL CONTENANT GENERALEMENT TOUT LES MOTS FRANCOIS TANT VIEUX QUE MODERNES, ET LES TERMES DE TOUTES LES SCIENCES ET DES ARTS (AEL, ABT 2; 17)
- DICTIONNAIRE UNIVERSEL
- DICTIONNAIRE UNIVERSEL, CONTENANT GENERALMENT TOUS LES MOTS FRANCOIS, TANT VIEUX QUE MODERNES, ET LES TERMES DES SCIENCES ET DES ARTS
- ESSAIS D'UN DICTIONNAIRE UNIVERSEL
- NOUVEAU RECUEIL DES FACTUMS DU PROCEZ

FUR-FARMING IN CANADA / Canada. Commission of Conservation. Committee on Fisheries, Game and Fur-Bearing Animals – By J. Walter Jones. Montreal: Gazette Printing Co. Ltd., 1913. viii, 166p. plates, maps, tables – 1 – us U.W. Library [636]
Furlong Cardiff, Guillermo *see*
- CARTOGRAFIA JESUISTICA DEL RIO DE LA PLATA...
- EL PADRE JOSE QUIROGA
- LA PERSONALIDAD Y LA OBRA DE TOMAS FALKNER. BUENOS AIRES, 1929

Furman, Hart, Botsford et al *see* SERMONS AND MISCELLANEOUS PAMPHLETS
FURMAN HISTORY – Publ. in the Greenville News, Greenville, SC, 15 Apr 1951 and 11 Nov 1958. 48p – 1 – 5.00 – us Baptist [240]
Furman, Richard *see* CORRESPONDENCE
Furman, Wood *see* A HISTORY OF CHARLESTON ASSOCIATION OF BAPTIST CHURCHES IN THE STATE OF SOUTH CAROLINA
Furmanov, Dmitrii *see*
- CHAPAEV
- ZA KOMMUNIZM

Furmanov, Dmitrii Andreevich *see* OPIS' DOKUMENTAL'NYKH MATERIALOV LICHNOGO FONDA NO.522
Furmer, B G *see* DE RERUM USU ET ABUSU
Furnas, Robert W *see* PAPERS
Furness, William H *see*
- REMARKS ON THE FOUR GOSPELS
- STORY OF THE RESURRECTION OF CHRIST TOLD ONCE MORE
- VEIL PARTLY LIFTED AND JESUS BECOMING VISIBLE

FURNITURE : ARCHITECTURE, APPLIED ARTS, STUDIO ARTS – (Individual titles not listed separately) – 29 catalogues on 33mf – 9 – £275.00 – uk Chadwyck [740]
FURNITURE – (Including Ormulu and musical instruments. Over 9,500 illustrations) – 165mf – 9 – $895.00 – 0-907006-22-1 – uk Mindata [740]
FURNITURE AND DECORATIVE ACCESSORIES (TIAM, PT 6) – (With printed catalogue ISBN: 0-914146-72-6 £30) – 35mf – 15 – £600.00 – uk Chadwyck [740]
FURNITURE AND UPHOLSTERY JOURNAL AND UNDERTAKERS GAZETTE – Toronto: J. Acton, [1895?-18– or 19–] – 9 – cn C.I.H.M. [680]
FURNITURE AND WOODWORK COLLECTION / Victoria and Albert Museum. London – (Over 6,500 illustrations) – 110mf – 9 – $585.00 – 0-907006-20-5 – uk Mindata [740]
THE FURNITURE LIBRARY COLLECTION – Significant monographs published since 1640 on the history of furniture making, decorative design, and interior decoration. Being published in three segments. Primarily European in nature, but also covers the Far and Middle East – 9 – us Readex [740]
FURNITURE NEWS *see* FDM
FURNITURE TODAY – 1978-79; 1985- – 1 – us UMI [073]
FURNITURE-TODAY – (1985-. 1,5,6) – 1976- – 9 – us UMI [073]
Furnivall, F J *see* THE STORY OF ENGLAND BY ROBERT MANNING OF BRUNNE (RS87)
Furrer, Reinhold *see* DIE HAFTUNG DES KOMMANDITISTEN IM VERGLEICH MIT DER HAFTUNG DES KOMPLEMENTARS AUF GRUNDLAGE DES FRANZOSISCHEN, SCHWEIZERISCHEN UND DEUTSCHEN HANDELSRECHTES
FURROW – 1894- 1; 1975- 5,6,9 – us UMI [630]
Furstenau, J A *see* DE FIDE HOSTI A PRIVATO DATA SERVANDA
FURTHER CORRESPONDENCE RELATIVE TO THE PROJECTED RAILWAY FROM HALIFAX TO QUEBEC / Canada. Gouverneur general – London: Printed by George Edward Eyre and William Spottiswoode, 1852. SEM105P120 – 2mf – 9 – Can$4.50 – cn Bibl Nat [380]
A FURTHER DEFENCE OF PRIESTCRAFT : BEING A PRACTICAL IMPROVEMENT OF THE SHAVER'S SERMON ON THE EXPULSION OF SIX YOUNG GENTLEMEN FROM THE UNIVERSITY OF OXFORD FOR PRAYING, READING AND EXPOUNDING THE SCRIPTURES,... / MacGowan, John – London, 5th ed 1768 – 1mf – 9 – MP-453/1 – ne IDC [240]
FURTHER ESSAYS ON BORDER BALLADS / Elliot, William Fitzwilliam – Edinburgh: Andrew Elliot, 1910 – 1 roll – 1 – 1-55879-523-5 – uk Libr Preservation [420]
FURTHER OBSERVATIONS ON THE EFFECT OF SEED ORIGIN ON COPPICE REGENERATION IN EUCALYPTUS CAMALDULENSIS DEHN / Israel. Ministry of Agriculture – By Clara Grunwald and R. Karschon. Bet-Dagan. Mar 1977. 9 p. Diagr – 9 – 2.00 – is I.T.T.I. [580]
FURTHER PAPERS RELATIVE TO THE AFFAIRS OF CANADA / Canada – London: Printed by W Clowes and Sons, 1849. SEM105P406 – 1mf – 9 – Can$2.25 – cn Bibl Nat [324]
A FURTHER REPORT FROM THE COMMITTEE OF SECRECY APPOINTED TO INQUIRE INTO THE CONDUCT OF ROBERT, EARL OF OXFORD / Great Britain. Parliament. House of Commons – London: T Leech, 1742. SEM16P3 – 1r – 5 – Can$9.00 – cn Bibl Nat [324]
FURTHER RESEARCHES INTO THE HISTORY OF THE FERRAR-GROUP / Harris, James Rendel – London: C.J. Clay, 1900.1 fiche – 9 – us A.T.L.A. [240]
FURTHER RESEARCHES INTO THE PHYSICAL REALITY OF SOME LONG-PERIODIC CYCLES IN THE BAROMETRIC PRESSURE OF BATAVIA / Boer, H J de – SE-6323 1. 1946? – 9 – ne IDC [530]
FURTHER STUDIES IN THE PRAYER BOOK / Dowden, John – London: Methuen, 1908 – 1mf – us A.T.L.A. [240]
Furttenbach, J *see*
- ARCHITECTURA CIVILIS
- ARCHITECTURA MARTIALIS
- ARCHITECTURA PRIVATA
- ARCHITECTURA RECREATIONIS
- ARCHITECTURA UNIVERSALIS
- MANNHAFFTER KUNST-SPIEGEL

FURUGH – Rasht. Sal-i 1, shumarah-i 1-12 (Day 1306-Aban va Azar 1308 [December 1927-October and November 1938]) – 1 reel – 1 – $80.00 – us MEDOC [950]
FUSAO DA FOLHA NOVA E BRASIL *see* DIARIO DE NOTICIAS

FUSE MAGAZINE – Toronto. v9-17. 1985/86-1993/94 – 9 – Can$20.00y – cn Micromedia [073]
FU-SHUN HSIEN-CHIH – 1777; 1882, 5, 1. BCH-730 2 – 8 – ne IDC [950]
Fusinato, G *see*
- DELL'EFFICACIA IN ITALIA DELLA SENTENZA ESTERA DI DIVORZIO
- L'ESECUZIONE DELLE SENTENZE STRANIERE...
- IL PRINCIPIO DELLA SCUOLA ITALIANA...

FUSION – (1985- 5,6,9) – 1977- – 1 – us UMI [621]
Fusslin, Johann C *see* WORKS
THE FUTILITY OF TECHNICAL, INDUSTRIAL, VOCATIONAL AND CONTINUATION SCHOOLS; A PAPER. / Crane, Richard Teller – Chicago, 1911. 13p – 1 – us U.W. Library [370]
THE FUTURE CENSUS(OCTOBER 1961) / Bhatta, Jitandra Nath – OF Indonesia. SE-3779 1 – 9 – ne IDC [310]
THE FUTURE GREAT CITY OF THE WORLD / Reavis, LU – Biographical sketches of representative men and women of St. Louis and Missouri. St. Louis: C.P. Barns, 1876. Missouri Reel 28. (The Cox Library Collection) – 5 – us Americana [978]
THE FUTURE GREAT STATE – CINCINNATI AND CLEVELAND / Comley & D'Eggville – Comley Brothers Manufacturing and Publ. Co., 1875. Mississippi Reel 4. (The Cox Library Collection) – 5 – us Americana [978]
THE FUTURE LEADERSHIP OF THE CHURCH / Mott, John Raleigh – New York: Student Dept., Young Men's Christian Association, 1908 – 1mf – us A.T.L.A. [240]
THE FUTURE OF AFRICA / Fraser, Donald – London: Student Volunteer Missionary Union, 1911 – 1mf – us A.T.L.A. [960]
FUTURE OF LIVESTOCK INDUSTRIES IN EAST AND SOUTHERN AFRICA : PROCEEDINGS OF THE WORKSHOP HELD AT KADOMA RANCH HOTEL, ZIMBABWE, 20-23 JULY 1992 / ed by Kategile, J A & Mubi, S – 1993 – 9 – Free – 92-9053-243-2 – et ILRI [338]
THE FUTURE OF MCGILL UNIVERSITY: ANNUAL UNIVERSITY LECTURE, SESSION 1880-81 / Dawson, John William – Montreal?: s.n., 1881?. 03666. (Pre-1900 Canadiana) – 9 – cn C.I.H.M. [971]
FUTURE OF SHIFTING CULTIVATION IN AFRICA AND THE TASK OF UNIVERSITIES : PROCEEDINGS OF THE INTERNATIONAL WORKSHOP ON SHIFTING CULTIVATION: TEACHING AND RESEARCH AT UNIVERSITY LEVEL. IBADAN, NIGERIA, 1982 – 1985 – 198p – it F.A.O. [631]
THE FUTURE OF THE DOMINION OF CANADA: A PAPER READ BEFORE THE ROYAL COLONIAL INSTITUTE (GROSVENOR GALLERY LIBRARY), JANUARY 25TH, 1881 – s.l.: s.n., 1881?. 03286. (Pre-1900 Canadiana) – 9 – cn C.I.H.M. [971]
THE FUTURE OF THE LEAGUE OF NATIONS – New York, n.d. – 2mf – 1 – ILM-4020/1 – ne IDC [327]
Future Political Status Commission [TTPI (U.S.)] *see*
- INTERIM REPORT TO THE CONGRESS OF MICRONESIA
- PAPERS OF THE 2ND MEETING
- REPORT TO THE CONGRESS OF MICRONESIA

FUTURE PROBATION : A SYMPOSIUM ON THE QUESTION "IS SALVATION POSSIBLE AFTER DEATH?" / Leathes, Stanley – London: James Nisbet, 1886 – 1mf – 9 – 0-8370-8835-6 – 1986-2835 – us A.T.L.A. [240]
FUTURE PROBATION AND FOREIGN MISSIONS : CERTAIN DUTIES AND USAGES AT THE ROOMS OF THE AMERICAN BOARD / Thompson, A C – Boston: Beacon Press, 1886 – 1mf – us A.T.L.A. [240]
FUTURE PUNISHMENT, OR, DOES DEATH END PROBATION: MATERIALISM, IMMORTALITY OF THE SOUL, CONDITIONAL IMMORTALITY OR ANNIHILATIONISM. / Cochrane, William – With illustrative notes from the writings of eminent British and American scientists and theologians; also additional papers...by the Rev. Wm. McLaren...illus. by...Gustave Dore. Brantford, Ont.: Bradley, Garretson, 1886. 00691. (Pre-1900 Canadiana) – 9 – cn C.I.H.M. [110]
FUTURE SPACE ACTIVITIES – (v40 1976, Science and Technology) – 1976 – 9 – $20.00 – us Univelt [629]
THE FUTURE TENSES OF THE BLESSED LIFE / Meyer, Frederick Brotherton – New York: Fleming H Revell, c1892 – 1mf – 9 – 0-8370-7174-7 – 1986-1174 – us A.T.L.A. [240]
THE FUTURE U.S. SPACE PROGRAM – (Suppl to v38, Advances) – 1979 – 6mf – 9 – $15.00 – 0-87703-129-0 – us Univelt [350]
FUTURES – (1982-. 1,5,6,9) – v1-. 1968- – 1 – us UMI [073]
FUTURES / Aroni, Julius – New Orleans, Gresham, 1882. 101 p. LL-439 – 1 – us L of C Photodup [340]
FUTURES OF CULTURES – 1994 – 167p – 9 – 92-3-103049-3 – fr UNESCO [306]
FUTURES RESEARCH QUARTERLY – v1-. 1985- – 1,5,6,9 – us UMI [073]
FUTURICS – v. 1- 1977- – 5,6,9 – us UMI [600]
FUTURISM / Plisko, N – Bol'shaia sovetskaia entsiklopediia. Ed. 1. M. 1935. BR-3578 2 – 8 – ne IDC [410]
FUTURISM : SUBJECT COLLECTIONS – (Individual titles not listed separately) – 10 catalogues on 12mf – 9 – £100.00 – uk Chadwyck [700]
FUTURISM, CONSTRUCTIVISM AND THE NEW CATHEDRALS FOR MAN – Pattee, University Park, PA. 1982 – 122p 5mf – 9 – $0.50f – us Lawrence Pub [720]
FUTURISTY / Chukovskii, K – Izd. "Poliarnaia Zvezda". Spb. 1922. BR-2027 2 – 8 – ne IDC [460]
FUTURISTY – Pervyi zhurnal russkikh futuristov. no. 1-2. M. 1914. B-1106 2 – 8 – ne IDC [460]
FUTURISTY – Rykaiushchii Parnas. Petrograd. 1914. BR-1849 2 – 8 – ne IDC [460]
FUTURISTY "GILEIA" – Sbornik dokhlaia luna. Moscow. 2v. 1913-14. BR-1840-2 – 8 – ne IDC [460]
FUTURISTY "GILEIA" – Sbornik moloko kobylits. Moscow, 1914. BR-3595-2 – 8 – ne IDC [460]
FUTURIZM / Maiakovskii, Vladimir – M. 1925. BR-967 2 – 8 – ne IDC [300]
FUTURIZM I VESHCH / Ivanov-Razumnik, R I – Kniga i revoliutsiia. nr. 8-9. 1921. BR-3564 2 – 8 – ne IDC [335]
FUTURIZM V LITERATURE. LITERATURNOKHUDOZHESTVENNYE ISKANIIA V KONTSE 19-NACHALE 20 VV / Red'ko, A M – Leningrad. 1924. "Seiatel". BR-2085 2 – 8 – ne IDC [460]
FUTURIZM V STIKHAKH BRIUSOVA / Shemshurin, A – M. 1913. BR-2119 2 – 8 – ne IDC [300]
O FUTURIZME / Gorkii, M – Zhurnal zhurnalov. Petrograd. nr. 1. 1915. BR-3561 2 – 8 – ne IDC [700]
FUTURO : PERIODICO LITTERARIO, NOTICIOSO E CRITICO – Manaos, Amazonas. 14 Abr-1 Out 1873 – 1,5,6 – bl Biblioteca [072]
EL FUTURO DE LA AGRICULTURA NACIONAL-SINDICALISTA / Falange Espanola Tradicionalista y de las Juntas Ofensivas nacional-Sindicalistas – n.p., 1937? Fiche W 870. (Blodgett Collection of Spanish Civil War Pamphlets) – 9 – us H.U. College Libr [946]
Fux, J J *see*
- GRADUS AD PARNASSUM
- GRADUS AD PARNASSUM. SALITA AL PARNASSO...NELL' IDIOMA ITALIANO DAL SACERDOTE ALESSANDRO MANFREDI...
- GRADUS AD PARNASSUM, SIVE MANUDUCTIO AS COMPOSITIONEM MUSICAE REGULAREN
- PRACTICAL RULES FOR LEARNING COMPOSITION
- SALITA AL PARNASSO....GRADUS AD PARNASSUM
- TRAITE DE COMPOSITION MUSICALE

Fux, Manfred *see* EIN BEITRAG ZUM ENTWURF VON ZEITREIHENREGLERN
Fuxhoffer, D, OSB *see* MONASTERIOLOGIAE REGNI HUNGARIAE
FUYUZAT – Baku, 1910-. Shumarah-'i 3-10 (1 Nov 1910-15 Mar 1911) – 1 reel – 1 – $25.00 – us MEDOC [950]
FUYUZAT – Istanbul, 1 sene, no. 1-3 (19 Tesrin II 1324-? [2 Dec. 1908-?]) – 4mf – 9 – $40.00 – us MEDOC [949]
FUZHOU WANBAO – Fuzhou Evending Post. -d. 1984-. M D66 – 1 reel/y – 1 – $55.00r – cc Microforms [072]
FUZULI / Sueleyman, Nazif – Istanbul, 1927 – $50.00 – us MEDOC [470]
Fuzuli *see* HADIKAT UEL-SU'ADA
FUZZY SETS AND SYSTEMS – v1-14. 1978-84 – 1,5,6,13 – sz Elsevier [510]
FV. PEDRO DE FERIA Y SU DOCTRINA ZAPOTECA. ESTUDIO BIBLIOGRAFICO / Salvador y Conde, Jose – Madrid: Missionalia Hispanica, 1947 – 1 – sp Bibl Santa Ana [240]
FVNDAMENTVM. EEN FONDAMENT / Simons, Menno – 1565. BME-294 1 – 9 – ne IDC [240]
FVNDAMENTVM. EIN FUNDAMENT VND KLARE ANWEISUNG VON DER SELIGMACHENDEN LEHRE VNSERS HERREN JESU CHRISTI. AUSZ NIDERL. SPRACH IN HOCHTEUTSCH GEBRACHT / Simons, Menno – 1575. BME-298 1 – 9 – ne IDC [240]
F.W. Beers and Co *see*
- HISTORY OF HERKIMER COUNTY
- HISTORY OF MONTGOMERY AND FULTON COUNTIES
- HISTORY OF WYOMING COUNTY

F.W. Faxon Company. Boston *see* CUMULATED MAGAZINE SUBJECT INDEX, 1907-1949
FYENS STIFTSBOG – 1969-92 (complete) – Inquire – 1 – ATLA S0760 – us A.T.L.A. [073]
Fyffe, David *see* THE ESSENTIALS OF CHRISTIAN BELIEF
Fynn, R *see* BRITISH CONSULS ABROAD...
FYRTIOFEMTE PSALMEN AF PSALTAREN OFVERSATTNING MED ANMARKNINGAR / Swartling, Karl – Upsala: Akademiska Boktryck, 1872. 1 fiche – 9 – us A.T.L.A. [240]
Fytche, A *see* BURMA, PAST AND PRESENT WITH PERSONAL REMINISCENCES OF THE COUNTRY
G. E. LESSINGS UEBERSETZUNGEN AUS DEM FRANZOESISCHEN FRIEDRICHS DES GROSSEN UND VOLTAIRES : IM AUFTRAG DER GESELLSCHAFT FUER DEUTSCHE LITTERATUR IN BERLIN / Lessing, Gotthold Ephraim; ed by Schmidt, Erich – Berlin: W Hertz, 1892 – 1r – 1 – us U.W. Library [430]
G FD *see* CAPTAIN LIGHTFOOT
G LP *see* LA VOIX PAYSANNE
G Maria de Alboraya, Domingo de *see* HISTORIA DEL MONESTARIO DE YUSTE
G, Mark *see* BOLSHE PRAVDY, CHIEM FANTAZII
G.A. GAPON PAMPHLET COLLECTION – 1906-1948 – 1 – CSUXANS0766-B – us Hoover Inst Photo [331]
G.A. Ogle and Co *see*
- COMPENDIUM OF HISTORY REMINISCENCE AND BIOGRAPHY OF LYON COUNTY
- MEMORIAL AND BIOGRAPHICAL RECORD
- MEMORIAL AND BIOGRAPHICAL RECORD OF BUTLER, POLK, SEWARD, YORK AND FILLMORE COUNTIES
- MEMORIAL AND BIOGRAPHICAL RECORD OF COLUMBIA, SAUK AND ADAMS COUNTIES
- MEMORIAL AND BIOGRAPHICAL RECORD OF SOUTH DAKOTA
- SOUTH DAKOTA BIOGRAPHICAL RECORD-1899

Gabba, C F *see*
- INTRODUZIONE AL DIRITTO CIVILE INTERNAZIONALE ITALIANO
- IL NUOVO DIRITTO INTERNAZIONALE...

Gabbert, John R *see* RIVERSIDE CITY AND COUNTY HISTORY
GABBS GABB – Las Vegas, NV. 1943; 1944 – 2r – 1 – $100.00 – U04856 – us Library Micro [071]
Gabelentz, H. C. von der *see*
- ELEMENTS DE LA GRAMMAIRE MANCHOUE
- MANDSCHUSINESISCHE GRAMMATIK NACH DEM SAN-HO-PIAN-LAN
- MANDSHU-MONGOLISCHE GRAMMATIK, AUS DEM SAN-HO-PIANLAN UEBERSETZT

Gabinete Psicopedagogico Sanchez Rodrigo *see* MANUAL DE LA BATERIA DE TEST GESAR
GABINETTO ARMONICO. DESCRIZIONE DEGL' ISTROMENTI ARMONICI / Bonanni, F – Seconda Ed. Riveduta, Corretta. French and Italian. 1776 – 9 – us Sibley [780]
GABINETTO ARMONICO PIENO D'INSTROMENTI SONORI / Bonanni, F – 1722 – 9 – us Sibley [780]
GABINETTO ARMONICO PIENO D'INSTROMENTI SONORI, INDICATI, SPIEGATI, E DI NUOVO CORRETTI / Bonanni, F – Roma. 1723. BP-644 1 – 9 – ne IDC [780]
GABINO MARQUEZ, S.J. DEBERES PATRIOTICOS / Meseguer, Pedro – Madrid: Razon y Fe, 1941 – sp Bibl Santa Ana [240]
GABINO TEJADO / Blanco Garcia, Francisco – Madrid: Saenz de Jubera, 1909 – sp Bibl Santa Ana [440]
GABLONZER TAGBLATT – Gablonz (Jablonec Nad Nisou), Czechoslovakia. 1 Mai 1935-31 Dec 1938 – 5r – 1 – gw Mikrofilm [072]
GABON : RAPPORT ANNUEL SUR LA SITUATION ECONOMIQUE, FINANCIERE ET SOCIALE DE LA REPUBLIQUE GABONAISE 1961-1971 / Gabon. Direction de la Statistique et des Etudes Economiques – (Coll title: African Official Statistical Serials, 1867-1982) – 29mf – 9 – £245.00 – uk Chadwyck [960]
Gabon *see*
- BULLETIN OFFICIEL
- ECONOMIE ET PLAN DE DEVELOPPEMENT
- JOURNAL OFFICIEL
- JOURNAL OFFICIEL DE LA REPUBLIQUE GABONAISE
- PLAN DE DEVELOPPEMENT ECONOMIQUE ET SOCIAL, 1966-1970
- PROGRAMME TRIENNAL INTERIMAIRE 1963-1965 PREPARATOIRE AU PLAN QUINQUENNAL DE DEVELOPPEMENT 1966-1970

Gabon. Direction de la Statistique et des Etudes Economiques *see* GABON
Gabon. Presidence *see* RESUME DU PLAN DE DEVELOPPEMENT ECONOMIQUE ET SOCIAL DU GABON, 66/70
Gabon. Republique Gabonaise *see* DEUXIEME PLAN DE DEVELOPPEMENT ECONOMIQUE ET SOCIAL, 1971-1975
Gabon-Congo *see* JOURNAL OFFICIEL
Gaboon and Corisco Mission. (Pres. Ch. in the U.S.A) *see* MINUTES AND RECORDS
Gabriel, Charles Nicolas *see* LE MARECHAL DE CAMP DESANDROUINS, 1729-1792: GUERRE DU CANADA 1756-1760: GUERRE DE L'INDEPENDANCE AMERICAINE 1780-1782
Gabriel de Jesus, C D *see* SERMON PREDICADO EN LA MISA NUEVA DEL PRESBITERO DON CONSTANTINO LANCHO SOLANA CELEBRADA EN LA IGLESIA PARROQUIAL DE SANTA MARINA, EN CANAVERAL (CACERES) POR EL FR
Gabriel de Talavera, Fray *see* HISTORIA... GUADALUPE
GABRIEL MARCEL ET KARL JASPERS / Ricoeur, P – Paris, 1947 – 8mf – 8 – ne Slangenburg [140]
Gabriel y Galan, Jose Maria *see*
- NUEVAS CASTELLANAS
- OBRAS COMPLETAS
- SOLO PARA MI LUGAR

Gabriel y Ruiz de Apodaca, Fernando de *see* POESIAS
Gabriel-de-l'Annonciation, Soeur *see* BIBLIOGRAPHIE ANALYTIQUE SUR LA METHODOLOGIE DE L'HISTOIRE DU CANADA (1950-1962)
Gabrielli, C de *see* MANUEL DU PROVENCAL
Gabungan Koperasi Batik Indonesia *see* SOMETHING ON BATIK TRADE
Gaby, Jean-Baptiste *see*
- RELATION DE LA NIGRITIE
- RELATION DE LA NIGRITIE. CONTENANT UNE EXACTE DESCRIPTION DE SES ROYAUMES ET DE LEURS GOUVERNEMENTS, LA RELIGION, LES MOEURS, COUSTUMES ET RARETES DE CE PAYS

LA GACETA / Costa Rica – San Jose. 1892-1948 – 1 – us NY Public [972]
LA GACETA : DIARIO OFICIAL – San Jose, Costa Rica, 1949-70 – 59r – 1 – us Ross [324]
LA GACETA : PERIODICO OFICIAL DE LA REPUBLICA DE HONDURAS – v74-95. 1949-70 – 24r – 1 – us Ross [324]
LA GACETA – Tampa. Fla. Oct 1922- – 1 – us P.K. Yonge [071]
GACETA ALGODONERA – Buenos Aires. v. 18, no. 213-v. 37, no. 433. Oct 1941-29 Feb 1960 – 1 – us NY Public [073]
GACETA DE LA HABANA / Cuba – Sept 4, 1800-June 1902 – 1 – 2231.00 – us L of C Photodup [324]
GACETA DE LOS TRIBUNALES / Chile – 1841-50 – 1 – 2,458.00 – us L of C Photodup [972]
GACETA DE LOS TRIBUNALES. – Santiago de Chile. On film: 1841-1950; indexes 1898-1902, 1905-12. LL-02005 – 1 – us L of C Photodup [340]
GACETA DE MADRID / Spain – Boletin oficiel. 1856-99; 1936-38 – 1 – 2940.00 – us L of C Photodup [324]
GACETA DE MEXICO, COMPENDIO DE NOTICIAS DE NUEVA ESPANA / Mexico – 1796-1809 – 1 – 54.00 – us L of C Photodup [340]
GACETA DE NICARAGUA – Managua. v62-71. 1958-67 – 13r – 1 – us Ross [324]

GACETA DE PAZ; DIARIO DE LA JUSTICIA DE PAZ Y DE INFORMACION JURIDICA GENERAL – v. 1-147. 1935-65. Includes indexes for v. 1-89. v. 132 33, 140-141, 144-145 wanting – 1 – 700.00 – us L of C Photodup [972]
GACETA DEL FORO – (Including "Diccionario de jurisprudencia") – Buenos Aires, Argentina. 3 Feb 1916-16 Apr 1964 – 104r – 1 – uk British Libr Newspaper [073]
GACETA DEL FORO. JURISPRUDENCIA-LEGISLACION-DOCTRINA – v v. 1-250. 1916-67 – 1 – 1,440.00 – us L of C Photodup [972]
GACETA DEL GOBIERNO / Bolivia – 1841-62 – 1 – 81.00 – us L of C Photodup [972]
GACETA DEL GOBIERNO / Mexico. (State) – Toluca. On film: 1851-1924. LL-02025 – 1 – us L of C Photodup [340]
GACETA DEL GOBIERNO DEL ECUADOR / Ecuador – (El 21 de Junio. 1845-46. El Nacional. 1846-49. 121.00; 1) – 1843-45 – us L of C Photodup [340]
GACETA DIARIO OFICIAL / Costa Rica – 1877-1957 – 1 – 4278.00 – us L of C Photodup [324]
GACETA DIARIO OFICIAL / Costa Rica – 1970- – 1 – us L of C Photodup [340]
LA GACETA DIARIO OFICIAL / Honduras – 1876-1949 – 1 – 1495.00 – us L of C Photodup [324]
LA GACETA DIARIO OFICIAL / Honduras – 1971- – 1 – us L of C Photodup [340]
LA GACETA DIARIO OFICIAL / Nicaragua – 1845-1946, 1962-69 – 1 – 1909.00 – us L of C Photodup [324]
LA GACETA DIARIO OFICIAL / Nicaragua – (Subject Index. 1970-74. 1) – 1970- – 1 – us L of C Photodup [340]
GACETA ESPANOLA – London, UK. Nov 1884; 7 Jan 1885-10 Mar 1886; 5 Jan-23 Mar 1887; 2 Jan 1889-20 May 1891; 11 Nov 1891 – 1 – uk British Libr Newspaper [072]
GACETA JUDICIAL – Tegucigalpa. Honduras. -w. 10 Feb 1900-12 Mar 1904, 2 Jul 1907-11 Apr 1911. (Imperfect). (2 reels) – 1 – uk British Libr Newspaper [072]
GACETA MEDICA DE MEXICO – (v.116 .1980 5,6,9) – v.1. 1864 – 1 – us UMI [073]
GACETA MUNICIPAL / Sucre. Venezuela (District) – Jan.-Sept. 1950 – 1 – us NY Public [324]
GACETA OFICIAL / Bolivia – 1911-15, 24-28, 43-44. 1970- – 1 – us L of C Photodup [972]
GACETA OFICIAL – Caracas. v88-98. 1960-70 – 22r – 1 – us Ross [324]
GACETA OFICIAL – Ciudad Trujillo, Dominican Republic. v78-91. 1957-70 – 15r – 1 – us Ross [324]
GACETA OFICIAL / Cuba – 1964-Feb 1969 very incomplete. Feb 1970- – 1 – us L of C Photodup [972]
GACETA OFICIAL / Cuba – Havana. 1902-1966 – 1 – us NY Public [972]
GACETA OFICIAL / Dominican Republic – 1865-1969 – 1 – $1,909.00 – us L of C Photodup [972]
GACETA OFICIAL / Dominican Republic – 1970-. LL-02087 – 1 – us L of C Photodup [340]
GACETA OFICIAL / Dominican Republic – Ciudad Trujillo. 1945-1966 – 1 – us NY Public [972]
GACETA OFICIAL – La Paz, Bolivia. 1960-68 – 4r – 1 – us Ross [324]
GACETA OFICIAL / Mexico. (Federal district) – 1943-1947 – 1 – us NY Public [324]
GACETA OFICIAL / Panama – 1970- – 1 – us L of C Photodup [340]
GACETA OFICIAL – Panama. v47-66. 1950-69 – 28r – 1 – us Ross [324]
GACETA OFICIAL / Paraguay – Asuncion. 1901-1903, 1918-1942, 1945, 1959-May 29, 1963 – 1 – us NY Public [324]
GACETA OFICIAL – v77. 1957 – 1r – 1 – us Ross [324]
GACETA OFICIAL / Venezuela – 1827-1969 – 1 – 4623.00 – us L of C Photodup [324]
GACETA OFICIAL / Venezuela – 1970- – 1 – us L of C Photodup [972]
GACETA OFICIAL / Vera Cruz. Mexico (State) – Jalapa-Enriquez. On film: 1853-1965. LL-02039 – 1 – us L of C Photodup [340]
GACETA OFICIAL AMERICANA – London, UK. 17 Jul 1873; 17 Apr 1874-29 Aug 1875 – 1 – uk British Libr Newspaper [072]
GACETA OFICIAL DE LA REPUBLICA DE CUBA – Havana, 1902-67 – 410r – 1 – us Ross [324]
GACETA OFICIAL DEL ESTADO / Sucre. Venezuela (State) – Cumana. Jan.-Nov. 1950 – 1 – us NY Public [972]
GACETA OFICIAL DEL ESTADO MIRANDA / Miranda. Venezuela – Los Teques. 1949-Apr. 1960 – 1 – us NY Public [324]
GACETA OFICIAL DEL ESTADO ZULIA / Zulia. Venezuela. (State) – Maracaibo. 1950-1966 – 1 – us NY Public [972]
LA GACETA PORTENA – Buenos Aires. 9 Mar 1984-. illus. -semim – 1 – us U.W. Library [073]
GACETA SUD AMERICANA Y DE ESPANA – London, UK. 8 Dec 1885-15 Dec 1886 – 1 – uk British Libr Newspaper [072]
Gache, Ferdinand Pierre *see* LA PHILOSOPHIE DU PEUPLE: L'HYGIENE, L'HABITATION
Gaches, R *see* DEUS SERMONS SUR LA PAIX...
Gaddi, G B *see* ROMA NOBILITATA NELLE SUE FABBRICHE DALLA SANTITA DI NOSTRO SIGNORE CLEMENTE XII
Gaddi, Giuseppe *see* POVERI BIMBI; LA BARBARIE DEI RIBELLI SPAGNUOLI
Gadeau de Kerville, H *see* LES INSECTS PHOSPOHORESCENTS...
GADIS TERATAI, SEBUAH DONGENG RAKJAT KOREA; DRAMA TIGA BABAK / Siregar, Bakri – SE 4569 1. 1962 – 9 – ne IDC [950]
GADJAH MADA – Djakarta. Incomplete. SE-587 1. 1950-1968 – 9 – ne IDC [073]
GADJAH MADA / Pratikto, Herman – SE-4559 1 – 9 – ne IDC [950]
GADOLINIUM-DTPA- UND TEMPERATURSTUDIEN ZUR INTERSTITIELLEN TUMORTHERAPIE FUER DIE INTERVENTIONELLE KERNSPINTOMOGRAPHIE / Franzen, Stefan – 1995 – 2mf – 9 – DM80.00 – 3-8267-2200-0 – gw Hänsel [616]
Gadomskii, A *see* UKAZATEL' K IZDANIIAM IMP. KAVKAZSKAGO MEDITSINSKAGO OBSHCHESTVA ZA DVADTSAT' PIAT LET EGO SUSHCHESTVOVANIIA
Gadsby, John *see*
- MEMOIRS OF THE PRINCIPAL HYMN-WRITERS AND COMPILERS OF THE 17TH, 18TH AND 19TH CENTURIES
- A VISIT TO CANADA AND THE UNITED STATES OF AMERICA: ALSO A SECOND VISIT TO SPAIN

Gadsby, William *see* THE WORKS OF THE LATE WILLIAM GADSBY
GADSDEN COUNTY TIMES – Quincy. Fl. -w. 1924-1933, 1942- – 1 – us P.K. Yonge [071]
Gadzhieva, S *see* DINAMIKA IZMENENIIA POLOZHENIIA DAGESTANSKOI ZHENSHCHINY I SEMIA
GAE UPDATE – Georgia Association of Educators – 1970- 1; 1975- 5,6,9 – us UMI [370]
Gaebelein, Arno Clemens *see*
- THE PROPHET JOEL
- PROPHET JOEL: AN EXPOSITION
- STUDIES IN ZECHARIAH

Gaebler, Joachim *see* INTERNATIONALE FREIZUEGIGKEIT DES KAPITALS UND UNTERENTWICKELTE LAENDER
Gaedertz, Karl Theodor *see* BEI GOETHE ZU GASTE
AN GAEDHEAL – Ireland.29 Jan-18 Mar 1916 – 1 – ie Microforms [072]
GAELIC AMERICAN – New York. v1-48. 1903-51 – 23r – 1 – us Ross [071]
THE GAELIC AMERICAN – New York. Sept 19 1903-Dec 15 1951 – 1 – us NY Public [071]
GAELIC CLUB, CLEVELAND, OHIO, RECORDS – (Minutes, membership rosters, and financial balance reports of this social and athletic club, located on Cleveland's West Side, serving Irish immigrants and Irish Americans) – Cleveland, Cuyahoga, OH. 1930-39 – 1r – 1 – us Western Res [790]
GAELIC FOLK TALES / O'Sheridan, Mary Grant – 1926 – 1 – us I.U. Libraries [390]
Gaertner, J *see*
- DE FRUCTIBUS ET SEMINBUS PLANTARUM
- DE FRUCTIBUS ET SEMINIBUS PLANTARUM

GAERTNERPOST *see* DEUTSCHE GAERTNERPOST
GAESTE IM PARADIES / Andres, Stefan Paul – (First publ in 1937 under title: Mosellaendische Novellen) – Muenchen: Paul List, c1937 – 1r – 1 – us U.W. Library [830]
Gaeterbock, F *see* OTTONIS MORENAE ET CONTINUATORUM HISTORIA FREDERICI 1 (MGH 6: 7.BD)
Gaeumann, E *see* BEITRAEGE ZU EINER MONOGRAPHIE DER GATTUNG PERONOSPORA CORDA
Gaffarel, Paul *see*
- ETUDE SUR LES RAPPORTS DE L'AMERIQUE ET DE L'ANCIEN CONTINENT AVANT CHRISTOPHE COLOMB
- LES IRLANDAIS EN AMERIQUE AVANT COLOMB: D'APRES LA LEGENDE ET L'HISTORIE: COLONISATION DE L'IRLAND IT MIKLA
- NUNEZ DE BALBOA
- VOYAGES DES FRANCAIS AU CANADA, DANS L'AMERIQUE CENTRALE ET AU BRESIL DANS LES PREMIERES ANNEES DU 16E SIECLE

GAFFNEY FIRST BAPTIST CHURCH. CHEROKEE COUNTY. SOUTH CAROLINA : CHURCH RECORDS – (WMU Minutes, 1977, 1981-1988. 250p) – Oct 1980-Sept 1986 – 1 reel – 1 – $11.25 – us Baptist [240]
Gaffurio, Franchino *see*
- ANGELICUM AC DIVINUM OPUS MUSICE..
- DE HARMONIA MUSICORUM INSTRUMENTORUM OPUS
- PRACTICA MUSICAE UTRIUSQUE CANTUS
- PRACTICA MUSICE
- THEORICA MUSICE FRANCHINI GAFURI LAUDENSIS

Gaffurius, F *see*
- ANGELICUM AC DIUINUM OPUS MUSICE FRANCHINI GAFURII LAUDENSIS REGII MUSICI
- FRANCHINI GAFURII LAUDENSIS REGII MUSICI PUBLICE PROFITENSIS
- PRACTICA MUSICAE VTRIUSQUE CATUS EXCELLETIS FRACHINI GAFFORI LAUDESIS
- THEORICA MUSICE FRANCHINI GAFURI LAUDENSIS

Gagalis, Zisis *see* EFFECTS OF LEG EXERCISE AND INSULIN INJECTION SITES ON BLOOD GLUCOSE IN PERSONS WITH INSULIN DEPENDENT DIABETES MELLITUS (IDDM)
Gagarin, G G *see* SBORNIK VIZANTIISKIKH I DREVNERUSSKIKH ORNAMENTOV
Gagarin, S P *see* VSEOBSHCHII GEOGRAFICHESKII I STATISTICHESKII SLOVAR'
GAGE COUNTY DEMOCRAT – Beatrice, NE. -w. Dec. 1879-Dec. 1909 – 1 – us NE Hist [071]
GAGE COUNTY DEMOCRAT – Beatrice. Neb. 1879-1909 – 1 – us UMI [071]
GAGE COUNTY HERALD – Beatrice, NE. -w. Jan. 1901-Jun. 1902; Aug. 1902-Feb. 1903; Apr. 1905 – 1 – us NE Hist [071]
Gage, Matilda Joslyn *see* WOMAN, CHURCH AND STATE
GAGE PAPERS – American mss. 1731-1874. BRRAM – 1 – uk Microform Academic [025]
Gage, Sandra L *see* MARKETING STRUCTURES, ACTIVITIES AND OUTCOMES AMONGST SELECTED NATIONAL SPORT ORGANIZATIONS
Gager, William *see* ULYSSES REDUX: TRAGOEDIA NOVA
GAGE'S SCHOOL EXAMINER AND MONTHLY REVIEW – Jan 1881- – 9 – cn C.I.H.M. [370]
Gagin, Dom. P *see* SACRAMENTAIRE GELASIEN D'ANGOULEME'
Gagliardi, Alfredo *see* CORRIERE ITALIANO
Gagne, Rolland *see* LA VOIX DE L'EST
Gagne, W H *see* L'ECHO DE SAINT-JUSTIN
Gagneius, Ioan. *see*
- IN QUATUOR SACRO-SANCTA IESU CHRISTI EVANGELIA. SCHOLIA
- IN QUATUOR SACRO-SANCTA IESU CHRISTI EVANGELIA..SCHOLIA

Gagnol, abbe *see* LE JANSENISME CONVULSIONNAIRE ET L'AFFAIRE DE LA PLANCHETTE
Gagnon, Charles-Octave *see* CHRONOLOGIE DE L'HISTOIRE DES ETATS-UNIS D'AMERIQUE
Gagnon, Ernest *see*
- CHANSONS POPULAIRES DU CANADA
- CHOSES D'AUTREFOIS
- LE FORT ET LE CHATEAU SAINT-LOUIS (QUEBEC): ETUDE ARCHEOLOGIQUE ET HISTORIQUE
- LE PALAIS LEGISLALIF DE QUEBEC: GOVERNMENT BUILDINGS IN QUEBEC

Gagnon, Ferdinand *see*
- ELOGE SUR LA VIE ET LES OEUVRES DE M. L'ABBE HYACINTHE MARTIAL: PRONONCE EVANT LES MEMBRES DE LA SOCIETE ST JEAN-BAPTISTE ET LES PAROISSIENS DE ST JOSEPHE GROSVENORDALE, CONN., LE 6 MAI, 1883
- FERDINAND GAGNON, SA VIE ET SES OEUVRES: NOTICE BIOGRAPHIQUE ET OEUVRES DE FERDINAND GAGNON...PAR M. LE CHANOINE J.-R. OUELLETTE, SUPERIEUR DU SEMINAIRE DE ST HYACINTHE, PROVINCE DE QUEBEC

Gagnon, Francoise *see* BIBLIOGRAPHIE ANALYTIQUE DE SIMONE BUSSIERES
Gagnon, Gilberte *see* BIBLIOGRAPHIE ANALYTIQUE DE LA LITTERATURE PEDAGOGIQUE CANADIENNE FRANCAISE DE 1790 A 1900
Gagnon, Huguette *see* BIBLIOGRAPHIE ANALYTIQUE DE ALAIN GRANDBOIS
Gagnon, Jacques Etiennette *see* BIBLIOGRAPHIE ANALYTIQUE DE L'OEUVRE DE OLIVETTE LAMONTAGNE
Gagnon, Jean-Louis *see*
- LE CANADA
- LE NOUVEAU JOURNAL
- LA REFORME
- VIVRE

Gagnon, J-L *see* LE CINQ TROIS UN SIX
Gagnon, Marcel-A *see* JOURNAL METROPOLE
Gagnon, Marcelle *see* BIBLIOGRAPHIE ANALYTIQUE DE MADAME HELENE B. BEAUSEJOUR
Gagnon, Yves *see* LE CANADA-FRANCAIS
Gahan, James Joseph *see*
- IRELAND'S POSITION EXPLAINED AND JUSTIFIED: THE RED HAND OF ULSTER
- VIVIAN: A TALE OF CHATEAU RICHER

Gahan, William *see* SERMONS AND MORAL DISCOURSES FOR ALL THE SUNDAYS AND PRINCIPLE FESTIVALS OF THE YEAR
GAI LE SAVOIR : OEUVRES POETIQUES – Nantes: [s.n.], 1885-1886 – 1 – F50.00 – fr Armell [810]
GAI SALLUSTI CRISPI BELLUM CATILINAE / Sallust – Sallust's Catiline with parallel passages from Cicero's orations against Cataline. Introd., notes, and vocabulary by Jared W. Scudder.Boston: Allyn and Bacon, (c1900). xx,126p – 1 – us U.W. Library [900]
GAI SOLLII APOLLINARIS SIDONII EPISTULAE ET CARMINA (MGH 1: 8.BD) / ed by Luetjohann, CH – (Accedunt Fausti Aliorumque Epistulae Ad Ruricium Aliosque. Ruricii Epistulae. Rec. Et Emend. B. Krusch) – 1887 – Dfl53.00 – ne Slangenburg [240]
LA GAIETE CANADIENNE – Montreal, Canada. 25 fev 1905-v1 n10. 28 avr 1905 – 1r – 1 – Can$25.00 – cn Can Microfilming [072]
Gaiffe, F *see* L'ART POETIQUE ABREGE DE CLAUDE DE BOISSIERE
Gail, Jean Francois *see* REFLEXIONS SUR LE GOUT MUSICAL EN FRANCE
Gailland, Maurice, S J *see* DIARY
Gaillard, Thomas *see* PRINCIPLES OF SURVEYING
Gaillardet, Frederic *see*
- L'ARISTOCRATIE EN AMERIQUE
- LE COURRIER DES ETATS-UNIS

Gaillardot, C *see* CATALOGUE DE L'HERBIER DE SYRIE
Gailly de Taurines, Charles *see* LA NATION CANADIENNE: ETUDE HISTORIQUE SUR LES POPULATIONS FRAN CAISES DU NORD DE L'AMERIQUE
Gailus-Doering, Sigrid *see* DIE IMAGINAERE UND DIE REALE HEXE
Gaimard *see* VOYAGE AUTOUR DU MONDE. EXECUTE SUR LES CORVETTES DE S.M. L'URANIE ET LA PHYSICIENNE, 1817-1820
GAIN OR LOSS?: AN APPRECIATION OF THE RESULTS OF RECENT BIBLICAL CRITICISM / Snell, Bernard Joseph – London: James Clarke, 1895. 1 fiche – 9 – us A.T.L.A. [240]
Gain, R *see*
- ETUDE SUR L'EVOLUTION DE LA NATIONALITE DES SOCIETES EN FRANCE
- LA NATIONALITE DES SOCIETES AVANT ET DEPUIS LA GUERRE 1914-18

GAINA-SUTRAS : PART 1: THE AKARANGA-SUTRA AND THE KALPA-SUTRA / ed by Mueller, Friedrich Max – (Translated from Prakrit by Herman Jacobi) – 1884 – 7mf – 8 – ne Slangenburg [280]

THE GAINA-SUTRAS : PART 2: THE UTTARADHYAYANA SUTRA, THE SUTRAKRITANGA SUTRA / ed by Mueller, Friedrich Max – (Translated from Prakrit by Hermann Jacobi) – 1895 – 9mf – 8 – ne Slangenburg [280]
Gainer *see* THE STORY OF OKLAHOMA CITY
GAINESVILLE FIRST BAPTIST CHURCH. GAINESVILLE, GEORGIA : WMU RECORDS – 1896-1954 – 1 – $39.84 – us Baptist [240]
GAINESVILLE SUN – Gainesville. Fla. 1903-81 – 1 – us P.K. Yonge [071]
GAINSBOROUGH EVENING NEWS – England.1954-83. 20 1/2 reels – 1 – uk British Libr Newspaper [072]
GAINSBOROUGH NEWS *see* RETFORD, WORKSOP ISLE OF AXHOLME AND GAINSBOROUGH NEWS
GAINSBOROUGH NEWS (MIDWEEK ED.) – 1986-89; Jan 29-Dec 18 1990; Jan-Dec 17 1991; Jan-Jun 1992; Jul 7-Dec 22 1992; Jan-Jun 1993; Jul 6-Dec 21 1993; Jan 11-Jun 28 1994; Jul 5-Dec 20 1994; Jan 10-Jun 27 1995; Jan-Dec 17 1996 – 11r – 1 – uk British Libr Newspaper [072]
GAINSBOROUGH STANDARD (FRIDAY EDN) – 1986-96 – 25r – 1 – uk British Libr Newspaper [072]
Gair, John R *see* FUN ON THE ROAD
Gairal, F *see* LE PROTECTORAT INTERNATIONAL
Gairdner, J *see*
- LETTERS AND PAPERS ILLUSTRATIVE OF THE REIGN OF RICHARD 3 AND HENRY 7 (RS24)
- MEMORIALS OF HENRY 7 (RS10)

Gairdner, James *see*
- ENGLAND
- THE HISTORICAL COLLECTION OF A CITIZEN OF LONDON IN THE FIFTEENTH CENTURY
- LOLLARDY AND THE REFORMATION IN ENGLAND
- THE REIGN OF HENRY 8 FROM HIS ACCESSION TO THE DEATH OF WOLSEY

Gairdner, William Henry Temple *see*
- D.M. THORNTON
- ECHOES FROM EDINBURGH, 1910

GAIRLOCH AND SURROUNDS 1851 CENSUS INDEX : ARGYLL AND WEST SCOTLAND CENSUS INDEX, PART 5 / Gibson, Peter – 1995 – 3mf – 9 – A$19.95 – 0-646-18029-0 – at Seanachas [920]
Gaisinskii, Mikhail Grigorevich *see* IAKOV MIKHAILOVICH SVERDLOV, EGO ZHIZN I DEIATELNOST
Gaismaier, Josef *see* JUSTINUS KERNERS SAEMTLICHE POETISCHE WERKE
Gaitanides, Johannes *see* GEORG RUDOLF WECKHERLIN
GAIZAO – La Rekonstruo. Sept 1920-Sept 1922. 2 reels. M C3A – 1 – $90.00 – cc Microforms [073]
GAJA BAHASA INDONESIA / Sabaruddin, Ahmad – SE 5261 1. 1959 – 9 – ne IDC [950]
GALAAY : OU, LA QUETE DE L'EPOUSE: CONTE WOLOF / Ndiaye, Moussa – 1987 – us Res Libr [390]
Galadee, M *see* THAILAND'S WALKING TEACHER PROJECT FOR FUNCTIONAL LITERACY
Galakhov, A D *see* ISTORIIA RUSSKOI SLOVESTNOSTI, DREVNEI I NOVOI
Galan, Leocadio *see*
- CIEN RAZONES (AUNQUE SEA TARDE)
- DIRSOS...!TENGO MADRE! COSAS DE UN RECLUTA

Galan Saval, Ricardo *see* ESCUELA ELEMANTAL DE TRABAJO Y DE CAPATACES AGRICOLAS DE CACERES
Galan y Galan, FG *see* DE MI VIEJA EXTREMADURA (PAGINAS MONTANCHEGAS)
Galant, H C *see* HISTOIRE POLITIQUE DE LA SECURITE SOCIALE FRANCAISE, 1945-1952
Galanus, Clemens *see* CONCILIATIONIS ECCLESIAE ARMENAE CUM ROMANA EX IPSIS ARMENORUM PATRUM ET DOCTORUM TESTIMONIIS IN DUAS PARTES
Galarza, J *see* CODEX MENDOZA
GALAS D'INAUGURATION / University of Montreal – (Includes: Bulletin des Anciens 1 jan-mai 1950) – Montreal, 3 jun 1943-46 – 1r – 1 – Can$28.75 – cn Can Microfilming [370]
Galasso, Norberto *see*
- LA IZQUIERDA NACIONAL Y EL FIP
- J.J. HERNANDEZ ARREGUI
- VIDA DE SCALABRINI ORTIZ

GALATEA – Zhurnal literatury, novostei i mod. v. 1-18. M. 1829-30. B-1413 2 – 8 – ne IDC [073]
GALATEA – Zhurnal nauk, iskusstv, literatury, novostei i mod. v. 1-6. M. 1839; v. 1-17. 1840. B-1730 2 – 8 – ne IDC [073]
LA GALATEA: EDICION PUBLICADA POR RODOLFO SCHEVILL Y ADOLFO BONILLA / Cervantes Saavedra, Miguel de – Madrid: Rodriguez, 1914.2v – 1 – us U.W. Library [830]
DER GALATERBRIEF : NACH SEINER ECHTHEIT UNTERSUCHT: NEBST KRITISCHEN BEMERKUNGEN ZU DEN PAULINISCHEN HAUPTBRIEFEN / Steck, Rudolf – (Includes bibliographical references) – Berlin: Georg Reimer, 1888 – 1mf – 9 – 0-8370-9421-6 – 1986-3421 – us A.T.L.A. [220]
GALATERBRIEF UND APOSTELGESCHICHTE / Zimmer, Friedrich – Hildburghausen: F.W. Gadow, 1882. 1 fiche – 9 – us A.T.L.A. [240]
Galatinus, P *see* DE ARCANIS CATHOLICI VERITATIS LIBRI 12
THE GALAX GATHERERS : THE GOSPEL AMONG THE HIGHLANDERS / Guerrant, Edward Owings; ed by Guerrant, Grace – (Includes index) – Richmond, VA: Onward Press, c1910 – 1mf – 9 – 0-8370-6059-1 – 1986-0059 – us A.T.L.A. [240]
Galaxy Publishing Co *see*
- BIOGRAPHICAL ENCYCLOPAEDIA OF OHIO OF THE 19TH CENTURY
- THE BIOGRAPHICAL ENCYCLOPEDIA OF ILLINOIS OF THE NINETEENTH CENTURY
- BIOGRAPHICAL ENCYCLOPEDIA OF PENNSYLVANIA

Galbraith, Francis J *see* FOURTH OF JULY MESSAGE
Galbraith, John *see* IN THE NEW CAPITAL, OR, THE CITY OF OTTAWA IN 1999
Galbraith, Thomas *see* A NEW CHAPTER ADDED TO POLITICAL ECONOMY: POINTING OUT A 100 MILLION DOLLARS CAPITAL THAT MAY BE MADE AVAILABLE TO CANADIAN INDUSTRIES BY THE ESTABLISHMENT OF A MORTGAGE BANK OF ISSUE
Gale, Charles James *see* A TREATISE ON THE LAW OF CASEMENTS
Gale, James Scarth *see*
- KOREA IN TRANSITION
- KOREAN SKETCHES
- THE VANGUARD

Gale, John T *see* ACCOUNT, GUIDE AND FORM BOOK FOR ADMINISTRATORS AND EXECUTORS IN THE STATE OF OHIO
Gale, Martha Tyler *see* WOMAN'S HIGH CALLING
Gale, Samuel *see* NERVA OR A COLLECTION OF PAPERS PUBLISHED IN THE "MONTREAL HERALD"
Gale, T *see*
- CERTAINE WORKES OF CHIRURGERIE
- AN EXCELLENT TREATISE OF WOUNDS MADE WITH GONNESHOT

Galeb, O *see* RECHERCHES SUR LES ENTOZOAIRES DES INSECTES: ORGANISATION ET DEVELOPPEMENT DES OXYURIDES
THE GALE-MORANT PAPERS – 1731-1825. BRRAM – 1 – uk Microform Academic [972]
Galen *see* OPERA OMNIA
Galen, Philipp *see* DER IRRE VON ST JAMES
Galeno *see* OPERA MEDICA
GALENO ILUSTRADO, AVICENA EXPLICADO Y DOCTORES DEFENDIDOS / Lopez Cornejo, A – Sevilla, 1699 – 6mf – 9 – sp Cultura [610]
Galenus *see* DE PLACITIS HIPPOCRATIS ET PLATONIS LIBRI NOVEM
Galeotti, H G *see* MEMOIRES SUR LES FOUGERES DE MEXIQUE
A GALERIA ILLUSTRADA – Curitiba, 20 Nov 1888-29 Sep 1889 – 1,5,6 – bl Biblioteca [072]
GALERIA UNIVERSITARIA. TOMO 1. CARACAS, 1934 / Dominguez, Rafael – Madrid: Razon y Fe, 1936 – 1 – sp Bibl Santa Ana [946]
Galerie L'Art francais *see* "L'ART FRANCAIS" PRESENTE... [...DU NOUVEAU AVEC MARC-AURELE FORTIN, A.R.C.A.]
GALERIE CHALETTE CATALOGUE – (Individual titles not listed separately) – New York, 1954-1970 – 30 catalogues on 31mf – 9 – £260.00 – uk Chadwyck [700]
GALERIE DES CONTEMPORAINS ILLUSTRES, PAR UN HOMME DE RIEN. 3E LIVRAISON (3E DU 10E VOL.) M. SPONTINI / Lomeni, L – Paris: A Rene et Cie, [1847] – 1 – us Sibley [780]
LA GALERIE DES OISEAUX / Vieillot, L J P & Oudart, PL – Z 1954. 2 v. 1820. 1825-1826 – 9 – ne IDC [590]
GALERIE HISTORIQUE / Dionne, Narcisse Eutrope – Quebec: Laflamme & Proulx, 1909-13. SEM105P497 – 25mf – 9 – Can$56.25 – cn Bibl Nat [971]
GALERIE UNIVERSELLE DES HOMMES QUI SE SONT ILLUSTRES: VOLTAIRE / Imbert de la Platiere, S – Paris. 1787 – 9 – fr Hachette [920]
Galeron, Frederic *see* STATISTIQUE DE L'ARRONDISSEMENT DE FALAISE
Galiani, F *see* DE' DOVERI DE' PRINCIPI NEUTRALI...
Galich, Iurii *see*
- KRASNY I KHOROVOD
- KRASNYI KHOROVOD
- VOLCHII SMEKH

GALICHANIN – Literaturnyi sbornik. v. 1-4. L'vov. 1862-63. BR-3385 2 – 8 – ne IDC [073]
GALICIA PAMPHLET COLLECTION – 1915-1931 – 1 – CSUXANL5641-B – us Hoover Inst Photo [946]
Galicia. Sejm *see* STENOGRAFICZNE SPRAWOZDANIA
Galiffe, J BG *see*
- QUELQUES PAGES D'HISTOIRE EXACTE
- LE REFUGE ITALIEN DE GENEVE

GALIGNANI'S MESSENGER – Paris. Daily Messenger. -d 15 Apr 1853-18 Sep 1870; 10 Mar 1871-31 Dec 1872; 1 Jan 1890-30 Jul 1904. Imperfect. 78 reels – 1 – uk British Libr Newspaper [072]
GALILEAN CHRISTIANITY / Elliott-Binns, L E – S.C.M. Press, 1956 – 9 – $10.00 – us I.R.C. [240]
GALILEAN GOSPEL / Bruce, Alexander Balmain – Cincinnati: Jennings & Graham, (18??). 1 fiche – 9 – us A.T.L.A. [240]
THE GALILEAN GOSPEL / Bruce, Alexander Balmain – Cincinnati: Jennings & Graham, [18–?] – 1mf – 9 – 0-8370-2483-8 – 1985-0483 – us A.T.L.A. [240]
Galilee, Madeleine-de *see* BIBLIOGRAPHIE ANALYTIQUE DE SON EXCELLENCE MONSEIGNEUR JEAN-MARIE FORTIER, EVEQUE DE GASPE
Galilei, Galileo *see* SYSTEMA COSMICUM, 1663; SYSTEMA COSMICUM, 1635; NOV-ANTIQUA, 1636
Galilei, V *see*
- DIALOGO DI VINCENTIO GALILEI NOBILE FIORENTINO DELLA MUSICA ANTICA, ET DELLA MODERNA
- DISCORSO DI VICENTIO GALILEI NOBILE FIORENTINO. ET ALTRI INPORTANTI PARTICOLARI ATTENENTI ALLA MUSICA
- DISCORSO DI VINCENTIO GALILEI, INTORNO ALL' OPERE DI MESSER GIOSEFFO ZARLINO DA CHIOGGIA

Galilei, Vincenzo *see* FROMINO, DIALOGO DI VINCENTIO GALILEI.....
GALILEISTUDIEN : HISTORISCH-THEOLOGISCHE UNTERSUCHUNGEN UEBER DIE URTHEILE DER ROEMISCHEN CONGREGATIONEN IM GALILEIPROCESS / Grisar, Hartmann – Regensburg, New York: F. Pustet, 1882 – 1mf – us A.T.L.A. [240]
GALILEO GALILEI AND THE ROMAN CURIA = GALILEO GALILEI UND DIE ROEMISCHE CURIE : FROM AUTHENTIC SOURCES / Gebler, Karl von – (Includes index) – London: C Kegan Paul, 1879 – 1mf – 9 – 0-8370-7294-8 – 1986-1294 – us A.T.L.A. [945]
Galimberti, Rodolfo *see* LA REVOLUCION PERONISTA
Galindez, Bartolome *see* APUNTES DE TRES REVOLUCIONES
Galindo Herrero, Santiago *see*
- DONOSO CORTES
- DONOSO CORTES EN LA ULTIMA ETAPA DE SU VIDA

Galinier *see* VOYAGE EN ABYSSINIE DANS LES PROVINCES DU TIGRE
Galion. Ohio. First Lutheran Church *see* RECORDS
Galion. Ohio. First United Methodist Church *see* RECORDS
Galion. Ohio. Peace Evangelical Lutheran Church *see* CHURCH RECORDS
Galion. Ohio. Peace United Church of Christ *see* RECORDS
Galisteo. Ayuntamiento *see*
- FERIAS Y FIESTAS DE NUESTRA SENORA DE LA ASUNCION DURANTE...AGOSTO 1962
- FERIAS Y FIESTAS DE NUESTRA SENORA DE LA ASUNCION LOS DIAS...AGOSTO 1960
- FERIAS Y FIESTAS EN HONOR DE NTRA. SRA. DE LA ASUNCION. 1971

GALITSKO-RUSSKII VESTNIK – Ezhemesiachnyi istorikoliteraturnyi i politicheskii zhurnal. V. 1-2. Spb. 1894. BR-3980 2 – 8 – ne IDC [320]
Gall, August, Freiherr von *see* ALTISRAELITISCHE KULTSTAETTEN
Gall, August, Frieherr von *see* DIE HERRLICHKEIT GOTTES
Gall, Frederick Beckles *see* GAZETTEER OF BAUCHI PROVINCE
Gall, James *see* PRIMEVAL MAN UNVEILED, OR, THE ANTHROPOLOGY OF THE BIBLE
Gall, M M *see* MATERNAL AND FETAL RESPONSES TO MAXIMAL EXERCISE DURING SWIMMING AND CYCLING
Gallagher & Gauthier *see* CATALOGUE ILLUSTRE ET DESCRIPTIF DES VIGNES, BAIES ET ROSES CULTIVEES ET EN VENTE AUX VIGNOBLES BEACONSFIELD (PRES LA POINTE-CLAIRE, P.Q.)
Gallagher, Margaret *see*
- BECOMING AWARE
- UNEQUAL OPPORTUNITIES

Gallagher, Mason *see* THE REGARD DUE TO THE VIRGIN MARY
Galland, Antoine *see*
- ALI-BABA OU LES QUARANTE VOLEURS ECTERMINES PAR UNE ESCLAVE
- JOURNAL D'ANTOINE GALLAND PENDANT SON SEJOUR A CONSTANTINOPLE: 1672-1673

Gallardo, B J *see* ENSAYO DE UNA BIBLIOTECA ESPANOLA DE LIBROS RAROS Y CURIOSOS
Gallardo, Bartolome Jose *see*
- AL ZURRIAGAZO ZURRIBANDA
- CATALOGO FORMADO POR...DE LOS PRINCIPALES ARTICULOS QUE COMPONEN LA SELECTA LIBRERIA DE D.J. BOEHL DE FABER
- ENSAYO...BIBLIOTECA...LIBROS RAROS

Gallardo Bonilla, Leandro *see* DESCRIPCION PROCLAMA...BADAJOZ...AL TRONO...REY D. FERNANDO 6
Gallardo de Alvarez, Isabel *see*
- CUENTOS DE LA ABUELITA
- NUESTRA SENORA DE FATIMA

Gallardo y Gomez, Manuela *see* MUCHACHAS EN FLOR. MADRID, 1946
Gallas, Heidrun *see* DIE SYNTHETISCHE EVOLUTIONSTHEORIE UND IHRE KRITIKER
Gallatin, Albert *see* THE PAPERS OF ALBERT GALLATIN
GALLATIN COUNTY JOURNAL – Belgrade. Mont. 1929-1933 – 1 – us UMI [071]
GALLATIN COUNTY REPUBLICAN – Bozeman. Mont. 1901-1905 – 1 – us UMI [071]
GALLATIN COUNTY TRIBUNE – Bozeman. Mont. -w. 1966- – 1 – us UMI [071]
THE GALLATIN DEBATE / Lipscomb-Griffin – 1872 – 1 – 5.00 – us Baptist [240]
GALLATIN DEMOCRAT – Shawneetown. Ill. 1957- – 1 – us UMI [071]
GALLATIN FARMER AND STOCKMAN – Belgrade. Mont. 1903-1906 – 1 – us UMI [071]
GALLATIN FIRST BAPTIST CHURCH. GALLATIN, TENNESSEE : CHURCH RECORDS – 1878-Sept 1987. 1354p – 1 – 60.93 – us Baptist [240]
Gallatin, Mississippi *see* MISCELLANEOUS EARLY NEWSPAPERS
Gallaudet College. Washington, DC *see* DICTIONARY CATALOG ON DEAFNESS AND THE DEAF
Galle, Emile *see* ECRITS POUR L'ART: FLORICULTURE, ART DECORATIF, NOTICES D'EXPOSITION, 1884-1889
Gallego, Ignacio *see* EL PROBLEMA CAMPESINO IN ANDALUCIA
Gallegos Rocafull, Jose Manuel *see*
- CRUSADE OR CLASS WAR?
- CRUSADE OR CLASS WAR? THE SPANISH MILITARY REVOLT

GALLEREIA PETRA VELIKAGO V IMPERATORSKOI PUBLICHNOI BIBLIOTEKE / Stasov, V – Spb. 1903. BR-11,257 1 – 9 – ne IDC [020]
GALLEREIA RUSSKIKH PISATELEI I KHUDOZHNIKOV S PUSHKINSKOI EPOKHI DO NASKIKH DNEI / Martov, N – Spb. 1901. BR-7144 2 – 8 – ne IDC [460]
GALLERIA CIVICA D'ARTE MODERNA CATALOGUE – Turin, 1939-74 – ca 27mf – 9 – uk Chadwyck [700]
GALLERIA DI PITTURE DELL'... TOMMASO RUFFO, VESCOVO DI PALESTRINA E DI FERRARA... / Agnelli, J – Ferrara, 1734 – 4mf – ne IDC [700]
Galleria Pesaro. Milan *see* LIBERO ANDREOTTI

A GALLERY OF DISTINGUISHED MEN / Barrass, Edward – Napanee, Ont.: Henry and Bros., c1870. 03378. (Pre-1900 Canadiana) – 9 – cn C.I.H.M. [971]
Gallet de Kulture, Achille *see* LE TSAR NICOLAS ET LA SAINTE RUSSIE
Galletti, Alfredo *see* LA POLITICA Y LOS PARTIDOS
Galley, Micheline *see* MARIA CALLEJA'S GOZO
Galley, Suzi-Lyn *see* THE EFFECTIVENESS OF MICROCURENT ELECTRICAL NERVE STIMULATION (M.E.N.S.) IN THE TREATMENT OF POST ACUTE LYMPHEDEMA IN ANKLE INJURIES
GALLIA CHRISTIANA *see*
– ARCHIEPISCOPATUS PARISIENSIS (GC 7)
– DE PROVINCIA REMENSI 1 (GC 9)
– DE PROVINCIA REMENSI 2 (GC 10)
– PROV. ALBIENSIS-AUSCIENSIS (GC 1)
– PROV. BITURICENSIS-BURDIGALENSIS (GC 2)
– PROV. CAMERACENSIS-COLONIENSIS-EBREDUNENSIS (GC 3)
– PROV. MECHLIENSIS ET MOGUNTINENSIS (GC 5)
– PROVINCIA LUGDUNENSIS (GC 4)
– PROVINCIA NARBONENSIS (GC 6)
– PROVINCIA ROTOMAGENSIS (GC 11)
– PROVINCIA TURONENSIS (GC 14)
– PROVINCIA VESUNTIONENSIS (GC 15)
– PROVINCIA VIENNENSIS (GC 16)
– PROVINCIAE SENONENSIS ET TARENTASIENSIS (GC 12)
– PROVINCIAE TOLOSANA ET TREVIRENSIS (GC 13)
– QUATUOR ECCLESIAE PARISIACAE SUFFRAGANEAE (GC 8)
GALLIA CHRISTIANA (GC) : OPERA ET STUDIO MONACHORUM CONGREGATIONIS S. MAURI O.S.B. / ed by Haureau, A B – (Vols listed individually) – Parisiis. v1-16. 1739-1865 – 726mf – 8 – Dfl2,541.00 coll – ne Slangenburg [240]
GALLIA CHRISTIANA IN PROVINCIAS ECCLESIASTICAS DISTRIBUTA / Sainte-Marthe, Denys de & Haureau, Barthelemy – (edition Palme) – Parisiis, 1715-1865. 16v – 9 – Bf59,000.00 set – 1-799-00702-2 – be Brepols [240]
GALLIA CHRISTIANA, IN PROVINCIAS ECCLESIASTICAS DISTRIBUTA.. – 1715-1865. SEM35P206 – 10r – 1 – Can$531.00 – cn Bibl Nat [240]
GALLIA JUDAICA, DICTIONNAIRE GEOGRAPHIQUE DE LA FRANCE... / Gross, H – Paris, 1897 – 9mf – ne IDC [270]
THE GALLICAN CHURCH : A HISTORY OF THE CHURCH OF FRANCE FROM THE CONCORDAT OF BOLOGNA, A.D. 1516, TO THE REVOLUTION : WITH AN INTRODUCTION / Jervis, W Henley – London: John Murray, 1872 – 3mf – us A.T.L.A. [240]
THE GALLICAN CHURCH : SKETCHES OF CHURCH HISTORY IN FRANCE / Lloyd, Julius – London: S.P.C.K., [1879?] – 1mf – us A.T.L.A. [240]
THE GALLICAN CHURCH AND THE REVOLUTION : A SEQUEL TO THE "HISTORY OF THE CHURCH OF FRANCE FROM THE CONCORDAT OF BOLOGNA TO THE REVOLUTION" / Jervis, W Henley – London: Kegan Paul, Trench, 1882 – 2mf – us A.T.L.A. [240]
Galliculus. Isagoge Ioannis Gallicvli *see* DE COMPOSICIONE CANTUS
Gallicus, Johann *see* LIBELLUS DE COMPOSITIONE CANTUS IOANNIS GALLICULI
Gallieni, Joseph-Simon *see*
– DEUX CAMPAGNES AU SOUDAN FRANCAIS, 1886-1888
– RAPPORT D'ENSEMBLE SUR LA PACIFICATION, L'ORGANISATION ET LA COLONISATION DE MADAGASCAR (OCTOBRE 1896 A MARS 1899)
GALLIONS REACH. LEIPZIG, 1928 / Tomlinson, H M; ed by Bayle, Constantino – Madrid: Razon y Fe, 1928 – 9 – sp Bibl Santa Ana [830]
GALLIPOLI : IZDANJE OBSHCHESTVA GALLIPOLI IT SEV – (Includes c.1: no.1 1923:Feb.15-no.2 (1923:Apr.8)) – Bielgrad: Obshchestvo, 1923- – 1 – CSUXAKG1810-S – us Hoover Inst Photo [947]
GALLIPOLIET S = GALLIPOLIETZ – (Includes c.1: no.1) – Paris: Izd. Soi uza gallipoli it sev vo Frant sii, 1927- – 1 – CSUXANR3285-S – us Hoover Inst Photo [947]
GALLIPOLIET S (PARIS, FRANCE: 1927) *see* GALLIPOLIET S
GALLIPOLIETZ *see* GALLIPOLIET S
Gallison, John *see* GALLISON'S REPORTS OF CASES IN THE FIRST CIRCUIT, 1812-1815
GALLISON'S REPORTS OF CASES IN THE FIRST CIRCUIT, 1812-1815 / Gallison, John – 2nd ed. Boston: Little-Brown. v1-2. 1845 (all publ) – 15mf – 9 – $22.50 – LLMC 81-452 – us L.L.M.C. [324]
Gallner, Bonifacius *see*
– REGULA EMBLEMATICA SANCTI BENEDICTI
EL GALLO – Denver, CO. 1968-88 – 11r – 1 – $550.00 – R04001 – us Library Micro [071]
Gallo, A *see* DECLARACION BREVE...Y SUMARIA DEL VALOR DEL ORO...
Galloe, O *see* FORBEREDENDE UNDERSOGELSER TIL EN ALMINDELIG LIKENOKOLOGI
LES GALLOIS EN AMERIQUE AU XIIE SIECLE / Beauvois, Eugene – 189-. 04067. (Pre-1900 Canadiana) – 9 – cn C.I.H.M. [970]
Gallop Organization *see* 1988 PRESIDENTIAL ELECTION POLLS
Gallopin, Gilberte C *see* PLANNING METHODS AND THE HUMAN ENVIRONMENT
Galloway, Charles B *see*
– CHRISTIANITY AND THE AMERICAN COMMONWEALTH, OR, THE INFLUENCE OF CHRISTIANITY IN MAKING THIS NATION
– THE EDITOR-BISHOP, LINUS PARKER
Galloway, George *see* STUDIES IN THE PHILOSOPHY OF RELIGION
GALL'S NEWSLETTER – Kingston, Jamaica. 7 Mar 1895-27 Mar 1899 (imperfect).-d. 14 reels – 1 – uk British Libr Newspaper [072]
GALLUP LOOKS AT THE MOVIES : AUDIENCE RESEARCH REPORTS, 1940-1953 – 1979 – 4r – 1 – $340.00 – S1853 – us Scholarly Res [790]
Gallus A Koenigsaal, O Cist. *see* DIALOGUS MALEGRANATUM
Gallus, Heidrun *see* UNTERSUCHUNGEN ZUR ANTHOCYANBIOSYNTHESE AN GENETISCH DEFINIERTEN BLUETEN UND ZELLKULTUREN DER DAHLIE UND DER SOMMERASTER
Gallus, N *see*
– CATECHISMVS PREDIGSWEISE GESTELT FUER DIE KIRCHE ZU REGENSPURG...
– EINE DISPVTATION VON MITTELDINGEN VND VON DEN ITZIGEN VERENDERUNGN IN KIRCHEN DIE CHRISTLICH VND WOL GEORDENT SIND...
– QVAESTIO
– WAECHTERSTIMME NIC. GALLI. WO VND IN WAS STUECKEN VNTER DEM NAMEN LUTHERI DER AUGSPURGISCHEN CONFESSION VND H. SCHRIFT...
GALOA OU EDONGO D'ANTAN / M'Beye, Ogoula – Port-Gentil, Gabon, 1957 – us Res Libr [960]
Galperin, S *see* NA PUTI K EDINOMU INTERNATSIONALU PROFSOIUZOV
Galpin, F W *see* ACCOUNT OF THE FLOWERING PLANTS, FERNS AND ALLIES OF HARLESTON
Galt, Alexander Tilloch *see*
– THE POLITICAL SITUATIONS: A LETTER TO THE HONORABLE JAMES FERRIER, SENATOR
– PROHIBITION: GREAT SPEECH OF SIR A. T. GALT, G.C.M.G
GALT HERALD – Galt, CA. 1912- – 70+ r – 1 – $3,500.00 ($100.00y) – C02264 – us Library Micro [071]
Galt, John *see* THE LIFE OF BENJAMIN WEST
GALT REPORTER – Cambridge, 1902-1920 – 10r – 1 – cn Preston [971]
GALT WEEKLY GAZETTE – Galt, CA. 1882-1911 – 7r – 1 – $350.00 – C03225 – us Library Micro [071]
Galtier, P *see* L'EGLISE ET LA REMISSION DES PECHES AUX PREMIERE SIECLES
Galton, Arthur *see*
– CHURCH AND STATE IN FRANCE, 1300-1907
– THE MESSAGE AND POSITION OF THE CHURCH OF ENGLAND
– OUR ATTITUDE TOWARDS ENGLISH ROMAN CATHOLICS AND THE PAPAL COURT
Galton, Francis *see* VACATION TOURISTS AND NOTES OF TRAVEL IN 1860 1861, 1862-3
Galtruchius, P *see* PHILOSOPHIAE, AC MATHEMATICAE TOTIUS...INSTITUTIO
Galvan Soto, F *see* LE CULTE DES SAINTS DANS LA BRENNE
Galvao, S de Vasconcellos *see* DICCIONARIO CHOROGRAPHICO, HISTORICO E ESTATISTICO DE PERNAMBUCO
Galvez, Manuel *see* ESPANA Y ALGUNOS ESPANOLES
Galvin *see* PEN PICTURES OF REPRESENTATIVE MEN OF OREGON
THE GALWAY AMERICAN – Galway. Ireland. -w. 12 Apr 1862-27 Jun 1863. (1 reel) – 1 – uk British Libr Newspaper [072]
GALWAY EXPRESS – Galway. Ireland. -w. 1853-1920. (31 reels) – 1 – uk British Libr Newspaper [072]
GALWAY FREE PRESS – Galway. Ireland. -w. 25 Jan 1832-28 Mar 1835. (2 reels) – 1 – uk British Libr Newspaper [072]
GALWAY INDEPENDENT PAPER – Galway. Ireland. -w. 3 Jan 1829-31 Mar 1832. (4 reels) – 1 – uk British Libr Newspaper [072]
GALWAY MERCURY AND CONNAUGHT WEEKLY ADVERTISER – Galway. Ireland. -w. 11 Oct 1844-10 Mar 1860. (6 reels) – 1 – uk British Libr Newspaper [072]
GALWAY OBSERVER – Ireland. 18 Nov, 23 Dec 1882; 20 Jan, 24 Feb, 3-17, 31 Mar, 7 Apr-2 Jun, 7, 28 Jul, 8 Sep, 20 Oct 1883; 17 May, 7, 14 Jun, 19 Jul 1884; 8 Jun 1889-Dec 1921; 11 Feb 1922-25; Aug 1923; 28 Feb 1925-1 Oct 1966 (1918 imperfect).-d. 19mqn reels – 1 – uk British Libr Newspaper [072]
GALWAY PACKET AND CONNAUGHT ADVOCATE – Galway. Ireland. -w. 24 Apr 1852-20 Dec 1854. (2 reels) – 1 – uk British Libr Newspaper [072]
GALWAY PATRIOT – Galway. Ireland. -w. 18 Jul 1835-23 Oct 1839. (3 reels) – 1 – uk British Libr Newspaper [072]
GALWAY PILOT AND CONNAUGHT ADVERTISER – Galway. Ireland. -w. 11 Feb 1905-12 Oct 1918. (6 reels) – 1 – uk British Libr Newspaper [072]
GALWAY PRESS – Galway. Ireland. -w. 17 Mar 1860-28 Dec 1861. (2 reels) – 1 – uk British Libr Newspaper [072]
GALWAY STANDARD – Galway. Ireland. -w. 21 Oct 1842-1 Dec 1843. (30 ft) – 1 – uk British Libr Newspaper [072]
GALWAY VINDICATOR – Galway. Ireland. -w. Jul 1841-Nov 1899. (Imperfect). (56 reels) – 1 – uk British Libr Newspaper [072]
GALWAY WEEKLY ADVERTISER – Galway. Ireland. -w. 4 Jan 1823-20 May 1843. (7 reels) – 1 – uk British Libr Newspaper [072]
Galzin, R *see* ECOLOGIE DES POISSONS RECIFAUX DE POLYNESIE FRANCAISE. VARIATIONS SPATIO-TEMPORELLES DES PEUPLEMENTS. DYNAMIQUE DES POPULATIONS DE TROIS ESPECES DOMINANTES DES LAGONS NORD DE MOOREA. EVALUATION DE LA PRODUCTION ICHTYOLOGIQUE D'UN SECTEUR RECIFO-LAGONAIRE
Gamaches, P E S de le *see* LES AGREMENS DU LANGAGE
GAMAIUN. IZBRANNYE STIKHI / Bal'mont, K D – Stockholm. 1921. BR-514 2 – 8 – ne IDC [460]
Gamarra, Abelardo M *see* RASGOS DE PLUMA
Gamazo, German *see* RECURSO DE CASACION...FERROCARRILES EXTREMENOS
Gambalo *see* NOVI FRUCTUS SACRORUM LAUDUM GUIBUS INSUNT DUAE MISSAE, SACRAE CANTIONES.
GAMBANG DJAKARTE; KUMPULAN / Firman Muntaco – SE-4666 1. v. 1 only. 1960- – 9 – ne IDC [950]
Gambarini, Elizabeth *see* LESSONS FOR THE HARPSICHORD, INTERMIX'D WITH ITALIAN AND ENGLISH SONGS, OPERA 2
Gambetta, C *see* SELECTED CHARACTERISTICS OF U.S. WHEELCHAIR BASKETBALL PLAYERS, THEIR SPORT PARTICIPATION AND THEIR ATTITUDES TOWARDS THEIR COACHES
GAMBIA : STATISTICAL SUMMARY 1964-1968 / Gambia. Parliament – (Coll title: African Official Statistical Serials, 1867-1982) – 4mf – 9 – £34.00 – uk Chadwyck [960]
Gambia *see*
– ANNUAL DEPARTMENTAL REPORTS
– THE GAMBIA GOVERNMENT DEVELOPMENT PROGRAMME, 1964-67
– THE GAMBIA GOVERNMENT DEVELOPMENT PROGRAMME, 1967/68 TO 1970/71
– GAMBIA REPORT ON DEVELOPMENT AND WELFARE, 1950-1952
– GOVERNMENT PUBLICATIONS
– REPORT ON DEVELOPMENT AND WELFARE, 1947
– REPORT ON DEVELOPMENT AND WELFARE, 1948
– REPORT ON DEVELOPMENT AND WELFARE, 1949
– REVISION OF THE DEVELOPMENT PROGRAMME, 1964/1967
– THIRD DEVELOPMENT PROGRAMME 1971/72-1973/74
THE GAMBIA : A PHYSICAL, REGIONAL AND ECONOMIC GEOGRAPHY / Jarrett, Harold Reginald – London, 1947 – 1 – us Res Libr [960]
THE GAMBIA ECHO – Bathurst, Gambia: The Gambia Echo Newspaper Syndicate, dec 1 1947; jan 12, mar 15-22 1948 – us Res Libr [072]
THE GAMBIA GOVERNMENT DEVELOPMENT PROGRAMME, 1964-67 / Gambia – (Sessional Paper No. 10 of 1964). Bathurst. 1964. BD-154 1 – 9 – ne IDC [338]
THE GAMBIA GOVERNMENT DEVELOPMENT PROGRAMME, 1967/68 TO 1970/71 / Gambia – Sessional Paper No. 4 of 1967. Bathurst. 1967 – 9 – ne IDC [338]
Gambia. Government Printer *see* FIVE YEAR PLAN FOR ECONOMIC AND SOCIAL DEVELOPMENT, JULY 1975-JUNE 1980
Gambia. Ministry of Economic Planning and Industrial Development *see*
– TIME SERIES OF SCHOOL POPULATION STATISTICS 1964/65, 1969/70 AND 1974/75-1979/80
– WORKING PAPERS FOR THE SECOND FIVE YEAR PLAN
Gambia. Ministry of Economic Planning and Industrial Development. Education Department *see* EDUCATION STATISTICS AND ANNUAL REPORT 1971/72-1984/85
Gambia. Ministry of Education, Youth, Sports and Culture *see* EDUCATION POLICY 1988-2003
THE GAMBIA OUTLOOK – Bathurst: Senegambian Press, mar 1961-jan 1962 – us Res Libr [072]
Gambia. Parliament *see* GAMBIA
GAMBIA REPORT ON DEVELOPMENT AND WELFARE, 1950-1952 / Gambia – D-1069 1. 1953 – 9 – ne IDC [338]
Gambier-Parry, T R *see* THE COLBERTINE BREVIARY
Gambini, Hugo *see*
– EL 17 [I.E. DIECISIETE] DE OCTUBRE
– EL LER GOBIERNO PERONISTA
Gamble, J S *see*
– BAMBUSEAE OF BRITISH INDIA
– FLORA OF THE PRESIDENCY OF MADRAS
– LIST OF THE TREES, SHRUBS AND LARGE CLIMBERS FOUND IN THE DARJEELING DISTRICT
– A MANUAL OF INDIAN TIMBERS
Gambrall, Theodore C *see*
– CHURCH LIFE IN COLONIAL MARYLAND
– STUDIES IN THE CIVIL, SOCIAL AND ECCLESIASTICAL HISTORY OF EARLY MARYLAND
Gambrell, James Bruton *see*
– THE BAPTIST GENERAL CONVENTION AND ITS WORK
– RECOLLECTIONS OF CONFEDERATE SCOUT SERVICE
GAMBURG NA BARRIKADAKH / Reisner, L – M. 1924. BR-1229 2 – 8 – ne IDC [947]
THE GAME AND THE CANDLE / Broughton, Rhoda – British Fiction Archive: Unit 4 – 9 – uk Bell [830]
THE GAME BIRDS OF INDIA, BURMA AND CEYLON / Hume, Allan O & Marshall, C H T – 24mf – 15 – $480.00 – us Ross [639]
THE GAME BIRDS OF INDIA, BURMAH AND CEYLON / Hume, Allan O & Marshall, C H T – 24mf – 15 – $480.00 – us Universal [590]
THE GAME BIRDS OF INDIA, BURMAH AND CEYLON / Hume, Allan O & Marshall, C H T – Z-272 2.m 1879-1881 – 8 – ne IDC [590]
THE GAMEKEEPER AT HOME : SKETCHES OF NATURAL HISTORY AND RURAL LIFE / Jefferies, Richard – London: Smith, Elder, 1878 – 1 roll – 1 – 1-55879-527-8 – uk Libr Preservation [500]
Games of the New Emerging Forces *see* GANEFO: GAMES OF THE NEW EMERGING FORCES (JEUX DES NOUVELLES FORCES MONTANTES); SES PRINCIPES, BUTS ET ORGANISATION
Games of the New Emerging Forces. 1st, Djakarta, 1963 *see*
– CLOSING CEREMONY: GENERAL PROGRAMME
– DOCUMENTS ON PREPARATIONS OF THE FIRST GANEFO AND CONFERENCE OF THE PREPARATORY COMMITTEE IN DJAKARTA

- GANEFO OPENS NEW ERA IN WORLD SPORTS; CHINESE SPORTS DELEGATION IN DJAKARTA

Games of the New Emerging Forces. Preparatory Conference, Djakarta, 1963 *see* DOCUMENTS OF THE PREPARATORY CONFERENCE FOR THE GANEFO HELD 27, 28 AND 29TH APRIL, 1963

Gamez, A *see*
- CENSURA SENCILLA DEL PAPEL QUE PUBLICO EN ESTA CORTE EL REVERENDO FRAY BUENAVENTURA ANGELERES CON EL TITULO DE DESENGANO DE LA FILOSOFIA REAL Y DESEMPENO DE LA MEDICINA SANATIVA
- DISCURSO DEL COMETA INOCENTE...
- DISCURSO FILOSOFICO, MEDICO E HISTORIAL...EN DEFENSA DE LA MEDICINA DOGMATICA Y SU SANGRIA...

GAMING TODAY – Las Vegas, NV. 1994 – 2+ r – 1 – $100.00 ($90.00y) – U04857 – us Library Micro [790]

Gamini, Hugo *see* EL PERONISMO Y LA IGLESIA

Gamitto, A C P *see* O MUATA CAZEMBE

DET GAMLE GRONLANDS NEYE PERLUSTRATION / Egede, H – Ed. by L. Bobe. nos. 96-97. Kobenhavn. 1741. MoG., v. 54. 1925. No. 97 trans. to: "A description of Greenland". London. 1745. Illus. BN-196 2 – 8 – ne IDC [550]

Gammell, William *see* A HISTORY OF AMERICAN BAPTIST MISSIONS IN ASIA, AFRICA, EUROPE AND NORTH AMERICA

DEN GAMMELTESTAMENTLIGE SKRIFTOVERLEVERING / Buhl, Frants – Kjobenhavn: Gyldendalske, 1885. 1 fiche – 9 – us A.T.L.A. [240]

Gammon, Samuel R *see* THE EVANGELICAL INVASION OF BRAZIL

Gams, Pius Bonifacius *see* DIE KIRCHENGESCHICHTE VON SPANIEN

GAN HA-MESHALIM VE-HA-HIDOT / Abulafia, T – Ed. by D. Yellin. v. 1. 1932; v. 2, pt. 1. 1934; v. 2, pt. 2. 1937. Jerusalem. 1932-37. BJ-421-76 1 – 9 – ne IDC [470]

LE GANA ET LE MALI / Delafosse, Maurice – 9 – 5.00 – fr Orientalistes [960]

Gana, Ujeng S *see* THE DEVELOPMENT OF THE TEACHING OF READING IN INDONESIA

GANADO KARAKUL / Carbonero Bravo, D – Madrid: Mag, 1954 – 1 – sp Bibl Santa Ana [946]

GANADO LANAR / Junta Provincial de Fomento Pecuario. Badajoz – Badajoz: Tip. La Minerva Extremena, 1963. Publ. no 14 – sp Bibl Santa Ana [946]

GANADO NEWS BULLETIN – 1947-48. (American Indian Periodicals in the Princeton University Library). 1 fiche – 9 – $45.00 – us UPA [305]

GANADO PORCINO EXTREMENO / Calles Mariscal, Juan & Calles Mariscal, Alfredo – Madrid: Artes Graficas J. San Martin, 1946 – sp Bibl Santa Ana [946]

Ganan Gonzalez, Felix *see* EJEMPLOS DE ORTOGRAFIA ESPANOLA...

GANAVARTA – Calcutta, India. 1957-62 – 6r – 1 – us L of C Photodup [072]

Gand, M *see* CODE DES ETRANGERS...

Gandara, F *see* ARMAS I TRIUNFOS...DE LOS HIJOS DE GALICIA...

Gandarias de Colmenares, Eusebio *see* RESENA DE VARIOS...MINAS DE VALDELAYEGUA

Gandavo, Henricus A *see* SUMMA THEOLOGICA AB HIERONYMUS SCARPARIO

Ganderias, Perfecto *see* TARDES DE LA QUINTA...CRISTIANO

GANDERSHEIMER KREISBLATT – Bad Gandersheim, Germany. 1 Jun 1983- – 5r per yr – 1 – gw Mikrofilm [072]

GANDHI AND ANARCHY / Sankaran Nair, Chettur – 2nd ed Madras: Tagore, (1922) 262p 1 reel.1247 – 1 – us U.W. Library [335]

Gandhi, Mahatma *see*
- INDIAN HOME RULE
- THE WISDOM OF GANDHI

GANDHI MARG – v. 1-8. New Delhi. 1957-64. – 57mf – 8 – ne IDC [280]

Gandia, Enrique de *see* LA REVISION DE LA HISTORIA ARGENTINA

Gando, Pere et Fils *see* OBSERVATIONS SUR LE TRAITE HISTORIQUE ET CRITIQUE DE MONSIEUR FOURNIER LE JEUNE

GANDRUNG PUTRI SALA; ROMAN ADI SAKA SURAKARTA – SE-3983 1. 1963 – 9 – ne IDC [950]

Ganduglia, Santiago *see*
- BASES SOCIALES DE LA CONSTITUCION JUSTICIALISTA
- DIGNIDAD DEL TRABAJO

GANEFO: GAMES OF THE NEW EMERGING FORCES (JEUX DES NOUVELLES FORCES MONTANTES); SES PRINCIPES, BUTS ET ORGANISATION / Games of the New Emerging Forces – SE-6467 1. 1965 – 9 – ne IDC [790]

GANEFO OPENS NEW ERA IN WORLD SPORTS; CHINESE SPORTS DELEGATION IN DJAKARTA / Games of the New Emerging Forces. 1st, Djakarta, 1963 – SE-4667 1 – 9 – ne IDC [790]

GANEFO SUATU KEHARUSAN SEDJARAH / Sukarno, Pres. Indonesia – SE 5451 1. 1964 – 9 – ne IDC [025]

DER GANG DER KIRCHE IN LEBENSBILDERN / Kahnis, Karl Friedrich August – Leipzig: Doerffling und Franke, 1881 – 2mf – us A.T.L.A. [240]

GANGAA – Nigeria: s.n., apr 1979 – 1r – 1 – us Res Libr [072]

THE GANGAS OF TALKAD: A MONOGRAPH ON THE HISTORY OF MYSORE FROM THE FOURTH TO THE CLOSE OF THE ELEVENTH CENTURY / Krishna Rao, MV – Madras: B.G. Paul, 1936.306p. ill. Bibliography – 1 – us U.W. Library [950]

Gange, C du *see* DESCRIPTIO MAGNAE ECCLESIAE SEU SANCTAE SOPHIAE (CBH 11,2)

Gangkofer, Manfred D *see* DENKEN UND SPRECHEN BEI GEISTIG BEHINDERTEN KINDERN

Ganglbauer, L *see* DIE KAEFER VON MITTELEUROPA

Gangoly, Ordhendra C *see* RUPAM

Gangstead, Sandra K *see*
- EFFECTS OF INSTRUCTION ON THE ANALYTICAL PROFICIENCY OF PHYSICAL EDUCATION MAJORS IN FUNDAMENTAL SPORT SKILLS ANALYSIS
- THE EFFECTS OF TWO INSTRUCTIONAL CONDITIONS ON SPORT SKILL SPECIFIC ANALYTIC PROFICIENCY OF PHYSICAL EDUCATION MAJORS

GANJINAH-I MA'ARIF – Tabriz. Sal-i 1, shumarah-i 1-8 (3 Rabi al-Avval 1341-8 Su'l Qa'dah 1341 [24 October 1922-23 June 1923]) – 1 reel – 1 – $90.00 – us MEDOC [950]

GANN – The Japanese Journal of Cancer Research. v. 1-47. 1907-56 – 1,5,6 – us Princeton Micro [610]

Gannett, Betty *see* PAPERS OF BETTY GANNETT, 1929-1970

Gannett, William C *see* CHILDHOOD OF JESUS

Gannett, William Channing *see* THE CHILDHOOD OF JESUS

Gano, Darwin Curtis *see* COMMERCIAL LAW

Gano, John *see*
- EVIDENCE OF GEORGE WASHINGTON'S RELIGION
- MEMOIRS

Gano-Overway, Lori A *see* GOAL PERSPECTIVES AND THEIR RELATIONSHIP TO BELIEFS, AFFECTIVE RESPONSES AND COPING STRATEGIES AMONG AFRICAN AND ANGLO AMERICAN ATHLETES

EEN GANS DUYTLIJCKE, ENDE BESCHEYDEN ANTWOORDT. AN". 1556. WT WAERHEYT ENDE CRACHT DER HEYLIGHEN GODLICKEN SCHRIFT GRONDLYCKEN VERUAETET, OP MARTINI MIKRONS ANTICHRISTISSCHE LEERE ENDE ONWAERACHTIGHE VALSCHE VERHAEL VAN DEN HANDEL OFTE BISPRECK / Simons, Menno – BME-288 1 – 9 – ne IDC [240]

Gans, Edgar Hilary *see* DIGEST OF MARYLAND STATUTES AND DECISIONS ON CRIMINAL LAW

EEN GANS GRONTLIJCKE ONDERWIJS OFT BERICHT, VAN DE EXCOMMUNICATIE, BANWTSLUYTINGE, OFTE AFSONDERINGE DER KERCKEN CHRISTI, WAT SY INDER CRACHT ZY / Simons, Menno – Datum by my M. S.. Anno 1558. den ii. Junij. 1558. BME-290 1 – 9 – ne IDC [240]

Ganschinietz, R *see* HIPPOLYTOS' CAPITEL GEGEN DIE MAGIER

Ganss, Henry George *see* MARIOLATRY, NEW PHASES OF AN OLD FALLACY

Gansser, Augustus H *see* HISTORY OF BAY COUNTY AND REPRESENTATIVE CITIZENS

GANSU RIBAO – Gansu Daily. 1982-, 1 reel/y. M D29 – 1 – $55.00r – cc Microforms [072]

EEN GANTS DUYTLIJCK ENDE BESCHEYDEN ANTWOORT AN. 1566. WT WAERHEYT ENDE CRACHT DER H. GODLICKER SCHRIFT / Simons, Menno – BME-355 1 – 9 – ne IDC [240]

DIE GANTSCHE LEERINGHE VAN DAUID IORISZOEN INT CORTE BEGREPEN, TOT NUT VANDEN ONPARTYDIGHEN / Blesdijk, Nicolaas M van – Stade. 1582. BME-263 1 – 9 – ne IDC [240]

Gantz, J L *see* DEVELOPMENT OF THE ATTITUDES TOWARD THE DISABLED IN PHYSICAL EDUCATION SCALE

DER GANZE PROLOG DES JOHANNESEVANGELIUMS IN SATZFOLGE UND -GLIEDERUNG WOERTLICHES CITAT AUS JESAIA : EINE STUDIE DES CHRISTUSBILDES NACH DER ANEINANDERHALTUNG BEIDER TESTAMENTE / Steinfuehrer, W – Leipzig: Doerffling & Franke, 1904 – 1mf – 9 – 0-8370-9307-4 – 1986-3307 – us A.T.L.A. [220]

GAO AUDITING STANDARDS : 1972, 1981 AND 1988 REVISIONS / General Accounting Office – Washington: GAO. 1v ea. 1972; 1881; 1988 – 4mf – 9 – $6.00 – LLMC 90-375A – us L.L.M.C. [340]

Gao, Jiaping *see* IN VIVO INSULIN ACTION ON WHOLE BODY AND INDIVIDUAL TISSUES IN OBESE SHHF/MCC-CP RATS WITH OR WITHOUT ACUTE EXERCISE

GAODENG XUEXIAO HUAXUE XUEBAO – Acta Chimica Scholarium Superiorum Sinensium. In Chinese but English abstracts to the main articles. F p190 – 9 – $4.50f – cc Microforms [073]

GAODENG XUEXIAO JISUAN SHUXE XUEBAO – Numerical Mathematics. A Journal of Chinese Universities. In Chinese but English abstracts to the main articles. F p191 – 9 – $4.50f – cc Microforms [073]

GAOFENZI TONGXUN – Bulletin of High Polymers. In Chinese but English abstracts to the main articles. F p133 – 9 – 4.00f – cc Microforms [073]

Gaon, M D *see*
- YEHUDEI HA-MIZRAH BE-EREZ-YISRA'EL

Gaon, S *see*
- RAV SAADYAH GAON, KOVEZ TORANI-MADDA'I
- SAADYA STUDIES

Gaona, Francisco *see* LA HEGEMONIA ARGENTINA EN EL PARAGUAY

DER GAONAEISCHE KOMMENTAR ZUR ORDNUNG TOHOROTH / Epstein, J N – Berlin. 1915. BJ-32-12 1 – 9 – ne IDC [270]

GAONENG WULI YU HE-WULI – (1983 $3.50f; 1986 $4.50f) – Physica Energiae Fortis et Physica Nuclearis. In Chinese but English abstracts to the main articles. F p132 – 9 – cc Microforms [073]

GAP HILL BAPTIST CHURCH. PICKENS COUNTY. SOUTH CAROLINA : CHURCH RECORDS – 1954-72 – 1 – 7.38 – us Baptist [240]

Gappmaier, Eduard *see* MAXIMAL EXERCISE TESTING AND AEROBIC TRAINING IN MULTIPLE SCLEROSIS

GAPWAY BAPTIST CHURCH. MARION COUNTY. SOUTH CAROLINA : CHURCH RECORDS – 1833-67 – 1 – 5.92 – us Baptist [240]

Garachanine, W *see* DROITS ET DEVOIRS DES NEUTRES...

Garanger, J *see* MARAE MARAE TA'ATA

Garant, J -Honorat *see* BIO-BIBLIOGRAPHIE DE MONSIEUR ELPHEGE BOIS, D.SC., DIRECTEUR DU DEPARTEMENT DE BIOCHIMIE DE LA FACULTE DES SCIENCES

Garasse, F *see*
- LA DOCTRINE CURIEUSE DES BEAUX ESPRITS DE CE TEMPS...
- LE RABELAIS REFORME PAR LES MINISTRES,...

Garat, M J *see* DE L'EXECUTION DES JUGEMENTS ET ACTES AUTHENTIQUES ETRANGERS...

Garat, P J *see* TROIS ROMANCES AVEC ACCOMPAGNEMENT DE PIANO OU HARPE... OEUVRE 5...

Garau, F *see* EL SABIO INSTRUIDO DE LA GRACIA...

Garavel, J *see* LES PAYSANS DE MORETTE

Garbe, R *see* VAITANA SUTRA

Garber, Klaus *see*
- ALLGEMEINE LITERATURGESCHICHTE
- DEUTSCHE DICHTUNG VON DER AELTESTEN BIS AUF DIE NEUESTE ZEIT
- DIE DEUTSCHE LITERATUR
- GESCHICHTE DER DEUTSCHEN LITERATUR
- GESCHICHTE DER DEUTSCHEN LITTERATUR
- GESCHICHTE DER DEUTSCHEN NATIONAL-LITTERATUR MIT PROBEN DER DEUTSCHEN DICHTKUNST UND BEREDSAMKEIT
- GESCHICHTE DER POESIE UND BEREDSAMKEIT SEIT DEM ENDE DES 13. JAHRHUNDERTS
- GESCHICHTE DER POETISCHEN NATIONAL-LITERATUR DER DEUTSCHEN
- GESCHICHTE UND KRITIK DER DEUTSCHEN POESIE UND BEREDSAMKEIT
- GRUNDRISS ZUR GESCHICHTE DER DEUTSCHEN NATIONALLITERATUR
- INNERE GESCHICHTE DER ENTWICKLUNG DER DEUTSCHEN NATIONAL-LITTERATUR
- VORLESUNGEN UEBER DIE GESCHICHTE DER DEUTSCHEN LITERATUR
- VORLESUNGEN UEBER DIE GESCHICHTE DER DEUTSCHEN NATIONAL-LITERATUR
- VORLESUNGEN UEBER DIE GESCHICHTE DER TEUTSCHEN NATIONAL-LITERATUR

Garbett, Edward *see*
- DOGMATIC FAITH: AN INQUIRY INTO... REVELATION AND DOGMA
- GOD'S WORD WRITTEN

Garbini *see* VOCABULAIRE LATIN-FRANCAIS

Garceau, Napoleon *see* LA JUSTICE

Garceran, Rafael *see* FALANGE DESDE FEBRERO DE 1936 AL GOBIERNO NACIONAL

Garces y Gonzales, Valeriano *see* VOCABULARIO DESCRIPTIVO...DICCIONARIO

Garcia, Alf. I *see*
- L'ADMINISTRACION DE SACRAMENTOS EN TOLEDO DESPUES DEL CAMBIO DE RITO
- EDICION TRIDENTINA DEL MANUAL TOLEDANO Y SU INCORPORACION AL RITUAL ROMANO
- EL MANUAL TOLENDANO PARA LA ADMINISTRATION DE SACRAMENTOS A TRAVERS DE LOS SIGLOS

Garcia Alonso, Francisco *see* FLORES DE HEROISMO. SEVILLA, 1939

Garcia, Antonio *see* NECROLOGIO DE LA PROVINCIA SERAFICA DE CARTAGENA DESDE SU RESTAURACION EN 1878. MURCIA, 1967

Garcia Arias, Luis *see* LAS EMBAJADAS DE DON JUAN ANTONIO DE VERA Y ZUNIGA EN ITALIA

Garcia Bermejo, Antonio *see*
- ORACION FUNEBRE...EXEQUIAS
- ORACION FUNEBRE...SAN ISIDRO

Garcia Blanco, Manuel *see* DE LAS ANDANZAS DE UNAMUNO POR TIERRAS EXTREMENAS

Garcia Bote, Eduardo *see* SERIE DE CONFERENCIAS EXPLICADAS EN DICHA CORPORACION DURANTE EL CURSO DE 1908-1909 (FEDERACION TAQUIGRAFA ESPANOLA)

Garcia Calderon K, Manuel *see* LA CAPACIDAD CAMBIARIA EN EL DERECHO INTERNACIONAL PRIVADO

Garcia Calderon, Ventura *see* VALE UN PERU

Garcia Camino, Victor Gerardo *see* APROXIMACION A UN ESTUDIO DE ANTONIO HURTADO COMO POETA

Garcia Caminos Burgos, Luis F *see* APROXIMACION A UN ESTUDIO DE ANTONIO HURTADO COMO POETA

Garcia Cantero, Gabriel *see* EL VINCULO DEL MATRIMONIO...

Garcia Carofalo, R *see* LA EJECUCION DE SENTENCIAS EXTRANJERAS ES MATERIA FEDERAL O DE LEGISLACION DE LOS ESTADOS?

Garcia Carrasco, Florencio *see*
- CUADERNO DE UNIDADES DIDACTICAS NO 4. NATURALEZA 1
- CUADERNO DE UNIDADES DIDACTICAS NO 4 NATURALEZA 2
- CUADERNO DE UNIDADES DIDACTICAS NO 4. VIDA SOCIAL 1
- CUADERNO DE UNIDADES DIDACTICAS NO 4 VIDA SOCIAL 2
- CUADERNO DE UNIDADES DIDACTICAS NO 4 VIDA SOCIAL 3

Garcia Carrasco, Florenico *see* CUADERNO DE UNIDADES DIDACTICAS NO 4 NATURALEZA 3

Garcia Carrasco, Francisco A *see*
- CUADERNO DE UNIDADES DIDACTICAS NO 4. NATURALEZA 1
- CUADERNO DE UNIDADES DIDACTICAS NO 4 NATURALEZA 2
- CUADERNO DE UNIDADES DIDACTICAS NO 4 NATURALEZA 3
- CUADERNO DE UNIDADES DIDACTICAS NO 4. VIDA SOCIAL 1
- CUADERNO DE UNIDADES DIDACTICAS NO 4 VIDA SOCIAL 2

- CUADERNO DE UNIDADES DIDACTICAS NO 4 VIDA SOCIAL 3

Garcia Carrasco, Francisco A et al *see* YO SOY... LENGUA ESPANOLA CURSO NO 6

Garcia Carrasco, Francisco Andres *see* EXTRACTO DE LA TESIS DE SOBRE LA ACCION CULTURAL DE ESPANA EN MARRUECOS

Garcia, Cesar Reinaldo *see* HISTORIA DE LOS GRUPOS Y PARTIDOS POLITICOS DE LA REPUBLICA ARGENTINA DESDE 1810 A 1983

Garcia, Clersida *see* A FIELDWORK STUDY OF HOW YOUNG CHILDREN LEARN FUNDAMENTAL MOTOR SKILLS AND HOW THEY PROGRESS IN THE DEVELOPMENT OF STRIKING

Garcia Costa, Victor O *see* EL PERIODISMO POLITICO

Garcia de Atocha, Jose *see*
- MEMORIA SOBRE...GUADALUPE
- RESPUESTAS...D. FELIPE ROSADO DE BELALCAZAR

Garcia de Diego, Jose A *see* ESCARCEOS DE TOPONIMIA EXTREMENA

Garcia de la Cuesta, Gregorio *see* MANIFIESTO QUE PRESENTA A EUROPA...EXTREMADURA

Garcia de la Fuente, P Arturo *see*
- EL CASO DEL OBISPO MARCIAL DE MERIDA
- EL CONCILIO 3 EMERITENSE

Garcia de la Huerta, Vicente *see*
- BIBLIOTECA MILITAR ESPANOLA
- ENDECASILABO CON MOTIVO DEL BOMBARDEO DE ARGEL
- LA ESCENA ESPANOLA...TEATRO
- LA FE TRIUNFANTE DEL AMOR
- LECCION CRITICA A LOS LECTORES DE LA MEMORIA DE COSME DAMIAN SOBRE EL TEATRO
- LECCION CRITICA A LOS LECTORES DEL PAPEL INTITULADO
- LECCION HISTORICA AL PROFESOR PAREDES
- POESIAS
- RAQUEL
- LA RAQUEL. TRAGEDIA
- THEATRO HESPANOL. TOMO 1
- THEATRO HESPANOL. TOMO 2
- THEATRO HESPANOL. TOMO 3
- THEATRO HESPANOL. TOMO 4

Garcia de la Vega, D de *see* GUIDE PRACTIQUE DES AGENTS POLITIQUES...

Garcia de Leon, Ma Antonia *see* LA OTRA UNIVERSIDAD

Garcia de Medrano *see* LA REGLA Y EL... SANTIAGO DEL ESPADA

GARCIA DE PAREDES / Llano y Persi, Manuel de – 1848 – 9 – 1.50f – sp Bibl Santa Ana [830]

Garcia de Soto, Jesus *see* NUEVAS APORTACIONES AL ESTUDIO DE LA NECROPOLIS ORIENTAL DE MERIDA

Garcia Della Costa, Fernando *see* EL PUEBLO AL PODER

Garcia, Eduardo Augusto *see* YO FUI TESTIGO ANTES, DURANTE Y DESPU ES DE LA SEGUNDA TIRANIA (MEMORIAS)

Garcia, Fernandez *see* LEXIC

Garcia Figueroa, Fernando *see* PLANO-GUIA-CALLEJERO DE CACERES

Garcia Flores, Juan Felipe (Don Felipe) *see*
- RESUMEN DE LA TEMPORADA TAURINA 1968 EN EXTREMADURA
- TOROS EN EXTREMADURA. AMPLIOS DETALLES DE LOS ESPECTACULOS TAURINOS CELEBRADOS EN LAS PLAZAS DE ESTA REGION DURANTE LA TEMPORADA DE 1969

Garcia Garces, Narciso *see* TITULOS Y GRANDEZAS DE MARIA

GARCIA GARCES, NARCISO. EXPOSICION DEL DOGMA CATOLICO / Marquez, Gabino – Madrid, 1943 – 1 – sp Bibl Santa Ana [240]

Garcia Garcia, A *see* MANUEL GERCIA GARRIDO

Garcia Garcia, Carmen *see* ELECCIONES Y PARTIDOS EN ASTURIAS

Garcia Garcia, Casimiro *see* ELEMENTOS DE RELIGION. LA DOCTRINA DE NUESTRO SENOR JESUCRISTO

Garcia Garcia, Juan *see* LOS BENFICIOS DEL TELEFONO

Garcia Garcia, Rafael *see*
- ARIAS MONTANO Y LA POLITICA DE FELIPE 2, EN FLANDES POR LUIS MORALES...
- LAS "ELUCIDATIONESIN EVANGELIA" DE BENITO ARIAS MONTANO

Garcia Gil, Manuel *see*
- CARTA PASTORAL
- CARTA PASTORAL. CONFIRMACION
- PASTORAL SOBRE EL SACRAMENTO DE LA CONFIRMACION

Garcia Gutierrez, Jesus *see* APUNTES PARA LA HISTORIA DEL ORIGEN Y DESENVOLVIMIENTO DEL REGIO PATRONATO INDIANO HASTA 1857

Garcia Hernandez, F *see* TRATADO DE FIEBRES MALIGNAS...

Garcia Herreros, E *see* EL DEPOSITO DE MUJER CASADA EXTRANJERA...

Garcia, Huecos *see* HECTOR ESTUDIOS DE HISTORIA COLONIAL VENEZOLANA...

Garcia Icazbalceta, Joaquin *see* CONQUISTA Y COLONIZACION DE MEJICO

Garcia, J *see* TEXTO DE DERECHO MARITIMO INTERNATIONAL...

Garcia Jalon, Miguel *see* A. POR EL EXCMO. SR. CONDE DE MONTIJO...SRA. DONA MARIANA ENRIQUEZ

Garcia Jimeno, Fernando *see*
- NOTA DEL DIA
- RIPIOS. POESIAS

Garcia Jimeno, Fernando y Jesus *see* EL VESTIDO LARGO

Garcia, Jose *see* PROYECTO...PAGAR LAS CONTRIBUCIONES

Garcia, Juan Justo *see*
- ELEMENTOS DE ARITMETICA
- ELEMENTOS DE ARITMETICA, ALGEBRA Y GEOMETRIA
- ELEMENTOS DE ARITMETICA.TOMO I
- ELEMENTOS DE...LOGICA
- NUEVOS ELEMENTOS DE GEOGRAFIA GENERAL ASTRONOMICA

GARCIA LASO DE LA VEGA / Salazar, Antonio – Badajoz: Imprenta Dipt. Provincial, 1963 – sp Bibl Santa Ana [946]

Garcia Lorca, Federico *see*
- ALOCUCION A LOS ACTORES ARGENTINOS. MANUSCRITO
- APUNTES SOBRE LA ESCENIFICACION DE LOS ROMANCES. MANUSCRITO
- CANCIONES Y OTROS POEMAS. MANUSCRITO
- LA CASA DE BERNARDA ALBA
- COMEDIA SIN TITULO. MS.
- LA COMEDIANTA. MS.
- CONFERENCIA RECITAL SOBRE EL ROMANCERO GITANO. MANUSCRITO
- CUADERNILLO DE MIGUEL PICAZO, MANUSCRITO
- LIBRO DE POEMAS (1918-1921)
- EL MALEFICIO DE LA MARIPOSA
- MARIANA PINEDA
- MARIANA PINEDA, FRAGMENTO MANUSCRITO
- POEMAS DEL CANTE JONDO. FRAGMENTO MANUSCRITO
- POETA EN NUEVA YORK. MANUSCRITO
- LOS SUENOS DE MI PRIMA AURELIA
- TITERES DE CACHIPORRA
- LA ZAPATERA PRODIGIOSA

Garcia, Lorenzo A *see* PLANIFICACION PERONISTA

Garcia Lupo, Rogelio *see* LA REBELION DE LOS GENERALES

Garcia, Manuel *see* DEPECHOS LEGALES... TIERRA SANTA

Garcia, Marcellan, Jose *see* CATALOGO DEL ARCHIVO DE MUSICA DE LA REAL CAPILLA DE PALACIO

Garcia Martinez, Carlos *see* LA GRANDEZA ARGENTINA

Garcia Matos, Manuel *see*
- L'ANTHOLOGIE DU FOLKLORE MUSICAL D'ESPAGUE
- LIRICA POPULAR DE LA ALTA EXTREMADURA

Garcia, Miguel *see* CAMPANA DE PORTUGAL...EXTREMADURA

Garcia Miranda, Vicenta *see* FLORES DEL VALLE

Garcia Monge, Eduardo *see* MIS PASATIEMPOS

Garcia Mora, Jose *see* ALEGACION EN DERECHO...VIRGEN DEL PUERTO...PLASENCIA

GARCIA MORENO : UN GOBERNANTE MODELO / Bayle, Constantino – Madrid: Razon y Fe, 1921 – 1 – sp Bibl Santa Ana [350]

Garcia Moreno, A *see* REVISTA DE DERECHO INTERNACIONAL...

GARCIA MORENO Y LA INSTRUCCION PUBLICA POR JULIO TOBAR DONOSO / Bayle, Constantino – Madrid: Razon y Fe, 1924 – 1 – sp Bibl Santa Ana [946]

Garcia Morente, Manuel *see* ORIGENES DEL NACIONALISMO ESPANOL

Garcia Morgado, Jose *see* POR LOS FUEROS DE LA VERDAD

Garcia Nieto, Jose *see* PREGON PRONUNCIADO POR D. JOSE GARCIA NIETO...EN LA MUY NOBLE Y MUY LEAL CIUDAD DE TRUJILLO

Garcia Oliver, Juan *see* EL FASCISMO INTERNACIONAL Y LA GUERRA ANTIFASCISTA ESPANOLA

Garcia Oro, J *see* SAN PEDRO DE ALCANTARA...MADRID, 1965

Garcia, Oscar J *see* EL SEGUNDA PLAN QUINQUENAL EN LA ENSENANZA MEDIA

Garcia Perez, Juan *see* LA DESAMORTIZACION DE LAS PROPIEDADES...VALENCIA DE ALCANTARA

Garcia, R *see* A COMPARISON OF GRIP STRENGTH IN YOUNG ATHLETES AND NON-ATHLETES

Garcia, Roberto *see* PATRIA SINDICAL VERSUS PATRIA SOCIALISTA

Garcia Rojo, D *see* MADRID. BIBLIOTECA NACIONAL. CATALOGO DE INCUNABLES

Garcia Romero de Tejada, Jose *see*
- EL LIBRO DEL JURADO
- LA PSICOLOGIA CON LA ONTOLOGIA

Garcia Romero de Tejada, Julio *see* LA PSICOLOGIA Y SU RELACION CON LA ONTOLOGIA

Garcia Romero, Diego *see* PROCEDIMIENTOS PRACTICOS MODERNOS PARA LAFABRICACION DE VINOS EN EXTREMADURA

Garcia Rubio, Manuel *see* SENCILLOS... GEOGRAFIA

Garcia Salinero, Fernando *see* UNA OMISION EN LA POLEMICA FORNERIANA

Garcia Sanchez, Federico *see* TE DEMU LANDANUS. LA BATALLA DE TERUEL...

Garcia Sanchez, Francisco *see*
- EL CASTILLO DE MEDELLIN EN LA RUTA DEL TURISMO
- MEDELLIN, RUTA DE TURISMO

Garcia Sandoval, Eugenio *see* EXCAVACIONES ARQUEOLOGICAS EN LA ZONA DE MERIDA

Garcia Santillan, Juan Carlos *see* LEGISLACION SOBRE INDIOS DEL RIO DE LA PLATA EN EL SIGLO 16TH. MADRID. 1928

Garcia, Susan C *see* VALIDITY OF THE SIT-AND-REACH TEST FOR MALE AND FEMALE ADOLESCENTS

Garcia, Telesforo *see* NAVEGAMTES Y DESCUBRIDORES ESPANOLES DEL MAR PACIFICO. VASCO NUNEZ DE BALBOA

Garcia Vazquez, Sebastian *see* EL PINTOR EUGENIO HERMOSO

Garcia Vidal, Ceferino *see* SEMINARIO DE PLASENCIA, EL. APUNTES HISTORICOS

Garcia y Bellido, Antonio *see*
- EL CULTO A MA-BELLONA EN LA ESPANA ROMANA
- EL JARRO RITUAL LUSITANO DE LA COLECCION CALZADILLA
- NOMBRES DE ARTISTAS EN LA ESPANA ROMANA

Garcia y Garcia, Antonio *see* LOS MANUSCRITOS JURIDICOS MEDIEVALES DE...

Garcia y Garcia, Casimiro *see*
- PROGRAMA DE 2ND CURSO DE RELIGION (3RD DEL BACHILLERATO) HISTORIA DE LA IGLESIA Y LITURGIA 1937-1938
- PROGRAMA DE RELIGION Y MORAL PARA LOS CURSOS 2ND, 4TH, 5TH Y 6TH DE BACHILLERATO 1937-1938

Garcia y Romero de Tejada, Jose *see* EL LIBRO DEL JURADO, 2ND PARTE

Garcia Zamor, Jean Claude *see* PUBLIC ADMINISTRATION AND SOCIAL CHANGES IN ARGENTINA, 1943-1955

Garcia-Parreno y Lopez, G *see* DICCIONARIO DE DERECHO MARITIMO

Garcilaso de la Vega (el Inca) *see* HISTOIRE DES INCAS, ROIS DU PEROU

Garcin de Tassy *see* HISTOIRE DE LA LITTERATURE HINDOUI ET HINDOUSTANI

Garcins, L *see* TRAITE DU MELO-DRAME, OU REFLEXIONS SUR LA MUSIQUE DRAMATIQUE

GARCONNE : JUNGGESELLIN – Berlin, 1930-32 n20/21 – 1r – 1 – Dist. gw Mikrofilm – gw Misc Inst [072]

LA GARDE BLANCHE – Organe national, contre-revolutionnaire. no. 1-8. Paris. mars-avr 1919 – 1 – fr A.C.R.P.P. [073]

LA GARDE INDEPENDANTE CHAMPLAIN – Quebec, Canada. 24 dec 1898 – 1r – 1 – Can$25.00 – cn Can Microfilming [072]

LE GARDE MOBILE – Paris: Leautey, aug 1848 – us Res Libr [072]

Garde, V *see* DEN DABSKE KONEBAADS-EXPEDITION TIL GRONLANDS OSTKUST

GARDEN – v. 1-. 1977- – 1,5,6,9 – us UMI [631]

GARDEN AND FIELD – Adelaide, Australia. -m. April 1894-Aug 1901; Sept 1903-Sept 1905. 5 reels – 1 – uk British Libr Newspaper [073]

The Garden Center of Greater Cleveland *see* FLOWERING PLANT INDEX OF ILLUSTRATION AND INFORMATION

Garden City Association. London, England *see* THE GARDEN CITY/GARDEN CITIES AND TOWN PLANNING

Garden City, Kansas *see* MISCELLANEOUS EARLY NEWSPAPERS

Garden City, Kansas. Community Congregational Church *see* RECORDS

Garden City, Michigan *see* MISCELLANEOUS NEWSPAPERS

GARDEN CITY SENTINEL – Kan. -w. 1884-1900 – 1 – us UMI [071]

THE GARDEN CITY/GARDEN CITIES AND TOWN PLANNING / Garden City Association. London, England – 1908-32. With printed Finding List – 1 – £35.00r – uk Altair [710]

GARDEN COUNTY NEWS – Oshkosh, NE. -w. Jul 1909 to date – 1 – us NE Hist [071]

GARDEN FERNS / Hooker, W J – or Coloured figures and descriptions. London. 1862. B-7199 2 – 8 – ne IDC [580]

Garden, G *see* CODE DIPLOMATIQUE...

Garden, Mary Gray Hogg *see* MEMORIALS OF JAMES HOGG, THE ETTRICK SHEPHERD

THE GARDEN OF ELOQUENCE / Peacham, Henry – 1577. 162p. (English Linguistics Series 1500-1800) – 9 – us UMI [400]

THE GARDEN OF ELOQUENCE / Peacham, Henry – 1593 – 9 – 15.00 – us Scholars' Facs [410]

GARDEN OF SPICES – 1899 – 1 – $50.00 – us Presbyterian [780]

GARDEN OF THE WORLD / Wentworth and Co – Boston, 1856. Oregon reel 7. (Cox Library Collection) – 5 – us Americana [978]

GARDEN OF THE WORLD OR SANTA CLARA COUNTY / Foote, H S – Chicago: Lewis Publ. Co., 1888. California Reel 32. (The Cox Library Collection) – 5 – us Americana [978]

THE GARDEN PLOT / Goldingham, Henry – 1825 – 1 – uk Microform Academic [810]

GARDENA VALLEY NEWS – Gardena, CA. 1950-Aug 1964; Nov 1964-65 – 36r – 1 – $1,800.00 – B02266 – us Library Micro [071]

GARDENERS' CHRONICLE – London, 1841-1873. v1-33. New York, 1874-1886, v1-26; S.3, 1887-1920, v1-68 – 2,709mf – 9 – 7351/1 – ne IDC [630]

GARDENERS DICTIONARY / Miller, P – ed. 4. abridged from the folio edition. London, 1754. 3 vols. B-465 2 – 8 – ne IDC [580]

GARDENERS DICTIONARY / Miller, P – ed. 7. London, 1759. B-250 2 – 8 – ne IDC [580]

GARDENERS DICTIONARY / Miller, P – ed. 8. London, 1768. B-251 2 – 8 – ne IDC [580]

GARDENERS DICTIONARY... / Miller, P – London. 3v. 1754 – 30mf – ne IDC [580]

THE GARDENER'S DICTIONARY / Miller, P – 1748 – 1 – uk Microform Academic [631]

GARDENER'S GAZETTE – London, UK. 1837. -m. 1 reel – 1 – uk British Libr Newspaper [073]

GARDENER'S MAGAZINE / ed by Loudon, J C – London, 1826-1843. v1-19 – 355mf – 9 – 7357/2 – ne IDC [630]

GARDENERS' NOTEBOOK / Rhode Island. Agricultural Extension Service – v. 1-9. 1961-69 – 1,5,6 – us Spaulding [630]

Gardenin, U *see*
- CHUZHIMI PUTIAMI
- INTERNATSIONAL I VOINA
- NASHIM OBVINITELI AM

LE GARDIEN PAROISSIAL – Ottawa, Ontario. 15 sep 1920 – 1r – 1 – Can$25.00 – cn Can Microfilming [072]

[Gardikas, K G] *see* SYMBOLE EIS TO DIETHNES POLNIKON DIKAION

Gardiner, A H *see* EGYPTIAN LETTERS TO THE DEAD. MAINLY FROM THE OLD AND MIDDLE KINGDOMS

Gardiner, A H, Weigall, A E P *see* A TOPOGRAPHICAL CATALOGUE OF THE PRIVATE TOMBS OF THEBES

Gardiner, Frederic *see* AIDS TO SCRIPTURE STUDY

GARDINER GAZETTE – Gardiner, OR. -w. 11 Dec 1903-24 Mar 1905. 1 roll – 1 – us U.O. Library [071]

Gardiner, H Norman *see* JONATHAN EDWARDS

GARDINER INDEX – Gardiner, OR. 11,18,25 Aug; 1-29 Sep 1916; 6 Oct-29 Dec 1916; 19,31 Jan 1917, 9 May, 26 Dec 1918. – us U.O. Library [071]

Gardiner, J S *see*
- THE FAUNA AND GEOGRAPHY OF THE MALDIVE AND LACCADIVE ARCHIPELAGOES
- A MONOGRAPH OF THE BRITISH EOCENE FLORA

Gardiner, Maine.West Gardiner Free Will Baptist Church/Spears Corner Free Will Baptist Church *see* RECORDS

Gardiner, Richard *see* MEMOIRS OF THE SIEGE OF QUEBEC, CAPITAL OF ALL CANADA, AND OF THE RETREAT OF MONSIEUR DE BOURLEMAQUE, FROM CARILLON TO THE ISLE AUX NOIX IN LAKE CHAMPLAIN

Gardiner, Robert William *see* MEMOIR OF ADMIRAL SIR GRAHAM MOORE

Gardiner, Samuel R *see*
- THE CONSTITUTIONAL DOCUMENTS OF THE PURITAN REVOLUTION, 1625-1660
- CROMWELL'S PLACE IN HISTORY
- HISTORY OF THE COMMONWEALTH AND PROTECTORATE, 1649-1656
- HISTORY OF THE GREAT CIVIL WAR, 1642-1649
- WHAT GUNPOWDER PLOT WAS

Gardiner, William *see* THE MUSIC OF NATURE.

GARDISTA – Bratislava, Czechoslovakia. Jul 1942-Mar 1945 (scattered Issues) – 4r – 1 – us L of C Photodup [072]

GARDNER 1737-1849 – (Mf 1T: Marriage Intentions 1786-1832. Mf 1T-2T: Marriages 1792-1829. Mf 2T-4T: Births & Deaths 1737-1847. Mf 4T: Marriages & Intentions 1836-42. Mf 4T-5T: Births 1842-49. Mf 5T: Marriages 1843-49. Mf 6T: Deaths 1843-49) – (mf ed 1996) – 6mf – 9 – 0-87623-251-9 – us Holbrook [920]

GARDNER 1762-1892 – (Mf 1-4: Births & Deaths 1762-1843. Mf 5: Births & Deaths 1785-96. Mf 6-7: Publishments 1786-1832. Mf 8-10: Intentions of Marriages 1839-79. Mf 11-12: B,M,D 1844-52. Mf 13-17: Births 1857-91. Mf 18-19: Index to Births 1857-91. Mf 20-23: Marriages 1853-92. Mf 24: Index to Marriages 1853-92. Mf 25-29: Deaths 1858-92. Mf 30-31: Index to Deaths 1858-92) – (mf ed 1986) – 31mf – 9 – 0-87623-037-0 – us Holbrook [920]

Gardner, Alice *see*
- THE CONFLICT OF DUTIES AND OTHER ESSAYS
- JULIAN, PHILOSOPHER AND EMPEROR
- THE LASCARIDS OF NICAEA
- STUDIES IN JOHN THE SCOT (ERIGENA)
- SYNESIUS OF CYRENE
- THEODORE OF STUDIUM
- WITHIN OUR LIMITS

Gardner, C E *see* LIFE OF FATHER GOREH

Gardner, E A *see*
- HISTORY OF FORD COUNTY TO 1908
- NAUKRATIS (MEES VOL 6)

Gardner, Edmund Garratt *see* THE KING OF COURT POETS; A STUDY OF THE WORK, LIFE AND TIME OF LODOVICO ARIOSTO

Gardner, Ella *see* LIFE IN JAPAN

Gardner, George *see* VIAGENS NO BRASIL

Gardner, George W *see* ECHOES FROM THE FLEETING YEARS

Gardner, Gregory A *see* CLINICAL INSTRUCTION IN ATHLETIC TRAINING

Gardner, J K *see* A COMPARISON OF OCCUPATIONAL STRESS AND RELATED VARIABLES AMONG SALESPERSONS, CLERICAL STAFF, SERVICE TECHNICIANS, AND MANAGERS OF THE MID-OHIO DISTRICT OF THE XEROX CORPORATION

Gardner, John M *see* AMERICAN NEGLIGENCE REPORTS, CURRENT SERIES

Gardner, Paul V *see* FREDERICK CARDER: A PORTRAIT OF A GLASSMAKER

Gardner, Percy *see*
- HISTORIC VIEW OF THE NEW TESTAMENT
- MODERNITY AND THE CHURCHES

Gardner, Robert G *see* JEREMIAH WALKER: GEORGIA GENERAL BAPTIST

Gardner, Washington *see* HISTORY OF CALHOUN COUNTY

GARDNER'S BAPTIST CHURCH. TAR RIVER ASSOCIATION. WARREN COUNTY. NORTH CAROLINA : CHURCH RECORDS – 1844-1930 – 1 – 9.90 – us Baptist [240]

Gardnier, Herbert Fairbairn *see* NOTHING BUT NAMES: AN INQUIRY INTO THE ORIGIN OF THE NAMES OF THE COUNTIES AND TOWNSHIPS OF ONTARIO

Gardthausen, V *see*
- CATALOGUS CODICUM GRAECORUM SINAITICORUM
- DIE GRIECHISCHEN SCHREIBER DES MITTELALTERS UND DER RENAISSANCE
- VOPROS O RUNAKH U SLAVIAN. GRECHESKOE PIS'MO IX-X STOLETII.

Gareis, Karl *see* INTRODUCTION TO THE SCIENCE OF LAW

Gareis, Reinhold *see* GESCHICHTE DER EVANGELISCHEN HEIDENMISSION

GARENGANZE : OR, SEVEN YEARS' PIONEER MISSION WORK IN CENTRAL AFRICA / Arnot, Frederick Stanley – Chicago: Fleming H Revell, [1889?] – 1mf – 9 – 0-8370-6321-3 – 1986-0321 – us A.T.L.A. [920]

GARFIELD COUNTY CALL – Eminence. Kan. 1887-93 – 1 – us UMI [071]

GARFIELD COUNTY JOURNAL – Edwards. Mont. 1924-1926 – 1 – us UMI [071]

GARFIELD HEIGHTS LEADER : WEEKLY CLEVELAND SUBURBAN NEWSPAPER – Garfield Heights, OH. 25 Feb 1971-20 Nov 1986 – 13r – 1 – us Western Res [071]

Garfield Heights. Ohio. St. John Evangelical Lutheran Church *see* CHURCH RECORDS

Garfield, James A *see* PAPERS

GARFIELD, JAMES A., FAMILY PAPERS MS 4575 – 1855-1938 – 2r – 1 – us Western Res [320]

GARFIELD NEWS – Chicago. Ill. 1956-1962 – 1 – us UMI [071]

Garfield, Viola E *see* VIOLA E. GARFIELD ALBUMS ON TOTEM ART

THE GARFIELDIAN – Chicago. Ill. 1935-1954; 1956-1966 – 1 – us UMI [071]

Garfinkel, Marian S *see* THE EFFECT OF YOGA AND RELAXATION TECHNIQUES ON OUTCOME VARIABLES ASSOCIATED WITH OSTEOARTHRITIS OF THE HANDS AND FINGER JOINTS

Garforth, C *see* GUIDE TO EXTENSION TRAINING

Garganta la Olla. Ayuntamiento *see* FIESTAS EN GARGANTA LA OLLA 1974

Gargasz, Kimberly L *see* PARTICIPATION IN WHITE WATER RAFTING INSTRUCTION BY ADULTS WITH DEVELOPMENTAL DISABILITIES

GARIBALDI NEWS – Garibaldi OR. Jan 8 1926-Dec 31 1931 – 1 – us U.O. Library [071]

GARIBALDI ROCKAWAY NEWS – Garibaldi OR. Jan 8 1932-May 29 1936 – 1 – us U.O. Library [071]

AL GARIDAH – Cairo, 1909-13 – 9r – 1 – us Ross [072]

Gariepy, Romuald *see* LA VARIOLE ET LA VACCINATION COMPULSOIRE

THE GARIES AND THEIR FRIENDS / Webb, Frank J – New York, 1857 – 1r – 1 – us Ross [975]

Garin, J *see* DES CONDITIONS REQUISES...

Garipuy, G *see* ETUDE DES ACTES INTERNATIONAUX...

Garlake, Peter S *see* THE KINGDOMS OF AFRICA

Garland, Augustus Hill *see*
- EXPERIENCE IN THE SUPREME COURT OF THE UNITED STATES, WITH SOME REFLECTIONS AND SUGGESTIONS AS TO THAT TRIBUNAL
- A TREATISE ON THE CONSTITUTION AND JURISDICTION OF THE UNITED STATES COURTS ON PLEADING, PRACTICE AND PROCEDURE THEREIN.

Garland, Bessie *see* THE OLD MAN'S DARLING: A SERIES OF CHARACTER SKETCHES

A GARLAND GATHERED AT MORN: A COLLECTION OF SHORT POEMS / Hazelwood, Hetty – Toronto: Hunter, Rose, 1871. 05526. (Pre-1900 Canadiana) – 9 – cn C.I.H.M. [810]

Garland, Hamlin *see* CRUMBLING IDOLS: TWELVE ESSAYS ON ART AND LITERATURE

GARLAND HERALD – Garland, NE. -w. Feb 1920-Dec 1921; Jan 1924-Apr 1934 – 1 – us NE Hist [071]

Garland, Nicholas Surrey *see* A COMPILATION OF THE LAWS AND AMENDMENTS THERETO RELATING TO BUILDING SOCIETIES, LOAN COMPANIES, JOINT STOCK COMPANIES, AND INTEREST ON MORTGAGES AND OTHER ACTS PERTAINING TO MONETARY INSTITUTIONS

GARMA C.C. CHANG COLLECTION – (Garma C.C. Chang Collection title list.-1mf. $1.00) – 504mf – $260.00 – us I.A.S.W.R. [090]

GARMA C.C. CHANG TIBETAN COLLECTION – Over 130 Tibetan works from the xylograph and manuscript collection. 504 fiches. Title list on 1 fiche available ($1.00) – 9 – $260.00 – us I.A.S.W.R. [280]

GARMENT WORKER – N.Y. v. 1-41. 1902-1945 – 1 – us UMI [331]

GARMENT WORKERS IN ACTION : HISTORY OF THE GARMENT WORKERS OF SOUTH AFRICA TO 1952 / Sachs, E S – Johannesburg: Eagle Press, 1957 – us Res Libr [960]

GARMENT WORKER'S UNION PAPERS – ((Case History)) – 30r – 1 – sa Microfile [331]

GARMISCH-PARTENKIRCHNER TAGBLATT – Garmisch-Partenkirchen. jan 2-apr 14 1945 – 1r – 1 – gw Mikrofilm [072]

Garneau, Alfred *see* POESIES

Garneau, F-X *see* L'ABEILLE CANADIENNE

Garneau, Marthe *see* BIBLIOGRAPHIE DE L'OEUVRE DE MONSIEUR GERARD MORISSET, MEMBRE DE LA SOCIETE ROYALE DU CANADA, 1950-1962

Garneau, Robert *see* BIBLIOGRAPHIE DE L'OEUVRE DE MONSIEUR ROLLAND DUMAIS, CONSEILLER PEDAGOGIQUE EN SCIENCES NATURELLES...

Garner *see* BIOGRAPHICAL AND PORTRAIT CYCLOPEDIA OF NIAGARA COUNTY

Garner, J Dianne *see* JOURNAL OF WOMEN AND AGING

Garner, J W *see* RECENT DEVELOPMENTS IN INTERNATIONAL LAW

A GARNER OF SAINTS : BEING A COLLECTION OF THE LEGENDS AND EMBLEMS USUALLY REPRESENTED IN ART / Hinds, Allen – New York: E.P. Dutton; London: J.M. Dent, 1900 – 1mf – us A.T.L.A. [700]

Garnett, Richard *see* ESSAYS OF AN EX-LIBRARIAN

Garnier, A *see* INTERNATIONALES EHESCHLIESSUNGSRECHT...

Garnier, Germain *see* DESCRIPTION GEOGRAPHIQUE, PHYSIQUE ET POLITIQUE DU DEPARTEMENT DE SEINE-ET-OISE

Garnier, J *see* INSTITUTIO GALLICAE LINGUAE

Garnier, Joseph *see* LE RECHERCHE DES FEUX EN BOURGOGNE AUX 14E ET 15E SIECLES

Garnier, L *see* QUATOUR, PREMIER GRAND, OP. 2

Garnier, T D *see* ZUR ENTWICKLUNGSGESCHICHTE DER NOVELLENDICHTUNG LUDWIG TIECK'S

Garofalo, R *see* LA ESECUTORIETA DELLE SENTENZE STRANIERE IN ITALIA

Garovaglio, S *see* BRYOLOGIA AUSTRIACA EXCURSORIA

Garrazin, General *see* GESCHICHTE DES KRIEGS IN SPANIEN

Garreau, Albert *see* SAINT ALBERT LE GRAND

GARRETT A. MORGAN PAPERS *see* MORGAN, GARRETT A., PAPERS, MS 3534

Garrett, Herbert G *see* THE LIFE INSURANCE ACT

Garrett, Herbert Leonard Offley *see*
- EVENTS AT THE COURT OF RANJIT SINGH, 1810-1817: TRANSLATED FROM THE PAPERS IN THE ALIENATION OFFICE, POONA
- THE PUNJAB A HUNDRED YEAR AGO AS DESCRIBED BY V. JACQUEMONT (1831) & A. SOLTYKOFF (1842)

Garrett, James L, Jr *see* BAPTIST CHURCH DISCIPLINE, BROADMAN PRESS, NASHVILLE, TENNESSEE

Garrett, John *see* A CLASSICAL DICTIONARY OF INDIA, ILLUSTRATIVE OF THE MYTHOLOGY, PHILOSOPHY, LITERATURE, ANTIQUITIES, ARTS, MANNERS, CUSTOMS, ETC. OF THE HINDUS

Garrett, John C *see* ST. MARK'S CHURCH: AN EXPLANATION AND APPEAL

Garrett, P *see* A DIGEST OF THE MINUTES OF THE METHODIST CONFERENCES, FROM THE FIRST,... BY THE LATE REV. JOHN WESLEY,... 1744, TO THE YEAR 1826

Garrett, William *see* PUBLIC MEN IN ALABAMA FOR 30 YEARS

Garrettsville. Ohio. Baptist Church *see* CHURCH RECORDS, MS 2087

Garrettsville. Ohio. Church of Christ *see* CHURCH RECORDS, MS 2843

Garrick Club. London *see* KEMBLE PROMPT BOOKS IN THE GARRICK CLUB, LONDON

GARRICK PAPERS / Victoria and Albert Museum. London – 1 – uk Microform Academic [920]

Garrido, Eduardo *see* RAZONES CONTRA ULTRAJES

Garrido Martin, Aurora *see* ELECCIONES Y PARTIDOS POLITICOS EN CANTABRIA

Garrido Santiago, Manuel *see*
- ARQUITECTURA RELIGIOSA DEL S. 16 DE LA TIERRA DE BARROS
- ARQUITECTURA RELIGIOSA DEL S. 16 EN LA TIERRA DE BARROS

GARRISON ARGUS – Garrison, NE. -w. Jun 1905-May 1907; Sep 1907-Nov 1907; Jan-Feb 1908 – 1 – us NE Hist [071]

Garrison, DR *see* OCCUPATIONAL STRESS AND JOB SATISFACTION RELATED TO MANAGEMENT STYLES OF AMERICAN- AND JAPANESE-OWNED COMPANIES IN AMERICA

GARRISON FORK BAPTIST CHURCH. BEECH GROVE, TENNESSEE : CHURCH RECORDS – 1809-1933 – 1 – 39.42 – us Baptist [240]

Garrison, J H *see* CHRISTIAN UNION

Garrison, W L *see* LIBERATOR

Garrison, William Lloyd *see* WILLIAM LLOYD GARRISON PAPERS, 1833-1881

Garrison, Winfred Ernest *see* ALEXANDER CAMPBELL'S THEOLOGY

Garrod, Heathcote William *see* THE RELIGION OF ALL GOOD MEN

Garrucci, R *see* STORIA DELLA ARTE CRISTIANA NEI PRIMI OTTO SECOLI DELLA CHIESA

Garsault *see* ARTE DEL BARBERO-PELUQUERO-BANERO, QUE CONTIENE EL MODO DE HACER LA BARBA, CONSTRUCCION DE PELUCAS... MODOS DE PEINADOS

GARSTANG COURIER – Lancashire – 1 – uk Microform Academic [072]

Garstin, J H *see* A MANUAL OF THE SOUTH ARCOTT DISTRICT

DER GARTEN VON VAUX-LE-VICOMTE / Bechter, Barbara – 1993 – 3mf – 9 – DM98.00 – 3-89349-850-8 – gw Hänsel [710]

GARTENFLORA – (v72, sept. 1922-dec. 1923 has not been published; Missing: 1937. v86(p. 241-end)) – Erlangen, 1852-1938. v1-87. Index 1852-1901 – 958mf – 9 – 7295/2 – ne IDC [580]

Gartenhof, Kaspar *see* DIE BEDEUTENDSTEN ROMANE PHILIPPS VON ZESEN UND IHRE LITERARGESCHICHTLICHE STELLUNG

DIE GARTENLAUBE : ILLUSTRIERTE FAMILIENZEITSCHRIFT – (Cont by: Die Neue Gartenlaube, 1935?) – Leipzig, 1853-1933 n50. 1934-41 n50. 1942-sep 1944 – 84r – 1 – gw Mikrofilm [073]

GARTENLAUBE *see* ILLUSTRIRTER DORFBARBIER

GARTENZEITUNG : MONATSSCHRIFT FUER GAERTNER UND GARTENFREUNDE – Berlin, 1882-1885 – 28mf – 9 – 8598/1 – ne IDC [630]

GARTH ANALYSIS: RESEARCH BY PENN AND SCHOEN ASSOCIATES. V1-. 1982- – 1,5,6,9 – us UMI [073]

GARTNER'S NOTES TO THE INTERSTATE COMMERCE COMMISSION REPORTS : VOLUMES 1-41 / U.S. Interstate Commerce Commission – Louisville: Banks. 3v. 1915-17 (all publ) – 5mf – 9 – $22.50 – LLMC 84-116 – us L.L.M.C. [324]

Garuda Indonesian Airways *see*
- GARUDA INDONESIAN AIRWAYS DURING 1958
- GIA SELAMA TAHUN 1955
- PLAN GARUDA INDONESIAN AIRWAYS, 1951-1955 (TRAFFIC ANALYSIS AND PRODUCTION PLAN)

GARUDA INDONESIAN AIRWAYS DURING 1958 / Garuda Indonesian Airways – SE-2818 1. 1959 – 9 – ne IDC [380]

Garvi, Petr Abramovich *see* KAPITAL PROTIV TRUDA

Garvie, Alfred Ernest *see* ROMANS

Gary *see* CENTENNIAL HISTORY OF RUSH COUNTY

Gary, Indiana *see* MISCELLANEOUS EARLY NEWSPAPERS

Gary, J M *see* EXAMEN CRITIQUE DU "DICTIONNAIRE DE L'ACADEMIE FRANCAISE."1873

Garzarella, L *see* PREDICTING BODY COMPOSITION OF HEALTHY FEMALES BY B-MODE ULTRASOUND

GAS – v1-49 1925-73 1; v47-49 1971-73 5,6 – us UMI [660]

GAS AND LIQUID CHROMATOGRAPHY ABSTRACTS – v16-27. 1973-84 – 1,5,6,13 – sz Elsevier [073]

GAS COMMITTEE / UN Economic Commission for Europe (ECE) – 1957-89 – E/F.100 E.536 F.443 R.425 – 9 – us U.N. Pubs [340]

GAS JOURNAL – v1-351 1849-1972 1; v349-351 1972 5,6 – us UMI [660]

GAS WAERME INTERNATIONAL – 1952- 1; 1977- 5,6,9 – us UMI [621]

Gasarabwe, E *see* ASPECTS DE L'UNIVERS MYSTIQUE DES RWANDAIS AU TEMPS DE LA ROYAUTE NYIGINYA

Gasco y Navarro, J M *see* ASSERTA APHORISTICA ET CHIRURGICA EX LIBRIS...

LE GASCON – Quebec, Canada. 3 mar 1858-27 mai 1858 – 1r – 1 – Can$30.00 – cn Can Microfilming [072]

Gascon y Miramon, Antonio *see* LOS CRIADEROS DE HIERRO DE BURGUILLOS (BADAJOS)

GASCONISMES CORRIGES / Lascoux, J B – 1823 – 9 – fr I.C.S. [440]

LES GASCONISMES CORRIGES / Desgrouais – 1766 – 9 – fr I.C.S. [440]

DAS GASEL IN DER DEUTSCHEN DICHTUNG UND DAS GASEL BEI PLATEN / Tschersig, Hubert – Leipzig: Quelle & Meyer, 1907 – 1 – us U.W. Library [430]

Gasiorowski, M *see* MIEDZYNARODOWE PRAWO ZEGLUGI RZECZNEJ

Gaskell, Elizabeth Cleghorn *see*
- COUSIN PHILLIS
- THE GREY WOMAN
- THE LIFE OF CHARLOTTE BRONTE
- THE MOORLAND COTTAGE
- RIGHT AT LAST

GASKIYA TA FI KWABO – Zaria, Nigeria: M Abubakar Iman Kagara, [aug 23 1950-dec 1957; aug 1959-dec 1972; 1973-nov 1981] – 1 – us Res Libr [072]

GASKIYA TA FI KWABO – Zaria: M. Abubakar Iman Kagara, sep 1974-dec 1982 – us Res Libr [960]

Gaskoin, Herman (Mrs) *see* CHILDREN'S TREASURY OF BIBLE STORIES

GASLIGHT – Osawatomie. Kan. -w. 1887-88 – 1 – us UMI [071]

EL GASODUCTO PRESIDENTE PERON A TRAVES DEL PERIODISMO NACIONAL Y EXTRANJERO / Argentina. Direccion General del Gas del Estado – [Buenos Aires], 1949 [i.e. 1950] – 1 – CSUXADH9021-B – us Hoover Inst Photo [660]

GASPAR CORTE-REAL: LA DATE EXACTE DE SA DERNIERE EXPEDITION AU NOUVEAU MONDE: D'APRES DEUX DOCUMENTS INEDITS.. / Harrisse, Henry – Paris: Leroux, 1883. (Pre-1900 Canadiana) – 9 – cn C.I.H.M. [910]

Gaspar de Segovia, Jose M *see* POR DON JUAN DE OVANDO...LAVADERO LANAS DE ALMENDRALEJO

Gaspar de Segovia, Joseph Manuel *see* POR LOS...MONASTERIOS DE...

GASPARD DE COLIGNY : ADMIRAL OF FRANCE / Whitehead, A W – London: Methuen, 1904 – 1mf – us A.T.L.A. [944]

GASPARD DE LA NUIT, FANTAISIE A LA MANIERE DE REMBRANDT ET DE CALLOT / Bertrand, Louis Jacques – Paris: Mercure de France, 1895. 250p. 3 fiches. (Literature Collection) – 9 – $8.00 – fr Bibl Nationale [830]

Gasparin, Agenor de *see*
- DE L'AFFRANCHISSMENT DES ESCLAVES ET DE SES RAPPORTS AVEC LA POLITIQUE ACTUELLE
- ESCLAVAGE ET TRAITE

Gasparin, de *see* RAPPORT AU ROI SUR LES HOPITAUX, LES HOSPICES ET LES SERVICES DE BIENFAISANCE PAR M. DE GASPARIN

Gasparini, F *see* SEI TRII PER 2 VIOLONCELLO

Gasparini, Francesco *see*
- L'ARMONICO PRATICO AL CIMBALO.... QUARTA IMPRESSIONE
- L'ARMONICO PRATICO AL CIMBALO: REGOLE, OSSERVAZIONI ED AVVERTIMENTI PER BEN SUONARE IL BASSO E ACCOMPAGNARE SOPRA IL CIMBALO SPINETTA ED ORGANI

Gasparini, Joseph *see* THE ATTRIBUTES OF CHRIST

Gasparini, L *see* LA MELODIA: GIORNALE MUSICALE LETTERARIO

GASPARO CONTARINI, 1483-1542 : EINE MONOGRAPHIE / Dittrich, Franz – Braunsberg: Ermlaendischen Zeitungs- Und Verlagsdruckerei, 1885 – 3mf – us A.T.L.A. [240]

Gasparotto, L *see* IL PRINCIPIO DI NAZIONALITA

THE GASPE GAZETTE – New-Carlisle, Canada. v4 n7. 13 fev 1851 – 1r – 1 – Can$25.00 – cn Can Microfilming [072]

THE GASPE MAGAZINE AND INSTRUCTIVE MISCELLANY – [New Carlisle, Quebec?: s.n. 1849-] – 9 – cn C.I.H.M. [420]

GASPESIANA / Saint-Denis, Soeur – 1963. SEM105P4 – 2mf – 9 – cn Bibl Nat [010]

LA GASPESIE, PROMENADES DANS LE GOLFE SAINT-LAURENT NOUVELLE ECOSSE, ILE DU PRINCE EDOUARD, NOUVEAU BRUNSWICK, LA BAIE DES CHALEURS, LA GASPESIE / Faucher de Saint-Maurice, Narcisse – 3e ed. Montreal. SEM16P38 – 1r – 5 – Can$9.00 – cn Bibl Nat [971]

LE GASPESIEN / ed by Marquis, Maurice – Gaspe, Canada. 4 oct 1930-v2 n45. 19 aut 1933 – 1r – 1 – Can$50.00 – cn Can Microfilming [072]

Gasquet, Abbot *see*
- EDWARD 6TH AND THE BOOK OF COMMON PRAYER
- ENGLISH MONASTIC LIFE
- HENRY THE THIRD AND THE CHURCH
- PARISH LIFE IN MEDIAEVAL ENGLAND

Gasquet, Francis Aidan *see*
- EDWARD 6 AND THE BOOK OF COMMON PRAYER
- ENGLAND UNDER THE OLD RELIGION
- HENRY 8 AND THE ENGLISH MONASTERIES
- THE LAST ABBOT OF GLASTONBURY AND OTHER ESSAYS
- THE OLD ENGLISH BIBLE

Gasquet, Francis Aidan, Cardinal *see* THE GREAT PESTILENCE (A.D. 1348-9)

Gass, J *see* UNE ORDONNANCE CURIEUSE

Gass, W *see*
- GENNADIUS UND PLETHO
- GESCHICHTE DER CHRISTLICHEN ETHIK
- GESCHICHTE DER PROTESTANTISCHEN DOGMATIK

Gasser, S P *see* DE IURE CEREMONIALI CIRCA LEGATOS

Gassette *see* HISTORY OF GREENE COUNTY

Gassol, Ventura *see* LES TOMBES FLAMEJANTS

Gast, E R *see* EMILIA GALOTTI

Gaster, M *see* OCCIDENT AND ORIENT IN HONOUR OF M. GASTER'S 80TH

Gastiazoro, Eugenio *see* ARGENTINA HOY

Gastius, I *see* DE ANNABAPTISMI EXORDIO, ERRORIBVS, HISTORIIS ABOMINANDIS

DAS GASTMAHL : NOVELLE / Klaehn, Friedrich Joachim – Muenchen: F Eher, 1943 – 1r – 1 – us U.W. Library [830]

GASTON DE LATOUR : AN UNFINISHED ROMANCE / Pater, Walter – London, New York: The Macmillan Company, 1896 – 1 roll – 1 – 1-55879-898-6 – uk Libr Preservation [830]

Gaston, Joseph *see*
- THE CENTENNIAL HISTORY OF OREGON
- PORTLAND, OREGON, ITS HISTORY AND BUILDERS

Gaston, William *see* WILLIAM GASTON PAPERS

GASTONIA FIRST BAPTIST CHURCH. GASTONIA, NORTH CAROLINA : CHURCH RECORDS – 1912-57 – 1 – 87.84 – us Baptist [240]

GASTOS SUNTUARIOS Y RECURSOS ECONOMICOS EN EL AFRICA ROMANA / Ramirez Sadaba, Jose Luis – 1mf – 9 – Pta1,000.00 – 84-85422-22-8 – sp Pentalfa [470]

GASTRIKLANDS TIDNING – Borlange, Sweden. 1979- – 1 – sw Kungliga [072]

GASTROENTEROLOGY AND ENDOSCOPY NEWS *see* AMERICAN JOURNAL OF PROCTOLOGY, GASTROENTEROLOGY AND COLON AND RECTAL SURGERY

GASTROENTEROLOGY & ENDOSCOPY NEWS – v36, no.3-. Mar 1985- – 1,5,6,9 – us UMI [073]

GASTROENTEROLOGY NURSING – (Formerly: SGA Journal) – v7-19. 1985-96 – 1,5,6,9 – $65.00r – us Williams [616]

GASTROINTESTINAL RADIOLOGY – A journal of diagnostic imaging.v.1-6, 1976-81. ISSN: 0364-2356 – 1,5,6,9,13 – 88.00v – us UMI [616]

GASTROINTESTINAL RADIOLOGY *see* ABDOMINAL IMAGING

GASTRONOMIE : RECITS DE TABLE / Monselet, Charles – Paris: Charpentier, 1874 – fr Armell [640]

Gasunas, Geraldine *see* THE PHYSIOLOGICAL RESPONSES OF THE ADDITION OF HAND HELD WEIGHTS TO STATIONARY BICYCLING

Gataker, Thomas *see* DE DIPHTHONGIS

GATCOMB'S MUSICAL GAZETTE, DEVOTED TO THE INTEREST OF BANJO, MANDOLIN AND GUITAR – v.1-12. 1887-99 – 1 – 23.00 – us L of C Photodup [780]

THE GATE AND THE CROSS, OR, PILGRIM'S PROGRESS IN ROMANS : AN EXCURSUS AND PARALLELISM / Peck, George Bacheler – Boston: Watchword Publ Co, 1889 – 1mf – 9 – 0-8370-4692-0 – 1985-2692 – us A.T.L.A. [220]

GATE CITY – Keokuk. Iowa. 1855-1927; 1949; 1955- – 1 – us UMI [071]

GATE CITY – Keokuk. Iowa. -w. 1862-72, 1876-95, 1897-1903 – 1 – us UMI [071]

A GATE OR DOOR TO THE HOLY TONGUE, OPENED IN ENGLISH / Robertson, William – 1653. 153p. (English Linguistics Series 1500-1800) – 9 – us UMI [400]

Gateau, M *see* LES MOULES A FROMAGE EN ROUMANIE

Gatenby, R M *see* SMALL RUMINANT BREED PRODUCTIVITY IN AFRICA

Gaterau *see* DESCRIPTION DES PLANTES QUI CROISSENT AUX ENVIRONS DE MONTAUBAN

GATES COUNTY INDEX – Gatesville. N.C. -w. 1955- – 1 – us UMI [071]

Gates, Errett *see*
- THE DISCIPLES OF CHRIST
- THE EARLY RELATION AND SEPARATION OF BAPTISTS AND DISCIPLES

Gates, Hartley Baxter *see* WOMAN'S RESOLVE, OR, ME, WOMAN VERSUS ME, MAN: A RALLYING SONG FOR WOMEN

Gates, Helen Dunn *see* A CONSECRATED LIFE

Gates, Henry Louis Jr *see* BLACK LITERATURE, 1827-1940

Gates, Horatio *see* HORATIO GATES PAPERS, 1726-1828

GATES INTO THE PSALM-COUNTRY / Vincent, Marvin Richardson – New York: Charles Scribner, 1878. 1 fiche – 9 – us A.T.L.A. [240]

Gates, Otis H *see* FEDERAL FOOD AND DRUG ACT DECISIONS

GATESHEAD AND TYNESIDE ECHO – England. -w. 24 Apr 1879-19 Jan 1880. (2 reels) – 1 – uk British Libr Newspaper [072]

GATESHEAD GUARDIAN – England. -w. 6 Jul 1895-23 Jun 1900. (Wanting 1896, 1897). (3 reels) – 1 – uk British Libr Newspaper [072]

GATESHEAD OBSERVER – England. -w. 18 Nov 1837-6 Oct 1886. (Wanting Jul 1870-Jul 1871). (59 reels) – 1 – uk British Libr Newspaper [072]

GATESHEAD POST – 1986-Jun 1988; Jul 7-Dec 29 1988; Jan-Jun 1989; Jul 6-Dec 28 1989; 1990-96 – 1 – uk British Libr Newspaper [072]

GATEWAY HERITAGE – v.1. 1980 – 1,5,6,9 – us UMI [073]

LA GATINEAU – Maniwaki, Canada. 2 nov 1955-25 dec 1968 – 1r – 1 – Can$50.00 – cn Can Microfilming [072]

THE GATINEAU BEAVER – Ottawa: Sergeant's Mess at the [D]rill Hall, [1899] – 9 – cn C.I.H.M. [320]

Gatlinburg, Tennessee *see* MISCELLANEOUS ISSUES OF EARLY NEWSPAPERS

EL GATO NEGRO – Caceres, 1923, 1924 y 1932 – 5 – sp Bibl Santa Ana [073]

GATOR – 1949 – 1 – us I.U. Libraries [390]

LOS GATOS MAIL *see* MISCELLANEOUS SARATOGA NEWSPAPERS

LOS GATOS TIMES *see* OBSERVER

GATOTKATJA GANDRUNG / Tjahya, T S – SE 4579 1. 1962 – 9 – ne IDC [950]

Gatsiskii, A S *see* NIZHEGORODSKII SBORNIK, IZDAVAEMYI NIZHEGORODSKIM GUBERNSKIM STATISTICHESKIM KOMITETOM

Gattel, C M *see* NOUVEAU DICTIONNAIRE PORTATIF DE LA LANGUE FRANCAISE

Gatti, A *see* SULLA LITISPENDENZA E SUL CONFLITTO DEI GIUDICATO...

Gatti de Gamond, Zoe *see* PAUPERISME ET ASSOCIATION

Gatti, L *see* LA ESECUTORIETA, IN ITALIA, DELLE SENTENZE ESTERE...

Gattine, M A de *see*
- RELATION CURIEUSE ET NOUVELLE D'UN VOYAGE DE CONGO FAIT LES ANNEES 1666 ET 1667
- RELATION D'UN VOYAGE AU CONGO FAIT LES ANNEES 1666 ET 1667

Gattula, Erasmus, OSB *see*
- AD HISTORIAM CASSINENSIS ACCESSIONES
- HISTORIA ABBATIAE CASSINENSIS

DIE GATTUNG ACAENA / Bitter, G – 8027 1. 1911 – 9 – ne IDC [580]

DIE GATTUNG LYSIMACHIA L., MONOGRAPHISCH BEARB / Klatt, Fritz – (Abhandl. des Naturw. Vereins in Hamburg. v. 4). Hamburg. 1862. B-5188 2 – 8 – ne IDC [580]

DIE GATTUNGEN DER FOSSILEN PFLANZEN / Goeppert, H R – 5354 2. 1841-1846 – 8 – ne IDC [560]

Gau, F von *see* GEGEN DIE ZIEBENBUERGER EHEN

GAUBOTE : NACHRICHTENBLATT FUER DEN GAU TEUTOBURGER WALD WESER-BERGLAND DES TOURISTENVEREINS "DIE NATURFREUNDE" – Bielefeld, 1926-33 n4 – 1r – 1 – Inquire at Mikrofilmarchiv for details – gw Misc Inst [790]

LA GAUCHE R.D.R – Journal du Rassemblement democratique revolutionnaire. Dir. Jean Ferniot. no. 1-13. Paris. mai 1948-mars 1949. mq no. 9-11 – 1 – fr A.C.R.P.P. [073]

LA GAUCHE REVOLUTIONNAIRE – Red. M. Pivert, M. Collinet, R. Lefeuvre. no. 1-14. Paris. oct 1935-janv 1937 – 1 – fr A.C.R.P.P. [073]

GAUDEAMUS! : LIEDER AUS DEM ENGEREN UND WEITEREN / Scheffel, Joseph Viktor von – Stuttgart: A Bonz, 1903 – 1r – 1 – us U.W. Library [780]

Gaudet-Smet, Francoise *see* PAYSANA

Gaudichaud, C *see* VOYAGE AUTOUR DU MONDE. EXECUTE SUR LES CORVETTES DE S.M. L'URANIE ET LA PHYSICIENNE, 1817-1820

Gaudig, H *see* PRINZ FRIEDRICH VON HOMBURG

GAUDIJ PASCHALES IESV CHRISTI REDIVIVI, IN GLORIOSISSIMAE RESURRECTIONIS EJUS LAETAM CELEBRATIONEM RELATIO HISTORIA, A QVATUOR EVANGELISTIS CONSIGNATA, ET MELODIA HARMONICA ADORNATA / Besler, Samuel – Breslae [i.e. Wroclaw] in officina typographica Baumanniana, [1612] – 1 – us Sibley [780]

Gaudin, J F A G P *see*
- AGROSTOLOGIA HELVETICA
- FLORA HELVETICA

Gaudio, Ricardo *see* ESTADO Y RELACIONES OBRERO-PATRONALES EN LOS ORIGENES DE LA NEGOCIACION COLECTIVA EN ARGENTINA

Gaugiran-Nanteuil *see* LA PETITE ECOLE DES PERES

GAUGUIN. CENTENAIRE / Reunion des musees nationaux. Paris – 1949. 24 illus. 2 fiches – 9 – fr Réunion [700]

LE GAULOIS : HOUDISTE / ed by Laflamme, J L K – Montreal, Canada. 26 aut 1933-28 jul 1934 – 1r – 1 – Can$30.00 – cn Can Microfilming [072]

LE GAULOIS – Litteraire et politique. Dir. H. de Pene. Paris. 5 juil 1868-30 mars 1929 – 1 – fr A.C.R.P.P. [073]

LE GAULOIS – Petite gazette, critique, satirique et anecdotique puis Journal hebdomadaire biographique illustre. Dir. Jean Dolent et Alfred Sirven. no. 1-140; n.s., no. 1-35. Paris. 10 nov 1857-1er sept 1861 – 1 – fr A.C.R.P.P. [073]

LE GAULOIS – (Issues filmed as pt of: Commune de Paris newspapers) – Paris: Impr de G Kugelman, [1868-]. jan 16-21,23,26-31, feb 1-4,7-8,15,20,22-25, mar 24-25,28-30 1871 – us Res Libr [072]

LE GAULOIS DU DIMANCHE – Supplement litteraire et illustre du Gaulois quotidien. Paris. 20 juin 1897-aout 1914 – 1 – fr A.C.R.P.P. [073]

Gaulot, Paul *see* A FRIEND OF THE QUEEN (MARIE ANTOINETTE-COUNT DE FERSEN)

Gault, Robert *see* POPERY

Gaultier, Bon *see* THE BOOK OF BALLADS

Gaultier, D Z *see* L'ALIENATION MENTALE DEVANT LA JUSTICE CRIMINELLE

Gaultier de Claubry, Charles Daniel *see* NOUVEL AVIS AUX MERES QUI VEULENT NOURRIR

Gaultier, J *see*
- L'ANATOMIE DU CALVINISME...
- TABLE CHRONOGRAPHIQUE DE L'ESTAT DU CHRISTIANISME

GAULT'S DECISIONS / Georgia – (No Pre-NRS cases) – 1v. 1820-1846 (all publ) – 1mf – 9 – $1.50 – LLMC 94-001 – us L.L.M.C. [340]

GAUMONT – Berlin. [1906/07?] – 1 – gw Mikrofilm [073]

Gaumont *see* KINEMATOGRAPHISCHE WOCHENSCHAU

Gaumont, Jean *see* MONOGRAPHIES COOPERATIVES: LE MOUVEMENT OUVRIER D'ASSOCIATION ET DE COOPERATION
Gauna, Adrian *see* CORRENTINO POR A
GAUNTLET – (Carlile). 1-60 (all publ). 1833-34 – 10mf – 9 – $65.00 – us UPA [900]
Gauss, J H *see*
- BIBLE'S AUTHORITY SUPPORTED BY THE BIBLE'S HISTORY
- THE BIBLE'S AUTHORITY SUPPORTED BY THE BIBLE'S HISTORY

Gauss, Karl *see* REFORMATIONSVERSUCHE IN DER BASLER BISCHOFSSTADT PRUNTRUT
Gaussen, L *see* THEOPNEUSTIC OU INSPIRATION PLENIERE DES SAINTES ECRITURES
THE GAUSS-JORDAN INVERSION FOR A SYMMETRIC NON-NEGATIVE DEFINITE MATRIX / Wang, Richard L C – 1978 – 9 – Can$15.00 – 0-88769-003-3 – cn Nash Info [510]
Gaussy, Fernand *see* LACLOS 1741-1803.
GAUTAMA BUDDHA / Law, N N – 25th Centenary Volume. 1956. BI-565 2 – 8 – ne IDC [280]
LOS GAUTES ESPANOLES. MADRID...1954 / Menendez Pidal Navascues, Fautismo – Hidalguia 11, Abril-junio, 1954 – 1 – sp Bibl Santa Ana [946]
Gautherot, Gustave *see* SEPTEMBRE 1792. HISTOIRE POLITIQUE DES MASSACRES...
Gauthier, Georges *see* BIBLIOGRAPHIE DE MADAME GABRIELLE ROY
Gauthier, H *see*
- DICTIONNAIRE DES NOMS GEOGRAPHIQUES CONTENUS DANS LES TEXTES HIEROGLYPHIQUES

Gautier, Emile Felix *see*
- L'AFRIQUE NOIRE OCCIDENTALE
- MISSIONS AU SAHARA

Gautier, Hubert *see* TRAITE DES PONTS, OU IL EST PARLE DE CEUX DES ROMAINS
Gautier, Lucien *see* LA MISSION DU PROPH ETE EZECHIEL
Gautier, Theophile *see*
- LA MUSIQUE
- VICTOR HUGO

Gauvin, A *see* LE JEAN-BAPTISTE
Gavagan, Joseph Andrew *see* POWERS OF THE UNITED STATES SUPREME COURT
GAVAKARI – Manamade, India. Jul-Sept 1966 – 1r – 1 – us L of C Photodup [072]
Gavalda y Cabre, Jose Maria de *see* REPARACION Y EJEMPLARIDAD...
Gavazzi, Alessandro *see* THE LECTURES COMPLETE OF FATHER GAVAZZI
Gaveaux *see* LEONORE OU L'AMOUR CONJUGAL
GAVEL / Milwaukee Bar Association – v1-35 and 1966 index. 1938-76 – 69mf – 9 – $103.00 – LLMC 84-607 – us L.L.M.C. [073]
THE GAVEL – Toronto: [R Ramsay, 1870-18–?] – 9 – cn C.I.H.M. [360]
GAVEL (MILWAUKEE) – v1-35. 1938-76 – 9 – $194.00 set – us Hein [340]
GAVEL (NORTH DAKOTA) – v15-41. 1970-94 – 9 – $173.00 set – us Hein [340]
Gavino Rodriguez, Martin *see* EXPOSICION DEL...AYUNTAMIENTO...BADAJOZ
Gavoy, L *see* FAUNULE COLEOPTEROLOGIQUE DU MONT-ALIRIC (AUDE)
Gavrilenko, K *see* ORGANIZATSIIA IURIDICHESKOI RABOTY UCHREZHDENII
Gavrilov, A V *see* OCHERKI ISTORII S. PETERBURGSKOI SINODAL'NOI TIPOGRAFII
GAVROCHE – Hebdomadaire litteraire, artistique, politique et social. Dir. Rene Lalou. Paris. nov 1944$mai 1948 – 1 – fr A.C.R.P.P. [073]
O GAVROCHE – Manaos, Amazonas. 18 Fev 1912 – 1,5,6 – bl Biblioteca [072]
GAWAN : EIN MYSTERIUM / Stucken, Eduard – 4. Aufl. Berlin: E Reiss, [1911] – 1r – 1 – us U.W. Library [430]
GAY COMMUNITY NEWS – -w. Boston, G.C.N., Inc – 1 – us U.W. Library [305]
Gay de Montella, R *see* EL ACCIDENTE DE ABORDAJE
Gay, George I *see* PUBLIC RELATIONS OF THE COMMISSION FOR RELIEF IN BELGIUM: DOCUMENTS
Gay, J E *see* ERYSIMORUM QUORUNDAM NOVORUM DIAGNOSES SIMULQUE ERYSIMI MURALIS DESCRIPTIONEM
GAY LIBERATOR – v1,no.11-. Sept 1971-. Detroit: Pansy Press.ill. Continues: Detroit Gay Liberator – 1 – us U.W. Library [305]
GAY LIFE – (Titles may vary: GayLife, Chicago's gay life, Chicago gay life) – Chicago, v1-11, no 31/32, June 20, 1975-Jan 30, 1986 – 10r – 1 – Can$865.00 – cn McLaren [305]
THE GAY LORD QUEX : A COMEDY IN FOUR ACTS / Pinero, Arthur Wing – London: W. Heinemann, 1900 – 1 roll – 1 – 1-55879-405-0 – uk Libr Preservation [820]
GAY NEWS – 1972-82.(Sexual Politics in Britain) – 9 – us Primary [305]
GAY NEWS – -bw. 1972-. London, England: Gay News Ltd – 1 – us U.W. Library [305]
GAY RENAISSANCE NEWSLETTER – Gay Center, Madison. 1979? -m. Ceased publ – 1 – us U.W. Library [305]
GAY STUDIES NEWSLETTER *see* GSN
GAY SUNSHINE – Berkeley, CA. nos 1-46. 1970-1980 – 1r – 1 – $50.00 – R04006 – us Library Micro [071]
Gay, Sydney Howard *see* JAMES MADISON
Gaya Nuno, Juan Antonio *see* ZURBARAN
Gaye, J W *see* CARTEGGIO INEDITO D'ARTISTI DEI SECOLI 14, 15, 16...
GAYE-I MILLIYE – Sivas, 1922 – 9 – $20.00 – us MEDOC [956]
Gayer, Christina D *see* PHYSIOLOGICAL DISCRIMINATORS OF ROWING PERFORMANCE IN MALE, CLUB ROWERS
Gaynor, William J A *see* CHRONOLOGICAL COLLECTION OF CARTOONS RELATING TO MR. GAYNOR PUBLISHED IN THE NEW YORK NEWSPAPERS
Gay-Para, P *see* CONTES DE LA MONTAGNE LIBANAISE
LE GAZ – Paris. -w.10 Feb 1857-15 Jun 1886 – 7r – 1 – uk British Libr Newspaper [622]
GAZA, A CITY OF MANY BATTLES : FROM THE FAMILY OF NOAH TO THE PRESENT DAY / Dowling, Theodore Edward – London: S.P.C.K.; New York: E.S. Gorham, 1913 – 1mf – us A.T.L.A. [930]
GAZAIR *see* AL-GAZA'IR
Gazaldun *see*
- DISEBERANG DJEMBATAN EMAS; DONGENG MODEREN
- DUA HATI JANG TAK PERNAH PUAS

Gazali *see* TATALAKSANA PRODUKSI; PRODUCTION MANAGEMENT JOGJAKARTA, FAKULTAS EKONOMI, UNIVERSITAS GADJAH MADA, 1963
GAZELLE. (SHIP) *see* DIE FORSCHUNGSREISE S.M.S. "GAZELLE" 1874 BIS 1876
A GAZETA – Cuiaba, 6 Jun-Nov 1889; Mar 1890; 16 Oct 1891 – 1,5,6 – bl Biblioteca [072]
A GAZETA : JORNAL NOTICIOSO – Rio Branco, Acre. 6 Ago 1968 – 1,5,6 – bl Biblioteca [072]
A GAZETA : ORGAO INDEPENDENTE, NOTICIOSO E POLITICO – Manaos, Amazonas. 25 Jul 1913 – 1,5,6 – bl Biblioteca [072]
A GAZETA : ORGAO NOTICIOSO DEDICADO AOS INTERESSES DO MUNICIPIO – Lavras, 24 Aug 1958 – 1,5,6 – bl Biblioteca [072]
A GAZETA – Rio Novo, Brazil. Jul 1952 – 1 – bl Biblioteca [072]
GAZETA BANKOWA – (Oct 1988-1998 2r per y $170/y) – Poland, 1999- – 2r per y – 1 – $160.00 standing order – us Ross [072]
GAZETA CHINOVNIKA – Russia, 1912-14 – 1r – 1 – us Ross [350]
GAZETA COMERCIAL DA BAHIA – '(s.l.')-BA, Brazil. 24 maio, out, nov 1833; dez 1835; jan, out 1836; out 1838; 27 jan 1843 – 1,5,6 – bl Biblioteca [072]
GAZETA COMMERCIAL : ORGAM DO COMMERCIO, LAVOURA E INDUSTRIA – Juiz de Fora, 6 Jun 1929; Feb, Jul, Dec 1953; Jul, Dec 1954; Sept, Nov 1958; Jan 1962; Jun, Aug 1963; 23-30 Dec 1977 – 1,5,6 – bl Biblioteca [072]
GAZETA DA BAHIA – '(s.l.')-BA, Brazil. 08 jan 1879-31 dez 1886 (incomplete) – 1,5,6 – bl Biblioteca [072]
GAZETA DE ALAGOAS : ORGAO DO PARTIDO CONSTITUCIONAL – Maceio, Alagoas. 28 Jan 1891; Fev 1892; 20 Ago 1895 – 1,5,6 – bl Biblioteca [072]
GAZETA DE AMSTERDAM – (Incomplete) – Amsterdam, 1674-1699 – 3mf – 9 – J-261-3/1 – ne IDC [943]
GAZETA DE ANNUNCIOS – Penedo, Alagoas. 1894 – 1,5,6 – bl Biblioteca [072]
GAZETA DE CARANGOLA – Carangola, 8 Sep-Oct 1956; Oct 1960; Jan-Dec 1979; Jan-May, Aug, Oct-20 Dec 1980 – 1,5,6 – bl Biblioteca [072]
GAZETA DE CATAGUAZES : ORGAM REPUBLICANO – Cataguazes, 31 Jan, 4 Jul 1897 – 1,5,6 – bl Biblioteca [072]
GAZETA DE CHRISTINA – Cristina, Brazil. Mar 1891; Aug, Oct 1892; May, Jul-Aug 1895 – 1 – bl Biblioteca [072]
GAZETA DE CURVELLO *see* BRASIL HODIERNO
GAZETA DE LEOPOLDINA – Leopoldina, 27 Sep 1896; Feb-Jul 1898; Jan, Mar, May, Jul-Sep, Dec 1912; Oct-Dec 1913; Feb, Sep 1915; Apr 1918; Jan, Dec 1922; Dec 1926; Jan-Apr 1927; Feb, Oct 1932; Apr, Jul-Dec 1933; Oct 1934; 18 Sep 1960 – 1,5,6 – bl Biblioteca [072]
GAZETA DE MACAO – Macao: M M D Pegado, jan-aug 1839 – us Res Libr [072]
GAZETA DE MACAO – Macao: Typographia do Governo, 1825-26 – 1r – 1 – us Res Libr [072]
GAZETA DE MACAU E TIMOR = AO-MEN HSIN-WEN CHIH – Macau: Typographia mercantil, [1872-]. sep 20 1872-apr 20 1874 – 1r – 1 – us Res Libr [072]
GAZETA DE MANAOS : ORGAO IMPARCIAL – Manaos, Amazonas. 13 Jun 1886 – 1,5,6 – bl Biblioteca [072]
GAZETA DE MANICORE : ORGAO DO PARTIDO CONSERVADOR – Manicore, Amazonas. 16 Jan 1887 – 1,5,6 – bl Biblioteca [072]
GAZETA DE MINAS – (Cont of: Gazeta de Oliveira) – Oliveira, 1 Jan-Dec 1899; Jan-May 1900; Jan, Sep 1901; Jul, Sep 1902; Apr-Jun 1903; Dec 1910; Jan, Mar 1911; Feb, Sep 1912; Jul 1917; May 1919; Nov 1921; Dec 1922; May, Aug 1923; Apr 1924; Aug 1926; Sep 1931; Jul 1932; Jan 1933; Jan 1939; Jun, Dec 1942; Dec 1944; Feb, Sep 1952; Aug-Dec 1979; Jan-25 Dec 1982 – 1,5,6 – bl Biblioteca [072]
GAZETA DE MINAS *see* GAZETA DE OLIVEIRA
GAZETA DE MOJI-MIRIM – Moji-Mirim, Brazil. Jan 1887-Nov 1895. Incomplete except 1888; 1890-92 complete – 1 – bl Biblioteca [072]
GAZETA DE MURIAE – Muriae, Brazil. Dec 1953 – 1 – bl Biblioteca [072]
GAZETA DE NANUQUE – Nanuque, Brazil. Sept, Nov 1967; Jan, May-Jun, Dec 1968 – 1 – bl Biblioteca [072]
GAZETA DE NOTICIAS : DEDICADO AOS INTERESES DO COMMERCIO, LAVOURA E INDUSTRIA – '(s.l.')-Sao Luiz, Brazil. 9 Apr-2 Oct 1883 – 1,5,6 – bl Biblioteca [072]
GAZETA DE NOTICIAS – Maceio, Alagoas. 22 Jul 1879; Abr-Maio 1880; Nov 1881; Jan-Mar, Maio-Jul 1882; 15 Fev 1883 – 1,5,6 – bl Biblioteca [072]
GAZETA DE NOTICIAS – Rio de Janeiro, 2 Aug 1875-Nov 1893; Jan 1894-Dec 1908; Mar 1914-31 Dec 1916 – 1,5,6 – bl Biblioteca [072]
GAZETA DE OLIVEIRA – (Cont as: Gazeta de Minas) – Oliveira, 8 Aug, Sep 1895; Apr 1897-25 Dec 1898 – 1,5,6 – bl Biblioteca [072]
GAZETA DE OLIVEIRA *see* GAZETA DE MINAS
GAZETA DE OURO FINO – Ouro Fino, Brazil. 1892-May 1925. Very scattered issues except 1892-94 complete – 1 – bl Biblioteca [072]
GAZETA DE OURO PRETO : ORGAO IMPARCIAL, NOTICIOSO E LITTERARIO – Ouro Preto, 8 Jan-31 Aug 1890 – 1,5,6 – bl Biblioteca [072]
GAZETA DE PANAMA : 1881 ENERO 27; PARNASO PANEMENO AND A COLLECTION OF LITERARY AND POLITICAL PAMPHLETS – Panama: Biblioteca Nacional de Panama, 1881 – 1r – 1 – us Ross [972]
GAZETA DE PANAMA – Panama: Biblioteca Nacional de Panama, 1889-1899 – 9r – 1 – $550.00 – us Ross [972]
GAZETA DE PANAMA – Panama: Ministerio de Education, 1878, 1881 – 1r – 1 – us Ross [972]
GAZETA DE PARAOPEBA : SEMANARIO INDEPENDENTE – Villa Paraopeba, 18 Jun 1916; Sep 1917; Jan-Apr 1927; Jan 1934-Oct 1935; Jan 1951; Aug-Sep 1954; Mar, 3-9 Apr 1955 – 1,5,6 – bl Biblioteca [072]
GAZETA DE PATROCINIO : ORGAO INFORMATIVO E CULTURAL DO ESTADO NOVO – Patrocinio, 2 Oct-Nov 1938; Jan-23 Dec 1979 – 1,5,6 – bl Biblioteca [072]
GAZETA DE QUELUZ – Queluz de Minas, 2 Sep 1906-Dec 1907; Feb 1908-Oct 1909; Apr, Jun, Sep 1910; Jan-May, Jul, Sep-25 Dec 1911 – 1,5,6 – bl Biblioteca [072]
GAZETA DE TOMBOS : PELA GRANDEZA DA LAVOURA, COMMERCIO E INDUSTRIA DO MUNICIPIO – Tombos, 8 Jul-Dec 1933; May-Dec 1937; Jan-Apr, Oct-Nov 1938; Apr 1939; Feb 1940; Mar-Jun, Aug-Sep, Nov-Dec 1941; Jan, Apr-Jul 1942; Feb 1943-Dec 1944; Jan 1945-23 May 1947 – 1,5,6 – bl Biblioteca [072]
GAZETA DE UBA : ORGAM DOS INTERESSES PUBLICOS – Cidade de Uba, 8-15 Sept 1895; Jul 1897; Aug 1908; 5 Dec 1912 – 1,5,6 – bl Biblioteca [072]
GAZETA DE UBERABA – Uberaba, 19 Mar 1888; Apr 1889; Nov 1901; Jan-Feb 1902; Mar, Dec 1906; May 1908; Feb, May, Jul 1912; Jan, Sep 1917; 19 Oct 1938 – 1,5,6 – bl Biblioteca [072]
GAZETA DE UBERABINHA – Uberlandia, Brazil. Nov 1901 – 1 – bl Biblioteca [072]
GAZETA DE VARGINHA – Varginha, Brazil. Dec 1977; 1978; Jan-May 1979 – 1 – bl Biblioteca [072]
GAZETA DE VICOSA – Vicosa, 6 Mar-Apr, 10 Nov 1938 – 1,5,6 – bl Biblioteca [072]
GAZETA DEVI ATAGO OKTI ABRI A – (Includes c.1: no.1) – Petrograd: Ispolnitelnai a kollegii a P.K.P.O.A. i F., [1917- – 1 – CSUXANR3222-S – us Hoover Inst Photo [947]
GAZETA DO ARACAJU : JORNAL POLITICO E NOTICIOSO – Aracaju, 4 Jun 1879; Aug, Dec 1880; Apr 1881; Oct 1882; Oct, Dec 1883; Jan 1885; Feb, 5-20 Sep 1888 – 1,5,6 – bl Biblioteca [072]
GAZETA DO BRASIL – Rio de Janeiro, 30 May 1827-5 Jan 1828 – 1,5,6 – bl Biblioteca [072]
A GAZETA DO C.S.U.-P10 : INFORMATIVOS COMUNITARIO – Manaos, Amazonas. Fev-Mar 1982 – 1,5,6 – bl Biblioteca [072]
GAZETA DO NORTE – Montes Claros, Brazil. June 1924-Mar 1949. Very scattered issues – 1 – bl Biblioteca [072]
GAZETA DO PENEDO : ORGAO DO PARTIDO CONSERVADOR DO BAIXO S. FRANCISCO – Penedo, Alagoas. 11 Set 1883 – 1,5,6 – bl Biblioteca [072]
GAZETA DO POVO – Maceio, Alagoas. 8 Maio 1887 – 1,5,6 – bl Biblioteca [072]
GAZETA DO POVO : ORGAO DO PARTIDO REPUBLICANO – Curityba, 23 Apr 1898; 15 Jan 1900 – 1,5,6 – bl Biblioteca [072]
GAZETA DO POVO – Sao Paulo, Brazil. 16 Oct 1879-Mar 1890 – 1 – bl Biblioteca [072]
GAZETA DO PURUS – Senna Madureira, Acre. 27 Jun-Jul, Nov-14 Dez 1918 – 1,5,6 – bl Biblioteca [072]
GAZETA DO RIO DE JANEIRO – Rio de Janeiro, 10 Sep 1808-31 Dec 1822 – 1,5,6 – bl Biblioteca [072]
GAZETA DO RIO NOVO – Rio Novo, Brazil. Dec 1901; May 1903 – 1 – bl Biblioteca [072]
GAZETA DO SUL *see* O BRAZIL
GAZETA DO SUL – Quilimane: [Alfredo de Aguiar, may 22-jul 20, dec 21 1889 – us Res Libr [072]
GAZETA DO SUL DE MINAS – Pocos de Caldas, 5 Nov 1961; 30 Jun 1963 – 1,5,6 – bl Biblioteca [072]
GAZETA DO TRIANGULO – Araguari, 1 Aug-Sep 1954; 3-24 Apr 1955 – 1,5,6 – bl Biblioteca [072]
GAZETA ESTUDANTINA : JORNAL LITTERARIO E NOTICIOSO – Manaos, Amazonas. 8 Jun-14 Jul 1915 – 1,5,6 – bl Biblioteca [072]
A GAZETA GASTRONOMICA – Manaus, Amazonas. 13 Dez 1907 – 1,5,6 – bl Biblioteca [072]
GAZETA GAZET (PETROGRAD, R.S.F.S.R.) – (Includes c.1: 1917:Mar.26) – Petrograd: Izd-vo "Gazeta gazet", 19uu – 1 – CSUXADP4948-S – us Hoover Inst Photo [947]
GAZETA HANDLOWA – Warsaw, Poland. 1950-70; 1972-78 – 17r – 1 – us L of C Photodup [943]
GAZETA KRAKOWSKA – (Backfile through 1998 $85/r) – Poland, 1999- – 6r per y – 1 – $480.00 standing order – us Ross [072]
GAZETA KRAKOWSKA – Krakow, Poland. Jun 1952-Apr 1976; 1978-1992 – 76r – 1 – us L of C Photodup [943]
GAZETA KUJAWSKA – (Some missing issues) – Inowroclaw, Poland. 1953-Jan 1960 – 12r – 1 – us L of C Photodup [943]

GAZETA LUDOWA – Warsaw. Poland. -d. Jul 1946-Nov 1949. (14 reels) – 1 – uk British Libr Newspaper [943]
GAZETA LUDOWA – Warsaw, Poland. Nov 1945-Nov 1949 – 5r – 1 – us L of C Photodup [943]
GAZETA MEDICA DA BAHIA – '(s.l.')-BA, Brazil. 10 jul 1866-jul 1870; out 1871; jan, ago-nov 1872;jan- mar 1873; maio, jul 1874; jan 1876-jun 1906 (incomplete) – 1,5,6 – bl Biblioteca [072]
GAZETA MINEIRA – S. Joao del-Rei, 29 Jan 1887 – 1,5,6 – bl Biblioteca [072]
GAZETA MORSKA – Gdansk, Poland. Sept 1-30 1945; July 14-31 1946 – 1r – 1 – us L of C Photodup [072]
GAZETA MUNICIPAL – Mar de Hespanha, 6 Mar 1898 – 1,5,6 – bl Biblioteca [072]
GAZETA NIEDZIELNA – London, UK. May 1949- – 1 – uk British Libr Newspaper [072]
GAZETA OFFICIAL DO IMPERIO DO BRASIL – Rio de Janeiro, 1 Set 1846-31 Jul 1848 – 1 – bl Biblioteca [324]
GAZETA OFICIAL / Panama – 1876-1969. Incomplete – 1 – 2599.00 – us L of C Photodup [324]
GAZETA OLSZTYNSKA – Olsztyn, Poland. Dec 1952-1957 (scattered issues); Feb 1959-1976 – 35r – 1 – us L of C Photodup [943]
GAZETA POLSKA – Warsaw, Poland. 25 Jan 1919; Apr-Dec 1934; Feb 1939; Jun-Sept 1939 – 4r – 1 – us L of C Photodup [943]
GAZETA POLSKA W CHICAGO – Chicago, IL: W Dyniewicz, 1888; 1890; jan 5 1905; 1907; 1909-10; 1912-jan 20 1917 – 14r – 1 – us Res Libr [071]
GAZETA POMORSKA – Bydgoszcz, Poland. Jul-Dec 1950; 1952-92 – 84r – 1 – us L of C Photodup [943]
GAZETA PORANNA – Warsaw, Poland. Jan-Feb 1919 – 1r – 1 – us L of C Photodup [943]
GAZETA POZNANSKA (GAZETA ZACHODNIA) – Poznan, Poland. Nov 1950-1973; Apr 1975-92 – 80r – 1 – us L of C Photodup [943]
GAZETA RABOCHEGO I KREST'IANSKOGO / Russia – St. Petersburg. 1917-18 – 1 – $19.00 – us L of C Photodup [324]
GAZETA RABOCHIKH I KRESTI AN : EZHENEDELNAI A GAZETA RABOCHIKH I KRESTI AN – (Includes c.1: 1921:Nov.7) – Kashira: Kashirskoe otd. Gosizdata, 1921- – 1 – CSUXAKG5896-S – us Hoover Inst Photo [947]
GAZETA ROBOTNICZA – London, UK. Aug 1948-Apr 1952 – 1 – uk British Libr Newspaper [072]
GAZETA ROBOTNICZA – (Missing: 1952) – Wroclaw, Poland. Apr 1951-1992 – 90r – 1 – us L of C Photodup [943]
GAZETA ROMANEASCA – Titre francais: La Gazette roumaine. 1 no. Paris. 1935 – 1 – fr A.C.R.P.P. [073]
GAZETA RURAL : DEDICADA AS CLASSES CONSERVADORAS DO ESTADO DE ALAGOAS – Maceio, Alagoas. 11 Jul, 7 Set 1900 – 1,5,6 – bl Biblioteca [072]
A GAZETA SABARENSE – Sabara, Brazil. Sept-Dec 1960; Jan, Apr-May, Jul-Dec 1961; Nov-Dec 1977 – 1 – bl Biblioteca [072]
GAZETA SADOWA WARSZAWSKA – Warsaw. On film: v2-65; 1874-1938. LL-0239 – 1 – us L of C Photodup [340]
GAZETA SERET – n.p. publ. twice a week by Austrians for the Russian Army. May-Dec. 1917; Jan.-Mar. 1918. Gaps – 1 – 35.00r – us Hoover Inst Photo [947]
GAZETA SUL-MINEIRA – Sao Goncalo do Sapucahy, 2 Oct 1887; Jul, Sep 1890; Jan, 18 Jul 1891 – 1,5,6 – bl Biblioteca [072]
GAZETA TARNOWSKA – Tarnow, Poland. 1953 – 1r – 1 – us L of C Photodup [943]
GAZETA TORUNSKA – Torun, Poland. 1953; Feb-Mar 1954; 1955-59 – 13r – 1 – us L of C Photodup [943]
GAZETA UFFICIALE / Sicily – Palermo. 1958-66 – 1 – us NY Public [945]
GAZETA VREMENNAGO – Rabochago i Krest'lanskago Pravitel'stva. Petrograd. Nov. 1, 23-Dec. 31, 1917; Jan. 4, 9, 19, Feb. 20, 28, Mar. 7-8, 10, 1918 – 1 – 35.00r – us Hoover Inst Photo [947]
GAZETA WARSZAWSKA – Warsaw, Poland. Jan-Feb 1919 – 1r – 1 – us L of C Photodup [943]
GAZETA WSPOLCZESNA – Bialystok, Poland. Feb-Sept 1916; 1953-90; 1992 – 65r – 1 – us L of C Photodup [943]
GAZETA WYBORCZA – (1989-90 6r per y $510/y. 1991 8r $680. 1992-98 12r per y $1,020/y) – Poland, 1999- – 12r per y – 1 – $960.00 standing order – us Ross [072]
GAZETA WYBORCZA – (Standing order available from De 1994 +. 12r per year. Sfr1,350.00y) – De 1989 a 1993 – 12r – 1 – Sfr1,440.00 – sz Infoprint [947]
GAZETA WYBORCZA – Warsaw, Poland. May 17 1989-Jan 1 1993 – 25r – 1 – us L of C Photodup [072]
GAZETA ZACHODNIA *see* GAZETA POZNANSKA (GAZETA ZACHODNIA)
GAZETA ZIELONOGORSKA – Zielona Gora, Poland. 1953-Jul 1954; Oct 1954-Feb 1955 (scattered issues); Jun 1955-Jun 1970 – 26r – 1 – us L of C Photodup [943]
GAZETA ZYDOWSKA = JEWISH GAZETTE – (In Yiddish) – Krakow, PL. v2 no37. 9 May 1941 – 1r – 1 – $25.00 – cn Can Microfilming [072]
GAZETA ZYRTARE – Tirane, Albania, 1959-68 – 3r – 1 – us Ross [324]
GAZETA ZYRTARE E RPS TE SHQIPERISE – Tirane, 1944-1991. jan 18 1955-83 – 13r – us Res Libr [072]
GAZETA-GRIVENNIK – (Includes c.1: 1917:Dec.11) – Petrograd: Tip. akt sionern. o-va izdatelskago di ela "Kopi e ika", 1917- – 1 – CSUXANR3154-S – us Hoover Inst Photo [947]
GAZETA-KOPI E IKA – (Includes c.1: 1914:Aug.6, 1917:Apr.22, July 18) – S-Peterburg: Tip. akt sionern. ob-va izdatelskago di ela "Kopi e ika", 1908 – 1 – CSUXANR4215-S – us Hoover Inst Photo [947]
GAZETI RASMI LA SERIKALI ZANZIBAR – Zanzibar. v66-74. 1957-65 – 6r – 1 – us Ross [324]
A GAZETINHA : ORGAO LITTERARIO, HUMORISTICO E NOTICIOSO – Oliveira, 15 Aug 1897 – 1,5,6 – bl Biblioteca [072]
A GAZETINHA : ORGAO SEMANAL – Manaos, Amazonas. 17-31 Jan 1904 – 1,5,6 – bl Biblioteca [072]
A GAZETINHA : PERIODICO CRITICO E LITTERARIO – Manaos, Amazonas. 20 Set-22 Nov 1885 – 1,5,6 – bl Biblioteca [072]
A GAZETINHA : PERIODICO LITTERARIO, CRITICO E NOTICIOSO – Maceio, Alagoas. 6 Maio 1884 – 1,5,6 – bl Biblioteca [072]
A GAZETINHA – Rio de Janeiro, 19 Nov 1880-18 Feb 1881 – 1,5,6 – bl Biblioteca [072]
GAZETINHA : ORGAM REPUBLICANO PARLAMENTARISTA DO CLUB "QUATRO DE MARCO" – Uberaba, 3-6 Sep 1896 – 1,5,6 – bl Biblioteca [072]
A GAZETINHA DE PASSOS : SEMANARIO IMPARCIAL, LITTERARIO, POETICO, COMMERCIAL E NOTICIOSO – Cidade de Passos, 8 May 1883 – 1,5,6 – bl Biblioteca [072]
GAZETINHA POPULAR – Paracatu, 5 Jul 1896 – 1,5,6 – bl Biblioteca [072]
GAZETNAIA LETOPIS' – Organ gosudarstvennoi bibliografii. v. 1-2. M. 1936-37. BR-3466 2 – 8 – ne IDC [460]
GAZETTA DE CAMPINAS – Campinas, Brazil. Oct 1869-Oct 1875 – 1 – bl Biblioteca [072]
GAZETTA ITALIANA DI LONDRA – London, UK. 20 Sept 1896-22 Sept 1900 – 1 – uk British Libr Newspaper [072]
GAZETTE – 1953-1959 – 1. 241-243 – £42.00r – uk Scot News [072]
GAZETTE – 1989-1991. G1-3. Continuation of Port Fairy Gazette – 3r – 1 – at Corangamite [072]
GAZETTE – Abilene. Kan. 1878-1889; 1894 – 1 – us UMI [071]
GAZETTE / Aligarh Institute – 13v. Aligarh. 1874-78. Lacking: 1874, v. 1-9; 1875-78, v. 10, 11, 12, 13, several numbers. BI-568 2 – 8 – ne IDC [073]
GAZETTE – Aliquippa. Pa. and Evening Times. 1929-46 – 1 – us UMI [071]
GAZETTE – Anaheim, CA. 1876-77; 1879-1882; 1944-64 – 22r – 1 RC02015 – $1,100.00 – us Library Micro [071]
GAZETTE – Anaheim. Calif. -w. 1944- – 1 – us UMI [071]
GAZETTE Antwerp, Ohio. 1871-78 – 2r – 1 – $32.50r – us Archival [071]
GAZETTE – Ashland. Neb. 1883-1886; 1893-1957 – 1 – us UMI [071]
GAZETTE – Ashland. Ohio. 1887-1901 – 1 – us UMI [071]
GAZETTE – Beaufort. S.C. 1892- – 1 – us UMI [071]
GAZETTE – Bedford. Pa. -d. and Inquirer. -W. 1966- – 1 – us UMI [071]
GAZETTE – Bedford. Pa. -w. 1899-1950 – 1 – us UMI [071]
GAZETTE – Bellevue. Ohio. 1904-1906; 1914-15; 1918-1922; 1950- – 1 – us UMI [071]
GAZETTE – Billings. Mont. 1883- – 1 – us UMI [071]
GAZETTE – Blantyre, Lanarkshire, Scotland, UK. 1935-7 Feb 1953; 13 Jun 1959-31 Jan 1964. -w.8 reels – 1 – uk British Libr Newspaper [072]
GAZETTE – Butte. Neb. 1893-1959 – 1 – us UMI [071]
GAZETTE – Cedar Rapids. Iowa. 1883- – 1 – us UMI [071]
GAZETTE – Charleston. West Virginia. 1891-1905; 1924- – 1 – us UMI [071]
GAZETTE – Chillicothe, Ohio. 1867-. And pred – 1 – us UMI [071]
GAZETTE – Cicero. Ind. 1876-1877 – 1 – us UMI [071]
GAZETTE – Clinton. Tenn. 1888-1904 – 1 – us UMI [071]
GAZETTE – Colfax. Wash. -w. 1900-32 – 1 – us UMI [071]
GAZETTE – Davenport. Iowa. 1853-1857; 1880-81; 1883-87 – 1 – us UMI [071]
GAZETTE – Davenport. Iowa. -w. 1841-47 – 1 – us UMI [071]
GAZETTE – Delaware. Ohio. 1967- – 1 – us UMI [071]
GAZETTE – Dunnville, 1884-1940 – 26r – 1 – cn Preston [971]
GAZETTE – Emporia. Kan. 1893- – 1 – us UMI [071]
GAZETTE – Emporia. Kan. -w. 1890-1930 – 1 – us UMI [071]
GAZETTE – Enugu, Eastern Region of Nigeria. v1-16. 1951-67 – 12r – 1 – us Ross [324]
GAZETTE – Evansville. Ind. 1822-1825 – 1 – us UMI [071]
GAZETTE – Fairbury. Neb. 1870-1958 – 1 – us UMI [071]
GAZETTE : FEUILLE OFFICIELLE D'ANNONCES JUDICIAIRES ET LEGALES / L'Hotel Drouot – Paris, 1929 – 1 – fr A.C.R.P.P. [073]
GAZETTE – Gastonia. N.C. 1900- – 1 – us UMI [071]
GAZETTE – Genoa, Ohio. 1925-66. 12 rolls – 1 – us Archival [071]
GAZETTE – Goleta. Calif. -w. 1955-67 – 1 – us UMI [071]
GAZETTE – Goodspring, NV. 29 Jul 1916; 11 May 1918; 1919-21 – 2r – 1 – $100.00 – U04568 – us Library Micro [071]
GAZETTE / Great Britain. Western Pacific High Commission – Sura. 1943-1967 – 1 – us NY Public [980]
GAZETTE – Haverhill. Mass. 1890- – 1 – us UMI [071]
GAZETTE – Haverhill. Mass. -w. 1821-95 – 1 – us UMI [071]
GAZETTE – Heppner. Or. -w. 1901-13 – 1 – us UMI [071]
GAZETTE – Hobart. Ind. -w. 1891-1932, 1934-40, 1949- – 1 – us UMI [071]
GAZETTE – Holly Springs. Miss. 1841-1847 – 1 – us UMI [071]
GAZETTE – Ibadan, Nigeria. v6-19. 1957-70 – 11r – 1 – us Ross [324]
GAZETTE : INTERNATIONAL JOURNAL OF MASS COMMUNICATION STUDIES – Deventer. v1-26. 1955-80 – 5,9 – Dfl2,080.00; Dfl80.00v – ne Swets [380]
GAZETTE – Janesville. Wis. 1854- – 1 – us UMI [071]
GAZETTE – Janesville. Wis. -w. 1845-65 – 1 – us UMI [071]
GAZETTE – Kaduna, Nigeria: Interim Common Services Agency. v7-19. 1958-70 – 9r – 1 – us Ross [324]
GAZETTE – Kalamazoo. Mich. 1876- – 1 – us UMI [071]
GAZETTE – Kalamazoo. Mich. -w. 1837-43, 1846-62, 1870-78, 1880-86, 1888-92, 1895-97 – 1 – us UMI [071]
GAZETTE – Kansas City. Kan. -w. 1888-1903, 1905-09 – 1 – us UMI [071]
GAZETTE – Kansas City. Mo. 1899; 1901-1905 – 1 – us UMI [071]
GAZETTE – Kissimmee. Fl. -w. 1940-1941, 1946- – 1 – us P.K. Yonge [071]
GAZETTE – Lawrence. Kan. -w. 1882-99 – 1 – us UMI [071]
GAZETTE – Lewistown. Pa. -w. 1846-50, 1856-58, 1860-67, 1870-71, 1878-87, 1890, 1893-1915, 1937, 1944 – 1 – us UMI [071]
GAZETTE – Lincoln. Mont. 1970- – 1 – us UMI [071]
GAZETTE – Lindsay. Calif. -w. 1945- – 1 – us UMI [071]
GAZETTE – McCook. Neb. 1924- – 1 – us UMI [071]
GAZETTE – Magnolia. Miss. 1881-1883; 1936-1952 – 1 – us UMI [071]
GAZETTE – Malawi. v1-7. 1964-70 – 6r – 1 – us Ross [324]
GAZETTE – Mariposa. Calif. -w. 1947-64 – 1 – us UMI [071]
GAZETTE – Martinsburg. West Virginia. 1810-1855 – 1 – us UMI [071]
GAZETTE – Missoula. Mont. 1890-1982 – 1 – us UMI [071]
GAZETTE – New Albany. Miss. 1937-1954 – 1 – us UMI [071]
GAZETTE – Niagara Falls. N.Y. 1854- – 1 – us UMI [071]
GAZETTE / Nigeria. Central-West State – Kaduna. v. 1, no. 1-v. 2. no. 5. Supplement. Jun. 15, 1967-Feb. 29, 1968 – 1 – us NY Public [324]
GAZETTE / Nigeria. North-Eastern State – Kaduna. v. 1, no. 1-v. 3, no. 50. Suppl. 15 Jun 1967-18 Dec 1969 – 1 – us NY Public [960]
GAZETTE / Nigeria. North-Western State – Kaduna. v. 1, no. 1-v. 3, no. 51. Suppl. 15 Jun 1967-26 Dec 1969 – 1 – us NY Public [960]
GAZETTE / Nigeria. Western Region – Ibadan. 1957-1966 – 1 – us NY Public [960]
GAZETTE – Olathe. Kan. 1879-83 – 1 – us UMI [071]
GAZETTE – Parkersburg. West Virginia. 1841-57; 1869-72 – 1 – us UMI [071]
GAZETTE – Pawtucket. R.I. and Chronicle. 1826-1912 – 1 – us UMI [071]
GAZETTE – Phoenix. Ariz. 1881- – 1 – us UMI [071]
GAZETTE – Pittsburgh. Pa. -w and sw. 1786-1833, 1844-45 – 1 – us UMI [071]
GAZETTE – Providence. R.I. -d. 1844-46 – 1 – us UMI [071]
GAZETTE – Providence. R.I. -w. 1762-1825, 1867-85 – 1 – us UMI [071]
GAZETTE – Raymond. Miss. 1845-1854 – 1 – us UMI [071]
GAZETTE – San Antonio. Tex. 1904-1909 – 1 – us UMI [071]
GAZETTE – Schenectady. N.Y. 1924- – 1 – us UMI [071]
GAZETTE – (Set incl. Gold Beach Gazette) – Wedderburn, OR. -w. 8 Nov 1895-28 Aug 1896. – 1r – 1 – us U.O. Library [071]
GAZETTE – St John's, Newfoundland, 1955-68 – 2r – 1 – us Ross [971]
GAZETTE – St. Joseph. Mo. -w. 1868-1900 – 1 – us UMI [071]
GAZETTE – Sterling. Ill. 1957- – 1 – us UMI [071]
GAZETTE – Stillwater. Minn. 1957- – 1 – us UMI [071]
GAZETTE – Stillwater. Okl. -w. 1953-54 – 1 – us UMI [071]
GAZETTE – Sumner. Iowa. 1973- – 1 – us UMI [071]
GAZETTE – Theophraste Renaudot. mai 1631-1761. devenu: Gazette de France. 1762-15 aout 1792. A paru ensuite sous des titres divers. Paris. mai 1631-1792. A partir de sept 1805 voir a Gazette de France – 1 – fr A.C.R.P.P. [073]
GAZETTE – Tifton. Ga. 1942-1951; 1954-1960 – 1 – us UMI [071]
GAZETTE – Tifton. Ga. -w. 1892-96, 1916, 1941-47, 1954-58, 1968-69 – 1 – us UMI [071]
GAZETTE – Turks and Caicos Islands. v114-120. 1964-69 – 1r – 1 – us Ross [324]
GAZETTE – Washington. Iowa. 1868-1903 – 1 – us UMI [071]
GAZETTE – Waukegan. Ill. 1897-1919 – 1 – us UMI [071]
GAZETTE – Wellsboro. Pa. 1968- – 1 – us UMI [071]
GAZETTE – Wellsburg. West Virginia. 1828-1833 – 1 – us UMI [071]
GAZETTE – Wheeling. West Virginia. 1826-1859 – 1 – us UMI [071]
GAZETTE – Winchester. Va. 1802-1813 – 1 – us UMI [071]
GAZETTE – Wyandotte. Kan. 1859-1888 – 1 – us UMI [071]
GAZETTE – Xenia. Ohio. -d, w, sw. 1868-1931, 1932, 1965- – 1 – us UMI [071]
GAZETTE – Zanesville. Ohio. 1831-1851 – 1 – us UMI [071]

THE GAZETTE – Basingstoke, England. Extra edition. -w. Aug-Dec 1980. 39 ft – 1 – uk British Libr Newspaper [072]
THE GAZETTE – Basingstoke, England. Mid-week edition. 1976-80. Lacking 1979. 8 reels – 1 – uk British Libr Newspaper [072]
THE GAZETTE – Basingstoke, England. Week-end edition. -w. 1976-81. Lacking 1979. 20 reels – 1 – uk British Libr Newspaper [072]
THE GAZETTE : COMMERCIAL AND FINANCIAL REVIEW FOR 1928 AND 1929 – Montreal, 4 jan 1929; 4 jan 1930 – 1r – 1 – Can$35.00 – cn Can Microfilming [072]
THE GAZETTE – Fair Oaks, CA. 1946-48 – 1r – 1 – $50.00 – C02233 – us Library Micro [071]
THE GAZETTE – Harrisville. West Virginia. 1936-1949 – 1 – us UMI [071]
THE GAZETTE : MEGANTIC EDITION – Lyster Station, Canada. 21 jun 1900-13 jan 1910 – 1r – 1 – Can$35.00 – cn Can Microfilming [072]
THE GAZETTE – Montreal, Quebec, CN. 1878- – 36r per yr – 1 – Can$53.00r – cn Commonwealth Micro [072]
THE GAZETTE : MONTREAL SUMMER ATTRACTIONS – Montreal, Canada. v129 n156. 30 jun 1900 – 1r – 1 – Can$25.00 – cn Can Microfilming [072]
THE GAZETTE – Montreal. v113 n79. 1 apr 1884-v113 n156. 30 jun 1884 – 1r – 1 – Can$25.00 – cn Can Microfilming [072]
THE GAZETTE – Portland, ME. apr 16 1798-apr 22 1799 – 1 – us Res Libr [071]
THE GAZETTE : SPECIAL ISSUE – Bonaventure Island, Canada. 26 jun 1925 – 1r – 1 – Can$25.00 – cn Can Microfilming [072]
THE GAZETTE *see* WEEKLY GAZETTE
THE GAZETTE AND BANKRUPTCY COURT REPORTER – v1 no 1-19. 1867-68 – 9 – LLMC 84-468 – us L.L.M.C. [073]
GAZETTE AND BULLETIN – Williamsport, PA., 1911 – 13 – $25.00r – us I.M.R. [071]
GAZETTE AND DAILY – York, PA., 1933-1970 – 13 – $25.00r – us I.M.R. [071]
GAZETTE AND DEMOCRAT – New Castle, PA. -w 1870-1874 – 13 – $25.00r – us I.M.R. [071]
GAZETTE AND HERALD DUSHORE – Dushore, PA., 1905-1925 – 13 – $25.00r – us I.M.R. [071]
GAZETTE AND PUBLIC LEDGER – Norfolk. Va. 1804-1816 – 1 – us UMI [071]
GAZETTE AND UNIVERSAL DAILY ADVOCATE – Philadelphia, PA., 1826-1834 – 13 – $25.00r – us I.M.R. [071]
GAZETTE ANECDOTIQUE, LITTERAIRE, ARTISTIQUE ET BIBLIOGRAPHIQUE – Paris. 1876-99 – 1 – fr A.C.R.P.P. [073]
LA GAZETTE CANADIENNE : REFORMISTE / ed by Quilliam, John – Montreal, Canada. 14 aut 1822-9 jul 1823 – 1r – 1 – Can$30.00 – cn Can Microfilming [072]
GAZETTE CONSTITUTIONNELLE DE L'ARRONDISSEMENT DE CAMBRAI – devenu: Gazette de Cambrai. 4 Ddec 1838-12 fevr 1839, 1848-27 mars 1852, avr 1863, 18 nov 1865-25 janv 1866. Cambrai – 1 – fr A.C.R.P.P. [073]
LA GAZETTE D'ARTHABASKA / ed by Leblanc, D & Tachereau, J-F – Arthabaska, Canada. 23 nov 1907-v7 n17. 9 mai 1914 – 1r – 1 – Can$50.00 – cn Can Microfilming [072]
LA GAZETTE DE BERTHIER – Berthier, Canada. 10 aut 1888-28 dec 1906 – 3r – 1 – Can$50.00r – cn Can Microfilming [072]
GAZETTE DE BONN – Bonn, 1789 n1-209 – 1r – 1 – Inquire at Mikrofilmarchiv for details – gw Misc Inst [943]
GAZETTE DE BRUXELLES – (Gazette francoise des Pays-Bas Gazette des Pays-Bas). Brussels. Belgium. -w. 30 Jul 1756-3 Feb 1763. (6 reels) – 1 – uk British Libr Newspaper [949]
GAZETTE DE CHAMPFLEURY – no. 1-10. Paris. nov-dec 1856 – 1 – fr A.C.R.P.P. [073]
GAZETTE DE FRANCE – Paris. A paru sous des titres divers. 23 sept 1805-juin 1841, 1842-sept 1919 – 1 – fr A.C.R.P.P. [073]
GAZETTE DE FRANCE – Paris. -d 31 Jan 1855-31 Dec 1864; 1 Jan 1869-22 Apr 1870; 1 Sep 1877-31 Oct 1900; 3 Jan 1906-19 Jun 1915. 90 reels – 1 – uk British Libr Newspaper [072]
GAZETTE DE GRANDE-BRETAGNE – London, UK. 19 Jul 1924-3 Aug 1929; 1931-30 Jul 1932 – 1 – uk British Libr Newspaper [072]
GAZETTE DE GUERNESEY – Saint Peter Port. 14 Oct 1837; 20 Apr 1839; 6 Jan 1894-28 Mar 1936 – 1 – uk British Libr Newspaper [072]
LA GAZETTE DE HOLLANDE – The Hague, Netherlands. -w. 1 Aug 1914-28 June 1922. 14 reels – 1 – uk British Libr Newspaper [949]
LA GAZETTE DE JOLIETTE – Joliette, Canada. 13 avr 1866-v30 n14. 31 dec 1895 – 8r – 1 – Can$50.00r – cn Can Microfilming [072]
GAZETTE DE LA GUADELOUPE – La Guadeloupe. I, no. 22-32, 39-52; II, no. 1. mai 1788-janv 1789 – 1 – fr A.C.R.P.P. [073]
LA GAZETTE DE LA PRESSE – Lille, France. v1 n6-7. 14 jun 1914 – 1 – cn Can Microfilming [072]
LA GAZETTE DE LA RIVE SUD – Longueuil, Canada. v1 n2. 15 jan 1916 – 1r – 1 – Can$25.00 – cn Can Microfilming [072]
GAZETTE DE LAUSANNE ET JOURNAL SUISSE – Lausanne: P Seguin, jan 3 1966-dec 31 1966/jan 1 1967 – 4r – 1 – us Res Libr [072]
GAZETTE DE L'EQUATEUR – Coquilhatville: L'Avenir belge, aug 1952-sep 1957 – 1r – 1 – us Res Libr [072]
LA GAZETTE DE L'ETAT / Pondicherry. India – Pondicherry. 1964-1966 – 1 – us NY Public [324]
LA GAZETTE DE L'HOTEL DROUOT : L'HEBDOMADAIRE DES VENTES PUBLIQUES – 1891-1988 – 99r – 1 – $9,820.00 – us UPA [700]
GAZETTE DE L'ILE DE JERSEY – Saint Helier. 5 Aug 1786-27 Dec 1788 – 1 – uk British Libr Newspaper [072]
LA GAZETTE DE LOUISEVILLE – Louiseville, Canada. 20 jun 1929 – 1r – 1 – Can$25.00 – cn Can Microfilming [072]
GAZETTE DE LYON – Lyon. 5 avr 1845-27 juil 1853 – 1 – fr A.C.R.P.P. [073]
LA GAZETTE DE MANIWAKI ET DE GATINEAU – Maniwaki, Canada. v31 n19. 24 nov 1960-v36 n36. 10 fev 1966 – 2r – 1 – Can$60.00r – cn Can Microfilming [072]
GAZETTE DE PARIS – Hebdomadaire puis Journal financier hebdomadaire. Red. en chef Arsene Houssaye. Paris. oct 1871-janv 1873 – 1 – fr A.C.R.P.P. [073]
GAZETTE DE PARIS – Paris. oct 1789-aout 1792 – 1 – fr A.C.R.P.P. [073]
LA GAZETTE DE PARIS, NON POLITIQUE – Dir. Dollingen. Paris. 6 avr 1856-1er avr 1860 avec un spec. de sept 1853. Interrompu du 29 sept au 30 nov 1859 – 1 – fr A.C.R.P.P. [073]
GAZETTE DE PRAGUE – Czechoslovakia. -w. 24 April 1920-29 Sept 1926. 4 reels – 1 – uk British Libr Newspaper [072]
GAZETTE DE PRAGUE – Prague, Czechoslovakia. Apr 1920-Sept 1926 – 4r – 1 – us L of C Photodup [072]
LA GAZETTE DE QUEBEC = THE QUEBEC GAZETTE – (French: 3 mai 1832-30 dec 1841 1r Can$60.00. English: v11 n1 7 nov 1833-v11 n54 30 oct 1834 1r Can$50.00. English: 3 jan 1834-24 nov 1873 21r Can$60.00. Centenary Illustrated Edition: v102 21 jun 1864 1r Can$25.00) – Quebec, Canada. bilingue: 21 jun 1764-27 avr 1832 – 12r – 1 – Can$60.00r – cn Can Microfilming [072]
GAZETTE DE SOREL – Sorel, Canada. 1862-73 – 6r – 1 – $390.00 – cn Library Assoc [971]
LA GAZETTE DE SOREL – Sorel, Canada. 13 aut 1857-25 mai 1883 – 9r – 1 – Can$80.00r – cn Can Microfilming [072]
GAZETTE DE ST-HYACINTHE – St-Hyacinthe, Canada. 13 aut 1868-v3 n97. 7 sep 1871 – 1r – 1 – Can$75.00 – cn Can Microfilming [072]
LA GAZETTE DE TOURCOING ET DES CANTONS – (Numerous missing numbers) – Quot. de Tourcoing (Nord), fevr. 1876-fevr. 1884 (ques dizaines de no. manq.) – 9r – 1 – F5,207.01 – fr Armell [072]
LA GAZETTE DE VALLEYFIELD – (Becomes: La Gazette de Valleyfield-Beauharnois 10 jan 1952-31 dec 1969) – Valleyfield, Canada. 22 mai 1936-3 jan 1952 – 25r – 1 – Can$65.00r – cn Can Microfilming [072]
LA GAZETTE DE VALLEYFIELD-BEAUHARNOIS *see* LA GAZETTE DE VALLEYFIELD
GAZETTE DEMOCRAT – (In German. Missing: Oct 1927-Oct 1928) – Philadelphia, PA. 1927-49 – 130r – 1 – $11,050.00 – D3384 – us Scholarly Res [071]
GAZETTE DES ARCHITECTES ET DU BATIMENT – 1853-86. 11 reels – 1 – $915.00 – us UPA [720]
GAZETTE DES ARDENNES – Journal des pays occupes paraissant quatre fois par semaine. Charleville. nov 1914-nov 1918 – 1 – fr A.C.R.P.P. [073]
GAZETTE DES BEAUX-ARTS – (Index 1859-63; 1864-68; 1859-1908) – v. 1-25. Paris. 1859-68; 2nd period. v. 1-38. 1869-88; 3rd period. v. 1-40 1889-1908; 4th period. v. 1-15. 1909-19; 5th period. v. 1-18. 1920-28 – 1,159mf – 9 – ne IDC [073]
GAZETTE DES BEAUX-ARTS – Paris. 1866-67, 1962 – 1 – fr A.C.R.P.P. [073]
LA GAZETTE DES CAMPAGNES – La Pocatiere, Canada. 21 sep 1861-22 avr 1895 – 9r – 1 – Can$75.00r – cn Can Microfilming [072]
LA GAZETTE DES CAMPAGNES – La Pocatiere, Canada. 2nd serie: 3 nov 1941-5 oct 1956 – 3r – 1 – Can$60.00r – cn Can Microfilming [072]
LA GAZETTE DES CHEVALIERS DE COLOMB DE LA P. DE Q – Granby. v1 n11. mai 1948-v1 n12. jun 1948 – 1r – 1 – Can$30.00 – cn Can Microfilming [072]
GAZETTE DES COURS DE L'EUROPE – Le royaliste, ami de l'humanite. 46 no. Paris. sept 1790-avr 1792 – 1 – fr A.C.R.P.P. [073]
GAZETTE DES ETRANGERS – Litterature, beaux-arts, sport, bourse, industrie, chronique de la Cour, de la ville et du theatre. Red. en chef H. de Pene. no. 2531-2750. Paris. juil-13 dec 1868 – 1 – fr A.C.R.P.P. [073]
LA GAZETTE DES FAMILLES CANADIENNES – Quebec, Ottawa, Canada. oct 1869-15 dec 1878 – 2r – 1 – Can$50.00r – cn Can Microfilming [072]
GAZETTE DES PETITES ANTILLES MARTINIQUE – French West Indies. 1774-1775 – 1 – us UMI [072]
GAZETTE DES TRIBUNAUX – Paris, France. -w. Jan 1850-1 March 1941; 11 July-31 Dec 1943; 22 April 1945-25 Dec 1955. 176 reels – 1 – uk British Libr Newspaper [072]
GAZETTE DES TRIBUNAUX – Port-au-Prince: Charles Heraux, 3eme annee n2-4e annee n16 15 janv 1887-15 aout 1888; 5e annee n1-n24 1 janv-15 dec 1889; 13e annee n1-n16 1 janv-15 aout 1902; 14e annee n1-16e annee n14 1 janv 1903-15 juil 1905; 17e annee n1-19e annee n21 1 janv 1906-1 nov 1908; 20e annee n1-n9; 22e annee n1-24e annee n51 – 30 sheets – 9 – us Res Libr [072]
GAZETTE DES TROIS-RIVIERES – Trois-Rivieres, Canada. v1 n4. 17 sep 1846-21 aut 1847 – 1r – 1 – Can$50.00 – cn Can Microfilming [072]
LA GAZETTE DES TROIS-RIVIERES / ed by Duvernay, Ludger – Trois-Rivieres, Canada. 25 jun 1817; 12 aut 1817-v2 n53. 17 aut 1819 – 1r – 1 – Can$35.00 – cn Can Microfilming [072]
LA GAZETTE DES TROIS-RIVIERES – Trois Rivieres, Canada. 1817-21 – 1 reel – 1 – $68.00 – cn Library Assoc [971]
LA GAZETTE D'OTTAWA : JOURNAL POLITIQUE, LITTERAIRE, AGRICOLE, INDUSTRIEL ET COMMERCIAL – Ottawa, Ontario. 27 dec 1878-28 fev 1898 – 15r – Can$100.00r – cn Can Microfilming [072]
GAZETTE DU BAS-LANGUEDOC – Nimes. Bihebd., quot. a partir du 1er dec 1849. 24 aout 1848-49, 1951 – 1 – fr A.C.R.P.P. [073]
GAZETTE DU BON TON – Paris, 1913-25 – 4r – 14 – £420.00 – uk Chadwyck [740]
GAZETTE DU CINEMA – Dir. Maurice Scherer, Eric Rohmer. no. 1-5. Paris. mai-nov 1950 – 1 – fr A.C.R.P.P. [790]
GAZETTE DU COMMERCE – puis Gazette du commerce, de l'agriculture et des finances; Gazette d'agriculture, commerce, arts et finances. Paris. 1763-83 – 1 – fr A.C.R.P.P. [073]
GAZETTE DU COMMERCE; ET D'AGRICULTURE – Saint Helier. 29 Apr 1837 – 1 – uk British Libr Newspaper [072]
LA GAZETTE DU COMMERCE ET DE L'INDUSTRIE – Quebec, Canada. 23 avr 1866-20 jul 1866 – 1r – 1 – Can$30.00 – cn Can Microfilming [072]
GAZETTE DU COMMERCE ET LITTERAIRE / ed by Mesplet, Fleury – (Includes: Gazette Litteraire 2 sep 1778-2 jun 1779) – Montreal, Canada. 3 jun 1778-19 aut 1778 – 1r – 1 – Can$30.00 – cn Can Microfilming [073]
GAZETTE DU COMMERCE ET LITTERAIRE – Montreal, Canada. 1778-79 – 1 reel – 1 – $68.00 – cn Library Assoc [971]
LA GAZETTE DU FRANC : LE CONSEILLER DE LA FAMILLE FRANCAISE – Nos 93-145. Paris. 1927 – 1 – fr A.C.R.P.P. [640]
LA GAZETTE DU LANGUEDOC – Memorial de Toulouse. Journal des interets provinciaux. Toulouse. juin 1831-52 – 1 – fr A.C.R.P.P. [073]
GAZETTE DU MIDI – Journal du soir. Marseille. 1848-51 – 1 – fr A.C.R.P.P. [073]
LA GAZETTE DU NORD *see* L'ABITIBI
GAZETTE DU PALAIS – Paris, France. -d. 5 June 1943-11 Jan, 3, 9 May 1944; 31 Dec 1955-Dec 1977. 84 reels – 1 – uk British Libr Newspaper [072]
GAZETTE EALING BOROUGH *see* MIDDLESEX COUNTY TIMES
GAZETTE & ECHO. (BEESTON & WEST NOTTS GAZETTE ECHO) – England. 1913-38, 1940, 1949-50. 24mqn reels – 1 – uk British Libr Newspaper [072]
GAZETTE (ENGLISH) – Quebec, 1840-1865 – 5r – 1 – cn Preston [971]
LA GAZETTE FINANCIERE – Vol 1, no. 1-52 (1909-1910) – 10mf – $75.00 – us MEDOC [332]
THE GAZETTE FOR ZANZIBAR AND EAST AFRICA / Zanzibar and East Africa – v. 1-17. 1892-1909 – 1 – uk Microform Academic [960]
GAZETTE GLOBE – Kansas City. Kan. 1909-1917 – 1 – us UMI [071]
THE GAZETTE (HEMEL HEMPSTEAD) *see* HEMEL HEMPSTEAD GAZETTE AND WEST HERTS ADVERTISER
THE GAZETTE (HITCHIN) *see* HITCHIN AND ROYSTON EXPRESS
GAZETTE LAW REPORTS – 54v. New Zealand. 1898-1952. N.Z. case reports of Court of Appeal, Supreme Court, Workers Compensation Court, Arbitration & Land Sales. Merged with New Zealand Law Reports in 1953 – 1,9 – $429.00 – at Butterworths [340]
GAZETTE LAW REPORTS OF NEW ZEALAND 1898-1952 – 54v set – nz Butterworths [340]
THE GAZETTE (LETCHWORTH AND BALDOCK) *see* CITIZEN GARDEN CITY RECORD AND ADVERTISING JOURNAL
GAZETTE LITTERAIRE *see* GAZETTE DU COMMERCE ET LITTERAIRE
LA GAZETTE LITTERAIRE / ed by Lavallee, G – Montreal, Canada. 8 fev-11 oct 1934 – 1r – 1 – Can$35.00 – cn Can Microfilming [072]
LA GAZETTE LITTERAIRE DE L'EUROPE – Paris. Par Arnaud et Suard. Mars 1764-1 mars 1766 (I-VIII) – 1 – fr A.C.R.P.P. [400]
GAZETTE MEDICALE : REVUE MENSUELLE MEDICO-CHIRURGICALE – Montreal, Canada. aut 1865-v1 n12. jul 1866 – 1 – Can$28.00 – cn Can Microfilming [610]
LA GAZETTE MEDICALE – Montreal, Canada. sep 1874 – 1r – 1 – Can$20.00 – cn Can Microfilming [610]
GAZETTE NATIONALE – Paris: Impr de A Gutot, jul 16-aug 13 1848 – us Res Libr [072]
GAZETTE NATIONALE OU LE MONITEUR UNIVERSEL – Paris, France. n283. 1 jul 1795-n100. 31 dec 1795 – 1r – 1 – Can$50.00 – cn Can Microfilming [072]
GAZETTE NEWS – Asheville. N.C. 1904-16 – 1 – us UMI [071]
GAZETTE OF INDIA / India – New Delhi. 1912-1942 – 1 – us NY Public [950]
GAZETTE OF INDIA – New Delhi, 1945-66 – 109r – 1 – us Ross [324]
GAZETTE OF PAKISTAN / Pakistan – 1967- – 1 – 65.00y – us L of C Photodup [950]
GAZETTE OF PAKISTAN – Pakistan, 1954-66 – 26r – 1 – us Ross [324]
GAZETTE OF THE UNITED REPUBLIC OF TANZANIA – Tanzania, 1960-70 – 11r – 1 – us Ross [324]

GAZETTE OF THE UNITED STATES – New York and Philadelphia. -d. 15 Apr 1789-14 Sep 1793, 23 Dec 1793-17 May 1797, 1 Aug-27 Dec 1798, 21-26 Nov 1803. (Imperfect). (4 reels) – 1 – uk British Libr Newspaper [071]
GAZETTE OF THE UNITED STATES – Philadelphia. Pa. 1789-1804. Includes N.Y., New York. Gazette of the U.S. 1789-1790 – 1,3 – us Readex [071]
GAZETTE OF THE UNITED STATES – Philadelphia. Pa. -d. 1794-96, 1798, 1820-30, 1833-38, 1840-47 – 1 – us UMI [071]
GAZETTE OF THE UNITED STATES – Philadelphia. Pa. -sw. 1789-93, 1805-10, 1812-18, 1825-38 – 1 – us UMI [071]
GAZETTE OF THE UNITED STATES – Philadelphia. Sept 1 1791-Dec 31 1792 – 1 – us NY Public [071]
GAZETTE OF THE UNITED STATES AND EVENING ADVERTISER – Philadelphia, 1791-94 – 1r – 1 – us Ross [071]
GAZETTE OFFICIELLE DE QUEBEC – Quebec. v85-101. 1953-69 – 40r – 1 – us Ross [324]
GAZETTE PATRIOTIQUE / ed by Lemaitre, Francois – Quebec, Canada. v1 n5. 9 aut 1823-v1 n13. 4 oct 1823 – 1r – 1 – Can$25.00 – cn Can Microfilming [072]
GAZETTE RANCHER FARMER – McCook. Neb. -w. 1954-58 – 1 – us UMI [071]
THE GAZETTE (STEVENAGE) *see* STEVENAGE GAZETTE
GAZETTE TRIBUNE – Sibley. Iowa. -w. 1951-59, 1961- – 1 – us UMI [071]
GAZETTE UNIVERSELLE – ou Papiers-nouvelles de tous les pays et de tous les jours. Paris. dec 1789-aout 1792 – 1 – fr A.C.R.P.P. [073]
GAZETTE-COMMONER – Colfax. Wash. -w. 1932-56 – 1 – us UMI [071]
GAZETTEER AND BIOGRAPHICAL RECORD OF GENESEE COUNTY 1788-1890 / Beers, F W – Syracuse, J. W. Vose and Co., 1890. New York Reel 16. (The Cox Library Collection) – 5 – us Americana [978]
GAZETTEER AND BUSINESS DIRECTORY OF CHEMUNG AND SCHUYLER COUNTIES 1868-69 / Child, Hamilton – Syracuse, 1868. New York Reel 11. The Cox Library Collection – 5 – us Americana [978]
GAZETTEER AND BUSINESS DIRECTORY OF FRANKLIN AND GRAND ISLE COUNTIES / Child, Hamilton – Syracuse, Printed at the Journal Office, 1883. Vermont Reel 7. (The Cox Library Collection) – 5 – us Americana [978]
GAZETTEER AND BUSINESS DIRECTORY OF LAMOILLE AND ORLEANS COUNTIES / Child, Hamilton – Syracuse, Printed at the Journal Office, 1883. Vermont Reel 7. (The Cox Library Collection) – 5 – us Americana [978]
GAZETTEER AND BUSINESS DIRECTORY OF NIAGARA COUNTY 1869 / Child, Hamilton – Syracuse, Journal Office, 1869. New York Reel 23. The Cox Library Collection – 5 – us Americana [978]
GAZETTEER AND BUSINESS DIRECTORY OF ORANGE COUNTY / Child, Hamilton – Syracuse, Syracuse Journal Co., 1888. Vermont Reel 7. (The Cox Library Collection) – 5 – us Americana [978]
GAZETTEER AND BUSINESS DIRECTORY OF RENSSELAER COUNTY, NEW YORK 1870/71 / Child, Hamilton – Syracuse, Journal Office, 1870. New York Reel 31. The Cox Library Collection – 5 – us Americana [978]
GAZETTEER AND BUSINESS DIRECTORY OF RUTLAND COUNTY / Child, Hamilton – Syracuse, Printed at the Journal Office, 1881. Vermont Reel 8. (The Cox Library Collection) – 5 – us Americana [978]
GAZETTEER AND BUSINESS DIRECTORY OF WINDHAM COUNTY / Child, Hamilton – Syracuse, Printed at the Journal Office, 1884. Vermont Reel 9. (The Cox Library Collection) – 5 – us Americana [978]
GAZETTEER OF BAUCHI PROVINCE / Gall, Frederick Beckles – (Filmed with: Gazetteer of Plateau Province by C G Ames) – London: Waterlow, 1920 – 1 – us Res Libr [960]
GAZETTEER OF CHESHIRE COUNTY 1736-1885 / Child, Hamilton – Syracuse, NY, 1885. New Hampshire Reel 3. (The Cox Library Collection) – 5 – us Americana [978]
GAZETTEER OF EASTERN EUROPE : ALPHABETICAL SEQUENCE – 8mf – 9 – $20.00 – us A.G.L.L. [910]
GAZETTEER OF EASTERN EUROPE : SOUNDEX SEQUENCE – 7mf – 9 – $17.50 – us A.G.L.L. [910]
GAZETTEER OF GRAFTON COUNTY 1709-1886 / Child, Hamilton – Syracuse, NY. New Hampshire Reel 3. (The Cox Library Collection) – 5 – us Americana [978]
GAZETTEER OF ILORIN PROVINCE – (Filmed with: Gazetteer of Bauchi Province by F B Gall) – London: Waterlow, 1921 – 1 – us Res Libr [960]
GAZETTEER OF KANO PROVINCE / Gowers, William Frederick – (Filmed with: Gazetteer of Bauchi Province by F B Gall) – London: Waterlow, 1921 – 1 – us Res Libr [960]
GAZETTEER OF MURI PROVINCE, UP TO DECEMBER 1919 / ed by Fremantle, John Morton – (Filmed with: Gazetteer of Bauchi Province by F B Gall) – [London: Waterlow, 1920] – 1 – us Res Libr [960]
GAZETTEER OF NUPE PROVINCE – (Filmed with: Gazetteer of Bauchi Province by F B Gall) – London: Waterlow, 1920 – 1 – us Res Libr [960]
GAZETTEER OF PLATEAU PROVINCE – (Filmed with: Gazetteer of Bauchi Province by F B Gall) – Lagos, 1933 – 1 – us Res Libr [550]
GAZETTEER OF SOKOTO PROVINCE / Arnett, Edward John – (Filmed with: Gazetteer of Bauchi Province by F B Gall) – London: Waterlow, 1920 – 1 – us Res Libr [910]
A GAZETTEER OF THE CENTRAL PROVINCE OF CEYLON, EXCLUDING WALAPANE / Lawrie, A Campbell – I-562 2. 2 v. 1896-98 – 8 – ne IDC [950]
GAZETTEER OF THE KONTAGORA PROVINCE : COMPILED FROM THE PROVINCIAL RECORDS / Duff, E C – (Filmed with: Gazetteer of Bauchi Province by F B Gall) – London: Waterlow, 1920 – 1 – us Res Libr [960]
GAZETTEER OF THE STATE OF NEW YORK / French, J H – Geography, general history, and history of every county, city, town and village. Syracuse, R. Pearsall Smith, 1860. New York Reel 1. (The Cox Library Collection) – 5 – us Americana [978]
GAZETTEER OF UTAH AND SALT LAKE CITY DIRECTORY 1874 / Sloan, Edward L – Salt Lake City: Salt Lake Herald Publ. Co., 1874. Utah reel 5. (Cox Library Collection) – 5 – us Americana [978]
GAZETTEER OF WASHINGTON COUNTY / Adams & Child, Hamilton – Syracuse, Syracuse Journal Co., 1889. Vermont Reel 9. (The Cox Library Collection) – 5 – us Americana [978]
GAZETTEER OF YOLA PROVINCE – (Filmed with: Gazetteer of Bauchi Province by F B Gall) – [Lagos: Govt Press, 1927] – 1 – us Res Libr [960]
GAZETTEER OF ZARIA PROVINCE / Arnett, Edward John – (Filmed with: Gazetteer of Bauchi Province by F B Gall) – [s.l: s.n.], 1920 – 1 – us Res Libr [910]
The Gazetteer Publishing and Printing Co *see*
- NEW MEXICO STATE BUSINESS DIRECTORY
- WYOMING STATE BUSINESS DIRECTORY 1929

GAZETTE.INDUSTRIELLE, MINIERE ET COMMERCIALE – London, UK. 8 Apr-20 May 1903 – 1 – uk British Libr Newspaper [072]
GAZETTE-JOURNAL – Hastings, NE. -d. Jan 1884-Jun 1888 – 1 – us NE Hist [071]
GAZETTE-TIMES – Heppner. Or. -w. 1912-51 – 1 – us UMI [071]
GAZETY MALAGASY *see* NY GAZETY MALAGASY
Gazier, Augustin Louis *see* HISTOIRE GENERALE DU MOUVEMENT JANSENISTE DEPUIS SES ORIGINES JUSQU'A NOS JOURS
GAZLEY'S BUSINESS DIRECTORY OF THE FIVE GREAT CITIES OF CALIFORNIA AND OREGON – West Coast. 1864-1865 – 1r – 1 – $50.00 – D119 – us Library Micro [978]
GAZOPHYLACIUM ANGLICANUM – anon. 1689. 569p. (English Linguistics Series 1500-1800) – 9 – us UMI [420]
GAZOPHYLACIUM MEDICO-PHYSICUM ODER SCHATZKAMMER / MEDICINISCH- UND NATUERLICHER DINGE...(AEL, ABT.3;2) / Woyt, Johann Jacob – Leipzig, 1709 (mf ed 1993) – 13mf – 9 – DM210.00 – 3-89131-151-6 – gw Fischer [610]
Gaztambide, Juan B *see* AN INTERIM PROGRAMME OF INDUSTRIAL ESTATES OF INDONESIA
Gaztelu, Teodoro *see* ESTABLECIMIENTO DE BANOS MINEROMEDICINALES DE ALANGE
Gazul, Arturo *see* EL LIBRO GRIS
Gazzam, Audley William *see* GAZZAM'S TREATISE ON THE BANKRUPT LAW
GAZZAM'S TREATISE ON THE BANKRUPT LAW / Gazzam, Audley William – 4th ed. Albany, N.Y.: Little, 1872. 789p. LL-579 – 1 – us L of C Photodup [340]
Gazzera, Miguel *see* PERONISMO
GAZZETA DE TORINO – Italy, 1793-96 – 5r – 1 – inquire – us Ross [945]
GAZZETA DEL POPOLO – Italy, 1848-1983 – 315r – 1 – inquire – us Ross [945]
GAZZETA DEL POPOLO DELLA SERA – Italy, 1931-35 – 5r – 1 – inquire – us Ross [945]
GAZZETA PIEMONTESE – Italy, 1797-1860 – 52r – 1 – inquire – us Ross [945]
GAZZETTA CHIMICA ITALIANA – v. 1-102. 1871-1972 – 1,5,6 – us Princeton Micro [540]
GAZZETTA DEL MASSACHUSETTS – Boston, MA: J M Gubitosi & Co, [aug 8 1903-1905; mar 23 1907-1911; 1915-1938] – 26r – 1 – us Res Libr [071]
GAZZETTA DEL POPOLO – 1893-1958 – 1 – L240,000 – sz Infoprint [072]
GAZZETTA DEL POPOLO – 1959-1983 – 1 – L480,000 – sz Infoprint [072]
GAZZETTA DEL POPOLO SERA – 1931-1935 – 1 – L400,000 – sz Infoprint [072]
GAZZETTA DELLE CAMPAGNE – Turin, Italy. 1876-80.-m. 1 reel – 1 – uk British Libr Newspaper [072]
GAZZETTA DELLO SPORT – 1896-1933 – 1 – L450,000 – sz Infoprint [072]
GAZZETTA DELLO SPORT – 1934-1973 – 1 – sz Infoprint [072]
GAZZETTA DELLO SPORT – 1974-1982 – 1 – L850,000 – sz Infoprint [072]
GAZZETTA DELLO SPORT – 1983-1995 – 1 – L1,200,000 – sz Infoprint [790]
GAZZETTA DI NAPOLI – Naples, Italy. -w. 5 Jan 1877-31 Dec 1887. 22 reels – 1 – uk British Libr Newspaper [072]
GAZZETTA DI PALERMO – Palermo, Italy. Gazzetta provinciale La Nuova gazzetta. -w. 1 April 1869-31 Dec 1887. 31 reels – 1 – uk British Libr Newspaper [072]
LA GAZZETTA DI SYRACUSE – Syracuse, NY: Ray Pub Co Inc, [mar 8 1918-mar 24 1939; jul 1940-feb 1952] – 1 – us Res Libr [071]
GAZZETTA DI TORINO – 1793-1796 – 1 – L100,000 – sz Infoprint [072]
GAZZETTA ITALIANO DI LONDRA – London, UK. 23 May-31 Dec 1871 – 1 – uk British Libr Newspaper [072]
GAZZETTA MUSICALE DI MILANO – Milan. 1842-1902. Lacking: v7-20; 24-26 – 24r – 1 – $459.00 – us L of C Photodup [780]
GAZZETTA PIEMONTESE – 1797-1860 – 1 – L100,000 – sz Infoprint [072]
GAZZETTA PRIVILEGIATA DI VENEZIA – Venice, Italy. Gazzetta di Venezia. Jan. 1847-Jun. 1920 and supplement – 1 – us NY Public [072]
GAZZETTA UFF. (ED. GEN.) – 1987-1995 – 4 times per yr – 6 – F2,800.00 – sz Infoprint [072]
GAZZETTA UFFICIALE – (1989-) – Italy, 1861-1988 – 1 – inquire – us Ross [945]
GAZZETTA UFFICIALE : ED. GENERALE – 1987-1995 – 4r per y – 5,6 – Sfr748.00 – sz Infoprint [072]
GAZZETTA UFFICIALE – Italy, 1987- – 4r per y – 5 – us Ross [072]
GAZZETTA UFFICIALE DELLA REPPUBBLICA ITALIANA / Italy – 1861-1894. 1899-1944. Turin, etc – 1 – us NY Public [945]
GAZZETTA UFFICIALE DELLA REPUBLICA ITALIANA – Italy. v85-109. 1944-68 – 203r – 1 – us Ross [324]
GAZZETTINO – London, UK. 3 May 1902 – 1 – uk British Libr Newspaper [072]
Gazzoli, Luis *see* CUANDO LOS MILITARES TENEMOS RAZON
GBU REPORTER – Pittsburgh, PA. v1.(1893):1-March 1980 – us I.H.R.C. [071]
G.C. LICHTENBERG'S BRIEFE AN DIETERICH, 1770-1798 = CORRESPONDENCE. SELECTIONS : ZUM 100. TODESTAGE LICHTENBERG'S / Lichtenberg, Georg Christoph; ed by Grisebach, Eduard – Leipzig: Dieterich, T Weicher, 1898 – 1r – 1 – us U.W. Library [920]
G/C/T (GIFTED/CREATIVE/TALENTED CHILDREN) – 1978 – 1,5,6,9 – us UMI [073]
GDA : ZEITSCHRIFT DES GEWERKSCHAFTSBUNDES DER ANGESTELLTEN – Berlin. 1920-jun 30, 1933 – 4r – 1 – gw Mikrofilm [360]
GDA : ZEITSCHRIFT DES GEWERKSCHAFTSBUNDES DER ANGESTELLTEN – Leipzig, 1925, 1927-28 – 1r – 1 – gw Mikrofilm [360]
GDE MOI DOM? OCHERKI (1920-1923) / Bal'mont, K D – Prague. 1924. BR-515 2 – 8 – ne IDC [460]
GDE NASTOIASHCHAIA SVOBODA? / Bukharin, Nikolai Ivanovich – Moskva: Gos. izd-vo, 1920 – 1 – CSUX89-B4523 – us Hoover Inst Photo [947]
GDR BULLETIN – -q. vol.1, no.1-2 (Apr. 1975)-. St. Louis, Mo.: Dept of Germanic Languages and Literature, Washington University, 1975-. Newletter for literature and culture in the German Democratic Republic – 1 – us U.W. Library [943]
G'DUD KEREN KAYEMETH – Amsterdam, 1927-1931 – 3mf – 9 – J-261-31/1 – ne IDC [943]
GE MIN WENG WU – Historical commentary. 1972-77.20 ill. HG12f – 9 – 70.00 – cc Globe [073]
DER GEAECHTETE : DIE BRUEDERSAGE / Kremer, Hannes – 2. Aufl. Muenchen: F Eher, 1943 – 1r – 1 – us U.W. Library [830]
Gear, Hiram Lewis *see* A TREATISE ON THE LAW OF LANDLORD AND TENANT WITH SPECIAL REFERENCE TO THE AMERICAN LAW
Geary County, KS *see* BIRTHS, DEATHS, AND MARRIAGE RECORD CARDS
GEAUGA COUNTY ENGINEER RECORDS – Geauga, OH. 1802-1951 – 6r – 1 – us Western Res [620]
Geauga County. Ohio. Russell Township *see* RECORDS, MS 3106
GEAUGA COUNTY RECORD : WEEKLY DEMOCRATIC NEWSPAPER – Chardon, OH. 22 Apr 1892-30 Dec 1904 – 2r – 1 – us Western Res [071]
GEAUGA DEMOCRATIC RECORD : WEEKLY DEMOCRATIC NEWSPAPER – Chardon, OH. 13 Jan 1887-28 Apr 1888 – 1r – 1 – us Western Res [071]
GEAUGA GAZETTE *see* CHARDON SPECTATOR AND GEAUGA GAZETTE
GEAUGA RECORD : WEEKLY DEMOCRATIC NEWSPAPER – (film also includes 12 May 1888) – Chardon, OH. 23 Dec 1886-6 Jan 1887 – 1r – 1 – us Western Res [071]
GEAUGA REPUBLIC : WEEKLY WHIG NEWSPAPER – Chardon, OH. 25 Dec 1849-17 Jan 1854 – 1r – 1 – us Western Res [071]
GEAUGA REPUBLICAN : WEEKLY REPUBLICAN NEWSPAPER – Chardon, OH. 1 Jan 1873-31 Dec 1873 – 1r – 1 – us Western Res [071]
GEAUGA REPUBLICAN AND WHIG : WEEKLY WHIG NEWSPAPER – Chardon, OH. 20 May 1843-16 Mar 1847 – 1r – 1 – us Western Res [071]
GEAUGA TIMES LEADER – Chardon. Ohio. 1955 – 1 – us UMI [071]
GEAUGA TIMES LEADER : WEEKLY INDEPENDENT NEWSPAPER – Chardon, OH. 6 Jan 1942-29 Dec 1950 – 5r – 1 – us Western Res [071]
DIE GEBAERDE; DER FREMDE / Wiechert, Ernst Emil – Zuerich: Im Verlag der Arche, 1947 – 1r – 1 – us U.W. Library [430]
GEBANNT UND ERLOEST / Werner, E – Philadelphia: Morwitz. 2v in 1. [1889?] – 1 – us U.W. Library [830]
GEBEN UND NEHMEN : SCHAUSPIEL IN FUENF AUFZUEGEN / Langen, Martin – Paris: A Langen [1902?] – 1r – 1 – us U.W. Library [820]
Gebertus, M *see* MONUMENTA VETERIS LITURGIAE ALEMANNICAE
DAS GEBET HIEREMIE DES PROPHETEN / Cresz, J – 1525. BME-29 1 – 9 – ne IDC [220]
DAS GEBET IN DER AELTESTEN CHRISTENHEIT : EINE GESCHICHTLICHE UNTERSUCHUNG / Goltz, Eduard von der – Leipzig: J.C. Hinrichs, 1901 – 1mf – us A.T.L.A. [240]
DAS GEBET: NACH DEN PAULINISCHEN SCHRIFTEN / Zimmer, Friedrich – Koenigsberg: Hartung, 1887. 1 fiche – 9 – us A.T.L.A. [240]
GEBET UND GOTTESDIENST IM NEUEN TESTAMENT / Nielen, J M – Freiburg i.Br., 1937 – 7mf – 8 – Dfl28.00 – ne Slangenburg [240]

GEBETE UND HYMNEN AN NERGAL / Boellenruecher, J – (Leipziger semitistische Studien, Band I, Heft 6). Leipzig. 1904. BNE-20,108 1 – 9 – ne IDC [290]
Gebhardt, C *see* DIE SCHRIFTEN DES URIEL DA COSTA
Gebhardt, Hermann *see* DOCTRINE OF THE APOCALYPSE
Gebhardt, Max *see* UNTERSUCHUNGEN ZUR BIOGRAPHIE PHILIPP ZESENS
Gebhardt, Oscar von *see*
- ACTA MARTYRUM SELECTA
- DIE AKTEN DER EDESSENISCHEN BEKENNER CURJAS, SAMONAS UND ABIBOS (T.U.U. 3-37/2)
- DIE EVANGELIEN DES MATTHAEUS UND DES MARCUS (T.U.U. 1-1/4A)
- PASSIO S. THECLAE VIRGINIS
- DIE PSALMEN SALOMO'S (T.U.U. 1-13/2)
- DER SOGENANNTE SOPHRONIUS (T.U.U. 1-14/1B)

Gebhart, Emile *see* L'ITALIE MYSTIQUE
GEBIET UND GEBIETSHOHEIT / Fricker, Karl Viktor – Tubingen: Verlage der H. Laupp'schen Buchhandlung, 1901. 112p. LL-4071 – 1 – us L of C Photodup [340]
DIE GEBIETSHOHEIT IM SCHWEIZERISCHEN STAATSRECHT... / Frey, J – Lachen, 1932 – 2mf – 1 – ILM-2168/1 – ne IDC [327]
Gebler, Karl von *see* GALILEO GALILEI AND THE ROMAN CURIA
DER GEBRAUCH DES ALTEN TESTAMENTS IN DEN NEUTESTAMENTLICHEN SCHRIFTEN / Clemen, August – Guetersloh: C Bertelsmann, 1895 – 1mf – 9 – 0-8370-2679-2 – 1985-0679 – us A.T.L.A. [220]
DER GEBRAUCH DES IMPERATIVISCHEN INFINITIVS IM GRIECHISCHEN / Wagner, Richard – [S.l.: s.n., 1891?] (Leipzig: Hesse & Becker) – 1mf – 9 – 0-8370-9197-7 – 1986-3197 – us A.T.L.A. [450]
GEBRAUCH UND MISSBRAUCH DES LATEINISCHEN SINGENS UND BETENS.. / Muscovius, Johannes – ca. 1695 – 9 – us Sibley [780]
GEBRUEDER HAGEDORN : SCHAUSPIEL IN FUENF AKTEN / Petersen, Johannes – Leipzig: Oswald Mutze, 1881 – 1r – 1 – us U.W. Library [820]
DIE GEBURTSGESCHICHTE JESU CHRISTI / Soltau, Wilhelm – (Includes bibliographical referenceS Inschriften zu Ehren des Augustus) – Leipzig: Dieterich, 1902 – 1mf – 9 – 0-8370-5327-7 – 1985-3327 – us A.T.L.A. [220]
DAS GEBURTSJAHR CHRISTI : GESCHICHTLICH-CHRONOLOGISCHE UNTERSUCHUNGEN / Zumpt, August Wilhelm – (Includes bibliographical references) – Leipzig: B G Teubner, 1869 – 1mf – 9 – 0-8370-9359-7 – 1986-3359 – us A.T.L.A. [220]
DIE GEBURTSSTUNDE...DE HEYELTE / Elias de Tejada, Francisco – Madrid: Arbor, 1953 – 1 – sp Bibl Santa Ana [946]
GEC ENGINEERING – v1-. 1983- – 1,5,6,9 – us UMI [621]
GEC JOURNAL OF RESEARCH – v1-. 1983- – 1,5,6,9 – us UMI [621]
GEC REVIEW – v1-. 1985- – 1,5,6,9 – us UMI [621]
GECMIS GUENLER / Uenaydin, Rusen Esref – [Istanbul]: Matbaa-yi Orhaniye, 1919 – $40.00 – us MEDOC [470]
GEDAECHTNISEFFEKTE BEI NICHTLINEAREN OSZILLATOREN / Suenner, Tobias – 1995 – 1mf – 9 – DM60.00 – 3-8267-2096-2 – gw Hänsel [530]
GEDAGTEN OVER DE BEGINSELEN EN ONDERWYZINGEN DES CLAVECIMBAALS / Frischmuth, L – Amsterdam. 1758. BP-276 1 – 9 – ne IDC [780]
Gedalia of Siemiatycze *see* SHA' ALU SHELOM YERUSHALAVIM
DER GEDANKE, 1. 1861-9. 1884 / ed by Michelet, Ludwig – 1861-1884 – 9 – DM358.00 – 3-89131-160-5 – gw Fischer [072]
GEDANKEN / Moltke, Helmuth Carl Bernhard; ed by Cochenhausen, Friedrich von – Berlin: Atlantis-Verlag, c1941 – 1r – 1 – us U.W. Library [943]
GEDANKEN GOETHES IN DER NEUZEITLICHEN BIOLOGIE / Loesche, Martin – Bremen: J Storm, 1949 – 1r – 1 – us U.W. Library [430]
GEDANKEN NACH ZWEI UHR NACHTS / Waescher, Aribert – Berlin: Buchwarte-Verlag L Blanvalet, 1939 – 1r – 1 – us U.W. Library [830]
GEDANKEN UEBER DIE VERSCHIEDENEN LEHRARTEN IN DER KOMPOSITION / Kirnberger, Johann P – 1793 – 9 – us Sibley [780]
GEDANKEN UEBER DIE VERSCHIEDENEN LEHRARTEN IN DER KOMPOSITION ALS VORBEREITUNG ZUR FUGENKENNTNISZ / Kirnberger, Johann P – Berlin. 1782. BP-343 1 – 9 – ne IDC [780]
GEDANKEN UEBER GOETHE / Hehn, Victor – (Includes index) – 3., verm. Aufl. Berlin: Borntraeger, 1895 – 1r – 1 – us U.W. Library [430]
GEDANKEN ZUM SEXUALPROBLEM MIT EINEM GELEITWORT VON DR. PLACZEK / Bang, Herman – Bonn, 1922 – 1mf – DM48.00 – 3-8267-3025-9 – gw Hänsel [150]
GEDANKENGANG DES V. FRANK'SCHEN SYSTEMS DER CHRISTLICHEN WAHRHEIT / Vollert, Wilhelm – Leipzig: A Deichert (Georg Boehme), 1895 – 1mf – 9 – 0-8370-5676-4 – 1985-3676 – us A.T.L.A. [230]
Geddes, Alexander *see* CRITICAL REMARKS ON THE HEBREW SCRIPTURES, CORRESPONDING WITH A NEW TRANSLATION OF THE BIBLE
Geddes, Thomas Edward *see* LA RESURRECTION DE JESU-CHRISTO, NUESTRO SENOR
Geden, Alfred Shenington *see*
- OUTLINES OF INTRODUCTION TO THE HEBREW BIBLE
- SELECT PASSAGES ILLUSTRATING MITHRAISM...WITH AN INTRODUCTION

GEDENBOEK VAN EEN VIJF-EN-TWINTIGJARIG ZENDELINGSLEVEN OP NIEUW-GUINEA (1862-1887) / Hasselt, J L van – 1888 – 1 – us A.T.L.A. [240]
GEDENKBOEK 1150-1940 : STUDIEN EN ESSAIS ONDER LEIDING VAN P. CLERINX C.SS.R. / Christina de Wonderbare – Leuven, 1950 – Dfl9.00 – ne Slangenburg [240]
GEDENKBOEK TER GELEGENHEID VAN HET HONDERDJARIG BESTAAN VAN HET NEDERLANDSCH-ISRAELIETISCH ARMBESTUUR, 1825-1925 / Philips, S J – Amsterdam. 1925. BJ-262-43 1 – 9 – ne IDC [360]
GEDENKBUCH / Luzzatto, S D – Berlin. 1900. BJ-100-26 1 – 9 – ne IDC [900]
GEDENKBUCH, ERINNERUNG AN KARL HEINZEN UND AN DIE ENTHUELLUNGSFEIER DES HEINZEN-DENKMALS AM 12. JUNI 1886 IN BOSTON, MASS. / Schmemann, Karl – (Includes bibliographical references) – Milwaukee, Wis.: Freidenker Pub. Co., 1887 – 1r – 1 – us U.W. Library [430]
GEDENKSCHRIFT FUER FERDINAND JOSEF SCHNEIDER, 1879-1954 / ed by Bischoff, Karl – (Includes bibliographical references) – Weimar: H. Boehlaus Nachfolger, 1956 – 1r – 1 – us U.W. Library [943]
GEDENKWAARDIGHEDEN UIT DE GESCHIEDENIS VAN GELDERLAND / Nijhoff, I A – Amsterdam. v1-6. 1830-1862 – Dfl284.00 – ne Slangenburg [240]
Gederici, V *see* DEH NUMI PIETOSI
GEDICHTBUECHELCHEN / Asmus, Georg – (Includes comedy: Der Blumenstrauss) – Leipzig: E H Mayer, 1891 – 1r – 1 – us U.W. Library [430]
GEDICHTE / Becker, Nicolaus – Koeln: M DuMont-Schauberg, 1841 – 1 – us U.W. Library [810]
GEDICHTE / Chamisso, Adelbert von; ed by Rauschenbusch, Wilhelm – 2. Aufl. Berlin: G Grote, 1876 – 1 – us U.W. Library [810]
GEDICHTE / Cornelius, Peter – Leipzig: C F Kahnt, 1890 – 1 – us U.W. Library [810]
GEDICHTE / Dahn, Felix – Leipzig: Breitkopf & Haertel. 3v. 1898-99 – 1 – us U.W. Library [810]
GEDICHTE / Deinhardstein, Johann Ludwig – Berlin: Duncker und Humblot, 1844 – 1 – us U.W. Library [810]
GEDICHTE / Droste-Huelshoff, Annette von – 3. Aufl. Paderborn: F Schoeningh, 1887 – 1 – us U.W. Library [810]
GEDICHTE / Droste-Huelshoff, Annette von – 6. Aufl. Paderborn: F Schoeningh, [1900] – 1 – us U.W. Library [810]
GEDICHTE / Droste-Huelshoff, Annette von – 7. Aufl. Paderborn: F Schoeningh, [1907?] – 1 – us U.W. Library [810]
GEDICHTE : GESAMTAUSGABE MIT EINEM LEBENSBILDE DES DICHTERS VON KARL WEINHOLD / Strachwitz, Moritz Graf – 8. Aufl. Breslau: E Trewendt, 1891 – 1r – 1 – us U.W. Library [810]
GEDICHTE / Gruen, Anastasius – 2. Aufl. Leipzig: Weidmann, 1838 – 1 – us U.W. Library [810]
GEDICHTE / Guenther, Johann Christian; ed by Litzmann, Berthold – (Includes bibliographical references) – Leipzig: P Reclam, [1880] – 1r – 1 – us U.W. Library [810]
GEDICHTE / Hassaurek, Friedrich – Cincinnati: M & R Burgheim, c1877 – 1r – 1 – us U.W. Library [810]
GEDICHTE / Huch, Ricarda – Leipzig: H Haessel, 1894 – 1r – 1 – us U.W. Library [810]
GEDICHTE / Lenau, Nikolaus – Berlin: G Hempel, [1879] – 1r – 1 – us U.W. Library [810]
GEDICHTE / Lexow, Friedrich – New York: E Steiger, 1872 – 1r – 1 – us U.W. Library [810]
GEDICHTE / Liliencron, Detlev, Freiherr von – Wiesbaden: Verlag des Volksbildungsvereins, 1909 – 1r – 1 – us U.W. Library [810]
GEDICHTE / Meissner, Alfred – 2., stark vermehrte Aufl. Leipzig: F L Herbig, 1846 – 1r – 1 – us U.W. Library [810]
GEDICHTE / Miegel, Agnes – Stuttgart: J G Cotta, 1935 – 1r – 1 – us U.W. Library [810]
GEDICHTE = POEMS / Hopfen, Hans – Berlin: A Hofmann, 1883 – 1r – 1 – us U.W. Library [810]
GEDICHTE = POEMS / Meyer, Conrad Ferdinand – 16. Aufl. Leipzig: H Haessel, 1900 – 1r – 1 – us U.W. Library [810]
GEDICHTE = POEMS / Moericke, Eduard Friedrich – 13. mit einem Nachtrag verm. Aufl. Leipzig: G J Goeschen, 1898 – 1r – 1 – us U.W. Library [810]
GEDICHTE / Prutz, Robert Eduard – Zuerich: Druck und Verlag des literarischen Comptoirs, 1843 – 1r – 1 – us U.W. Library [810]
GEDICHTE / Schack, Adolf Friedrich von – 3. Aufl. Stuttgart: J G Cotta, 1874 – 1r – 1 – us U.W. Library [810]
GEDICHTE / Scriba, Carl – 2. Aufl. Butzbach: M Kuhl, 1850 – 1r – 1 – us U.W. Library [810]
GEDICHTE / Simrock, Karl Joseph – Leipzig: Hahn, 1844 – 1r – 1 – us U.W. Library [810]
GEDICHTE / Storm, Theodor – 13. Auflage. Berlin: Gebrueder Paetel, 1903 – 1r – 1 – us U.W. Library [810]
GEDICHTE / Strodtmann, Adolf – 3. und verm. Gesammt-Ausg. Leipzig: P Reclam, [18–?] – 1r – 1 – us U.W. Library [810]
GEDICHTE / Strodtmann, Adolf – 3., verm. Ges.-Ausg. Leipzig: P Reclam, [18–?] – 1 – us U.W. Library [810]
GEDICHTE / Viereck, George Sylvester – (Appendix: George Sylvester Viereck: an appreciation) – Leipzig: Hesse & Becker, 1922 – 1r – 1 – us U.W. Library [810]
GEDICHTE / Weckherlin, Georg Rodolf; ed by Goedeke, Karl – Leipzig: Brockhaus, 1873 – 1 – us U.W. Library [810]
GEDICHTE / Weckherlin, Georg Rudolf; ed by Goedeke – Leipzig: Brockhaus, 1873 – 1r – 1 – us U.W. Library [810]
GEDICHTE / Werfel, Franz – Berlin: P Zsolnay, 1927 – 1r – 1 – us U.W. Library [810]
GEDICHTE / Werfel, Franz – Berlin: P Zsolnay, 1927 – 1 – us U.W. Library [810]
GEDICHTE / Wilbrandt, Adolf von – Wien: L Rosner, 1874 – 1r – 1 – us U.W. Library [810]
GEDICHTE AUS DREISSIG JAHREN / Werfel, Franz – Stockholm: Bermann-Fischer Verlag, 1939 – 1r – 1 – us U.W. Library [810]
GEDICHTE DER GEBRUEDER WOLF : EINE AUSWAHL / Wolf, Johann Theobald; ed by Mueller, Eugen – Strassburg: K J Truebner, 1916 – 1r – 1 – us U.W. Library [810]
GEDICHTE DER GEFANGENEN : EIN SONETTENKREIS / Toller, Ernst – 2. Aufl. Muenchen: K Wolff, 1923 – 1r – 1 – us U.W. Library [810]
GEDICHTE GOETHES VERANSCHAULICHT NACH FORM- UND STRUKTURWANDEL / Meschke, Waltraut – (Includes bibliographical references) – Berlin. Akademie-Verlag, 1957 – 1r – 1 – us U.W. Library [430]
GEDICHTE IN HOCHDEUTSCHER MUNDART / Stoltze, Friedrich – Frankfurt a.M.: H Keller, 1862 – 1r – 1 – us U.W. Library [390]
GEDICHTE IN SCHWAEBISCHER MUNDART / Heerbrandt, Gustav – New York: Selbstverlag von G Heerbrandt, 1892 – 1r – 1 – us U.W. Library [810]
GEDICHTE IN ZWEI TEILEN : KRITISCH DURCHGESEHENE UND ERLAEUTERTE AUSGABE / Buerger, Gottfried August; ed by Consentius, Ernst – Berlin: Bong. 2v. [1914] – 1 – us U.W. Library [810]
GEDICHTE UND GEDANKEN / Thoma, Hans; ed by Eberlein, Karl – (Includes Bibliographical References) – Konstanz: Reuss & Itta, 1919 – 1r – 1 – us U.W. Library [800]
GEDICHTEN; MET VEELE KOPERE KUNSTPLATEN VERSIERT / Zeeus, J – O 807. 1737 – 9 – ne IDC [810]
GEDICHTEN VAN JACOB ZEEUS, MET VEELE KOPERE KUNSTPLATEN VERSIERT / Zeeus, J – 1st ed. Delft, 1721 – 7mf – 9 – ne IDC [810]
Gedik, S *see*
- ANTIPISTORIUS, ORDER WIDERLEGUNG DES CALVINISCHEN POLITICI SIMONIS ULRICH PISTORIS IN SEUSELITZ...
- CALVINIANA RELIGIO, ODER CALVINISTEREY, SO FAELSCHLICH DIE REFORMIRTE RELIGION GENENNET WIRD...
- DREY CHRISTLICHE VND IN GOTTES WORT VND DER ALTEN LEHRER SCHRIFFTEN WOLGEGRUENDTE PREDIGTEN
- POSTILLA DAS IST AVSZLEGUNG DER EUANGELIEN DURCHS GANTZE JAHR...
- VON BILDERN VND ALTARN JN DEN EUANGELISCHEN KIRCHEN AUGSPURGISCHER CONFESSION
- VON DEN CEREMONIEN BEY DEM HEILIGEN ABENDMAHL

Gedike, Friedrich *see* BERLINISCHE MONATSSCHRIFT 1783-96; BERLINISCHE BLAETTER 1797-98; NEUE BERLINISCHE MONATSSCHRIFT 1799-1811
DAS GEDOPPELTE TUN : BEITRAEGE ZUR ANALYSE DES VERHAELTNISSES ZWISCHEN MAENNERN UND FRAUEN IN EINER ANTAGONISTISCHEN GESELLSCHAFT / Mueller, Hannelore – 1995 – 3mf – 9 – DM98.00 – 3-8267-2103-9 – gw Hänsel [305]
Gee, Henry *see*
- DOCUMENTS ILLUSTRATIVE OF ENGLISH CHURCH HISTORY
- THE ELIZABETHAN CLERGY AND THE SETTLEMENT OF RELIGION, 1558-1564
- THE ELIZABETHAN PRAYER-BOOK AND ORNAMENTS
- THE REFORMATION PERIOD

GEELONG ADVERTISER – Australia. -d. 23 Jan-15 Nov 1841; 19 Sept 1844-31 Dec 1860; 2 Oct 1866; 25, 27 July, 26 Oct 1867; 28 March 1868; 5 Sept 1892-30 Oct 1918; 21 June 1919-30 April 1940. 228 reels – 1 – uk British Libr Newspaper [072]
GEELONG TELEPHONE DIRECTORY – 1938-1941. GTD1 – 1r – 1 – at Corangamite [920]
GEELONG WEST CITY COUNCIL RATES – 1875-1959. 1880-83 lost. GWR1-14 – 14r – 1 – at Corangamite [910]
GEELONG WEST CITY COUNCIL RATES – 1960-78/79 – 229r – 5 – at Corangamite [910]
Geer, C de *see* MEMOIRES POUR SERVIR A L'HISTOIRE DES INSECTES
Geer, George Jarvis *see*
- THE CONVERSION OF ST PAUL
- CONVERSION OF ST PAUL: THREE DISCOURSES

GEER MEMORIAL BAPTIST CHURCH. EASLEY, SOUTH CAROLINA : CHURCH RECORDS – Pickens County, Nov 1902-Sept 1985. Piedmont Assoc. Membership Rolls to Feb 1960. 1306p – 1 – 100.13 – us Baptist [978]
HET GEESTELYCK JUBILEE VAN HET JAER O.H. M.D.C.L.... / Sambeeck, J – Antwerpen, 1663 – 5mf – 9 – ne IDC [700]
HET GEESTELYCK KAERT-SPEL MET HERTEN TROEF, OFT HET SPEL DER LIEFDE / Joseph a Sancta Barbara – Den derden druck. Antwerpen, [c1666] – 6mf – 9 – O-3097/1 – ne IDC [760]
HET GEESTELYCK KAERT-SPEL MET HERTEN TROEF, OFT HET SPEL DER LIEFDE / Joseph a Sancta Barbara – (First part of dedication missing) – Den derden druck. Antwerpen, 1712 – 6mf – 9 – O-3096/1 – ne IDC [760]
DER GEFAELSCHTE BRIEF DES BISCHOFS THEONAS AN DEN OBERKAMMERHERRN LUCIAN (T.U.U. 2-24/3C) / Harnack, Adolf von – Leipzig, 1903 – 1mf – 9 – ne Slangenburg [240]

DAS GEFAENGNIS ZUM PREUSSISCHEN ADLER : EINE SELBSTERLEBTE SCHILDBUERGEREI / Wille, Bruno – Jena: E Diederichs, 1914 – 1 – us U.W. Library [890]

DIE GEFAESSBUENDEL IM STIPES DER FARRN / Presl, K B – Heft 1. Prag. 1847. (Abhandl. K. Boehm. Ges. Wissensch. Folge 5. 1848). v. 5. Prag. 1848. B-7248 1 – 9 – ne IDC [580]

Geffcken, F H *see* LA QUESTION DU DANUBE

Geffcken, F Heinrich *see* DIE VOELKERRECHTLICHE STELLUNG DES PAPSTES

Geffcken, Heinrich *see* CHURCH AND STATE

Geffcken, J *see* KOMPOSITON UND ENTSTEHUNGSZEIT DER ORACULA SIBYLLINA (T.U.U. 2-23/1)

Geffcken, Johannes *see*
- AUS DER WERDEZEIT DES CHRISTENTUMS
- KAISER JULIANUS
- SOKRATES UND DAS ALTE CHRISTENTUM
- ZWEI GRIECHISCHE APOLOGETEN

Geffner, Robert A *see*
- JOURNAL OF CHILD SEXUAL ABUSE
- JOURNAL OF EMOTIONAL ABUSE

Geffroy, Gustave *see* PAYS D' OUEST

GEFLE DAGBLAD – Gavle, Sweden. 1895-1978 – 450r – 1 – sw Kungliga [072]

GEFLE DAGBLAD – Gavle, Sweden. 1979- – 1 – sw Kungliga [072]

GEFLEPOSTEN – Gavle, Sweden. 1864-1941 – 1 – sw Kungliga [072]

DER GEFRORENE DIONYSUS : ERZAEHLUNG / Andres, Stefan Paul – (Later publ under title: Die Liebesschaukel) – Berlin: Ulrich Riemerschmidt, c1942 – 1r – 1 – us U.W. Library [830]

Gefshtetter, Ippolit *see* V KHAOSIE SOBYTII

GEGEN DEN MILITARISMUS UND GEGEN DIE NEUEN STEUERN / Liebknecht, Wilhelm & Bebel, A – Berlin, 1893 – 1 – DM30.00 – gw Mikro Press [943]

GEGEN DEN STROM – (Cont by: Der Internationale Klassenkampf. Organ der KPD (Opposition) in 1936. Cont: Gegen den Strom, Berlin) – Paris, FR. 1933-1935 (incl Inhaltsverz 1-8 Jg) – 1r – 1 – gw Mikrofilm [072]

GEGEN DEN STROM : LYRISCHES UND SATYRISCHES / Palmer, Albert – 2. Aufl. Leipzig: O Wigand, 1884 – 1r – 1 – us U.W. Library [430]

GEGEN DEN STROM – New York, NY. Mar 1938-Oct-Nov 1939 – 1r – 1 – gw Mikrofilm [071]

GEGEN DEN STROM : ZENTRALORGAN DER KPD-OPPOSITION – (Incl table of contents for v1-8. Cont by: Der Internationale Klassenkampf, 1936. Publ in Breslau 1928, in Paris since may 1933.) – Berlin, nov 17 1928-35 n5 (incomplete) – 4r – 1 – Dist. gw Mikrofilm – gw Misc Inst [072]

GEGEN DEN STROM, BERLIN *see* GEGEN DEN STROM

GEGEN DIE ZIEBENBUERGER EHEN / Gau, F von – Wien, 1893 – 1mf – 1 – ILM-3384/1 – ne IDC [327]

DER GEGEN-ANGRIFF : ANTIFASCHISTISCHE WOCHENSCHRIFT – (Cont by: Deutsche Volkszeitung, Prag) – Prag-Zurich-Paris. Apr 1933-14 Mar 1936 – 3r – 1 – gw Mikrofilm [072]

DER GEGENANGRIFF – Anti-faschistische Zeitschrift. Prague, Zurish, Paris. avr 1933-mars 1936 – 1 – fr A.C.R.P.P. [073]

Gegenbaur, C von *see* MORPHOLOGISCHES JAHRBUCH

DIE GEGENREFORMATION IN SCHLESIEN / Ziegler, Heinrich – Halle a.S.: Verein fuer Reformationsgeschichte, [1888?] ([Schriften des Vereins fuer Reformationsgechichte; Bd.24]) – 1mf – us A.T.L.A. [240]

DER GEGENSATZ DES KATHOLICISMUS UND PROTESTANTISMUS : NACH DEN PRINCIPIEN UND HAUPTDOGMEN DER BEIDEN LEHRBEGRIFFE: MIT BESONDERER RUECKSICHT AUF HERRN DR. MOEHLER'S SYMBOLIK / Baur, Ferdinand Christian – Tuebingen: L.F. Fues, 1836 – 2mf – us A.T.L.A. [230]

GEGENSEITIGEN BEZIEHUNGEN ZWISCHEN DER MODERNEN MISSION UND CULTUR = MODERN MISSIONS AND CULTURE: THEIR MUTUAL RELATIONS / Warneck, Gustav – (In English) – New ed. Edinburgh: James Gemmell, 1888 – 1mf – 9 – 0-8370-6446-5 – 1986-0446 – us A.T.L.A. [240]

DIE GEGENWAERTIGE SITUATION IN DER ALTENHILFE / Klaehn, Simone – 1994 – 1mf – 9 – DM98.00 – 3-930263-65-3 – gw Böhner [360]

GEGENWAERTIGER ZUSTAND DER BESITZUNGEN DER EUROPAEER IN OSTINDIEN / Hennings, A – Kopenhagen, 1784-1786. v1-3 – 32mf – 9 – ne IDC [950]

DIE GEGENWART : EINE HALBMONATSSCHRIFT – Freiburg u. Frankfurt-Main, West Germany. 1946-58 – 8r (incl Jahresregister) – 1 – gw Mikrofilm [072]

DIE GEGENWART : EINE HALBMONATSSCHRIFT – (Mit Jahresregistern, alles erschienene) – Freiburg/Frankfurt M., 1946-58 – 8r – 1 – DM680.00 – gw Mikro Press [072]

DIE GEGENWART – Organ fuer die Interessen des Judenthums. Prague. v1-3, 1867-70. Incomplete. 1 reel. B-HUC (Leo Baeck Institute. German-Jewish Periodicals, Pt 2) – 1 – $75.00 – us UPA [290]

DIE GEGENWART, LEIPZIG 1848-1856 : EINE ENZYKLOPAEDISCHE DARSTELLUNG DER NEUESTEN ZEITGESCHICHTE FUER ALLE STAENDE – 1985 – 26mf (1:42) – 9 – diazo DM498.00 – 3-598-30671-7 – gw Saur [943]

DER GEGNER : BLAETTER ZUR KRITIK DER ZEIT – Berlin, apr 1 1919-mar 25 1922 – 1 – Dist. gw Mikrofilm – gw Misc Inst [072]

DIE GEGNER "EDGARS" : UND IHRE LEISTUNGEN / Hammerstein, Ludwig von – Trier: Paulinus-Druckerei, 1887 – 1mf – 9 – 0-8370-7152-6 – 1986-1152 – us A.T.L.A. [230]

GEHEIME CORRESPONDENZ JOSEFS 2. MIT SEINEM MINISTER IN DEN OESTERREICHISCHEN NIEDERLANDEN...1787-1789 / ed by Schlitter, H – Wien, 1902 – 10mf – 9 – ne IDC [943]

[GEHEIME STAATSPOLIZEI (GESTAPO) PAMPHLET COLLECTION] – 19?? – 1 – CSUXANS0337-B – us Hoover Inst Photo [360]

GEHEIME UNTERREDUNGEN ZWISCHEN ZWEYEN VERTRAUTEN FREUNDEN, EINEM THEOLOGO PHILOSOPHIZANTE UND PHILOSOPHO THEOLOGIZANTE, VON MAGIA NATURALI. ZUM DRUCK GEGEBEN VOM COLLEGIO CURIOSORUM IN DEUTSCHLAND – Cosmopoli, 1702 – 1 – us U.W. Library [240]

DAS GEHEIMNIS DER UNIVERSITAET / Rosenstock-Huessy, Eugen – Stuttgart, 1958 – 6mf – 8 – ne Slangenburg [100]

DAS GEHEIMNIS UND DIE INNERE EINHEIT DER DREY GOETHE'SCHEN BALLADEN : DER FISCHER, DER ERLKOENIG UND DER TODTENTANZ / Schrader, Hermann – Berlin: H Dolfuss, 1881 – 1r – 1 – us U.W. Library [430]

DIE GEHEIMNISSE DES GLAUBENS / Schoeberlein, Ludwig – Heidelberg: Carl Winter, 1872 – 1mf – 9 – 0-8370-5312-9 – 1985-3312 – us A.T.L.A. [240]

GEHEIMNISSE EINIGER PHILOSOPHEN UND ADEPTEN: AUS DER VERLASSENSCHAFT EINES ALTEN MANNES – Erster theil. Leipzig: C.G. Hilscher, 1780. 1 reel. 1203 – 1 – us U.W. Library [540]

DER GEHEIMNISVOLLE HOF : EINE ERZAEHLUNG AUS DEM NORDEN / Asbeck, Wilhelm Ernst – Dresden: Meinhold, c1940 – 1r – 1 – us U.W. Library [430]

DIE GEHEIMPOLIZEI AUF DEM WIENER KONGRESS : EINE AUSWAHL AUS IHREN PAPIEREN / Fournier, A – Wien, Leipzig, 1913 – 6mf – 9 – ne IDC [943]

GEHETZT UEBERS MEER / Korn, Heinz – 5. und 6. Aufl. Berlin: Junge Generation Verlag, [1944] – 1r – 1 – us U.W. Library [830]

Gehin, J J B *see*
- CATALOGUE DES COLEOPTERES CARABIQUES DE LA TRIBU DES CARABIDES
- CATALOGUE DES COLEOPTERES DE LA COLLECTION DE J.B. GEHIN...

Gehler, ST *see* JOHANN SAMUEL TRAUGOTT GEHLERS PHYSIKALISCHES WOERTERBUCH

Gehre, Horst *see* DIE ENTWICKLUNG DER AMTSHAFTUNG IN DEUTSCHLAND SEIT DEM 19. JAHRHUNDERT

Gehrig, Hans *see* DIE GENFAMILIE DER BANDE 3 UND BANDE 3-VERWANDTEN ANIONENAUSTAUSCHPROTEINE

Gehrig, Pearl S *see* HISTORY OF CHARITON AND HOWARD COUNTIES

Geider, Stefan *see* DIE HISTORISCHE ENTWICKLUNG DER INTERDEPENDENZ VON ATMUNG UND HERZ-KREISLAUFSYSTEM UND DER EINFLUß DER ATMUNG AUF DIE HERZZEITINTERVALLE UNTER BESONDERER BERUECKSICHTIGUNG DER KOERPERPOSITION

Geiersbach, H *see* STAATSANGEHOERIGKEITS-FRAGEN IM SAARGEBIET

Geiger, Abraham *see*
- JUDAISM AND ITS HISTORY
- JUEDISCHE ZEITSCHRIFT FUER WISSENSCHAFT UND LEBEN
- LEHR- UND LESEBUCH ZUR SPRACHE DER MISCHNAH
- NACHGELASSENE SCHRIFTEN

Geiger, Ludwig *see*
- CHARLOTTE VON SCHILLER UND IHRE FREUNDE
- DEUTSCHE SATIRIKER DES 16. JAHRHUNDERTS
- GOETHE IN FRANKFURT AM MAIN 1797
- GOETHE UND DIE SEINEN
- JOHANN REUCHLIN
- RENAISSANCE UND HUMANISMUS IN ITALIEN UND DEUTSCHLAND
- DAS STUDIUM DER HEBRAEISCHEN SPRACHE IN DEUTSCHLAND
- ZEITSCHRIFT FUER DIE GESCHICHTE DER JUDEN IN DEUTSCHLAND

Geiger, Michael *see* PERSOENLICHKEITSEN-TWICKLUNGEN IN ZERFALLENDER TRADITION

Geiger, Paul *see* DEUTSCHES VOLKSTUM IN SITTE UND BRAUCH

Geiger, W *see* DIE PEHLEVIVERSION DES ERSTEN CAPITELS DES VENDIDAED

Geigle y Zenon, J *see* BIBLIOGRAFIA PUERTORRIQUENA, ESCRITA EN 1892-1894

Geijer, Eric Gustave *see* THE HISTORY OF THE SWEDES

Geikie, John Cunningham *see* THE HOLY LAND AND THE BIBLE

GEIKIE'S LITERARY NEWS – Toronto: J.C. Geikie, [1856-18–] – 9 – cn C.I.H.M. [400]

Geiler, K *see* DIE SCHWEIZERISCHEN GOLDHYPOTHEKEN IN DEUTSCHLAND...

GEILLUSTREERD HANDBOEK DER JAVAANSCHE THEEONKRUIDEN EN HUNNE BETEEKENIS VOOR DE CULTUUR / Backer, C A – Batavia, 1924 – 7mf – 9 – ne IDC [580]

DE GEILLUSTREERDE JOODSCHE POST – Amsterdam, 1921. v1(1-40) – 23mf – 9 – J-261-32/1 – ne IDC [943]

Geisel, Judith Charlotte *see* TASSO UND SEIN GEFOLGE

DIE GEISHA O-SEN : GEISHA-LIEDER NACH JAPANISCHEN MOTIVEN / Klabund – Muenchen: Roland-Verlag A Mundt, 1918 – 1r – 1 – us U.W. Library [480]

Geisler *see* UEBER DIE SCHRIFTSTELLERISCHE THAETIGKEIT THOMAS ABBT'S

Geisler, PR *see* TISSUE DEGRADATION MARKERS AND SUBJECTIVE REPORTS OF PAIN AS A RESULT OF ECCENTRIC MUSCULAR CONTRACTIONS

Geisler, S A *see* ECCENTRIC PEAK TORQUE AND MAXIMAL REPETITION WORK PERCENTAGES OF THE DOMINANT EXTERNAL ROTATORS IN COLLEGE DIVISION 1 BASEBALL PLAYERS

Geisler, Victor *see* HERMANN SIEBECK'S RELIGIONSPHILOSOPHIE DARGESTELLT UND BEURTEILT

GEISLINGER ZEITUNG : BA DER SUEDWEST-PRESSE – Geislingen-Ulm, Germany. 1987-1989 – 6r per yr – 1 – gw Mikrofilm [072]

Geissler, Horst Wolfram *see* GRILLPARZER UND SCHOPENHAUER

Geissler, Patricia *see* ICONES HEPATICARUM

GEIST DER GOETHEZEIT : VERSUCH EINER IDEELLEN ENTWICKLUNG DER KLASSISCH-ROMANTISCHEN LITERATURGESCHICHTE / Korff, Hermann August – Leipzig: Koehler und Amelag. 5v. 1964-66 – 2r – 1 – us U.W. Library [430]

DER GEIST DER LUTHERISCHEN THEOLOGEN WITTENBERGS IM VERLAUFE DES 17. JAHRHUNDERTS : THEILWEISE NACH HANDSCHRIFTLICHEN QUELLEN / Tholuck, August – Hamburg: F. und A. Perthes, 1852 – 1mf – us A.T.L.A. [240]

DER GEIST DES CHRISTENTHUMS:... PROTESTANTISCHE BRIEFE / Hanne, Johann Wilhelm – Elberfeld: R.L. Friderichs, 1867. 1 fiche – 9 – us A.T.L.A. [240]

DER GEIST DES HOHEN LIEDES : GESCHICHTE, KRITIK UND UEBERSETZUNG / Altschul, Jakob – Wien: Wilhelm BraumUeller, 1874 – 1mf – 9 – 0-8370-2082-4 – 1985-0082 – us A.T.L.A. [220]

GEIST DES MUSIKALISCHEN KUNSTMAGAZINS / Reichardt, Johann F – 1791 – 9 – us Sibley [780]

DER GEIST GOTTES UND DIE VERWANDTEN ERSCHEINUNGEN IM ALTEN TESTAMENT UND IN ANSCHLIESSENDEN JUDENTUM / Volz, Paul – Tuebingen. 1910. BNE-20,010 1 – 9 – ne IDC [220]

GEIST UND FORM : AUFSAETZE ZUR DEUTSCHEN LITERATURGESCHICHTE / Vietor, Karl – (Includes bibliographical references and index) – Bern: A Francke, c1952 – 1 – us U.W. Library [430]

GEIST UND GESELLSCHAFT : UEBER DIE AUFLOESUNG DER STAENDISCHEN GESELLSCHAFT IM EPISCHEN WERK VON KARL GUTZKOW / Kramp, Willy – (Includes bibliographical references (p. 68-70)) – Wuerzburg: K Triltsch, 1937 – 1r – 1 – us U.W. Library [430]

GEIST UND LEBEN – 20(1947)-31(1958) – 105mf – 9 – Dfl368.00 – ne Slangenburg [073]

GEIST UND LEBEN : VORTRAGE UND AUFSAETZE / Koch, Franz – (Includes bibliographical references) – Hamburg: Hanseatische Verlagsanstalt, [c1939] – 1r – 1 – us U.W. Library [430]

GEIST UND SCHRIFT BEI SEBASTIAN FRANCK : EINE STUDIE ZUR GESCHICHTE DES SPIRITUALISMUS IN DER REFORMATIONSZEIT / Hegler, Alfred – Freiburg i.B.: J.C.B. Mohr, 1892 – 1mf – us A.T.L.A. [240]

Geistdoerfer, Patrick *see* ECOLOGIE ALIMENTAIRE DES MACROURIDAE (TELEOSTEENS GADIFORMES)

DER GEISTERBESCHWOERER : VOLKSSCHAUSPIEL IN 4 AKTEN / Zwerenz, Carl – Wien: F S Hummel, 1869 – 1r – 1 – us U.W. Library [820]

DER GEISTERSEHER : AUS DEN PAPIEREN DES GRAFEN O– / Schiller, Friedrich von – (1st pt ed by Friedrich Schiller. 2nd pt ed by Hanns Heinz Ewers) – Muenchen: Georg Mueller, 1922 – 1r – 1 – us U.W. Library [430]

DIE GEISTERWELT IM GLAUBEN DES PAULUS / Dibelius, Martin – Goettingen: Vandenhoeck & Rup., 1909. 1 fiche – 9 – us A.T.L.A. [240]

GEISTESGESCHICHTLICHE ASPEKTE DES GENOSSENSCHAFTLICHEN BILDUNGSGEDANKENS : UNTER BESONDERER BERUECKSICHTIGUNG VON V. A. HUBERS SCHRIFTEN / Jansen, Brigitte E S – 1995 – 3mf – 9 – DM98.00 – 3-8267-2100-4 – gw Hänsel [370]

DIE GEISTIGE EINWIRKUNG DER PERSON JESU AUF PAULUS : EINE HISTORISCHE UNTERSUCHUNG / Koelbing, Paul – Goettingen: Vandenhoeck & Ruprecht, 1906 – 1mf – 9 – 0-8370-3959-2 – 1985-1959 – us A.T.L.A. [920]

DIE GEISTIGE OFFENBARUNG GOTTES IN DER GESCHICHTLICHEN PERSON JESU / Steinmann, Theophil – (Includes bibliographical references) – Goettingen: Vandenhoeck & Ruprecht, 1903 – 1mf – 9 – 0-8370-55431 – 1985-3543 – us A.T.L.A. [240]

DAS GEISTIGE UNGARN; BIOGRAFICHES LEXIKON / Kruecken, O von & Parlagi, I – Ed. by O. von Kruecken and I. Parlagi. Wien, Leipzig. 1918. BR-5346 2 – 8 – ne IDC [920]

DIE GEISTLICHE GESTALT EINES EVANGELISCHEN LEHRERS, NACH DEM SINN UND EXEMPEL DER ALTEN, AUS LICHT GESTELLET / Arnold, Gottfried – 2v. in 1. 1723 – 1 – us A.T.L.A. [240]

GEISTLICHE HERZENS EINBILDUNGEN INN ZWEIHUNDERT UND FUENFZIG BIBLISCHEN FIGURSPRUECHEN ANGEDEUTET / Mattsperger, M & Bodenehr, H G – O-1135 1. 1685 – 9 – ne IDC [240]

GEISTLICHE SELBSTBEKENNTNISSE UEBER DAS WESEN UND LEBEN DER EVANGELISCH-LUTHERISCHEN KIRCHE : EIN HINTERLASSENES RELIGIOESES VERMAECHTNISS AN ALLE EVANGELISCHEN CHRISTEN / Appelius, Karl Theodor – Leipzig: Eduard Kummer, 1867 – 1mf – 9 – 0-8370-8644-2 – 1986-2644 – us A.T.L.A. [240]

DIE GEISTLICHEN UEBUNGEN DES IGNATIUS VON LOYOLA : EINE PSYCHOLOGISCHE STUDIE / Holl, Karl – Tuebingen: J.C.B. Mohr, 1905 – 1mf – us A.T.L.A. [150]

GEISTREICHES FAEST- UND NACHTMAHLBUECHLEIN... – Zuerich: Buercklischer Truckerey – 5mf – 8 – Dfl22.00 – ne Slangenburg [240]
Geitler, L *see* DIE ALBANESISCHEN UND SLAVISCHEN SCHRIFTEN
Gekkel', A *see* BIBLIOGRAFICHESKII UKAZATEL' RUSSKOI I INOSTRANNOI LITERATURY PO VZRYVCHATYM VESHCHESTVAM S 1529 PO 1882 G
GELAEHMTE SCHWINGEN : LUSTSPIEL IN EINEM AUFZUGE / Thoma, Ludwig – Muenchen: A Langen, c1918 – 1r – 1 – us U.W. Library [820]
GELANGGANG REPOLUSI; 10 TAHUN PROKLAMASI / Tjarly, S T – SE 4655 1. 1955 – 9 – ne IDC [950]
GELBE HEFTE; HISTORISCHE UND POLITISCHE ZEITSCHRIFT FUER DAS CHRISTLICHE DEUTSCHLAND – Munich. v. 1-17; 1924-41. Supersedes Historisch-politische Blaetter fuer das katholische Deutschland. Film Mas C 721 – 1 – us H.U. Library [073]
DIE GELBE POST : OSTASIATISCHE HALBMONATSSCHRIFT – Shanghai, China. 1 May-1 Nov 1939 – 1r – 1 – gw Mikrofilm [072]
DER GELBE SEEDIEB : ROMAN / Seeliger, Ewald Gerhard – Berlin: Ullstein, 1915 – 1r – 1 – us U.W. Library [830]
Gelber, N M *see*
- LE-TOLEDOT YISSUD BEIT HA-SEFER "LAEMEL" BI-YERUSHALAYIM
- SHE'ELAT EREZ-YISRA'EL BI-SHENOTH 1840-1842

GELD UND GEIST / Gotthelf, Jeremias; ed by Bloesch, Hans – Muenchen; Bern: E Rentsch, 1930 – 1 – us U.W. Library [890]
Geldner, F *see* DIE STAATSAUFFASSUNG...DES ERASMUS...
DER GELDSTAG : ODER, DIE WIRTSCHAFT NACH DER NEUEN MODE / Gotthelf, Jeremias; ed by Hunziker, Rudolf & Baehler, Eduard – Erlenbach, Zuerich: E Rentsch, 1923 – 1 – us U.W. Library [830]
GELDTHEORIE UND WIRTSCHAFTSWACHSTUM : NEUERE METHODIK UND DEUTUNGEN / Gruner, Hans – Heidelberg, 1961 – 2mf – 9 – DM48.00 – 3-89349-391-3 – gw Hänsel [332]
GELEGENHEITSGEDICHTE UND PROLOGE FUER ARBEITERFESTE : MIT EINEM ANHANG, WINKE FUER REDNER / Wittich, Manfred – 2. durchgesehene und verm. Aufl. Muenchen: M Ernst, 1894 – 1r – 1 – us U.W. Library [810]
DAS GELEHRTE HANNOVER / Rotermund, Heinrich Wilhelm – Bremen, 1823. 2v. Zusaetze und Nachtraege von A-K. Mehr nicht erschienen. Hildesheim, 1983 – 19mf – 9 – DM160.00 diazo DM180.00 silver – gw Olms [430]
DAS GELEHRTE SCHWABEN / Gradmann, Johann Jacob – Ravensburg, 1802. Hildesheim, 1983 – 10mf – 9 – DM80.00 diazo DM100.00 silver – gw Olms [430]
GELEHRTES FUERSTENTHUM BAIREUT / Fikenscher, Georg Wolfgang Augustin – Erlangen und Nuernberg, 1801-05. Hildesheim, 1983. – 34mf – 9 – DM250.00 diazo DM300.00 silver – gw Olms [430]
Gelesnoff (Zhelieznov), Vladimir *see* THE PATHWAY OF FAITH
Gelfand, Mark I *see* THE WAR ON POVERTY, 1964-68
Gelfer, A *see* CHTO TAKOE SOTSIALNOE STRAKHOVANIE, DLIA CHEGO ONO NUZHNO I KAK EGO PROVODIT V ZHIZN
Geliboeluelue, Mustafa Ali b. Ahmed *see* KUENH UEL-AHBAR
GELIEBETER JAN : BRIEFE GEHEN NACH DEM OSTEN / Loeff, Friedel – Berlin: M Warneck, 1944 – 1r – 1 – us U.W. Library [860]
Gelineau, J *see* CHANT ET MUSIQUE DANS LE CULTE CHRETIEN
Gelinek, J *see*
- [2] SELECT AIRS WITH VARIATIONS
- AIR [SAXON] WITH VARIATIONS FOR THE PIANO
- MARCHE DE L'OPERA D'ACHILLE
- VARIATIONS POUR LE PIANOFORTE SUR UNE WALZE FAVORITE DE MOZART

Gella Iturriaga, Jose *see* REFRANERO DEL MAR. MADRID, 1944
Geller, G M *see* SEZONNOST RUSSKOGO EKSPORTA DO VO INY I V NSTOI ASHCHEE VREMI A
GELLIVAREBLADET – Lulea, Sweden. 1899-1901 – 1 reel – 1 – sw Kungliga [072]
GELMINTOZY CHELOVEKA, ZHIVOTNYKH, RASTENII I MERY BORBY S NIMI : TEZISY DOKLADOV KONFERENTSII VSESOIUZNOGO OBSHCHESTVA GELMINTOLOGOV AN SSSR, MOSKVA, 27-29 IANVARIA 1981 G / ed by Filippov, V V – Moskva: Obshchestvo, 1980 – us Res Libr [072]
GELORA KONFRONTASI MENGGANJANG MALAYSIA / Indonesia. Departemen Penerangan – 1964. In Indonesian and English. SE-4797-1 – 9 – ne IDC [324]
GELRE : BIJDRAGEN EN MEDEDEELINGEN – (Index: 1-40 (1897-1937) 5mf. Dfl22.00) – 1(1898)-49(1949) – 328mf – 9 – Dfl148.00 – ne Slangenburg [073]
Gelzer, Heinrich *see*
- AUSGEWAEHLTE KLEINE SCHRIFTEN
- BYZANTINISCHE KULTURGESCHICHTE

GEM – 1829-32 – 12mf – 9 – £100.00 – uk Chadwyck [800]
THE GEM – Saint John, N.B.: R and E Armstrong, [1879-1886?] – 9 – cn C.I.H.M. [072]
GEMA TANAH AIR, PROSA DAN PUISI 1942-1948 / Jassin, Hans Bague – SE-12,191 1. 1959 – 9 – ne IDC [950]
GEMBIRA BERNJANJI / Sutigna, Daeng – SE 4577 1. 1956 – 9 – ne IDC [950]
Gemblacensis, Guibertus *see* EPISTOLAE
Gemci, Tevfik *see* PARTIKELABSCHEIDUNG IN NASSENTSTAUBERN UNTER BERUECKSICHTIGUNG VON WAERME- UND STOFFAUSTAUSCHVORGAENGEN
GEMEENSCHAP TUSSEN DE GOTTISCHE SPRAEKE EN DE NEDERDUYTSCHE VERTOONT / Kate, L ten – Amsterdam, 1710 – 1mf – 9 – ne IDC [430]
DIE GEMEINDE – Halbmonatsschrift fuer sozialistische Arbeit in Stadt und Land. Berlin. Jahrg. 1-7; 1924-30. No more published after 1933. Film Mas C 715 – 1 – us H.U. Library [073]
DIE GEMEINDE : ORGAN DES BUNDES EVANGELISCH-FREIKIRCHLICHER GEMEINDEN – 1965-92 (complete) – Inquire – 1 – ATLA S0379 – us A.T.L.A. [073]
DIE GEMEINDE. (THE CHURCH) – German Baptist. 1946-60 – 1 – 269.92 – us Baptist [240]
DIE GEMEINDE UNTERM KREUZ : ODER, BOTSCHAFTER DES HEILS IN CHRISTO – v1-4. 1885-88 (complete) – 1r – 1 – ATLA 1994-S019 – us A.T.L.A. [073]
GEMEINDEBLATT / Der Juedischen Gemeinde zu Berlin – Berlin. Jarg. 1-28. no. 45. Jan. 13, 1911-Nov. 6, 1938 – 1 – us NY Public [072]
GEMEINDEBLATT DER DEUTSCH-ISRAELITISCHEN GEMEINDE ZU HAMBURG – Juedisches Gemeindeblatt fuer das Gebiet der Hansestadt Hamburg. v1-14. 1925-1938. Lacking misc. issues. 1 reel. B444 (Leo Baeck Institute. German-Jewish Periodicals, Pt 1) – 1 – $75.00 – us UPA [270]
GEMEINDEBLATT DER ISRAELITISCHEN RELIGIONSGEMEINDE DRESDEN – Dresden. v1-14. 1925-38. Lacking: v9, 1933 and misc. issues. 2 reels. B438 (Leo Baeck Institute. German-Jewish Periodicals, Pt 1) – 1 – $135.00 – us UPA [270]
GEMEINDEBLATT DER JUEDISCHEN GEMEINDE ZU BERLIN – Berlin. v. 1-28 no. 45. Jan 13 1911-Nov 6 1938 – 1 – us NY Public [305]
GEMEINDEBLATT FUER DIE JUEDISCHEN GEMEINDEN PREUSSENS *see* VERWALTUNGSBLATT DES PREUSSISCHEN LANDESVERBANDES JUEDISCHER GEMEINDEN
DIE GEMEINDEGESAENGE DER HEILIGEN MESSE / Winterswyl, L A & Messerschmid, F – Wuerzburg, 1940 – 1mf – 8 – Dfl6.00 – ne Slangenburg [240]
GEMEINDEGRUSS – 1967-92 (complete) – Inquire – 1 – ATLA S0646 – us A.T.L.A. [073]
GEMEINDE-UNTERWEGS – v1-12. 1974-85 (complete) – 3r – 1 – ATLA S0427 – us A.T.L.A. [240]
GEMEINNUETZIGE DANZIGER ANZEIGEN, ERFAHRUNGEN UND ERLAEUTERUNGEN – Danzig (Gdansk), Poland. 1755-57 – 1 – gw Mikrofilm [943]
GEMEINNUETZIGE NACHRICHTEN FUER DIE PROVINZ OSTFRIESLAND – Aurich, 1805-08 – 2r – 1 – Dist. gw Mikrofilm – gw Misc Inst [943]
GEMEINNUETZIGE STADT- UND LAND ZEITUNG – Cahla bei Jena, Germany. Okt 1799-1801 (incomplete) – 1r – 1 – gw Mikrofilm [072]
GEMEINNUETZIGES WOCHENBLATT – (Also known as: Bernkast'ler Tageblatt, Bernkasteler Zeitung) – Bernkastel, Germany. 1849 – 1r – 1 – gw Mikrofilm [072]
GEMEINNUETZIGES WOCHENBLATT : FUER GEILENKIRCHEN, HEINSBERG UND DIE UMGEBUNG – Geilenkirchen, Germany. 1845 – 1 – gw Mikrofilm [072]
GEMEINNUETZIGES WOCHENBLATT – (Title changes: Intelligenzblatt, 4 Aug 1840; Der Bote vom Remsthale, 6 Dec 1842; Der Remsthalbote, 2 Jan 1864; Rems-Zeitung, 1873; Schwaebische Rundschau, 1 Jul 1936) – Schwaebisch Gmuend, West Germany. 1977- – 1 – gw Mikrofilm [072]
GEMEINNUETZIGES WOCHENBLATT *see* BERNKASTELER ZEITUNG
GEMEINNUETZIGES WOCHENBLATT FUER FRIEDBERG UND DIE GEGEND *see* ALLGEMEINES FRIEDBERGER WOCHENBLATT FUER STADT- UND LANDLEUTE
GEMEINNUETZLICHES ELEMENTARWERK DER HARMONIE UND DES GENERALBASSES. / Knecht, J H – 4vol. 1792-97 – 9 – us Sibley [780]
GEMEINNUTZIGE BETRACHTUNG DER NEUESTEN SCHRIFTEN – 1776-78 (complete) – 2r – 1 – ATLA S0888 – us A.T.L.A. [073]
GEMEINNUTZIGE BETRACHTUNGEN DER NEUESTEN SCHRIFTEN – 1779-1800 (incomplete) – 8r – 1 – ATLA S0888A – us A.T.L.A. [073]
DIE GEMEINSCHAFT – (Cont by: Der Beamtenbund) – Berlin, 1917-22 – 1 – Dist. gw Mikrofilm – gw Misc Inst [072]
DIE GEMEINSCHAFT – Hefte fuer die religioese Erstaerkung des Judenthums. Berlin. v1-22. 1925-33. 1 reel. Incomplete. B85 (Leo Baeck Institute. German-Jewish Periodicals, Pt 2) – 1 – $60.00 – us UPA [270]
DIE GEMEINSCHAFT : HEFTE FUER DIE RELIGIOESE ERSTARKUNG DES JUDENTUMS – Berlin, 1925-33 (incomplete) – 1r – 1 – Dist. gw Mikrofilm – gw Misc Inst [270]
DIE GEMEINSCHAFT DER EIGENEN – Berlin, 1919-1924/25 n7 – 1r – 1 – Dist. gw Mikrofilm – gw Misc Inst [072]
GEMEINSCHAFT UND EINZELMENSCH / Welty, E O – Salzburg, Leipzig, 1935 – 6mf – 8 – ne Slangenburg [140]
GEMEINSCHAFTSBLATT *see* DER KOMET
GEMINGSHI ZILIAO – Materials on Revolutionary History. 4v. Comp. by The Research Office of Historical and Cultural Materials. 9 fiches. F H11 – 9 – $70.00 – cc Microforms [950]
Geminiani, Francesco *see*
- L'ART DE JOUER LE VIOLON. OPERA IX
- THE ART OF ACCOMPANIAMENT
- THE ART OF ACCOMPANIAMENT. OPERA 11
- THE ART OF PLAYING ON THE VIOLIN CONTAINING ALL THE RULES NECESSARY TO ATTAIN TO A PERFECTION ON THAT INSTRUMENT
- COMPLEAT INSTRUCTIONS FOR THE VIOLIN
- CONCERTI GROSSI [NOS. 1-6] CON DUE VIOLINE, VIOLA E VIOLONCELLE DO CONCERTINO OBBLIGATI, E DUE ALTRI VIOLINI E BASSO DI CONCERTO GROSSE...
- CONCERTI GROSSI [NOS. 7-12] CON DUE VIOLINI, VIOLA E VIOLONCELLO DI CONCERTINO OBBLIGATI, E DUE ALTRI VIOLINI E BASSE DI CONCERTO GROSSO...OP. 2
- DICTIONAIRE HARMONIQUE OU GUIDE SUR POUR LA VRAI MODULAISON
- DICTIONAIRE HARMONIQUE OU GUIDE SUR POUR LA VRAIE MODULAISON
- GUIDA ARMONICA O DIZIONARIO ARMONICO, BEING A SURE GUIDE TO HARMONY AND MODULATION. OPERA X
- THE INCHANTED FORREST
- RULES FOR PLAYING IN A TRUE TASTE ON THE VIOLIN, GERMAN FLUTE, VIOLONCELLO, AND HARPSICHORD, PARTICULARLY THE THOROUGH-BASS. OPERA 8
- RULES FOR PLAYING IN A TRUE TASTE ON THE VIOLIN, GERMAN FLUTE, VIOLONCELLO AND HARPSICORD PARTICULARLY THE THOROUGH BASS EXEMPLIFY'D IN A VARIETY OF COMPOSITIONS
- A TREATISE OF GOOD TASTE IN THE ART OF MUSICK

Geminova, N V et al *see* ANGLO-RUSSKII SEL'SKOKHOZIAIST VENNYI SLOVAR'
Geminus, T *see*
- COMPENDIOSA ANATOMIAE DELINEATIO

Gemmill, J F *see* THE TERATOLOGY OF FISHES
Gemmill, John Alexander *see* THE PRACTICE OF THE PARLIAMENT OF CANADA UPON BILLS OF DIVORCE: INCLUDING AN HISTORICAL SKETCH OF PARLIAMENTARY DIVORCE AND SUMMARIES OF ALL THE BILLS OF DIVORCE PRESENTED TO PARLIAMENT FROM 1867 TO 1888, ALSO NOTES ON THE PROVINCIAL DIVORCE COURTS, &C
Gemminger, M *see* CATALOGUS COLEOPTERORUM HUCUSQUE DESCRIPTORUM SYNONYMICUS ET SYSTEMATICUS
THE GEMMOLOGIST – 1931-62 – 1 – uk Microform Academic [740]
GEMS OF HOPE: IN MEMORY OF THE FAITHFUL DEPARTED / Bate, Fanny – Selected and arranged by Fanny Bate. Toronto: W. Briggs, 1896. 00901. (Pre-1900 Canadiana) – 9 – cn C.I.H.M. [240]
GEMUETHS-SCHAETZE : HINTERLASSENE GEDICHTE / Hiller, Louise – New York: [s.n.], 1883 – 1r – 1 – us U.W. Library [810]
GEMUL ATALIAH / Franco-Mendes, D – Amsterdam. 1770. BJ-422-21 1 – 9 – ne IDC [240]
DIE GEMUTSART JESU : NACH JETZIGER WISSENSCHAFTLICHER, INSBESONDERE JETZIGER PSYCHOLOGISCHER METHODE / Baumann, Julius – Leipzig: Alfred Kroner, 1908 – 1mf – 9 – 0-8370-2211-8 – 1985-0211 – us A.T.L.A. [150]
Genand, J A *see* NOTES DE VOYAGE: LE GOLFE ET LES PROVINCES MARITIMES
GENC KALEMLER – Selanik. Mueduer-i Mes'ul ve Sahib-i Imtiyaz: Nesimi Sarim, 1910-1912. II. cilt, nos. 1 (8 Nisan 1327 [1911]), 5 (19 Haziran 1327 [1911]) – 9 – $25.00 – us MEDOC [956]
Gence, Comtesse de *see* LE CABINET DE TOILETTE D'UNE HONNETE FEMME
Gence, E *see* DE LA REPRESSION...
Gench, Barbara E *see*
- BONE DENSITY PATTERNS IN ADULT FEMALES WITH A HISTORY OF ANOREXIA NERVOSA
- EFFECT OF AGE ON REACTION AND MOVEMENT TIMES IN GIRLS AND WOMEN
- MOTOR ABILITY TESTING OF SPEECH HANDICAPPED PRESCHOOL CHILDREN

GENCLIK – (Sahib-i Imtiyaz ve mueduer-i mes'ul: Cemal Ankara: Resimli Ay Matbaasi) – 1928 – 2mf – 9 – $40.00 – us MEDOC [949]
Gendarme de Bevotte, Georges *see* LA LEGENDE DE DON JUAN
Gendarme, R *see* L'ECONOMIE DE L'ALGERIE
GENDER AND EDUCATION – 1989- 5v – 9 – £164.00 – 0954-0253 – uk Carfax [370]
GENDER CLASSIFICATIONS OF FEMALE ATHLETES AND NONATHLETES AT WOMEN'S AND COEDUCATIONAL COLLEGES / Chick, Susan A & Murray, Mimi – 1992 – 2mf – $8.00 – us Microform Publ [150]
GENDER DIFFERENCES IN OVERT COACHING BEHAVIORS OF HIGH SCHOOL SOCCER COACHES / Millard, Linda & Brockmeyer, Gretchen A – 1992 – 2mf – 9 – $8.00 – us Microform Publ [150]
GENDER DIFFERENCES IN PEAK BLOOD LACTATE CONCENTRATION AND BLOOD LACTATE REMOVAL FOLLOWING STRENUOUS EXERCISE / Zhang, Q – 1991 – 2mf – 9 – $8.00 – us Microform Publ [612]
GENDER DIFFERENCES IN RUNNING ECONOMY / Davies, Michael J & Mahar, Matthew T – 1992 – 2mf – $8.00 – us Microform Publ [612]
GENDER DIFFERENCES IN SPORT CENTRALITY / Allan, Diane E & Boydell, Cary – 1992 – 2mf – $8.00 – us Microform Publ [150]
GENDER DIFFERENCES IN SPORT ORIENTATION AND GOAL ORIENTATION / Kleppinger, Alison – Springfield College, 1995 – 2mf – 9 – $8.00 – PSY1848 – us Microform Publ [150]
GENDER DIFFERENCES IN SPORT PARTICIPATION AND INCENTIVE MOTIVATION OF FORMER COLLEGE BASKETBALL PLAYERS AND SWIMMERS / Schwartz, Diana L – Springfield College, 1995 – 2mf – 9 – $8.00 – PSY1862 – us Microform Publ [150]
GENDER DIFFERENCES IN SUBSTRATE METABOLISM AND THERMOREGULATION DURING REST AND EXERCISE IN COLD AND WARM WATER / Shea, Kyla – 1993 – 2mf – $8.00 – us Microform Publ [612]

GENDER DIFFERENCES IN THE RELATIONSHIPS AMONG SELF-CONFIDENCE, GENDER-APPROPRIATENESS, AND VALUE / Clifton, Robert T & Gill, Diane L – 1992 – 2mf – 9 – $8.00 – us Microform Publ [150]
GENDER DIFFERENCES IN WALKING WITH RESPECT TO MOVEMENT OF THE PELVIS / Johansen, Michelle K – University of British Columbia, 1996 – 1mf – 9 – PE 3656 – us Microform Publ [612]
GENDER DIFFERENCES REGARDING KNOWLEDGE OF CHILD HEALTH AND DEVELOPMENT AMONG HIGH SCHOOL STUDENTS / Roeschlein, Debra L & Gilbert, Kathleen R – 1992 – 2mf – 9 – $8.00 – us Microform Publ [613]
GENDER PLACE AND CULTURE : A JOURNAL OF FEMINIST GEOGRAPHY – 1995, Vol 2 – £94.00 – uk Carfax [305]
GENDER RELATED DIFFERENCES IN PERFORMANCE LEVELS OF TRIATHLETES / Santanello, T – 1992 – 2mf – 9 – $8.00 – us Microform Publ [150]
Gendron, F *see* RECHERCHE SUR LA TOXICITE DES PEINTURES ANTISALISSURES A BASE D'ORGANOSTANNIQUES ET DE L'OXYDE DE TRIBUTYLETAIN VIS-A-VIS DE L'HUITRE CRASSOSTREA GIGAS
Gendry, Jules *see* PIE 6
Gendt, W G J van *see* DE AEQUALITATE IN CONTRACTIBUS PRAESERTIM ONEROSIS...
GENE – v1-31. 1977-84 – 1,5,6,13 – sz Elsevier [575]
GENEALOGIA DE LA CASA DE URRIES, DEL MARQUES DE VELILLA DE EBRO / T'Serclaes, Duque de – Madrid: Tip. Arch., Bibl. y Mus, 1930. B.R.A.H. 97, pp. 12-13 – sp Bibl Santa Ana [920]
GENEALOGIA DE LOS CONQUISTADORES DE CUYO / Morales Guinazu, Fernando – Buenos Aires, 1932; Madrid: Razon y Fe, 1933 – 1 – sp Bibl Santa Ana [920]
GENEALOGIAS DEL NUEVO REYNO DE GRANADA. 2 VOL. BOGOTA, 1943 / Florez de Ocariz, Juan – Madrid: Razon y Fe, 1947 – 1 – sp Bibl Santa Ana [920]
GENEALOGICAL AND BIOGRAPHICAL ANNALS OF NORTHUMBERLAND COUNTY / Floyd, J. L. and Co – Chicago, 1911. Pennsylvania Reel 34. (The Cox Library Collection) – 5 – us Americana [920]
GENEALOGICAL AND BIOGRAPHICAL HISTORY OF KEOKUK COUNTY – Chicago: 1903. Iowa Reel 24. (The Cox Library Collection) – 5 – us Americana [978]
GENEALOGICAL AND BIOGRAPHICAL RECORD OF MIAMI COUNTY – Chicago: 1900. Ohio Reel 49. (The Cox Library Collection) – 5 – us Americana [978]
GENEALOGICAL AND BIOGRAPHICAL RECORD OF NEW LONDON COUNTY, CONNECTICUT / J.H. Beers and Co – Chicago, 1905. Connecticut Reel 6. The Cox Library Collection – 5 – us Americana [978]
GENEALOGICAL AND BIOGRAPHICAL RECORD OF NORTHEASTERN KANSAS – Chicago, 1900. Kansas Reel 5. (The Cox Library Collection) – 5 – us Americana [978]
GENEALOGICAL AND BIOGRAPHICAL RECORD OF WILL COUNTY – Chicago, 1900. (Illinois Reel 62). (The Cox Library Collection) – 5 – us Americana [978]
GENEALOGICAL AND FAMILY HISTORY OF CENTRAL NEW YORK / Cutter, William Richard – New York, Lewis Historical Publ. Co., 1912. Vols. 1-3. New York Reel 3. (The Cox Library Collection) – 5 – us Americana [978]
GENEALOGICAL AND FAMILY HISTORY OF EASTERN OHIO / Summers, Ewing – Chicago: Lewis Publ. Co., 1903. Mississippi Reel 4. (The Cox Library Collection) – 5 – us Americana [978]
GENEALOGICAL AND FAMILY HISTORY OF JEFFERSON COUNTY / Oakes, R A – New York, Lewis Publ. Co., 1905. Vols. 1-2. New York Reel 18. (The Cox Library Collection) – 5 – us Americana [978]
GENEALOGICAL AND FAMILY HISTORY OF NEW HAMPSHIRE / Stearns, Ezra Scollay et al – New York, Lewis Publ. Co., 1908. Vols. 1-2, New Hampshire Reel 1; Vols. 3-4, New Hampshire Reel 2. (The Cox Library Collection) – 5 – us Americana [978]
GENEALOGICAL AND FAMILY HISTORY OF NORTHERN NEW YORK / Cutter, William Richard – New York, Lewis Historical Publ. Co., 1910. Vol. 1. New York Reel 2; Vols. 2-3. New York Reel 3. (The Cox Library Collection) – 5 – us Americana [978]
GENEALOGICAL AND FAMILY HISTORY OF SOUTHERN NEW YORK AND HUDSON RIVER VALLEY / Reynolds, Cuyler – New York, Lewis Historical Publ. Co., 1914. Vols. 1-3. New York Reel 4. (The Cox Library Collection) – 5 – us Americana [978]
GENEALOGICAL AND FAMILY HISTORY OF THE STATE OF CONNECTICUT – New York, 1911. 4V. Connecticut Reel 1. (The Cox Library Collection) – 5 – us Americana [978]
GENEALOGICAL AND FAMILY HISTORY OF THE STATE OF MAINE / Little, George T – New York, Lewis Historical Publ. Co., 1909. Vol. 1. (Maine Reel 1); Vols. 2-4. (Maine Reel 2). (The Cox Library Collection) – 5 – us Americana [978]
GENEALOGICAL AND FAMILY HISTORY OF THE STATE OF NEW HAMPSHIRE / Stearns, Ezra Scollay – 4v. 1908 – 1 – 46.00 – us L of C Photodup [920]
GENEALOGICAL AND FAMILY HISTORY OF THE STATE OF VERMONT / Carleton, Hiram – New York, Lewis Publishing Co., 1903. Vols. 1-2. Vermont Reel 4. (The Cox Library Collection) – 5 – us Americana [978]
GENEALOGICAL AND FAMILY HISTORY OF WESTERN NEW YORK / Cutter, William Richard – New York, Lewis Historical Publ. Co., 1912. Vols. 1-2. New York Reel 4; Vol. 3. New York Reel 5. (The Cox Library Collection) – 5 – us Americana [978]
GENEALOGICAL AND FAMILY HISTORY OF WYOMING AND LACKAWANNA VALLEYS / Hayden, Hand – New York: Lewis Publ. Co., 1906. v1-2. Pennsylvania Reel 4. The Cox Library Collection – 5 – us Americana [978]
GENEALOGICAL AND FAMILY MEMOIRS OF THE HUDSON AND MOHAWK – New York, 1911. Vols. 1-4. New York Reel 5. (The Cox Library Collection) – 5 – us Americana [978]
GENEALOGICAL AND MEMORIAL ENCYCLOPEDIA OF THE STATE OF MARYLAND / Spencer, Richard H – New York, American Historical Society, 1919. Vols. 1-2. Maryland Reel 2. (The Cox Library Collection) – 5 – us Americana [978]
GENEALOGICAL AND PERSONAL HISTORY OF ALLEGHENY VALLEY / Jordan, J W – New York, Lewis Historical Publ. Co., 1913. Vols. 1-3, Pennsylvania Reel 8. (The Cox Library Collection) – 5 – us Americana [978]
GENEALOGICAL AND PERSONAL HISTORY OF FAYETTE COUNTY / Jordan, J W & Hardin – New York: Lewis Historical Publ. Co., 1912. v1-3. Pennsylvania Reel 22. (The Cox Library Collection) – 5 – us Americana [978]
GENEALOGICAL AND PERSONAL MEMORIAL OF MERCER COUNTY / Lee, Francis B – New York, Lewis Publ. Co., 1907. Vols. 1-2. New Jersey Reel 4. (The Cox Library Collection) – 5 – us Americana [978]
GENEALOGICAL COLLECTION – Early California records. 3 rolls. Individual rolls available – 5 – 75.00 – uk Libr Preservation [920]
GENEALOGICAL COLUMN, 1896-1941 / Boston Transcript – 9 – $325.00 – us Godfrey [920]
GENEALOGICAL DICTIONARY OF THE FIRST SETTLERS OF NEW ENGLAND – Showing three generations of those who came before May 1692, v1-4, A-Z, by James Savage, 1860.Item A-D. SW16-0004 – 5 – us A.G.L.L. [920]
GENEALOGICAL FAMILY HISTORY OF AND BIOGRAPHY OF SCHUYLKILL COUNTY / J.H. Beers and Co – Chicago, 1916. v1-2. Pennsylvania Reel 38. The Cox Library Collection – 5 – us Americana [920]
GENEALOGICAL & FAMILY HISTORY OF THE STATE OF CONNECTICUT – 4v, 1911. Items A-D. Indexes in v4. SW16-0147 – 5 – us A.G.L.L. [920]
A GENEALOGICAL HISTORY OF THE MILESIAN FAMILIES OF IRELAND, WITH THE MONUMENT TO BRIAN BOROIMHE: THE CHART OF THE ARMORIAL BEARINGS OF THE SAME FAMILIES / De Courcy, B W – Cincinnati: W.F. Overdiek & M.L. Riegel, 1880. 77p – 1 – us U.W. Library [920]
THE GENEALOGICAL INDEX / Newberry Library. Chicago – 1960.-512,000 entries 8 reels.-ISBN: 0-8161-1317-3; or 109mf.-ISBN: 0-8161-1771-3 – 1,9 – $380.00 – uk Hall [920]
THE GENEALOGICAL INDEX OF THE NEWBERRY LIBRARY / Newberry Library. Chicago – (Also 109 microfiche. $345.00 export $415.00. ISBN 0-8161-1771-3) – 1960 – 8r – 1 – $345.00 export $415.00 – 0-8161-1317-3 – uk Hall [920]
GENEALOGICAL MATERIAL, MS 1826 / Spooner Family – 1879-1935 – 4r – 1 – us Western Res [920]
GENEALOGICAL MATERIAL, MS 2500 / Oberholtzer Family – Excerpts – 3r – 1 – us Western Res [920]
GENEALOGICAL MEMORANDA : SNIVELY / Snively, William Andrew – (Original in the Library of Congress) – Brooklyn, NY, 1883 – 1r – 1 – us Western Res [920]
A GENEALOGICAL NARRATIVE OF THE DANIEL HAIGHT FAMILY / Haight, Canniff – Toronto: Rowsell & Hutchison, 1899. 05148. (Pre-1900 Canadiana) – 9 – cn C.I.H.M. [920]
GENEALOGICAL NOTES ON CAPE COD FAMILIES, 1620-1901 / Brownson, Lydia B et al – 8r – 1 – $680.00 – S1831 – us Scholarly Res [978]
GENEALOGICAL NOTES, OR CONTRIBUTIONS TO THE FAMILY HISTORY OF SOME OF THE FIRST SETTLERS OF CONNECTICUT & MASSACHUSETTS – By Nathaniel Goodwin, 1969. Orig. publ., 1856. Indexed. 6 fiches. F-0870 – 9 – us A.G.L.L. [978]
GENEALOGICAL PAPERS / White-Synder Family – 600-1994 – 2r – 1 – $32.50r – us Archival [978]
Genealogical Publishing Co *see*
– BIOGRAPHICAL ANNALS OF CUMBERLAND COUNTY
– MEMORIAL AND FAMILY HISTORY OF ERIE COUNTY
GENEALOGICAL QUERIES OF CENTRAL STATES MISSION – 1958. Item R. SW16-0043 – 5 – us A.G.L.L. [920]
A GENEALOGICAL RECORD: FORSYTH OF NYDIE / Fronsac, Frederic Gregory Forsyth – New Market, Va.: Henkel & Co., 1888. 04328. (Pre-1900 Canadiana) – 9 – cn C.I.H.M. [971]
GENEALOGICAL RECORDS / Gibbes Family – ca.1885. 3 fiches – 9 – us South Carolina Historical [920]
GENEALOGICAL RECORDS OF HANOVER, NEW HAMPSHIRE / Saunders, Mildred L & Hurd, John; ed by Frost, Gilman Dubois – 15r – 1 – $150.00 – us Dartmouth [920]
GENEALOGICAL REGISTER OF THE DESCENDANTS : OF JOHN SCANTON OF GUILDFORD, CONNECTICUT, WHO DIED IN THE YEAR 1651 / Scranton, Erastus – Hartford: Press of Case, Tiffany & Co, 1855 – 1r – 1 – us Western Res [920]
GENEALOGICAL RESEARCH KIT – (Made up of 4 stages) – Sydney: Archives Authority of NSW, 1984- – 523r 416mf – 1,9 – A$19,885.00 – at N.S.W. Archives [920]
GENEALOGICAL SERVICES / American Genealogical Lending Library – Over 100,000 titles for loan or purchase. Includes: Complete Federal Census Records, 1790-1910; Military Records; Ship Passenger Lists; Selected State Censuses; Slave Schedules; Vital Records; Family and County Histories; bibliographies and indexes – 1 – us A.G.L.L. [920]
Genealogical Society of the Northern Territory *see*
– ANNUAL SINGLE NUMBERS SERIES ALPHABETICAL INDEX
GENEALOGIE DE LA FAMILLE ARCHAMBAULT, 1620-1890: TABLEAU ET NOTES HISTORIQUES / Archambault, Louis Missael – Montreal: E. Senecal, 1891. 00821. (Pre-1900 Canadiana) – 9 – cn C.I.H.M. [920]
GENEALOGIE DE LA FAMILLE FILTEAU / Filteau, Louis Honore – Ottawa: A. Bureau, 1895. 03103. (Pre-1900 Canadiana) – 9 – cn C.I.H.M. [971]
GENEALOGIE DE LA MAISON DE BERTHOU EN BRETAGNE / Berthou, maison de – Nantes: Deroual, Joubin et Cie, 1896 – 1 – F52.18 – fr Armell [920]
GENEALOGIE DE LA MAISON DU BELLAY... – S.d. – fr Armell [920]
LA GENEALOGIE DU GRANT TURC A PRESENT REGNANT – N.p., 1519 – 2mf – 9 – H-8135/1 – ne IDC [956]
GENEALOGIE VORSTELIJKE FAMILIE VAN DJOHOR DOOR L.C. VAN RANZOW, 1827 – KITLV,H 369. BSD-102/1 – 45mf – 9 – ne IDC [920]
GENEALOGIES DE BELEP / Dubois, M J – 9 – F50.00 – fr Ethnologie [520]
GENEALOGIES DE L'ILE DES PINS / Dubois, M J – 9 – F60.00 – fr Ethnologie [920]
GENEALOGIES DE MARE / Dubois, M J – 9 – F100.00 – fr Ethnologie [920]
LES GENEALOGIES DE SOIXANTE ET SEPT TRES NOBLES ET TRES ILLUSTRES MAISONS, PARTIE DE FRANCE, PARTIE ESTRAGERES, YSSUES DE MEROUEE / Lusignano, S di – Paris, 1587 – 1mf – 9 – H-8369/1 – ne IDC [920]
LES GENEALOGIES DE SOIXANTE ET SEPT TRES-NOBLES ET TRES-ILLUSTRES MAISONS, PARTIE DE FRANCE, PARTIE ESTRAGERES... / Lusignan de Cypre, E de – Paris, 1586 – 4mf – ne IDC [920]
GENEALOGIES OF THE SHEPHERD ISLANDS, VANUATU : (BY ISLAND, VILLAGE AND FAMILY) – 1930s – 1r – 1 – PMB 1132 – at Pacific Mss [980]
GENEALOGIES OF THE TRIBES OF BRITISH SOMALILAND AND MIJERTEIN – [Hargeisa?]: publ under the auspices of the Military Govt, Somaliland Protectorate, 1944 – 1 – us Res Libr [960]
GENEALOGISCHES TASCHENBUCH DER ADELIGEN HAEUSER – Brunn. v. 1-19. 1870-94. (Wanting v. 2, 12) – 1 – 60.00 – us L of C Photodup [920]
THE GENEALOGIST'S GUIDE / Marshall, G W – 1903 – 1 – uk Microform Academic [920]
GENEALOGY / Bobo and Ray Families. South Carolina – 1744-1946. 251p – 1 – us Baptist [920]
GENEALOGY AND LOCAL HISTORY – (Parts available separately) – 9 – $129,200.00 Parts 1-19 – us UMI [920]
Genealogy Division, Indiana State Library *see* 1840 FEDERAL POPULATION CENSUS, INDIANA
THE GENEALOGY OF CREATION...FROM THE UNPOINTED HEBREW TEXT OF... GENESIS / Pratt, Henry F A – London: John Churchill, 1861. 1 fiche. 8370-4790-0 – 9 – us A.T.L.A. [240]
GENEALOGY OF NEW ENGLAND – v1. p1-61 vandalized before filming. 10 fiches. F-0770 – 9 – us A.G.L.L. [920]
GENEALOGY OF SOME EARLY AMERICAN FAMILIES IN PRESTON COUNTY / King, Edward T – Thorpe Family of Fayette County, Penn. and Cunningham Family of Somerset County, Penn. 1933. West Virginia Reel 5. (The Cox Library Collection) – 5 – us Americana [978]
THE GENEALOGY OF THE CUSHING FAMILY / Cushing, Lemuel – Montreal: Lovell, 1877. 02252. (Pre-1900 Canadiana) – 9 – cn C.I.H.M. [971]
GENEALOGY OF THE FAMILY NORMANDEAU, DIT DESLAURIERS / Filteau, Louis Honore – Ottawa: A. Bureau, 1894. 05458. (Pre-1900 Canadiana) – 9 – cn C.I.H.M. [971]
GENEALOGY OF THE LYMAN FAMILY / Coleman, Lyman – 1872 – 1 – $50.00 – us Presbyterian [920]
GENEALOGY OF THE MERRICK FAMILY / Merrick, George B – Madison, WI: Tracy, Gibb & Co, 1902 – 1r – 1 – us Western Res [920]
Genebrardus, Gilb. *see*
– CHRONOGRAPHIAE LIBRI QUATUOR
– PSALMI DAVIDIS
Y GENEDL GYMREIG – Caernarvon, Wales. Feb 1877-1909 – 27 1/2r – 1 – uk British Libr Newspaper [072]
Gener, J B *see* THEOLOGIA DOGMATICO-SCHOLASTICA...
THE GENERA AND SPECIES OF ORCHIDACEOUS PLANTS / Lindley, J – London. 1830-40. B-5297 2 – 8 – ne IDC [580]
GENERA AROIDEARUM EXPOSITA / Schott, H W – Vindobonae. 1858. B-1034 2 – 8 – ne IDC [580]
GENERA AVIUM / Wytsman, P A G – Bruxelles, 1905-1914 – 31mf – ne IDC [590]
GENERA AVIUM / Wytsman, P A G – Z 1965. 1905-1914 – 9 – ne IDC [590]
GENERA DES INSECTES / Guerin-Meneville, Felix Edouard & Percheron, A R – Paris, Londres, 1835. Z/1320/2 – 8 – ne IDC [590]
GENERA ET INDEX METHODICUS EUROPAEORUM LEPIDOPTERORUM / Boisduval, J B A D de – Parisiis, 1840. vii,238p. Z-1078/2 – 8 – ne IDC [590]
GENERA ET SPECIES ASTEREARUM / Nees von Esenbeck, C G D – Norimbergae, 1833. 309 pp. B-763 2 – 8 – ne IDC [580]

GENERA ET SPECIES GENTIANEARUM / Grisebach, A – Stuttgartiae et Tubingae. 1839. B-5940 2 – 8 – ne IDC [580]
GENERA ET SPECIES MUSCORUM SYSTEMATICE DISPOSITA SEU ADUMBRATIO FLORAE MUSCORUM / Jaeger, H & Sauerbeck, F – (Bericht ueber die Thaetigkeit der Sanct Gallischen Naturw. Gesellschaft, 1869-79). B-1511 2 – 8 – ne IDC [590]
GENERA ET SPECIES ORCHIDEARUM ET ASCLEPIADEARUM / Breda, J S G van – Gandavi. 1827, 1828-29. B-5026 2 – 8 – ne IDC [580]
GENERA ET SPECIES PLANTARUM, QUAE AUT NOVAE SUNT, AUT NONDUM RECTE COGNOSCUNTUR / Lagasca y Segura, M – Matriti. 1816. B-6000 2 – 8 – ne IDC [580]
GENERA ET SPECIES PLANTARUM VOCABULIS CHARACTERISTICIS DEFINITA / Wolf, N M von – (Additamentum alterum Sibiricae. Pallas et aliae quaedam. Genera plantarum vocabulis characteristics definita. 1776. Concordantia botanica). Marienwerder. 1781. B-5821 2 – 8 – ne IDC [580]
GENERA ET SPECIES STAPHYLINORUM INSECTORUM COLEOPTERORUM FAMILAE / Erichson, W F – Berolini, 1840. viii,954p.,5 pls. Z/1216/2 – 8 – ne IDC [590]
GENERA FILICUM / Hooker, W J & Bauer, F – London. 1842. B-5083 2 – 8 – ne IDC [580]
GENERA FILICUM / Schott, H W – Vindobonae. 1834-36. B-5150 2 – 8 – ne IDC [580]
GENERA FLORAE AMERICAE BOREALIORIENTALIS ILLUSTRATA / Gray, A – v. 1. Boston. 1848; v. 2. Boston. 1849. B-5130 2 – 8 – ne IDC [580]
GENERA INSECTORUM... / ed by Wytsman, P A G – Bruxelles, 1902-1935. v1-203 – 712mf – 9 – Z-1736/2 – ne IDC [073]
GENERA INSECTORUM LINNAEI ET FABRICII ICONIBUS ILLUSTRATA / Roemer, J J – Vitoduri Helvetorum, 1789. viii,86p. 37 pls. Z-1577/2 – 8 – ne IDC [590]
GENERA MORBORUM / Linnaeus, Carl – Upsaliae. 1763. B-165 2 – 8 – ne IDC [580]
GENERA NOVA MADAGASCARIENSIA / Du Petit-Thouars, L M A A – Paris. 1806. B-5531 2 – 8 – ne IDC [580]
GENERA OF BIRDS / Pennant, T – 2108 2. 1773 – 8 – ne IDC [590]
GENERA OF BIRDS / Pennant, T – 2182 2. 1781 – 8 – ne IDC [590]
THE GENERA OF BIRDS / Gray, G R – 2089 2. 3 v. plus appendix. 1844-1849 – 8 – ne IDC [590]
THE GENERA OF DIURNAL LEPIDOPTERA / Doubleday, E & Westwood, J O – London: 1846-52.2v. Z/1195/2 – 8 – ne IDC [590]
THE GENERA OF FISHES FROM LINNAEUS TO CUVIER, 1758-1833 / Jordan, D S – 2132 2. 4 pts. 1917-1920 – 8 – ne IDC [590]
THE GENERA OF GRASSES OF THE UNITED STATES / Hitchcock, A S – 7557 2. 1920 – 8 – ne IDC [580]
THE GENERA OF NORTH AMERICAN PLANTS / Nuttall, T – 2v. Philadelphia. 1818. B-5070 2 – 8 – ne IDC [580]
THE GENERA OF PLANTS / Salisbury, R A – Fragment contains part of Liriogamae. 301. 1866 – 9 – ne IDC [580]
THE GENERA OF RECENT MOLLUSCA / Adams, H & Adams, Andrew Leith – 2V. 2251 2. 1853-1858 – 9 – ne IDC [590]
THE GENERA OF SOUTH AFRICAN PLANTS / Harvey, W H – Cape Town. 1838. B-5133 2 – 8 – ne IDC [580]
THE GENERA OF SOUTH AFRICAN PLANTS / Harvey, W H – ed 2. Cape Town. 1868. B-6119 2 – 8 – ne IDC [580]
GENERA PLANTARUM / Bentham, G & Hooker, J D – 3V. London. 1862-83. B-35 2 – 8 – ne IDC [580]
GENERA PLANTARUM / Endlicher, S L & Fenzl, E – Vindobonae. 1836-1840-50. B-5521 2 – 8 – ne IDC [580]
GENERA PLANTARUM / Jussieu, A H L de – Parisiis. 1789. B-232 2 – 8 – ne IDC [580]
GENERA PLANTARUM / Linnaeus, Carl – 556. 1737 – 9 – ne IDC [580]
GENERA PLANTARUM / Linnaeus, Carl – curante C. Sprengel. 2 v. ed. 9. Gottingae. 1830-31. B-229 2 – 8 – ne IDC [580]
GENERA PLANTARUM / Linnaeus, Carl – curante J. C. D. Schreber. 2 v. ed. 8. Francofurti ad Moenum. 1789-91. B-237 2 – 8 – ne IDC [580]
GENERA PLANTARUM / Linnaeus, Carl – ed. 2. Lugduni Batavorum. 1742. B-557 2 – 8 – ne IDC [580]
GENERA PLANTARUM / Linnaeus, Carl – ed. 6. Holmiae. 1764. B-166 2 – 8 – ne IDC [580]
GENERA PLANTARUM / Wernischeck, J J – ed. 1. Vindobonae. 1763; ed. 2. Vindobonae. 1764. B-5806 2 – 8 – ne IDC [580]
GENERA PLANTARUM FLORAE GERMANICAE / Nees von Esenbeck, C G D – 1835-45 – 5 – uk Microform Academic [580]
GENERA PLANTARUM METHODO NATURALI DISPOSITA / Trattinick, L – Vindobonae. 1802. B-5486 2 – 8 – ne IDC [580]
GENERA PLANTARUM ODER DIE PLFANZEN-GATTUNGEN DER IN DEN RUSSISCHEN OSTSEEPROVINZEN ESTH-, LIV- UND KURLAND WILDWACHSENDEN PFLANZEN / Engelmann, CW – Mitau-Leipzig, 1844 – 3mf – 9 – ne IDC [580]
GENERA PLANTARUM SECUNDUM CHARACTERES DIFFERENTIALES AD MIRBELII EDITIONEM / Hedwig, R A – Lipsiae. 1806. B-106 2 – 8 – ne IDC [580]
GENERA PLANTARUM UMBELLIFERARUM / Hoffmann, G F – ed. 2. M. 1816. B-5018 2 – 8 – ne IDC [580]
GENERA PLANTARUM UMBELLIFERARUM / Hoffmann, G F – M. 1814. B-5057 2 – 8 – ne IDC [580]
GENERA SIPHONOGAMARUM / Dalla Torre, K W von & Harms, H – Lipsiae. 1900-07. B-69 2 – 8 – ne IDC [580]
GENERA, SPECIES ET SYNONYMA CANDOLLEANA ALPHABETICO ORDINE DISPOSITA, SEU INDEX GENERALIS ET SPECIALIS AD A. P. DE CANDOLLE (ET A. DE CANDOLLE) / Bueck, H W – Prodromum systematis naturalis Regni Vegetabilis. 4 v. Berolini. Hamburgi. 1840, 1842-74. B-45 – 8 – ne IDC [580]
THE GENERA VERMIUM OF LINNAEUS EXEMPLIFIED BY VARIOUS SPECIMENS OF THE ANIMALS / Barbut, J – Z-391 2. 1783-1788 – 8 – ne IDC [590]
LA GENERACION ESPANOLA QUE VIVIO LA DERROTA / Sanchez Montes, Juan – Madrid: Arbor, 1949 – 1 – sp Bibl Santa Ana [946]
GENERAELE BEMERCKINGEN...TRACTAET VAN BARRIERE VAN DE NEDERLANDEN...1716 – N.p., n.d. – 1mf – 1 – ILM-833/1 – ne IDC [327]
GENERAL ABDUL HARRIS NASUTION; BIOGRAPHICAL NOTE. PROGRESS IN EFFORTS TO RESTORE SECURITY IN INDONESIA / Indonesia. Kedutaan Besar. Great Britain – SE-3543 1. 1961 – 9 – ne IDC [324]
A GENERAL ABRIDGEMENT OF LAW AND EQUITY : ALPHABETICALLY DIGESTED UNDER THE PROPER TITLES; WITH NOTES AND REFERENCES TO THE WHOLE / Viner, Charles – 2nd ed. London: G G J, J Robinson etc, Dublin. v1-124. 1791-94 (all publ) – 176mf – 9 – $264.00 – LLMC 95-245 – us L.L.M.C. [324]
A GENERAL ABRIDGEMENT OF LAW AND EQUITY; ALPHABETICALLY DIGESTED UNDER PROPER TITLES, WITH NOTES AND REFERENCES TO THE WHOLE / ed by Viner, Charles – Aldershot, 1741-1753. 23v. Index – 155mf – 9 – H-1847/1 – ne IDC [340]
General Accounting Office *see* GAO AUDITING STANDARDS
GENERAL ADMINISTRATION AND AUDITOR'S REPORTS / Syria. Banque Agricole de Syrie – 1947-59. (lacking 1948-59). BNE-9688 1 – 9 – ne IDC [350]
GENERAL ADVERTISER – Limerick. Ireland. - tw. 17 Sep 1804-10 Nov 1820. (16 reels) – 1 – uk British Libr Newspaper [072]
GENERAL ADVERTISER – Philadelphia. Pa. 1790-1794 – 1,3 – us Readex [071]
GENERAL ALPHABETICAL SEQUENCE – 614mf – $3,600.00 – 1-900853-00-0 – uk Mindata [700]
A GENERAL AND RATIONAL GRAMMAR / Arnauld, Antoine & Lancelot, Claude – 1753. 174p. (English Linguistics Series 1500-1800) – 9 – us UMI [400]
GENERAL AND SPECIAL INDEXES TO THE GENERAL CORRESPONDENCE OF THE OFFICE OF THE SECRETARY OF THE NAVY / U.S. Secretary of the Navy – Jul 1897 – Aug 1926. 119 rolls. M1052 – 1 – us Nat'l Archives [324]
GENERAL AND SPECIAL ORDERS, DEPARTMENT OF TEXAS, 1878-93 / United States Adjutant-General's Office – Washington: National Archives and Records Service, 1974. reel 8: v530, 532-533; reel 9: v534-537; reel 10: v538-540; reel 11: v541-542 – 4r – 1 – us Res Libr [324]
GENERAL ARMORY : ITEM V: A REGISTRY OF AMERICAN FAMILIES ENTITLED TO COAT ARMOR / ed by Crozier, William Armstrong – 155p. SW16-0080 – 5 – us A.G.L.L. [920]
GENERAL ASSEMBLY / United Nations – (Official Records 9300mf $17,000.00 $1.90f; Official Records, General Distribution Meeting Documents $20,000mf $38,000.00 $1.90f; Indexes to Proceedings of the General Assembly 199mf $380.00 $1.90f) – 9 – uk UNIMICRO [900]
GENERAL ASSEMBLY OFFICIAL RECORDS : ANNEXES / United Nations – (1st Sess. 3rd Sess.: 1946-1949. E/F.25 S.14; 4th Sess. 40th Sess.: 1949-1985. E.690 F.714 S.730; 1st Spec. Sess. 2nd Spec. Sess.: 1947-1948. E/F.2 S.2; 3rd Spec. Sess. 15th Spec. Sess.: 1961-1988. E.68 F.65 S.66; 1st Emerg. Spec. Sess. 9th Emerg. Spec. Sess.: 1956-1982. E.17 F.18 S.18; 35th Session is not yet available in microfiche; 7th Emerg. Spec. Sess. is not yet available in microfiche) – 9 – us U.N. Pubs [324]
GENERAL ASSEMBLY OFFICIAL RECORDS : RESOLUTIONS AND DECISIONS / United Nations – (1st Sess., 2nd Pt 3rd Sess., 2nd Pt: A/RES/session/ 1946-1948. F/F 12 S.7 R.7; 1st Sess., 1st Pt; 4th Sess. 44th Sess.: A/RES/session/1946; 1949-1989. E.158 F.169 S.176 R.178; 1st Spec. Sess. 2nd Spec. Sess.: A/RES/session/ 1947-1948. E/F.2 S.2 R.2; 3rd Spec. Sess. 15th Spec. Sess.: A/RES/session/ 1961-1988. E.13 F.13 S.12 R.13; 1st Emerg. Spec. Sess. 9th Emerg. Spec. Sess.: A/RES/session/ 1956-1982. E.9 F.9 S.9 R.9) – 9 – us U.N. Pubs [324]
GENERAL ASSEMBLY OFFICIAL RECORDS : SUPPLEMENTS / United Nations – (No suppl were issued for 1st, 3rd, 4th & 7th Special Sessions) – 1st Sess: A/session/ 1946 E/ F14 S7; 2nd & 44th Sess: A/session/ 1947-89 E3788 F3892 S3819; 2nd & 15th Spec Sess: A/session/ 1948-88 E99 F101 S101; 1st & 9th Emerg Spec Sess: A/session/ 1956-82 E9 F9 S9 – 9 – us U.N. Pubs [324]
GENERAL ASSEMBLY OFFICIAL RECORDS : VERBATIM RECORDS OF THE PLENARY MEETINGS / United Nations – (1st Sess. 3rd Sess.: A/PV. 1946-1949. E/F.87 R.42; 4th Sess. 38th Sess.: A/session/PV. 1949-1983. E.884 F.912 S.958; 1st Spec. Sess. 2nd Spec. Sess.: A/session/PV. 1947-1948. E.6 S.3; 3rd Spec. Sess. 15th Spec. Sess.: A/session/PV. 1961-1986. E.79 F.77 S.75; 1st Emerg. Spec. Sess. 9th Emerg. Spec. Sess.: A/session/PV. 1956-1982. E.33 F.34 S.34; 7th Emerg. Spec. Sess. is not yet available in microfiche; French and Spanish for the 15th sess. is not yet available in microfiche) – 9 – us U.N. Pubs [324]
GENERAL ASSEMBLY PROVISIONAL RECORDS : VERBATIM RECORDS OF MEETINGS / United Nations – 43rd Sess: 1988 A/43/PV1-96 E72; 44th Sess: 1989 A/44/PV1-95 E66; 45th Sess: 1990 A/45/PV1-79 E50 – 9 – us U.N. Pubs [324]
GENERAL BAPTIST MESSENGER – Owensville, IN/Poplar Bluff,MO. 1914-15, 1928-66. Single reels available – 1 – 596.20 – us A.B.H.S. [073]
GENERAL BUDGET 1968-1970 / South Yemen. Southern Yemen Ministry of Finance – 2v. BNE-9628 1 – 9 – ne IDC [350]
GENERAL BUDGET FOR THE FIFTH GOVERNORATE / South Yemen. Ministry of Finance – 3v. 1968-71 – 9 – ne IDC [350]
GENERAL BUDGET, SUPPLEMENTARY AND INDEPENDENT BUDGETS / Syria. Ministry of Finance – 9v. 1957-67. (lacking 1958 59). BNE-9718 1 – 9 – ne IDC [336]
GENERAL BUSINESS AND MINING DIRECTORY – State of California. 1875 – 1r – 1 – $50.00 – D110 – us Library Micro [978]
GENERAL CATALOGUE OF ALL PUBLICATIONS OF THE GOVERNMENT OF BOMBAY (INCLUDING SIND) – Bombay, Govt Print and Stationery. n4 1927; n9 1933; n12 1938; 1958 – us Res Libr [324]
GENERAL CATALOGUE OF ALL PUBLICATIONS OF THE GOVERNMENT OF INDIA AND LOCAL GOVERNMENTS AND ADMINISTRATIONS – Calcutta. n23-37. 1915-1922 – us Res Libr [324]
LE GENERAL CAVAIGNAC DEVANT L'ASSEMBLEE NATIONALE – Paris [1848?] – us Res Libr [324]
A GENERAL COLLECTION OF TREATYS... – Ed 2. London, 1732 – 5mf – 1 – ILM-689/1 – ne IDC [327]
GENERAL CONCHOLOGY, OR A DESCRIPTION OF SHELLS ARRANGED ACCORDING TO THE LINNEAN SYSTEM / Wood, W – Z 880 2. 1835 – 8 – ne IDC [590]
GENERAL CONDITIONS OF EMPLOYMENT IN ISRAEL FOR PROFESSIONALS / Israel. Ministry of Immigrant Absorption – 3rd rev. ed. Dec 1975. 45 p., illus. In cooperation with the Jewish Agency, Department for Aliyah and Absorption – 9 – 2.00 – is I.T.T.I. [331]
GENERAL CONFERENCE MENNONITE CHURCH : HANDBOOK OF INFORMATION – 1951-56 (complete) – 1r – 1 – ATLA 1993-S008 – us A.T.L.A. [240]
General Conference of the Protestant Missionaries of China (1890 : Shangai, China) *see* RECORDS OF THE GENERAL CONFERENCE OF THE PROTESTANT MISSIONARIES OF CHINA
General Conference of the Protestant Missionaries of Japan *see* PROCEEDINGS OF THE GENERAL CONFERENCE OF THE PROTESTANT MISSIONARIES OF JAPAN
General Convention for Religious Liberty *see* MINUTES, 1766-75; PRESBYTERIAN CHURCH IN THE U.S.A., RECORDS, 1706-88
GENERAL CONVENTION OF CONGREGATIONAL MINISTERS AND CHURCHES OF VERMONT : MINUTES / Congregational Ministers and Churches of Vermont – 1855-98 (complete) – 3r – 1 – ATLA S0608 – us A.T.L.A. [240]
THE GENERAL CORPORATION ACT OF NEW JERSEY. / New Jersey. Laws, Statutes, etc – 4th ed., with the amendments of 1902. Trenton? 1902. 240 (i.e. 250)p. LL-962 – 1 – us L of C Photodup [340]
THE GENERAL CORPORATION LAW OF PENNSYLVANIA, APPROVED 29 APRIL, 1874. / Freedley, Angelo Tillinghast – Philadelphia: Johnson, 1882. 141p. LL-75 – 1 – us L of C Photodup [340]
THE GENERAL CORPORATION LAW, THE STOCK CORPORATION LAW, THE TRANSPORTATION CORPORATIONS LAW, AND THE BUSINESS CORPORATION LAW, OF THE STATE OF NEW YORK. / Haviland, Charles Tappan – (New York: Diossy, 1892. 187p. LL-693) – New York: Diossy, 1891. 155p. LL-694 – 1 – us L of C Photodup [340]
GENERAL CORRESPONDENCE BEFORE 1906, ARCHIVES OF CONFERENCES, CONTINENT 1813-1822 / Great Britain. Foreign Office – FO 139 – 14r – 1 – us Ross [941]
GENERAL CORRESPONDENCE BEFORE 1906, CHINA, 1815-1905 / Great Britain. Foreign Office – FO 17. 1-1306. 1815-85 – 568r – 1 – us Ross [941]
GENERAL CORRESPONDENCE BEFORE 1906, CONTINENT, CONFERENCES, 1814-1822 / Great Britain. Foreign Office – FO 92 – 16r – 1 – us Ross [941]
GENERAL CORRESPONDENCE BEFORE 1906, SLAVE TRADE-AFRICA. 1816-1892 / Great Britain. Foreign Office – FO 84. 1-1939. 1816-92 – 1223r – 1 – us Ross [941]
GENERAL CORRESPONDENCE BEFORE 1906, SUPPLEMENT TO GENERAL CORRESPONDENCE 1780-1905 / Great Britain. Foreign Office – FO 97. 120-155. Denmark. The Schleswig-Holstein Question, 1851-64 – 15r – 1 – us Ross [941]
GENERAL CORRESPONDENCE BEFORE 1906, UNITED STATES OF AMERICA / Great Britain. Foreign Office – (Series 2: 1793-1905. FO 5-1334-1351, 1427, 1535, 1556, 1599, 1706-7, 1745-6, 1776-80, 1816-20, 1861-3, 1928-32, 1975, 2044, 2359. The Fenian Brotherhood. 28r) – FO 4. Series 1: 1782-95 – 10r – 1 – us Ross [941]
GENERAL CORRESPONDENCE OF THE ALASKAN TERRITORIAL GOVERNOR / U.S. Department of State – 1909-58. 378 rolls. M939 – 1 – us Nat'l Archives [324]
GENERAL COURT MARTIAL OF GENERAL GEORGE ARMSTRONG CUSTER, 1867 / U.S. Army. Judge Advocate General – 1roll. T1103 – 1 – us Nat'l Archives [324]

GENERAL DECORATIVE AND APPLIED ART – (Including sculpture, arms and armour, clocks, antiquities, tribal art, tapestries and icons. Over 15,000 reproductions) – 171mf – 9 – $930.00 – 0-907006-42-6 – uk Mindata [700]

A GENERAL DICTIONARY OF THE ENGLISH LANGUAGE / Sheridan, Thomas – 1780. 2v. (English Linguistics Series 1500-1800) – 9 – us UMI [420]

GENERAL DIRECTORY OF UPPER CALIFORNIA – West Coast. 1866 – 1r – 1 – $50.00 – D123 – us Library Micro [978]

GENERAL DISCUSSIONS. DISCUSSIONS ON DIELECTRICS AND ON SWELLING AND SHRINKING / Faraday Society. London – 1946 – 1,5,6 – us Princeton Micro [621]

GENERAL DOCUMENTATION, 1969-73 : STUDY PROJECT ON CHRISTIANITY IN APARTHEID SOCIETY – Johannesburg, [19–?] – us Res Libr [240]

THE GENERAL ECCLESIASTICAL CONSTITUTION OF THE AMERICAN CHURCH : ITS HISTORY AND RATIONALE / Perry, William Stevens – New York: T. Whittaker, 1891 – 1mf – us A.T.L.A. [240]

GENERAL ECONOMIC BACKGROUND INFORMATION / Libya – Tripoli. 30 May 1971. BNE-518 1 – 9 – ne IDC [338]

GENERAL ECONOMIC CONDITIONS IN INDONESIA / Schacht, Hjalvar – Report to Indonesian govt. translated. SE 4893 1. 1951? – 9 – ne IDC [338]

THE GENERAL EDUCATION BOARD : SERIES 1: APPROPRIATIONS; SUBSERIES 1: THE EARLY SOUTHERN PROGRAM – (States in coll also listed separately. Printed guide for entire collection. Also sold separately $25.00 S3298.G) – 159r – 1 – $85.00r $13,515.00 coll – S3298 – Co-publ with Rockefeller Archive Centre, North Tarrytown – us Scholarly Res [370]

THE GENERAL EDUCATION BOARD ARCHIVES : SERIES 1: APPROPRIATIONS; SUBSERIES 3: NEW SOUTHERN PROGRAM AND RELATED PROGRAMS, 1931-1961 – (Guide available Dec 1996 and only sold separately unless entire collection is purchased S3350.G $35.00) – 201r – 1 – $17,085.00 – S3350 – Co-publ with the Rockefeller Archive Center, North Tarrytown, NY, A Division of the Rockefeller univ – us Scholarly Res [370]

GENERAL EDUCATION BOARD: THE EARLY SOUTHERN PROGRAM *see*
- ALABAMA
- ARKANSAS
- DISTRICT OF COLUMBIA
- FLORIDA
- GEORGIA
- KENTUCKY
- LOUISIANA
- MINNESOTA
- MISSISSIPPI
- MISSOURI AND NEW MEXICO
- NEW YORK
- NORTH CAROLINA
- OKLAHOMA
- SOUTH CAROLINA
- TENNESSEE
- TEXAS
- VIRGINIA
- WEST VIRGINIA

THE GENERAL EFFECT OF MANDATORY MINIMUM PRISON TERMS / Meierhoefer, Barbara S – Washington: FJC, 1992 – 1mf – 9 – $1.50 – LLMC 95-830 – us L.L.M.C. [340]

GENERAL ELECTRIC FORUM – 1958-63 – 1 – 41.00 – us L of C Photodup [621]

GENERAL ELECTRIC REVIEW – v. 1-48. 1903-1945 – 1,5,6 – us Princeton Micro [621]

THE GENERAL EPISTLE OF ST JAMES / Plumptre, Edward Hayes – Cambridge: University Press, 1878. 1 fiche – 9 – us A.T.L.A. [240]

THE GENERAL EPISTLES : JAMES, PETER, JOHN, AND JUDE. INTRODUCTION, AUTHORIZED VERSION, REVISED VERSION, WITH NOTES, INDEX AND MAP / ed by Bennett, William Henry – (Includes index) – NY: Henry Frowde, 1901 – 1mf – 9 – 0-8370-2268-1 – 1985-0268 – us A.T.L.A. [220]

GENERAL EPISTLES: JAMES, PETER, JOHN AND JUDE / Bennett, William Henry – New York: Henry Frowde, 1901. 1 fiche – 9 – us A.T.L.A. [240]

THE GENERAL EPISTLES OF SS. JAMES, PETER, JOHN, AND JUDE : WITH NOTES CRITICAL AND PRACTICAL / Sadler, Michael Ferrebee – London: George Bell, 1891 – 1mf – 9 – 0-8370-5024-3 – 1985-3024 – us A.T.L.A. [220]

THE GENERAL EPISTLES OF ST JAMES AND ST JUDE / Plummer, Alfred – New York: A.C. Armstrong, 1891. 2 fiches – 9 – us A.T.L.A. [240]

UN GENERAL ESPANOL DEL SIGLO 27, DON JOSE DE GARRO / Arrillaga, Enrique de – Madrid: Razon y Fe, 1935 – 1 – sp Bibl Santa Ana [920]

GENERAL EVENING POST – Dublin. Ireland. -sw. 3 Jan 1782-31 May, 24 Jun-10 Jul, 30 Sep, 30 Oct, 13 Nov-30 Dec 1783. (1 reel) – 1 – uk British Libr Newspaper [072]

LE GENERAL FAIDHERBE / Brunel, Ismael-Matthieu – Paris: C Delagrave, 1890 – 1 – us Res Libr [920]

GENERAL FISHERIES COUNCIL FOR THE MEDITERRANEAN – it F.A.O. [338]

GENERAL FRAME OF THE 5-YEAR PLAN FOR ECONOMIC AND SOCIAL DEVELOPMENT, JUL 1960-JUN 1965 / United Arab Republic. National Planning Committee – Cairo. 1960 – 9 – ne IDC [338]

GENERAL GUIDELINES TO THE ANALYSIS OF AGRICULTURAL PRODUCTION PROJECTS – 1975 – 119p – it F.A.O. [338]

General Headquarters, Southwest Pacific Area *see* CHRONOLOGICAL INDEX AND SUMMARY OF COMMUNICATIONS, 1941-45

A GENERAL HISTORY AND COLLECTION OF VOYAGES AND TRAVELS, ARRANGED IN SYSTEMATIC ORDER : FORMING A COMPLETE HISTORY OF THE ORIGIN AND PROGRESS OF NAVIGATION, DISCOVERY, AND COMMERCE, BY SEA AND LAND, FROM THE EARLIEST AGES TO THE PRESENT TIME / ed by Kerr, Robert – Edinburgh. 18v. 1811-24 – 3r – 1 – us Ross [910]

GENERAL HISTORY OF AFRICA / ed by Ki-Zerbo, J et al – 9 – Co-publication with Heinemann Educational Books (exclusive rights UK & Commonwealth) & University of California Press (exclusive rights N, C, S America) – fr UNESCO [960]

GENERAL HISTORY OF MACON COUNTY / Henry Taylor and Co – Chicago, 1910. Missouri Reel 24. The Cox Library Collection – 5 – us Americana [978]

A GENERAL HISTORY OF MUSIC FROM THE EARLIEST AGES TO THE PRESENT PERIOD / Burney, Charles – P 650. 1782 – 9 – ne IDC [780]

GENERAL HISTORY OF SEWARD COUNTY, NEBRASKA / Waterman, John H – Beaver Crossing, 1914-20. Nebraska Reel 12. (The Cox Library Collection) – 5 – us Americana [978]

GENERAL HISTORY OF SHELBY COUNTY / Henry Taylor and Co – Chicago, 1911. Missouri Reel 32. The Cox Library Collection – 5 – us Americana [978]

A GENERAL HISTORY OF THE BAPTIST DENOMINATION IN AMERICA AND OTHER PARTS OF THE WORLD / Benedict, David – New York: Lewis Colby, 1848 – 3mf – us A.T.L.A. [240]

A GENERAL HISTORY OF THE DICHLAMYDEOUS PLANTS / Don, G – 4v. London. 1831-38 – 8 – ne IDC [580]

A GENERAL HISTORY OF THE SCIENCE AND PRACTICE OF MUSIC / Hawkins, J – 1776. 5v – 9 – us Sibley [780]

A GENERAL HISTORY OF THE SCIENCE AND PRACTICE OF MUSIC / Hawkins, J – P 693. 5 v. 1776 – 9 – ne IDC [780]

GENERAL HISTORY OF THE STATE OF MICHIGAN / Tuttle, Charles R – R.D.S. Tyler and Co., 1873. Michigan Reel 1. (The Cox Library Collection) – 5 – us Americana [978]

GENERAL HOSPITAL PSYCHIATRY – v1-6. 1979-84 – 1,5,6,13 – sz Elsevier [616]

GENERAL IDEA OF THE REVOLUTION IN THE NINETEENTH CENTURY / Proudhon, Pierre-Joseph – 1851. 300p. 1 fiche (24x) – 9 – 1.00f – at Libertarian Micro [320]

GENERAL INDEX OF ALL PUBLICATIONS 1710-1899, OF "ABHANDLUNGEN" 1710-1870, OF "BERICHT" AND "MONATSBERICHT" 1836-58, 1859-73, 1874-81 / Akademie der Wissenschaften. Berlin – 1 – us Schnase [500]

GENERAL INDEX TO BIRTHS / Van Wert County. Ohio. Probate Court – 1867-1908 – 1r – 1 – $32.50r – us Archival [324]

GENERAL INDEX TO BIRTHS/DEATHS / Hardin County, Ohio. Probate Court – 1867-1908 – 1r – 1 – $32.50r – us Archival [920]

GENERAL INDEX TO COMPILED MILITARY SERVICE RECORDS OF REVOLUTIONARY WAR SOLIDERS / U.S. War Department. Collection of Revolutionary War Records – M860 – 58r – 1 – us Nat'l Archives [324]

GENERAL INDEX TO COMPILED SERVICE RECORDS OF VOLUNTEER SOLDIERS WHO SERVED DURING THE WAR WITH SPAIN / U.S. War Department. Adjutant General's Office – M871 – 126r – 1 – us Nat'l Archives [324]

GENERAL INDEX TO DEATHS / Van Wert County. Ohio. Probate Court – 1867-1908 – 1r – 1 – $32.50r – us Archival [324]

GENERAL INDEX TO MORTGAGES / Wyandot County. Ohio. Recorder – 1845-1888 – 2r – 1 – $32.50r – us Archival [324]

GENERAL INDEX TO PENSION FILES, 1861-1934 / U. S. Veterans Administration – 544 rolls. T288 – 5 – us Nat'l Archives [324]

GENERAL INDEX TO THE 43 VOLUMES OF THE REGISTER. / Kentucky State Historical Society – 1903-1945. By Bayless E. Hardin. 1 fiche. F-1055 – 9 – us A.G.L.L. [920]

GENERAL INDEX TO THE JOURNALS OF THE LEGISLATIVE ASSEMBLY OF CANADA : ALPHABETICAL INDEX – 1ST, 2ND AND 3RD PARLIAMENTS / Canada. Parliament. Legislative Assembly – Montreal, 1841-51; Ottawa, 1852-1866 – 1r – 1 – Can$60.00 – cn Can Microfilming [350]

GENERAL INDEX TO THE STATUTES...,PUBLIC AND PRIVATE, PASSED DURING THE YEARS 1869-1919 (BOTH INCLUDED) / Prince Edward Island. Laws, Statutes, etc – Charlottetown: Dillon, 1918. 116p. LL-2331 – 1 – us L of C Photodup [340]

GENERAL INDEXES / Huron County. Ohio. Common Pleas. Civil Division – 1826-1850 – 2r – 1 – $32.50r – us Archival [324]

GENERAL INDEXES / Putnam County. Ohio. Probate Court – 1851-1984 – 2r – 1 – $32.50r – us Archival [324]

GENERAL INDEXES / Wyandot County. Ohio. Common Pleas. Civil Division – 1845-1886 – 1r – 1 – $32.50r – us Archival [324]

GENERAL INSTRUCTIONS FOR MAKING THE METEOROLOGICAL OBSERVATIONS AT THE SENIOR COUNTY GRAMMAR SCHOOLS IN UPPER CANADA / Canada. Departement de l'Instruction Publique pour le Haut-Canada – Toronto: Printed for the Department of Public Instruction for Upper Canada by Lovell and Gibson, 1857. SEM105P337 – 1mf – 9 – Can$2.25 – cn Bibl Nat [550]

GENERAL INSTRUCTIONS IN MUSIC, CONTAINING PRECEPTS AND EXAMPLES IN EVERY BRANCH OF THE SCIENCE / Bemetzrieder, A – CA.1785 – 9 – us Sibley [780]

GENERAL INSURANCE GUIDE – (1979 5,6,9) – 1936 – 1 – us UMI [073]

THE GENERAL INTRODUCTION AND SUPPLEMENT TO THE TWO TRACTS ON CIVIL LIBERTY, THE WAR WITH AMERICA, AND THE FINANCES OF THE KINGDOM / Price, R – London, 2nd ed 1778 – 1mf – 9 – ne IDC [320]

GENERAL INTRODUCTION TO STATISTICAL ACCOUNT OF UPPER CANADA / Gourlay, Robert – London: Published by Simpkin and Marshall...and J.M. Richardson, 1822. SEM105P374 – 6mf – 9 – Can$13.50 – cn Bibl Nat [310]

GENERAL INTRODUCTION TO THE OLD TESTAMENT / Green, William Henry – New York: Charles Scribner, 1899 – 9 – us A.T.L.A. [220]

GENERAL INTRODUCTION TO THE PROPHETIC WRITINGS OF THE OLD TESTAMENT : AND ESPECIALLY TO THE MINOR PROPHETS / Elliott, Charles – New York: Charles Scribner, c1874 – 1mf – 9 – 0-8370-6040-0 – 1986-0040 – us A.T.L.A. [220]

GENERAL INTRODUCTION TO THE STUDY OF HOLY SCRIPTURE / Briggs, Charles Augustus – New York: Scribner's, 1899. 2 fiches – 9 – us A.T.L.A. [240]

GENERAL INTRODUCTION TO THE TECHNIQUES OF INFORMATION AND DOCUMENTATION WORK – 1983 – 360p – 9 – 92-3-101860-4 – fr UNESCO [020]

GENERAL JACKSON'S FINE : AN EXAMINATION INTO THE QUESTION OF MARTIAL LAW / Ingersoll, Charles Jared – Washington, Blair and Rives, 1843. LL-380 – 88p – 1 – us L of C Photodup [340]

GENERAL JAMES WILKINSON'S ORDER BOOK, DECEMBER 31, 1796-MARCH 8, 1808 / U.S. War Department. Adjutant General's Office – 3rolls. M654. Printed guide – 5 – us Nat'l Archives [324]

GENERAL LAND OFFICE CIRCULARS AND GENERAL REGULATIONS / Fisher, CG – Washington: GPO, 1930 – 18mf – 9 – $27.00 – LLMC 85-303 – us L.L.M.C. [340]

THE GENERAL LAW OF PARTNERSHIP AS APPLIED TO COMMERCIAL AND BUSINESS LIABILITIES / Button, Charles P – New York, Hassel, 1881. 16 p. LL-574 – 1 – us L of C Photodup [340]

GENERAL LEGAL FORMS AND PRECEDENTS, FOR ORDINARY USE AND WITH EXPLANATORY CHANGES ADAPTED TO SPECIAL CASES. / Jones, James – Chicago, Myers, 1894. 929 p. LL-1410 – 1 – us L of C Photodup [340]

THE GENERAL MAGAZINE OF ARTS AND SCIENCES, PHILOSOPHICAL, PHILOLOGICAL, MATHEMATICAL, AND MECHANICAL. – London, 1755-65 – 3 – us Readex [500]

GENERAL MEMORANDUM ON THE 1950/51 AND 1951/52 PROGRAMMES / Organization for European Economic Cooperation – Paris. 1950. BD-1735 1 – 9 – ne IDC [940]

GENERAL MEMORANDUM ON THE 1950/51 AND 1951/52 PROGRAMMES. AUSTRIA / Organization for European Economic Cooperation – Paris. Apr 1950. BD-1611 1 – 9 – ne IDC [943]

GENERAL MEMORANDUM ON THE 1950/51 AND 1951/52 PROGRAMMES. DENMARK / Organization for European Economic Cooperation – Paris. Apr 1950 – 9 – ne IDC [948]

GENERAL MEMORANDUM ON THE 1950/51 AND 1951/52 PROGRAMMES. ICELAND / Organization for European Economic Cooperation – Paris. Apr 1950 – 9 – ne IDC [948]

GENERAL MEMORANDUM ON THE 1950/51 AND 1951/52 PROGRAMMES. ITALY / Italy. Organization for European Economic Cooperation – Paris. Apr 1950. BD-1673 1 – 9 – ne IDC [338]

GENERAL MEMORANDUM ON THE 1950/51 AND 1951/52 PROGRAMMES. SWEDEN / Organization for European Economic Cooperation – Paris. Apr 1950. BD-1749 1 – 9 – ne IDC [948]

GENERAL MEMORANDUM ON THE 1950/51 AND 1951/52 PROGRAMMES. UNITED KINGDOM / United Kingdom. Organization for European Economic Cooperation – Paris. 1950. BD-1777 1 – 9 – ne IDC [338]

GENERAL MISSION CONVENTION / Methodist Episcopal Church – Cleveland, 1902.New York: Eaton & Mains, 1903.viii,404p. 1 fiche – 9 – us A.T.L.A. [240]

General Missionary Convention of the Methodist Episcopal Church. 1st *see* THE OPEN DOOR

GENERAL ORDERS AND CIRCULARS OF THE CONFEDERATE WAR DEPARTMENT / Confederate States of America – 1861-1865. 1 roll. M901 – 1 – us Nat'l Archives [324]

GENERAL ORDERS AND CIRCULARS OF THE WAR DEPARTMENT AND HEADQUARTERS OF THE ARMY, 1809-1860 / U.S. Army. Adjutant General's Office – RG 94. M1094. 8 rolls – 1 – us Nat'l Archives [355]

GENERAL ORDERS, GENERAL FIELD ORDERS AND CIRCULARS, 1861-62 / United States Army Dept of Missouri and Mississippi – Washington, DC: National Archives and Records Service, 1977 – us Res Libr [355]

GENERAL ORDERS KEPT BY GENERAL WILLIAM HEATH, MAY 23, 1777-OCT 20, 1778 / U.S. War Department. Collection of Revolutionary War Records – 1roll. T42 – 1 – us Nat'l Archives [324]

General Organization of the Jewish Workers of Palestine (Histadrut) *see* REPORT TO THE 3RD CONVENTION (1927), 4TH CONVENTION (1932), 7TH CONVENTION (1948)

General Organization of the Jewish Workers of Palestine. (Histadrut) *see*
- PROCEEDINGS OF THE 3RD CONVENTION
- RESOLUTIONS OF THE FOUNDATION CONVENTION

GENERAL OT PORAZHENI I V.A. SUKHOMLINOV / Apushkin, Vladimir Aleksandrovich – Leningrad: "Byloe", 1925 – 1 – CSUX89-B7287 – us Hoover Inst Photo [355]

THE GENERAL OUTLINE OF THE FIVE-YEAR ECONOMIC AND SOCIAL DEVELOPMENT PLAN OF IRAQ FOR THE YEARS 1970-74 / Iraq. Planning Board – D-889 1. 1969 – 9 – ne IDC [338]

A GENERAL OUTLINE OF THE INDONESIAN YOUTH MOVEMENTS IN PREWAR TIME / Sutardjo, Nurdjana – SE 3754 1. 1946? – 9 – ne IDC [360]

GENERAL PHARMACOLOGY – (Formerly: Comparative and General Pharmacology) – v1- 1970- – 5,6,9 – us UMI [073]

GENERAL PHOTOGRAPHS OF THE BUREAU OF SHIPS, 1914 – 1,100r – 1 – M1222 – us Nat'l Archives [355]

GENERAL POPULATION CENSUS 1964 / Libya. Ministry of Economy and Trade. Census and Statistical Department – Tripoli. BNE-508 1 – 9 – ne IDC [304]

GENERAL POPULATION CENSUS OF LIBYA, 1954. REPORT AND TABLES / Libya. Economic Social Development (incl. Planning, Literacy) – 1959. BNE-718 1 – 9 – ne IDC [304]

GENERAL PRACTISE OF PHYSICKE / Wirtzung, C – London, 1617 – 25mf – 9 – ne IDC [610]

GENERAL PRICE CURRENT, MERCANTILE REGISTER, AND SHIPPING LIST – (Filmed consecutively with: Hongkong register, jan 3-aug 22 1845) – Hong Kong: John Cairns, jan 3-aug 22, 1845 – us Res Libr [380]

GENERAL PRIMARY CURRICULUM COMMITTEE MEETING, HOUSE OF ASSEMBLY, PORT MORESBY 1971 : RESOLUTIONS AND RECOMMENDATIONS / Papua New Guinea. Department of Education – Konedobu, 1971 – 1mf – 9 – DE-243/1 – ne IDC [370]

THE GENERAL PRINCIPLES OF CONSTITUTIONAL LAW IN THE UNITED STATES / Cooley, Thomas McIntyre – 3rd ed. Boston: Little, Brown, 1898 – 5mf – 9 – $7.50 – LLMC 95-064 – us L.L.M.C. [323]

THE GENERAL PRINCIPLES OF GRAMMAR / Collyer, John – 1735. 141p. (English Linguistics Series 1500-1800) – 9 – us UMI [420]

THE GENERAL PRINCIPLES OF THE LAW OF CONTRACT / Hammon, Louis Lougee – Saint Paul, Keefe-Davidson, 1902. 1233 p. LL-340 – 1 – us L of C Photodup [340]

THE GENERAL PRINCIPLES OF THE LAW OF INSURANCE / Peele, Stanton Canfield – Washington, D.C.: Tibbetts, 1901. 69 1p. LL-1204 – 1 – us L of C Photodup [340]

GENERAL PRINCIPLES OF THE PHILOSOPHY OF NATURE / Stallo, John Bernard – 1848 – 1 – us Res Libr [140]

GENERAL PUBLIC ACTS OF CONGRESS RESPECTING THE SALE AND DISPOSITION OF PUBLIC LANDS : WITH A.G. OPINIONS, 1776-1838 – Washington: Gales & Seaton. 2v. 1838 – 19mf – 9 – $28.50 – LLMC 82-101-1 – us L.L.M.C. [340]

GENERAL PUBLICATIONS / Alabama. Agricultural Experiment Station – 1953-61 – 1,5,6 – us Spaulding [630]

GENERAL PUBLICATIONS / Auburn University. Extension Service – 1941-57 – 1,5,6 – us Spaulding [630]

GENERAL PUBLICATIONS OF THE VENICE BIENNALE WITH LA BIENNALE DI VENEZIA (PVB 1895-1977, PT 5) – (With printed bibliography & subject index) – 157mf – 9 – £620.00 – uk Chadwyck [700]

A GENERAL REGISTER OF H.E.I.C. CIVIL SERVANTS / Prinsep, H T – Bengal Establishment, 1790-1842. Calcutta. 1844. BI-354 2 – 8 – ne IDC [950]

GENERAL REGISTER...1899-1902; CONSTITUTION / Society of Colonial Wars – 1902. Indexed. F-1037 – 17mf – 9 – us A.G.L.L. [060]

General Registry Office *see*
- BOOKS OF ENROLLED CERTIFICATES OF NATURALIZATION, ISSUED 1848-1858, ENROLLED 1850-1888, 1850-1889
- ENROLLED CERTIFICATES OF NATURALIZATION AND MEMORIALS, 1859-1866
- VOLUMES OF ENROLLED LETTERS OF NATURALIZATION, 1865-1903

GENERAL REGULATIONS AND PRIZE LIST / Agricultural and Industrial Exhibition (1878: Truro, Nova Scotia) – 1878. 06917. (Pre-1900 Canadiana) – 9 – cn C.I.H.M. [630]

GENERAL REGULATIONS AND PRIZE LIST / Agricultural and Industrial Exhibition (1880: Kentville, Nova Scotia) – Kentville, N.S.: Western Chronicle Office, 1880. 06915. (Pre-1900 Canadiana) – 9 – cn C.I.H.M. [630]

GENERAL REGULATIONS FOR THE EXECUTION OF THE MORTGAGE LAWS FOR CUBA, PUERTO RICO AND THE PHILIPPINES, 1893 – Washington: GPO, 1899 – 2mf – 9 – $3.00 – LLMC 92-313 – us L.L.M.C. [340]

GENERAL RELATIVITY AND GRAVITATION – v1-26. 1970-94 – 1,5 – $150.00v – us UMI [530]

GENERAL REPORT AND MINUTES OF EVIDENCE / Great Britain. Royal Commission on the State of the Universities of Scotland – 1830. Command No. 310 – 9 – uk Microform Academic [324]

GENERAL REPORT IN REGARD TO THE SHARE AND LOAN CAPITAL, THE TRAFFIC IN PASSENGERS AND GOODS, AND THE WORKING EXPENDITURE OF THE RAILWAY COMPANIES IN THE UNITED KINGDOM 1871-1901 – (Coll title: British Government Publications...1801-1977, Transport) – 1r – 1 (£590.00 transport set of 12mf + 9r) – uk Chadwyck [380]

A GENERAL REPORT OF THE HOSPITAL AT KUM-LE-FAU, IN CANTON / Hobson, B – Canton, 1850 – 1mf – 9 – ne IDC [360]

GENERAL REPORT ON THE COMMERCIAL, INDUSTRIAL, & ECONOMIC SITUATION OF CHINA IN JUNE, 1921 / Fox, Harry Halton – London: His Majesty's Stationery Office, 1921. 64p. illus – 1 – us U.W. Library [950]

GENERAL REPORT ON THE GROUND-WATER INVESTIGATION OF THE AZRAQ BASIN PREPARED FOR THE GOVERNMENT OF JORDAN / Jordan. U.N. Development Programme – 1966. BNE-9815 1 – 9 – ne IDC [627]

GENERAL RULE.. / Apostolic Union of Secular Priests – Office of the Messenger of the Sacred Heart. 1880?. 07062. (Pre-1900 Canadiana) – 9 – cn C.I.H.M. [240]

[GENERAL RULES, 1824] : LARGE MINUTES OF THE PRIMITIVE METHODIST CONNEXION / Primitive Methodist Connexion – Bemersley, 1824 – 1mf – 9 – ne IDC [240]

GENERAL RULES AND ORDERS. / New Brunswick. Canada. Supreme Court – Toronto and Edinburgh: Carswell, 1881. 287, 1p. LL-2381 – 1 – us L of C Photodup [340]

GENERAL RULES FOR THE GOVERNMENT OF THE NEW CONNEXION OF METHODISTS / Methodist New Connexion – Leeds, 1803. 32p – 1mf – 9 – ne IDC [240]

GENERAL RULES OF THE QUEBEC BENEVOLENT SOCIETY, PASSED 7TH AUG 1805 / Quebec Benevolent Society – Quebec: John Neilson, 1805. SEM16P197 – 1r – 5 – Can$9.00 – cn Bibl Nat [360]

GENERAL SEMANTICS BULLETIN – (v.46 .1979 5,6,9) – v.1. 1949 – 1 – us UMI [400]

GENERAL SERIES / Colorado. Agricultural Experiment Station. Fort Collins – nos.1-424. 1936-49 – 1,5,6 – us Spaulding [630]

GENERAL SERIES DOCUMENTS / United Nations – General distribution. 252 fiches – 9 – 490.00; 1.90f – uk UNIMICRO [900]

GENERAL SERIES DOCUMENTS / United Nations. International Law Commission – General distribution – 654mf – 9 – $1200.00; $1.90f – uk UNIMICRO [340]

General State Archives of the Netherlands *see*
- WAR AND DECOLONIZATION IN INDONESIA, 1940-1950

General State Archives, The Hague *see*
- INDONESIA: MEMORIES VAN OVERGAVE
- SOURCES FOR THE CULTURE AND ETHNOLOGY OF NETHERLANDS NEW GUINEA (IRIAN JAYA)

GENERAL STATEMENT OF THE ANNUAL REVENUE AND EXPENDITURE OF THE PROVINCE OF CANADA.. / Canada – Toronto: Printed by Rollo Campbell, 1850. SEM105P434 – 1mf – 9 – Can$2.25 – cn Bibl Nat [336]

THE GENERAL STATUTES OF THE STATE OF MINNESOTA AS AMENDED BY SUBSEQUENT LEGISLATION. / Minnesota. Laws, Statutes, etc – St. Paul: West, 1894. 2v. L.C. set incomplete: v.1, p. 1273-1274 wanting. LL-967 – 1 – us L of C Photodup [340]

THE GENERAL STORE – Salinas, CA. Aug 1979-1980 – 2r – 1 – $100.00 – B02752 – us Library Micro [071]

General Store (Tymochtee, Ohio) *see* LEDGERS

GENERAL STRIKE – London. Issued by the International Libertarian Group of Correspondence. 1 Oct 1903. 3 ft – 1 – uk British Libr Newspaper [072]

GENERAL STUDY OF LIBYA / Libya. Direction de la Documentation – (Doc. Francaise. Notes et Etudes Documentaires, No. 3740-3741). Paris. 1970. Gaudio, A. BNE-526 1 – 9 – ne IDC [956]

GENERAL SUMMATION / International Military Tribunal for the Far East – Tokyo. LL-028 – 1 – us L of C Photodup [340]

A GENERAL SURVEY AND STUDY OF THE MEANS OF COMMUNICATIONS. TRANSPORT IN LIBYA / Libya. Ministry of Planning and Development – (Document DOX-LIB-A 23 (20 Mar 1965). 2 v. BNE-515 1 – 9 – ne IDC [380]

GENERAL TEN-YEAR PLAN OF DEVELOPMENT AND WELFARE, 1947-56 / British Guiana – (Legislative Council Paper no. 8 1947 and 11 1948). 2 v. Georgetown. 1947-48 – 9 – ne IDC [338]

GENERAL THEATRICAL PROGRAMME – (Theatrical Programme). London. -w. Dec 1883-Feb 1886. (2 reels) – 1 – uk British Libr Newspaper [790]

GENERAL THEOLOGICAL LIBRARY : BULLETIN – v1-77. 1908-83 (complete) – 3r – 1 – ATLA S0631 – us A.T.L.A. [073]

GENERAL THEORY OF LAW / Korkunov, N M – N.Y.: The Macmillan Co, 1909 (reprint 1922) – 6mf – 9 – $9.00 – LLMC 95-180 – us L.L.M.C. [340]

GENERAL TOPOGRAPHICAL INDEX TO THE TOWNLANDS AND TOWNS OF IRELAND / Great Britain. Parliament. House of Commons – (Issued with Irish census returns). 1901 – 9 – ie Microforms [920]

GENERAL TRADING COMPANIES : A COMPARATIVE AND HISTORICAL STUDY / ed by Yonekawa, Shin'ichi – 9 – $14.00 – 92-808-0532-0 – ja U.N. Univ [338]

A GENERAL TREATISE ON KANSAS PLEADING AND PRACTICE UNDER THE CODE OF CIVIL PROCEDURE / Taylor, Irwin – Topeka, Kan., Crane, 1888. 662 p. LL-568 – 1 – us L of C Photodup [340]

A GENERAL TREATISE ON THE DISEASES OF INFANTS AND CHILDREN / Pechey, J – M 387. 1697 – 9 – ne IDC [616]

GENERAL UNDERGRADUATE CATALOG 1985-1987 / Kuwait. Kuwait University – Safat – 5mf – 9 – DE-652/1 – ne IDC [370]

A GENERAL VIEW OF ENGLISH PRONUNCIATION – Anon. 1784. 94p. (English Linguistics Series 1500-1800) – 9 – us UMI [420]

A GENERAL VIEW OF THE CRIMINAL LAW OF ENGLAND / Stephen, James Fitzjames – (2nd ed. London: Macmillan, 1890 5mf $7.50 84-807B) – 1st ed. London: Macmillan, 1863 – 6mf – 9 – $9.00 – LLMC 84-807A – us L.L.M.C. [340]

A GENERAL VIEW OF THE HISTORY OF THE ENGLISH BIBLE / Westcott, Brooke Foss – London: Macmillan, 1872.1 fiche – 9 – us A.T.L.A. [240]

A GENERAL VIEW OF THE RISE, PROGRESS, AND CORRUPTIONS OF CHRISTIANITY. / Whately, Richard – (With a sketch of the life of the author and a catalogue of his writings) – New York: William Gowans, 1860 – 1mf – 9 – 0-8370-5763-9 – 1985-3763 – us A.T.L.A. [240]

A GENERAL VIEW OF THE WRITINGS OF LINNAEUS / Pulteney, R – London, 1805 – 11mf – ne IDC [580]

GENERAL WOLFE : A FAVORITE SONG / Smart, Thomas – Covent Garden, [London]: Printed for G Goulding, [ca 1770]. SEM105P909 – 1mf – 9 – Can$2.25 – cn Bibl Nat [780]

[GENERAL WORKS ON WORLD WAR 1 PAMPHLET COLLECTION] – 1915-1955 – 4r – 1 – CSUXAML4757-B – us Hoover Inst Photo [355]

GENERAL Y NATURAL HISTORIA DE LAS INDIAS / Fernandez de Oviedo Valdes, Gonzalo – Sevilla: Juan Cromberger, 1535 – 1 – sp Bibl Santa Ana [950]

GENERAL-ANZEIGER – (Title change: General-Anzeiger/Rote Erde, 3 May 1933; Westfaelische Landeszeitung/Rote Erde, 30 Jan 1934) – Dortmund, Germany. 2 Oct 1889-1907; Apr 1908-Nov 1915; 1916-Jun 1924; Aug 1924-1925; Feb 1926-Dez 1927; Febr 1927-Nov 1930; 1931; 1932 (incomplete); 1933-13 Apr 1945 – 185r – 1 – gw Mikrofilm [072]

GENERAL-ANZEIGER *see*
- GENERALANZEIGER DER STADT WUPPERTAL
- DER PFORZHEIMER BEOBACHTER
- WOECHENTLICHES FRAG- UND KUNDSCHAFFTS-BLATH

GENERALANZEIGER – (Cont by: Luebecker Generalanzeiger, jan 1 1899) – Luebeck, jul 1-sep 30 1890, jan 3 1894-96, jul 1 1897-jun 30 1898, jan 1-jun 30 1899, jul 1 1900-jun 30 1901, 1902-07, jan 1-jun 30 1909, 1910-apr 1 1942 – 186r – 1 – gw Mikrofilm [072]

GENERAL-ANZEIGER – Joliet, IL: [R Zintzch & Co], feb 1896-feb 1897; sep 1917; oct 1917-sep 1937 – 20r – 1 – us Res Libr [071]

GENERALANZEIGER DER STADT WUPPERTAL – (Title changes: General-Anzeiger, 16 Aug 1971; WZ/Westdeutsche Zeitung (General Anzeiger), 16 Oct 1978) – Wuppertal, West Germany. 1992- – 10r per yr – 1 – gw Mikrofilm [072]

GENERAL-ANZEIGER FUER BONN UND UMGEBUNG – (Called: Bonner Nachrichten, aug 16 1944-mar 2 1945) – Bonn, dec 1 1889-mar 2 1945, oct 1 1949- – 1 – Inquire at Mikrofilmarchiv for details – gw Misc Inst [943]

GENERAL-ANZEIGER FUER BONN UND UMGEBUNG – (Title change: Bonner Nachrichten, 16 Aug 1944-2 Mar 1945) – Bonn, West Germany. 1 Oct 1891-21 Feb 1930; 1931-2 Mar 1945; 1992- – 16r per yr – 1 – gw Mikrofilm [072]

GENERALANZEIGER FUER DAS UNTERWESERGEBIET – Bremerhaven-Wesermuende, apr 8, 18, 22, 24-27, 29 1933 – 1 – Inquire at Mikrofilmarchiv for details – gw Misc Inst [072]

GENERAL-ANZEIGER FUER DIE GESAMTEN INTERESSEN DES JUDENTUMS – Berlin, 1902-03, 1906, 1907 (incomplete), 1908-10, 1911 (incomplete) – 4r – 1 – Dist. gw Mikrofilm – gw Misc Inst [072]

GENERALANZEIGER FUER DIE GESAMTEN INTERESSEN DES JUDENTUMS – Berlin. 1902-10. Lacking: 1902; 1905; 1906 (26-52); 1909; 1910 (1-3). – 89mf – 9 – ne IDC [305]

GENERAL-ANZEIGER FUER GROSS-LICHTERFELDE – (Cont by: Buerger-Zeitung fuer Gross-Lichterfelde und Dahlem, jan 20 1919) – Berlin, jul 1913-20 – 1 – Dist. gw Mikrofilm – gw Misc Inst [072]

GENERALANZEIGER FUER KOESLIN UND UMGEBUNG – Koeslin, (Koszalin) Germany. 1891 (incomplete); 1893, Nrn. 152-306 – 1 – gw Mikrofilm [072]

GENERAL-ANZEIGER/ROTE ERDE *see* GENERAL-ANZEIGER

DER GENERAL-BASS IN DER COMPOSITION / Heinichen, J D – Herausgegeben von Johann David Heinichen. 1728 – 9 – us Sibley [780]

GENERAL-BASS IN DREY ACCORDEN / Daube, J F – 1756 – 9 – us Sibley [780]

LA GENERALE – Paris. Imprimerie du Cercle Social. 1791 – 9 – fr Hachette [321]

GENERALE KERCKELYCKE HISTORIE VAN DEN GHEBOORTE ONZES H. IESU CHRISTI TOT HET IAER 1624. H. ROSWEYDUS : KERCKELYCKE HISTORIE VAN NEDER-LANDT / Baronius, C & Spondanus, H – Antwerpen, 1623 – Dfl420.00 – ne Slangenburg [240]

GENERALE LEGENDE DER HEYLIGHEN MET HET LEVEN IESU CHRISTI ENDE MARIE : VERGADERT WT DE H. SCHRIFTURE, OUDE VADERS ENDE REGISTERS DER H KERCKE / Ribadineira, P & Rosweydus, H – 2e Druck. Antwerpen. Tom 1-2. 1629 – Dfl324.00 – ne Slangenburg [240]

DIE GENERALIN : ERZAEHLUNG / Heuschele, Otto – Leipzig: Bong, 1943 – 1r – 1 – us U.W. Library [830]

GENERALIS COLLECTIONIS, OMNIUM OPERUM ILLUSTRISSIMI AC REVERENDISSIMI DOMINI... / Wellens, J – Antwerpen, 1784 – 4mf – 9 – ne IDC [700]

GENERALIS TOTIUS ORDINIS CLERICORUM CANONICORUM HISTORIA / Pennotto, Gabr. – Romae, 1624 – Dfl175.00 – ne Slangenburg [240]

GENERALIS TOTIUS SACRI ORDINIS CLERICORUM CANONICORUM HISTORIA / Pennotto, Gabr. – Romae, 1624 – 50mf – 8 – Dfl175.00 – ne Slangenburg [240]
EL GENERALISIMO TRUJILLO. / Fernandex Mato, Romas – Ciudad Trujillo. 1944 – 1 – us Res Libr [920]
GENERALISIMUS KNIAZ SUVOROV / Petrushevskii, A – Ed. 2. Spb. 1900. BR-10,528 1 – 9 – ne IDC [920]
Generalkommission der Gewerkschaften Deutschlands *see* RECHENSCHAFTSBERICHT
GENERAL-LEITENANT VLADIMIR OSKAROVICH KAPPEL – [Vladivostok]: Izd. Tikho-Okeanskago t.-p. t-va, [1920?] – 1 – CSUX89-B4222 – us Hoover Inst Photo [355]
GENERALMAJOR V. STILLE UND FRIEDRICH DER GROSSE CONTRA LESSING / Fisch, Richard – Berlin: Weidmann, 1885 – 1r – 1 – us U.W. Library [430]
General'nyi shtab Vooruzhennykh Sil SSSR, Glavnoe voenno-nauchnoe upravlenie *see* SBORNIK VOENNO-ISTORICHESKIKH MATERIALOV VELIKOI OTECHESTVENNOI VOINY
General'nyi shtab Vooruzhennykh Sil SSSR, Otdel Upravlenie izucheniia opyta *see* SBORNIK MATERIALOV PO IZUCHENIIU OPYTA VOINY
General'nyi shtab Vooruzhennykh Sil SSSR, Upravlenie izucheniia opyta voiny *see* SBORNIK BOEVYKH DOKUMENTOV'VELIKOI OTECHESTVENNOI VOINY [1947]
GENERAL-POST-OFFICE-ADVERTISER – Dublin, Ireland. 22 July, 26 Oct 1741. 3 ft – 1 – uk British Libr Newspaper [072]
THE GENERAL'S LETTERS, 1885 / Booth, William – London: Salvation Army, 1890. 204p – 1 – us U.W. Library [941]
GENERATION HARMONIQUE, OU TRAITE DE MUSIQUE THEORIQUE ET PRATIQUE / Rameau, Jean-Phillippe – 1737 – 9 – us Sibley [780]
GENERIS ASPARAGI HISTORIA NATURALIS ATQUE MEDICA / Bresler, M – Berlin, [1826] – 1mf – 9 – ne IDC [615]
LA GENESE DES MYTHES / Krappe, Alexander Haggerty – 1938 – 1 – us I.U. Libraries [390]
LA GENESE ET LA REDACTION DE L'EMILE / Jimack, Peter D – (Studies on Voltaire and the eighteenth century, v13) – Oxford. 1960 – 9 – $45.00 – 0-7294-0067-0 – uk Voltaire [440]
GENESEE COUNTY HERALD – Flint. Mich. 1946-1969 – 1 – us UMI [071]
GENESEE DEMOCRAT – Flint. Mich. 1878-1904 – 1 – us UMI [071]
GENESEE FARMER *see* AMERICAN AGRICULTURIST AND THE RURAL NEW YORKER
Genesee Synod. (Pres. Ch. in the U.S.A.) *see* MINUTES, 1821-1870
GENESEE VALLEY FREE PRESS – Belmont. N.Y. 1863-1870; 1879-1880 – 1 – us UMI [071]
GENESEE VALLEY POST – Belmont. N.Y. 1881-1892 – 1 – us UMI [071]
Genesee Valley. Presbytery. (Pres. Ch. in the U.S.A.) *see* MINUTES, 1858-1886
GENESEE WHIG – Flint. Mich. (title varies). 1850-1911 – 1 – us UMI [071]
LA GENESI: CON DISCUSSIONI CRITICHE / Minocchi, Salvatore – Firenze: Bibl. scient.-relig., 1908. 1 fiche – 9 – us A.T.L.A. [240]
DIE GENESIS / Delitzsch, Franz – Leipzig: Doerffling und Franke, 1852 – 1mf – 9 – 0-8370-9374-0 – 1986-3374 – us A.T.L.A. [220]
DIE GENESIS / Dillmann, August – 4. Aufl. Leipzig: S Hirzel, 1882 – 2mf – 9 – 0-8370-9461-5 – 1986-3461 – us A.T.L.A. [220]
GENESIS / Gunkel, Hermann – (Includes index) – 2. verb Aufl. Goettingen: Vandenhoeck und Ruprecht, 1902 – 2mf – 9 – 0-8370-9476-3 – 1986-3476 – us A.T.L.A. [220]
GENESIS / Holzinger, Heinrich – (Includes appendix) – Freiburg i.B.: J C B Mohr, 1898 – 1mf – 9 – 0-8370-3647-X – 1985-1647 – us A.T.L.A. [220]
GENESIS / Mitchell, Hinckley Gilbert – New York: Macmillan, 1909. 1 fiche – 9 – us A.T.L.A. [240]
GENESIS AND GEOLOGY: THE HARMONY OF THE SCRIPTURAL AND GEOLOGICAL RECORDS / Hughes, Nicholas Collin – Chocowinity, NC: N.C. Hughes, 1887. 1 fiche – 9 – us A.T.L.A. [240]
GENESIS AND MODERN SCIENCE / Perce, Warren Raymond – New York: J. Pott, 1897. 362p. illus., plates, diagrs – 1 – us U.W. Library [500]
GENESIS AND MODERN SCIENCE / Perce, Warren Raymond – New York: James Pott, 1897. 1 fiche. 8370-4700-5 – 9 – us A.T.L.A. [240]
GENESIS AND SEMITIC TRADITION / Davis, John D – (Includes bibliographical references) – New York: Charles Scribner, 1894 – 1mf – 9 – 0-8370-6105-9 – 1986-0105 – us A.T.L.A. [220]
GENESIS, CRITICALLY AND EXEGETICALLY EXPOUNDED / Dillmann, August – Edinburgh: T. & T. Clark, 1897. 1 fiche – 9 – us A.T.L.A. [220]
GENESIS DE ESTADO MODERNO EN ESPANA / Sanchez Bella, Ismael – Pamplona. 1956 – 1 – us Res Libr [946]
GENESIS DISCLOSED : BEING THE DISCOVERY OF A STUPENDOUS ERROR WHICH CHANGES THE ENTIRE NATURE OF THE ACCOUNT OF THE CREATION OF MANKIND / Davies, Thomas Alfred – New York: G W Carleton, 1874 – 1mf – 9 – 0-8370-2844-2 – 1985-0844 – us A.T.L.A. [220]
GENESIS I AND MODERN SCIENCE / Warring, Charles Bartlett – New York: Hunt & Eaton, 1892. 1 fiche – 9 – us A.T.L.A. [240]
DIE GENESIS: MIT AUSSERER UNTERSCHEIDUNG DER QUELLENSCHRIFTEN / Kautzsch, E – Freiberg i.B.: J.C.B. Mohr, 1891. 1 fiche – 9 – us A.T.L.A. [220]
THE GENESIS OF AMERICAN ANTI-MISSIONISM / Carroll, BH – 1902 – 1 – 8.26 – us Baptist [240]
THE GENESIS OF AMERICAN ANTI-MISSIONISM / Carroll, BH – Louisville, Ky.: Baptist Book Concern, 1902 – 1mf – us A.T.L.A. [240]
THE GENESIS OF CALIFORNIA'S FIRST CONSTITUTION, 1846-1849 / Rockwell et al – CA, 1895 – 1 – $50.00 – B50525 – us Library Micro [323]
THE GENESIS OF GENESIS: A STUDY OF THE DOCUMENTARY SOURCES / Bacon, Benjamin Wisner – Hartford: Student Pub. Co., 1892. 1 fiche – 9 – us A.T.L.A. [240]
THE GENESIS OF LIFE AND THOUGHT / Musick, Thomas Hubbard – New York: John B. Alden, 1892. 1 fiche.8370-4547-9 – 9 – us A.T.L.A. [240]
GENESIS OF THE FEDERAL JUDICIARY SYSTEM; ADDRESS BEFORE VIRGINIA STATE BAR ASSOCIATION, AUGUST 2, 1904 / Richards, Walter Buck – Richmond: Everett Waddey, 1904. 36p LL-11217 – 1 – us L of C Photodup [340]
GENESIS OF THE HEAVENS AND THE EARTH AND ALL THE HOST OF THEM / Dana, James Dwight – Hartford: Student Publ. Co., 1890. 1 fiche – 9 – us A.T.L.A. [240]
THE GENESIS OF THE HEAVENS AND THE EARTH AND ALL THE HOST OF THEM / Dana, James Dwight – Hartford:Student Publ. Co., 1890 – 1mf – 9 – 0-8370-2821-3 – 1985-0821 – us A.T.L.A. [220]
THE GENESIS OF THE NEW ENGLAND CHURCHES / Bacon, Leonard – New York: Harper, 1874 – 2mf – us A.T.L.A. [240]
THE GENESIS OF THE UNITED STATES / ed by Alexander Brown 1890 – Collected, arranged and Item A. 2v in one. The settlement of North America by the English – 5 – us A.G.L.L. [978]
GENESIS PRINTED IN COLORS / Bissell, Edwin Cone – Hartford: Belknap & Warfield, 1892. 1 fiche – 9 – us A.T.L.A. [220]
Genesius, J *see* DE REBUS CONSTANTINOPOLITANIS LIBRI 4 (CBH30,1)
Genesius, W *see* THESAURUS PHILOLOGICUS CRITICUS LINGUAE HEBRAEAE ET CHALDAEAE V.T.
Genest, J *see* SOME ACCOUNT OF THE ENGLISH STAGE, 1660-1830
Genet, Edmond C *see* PAPERS
THE GENETIC ENGINEER AND BIOTECHNOLOGIST : THE BIOPAPERS JOURNAL – 13v- – 9 – £163.00 – 0959-020X – uk Carfax [575]
GENETIC ENGINEERING NEWS – v1- 1981- Ten times a year – 9 – $250.00 (Free to customers in the Biotech Industry) – us Genetic Eng [575]
A GENETIC HISTORY OF THE NEW ENGLAND THEOLOGY / Foster, Frank Hugh – Chicago: University of Chicago Press, 1907 – 2mf – us A.T.L.A. [240]
GENETIC IMPROVEMENT OF HAIR SHEEP IN THE TROPICS – 1992 – 180p – it F.A.O. [636]
GENETIC THEORY OF REALITY : BEING THE OUTCOME OF GENETIC LOGIC AS ISSUING IN THE AESTHETIC THEORY OF REALITY CALLED PANCALISM; WITH AN EXTENDED GLOSSARY OF TERMS / Baldwin, James Mark – New York: G.P. Putnam, 1915 – 1mf – us A.T.L.A. [160]
GENETICA : NEDERLANDSCH TIJDSCHRIFT VOOR ERFELIJKHEIDS- EN AFSTAMMINGSLEER – 's-Gravenhage, 1919-1941. v1-22 – 168mf – 9 – 7699c/1 – ne IDC [575]
GENETICS : A PERIODICAL RECORD OF INVESTIGATIONS BEARING ON HEREDITY AND VARIATION – New York, 1916-1941. v1-26 – 222mf – 9 – 7706c/1 – ne IDC [575]
GENETICS – v1-102. 1916-82 – 1,5,6 – us Princeton Micro [575]
GENETICS – (v.97-. 1981-. 5,6,9) – v.1-. 1916- – 1 – us UMI [575]
GENETICS ABSTRACTS – 9 – us C.S.A. [575]
DIE GENETISCHE ANLAGE DES CHRISTLICHEN LEBENS / Beck, Johann Tobias; ed by Lindenmeyer, Julius – Guetersloh: Bertelsmann, 1882 – 1mf – us A.T.L.A. [240]
GENETISCHE ENTWICKLUNG DER VORNEHMSTEN GNOSTISCHEN SYSTEME / Neander, August – Berlin: F. Duemmler, 1818 – 1mf – us A.T.L.A. [200]
GENEVA : A MONTHLY REVIEW OF WORLD AFFAIRS – 1930-36. Formerly: League of Nations in Review, Jun 1930-31. Formerly: League of Nations, Mar-May 1930 – 12mf – 9 – $60.00 – us UPA [327]
GENEVA GAZETTE – Geneva, NE. -w. Nov 1895-Oct 1896 scattered issues missing; Dec 1896-Aug 1898; Oct 1898-Jan 1902, scattered issues missing; Aug 1902-Apr 1911 – 1 – us NE Hist [071]
GENEVA PAPERS ON RISK AND INSURANCE – (v.18-. 1981-. 5,6,9) – v.1-. 1976- – 1 – us UMI [336]
GENEVA, PAST AND PRESENT : AN HISTORICAL AND DESCRIPTIVE GUIDE FOR THE USE OF FOREIGN VISITORS IN GENEVA / Doumergue, Emile – Geneva: Atar, [1909?] – 1mf – us A.T.L.A. [949]
Geneva. Presbytery (Pres. Ch. in the U.S.A.) *see* MINUTES
Geneva. Synod (Pres. Ch. in the U.S.A.) *see* MINUTES, 1812-1881
GENEVE PLAGIAIRE, ... / Coton, P – Paris, 1618 – 21mf – 9 – CA-121/1 – ne IDC [240]
GENEVIEVE TAGGARD : COMPLETE WORKS – 3r – 1 – us UMI [920]
DIE GENFAMILIE DER BANDE 3 UND BANDE 3-VERWANDTEN ANIONENAUSTAUSCHPROTEINE : VOLLSTAENDIGE PRIMAERSTRUKTUR DES AE2-PROTEINS UND NACHWEIS DER AE3-GENEXPRESSION IN DER MENSCHLICHEN NIERE / Gehrig, Hans – 1994 – 3mf – 9 – DM98.00 – 3-89349-867-2 – gw Hänsel [574]
Geng, Lizhong *see* A PERSPECTIVE OF SPORT CONSUMER BEHAVIOR IN THE PEOPLE'S REPUBLIC OF CHINA
GENGANGAREN – Vadstena, Sweden. 1844-54 – 1 – sw Kungliga [072]
GENGTIE – Iron and Steel. In Chinese, with English abstracts to the main articles – 9 – 4.00f – cc Microforms [670]
GENGZI JISHI – Historical Records of 1840. Comp. by the Institute of Modern History, Chinese Academy of Social Sciences. 3 fiches. F H89 – 9 – $24.50 – cc Microforms [950]
LE GENIE DE LA LANGUE FRANCOISE / Aisy, J – 1685 – 9 – fr I.C.S. [440]
LA GENIE DE L'ARCHITECTURE OU L'ANALOGIE DE CET ART AVEC NOS SENSATIONS / Le Camus de Mezieres, Nicolas – Paris, 1780. 8 fol., vii, 276p., ill. (Architecture Series) – 9 – fr Hachette [720]
LE GENIE DE VIRGILE / Malfilatre, J C L de – Paris: Maradon, 1810. 4v. 24 fiches. (Literature Collection) – 9 – 59.00 – fr Bibl Nationale [450]
LE GENIE DE VOLTAIRE / Palissot de Montenoy, Charles – Apprecie dans tous ses ouvrages. Volume destine a servir de supplement a toutes les editions de cet illustre ecrivain. Paris. C.-F. Patris. 1806. XI – 9 – fr Hachette [440]
GENII VREMENI – Istoricheskii i politicheskii zhurnal. Spb. 1807-09. Lacking: 1807 (1), 1809 (1). B-1731 2 – 38mf – 8 – ne IDC [947]
Genin, F *see* DES VARIATIONS DU LANGAGE FRANCAIS DEPUIS LE 12E SIECLE
GENIO CONSTITUCIONAL – Porto (Portugal)/Rio de Janeiro, Oct-Dec 1820; 14 Nov 1821 – 1,5,6 – bl Biblioteca [072]
GENIO DE LA ARGENTINA : DEBERES FRENTE A LA CRISIS POLITICO SOCIAL DE NUESTRO PUEBLO / Carulla, Juan Emiliano – Buenos Aires, Distribuidores: R. Medina, [1st ed] 1943 – 1 – CSUXADQ6404-B – us Hoover Inst Photo [320]
EL GENIO LITERARIO DE EXTREMADURA. APUNTES DE LITERATURA REGIONAL / Lopez Prudencio, Jose – Badajoz: Imp. Vicente Rodriguez, 1912 – 1 – sp Bibl Santa Ana [440]
GENITOURINARY MEDICINE – v61-. Feb 1985- – 1,5,6,9 – us UMI [073]
GENIUS – Munich, 1919-21 – 1r + 23 col slides – 1 – £120.00 – uk Chadwyck [700]
THE GENIUS AND MISSION OF METHODISM : EMBRACING WHAT IS PECULIAR IN DOCTRINE, GOVERNMENT, MODES OF WORSHIP, ETC. / Strickland, William Peter – Boston: C.H. Peirce, 1851 – 1mf – us A.T.L.A. [240]
THE GENIUS AND MISSION OF THE PROTESTANT EPISCOPAL CHURCH IN THE UNITED STATES / Colton, Calvin – New York: Stanford & Swords, 1853 – 1mf – us A.T.L.A. [240]
DER GENIUS DER MENSCHHEIT. FRAUENWIRKEN IM DIENSTE DER HUMANITAT. EINE GABE FUR MADCHEN UND FRAUEN / Otto, Louise – Pest: A. Hartleben, 1870 – 1 – us U.W. Library [920]
THE GENIUS OF CHRISTIANITY, OR, THE SPIRIT AND BEAUTY OF THE CHRISTIAN RELIGION / Chateaubriand, Francois-Rene de – Baltimore: John Murray, 1856 – 2mf – us A.T.L.A. [240]
GENIUS OF LIBERTY – Uniontown. Pa. 1805-1859; 1861-1865; 1868-1909 – 1 – us UMI [071]
THE GENIUS OF PROTESTANTISM : A BOOK FOR THE TIMES / Edgar, Robert McCheyne – (Includes bibliographical references and index) – 2nd ed. Edinburgh: Oliphant, Anderson & Ferrier, 1900 – 1mf – 9 – 0-8370-8666-3 – 1986-2666 – us A.T.L.A. [240]
GENIUS OF TEMPERANCE – New York, New York. 1827-1834 – 2r – 1 – $32.50r – us Archival [071]
THE GENJAM DISTRICT MANUAL / Maltby, T J – I-150-6 2. 1882 – 8 – ne IDC [960]
Genkin, *see* ZAKONODATEL'STVO O PROMYSLOVOI KREDITNOI KOOPERATSII
Genkin, Aleksandr Borisovich *see* KROVAVYI OPYT
Genkin, D M *see*
- KHOZRASCHET V PROMKOOPERATSII
- NOVYI ZAKON O PROMYSLOVOI KOOPERATSII 11 MAIA 1927 G. S POSTATEINYMI RAZ"IASNENIIAMI
- SBORNIK POSTANOVLENII O PROMYSLOVOI KOOPERATSII I KUSTARNOI PROMYSHLENNOSTI

Genkin, Iosif Isaevich *see*
- IZ VOSPOMINANI I POLITICHESKOGO KATORZHANINA
- PO TIURMAM I ETAPAM
- SREDI POLITKATORZHAN

Gennadi, G *see*
- LES ECRIVAINS FRANCO-RUSSES. BIBLIOGRAPHIE DES OUVRAGES FRANCAIS PUBLIES PAR DES RUSSES
- LITERATURA RUSSKOI BIBLIOGRAFII
- PRILOZHENIIA K SOCHINENIIAM A.S. PUSHKINA, IZDANNYM A.A. ISAKOVYM
- SPISOK KNIG O RUSSKIKH MONASTYRIAKH I TSERKVAKH

GENNADIUS UND PLETHO : ARISTOTELISMUS UND PLATONISMUS IN DER GRIECHISCHEN KIRCHE: NEBST EINER ABHANDLUNG UEBER DIE BESTREITUNG DES ISLAM IM MITTELALTER / Gass, W – Breslau: A. Goschorsky, 1844 – 1mf – us A.T.L.A. [240]
Gennep, Arnold van *see* LE FOLKLORE
Gennrich, Paul *see* DER KAMPF UM DIE SCHRIFT IN DER DEUTSCH-EVANGELISCHEN KIRCHE DES NEUNZEHNTEN JAHRHUNDERTS
Gennuso, Giuseppo *see* LA QUESTION SICILIANA

GENOA ENTERPRISE – Genoa, NV. 1992 – 2+ r – 1 – $100.00 ($50.00y) – U04844 – us Library Micro [071]
GENOA LEADER-TIMES – Genoa, NE. -w. Oct 1895-Sept 1902, scattered issues missing; Dec 1908 to date – 1 – us NE Hist [071]
GENOA TIMES – Genoa, NE. -w. Jan 1902-Jun 1926 – 1 – us NE Hist [071]
GENOME – (v31 and 32 publ in 1989. Cont: Canadian Journal of Genetics and Cytology at v29 1987) – Ottawa. v29-37. 1987-94 – 9 – Can$37.00y – cn Micromedia [575]
GENOME *see* CANADIAN JOURNAL OF GENETICS AND CYTOLOGY
DER GENOSSENSCHAFTSBAUER – Berlin, Jan 1961-Dec 1964 – 8r – 1 – uk British Libr Newspaper [072]
DER GENOSSENSCHAFTSBAUER – (Cont by: Neue Deutsche Bauernzeitung, nov 4 1960) – Berlin, aug 1955-90 – 49r – 1 – Dist. gw Mikrofilm – gw Misc Inst [072]
DER GENOSSENSCHAFTSBAUER *see* NEUE DEUTSCHE BAUERNZEITUNG
DIE GENOSSIN – Berlin, 1924-27, 1928 (incomplete), 1929-30, 1931 (incomplete), 1932-33 – 2r – 1 – Dist. gw Mikrofilm – gw Misc Inst [072]
Genouy, Oswald *see* VERS LA RELIGION ETERNELLE
Genov, G P *see* IZTOCHNIIAT VAPROS; POLITICHESKA I DIPLOMATICHESKA ISTORIIA
GENQO KENYKU = JOURNAL OF THE LINGUISTIC SOCIETY OF JAPAN / Linguistic Society of Japan – Tokyo. Incomplete. CH405. 1939-1969 – 9 – ne IDC [400]
LE GENRE ALEURITES FOR (EUPHORBIACEES). SYSTEMATIQUE, ANATOMIE-PHARMACOLOGIE / Langeron, M – Paris. 1902. B-157 2 – 8 – ne IDC [580]
GENRES DES MOUCHES DIPTERES REPRESENTES EN 42 PLANCHES, PROJETTEES ET DESSINEES / Schellenberg, J R – Zuerich, 1803. 95p, 42 pls. Z-1606/2 – 8 – ne IDC [590]
LES GENRES LITTERAIRES YAKA, REPUBLIQUE DU ZAIRE / Ifwanga, WP – 9 – F40.00 – fr Ethnologie [490]
GENSEE COUNTY HERALD – Mount Morris. Mich. 1946-1969 – 1 – us UMI [071]
GENTE – 1987-1995 – 2r per y – 5,6 – Sfr588.00 – sz Infoprint [072]
GENTE NOSTRA – Rome, Italy. -w. 1 Jan 1933-1 Dec 1935. 3 reels – 1 – uk British Libr Newspaper [072]
GENTE NUEVA – Montijo, 1920 – 5 – sp Bibl Santa Ana [073]
Gentet, F *see* ETUDES LES QUESTION D'ETAT ET DE CAPACITE...
Gentil, Emile *see* LA CHUTE DE L'EMPIRE DE RABAH
Gentile, Dina *see* THE PERCEPTIONS OF SPORT MANAGEMENT STUDENTS TOWARD THE MARKET ABILITY OF PROFESSIONAL ATHLETES
Gentile, E *see* IL TRIBUNALE DELL'AMMIRAGLIATO E CONSOLATO [1783-1808]
Gentile, Giovanni *see* IL MODERNISMO
Gentili, A *see*
- DE ARMIS ROMANIS...
- DE IURE BELLI, LIBRI III
- DE LEGATIONIBUS LIBRI TRES...
- HISPANICAE ADVOCATIONIS

Gentiluomo, Federico A *see*
- DESAFIO A LA REVOLUCION ARGENTINA
- PERON, EL EJERCITO Y LA IGLESIA

THE GENTLE ART OF MAKING ENEMIES : AS PLEASINGLY EXEMPLIFIED IN MANY INSTANCES, WHEREIN THE SERIOUS ONES OF THIS EARTH, CAREFULLY EXASPERATED, HAVE BEEN PRETTILY SPURRED ON TO UNSEEMLINESS AND INDISCRETION, WHILE OVERCOME BY AN UNDUE SENSE OF RIGHT / Whistler, James Abbott McNeill – London: W. Heinemann, 1890 – 1 roll – 1 – 1-55879-388-7 – uk Libr Preservation [880]
GENTLEMAN DICK OF THE GREYS: AND OTHER POEMS / Cockin, Hereward Kirby – Toronto: C. Robinson, 1889. 00693. (Pre-1900 Canadiana) – 9 – cn C.I.H.M. [810]
A GENTLEMAN OF PEMBROKE COLLEGE, OXON : A LETTER TO THE REVEREND MR. WHITEFIELD,... – London, [1744] – 1mf – 9 – MP-311/1 – ne IDC [240]
GENTLEMAN'S MAGAZINE – London. v. 1-103. 1731-1833; n.s. v. 1-20. 1834-43 – 1 – us Princeton Micro [800]
GENTLEMAN'S MAGAZINE: INDEX – 1731-1818 – 1 – uk Microform Academic [073]
THE GENTLEMAN'S MATHEMATICAL COMPANION, FOR...1798-1827; CONTAINING ANSWERS TO THE LAST YEAR'S ENIGMAS, CHARADES, REBUSES, QUERIES, AND QUESTIONS, ALSO NEW ENIGMAS, CHARADES, REBUSES, QUERIES, AND QUESTIONS – London, 1798-1826? – 3 – us Readex [510]
GENTLEMANS VODE MECUM – Philadelphia, PA., 1827-1836 – 13 – $25.00r – us I.M.R. [071]
THE GENTLEMENS AMUSEMENT / Shaw, R & Carr, B – A Selection of solos, duetts, overtures, arranged as duetts, rondos & romances. Philadelphia: B. Carr 1794-96. MUSIC 123, Item 14 – 1 – us L of C Photodup [780]
THE GENTLEMEN'S BOOK OF ETIQUETTE; AND MANUEL OF POLITENESS. / Hartley, Cecil B – Boston: DeWolfe, Fiske & Co., 1873. 332p – 1 – us U.W. Library [390]
THE GENTLEMEN'S HANDBOOK ON POKER / Florence, William James – New York: G. Routledge, 1892. xi,195p. illus – 1 – us U.W. Library [790]
Gentz, Friedrich von *see* DEUTSCHE MONATSSCHRIFT/NEUE DEUTSCHE MONATSSCHRIFT
Gentz, G *see* DIE KIRCHENGESCHICHTE DER NICEPHORUS CALLISTUS XANTHOPUPOS UND IHRE QUELLEN (T.U.U. 5-98)
THE GENUINENESS AND AUTHORSHIP OF THE PASTORAL EPISTLES / James, J D – (Includes index) – London: Longmans, Groon, 1906 – 1mf – 9 – 0-8370-3763-8 – 1985-1763 – us A.T.L.A. [220]
Genung, George F *see* FOURFOLD STORY: A STUDY OF THE GOSPELS
Genung, George Frederick *see*
- THE FOURFOLD STORY
- THE MAGNA CHARTA OF THE KINGDOM OF GOD

Genung, John Franklin *see*
- ECCLESIASTES
- THE HEBREW LITERATURE OF WISDOM IN THE LIGHT OF TO-DAY
- THE HEBREW LITERATURE OF WISDOM IN THE LIGHT OF TO-DAY; A SYNTHESIS

THE GENUS HALIMEDA / Barton, E S – Leyden, 1901. 32p, 4pls. Siboga-Expeditie, Monogr. 60, Livr. 2 – 8 – ne IDC [580]
GEO. BATTEN AND CO.'S DIRECTORY OF THE RELIGIOUS PRESS OF THE UNITED STATES : A LIST OF NEARLY ALL RELIGIOUS PERIODICALS WITH THEIR DENOMINATION OR CLASS, FREQUENCY OF ISSUE, NUMBER OF PAGES, SIZE OF PAGES, WHETER... – New York: Geo. Batten 1897 – 1mf – 9 – us A.T.L.A. [240]
GEOCHEMISTRY INTERNATIONAL – (v21-. 1984-. 5,6,9) – v1-. 1964- – 1 – us UMI [073]
GEOCHIMICA ET COSMOCHIMICA ACTA – v1-1950- – 5,6,9 – us UMI [550]
GEODERMA – v1-34. 1967-84 – 1,5,6,13 – sz Elsevier [550]
GEODESY, MAPPING AND PHOTOGRAMMETRY – (v1-3 1959-61 $50.00 set. v4-15 1962-73 $20.00y. v16 1974 $30.00. v17 1975 $30.00. v18 1976 $35.00. v19 1977 $50.00. v20 1978 $40.00) – v1-3, 1959-61 bimonthly as Geodesy and Cartography; v4-14, 1962-72 bimonthly as Geodesy and Aerophotography. Quarterly under present title. In English – 1,5,6 – us A.G.U. [550]
GEOEXPLORATION – v1-22. 1963-84 – 1,5,6,13 – sz Elsevier [550]
GEOFFREY DE MANDEVILLE / Round, J H – H 1156 2. 1892 – 8 – ne IDC [910]
Geoffrey Gaimar *see* LESTORIE DES ENGLES SOLUM LA TRANSLACION MAISTRE GEFFREI GAIMAR (RS91)
Geoffrion, Leo D *see* LANGUAGE, READING AND DEAFNESS
Geoffrion, Louis Philippe *see* REGLEMENT ANNOTE DE L'ASSEMBLEE LEGISLATIVE CONTENANT LES TEXTES FRANCAIS ET ANGLAIS DU REGLEMENT..
Geoffroy de Villeneuve, Rene C *see* L'AFRIQUE, OU HISTOIRE, MOEURS, USAGES ET COUTUMES DES AFRICAINS
Geoffroy, E L *see* HISTOIRE ABREGEE DES INSECTES QUI SE TROUVENT AUX ENVIRONS DE PARIS...
Geoffroy, Julien Louis *see* MANUEL DRAMATIQUE: A L'USAGE DES AUTEURS ET DES ACTEURS, ET NECESSAIRE AUX GENS DU MONDE QUI AIMENT LES IDEES TOUTES TROUVEES, ET LES JUGEMENS TOUT FAITS
Geoffroy Saint-Hilaire, Etienne *see* PHILOSOPHIE ANATOMIQUE DES ORGANES RESPIRATOIRES SOUS LE RAPPORT DE LA DETERMINATION ET DE L'IDENTITE DE LEURS PIECES OSSEUSES
Geoffroy Saint-Hilaire, Isidore *see* VIE, TRAVAUX ET DOCTRINE SCIENTIFIQUE D'ETIENNE GEOFFROY SAINT-HILAIRE
GEOFORUM – v1- 1970- – 5,6,9 – us UMI [550]
GEOGNOSIA. COMPONENTES DE LA CORTEZA TERRESTRE / Gil Calvo, Joaquin – Villafranca de los Barros (Badajoz): Graficas Crasferv, 1964 – 1 – sp Bibl Santa Ana [240]
GEOGRAFI INDONESIA / Djenen – SE-5511 1. v. 2 only. 1966 – 9 – ne IDC [950]
GEOGRAFIA : GUIA Y PLAN PARA SU ESTUDIO, CON APLICACION ESPECIAL A LA ECONOMIA POLITICA, TOMO 1 / Beltran y Rozpide, Ricardo – Madrid: Razon y Fe, 1926 – 1 – sp Bibl Santa Ana [330]
GEOGRAFIA ANTIGUA / Ramirez de Arellano, Rafael – Madrid: Fortanet, 1915. B.R.A.H. lxvi/pp. 110-115 – 1 – sp Bibl Santa Ana [900]
GEOGRAFIA DE BOLIVIA Y PERU / Sievers, Wilhelm – (Tambien de Ecuador, Colombia y Venezuela) – Madrid: Razon y Fe, 1931 – 1 – sp Bibl Santa Ana [972]
GEOGRAFIA DE ESPANA... / Martin Echevarria, L; ed by Bayle, Constantino – Madrid: Razon y Fe, 1928 – 9 – sp Bibl Santa Ana [910]
GEOGRAFIA DE LAS ISLAS BRITANICAS. BARCELONA, 1929 / Moscheles, J – Madrid: Razon y Fe, 1930 – 1 – sp Bibl Santa Ana [941]
GEOGRAFIA DE SUIZA. BARCELONA, 1929 / Walser, H – Madrid: Razon y Fe, 1930 – 1 – sp Bibl Santa Ana [946]
GEOGRAFIA DE...BADAJOZ / Franco y Lozano, Francisco – 1894 – 9 – 1.50f – sp Bibl Santa Ana [910]
GEOGRAFIA DE...BADAJOZ / Munoz de Rivera, Antonio – 1894 – 9 – 1.50f – sp Bibl Santa Ana [910]
GEOGRAFIA DEL JAPON. BARCELONA, 1929 / L Ehmann, FV Paul – Madrid: Razon y Fe, 1930 – 1 – sp Bibl Santa Ana [950]
GEOGRAFIA ECONOMICA / Schmidt, Walter; ed by Bayle, Constantino – Madrid: Razon y Fe, 1928 – 9 – sp Bibl Santa Ana [330]
GEOGRAFIA ECONOMICO-SOCIAL ARGENTINA : SOMOS UNA NACION? / Hojvat, Carlos – Buenos Aires: El Ateneo, [1947] – 1 – CSUXAHZ5786-B – us Hoover Inst Photo [330]
GEOGRAFIA POLITICA. BARCELONA, 1929 / Dix, Arthur – Madrid: Razon y Fe, 1930 – 1 – sp Bibl Santa Ana [320]
GEOGRAFIA...DISTINTA IN 12 LIBRI : NE' QUALI; OLTRA L'ESPLICATIONE DI MOLTI LUOGHI DI TOLOMEO, E DELLA BUSSOLA, E DELL' AGUGLIA / Sanuto, L – Vinegia, 1588 – 10mf – 9 – H-8411/1 – ne IDC [956]
GEOGRAFICA DESCRIPCION / Burgoa, Francisco de – Mexico: Talleres graficos de la nacion, 1934. Includes reproduction of t.p. of original edition. Sequel to the author's Palestra historial – 1 – us U.W. Library [910]
GEOGRAFICA DESCRIPCION DE LA PARTE SEPTENTRIONAL DEL POLO ARTICO DE LA AMERICA Y NUEVA IGLESIA DE LAS INDIAS OCCIDENTALES...2 VOL. MEXICO, 1934 / Burgoa, Francisco de – Madrid: Razon y Fe, 1936 – 1 – sp Bibl Santa Ana [970]
GEOGRAFICHESKIE IZVESTIIA, VYDAVAEMYE OT RUSSKOGO GEOGRAFICHESKOGO OBSHCHESTVA – v. 1-17. Spb. 1848-50. Available: 1848-49, v. 1-7. B-1732 2 – 8 – ne IDC [910]
GEOGRAFICHESKII LEKSIKON / ed by Bashkatovym, A – M., 1830 – 4mf – 9 – R-8388/2 – ne IDC [947]
GEOGRAFICHESKII LEKSIKON ROSSIISKOGO GOSUDARSTVA / Polunin, F – M., 1773 – 9mf – 9 – R-8401/2 – ne IDC [947]
GEOGRAFICHESKII SLOVAR' ZAPADNOSLAVIANSKIKH I IUGOSLAVIANSKIKH ZEMEL'I PRINADLEZHSHCHIKH STRAN / Golovatskii, I A – Vil'na, 1884 – 8mf – 9 – R-8389/2 – ne IDC [947]
GEOGRAFICHESKIIA KARTY ROSSII XV-XIX STOLETTII – Spb. 1892. BR-7105 2 – 8 – ne IDC [910]
GEOGRAFICHESKO-STATISTICHESKII SLOVAR' AMURSKOI PRIMORSKOI OBLASTEI / Kirillov, A – Blagoveshchensk, 1894 – 10mf – 9 – R-8394/2 – ne IDC [304]
GEOGRAFICHESKO-STATISTICHESKII SLOVAR' ROSSIISKOI IMPERII / Semenov, P P – Spb., 1863-1885. 5 vols – 115mf – 9 – 1279/2 – ne IDC [304]
GEOGRAPHIC CUTTERS / U.S. Library of Congress – (Lists of geographic cutters for U.S. cities, counties, and regions) – 24mf – 9 – $50.00 – us L of C Cataloging [020]
GEOGRAPHIC INDEX TO CORRESPONDENCE OF THE MILITARY INTELLIGENCE DIVISION OF THE WAR DEPARTMENT GENERAL STAFF, 1917-1941 – 17r – 1 – M1474 – us Nat'l Archives [355]
A GEOGRAPHIC STUDY OF THE EARLY HISTORY OF THE ALGONQUIAN INDIANS / Birket-Smith, K – BN 127 2. 1918 – 8 – ne IDC [304]
A GEOGRAPHICAL, AGRICULTURAL AND MINERALOGICAL SKETCH – Quebec: Printed at "Le Canadien" Office, 1865 – 1mf – 9 – Can$2.25 – cn Bibl Nat [971]
A GEOGRAPHICAL DESCRIPTION OF SOUTHAMPTON ISLAND AND NOTES ON THE ESKIMO / Comer, G – BN 174 2. 1910 – 8 – ne IDC [910]
GEOGRAPHICAL DICTIONARY OR GAZETTEER OF THE AUSTRALIAN COLONIES 1848 – 6mf – 9 – A$30.00 – at State Libr Vic [980]
GEOGRAPHICAL GUIDE TO FLORAS OF THE WORLD / Blake, S F & Atwood, A C – Pt. I: Africa, Australia, North America, South America and islands of the Atlantic, Pacific, and Indian Oceans. (U.S. Dept. of Agriculture, Misc. Publ. 401). Washington. 1942. B-5024 2 – 8 – ne IDC [580]
A GEOGRAPHICAL HANDBOOK OF ALL THE KNOWN FERNS, WITH TABLES TO SHOW THEIR DISTRIBUTION / Lyell, K M – London, 1870. 225 pp. B-7219 prSF 16,00 IDC 9 – ne IDC [580]
GEOGRAPHICAL HANDBOOK OF THE COUNTY OF GREY / Campbell, N W – Hanover Ont.: J. Mitchell, 1895. 00393. (Pre-1900 Canadiana) – 9 – cn C.I.H.M. [971]
GEOGRAPHICAL HANDBOOK: PALESTINE AND TRANSJORDAN / U. S. Naval Intelligence – 1943 – 9 – $24.00 – us I.R.C. [910]
A GEOGRAPHICAL HISTORIE OF AFRICA : BEFORE WHICH OUT OF THE BEST ANCIENT AND MODERN WRITERS IS PREFIXED A GENERAL DESCRIPTION OF AFRICA, AND ALSO A PARTICULAR TREATISE OF ALL THE MAINE LANDS AND ISLES UNDESCRIBED / Leo, John – (In Arabicke and Italian. Filmed with: Blyden, E W Christianity, Islam and the Negro race) – Londini: G Bishop, 1600 – us Res Libr [960]
GEOGRAPHICAL INFORMATION SYSTEM TO PLAN FOR AQUACULTURE : A F.A.O.-UNEP-GRID STUDY IN COSTA RICA – 1987 – 56p – it F.A.O. [639]
GEOGRAPHICAL INFORMATION SYSTEMS AND REMOTE SENSING IN INLAND FISHERIES AND AQUACULTURE – 1991 – 285p – it F.A.O. [639]
GEOGRAPHICAL JOURNAL – v1- 1893- 1; v135- 5,6; v141- 9 – us UMI [910]
THE GEOGRAPHICAL MAGAZINE – London, 1935-93. Continued annually – 1,14 – £3,250.00 – uk World [910]
GEOGRAPHICAL REVIEW – v1- 1916- 1; v58- 5,6; v65- 9 – us UMI [910]
GEOGRAPHICAL REVIEW – v. 1-30. 1916-1940 – 1 – us Princeton Micro [910]
GEOGRAPHICAL REVIEW *see* BULLETIN
GEOGRAPHICAL REVIEW OF INDIA / Calcutta Geographical Society – v. 1-26. Calcutta. 1936-64. – 108mf – 8 – ne IDC [910]
A GEOGRAPHICAL STUDY OF HUMAN SETTLEMENT IN THE EASTERN PROVINCE OF THE GOLD COAST COLONY WEST OF THE VOLTA DELTA / Boateng, Ernest Amano – Oxford, 1954 – us Res Libr [960]
GEOGRAPHICAL SYSTEMS : AN INTERNATIONAL JOURNAL OF GEOGRAPHICAL INFORMATION, ANALYSIS, THEORY AND DECISION / ed by Fischer, Manfred et al – 9,5,1 – us Gordon [900]
LA GEOGRAPHIE – Paris. v1-32; 62-72. 1900-18-19; 1934-39 – 1 – 207.00 – us L of C Photodup [910]
GEOGRAPHIE A L'USAGE DES ECOLIERS DU PETIT SEMINAIRE DE QUEBEC – Quebec: J Neilson, 1804. SEM16P142 – 1r – 5 – Can$9.00 – cn Bibl Nat [910]

GEOGRAPHIE DE LA PALESTINE : TOM.1-2 (ETB) / Abel, F M – Paris. Tom. 1-2. 1933-1938 – Dfl77.00 – ne Slangenburg [220]
DIE GEOGRAPHIE DER FARNE / Christ, H – Jena. 1910. B-7173 1 – 9 – ne IDC [580]
GEOGRAPHIE MYTHIQUE ET TRADITIONELLE DE L'ILE DE MARE, ILES LOYAUTE, NOUVELLE-CALEDONIE / Dubois, M J – 9 – F190.00 – fr Ethnologie [910]
GEOGRAPHISCHE BERICHTE *see* ZEITSCHRIFT FUER GEOPHYSIK
Geographische Gesellschaft. Munich *see* MITTEILUNGEN
GEOGRAPHISCHE UND ETHNOGRAPHISCHE STUDIEN ZUM 3. UND 4. BUCHE DER KOENIGE / Doeller, Johannes – Wien: Mayer. 1904. 1 fiche – 9 – us A.T.L.A. [220]
GEOGRAPHISCHE ZEITSCHRIFT / ed by Hettner, Alfred – (From 1937 ed by Schmitthenner, Heinrich) – Leipzig, 1895-1944 – 380mf – 9 – subsc: DM2,100.00 diazo DM2,500.00 silver – gw Olms [910]
DIE GEOGRAPHISCHEN UND VOELKERKUNDLICHEN QUELLEN UND ANSCHAUUNGEN IN HERDERS "IDEEN ZUR GESCHICHTE DER MENSCHHEIT" / Grundmann, Johannes – (Includes bibliographical references) – Berlin: Weidmann, 1900 – 1r – 1 – us U.W. Library [100]
GEOGRAPHISCHES REGISTER ZU "KATALOG DER SALO COHN'SCHEN SCHENKUNGEN", WIEN, 1911, 1914 / Wachstein, B – Wien, 1934 – 1mf – ne IDC [943]
GEOGRAPHISCH-HISTORISCHES WOCHENBLATT ZUR ERLAEUTERUNG DER BEGEBENHEITEN DES TAGES – Bremen, 1798-1801 – 1r – 1 – Inquire at Mikrofilmarchiv for details – gw Misc Inst [900]
A GEOGRAPHY AND ATLAS OF PROTESTANT MISSIONS. VOLUME I, GEOGRAPHY : THEIR ENVIRONMENT, FORCES, DISTRIBUTION, METHODS, PROBLEMS, RESULTS AND PROSPECTS AT THE OPENING OF THE TWENTIETH CENTURY / Beach, Harlan P – New York: Student Volunteer Movement for Foreign Missions, 1901 – 2mf – us A.T.L.A. [240]
GEOGRAPHY OF HUDSON'S BAY – Hakluyt Society – 7 – uk Microform Academic [910]
THE GEOGRAPHY OF HUDSON'S BAY / Coats, W – BN 165 2. 1852 – 8 – ne IDC [910]
THE GEOGRAPHY OF INDONESIA / Indonesia. Kedutaan Besar. U.S – SE-6728 1. 1967 – 9 – ne IDC [910]
GEOJOURNAL – (1984-. 5,6,9) – 1977- – 1 – us UMI [910]
GEOKHIMICHESKIE ISSLEDOVANIIA – Moskva: IMGRE, [1970-] v2. 1972 – us Res Libr [947]
GEOKHIMIYA TRANSLATIONS – (1984-. 5,6,9) – 1964- – 1 – us UMI [073]
GEOLOGI / Katili, John A – Djakarta, Departemen Urusan Research Nasional. 196-. xliii,855p. illus.SEM-10171-10186/1 – 9 – ne IDC [550]
GEOLOGIA Y METALURGIA – 1978- – 1 – us UMI [550]
THE GEOLOGICAL EVIDENCES OF THE ANTIQUITY OF MAN : WITH REMARKS ON THEORIES OF THE ORIGIN OF SPECIES BY VARIATION / Lyell, Charles – London: J. Murray, 1863 – 1 roll – 1 – 1-55879-959-1 – uk Libr Preservation [575]
THE GEOLOGICAL HISTORY OF LAKE SUPERIOR / Bell, Robert – Toronto: Murray, 1899. 03554. (Pre-1900 Canadiana) – 9 – cn C.I.H.M. [550]
GEOLOGICAL MAGAZINE – v1- 1864- 1; v108- 5,6; v114- 9 – us UMI [550]
THE GEOLOGICAL RECORD FOR...: AN ACCOUNT OF WORKS ON GEOLOGY, MINERALOGY AND PALAEONTOLOGY PUBLISHED DURING THE YEARS 1874-84 – London, 1875-89 – 3 – us Readex [550]
Geological Society of America *see*
- BULLETIN
- GEOLOGY OF THE GRAND CANYON
Geological Society of London *see*
- PROCEEDINGS OF THE GEOLOGICAL SOCIETY OF LONDON
- QUARTERLY JOURNAL
Geological Society of South Africa *see* TRANSACTIONS
GEOLOGICAL SURVEY AND MARINE CORPS SURVEYS AND MAPS OF THE DOMINICAN REPUBLIC, 1919-23 / U. S. Geological Survey – 6rolls. T282 – 1 – us Nat'l Archives [550]
GEOLOGICAL SURVEY OF CANADA – Montreal: printed by John Lovell, 1863. SEM105P1684 – 1mf – 9 – Can$2.25 – cn Bibl Nat [550]
GEOLOGICAL SURVEY OF VICTORIA. OBSERVATIONS ON NEW VEGETABLE FOSSILS OF THE AURIFEROUS DRIFTS / Mueller, Ferdinand Jakob Heinrich von – n.p. 1874. B-8055 1 – 9 – ne IDC [580]
GEOLOGIE EN MIJNBOUW – The Hague. v1-46. 1923-67 – 5,9 – Dfl1,720.00; Dfl140.00v – ne Swets [550]
GEOLOGISCHE UND PALAEONTOLOGISCHE ABHANDLUNGEN *see* PALAEONTOLOGISCHE ABHANDLUNGEN
GEOLOGISCHES ZENTRALBLATT – Leipzig, 1901-1931. v1-45 – 583mf – 9 – 2530/2 – ne IDC [550]
THE GEOLOGIST: A POPULAR MONTHLY MAGAZINE OF GEOLOGY – v. 1-7. 1858-64 – 3 – us Readex [550]
GEOLOGY – (1981-. 1,5,6,9) – v1-. 1973- – 1 – us UMI [550]
GEOLOGY – 56 serials – 9 – ne IDC [550]
GEOLOGY AND BAUXITE DEPOSITS OF THE CENTRAL RIAU ISLANDS, INDONESIA / Johnson, Robert F – Bandung, 1963.54p. maps. SEM-13098-13099/1 – 9 – ne IDC [550]
GEOLOGY AND WATER RESOURCES OF PALESTINE / Palestine. Department of Land Settlement and Water Commissioner – (G. S. Blake and M. J. Goldschmidt). 3 v. Illus. Appendix. Rainfall in Palestine and Trans-Jordan. (R. Feige and E. Rosenau). Jerusalem. 1947. BJ-28-114 1 – 9 – ne IDC [550]
THE GEOLOGY OF RUSSIA IN EUROPE AND THE URAL MOUNTAINS / Murchison, R I de & Verneuil, E de & Keyserling, A – 2549 2. 2 v. 1845 – 9$31.00 – ne IDC [550]
THE GEOLOGY OF THE ALBUQUERQUE SHEET / Herrick, C L & Johnson, D W – G-165 2. 1900 – 8 – ne IDC [550]
GEOLOGY OF THE GRAND CANYON : AN ANNOTATED BIBLIOGRAPHY, ALONG WITH AN ANNOTATED CATALOGUE OF GRAND CANYON TYPE FOSSILS, VOL 4 / Geological Society of America; ed by Spamer, Earle E – 1990 – 9 – $6.50 – 0-8137-6020-8 – us Geological Soc [550]
GEOLOGY OF THE GRAND CANYON : A GUIDE AND INDEX TO PUBLISHED GRAPHIC AND TABULAR DATA (EXCLUDING PALEONTOLOGY) / Geological Society of America; ed by Spamer, Earle E – 1990 – 9 – $23.75 – 0-8137-6021-6 – us Geological Soc [550]
GEOLOGY OF THE PACIFIC OCEAN / ed by Shilo, N A – 9,5,1 – us Harwood [550]
GEOLOGY OF TUNGSTEN / ed by Beus, Alexei A – 1986 – 284p – 9 – 92-3-102195-8 – fr UNESCO [550]
GEOLOGY REVIEWS / ed by Semikhatov, M A & Sokolov, B S – 9,5,1 – us Harwood [550]
GEOMETRIAE DEDICATA – (1984-. 5,6,9) – 1972- – 1 – us UMI [073]
GEOMETRIE, TOISE ET LE TABLEAU STEREOMETRIQUE: LECTURE FAITE...DU QUEBEC 20 MARS 1872 / Baillairge, Charles – Quebec: C. Darveau, 1873. 00055. (Pre-1900 Canadiana) – 9 – cn C.I.H.M. [510]
GEOMETRISCHE ZUORDNUNG SEQUENTIELLER ROENTGENBILDER MIT HILFE DREHUNGS-UND MASSTABSINVARIANTER BILDMUSTER-MERKMALE / Harendt, Norbert – 1995 – 2mf – 9 – DM80.00 – 3-8267-2204-3 – gw Hänsel [530]
GEOMETRY, ANALOGUES AND ARCHITECTURE – Pattee, University Park, PA. n.d – 111p 5mf – 9 – $0.50f – us Lawrence Pub [720]
GEOMETRY, MENSURATION AND THE STEREOMETRICAL TABLEAU: LECTURE READ...20TH MARCH 1872 / Baillairge, Charles – Quebec: C. Darveau, 1873. 00809. (Pre-1900 Canadiana) – 9 – cn C.I.H.M. [510]
GEOMICROBIOLOGY JOURNAL – v. 1-. 1978- – 1,5,6,9 – us UMI [576]
GEOPHYSICAL ABSTRACTS – NOS. 1-299. 1929-1971 – 1,5,6 – us Princeton Micro [530]
GEOPHYSICAL ABSTRACTS INDEXES – (Cumulative). Years: 1929-1970 – 1,5,6 – us Princeton Micro [530]
GEOPHYSICAL AND ASTROPHYSICAL FLUID DYNAMICS / ed by Soward, A M et al – 1970- – 1,5,9 – us Gordon [550]
GEOPHYSICAL JOURNAL / ed by Chekunov, A V – 1982 – 1,5,9 – us Gordon [550]
GEOPHYSICAL MEMOIRS – London. v1-14. 1912-63 – 5,9 – Dfl700.00; Dfl50.00v – ne Swets [530]
GEOPHYSICAL RESEARCH LETTERS – (v1-3 1974-76 $25.00y 1,5,6,9,13. v4 1977 $25.00 1,5,6,13 $35.00 9. v5 1978 $30.00 1,5,6,13 $40.00 9. v6 1979 $35.00 1,5,6,1,3 $50.00 9. v7 1980 $35.00 1,5,6,13 $65.00 9. v8 1981 $35.00 1,5,6,13 $105.00 9. v9 1982 $70.00 1,5,6,13 $145.00 9 v19. 1992 $480.00. v20 1993 $498.00. v21 $590.00 10. v22 1995 $680.00) – v1- 1974-. Semi-monthly since 1992 – us A.G.U. [550]
GEOPHYSICAL SURVEYS – (v7-. 1984-. 5,6,9) – v1-. Sept 1972- – 1 – us UMI [550]
GEOPHYSICS – 1-22. 1936-57 – 2 – 116.50 – us UMI [550]
GEOPHYSICS – (v30- 1965- 5,6. v35- 1970-9) – v1- 1936- – 1 – us UMI [550]
GEOPOLITICA IMPERIALISTA Y LA NUEVA ARGENTINA / Cattaneo, Atilio E – Buenos Aires: [s.n.], 1948 – 1 – CSUXADM8349-B – us Hoover Inst Photo [320]
GEOPOLITIEK ASIA TIMOER RAJA; KOETIPAN PIDATO / Bekki, A – Djakarta, Djawa Shimbun Sha, 2604. 48p. maps – 24mf – 9 – ne IDC [320]
GEO-POLITIK INDONESIA; POLITIK BOEMI INDONESIA / Chairul Basri – SE-11,777 1. 1946? – 9 – ne IDC [320]
GEORG : EINE DORFGESCHICHTE AUS DEM RIES / Meyr, Melchior – Bayreuth: Gauverlag Bayreuth, 1944 – 1r – 1 – us U.W. Library [390]
GEORG BUECHNER : EINE BIOGRAPHISCHE ERZAEHLUNG / Bauer, Franz – Berlin: Neues Leben, c1949 – 1 – us U.W. Library [830]
GEORG BUECHNER IN SELBSTZEUGNISSEN UND BILDDOKUMENTEN / Johann, Ernst – (Includes bibliographical references) – Hamburg: Rowohlt, 1958 – 1 – us U.W. Library [920]
GEORG BUECHNER UND DER DANDYSMUS / Gunkel, Richard – (Includes bibliographical references and index) – Utrecht: Kemink, 1953 – 1 – us U.W. Library [430]
GEORG BUECHNERS AESTHETISCHE ANSCHAUUNGEN / Nahke, Heinz – Dresden: Verlag der Kunst, 1955 – 1 – us U.W. Library [430]
GEORG ENACH = JUERG JENATCH : IZ EPOKI BOR BY SHVEITSARSKOGO NARODA ZA NEZAVISIMOST / Meyer, Conrad Ferdinand – Petrograd: Tipografiia im. N Bukharina, 1923 – 1 – us U.W. Library [430]
GEORG FRIDERICH HAENDELS LEBENSBESCHREIBUNG / Mainwaring, J – 1761 – 9 – us Sibley [780]
GEORG FRIEDRICH HAENDELS LEBENSBESCHREIBUNG, NEBST EINEM VERZEICHNISSE SEINER AUSUEBUNGSWERKE UND DEREN BEURTEILUNG... / Mattheson, J – Hamburg, 1761 – 2mf – ne IDC [780]
Georg, Graf *see*
- CATALOGUE DE MANUSCRITS ARABES CHRETIENS CONSERVES AU CAIRE
- GESCHICHTE DER CHRISTLICHEN ARABISCHEN LITERATUR
Georg, Manfred *see* GRABBES DOPPELTES GESICHT
GEORG RUDOLF WECKHERLIN : THE EMBODIMENT OF A TRANSITIONAL STAGE IN GERMAN METRICS / Schaffer, Aaron – (Includes bibliographical references) – Baltimore: The Johns Hopkins Press, 1918 – 1 – us U.W. Library [430]
GEORG RUDOLF WECKHERLIN : VERSUCH EINER PHYSIOGNOMISCHEN STILANALYSE / Gaitanides, Johannes – (Includes bibliographical references) – [S.l.: s.n.], 1936 – 1r – 1 – us U.W. Library [430]
GEORG SCHWARTZERDT, DER BRUDER MELANCHTHONS UND SCHULTHEISS ZU BRETTEN : FESTSCHRIFT ZUR FEIER DES 25JAEHRIGEN BESTEHENS DES VEREINS FUER REFORMATIONSGESCHICHTE / Mueller, Nikolaus – Leipzig: Verein fuer Reformationsgeschichte; 25. Jahrg., Schrift 96/97) – 1mf – us A.T.L.A. [240]
GEORG TRAKL / Jaspersen, Ursula – (Includes bibliographical references) – Hamburg: Hansischer Gildenverlag, 1947 – 1r – 1 – us U.W. Library [430]
GEORG WILHELM FRIEDRICH HEGEL PAMPHLET COLLECTION – 1967 – 1 – CSUXAMJ4537-B – us Hoover Inst Photo [190]
GEORG WITZEL, EIN ALTKATHOLIK DES 16. JAHRHUNDERTS / Schmidt, G L – Wien: W. Braumueller, 1876 – 1mf – us A.T.L.A. [240]
THE GEORGE A. MYERS PAPERS / Myers, George A – (With printed guide) – 8r – 1 – $680.00 – D3169 – us Scholarly Res [320]
GEORGE A. SMATHERS, U.S. SENATOR FROM FLORIDA 1951-1969 – 4mf – 9 – $20.00 – us Scholarly Res [320]
THE GEORGE ADVERTISER – George, South Africa. 1 Dec 1864-28 Dec 1870. 3 reels – 1, 16 diazo available at reduced price – sa SA Libr [072]
GEORGE AND KNYSNA HERALD – (Cont as: The South Western Herald, 1971-) – George, South Africa. 21 Dec 1881-23 Dec 1975 – 55r – 1 – sa SA Libr [072]
GEORGE BANCROFT PAPERS / Bancroft, George – 7r – 1 – $515.00 – us UMI [976]
THE GEORGE BRINTON MCCLELLAN PAPERS – 82r – 1 – $2,870.00 – Dist. us Scholarly Res – us L of C Photodup [355]
GEORGE BROWN, D.D., PIONEER-MISSIONARY AND EXPLORER : AN AUTOBIOGRAPHY: A NARRATIVE OF FORTY-EIGHT YEARS' RESIDENCE AND TRAVEL IN SAMOA, NEW BRITAIN, NEW IRELAND, NEW GUINEA, AND THE SOLOMON ISLANDS / Brown, George – London: Hodder and Stoughton, 1908 – 2mf – us A.T.L.A. [240]
GEORGE BUCHANAN / Wallace, Robert & Smith, Campbell – Edinburgh: Oliphant, Anderson and Ferrier, [1899?] – 1mf – us A.T.L.A. [240]
GEORGE BUCHANAN, HUMANIST AND REFORMER : A BIOGRAPHY / Brown, Peter Hume – Edinburgh: D. Douglas, 1890 – 1mf – us A.T.L.A. [240]
GEORGE BUCHANAN, HUMANIST AND REFORMER.. / Brown, Peter Hume – Edinburgh: D. Douglas, 1890. xvii,1 leaf,388p – 1 – us U.W. Library [920]
George, C *see* CHRONICA DEL ESFORCADO PRINCIPE Y CAPITAN IORGE CASTRIOTO REY DE EPIRO, O ALBANIA
GEORGE CANTERBURY'S WILL / Wood, Ellen – British Fiction Archive: Unit 1 – 9 – uk Bell [830]
THE GEORGE CHALMERS COLLECTION – 8r – 1 – $280.00 – Dist. us Scholarly Res – us L of C Photodup [975]
GEORGE COUNTY TIMES – Lucedale. Miss. 1915-1924; 1936- – 1 – us UMI [071]
George, CS *see* BUDDHIST SANSKRIT MANUSCRIPTS
GEORGE DIOCESAN MAGAZINE – (Missing some pgs) – Durban, 1937-49 – 1r – 1 – ATLA S0700 – us A.T.L.A. [073]
GEORGE EASTMAN HOUSE NEWSLETTERS – Rochester, NY. 1979-1993 – 6r – 1 – $300.00 – R04152 – us Library Micro [770]
GEORGE ELIOT / Blind, Mathilde – Boston: Little, Brown, 1904 – 1 roll – 1 – 1-55879-680-0 – uk Libr Preservation [420]
GEORGE ELIOT / Thomson, Clara Linklater – London: K. Paul, Trench, Trbner & Co., [1901] – 1 roll – 1 – 1-55879-708-4 – uk Libr Preservation [420]
George Fisher and Co *see* BIOGRAPHICAL DIRECTORY OF THE VOTERS AND TAXPAYERS OF KENDALL COUNTY, ILLINOIS
GEORGE FOX / Hodgkin, Thomas – London: Methuen, 1896 – 1mf – us A.T.L.A. [240]
THE GEORGE GORDON MEADE COLLECTION, 1793-1896 – (With Guide) – ca 13r – 1 – ca $1,105.00 – S3360 – Co-publ with the Historical Society of Pennsylvania. Available Spring, 1997 – us Scholarly Res [975]
George, H B *see* HISTORICAL EVIDENCE
GEORGE H.C. MACGREGOR, M. A., A BIOGRAPHY / Macgregor, Duncan Campbell – 1901 – 1 – us A.T.L.A. [920]
George, Henry *see*
- THE LABOUR QUESTION
- A PERPLEXED PHILOSOPHER
- PROTECTION OR FREE TRADE
GEORGE HUBBARD PEPPER PAPERS, 1895-1918 / Pepper, George Hubbard – (With printed guide) – ca 8r – 1 – $750.00 – us Ross [930]
George, James *see* THOUGHTS ON HIGH THEMES: BEING A COLLECTION OF SERMONS FROM THE MSS. OF THE LATE REV. JAMES GEORGE

George, Jody et al *see* HANDBOOK ON JURY USE IN THE FEDERAL COURTS

GEORGE MASON UNIVERSITY CIVIL RIGHTS LAW JOURNAL – v1-5. 1990-95 – 9 – $59.00 set – us Hein [340]

GEORGE MEREDITH : SOME CHARACTERISTICS. WITH A BIBLIOGRAPHY BY JOHN LANE / Le Gallienne, Richard – London, New York: The Bodley head, 1900 – 1 roll – 1 – 1-55879-789-0 – uk Libr Preservation [420]

GEORGE MEREDITH : SOME EARLY APPRECIATIONS / Forman, Maurice Buxton – London: Chapman & Hall, Ltd, 1909 – 1 roll – 1 – 1-55879-531-6 – uk Libr Preservation [420]

GEORGE MUELLER OF BRISTOL AND HIS WITNESS TO A PRAYER-HEARING GOD / Pierson, Arthur Tappan – New York: Baker and Taylor, 1899. 462p.2 fiches – 9 – us A.T.L.A. [240]

George Munro Grant *see* FRENCH CANADIAN LIFE AND CHARACTER: WITH HISTORICAL AND DESCRIPTIVE SKETCHES OF THE SCENERY AND LIFE IN QUEBEC, MONTREAL, OTTAWA, AND SURROUNDING COUNTRY

THE GEORGE R SIMS COLLECTION OF PLAYSCRIPTS – (With printed index) – 106mf – 9 – $266.00 – 1-869934-34-2 – uk Emmett [790]

GEORGE RIPLEY / Frothingham, Octavius Brooks – Boston: Houghton, Mifflin, c1882. (American men of letters) – 1mf – us A.T.L.A. [240]

GEORGE S. FRARY DIARY *see* FRARY, GEORGE S., DIARY, MS 3079

George, Stefan *see* DEUTSCHE DICHTUNG

GEORGE TAMES : PROFESSIONAL PHOTOGRAPHER WHO SPECIALIZED IN CAPITOL HILL – 3mf – 9 – $15.00 – us Scholarly Res [320]

GEORGE W. CRILE PAPERS *see* CRILE, GEORGE W., PAPERS, MS 2806

GEORGE WASHINGTON CARVER – 1 – us Ross [975]

GEORGE WASHINGTON JOURNAL OF INTERNATIONAL LAW AND ECONOMICS – (v1-18 1966-84 on reel $230.00. v19-27 1985-94 on mf $194.00. Title varies: v1-2 1966-68 as Studies in Law and Economic Development. v3-5 1968 -71 as Journal of Law and Economic Development. v6-15 1971-81 as Journal of International Law and Economics) – v1-27. 1966-94 – 5,6,9 – $424.00 set – us Hein [340]

GEORGE WASHINGTON LAW REVIEW – (v1-53 1932-85 on reel or mf $1,040.00. v54-62 1985-94 on mf $256.00) – v1-62. 1932-94 – 5,6,9 – $1,296.00 set – us Hein [340]

GEORGE WASHINGTON PAPERS – 124r – 1 – $4,340.00 – Dist. us Scholarly Res – us L of C Photodup [975]

George Washington University. Department of Law *see* EXAMINATION QUESTIONS GIVEN IN THE LAW SCHOOL OF COLUMBIAN UNIVERSITY

GEORGE WHITEFIELD : A BIOGRAPHY, WITH SPECIAL REFERENCE TO HIS LABORS IN AMERICA / Belcher, Joseph – New York: American Tract Society, [1857?] – 2mf – us A.T.L.A. [240]

GEORGES BIDAULT PAMPHLET COLLECTION – 1945 – 1 – CSUXANQ4923-B – us Hoover Inst Photo [944]

GEORGES CLEMENCEAU PAMPHLET COLLECTION – 1918-1921 – 1 – CSUXANQ4897-B – us Hoover Inst Photo [944]

GEORGE'S CREEK BAPTIST CHURCH. PICKENS COUNTY. SOUTH CAROLINA : CHURCH RECORDS – 1859-1909, 1916, 1941-58, 1965-69 – 1 – $17.82 – us Baptist [240]

Georges, Karl August *see* FRIEDRICH MELCHIOR GRIMM ALS KRITIKER DER ZEITGENOESSISCHEN LITERATUR IN SEINER "CORRESPONDANCE LITTERAIRE" (1753-1770)

GEORGES POMPIDOU PAMPHLET COLLECTION – 1970-1974 – 1 – CSUXANQ5618-B – us Hoover Inst Photo [944]

Georges-Andre, Soeur *see* BIO-BIBLIOGRAPHIE ANALYTIQUE, 1941-1957, DE MONSIEUR L'ABBE PIERRE GRAVEL, CURE DE BOISCHATEL

GEORGETOWN 1639-1905 – (Mf 1-6: Births 1639-1888 A-Y. Mf 6-8: Marriage 1836-88 A-Y. Mf 8-13: Paupers & Accounts 1841-1915. Mf 14-18: Tax Assessments 1863-65. Mf 18-20: Rebellion Record 1861-65. Mf 21-22: Birth Index 1825-97. Mf 22-24: Birth Index 1898-1996. Mf 25-28: Groom Index 1836-97. Mf 28-30: Marriage Index 1898-1996. Mf 31-33: Death Index 1836-1996. Mf 34-35,44: Publishments 1838-1907. Mf 36: Births 1825-51. Mf 37: Deaths 1836-49, 1859. Mf 37: Marriages 1836-49+. Mf 38-39: Births 1837-70. Mf 39: Marriages 1844-51; Deaths 1844-58. Mf 40-41: Births 1870-1905. Mf 42-44: Marriages 1852-97. Mf 45: Marriages 1898-1905. Mf 46-50: Deaths 1860-94. Mf 51-53: Deaths 1895-1909) – (mf ed 1998) – 53mf – 9 – 0-87623-395-7 – us Holbrook [920]

GEORGETOWN 1779-1849 – (Mf 1T: Births 1780-1851; Marriage 1779; Deaths 1838-49. Mf 2T: Intentions 1838-49; Marriages 1836-49. Mf 3T. Births 1837-49; Marriages 1843-49; Deaths 1844-49) – (mf ed 1996) – 3mf – 9 – 0-87623-252-7 – us Holbrook [920]

GEORGETOWN BAPTIST CHURCH. GEORGETOWN COUNTY. SOUTH CAROLINA : CHURCH RECORDS – 1909-21, 1953-72 – 1 – 17.87 – us Baptist [240]

GEORGETOWN BAPTIST CHURCH. GEORGETOWN, GEORGIA : CHURCH RECORDS – 1843-1964 – 1 reel – 1 – $8.46 – us Baptist [240]

Georgetown College *see* HISTORICAL CATALOG AND HISTORY

Georgetown College. Georgetown, Ky *see* CATALOG

Georgetown County. South Carolina. Church of the Messiah (Episcopal) *see* RECORDS

THE GEORGETOWN COURIER – Georgetown, [i.e. Washington] DC: J D McGill, 1865-76 – 1 – us Res Libr [071]

GEORGETOWN FIRST BAPTIST CHURCH. GEORGETOWN, SOUTH CAROLINA : CHURCH RECORDS – 1805-21 – 1 – 5.00 – us Baptist [240]

GEORGETOWN GAZETTE – Georgetown, CA. 1880-1924; 1933-35 – 10r – 1 BC02267 – $500.00 – us Library Micro [071]

GEORGETOWN IMMIGRATION LAW JOURNAL – v1-9. 1985-95 – 9 – $197.00 set – us Hein [340]

GEORGETOWN INTERNATIONAL ENVIRONMENTAL LAW REVIEW – v1-7. 1988-95 – 9 – $115.00 set – us Hein [340]

GEORGETOWN JOURNAL OF LEGAL ETHICS – v1-8. 1987-95 – 9 – $188.00 set – us Hein [340]

GEORGETOWN JOURNAL ON FIGHTING POVERTY – v1-2. 1993-95 – 9 – $32.00 set – us Hein [360]

GEORGETOWN LAW JOURNAL – v1-84. 1912-96 – 1,5,6,9 – $2,160.00 – us Hein [073]

GEORGETOWN LAW JOURNAL – (v7 1918/19 was never published. Add vols as copyright expires) – v1-8. 1912/13-1919/20 – 14mf – $21.00 – LLMC 95-105 – us L.L.M.C. [073]

GEORGETOWN NEWS – Georgetown, CA. 1854-56 – 1r – 1 – $50.00 – C02268 – us Library Micro [071]

GEORGI DIMITROV PAMPHLET COLLECTION – 1946-1947 – 1 – CSUXANL7456-B – us Hoover Inst Photo [949]

Georgi, I G *see*
- BEMERKUNGEN EINER REISE IM RUSSISCHEN REICH IM JAHRE 1772
- BESCHREIBUNG ALLER NATIONEN DES RUSSISCHEN REICHES
- OPISANIE ROSSIISKO-IMPERATORSKOGO STOLICHNOGO GORODA SANKTPETERBURGA I DOSTOPAMIATNOSTEI V OKRESTNOSTIAKHONOGO

GEORGIA – 28r – 1 – $2,240.00 – us Scholarly Res [370]

GEORGIA : CODE OF GEORGIA ANNOTATED – Norcross: The Harrison Co, 1936-Mar 1996 update – 9 – $3,420.00 set – us Hein [340]

GEORGIA : SESSION LAWS OF AMERICAN STATES AND TERRITORIES – 1787-1995 – 9 – $3,579.00 set – us Hein [340]

Georgia *see*
- THE COLONIAL RECORDS OF THE STATE OF GEORGIA
- THE CONFEDERATE RECORDS OF THE STATE OF GEORGIA
- GAULT'S DECISIONS
- GEORGIA APPELLATE REPORTS
- GEORGIA'S OFFICIAL REGISTER
- GUIDE TO PUBLIC VITAL STATISTICS RECORDS IN GEORGIA
- REPORTS AND OPINIONS (A-G)
- REPORTS, POST-NRS
- REPORTS, PRE-NRS
- THE REVOLUTIONARY RECORDS OF THE STATE OF GEORGIA
- SUPERIOR COURT DECISIONS

THE GEORGIA 'AG ENGINEER' / Georgia. University. College of Agriculture – 1930-69 – 1,5 – us Spaulding [630]

Georgia. Agricultural Experiment Station. Athens *see*
- AG-RESEARCH BRIEFS
- BULLETIN
- CIRCULAR
- FIELD CROPS VARIETY TRIALS
- GEORGIA AGRICULTURAL RESEARCH
- INFORMATION LEAFLET
- LEAFLET
- MIMEOGRAPH SERIES
- MIMEOGRAPHED SERIES
- REPORT
- REPORT "SERVING GEORGIA THROUGH RESEARCH"
- RESEARCH NEWS
- RESEARCH REPORT
- TECHNICAL BULLETIN

GEORGIA AGRICULTURAL RESEARCH / Georgia. Agricultural Experiment Station. Athens – v. 1-11. 1959-69 – 1,5,6 – us Spaulding [630]

GEORGIA AGRICULTURAL RESEARCH / University of Georgia. Agricultural Experiment Station – v11,no3-v22,no4.1070 82. 11 fiches – 9 – us Spaulding [630]

GEORGIA ANALYTICAL REPOSITORY – Ed. by Henry Holcombe. 1802-03 – 1 – 10.29 – us Baptist [240]

GEORGIA ANALYTICAL REPOSITORY – Savannah. 1802-03 – 1 – 15.50 – us A.B.H.S. [073]

GEORGIA APPELLATE REPORTS /, Georgia – (No Pre-NRS vols. Updates planned as copyright ends) – v1-24. 1907-20 – 37mf (1:42) 153mf (1:24) – 9 – $396.00 – LLMC 84-130 – us L.L.M.C. [340]

GEORGIA APPELLATE REPORTS *see*
- GAULT'S DECISIONS
- SUPERIOR COURT DECISIONS

GEORGIA ATTORNEY GENERAL REPORTS AND OPINIONS – (6 1878-1881, 1885-1979 $245.00. 9 1980-1994 + tables and indexes $250.00) – 1878-1994 + tables and indexes – 6,9 – $505.00set – us Hein [340]

GEORGIA BAPTIST – Augusta/Atlanta.General Missionary Baptist Convention of Georgia. 1898-1900, 1902, 1918, 1927-31, 1936-49. Single reels available – 1 – 130.20 – us A.B.H.S. [073]

GEORGIA BAPTIST – (Vols 1-3; Pub.No 6525) – Vidalia, Georgia: 1905-1907, incomplete – 1 reel – 1 – $12.88 – us Baptist [240]

GEORGIA BAPTIST ASSOCIATION : WOMAN'S MISSIONARY UNION SCRAPBOOK AND HISTORIES / Davison, Annie – (Also includes church histories, biographies, and an historical table, 1890-1936) – 1 reel – 1 – $13.12 – us Baptist [240]

Georgia Baptist Associations *see* HISTORICAL MATERIALS

GEORGIA BAPTIST CONVENTION BOARD MINUTES – 1816-64. 598p – 1 – us Baptist [240]

GEORGIA BAPTISTS: HISTORICAL & BIOGRAPHICAL / Campbell, J H – 1874. 8 fiches.F-0092 – 9 – us A.G.L.L. [920]

GEORGIA BAR ASSOCIATION ANNUAL REPORTS – (Lacking: 1959) – 1884-1962 – 301mf – 9 – $451.00 – LLMC 84-469 – us L.L.M.C. [340]

GEORGIA BAR JOURNAL *see* GEORGIA STATE BAR JOURNAL

GEORGIA BAR JOURNAL (MACON) – (Superseded by: Georgia State Bar Journal) – v1-26. 1938-64 (all publ) – 9 – $292.00 set – us Hein [340]

GEORGIA BAR JOURNAL (NS.) – v1. 1995-96 – 9 – us Hein [340]

THE GEORGIA BATTALION IN THE TEXAS REVOLUTION: A CRITICAL STUDY / Scarborough, Jewel Davis – 1960. Reprinted from The Southwestern Historical Quarterly, v63, Apr 1960, no.4. 1 fiche. F-0638 – 9 – us A.G.L.L. [920]

Georgia. Black Baptist Associations *see* MINUTES

GEORGIA: CENSUS – (Mortality Schedules, 1850. Includes index.T655-0007. Mortality Schedules, 1860. Includes index.T655-0008. Mortality Schedules, 1870. Includes index.T655-0009. Mortality Schedules, 1880. Appling-Franklin Co. T655-0010. Mortality Schedules, 1880. Fulton-Pulaski Co. T655-0011. Mortality Schedules, 1880. Putnam-Worth Co. T655-0012) – 1 – us A.G.L.L. [920]

Georgia. Coastal Plain Experiment Station. Tifton *see*
- BULLETIN
- CIRCULAR
- MIMEOGRAPH PAPER
- REPORT
- TECHNICAL MIMEOGRAPH PAPER

GEORGIA DECISIONS / Georgia. Supreme Court – (A Pre-NRS title) – pts1-2. 1842-1843 (all publ) – 3mf – 9 – $4.50 – LLMC 94-003 – us L.L.M.C. [340]

Georgia. Experiment Station *see* RESEARCH BULLETIN. V.1-71. 42 FICHES

Georgia. Experiment Station. Athens *see* TECHNICAL BULLETIN

Georgia. Experiment Station. Experiment *see*
- BULLETIN
- CIRCULAR
- MIMEO SERIES
- MISCELLANEOUS PAPERS
- PRESS BULLETIN
- REPORT
- TECHNICAL BULLETIN

THE GEORGIA FORM BOOK. / Silman, James B – Atlanta: Harrison, 1882. 396p. LL-127 – 1 – us L of C Photodup [340]

GEORGIA GAZETTE – Savannah. Ga. 1763-1770 – 1,3 – us Readex [071]

GEORGIA GAZETTE, 1763-1770 – (Complete run from 7 Feb 1763 – May 23 1770) – Massachusetts Historical Society – 2r – 1 – $150.00 – us UMI [071]

THE GEORGIA GENEALOGICAL MAGAZINE – Nos. 1-24, 1961-67. F-1019/F-1024 – 9 – us A.G.L.L. [920]

THE GEORGIA GENEALOGICAL SOCIETY QUARTERLY – v1,2,4, 1964, 1965, 1967/68. F-0940/F-0942 – 9 – us A.G.L.L. [920]

GEORGIA HISTORICAL QUARTERLY – v1-1917- 1; v55- 5,6; v60- 9 – us UMI [970]

GEORGIA HISTORICAL QUARTERLY – v. 11-56. 1927-1972 – 1,5,6 – us Princeton Micro [073]

Georgia Historical Society *see* COLLECTIONS

GEORGIA JOURNAL OF INTERNATIONAL AND COMPARATIVE LAW – (v4- 1974- 5,6 v5-1975- 9) – v1- 1970- – 1 – us UMI [340]

THE GEORGIA JURIST – v1 no 1-3. 1938 (all publ) – 1mf – 9 – $1.50 – LLMC 84-470 – us L.L.M.C. [073]

THE GEORGIA LAW REPORTER – v1. 1885-86 (all publ) – 3mf – 9 – $13.50 – LLMC 84-472 – us L.L.M.C. [073]

GEORGIA LAW REVIEW – v1 no 1-3. 1927-28 – 1mf – 9 – $1.50 – LLMC 84-471 – us L.L.M.C. [073]

GEORGIA LAW REVIEW – v1-29. 1966-95 – 1,5,6 – $720.00 – us Hein [073]

GEORGIA LAWYER (MACON) – v1-2. 1930-32 (all publ) – 9 – $12.00 set – us Hein [340]

Georgia. New Sunbury Baptist Association. Savannah Extension Board *see* RECORD BOOK, 1935-49

GEORGIA PENSION LIST OF ALL WARS FROM THE REVOLUTION DOWN TO 1883 – Comp. by Lucy Kate McGhee. Indexed. 2 fiches. F-0131 – 9 – us A.G.L.L. [920]

GEORGIA PIONEERS GENEALOGICAL MAGAZINE – v5, 1968. 1 fiche. F-0136 – 9 – us A.G.L.L. [920]

Georgia. Presbytery (Cum. Pres. Ch.) *see* MINUTES, 1880-1899

GEORGIA REPORTER – v.1-2. 1968-69. Superseded by yGeorgia Social Science Journal – 1 – us UMI [073]

GEORGIA REVIEW – v1- 1947- 1; v25- 5,6; v30- 9 – us UMI [978]

GEORGIA SOCIAL SCIENCE JOURNAL – (v.11-. 1980 5,6,9) – v.2-. 1970- – 1 – us UMI [073]

Georgia. State Bar Association *see* PROCEEDINGS 1884-1962

GEORGIA STATE BAR JOURNAL – (Supersedes: Georgia Bar Journal) – v1-31. 1964-95 – 9 – $290.00 set – us Hein [340]

GEORGIA STATE BAR JOURNAL *see* GEORGIA BAR JOURNAL (MACON)

Georgia. Supreme Court *see*
- DUDLEY'S REPORTS
- GEORGIA DECISIONS
- GEORGIA SUPREME COURT REPORTS
- ROBERT M. CHARLTON'S REPORTS
- THOMAS T.U.P. CHARLTON'S REPORTS

GEORGIA SUPREME COURT REPORTS / Georgia. Supreme Court – (Pre-NRS: v1-22 1846-86 168mf $252.00. Updates not poss before year 2006) – v1-149. 1846-1920 – 1411mf – 9 – $2,116.00 – LLMC 82-982 – us L.L.M.C. [340]

GEORGIA SUPREME COURT REPORTS *see*
- DUDLEY'S REPORTS
- GEORGIA DECISIONS
- ROBERT M. CHARLTON'S REPORTS
- THOMAS T.U.P. CHARLTON'S REPORTS

GEORGIA TREND – v1-. 1985- – 1,5,6,9 – us UMI [330]

Georgia. University *see* PHELPS-STOKES FELLOWSHIP FUND

Georgia. University. Agricultural Extension Service *see*
- BULLETIN
- CIRCULAR
- FARM ECONOMIC BRIEFS
- GEORGIA'S AGRICULTURE: MANAGEMENT AND MARKETING
- LEAFLET
- REPORT
- SERVICE BULLETIN
- VETERINARY NEWSLETTER

Georgia. University. College of Agriculture *see*
- THE GEORGIA 'AG ENGINEER'
- REPORT OF THE CONGRESS DISTRICT AGRICULTURAL SCHOOL OF GEORGIA
- RESEARCH AND INVE ACT. ANNUAL REPORT

Georgia. University. Department of Agriculture Economics *see* SPECIAL REPORT

Georgia. University. Department of Agriculture Education *see* VOCATIONAL EDUCATION IN AGRICULTURE RESEARCH SERIES: BULLETIN

Georgia. University. George Foster Peabody School of Forestry *see*
- BULLETIN
- LEAFLET

Georgia. University. Southern Cooperative Series *see* BULLETIN

GEORGIAN ARCHITECTURE / ed by Bruchhaus, G – (The complete collection consists of 8 volumes) – ca 960mf – 9 – GA-1 – ne IDC [720]

THE GEORGIAN ERA: MEMOIRS OF THE MOST EMINENT PERSONS, WHO HAVE FLOURISHED IN GREAT BRITAIN, FROM THE ACCESSION OF GEORGE THE FIRST TO THE DEMISE OF GEORGE THE FOURTH. – London: Vizetelly, Branston and Co., 1832-34. 4v. By ....Clarke, Brit. Museum – 1 – us U.W. Library [920]

Georgian S.S.R. *see* LAWS, ETC

GEORGIA'S AGRICULTURE: MANAGEMENT AND MARKETING / Georgia. University. Agricultural Extension Service – 1965-68 – 1,5,6 – us Spaulding [630]

GEORGIA'S OFFICIAL REGISTER / Georgia – (1923. 4 fiches. F-0617. 1925. 8 fiches. F-0618. 1927. Indexed. 9 fiches. F-0619. 1929. Indexed. 9 fiches. F-0620. 1931. Indexed. 14 fiches.F-0621. 1951-1952. 13 fiches. F-0622) – By state of Georgia. Department of Archives and History – 9 – us A.G.L.L. [920]

GEORGIA'S ROSTER OF THE REVOLUTION – Comp. by Lucian Lamar Knight. Indexed. 10 fiches. F-0132 – 9 – us A.G.L.L. [976]

Georgiev, E *see*
- NACHALOTO NA SLAVIANSKATA PISMENNOST' V BALGARIIA
- SLAVIANSKAIA PISMENNOST DO KIRILLA I MEFODIIA

GEORGIEVSKI I DEN – (Includes c.1: 1932:Dec.9) – Kharbin: [s.n.], 19uu – 1 – CSUXAKGO797-S – us Hoover Inst Photo [947]

GEORGIEVSKI I KAVALER – (Includes c.1: 1938:Dec.9) – Kharbin: Dalnevostochny i soi uz voennykh, 193u – 1 – CSUXAKF0435-S – us Hoover Inst Photo [947]

Georgievskii, G *see* OCHERKI PO ISTORII KRASNOI GVARDII

Georgievskii, G P *see*
- DREVNE RUSSKAIA MINIATIURA
- RUKOPISI T.F. BOL'SHAKOVA, KHRANIASHCHIESIA V IMP. MOSKOVSKOM I HUMIANTSEVSKO MUZEE

GEORGII IVANOV / Gul', R – Novyi zhurnal. New York. 1955. BR-3660 – 8 – ne IDC [073]

GEORGII VALLAE PLACENTINI VIRI CLARISS.. / Valla, G – 1501 – 9 – us Sibley [780]

LES GEORGIQUES CHRETIENNES: POEME COURONNE PAR L'ACADEMIE FRANCAISE / Jammes, Francis – 5th ed. Paris: Mercure de France, 1914.216p – 1 – us U.W. Library [810]

GEOS / Canada. Department of Energy, Mines and Resources – (Ceased v21 no 1 1992) – Ottawa. v1-21. 1972-92 – 9 – Can$20.00y – cn Micromedia [550]

GEOSCIENCE CANADA – v1- 1974- 1,5,6; v2- 1975- 9 – us UMI [550]

GEOTECHNICA – Praha: Ceskoslovenske akademie ved. v25. 1959 – us Res Libr [072]

GEOTECHNICAL TESTING JOURNAL – v. 1-. 1978- – 1,5,6,9 – us UMI [550]

GEOTECHNIQUE : INTERNATIONAL JOURNAL ON SOIL MECHANICS AND ENGINEERING GEOLOGY – (v1-14 $246.00v; v15-23 $249.00v) – London. v1-23 1948/49-73 – 9 – $24,165.00 – uk Dawson [550]

GEOTHERMAL ENERGY : REVIEW OF RESEARCH AND DEVELOPMENT / ed by Christopher, H & Armstead, H – 3rd ed 1977 – 186p – 9 – 92-3-101063-8 – fr UNESCO [333]

GEOTHERMAL ENERGY – v12-. 1984- – 1,5,6,9 – us UMI [621]

GEOTHERMAL SCIENCE AND TECHNOLOGY : THE OFFICIAL PEER-REVIEWED JOURNAL OF THE GEOTHERMAL RESOURCES COUNCIL / Flynn, Thomas et al; ed by Bresee, James C – 9,5,1 – us Gordon [550]

GEOTHERMICS – v1- 1972- – 5,6,9 – us UMI [550]

GEOTIMES – v1- 1956- 1; v17- 5,6; v20- 9 – us UMI [550]

Geouffre de la Pradelle, A de *see* LA MER

Gepp, A *see* THE CODIACEAE OF THE SIBOGA EXPEDITION

Gepp, E S *see* THE CODIACEAE OF THE SIBOGA EXPEDITION

Ger y Lobez, Florencio *see*
- TRATADO DE CONSTRUCCION CIVIL
- TRATADO DE CONSTRUCCION CIVIL. ATLAS

DER GERADE WEG/ILLUSTRIERTER SONNTAG : DEUTSCHE ZEITUNG FUER WAHRHEIT UND RECHT – (Dazu Beilage: Romanblaetter) – Muenchen, 31 Mar 1929-8 Mar 1938 – 4r – 1 – DM300.00 – gw Mikro Press [072]

GERAKAN KEBERSIHAN NASIONAL / Sukarno, Pres. Indonesia – SE 1216 1. 1958 – 9 – ne IDC [025]

GERAKAN PEMBEBASAN NASIONAL DI TIMUR / Lenin, Vladimir Ilyich – SE-10,820 1. v. 1 only. 1965- – 9 – ne IDC [335]

GERALDINE: A SOUVENIR OF THE ST LAWRENCE / Hopkins, Alphonso Alva – Boston: J.R. Osgood, 1881. 06840. (Pre-1900 Canadiana) – 9 – cn C.I.H.M. [971]

GERALDTON-MURCHISON TELEGRAPH – Geraldton, Australia. Sep 1892-Jan 1899.-w. 6 reels – 1 – uk British Libr Newspaper [072]

GERALTON-LONGLAC TIMES-STAR – 1937-1986 – cn Commonwealth Micro [072]

Gerando, J M de *see*
- DE LA BIENFAISANCE PUBLIQUE
- LE VISITEUR DU PAUVRE

Gerando, Joseph-M de *see* CONSIDERATIONS SUR LES DIVERSES METHODES A SUIVRE DANS L'OBSERVATION DES PEUPLES SAUVAGES

GERANIACEAE / Sweet, R – 1820-28; Supplement 1828-30 – 5 – uk Microform Academic [580]

GERANIACEAE. THE NATURAL ORDER OF GERANIA / Sweet, R – 5056. 5 V. 1820-1830 – 9 – ne IDC [580]

GERANIOLOGIA, SEU ERODII, PELARGONII, GERANII, MONSONIAE ET GRIELI HISTORIA ICONIBUS ILLUSTRATA / L'Heritier de Brutelle, C L Cornus – Parisiis, 1787-88; 1792 – 8 – B-6021 2 – ne IDC [580]

GERANIUMS / Andrews, H C – London, 1805. B-7375 2 – 8 – ne IDC [760]

Gerard, Alexander *see* AN ESSAY ON TASTE 1759, TOGETHER WITH

Gerard, Arsene Gilbert *see* ITINERAIRE DE QUEBEC A CHICAGO

Gerard de Reyneval, J M *see*
- DE LA LIBERTE DES MERS
- INSTITUTIONS DU...

GERARD GROTE (1340-1384) ET LES DEBUTS DE LA DEVOTION MODERNE / Epiney-Burgard, G – Wiesbaden, 1970 – 9mf – 8 – Dfl32.00 – ne Slangenburg [240]

Gerard, James Watson *see* TITLES TO REAL ESTATE IN THE STATE OF NEW YORK

Gerard, L *see* FLORA GALLO-PROVINCIALIS

GERARD, OR THE WORLD, THE FLESH AND THE DEVIL / Braddon, Mary Elizabeth – British Fiction Archive: Unit 5 – 9 – uk Bell [830]

Gerarde, J *see* THE HERBALL OR GENERAL HISTORIE OF PLANTES

Gerardo Marquez, D *see* DERECHO INTERNACIONAL

Gerasimenko, N V *see* BATKO MAKHNO

Gerasimov, Mikhail Prokopevich *see* ELEKTRIFIKATSIIA

Gerasimov, P V *see* NOVYI STROI I PRAVA SVOBODNYKH GRAZHDAN

Gerathewohl, Fritz *see* GOETHE IN HEUTIGER SICHT

Geraud, Jules *see* PATENT LAWS OF LATIN AMERICA (SOUTH AND CENTRAL AMERICA)

Geraudie, J *see* CONTROLES MORPHOGENETIQUES DU DEVELOPPEMENT ET DE LA REGENERATION DES NAGEOIRES PAIRES DES TELEOSTEENS

LA GERBE – Hebdomadaire de la volonte francaise. Dir. A. de Chateaubriant. no. 1-214. Paris. 11 juil 1940-17 aout 1944 – 1 – fr A.C.R.P.P. [073]

LA GERBE – Petite revue artistique, litteraire et scientifique. no. 1-2. nov 1885. devenu: Le Sans-titre. Petite revue artistique. no. 3-5. dec 1885-janv 1886. devenu: La Revue blanche, artistique, litteraire et scientifique. no. 6-14. Paris. fevr-juin 1886 – 1 – fr A.C.R.P.P. [073]

Gerber, E L *see*
- HISTORISCH-BIOGRAPHISCHES LEXICON DER TONKUENSTLER
- HISTORISCH-BIOGRAPHISCHES LEXICON DER TONKUENSTLER, WELCHES NACHRICHTEN VON DEM LEBEN UND WERKEN MUSKALISCHER SCHRIFTSTELLER, BERUEMTER COMPONISTEN, SAENGER...

THE GERBER STAR – Gerber, CA. 1924-39 – 5r – 1 BC02271 – $250.00 – us Library Micro [071]

Gerberon, Dom Gabriel *see* HISTOIRE GENERAL DU JANSENISME

Gerbert, Martin *see*
- DE CANTU ET MUSICA SACRA A PRIMA ECCLESIAE AETATE USQUE AD PRAESENS TEMPUS
- DE CANTU ET MUSICA SACRA A PRIMA ECCLESIAE AETATE USQUE AD PRAESENS TEMPUS AUCTORE MARTINO GERBERTO
- SCRIPTORES ECCLESIASTICI DE MUSICA SACRA POTISSIMUM

Gerberti *see* SILVESTRI 2 PAPAE OPERA MATHEMATICA

Gerbertus, M *see* VETUS LITURGIA ALEMANICA

Gerbner, George *see* VIOLENCE AND TERROR IN THE MASS MEDIA

GERBOVED – Spb. 1913-14. BR-3384 2 – 8 – ne IDC [073]

Gerbrandy, P S *see* AMBON EN DE A.R. PARTIJ. DE VRIJHEIDSSTRIJD VAN DE REPUBLIEK DER ZUID-MOLUKKEN

Gerdener, G B A *see* STUDIES IN THE EVANGELISATION OF SOUTH AFRICA

Gerder, FE fon *see* SISTEMATICHESKII KATALOG BIBLIOTEKI IMP. S.-PETERBURGSKAGO BOTANICHESKAGO SADA

Gerdes, Dan *see* FLORILEGIUM HISTORICO-CRITICUM LIBRORUM RARIORUM

Gerdes, Gerriet *see*
- UNTERSUCHUNGEN UEBER DIE WIRKUNG VON ALUMINIUM- UND H-IONEN AUF DIE SPROSSZELLEN CALCICOLER UND CALCIFUGER ARTEN
- UNTERSUCHUNGEN UEBER VERSCHIEDENE SYSTEME DES WASSERREISANBAUS MIT DEM ALGENFARN AZOLLA UND DESSEN WIRKUNGEN AUF UNKRAUTFLORA UND ERTRAGSPARAMETER

Gerding *see* DIE BAHN SWAKOPMUND-WINDHOEK

Gere, Vladimir Ivanovich *see* PERVAI A RUSSKAI A GOSUDARSTVENNAI A DUMA

DIE GERECHTEN VON KUMMEROW : ROMAN / Welk, Ehm – Berlin: Deutscher Verlag c1943 – 1r – 1 – us U.W. Library [830]

GERECHTIGKEIT / International Ladies Garment Workers' Union – New York, N.Y. Yiddish edition of Justice. v. 1-40. 1919-Jan 1958 – 1 – us NY Public [071]

GERECHTIGKEIT – v1-40. 1919-58 – 11r – 1 – us Ross [330]

DE GEREFORMEERDE KERKEN IN NEDERLAND – 1950-92 (complete) – Inquire – 1 – ATLA S0675 – us A.T.L.A. [073]

GEREGTELIKE NADOODSE ONDERSOEK NA DIE DOOD VAN STEPHEN BANTU BIKO GEHOU IN DIE SINAGOGE, PRETORIA : EXTRACTS FROM THE EVIDENCE [...] AT THE OLD SYNAGOGUE, PRETORIA, DURING THE INQUEST INTO THE DEATH OF STEPHEN BANTU BIKO, NOV-DEC 1, 1977 – Johannesburg,[19–?] – us Res Libr [960]

HET GEREINIGT HERTE DOOR 'T GELOOF / Dulken, G van – 1st ed. Amsterdam, 1715 – 3mf – 9 – ne IDC [700]

HET GEREINIGT HERTE DOOR 'T GELOOF / Dulken, G van – Amsterdam, 1739 – 3mf – 9 – ne IDC [700]

GEREKHIGKAYT = JUSTICE – Jersey City, NJ. v19 no 3, v42 no 9. 1937-1960 – 2r – Can$60.00r – cn Can Microfilming [071]

Gerest, Regis *see* VERITAS. LA VIE CHRETIENNE RAISONNEE ET MEDITEE 4. LA MAISON PATERNELLE 1933

LE GERFAUT : REVUE DE LA SOCIETE ORNITHOLOGIQUE DU CENTRE DE LA BELGIQUE – Bruxelles, 1911-1942. v1-32 – 92mf – 9 – Z-2019c/2 – ne IDC [590]

Gerhard, J *see*
- COMMENTARIUS SUPER GENESIN, IN QUO TEXTUS DECLARATUR, QUAESTIONES DUBIAE SOLVUNTUR, OBSERVATIONES ERUUNTUR,...
- HOMILIARUM SACRARUM IN PERICOPAS EVANGELIORUM DOMINICALIUM...
- EIN VND FUENFFTZIG GOTTSELIGE, CHRISTLICHE EVANGELISCHE ANDACHTEN ODER GEISTREICHE BETRACHTUNGEN...

Gerhard, Johann *see* ERKLAERUNG DER HISTORIE DES LEIDENS UND STERBENS UNSERS HERRN CHRISTI JESU

GERHARD SCHRODER: PAMPHLET COLLECTION – 1955-1968 – 1 – CSUXANS3224-B – us Hoover Inst Photo [943]

Gerhard, Wilhelm *see* HISTORIEN DER ALDEN E

Gerhards, Marty D *see* HANDRAIL ASSISTED VERSUS NONHANDRAIL ASSISTED STAIRMASTER GAUNTLET ERGOMETRY

GERHART HAUPTMANN : KRITISCHE STUDIEN / Kutscher, Artur – (Includes bibliographical references) – Hirschberg: O Reier, [1909?] – 1r – 1 – us U.W. Library [430]

GERHART HAUPTMANN : EINE STUDIE / Behl, CF W – Berlin: W Borngraeber, [1913?] – 1r – 1 – us U.W. Library [430]

GERHART HAUPTMANN / Sulger-Gebing, Emil – (Includes bibliographical references) – 3. verb. & verm. Aufl. Leipzig: B G Teubner, 1922 – 1r – 1 – us U.W. Library [430]

GERHART HAUPTMANN / Woerner, U C – 2. verb. & verm. Aufl. Berlin: A Duncker, 1901 – 1r – 1 – us U.W. Library [430]

GERHART HAUPTMANN AND JOHN GALSWORTHY : A PARALLEL / Trumbauer, Walter H R – (Includes bibliographical references) – Philadelphia, PA: [s.n.], 1917 – 1r – 1 – us U.W. Library [410]

GERHART HAUPTMANN – AUS DEM LEBEN DES DEUTSCHEN GEISTES IN DER GEGENWART : FUENF REDEN / Kuehnemann, Eugen – Muenchen: Beck, 1922 – 1r – 1 – us U.W. Library [430]

GERHART HAUPTMANNS "EMANUEL QUINT" : EINE STUDIE / Faesi, Robert – Zuerich: Schulthess, 1912 – 1r – 1 – us U.W. Library [430]

GERHART HAUPTMANNS "TILL EULENSPIEGEL" : EIN STUDIE / Enking, Ottomar – 1. und 2. Aufl. Berlin: S Fischer, 1930, c1929 – 1r – 1 – us U.W. Library [430]

GERHART HAUPTMANNS "TILL EULENSPIEGEL" : VERSUCH EINER IDEENGEHALTLICHEN, FORMALAESTHETISCHEN UND LITERARHISTORISCHEN WUERDIGUNG / Schwager, Lothar Helmut – (Includes bibliographical references) – Leipzig: Schwarzenberg & Schumann, [1930] – 1 – us U.W. Library [430]

GERHART HAUPTMANNS VELAND : SEINE ENTSTEHUNG UND DEUTUNG / Hemmerich, Karl – (Includes bibliograpical references) – Wuerzburg: Druck von Memminger, 1935 – 1r – 1 – us U.W. Library [430]

Gerhart, Isaac *see* CHORAL HARMONIE. ENTHALTEND KIRCHEN-MELODIEN

GERIATRIC NURSING – v.1. 1980 – 1,5,6,9 – us UMI [073]

GERIATRICS – v39-. Dec 1984- – 1,5,6,9 – us UMI [618]

DER GERICHTSSAAL; ZEITSCHRIFT FUER ZIVIL-UND MILITARSTRAFRECHT UND STRAFPROZESSRECHT SOWIE DIE ERGANZENDEN DISZIPLINEN – Stuttgart. On film: v1-116; 1849-1942. LL-0224 – 1 – us L of C Photodup [340]

DER GERICHTSTAG : IN FUENF BUECHERN / Werfel, Franz – Leipzig: K Wolff, 1923, c1919 – 1r – 1 – us U.W. Library [810]

GERICHTS-ZEITUNG – Wien, Manz etc. v.1-82; 1850-1931. Missing: v76-78; 1925-27. LL-0200 – 1 – 690.00 – us L of C Photodup [073]

GERICHTSZEITUNG *see* HAMBURG-ALTONAER VOLKSBLATT

GERIFALTES EXTREMENOS. ANGEL MARINA, EL JUGLAR DE LA VIRGEN MORENA / Gutierrez Macias, Valeriano – Badajoz: Dip. Provincial, 1974. Sep. REE – 1 – sp Bibl Santa Ana [946]

LOS GERIFALTES MARXISTAS POR... / Gonzalez Alvarez, Claudio – Caceres: Tip. Floriano, 1939 – 1 – sp Bibl Santa Ana [335]

Gerig, B *see* THE OPEN DOOR AND...

Gerin, Leon *see* TROIS TYPES DE L'HABITANT CANADIEN-FRANCAIS

GERING COURIER – Gering, NE. -w. Apr 1887-Oct 1898; Dec 1898-Sept 1899, scattered issues missing; Oct 1900 to date – 1 – us NE Hist [071]

GERING MIDWEST – Gering, NE. -w. Jan 1919-Dec 1922; Jan 1925-Jul 1927 – 1 – us NE Hist [071]

Gerini, G E *see* RESEARCHES ON PTOLEMY'S GEOGRAPHY OF EASTERN ASIA

Gerin-Lajoie, Antoine *see* JEAN RIVARD

Gerin-Lajoie, Marie *see* A TREATISE ON EVERYDAY LAW

Gerke, F *see* DIE STELLUNG DES ERSTEN CLEMENSBRIEFES, INNERHALB DER ENTWICKLUNG DER ALTCHRISTLICHEN GEMEINDEVERFASSUNG UND DES KIRCHENRECHTS (T.U.U. 4-47/1)

Gerlach, Andreas *see* DIE WECHSELWIRKUNG ORGANISCHER MOLEKUELE MIT SUPRA-MOLEKULAREN VERBINDUNGEN

GERLACH EXPRESS – Gerlach, NV. 19 Jun 1964 – 1r – 1 – $45.00 – U04572 – us Library Micro [071]

Gerlach, Hermann *see* DIE LETZTEN DINGE

Gerlach, Martin von *see* DER MENSCH IM STANDE DER SCHULD NACH DEM BUCHE JESAJA

GERLANDS BEITRAEGE ZUR GEOHYSIK / ed by Conrad, V – Leipzig, 1935-1941. v44-57 – 121mf – 9 – G-164c/2 – ne IDC [550]

Germain, Dom Michel OSB *see* MONASTICON GALLICANUM

Germain, Nicole *see* LE CINQ TROIS UN SIX

Germaine-Marie, Soeur *see* BIBLIOGRAPHIE DE LA PSYCHOLOGIE RATIONNELLE AU CANADA FRANCAIS, 1945-1963

GERMAN 19TH CENTURY PART SONGS BY TAUBERT, REICHARDT, BERGER, LOEWE, ZELTER, AND PEROTTI – Binder's collection – 9 – us Sibley [780]

[GERMAN AERIAL OPERATIONS DURING WORLD WAR 2 PAMPHLET COLLECTION] – 194?-1943 – 1 – CSUXANM9841-B – us Hoover Inst Photo [355]

GERMAN AFFAIRS – London. 6 Nov 1947-14 Jun 1948 – 1r – 1 – gw Mikrofilm [072]

GERMAN AIR FORCE REPORT : LUFTGAUKOMMANDOS, FLAK, DEUTSCHE LUFTWAFFENMISSION IN RUMANIEN – T405 – 64r – $1,472.00 – us Nat'l Archives [350]

GERMAN ALLIED TROOPS IN THE NORTH AMERICAN WAR OF INDEPENDENCE – 1776-83.By J.G. Rosengarten, 1893. Item E. Trans. and abr. from the German of Max von Elking, Captain Saxon-Meiningen Army. Indexed, 351p. SW16-0052 – 5 – us A.G.L.L. [920]

[GERMAN ALMANACS PAMPHLET COLLECTION] – 1847-1930 – 1 – CSUXAMJ4503-B – us Hoover Inst Photo [030]

THE GERMAN AMERICAN – New York. May 1942-Mar 1952 – 2r – 1 – gw Mikrofilm [071]

GERMAN AMERICAN LAW JOURNAL – v1-5. 1991-1996 – 9 – $40.00set – us Hein [340]

[GERMAN AMERICANS DURING WORLD WAR 1 PAMPHLET COLLECTION] – 1917-1918 – 2r – 1 – CSUXANL3031-B – us Hoover Inst Photo [305]

GERMAN AND AUSTRIAN DRAMA : THE DEVELOPMENT OF VIENNESE THEATRE – 1740-1790. Based on the holdings of the Houghton Library, Harvard University – 1 – us Primary [790]

THE GERMAN AND SWISS SETTLEMENTS OF COLONIAL PENNSYLVANIA : A STUDY OF THE SO-CALLED PENNSYLVANIA DUTCH / Kuhns, Oscar – New York: H. Holt, 1901, c1900 – 1mf – us A.T.L.A. [305]

GERMAN ARCHITECTURAL PERIODICALS – 9 – ne IDC [073]

THE GERMAN ARMY HIGH COMMAND, 1938-1945 / Germany. Heer. Oberkommando – An original microform collection of 42 archival titles written by former Oberkommando officers under Allied supervision at the Interrogation Enclosure in Neustadt, Germany, giving the inside history of the German Army command structure. Translated into English – 1 – $380.00 – 0-89093-107-0 – us UPA [940]

GERMAN ARTISTS / Courtauld Institute of Art – (Printed index of 8,200 artists included) – 1994 – 1794mf – 9 – $10,153.00 – 1-869934-98-9 – uk Emmett [700]

[GERMAN ASPECTS OF WORLD WAR 1 PAMPHLET COLLECTION] – 1914-1918 – 4r – 1 – CSUXANM0157-B – us Hoover Inst Photo [355]

[GERMAN ATROCITIES AND WAR CRIMES DURING WORLD WAR 2 PAMPHLET COLLECTION] – 1940-1987 – 1 – CSUXANN0292-B – us Hoover Inst Photo [360]

German Aviation Society *see* DIE LUFTFLOTTE

German Baptist Convention *see*
– ANNUAL
– JAHRBUCH DES BUNDES

GERMAN BAROQUE LITERATURE : YALE COLLECTION – Titles from the von Faber du Faur Collection – 1 – us Primary [430]

GERMAN BOOKS AND PERIODICALS FROM THE WILHELM SCHERER COLLECTION – From the holdings of the Freiberger Library of Case Western Reserve University – 1 – us Primary [430]

GERMAN BOOKS BEFORE 1601 – (Group 1: The Incunabula 1440-1500 290r. Group 2: Books Printed 1501-1550 180r. Group 3: Books Printed 1551-1600 130r. Catalog cards also available. Annual instalments of 20r each. Each instalment supplied with short-title listing) – 643r – 1 – ne IDC [430]

THE GERMAN CHURCH ON THE AMERICAN FRONTIER / Schneider, Carl Edward – A Study in the Rise of Religion Among the Germans of the West.... 1840-1866. 1939 – 1 – us A.T.L.A. [240]

GERMAN "COLONISATION" BEGUN IN SPAIN – NY, 1937. Fiche W 910. (Blodgett Collection of Spanish Civil War Pamphlets) – 9 – us H.U. College Libr [946]

[GERMAN CULTURE AND CIVILIZATION IN THE 19TH CENTURY PAMPHLET COLLECTION] – 1869 – 1 – CSUXANQ7832-B – us Hoover Inst Photo [306]

[GERMAN CULTURE AND CIVILIZATION IN THE 20TH CENTURY PAMPHLET COLLECTION] – 1910-1958 – 4r – 1 – CSUXANQ7836-B – us Hoover Inst Photo [306]

THE GERMAN DEMAND FOR COLONIES / Glahn, Gerhard Ernst Ludwig Von – Evanston, 1939 – us Res Libr [943]

GERMAN (DIN) STANDARDS – 1979. 1v. Microfilm 5 sections updated every 2 months; microfiche 27 sections updated monthly – 5,9 – uk Tech [380]

GERMAN DOCUMENTS AMONG THE WAR CRIMES RECORDS OF THE JUDGE ADVOCATE DIVISION, HEADQUARTERS, U.S. ARMY, EUROPE / U.S. Army. Commands – 20r. T1021 – 1 – us Nat'l Archives [324]

GERMAN DRAMA – 1961- – 19,917mf – 9 – $59,000.00 $1,280.00y – us OmniSys [430]

GERMAN DRAMA – (Annual instalments of 325mf. Each instalment supplied with short-title listing) – 19,592mf coll – 9 – ne IDC [820]

THE GERMAN ELEMENT IN THE UNITED STATES : WITH SPECIAL REFERENCE TO ITS POLITICAL, MORAL, SOCIAL, AND EDUCATIONAL INFLUENCE / Faust, Albert Bernhardt – Boston: Houghton Mifflin, 1909 – 3mf – us A.T.L.A. [305]

GERMAN ENAMELLED GLASS: THE EDWIN J. BEINECKE COLLECTION AND RELATED PIECES / Saldern, Axel von – 1965. 474p. 470 illus.10 fiches. Fiche No.1265 – 9 – $15.00 – us Corning Mus [740]

GERMAN FOREIGN MINISTRY ARCHIVES, 1867-1920 / Germany. Foreign Office. Archives – Filmed by the American Historical Association. T149 – 434r – 1 – us Nat'l Archives [324]

[GERMAN FOREIGN RELATIONS–1888-1918–PAMPHLET COLLECTION] – 1913-1920 – 1 – CSUXANR3414-B – us Hoover Inst Photo [320]

[GERMAN FOREIGN RELATIONS–1918-1945–PAMPHLET COLLECTION] – 19??-1965 – 1 – CSUXANR9414-B – us Hoover Inst Photo [320]

[GERMAN GENERALS PAMPHLET COLLECTION] – 1915?-19?? – 1 – CSUXANR2670-B – us Hoover Inst Photo [355]

[GERMAN GUIDEBOOKS PAMPHLET COLLECTION] – 1915-1938 – 1 – CSUXANQ7807-B – us Hoover Inst Photo [943]

[GERMAN HISTORY–1945 TO THE PRESENT–PAMPHLET COLLECTION] – 1945-1979? – 2r – 1 – CSUXANS1068-B – us Hoover Inst Photo [943]

[GERMAN HISTORY–1918-1933–PAMPHLET COLLECTION] – 1919-1963 – 3r – 1 – CSUXANR3454-B – us Hoover Inst Photo [943]

[GERMAN HISTORY–1933-1945–PAMPHLET COLLECTION] – 1938?-1985 – 1 – CSUXANS0333-B – us Hoover Inst Photo [943]

GERMAN KEYBOARD MUSIC OF THE BAROQUE – 88mf – 9 – MS-g – ne IDC [780]

GERMAN LANGUAGE NOVELS OF THE EDITION CORVEY : LITERARY WORKS OF THE 18TH AND 19TH CENTURY – (Silver halide microfiche on request) – Wildberg: BELSER WISS. DIENST, 1990-1992 – 3,146mf – 9 – DM24,300.00 diazo – 3-628-04001-9 – gw Belser Wiss [430]

GERMAN LANGUAGE TITLES OF THE EDITION CORVEY : LITERARY WORKS OF THE 18TH AND 19TH CENTURY – (Silver halide microfiche on request) – Wildberg: BELSER WISS. DIENST, 1990-1992 – 6,862mf – 9 – DM52,240.00 diazo – 3-628-04000-0 – gw Belser Wiss [430]

GERMAN LITERATURE OF THE MID-NINETEENTH CENTURY IN ENGLAND AND AMERICA : AS REFLECTED IN THE JOURNALS, 1840-1914 / Hathaway, Lillie Vinal – Boston: Chapman & Grimes, c1935 – 1 – us U.W. Library [430]

GERMAN LITERATURE THROUGH NAZI EYES / Atkins, Henry Gibson – (Includes bibliographical references and index) – London: Methuen, 1941 – 1r – 1 – us U.W. Library [430]

GERMAN MILITARY AND TECHNICAL MANUALS, 1910-45 / Germany – 126r – 1 – T283 – us Nat'l Archives [324]

[GERMAN NAVAL OPERATIONS DURING WORLD WAR 1 PAMPHLET COLLECTION] – 1915-1918 – 2r – 1 – CSUXANL2789-B – us Hoover Inst Photo [355]

[GERMAN OCCUPATION AND UNDERGROUND MOVEMENTS IN BELGIUM DURING WORLD WAR 2 PAMPHLET COLLECTION] – 1941-1948 – 1 – CSUXANM9874-B – us Hoover Inst Photo [355]

[GERMAN OCCUPATION AND UNDERGROUND MOVEMENTS IN DENMARK DURING WORLD WAR 2 PAMPHLET COLLECTION] – 1943 – 1 – CSUXANM9878-B – us Hoover Inst Photo [355]

GERMAN PERIODICAL ON CONTEMPORARY HISTORY *see* DIE GEGENWART, LEIPZIG 1848-1856

[GERMAN PHILOSOPHY PAMPHLET COLLECTION] – 1946 – 1 – CSUXAMJ4546-B – us Hoover Inst Photo [190]

THE GERMAN PIETISTS OF PROVINICIAL PENNSYLVANIA, 1694-1708 / Sachse, Julius Friedrich – Philadelphia: Printed for the author, 1895 – 2mf – us A.T.L.A. [240]

GERMAN POLITICKS, OR, THE MODERN SYSTEM... – London, 1744 – 2mf – 1 – ILM-876/1 – ne IDC [327]

[GERMAN POLITICS AND GOVERNMENT IN THE 19TH CENTURY PAMPHLET COLLECTION] – 1849-1961 – 1 – CSUXANR3402-B – us Hoover Inst Photo [320]

[GERMAN POLITICS AND GOVERNMENT PAMPHLET COLLECTION] – 1916?-1947 – 1 – CSUXANR2678-B – us Hoover Inst Photo [320]

[GERMAN POLITICS AND GOVERNMENT–1945 TO THE PRESENT–PAMPHLET COLLECTION] – 1947-1970 – 2r – 1 – CSUXANS1079-B – us Hoover Inst Photo [320]

[GERMAN POLITICS AND GOVERNMENT–1888-1918–PAMPHLET COLLECTION] – 1896-1918 – 1 – CSUXANR3410-B – us Hoover Inst Photo [320]

[GERMAN POLITICS AND GOVERNMENT–1933-1945–PAMPHLET COLLECTION] – 1934-1986 – 2r – 1 – CSUXANS0359-B – us Hoover Inst Photo [320]

GERMAN POPULAR STORIES / Grimm, Jacob – London: Published by C. Baldwyn, 1823 – 1 roll – 1 – 1-55879-740-8 – uk Libr Preservation [390]

GERMAN POW CAMP NEWSPAPERS – L110093 – 15r – 1 – $525.00 – us L of C Photodup [350]

[GERMAN PRAYER-BOOKS AND DEVOTIONS FOR CHRISTMAS DURING WORLD WAR 1 PAMPHLET COLLECTION] – 1914-1917 – 1 – CSUXANM2711-B – us Hoover Inst Photo [240]

[GERMAN PROPAGANDA DURING WORLD WAR 2 PAMPHLET COLLECTION] – 1937-1944 – 4r – 1 – CSUXANN2800-B – us Hoover Inst Photo [320]

GERMAN PSYCHOLOGY OF TODAY, THE EMPIRICAL SCHOOL / Ribot, Theodule Armand – Trans. from 2nd French ed. by James Mark Baldwin. New York: Scribner, c1886. xxi,307p – 1 – us U.W. Library [150]

German Publications Ltd *see* KITCHENER JOURNAL

GERMAN QUARTERLY – v. 1-44. 1928-1971 – 1,5,6 – us Princeton Micro [370]

GERMAN QUARTERLY – (v.52 .1979 5,6,9) – v.1. 1928 – 1 – us UMI [073]

GERMAN RATIONALISM : IN ITS RISE, PROGRESS, AND DECLINE, IN RELATION TO THEOLOGIANS, SCHOLARS, POETS, PHILOSOPHERS, AND THE PEOPLE... / Hagenbach, K R; ed by Stuckenberg, John Henry Wilburn – Edinburgh: T.& T. Clark, 1865 – 1mf – us A.T.L.A. [140]

GERMAN RELIGIOUS LIFE IN COLONIAL TIMES / Bittinger, Lucy Forney – Philadelphia: J.B. Lippincott, 1906 – 1mf – us A.T.L.A. [306]

[GERMAN RELIGIOUS TRACTS PUBLISHED DURING WORLD WAR 1 PAMPHLET COLLECTION] – 1914-1918 – 10r – 1 – CSUXANM0100-B – us Hoover Inst Photo [240]

[GERMAN REPARATIONS FOR WORLD WAR 1 PAMPHLET COLLECTION] – 1919-1932 – 2r – 1 – CSUXANM5408-B – us Hoover Inst Photo [355]

[GERMAN REUNIFICATION QUESTION PAMPHLET COLLECTION] – 1947-1992 – 2r – 1 – CSUXANS1074-B – us Hoover Inst Photo [320]

THE GERMAN SECTARIANS OF PENNSYLVANIA, 1708-1800 : A CRITICAL AND LEGENDARY HISTORY OF THE EPHRATA CLOISTER AND THE DUNKERS / Sachse, Julius Friedrich – Philadelphia: Printed for the author, 1899-1900 – 3mf – us A.T.L.A. [240]

[GERMAN SERMONS DURING WORLD WAR 1 PAMPHLET COLLECTION] – 1914-1921 – 9r – 1 – CSUXANM0140-B – us Hoover Inst Photo [240]

GERMAN SIXTEENTH CENTURY IMPRINTS FROM THE REFORMATION PERIOD – 1520-1666 – 1 – 325.50 – us Baptist [240]

GERMAN SOCIAL REPORT – 1963-1970 – 1 – us UMI [300]

[GERMAN SONGS AND MUSIC DURING WORLD WAR 1 PAMPHLET COLLECTION] – 1914-1918 – 2r – 1 – CSUXANM2745-B – us Hoover Inst Photo [780]

GERMAN STUDIES PRESENTED TO LEONARD ASHLEY WILLOUGBY : BY PUPILS, COLLEAGUES AND FRIENDS ON HIS RETIREMENT – (Includes bibliographical references) – Oxford: B. Blackwell, 1952 – 1 – us U.W. Library [430]

GERMAN STUDIES PRESENTED TO PROFESSOR H.G. FIEDLER, M.V.O., BY PUPILS, COLLEAGUES, AND FRIENDS ON HIS SEVENTY-FIFTH BIRTHDAY, 28 APRIL 1937 – (Includes bibliographical references) – Oxford: Clarendon Press, 1938 – 1r – 1 – us U.W. Library [943]

GERMAN, SWISS AND AUSTRIAN BOOKS BEFORE 1601 – 1965- – 643r – 1 – $39,600.00 $1,200.00y – us OmniSys [430]

GERMAN TRIBUNE – Hamburg, Germany. -w. 10 Feb 1970-Dec 1976. 7 reels – 1 – uk British Libr Newspaper [072]

GERMAN UNIVERSITIES : A NARRATIVE OF PERSONAL EXPERIENCE, TOGETHER WITH RECENT STATISTICAL INFORMATION, PRACTICAL SUGGESTIONS, AND A COMPARISON OF THE GERMAN, ENGLISH AND AMERICAN SYSTEMS OF HIGHER EDUCATION / Hart, James Morgan – New York: Putnam, 1874 – 1mf – us A.T.L.A. [370]

THE GERMAN UNIVERSITIES : THEIR CHARACTER AND HISTORICAL DEVELOPMENT / Paulsen, Friedrich – New York: Macmillan, 1895 – 1mf – us A.T.L.A. [370]

[GERMAN YEARBOOKS PAMPHLET COLLECTION] – 1921-1924 – 1 – CSUXANQ7799-B – us Hoover Inst Photo [943]

GERMAN-AMERICAN STUDIES – v1-10. 1969-75 – 1 – us UMI [073]

GERMAN-ENGLISH DICTIONARY FOR FORESTERS – 1939 – 7 – uk Microform Academic [430]

GERMANEREN / Germanske S S Norge – Kamporgan for Germanske SS. Norge. Oslo, Norway. -w. Oct. 1942-Apr. 1945. (very imperfect, 1 reel) – 1 – uk British Libr Newspaper [072]

DIE GERMANIA – Upper Sandusky, Ohio. 1886-96 – 4r – 1 – $32.50r – us Archival [071]

GERMANIA – 1871-1938 – Cumul – 1 – DM16,000.00 – sz Infoprint [072]

GERMANIA – Berlin, 1871-1938 – 196r – 1 – DM14,700.00 – gw Mikro Press [072]

GERMANIA – Berlin, Germany. Apr-Jul 1936 – 1r – 1 – us L of C Photodup [072]

GERMANIA – Cleveland, Ohio. -d. Jan 1889-Jun 1889 – 1 – us Western Res [071]

GERMANIA : KORRESPONDENTBLATT DER ROEMISCH-GERMANISCHEN KOMMISSION – Frankfurt M., 1917-63 – 6r – 1 – DM660.00 – gw Mikro Press [073]

GERMANIA – London, UK. 9 Apr-7 May 1859 – 1 – uk British Libr Newspaper [072]

GERMANIA – Milwaukee. Wis. -d. 1873-74, 1877-78, 1891-1912 – 1 – us UMI [071]

GERMANIA : VIERTELJAHRESSCHRIFT FUER DEUTSCHE ALTERTUMSKUNDE / ed by Pfeiffer, Franz & Bartsch Karl et al – Wien, 1856-92 – 225mf – 9 – subsc: DM1,300.00 diazo DM1,500.00 silver – gw Olms [930]

GERMANIA : ZEITUNG FUER DAS DEUTSCHE VOLK (ZENTRUM) – (These suppl are also available: Kirche und Welt, sep 24 1911-aug 2 1914. Sonntagsblatt, may 30 1897-sep 11 1898) – Berlin, 1871-1938 – 1 – Dist. gw Mikrofilm – gw Misc Inst [072]

GERMANIA *see* KATHOLISCHE VOLKSZEITUNG

THE GERMANIA; A COLLECTION OF THE MOST FAVORITE OPERATIC AIRS, MARCHES, POLKAS, WALTZES, DANCES, AND MELODIES OF THE DAY / Burditt, B A – Arranged in an easy and familiar style, for four, five, and six instruments. Boston: Oliver Ditson, 1855. MUSIC 1991, Item 1 – 1 – us L of C Photodup [780]

GERMANIA – ZEITUNG FUER DAS DEUTSCHE VOLK : BEILAGE: KIRCHE UND WELT – Berlin. sep 24, 1911-aug 2, 1914 – 1 – gw Mikrofilm [072]

GERMANIA – ZEITUNG FUER DAS DEUTSCHE VOLK : BEILAGE: SONNTAGSBLATT – Berlin. may 30, 1897-sep 11, 1898 – 1 – gw Mikrofilm [073]

GERMANIA-HERALD – Milwaukee. Wis. 1913-1919 – 1 – us UMI [071]

GERMANIC NOTES – v1-17. 1970-87 – 3r – 1 – $225.00 – us OmniSys [430]

GERMANIC REVIEW – v. 1-21. 1939-1946 – 1 – us Princeton Micro [430]

GERMANIC REVIEW – (v45-57. 1970-82. 5,6. v51-57. 1976-82. 9) – v. 1-57. 1926-82 – 1 – us UMI [430]

GERMANIEN – Berlin, 1933 n1, 1937, 1939 n4 – 1 – Dist. gw Mikrofilm – gw Misc Inst [072]

GERMANIEN, HEILIG HERZ EUROPAS : DER GERMANISCHE GEDANKE BEI ERNST MORITZ ARNDT, 1769-1860 / Zander, Alfred – Berlin-Grunewald: Der Reichsfuehrer SS, SS-Hauptamt, [194-?] – 1r – 1 – us U.W. Library [943]

GERMANIIA / Heine, Heinrich – Moskva: Gos. Izd-vo "Khudozhestvennaia Literatura", 1938 – 1 – us U.W. Library [830]

GERMANIIA, ANTANTAI SSSR / Erusalimskii, Arkadii Samsonovich – Moskva: Izd-vo Kommunistichesko i akademii, 1928 – 1 – CSUX88-B8719 – us Hoover Inst Photo [943]

GERMANISCHE ALTERTHUEMER. MIT TEXT, UEBERSETZUNG UND ERKLAERUNG VON TACITUS GERMANIA / Holtzmann, Adolf – Ed. by Alfred Holder. Leipzig: B.G. Teubner, 1873. iv,313p – 1 – us U.W. Library [943]

Germanische Fuerstentochter *see* EINE GERMANISCHE FUERSTENTOCHTER – DIE LIEBE SIEGT

EINE GERMANISCHE FUERSTENTOCHTER – DIE LIEBE SIEGT : ZWEI ERZAEHLUNGEN / Germanische Fuerstentochter – Milwaukee, Wis.: Germania, 1913 – 1r – 1 – us U.W. Library [830]

GERMANISCHE HELDENSAGE / Schneider, Hermann – (Publ out of sequence. Includes bibliographical references and index to all vols) – Berlin: W de Gruyter, 1933-1962 – 1 – us U.W. Library [390]

GERMANISCHE MYTHOLOGIE / Mogk, Eugen – Leipzig: C.J. Goeschen, 1906. 129p – 1 – us U.W. Library [390]

GERMANISCH-ROMANISCHE MONATSSCHRIFT – Heidelberg, 1909-1920. v1-8 – 61mf – 9 – H-10027/1 – ne IDC [943]

GERMANIZATSIIA BALTIISKIKH SLAVIAN / Pervol'f, I – Spb., 1876 – 3mf – 9 – ne IDC [460]

GERMAN-JEWISH PERIODICALS / Leo Baeck Institute, New York – (Pt 1: 52 titles. 113 reels. $7,365.00; Pt 2. 36 titles. 51 reels. $3,330.00; Pt 3. 56 titles. $6,820.00) – 1768-1938. Individual titles available – us UPA [073]

Germann, W *see*
- DIE KIRCHE DER THOMASCHRISTEN
- MISSIONAR CHRISTIAN FRIEDRICH SCHWARTZ

DIE GERMANOMANIE / Ascher, S – Berlin. 1815. BJ-23-103 1 – 9 – ne IDC [190]

THE GERMANS / Wylie, Ida Alena Ross – Indianapolis: The Bobbs-Merrill Company, 1911. 4+361p. Plates. Illus.Publ. 1910 by Mills & Boon, London, under title: My German Year. With a different set of illus.1 reel. 1260 – 1 – us U.W. Library [390]

[GERMANS IN CZECHOSLOVAKIA PAMPHLET COLLECTION] – 1914-1968 – 1 – CSUXANL5030-B – us Hoover Inst Photo [305]

[GERMANS IN ROMANIA PAMPHLET COLLECTION] – 1976 – 1 – CSUXANL8118-B – us Hoover Inst Photo [305]

[GERMANS IN RUSSIA PAMPHLET COLLECTION] – 1916-1962 – 1 – CSUXANR3588-B – us Hoover Inst Photo [305]

[GERMANS IN THE SOVIET UNION PAMPHLET COLLECTION] – 1986?-1987? – 1 – CSUXANR3606-B – us Hoover Inst Photo [305]

[GERMANS IN YUGOSLAVIA PAMPHLET COLLECTION] – 1920-1925? – 1 – CSUXANQ5649-B – us Hoover Inst Photo [305]

Germanske S S Norge *see* GERMANEREN

GERMANTOWN GLEANER – Germantown, NE. -w. Nov 1895-Apr 1896; Aug 1896-Aug 1897 – 1 – us NE Hist [071]

Germanus *see* LERCHENSANG UND SCHWERTERKLANG

GERMANY : FOREIGN AFFAIRS, 1930-39 / U.S. Department of State – (Series: Confidential US State Department Central Files) – 12r – 1 – $1,430.00 – 0-89093-427-4 – us UPA [320]

GERMANY : FOREIGN AFFAIRS, 1940-1944 / U. S. State Department – (Series: Confidential US State Department Central Files. With printed guides) – 5r – 1 – $595.00 – 0-89093-428-2 – us UPA [320]

GERMANY : INTERNAL AFFAIRS, 1930-1941 / U.S. Department of State – (Series: Confidential US State Department Central Files: Germany) – 59r – 1 – $7,030.00 – 0-89093-637-4 – us UPA [943]

GERMANY : INTERNAL AFFAIRS, 1942-1944 / U. S. State Department – (Series: Confidential US State Department Central Files: Germany. With printed guide) – 35r – 1 – $4,170.00 – 0-89093-429-0 – us UPA [943]

GERMANY : INTERNAL AFFAIRS, 1945-1949 / U. S. State Department – (Pt 1: Political, Governmental and National Defense Affairs 41r $4,885.00 ISBN 0-89093-430-4. Pt 2: Social, Economic and Industrial Affairs 68r $8,095.00 ISBN 0-89093-431-2. Series: Confidential US State Department Central Files: Germany) – 1 – us UPA [320]

GERMANY : INTERNAL AFFAIRS AND FOREIGN AFFAIRS, 1950-1954 / U. S. State Department – (Series: Confidential US State Department Central Files. With printed guides) – 45r – 1 – $5,360.00 – 1-55655-193-2 – us UPA [320]

GERMANY : INTERNAL AND FOREIGN AFFAIRS, 1955-1959 / U.S. Department of State – (Series: Confidential US State Department Central Files: Germany) – 37r – 1 – $4,405.00 – 1-55655-194-0 – us UPA [943]

GERMANY : ITS UNIVERSITIES, THEOLOGY AND RELIGION / Schaff, Philip – Philadelphia: Lindsay & Blakiston; New York: Sheldon, Blakeman, 1857 – 1mf – us A.T.L.A. [943]

GERMANY : MONTHLY REPORTS BY THE EXECUTIVE COMMITTEE OF THE SOCIAL DEMOCRATIC PARTY OF GERMANY – (Englische Ausgabe der Deutschland-Berichte der SoPaDe) – Prag (Praha), Czechoslovakia-Paris, France. Jun 1937-Mar 1940 – 3r – 1 – gw Mikrofilm [072]

Germany *see*
- DEUTSCHER REICHS-ANZEIGER UND PREUSSISCHER STAATS-ANZEIGER
- GERMAN MILITARY AND TECHNICAL MANUALS, 1910-45
- GUIDE TO CAPTURED GERMAN DOCUMENTS
- JOURNAUX PUBLIES PAR LES PRISONNIERS DE GUERRE ALLEMANDS EN FRANCE 1946-1948
- MISCELLANEOUS GERMAN RECORDS COLLECTION
- PRUSSIAN MOBILIZATION RECORDS, 1866-1918
- RECORDS OF GERMAN AND JAPANESE EMBASSIES AND CONSULATES, 1890-1945
- RECORDS OF THE ROYAL BAVARIAN WAR MINISTRY AND OTHER BAVARIAN MILITARY AUTHORITIES, 1866-1913

GERMANY, 1919-41 : REPORTS / U.S. Military Intelligence; ed by Kesaris, Paul – (With printed guide. Series: US Military Intelligence Reports) – 1982 – 28r – 1 – $2,825.00 – 0-89093-426-6 – us UPA [355]

GERMANY, 1941-44 : REPORTS / U.S. Military Intelligence – (Pt 1: Geography, Population and Social Conditions, Politics and Government, Economy and Finance 42r $4,255.00 ISBN 0-89093-475-4. Pt 2: National Defense, Army, Navy and Military Aviation 37r $3,745.00 ISBN 0-89093-476-2. With printed guides. Series: US Military Intelligence Reports) – 79r – 1 – $7,590.00 coll – us UPA [355]

Germany. Air Force *see* ...RECORDS

Germany. Air Force High Command. Headquarters *see* RECORDS...(OBERKOMMANDO DER LUFTWAFFE-OKL)

GERMANY AND ITS OCCUPIED TERRITORIES DURING WORLD WAR 2 / U.S. Office of Strategic Services – (Series: OSS State Department Intelligence and Research Reports, Pt 4) – 1977 – 1 – $2,115.00 – 0-89093-120-8 – us UPA [943]

[GERMANY AND THE CAUSES AND ORIGINS OF WORLD WAR 1 PAMPHLET COLLECTION] – 1914-1929 – 6r – 1 – CSUXAML2952-B – us Hoover Inst Photo [320]

Germany. Armed Forces High Command. Headquarters *see* RECORDS

Germany. Army *see*
- RECORDS OF GERMAN ARMY AREAS
- RECORDS OF GERMAN FIELD COMMANDS: REAR AREAS, OCCUPIED TERRITORIES AND OTHERS

Germany. Army High Command. Headquarters *see* RECORDS

Germany. Auswaertiges Amt *see* DIE GROSSE POLITIK DER EUROPAEISCHEN KABINETTE

Germany. Berlin Documents Center *see*
- DOCUMENTATION CONCERNING JEWS IN THE BERLIN DOCUMENTS CENTER
- NAME INDEX OF JEWS WHOSE GERMAN NATIONALITY WAS ANNULLED BY THE NAZI REGIME

Germany. Democratic Republic *see*
- GESETZ UEBER DEN 2. FUENFJAHRPLAN. 1956-1960 (VOM 9 JAN 1958)
- GESETZ UEBER DEN FUENFJAHRPLAN. (1951-1955)
- GESETZ UEBER DEN PERSPEKTIVPLAN ZUR ENTWICKLUNG DER WOLKSWIRTSCHAFT DER D.D.R. BIS 1970 (VOM 26 MAI 1967)
- GESETZ UEBER DEN SIEBENJAHRPLAN. 1959 BIS 1965 (VOM 1. OKT 1959)
- GESETZ UEBER DEN VOLKSWIRTSCHAFTSPLAN 1950, DAS ZWEITE JAHR DES ZWEIJAHRPLANES DER DEUTSCHEN DEMOKRATISCHEN REPUBLIC
- GESETZ UEBER DEN VOLKSWIRTSCHAFTSPLAN 1951, DAS ERSTE JAHR DES FUENFJAHRPLANES DER D.D.R. (VON 14 MAR 1951)
- GESETZ UEBER DEN VOLKSWIRTSCHAFTSPLAN 1953, DAS DRITTE JAHR DAS FUENFJAHRPLANES. (VOM 17. DEZ 1952)
- GESETZ UEBER DEN VOLKSWIRTSCHAFTSPLAN 1965 (VOM 14. JAN 1965)
- GESETZ UEBER DEN VOLKSWIRTSCHAFTSPLAN 1967 (VOM 9. DEZ 1966)
- GESETZ UEBER DEN VOLKSWIRTSCHAFTSPLAN 1968 (VOM 15. DEZ 1967)
- LAW ON THE SEVEN YEAR PLAN FOR THE DEVELOPMENT OF THE GERMAN NATIONAL ECONOMY FROM 1959 TO 1965
- STATUTES

Germany. Democratic Republic. Amt fuer Information *see*
- DIE GESETZLICHEN BESTIMMUNGEN ZUM VOLKSWIRTSCHAFTSPLAN, 1950
- DER VOLKSWIRTSCHAFTSPLAN, 1950
- DER VOLKSWIRTSCHAFTSPLAN, 1951 DAS ERSTE JAHR DES FUENFJAHRPLANES DER DEUTSCHEN DEMOKRATISCHEN REPUBLIK

Germany. Democratic Republic. Ausschuss fuer Deutsche Einheit *see* DDR: DREIHUNDERT FRAGEN, 300 ANTWORTEN

Germany. Democratic Republic. Volkskammer *see* VOLKSKAMMER..

[GERMANY DURING WORLD WAR 1 AND THE REVOLUTION OF 1918 PAMPHLET COLLECTION] – 1914-19?? – 3r – 1 – CSUXANR3421-B – us Hoover Inst Photo [320]

Germany. Embassy. Washington, DC *see* ARCHIVES...(AMERICAN HISTORICAL ASSOC. PROJECT I)

Germany. Federal Republic *see*
- BUNDESANZEIGER
- BUNDESGESETZBLATT
- DEUTSCHER WETTERDIENST

Germany. Federal Republic. Bundesrat *see* VERHANDLUNGEN DES DEUTSCHEN BUNDESRATES, 1949-1995

Germany. Federal Republic. Bundesregierung *see* BULLETIN DES PRESSE- INFORMATIONSAMTES..

Germany. Federal Republic. Bundestag *see*
- VERHANDLUNGEN DES DEUTSCHEN BUNDESTAGES, 1949-1995
- VERHANDLUNGEN, STENOGRAPHISCHE BERICHTE

Germany. Foreign Ministry *see* RECORDS... PERTAINING TO CHINA, 1919-35

Germany. Foreign Office *see*
- A CATALOG OF FILES AND MICROFILMS OF THE GERMAN FOREIGN MINISTRY ARCHIVES, 1867-1920
- RECORDS...FILMED FOR THE UNIV. OF LONDON
- RECORDS...RECEIVED BY THE DEPT. OF STATE (U.S.A.)
- RECORDS...RECEIVED BY THE DEPT. OF STATE (U.S.A.) FROM ANTONY'S COLLEGE
- RECORDS...RECEIVED BY THE DEPT. OF STATE (U.S.A.) FROM THE UNIV. OF CALIFORNIA (PROJECT I)

Germany. Foreign Office. Archives *see* GERMAN FOREIGN MINISTRY ARCHIVES, 1867-1920

Germany. (formerly Democratic Republic). Staatliche Zentralverwaltung fuer Statistik *see* GERMANY (FORMERLY DEMOCRATIC REPUBLIK)

GERMANY (FORMERLY DEMOCRATIC REPUBLIK) : STATISTISCHES JAHRBUCH DER DEUTSCHEN DEMOKRATISCHEN REPUBLIK 1955-1965 / Germany. (formerly Democratic Republic). Staatliche Zentralverwaltung fuer Statistik – (Coll

title: European Official Statistical Serials, 1841-1984) – 75mf – 9 – £550.00 – uk Chadwyck [943]
GERMANY (FORMERLY FEDERAL REPUBLIC) : STATISTISCHES JAHRBUCH FUER DAS DEUTSCHE REICH 1880-1942 / Germany. (formerly Federal Republic). Statistisches Reichsamt – (Cont by: Statistisches Jahrbuch fuer die Bundesrepublik Deutschland 1952- 1965. Coll title: European Official Statistical Serials, 1841-1984) – 334mf – 9 – £4.00f (set £2,400.00 458mf) – uk Chadwyck [943]
Germany. (formerly Federal Republic). Statistische Bundesamt *see* GERMANY (FORMERLY FEDERAL REPUBLIK)
Germany. (formerly Federal Republic). Statistisches Reichsamt *see* GERMANY (FORMERLY FEDERAL REPUBLIC)
GERMANY (FORMERLY FEDERAL REPUBLIK) : STATISTISCHES JAHRBUCH FUER DIE BUNDESREPUBLIK DEUTSCHLAND 1952-1965 / Germany. (formerly Federal Republic). Statistische Bundesamt – (Cont: Statistisches Jahrbuch fuer das Deutsche Reich 1880-1942. Coll title: European Official Statistical Serials, 1841-1984) – 124mf – 9 – £5.00f (set £2,400.00 458mf) – uk Chadwyck [943]
Germany. Heer. Oberkommando *see*
- THE GERMAN ARMY HIGH COMMAND, 1938-1945
- OBERKOMMANDO DES HEERES

Germany. Kingdom of Prussia *see* STATE ARCHIVES-BAPTISTS
Germany. Kriegsmarine Oberkommando *see* FUEHRER CONFERENCES ON MATTERS DEALING WITH THE GERMAN NAVY, 1939-1945
Germany. Laws, Statutes etc *see* ALIEN LAW
[GERMANY NATIONALISM PAMPHLET COLLECTION] – 19?? – 1 – CSUXANQ7848-B – us Hoover Inst Photo [320]
Germany. Navy *see* RECORDS OF THE GERMAN NAVY,1850-1945, RECEIVED FROM THE U.S. NAVAL HISTORY DIVISION
Germany. Navy High Command. Headquarters *see* RECORDS
Germany. Navy. Operations Division. Staff *see* WAR DIARY, OPERATIONS DIVISION, GERMAN NAVAL STAFF, 1939-45
Germany. North German Confederation, 1866-70. Reichstag *see* STENOGRAPHISCHE BERICHTE UND ANLAGEN UEBER DIE VERHANDLUNGEN DES REICHSTAGES DES NORDDEUTSCHEN BUNDES
Germany. Office of the Deputy for Serbian Economy *see* RECORDS
Germany. Reich Commissioner for the Strengthening of Germandom *see* RECORDS
Germany. Reich Ministry for Armaments and War Production *see* RECORDS
Germany. Reich Ministry for Public Enlightenment and Propaganda *see* RECORDS, 1936-44
Germany. Reich Ministry of Economics *see* RECORDS
Germany. Reich SS. and German Police *see* RECORDS OF THE REICH LEADER OF THE SS AND CHIEF OF THE GERMAN POLICE
Germany. Reichsamt fuer Bodenforschung *see* PAPERS
Germany. Reichsarbeitsministerium. Hauptabteilung *see* DER ARBEITSEINSATZ IM DEUTSCHEN REICH
Germany. Reichskommissar fuer das Ostland *see* RECORDS OF THE REICH COMMISSIONER FOR THE BALTIC STATES, 1941-45
Germany. Reichsluftfahrtministerium. (Reich Air Ministry) *see* RECORDS
Germany. Reichsministerium des Innern *see* HANDBUCH FUER DAS DEUTSCHE REICH
Germany. Reichsministerium fuer Wissenschaft, Erziehung und Volksbildung *see* RICHTLINIEN FUER DIE LEIBERSERZIEHUNG IN JUNGENSCHULEN
Germany. Reichstag *see*
- VERHANDLUNGEN. LEGISLATURPERIODE
- VERHANDLUNGEN. STENOGRAPHISCHE

Germany. Statistiches Reichsamt *see* STATISTISCHES JAHRBUCH FUER DAS DEUTSCHE REICH
GERMANY (TERRITORY UNDER ALLIED OCCUPATION, 1945-1955, RUSSIAN ZONE) HAUPTVERWALTUNG ARBEIT UND SOZIALFURSORGE – Jahrbuch: arbeit und sozialfursorge. Berlin – 1 – us U.W. Library [943]
GERMANY (TERRITORY UNDER ALLIED OCCUPATION 1945-1955, RUSSIAN ZONE) STATISTISCHES ZENTRALAMT. VOLKS-UND BERUFSZAHLUNG VOM 29. OKTOBER 1946 IN DER SOWJETISCHEN BESATZUNGSZONE DEUTSCHLANDS – Berlin: Deutscher Zentralverlag, 1948 – 1 – us U.W. Library [943]
GERMANY TO-DAY – (Suppl.: Austria to-day; Cont by: Inside Nazi Germany, London) – London. Jan 1938-Sep 1939 – 1 – gw Mikrofilm [072]
GERMANY TODAY : NEWSLETTER – New York. 21 Jun 1945-7 Dec 1946 – 1r – 1 – gw Mikrofilm [071]
Germany. Todt Organization *see* RECORDS
[GERMANY'S FOREIGN RELATIONS WITH THE NETHERLANDS PAMPHLET COLLECTION] – 1921-1957 – 1 – CSUXANR2734-B – us Hoover Inst Photo [320]
[GERMANY'S POLITICAL RELATIONS WITH AUSTRIA PAMPHLET COLLECTION] – 1956-1957 – 1 – CSUXANR2688-B – us Hoover Inst Photo [320]
[GERMANY'S POLITICAL RELATIONS WITH BELGIUM PAMPHLET COLLECTION] – 19??-1954 – 1 – CSUXANR2692-B – us Hoover Inst Photo [320]
[GERMANY'S POLITICAL RELATIONS WITH CZECHOSLOVAKIA PAMPHLET COLLECTION] – 1949 – 1 – CSUXANR2698-B – us Hoover Inst Photo [320]
[GERMANY'S POLITICAL RELATIONS WITH DENMARK PAMPHLET COLLECTION] – 1958 – 1 – CSUXANR2706-B – us Hoover Inst Photo [320]
[GERMANY'S POLITICAL RELATIONS WITH FRANCE PAMPHLET COLLECTION] – 19??-1991 – 1 – CSUXANR2712-B – us Hoover Inst Photo [320]
[GERMANY'S POLITICAL RELATIONS WITH GREAT BRITAIN PAMPHLET COLLECTION] – 1911-1968 – 1 – CSUXANR2719-B – us Hoover Inst Photo [320]
[GERMANY'S POLITICAL RELATIONS WITH HUNGARY PAMPHLET COLLECTION] – 1955 – 1 – CSUXANR2722-B – us Hoover Inst Photo [320]
[GERMANY'S POLITICAL RELATIONS WITH INDONESIA PAMPHLET COLLECTION] – 1957 – 1 – CSUXANR2724-B – us Hoover Inst Photo [320]
[GERMANY'S POLITICAL RELATIONS WITH LUXEMBOURG PAMPHLET COLLECTION] – 1957 – 1 – CSUXANR2731-B – us Hoover Inst Photo [320]
[GERMANY'S POLITICAL RELATIONS WITH POLAND PAMPHLET COLLECTION] – 1916-1958 – 1 – CSUXANR2738-B – us Hoover Inst Photo [320]
[GERMANY'S POLITICAL RELATIONS WITH RUSSIA PAMPHLET COLLECTION] – 1921-1955? – 1 – CSUXANR2747-B – us Hoover Inst Photo [320]
[GERMANY'S POLITICAL RELATIONS WITH SCANDINAVIA PAMPHLET COLLECTION] – 1962 – 1 – CSUXANR2752-B – us Hoover Inst Photo [320]
[GERMANY'S POLITICAL RELATIONS WITH SWEDEN PAMPHLET COLLECTION] – 1958 – 1 – CSUXANR2757-B – us Hoover Inst Photo [320]
[GERMANY'S POLITICAL RELATIONS WITH THE UNITED STATES PAMPHLET COLLECTION] – 1917-1981 – 1 – CSUXANR2759-B – us Hoover Inst Photo [320]
Germar, E F *see*
- FAUNA INSECTORUM EUROPAE
- MAGAZIN DER ENTOMOLOGIE
- ZEITSCHRIFT FUER DIE ENTOMOLOGIE

O GERMEN : PERIODICO LITTERARIO – Penedo, Alagoas. 15 Jul 1901 – 1,5,6 – bl Biblioteca [072]
GERMINAL – Chicago, IL, 1913 – 1mf or 1r – 1,9 – us I.H.R.C. [978]
GERMINAL : ORGAO DOS ALUMNOS DO INSTITUTO ALAGOANO – Maceio, Alagoas. 10 Jul 1904 – 1,5,6 – bl Biblioteca [072]
GERMINAL : ORGAO LITTERARIO E NOTICIOSO – Penedo, Alagoas. 25 Jul-Dez 1909 – 1,5,6 – bl Biblioteca [072]
GERMINAL – Tout pour la Republique. Red. en chef P. Grousset. I, no. 1; II, no. 1-220. Paris. 18 dec 1892, 29 janv-6 sept 1893 – 1 – fr A.C.R.P.P. [073]
GERMINAL! – Messina, Italy, 1906 (May 6, July 22) – 3r – 1 – us I.H.R.C. [945]
GERMISTON ADVOCATE – Germiston, South Africa. 1923-82 – 1 – sa State Libr [072]
Germoni, A *see* DE LEGATIS PRINCIPUM,...
Gerock, C F *see* VERSUCH EINER DARSTELLUNG DER CHRISTOLOGIE DES KORAN
GERODONTOLOGY – v1-. Summer 1982- – 1,5,6,9 – us UMI [073]
GEROI I ZHERTVY REVOLIUTSII / ed by Maliakovskogo, Vladimira – Petrograd: Izd. Otdela izobrazitelnykh iskusstv Komissariata narodnogo prosveshchenii a, [1918?] – 1 – CSUX88-B4220 – us Hoover Inst Photo [947]
GEROI NE- REVOLIUTSII : FELETONY / Chaprusha – Aleksandropol: Tip. "Svoboda", 1917 – 1 – CSUX88-B6979 – us Hoover Inst Photo [947]
GEROI ROMANA / Ivnev, R – L. 1928. BR-1069 2 – 8 – ne IDC [460]
GEROICHESKII KHARAKTER RUSSKOI LITERATURY / Vengerov, S A – (Sobranie Sochinenii t.I). St. Petersburg, 1911. BR-2190/2 – 8 – ne IDC [460]
Gerok, Karl *see* DER WANDSBECKER BOTE
GERONIMO CASTILLO DE BOVADILLA / Elias de Tejada Spinola, Francisco – Madrid: Grafica Universal, 1939 – sp Bibl Santa Ana [940]
GERONTOLOGIST – (v10-. 1970-. 5,6,9) – v. 1- 1961- – 1 – us UMI [360]
GERONTOLOGY – v1-. 1957- – 1,5,9 – us UMI [073]
GERONTOLOGY AND GERIATRIC EDUCATION – 1980 – 1,5,6,9 – us UMI [618]
GERONTOLOGY AND GERIATRICS EDUCATION / ed by Dawson, Grace D – v1- . 1980- . q – 1, 9 ($200.00 in US $280.00 outside hardcopy subsc) – us Haworth [618]
GERONTOLOGY AND GERIATRICS TRAINING MATERIALS *see* MICROFICHE LIBRARY OF GERONTOLOGY AND GERIATRICS
GERONTOPICS – (1983-. 1,5,6,9) – v1-. 1977- – 1 – us UMI [073]
GERPOLEK: GERILA POLITIK EOKONOMI / Tan Malaka – SE 5154 1. 1964 – 9 – ne IDC [338]
Gerrald, J *see* A CONVENTION THE ONLY MEANS OF SAVING US FROM RUIN...
THE GERRARD STREET MYSTERY AND OTHER WEIRD TALES / Dent, John Charles – Toronto: Rose, 1888. 02639. (Pre-1900 Canadiana) – 9 – cn C.I.H.M. [830]
Gerretson, Frederik Carel *see* COENS EERHERSTEL
GERRIT SMITH : A BIOGRAPHY / Frothingham, Octavius Brooks – New York: G.P. Putnam, 1878, c1877 – 1mf – us A.T.L.A. [240]
GERRITSEN COLLECTION OF WOMEN'S HISTORY, 1543-1945 – (4471 monographs and pamphlets in English, French, German, and 12 other languages; 265 periodical titles. Parts available separately) – 17,556mf + 244r – 1 + 9 – $43,325.00 – us UMI [900]
Gerritsz, Hessell *see* DESCRIPTIO AC DELINEATIO GEOGRAPHICA DETECTIONIS FRETI, SIVE, TRANSITUS AD OCCASUM, SUPRA TERRAS AMERICANAS, IN CHINAM ARQ;...
Gerry, Elbridge *see* ELBRIDGE GERRY PAPERS
Gersdorf, F G *see* REPERTORIUM DER GESAMMTEN DEUTSCHEN LITERATUR
Gershenson, M *see* PEREPISKA IZ DVUKH UGLOV
Gershuni, Grigorii Andreevich *see* IZ NEDAVNIAGO PROSHLAGO
Gerson, Adolf *see* DER CHACHAM KOHELET ALS PHILOSOPH UND POLITIKER
Gerson, J *see* OM DYAEFWLSENS FRAESTILSE. JOHANNES FABRI
Gerson, Joh. *see* TRAKTAT UEBER DIE HINFUEHRUNG DER KLEINEN ZU CHRISTUS
Gerson, John *see* OPERA OMNIA
Gerstaecker, C E A *see* RHIPIPHORIDUM COLEOPTERORUM FAMILIAE DISPOSITIO SYSTEMATICA
Gerstaecker, Friedrich *see*
- GESAMMELTE SCHRIFTEN
- THE LITTLE WHALER; OR, THE ADVENTURES OF CHARLES HOLLBERG

Gerstenberg, Heinrich *see*
- DEUTSCHLAND, DEUTSCHLAND UEBER ALLES!
- HOFFMANN VON FALLERSLEBEN UND SEIN DEUTSCHES VATERLAND

Gerstenberg, Heinrich Wilhelm von et al *see* BRIEFE UEBER MERKWUERDIGKEITEN DER LITTERATUR
Gerstenhauer, Arthurius *see* DE ALCAEI ET SAPPHONIS COPIA VOCABULORUM
GERTRUD VON LODEN : EINE ERZAEHLUNG AUS DER SCHWEDENZEIT / Quandt, Clara – Braunschweig: Benno Goeritz, 1891 – 1r – 1 – us U.W. Library [830]
GERTRUDE OF WYOMING : A PENNSYLVANIAN TALE AND OTHER POEMS / Campbell, Thomas – London: Printed by T. Bensley, published for the author by Longman, Hurst, Rees, and Orme, 1809 – 1 roll – 1 – 1-55879-642-8 – uk Libr Preservation [810]
Gertsen, Aleksandr Ivanovich *see* OPIS' DIKUMENTAL'NYKH MATERIALOV FONDA NO.129
GERTSEN, OGAREV I IKH OKRUZHENIE – Rukopisi, perepiska i dokumenty. Moscow, 1940. 440p. Covers material now in TsGALI SSSR. BR-10,702/1 – 9 – ne IDC [335]
Gerua, Aleksandr Vladimirovich *see* K POZNANII U ARMII
Gervais, Albert *see* JOLIETTE ILLUSTRE: NUMERO SOUVENIR DE SES NOCES D'OR, 1843-93
Gervais, F L P *see* VOYAGE AUTOUR DU MONDE. LES ANNEES 1830, 1831, 1832
GERVAIS STAR – Gervais, OR. -w. 9 Jul 1926-16 Jan 1948. 7 rolls – 1 – us U.O. Library [071]
GERVAIS WEEKLY STAR – Gervais, OR. 1901-26 – 1 – 113.00 – us Oregon Hist [071]
Gervase Of Canterbury *see* HISTORICAL WORKS, THE CHRONICLE OF THE REIGNS OF STEPHEN, HENRY 2 AND RICHARD 1 (RS73)
Gervinus, Georg Gottfried *see* GESCHICHTE DER POETISCHEN NATIONAL-LITERATUR DER DEUTSCHEN
Gerwerkschaftsbund der Angestellten *see*
- BERICHT
- ORDENTLICHER BUNDESTAG

Gerz, Alfred *see* MEISTER MARTIN DER KUEFNER UND SEINE GESELLEN
GESAENGE AUS DEN DREI REICHEN : AUSGEWAEHLTE GEDICHTE / Werfel, Franz – 2. Aufl. Leipzig: K Wolff, c1917 – 1r – 1 – us U.W. Library [810]
GESAENGE MIT BEGLEITUNG DER FORTEPIANO / Schroeter, C – Weimar: in commission bey dem Industrie Comptoir, 1794 – 1 – us Sibley [780]
GESAMMELTE AUFSAETZE / Zuckermandel, M – v. 1-2. 2 v. Frankfurt a.M. 1911-15. Lacking: 1911, v. 1. BJ-100-12 1 – 9 – ne IDC [956]
GESAMMELTE DICHTUNGEN / Wagner, Christian; ed by Guentter, Otto – 1. Ausg. Stuttgart: Strecker und Schroeder, 1918 – 1r – 1 – us U.W. Library [810]
GESAMMELTE ERZAEHLUNGEN = SHORT STORIES / Raabe, Wilhelm Karl – Berlin: O. Janke, 1896-1900 – 1 – us U.W. Library [830]
GESAMMELTE GEDICHTE / Keller, Gottfried – Berlin: W Hertz, 1883 – 1 – us U.W. Library [810]
GESAMMELTE GEDICHTE / Sallet, Friedrich von – Leipzig: P Reclam, [18–?] – 1r – 1 – us U.W. Library [810]
GESAMMELTE GESCHICHTEN UND NOVELLEN = SHORT STORIES / Riehl, Wilhelm Heinrich – Stuttgart: J G Cotta, 1879 – 1 – us U.W. Library [830]
GESAMMELTE NOVELLEN UND ERZAEHLUNGEN / Birch-Pfeiffer, Charlotte – Leipzig: Reclam. 3v. 1863-65 – 1 – us U.W. Library [830]
GESAMMELTE PATRISTISCHE UNTERSUCHUNGEN / Draeseke, Johannes – Altona: A.C. Reher, 1889 – 1mf – us A.T.L.A. [240]
GESAMMELTE SCHRIFTEN / Berliner, Abraham – Frankfurt a.M. 1913. BJ-100-2 1 – 9 – ne IDC [920]
GESAMMELTE SCHRIFTEN / Birmann, Martin – Basel, Reich, 1894. 2 v. in 1. Film Mas 8765 – 1 – us H.U. Library [080]
GESAMMELTE SCHRIFTEN / Boerne, Ludwig – Vollsaendige Ausgabe. Wien, Tendler & Comp. (J. Grosser), 1868, 12 v. Film Mas 8592 – 1 – us H.U. Library [080]
GESAMMELTE SCHRIFTEN / Erter, I – Ed. 2. Vienna. 1864. BJ-422-15 1 – 9 – ne IDC [800]
GESAMMELTE SCHRIFTEN / Freud, Sigmund – t. I-XII). Wien – 1 – fr A.C.R.P.P. [150]
GESAMMELTE SCHRIFTEN / Gerstaecker, Friedrich – Jena. 43v. 1872-79 – 1 – $184.00 – us L of C Photodup [800]
GESAMMELTE SCHRIFTEN / Meissner, Alfred – Leipzig, Grunow, 1871-72. 18 v. Film Mas C 472 – 1 – us H.U. Library [080]

GESAMMELTE SCHRIFTEN / Mommsen, Theodor – Berlin. v. 1-8. 1905-1913 – 87mf – 8 – ne IDC [400]
GESAMMELTE SCHRIFTEN / Schlieffen, Alfred, Graf von – Berlin. Mittler. 1913. xiiii, 266p; vii, 460 p. (Strategy of War Series) – 9 – fr Hachette [355]
GESAMMELTE SCHRIFTEN / Seidel, Heinrich – 20 v. Film Mas C 419 – 1 – us H.U. Library [080]
GESAMMELTE SCHRIFTEN / Steinschneider, M – Berlin. 1925. BJ-100-11 1 – 9 – ne IDC [956]
GESAMMELTE SCHRIFTEN / Zschokke, Heinrich – 2., vermehrte Ausgabe. Aarau, H. R. Sauerlaender, 1865. 10 v. in 5. Film Mas 8653 – 1 – us H.U. Library [800]
GESAMMELTE SCHRIFTEN / Zunz, L – 3v. Berlin. 1875-76. BJ-23-120 1 – 9 – ne IDC [270]
GESAMMELTE SCHRIFTEN IN 15 (16) BAENDEN = WORKS / Laube, Heinrich – Wien: W Braumueller, 1875-82 – 1 – us U.W. Library [800]
GESAMMELTE SCHRIFTEN: VOLKS- UND FAMILIEN-AUSGABE / Schmid, Hermann von – Leipzig, Keil, 18 . 50v. Film Mas C 438 – 1 – us H.U. Library [900]
GESAMMELTE SCHRIFTEN VON DAVID KAUFMANN / Kaufmann, David – 3v. Frankfurt a.M. 1908-15. BJ-100-7 1 – 9 – ne IDC [900]
GESAMMELTE SCHRIFTEN VON G. RIESSER / Riesser, G – 4v. Frankfurt a.M. 1867-68. BJ-23-116 1 – 9 – ne IDC [940]
GESAMMELTE SCHRIFTEN VON L. LOEW / Loew, L – 5v. Szegedin. 1889-1900. BJ-100-9 1 – 9 – ne IDC [900]
GESAMMELTE SCHRIFTEN ZUR MINDERHEITENFRAGE / Bruns, C G – Berlin, 1933 – 4mf – 1 – ILM-1578/1 – ne IDC [327]
GESAMMELTE WERKE / Anzengruber, Ludwig – Stuttgart. 1890. 10v. in 5. Film Mas 8276 – 1 – us H.U. Library [080]
GESAMMELTE WERKE : BAND 1-5 / Braun, Lily – (1. Band: Im Schatten der Titanen und Julie Vogelstein: Lily Braun. Ein Lebensbild 6mf DM90.00 ISBN 3-8267-3173-5. 2. Band: Memoiren einer Sozialistin. Lehrjahre. Roman 6mf DM90.00 ISBN 3-8267-3174-3. 3. Band: Memoiren einer Sozialistin. Kampfjahre. Roman 6mf DM90.00 ISBN 3-8267-3175-1. 4. Band: Lebensucher. Roman und: Mutter Maria. Eine Tragoedie in fuenf Akten 6mf DM90.00 ISBN 3-8267-3176-X. 5. Band: Die Liebesbriefe der Marquise. Madeleine Guimard. Eine lyrische Oper in drei Akten 5mf DM80.00 ISBN 3-8267-3177-8) – 1995 – 29mf – 9 – DM380.00 – 3-8267-3178-6 – gw Hänsel [943]
GESAMMELTE WERKE / Chamisso, Adelbert von; ed by Koch, Max – (Includes bibliographical references and index) – Stuttgart: J G Cotta. 4v. [1882?] – 1 – us U.W. Library [800]
GESAMMELTE WERKE : ERSTE SERIE / Zahn, Ernst – Stuttgart: Deutsche Verlags-Anstalt. 10v. [192-?] – 1 – us U.W. Library [800]
GESAMMELTE WERKE / Freytag, Gustav – Leipzig, S. Hirzel, 1887-88. 32 v. Film Mas C 541 – 1 – us H.U. Library [080]
GESAMMELTE WERKE / Hoelderlin, Friedrich; ed by Boehm, Wilhelm – Jena: E Diederichs. 3v. 1905 – 1 – us U.W. Library [800]
GESAMMELTE WERKE / MacKay, John Henry – Treptow bei Berlin, B. Zack, 1911. 8 v. Film Mas 8193 – 1 – us H.U. Library [080]
GESAMMELTE WERKE / Mosenthal, Salomon Hermann von – Stuttgart, etc., E. Hallberger, 1878, 6v. Film Mas 8518 – 1 – us H.U. Library [080]
GESAMMELTE WERKE / Stehr, Hermann; ed by Tau, Max – Trier: F Lintz, 1924 – 2r – 1 – us U.W. Library [800]
GESAMMELTE WERKE = WORKS / Rosegger, Peter – (Includes index) – Neub. und neueingeleit. Ausg. Leipzig: L Staackmann, 1922-1924 – 1 – us U.W. Library [800]
GESAMMELTE WERKE = WORKS. 1911 / Wildenbruch, Ernst von; ed by Litzmann, Berthold – (Includes bibliographical references) – Berlin: G Grote. 6v. 1911-1924 – 5r – 1 – us U.W. Library [800]
GESAMMELTE WERKE VON LUDWIG ANZENGRUBER / Anzengruber, Ludwig; ed by Bettelheim, Anton et al – Stuttgart: J G Cotta, 1897-1898 – 10v – 1 – us U.W. Library [800]
DIE GESAMMELTEN GEDICHTE / Lasker-Schueler, Else – 2. Aufl. Leipzig: K Wolff, [19-?] – 1r – 1 – us U.W. Library [810]
GESAMMTGESCHICHTE DES NEUEN TESTAMENTS ODER NEUTESTAMENTLICHE ISAGOGIK / Guericke, H E F – Leipzig 2. Auflage 1854 – 13mf – 8 – ne Slangenburg [220]
GESAMMT-REGISTER ZU AMTSBLATT AND GESETZESSAMMLUNGEN DES KANTONS ZURICH / Zurich. (Canton). Laws, Statutes, etc. (Indexes) – Zurich. Genossenschaftsbuchdruckerei, 1882. 182 p. LL-4085 – 1 – us L of C Photodup [340]
GESAMMT-VERLAGS-KATALOG DES DEUTSCHEN BUCHHANDELS UND DES MIT IHM IM DIREKTEN VERKEHR STEHENDEN AUSLANDES = COMPLETE PUBLISHERS' CATALOGUE OF THE GERMAN BOOK TRADE AND FOREIGN COUNTRIES IN CONTACT WITH IT / ed by Russell, Adolph & Basch, Johannes – 1986 – 217mf (1:24) – 9 – silver DM1,600.00 – 3-598-10625-4 – gw Saur [070]
GESAMTVERANTWORTUNG UND SPEZIFIK: DIE CDU-PRESSE IN DER ENTWICKLUNG DES DDR-JOURNALISMUS 1957 BIS 1961 / Fischer, Gerhard – Berlin: Union Verlag, 1971. 175p – apply; – us U.W. Library [070]
Gesamtverband der Arbeiternehmer der offentlichen betriebe und des Personen- und verkehrs *see* JAHRBUCH
GESAMTVERBAND DER CHRISTLICHEN GEWERKSCHAFTEN DEUTSCHLANDS – Krefeld, Germany. 1901-04 – 1 – gw Mikrofilm [072]
Gesamtverband der Christlichen Gewerkschaften Deutschlands *see* JAHRBUCH..
GESAMTVERZEICHNIS DES DEUTSCHSPRACHIGEN SCHRIFTTUMS 1700-1910 = BIBLIOGRAPHY OF GERMAN-LANGUAGE PUBLICATIONS / ed by Schmuck, Hilmar & Gorzny, Willi – 1986 – 795mf (1:24) – 9 – diazo DM5,600.00 (silver DM6,200.00 ISBN: 3-598-30595-8) – 3-598-30590-7 – gw Saur [010]
GESAMTVERZEICHNIS DES DEUTSCHSPRACHIGEN SCHRIFTTUMS, 1911-1965 = BIBLIOGRAPHY OF GERMAN-LANGUAGE PUBLICATIONS, 1911-1965 / ed by Oberschlep, Reinhard – 1984 – 400mf (1:42) – 9 – diazo DM5,600.00 silver DM6,200.00 – gw Saur [010]
GESANG DES DEUTSCHEN / Hoelderlin, Friedrich – Frankfurt (Main): Hausdruckerei der Bauerschen, [1925?] – 1 – us U.W. Library [810]
GESCH. D. GOTTES BEWEISE IM MA BIS Z. AUSGANG D. HOCHSCHOLASTIK : BGPHMA 6/3 / Grunwald, G – Muenster, 1907 – 3mf – 9 – ne Slangenburg [240]
GESCH. D. GOTTES BEWEISE IM MA BIS Z. AUSGANG D. HOCHSCHOLASTIK / Grunwald, G – Muenster, 1907 – 3mf – 8 – ne Slangenburg [290]
DIE GESCHAEFTIGE MARTHA *see* DER FROEHLICHE BOTSCHAFTER
GESCHAEFTS- UND KASSENBERICHT / Zentralverband christlicher Lederarbeiter Deutschlands – 1907/09. Includes Protokoll der V. Generalversammlung, 1909. (Serial publications of German trade unions in the Memorial Library, University of Wisconsin-Madison) – 1 – us U.W. Library [330]
GESCHAEFTS- UND UNTERHALTUNGS-BLATT FUER GLADBACH UND DESSEN UMGEBUNG – 1837-1838 – 1r – 1 – DM75.00 – gw Mikro Press [072]
GESCHAEFTSBERICHT / Allgemeiner deutscher Gewerkschaftsbund. Ortsausschuss Berlin – Berlin. v15, 20, 27, 29-40. 1903-31. Includes Bericht des Arbeitersekretariats. (Serial publications of German trade unions in the Memorial Library, University of Wisconsin-Madison) – 1 – us U.W. Library [073]
GESCHAEFTSBERICHT / Arbeiter-Sekretariat. Halle – Halle. v2,4. 1901-03. (Serial publications of German trade unions in the Memorial Library, University of Wisconson-Madison) – 1 – us U.W. Library [330]
GESCHAEFTSBERICHT / ed by Club der Filmindustrie – Berlin. 1916. 1918 – 1 – gw Mikrofilm [650]
GESCHAEFTSBERICHT / Deutscher Arbeitgeberbund fuer das Baugewerbe – Berlin. 1926/27, 1929/30. (Serial Publications of German trade unions in the Memorial Library, University of Wisconsin-Madison.) – 1 – us U.W. Library [073]
GESCHAEFTSBERICHT / Deutscher Handels- und Industrieangestellten-Verband – 1927-28. (Serial publications of German trade unions in the Memorial Library, University of Wisconsin-Madison.) – 1 – us U.W. Library [330]
GESCHAEFTSBERICHT / Deutscher Werkmeister-Verband – Duesseldorf. 1924-25, 1926-27, 1928-29, 1930-31. (Serial publications of German trade unions in the Memorial Library, University of Wisconsin-Madison.) – 1 – us U.W. Library [330]
GESCHAEFTSBERICHT / Deutscher Wirtschaftsbund fuer das Baugewerbe – Berlin. 1928-29, 1930-31. (Serial publications of German trade unions in the Memorial Library, University of Wisconsin-Madison.) – 1 – us U.W. Library [330]
GESCHAEFTSBERICHT / Freier Deutscher Gewerkschaftsbund. Berlin – 1946. 431p. illus. map, ports – 1 – us U.W. Library [330]
GESCHAEFTSBERICHT / Verband der Bergarbeiter Deutschlands – Bochum. 1913/14. (Serial publications of German trade unions in the Memorial Library, University of Wisconsin-Madison) – 1 – us U.W. Library [330]
GESCHAEFTSBERICHT / Verband der Buchbinder und Papierverarbeiter Deutschlands – Berlin. 1906, 1921, 1925-31. Title varies: Bericht. (Serial publications of German trade unions in the Memorial Library, University of Wisconsin-Madison.) – 1 – us U.W. Library [330]
GESCHAEFTSBERICHT / Verband der Gaertner und Gaertnereiarbeiter – 1920/25. s.l.: s.n. Until 1919, organization called Allgemeiner deutscher Gaertnerverein. Some vols. also include ITS: Verhandlungsbericht des Verbandstages. (Serial publications of German trade unions in the Memorial Library, University of Wisconsin-Madison.) – 1 – us U.W. Library [330]
GESCHAEFTSBERICHT / Verband der Gemeinde- und Staatsarbeiter – Berlin. 1922/23, 1926, 1928. (Serial publications of German trade unions in the Memorial Library, University of Wisconsin-Madison.) – 1 – us U.W. Library [330]
GESCHAEFTSBERICHT / Verband der Graphischen Hilfsarbeiter und -arbeiterinnen Deutschlands – 1927. Berlin. (Serial publications of German trade unions in the Memorial Library, University of Wisconsin-Madison.) – 1 – us U.W. Library [330]
GESCHAEFTSBERICHT / Verband deutscher Arbeitsnachweise – 1898/99. Berlin. (Serial publications of German trade unions in the Memorial Library, University of Wisconsin-Madison) – 1 – us U.W. Library [330]
GESCHAEFTSBERICHT / Verband deutscher Textilarbeiter – 1906/07. Berlin. (Serial publications of German trade unions in the Memorial Library, University of Wisconsin-Madison.) – 1 – us U.W. Library [330]
GESCHAEFTSBERICHT / Vereinigung der deutschen Arbeitgeberverbaende – Berlin. 1921/22, 1927/29. (Serial publications of German trade unions in the Memorial Library, University of Wisconsin-Madison.) – 1 – us U.W. Library [330]
GESCHAEFTSBERICHT / Zentralverband der Angestellten – 1919/20, 1924/25, 1928/30. Berlin. (Serial publications of German trade unions in the Memorial Library, University of Wisconsin-Madison.) – 1 – us U.W. Library [330]
GESCHAEFTSBERICHT / Zentralverband der Arbeitnehmer oeffentlicher Betriebe und Verwaltungen – Koeln. 1925 27. (Serial publications of German trade unions in the Memorial Library, University of Wisconsin-Madison.) – 1 – us U.W. Library [330]
GESCHAEFTSBERICHT / Zentralverband der Handlungsgehilfen – 1912. (Serial publications of German trade unions in the Memorial Library, University of Wisconsin-Madison.) – 1 – us U.W. Library [330]
GESCHAEFTSBERICHT / Zentralverband der Lederarbeiter und Arbeiterinnen Deutschlands – 1905-07. Berlin. (Serial publications of German trade unions in the Memorial Library, University of Wisconsin-Madison.) – 1 – us U.W. Library [330]
GESCHAEFTSBERICHT.. / Arbeiterwohlfahrt Hauptausschuss – 1926. (Serial publications of German trade unions in the Memorial Library, University of Wisconsin-Madison) – 1 – us U.W. Library [073]
GESCHAEFTSBERICHT.. / Gewerkschaft deutscher Eisenbahner – v4-5. 1928-31. (Serial publications of German trade unions in the Memorial Library, University of Wisconsin-Madison.) – 1 – us U.W. Library [330]
GESCHAEFTSBERICHT.. / Gewerkverein christlicher Bergarbeiter Deutschlands – Essen. 1911/12, 1921/25, 1928/29. Title varies. (Serial publications of German trade unions in the Memorial Library, University of Wisconsin-Madison) – 1 – us U.W. Library [330]
GESCHAEFTSBERICHT DER KONZENTRATION – Berlin, 1925-29 – 1 – Dist. gw Mikrofilm – gw Misc Inst [072]
GESCHAEFTSBERICHT DES RHEINISCH-WESFAELISCHEN KOHLENSYNDIKATS – Essen-Ruhr, 1893-1939/40 – 2r – 1 – DM220.00 – gw Mikro Press [072]
GESCHAEFTSBERICHT DES VORSTANDES / Zentralverband aller in der Schmiederei beschaeftigten Personen – 1906. Hamburg. (Serial publications of German trade unions in the Memorial Library, University of Wisconsin-Madison.) – 1 – us U.W. Library [330]
GESCHAEFTSBERICHT DES ZENTRALVORSTANDES / Zentralverband der Schuhmacher Deutschlands – 1908/09, 1910/11. Nuernberg. (Serial publications of German trade unions in the Memorial Library, University of Wisconsin-Madison.) – 1 – us U.W. Library [330]
GESCHAEFTSBERICHTE DER BEZIRKE/ LANDESVERBAENDE / Sozialdemokratische Partei Deutschlands – 1946-1968 – 1 – DM890.00 – gw Mikro Press [943]
GESCHAEFTSBERICHTE DEUTSCHER UNTERNEHMEN 1981 BIS 1990 – (Einer Auswahl von 54 der groeßten Industrieunternehmen, Banken, Versicherungen und Dienstleistern) – 448mf – 9 – DM5,400.00 – gw Keip [650]
GESCHAEFTSBRIEFE SCHILLER'S / ed by Goedeke, Karl – Leipzig: Veit, 1875 – 1r – 1 – us U.W. Library [920]
DIE GESCHAEFTS-ORDNUNG DES CONCILS VON TRIENT : AUS EINER HANDSCHRIFT DES VATICANISCHEN ARCHIVES ZUM ERSTENMALE GENAU UND VOLLSTAENDIG AN'S LICHT GESTELLT: SAMMT EINEM VORBERICHTE – Wien: Carl Gerold, 1871 – 1mf – 9 – 0-8370-8331-1 – 1986-2331 – us A.T.L.A. [240]
GESCHICHT (EYN NEW WARHAFFTIG) ODER HYSTORI. VON JOERGEN WAGNER ALS EYN KETZER VERBRANDT IM JAR M.D.XXVIJ – n.d. BME-9 1 – 9 – ne IDC [240]
GESCHICHTE DER ALTBULGARISCHEN KUNST BIS ZUR EROBERUNG DES BULGARISCHEN REICHES DURCH DIE TUERKEN / Filov, B D – Berlin. 1932. BR-3820 2 – 8 – ne IDC [949]
GESCHICHTE DER ALTHEBRAEISCHEN LITTERATUR (MIT) APOKRYPHEN UND PSEUDEPIGRAPHEN / Budde, Karl – Leipzig: C.F. Amelang, 1906. 1 fiche – 9 – us A.T.L.A. [220]
GESCHICHTE DER ALTKIRCHLICHEN LITTERATUR / Bardenhewer, Otto – Freiburg, 1902-1924. Band 1-4 – 69mf – 8 – ne Slangenburg [240]
GESCHICHTE DER ALTTESTAMENTLICHEN WEISSAGUNG, THEILE 1 : DIE VORGESCHICHTE DER ALTTESTAMENTLICHEN WEISSAGUNG / Baur, Gustav – (No further parts were published) – Giessen:J Ricker, 1861 – 1mf – 9 – 0-8370-2216-9 – 1985-0216 – us A.T.L.A. [220]
GESCHICHTE DER ATTRIBUTENLEHRE : IN DER JUEDISCHEN RELIGIONSPHILOSOPHIE DES MITTELALTERS VON SAADJA BIS MAIMUENI / Kaufmann, David – Gotha: F.A. Perthes, 1877 – 2mf – 9 – us A.T.L.A. [270]
GESCHICHTE DER ATTRIBUTENLEHRE IN DER JUEDISCHEN RELIOGIONSPHILOSOPHIE VON SAADIA BIS MAIMUNI / Kaufmann, David – Gotha. 1877. BJ-33-4 1 – 9 – ne IDC [180]
DIE GESCHICHTE DER AUFERWECKUNG DES LAZARUS / Steinmeyer, Franz Ludwig – (Includes bibliographical references) – Berlin: Wiegandt und Grieben, 1888 – 1mf – 9 – 0-8370-5389-7 – 1985-3389 – us A.T.L.A. [240]

GESCHICHTE DER AUFLOESUNG DER ALTEN GOTTESDIENSTLICHEN KIRCHE DEUTSCHLANDS / Graff, P – Goettingen. v1-2. 1937-1939 – Dfl53.00 – ne Slangenburg [240]

GESCHICHTE DER AUFTEILUNG...AFRIKAS... / Darmstaedter, P – Berlin, Leipzig, 1913-20 – 6mf – 1 – ILM-850/1 – ne IDC [327]

GESCHICHTE DER AUGENHEILKUNDE / Hirschberg, J – Leipzig, 1899-1918 – 93mf – 9 – ne IDC [617]

GESCHICHTE DER BERLINER MISSIONGESELLSCHAFT UND IHRER ARBEITEN IN SUEDAFRICA / Wangemann, Hermann Theodor – Berlin, 1872-77.4v in 6. (Religion Series) – 9 – 87.00 – fr Bibl Nationale [240]

GESCHICHTE DER BERLINER MISSIONSGESELLSHAFT UND IHRER ARBEITEN IN SUDAFRICA, MIT EINER UEBERSICHTSKARTE UND VIELEN BILDERN / Wangemann, Hermann Theodor – 5V. 1872-77 – 1 – us A.T.L.A. [240]

GESCHICHTE DER BOEHMISCHEN REFORMATION IM FUENFZEHNTEN JAHRHUNDERT / Krummel, L – Gotha: F.A. Perthes, 1866 – 2mf – us A.T.L.A. [943]

GESCHICHTE DER BOTANIK / Meyer, E H F – 4v. Koenigsberg. 1854-57. B-8317 1 – 9 – ne IDC [580]

GESCHICHTE DER BOTANIK UNSERER ZEITEN / Medikus, F K – Mannheim. 1793. B-8141 1 – 9 – ne IDC [580]

GESCHICHTE DER BULGAREN / Jirecek, C J – Prague. 1876. BR-3878 2 – 8 – ne IDC [940]

GESCHICHTE DER BULGARISCHEN KUNST UNTER DER TUERKISCHEN HERRSCHAFT UND IN DER NEUEREN ZEIT / Filov, B D – Berlin. 1933. BR-3821 2 – 8 – ne IDC [949]

GESCHICHTE DER BULGARISCHEN SPRACHE / Mladenov, S – Berlin, Leipzig. 1929. BR-3968 2 – 8 – ne IDC [460]

GESCHICHTE DER CHRISTLICHEN ARABISCHEN LITERATUR : BAND 1: DIE UEBERSETZUNGEN / Georg, Graf – 1944 – 18mf – 8 – ne Slangenburg [240]

GESCHICHTE DER CHRISTLICHEN ARABISCHEN LITERATUR : BAND 2: DIE SCHRIFTSTELLER... / Georg, Graf – 1947 – 14mf – 8 – ne Slangenburg [240]

GESCHICHTE DER CHRISTLICHEN ARABISCHEN LITERATUR : BAND 3: DIE SCHRIFTSTELLER... / Georg, Graf – 1949 – 14mf – 8 – ne Slangenburg [240]

GESCHICHTE DER CHRISTLICHEN ARABISCHEN LITERATUR : BAND 4: DIE SCHRIFTSTELLER... / Georg, Graf – 1951 – 10mf – 8 – ne Slangenburg [240]

GESCHICHTE DER CHRISTLICHEN ETHIK / Gass, W – Berlin: G. Reimer, 1881-87 – 3mf – us A.T.L.A. [240]

GESCHICHTE DER DEUTSCHEN ARBEITSBEWEGUNG IN 15 KAPITELN / Berlin. Institut fuer Marxismus-Leninismus – Autorenkollektiv: Walter Ulbricht et al.1966-69. 15v – 1 – us U.W. Library [335]

GESCHICHTE DER DEUTSCHEN DICHTUNG / Pfeiffer-Belli, Wolfgang – (Includes bibliographical references and index) – Freiburg: Herder, 1954 – 1r – 1 – us U.W. Library [430]

GESCHICHTE DER DEUTSCHEN DICHTUNG / Roehl, Hans – (Includes bibliographical references and index) – Leipzig: B G Teubner, 1914 – 1r – 1 – us U.W. Library [430]

GESCHICHTE DER DEUTSCHEN DICHTUNG NACH IHREN EPOCHEN DARGESTELLT / Schneider, Hermann – Bonn: Athenaeum-Verlag, 1949-50 – 1r – 1 – us U.W. Library [430]

GESCHICHTE DER DEUTSCHEN DICHTUNG NACH IHREN EPOCHEN DARGESTELLT / Schneider, Hermann – (Includes bibliographical references and index) – Bochum: Deutscher Buchklub, [1952?] – 1r – 1 – us U.W. Library [430]

GESCHICHTE DER DEUTSCHEN DICHTUNG VON DEN AELTESTEN DENKMAELERN BIS AUF DIE NEUZEIT / Roquette, Otto – (Includes index) – 3. durchgesehene Aufl, neue unveraenderte Ausg. Frankfurt a.M.: Literarische Anstalt Ruetten & Loening, 1882 – 1 – us U.W. Library [430]

GESCHICHTE DER DEUTSCHEN EVANGELISCHEN SYNODE VON NORD-AMERIKA : IM AUFTRAGE DER SYNODE ZU IHREM FUENFUNDSIEBZIGJAEHRIGEN JUBILAEUM / Muecke, Albert – St. Louis, Mo.: Eden Publishing House, 1915 – 1mf – us A.T.L.A. [240]

GESCHICHTE DER DEUTSCHEN FRAUENDICHTUNG SEIT 1800 / Spiero, Heinrich – Leipzig, 1913 – 139p – 9 – DM48.00 – 3-89349-109-0 – gw Hänsel [430]

GESCHICHTE DER DEUTSCHEN GOETHE-BIOGRAPHIE : EIN KRITISCHER ABRISS / Mayne, Harry Wilhelm – 2. Abdruck. Leipzig: H Haessel, 1914 – 1 – us U.W. Library [430]

GESCHICHTE DER DEUTSCHEN LITERATUR / Bartels, Adolf – (Includes indexes) – Leipzig: H Haessel, 1924-1928 – 1 – us U.W. Library [430]

GESCHICHTE DER DEUTSCHEN LITERATUR / Fechter, Paul – (Includes index) – [Guetersloh]: C Bertelsmann, 1952 – 1r – 1 – us U.W. Library [430]

GESCHICHTE DER DEUTSCHEN LITERATUR / Fechter, Paul – (Includes index) – [Guetersloh]: S Mohn, [1960] – 1r – 1 – us U.W. Library [430]

GESCHICHTE DER DEUTSCHEN LITERATUR / Grabert, Willy – (Includes index) – Muenchen: Bayerischer Schulbuch-Verlag, 1953 – 1 – us U.W. Library [430]

GESCHICHTE DER DEUTSCHEN LITERATUR / Howald, Johann – (Includes index) – Konstanz: C Hirsch, [1903] – 1r – 1 – us U.W. Library [430]

GESCHICHTE DER DEUTSCHEN LITERATUR / Kurz, Heinrich; ed by Garber, Klaus – Leipzig. 3v. 1853-59 – 27mf – 9 – subsc: DM190.00 diazo DM250.00 silver – gw Olms [430]

GESCHICHTE DER DEUTSCHEN LITERATUR / Laube, Heinrich; ed by Garber, Klaus – Stuttgart. 3v. 1839-40 – 15mf – 9 – DM130.00 diazo – gw Olms [430]

GESCHICHTE DER DEUTSCHEN LITERATUR : MIT EINEM ABRISS DER GESCHICHTE DER DEUTSCHEN SPRACHE UND METRIK / Boetticher, Gotthold & Kinzel, K – (Includes bibliographical references and index) – Halle a.S.: Buchhandlung des Waisenhauses, 1896 – 1r – 1 – us U.W. Library [430]

GESCHICHTE DER DEUTSCHEN LITERATUR / Scherer, Wilhelm & Walzel, Oskar – (Includes bibliographical references and indexes) – 4. Aufl. Berlin: Askanischer Verlag, C A Kindle, 1928 – 1 – us U.W. Library [430]

GESCHICHTE DER DEUTSCHEN LITERATUR / Scherer, Wilhelm & Walzel, Oskar – (Includes bibliographical references and indexes) – 4. Aufl. Berlin: Askanischer Verlag, C A Kindle, 1928 – 1r – 1 – us U.W. Library [430]

GESCHICHTE DER DEUTSCHEN LITERATUR BIS ZUR MITTE DES ELFTEN JAHRHUNDERTS / Unwerth, Wolf von – (Includes bibliographical references and index) – Berlin: Vereinigung wissenschaftlicher Verleger, 1920 – 1r – 1 – us U.W. Library [430]

GESCHICHTE DER DEUTSCHEN LITERATUR VON DEN ANFAENGEN BIS ZUR GEGENWART / Linden, Walther – (Includes index) – 5. Aufl. Leipzig: P Reclam, 1944, c1937 – 1r – 1 – us U.W. Library [430]

GESCHICHTE DER DEUTSCHEN LITTERATUR / Scherer, Wilhelm; ed by Garber, Klaus – Berlin, 1883 – 9mf – 9 – DM90.00 – gw Olms [430]

GESCHICHTE DER DEUTSCHEN LITTERATUR VON DEN AELTESTEN ZEITEN BIS ZUR GEGENWART / Vogt, Friedrich Hermann Traugott & Koch, Max – (Includes index) – Leipzig: Bibliographisches Institut, 1897 – 1 – us U.W. Library [430]

GESCHICHTE DER DEUTSCHEN LITTERATUR VON IHREN ANFAENGEN BIS AUF DIE NEUESTE ZEIT / Hirsch, Franz – Leipzig, W. Friedrich 1883-85. 3.v. (Geschichte der Weltlitteratur in Einzeldarstellungen, Bd. v.) Film Mas 8652 – 1 – us H.U. Library [430]

GESCHICHTE DER DEUTSCHEN MYSTIK IM MITTELALTER / Preger, W – (1st Teil.-Leipzig, 1874.-9mf; 2nd Teil.-Leipzig, 1881.-8mf; 3rd Teil.- Leipzig, 1893.-8mf) – 8 – ne Slangenburg [290]

GESCHICHTE DER DEUTSCHEN NATIONAL-LITERATUR : ZUM GEBRAUCH AN HOEHEREN UNTERRICHTSANSTALTEN UND ZUM SELBSTSTUDIUM / Kluge, Hermann – (Includes bibliographical references and index) – 21. verb. Aufl. Altenburg: O Bonde, 1890 – 1r – 1 – us U.W. Library [430]

GESCHICHTE DER DEUTSCHEN NATIONAL-LITTERATUR MIT PROBEN DER DEUTSCHEN DICHTKUNST UND BEREDSAMKEIT / Herzog, Karl; ed by Garber, Klaus – Jena, 1831 – 4mf – 9 – subsc: DM40.00 – gw Olms [430]

GESCHICHTE DER DEUTSCHEN SPRACHE – Mit Texten und Uebersetzungshilfen. Berlin: Verlag Volk und Wissen, 1969. 428p. with illus. and 4 folding tables (in pocket) – 1 – us U.W. Library [430]

DIE GESCHICHTE DER DOGMATISCHEN FLORILEGIEN VOM 5.-8. JAHRHUNDERT (T.U.U. 2-28/1) / Schermann, Theodor – Leipzig, 1904 – 2mf – 9 – ne Slangenburg [240]

GESCHICHTE DER DOMSCHULE ZU REVAL : 1319-1939 / Thomson, Erik – (Includes bibliographical references and index) – Wuerzburg: Holzner Verlag, 1969 – 1 – us U.W. Library [370]

GESCHICHTE DER EINFUEHRUNG DES CHRISTENTUMS IM SUEDWESTLICHEN DEUTSCHLAND : BESONERS IN WUERTEMBERG / Hefele, C J – Tuebingen: H. Laupp, 1837 – 1mf – us A.T.L.A. [240]

GESCHICHTE DER ENTSTEHUNG UND AUSBILDUNG DES KIRCHENSTAATES / Sugenheim, Samuel – Leipzig: F.A. Brockhaus, 1854 – 2mf – us A.T.L.A. [240]

GESCHICHTE DER EVANGEL. KIRCHE DEUTSCHLANDS : IN DER ERSTEN HAELFTE DES 19. JAHRHUNDERTS / Tischhauser, Christian – Basel: S. Reich, 1900 – 2mf – us A.T.L.A. [240]

GESCHICHTE DER EVANGELISCHEN HEIDENMISSION : MIT BESONDERER BERUECKSICHTIGUNG DER DEUTSCHEN / Gareis, Reinhold – (Includes index) – Konstanz: Carl Kirsch, [1901?] – 2mf – 9 – 0-8370-7141-0 – 1986-1141 – us A.T.L.A. [240]

GESCHICHTE DER EVANGELISCHEN KIRCHENVERFASSUNG IN DEUTSCHLAND / Richter, Ludwig – Leipzig: Bernh. Tauchnitz, 1851 – 1mf – us A.T.L.A. [240]

GESCHICHTE DER EVANGEL.-LUTH. SYNODE VON IOWA UND ANDEREN STAATEN / Deindoerfer, Johannes – Chicago, Ill.: Wartburg Pub. House, 1897 – 2mf – us A.T.L.A. [240]

DIE GESCHICHTE DER FAMILIE LESSING / Buchholtz, Arend; ed by Lessing, Carl Robert – Berlin: Druck von O v Holten. 2v. 1909 – 1 – us U.W. Library [920]

GESCHICHTE DER FANATISCHEN UND ENTHUSUASTISCHEN WIEDERTAEUFER VORNEHMLICH IN NIEDERDEUTSCHLAND. MELCHIOR HOFMANN UND DIE SECTE DER HOFMANNIANER / Krohn, Barthold N – 1 – us A.T.L.A. [240]

DIE GESCHICHTE DER FESTUNG GLATZ / Koehl, Eduard – (Includes bibliographical references and index) – Wuerzburg: Holzner Verlag, 1972 – 10r – 1 – us U.W. Library [943]

DIE GESCHICHTE DER FESTUNG KOENIGSBERG/PR., 1257-1945 / Ehrhardt, Traugott – (Includes bibliographical references) – Wuerzburg: Holzner, 1960 – 10r – 1 – us U.W. Library [943]

GESCHICHTE DER FRANZOESISCHEN ARBEITER ASSOCIATIONEN / Englaender, Sigmund – 1864. 1031p. 2 fiches (29x) – 9 – 1.00f – at Libertarian Micro [320]

GESCHICHTE DER FRIEDRICHSSCHULE ZU GUMBINNEN : EIN BEITRAG ZUR KULTUR- UND BILDUNGSGESCHICHTE OSTPREUSSENS / Kirrinnis, Herbert – (Includes bibliographical references) – Wuerzburg: Holzner Verlag, 1963 – 1 – us U.W. Library [370]

GESCHICHTE DER GELEHRTHEIT / Wieland, Christoph Martin; ed by Hirzel, Ludwig – (Includes bibliographical references) – Frauenfeld: J Huber, 1891 – 1r – 1 – us U.W. Library [000]

GESCHICHTE DER GRUENDUNG DER ARMENISCH-EVANGELISCHEN GEMEINDE IN SCHAMACHI : EIN LEBENSBILD AUS DER ARMENISCHEN KIRCHE UND BASLER MISSION / Eppler, CF – Basel: Verlag des Missionskomptoirs, 1873 – 1mf – us A.T.L.A. [240]

GESCHICHTE DER HEBRAISCHEN SPRACHE UND SCHRIFT / Gesenius, W – Leipzig. 1815. BNE-483 1 – 9 – ne IDC [470]

GESCHICHTE DER HEILIGEN MONIKA / Bougaud, Emile – Mainz: Franz Kirchheim; Milwaukee: Hoffman [distributor], 1870 – 1mf – 9 – 0-8370-6887-8 – 1986-0887 – us A.T.L.A. [920]

DIE GESCHICHTE DER HEILIGEN SCHRIFTEN NEUEN TESTAMENTS / Reuss, Eduard – Braunschweig 6 Ausgabe 1887 – 12mf – 8 – ne Slangenburg [220]

GESCHICHTE DER IRISCHEN KIRCHE VON ANFANG BIS ZUM 12. JH. / Delius, W – Basel, 1954 – Dfl19.00 – ne Slangenburg [240]

GESCHICHTE DER ISRAELITISCHEN RELIGION / Marti, Karl – (Includes bibliographical references and indexes) – 5. Aufl. Strassburg: Friedrich Bull, 1907 – 1mf – 9 – 0-8370-9488-7 – 1986-3488 – us A.T.L.A. [220]

GESCHICHTE DER ITALIAENISCHEN OPER / Arteaga, Stefano – 2v. 1789 – 9 – us Sibley [780]

GESCHICHTE DER JUDEN VON DEN AELTESTEN ZEITEN BIS AUF DIE GEGENWART / Graetz, H – (Band 1 Leipzig 1874 10mf; Band 2,1 Leipzig 1875 9mf; Band2,2 Leipzig 1876 9mf) – 8 – ne Slangenburg [270]

GESCHICHTE DER KARTAGER / Meltzer, Otto – Berlin. 1879-1913. xii, 530; xii, 510; xi, 800p. Cartes. (Historical Studies Series) – 9 – 63.00 – fr Bibl Nationale [900]

GESCHICHTE DER KATHOLISCHEN KIRCHE : VON DER MITTE DES 18. JAHRHUNDERTS BIS ZUM VATIKANISCHEN KONZIL / Mirbt, Carl – Berlin: G.J. Goeschen, 1913 – 1mf – us A.T.L.A. [240]

GESCHICHTE DER KATHOLISCHEN KIRCHE IN DEUTSCHLAND IM NEUNZEHNTEN JAHRHUNDERT : MAINZ 1902. 1. BAND: VOM BEGINNE DES 19: JAHRHUNDERTS BIS ZU DEN CONCORDATSVERHANDLUNGEN / Brueck, Heinrich – 1994 – 6mf – DM500.00 – 3-89349-184-8 – gw Hänsel [240]

GESCHICHTE DER KATHOLISCHEN KIRCHE IN SCHOTTLAND : VON DER EINFUEHRUNG DES CHRISTENTUMS BIS AUF DIE GEGENWART / Bellesheim, Alphons – (Includes index) – Mainz: Franz Kirchheim. 2v. 1883 – 4mf – 9 – 0-8370-6800-2 – 1986-0800 – us A.T.L.A. [240]

GESCHICHTE DER KATHOLISCHEN LITERATUR DEUTSCHLANDS VOM 17. JAHRHUNDERT BIS ZUR GEGENWART / Bruehl, I A – Wien, Leipzig, 1861 – 9 – DM148.00 – 3-89349-124-4 – gw Hänsel [430]

GESCHICHTE DER KIRCHENVERFASSUNG DEUTSCHLANDS IM MITTELALTER / Werminghoff, Albert – Leipzig: B.G. Teubner, 1905 – 1mf – us A.T.L.A. [240]

GESCHICHTE DER KIRCHLICHEN LITURGIE DES BISTHUMS AUGSBURG / Hoeynck, F A – Augsburg, 1889 – 8mf – 8 – Dfl30.00 – ne Slangenburg [943]

GESCHICHTE DER KIRCHLICHEN TRENNUNG ZWISCHEN DEM ORIENT UND OCCIDENT: VON DEN ERSTEN ANFAENGEN BIS ZUR JUENGSTEN GEGENWART / Pichler, A – Muenchen: M. Rieger, 1864-1865 – 4mf – us A.T.L.A. [240]

GESCHICHTE DER KOSMOLOGIE IN DER GRIECHISCHEN KIRCHE BIS AUF ORIGINES : MIT SPECIALUNTERSUCHUNGEN UEBER DIE GNOSTISCHEN SYSTEME / Moeller, E Wilhelm – Halle: Fricke, 1860 – 2mf – us A.T.L.A. [110]

GESCHICHTE DER LATEINISCHEN LITERATUR DES MITTELALTERS / Manitius, M – v. 1-2. Muenchen. 1911-23. B-202 2 – 8 – ne IDC [450]

GESCHICHTE DER LATEINISCHEN SPRACHE / Stolz, Friedrich – Leipzig, 1910 – 147p – 9 – DM48.00 – 3-89349-114-7 – gw Hänsel [450]

GESCHICHTE DER LOGIK IM ABENDLANDE / Prantl, Carl – Leipzig: S. Hirzel, 1855-1870 – 5mf – us A.T.L.A. [160]

GESCHICHTE DER LUTHERISCHEN KIRCHE IN AMERICA / Graebner, A L – St. Louis, Mo.: Concordia Publishing House, 1892 – 2mf – us A.T.L.A. [240]

GESCHICHTE DER MESSGEWAENDER / Papas, T – Muenchen, 1965 – 6mf – 8 – Dfl25.00 – ne Slangenburg [240]

GESCHICHTE DER MITTELHOCHDEUTSCHEN LITERATUR / Vogt, Friedrich Hermann Traugott – (Includes bibliographical references) – 3. umgearb. Aufl. Berlin; Leipzig: Vereinigung Wissenschaftlicher Verleger, 1922 – 1 – us U.W. Library [430]

GESCHICHTE DER NIEDERFRAENKISCHEN GESCHAEFTSSPRACHE / Heinzel, Richard – Paderborn: Schoeningh, 1874. 464p – 1 – us U.W. Library [430]

GESCHICHTE DER OPTIK / Wilde, E – 1838. v1: From Aristotle to Newton – 1 – uk Microform Academic [530]

GESCHICHTE DER ORIENTALISCHEN KIRCHEN VON 1453-1898 / Kyriakos, A Diomedes – Leipzig: A. Deichert, 1902 – 1mf – us A.T.L.A. [240]

DIE GESCHICHTE DER PAN-AMERIKANISCHEN BEWEGUNG / Buechi, R; ed by Schuecking, W – Breslau, 1914 – 3mf – 1 – ILM-4079/1 – ne IDC [327]

GESCHICHTE DER PERSER UND ARABER ZUR ZEIT DER SASANIDEN / Noeldeke, Theodor – Aus der arabischen Chronik des Tabari ueberzetzt und mit ausfuehflichen Erlaeuterungen und Ergaenzungen versehen. Leiden. 1879. BU-584 2 – 8 – ne IDC [956]

GESCHICHTE DER PFLANZUNG UND LEITUNG DER CHRISTLICHEN KIRCHE DURCH DIE APOSTEL / Neander, August – (Band 1 Hamburg 1832 8mf; Band 2 Hamburg 1833 7mf) – 8 – ne Slangenburg [220]

GESCHICHTE DER PHILOSOPHIE / Schwegler, A – Tuebingen, 1870 – 8mf – 8 – ne Slangenburg [100]

GESCHICHTE DER PHILOSOPHIE / Stoeckle, A – Mainz, 1875 – 24mf – 8 – ne Slangenburg [100]

GESCHICHTE DER POESIE UND BEREDSAMKEIT SEIT DEM ENDE DES 13. JAHRHUNDERTS : GESCHICHTE DER DEUTSCHEN LITERATUR / Bouterwek, Friedrich; ed by Garber, Klaus – Goettingen. v9-12. 1812-19 – 18mf – 9 – subsc: DM150.00 diazo DM180.00 silver – gw Olms [430]

GESCHICHTE DER POETISCHEN LITTERATUR DER DEUTSCHEN / Hahn, Werner; ed by Kreyenberg, Gotthold – (Includes index) – Berlin: W Hertz, 1897 – 1r – 1 – us U.W. Library [430]

GESCHICHTE DER POETISCHEN NATIONAL-LITERATUR DER DEUTSCHEN / Gervinus, Georg Gottfried; ed by Garber, Klaus – Leipzig, 1835-42 – 33mf – 9 – subsc: DM200.00 diazo DM240.00 silver – gw Olms [430]

GESCHICHTE DER POLITISCHEN IDEEN IN POLEN SEIT DESSEN TEILUNGEN / Feldman, W – (1795-1914). Muenchen, Berlin. 1917. BR-5492 2 – 8 – ne IDC [943]

DIE GESCHICHTE DER PREDIGT IN DEUTSCHLAND BIS AUF KARL DEN GROSSEN, 600-814 : LATEINISCHE PREDIGTEN VON VERFASSERN FREMDLAENDISCHER HERKUNFT / Albert, F R – Guetersloh: C. Bertelsmann, 1892. (Die Geschichte der Predigt in Deutschland bis Luther / von F.R. Albert; 1. T.) – 1mf – us A.T.L.A. [240]

GESCHICHTE DER PRESBYTERIAL- UND SYNODALVERFASSUNG : SEIT DER REFORMATION / Lechler, G V – Leiden: D. Noothoven van Goor, 1854 – 1mf – us A.T.L.A. [240]

GESCHICHTE DER PROTESTANTISCHEN DOGMATIK : IN IHREM ZUSAMMENHANGE MIT THEOLOGIE UEBERHAUPT / Gass, W – Berlin: G. Reimer, 1854-1867 – 5mf – us A.T.L.A. [240]

GESCHICHTE DER PROTESTANTISCHEN KIRCHENVERFASSUNG / Sehling, Emil – Leipzig: B.G. Teubner, 1914 – 1mf – us A.T.L.A. [240]

GESCHICHTE DER PROTESTANTISCHEN THEOLOGIE / Frank, Gustav – Leipzig: Breitkopf und Haertel, 1862-1905 – 5mf – us A.T.L.A. [240]

GESCHICHTE DER PROTESTANTISCHEN THEOLOGIE : VON DER KONKORDIENFORMAL AN BIS IN DIE MITTE DES ACHTZEHNTEN JAHRHUNDERTS / Planck, G J – Goettingen: Vandenhoeck und Ruprecht, 1831 – 1mf – us A.T.L.A. [240]

DIE GESCHICHTE DER QUELLEN UND LITERATUR DES CANONISCHEN RECHTS / Schulte, Johann Friedrich von – (Band 1: Stuttgart, 1875.-7mf; Band 2: Stuttgart, 1877.-15mf; Band 3: Stuttgart, 1880.-31mf) – 8 – ne Slangenburg [240]

GESCHICHTE DER QUIETISTISCHEN MYSTIK IN DER KATHOLISCHEN KIRCHE / Heppe, Heinrich – Berlin: Wilhelm Hertz, 1875 – 2mf – us A.T.L.A. [240]

GESCHICHTE DER REFORMATION IM ELSASS UND BESONDERS IN STRASBURG, NACH GLEICHZEITIGEN QUELLEN / Roehrich, T W – 2v. 1830-32 – 1 – us A.T.L.A. [240]

GESCHICHTE DER REFORMATION IN DER GRAFSCHAFT OETTINGEN, 1522-1569 / Herold, Reinhold – Halle: Verein fuer Reformationsgeschichte, 1902. (Schriften des Vereins fuer Reformationsgeschichte; 20. Jahrg., Schrift 75) – 1mf – us A.T.L.A. [240]

GESCHICHTE DER REFORMATION IN POLEN / Wotschke, T – In: Studien zur Kultur und Geschichte der Reformation. v. 1. Leipzig. 1911. BR-5486 2 – 8 – ne IDC [943]

GESCHICHTE DER REFORMATION IN VENEDIG / Benrath, Karl – Halle: Verein fuer Reformationsgeschichte, 1887. ('(Schriften des Vereins fuer Refomationsgeschichte; Bd. 18]) – 1mf – us A.T.L.A. [240]

GESCHICHTE DER REFORMIRTEN KIRCHEN IN LITHAUEN / Kudaszewicz, Joseph – Leipzig: Dyk, 1848-1850 – 2mf – us A.T.L.A. [240]

GESCHICHTE DER RITTER DES ORDENS POUR LA MERITE IM WELTKRIEG / ed by Moeller-Witten, Hanns – Berlin: Bernard & Graefe, 1935. 2v – 1 – us U.W. Library [943]

GESCHICHTE DER SCHWEIZERISCH-REFORMIERTEN KIRCHEN / Bloesch, E – Bern: Schmid & Francke, 1898-1899 – 3mf – us A.T.L.A. [240]

GESCHICHTE DER SLAVENAPOSTEL KONSTANTINUS (KYRILLUS) UND METHODIUS / Goetz, Leopold Karl – Gotha: F.A. Perthes, 1897 – 1mf – us A.T.L.A. [240]

GESCHICHTE DER SPANISCH-PORTUGIESISCHEN JUDEN IN AMSTERDAM IM 17. JAHRHUNDERT / Ullmann, S – Inaugural Dissertation. Frankfurt a.M. 1908. BJ-262-62 1 – 9 – ne IDC [949]

GESCHICHTE DER STADT HOHENSTEIN IN OSTPREUSSEN / Hartmann, Ernst of Osterode – Wuerzburg: Holzner-Verlag, 1959 – 10r – 1 – us U.W. Library [910]

GESCHICHTE DER STADT LIEBEMUEHL / Hartmann, Ernst of Osterode – (Includes bibliographical references and index) – Wuerzburg: Holzner, 1964 – 1r – 1 – us U.W. Library [910]

GESCHICHTE DER STADT SCHNEIDEMUEHL / Boese, Karl – 2. vollstaendige umgearb. und erweiterte Aufl. Wuerzburg: Holzner Verlag, 1965 – 10r – 1 – us U.W. Library [910]

DIE GESCHICHTE DER SYNAGOGEN-GEMEINDE ZU STETTIN : EINE STUDIE ZUR GESCHICHTE DES POMMERSCHEN JUDENTUMS / Peiser, Jacob – (Includes bibliographical references) – 2., bearb. und erw. Aufl. Wuerzburg: Holzner Verlag, 1965 – 1 – us U.W. Library [270]

GESCHICHTE DER TECHNOLOGIE SEIT DER WIEDERHERSTELLUNG DER WISSENSCHAFTEN AM ENDE DES 18. JHDTS – Band 1-3. Gottingen. 1807, 1810, 1811 – 1 – DM80.00 – gw Mikro Press [500]

GESCHICHTE DER UNGARISCHEN LITTERATUR / Schwicker, J H – v. 10. Leipzig. 1889. BR-5351 2 – 8 – ne IDC [490]

GESCHICHTE DER UNION DER RUTHENISCHEN KIRCHE MIT ROM VON DEN ALTESTEN ZEITEN BIS AUF DIE GEGENWART / Pelesh, Iuliian – Wien: Mechitharliste Buchdruckerei, 1878.Includes bibliog. references – 1 – us U.W. Library [240]

GESCHICHTE DER WIEDERTAEUFER IN DER SCHWEIZ ZUR REFORMATIONSZEIT / Nitsche, Richard – Einsiedeln, New York, Cincinnati, St. Louis, 1885 – 2mf – 9 – DM62.00 – 3-89349-296-8 – gw Hänsel [943]

GESCHICHTE DER WIEDERTAEUFER UND IHRES REICHS ZU MUENSTER / Keller, Ludwig – Muenster: Coppenrath, 1880 – 1mf – us A.T.L.A. [240]

GESCHICHTE DER WIEDERTAEUFER ZU MUENSTER : NACH URKUNDEN UND BERICHTEN VON ZEITGENOSSEN DEM DEUTSCHEN VOLKE / Faesser, Johann Chr – 2., gaenzlich umgearb Aufl. Muenster: E C Brunn, [1861?] – 1mf – 9 – 0-8370-8898-4 – 1986-2898 – us A.T.L.A. [240]

GESCHICHTE DES ALTERTHUMS / Duncker, Maximilian Wolfgang – Leipzig, Duncker & Humblot, 1874-86. 9 v. Film Mas C 665 – 1 – us H.U. Library [900]

DIE GESCHICHTE DES ALTTESTAMENTLICHEN PRIESTERTUMS / Baudissin, Wolf Wilhelm, Graf – Leipzig: S. Hirzel, 1889. 1 fiche – 9 – us A.T.L.A. [240]

GESCHICHTE DES APOSTOLISCHEN ZEITALTERS ZUR ZERSTOERUNG JERUSALEM'S / Ewald, Heinrich – Goettingen 3. Ausgabe 1868 – 14mf – 8 – ne Slangenburg [240]

GESCHICHTE DES BAIERISCHEN ERBFOLGESTREITS... – Frankfurt, Leipzig, 1779 – 1mf – 1 – ILM-2790/1 – ne IDC [327]

GESCHICHTE DES CHRISTLICHEN GOTTESDIENSTES : EIN HANDBUCH FUER VORLESUNGEN UND UEBUNGEN IM SEMINAR / Koestlin, Heinrich Adolf – Freiburg i.B.: J.C.B. Mohr, 1887 – 1mf – us A.T.L.A. [240]

GESCHICHTE DES DEUTSCHEN KIRCHENLIEDES BIS AUF LUTHERS ZEIT / Fallersleben, Hoffmann von – Hannover, 1861 – 10mf – 8 – Dfl35.00 – ne Slangenburg [780]

GESCHICHTE DES DEUTSCHEN VOLKES SEIT DEM AUSGANG DES MITTELALTERS / Jannsen, Johannes – St. Louis, MO: Herder, (1893-1901). 8v.3 reels. 1259 – 1 – us U.W. Library [943]

GESCHICHTE DES ENGLISCH-CHINESISCHEN KRIEGES / Neumann, C F – ed 2 enlarged. Leipzig. 1855. BCH-824 2 – 8 – ne IDC [941]

GESCHICHTE DES ENGLISCHEN DEISMUS / Lechler, Gotthard Victor – Stuttgart: J.G. Cotta, 1841 – 2mf – us A.T.L.A. [240]

GESCHICHTE DES ENGLISCHEN REICHES IN ASIEN / Neumann, C F – 2v. Leipzig. 1857. BCH-825 2 – 8 – ne IDC [941]

GESCHICHTE DES HELLENISMUS / Droysen, Johann Gustav – Von Joh. Gust. Droysen. 2 Aufl. Gotha, F. A. Perthes, 1877-78. 3 v. in 4. Film Mas 9043 – 1 – us H.U. Library [900]

DIE GESCHICHTE DES HUSSITENTHUMS UND PROF. CONSTANTIN HOEFLER : KRITISCHE STUDIEN / Palacky, Franz – Prag: F. Tempsky, 1868 – 1mf – us A.T.L.A. [240]

DIE GESCHICHTE DES JUEDISCHEN VOLKES UND SEINER LITERATUR VOM BABYLONISCHEN EXILE BIS AUF DIE GEGENWART MIT EINEM ANHANGE : PROBEN DER JUEDISCHEN LITERATUR / Baeck, Samuel – 1996 – 8mf – 9 – DM146.00 – 3-8267-3187-5 – gw Hänsel [270]

GESCHICHTE DES KATHOLISCHEN MODERNISMUS / Kuebel, Johannes – (Includes index) – Tuebingen: J C B Mohr, 1909 – 1mf – 9 – 0-8370-8916-6 – 1986-2916 – us A.T.L.A. [240]

GESCHICHTE DES KIRCHENRECHTS / Ploechl, W M – Band 1-5 (1953)-(1969) – 42mf – 8 – ne Slangenburg [240]

GESCHICHTE DES KRIEGS IN SPANIEN / Garrazin, General – 1815 – 9 – 1.50f – sp Bibl Santa Ana [946]

DIE GESCHICHTE DES MEHRSTIMMIGEN PROPRIUM MISSAE / Lipphardt, W – Heidelberg, 1950 – 2mf – 8 – ne Slangenburg [240]

DIE GESCHICHTE DES MONTANISMUS / Bonwetsch, G N – Erlangen: A. Deichert, 1881 – 1mf – us A.T.L.A. [240]

GESCHICHTE DES OESTLICHEN ASIENS. V. 1 DIE MANDSCHUREY: V. 2 DIE VOELKER DER MANDSCHUREY / Plath, J H – 2v. Goettingen. 1830-31. BU-613 2 – 8 – ne IDC [950]

DIE GESCHICHTE DES PIETISMUS / Schmid, Heinrich – (Includes bibliographical references) – Noerdlingen: C H Beck, 1863 – 2mf – 9 – 0-8370-8865-8 – 1986-2865 – us A.T.L.A. [240]

GESCHICHTE DES PIETISMUS IN DER LUTHERISCHEN KIRCHE DES 17. UND 18. JAHRHUNDERTS / Ritschl, Albrecht Benjamin – Bonn: A. Marcus, 1884-1886 – 3mf – us A.T.L.A. [240]

GESCHICHTE DES PIETISMUS IN DER REFORMIERTEN KIRCHE / Ritschl, Albrecht Benjamin – Bonn: A. Marcus, 1880 – 2mf – us A.T.L.A. [240]

GESCHICHTE DES PIETISMUS UND DER MYSTIK IN DER REFORMIERTEN KIRCHE : NAMENTLICH DER NIEDERLANDE / Heppe, Heinrich – Leiden: E.J. Brill, 1879 – 2mf – us A.T.L.A. [240]

GESCHICHTE DES PREUSSISCHEN TRUCKVERBOTS / Anton, Guenther K – c1890-1900, 1953. 30S – 9 – 1.00f – at Libertarian Micro [335]

GESCHICHTE DES PRINZEN BIRIBINKER / Wieland, Christoph Martin – Leipzig: G H Wigand, [1902?] – 1r – 1 – us U.W. Library [830]

GESCHICHTE DES PROTESTANTISMUS IN OESTERREICH : IN UMRISSEN / Loesche, Georg – Tuebingen: Mohr, 1902 – 1mf – us A.T.L.A. [240]

GESCHICHTE DES RATIONALISMUS. ERSTE ABTHEILUNG, GESCHICHTE DES PIETISMUS UND DES ERSTEN STADIUMS DER AUFKLAERUNG / Tholuck, August – (No more published. Includes bibliographical references) – Berlin: Wiegandt und Grieben, 1865 – 1mf – 9 – 0-8370-8870-4 – 1986-2870 – us A.T.L.A. [210]

GESCHICHTE DES REICHES GOTTES BIS AUF JESUS CHRISTUS / Koenig, Eduard – (Includes bibliographical references and index) – Berlin: Martin Warneck, 1908 – 1mf – 9 – 0-8370-3968-1 – 1985-1968 – us A.T.L.A. [220]

GESCHICHTE DES RELIGIONSUNTERRICHTS IN DER EVANGELISCHEN VOLKSSCHULE WUERTTEMBERGS / Weisenboehler, Oskar – Marbach: A Remppis, 1903 – 1mf – 9 – 0-8370-7598-X – 1986-1598 – us A.T.L.A. [370]

DIE GESCHICHTE DES RICHTERS VON ORB / Weismantel, Leo – (Cover title: Johann Christin: der Richter von Orb) – Freiburg im Breisgau: Herder, 1927 – 1r – 1 – us U.W. Library [830]

GESCHICHTE DES SEMITISCHEN ALTERTUMS IN TABELLEN / Floigl, Victor – Leipzig:Wilhelm Friedrich, 1882 – 1mf – 9 – 0-8370-3155-9 – 1985-1155 – us A.T.L.A. [270]

GESCHICHTE DES SLAWISCHEN SPRACHE UND LITERATUR NACH ALLEN MUNDARTEN / Schaffarik, P J – Ofen. 1826. BR-5011 2 – 8 – ne IDC [460]

GESCHICHTE DES SONETTES IN DER DEUTSCHEN DICHTUNG : MIT EINER EINLEITUNG UEBER HEIMAT, ENTSTEHUNG UND WESEN DER SONETTFORM / Welti, Heinrich – (Includes bibliographical references and index) – Leipzig: Veit, 1884 – 1r – 1 – us U.W. Library [430]

GESCHICHTE DES SOZIALISMUS UND KOMMUNISMUS / Adler, Georg – 1899 – 9 – 1.00f – at Libertarian Micro [320]

GESCHICHTE DES SPANISCHEN PROTESTANTISMUS IM SECHSZEHNTEN JAHRHUNDERT / Wilkens, C A – Guetersloh: C. Bertelsmann, 1888 – 1mf – us A.T.L.A. [240]

GESCHICHTE DES UNTERGANGS DER ANTIKEN WELT / Seeck, Otto – Stuttgart, J. B. Metzler, 1920-23. 6 v. in 12. Film Mas C 670 – 1 – us H.U. Library [930]

GESCHICHTE DES VOLKES ISRAEL : 1. BAND: EINLEITUNG IN DIE GESCHICHTE DES VOLKES ISRAEL / Ewald, Heinrich – Goettingen 3. Ausgabe 1864 – 11mf – 8 – ne Slangenburg [270]

GESCHICHTE DES WACHSTUMS UND DER ERFINDUNGEN DER CHEMIE, IN DER NEUERN ZEIT / Wiegleb, Johann Christian – Berlin, 1790-91. 2v – 1 – us U.W. Library [540]

GESCHICHTE DES WEINBAUS UNTER BESONDERER BERUECKSICHTIGUNG DER BAYERISCHEN RHEINPFALZ / Basserman-Jordan, F – 3v. Frankfurt. 1907 – 9 – ne IDC [630]

GESCHICHTE DES ZUERCHERISCHEN SCHULWESENS : BIS GEGEN DAS ENDE DES SECHZEHNTEN JAHRHUNDERTS / Ernst, Ulrich – Winterthur: Bleuler-Hausheer, 1879 – 1mf – 9 – 0-8370-7630-7 – 1986-1630 – us A.T.L.A. [370]

DIE GESCHICHTE DEUTSCH-JUEDISCHER REFUGEES IN SCHOTTLAND / Koelmel, Rainer – Heidelberg, 1979 – 4mf – DM90.00 – 3-89349-837-0 – gw Hänsel [320]

DIE GESCHICHTE EINES GENIES : NOVELLE / Schubin, Ossip – 2. Aufl. Berlin: Paetel, 1890 – 1 – us U.W. Library [830]

GESCHICHTE EINES KNABEN / Wiechert, Ernst Emil – Tuebingen: R Wunderlich, [194-?] – 1r – 1 – us U.W. Library [830]

GESCHICHTE MASURENS / Toeppen, Max – Danzig, 1870 – 1r – 1 – gw Mikro Press [943]

GESCHICHTE RUECKWAERTS? / Wolff, Eugen – Kiel: Lipsius und Tischer, 1892 – 1r – 1 – us U.W. Library [943]

GESCHICHTE SICILIENS IM ALTERTHUM / Holm, Adolf – Leipzig, W. Engelmann, 1880-98. 3 v. Film Mas 9096 – 1 – us H.U. Library [940]

GESCHICHTE, SYSTEMATIK UND LITERATUR DES INSEKTENKUNDE, VON DEN AELTESTEN ZEITEN BIS AUF DIE GEGENWART / Eiselt, J N – Leipzig, 1836. viii,255p. 2 pls. Z/1213/2 – 8 – ne IDC [590]

GESCHICHTE UND BESIEDLUNG DES RATIBORER LANDES : MIT BEITRAEGEN VON GEORG RASCHKE UND FERDINAND HUETTEROTH / Hyckel, Georg – (Includes bibliographical references) – Wuerzburg: Holzner, 1961 – 1 – us U.W. Library [943]

GESCHICHTE UND BIBLIOGRAPHIE DER ANATOMISCHEN ABBILDUNG / Choulant, J L – Leipzig, 1852 – 6mf – ne IDC [611]

GESCHICHTE UND DARSTELLUNG DES JUEDISCHEN CULTUS / Duschak, Moritz – Mannheim: J. Schneider, 1866. 1 fiche – 9 – us A.T.L.A. [270]

GESCHICHTE UND DOGMATIK : EINE ERKENNTNISTHEORETISCHE UNTERSUCHUNG / Vowinckel, Ernst – (Includes bibliographical references) – Leipzig: A Deichert (Georg Boehme), 1898 – 1mf – 9 – 0-8370-6444-9 – 1986-0444 – us A.T.L.A. [110]

GESCHICHTE UND GESCHICHTSWISSENSCHAFT IN DER METHODOLOGISCHEN DISKUSSION DER GEGENWART / Rhein, Monika – Frankfurt a.M., 1983 – 3mf – 9 – DM76.00 – 3-89349-393-X – gw Hänsel [943]

GESCHICHTE UND KIRCHE / Doellinger, Johann Joseph Ignaz von – 1995 – 2mf – 9 – DM62.00 – 3-8267-3152-2 – gw Hänsel [240]

GESCHICHTE UND KRITIK DER DEUTSCHEN POESIE UND BEREDSAMKEIT / Horn, Franz; ed by Garber, Klaus – Berlin, 1805 – 3mf – 9 – subsc: DM30.00 – gw Olms [430]

GESCHICHTE UND LITTERATUR DER LICHENOLOGIE VON DEN AELTESTEN ZEITEN BIS ZUM SCHLUSSE DES JAHRES 1865 / Krempelhuber, A von – 3v. Muenchen. 1867-72. B-582 2 – 8 – ne IDC [580]

GESCHICHTE UND OFFENBARUNG IM ALTEN TESTAMENT / Lotz, Wilhelm – Leipzig: J.C. Hinrichs, 1891. 1 fiche – 9 – us A.T.L.A. [240]

GESCHICHTE UND POLITIK – Berlin, 1802-04 – 3r – 1 – Dist. gw Mikrofilm – gw Misc Inst [072]

GESCHICHTE UND SYSTEM DES IRANISCHEN STRAFRECHTS / Daftary, Ali Akkbar Khan – Halle-Wittenberg, 1935 – 2mf – DM62.00 – 3-8267-3000-3 – gw Hänsel [340]

DIE GESCHICHTE UNSERES VOLKS. BILDER AUS DER VERGANGENHEIT UND GEGENWART DER DEUTSCHEN IN RUMAENIEN / Mueller-Langenthal – Hermannstadt – 1 – DM30.00 – gw Mikro Press [943]

DIE GESCHICHTE VOM ALTEN BLUTE UND VON DER UNGEHEUREN VERLASSENHEIT : ERZAEHLUNG / Grimm, Hans – Berlin: Deutsche Buch-Gemeinschaft, c1931 – 1r – 1 – us U.W. Library [830]

GESCHICHTE VON HALITSCH UND WLADIMIR BIS 1772.. / Engel, Johann Christian von – Wien: Franz Jakob Kaiserer, 1792. 2v in 1. 1 reel. 1245 – 1 – us U.W. Library [947]

DIE GESCHICHTE VON JOSEPH DEM ZIMMERMANN (T.U.U. 5-56) / Morenz, S – Berlin, 1951 – 3mf – 9 – ne Slangenburg [240]

DIE GESCHICHTEN DES MAJORS / Hopfen, Hans – 3. Aufl. Berlin: Richard Wilhelmi, 1882 – 1r – 1 – us U.W. Library [830]

GESCHICHTEN UND NOVELLEN: GESAMTAUSGABE / Riehl, Wilhelm Heinrich – (v. 1. Kulturgeschichtliche Novellen. v. 2-3. Geschichten aus alter Zeit. v. 4. Neues Novellenbuch. v. 5. Auf der Ecke; sieben Novellen. v. 6. Am Feierabend; sechs neue Novellen. v. 7. Lebensraetsel; fuenf Novellen) – Stuttgart, Cotta, 1923. 7 v. Film Mas 8596 – 1 – us H.U. Library [830]

GESCHICHTLICHE AUFSAETZE UND GEDICHTE / Leibniz, Gottfried Wilhelm von; ed by Pertz, G H – Hannover, 1847 – Dfl28.00 – ne Slangenburg [240]

DER GESCHICHTLICHE CHRISTUS : EINE REIHE VON VORTRAEGEN MIT QUELLENBEWEIS UND CHRONOLOGIE DES LEBENS JESU / Keim, Theodor – (Includes bibliographical references) – 3., vielfach erw Aufl. Zuerich: Orell, Fuessli, 1866 – 1mf – 9 – 0-8370-3869-3 – 1985-1869 – us A.T.L.A. [240]

DIE GESCHICHTLICHE ENTWICKLUNG DES DEUTSCHEN REALSCHULWESENS : ABSCHNITT 6: BESTREBUNGEN AUF DEM GEBIET DER SCHULREFORM IN DEN JAHREN 1882-1890 / Wetzstein, O – Neustrelitz, 1911 – 1mf – 9 – DM38.00 – 3-89349-312-3 – gw Hänsel [370]

DIE GESCHICHTLICHE ENTWICKLUNG DES REALSCHULWESENS IN DEUTSCHLAND : ABSCHNITT 1: DIE ENTSTEHUNG DEUTSCHER REALSCHULEN IM 18. JAHRHUNDERT / Wetzstein, O – Neustrelitz, 1906 – 1mf – 9 – DM38.00 – 3-89349-313-1 – gw Hänsel [370]

DIE GESCHICHTLICHEN BUECHER DES ALTEN TESTAMENTS / Graf, Karl Heinrich – Leipzig: T.O. Weigel, 1866. 1 fiche – 9 – us A.T.L.A. [220]

DIE GESCHICHTLICHKEIT DES PENTATEUCHS... PRUEFUNG DER WELLHAUSEN'SCHEN HYPOTHESE / Roos, Friedrich – Stuttgart: J.F. Steinkopf, 1883.1 fiche – 9 – us A.T.L.A. [240]

DIE GESCHICHTLICHKEIT DES SINAIBUNDES / Giesebrecht, Friedrich – (Includes bibliographical references) – Koenigsburg i. Pr: Thomas & Oppermann, 1900 – 1mf – 9 – 0-8370-3273-3 – 1985-1273 – us A.T.L.A. [240]

Geschichts- und Altertumforschender Verein. Eisenberg *see* MITTEILUNGEN

GESCHICHTSBETRACHTUNG UND GESCHICHTLICHE UEBERLIEFERUNG...PROPHETEN / Procksch, Otto – Leipzig: J.C. Hinrichs, 1902. 1 fiche – 9 – us A.T.L.A. [240]

GESCHICHTSBLAETTER FUER STADT UND LAND MAGDEBURG – Magdeburg. Jahrg. 1-74 75; 1866-1939 41. "Mitteilungen des Vereins fuer Geschichte und Altertumskunde des Herzogtums und Erzstifts Magdeburg." Film Mas C 315 – 1 – us H.U. Library [073]

DIE GESCHICHTSCHREIBUNG DER REFORMATION UND GEGENREFORMATION : BODIN UND DIE BEGRUENDUNG DER GESCHICHTSMETHODOLOGIE DURCH BARTHOLOMAEUS KECKERMANN / Menke-Glueckert, Emil – Leipzig: J.C. Hinrichs, 1912 – 1mf – us A.T.L.A. [940]

DIE GESCHICHTSPHILOSOPHIE IN DEN HISTORISCHEN DRAMEN JULIUS MOSENS : BEITRAG ZUR ENTWICKLUNGSGESCHICHTE DER DICHTERPERSOENLICHKEIT / Fehn, Andreas – (Includes bibliographcal references) – Bamberg: Buchner, 1915 – 1r – 1 – us U.W. Library [430]

GESCHICHTSPHILOSOPHISCHE ANSAETZE IN DER FRUEHROMANTIK / Klawon, Dieter – Frankfurt a.M., 1977 – 3mf – 9 – DM76.00 – 3-89349-673-4 – gw Hänsel [190]

GESCHICHTSSCHREIBUNG UND GESCHICHTSAUFFASSUNG IM ELSASS ZUR ZEIT DER REFORMATION : VORTRAG / Lenz, Max – Halle: Verein fuer Reformationsgeschichte, 1895. ([Schriften des Vereins fuer Reformationsgeschichte; Bd. 49]) – 1mf – us A.T.L.A. [900]

GESCHIED-EN TIJDREKENKUNDIG OVERZICHT VAN HET GOUVERNEMENT MAKASAR DOOR A. LIGTVOET – 1669-1846. 3v. KITLV,H 226(I-III). BSD-103/1 mf. 1-18 – 9 – ne IDC [950]

GESCHIEDENIS DER DOOPSGEZINDEN IN FRIESLAND : VAN DERZELVER ONTSTAAN TOT DEZEN TYD / Cate, S Blaupot ten – Leeuwarden: W. Eekhoff, 1839 – 1mf – us A.T.L.A. [240]

GESCHIEDENIS DER DOOPSGEZINDEN IN HOLLAND, ZEELAND, UTRECHT EN GELDERLAND : VAN DERZELVER ONTSTAAN TOT OP DEZEN TIJD, UIT OORSPRONKELIJKE STUKKEN EN ECHTE BERIGTEN / Cate, S Blaupot ten – Amsterdam: P.N. van Kampen, 1847 – 2mf – us A.T.L.A. [240]

GESCHIEDENIS DER JODEN IN NEDERLAND / Brugmans, H & Frank, A – v. 1. Amsterdam. 1940. BJ-262-10 1 – 9 – ne IDC [949]

GESCHIEDENIS DER JODEN IN NEDERLAND / Koenen, H J – Utrecht. 1843. BJ-262-31 1 – 9 – ne IDC [900]

DE GESCHIEDENIS DER KERKMUZIEK IN DE NEDERLANDEN SEDERT DE HERVORMING / Kat, A I M – Hilversum, 1939 – 7mf – 8 – Dfl28.00 – ne Slangenburg [240]

GESCHIEDENIS DER PORTUGEESCHE JODEN TE AMSTERDAM, 1593-1925 / Silva Rosa, J S da – Amsterdam. 1925. BJ-262-57 1 – 9 – ne IDC [949]

GESCHIEDENIS VAN DE DOOPSGEZINDEN TE STRAATSBURG VAN 1525 TO 1557 / Hulshof, Abraham – Amsterdam: J. Clausen, 1905 – 1mf – us A.T.L.A. [240]

GESCHIEDENIS VAN DE HERVORMING EN DE HERVORMDE KERK DER NEDERLANDEN / Reitsma, J – Groningen, 1916 – Dfl56.00 – ne Slangenburg [240]

GESCHIEDENIS VAN DE VORSTEN VAN PALEMBANG – n.d. KITLV,H 184. BSD-102/1 – 2mf – 9 – ne IDC [950]

GESCHIEDENIS VAN DEN OORSPRONG, DE INVOERING EN DE LOTGEVALLEN VAN DEN HEIDELBERGSCHEN CATECHISMUS / Schotel, G D J – Amsterdam: W.H. Kirberger, 1863 – 1mf – us A.T.L.A. [240]

GESCHIEDENISSEN ENDE HANDELINGEN.DER NEDERDUYTSCHE NATIE IN ENGELANT (DE WERKEN..3,1) / ed by Toorenbergen, J J van – Utrecht, 1873 – Dfl32.00 – ne Slangenburg [240]

GESCHIEDKUNDIG ONDERZOEK NAAR DEN WALDENZISCHEN OORSPRONG VAN DE NEDERLANDSCHE DOOPSGEZINDEN / Cate, S Blaupot ten – Amsterdam: F. Muller, 1844 – 1mf – us A.T.L.A. [240]

GESCHIEDKUNDIGE AANTEEKENINGEN BETREFFENDE DE PORTUGESCHE ISRAELIETEN IN DEN HAAG EN HUNNE SYNAGOGEN ALDAAR / Pimentel, M H – 's-Gravenhage. 1876. BJ-262-44 1 – 9 – ne IDC [949]

EIN GESCHLECHT : TRAGOEDIE / Unruh, Fritz von – Muenchen: Kurt Wolff Verlag, 1922, c1917 – 1r – 1 – us U.W. Library [430]

GESCHLECHT UND GESELLSCHAFT (HQ 3) / Vanselow, Karl et al – v1-14. 1906-1926/27. Berlin, Leipzig, Wien, spaeter: Muenchen, Dresden, Leipzig (mf ed 1991) – 94mf – 9 – DM760.00 – 3-89131-044-7 – gw Fischer [305]

GESCHRIFTEN UITGEGEVEN VANWEGE DEN NEDERLANDSCHEN PROTESTANTENBOND, 6 *see* DE BERGREDE

DER GESCHWINDE RECHNER, ODER DES HAENDLERS NUETZLICHER GEHUELFE... – Chesnut-Hill, 1793 – 1mf – DM48.00 – 3-8267-3028-3 – gw Hänsel [510]

GESCHWISTER : ROMAN / Huch, Friedrich – Berling: S Fischer, [1921] – 1r – 1 – us U.W. Library [830]

DIE GESELLSCHAFT : INTERNATIONALE REVUE FUER SOZIALISMUS UND POLITIK – Berlin, 1924-33 – 5r – 1 – DM600.00 – gw Mikro Press [072]

DIE GESELLSCHAFT : INTERNATIONALE REVUE FUER SOZIALISMUS UND POLITIK – Berlin, 1924-mar 1933 – 5r – 1 – Dist. gw Mikrofilm – gw Misc Inst [072]

Gesellschaft fuer aeltere Deutsche Geschichtskunde *see* NEUES ARCHIV

GESELLSCHAFT FUER BEDROHTE VOELKER = SOCIETY FOR ENDANGERED PEOPLES – (Missing: Doc 186) – Goettingen. 189 docs. 1980-1991 – 164mf – 9 – ne IDC [320]

Gesellschaft fuer Geschichte des Landvolks und der Landwirtschaft *see* ZUR OSTDEUTSCHEN AGRARGESCHICHTE

GESELLSCHAFT FUER MUSIKFORSCHUNG – v. 1-29. 1870-1905 – 1 – 55.00 – us L of C Photodup [780]

Gesellschaft fuer Musikforschung *see* MONATSHEFTE FUER MUSIK-GESCHICHTE

Gesellschaft fuer Pommersche Geschichte, Altertumskunde und kunst *see* MONATSBLAETTER

Gesellschaft fuer Salzburger Landeskunde *see* MITTEILUNGEN

Gesellschaft fuer Wiener Theaterforschung *see* FESTSCHRIFT FUER EDUARD CASTLE ZUM ACHTZIGSTEN GEBURTSTAG

Gesellschaft Naturforschender Freunde. Berlin *see* SITZUNGSBERICHTE

Gesellschaft rheinlaendischer Gelehrter *see* RHEINISCHES CONVERSATIONS-LEXICON ODER ENCYCLOPAEDISCHES HANDWOERTERBUCH FUER GEBILDETE STAENDE (AEL, ABT 1;20)

GESELLSCHAFT UND ORGANISATION : ZUR SOZIOLOGISCHEN THEORIE VON ORGANISATIONEN / Herrmann, Peter – 1993 – 7mf – 9 – DM148.00 – 3-89349-684-X – gw Hänsel [303]

GESELLSCHAFT ZUR ERFORSCHUNG JUEDISCHER KUNSTDENKMAELER E.V. – Frankfurt a.M. Mitteilungen. Duesseldorf. v1-8. 1900-15. 1 reel. B88 (Leo Baeck Institute. German-Jewish Periodicals, Pt 2) – 1 – $75.00 – us UPA [270]

DER GESELLSCHAFTER – Litterarische Monatsschrift. Erfurt etc. 1.-3. Jahrg.; 1. Oct 1894-1 Mar 1897. Film Mas 8776 – 1 – us H.U. Library [430]

DER GESELLSCHAFTER : ODER BLAETTER FUER GEIST UND HERZ – Berlin, 1849-50 – 1 – Dist. gw Mikrofilm – gw Misc Inst [072]

DER GESELLSCHAFTER : ODER BLAETTER FUER GEIST UND HERZ – (Missing issues: sep 20-dec 27 1820, apr 1-jun 29 1822, oct 2 1822-may 2 1823) – Berlin, jan 1-jun 30 1817, 1820-may 31 1823, 1825 n7, aug 11 1828, 1848 – 3r – 1 – Dist. gw Mikrofilm – gw Misc Inst [072]

GESELLSCHAFTER – London, UK. 1890-91 – 1 – uk British Libr Newspaper [072]

Gesenhoff, Georgia *see* UNTERSUCHUNGEN ZUM GRIECHISCHEN SCHMUCK AN BEISPIELEN DES 7. UND 6. JAHRHUNDERTS V. CHR

Gesenius, G *see* THESAURUS PHILOLOGICUS CRITICUS LINGUAE HEBRAEAE ET CHALDAEAE V.T.

Gesenius, H *see* HEBREW GRAMMAR

Gesenius, W *see*
- GESCHICHTE DER HEBRAISCHEN SPRACHE UND SCHRIFT
- THESAURUS PHILOLOGICUS CRITICUS LINGUAE HEBRAICAE ET CHALDAICAE VETERIS TESTAMENTI

DAS GESETZ DER FORM : BRIEFE AN TOTE / Hefele, Herman – Jena: E Diederichs, 1921 – 1 – us U.W. Library [840]

DAS GESETZ DES HERRN : ODER, DIE HEILIGEN ZEHN GEBOTE / Seeberg, P – 2. verm. Aufl. Berlin:Eduard Beck, 1867 – 1mf – 9 – 0-8370-5206-8 – 1985-3206 – us A.T.L.A. [220]

GESETZ UBER DIE VERWALTUNGSGERICHTS-BARKEIT IN BAYERN, WURTTEMBERG-BADEN UND HESSEN, MIT KOMMENTAR VON PAULUS VAN HUSEN / Bavaria. Laws, Statutes, etc – Stuttgart, Poeschel 1947 177 p. LL-4088 – 1 – us L of C Photodup [340]

GESETZ UEBER DEN 2. FUENFJAHRPLAN. 1956-1960 (VOM 9 JAN 1958) / Germany. Democratic Republic – Gesetzblatt der D.D.R. Berlin. pt. 1, (5), 20 Jan 1958, 41-55. BD-739 1 – 9 – ne IDC [338]

GESETZ UEBER DEN FUENFJAHRPLAN. (1951-1955) / Germany. Democratic Republic – Berlin. 1951 – 9 – ne IDC [338]

GESETZ UEBER DEN PERSPEKTIVPLAN ZUR ENTWICKLUNG DER WOLKSWIRTSCHAFT DER D.D.R. BIS 1970 (VOM 26 MAI 1967) / Germany. Democratic Republic – Gesetzblatt der D.D.R. (Berlin). 7 Jun 1967 – 9 – ne IDC [338]

GESETZ UEBER DEN SIEBENJAHRPLAN. 1959 BIS 1965 (VOM 1. OKT 1959) / Germany. Democratic Republic – Gesetzblatt der D.D.R. (Berlin). 17 Oct 1959 – 9 – ne IDC [338]

GESETZ UEBER DEN VATERLANDISCHEN HILFSDIENST / Konferenz von Vertretern der gewerkschaftlichen Organisationen und Angestelltenverbande – 1917. 78p. Generalkommission der Gewerkschaften Deutschlands. (Serial publications of German trade unions in the Memorial Library, University of Wisconsin-Madison.) – 1 – us U.W. Library [331]

GESETZ UEBER DEN VOLKSWIRTSCHAFT-SPLAN 1950, DAS ZWEITE JAHR DES ZWEIJAHRPLANES DER DEUTSCHEN DEMOKRATISCHEN REPUBLIC / Germany. Democratic Republic – Berlin. 1950 – 9 – ne IDC [338]

GESETZ UEBER DEN VOLKSWIRTSCHAFT-SPLAN 1951, DAS ERSTE JAHR DES FUENFJAHRPLANES DER D.D.R. (VON 14 MAR 1951) / Germany. Democratic Republic – Gesetzblatt der D.D.R. (Berlin). 19 Mar 1951 – 9 – ne IDC [338]

GESETZ UEBER DEN VOLKSWIRTSCHAFT-SPLAN 1953, DAS DRITTE JAHR DAS FUENFJAHRPLANES. (VOM 17. DEZ 1952) / Germany. Democratic Republic – Gesetzblatt der D.D.R. (Berlin). 22 Dec 1952 – 9 – ne IDC [338]

GESETZ UEBER DEN VOLKSWIRTSCHAFTS-PLAN 1965 (VOM 14. JAN 1965) / Germany. Democratic Republic – Gesetzblatt der D.D.R. (Berlin). 14 Jan 1965 – 9 – ne IDC [338]

GESETZ UEBER DEN VOLKSWIRTSCHAFTS-PLAN 1967 (VOM 9. DEZ 1966) / Germany. Democratic Republic – Geseztblatt der D.D.R. Berlin. T. 1, (16), 12 Dec 1966, 159-163. BB-763 1 – 9 – ne IDC [338]

GESETZ UEBER DEN VOLKSWIRTSCHAFTS-PLAN 1968 (VOM 15. DEZ 1967) / Germany. Democratic Republic – Gesetzblatt der D.D.R. Berlin. T. 1, (18), 18 Dec 1967, 137-151. BD-761 1 – 9 – ne IDC [338]

DAS GESETZ UEBER DIE PRESSE VOM 12. MAI 1851, AUS DER ENTSTEHUNGSGESCHICHTE, DER RECHTSLEHRE UND DER ENTSCHEIDUNGEN DES KOENIGLICHEN OBER-TRIBUNALS ERLAUTERT. / Hartmann, L – Berlin: Decker, 1865 2 347 1p. LL-4104 – 1 – us L of C Photodup [340]

GESETZ ZUR BEFREIUNG VON NATIONALSOZIALISMUS UND MILITARISMUS MIT DEN AUSFUEHRUNGSVORSCHRIFTEN UND FORMULAREN / ed by Schullze, Erich – 1995 – 3mf – 9 – DM148.00 – 3-8267-3147-6 – gw Hänsel [340]

GESETZBLATT BADEN-WUERTTEMBERG/ GEMEINSAMES AMTSBLATT BADEN-WUERTTEMBERG – (mit Folgelieferungen zum Preis von DM 13,-/Fiche) – saemtl. Jahrgaenge bis einschl. 1991, mit 2 Sammelordnern und Kompakt-Lesegeraet – DM1,973.00 – gw Boorberg [340]

GESETZBLATT DER DDR – 1949-1989 – 1,797mf – 1 – DM10,242.90 – gw Mikro Press [340]

GESETZBLATT DER DEUTSCHEN DEMOKRATISCHEN REPUBLIK – Berlin, 1973-1988(2) – 227mf – 9 – H-1110/1 – ne IDC [340]

GESETZBLATT DER DEUTSCHEN DEMOKRATISCHEN REPUBLIK – (Supplemented: 1989(1)-1990(2)) – Berlin, 1973-1990(2) – 275mf – 9 – H-1110/1 – ne IDC [340]

DAS GESETZESFREIE EVANGELIUM DES PAULUS: NACH SEINEM WERDEGANG / Feine, Paul – Leipzig: J.C. Hinrichs, 1899. 1 fiche – 9 – us A.T.L.A. [240]

DIE GESETZESSAMMLUNG (ULOZENIE) VON 1649 UND IHRE AUSWIRKUNGEN AUF DIE KIRCHE IN DER AERA NIKONS : UNTERSUCHUNGEN ZUM VERHAELTNIS ZWISCHEN STAAT UND KIRCHE IM MOSKAUER RUSSLAND / Heise, Christoph Ulrich – Heidelberg, 1972 – 2mf – 9 – DM62.00 – 3-89349-769-2 – gw Hänsel [340]

DIE GESETZESSCHRIFT DES KOENIGS JOSIA : EINE KRITISCHE UNTERSUCHUNG / Fries, Samuel Andreas – Leipzig: A Deichert, 1903 – 1mf – 9 – 0-8370-3206-7 – 1985-1206 – us A.T.L.A. [220]

GESETZES-UND VERORDUNGSBLATT / Evangelische Landeskirche in Baden – 1969-85 – 1 – us A.T.L.A. [240]

DIE GESETZLICHEN BESTIMMUNGEN ZUM VOLKSWIRTSCHAFTSPLAN, 1950 / Germany. Democratic Republic. Amt fuer Information – Berlin. 1950. BD-736 1 – 9 – ne IDC [338]

GESHIKHTE FUN YIDISHE GEZELSHAFTLIEKHE SHTREMUNGEN IN RUSLAND / Sosis, Y – Minsk. 1929. BJ-290-23 1 – 9 – ne IDC [940]

DI GESHIKHTE FUN YIDISHER ARBAYTER BAWEGUNG IN RUSLAND / Buchbinder, N – Vilna. 1931. BJ-290-25 1 – 7mf – 9 – ne IDC [940]

GESHIKTE FUN IDN IN RUSLAND / Margolis, A – Moscow. 1930. BJ-290-24 1 – 9 – ne IDC [956]

GESICHTER UND GESICHTE / Usinger, Fritz – Darmstadt: E Roether, 1965 – 1r – 1 – us U.W. Library [430]

GESKIEDENIS VAN DIE SUID-AFRIKAANSE REPUBLIEK / Pelzer, Auguste – Kaapstad: A A Balkema, 1950 – 1 – us Res Libr [960]

GESLACHTKUNDIGE AANTEEKENINGEN : T.A.V.D.GECOMMITEERDEN TEN LANDDAGE VAN OVERIJSSEL ZEDERT 1610-1794 / Doorninck, J van – Deventer, 1871 – Dfl60.00 – ne Slangenburg [920]

GESLAGT-LYSTE DER NAKOMELINGEN VAN DER VERMAERDEN CHRISTOFFEL PLANTIN / Straelen, J B van der – Antwerpen, 1858 – 9 – ne IDC [700]

Geslin, P *see* LES JADES OLMEQUES

Geslison, Jeannette E K *see* A COMPARISON OF VILLAGE AND STAGED VERSIONS OF SELECTED HUNGARIAN DANCE STYLES

GESNALDA DELLO SPIRITO SANCTO. SANTA GEMA GALGANI / Bayle, Constantino – Madrid: Razon y Fe, 1944 – 1 – sp Bibl Santa Ana [240]

Gesner, C *see*
- HISTORIA ANIMALIUM. LIBRI 1 DE QUADRUPEDIBUS VIVIPARIS...
- HISTORIA ANIMALIUM. LIBRI 2 DE QUADRUPEDIBUS VIVIPARIS...
- HISTORIA ANIMALIUM. LIBRI 3 DE DE AVIUM NATURA...
- HISTORIA ANIMALIUM. LIBRI 4 DE PISCIUM ET AQUATILIUM...
- HISTORIA ANIMALIUM. LIBRI 5 DE SERPENTIUM NATURA...
- HISTORIAE ANIMALIUM
- HISTORIAE INSECTORUM LIBELLUS QUI EST DE SCORPIONE
- A NEW BOOKE OF DESTILLATYON
- OPERA BOTANICA PER DUO SAECULA
- THE PRACTISE OF. PHISICKE

Gesner, S *see*
- CONTROVERSIAE INTER THEOLOGOS VVITTENBERGENSES DE REGENERATIONE ET ELECTIONE DILVCIDA EXPLICATIO D.D. EGIDII HVNNII, POLYCARPI LEYSERI, SALOMONIS GESNERI,...
- PRO SANCTISSIMO LIBRO CHRISTIANAE CONCORDIAE DISPVTATIO PRIMA SEX CAPITVM:...

GESNERACEAE CENTRO-AMERICANAE. CENTRALAMERICAS GESNERACEER, ET SYSTEMATISK, PLANTEGEOGRAPHISK BIDRAG TIL CENTRALAMERICAS FLORA / Oersted, A S – Kjobenhavn. 1858. B-6162 2 – 8 – ne IDC [580]

GESPRACHE IN DEM REICHE DERER WELT-WEISSEN, IN ACHT VERSCHIEDENEN THEILEN ZUSAMMEN GEFASSET, UND MIT EINER VORREDE VOM DEM VORZUGE DER NEUERN.. – Halle, 1722 – 1 – us U.W. Library [400]

GESPRAECH (EIN CHRISTENLICH) GEHALLTEN ZU BERNN ZWUESCHEN DEN PREDICANTEN VND HANSEN PFYSTER MEYER VON AROUW, DEN WIDERTOUFF, EYD, OBERKEYT VND ANDERE WIDERTOEUFFERISCHE ARTICKEL BETREFFENDE – 1531. BME-121 1 – 9 – ne IDC [240]

DAS GESPRAECH UEBER GEDICHT / Hofmannsthal, Hugo von – Berlin: Hyperionverlag, 1918 – 1r – 1 – us U.W. Library [430]

GESPRAECH UND DISCURSEN ... / Boccalinus, T – N.p, 1680 – 1mf – 9 – ILM-1051/1 – ne IDC [327]

GESPRAECH VON DER MUSIK, ZWISCHEN EINEM ORGANISTEN UND ADJUVATEN / Voigt, J C – 1742 – 9 – us Sibley [780]

GESPRAECH ZWISCHEN EINEM MUSICO THEORETICO / Sorge, G A – 1748 – 9 – us Sibley [780]

GESPRAECH ZWISCHEN EINEM MUSICO THEORETICO UND EINEM STUDIOSO MUSICES VON DER PRAETORIANISCHEN / Sorge, G A – Lobenstein. 1748. BP-760 1 – 9 – ne IDC [780]

GESPRAECHE JESU MIT SEINEN JUENGERN NACH DER AUFERSTEHUNG : EIN KATHOLISCH-APOSTOLISCHES SENDERSCHREIBEN DES 2. JAHRHUNDERTS (T.U.U. 3-43) / Schmidt, Carl – Leipzig, 1919 – 12mf – 9 – ne Slangenburg [240]

GESPRAECHE MIT GOETHE IN DEN LETZTEN JAHREN SEINES LEBENS / Eckermann, Johann Peter; ed by Castle, Eduard – (Includes index) – Berlin: Bong, [19–?] – 1r – 1 – us U.W. Library [920]

GESPRAECHSBEFAEHIGUNG IM BERUFSBEZOGENEN PORTUGIESISCHUNTERRICHT / Groeschl, Juergen – 1993 – 3mf – 9 – DM98.00 – 3-89349-760-9 – gw Hänsel [440]

AIN GESPRECH ETLICHER PREDICANTEN ZU BASEL / Oecolampad, J & Ecolampadius, J – 1525. BME-89 1 – 9 – ne IDC [240]

Gessa *see* MANUAL DE APLICACION Y CORRECION DE LA BATERIA "C"

Gessen, I Ulii *see* O ZHIZNI EVREEV V ROSSII

Gessen, I V *see* KONSTITUTSIONNOE GOSUDARSTVO

Gessner, C *see*
- BIBLIOTHECA UNIVERSALIS,...
- CATALOGUS PLANTARUM LATINE, GRAECE, GERMANICE AND GALLICE
- LEXICON GRAECOLATINUM
- LEXICON GRAECOLATINUM...
- LEXICON GRAECOLATINUM DENUO IMPRESSUM..., NOVISSIME PER ADRIANUM IUNIUM... LOCUPLETATUM...
- NOMENCLATOR INSIGNIUM SCRIPTORUM,...
- OPERA BOTANICA

Gessner, C (D Kyber) *see* LEXICON REI HERBARIAE TRILINGUAE,...

Gessner, C (Hieronymus Tragus) *see* DE STIRPIUM...

Gessner, C (Jacques Houllier) *see* VIATICUM NOVUM

Gessner, C Josua Maler *see* DICTIONARUM GERMANICO LATINUM...

Gessner, Conrad *see* MITHRIDATES, SIVE DE DIFFERENTIIS LINGUARUM

Gessner, L *see* LE DROIT DES NEUTRES SUR MER

Gessner, Salomon *see* LA MORT D'ABEL

Gessner, Th *see* PROGRAMM DER HOEHEREN BUERGERSCHULE ZU QUAKENBRUECK DEN 26 MAERZ 1874...RATHHAUSES

GESTA ABBATUM FONTANELLENSIUM (MGH 7: 28.BD) – 1886 – Dfl6.00 – ne Slangenburg [240]

GESTA ABBATUM MONASTERII S. ALBANI (CHRONIA..4) / Thomas Walsingham – (v1 1867 Dfl35.00. v2 1867 Dfl35.00. v3 1869 Dfl46.00) – ne Slangenburg [240]

GESTA CHRISTI, OR, A HISTORY OF HUMANE PROGRESS UNDER CHRISTIANITY / Brace, Charles Loring – New York: A.C. Armstrong, 1884, c1882 – 2mf – us A.T.L.A. [240]

GESTA EPISCOPORUM. HISTORIAE (SUPPL. TOM. 1-12, PARS 2) (MGH 5: 14.BD) : SUPPL. TOMI 13 – 1883 – Dfl63.00 – ne Slangenburg [240]

GESTA FREDERICI I. IMPERATORIS IN LOMBARDIA AUCTORE CIVE MEDIOLANENSI (MGH 7: 27.BD) : ACCEDUNT GESTA FREDERICI 1 IN EXPEDITIONE SACRA – 1892 – Dfl9.00 – ne Slangenburg [240]

GESTA GREYORUM... : HENRY, PRINCE OF PURPOOLE / England. Inns of Court – (Account of Gray's Inn revels under Henry Helmes, "Prince of Purpoole") – London, 1688 – 2mf – 9 – $3.00 – LLMC 84-282 – us L.L.M.C. [941]

GESTA SAEC. 13 (MGH 5: 25.BD) – 1880 – Dfl88.00 – ne Slangenburg [240]

GESTA STEPHANI REGIS ANGLORUM (CHRONICLES..3) – ne Slangenburg [941]

DIE GESTALT DER WORTFORM UND DES SATZES UNTER EINWIRKUNG DES RHYTHMUS BEI CHAUCER UND GOWER / Bihl, Josef – Tuebingen, 1915 – 2mf – DM62.00 – 3-8267-3043-7 – gw Hänsel [420]

DIE GESTALT DES BILDENDEN KUENSTLERS IN DER DICHTUNG / Laserstein, Kaete – (Includes bibliographical references and index) – Berlin: W de Gruyter & Co, 1931 – 2r – 1 – us U.W. Library [430]

GESTALTEN DEUTSCHER DICHTUNG : EINE LITERATURGESCHICHTE / Denecke, Rolf – (Includes index) – Frankfurt am Main: Hirschgraben-Verlag, 1965 – 1 – 1 – us U.W. Library [430]

GESTALTEN UND PROBLEME / Winkler, Eugen Gottlob – Leipzig-Markkleeberg: Karl Rauch Verlag, c1937 – 1 – us U.W. Library [840]

GESTALTUNG, UMGESTALTUNG : FESTSCHRIFT ZUM 75. GEBURTSTAG VON HERMANN AUGUST KORFF / ed by Mueller, Joachim – (In German; one article in English. Includes bibliographical references) – Leipzig: Koehler & Amelang, 1957 – 1 – us U.W. Library [430]

GESTALTUNGEN DES FRAUEN-BILDES IN DEUTSCHER LYRIK / Schukart, Hanns – (Includes bibliographical references) – Bonn a. Rh.: L Roehrscheid, 1933 – 1r – 1 – us U.W. Library [430]

GESTALTUNGSMITTELANALYSE BEI DIENSTLEISTUNGEN / Willms, Jens-Peter – 1995 – 2mf – 9 – DM80.00 – 3-8267-2085-7 – gw Hänsel [650]

LA GESTE TIEDO / Sy, Amadou Abel – 1980 – us Res Libr [390]

GESTERN : DRAMATISCHE STUDIE IN EINEM AKT IN VERSEN / Hofmannsthal, Hugo von – 3. Aufl. Berlin: S Fischer, 1909 – 1r – 1 – us U.W. Library [810]

GESTES DE LA VIE QUOTIDIENNE DANS LE CONSTANTINOIS / Abel, F – 7mf – 9 – F100.00 – fr Ethnologie [306]

DER GESTIEFELTE KATER – DAS ROTKAEPPCHEN : ZWEI MAERCHENSPIELE MIT MUSIK UND REIGEN / Herrmann, Emil Alfred; ed by Benz, Richard – Jena: E Diederichs, 1911 – 1r – 1 – us U.W. Library [790]

GESTIRN DES KRIEGES : GEDICHTE / Schuett, Bodo – Jena: E Diederichs, 1941 – 1 – us U.W. Library [810]

DIE GESTOHLENE SEELE : EINE ERZAEHLUNG AUS CHILE / Vegesack, Siegfried von – Muehlacker: E Haendle, [194-?] – 1r – 1 – us U.W. Library [830]

Gestoso y Perez, Jose *see* DE SEVILLA A GUADALUPE. BREVES APUNTES TOMADOS A VUELA PLUMA

GESU CRISTO NELLA LETTERATURA CONTEMPORANEA STRANIERA E ITALIANA / Labanca, Baldassare – Torino: Fratelli Bocca, 1903. 1 fiche – 9 – us A.T.L.A. [240]

GESUNDHEITSFOERDERUNG ALS ARBEITSFELD SOZIALER THERAPIE / Weil, Thomas – 1995 – 3mf – 9 – DM98.00 – 3-8267-2164-0 – gw Hänsel [360]

DIE GESUNDHEITSFUEHRUNG – Berlin, 1939 n1-3, 1940-45 n2 – 1 – Dist. gw Mikrofilm – gw Misc Inst [613]

GETE V RUSSKOI LITERATURE / Zhirmunskii, V M – L. 1937. BR-7987 2 – 8 – ne IDC [460]

GETHSEMANE AND AFTER : A NEW SETTING OF AN OLD STORY / Brady, Cyrus Townsend – New York: Moffat, Yard, 1907 – 1mf – 9 – 0-8370-2436-6 – 1985-0436 – us A.T.L.A. [790]

GETHSEMANE BAPTIST CHURCH. CALHOUN COUNTY. SOUTH CAROLINA : CHURCH RECORDS – (914p) – 1894-Sept 1928, 1940-Nov 1949, Oct 1954-1985 – 1 reel – 1 – $41.13 – us Baptist [240]

Getino, Luis A *see* MANIPUELO DE FLORES DEL MAESTRO FR. FRANCISCO DE VITORIA

Getino, Luis G *see* JUSTICIA Y CARACTER DE LA GUERRA NACIONAL ESPANOLA

GETLEKH LID – Prague. c.1650? BJ-43-19 1 – 9 – ne IDC [956]

GETREIDE-ZEITUNG – Bremen, 1852-53 – 2r – 1 – Inquire at Mikrofilmarchiv for details – gw Misc Inst [631]

GETREIDE-ZEITUNG – Bremen, Germany. 1852-53 – 2r – 1 – gw Mikrofilm [072]

GETRENNT MARSCHIEREN : ERZAEHLUNG / Hohlbaum, Robert – Muenchen: A Langen/G Mueller, 1935 – 1r – 1 – us U.W. Library [830]

DIE GETRENNTEN : GEDICHTE / Gstettner, Hans – Berlin: Suhrkamp, 1944 – 1r – 1 – us U.W. Library [810]

GETREUE DARSTELLUNG UND BESCHREIBUNG DER IN DER ARZNEYKUNDE GEBRAUECHLICHEN GEWAECHSE / Hayne, FG – (Missing: 1843-1846. V.14(1-2)) – Berlin, 1805-1846. 14v. [in 8] – 34mf – 9 – ne IDC [615]

DER GETREUE MUSIC-MEISTER...DURCH TELEMANN – 1728. Contains works of (C.P.E. Bach, E.T.Baron, Dirnflot, J.G. Kreysing, et al – 9 – us Sibley [780]

DEN GETRUEWEN VND VSSERWELTEN BRUEDERN VND SCHWOESTERN IN CHRISTO JHESU, WUENSCHT L. HAETZER ERLOESUNG / Haetzer, L – 1523. BME-50 – 9 – ne IDC [240]

Getting, Milan *see* AMERICKI SLOVACI

GETTING TOGETHER:...FRIENDS...ON THE REGULATIVE IDEAS OF RELIGIOUS THOUGHT / Whiton, James Morris – New York: Sturgis & Walton, 1913. 1 fiche – 9 – us A.T.L.A. [240]

GETTING WHAT WE WANT; HOW TO APPLY PSYCHOANALYSIS TO YOUR OWN PROBLEMS / Edson, David Orr, M D – New York, London: Harper & Brothers, (c1921). 4p,l,286,(1)p. Fold. form – 1 – us U.W. Library [150]

Gettysburg, Pennsylvania *see* MISCELLANEOUS EARLY NEWSPAPERS

GETTYSBURG SEMINARY BULLETIN / Lutheran Theological Seminary. Gettysburg, PA – v6-20. 1927-41 – 1 – us UMI [240]

GETULIO VARGAS, MEU PAI / Peixoto, Alzira Vargas do Amaral – Rio de Janeiro, Editora Globo 1960 – 1 – us U.W. Library [920]

Getze, J *see* THE YOUNG ORGANIST: A COMPLETE INSTRUCTOR

Geuer, F *see* DIE KIRCHENPOLITIK DES KANZLERS MICHEL DE L'HOSPITAL

Geuffroy, A *see*
- BRIEFUE DESCRIPTIO DE LA COVRT DV GRANT TVRC ET VNG SOMMAIRE DU REGNE DES OTHMANS AUEC VN ABREGE DE LEURS FOLLES SUPERSTITIONS
- PARS 1: AULAE TURCICAE, OTHOMANNICIQ'VE IMPERII DESCRIPTIO: ...PARS 2: SOLYMANNI 12. ET SELYMI 13. TVRCAR. IMPP. CONTRA CHRISTIANOS

GE'ULLAH IN THE BOOK OF RUTH / Bewer, Julius A – Chicago: University of Chicago: (1903). 1 fiche – 9 – us A.T.L.A. [220]

GEVATTER TOD : FUER DIE MAERCHENSPIELE DER KUENSTLERISCHEN VOLKSBUEHNE NACH GRIMMS MAERCHEN IN REDE UND HANDLUNG GESETZT / Guembel-Seiling, Max – Leipzig: Breitkopf & Haertel, 1918 – 1r – 1 – us U.W. Library [820]

Gevers Deynoot, W T *see* DE MAGNO SIVE HALECUM PISCATU BELGICO,...

Gevers, P *see* DE JURE EORUM, QUI INAEQUALI FOEDERI JUNCTI SUNT

GEVEZE – (Nos. 6-36, 38, 41, 43 (23 Tesrinisani 1324-2 Nisan 1325[1908-1909])) – Istanbul: Asir Matbassi. Sahib-i Imtiyaz: Kirkor Faik, 1908-1909 – 3mf – 9 – $65.00 – us MEDOC [949]

DIE GEWAEHRUNG LANGFRISTIGER KREDITE NACH DEM VERRECHNUNGSPRINZIP / Beckerath, Ulrich von – 9 – 1.00f – at Libertarian Micro [335]

GEWALT AN FRAUEN : ZUR SOZIAL-PAEDAGOGISCHEN HANDLUNGSKOMPETENZ IN DER ARBEIT MIT BETROFFENEN ALS NOTWENDIGE GRUNDLAGE ZUKUNFTSWEISENDER PSYCHO-SOZIALER/THERAPEUTISCHER/ GESUNDHEITSFOERDERNDER AUSBILDUNG / Ragoss, Silvia – 1950 – 3mf – 9 – DM98.00 – 3-8267-2132-2 – gw Hänsel [360]

GEWERBE- UND HANDELSZEITUNG – Prag (Praha), Czechoslovakia. Sept 1930-31 Mar 1938 – 4r – 1 – gw Mikrofilm [072]

GEWERBE-ZEITUNG – Leipzig, Germany. Apr 1846-Mar 1847 – 1r – 1 – gw Mikrofilm [072]

GEWERBLICHER RECHTSSCHUTZ UND URHEBERRECHT : INALND. ZEITSCHRIFT DER DEUTSCHEN VEREINIGUNG FUER GEWERBLICHEN RECHTSSCHUTZ UND URHEBERRECHT – v50-98. 1948-96 – 1,5,6,13 – us V.C.H. [340]

GEWERBLICHER RECHTSSCHUTZ UND URHEBERRECHT = JOURNAL OF THE GERMAN ASSOCIATION FOR THE PROTECTION OF INDUSTRIAL PROPERTY AND COPYRIGHT : INTERNATIONALER TEIL – v1-45. 1952-96 – 1,5,6,13 – us V.C.H. [340]

Gewerkschaft der Angestellten *see* ZEITSCHRIFT

Gewerkschaft deutscher Eisenbahner *see* GESCHAEFTSBERICHT..

DER GEWERKSCHAFTER : MITTEILUNGSBLATT DER GEWERKSCHAFT HESSEN-PFALZ – Neustadt-Haardt, West Germany. 1946-1949 – 1r – 1 – gw Mikrofilm [331]

DER GEWERKSCHAFTLER : MITTEILUNGSBLATT DER GEWERKSCHAFT HESSEN-PFLAZ – Neustadt/Haardt, 1946-1949 – 1r – 1 – DM75.00 – gw Mikro Press [072]

GEWERKSCHAFTLICHE FRAUENZEITUNG – Berlin, 1916-27 – 3r – 1 – Dist. gw Mikrofilm – gw Misc Inst [072]

GEWERKSCHAFTLICHE FRAUENZEITUNG – Berlin. v7. 1922. (Serial publications of German trade unions in the Memorial Library, University of Wisonsin-Madison.) – 1 – us U.W. Library [331]

GEWERKSCHAFTLICHE INFORMATIONEN – (Cont as: Gewerkschaftliche Praxis 1949) – Koeln, Bielefeld, Duesseldorf. 1946-1948 – 1r – 1 – DM75.00 – gw Mikro Press [072]

GEWERKSCHAFTLICHE INFORMATIONEN – (Title change: Gewerkschaftliche Praxis, 1949) – Koeln-Bielefeld-Duesseldorf, West Germany. 24 Oct 1946-1949 (incomplete) – 1r – 1 – gw Mikrofilm [380]

GEWERKSCHAFTLICHE KOOPERATION AUF BETRIEBLICHER EBENE INNERHALB EINES MULTINATIONALEN KONZERNS : DAS BEISPIEL VON VOLKSWAGEN DE MEXICO INNERHALB DES VOLKSWAGENKONZERNS / Mertens, Volker – 1991 – 171p – 9 – DM98.00 – 3-89349-436-7 – gw Hänsel [338]

GEWERKSCHAFTLICHE PRAXIS *see* GEWERKSCHAFLICHE INFORMATIONEN

GEWERKSCHAFTS-ARCHIV – Jena. v1-18. 1924-33. (Serial publications of German trade unions in the Memorial Library, University of Wisconsin-Madison.) – 1 – us U.W. Library [331]

GEWERKSCHAFTSEINHEIT : INFORMATIONSBLATT DER EINHEITSGEWERKSCHAFT FUER DEN BEZIRK KOBLENZ-TRIER – Koblenz, Trier. Sept-Dec 1945 – 1r – 1 – DM75.00 – gw Mikro Press [072]

GEWERKSCHAFTSEINHEIT : INFORMATIONSBLATT DER EINHEITSGEWERKSCHAFT FUER DEN BEZIRK KOBLENZ-TRIER – Koblenz Trier, West Germany. 5 Sep-12 Dec 1945 – 1r – 1 – gw Mikrofilm [331]

Gewerkschaftskommission. Berlin *see* RECHENSCHAFTS-BERICHT

GEWERKSCHAFTSLEBEN – No.1-. Jan 1981-. -m. Monatsschrift des FDGB – 1 – us U.W. Library [331]

Gewerkschaftspropaganda und Kulturarbeit *see* BULLETIN DER AGITPROPABTEIL DER RGI

DIE GEWERKSCHAFTSSTIMME – Aschaffenburg, 1910-33 – 16r – 1 – Dist. gw Mikrofilm – gw Misc Inst [360]

GEWERKSCHAFTS-ZEITUNG : FUER DAS GEBIET SUEDWUERTTENBERG UND HOHENZOLLERN – (Titelaenderung ab Nr. 3: Die Schaffenden 1948-49) – Tuttlingen, 1946-49 – 1r – 1 – DM75.00 – gw Mikro Press [072]

GEWERKSCHAFTS-ZEITUNG : INFORMATIONSBLATT DER EINHEITSGEWERKSCHAFTEN RHEINLAND-HESSEN-NASSAU – Koblenz, 1946-1949 – 1r – 1 – DM75.00 – gw Mikro Press [072]

GEWERKSCHAFTS-ZEITUNG : ORGAN DER BAYERISCHEN GEWERKSCHAFTEN – Muenchen, 10 Jan-25 Dec 1947 – 1r – 1 – DM75.00 – gw Mikro Press [072]

GEWERKSCHAFTS-ZEITUNG : ORGAN DER BAYERISCHEN GEWERKSCHAFTEN – Muenchen, DE. 10 Jan-25 Dec 1947 – 1r – 1 – gw Mikrofilm [380]

GEWERKSCHAFTS-ZEITUNG : ZEITSCHRIFT DER FREIEN GEWERKSCHAFT IN DER BRITISCHEN ZONE – Hamburg, 1946-47 – 1r – 1 – DM75.00 – gw Mikro Press [072]

GEWERKSCHAFTS-ZEITUNG : ZEITSCHRIFT DER FREIEN GEWERKSCHAFT IN DER BRITISCHEN ZONE – Hamburg, West Germany. Feb 1946-April 1947 – 1r – 1 – gw Mikrofilm [331]

GEWERKSCHAFTSZEITUNG : INFORMATIONSBLATT DER EINHEITSGEWERKSCHAFT RHEINLAND-HESSEN-NASSAU – Koblenz, West Germany. 1 Jun 1946-25 Dec 1949 (incomplete) – 1r – 1 – gw Mikrofilm [331]

GEWERKSCHAFTS-ZEITUNG FUER DAS GEBIET SUEDWUERTTEMBERG UND HOHENZOLLERN – (Title change: Die Schaffenden, Feb 1948) – Tuttlingen, West Germany. 15 Sep 1946-Jan 1948; 18 Feb 1948-Dec 1949 – 1r – 1 – gw Mikrofilm [331]

DER GEWERKVEREIN – Berlin, 1869-73, 1908-nov 30 1918 – 1 – Dist. gw Mikrofilm – gw Misc Inst [331]

DER GEWERKVEREIN – Berlin, 1877-89, 1906-19 – 1r – 1 – Dist. gw Mikrofilm – gw Misc Inst [331]

DER GEWERKVEREIN – Berlin. v34-50. 1908-18 – 3r – 1 – DM225.00 – gw Mikro Press [072]

Gewerkverein christlicher Bergarbeiter Deutschlands *see*
- GESCHAEFTSBERICHT..
- PROTOKOLL...

GEWISSEN – Berlin, 1928-1929 – 1r – 1 – DM75.00 – gw Mikro Press [072]

GEWISSEN – Berlin. apr 9, 1919-20 – 1r – 1 – gw Mikrofilm [072]

GEWISSEN – Potsdam, Berlin. 1921-mar 1929 – 3r – 1 – Dist. gw Mikrofilm – gw Mikrofilm [072]

DAS GEWISSEN UND DIE GEWISSENSFREIHEIT : ZEHN VORTRAEGE / Simar, Hubert Theophil – (Includes bibliographical references) – Freiburg i.B.; St Louis, MO: Herder, 1874 – 1mf – 9 – 0-8370-7264-6 – 1986-1264 – us A.T.L.A. [240]

GEWISSENSFRAGEN: RELIGIOESE BRIEFE AUS DER GEGENWART FUER DIE GEGENWART / Wimmer, Richard – Tuebingen: J.C.B. Mohr, 1902. 1 fiche – 9 – us A.T.L.A. [240]

GEWORDENE LITURGIE / Jungmann, J A – Innsbruck, 1941 – 7mf – 8 – Dfl28.00 – ne Slangenburg [240]

Gey van Pittius, E F W *see* NATIONALITY WITHIN THE BRITISH COMMONWEALTH...

Geyer, Carl-Friedrich *see* KRITISCHE THEORIE UND METAPHYSIK

Geyer, Mauritius *see* OBSERVATIONES EPIGRAPHICAE DE PRAEPOSITIONUM GRAECARUM

Geyer, Ursula *see* DER ADLERFLUG IM ROMISCHEN KONSERKRATIONSZEREMONIELL

GEYER'S OFFICE EQUIPMENT DIGEST *see* ADMINISTRATIVE MANAGEMENT

Geyr, M H J A de *see* DE PRAESCRIPTIONE JURIS GENTIUM,...

GEYSERVILLE PRESS – Geyserville, CA. 1940-60 – 7r – 1 – $350.00 – B02273 – us Library Micro [071]

Geza, M *see* A MAGYAR POLGARY PERJOG NEMZETKOEZI VONATKOZASAI

DE GEZAGHEBBERS DER OOST-INDISCHE COMPAGNIE OP HARE BUITEN-COMPTOIREN IN AZIE / Wijnaendts van Resandt, Willem – Amsterdam: Liebaert, 1944 – 1r – 1 – us U.W. Library [380]

Geze, Francois *see* ARGENTINE, REVOLUTION ET CONTRE-REVOLUTIONS

THE GEZIRA SCHEME FROM WITHIN: A COLLECTION OF ARTICLES BY HEADS OF DEPARTMENTS / Sudan. Gezira Board – 1963 – 9 – ne IDC [330]

GF *see* ABRASIVE ENGINEERING

G.F.C.M. *see*
- REPORT OF THE 1ST SESSION OF THE WORKING GROUP ON ARTIFICIAL REEFS AND MARICULTURE
- REPORT OF THE 1ST SESSION OF THE WORKING PARTY ON FISHERIES ECONOMICS AND STATISTICS
- REPORT OF THE 2ND GFCM TECHNICAL CONSULTATION ON RED CORAL OF THE MEDITERRANEAN
- REPORT OF THE 2ND TECHNICAL CONSULTATION ON STOCK ASSESSMENT IN THE CENTRAL MEDITERRANEAN. MAZARA DEL VALLO, ITALY, 1985
- REPORT OF THE 2ND TECHNICAL CONSULTATION ON STOCK ASSESSMENT IN THE EASTERN MEDITERRANEAN
- REPORT OF THE 2ND TECHNICAL CONSULTATION ON THE UTILIZATION OF SMALL PELAGIC SPECIES IN THE MEDITERRANEAN AREA. ZADAR, YUGOSLAVIA, 1985
- REPORT OF THE 3RD TECHNICAL CONSULTATION ON UTILIZATION OF SMALL PELAGIC SPECIES IN THE MEDITERRANEAN AREA
- REPORT OF THE 4TH SESSION OF THE TECHNICAL CONSULTATION ON STOCK ASSESSMENT IN THE EASTERN MEDITERRANEAN
- REPORT OF THE 4TH TECHNICAL CONSULTATION ON STOCK ASSESSMENT IN THE BALEARIC AND GULF OF LIONS STATISTICAL DIVISIONS. SIDI-FEDJ, ALGERIA, 1985
- REPORT OF THE 5TH TECHNICAL CONSULTATION ON STOCK ASSESSMENT IN THE ADRIATIC AND THE IONIAN SEAS. BARI, ITALY, JUNE 1987
- REPORT OF THE 6TH SESSION OF THE COMMITTEE ON RESOURCE MANAGEMENT. ROME, 1986
- REPORT OF THE 7TH SESSION OF THE COMMITTEE ON RESOURCES MANAGEMENT
- REPORT OF THE 8TH SESSION OF THE COMMITTEE ON FISHERIES MANAGEMENT
- REPORT OF THE TECHNICAL CONSULTATION ON FISHING TECHNOLOGY AND ITS SOCIO-ECONOMIC ASPECTS. ANCONA, 1986
- REPORT OF THE TECHNICAL CONSULTATION ON METHODS OF EVALUATING SMALL-SCALE FISHERIES IN THE EASTERN MEDITERRANEAN. SETE, FRANCE, 1986
- REPORT OF THE TECHNICAL CONSULTATION ON OPEN SEA SHELLFISH CULTURE IN ASSOCIATION WITH ARTIFICIAL REEFS. ANCONA, ITALY, 1986
- REPORT OF THE TECHNICAL CONSULTATION ON STOCK ASSESSMENT IN THE EASTERN MEDITERRANEAN. ROME, 1986

Gfoerer, AF *see* UNTERSUCHUNG UEBER ALTER, URSPRUNG, ZWECK DER DEKRETALEN DES FALSCHEN ISIDORUS

Gfroerer, August *see* PHILO UND DIE ALEXANDRINISCHE THEOSOPHIE, ODER, VOM EINFLUSSE DER JUEDISCH-AEGYPTISCHEN SCHULE AUF DIE LEHRE DES NEUEN TESTAMENTS

THE GHADR DIRECTORY : CONTAINING THE NAMES OF PERSONS WHO HAVE TAKEN PART IN THE GHADR MOVEMENT IN AMERICA, EUROPE, AFRICA AND AFGHANISTAN AS WELL AS INDIA / India. Intelligence Bureau – New Delhi: Govt of India Press, 1934 – 1 – us Res Libr [950]

Ghana *see*
- ONE-YEAR DEVELOPMENT PLAN
- SECOND DEVELOPMENT PLAN, 1959-64
- SUBSIDIARY LEGISLATION – SUPPLEMENT
- WHITE PAPER ON THE REPORT OF THE COMMITTEE OF ENQUIRY INTO THE DISTURBANCES AT THE UNIVERSITY OF GHANA CAMPUS, LEGON, 17TH JANUARY 1975
- WHITE PAPER ON THE REPORT OF THE EDUCATION REVIEW COMMITTEE

LE GHANA : NAISSANCE D'UN ETAT AFRICAIN. LA GOLD COAT DE LA COLONISATION A L'INDEPENDANCE / Boyon, J – F50.00 – fr Ethnologie [960]

GHANA AGRICULTURE, 1890-1962 : A BIBLIOGRAPHY OF CROP AND STOCK,CO-OPERATION AND FORESTRY, FOOD AND FISHERY / Tetteh, S N – Accra, Government Printing Office [1962] – us Res Libr [960]

GHANA ARCHIVE / The Basel Mission – 1829-1917 – 1 – uk Microform Academic [240]

Ghana. Central Bureau of Statistics *see* EXTERNAL TRADE STATISTICS OF GHANA

GHANA DAILY EXPRESS – Accra: Ausco Press and Pub Co, feb 1954-mar 1955] – us Res Libr [072]

GHANA DAILY MAIL – Accra: Amalgamated Press Ltd, jul 1957-apr 1958] – us Res Libr [072]

Ghana. Education Review Committee *see* REPORT OF THE ... COMMITTEE

THE GHANA EVENING NEWS – Accra: Heal Press, mar 1954-aug 1958 – us Res Libr [072]

GHANA (FORMERLY GOLD COAST) : STATISTICAL YEARBOOK 1961-1970 / Ghana (formerly Gold Coast). Central Bureau of Statistics – (Coll title: African Official Statistical Serials, 1867-1982) – 23mf – 9 – £195.00 – uk Chadwyck [960]

Ghana (formerly Gold Coast). Central Bureau of Statistics *see* GHANA (FORMERLY GOLD COAST)

GHANA GAZETTE – Accra, 1957-69 – 7r – 1 – us Ross [324]

Ghana. Ministry of Education *see* THE NEW STRUCTURE AND CONTENT OF EDUCATION FOR GHANA

Ghana. Ministry of Education, National Family Planning Programme *see* REPORT ON POPULATION AND FAMILY LIFE EDUCATION SURVEY IN SCHOOLS AND COLLEGES

Ghana. Ministry of Finance *see* THE CONSOLIDATION DEVELOPMENT PLAN (1957/58-1958/59)

Ghana. National Consultative Committee on Education *see* FINANCE, SEPTEMBER 1974-JANUARY 1975

GHANA NATIONALIST – Accra: Fortitude Press & Pub Co, mar 1953-apr 1955 – us Res Libr [072]

Ghana. Planning Commission *see* SEVEN-YEAR DEVELOPMENT PLAN A BRIEF OUTLINE

THE GHANA REPORT : ECONOMIC DEVELOPMENT AND INVESTMENT OPPORTUNITIES, LEGAL PROBLEMS RELATIVE TO INVESTMENT, SOCIOLOGICAL FACTORS RELATIVE TO GENERAL ECONOMIC DEVELOPMENT – New York, 1959 – us Res Libr [338]

GHANA STATESMAN – Accra. Ghana. Sept. 10, 17; Oct. 1, 1948 – 1 – us NY Public [072]

GHANA TIMES – Accra: Star Pub Co, oct 4, 1958-jun 30, 1960 – us Res Libr [072]

Ghana. Vocational Training Institute *see* NATIONAL VOCATIONAL TRAINING ACT 1970

GHANAIAN LANGUAGE MATERIALS AND MISCELLANEA, 1966-68 – Chicago, University of Chicago, Photodup Dept, 1973 – us Res Libr [470]

THE GHANAIAN TIMES – Accra: Star Pub Co, jul 1960-sep 20 1962 – us Res Libr [072]

GHARBANDHU – v58-63. 1934-40 (complete) – 1r – 1 – ATLA S0525 – us A.T.L.A. [073]

Ghassemlou, Abdul Rahman *see* KURDISTAN AND THE KURDS
Ghazzali *see* AD-DOURRA AL-FAAKHIRA. PREMI ERE PARTIE
GHEBRUIK, EN ONGHEBRUIK VAN 'T ORGHEL, IN DE KERKEN DER VEREENIGHDE NEDERLANDEN / Huigens, C – Amsterdam. 1660. BP-701 1 – 9 – ne IDC [780]
DEN GHEESTELIJCKEN NACHTEGAEL / Salomon, Th – Antwerpen. 1634. BP-779 1 – 9 – ne IDC [780]
GHEESTELYCKE SERMOONEN : DE NAEVOLGHINGHE DES ARMEN LEVEN CHRISTI – HET MERCH DER ZIELEN / Tauler, Johannes – Antwerpen, 1707 – 28mf – 8 – ne Slangenburg [240]
Ghellinck, J de *see*
- L'ESSOR DE LA LITTERATURE LATINE AU 12TH SIECLE
- LITTERATURE LATINE AU MOYEN AGE
- PATRISTIQUE ET MOYEN AYGE

Ghenadieff, M *see* LA JURIDICTION DES EGLISES ET LES CONFLICTS DE LOIS EN MATIERE DE MARIAGE EN BULGARIE
Gherardi, Alessandro *see* LE LETTERE DI SANTA CATERINA DE'RICCI
Gherardius, P *see* IN FOEDVS ET VICTORIAM CONTRA TVRCAS
Ghesquiere, Henri J *see* LA MINE ET LES MINEURS
Ghesquiere, J *see* ACTA SANCTORUM BELGII SELECTA
HET GHETTO / Praag, S van – Zutphen. 1930. BJ-262-50 1 – 9 – ne IDC [949]
GHETTO TRAGEDIES / Zangwill, Israel – London: McClure & Co., Simpkin, Marshall, 1893 – 1 roll – 1 – 1-55879-565-0 – uk Libr Preservation [830]
GHETTO TSEITUNG = GHETTO JOURNAL – (In Yiddish) – Litz, PL. no1 7 Mar 1941-no18 21 Sep 1941 – 1r – 1 – $35.00 – cn Can Microfilming [072]
Ghiliani, V *see* MATERIALI PER SERVIRE ALLA COMPILAZIONE DELLE FAUNA ENTOMOLOGICA ITALIANA
Ghioldi, Americo *see*
- EL "ANTIIMPERIALISMO" DE PERON
- BASES DE LA PEDAGOGIA CONSTITUCIONAL
- CONCIENCIA OBRERA Y FRACASO PERONISTA
- DE LA TIRANIA A LA DEMOCRACIA SOCIAL
- DOS FECHAS, 4 DE JUNIO-24 DE FEBRERO
- HISTORIA CRITICA DE LA REVOLUCION DEL 43
- MAS ALL A DE LA REVOLUCION
- EL MITO DE EVA DUARTE
- LA SITUACION ECONOMICA
- EL SOCIALISMO Y LA ACTUAL CRISIS ARGENTINA
- LOS TRABAJADORES, EL SENOR PERON Y EL PARTIDO SOCIALISTA

Ghirardini, C *see* LA SOVRANITA TERRITORIALE...
Ghonemy, M R El et al *see* STUDIES ON AGRARIAN REFORM AND RURAL POVERTY
Ghose, Aurobindo *see* IDEAL AND PROGRESS; ESSAYS
Ghulam Husain Khan Tuba Tubee *see* SIYAR AL-MUT'AKHKHIRIN
Ghulam Murtada *see* BASATIN AL-SALATIN
Ghyvelde, Frederic de *see*
- ALBUM DE TERRE-SAINTE
- LA BONNE STE. ANNE
- LE CIEL, SEJOUR DES ELUS
- SAINT FRANCOIS D'ASSISE
- VIE DE SAINT ANTOINE DE PADOUE
- LA VIERGE IMMACULEE

GI CANCER : AN INTERNATIONAL JOURNAL OF GASTROINTESTINAL ONCOLOGY / ed by Fielding, John W L – 9,5,1 – us Harwood [616]
GI STORIES OF THE GROUND, AIR AND SERVICE FORCES IN THE EUROPEAN THEATER OF OPERATIONS – 53 unit histories – 1 – us NY Public [940]
GI STORIES OF THE GROUND, AIR AND SERVICE FORCES IN THE EUROPEAN THEATER OF OPERATIONS – Paris. 53v. 1944-45 – 1r – 1 – us Ross [977]
GIA SELAMA TAHUN 1955 / Garuda Indonesian Airways – SE-10,082 1. 1956 – 9 – ne IDC [380]
Giaccone, E *see* IL CANALE DI PANAMA...
GIA-DINH BAO – Saigon. 1865, 1872, 1874-76, 1893, 1895, 1897-1909. LO. Per. 552 – 1 – fr A.C.R.P.P. [950]
GIAI PHONG : CO QUAN CU MAT TRAN DAN TOC GIAI PHONG MIEN NAM VIET NAM – [Hanoi: s.n, sep 1975-jun 1976] – 1 – us Res Libr [072]
Giambelluca, Christopher *see* REDUCING ANTERIOR SHEAR DURING KNEE EXTENSION
Giamberandini, G *see* LA CONSACRAZIONE EUCHARISTICA NELLA CHIESA COPTA
Giannini, A *see*
- CAMBIALE E ASSEGNO BANCARIO...
- LE CONVENTIONI INTERNAZIONALI DI DIRITTO MARITTIMO
- IL MOVIMENTO INTERNAZIONALE PER L'UNIFICAZIONE DEL DIRITTO COMMERCIALE

Giannini, Amedeo *see* LO STATO GIURIDICO DELLA GENTE DELL'ARIA, DIRITTO INTERNAZIONALE ED INTERNO
Giannini Foundation of Agricultural Economics *see* DICTIONARY CATALOG OF THE GIANNINI FOUNDATION OF AGRICULTURAL ECONOMICS LIBRARY UNIVERSITY OF CALIFORNIA AT BERKELEY
Giannotti, Donati *see* OPERE POLITICHE E LETTERARIE.
THE GIANT CITIES OF BASHAN / Porter, Josias Leslie – 1844 – 9 – us A.T.L.A. [240]
Giardini, F de *see* SEI SRIE WITH CHAMBER MUSIC ACCONPANIMENT, OP. 4
Giauque, Florien *see*
- THE LAWS RELATING TO ROADS AND DITCHES, BRIDGES AND WATERCOURSES IN THE STATE OF OHIO.
- A MANUAL FOR GUARDIANS AND TRUSTEES OF MINORS, INSANE PERSONS, IMBECILES, IDIOTS, DRUNKARDS, AND FOR GUARDIANS AD LITEM, RESIDENT AND NON-RESIDENT, AFFECTED BY THE LAWS OF OHIO
- A MANUAL FOR NOTARIES PUBLIC, GENERAL CONVEYANCERS, COMMISSIONERS, JUSTICES, MAYORS, CONSULS.
- THE SETTLEMENT OF ESTATES OF DECEASED PERSONS, INCLUDING THE SUBJECTS OF WILLS, EXECUTORS, ADMINISTRATORS, TESTAMENTARY TRUSTEES...WITH SUCH ESTATES IN OHIO

Gib, A *see* A WARNING AGAINST COUNTENANCING THE MINISTRATIONS OF MR. GEORGE WHITEFIELD PUBLISHED IN THE NEW CHURCH AT BRISTOW UPON SABBATH, JUNE 6, 1742,...
Gibb, A D *see* INTERNATIONAL PRIVATE LAW IN SCOTLAND...
Gibb, Alexander *see* THE ECONOMIC DEVELOPMENT OF SYRIA; REPORT, 1947
Gibb, H A R *see*
- THE ARAB CONQUESTS IN CENTRAL ASIA
- THE CONQUEST IN CENTRAL ASIA

Gibb, H O *see* "TORHEIT" UND "RAETSEL" IM NEUEN TESTAMENT
Gibb, Sir Alexander and Partners, Consulting Engineers, London *see* ESTIMATION OF IRRIGABLE AREAS IN THE SUDAN, 1951-1953
Gibbens *see* PROMINENT MEN OF WEST VIRGINIA
Gibberd, K *see* THE LEAGUE IN OUR TIME
Gibbes Family *see* GENEALOGICAL RECORDS
Gibbes, James Shoolbred *see* LETTERBOOKS
Gibbes, Lewis R *see* PAPERS
GIBBON / Morison, James Cotter – New York: Harper, 1879 – 1mf – us A.T.L.A. [900]
Gibbon, Guy E *see* THE MISSISSIPPIAN OCCUPATION OF THE RED WING AREA
GIBBON REPORTER – Gibbon, NE. -w. Jun 1892-Nov 1898, scattered issues missing; Feb 1900-Dec 1912; Jun 1914 to date – 1 – us NE Hist [071]
Gibbons, James *see*
- THE FAITH OF OUR FATHERS
- OUR CHRISTIAN HERITAGE

Gibbons Mortuary (GSU), Coffey County, KS *see* FUNERAL RECORDS
Gibbons, Ruth E G *see* A PRISMATIC APPROACH TO THE ANALYSIS OF STYLE IN DANCE
Gibbons, Thomas *see* RHETORIC, OR A VIEW OF ITS PRINCIPAL TROPES AND FIGURES
Gibbs, Antony *see* THE GIBBS ARCHIVE: THE PAPERS OF ANTONY GIBBS & SONS
THE GIBBS ARCHIVE: THE PAPERS OF ANTONY GIBBS & SONS / Gibbs, Antony – 1744-1953. Guildhall Library Manuscripts 11021-96, 11107-40, etc. With printed index – 120r – 1 – £16,995.00 – uk World [941]
Gibbs, G *see* NOTES ON THE TINNEH OF CHEPEWYAN INDIANS OF BRITISH AND RUSSIAN AMERICA
Gibbs, George *see* THE JUDICIAL CHRONICLE, BEING A LIST OF THE JUDGES OF THE COURTS OF COMMON LAW AND CHANCERY IN ENGLAND AND AMERICA AND OF THE CONTEMPORARY REPORTS
Gibbs, Josiah Willard *see*
- DIAGRAMMES ET SURFACES THERMODYNAMIQUES
- PHILOLOGICAL STUDIES WITH ENGLISH ILLUSTRATIONS

Gibbs, Nanette *see* AMERICAN BIOGRAPHICAL ARCHIVE (ABA 1)
GIBEL' SOLOV'INOGO SADA A. BLOKA / Gorelov, A – (Podvig russkoi literatury). "Sov. pisatel'". L. 1957. BR-3265 2 – 8 – ne IDC [460]
Gibelius, O *see*
- INTRODUCTIO MUSICAE THEORETICAE DIDACTICAE, IN QUA PRAICIPUA EJUS PRINCIPIA, CUM PRIMIS VERO MATHEMATICA
- PROPOSITIONES MATHEMATICO-MUSICAE

Giberga, E *see* EL PAN-AMERICANISMO Y EL PAN-HISPANISMO
Gibernau, Jose *see*
- SOLUTION FOR THE IBERIAN PUZZLE; NOTES FOR A FURTHER STUDY
- SPAIN AND THE WORLD

Gibert, B *see*
- DE LA VERITABLE ELOQUENCE
- REFLEXIONS SUR LA RHETORIQUE

Gibert, E G *see* OBSERVATIONS SUR LES ECRITS DE M. DE VOLTAIRE
Gibert, Frederic *see* LES PAYS D'ALBANIE ET LEUR HISTOIRE...
Gibner, N P *see* SISTEMA KOOPERATSII
Gibraltar *see* GIBRALTAR CHRONICLE AND OFFICIAL GAZETTE
GIBRALTAR CHRONICLE – Gibraltar. -w. Jan 1944-June 1945; Jan 1948-June 1949; Jan 1950-Dec 1972. 32 1 2 reels – 1 – uk British Libr Newspaper [072]
GIBRALTAR CHRONICLE AND OFFICIAL GAZETTE / Gibraltar – no. 27344-32231. 1926-41. nos. 31193-31218, 31659-31687, 31788-31869, 31926-32164 And Other Scattered numbers missing – 1 – 445.00 – us L of C Photodup [324]
GIBRALTAR E OLIVENOA / Veiga, Estacio – 1863 – 9 – 1.50f – sp Bibl Santa Ana [946]
GIBRALTAR GAZETTE – Gibralta. v1-5 1949-53; v9-21 1957-69 – 5r – 1 – us Ross [324]
GIBRALTAR POST – Gibraltar. -w. Jan 1958-Dec 1968. 4 reels – 1 – uk British Libr Newspaper [072]
Gibran, Kahlil *see* AN NABI
Gibson, A *see* THE BOMBAY FLORA
Gibson Bowles, T *see* MARITIME WARFARE
Gibson, E *see*
- THE BISHOP OF LONDON'S PASTORAL LETTER TO THE PEOPLE OF HIS DIOCESE,...
- DIRECTIONS GIVEN TO THE CLERGY OF THE DIOCESE OF LONDON IN THE YEAR 1724 BY THE RIGHT REVEREND FATHER IN GOD, EDMUND LORD BISHOP OF LONDON;...
- OBSERVATIONS UPON THE CONDUCT AND BEHAVIOUR OF A CERTAIN SECT USUALLY DISTINGUISHED BY THE NAME OF METHODISTS

Gibson, Edgar Charles Sumner *see* THE OLD TESTAMENT IN THE NEW
Gibson, Edgar CS *see*
- BOOK OF JOB
- OLD TESTAMENT IN THE NEW

Gibson, John *see*
- COMMERCIAL MESSENGER AND BRITISH CANADIAN LITERARY GAZETTE
- HISTORY OF YORK COUNTY

Gibson, John Campbell *see* MISSION PROBLEMS AND MISSION METHODS IN SOUTH CHINA
Gibson, John Monro *see*
- THE AGES BEFORE MOSES
- AGES BEFORE MOSES: A SERIES OF LECTURES ON THE BOOK OF GENESIS
- CHRISTIANITY ACCORDING TO CHRIST: A SERIES OF PAPERS
- THE FOUNDATIONS
- FOUNDATIONS: A SERIES OF LECTURES ON THE EVIDENCES OF CHRISTIANITY
- THE GOSPEL OF ST MATTHEW
- PROTESTANT PRINCIPLES
- THE UNITY AND SYMMETRY OF THE BIBLE

Gibson, John W *see* THE COLORED AMERICAN FROM SLAVERY TO HONORABLE CITIZENSHIP
Gibson, Margaret Dunlop *see*
- HOW THE CODEX WAS FOUND
- THE PALESTINIAN SYRIAC LECTIONARY OF THE GOSPELS
- STUDIA SINAITICA 2

Gibson, Peter *see*
- THE BLACK ISLE 1851 CENSUS INDEX
- CENTRAL INVERNESS 1851 CENSUS INDEX
- COUNTY OF BUTE 1851 CENSUS INDEX
- DINGWALL AND SURROUNDS 1851 CENSUS INDEX
- DISTRICT OF INVERNESS 1851 CENSUS INDEX
- GAIRLOCH AND SURROUNDS 1851 CENSUS INDEX
- ISLE OF ISLAY 1851 CENSUS INDEX
- ISLE OF SKYE (NORTH) 1851 CENSUS INDEX
- ISLE OF SKYE (SOUTH) AND THE SMALL ISLES 1851 CENSUS INDEX
- SPEYSIDE INVERNESS 1851 CENSUS INDEX
- TAIN AND SURROUNDS 1851 CENSUS INDEX
- WESTER ROSS PART 2 1851 CENSUS INDEX
- WESTERN INVERNESS 1851 CENSUS INDEX

THE GIBSON REPORT – v7-21. 1966-81 – 1 – us UMI [073]
THE GIBSON REPORT ON THE NEGRO MARKET – v3-6. 1963-66 – 1 – us UMI [073]
Gibson, T *see* THE ANATOMY OF HUMANE BODIES
Gibson, William *see*
- THE YEAR OF GRACE

Gibson, William Ralph Boyce *see* GOD WITH US
GIBSON'S LAW NOTES *see* LAW NOTES
GIBSON'S MONTHLY – Cowansville, Canada. jun; n2 jul 1899 – 1r – 1 – Can$25.00 – cn Can Microfilming [073]
DER GICHTSCHWAMM MIT GRUENSCHLEIMIGEM HUTE / Schaeffer, J C – Regensburg. 1760. B-6312 2 – 8 – ne IDC [580]
Gicquel, Francisque *see* LES PECHERIES FRANCAISES SUR LES COTES D'ISLANDE
Giddings, Joshua R *see* PAPERS
Giddins, Kevin J *see* INFLUENCING A BROADER UNDERSTANDING OF JAZZ DANCE
Gide, Andre Paul Guillaume *see* LETTRES A ANGELE
Gidel, G *see* LE DROIT INTERNATIONAL PUBLIC DE LA MER...
Gidel, G C *see* DE L'EFFICACITE EXTRATERRITORIALE...
GIDIK – Istanbul Selanik Matbassi. Sahib-i Imtiyaz: H. Seyfeddin, Mueduer-i Mes'ul: M. Hazim, Arif Hikmet. No. 1 (21 Tesrinievvel 1326 [1910]) – 1mf – 9 – $12.00 – us MEDOC [949]
Gidney, William Thomas *see*
- THE HISTORY OF THE LONDON SOCIETY FOR PROMOTING CHRISTIANITY AMONGST THE JEWS
- THE JEWS AND THEIR EVANGELIZATION

GIDROGEOLOGIIA SSSR / ed by Sidorenko, A V – Moskva: Nedra, [1966-] – us Res Libr [550]
GIDS OP MIKROFILMS IN DIE TRANSVAALSE ARGIEFBEWAARPLEX, PRETORIA = GUIDE TO MICROFILMS IN THE TRANSVAAL ARCHIVES DEPOT, PRETORIA – 4th ed. Pretoria: State Archives Service, April 1996 – 1,5 – R9.50 – 0-7970-3294-0 – sa State Archives [025]
GIDS OP MIKROFILMS IN DIE VRYSTAATSE ARGIEFBEWAARPLEX, BLOEMFONTEIN = GUIDE TO MICROFILMS IN THE FREE STATE ARCHIVES DEPOT, BLOEMFONTEIN – 4th ed. Pretoria: State Archives Service, August 1994 – 1,5 – R2.00 – 0-7970-3049-2 – sa State Archives [025]
GIDS VOOR INDONESIE – Djakarta, 1952-1953 – 8mf – 9 – SE-1493/1 – ne IDC [950]
Gidulianov, Pavel Vasilevich *see* KODEKS ZAKONOV O BRAKE, SEME I OPEKE
Giebel, C *see* REPERTORIUM ZU GOLDFUSS' PETREFAKTEN DEUTSCHLANDS
Giebel, CG A *see* THESAURUS ORNITHOLOGIAE
Gieben, Claartje *see* MUSIC AND DANCE IN SURINAM
Gieben, Joseph *see* CHRISTIAN DIETRICH GRABBE IN DER NACHSCHILLERISCHEN ENTWICKELUNG
Gierke, Otto *see* POLITICAL THEORIES OF THE MIDDLE AGE
Giertych, Jedrzej *see* TRAGIZM LOSOW POLSKI
Gies, L *see* ELTEN, LAND UND LEUTE

Giese, F *see* FESTSCHRIFT FRIEDRICH GIESE AUS ANLASS DES SIEBZIGSTEN GEBURTSTAGS UEBERREICHT VON FREUNDEN UND SCHUELERN
Giese, Friedrich *see*
- ALTOSMANISCHEN ANONYMEN CHRONIKEN
- TEVARIH-I AL-I OSMAN [ASIKPASAZADE TARIHI]

Giesebrecht, Franz *see* EIN DEUTSCHER KOLONIALHELD
Giesebrecht, Friedrich *see*
- DIE ALTTESTAMENTLICHE SCHAETZUNG DES GOTTESNAMENS
- BEITRAEGE ZUR JESAIAKRITIK
- DIE BERUFSBEGABUNG DER ALTTESTAMENTLICHEN PROPHETEN
- DAS BUCH JEREMIA
- DIE DEGRADATIONSHYPOTHESE UND DIE ALTTESTAMENTLICHE GESCHICHTE
- DIE GESCHICHTLICHKEIT DES SINAIBUNDES
- DIE HEBRAEISCHE PRAEPOSITION LAMED
- JEREMIAS METRIK
- DER KNECHT JAHVES DES DEUTEROJESAIA

Gieseler, Johann Carl Ludwig *see*
- DIE PROTESTANTISCHE KIRCHE FRANKREICHS VON 1787 BIS 1846
- A TEXT-BOOK OF CHURCH HISTORY

Giesen, Adolf *see* EBERHARD VON GROOTE
Giesenhagen, K F G *see* DIE FARNGATTUNG NIPHOBOLUS
Giessen *see* SEMINA IN HORTO BOTANICO ACAD. LUDOVIC
GIESSENER ALLGEMEINE – Giessen, West Germany. 4 May 1976- – ca 11r per yr – 1 – gw Mikrofilm [072]
GIESSENER ANZEIGER – Giessen, West Germany. 1969- – ca 11r per yr – 1 – gw Mikrofilm [072]
GIESSEREI – v39-52 1952-65 – 1,5,6 – us Princeton Micro [670]
GIESSEREI-ZEITUNG – Berlin, jan 1 1904-dec 15 1909 – 6r – 1 – uk British Libr Newspaper [670]
Gietmann, Gerhard *see* DE RE METRICA HEBRAEORUM
Gifford, Edwin Hamilton *see*
- THE INCARNATION
- VOICES OF THE PROPHETS: TWELVE LECTURES

Gifford, John *see* ORANGE, A POLITICAL RHAPSODY IN THREE CANTOS
Gifford, William *see* THE BAVIAD, AND MAEVIAD
THE GIFT ADDRESSED TO THE SPIRIT OF THE PROPHET,BY A. H. JOHNS. (ORIENTAL MONOGRAPH SERIES, NO. 1). ARABIC, JAVANESE AND ENGLISH. SE-11,438/1. 1965 / Al-Burhanpuri, Muhammad ibn Fadl Allah al-Hindi – 9 – ne IDC [260]
GIFT BASKET IDEA ENCYCLOPAEDIA / Alpha Pyram's Publishing – 1990 – $10.95 – us Continnuus [640]
A GIFT FROM ST NICHOLAS – 1969. 8p. 6 illus. Fiche no. 2290 – 9 – $2.50 – us Corning Mus [700]
GIFT FROM THE MINISTRY OF FOREIGN AFFAIRS AND EXTERNAL COMMERCE OF BELGIUM. (RECORDS RELATING TO THE U.S.) / Belgium. Ministry of Foreign Affairs – 30 rolls. T1113 – 1 – us Nat'l Archives [949]
THE GIFT OF THE HOLY GHOST ACCORDING TO THE TEACHING OF THE SCRIPTURE / Morgan, John – Oberlin: E.J. Goodrich, 1875. 1 fiche. 8370-4490-1 – 9 – us A.T.L.A. [240]
GIFTED CHILD QUARTERLY – (v15- 1971-5,6) – v1- 1958- – 1 – us UMI [305]
GIFU NICHINICHI SHIMBUN – (Yrly reel count varies) – Japan. 1937- – 1 – inquire – us Ross [950]
GIFU SHIMBUN – (1995- 24r per yr Y240,000) – March 1937-December 1994 – 886r – 1 – Y8,860,000 – ja Japan Micro [950]
Giger, George Musgrave *see* SERMONS
GIGIENA I EPIDEMIOLOGII A – (Library has: 1922, no. 1) – Moskva: San epid: otdel N.K.Zdr., 1922- – 1 – CSUX89-S777 – us Hoover Inst Photo [947]
GIGIENA I SANITARII A (1943) – (Library has: 1945, no. 3) – Moskva: Narkomzdrav SSSR, Medgiz, 1943 – 1 – CSUX89-S797 – us Hoover Inst Photo [947]
GIGIENA I SANITARNOE DELO – Petrograd. 1914-16. BR-9275 2 – 8 – ne IDC [073]
GIGIENA TRUDA I PROFESSIONALNYE ZABOLEVANIIA / Ministerstvo zdravookhraneniia Soiuza SSR – Moskva: Medgiz, [1957-]. v10. 1966 – 1r – 1 – us Res Libr [947]
Gignac, Francoise *see* BIBLIOGRAPHIE ANALYTIQUE DE MADEMOISELLE SIMONE PARE, M.S.S., PROFESSEUR A L'ECOLE DE SERVICE SOCIAL, FACULTE DES SCIENCES SOCIALES, UNIVERSITE LAVAL
Gihl, T *see* GRAENSEN FOER SVERIGES TERRITORIALVATTEN...
GIJIG-ANANG MEKATEOKONAIE, S.J. O GAGIKWEWINAN / Artus, Gaston Andre – Tours France: Impr. A. Mame, 1898. 00033. (Pre-1900 Canadiana) – 9 – cn C.I.H.M. [240]
Gijselaar, N C de *see* HET PANAMA-KANAAL
Gil, Alexander *see* LOGONOMIA ANGLICA
Gil Ayuso, F *see* NOTICIAS BIBLIOGRAFICAS DE TEXTOS Y DISPOSIONES LEGALES DE LOS REINOS DE CASTILLA...
Gil Becerra, Benito *see*
- ASSERTA THEO-SUBTITULIA...EFFICACIA
- AVE MARIA. CUARESMA
- AVE MARIA. PARAISO
- AVE MARIA. PARAISO DE ORACIONES SAGRADAS EN...

GIL BECERRA, BENITO, EN LA INMACULADA EN LA LITERATURA FRANCISCANO-ESPANOLA / Uribe, Angel – Archivo Ibero Americano, 1955 – 1 – sp Bibl Santa Ana [240]
GIL BLAS – Madrid, Spain. -w. 3 Nov 1864-29 Sept 1872. 3 reels – 1 – uk British Libr Newspaper [072]
GIL BLAS – Paris. nov 1879-4 aout 1914, 20 janv, 9 juil, 31 dec 1921, 1er juil 1922, juin 1931, 8 nov 1937-12 janv 1938 – 1 – fr A.C.R.P.P. [073]
GIL BLAS – Paris.-w. 1 Jan 1897-23 Sep 1898; 6-20 Jan 1899. 1 reel – 1 – uk British Libr Newspaper [072]
GIL BLAS ILLUSTRE – Paris, France. -w. 28 June 1891-25 Dec 1896. 3 reels – 1 – uk British Libr Newspaper [072]
GIL BLAS ILLUSTRE. SUPPLEMENT – Paris. mai 1891-aout 1903 – 1 – fr A.C.R.P.P. [073]
Gil Calvo, Joaquin *see* GEOGNOSIA. COMPONENTES DE LA CORTEZA TERRESTRE
Gil de Godoy, Juan *see* EL MEJOR GUZMAN DE LOS BUENOS
Gil, F *see* DISERTACION FISICO-MEDICA..., PARA PRESERVAR...DE VIRUELA
Gil Farres, Octavio *see*
- EXTENSION URBANA DE LA MERIDA ROMANA
- LUCERNAS ROMANAS DECORADAS DEL MUSEO EMERITENSE

Gil Garcia, Bonifacio *see*
- CANCIONERO POPULAR DE EXTREMADURA. CONTRIBUCION AL FOLKLORE MUSICAL DE LA REGION
- EL CANTO DE RELACION EN EL FOLKLORE INFANTIL DE EXTREMADURA
- LAS FLORES EN LA TRADICION EXTREMENA
- FOLKLORE EXTREMENO. EXTREMADURA Y LA POSIBLE REGIONALIZACION DE SU MUSICA POPULAR. LA TRADICION EN LA CANCION EXTREMENA Y SU EVOLUCION
- HALLAZGO DE VEINTIOCHO CANCIONES POPULARES DE EXTREMADURA, RECOGIDAS EN LOS ANOS 1884-85
- EL PAJARILLO DE LA TRADICION EXTREMENA

Gil Julian, Juan *see* PERGAMINOS DEL MUSEO ARQUEOLOGICO PROVINCIAL DE BADAJOZ
Gil, M *see* TESIS
Gil Sanz, J *see* EL TRIUMPHO VINDICADO DE LA CALUMNIA, IMPOSTURA E IGNORANCIA CONTRA LA MEDICINA...
Gil y de Pina, J *see* TRATADO BREVE DE LA CURACION DEL GARROTILLO
Gilabert, A G *see* DURRUTI UN ANARQUISTA INTEGRO
Gilarov-Platonov, N P *see* UNIVERSITETSKII VOPROS
Gilbert and Ellice Islands Colony *see* DEVELOPMENT PLAN, 1970-1972
Gilbert and Ellice Islands. Ministry of Education, Training and Culture *see* REPORT 1974-1975
Gilbert, David W *see* MEMORANDA AND NOTEBOOKS
Gilbert, E W *see* PIETY HONORED AFTER DEATH...ON THE DEATH OF ROBERT PORTER
Gilbert, Emile *see* SORCIERS ET MAGICIENS
Gilbert, Frank *see* RAILWAY LAW IN ILLINOIS
Gilbert, Frank G *see* STREET RAILWAY REPORTS, ANNOTATED
Gilbert, G T *see* CHARTULARIES OF ST MARY'S ABBEY, DUBLIN (RS80)
Gilbert, George Holley *see*
- THE FIRST INTERPRETERS OF JESUS
- THE REVELATION OF JESUS
- A SHORT HISTORY OF CHRISTIANITY IN THE APOSTOLIC AGE
- A SHORT HISTORY OF CHRISTIANITY... APOSTOLIC AGE
- THE STUDENT'S LIFE OF JESUS
- THE STUDENT'S LIFE OF PAUL

Gilbert, Georges *see* ESSAI DE CRITIQUE MILITAIRE
GILBERT H. GROSVENOR COLLECTION OF PHOTOGRAPHS OF THE ALEXANDER GRAHAM BELL FAMILY / U.S. Library of Congress. Prints and Photographs Division – 28,000 images. 3 reels. P&P11533 – 1 – $23.00r – us L of C Photodup [770]
Gilbert, J T *see* REGISTER OF THE ABBEY OF ST THOMAS THE MARTYR, DUBLIN (RS94)
Gilbert, Jesse S *see* BLESSED ARE THEY, OR, THOUGHTS ON THE BEATITUDES
Gilbert, John Th *see* HISTORIC AND MUNICIPAL DOCUMENTS, IRELAND, A.D. 1172-1320 (RS53)
Gilbert, Kathleen R *see*
- GENDER DIFFERENCES REGARDING KNOWLEDGE OF CHILD HEALTH AND DEVELOPMENT AMONG HIGH SCHOOL STUDENTS
- THE RELATIONSHIP BETWEEN IDENTITY STATUS AND CONTRACEPTIVE PRACTICES OF COLLEGE STUDENTS

Gilbert, Pamela *see* BRITISH MUSEUM ENTOMOLOGICAL LITERATURE, 1800-1864
Gilbert, Paul James *see* THE KING'S GREATEST BUSINESS
Gilbert, Paul S ET A L *see* BEGINNING SOMALI HISTORY
Gilbert, R P *see*
- APPLICABLE ANALYSIS
- COMPLEX VARIABLES

Gilbert, Stephen *see* CLEVELAND, OHIO, TAXES, MS V.F. O
Gilbert, W S *see* FIFTY "BAB" BALLADS
THE GILBERTINE RITE / Woolley, R M – 2v. 1921-1923 – 9mf – 8 – ne Slangenburg [240]
Gilbertson, A N *see* SOME ETHICAL PHASES OF ESKIMO CULTURE
GILBOA GAZETTE – Gilboa, Ohio. 1978-81 – 1r – 1 – $32.50r – us Archival [071]
Gilbreth, Frank B *see* FRANK B. GILBRETH PAPERS
Gilburth, Kenneth Riley *see* AN INVESTIGATION OF THE PROCESS OF CHANGE IN THE MAJOR CONTEMPORARY SCHOOLS OF PSYCHOTHERAPY
Gilchevskii, Konstantin Lukich *see* BOEVYE DEISTVIIA VTOROOCHEREDNYKH CHASTEI V MIROVUIU VOINU
Gilchrist, Anne Burrows *see* MARY LAMB
Gilchrist, Beth Bradford *see* THE LIFE OF MARY LYON
GILCHRIST COUNTY JOURNAL – Trenton. Fl. -w. 1934-1941, 1943- – 1 – us P.K. Yonge [071]
Gilchrist, H *see* IMPERIALISM AND THE MANDATES SYSTEM
Gilchrist, John Borthwick *see* A GRAMMAR OF THE HINDOOSTANEE LANGUAGE
THE GILD MERCHANT / Gross, C – (British Municipal History). H-1273 2. 2 v. 1890 – 8 – ne IDC [941]
Gildon, Charles *see* A GRAMMAR OF THE ENGLISH TONGUE
GILEAD BAPTIST CHURCH. HETTICK, ILLINOIS : CHURCH RECORDS – 1869-Jun 1986. History, 1869-1969. 1752p – 1 – 78.84 – us Baptist [240]
GILEAD BAPTIST CHURCH. UNION COUNTY. JOHNSVILLE, SOUTH CAROLINA : CHURCH RECORDS – 1838-Feb 1953 – 1 – 29.16 – us Baptist [240]
Giles, Chauncey *see* THE TRUE AND FALSE THEORY OF EVOLUTION
Giles, Herbert Allen *see*
- CONFUCIANISM AND ITS RIVALS
- A GLOSSARY OF REFERENCE ON SUBJECTS CONNECTED WITH THE FAR EAST

GILES OF ROME ON BOETHIUS : "DIVERSUM EST ESSE ET ID QUOD EST" / Nash – 1950 – 1mf – 8 – ne Slangenburg [190]
Giles, Scott L *see* AN INVESTIGATION OF THE CAREER MOBILITY PATTERNS OF NCAA DIVISION 1-A HEAD FOOTBALL COACHES
GILFIELD BAPTIST CHURCH, PETERSBURG, VIRGINIA, 1803-1903 / Kennard, Richard – 1 – 5.00 – us Baptist [240]
GIL'GAMESH / Gumilev, Nikolai Sepanovich – Vavilonskii epos. Spb. 1919. BR-3618 2 – 8 – ne IDC [460]
Gilhodes, C *see* THE KACHINS
Gilibert, Jean Emmanuel *see*
- L'ANARCHIE MEDICINALE OU LA MEDECINE CONSIDEREE COMME NUISIBLE A LA SOCIETE
- EXERCITIA PHYTOLOGICA
- SYSTEMA PLANTARUM EUROPAE EXHIBENS CHARACTERES NATURALES GENERUM

GILJAKI, OROCI, GOL'DY, NEGIDAL'CY, AJMI... / Sternberg, Lev J – Khabarovsk: Dal'giz, 1933 – 1 – F387.11 – fr Armell [306]
Gilkey, Langdon *see* REAPING THE WHIRLWIND
GILL 1719-1849 – (Mf 1T-2T: Births & Deaths 1719-1845. Mf 2T: Marriages & Intentions 1794-1843. Mf 3T: Intentions 1795-1805, 1837-49; Out-of-Town Marriages 1794-98. Mf 4T: Vital Records 1843-49) – (mf ed 1996) – 4mf – 9 – 0-87623-253-5 – us Holbrook [920]
GILL 1754-1895 – (Mf 1-4: Births & Deaths 1754-1810. Mf 5-7: Births & Deaths 1804-44. Mf 8-9: Town Records 1793-1824. Mf 10-11: Index to Births 1843-1930. Mf 12-13: Index to Marriages 1843-1930. Mf 14: Index to Deaths 1843-1930. Mf 15-16: B,M,D 1843-63. Mf 17-19: B,M,D 1860-92) – (mf ed 1987) – 19mf – 9 – 0-87623-057-5 – us Holbrook [920]
GILL AND JOHNSON'S LAW REPORTS / Maryland. Court of Appeals – (A Pre-NRS title) – v1-12. 1829-43 (all publ) – 24mf – 9 – $108.00 – LLMC 84-149 – us L.L.M.C. [340]
Gill, Charles *see*
- NOTES ADDITIONNELLES A L'HISTOIRE DE LA FAMILLE GILL
- NOTES HISTORIQUES SUR L'ORIGINE DE LA FAMILLE GILL DE SAINT FRANCOIS DU LAC ET SAINT THOMAS DE PIERREVILLE: ET HISTOIRE DE MA PROPRE FAMILLE
- NOTES SUR DE VIEUX MANUSCRITS ABENAKIS
- NOUVELLES NOTES SUR L'HISTOIRE DE LA FAMILLE GILL

Gill, Diane L *see*
- EFFECT OF AN ACTIVE ATTENTIONAL STRATEGY ON RUNNING ECONOMY OF LOW ECONOMICAL RUNNERS
- GENDER DIFFERENCES IN THE RELATIONSHIPS AMONG SELF-CONFIDENCE, GENDER-APPROPRIATENESS, AND VALUE
- AN INVESTIGATION OF SELF-EFFICACY AND CONTROL THEORY WITH ELITE DISTANCE RUNNERS
- PSYCHOLOGICAL AND PHYSIOLOGICAL CHANGES ASSOCIATED WITH A PERIOD OF INCREASED TRAINING

GILL E.D. GEOLOGICAL NOTES – 1949-1986. GNB1-4 – 4mf – 9 – at Corangamite [550]
Gill, Everett *see* PROTESTANTS OF THE EAST
Gill, J *see*
- THE DOCTRINE OF PREDESTINATION STATED AND SET IN THE SCRIPTURE-LIGHT, IN OPPOSITION TO MR. WESLEY'S 'PREDESTINATION CALMLY CONSIDER'D',...
- THE DOCTRINE OF THE SAINTS FINAL PERSEVERANCE ASSERTED AND VINDICATED, IN ANSWER TO A LATE PAMPHLET CALLED 'SERIOUS THOUGHTS' ON THAT SUBJECT

Gill, James V *see* 1820 FEDERAL CENSUS OF ILLINOIS
Gill, John *see* NOTICES OF THE JEWS BY THE CLASSIC WRITERS OF ANTIQUITY; BEING A COLLECTION OF FACTS AND OPINIONS FROM THE WORKS OF ANCIENT HEATHEN AUTHORS PREVIOUS TO A.D. 500
Gill, W N et al *see* CHEMICAL ENGINEERING COMMUNICATIONS
Gill, William Hugh *see*
- ESTHER
- THE INCARNATE WORD

Gill, William Icrin *see* CHRISTIAN CONCEPTION AND EXPERIENCE
Gillanders, A T *see* FOREST ENTOMOLOGY
Gillemot, LF *see* MATERIAL TESTING LABORATORIES
Gillentine, John A *see* A COMPARISON OF THE SPORTSMANSHIP ATTITUDES AND/OR MORAL REASONING OF INTERSCHOLASTIC COACHES
GILLES DE RAIS : ENSEMBLE DE 15 MSS CONSERVES A LA BIBL. MUNIC. DE NANTES: ORIGINAUX OU COPIES D'ACTES, TRAVAUX D'HISTORIENS, ETC / Rais, Gilles de – 14-19th cent – 2r – 1 – F845.18 – fr Armell [944]

GILLES DE RAIS MARECHAL DE FRANCE... / Bossard, abbe Eugene – Paris: Champion, 1885 – 1 – F211.18 – fr Armell [920]
Gilles, P *see*
- DE BOSPORO THRACIO LIBRI 3
- DE TOPOGRAPHIA CONSTANTINOPOLEOS, ET DE ILLIVS ANTIQVITATIBVS LIBRI QVATVOR
Gillespie, Charles George Knox *see* SANITARY CODE OF THE PENTATEUCH
Gillespie, David F *see* JOURNAL OF SOCIAL SERVICE RESEARCH
Gillespie, R *see* MANUAL ON EVALUATION OF POPULATION COMMUNICATION PROGRAMMES
Gillespie, Richard *see* SOLDIERS OF PERON
Gillespie, William Honyman *see* THE ARGUMENT
Gillet *see* QUELQUES REFLEXIONS SUR L'EMPLOI DES ENFANTS DANS LES FABRIQUES ET SUR LES MOYENS D'EN PREVENIR LES ABUS
Gillet, F *see* LE CARACTERE HOSTILE...
Gillet, Joseph E *see*
- PROPALLADIA AND OTHER WORKS OF...
Gillet, Joseph H E *see* PROPALLADIA AND OTHER WORKS OF...
Gillet, Martin Stanislaus *see* L'EDUCATION DU CARACTERE
Gillett, E H *see*
- ANCIENT CITIES AND EMPIRES
- ENGLAND TWO HUNDRED YEARS AGO
Gillett, Ezra Hall *see*
- HISTORY OF THE PRESBYTERIAN CHURCH IN THE UNITED STATES OF AMERICA
Gillieron, J *see*
- ATLAS LINGUISTIQUE DE LA FRANCE
- ETUDES DE GEOGRAPHIE LINGUISTIQUE D'APRES L'ATLAS LINGUISTIQUE DE LA FRANCE
Gillies, James Robertson *see* JEREMIAH
Gilliland, Thaddeus S *see* HISTORY OF VAN WERT COUNTY AND REPRESENTATIVE CITIZENS
Gillingwater, D *see* TRANSPORTATION PLANNING AND TECHNOLOGY
Gilliodts-Van Severen, Louis *see* CARTULAIRE DE L'ANCIEN CONSULAT D'ESPAGNE A BRUGES
GILLISONVILLE BAPTIST CHURCH (CALLED COOSAWHATCHIE, 1832-85). JASPER COUNTY. SOUTH CAROLINA : CHURCH RECORDS – 1873-98; 1950-81 – 1 – 107.19 – us Baptist [240]
Gillmore, Parker *see*
- ACCESSIBLE FIELD SPORTS: THE EXPERIENCES OF A SPORTSMAN IN NORTH AMERICA
- LEAVES FROM A SPORTSMAN'S DIARY
Gillow & Company *see* ARCHIVES
Gillow, Joseph *see* THE HAYDOCK PAPERS
GILL'S LAW REPORTS / Maryland. Court of Appeals – (A Pre-NRS title) – v1-9. 1843-51 (all publ) – 18mf – 9 – $81.00 – LLMC 84-150 – us L.L.M.C. [340]
Gilman, Charlotte Perkins *see* WOMEN AND ECONOMICS; A STUDY OF THE ECONOMIC RELATION BETWEEN MEN AND WOMEN AS A FACTOR IN SOCIAL EVOLUTION
Gilman, Samuel C *see* THE CONQUEST OF THE SIOUX
Gilmantown, New Hampshire. Gilmantown Baptist Church *see* RECORDS
GILMER FIRST BAPTIST CHURCH. GILMER, TEXAS : CHURCH RECORDS – (2,968p) – 1899-1988 – 2r – 1 – $133.56 – us Baptist [240]
GILMER FIRST BAPTIST CHURCH. GILMER, TEXAS : CHURCH RECORDS – (3,630p) – Newsletter, Vols 1-17, 19-35, Apr 1955-1989 – 3r – 1 – $163.35 – us Baptist [240]
Gilmer, George R *see* SKETCHES OF SOME OF THE FIRST SETTLERS OF UPPER GEORGIA, OF THE CHEROKEES, AND THE AUTHOR
Gilmore, Andrew *see*
- THE HISTORIC GARRISON AT ANNAPOLIS ROYAL: SOME OF ITS EARLY HISTORY AS TOLD BY ANDREW GILMORE: THE LAST BRITISH SOLDIER THAT STOOD SENTRY ON THE OLD GARRISON GATE
- THE HISTORIC GARRISON AT ANNAPOLIS ROYAL: SOME OF ITS EARLY HISTORY AS TOLD BY ONE OF ITS DEFENDERS
Gilmore, Carole A *see* AN EXAMINATION OF THE ACADEMIC PERFORMANCE OF STUDENT-ATHLETE ADMISSION EXCEPTIONS AT A DIVISON 1-A INSTITUTION
Gilmore, Eugene Allen *see* HANDBOOK ON THE LAW OF PARTNERSHIP, INCLUDING LIMITED PARTNERSHIPS
Gilmore, Gary D *see* THE IMPACT OF THE LA CROSSE WELLNESS PROJECT ON THE HEALTH PROMOTION INVOLVEMENT OF COLLEGE STUDENTS RESIDING ON THE CAMPUS OF THE UNIVERSITY OF WISCONSIN-LA CROSSE
Gilmore, George W *see*
- JOHANNEAN PROBLEM: A RESUME FOR ENGLISH READERS
- KOREA FROM ITS CAPITAL
Gilmore, George William *see* THE CHURCH, THE PEOPLE, AND THE AGE
Gilmore, James Houston *see* NOTES OF A COURSE OF LECTURES ON SMITH'S MERCANTILE LAW
Gilmour, James *see* JAMES GILMOUR OF MONGOLIA
Gilow, Hermann *see* DIE GRUNDGEDANKEN IN HEINRICH VON KLEISTS "PRINZ FRIEDRICH VON HOMBURG"
Gilpin, Edwin *see* THE GOLD FIELDS OF NOVA SCOTIA
Gilpin, H D *see* GILPIN'S REPORTS OF CASES IN THE EASTERN DISTRICT OF PENNSYLVANIA, 1828-1826
Gilpin, Richard *see* DAEMONOLOGIA SACRA; OR, A TREATISE OF SATAN'S TEMPTATIONS
Gilpin, W *see* AN ESSAY UPON PRINTS
GILPIN'S REPORTS OF CASES IN THE EASTERN DISTRICT OF PENNSYLVANIA, 1828-1826 / Gilpin, H D – Philadelphia: Nicklin. 1v. 1837 (all publ) – 7mf – 9 – $10.50 – LLMC 81-453 – us L.L.M.C. [340]
Gil-Robles y Quinones, Jose Maria *see* SPAIN IN CHAINS
GILROY ADVOCATE – Gilroy, CA. 1886-1946 – 24r – 1 RC02274 – $1,200.00 – us Library Micro [071]
GILROY DISPATCH – Gilroy, CA. 1981-1983 – 1r – 1 – $50.00 – R04029 – us Library Micro [071]
THE GILROY DISPATCH – Gilroy, CA. 1925 – 202+ r – 1 RC02275 – $10,100.00 ($360.00y) – us Library Micro [071]
Gilson, J P *see* THE MOZARABIC PSALTER
Gil'Terbrandt, P *see* RUKOPISNOE OTDELENIE VILENSKOI PUBLICHNOI BIBLIOTEKI
GILTNER GAZETTE – Giltner, NE. -w. Jan 1918-Dec 1962 – 1 – us NE Hist [071]
GILYONOT – v. 1-31. Tel Aviv. 1934-54. Index. 1933-55. BJ-91-6 1 – 9 – ne IDC [956]
Gimenez Caballero, Ernesto *see* ESPANA Y FRANCO
Gimenez de la Torre, Pelayo *see* TRATADO PRACTICO SOBRE EL MAL ROJO DEL CERDO
Gimeno, Jose Blat *see* EDUCATION IN LATIN AMERICA AND THE CARIBBEAN
GIMLI BALOUR – (In Icelandic) – Canada, 1903-1909 – 1r – 1 – cn Commonwealth Micro [072]
GIMLI GIMLUNGUR – (In Icelandic) – Canada, 1909-1911 – 1r – 1 – cn Commonwealth Micro [072]
Gimmerthal, Armin *see* HINTER DER MASKE
GIMSON AND BARNSLEY'S DESIGNS AND DRAWINGS IN CHELTENHAM ART GALLERY AND MUSEUM – 4r – 1,14 – £220.00 – uk World [740]
GIMTASIS KRASTAS – 1991-1993 – 1 – Sfr240.00 – sz Infoprint [947]
Gin, Pierre L C *see*
- DES CAUSES DE NOS MAUX, DE LEURS PROGRES ET DES MOYENS D'Y REMEDIER
- DISCOURS: 21 AOUT 1804: DISCOURS PRONONCES A L'UNIVERSITE DE JURISPRUDENCE
O GINASIANO : BOLETIM CULTURAL DO GREMIO DE ESTUDOS "PLACIDO DE CASTRO" DO CORPO DISCENTE DO GINASIO ACREANO – Rio Branco, Acre. 21 Ago-6 Set 1950 – 1,5,6 – bl Biblioteca [072]
O GINASIANO : JORNAL ESTUDANTIL – Cataguazes, Aug 1961 – 1,5,6 – bl Biblioteca [072]
Gindely, Anton *see* HISTORY OF THE THIRTY YEARS' WAR
Gindert, Christine *see* TEXTVERWALTUNG ALS AUFGABE DER MENSCH-COMPUTER-INTERAKTION
Gindraux, Jules *see* HISTOIRE DU CHRISTIANISME DANS LE MONDE PAIEN
Gineitis, Kazys *see* AMERIKA IR AMERIKOS LIETUVIAI
Giner de los Rios, Francisco *see* ESTUDIOS FILOSOFICOS Y RELIGIOSOS
Gingerich, Melvin *see* THE MENNONITES IN IOWA
Gingras, Apollinaire *see* LE CHANT POPULAIRE DANS NOS EGLISES: DOUZE CANTIQUES NOUVEAUX: EMBELISSONS NOS CIMITIERES
Gingras, Isaie *see* PREUVE TESTIMONIALE DANS L'AFFAIRE DES SYNDICS DE LA VILLE DE LONGUEUIL..
Gingras, Jean-Jules *see* BIBLIOGRAPHIE ANALYTIQUE DE L'OEUVRE DE MONSIEUR LE CHANOINE PAUL-EMILE CREPEAULT, 1944-1964
Gingras, Jules Fabien *see* MANUEL DES EXPRESSIONS VICIEUSES LES PLUS FREQUENTES
Ginguene, P L *see* NOTICE SUR LA VIE ET LES OUVRAGES DE NICOLAS PICCINNI
Ginguene, Pierre-Louis *see* ENCYCLOPEDIE METHODIQUE MUSIQUE
Ginius, L *see* AD CHRISTIANOS PRINCIPES DE SVSCEPTO PRO CHRISTIANA REP. CONTRA TURCAS BELLO COMMUNITER CONFICIENDO...
GINKO SORAN = ANNUAL DIRECTORY OF BANKS IN JAPAN: THE BANKING BUREAU OF THE MINISTORY OF FINANCE – 1st-49th (1895-1942) – 18r – 1 – Y178,000.00 – ja Yushodo [332]
Ginlein, R E *see* ADRESNAIA KNIGA KNIGOPRODAVTSEV, IZDATELEI, TORGOVTSEV NOTAMI, REDAKTSII GAZET I ZHURNALOV, BIBLIOTEK DLIA CHTENIIA I ZAVEDENII PECHATI V ROSSII
Ginsberg, Hyman *see* QUESTIONS AND ANSWERS TO PAST BAR EXAMINATION QUESTIONS
Ginsburg, Christian David *see* THE ESSENES
Ginsburg, S L *see* A WANDERING JEW IN BRAZIL
Ginsburger, M *see* THARGUM JONATHAN BEN USIEEL ZUM PENTATEUCH
Gintsburg, L Ia *see* SOVETSKOE KHOZIAISTVENHOE ZAKONODATEL'STVO..
Gintse, G E *see* DOPOLNENIE VTOROE K PODROBNOMU SISTEMATICHESKOMU UKAZATELIU KNIG D. S. PONOMAREVA. GODA 1892-1894
Ginzberg, L *see*
- THE LEGENDS OF THE JEWS
- SEFER HA-YOVEL LE-LEVI GINZBERG
- STUDENTS, SCHOLARS AND SAINTS
Ginzburg, M A *see*
- DEVIR
- MAGGID EMET
Ginzburg, Vul'f Veniaminovich *see* GORNYE TADZHIKI
GINZEI OXFORD / Edelmann, Z H & Dukes, J L – London. 1850-51. BJ-421-34 1 – 9 – ne IDC [400]
Gionnais Gianquinto, G de *see* LA QUISTIONE INTERNAZIONALE DELL' AUNIS
Giordani, G *see* CARO MIA BEN
GIORDANO BRUNO / McIntyre, James Lewis – London, New York: The Macmillan Co., 1903 – xvi/365p – 1 – us U.W. Library [190]
GIORDANO BRUNO : TRAUERSPIEL IN DREI AUFZUEGEN / Wilbrandt, Adolf von – Wien: L Rosner, 1874 – 1r – 1 – us U.W. Library [820]
GIORDANO BRUNO AND THE RELATION OF HIS PHILOSOPHY TO FREE THOUGHT; A LECTURE...NEW YORK LIBERAL CLUB, OCT. 30, 1885 / Davidson, Thomas – Boston: Index Assoc., 1886. 45p – 1 – us U.W. Library [180]
GIORDANO BRUNO: PHILOSOPHER AND MARTYR / Brinton, Daniel Garrison – Two addresses. Philadelphia: D. McKay, 1890. 68p – 1 – us U.W. Library [180]
GIORDANO BRUNOS EINFLUSS AUF GOETHE UND SCHILLER : VORTRAG GEHALTEN IN DER RICHARD WAGNER-GESELLSCHAFT ZU BERLIN AM 25. OKTOBER 1906 / Kuhlenbeck, L – (Includes bibliographical references) – Leipzig: T Thomas, 1907 – 1r – 1 – us U.W. Library [430]
GIORNALE – 1974-1981 – 1 – L480,000 – sz Infoprint [072]
GIORNALE – 1982-1993 – 1 – L960,000 – sz Infoprint [072]
IL GIORNALE – 1974-1995 – 4r per y – 5,6 – Sfr1,123.00 – sz Infoprint [072]
IL GIORNALE – (Standing orders available) – Roma, 1974- – inquire – us Ross [072]
GIORNALE ARALDICO-GENEALOGICO-DIPLOMATICO – Fermo. v1-28 1874-1905 – 1 – $161.00 – us L of C Photodup [920]
GIORNALE BOTANICO ITALIANO – 4v. Firenze. 1844-47. Cont. as: Nuovo Giornale Botanico. Firenze. 25 v. and index. 1869-98; n.s. 27 v. Firenze. 1898-1920. Lacking: 1845-47, v. 2 (2-3?)-v. 4. B-7417 1 – 9 – ne IDC [580]
IL GIORNALE DE SICILIA – 1988-1995 – 4r per y – 5,6 – Sfr962.00 – sz Infoprint [072]
GIORNALE DELLE ARTI E DELLE INDUSTRIE – Turin, Florence, Italy. -w. Jan 1861-Dec 1865; 1871-89. 20 reels – 1 – uk British Libr Newspaper [073]
GIORNALE DI ENTOMOLOGIA / Redia – (1929-1931. v17-19. Sfr74.00) – Florence, 1903-1927. v1-16 – 8 – ne IDC [590]
GIORNALE DI FISICA, CHIMICA E STORIA NATURALE – Pavia, 1808-27 – 3 – us Readex [500]
GIORNALE DI MALACOLOGIA / Stobel, P – Pavia, 1853-1854. 2v – 7mf – 9 – Z-900/2 – ne IDC [590]
IL GIORNALE DI NAPOLI – 1992-1995 – 3r per y – 5,6 – Sfr962.00 – sz Infoprint [945]
GIORNALE DI SICILIA – 1988-1995 – 4 times per yr – 6 – F3,600.00 – sz Infoprint [072]
IL GIORNALE DI TORONTO – v1-13, 1967-79 – 1 – 865.00 – cn McLaren [971]
IL GIORNALE D'ITALIA – 1974-1995 – 3r per y – 5,6 – Sfr962.00 – sz Infoprint [945]
IL GIORNALE D'ITALIA – Roma: L'Unione publicita italiana SA, jun 1939; dec 1938-jun 7 1944 – 1 – us Res Libr [072]
IL GIORNALE D'ITALIA – Roma: Societa per la pubblicita la Italia, 1949-52 – us Res Libr [072]
IL GIORNALE ITALIANO – New York: Italian Press Pub. Association, jan-sep 27 1919 – us Res Libr [072]
GIORNALE ITALIANO DI CHEMIOTERAPIA – 1954- – 1. – apply; v.22- 1975- 5,6,9 – us UMI [615]
IL GIORNALE ITALO-CANADESE – Montreal, Canada. 1 aut 1940-v1 n7,8,9. 28 oct 1940 – 1r – 1 – Can$25.00 – cn Can Microfilming [072]
GIORNALE PATRIOTTICO DI CORSICA / ed by Buonarroti, Filippo – v1-2. Apr-Nov 1790 – 4mf – 9 – $45.00 – us UPA [360]
GIORNALE STORICO DELLA LETTERATURA ITALIANA – v. 1-140, SUPPS. 1-28. Index v. 1-100. 1883-1963 – 1 – 1,250.00 – us L of C Photodup [440]
GIORNO – 1978-1981 – 1 – sz Infoprint [072]
IL GIORNO – 1987- – 4r per y – 5 – inquire – us Ross [072]
IL GIORNO – 1987-1995 – 4r per y – 5,6 – Sfr1,123.00 – sz Infoprint [072]
IL GIORNO – Italy, 1978-1981 – 48r – 1 – inquire – us Ross [072]
IL GIORNO. (L'ELETTRICITA) – Milan, Italy. 1 May 1882-24 Dec 1908.-w. 29 reels – 1 – uk British Libr Newspaper [073]
GIOUSUE CARDUCCI, L'HOMME ET LE POETE / Jeanroy, A – Paris. 1911 – 1 – us Res Libr [920]
GIOVANNI CASSIANO ED EVAGRIO PONTICO / Marsili, S – 1936 – 4mf – 8 – ne Slangenburg [240]
GIOVANNI GENTILES PHILOSOPHIE UND PAEDAGOGIK / Baur, Johannes – Muenchen, 1935 – xv/338p – 9 – DM48.00 – 3-89349-009-4 – gw Hänsel [100]
Giovio, P *see*
- COMMENTARIO DE LE COSE DE TVRCHI, DI PAVLO IOVIO, VESCOVO DI NOCERA, A CARLO QVINTO IMPERADORE AVGVSTO
- COMMENTARIO DE LE COSE DE TVRCHI, DI PAVLO IOVIO, VESCOVO DI NOCERE, A CARLO QVINTO IMPERADORE AVGVSTO
- COMMENTARIO DE LE COSE DE TVRCHI, ET DEL S. GEORGIO SCANDERBEG, PRINCIPE DI EPYRRO
- COMMENTARIUS CAPTAE VRBIS, DVCTORECAROLO BORBONIO, AD EXQUISITUM MODUM CONFECTUS
- DE ROMANIS PISCIBUS LIBELLUS
- HISTOIRE...SVR LES CHOSES FAICTES ET AUENUES DE SON TEMPS EN TOUTES LES PARTIES DU MONDE
- OPERA QVOTQVOT EXTANT OMNIA
- TURCICARUM RERVM COMMENTARIVS
- VRSPRUNG DES TURKISCHEN REICHS BIS AUFF DENITZIGEN SOLYMAN
Giovio, Paolo *see*
- DIALOGO DELL'IMPRESE MILITARI ET AMOROSE

- DIALOGO DELL'IMPRESE MILITARI ET AMOROSE, DI MONSIGNOR GIOVIO VESCOVO DI NOCERA

GIPERBOREI – Ezhemesiachnik stikhov i kritiki. nrs. 1-8. Spb. Noiabr' 1912-Oktiabr' 1913. Lacking: nrs. 1, 3, 5, 7. BR-1850 2 – 8 – ne IDC [460]

GIPHANTIE / Tiphaigne de la Roche, Charles-Francois – (Utopias in the Enlightenment series). 1760 – 9 – fr Hachette [800]

Gippius Andrei *see* ZAPISKI GLAVNOUGOVARIVAI USHCHEGO 293 PEKHOTNOGO IZHORSKOGO POLKA

Gippius, Z N *see*
- CHERNOE PO BELOMU
- CHERTOVA KUKLA
- LITERATURNYI DNEVNIK
- LUNNYE MURAV'I, SHESTAIA KNIGA RAZSKAZOV
- MAKOV TSVET
- NEBESNYIA SLOVA I DRUGIE RAZSKAZY
- NOVYE LIUDI
- POSLEDNIE STIKHI
- RAZSKAZY (4-AIA KNIGA)
- ROMAN TSAREVICH
- SIIANIIA
- SINIAIA KNIGA. PETERBURGSKII DNEVNIK 1914-1918
- SOBRANIE STIKHOV
- STIKHI
- TRET'IA KNIGA RAZSKAZOV
- ZERKALA
- ZHIVYIA LITSA

Gippius-Merezhkovskaia, Z *see* DMITRII MEREZHKOVSKII

GIPPOKRATOVO LITSO / Lelevich, G – Krasnaia nov', 1. nr. 1. 1925. BR-3670 2 – 8 – ne IDC [610]

GIPPSLAND MERCURY – 1901-1920. GM1-20 – 20r – 1 – at Corangamite [072]

GIPS ALS HISTORISCHER AUSSENBAUSTOFF IN DER WINDSHEIMER BUCHT : VERBREITUNG, GEWINNUNG UND BESTAENDIGKEIT IM VERGLEICH ZU ANDEREN OERTLICHEN NATURWERKSTEINEN / Lucas, Hans Guenter – 1994 – 4mf – 9 – DM112.00 – 3-89349-871-0 – gw Hänsel [550]

THE GIPSY SMITH MISSIONS IN AMERICA.. / Bayliss, Edward E – Boston: Interdenominational Pub., 1907. 158p. 1 fiche – 9 – us A.T.L.A. [240]

GIRALDI CAMBRENSIS OPERA, VOLS 8 (RS21) : DE PRINCIPIS INSTRUCTIONE LIBER / Giraldus; ed by Warner, G F – (With index to v1-4 + 8 1891 Dfl32.00) – ne Slangenburg [240]

GIRALDI CAMBRENSIS OPERA, VOLS 1-4 (RS21) / Giraldus; ed by Brewer, J S – (v1: Invectionum Libellus; Symbolum Elect 1861 Dfl35.00. v2: Gemma Ecclesiastica 1862 Dfl30.00. v3: De Invectionibus, Lib. 4, De Menevensi Eccl. Dialogus; Vita S. David 1863 Dfl 32.00) – ne Slangenburg [240]

GIRALDI CAMBRENSIS OPERA, VOLS 5-7 (RS21) / Giraldus; ed by Dimock, J F – (v4: Speculum Ecclesiae; De Vita Galfridi Archiepiscopi Eboracensis Sive Certamina Galfridi Eb. Archiepisc 1873 Dfl32.00. v5: Topographia Hibernica, Et Expugnati Hibernica 1867 Dfl35.00. v6: Itinerarium Kambriae, Et Descriptio Kambriae 1868 Dfl28.00. v7: Vita S. Remigii, Et Vita S. Hugonis 1877 Dfl30.00) – ne Slangenburg [240]

Giraldo, Juan Manuel *see* VIDA Y...DON DIEGO DE ARCE REYNOSO

Giraldus *see*
- GIRALDI CAMBRENSIS OPERA, VOLS 8 (RS21)
- GIRALDI CAMBRENSIS OPERA, VOLS 1-4 (RS21)
- GIRALDI CAMBRENSIS OPERA, VOLS 5-7 (RS21)

Giralt Thovar, Arturo *see* NORMAS DE CULTIVO PARA OBTENER BENEFICIO CON LOS MAICES...

Giran, Etienne *see* JESUS OF NAZARETH: AN HISTORICAL AND CRITICAL SURVEY OF HIS LIFE AND TEACHING

Girard *see*
- LA JUSTESSE DE LA LANGUE FRANCOISE
- L'ORTOGRAFE FRANCAISE
- SYNONYMES FRANCOIS
- LES VRAIS PRINCIPES DE LA LANGUE FRANCOISE

Girard, CF *see* BIBLIOGRAPHIA AMERICANA HISTORICO-NATURALIS... FOR 1851

GIRARD COSMOPOLITE – Girard, PA. -w 1899-1910 – 13 – $25.00r – us I.M.R. [071]

Girard de Rialle, Julien *see* MONUMENTS MEGALITHIQUES DE TUNISIE

Girard, Gabriel *see* A NEW GUIDE TO ELOQUENCE

Girard, Louis *see* LA POLITIQUE DES TRAVAUX PUBLICS DU SECOND EMPIRE

GIRARD WEEKLY JOURNAL : WEEKLY REPUBLICAN NEWSPAPER – Girard, OH, 4 Jan 1910-24 Mar 1911 – 1r – 1 – us Western Res [071]

Girardeau, John Lafayette *see*
- CALVINISM AND EVANGELICAL ARMINIANISM
- THEOLOGY AS A SCIENCE, INVOLVING AN INFINITE ELEMENT

Girardet, R *see* LA CRISE MILITAIRE FRANCAISE 1945-1962

Girardi, Francesco *see* RADIOACTIVE WASTE MANAGEMENT AND ENVIRONMENTAL RESTORATION

Girardi, Rene Ulises *see* RADICALISMO, LIBERACION Y CAMBIA

Girardin, Emile de *see* L'ABOLITION DE LA MISERE PAR L'ELEVATION DES SALAIRES

Girardon, Rene Louis de *see* DE LA COMPOSITION DES PAYSAGES OU DES MOYENS D'EMBELLIR LA NATURE AUTOUR DES HABITATIONS

Giraud, Augustin *see* CULTURAL DEVELOPMENT

Giraud, C *see* TRATADO DE UTRECHT

Giraud, Leon *see* LE ROMAN DE LA FEMME CHRETIENNE

Giraud, M *see* LE METIS CANADIEN

Giraud, Philippe *see*
- L'ABEILLE
- IS THIS PAUL AT ATHENS IN THE MIDST OF THE AREOPAGUS? (ACTS XVIII, V22-15 (SIC): NO, IT IS FATHER GIRAUD IN THE PROVINCE OF QUEBEC BEFORE THE CRIMINAL COURT

Giraudet, E *see* TRAITE DE LA DANSE

Girauld de Montpellier, A *see* UTILISSIM, PROMT...Y FACIL REMEY E MEMORIAL PARA PRESERVARSE Y CURAR DE LA PESTE

Girault, L *see*
- LE RITUEL POPULAIRE DANS LES REGIONS ANDINES DE BOLIVIE
- LA SYRINX DANS LES REGIONS ANDINES DE BOLIVIE

Girault-Duvivier, Ch *see* GRAMMAIRE DES GRAMMAIRES

Girdlestone, Robert B *see* HOW TO STUDY THE ENGLISH BIBLE

Girdlestone, Robert Baker *see*
- THE FOUNDATIONS OF THE BIBLE
- OLD TESTAMENT THEOLOGY AND MODERN IDEAS

Girdvainis, J V *see* AUSRININKAS (HY. JONAS SLIUPA)

Girerd, Sylvain *see* L'OEUVRE MILITAIRE DE LA GALISSONIERE AU CANADA

Girgensohn, G K *see* NATURGESCHICHTE DER LAUB- UND LEBERMOOSE LIV-, ESTH- UND KURLANDS

Girgensohn, Karl *see* DIE RELIGION, IHRE PSYCHISCHEN FORMEN UND IHRE ZENTRALIDEE

THE GIRL I CAN'T FORGET = CELLE QU'ON OUBLIE PAS / Carbonneau, Fred – Montreal: The Popular Music Pub Co, 1926. SEM105P926 – 1mf – 9 – Can$2.25 – cn Bibl Nat [780]

THE GIRL IN THE POSTER: FOR A DESIGN BY MISS ETHEL REED / Carman, Bliss – 1897. 00486. (Pre-1900 Canadiana) – 9 – cn C.I.H.M. [830]

GIRLHOOD'S HAND-BOOK OF WOMAN / ed by Donnelly, Eleanor C – 3rd ed. St Louis, MO: B Herder, 1914 – 1mf – 9 – 0-8370-6897-5 – 1986-0897 – us A.T.L.A. [305]

THE GIRL'S OWN PAPER – Toronto: Warwick Bro's and Rutter, [1880-1907] – 9 – cn C.I.H.M. [073]

Girl's Rodeo Association *see* GRA NEWS

Girod, Roger *see* PROBLEMS OF SOCIOLOGY IN EDUCATION

Giron, Pedro *see* CRONICA EL EMPERADOR CARLOS 5TH. EDICION DE JUAN SANCHEZ MONTES. PROLOGO DE PETER RASOW. MADRID, 1964

Gironcourt, George R de *see* MISSIONS DE GIRONCOURT EN AFRIQUE OCCIDENTALE, 1908/1909/1912

LA GIRONDE – Bordeaux. 1858-1926 – 1 – fr A.C.R.P.P. [073]

LE GIRONDIN – Paris: Impr de E Briere, feb 29-mar 1 1848 – us Res Libr [072]

Girouard, Desire *see*
- THE BILLS OF EXCHANGE ACT, 1890: AN ACT TO CODIFY THE LAWS RELATING TO BILLS OF EXCHANGE, CHEQUES AND PROMISSORY NOTES, PASSED BY THE PARLIAMENT OF CANADA, 53 VIC., CH33, WITH NOTES AND COMMENTS
- CONSIDERATIONS SUR LES LOIS CIVILES DU MARIAGE
- LA FAMILLE COUSINEAU
- LA FAMILLE GIROUARD
- LAKE ST LOUIS OLD AND NEW: ILLUSTRATED: AND CAVELIER DE LA SALLE
- LE VIEUX LACHINE: ET LE MASSACRE DU 5 AOUT 1689: CONFERENCE DONNEE DEVANT LA PAROISSE DE LACHINE, LE 6 AOUT 1889

LA GIROUETTE DE SAINT-CLOUD / Barre, Radet, Desfontaines, Bourgueil, Maurice et Dupaty – (French Theatre Series). Paris. Chez le libraire "Au Theatre du Vaudeville." an VIII. 1799 – 9 – fr Hachette [820]

Giroux, Henri *see*
- GUIDE ILLUSTRE DE MONTREAL ET DE SES INSTITUTIONS CATHOLIQUES AVEC PROGRAMME DE LA ST JEAN BAPTISTE POUR 1884
- HISTOIRE ET STATISTIQUES DES INSTITUTIONS CATHOLIQUES DE MONTREAL

Giroux, Henry *see* REVIEW OF EDUCATION/ PEDAGOGY/CULTURAL STUDIES

Giroux, Pauline *see* BIBLIOGRAPHIE ANALYTIQUE DU DOCTEUR LOUIS-GEORGES GODIN (1897-1932)

Giroux, Yvette *see* BIBLIOGRAPHIE ANALYTIQUE DE MONSIEUR ANDRE GIROUX, PUBLICISTE AU MINISTERE DE L'INDUSTRIE ET DU COMMERCE

Giry, A *see*
- MANUEL DE DIPLOMATIQUE
- MANUEL DE DIPLOMATIQUE (DONNE LES CONCORDANCES DE DATES ANCIEN STYLE ET NOUVEAN STYLE)

Giry, F *see* LA VIE DE M. JEAN-JACQUES OLIER

GISBERTUS VOETIUS / Duker, A C – Leiden: Brill, 1897-1915 – 4mf – us A.T.L.A. [240]

GISBERTUS VOETIUS / Duker, A C – Leiden. v1-3. 1897-1914 – 23mf – 8 – Dfl95.00 – ne Slangenburg [240]

Gisborne, Thomas *see* WALKS IN A FOREST

GISLEBERTI CHRONICON HANONIENSE (MGH 7: 29.BD) – 1869 – Dfl25.00 – ne Slangenburg [240]

Gislenius, A *see* INITERA CONSTANTINOPOLITANVM ET AMASIANVM...

Gismondi, Enrico *see* LINGUAE SYRIACAE

Gisneros y Sevillano, Juan *see* EXTIRPACION TOTAL DE LA LARINGE POR CACINOMA

Gissing, G *see* WORKERS IN THE DAWN

Gissing, George Robert *see*
- BY THE IONIAN SEA
- THE CROWN OF LIFE
- DEMOS, A STORY OF ENGLISH SOCIALISM
- DENZIL QUARRIER
- SLEEPING FIRES
- THE UNCLASSED
- THE WHIRLPOOL
- WILL WARBURTON

Gistl, J von N FX. *see*
- ENUMERATIO COLEOPTERORUM AGRI MONACENSIS
- LEXIKON DER ENTOMOLOGISCHEN WELT
- SYSTEMA INSECTORUM

G-I-T : GLAS UND INSTRUMENTEN-TECHNIK – Darmstadt: Hoppenstedt Wirtschaftsverlag GmbH. v32 n6. jun 1988 – 1r – 1 – us Res Libr [660]

LA GITANA EXTREMENA Y OTROS POEMAS / Alvarez Joven, Arturo – Salamanca: Imprenta Comercial Salmantina, 1949 – sp Bibl Santa Ana [810]

GITANOS, GITANERIAS. CANTOS, BAILES Y COSAS DE LOS GITANOS DE ESPANA / Lopez Martinez, Antonio – Merida, 1950 – sp Bibl Santa Ana [946]

GITARIST – Moscow. n1-12 1904; n1-12 1905; n1-12 1906 (monthly) – 18mf – 9 – $105.00 – us Ross [780]

Gitsham, Ernest *see* A FIRST ACCOUNT OF LABOUR ORGANISATION IN SOUTH AFRICA

Gitteridge, William H *see* A BRIEF HISTORY OF THE TOWN OF MAYNARD, MASSACHUSETTS

GITTIT – Minneapolis, 1892-1903 – 1 – £60.00 – uk Chadwyck [780]

Gitto, Anita T *see* RELATIONSHIP OF EXCESS POST-EXERCISE OXYGEN CONSUMPTION TO VO2MAX AND RECOVERY RATE

GIU GOU SHIBAO – (Au Secours de la Patrie, National Salvation Times). China. Dec 1935-Feb 1938. M B13 – 1 – $50.00 – cc Microforms [072]

GIUBILEO SACERDOTALE DI MONSIGNOR BOURGET, VESCOVO DI MONTREALE, NEL CANADA – Roma: Cuggiana, Santini, 1872. 02525. (Pre-1900 Canadiana) – 9 – cn C.I.H.M. [240]

Giudice, Fiorangel del *see* PERON

Giudici, Ernesto *see* CARTA A MIS CAMARADAS

Giudici, Roberto B *see* LOS FUNDAMENTOS DEL BATTLISMO

IL GIUDIZIO DI DELIBAZIONE / Arduino, M – Milano, Roma, 1909 – 4mf – 9 – ILM-2240/1 – ne IDC [340]

GIULIO SABINO. CARI FIGLI UN'ALTRO AMPLESSO / Sarti, G – London: Longman & Broderip, [1778?] – 1 – us Sibley [780]

GIUSEPPE GARIBALDI – Philadelphia, PA, July 7, 1907 – 3r – 1 – us I.H.R.C. [978]

Giuseppe, Maria *see* THE LIVES OF THE BLESSED LEONARD OF PORT MAURICE AND OF THE BLESSED NICHOLAS FATTORE

Giussani, Pablo *see* MONTONEROS

Giustiniani, A *see* CASTIGATISSIMI ANNALI CON LA LORO COPIOSA TAVOLA DELLA ECCELSE ET ILLUSTRISSIMA REPUBLI. DI GENOA, DA FIDELI ET APPROUATI SCRITTORE, ...

GIUSTIZIA / International Ladies Garment Workers' Union – Organo Ufficiale. New York etc. v1-29 Jan 18 1919-1946 – 1 – us NY Public [331]

GIUSTIZIA – New York. v1-29. 1919-46 – 6r – 1 – us Ross [330]

GIUSTIZIA E LIBERTA – Paris, France. -w. 18 May 1934-8 Sept 1939. 2 reels – 1 – uk British Libr Newspaper [072]

LA GIUSTIZIA FRA INTRIGHI E TRADIMENTI / Conti, Giovanni – 2nd ed. Roma, Casa, 1952. 115 p. LL-4069 – 1 – us L of C Photodup [340]

LA GIUSTIZIA NELLA SOMALIA, GUGLIELMO CIAMARRA. RACCOLTA DI GIURISPRUDENZA COLONIALE. / Ciamarra, Guglielmo – Napoli: Giannini, 1914. 421p. LL-12011 – 1 – us L of C Photodup [340]

Giuzal'ian, LT *see* RUKOPISI SHAKH-NAME V LENINGRADSKIKH SOBRANIIAKH

Given, John James *see* THE TRUTH OF SCRIPTURE

Givens, Nick K *see* ECHOES FROM HELL

GIVSTINO HISTORICO... / Trogus, Pompeius – Vinegia, 1561 – 3mf – 9 – H-8408/1 – ne IDC [956]

Gizetti, A *see*
- BIBLIOGRAFICHESKII UKAZATEL' PECHATANNYM NA RUSSKOM IAZYKE SOCHINENIIAM I STAT'IAM O VOENNYKH DEISTVIIAKH RUSSKIKH VOISK NA KAVKAZE
- TRI DUSHI (STIKHI N. L'VOVOI, A. ACHMATOVOI, M. MORAVSKOI)

GIZLI EL / Guentekin, Resat Nuri – Dersaadet: Sems Matbaasi, 1925 – $42.00 – us MEDOC [470]

Gjandschezian, L *see* VERZEICHNIS DER ARMENISCHEN HANDSCHRIFTEN DER KOENIGLICHEN UNIVERSITAETSBIBLIOTHEK ZU TUEBINGEN

Gjellerup, Karl *see* DIE HUEGELMUEHLE

GJENTAGELSEN : ET FORSOG I DEN EXPERIMENTERENDE PSYCHOLOGI / Constantius, Constantin – Kjobenhavn: C.A. Reitzel, 1843 – 1mf – us A.T.L.A. [150]

G.K. Hall and Co. *see* CUMULATED SUBJECT INDEX TO PSYCHOLOGICAL ABSTRACTS, 1927-1960

GK'S WEEKLY – London. March 21, 1925-March 12, 1927 – 1 – us NY Public [073]

GL' ANNALI AVERO LE VITE DE' PRINCIPI ET SIGNORI DELLA CASA OTHOMANA / Sansovino, F – Venetia, 1571 – 3mf – 9 – H-8318/1 – ne IDC [956]

Gla, Dietrich *see* DIE ORIGINALSPRACHE DES MATTHAEUSEVANGELIUMS

GLACIAL AND INTER-GLACIAL DEPOSITS NEAR TORONTO / Coleman, Arthur Philemon – Chicago: University of Chicago Press, 1895?. 00704. (Pre-1900 Canadiana) – 9 – cn C.I.H.M. [550]

GLACIATION OF HIGH POINTS IN THE SOUTHERN INTERIOR OF BRITISH COLUMBIA / Dawson, George M – London?: s.n., 1889. 02278. (Pre-1900 Canadiana) – 9 – cn C.I.H.M. [971]

GLACIER – Hood River. Or. 1899-1933 – 1 – us UMI [071]

GLACIER COUNTY CHIEF – Browning. Mont. 1935-1936 – 1 – us UMI [071]

GLACIER REPORTER – Browning. Mont. 1954-1959; 1966- – 1 – us UMI [071]
THE GLACIERS OF THE ALPS : BEING A NARRATIVE OF EXCURSIONS AND ASCENTS, AN ACCOUNT OF THE ORIGIN AND PHENOMENA OF GLACIERS AND AN EXPOSITION OF THE PHYSICAL PRINCIPLES TO WHICH THEY ARE RELATED / Tyndall, John – London: J. Murray, 1860 – 1 roll – 1 – 1-55879-827-7 – uk Libr Preservation [550]
Glackemeyer, Edouard Claude *see* TABLEAU ALPHABETIQUE DES CITES, VILLES, VILLAGES, PAROISSES ET CANTONS DANS CHAQUE COMTE DE LA PROVINCE DE QUEBEC
GLAD TIDINGS – [S.1: s.n. 1864?-18–] – 9 – cn C.I.H.M. [200]
GLADBACHER KREIS-BLATT FUER GESCHAEFTE, POLITIK UND UNTERHALTUNG – Moenchengladbach, Germany. 4 Jan-30 Dec 1849 – 1r – 1 – gw Mikrofilm [072]
Gladden, Ted *see* THE NORTH DAKOTA JUDICIAL EDUCATION PLAN
Gladden, Washington *see*
- APPLIED CHRISTIANITY
- THE CHURCH AND MODERN LIFE
- THE CHURCH AND THE KINGDOM
- THE GREAT WAR
- HOW MUCH IS LEFT OF THE OLD DOCTRINES?
- THE LABOR QUESTION
- THE LORD'S PRAYER
- PAPERS
- RECOLLECTIONS
- RULING IDEAS OF THE PRESENT AGE
- SEVEN PUZZLING BIBLE BOOKS
- SOCIAL FACTS AND FORCES
- WHERE DOES THE SKY BEGIN
- WHO WROTE THE BIBLE?
- WHO WROTE THE BIBLE? A BOOK FOR THE PEOPLE
- WORKING PEOPLE AND THEIR EMPLOYERS
- THE YOUNG MEN AND THE CHURCHES

GLADES COUNTY DEMOCRAT – Moore Haven. Fl. -w. 1940-42, 1946- – 1 – us P.K. Yonge [071]
O GLADIANTE : ORGAM DA SOCIEDADE "GLADIANTES" – Maceio, Alagoas. 15 Nov 1903 – 1,5,6 – bl Biblioteca [072]
O GLADIANTE : ORGAO DA S. GLADIANTES – Maceio, Alagoas. 30 Abr-23 Maio 1908 – 1,5,6 – bl Biblioteca [072]
GLADIO – Oliveira, 19 Apr, May, 13 Jun 1943 – 1,5,6 – bl Biblioteca [072]
GLADIUS ECCLESIAE : CHURCH LESSONS FOR YOUNG CHURCHMEN / Titcomb, Jonathan Holt – (Includes index) – 6th ed. London: Church of England Sunday School Institute, [18–?] – 1mf – 9 – 0-8370-8795-3 – 1986-2795 – us A.T.L.A. [240]
Gladkov, I A *see* ELEKTRIFIKATSII A SSSR
GLADNESS IN JESUS / Boardman, William Edwin – Boston: Willard Tract Repository, c1870 – 1mf – us A.T.L.A. [240]
GLADSTONE AGE PRESS – Manitoba, CN. Oct 1981-Jun 1988 – 8r – 1 – cn Commonwealth Micro [072]
GLADSTONE AND OTHER ADDRESSES / Tupper, Kerr B – 1898 – 1 – 9.55 – us Baptist [240]
Gladstone, William Ewart *see*
- CONTEMPORARY ESTIMATES OF HIS LIFE AND CHARACTER
- CORRESPONDANCE ON CHURCH AND RELIGION SELECTED AND ARRANGED BY D.C. LATHBURY
- CORRESPONDENCE ON CHURCH AND RELIGION OF WILLIAM EWART GLADSTONE
- THE CREATION STORY
- ECCE HOME
- THE IMPREGNABLE ROCK OF HOLY SCRIPTURE
- ROME AND THE NEWEST FASHIONS IN RELIGION
- THE VATICAN DECREES IN THEIR BEARING ON CIVIL ALLEGIANCE; A POLITICAL EXPOSTULATION. TO WHICH ARE ADDED: A HISTORY OF THE VATICAN COUNCIL; TOGETHER WITH THE LATIN AND ENGLISH TEXT OF THE PAPAL SYLLABUS AND THE VATICAN DECREES

Gladwell, G M L *see* INVERSE PROBLEMS IN ENGINEERING
Glaeser, K *see* ERWERB UND VERLUST DER STAATSANGEHOERIGKEIT IN HISPANO-AMERIKA
Glahn, Gerhard Ernst Ludwig Von *see* THE GERMAN DEMAND FOR COLONIES
Glahn, H C *see*
- DAGBOAGER
- FORSOG TIL EN AFHANDLING OM GRONLAENDERNES SKIKKE VED HVALFISKERIET

Glaisher, James *see* TRAVELS IN THE AIR
GLAIVE DE L'ESPRIT – London, UK. 20 Dec 1940; 17 Jan, 14 Mar-Aug 1941 – 1 – uk British Libr Newspaper [072]
LE GLAIVE DE L'ESPRIT – Dir. Cardinal Hinsley, Jacques Maritain. no. 8-10. Londres. 28 juil-sept 1941 – 1 – fr A.C.R.P.P. [073]
Glamorgan. County Council *see* COUNTY HALL RECORDS
GLAMORGAN GAZETTE – Bridgend, Wales. -w. April 1894-Dec 1977. Lacking 1896; July-Dec 1897; 1899. 77 1 2 reels – 1 – uk British Libr Newspaper [072]
GLAMORGAN GAZETTE – Maesteg, Wales. -w. Jan-Dec 1979. 3 reels – 1 – uk British Libr Newspaper [072]
GLAMOUR – 1- 1939- – 1. ; 5,6. ; 9 – apply; v.65-; v.73- – us UMI [073]
THE GLAMOUR AND TRAGEDY OF THE ZULU WAR / Clements, W H – London: J Lane, [1936] – 1 – us Res Libr [960]
A GLANCE AT THE ECCLESIASTICAL COUNCILS OF NEW ENGLAND / Dexter, Henry Martyn – Boston: Wiggin & Lunt, 1867 – 1mf – us A.T.L.A. [240]
A GLANCE BACKWARD AT FIFTEEN YEARS OF MISSIONARY LIFE IN NORTH INDIA / Warren, Joseph – Philadelphia: Presbyterian Board of Publ, 1856 – 1mf – 9 – 0-8370-6630-1 – 1986-0630 – us A.T.L.A. [920]
THE GLANDS OF DESTINY (A STUDY OF THE PERSONALITY) / Cobb, Ivo Geikie – New York: MacMillan, 1928. vii,295p. Bibliog – 1 – us U.W. Library [150]
GLANES PALEOLITHIQUES ANCIENNES DANS LE BASSIN DU GUADIANA / Brenil, H – 1917 – 1 – sp Bibl Santa Ana [560]
LE GLANEUR : RECUEIL LITTERAIRE DES JEUNES – Montreal: P J Bedard, 10 juin-10 oct 1892. SEM16P360 – 1r – 5 – Can$11.00 – cn Bibl Nat [073]
LE GLANEUR – St-Charles, Canada. dec 1836-sep 1837 – 1r – 1 – Can$25.00 – cn Can Microfilming [072]
LE GLANEUR – Port-au-Prince: [Impr V Pierre-Noel, 1ere annee, n1-n5. sep 1925-janv 1926 – 1 sheet – 9 – us Res Libr [072]
LE GLANEUR – Port-au-Prince: Imp H Amblard, jan 24, jan 30-feb 3 1900 – 1 sheet – 9 – us Res Libr [072]
LE GLANEUR DU HAUT-RHIN – Colmar. 1848-53 – 1 – fr A.C.R.P.P. [073]
LE GLANEUR (LEVIS, QUEBEC) – Levis: [s.n.] v1 no 1-12. 1890-92. SEM16P361 – 1r – 5 – Can$11.00 – cn Bibl Nat [073]
LA GLANEUSE – Journal des salons et des theatres. puis Journal populaire. Red. en chef J.-A. Granier. no. 1-318. Lyon. juin 1831-mars 1834 – 1 – fr A.C.R.P.P. [410]
Glanvill, Joseph *see*
- PLUS ULTRA
- SADUCISMUS TRIUMPHATUS; OR, FULL AND PLAIN EVIDENCE CONCERNING WITCHES AND APPARITIONS

Glanz, R *see* DEUTSCH-RUSSISCHES VERTRAGSWERK...1925
Glard, I *see* DROIT ROMAIN
Glarean, Heinrich *see*
- AUSS GLAREANI MUSICK EIN USSZUG
- GLAREANI DODECACHORDO
- ISAGOGE IN MUSICEN HENRICI GLAREANI
- MUSICAE EPITOME SIVE COMPENDIUM EX GLAREANI DODECACHORDO

GLAREANI DODECACHORDO / Glarean, Heinrich – 1547 – 9 – us Sibley [780]
Glareanus, H L *see*
- DODEKACHORDON
- ISAGOGE IN MUSICEN HENRICI GLAREANI HELVETII POE. LAV. E QUIBUSQUARBONIS AUTHORIBUS

GLAS – Belgrade, Yugoslavia. Sept 1944-Feb 1952 – 8r – 1 – us L of C Photodup [949]
GLAS CRNOGORCA – Cetinje, Yugoslavia. -d. Jan 1893-Dec 1913. 4 reels – 1 – uk British Libr Newspaper [949]
GLAS ISTRE – Pula, Yugoslavia. 7 Nov 1947; Mar 1955-Jun 1957 (scattered issues) – 2r – 1 – us L of C Photodup [949]
GLAS JUGA – Skopje, Yugoslavia. Mar 1941 (scattered issues) – 1r – 1 – us L of C Photodup [949]
GLAS NARODA – New York, NY, 1893-1950 (incomplete) – 23mf or 1 reel – 9,1 – us I.H.R.C. [975]
GLAS NARODA – New York, NY, 1912, 1916-1917, 1919-1921 – 10r – 1 – us I.H.R.C. [975]
GLAS NARODA – New York: Slovenic Pub Co, 1924-1940; 1946-oct 24 1963 – us Res Libr [071]
GLAS SLAVONIJE – Osijek, Yugoslavia. Jan 1955; 1956-Jun 1957 – 4r – 1 – us L of C Photodup [949]
GLAS SV. ANTUNA – Buenos Aires, Argentina. -m. Oct 1947-June 1955. 2 reels – 1 – uk British Libr Newspaper [072]
GLAS SVOBODE – Chicago, IL, 1907, 1908, 1910, 1911, 1918, 1922 – 10mf or 1 reel – 9,1 – us I.H.R.C. [975]
GLAS SVOBODE – Pueblo, CO, 1902-1907 – 3r – 1 – us I.H.R.C. [975]
GLAS SVOBODE – Chicago: M V Konda, aug 1917-apr 1927 – 9r – 1 – us Res Libr [071]
DER GLASBERG : ROMAN EINER JUGEND, DIE HINAUF WOLLTE / Wille, Bruno – Berlin, Ullstein, c1920 – 1r – 1 – us U.W. Library [830]
Glascock, William Nugent *see* THE NAVAL SERVICE
Glaser, Eduard *see* JEHOWAH-JOVIS UND DIE DREI SOEHNE NOAH'S
Glasgow. Anderston Old Church *see* REGISTERS OF BURIALS
GLASGOW EAST INDIA ASSOCIATION MINUTES (1812-14, 1829-47) AND LETTER BOOKS – 7r – 1 – £300.00 – uk Altair [380]
GLASGOW EVENING NEWS – Scotland, UK. 1893. -d. 2 reels – 1 – uk British Libr Newspaper [072]
GLASGOW EXAMINER – Scotland. -w. Jan 1858-3 Sept 1864. 6 1 reels – 1 – uk British Libr Newspaper [072]
Glasgow. Faculty of Procurators *see* REPORT BY COMMITTEE OF THE FACULTY OF PROCURATORS IN GLASGOW APPOINTED TO CONSIDER AND REPORT UPON A BILL (AS AMENDED IN COMMITTEE) TO CONSOLIDATE AND AMEND THE LAWS RELATING TO PROCEDURE IN THE COURT OF SESSION IN SCOTLAND...
GLASGOW HERALD – 1806- – 24r per y – 1 – inquire for standing orders – us Ross [072]
GLASGOW HERALD *see* HERALD
GLASGOW MERCANTILE ADVERTISER – Scotland. Mercantile Advertiser & Shipping Gazette. -w. 1853, 1858, 1863, 1868, 1873, 1878. 6 reels – 1 – uk British Libr Newspaper [072]
Glasgow. Natural History Society *see*
- GLASGOW NATURALIST
- TRANSACTIONS AND PROCEEDINGS

GLASGOW NATURALIST / Glasgow. Natural History Society – (Journal of the Natural History Society of Glasgow). Series 3. v. 1-8. 1908-1926 – 1,5,6 – us Princeton Micro [574]
Glasgow. North Street Cemetery *see* REGISTER OF BURIALS
Glasgow. Public Library *see* WILLIAM SMEAL COLLECTION
Glasgow. Ramshorn Churchyard, Ingram Street *see* REGISTERS OF BURIALS
GLASGOW SATURDAY POST – Scotland. -w. May 1840-Apr 1843, Feb 1844-Jan 1845. (2 reels) – 1 – uk British Libr Newspaper [072]
GLASGOW SENTINEL – Scotland. -w. 1850-77. (40 reels) – 1 – uk British Libr Newspaper [072]
Glasgow. Sighthill *see* REGISTER OF BURIALS
GLASGOW SOUTH AND EASTWOOD EXTRA – 1 – £42.00r – uk Scot News [072]
Glasgow, W. Melanchthon *see* HISTORY OF THE REFORMED PRESBYTERIAN CHURCH
GLASGOW WEST INDIA ASSOCIATION MINUTE BOOKS, 1807-1969 – 5r – 1 – £220.00 – uk Altair [380]
Glasgow, William Melancthon *see*
- CYCLOPEDIC MANUAL OF THE UNITED PRESBYTERIAN CHURCH OF NORTH AMERICA
- HISTORY OF THE REFORMED PRESBYTERIAN CHURCH IN AMERICA

GLASILO K.S.K. JEDNOTE – Chicago, IL, 1915 – 3mf or 1 reel – 9,1 – us I.H.R.C. [975]
GLASILO K.S.K. JEDNOTE – Chicago, IL, 1915-1945 – 16r – 1 – us I.H.R.C. [975]
GLASILO SNPJ – Chicago, IL, 1910, 1911, 1913, 1914 – 6mf or 1 reel – 9,1 – us I.H.R.C. [975]
GLASILO SNPJ – Chicago, IL, 1910-1915 – 2r – 1 – us I.H.R.C. [975]
GLASMACHER : FUENF ERZAEHLUNGEN / Leutelt, Gustav – Karlsbad: A Kraft, [1944] – 1r – 1 – us U.W. Library [830]
GLASNIK – Calumet, MI, 1901 – 66mf or 1 reel – 9,1 – us I.H.R.C. [975]
Glasow, Catharina von *see* EIN BEITRAG ZUR KENNTNIS DER GENSTRUKTUR DER PHOSPHOENOLPYRUVAT-CARBOXYLASE HOEHERER PFLANZEN
GLASS – 1973- – 9 – us UMI [073]
GLASS : A POCKET DICTIONARY OF TERMS COMMONLY USED TO DESCRIBE GLASS AND GLASSMAKING / ed by Whitehouse, David – 1993. 88p. col., ill. Fiche no. 14,314 – 2mf – 9 – $5.00 – us Corning Mus [740]
GLASS 1959 – 1959. 329p., 295 illus. 6 fiche. Fiche no. 387 – 9 – $10.00 – us Corning Mus [730]
GLASS AND CERAMICS – v13-51. 1956-94 – 1,5 – $80.00v – us UMI [660]
GLASS AND GLASSMAKING IN ANCIENT MESOPOTAMIA / Oppenheim, A Leo & Brill, Robert H & Barag, Dan & Saldern, Axel von – 1970. 242p. 152 illus. 5 fiche. Fiche no. 965 – 9 – $8.75 – us Corning Mus [730]
Glass, Charles Gordon *see* STRAY LEAVES FROM SCOTCH AND ENGLISH HISTORY: WITH THE LIFE OF SIR WILLIAM WALLACE, SCOTLAND'S PATRIOT, HERO, AND POLITICAL MARTYR
GLASS COLLECTIONS IN THE UNITED STATES AND CANADA – 1982. 224p. 141 illus. 5 fiche. Fiche no. 6665 – 9 – $8.75 – us Corning Mus [730]
GLASS CRAFT NEWS – 1983-85 – 1,9 – us UMI [740]
GLASS DIGEST – (See also: Glaziers Journal) – 1927- – 1. – apply; v.57- 1978- 5,6,9 – us UMI [740]
GLASS DRINKING VESSELS FROM THE COLLECTIONS OF JEROME STRAUSS AND THE RUTH BRYAN STRAUSS MEMORIAL FOUNDATION – 1955. 140p. 73 illus. 3 fiches. Fiche No.1035 – 9 – $6.25 – us Corning Mus [740]
GLASS FROM THE ANCIENT WORLD: THE RAY WINFIELD SMITH COLLECTION – 1957. 298p. 418 illus.6 fiches. Fiche No. 163 – 9 – $10.00 – us Corning Mus [740]
GLASS FROM THE CORNING MUSEUM OF GLASS / Corning Museum of Glass – (1958. 96p., 126 illus. 2 diazo copies. Fiche no. 962. 5.00; 9. 1965. 99p., 141 illus. 2 diazo copies. Fiche no. 963. 5.00; CMG; 9. 1974. 105p., 153 illus. 2 diazo copies. Fiche no. 964. 5.00; CMG; 9) – 1955. 77p., 91 illus. 2 fiche – 9 – $5.00 – us Corning Mus [730]
GLASS FROM WORLD'S FAIRS, 1851-1904 / Spillman, Jane Shadel – 1986. 59p. 2 fiches. Fiche No. 9189 – 9 – $5.00 – us Corning Mus [730]
Glass, Henry Alexander *see*
- THE BARBONE PARLIAMENT
- THE STORY OF THE PSALTERS

THE GLASS INDUSTRY – (Vol 4 1969-70 of Glass Industry International Directory) – v51-52. 1970-71 – 16mf – 9 – $5.00f – us Ross [338]
GLASS, MOSAICS AND JEWELRY : ARCHITECTURE, APPLIED ARTS, STUDIO ARTS – (Individual titles not listed separately) – 8 catalogues on 12mf – 9 – £100.00 – uk Chadwyck [740]
THE GLASS OF FASHION UP TO DATE – Toronto: Delineator Pub. Co, 18– -189- or 19–] – 9 – cn C.I.H.M. [740]
GLASS OF THE ROMAN EMPIRE / Whitehouse, David – Corning, NY: The Corning Museum of Glass, 1988. 60p. Fiche No.11,910 – 2mf – 9 – $5.00 plus $0.55 postage and handling plus N.Y. State sales tax – 0-87290-118-1 – us Corning Mus [740]
Glass, Paul *see* DER KREIS SENSBURG
GLASS PHYSICS AND CHEMISTRY – (Cont: Soviet Journal of Glass Physics and Chemistry) – v1-19. 1975-93 – 1,5 – $65.00v – us UMI [540]
GLASS STUDIO – 1978- – 9 – us UMI [740]
GLASS TECHNOLOGY – v1-13. Sheffield. 1960-72 – 9 – uk Dawson [660]
GLASS VESSELS IN DUTCH PAINTING OF THE 17TH CENTURY / Buechner, Thomas S – 1952. 31p., 10 illus. 1 fiche. Fiche no. 1038 – 9 – $2.50 – us Corning Mus [750]
Glassbrenner, Adolf *see* FREIE BLAETTER
GLASSMAKING: AMERICA'S FIRST INDUSTRY / Spillman, Jane Shadel – 1976. 35p. Fiche No. 4899 – 1mf – 9 – $2.50 – us Corning Mus [660]

Glassman, I et al *see* COMBUSTION SCIENCE AND TECHNOLOGY
GLASTONBURY ABBEY DOCUMENTS AT LONGLEAT – Court and Compotus vellum rolls. 13th-16th cent. Indexed. Printed summary of contents of each court and compotus roll. Partial sets available – 1 – £800.00 – uk Chivers [941]
GLASTONBURY FOR TWO HUNDRED YEARS: A CENTENNIAL DISCOURSE / Hartford County. Connecticut – By Rev. Alonzo B. Chapin, 1853. Hist. and statistical papers. F-0083 – 4mf – 9 – us A.G.L.L. [920]
GLASUL BUCURE STILOR *see* GOLOS BUKHARESTA
Glatthaar, Joseph T *see* CONFEDERATE MILITARY MANUSCRIPTS
Glatzel, Max *see* JULIUS LEOPOLD KLEIN ALS DRAMATIKER
Glatzel, W *see* VOELKERRECHTLICHE GRENZEN...
DER GLAUBE AN JESUS CHRISTUS : EIN VORTRAG / Bassermann, Heinrich – Frankfurt a.M: M Diesterweg, 1881 – 1mf – 9 – 0-8370-2573-7 – 1985-0573 – us A.T.L.A. [240]
DER GLAUBE DER MODERNEN WISSENSCHAFT GEGENUEBER / Segur, Louis Gaston – Mainz:Franz Kirchheim, 1874 – 1mf – 9 – 0-8370-5219-X – 1985-3219 – us A.T.L.A. [210]
GLAUBE, HISTORIE UND SITTLICHKEIT... / Browarzik, Ulrich – 1 – us A.T.L.A. [240]
GLAUBE IN DER 2. WELT – v1-22. 1973-94 (complete) – 8r – 1 – ATLA S0471 – us A.T.L.A. [073]
GLAUBE UND ERFAHRUNG : SAETZE AUS DEN WERKEN / Grimm, Hans – Muenchen: A Langen/G Mueller, 1937 – 1r – 1 – us U.W. Library [430]
GLAUBE UND GEWISSEN – (Includes indexes) – 1960-72 (complete) – 3r – 1 – ATLA S0640A – us A.T.L.A. [073]
GLAUBE UND HEIMAT : EVANGELISCHES SONNTAGSBLATT FUER THUERINGEN – (Some issues missing) – v21-46. 1966-91 – Inquire – 1 – ATLA S0429 – us A.T.L.A. [073]
DER GLAUBE UND SEINE BEDEUTUNG FUER ERKENNTNIS, LEBEN UND KIRCHE : MIT RUECKSICHT AUF DIE HAUPTFRAGEN DER GEGENWART / Koestlin, Julius – (Includes bibliographical references) – Berlin:Reuther & Reichard, 1895 – 1mf – 9 – 0-8370-4422-7 – 1985-2422 – us A.T.L.A. [210]
GLAUBEN UND WISSEN BEI DEN GROSSEN DENKERN DES MITTELALTERS / Betzendoerfer, W – Gotha, 1931 – 5mf – 8 – ne Slangenburg [290]
DER GLAUBENSACT DES CHRISTEN : NACH BEGRIFF UND FUNDAMENT / Koenig, Eduard – (Includes bibliographical references) – Erlangen:Andr. Deichert (Georg Boehme), 1891 – 1mf – 9 – 0-8370-4433-2 – 1985-2433 – us A.T.L.A. [210]
GLAUBENSLEHRE UND GEBRAEUCHE DER AELTEREN ABESSINISCHEN KIRCHE / Kromrei, Ernst – Leipzig: A Th Engelhardt, 1895 – 1mf – 9 – 0-8370-7641-2 – 1986-1641 – us A.T.L.A. [240]
Glauber, Johann *see* THE WORKS OF THE HIGHLY EXPERIENCED AND FAMOUS CHYMIS
DIE GLAUBWUERDIGKEIT DES IRENAEISCHEN ZEUGNISSES UEBER DIE ABFASSUNG DES VIERTEN KANONISCHEN EVANGELIUMS / Gutjahr, F S – Graz, 1904 – 4mf – 8 – ne Slangenburg [240]
GLAUCOM, ESSENTIELLE PHTHISIS BULBI. HB. GES. AUGENHK / Schmidt, H – M-5 2. 1877 – 8 – ne IDC [610]
GLAUCOMA DISCUSSION MEETINGS & REPORTS / National Society for the Prevention of Blindness – 1957-58, 1960-64. M-11/2 – 8 – ne IDC [610]
GLAUCOMA; PATHOGENESIS, SYMPTOMS COURSE AND TREATMENT / Smith, P – M 2 2. 1898 – 8 – ne IDC [616]
GLAUKOM UND OPHTHALMOMALACIE. HB. GES. AUGENHK / Schmidt-Rimpler, H – M-4 2. 1908 – 8 – ne IDC [610]
Glaumont, G *see*
- ETUDE SUR L'AGE DE LA PIERRE EN NOUVELLE-CALEDONIE. DECOUVERTE DE MONUMENTS GRAVES
- MOEURS ET COUTUMES DES NATURELS DE LA NOUVELLE-BRETAGNE
- TROIS MOIS AUX NOUVELLES-HEBRIDES

Glauning, O *see* DEUTSCHE SCHRIFTTAFELN DES 9. BIS 16. JAHRHUNDERTS AUS HANDSCHRIFTEN DER K. HOF- UND STAATSBIBL. IN MUENCHEN
Glavnago Shtaba Library. Saint Petersburg *see* SISTEMATICHESKII KATALOG BIBLIOTEKI GLAVNAGO SHTABA. 1-2
GLAVNE ISHIE SVEDENII A PO GOSUDARSTVENNOMU BI UDZHETU I DENEZHNOMU OBRASHCHENII U ZA 1923-24 BI UDZHETNY I GOD / Narodny i komissariat finansov et al – Moskva: Komissariat, 1924 – 1 – CSUX90-B5654 – us Hoover Inst Photo [332]
GLAVNI KATALOG CELOKUPNE SRPSKE KNJIZEVNOSTI – Ed. 4. Beograd. 1912. BR-4712 2 – 8 – ne IDC [010]
Glavnoe upravlenie po toplivu *see* TOPLIVNOE DELO
Glavnogo khlopkovogo komiteta i Vsesoiuznogo tsentra khlopkovodchesko i kooperatsii *see* ZA KHLOPKOVUI U NEZAVISIMOST
Glavnyi Morskoi shtab NKBMF SSSR *see* SBORNIK MATERIALOV PO OPYTU BOEVOI DEIATEL'NOSTI VOENNO-MORSKOGO FLOTA SSSR
Glavpoliprosvet (RSFSR) *see* CHTO GOVORI AT TSIFRY O GOLODE?
Glavpolitprosvet (RSFSR) *see*
- PLAN RABOTY GLAVPOLITPROSVETA NA SENTI ABRDEKABR 1921 G
- PLAN RABOTY GLAVPOLITPROSVETA NA SENTIABRDEKABR 1921 G

Glavprofobr (RSFSR) *see* PROFESSIONALNO-TEKHNICHESKOE OBRAZOVANIE V ROSSII ZA 1917-1921 GG
Glay, [A JC] Le *see* NEGOCIATIONS DIPLOMATIQUES ENTRE LA FRANCE ET L'AUTRICHE DURANT LES TRENTE PREMIERES ANNEES DU 16 SIECLE
Glazer, A M et al *see* PHASE TRANSITIONS
Glazer, A R *see* EFFECTS OF SUBMAXIMAL EXERCISE ON THE MOOD OF FEMALE BULIMICS
Glazier, Kenneth M *see*
- AFRICA SOUTH OF THE SAHARA
- A CHECKLIST OF SERIALS FOR AFRICAN STUDIES

GLAZIERS JOURNAL – (See also: Glass Digest) – 1923-1927 – 1 – us UMI [740]
Glazunova, M P *see*
- REESTR ROSSIISKIM KNIGAM IMP. PUBLICHNOI BIBLIOTEKI
- REESTR ROSSIISKIM KNIGAM, PRODAIUSHCHIMSIA V KNIZHNOM MAGAZINE

GLEANER – Chatham, Canada. 1829-80 – 17r – 1 – $1,105.00 – cn Library Assoc [971]
THE GLEANER – Brantford, Ont: T Somerville, [1886?-19–] – 9 – cn C.I.H.M. [971]
THE GLEANER – Chatham, New Brunswick. ns: v15. 20 nov 1858; 11 dec; 18 dec 1858 – 1r – 1 – Can$25.00 – cn Can Microfilming [072]
THE GLEANER – (Filmed with: The Weekly Gleaner v2 n16 4 avr 1848-v2 n50 26 dec 1848) – Philipsburg, Canada. v1 n12. 3 fev 1847-v1 n25. 4 jun 1847 – 1r – 1 – Can$30.00 – cn Can Microfilming [072]
THE GLEANER – San Francisco, CA; Portland, OR.1865 – 1 – us A.J.P.C. [071]
THE GLEANER *see* CANADIAN GLEANER / THE GLEANER
THE GLEANER – Kingston: The Gleaner Co Ltd, dec 7 1992- – us Res Libr [072]
THE GLEANER AND DE CORDOVA'S ADVERTISING SHEET – Kingston. Jamaica. -sw. 8 Sep, 8, 24 Nov, 25 Dec 1866, 8, 24 Jan, 9, 25 Feb, 11, 13 Mar, 24 Apr, 24 Oct 1867, 26 Mar 1868, 27 May, 9, 18 Jun 1875. (13 ft) – 1 – uk British Libr Newspaper [072]
GLEANINGS – v1-30. 1895-1925 (incomplete) – 1r – 1 – ATLA S0695 – us A.T.L.A. [073]
GLEANINGS FROM MY PORTFOLIO: ORIGINAL POEMS / Clark, Katherine A – (Toronto?, 1894). 00667. (Pre-1900 Canadiana) – 9 – cn C.I.H.M. [810]
GLEANINGS FROM THE CHURCH-YARD: A SELECTION OF OLD INSCRIPTIONS / Fordyce, Alexander Dingwall – Arranged with brief comments by A. D. Fordyce. s.l.: s.n., 1880. 03147. (Pre-1900 Canadiana) – 9 – cn C.I.H.M. [971]
GLEANINGS IN HOLY FIELDS / MacMillan, Hugh – London. 1899 – 9 – us A.T.L.A. [240]
Gleason, Arthur H *see* PAPERS
Gleason, William J *see* HISTORY OF SOLDIERS' AND SAILORS' MONUMENT
GLEBE – New York. v. 1-2. Sept 1913-Nov 1914. Incomplete – 1 – us NY Public [073]
Glebova, N *see* SUD NAD DELEGATKOI

Gleditsch, J G *see* METHODUS FUNGORUM EXHIBENS GENERA, SPECIES ET VARIETATES
Gleichen-Russwurm, Alexander von *see* KLASSISCHE SCHOENHEIT
GLEICHES RECHT : SOZIALES DRAMA IN VIER AKTEN / Grelling, Richard – Berlin: H Steinitz, 1892 – 1r – 1 – us U.W. Library [820]
DIE GLEICHHEIT – Berlin, Stuttgart, 1892-1922 – 8r – 1 – DM600.00 – gw Mikro Press [072]
DIE GLEICHHEIT – New York. N.Y. (Equality). 1913-19 – 1 – us A.J.P.C. [071]
GLEICHHEIT – New York. v. 1-5. Dec 5 1913-Jan 11 1919 – 1 – us NY Public [071]
Gleig, George Robert *see* THE GREAT PROBLEM
Glen Covenant, New Hampshire. Glen Covenant Free Will Baptist Church *see* RECORDS
GLEN ELLY – THE STORY OF AN OLD TOWN / Harmon, Ada D, Compiler; ed by Harmon, Ada D – Anon Harmon Charter D.A.R., 1928. Illinois Reel 23. (The Cox Library Collection) – 5 – us Americana [978]
Glen, Francis Wayland *see* ANNEXATION: THE IDEAS OF THE LATE WILLIAM H. SEWARD
Glen, John *see* ENTRIES IN THE FAMILY BIBLE
GLEN PARK NEWS – Gary. Ind. 1928-32 – 1 – us UMI [071]
THE GLENBOW COLLECTION – (Write for the complete list of the Glenbow Collection) – 1 – cn Commonwealth Micro [971]
GLENCOE BAPTIST CHURCH. GLENCOE, KENTUCKY : CHURCH RECORDS – 1878-Nov 1956 – 1 – 42.84 – us Baptist [240]
GLENCOE TRANSCRIPT – Ontario Prov., Canada. Apr 1873-1914 – 1 – cn Commonwealth Micro [072]
GLENDALE – 1923-50; 1986; 1988 – 19r – 1 – $950.00 – P00031 – us Library Micro [910]
GLENDALE BAPTIST CHURCH. NASHVILLE, TENNESSEE : CHURCH RECORDS – 1950-69. (Includes bulletins and newsletters) – 1 – 135.32 – us Baptist [240]
GLENDALE EVENING NEWS – Glendale, CA. 1914; Anniversary Issue-Fall of 1914; 1915; 1921-1928 – 73r – 1 – $3,650.00 – H04012 – us Library Micro [071]
GLENDALE LOG – Glendale, OR. -w. 2 Dec 1926-3 Sept 1942. – 1 – us U.O. Library [071]
GLENDALE NEWS – Glendale, CA. 1905; 1906-1913; 1920-1928 – 63r – 1 – $3,150,00 – H03229 – us Library Micro [071]
GLENDALE NEWS-PRESS – Glendale, CA. 1928-1931; 1933-1981; 1983 – 842+ r – 1 – $42,100.00 – H04013 – us Library Micro [071]
GLENDALE SCENE – Glendale, CA. 1964 – 1r – 1 – $50.00 – H03228 – us Library Micro [071]
GLENDALE/BURBANK – 1987; 1991- – 7+ r – 1 – $350.00 – P00032 – us Library Micro [910]
GLENDORA MAGAZINE – Glendora, CA. 1983 – 3+ r – 1 – $150.00 ($50.00y) – R04030 – us Library Micro [071]
GLENDORA PRESS – Glendora, CA. 1926 – 5+ r – 1 – $250.00 ($50.00y) – RH03230 – us Library Micro [071]
GLENDORA SIGNAL – Glendora, CA. 1887 – 2+ r – 1 – $100.00 ($50.00y) – RC03600 – us Library Micro [071]
Glenelg, Lord *see* LORD GLENELG'S DESPATCHES TO SIR F.B. HEAD, BART. DURING HIS ADMINISTRATION OF THE GOVERNMENT OF UPPER CANADA
GLENELG REGIONAL SOCIAL PROFILE – 1984. Statistics. GRSP1 – 1r – 1 – at Corangamite [910]
GLENGLEESON STATION LETTER BOOK – 1878-1890. GSLB1 – 1r – 1 – at Corangamite [910]
Glenn, Allen *see* HISTORY OF CASS COUNTY
Glenn, Cherie A *see* ATTITUDES OF THERAPEUTIC RECREATION PROFESSIONALS TOWARD PERSONS WITH AIDS AND THE RELATIONSHIP OF THEIR ATTITUDE TO THEIR KNOWLEDGE OF AIDS
Glenn, E F *see* HANDBOOK OF INTERNATIONAL LAW
GLENN TRANSCRIPT – Willows, CA. 1902-08 – 1r – 1 – $100.00 – B03106 – us Library Micro [071]

Glennie, Alexander *see* METEOROLOGICAL RECORDS
GLENN/TEHAMA COUNTIES – 1916-33; 1992- – 20+ r – 1 – $1,000.00 – P00033 – us Library Micro [910]
GLENROCK ITEM – Glenrock, PA. -w 1874-1886; 1886-1943 – 13 – $25.00r – us I.M.R. [071]
GLENROTHES GAZETTE – 1969-1971 – 1. 190-196 – £42.00r – uk Scot News [072]
GLENVIL GLOBE – Glenville, NE. -w. Feb 1915-Sept 1918 – 1 – us NE Hist [071]
GLENVILLE BEE – Glenville, NE. -w. Nov 1899-Aug 1900; Oct 1900-Jan 1901 – 1 – us NE Hist [071]
Glick, Jeffrey *see* A CASE STUDY OF SELECTED EFFECTS OF AN ORGANIZED SUMMER RESIDENTIAL CAMP UPON STAFF MEMEBERS
Glikson, M *see* OLAMENU
GLIM / Inns of Court Students Union. London – v1-4 nos 11-31 (all publ?) – 54mf – 9 – $81.00 – LLMC 84-283 – us L.L.M.C. [340]
GLIMPSES ALONG THE SOUTH COAST: SUMMER-LAND BY THE SEA – Yarmouth, N.S.: Coast Railway Company of Nova Scotia, 1897. 03208. (Pre-1900 Canadiana) – 9 – cn C.I.H.M. [910]
GLIMPSES IN PIONEER LIFE ON PUGET SOUND / Atwood, A – Seattle: Denny-Corvall Co., 1903. Washington reel 8. (Cox Library Collection) – 5 – us Americana [978]
GLIMPSES OF AFRICA, WEST AND SOUTHWEST COAST : CONTAINING THE AUTHOR'S IMPRESSIONS AND OBSERVATIONS DURING A VOYAGE OF SIX THOUSAND MILES... / Smith, CS – Nashville, Tenn.: Publishing House A.M.E. Church Sunday School Union, 1895 – 1mf – us A.T.L.A. [240]
GLIMPSES OF CULTURAL HISTORY OF INDONESIA / Sutjipto Wirjosunparto, R M – SE 4852 1. 1964 – 9 – ne IDC [950]
GLIMPSES OF INDONESIAN EDUCATION AND CULTURE / Prijono – SE-10,711 1. 1964 – 9 – ne IDC [370]
GLIMPSES OF THE AGES / Scholes, Theophilus E Samuel – (Filmed with: Fournier, G La raza negra es la mas antigua de las razas humanas) – or, The "superior" and "inferior" races, so-called discussed in the light of science and history – us Res Libr [573]
GLIMPSES OF THE PAST – v.1-10. 1933-43. Superseded by yBulletin: Missouri Historical Society – 1 – us UMI [073]
GLIMPSES OF THE SUPERNATURAL : BEING FACTS, RECORDS AND TRADITIONS RELATING TO DREAMS, OMENS, MIRACULOUS OCCURRENCES, APPARITIONS, WRAITHS, WARNINGS, SECOND-SIGHT, WITCHCRAFT, NECROMANCY, ETC / ed by Lee, Frederick George – New York: G.W. Carleton, 1875 – 1mf – us A.T.L.A. [130]
GLINIANYE GOLUBKI / Kuzmin, M – Tret'ia kniga stikhov. Ed. 2 in v. III of Sobranie sochinenii, I-XI. Spb. 1914-18. BR-3624 – 8 – ne IDC [460]
GLINIANYIA GOLUBKI / Kuzmin, M – Tret'ia kniga stikhov. Spb. 1914. BR-1191 2 – 8 – ne IDC [460]
Glinstra Bleeker, R J P van *see*
- A TENTATIVE STRATEGY OF DEVELOPMENT FOR LIBYA

GLIRICIDIA SEPIUM (JACQ.) STEUD : A SELECTED BIBLIOGRAPHY / Sumberg, J E – 1986 – 9 – $4.00 – 92-9053-152-5 – et ILRI [631]
Glisson, F *see*
- ANATOMIA HEPATIS
- DE RACHITIDE SIVE MORBO PUERILI, QUI VULGO THE RICKETS DICITUR
- A TREATISE OF THE RICKETS

Gliwicowna, Marja *see* DROGI EMIGRACJI
Gloag, Paton J *see* MESSIANIC PROPHECIES
Gloag, Paton James *see*
- INTRODUCTION TO THE CATHOLIC EPISTLES
- INTRODUCTION TO THE JOHANNINE WRITINGS
- INTRODUCTION TO THE SYNOPTIC GOSPELS

GLOBAL BIOGEOCHEMICAL CYCLES – (v6 1992 $135.00. v8 1994 $185.00. v9 1995 $250.00) – Quarterly. – $148.00 – us A.G.U. [550]
GLOBAL COMMUNICATIONS – v.1. 1979 – 1,5,6,9 – us UMI [073]

GLOBAL COMMUNICATIONS SATELLITE POLICY: INTELSAT, POLITICS AND FUNCTIONALISM / Pelton, Joseph N – 1974. 183p. ISBN: 0-912338-33-4 – 9 – 11.50 – us Lomond [621]
GLOBAL ENVIRONMENTAL CHANGE : THE ROLE OF SPACE IN UNDERSTANDING EARTH – (Suppl to vol 76, Science and Technology) – 1990 – 1mf – 9 – $10.00 – 0-87703-324-2 – us Univelt [550]
GLOBAL GEOCHEMICAL DATABASE FOR ENVIRONMENTAL AND RESOURCE MANAGEMENT : FINAL REPORT OF IGCP PROJECT 259 – 1995 – 122p – 9 – 92-3-103085-X – fr UNESCO [333]
GLOBAL GOVERNANCE – v1. 1995 – 9 – $25.00 – us Hein [340]
GLOBAL SOCIETY *see* PARADIGMS
GLOBAL TRADE *see* AMERICAN IMPORT/ EXPORT GLOBAL TRADE
GLOBAL TRADE EXECUTIVE *see*
– AMERICAN IMPORT-EXPORT MANAGEMENT'S GLOBAL TRADE EXECUTIVE
THE GLOBAL TRADE WHITE PAGES – (Updated annually in February) – 8mf – 9 – $80.00 – us UMI [380]
GLOBALE KONVERGENZ VON ZUFALLSSTRATEGIEN IN DER OPTIMIERUNG : EINE ANALYSE DER UEBERGANGSWAHRSCHEINLICHKEITEN IN MARKOV-KETTEN AUF DIE BEDINGUNG DER GLOBAL ASYMPTOMISCHEN KONVERGENZ UND DIE ENTWICKLUNG EINER NEUEN OPTIMIERUNGSSTRATEGIE EVOLUTIONARY ACCEPTING / Krimphove, Frank – 1995 – 1mf – 9 – DM60.00 – 3-8267-2272-8 – gw Hänsel [000]
GLOBE – Atchison. Kan. 1879- – 1 – us UMI [071]
GLOBE – Auburn. Wash. 1914-1915 – 1 – us UMI [071]
GLOBE – Dodge City. Kan. 1912- – 1 – us UMI [071]
GLOBE – Dodge City. Kan. -w. 1910-14 – 1 – us UMI [071]
GLOBE – El Reno. Okl. 1894-1904 – 1 – us UMI [071]
GLOBE – Elk City. Kan. 1882-87 – 1 – us UMI [071]
GLOBE – Flint. Mich. -d. 1900-02 – 1 – us UMI [071]
GLOBE – Flint. Mich. -w, sw. 1900-02, 1904-06 – 1 – us UMI [071]
GLOBE – Ironwood. Mich. 1920- – 1 – us UMI [071]
GLOBE – Joplin. Mo. 1942- – 1 – us UMI [071]
GLOBE : JOURNAL PHILOSOPHIQUE ET LITTERAIRE – v1-8 Paris 1824-30. Lacking: 1830, v8 (161, 254, 255, 283, 297, 298, 303, 310). – 210mf – 8 – ne IDC [100]
GLOBE – Kansas City. Kan. 1905-09 – 1 – us UMI [071]
GLOBE – Saginaw. Mich. 1893-1898 – 1 – us UMI [071]
GLOBE – Schoharie. Kan. -w. 1883-84 – 1 – us UMI [071]
GLOBE – Shelby. Ohio. 1900-19; 1950- – 1 – us UMI [071]
GLOBE – Toronto, Canada. 1844-49 1858-69 – 50r – 1 – $3,250.00 – cn Library Assoc [971]
GLOBE – Waukesha. Wis. 1854-55 – 1 – us UMI [071]
LE GLOBE – Journal des interets economiques, puis Revue economique hebdomadaire. Dir., A. Coste, puis A. Burdeau. Paris. quot., puis hebd. 1871-85 – 1 – fr A.C.R.P.P. [330]
LE GLOBE – Politique, litteraire et financier. Red. en chef H. Mille-Noe. no. 1-33. Paris. 15 janv-16 fevr 1868 – 1 – fr A.C.R.P.P. [073]
THE GLOBE : FIRST PENNY DAILY – Montreal, Canada. 17 avr-28 avr 1837 – 1r – 1 – Can$30.00 – cn Can Microfilming [072]
THE GLOBE – London. -d. 1822-99, 228mqn reels – 1 – uk British Libr Newspaper [072]
THE GLOBE – New York, 1873-76 – 1 – £60.00 – uk Chadwyck [780]
THE GLOBE – Sydney, Australia. 28 Jan 1886-14 Jun 1887.-d. 6 reels – 1 – uk British Libr Newspaper [072]
THE GLOBE – Toronto, Canada. -d. 1870-73 – 8r – 1 – uk British Libr Newspaper [072]
THE GLOBE – Toronto, Canada. Weekly Globe and Canada Farmer. -w. Jan 1871-Feb 1909 – 44r – 1 – uk British Libr Newspaper [072]
GLOBE AND CANADA FARMER *see* CANADA FARMER
GLOBE AND COMMERCIAL ADVERTISER – New York, 1797-191235 reels – 35r – 1 – us Ross [071]
GLOBE AND MAIL : FINAL EDITION – Toronto, 1849-1992 – 1280r – 1 – cn Preston [971]
GLOBE AND MAIL : NATIONAL EDITION – Toronto, 1980-1992 – 155r – 1 – cn Preston [971]
GLOBE AND MAIL : R.O.B. – Toronto, 1959-1992 – 133r – 1 – cn Preston [971]
GLOBE AND MAIL : R.O.B. MAGAZINE – Toronto, 1985-1992 – 15r – 1 – cn Preston [971]
THE GLOBE AND MAIL – (Back Files. Can$80.00r Vesicular Can$85.00 Negative or Positive Silver; High school rate. Can$650.00) – Toronto 1849- – 1,277r – 1 – Can$1,350.00 Vesicular Can$1,650.00 Negative or Positive Silver – cn Globe Info [072]
THE GLOBE AND MAIL – (Yrly reel count varies) – 1849- – 1 – inquire – us Ross [072]
THE GLOBE AND MAIL – Toronto: The Globe Print Co, [1936-]. jun 1938-feb 1946 – us Res Libr [072]
GLOBE GAZETTE – Mason City. Iowa. 1925- – 1 – us UMI [071]
GLOBE JOURNAL – Falls City. Neb. 1878-1908 – 1 – us UMI [071]
LE GLOBE: JOURNAL PHILOSOPHIQUE ET LITTERAIRE – Paris. Biweekly, later daily. 15 Sep 1824-20 Apr 1832 – 1 – fr A.C.R.P.P. [100]
GLOBE LIVESTOCK JOURNAL – Dodge City. Kan. 1884-88 – 1 – us UMI [071]
GLOBE MAGAZINE – Toronto, 1957-1979 – 27r – 1 – cn Preston [971]
GLOBE POST – LeMars. Iowa. -w. 1951- – 1 – us UMI [071]
Globe Publishing Co *see* HISTORY OF WAYNE AND CLAY COUNTIES
GLOBE REPUBLICAN – Dodge City. Kan. -w. 1889-1902 – 1 – us UMI [071]
GLOBE (TORONTO, ONT.) *see* CANADA FARMER
GLOBE-CITIZEN – Omaha, NE -w. Mar 1908-Aug 1909; Dec 1909-Mar 1910 – 1 – us NE Hist [071]
GLOBE-DEMOCRAT – St. Louis. Mo. 1853- – 1 – us UMI [071]
GLOBE-REPUBLICAN – Auburn. Wash. 1916-1917 – 1 – us UMI [071]
IL GLOBO – Rome, Italy. -d. 1 June 1946-18 May 1947; 1 Aug 1950-30 Dec 1951; 2 Jan-31 Dec 1957. 10 reels – 1 – uk British Libr Newspaper [072]
O GLOBO : JORNAL DIARIO – '(s.l.')-Sao Luis, Brazil. 7 Sept 1889-3 Jun 1890 – 1,5,6 – bl Biblioteca [072]
O GLOBO : ORGAO DEDICADO AOS INTERESSES DO COMMERCIO, LAVOURA E INDUSTRIA – Rio de Janeiro, 10 Aug 1874-Mar 1878; Sep 1881-23 Mar 1883 – 1,5,6 – bl Biblioteca [072]
O GLOBO – '(s.l.')-Sao Luis, Brazil. 20 Jan 1852-Sep 1855. Jul 1858-30 Dec 1859 – 1,5,6 – bl Biblioteca [072]
GLOBS – Israel, 1983- – 9 – $320.00y – us Ross [072]
DER GLOBUS – Berlin, 1941 n5, 7, 9-18; 1942 n19-27 – 1 – Dist. gw Mikrofilm – gw Misc Inst [900]
GLOBUS – Warsaw. v. 1-2. July 1932-Nov 1933 – 1 – us NY Public [947]
GLOBUS – Warsaw. v1-2. 1932-33 – 1r – 1 – us Ross [073]
GLOBUS – Zagreb. Yugoslavia. -w. 3 Jan 1960-12 May 1963. (7 reels) – 1 – uk British Libr Newspaper [949]
DIE GLOCKE – (Ausgabe D/E (Guetersloh) der Glocke in Oelde) – Guetersloh, West Germany. 1992- – 8r per yr – 1 – gw Mikrofilm [072]
DIE GLOCKE – Leipzig, Germany. 1859-1860 – 1 – gw Mikrofilm [072]
DIE GLOCKE – Muenchen, Berlin, 1915-1925 – 7r – 1 – DM840.00 – gw Mikro Press [072]
DIE GLOCKE : WOCHENSCHRIFT FUER POLITIK, FINANZWIRTSCHAFT UND KULTUR – Muenchen, Berlin, DE. 1 Sep 1915-26 Sop 1925 – 7r – 1 – gw Mikrofilm [072]
GLOCKE – London, UK. 15 May 1881 – 1 – uk British Libr Newspaper [072]
Glockmann, G *see* HOMER IN DER FRUEHCHRISTLICHEN LITERATUR BIS JUSTININ (T.U.U. 5-105)
Gloeckner, O *see* KELSUS TEXTE
Gloel, Heinrich *see* DER WETZLARER GOETHE
Gloel, Johannes *see*
– DER HEILIGE GEIST IN DER HEILSVERKUENDIGUNG DES PAULUS
– DIE JUENGSTE KRITIK DES GALATERBRIEFES
Glogau, Gustav *see* DIE IDEALE DER SOCIALDEMOKRATIE UND DIE AUFGABE DES ZEITALTERS
A LA GLOIRE DE LA MARINE A VOILE DU 16E AU 19E SIECLE. 1935. 16 ILLUS. 3 FICHES / Reunion des musees nationaux. Paris – 9 – fr Réunion [700]
Glonti, Fedor Zurabovich *see* AZII ATSKAI A POLITIKA BOLSHEVIKOV
GLORIA CHRISTI : AN OUTLINE STUDY OF MISSIONS AND SOCIAL PROGRESS / Lindsay, Anna Robertson Brown – (Includes index) – New York: Macmillan, 1907 – 1mf – 9 – 0-8370-6141-5 – 1986-0141 – us A.T.L.A. [240]
GLORIA DEI LUTHERAN CHURCH – Hancock, Michigan. 1884-1970 – 16r – 1 – us I.H.R.C. [240]
GLORIA PATRI : OUR TALKS ABOUT THE TRINITY AND THE NEW TRINITARIANISM / Whiton, James Morris – 2nd ed. New York: Thomas Whittaker, 1904, c1892 – 1mf – 9 – 0-8370-5760-4 – 1985-3760 – us A.T.L.A. [240]
GLORIAS DE ASTURIAS / Leon Gutierrez, Florencio – 1896 – 9 – 1.50f – sp Bibl Santa Ana [946]
GLORIAS DE ESPANA. HERNANDO CORTES / Sandoval, M de – 1898 – 9 – 1.50f – sp Bibl Santa Ana [946]
GLORIAS...HERNANDO CORTES / Sandoval, M de – 18-8 (sic) – 9 – 1.50f – sp Bibl Santa Ana [946]
GLORIES OF THE CATHOLIC CHURCH IN ART, ARCHITECTURE AND HISTORY – Chicago, IL. 1895 – 1r – 1 – Can$40.00 – cn Can Microfilming [240]
Glorieux, P *see*
– AUX ORIGINES DE LA SORBONNE
– LA LITTERATURE QUODLIBETIQUE 2
– LA LITTERATURE QUODLIBETIQUE DE 1260 A 1320
– REPERTOIRE DES MAITRES EN THEOLOGIE DE PARIS AU 13TH SIECLE
LA GLORIOSA ET FELICE VITTORIA CONSEGVITA DALL' ARMATA CHRISTIANA CONTRA QUELLA DEL TURCHO – Venetia, 1571 – 1mf – 9 – H-8177/1 – ne IDC [956]
A GLORIOSA SOTAINA DO PRIMEIRO IMPERIO / Brito, Lemos – Sao Paulo, 1937 – 7mf – 8 – ne Slangenburg [972]
THE GLORIOUS COMPANY OF THE APOSTLES : BEING STUDIES IN THE CHARACTERS OF THE TWELVE / Jones, John Daniel – London: J Clarke; New York: [distr by] Thomas Whittaker, 1904 – 1mf – 9 – 0-8370-3798-0 – 1985-1798 – us A.T.L.A. [220]
THE GLORIOUS LORD / Meyer, Frederick Brotherton – Chicago: Fleming H Revell, c1896 – 1mf – 9 – 0-8370-7175-5 – 1986-1175 – us A.T.L.A. [240]
GLORIOUS RECOVERY BY THE VAUDOIS OF THEIR VALLEYS, FROM THE ORIGINAL WITH A COMPENDIOUS HISTORY OF THAT PEOPLE, PREVIOUS AND SUBSEQUENT TO THAT EVENT, BY HUGH DYKE ACLAND / Arnaud, Henri & Acland, Hugh Dyke – London: John Murray, Albemarle-Street, 1827 – 1r – 1 – $16.72 – us Baptist [240]
THE GLORY AND DIVINITY OF THE HOLY BIBLE AND ITS SPIRITUAL SENSE : A LECTURE / Hyde, John – London: James Speirs, 1889 – 1mf – 9 – 0-8370-3712-3 – 1985-1712 – us A.T.L.A. [220]
THE GLORY OF THE REDEEMER IN HIS PERSON AND WORK / Winslow, Octavius – (Includes index) – 4th ed. Philadelphia: Lindsay & Blakiston, 1859 – 1mf – 9 – 0-8370-5438-9 – 1985-3438 – us A.T.L.A. [240]
GLOS ANGLII – Cracow. Poland. -w. 9 Nov 1946-2 Apr 1949. (Imperfect). 3 reels – 1 – uk British Libr Newspaper [943]
GLOS BUNDU – (In Polish) – Warsaw, PL. v1 no2-3 Oct 1946-v2 no3 May 1948 – 1r – 1 – $25.00 – cn Can Microfilming [072]
GLOS GMINY ZYDOWSKIEJ – Warsaw. v. 1-3. 1937-1939 – 1 – us NY Public [073]
GLOS KONFEDERACJI – London, UK. Sept 1953-Mar/Oct 1960 – 1 – uk British Libr Newspaper [072]
GLOS KOSZALINSKI *see* GLOS POMORZA
GLOS LUDU – Lublin, Poland. Nov 1944-Jan 1945 – 1r – 1 – us L of C Photodup [943]
GLOS LUDU – Warsaw, Poland. Feb 1945-1948 – 9r – 1 – us L of C Photodup [943]
GLOS LUDU – Warsaw. Poland. -w. 28 May 1946-12 Jul 1947. (12 reels) – 1 – uk British Libr Newspaper [943]
GLOS NARODU – Czestochowa, Poland. Aug-Sept 1945 – 1r – 1 – us L of C Photodup [943]
GLOS NARODU – Jersey City, NJ. -w. 19 Oct 1950-23 June 1955. Imperfect. 3 reels – 1 – uk British Libr Newspaper [071]
GLOS POLEK – Chicago, IL: Women's Voice Pub Co, 1902-03; 1910-73 – 26r – 1 – us Res Libr [071]
GLOS POLSKI – (In Polish) – Canada, 1938- – 1 – cn Commonwealth Micro [072]
GLOS POLSKI – Liverpool. 1911-Jun 1912 – 1 – uk British Libr Newspaper [072]
GLOS POLSKI – Paris, France. -w. 25 Nov 1939-9 June 1940. 1 reel – 1 – uk British Libr Newspaper [072]
GLOS POLSKI W LONDYNIE – London, UK. Sept 1940; 1944 – 1 – uk British Libr Newspaper [072]
GLOS POMORZA – (Previously: Glos Koszalinski) – Koszalin, Poland. 1953-79 – 43r – 1 – us L of C Photodup [943]
GLOS PORANNY *see* GLOS ROBOTNICZY
GLOS PRACY – Krakow, Poland. Aug 19-Nov 1945 – 1r – 1 – us L of C Photodup [072]
GLOS PRACY – Warsaw, Poland. Feb 1951-1981 – 61r – 1 – us L of C Photodup [943]
GLOS ROBOTNICZY – (Cont as: Glos Poranny as of 30 Jan 1990) – Lodz, Poland. Jul 1950-1992 – 91r – 1 – us L of C Photodup [943]
GLOS SZCZECINSKI – Szczecin, Poland. 31 Dec 1952-1992 – 79r – 1 – us L of C Photodup [943]
GLOS WIELKOPOLSKI – Poznan, Poland. 18 Aug 1945-Jun 1970 – 32r – 1 – us L of C Photodup [943]
GLOS WYBRZEZA – Gdansk, Poland. 14,18,27 Sept 1951; 1953-92 – 84r – 1 – us L of C Photodup [943]
LA GLOSA QUE...CODIGO...PARTIDAS / Lopez de Tovar, Gregorio – (Tomos II-VI. 1878. 1.50f; 9) – 1878 – 9 – 1.50f – sp Bibl Santa Ana [946]
GLOSANDO A BENITO ARIAS MONTANO. LA FUNCION SOCIAL DEL INGENIO / Goni, Blas – Malaga: Revista Espanola de Estudios Biblicos, 1928 – 1 – sp Bibl Santa Ana [946]
GLOSAS / Sanchez-Arjona, Vicente – Sevilla: Editorial Franciscana de San Antonio, 1950 – 1 – sp Bibl Santa Ana [810]
GLOSSA IN QUATTUOR LIBROS / Alexander de Hales – (Sententiarum Vol 1.-Quaracchi, 1951.-17mf; Vol 2.-Quaracchi, 1952.-13mf; Vol 3.-Quaracchi, 1954.-17mf; Vol 4.-Quaracchi, 1957.-18mf) – 8 – ne Slangenburg [290]
GLOSSA IN QUATTUOR LIBROS SENTENTIARUM / Hales, Alexander de – (Vol. 1: Quaracchi, 1951. 17mf; Vol. 2: Quaracchi, 1952. 13mf; Vol 3: Quaracchi, 1954. 17mf; Vol 4: Quaracchi, 1957. 18mf) – 8 – ne Slangenburg [240]
GLOSSAIRE DU CENTRE DE LA FRANCE / Jaubert, H F – 1864-69 – 9 – fr I.C.S. [440]
GLOSSAIRE DU DROIT FRANCAIS / Ragueau, F – 1701 – 9 – fr I.C.S. [340]
GLOSSAIRE DU PATOIS ROCHELAIS / Burgaud des Marets, J H – 1861 – 9 – fr I.C.S. [440]
GLOSSAIRE ETYMOLOGIQUE MONTOIS / Sigart, J D – 2E ED – 9 – fr I.C.S. [440]
GLOSSAIRE FRANCO-CANADIEN / Dunn, Oscar – 1880 – 9 – fr I.C.S. [440]
GLOSSAIRE FRANCO-CANADIEN ET VOCABULAIRE DE LOCUTIONS VICIEUSES USITEES AU CANADA / Dunn, Oscar – Quebec: Imprimerie A Cote, 1880. SEM16P136 – 1r – 5 – Can$9.00 – cn Bibl Nat [440]
GLOSSAIRE FRANCO-CANADIEN: ET VOCABULAIRE DE LOCUTIONS VICIEUSES USITEES AU CANADA / Dunn, Oscar – Avec une introduction de M. Frechette. Quebec: s.n., 1880 (Quebec: A. Cote). 02800. (Pre-1900 Canadiana) – 9 – cn C.I.H.M. [971]

GLOSSAIRE GENEVOIS – 1827 – 9 – fr I.C.S. [440]
GLOSSAIRE NAUTIQUE / Jal, A – 1848 – 9 – fr I.C.S. [623]
GLOSSAIRE VAUDOIS / Callet, P M – 1861 – 9 – fr I.C.S. [440]
GLOSSARIUM GERMANICUM CONTINENS ORIGINES ET ANTIQUITATES TOTIUS LINGUAE GERMANICAE... / Wachter, J G – Lipsiae. 2v. 1737 – 20mf – ne IDC [430]
GLOSSARIUM LATINO-GERMANICUM MEDIAE ET INFIMAE AETATIS / ed by Diefenbach, L – Francofurti ad Moenum, 1857 – 22mf – ne IDC [450]
GLOSSARIUM MEDIAE ET INFIMAE LATINATIS CONDITUM A CARCLO DU FRESNE / Du Cange, Charles d. Fresne – 10v. 1883-87 – 1 – 95.00 – us L of C Photodup [450]
GLOSSARIUM MEDIAE ET INFIMAE LATINITATIS / ed by Du Cange, Charles d. Fresne – (Index included) – Paris. 1937-38. – 193mf – 9 – ne IDC [450]
GLOSSARIUM MEDIAE ET INFIMAE LATINITATIS. ED. NOVA / Cange, Ch. Dufresne Du – Parisiis. Tome 1-9. 1883-1887 – 156mf – 8 – ne Slangenburg [450]
GLOSSARIUM NOVUM AD SCRIPTORES MEDII AEVI / C A RP ENTIER POSB – Parisiis Tomi 1-4. 1766 – 9 – Dfl357.00 – ne Slangenburg [220]
GLOSSARIUM SUIOGOTHICUM... / Ihre, J – Upsaliae. 2v. 1769 – 22mf – ne IDC [490]
GLOSSARY OF EDUCATIONAL TECHNOLOGY TERMS : ENGLISH/SPANISH EDITION – 1986 – 243p – 9 – 92-3-002436-8 – fr UNESCO [370]
GLOSSARY OF EDUCATIONAL TECHNOLOGY TERMS = GLOSSAR ZUR BILDUNGSTECHNOLOGIE : ENGLISH/GERMAN EDITION – 1992 – 276p – 9 – 92-3-002790-1 – fr UNESCO [370]
GLOSSARY OF INLAND FISHERY TERMS – 1978 – 129p – it F.A.O. [636]
A GLOSSARY OF LITURGICAL AND ECCLESIASTICAL TERMS / Lee, Frederick George – London: Bernard Quaritch, 1877 – 2mf – us A.T.L.A. [240]
GLOSSARY OF PHYSICAL EDUCATION TERMS, PART 1 / College Physical Education Association Committee on Terminology – 1937 – 9 – 2.00 – us Microform Publ [790]
A GLOSSARY OF REFERENCE ON SUBJECTS CONNECTED WITH THE FAR EAST / Giles, Herbert Allen – Hongkong: Lane, Crawford, c1878.iii,182p – 1 – us U.W. Library [950]
GLOSSARY OF TECHNICAL TERMS, PHRASES, AND MAXIMS OF THE COMMON LAW / Stimson, Frederic Jesup – Boston, Little, Brown, 1881. 305 p. LL-318 – 1 – us L of C Photodup [340]
GLOSSARY OF TERMS FOR AGRICULTURAL INSURANCE AND RURAL FINANCE – 1992 – 157p – it F.A.O. [360]
A GLOSSARY OF THE TRIBES AND CASTES OF THE PUNJAB AND THE NORTH-WEST FRONTIER PROVINCE / Rose, H A – 3v. Lahore. 1911-14. BI-480 2 – 8 – ne IDC [306]
GLOSSARY OF THE WEST SAXON GOSPELS : LATIN-WEST SAXON AND WEST-SAXON LATIN / Harris, Mattie Anstice – Boston: Lamson, Wolffe, 1899 – 1mf – 9 – 0-8370-3498-1 – 1985-1498 – us A.T.L.A. [220]
A GLOSSARY OF WORDS AND TERMS USED IN THE CONSTITUTION – Saipan: Education for Self-Government, 1976 – 1mf – 9 – $1.50 – LLMC 82-100F, Title 104 – us L.L.M.C. [323]
GLOSSOGRAPHIA / Blount, Thomas – 1656. 694p. (English Linguistics Series 1500-1800) – 9 – us UMI [420]
GLOSSOLALIA / Lovekin, Arthur A – 1962 – 1 – us A.T.L.A. [240]
GLOSSOLALIIA / Belyi, A – Izd. Epokha. Berlin. 1922. BR-562 2 – 8 – ne IDC [400]
GLOSSOP CHRONICLE – Glossop, England. 1986- – 34+ r – 1 – uk British Libr Newspaper [072]
GLOSSOP RECORD *see* THE RECORD
GLOSSOP-DALE CHRONICLE – Glossop. England. -w. Nov 1859-Jul 1861, Jul 1869-Dec 1894. (24 reels) – 1 – uk British Libr Newspaper [072]
GLOUCESTER 1634-1895 – (Mf 1-27: Church Records 1703-1835. Mf 28-47: Town Records 1642-1752. Mf 48-68: Land Grants 1707-1820. Mf 69-93: B,M,D 1643-1794. Mf 94-107: B,I,M,D 1772-1807. Mf 108-116: B,I,M,D 1797-1828. Mf 117-140: B,I,M,D 1740-1848. Mf 141-154: B,M,D 1843-50. Mf 154-156: Marriages & Intentions 1839-61. Mf 157-164: Deaths 1851-64. Mf 165-169: Deaths 1865-73. Mf 170-180: Deaths 1874-83. Mf 181-199: Deaths 1884-93. Mf 200-220: Deaths 1894-1903. Mf 221-228: Marriages 1851-69. Mf 229-231: Marriages & Intents 1861-74. Mf 232-235: Intentions 1861-74. Mf 236-286: Marriages & Intents 1874-1903. Mf 287-294: Intentions 1890-95. Mf 295-315: Births 1851-68. Mf 316-324: Births 1868-73. Mf 325-330: Births 1873-76. Mf 331-344: Births 1874-1883. Mf 345-361: Births 1884-93. Mf 362-369: Births 1893-98. Mf 370-375: Births 1894-95) – (mf ed 1989) – 375mf – 9 – 0-87623-093-1 – us Holbrook [920]
GLOUCESTER 1641-1849 – (Mf 1T-5T: Vital Records 1641-1727. Mf 5T-10T: Vital Records 1716-39. Mf 10T-20T: Vital Records 1722-99. Mf 20T-26T: Vital Records 1767-1840. Mf 27T-32T: Vital Records 1775-1842. Mf 32T-36T: Marriages 1827-39. Mf 36T-40T: Vital Records 1764-1858. Mf 40T-42T: Marriages 1839-49. Mf 43T: Out-of-Town Marriages 1676-1799. Mf 43T-44T: Marriages 1844-50. Mf 45T-49T: Births 1843-49. Mf 50T-53T: Deaths 1843-50. Mf 54T: Vital Records 1751-1849) – (mf ed 1996) – 54mf – 9 – 0-87623-254-3 – us Holbrook [920]
GLOUCESTER ADVOCATE – Jan 6 1925-Dec 28 1926; Jan 6 1928- Dec 20 1946 – 9 – at Pascoe [072]
Gloucester Cathedral *see* REGISTERS, MS
Gloucester. England *see* WARD LISTS AND OTHER RECORDS OF THE CITY OF GLOUCESTER
Gloucester. England. City Library *see*
– GLOUCESTERSHIRE COLLECTION: CATALOGUE OF ADDITIONAL VOLUMES
– GLOUSTERSHIRE COLLECTION: CATALOGUE
GLOUCESTERHIRE (INCLUDING BRISTOL), 1889 : BRITISH ISLES CENSUS DIRECTORIES PROJECT, ENGLAND – (In prep) – at Vine [941]
GLOUCESTERSHIRE, 1830 : BRITISH ISLES CENSUS DIRECTORIES PROJECT, ENGLAND – at Vine [941]
GLOUCESTERSHIRE, 1863 : BRITISH ISLES CENSUS DIRECTORIES PROJECT, ENGLAND – (In prep) – at Vine [941]
GLOUCESTERSHIRE CHRONICLE – England.6 Jul 1833-1848. -w. 6 reels – 1 – uk British Libr Newspaper [072]
GLOUCESTERSHIRE COLLECTION: CATALOGUE OF ADDITIONAL VOLUMES / Gloucester. England. City Library – 1928-55. Original typescript – 1 – uk Microform Academic [941]
GLOUCESTERSHIRE (EXC BRISTOL), 1822 : BRITISH ISLES CENSUS DIRECTORIES PROJECT, ENGLAND – at Vine [941]
GLOUCESTERSHIRE (EXC BRISTOL), 1894 : BRITISH ISLES CENSUS DIRECTORIES PROJECT, ENGLAND. VOL 47 – 8mf – 9 – A$51.00 – at Vine [941]
GLOUCESTERSHIRE (EXC BRISTOL), 1902 : BRITISH ISLES CENSUS DIRECTORIES PROJECT, ENGLAND. VOL 95 – 8mf – 9 – A$51.00 – at Vine [941]
GLOUCESTERSHIRE (EXC BRISTOL), 1914 : BRITISH ISLES CENSUS DIRECTORIES PROJECT, ENGLAND. VOL 92 – 7mf – 9 – A$45.00 – at Vine [941]
GLOUCESTERSHIRE (GLOUCESTER), 1847 : BRITISH ISLES CENSUS DIRECTORIES PROJECT, ENGLAND – at Vine [941]
GLOUCESTERSHIRE (INC BRISTOL), 1852 : BRITISH ISLES CENSUS DIRECTORIES PROJECT, ENGLAND. VOL 158 – 3mf – 9 – A$21.00 – at Vine [941]
GLOUCESTERSHIRE (INC BRISTOL), 1858 : BRITISH ISLES CENSUS DIRECTORIES PROJECT ENGLAND, VOL 31 – 3mf – 9 – A$21.00 – at Vine [941]
GLOUCESTERSHIRE (INC BRISTOL), 1870 : BRITISH ISLES CENSUS DIRECTORIES PROJECT ENGLAND, VOL 121 – 6mf – 9 – A$39.00 – at Vine [941]
GLOUCESTERSHIRE (INC BRISTOL), 1927 : BRITISH ISLES CENSUS DIRECTORIES PROJECT, ENGLAND. VOL 229 – 8mf – 9 – A$51.00 – at Vine [941]
GLOUCESTERSHIRE (INCLUDING BRISTOL) : BRITISH ISLES CENSUS DIRECTORIES PROJECT, ENGLAND – (In prep) – 1880 – at Vine [941]
GLOUCESTERSHIRE (INCLUDING BRISTOL), 1844 : BRITISH ISLES CENSUS DIRECTORIES PROJECT, ENGLAND – (In prep) – at Vine [941]
GLOUSTERSHIRE COLLECTION: CATALOGUE / Gloucester. England. City Library – 1928. Comp. by R. Austin – 1 – uk Microform Academic [941]
Glover, Edward *see* FREUD OR JUNG
Glover, Elizabeth Rosetta Scott *see*
– LIFE OF SIR JOHN HAWLEY GLOVER
Glover, J *see* LE LIVERE DE REIS DE BRITTANIE E LE LIVERE DE REIS DE ENGLETERRE (RS42)
Glover, L H *see* A 20TH CENTURY HISTORY OF CASS COUNTY
Glover, Octavius *see* DOCTRINE OF THE PERSON OF CHRIST
Glover, Robert *see* THE VISITATION OF YORKSHIRE, MADE IN THE YEARS 1584-85, BY ROBERT GLOVER, SOMERSET HERALD..
Glover, Terrot Reaveley *see* LIFE AND LETTERS IN THE FOURTH CENTURY
Glover, W B *see* EVANGELICAL NONCONFORMISTS AND HIGHER CRITICISM IN THE NINETEENTH CENTURY
THE GLOWWORM – Toronto: [s.n. 1891-189-?] – 9 – cn C.I.H.M. [971]
GLQ : A JOURNAL OF LESBIAN AND GAY STUDIES / ed by Dinshaw, Carolyn & Halperin, David M – 9,5,1 – us Gordon [305]
Gluck, CW *see* ALCESTE-TRAGEDIE
Gluck, James Fraser *see* THE LAW OF RECEIVERS OF CORPORATIONS INCLUDING NATIONAL BANKS.
Gluck, Paisiello *see* [OLIMPIADE] THE FAVORITE SONGS IN THE OPERA
GLUCK-JAHRBUCH – Berlin, 1913-1918. v1-4 – 9mf – 9 – P.580/1 – ne IDC [943]
Gluckman, M *see*
– ANALYSIS OF A SOCIAL SITUATION IN MODERN ZULULAND
– THE ECONOMY OF THE CENTRAL BAROTSE PLAIN
– ESSAYS ON LOZI LAND AND ROYAL PROPERTY
– MALINOWSKI'S SOCIOLOGICAL THEORIES
GLUCOREGULATION AND WORK PERFORMANCE IN GLUCONEOGENESIS-INHIBITED IRON DEFICIENT RATS / Linderman, J K – 1991 – 2mf – 9 – $8.00 – us Microform Publ [590]
GLUECK AUF! / Werner, E – Philadelphia: Morwitz. 2v. [1889?] – 1 – us U.W. Library [830]
DAS GLUECK DIESES SOMMERS : NOVELLE / Sturm, Stefan – 5. Aufl. Guetersloh: C Bertelsmann, 1943 – 1r – 1 – us U.W. Library [830]
Glueck, Hermann *see* DER DIALEKT IN DEN DORFGESCHICHTEN BERTHOLD AUERBACHS UND MELCHIOR MEYRS
Glueck, Sheldon *see* THE SHELDON GLUECK PAPERS
GLUECKAUF : BERG- UND HUETTENMAENNISCHE ZEITSCHRIFT – Essen, 1865-1918 – 48r – 1 – DM3,600.00 – gw Mikro Press [790]
GLUECKAUF : BERG- UND HUETTENMAENNISCHE ZEITUNG FUER DEN NIEDERRHEIN UND WESTFALEN – (Suppl.: Essener Zeitung) – Essen, Germany. 1865-1918 – 48r – 1 – gw Mikrofilm [072]
GLUECKAUF – (Cont by: Deutsche Berg- und Huettenarbeiter-Zeitung) – Bochum, Germany. 16 Mar 1889-28 Dec 1907 – 8r – 1 – gw Mikrofilm [622]
GLUECKAUF! – (Publ under various titles, eg: Deutsche Berg- und Huettenarbeiter-Zeitung; Deutsche Bergarbeiter-Zeitung, since 1903; Bergarbeiter-Zeitung, since 1905; Die Bergbau-Industrie, since 1931; Der deutsche Bergknappe, 1933) – Dortmund, Gelsenkirchen, Bochum. mar 16 1889-1933 – 13r – 1 – Inquire at Mikrofilmarchiv for details – gw Misc Inst [622]
GLUECKLICHE MENSCHEN : ROMAN / Polenz, Wilhelm von – 3. Aufl. Berlin: F Fontane, 1905 – 1r – 1 – us U.W. Library [830]
DAS GLUECKSKIND : FUER DIE MAERCHENSPIELE DER KUENSTLERISCHEN VOLKSBUEHNE SCHLICHT UND GETREU IN REDE UND HANDLUNG GEBRACHT NACH DEM MAERCHEN DER GEBRUEDER GRIMM "DER TEUFEL MIT DEN DREI GOLDENEN HAAREN" / Guembel-Seiling, Max – Leipzig: Breitkopf & Haertel, 1918 – 1r – 1 – us U.W. Library [820]
GLUEHENDER TAG : MAENNER IN DER BEWAEHRUNG / Goote, Thor – 7. Aufl. Guetersloh: C Bertelsmann, 1943 – 1r – 1 – us U.W. Library [830]
Glukhikh, V A *see* PLASMA DEVICES AND OPERATIONS
Glushkov, T P *see* KATALOG RUKOPISEI
Gluth, Oskar *see* LENZ ALS DRAMATIKER
Glycae, Michaelis *see*
– ANNALES A MUNDI EXORDIO USQUE AD OBITUM ALEXII COMMENI IMPER. (CBH 9)
– ANNALES (CSHB 27)
GLYCOSYLATED HEMOGLOBIN AND THE OXYGEN KINETICS IN INDIVIDUALS WITH TYPE 2 DIABETES / Dwyer, Gregory B & Wallace, Janet P, – 1992 – 2mf – 9 – $8.00 – us Microform Publ [613]
GMB JOURNAL – General, Municipal, Boilermakers & Allied Trades Union, 1983-. -m. Continues: GMW Journal – 1 – us U.W. Library [330]
Gmelin, J F *see* ONOMATOLOGIA BOTANICA COMPLETE
Gmelin, J G *see*
– FLORA SIBIRICA SIVE HISTORIA PLANTARUM SIBIRIAE
– REISE DURCH SIBIRIEN VOM DEM JAHRE 1733 BIS 1743
Gmelin, S G *see* HISTORIA FUCORUM
GMINA WYZNANIOWA ZYDOWSKA W WARSZAWIE I JEJ INSTYTUCJE – Warszawa: Gmina, 1927 – us Res Libr [072]
GMUENDER TAGESPOST : BA DER SUEDWEST-PRESSE – Schwaebisch Gmuend-Ulm, Germany. 1 Jan 1980- – 1 – gw Mikrofilm [072]
GMW JOURNAL – v34, no.12 (Dec 1971)-v37, no.2 (Feb 1974); n.s. Sept 1981; tabloid Oct Nov 1981-Nov Dec 1982. Esher, Surrey: General and Municipal Workers' Union. illus. semimonthly. Continued by: GMB Journal – 1 – us U.W. Library [330]
Gnad, Ernst *see* UEBER ROBERT HAMERLINGS LYRIK
DAS GNADENBILD DER MATER TER ADMIRABILIS VON INGOLSTADT IN BAYERN : GESCHICHTLICHER BERICHT UND GEBETE / Hattler, Franz – 2. Aufl. Freiburg i.B.: Herder, 1880 – 1mf – 9 – 0-8370-9789-4 – 1986-3789 – us A.T.L.A. [240]
DIE GNADENLEHRE DES PETRUS LOMBARDUS / Schupp, J – 1932 – 6mf – 8 – ne Slangenburg [290]
DIE GNAEDIGE FRAU VON PARETZ : DRAMOLET IN EINEM AUFZUG / Wichert, Ernst – 2. Aufl. Leipzig: P Reclam jun., [1894?] – 1r – 1 – us U.W. Library [820]
GNAEDIGST PRIVILEGIRT ONOLZBACHISCHE WOCHENTLICHE FRAG- UND ANZEIGUNGSNACHRICHTEN – Ansbach, 1773-78 – 1r – 1 – Dist. gw Mikrofilm – gw Misc Inst [943]
Gnedich, P P *see* KNIGA ZHIZNI
Gneisenau, August von *see* PAPERS
Gneisse, Karl *see* DER BEGRIFF DES KUNSTWERKS IN GOETHES AUFSATZ VON DEUTSCHER BAUKUNST (1772) UND IN SCHILLERS AESTHETIK
Gnerich, Ernst *see* ANDREAS GRYPHIUS UND SEINE HERODES-EPEN
GNESTA TIDNING *see* TROSA TIDNING
GNISTAN – Stockholm, Sweden. 1967-78 – 7r – 1 – sw Kungliga [072]
GNISTAN – Stockholm, Sweden. 1979-86 – 1 – sw Kungliga [072]
DER GNOM – Duesseldorf, Germany. Wochenschrift fuer den gesammten Bergbau. -w. July 1898-June 1901. 2 reels – 1 – uk British Libr Newspaper [072]
GNOMEN OF THE NEW TESTAMENT / Bengel, Johann Albrecht – 5v. 1860 – 1 – us A.T.L.A. [240]
GNOMIC LITERATURE IN BIBLE AND APOCYRPHA : WITH SPECIAL REFERENCE TO THE GNOMIC FRAGMENTS AND THEIR BEARING ON THE PROVERB COLLECTIONS / Levi, Gerson Baruch – (Includes index of biblical citations) – 1mf – 9 – 0-8370-9714-2 – 1986-3714 – us A.T.L.A. [270]
GNOMON : KRITISCHE ZEITSCHRIFT FUER DIE GESAMTE KLASSICHE ALTERTUMSWISSENSCHAFT – Berlin, 1925-40. v1-16. – 8 – ne IDC [930]
GNOSEOLOGIA DE LA GRAMATICA GENERATIVA / Velarde Lombrana, Julian – 1mf – 9 – Pta1,000.00 – 84-85422-06-6 – sp Pentalfa [440]

THE GNOSTICS AND THEIR REMAINS, ANCIENT AND MEDIEVAL / King, C W – New York: G.P. Putnam, 1887 – 2mf – us A.T.L.A. [240]

LE GNOSTIQUE DE CLEMENT D'ALEXANDRIE. OPUSCULE INEDIT DE FENELON / Dudon, P – Paris, 1930 – 6mf – 8 – ne Slangenburg [240]

GNOSTIQUES ET GNOSTICISME : ETUDE CRITIQUE DES DOCUMENTS DU GNOSTICISME CHRETIEN AUX IIE ET IIIE SIECLES / Faye, Eugene de – Paris: E. Leroux, 1913. (Bibliotheque de l'Ecole des Hautes Etudes, Sciences religieuses; 27e v) – 2mf – us A.T.L.A. [240]

GNOSTISCHE SCHRIFTEN IN KOPTISCHER SPRACHE AUS DEM CODEX BRUCIANUS (T.U.U. 1-8/1.2.) / Schmidt, Carl – Leipzig, 1892 – 11mf – 9 – ne Slangenburg [240]

DIE GNOSTISCHEN QUELLEN HIPPLOYTIS (T.U.U. 1-6/3A) / Staehelin, H – Leipzig, 1890 – 2mf – 9 – ne Slangenburg [240]

DIE GNOSTISCHEN SCHRIFTEN DES KOPTISCHEN PAPYRUS BEROLINENSIS 8502 (T.U.U. 5-60) / Till, W – Berlin, 1955 – 6mf – 9 – ne Slangenburg [240]

Gnueg, Hiltrud *see* LITERARISCHE UTOPIE-ENTWUERFE

GO – 1962-67 (complete) – 1r – 1 – ATLA S0521 – us A.T.L.A. [073]

Go, Ban Hong *see* ON THE MINERAL NUTRITION OF LOWLAND RICE

GO DOWN, MOSES – Concordance to the novel – 10mf – 9 – us UMI [420]

GO, RENEW THE FACE OF THE LAND.' / Israel. Ministry of Agriculture – An account of Israel. By N. Rosenzweig. 115 p. Illus – 9 – 3.00 – is I.T.T.I. [956]

GO THE RIGHTS WAY, DO THE RIGHTS THING, A POLICY STATEMENT / Cleary, N P – 1984. 9 points – 9 – 1.00f – at Libertarian Micro [323]

Goa *see* BOLETIM OFICIAL DO ESTADO DA INDIA

Goa. India *see*
- PLANO DE FOMENTO 1953-1958
- PLANO DE FOMENTO 1959-1964

Goa. India. Presidencia do Conselho *see* PLANO INTERCALAR DE FOMENTO PARA 1965-1967

GOAD COMPANY *see*
- INSURANCE PLAN OF THE CITY OF MONTREAL
- INSURANCE PLAN OF THE CITY OF QUEBEC, CANADA

Goad, George Washington *see* INSTRUCTIONS TO JURIES ESPECIALLY ADAPTED TO THE LAWS OF TEXAS

GOAL ORIENTATION AND MORAL ATMOSPHERE IN YOUTH SPORT : AN EXAMINATION OF LYING, HURTING, AND CHEATING BEHAVIOR IN GIRLS' SOCCER / Stephens, Dawn E & Bredemeier, Brenda Jo Light – 1993 – 3mf – 9 – $12.00 – us Microform Publ [150]

GOAL PERSPECTIVES AND THEIR RELATIONSHIP TO BELIEFS, AFFECTIVE RESPONSES AND COPING STRATEGIES AMONG AFRICAN AND ANGLO AMERICAN ATHLETES / Gano-Overway, Lori A – Purdue University, 1995 – 2mf – 9 – $8.00 – PSY1844 – us Microform Publ [150]

GOALS OF DEVELOPMENT – 1988 – 196p – 9 – 92-3-102541-4 – fr UNESCO [307]

Goar, J *see*
- CHRONOGRAPHIA
- DE OFFICIIS MAGNAE ECCLESIAE ET AULAE CONSTANTINOPO- LITANAE (CBH 18)
- RITUALE GRAECORUM

GOBANKATA DAIDAIKI = DIRECTORY OF MILITARY OFFICIALS IN THE TOKUGAWA REGIME / ed by Kikuchi, Yoshio – In 1584-1819 handwriting, 394 books – 52r – 1 – Y540,000 – ja Yushodo [950]

Gobat, Samuel *see*
- JOURNAL OF A THREE YEARS' RESIDENCE IN ABYSSINIA
- SAMUEL GOBAT

LES GOBELINS. 3 SIECLES DE TAPISSERIE / Mobilier National. Paris – 1966. 53 illus. 2 fiches – 9 – fr Réunion [740]

GOBERNADORES DE ANTIOQUIA 1571-1819. BOGOTA, 1932 / Restrepo Saenz, Jose Ma. – Madrid: Razon y Fe, 1934 – 1 – sp Bibl Santa Ana [946]

LOS GOBERNANTES DE MEXICO : HERNANDO CORTES / Rivera Cambas, Manuel – Tabucaya: (Mexico. Editorial Cttp apte), 1962 – sp Bibl Santa Ana [320]

Gobet, Nicholas *see* LES ANCIENS MINERALOGISTES DU ROYAUME DE FRANCE

GOBHILIYA GRIHYA SUTRA – Calcutta. 1908. BI-499 2 – 8 – ne IDC [280]

Gobierno Civil *see* PROTOCOLO

EL GOBIERNO DE FACTO / Anderson, L – San Jose, 1925 – 1mf – 9 – ILM-1529/1 – ne IDC [340]

EL GOBIERNO DE MAURA DE 1921 / Gomez Ochoa, Fidel – 2mf – 9 – Pta1,500.00 – 84-85422-69-4 – sp Pentalfa [320]

EL GOBIERNO, EL ESTADO Y LAS ORGANIZACIONES LIBRES DEL PUEBLO, LA COMUNIDAD ORGANIZADA : TRABAJOS, ALOCUCIONES Y ESCRITOS DEL GENERAL JUAN DOMINGO PERON QUE FUNDAMENTAN LA CONCEPCION JUSTICIALISTA DE LA COMUNIDAD / Peron, Juan Domingo – Buenos Aires: Editorial de la Reconstruccion, [1975] – 1 – CSUXAHZ5063-B – us Hoover Inst Photo [350]

GOBIERNO PERONISTA – (Includes c.1: no.1 1973:July 12-no.5 (1973:Aug. 9); no.7 1973:Aug. 23; no.9 1973:Sept. 6-no.13 (1973:Oct. 4); no.15 1973:Oct 18)) – 1973 – 1 – CSUXAHZ5739-S – us Hoover Inst Photo [073]

UN GOBIERNO POPULAR SIN DEMAGOGIA : (LA ARGENTINA DEL GENERAL PERON) / Gonzalez Blanco, Pedro – Mexico: "Editorial Galatea", 1951 – 1 – CSUXAHZ7366-B – us Hoover Inst Photo [320]

Gobillon, N *see* LA VIE DE LA VENERABLE LOUISE DE MARILLAC, VEUVE DE M. LEGRAS

Gobineau, Joseph A *see* SOUVENIRS DE VOYAGE

GOCE DELCEV PAMPHLET COLLECTION – 1972 – 1 – CSUXANQ9972-B – us Hoover Inst Photo [080]

Gochet, Alexis Marie *see*
- SOLDATS ET MISSIONAIRES AU CONGO DE 1891 A 1894
- LA TRAITE DES NEGRES ET LA CROISADE AFRICAINE.

GOCKEL, HINKEL UND GACKELEIA : EIN MAERCHEN / Brentano, Clemens – 2. Aufl. Berlin: Morawe & Scheffelt, 1912 – 1 – us U.W. Library [830]

GOD – Istoriko-politicheskoe obozrenie Vestnika Evropy. v. 1-2. Spb. 1872-74. BR-3383 2 – 8 – ne IDC [947]

GOD AGAINST SLAVERY : AND THE FREEDOM AND DUTY OF THE PULPIT TO REBUKE IT AS A SIN AGAINST GOD / Cheever, George B – New York: J.H. Ladd, 1857 – 1mf – us A.T.L.A. [240]

GOD: AN ENQUIRY INTO THE NATURE OF MAN'S HIGHEST IDEAL...FROM THE STANDPOINT OF SCIENCE / Carus, Paul – Chicago: Open Court, 1908. 1 fiche – 9 – us A.T.L.A. [240]

GOD AND AMN : PHILOSOPHY OF THE HIGHER LIFE / Shumaker, Elmer Ellsworth – New York: G P Putnam, 1909 – 1mf – 9 – 0-8370-5603-9 – 1985-3603 – us A.T.L.A. [210]

GOD AND CHRIST : SERMONS PREACHED IN BEDFORD CHAPEL / Brooke, Stopford Augustus – London: P. Green, 1894 – 1mf – us A.T.L.A. [240]

GOD AND FREEDOM IN HUMAN EXPERIENCE : CONTAINING THE DONNELLAN LECTURES FOR THE YEAR 1913-14 / D'Arcy, Charles Frederick – London: E. Arnold, 1915 – 1mf – us A.T.L.A. [210]

GOD AND HIS BOOK / Saladin – London: W. Stewart, 18–. 1 fiche – 9 – us A.T.L.A. [240]

GOD AND MAN: CONFERENCES DELIVERED AT NOTRE DAME IN PARIS / Lacordaire, Henri Dominique – New York: Scribner, 1872. 1 fiche – 9 – us A.T.L.A. [240]

GOD AND REASON: LECTURES UPON THE PRIMARY TRUTHS OF NATURAL RELIGION / Preston, Thomas Scott – New York: Robert Coddington, 1884. 1 fiche. 8370-4796-X – 9 – us A.T.L.A. [240]

GOD AND THE BIBLE : A REVIEW OF OBJECTIONS TO "LITERATURE AND DOGMA" / Arnold, Matthew – (Includes bibliographical references) – New York: Macmillan, 1903 – 1mf – 9 – 0-8370-9440-2 – 1986-3440 – us A.T.L.A. [230]

GOD AND THE BIBLE : A REVIEW OF OBJECTIONS TO LITERATURE AND DOGMA / Arnold, Matthew – London: Smith, Elder, 1875 – 1 roll – 1 – 1-55879-166-3 – uk Libr Preservation [240]

GOD AND THE FUTURE LIFE : THE REASONABLENESS OF CHRISTIANITY / Nordhoff, Charles – NY: Harper, c1883 – 1mf – 9 – 0-8370-4598-3 – 1985-2598 – us A.T.L.A. [210]

GOD AND THE SOUL : AN ESSAY TOWARDS FUNDAMENTAL RELIGION / Armstrong, Richard Acland – London: Philip Green, 1896 – 1mf – 9 – 0-8370-2113-8 – 1985-0113 – us A.T.L.A. [210]

GOD (CCC163) / Horton, Walter M – (In Chinese) – 1st ed. Hong Kong: Council on Christian Literature for Overseas Chinese, 1957 – 1r – 1 – 1984-B500 – us A.T.L.A. [210]

GOD IN CHRIST / Bushnell, Horace – 1903 – 9 – us A.T.L.A. [240]

GOD IN HIS PROVIDENCE / Fernald, Woodbury M – 1859 – 9 – us A.T.L.A. [240]

GOD IN HIS WORLD: AN INTERPRETATION / Alden, Henry Mills – New York: Harper, 1890. 1 fiche – 9 – us A.T.L.A. [240]

GOD IS IN HEAVEN : AN INVESTIGATION OF THE CONCEPT OF GOD IN THE BOOK OF ECCLESIASTES / Estes, Henry B 2 – 1982 – 1 – $7.84 – us Baptist [240]

GOD IS SPIRIT, GOD IS LOVE : A TREATISE ON SPIRITUAL UNITARIANISM / Elliot, George – London: Philip Green, 1895 – 1mf – 9 – 0-8370-8811-9 – 1986-2811 – us A.T.L.A. [210]

THE GOD MAN / Dixon, Amzi Clarence – Baltimore: Wharton, Barron, c1891 – 1mf – 9 – 0-8370-2929-5 – 1985-0929 – us A.T.L.A. [240]

THE GOD OF ISRAEL : A PAPER READ BEFORE THE INTERNATIONAL POSITIVIST CONGRESS AT NAPLES, 27TH APRIL-3RD MAY 1908 / Levy, Joseph Hiam – (Includes bibliographical references) – London: Lawrence Nelson, [1908?] – 1mf – 9 – 0-8370-4094-9 – 1985-2094 – us A.T.L.A. [210]

GOD PROLETARSKO I DIKTATURY : I UBILE INY I SBORNIK. 1917.25.7-10.11.1918: GOD PROLETARSKO I DIKTATURY – Nizhni i-Novgorod: Izd. Nizhegorodskogo gub. kom-ta R.K.P., [1918 or 1919] – 1 – CSUX88-B6471 – us Hoover Inst Photo [320]

GOD PROLETARSKO I REVOLIUTSI I – (Includes c.1: 1918:Nov.9) – Petrograd: 14-i a gos. tip., 1918 – 1 – CSUXANR4310-S – us Hoover Inst Photo [947]

GOD PUTI : ZHIZN DOBROVOLCHESKOI ARMII / Ilovaiskii, Vladimir – Rostov n.D.: Tip. t-va "Obnovlenie", 1919 – 1 – CSUX88-B7684 – us Hoover Inst Photo [947]

GOD RABOTY PO SNABZHENIIU ZHELEZNYKH DOROG TOPLIVOM : OBZOR DEIATELNOSTI ZHELESKOMOV V 1919-20 OPERAT SIONNOM GODU / ed by Derevenko, N N & Rudkovskogo, V I – Moskva: Gos. izd-vo, 1920. 2v – 1 – CSUX90-B6205 – us Hoover Inst Photo [380]

GOD RABOTY PRAVITELSTVA RSFSR – (Includes c.1: 1926/1927-1927/1928) – Moskva: Izd. VT SIK i SNK RSFSR, 1928-1929. 2v – 1 – CSUXAKZ3613-S – us Hoover Inst Photo [947]

GOD SLUZHBY "SOTSIALISTOV" KAPITALISTAM : OCHERKI PO ISTORII KONTRREVOLIUTSII V 1918 GODU / Vladimirova, V; ed by Iakovlev, I A – M., 1927. 386p – 5mf – 9 – ne IDC [320]

GOD SPAKE ALL THESE WORDS / Brookes, James Hall – [s.l.]: J T Smith; St Louis: Rev J W Allen, Presbyterian Bd of Publ [distributor], c1895 – 1mf – 9 – 0-8370-2468-4 – 1985-0468 – us A.T.L.A. [220]

GOD, THE SOUL, AND A FUTURE STATE: A TWOFOLD POPULAR TREATISE / Cooper, Thomas – London: Hodder and Stoughton, 1874. 1 fiche – 9 – us A.T.L.A. [240]

GOD V SELSKO-KHOZI A ISTVENNOM OTNOSHENII – (Includes c.1: 1922/1923) – Moskva: Izd. T SSU, 1927 – 1 – CSUXAKY9925-S – us Hoover Inst Photo [947]

GOD VOINY S 19-GO IIULI A 1914 G. PO 19-E IIULIA 1915 G – Moskva: Izd. D.I A. Makovskago, 1915 – 1 – CSUX89-B1606 – us Hoover Inst Photo [355]

GOD WITH US : A STUDY IN RELIGIOUS IDEALISM / Gibson, William Ralph Boyce – London: Adam and Charles Black, 1909 – 1mf – 9 – 0-8370-3267-9 – 1985-1267 – us A.T.L.A. [200]

GOD WITH US, OR, THE PERSON AND WORK OF CHRIST : WITH AN EXAMINATION OF "THE VICARIOUS SACRIFICE" OF DR. BUSHNELL / Hovey, Alvah – 2nd ed. Boston: Gould and Lincoln; New York: Sheldon, 1872 – 1mf – 9 – 0-8370-4855-9 – 1985-2855 – us A:T.L.A. [240]

Godard, B *see* CHANT ET BAISER

Godard, J *see* LA LANGUE FRANCAISE

Godart, Felix *see* LA REFORME JUDICIAIRE DE 1789 A 1794 D'APRES CAMILLE DESMOULINS ET LA LEGISLATION

Godart, J B *see* HISTOIRE NATURELLE DES LEPIDOPTERES, OU PAPILLONS DE FRANCE

Godbey, Geoffrey C *see*
- THE RELATION OF SELF-ESTEEM TO CONSTRAINTS ON LEISURE AMONG ADOLESCENTS
- TOURIST TRAVEL MOTIVATIONS AND SATISFACTION STUDY OF CHINA/YANGZTE RIVER ADVENTURE TOURS

Goddard D'Aucourt de Saint-Just *see* JEAN DE PARIS

Goddard, Dwight *see* WAS JESUS INFLUENCED BY BUDDHISM. A COMPARATIVE STUDY OF THE LIVES AND THOUGHTS OF GAUTAMA AND JESUS

Goddard, Harold Clarke *see* STUDIES IN NEW ENGLAND TRANSCENDENTALISM

Goddard, Pliny E *see* ETHNOLOGY OF THE NORTH CALIFORNIA COAST INDIAN TRIBES HUPA WYOT POMO MIWAK

HET GODDELYCK HERTE, OFTE DE WOONSTE GODTS IN HET HERTE / Bottens, Fulg. OF M – Ghendt. Deel 1-3. 1716 – 33mf – 8 – ne Slangenburg [240]

GODDELYCKE AANDACHTEN OFTE VLAMMENDE BEGEERTEN EENS BOETVAERDIGE GEHEIJLIGD EN LIEF-RIJCKE ZIELE / Serrarius, P – Amsterdam, 1653 – 2mf – 9 – ne IDC [700]

GODDELYCKE WENSCHEN VERLICHT MET SINNEBEELDEN EN VIERIGE UYTSPRAKEN DER OUT-VADERS / Hugo, H – [Antwerpen], 1645 – 5mf – 9 – O-3091/1 – ne IDC [760]

GODDELYCKEWENSCHEN. TRANS. BY J. DE HARDUYN. O 640. 1629 / Hugo, H – 9 – ne IDC [240]

GODDELYKE LIEFDE-VLAMMEN OF VERVOLG VAN JESUS EN DE ZIELE, HANDELENDE VAN EEN BOETVAERDIGE, GEHEILIGDE, LIEFHEBBENDE, EN HAAR ZELFSTERVENDE ZIELE, IN DRIE DEELEN, MET KOOPERE AFBEELDINGEN VERCIERT : NEVENS HAAR VAARSEN, AANMERKINGEN, EN ZIELZUCHTINGEN / Luyken, J – Amsterdam, 1736 – 3mf – 9 – O-3032/1 – ne IDC [760]

GODDELYKE LIEFDE-VLAMMEN, VAN EEN BOETVAARDIGE, GEHEILIGDE, LIEFHEBBENDE, EN AAN HAAR SELFS-STERVENDE ZIELE, IN DRIE DEELEN VERDEELT : AFGEBEELD DOOR VIJFTIG NETTE KOOPERE FIGUUREN / Luyken, J – 1st ed. Amsterdam, 1691 – 3mf – 9 – O-3033/1 – ne IDC [760]

Godden, G M *see* COMMUNIST ATTACK IN GREAT BRITAIN, LONDON 1938

Godden, Gertrude M *see*
- COMMUNISM IN SPAIN, 1931-36
- COMMUNIST OPERATIONS IN SPAIN
- NEW SPAIN; ITS PEOPLE, ITS RULER

Godden, John *see* NOTES AND REMINISCENCES OF A JOURNEY TO ENGLAND

Goddyn, M *see* LE DROIT CRIMINEL BELGE...

Gode, Antonio *see* ASEDIO DE HUESCA; 18 JULIO 1936, 25 MARZO 1938

Gode, P K *see* NEW INDIAN ANTIQUARY

GODEFRIDUS ABBAS ADMONTENSIS OLIM WEINGARTTENSIS, HOMILIAE : OPERA ET STUDIO B. PEZ O.S.B. AUG – Vindelicorum, 1725 – Dfl133.00 – ne Slangenburg [240]

Godefroy, FE *see*
- DICTIONNAIRE DE L'ANCIENNE LANGUE FRANCAISE
- LEXIQUE COMPARE DE LA LANGUE DE CORNEILLE, ET DE LA LANGUE DU XVIIE

Godefroy, Frederic *see* DICTIONNAIRE DE L'ANCIENNE LANGUE FRANCAISE DU IXEME AU XVEME SIECLE

Godefroy, J *see* BIBLIOTHEQUE DES BENEDICTINS DE LA CONGREGATION DE SAINT-VANNE ET SAINT-HYDULPHE

LE GODENDARD : HUMORISTIQUE, ILLUSTRE – Sorel, Canada. 4-18 mai 1889 – 1r – 1 – Can$25.00 – cn Can Microfilming [072]

Goderich, Frederick John Robinson, Viscount *see*
- COPY OF A DESPATCH FROM LORD GODERICH TO LORD AYLMER
- MESSAGE

GODESBERGER VOLKSZEITUNG – (Also suppl available: Drachenfelser Echo, Wochenblatt fuer Mehlem und Umgebung, apr 1-nov 27 1931, 1932-sep 22 1933, oct 20 1933, 2r. Cont by: Deutsche Reichszeitung, jan 2 1934; Mittelrheinische Landes-Zeitung, oct 1 1934) – Bonn, jul-dec 1913, jan-jun 1920, 1921-jun 1923, 1924-27, jul 1928-mar 1941 – 49r – 1 – Inquire at Mikrofilmarchiv for details – gw Misc Inst [943]

Godet, Frederic Louis *see*
- BIBLISKA STUDIER
- CONFERENCES APOLOGETIQUES
- ETUDES BIBLIQUES
- ETUDES BIBLIQUES. DEUXIEME SERIE: NOUVEAU TESTAMENT
- FREDERIC GODET (1812-1900): D'APRES SA CORRESPONDANCE ET D'AUTRES DOCUMENTS INEDITS
- HISTOIRE DE LA REFORMATION ET DU REFUGE DANS LE PAYS DE NEUCHATEL
- INTRODUCTION TO THE NEW TESTAMENT
- LECTURES IN DEFENCE OF THE CHRISTIAN FAITH
- STUDIES OF CREATION AND LIFE
- STUDIES ON THE EPISTLES
- STUDIES ON THE NEW TESTAMENT
- STUDIES ON THE OLD TESTAMENT

Godet, Michel *see* FROM ANTICIPATION TO ACTION

Godey, P *see* LA MER COTIERE

GODEY'S LADY'S BOOK – 1830-1898 – 1 – us UMI [073]

Godfrey *see* EARLY HISTORY OF MICHIGAN

Godfrey, Carlos E *see* LES METHODES SCIENTIFIQUES DANS L'ETUDE ET LA CONSERVATION DES OEUVRES D'ART

Godinez de la Paz, Carlos *see* CONSIDERA-CIONES...FERROCARRILES...CACERES

Goding, MW *see* STATEMENT OF OBJECTIVES AND POLICIES OF THE TRUST TERRITORY OF THE PACIFIC ISLANDS (TTPI)

Godinho, Manuel *see* RELACAO DO NOVO CAMINHO QUE FEZ POR TERRA E MAR VINDO DE INDIA PARA PORTUGAL...

Godio, Julio *see*
- LA CAIDA DE PERON, DE JUNIO A SETIEMBRE DE 1955
- EL ULTIMO ANO DE PERON

Godkin, Edwin L *see* UNFORESEEN TENDENCIES OF DEMOCRACY

Godkin, James *see*
- IRELAND AND HER CHURCHES
- THE RELIGIOUS HISTORY OF IRELAND, PRIMITIVE, PAPAL AND PROTESTANT..

DE GODLIEVENDE ZIEL VERTOONT IN ZINNEBEELDEN / Hugo, H & Veen, O van – O 641. 1724 – 9 – ne IDC [240]

DE GODLIEVENDE ZIEL VERTOONT IN ZINNEBEELDEN / Hugo, H & Veen, O van – O 642. 1749 – 9 – ne IDC [240]

THE GODLY PASTOR : LIFE OF THE REV. JEREMIAN HALLOCK, OF CANTON, CONN.: TO WHICH IS ADDED A SKETCH OF THE LIFE OF THE REV. MOSES HALLCOCK, OF PLAINFIELD, MASS. / Yale, Cyrus – New York: American Tract Society, [1854?] – 1mf – us A.T.L.A. [240]

GODLY UNION AND CONCORD : SERMONS PREACHED MAINLY IN WESTMINSTER ABBEY IN THE INTEREST OF CHRISTIAN FRATERNITY / Henson, H Hensley – London: J. Murray, 1902 – 1mf – us A.T.L.A. [240]

THE GODOLPHIN / Paisible, J – Hoboy on London bridge, [1714] – 1 – us Sibley [780]

GODOVO I OTCHET N.K.I.D. K...S"EZDU SOVETOV... – (Includes c.1: 1919/1920) – Moskva: Narkomindel, 191u – 1 – CSUXAKY5530-S – us Hoover Inst Photo [947]

GODOVOI PLAN GOSUDARSTVENNOGO SNABZHENIIA NA 1921-1922 G : STATI I MATERIALY UPRAVLENIIA RASPREDELENIIA NARKOMPRODA I TSENTRALNOI KOMISSII PO SNABZHENIIU RABOCHIKH – Moskva: Mosk. Sov. Nar. Khoz., 1921 – 1 – CSUX90-B5431 – us Hoover Inst Photo [330]

GODOY / Izquierdo Hernandez, Manuel – Badajoz: Dip. Provincial, 1967 – sp Bibl Santa Ana [946]

Godoy, Manuel *see*
- CARLOS 4 Y MARIA LUISA, DE JUAN PEREZ DE GUZMAN Y GALLO
- CARTA AL MARQUES DE SAN SIMON
- CUENTA...MEMORIAS CRITICAS Y APOLOGETICAS...CARLOS 4 DE BORBON
- DISPUTATIONES...THOMAE EIDEM ANGELICO
- MANIFIESTO...ARANJUEZ, MADRID Y BAYONA
- MEMORIAS

Godoy, Pedro de *see*
- DISPUTATIONES THEOLOGICAE. IN PRIMAN PARTEM DIVI THOMAE. TOMUS SECUNDUS
- DISPUTATIONES THEOLOGICAE IN TERTIAM PARTEM DIVI THOMAE
- DISPUTATIONES THEOLOGICAE INTERTIAM PARTEM DIVI THONAE...
- DISPUTATIONES THEOLOGICAE INTERTIAN PASTEM DIVI THONAE...

GODOY. PRINCIPE DE LA PAZ Y DE BASSANO / Taxonera, Luciano de – Barcelona: Edit. Juventud, 1946 – 9 – sp Bibl Santa Ana [940]

Godron, D A *see* FLORULA JUVENALIS

Godrycz, John A *see* THE DOCTRINE OF MODERNISM AND ITS REFUTATION

GODS AND FIGHTING MEN : THE STORY OF TUATHA DE DANANN AND OF THE FIANNA OF IRELAND / Gregory, Lady – London: John Murray, 1910 – 1 roll – 1 – 1-55879-545-6 – uk Libr Preservation [390]

THE GODS AND OTHER LECTURES / Ingersoll, Robert Green – Washington, DC: C P Farrell, 1879, c1874 – 1mf – 9 – 0-8370-3724-7 – 1985-1724 – us A.T.L.A. [210]

GOD'S BALANCE OF FAITH AND FREEDOM : BEING THE MARY FITCH PAGE LECTURES AT THE BERKELEY DIVINITY SCHOOL, 1910 / Waterman, Lucius – Milwaukee: Young Churchman, c1911 – 1mf – us A.T.L.A. [240]

GOD'S FOLLY: THE GREAT FLOOD / Arrigoni, Enrico – Biblical Fairy Tales, No.3 – 9 – 1.00f – at Libertarian Micro [335]

GOD'S GOOD MAN / Corelli, Marie – British Fiction Archive: Unit 1 – 9 – uk Bell [830]

GOD'S HAND IN AMERICA / Cheever, George Barrell – New York: M.W. Dodd; London: Wiley & Putnam, 1841 – 1mf – us A.T.L.A. [240]

GOD'S IMAGE IN MAN : SOME INTUITIVE PERCEPTIONS OF TRUTH / Wood, Henry – 6th ed. Boston: Lee and Shepard, 1894, c1892 – 1mf – 9 – 0-8370-5749-3 – 1985-3749 – us A.T.L.A. [210]

GOD'S IRON : A LIFE OF THE PROPHET JEREMIAH / Birmingham, G A – London, 1956 – 5mf – 8 – ne Slangenburg [240]

GODS MERCIE MIXED WITH HIS JUSTICE, OR HIS PEOPLES DELIVERANCE IN TIMES OF DANGER / Cotton, John – 1641 – 9 – 10.00 – us Scholars' Facs [240]

GOD'S MESSAGE TO THE HUMAN SOUL... THE BIBLE IN THE LIGHT OF THE NEW KNOWLEDGE / Maclaren, Ian – New York: Fleming H. Revell, 1907. 1 fiche. 8370-5723-X – 9 – us A.T.L.A. [240]

GOD'S METHOD WITH MAN / Gorham, Barlow Weed – 1879 – 9 – us A.T.L.A. [240]

GOD'S MISSIONARY PLAN FOR THE WORLD / Bashford, James Whitford – (With index) – New York: Young People's Missionary Movt, 1908 – 1mf – 9 – 0-8370-6011-7 – 1986-0011 – us A.T.L.A. [240]

GOD'S OATH: A STUDY OF AN UNFULFILLED PROMISE OF GOD / Ottman, Ford Cyrinde – New York: Pub. Office Our Hope, 1911. 278,iiip.1 fiche – 9 – us A.T.L.A. [240]

THE GODS OF INDIA; A BRIEF DESCRIPTION OF THEIR HISTORY, CHARACTER & WORSHIP / Martin, Edward Osborn – London: J.M. Dent; New York: E.P. Dutton, 1914. 330p. ill – 1 – us U.W. Library [280]

GODS OF MODERN GRUB STREET : IMPRESSIONS OF CONTEMPORARY AUTHORS / Adcock, Arthur John – New York: Frederick A. Stokes Company, 1923. viii/326p Ports – 1 – us U.W. Library [070]

GOD'S OTHER CHILDREN AND OTHER SKETCHES / Manganyi, M C – (Filmed with: The politics of separate freedoms) – New Haven, 1973 – us Res Libr [240]

GOD'S PLAN FOR SOUL-WINNING / Hogben, Thomas – [2nd ed]. Toronto: A Sims, 1907 – 1mf – 9 – 0-8370-6264-0 – 1986-0264 – us A.T.L.A. [240]

GOD'S PLAN FOR WORLD REDEMPTION : AN OUTLINE STUDY OF THE BIBLE AND MISSIONS / Watson, Charles Roger – Philadelphia, Pa.: Board of Foreign Missions of the United Presbyterian Church of N.A., c1911 – 1mf – us A.T.L.A. [240]

GOD'S RESCUES : OR, THE LOST SHEEP, THE LOST COIN, AND THE LOST SON: THREE DISCOURSES ON LUKE 15 / Williams, William R – New York: Anson D F Randolph, 1871 – 1mf – 9 – 0-8370-7353-7 – 1986-1353 – us A.T.L.A. [220]

GOD'S REVELATIONS OF HIMSELF TO MEN : AS SUCCESSIVELY MADE IN THE PATRIARCHAL, JEWISH, AND CHRISTIAN DISPENSATIONS AND IN THE MESSIANIC KINGDOM / Andrews, Samuel James – (Includes appendix on higher criticism, notes for revision and analysis of each chapter at the end of the book) – 2nd rev enl ed. New York: Putnam's, 1901 – 1mf – 9 – 0-8370-2103-0 – 1985-0103 – us A.T.L.A. [220]

GOD'S REVIVALIST – 1890-1974 (complete) – 35r – 1 – ATLA S0295 – us A.T.L.A. [073]

GOD'S TRUTH AND MAN'S INFIDELITY, OR, FAITH AND SIGHT CONTRASTED: A BOOK FOR "THOSE LAST DAYS" / Foote, LeRoy – s.l.: s.n., 1881 (Ottawa: A. Woodburn). 03144. (Pre-1900 Canadiana) – 9 – cn C.I.H.M. [971]

GOD'S TWO BOOKS : OR, NATURE AND THE BIBLE HAVE ONE AUTHOR / Balfour, Thomas Alexander Goldie – London: James Nisbet, 1861 – 1mf – 9 – 0-8370-2166-9 – 1985-0166 – us A.T.L.A. [210]

GOD'S WAY OF HOLINESS / Bonar, Horatius – New York: Robert Carter, 1867. 1 fiche – 9 – us A.T.L.A. [240]

GOD'S WHITE THRONE : A RATIONAL EVANGELICAL THEODICY / Palmer, Byron – 3rd ed. Cincinnati: Jennings and Graham, 1904 – 1mf – 9 – 0-8370-3973-8 – 1985-1973 – us A.T.L.A. [210]

GOD'S WITNESS IN PROPHECY AND HISTORY : BIBLE STUDIES ON THE HISTORICAL FULFILMENTS OF JACOB'S PROPHETIC BLESSINGS ON THE TWELVE TRIBES CONTAINED IN GENESIS 49: WITH A SUPPLEMENTARY ENQUIRY INTO THE HISTORY OF THE LOST TRIBES / Bellett, John Crosthwaite – (Includes bibliographical references and index and appendixes containing different versions of genesis 49 and Deuteronomy 33, 6-25) – London: J Masters, 1884 – 1mf – 9 – 0-8370-6162-8 – 1986-0162 – us A.T.L.A. [220]

GOD'S WITNESS TO HIS OWN WORD / Bryan, R G – London: Skeffington, 1892 – 1mf – 9 – 0-8370-2502-8 – 1985-0502 – us A.T.L.A. [220]

GOD'S WORD : MAN'S LIGHT AND GUIDE: A COURSE OF LECTURES / Taylor, William M et al – New York: American Tract Society, c1877 – 1mf – 9 – 0-8370-3316-0 – 1985-1316 – us A.T.L.A. [220]

GOD'S WORD IN MAN'S LANGUAGE / Nida, E – New York – 3mf – 8 – ne Slangenburg [210]

GOD'S WORD WRITTEN : THE DOCTRINE OF THE INSPIRATION OF HOLY SCRIPTURE / Garbett, Edward – Boston: American Tract Society, [1868] – 1mf – 9 – 0-8370-3230-X – 1985-1230 – us A.T.L.A. [220]

GOD'S WORLD AND OTHER SERMONS / Mills, Benjamin Fay – 1894 – 9 – us A.T.L.A. [240]

DE GODSDIENST UIT...EN DE GELOOFSVOORSTELLING UIT DICHTENDE VERBEELDING GEBOREN? / Cannegieter, Tjeerd – Leiden: E.J. Brill, 1890. 1 fiche – 9 – us A.T.L.A. [240]

DE GODSLEER DER MIDDELEEUWSCHE JODEN / Muller, P J – Groningen: J.B. Wolters, 1898. 1 fiche – 9 – us A.T.L.A. [240]

DE GODSPRAKEN VAN AMOS / Gunning, J H – Leiden: E.J. Brill, 1885 – 9 – us A.T.L.A. [240]

EEN GODTLIJCKE ANTWOORDT VNDE CORT ONDERWIJS / Joris, David – BME-376 1 – 9 – ne IDC [240]

HET GODTVRUCHTICH HERTE : DEN KONINGHLIJCKEN THROON VAN JESYS DEN VREEDSAMIGHEN SALOMON / Luzvic, S – (78 (6th emblem) partly destroyed) – 2nd issue of 1st ed. Antwerpen, 1627 – 3mf – 9 – O-3118/1 – ne IDC [760]

Godwin, Benjamin *see*
- THE JUBILEE MEMORIAL OF HORTON COLLEGE, BRADFORD, CONTAINING THE SERMON PREACHED AT THE JUBILEE SERVICE, 2 AUG 1854; ALSO
- LECTURES ON THE ATHEISTIC CONTROVERSY, 1836, DELIVERED AT SION CHAPEL, BRADFORD, YORKSHIRE

Godwin, John Henry *see*
- CHRISTIAN FAITH
- THE EPISTLE OF THE APOSTLE PAUL TO ROMANS

Godwin, Parke *see*
- THE HISTORY OF FRANCE
- TALES FROM THE GERMAN OF HEINRICH ZSCHOKKE

Godwin, William *see*
- THE ENQUIRER
- ESSAY ON SEPULCHRES
- FABLES ANCIENT AND MODERN
- FOUR EARLY PAMPHLETS, 1783-84
- LIVES OF THE NECROMANCERS...
- LIVES OF THE NECROMANCERS: OR, AN ACCOUNT OF THE MOST EMINENT PERSONS IN SUCCESSIVE AGES WHO HAVE CLAIMED...OR TO WHOM HAS BEEN IMPUTED...THE EXERCISE OF MAGICAL POWER
- ST. LEON
- SKETCHES OF HISTORY
- THOUGHTS ON MAN, HIS NATURE, PRODUCTIONS, AND DISCOVERIES

Godwin-Austen, H H *see* LAND AND FRESHWATER MOLLUSCA OF INDIA

GODY : OCHERKI PI ATILI ETNE I BORBY / Davatts, Vladimir Khristianovich – Bielgrad: Russkai a tip., 1926 – 1 – CSUX88-B9150 – us Hoover Inst Photo [999]

GODY STRANSTVII / Chulkov, G I – Izd. "Federatsiia". M. 1930. BR-2038 2 – 8 – ne IDC [460]

Goebbels, Joseph *see*
- UN DISCURSO DEL DR. GOEBBELS, MINISTRO DE PROPAGANDA DE ALEMANIA
- THE TRUTH ABOUT SPAIN
- LA VERDAD SOBRE ESPANA
- DIE WAHRHEIT UEBER SPANIEN

Goebel, BM *see* THE EFFECTS OF SUPERVISED CARDIAC REHABILITATION ON SELECTED CORONARY ARTERY DISEASE RISK FACTORS FOLLOWING CORONARY ARTERY BYPASS GRAFT SURGERY

Goebel, H *see* DIE VOEGEL DES KREISES UMAN

Goebel, Julius *see* HOFFMANN VON FALLERSLEBENS "TEXANISCHE LIEDER"

Goebel, K von *see* WILHELM HOFMEISTER: THE WORKS AND LIFE OF A NINETEENTH CENTURY BOTANIST

Goebel, Kaete *see* DIE QUELLEN UND DIE ENTSTEHUNGSZEIT VON THOMAS HEYWOOD'S "IRON AGE"

Goebel, Siegfried *see* DIE PARABELN JESU, METHODISCH AUSGELEGT

GOEBEL'S PROBATE REPORTS / Ohio. Supreme Court – Hamilton County. 1v. 1885-90 (all publ) – 4mf – 9 – $6.00 – LLMC 84-183 – us L.L.M.C. [340]

Goede, Arian de *see* OUD-NEDERLANDSCH PROCESRECHT

Goedeke *see* GEDICHTE

Goedeke, Karl *see*
- GEDICHTE
- GESCHAEFTSBRIEFE SCHILLER'S
- SCHILLERS SAEMMTLICHE SCHRIFTEN

Goedeke, Karl, 1814-87 *see* GOETHES LEBEN..

Goedings, Peter *see* DER MINERALSTOFFHAUSHALT IN VISCUM ALBUM L. (WEISSBEERIGE MISTEL)

Goehl, Bo *see* TROPICAL FEEDS

Goehler, Georg *see* CORNELIUS FREUNDT

GOEHNER NEWS – Goehner, NE. -w. Sept 1899-Apr 1900. Scattered issues missing – 1 – us NE Hist [071]

Goehringer, Diane M *see* A STUDY OF THE PERCEIVED EFFECTS OF THE REPEAL OF THE PENNSYLVANIA INTERSCHOLASTIC ATHLETIC ASSOCIATION CONSTITUTIONAL BYLAW ARTICLE 11, SECTION 2

Goei, Bian Sioe (The) *see* OBAT-OBAT JANG HARUS DIKETAHUI

Goeje, M J de *see* HISTORIA KHALIFATUS OMARI 2, JAZIDI 2 ET HISCHAMI

Goekalp, Ziya *see* TUERK MEDENIYET TARIHI

Goeken, Walther *see* HERDER ALS DEUTSCHER

Goel, N S et al *see* REMOTE SENSING REVIEWS

Goeldlin de Tiefenau, E *see* L'EXISTENCE A L'ETRANGER DES SOCIETES RUSSES

Goepp, Edouard *see* LES GRANDS HOMMES DE LA FRANCE: HOMMES DE GUERRE (CINQUIEME SERIE): MONTCALM

Goeppert, H R *see*
- DIE GATTUNGEN DER FOSSILEN PFLANZEN
- DIE TERTIAERFLORA AUF DER INSEL JAVA,...

Goeranzon, Bop *see* PRACTICAL INTELLECT

Goeree, W *see* INLEYDINGE TOT DE ALGEMEENE TEYKENKONST
Goeres, Joern *see*
- ABRISS DER DEUTSCHEN LITERATURGESCHICHTE IN TABELLEN
Goerg, O *see* ECHANGES, RESEAUX, MARCHES: L'IMPACT COLONIAL EN GUINEE
Goering, Reinhard *see*
- SEESCHLACHT
- DIE SUEDPOLEXPEDITION DES KAPITAENS SCOTT
Goeringer, H *see* VERGLEICH ZWISCHEN DEM ENGLISCHEN UND DEUTSCHEN WECHSELRECHT...1927
GOERRES / Sepp, Johann Nepomuk – Berlin: E Hofmann, 1896 – 1r – 1 – us U.W. Library [920]
Goerres, Guido *see* DER HEILIGE STUHL
Goerres, J *see* ATHANASIUS
Goerres, Joseph *see*
- CHARAKTERISTIKEN UND KRITIKEN VON JOSEPH GOERRES
- CHARAKTERISTIKEN UND KRITIKEN VON JOSEPH GOERRES AUS DEN JAHREN 1804 UND 1805
- DER DOM VON KOELN UND DAS MUENSTER VON STRASSBURG
- EUROPA UND DIE REVOLUTION
- TEUTSCHLAND UND DIE REVOLUTION
- DIE TRIARIER
Goerres, Joseph von *see* EUROPA UND DIE REVOLUTION
GOERRES UND SEIN "ROTHES BLATT" / Nothardt, Fritz – (Includes bibliographical references) – [s.l.: s.n.] 1932 – 1r – 1 – us U.W. Library [943]
Goes, Albrecht *see*
- MOERIKE
- UEBER DAS GESPRAECH
Goes, D de *see* CHRONICA DO SERENISSIMO SENHOR REI D. MANOEL...
Goesbriand, Louis de *see* VOYAGE EN TERRE SAINTE
Goessell, I C *see* DE LEGATO PACIS GRATIA...
Goeßl, Manfred M *see* DIE WIRTSCHAFTLICHKEIT VON ERSATZINVESTITIONEN. INVESTITIONSRECHNUNG IN DER BETRIEBSWIRTSCHAFTLICHEN PRAXIS
GOETEBORGS MARKNADSBERAETTELSE – Goeteborg, 1880-84, 1886-1913 – 9 – sw Kungliga [072]
GOETEBORGS NYHETER – Goeteborg, 1884-85 – 9 – sw Kungliga [072]
Goeters, Wilhelm *see*
- DIE VORBEREITUNG DES PIETISMUS
- DIE VORBEREITUNG DES PIETISMUS IN DER REFORMIERTER KIRCHE DER NIEDERLAENDE
GOETHE / Charpentier, John – (Includes bibliographical references) – Paris: J Tallandier, 1943 – 1r – 1 – us U.W. Library [920]
GOETHE : DISCORSI PRONUNCIATI A WEIMAR E A ROMA 24 MARZO E 2 APRILE 1932-X / Farinelli, Arturo – Roma: Reale Accademia d'Italia, 1933 – 1r – 1 – us U.W. Library [430]
GOETHE : DREI REDEN / Schweitzer, Albert – Muenchen: Biederstein, 1949 – 1r – 1 – us U.W. Library [430]
GOETHE : ENSAYOS POETICOS / Gonzalez Serrano, Urbano – Madrid: Lib. Int. de Fdez. Villegary Cia s.a. 3rd ed – 9 – sp Bibl Santa Ana [430]
GOETHE : GEDENKREDE GEHALTEN BEI DER FEIER DER 100. WIEDERKEHR SEINES TODESTAGES IN SEINER VATERSTADT FRANKFURT A.M. AM 22. MAERZ 1932 / Schweitzer, Albert – Muenchen: C H Beck, 1933 – 1r – 1 – us U.W. Library [430]
GOETHE / Hauptmann, Gerhart – New York: Columbia University Press, 1932 – 1r – 1 – us U.W. Library [430]
GOETHE / Heinemann, Karl – Leipzig: E A Seemann, 1895 – 1r – 1 – us U.W. Library [430]
GOETHE / Herford, Charles Harold – London: T C & E C Jack, [19–?] – 1r – 1 – us U.W. Library [430]
GOETHE : LEBEN, GEDANKEN, BILDNISSE / Langewiesche, Wilhelm & Langewiesche, Karl Robert – Koenigstein im Taunus: Verlag der eiserne Hammer, c1932 – 1r – 1 – us U.W. Library [430]
GOETHE : EIN PROFIL / Paasche, Fredrik – Stuttgart: Greiner und Pfeiffer, 1922 – 1r – 1 – us U.W. Library [430]
GOETHE : DER ROMAN VON SEINER ERWECKUNG / Trentini, Albert – Muenchen: G D W Callwey, 1923 – 1r – 1 – us U.W. Library [430]
GOETHE : SKIZZEN ZU DES DICHTERS LEBEN UND WERKEN / Graf, Hans Gerhard – (Includes bibliographical references) – Leipzig: H Haessel, 1924 – 1r – 1 – us U.W. Library [430]
GOETHE : VIER REDEN / Schweitzer, Albert – 3. erw. Aufl. Muenchen: C H Beck, 1950 – 1 – us U.W. Library [430]
GOETHE / Wolff, Max Josef – Leipzig: B G Teubner, 1921 – 1r – 1 – us U.W. Library [430]
GOETHE ALS BILDENDER KUENSTLER : MIT 60 LICHTDRUCKBILDERN / Federmann, Arnold – (Includes bibliographical references) – Stuttgart: J G Cotta, 1932 – 1r – 1 – us U.W. Library [700]
GOETHE ALS ERBE SEINER AHNEN / Bradish, Joseph Arno von – Berlin, New York: B Westermann, 1933 – 1 – us U.W. Library [430]
GOETHE ALS ERZIEHER NIETZSCHES / Saleski, Maria Agnes – (Includes bibliographical references) – Leipzig: Schwarzenberg & Schumann, [1929] – 1r – 1 – us U.W. Library [943]
GOETHE ALS FREIMAURER / Deile, Gotthold – (Includes bibliographical references) – Berlin: E S Mittler, 1908 – 1r – 1 – us U.W. Library [430]
GOETHE ALS GESCHICHTSPHILOSOPH UND DIE GESCHICHTSPHILOSOPHISCHE BEWEGUNG SEINER ZEIT / Menke-Glueckert, Emil – Leipzig: R Voigtlaender, 1907 – 1r – 1 – us U.W. Library [430]
GOETHE ALS MENSCH UND DEUTSCHER / ed by Heyd, Guenther – Potsdam: Ruetten & Loening, c1937 – 1r – 1 – us U.W. Library [920]
GOETHE ALS NATURFORSCHER / Strunz, Franz – Wien: Verlag des Volkbildungshauses Wiener Urania, 1917 – 1r – 1 – us U.W. Library [500]
GOETHE ALS NATURFORSCHER UND HERR DU BOIS-REYMOND ALS SEIN KRITIKER : EINE ANTIKRITIK / Kalischer, Salomon – Berlin: G Hempel, 1883 – 1r – 1 – us U.W. Library [430]
GOETHE ALS NATURFORSCHER UND IN BESONDERER BEZIEHUNG AUF SCHILLER / Virchow, Rudolf – Berlin, 1861 – 9 – DM48.00 – 3-89349-260-7 – gw Hänsel [500]
GOETHE ALS PAEDAGOG : VORTRAG GEHALTEN IM BRUENNER LEHRERVEREINE AM 22. MAERZ 1880 – Leipzig: H Pfeil, 1880 – 1r – 1 – us U.W. Library [370]
GOETHE ALS PATIENT / Veil, Wolfgang Heinrich – (Includes bibliographical references) – Jena: G Fischer, 1939 – 1r – 1 – us U.W. Library [920]
GOETHE ALS RAETSELDICHTER : MIT EINEM BISHER UNBEKANNTEN GOETHEBILD VON JAGEMANN / Biedermann, Flodoard, Freiherr von – Berlin: H Berthold AG, Abt. Privatdrucke, 1924 – 1 – us U.W. Library [430]
GOETHE ALS RECHTSANWALT / Wieruszowski, Alfred – (Includes bibliographical references) – Coeln a. Rhein: P Neubner, [1909?] – 1r – 1 – us U.W. Library [340]
GOETHE ALS RELIGIOESER CHARAKTER / Loew, Wilhelm – Muenchen: Ch Kaiser, 1924 – 1r – 1 – us U.W. Library [430]
GOETHE ALS REPRAESENTANT DES BUERGERLICHEN ZEITALTERS : REDE ZUM 100. TODESTAG GOETHES GEHALTEN AM 18. MAERZ 1932 IN DER PREUSSISCHEN AKADEMIE DER KUENSTE ZU BERLIN / Mann, Thomas – Berlin: S Fischer, c1932 – 1r – 1 – us U.W. Library [430]
GOETHE ALS SEELENFORSCHER / Klages, Ludwig – Leipzig: Verlag von J A Barth, 1932 – 1r – 1 – us U.W. Library [430]
GOETHE ALS VATER EINER NEUEN AESTHETIK / Steiner, Rudolf – Duesseldorf: Deibele & Teubig, 1948 – 1r – 1 – us U.W. Library [110]
GOETHE ALS ZEICHNER : EIN BEITRAG ZUM BILDE SEINER PERSOENLICHKEIT / Drost, Willi – (Includes bibliographical references) – 2. verm. Aufl. Potsdam: Akademische Verlagsgesellschaft Athenaion, [1938] – 1r – 1 – us U.W. Library [430]
GOETHE AND AUGUST VON KOETZEBUE / Stenger, Gerhard – (Includes bibliographical references) – Breslau: F Hirt, 1910 – 1 – us U.W. Library [430]
GOETHE AND DEMOCRACY : ADDRESS DELIVERED IN THE COOLIDGE AUDITORIUM IN THE LIBRARY OF CONGRESS ON MAY 2, 1949 / Mann, Thomas – Washington, D.C.: [Library of Congress], 1950 – 1r – 1 – us U.W. Library [430]
GOETHE AND SCHILLER'S XENIONS / ed by Carus, Paul – (In English/German) – Chicago: Open Court, 1896 – 1r – 1 – us U.W. Library [430]
GOETHE AND THE TWENTIETH CENTURY / Robertson, John George – (Includes index) – Cambridge [Engl.]: The University Press; New York: G P Putnam, 1912 – 1r – 1 – us U.W. Library [430]
THE GOETHE CENTENARY AT THE UNIVERSITY OF WISCONSIN : A MEMORIAL VOLUME OF ADDRESSES AND SOME OTHER CONTRIBUTIONS / ed by Hohlfeld, A R – Madison, Wis.: University of Wisconsin, 1932 – 1r – 1 – us U.W. Library [430]
GOETHE DER BILDNER / Thode, Henry – Heidelberg: C Winter, 1906 – 1r – 1 – us U.W. Library [430]
GOETHE DER GROSSE HUMANIST / Fischer, Ernst – Wien: Globus-Verlag, 1949 – 1r – 1 – us U.W. Library [430]
GOETHE ET LA LITTERATURE FRANCAISE / Caumont, Armand – Frankfurt a.M.: Mahlau & Waldschmidt, 1885 – 1r – 1 – us U.W. Library [430]
GOETHE ET SCHILLER : LA LITTERATURE ALLEMANDE A WEIMAR, LA JEUNESSE DE SCHILLER, L'UNION DE GOETHE ET DE SCHILLER, LA VIEILLESSE DE GOETHE / Bossert, Adolphe – (Includes bibliographical references) – 5 rev ed. Paris: Hachette, 1903 – 1r – 1 – us U.W. Library [430]
GOETHE IM GESPRAECH / ed by Deibel, Franz & Gundelfinger, Friedrich – (Includes bibliographical references) – Leipzig: Insel-Verlag, 1906 – 1r – 1 – us U.W. Library [920]
GOETHE IN DORNBURG / Sternaux, Ludwig Friedrich – Berlin: E Runge, 1919 – 1r – 1 – us U.W. Library [430]
GOETHE IN FRANKFURT AM MAIN 1797 : AKTENSTUECKE UND DARSTELLUNG / Geiger, Ludwig – Frankfurt a.M.: Ruetten & Loening, 1899 – 1r – 1 – us U.W. Library [430]
GOETHE IN HEUTIGER SICHT / Gerathewohl, Fritz – (Includes bibliographical references (p. 51-52)) – Muenchen, Berlin: R Oldenbourg, 1942 – 1r – 1 – us U.W. Library [430]
GOETHE IN VERTRAULICHEN BRIEFEN SEINER ZEITGENOSSEN : AUCH EINE LEBENSGESCHICHTE / ed by Bode, Wilhelm – (Includes bibliographical references) – Berlin: E S Mittler, 1921 – 1r – 1 – us U.W. Library [920]
GOETHE IN ZUERICH / Zollinger, Friedrich – Zuerich: Atlantis-Verlag, 1932 – 1r – 1 – us U.W. Library [920]
Goethe, Johann Wolfgang von *see*
- FAUST
- FAUST, A TRAGEDY
- FAUST, FIRST PART
- GOETHE, SCHILLER: UEBER DAS THEATER; EINE AUSWAHL AUS IHREN SCHRIFTEN
- GOETHE UND UVAROV UND IHR BRIEFWECHSEL
- GOETHE-BRIEFE
- GOETHES BRIEFE
- GOETHES FAUST
- GOETHES ROEMISCHE ELEGIEN
- GOETZ VON BERLICHINGEN MIT DER EISERNEN HAND
- HERMANN AND DOROTHEA
- HERMANN UND DOROTHEA
- ITALIENISCHE REISE
- JURISTISCHE ABHANDLUNG UEBER DIE FLOEHE
- MIT GOETHE DURCH DIE SCHWEIZ
- DAS TAGEBUCH (1810)
- WEST-OESTLICHER DIVAN
- WILHELM MEISTERS THEATRALISCHE SENDUNG
- WILHELM MEISTERS WANDERJAHRE
- ZUR MORPHOLOGIE
GOETHE, KARL AUGUST UND OTTOKAR LORENZ : EIN DENKMAL / Duentzer, Heinrich – Dresden: Dresdener Verlagsanstalt, 1895 – 1r – 1 – us U.W. Library [430]
GOETHE OG WERTHER / Enault, Louis – (Includes bibliographical references) – Kjøbenhavn: V Pontoppidan, 1889 – 1r – 1 – us U.W. Library [430]
GOETHE, SCHILLER: UEBER DAS THEATER; EINE AUSWAHL AUS IHREN SCHRIFTEN / Goethe, Johann Wolfgang von; ed by Eggebrecht, Axel – Berlin: B. Henschel, 1949. vii,495p – 1 – us U.W. Library [430]
GOETHE, UN HOMME FACE A LA VIE : ESSAI DE BIOGRAPHIE INTERIEURE / Fuchs, Albert – (Includes bibliographical references) – Paris: Aubier, 1946 – 1r – 1 – us U.W. Library [920]
GOETHE UND ARISTOTELES / Petersen, Peter – (Includes bibliographical references) – Braunschweig: G Westermann, 1914 – 1r – 1 – us U.W. Library [410]
GOETHE UND AUGUST VON KOTZEBUE / Stenger, Gerhard – (Includes bibliographical references) – Breslau: F Hirt, 1910 – 1 – us U.W. Library [430]
GOETHE UND BEETHOVEN / Engelsmann, Walter – Augsburg: B Filser, c1931 – 1r – 1 – us U.W. Library [430]
GOETHE UND CHARLOTTE V. STEIN / Hoefer, Edmund – 2. Aufl. Leipzig: Xenien-Verlag, 1911 – 1r – 1 – us U.W. Library [430]
GOETHE UND CHRISTENTUM : DIE RELIGION UND ETHIK GOETHES UND DER HAUPTVERTRETER DES CHRISTENTUMS / Fliedner, Wilhelm – Gotha: L Klotz, 1930 – 1r – 1 – us U.W. Library [430]
GOETHE UND DAS CHRISTENTUM / Kahle, Wilhelm – Duelmen i.Westf.: A Laumann, 1949 – 1r – 1 – us U.W. Library [430]
GOETHE UND DAS CLASSISCHE ALTERTHUM : DIE EINWIRKUNG DER ANTIKE AUF GOETHES DICHTUNGEN IM ZUSAMMENHANGE MIT DEM LEBENSGANGS DES DICHTERS / Thalmayr, Franz – (Includes bibliographical references) – Leipzig: G Fock, 1897 – 1r – 1 – us U.W. Library [430]
GOETHE UND DAS WEIMARER HOFTHEATER : MIT VIELEN BILDERN NACH ALTEN VORLAGEN / Hoeffner, Johannes – Weimar: G Kiepenheuer, 1913 – 1r – 1 – us U.W. Library [430]
GOETHE UND DER KATHOLIZISMUS / Hammerschmidt, Ferdinand – Breslau: O Borgmeyer, [1932] – 1r – 1 – us U.W. Library [430]
GOETHE UND DER OKKULTISMUS / Seiling, Max – Leipzig: O Mutze, [1901?] – 1r – 1 – us U.W. Library [130]
GOETHE UND DER ORIENT / Krueger-Westend, Herman – Weimar: H Boehlau, 1903 – 1r – 1 – us U.W. Library [430]
GOETHE UND DIE BILDENDE KUNST : FESTREDE, GEHALTEN IN DER OEFFENTLICHEN SITZUNG DER BAYERISCHEN AKADEMIE DER WISSENSCHAFTEN ZUR FEIER DES 173. STIFTUNGSTAGES AM 11. MAI 1932 / Pinder, Wilhelm – Muenchen: Verlag der Bayerischen Akademie der Wissenschaften: C H Beck, 1933 – 1r – 1 – us U.W. Library [700]
GOETHE UND DIE BILDENDE KUNST / Stelzer, Otto – Braunschweig: Vieweg, 1949 – 1r – 1 – us U.W. Library [700]
GOETHE UND DIE DESCENDENZLEHRE / Wasielewski, Waldemar von – (Includes bibliographical references) – Frankfurt a.M.: Ruetten & Loening, 1903 – 1r – 1 – us U.W. Library [920]
GOETHE UND DIE DEUTSCHE GEGENWART / Linden, Walther – Berlin: Bong, c1932 – 1r – 1 – us U.W. Library [430]
GOETHE UND DIE JUDEN / Teweles, Heinrich – (The "Register" includes brief biographical notices) – Hamburg: W Gente, 1925 – 1r – 1 – us U.W. Library [320]
GOETHE UND DIE MUSIK / Abert, Hermann – (Includes bibliographical references) – Stuttgart: J Engelhorn, 1922 – 1r – 1 – us U.W. Library [780]
GOETHE UND DIE NATURWISSENSCHAFTEN / Walden, Paul – Bremen: G A v Halem, c1933 – 1r – 1 – us U.W. Library [500]
GOETHE UND DIE PHYSIK : VORTRAG GEHALTEN IN DER MUENCHNER UNIVERSITAET AM 9. MAI 1923 / Wien, Wilhelm – (Includes bibliographical references) – Leipzig: J A Barth, 1923 – 1r – 1 – us U.W. Library [530]
GOETHE UND DIE SEINEN : QUELLENMAESSIGE DARSTELLUNGEN UEBER GOETHES HAUS / Geiger, Ludwig – (Includes bibliographical references) – Leipzig: R Voigtlaender, 1908 – 1r – 1 – us U.W. Library [430]

GOETHE UND DIE WERTHERZEIT : EIN VORTRAG / Knortz, Karl – Zuerich: Verlags-Magazin (J Schabelitz), 1885 – 1r – 1 – us U.W. Library [430]

GOETHE UND DIE WIRTSCHAFT / Dantz, Antonie – (Includes bibliographical references) – Borna-Leipzig: R Noske, 1935 – 1r – 1 – us U.W. Library [430]

GOETHE UND FRAU V. STEIN / Adler, Emma – Leipzig: Toeplitz & Deuticke, 1887 – 1r – 1 – us U.W. Library [430]

GOETHE UND GROSSBRITANNIEN / Vollrath, Wilhelm – (Includes bibliobraphical references) – Erlangen: Palm & Enke, 1932 – 1r – 1 – us U.W. Library [430]

GOETHE UND HEBBEL : EINE ANTITHESE: FESTVORTRAG ZUR DEZENNARFEIER DES WUERTTEMBERGISCHEN GOETHEBUNDES AM 22. NOVEMBER 1910 IM BUERGERMUSEUM ZU STUTTGART / Zinkernagel, Franz – Tuebingen: J C B Mohr, 1911 – 1r – 1 – us U.W. Library [430]

GOETHE UND HEINRICH LEOPOLD WAGNER : EIN WORT DER KRITIK AN UNSERE GOETHE-FORSCHER / Froitzheim, Johann – Strassburg: J H E Heitz (Heitz & Muendel), 1889 – 1r – 1 – us U.W. Library [430]

GOETHE UND KARL AUGUST : STUDIEN ZU GOETHES LEBEN / Duentzer, Heinrich – (Includes indexes) – 2. neubearb. und vollend. Aufl. Leipzig: Dyk, 1888 – 1r – 1 – us U.W. Library [430]

GOETHE UND KEIN ENDE / Du Bois-Reymond, Emil Heinrich – (Includes bibliographical references) – Leipzig: Veit, 1883 – 1r – 1 – us U.W. Library [430]

GOETHE UND LAVATER : ZEUGNISSE IHRER FREUNDSCHAFT – Zuerich: Rascher, 1918 – 1r – 1 – us U.W. Library [920]

GOETHE UND SCHOPENHAUER : EIN BEITRAG ZUR ENTWICKLUNGSGESCHICHTE DER SCHOPENHAUERSCHEN PHILOSOPHIE / Doell, Heinrich – Berlin: E Hofmann, 1904 – 1r – 1 – us U.W. Library [430]

GOETHE UND SEIN SOHN : WEIMARER ERLEBNISSE IN DEN JAHREN 1827-1831 / Holtei, Karl von – 1. Ausgabe in Auswahl nach Holteis Lebenserinnerungen "Vierzig Jahre". Hamburg: Vera-Verlag, c1924 – 1r – 1 – us U.W. Library [430]

GOETHE UND SEINE ELTERN / Krueger-Westend, Herman – Weimar: H Boehlau, 1904 – 1r – 1 – us U.W. Library [430]

GOETHE UND SEINE FREUNDE IM BRIEFWECHSEL / ed by Meyer, Richard M – Berlin: G Bondi, 1909-11 – 1r – 1 – us U.W. Library [920]

GOETHE UND SEINE ZEIT / Alt, Karl Hermann – (Includes bibliographical references) – Leipzig: Quelle & Meyer, 1911 – 1r – 1 – us U.W. Library [430]

GOETHE UND TOLSTOI / Mann, Thomas – Aachen: Verlag "Die Kuppel", 1923 – 1r – 1 – us U.W. Library [430]

GOETHE UND UVAROV UND IHR BRIEFWECHSEL / Goethe, Johann Wolfgang von – (Includes bibliographical references) – St. Petersburg: H Schmitzdorff, 1888 – 1r – 1 – us U.W. Library [920]

GOETHE UND WEIMAR : MIT EINEM GOETHEBILDNIS VON KARL BAUER / Schrumpf, Ernst – Muenchen: C H Beck, 1912 – 1r – 1 – us U.W. Library [430]

GOETHE VON SCHILLER IN BRIEFEN / Voss, Heinrich; ed by Graf, Hans Gerhard – (Includes bibliographical references (p.[126]) – Leipzig: Philipp Reclam, [1895] – 1r – 1 – us U.W. Library [430]

GOETHE, WEIMAR UND JENA IM JAHRE 1806 : NACH GOETHES PRIVATACTEN: AM FUENFZIGJAEHRIGEN TODESTAGE GOETHES / Keil, Robert; ed by Keil, Richard & Keil, Robert – (Includes bibliographical references) – Leipzig: E Schloemp, 1882 – 1r – 1 – us U.W. Library [430]

DIE GOETHE-BILDNISSE : BIOGRAPHISCH-KUNSTGESCHICHTLICH DARGESTELLT; MIT 78 HOLZSCHNITTEN, 8 RADIERUNGEN UND 2 HELIOGRAVUREN / Rollett, Hermann – (Includes bibliographical references) – Wien: W Braumueller, 1883 – 1 – us U.W. Library [760]

GOETHE-BRIEFE : MIT EINLEITUNGEN UND ERLAEUTERUNGEN / Goethe, Johann Wolfgang von; ed by Stein, Philipp – (Includes bibliographical references) – Berlin: O Elsner, 1902-05 – 2r – 1 – us U.W. Library [920]

GOETHE-FESTWOCHE 1946 IN BREMEN : VERANSTALTET VON DER BREMER ORTSVEREINIGUNG DER GOETHE-GESELLSCHAFT IN WEIMAR VOM 25. BIS 31. AUGUST 1946 – Bremen: F Truejen, 1947 – 1r – 1 – us U.W. Library [430]

GOETHE-HANDBUCH – 3v. Stuttgart: J.B. Metzler, 1916-18. 1 reel. 1221 – 1 – us U.W. Library [430]

DAS GOETHEHAUS AM FRAUENPLAN : DIE GESCHICHTE DES HAUSES VON DER ERBAUUNG BIS ZU GOETHES ZEIT / Weichberger, Alexander – (Includes bibliographical references) – Weimar: H Boehlau, 1932 – 1r – 1 – us U.W. Library [430]

GOETHE-PROBLEME / Wukadinovic, Spiridion – (Includes bibliographical references) – Halle (Saale): M Niemeyer, 1926 – 1r – 1 – us U.W. Library [430]

GOETHES BEITRAEGE ZU DEN FRANKFURTER GELEHRTEN ANZEIGEN VON 1772 : ZUGLEICH BEITRAG ZUR KENNTNIS DER SPRACHE DES JUNGEN GOETHE / Modick, Otto – (Includes bibliographical references (p.[126])) – Borna-Leipzig: R Noske, 1913 – 1r – 1 – us U.W. Library [430]

GOETHES BRIEFE / Goethe, Johann Wolfgang von; ed by Hellen, Eduard von der – (Includes bibliographical references) – Stuttgart: J G Cotta, [1901-13] – 1r – 1 – us U.W. Library [920]

GOETHE'S BRIEFE AN CHARLOTTE VON STEIN / ed by Borcherdt, Hans Heinrich – Berlin: Deutsche bibliothek, [19] – 1r – 1 – us U.W. Library [920]

GOETHE'S BRIEFE AN CHARLOTTE VON STEIN / ed by Fraenkel, Jonas – Jena: E Diederichs, 1908 – 1r – 1 – us U.W. Library [920]

GOETHES BRIEFE AN E. TH. LANGER / ed by Zimmermann, Paul – (Includes bibliographical references) – Wolfenbuettel: J Zwissler, 1922 – 1r – 1 – us U.W. Library [920]

GOETHES BRIEFE AN FRAU VON STEIN / ed by Schoell, Adolf & Wahle, Julius – Frankfurt a.M.: Ruetten & Loening, 1899 – 1r – 1 – us U.W. Library [920]

GOETHES BRIEFWECHSEL MIT ANTONIE BRENTANO 1814-1821 / ed by Jung, Rudolf – Weimar: H Boehlaus Nachf., 1896 – 1r – 1 – us U.W. Library [920]

GOETHE'S BRIEFWECHSEL MIT EINEM KINDE : SEINEM DENKMAL / ed by Grimm, Herman Friedrich – 4. Aufl. Berlin: W Hertz, 1890 – 1r – 1 – us U.W. Library [920]

GOETHES BRIEFWECHSEL MIT FRIEDRICH ROCHLITZ / ed by Biedermann, Woldemar Freiherr von – (Includes bibliographical references) – Leipzig: F W v Biedermann, 1887 – 1r – 1 – us U.W. Library [920]

GOETHES BRIEFWECHSEL MIT SEINER FRAU / ed by Graf, Hans Gerhard – Frankfurt a.M.: Ruetten & Loening, 1916 – 1r – 1 – us U.W. Library [920]

GOETHES BRIEFWECHSEL MIT THOMAS CARLYLE / ed by Hecht, Georg – (Includes the English text of Carlyle's letters to Goethe) – Dachau: Einhorn-Verlag, [1913] – 1 – us U.W. Library [920]

GOETHES BUEHNENBEARBEITUNG VON "ROMEO UND JULIA" / Wendling, Emil – (Includes bibliographical references) – Zabern: [s.n.], 1907 – 1 – 1 – us U.W. Library [790]

GOETHES CHARAKTER : EINE SEELENSCHILDERUNG / Saitschick, Robert – Stuttgart: F Frommann (E Hauff), 1898 – 1r – 1 – us U.W. Library [430]

GOETHE'S DEUTSCHE GESINNUNG : EIN BEITRAG ZUR GESCHICHTE SEINER ENTWICKLUNG / Winter, Friedrich Gotthard – (Includes bibliographical references) – [S.l.: s.n.], 1880 Leipzig: Druck der Rossberg'schen Buchdruckerei – 1r – 1 – us U.W. Library [430]

GOETHES DEUTSCHE SENDUNG : EINE FESTREDE / Korff, Hermann August – Leipzig: J J Weber, 1932 – 1r – 1 – us U.W. Library [430]

GOETHES EHE / Hofer, Klara – 1.-3. Aufl. Stuttgart, Berlin: J G Cotta, 1920 – 1r – 1 – us U.W. Library [920]

GOETHES EINFLUSS AUF GEORGE MEREDITH / Wilcox, Richard – Frankfurt a.M., 1976 – 3mf – DM76.00 – 3-89349-941-5 – gw Hänsel [420]

GOETHES EINFLUSS AUF NOVALIS HEINRICH VON OFTERDINGEN / Woltereck, Kaete A – (Includes bibliographical references) – Weida i.Th.: Thomas & Hubert, 1914 – 1 – us U.W. Library [430]

GOETHE'S EINFLUSS AUF UHLAND / Sintenis, Franz – (Includes bibliographical references) – Dorpat: C Mattiesen, 1871 – 1r – 1 – us U.W. Library [430]

GOETHES ETHISCHE ANSICHTEN : EIN BEITRAG ZUR GESCHICHTE DER PHILOSOPHIE UNSERER DICHTERHEROEN / Melzer, Ernst – (Includes bibliographical references) – Neisse: J Graveur, 1890 – 1r – 1 – us U.W. Library [430]

GOETHES FAUST / Goethe, Johann Wolfgang von; ed by Petsch, Robert – (Includes bibliographical references) – 2. Ausg. Leipzig: Bibliographisches Institut, [1925?] – 1 – us U.W. Library [820]

GOETHES FAUST UND DIE BILDENDE KUNST / Storck, Willy F – (Includes bibliographical references) – Leipzig: Xenien-Verlag, 1912 – 1r – 1 – us U.W. Library [430]

GOETHES GESCHICHTLICHER SINN / Tellenbach, Gerd – (Includes bibliographical references) – [Freiburg i.B.]: Selbstverlag der Universitaet, 1949 – 1r – 1 – us U.W. Library [430]

GOETHES GESUNDHEITSPFLEGE : ESSEN UND TRINKEN – ZWEI KAPITEL AUS "GOETHES LEBENSKUNST" / Bode, Wilhelm – Berlin: E S Mittler, 1913 – 1r – 1 – us U.W. Library [920]

GOETHES INTUITION / Emrich, Hermann – Tuebingen: J C B Mohr, 1928 – 1r – 1 – us U.W. Library [430]

GOETHES LAUFBAHN ALS SCHRIFTSTELLER / Mann, Thomas – Muenchen: R Oldenbourg, c1933 – 1r – 1 – us U.W. Library [430]

GOETHES LEBEN / Bode, Wilhelm – Berlin: E S Mittler, 1920-1927 – 2r – 1 – us U.W. Library [430]

GOETHES LEBEN : EINE KRANKENGESCHICHTE / Lorenz, Friedrich – (Includes bibliographical references) – Jena: G Neuenhahn, 1938 – 1 – us U.W. Library [920]

GOETHES LEBEN.. / Goedeke, Karl, 1814-87 – Suppl. zu den Werken des Dichters. Stuttgart: J.G. Cotta, (1883). 187p. Illus. With: Laerdal og Borgund by J.A. Laberg. 1 reel. 1291 – 1 – us U.W. Library [430]

GOETHES LEBEN IM GARTEN AM STERN / Bode, Wilhelm – Berlin, 1917 – 4mf – DM90.00 – 3-8267-3015-1 – gw Hänsel [430]

GOETHES LEBEN IN SEINEN BRIEFEN / ed by Bab, Julius – Berlin: Deutsche Buch-Gemeinschaft, [1929-31] – 1r – 1 – us U.W. Library [920]

GOETHE'S LEBEN, LEISTEN UND LEIDEN : IN GOETHE'S BILDERSPRACHE / Schauffler, Theodor – (Includes index) – Heidelberg: C Winter, 1913 – 1r – 1 – us U.W. Library [430]

GOETHES LEIPZIGER KRANKHEIT UND "DON SASSAFRAS" / Hansen, Adolfph – (Includes bibliographical references) – Leipzig: J Woerner, 1911 – 1r – 1 – us U.W. Library [430]

GOETHE'S NATURWISSENSCHAFTLICHE CORRESPONDENZ : (1812-32) / ed by Bratranek, F T H – (Includes indexes) – Leipzig: F A Brockhaus, 1874-76 – 1r – 1 – us U.W. Library [920]

GOETHE'S PAEDAGOGIK : VORTRAG GEHALTEN ZUM BESTEN DER WILHELM-AUGUSTA-STIFTUNG FUER FRANKFURTER LEHRERKINDER AM 7. FEBRUAR 1881 / Eiselen, F – Frankfurt a.M.: M Diesterweg, 1881 – 1r – 1 – us U.W. Library [430]

GOETHES PAEDAGOGISCHE PROVINZ : EINE DEUTUNG VON GOETHES ERZIEHUNGSBILD / Nitschke, Otfried – (Includes bibliographical references (p. 80-84)) – Wuerzburg: K Triltsch, 1937 – 1r – 1 – us U.W. Library [430]

GOETHES PERSOENLICHKEIT : DREI REDEN DES KANZLERS FRIEDRICH V. MUELLER, GEHALTEN IN DEN JAHREN 1830 UND 1832 / Mueller, Friedrich von; ed by Bode, Wilhelm – Berlin: Mittler, 1901 – 1r – 1 – us U.W. Library [430]

GOETHES PROPYLAEEN / Boehlich, Ernst – Stuttgart: Metzler, 1915 – 1r – 1 – us U.W. Library [430]

GOETHES REIM / Wehnert, Bruno – Berlin: B Paul, 1899 – 1r – 1 – us U.W. Library [430]

GOETHES RELIGIOESE JUGENDENTWICKLUNG / Schubert, Hans von – Leipzig: Quelle & Meyer, 1925 – 1r – 1 – us U.W. Library [240]

GOETHES RELIGIOESES ERLEBEN IM ZUSAMMENHANG SEINER INTUITIV-ORGANISCHEN WELTANSCHAUUNG / Neubauer, Ernst – (Includes bibliographical references (p. 79-84)) – Tuebingen: J C B Mohr (P Siebeck), 1925 – 1r – 1 – us U.W. Library [430]

GOETHES ROEMISCHE ELEGIEN : NACH DER AELTESTEN REINSCHRIFT / Goethe, Johann Wolfgang von; ed by Leitzmann, Albert – Bonn: A Marcus und E Weber, 1912 – 1 – us U.W. Library [810]

GOETHES SCHOENE SEELE SUSANNA KATHARINA V. KLETTENBERG : EIN LEBENSBILD IM ANSCHLUSSE AN EINE SONDERAUSGABE DER BEKENNTNISSE EINER SCHOENEN SEELE / Dechent, Hermann – Gotha: F A Perthes, 1896 – 1r – 1 – us U.W. Library [920]

GOETHES "SELIGE SEHNSUCHT" : EIN GESPRAECH UM DIE MOEGLICHKEIT EINER CHRISTLICHEN DEUTUNG / Rang, Florens Christian & Rang, Bernhard – Freiburg: Herder, 1949 – 1r – 1 – us U.W. Library [430]

GOETHE'S SPRACHE UND DIE ANTIKE : STUDIEN ZUM EINFLUSS DER KLASSISCHEN SPRACHEN AUF GOETHE'S POETISCHEN STIL / Olbrich, Carl – Leipzig: F W v Biedermann, 1891 – 1r – 1 – us U.W. Library [430]

GOETHES SPRACHE UND STIL IM ALTER / Knauth, Paul – (Includes bibliographical references and index) – Leipzig: E Avenarius, 1898 – 1r – 1 – us U.W. Library [430]

GOETHE'S STELLUNG ZUM CHRISTENTHUM : EIN LITERARISCHER BEITRAG / Oosterzee, Johannes Jacobus van – (Includes bibliograhical references) – Bielefeld: Velhagen und Klasing, 1858 – 1r – 1 – us U.W. Library [210]

GOETHES STELLUNG ZUR FRANZOESISCHEN ROMANTIK / Wadepuhl, Walter – (Includes bibliographical references) – [S.l.: s.n.], 1924 – 1r – 1 – us U.W. Library [410]

GOETHE'S STELLUNG ZUR RELIGION / Filtsch, Eugen – Langensalza, 1879 – 98p – 9 – DM48.00 – 3-89349-116-3 – gw Hänsel [200]

GOETHES THEATER-ROMAN : FESTTAGSGRUSS AN KONRAD ZWIERINA / Seuffert, Bernhard – Graz: Leuschner und Lubensky, 1924 – 1r – 1 – us U.W. Library [430]

GOETHES TYPUSBEGRIFF / Spinner, Heinrich – (Includes bibliographical references) – Horgen-Zuerich: Verlag der Muenster-Presse, 1933 – 1r – 1 – us U.W. Library [500]

GOETHES URTEILE UEBER SHAKESPEARE AUS SEINER PERSOENLICHKEIT ERKLAERT / Eckert, Georg Heinrich – (Includes bibliographical references) – [S.l.: s.n.] Goettingen: Druck von L Hofer, 1918 – 1r – 1 – us U.W. Library [410]

GOETHES VATER : EINE STUDIE / Ewart, Felicie – Hamburg: L Voss, 1899 – 1r – 1 – us U.W. Library [920]

GOETHE'S VERHAELTNIS ZU DEN ORGANISCHEN NATURWISSENSCHAFTEN : VORTRAG GEHALTEN IM WISSENSCHAFTLICHEN VEREIN ZU BERLIN / Schmidt, Oscar – Berlin: W Hertz, 1853 – 1r – 1 – us U.W. Library [500]

GOETHES VERHAELTNIS ZU HANS SACHS : BEILAGE ZUM 30. JAHRESBERICHT DES HOHENZOLLERN-GYMNASIUMS ZU SCHWEDT A.O. / Cleve, Karl – Schwedt a.O.: F Freyhoff, 1911 – 1r – 1 – us U.W. Library [430]

GOETHES VERHAELTNIS ZU KLOPSTOCK : IHRE GEISTIGEN, LITTERARISCHEN UND PERSOENLICHEN BEZIEHUNGEN / Lyon, Otto – (Includes bibliographical references) – Leipzig: T Grieben (L Fernau), 1882 – 1r – 1 – us U.W. Library [430]

GOETHES VERMAECHTNIS AN AMERIKA : VORTRAG GEHALTEN IM DEUTSCHEN GESELLIG-WISSENSCHAFTLICHEN VEREIN VON NEW YORK AM 12. OKTOBER 1899 / Francke, Kuno – [S.l.: s.n.], 1899 – 1r – 1 – us U.W. Library [430]

GOETHES WEG ZUR HOEHE : NEUE BEARBEITUNG VON "GOETHES BESTEM RAT" / Bode, Wilhelm – Berlin: E S Mittler, 1912 – 1r – 1 – us U.W. Library [430]

GOETHES WELT- UND LEBENSANSCHAUUNG / Menzel, Alfred – Hamburg: Pfadweiser-Verlag, 1919 – 1r – 1 – us U.W. Library [430]

GOETHES WELT- UND LEBENSANSCHAUUNG / Ziegler, Theobald – Berlin: G Reimer, 1914 – 1r – 1 – us U.W. Library [140]
GOETHES WELTWENDE-SCHICKSAL : FESTVORTRAG ZUR FEIER DER 100. WIEDERKEHR VON GOETHES TODESTAG GEHALTEN IN DER AULA DER VEREINIGTEN FRIEDRICHS-UNIVERSITAET HALLE-WITTENBERG AM 18. FEBRUAR 1932 / Schneider, Ferdinand Josef – Halle (Saale): M Niemeyer, 1932 – 1r – 1 – us U.W. Library [430]
GOETHES "WERTHER" IM URTEIL DES 19. JAHRHUNDERTS : ROMANTIK BIS NATURALISMUS 1830-1880 / Bickelmann, Ingeborg – (Includes bibliographical references) – [S.l.: s.n.], 1937 Gelnhausen: Dissertationsdruckerei F W Kalbfleisch – 1r – 1 – us U.W. Library [430]
GOETHES 'WERTHER' IN DER NIEDERLAENDISCHEN LITERATUR : EIN BEITRAG ZUR VERGLEICHENDEN LITERATURGESCHICHTE / Menne, Karl Johannes Joseph – (Includes bibliographical references and index) – Leipzig: M Hesse, 1905 – 1 – us U.W. Library [410]
GOETHES WILHELM MEISTER UND DIE AESTHETISCHE DOCTRIN DER AELTEREN ROMANTIK / Prodnigg, Heinrich – Graz: Verlag der Steierm. Landes-Oberrealschule, 1891 – 1 – us U.W. Library [430]
DIE GOETHEZEIT IN DEUTSCHLAND : SIEBEN SKIZZEN / Herse, Wilhelm – Hannover: Wissenschaftliche Verlagsanstalt, 1949 – 1 – us U.W. Library [430]
GOETHEZEIT UND KATHOLIZISMUS IM WERK IDA HAHN-HAHNS : EIN BEITRAG ZUR GEISTESGESCHICHTE DES 19. JAHRHUNDERTS / Guntli, Lucie – Emsdetten, 1931 – 97p – 9 – DM48.00 – 3-89349-043-4 – gw Hänsel [430]
GOETTER, BILDER UND SYMBOLE NACH DEN TRAKTATEN UEBER FREMDEN DIENST / Blaufuss, H – (Aboda zara) in Mischna, Tosefta, Jerusalemer und babylonischen Talmud. 1910? BJ-32-59 1 – 9 – ne IDC [470]
DAS GOETTERDEKRET UEBER DAS ABATON / Junker, H – Wien, 1913. BNE-20,024/1 – 9 – ne IDC [390]
GOETTERNAMEN : VERSUCH EINER LEHRE VON DER RELIGIOESEN BEGRIFFSBILDUNG / Usener, Hermann – Bonn: F. Cohen, 1896 – 1mf – us A.T.L.A. [230]
DIE GOETTERWELT DER ALTEN DEUTSCHEN / Kaiser, W – Prag: Verlag des deutschen Vereines zur Verbreitung gemeinnuetziger Kenntnisse, 1880 – 1r – 1 – us U.W. Library [390]
GOETTI UND GOTTELI : BERNDEUTSCHE NOVELLE / Tavel, Rudolf von – 6. Aufl. Bern: A Francke, 1931 – 1 – us U.W. Library [830]
GOETTINGENSCHES WOCHENBLATT – (Cont by: Goettinger Tageblatt, jan 2, 1868) – Goettingen. jan 2-nov 4, 1870 (incomplete) – 1r – 1 – gw Mikrofilm [943]
GOETTINGER ANZEIGENBLAETTER – Goettingen. nov 15, 1931-feb 25, 1933 – 1r – 1 – gw Mikrofilm [072]
GOETTINGER ANZEIGER – (Cont by: Goettinger Freie Presse, oct 1, 1882. Goettinger Anzeiger, jan 1, 1891) – Goettingen. jan 1-jun 30, 1893 – 1r – 1 – gw Mikrofilm [943]
Goettinger Arbeitskreis *see* EIN OSTPREUSSISCHES PFARRERLEBEN
GOETTINGER BLICK – Goettingen. jan 15, 1969-92 – 20r – 1 – gw Mikrofilm [072]
GOETTINGER DEUTSCHER BOTE – Goettingen. jan 26, feb 6, aug 1-dec 31, 1907 – 1r – 1 – gw Mikrofilm [943]
GOETTINGER ECHO AM FREITAG – Goettingen. apr 10-oct 2, 1970 – 1r – 1 – gw Mikrofilm [072]
GOETTINGER FREIE PRESSE *see* GOETTINGER ANZEIGER
GOETTINGER FREIZEIT-MAGAZIN – Goettingen. jul 30, 1983-jun 12, 1991 – 4r – 1 – gw Mikrofilm [790]
GOETTINGER LEBEN – Goettingen. oct 1, 1925-jun 28, 1936 – 2r – 1 – gw Mikrofilm [072]
GOETTINGER TAGEBLATT – Goettingen. aug 6, 1889-1905. oct 27, 1949-75 – ca 8r a yr – 1 – gw Mikrofilm [072]
GOETTINGER TAGEBLATT *see* GOETTINGENSCHES WOCHENBLATT
GOETTINGER WOCHE – Goettingen. jun 28, 1985-oct 12, 1990 – 2r – 1 – gw Mikrofilm [072]
GOETTINGER ZEITUNG : BEILAGE: ALT-GOETTINGEN – Goettingen. sep 29, 1933-apr 20, 1935 – 1r – 1 – gw Mikrofilm [943]
GOETTINGER ZEITUNG : BEILAGE: GOETTINGEN HEUTE – Goettingen. jul 6, 1934-mar 28, 1935 – 1r – 1 – gw Mikrofilm [072]
GOETTINGER ZEITUNG – Goettingen. jul 1-dec 27, 1869. jul 1-dec 31, 1870. jul 1, 1874-78. jan 2-dec 31, 1890. 1922 – 9r – 1 – gw Mikrofilm [943]
GOETTINGISCHE ANZEIGEN VON GELEHRTEN SACHEN – (Angefangen unter dem Titel: Goettingische Zeitungen von Gelehrten Sachen, Goettingen, 1739-52. Hildesheim, 1980 183mf DM1,280.00) – Goettingen, 1739-1801. Hildesheim, 1980 – 1327mf – 9 – DM7,500.00 diazo DM8,400.00 silver – gw Olms [943]
GOETTINGISCHE GELEHRTE ANZEIGEN *see* GOETTINGISCHE ZEITUNGEN [ANZEIGEN] VON GELEHRTEN SACHEN
GOETTINGISCHE ZEITUNGEN : ANZEIGEN VON GELEHRTEN SACHEN – (Cont. as: GOETTINGSCHE GELEHRTE ANZEIGEN) – Goettingen. 1802-92. Lacking: 1739-51 – 4,119mf – 8 – ne IDC [100]
GOETTINGISCHE ZEITUNGEN [ANZEIGEN] VON GELEHRTEN SACHEN – (Cont as; Goettingische gelehrte Anzeigen) – Goettingen, 1739-1801 – 4119mf – 9 – ne IDC [500]
DAS GOETTLICHE REICH ALS WELTREICH: NACH DER HEILIGEN SCHRIFT / Lindenmeyer, Julius – Tuebingen: Osiander, 1869. 1 fiche – 9 – us A.T.L.A. [240]
DIE GOETTLICHE VORHERBESTIMMUNG BEI PAULUS UND IN DER POSIDONIANISCHEN PHILOSOPHIE / Liechtenhan, R – Goettingen, 1922 – 3mf – 8 – ne Slangenburg [220]
Goetz, Karl *see* DIE HEIMSTAETTER
Goetz, KG *see* DER ALTE ANFANG UND DIE URSPRUENGLICHE FORM VON CYPRIANS SCHRIFT AD DONATUM (T.U.U. 2-19/1C)
Goetz, L K *see* DEUTSCH-RUSSISCHE HANDELSVERTRAEGE DES MITTELALTERS
Goetz, Leopold Karl *see*
- GESCHICHTE DER SLAVENAPOSTEL KONSTANTINUS (KYRILLUS) UND METHODIUS
- GOSUDARSTVO I TSERKOV V DREVNEI ROSSII
- IGNATIUS VON LOYOLA UND DER PROTESTANTISMUS
- LEO 13.
- DER ULTRAMONTANISMUS ALS WELTANSCHAUUNG

GOETZ VON BERLICHINGEN MIT DER EISERNEN HAND : EIN SCHAUSPIEL / Goethe, Johann Wolfgang von – (Includes bibliographical references) – Paris: L Cerf, 1885 – 1r – 1 – us U.W. Library [820]
Goetz, Walter *see* DIE QUELLEN ZUR GESCHICHTE DES HL. FRANZ VON ASSISI
Goetz, Wolfgang *see*
- ROBERT EMMET
- SCHILLER
- SCHILLER – ANEKDOTEN ERZAEHLT VON SEINEN ZEITGENOSSEN

Goetze, Robert *see* H. HEINE'S 'BUCH DER LIEDER' UND SEIN VERHAELTNIS ZUM DEUTSCHEN VOLKSLIED
DER GOETZENDIENST GOETHE / Lutz, Joseph Maria – (Includes bibliographical references) – Muenchen: Drei Eulen-Verlag, 1925 – 1r – 1 – us U.W. Library [430]
Goetz-Girey, R *see* LA PENSEE SYNDICALE FRANCAISE. MILITANTS ET THEORICIENS
Goetzinger, Ernst *see* JOACHIM VADIAN, DER REFORMATOR UND GESCHICHTSSCHREIBER VON ST GALLEN
Goeurot, J *see* THE REGIMENT OF LIFE
Goffinet, Hippolyte *see* CARTULAIRE DE L'ABBAYE D'ORVAL
Goffstown, New Hampshire. Goffstown Baptist Church *see* RECORDS
Gofman, M *see* KNIGA O RUSSKIKH POETAKH POSLEDNIAGO DESIATILETIIA
Gogarten, F *see* FICHTE ALS RELIGIOESER DENKER
LE GOGLU / ed by Arcand, Adrien & Menard, Adjutor – (Also: Le Goglu: v5 n1 30 nov 1946-22 fev 1947) – Montreal, Canada. 8 aut 1929-10 mar 1933 – 1r – 1 – Can$40.00 – cn Can Microfilming [072]
LA GOGNA – Kensington, IL, Nov. 1909 – 3r – 1 – us I.H.R.C. [978]
GOGOL' / Merezhkovskii, Dimitrii – Spb. 1909. BR-763 2 – 8 – ne IDC [460]
GOGOL' I CHORT / Merezhkovskii, Dimitrii – Issledovanie. M. 1906. BR-764 2 – 8 – ne IDC [460]
Gogol, Nikolai Vasilievich *see*
- GOGOLEVSKIE TEKSTY
- OPIS' DOKUMENTAL'NYKH MATERIALOV LICHNOGO FONDA NO.139

GOGOLEVSKIE TEKSTY / Gogol, Nikolai Vasilievich – S. Petersburg: Izd. Otdniia russkago iazyka i slovesnosti Imp. akademii nauk, 1910 – 1 – us U.W. Library [460]
Goguel, F et al *see* SOCIOLOGIE ELECTORALE
Goguel, Maurice *see*
- LES CHRETIENS ET L'EMPIRE ROMAIN A L'EPOQUE DU NOUVEAU TESTAMENT
- L'EUCHARISTIE
- L'EVANGILE DE MARC ET SES RAPPORTS AVEC CEUX DE MATHIEU ET DE LUC
- INTRODUCTION AU NOUVEAU TESTAMENT
- LA NOTION JOHANNIQUE DE L'ESPRIT ET SES ANTECEDENTS HISTORIQUES

Gohier, Louis *see* LA MORT DE CESAR
Gohiet, Francois *see* L'OEUVRE DU PAIN DES PAUVRES: DISCOURS POUR LA BENEDICTION D'UNE STATUE DE SAINT ANTOINE DE PADOUC:..
Goicoechea, A *see* EL PROBLEMA DE LAS LIMITACIONES DE LA SOBERANIA...
GOIN BUNKO INOUE KOWASHI MONJO = THE VISCOUNT KOWASHI INOUE RECORDS / Inoue, Kowashi Viscount – Original materials concerning the Meiji modernization in Japan, especially of the constitutional and educational systems. 5594 mss., 112,326p. Now in the library of Kokugakuin University, Tokyo. Classified catalog – 94r – 1 – Y792,000.00 – ja Yushodo [950]
GOING PLACES – 1977- – 1,5,6,9 – us UMI [910]
Goirand, H *see* ETUDE SUR LES CONDITIONS DE VALIDITE DU TESTAMENT...
Goirand, L *see*
- DIE DEUTSCHEN, OESTERREICHISCHEN UND UNGARISCHEN ACTIEN-GESELLSCHAFTEN IM FRANZOESISCHEN RECHT
- LES SOCIETES ANONYMES BELGES DEVANT LA LOI FRANCAISE

Goitein, Hirsch *see* DAS PROBLEM DER THEODICEE IN DER AELTEREN JUEDISCHEN RELIGIONSPHILOSOPHIE
Gokel, George W *see* SUPRAMOLECULAR CHEMISTRY
Golan, Ron *see* EFFECTS OF THYMOPENTIN ON THE RESPONSES OF HYPOTHALAMIC-PITUITARY-ADRENAL AXIS TO A HIGH INTENSITY DYNAMIC EXERCISE PROTOCOL
Golash, Deirdre *see* THE BAIL REFORM ACT OF 1984
Golbery, Sylvain M X de *see* TRAVELS IN AFRICA PERFORMED DURING THE YEARS 1785, 1786 AND 1787
Golbery, Sylvain M X. de *see*
- FRAGMENS D'UN VOYAGE EN AFRIQUE
- FRAGMENTS D'UN VOYAGE EN AFRIQUE FAIT PENDANT LES ANNEES 1785, 1786, ET 1787 DANS LES CONTREES OCCIDENTALES DE CE CONTINENT, COMPRISES ENTRE LE CAP BLANC DE BARBARIE ET LE CAP DES PALMES

DAS GOLD ALS WERTMESSER, ALS ZAHLUNGSMMITTEL UND ALS KAPITAL / Beckerath, Ulrich von – 9 – 1.00f – at Libertarian Micro [335]
GOLD AND INCENSE / Pearse, Mark Guy – 1895 – 9 – us A.T.L.A. [240]
GOLD AND SILVER: THE BEST TWENTY POEMS AND THOUGHTS EXTANT, SELECTED WITH SOME APPROACH TO ANALYTICAL CERTAINTY / Emberson, Frederick C & Ogilvy, Maud – Montreal: W. Drysdale, 18??. 02912. (Pre-1900 Canadiana) – 9 – cn C.I.H.M. [810]
GOLD BEACH GAZETTE – Gold Beach OR. Feb 21 1888-Sep 13 1895 – 1 – us U.O. Library [071]
GOLD BEACH GLOBE – Gold Beach, OR. -w. 11 Sept 1906; 7 Jan 1908-6 Jun 1916. 1 roll – 1 – us U.O. Library [071]
GOLD BEACH REPORTER – Gold Beach OR. Aug 3 1916-Nov 29 1923 – 1 – us U.O. Library [071]
Gold, Charles E *see* A STUDY OF THE GOSPEL SONG
Gold Coast *see*
- THE DEVELOPMENT PLAN, 1951: FOR ECONOMIC AND SOCIAL DEVELOPMENT OF THE GOLD COAST 1951-1956
- GOLD COAST GAZETTE
- GOLD COAST GAZETTE SUPPLEMENTS
- GOVERNMENT PUBLICATIONS

GOLD COAST ABORIGINE – Cape Coast. Ghana. -w. Jan 1898-Jun 1902. (48 ft) – 1 – uk British Libr Newspaper [072]
Gold Coast and British Togoland *see* ANNUAL DEPARTMENTAL REPORTS
THE GOLD COAST AND THE FANTIS : A COMPLETE COMPENDIUM FOR MINERS, TRADERS, AND STUDENTS OF NATIVE LIFE / Foot, Lionel R & Jones, T F E – London: Gold Coast Globe Pub Co, 1903 – us Res Libr [960]
GOLD COAST ASSIZE – Cape Coast. Ghana. -m. Nov 1883-Feb 1884. (3 ft) – 1 – uk British Libr Newspaper [072]
GOLD COAST CHRONICLE – Accra. Ghana. -f. Jun 1894-Dec 1901. (1 reel) – 1 – uk British Libr Newspaper [072]
Gold Coast. (Colony). Legislative Council *see* MINUTES
GOLD COAST DAILY MAIL – Accra: Amalgamated Press Ltd, jul 18, 21, 23, 1956 – us Res Libr [072]
GOLD COAST ECHO – Cape Coast. Ghana. -irr. Jan, Jul-Dec 1888. (12 ft) – 1 – uk British Libr Newspaper [072]
GOLD COAST EXPRESS – Accra. Ghana. -w. Jul-Dec 1897, Sep 1899-May 1900. (1 reel) – 1 – uk British Libr Newspaper [072]
GOLD COAST EXPRESS – (Library has 43 no. issued between Dec. 21, 1948 and March 9, 1951) – Accra, Ghana: Gold Coast Express, 193u – 1 – CSUX86-S82 – us Hoover Inst Photo [960]
GOLD COAST FREE PRESS – Accra. Ghana. -m. Aug-Nov 1899. (6 ft) – 1 – uk British Libr Newspaper [072]
GOLD COAST GAZETTE / Gold Coast – 1917-1937, 1947-1957. Gaps – 1 – 35.00r – us Hoover Inst Photo [960]
GOLD COAST GAZETTE / Gold Coast – and GAZETTE SUPPLEMENTS. (Including Legislative Supplements). Gazette. 1917-37, 1947-57; Supplements. 1933-37, 1947-57. Issues missing – 1 – 35.00r – us Hoover Inst Photo [324]
GOLD COAST GAZETTE / Gold Coast – Concessions Supplement. 1937, 1947-1950. Missing: nos. 1-2, 1948 – 1 – 35.00r – us Hoover Inst Photo [960]
GOLD COAST GAZETTE / Gold Coast – Trade Supplements. 1927-1937. 1947-1950. Missing: nos. 11-12, 1933 – 1 – 35.00r – us Hoover Inst Photo [960]
GOLD COAST GAZETTE SUPPLEMENTS / Gold Coast – Including Legislative Supplements. 1933-1937, 1947-1957 – 1 – 35.00r – us Hoover Inst Photo [960]
GOLD COAST INDEPENDENT – Accra. Ghana. -w. 14, 21 Dec 1895, 6 Jun 1896-19 Feb, 30 Sep 1898. (Imperfect). (36 ft) – 1 – uk British Libr Newspaper [072]
GOLD COAST INDEPENDENT – Accra. Ghana. -w. Jun 1922-Jan 1940, Feb-Mar 1941, Mar 1942-Sep 1947, Jun 1948. (Imperfect). (32 reels) – 1 – uk British Libr Newspaper [072]
THE GOLD COAST INDEPENDENT – Accra: Independent Press Ltd, apr 9, aug 9, 21, sep 11 1954 – us Res Libr [072]
GOLD COAST LEADER – Cape Coast. Ghana. -w. Jun 1902-Aug 1929. (9 reels) – 1 – uk British Libr Newspaper [072]
Gold Coast. Legislative Council *see* DEBATES
GOLD COAST METHODIST – Cape Coast. Ghana. -m. Dec 1886. (2 ft) – 1 – uk British Libr Newspaper [072]
GOLD COAST METHODIST TIMES – Cape Coast. Ghana. -m. Jul-Dec 1897. (9 ft) – 1 – uk British Libr Newspaper [072]
GOLD COAST NATION – Cape Coast. Ghana. -w. Mar 1912-Dec 1920. (Imperfect). (3 reels) – 1 – uk Britich Libr Newspaper [072]
GOLD COAST NEWS – Cape Coast. Ghana. -w. Mar-Aug 1885. (Imperfect). (8 ft) – 1 – uk British Libr Newspaper [072]
THE GOLD COAST OBSERVER – Cape Coast. Ghana. may 16-23, 30; June 27; July 4, 11, 1941 – 1 – us NY Public [072]
GOLD COAST OBSERVER AND WEEKLY ADVERTISER – (Library has holdings (incomplete) from between July 2, 1943 and Mar. 9, 1951) – Cape Coast, Ghana: Observer Printing and Publishing Co., 193u – 1 – CSUX86-S86 – us Hoover Inst Photo [960]
GOLD COAST OBSERVER AND WEEKLY ADVERTISER – Cape Coast: F G Mensah, sep 19-27 1952; apr 9 1954 – us Res Libr [072]

GOLD COAST PEOPLE – Cape Coast. Ghana. -w. 26 Oct 1891. (4 ft) – 1 – uk British Libr Newspaper [072]
GOLD COAST PIONEER – Accra. Ghana. -m. Feb 1921. (5 ft) – 1 – uk British Libr Newspaper [072]
GOLD COAST RECORDS / United Society for the Propagation of the Gospel – 1753-1933 – 1 – uk Microform Academic [240]
GOLD COAST REVIEW – Accra, Govt Printer. v2-5 n2. 1926-31 – us Res Libr [072]
GOLD COAST SPECTATOR – Accra. Ghana. -w. Oct 1937-Sep 1938. (2 reels) – 1 – uk British Libr Newspaper [072]
GOLD COAST TIMES – Cape Coast. Ghana. may 22; June 19, 26; July 3, 17; Aug. 7, 14; Sept. 11, 18, 25; Oct. 2, 9, 23; Nov. 6, 13, 20, 27, 1926 – 1 – us NY Public [072]
GOLD COAST TIMES – Cape Coast. Ghana. -w. 28 Mar 1874-31 Mar 1875, 22 May-11 Sep 1875, 17 Nov 1877-25 Jan 1878, 11 Feb, 9, 30 Jul 1881-12 Feb 1885. (Imperfect). (1 reel) – 1 – uk British Libr Newspaper [072]
GOLD COAST TIMES – Cape Coast. Ghana. -w. 4 Jan 1930-23 May 1936, 28 Nov 1936-6 Jul 1940. (6 reels) – 1 – uk British Libr Newspaper [072]
THE GOLD FIELDS MERCURY – Pilgrim's Rest, South Africa. 30 Jun 1876-7 Feb 1878 – 1r – 1, 16 diazo available – sa SA Libr [960]
GOLD FIELDS NEWS – Barberton. South Africa. 1888-1947 – 1 – sa State Libr [072]
THE GOLD FIELDS OF CANADA AND HOW TO REACH THEM: BEING AN ACCOUNT OF THE ROUTES AND MINERAL RESOURCES OF NORTH-WESTERN CANADA / Dyer, E Jerome – London: G. Philip, 1898. 02812. (Pre-1900 Canadiana) – 9 – cn C.I.H.M. [971]
THE GOLD FIELDS OF NEW ONTARIO: COMPRISING THE LAKE OF THE WOODS, RAINY LAKE, SEINE RIVER, THE MANITOU AND MICHIPICOTON DISTRICTS.. – s.l., s.n., 1899. 00456. (Pre-1900 Canadiana) – 9 – cn C.I.H.M. [622]
THE GOLD FIELDS OF NOVA SCOTIA / Gilpin, Edwin – Newcastle-upon-Tyne: A. Reid, 1882. 02506. (Pre-1900 Canadiana) – 9 – cn C.I.H.M. [971]
THE GOLD FIELDS OF THE KLONDIKE: ILLUSTRATING ALL THE INCIDENTS / Goldie, John – Douglas, Alaska: J.B. Prather, 1899. 03460. (Pre-1900 Canadiana) – 9 – cn C.I.H.M. [622]
GOLD FIELDS TIMES – Barberton. South Africa. 1886-88 – 1 – sa State Libr [072]
GOLD HILL NEWS – Gold Hill, OR. -w. 29 Jan 1897-17 Sept 1942. 6 rolls – 1 – us U.O. Library [071]
GOLD HILL NEWS – Virginia City, NV. 1974-1977 – 2r – 1 – $100.00 – N04791 – us Library Micro [071]
GOLD HILL NUGGET – Gold Hill OR. Jan 6 1949 – 1 – us U.O. Library [071]
GOLD HILL RENO, CARSON CITY, SILVER CITY AND VIRGINIA CITY DIRECTORY – State of Nevada. 1878-1879 – 1r – 1 – $50.00 – D117 – us Library Micro [910]
GOLD IN CANADA: THE CHAUDIERE VALLEY AND ITS MINERAL WEALTH – Quebec: Morning Chronicle, 1880. 00586. (Pre-1900 Canadiana) – 9 – cn C.I.H.M. [622]
GOLD, IRVING, SCRAPBOOK – (Scrapbook, consisting of posters, clippings, photographs, telegrams, and sheet music relating to Gold's early career as a dance band musician and booking agent in around Cleveland) – Cleveland, Cuyahoga, OH. 1930-36 – 1r – 1 – us Western Res [920]
THE GOLD MEASURES OF NOVA SCOTIA AND DEEP MINING: PAPER READ BEFORE THE CANADIAN MINING INSTITUTE, MARCH, 1899 / Faribault, Eugene Rodolphe – Ottawa: Published by the Mining Society of Nova Scotia, 1899 (Ottawa: Mortimer Co.). 02948. (Pre-1900 Canadiana) – 9 – cn C.I.H.M. [971]
GOLD MINES OF BEAUCE / Chapman, William – Quebec: Mercier, 1881. 00574. (Pre-1900 Canadiana) – 9 – cn C.I.H.M. [622]
GOLD OR LAUREL : THE OLYMPIC TRADITION IN A CHANGING WORLD – (Series: United States Olympic Academy, 14) – Emory University, 1990 – 4mf – 9 – $16.00 – us Microform Publ [790]
GOLD SPRING DIARY : DIARY OF JOHN JOLLY IN GOLDFIELDS / Jolly, John – 1854-55 – 1r – 1 – $50.00 – B40014 – us Library Micro [910]
GOLD UND REIHERFEDERN : GESTALTEN UND ERLEBNISSE AUS ECUADOR / Uden, Horst – Salzburg: Verlag "Das Bergland-Buch", 1942 – 1r – 1 – us U.W. Library [390]
Goldammer, Kurt *see* NOVALIS UND DIE WELT DES OSTENS
Goldammer, Peter *see* BEGEGNUNGEN UND WUERDIGUNGEN
Gol'danskii, V I *see* CHEMICAL PHYSICS REPORTS
Goldar, Ernesto *see* EL PERONISMO EN LA LITERATURA ARGENTINA
Goldbeck, Eduard *see* DER ROTE LEUTNANT
GOLDBECK'S MUSICAL INSTRUCTOR – St Louis, 1882-85 – 1 – £60.00 – uk Chadwyck [780]
Goldberg, Edward D *see* COASTAL ZONE SPACE
Goldberg, Isaac *see* HAVELOCK ELLIS: A BIOGRAPHICAL AND CRITICAL SURVEY
Goldberger, Michael *see* THE EFFECTS OF CONTEXTUAL INTERFERENCE AND THREE LEVELS OF DIFFICULTY ON THE ACQUISITION, RETENTION, AND TRANSFER OF HOCKEY STRIKING SKILLS BY SECOND GRADE CHILDREN
Goldberger, Philipp *see* DIE ALLEGORIE IN IHRER EXEGETISCHEN ANWENDUNG BEI MAIMONIDES
GOLDBURGFRIEDE U. INTERNATIONALES CLEARING / Milhaud, Edgar – 1933. 1 fiche (24x) – 9 – 1.00f – at Libertarian Micro [320]
Golde, I U *see* ZEMELNOE USTROISTVO TRUDI ASHCHIKHSI A EVREEV
GOLDEN – (1985-. 5,6,9) – 1983- – 1 – us UMI [073]
THE GOLDEN AGE OF VIOLIN DUETS : 1770-1820 – 136mf – 9 – MS-j – ne IDC [780]
THE GOLDEN APHRODITIS AND GRANGES GARDEN OF VERSE / Grange, John – 1577 – 9 – 10.00 – us Scholars' Facs [810]
GOLDEN BELT – Red Cloud, NE. -w. May-Dec 1893; Jul 1894-Oct 1896 – 1 – us NE Hist [071]
THE GOLDEN BOUGH, A STUDY IN MAGIC AND RELIGION / Frazer, James George – London, New York: Macmillan, 2nd rev enl ed 1900 – 2 rolls – 1 – 1-55879-231-7 – uk Libr Preservation [390]
THE GOLDEN CALF / Braddon, Mary Elizabeth – British Fiction Archive: Unit 5 – 9 – uk Bell [830]
GOLDEN COAST NEWS FORECAST – Santa Barbara. Calif. 1964-1967 – 1 – us UMI [071]
THE GOLDEN CRUSADER – Montreal, Canada. v1 n3. oct 1893-v1 n10. jul 1894 – 1r – 1 – Can$25.00 – cn Can Microfilming [072]
GOLDEN DAYS FOR BOYS & GIRLS – Philadelphia. 6 mar 1880-28 Nov 1885; 13 Mar 1886-13 Nov 1897; 18 Nov 1899-8 Nov 1902.-w. 21 reels – 1 – uk British Libr Newspaper [800]
THE GOLDEN ERA – San Francisco. Calif. 1860-1871 – 1 – us UMI [071]
Golden Gate Baptist Theological Seminary *see* BULLETINS, CATALOGS AND OTHER MATERIAL
GOLDEN GATE BRIDGE : NEWSPAPER CLIPPINGS – San Francisco, 1932-58 – 1r – 1 – $50.00 – B40307 – us Library Micro [978]
GOLDEN GATE LAW REVIEW – (See also: Golden Gate University Law Review) – v1-5. 1971-1975 – 1 – us UMI [340]
GOLDEN GATE LAW REVIEW *see* GOLDEN GATE UNIVERSITY LAW REVIEW
THE GOLDEN GATE; SPARKLING JEWELS; GOSPEL TRUMPET; SHINING PEARLS / Shaw, Knowles – 1 – 10.85 – us Baptist [240]
GOLDEN GATE UNIVERSITY LAW REVIEW – v. 6-. 1975- – 1,5,6,9 – us UMI [340]
GOLDEN GATE UNIVERSITY LAW REVIEW – (v1-14 1971-984 on reel $184.00. v15-26 1985-96 on mf $213.00. Title varies: v1-5 1971-75 as Golden Gate Law Review) – v1-26. 1971-96 – 5,6,9 – $391.00 set – us Hein [340]
GOLDEN GATOR – (Also known as: The Vigilante; Bay Leaf; Zengers) – San Francisco, CA. SF State University: 1922-1966; 1967-1970; 1971 – 23+ r – 1 – $1,150.00 ($50.00y) – B03717 – us Library Micro [370]
THE GOLDEN HIND – London, 1922-24 – 1r – 1 – £60.00 – uk Chadwyck [760]
Golden, Jane E et al *see* RESPONSES TO GRADED EXERCISE TESTING IN NORMAL CHILDREN AND ADOLESCENTS WITH HIGH AND LOW LEFT VENTRICULAR MASS
THE GOLDEN LION OF GRANPERE / Trollope, Anthony – London: Tinsley brothers, 1872 – 1 roll – 1 – 1-55879-891-9 – uk Libr Preservation [830]
GOLDEN RAIN NEWS, LEISURE WORLD – Seal Beach, CA. 1963 – 50+ r – 1 – $2,500.00 ($100.00y) – R04114 – us Library Micro [071]
"GOLDEN RULE" PAPERS 1896-1904 / Jones, Samuel M – Toledo (Ohio) Public Library. 15 roll 35mm set – 1 – us Ohio Hist [978]
GOLDEN STAR – British Columbia, CN. Oct 1963-1980 – 24r – 1 – cn Commonwealth Micro [072]
GOLDEN TEMPLE AT AMRITSAR, PUNJAB / India. Preservation of National Monuments; ed by Cole, H H – Calcutta, 1884. BI-682 2 – 8 – ne IDC [720]
THE GOLDEN TRADE OR A DISCOVERY OF THE RIVER GAMBRA / Jobson, R – London. 1932. BA-319 2 – 8 – ne IDC [910]
THE GOLDEN TREASURY OF THE BEST SONGS AND LYRICAL POEMS IN THE ENGLISH LANGUAGE : SELECTED AND ARRANGED WITH NOTES / Palgrave, Francis Turner – London, New York: Macmillan, rev enl ed 1892 – 1 roll – 1 – 1-55879-418-2 – uk Libr Preservation [810]
THE GOLDEN YEARS – 1929-41. Kine Weekly – 1,14 – £1,900.00 – uk World [073]
Goldenberg, C F *see* FLORA SARAEPONTANA FOSSILS
DIE GOLDENE BULLE KARLS 4. VOM JAHRE 1356 (MGH LEGES 4: 11.BD) – Dfl13.00 – ne Slangenburg [240]
DER GOLDENE CHERSONES / Bishop, IL (Bird) – Leipzig, 1884 – 5mf – 9 – ne IDC [950]
DAS GOLDENE VLIES : DRAMATISCHES GEDICHT IN DREI ABTEILUNGEN / Grillparzer, Franz – Stuttgart, Berlin: Cotta, 1906 – 1r – 1 – us U.W. Library [810]
THE GOLDENROD / Wayne State College – 1911-60 – 1 – us UMI [370]
Goldenveizer-Liubimov, Nikolai *see* DA ZDRAVSTVUET EMIGRATSIIA
Golder, Christian *see* HISTORY OF THE DEACONESS MOVEMENT IN THE CHRISTIAN CHURCH
Golder, F A *see*
- BERING'S VOYAGES
- GUIDE TO MATERIALS FOR AMERICAN HISTORY IN RUSSIAN ARCHIVES
- SONGS AND STORIES OF THE ALEUTS
- TALES FROM KODIAK ISLAND

Goldfaden, A *see* BLUMENLESE
GOLDFIELD GOSSIP WEEKLY *see* GOSSIP
GOLDFIELD NEWS – Goldfield, NV. 1904-10; 1946-47 (broken series) – 3r – 1 – $150.00 – U04556 – us Library Micro [071]
THE GOLDFIELDS OF MASHONALAND / Sawyer, Arthur Robert – Manchester: J. Heywood, 1894. 99p. fold. maps – 1 – us U.W. Library [622]
Goldflies, David G *see* THE RELATIONSHIP BETWEEN HABITUAL DIET AND BLOOD PRESSURE AMONG BLACK AND WHITE ADULTS
GOLD-FOIL : HAMMERED FROM POPULAR PROVERBS / Holland, Josiah Gilbert – New York: Charles Scribner, 1883, c1881 – 1mf – 9 – 0-8370-7513-0 – 1986-1513 – us A.T.L.A. [240]
Goldfrank, Esther *see* THE ARTIST OF "ISLETA PAINTINGS" IN PUEBLO SOCIETY
Goldfuss, F *see* SYMBOLAE AD ORTHOPTERORUM QUORUNDAM OECONOMIAM
Goldfuss, G A *see* PETREFACTA GERMANIAE...
THE GOLDHEADED CANE / Macmichael, W – London, 1827 – 4mf – ne IDC [610]
Goldie, John *see*
- DIARY OF A JOURNEY THROUGH UPPER CANADA AND SOME OF THE NEW ENGLAND STATES, 1819
- THE GOLD FIELDS OF THE KLONDIKE: ILLUSTRATING ALL THE INCIDENTS

Goldingham, Henry *see* THE GARDEN PLOT
Goldman, F du Cane *see* A MONOGRAPH OF THE PETRELS (ORDER TUBINARES)
Goldman, Jerry *see* THE SEVENTH CIRCUIT PREAPPEAL PROGRAM
Gol'dman, L I *see* POLITICHESKIE PROTSESSY V ROSSII (1901-1917)
Goldman-Liber, M *see* ZADACHI RABOCHAGO KLASSA V RUSSKO I REVOLIUTSII
Goldmann, I *see* SHANIM KADMONIYYOT
Goldmann, J *see* SHEAR YASHUV
Goldmann, Karl *see* RICHARD VOSS
Goldmark, C *see* DIE KOENINGEN VON SABA...OP. 27
DER GOLDNE TOPF : EIN MAERCHEN AUS DER NEUEN ZEIT / Hoffmann, Ernst Theodor Amadeus – Wiesbaden: Herta Hartmanshenn, [1947?] – 1 – us U.W. Library [830]
Goldney, E *see* SCRIPTURAL REMEDIES FOR HEALING THE UNHAPPY DIVISIONS IN THE CHURCH OF ENGLAND, PARTICULARLY OF THOSE PEOPLE CALLED METHODISTS
GOLDRUSH GAZETTE – Jacksonville OR. 1959 – 1 – us U.O. Library [071]
Goldschmidt, L *see*
- BABYLONISCHE TALMUD, HEBRAEISCH UND DEUTSCH MIT EINSCHLUSS DER VOLLSTAENDIGE MISNAH
- BIBLIOTHECA AETHIOPICA

Goldschmidt, Lazarus *see* SEFER YETSIRAH
Goldschmit, Rudolf K *see* HEIDELBERG ALS STOFF UND MOTIV DER DEUTSCHEN DICHTUNG
Goldshtein, ML *see*
- PECHAT' PERED SUDOM RECHI PO DELAM "RUSI", "NASHEI ZHIZNI" I "SYNA OTCHESTVA"
- RECHI I STAT'I

Goldsmith, F H *see* JOHN AINSWORTH, PIONEER KENYA ADMINISTRATOR, 1864-1946
Goldsmith, L *see* AN EXPOSITION OF THE CONDUCT OF FRANCE TOWARDS AMERICA
Goldsmith, Lewis *see* HISTORIA SECRETA DEL GABINETE DE NAPOLEON (ANNO 1811)
Goldsmith, Oliver *see*
- ESSAYS AND CRITICISMS
- THE POEMS OF OLIVER GOLDSMITH

Goldsmith, William M *see* THE PUBLIC PAPERS OF LOUIS DEMBITZ BRANDEIS IN THE JACOB AND BERTHA GOLDFARB LIBRARY OF BRANDEIS UNIVERSITY
GOLDSMITHS'-KRESS LIBRARY OF ECONOMIC LITERATURE – (Subject break-outs available) – Combines the pre-1850 monographic and pre-1906 serials holdings of the Goldsmiths' Library of Economic Literature at the University of London and the Kress Library of Business and Economics at the Harvard Graduate School of Business Administration. Supplemented with material from Seligman Collection, Butler Library, Columbia Univ. and Sterling Library at Yale – 1 – us Primary [330]
Goldstein, Harvey *see* INTERPRETING INTERNATIONAL COMPARISONS OF STUDENT ACHIEVEMENT
Goldstein, Joseph M *see*
- PANAMSKI I KANAL, PADENIE KHLI EBNYKH T SI EN, VO INA I NASHI TORGOVYE DOGOVORY
- PANAMSKI I KANAL, PADENIE KHLI EBNYKH T SIE EN, VO INA I NASHI TORGOVYE DOGOVORY
- UGROZHAET LI NASHEI PROMYSHLENNOSTI KRAKH?

Goldstein, Sidney M *see*
- CAMEO GLASS, MASTERPIECES FROM 2000 YEARS OF GLASSMAKING
- PRE-ROMAN AND EARLY ROMAN GLASS IN THE CORNING MUSEUM OF GLASS

Goldstein, Walter Benjamin *see* WASSERMANN
GOLDWIN SMITH AND THE JEWS / Bendavid, Isaac Besht – 1891?. 02322. (Pre-1900 Canadiana) – 9 – cn C.I.H.M. [270]
GOLDWIN SMITH PAPERS, 1823-1910 / Smith, Goldwin – 28r – 1 – $2080.00 – us UMI [920]
Goldziher, I *see*
- BIBLIOGRAPHIE DE [SES] OUEVRES
- SEFER ZIKKARON LE-YIZHAK YEHUDAH GOLDZIHER

Golecek, V *see* CHEKHOSLOVAT SKOE VO ISKO V ROSSII
Golembiewski, Robert *see* HUMANIZING PUBLIC ORGANIZATIONS
Golenischeff, W *see*
- PAPYRUS HIERARIQUES, NOS. 58001-58036
- LES PAPYRUS HIERATIQUES NO 1115, 1116 A ET 1116 B DE L'ERMITAGE IMPERIAL A ST-PETERSBOURG

GOLETA EL GAUCHO – Goleta. Calif. 1960- – 1 – us UMI [071]
GOLF BUSINESS – (See also: Golfdom) – v50. 1976 – 1 – us UMI [790]

GOLF DIGEST – (1979-. 9. 1983-. 5,6) – 1971- – 1 – us UMI [790]
GOLF JOURNAL – v. 1-. 1948- – 1. ; 5,6,9 – apply; v.29- – us UMI [790]
GOLFDOM – (See also: Golf Business) – v1-50. 1927-1976 – 1 – us UMI [790]
GOLGOTHA AND THE CHURCH OF THE HOLY SEPULCHRE / Parrot, Andre – S.C.M. Press, 1957 – 9 – $10.00 – us I.R.C. [930]
LE GOLI. CONTRIBUTION A L'ETUDE DES MASQUES BAOULE / Lafargue, Fernand – (Africa series). 1970 – 9 – fr Hachette [730]
GOLIATH SLAIN, BEING A REPLY TO THE REVEREND DR. NOWELL'S ANSWER TO 'PIETAS OXONIENSIS',... / Hill, Richard – London, 1768 – 3mf – MP-448/1 – ne IDC [240]
Golightly, Charles Portales *see* THE POSITION OF THE RIGHT REV. SAMUEL WILBERFORCE, D.D., LORD BISHOP OF OXFORD, IN REFERNCE TO RITUALISM
Golikov, I I *see* DEIANIIA PETRA VELIKAGO, MUDRAGO PREOBRAZITELIA ROSSII, SOBRANNYIA IZ DOSTOVERNYKH ISTOCHNIKOV I RAZPOLOZHENNYI PO GODAM
Golikov, Pla. *see* CHTO TAKOE PROIZVODITEL'NO-TRUDOVAIA ARTEL' I KAK EE ORGANIZOVAT'
Golitsyn, N N *see* BIBLIOGRAFICHESKII SLOVAR' RUSSKIKH PISATEL'NITS
Golitsyn-Muravlin *see* NA POROGIE NOVYKH MYSLEI
Gollan, Josue *see* LA UNIVERSIDAD AL SERVICIO DE LA DEMOCRACIA, UNA EXPERIENCIA EN POLITICA UNIVERSITARIA
Gollancz, H *see* SHEKEL HAKODESH
Gollancz, Hermann *see* DAS BUCH HENOCH: AUS DEM AETHIOPISCHEN
Gollenperger, Dr. *see* RADIKALE LIEDER
Gollerbakh, E *see* RUSSKAIA SATIRA PERVOI REVOLIUTSII 1905-1906
Gollnhofer, O *see* BOKUDU ETHNO-HISTOIRE GHETSOGHO
GOLOD 1921-1922 : SBORNIK – Niu-Iork: Izd. Predstavitelstva Rossi iskogo obshchestva Krasnogo kresta v Amerike, [1923?] – 1 – CSUX89-B1634 – us Hoover Inst Photo [947]
GOLOD I TSERKOVNYE BOGATSTVA – Moskva: Gosizdat, 1922 – 1 – CSUX91-B382 – us Hoover Inst Photo [947]
GOLODNY I POKHOD ORENBURGSKO I ARMII : IZ VOSPOMINAI I UCHASTNIKA POKHODA / Elovksii, I – Pekin: Tip. Uspenskago monastyri a pri Russko i dukhovno i missii, 1921 – 1 – CSUX88-B6857 – us Hoover Inst Photo [947]
GOLOS – (Missing: Many numbers) – 1863-1883 – 53r – 1 – RF-3/3 – ne IDC [072]
GOLOS ANARKHISTA – (Includes c.1: no.1(1918:Mar.11)) – Ekaterinoslav: Bi uro anarkhistov Donet skago basse ina, 1918- – 1 – CSUXANR4249-S – us Hoover Inst Photo [947]
GOLOS AZII – (Includes c.1: 1932:Apr.2-1933:Feb.14//; LACKS many issues) – [Tiantszin]: I U. Koiama, -1933 – 1 – CSUXAKB0406-S – us Hoover Inst Photo [947]
GOLOS BUKHARESTA – (Includes c.1: v.1:no.1 1933:Aug.13-v.1:no.13 (1933:Nov.19/26)) – Bucuresti: [s.n.], 1933- – 1 – CSUXAKG1977-S – us Hoover Inst Photo [947]
GOLOS KOOPERATORA – Stavropol', 1916-17 n4 – 3mf – 9 – COR-576/1 – ne IDC [334]
GOLOS KOOPERATORA *see* BIULLETEN' GUBSOIUZA
GOLOS KOOPERATSII – Kiev, 1918-19 n7 – 5mf – 9 – COR-577/1 – ne IDC [334]
GOLOS MINUVSHAGO – Zhurnal istorii i istorii literatury. M. 1913-23. Lacking: 1923 (2, 4). B-1193 2 – 8 – ne IDC [900]
GOLOS MINUVSHAGO NA CHUZHOI STORONE – Zhurnal istorii i istorii literatury. v. 1-6. Paris. 1926-28. BR-3386 2 – 8 – ne IDC [900]
GOLOS MINUVSHEGO – Moscow. Jan. 1913-Jan. Feb. 1923 – 1 – 35.00r – us Hoover Inst Photo [073]
GOLOS MOSKVY – Moskva: Moskovskoe tovarishchestvo dlia izdaniia knig i gazet. n2-25 jan 3-31 1912; n26-49 feb 1-29 1912 – 1 – us Res Libr [947]
GOLOS NARODA (PECHORY, R.S.F.S.R.) – (Includes c.1: no.1 1927:Mar.15) – Pechery: A. Grechanov, 1927- – 1 – CSUXAKG0839-S – us Hoover Inst Photo [947]
GOLOS NARODA (PRAGUE, CZECH REPUBLIC) – (Includes c.1: 1920:June 26, July 6) – Praga: J. Vodicka – 1 – CSUXANR4341-S – us Hoover Inst Photo [947]
GOLOS NIZHNE-VOLZHSKOGO KOOPERATORA *see* BIULLETEN' GUBSOIUZA
GOLOS PRAVDY – New York: Golos Pravdy Pub Co. v1-8. mar 1938-dec 1945 – 1 – us Res Libr [073]
GOLOS RODINY (HAGUE, NETHERLANDS) – (Includes c.1: 1918:June 2-1919:Mar.15, 18-July 12, 14-31) – Gaaga: [s.n.], 1918- – 1 – CSUXADQ1577-S – us Hoover Inst Photo [949]
GOLOS RODINY (VLADIVOSTOK, R.S.F.S.R.) – (Includes c.1: 1919:Sept.27, Oct.1, 23-25) – Vladivostok: T-vo "Svobodnai a Rossii a", 1919 – 1 – CSUXAKG3995-S – us Hoover Inst Photo [947]
Golos rodiny (Vladivostok, RSFSR) *see* DIEISTVIIA IAPONII V PRIAMURSKOM KRAIE
GOLOS RONDA = ORGAN DER RUSSISCHEN NATIONAL-SOZIALISTISCHEN BEWEGUNG : ORGAN ROSSI ISKOGO OSVOBODITELNOGO NARODNOGO DVIZHENII A (ROSSI ISKOE NATSIONAL-SOTSIALISTICHSKOE DVIZHENIE TRUDI ASHCHIKHSI A) – (Includes c.1: no.1 1933:June 8) – Berlin: Verlag ROND, 1933- – 1 – CSUXADP4158-S – us Hoover Inst Photo [947]
GOLOS ROSSII – Sofia, Bulgaria. Jun 1936-Aug 1938 – 1r – 1 – us L of C Photodup [949]
GOLOS RUSI – (Includes c.1: no.194 1914: Aug.3suppl.-no.196 (1914:Aug.5) suppl.; no.200 1914:Aug.9 suppl., no.273 (1914:Oct.22)suppl)) – S.-Petersburg: [s.n.], 19uu – 1 – CSUXADQ1029-S – us Hoover Inst Photo [947]
GOLOS RUSSKO I MOLODEZHI = VOIX DE LA JEUNESSE RUSSE – (Includes c.1: no.6 1939:May-no.8 (1939:July)) – Geneve: Russkoe trudovoe khristianskoe dvizhenie, 193u – 1 – CSUXAKG1241-S – us Hoover Inst Photo [947]
GOLOS (SHANGHAI, CHINA) – (Includes c.1: no.3 1931:Feb.2-no.45 (1932:Sept.20); Lacks many issues) – Shankhai: "Golos", 1931 – 1 – CSUXAKG5691-S – us Hoover Inst Photo [950]
GOLOS SIBIRI (KRASNOIARSK, R.S.F.S.R.) – (Includes c.1: 1906:May 10, 17, 24) – Krasnoiarsk: Golos Sibiri, 1906 – 1 – CSUXADP4373-S – us Hoover Inst Photo [947]
GOLOS SIMBIRSKOI KOOPERATSII – (Missing: 1918: n1-4, 6-8; 1919: n1-4) – Simbirsk, 1918-19 n5/6 – 4mf – 9 – COR-579/1 – ne IDC [334]
GOLOS SOTSIAL'DEMOKRATA – Geneva etc. v. 1-5 no. 1-26. Feb 1908-Dec 1911 – 1 – us NY Public [335]
GOLOS SOTSIAL-DEMOKRATA – Geneva-Paris. 1908-1911, nos. 1-26 – 1 – 35.00r – us Hoover Inst Photo [073]
GOLOS STUDENCHESTVA – (Includes c.1: no.3 1910:Sept.30) – Moskva: [s.n.], 19uu – 1 – CSUXADP4263-S – us Hoover Inst Photo [947]
GOLOS TEKSTILE I : ORGAN T SK SOI UZA RABOCHIKH KHLOPCHATOBUMAZHNO I PROMYSHLENNOSTI, T SK SOI UZA RABOCHIKH LNOPENKODZHUTOVO I PROMYSHLENNOSTI I T SK SOI UZA RABOCHIKH SHERSTI ANO I, SHELKOVO I I TRIKOTAZHNO I PROMYSHLENNOSTI – (Includes c.1: v.10:no.251 = no.1852 1931:Oct.25) – Moskva: T SK soi uzov, 19uu – 1 – CSUXADP4239-S – us Hoover Inst Photo [947]
GOLOS TRUDA : IZDANIE ALEKSANDROVSKOGO, I UREV-POLSKOGO, PERESLAVL-ZALESSKOGO I KIRZHACHSKOGO ISPOLNITELNYKH KOMITETOV SOVETOV RABOCHIKH, KRESTI ANSKIKH I KRASNOARME ISKIKH DEPUTATOV – (Includes c.1: 1919:Nov.7) – Aleksandovsk: [s.n.], 1917 – 1 – CSUXADP4831-S – us Hoover Inst Photo [947]
GOLOS TRUDA – (Library has holdings (incomplete) from between June 25, 1918 and May 1, 1930) – Buenos Aires: Federatsii a rossi iskikh rabochikh organizatsi i I Uzhno i Ameriki, 1918- – 1 – CSUX86-S445 – us Hoover Inst Photo [972]
GOLOS TRUDA : ORGAN RUSSKAGO OBSHCHE-TRUDOVOGO SOI UZA V BOLGARII – (Includes c.1: no.77 1934:Apr.21-no.92 (1934:Aug.23); no.94 1934:Sept.6-no.121 (1935:Mar.29); no.123 1935:Apr.12-no.165 (1936:May 28)) – Sofiia: [Soi uz], 19uu – 1 – CSUXADP4337-S – us Hoover Inst Photo [947]
GOLOS TRUDA (ALEKSANDROVSK, MURMANSKAI A OBLAST (R.S.F.S.R.) *see* GOLOS TRUDA
GOLOS TRUDA (SAMARA, R.S.F.S.R.) – (Includes c.1: no.1 1916:June 21-no.2 (1916:July 3)) – Samara: E.A. Medvi edeva, 1916- – 1 – CSUXAKP3669-S – us Hoover Inst Photo [947]
GOLOS TRUDA (SOFIA, BULGARIA) *see* GOLOS TRUDA
GOLOS TRUDOVOGO KRESTI ANSTVA : ORGAN KRESTI ANSKO I SEKT SII VSEROSSI ISKAGO T SENTRALNAGO ISPOLNITELNAGO KOMITETA SOVI ETOV – (c.1 Library lacks many issues; c.1: 1918:Mar.2-Nov.30) – Petrograd: Sekt s-ii a, 191u – 1 – CSUXANRO193-S – us Hoover Inst Photo [947]
GOLOS UDARNIKA (OZERY, R.S.F.S.R.) – (Library has: no. 108-109 (Sept. 8, 11, 1945)) – Ozery: "Golos udarnika", 1934- – 1 – CSUX88-S498 – us Hoover Inst Photo [947]
GOLOS UKRAINY – (Backfile through 1998 $85r) – 1999- – 3r per y – 1 – $240.00 standing order – us Ross [072]
GOLOS UKRAINY – Kiev: Verkhovnyi Sovet Ukrainy, 1991- – 3mf per year – 9 – $229.95y – us East View [320]
GOLOS ZHIZNI – Ezhenedel'nyi zhurnal. M. 1905-06. BR-4166 2 – 8 – ne IDC [073]
GOLOSA IZ ROSSII – (2nd Edition). London. v. 1-9. 1858-1859 – 1 – us NY Public [947]
GOLOSA IZ ROSSII – London. pts1-9. 1858-60 – 1r – 1 – us Ross [947]
GOLOS-ROSSII (BERLIN, GERMANY) – (Includes c.1: 1919:Mar.15; 1920:Apr.28, May 20, 23, 28; 1921:Dec.3-25, 29-31; 1922:Feb.22, 25, June 27, 30-July 18, 20-25, 27, Aug.8, 13, 27, Sept.28) – Berlin: "Golos Rossii", 1919 – 1 – CSUXANR4444-S – us Hoover Inst Photo [943]
Golovatskii, I A *see* GEOGRAFICHESKII SLOVAR' ZAPADNOSLAVIANSKIKH I IUGOSLAVIANSKIKH ZEMEL'I PRINADLEZHSHCHIKH STRAN
Golovin, Nikolai Nikolaevich *see*
- MYSLI OB USTROISTVIE BUDUSHCHEI ROSSIISKO I VOORUZHENNOI SILY
- SOVREMENNAIA KONNITSA

Golovine, Ivan G *see* AUTOCRATIC RUSSE
Golovkin, F *see* DVOR I TSARSTVOVANIE PAVLA I
Golstunskii, K F *see* MONGOLO-OIRATSKIE ZAKONY 1640 GODA, DOPOLNITEL'NYE GALDAN-KHUN- TAIDZHIIAI ZAKONYM SOSTAVLENNYE DLIA VOLZHSKIKH KALMYKOV PRI KALMYTSKOM KHANE DONDUK-DASHI
Golterman, H L et al *see* STUDY OF THE RELATIONSHIP BETWEEN WATER QUALITY AND SEDIMENT TRANSPORT
Golther, Wolfgang *see*
- PARZIVAL IN DER DEUTSCHEN LITERATUR
- DIE SAGENGESCHICHTLICHEN GRUNDLAGEN DER RINGDICHTUNG RICHARD WAGNERS
- TRISTAN UND ISOLDE IN DER FRANZOESISCHEN UND DEUTSCHEN DICHTUNG DES MITTELALTERS UND DER NEUZEIT
- ZUR DEUTSCHEN SAGE UND DICHTUNG

Gol'tsev, V A *see*
- BRIUSOV I BLOK
- VOPROSY DNIA I ZHIZNI

Goltz, Colmar von der *see* LA NATION ARMEE, ORGANIZATION MILITAIRE ET GRANDE TACTIQUE MODERNE
Goltz, Eduard von der *see*
- DER DIENST DER FRAU IN DER CHRISTLICHEN KIRCHE
- DAS GEBET IN DER AELTESTEN CHRISTENHEIT
- IGNATIUS VON ANTIOCHIEN ALS CHRIST UND THEOLOGE (T.U.U. 1-12/3A)
- LOGOS SOTERIAS PROS TEN PARTHENON (DE VIRGINITATE)
- LOGOS SOTERIAS PROS TEN PARTHENON – DE VIRGINITATE
- EINE TEXTKRITISCHE ARBEIT DES ZEHNTEN BEZW. SECHSTEN JAHRHUNDERTS (T.U.U. 2-17/4)
- TISCHGEBETE UND ABENDMAHLSGEBETE IN DER ALTCHIRSTLICHEN UND IN DER GRIECHISCHEN KIRCHE
- TISCHGEBETE UND ABENDMAHLSGEBETE IN DER ALTCHRISTLICHEN UND IN DER GRIECHISCHEN KIRCHE (T.U.U. 2-29/2B)

Goltz, Hermann, Freiherr von der *see* DIE REFORMIRTE KIRCHE GENF'S IM NEUNZEHNTEN JAHRHUNDERT
Goltz, Hermann von der *see* DIE CHRISTLICHEN GRUNDWAHRHEITEN
Goltz, Joachim, Freiherr von der *see*
- EINST AUF DER LORETTOHOEHE
- EWIG WIEDERKEHRT DIE FREUDE
- VATER UND SOHN
- VON MANCHERLEI HOELLE UND SELIGKEIT

Der Goltz Pasa *see* HARBIN SEVK VE IDARESI
Golubev, A *see* RUSSKAIA BIBLIOGRAFIIA, GOD PERVYI (1878)
Golubeva, O D *see* LITERATURNO-KHUDOZHESTVENNYE AL' MANAKHI I SBORNIKI
Golubinskii, E E *see* K NASHEI POLEMIKIE S STAROOBRIADISAMI
Golubkova, SN *see* KACHESTVO I STANDART V PROMKOOPERATSII
Golubov, S *see* ORGANIZATSIIA IURIDICHESKOI RABOTY UCHREZHDENII
Golubovich, PG *see*
- BIBLIOTECA BIOBIBLIOGRAFICA DELLA TERRA SANTA E DELL'ORIENTE FRANCESCANO
- BIBLIOTHECA BIO-BIBLIOGRAFICA DELLA TERRA-SANTA E DELL' ORIENTE FRANCESCANO

Golubovskii, I V *see* MUZYKAL'NYI LENINGRAD, 1917-1957
Golubovskii, P *see* PECHENEGI, TORKI I POLOVTSY DO NASHESTVIIA TARTAR
Golubykh, M *see* URALSKIE PARTIZANY
Golunskii, Sergei Aleksandrovich *see* SUDOUSTROISTVO SSSR; UCHEBNIK DLIA IURIDICHESKIKH SHKOL
GOLUS : ZEITSCHRIFT FUER JUEDISCHEN EMIGRATION AUS DEUTSCHLAND – Prag (Praha), Czechoslovakia. Aug 1933, No 1 – 1 – gw Mikrofilm [073]
Golz, Bruno *see* ZWEI SCHWAEBISCHE ERZAEHLER
Goma, Isidoro *see*
- LA EUCARISTIA Y LA VIDA CRISTIANA. 2ND ED. 2 TOMOS. BARCELONA, 1934
- LA FAMILIA, SEGUN EL DERECHO NATURAL Y CRISTIANO...
- JESUCRISTO REDENTOR
- LAS MODAS Y EL LUJO, ANTE LA LEY CRISTIANA, LA SOCIEDAD Y EL ARTE. 3RD ED SAN SEBASTIAN, 1935

Goma Tomas, Isidro *see* ANTILAICISMO. 2 VOL. BARCELONA, 1935
Goma y Tomas, Isidro *see* EL EVANGELIO EXPLICADO, VOL 1, BARCELONA, 1930
GOMANTAK – Panjim, India. Jul 1966-1993 – 86r – 1 – us L of C Photodup [072]
Gomara, Francisco Lopez de *see* THE CONQUEST OF THE WEAST INDIA
Gomarus, F *see* OPERA THEOLOGICA OMNIA...
Gomes da Silva, A J *see* REGRAS DE ACOMPANHAR PARA CRAVO OU ORGAO, E AINDA TAMBEM PARA QUALQUER OUTRO INSTRUMENTO DE VOZES, REDUZIDAS A BREVE METHODO, E FACIL PERCEPECAO
Gomes, Ruy Cinatti Vaz Monteiro *see* EXPLORACOES BOTANICAS EM TIMOR
Gomez Acedo, Francisco *see* NOVENA DE NUESTRA SENORA DE SOPETRAN ORDENADA DE NUEVE PRECIOSAS PIEDRAS DE QUE SE COMPONE EL NOMBRE SOPETRANA...
Gomez, Antonio *see*
- DISCURSOS EVANGELICOS
- SERMON DEL DOCTOR SERAPHICO S. BUENAVENTURA...

Gomez Ballesteros, Francisco *see* EL LIBERALISMO EL SOCIALISMO Y LA SOLUCION NACIONALSINDICALISTA
Gomez Barrientos, Estanislao *see* 25 ANOS A TRAVES DEL ESTADO DE ANTIOQUIA
Gomez Bravo, Juan *see*
- ADVERTENCIAS A LA ISTORIA (SIC) DE MERIDA
- CATALOGO DE LOS OBISPOS DE CORDOBA. 1ST PARTE
- CATALOGO... OBISPOS DE CORDOBA

Gomez Bravo, Vicente *see*
- AESTHETICA. NOCIONES DE LA BELLEZA Y DE LAS ARTES
- AQUAVIVA
- ESPANA EN AMERICA. DOS VELADAS LITERARIAS CELEBRADAS EN LA CIUDAD DE BURGOS 1892-1893, CON MOTIVO DEL CUARTO CENTENARIO DE COLON
- GRAMATICA HISTORICA ESPANOLA Y ANTOLOGIAS
- UNA HIJA DE MARIA (MARIA PEREZ DE GUZMAN Y SANJUAN)

- LYRA HISPANA...
- LYRA HISPANA. CUESTOMATIA ESCOLAR PARA LECTURA Y ANALISIS LITERARIO
- LYRA HISPANA. PROSA SELECTA
- LYRA HISPANA. PROSA SELECTA. SILVA DRAMATICA
- NOCHE-BUENA EN FAMILIA
- PROSA SELECTA DE AUTORES ESPANOLES PARA LECTURA Y ANALISIS LITERARIO
- SILVA DRAMATICA...
- SILVA DRAMATICA. ASUNTOS DEL TEATRO ESPANOL DISPUESTOS PARA ESTUDIO LITERARIO
- SUBPLEMENTO AL TESORO POETICO CASTELLANO DEL SIGLO 19
- TESORO POETICO CASTELLANO DEL SIGLO 19

Gomez, C F *see* CIUDADANIA Y NACIONALIZACION
Gomez Canedo, Lino *see* DON JUAN DE CARVAJAL. UN ESPANOL AL SERVICIO DE LA SANTA SEDE. MADRID, 1947
Gomez Canedo, Luis *see* UN ESPANOL AL SERVICIO DE LA SANTA SEDE. DON JUAN DE CARVAJAL, CARDENAL DE SANT'ANGELO, LUGADO EN ALEMANIA Y HUNGRIA (1.399-1.469)
Gomez Castanos, Marcial *see* MOCION PRESENTADA AL AYUNTAMIENTO DE OLIVENZA
Gomez de Arteche, Jose *see* LA CONQUISTA DE MEJICO
Gomez de Avellaneda, Gertrudis *see* GUATIMOZIN. TOMO 2
Gomez de Cervantes, Gonzalo *see* LA VIDA ECONOMICA SOCIAL DE NUEVA ESPANA AL FINALIZAR EL SIGLO 16. PROLOGO Y NOTAS DE ALBERTO MA CARRENO. MEXICO, 1944
Gomez de la Parra, A *see* POLYANTHEA MEDICIS SPECIOSA CHIRURGIS MIRIFICA MYREPSICIS VALDE UTILIS ET NECESSARIA
Gomez de la Serna, Ramon *see* MI TIA CAROLINA CORONADO
Gomez de Mercado y Miguel, F *see* ISABEL 1, REINA DE ESPANA Y MADRE DE AMERICA. MADRID, 1943
Gomez de Santana, Indalecio *see*
- MEMORIA LEIDA EL DIA 16 DE SEPTIEMBRE EN LA APERTURA DEL CURSO DE 1867 A 1868 EN EL INSTITUTO DE SEGUNDA ENSENANZA DE CACERES, POR...
- MEMORIA...23 DE SEPTIEMBRE...DE 1867 A 1868...COLEGIO DE ISABEL 2...
- MEMORIA...CACERES
- MEMORIA...INSTITUTO DE 2A ENSENANZA

Gomez, Florencio *see* DISCURSO-POLITICO... COLERO NORBO
Gomez Gomez, P A *see* LA PROPIEDAD DE LAS MINAS Y SU ADQUISICION POR EXTRANJEROS
Gomez Guillen, Roman *see* JUAN VAZQUEZ EN LA CATEDRAL DE PLASENCIA
Gomez Hermosilla, Jose *see* ARTE DE HABLAR...VERSO
Gomez Jara, Francisco *see* DISCURSO PRONUNCIADO EN LA COLABORACION DE GRADOS DE LICENCIADOS EN JURISPRUDENCIA...
Gomez Jara y Herrera, Juan de la Cruz *see* APUNTES HISTORICOS...VILLA DE FUENTE DEL MAESTRE DESDE..
Gomez, M *see* ...DE QUE EL AFORISMO PRIMERO DE HIPOCRATES...SIRVE A LA MILICIA COMO A LA MEDICINA...
Gomez Miedes, B *see*
- ENCHIRIDION O MANUAL INSTRUMENTO DE SALUD CONTRA EL MORBO ARTICULAR QUE LLAMAN GOTA...
- ENQUIRIDION CONTRA EL MORBO ARTICULAR

GOMEZ MONSEGU C.P., BERNARDO Y ELIAS DE TEJADA, F. LA RIQUEZA ESPIRITUAL DE ESPANA / Elordury, E – Madrid: Razon y Fe, 1944 – 1 – sp Bibl Santa Ana [240]
Gomez Morales, Alfredo *see*
- CURSO DE POLITICA ECONOMICA PERONISTA
- POLITICA ECONOMICA PERONISTA

Gomez Nogales, Salvador *see*
- LA FILOSOFIA DE LA NATURALEZA Y LA PSICOLOGIA SEGUN IBN HAZM
- HORIZONTE DE LA METAFISICA ARISTOTELICA

Gomez Ochoa, Fidel *see* EL GOBIERNO DE MAURA DE 1921
Gomez Ortega, Casimiro *see*
- CURSO ELEMENTAL DE BOTANICA
- ELOGIO DE CARLOS 3
- INSTRUCCION SOBRE MODO DE TRANSPORTAR PLANTAS VIVAS
- TABLAS BOTANICAS

Gomez, P *see* SATISFACCION AL PUBLICO CONTRA LA ADICION APOLOGETICA QUE A SU DISSERTACION MEDICO-MORAL DEL PRIMER TOMO DE LA PALESTRA CRITICA. MEDICA
Gomez Restrepo, Antonio *see* BOGOTA
Gomez Rodeles, Cecilio *see* HISTORIA DE LA PUBLICACION MONUMENTA HISTORICA SOCIETATIS JESU
Gomez Villafranca, Ramon *see*
- COOPERACION DE ROMAN GOMEZ VILLAFRANCA A LA BIBLIOGRAFIADE ARIAS MONTANO. N° 1
- EXTREMADURA EN LA GUERRA DE LA INDEPENDENCIA ESPANOLA
- LOS EXTREMANOS EN LAS CORTES DE CADIZ
- SEMINARIO CONCILIAR DE SAN ATON. GABINETE NUMISMATICO. CATALOGO

Gomez-Bravo, Vicente *see*
- ESTETICA SIEMPREVIVAS Y ENSAYOS
- EN FAMILIA. VERSOS VIEJOS

Gomez-Moreno, M *see* IGLESIAS MOZARABES
Gomez-Pompa, A et al *see* RAIN FOREST REGENERATION AND MANAGEMENT
Gomis, Juan B *see* MAGISTERIO DE AMOR FRAY JUAN DE LOS ANGELES (1536-1610)
Gomont, M *see* MONOGRAPHIE DES OSCILLARIES
Gomperz, T *see* GRIECHISCHE DENKER
GONAECIERUM LIBRI 3. DE MORBIS MULIERUM COMMUNIBUS... / Mercado, Luys de – Basilea, 1588 – 9 – sp Cultura [610]
Goncalves, J A *see*
- DICCIONARIO CHINA-PORTUGUEZ
- DICCIONARIO PORTUGUEZ-CHINA...
- LEXICON MAGNUM LATINO-SINICUM...
- LEXICON MANUALE LATINO-SINICUM...
- VOCABULARIUM LATINO-SINICUM

Goncharov, Ivan *see* THE PRECIPICE
Gontcharskaia, S *see* 1905 GOD V DEREVNE
Goncourt, Edmond et Jules *see* LA FEMME AU DIX-HUITIEME SIECLE
GONDLA / Gumilev, Nikolai Sepanovich – Dramaticheskaia poema. Berlin. 1936. BR-1139 2 – 8 – ne IDC [460]
Gondokusumo, Djody *see* PSYCHOLOGIE
Gondon, G *see* L'IMITATEUR DE JESUS-CHRIST, OU LA VIE DU VENERABLE PERE ANTOINE YVAN
Gondon, Jules *see* NOTICE BIOGRAPHIQUE SUR LE R.P. NEWMAN DE L'ORATOIRE DE SAINT-PHILIPPE DE NERI
GONE FICHING-FOR LIBERTY – 52p. on microfiche reading and publishing for libertarians – 9 – 1.00f – at Libertarian Micro [320]
Gonet, J B *see*
- CLYPEUS THEOLOGIAE THOMISTICAE CONTRA NOVOS EIUS IMPUGNATOURS
- MANUALE THOMISTARUM SEU BREVIS THEOLOGIAE CURSUS...

GONG CAN DANG – Nov 1920-Jul 1927. 6 ill. DL47f – 9 – 30.00 – cc Globe [073]
GONG CAN DANG REN – China. A Central Committee Party newspaper published during the war with Japan. Oct 1939-Aug 1941. 20 ill. DL56f – 9 – 80.00 – cc Globe [072]
GONG CHAN DANG – Communist. Nov 1920-Jul 1921. 1 reel. M C66 – 1 – $28.00 – cc Microforms [073]
GONGCHAN DANG REN – Communists. Oct 1939-Aug 1941. 1 reel.M/C 89 – 1 – $55.00 – cc Microforms [073]
GONGCHENG JIXIE – Construction Machinery and Equipment. 1982-. F P241 – 9 – $4.50f – cc Microforms [073]
GONGCHENG KANCHA – Engineering Prospecting. 1981-. F P228 – 9 – $4.50f – cc Microforms [620]
GONGCHENG RE-WULI XUEBAO – (1983 $3.50f; 1980-81, 1984 $4.50f) – Chinese Journal of Engineering Thermo-Physics. In Chinese but English abstracts to the main articles. F p98 – 9 – cc Microforms [073]
GONGREN BAOJIAN – Mirror of Worker. 1929. F C20. In Chinese – 9 – $4.50f – cc Microforms [073]
GONGREN RIBAO – Workers Daily. China. In Chinese. Current Subscription. Annual Delivery. Oct 1978-Dec 1979. 1 reel; 1980-. 1 reel per yr. M D3 – 1 – $55.00r – cc Microforms [072]
GONGREN ZHI LU – The Road of Worker. Jun 1925-Jan 1927. M C21. In Chinese – 1 – $68.00 – cc Microforms [073]
Goni, Blas *see* GLOSANDO A BENITO ARIAS MONTANO. LA FUNCION SOCIAL DEL INGENIO
Goni Moreno, Jose Maria *see* LA HORA DECISIVA

GONIEC KRAKOWSKI – Krakow, Poland. Aug 1940-Jan 1945 – 6r – 1 – us L of C Photodup [943]
GONIEC POLSKI – South Bend: Goniec Polski Pub Co, jun 27 1896-1927; 1928-64 – 57r – 1 – us Res Libr [071]
GONKONG V SISTEME MIROVYKH EKONOMICHESKIKH SVIAZEI / Kukolevskii, A G; ed by Medovogo, A I – Moskva: Izd-vo "Mezhdunarodnye otnosheniia", 1972 – us Res Libr [947]
Gonne, J G *see* DE IURE NEUTRALITATIS STATUUM...
Gonnermann, WE *see* MYCOLOGIA EUROPAEA
Gontaut Biron, R de *see* SUR LES ROUTES DE SYRIE...
Gontery, J *see* LA PIERRE DE TOUCHE, OU LA VRAYE METHODE POUR DESABUSER LES ESPRITS
Gonthier, Dominique C *see* LE REGNE DE JESUS CHRIST
GONZAGA LAW REVIEW – (v1-20 1966-85 on reel $300.00. v21-30 1985-95 on mf $225.00) – v1-30. 1967-95 – 5,6,9 – $525.00 set – us Hein [340]
Gonzaga, Mary *see* THE MYSTICISM OF JOHANN JOSEPH VON GOERRES AS A REACTION AGAINST RATIONALISM
Gonzales Borreguero, G *see* LA CAZA DE LA PERDIZ CON RECLAMO
Gonzales de la Calle, Pedro Urbano *see* VARIAS NOTAS Y APUNTES SOBRE TEMAS DE LETRAS CLASICAS
Gonzales de Mendoza, Juan *see* HISTORIA DE LAS COSAS MAS NOTABLES DEL GRAN REYNO DE CHINA
Gonzales, Jose Maria *see*
- EL DIA DE COLON Y DE LA PAZ. 12 DE OCTUBRE DE 1492-12 DE OCTUBRE DE 1918 2ND ED OVIEDO, 1933
- EL DIA DE COLON Y LA PAZ. MADRID, 1930

Gonzales Llubera, Ignacio *see* VIAJES DE BENJAMIN DE TUDELA. 1160-1173
Gonzales, Manuel G *see* ANDREA COSTA AND THE RISE OF SOCIALISM IN THE ROMAGNA, 1871-1892
Gonzales Pintado, Gaspar *see* LOS MARTIRES DE LAS MISIONES DEL PARAGUAY. BILBAO, 1934. MADRID, 1934
Gonzales y Gomez de Soto, Juan Jose *see* BREVE HISTORIAL DE LAS SAGRADAS RELIQUIAS QUE SE VENERAN EN LAS PARROQUIAS DE SANTA EULALIA Y STA. MARTA LA MAYOR DE MERIDA
Gonzalez Alberdi, Paulino *see*
- A DONDE NOS LLEVA ESTA DICTADURA? Y QUE DEBEMOS HACER?
- POR QUE ESTA EN CRISIS LA ECONOMIA ARGENTINA

Gonzalez Alonso, Diego *see* EL TEMPLO DE AMMON Y LOS PITAGORICOS
Gonzalez Alvarez, Claudio *see* LOS GERIFALTES MARXISTAS POR...
Gonzalez, Antonio *see* CAPSULAS GELATINOSAS
Gonzalez Arzac, Alberto Ricardo *see* LA CONSTITUCION "JUSTICIALISTA" DE 1949
Gonzalez Blanco, Pedro *see* UN GOBIERNO POPULAR SIN DEMAGOGIA
Gonzalez Calderon, Juan Antonio *see* NO HAY JUSTICIA SIN LIBERTAD
Gonzalez Castell, Rafael *see* ENTRE MIS CUATRO PAREDES
Gonzalez, Castro *see* COMPENDARIA IN GRAECAM VIA
Gonzalez Castro, Jose *see* MEDICO DE GUIJO DE SANTA BARBARA. TRATAMIENTO DE LA NEURALGIA CIATICA POR LA CAUTERIZACION DEL HELIX
Gonzalez, Ceferino *see*
- LA REBELLION MILITAIRE EN ESPAGNE ET L'INCOMPREHENSION DES DEMOCRATIES EUROPEENNES DEVANT UN AUSSI GRAVE PROBLEME
- VOIE LIBRE A LA VERITE

Gonzalez Cuadrado, Antonio *see*
- INSTITUTO GENERAL TECNICO DE BADAJOZ. MEMORIA DEL CURSO DE 1904 A 1905...
- MEMORIA...CURSO DE 1889 A 1890...
- MEMORIA...INSTITUTO DE BADAJOZ
- PROGRAMA DE GEOGRAFIA

Gonzalez de Carreras, Diego *see* TERTIUS ARTICULUS QUE...
Gonzalez de Cellorigo, M *see* MEMORIAL DE LA POLITICA NECESARIO Y UTIL RESTAURACION A LA REPUBLICA DE ESPANA

Gonzalez de la Calle, Pedro Urbano *see*
- ARIAS MONTANO, HUMANISTA
- CONSIDERACIONES ACERCA DE LA SEGUNDA PARADOJA DE EL BROCENSE
- VIDA PROFESIONAL Y ACADEMICA DE FRANCISCO DE SANCHEZ DE LAS BROZAS

Gonzalez de Manuel, Thomas *see* VERDADERA RELACION...LAS BATUECAS
Gonzalez de Mendoza, J *see* HISTORIA DELAS COSAS MAS NOTABLES, RITOS Y COSTUMBRES, DEL GRAN REYNO DELA CHINA,...
Gonzalez de Salcedo, P *see* TRATADO IURIDICO-POLITICO DEL CONTRA-BANDO
Gonzalez, Ernesto *see* ASCENSO Y CAIDA DEL PERONISMO
Gonzalez Escudero, Santiago *see* EPICURO Y MARX
Gonzalez, F A *see* EL DIVORCIO A LA LUZ DEL DERECHO INTERNACIONAL...
Gonzalez, F et al *see* CARACTERIZACION Y PROPIEDADES DE UNA VERMICULITA DE BADAJOZ
Gonzalez Fernandez, Carlos *see* ESTUDIO DE LA ATMOSFERA DE UN NUCLEO URBANO EMPLEANDO EL RADON
Gonzalez, Fray Diego *see* POESIAS
Gonzalez Gonzalez, Valeriano *see* ROSA, LA DE VILLAMBRO
Gonzalez Gutierez, E *see* EL TRATADO SOBRE BELICE Y LA DOCTRINA MONROE
Gonzalez Hernandez, Juan *see*
- LA S SOCIEDADES DE CREDITO Y LOS FERROCARRILES EXTREMENOS
- LAS SOCIEDADES DE CREDITO Y LOS FERROCARRILES EXTREMENOS

Gonzalez Hernandez, Ma Jesus *see* MAURA Y EL MAURISMO
Gonzalez Holguin, Diego *see* GRAMATICA Y...EL PERU
Gonzalez, J de M *see* LOS HIJOS DE LA FORTUNA. NOVELA ORIGINAL DE COSTUMBRES ESPANOLAS
Gonzalez Janzen, I *see* ARGENTINA, 20 [I.E. VEINTE] ANOS DE LUCHAS PERONISTAS
GONZALEZ, JULIO. ALFONSO 9TH. MADRID, 1944 / Cereceda, F – Madrid: Razon y Fe, 1946 – 1 – sp Bibl Santa Ana [946]
Gonzalez, Julio V *see* NACIONALIZACION DEL PETROLEO
Gonzalez Menendez-Reigada, Albino *see* CATECISMO PATRIOTICO ESPANOL
Gonzalez Palencia, A *see* MADRID. ARCHIVO HISTORICO NACIONAL. EXTRACTO DEL CATALOGO DE DOCUMENTOS DEL CONSEJO DE INDIAS...
Gonzalez, Palencia Angel *see* THE FLAME OF HISPANICISM
Gonzalez Paz, Amancio *see* LA REVOLUCION Y LAS REVOLUCIONES
Gonzalez Pintado, Gaspar *see* PAJE, MISIONERO Y MARTIR
Gonzalez, R *see* IMPORTANTE CUESTION DE DERECHO INTERNACIONAL...
Gonzalez, Rafael *see* SOCIEDAD EXTREMENA DE FOMENTO-REFORMA DE PROYECTO BANCO HIPITECARIO
Gonzalez Ramos, Vicente *see* PREGON DE LA SANTISIMA VIRGEN DE LA VICTORIA
Gonzalez Revilla, L *see* LA PATRIA POTESTAD Y LA NACIONALIZACION...
Gonzalez Roura, Octavio *see* EL "AFFAIRE" DE LA CORTE SUPREMA ARGENTINA
Gonzalez Ruiz, Nicolas *see* HERNANDO CORTES Y FRANCISCO PIZARRO
Gonzalez Serrano, Urbano *see*
- EN PRO Y EN CONTRA (CRITICAS)
- ESTUDIOS CRITICOS
- GOETHE
- PREOCUPACIONES SOCIALES
- LA PSICOLOGIA DEL AMOR
- LA PSICOLOGIA FISIOLOGICA

Gonzalez, T *see* CENSO DE POBLACION DE LAS PROVINCIAS Y PARTIDOS DE LA CORONA DE ARAGON EN EL SIGLO 16
Gonzalez Trejo, Horacio *see* ARGENTINA
Gonzalez Trillo, Enrique *see* CULTURA CIUDADANA
Gonzalez Valcarcel, Jose Manuel *see* TREINTA ANOS DE RESTAURACION MONUMENTAL EN CACERES
Gonzalez, Valentin *see* EL CAMPESINO
Gonzalez y Centeno, V *see* MEMORIAS ACADEMICAS DE LA REAL SOCIEDAD DE MEDICINA...
Gonzalez y Gomez de Soto, Juan Jose *see*
- CORRESPONDIENTE EN MERIDA DE LA R.A. DE LA HISTORIA
- EMERITA AUGUSTA. APUNTES MONOGRAFICOS ACERCA DE LA CATEDRAL METROPOLITANA DE SANTA MARIA JERUSALEN

- EPITOME HISTORICO DE MERIDA
Gonzalez y Gonzalez, Valeriano *see* PRIMICIAL (LA DESGRACIA PUDO MAS...ODISEA...EL DOCTOR AMORES...!PERO NO AL AXILO!)
Gonzalez y Grez, Juan J *see*
- ESTUDIO...VIRGEN MARIA...ALMOHARIN (CACERES)
- EL OBRERO
Gonzolo Picon, Febres *see* OBRAS COMPLETAS...
Gooch, G P *see*
- HISTORY AND HISTORIANS IN THE NINETEENTH CENTURY
- THE HISTORY OF ENGLISH DEMOCRATIC IDEAS IN THE SEVENTEENTH CENTURY
GOOCHLAND GAZETTE – Sabot. Va. -w. 1955- – 1 – us UMI [071]
Good, Adolphus Clemens *see* JOURNAL
Good, DL *see* COLLEGE WOMEN, ALCOHOL CONSUMPTION, AND NEGATIVE SEXUAL OUTCOMES
GOOD FORM FOR ALL OCCASIONS; A MANUAL OF MANNERS, DRESS AND ENTERTAINMENT FOR BOTH MEN AND WOMEN / Hall, Florence Marion Howe – New York, London: Harper, 1914. vii,228p – 1 – us U.W. Library [390]
GOOD FORTUNE – Brooklyn, NY. 1981-86 – 1 – us A.J.P.C. [071]
GOOD HEALTH TO INDONESIA; REPORT OF JOINT REVIEW OF NEEDS OF THE PHARMACEUTICAL INDUSTRY OF INDONESIA / U.S. Operations Mission to Indonesia – SE 11,619 1. 2 v. in 1. 1961 – 9 – ne IDC [324]
GOOD HOUSEKEEPING – (v158- 1964- 5,6 v182- 1976- 9) – v1- 1885- – 1 – us UMI [640]
GOOD HOUSEKEEPING'S COUNTRY LIVING – v1-4. 1978-Jan 1982 – 1 – us UMI [073]
GOOD HOUSEKEEPING'S VICTORIA *see* VICTORIA
Good, James I *see*
- FAMOUS MISSIONARIES OF THE REFORMED CHURCH
- THE HEIDELBERG CATECHISM IN ITS NEWEST LIGHT
- HISTORICAL HAND-BOOK OF REFORMED CHURCH IN THE UNITED STATES
- HISTORY OF THE REFORMED CHURCH IN THE U.S. IN THE NINETEENTH CENTURY
- HISTORY OF THE SWISS REFORMED CHURCH SINCE THE REFORMATION
- JOHN HUSS AND THE PRESBYTERIANS AND REFORMED
- LIFE OF REV. BENJAMIN SCHNEIDER, D.D.
- LIFE PICTURES OF JOHN CALVIN
- THE ORIGIN OF THE REFORMED CHURCH IN GERMANY
- WOMEN OF THE REFORMED CHURCH
Good, James Isaac *see*
- FAMOUS PLACES OF THE REFORMED CHURCHES
- HISTORY OF THE REFORMED CHURCH OF GERMANY, 1620-1890
- RAMBLES ROUND REFORMED LANDS
Good, John Booth *see* A VOCABULARY AND OUTLINES OF GRAMMAR OF THE NITLAKAPAMUK OR THOMPSON TONGUE... TOGETHER WITH A PHONETIC CHINOOK DICTIONARY..
Good, John Mason *see* MEMOIRS OF THE LIFE AND WRITINGS OF THE REVEREND ALEXANDER GEDDES, LL.D
GOOD MORNING – 1-3 (all publ). 1919-1921 – 7mf – 9 – $50.00 – us UPA [073]
GOOD NEIGHBOURSHIP AMONG NATIONS = RUKUN BANGSA-BANGSA – Djakarta, Ikatan Indonesia Untuk Perserikatan Bangsa-Bangsa. 1955-1957 (1-10). TEN 1858 Lacking: 1955 (1-2); 1956/57 (6/8) – 9 – ne IDC [950]
GOOD NEWES FROM VIRGINIA / Whitaker, Alexander – 1613 – 9 – 5.00 – us Scholars' Facs [978]
GOOD NEWS – Nashville. 1970-76. 2 reels – 1 – 36.00 – us L of C Photodup [780]
GOOD NEWS – New York. v1-4. 1890-92 – 2r – 1 – us Ross [073]
THE GOOD NEWS – Prescott, C.W. [Ont: Printed and pub. at the "Evangelizer Office", [1861?-18– or 19–] – 9 – cn C.I.H.M. [240]
THE GOOD NEWS (CCC323) / Wickings, H F – (In Chinese) – 1st ed. Hong Kong: Bible Book and Tract Depot, 1952 – 1r – 1 – 1984-6662 – us A.T.L.A. [220]
THE GOOD OLD TIMES IN MC LEAN COUNTY / Duis, E – Biographical sketches. Bloomington: Leader Publ. and Printing House. Illinois Reel 44. (The Cox Library Collection) – 5 – us Americana [978]
THE GOOD OLD TIMES; THE STORY OF THE MANCHESTER REBELS OF '45 / Ainsworth, William Harrison – London: Tinsley, 1873. 3v – 1 – us U.W. Library [941]
GOOD OUT OF AFRICA / Culwick, A T – 7 – uk Microform Academic [960]
GOOD REASONS FOR NOT BEING A CONGREGATIONALIST OR THE ANSWER TO THE QUESTION, WHY AM I NOT A CONGREGATIONALIST? – 1 – 5.00 – us Baptist [240]
GOOD SAMARITAN – (In Chinese) – 1947-51 (incomplete) – 1r – 1 – ATLA S0296H – us A.T.L.A. [073]
A GOOD SPEED TO VIRGINIA / Gray, Robert – 1609. Bound with Richard Rich, Newes from Virginia. 1610 – 9 – 5.00 – us Scholars' Facs [978]
GOOD STORIES / Reade, Charles L – British Fiction Archive: Unit 2 – 9 – uk Bell [830]
GOOD TEMPLAR – Gerardstown. West Virginia. 1884-85 – 1 – us UMI [071]
GOOD TEMPLAR – Glasgow, Scotland, UK. 1892-1907. -w. 4 reels – 1 – uk British Libr Newspaper [072]
Good, Thomas *see* A BRIEF ENGLISH TRACT OF LOGICK
GOOD TIME COMING *see* AGE OF FREEDOM
GOOD TIMES – (Index available) – Santa Cruz, CA. Apr 1975-94 – 38r – 1 – $1,900.00 – B02952 – us Library Micro [071]
GOOD TIMES – Santa Cruz, Washington, DC. 1975-1985 – 1r – 1 – $50.00 – B02952 – us Library Micro [071]
GOOD WILL / Pearse, Mark Guy – 187- – 9 – us A.T.L.A. [240]
GOOD WORK *see* AMERICAN BAPTIST
GOOD YEARS = HUA NIEN – (In Chinese) – v1-2. 1932-33 (complete) – 1r – 1 – ATLA S0308 – us A.T.L.A. [073]
Goodall, Edward Basil Herbert *see* SOME WEMBA WORDS
GOOD-BYE / Aberdeen and Temair, Ishbel Gordon – November 12th, 1898. 1898? 00267. (Pre-1900 Canadiana) – 9 – cn C.I.H.M. [971]
GOOD-BYE SWEETHEART: A TALE / Broughton, Rhoda – British Fiction Archive: Unit 4 – 9 – uk Bell [830]
Goodchild, R G *see*
- THE LIMES TRIPOLITANUS IN THE LIGHT OF RECENT DISCOVERIES
- ROMAN TRIPOLITANIA: RECONNAISANCE IN THE DESERT FRONTIER ZONE
Goode, C B *see* OCEANIC ICHTHYOLOGY
Goode, Christine Mary *see* PREPARATION AND NEGOTIATION
Goode, G B *see* OCEANIC ICHTHYOLOGY
Goode, J F *see* HISTORY OF TUGALO BAPTIST ASSOCIATION, GEORGIA
Goode, William H *see* OUTPOSTS OF ZION WITH LIMNINGS OF MISSION LIFE
Goodell, Charles Le Roy *see* PASTORAL AND PERSONAL EVANGELISM
Goodell, Thomas Dwight *see* A SCHOOL GRAMMAR OF ATTIC GREEK
Goodell, William *see*
- THE AMERICAN SLAVE CODE IN THEORY AND PRACTICE
- SELECTED WORKS
Goodelman, E DH *see* POEZYE
Gooden, G M *see* CONFLICT IN SPAIN 1920-1937
Goodenow, Smith B *see* WOMAN'S VOICE IN THE CHURCH
Goodenow, Smith Bartlett *see* BIBLE CHRONOLOGY CAREFULLY UNFOLDED...
GOODFELLOW NEWSLETTER – (See also: Goodfellow Review of Crafts) – v1-3. 1973-1975 – 1 – us UMI [740]
GOODFELLOW REVIEW OF CRAFTS – v1- 1975- – 1 – us UMI [740]
GOODFELLOWS CHARITY EDITION – Toledo, Ohio, 1933-1990 – 1r – 1 – $32.50r – us Archival [978]
Goodger, D R *see* PAPUA NEW GUINEA PATROL REPORTS AND RELATED CORRESPONDENCE, 1954-1963
Goodhart et al *see* COUNTDOWN TO 1997
Goodison, Nicholas Sir *see* INDUSTRIAL REVOLUTION: A DOCUMENTARY HISTORY
Goodkind, Herbert S *see* VIOLIN ICONOGRAPHY
Goodman, George *see* THE CHURCH IN VICTORIA DURING THE EPISCOPATE OF THE RIGHT REVEREND CHARLES PERRY
Goodman, Paul *see* SYNAGOGUE AND THE CHURCH: BEING A CONTRIBUTION TO THE APOLOGETICS OF JUDAISM
Goodmann, Gustav *see* PROBATE PROCEEDINGS AND ADMINISTRATION OF ESTATES
THE GOODNESS OF GOD / Bascom, John – New York: G P Putnam; London: Knickerbocker Press, 1901 – 1mf – 9 – 0-8370-2563-X – 1985-0563 – us A.T.L.A. [210]
Goodnow, Frank Johnson *see*
- SELECTED CASES ON GOVERNMENT AND ADMINISTRATION
- SOCIAL REFORM AND THE CONSTITUTION
Goodnow, Josephine A B *see* GREAT MISSIONARIES OF THE CHURCH
Goodrich, Arthur et al *see* THE STORY OF THE WELSH REVIVAL
GOODRICH BAPTIST CHURCH. CHARLESTON COUNTY, SOUTH CAROLINA : CHURCH RECORDS – 1963-1980 – 1r – 1 – $5.00 – us Baptist [240]
Goodrich, Charles Augustus *see* THE ECCLESIASTICAL CLASS BOOK
Goodrich, Charles B *see* THE SCIENCE OF GOVERNMENT AS EXHIBITED IN THE INSTITUTIONS OF THE U.S.
Goodrich, Samuel G *see* POPULAR BIOGRAPHY: EMBRACING THE MOST EMINENT CHARACTERS OF EVERY AGE, NATION, AND PROFESSION.
Goodrich, William Winton *see* LEGAL ETHICS, THE DUTY OF THE HOUR; LECTURE DELIVERED BEFORE THE STUDENTS OF LAW DEPARTMENT OF UNION UNIVERSITY
Goodsell, Fred Field *see* THE AMERICAN BOARD IN CHINA 1830-1950
Goodsir, Joseph Taylor *see* THE WESTMINSTER CONFESSION OF FAITH EXAMINED ON THE BASIS OF THE OTHER PROTESTANT CONFESSIONS
Goodspeed *see*
- COUNTIES OF PORTER AND LAKE
- COUNTIES OF WHITELY AND NOBLE
- COUNTY OF WILLIAMS
Goodspeed, Calvin *see* THE BOOK OF GENESIS
Goodspeed, Edgar J *see*
- DIE AELTESTEN APOLOGETEN
- INDEX APOLOGETICUS, SIVE, CLAVIS IUSTINI MARTYRIS OPERUM
- INDEX PATRISTICUS, SIVE, CLAVIS PATRUM APOSTOLICORUM OPERUM
Goodspeed, Edgar Johnson *see*
- THE EPISTLE TO THE HEBREWS
- THE NEWBERRY GOSPELS
Goodspeed, George Stephen *see* ISRAEL'S MESSIANIC HOPE TO THE TIME OF JESUS
Goodspeed, K C *see* HISTORY OF DUBUQUE COUNTY
Goodspeed, W A *see* HISTORY OF DUBUQUE COUNTY
GOODWAY HYMNS AND SONGS FOR GENERAL USE IN ALL HOLINESS MEETINGS – 1 – $50.00 – us Presbyterian [780]
Goodwin, Daniel Raynes *see* NOTES ON THE LATE REVISION OF THE NEW TESTAMENT VERSION
Goodwin, E P et al *see* JEW AND GENTILE
Goodwin, Edward Lewis *see* THE COLONIAL CHURCH IN VIRGINIA
Goodwin, Frank J *see* HARMONY OF THE LIFE OF ST PAUL ACCORDING TO THE ACTS...AND THE PAULINE EPISTLES
Goodwin, Harvey et al *see* CREDENTIALS OF CHRISTIANITY
Goodwin, Henry Martyn *see* CHRIST AND HUMANITY
Goodwin, Jeff E *see* BANDWIDTH KNOWLEDGE OF RESULTS IN MOTOR SKILL PERFORMANCE AND LEARNING
Goodwin, John A *see* THE PILGRIM REPUBLIC
Goodwin, John Albert Reed *see* LONG RANGE PLANNING IN THE FACE OF CHANGE
Goodwin, Nolan W *see* WINTERTON REMEMBERED
Goodwin, Thomas A *see* LOVERS THREE THOUSAND YEARS AGO: AS INDICATED BY THE SONG OF SOLOMON
Goodwin, W L *see* LE MONITEUR
Goodwin, William W *see* GREEK READER
GOODWIN'S TOWN OFFICER / Thomas, Benjamin F – (Covers the range of duties and legal responsibilities of various municipal officers in early 19th century Massachusetts) – 4th ed. Worchester (Mass.): Dorr, Howland & Co, 1837 – 4mf – 9 – $6.00 – LLMC 96-065 – us L.L.M.C. [350]
Gool, J van *see*
- DE NIEUWE SCHOUBOURGH DER NEDERLANTSCHE KUNSTSCHILDERS EN SCHILDERESSEN...
- DE NIEUWE SCHOUBURGH DER NEDERLANTSCHE KUNSTSCHILDERS EN SCHILDERESSEN
Goonasekera, Anura *see* TV TRANSNATIONALIZATION – EUROPE AND ASIA
Goonetileke, H A I *see* A BIBLIOGRAPHY OF CEYLON
Goonewardene, T W *see* SINHALESE DIARY, 1893
Goote, Thor *see*
- GLUEHENDER TAG
- 'RANGEHEN IST ALLES!
- SIE WERDEN AUFERSTEHEN!
- WIR TRAGEN DAS LEBEN
Gopinatha, Diksita, Bhatta *see* BHATTAGOPINATHADIKSITAVIRACITA SAMSKARARATNAMALA
Gopinatha Rao, T A *see* ELEMENTS OF HINDU ICONOGRAPHY
Gorbachev, I A *see* TOVARICHESTVA POLNYE, NA VERE, KREDITNYE, SSUDO-SBEREGATEL'NYE, TRUDOVYE I S PEREMENNYM KAPITALOM
Gorbachevskii, N *see* SLOVAR' DREVNEGO AKTOVOGO IAZYKA SEVERO-ZAPADNOGO KRAIA I TSARSTVA POL'SKOGO
Gorbov, D *see* LITERATURA REVOLIUTSIONNOGO DESIATILETIIA 1917-1927
Gorchakov, D P *see* SOCHINENIIA
Gorchakov, Mikhail Konstantinovich *see* ITOGI POLITIKI MITROPOLITOV SERGII A I EVLOGII A
THE GORDIAN KNOT, OR, THE PROBLEM WHICH BAFFLES INFIDELITY / Pierson, Arthur Tappan – New York: Funk & Wagnalls, 1902.1 fiche – 9 – us A.T.L.A. [240]
Gordimer, Nadine *see* THE BLACK INTERPRETERS
Gordlevskii, V A *see* GOSUDARSTVO SEL'DZHYKUDOV MALOI AZII
Gordo Moreno, Angel *see*
- A LA LEGION CANTOS DE AMOR Y DE DOLOR DE ESPANA POR...
- MIS CANTARES
Gordon, Adoniram Judson *see*
- THE HOLY SPIRIT IN MISSIONS
- THE MINISTRY OF WOMEN
- THE TWOFOLD LIFE
Gordon, Alex *see* EXPOSE HISTORIQUE ET PHILOSOPHIQUE PLACE EN REGARD DE LA DOCTRINE SAINT-SIMONIENNE
Gordon, Alexander R *see* EARLY TRADITIONS OF GENESIS
Gordon, Andrew *see* OUR INDIA MISSION
Gordon, Andrew R *see* RAPPORT SUR L'EXPEDITION A LA BAIE D'HUDSON EN 1886
Gordon, Ann *see* THE PAPERS OF ELIZABETH CADY STANTON AND SUSAN B. ANTHONY
Gordon, Anna Adams *see* THE BEAUTIFUL LIFE OF FRANCIS E. WILLARD
Gordon, Bert *see* JOURNAL OF CHROMATOGRAPHIC SCIENCE
Gordon, D *see* HEGYONEI HA-MAGGID
Gordon, D M *see* INTELLIGENTSIIA DLIA KOGO SKAZKA, DLIA KOGO BYL
Gordon, Elizabeth Anna *see* WORLD-HEALERS; OR, THE LOTUS GOSPEL AND ITS BODHISATTVAS, COMPARED WITH EARLY CHRISTIANITY.
Gordon, Ernest B *see* ADONIRAM JUDSON GORDON
GORDON FALLS GAZETTE – Portland OR. July 17 1908 – 1 – us U.O. Library [071]
Gordon, George A *see*
- THE MISSION OF THE PROPHET
- RELIGION AND MIRACLE
Gordon, George Angier *see* THE CHRIST OF TO-DAY
Gordon, George Hamilton *see* COPY OF A DESPATCH, AND ITS ENCLOSURES, ADDRESSED TO EARL AMHERST BY THE EARL OF ABERDEEN, ON THE 2ND APRIL 1835
Gordon, I *see* LITURGIA ET POTESTAS IN RE LITURGICA
Gordon, J *see* CONTROVERSIARUM EPITOMES...
Gordon, J L *see* IGGAROT
Gordon, James B *see* AN HISTORICAL AND GEOGRAPHICAL MEMOIR OF THE NORTH-AMERICAN CONTINENT, ITS NATIONS AND TRIBES

GORDON JOURNAL – Gordon, NE. -w, -sw (1919). Oct 1892; Jan 1896; May 1896-Dec 1900; Apr-Nov 1901; Feb 1902-Apr 1905; Mar 1907-Nov 1910; Mar 1911; Jan 1912 to date – 1 – us NE Hist [071]

Gordon, L et al *see* ETAPY ZHIZNENNOGO TSIKLA I BYT RABOTAIUSHCHEI ZHENSHCHINY

Gordon, Maks *see* OCHERK EKONOMICHSKO I BORBY RABOCHIKH V ROSSII

GORDON REVIEW – v.1-11. 1955-70 – 1 – us UMI [073]

Gordon, Robert Winslow *see*
- AMERICAN FOLKSONG TEXTS
- FOLK-SONGS OF AMERICA

Gordon, Saint A J *see* THE WATCHWORD

Gordon, Samuel D *see* QUIET TALKS ABOUT JESUS

Gordon, Saul *see* GORDON'S ANNOTATED FORMS OF AGREEMENT

THE GORDON W. PRANGE COLLECTION, 1945-1949 *see* SENRYO-GUN KEN-ETSU ZASSI

Gordon, William N *see* THE LEISURE ACTIVITY SELECTION PROCESS

Gordon, William R *see* SCIENCE OF REVEALED TRUTH IMPREGNABLE

Gordon, William Robert *see* THE SCIENCE OF REVEALED TRUTH IMPREGNABLE

Gordon, Wolff von *see* DIE DRAMATISCHE HANDLUNG IN SOPHOKLES' "KOENIG OIDIPUS" UND KLEISTS "DER ZERBROCHENE KRUG"

GORDON'S ANNOTATED FORMS OF AGREEMENT / Gordon, Saul – New York: Prentice-Hall, 1923. 904p. LL-401 – 1 – us L of C Photodup [340]

Gore, Charles *see*
- THE CLERGY AND THE CREEDS
- THE INCARNATION OF THE SON OF GOD; BEING THE BAMPTON LECTURES FOR THE YEAR 1891
- LEO THE GREAT
- THE NEW THEOLOGY AND THE OLD RELIGION
- ORDERS AND UNITY
- THE QUESTION OF DIVORCE
- THOUGHTS ON RELIGION

GORE GAZETTE – Dundas, Mr1827-1829Jn – 1r – 1 – cn Preston [971]

GORE GAZETTE AND ANCASTER, HAMILTON, DUNDAS AND FLAMBOROUGH ADVERTISER – Ancaster, Canada. 1827-29 – 1 reel – 1 – $68.00 – cn Library Assoc [971]

Gore, John *see* KING CHARLES 5, A PERSONAL MEMOIR

Gorecki, P *see* LE FOUR ET LA PANIFICATION DU SUD-EST DE LA GRANDE POLOGNE

GOREE-ISLAND OF MEMORIES : INTERNATIONAL CAMPAIGN FOR THE SAFEGUARDING OF GOREE – 1986 – 56p – 9 – 92-3-102348-9 – fr UNESCO [960]

Gorelov, A *see* GIBEL' SOLOV'INOGO SADA A. BLOKA

GORENIE I VZRYV : MATERIALY CHETVERTOGO VSESOIUZNOGO SIMPOZIUMA PO GORENIIU I VZRYVU, 23-27 SENTIABRIA 1974 G. / Akademiia nauk SSSR, Otdelenie ordena Lenina Instituta khimicheskoi fiziki; ed by Stesik, L N – Moskva: Nauka, 1977 – us Res Libr [947]

GORESTNYI A ZAMIETY : OCHERKI KRASNAGO PETROGRADA / Amfiteatrov, Aleksandr – Berlin: "Grani", 1922 – 1 – CSUX88-B1979 – us Hoover Inst Photo [947]

Gorev, Mikhail *see*
- OTKUDA NEUROZHAI I GOLODOVKI
- TSERKOVNYE BOGATSTVA I GOLOD V ROSII

GOREY CORRESPONDENT – Ireland. -w. 1867-69. (1 reel) – 1 – uk British Libr Newspaper [072]

Gorfein, G M *see* ARKHIVOVEDENIE UCHEBNOE POSOBIE

Gorfinkel, E S *see* SSSR V SISTEME MIROVOGO KHOZIAISTVA

THE GORGIANIC FIGURES IN EARLY GREEK PROSE / Robertson, J C – H 198 2. 1893 – 8 – ne IDC [450]

GORGON – 1-49 (all publ). 1818-1819 – 5mf – 9 – $65.00 – us UPA [335]

Gorham, Barlow Weed *see*
- CAMP MEETING MANUAL
- CONCERNING THEM THAT ARE ASLEEP
- GOD'S METHOD WITH MAN

Gorham, Charles Turner *see*
- ETHICS OF THE GREAT RELIGIONS
- THE FIRST EASTER DAWN
- FIRST EASTER DAWN: AN INQUIRY INTO THE EVIDENCE FOR THE RESURRECTION OF JESUS

Gorham, George Cornelius *see* EXAMINATION BEFORE ADMISSION TO A BENEFICE BY THE BISHOP OF EXETER

Gori, A F *see* SYMBOLAE LITTERARIAE

Goriaev, N V *see* SRAVNITEL'NYI ETIMOLOGICHESKII SLOVAR' LITERATURNOGO RUSSKOGO IAZYKA

Goriainov, S M *see*
- 1812: DOKUMENTY GOSUDARSTVENNOGO I S. PETERSBURGSKOGO GLAVNOGO ARKHIVOV
- GOSUDARSTVENNYI ARKHIV. RAZRIAD 2. "DELA SOBSTVENNO DO IMPERATORSKOI FAMILII OTNOSIASHCHIIASIA"

Goriainow, S *see* LE BOSPHORE ET LES DARDANELLES

GORIASHCHIIA ZDANIIA. LIRIKA SOVREMENNOI DUSHI / Bal'mont, K D – M. 1900. BR-516 2 – 8 – ne IDC [460]

Gorielov, M *see*
- CHORT ZA RULEM
- NARI EKAKH VAVILONSKIKH

DES GORILLES, DES NAINS ET MEME...DES HOMMES : HISTOIRE DE LA GRANDE FORET, DE LA BROUSSE ET DE LA COTE AFRICAINES / Gouzy, Rene – Lausanne, 1919 – 1 – us Res Libr [590]

Gorin, Pavel Osipovich *see*
- OCHERKI PO ISTORII SOVETOV RABOCHIKH DEPUTATOV V 1905 G
- PROLETARIAT V 1917 G. V BORBE ZA VLAST

Goris, R *see* BALI, CULTS AND CUSTOMS

Gorkii, A M *see* A.M. GORKII I SOZDANIE ISTORII FABRIK I ZAVODOV

Gorkii, M *see* O FUTURIZME

Gorkov, Mikhail *see* FINANSIROVANIE VNESHNE I TORGOVLI SSSR (1920-1924 G.)

GORKOVSKI I KRA I: BEZHEMESI ACHNY I ZHURNAL KRA IPLANA – (Includes c.1: no.5/6 1934) – Gorki i: Gorkovskoe kraevoe izd-vo, 1932 – 1 – CSUXAKZ6888-S – us Hoover Inst Photo [947]

Gorky, Maksim *see*
- 9-OE IANVARIA
- O EVREIAKH
- REVOLIUTSII A I KULTURA

Gorman, Monica E *see* TEST-RETEST STUDY OF THE BIODEX CLOSED KINETIC CHAIN ATTACHMENT FOR THE UPPER EXTREMITY

GORNAIA TROPA. VTORAIA KNIGA STIKHOV / Baltrushaitis, Iu – Skorpion. 1912. BR-557 2 – 8 – ne IDC [460]

Gornberg, B *see* PROFSOIUZYI KHOZIAISTVENNOE STROITELSTVO

GORNIK CODZIENNY = THE MINER'S DAILY – Wilkes-Barre, PA: Gornik Pub Co, apr 1-jun 19 1922 – 1r – 1 – us Res Libr [071]

GORNITSA / Ivanov, G – Kniga stikhov. Spb. 1914. BR-1176 2 – 8 – ne IDC [460]

Gornitskii, KS *see* SPISOK RUSSKIKH I NEMNOGIKH INORODCHESKIKH NAZVANII RASTENII. DOPOLNENIE K "BOTANICHESKOMU SLOVARIU"

GORNYE TADZHIKI / Ginzburg, Vul'f Veniaminovich – 1937 – 1 – us I.U. Libraries [390]

GORNYI KLIUCH / Lozinskii, M – Spb. 1916. BR-3628 2 – 8 – ne IDC [460]

GORNYIA VERSHINY. SBORNIK STATEI / Bal'mont, K D – Kn. I., M. 1904. BR-517 2 – 8 – ne IDC [460]

GOROD – Sotsial'no-ekonomicheskii, nauchnoobshchestvennyi i literaturnyi zhurnal. v. 1, nr. 1. Spb. 1907. BR-4119 2 – 8 – ne IDC [300]

GOROD I DEREVNIA – Moscow, 1923-27 n13/14 – 91mf – 9 – COR-580/1 – ne IDC [334]

GORODA I GODY : ROMAN / Fedin, Konstantin – Izd. 3-e. Leningrad: "Pribo i", [192?] – 1 – CSUX88-B7527 – us Hoover Inst Photo [830]

Gorodetskii, S *see*
- CHETYRNADTSATYI GOD
- DAL'NIIA MOLNII
- DIKAIA VOLIA
- DNI LIUBVI
- IAR'. STIKHI LIRICHESKIE I LIROEPICHESKIE
- IVA. PIATAIA KNIGA STIKHOV
- IZBORNIK
- NA ZEMLE
- PERUN. STIKHOTVORENIIA LIRICHESKIIA I LIRO-EPICHESKIIA
- RAZSKAZY
- RUS'. PESNI I DUMY
- SERP. DVENADTSATAIA KNIGA STIKHOV
- SOBRANIE STIKHOV
- STARYIA GNEZDA
- STIKHI
- STIKHOTVORENIIA
- TSVETUSHCHII POSOKH
- VOSPOMINANIIA O BLOKE

Gorodetskii, V D *see* BIBLIOGRAFIIA TURKESTANA 1

Gorodnev, A *see*
- OCHERKI KRASNOI ARMII

GORODSKOE DELO – Spb., Petrograd. 1909-17. Lacking: 1909 (24); 1914 (21); 1915 (20); 1916 (2-3); 1917 (4-24). BR-2348 2 – 8 – ne IDC [073]

O GORODSKOM, RAIONNOM V GORODE SOVETE DEPUTATOV TRUDI ASHCHIKHSIA ESTONSKOI SSR : OFITSIALNY I TEKST S IZMENEII AMI I DOPOLNENII AMI NA 21 DEK. 1973 G – Tallin: E esti raamat, 174 – 1 – CSUX91-B2620 – us Hoover Inst Photo [947]

O GORODSKOM, RAIONNOM V GORODE SOVETE DEPUTATOV TRUDI ASHCHIKSHIA ESTONSKOI SSR : PRINI AT 14 II ULI A 1971 G – Tallin: E esti raamat, 1971 – 1 – CSUX91-B2772 – us Hoover Inst Photo [947]

Goron, Marie Francois *see* L'AMOUR A PARIS, NOUVEAUX MEMOIRES

Goropius, J (Called Becanus) *see* OPERA, HACTENUS IN LUCEM NON EDITA

Gorovtsov', A M *see* SLOVAR' KRATKOI ENTSIKLOPEDII MEZHDUNARODNOGO PRAVA

Gorozhanskii, Ia. I *see* DAMASKIN SEMENOV-RUDNEV, OPISKOP NIZHEGORODSKII (1737-1795)

Gorp, J van *see* ORIGINES ANTWERPIANAE...; NOVEM LIBROS COMPLEXA...

Gorraeus, Ioannis *see* DEFINITIONUM MEDICARUM LIBRI 24 LITERIS GRAECIS DISTINCTI (AEL, ABT 3;1)

GORRELL'S HISTORY OF THE AMERICAN EXPEDITIONARY FORCES AIR SERVICE / U.S. Army. Air Force – 1917-19. 58 rolls. M990 – 1 – us Nat'l Archives [355]

Gorrequer, Gideon, Lt. Col *see* THE OFFICIAL AND PRIVATE PAPERS OF LT. COL. GIDEON GORREQUER

Gorrie, P Douglas *see*
- THE LIVES OF EMINENT METHODIST MINISTERS
- THE LIVES OF EMINENT METHODIST MINISTERS; CONTAINING BIOGRAPHICAL SKETCHES, INCIDENTS, ANECDOTES, RECORDS OF TRAVEL, REFLECTIONS,...

Gorrie, P Douglass *see*
- THE CHURCHES AND SECTS OF THE UNITED STATES
- EPISCOPAL METHODISM AS IT WAS AND IS, OR, AN ACCOUNT OF THE ORIGIN, PROGRESS, DOCTRINES, CHURCH POLITY, USAGES, INSTITUTIONS, AND STATISTICS OF THE METHODIST EPISCOPAL CHURCH IN THE UNITED STATES
- THE LIVES OF EMINENT METHODIST MINISTERS

EL GORRO DE DORMIR / Vargas, Adolfo de – 1876 – 9 – 1.50f – sp Bibl Santa Ana [830]

Gorschboth, P *see* DIE "HESPERIDINE" IN DEN ACHAENEN DER KOMPOSITEN

GORSKAI A PRAVDA : ORGAN GORSKOGO OBLASTN. KOMITETA R.K.P. (B) I GORSKOGO T SENTRALNOGO ISPOLNITELNOGO KOMITETA SOVETOV RAB.KRESTI AN. KRASN. KAZ. GORSK. TRUD. DEPUTATOV G.S.S.R. – (Includes c.1: 1922:Mar.12) – Vladikavkaz: Gorskoe otd-nie gos. izd-va, 19uu – 1 – CSUXADP5035-S – us Hoover Inst Photo [947]

Gorskii, A V *see*
- OPISANIE SLAVIANSKIKH RUKOPISEI MOSKOVSKOI SINODAL'NOI (PATRIARSHEI) BIBLIOTEKI
- OPISANIE VELIKIKH CHETIKH-MINEI MAKARIIA MITROPOLITA VSEROSSIISKAGO

Gorter, D de *see* CATALOGUS PLANTARUM HORTI ULENPASSIANI

Gorter, James Polk *see* LAW OF EVIDENCE

O GORUTUBA – Janauba, 6 Jan-25 Dec 1980 – 1,5,6 – bl Biblioteca [072]

Gory, H L *see* HISTOIRE NATURELLE ET ICONOGRAPHIE DES INSECTES COLEOPTERES

Gorzny, Willi *see* GESAMTVERZEICHNIS DES DEUTSCHSPRACHIGEN SCHRIFTTUMS 1700-1910

Gosche, Richard *see* ARCHIV FUER LITERATURGESCHICHTE

GO-SET – 1966-1974. GS1-9 – 9r – 1 – at Corangamite [999]

GOSFORD TIMES – Jul 7-Dec 29 1911; Jan 3-Mar 28 1929; Jan 15-Dec 17 1931; Jul 14 1932-Dec 19 1935; Jul 1 1937-Dec 24 1940; Sep 2 1887; Jun 13 1890; Nov 1 1895; Aug 21 1919; Nov 24 1921; Dec 1 1921; Sep 22 1927; Sep 5 1929; Jun 16 1932; Oct 28 1952 – 9 – at Pascoe [072]

GOSHEN 1781-1898 – (Mf 1-2: Early Records 1781-1820. Mf 3: Early Records 1821-43. Mf 4: M,B,D,Intention 1822-53. Mf 5-6: B,M,D 1844-98) – (mf ed 1983) – 6mf – 9 – 0-931248-34-5 – us Holbrook [920]

GOSHEN AND THE SHRINE OF SAFT EL HENNEH (MEES VOL 4) : (1885) / Naville, E – London, 1887 – 3mf – 8 – Dfl13.00 – ne Slangenburg [720]

GOSHEN BAPTIST CHURCH. LINCOLN COUNTY. GEORGIA : CHURCH RECORDS – 1802-67 – 1 – 9.72 – us Baptist [240]

Goshen, New Hampshire. Goshen Baptist Church *see* RECORDS

GOSLARSCHE ZEITUNG – Goslar, West Germany. 1976- – ca 8r per yr – 1 – gw Mikrofilm [072]

Gosling, W G *see* LABRADOR: ITS DISCOVERY, EXPLORATION AND DEVELOPMENT

THE GOSPEL ACCORDING TO DARWIN / Hutchinson, Woods – Chicago: Open Court, 1898 – 1mf – 9 – 0-8370-3702-6 – 1985-1702 – us A.T.L.A. [210]

THE GOSPEL ACCORDING TO LUKE / Luce, H K – 1936 – 9 – $15.00 – us I.R.C. [240]

THE GOSPEL ACCORDING TO LUKE / Riddle, Matthew Brown – New York: Charles Scribner, 1882, c1881 – 1mf – 9 – 0-8370-9731-2 – 1986-3731 – us A.T.L.A. [220]

THE GOSPEL ACCORDING TO MARK / Hort, A F – 1914 – 9 – $10.00 – us I.R.C. [240]

THE GOSPEL ACCORDING TO MARK / Riddle, Matthew Brown – New York: Charles Scribner, 1881 – 1mf – 9 – 0-8370-9732-0 – 1986-3732 – us A.T.L.A. [220]

THE GOSPEL ACCORDING TO MATTHEW = EVANGELIUM NACH MATTHAEUS : TOGETHER WITH A GENERAL THEOLOGICAL AND HOMILETICAL INTRODUCTION TO THE NEW TESTAMENT / Lange, Johann Peter – (In English. Includes bibliographies) – New York: Charles Scribner, 1865, c1864 – 2mf – 9 – 0-8370-6750-2 – 1986-0750 – us A.T.L.A. [220]

THE GOSPEL ACCORDING TO MATTHEW / McNeile, Alan Hugh – 1915 – 9 – $18.00 – us I.R.C. [240]

THE GOSPEL ACCORDING TO MATTHEW / Schaff, Philip – New York: Charles Scribner, 1882, c1881 – 1mf – 9 – 0-8370-9740-1 – 1986-3740 – us A.T.L.A. [220]

THE GOSPEL ACCORDING TO MATTHEW / Williams, Nathaniel Marshman – Boston: Gould & Lincoln, 1873, c1870 – 1mf – 9 – 0-8370-5858-9 – 1985-3858 – us A.T.L.A. [220]

THE GOSPEL ACCORDING TO MATTHEW...FOR BIBLE READERS & FOR SUNDAY SCHOOL TEACHERS / Whiton, James Morris – Boston: W.A. Wilde, 1879. 1 fiche. 8370-5829-5 – 9 – us A.T.L.A. [240]

THE GOSPEL ACCORDING TO SAINT MATTHEW : WITH MAPS, NOTES AND INTRODUCTION / Carr, Arthur – (Includes indexes) – Cambridge: University Press, 1894 – 1mf – 9 – 0-8370-9768-1 – 1986-3768 – us A.T.L.A. [220]

THE GOSPEL ACCORDING TO SAINT MATTHEW AND PART OF SAINT MARK – Translated by Sir John Cheke. Prefixed is an introductory account of the nature and object of the translation, by James Goodwin. 1843 – 1 – us A.T.L.A. [240]

GOSPEL ACCORDING TO SAINT PAUL / Du Bose, William Porcher – New York: Longmans, Green, 1907.1 fiche – 9 – us A.T.L.A. [240]

GOSPEL ACCORDING TO SATAN / Grey, Standish – London: Kerby & Endean, 1881 – 9 – us A.T.L.A. [240]

THE GOSPEL ACCORDING TO SATAN / Grey, Standish – 4th ed. London:Kerby & Endean ; New York:James Pott, 1881 – 1mf – 9 – 0-8370-3393-4 – 1985-1393 – us A.T.L.A. [230]

THE GOSPEL ACCORDING TO ST JOHN – B. F. Westcott. Authorised. 1902 – 9 – us A.T.L.A. [240]

THE GOSPEL ACCORDING TO ST JOHN: WITH MAPS, NOTES AND INTRODUCTION / Plummer, Alfred – Cambridge: University Press, 1892. 1 fiche – 9 – us A.T.L.A. [240]

THE GOSPEL ACCORDING TO ST LUKE / Lindsay, Thomas M – New York: Scribner & Welford, 1887 – 1mf – 9 – us A.T.L.A. [240]

THE GOSPEL ACCORDING TO ST LUKE : WITH MAPS, NOTES AND INTRODUCTION / Farrar, Frederic William – (Includes indexes) – Cambridge: University Press; London: C J Clay, 1891 – 1mf – 9 – 0-8370-3097-8 – 1985-1097 – us A.T.L.A. [220]

THE GOSPEL ACCORDING TO ST. LUKE / Plumptre, Edward Hayes; ed by Ellicott, Charles John – (Includes indexes) – London; New York: Cassell, [18–?] – 2mf – 9 – 0-8370-6834-7 – 1986-0834 – us A.T.L.A. [220]

THE GOSPEL ACCORDING TO ST MARK / Chadwick, George Alexander – New York: A.C. Armstrong, 1887. 2 fiches – 9 – us A.T.L.A. [240]

THE GOSPEL ACCORDING TO ST MARK / ed by Plummer, Alfred – (Includes index) – Cambridge:University Press, 1915 – 1mf – 9 – 0-8370-5448-6 – 1985-3448 – us A.T.L.A. [220]

THE GOSPEL ACCORDING TO ST MARK / Swete, Henry Barclay – The Greek text with introductions, notes, and indices. 3d ed. 1909 – 1 – us A.T.L.A. [240]

THE GOSPEL ACCORDING TO ST. MARK : THE GREEK TEXT / ed by Hort, Arthur – Cambridge: University Press; New York: Macmillan [distributor], 1902 – 1mf – 9 – 0-8370-7157-7 – 1986-1157 – us A.T.L.A. [220]

THE GOSPEL ACCORDING TO ST. MARK : WITH MAPS, NOTES AND INTRODUCTION / Maclear, George Frederick – (Discussion in English; text in Greek. Includes indexes) – 1st ed. Cambridge: University Press, 1883 – 1mf – 9 – 0-8370-9803-3 – 1986-3803 – us A.T.L.A. [220]

GOSPEL ACCORDING TO ST PAUL: STUDIES IN THE FIRST EIGHT CHAPTERS OF... ROMANS / Dykes, James Oswald – New York: Robert Carter, 1888. 1 fiche – 9 – us A.T.L.A. [240]

THE GOSPEL AMONG THE SLAVES : A SHORT ACCOUNT OF MISSIONARY OPERATIONS AMONG THE AFRICAN SLAVES OF THE SOUTHERN STATES / Harrison, W P – Nashville, Tenn.: Publishing House of the M.E. Church, South, 1893 – 1mf – us A.T.L.A. [976]

THE GOSPEL AND FRONTIER PEOPLES : A REPORT OF A CONSULTATION DECEMBER 1972 / ed by Pierce Beaver, R – South Passadena, 1973 – 9mf – 8 – ne Slangenburg [290]

THE GOSPEL AND HUMAN NEEDS : BEING THE HULSEAN LECTURES DELIVERED BEFORE THE UNIVERSITY OF CAMBRIDGE, 1908-9, WITH ADDITIONS / Figgis, John Neville – London; New York: Longmans, Green, 1909 – 1mf – us A.T.L.A. [240]

THE GOSPEL AND ITS EARLIEST INTERPRETATIONS / Cone, Orello – New York: Putnam, 1893. 1 fiche – 9 – us A.T.L.A. [240]

THE GOSPEL AND ITS MINISTRY / Anderson, Robert – 2nd ed. Bososton: Believers' Book-Rooms, [18–] – 1mf – 9 – 0-8370-2497-8 – 1985-0497 – us A.T.L.A. [240]

THE GOSPEL AND ITS WITNESSES : SOME OF THE CHIEF FACTS IN THE LIFE OF OUR LORD AND THE AUTHORITY OF THE EVANGELICAL NARRATIVES CONSIDERED IN LECTURES CHIEFLY PREACHED AT ST. JAMES'S WESTMINSTER / Wace, Henry – (Includes bibliographical references) – 2nd ed. London: John Murray, 1884 – 1mf – 9 – 0-8370-9336-8 – 1986-3336 – us A.T.L.A. [220]

THE GOSPEL AND PHILOSOPHY : SIX LECTURES PREACHED IN TRINITY CHAPEL, NEW YORK / Dix, Morgan – New York: E & J B Young, 1886 – 1mf – 9 – 0-8370-2927-9 – 1985-0927 – us A.T.L.A. [230]

GOSPEL BANNER – v1-92. 1878-1969 (gaps) – 43r – 1 – ATLA 1994-S004 – us A.T.L.A. [073]

THE GOSPEL BANNER – 1854-55 (complete) – 1r – 1 – ATLA R0136 – us A.T.L.A. [073]

THE GOSPEL BANNER : GOSPEL WORKER EDITION – v23 no13-v24; v26 nos2-24. 1900-01; 1903 (gaps) – 2r – 1 – ATLA 1994-S030 – us A.T.L.A. [073]

THE GOSPEL DEVELOPED THROUGH THE GOVERNMENT AND ORDER OF THE CHURCHES OF JESUS CHRIST / Johnson, William B – 1846 – 1 – 8.05 – us Baptist [240]

THE GOSPEL FOR A WORLD OF SIN : A COMPANION-VOLUME TO "THE GOSPEL FOR AN AGE OF DOUBT" / Van Dyke, Henry – (Includes bibliographical references) – New York: Macmillan, 1900, c1899 – 1mf – 9 – 0-8370-5642-X – 1985-3642 – us A.T.L.A. [240]

THE GOSPEL FOR ALL (CCC87) / Ch'en, Chi-yun – (In Chinese) – Shanghai: Christian Literature Society, 1949 – 1r – 1 – 1984-B500 – us A.T.L.A. [220]

GOSPEL HERALD – Beamsville, 1937-92 – 16r – 1 – cn Commonwealth Micro [073]

GOSPEL HERALD – v1-48. 1908-55 (complete) – 48r – 1 – ATLA 1990-S000 – us A.T.L.A. [073]

THE GOSPEL HERALD – (Cumulative index 1969-84) – Ontario, CN. 1937-91 – 15r – 1 – $65.00r – cn Commonwealth Micro [072]

GOSPEL HISTORY : A SYLLABUS OF PROFESSOR C.W. HODGE'S GOSPEL HISTORY / Hodge, Caspar Wistar – Princeton:Charles S. Robinson, 1879 – 1mf – 9 – 0-8370-3605-4 – 1985-1605 – us A.T.L.A. [220]

GOSPEL HISTORY: A SYLLABUS OF PROFESSOR C.W. HODGE'S GOSPEL HISTORY / Hodge, Caspar Wistar – Princeton: Charles S. Robinson, 1879. 1 fiche – 9 – us A.T.L.A. [240]

GOSPEL HOLINESS / Dayton, A C – 1879 – 1 – 5.00 – us Baptist [240]

GOSPEL HYMNS AND SACRED SONGS / Bliss, PO & Sankey, Ira D – 1875 – 1 – 5.00 – us Baptist [240]

THE GOSPEL IN BURMAH : THE STORY OF ITS INTRODUCTION AND MARVELLOUS PROGRESS AMONG THE BURMESE AND KARENS / Wylie, Macleod (Mrs) – New York: Sheldon; Boston: Gould & Lincoln, 1860 – 1mf – 9 – 0-8370-6553-4 – 1986-0553 – us A.T.L.A. [240]

THE GOSPEL IN CENTRAL AMERICA, PUBLISHED IN LONDON IN 1850 / Crowe, Frederick – 1 – 21.80 – us Baptist [240]

THE GOSPEL IN ENOCH, OR, TRUTH IN THE CONCRETE : A DOCTRINAL AND BIOGRAPHICAL SKETCH / Tucker, Henry Holcombe – (Includes appendix) – Philadelphia: J B Lippincott, 1869 – 1mf – 9 – 0-8370-5583-0 – 1985-2289 – us A.T.L.A. [220]

GOSPEL IN EZEKIEL: ILLUSTRATED IN A SERIES OF DISCOURSES / Guthrie, Thomas – New York: E.B. Treat, (1891). 1 fiche – 9 – us A.T.L.A. [240]

THE GOSPEL IN ISAIAH:...EXPOSITIONS...UPON THE SIXTH CHAPTER / Robinson, Charles Seymour – Chicago: Fleming H. Revell, 1895. 1 fiche – 9 – us A.T.L.A. [240]

THE GOSPEL IN LATIN LANDS : OUTLINE STUDIES OF PROTESTANT WORK IN THE LATIN COUNTRIES / Clark, Francis Edward – (Includes bibliographies & index) – New York: Macmillan, 1909 – 1mf – 9 – 0-8370-6095-8 – 1986-0095 – us A.T.L.A. [240]

THE GOSPEL IN LEVITICUS : OR, AN EXPOSITION OF THE HEBREW RITUAL / Seiss, Joseph Augustus – Philadelphia:Lindsay & Blakiston, 1860, c1859 – 1mf – 9 – 0-8370-5221-1 – 1985-3221 – us A.T.L.A. [220]

THE GOSPEL IN NATURE: SCRIPTURE TRUTHS ILLUSTRATED BY FACTS OF NATURE / McCook, Henry Christopher – Philadelphia: Geo. W. Jacobs, 1895 – 1mf – 9 – us A.T.L.A. [240]

THE GOSPEL IN PAGAN RELIGIONS : SOME THOUGHTS SUGGESTED BY THE WORLD'S PARLIAMENT OF RELIGIONS TO AN ORTHODOX CHRISTIAN – Boston: Arena Publ Co, 1894 – 1mf – 9 – 0-8370-3348-9 – 1985-1348 – us A.T.L.A. [230]

GOSPEL IN PAGAN RELIGIONS: SOME THOUGHTS SUGGESTED BY THE WORLD'S PARLIAMENT OF RELIGIONS – Boston: Arena Publ. Co., 1894. 1 fiche – 9 – us A.T.L.A. [230]

GOSPEL IN RUSSIA – (Filmed with: Friends of Russia) – 1936-46 (complete) – 1r – 1 – ATLA S0702B – us A.T.L.A. [073]

GOSPEL IN RUSSIA *see* FRIENDS OF RUSSIANS

THE GOSPEL IN RUSSIA – (Printed by the All-Russian Evangelical Christian Union, U.S.A. Nov. 1926, Oct. 1928, July-Oct. 1930, Jan. & Apr. 1931, Oct. 1933, Jan. 1935) – New York – 1r – 1 – $5.00 – us Baptist [240]

THE GOSPEL IN THE PSALMS : A SERIES OF EXPOSITIONS BASED ON REVISED TRANSLATION / M'Lean, Daniel – Edinburgh: Andrew Elliot, 1875 – 1mf – 9 – us A.T.L.A. [240]

THE GOSPEL IN WATER, OR CAMPBELLISM / Jarrel, Willis Anselm – 1886 – 1 – 22.47 – us Baptist [240]

THE GOSPEL ITS OWN WITNESS / Leathes, Stanley – 1874 – 9 – us A.T.L.A. [240]

THE GOSPEL MESSAGE : OR, ESSAYS, ADDRESSES, SUGGESTIONS, AND WARNINGS ON THE DIFFERENT ASPECTS OF CHRISTIAN MISSIONS TO NON-CHRISTIAN RACES AND PEOPLES / Cust, Robert Needham – (Includes index) – London: Luzac, 1896 – 2mf – 9 – 0-8370-6661-1 – 1986-0661 – us A.T.L.A. [240]

GOSPEL MESSENGER – (Lacking some issues) – v21-113. Jul 1883-1964 – 81r – 1 – ATLA S0232 – us A.T.L.A. [073]

GOSPEL MESSENGER, OR, UNIVERSALIST ADVOCATE – London, C.W. [Ont]: J.R. Lavell, [1849?-18–] – 9 – cn C.I.H.M. [240]

THE GOSPEL MIRACLES IN THEIR RELATION TO CHRIST AND CHRISTIANITY / Taylor, William Mackergo – (Includes bibliographical references) – New York: A D F Randolph, 1880 – 1mf – 9 – 0-8370-5487-7 – 1985-3487 – us A.T.L.A. [240]

GOSPEL NEWS REPORT = FU YIN HSIN PAO – (In Chinese) – no 32. Jul 1877 (incomplete) – 1r – 1 – ATLA S0296I – us A.T.L.A. [073]

GOSPEL OF A RISEN SAVIOUR / Edgar, Robert McCheyne – Edinburgh: T. & T. Clark, 1892. 1 fiche – 9 – us A.T.L.A. [240]

THE GOSPEL OF BARNABAS / Ragg, Lonsdale & Ragg, Lara – Oxford, 1907 – 12mf – 8 – ne Slangenburg [220]

THE GOSPEL OF COMMON SENSE : AS CONTAINED IN THE CANONICAL EPISTLE OF JAMES / Deems, Charles Force – New York: Wilber B Ketcham, c1888 – 1mf – 9 – 0-8370-2859-0 – 1985-0859 – us A.T.L.A. [220]

THE GOSPEL OF JESUS THE SON OF GOD : AN INTERPRETATION FOR THE MODERN MAN / Knox, George William – Boston: Houghton, Mifflin, 1909 – 1mf – 9 – 0-8370-4442-1 – 1985-2442 – us A.T.L.A. [240]

THE GOSPEL OF JOY / Brooke, Stopford Augustus – London: Isbister, 1898 – 1mf – us A.T.L.A. [240]

THE GOSPEL OF LABOR / Stelzele, Charles – New York: F.H. Revell, c1912 – 1mf – us A.T.L.A. [240]

THE GOSPEL OF LAW : A SERIES OF DISCOURSES UPON FUNDAMENTAL CHURCH DOCTRINES / Stewart, Samuel James – Boston: George H Ellis, 1882 – 1mf – 9 – 0-8370-5544-X – 1985-3544 – us A.T.L.A. [210]

THE GOSPEL OF LIFE : THOUGHTS INTRODUCTORY TO THE STUDY OF CHRISTIAN DOCTRINE / Westcott, Brooke Foss – 2nd ed. London; New York: Macmillan, 1895 – 1mf – 9 – 0-8370-5806-6 – 1985-3806 – us A.T.L.A. [230]

GOSPEL OF PAUL / Everett, Charles Carroll – Boston: Houghton, Mifflin, 1893.1 fiche – 9 – us A.T.L.A. [240]

THE GOSPEL OF PAUL / Everett, Charles Carroll – (Includes index) – Boston:Houghton, Mifflin, 1893 – 1mf – 9 – 0-8370-3083-8 – 1985-1083 – us A.T.L.A. [220]

THE GOSPEL OF RECONCILIATION, OR, AT-ONE-MENT / Walker, William Lowe – Edinburgh: T.& T. Clarke, 1909. 1 fiche – 9 – us A.T.L.A. [240]

THE GOSPEL OF RIGHTNESS: A STUDY IN PAULINE PHILOSOPHY / Woods, Charlotte Elizabeth – London: Williams & Norgate, 1909. 1 fiche – 9 – us A.T.L.A. [240]

THE GOSPEL OF ST JOHN / Dods, Marcus – New York: A.C. Armstrong, 1896. 2 fiches – 9 – us A.T.L.A. [240]

GOSPEL OF ST JOHN AND THE SYNOPTIC GOSPELS / Barth, Fritz – New York: Eaton & Mains, 1907. 1 fiche – 9 – us A.T.L.A. [240]

THE GOSPEL OF ST. JOHN AND THE SYNOPTIC GOSPELS / Barth, Fritz – New York: Eaton & Mains, c1907 – 1mf – 9 – 0-8370-2194-4 – 1985-0194 – us A.T.L.A. [220]

THE GOSPEL OF ST. LUKE / Maclaren, Alexander – 2nd ed. London: Hodder & Stoughton, 1898 – 1mf – 9 – 0-8370-6213-6 – 1986-0213 – us A.T.L.A. [220]

THE GOSPEL OF ST MATTHEW / Gibson, John Monro – New York: A C Armstrong, [1890] – 2mf – 9 – 0-8370-2289-4 – 1985-0289 – us A.T.L.A. [220]

THE GOSPEL OF THE ATONEMENT / Wilson, James Maurice – London: Macmillan, 1899.1 fiche – 9 – us A.T.L.A. [240]

THE GOSPEL OF THE DIVINE SACRIFICE : A STUDY IN EVANGELICAL BELIEF: WITH SOME CONCLUSIONS TOUCHING LIFE / Hall, Charles Cuthbert – New York: Dodd, Mead, 1897, c1896 – 1mf – 9 – 0-8370-4728-5 – 1985-2728 – us A.T.L.A. [240]

GOSPEL OF THE KINGDOM *see* SOCIAL PROGRESS

THE GOSPEL OF THE KINGDOM OF HEAVEN... LECTURES ON THE GOSPEL OF ST LUKE / Maurice, Frederick Denison – London: Macmillan, 1888.1 fiche – 9 – us A.T.L.A. [240]

THE GOSPEL OF THE SECULAR LIFE : SERMONS PREACHED AT OXFORD, WITH A PREFATORY ESSAY / Fremantle, W H – New York: Scribner, 1883 – 1mf – us A.T.L.A. [240]

THE GOSPEL OF WEALTH / Carnegie, Andrew – 1906 – 9 – 1.00f – at Libertarian Micro [320]

THE GOSPEL PLAN...DOCTRINES OF SALVATION, SPIRITUAL LIFE, OR, REGENERATION... *see* THEOLOGICAL MISCELLANY 1

GOSPEL PUBLISHER – Harrisburg, PA. 1835-45 – 3r – 1 – $32.50r – us Archival [071]

THE GOSPEL REFLECTOR – Philadelphia. v. 1 no. 1-12. June 15 1845 – 1 – us NY Public [240]

THE GOSPEL TEACHER – v1 no11-v37. Nov 1891-1931 (complete) – Inquire – 1 – ATLA 1994-S016 – us A.T.L.A. [073]

GOSPEL TEMPERANCE HERALD AND BLUE RIBBON OFFICIAL GAZETTE – The Blue Ribbon Official Gazette and Gospel Temperance Herald The Signal. London. -w. 5 Apr 1882-9 Feb 1910. Wanting 12 Jun 1901-29 Jun 1902 – 11r – 1 – uk British Libr Newspaper [073]

GOSPEL TIDINGS – v31-32. 1941-1953 (complete) – Inquire – 1 – ATLA 1994-S032 – us A.T.L.A. [073]

THE GOSPEL TRIBUNE AND CHRISTIAN COMMUNIONIST – Toronto: R Dick, v3 no 1(May 1856-) – 9 – cn C.I.H.M. [220]

THE GOSPEL TRIBUNE FOR ALLIANCE AND INTERCOMMUNION THROUGHOUT EVANGELICAL CHRISTENDOM – Toronto: R Dick, 1854-1856 – 9 – cn C.I.H.M. [220]

GOSPEL TRUMPET *see* VITAL CHRISTIANITY

GOSPEL TRUTHS – v1 no7-nos8, 13-14. 1902 (complete) – 1r – 1 – ATLA 1994-S020 – us A.T.L.A. [073]

THE GOSPEL WALL, OR, LESSONS FROM NEHEMIAH / Lockhart, W P – London: James Nisbet, 1879. 1 fiche – 9 – us A.T.L.A. [240]

GOSPEL WITNESS – (Title varies: Gospel Witness and Protestant Advocate) – Toronto. v1-58. 1922-80 (complete) – 23r – 1 – ATLA RS0148 – us A.T.L.A. [073]

THE GOSPEL WITNESS – 1838-39 (complete) – 1r – 1 – ATLA R0126 – us A.T.L.A. [240]

THE GOSPEL WITNESS – Toronto, April 9, 1931, February 11 and 18, 1932. Publ. No. 2204-4 g. One of several items on a reel – 1 – us Baptist [240]

THE GOSPEL WITNESS – v1-3. 1905-08 (complete) – 2r – 1 – ATLA 1991-S000 – us A.T.L.A. [073]

GOSPEL WITNESS AND PROTESTANT ADVOCATE *see* GOSPEL WITNESS

GOSPEL-CRITICISM AND HISTORICAL CHRISTIANITY / Cone, Orello – New York: G.P. Putnam, 1891. 1 fiche – 9 – us A.T.L.A. [240]

THE GOSPELS AS HISTORICAL DOCUMENTS / Stanton, Vincent Henry – 1903-20 – 1 – us A.T.L.A. [240]

THE GOSPELS IN THE SECOND CENTURY: AN EXAMINATION OF...SUPERNATURAL RELIGION / Sanday, William – London: Macmillan, 1876.1 fiche – 9 – us A.T.L.A. [240]

GOSPELS OF YESTERDAY : DRUMMOND, SPENCER, ARNOLD / Watson, Robert Alexander – (Includes bibliographical references) – 3rd ed. London: James Nisbet, 1889 – 1mf – 9 – 0-8370-5706-X – 1985-3706 – us A.T.L.A. [210]
THE GOSPEL-SHOP : A COMEDY OF FIVE ACTS, WITH A NEW PROLOGUE AND EPILOGUE,... / Hill, Richard – [London, 1778] – 1mf – 9 – MP-529/1 – ne IDC [820]
GOSPER COUNTY ENTERPRISE – Elwood, NE. -w. Jun. 1899-Mar. 1901 – 1 – us NE Hist [071]
GOSPODARSTVO – Buenos Aires, Argentina, 1926 – 1mf or 1 reel – 9,1 – us I.H.R.C. [972]
GOSPORT & FAREHAM EXPRESS & STANDARD – Ennisworth, England. Aug-Dec 1982; 1983-May 1986. -w. 3 reels – 1 – uk British Libr Newspaper [072]
GOSPORT JOURNAL – Portsmouth, England. 3 Jan-28 Mar 1958; 4 Jul-24 Dec 1958; 2 Jan-19 Jun 1959; 14 Aug-23 Dec 1959; 1960-64. -w. 10 reels – 1 – uk British Libr Newspaper [072]
GOSPORT STANDARD – England.Nov-Dec 1976; 17, 24 Mar, 12 May-22 Dec 1977; Jan-Aug, 21 Sept-21 Dec 1978; 1979-24 Dec 1980; 8 Jan 1981-5 Aug 1982 – 1 – uk British Libr Newspaper [072]
Goss, C C *see* STATISTICAL HISTORY OF THE FIRST CENTURY OF AMERICAN METHODISM
Goss, CW F *see* THE LONDON DIRECTORIES
Goss, Dwight *see* HISTORY OF GRAND RAPIDS AND ITS INDUSTRIES
Gossalbes, Jose *see* INFORMACION QUE DA AL PUBLICO EL DR. JOSE GOSSALBES... SOBRE LA ULTIMA ENFERMEDAD...
Gosse, Abbe *see* EXPOSITION RAISONNEE DES PRINCIPES DE L'UNIVERSITE, RELATIVEMENT A L'EDUCATION
Gosse, Edmund *see*
- CRITICAL KIT-KATS
- JEREMY TAYLOR
- THE POETICAL WORKS OF THOMAS LOVELL BEDDOES

Gosse, Etienne *see* LA MORT DE VINCENT MALIGNON, AGENT NATIONAL DE LA COMMUNE DE CLAYS(...)EN UN ACTE ET EN VERS(...)
Gosse, P H *see*
- THE BIRDS OF JAMAICA
- NATURAL HISTORY. MOLLUSCA

Gosselet, A *see* STATISTIQUE ADMINISTRATIVE ET MEDICALE DE L'ASILE PUBLIC DES ALIENEES DE LILLE, POUR LES ANNEES 1847 A 1851: RAPPORT? MR. LE PREFET DE DEPART. DU NORD
Gosselin, Auguste *see*
- LE 19. SIECLE: TABLEAUX DES PREMIERES ANNEES
- L'ENGLISE (SIC) DU CANADA
- JURIDICTION EXERCEE PAR L'ARCHEVEQUE DE ROUEN
- M. JEAN LE SUEUR: ANCIEN CURE DE SAINT-SAUVEUR-DE-THURY, PREMIER PRETRE SECULIER DU CANADA, 1634-68
- LE VENERABLE FRANCOIS DE LAVAL, PREMIER EVEQUE DE QUEBEC ET APOTRE DU CANADA: SA VIE ET SES VIRTUS

Gosselin, Charles *see* PETIT TRAITE DE GRAMMAIRE ANGLAISE A L'USAGE DES ECOLES PRIMAIRES
Gosselin, Charles-Robert *see* PLAN D'EDUCATION EN REPONSE AUX ACADEMIES DE MARSEILLE ET DE CHALONS
Gosselin, David *see* LE CATECHIME DES COMMENCANTS
Gosselin, L *see* MONTREAL MUSEUM
Gosselin, M *see* THE POWER OF THE POPE DURING THE MIDDLE AGES, OR, AN HISTORICAL INQUIRY INTO THE ORIGIN OF THE TEMPORAL POWER OF THE HOLY SEE, AND THE CONSTITUTIONAL LAWS OF THE MIDDLE AGES RELATING TO THE DEPOSITION OF SOVEREIGNS
Gosset, P *see* LA BANQUE DE FRANCE EXPROPRIEE, LIQUIDEE POUR CAUSE D'UTILITE PUBLIQUE.
GOSSIP – (Also known as: Goldfield Gossip Weekly) – Goldfield, NV. 1906-07 – 2r – 1 – $100.00 – U04553 – us Library Micro [071]
GOSSIP – Montreal, Canada. v2 n14. 13 jun-18 jul 1885 – 1r – 1 – Can$30.00 – cn Can Microfilming [072]
THE GOSSIP – Ottawa: Gossip Pub. Co, [1887] – 9 – cn C.I.H.M. [073]
Gossman, Stephen J *see* FARM LABOR CAMP DESIGN IN RURAL MARION COUNTY
GOSSNERS MISSION UNTER HINDUS UND KOLHS UM NEUJAHR 1878 / Plath, Karl Heinrich Christian – Berlin: Gossnerischen Mission, 1879 – 1mf – us A.T.L.A. [240]
Gossot, Emile *see* ESSAI CRITIQUE SUR L'ENSEIGNEMENT PRIMAIRE EN FRANCE DE 1800 A 1900
GOST' = THE GUEST – (From years 1923, 1925, 1929, 1930, 1935 (incomplete)) – Riga, Warsaw – 1r – 1 – $12.80 – us Baptist [240]
GOSTA BERLINGS SAGA...2. UPPLAGAN / Lagerlof, Selma – Stockholm, 1895. 2v – 1 – us U.W. Library [830]
Gostling, George *see* EXTRACTS FROM THE TREATIES BETWEEN GREAT BRITAIN AND OTHER KINGDOMS AND STATES OF SUCH ARTICLES AS RELATE TO THE DUTY AND CONDUCT OF THE COMMANDERS OF HIS MAJESTY'S SHIPS OF WAR
Gostling, William *see* MUSIC PART-BOOKS
Gostwick, Joseph *see* OUTLINES OF GERMAN LITERATURE
GOSUDAREV PECHATNYI DVOR I SINODAL' NAIA TIPOGRAFIIA V MOSKVE – Istoricheskaia spravka. M. 1903. BR-4567 2 – 8 – ne IDC [070]
GOSUDARSTVENNAI A PROMYSHLENNOST DALNEGO VOSTOKA ZA 1923-1925 GODY – Khabarovsk: Izd. Dalprombi uro, 1925 – 1 – CSUX91-B235 – us Hoover Inst Photo [338]
GOSUDARSTVENNAIA AKADEMIIA ISTORII MATERIAL'NOI KULTURY – Soobshcheniia. v. 1-2. L. 1926-29. BR-3801 2 – 8 – ne IDC [947]
Gosudarstvennaia Biblioteka SSSR im V.I. Lenina. Moscow *see* BIBLIOGRAFIIA DISSERTATSII. 1941-1945
GOSUDARSTVENNAIA DUMA PERVAGO SOZYVA / Ezerskii, Nikolai Fedorovich – Penza: Tipo-lit. E M Grushet sko i, 1907 – 1 – CSUX89-B431 – us Hoover Inst Photo [947]
GOSUDARSTVENNAIA DUMA. STENOGRAMMA ZASEDANII – Moscow: Parlament Rossiiskoi Federatsii, 1994- – 75mf – 9 – $279.00y – us East View [320]
GOSUDARSTVENNAIA DUMA V ROSSII : SB. DOKUMENTOV I MATERIALOV / Kalinychev, F I – M., 1957. 646p – 7mf – 9 – ne IDC [320]
GOSUDARSTVENNAIA KREDITNAIA POMOSHCH KOLKHOZAM I KOLKHOZNIKAM ZA PERIOD OT 6 DO 7 SEZDA SOVETOV SSSR – Moskva: Gosfinizdat, 1935 – 1 – CSUX90-B9143 – us Hoover Inst Photo [330]
Gosudarstvennaia Planovaia Komissiia *see*
- PLAN

GOSUDARSTVENNAIA PROMYSHLENNOST S.S.S.R. V 1921-23 G.G. I EE FINANSOVOE POLOZHENIE : OPYT IZUCHENII A DINAMIKI VAZHNE ISHIKH OTRASLE I RUSSKO I PROMYSHLENNOSTI / ed by Gromana, V G – Moskva: Gos. izd-vo, [1925?] – 1 – CSUX88-B8763 – us Hoover Inst Photo [338]
Gosudarstvennaia Publichnaia biblioteka im. M.E. Saltykova-Shchedrina *see* TRUDY
GOSUDARSTVENNAIA PUBLICHNAIA BIBLIOTEKA IM. M.E. SALTYKOVA-SHCHEDRINA V 1954 G.-...V 1961 – (1962-63, Leningrad, 1964. 1964-68, Leningrad, 1969) – Leningrad, 1955-62. 8v. BR-10,850/1 – 9 – ne IDC [010]
Gosudarstvennoe izdatelstvo (R.S.F.S.R.) *see* 1905, K GODOVSHCHINE PERVO I RUSSKO I REVOLIUTSII
GOSUDARSTVENNOE KHOZIAISTVO ROSSII V PERVOI CHETVERTI XVIII STOLETIIA I REFORMA PETRA VELIKOGO / Miliukov, P N – Spb. 1892. BR-7698 2 – 8 – ne IDC [947]
GOSUDARSTVENNOE PREDPRIIATIE : TRESTY, ZAVODY, FABRIKI, PROMKOMBINATY, AKTSIONERNYE OBSHCHESTVA, SINDIKATY, TORGI, STROITELSTVO: SISTEMATICHESKII SBORNIK DEISTVUIUSHCHEGO ZAKONODATELSTVA I VEDOMSTVENNYKH RASPORIAZHENII – Moskva: I Urid. izd-vo NKI U RSFSR, 1929 – 1 – CSUX88-B8675 – us Hoover Inst Photo [330]
GOSUDARSTVENNOE SOVESHCHANIE PO STATISTIKE NARODNOGO OBRAZOVANII A (1919: MOSCOW, R.S.F.S.R.) DOKLADY – Moskva: Statisticheski i otdel Narodnogo komissariata po prosveshchenii u, 1919 – 1 – CSUX91-B643 – us Hoover Inst Photo [330]
GOSUDARSTVENNOE UPRAVLENIE; KODIFITSIROVANNYI SBORNIK ZAKONODATEL'STVA RSFSR NA 1 IANVARIA 1934 GODA – Moscow, 1934. 108p. BR-8457/1 – 9 – ne IDC [340]
O GOSUDARSTVENNOM PLANE RAZVITII A NARODNOGO KHOZI A ISTVA SSSR – (Includes c.1: 1957-1958, 1960, 1965-1969, 1974) – Moskva: Politizdat, 19uu – 1 – CSUXAKZ2639-S – us Hoover Inst Photo [947]
Gosudarstvenny i bank RSFSR *see*
- MESI AT S RABOTY PRAVLENII A GOSUDARSTVENNOGO BANKA R.S.F.S.R.
- THE RUSSIAN STATE BANK

Gosudarstvenny i bank RSFSR. Vserossi iski i sezd upravli ai ushchikh mestnymi uchrezhdenii ami (1922: Moscow, R.S.F.S.R.) *see* STENOGRAFICHESKI I OTCHET PLENARNYKH ZASEDANI I VSEROSSI ISKOGO SEZDA UPRAVLI AI USHCHIKH MESTNYMI UCHREZHDENII AMI GOSUDARSTVENNOGO BANKA, 19-22 DEKABRI A 1922 G
Gosudarstvenny i bank SSSR *see*
- GOSUDARSTVENNY I BANK SSSR K 7 VSESOI UZNOMU SEZDU SOVETOV
- THE STATE BANK OF THE U.S.S.R.

GOSUDARSTVENNY I BANK SSSR K 7 VSESOI UZNOMU SEZDU SOVETOV / Gosudarstvenny i bank SSSR – Moskva: Gosbank, 1935 – 1 – CSUX90-B9587 – us Hoover Inst Photo [332]
Gosudarstvenny i komitet Soveta Ministrov SSSR po voprosam truda i zarabotno i platy *see* EDINYI TARIFNO-KVALIFIKATSIONNYI SPRAVOCHNIK RABOTI PROFESSII RABOCHIKH
GOSUDARSTVENNYE ARKHIVY SOIUZA SSR – Kratkii spravochnik. Moscow, 1956. 507p. BR-3533/2 – 8 – ne IDC [947]
GOSUDARSTVENNYE FINANSY. TOVARNYE T SENY : STATISTICHESKI I SBORNIK – Moskva: Redaktsion. izdatelsk. otdel Fin.-ekonom.-biuro N.K.F., 1922 – 1 – CSUX90-B9539 – us Hoover Inst Photo [330]
GOSUDARSTVENNYE IZBIRATELNYE ZAKONY : AGRARNY I PEREVOROT: SELSKI I SUD / Dashkevich, Leonid Viacheslavovich – Moskva: Tip. Russkago t-va pechatn. i izdat. di ela, 1909 – 1 – CSUX89-B3844 – us Hoover Inst Photo [630]
GOSUDARSTVENNYE UNIVERSITETY = STATE UNIVERSITIES / Narodny i komissariat prosveshchenii a RSFSR – Moskva: Ogiz: Izogiz, 1934 – 1 – CSUX90-B6203 – us Hoover Inst Photo [370]
GOSUDARSTVENNYI ARKHIV OKTIABR'SKOI REVOLIUTSII I SOTSIALISTICHESKOGO STROITEL'STVA LENINGRADSKOI OBLASTI – Kratkii putevoditel'. Leningrad, 1962. 183p. BR-10,943/1 – 9 – ne IDC [947]
GOSUDARSTVENNYI ARKHIV OKTIABR'SKOI REVOLIUTSII I SOTSIALISTICHESKOGO STROITEL'STVA MOSKOVSKOI OBLASTI – Kratkii spravochnik. Moscow, 1962. 77p. BR-10,938/1 – 9 – ne IDC [947]
GOSUDARSTVENNYI ARKHIV. RAZRIAD 2. "DELA SOBSTVENNO DO IMPERATORSKOI FAMILII OTNOSIASHCHIIASIA" / Goriainov, S M – Spb. 1913. (mid) BR-10,708/1 – 9 – ne IDC [947]
Gosudarstvennyi Bank. S.S.S.R *see* ECONOMIC SURVEY
Gosudarstvennyi Istoricheski Muzei. Moscow *see* TRUDY
GOSUDARSTVENNYI ISTORICHESKII ARKHIV LENINGRADSKOI OBLASTI – Kratkii putevoditel'. Leningrad, 1960. 107p. BR-10,944/1 – 9 – ne IDC [947]
GOSUDARSTVENNYI ISTORICHESKII ARKHIV MOSKOVSKOI OBLASTI – Putevoditel'. Moscow, 1961. 345p. BR-10,940/1 – 9 – ne IDC [947]
Gosudarstvennyi komitet SSSR po statistike *see*
- ITOGI VSESOIUZNOI PEREPISI NASELENIIA 1989 GODA

GOSUDARSTVENNYI MUZEI IZOBRAZITELNYKH ISKUSSTV IM. A.S. PUSHKINA – Moscow, 1962. 352p. BR-11,030/1 – 9 – ne IDC [060]
GOSUDARSTVENNYI PEREVOROT ADMIRALA KOLCHAKA V OMSKI E 18 NOIABRIA 1918 GODA : SBORNIK DOKUMENTOV – Parizh: Tip. I. Rirakhovskago, 1919 – 1 – CSUX88-B6774 – us Hoover Inst Photo [355]
GOSUDARSTVENNYI PIATILETNII PLAN RAZVITIIA NARODNOGO KHOZIAISTVA SSSR NA 1971-1975 GG / USSR. Gosplan – (Izd-vo Politicheskoi literatury). M. 1972. BD-1793 1 – 9 – ne IDC [947]
GOSUDARSTVENNYI SOVET – Arkhiv Gosudarstvennago soveta. v. 1-5 (1). Spb. 1869-1904. BR-4242 2 – 8 – ne IDC [947]
GOSUDARSTVENNYI SOVYET, OPIS. DYEL ARKHIVA – Leningrad. v1-21. 1908-14 – 3r – 1 – us Ross [947]
GOSUDARSTVENNYI TRUD-GUZH-NALOG I KRESTIANSKOE KHOZIAISTVO : S PRILOZHENIEM I RAZI ASNENIEM DEKRETOV I POSTANOVLENIIO TRUD-GUZH-NALOGE / Grandov, M – Moskva: Gos. izd-vo, 1922 – 1 – CSUX89-B7335 – us Hoover Inst Photo [630]
GOSUDARSTVO I PRAVO (OPYT IZLOZHENIIA MARKSISTSKOGO UCHENIIA O SUSHCHESTVE GOSUDARSTVA I PRAVA). S PREDISLOVIEM N. V. KRYLENKO / Ksenofontov, F – Moskva, IUridicheskoe izdatel'stvo N. K. IU., 1924. 171 p. LL-4002 – 1 – us L of C Photodup [340]
GOSUDARSTVO I TSERKOV V DREVNEI ROSSII : KIEVSKII PERIOD 988-1240 / Goetz, Leopold Karl – Berlin: Duncker, 1908 – 1mf – us A.T.L.A. [947]
GOSUDARSTVO SEL'DZHYKUDOV MALOI AZII / Gordlevskii, V A – (Izbrannye sochineniia). v1. 1960 – 8 – BU-655 2 – ne IDC [947]
GOTA – Vadstena, Sweden. 1853-56 – 1 – sw Kungliga [072]
GOTA ALVDALSNYHETERNA *see* ALINGSAS TIDNING
GOTEBORG – Goteborg, Sweden. 1886 – 1 – sw Kungliga [072]
GOTEBORGS AFTONBLAD – Goteborg, Sweden. 1888-95, 1902 – 21r – 1 – sw Kungliga [072]
GOTEBORGS HANDELS- OCH SJOFARTSTIDNING – Goteborg, Sweden. 1832-1973 – 748r – 1 – sw Kungliga [072]
GOTEBORGS HANDELS- OCH SJOFARTSTIDNING – Goteborg, Sweden. 1974-85 – 1 – sw Kungliga [072]
GOTEBORGS MORGONPOST – (Suppl: Vy och Revy, 1910-11) – Goteborg, Sweden. 1896-1950 – 298r – 1 – sw Kungliga [072]
GOTEBORGSKURIREN – Uddevalla, Sweden. 1979-86 – 1 – sw Kungliga [072]
GOTEBORGSNYTT – Molndal, Sweden. 1979-84 – 1 – sw Kungliga [072]
GOTEBORGSPOSTEN – Goteborg, Sweden. 1858-1978 – 976r – 1 – sw Kungliga [072]
GOTEBORGSPOSTEN – Goteborg, Sweden. 1979- – 1 – sw Kungliga [072]
GOTEBORGSTIDNINGEN – Goteborg, Sweden. 1902-67. GT, 1967-78 – 515r – 1 – sw Kungliga [072]
DER GOTHA, 1763-1944 – 1982-1984 – 496mf (1:24) – 9 – silver DM12,990.00 – 3-598-30330-0 – gw Saur [920]
DER GOTHA SUPPLEMENT : DIE OESTERREICH-ABTEILUNG. JAHRBUCH DES DEUTSCHEN ADELS, HANDBUCH DES PREUSSISCHEN ADELS U. GENEALOGISCHES TASCHENBUCH DES URADELS – (Diazo DM3,600 ISBN: 3-598-30358-0. DM2,980 (fuer Bez. d. Hauptwerkes)) – 1997 – ca 127mf (1:24) – 9 – silver DM4,500.00 (DM3,480.00 (fuer Bez. d. Gotha)) – 3-598-30359-9 – gw Saur [920]
GOTHAISCHES GENEALOGISCHES TASCHENBUCH DER FREIHERRLICHEN HAUSER – 1920-25 – 1 – 46.00 – us L of C Photodup [920]
GOTHEBORGSKA NYHETER – Goteborg, Sweden. 1765-1848 – 16r – 1 – sw Kungliga [072]
GOTHEBORGSPOSTEN – Goteborg, Sweden. 1813-32. 4 reels. 1850-51. 1 reel – 1 – sw Kungliga [072]
Gothein, Eberhard *see*
- IGNATIUS VON LOYOLA
- IGNATIUS VON LOYOLA UND DIE GEGENREFORMATION
- POLITISCHE UND RELIGIOESE VOLKSBEWEGUNGEN VOR DER REFORMATION

GOTHENBURG INDEPENDENT – Gothenburg, NE. -w. Jun 1892; Oct 1895-June 1905; Aug 1908-Jan 1925 – 1 – us NE Hist [071]
GOTHENBURG SUN – Gothenburg, NE. -w. Apr 1901-Jan 1902; May 1902-Dec 1904 – 1 – us NE Hist [071]
GOTHENBURG TIMES – Gothenburg, NE. -w. Aug 1896-Sept 1897 – 1 – us NE Hist [071]
GOTHENBURG TIMES – Gothenburg, NE. -w. Jul 1908 to date – 1 – us NE Hist [071]
GOTIFREDI VITERBIENSIS GESTA FRIDERICI I ET HENRICI 4 IMPERATORUM METRICE SCRIPTA (MGH 7: 30.BD) – 1870 – Dfl9.00 – ne Slangenburg [240]

GOTLAND – Visby, Sweden. 1886-99 – 1 – sw Kungliga [072]

GOTLANDS ALLEHANDA – Visby, Sweden. 1873-1953 – 1 – sw Kungliga [072]

GOTLANDS ALLEHANDA – Visby, Sweden. 1954-78 – 160r – 1 – sw Kungliga [072]

GOTLANDS ALLEHANDA – Visby, Sweden. 1979- – 1 – sw Kungliga [072]

GOTLANDS FOLKBLAD – Visby, Sweden. 1928-32, 1954-78 – 175r – 1 – sw Kungliga [072]

GOTLANDS FOLKBLAD – Visby, Sweden. 1979-83 – 1 – sw Kungliga [072]

GOTLANDS LAENS TIDNING – Visby, 1849-58 – 9 – sw Kungliga [072]

GOTLANDS TIDNING – Visby, 1858-65, 1867-88 – 9 – sw Kungliga [072]

GOTLANDS TIDNINGAR – Visby, Sweden. 1983- – 1 – sw Kungliga [072]

GOTLANNINGEN – Visby, Sweden. 1954-78 – 155r – 1 – sw Kungliga [072]

GOTLANNINGEN *see* GOTLANDS FOLKBLAD

Goto, Shimpei *see* GOTO SHIMPEI MONJO

GOTO SHIMPEI MONJO = THE COUNT SHIMPEI GOTO RECORDS / Goto, Shimpei – 1857-1929. All of his papers in chronological sequence – 88r – 1 – Y880,000.00 – ja Yushodo [025]

GOTONGROYONG,OR / Dey, Sushil Kumar – Alang Alang? (Draft scheme for community development programme in Indonesia. SE-1170 1. 1955 – 9 – ne IDC [338]

Gotschlich, Emil *see* LESSING'S ARISTOTELISCHE STUDIEN UND DER EINFLUSS DERSELBEN AUF SEINE WERKE

GOTT UND DIE WISSENSCHAFT / Buechner, Ludwig – Leipzig: Theod. Thomas, 1897 – 1mf – 9 – 0-8370-2519-2 – 1985-0519 – us A.T.L.A. [210]

GOTT UND SEIN REICH : PHILOSOPHISCHE DARLEGUNG DER FREIEN GOETTLICHEN SELBSTENTWICKLUNG ZUM ALLUMFASSENDEN ORGANISMUS / Meyr, Melchior – Stuttgart:Gebrueder Maentler (A. Kroener), 1860 – 1mf – 9 – 0-8370-4421-9 – 1985-2421 – us A.T.L.A. [210]

GOTT UND SEINE OFFENBARUNGEN IN NATUR UND GESCHICHTE / Hamberger, Julius – Guetersloh: C. Bertelsmann, 1882. 1 fiche – 9 – us A.T.L.A. [240]

DAS GOTTERLEBNIS DES GERMANISCHEN MENSCHEN : WELTANSCHAULICHES IN DER DICHTUNG VON HANS FR. BLUNCK / Etscheid, Lisel – (Includes bibliographical references) – Bonn a. Rh.: L Roehrscheid, 1932 – 1 – us U.W. Library [430]

GOTTES DASEIN BEWIESEN AM WISSEN UND SEIN : EIN BEITRAG ZUR RECHENSCHAFT UNSRES GLAUBENS / Doederlein, Julius – Erlangen: Eduard Besold, 1871 – 1mf – 9 – 0-8370-2943-0 – 1985-0943 – us A.T.L.A. [210]

DAS GOTTES KIND : EIN WEIHNACHTSSPIEL / Herrmann, Emil Alfred – Jena: E Diederichs, 1912 – 1r – 1 – us U.W. Library [820]

DIE GOTTESANREDE IM ANTE-SANCTUS / Beckman, S – Muenster, 1932 – 2mf – 8 – Dfl9.00 – ne Slangenburg [240]

DIE GOTTESBEWEISE BEI FRANZ BRENTANO / Seiterich, Eugen – Freiburg i.B., 1936 – xv/240p – 9 – DM48.00 – 3-89349-067-1 – gw Hänsel [240]

DIE GOTTESBEZEICHNUNGEN IN DEN LITURGIEN DER OSTKIRCHEN / Buckel, A – Wuerzburg, 1938 – 3mf – 8 – Dfl13.00 – ne Slangenburg [240]

GOTTESDIENST UND KIRCHENMUSIK – 1957-91 (complete) – Inquire – 1 – ATLA S0572 – us A.T.L.A. [073]

DAS GOTTESDIENSTLICHE JAHR DER JUDEN / Schaerf, Theodor – (Includes bibliographical references) – Leipzig:J C Hinrichs, 1902 – 1mf – 9 – 0-8370-5067-7 – 1985-3067 – us A.T.L.A. [270]

DIE GOTTESDIENSTLICHE SCHRIFTLESUNG 1 : STAND UND AUFGABEN DER PERIKOPENFORSCHUNG / Kunze, G – Goettingen, 1947 – 4mf – 8 – Dfl19.00 – ne Slangenburg [240]

DER GOTTESDIENSTLICHE VOLKSGESANG IM JUEDISCHEN UND CHRISTLICHEN ALTERTUM / Leitner, Franz – Freiburg i. Br., 1906 – 6mf – 8 – Dfl25.00 – ne Slangenburg [240]

DAS GOTTESERLEBNIS IN HEBBELS DRAMEN / Blaustein, Leopold – (Includes bibliographical references) – Berlin: Reuther & Reichard, 1929 – 1r – 1 – us U.W. Library [430]

GOTTESFRIEDE UND TREUGA DEI (MGH SCHRIFTEN..: 20.BD) / Hoffmann, H – 1964 – Dfl28.00 – ne Slangenburg [240]

DIE GOTTESIDEE IN RELIGIOESER UND SPEKULATIVER RICHTUNG / Walthoffen, Hippolyt Walter von – Wien: Wilhelm Braumueller, 1904.1 fiche – 9 – us A.T.L.A. [240]

GOTTESKNECHT DES DEUTEROJESAJA: EIN KRITISCH-EXEGETISCHE UND BIB.-THEOL. STUDIE / Fuellkrug, Gerhard – Goettingen: Vandenhoeck & Rup., 1899. 1 fiche – 9 – us A.T.L.A. [240]

DIE GOTTESLEHRE DES IRENAEUS / Kunze, Johannes – Leipzig: Doerffling und Francke, 1891 – 1mf – us A.T.L.A. [240]

DIE GOTTESOFFENBARUNG IN JESU CHRISTO : NACH WESEN, INHALT UND GRENZEN: UNTER DEM GESCHICHTLICHEN, PSYCHOLOGISCHEN UND DOGMATISCHEN GESICHTSPUNKTE / Schwartzkopff, Paul – (Includes bibliographical references) – Giessen: J Ricker, 1896 – 1mf – 9 – 0-8370-5610-1 – 1985-3610 – us A.T.L.A. [240]

GOTTFRIED EPHRAIM MUELLERS A.M. HISTORISCH-PHILOLOGISCHES SENDSCHREIBEN AN EINEN HOHEN GOENNER, VON ORGELN, IHREM URSPRUNGE UND GEBRAUCHE IN DER ALTEN UND NEUEN KIRCHE GOTTES / Mueller, Gottfried Ephraim – Dresden. 1748. BP-413 1 – 9 – ne IDC [780]

GOTTFRIED KELLER / Enders, Carl Friedrich – Leipzig: P Reclam, c1921 – 1r – 1 – us U.W. Library [920]

GOTTFRIED KELLER : FESTVORTRAG BEI DER AM 19. JULI 1919 VON DER UNIVERSITAET BERN IN IHRER AULA VERANSTALTETEN KELLER-HUNDERT-JAHRFEIER / Maync, Harry Wilhelm – (Includes bibliographical references) – Bern: K J Wysz, 1919 – 1r – 1 – us U.W. Library [430]

GOTTFRIED KELLER : EIN LITERARISCHER ESSAY / Brahm, Otto – Berlin: A B Auerbach, 1883 – 1 – us U.W. Library [430]

GOTTFRIED KELLER / Rosenfeld, W – (Includes bibliographical references) – Leipzig: Sphinx-Verlag, [1907?] – 1r – 1 – us U.W. Library [920]

GOTTFRIED KELLER : SECHS VORTRAEGE / Steiner, Gustav – Basel: Helbing & Lichtenhahn, 1918 – 1r – 1 – us U.W. Library [430]

GOTTFRIED KELLER : ZU SEINEM HUNDERTSTEN GEBURTSTAGE (19. JULI 1919) / Arx, Walther von – Basel: Verein fuer Verbreitung guter Schriften, 1919 – 1 – us U.W. Library [430]

GOTTFRIED KELLER IM EUROPAEISCHEN GEDANKEN / Hochdorf, Max – Zuerich: Rascher, 1919 – 1r – 1 – us U.W. Library [430]

GOTTFRIED KELLER IM SPIEGEL SEINER ZEIT : URTEILE UND BERICHTE VON ZEITGENOSSEN UEBER DEN MENSCHEN UND DICHTER / ed by Zaech, Alfred – Zuerich: Scientia, 1952 – 1 – us U.W. Library [430]

GOTTFRIED KELLER UND DIE FRAUEN : EIN STUECK HERZENSTRAGIK / Huber, Walther – 2. Aufl. Bern: F Wyss, 1919 – 1r – 1 – us U.W. Library [430]

GOTTFRIED KELLER UND J V WIDMANN : BRIEFWECHSEL / ed by Widmann, Max – (Includes bibliographical references and index) – Basel: Rhein-Verlag, 1922 – 1 – us U.W. Library [920]

GOTTFRIED KELLERS DRAMATISCHE BESTREBUNGEN / Preitz, Max – (Includes bibliographical references (5th prelim. leaf)) – Marburg a.L.: N G Elwert, 1909 – 1r – 1 – us U.W. Library [430]

GOTTFRIED KELLERS GLAUBE : EIN BEKENNTNIS ZU SEINEM PROTESTANTISMUS / Buri, Fritz – Bern: P Haupt, 1944 – 1 – us U.W. Library [430]

GOTTFRIED KELLERS "GRUENER HEINRICH" VON 1854/5 UND 1879/80 : BEITRAEGE ZU EINER VERGLEICHUNG / Leppmann, Franz – (Includes bibliographical references) – Berlin: E Ebering, [1902] – 1r – 1 – us U.W. Library [430]

GOTTFRIED KELLERS POLITISCHE ANSCHAUUNGEN / Schlomer, Harm Henry – (Includes bibliographical references) – Heidelberg-Handschuhsheim: H Fahrer, 1936 – 1r – 1 – us U.W. Library [430]

GOTTFRIED WILHELM SACER'S "REIME DICH, ODER ICH FRESSE DICH...NORTHAUSEN 1673" / Pfeil, Leopold – 1995 – 2mf – 9 – DM62.00 – 3-8267-3139-5 – gw Hänsel [430]

DIE GOTTGEWEIHTEN IN DER ALTTESTAMENTLICHEN RELIGION / Duhm, Bernhard – Tuebingen: J.C.B. Mohr, 1905. 1 fiche – 9 – us A.T.L.A. [240]

Gottheil, Gustav *see* HYMNS AND ANTHEMS ADAPTED FOR JEWISH WORSHIP

Gotthelf, Jeremias *see*
- ALBERT BITZIUS
- DIE ARMENNOT; EIN SYLVESTERTRAUM; EINES SCHWEIZERS WORT
- DER BAUERN-SPIEGEL
- BAUERNSPIEGEL
- DER BAUERN-SPIEGEL, ODER, LEBENSGESCHICHTE DES JEREMIAS GOTTHELF
- BILDER AUS DER SCHWEIZ
- ERLEBNISSE EINES SCHULDENBAUERS
- GELD UND GEIST
- DER GELDSTAG
- JAKOBS, DES HANDWERKSGESELLEN WANDERUNGEN DURCH DIE SCHWEIZ
- DIE KAESEREI IN DER VEHFREUDE
- KAETHI DIE GROSSMUTTER
- KAETHI, DIE GROSSMUTTER, ODER, DER WAHRE WEG DURCH JEDE NOT
- KALENDERGESCHICHTEN
- KLEINERE ERZAEHLUNGEN
- LEIDEN UND FREUDEN EINES SCHULMEISTERS
- SAEMTLICHE WERKE IN 24 BAENDEN
- ULI DER PAECHTER
- VOLKSAUSGABE SEINER WERKE IM URTEXT
- DIE WASSERNOT IM EMMENTAL; DIE ARMENNOT; EINES SCHWEIZERS WORT
- DIE WASSERNOT IM EMMENTHAL; FUENF MAEDCHEN; DURSLI DER BRANNTWEINLAEUTER
- DIE WASSERSNOT IM EMMENTAL AM 13. AUGUST 1837
- WIE ANNE BAEBI JOWAEGER HAUSHALTET UND WIE ES IHM MIT DEM DOKTERN GEHT
- WIE ULI DER KNECHT, GLUECKLICH WIRD
- WIE ULI DER KNECHT GLUECKLICH WIRD
- ZEITGEIST UND BERNERGEIST

GOTTHOLD EPHRAIM LESSING : EINE EINFUEHRUNG IN SEIN LEBEN UND WERK / Seidel, Siegfried – (Includes bibliographical references & index) – Berlin: Verlag Neues Leben, 1963 – 1r – 1 – us U.W. Library [430]

GOTTHOLD EPHRAIM LESSING / ed by Vorbrodt, Walther – Berlin: Union Deutsche Verlagsgesellschaft, 1920 – 1r – 1 – us U.W. Library [920]

GOTTHOLD EPHRAIM LESSINGS SAEMTLICHE SCHRIFTEN = WORKS / Lessing, Gotthold Ephraim; ed by Lachmann, Karl – (Includes bibliographical references & index) – 3. durchges. verm. Aufl. Stuttgart: G J Goeschen, 1866-1924 – 1 – us U.W. Library [800]

GOTTLOB DAVID HARTMANN : EIN LEBENSBILD AUS DER STURM- UND DRANGZEIT / Lang, Wilhelm – Stuttgart: W Kohlhammer, 1890 – 1r – 1 – us U.W. Library [430]

Gottlober, A B *see* KOL SHIREI MAHALALEL

Gottmann, Jet al *see* L'AMENAGEMENT DE L'ESPACE

GOTT-NATUR : GOETHES NATURANSCHAUUNG IM LICHTE SEINER FROEMMIGKEIT / Fischer, Paul – Weimar: H Boehlaus Nachfolger, 1932 – 1r – 1 – us U.W. Library [430]

Gottschald, Max *see* DEUTSCHE NAMENKUNDE; UNSERE FAMILIENNAMEN NACH IHRER ENTSTEHUNG UND BEDEUTUNG

Gottschalk, Hanns *see* SCHICHT UND SCHACHT

Gottschalk, L M *see*
- 6EME BALLADE...OP. 85
- 7EME BALLADE...OP. 87
- 8EME BALLADE...OP. 90
- APOTHEOSE
- BAMBOULA, DANSE DE NEGRES
- SOUVENIR DES ARDENNES, MAZURKA DE SALON

Gottschall, Rudolf von *see*
- CHRISTIAN DIETRICH GRABBE
- DIE DEUTSCHE NATIONALLITTERATUR DES NEUNZEHNTEN JAHRHUNDERTS

GOTTSCHALL'S REPORTS / Ohio. Montgomery County. Dayton – 1v. 1865-73 (all publ) – 6mf – 9 – $9.00 – LLMC 84-184 – us L.L.M.C. [340]

Gottsche, C M *see* SPECIES HEPATHICARUM

Gottsche, C M et al *see* SYNOPSIS HEPATICARUM

GOTTSCHED : BIOGRAPHISCHE SKIZZE / Reichel, Eugen – (Includes bibliographical references) – Berlin: Gottsched-Verlag, 1900 – 1r – 1 – us U.W. Library [920]

Gottsched, Johann Christoph *see*
- BEYTRAEGE ZUR CRITISCHEN HISTORIE DER DEUTSCHEN SPRACHE, POESIE UND BEREDSAMKEIT
- JOH. CHR. GOTTSCHEDS STERBENDER CATO
- NEUER BUECHERSAAL DER SCHOENEN WISSENSCHAFTEN UND FREYEN KUENSTE

GOTTSCHED UND DIE REFORM DER DEUTSCHEN LITERATUR IM ACHTZEHNTEN JAHRHUNDERT / Koch, Max – (Includes bibliographical references) – Hamburg: J F Richter, 1887 – 1r – 1 – us U.W. Library [430]

DER GOTTSCHEDKREIS UND RUSSLAND : DEUTSCH-RUSSISCHE LITERATURBEZIEHUNGEN IM ZEITALTER DER AUFKLAERUNG / Lehmann, Ulf – (Includes bibliographical references) – Berlin: Akademie-Verlag, 1966 – 1r – 1 – us U.W. Library [430]

GOTTSCHEDS BEDEUTUNG FUER DIE GESCHICHTE DER DEUTSCHEN PHILOLOGIE / Lachmann, Hans – (Includes bibliographical references) – Leipzig: Kommissionsverlag von Alfred Lorentz, 1931 – 1r – 1 – us U.W. Library [430]

GOTTSCHEER ZEITUNG – Kocevje, Yugoslavia. 20 Aug 1924; Feb 1925-1941 – 3r – 1 – us L of C Photodup [949]

Gottschick, Johannes *see* DIE KIRCHLICHKEIT DER S.G. KIRCHLICHEN THEOLOGIE

Gouan, A *see*
- FLORA MONSPELIACA, SISTENS PLANTAS NO. 1850
- HISTORIA PISCIUM
- HORTUS REGIUS MONSPELIENSIS

Gouault, J *see* COMMENT LA FRANCE EST DEVENUE REPUBLICAINE

Gouaux, M *see* EVOLUTION DES COUTUMES LIEES AUX FETES DE PAQUES EN CONFLENS

Goubier, J *see* BIOGEOGRAPHIE, BIOMETRIE ET BIOLOGIE DU SANDRE, LUCIOPERCA LUCIOPERCA (L.) OSTEICHTHYEN PERCIDE

GOUCHER BAPTIST CHURCH. SOUTH CAROLINA : CHURCH RECORDS – 20 Jan 1810-19 Nov 1859 – 1 – 11.44 – us Baptist [240]

Goudar, A *see* LE BRIGANDAGE DE LA MUSIQUE ITALIENNE

Goudge, Henry Leighton *see* FIRST EPISTLE TO THE CORINTHIANS

Goudin, A *see* PHILOSOPHIA IUXTA INCONCUSSA TUTISSIMAQUE DIVI THOMAE DOGMATA...

Goudy, H *see* THE MARRIAGE LAWS

Gougaud, L *see*
- ANCIENNES COUTUMES CLAUSTRALES
- CHRISTIANITY IN CELTIC LANDS
- EREMITES ET RECLUS
- ERMITES ET RECLUS

Gougaud, Louis *see* LES CHRETIENTES CELTIQUES

Gouge, William *see* THE SAINTS' SACRIFICE, OR, A COMMENTARY ON PSALM 116

Gouges, Olympe de *see* RECUEIL FACTICE DE 16 OPUSCULES

Gough, James *see* A PRACTICAL GRAMMAR OF THE ENGLISH TONGUE

Gough, John B *see*
- AUTOBIOGRAPHY AND PERSONAL RECOLLECTIONS OF JOHN B. GOUGH
- PLATFORM ECHOES, OR, LIVING TRUTHS FOR HEAD AND HEART:...DRAWN FROM THE HUMOR AND PATHOS OF LIFE

Gough, Robert E *see* JOURNAL OF SMALL FRUIT AND VITICULTURE

Goujet, C P *see* BIBLIOTHEQUE FRANCOISE OU HISTOIRE DE LA LITTERATURE FRANCOISE

Goulart, S *see* THEATRE DU MONDE, CONTENANT DIVERS EXCELLENS TABLEAUX DE LA VIE HUMAINE

Goulart, Simon *see* MEMOIRE DE LA LIGUE, CONTENANT LES EVENEMENTS LES PLUS REMARQUABLES DEPUIS 1576, JUSQU'A LA PAIX ACCORDEE ENTRE LE ROI DE FRANCE ET LE ROI D'ESPAGNE, EN 1598

Goulburn, Edward Meyrick *see*
- ACTS OF THE DEACONS: BEING A COURSE OF LECTURES...ON ACTS
- JOHN WILLIAM BURGON

GOULBURN EVENING PENNY POST – Australia. 31 Jan 1911-29 Jun 1922. -d. 12 reels – 1 – uk British Libr Newspaper [072]

Gould *see* THE HISTORY OF NEW IPSWICH

GOVERNMENT PUBLICATIONS / Gold Coast – 1846-1957 – 1 – uk Microform Academic [960]
GOVERNMENT PUBLICATIONS / Kenya – 1897-1963 – 1 – uk Microform Academic [960]
GOVERNMENT PUBLICATIONS / Natal Colony – 1 – uk Microform Academic [960]
GOVERNMENT PUBLICATIONS / Nigeria – 1862-1960 – 1 – uk Microform Academic [960]
GOVERNMENT PUBLICATIONS / Nyasaland – 1 – uk Microform Academic [960]
GOVERNMENT PUBLICATIONS / Rhodesia. Northern – 1 – uk Microform Academic [960]
GOVERNMENT PUBLICATIONS / Rhodesia. Southern – 1890-1963 – 1 – uk Microform Academic [960]
GOVERNMENT PUBLICATIONS / Sierra Leone – 1808-1961 – 1 – uk Microform Academic [960]
GOVERNMENT PUBLICATIONS / Tanganyika – 1919-61 – 1 – uk Microform Academic [960]
GOVERNMENT PUBLICATIONS / Uganda – 1900-1962 – 1 – uk Microform Academic [960]
GOVERNMENT PUBLICATIONS / Zanzibar – 1873-1963 – 1 – uk Microform Academic [960]
GOVERNMENT PUBLICATIONS AND ANNUAL DEPARTMENTAL REPORTS RELATING TO AFRICAN COUNTRIES PRIOR TO INDEPENDENCE / Africa – 1 – uk Microform Academic [960]
GOVERNMENT PUBLICATIONS CATALOGUE / Canada – 1891- – 9 – cn Micromedia [971]
GOVERNMENT PUBLICATIONS LISTS / Israel State Archives – 1948-74. English or Hebrew text. Individual titles available – 9 – is I.T.T.I. [324]
GOVERNMENT PUBLICATIONS RELATING TO NYASALAND, 1891-1964 – 69r – 1 – uk Microform Academic [324]
GOVERNMENT PUBLICATIONS REVIEW – v1-1974- – 5,6,9 – us UMI [320]
GOVERNMENT PUBLICATIONS REVIEW *see* JOURNAL OF GOVERNMENT INFORMATION
GOVERNMENT RED TAPE COSTS PUT AT EIGHTY BILLION A YEAR / Bowden, Robert – The Australian, 20 May 1986. 1p – 9 – 1.00f – at Libertarian Micro [335]
GOVERNMENT REGULATIONS ON MINING AND THE EXTRACTION OF OIL AND NATURAL GAS / Indonesia. Laws, Statutes, etc – SE-6868 1. 1961 – 9 – ne IDC [324]
GOVERNMENT REPORTS ANNOUNCEMENTS – v1-83. 1946-83.Continues: U.S. Government Research and Development Reports (1965-69); U.S. Government Research Reports (1954-64); Bibliography of Technical Reports (1949-54); Bibliography of Scientific and Technical Reports (1946-49) – 1,5,6 – us Princeton Micro [324]
GOVERNMENT REPORTS ANNOUNCEMENTS AND INDEX – v. 1- 1946- – 1. ; 5,6. ; 9 – apply; v.41-; v.76- – us UMI [073]
GOVERNMENT REPORTS INDEX – (Annual subscription. 81.00; 1,5,6) – v1-83. 1946-83 – 1,5,6 – us Princeton Micro [324]
GOVERNMENT RISK MANAGEMENT REPORTS – (v.3-. 1981-. 5,6,9) – v.1-. 1979- – 1 – us UMI [336]
GOVERNMENT TECHNICAL REPORTS – More than 60,000 available each year in microfiche. Sources include U.S. and foreign government agencies and contractors – 9 – $9.00 – us N.T.I.S. [600]
GOVERNMENT UNION REVIEW – v.1. 1980 – 1,5,6,9 – us UMI [073]
GOVERNMENTAL FINANCE – v. 1- 1972- – 1. ; 5,6,9 – apply; v.5- – us UMI [336]
THE GOVERNMENT'S PROGRAM ON INDUSTRIES; A PROGRESS REPORT / Jakarta. Universitas Indonesia – SE-3149 1. 1954? – 9 – ne IDC [380]
"GOVERNOR FRED HALL, A STUDY OF A POLITICAL PERSONALITY" / Green, Robert – undated – 1 – us KS Hist [320]
THE GOVERNOR GENERAL TRANSMITS FOR THE INFORMATION...RELATING TO THE COMMUTATION OF THE SENTENCE OF DEATH PASSED ON AMBROISE LEPINE, FOR THE MURDER OF THOMAS SCOTT, AT FORT GARRY – (In French 1mf SEM105P643) – Ottawa, 1875. SEM105P642 – 1mf – 9 – Can$2.25 – cn Bibl Nat [971]
GOVERNOR JONATHAN BELCHER LETTERBOOKS, 1723-1754 / Belcher, Jonathan – Massachusetts Historical Society – 11r – 1 – $830.00 – us UMI [920]
Governors' Conference *see* PROCEEDINGS
GOVERNOR'S CORRESPONDENCE RELATING TO LUKE SHORT / Kansas. Governor, 1883-85 (Governor Glick) – May-Jun 1883 – 1 – us KS Hist [978]
GOVERNOR'S DISPATCHES / Trinidad. Governor – 1814-1845 – 1 – us UMI [324]
Govett, James R *see* THE RELATIVE IMPORTANCE OF PROPRIOCEPTION, LIGAMENT LAXITY AND STRENGTH ON FUNCTIONAL PERFORMANCE IN THE ACL DEFICIENT AND ACL RECONSTRUCTED KNEE
Govin, Trelles *see*
- BIBLIOGRAFIA CUBANA DE LES SIGLOS 17 Y 18
- BIBLIOTECA HISTORICA CUBANA

Gow, Andrew J *see*
- THE EFFECT OF EXERCISE ON GLYCERALDEHYDE-3-PHOSPHATE DEHYDROGENASE AND SUPEROXIDE DISMUTASE ACTIVITIES IN THE POST-ISCHEMIC HEART
- EFFECT OF SPRINT TRAINING UPON SARCOPLASMIC RETICULUM CA2+ ATPASE AND NA+-CA2+ EXCHANGER MRNA EXPRESSION IN RAT MYOCARDIUM

GOWANSVILLE BAPTIST CHURCH. GOWANSVILLE, SOUTH CAROLINA : CHURCH RECORDS – 1835-83.Formerly: Cross Roads Baptist Church – 1 – 76.50 – us Baptist [240]
Gowers, William Frederick *see* GAZETTEER OF KANO PROVINCE
Gowon, Yakubu *see* FAITH IN UNITY
Goy, Ina *see* LEXIKOLOGISCHE UNTERSUCHUNGEN ZUM FACHWORTSCHATZ DER OEKOLOGIE UND DES UMWELTSCHUTZES IM NEUGRIECHISCHEN
GOYA, MORATIN, MELENDEZ VALDES Y DONOSO CORTES. RESENA HISTORICA DE LOS ANTERIORES ENTERRAMIENTOS Y TRASLACIONES DE SUS RESTOS MORTALES HASTA SU INHUMACION EN EL MAUSOLEO DEL CEMENTERIO DE SAN ISIDRO EL DIA 11 DE MAYO DE 1900 / Mesonero Romanos, Manuel – Madrid: Imp. Hijos de M.G. Hernandez, 1900 – sp Bibl Santa Ana [946]
Goyat, Michel *see* LE CODE DU TRAVAIL MALGACHE
Goyau, Lucie Faure *see* L'EVOLUTION FEMININE: LA FEMME AU FOYER ET DANS LA CITE
Goyau, Lucie Felix-Faure *see* NEWMAN
GOZOY LITURGIA DE LA SANTA MISA / Aradillas Agudo, Antonio – Barcelona: Juan Flors, editor, 1960 – 1 – sp Bibl Santa Ana [240]
Gozzadini, Giovanni *see* DELLE TORRI GENTILIZIE DI BOLOGNA E DELLA FAMIGLIE ALLE QUALI PRIMA APPARTENNERO
GP *see*
- AMERICAN FAMILY PHYSICIAN
- AMERICAN FAMILY PHYSICIAN/GP

GP (KANSAS CITY) – v. 1-40. 1950-1969 – 1,5,6 – us Princeton Micro [610]
GPA (GAS PROCESSORS ASSOCIATION) – Printed index. Updated every 60 days – 6,9 – us Info Handling [622]
GPO COM CATALOG ON ROLLFICHE – Four sections: Author-Title; Subject; Sudocs number; Report number. Notes and references from the LC Name and Subject Authority Files. Sudocs number section indexed by MARC fields 086 or 099, provides main entry and title verification. Report number section-MARC fields 027 and 088. Totally cumulated. Issued monthly – 9 – us Auto-Graphics [025]
GPO SALES PUBLICATIONS REFERENCE FILE / U.S. Government Printing Office – Bimonthly and monthly suppl. "Documents in Print" catalog – 9 – $125.00y in US $156.25y outside – S-N 721-002-00000-4. Sub-list ID-PRF – us Gov't Printing [324]
GRA NEWS / Girl's Rodeo Association – (v. 7- 1979- 9) – v. 1-. 1973- – 1,5,6 – us UMI [790]
Graaf, H J de *see* DE BAND TUSSEN AMBON EN NEDERLAND
Graaf, R de *see* DE MULIERUM ORGANIS GENERATIONI INSERVIENTIBUS
THE GRAAFF-REINET HERALD – Graaff-Reinet, South Africa. 25 Aug 1852-27 Aug 1884. 12 reels – 1, 16 diazo available at reduced price – sa SA Libr [072]
GRAAFF-REINETTER, DE – Graaff-Reinet, South Africa. 6 Jan 1890-27 Nov 1902. 13 reels. Suspended: 9 Apr-31 Dec 1900 – 1, 16 diazo available at reduced price – sa SA Libr [072]
Graah, WA *see*
- NARRATIVE OF AN EXPEDITION TO THE EAST COAST OF GREENLAND
- UNDERSOGELSES-REISE TIL OSTKYSTEN AF GRONLAND

Graap, Paul-Gerhard *see* RICHARD WAGNERS DRAMATISCHER ENTWURF JESUS VON NAZARETH
Graauwhart, Hendrik *see*
- CHRISTELYKE BEDENKINGEN EN VOORBEELDLYKE ZEEDELESSEN AFGELEID UIT 'S WERELDS EERSTE TOESTAND
- LEERZAME ZINNEBEELDEN, BESTAANDE IN CHRISTELYKE BEDENKINGEN DOOR VERGELYKINGE EENIGER SCHEPSELEN, ALS DIEREN, VOGELS, GEWASSEN, ETC.
- LEERZAME ZINNEBEELDEN; BESTAANDE IN CHRISTELYKE BEDENKINGEN DOOR VERGELYKINGE EENIGER SCHEPSELEN, ALS DIEREN, VOGELS, GEWASSEN ETC.
- VOORBEELDLYKE ZEEDE-LESSEN, GENOOMEN UYT DEN EERSTEN TOESTAND DES WERELDS, DES MENSCHEN LEVEN, AMPTEN, STAATEN, KONSTEN, EN NEYGINGEN DES GEMOEDS

GRAB- UND WEIHDENKMAELER AUS DEN TERRITORIEN VON AUGUSTA TRAIANA UND KABYLE VOM 1. BIS 3. JAHRHUNDERT N. CHR / Conrad, Sven – (Abbildungsteil: 1mf. DM60.00. ISBN: 3-89349-863-X) – 1994 – 3mf – 9 – DM98.00 – 3-89349-862-1 – gw Hänsel [930]
Grabar, A *see* LA PEINTURE RELIGIEUSE EN BULGARIE
Grabar, Oleg *see* THE ILLUSTRATIONS OF THE MAQAMAT
Grabar', VE *see* CATALOGUS (DE LEGATORUM JURE TRACTATUUM) COMPLETUS AB ANNO 1625 USQUE AD ANNUM 1700
GRABBE / Krack, Otto – Berlin, Leipzig: Schuster & Loeffler, [1904?] – 1r – 1 – us U.W. Library [430]
GRABBE ALS KRITIKER / Els, Hans van – Marburg, 1914 – 2mf – DM62.00 – 3-8267-3096-8 – gw Hänsel [430]
DAS GRABBE-BUCH / ed by Freidrich, Paul & Ebers, Fritz – (Includes bibliographical references) – Detmold: Meyer (M Staercke), 1923 – 1r – 1 – us U.W. Library [920]
GRABBES DOPPELTES GESICHT / Georg, Manfred – (Includes bibliographical references) – Berlin-Lichterfelde: E Runge, [1922?] – 1r – 1 – us U.W. Library [920]
DAS GRABDENKMAL DES KOENIGS CHEPHREN / Hoelscher, U – (Veroeffentlichungen der Ernst von der Sieglin Expedition in AEgypten. Leipzig, 1912). BNE-394 1 – 9 – ne IDC [930]
Grabe, Sven *see* EVALUATION MANUAL
Grabenhorst, Georg *see*
- REGIMENTSTAG
- SPAETE HEIMKEHR

GRABENZEITUNG – Berlin, mar 17-apr 10 1945 – 1 – Dist. gw Mikrofilm – gw Misc Inst [943]
Graber, V *see* DIE INSEKTEN
Grabert, Willy *see* GESCHICHTE DER DEUTSCHEN LITERATUR
DIE GRABESSCHULD : NACHGELASSENE ERZAEHLUNG / Sealsfield, Charles; ed by Meissner, Alfred – Leipzig: E J Guenther, 1873 – 1r – 1 – us U.W. Library [830]
Grabmann, M *see*
- MITTELALTERLICH GEISTESLEBEN
- DIE THEOLOGISCHE ERKENNTNIS- UND EINLEITUNGSLEHRE DES H. THOMAS VON AQUIN

DER GRABPALAST DES PATUAMENAP IN DER THEBANISCHEN NEKROPOLIS / Duemichen, J – 3v. Leipzig. 1884-94. BNE-371 1 – 9 – ne IDC [930]
GRACE BAPTIST CHURCH. LEXINGTON, KENTUCKY : CHURCH RECORDS – 1924-73.History, 1924-64 – 1 – 110.88 – us Baptist [240]
GRACE JOURNAL – v1-14. 1960-73 (complete) – 2r – 1 – ATLA S0325 – us A.T.L.A. [073]
Grace, M R *see* CASSAVA PROCESSING
Grace, Marie de la *see* BIBLIOGRAPHIE DE L'HOTEL-DIEU ST-VALLIER DE CHICOUTIMI, 1879-1889
GRACE THEOLOGICAL JOURNAL – (1985-. 5,6,9) – v1-. 1980- – 1 – us UMI [240]
THE GRACES : A CLASSICAL ALLEGORY, INTERSPERSED WITH POETRY, AND ILLUSTRATED BY EXPLANATORY NOTES: TOGETHER WITH A POETICAL FRAGMENT ENTITLED PSYCHE AMONG THE GRACES / Wieland, Christoph Martin – (Includes bibliographical references) – London: G and W B Whittaker, 1823 – 1 – us U.W. Library [810]
Gracey, Annie Ryder *see* MEDICAL WORK OF THE WOMAN'S FOREIGN MISSIONARY SOCIETY
Gracey, Mrs J T *see* EMINENT MISSIONARY WOMEN
Gracia Villacampa, Carlos *see*
- UNA COMISION DE CARLOS 5TH AL...P. FRANCISCO DE LOS ANGELES QUINONES (DESPUES OBISPO DE CORIA)
- FUNDACIONES TESTAMENTARIAS DE FR. MIGUEL DE MEDINA, JERONIMO DE GUADALUPE EN EL CONVENTO DE SAN FRANCISCO DE MEDINA DE POMAR, BURGOS, 1915

LA GRACIA Y EL SACERDOCIO DE CRISTO – Francisco Navares Merino Lima: Facultad de Teologia Pontificia y Civil de Lima, 1967 – us Res Libr [972]
Gracian *see* DE KONST DER WIJSHEID
Graciarena, Jorge *see* PODER Y CLASSES SOCIALES EN EL DESARROLLO DE AMERICA LATINA
Gracza, Gyorgy *see* AZ 1848-49-IKI MAGYAR SZABADSAGHARZ TOERTENETE
GRADE SCHOOL REGISTER / Monroe County. Mich, Bedford Township. Board of Education – 1893-1897 – 1r – 1 – $32.50r – us Archival [324]
GRADED BIBLE LESSONS AND MATERIALS / Presbyterian Church in the U.S.A. Board of Christian Education – 1937-1948 – 1 – $50.00 – us Presbyterian [240]
GRADED ELEMENTARY MAGAZINE – Oct 1930-Sep 1933 – 1 – 45.99 – us Baptist [240]
GRADED JUNIOR PUPIL, YEARS 1-4 – 1943 – 1 – 32.13 – us Baptist [240]
GRADED JUNIOR TEACHER, YEARS 1-4 – 1943 – 1 – 49.42 – us Baptist [240]
GRADED LESSON HELPER – Apr 1926-Sep 1930 – 1 – 77.35 – us Baptist [240]
THE GRADED SCHOOL. A GRADED COURSE OF INSTRUCTION FOR PUBLIC SCHOOLS / Wells, William Harvey – New York: A.S. Barnes & Co., 1867. 200p. fold. forms – 1 – us U.W. Library [370]
Grader, Ch. J *see* LAND MANAGEMENT IN TIMOR; ORIENTING NOTES
Gradis, Gaston *see* A LA RECHERCHE DU GRAND-AXE
Gradmann, Johann Jacob *see* DAS GELEHRTE SCHWABEN
Gradovskii, A *see* O SVOBODE RUSSKOI PECHATI
Gradstein, F M et al *see* QUANTITATIVE STRATIGRAPHY
GRADUAL ROMANUM... – Early 18th C ms – 1 – us Sibley [780]
GRADUALE AD USUM ORDINIA PRAEDICATORUM. – French illum. mss., Dominican Gradual, inc. Scripture Lessons and Offices. Some missing leaves at beginning and end. Between 1253-1262? – 9 – us Sibley [780]
GRADUALE ROMANUM : PROPRIUM DE TEMPERE ADVENTUS AD SABBATUM SANCTUM – 16th [?] century manuscript – 1 – us Sibley [780]
GRADUATE EMPLOYMENT AND HIGHER EDUCATION IN WEST BENGAL / Sanyal, B C et al – Paris, New Delhi, 1983 – 4mf – 9 – DE-141/1 – ne IDC [370]
GRADUATE WOMAN *see* AAUW JOURNAL
GRADUATING ENGINEER – 1979- – 1,5,6,9 – us UMI [620]
GRADUATION DAY FAKULTAS EKONOMI AND AKADEMI PEMIMPIN PERUSAHAAN DAN AKUNTANSI / Pematang Siantar, Indonesia – SE-10,956 1. 1964 – 9 – ne IDC [370]
GRADUS AD PARNASSUM / Fux, J J – 1725 – 9 – us Sibley [780]
GRADUS AD PARNASSUM. SALITA AL PARNASSO...NELL' IDIOMA ITALIANO DAL SACERDOTE ALESSANDRO MANFREDI... / Fux, J J – Carpi: Carmignani, 1761 – 6mf – 2 – us Sibley [780]
GRADUS AD PARNASSUM, SIVE MANUDUCTIO AS COMPOSITIONEM MUSICAE REGULAREN / Fux, J J – 1725. P 279 – 9 – ne IDC [780]

LE GRADUS FRANCAIS OU DICTIONNAIRE DE LA LANGUE POETIQUE / Carpentier, L J M – 1822 – 9 – fr I.C.S. [440]
GRADWELL LETTERS, 1777-1833, FROM THE ARCHIVES OF THE ARCHBISHOP OF WESTMINSTER / Westminster Cathedral. Archives – Ms. with index – 1 – uk Microform Academic [240]
GRAE ACTUALITES – [s.l.]: Publie par le Departement des relations exterieures du Gouvernement revolutionnaire de l'Angola en exil. n1-3 – us Res Libr [327]
Graeber, H J *see* DIE KONFESSIONELLE SCHULE
Graebner, A L *see* GESCHICHTE DER LUTHERISCHEN KIRCHE IN AMERICA
Graebner, C O R *see* SYNOPSIS DER MITTELEUROPAEISCHEN FLORA
GRAECA LATINA / Schulze, Wilhelm – (Includes bibliographical references) – Gottingae: Officina Academica Dieterichiana, 1901 – 1mf – 9 – 0-8370-9178-0 – 1986-3178 – us A.T.L.A. [450]
GRAECO-BUDDHIST SCULPTURES FROM YUSUFZAI / India. Preservation of National Monuments; ed by Cole, H H – Calcutta, 1885. BI-690 2 – 8 – ne IDC [730]
Graef, Hermann *see* HEINRICH VON KLEIST
Graef, Juan Enrique *see* DISCURSOS MERCURIALES, NO 7 AL 13
Graef, Peter Leo *see* HILFE, DIE NICHT ANKOMMT
Graefe, A von *see*
- CLINICAL LECTURES ON AMBLYOPIA AND AMAUROSIS, AND THE EXTRACTION OF CATARACT
- THREE MEMOIRS ON IRIDECTOMY IN CERTAIN FORMS OF IRITIS, CHOROIDITIS AND GLAUCOMA

Graefe, Alan R *see*
- AN EXAMINATION OF ENVIRONMENTAL ATTITUDES AMONG COLLEGE STUDENTS
- THE IMPACTS OF MARINE DEBRIS, WEATHER CONDITIONS, AND UNEXPECTED EVENTS ON RECREATIONAL BOATER SATISFACTION ON THE DELAWARE INLAND BAYS
- OUTDOOR RECREATION PARTICIPATION OF MARYLAND RESIDENTS IN MARYLAND STATE FORESTS AND PARKS
- A SIMULATION APPROACH TO CROWDING IN OUTDOOR RECREATION

Graefe, CF v. *see* ENCYCLOPAEDISCHES WOERTERBUCH DER MEDICINISCHEN WISSENSCHAFTEN (AEL, ABT 3;13)
Graefe, J F *see* SAMLUNG VERSCHIEDENER UND AUSERLESENER...1. THEIL
Graefe, Johanna *see* UEBER DEN "ZAUBERBERG" VON THOMAS MANN
GRAEFES ARCHIV FUER KLINISCHE U. EXPERIMENTELLE OPHTHALMOLOGIE – v. 148-214. 1947-80 – 1,5,9 – 7839.00 – us UMI [617]
Graeffer, Franz *see* OESTERREICHISCHE NATIONAL-ENZYKLOPAEDIE ODER ALPHABETISCHE DARLEGUNG DER WISSENSWUERDIGSTEN EIGENTHUEMLICHKEITEN DES OESTERREICHISCHEN KAISERTUMS (AEL, ABT.1;10)
GRAEFIN ERIKA LEHR- UND WANDERJAHRE / Schubin, Ossip – Braunschweig: G Westermann, c1921 – 1 – us U.W. Library [830]
GRAEFLICH ERBACHISCHES WOCHEN-BLATT FUER DEN LANDKREIS ERBACH : BA DES DARMSTAEDTER TAGBLATT – (Title changes: Erbacher Kreisblatt, 1867; Centralanzeiger fuer den Odenwald, 1900; Odenwaelder Heimatzeitung, 1 Aug 1949) – Erbach-Michelstadt, West Germany. 1977- – 7r per yr – 1 – gw Mikrofilm [072]
GRAENSEN FOER SVERIGES TERRITORIALVATTEN... / ed by Gihl, T – Stockholm, 1930 – 4mf – 1 – ILM-2940/1 – ne IDC [327]
GRAENZBOTE *see* SCHWAEBISCHES TAGBLATT
Graesse, J GT *see* ORBIS LATINUS ODER VERZEICHNIS DER WICHTIGSTEN LATEINISCHEN ORTS- UND LAENDERNAMEN. ED. 3
Graessner, Gernot Heinrich Willi *see* DEUTSCHLAND UND DIE NATIONALSOZIALISTEN IN DEN VEREINIGTEN STAATEN VON AMERIKA
Graetz, H *see*
- ATERET ZEVI. JUBELSCHRIFT ZUM SIEBZIGSTEN GEBURTSTAGE
- GESCHICHTE DER JUDEN VON DEN AELTESTEN ZEITEN BIS AUF DIE GEGENWART

Graetz, Heinrich *see*
- KOHELET
- SCHIR HA-SCHIRIM

Graevenitz, George von *see* ITALIENISCHE REISE
GRAF ADOLF FRIEDRICH VON SCHACK : EIN LITERARISCHER ESSAY / Brenning, Emil – (Includes bibliographical references) – Bremen: Carl Rocco, 1885 – 1r – 1 – us U.W. Library [840]
GRAF ADOLF FRIEDRICH VON SCHACK : EIN LITERARISCHES PORTRAIT / Babel, Eugen – Wien: Carl Gerold's Sohn, 1885 – 1r – 1 – us U.W. Library [920]
GRAF ALFRED KEYSERLING ERZAEHLT / Keyserling, Alfred – Kaunas und Leipzig: Pribacis, 1937. xii,399p – 1 – us U.W. Library [947]
Graf, Arturo *see* UN MONTE DI PILATO IN ITALIA
GRAF DMITRII ALEKSEVICH MILIUTIN / Baiov, A K – St. Petersburg, 1912. B-2233 2 – 8 – ne IDC [920]
GRAF ESSEX / Laube, Heinrich – 8. Aufl. Leipzig: J J Weber, [1898?] – 1 – us U.W. Library [820]
Graf, G *see*
- DIE CHRISTLICH-ARABISCHE LITTERATUR BIS ZUR FRAENKISCHEN ZEIT...
- EIN REFORMVERSUCH INNERHALB DER KOPTISCHEN KIRCHE IM 12.JH.

Graf, Hans Gerhard *see*
- GOETHE
- GOETHE VON SCHILLER IN BRIEFEN
- GOETHES BRIEFWECHSEL MIT SEINER FRAU

GRAF JULIUS ANDRASSY. SEIN LEBEN UND SEINE ZEIT / Wertheimer, E von – 3v. Stuttgart. 1910-13. BR-5300 2 – 8 – ne IDC [920]
Graf, Karl Heinrich *see* DIE GESCHICHTLICHEN BUECHER DES ALTEN TESTAMENTS
GRAF L. N. TOLSTOI KAK PISATEL' VSEMIRNYI I RASPROSTRANENIE EGO PROIZVEDENII V ROSSII I ZA GRANITSEI / Draganov, P D – Spb. 1903. BR-5890 2 – 8 – ne IDC [460]
GRAF P. A. STROGANOV, 1774-1817 / Nikolai Mikhailovich, Vel. Kn – v. 1-3. Spb. 1903. BR-7730 2 – 8 – ne IDC [920]
GRAF PHILIPP COBENZL UND SEINE MEMOIREN / ed by Arneth, A von – Wien, 1885 – 2mf – 9 – ne IDC [943]
DER GRAF VON CHAROLAIS : EIN TRAUERSPIEL / Beer-Hofmann, Richard – 4. Aufl. Berlin: S Fischer, 1906 – 1r – 1 – us U.W. Library [820]
DER GRAF VON ESSEX IM DEUTSCHEN DRAMA / Baerwolf, Walther – Tuebingen, 1919 – 1mf – DM48.00 – 3-8267-3010-0 – gw Hänsel [430]
Grafe, Eduard *see* DIE PAULINSCHE LEHRE VOM GESETZ: NACH DEN VIER HAUPTBRIEFEN
Grafenstein, Andreas *see* MOEGLICHKEITEN UND GRENZEN EINER ERHOEHUNG DER STAATSWIRTSCHAFTLICHEN PLANUNGSRATIONALITAET DURCH CUTBACK-MANAGEMENT-TECHNIKEN UND ERFOLGSKONTROLLEN
Graff, L von *see* MONOGRAPHIE DER TURBELLARIEN
Graff, P *see* GESCHICHTE DER AUFLOESUNG DER ALTEN GOTTESDIENSTLICHEN KIRCHE DEUTSCHLANDS
Graff, Sigmund *see* DIE ENDLOSE STRASSE
Graffenauer, Jean Philippe *see* TOPOGRAPHIE PHYSIQUE ET MEDICALE DE LA VILLE DE STRASBOURG
Graffin, B *see* APHRAETES
GRAFINIA EKATERINA IVANOVNA GOLOVKINA I EE VREMIA / Khmyrov, M D – 1701-91 GODA. Istoricheskii ocherk po arkhivnym dokumentam. Spb. 1867. BR-6006 2 – 8 – ne IDC [460]
GRAFSCHAFTER NACHRICHTEN – Nordhorn, West Germany. 1978- – ca 7r per yr – 1 – gw Mikrofilm [072]
GRAFTON 1693-1849 – (Mf 1T: Births, Intentions, Marriages 1693-1766. Mf 2T: Vital Records 1721-82. Mf 3T-6T: Marriages & Intentions 1781-1849. Mf 7T: Marriages & Births 1735-1824. Mf 8T-9T: Births & Deaths 1756-1849. Mf 10T: Births 1791-1846. Mf 11T: Births & Deaths 1788-1850. Mf 12T: Births 1846-48. Mf 13T: Births 1848-49; Marriages 1844-45. Mf 14T: Marriages 1845-49; Deaths 1844-47. Mf 15T: Deaths 1847-49) – (mf ed 1996) – 15mf – 9 – 0-87623-255-1 – us Holbrook [920]
GRAFTON 1693-1900 – (Mf 1-5: Birth Index 1693-1900. Mf 6-15: Births 1693-1900. Mf 16-20: Marriage Index 1729-1900. Mf 21-29: Marriages 1729-1905. Mf 30-33: Death Index 1721-1900. Mf 34-40: Deaths 1721-1900. Mf 41-44: Birth Index 1693-1934. Mf 45-48: Death Index 1721-1934. Mf 49-56: Birth, Death 1693-1851. Mf 57-60: Birth, Death 1744-1843. Mf 61-67: Birth, Death 1779-1856. Mf 68-78: Proprietors 1728-1775. Mf 79-83: Town Records 1735-1782. Mf 84-90: Town Records 1752-89. Mf 84-90: Town Records 1752-89. Mf 91-97: Town Records 1779-1800. Mf 98-107: Town Records 1799-1820. Mf 108-114: Town Record 1820-39. Mf 115-124: Town Record 1821-48. Mf 125-138: Intentions 1735-1900. Mf 139-141: Death Index 1844-84. Mf 142-150: Deaths 1844-1905. Mf 151-152: Marriage Index 1844-85. Mf 153-159: Marriages 1844-1900. Mf 160-161: Birth Index 1844-62. Mf 162-166: Births 1844-84. Mf 167-169: Birth 1885-1900) – (mf ed 1993) – 169mf – 9 – 0-87623-164-4 – us Holbrook [920]
GRAFTON AND COOS COUNTIES BAR ASSOCIATION ANNUAL MEETINGS – New Hampshire. 3v in 5 books. 1882-98 – 24mf – 9 – $36.00 – LLMC 84-476 – us L.L.M.C. [340]
GRAFTON ARGUS – Nov 3 1879-Aug 28 1882 – 9 – at Pascoe [072]
Grafton, Charles Chapman *see* DIFFICULTIES OF FAITH
Grafton County. New Hampshire. Bar *see* PROCEEDINGS OF THE GRAFTON COUNTY BAR, ON THE DEATH OF THE HON. HARRY HIBBARD.
GRAFTON SUN – Grafton, NE. -w. Mar-May 1898; Jan 1899-Feb 1902 – 1 – us NE Hist [071]
Grafton, Thomas W *see* ALEXANDER CAMPBELL
GRAFT-TRANSMISSIBLE DISEASES OF CITRUS : HANDBOOK FOR DETECTION AND DIAGNOSIS – 1991 – 300p – it F.A.O. [660]
GRAFY NIKITA I PETR PANINY / Lebedev, P S – Spb. 1863. BR-4227 2 – 8 – ne IDC [920]
Gragera Vega, Silverio *see* PROCURADORES DE LOS TRIBUNALES EJERCIENTES EN ESPANA
Gragger, Robert *see* PREUSSEN, WEIMAR UND DIE UNGARISCHE KOENIGSKRONE, MIT DEM FAKSIMILE EINES GOETHE-BRIEFES
Graham *see* HISTORY OF THE SOMONAUK UNITED PRESBYTERIAN CHURCH
Graham, A A *see*
- HISTORY OF FAIRFIELD AND PERRY COUNTIES
- HISTORY OF RICHLAND COUNTY ITS PAST AND PRESENT

Graham, Angela H *see* THE NATIONAL ENDOWMENT FOR THE ARTS DANCE PROGRAM, 1965-1971
GRAHAM BAPTIST CHURCH. SUMTER COUNTY. SOUTH CAROLINA : CHURCH RECORDS – 1886-1924. Roll. 1952-59 – 1 – 7.92 – us Baptist [240]
Graham, Bruce J *see* A COMPARISON OF HYDROSTATIC WEIGHING AND DISPLACEMENT PLETHYSMOGRAPHY FOR DETERMINING BODY DENSITY OF YOUNG ELITE FEMALE GYMNASTS
Graham County. Arizona *see* CEMETERY RECORD OF THE FRANKLIN WARD, GRAHAM COUNTY, ARIZONA
Graham, David *see* A TREATISE ON THE LAW OF NEW TRIALS IN CASES CIVIL AND CRIMINAL
Graham, Gabriela Cunninghame *see* SANTA TERESA
Graham, H Q. *see* PASTORAL REGISTER
Graham, Isabella Marshall *see* THE POWER OF FAITH: EXEMPLIFIED IN THE LIFE AND WRITINGS OF THE LATE MRS. ISABELLA GRAHAM
Graham, J *see* A CATALOGUE OF THE PLANTS GROWING IN BOMBAY AND ITS VICINITY
Graham, J A *see* ON THE THRESHOLD OF THREE CLOSED LANDS
Graham, J Miller *see* EAST OF THE BARRIER
Graham, James *see* INTERVIEWS FROM VILLAGES IN THE NJOMBE DISTRICT, TANZANIA
Graham, John Anderson *see* MISSIONARY EXPANSION SINCE THE REFORMATION
Graham, M W *see*
- IN QUEST OF A LAW OF RECOGNITION
- THE LEAGUE OF NATIONS AND THE RECOGNITION OF STATES

Graham, Mary Jane *see* TRUTH AND GRACE, OR, THE WORKS OF MARY JANE GRAHAM
Graham, Ralph E *see* THE RELATIONSHIP OF AEROBIC FITNESS, TYPE A BEHAVIOR PATTERN, AND HOSTILITY TO BAROREFLEX RESPONSES AND CARDIOVASCULAR REACTIVITY TO NONEXERTIONAL STRESSORS
Graham, Rose *see* ST. GILBERT OF SEMPRINGHAM AND THE GILBERTINES. A HISTORY OF THE ONLY ENGLISH MONASTIC ORDER
Graham, Stephen *see*
- CHANGING RUSSIA
- THE WAY OF MARTHA AND THE WAY OF MARY
- WITH POOR IMMIGRANTS TO AMERICA
- WITH THE RUSSIAN PILGRIMS TO JERUSALEM

Graham, William *see* THE ONE POUND NOTE/ SCOTLAND/ ENGLAND
Graham, William A *see* ISLAM-FICHE
Grahame, James *see* THE POETICAL WORKS OF HENRY KIRKE WHITE AND JAMES GRAHAME
THE GRAHAMSTOWN JOURNAL – (Title varies: The Journal 1864-1920) – Grahamstown, South Africa. 1 Jul 1913-30 Dec 1919 – 13r – 1, 16 diazo available at reduced price – sa SA Libr [072]
THE GRAHAMSTOWN OBSERVER – Grahamstown, South Africa. 3 Jul-25 Dec 1933. 1 reel – 1, 16 diazo available at reduced price – sa SA Libr [072]
GRAHAMSTOWN (SOUTH AFRICA) DIOCESAN RECORDS / United Society for the Propagation of the Gospel. Archives – 19th Century – 1 – uk Microform Academic [025]
GRAHAN COUNTY LEVER – Gettysburg. Kan. 1879-81 – 1 – us UMI [071]
GRAIN GROWERS GUIDE – Winnipeg, 1908-28 – 13r – 1 – cn Commonwealth Micro [073]
GRAIN SORGHUM VARIETIES / Alabama. Agricultural Experiment Station – 1956-60. 1 fiche – 9 – us Spaulding [630]
GRAINS DE BON SENS – 15e Mille. Montreal: Imprimerie du Messager, 1918. SEM105P1212 – 3mf – 9 – Can$6.75 – cn Bibl Nat [240]
GRAIUL NOU – Bucharest. Rumania. -sw. 18 Dec 1944-22 Feb 1948. (Very imperfect). (2 reels) – 1 – uk British Libr Newspaper [949]
Grajewski, A L *see* MI-GINZEI YERUSHALAYIM
Grajewski, P *see* MILHEMET HA-YEHUDIM BA-MISSION MI-SHENAT 5584 AD HA-YOM HA-ZEH
Grajon, Nicole *see* DE LA REPETITION DANS LES TEXTES LITTERAIRES SITUATION HISTORIQUE ET APPROCHE STRUCTURALE
Gram, Hans *see*
- AMERICA–A NEW MARCH
- THE DEATH SONG OF AN INDIAN CHIEF, FROM "OUABI."

Gramain, P *see* LES DROITS INTERNATIONAUX DE L'HOMME
GRAMATICA CASTELLANA / Castillo, Manuel – 1898 – 9 – 1.50f – sp Bibl Santa Ana [440]
GRAMATICA DE LA LENGUA ARABIGA / Moreno Nieto, Jose – 1872 – 9 – $1.50f – sp Bibl Santa Ana [470]
GRAMATICA DE LA LENGUA CASTELLANA / Academia Espanola – 1771 – 1mf – 9 – Pta1,000.00 – 84-7848-129-X – sp Pentalfa [440]
GRAMATICA DE LA LENGUA ESPANOLA / Real Academia Espanola – Nueva ed. reformada. Madrid: Perlado, Paez y Compania, 1924. 564p. 1 reel. 1283 – 1 – us U.W. Library [440]
GRAMATICA ELEMENTAL DE LA LENGUA LATINA Y CASTELLANA / Lama y Lena, Rafael & Lozano, Francisco Franco – Gijon: Imprenta de Mussel, 2nd ed 1894 – 1 – sp Bibl Santa Ana [440]
GRAMATICA FRANCESA / Nunez Coronado, J – Badajoz: Imp. Grafica Iberia, 2nd ed 1945 – 1 – sp Bibl Santa Ana [440]
GRAMATICA FRANCESA / Nunez Coronado, J – Badajoz: La Minerva Extremena, 3rd ed 1946 – 1 – sp Bibl Santa Ana [440]
GRAMATICA GRAECA / Sanchez de las Brozas, Francisco – 1592 – 9 – 1.50f – sp Bibl Santa Ana [450]
GRAMATICA HISTORICA ESPANOLA Y ANTOLOGIAS / Gomez Bravo, Vicente – Medieval y del siglo 15. Madrid: Graficas Nebrija, 1957 – 1 – sp Bibl Santa Ana [440]

GRAMATICA ILOCANA / Lopez, Francisco, Fr; ed by Carro, P – 3rd ed. Malabon: Estab tip del Asilo de huerfanos de Malabon, a cargo de pp. Agustinos calzados, 1895 – us Res Libr [400]

GRAMATICA LATINA / Iriarte, Juan de – 1771 – 2mf – 9 – Pta1,500.00 – 84-7848-182-6 – sp Pentalfa [450]

GRAMATICA LATINA / Santos Coco, Francisco – Badajoz: Tip. Artes Graficas, 1932 – 1 – sp Bibl Santa Ana [440]

GRAMATICA LATINA (I. 1468) / Mates, Bartolome – Barcelona – 1r – 5,6 – sp Cultura [450]

GRAMATICA Y DICCIONARIO DE LA LENGUA PEMON (AREKUNA, TAUREPAN, KAMARAKOTO) (FAMILIA CARIBE) POR EL R.P. -, MISIONERO CAPUCHINO / Armellada, Cesareo de – Caracas: Coop. A Artes Graficas. 2v. 1943-44 – 7mf – 9 – CIDOC-26240/1 – ne IDC [054]

GRAMATICA Y...EL PERU / Gonzalez Holguin, Diego – 1842 – 9 – 1.50f – sp Bibl Santa Ana [440]

GRAMATICES...FALLACES E PROLIXAE / Sanchez de las Brozas, Francisco – 1595 – 9 – 1.50f – sp Bibl Santa Ana [450]

GRAMATICUS LATINAE INSTITUTIONES / Sanchez de las Brozas, Francisco – 1576 – 9 – 1.50f – sp Bibl Santa Ana [450]

GRAMATYKA HISTORYCZNA JEZYKA CZESKIEGO / Lehr-Sptawinski, Tadeusz – Warszawa: Panstwowe Wydawn, Naukowe, 1957-. Map. Bibliog. 1 reel. 1287 – 1 – us U.W. Library [460]

GRAMATYKA JEZYKA POLSKIEGO / Benni, T et al – Krakow. 1923. B-1472 2 – 8 – ne IDC [460]

GRAMATYKA JEZYKA POLSKIEGO / Lazowski, D – Krakow. 1848. BR-8011 2 – 8 – ne IDC [460]

GRAMATYKA JEZYKA POLSKIEGO / Muczkowski, J – Wyd. 3. Krakow. 1849. BR-4850 2 – 8 – ne IDC [460]

Gramberg, Frank *see* STRATEGISCHE ALLIANZEN

Grambert, Joseph *see* LA VOLTAIRIADE

GRAMERA MALAGASY : DINGANA FAHAROA / Rajaobelina, Prosper – [Tananarive]: Edisiona Salohy, 1960 – 1 – us Res Libr [490]

GRAMERE / Ramus, Peter – 1562 – 9 – fr I.C.S. [440]

Graminaeus, Diederich *see* MYSTICUS AQUILO, SIVE DECLARATION VATICINII JEREMIE PROPHETAE

GRAMINUM MONOGRAPHIAE / Fluegge, D J – 8028 1. 1810 – 9 – ne IDC [580]

GRAMMAIRE / Ramus, Peter – 1572 – 9 – fr I.C.S. [440]

GRAMMAIRE ANGLOISE / Mason, George – 1633. 112p. (English Linguistics Series 1500-1800) – 9 – App – us UMI [420]

GRAMMAIRE CATEGORIELLE DU FRANCAIS. ETUDE THEORIQUE ET IMPLANTATION. LE SYSTEME GRACE (GRAMMAIRE CATEGORIELLE ETENDUE) / Segond, Frederique – 1mf – 9 – 10065 – fr Atelier National [440]

GRAMMAIRE COMPLETE DE LA LANGUE DES NAMAS / Schils, G H – Louvain, Imprimerie Lefever freres et soeurs. 1891 – 9 – $5.00 – fr Orientalistes [490]

GRAMMAIRE DE LA LANGUE PONGOUEE / Le Berre – Paris, Imprimerie Simon Racon et Cie. 1873 – 9 – $7.50 – fr Orientalistes [490]

GRAMMAIRE DE LA LANGUE SERERE AVEC DES EXEMPLES ET DES EXERCICES / Lamoise – St-Joseph de Ngasobil, Imprimerie de la Mission. 1873 – 9 – $10.00 – fr Orientalistes [490]

GRAMMAIRE DE LA LANGUE TURQUE / Deny, J – (dialecte osmanli). Paris. 1921. BU-302 2 – 8 – ne IDC [490]

GRAMMAIRE DE LA LANGUE VOLOFE / Kobes, Alois – Saint Joseph de Ngasobil, Imprimerie de la Mission. 1869 – 9 – $10.00 – fr Orientalistes [490]

GRAMMAIRE DE LA LANGUE WOLOFFE / Boilat, P D – Paris, Imprimerie Imperiale. 1858 – 9 – $12.50 – fr Orientalistes [490]

GRAMMAIRE DEMOTIQUE / Lexa, F – 7v. Prague. 1949-51. BNE-20.061 1 – 9 – ne IDC [450]

GRAMMAIRE DES GRAMMAIRES / Girault-Duvivier, Ch – 1853 – 9 – fr I.C.S. [400]

GRAMMAIRE ELEMENTAIRE DE LA LANGUE VOLOFE / Speisser, F L – St-Joseph de Ngasobil, Imprimerie de la Mission. 1884 – 9 – $10.00 – fr Orientalistes [490]

GRAMMAIRE ESQUIMAUDE DU SOUS-DIALECTE DE L'UNGAVA / Schneider, Lucien – Quebec: Ministere des Richesses naturelles, 1968? SEM105P937 – 2mf – 9 – Can$4.50 – cn Bibl Nat [490]

GRAMMAIRE ET SYNTAXE FRANCOISE / Maupas, Ch – 3e ed. 1632 – 9 – fr I.C.S. [440]

GRAMMAIRE ET VOCABULAIRE DE LA LANGUE POUL / Faidherbe, Louis Leon Cesar – 2ed. Paris, Maisonneuve et Cie. 1882 – 9 – $5.00 – fr Orientalistes [490]

GRAMMAIRE FIOTE / Visseq, Alexandre – Paris, Maison-Mere, Rue Lhomond. 1889 – 9 – $5.00 – fr Orientalistes [490]

LA GRAMMAIRE FRANCAISE ET LES GRAMMAIRIENS DU XVIE SIECLE / Livet, C L – 1859 – 9 – fr I.C.S. [440]

GRAMMAIRE FRANCOISE – Montreal: J Brown, 1811. SEM16P46 – 1r – 5 – Can$9.00 – cn Bibl Nat [440]

GRAMMAIRE FRANCOISE / Vallart, J – 1744 – 9 – fr I.C.S. [440]

GRAMMAIRE FRANCOISE RAISONNEE / Vallange, de – 1721 – 9 – fr I.C.S. [440]

GRAMMAIRE FRANCOISE, RAPPORTEE AU LANGAGE DU TEMPS. REVUEE ET AUGMENTEE DE BEAUCOUP EN CETTE SECONDE EDITION / Oudin, A – 2E ED. 1640 – 9 – fr I.C.S. [440]

GRAMMAIRE FRANCOISE SIMPLIFIEE / Domergue, U – 1778 – 9 – fr I.C.S. [440]

GRAMMAIRE FRANCOISE SUR UN PLAN NOUVEAU / Buffier, Cl – 1709 – 9 – fr I.C.S. [440]

GRAMMAIRE GENERALE / Beauzee, N – 1767 – 9 – fr I.C.S. [440]

GRAMMAIRE GENERALE ET RAISONNEE / Arnauld, Antoine & Lancelot, Claude – 1660 – 9 – fr I.C.S. [440]

GRAMMAIRE GENERALE ET RAISONNEE / Arnauld, Antoine & Lancelot, Claude – 1754 – 9 – fr I.C.S. [440]

GRAMMAIRE GENERALE ET RAISONNEE / Fromant, Abbe – 3e ed. 1769 – 9 – fr I.C.S. [400]

GRAMMAIRE GENERALE ET RAISONNEE / Lancelot, Claude & Arnauld, Antoine – Linguistic series. 1754 – 9 – fr Hachette [400]

GRAMMAIRE GENERALE, OU EXPOSITION RAISONNEE DES ELEMENTS NECESSAIRES DU LANGAGE / Bezauzee, N – (Linguistics series). 2 v. 1767 – 9 – fr Hachette [440]

GRAMMAIRE HEBRAEIQUE : PRECEDEE D'UN PRECIS HISTORIQUE SUR LA LANGUE HEBRAEIQUE / Preiswerk, Samuel – 3e rev et corr ed. Bale: H Georg, 1871 – 1mf – 9 – 0-8370-9263-9 – 1986-3263 – us A.T.L.A. [470]

GRAMMAIRE KISWAHILI / Delaunay – Imprimerie F. Leve. 1885 – 9 – $5.00 – fr Orientalistes [490]

GRAMMAIRE LATINE – Montreal: J Brown, 1811. SEM16P48 – 1r – 5 – Can$9.00 – cn Bibl Nat [450]

LA GRAMMAIRE LOGIQUE: RESOLVANT TOUTES LES DIFFICULTES / Brisset, Pierre – Paris: E. Leroux, 1883. 176p. 2 fiches. (Language Collection) – 9 – 6.00 – fr Bibl Nationale [400]

GRAMMAIRE MALGACHE FONDEE SUR LES PRINCIPES DE LA GRAMMAIRE JAVANAISE : SUIVIE D'EXERCICES ET D'UN RECUEIL DE CENT ET UN PROVERBES / Marre-de Marin – Paris: Chez Maisonneuve et Cie, 1876 – 1 – us Res Libr [490]

GRAMMAIRE MALGACHE FONDEE SUR LES PRINCIPES DE LA GRAMMAIRE JAVANAISE SUIVIE D'EXERCICES ET D'UN RECUEIL DE CENT ET UN PROVERBES / Marre, Aristide – Paris, Maisonneuve et Cie. 1876 – 9 – $5.00 – fr Orientalistes [490]

GRAMMAIRE MALGACHE FONDEE SUR LES PRINCIPES DE LA GRAMMAIRE JAVANAISE, SUIVIE D'EXERCICES ET D'UN RECUEIL DE CENT ET UN PROVERBES / Marin, Marre-de – Paris: Maisonneuve, 1876 – us Res Libr [470]

GRAMMAIRE MALGACHE (SAKALAVE) REDIGEE PAR LES MISSIONNAIRES DE MADAGASCAR – Ile Bourbon: Notre Dame de la Ressource. 1855 – 9 – $5.00 – fr Orientalistes [490]

GRAMMAIRE METHODIQUE ET RAISONNEE / Boniface, A – 1843 – 9 – fr I.C.S. [440]

GRAMMAIRE OUOLOVE / Lambert, M – Paris. 1842 – 9 – $5.00 – fr Orientalistes [490]

GRAMMAIRE RONGA SUIVIE D'UN MANUEL DE CONVERSATION ET D'UN VOCABULAIRE RONGA-PORTUGAIS-FRANCAIS-ANGLAIS / Junod, Henri A – Laus sanne, Imprimerie Georges Bridel et Cie. 1896 – 9 – $10.00 – fr Orientalistes [490]

GRAMMAIRE WOLOFE OU METHODE POUR ETUDIER LA LANGUE DES NOIRS QUI HABITENT LES ROYAUMES DE BOURBA-YOLOF / Dard, J – Paris, Imprimerie Royale. 1826 – 9 – $7.50 – fr Orientalistes [490]

LES GRAMMAIRIENS FRANCAIS / Telle, J A – 2e ed. 1874 – 9 – fr I.C.S. [440]

GRAMMAR AND VOCABULARY OF THE BULLOM LANGUAGE / Nylander, Gustavus Reinhold – London: Printed for the Church missionary society, by Ellerton and Henderson, 1814 – us Res Libr [470]

GRAMMAR AND VOCABULARY OF THE ESKIMO LANGUAGE / Hinz, J – Bethlehem, Pa. 1944. BN-250 2 – 8 – ne IDC [490]

A GRAMMAR AND VOCABULARY OF THE SUSCO LANGUAGE : TO WHICH ARE ADDED THE NAMES OF SOME OF THE SOSOO TOWNS / Brunton, E – Edinburgh: Printed by J Ritchie, 1802 – 1 – us Res Libr [490]

A GRAMMAR FOR LEARNING THE PRINCIPLES OF THE MALABAR LANGUAGE / Fabricus, Johann P & Breithaupt, Christian – 1789. 70p. (English Linguistics Series 1500-1800) – 9 – us UMI [490]

GRAMMAR MADE EASIE / Watt, Thomas – 1704. 126p. (English Linguistics Series 1500-1800) – 9 – us UMI [420]

A GRAMMAR OF CHINYANJA : A LANGUAGE SPOKEN IN BRITISH CENTRAL AFRICA ON AND NEAR THE SHORES OF LAKE NYASA – Aberdeen: G & W Fraser, 1891 – 1 – us Res Libr [490]

A GRAMMAR OF HIGH TAMIL / Beschi, Constantino Giuseppe – (Latin text publ for the first time by L Besse) – Trichinopoly: St Joseph's Industrial School Press, 1917 – 1 – us Res Libr [490]

GRAMMAR OF NEW TESTAMENT GREEK = GRAMMATIK DES NEUTESTAMENTLICHEN GRIECHISCH / Blass, Friedrich – (Includes indexes) – 2nd rev enl ed. London; New York: Macmillan, 1905 – 1mf – 9 – 0-8370-9365-1 – 1986-3365 – us A.T.L.A. [450]

THE GRAMMAR OF SCIENCE / Pearson, Karl – 2nd ed., rev. and enl. London: A. and C. Black, 1900. xviii,548p. Bibliography. tabls. diagr – 1 – us U.W. Library [500]

THE GRAMMAR OF SCIENCE / Pearson, Karl – London: A. and C. Black, 2nd rev enl ed 1900 – 1 roll – 1 – 1-55879-577-4 – uk Libr Preservation [600]

THE GRAMMAR OF SCIENCE / Pearson, Karl – London: W. Scott, 1892. xvi,493p. (The Contemporary Science Series) – 1 – us U.W. Library [500]

A GRAMMAR OF THE ANCIENT DIALECT OF THE CANARESE LANGUAGE – 2nd rev enl ed. Bangalore: Basel Mission Book & Tract Depository, 1889 – 1 – us Res Libr [490]

A GRAMMAR OF THE ARABIC LANGUAGE / Caspari, Carl P – 1862 – 9 – $27.00 – us I.R.C. [470]

A GRAMMAR OF THE ARABICK LANGUAGE / Richardson, John – 1776. 231p. (English Linguistics Series 1500-1800) – 9 – us UMI [470]

A GRAMMAR OF THE BECHUANA LANGUAGE / Archbell, James – Graham's Town, Cape of Good Hope: Meurant & Godlonton, 1837 – 1 – us Res Libr [490]

A GRAMMAR OF THE BENGA LANGUAGE / Mackey, James L – New York: Mission House, 1855 – 1 – us Res Libr [490]

A GRAMMAR OF THE BENGAL LANGUAGE / Halhed, Nathaniel Brassey – 1778. 256p. (English Linguistics Series 1500-1800) – 9 – us UMI [490]

A GRAMMAR OF THE CHINYANJA LANGUAGE AS SPOKEN AT LAKE NYASSA : WITH CHINYANJA-ENGLISH AND ENGLISH-CHINYANJA VOCABULARIES / Riddel, Alexander – Edinburgh: J Maclaren, 1880 – 1 – us Res Libr [490]

GRAMMAR OF THE CLASSICAL ARABIC LANGUAGE / Howell, M S – 19th century – 1 – uk Microform Academic [470]

A GRAMMAR OF THE CREE LANGUAGE / Howse, Joseph – 1865 – 1 – us I.U. Libraries [490]

A GRAMMAR OF THE ENGLISH LANGUAGE : IN A SERIES OF LETTERS. INTENDED FOR THE USE OF SCHOOLS AND OF YOUNG PERSONS IN GENERAL; BUT, MORE ESPECIALLY FOR THE USE OF SOLDIERS, SAILORS, APPRENTICES AND PLOUGH-BOYS / Cobbett, William – New York: Printed for the author by Clayton and Kingsland, 1818 – 1 roll – 1 – 1-55879-336-4 – uk Libr Preservation [420]

A GRAMMAR OF THE ENGLISH LANGUAGE, IN A SERIES OF LETTERS / Cobbett, William – London, 1819 – 2mf – 9 – ne IDC [420]

A GRAMMAR OF THE ENGLISH TONGUE / Brightland, John & Gildon, Charles – 1711. 206p. (English Linguistics Series 1500-1800) – 9 – us UMI [420]

GRAMMAR OF THE FULDE LANGUAGE / Reichardt, Charles August Ludwig – (With appendix of some original traditions & portions of Scripture transl into Fulde, together with 8 chapters of the book of Genesis) – London: Church Missionary House, 1876 – 1 – us Res Libr [490]

A GRAMMAR OF THE GREEK LANGUAGE / Crosby, Alpheus – 23rd ed.Boston: Phillips, Sampson and Co., 1858. xiv,464,viiip – 1 – us U.W. Library [450]

A GRAMMAR OF THE HEBREW LANGUAGE / Green, William Henry – (Includes indexes) – 3rd ed. New York: John Wiley, 1865, c1861 – 1mf – 9 – 0-8370-9150-0 – 1986-3150 – us A.T.L.A. [470]

A GRAMMAR OF THE HINDI LANGUAGE...HIGH HINDI, BRAJ, EASTERN HINDI...ALSO COLLOQUIAL DIALECTS OF RAJPUTANA, KUMAON, AVADH, RIWA, BHOJPUR, MAGADHA, MAITHILA, ETC / Kellogg, SH – 2nd ed., 1893 – 1 – us A.T.L.A. [490]

A GRAMMAR OF THE HINDOOSTANEE LANGUAGE / Gilchrist, John Borthwick – 1796. 347p. (English Linguistics Series 1500-1800) – 9 – us UMI [490]

A GRAMMAR OF THE HINDUSTANI LANGUAGE IN THE ORIENTAL AND ROMAN CHARACTER.. / Forbes, Duncan – New ed. London: W.H. Allen, 1855. c232p. 14 leaves of plates.ill – 1 – us U.W. Library [490]

A GRAMMAR OF THE IDIOM OF THE NEW TESTAMENT, PREPARED AS A SOLID BASIS FOR THE INTERPRETATION OF THE NEW TESTAMENT / Winer, Georg Benedikt – 7th ed. enl. and improved by Gottlieb Luenemann.Andover: W.F. Draper, 1897, c1874.xviii,728p. Ed. by J.H. Thayer – 1 – us U.W. Library [450]

A GRAMMAR OF THE MASKOKE, OR CREEK LANGUAGE / Bucknew, H F – 140 p. 4516 – 1 – 5.00 – us Baptist [490]

A GRAMMAR OF THE PERSIAN LANGUAGE / Jones, William – 1771. 194p. (English Linguistics Series 1500-1800) – 9 – us UMI [490]

GRAMMAR OF THE PHOENECIAN LANGUAGE / Harris, Z S – 1936 – 9 – $10.00 – us I.R.C. [470]

A GRAMMAR OF THE SAMARITAN LANGUAGE : WITH EXTRACTS AND VOCABULARY / Nicholls, G F – London: Samuel Bagster, [1858?] – 1mf – 9 – 0-8370-7654-4 – 1986-1654 – us A.T.L.A. [470]

A GRAMMAR OF THE SEPTUAGINT / Thackeray, Henry St John – Cambridge. 1900 – 9 – $21.00 – us I.R.C. [220]

A GRAMMAR OF THE TURKISH LANGUAGE / Vaughan, Thomas – 1709. 132p. (English Linguistics Series 1500-1800) – 9 – us UMI [490]

A GRAMMAR OF THE VULGATE / Plate, WE & White, H J – Oxford, 1926 – 3mf – 8 – ne Slangenburg [220]

THE GRAMMAR OF TIV / Abraham, Roy Clive – Kaduna, Nigeria: Printed by the Govt Printer, 1933 – 1 – us Res Libr [490]

Grammatic, Leonis *see* CHRONOGRAPHIA (CSHB 44)

GRAMMATICA ANGLICANA / Greaves, Paul – 1594. 88p. (English Linguistics Series 1500-1800) – 9 – us UMI [420]

GRAMMATICA ANGLO-LATINA / Shirley, James – 1651. 189p. (English Linguistics Series 1500-1800) – 9 – us UMI [450]

GRAMMATICA ANGLO-ROMANA: OR,A SYNCRITICAL GRAMMAR, TEACHING ENGLISH YOUTH THE LATIN TONGUE / Shaw, Samuel – 1687. 247p. (English Linguistics Series 1500-1800) – 9 – us UMI [450]

GRAMMATICA ANGLO-SAXONICA EX HICKESIANO / Hickes, George – 1711. 60p. (English Linguistics Series 1500-1800) – 9 – us UMI [420]

GRAMMATICA ARABICA / Postel, G – Parisiis, [1540] – 1mf – 9 – H-8266/1 – ne IDC [470]

GRAMMATICA BRITANNICA / Salesbury, Henry – 1593. 99p. (English Linguistics Series 1500-1800) – 9 – us UMI [420]

GRAMMATICA BURLESA / Burles, Edward – 1652. 439p. (English Linguistics Series 1500-1800) – 9 – us UMI [400]

GRAMMATICA, ETC / Priscianus – 14 and 15th cents. Holkham mss. 406, 423. Holkham Hall, Norfolk, England – 1 – uk Microform Academic [760]

GRAMMATICA GROENLANDICA-DANICO-LATINA / Egede, P – BH-179 2. 1760 – 8 – ne IDC [450]

GRAMMATICA LATINO-FRANCICA / Ramus, Peter – 1583 – 9 – fr I.C.S. [400]

...GRAMMATICA LINGUAE AMHARICAE. / Ludolf, Hiob – Frankfort. 1698 – 1 – us Res Libr [470]

GRAMMATICA LINGUAE AMHARICAE : QUAE VERNACULA EST HABESSIHORUM, IN USUM EORUM QUI CUM ANITQUA BAC ET PRAECLARE NATIONE CHRISTIANA CONVERSARI VOLENT, EDITA: PLURA HABES IN PRAEFATIONE / Ludolfo, Iobo – (Filmed with Ludolf, Hiob. Lexicon ambarico-latinum) Francofurti ad Moenum: Prostat apud Johannem David. Zunnerum: Impressit Martinus Jacquetus, 1698 – us Res Libr [470]

GRAMMATICA LINGUAE ANGLICANAE / Cooper, Christopher – 1685. 251p. (English Linguistics Series 1500-1800) – 9 – us UMI [420]

GRAMMATICA LINGUAE ANGLICANAE / Wallis, John – 1653. 159p. (English Linguistics Series 1500-1800) – 9 – us UMI [420]

GRAMMATICA NOVA IN USUM JUVENTUTIS SCOTICAE / Hume, Alexander – 1612.236p. (English Linguistics Series 1500-1800) – 9 – us UMI [450]

GRAMMATICA QUADRILINGUIS: OR, BRIEF INSTRUCTIONS FOR THE FRENCH, ITALIAN, SPANISH, AND ENGLISH TONGUES / Smith, J – 1674. 278p. (English Linguistics Series 1500-1800) – 9 – us UMI [400]

GRAMMATICAE LATINAE INSTITUTIONES / Sanchez de las Brozas, Francisco – 1595 – 9 – 1.50f – sp Bibl Santa Ana [450]

GRAMMATICAL COMMENTARIES / Johnson, Richard – 1706. 477p. (English Linguistics Series 1500-1800) – 9 – us UMI [420]

GRAMMATICAL FUNDAMENTS OF THE INNUIT LANGUAGE AS SPOKEN BY THE ESKIMO OF THE WESTERN COAST OF ALASKA / Barnum, F – BN 114 2. 1901 – 8 – ne IDC [490]

A GRAMMATICAL INSTITUTE OF THE ENGLISH LANGUAGE / Webster, Noah – 1783. Part I. 127p. (English Linguistics Series 1500-1800) – 9 – us UMI [420]

A GRAMMATICAL INSTITUTE OF THE ENGLISH LANGUAGE / Webster, Noah – 1784. Part 2. 144p. (English Linguistics Series 1500-1800) – 9 – us UMI [420]

GRAMMATICAL INSTITUTES / Ash, John – 1763. 157p. (English Linguistic Series 1500-1800) – 9 – us UMI [400]

GRAMMATICAL OUTLINE AND VOCABULARY OF THE OJI LANGUAGE : WITH ESPECIAL REFERENCE TO THE AKWAPIM-DIALECT, TOGETHER WITH A COLLECTION OF PROVERBS OF THE NATIVES / Riis, Hans Nicolaus – Basel: Bahmaier, 1854 – 1 – us Res Libr [490]

GRAMMATICAL REMARKS ON THE PRACTICAL AND VULGAR DIALECT OF THE INDOSTAN LANGUAGE / Hadley, George – 1772. 154p. (English Linguistics Series 1500-1800) – 9 – us UMI [490]

GRAMMATICALL MISCELLANIES / Merriott, Thomas – 1660. 210p. (English Linguistics Series 1500-1800) – 9 – us UMI [420]

GRAMMATICI LATINI / ed by Keil, Heinrich – (Supplement included) – Lipsiae. v. 1-7. 1857-1880. – 95mf – 8 – ne IDC [450]

GRAMMATIK DER ARAMAEISCHEN MUTTERSPRACHE JESU / Schultze, Martin – (Includes bibliographical references) – Berlin: S Calvary, 1899 – 1mf – 9 – 0-8370-7261-1 – 1986-1261 – us A.T.L.A. [470]

GRAMMATIK DER BIBLISCH-CHALDAEISCHEN SPRACHE UND DES IDIOMS DES THALMUD BABLI = ELEMENTI GRAMMATICALI DEL CALDEO BIBLICO E DEL DIALETTO TALMUDICO BABILONESE : EIN GRUNDRISS / Luzzatto, Samuel David – (In German. Includes bibliographical references) – Breslau [Wroclau]: Schletter, 1873 – 1mf – 9 – 0-8370-9294-9 – 1986-3294 – us A.T.L.A. [470]

GRAMMATIK DER ESKIMO-SPRACHE. / Bourquin, Theodor – London: Moravian Mission Agency, 1891. 00217. (Pre-1900 Canadiana) – 9 – cn C.I.H.M. [490]

GRAMMATIK DER GRIECHISCHEN VULGARSPRACHE IN HISTORISCHER ENTWICKLUNG / Mullach, Friedrich Wilhelm August – (Includes indexes) – Berlin: Ferd. Duemmler, 1856 – 1mf – 9 – 0-8370-9299-X – 1986-3299 – us A.T.L.A. [450]

GRAMMATIK DER GROENLAENDISCHEN SPRACHE / Kleinschmidt, Samuel P – BN 282 2. 1851 – 8 – ne IDC [430]

GRAMMATIK DER NEUHEBRAEISCHEN SPRACHE / Siegfried, Carl – (Includes bibliographischer Abriss der neuhebraeischen Litteratur und der Hilfsmittel zum Verstaendnisse derselben von Herm. L. Strack) – Karlsruhe: H Reuther; New York: B Westermann, 1884 – 1mf – 9 – 0-8370-9271-X – 1986-3271 – us A.T.L.A. [470]

GRAMMATIK DER SEPTUAGINTA : LAUT- UND WORTLEHRE / Helbing, Robert – Goettingen: Vandenhoeck und Ruprecht, 1907 – 1mf – 9 – 0-8370-9288-4 – 1986-3288 – us A.T.L.A. [450]

GRAMMATIK DES JUEDISCH-PALAESTINISCHEN ARAMAEISCH : NACH DEN IDIOMEN DES PALAESTINISCHEN TALMUD, DES ONKELOSTARGUM UND PROPHETENTARGUM, UND DER JERUSALEMISCHEN TARGUME / Dalman, Gustaf – (Includes index) – 2. Aufl, verm und vielfach umgearb. Leipzig: J C Hinrichs, 1905 – 1mf – 9 – 0-8370-9220-5 – 1986-3220 – us A.T.L.A. [470]

GRAMMATIKA NANAISKOGO JAZYKA / Avrorin, V A – V. I. Foneticheskoe vvedenie i morfologiia imennykh chastei rechi. Moscow, Leningrad. 1959. 282p. BU-457 2 – 8 – ne IDC [400]

GRAMMATISCHE UNTERSUCHUNGEN UEBER DIE BIBLISCHE GRAECITAET : UEBER DIE LESEZEICHEN / Lipsius, Karl Heinrich Adelbert – (Includes bibliographical references) – Leipzig: J C Hinrichs, 1863 – 1mf – 9 – 0-8370-9292-2 – 1986-3292 – us A.T.L.A. [450]

DIE GRAMMATISCHEN SCHULEN DER ARABER : ERSTE ABTHEILUNG, DIE SCHULEN VON BASRA UND KUFA UND DIE GEMISCHTE SCHULE / Fluegel, Gustav – (In German and Arabic. No more published. Includes bibliographical references) – Leipzig: In Commission bei F A Brockhaus, 1862 – 1mf – 9 – 0-8370-7697-8 – 1986-1697 – us A.T.L.A. [470]

GRAMMATYKA JEZYKA POLSKIEGO / Deszkiewicz, J N – Rzeszow. 1846. BR-8008 2 – 8 – ne IDC [460]

GRAMMATYKA JEZYKA POLSKIEGO / Jakubowicz, M – Wilno. 2v. 1825 – 9mf – 9 – ne IDC [947]

GRAMMATYKA JEZYKA POLSKIEGO / Muczkowski, J – Wyd. 2-ie. Krakow. 1836. BR-4849 2 – 8 – ne IDC [460]

A GRAMMER OR INTRODUCTION TO THE ITALIAN TONGUE / Sanford, John – 1605. 56p. (English Linguistics Series 1500-1800) – 9 – us UMI [440]

GRAMMOFON I FONOGRAF – (Title changed in 1905-1906 to Svet i zvuk. In aug-sep 1906 to Grammofon i Fotografiia) – St Petersburg. n1-3 1902; n1-13, 16-17 1903; n1-12 1904; n1 1907 – 14mf – 9 – $85.00 – us Ross [780]

GRAMMOFON I FOTOGRAFIIA – aug-sep 1906 (monthly) – 2mf – 9 – $25.00 – us Ross [780]

GRAMMOFON I FOTOGRAFIIA *see* GRAMMOFON I FONOGRAF

GRAMMOFONNAIA ZHIZN' – Moscow. n1-18 1911; n19-31 1912 (biweekly) – 14mf – 9 – $85.00 – us Ross [780]

GRAMMOFONNYI MIR = DIE GRAMMOFON-WELT – St Petersburg. n1-12 1910; n1-23 1911; n1-20 1912; n1-20 1913; n1-14 1914; from 1915 on in Russian only n1-5,7-8 1915; n1-12 1916; n1-2,6-8 1917 (monthly) – 48mf – 9 – $290.00 – us Ross [780]

Grammont, Henri Delmas de *see* HISTOIRE D'ALGER SOUS LA DOMINATION TURQUE

GRAMOPHONE – 1- 1923- – 1. ; 5,6. ; 9 – apply; v.49-; v.53- – us UMI [780]

GRAN BRETANA, ESTADOS UNIDOS Y LA DECLINACION ARGENTINA 1942-1949 / Escude, Carlos – Buenos Aires: Editorial de Belgrano, 2nd ed 1983 – 1 – CSUXAHZ6411-B – us Hoover Inst Photo [972]

GRAN BRETANA MERCANTIL E INDUSTRIAL – London, UK. Sept 1926 – 1 – uk British Libr Newspaper [072]

EL GRAN CARDINAL DE ESPANA, DON PEDRO GONZALEZ DE MENDOZA / La Cadena, Ramon Lacadena y Brualla – Madrid, 2nd ed 1942 – 1 – us Res Libr [920]

GRAN DICCIONARIO HISTORICO. TOMO 1 / Moreri, Louis – 1753 – 8mf – 9 – Pta4,500.00 – 84-7848-382-9 – sp Pentalfa [946]

GRAN DICCIONARIO HISTORICO. TOMO 2 / Moreri, Louis – 1753 – 8mf – 9 – Pta4,500.00 – 84-7848-383-7 – sp Pentalfa [946]

GRAN DICCIONARIO HISTORICO. TOMO 3, 1ST PARTE / Moreri, Louis – 1753 – 5mf – 9 – Pta3,000.00 – 84-7848-384-5 – sp Pentalfa [946]

GRAN DICCIONARIO HISTORICO. TOMO 3, 2ND PARTE / Moreri, Louis – 1753 – 5mf – 9 – Pta3,000.00 – 84-7848-385-3 – sp Pentalfa [946]

GRAN DICCIONARIO HISTORICO. TOMO 4 / Moreri, Louis – 1753 – 8mf – 9 – Pta4,500.00 – 84-7848-386-1 – sp Pentalfa [946]

GRAN DICCIONARIO HISTORICO. TOMO 5 / Moreri, Louis – 1753 – 7mf – 9 – Pta4,000.00 – 84-7848-387-X – sp Pentalfa [946]

GRAN DICCIONARIO HISTORICO. TOMO 6 / Moreri, Louis – 1753 – 9mf – 9 – Pta5,000.00 – 84-7848-388-8 – sp Pentalfa [946]

GRAN DICCIONARIO HISTORICO. TOMO 7 / Moreri, Louis – 1753 – 8mf – 9 – Pta4,500.00 – 84-7848-389-6 – sp Pentalfa [946]

GRAN DICCIONARIO HISTORICO. TOMO 8, 1ST PARTE / Moreri, Louis – 1753 – 5mf – 9 – Pta3,000.00 – 84-7848-390-X – sp Pentalfa [946]

GRAN DICCIONARIO HISTORICO. TOMO 8, 2ND PARTE / Moreri, Louis – 1753 – 5mf – 9 – Pta3,000.00 – 84-7848-391-8 – sp Pentalfa [946]

LA GRAN EXTREMADURA, UNA UTOPIA / Sanchez Morales, Narciso – Badajoz: Imp. Diput. Provincial, 1968 – sp Bibl Santa Ana [946]

GRAN MATEMATICO Y FECUNDO POETA. ARSENIO GALLEGO HERNANDEZ / Fernandez Sanchez, Teodoro – Badajoz: Dip. Provinicial, 1974. Sep. REE – 1 – sp Bibl Santa Ana [510]

LA GRAN NOCHE DEL MUNDO / Perez Lozano, Jose Maria – Madrid: PPC, 1962 – 1 – sp Bibl Santa Ana [946]

A UN GRAN PARTIDO, UNA GRAN ORGANIZACION – (Checa, Pedro). Barcelona, 1937. Fiche W 794. (Blodgett Collection of Spanish Civil War Pamphlets) – 9 – us H.U. College Libr [946]

GRAN QUIVIRA : EXCAVATIONS IN A 17TH CENTURY JUMANO PUEBLO / Vivian, R Gordon; ed by Valkenburgh, Sallie van – 1964 – 4mf – 9 – $5.00f – us Ross [970]

Granados, Anastasio *see* EL CARDENAL GOMA, PRIMADO DE ESPANA. MADRID, 1969

Granau, Johannes *see* LEISE BESCHWOERUNG

Granbery, John C *see* EXPERIENCE, THE CROWNING EVIDENCE OF THE CHRISTIAN RELIGION

Granbery, John Cowper *see* OUTLINE OF NEW TESTAMENT CHRISTOLOGY: A STUDY OF GENETIC RELATIONSHIPS

GRANBY 1710-1900 – (Mf 1-7,9: Town Records 1765-1845. Mf 7-11: Vital Records 1710-1863. Mf 12-17: Tax Lists 1782-1824. Mf 18-29: Tax Lists 1824-49. Mf 30: Vital Records 1843-60. Mf 31: Births 1860-93. Mf 32: Marriages 1860-93. Mf 33: Deaths 1860-93. Mf 34: Deaths 1894-1903. Mf 35: Marriages 1894-1904. Mf 36: Births 1894-1902) – (mf ed 1993) – 36mf – 9 – 0-87623-171-7 – us Holbrook [920]

GRANBY ECHO – Granby, Canada. 15 nov. 1911-v1 n8. 10 jan 1912 – 1r – 1 – Can$25.00 – cn Can Microfilming [072]

GRANBY GAZETTE – Granby, Canada. v2 n547. 29 jun 1866-v23 n4. 26 jan 1877 – 1r – Can$30.00 – cn Can Microfilming [072]

GRANBY GAZETTE AND SHEFFORD COUNTY ADVERTISER – Granby, Canada. 1855-77 – 2r – 1 – $136.00 – cn Library Assoc [971]

THE GRANBY LEADER – Granby, Canada. v1 n17. 10 sep 1891-v9 n499. 25 jan 1901 – 1r – 1 – Can$35.00 – cn Can Microfilming [072]

GRANBY LEADER AND EASTERN TOWNSHIPS RECORD – Granby, Canada. 1891-1901 – 1 reel – 1 – $68.00 – cn Library Assoc [971]

THE GRANBY LEADER MAIL – Granby, 5 avr 1901-22 jun 1977f – 28r – 1 – Can$60.00 – cn Can Microfilming [072]

THE GRANBY LEADER MAIL *see* THE MAIL

GRANBY LEADER-MAIL – Granby, Canada. 1901-10 – 3r – 1 – $204.00 – cn Library Assoc [971]

THE GRANBY MAIL – Granby, 3 jan 1900-13 fev 1901 – 1r – 1 – Can$60.00 – cn Can Microfilming [072]

THE GRANBY MAIL *see* THE MAIL

LE GRANBYEN – Granby, Canada. 19 sep 1963-v1 n7. 23 oct 1963 – 1r – 1 – Can$25.00 – cn Can Microfilming [072]

Grancini, M *see* MUSICA ECCLESIASTICA DA CAPELLA, A QUATTRO VOCI DIVISA IN MESSE, MOTETTI

Grancolas, M J *see*
- LES ANCIENNES LITURGIES 2. L'ANCIEN SACRAMENTAIRE DE L'EGLISE 1
- LES ANCIENNES LITURGIES 3. L'ANCIEN SACRAMENTAIRE DE L'EGLISE 2

Grand, A le *see* LES IMMUNITES DES CONSULS

LE GRAND ALMANACH MANCEAU – Annuel, Le Mans (Sarthe), 1866-1942 – 16r – 1 – F9,503.18 – fr Armell [073]

LE GRAND ALPHABET FRANCOIS DIVISE PAR SYLLABLES (SIC) – Nouv. ed. Quebec: Imprime a la Nouvelle Imprimerie, 1806. SEM16P152 – 1r – 5 – Can$9.00 – cn Bibl Nat [440]

GRAND ARMY JOURNAL – Washington, DC, 30 Apr 1870-15 July 1871 – 1 reel – 1 – us Western Res [355]

Grand Army of the Republic. Department of the Potomac *see* JOURNAL OF THE ANNUAL ENCAMPMENT

Grand Army of the Republic. District of Kansas *see* RECORDS

Grand Army of the Republic. Norris Post No27 (Fostoria, OH) *see* PERSONAL WAR SKETCHES

Grand Army of the Republic. Post 332. White Cloud, Kansas *see* MINUTES

Grand Army of the Republic. Post No. 69 (O.M. Mitchell), Osborne, KS *see* MINUTES AND ROSTER

Grand Army of the Republic. Robbins Post No91 (Upper Sandusky, OH) *see* RECORDS

Grand Army Publishing Co *see* SOLDIERS AND CITIZENS ALBUM OF WISCONSIN

GRAND BAHAMA TRIBUNE – Nassau. Bahamas. 1969- – 1 – us UMI [072]

LE GRAND BAPTEME DU FAUBOURG SAINT-ANTOINE FAIT AU CIRQUE NATIONAL LE 18 FEVRIER DE L'AN 1791 – Paris. Imprimerie du Cercle Social – 9 – fr Hachette [321]

LE GRAND CALENDRIER ET COMPOST DES BERGERS COMPOSE PAR LE BERGER DE LA GRANDE MONTAIGNE – Rouen – 9 – fr Hachette [360]

Grand Canyon College. Phoenix, Arizona *see* CATALOGS AND COLLEGE RECORDS

GRAND CARREFOUR – Riviere-du-Loup – 2r – 1 – Can$65.00 – cn Can Microfilming [072]

UN GRAND CHEF BERBERE : LE CAID GOUNDAFI / Justinard, Leopold Victor – Casablanca: Editions Atlantides, [1951] – 1 – us Res Libr [920]

GRAND CONCERT [K.414] POUR LE CLAVECIN OU FORTE PIANO, AVEC L'ACCOMPAGNEMENT DES PLUSIERS INSTRUMENTS / Mozart, Wolfgang Amadeus – (9 parts) – Amsterdam: J Schmitt, [1782?] – 1 – us Sibley [780]

GRAND CONCERTO A LA CHASSE, OP. 64 / Steibelt, Daniel – London: printed by Joseph Dale & Son...[180-?] – 1 – us Sibley [780]

A GRAND CONCERTO FOR THE PIANOFORTE, OP. 33 / Steibelt, Daniel – London: Muzio Clementi & Co, 26 Cheapside, [180-?] – 1 – us Sibley [780]

LE GRAND DESERT, OU ITINERAIRE D'UNE CARAVANE DU SAHARA AU PAYS DES NEGRES... / Daumas, Gal Eugene – Paris: Chaix, 1848 – 1 – F237.20 – fr Armell [910]

LE GRAND DICTIONNAIRE DES PRETIEUSES / Somaize, A Baudeau, sieur de – 1661 – 9 – fr I.C.S. [440]

GRAND DICTIONNAIRE DES RIMES FRANCAISES / Morandini d'Eccatage, F – 1886 – 9 – fr I.C.S. [440]

LE GRAND DICTIONNAIRE DES RIMES FRANCOISES / La Noue, O de – 1623 – 9 – fr I.C.S. [440]

GRAND DICTIONNAIRE FRANCOIS ET LATIN / Danet, P – 1735 – 9 – fr I.C.S. [450]

LE GRAND DICTIONNAIRE FRANCOIS-LATIN / Brosses, P de – 1625 – 9 – fr I.C.S. [440]

LE GRAND DICTIONNAIRE FRANCOIS-LATIN / Poille, G – 1614 – 9 – fr I.C.S. [450]

GRAND DICTIONNAIRE GENERAL ET GRAMMATICAL DES DICTIONNAIRES FRANCAIS / Landais, N – 1853 – 9 – fr I.C.S. [440]

LE GRAND DICTIONNAIRE HISTORIQUE OU LE MELANGE CURIEUX DE L'HISTOIRE SACREE ET PROFANE / Moreri, Louis – Paris: Chez Jean Baptiste Coignard, 1718. SEM35P186 – 4r – 1 – Can$183.00 – cn Bibl Nat [944]

GRAND DICTIONNAIRE UNIVERSEL FRANCAIS / Larousse, Pierre – 1865-90 – 9 – fr I.C.S. [440]

LA GRAND DUCHESSE DE GEROLSTEIN : OPER IN 3 ACTEN UND 4 BILDERN / Offenbach, J – (Score, 3 vols and libretto[many notes and additions]) – Manuscript in scribal hand, 1887? – 1 – us Sibley [780]

LE GRAND ELECTEUR ET LOUIS XIV, 1660-1688 / Pages, G – H-555 2. 1905 – 8 – ne IDC [944]

GRAND FORKS GAZETTE – Grand Forks, British Columbia, CN. Apr 1905-Dec 1970 – 26r – 1 – cn Commonwealth Micro [072]

GRAND FORKS MINER AND NEWS GAZETTE – Grand Forks, British Columbia, CN. May 1889-Dec 1905 – 1r – 1 – cn Commonwealth Micro [072]

GRAND ISLAND DAILY INDEPENDENT – Grand Island, NE. Jan 1884 to date – 1 – us NE Hist [071]

GRAND ISLAND DAILY PRESS – Grand Island, NE. Jul 1897-Oct 1902 – 1 – us NE Hist [071]

GRAND ISLAND DEMOCRAT – Grand Island, NE. -w. Mar 1891-Dec 1892, scattered issues missing; Aug 1895-Jan 1896; Mar 1896-Dec 1898; Feb 1899; Jan 1901; Mar 1901-Nov 1908 – 1 – us NE Hist [071]

GRAND ISLAND HERALD – Grand Island, NE. -w. Jul 1918-Sept 1942 – 1 – us NE Hist [071]

GRAND ISLAND HERALD – Grand Island, NE. -w. Sept 1886-Dec 1887 – 1 – us NE Hist [071]

GRAND ISLAND INDEPENDENT – Grand Island, NE. -w, -sw (1892-99). Aug 1873-Apr 1890, scattered issues missing; Jan 1891-Nov 1899 – 1 – us NE Hist [071]

GRAND ISLAND TIMES – Grand Island, NE. -w, (-sw 1882-92). Jul 1873-Dec 1887; Mar 1889; Sept 1891-Sept 1892 – 1 – us NE Hist [071]

LE GRAND JEU – Roger Gilbert-Lecomte, Rene Daumal. no. 1-3. Paris. ete 1928-automne 1930. Reconstitution du no. 4 qui devait paraitre en 1932. Collection privee. Disponible en reimpression – 1 – fr A.C.R.P.P. [073]

LE GRAND JOURNAL – Moniteur de la semaine. Dir. H. de Villemessant. Paris. 14 fevr, 3 avr 1864-25 nov 1866 – 1 – fr A.C.R.P.P. [073]

LE GRAND JOURNAL ILLUSTRE – Montreal. v2-18. 1968-1985. SEM35P103 – 33r – 1 – Can$1,490.00 – cn Bibl Nat [971]

LE GRAND JUBILE DE 1875: CATECHISME, PRIERES SPECIALES ET PIEUX EXERCICES A L'USAGE DE TOUS LES FIDELES – 1875. 04381. (Pre-1900 Canadiana) – 9 – cn C.I.H.M. [240]

THE GRAND MILITARY CONCERTO FOR THE PIANOFORTE, OP. 40 / Dussek, J L – (Piano part only) – London: Clementi & Co, 180- – 1 – us Sibley [780]

DAS "GRAND MINISTERE" LEON GAMBETTAS 10. NOVEMBER 1881 – 26. JANUAR 1882 : EIN BEITRAG ZUR PARLAMENTSGESCHICHTE DER DRITTEN REPUBLIK / Pfeiffer, Peter – Heidelberg, 1974 – 3mf – 9 – DM76.00 – 3-89349-376-X – gw Hänsel [320]

LE GRAND MIRACLE ARRIVE EN LA VILLE DE LOUDUN, EN LA PERSONNE D'ISABELLE BLANCHARD FILLE SECULIERE RECEVANT LE S. SACREMENT DE L'AUTEL – Poitiers. 1934 – 9 – fr Hachette [360]

UN GRAND PEUPLE DE L'AFRIQUE EQUATORIALE : ELEMENTS D'UNE MONOGRAPHIE SUR L'URUNDI ET LES WARUNDI / Burgt, Johannes Michael M van der – Bois-le-Duc, Netherlands: Societe "L'illustration catholique," 1903 – 1 – us Res Libr [960]

GRAND QUATOUR, OP. 18 / Brandl, J – (Parts) – Offenbach s/M: J Andre, 181- – 1 – us Sibley [780]

GRAND RAPIDS DAILY LEADER – Wisconsin Rapids. Wis. 1917-1919 – 1 – us UMI [071]

THE GRAND RAPIDS FURNITURE JOURNAL – (With printed index) – 1880-1930 – 70r – 1 – $5,600.00 – us Ross [680]

Grand Rapids. Ohio. First Presbyterian Church *see* RECORDS

THE GRAND REPOSITORY OF THE ENGLISH LANGUAGE / Spence, Thomas – 1775. 385p. (English Linguistics Series 1500-1800) – 9 – us UMI [420]

GRAND RIVER EAGLE – Grand Rapids. Mich. -w. 1847-51 – 1 – us UMI [071]

Grand River. Ohio. Grand River Baptist Association *see* CHURCH RECORDS

Grand River. Ohio. Presbytery of Grand River *see* CHURCH RECORDS, MS 500

GRAND RIVER SACHEM – Caledonia, Canada. 1866-68 – 1 reel – 1 – $68.00 – cn Library Assoc [971]

UN GRAND ROMANCIER D'AMOUR ET D'AVENTURE AU 13E SIECLE. CHRETIEN DE TROYES. / Cohen, Gustave – Paris. 1931 – 1 – us Res Libr [440]

GRAND RONDE CHRONICLE – LaGrande OR. Sep 18 1891, Mar 18 Apr 8 1892 – 1 – us U.O. Library [071]

GRAND ROUNDS – [Halifax, N.S.: s.n.], 1876 – 9 – cn C.I.H.M. [420]

GRAND SONATA POUR PIANO, VIOLON, VIOLONCELLE OU BASSOON, OP. 69 / Steibelt, Daniel – Paris: Richault, [ca. 1819] – 1 – us Sibley [780]

GRAND TRAVERSE HERALD – Traverse City. Mich. -w, sw. 1858-1913 – 1 – us UMI [071]

GRAND TRIO POUR PIANO, VIOLON ET VIOLONCELLE, OEUVRE 49 / Mendelssohn, Felix – (Score and parts) – Leipsic: Breitkopf & Haertel, [18–] – 1 – us Sibley [780]

Grand Trunk Railway Company of Canada *see*
- CORRESPONDENCE BETWEEN THE COMPANY AND THE DOMINION GOVERNMENT RESPECTING ADVANCES TO THE CANADIAN PACIFIC RAILWAY COMPANY
- THE GRAND TRUNK RAILWAY OF CANADA: A FINANCIAL REVIEW

THE GRAND TRUNK RAILWAY OF CANADA: A FINANCIAL REVIEW / Grand Trunk Railway Company of Canada – London: E. Wilson, 1887.02259.(Pre-1900 Canadiana) – 9 – cn C.I.H.M. [971]

GRAND TRUNK RAILWAY OF CANADA: THE GREAT INTERNATIONAL ROUTE BETWEEN EAST AND WEST – Toronto: A. Dixon, 18–.03713.(Pre-1900 Canadiana) – 9 – cn C.I.H.M. [971]

GRAND VALLEY STAR AND VIDETTE – Ontario, CN. 1902- – 1r per yr – 1 – Can$57.00r – cn Commonwealth Micro [072]

LA GRAND VICTOIRE DV TRESILLVSTRE ROY DE POLOINE, CONTRE DAYEUODE DUC DE MULDAUIE... – Paris, 1531 – 1mf – 9 – H-8140/1 – ne IDC [956]

LE GRAND VOYAGE AU PAYS DES HURONS / Sagard, G – Paris, France. 1v. 1632 – 1r – 1 – cn Can Microfilming [910]

Grand-Carteret, John *see*
- L'ENSEIGNE
- LA FEMME EN CULOTTE

LE GRAND-DUCHE DE BERG (1806-1813) : ETUDE SUR LA DOMINATION FRANCAISE EN ALLEMAGNE SOUS NAPOLEON 1ER / Schmidt, Charles – Paris, 1905 – xvi/528p – 9 – DM48.00 – 3-89349-021-3 – gw Hänsel [320]

LA GRANDE BATAILLE – La France aux republicains. Red. en chef Lissagaray (1893) puis Organe republicain. Politique, financier, industriel, commercial. Dir. F. Fourcroy. Paris. Quot. puis irr. 19 janv-7 juin 1893. quelques no. en 1912-16, 1920-21, 1926-30, 1935 – 1 – fr A.C.R.P.P. [073]

LA GRANDE BATAILLE – Organe de la ligue des anti-clericaux francais. Rev. en chef Philibert Roger. Paris. 21 aout 1898-12 avr 1899 – 1 – fr A.C.R.P.P. [073]

LA GRANDE CHRONIQUE DE BOMU / Lotar, L – Bruxelles: G van Campenhout, 1940 – 1 – us Res Libr [960]

LA GRANDE CHRONIQUE DE L'UBANGI / Lotar, L – Bruxelles: G van Campenhout, 1937 – 1 – us Res Libr [960]

LA GRANDE COLERE DE LA MERE DUCHENE – Paris: Impr. de Beaule et Maignand, may 1849 – us Res Libr [944]

LA GRANDE COMORE / Fontoynont, Antoine Maurice & Raomandahy – Tananarive: Impr moderne de l'Emyrne, Pitot de la Beaujardiere, 1937 – 1 – us Res Libr [960]

LA GRANDE COMORE PAR LE DOCTEUR FONTOYONT ET RAOMANDAHY, MEDICIN INDIGENE – Tananarive, Imprimerie moderne de l'Emyrne, Pitot de la Beaufardiere, 1937 – us Res Libr [610]

LA GRANDE ENCYCLOPEDIE (AEL, ABT.1;3) – 31v. 1886-1902 (mf ed 1992) – 404mf – DM2,620.00 – 3-89131-054-4 – gw Fischer [030]

LA GRANDE ET MERUEIILEUSE, ET TRESCRUELLE OPPUGNATIO DE LA NOBLE CITE DE RHODES, ... / Bourbon, J de – [Paris], 1527 – 1mf – 9 – H-8235/1 – ne IDC [910]

LA GRANDE EVENING OBSERVER – LaGrande, OR. -d. 21 May 190413-26 May 1959; 22,23 Feb 1954. – 1 – us U.O. Library [071]

LA GRANDE FETE BOBONGO CHEZ LES EKONDA, ZAIRE / Vangroenweghe, D – 9 – F100.00 – fr Ethnologie [306]

LA GRANDE FRANCE – Art, litterature sociale, colonies. no. 1-4, 6-7, 13-15, 17-44. Paris. 1900-03 – 1 – fr A.C.R.P.P. [073]

LA GRANDE GREVE / Malato de Corne, Charles A – Paris. 1905. (La Condition Ouvriere. Part Two.) – 9 – 15.00 – fr Bibl Nationale [360]

LA GRANDE GREVE DE MAI 1920 / Brecot, Jean – Paris. n.d. (La Condition Ouvriere. Part Two.) – 9 – 2.50 – fr Bibl Nationale [360]

LA GRANDE GUERRE ET L'EFFORT BRITANNIQUE : VOYAGE DES JOURNALISTES CANADIENS EN ANGLETERRE ET EN FRANCE, CONFIANCE GENERALE EN UNE VICTOIRE PROCHAINE / Robillard, Charles – [Montreal ?: s.n.], 1918. SEM105P1664 – 1mf – 9 – Can$2.25 – cn Bibl Nat [971]

GRANDE PRAIRIE NORTHERN TRIBUNE – Alberta, CN. Jun 1932-Dec 1939 – 3r – 1 – cn Commonwealth Micro [072]

LA GRANDE REVUE – Montreal: Arthur Saint-Pierre, 21 avr-26 mai 1917. SEM35P194 – 1r – 1 – Can$15.00 – cn Bibl Nat [073]

LA GRANDE REVUE – Paris, 1897-1921 – 28r – 1 – us Ross [073]

LA GRANDE REVUE – Paris. 1898-1940 – 1 – fr A.C.R.P.P. [073]

GRANDE RONDE SENTINEL – LaGrande OR. May 2 1868-Feb 19 1870 – 1 – us U.O. Library [071]

GRANDE RONDE TIMES – LaGrande OR. June 24 1874 – 1 – us U.O. Library [071]

GRANDE SONATE POUR LE PIANOFORTE / Cramer, Johann Baptist – Leipzig: C F Peters, [182-] – 1 – us Sibley [780]

LA GRANDE TRONICIADE OU ITINERAIRE DE QUEBEC A LA RIVIERE-DU-LOUP: POEME BADIN / Cassegrain, Arthur – Ottawa: G. Desbarats, 1866. 02540. (Pre-1900 Canadiana) – 9 – cn C.I.H.M. [910]

LA GRANDE WEEKLY OBSERVER – La Grande, OR. 1905-14 – 1 – 96.00 – us Oregon Hist [071]

LA GRANDE WEEKLY OBSERVER-STAR – La Grande, OR. 1914-21 – 1 – 96.00 – us Oregon Hist [071]

LA GRANDE WEEKLY STAR – La Grande, OR. 1909 – 1 – 17.00 – us Oregon Hist [071]

Grande-Bretagne. Colonial Office *see*
- COMMUNICATIONS BETWEEN THE COLONIAL OFFICE AND THE GOVERNORS OF UPPER AND LOWER CANADA, ON THE SUBJECT OF THE CIVIL GOVERNMENT OF CANADA,...
- HUDSON BAY COMPANY

Grande-Bretagne. Parliament. House of Commons *see* A BILL, AS AMENDED BY THE COMMITTEE, TO MAKE TEMPORARY PROVISION FOR THE GOVERNMENT OF LOWER CANADA

Grande-Bretagne. Parliament. House of Commons. Select Committee Appointed in the Year 1834 on the Affairs of Lower Canada *see* LOWER CANADA

Grande-Bretagne. Parliament. House of Commons. Select Committee on the Affairs of Lower Canada *see* REPORT FROM SELECT COMMITTEE ON LOWER CANADA

Grande-Bretagne, Privy Council Judicial Committee *see* JUGEMENT DES LORDS DU COMITE JUDICIAIRE DU CONSEIL PRIVE SUR L'APPEL DE DAME HENRIETTE BROWN...

LES GRANDES COMPAGNIES DE COMMERCE: ETUDE POUR SERVIR A L'HISTOIRE DE LA COLONISATION / Bonnassieux, Pierre – Paris: Plon. Nourrit, 1892. 00179. (Pre-1900 Canadiana) – 9 – cn C.I.H.M. [971]

GRANDES DE ESPANA. PRIMERA SERIE : CAPITANES. BIOGRAFIA DE ORELLANA / Anonimo – Madrid: Ediciones de la Vicesecretaria de Educacion Popular, 1945 – 1 – sp Bibl Santa Ana [920]

LES GRANDES ET EFFROIABLES MERVEILLES VUES LE IOUR DU MOIS DE IUIN, PRES LA VILLE DE AUTHUN – Rouen. 1582 – 9 – fr Hachette [360]

GRANDES FERIAS DE GANADO DE TODAS CLASES...LOS DIAS 18, 19, 20 DE JUNIO... 1960 / Logrosan. Ayuntamiento – Caceres: Tip. La Minvera, 1960 – 1 – sp Bibl Santa Ana [630]

GRANDES FERIAS DE GANADOS DE TODAS CLASES EN LOGROSAN (CACERES) – Caceres: Tip. La Minerva, 1962 – 1 – sp Bibl Santa Ana [946]

GRANDES FERIAS DE GANADOS DE TODAS CLASES EN...JUNIO 1959 / Logrosan. Ayuntamiento – Caceres: Imprenta La Minerva, 1959 – 1 – sp Bibl Santa Ana [390]

GRANDES FIESTAS 1976. DIAS 12, 13, 14, 15 Y 16 DE SEPTIEMBRE EN HONOR DEL SANTISIMO CRISTO, PATRONO DE ESTA VILLA – Caceres: Imp. La Minerva, 176 – 1 – sp Bibl Santa Ana [240]

GRANDES FIESTAS, 1976 EN HONOR DEL SANTISIMO CRISTO...CACERES... – Caceres: Tip. La Minerva, 1975 – 1 – sp Bibl Santa Ana [240]

GRANDES FIESTAS DE SAN BARTOLOME. AGOSTO 1972 – Trujillo: Imp. Gexme, 1972 – 1 – sp Bibl Santa Ana [390]

GRANDES FIESTAS DE SANTIAGO DE TODA CLASE DE GANADOS Y GENEROS DE COMERCIO...24, 25 Y 26 DE JULIO, 1960 / Casatejada. Ayuntamiento – Caceres: Tip. Minerva, 1960 – 1 – sp Bibl Santa Ana [630]

GRANDES FIESTAS EN HONOR DE LA SANTISIMA VIRGEN DEL ROSARIO. 1974 / Alcuescar. Ayuntamiento – Caceres: Imp. La Minerva, 1974 – 1 – sp Bibl Santa Ana [390]

GRANDES FIESTAS EN HONOR DE LA SANTISIMA VIRGEN DEL ROSARIO 1975 – Caceres: Imp. La Minerva, 1975 – 1 – sp Bibl Santa Ana [240]

GRANDES FIESTAS EN HONOR DE LA SANTISIMA VIRGEN DEL ROSARIO 1976 – Caceres: Tip. La Minerva, 1976 – 1 – sp Bibl Santa Ana [240]

GRANDES FIESTAS EN HONOR DE LA SANTISIMA VIRGEN DEL ROSARIO. SEPTIEMBRE OCTUBRE 1972 – Caceres: Imp. La Minerva, 1972 – 1 – sp Bibl Santa Ana [240]

GRANDES FIESTAS EN HONOR DE LA VIRGEN DE LA SALUD – Merida: Imp. J. Rejas, 1970 – 1 – sp Bibl Santa Ana [240]

GRANDES FIESTAS EN HONOR DE LA VIRGEN DEL ROSARIO, 1977 / Alcuesca R. Ayuntamiento – Caceres: Imp. La Minerva, 1977 – sp Bibl Santa Ana [390]

GRANDES FIESTAS EN HONOR DE SAN FERNANDO. ESTACION DE LA RENFE...JULIO, 1959 / Valencia de Alcantara. Estacion de Renfe – Caceres: Tip. El Noticiero S.L., 1959 – 1 – sp Bibl Santa Ana [390]

GRANDES FIESTAS EN HONOR DE SAN JUAN BAUTISTA, 1974 / Herreruela. Ayuntamiento – Caceres: Tip. La Minerva, 1974 – 1 – sp Bibl Santa Ana [390]

GRANDES FIESTAS EN HONOR DE SAN JUAN BAUTISTA 1975 – Caceres: Tip. La Minerva, 1975 – 1 – sp Bibl Santa Ana [240]
GRANDES FIESTAS EN HONOR DEL EMIGRANTE 1974 – Caceres: Tip. La Minverva, 1974 – 1 – sp Bibl Santa Ana [390]
GRANDES FIESTAS EN HONOR DE...LA VIRGEN DE LA SOTERRANA. 1972 – Trujillo: Imp. Gexme, 1972 – 1 – sp Bibl Santa Ana [240]
GRANDES FIESTAS PATRONALES EN HONOR DE NTRA. SRA. DEL CONSUELO. 1972 / Logrosan. Ayuntamiento – Caceres: Imp. La Minerva, 1972 – 1 – sp Bibl Santa Ana [390]
GRANDES FIESTAS PATRONALES EN HONOR DE NUESTRA SENORA DEL CONSUELO. SEPTIEMBRE-OCTUBRE 1973 – Caceres: Imp. La Minerva, 1973 – 1 – sp Bibl Santa Ana [240]
GRANDES FIESTAS QUE LA REAL VILLA DE... CELEBRA EN HONOR DE SUS PATRONOS SAN FULGENCIO Y SANTA FLORENTINA. AGOSTO 1973 – Caceres: Imp. La Minerva, 1973 – 1 – sp Bibl Santa Ana [390]
LES GRANDES LIGNES DES MIGRATIONS DES BANTOUS DE LA PROVINCE ORIENTALE DU CONGO BELGE / Moeller, A – Bruxelles: G van Campenhout, 1936 – 1 – us Res Libr [300]
GRANDES QUATUORS, TROIS, 2E LIVRE / Rolla, A – (Pts.) – Paris: Janet et Cotelle, 181- – 1 – us Sibley [700]
LOS GRANDES SABIOS / Munoz de la Pena, Arsenio – Madrid: Aguilar, 1964 – 1 – sp Bibl Santa Ana [946]
GRANDES SONATAS, TROIS, POUR LE FORTEPIANO AVEC ACCOMPAGNEMENT DE VIOLON ET VIOLONCELLE, OP. 33. 3E LIVRE / Pleyel, Ignaz J – (Pts) – Augsbourg: Gombart, ca 1800 – 1 – us Sibley [780]
GRANDEUR ET MISERE DE LA FEMME / Nayrac, Jean Paul – Paris: Michalon, 1905. 171p. (Les Femmes Collection) – 2mf – 9 – $6.00 – fr Bibl Nationale [305]
LA GRANDEZA ARGENTINA / Garcia Martinez, Carlos – Buenos Aires: Editorial Sudamericana, c1983 – 1 – CSUXADJ0673-B – us Hoover Inst Photo [972]
GRANDEZAS DE LA CIUDAD DE DIOS / Moreno Maldonado, Jose – Madrid: Razon y Fe, 1927 – 1 – sp Bibl Santa Ana [910]
GRANDEZAS Y MISERIAS DE LA REVOLUCION SOCIAL ESPANOLA / Marti-Ibanez, Felix – Barcelona, 1937? Fiche W 1028. (Blodgett Collection of Spanish Civil War Pamphlets) – 9 – us H.U. College Libr [946]
GRANDEZZE DELLA CITA DI ROMA / Mari, G – O-1044 1. 1625 – 9 – ne IDC [945]
GRANDFATHER'S CHAIR & BIOGRAPHICAL STORIES / Hawthorne, Nathaniel – 1896. Biog. sketches of Hawthorne, Benjamin West, Sir Isaac Newton, Samuel Johnson, Oliver Cromwell, Benjamin Franklin & Queen Christina. 6 fiches. F-1574 – 9 – us A.G.L.L. [920]
GRANDFIELD FIRST BAPTIST CHURCH. GRANDFIELD, OKLAHOMA : CHURCH RECORDS – 1916-66 – 1 – 63.81 – us Baptist [240]
Grandgagnage, Ch. *see* DICTIONNAIRE ETYMOLOGIQUE DE LA LANGUE WALLONNE
Grandgaignage, E *see* HISTOIRE DU PEAGE DE L'ESCAUT
Grandgeorge, L *see* SAINT AUGUSTIN ET LE NEO-PLATONISME
Grandidier, Alfred *see*
- ETHNOGRAPHIE DE MADAGASCAR
- HISTOIRE PHYSIQUE, NATURELLE ET POLITIQUE DE MADAGASCAR

Grandidier, Alfred et al *see* COLLECTION DES OUVRAGES ANCIENS CONCERNANT MADAGASCAR
Grandidier, Guillaume *see*
- BIBLIOGRAPHIE DE MADAGASCAR
- BIBLIOGRAPHIE DE MADAGASCAR 1904-1933
- ETHNOGRAPHIE DE MADAGASCAR
- EXPRESSIONS FIGUREES DE LA LANGUE MALGACHE

GRANDIN COURT BAPTIST CHURCH. ROANOKE, VIRGINIA : CHURCH RECORDS – 1945-Sep 1966 – 1 – 77.40 – us Baptist [240]
Grandin, Leonce *see* LE DAHOMEY, A L'ASSAUT DU PAYS DES NOIRS
Grandmaison, Charles *see* DICTIONNAIRE HERALDIQUE
Grandmoulin, J *see* TRAITE ELEMENTAIRE DE DROIT CIVIL EGYPTIEN INDIGENE ET MIXTE COMPARE AVEC LE DROIT FRANCAIS, CONFORME AUX PROGRAMMES DE L'ECOLE KHEDIVIALE ET DES FACULTES FRANCAISES DE DROIT
Grandov, M *see* GOSUDARSTVENNYI TRUD-GUZH-NALOG I KRESTIANSKOE KHOZIAISTVO
GRAND-PRAIRIE DAILY HERALD-TRIBUNE – Alberta, CN. 1964- – 6r per yr – 1 – Can$55.00r – cn Commonwealth Micro [072]
Grandpre, Louis de *see*
- VOYAGE A LA COTE OCCIDENTALE D'AFRIQUE
- VOYAGE A LA COTE OCCIDENTALE D'AFRIQUE DANS LES ANNEES 1786 ET 1787 CONTENANT LA DESCRIPTION DES MOEURS, USAGES, LOIS, GOUVERNEMENT ET COMMERCE DES ETATS DU CONGO, FREQUENTES PAR LES EUROPEENS, ET UN PRECIS DE LA TRAITE DES NOIRS

LES GRANDS ESQUIMAUX. 6, 307P., ILLUS., MAP / Petitot, E – BN 344 2. 1887 – 8 – ne IDC [306]
GRANDS FIESTAS EN HONOR DEL SANTISIMO CRISTO PATRONO DE ESTA VILLA – Caceres: Imp. La Minerva, 1972 – 1 – sp Bibl Santa Ana [240]
GRANDS GERMAND HERALD – Philadelphia, PA., 1840 – 13 – $25.00r – us I.M.R. [071]
LES GRANDS HOMMES DE LA FRANCE: HOMMES DE GUERRE (CINQUIEME SERIE): MONTCALM / Goepp, Edouard – Paris: P. DuCrocq, 1888.04375.(Pre-1900 Canadiana) – 9 – cn C.I.H.M. [971]
GRANDS HOMMES EN ROBE DE CHAMBRE / Buet, Charles – Paris, 1897. 33p. 4 fiches. (Literature Collection) – 9 – 10.00 – fr Bibl Nationale [830]
LES GRANDS NEGOCIANTS BORDELAIS AU XVIIIE SIECLE / Communay, Arnaud – Bordeaux, France: A. Moquet, 1888. 04159. (Pre-1900 Canadiana) – 9 – cn C.I.H.M. [380]
LES GRANDS PRETRES – 1882?. 03498. (Pre-1900 Canadiana) – 9 – cn C.I.H.M. [240]
LES GRANDS SERVICES DE SEVRES / Reunion des musees nationaux. Paris – 1951. 6 illus. 1 fiche – 9 – fr Réunion [700]
LES GRANDS TRAITES DE LA GUERRE DE CENT ANS / Cosneau, E – Paris, 1889 – 3mf – 1 – ILM-657/1 – ne IDC [327]
LES GRANDS TRAITES POLITIQUES ... DEPUIS 1815 JUSQU'A NOS JOURS / Albin, P – Paris, 1911 – 7mf – 9 – ILM-2462/1 – ne IDC [340]
LES GRANDS TRAITES POLITIQUES RECUEIL DES PRINCIPAUX TEXTES DIPLOMATIQUES DE 1815 A 1914 AVEC DES NOTICES HISTORIQUES ET DES NOTES / Albin, P – Ed 3. Paris, 1923 – 7mf – 9 – ILM-3625/1 – ne IDC [340]
LES GRANDS TRAITES POLITIQUES RECUEIL DES PRINCIPAUX TEXTES DIPLOMATIQUES DEPUIS 1815 JUSQU'A NOS JOURS AVEC DES NOTICES HISTORIQUES ET DES NOTES / Albin, P – Ed 2. Paris, 1912 – 7mf – 9 – ILM-3622/1 – ne IDC [340]
LES GRANDS TYPES DE COMPLEXES INDUSTRIELS / Chardonnet, J – 4mf – 9 – F60.00 – fr Ethnologie [338]
LES GRANDS VOYAGEURS CONTEMPORAINS : OUVRAGE CONTENANT CENT QUARANTE ET UN DESSINS GRAVEES SUR BOIS, TRENTE ET UN PORTRAITS DE VOYAGEURS ET VINGT-SEPT CARTES ITINERAIRES / Meissas, G – Paris: Hatchette, 1894 – 1 – us Res Libr [910]
Grandval, M F *see* MAZEPPA. OPERA EN 5 ACTES ET 6 TABLEAUX...
Granet, Marcel *see* LA POLYGINIE SORORALE ET LE SORORAT DANS LA CHINE FEODALE
GRANGE BULLETIN – Toronto: [s.n. 1881?-18– or 19–] – 9 – cn C.I.H.M. [630]
THE GRANGE GARDEN / Kingsley, Henry – British Fiction Archive: Unit 2 – 9 – uk Bell [830]
LA GRANGE GAZETTE – Goldsburg. N.C. 1972- – 1 – us UMI [071]
Grange, John *see* THE GOLDEN APHRODITIS AND GRANGES GARDEN OF VERSE
GRANGE NEWS – Kalispell. Mont. 1945-1951; 1956-1959; 1961- – 1 – us UMI [071]
Grangent, Stanislas V *see* DESCRIPTION ABREGEE DU DEPARTEMENT DU GARD
GRANGER – Auburn, NE. -w. Sep. 1872-Dec. 1880. Incomplete; Jan. 1882-Dec. 1915 – 1 – us NE Hist [071]
THE GRANGER – and pred. Auburn. Neb. 1872-1915 – 1 – us UMI [071]
THE GRANGER – (Cont by: The Canadian Granger) – London, Ont: [s.n. 1875-1876] – 9 – cn C.I.H.M. [630]
Granger, Frank Stephen *see* THE WORSHIP OF THE ROMANS, VIEWED IN RELATION TO THE ROMAN TEMPERAMENT
Granger, Thomas *see* SYNTAGMA GRAMMATICUM, OR AN EASIE AND METHODICALL EXPLANATION OF LILLIES GRAMMAR
Grangeron, Henri *see* RELATION DE L'ETAT DE QUELQUES PERSONNES PRETENDUES POSSEDEES
Granges de Surgeres, Anatole de *see* RECUEIL DE 28 BROCHURES, SURTOUT HISTORIQUES, PUBL. PAR CET AUTEUR ENTRE 1878 ET 1902
GRANI – No.64-134, 1967-84 – 1 – us I.U. Libraries [073]
GRANI : ZHURNAL LITERATURY, ISKUSSTVA, NAUKI I OBSHCHESTVENNOI MYSLI – v1-32. 1946-56 – 2r – 1 – us Ross [460]
GRANI – Zhurnal Literatury, Iskusstvo; Obshchestvennoi Mysli. Limburg-Lahn Western Germany etc. v. 1-62. July 1946-1966 – 1 – us NY Public [700]
GRANIA / Lawless, Emily – British Fiction Archive: Unit 4 – 9 – uk Bell [830]
Granier, Camille *see* ESSAI DE BIBLIOGRAPHIE CHARITABLE
Granier, Jacquelin P *see* HUMAN RIGHTS, THE HELSINKI ACCORDS AND THE UNITED STATES
Granier, Jacqueline P *see* HUMAN RIGHTS, EUROPEAN POLITICS, AND THE HELSINKI ACCORD
Granin, A *see* LITERATURNYE STUDII ROSS. KOMM. SOI UZA MOLODEZHI, IKH T SELI I ZADACHI
GRANITE BOULDER – Granite OR. Feb 23 July 7 1900 – 1 – us U.O. Library [071]
Granite City. Illinois. First Baptist Church *see* NEWSPAPER
GRANITE COUNTY NEWS – Drummond. Mont. 1912-1915 – 1 – us UMI [071]
GRANITE GEM – Granite OR. Aug 14 1903 – 1 – us U.O. Library [071]
GRANMA : ENGLISH EDITION – Havana, CU. 1966-1993 – 28r – $1,400.00 – R60607 – us Library Micro [320]
GRANMA : SPANISH EDITION – Havana, CU. 1971-1978 – 23r – $1,200.00 – R04202 – us Library Micro [320]
Granniss, Ruth Shepard *see* A DESCRIPTIVE CATALOGUE OF THE FIRST EDITIONS IN BOOK FORM OF THE WRITINGS OF PERCY BYSSHE SHELLEY
GRANOS DE ARENA / Sanchez-Arjona, Vicente – Sevilla: Imp. Carlos Acuna, Tomo 3. 1953 – 1 – sp Bibl Santa Ana [810]
GRANOS DE ARENAS / Sanchez-Arjona, Vicente – Sevilla: Graficas La Gavidia, Tomo 1. 1952 – 1 – sp Bibl Santa Ana [810]
GRANOS DE ARENAS / Sanchez-Arjona, Vicente – Sevilla: Graficas Tirvia, Tomo 2. 1953 – 1 – sp Bibl Santa Ana [810]
Granstrem, E E *see* KATALOG GRECHESKIKH RUKOPISEI LENINGRADSKIKH KHRANILISHCH
Grant, A *see*
- A CATALOGUE OF NATIVE PUBLICATIONS IN THE BOMBAY PRESIDENCY
- CATALOGUE OF NATIVE PUBLICATIONS IN THE BOMBAY PRESIDENCY UP TO 31ST DECEMBER, 1864

GRANT ALLEN: A MEMOIR, WITH A BIBLIOGRAPHY / Clodd, Edward – London: G. Richards, 1900. 03011. (Pre-1900 Canadiana) – 9 – cn C.I.H.M. [920]
Grant, Anthony *see* THE PAST AND PROSPECTIVE EXTENSION OF THE GOSPEL BY MISSIONS TO THE HEATHEN
Grant, Asahel *see* THE NESTORIANS, OR, THE LOST TRIBES
Grant, B *see* THE ORCHIDS OF BURMA
Grant, Charles Baron Glenelg *see*
- EXTRACT OF A DESPATCH FROM LORD GLENELG TO THE EARL OF DURHAM, G.C.B., DATED DOWNING-STREET, 20TH JANUARY 1838
- LOWER CANADA

GRANT COUNTY BLUE MOUNTAIN EAGLE – John Day OR. Aug 27 1948-July 13 1972 – 1 – us U.O. Library [071]
GRANT COUNTY JOURNAL – Prairie City, OR. -w. 12 Dec 1913-28 May 1942. 6 rolls – 1 – us U.O. Library [071]
GRANT COUNTY NEWS – Canyon City, OR. -w. 19 May 1887-13 Nov 1890. – 1 – us U.O. Library [071]
GRANT COUNTY NEWS – Hyannis, NE. -w. Oct 1970 to date – 1 – us NE Hist [071]
GRANT COUNTY NEWS – John Day, OR. -w. 20 Aug 1903; 3 Dec 1908-9 Jul 1908 – 1 – us U.O. Library [071]
GRANT COUNTY PRESS – Petersburg. West Virginia. 1897-1966 – 1 – us UMI [071]
GRANT COUNTY TRIBUNE – Hyannis, NE. -w. May 1890-Mar 1893; Jan 1894-Jun 1895; Aug 1895-Jul 1898; Dec 1899-Jan 1902, scattered issues missing; Oct 1902-Dec 1910; Aug 1911; Jun 1912-Jan 1913; Mar 1913-Dec 1915; May 1916-Sep 1919; Dec 1919-Aug 1969 – 1 – us NE Hist [071]
Grant, David *see* SERMONS
Grant, Elihu *see* PEASANTRY OF PALESTINE
GRANT ET VRAY ART DE PLEINE RHETORIQUE / Fabri – 1889-90 – 9 – fr I.C.S. [410]
Grant, George *see* ACCOUNT BOOK
Grant, George Monro *see*
- ADVANTAGES OF IMPERIAL FEDERATION: A LECTURE DELIVERED...JANUARY 30TH, 1891..
- IMPERIAL FEDERATION: A LECTURE DELIVERED...SEPTEMBER 13TH, 1889
- OUR PICTURESQUE NORTHERN NEIGHBOR: HISTORICAL AND DESCRIPTIVE SKETCHES OF THE SCENERY AND LIFE...TORONTO...CANADIAN SHORE OF LAKE HURON...NORTHWEST TERRITORIES...BRITISH COLUMBIA
- PRINCIPAL GRANT'S LETTERS ON PROHIBITION: AS THEY APPEARED IN THE TORONTO DAILY GLOBE, DECEMBER 1897, JANUARY, 1898

Grant, Gillian *see* HISTORICAL PHOTOGRAPHS OF THE MIDDLE EAST
Grant, J A *see* THE BOTANY OF THE SPEKE AND GRANT EXPEDITION
Grant, James F *see* HISTORY OF SEATTLE
Grant, Percy Stickney *see* SOCIALISM AND CHRISTIANITY
Grant, President *see* THE AGENCY OF A.B. STEINBERGER IN THE SAMOAN ISLANDS
Grant, Ulysses *see*
- PAPERS
- RAPPORT OFFICIEL DU LIEUTENANT-GENERAL GRANT A L'HONORABLE E. M. STANTON

LE GRANT VOYAGE DE HIERUSALEM DIUISE EN DEUX PARTIES / Le Huen, N – Paris. 2pts. 1522 – 5mf – 9 – H-8229/1 – ne IDC [910]
Grant, W L *see* ACTS OF THE PRIVY COUNCIL OF ENGLAND
GRANTHAM AND MELTON POST *see* GRANTHAM AND MELTON TRADER NEWS
GRANTHAM AND MELTON TRADER *see* GRANTHAM AND MELTON TRADER NEWS
GRANTHAM AND MELTON TRADER NEWS – (Also known as: Grantham and Melton Post; Grantham and Melton Trader; Grantham Post) – 1986; Jan 8-Jul 2, Sep 10-Dec 1987; 1988-91; Jan 9-Jun 25 1992; Jul 1992-96 – 16 3/4r – 1 – uk British Libr Newspaper [072]
Grantham, David B *see* PARENTS SUCCESSFULLY SEPARATING FROM ADOLESCENTS: A STUDY IN THE PHENOMENON OF SEPARATION
GRANTHAM JOURNAL – England, Feb 1854-Jul 1855; 1857; 1862; 1871; 1877; 1889-1914; 1918; 1950; 1986- – 73+ r – 1 – uk British Libr Newspaper [072]
GRANTHAM POST *see* GRANTHAM AND MELTON TRADER NEWS
Granthan, Henry *see* AN ITALIAN GRAMMAR WRITTEN IN LATIN BY SCIPIO LENTULO A NEAPOLITANE: AND TURNED IN ENGLISHE
GRANT'S CASES / Pennsylvania. Superior Court – (A Pre-NRS title) – v1-3. 1814-63 (all publ) – 20mf – 9 – $30.00 – LLMC 84-196 – us L.L.M.C. [340]
GRANT'S ONTARIO ERROR AND APPEAL REPORTS / Ontario. Canada – v1-3. 1846-66 (all publ) – 16mf – 9 – $24.00 – LLMC 81-044 – us L.L.M.C. [340]
GRANTS PASS BULLETIN – Grants Pass, OR. -w. 8 Mar 1924-28 May 1970. 16 rolls – 1 – us U.O. Library [071]
GRANTS PASS COURIER – Grants Pass OR. Apr 3 1885-May 28 1886 – 1 – us U.O. Library [071]
GRANTS PASS DAILY COURIER – Grants Pass, OR. 1929-52 – 1 – 1217.00 – us Oregon Hist [071]
GRANTS PASS DAILY COURIER – Grants Pass, OR. -w. 2 Jan 1919-31 Dec 1929; 2 Jan 1953 – 1 – us U.O. Library [071]
GRANTS PASS HERALD – Grants Pass OR. Oct 12 1904, July 14 1905 – 1 – us U.O. Library [071]

GRANT'S UPPER CANADA CHANCERY REPORTS / Ontario. Canada – v1-29. 1849-82 (all publ) – 226mf – 9 – $339.00 – LLMC 81-045 – us L.L.M.C. [340]

GRANTSMANSHIP CENTER NEWS – (v.5 .1979 5,6,9) – v.1. 1973 – 1 – us UMI [073]

Granucci, N *see* L'EREMITA, LA CARCERE, E L' DIPORTO

GRANVILLE 1732-1902 – (Mf 1-3: Town & Vital Records 1751-96. Mf 4-7: Town Records 1751-88. Mf 7-8: Marriages & Intentions 1787-99. Mf 9-13: Town & Vital Records 1757-1836. Mf 14-16: Baptisms, Marriages, Deaths 1739-1861. Mf 17: Estate Valuations in 1853. Mf 18: Rebellions 1861-65. Mf 19-20: Index: B,M,D 1855-90. Mf 21-22: B,M,D 1843-58. Mf 23-27: B,M,D 1855-90. Mf 28: Intentions of Marriage 1906-40. Mf 29-31: Deaths 1891-1951. Mf 32: Marriages & Births 1891-1902) – (mf ed 1988) – 32mf – 9 – 0-87623-089-3 – us Holbrook [920]

GRANVILLE 1735-1849 – (Mf 1T-2T: Vital Records 1735-99. Mf 2T-3T: Marriage & Intentions 1787-99. Mf 3T: Births & Deaths 1757-1836. Mf 3T-6T: Marriages & Intentions 1796-1831. Mf 6T: Births 1792-1804, 1843-49; Marriages 1843-49; Deaths 1843-49) – (mf ed 1996) – 6mf – 9 – 0-87623-256-X – us Holbrook [920]

Granville, George Leveson-Gower *see* THE GRANVILLE PAPERS, 1870-1874

Granville, Joseph Mortimer *see* THE SECRET OF A GOOD MEMORY

THE GRANVILLE PAPERS, 1870-1874 / Granville, George Leveson-Gower – (Orig. publ. by Michael Glazier Inc) – 2r – 1 – $170.00 – D3265 – us Scholarly Res [327]

GRAO TUTU : PERIODICO CRITICO E CARICATO – Maceio, Alagoas. 7 Fev 1878 – 1,5,6 – bl Biblioteca [072]

GRAPE BELT – Dunkirk. N.Y. -w. 1893-1960 – 1 – us UMI [071]

THE GRAPEVINE INDEPENDENT – Rancho Cordova, CA. 1993 – 2+ r – 1 – $100.00 ($90.00y) – B06049 – us Library Micro [071]

GRAPHIC – Atkinson. Neb. 1882-1960 – 1 – us UMI [071]

GRAPHIC – Beloit. Wis. 1877-1880 – 1 – us UMI [071]

GRAPHIC – Eureka. Kan. -w. 1881-82 – 1 – us UMI [071]

GRAPHIC – Greenwich. Conn. 1881-1882; 1884-1913 – 1 – us UMI [071]

GRAPHIC – Harper. Kan. -w., sw. 1883-88, 1890-92 – 1 – us UMI [071]

GRAPHIC – Kinsley. Kan. 1877-1940 – 1 – us UMI [071]

GRAPHIC – Wheatland. Calif. 1882-1885 – 1 – us UMI [071]

GRAPHIC *see* WHEATLAND NEWSPAPERS

THE GRAPHIC – Chicago, IL. 4 Jul 1891-30 Jun 1894 – 3r – 1 – uk British Libr Newspaper [071]

THE GRAPHIC – Dinuba, CA. 1895-1896 – 1r – 1 – $50.00 – B06021 – us Library Micro [071]

THE GRAPHIC – London, England. Jan 1873-Dec 1874; Jan 1877-Jun 1878 – 7r – 1 – uk British Libr Newspaper [072]

GRAPHIC ART / Victoria and Albert Museum. London – (9900 captioned illustrations: miniatures, engravings, illuminated mss., posters, historic photographs, oriental paintings, drawings, prints. With printed index) – 165mf – 9 – $915.00 – 0-907006-40-X – uk Mindata [760]

THE GRAPHIC ARTS : A MAGAZINE FOR PRINTERS AND USERS OF PRINTING – Boston, Mass.: National Arts Pub Co, [1911-]. v4. jul 1912-jun 1913 – us Res Libr [680]

GRAPHIC ARTS MONTHLY AND THE PAINTING INDUSTRY – 1- 1929- – 1. ; 5,6. ; 9 – apply; v.41-; v.47- – us UMI [760]

GRAPHIC NEWS – Osawatomie. Kan. and pred. 1888-1965 – 1 – us UMI [071]

GRAPHIC SCENES IN AFRICAN STORY : SETTLERS – SLAVERY – MISSIONS AND MISSIONARIES – BATTLE-FIELDS / Bruce, Charles – Edinburgh: W P Nimmo, Hay & Mitchell, [188-?] – 1mf – 9 – 0-8370-6248-9 – 1986-0248 – us A.T.L.A. [960]

GRAPHICAL JOURNAL – v.1-4. 1964-67. Superseded by yPrint – 1 – us UMI [760]

THE GRAPHICS : WESTERN GRAPHIC – San Francisco. v6-7 1899; v9 July-Dec 1900; v33-34. 4 Jun 1910-27 May 1911 – 3r – 1 – $150.00 – B06102 – us Library Micro [978]

GRAPHIDEAE FEEANAE / Mueller, J A – Genea6ve, 1887. 80 pp. (Mea1m. Soc. Phys. Hist. Nat. de Genea6ve, v. 29). B-625 2 – 8 – ne IDC [580]

GRAPHISCHE REQUISITEN UND ERZEUGNISSE BEI DEN JUDEN / Loew, L – v. 1-2. Leipzig. 1869-1870, 1870-71. BJ-32-57 – 9 – ne IDC [760]

Grapin, P *see* VALEUR INTERNATIONALE DES...

Grappe, Georges *see* J.-H. NEWMAN

Grasedieck, Brunhild *see* "MARY HAMILTON", EINE KRITISCHE UNTERSUCHUNG DER VARIANTEN

GRASP YOUR NETTLE : A NOVEL / Linton, Elizabeth Lynn – London: Smith, Elder, 1891 – 1 roll – 1 – 1-55879-547-2 – uk Libr Preservation [830]

GRASS COVER OF AFRICA / Rattray, J M – 3rd printing 1978 – 168p – it F.A.O. [634]

Grass, K *see* VOM JUEDISCHEN KRIEGE

Grass, Karl Konrad *see*
- DIE RUSSISCHEN SEKTEN
- ZUR LEHRE VON DER GOTTHEIT JESU CHRISTI

GRASS VALLEY AND NEVADA CITY DIRECTORIES – Nevada Co, CA. 1861; 1865 – 2r – 1 – $100.00 – D065 – us Library Micro [910]

GRASS VALLEY JOURNAL – Grass Valley, OR. -w. 7 Oct 1898-27 Feb 1931. 5 rolls – 1 – us U.O. Library [071]

GRASS VALLEY NATIONAL *see* NEVADA NATION

GRASS VALLEY TELEGRAPH – Grass Valley, CA. Jul 1853-Oct 1858 (broken file) – 1r – 1 – $50.00 – C02276 – us Library Micro [071]

GRASS VALLEY/NEVADA CITY – 1992- – 3+ r – 1 – $150.00 – P00034 – us Library Micro [910]

Grassal, Georges *see* TROIS ARTISTES ETRANGERS

GRASSES IN AGRICULTURE / Whyte, R O et al – 5th printing 1975 – 418p – it F.A.O. [634]

GRASSES OF NORTH AMERICA / Beal, William James – 2v. 7508 2. 1896 – 8 – ne IDC [580]

GRASSES OF NORTH AMERICA, V1:...PHYSIOLOGY, COMPOSITION, SELECTION, IMPROVING AND CULTIVATION .. / Beal, William James – New York: Holt, 1896, c1887. 05301. (Pre-1900 Canadiana) – 9 – cn C.I.H.M. [580]

GRASSES OF NORTH AMERICA, V2: THE GRASSES CLASSIFIED, DESCRIBED AND EACH GENUS ILLUSTRATED.. / Beal, William James – New York: Holt, 1896. 05302. (Pre-1900 Canadiana) – 9 – cn C.I.H.M. [580]

Grasset de Saint-Saveur, J *see* ENCYCLOPEDIE DES VOYAGES

Grasset-Saint-Sauveur, Andre *see* VOYAGE HISTORIQUE, LITTERAIRE ET PITTORESQUE DANS LES ISLES ET POSSESSIONS CI-DEVANT VENITIENNES DU LEVANT; SAVOIR: CORFOU, PAXO, BUCINTRO, PARGA, PREVESA, VONIZZA, SAINTE-MAURE, THIAQUI, CEPHALONIE, ZANTE...

Grassineau, J *see* A MUSICAL DICTIONARY

GRASSLAND NEWS – Thedford, NE. -w. Jan 1854-Sept 1955 – 1 – us NE Hist [071]

Grassmann, Robert *see* DIE VERFLUCHUNGEN UND BESCHIMPFUNGEN DES HERRN CHRISTUS UND DER CHRISTEN DURCH DIE PAEPSTE, BISCHOEFE UND PRIESTER DER ROEMISCHEN KRICHE UND DIE PFLICHT JEDES CHRISTEN DIESEN VERSUCHUNGEN GEGENUEBER

GRASSMERE STATE SCHOOL RECORDS – 1877-1985. GSS1 – 1r – 1 – at Corangamite [920]

GRASSROOTS – Cape Town, South Africa: Grassroots Publications. 1 Mar 1980- 31 Dec 1987 – 1r – 1, 16 diazo available – sa SA Libr [960]

GRASSROOTS DEVELOPMENT : JOURNAL OF THE INTER-AMERICAN FOUNDATION – (1985-5,6,9) – v6- 1982- – 1 – us UMI [970]

GRASSY COVE AND MT. PLEASANT BAPTIST CHURCH. CUMBERLAND COUNTY. TENNESSEE : CHURCH RECORDS – 1833-1924 – 1 – 5.00 – us Baptist [240]

GRASSY POND BAPTIST CHURCH. GAFFNEY, SOUTH CAROLINA : CHURCH RECORDS – 9Feb 1879-27 Sep 1959, 1965-1987 (Lacking 1944-24 Sep 1950). Roll Book. 1958-Mar 1965 – 1 – $50.58 – us Baptist [240]

Graswinckel, T J F *see* MARIS LIBERI VINDICIAE:...

Gratacap, LP *see* PHILOSOPHY OF RITUAL

Gratama, H *see* DISPUTATIO...QUA HUGONIS GROTII MEMORIA VINDICATUR...

Grateloup, J P S de *see* MEMOIRE SUR PLUSIEURS ESPECES DE COQUILLES NOUVELLES, OU PEU CONNUES

Gratieux, L *see* L'AMI DE LA JEUNESSE OU PLAN DE REFORME DANS LES PENSIONS

Graton, John R *see* CORRESPONDENCE

Gratry, A *see* LA PAIX MEDITATIONS HISTORIQUES ET RELIGIEUSES

Gratsianov, PK *see* DOMASHNIE PTITSY, UKHOD ZA NIMI I SPOSOBY SOKHRANENIIA IAITS

DIE GRATULANTEN KOMMEN : EDVARD GRIEG ZUM 150. GEBURTSTAG / Christensen, Mogens et al; ed by Oelmann, Klaus Henning – 1993 – 2mf – 9 – DM80.00 – 3-89349-814-1 – gw Hänsel [780]

Grau, Rudolf Friedrich *see* SEMITEN UND INDOGERMANEN IN IHRER BEZIEHUNG ZU RELIGION UND WISSENSCHAFT

Graul, Karl *see* DIE UNTERSCHEI-DUNGSLEHREN DER VERSCHIEDENEN CHRISTLICHEN BEKENNTNISSE IM LICHTE GOETTLICHEN WORTS

Graupner, Ludwig *see* DIE AMERIKAWANDERUNG IN GUESSIGER BEZIRK

Graux, Lucien *see* LA TUBERCULOSE ET L'HABITATION URBAINE

Grava, S *see* DOSSIERS D'ETHNOLOGIE PROVENCALE, NO. 2. CULTES ET REPRESENTATIONS DE SAINT-JOSEPH EN PROVENCE

Grave, P de la *see* LE TOSCIN MARITIME CONTRE LE PRETENTION DES ROIS D'ANGLETERRE, A L'EMPIRE DE LA MER

GRAVEL AND GOLD DUST / Monash University Library. South-East Asia Pamphlet Collection – Inventory Listing. 2 v. Zug. 1975. BSE-20.106 1 – 9 – ne IDC [080]

GRAVEL RIDGE FIRST BAPTIST CHURCH. NORTH LITTLE ROCK, ARKANSAS : CHURCH RECORDS – Mar 1949, Feb 1965 – 1 – 23.85 – us Baptist [240]

Gravenhorst, J L C *see*
- COLEOPTERA MICROPTERA BRUNSVICENSIA
- MONOGRAPHIA COLEOPTERORUM MICROPTERORUM

Graves, Mrs. *see* PERSONAL TESTIMONIES OF

Graves, Absalom *see* HYMNS, PSALMS AND SPIRITUAL SONGS

Graves, C B *see* CATALOGUE OF THE FLOWERING PLANTS AND FERNS OF CONNECTICUT

Graves, Charles Alfred *see* REAL PROPERTY

GRAVES CREEK BAPTIST CHURCH. HENDERSON COUNTY. KENTUCKY : CHURCH RECORDS – 1810-1941 – 1 – 61.20 – us Baptist [240]

Graves, F A *see* PERSONAL TESTIMONIES OF

Graves, Frank Pierrepont *see*
- GREAT EDUCATORS OF THREE CENTURIES
- A HISTORY OF EDUCATION BEFORE THE MIDDLE AGES
- A HISTORY OF EDUCATION DURING THE MIDDLE AGES
- A HISTORY OF EDUCATION IN MODERN TIMES
- PETER RAMUS AND THE EDUCATIONAL REFORMATION OF THE SIXTEENTH CENTURY

Graves, G *see* BRITISH ORNITHOLOGY: BEING THE HISTORY OF EVERY KNOWN SPECIES OF BRITISH BIRDS

Graves, J *see* ROLL OF THE PROCEEDINGS OF THE KING'S COUNCIL IN IRELAND (RS69)

Graves, J R *see*
- THE GREAT IRON WHEEL
- THE LITTLE SERAPH
- THE NEW GREAT IRON WHEEL
- OLD LANDMARKISM: WHAT IS IT?
- OLD LANDMARKISM, WHAT IS IT?
- SOUTHERN BAPTIST ALMANAC AND ANNUAL REGISTER
- THE SOUTHERN PSALMIST
- TRIAL OF, BEFORE THE FIRST BAPTIST CHURCH OF NASHVILLE, TENNESSEE
- THE TRI-LEMMA
- THE WORK OF CHRIST IN THE COVENANT OF REDEMPTION

Graves, Norman J *see* NEW UNESCO SOURCE BOOK FOR GEOGRAPHY TEACHING

THE GRAVES OF MYLES STANDISH AND OTHER PILGRIMS / Huiginn, E J V – Beverley, Mass.: E.J.V. Huiginn, 1914 – 1mf – us A.T.L.A. [975]

Graves, R *see* THE SPIRITUAL QUIXOTE

GRAVESEND AND MILTON JOURNAL – England, 23 Aug 1834-25 Nov 1837 – 1r – 1 – uk British Libr Newspaper [072]

GRAVESEND ARGUS – England, 15 May 1880-9 May 1885 – 3r – 1 – uk British Libr Newspaper [072]

GRAVESEND JOURNAL ETC – Gravesend, England. 6 Jul 1864-1876; 1878-1892.-w. 16 reels – 1 – uk British Libr Newspaper [072]

GRAVESEND & NORTHFLEET STANDARD – England.8 Apr 1892-1915. -w. 23 reels – 1 – uk British Libr Newspaper [072]

GRAVESEND & NORTHFLEET STANDARD, ETC. (FOOTBALL ED.) – England.5 Jan-6 Apr, 21 Sept-28 Dec 1895; 4 Jan-11 Apr, 26 Sept-26 Dec 1896. -w.1/2 reel – 1 – uk British Libr Newspaper [072]

GRAVESEND REPORTER – (Gravesend and Dartford Reporter). England. -w. 2 Feb 1856-Dec 1969. (160 reels) – 1 – uk British Libr Newspaper [072]

Gravier, Gabriel *see*
- DECOUVERTE DE L'AMERIQUE PAR LES NORMANDS AU 10E SIECLE
- VOYAGE A SEGOU, 1878-1879

Gravil, Roger *see* THE ANGLO-ARGENTINE CONNECTION, 1900-1939

GRAVURE *see* PACKAGE PRINTING AND DIECUTTING

LA GRAVURE FRANCAISE EN COULEURS AU XVIIIE SIECLE / Reunion des musees nationaux. Paris – 1938. 1 fiche – 9 – fr Réunion [760]

GRAVURE MAGAZINE – v1-20. 1955-1974 – 1 – us UMI [760]

Grawe, J F *see* HISTORY OF BREMER COUNTY

Grawert, Rolf *see* VERWALTUNGSABKOMMEN ZWISCHEN BUND UND LANDERN IN DER BUNDESREPUBLIK DEUTSCHLAND. EINE KRITISCHE UNTERSUCHUNG DER GEGENWARTIGEN STAATSPRAXIS MIT EINE-ZUSAMMENSTELLUNG DER ZWISCHEN BUND UND LANDERN ABGESCHLOSSENEN ABKOMREN

Gray, A *see*
- CONTRIBUTIONS TO NORTH AMERICAN BOTANY
- A FLORA OF NORTH AMERICA
- GENERA FLORAE AMERICAE BOREALIORIENTALIS ILLUSTRATA
- A MANUAL OF THE BOTANY OF THE NORTHERN UNITED STATES
- PLANTAE WRIGHTIANAE TEXANO-NEO-MEXICANAE
- SYNOPTICAL FLORA OF NORTH AMERICA

Gray, Arthur R *see* AN INTRODUCTION TO THE STUDY OF CHRISTIAN APOLOGETICS

Gray, Carol *see* HUMAN EXPERIMENTATION

Gray, Clifton Daggett *see* THE SAMAS RELIGIOUS TEXTS

Gray, Cochard *see* VOYAGE DANS L'AFRIQUE OCCIDENTALE, PENDANT LES ANEES 1818, 1819, 1820 ET 1821, DEPUIS LA RIVIERE GAMBIE JUSQU'AU NIGER. V. V. V

Gray, Edward A *see* A HOLISTIC ANALYSIS OF STRESS WITH IMPLICATIONS FOR STRESS MANAGEMENT AS A FUNCTION OF PASTORAL COUNSELING

Gray, Elizabeth (nee McEwen) *see* JOURNAL AND CORRESPONDENCE, 1882-1886

Gray, G R *see*
- DESCRIPTIONS AND FIGURES OF SOME NEW LEPIDOPTEROUS INSECTS. CHIEFLY FROM NEPAL
- THE ENTOMOLOGY OF AUSTRALIA
- THE GENERA OF BIRDS
- A LIST OF THE GENERA OF BIRDS
- SYNOPSIS OF THE SPECIES OF INSECTS BELONGING TO THE FAMILY OF PHASMIDAE

Gray, George Buchanan *see*
- DIVINE DISCIPLINE OF ISRAEL...LECTURES ON THE GROWTH OF IDEAS IN THE OLD TESTAMENT
- THE FORMS OF HEBREW POETRY
- SACRIFICE IN THE OLD TESTAMENT
- STUDIES IN HEBREW PROPER NAMES

Gray, George Zabriskie *see* THE CHURCH'S CERTAIN FAITH GRAY

Gray, Georgina L *see* OXYGEN CONSUMPTION DURING KAYAK PADDLING

GRAY HERBARIUM INDEX / Harvard University. Gray Herbarium Library – 1968.-259,000 cards 10 reels.-ISBN: 0-8161-1540-0 – 1 – $945.00 – uk Hall [580]

Gray, J E *see*
- ILLUSTRATIONS OF INDIAN ZOOLOGY(CHIEFLY FROM COLLECTION OF MAJOR-GENERAL HARDWICKE). Z-307/2. 1830-1834(-35)

- THE ZOOLOGY OF THE VOYAGE OF H.M.S. EREBUS AND TERROR, 1839-1843
Gray, J M *see* MUTESA OF BUFANDA
Gray, James Comper *see* BIBLE LORE
Gray, John *see* FILE OF CORRESPONDENCE RELATING TO EMIN PASHA EXTRACTED FROM THE ZANZIBAR ARCHIVES
Gray, Marvin *see* CATASTROPHE MODEL OF ANXIETY AND PERFORMANCE
GRAY PANTHER NETWORK – Philadelphia, PA. 1982-1983 – 1r – 1 – $50.00 – R04992 – us Library Micro [071]
GRAY PANTHER NETWORK; AGE AND YOUTH IN ACTION / Gray Panther Project Fund – Philadelphia, PA, Quarterly, 1977-78; bimonthly 1979- – 1 – us U.W. Library [073]
Gray Panther Project Fund *see* GRAY PANTHER NETWORK; AGE AND YOUTH IN ACTION
GRAY PANTHERS NETWORK – 1972-87 – 1 – $50.00 – us Presbyterian [073]
Gray, R *see* THE BIRDS OF THE WEST OF SCOTLAND
Gray, Robert *see*
- A GOOD SPEED TO VIRGINIA
- JUDGEMENT
Gray, S F A *see* NATURAL ARRANGEMENT OF BRITISH PLANTS ACCORDING TO THEIR RELATIONS TO EACH OTHER, AS POINTED OUT BY JUSSIEU, DE CANDOLLE, BROWN
Gray, W H *see* A HISTORY OF OREGON, 1792-1849
Gray, William *see*
- DIARIES, CORRESPONDENCE AND MISCELLANEOUS PAPERS, 1882-1937
- JOURNAL, REPORT AND LETTERBOOK, 1882-1906
- PRESS CUTTINGS, PAMPHLETS AND ARTICLES ON KANAKA LABOUR TRAFFIC AND MISSIONARY LIFE IN THE NEW HEBRIDES
- VOYAGE DANS L'AFRIQUE OCCIDENTALE, PENDANT LES ANEES 1818, 1819, 1820 ET 1821, DEPUIS LA RIVIERE GAMBIE JUSQU'AU NIGER. V. V. V
GRAYA : A MAGAZINE FOR CIRCULATION AMONG MEMBERS OF GRAY'S INN – nos 1-86. 1927-82 (all publ) – 88mf – 9 – $132.00 – LLMC 84-283 – us L.L.M.C. [073]
GRAYS EINFLUSS AUF DIE DEUTSCHE LYRIK IM ACHTZEHNTEN JAHRHUNDERT / Uebel, Otto – Heidelberg, 1914 – 1mf – DM38.00 – 3-8267-3098-4 – gw Hänsel [430]
GRAY'S INN : COMMEMORATION OF THE TERCENTENERY OF FRANCIS BACON / Gray's Inn. London – London: Printed by order of the Masters of the Bench, – 1mf – 9 – $1.50 – LLMC 84-286 – us L.L.M.C. [920]
GRAY'S INN : NOTES ILLUSTRATIVE OF ITS HISTORY AND ANTIQUITIES / Douthwaite, William R – London: Benson & Page, 1876 – 2mf – 9 – $3.00 – LLMC 84-281 – us L.L.M.C. [340]
GRAY'S INN AND LINCOLN'S INN / Bellot, Hugh Hale L – London: Methuen & Co, 1925? – 3mf – 9 – $4.50 – LLMC 84-273 – us L.L.M.C. [340]
THE GRAY'S INN JOURNAL / Murphy, Arthur – (A repr of 101 papers by Charles Ranger (pseud. of Arthur Murray), of which some appeared in The Craftsman and some after 1753, were issued separately. On republ in Gemtleman's Magazine, the 101 nos were extended to 104 with major alterations) – 4mf – 9 – $6.00 – LLMC 84-285 – us L.L.M.C. [340]
GRAY'S INN LIBRARY : CATALOGUE OF BOOKS / Severn, M D – London: Witherby & Co, 1906 – 11mf – 9 – $16.50 – LLMC 84-288 – us L.L.M.C. [340]
Gray's Inn. London *see*
- GRAY'S INN
- GRAY'S INN PENSION BOOK
Gray's Inn. London. Library *see*
- GRAY'S INN LIBRARY
- MR BALDWIN'S VISIT
GRAY'S INN PENSION BOOK : THE RECORDS OF THE HONORABLE SOCIETY / Gray's Inn. London – London: Chiswick. 2v. 1901-10 – 12mf – 9 – $18.00 – LLMC 84-291 – us L.L.M.C. [340]
GRAY'S NEW ENGLAND REAL ESTATE JOURNAL – Boston, MA. v23 n1. apr 1892 – 1r – 1 – Can$25.00 – cn Can Microfilming [073]
GRAZDANSKOE PRAVO I PRAKTIKA EGO PRIMENENIIA / Stuchka, Petr Ivanovich – M., 1929 – 1mf – 9 – ne IDC [340]
GRAZHDANKII KODEKS AZERBAIDZHANSKOI SSR : OFITSIALNYI TEKST SOVSEMI IZMENENIIAMI I DOPOLNENIIAMI NA 1-E I ANV. 1956 G. AZARBAIJAN SSR MULKI M AY ALL ASI / Azerbaijan S.S.R. – Baku: Azerba idzhanskoe gos. izd-vo, 1956 – 1 – CSUX91-B2245 – us Hoover Inst Photo [947]
GRAZHADANSKAI A AVIAT SII A – (Library has: Feb., Mar., May-June, Aug.-Nov. 1936; Jan.-Nov.1939; Apr./May-Dec.1940; Nov-Dec.1963; Feb.1964-Dec.1967) – Moskva, 1931 – 1 – CSUX90-S1 – us Hoover Inst Photo [947]
GRAZHDANIN (SAINT PETERSBURG, RUSSIA) – (Includes c.1: 1890:Mar.25-1891:Aug.21; Lacks many issues) – S.-Petersburg: Kn. V. Meshcherski i, 1872 – 1 – CSUXAKF0380-S – us Hoover Inst Photo [947]
GRAZHDANKAI A VO INA NA VOLGE V 1918 G – (Includes v.1, 1930) – Praha: Izd. Obshchestva uchastnikov volzhskogo dvizhenii a, 1930 – 1 – CSUX88-S349 – us Hoover Inst Photo [947]
GRAZHDANSKAIA AVIATSIIA – Moskva: Gos obedinennoe nauch-tekhn. izd-vo. 1967-1972 – us Res Libr [072]
GRAZHDANSKAIA VOINA V ROSSII (1918-1921 G.G.) : KRESTOMATIIA / Piontkovskii, S – Moskva: Izd. Kommunistich. un-ta im. I A.M. Sverdlova, 1925 – 1 – CSUX88-B7360 – us Hoover Inst Photo [947]
GRAZHDANSKAIA VOINA V SIBIRII SEVERNOI OBLASTI / Alekseev, S A; ed by Meshcheriakova, N L – Moskva: Gos. izdvo, 1927 – 1 – CSUX88-B6957 – us Hoover Inst Photo [947]
GRAZHDANSKI I KODEKS ESTONSKO I SSR : OFITSIALNY I TEKST S IZMENENII AMI I DOPOLNENII AMI NA 1 MARTA 1973 GODA – Tallin: E esti raamat, 1973 – 1 – CSUX91-B2545 – us Hoover Inst Photo [340]
GRAZHDANSKIE KODEKSY SOIUZNYKH RESPUBLIK / Bakhchisaraitsev, Khr. & Drabkin, S – Moskva: Iurid. izdvo NKI U RSFSR, 1928 – 1 – CSUX90-B6006 – us Hoover Inst Photo [340]
GRAZHDANSKII KODEKS ARMIANSKOI SOVETSKOI SOTSIALISTICHESKOI RESPUBLIKI : PRINIATNA TRETEI SESSII VERKHOVNOGO SOVETA ARMIANSKOI SSR SHESTOGO SOZYVA 4 II UNI A 1964 GODA / Armenian SSR – Erevan: Aiastan, 1964 – 1 – CSUX91-B2692 – us Hoover Inst Photo [947]
GRAZHDANSKII KODEKS AZERBA IDZHANSKOI SSR : AZARBAIJAN SSR MULKI M AJ ALL ASI / Azerbaijan S.S.R. – Baku: Verkhovny i Sovet Azerba idzhansko i SSR, 1964 – 1 – CSUX91-B2255 – us Hoover Inst Photo [947]
GRAZHDANSKII KODEKS GRUZINSKOI SOVETSKOI SOTSIALISTICHESKOI RESPUBLIKI : PRINIATNA CHETVERTOI SESSII VERKHOVNOGO SOVETA GRUZINSKOI SSR SHESTOGO SOZYVA 26 DEK. 1964 G – Tbilisi: Sabchota Sakartvelo, 1965 – 1 – CSUX91-B2010 – us Hoover Inst Photo [947]
GRAZHDANSKII KODEKS RSFSR S POSTATEINO-SISTEMATIZIROVANNYMI MATERIALAMI / ed by Aleksandrovskii, S V – 2nd rev. ed., Moscow, 1926. 958p. BR-9104 1 – 9 – ne IDC [340]
GRAZHDANSKII KODEKS SOVETSKIKH RESPUBLIK : TEKST I PRAKTICHESKI I KOMMENTARI I / ed by Malitskogo, AL – Izd. 3-e, ispr. i dop. [Kharkov]: Iurid. izdvo NKI U USSR, 1927 – 1 – CSUX90-B8935 – us Hoover Inst Photo [340]
GRAZHDANSKII PROTSESSUALNYI KODEKS ARMIANSKOI SOVETSKOI SOTSIALISTICHESKOI RESPUBLIKI : PRINIATNA TRETEI SESSII VERKHOVNOGO SOVETA ARMIANSKOI SSR SHESTOGO SOZYVA 4 IUNIA 1964 G / Armenian SSR – Erevan: Aiastan, 1964 – 1 – CSUX91-B2704 – us Hoover Inst Photo [947]
GRAZHDANSKII PROTSESSUALNYI KODEKS AZERBAIDZHANSKOI SSR / Azerbaijan S.S.R. – Baku: Verkhovny i Sovet Azerba idzhansko i SSR, 1964 – 1 – CSUX91-B1732 – us Hoover Inst Photo [947]
GRAZHDANSKII PROTSESSUALNYI KODEKS GRUZINSKOI SSR : OFITSIALNYI TEKST S IZMENENIIAMI NA L SENT. 1957 G – Tbilisi: "Sabchota Sakratvelo", 1958 – 1 – CSUX91-B2008 – us Hoover Inst Photo [947]
GRAZHDANSKOE PRAVO / Tiutrimov, IM – Iur'ev, 1922 – 10mf – 9 – ne IDC [340]
GRAZHDANSKOE PRAVO. UKAZATEL' LITERATURY / Nikonov, S P – 1v. Khar'kov. 1904. BR-11,143 2 – 8 – ne IDC [460]
GRAZHDANSKOE PROTSESSUAL'NOE ZAKONODATEL'STVO SSSR; SOIUZNYKH RESPUBLIK / Chapurskii, VP; ed by Chapurskii, V P – Moscow, 1957. BR-8771 1 – 9 – ne IDC [335]
GRAZIA – 1988-1995 – 3r per y – 5,6 – Sfr748.00 – sz Infoprint [945]
GRAZIA E GIUSTIZIA / Italy. Ministero di Giustizia e dei Culti – Annuario. Roma. 1864-1919 – 1 – us NY Public [324]
THE GREAT ABUSE OF MUSICK / Bedford, A – Containing an account of the use and design of Musick among the antient Jews, Greeks, Romans, and others. P-637. 1711 – 9 – ne IDC [930]
GREAT AMERICAN DRAMA – (Lists 74 productions) – 88mf – 9 – £425.00 – uk Chadwyck [790]
GREAT AMERICAN LAWYERS / Lewis, W D – Philadelphia: John C. Winston Co. v1-8 + index. 1907-09 – 54mf – 9 – $81.00 – LLMC 81-407 – us L.L.M.C. [340]
GREAT ANIMAL REFUGES – 1993 – 36p – 9 – 92-3-102588-0 – fr UNESCO [630]
THE GREAT APOSTASY : CONSIDERED IN THE LIGHT OF SCRIPTURAL AND SECULAR HISTORY / Talmage, James Edward – Salt Lake City, Utah: Deseret News, 1909 – 1mf – us A.T.L.A. [240]
THE GREAT AWAKENING : A HISTORY OF THE REVIVAL OF RELIGION IN THE TIME OF EDWARDS AND WHITEFIELD / Tracy, Joseph – Boston: Tappan & Dennet, 1842, c1841 – 2mf – us A.T.L.A. [240]
THE GREAT AWAKENING IN COLUMBUS, OHIO / Stauffer, Henry – 1895 – 9 – us A.T.L.A. [240]
GREAT BARRINGTON 1741-1849 – (Mf 1T: Births 1741-1813; Marriage Intentions 1761-1802. Mf 1T-2T: Marriages 1795-1844. Mf 2T: Out-of-Town Marriages 1762-99. Mf 2T-3T: Births 1847-49. Mf 3T: Marriages 1843-49; Deaths 1843-49) – (mf ed 1996) – 3mf – 9 – 0-87623-257-8 – us Holbrook [920]
GREAT BARRINGTON 1745-1903 – (Mf 1-2: Vital & Church Records 1770-1856. Mf 3: Sheffield North Parish Meetings 1745-61. Mf 4-8: Town Minutes 1761-91. Mf 9-11: B,D,M 1794-1855. Mf 12-15: B,M,D 1843-68. Mf 16-17: Index to Marriage Intents 1850-80. Mf 18-20: Marriage Intentions 1850-80. Mf 21-25: Index to Deaths 1850-1960. Mf 26-28: Deaths 1863-1903. Mf 29-34: Index to Marriages 1848-1959. Mf 35-39: Marriages 1843-1901. Mf 40-42: Marriages 1880-94. Mf 43-49: Index to Births 1848-1959. Mf 50-51: Births 1867-90) – (mf ed 1990) – 51mf – 9 – 0-87623-104-0 – us Holbrook [920]
THE GREAT BOOK OF SUFFERINGS / Library of the Society of Friends, London – 1650-1790. 29 reels with printed guide. Accounts of Prosecutions against Quakers – £1,140.00 – uk World [240]
GREAT BRITAIN : BOARD OF TRADE/ OVERSEAS DEPARTMENT ECONOMIC SURVEYS, 1921-1961 – (Individual rpts available separately. 806 economic rpts on 125 countries: Africa 107mf £675; Asia 144mf £910; Australasia 51mf £375; Europe and the Near East 422mf £2,215; Latin America and the Caribbean 256mf £1,345; Middle East 61mf £450; North America 70mf £515) – 1113mf – 9 – £4,185.00 coll – uk Chadwyck [330]
Great Britain *see*
- AGREEMENT BETWEEN H.M.'S GOVERNMENT AND THE FRENCH GOVERNMENT RESPECTING THE BOUNDARY LINE BETWEEN SYRIA AND PALESTINE FROM THE MEDITERRANEAN TO EL HAMME
- ANNUAL ABSTRACT OF STATISTICS OF THE U.K
- BRITISH GAZETTE
- CARRINGTON AND KIRWAN'S REPORTS
- CARRINGTON AND MARSHMAN'S REPORTS
- CARRINGTON AND PAYNE'S REPORTS
- CORRESPONDENCE BETWEEN SIR HENRY MCMAHON, HIS MAJESTY'S HIGH COMMISSIONER AT CAIRO, AND THE SHERIF HUSSEIN OF MECCA JUL 1915-MAR 1916
- EDUCATION ENQUIRY: ABSTRACT OF ANSWERS AND RETURNS
- ENGLISH STATE TRIALS, 1163-1858
- HOUSEHOLD ACCOUNTS AND EXPENSES OF EDWARD 5, RICHARD 3, HENRY 7 AND JAMES 1
- HOUSEHOLD ACCOUNTS AND EXPENSES OF HENRY 6 (1452-3), THE THIRD EARL OF STAFFORD (1370-2), THE THIRD DUKE OF BUCKINGHAM (1506), WILLIAM MALVERN, ABBOT OF ST PETER'S GLOUCESTER (1524-5) AND FRANCES DEVEREUX (1641-2)
- HOUSEHOLD ACCOUNTS AND EXPENSES OF THE EARL OF WARWICK, (1420-1), DUKE OF RICHMOND (1527-8), DUKE OF BUCKINGHAM (1506-7) AND EDWARD SEYMOUR (1538-41) 15TH/16TH
- THE JURIST, NEW SERIES
- THE JURIST, OLD SERIES
- KING JAMES 1 OF ENGLAND TO KING CHRISTIAN 4 OF DENMARK: ROYAL CORRESPONDENCE, 1603-1625
- LONDON GAZETTE
- POLITICAL HISTORY OF PALESTINE UNDER BRITANNIC ADMINISTRATION
- PUBLIC GENERAL ACTS, 1801-1922
- REPORT OF THE COMMISSION APPOINTED BY H.M. GOVERNMENT IN THE UNITED KINGDOM OF GREAT BRITAIN AND NORTHERN IRELAND, WITH THE APPROVAL OF THE COUNCIL OF THE LEAGUE OF NATIONS
- RETURN OF ENDOWED GRAMMAR SCHOOLS
- RETURNS FOR EACH PUBLIC ELEMENTARY SCHOOL
- RETURNS RELATING TO ELEMENTARY EDUCATION (CIVIL PARISHES)
- ROYAL ARCHIVES AT WINDSOR CASTLE
- SCHOOL CERTIFICATE EXAMINATION: REPORT OF THE PANEL OF INVESTIGATORS
- UNITED KINGDOM WRECK REGISTERS, 1855-98
- YEARBOOKS
Great Britain. Admiralty *see* PAPERS DELIVERED FROM THE ADMIRALTY RELATIVE TO THE WAR WITH AMERICA
Great Britain. Advisory Committee on Handicapped Children *see* CHILDREN WITH SPECIFIC READING DIFFICULTIES
Great Britain. Advisory Council for Education in Northern Ireland on Secondary Education in Northern Ireland *see* REPORT
Great Britain. Advisory Council on Art Education *see* 1ST REPORT
Great Britain. Air Ministry Aeronautical Research Committee *see* REPORTS AND MEMORANDA
GREAT BRITAIN AND THE CAUSES AND ORIGINS OF WORLD WAR 1 PAMPHLET COLLECTION – 1914-1919 – 4r – 1 – CSUXAML2964-B – us Hoover Inst Photo [355]
GREAT BRITAIN AND THE PANAMA-CANAL / Butte, G C – n.p., 1913 – 1mf – 9 – ILM-2368/1 – ne IDC [327]
Great Britain. Atomic Energy Authority *see*
- ANNUAL REPORT AND STATEMENT OF ACCOUNTS
- UNCLASSIFIED AND DECLASSIFIED REPORTS
Great Britain. Board of Agriculture *see* COUNTY REPORTS
Great Britain. Board of Trade *see*
- JOURNAL
- REPORT OF UNITED KINGDOM TRADE MISSION TO EGYPT, THE SUDAN AND ETHIOPIA, FEBRUARY 1955
Great Britain. British Railways Board *see* ANNUAL REPORT AND STATEMENT OF ACCOUNTS
Great Britain. British Transport Commission *see* ANNUAL REPORT AND STATEMENT OF ACCOUNTS
Great Britain. British Waterways Board *see* ANNUAL REPORT AND STATEMENT OF ACCOUNTS
Great Britain. Cabinet Office *see*
- CABINET MINUTES
- CABINET MINUTES AND MEMORANDA
- MEMORANDA
- RECORDS
Great Britain. Cabinet Secretariat *see* MANDATE FOR PALESTINE
Great Britain. Census Office *see* CENSUS OF ENGLAND AND WALES, 1871
Great Britain. Central Advisory Committee for England *see*
- CHILDREN AND THEIR PRIMARY SCHOOLS
- HALF OUR FUTURE: REPORT OF THE CENTRAL ADVISORY COUNCIL FOR ENGLAND
Great Britain. Central Advisory Council for Education *see*
- 15 TO 18: REPORT
- EARLY LEAVING: REPORT OF THE CENTRAL ADVISORY COUNCIL FOR EDUCATION

- LAW REPORTS: PRE-1865: ENGLISH NOMINATIVES
- LOCAL, PERSONAL, AND PRIVATE ACTS
- PRIVATE ACTS
- PUBLIC ELEMENTARY EDUCATION IN ENGLAND AND WALES. BILL 33
- PUBLIC GENERAL ACTS, 1714-1933
- REGULATIONS FOR SECONDARY SCHOOLS, INCLUDING SUPPLEMENTARY REGULATIONS FOR SECONDARY SCHOOLS
- THE STATUTES AT LARGE (PICKERING'S STATUTES), 1225-1869
- STATUTES D'ANGLETERRE
- STATUTES OF THE REALM

Great Britain. Local Government Board *see* URBAN AND RURAL SOCIAL CONDITIONS IN INDUSTRIAL BRITAIN, SERIES 2

Great Britain. Medical Officers of Health *see* URBAN AND RURAL SOCIAL CONDITIONS IN INDUSTRIAL BRITAIN, SERIES 3

Great Britain. Ministry of Education *see*
- EDUCATION, A FRAMEWORK FOR EXPANSION
- THE EDUCATION OF DEAF CHILDREN
- EDUCATIONAL RECONSTRUCTION
- NINTH REPORT ON THE DEMAND FOR AND SUPPLY OF TEACHERS
- PRIMARY EDUCATION TEACHER'S GUIDE
- PUBLIC ELEMENTARY SCHOOL: SUGGESTIONS FOR THE CONSIDERATION OF TEACHERS AND OTHERS CONCERNED IN THE WORK
- SECONDARY EDUCATION WITH SPECIAL REFERENCE TO GRAMMAR SCHOOLS AND TECHNICAL HIGH SCHOOLS
- TEACHERS AND YOUTH LEADERS: REPORT OF THE COMMITTEE APPOINTED BY THE PRESIDENT OF THE BOARD OF EDUCATION TO CONSIDER THE SUPPLY, RECRUITMENT AND TRAINING OF TEACHERS AND YOUTH LEADERS

Great Britain. Ministry of Education Committee on Day Release *see* REPORT

Great Britain. Ministry of Labour *see* REPORT ON THE ESTABLISHMENT AND PROGRESS OF JOINT INDUSTRIAL COUNCILS SET UP IN ACCORDANCE WITH THE RECOMMENDATIONS OF THE COMMITTEE ON RELATIONS BETWEEN EMPLOYERS AND EMPLOYED "THE WHITLEY" COMMITTEE

Great Britain. National Coal Board *see* ANNUAL REPORT AND STATEMENT OF ACCOUNTS

Great Britain. National Economic Development Council *see*
- CONDITIONS FAVOURABLE TO FASTER GROWTH (1961-1966)
- GROWTH OF THE UNITED KINGDOM ECONOMY, 1961-1966

Great Britain. Naval Office *see*
- SHIPPING LISTS FOR EAST FLORIDA
- SHIPPING LISTS FOR GEORGIA
- SHIPPING LISTS FOR HALIFAX, NOVA SCOTIA
- SHIPPING LISTS FOR JAMAICA
- SHIPPING LISTS FOR MARYLAND
- SHIPPING LISTS FOR MASSACHUSETTS
- SHIPPING LISTS FOR NEW HAMPSHIRE
- SHIPPING LISTS FOR NEW JERSEY
- SHIPPING LISTS FOR NEW YORK, 1713-65
- SHIPPING LISTS FOR SOUTH CAROLINA
- SHIPPING LISTS FOR VIRGINIA
- SHIPPING LISTS FOR WEST INDIES (EXCLUDING JAMAICA)

Great Britain. Organization for European Economic Cooperation *see* REPORT TO THE ECONOMIC COOPERATION ADMINISTRATION ON THE 1949/50 PROGRAMME. V. 2. UNITED KINGDOM

Great Britain. Palestine *see* CORRESPONDENCE WITH THE PALESTINE ARAB DELEGATION AND THE ZIONIST ORGANISATION

GREAT BRITAIN, PALESTINE AND THE JEWS – New York, 1918 – 1mf – 1 – ILM-2481/1 – ne IDC [327]

Great Britain. Parliament *see*
- DEBATES
- INDEX TO THE ROLLS OF PARLIAMENT, 1832
- ORD REPORT ON THE WEST COAST OF AFRICA
- PARLIAMENTARY REPORTS AND PAPERS RELATING TO EDUCATION
- PARLIAMENTARY REPORTS AND PAPERS RELATING TO THE NAVY
- PARLIAMENTARY RETURNS
- RECORDS OF THE PARLIAMENT HOLDEN AT WESTMINSTER, 28 FEBRUARY IN THE 33RD YEAR OF THE REIGN OF EDWARD 1 (1305) (RS98)

Great Britain. Parliament. High Court *see* REPORTS OF CASES UPON APPEALS AND WRITS OF ERROR DETERMINED IN THE HIGH COURT OF PARLIAMENT

GREAT BRITAIN. PARLIAMENT. HOUSE OF COMMONS *see* LATIN AMERICA BRITISH DIPLOMATIC BLUE BOOKS

Great Britain. Parliament. House of Commons *see*
- BRITISH DIPLOMATIC BLUE BOOKS CONCERNING CENTRAL AND SOUTH AMERICA
- DEBATES
- DEVON COMMISSION REPORT
- DIVISION LISTS
- A FURTHER REPORT FROM THE COMMITTEE OF SECRECY APPOINTED TO INQUIRE INTO THE CONDUCT OF ROBERT, EARL OF OXFORD
- GENERAL TOPOGRAPHICAL INDEX TO THE TOWNLANDS AND TOWNS OF IRELAND
- JOURNAL
- JOURNAL. 75 V
- PARLIAMENTARY PAPERS, RELATING TO THE EAST INDIES
- POPULATION OF ENGLAND AND WALES, 1911
- REPORT ON THE VISIT BY AN ALL PARTY GROUP OF MEMBERS OF PARLIAMENT TO SPAIN
- SESSIONAL PAPERS

Great Britain. Parliament. House of Commons. Select Committee on the Affairs of Lower Canada *see* REPORT FROM SELECT COMMITTEE ON LOWER CANADA

Great Britain. Parliament. House of Lords *see*
- CASES SUBMITTED TO THE HOUSE OF LORDS ON APPEAL FROM THE COURTS OF ENGLAND, SCOTLAND, AND NORTHERN IRELAND
- DEBATES
- MATERIAL RELATING TO AMERICA
- POLITICS AND STATECRAFT IN EARLY MODERN ENGLAND: THE MAIN PAPERS OF THE HOUSE OF LORDS
- SESSIONAL PAPERS

Great Britain. Planning and Development in Scotland 1973 74 *see* REPORTS OF THE SCOTTISH ECONOMIC PLANNING DEPARTMENT AND THE SCOTTISH DEVELOPMENT DEPARTMENT

Great Britain. Poor Law Commissioners *see* REPORT

Great Britain. Prime Minister *see*
- PAPERS OF THE PRIME MINISTERS OF GREAT BRITAIN, SERIES 1
- PAPERS OF THE PRIME MINISTERS OF GREAT BRITAIN, SERIES 2
- PAPERS OF THE PRIME MINISTERS OF GREAT BRITAIN, SERIES 3
- PAPERS OF THE PRIME MINISTERS OF GREAT BRITAIN, SERIES 4
- PAPERS OF THE PRIME MINISTERS OF GREAT BRITAIN, SERIES 5
- PAPERS OF THE PRIME MINISTERS OF GREAT BRITAIN, SERIES 6
- PAPERS OF THE PRIME MINISTERS OF GREAT BRITAIN, SERIES 7

Great Britain. Privy Council *see*
- ACTS OF THE PRIVY COUNCIL OF ENGLAND
- LAW REPORTS: INDIAN APPEALS
- MOORE'S PRIVY COUNCIL CASES
- RECORDS AND BRIEFS OF CASES SUBMITTED ON APPEAL TO THE PRIVY COUNCIL

Great Britain. Public Record Office *see*
- AMBASSADORIAL AND SECRET SERVICE REPORTS ON REVOLUTIONARY AND NAPOLEONIC FRANCE, 1781-1815
- THE BRITISH TREASURY, ECONOMIC DEPRESSION, AND INTERNATIONAL FINANCE
- CALENDAR OF ENTRIES IN THE PAPAL REGISTERS RELATING TO GREAT BRITAIN AND IRELAND. PAPAL LETTERS
- CALENDAR OF STATE PAPERS, DOMESTIC SERIES OF THE REIGN OF CHARLES I, 1625-1649
- THE CLARENDON PAPERS, 1867-1870
- THE COMPLETE STATE PAPERS DOMESTIC, SERIES 1
- THE COMPLETE STATE PAPERS DOMESTIC, SERIES 2
- THE COMPLETE STATE PAPERS DOMESTIC, SERIES 3
- THE COMPLETE STATE PAPERS REGENCIES
- CONDITIONS AND POLITICS IN OCCUPIED WESTERN EUROPE, 1940-45, PART 6/B
- CONFLICT AND CONSENSUS IN BRITISH INDUSTRIAL RELATIONS
- CUSTOMS 3. 1696-1780
- CUSTOMS 16 AMERICA 1768-72
- CUSTOMS 17
- DISCONTENT AND AUTHORITY 1820-40
- THE GRANVILLE PAPERS, 1870-1874
- HAND-BOOK TO THE PUBLIC RECORDS
- HOME OFFICE PAPERS AND RECORDS: ORDER AND AUTHORITY IN ENGLAND, SERIES 1
- LETTERS OF MARQUE 1777-1783; DECLARATIONS AGAINST AMERICA
- MEDITERRANEAN PASSES
- NATIONAL ARCHIVES
- POLITICS AND SOCIETY IN INTER-WAR BRITAIN
- PUBLIC ORDER, DISCONTENT AND PROTEST IN NINETEENTH CENTURY ENGLAND, 1820-1850 (PRO CLASS HO 52)
- STATE PAPERS (FOREIGN) OF EDWARD 6TH, 1547-1553
- STATE PAPERS (FOREIGN) OF MARY 1ST, 1553-1558
- STATE PAPERS MEDIEVAL AND OTHER RECORDS
- THE STATE PAPERS OF QUEEN ANNE
- UNCALENDARED STATE PAPERS FOREIGN OF ELIZABETH 1 (MAY 1592-MAR 1603)

Great Britain. Public Schools Commission *see*
- FIRST REPORT
- SECOND REPORT

Great Britain. Royal Air Force *see* ROYAL AIR FORCE FINAL REPORTS ON OPERATIONS

Great Britain. Royal Archives *see* THE ORIENTAL QUESTION, 1840-1900

Great Britain. Royal Army *see* ROYAL MILITIA AND YEOMANRY CAVALRY: THE ARMY LIST, 1850

Great Britain. Royal Commission and Select Committee *see* LABOUR AND TRADES UNIONISM

Great Britain. Royal Commission for the Advancement of Science *see* DEVONSHIRE REPORT

Great Britain. Royal Commission into Schools in Scotland *see* REPORT

Great Britain. Royal Commission on Legal Services *see* THE PUBLIC EVIDENCE PRESENTED TO THE ROYAL COMMISSION ON LEGAL SERVICES, 1979

Great Britain. Royal Commission on Poor Law *see* REPORT

Great Britain. Royal Commission on Secondary Education *see* REPORT

Great Britain. Royal Commission on Technical Instruction *see* FIRST AND SECOND REPORTS

Great Britain. Royal Commission on the Railways of Gt. Britain and Ireland *see* APPENDICES, INDICES AND REPORTS IN RESPECT OF THE ROYAL COMMISSION

Great Britain. Royal Commission on the State of the Universities of Scotland *see* GENERAL REPORT AND MINUTES OF EVIDENCE

Great Britain. Royal Commission upon Decentralisation in India *see* REPORT 1908

Great Britain. Royal Commissioners Appointed to Enquire into Popular Education in England. The Newcastle Commission *see* REPORT

Great Britain. Royal Commissioners for Taking a Census of Great Britain on Education *see* REPORT

Great Britain. Royal Commissioners into the Means of Education in Wales *see* REPORT

Great Britain. Royal Commissions on Ancient and Historical Monuments and Constructions *see*
- HISTORIC BUILDINGS IN BRITAIN
- HISTORIC BUILDINGS IN BRITAIN. INVENTORY
- WALES

Great Britain. Royal Photographic Society *see* THE JOURNAL OF THE PHOTOGRAPHIC SOCIETY

Great Britain. Schools Inquiry Commission. Taunton Commission *see* REPORT

Great Britain. Secondary School Examinations Council on Secondary School Examinations other than G. C. E *see* BELOE REPORT

Great Britain. Selbourne Commission *see* DURHAM UNIVERSITY ACT 1861: REPORT ON THE ADVANCEMENT OF HIGHER EDUCATION IN LONDON

Great Britain. Select Committee for Giving Instruction in Theoretical and Applied Science to Industrial Classes *see* REPORT

Great Britain. Select Committee into the Education of the Poor *see* A DIGEST OF PAROCHIAL RETURNS

Great Britain. Select Committee on Education in England and Wales *see* REPORT

Great Britain. Select Committee on Public Libraries *see* REPORT

Great Britain. Select Committee on Schools of Art *see* REPORT

Great Britain. Select Committee on the Education of the Lower Orders *see* REPORT

Great Britain. Select Committee on the Education of the Poorer Classes *see* REPORT

Great Britain. Select Committee on the State of Education *see* REPORT

Great Britain. Select Committee on the West Coast of Africa *see* REPORT

Great Britain. Select Committee on West African Settlements *see* REPORT: THE AIMS OF BRITISH POLICY IN WEST AFRICA

Great Britain. South East Economic Planning Council *see* A STRATEGY FOR THE SOUTH EAST

Great Britain. Standing Joint Committee on A Provisional minimum scale of salaries for teachers in Public Elementary Schools *see* REPORT

Great Britain. State Papers *see* MILITARY EXPEDITIONS 1695-1763

Great Britain. Stationery Office *see*
- ANNUAL CATALOGUES OF BRITISH OFFICIAL AND PARLIAMENTARY PUBLICATIONS, 1894-1909
- ANNUAL CATALOGUES OF BRITISH OFFICIAL AND PARLIAMENTARY PUBLICATIONS, 1910-1919

Great Britain. Study Group on the Government of Colleges of Education *see* REPORT

Great Britain. Superior Courts of Equity and Law *see* THE WEEKLY REPORTER

Great Britain. Teaching Council for England and Wales *see* REPORT OF A WORKING PARTY

Great Britain. Treasury Solicitor *see* THE 1745 REBELLION PAPERS, 1745-1753

Great Britain. Uganda Development Commission, 1920 and Cotton Commissions, 1929, 1938 and 1948 *see* REPORTS

Great Britain. Unemployment Assistance Board *see* ORIGINS OF THE WELFARE STATE IN BRITAIN

Great Britain. War Office *see*
- INTER-ALLIED ARMISTICE COMMISSION, 1918-1920
- ROUTE BOOKS, MILITARY REPORTS AND INFORMATION PRECIS FOR BRITISH AFRICA

Great Britain. War Office. General Staff *see*
- MILITARY REPORT ON THE GOLD COAST, ASHANTI AND THE NORTHERN TERRITORIES
- ROUTE BOOK OF THE GOLD COAST COLONY, ASHANTI AND THE NORTHERN TERRITORIES

Great Britain. War Office. General Staff. Geographical Section *see* THE ANGLO-EGYPTIAN SUDAN

Great Britain. War Office. Intelligence Division *see* MILITARY REPORT ON SOMALILAND, 1907

Great Britain. Western Pacific High Commission *see* GAZETTE

Great Britain. York Court of High Commission *see* FROM THE REFORMATION TO THE PURITAN REVOLUTION

GREAT BUDDHIST TOPE AT SANCHI / India. Preservation of National Monuments; ed by Cole, H H – Calcutta, 1885. BI-687 2 – 8 – ne IDC [720]

GREAT CHARTER OF CHRI..STUDIES IN THE SERMON ON THE MOUNT / Carpenter, William Boyd – New York: T. Whittaker, 1896. 1 fiche – 9 – us A.T.L.A. [240]

THE GREAT CIVIL WAR IN DORSET, 1642-1660 / Bayley, Arthur Rutter – Taunton: Barnicott and Pearce: Wessex Press, 1910 – 1 – us U.W. Library [941]

GREAT COHARY BAPTIST CHURCH. EASTERN ASSOCIATION. NORTH CAROLINA : CHURCH RECORDS – 1790-1855 – 1 – 7.92 – us Baptist [240]

THE GREAT CONFLICT : A DISCOURSE CONCERNING BAPTISTS, AND RELIGIOUS LIBERTY / Lorimer, George Claude – (Includes bibliographical references) – Boston: Lee and Shepard; New York: Charles T Dillingham, 1877 – 1mf – 9 – 0-8370-8921-2 – 1986-2921 – us A.T.L.A. [240]

THE GREAT CONQUEST : OR, MISCELLANEOUS PAPERS ON MISSIONS / Ellinwood, Frank Field – New York: William Rankin, 1876 – 1mf – 9 – 0-8370-6113-X – 1986-0113 – us A.T.L.A. [240]

GREAT CRISIS: EIGHTEEN HUNDRED FORTY-THREE – v. 1. 1842 – 1 – us UMI [240]

THE GREAT CYLINDER INSCRIPTIONS A AND B OF GUDEA / Price, J M – (Assyriologische Bibl. v15, 26). Leipzig, 1899, 1927. BNE-20,032 1 – 9 – ne IDC [410]

THE GREAT DENE RACE / Morice, Adrien G – BN 320 2. 1906 – 8 – ne IDC [306]

THE GREAT DIDACTIC OF JOHN AMOS COMENIUS = DIDACTICA MAGNA : NOW FOR THE FIRST TIME ENGLISHED / ed by Keatinge, Maurice Walter – (Includes bibliographical references) – London: Adam and Charles Black, 1896 – 2mf – 9 – 0-8370-7615-3 – 1986-1615 – us A.T.L.A. [370]

THE GREAT EASTERN – Grahamstown, South Africa. 2 Feb 1864-9 Sept 1868. 8 reels – 1, 16 diazo available at reduced price – sa SA Libr [072]

GREAT EDUCATORS OF THREE CENTURIES : THEIR WORK AND ITS INFLUENCE ON MODERN EDUCATION / Graves, Frank Pierrepont – New York: Macmillan, 1912 – 1mf – us A.T.L.A. [370]

THE GREAT ELECTION / Campbell, John – Montreal: J. Lovell, 1894. 00375. (Pre-1900 Canadiana) – 9 – cn C.I.H.M. [971]

A GREAT EMERGENCY / Ewing, Juliana Horatia – British Fiction Archive: Unit 1 – 9 – uk Bell [830]

THE GREAT ENIGMA / Lilly, William Samuel – London: John Murray, 1893. 1 fiche – 9 – us A.T.L.A. [240]

GREAT EXHIBITION *see*
- PALAIS DE CRISTAL
- PILOTE DE LONDRES

THE GREAT EXHIBITION OF 1851: PROSPECTUSES OF EXHIBITORS – (Ca 900 prospectuses in four sections: Raw Materials, Machinery, Manufactures, and Fine Arts) – Includes index – 9r – 1 – $660.00 – us UMI [900]

THE GREAT GULF (CCC18) = HUNG KOU / Chang, Wan-Ju – (In Chinese) – Shanghai: Christian Literature Society, 1935 – 1r – 1 – 0-8370-1718-1 – 1984-6087 – us A.T.L.A. [240]

THE GREAT HISTORICAL PROCESS AGAINST FASCISM / Spain. Embajada. United States – Washington, DC, n.d. Fiche W1179. (Blodgett Collection of Spanish Civil War Pamphlets) – 9 – us H.U. College Libr [946]

GREAT HYMNS AND HYMN WRITERS (CCC317) = SHENG SHIH TIEN K'AO / Wang, Stephen – (In Chinese) – 1st ed. Hong Kong: Council on Christian Literature for Overseas Chinese, 1955 – 1r – 1 – 1984-6656 – us A.T.L.A. [780]

THE GREAT IRON WHEEL / Graves, J R – 1856 – 1 – 20.58 – us Baptist [240]

THE GREAT JOY OF SAINTS / Simson, John – 1654- – 1 – 16.31 – us Baptist [240]

A GREAT JUDICIAL CHARACTER, ROGER BROOKE TANEY / Gregory, Charles Noble – New Haven, CT: Field 1908. 18p. LL-490 – 1 – us L of C Photodup [340]

THE GREAT LAKE BASINS OF THE ST LAWRENCE / Drummond, Andrew Thomas – s.l.: s.n., 1889?. 02769. (Pre-1900 Canadiana) – 9 – cn C.I.H.M. [971]

GREAT LAKES SEAFARER – River Rouge, MI. v7-11. 1959-64 – 1r – 1 – us Ross [071]

THE GREAT LAKES SEAFARER – Detroit. v. 7-10. Mar 1959-Jan 1964. Incomplete – 1 – us NY Public [978]

THE GREAT MATCH, AND OTHER MATCHES – Boston: Roberts Brothers, 1877. 293p., illus. (No name series) – 1 – us U.W. Library [999]

THE GREAT MEANING OF METANOIA : AN UNDEVELOPED CHAPTER IN THE LIFE AND TEACHING OF CHRIST / Walden, Treadwell – New York: Thomas Whittaker, 1896 – 1mf – 9 – 0-8370-5683-7 – 1985-3683 – us A.T.L.A. [240]

GREAT MEN OF THE CHRISTIAN CHURCH / Walker, Williston – Chicago: University of Chicago Press, 1908 – 1mf – us A.T.L.A. [240]

GREAT MISSIONARIES OF THE CHURCH / Creegan, Charles Cole & Goodnow, Josephine A B – New York: Thomas Y Crowell, c1895 – 1mf – 9 – 0-8370-6484-8 – 1986-0484 – us A.T.L.A. [920]

Great Northern and Northern Pacific Railway Companies *see* STEAM LOCOMOTIVE DRAWINGS

Great Northern Railway Company *see*
- ANNUAL REPORTS
- PAPERS OF THE GREAT NORTHERN RAILWAY COMPANY, PART 1

Great Northern Railway Company. Advertising and Publicity Dept *see* MAGAZINE AND NEWSPAPER ADVERTISEMENTS AND ARTICLES AND OTHER PUBLICITY

Great Northern Railway Company. Personnel Dept *see* INDEX TO PERSONNEL FILES

Great Northern Railway of Canada *see* PROSPECTUS..

GREAT OPINIONS BY GREAT JUDGES / Snyder, William Lamartine – New York, Baker, Voorhis, 1883. 792 p. LL-1082 – 1 – us L of C Photodup [340]

THE GREAT PESTILENCE (A.D. 1348-9) : NOW COMMONLY KNOWN AS THE BLACK DEATH / Gasquet, Francis Aidan, Cardinal – (Includes bibliographical references and index) – London: Simpkin Marshall, Hamilton, Kent, 1893 – 1mf – 9 – 0-8370-6905-X – 1986-0905 – us A.T.L.A. [941]

THE GREAT PROBLEM : CAN IT BE SOLVED? / Gleig, George Robert – Edinburgh: William Blackwood, 1876 – 1mf – 9 – 0-8370-3308-X – 1985-1308 – us A.T.L.A. [230]

THE GREAT QUESTION, WILL YOU CONSIDER THE SUBJECT OF PERSONAL RELIGION? / Boardman, Henry Augustus – Philadelphia: American Sunday-School Union, c1855 – 1mf – us A.T.L.A. [240]

THE GREAT REDEMPTION / Moody, Dwight Lyman – 1889 – 9 – us A.T.L.A. [240]

THE GREAT REGISTER OF PLACER COUNTY – Placer Co, 1867-82 – 1r – 1 – $50.00 – C40250 – us Library Micro [978]

THE GREAT REGISTER OF PLUMAS COUNTY – Plumas Co, 1867; 1879; 1896 – 1r – 1 – $50.00 – B40251 – us Library Micro [978]

THE GREAT REGISTER OF SAN FRANCISCO CITY AND COUNTY – San Francisco, 1866; 1867; 1869; 1871 – 1r – 1 – $50.00 – C40308 – us Library Micro [978]

GREAT REGISTER OF SISKIYOU COUNTY – Siskiyou Co, Oct 24 1892 – 1r – 1 – $50.00 – B40271 – us Library Micro [978]

GREAT REGISTER OF THE COUNTY OF ALAMEDA – Oakland, 1894. California Reel 9. (The Cox Library Collection) – 5 – us Americana [978]

GREAT REGISTER OF VOTERS FOR FRESNO COUNTY – Fresno Co, 1867-77; AA-LY (1890); MA-ZO (1890); A-E (1892-95); F-L (1892-95); M-R (1892-95); S-Z (1892-95) – 8r – 1 – $400.00 – B06094 – us Library Micro [324]

GREAT REGISTER OF YUBA COUNTY – Yuba Co, 1867-96 – 1r – 1 – $50.00 – C40288 – us Library Micro [978]

THE GREAT REVIVAL OF 1800 / Speer, William – Philadelphia: Presbyterian Board of Publication, c1872 – 1mf – us A.T.L.A. [240]

THE GREAT REVIVAL OF THE EIGHTEENTH CENTURY / Hood, Edwin Paxton – w index. Philadelphia. 1882 – 9 – us A.T.L.A. [240]

GREAT REVIVALS AND THE GREAT REPUBLIC / Candler, Warren A – 1904 – 9 – us A.T.L.A. [240]

THE GREAT RUSSIAN REVOLUTION / Chernov, Viktor Mikhailovich – Trans. and abridged by Philip E. Mosely.New Haven: Yale University Press, 1936. viii,466p. plates, ports – 1 – us U.W. Library [947]

GREAT SOUTHERN STAR – 1889-1899 – 3mf – 9 – at Corangamite [980]

GREAT SOUTHWEST – Richfield. Kan. 1886-87 – 1 – us UMI [071]

GREAT SPECKLED BIRD – Atlanta, GA, 1972-1974 – 10r – 1 – $500.00 – R04143 – us Library Micro [071]

GREAT SPEECHES BY GREAT LAWYERS : A COLLECTION OF ARGUMENTS AND SPEECHES BEFORE COURTS AND JURIES BY EMINENT LAWYERS / Snyder, William Lamartine – New York: Baker, Voorhis & Co, 1892 – 8mf – 9 – $12.00 – LLMC 92-131 – us L.L.M.C. [340]

THE GREAT STANDARD OIL MONOPOLY CASE : THE UNITED STATES OF AMERICA V. STANDARD OIL COMPANY OF NEW JERSEY / U.S. Supreme Court – Anti-trust case against John D. Rockefeller's Standard Oil Company in 1911. 6 reels with guide. – 1 – $580.00 – 0-89093-018-X – us UPA [340]

A GREAT SUCCESS / Ward, Mary Augusta – British Fiction Archive: Unit 2 – 9 – uk Bell [830]

THE GREAT SUPPER OF GOD = COMMUNION HEBDOMADAIRE : OR, DISCOURSES ON WEEKLY COMMUNION / Coube, Stephen; ed by Brady, F X – New York: Benziger, 1901 – 1mf – 9 – 0-8370-6811-8 – 1986-0811 – us A.T.L.A. [240]

GREAT TEMPLE TO SIVA AND HIS CONSORT AT MADURA / India. Preservation of National Monuments; ed by Cole, H H – Calcutta, 1884. BI-684 2 – 8 – ne IDC [720]

GREAT THOUGHTS OF THE BIBLE / Reid, John – (Includes index) – New York: Wilbur B Ketcham, c1891 – 1mf – 9 – 0-8370-3986-X – 1985-1986 – us A.T.L.A. [220]

THE GREAT VALUE AND SUCCESS OF FOREIGN MISSIONS : PROVED BY DISTINGUISHED WITNESSES / ed by Liggins, John – (Includes appendix) – New York: Baker & Taylor, c1888 – 1mf – 9 – 0-8370-6139-3 – 1986-0139 – us A.T.L.A. [230]

THE GREAT VOLCANO / Bentley-Taylor, David – SE-5341 1. 1965 – 9 – ne IDC [550]

THE GREAT WAR : SIX SERMONS / Gladden, Washington – Columbus, Ohio: McClelland, [1915?] – 1mf – us A.T.L.A. [240]

Great Western Railway Company of Canada *see* REPLY OF THE DIRECTORS TO THE REPORT OF THE COMMITTEE...30TH OCTOBER 1873:...TO BE SUBMITTED...IN LONDON, WEDNESDAY, 26TH AUGUST, 1874

GREAT-BRITAIN'S TRUE SYSTEM : WHEREIN IS CLEARLY SHEWN...THAT AN INCREASE OF THE PUBLIC DEBTS AND TAXES... / Postlethwayt, M – London, 1757 – 6mf – 9 – ne IDC [320]

GREATE HERBALL – London. 1561. BM-370 2 – 8 – ne IDC [615]

GREATER ASIA – Rangoon, Burma. 7 Feb 1943-21 Apr 1945 – 1r – 1 – us L of C Photodup [072]

GREATER BRITAIN *see* BRITISH FOREIGN AND COLONIAL JOURNAL

GREATER CLEVELAND RAPID TRANSIT AUTHORITY RECORDS *see* RTA RECORDS, LR-RA 0001, 1848-1958

GREATER CLEVELAND REGIONAL TRANSIT AUTHORITY RECORDS, LR-RA 0001 – (Records of several plank toll road and street car companies, predecessors to the Cleveland Railway Co, of the CRC, of the Shaker Heights Rapid Transit, and copies of the Tayler Grant negotiations and settlement) – 1848-1958 – 25r – 1 – us Western Res [978]

GREATER DALLAS AND VICINITY / Lindsley, Philip – Chicago: Lewis Publ. Co., 1909. v1, Texas Reel 10. v2, Texas Reel 11. (The Cox Library Collection) – 5 – us Americana [978]

GREATER ENTERPRISE NEWS – Portland OR. Sep 9 1964-Feb 22 1967 – 1 – us U.O. Library [071]

THE GREATER ILLUSION, A CRITICAL REVIEW OF AUSTRALIA'S FISCAL POLICY / Alford, F S – 1934. 198p – 9 – 1.00f – at Libertarian Micro [320]

GREATER INDIANAPOLIS / Dunn, Jacob Pratt – Historical and biographical sketches. Chicago: Lewis Publishing Co., 1910. 2v. Indiana Reel 21. (The Cox Library Collection) – 5 – us Americana [978]

GREATER LAWRENCE JEWISH NEWS – (Lawrence, Mass.) V34, no. 3 (Dec. 1963) ; v34, no. 5 (Feb. 1964)-v34, no. 7 (Apr.1964) – us A.J.P.C. [270]

THE GREATER LIFE AND WORK OF CHRIST : AS REVEALED IN SCRIPTURE, MAN, AND NATURE / Patterson, Alexander – Chicago: Fleming H Revell, c1896 – 1mf – 9 – 0-8370-3982-7 – 1985-1982 – us A.T.L.A. [240]

GREATER OREGON – Albany, OR. -w 17 Jan 1929-25 May 1978. – 1 – us U.O. Library [071]

GREATER PORTLAND NEWS – Portland OR. Sep 29 1955-Mar 8 1956 – 1 – us U.O. Library [071]

GREATER SAFETY AT SEA... / Field, D D – New York, [1875] – 1mf – 1 – ILM-3586/1 – ne IDC [327]

GREATER TERRE HAUTE AND VIGO COUNTY / Oakey, C C – Chicago: Lewis Publishng Co., 1908. 2v. Indiana Reel 29. (The Cox Library Collection) – 5 – us Americana [978]

THE GREATEST WORK IN THE WORLD : OR, THE EVANGELIZATION OF ALL PEOPLES IN THE PRESENT CENTURY / Pierson, Arthur Tappan – 4th rev ed. New York: Fleming H Revell, c1891 – 1mf – 9 – 0-8370-7253-0 – 1986-1253 – us A.T.L.A. [240]

Greathead, Henry *see* THE REPORT OF THE EVIDENCE, AND OTHER PROCEEDINGS IN PARLIAMENT RESPECTING THE INVENTION OF THE LIFE-BOAT

Greatwood, Edward Albert *see* DIE DICHTERISCHE SELBSTDARSTELLUNG IM ROMAN DES JUNGEN DEUTSCHLAND

Greaves, A B *see* A LETTER ADDRESSED TO MINISTERS OF STATE, BISHOPS, MAGISTRATES AND OTHERS RESPECTING THE BODY OF MEN GENERALLY TERMED METHODIST PREACHERS,...

Greaves, Paul *see* GRAMMATICA ANGLICANA

Grebe, Walter *see* DIE ERZAEHLUNGSTECHNIK VIKTOR SCHEFFELS

Grebenshchikov, A V *see*
- MAN'CHZHURY, IKH IAZYKH I PIS'MENNOST'
- OCHERK IZUCHENIIA MAN'CHZHURSKAGO IAZYKA V KITAE

Greber, J *see* NACH WELCHEM OERTLICHEN RECHT...

LE GREC, LE LATIN: LEUR UTILITE POUR APPRECIER LA SIGNIFICATION DES MOTS ACTUELS DE LA LANGUE.. / Baillairge, Charles – 1899?. 04355. (Pre-1900 Canadiana) – 9 – cn C.I.H.M. [450]

Grech Delicata, G C *see*
- FLORA MELITENSIS
- PLANTAE MELITAE LECTAE

Grech, N I *see* UCHEBNAIA KNIGA ROSSIISKOI SLOVESNOSTOSTI

Grechko, A M *see* ORGANIZATSIIA NARODNOGO KHOZIAISTVA I KOOPERATSIIA

Gredeskul', N A *see* ROSSIIA I EIA NARODY

Gredeskul, Nikolai Andreevich *see* NA TEMY DNIA

Gredler, P V *see* ZUR CONCHYLIEN-FAUNA VON CHINA

GREECE = ANNUAIRE STATISTIQUE DE LA GRECE 1930-1939 : STATISTIKE EPETERIS TES HELLADOS 1930-1939 / Greece. Ethnike Statisstike Hyperesia – (Coll title: European Official Statistical Serials, 1841-1984) – 63mf – 9 – £6.00f (set £630.00 100mf) – uk Chadwyck [949]

GREECE = STATISTIKE EPETERIS TES HELLADOS 1954-1965 : STATISTICAL YEARBOOK OF GREECE 1954-1965 / Greece. Ethnike Statisstike Hyperesia – (1954-56, 1965 not available. Coll title: European Official Statistical Serials, 1841-1984) – 37mf – 9 – £7.00f (set £630.00 100mf) – uk Chadwyck [949]

Greece *see*
- GREECE ON THE ROAD TO PROSPERITY THE PRELIMINARY FIVE YEAR PROGRAMME
- OEEC. GENERAL MEMORANDUM ON THE 1950/51 AND 1951/52 PROGRAMME
- OEEC. REPORT TO ECONOMIC COOPERATION ADMINISTRATION ON THE 1949/50 PROGRAMME, V. 2 – GREECE
- PRELIMINARY FIVE-YEAR PROGRAMME FOR ECONOMIC DEVELOPMENT OF GREECE (1959-1963)

GREECE, ANCIENT AND MODERN / Felton, Cornelius Conway – Lectures before the Lowell Institute. 7th ed. Boston: Houghton, Mifflin, 1886.2v in 1 – 1 – us U.W. Library [450]

GREECE AND BABYLON : A COMPARATIVE SKETCH OF MESOPOTAMIAN, ANATOLIAN AND HELLENIC RELIGIONS / Farnell, Lewis R – Edinburgh: T. & T. Clark, 1911 – 1mf – us A.T.L.A. [230]

GREECE AND THE GOLDEN HORN / Olin, Stephen – 1854 – 9 – us A.T.L.A. [240]

GREECE AND THE GREEKS OF THE PRESENT DAY / About, Edmond – New York: Dix, Edwards & Co., 1857. xvi,360p – 1 – us U.W. Library [949]

Greece. Center of Planning and Economic Development, Athens *see* DRAFT OF THE FIVE-YEAR ECONOMIC DEVELOPMENT PLAN (1966-1970)

GREECE DURING WORLD WAR 2 PAMPHLET COLLECTION – 1941 – 1 – CSUXANL2974-B – us Hoover Inst Photo [355]

Greece. Ethnike Statisstike Hyperesia *see* - GREECE

Greece. Greek Board of Reconstruction *see* PROGRAM OF RECONSTRUCTION

Greece. Ministere de la Coordination *see* MEMORANDUM SUR LE PROGRAMME DE DEVELOPPEMENT ECONOMIQUE DE LA GRECE

Greece. Ministry of Coordination *see*
- ECONOMIC DEVELOPMENT PLAN FOR GREECE, 1968-1972
- FIVE-YEAR PROGRAMME FOR THE ECONOMIC DEVELOPMENT OF GREECE, 1960-1964
- PRELIMINARY FIVE YEAR PROGRAMME FOR THE ECONOMIC DEVELOPMENT OF GREECE

Greece. Ministry of Economic Coordination *see* ECONOMIC DEVELOPMENT PLAN, 1968-1972

Greece, New York. Greece Baptist Church *see* RECORDS

GREECE ON THE ROAD TO PROSPERITY THE PRELIMINARY FIVE YEAR PROGRAMME / Greece – Athens. 1959 – 9 – ne IDC [338]

THE GREEK AND EASTERN CHURCHES / Adeney, Walter Frederic – (Includes bibliographical references and index) – New York: Charles Scribner, 1908 – 2mf – 9 – 0-8370-7600-5 – 1986-1600 – us A.T.L.A. [240]

A GREEK AND ENGLISH LEXICON TO THE NEW TESTAMENT. / Parkhurst, John – New ed., cor., enl., and improved. London, 1825. 712p – 1 – us U.W. Library [240]

GREEK CANADIAN TRAVEL NEWS – Montreal, jul 1963 – 1r – 1 – Can$25.00 – cn Can Microfilming [910]

THE GREEK CATHOLIC SOWER – [Joliet, IL: Pittsburgh Byzantine Diocesan Press. v1 n1-n7 mar-sep 1949; v2 n1-6 jan-jun 1950] – 1 – us Res Libr [240]

GREEK CATHOLIC UNION MESSENGER = VIESTNIK GREKO KAFT: SOJEDINENIJA – Homestead, PA: Greek Catholic Union, 1952-76, 1953-75 – 1 – us Res Libr [071]

THE GREEK CHRISTIAN POETS AND THE ENGLISH POETS / Browning, Elizabeth Barrett – London: Chapman and Hall, 1863 – 1 roll – 1 – 1-55879-837-4 – uk Libr Preservation [410]

GREEK CIVILIZATION AND CULTURE PAMPHLET COLLECTION – 1946 – 1 – CSUXANL5833-B – us Hoover Inst Photo [306]

GREEK COINS; POEMS...WITH MEMORABILIA BY FLOYD DELL, EDNA KENTON AND SUSAN GLASPELL / Cook, George Cram – New York, (c1925). 142p. With: The Royal Woman by H. Mann. 1 reel. 1297 – 1 – us U.W. Library [810]

GREEK FOLK SONGS FROM THE OTTOMAN PROVINCES OF NORTHERN HELLAS – 1888 – 1 – us I.U. Libraries [390]

THE GREEK GRAMMAR OF ROGER BACON AND A FRAGMENT OF HIS HEBREW GRAMMAR / Bacon, Roger; ed by Nolan, Edmond & Hirsch, Samuel Abraham – (In Latin, English and Greek. Includes index) – Cambridge: University Press, 1902 – 1mf – 9 – 0-8370-9682-0 – 1986-3682 – us A.T.L.A. [450]

GREEK LEARNING IN THE WESTERN CHURCH DURING THE SEVENTH AND EIGHTH CENTURIES, A.D. / Lumby, Joseph Rawson – Cambridge: [s.n.], 1878 (J. Palmer) – 1mf – us A.T.L.A. [240]

GREEK LEXICON OF THE ROMAN AND BYZANTINE PERIODS / Sophocles, Evangelinus Apostolides – 1900 – 9 – $39.00 – us I.R.C. [450]

GREEK LIFE AND THOUGHT; A PORTRAYAL OF GREEK CIVILIZATION / Van Hook, Larue – New York: Columbia University Press, 1923. xiv,329p. front., illus., plates, map – 1 – us U.W. Library [900]

THE GREEK LITURGIES : CHIEFLY FROM ORIGINAL AUTHORITIES / ed by Swainson, Charles Anthony – (With an appendix containing the Coptic ordinary canon of the Mass from 2 mss in the British Museum, ed & transl by C Bezold) – Cambridge: University Press, 1884 – 2mf – 9 – 0-8370-5839-2 – 1985-3839 – us A.T.L.A. [240]

GREEK MANUALS OF CHURCH DOCTRINE / Duckworth, H T F – London: Published for the Eastern Church Association [by] Rivingtons, 1901 – 1mf – us A.T.L.A. [240]

GREEK POLITICS AND GOVERNMENT PAMPHLET COLLECTION – 1946-1986 – 1 reel – 1 – CSUXANL6479-B – us Hoover Inst Photo [320]

GREEK POTTERY / Lane, Arthur – Faber & Faber. 1948 – 9 – $10.00 – us I.R.C. [930]

GREEK READER : CONSISTING OF SELECTIONS FROM XENOPHON, PLATO, HERODOTUS, AND THUCYDIDES: WITH NOTES ADAPTED TO GOODWIN'S GREEK GRAMMAR, PARALLEL REFERENCES TO CROSBY'S AND HADLEY'S GRAMMARS, AND COPPERPLATE MAPS / ed by Goodwin, William W & Allen, Joseph H – (Texts in Greek; notes in English) – rev ed. Boston: Ginn and Heath, 1877, c1871 – 1mf – 9 – 0-8370-9236-1 – 1986-3236 – us A.T.L.A. [450]

GREEK STUDIES : A SERIES OF ESSAYS / Pater, Walter – New York, London: Macmillan and Co., 1895 [c1894] – 1 roll – 1 – 1-55879-880-3 – uk Libr Preservation [450]

GREEK TESTAMENT LESSONS FOR COLLEGES, SCHOOLS, AND PRIVATE STUDENTS / Smith, John Hunter – Edinburgh: William Blackwood, 1884. 1 fiche – 9 – us A.T.L.A. [240]

THE GREEK TESTAMENT: WITH A CRITICALLY REVISED TEXT; A DIGEST OF VARIOUS READINGS: MARGINAL REFERENCES TO VERBAL AND IDIOMATIC USAGE: PROLEGOMENA: AND A CRITICAL AND EXEGETICAL COMMENTARY – By Henry Alford.London: Rivingtons, 1871-74. 4v. folding tab – 1 – us U.W. Library [240]

GREEK THOUGHT AND THE ORIGINS OF THE SCIENTIFIC SPIRIT / Robin, Leon – London: K. Paul, Trench, Trubner & Co; New York: A.A. Knopf, 1928. Trans. from the French by M.R. Dobie – xx/409p – 1 – us U.W. Library [180]

GREEK-ENGLISH WORD-LIST : CONTAINING ABOUT 1000 MOST COMMON GREEK WORDS: SO ARRANGED AS TO BE MOST EASILY LEARNED AND REMEMBERED / Baird, Robert – (Includes index) – Boston: Ginn, 1893 – 1mf – 9 – 0-8370-9202-7 – 1986-3202 – us A.T.L.A. [450]

GREEKS AND LATINS : BEING A FULL AND CONNECTED HISTORY OF THEIR DISSENSIONS AND OVERTURES FOR PEACE DOWN TO THE REFORMATION / Ffoulkes, Edmund S – Pt 2. London: Longmans, Green, 1867. (Christendom's divisions) – 2mf – us A.T.L.A. [240]

GREEKS IN AMERICA : AN ACCOUNT OF THEIR COMING, PROGRESS, CUSTOMS, LIVING, AND ASPIRATIONS: WITH AN HISTORICAL INTRODUCTION AND THE STORIES OF SOME FAMOUS AMERICAN-GREEKS / Burgess, Thomas – Boston: Sherman, French, 1913 – 1mf – us A.T.L.A. [305]

GREEKS IN CYPRUS PAMPHLET COLLECTION – 1974?-1980 – 1 reel – 1 – CSUXANR0380-B – us Hoover Inst Photo [949]

GREEKS LEXICON OF THE ROMAN AND BYZANTINE PERIODES (FROM B.C. 146 TO A.D. 1100) / Sophocles, Evangelinus Apostolides – Cambridge, 1914 – 21mf – 8 – ne Slangenburg [930]

Greeley, A W *see* THREE YEARS OF ARCTIC SERVICE

GREELEY CITIZEN – Greeley, NE. -w. Oct 1895-Nov 1898, scattered issues missing; July 1900-Feb 1919; Feb 1920 to date – 1 – us NE Hist [071]

GREELEY HERALD – Greeley, NE. -w. Dec 1883-Sept 1892 – 1 – us NE Hist [071]

Greeley, Horace *see*
- THE AMERICAN CONFLICT
- A HISTORY OF THE STRUGGLE FOR SLAVERY EXTENSION OR RESTRICTION IN THE UNITED STATES

GREELEY INDEPENDENT – Greeley, NE. -w. Nov 1886-Mar 1888 – 1 – us NE Hist [071]

Green, Arnold *see* OHIO SUPREME COURT PRACTICE; CONTAINING THE LAW, DECISIONS AND FORMS, WITH FULL DIRECTIONS FOR PROCEEDING IN MANDAMUS, QUO-WARRANTO, HABEAS CORPUS.

Green, Arthur George *see* A SYSTEMATIC SURVEY OF THE ORGANIC COLOURING MATTERS, FOUNDED ON THE GERMAN OF DR. G. SCHULTZ AND P. JULIUS

Green, Ashbel *see* THE LIFE OF ASHBEL GREEN, V.D.M.

THE GREEN BAG – (Index included) – v1-26. 1889-1914 (all publ) – 62mf – 9 – $279.00 – LLMC 82-925 – us L.L.M.C. [073]

GREEN BAYS : VERSES AND PARODIES / Quiller-Couch, Arthur Thomas – London: Methuen, 1893 – 1 roll – 1 – 1-55879-820-X – uk Libr Preservation [810]

THE GREEN BOOK OF THE BARDS / Carman, Bliss – Cambridge, Mass.: University Press, 1898. 00488. (Pre-1900 Canadiana) – 9 – cn C.I.H.M. [810]

GREEN BRIER BAPTIST CHURCH. CLAIBORNE COUNTY. MISSISSIPPI : CHURCH RECORDS – 1884-Jun 1902 – 1 – 5.09 – us Baptist [240]

Green, C P *see* A MIRROR OF HANNIBAL

Green, C R *see* LYNDON-"US" AND OUR NEIGHBORS

THE GREEN CURTAIN / Braddon, Mary Elizabeth – British Fiction Archive: Unit 5 – 9 – uk Bell [830]

Green, Duff *see* DUFF GREEN PAPERS

Green, E E *see* THE COCCIDAE OF CEYLON

Green, Edmund S *see*
- GREEN'S DIGEST OF ANNOTATED CASES
- GREEN'S DIGEST OF THE CASES IN THE AMERICAN STATE REPORTS

THE GREEN FLAG AND OTHER STORIES OF WAR AND SPORT / Doyle, Arthur Conan – London: Smith, Elder, 1900 – 1 roll – 1 – 1-55879-549-9 – uk Libr Preservation [830]

Green, Mrs. Frederic *see* STORY OF THE BEGINNING: GENESIS IN THE LIGHT OF RECENT RESEARCH

Green, Frederick *see* A BRIEF REVIEW OF CRIMINAL CASES IN THE SUPREME COURT FOR THE PAST YEAR

Green, H *see* THE MIRROUR OF MAIESTIE

GREEN HILL BAPTIST CHURCH. MOUNT JULIET, TENNESSEE : CHURCH RECORDS – 1900-Sep 1967 – 1 – 12.33 – us Baptist [240]

Green, J *see* AN APPEAL TO THE ORACLES OF GOD

Green, John P *see*
- JOHN P. GREEN PAPERS, MS 3379
- PAPERS

Green, Katharine R *see* ROBERT MORRISON, 1782-1934 (CCC250)

GREEN LANTERN – Issue Nos. 1-5 Fall 41-Fall 42 – 5mf – 15 – $31.95 – us Comics [760]

GREEN LANTERN – Issue Nos. 6-10 Winter 43-Winter 44 – 5mf – 15 – $31.95 – us Comics [760]

GREEN MOUNTAIN DAIRYING / Vermont. Agricultural Extension Service – v. 1-4. 1965-70 – 1,5,6 – us Spaulding [636]

GREEN MOUNTAIN GROWER / Vermont. Agricultural Extension Service – v. 1-48. 1963-69 – 1,5,6 – us Spaulding [636]

THE GREEN MOUNTAIN PATRIOT – Peacham. Vt. 1798-1807, 1809-1810 – 1,3 – us Readex [071]

Green, Nicholas John *see* CRIMINAL LAW REPORTS

Green, Oscar Olin *see* NORMAL EVANGELISM

GREEN PASTURES AND PICCADILLY / Black, William – British Fiction Archive: Unit 4 – 9 – uk Bell [830]

GREEN POND BAPTIST CHURCH. SPARTANBURG COUNTY. WOODRUFF, SOUTH CAROLINA : CHURCH RECORDS – 1804-1971 – 1 – 5.00 – us Baptist [240]

Green, R *see*
- ANTI-METHODIST PUBLICATIONS ISSUED DURING THE EIGHTEENTH CENTURY...
- THE WORKS OF JOHN AND CHARLES WESLEY

Green, Richard *see*
- THE MISSION OF METHODISM
- WESLEY BIBLIOGRAPHY

Green, Robert *see* "GOVERNOR FRED HALL, A STUDY OF A POLITICAL PERSONALITY"

GREEN ROOM – Sydney. v1-17. 1919-27 – 3r – 1 – us Ross [420]

Green, Samuel Gosnell *see*
- A BRIEF INTRODUCTION TO NEW TESTAMENT GREEK
- A HANDBOOK TO OLD TESTAMENT HEBREW

GREEN SHEET – Watsonville, CA. 1976-86 – 21r – 1 – $1,050.00 – R03084 – us Library Micro [071]

Green, T *see*
- A DISSERTATION ON ENTHUSIASM, SHEWING THE DANGER OF ITS LATE INCREASE AND THE GREAT MISCHIEFS IT HAS OCCASIONED, BOTH IN ANCIENT AND MODERN TIMES;...
- THE UNIVERSAL HERBAL

Green, Thomas Andre *see* COLORADO ADDENDUM TO GREEN'S PLEADING AND PRACTICE

Green, Thomas S *see* CRITICAL NOTES ON THE NEW TESTAMENT: SUPPLEMENTARY TO...GRAMMAR OF THE NEW TESTAMENT DIALECT

Green, William *see*
- A DIALOGUE BETWEEN THE PULPIT AND READING DESK
- PAPERS

Green, William Henry *see*
- THE ARGUMENT OF THE BOOK OF JOB UNFOLDED
- AN ELEMENTARY HEBREW GRAMMAR
- GENERAL INTRODUCTION TO THE OLD TESTAMENT
- A GRAMMAR OF THE HEBREW LANGUAGE
- A HEBREW CHRESTOMATHY, OR, LESSONS IN READING AND WRITING HEBREW
- HEBREW FEASTS IN THEIR RELATION TO...HYPOTHESES CONCERNING THE PENTATEUCH
- HIGHER CRITICISM OF THE PENTATEUCH
- MOSES AND THE PROPHETS: THE OLD TESTAMENT IN THE JEWISH CHURCH... REVIEWED
- OLD TESTAMENT CANON AND PHILOLOGY
- OLD TESTAMENT LITERATURE: LECTURES ON THE POETICAL BOOKS OF THE OLD TESTAMENT
- PROPHETS AND PROPHECY: A COMPILATION...OF THE LECTURES BEFORE THE SENIOR CLASS

Greenaway, Frank et al *see* TIME AND THE SCIENCES

Greenberg, Doreen L *see* THE EFFECT OF THE PARADOXICAL INTERVENTION OF SYMPTOM PRESCRIPTION ON STATE ANXIETY LEVELS AND PERFORMANCE IN YOUNG COMPETITIVE SWIMMERS

GREENBRIAR DISPATCH – East Rainelle. West Virginia. -w. 1946-66 – 1 – us UMI [071]

GREENBRIER FIRST BAPTIST CHURCH. GREENBRIER, TENNESSEE : CHURCH RECORDS – 1885-1973. Records. 1905-75 – 1 – 73.53 – us Baptist [240]

GREENBRIER INDEPENDENT – Lewisburg. West Virginia. 1932-1959; 1960-67 – 1 – us UMI [071]

GREENCASTLE PRESS – Greencastle, PA. -w 1889-1912 – 13 – $25.00r – us I.M.R. [071]

Greene, Carol *see* A PHYSIOLOGICAL PROFILE OF CHAMPION LEVEL FEMALE TRIATHLETES

GREENE COUNTY DEMOCRAT – Waynesburg, PA. -w 1889-1904; 1905-1912 – 13 – $25.00r – us I.M.R. [071]

Greene, Daniel *see* PUBLIC LAND STATUTES OF THE UNITED STATES

Greene, Daniel Crosby *see* DREISSIG JAHRE PROTESTANTISCHER MISSION IN JAPAN

Greene, E A *see* SAINTS AND THEIR SYMBOLS: A COMPANION IN THE CHURCHES AND PICTURE GALLERIES OF EUROPE

Greene, E L *see* LEAFLETS OF BOTANICAL OBSERVATION AND CRITICISM

Greene, Francis Vinton *see* SKETCHES OF ARMY LIFE IN RUSSIA

Greene, JG *see* TIFFANY'S TRANSCRIPT APPEALS

Greene, John Bulkley *see* MONUMENTS, LANDSCAPES

Greene, M *see* DEBORAH AND BARAK. AN ORATORIO FOR SOLO VOICES, CHORUS, AND ORCHESTRA

Greene, M Louise *see* THE DEVELOPMENT OF RELIGIOUS LIBERTY IN CONNECTICUT

Greene, Maine. Free Will Baptist Church *see* RECORDS

Greene, Nathanael *see*
- NATHANAEL GREENE PAPERS
- THE PAPERS OF GENERAL NATHANAEL GREENE

Greene, Nelson *see* HISTORY OF THE HUDSON RIVER VALLEY (RIVER OF DESTINY)

Greene, Nelson Lewis *see* AN HISTORICAL CHART OF GERMAN LITERATURE FOR USE IN SCHOOLS AND COLLEGES

Greene, Robert *see*
- CICERONIS AMOR: TULLIES LOVE
- THE HISTORY OF ORLANDO FURIOSO, 1594..

Greene, William B *see* MUTUAL BANKING

Greene, William Brenton *see* CHRISTIAN DOCTRINE

GREENE'S REPORTS – (A Pre-NRS title) – v1-4. 1847-54 (all publ) – 28mf – 9 – $42.00 – LLMC 94-006 – us L.L.M.C. [340]

Gregory, Saint, Bishop of Tours *see* HISTOIRE DES FRANCS, TEXTES DE MANUSCRITS DE CORBIE ET DE BRUXELLES

Gregory the Great *see* MORALIA

Gregory, Tom *see*
- HISTORY OF SOLANO AND NAPA COUNTIES, CALIFORNIA
- HISTORY OF SONOMA COUNTY

Grei, I *see* RABOCHII VOPROSI ZEMELNAIA REFORMA

Greif, Martin *see* SCHILLERS DEMETRIUS

GREIFSWALDER STUDIEN: THEOLOGISCHE ABHANDLUNGEN HERMANN CREMER / Oettlie, Sam – Guetersloh: C. Bertelsmann, 1895. 1 fiche – 9 – us A.T.L.A. [240]

Greig, Peter E *see* FLEURY MESPLET (1734-1794); THE FIRST FRENCH PRINTER IN THE DOMINION OF CANADA

Greiner, Leo *see*
- LENAU
- DAS TAGEBUCH

Greiner, Wilhelm *see* DIE ERSTEN BNOVELLEN OTTO LUDWIGS UND IHR VERHAELTNIS ZU LUDWIG TIECK

Greinz, Rudolf *see* HEINRICH HEINE UND DAS DEUTSCHE VOLKSLIED

GREKO-KAFTOLICESKE SOJEDINENIJE V SSA. KALENDAR' – 1912-1937, 1939-1943, 1945-1977 – 1 – us Res Libr [520]

Grekov, Mitrofan Borisovich *see* OPIS' DOKUMENTAL'NYKH MATERIALOV LICHNOGO FONDA NO. 1996

Grell, Guenther *see* WIJ BOUWEN ZEEDIJKEN

Grelling, Richard *see* GLEICHES RECHT

O GREMIO : ORGAO DE DIVULGACAO DO GREMIO ESTUDANTIL "PADRE ANDRE" – Rio Branco, Acre. 1 Ago 1964 – 1,5,6 – bl Biblioteca [072]

O GREMIO : ORGAO DO GREMIO FAMILIAR AMAZONENSE – Manaos, Amazonas. 1 Set 1909; 10 Jul 1910 – 1,5,6 – bl Biblioteca [072]

EL GREMIO DE PLATEROS EN LAS INDIAS OCCIDENTALES / Torre Revello, Jose – Buenos Aires, 1932; Madrid: Razon y Fe, 1933 – 1 – sp Bibl Santa Ana [972]

Gremio Oficial de Exportadores de Pimenton *see* EL PIMENTON DE LA VERA EN SU COCINA

Grenada *see*
- ECONOMIC SURVEY AND DEVELOPMENT PLAN
- FIVE-YEAR DEVELOPMENT PLAN
- FIVE-YEAR DEVELOPMENT PLAN 1967-1971
- GRENADA GOVERNMENT GAZETTE

GRENADA: 1860-1938 – Oct 1991, M.A.P. East Ardsley, west yorks – 16r – 1 – uk Microform Academic [972]

GRENADA GOVERNMENT GAZETTE / Grenada – Saint George. 1957-1968- – 1 – us NY Public [972]

Grenada. Ministry of Education *see* EDUCATIONAL DIRECTORY AND BASIC EDUCATIONAL STATISTICS 1969/70-1978/79

Grenada, Mississippi *see* MISCELLANEOUS EARLY NEWSPAPERS

THE GRENADIAN VOICE – St. Georg's, Grenada. June 13 1981-1991 – 6r – 1 – us L of C Photodup [072]

Grenand, F *see*
- L'ART ET LES TECHNIQUES CULINAIRES DES INDIENS WAYAPI DE GUYANE FRANCAISE
- LE MANIOC CHEZ LES INDIENS WAYANA ET WAYAPI DE GUYANE FRANCAISE ET DU BRESIL

Grenand, P *see* LES RELATIONS INTERTRIBALES EN HAUTE-GUYANE DU XVIIIEME SIECLE A NOS JOURS

GRENFELL RECORD – May 29 1875-Dec 22 1877; Jan 1 1898-Dec 21 1939 – 9 – at Pascoe [072]

Grenfell, W T *see* LABRADOR: THE COUNTRY AND THE PEOPLE

Grenier, A *see* CATALOGUE DES COLEOPTERES DE FRANCE

Grenier, Henry Napoleon *see* LECONS DE PHOTOGRAPHIE

Grenier, J C M *see* MONOGRAPHIA DE CERASTIO

Grenier, WA *see* LA SCIENCE DE LA RECLAME

GRENIER'S RUBBER NEWS – Kuala Lumpur. Malaysia. -w. Oct 1909-Sep 1918, Jan 1919-Jun 1920. (9 reels) – 1 – uk British Libr Newspaper [073]

GRENNA TIDNING – Granna, Sweden. 1857-1964 – 1 – sw Kungliga [072]

GRENNAPOSTEN – Graenna, 1992, 1993 – 9 – sw Kungliga [072]

Grenon, P *see* DOCUMENTOS HISTORICOS COLECCIONADOS PO...SECCION GEOGRAFIA...

GRENVILLE ADVOCATE – (Incomplete) – 1862-1874 – 1mf – 9 – at Corangamite [980]

GRENVILLE SHIRE COUNCIL MINUTES – (1872-99 Lost) – 1963-1940 – 3mf – 9 – at Corangamite [350]

GRENZBOTE – Bratislava, Czechoslovakia. May-Jul 1941; Nov 1943-Mar 1945 – 5r – 1 – us L of C Photodup [072]

GRENZ-ECHO – Eupen, Belgium. 1972- – 1 – gw Mikrofilm [949]

GRENZEN DER DEUTSCHEN GEBIETSHOHEIT... / Badenhoop, W – Gelnhausen, 1934 – 1mf – 9 – ILM-1689/1 – ne IDC [340]

GRENZLAND / Deutschen Schulvereines Sua5dmark – Vienna, Graz. Published until May 1925 as Sua5dmark Bundeszeitung. Superseded by Volkstum in Sua5d-Osten, Jan. 1939. 1924-1938. Missing: July 1925; Aug.-Dec. 1928 – 1 – 35.00r – us Hoover Inst Photo [073]

GRENZLAND – Saarbruecken. dec 1934. suite de: WESTLAND voir a ce titre – 1 – fr A.C.R.P.P. [073]

GRENZLAND *see* WESTLAND

GRENZLAND-BOTE : WYRZYSKER ZEITUNG – Wyrzysk (Wirsitz), Poland. 19 Jan-23 Apr 1932; 2 May 1935-29 Jun 1939 – 2r – 1 – gw Mikrofilm [943]

GRENZLAND-ZEITUNG – Grottau (Hradek nad Nisou), Czechoslovakia. 4 Jan 1929/30 31 Dec 1937 – 4r – 1 – gw Mikrofilm [072]

Grenzmann, Wilhelm *see* DIE JUNGFRAU VON ORLEANS IN DER DICHTUNG

DER GRENZMARK-RAPPE : GRENZMAERKISCHE SAGEN, ERZAEHLUNGEN, BALLADEN UND GEDICHTE / Menzel, Herybert – Hamburg: Hanseatische Verlagsanstalt, 1933 – 1r – 1 – us U.W. Library [800]

GRENZPOLIZIST – Berlin, 1956, jan 6 1961 – 1 – Dist. gw Mikrofilm – gw Misc Inst [350]

GRENZPOST – Zwittau (Svitavy), Czechoslovakia. 17 Aug 1929-1938 – 4r – 1 – gw Mikrofilm [072]

GRENZWACHT – Osijek, Yugoslavia. 1942-43 – 1r – 1 – us L of C Photodup [949]

GRENZWARTE – Bocholt. 1927. jan 3-mar 30, 1929. feb 25, 1930-apr 29, 1931. apr 1-jun 30, 1932. 1933-feb 9, 1934 – 7r – 1 – gw Mikrofilm [072]

GRESHAM GAZETTE – Gresham, NE. -w. May 1896-Jul 1907, scattered issues missing; Mar 1908 to date – 1 – us NE Hist [071]

Gresham, J *see* HISTORICAL AND BIOGRAPHICAL RECORD OF DOUGLAS COUNTY

GRESHAM OUTLOOK – Gresham, OR. 1913 – 1 – 24.00 – us Oregon Hist [071]

GRESHAM OUTLOOK – Gresham, OR. -w,-sw. 3 Mar 1911-. – 1 – us U.O. Library [071]

Gresham Publishing Co *see* HISTORY AND BIOGRAPHY OF WASHINGTON COUNTY AND THE TOWN OF QUEENSBURY

Gresham, William G *see* HISTORY OF NICOLLET AND LE SUEUR COUNTIES

Gresley, J -E Le *see* BIBLIOGRAPHIE ANALYTIQUE DE MONSIEUR ALPHONSE DESILETS

Gresset, J -B *see* DISCOURS SUR L'HARMONIE

Gressmann, H *see*
- NONNENSPIEGEL UND MOENCHSSPIEGEL DES EUAGRIOS PONTIKOS (T.U.U. 3-39/4B)
- STUDIEN ZU EUSEBS THEOPHANIE (T.U.U. 2-23/3)

Gressmann, Hugo *see* UEBER DIE IN JESUS CHRIST 56-66 VORAUSGESETZTEN ZEITGESCHICHTLICHEN VERHAELTNISSE

Greswell, William Henry Parr *see* OUR SOUTH AFRICAN EMPIRE

GRETA AND BRANXTON GAZETTE – Jan 3 1891-Jun 25 1892 – 9 – at Pascoe [072]

GRETE HERBALL – The grete herball whiche geueth parfyt knowlege and vnderstandyng of all maner of herbes & there gracyous vertues...London, 1526 – 1 – us U.W. Library [631]

Grethenbach, Constantine *see* SECULAR VIEW OF THE BIBLE

GRETNA BREEZE – Gretna, NE. -w. Jun 1899-Dec 1935; Jan 1938 to date – 1 – us NE Hist [071]

GRETNA GUIDE AND NEWS – Gretna, NE. -w. Jan 1964 to date – 1 – us NE Hist [071]

Gretre *see* MEMOIRE SUR L'ETAT DU DEPARTEMENT DE L'INDRE

Gretry *see* ELISCA OU L'AMOUR MATERNEL

Gretry, A *see* OUVERTURE DE LA CARAVANE. ARRANGEE POUR LE CLAVECIN OU LE FORTEPIANO AVEC VIOLON AD LIB PAR M. CESAR...

Gretry, Andre E M *see*
- COLLECTION COMPLETE DES OEUVRES DE GRETRY PUBLIEE PAR LE GOUVERNEMENT BELGE
- MEMOIRES OU ESSAIS SUR LA MUSIQUE
- MEMOIRES OU ESSAIS SUR LA MUSIQUE..

Gretser, J *see* DE OFFICIIS MAGNAE ECCLESIAE ET AULAE CONSTANTINOPO-LITANAE (CBH 18)

Gretton, R *see* AGRICULTURAL COOPERATIVE MARKETING

GREUEL IN SPANIEN. LA TERREUR EN ESPAGNE – Olten, 1936? Fiche W930. (Blodgett Collection of Spanish Civil War Pamphlets) – 9 – us H.U. College Libr [946]

Greulich, Oskar *see* PLATENS LITTERATUR-KOMOEDIEN

LA GREVE DES MACHINES / Seuhl, Antonin – Paris. 1924. (La condition Ouvriere. Part Two.) – 9 – 7.50 – fr Bibl Nationale [360]

GREVE GENERALE – London, UK. 18 Mar-2 Jun 1902 – 1 – uk British Libr Newspaper [072]

LA GREVE GENERALE / Congres National des Chambres Syndicales et Groupes Corporatifs – Organe du Comite d'organisation de la greve generale. 2e annee, no. 1-7. Paris. 13 janv 18 mars 1894; 3e annee, no. 1-14. mars 1899-sept 1900. mq no. 3, 9, 11 – 1 – fr A.C.R.P.P. [331]

Greve, H E *see* DE BRONNEN VAN CAREL VAN MANDER VOOR "HET LEVEN DER DOORLUCHTIGHE NEDERLANDTSCHE EN HOOGDUYTSCHE SCHILDERS"

Greven, Joseph *see* DIE ANFAENGE DER BEGINEN

GREVES DE FLOTTEURS SUR L'YONNE AUX 18E ET 19E SIECLES / Cornu, Paul – Nevers. 1911. (La Condition Ouvriere. Part Two.) – 9 – 2.50 – fr Bibl Nationale [360]

LES GREVES ET LA LOI SUR LES COALITIONS / Barberet, J – (Condition of 19th C. French working class series). 1873 – 9 – fr Hachette [331]

GREVILLAE : A QUARTERLY RECORD OF CRYPTOGAMIC BOTANY AND ITS LITERATURE – London, 1872/1873-1894. v1-22 – 74mf – 9 – 93/2 – ne IDC [580]

Greville, R K *see*
- ALGAE BRITANNICAE
- FLORA EDIENSIS
- FLORA EDINENSIS
- ICONES FILICUM
- SCOTTISH CRYPTOGAMIC FLORA
- TENTAMEN METHODI MUSCORUM

Grevinchovius, Casp *see* GRONDELIJE BERICHT VANDEN DOOPE ENDE WEDERDOOPE

Grew, N *see*
- THE ANATOMY OF PLANTS
- THE ANATOMY OF VEGETABLES BEGUN
- A DISCOURSE
- EXPERIMENTS
- MUSAEUM

THE GREY BOOKS INDEX : RIBA MEMBERS' WORK ILLUSTRATED IN ARCHITECTURAL PERIODICALS 1900-1974 / Royal Institute of British Architects – (Pt A: Index to members' work in periodicals 1900-19 fiches 1-12. Pt B: Index to members' work in periodicals 1920-74 fiches 13-269. With printed guide) – 2pts 269mf – 9 – £1,300.00 – uk World [720]

THE GREY PAPERS – Some papers of the Grey Family of Howick – 1 – uk Microform Academic [025]

Grey, Standish *see*
- THE GOSPEL ACCORDING TO SATAN
- GOSPEL ACCORDING TO SATAN

Grey, W *see* CATALOGUS INSECTARUM

THE GREY WOMAN : AND OTHER TALES / Gaskell, Elizabeth Cleghorn – London: Smith, Elder, 1865 – 1 roll – 1 – 1-55879-695-9 – uk Libr Preservation [830]

Grey, Z *see* THE QUAKER AND METHODIST COMPARED IN AN ABSTRACT OF GEORGE FOX'S JOURNAL,...

Grey, Zachary *see* A SERIOUS ADDRESS TO LAY METHODISTS TO BEWARE OF THE FALSE PRETENCES OF THEIR TEACHERS;...

Greyerz, O von *see* BLUMENLESE AUS DEN SAEMMTLICHEN WERKEN VON JOHANN RUDOLF WYSS DEM JUENGERN

Greyffenberger, H *see*
- EINE CHRISTENLICHE ANTWORDT DENEN
- DISZ BIECHLIN ZAIGT AN DIE FALSCHEN PROPHETEN
- EIN KURTZER BEGRIFF VON GUTEN WERCKEN
- EIN WARNUNG VOR DEM TEUEFFEL

GREYHOUND – Worcester, MA. v4 n1. 1 dec 1941-v4 n4. 9 mai 1942 – 1r – 1 – Can$25.00 – cn Can Microfilming [071]

GREYTOWN GAZETTE – Greytown, South Africa. 1903-88 – 1 – sa State Libr [072]

GREZA – Khudozhestvenno-literaturnyi zhurnal. v. 1-12. Spb. 1907. B-1734 2 – 8 – ne IDC [073]

GRI ADUSHCHAI A ROSSII A = DAS ZUKUNFTIGE RUSSLAND – (Includes c.1: 1921:Sept.29-Oct.13, Dec.15) – Berlin: Evgeni i Efimovski i, 19uu – 1 – CSUXANR4698-S – us Hoover Inst Photo [947]

GRI ADUSHCHAI A ROSSII A (BERLIN, GERMANY) *see* GRI ADUSHCHAI A ROSSII A

GRIADUSHCHII KHAM / Merezhkovskii, Dimitrii – Spb. 1906. BR-765 2 – 8 – ne IDC [460]

Griaule, M *see*
- MASQUES DOGONS
- NOTES DE TERRAIN, DOGON, OGOTEMMELI

Griaznov, M P *see* ISTORIIA DREVNIKH PLEMEN VERKHENI OBI PO RASKOPKAM BLIZ S. BOL'SHAIA RECHKA

Gribanovskii, N N *see* BIBLIOGRAFIIA IAKUTII

Gribble, Cecil F *see* COLLECTION OF PAMPHLETS RELATING TO THE METHODIST CHURCH IN FIJI, 1878-1970

Gribble, Francis Henry *see* THE COMEDY OF CATHERINE THE GREAT

Gribble, J D B *see* A MANUAL OF THE DISTRICT OF CUDDAPAH IN THE PRESIDENCY OF MADRAS

Gribetz, L J *see* THE CASE FOR THE JEWS

Gribovskii, Viacheslav Mikhailovich *see* MATER IALY DLIA ISTORII VYSSHAGO SUDA I NADZORA V PERVUIU POLOVINU..

THE GRIDIRON : HUMORISTIQUE – Quebec, Canada. v1 n12. 8 oct 1859 – 1r – 1 – Can$25.00 – cn Can Microfilming [073]

GRIDLEY HERALD – Gridley, CA. 1880-85; 1888-92; 1902- – 65+ r – 1 – $3,250.00 ($50.00y) – B02281 – us Library Micro [071]

IL GRIDO DEL POPOLO – Denver, Colorado Springs, Colorado. 1907-1910 – us I.H.R.C. [071]

IL GRIDO DELLA FOLLA – Milano, Italy, May 20, 1905 – 3r – 1 – us I.H.R.C. [945]

IL GRIDO DELLA FOLLA – New York, 1916 (May 20-June 15) – 2mf or 1r – 1,9 – us I.H.R.C. [978]

GRIECHENTUM UND CHRISTENTUM : ZWOELF HIBBERTVORLESUNGEN UEBER DEN EINFLUSS GRIECHISCHER IDEEN UND GEBRAEUCHE AUF DIE CHRISTLICHE KIRCHE / Hatch, Edwin – Freiburg i.B.: J.C.B. Mohr, 1892 – 1mf – us A.T.L.A. [240]

GRIECHISCH-BYZANTINISCHE GESPRAECHSBUECHER UND VERWANDTES AUS SAMMELHANDSCHRIFTEN / ed by Heinrici, Carl Friedrich Georg – Leipzig: B.G. Teubner, 1911. (Abhandlungen der Koeniglich Saechsischen Gesellschaft der Wissenschaften; 60. Bd., [no. 8]) (Des XXVIII. Bandes der Abhandlungen der philologisch-historischen Klasse der Koenigl. Saechsischen Gesellschaft der Wissenschaften; no. 8) – 1mf – us A.T.L.A. [450]

GRIECHISCHE CHRISTLICHE SCHRIFTSTELLER DER ERSTEN DREI JAHRHUNDERTE – Leipzig. v1-40. 1897-1935 – 390mf – ne IDC [450]

GRIECHISCHE DENKER / Gomperz, T – (Leipzig, 1896.-1st Bd.-10mf; Leipzig, 1902.-2nd Bd.-13mf; Leipzig, 1909.-3rd Bd.-10mf) – 8 – ne Slangenburg [180]

GRIECHISCHE EXCERPTE AUS HOMILIEN DES ORIGENES (T.U.U. 1-12/3B) / Klostermann, Erich – Leipzig, 1894 – 1mf – 9 – ne Slangenburg [240]

GRIECHISCHE GESCHICHTE VON IHREM URSPRUNGE BIS ZUM UNTERGANGE DER SELBSTAENDIGKEIT DES GRIECHISCHEN VOLKES / Holm, Adolf – Berlin, S. Calvary & co., 1886-94. 4 v. (Calvary's philologische u. archaeologische Bibliothek, 81-85, 89-99, 107-114, i.). Film Mas 9111 – 1 – us H.U. Library [930]

GRIECHISCHE MYTHOLOGIE / Preller, Ludwig – 4th ed. ed by Carl Robert. Berlin: Weidmann, 1894-1926.2v in 3 – 1 – us U.W. Library [250]

GRIECHISCHE SCHULGRAMMATIK : AUF GRUND DER ERGEBNISSE DER VERGLEICHENDEN SPRACHFORSCHUNG / Koch, Ernst – (Includes glossary and index) – 8. Aufl. Leipzig: B G Teubner, 1881 – 1mf – 9 – 0-8370-9253-1 – 1986-3253 – us A.T.L.A. [450]

GRIECHISCHE SCHULGRAMMATIK / Curtius, Georg – (Includes indexes) – 5. Aufl. Prag: F Tempsky, 1862 – 1mf – 9 – 0-8370-9219-1 – 1986-3219 – us A.T.L.A. [450]

DIE GRIECHISCHE SPRACHE IM ZEITALTER DES HELLENISMUS : BEITRAEGE ZUR GESCHICHTE UND BEURTEILUNG DER KOINE / Thumb, Albert – (Includes bibliographical references and indexes) – Strassburg: Karl J Truebner, 1901 – 1mf – 9 – 0-8370-9317-1 – 1986-3317 – us A.T.L.A. [450]

DIE GRIECHISCHE UEBERSETZUNG DER VIRI INLUSTRES DES HIERONYMUS (T.U.U. 1-13/3) / Wentzel, G – Leipzig, 1895 – 1mf – 9 – ne Slangenburg [240]

DIE GRIECHISCHE UEBERSETZUNG DES APOLOGETICUS TERTULLIAN'S (T.U.U. 1-8/4A) / Harnack, Adolf von – Leipzig, 1892 – 1mf – 9 – ne Slangenburg [240]

EINE GRIECHISCHE UEBERSETZUNG DES ITALIENISCHEN APOKALYPSENKOMMENTARS VON FEDERIGO DA VENEZIA O.P. (T.U.U. 4-48/2) / Stadtmueller, G – Leipzig, 1936 – 1mf – 9 – ne Slangenburg [240]

GRIECHISCHE UND LATEINISCHE LEHNWOERTER IM TALMUD, MIDRASCH UND TARGUM / Krauss, S – Berlin 2 Teile 1898-99 – 18mf – 8 – ne Slangenburg [270]

GRIECHISCHE UND LATEINISCHE LEHNWOERTER IM TALMUD, MIDRASCH UND TARGUM / Krauss, S – Berlin. 2v. 1898–1899 – 14mf – ne IDC [450]

GRIECHISCHE ZAUBERPAPYRI UND DAS GEMEINDE- UND DANKGEBET IM 1. KLEMENSBRIEFE (T.U.U. 3-34/2B) / Schermann, Theodor – Leipzig, 1909 – 2mf – 9 – ne Slangenburg [240]

GRIECHISCHE-KULTURGESCHICHTE / Burckhardt, Jakob – hrsg. von Jakob Oeri. Berlin 1898-1902. 4 v. Bd. 1-2 are 3.Aufl. Film Mas 9023 – 1 – us H.U. Library [930]

DIE GRIECHISCHEN CHRISTLICHEN SCHRIFTSTELLER DER ERSTEN JAHRHUNDERTE – (Individual titles not listed. Please apply to publisher for a complete list) – 547mf – 8 – ne Slangenburg [240]

DIE GRIECHISCHEN HANDSCHRIFTEN DES NEUEN TESTAMENTS / Gregory, Caspar Rene – Leipzig: J C Hinrichs, 1908 – 1mf – 9 – 0-8370-3386-1 – 1985-1386 – us A.T.L.A. [220]

DIE GRIECHISCHEN HANDSCHRIFTEN DES NEUEN TESTAMENTS IN DER UDSSR (T.U.U. 5-91) / Treu, K – Berlin, 1966 – 7mf – 9 – ne Slangenburg [220]

DIE GRIECHISCHEN SCHREIBER DES MITTELALTERS UND DER RENAISSANCE / Vogel, M & Gardthausen, V – Leipzig, 1909 – 9mf – 8 – ne Slangenburg [450]

GRIECHISCHES ERBE; DAS URBILD DER ANTIKE IM WIDERSCHEIN DES HEUTIGEN LEBENS / Klatt, Fritz – Berlin: W. de Gruyter & Co., 1943. 100p. 20 pl. 1 reel. 1293 – 1 – us U.W. Library [900]

Grieg, E *see*
- AN DEN FRUHLING, OP. 43, NO. 6
- PEER GYNT NO. 1, OP. 46

Grierson, G A *see*
- LINGUISTIC SURVEY OF INDIA
- THE PISACA LANGUAGES OF NORTH WESTERN INDIA

GRIESBACH'S NEW TESTAMENT / Buckminster, Joseph Stevens – (The Monthly Anthology and Boston Review, v. 10, Feb., June, 1811, p. 107-114, 403-421) – 9 – us A.T.L.A. [240]

Griese, Friedrich *see*
- FRITZ REUTER
- DER HEIMLICHE KOENIG
- DAS KIND DES TORFMACHERS
- MEIN LEBEN
- MENSCH AUS ERDE GEMACHT
- DER RUF DES SCHICKSALS

Griesheimer, Friedrich *see* VERGLEICH DEUTSCHER SONDERSTRAFNORMEN MIT DEN ENTSPRECHENDEN OESTERREICHISCHEN BESTIMMUNGEN

Grießhaber, Christoph *see* EUROPAFAEHIGKEIT DER SCHWEIZERISCHEN ALTERS- UND HINTERLASSENENVERSICHERUNG (AHV) MIT BLICK AUF EINEN BEITRITT ZUR EUROPAEISCHEN UNION

DER GRIFF INS ALL : ANEKDOTEN UND KURZE GESCHICHTEN / Lerbs, Karl – Berlin: T Knaur, 1943 – 1r – 1 – us U.W. Library [830]

LA GRIFFE – Montreal, Canada. numero souvenir: 24 aut 1931 – 1r – 1 – Can$25.00 – cn Can Microfilming [072]

GRIFFIN BAPTIST CHURCH. PICKENS COUNTY. SOUTH CAROLINA : CHURCH RECORDS – 1857-1972 – 1 – 46.22 – us Baptist [240]

Griffin, G *see* CONCERTO (NO 1) FOR PIANOFORTE, OP. 1

Griffin, Gilderoy Wells *see* NEW SOUTH WALES: HER COMMERCE AND RESOURCES

Griffin, H J *see*
- ANCIENT HEBREW AND SOLOMONIC BUILDING CONSTRUCTION
- A COMPARATIVE HISTORY OF METROLOGY

Griffin, Levi Thomas *see*
- CASES ON PERSONAL PROPERTY.
- SPRAGUE'S ILLUSTRATIVE CASES ON PERSONAL PROPERTY

Griffin, Lisa M *see* AN EXAMINATION OF THE RELATIONSHIP BETWEEN TEACHER ENTHUSIASM AND ALT-PE

Griffing, James Sayre *see*
- PAPERS

Griffini, A *see*
- IMENOTTERI, NEUROTTERI, PSEUDO-NEUROTTERI, ORTOTTERI ET RINCHOTI ITALIANI
- LEPIDOTTERI ITALIANI

Griffis, William Elliot *see*
- AMERICAN IN THE EAST
- LILY AMONG THE THORNS: A STUDY OF THE BIBLICAL DRAMA ENTITLED THE SONG OF SONGS
- THE LILY AMONG THORNS
- A MAKER OF THE NEW ORIENT
- VERBECK OF JAPAN

Griffis, William Elliott *see* DUX CHRISTUS

Griffith, Coleman R *see*
- PSYCHOLOGY AND ATHLETICS
- THE PSYCHOLOGY OF COACHING

Griffith, D W *see* D.W. GRIFFITH PAPERS

Griffith, F L *see* HIERATIC PAPYRI FROM KAHU AND GUROB

Griffith, Fl *see* EL BERESH, PART 2

Griffith, FL *see* BENI-HASAN, 4: ZOOLOGICAL AND OTHER DETAILS

Griffith, FL L *see* STORIES OF THE HIGH PRIESTS OF MEMPHIS

GRIFFITH GAUNT / Reade, Charles L – British Fiction Archive: Unit 2 – 9 – uk Bell [830]

Griffith, Joseph B *see* CAUSAL ATTRIBUTIONS AND TASK PERSISTENCE OF LEARNED-HELPLESS AND MASTERY-ORIENTED SIXTH GRADERS IN MATH, PHYSICAL EDUCATION, AND READING

Griffith, Thomas *see* FUNDAMENTALS, OR, BASES OF BELIEF CONCERNING MAN, GOD, AND THE CORRELATION OF GOD AND MEN

Griffith, W *see*
- ICONES PLANTARUM ASIATICARUM
- INTERNATIONAL LAW:...
- ITINERARY NOTES OF PLANTS
- MUSCOLOGIA ITINERIS ASSAMICI
- NOTULAE AD PLANTAS ASIATICAS
- ON THE HIGHER CRYPTOGAMOUS PLANTS

Griffith, William *see* A TREATISE ON THE JURISDICTION AND PROCEEDINGS OF JUSTICES OF THE PEACE IN CIVIL SUITS

Griffith, William Brandford *see* A DIGEST OF AND INDEX TO THE REPORTS OF CASES DECIDED IN THE SUPREME COURT OF THE GOLD COAST COLONY. 1844-1931

Griffith, William Herbert *see* THE EFFECTS OF COUPLE COMMUNICATION TRAINING ON MARITAL PERCEPTIONS

Griffith-Jones, E *see* FAITH AND VERIFICATION, WITH OTHER STUDIES IN CHRISTIAN THOUGHT AND LIFE

Griffith-Jones, Ebenezer *see*
- THE CHALLENGE OF CHRISTIANITY TO A WORLD AT WAR
- ECONOMICS OF JESUS, OR, WORK AND WAGES IN THE KINGDOM OF GOD

Griffiths, Anselm John *see* OBSERVATIONS ON SOME POINTS OF SEAMANSHIP, WITH PRATICAL HINTS ON NAVAL ECONOMY

Griffiths, E *see* THE SCHOOL FOR RAKES, A COMEDY

Griffiths, Frederick A *see* NOTES ON MILITARY LAW

GRIFFITH'S VALUATION : GENERAL VALUATION OF RATEABLE PROPERTY IN IRELAND 1846-1880 – (373mf without index; index consists of 89mf) – 462f – Ir£600.00 Ir£700.00 complete with index – ie Microforms [650]

Grigg, H B *see* A MANUAL OF THE NILGIRI DISTRICT IN THE PRESIDENCY OF MADRAS

Grignon, C-Henri *see* EN AVANT

Grignon, J-J *see* LE BULLETIN

Grignon, Joseph-Jerome *see*
- LE LUXE DE NOTRE EPOQUE
- LE VIEUX TEMPS

Grignon, Wilfrid *see* CONFERENCE DU DR. GRIGNON: LE FONCTIONNEMENT DES SOCIETES D'AGRICULTURE PAR LES CERCLES AGRICOLES

Grigorev, Rafail *see* OTRAZHENIIA RUSSKOI REVOLIUTSII NA ZAPADIE

Grigorian, R *see* VLADIMIR MAIAKOVSKII

Grigor'iants, T S *see* ODNODNEVNYE GAZETY SSSR 1917-1983

GRIGORII NIKOLAEVICH GENNADI / Ivask, U G – (Obzor zhizni i trudov). M. 1913. BR-5906 2 – 8 – ne IDC [920]

GRIGORII RASPUTIN : IZ ZAPISOK / Beletskii, S P – Petrograd, 1923 – 1 – $35.00r – us Hoover Inst Photo [920]

Grigsby, James Edward *see* THE CRIMINAL LAW, INCLUDING THE FEDERAL PENAL CODE.

GRIHYA A SUTRA OF A'S'VALA'YANA – Calcutta. 1869. BI-498 2 – 8 – ne IDC [280]

THE GRIHYA-SUTRAS, RULES OF VEDIC DOMESTIC CEREMONIES : PART 1: SANKHAYANA, ASVALAYANA, PARASKARA, KHADIRA / ed by Mueller, Friedrich Max – (Translated by Hermann Oldenberg) – 1886 – 8mf – 8 – ne Slangenburg [280]

THE GRIHYA-SUTRAS, RULES OF VEDIC DOMESTIC CEREMONIES : PART 2: GOBHILA, HIRANYAKESIN, APASTAMBA / ed by Mueller, Friedrich Max – (Translated by Hermann Oldenberg. Apastamba, Yagna-paribhasha-sutras. Translated by F. Max Mueller) – 1892 – 7mf – 8 – ne Slangenburg [280]

Grill, Julius *see*
- DER ACHTUNDSECHZIGSTE PSALM:...UND NEUEREN AUSLEGER
- DIE PERSISCHE MYSTERIENRELIGION IM ROEMISCHEN REICHE UND DAS CHRISTENTUM

DIE GRILLE, 1811-1812 / ed by Kotzebue, August von – 1811-12 (mf ed 1997) – 7mf – 9 – DM220.00 – 3-89131-233-4 – gw Fischer [305]

GRILLPARZER / Hohlbau, Robert – Stuttgart: J G Cotta, 1938 – 1r – 1 – us U.W. Library [430]

GRILLPARZER ALS ARCHIVDIRECTOR / Wolf, Gerson – Wien: Winter, 1874 – 1r – 1 – us U.W. Library [920]

GRILLPARZER, DER TRAGIKER DER SCHULD / Sprengler, Joseph – Lorch: A Buerger, 1947 – 1r – 1 – us U.W. Library [430]

Grillparzer, Franz *see*
- DIE AHNFRAU
- EURIPIDES MEDEA UND DAS GOLDENE VLIESS VON GRILLPARZER
- DAS GOLDENE VLIES
- KOENIG OTTOKARS GLUECK UND ENDE
- DES MEERES UND DER LIEBE WELLEN
- SAPPHO
- EL SUENO ES VIDA

GRILLPARZER UND DIE WISSENSCHAFT : DREI VORTRAEGE / Redlich, Oswald – (Includes bibliographical references) – Wien: A Hartleben, [1925?] – 1r – 1 – us U.W. Library [500]

GRILLPARZER UND SCHOPENHAUER / Geissler, Horst Wolfram – (Includes bibliographical references) – [S.l.: s.n.] 1915 (Weimar: G Uschmann) – 1r – 1 – us U.W. Library [943]

GRILLPARZER UND SEINE WERKE / Paoli, Betty – Stuttgart: J G Cotta, 1875 – 1r – 1 – us U.W. Library [430]

GRILLPARZER UNTER GOETHE'S EINFLUSS / Waniek, Gustav – (Includes bibliographical references) – Bielitz: Im Verlage des k. k. Staats-Obergymnasiums, 1893 – 1r – 1 – us U.W. Library [430]

GRILLPARZERS "AHNFRAU" UND DIE SCHICKSALSIDEE / Terlitza, Victor – Bielitz: Verlag der k. k. Staats-Oberrealschule, 1883 – 1r – 1 – us U.W. Library [430]

GRILLPARZERS "AHNFRAU" UND DIE WIENER VOLKSDRAMATIK / Mueller, Curt – (Includes bibliographical references) – Leipzig: E Wiegandt, 1911 – 1r – 1 – us U.W. Library [430]

GRILLPARZERS KUNSTPHILOSOPHIE / Reich, Emil – Wien: Manz, 1890 – 1r – 1 – us U.W. Library [700]

GRILLPARZERS LYRIK ALS AUSDRUCK SEINES WESENS / Zausmer, Otto – (Includes bibliographical references) – Wien, Leipzig: Deutscher Verlag fuer Jugend und Volk, c1933 – 1r – 1 – us U.W. Library [430]

GRILLPARZERS MENSCHENAUFFASSUNG / Mueller, Joachim – Weimar: H Boehlau, 1934 – 1r – us U.W. Library [430]

GRILLPARZERS VERHAELTNIS ZU SHAKESPEARE / Braun, Hanns – (Includes bibliographical references) – [S.l: s.n.] 1916 (Nuernberg: Gedruckt bei H Lotter) – 1r – 1 – us U.W. Library [410]

GRILLPARZERS VERHAELTNIS ZUR POLITIK SEINER ZEIT : EIN BEITRAG ZUR WUERDIGUNG SEINES SCHAFFENS UND SEINER PERSOENLICHKEIT / Buecher, Wilhelm – (Includes bibliographical references and index) – Marburg a.L.: N G Elwert, 1913 – 1r – 1 – us U.W. Library [430]

GRILLPARZERS VERHAELTNIS ZUR POLITISCHEN TENDENZLITERATUR SEINER ZEIT / Beste, Konrad – (Includes bibliographical references) – [S.l.: s.n.] 1915 (Wolfenbuettel: Druck von R Angermann) – 1 – us U.W. Library [430]

Grima y Villa-Senor Gabriel de *see* CEREMORIAS EN EL COLEGIO MILITAR DE NUESTRA SRA. STA. MARIA DE TUDIA DEL ORDEN DE SANTIAGO DE LA UNIVERSIDAD DE SALAMANCA

Grima y Villa-Senor, Gabriel de *see* CEREMONIA DEL...SANTA MARIA DE TUDIA

Grimal de Guiraudon, T *see* MANUEL DE LA LANGUE TOULE

Grimarest, J L le Gallois *see*
- ECLAIRCISSEMENTS SUR LES PRINCIPES DE LA LANGUE FRANCAISE
- TRAITE DU RECITATIF

Grimball, John *see* LOG

Grimblot, Paul *see* LETTERS OF WILLIAM 3 AND LOUIS 14 AND THEIR MINISTERS

Grime, Elder J H *see* MANUSCRIPTS AND PAMPHLETS

Grime, J H *see* WHAT IS AN ORTHODOX BAPTIST?

Grimke, Angelina Emily *see*
- APPEAL TO THE CHRISTIAN WOMEN OF THE SOUTH
- AN APPEAL TO THE WOMEN OF THE NOMINALLY FREE STATES
- LETTERS TO CATHERINE E. BEECHER

Grimke, Archibald H *see* WILLIAM LLOYD GARRISON, THE ABOLITIONIST

Grimke Family *see* PAPERS

Grimke, Sarah *see* AN EPISTLE TO THE CLERGY OF THE SOUTHERN STATES

THE GRIMKE SISTERS: SARAH AND ANGELINA GRIMKE, THE FIRST AMERICAN WOMEN ADVOCATES OF ABOLITION AND WOMEN'S RIGHTS / Birney, Catherine H – 1885 – 9 – us A.T.L.A. [920]

Grimm, Ervin Davidovich *see* KAK BOLSHEVIKI ZAKHVATILI VLAST NA RUSI

Grimm, Hans *see*
- DIE DREI LACHENDEN GESCHICHTEN
- DIE GESCHICHTE VOM ALTEN BLUTE UND VON DER UNGEHEUREN VERLASSENHEIT
- GLAUBE UND ERFAHRUNG
- DIE OLEWAGEN SAGA
- DIE OLEWAGEN-SAGA
- WIE GRETE AUFHOERTE EIN KIND ZU SEIN
- DER ZUG DES HAUPTMANNS VON ERCKERT

Grimm, Herman Friedrich *see* GOETHE'S BRIEFWECHSEL MIT EINEM KINDE

Grimm, Hermann Friedrich *see*
- DEMETRIUS
- DAS KIND
- DAS LEBEN GOETHES

Grimm, Jacob *see*
- DER DEUTSCHE GEDANKE BEI JAKOB GRIMM
- DREI REDEN JAKOB GRIMMS
- GERMAN POPULAR STORIES
- ROTKAEPPCHEN

Grimm, Karl Josef *see* EUPHEMISTIC LITURGICAL APPENDIXES IN THE OLD TESTAMENT

Grimm, Wilibald *see* KURZGEFASSTE GESCHICHTE DER LUTHERISCHEN BIBELUEBERSETZUNG BIS ZUR GEGENWART

Grimme, Hubert *see*
- DAS ISRAELITISCHE PFINGSTFEST UND DER PLEJADENKULT
- PSALMENPROBLEME

GRIMMELSHAUSEN, ERLOESUNG UND BAROCKER GEIST / Burkhard, Werner – (Includes bibliographical references) – Frankfurt am Main: M Diesterweg, 1929 – 1r – 1 – us U.W. Library [430]

Grimmelshausen, Hans Jakob Christoph von *see*
- DER ABENTEUERLICHE SIMPLICISSIMUS
- DER SELTSAME SPRINGINSFELD

GRIMMELSHAUSENS SPRICHWOERTER UND REDENSARTEN / Lenschau, Martha – (Includes bibliographical references) – Frankfurt am Main: M Diesterweg, 1924 – 1 – us U.W. Library [430]

GRIMMER KREIS-WOCHENBLATT – Grimmen, Germany. 1855-56 – 1r – 1 – gw Mikrofilm [073]

Grimm,J *see* DEUTSCHE MYTHOLOGIE

Grimoard, P H de *see* ESSAI THEORIQUE ET PRATIQUE SUR LES BATAILLES

GRIMSBY EVENING AND SATURDAY TELEGRAPH – Humberside. 1952 to date – 1 – uk Microform Academic [072]

GRIMSBY GUARDIAN – England. -w. 9 Oct 1857-8 Nov 1867. (4 reels) – 1 – uk British Libr Newspaper [072]

GRIMSBY HERALD – England. -w. 31 Jul 1863-1 Oct 1881. (1872 imperfect). (8 reels) – 1 – uk British Libr Newspaper [072]

GRIMSBY INDEPENDENT AND ADVERTISER – (Grimsby and North Lincolnshire Advertiser Grimsby Advertiser). England. -w. 7 Jun 1861-22 Oct 1887. (12 reels) – 1 – uk British Libr Newspaper [072]

GRIMSBY INDEPENDENT, LINDSEY AND GENERAL ADVERTISER – England. -w. 4 Jun 1858-27 May 1859. (33 ft) – 1 – uk British Libr Newspaper [072]

Grimsdell, J R *see* LOW LEVEL AERIAL SURVEY TECHNIQUES

Grimshaw, W *see* DIARY, 1755-1757

Grimshaw, William *see* THE MERCHANTS' LAW BOOK; BEING A TREATISE ON THE LAW OF ACCOUNT RENDER, ATTACHMENT, BAILMENT, BILLS OF EXCHANGE AND PROMISSORY NOTES.

Grimsted, Patricia Kennedy *see*
- ARCHIVES AND MANUSCRIPT COLLECTIONS IN THE USSR
- ARCHIVES AND MANUSCRIPT REPOSITORIES IN THE USSR

Grimwood, BE *see* COCONUT PALM PRODUCTS

Grimwood-Jones, Diana *see*
- MIDDLE EAST AND ISLAM: A BIBLIOGRAPHICAL INTRODUCTION
- SOURCES FOR THE HISTORY OF THE BRITISH IN THE MIDDLE EAST

Grinberg, B Ia. *see* UKAZATEL'-SPRAVOCHNIK PROMYSLOVOI KOOPERATSII MOSKOVSKOI OBLASTI

Grinberg-Vinaver, S *see* DU DOMICILE EN DROIT INTERNATIONAL PRIVE

GRINCHUCKLE : CARICATURES – Montreal, Canada. 23 sep 1869-24 fev 1870 – 1r – 1 – Can$35.00 – cn Can Microfilming [072]

GRINCHUCKLE – Montreal. 1869-70 – 1 – 60.00 – cn McLaren [800]

GRINDING AND FINISHING *see* ABRASIVE ENGINEERING

GRINDING/FINISHING *see* ABRASIVE ENGINEERING

Grindrod, E *see* A COMPENDIUM OF THE LAWS AND REGULATIONS OF WESLEYAN METHODISM, WITH NOTES AND AN APPENDIX

Grinell, DeWitt Clinton *see* DIARY; PAPERS

Grinevetskii, Vasilii Ignatevich *see*
- POSLEVOENNYE PERSPEKTIVY RUSSKOI PROMYSHLENNOSTI
- POSLIEVOENNYIA PERSPEKTIVY RUSSKOI PROMYSHLENNOSTI

Grinevskaia, I *see* PRAVO KNIGI

Gringmut, V A *see* SOBRANIE STATEI

GRINGOIRE – Le grand hebdomadaire parisien, politique, litteraire. Paris. nov 1928-mai 1944 – 1 – fr A.C.R.P.P. [800]

Gringolts, A *see* ZAKONY O TRUDEI SOTSIALNOM STRAKHOVANII NA STROITELNYKH RABOTAKH

Grinstead, E D *see* TANGUT STUDIES

Grinstead, William *see* ACCOUNT BOOK

Grinten, Willem Christiaan Leonard van der *see* DE VERPLICHTINGEN VAN DEN WERKGEVER, KRACHTENS DE VERSCHILLENDE SOCIALE VERZEKERINGSWETTEN EN DE BESLUITEN, VEREVENINGSHEFFING, LOONBELASTING EN COMMISSARISSENBELASTING

Grinter, Moses *see* ACCOUNT BOOK

LES GRIOTS : LA REVUE SCIENTIFIQUE ET LITTERAIRE D'HAITI – Port-au-Prince: [s.n., v1 n1-v2 n2/3 jul/aug/sep 1938- oct/nov/dec 1939/jan/feb/mar 1940 – 15r – 1 – us Res Libr [073]

GRIP – v. 1-42. 24 May 1873-29 Dec 1894 – 1 – 385.00 – cn McLaren [971]

GRIP – v4-42. May 24, 1873-Dec. 29, 1894 – 1 – cn Precision [073]

THE GRIP – Williamsport, PA., 1889 – 13 – $25.00r – us I.M.R. [071]

THE GRIP CARTOONS, FROM MAY 1873 TO MAY 1874 / Bengough, John Wilson – 2v. Toronto: Rogers & Larminie, 1875. 00128. (Pre-1900 Canadiana) – 9 – cn C.I.H.M. [971]

GRIP STRENGTH PROFILES OF ELEMENTARY AGED MALES AND FEMALES / Svehla, B G – 1991 – 1mf – 9 – $4.00 – us Microform Publ [790]

GRIPEN – Sodertalje, Sweden. 1880-90 – 6r – 1 – sw Kungliga [072]

GRIP'S COMIC ALMANAC – 1880-93 – 9 – 75.00 – cn McLaren [073]

GRIP'S OWN LIBRARY – 1887 – 9 – 12.50 – cn McLaren [073]

THE GRIP-SACK – A receptacle of light literature, fun and fancy. v. 1-2. 1882-83 – 1 – 35.00 – cn McLaren [971]

GRIQUALAND WEST GOVERNMENT GAZETTE *see* THE DIAMOND NEWS

Grisanti, C F *see* LA NACIONALIDAD A LA LUZ DE LA LEGISLACION VENEZOLANA

Grisar, Erich *see* MONTEUR KLINKHAMMER

Grisar, Hartmann *see*
- GALILEISTUDIEN
- DIE ROEMISCHE KAPELLE SANCTA SANCTORUM UND IHR SCHATZ

Grisebach, A *see*
- CATALOGUS PLANTARUM CUBENSIUM
- FLORA OF THE BRITISH WEST INDIAN ISLANDS
- FLORA OF THE BRITISH WEST INDIES
- GENERA ET SPECIES GENTIANEARUM
- PLANTAE LORENZIANAE
- SPICILEGIUM FLORAE RUMELICAE ET BITHYNICAE EXHIBENS SYNOPSIN PLANTARUM
- SYMBOLAE AD FLORAM ARGENTINAM

Grisebach, Eduard *see* G.C. LICHTENBERG'S BRIEFE AN DIETERICH, 1770-1798

GRISELDA / Hauptmann, Gerhart – 2. Aufl. Berlin: S Fischer, 1909 – 1r – 1 – us U.W. Library [820]

GRISELDIS : DRAMATISCHE DICHTUNG IN EINEM VORSPIEL UND DREI AKTEN / Stach, Ilse von – Kempten: J Koesel & F Pustet, 1921 – 1r – 1 – us U.W. Library [810]

GRISELDIS : DRAMATISCHES GEDICHT IN FUENF AKTEN / Halm, Friedrich – 11. Aufl. Wien: C Gerold, 1896 – 1r – 1 – us U.W. Library [810]

Grishin, Z Z *see* SOVETSKOE TRUDOVOE PRAVO

Grishin, Zin *see* PRAVOVOE POLOZHENIE IUNOSHESKOGO TRUDA V SSSR

Grishinskii, A S *see* ISTORIIA RUSSKOI ARMII I FLOTA

Grishinskii, A S et al *see* ISTORIIA RUSSKOI ARMII I FLOTA

Grismer, Karl H *see* HISTORY OF ST PETERSBURG, FLORIDA

Grisson, Rudolf Hermann Rulemann *see* BEITRAEGE ZUR AUSLEGUNG VON RICHARD WAGNERS "RING DES NIBELUNGEN"

Griswold, Luther D *see* LUTHER D. GRISWOLD PAPERS, MS P.P.

Griswold, Rufus Wilmot *see* THE POETS AND POETRY OF ENGLAND

THE GRIT – Toronto. 1917 – 1 – 35.00 – cn McLaren [971]

EL GRITO – Las Vegas, NV. 1968-1973 – 2r – 1 – $100.00 – R04147 – us Library Micro [071]

O GRITO – Manaus, Amazonas. Nov-Dez 1964; Jan-Maio, Ago 1965 – 1,5,6 – bl Biblioteca [072]

O GRITO – Nanuque, Brazil. Nov 1968 – 1 – bl Biblioteca [072]

GRITO DA RAZAO – Bahia, Brazil. 13 Feb 1824-Aug 1825 – 1 – bl Biblioteca [072]

O GRITO DA RAZAO NA CORTE DO RIO DE JANEIRO – Rio de Janeiro, 23 Feb-22 Mar 1825 – 1,5,6 – bl Biblioteca [072]

EL GRITO DEL PUEBLO – Manila: P H Pobiete, jan 13 1900; mar 30 1901; jan 9 1902 – us Res Libr [072]

Gritsenko, I F *see* SISTEMATICHESKII UKAZATEL' RUSSKOI LITERATURY PO KOOPERATSII 1856-1924 GG

THE GRIZZLY – Big Bear Lake, CA. May 1941-1961 – 13r – 1 – $650.00 – R02065 – us Library Micro [071]

GROANLAND, ILL, SKILDRING AF DEN DANSKE LITERAERE GROANL. EXP / Mylius-Erichsen, L & Moltke, H – Koabenhavn, 1906. 628 pp., index, pls. maps. BH-487 2 – $30.00 – ne IDC [430]

Groat, George Gorham *see* ATTITUDE OF AMERICAN COURTS IN LABOR CASES; A STUDY IN SOCIAL LEGISLATION

Grob, F *see* DIE KOMPETENZEN DES VOELKERBUNDSRATES UND DER VOELKERBUNDSVERSAMMLUNG...

Grob, Johann *see* EPIGRAMME

DAS GROBE HEMD : VOLKSSTUECK IN VIER ACTEN / Karlweis, C – [Wien]: Wiener Verlag, 1901 – 1r – 1 – us U.W. Library [820]

Grobes *see* THE ENCYCLOPEDIA OF TEXAS

GROCOTT'S DAILY MAIL *see* GROCOTT'S MAIL

GROCOTT'S FREE PRESS *see* GROCOTT'S MAIL

GROCOTT'S MAIL – Grahamstown, South Africa. 4 Jan-20 Dec 1871. 1 reel. Title varies: Grocott's Free Press, 1870-71; Grocott's Penny Mail, 1872-Feb 1899, 1901-20; Grocott's Daily Mail, Feb-Dec 1899, 1920-64 – 1, 16 diazo available at reduced price – sa SA Libr [072]

GROCOTT'S PENNY MAIL *see* GROCOTT'S MAIL

GRODNER MOMENT = GRODNO MOMENT – (Yiddish daily) – Grodno, PL. no1 1 Jan-no100 1 May 1925 – 1r – 1 – $45.00 – cn Can Microfilming [072]

GRODSKIE I ZEMSKIE AKTY-VAZNEISHII ISTOCHNIK PO AGRARNOI ISTORII RECHI POSPOLITOI V XVI-XVIII VV / Isaevich, I D – (Ezhegodnik po agrarnoi istorii Vostochnoi Evropy na 1961 g). Riga. 1963. BR-9829 1 – 9 – ne IDC [947]

Groene, V *see*
- DER ABLASS
- COMPENDIUM DER KIRCHENGESCHICHTE

Groener, Wilhelm *see* PAPERS

Groenewegen, H *see* HIEROGLYPHICA; ANDERS, EMBLEMATA SACRA

Groenewegen, H Ij *see* DE EVOLUTIELEER EN HET GODSDIENSTIG GELOOF

DIE GROENINGER THEOLOGEN = GRONINGER GODGELEERDEN : SEINEN FRUEHERN UND JETZIGEN ZUHOERERN AM 25-JAEHRIGEN JUBELFESTE SEINES AMTSANTRITTES / Hofstede de Groot, Petrus – (Includes bibliographical references) – Gotha: Friedrich Andreas Perthes, 1863 – 1mf – 9 – 0-8370-8679-5 – 1986-2679 – us A.T.L.A. [240]

GROENLANDS HISTORISKE MINDESMAERKER : DET KONGELIGE NORDISKE OLDSKRIFT SELSKAB – Kobenhavn. v. 1-3. 1838-1845 – 46mf – 8 – ne IDC [948]

Groesbeck, John *see* THE CRITTENDEN COMMERCIAL ARITHMETIC AND BUSINESS MANUAL...

Groeschl, Juergen *see* GESPRAECHSBEFAEHIGUNG IM BERUFSBEZOGENEN PORTUGIESISCHUNTERRICHT

GROESSE UND GRENZEN DER KLEINBUERGERLICH-DEMOKRATISCHEN BEWEGUNG IN DER REVOLUTION VON 1848-49 IN DEUTSCHLAND – Berlin: Sekretariat des Zentralvorstandes der Liberal-Demokratischen Partei Deutschlands, 1968. 153p. Bibliog – 1 – us U.W. Library [943]

Groessel, Wolfgang *see* DIE STELLUNG DER LUTHERISCHEN KIRCHE DEUTSCHLANDS ZUR MISSION IM 17. JAHRHUNDERT

GROESSENWAHN : PATALOGISCHER ROMAN / Bleibtreu, Karl – Leipzig: W Friedrich, 1888 – 1r – 1 – us U.W. Library [830]

DIE GROESSEREN DICHTUNGEN VON JAMES MONTGOMERY / Wissmann, Paul – Koenigsberg i. Pr., 1913 – 1mf – DM48.00 – 3-8267-3049-6 – gw Hänsel [420]

GROESSTE DENKWUERDIGKEITEN DER WELT ODER SOGENANNTE RELATIONES CURIOSAE / ed by Happel, Eberhard G – Hamburg. bd 1-5. 1683-91 (mf ed 1993) – 28mf – 9 – DM520.00 – 3-89131-094-3 – gw Fischer [943]

Grogan, Jennifer *see* THE MEASUREMENT OF PERCEIVED-SELF AND PERCEIVED-PARENTAL GENDER-ROLE ORIENTATION

Grogan, Kevin *see* A COLLECTION IN THE MAKING

LE GROGNARD : HUMORISTIQUE AVEC CARICATURES / ed by Berthelot, Hector – Montreal, Canada. 12 nov 1881-8 mar 1884 – 1r – 1 – Can$35.00 – cn Can Microfilming [072]

LE GROGNARD – Quebec, Canada. 27 sep 1862 – 1r – 1 – Can$25.00 – cn Can Microfilming [072]

Grohmann, Wilhelm *see* LUTHERISCHE METAPHYSIK

Grohmann, Willy *see* VERS ODER PROSA IM HOHEN DRAMA DES ACHTZEHNTEN JAHRHUNDERTS

Groizard y Coronado, Carlos *see* CUARTILLAS

DEN GRØLANDSKE ORDBOG / Kleinschmidt, Samuel P – København, 1871 – 9mf – ne IDC [490]

Grolier, Eric de *see*
- DIRECTORY OF DOCUMENTATION, LIBRARIES AND ARCHIVES SERVICES IN AFRICA
- ORGANIZATION OF INFORMATION SYSTEMS FOR GOVERNMENT AND PUBLIC ADMINISTRATION

Gromachevskii, S G *see* BIBLIOGRAFICHESKII UKAZATEL'LITERATURY PO RUSSKOI NUMISMATIKE

GROMADA – Warsaw, Poland. 4 Jul 1951; Jan-May 1952 – 1r – 1 – us L of C Photodup [943]

GROMADA ROLNIK POLSKI – Warsaw, Poland. Jun 1952-Jun 1958; 1959; 1961-May 1979 – 29r – 1 – us L of C Photodup [943]

Gromana, V G *see* GOSUDARSTVENNAIA PROMYSHLENNOST S.S.S.R. V 1921-23 G.G. I EE FINANSOVOE POLOZHENIE

GROMBOLAN GAGAK MATARAM – In Javanese. SE-5219 1. 1963 – 9 – ne IDC [950]

GROMOKIPIASHCHII KUBOK. POEZY / Severianin, I – ed. 2. M. 1913. BR-1027 2 – 8 – ne IDC [460]

Gronau, K *see* POSEIDONIOS UND DIE JUEDISCH-CHRISTLICHE GENESISEXEGESE

Grondel, A H *see* ENKELE OPMERKINGEN NAAR AANLEIDING VAN DE ENQUETE INZAKE

EEN GRONDELIJCKE VERCLARINGHE: VAN DEN ECHTELIJCKEN STAET. IN TWEE GHESPRAKEN GHESTELT / Honich, T C – BME-226 1 – 9 – ne IDC [240]

GRONDELIJE BERICHT VANDEN DOOPE ENDE WEDERDOOPE / Grevinchovius, Casp – Rotterdam, J. v. Waesberghe. 1599. BME-217 1 – 9 – ne IDC [240]

EEN GRONDICH BEWIJS WT DE GODLIJCKE SCHRIFTUERE VERTOONT, DAT GODS GEMEYNTE, DE GHELOOUIGEN OP AERDEN / Claes Ganglofs – 1599. BME-223 1 – 9 – ne IDC [240]

GRONDIG ONDERSOEK VAN DE TOONEN DER MUSIJK / Douwes, C – Franeker. 1699. BP-247 1 – 9 – ne IDC [780]

GRONDIG ONDERWYS IN DE GREGORIAANSCHE CHOORZANG OF CHORAL / Juerrns, J F – 1789 – 9 – us Sibley [780]

GRONDIG ONDERWYS IN HET BEHANDELEN DER VIOOL / Mozart, L – P 412. 1766 – 9 – ne IDC [780]

GRONDIGHE WEDERLEGGINGHE, VAN SEKER GHESCHRIFT, EERST BY JACOB JANSZ. GHESTELT / Pieter Cornelisz – Amsterdam, Laurens Jacobsz. 1597. BME-222 1 – 9 – ne IDC [240]

GRONDSLAG VAN HET VOCAAL MUZYK / Hoogh, D. van der – P 328. 1770 – 9 – ne IDC [780]

Gronemann, S *see* DIE JONATHAN'SCHE PENTATEUCH-UEBERSETZUNG IN IHREM VERHAELTNISSE ZUR HALACHA

GRONLAND GEOGRAPHISK OG STATISTISK BESKREVET / Rink, H J – I: Det nordre inspectorat. II: Det sondre inspectorat. Kjobenhavn. 1857. BH-497 2 – 8 – ne IDC [910]

GRONLAND I TOHUNDREDAARET FOR HANS EGEDES LANDING – (Medd. om Gronland, Bd. LX og LXI). 2 v. Kobenhavn. 1921. BH-478 2 – 8 – ne IDC [910]

GRONLAND LANGS POLHAVET / Rasmussen, Knud – BN 359 2.1919 – 8 – ne IDC [910]

GRONLAND PA VEJ MOD 1970: INVESTERINGSPLANNEN 1966-70 / Greenland. Ministeriet for Gronland – (Greenland on the way to 1970: investment plan 1966-70). Copenhagen. 1967 – 9 – ne IDC [330]

GRONLANDSBOGEN 1-2 / Birket-Smith, K – BN 138 2. 1950 – 8 – ne IDC [948]

GRONLANDSK GRAMMATICA / Fabricius, O – BN 206 2. 1801 – 8 – ne IDC [430]

GRONLANDSK REJSPARLOR / Bugge, A – A Greenlandic-Danish Phrase Book. Kjobenhavn. 1952. BN-460 2 – 8 – ne IDC [400]
GRONLANDSK SPROGLAERE / Rasmussen, Knud – BH 180 2.1888 – 8 – ne IDC [910]
DEN GRØNLANDSKE ORDBOG. / Fabricius, O – Kjøbenhavn, 1804 – 14mf – ne IDC [490]
DEN GRONLANDSKE ORDBOG / Kleinschmidt, Samuel P – BH-177 2. 1871 – 8 – ne IDC [910]
DEN GRONLANDSKE ORDBOG / Kleinschmidt, Samuel P – Kobenhjavn: Bogtrykkeri, 1871 – 1 – F238.15 – fr Armell [948]
DEN GRØNLANDSKE ORDBOG. GRØNLANDSK-DANSK / Schultz-Lorentzen, C W – København. [4], 360 pp. 1926 – 7mf – ne IDC [490]
GRONLANDSKE RELATIONER / Dalager, L – BN 183 2. 1915 – 8 – ne IDC [910]
Gronlund, Laurence *see*
- CA IRA; OR, DANTON IN THE FRENCH REVOLUTION; A STUDY
- THE COOPERATIVE COMMONWEALTH IN ITS OUTLINES. AN EXPOSITION OF MODERN SOCIALISM

Gronovius, J F *see*
- FLORA ORIENTALIS SIVE RECENSIO PLANTARUM QUAS BOTANICORUM CORYPHAEUS LEONHARDUS RAUWOLFFUS
- FLORA VIRGINICA

Groome, F H *see* AN ORDNANCE GAZETTEER OF SCOTLAND
Groos, Karl *see* THE PLAY OF MAN
Grooss, K S *see* THE LIBRARY OF MEDICAL HISTORY ON MICROFICHE
Groot, H de *see* AENMERKINGE OP DE MISSIVE VAN PARNAS,...
Groot, Hugo de *see*
- LE DROIT DE LA GUERRE ET DE LA PAIX, NOUVELLE TRADUCTION PAR JEAN BARBEYRAC
- HUGONIS GROTII DE JURE BELLI AC PACIS LIBRI 3...

Groot, J J M de *see*
- CHINESISCHE URKUNDEN ZUR GESCHICHTE ASIENS
- LES FETES ANNUELLEMENT CELEBREES A EMOUI (AMOY). ETUDE CONCERNANT LA RELIGION POPULAIRE DES CHINOIS
- THE RELIGION OF THE CHINESE
- THE RELIGIOUS SYSTEM OF CHINA

Groot, L de *see* MAIK DAN MADJU
HET GROOT NATUUR-EN ZEDEKUNDIGH WERELTTONEEL / Poot, H K zn – O 406. 3 v. 1743-1750 – 9 – ne IDC [580]
Groot, O O *see* DE CAPTIS IN BELLO,...
GROOT SCHILDERBOEK / Lairesse, Gerard de – O-334. 2 v. 1740 – 9 – ne IDC [700]
DE GROOTE SCHOUBURGH DER NEDERLANTSCHE KONSTSCHILDERS EN SCHILDERESSEN... / Houbraken, Arnold – Amsterdam. 3v. 1718-1721 – 15mf – ne IDC [700]
Gropp, I OSB *see* HISTORIA MONASTERII AMORBACENSIS ORD. S. BENEDICTI
Gros, K H *see* LEHRBUCH DER PHILOSOPHISCHEN RECHTSWISSENSCHAFT...
Gros, L *see* HISTOIRE DE NOTRE DAME DE LOURDES
Grosart, Alexander Balloch *see*
- THE PRINCE OF LIGHT AND THE PRINCE OF DARKNESS IN CONFLICT
- PRINCE OF LIGHT AND THE PRINCE OF DARKNESS IN CONFLICT

Grosch, Rudolf *see* DIE JUGENDDICHTUNG FRIEDRICH HOELDERLINS
Grose, F *see* RULES FOR DRAWING CARICATURES: WITH AN ESSAY ON COMIC PAINTING
Grose, Francis *see*
- A CLASSICAL DICTIONARY OF THE VULGAR TONGUE
- A PROVINCIAL GLOSSARY

Grose, Howard B *see*
- ALIENS OR AMERICANS?
- THE INCOMING MILLIONS
- THE JUDSON CENTENNIAL, 1814-1914

Grose, Howard Benjamin *see* ADVANCE IN THE ANTILLES: THE NEW ERA IN CUBA AND PORTO RICO
Groser, William H *see*
- BIBLE MONTHS, OR, THE SEASONS IN PALESTINE: AS ILLUSTRATIVE OF SCRIPTURE
- A HUNDRED YEARS WORK FOR CHILDREN, 1803-1903
- SCRIPTURE NATURAL HISTORY: I: THE TREES AND PLANTS MENTIONED IN THE BIBLE
- TEACHER'S MODEL AND THE MODEL TEACHER

Groser, William Howse *see* THE TEACHER'S MODEL AND THE MODEL TEACHER
Gross, Alexander *see* SON OF MAN: STUDIES IN HIS LIFE AND TEACHINGS
Gross, C *see* THE GILD MERCHANT
Gross, Ch. *see* THE SOURCES AND LITERATURE OF ENGLISH HISTORY
Gross, Fred Louis *see* THE LAW OF REAL ESTATE BROKERS, WITH 1917 SUPPLEMENT.
Gross, H *see*
- GALLIA JUDAICA, DICTIONNAIRE GEOGRAPHIQUE DE LA FRANCE...
- DIE SATIRE IN DER JUEDISCHEN LITERATUR

Gross, Lewis M *see* PAST AND PRESENT OF DE KALB COUNTY, ILLINOIS
Gross, S *see* MENAHEM BEN SARUK
Gross, Samuel *see* CANCER RESEARCH, THERAPY AND CONTROL
GROSSBRITANNIENS CONFERVEN / Weber, F & Mohr, D M H – (Dillwyn, Rev.). 4 v. Goettingen. 1803-05. B-6418 2 – 8 – ne IDC [580]
GROSSBRITTANIENS. MINERAL-CONCHOLOGIE / Sowerby, J – Z 806 2. 1837-1844 – 8 – ne IDC [590]
"GROSSDEUTSCHLAND IM WELTGESCHEHEN." / U.S. Library of Congress. Prints and Photographs Division – Four annual news photo compilations, published for the Reichsministerium fuer Volksaufklaerung und Propaganda. 1939-42. Approx. 1325 photos. 1 reel. P&P2651 – 1 – 23.00r – us L of C Photodup [080]
DER GROSSE BAUM : ERZAEHLUNG / Hoerner, Herbert von – Stuttgart: J Engelhorns Nachf. A Spemann, 1940, c1938 – 1r – 1 – us U.W. Library [830]
DER GROSSE BERGARBEITER-STREIK DES JAHRES 1889 IM RHEINISCH-WESTFAELISCHEN KOHLENREVIER : EIN WORT ZUR ABWEHR / Lensing, L – Dortmund 1889 – 1 – DM30.00 – gw Mikro Press [943]
DAS GROSSE CONVERSATIONSLEXIKON FUER GEBILDETE STAENDE (AEL, ABT.1;5) / Meyer, Josef – 1993. Hildburghausen, 1840-55 – 399mf – 9 – DM5,200.00 – 3-89131-068-4 – gw Fischer [030]
DIE GROSSE DER MUSIKALISCHE INTERVALLE ALS GRUNDLAGE DER HARMONIE / Bellermann, H – Berlin: J Springer, 1873 – 1 – us Sibley [780]
GROSSE DEUTSCHE LEXIKA : AUFKLAERUNG UND FRUEHES NEUNZEHNTES JAHRHUNDERT / ed by Killy, Walther – (Universal-Lexikon oder vollstaendiges Encyclopaedisches Woerterbuch. Altenburg: Literatur-Comptoir 1835-1836, Bd. 1-26. 211mf. DM5,800.00. ISBN 3-598-40621-5; Allgemeine Deutsche Real-Encyklopaedie fuer die gebildeten Staende: (Conversations-Lexikon). Leipzig: Brockhaus, 1827. 113mf. DM2,980.00. ISBN 3-598-40622-3; Huebner, Johann: Reales Staats-, Zeitungs- und Conversations-Lexicon. Leipzig: Gleditsch, 1737. 14mf. DM390.00. ISBN 3-598-40623-1; Huebner, Johann: Reales, Staats-, Zeitungs-, und Conversations-Lexicon. Leipzig: Glegitsch, 1795. 15mf. DM450.00. ISBN 3-598-40624-X; Hederich, Benjamin: Reales Schul-Lexicon. Leipzig, Gleditsch, 1717. 16mf. DM485.00. ISBN 3-598-40625-8; Hederich, Benjamin: Gruendliches Lexicon Mythologicum. Leipzig, Gleditsch, 1741. 11mf. DM280.00. ISB 3-598-40626-6; Hederich, Benjamin: Gruendliches Antiquitaeten-Lexicon. Leipzig, Gleditsch, 1743. 17mf. DM515.00. ISBN 3-598-40627-4; Walch, Johann Georg: Philosophisches Lexicon. Leipzig, Gleditsch, 1775. 25mf. DM560.00. ISBN 3-598-40628-2) – 1993 – 421mf (1:24) – 9 – silver DM9,200.00 – 3-598-40620-7 – gw Saur [430]
DIE GROSSE ENTSCHEIDUNG : DRAMA / Klass, Gert von – Wiesbaden: Verlag Der Greif, c1944 – 1r – 1 – us U.W. Library [820]
GROSSE GENERAL-BASS-SCHULE.. / Mattheson, J – 460p. 1731 – 2 – us Sibley [780]
GROSSE GENERAL-BASS-SCHULE. ODER: DER EXEMPLARISCHEN ORGANISTEN-PROBE / Mattheson, J – 1731. 484p – 9 – us Sibley [780]
DAS GROSSE ILLUSTRIERTE KRAUETERBUCH / Mueller, Ferdinand Jakob Heinrich von – ed. 8. Ulm. 1860. B-8043 1 – 9 – ne IDC [580]
DER GROSSE JANJA : EIN KATTOWITZER ROMAN / Ulitz, Arnold – Breslau: W G Korn, c1939 – 1r – 1 – us U.W. Library [830]
GROSSE JUEDISCHE NATIONAL-BIOGRAPHIE / ed by Wininger, S – Czernowitz. 7v. 1925-1936 – 83mf – ne IDC [320]
Grosse, Julius *see* GUDRUN
DAS GROSSE LEBEN : GOETHES BRIEFE / ed by Hartung, Ernst – Ebenhausen bei Muenchen: W L Brandt, 1924 – 1r – 1 – us U.W. Library [920]
DIE GROSSE POLITIK DER EUROPAEISCHEN KABINETTE / Germany. Auswaertiges Amt – 1871-1914 – 1 – us UMI [900]
GROSSE POLITIK DER EUROPAEISCHEN KABINETTE, 1871-1914 – Berlin. v. 1-40. 1922-27. – 413mf – 8 – ne IDC [900]
DIE GROSSE POLITIK DER EUROPAISCHEN KABINETTE – Berlin. 1871-1914 (complete) – 1 – 35.00r – us Hoover Inst Photo [073]
DAS GROSSE SCHERMESSER *see* DAMIAN, ODER, DAS GROSSE SCHERMESSER
DAS GROSSE SIGNAL : JUNGEN IM VERRATENEN RHEINLAND / Lux, Hanns Maria – (Includes "Geschichtliches Nachwort" by Hans Bellinghausen) – Berlin: W Limpert – 1r – 1 – us U.W. Library [830]
DIE GROSSE STUNDE : ERZAEHLUNGEN / Helke, Fritz – Stuttgart: Union Deutsche Verlagesgesellschaft, 1943 – 1r – 1 – us U.W. Library [830]
DIE GROSSE TOUR *see* AN INQUIRY INTO THE SOURCES OF CHARLES SEALSFIELD'S NOVEL MORTON, ODER, DIE GROSSE TOUR
DIE GROSSE WOGE : ROMAN / Baudissin, Eva Fanny Bernhardine Tuerk, Graefin von – Stuttgart: J Engelhorn, 1919 – 1r – 1 – us U.W. Library [830]
DIE GROSSE WOLTHAT : SO UNSER HERRE GOTT DURCH...D. MARTINUM LUTHER...DER WELT ERZEIGET...IN REIMEN KUERTZLICH ZUSAMMEN GEFASSET / Alber, E – N.p. [1546] – 1mf – 9 – ne IDC [240]
DIE GROSSEN KRIEGE IN DER GESCHICHTE DES DEUTSCHEN VOLKES / Jacob, Karl – Tuebingen: Kloeres, 1915. 28p – 1 – us U.W. Library [943]
Grosser, Guenther *see* DAS BUENDNIS DER PARTEIEN: HERAUSBILDUNG UND ROLLE DES MEHRPARTEIENSYSTEMS IN DER EUROPAEISCHEN SOZIOLISTISCHEN LAENDERN
GROSSES VOLLSTAENDIGES UNIVERSAL-LEXIKON ALLER WISSENSCHAFTEN UND KUENSTE (AEL, ABT 1;32) / Zedler, Johann Heinrich – Halle, Leipzig. 64 bde + 4 suppl-bde. 1732-1754 (mf ed 1995) – 630mf – 9 – DM7,732.00 – 3-89131-213-X – gw Fischer [030]
Grosseteste, Robert *see*
- ROBERTI GROSSETESTE EPISCOPI QUONDAM LINCOLNIENSI EPISTOLAE (RS25)
- SERMONS

DIE GROSSFALTER (MACROLEPIDOPTERA) KURLANDS, LIVLANDS, ESTLANDS UND OSTPREUSSENS... / Slevogt, B – Riga, 1910 – 7mf – 9 – ne IDC [574]
DIE GROSSFUERSTIN : ROMAN / Samarow, Gregor – 2. Aufl. Stuttgart: Deutsche Verlags-Anstalt – 1r – 1 – us U.W. Library [830]
GROSSHERZOGLICH BADISCHES ANZEIGE-BLATT FUER DEN SEEKREIS – (Publ at various places) – 1821-25 – 1 – Dist. gw Mikrofilm – gw Misc Inst [072]
GROSSHERZOGLICH BADISCHES PRIVILEGIRTES FREYBURGER WOCHENBLATT *see* FREIBURGER ZEITUNG
GROSSHERZOGLICH HESSISCHE LANDZEITUNG *see* HESSEN-DARMSTAEDTISCHE PRIVILEGIRTE LANDES-ZEITUNG
GROSSHERZOGLICH HESSISCHE ZEITUNG *see* HESSEN-DARMSTAEDTISCHE PRIVILEGIRTE LANDES-ZEITUNG
Grossman, George S *see* OMNIBUS COPYRIGHT REVISION: LEGISLATIVE HISTORY
Grossman, L *see*
- BOR'BA ZA STIL'
- OT PUSHKINA DO BLOKA

GROSSMAN, MARY B, PAPERS, MS 3660 – 1923-1972 – 1 reel – 1 – us Western Res [340]
Grossman, V IA *see* NALOGOVYI SPRAVOCHNIK DLIA KUSTAREI I REMESLENNIKOV I IKH PERVICHNIKH OB"EDINENII
Grossmann, K *see* JACOB UNREST (MGH 6: 11.BD)
Grossmann, Louis *see*
- MAIMONIDES
- SELECTED WRITINGS OF ISAAC M. WISE
- SOME CHAPTERS ON JUDAISM AND THE SCIENCE OF RELIGION

Grosz, Georg *see* ABRECHNUNG FOLGT
Grot, Ia. K *see* TRUDY FILOLOGICHESKIIA RAZYSKANIIA
Grot, K I *see* KONSTANTIN KARLOVICH GROT KAK GOSUDARSTVENNYI OBSHCHESTVENNYI DEIATEL'
Grot, Nikolaus *see* NIETZSCHE UND TOLSTOI
Grote, A R *see* NORTH AMERICAN ENTOMOLOGIST
Grote, Augustus Radcliffe *see*
- LIST OF THE LEPIDOPTERA OF NORTH AMERICA
- NORTH AMERICAN LEPIDOPTERA

Grote, F von *see* BEITRAEGE ZUM RECHT DER LUFTSCHIFFAHRT
Grote, Hans Henning, Freiherr *see* DER HAUPTMANN
Grotefend, Otto *see* URKUNDEN DER FAMILIE VON SALDERN
DAS GROTESKE IN DER FRUEHEN PROSA V.A. KAVERINS (1920-1931) / Suchy, Joerg – 1994 – 2mf – DM80.00 – 3-8267-2013-X – gw Hänsel [460]
Groth, Klaus *see* LEBENSERINNERUNGEN
Grotius, H *see*
- ANNALES ET HISTORIAE DE REBUS BELGICIS
- THE FREEDOM OF THE SEAS...
- MARE LIBERUM SIVE DE JURE QUOD BATAVIS...

Grotius, Hugo *see* A DEFENCE OF THE CATHOLIC FAITH
Grotius, Hugo de *see*
- OPERA OMNIA THEOLOGICA...
- THE RIGHTS OF WAR AND PEACE

GROTJAN'S PHILADELPHIA PUBLIC-SALE REPORT – Philadelphia. Pennsylvania. 1812-1820 – 3 – us Readex [071]
Groto, L *see* ORATIONE...FATTA IN VINEGIA, PER L'ALLEGREZZA DELLA UITTORIA OTTENUTA CONTRA TURCHI DALLA SANTISSIMA LEGA
GROTON 1640-1900 – (Mf 1-4: Vital Records 1656-1829. Mf 5-11: Vital Records 1640-1853. Mf 12-14: Vital Records 1674-1758. Mf 15-24: Vital Records 1674-1758. Mf 25-42: Proprietors 1711-1829. Mf 43-48: Land Records 1662-1772. Mf 49-58: Town Records 1655-1797. Mf 59: Births 1829-43. Mf 59-78: Town Records 1740-1825. Mf 79-88: Town Meetings 1813-35. Mf 89-101: Town Orders 1789-1808. Mf 101-102: Boundaries 1828-29. Mf 103-105: Town Records 1815-48. Mf 106-107: Paupers 1854-1902. Mf 108: Dogs 1858-69. Mf 108-110: Taxes 1863, 1879. Mf 110-113: Veterans 1861-83. Mf 114-115: Birth Index 1843-1901. Mf 115-116: Death Index 1843-1901. Mf 117-118: Marriage Index 1843-1901. Mf 119-120: Births 1843-53. Mf 120: Marriages 1843-55. Mf 121: Deaths 1843-52. Mf 122-126: Births 1854-1901. Mf 126-129: Marriages 1856-1901. Mf 130-133: Deaths 1853-1901) – (mf ed 1995) – 133mf – 9 – 0-87623-381-7 – us Holbrook [920]
GROTON 1648-1849 – (Mf 1T-3T. Births & Marriages 1674-1753. Mf 1T-5T: Deaths 1734-1829. Mf 3T-5T: Births 1689-1795. Mf 6T-7T: Marriages 1732-72. Mf 7T-8T: Births & Deaths 1648, 1714-1843. Mf 9T-12T: Births & Deaths 1701-1851. Mf 12T-13T: Marriages 1772-98; Births & Deaths 1771-1850. Mf 13T: Out-of-Town Marriages 1685-1799. Mf 14T-16T: Marriages & Intentions 1795-1849. Mf 16T-17T: Births 1843-49. Mf 18T: Marriages 1843-49. Mf 19T: Deaths 1843-49) – (mf ed 1996) – 19mf – 9 – 0-87623-259-4 – us Holbrook [920]
LA GROTTA DI TROFONIO. OPERA COMICA... / Salieri, A – Wien: Artaria & Co, [1786] – 1 – us Sibley [780]
Grou, Jean Nicholas *see* MANUAL FOR INTERIOR SOULS
Grouard, Auguste Antoine *see* STRATEGIE, OBJET, ENSEIGNEMENT, ELEMENTS
Groulx, Lionel *see* L'ACTION FRANCAISE
THE GROUND OF WOMAN'S ELIGIBILITY – Methodist Review, 73, 1891 – 9 – us A.T.L.A. [240]

THE GROUND PLAN OF THE ENGLISH PARISH CHURCH / Hamilton Thompson, A – H-1287 2. 1913 – 8 – ne IDC [240]
GROUND WATER – (1974-. 5,6. 1975-. 9) – v. 1-. 1963- – 1 – us UMI [550]
THE GROUNDS OF FAITH : FOUR LECTURES / Manning, Henry Edward – London: Burns and Lambert, 1852 – 1mf – 9 – 0-8370-6820-7 – 1986-0820 – us A.T.L.A. [230]
GROUNDS OF GRAMMER PENNED AND PUBLISHED / Bird, John – 1639. 197p. (English Linguistics Series 1500-1800) – 9 – us UMI [400]
THE GROUNDS OF THE FRENCH TONGUE / Miege, Guy – 1687. 185p. (English Linguistics Series 1500-1800) – 9 – us UMI [440]
THE GROUNDS OF THEISTIC AND CHRISTIAN BELIEF / Fisher, George Park – New York: Scribner, 1915, c1911 – 2mf – us A.T.L.A. [240]
GROUNDWATER MODELS – 1978 – 198p – it F.A.O. [550]
GROUNDWATER POLLUTION – 1979 – 149p – it F.A.O. [360]
GROUNDWATER PROBLEMS IN COASTAL AREAS : A CONTRIBUTION TO THE INTERNATIONAL HYDROLOGICAL PROGRAMME / Custodio, E et al – 1987 – 596p – 9 – 92-3-102415-9 – fr UNESCO [550]
GROUND-WATER STUDIES. SUPPLEMENT 3 – (Chapters 7 (Section 7.6), 8 (Section 8.5) and 15 (with binder)) – 1977 – 9 – 92-3-101471-4 – fr UNESCO [550]
GROUND-WATER STUDIES. SUPPLEMENT 4 – 44p – 9 – 92-3-102087-0 – fr UNESCO [550]
THE GROUND-WORK OF FOUNDATION LAID... FOR THE FRAMING OF A NEW PERFECT LANGUAGE / Lodowyck, Francis – 1652. 29p. (English Linguistics Series 1500-1800) – 9 – us UMI [400]
GROUP – (1985-. 5,6,9) – v1-. 1974- – 1 – us UMI [073]
GROUP AND ORGANIZATION STUDIES – v. 1-. 1976- – 1,5,6,9 – us UMI [310]
THE GROUP AREAS ACT – Cape Town: Juta, 1953 – 1 – us Res Libr [960]
GROUP COHESION AND PERCEPTIONS OF PRESSURE TO CONFORM IN A UNIVERSITY RESIDENCE / Ramsay, Michael C – 1994 – 1mf – $4.00 – us Microform Publ [150]
A GROUP OF NOBLE DAMES... / Hardy, Thomas – [London]: James R. Osgood, McIlvaine, 1891 – 1 roll – 1 – 1-55879-817-X – uk Libr Preservation [920]
GROUP PSYCHOTHERAPY AND PSYCHODRAMA *see* HANDBOOK OF INTERNATIONAL SOCIOMETRY
GROUP PSYCHOTHERAPY, PSYCHODRAMA AND SOCIOMETRY *see* HANDBOOK OF INTERNATIONAL SOCIOMETRY
GROUPE DE PRODUCTION ET NIVEAU DE REVENU DANS LA ZONE DENSE DE L'OUEST DE BOUAKE / Michotte, J – (Africa series). 1969 – 9 – fr Hachette [338]
Groupe des Etudiants Socialistes *see* LA JEUNESSE SOCIALISTE
Groupe du Bas-Languedoc de l'Association Sully *see* BULLETIN
Groupe Parlementaire francais de l'Arbitage International *see* ANNEE 1907. LA DEUXIEME CONFERENCE DE LA HAYE
LES GROUPES DE PRESSION EN FRANCE / Meynaud, J – F60.00 – fr Ethnologie [320]
Grout, Lewis *see* ZULU-LAND, OR, LIFE AMONG THE ZULU-KAFIRS
Grouvelle, A *see* MEMOIRES ENTOMOLOGIQUES.ETUDES SUR LES COLEOPTERES
Grovalet, C *see* LA NAVIGATION AERIENNE...
GROVE BOOKLET ON MINISTRY AND WORSHIP / Church of England – Church of England. nos 1-34. 1972- (complete) – 1r – 1 – ATLA S0279 – us A.T.L.A. [073]
Grove, C A *see* THE EFFECTS OF HIGH IMPACT EXERCISE VERSUS LOW IMPACT EXERCISE ON BONE DENSITY IN POSTMENOPAUSAL WOMEN
GROVE LEVEL BAPTIST CHURCH. DALTON, GEORGIA : CHURCH RECORDS – Sept 1853 – Mar 1952. Incomplete – 1 – 49.86 – us Baptist [240]
Grover, Alonzo J *see* ROMANISM
GROVER CLEVELAND PAPERS – (With guide) – 164r – 1 – $5,740.00 – Dist. us Scholarly Res – us L of C Photodup [975]
GROVER FIRST BAPTIST CHURCH. KINGS MOUNTAIN ASSOCIATION. GROVER, NORTH CAROLINA : CHURCH RECORDS – 1897-1963 – 1 – 31.68 – us Baptist [240]
GROVER HILL NEWS – Grover Hill, Ohio. 1947-72 – 8r – 1 – $32.50r – us Archival [071]
GROVER W. ENSLEY, SENATE SERVICE 1949-1957 : EXECUTIVE DIRECTOR, JOINT ECONOMIC COMMITTEE – 2mf – 9 – $10.00 – us Scholarly Res [320]
Groves, J *see*
– THE BRITISH CHAROPHYTA
Groves, Michelle D *see* DYNAMIC FUNCTIONAL ASSESSMENT OF THE LOWER EXTREMITY IN THE NON-VARSITY ATHLETIC POPULATION
THE GROWLER – Toronto. 1864 – 1 – 45.00 – cn McLaren [971]
GROWLS FROM UGANDA / Critolaus – London: E Stock, 1909 – 1 – us Res Libr [960]
GROWTH : A JOURNAL FOR STUDIES OF DEVELOPMENT AND INCREASE – Menasha, WI. v1-5. 1937-41. – 44mf – 8 – ne IDC [073]
GROWTH – v. 1-32. 1937-1968 – 1,5,6 – us Princeton Micro [574]
GROWTH AND CHARACTERIZATION OF ELECTRONIC MATERIALS / Haidemenakis, E D – (Chania International Conference). v1. 1979. 374p. v2. 1979. 328p – 1,5,9 – us Gordon [621]
GROWTH AND EDUCATION / Tyler, John M – 1907 – 4mf – 9 – $12.00 – us Microform Publ [370]
GROWTH AND STRUCTURE OF THE ENGLISH LANGUAGE / Jespersen, Otto – Leipzig: B.G. Teubner; New York: G.E. Stechert, 1905 – 1 roll – 1 – 1-55879-903-6 – uk Libr Preservation [420]
GROWTH FACTORS / ed by Baird, Andrew et al – 1,5,9 – us Gordon [574]
THE GROWTH HORMONE RESPONSE TO EXERCISE AT DIFFERENT TIMES OF THE DAY / Bullard, J M – 1991 – 1mf – 9 – $4.00 – us Microform Publ [613]
THE GROWTH OF A CENTURY OF THE COUNTY OF JEFFERSON 1793-1894 / Haddock, John A – Philadelphia, Sherman and Co., 1894. New York Reel 17. (The Cox Library Collection) – 5 – us Americana [978]
THE GROWTH OF AFRICAN LITERATURE : A SURVEY OF THE WORKS PUBLISHED BY AFRICAN WRITERS / Joseph, Stanislaus – (In English and French) – Montreal, 1952 – us Res Libr [470]
GROWTH OF LABOR LAW IN THE UNITED STATES : 1962 EDITION / U.S. Dept of Labor – Washington: GPO, 1962 (all publ) – 4mf – 9 – $6.00 – LLMC 95-009A – us L.L.M.C. [340]
GROWTH OF LABOR LAW IN THE UNITED STATES : 1967 EDITION / U.S. Dept of Labor – Washington: GPO, 1967 (all publ) – 4mf – 9 – $6.00 – LLMC 95-009B – us L.L.M.C. [340]
THE GROWTH OF THE CHURCH IN ITS ORGANIZATION AND INSTITUTIONS : BEING THE CROALL LECTURES FOR 1886 / Cunningham, John – London: Macmillan, 1886 – 1mf – us A.T.L.A. [240]
THE GROWTH OF THE CONSTITUTION IN THE FEDERAL CONVENTION OF 1787 : AN EFFORT TO TRACE THE ORIGIN AND DEVELOPMENT OF EACH SEPARATE CLAUSE FROM ITS FIRST SUGGESTION IN THAT BODY TO THE FORM FINALLY APPROVED / Meigs, William M – 2nd ed. Philadelphia/London: J B Lippincott Co, 1900 – 5mf – 9 – $7.50 – LLMC 90-358 – us L.L.M.C. [323]
THE GROWTH OF THE ECONOMY (1961-1966) / United Kingdom. National Economic Development Council – London. 1964. BD-1779 1 – 9 – ne IDC [338]
THE GROWTH OF THE IDYLLS OF THE KING / Jones, Richard – Philadelphia: Lippincott, 1895, [c1894] – 1 roll – 1 – 1-55879-539-1 – uk Libr Preservation [820]
GROWTH OF THE UNITED KINGDOM ECONOMY, 1961-1966 / Great Britain. National Economic Development Council – London. 1963 – 9 – ne IDC [338]
THE GROWTH OF WORLD INDUSTRY / United Nations – (ST/STAT/Ser.P/1-3. E/F.32; ST/STAT/Ser.P/4. E.11; 1967-1971. ST/STAT/Ser.P/5-9. E/F.45; 1967-1971. ST/STAT/Ser.P/5-9. E.40; 1972-1973. ST/ESA/STAT/Ser.P/10-11. E.47) – 9 – us U.N. Pubs [338]
GROWTH PROSPECTS FOR THE FINNISH ECONOMY UP TO 1980 / Finland. Economic Planning Centre – Helsinki. 1972. BD-1649 1 – 9 – ne IDC [339]
DER GROYSER KUNDES *see* THE BIG STICK
Groznenski i okrug (R.S.F.S.R.). Otdel zdravookhranenii a *see* OBZOR DEI ATELNOSTI GROZNENSKOGO OKRUZHNOGO OTDELA ZDRAVOOKHRANENII A ZA...BI UDZHETNY I GOD
GROZNENSKI I RABOCHI I – (Includes c.1: 1928:Dec.29) – Grozny i: [s.n.], 1924 – 1 – CSUXANR5051-S – us Hoover Inst Photo [947]
GROZNYI SMEKH / Maiakovskii, Vladimir – M., L. 1932. BR-968 2 – 8 – ne IDC [460]
GRRRANDE PECHE AU GOUJON ELECTORAL : OU, BLAGEURS TAISEZ-VOUS! – Paris [1848?] – us Res Libr [944]
Grub, George *see* AN ECCLESIASTICAL HISTORY OF SCOTLAND
Grubb, A P *see* A POPULAR HANDBOOK OF METHODIST LAW AND USAGE
Grubb, Edward *see*
– AUTHORITY AND THE LIGHT WITHIN
– SOCIAL ASPECTS OF THE QUAKER FAITH
Grubb, I C *see* THE COLONIAL AND STATE JUDICIARY OF DELAWARE
Grube, K *see*
– DES AUGUSTINERPROPSTES IOANNES BUSCH
– CHRONICON WINDESHEMENSE UND LIBER DE REFORMATIONE MONASTICA DES AUGUSTINERPROPSTES JOH. BUSCH
Grubenmann, Yvonne de Athayde *see* UN COSMOPOLITE SUISSE
Gruber, J G *see*
– ALLGEMEINE ENCYCLOPAEDIE DER WISSENSCHAFTEN UND KUENSTE
– ALLGEMEINE ENCYCLOPAEDIE DER WISSENSCHAFTEN UND KUENSTE (AEL, ABT 1; 33)
Gruber, J S *see*
– LITERATUR DER MUSIK, ODER SYSTEMATISCHE ANLEITUNG ZUR KENNTNIS DER VORZUEGLICHEN MUSIKALISCHEN BUECHER,...
– LITTERATUR DER MUSIK, ODER SYSTEMATISCHE ANLEITUNG ZUR KENNTNISS DER VORZUEGLICHEN MUSIKALISCHEN BUECHER
Gruber, Johann Sigmund *see* BEYTRAEGE ZUR LITTERATUR DER MUSIK HERAUSGEGEBEN VON JOHANN SIGMUND GRUBER
Grudzinski, Herbert *see* SHAFTESBURYS EINFLUSS AUF CHR. M. WIELAND
Gruebler, R *see* DIE VOLLSTRECKUNG AUSLAENDISCHER CIVILURTEILE IN DER SCHWEIZ
Gruel, Guillaume *see* LA CHRONIQUE DE TRES HAULT ET TRES EXCELLANT PRINCE DE BON MEMOIRE ARTHUR, DEUXZIESME DE CE NOM...
Gruen, Anastasius *see*
– ANASTASIUS GRUEN'S GESAMMELTE WERKE
– GEDICHTE
– IN DER VERANDA
– NIKOLAUS LENAU'S DICHTERISCHER NACHLASS
Gruen, Ferdinand Bernard *see* ENGLISH GRAMMAR IN AMERICAN HIGH SCHOOLS SINCE 1900
Gruenanger, Carlo *see* STORIA DELLA LETTERATURA TEDESCA MEDIOEVALE
Gruenau, W von *see* DIE STAATS- UND VOELKERRECHTLICHE STELLUNG AEGYPTENS
Gruenbaum, Max *see* NEUE BEITRAEGE ZUR SEMITISCHEN SAGENKUNDE
Gruenberg, Benjamin C in collaboration with U.S Bureau *see* HIGH SCHOOLS AND SEX EDUCATION
Gruenberg, C *see* ARCHIV FUER DIE GESCHICHTE DES SOZIALISMUS UND DER ARBEITERBEWEGUNG
Gruenberg, Gottfried *see* WIR KAEMPFEN UND SIEGEN FUER DICH FREIHEIT
Gruenberg, Paul *see* DIE EVANGLISCHE KIRCHE
GRUENDLICHE ABLEINUNG FUENFFZIG STATLICHER AUSSERLESENER VND IN ALLE EWIGE EWIGKEIT UNERWEISSLICHER CALVINISCHER ERTZ-VND HAUPTLUEGEN... / Hoenegg, M Hoe von – Leipzig, 1621 – 1mf – ne IDC [240]
GRUENDLICHE ANWEISUNG ZUR COMPOSITION / Albrechtsberger, Johann G – Leipzig. 1790. BP-122 1 – 9 – ne IDC [780]
GRUENDLICHE EINLEITUNG IN DIE ANFANGSLEHREN DER TONKUNST / Albrecht, J L – 1761 – 9 – us Sibley [780]
GRUENDLICHE KURTZ VERFASTE HISTORIA VON MUENSTERISCHEN WIDERTAUFFERN / Erhard, Chr – Muenchen. A. Berg. 1588. BME-141 1 – 9 – ne IDC [240]
GRUENDLICHE, SUMMARISCHE, APOSTOLISCHE AUSFUEHRUNG, DER GANTZEN REINEN CATHOLISCHEN EVANGELISCHEN LEHRE... IN FUNFFZIG PREDIGTEN VERFASSET / Hoenegg, M Hoe von – Leipzig, 1611 – 9mf – ne IDC [240]
GRUENDLICHER BERICHT, AUFF DIE VON DEN CALVINISTEN EINGEGEBENE KLAEGLICHE SUPPLIKATION, DARINNEN DIE HIMMELSCHE GOETTLICHE WAHRHEIT,... / Hoenegg, M Hoe von – Leipzig, 1605 – 4mf – ne IDC [240]
AIN GRUENDTLICHER BERICHT VOM CHRISTLICHEN TAUFF / Landtsperger, J – 1526. BME-63 1 – 9 – ne IDC [240]
GRUENDTLICHER BERICHT...AUFF JOHANN STURMIJ... / Andreae d.A E, J – Tuebingen, 1581 – 4mf – 9 – ne IDC [240]
GRUENDTLICHER WARHAFFTIGER VND BESTENDIGER BERICHT: VON CHRISTLICHER EINIGKEIT DER THEOLOGEN VND PREDICANTEN... / Andreae d.A E, J – Wolffenbuettel, 1570 – 2mf – 9 – ne IDC [240]
GRUENDUNG UND ENTWICKLUNG DER KREDITINSTITUTE IN MANNHEIM UND LUDWIGSHAFEN VON DER MITTE DES 19. JAHRHUNDERTS BIS 1911 / Wuestenhoff, Conrad Kleefeld von – Heidelberg, 1967 – 3mf – 9 – DM76.00 – 3-89349-757-9 – gw Hänsel [332]
GRUENDUNGSGESCHICHTE DER STIFTER...DES ALTEN BISTUMS MUENSTER / Tibus, A – Muenster, 1867 – 5mf – 8 – Dfl22.00 – ne Slangenburg [240]
GRUENE BRUECHE : SCHILDERUNGEN UND ERZAEHLUNGEN AUS DEM WILD- UND WAIDMANNSLEBEN DES HOCHGEBIRGES / Achleitner, Arthur – Stuttgart: Adolf Bonz, 1894 – 1r – 1 – us U.W. Library [830]
DER GRUENE HEINRICH : STUDIEN-AUSGABE DER ERSTEN FASSUNG VON 1854/55 / Keller, Gottfried; ed by Ermatinger, Emil – (Includes bibliographical references) – 2. u. 3. Aufl. Stuttgart: J G Cotta'sche Buchhandlung Nachfolger. 2v. 1914 – 1 – us U.W. Library [830]
Gruenebaum, GE von *see* MODERN ISLAM
Grueneisen, Carl *see* DER AHNENKULTUS UND DIE URRELIGION ISRAELS
GRUENENTHAL WAAGE *see* WAAGE
Gruenwald, F *see* DAS LUFTSCHIFF IN VOELKERRECHTLICHER UND STRAFRECHTLICHER BEZIEHUNG
Gruenwedel, A *see*
– ALTBUDDHISTISCHE KULSTAETTEN IN CHINESISCH-TURKISTAN
– BERICHT UEBER ARCHAEOLOGISCHE ARBEITEN IN IDIKUTSCHARI UND UMGEBUNG, IM WINTER 1902-1903
– BUDDHISTISCHE KUNST IN INDIEN
– MYTHOLOGIE DES BUDDHISMUS IN TIBET UND DER MONGOLEI
Gruetzmacher, Richard H *see*
– JUNGFRAUENGEBURT
– THE VIRGIN BIRTH
Gruetzmacher, Richard Heinrich *see*
– IST DAS LIBERALE JESUSBILD MODERN?
– WORT UND GEIST
Grulev, Mikhail Vladimirovich *see* ZAPISKI GENERALA-EVREIA
Grumbine, Jesse Charles Fremont *see* EVOLUTION AND CHRISTIANITY
THE GRUMBLER – Toronto. 1858-69 – 1 – 45.00 – cn McLaren [971]
Grum-Grzhimailo, G E *see* ZAPADNAIA MONGOLIIA I URIANKHANSKII KRAI
DIE GRUNDBEDEUTUNG DES GROENLAENDISCHEN SUBJECTIVS / Finck, N F – BN 209 2. 1905 – 8 – ne IDC [430]
GRUNDBEGRIFFE DER NATURPHILOSOPHIE BEI WILHELM VON OCKHAM / Moser, S – Innsbruck, 1932 – 4mf – 8 – ne Slangenburg [100]
DAS GRUNDDOGMA DES ROMANISMUS : ODER, DIE LEHRE VON DER KIRCHE / Delitzsch, Johannes – Gotha: Rud. Besser, 1875 – 1mf – 9 – 0-8370-5910-0 – 1985-3910 – us A.T.L.A. [240]
Grundemann, R *see* DIE ENTWICKLUNG DER EVANGELISCHEN MISSION

GRUNDFORMEN VOLKSTUEMLICHER ERZAEHLERKUNST IN DEN KINDER- UND HAUSMAERCHEN DER BRUEDER GRIMM : EIN STILKRITISCHER VERSUCH / Berendsohn, Walter Arthur – (Includes bibliographical references) – Hamburg: W Gente, 1921 – 1r – 1 – us U.W. Library [430]

GRUNDFRAGEN DER MOTOLOGIE : EINE UNTERSUCHUNG DER GANZHEITLICHKEIT AM BEISPIEL VON KINDLICHER ENTWICKLUNG UND ANGST / Haegele, Sigurd – 1993 – 3mf – 9 – DM98.00 – 3-89349-792-7 – gw Hänsel [150]

GRUNDFRAGEN DER VERGLEICHENDEN TEKTONIK / Stille, H – 1924 – 8 – G-116 2 – ne IDC [550]

GRUNDGEDANKEN EINES LUFTRECHTS / Fleischmann, M – Muenchen, 1910 – 1mf – 1 – ILM-1658/1 – ne IDC [327]

DIE GRUNDGEDANKEN IN HEINRICH VON KLEISTS "PRINZ FRIEDRICH VON HOMBURG" / Gilow, Hermann – Berlin: R Gaertner, 1893 – 1r – 1 – us U.W. Library [430]

GRUNDIDEEN, ERSCHEINUNGSFORMEN UND URSACHEN POLITISCHEN HINDU-FUNDAMENTALISMUS IN INDIEN VON 1875 BIS HEUTE AUS MODERNISIERUNGSTHEORETISCHER SICHT / Schworck, Andreas – 1995 – 1mf – 9 – DM60.00 – 3-8267-2099-7 – gw Hänsel [320]

DIE GRUNDLAGE DES VOELKERRECHTS / Cathrein, V – Freiburg, 1918 – 2mf – 1 – ILM-1741/1 – ne IDC [327]

GRUNDLAGE EINER EHREN-PFORTE / Mattheson, J – 1740 – 9 – us Sibley [780]

GRUNDLAGE ZU EINER HESSISCHEN GELEHRTEN- UND SCHRIFTSTELLER-GESCHICHTE / Strieder, Friedrich Wilhelm et al – Kassel und Marburg, 1781-1868. Hildesheim, 1983. – 117mf – 9 – DM820.00 diazo DM930.00 silver – gw Olms [430]

GRUNDLAGEN DER AEGYPTISCH-SEMITISCHEN WORTVERGLEICHUNG / Calice, F – (Beihefte zur "Wiener Zeitschrift fuer die Kunde des Morgenlandes." heft 1). Wien. 1936. BNE-470 1 – 9 – ne IDC [470]

DIE GRUNDLAGEN DES LUTHERISCHEN KIRCHENREGIMENTES / Mejer, Otto – Rostock: Stiller, 1864 – 1mf – us A.T.L.A. [240]

GRUNDLAGEN, STILE, GESTALTEN DER DEUTSCHEN LITERATUR : EINE GESCHICHTLICHE DARSTELLUNG / Hoffmann, G F & Roesch, Herbert – (Includes index) – Frankfurt am Main: Hirschgraben, 1968 – 1r – 1 – us U.W. Library [430]

GRUNDLINIEN DER KIRCHENGESCHICHTE : IN DER FORM VON DISPOSITIONEN FUER SEINE VORLESUNGEN / Loofs, Friedrich – Halle a.S.: M. Niemeyer, 1910 – 2mf – us A.T.L.A. [240]

GRUNDLINIEN DER SYSTEMATISCHEN THEOLOGIE : ZUM GEBRAUCHE BEI VORLESUNGEN / Bachmann, Philipp – Leipzig:A. Deichert (Georg Boehme), 1908 – 1mf – 9 – 0-8370-2540-0 – 1985-0540 – us A.T.L.A. [240]

GRUNDLINIEN DER SYSTEMATISCHEN THEOLOGIE: ZUM GEBRAUCHE BEI VORLESUNGEN / Bachmann, Philipp – Leipzig: A. Deichert, 1908. 1 fiche – 9 – us A.T.L.A. [240]

GRUNDLINIEN EINER ERKENNTNISTHEORIE DER GOETHESCHEN WELTANSCHAUUNG MIT BESONDERER RUECKSICHT AUF SCHILLER : ZUGLEICH EINE ZUGABE ZU GOETHES "NATURWISSENSCHAFTLICHEN SCHRIFTEN" IN KUERSCHNERS DEUTSCHER NATIONAL-LITERATUR / Steiner, Rudolf – erw. Aufl. Stuttgart: Der Kommende Tag, 1924 – 1r – 1 – us U.W. Library [430]

Grundmann, Johannes *see* DIE GEOGRAPHISCHEN UND VOELKERKUNDLICHEN QUELLEN UND ANSCHAUUNGEN IN HERDERS "IDEEN ZUR GESCHICHTE DER MENSCHHEIT"

GRUND-RICHTIGER, KURTZ, LEICHT UND NOETHIGER, (JETZT WOHLVERMEHRTER) UNTERRICHT DER MUSICALISCHEN KUNST / Speer, D – Ulm. 1697. BP-478 1 – 9 – ne IDC [780]

GRUND-RICHTIGER, KURTZ-, LEICHT- UND NOETHIGER, JETZT WOL-VERMEHRTER UNTERRICHT DER MUSICALISCHEN KUNST / Speer, D – 1697 – 9 – us Sibley [780]

GRUND-RICHTIGER, KURTZ, LEICHT UND NOETHIGER UNTERRICHT DER MUSICALISCHEN KUNST / Speer, D – 1687. Herausgegeben von Daniel Speeren – 9 – us Sibley [780]

GRUNDRISS DER BIBLISCHEN HERMENEUTIK / Lange, Johann Peter – Heidelberg: C. Winter, 1878. 1 fiche – 9 – us A.T.L.A. [240]

GRUNDRISS DER CHRISTLICHEN APOLOGETIK : ZUM GEBRAUCHE BEI AKADEMISCHEN VORLESGUNGEN / Schultz, Hermann – (Includes bibliographical references) – Goettingen: Vandenhoeck & Ruprecht, 1894 – 1mf – 9 – 0-8370-5646-2 – 1985-3646 – us A.T.L.A. [230]

GRUNDRISS DER CHRISTLICHEN DOGMENGESCHICHTE / Nitzsch, Friedrich – Berlin: E.S. Mittler, 1870 – 1mf – us A.T.L.A. [240]

GRUNDRISS DER CHRISTLICHEN ETHIK / Lange, Johann Peter – (Includes bibliographical references) – Heidelberg: Carl Winter, 1878 – 1mf – 9 – 0-8370-2094-8 – 1985-0094 – us A.T.L.A. [230]

GRUNDRISS DER CHRISTLICHEN GLAUBENS- UND SITTENLEHRE : ALS COMPENDIUM FUER STUDIRENDE UND ALS LEITFADEN FUER DEN UNTERRICHT AN HOEHEREN SCHULEN / ed by Pfleiderer, Otto – (Includes bibliographical references) – 4. Aufl. Berlin:Georg Reimer, 1888 – 1mf – 9 – 0-8370-5450-8 – 1985-3450 – us A.T.L.A. [240]

GRUNDRISS DER DEUTSCHEN LITERATURGESCHICHTE – (No more publ? Includes bibliographic references and index) – Berlin: Vereinigung Wissenschaftlicher Verleger. 2v. 1920-22 – 1 – us U.W. Library [430]

GRUNDRISS DER ENCYCLOPAEDIE DER THEOLOGIE / Dorner, Isaak August – Berlin: Georg Reimer, 1901 – 1mf – 9 – 0-8370-2953-8 – 1985-0953 – us A.T.L.A. [240]

GRUNDRISS DER EVANGELISCHEN DOGMATIK : ZUM GEBRAUCHE BEI AKADEMISCHEN VORLESUNGEN / Schultz, Hermann – (Includes bibliographical references) – 2. erw. Aufl. Goettingen: Vandenhoek & Ruprecht, 1892 – 1mf – 9 – 0-8370-5616-0 – 1985-3616 – us A.T.L.A. [240]

GRUNDRISS DER EVANGELISCHEN ETHIK : ZUM GEBRAUCHE BEI AKADEMISCHEN VORLESUNGEN / Schultz, Hermann – (Includes bibliographical references) – Goettingen: Vandenhoeck & Ruprecht, 1891 – 1mf – 9 – 0-8370-6367-1 – 1986-0367 – us A.T.L.A. [230]

GRUNDRISS DER GESCHICHTE DES NEUTESTAMENTLICHEN KANONS : EINE ERGAENZUNG ZU DER EINLEITUNG IN DAS NEUE TESTAMENT / Zahn, Theodor – (Includes bibliographical references) – 2. verm vielfach bearb Aufl. Leipzig: A Deichert (Georg Boehme), 1904 – 1mf – 9 – 0-8370-6556-9 – 1986-0556 – us A.T.L.A. [220]

GRUNDRISS DER GRIECHISCHEN LITTERATUR / Bernhardy, Gottfried – Erster Theil: Innere Geschichte der griechischen Litteratur. (Einleitung und allgemeine Uebersicht.) Fua5nfte Bearbeitung, von Richard Volkmann. Halle: E. Anton, 1892, xvi, 844 p. Film Mas 8651 – 1 – us H.U. Library [450]

GRUNDRISS DER GRIECHISCHEN LITTERATUR / Bernhardy, Gottfried – Halle, E. Anton, 1876-80 2 pt. in 3 v. Film Mas 8616 – 1 – us H.U. Library [450]

GRUNDRISS DER KRAEUTERKUNDE ZU VORLESUNGEN ENTWORFEN / Willdenow, C L – Berlin. 1792. B-5814 2 – 8 – ne IDC [580]

GRUNDRISS DER PATROLOGIE / Rauschen, G – Freiburg, 1906 – 4m – 9 – ne Slangenburg [240]

GRUNDRISS DER POLNISCHEN VERFASSUNGSGESCHICHTE / Kutrzeba, S – Berlin. 1912. BR-5464 2 – 8 – ne IDC [943]

GRUNDRISS DER RELIGIONSPHILOSOPHIE / Puenjer, Georg Christian Bernhard – Braunschweig: C.A. Schwetschke, 1886. 1 fiche – 9 – us A.T.L.A. [240]

GRUNDRISS DER THEOLOGISCHEN ENCYKLOPAEDIE: MIT EINSCHLUSS DER METHODOLOGIE / Lange, Johann Peter – Heidelberg: Carl Winter, 1877. 1 fiche – 9 – us A.T.L.A. [240]

GRUNDRISS DER THEOLOGISCHEN WISSENSCHAFT *see* THEOLOGISCHE ENCYKLOPAEDIE

GRUNDRISS DES RECHTS DER NATUR / Claproths, J C – Goettingen, 1749 – 3mf – 1 – ILM-807/1 – ne IDC [327]

GRUNDRISS DES ... SEERECHTS / Bischof, H – Graz, 1868 – 1mf – 9 – ILM-1641/1 – ne IDC [327]

GRUNDRISS ZUR GESCHICHTE DER DEUTSCHEN NATIONALLITERATUR / Koberstein, August; ed by Garber, Klaus – Leipzig, 1827 – 4mf – 9 – subsc: DM36.00 diazo DM40.00 silver – gw Olms [430]

GRUND-SAESSE DES VOELCKER-RECHTS... / Kemmerich, D H – Christian, Eralng, [1710] – 1mf – 9 – ILM-1362/1 – ne IDC [327]

GRUNDSAETZE DES GENERAL-BASSES ALS ERSTE LINIEN ZUR COMPOSITION / Kirnberger, Johann P – Amsterdam. BP-344 1 – 9 – ne IDC [780]

GRUNDSAETZE DES GENERALBASSES ALS ERSTE LINIEN ZUR COMPOSITION / Kirnberger, Johann P – Nebst XXXV Kupfertafeln. ca.1781 – 9 – us Sibley [780]

GRUNDSAETZE EINER EUROPAEISCHENARMEE GEGENUEBER DEN GEZWUNGENERMASSEN AUF RUSSISCHER SEITE KAEMPFENDEN / Beckerath, Ulrich von – 9 – 1.00f – at Libertarian Micro [335]

GRUNDSAETZE EVANGELISCH-LUTHERISCHER KIRCHENVERFASSUNG / Hoefling, J W – Erlangen: T. Blaesing, 1853 – 1mf – us A.T.L.A. [240]

GRUNDSAETZE REFORMIERTER KIRCHENVERFASSUNG / Rieker, Karl – Leipzig: C.L. Hirschfeld, 1899 – 1mf – us A.T.L.A. [240]

DIE GRUNDSAETZLICHE BEURTEILUNG DER RECHTE AN BEWEGLICHEN SACHEN... / Elten, H – Halle, 1914 – 1mf – 1 – ILM-3461/1 – ne IDC [327]

DER GRUNDSATZ DER NATIONALITAET UND DAS EUROPAEISCHE STAATENSYSTEM – Berlin, 1860 – 1mf – 1 – ILM-2484/1 – ne IDC [327]

DAS GRUNDSCHULWESEN IN DEN PROVINZEN DES OSMANISCHEN REICHES WAEHREND DER HERRSCHAFTSPERIODE ABDUELHAMIDS 2 (1876-1908) / Somel, Aksin – 1995 – 5mf – 9 – DM118.00 – 3-8267-2115-2 – gw Hänsel [470]

Grundt, Friedrich Immanuel *see* HEBRAEISCHE ELEMENTARGRAMMATIK

DER GRUNDTON IN GOETHES LEBENSANSCHAUUNG / Vogt, Paul – (Includes bibliographical references) – Weimar: H Boehlau, 1932 – 1r – 1 – us U.W. Library [140]

Grundtvig, N F S *see* SKAL DEN LUTHERSKE REFORMATION VIRKELIG FORTSOETTES?

GRUNDVORSTELLUNGEN DER AMERIKANISCHEN WIRTSCHAFTS-ETHIK : ZUR IDEOLOGIE DER "PROSPERITY" / Koenigsgarten, Hugo F – 1995 – 2mf – 9 – DM62.00 – 3-8267-3160-3 – gw Hänsel [330]

DIE GRUNDWAHRHEITEN DER CHRISTLICHEN RELIGION : EIN AKADEMISCHES PUBLIKUM IN SECHZEHN VORLESUNGEN... / Seeberg, Reinhold – 4. verb. Aufl. Leipzig: A Deichert (Georg Boehme), 1906 – 1mf – 9 – 0-8370-5209-2 – 1985-3209 – us A.T.L.A. [240]

GRUNDY COUNTY DIRECTORY / Lawrence & Thompson – Morris: Morris Reformer Office, 1877. Illinois Reel 26. (The Cox Library Collection) – 5 – us Americana [978]

GRUND-ZATSE DES EUROPAEISCHEN SEE-RECHTS / Gurland, J – Hanover, 1750 – 2mf – 1 – ILM-1132/1 – ne IDC [327]

DIE GRUNDZUEGE DER LEHRE VON TEMPUS UND MODUS IM GRIECHISCHEN / Aken, Adolf Friedrich – (Includes indexes) – Rostock: Stiller, 1861 – 1mf – 9 – 0-8370-9200-0 – 1986-3200 – us A.T.L.A. [450]

GRUNDZUEGE DER LITERATURGESCHICHTE / Lechner, Hermann – (Includes index) – Erw. Aufl. Innsbruck: Tyrolia-Verlag, 1947 – 1r – 1 – us U.W. Library [430]

GRUNDZUEGE DER NEUTESTAMENTLICHEN GRAECITAET : NACH DEN BESTEN QUELLEN FUER STUDIERENDE DER THEOLOGIE UND PHILOLOGIE / Schirlitz, Samuel Christoph – (Includes indexes) – Giessen: Ferber, 1861 – 1mf – 9 – 0-8370-9177-2 – 1986-3177 – us A.T.L.A. [450]

GRUNDZUEGE DER PHYSIOLOGISCHEN OPTIK / Aubert, Hermann – Leipzig, 1876 – 1 – DM30.00 – gw Mikro Press [612]

GRUNDZUEGE DER RELIGIONSWIS-SENSCHAFT : EINE KURZGEFASSTE EINFUEHRUNG IN DAS STUDIUM DER RELIGION UND IHRER GESCHICHTE / Tiele, Cornelius Petrus – Tuebingen: J C B Mohr, 1904 – 1mf – 9 – 0-8370-5534-2 – 1985-3534 – us A.T.L.A. [200]

GRUNDZUEGE DER SUMERISCHEN GRAMMATIK / Poebel, A – H 355 2. 1923 – 8 – ne IDC [490]

GRUNDZUEGE DES HEBRAEISCHEN RHYTHMUS UND SEINER FORMENBILDUNG / Rothstein, Johann Wilhelm – Leipzig: J.C. Hinrichs, 1909. 1 fiche – 9 – us A.T.L.A. [220]

GRUNDZUEGE EINER JURISTISCHEN CONSTRUCTION... / Franzinger, D – Freiburg, 1868 – 1mf – 1 – ILM-170/1 – ne IDC [327]

GRUNDZUEGE EINER TUNGUSISCHEN SPRACHLEHRE NEBST KURZEM WOERTERVERZEICHNISS / Castren, M A; ed by Schiefner, A – St. Petersburg, 1856.BU-448/2 – 8 – ne IDC [490]

Gruner, Hans *see* GELDTHEORIE UND WIRTSCHAFTSWACHSTUM

Grunert, Johann August *see* ARCHIV DER MATHEMATIK UND PHYSIK

Grunow, A *see* SUESSWASSER-DIATOMACEEN UND DESMIDIACEEN VON DER INSEL BANKA

Grunwald, G *see*
- GESCH. D. GOTTES BEWEISE IM MA BIS Z. AUSGANG D. HOCHSCHOLASTIK

Grupe-Loercher, Erica *see* DER WEG UEBER DEN VULKAN

GRUPO DE DOLMENES EN TERMINO DE BARCARROTA, PROVINCIA DE BADAJOZ / Melida, Jose Ramon – Etnografia y Prehistoria. T.III. Madrid, Museo Antropologico. 1924 – 1 – sp Bibl Santa Ana [946]

Grupo sindical de colonization num. 7959 *see* ORDENANZAS DE REGIMEN INTERIOR

Grupp, Georg *see* KULTURGESCHICHTE DER ROEMISCHEN KAISERZEIT

"GRUPPA OSVOBOZHDENIE TRUDA" – Moscow. no. 1-6. 1924-1928 – 1 – us NY Public [073]

Gruppa "Osvobozhdenie Truda. Moscow *see* SBORNIK

Grußendorf, Hermann *see* DER MONOLOG IM DRAMA DES STURM UND DRANG

Grutze, Albert Lewis *see* A COLLECTION OF WILLS

Gruver, BM *see* THE SOCIAL CONSTRUCTION OF LEISURE FOR WOMEN IN ACADEME

Gruys, J A *see* BOOK SALES CATALOGUES OF THE DUTCH REPUBLIC, 1599-1800

Gruyter, P de *see* REPORT TO THE GOVERNMENT OF SYRIA ON SOME ASPECTS OF THE GHAB RECLAMATION

A GRUZ – Maceio, Alagoas. 7 Out 1900; Mar-12 Abr 1903 – 1,5,6 – bl Biblioteca [072]

Gruzdev, I *see* RUSSKAIA POEZIIA 1918-1923 G

GRUZINSKAIA KONTR-REVOLIUTSIIA / Drabkina, Elizaveta – Leningrad: Pribo i, 1928 – 1 – CSUX89-B5596 – us Hoover Inst Photo [947]

GRUZINSKIE DOKUMENTY INSTITUTA NARODOV AZII AN SSSR / Kakabadze, S S – Moscow, 1967. 512p. BR-10,977/1 – 9 – ne IDC [950]

GRUZINSKIE LIRIKI / Pasternak, B – M. 1937. BR-1014 2 – 8 – ne IDC [460]

GRUZINSKIE RUKOPISI INSTITUTA VOSTOKOVEDENIIA – v1. Moscow, Leningrad, 1956. 214p. BR-10,976/1 – 9 – ne IDC [947]

Grygier, T et al *see* POLSKI SLOWNIK ARCHIWALNY

GRYLL GRANGE... / Peacock, Thomas Love – London: Parker, Son, and Bourn, 1861 – 1 roll – 1 – 1-55879-667-3 – uk Libr Preservation [830]

Grynaeus, S *see* NOVVS ORBIS REGIONVM AC INSVLARVM VETERIBVS INCOGNITARVM, UNA CUM TABULA COSMOGRAPHICA, ET ALIQUOT ALIJS CONSIMILIS ARGUMENTI LIBELLIS, QUORUM OMNIUM CATALOGUS SEQUENTI PATEBIT PAGINA

Gryphius, Andreas *see*
- LATEINISCHE UND DEUTSCHE JUGENDDICHTUNGEN
- OLIVETUM
- SONN- UND FEIERTAGS-SONETTE
- SONNETTE

Gryseels, G *see* RESEARCH ON FARM AND LIVESTOCK PRODUCTIVITY IN THE CENTRAL ETHIOPIAN HIGHLANDS
GRYTHYTTE TIDNING – Nora, Sweden. 1885-1907 – 1 – sw Kungliga [072]
Gryzynski, Waclaw *see* CO DALI BOLSZEWICY LUDOWI W ROSJI?
Gsell, S *see* HISTOIRE ANCIENNE DE L'AFRIQUE DU NORD
Gsell, Stephane *see* HISTOIRE ANCIENNE DE L'AFRIQUE DU NORD
Gsell-Truempi, F *see* ZUR RECHTLICHEN NATUR DER VOELKERBUNDSMANDATE
GSN : GAY STUDIES NEWSLETTER – (Superseded by: Lesbian and Gay Studies Newsletter) – Toronto. v1-16 n1. Apr 1974-Mar 1989 – 1r – 1 – Can$85.00 – cn McLaren [305]
Gstettner, Hans *see* DIE GETRENNTEN
GT – Goeteborg, Malmoe. 1995- – 9 – sw Kungliga [072]
GT – Goteborg, Sweden. 1979-89 – 1 – sw Kungliga [072]
GT *see* GOTEBORGSTIDNINGEN
GTE AUTOMATIC ELECTRIC WORLD-WIDE COMMUNICATIONS JOURNAL – v17, no.6-v21, no.2. Nov 1979-2nd quarter 1983 – 1,5,6,9 – us UMI [073]
GTE NETWORK SYSTEMS WORLD-WIDE COMMUNICATIONS JOURNAL – v21, no.3-4. 3rd, 4th quarters 1983 – 1,5,6,9 – us UMI [073]
GUADALAJARA, 8-23 MARZO, 1937 / Tedeschi, Paolo – Con i prigionieri italiani, dopo la vittoria dell'escrito populare spagnolo. Parigi, 1937. Fiche W1222. (Blodgett Collection of Spanish Civil War Pamphlets) – 9 – us H.U. College Libr [946]
GUADALAJARA; PALACIO DEL INFANTADO – n.p.,1936. Fiche W932. (Blodgett Collection of Spanish Civil War Pamphlets) – 9 – us H.U. College Libr [946]
GUADALUPE – Caceres, 1906-1909 – 5 – sp Bibl Santa Ana [073]
GUADALUPE – Caceres, 1914 y 1915 – 5 – sp Bibl Santa Ana [073]
GUADALUPE, ARTE, DEVOCION Y... / Alvarez, Arturo – Madrid: Archivo Ibero Americano, 1965 – 1 – sp Bibl Santa Ana [240]
GUADALUPE (CACERES) / Junta Provincial de Turismo – (Fotos Mas) – Vitoria: Tip. Fournier, s.a. – 1 – sp Bibl Santa Ana [338]
GUADALUPE DE EXTREMADURA EN INDIAS / Bayle, Constantino – Madrid: Razon y Fe, 1928 – 9 – sp Bibl Santa Ana [972]
GUADALUPE EN LA AMERICA ANDINA. MADRID, 1969 / Meseguer Fernandez, Juan & Alvarez, Arturo – Madrid: Graf. Calleja, 1969 – 1 – sp Bibl Santa Ana [972]
GUADALUPE EN LOS SIGLOS 17; 18 / Jimenez Priego, Teresa – Badajoz: Dip. Provincial, 1975. Sep. REE – 1 – sp Bibl Santa Ana [946]
GUADALUPE, IMPRESIONES ARTISTICO-RELIGIOSAS / Pedrajas y Nunez-Romero, Eloy – Badajoz: Uceda Hermanos, 1902 – 1 – sp Bibl Santa Ana [240]
GUADELOUPE : ANNUAIRE STATISTIQUE DE LA GUADELOUPE 1949/53-1967/70 / France. Institut National de la Statistique et des Etudes Economiques – (1949-53 not available. Coll title: Latin American and Caribbean Official Statistical Serials, 1821-1982) – 11mf – 9 – £92.00 – uk Chadwyck [972]
Guadeloupe. French West Indies *see*
– JOURNAL OFFICIEL DE LA GUADELOUPE
– RECUEIL DES ACTS, ADMINISTRATIFS ET D'INFORMATION DE LA PREFECTURE
Guadelupe, Andres *see*
– COMMENTARIA IN HOSSEAN PROPHETAM
– HISTORIA...DE LOS ANGELES
– MYSTICA THEOLOGIA
Guadet, Julien *see* ELEMENTS ET THEORIE DE L'ARCHITECTURE.
GUADIANA – Badajoz, 1946 – 5 – sp Bibl Santa Ana [073]
GUADIANA. SEMINARIO DE ACTUALIDADES EXTREMENAS – Badajoz, 1946 (1 a 11) – sp Bibl Santa Ana [946]
Guagnino, A *see*
– SARMATIAE EUROPEAE DESCRIPTIO/ QUAE REGNUM POLONIAE, LITVANIAM SAMOGITIAM, RUSSIAM, MASSOVIAM, PRUSSIAM, POMERANIAM, LIVONIAM ET MOSCHOVIAE TARTARIAEQUE PARTEM COMPLECTITUR
– SARMATIAE EUROPEAE DISCRIPTIO...
O GUAJAJARA – '(s.l.')-Sao Luis, Brazil. 1 Apr-Aug, Oct 1840 – 1,5,6 – bl Biblioteca [072]
Gual Villalbi, P *see* TRATADO DE DERECHO MERCANTIL INTERNACIONAL
Gualtieri, F *see* CORONA PER LA VITTORIA DEL SERENISS. DON GIO. D'AVSTRIA
Gualtieri, G *see* RELATIONI DELLA VENVTA DE GLI AMBASCIATORI GIAPONESI A ROMA, SINO ALLA PARTITA DI LISBONA
Gualtieri, N *see* INDEX TESTARUM CONCHYLIORUM QUAE AD SERVANTUR IN MUSEO N. GUALTIER
GUAM : PROCEEDINGS OF THE CONSTITUTIONAL CONVENTION, 1977 – Agana: The Territory of Guam, Mar 1979 – 16mf – 9 – $24.00 – LLMC 82-100B Title 35 – us L.L.M.C. [323]
GUAM : PROCEEDINGS OF THE FIRST CONSTITUTIONAL CONVENTION, 1969-1970 – Agana: Garrison & McCarter Inc, n.d. – 28mf – 9 – $42.00 – LLMC 82-100B Title 32 – us L.L.M.C. [340]
GUAM : SESSION LAWS OF AMERICAN STATES AND TERRITORIES – 1975-94 – 9 – $185.00 set – us Hein [340]
Guam *see* GUAM NEWS LETTER
GUAM ADMINISTRATIVE RULES, 1991 / Guam. Office of the Attorney General, Division of the Compiler of Laws – (Updates planned) – 1v titles 1-6. Agana: Govt of Guam, 1991 – 8mf – 9 – $12.00 – LLMC 82-100B Title 36 – us L.L.M.C. [324]
Guam. (Commonwealth) *see*
– ADMINISTRATIVE RULES AND REGULATIONS OF THE GOVERNMENT OF GUAM, 1975
– ANNUAL REPORTS OF THE GOVERNOR OF GUAM, 1938-1981
– CIVIL REGULATIONS WITH THE FORCE AND EFFECT OF LAW IN GUAM, 1947
– THE GUAM RECORDER, OLD SERIES
Guam. (Commonwealth). 1st Legislature *see* STATUTES AND AMENDMENTS TO THE CODES OF THE TERRITORY OF GUAM, 1951-1952
Guam. (Commonwealth). 5th Legislature *see* THE GOVERNMENT CODE OF GUAM, 1961
Guam. (Commonwealth). 10th Legislature *see* THE CIVIL CODE OF THE TERRITORY OF GUAM, 1970
Guam. (Commonwealth). Laws, Statutes, etc *see*
– THE CIVIL AND PENAL CODES OF THE TERRITORY OF GUAM, 1953
– THE CIVIL CODE OF GUAM, 1947
– THE CODE OF CIVIL PROCEDURE AND PROBATE CODE OF GUAM, 1953
– THE CODE OF CIVIL PROCEDURE AND PROBATE CODE OF GUAM, 1970
– THE CODE OF CIVIL PROCEDURE OF GUAM, 1947
– THE GOVERNMENT CODE OF GUAM, 1970
– THE PENAL CODE OF GUAM, 1947
– THE PENAL CODE OF THE TERRITORY OF GUAM, 1970
– THE PROBATE CODE OF GUAM, 1947
Guam. (Commonwealth). Legislative Counsel *see* THE GOVERNMENT CODE OF GUAM, 1952
Guam. Federal-Territorial Commission *see* "LONG-RANGE ECONOMIC DEVELOPMENT PLAN" D-1316/1. 1966
Guam Govt *see* GUAM NAVAL GOVERNMENT BRIEF EXTRACTS, 1905
Guam Law Revision Commission *see* GUAM ORGANIC ACT AND RELATED FEDERAL LAWS THRU JUNE 5, 1979
Guam Legislature *see* SESSION LAWS OF GUAM, 1975/76-1991/92
GUAM NAVAL GOVERNMENT BRIEF EXTRACTS, 1905 : BRIEF EXTRACTS RELATIVE TO THE ISLAND OF GUAM FROM PUBLICATIONS, MEMORANDA FURNISHED TO CONGRESS, GENERAL ORDERS AND ANNUAL REPORTS FOR 1901-1904 / Guam Govt – Washington: GPO, 1905 – 2mf – 9 – $3.00 – LLMC 82-100B Title 31 – us L.L.M.C. [324]
GUAM NEWS LETTER / Guam – Agana. 1909-1922 – 1 – us NY Public [072]
Guam. Office of the Attorney General *see* GUAM ORGANIC ACT AND RELATED FEDERAL LAWS THRU AUGUST 31, 1984
Guam. Office of the Attorney General, Division of the Compiler of Laws *see* GUAM ADMINISTRATIVE RULES, 1991
GUAM ORGANIC ACT AND RELATED FEDERAL LAWS THRU AUGUST 31, 1984 / Guam. Office of the Attorney General – Agana: Office of the Attorney General, Div of Compiler of Laws, 1984 – 1mf – 9 – $1.50 – LLMC 82-100B Title 25 – us L.L.M.C. [340]
GUAM ORGANIC ACT AND RELATED FEDERAL LAWS THRU JUNE 5, 1979 / Guam Law Revision Commission – Agana, 1979 – 1mf – 9 – $1.50 – LLMC 82-100B Title 27 – us L.L.M.C. [323]
THE GUAM RECORDER – Agana. v. 1-17, no. 2. 1924-May 1940 – 1 – us NY Public [072]
THE GUAM RECORDER, NEW SERIES – Univ of Guam, Micronesia Research Centre. v1-9. Oct/Dec 1971-79 (all publ?) – 16mf – 9 – $24.00 – LLMC 82-100B Title 22 – us L.L.M.C. [972]
THE GUAM RECORDER, OLD SERIES / Guam. (Commonwealth) – (Includes index) – v12-18. Mar 1924-Nov 1941 – 48mf – 9 – $72.00 – LLMC 82-100B Title 21 – us L.L.M.C. [972]
Guam. US Congress *see*
– ALIEN LABOR PROGRAM IN GUAM
– AMENDMENT TO THE ORGANIC ACT OF GUAM
– NON-VOTING DELEGATES, GUAM AND THE VIRGIN ISLANDS
– PROPOSED CONSTITUTION FOR GUAM
– PROVIDING FOR THE ESTABLISHMENT OF A CONSTITUTION FOR GUAM
O GUANABARA : REVISTA MENSAL ARTISTA, SCIENTIFICA E LITTERARIA – Rio de Janeiro, 1850-1851; 1854-1855 – 1,5,6 – bl Biblioteca [072]
Guanajuato. Mexico (State) *see* PERIODICO OFICIAL
GUANG DONG QUN BAO – China. 1921-22 – 9 – 300.00 – cc Globe [072]
Guangdong Province. China *see*
– JIAJING HUI ZHILUE, 1560
– JIAJING HUIZHOU FU ZHI, 1556
– JIAJING QINZHOU ZHI, APPROX. 1529
– JIAJING RENHUA XIAN ZHI, APPROX. 1529
– JIAJING WENGYUAN XIAN ZHI, APPROX. 1529
– LONGQING CHAOYANG XIAN ZHI, 1572
– ZHENGDE QIONGTAI ZHI, 1521
GUANGDONG QIAOBAO – Guangdong Overseas Chinese Journal. -w. 1983-. M D48 – 1 reel/y – 1 – $28.00r – cc Microforms [072]
GUANGMING RIBAO – 1949- – 1r per y – 1 – inquire – us Ross [072]
GUANGMING RIBAO – (Jun 1949-Feb 1967, 45r. 1967-76, 3r per yr. $67.50r; 1977- , 1r per yr. $55.00r) – Guangming Daily. China. In Chinese. Current Subscription. Annual Delivery. M D2 – 1 – cc Microforms [072]
GUANGMING RIBAO SUOYIN – Index to Guangming Daily. 1977-. F D2A – 9 – $4.50f – cc Microforms [072]
GUANGXI RIBAO – 1986- – 2r per y – 1 – inquire – us Ross [072]
GUANGXI RIBAO – Guangxi Daily. 1986- . M/D 114 – 1 – $55.00r – cc Microforms [072]
GUANGXUE XUEBAO – Acta Optica Sinica. In Chinese but English abstracts to the main articles. F p130 – 9 – $4.50f – cc Microforms [072]
GUANGZHOU RIBAO – Guangzhou Daily. 1983-86, 1 reel/y; 1987-91, 2 reels/y. M D46 – 1 – $55.00r – cc Microforms [072]
O GUARANY – Curitiba, 21 Jan-5 Aug 1981 – 1,5,6 – bl Biblioteca [072]
O GUARANY : JORNAL PARA TODOS – Aracaju, 27 Mar, May, Sep, Oct 1879; May, Jul 1880; Jan, May, Jun 1881; Feb-Dec 1883; Feb-Dec 1884 – 1,5,6 – bl Biblioteca [072]
O GUARANY – Laranjeiras, Brazil. 1 Oct-12 Nov 1847. Incomplete – 1 – bl Biblioteca [072]
O GUARANY : ORGAO DO GREMIO DRAMATICO TABORDA – Manaos, Amazonas. 10 Ago-8 Set 1900 – 1,5,6 – bl Biblioteca [072]
O GUARANY : PERIODICO CRITICO E JOCO-SERIO – Maceio, Alagoas. 22 Set, 25 Nov 1879 – 1,5,6 – bl Biblioteca [072]
O GUARANY : SEMANARIO INDEPENDENTE – Poco, Alagoas. 3 Set 1911 – 1,5,6 – bl Biblioteca [072]
GUARD – Holly Springs. Miss. 1842-1846 – 1 – us UMI [071]
GUARDIAN – (1964-1992.-111r) – Brampton, 1993 – 6r – 1 – cn Preston [971]
GUARDIAN – (1993.-16r; 1958-1961.-24r) – Charlottetown, 1974-1992 – 235r – 1 – cn Preston [971]
GUARDIAN – Aurora. Ill. -w. 1852-57 – 1 – us UMI [071]
GUARDIAN – Bahamas. 1849-1961 – 1 – us UMI [072]
GUARDIAN – Cape Town. Republic of South Africa. v. 1, no. 1-v. 16, no. 14. Feb 1937-May 1952. Missing: 15 Mar 1945 – 1 – 35.00r – us Hoover Inst Photo [072]
GUARDIAN – Cape Town, South Africa.1937-62. Title varies: Clarion, 1952; People's World, 1952; Advance, 1952-54; New Age, 1954-62 – 20r – 1, 16 diazo available at reduced price – sa SA Libr [072]
GUARDIAN – Charlottetown, Canada. (Daily and Morning). 1890-1903 – 24r – 1 – $1,560.00 – cn Library Assoc [971]
GUARDIAN – Dominica. 1893-1924 – 1 – us UMI [072]
GUARDIAN – Manchester. 1821- – 1 – us UMI [072]
GUARDIAN – Nassau. Bahamas. 1849-1854; 1863-1961 – 1 – us UMI [072]
GUARDIAN – New York. 1- 1948- – 1 – us UMI [073]
GUARDIAN – Rangoon, Burma. 1973-Aug 1988 – 50r – 1 – us L of C Photodup [072]
GUARDIAN – Sydney, 1844 – 1r – 1 – A$31.00 silver A$27.00 vesicular – at Pascoe [072]
GUARDIAN – The Entrance, Mar 4 1933-Feb 12 1959 (impf) – 9 – at Pascoe [072]
GUARDIAN *see* NEW AGE, 1955-62
GUARDIAN – Cape Town: Stewart Printing Co. jun 18-dec 1937 (1r); MF-6505 CAMP (12r) 1938-may 22 1952 – us Res Libr [072]
THE GUARDIAN – Boston, Mass. Black newspaper ed. by Wm. Monroe Trotter. 1902-13. no. 80-83. Incomplete. 2 reels – 1 – 50.00 – us Partington [071]
THE GUARDIAN – Dublin. Ireland. -w. 31 Oct 1846-30 Jan 1847. (10 ft) – 1 – uk British Libr Newspaper [072]
THE GUARDIAN – Durban, South Africa. 1921-24 – 1 – sa State Libr [072]
THE GUARDIAN – London. -w. 1852; 1860-65. (13 reels) – 1 – uk British Libr Newspaper [072]
THE GUARDIAN – Madras. India. v. 21, no. 17-36. 29 Apr-9 Sep 1943 – 1 – us NY Public [072]
THE GUARDIAN – New Castle, PA. -w 1889-1901 – 13 – $25.00r – us I.M.R. [071]
THE GUARDIAN – Rangoon: The Guardian Press, 1959-apr 1973; jan-apr 1975; jan-aug 1977 – 1 – us Res Libr [072]
THE GUARDIAN – Saint John, N.B.: [s.n. 1860] – 9 – cn C.I.H.M. [370]
THE GUARDIAN – Verdun. v2 n31. 23 jan 1931-v6 n52. 28 dec 1934 – 3r – 1 – Can$65.00 – cn Can Microfilming [072]
THE GUARDIAN – Wexford. Ireland. -w. 20 Nov 1847-30 Dec 1848. (37 ft) – 1 – uk British Libr Newspaper [072]
THE GUARDIAN *see* WALTHAMSTOW AND LEYTON GUARDIAN
THE GUARDIAN – Manchester: Manchester Guardian and Evening News Ltd, aug 1959-dec 1972 – us Res Libr [072]
THE GUARDIAN AND CONSTITUTIONAL ADVOCATE – Belfast. Ireland. -sw. 19 Jun 1827-25 Mar 1936. (8 reels) – 1 – uk British Libr Newspaper [072]
THE GUARDIAN INDEX 1842-1928, PART 1 : 1842-1880 – (Part 2: 1881-1904. 23 reels. $2,600.00; Part 3: 1905-1928. 24 reels. $2,700.00) – Marlborough: Adam Matthew Publications, 1994 – 18r – 1 – $2,000.00 – uk Matthew [072]
THE GUARDIAN INDEX, 1929-1972 : PART 1: 1929-1935 – (Part 2: 1936-1945, 479mf. $3,500.00, 1993. Part 3: 1946-1955, 474mf. $3,500.00, 1993. Part 4: 1956-1962, 429mf. $3,200.00, 1994; Part 5: 1963-1972, 513mf. $4,000.00, 1995) – Marlborough: Adam Matthew Publications, 1993 – 474mf – 9 – $3,500.00 – uk Matthew [072]
THE GUARDIAN INDEX, 1973-1985, PART 1 : 1973-1978 – (Part 2: 1979-1985. 153mf. $1,250.00) – Marlborough: Adam Matthew Publications – 184mf – 9 – $1,950.00 – uk Matthew [072]
GUARDIAN JOURNAL – Nottingham, England. Feb 1962. -w. 1/2 reel – 1 – uk British Libr Newspaper [072]
GUARDIAN OF TRUTH = WEI LI PAO – (In Chinese) – v7-9. 1956-58 (incomplete) – 1r – 1 – ATLA S0296R – us A.T.L.A. [073]

GUARDIAN RECORD / Williams. County, Ohio. Probate Court – 1878 – 1r – 1 – $32.50r – us Archival [324]
GUARDIAN REVIEW – Garden City. Mich. 1960-1967 – 1 – us UMI [071]
GUARDIAN TODAY : THE VOICE OF THE MALAWI CONGRESS PARTY – Lilongwe: The Party, apr 7/13-jun 11/15, jun 25/30, jul 5, 9, 16, 1993; jul 30/aug 5 1993-jan 28/feb 3 1994; feb 11/17-mar 25/31, apr 8/14-apr 29/may 5, may 13/19 1994 – 1r – 1 – us Res Libr [072]
GUARDIAN WEEKLY – (v. 120- 1979- 5,6,9) – v. 1- 1919- – 1 – us UMI [072]
Guardo, Ricardo C *see* HORAS DIFICILES
THE GUARDSMAN – San Francisco, CA: City College, 1935-80 – 5r – 1 – $250.00 – B02818 – us Library Micro [370]
Guarena. Ayuntamiento *see* ORDENANZAS MUNICIPALES
Guarini, M A *see* COMPENDIO HISTORICO DI FERRARA
Guarnello, A *see* CANZONE NELLA FELICISSIMA VITTORIA CHRISTIANA CONTRA INFIDELI AL SERENISS. D. GIO. D'AVSTRIA
Guastaferri, Fabritio *see* LETTERA DI FABRITIO GUASTAFERRI AL SIG. GIO. FRANCESCO SALITTI..
GUATEMALA : ANUARIO DE LA DIRECCION GENERAL DE ESTADISTICA 1898 / Guatemala. Direccion General de Estadistica – (Coll title: Latin American and Caribbean Official Statistical Serials, 1821-1982) – 3mf – 9 – £7.00f (set £300.00 36mf) – uk Chadwyck [972]
GUATEMALA : ANUARIO ESTADISTICO 1970 / Guatemala. Direccion General de Estadistica – (Coll title: Latin American and Caribbean Official Statistical Serials, 1821-1982) – 3mf – 9 – £7.00f (set £300.00 36mf) – uk Chadwyck [972]
GUATEMALA : GUATEMALA EN CIFRAS 1955-1969 / Guatemala. Direccion General de Estadistica – (Coll title: Latin American and Caribbean Official Statistical Serials, 1821-1982) – 28mf – 9 – £7.00f (set £300.00 36mf) – uk Chadwyck [972]
GUATEMALA : REPUBLICA DE GUATEMALA: SINTESIS GEOGRAFICA-ESTADISTICA 1948 / Guatemala. Direccion General de Estadistica – (Coll title: Latin American and Caribbean Official Statistical Serials, 1821-1982) – 2mf – 9 – £7.00f (set £300.00 36mf) – uk Chadwyck [972]
Guatemala *see*
– DIARIO DE CENTRO AMERICA. GUATEMALA
– EL GUATEMALTECO DIARIO DE CENTRO AMERICA
– PLAN DE DESARROLLO ECONOMICO DE GUATEMALA, 1955-1960
– PLAN DE DESARROLLO ECONOMICO Y SOCIAL DE CORTO PLAZO, 1967-70
– PLAN NACIONAL DE EDUCACION PARA LA REP. DE GUATEMALA
Guatemala. Con. Nac. de Plan. Econ *see*
– DESARROLLO ECONOMICO DE GUATEMALA
– PLAN DE INVERSIONES PUBLICAS, 1960-1964
– PLAN NACIONAL DE DESARROLLO ECONOMICO Y SOCIAL DE GUATEMALA 1965-1969
Guatemala. Direccion General de Estadistica *see*
– GUATEMALA
Guatemala. Inter-American Economic and Social Council *see* EVALUACION DEL PLAN. DE GUATEMALA, 1965-1969
GUATEMALA NEWS AND INFORMATION BUREAU (GNIB) – Oakland. 79 docs. 1980-1991 – 18mf – 9 – ne IDC [360]
Guatemala. Sec. General del Con. Nac. De Plan. Econ *see* PLAN DE DESARROLLO 1971-1975
Guatemala. Secretaria de relaciones exteriores *see* CONVENCION Y REGLAMENTOS...
Guatemala. Unidad Sectorial de Investigacion y Planification Educativa. Division Documentacion y Estadistica *see* ESTADISTICAS EDUCACIONALES 1988
EL GUATEMALTECO DIARIO DE CENTRO AMERICA / Guatemala – (Index. 1971-76. 1) – 1970- – 1 – us L of C Photodup [340]
GUATIMOZIN. TOMO 2 / Gomez de Avellaneda, Gertrudis – 1846 – 9 – $1.50f – sp Bibl Santa Ana [946]
Guay, A *see* LE PROGRES DU SAGUENAY
Guay, J D *see* LE PROGRES DU SAGUENAY
Guay, Marcel *see* BIBLIOGRAPHIE DE PAUL-ANDRE LAMONTAGNE
Guazzo, M *see*
– HISTOIRE...DI TVTTI I FATTI DEGNI DI MEMORIA NEL MONDO SVCCESSI DELL' ANNO M.D.24
– HISTORIE...CONTENENO LE GVERRE DI MAHOMETTO IMPERATORE DE TURCHI
Guback, Thomas *see* TRANSNATIONAL COMMUNICATION AND CULTURAL INDUSTRIES
Gubareva, MN *see* CHTO CHITAT' PO ISTORII KOMMUNISTICHESKOI PARTII SOVETS-KOGO SOIUZA
Gubel'man, M I *see* SMYCHKA
GUBENER ANZEIGER – Guben, Germany. 1884-86 – 1 – gw Mikrofilm [072]
GUBENER TAGEBLATT – Guben, Germany. No.231-306, 1906 – 1 – gw Mikrofilm [072]
GUBENER ZEITUNG – Guben, Germany. 1874 – 1 – gw Mikrofilm [072]
Gubernatis, Alessandro de *see* LE TRADIZIONI POPOLARI DI S. STEFANO DI CALCINAIA
Gubernskii sezd uezdnykh otdelov narodnogo khoziaistva (1920: Leningrad, R.S.F.S.R.) *see* ORGANIZATSIIA KHOZIAISTVENNOI ZHIZNI PETROGRADSKOI GUBERNII
GUBERNSKIIA VIEDOMOSTI / Russia – 1838-1906 – 1 – $1,531.00 – us L of C Photodup [073]
Guberti, Nikolai V *see* MATERIALY DLIA RUSSKOI BIBLIOGRAFII. KHRONOLOGICHESKOE OBOZRENIE REDKIKH I ZAMECHATEL'NYKH KNIG XVIII...1725-1800
Gubskii, N P *see* REVOLIUTSIIA I VNIESHNIAIA POLITIKA ROSSII
Guchkov, Aleksandr Ivanovich *see* A.I. GUCHKOV V TRETEI GOSUDARSTVENNOI DUMIE, 1907-1912 GG
Gude, Carl *see* GUDES ERLAEUTERUNGEN DEUTSCHER DICHTUNGEN
GUDES ERLAEUTERUNGEN DEUTSCHER DICHTUNGEN : AUSGEFUEHRTE ANLEITUNGEN ZUR AESTHETISCHEN WUERDIGUNG UND UNTERRICHTLICHEN BEHANDLUNG / Gude, Carl; ed by Linde, Ernst – (Vol publ out of sequence and in different editions) – Leipzig: F Brandstetter. 10v. 1910-1928 – 1 – us U.W. Library [430]
Gudgeon, T W *see* DEFENDERS OF NEW ZEALAND
Gudin de la Brenellerie, Paul P *see* SUPPLEMENT AU CONTRAT SOCIAL
GUDKI – Ezhenedel'nik Moskovskogo proletkul'ta. v. 1-6. M. 1919. Lacking: 1919 (2). BR-3425 2 – 8 – ne IDC [460]
GUDOK – Gazeta Ts. K. Soiuza Zheleznodorozhnogo i Vodnogo Transporta. Moscow. May 11, 1920-Feb. 3, 1922, nos. 1-519; Aug. 2, 1959, no. 175 (2761). Gaps – 1 – 35.00r – us Hoover Inst Photo [073]
GUDOK – Iumoristichesko-satiricheskii zhurnal. V. 1-22. Spb. 1859. BR-3981 2 – 8 – ne IDC [073]
GUDOK – Moscow. U.S.S.R. 1945- – 1 – us UMI [620]
GUDOK – Moscow, USSR. 1962-1981 – 20r – $1,000.00 – B63590 – us Library Micro [072]
GUDRUN : EIN SCHAUSPIEL / Strauss und Torney, Viktor Friedrich von – Frankfurt a.M.: K T Voelcker, 1851 – 1r – 1 – us U.W. Library [820]
GUDRUN : SCHAUSPIEL IN FUENF AUFZUEGEN / Grosse, Julius – Leipzig: J J Weber, 1870 – 1r – 1 – us U.W. Library [820]
GUDRUNS TOD : TRAGOEDIE / Schumann, Gerhard – Wien: K H Bischoff, 1943 – 1r – 1 – us U.W. Library [890]
DIE GUDRUNSAGE : DREI VORTRAEGE UEBER IHRE ERSTE GESTALT UND IHRE WIEDERBELEBUNG, GEHALTEN IN SCHLESWIG IM JANUAR 1867 / Keck, Karl Heinrich – Leipzig: B G Teubner, 1867 – 1r – 1 – us U.W. Library [390]
GUDSTRONS UPPKIMST / Soederblom, Nathan – Stockholm: H. Gebers, 1914 – 1mf – us A.T.L.A. [240]
Gudzii, N *see*
– IZ ISTORII RANNEGO RUSSKOGO SIMVOLIZMA
– TIUTCHEV V POETICHESKOI KUL'TURE RUSSKOGO SIMVOLIZMA
Guede, Lisardo *see*
– FRAY PEDRO NUNEZ MACHADO (ZAFRA 1550-BURGOS 1609)
– LA MERCED (COMPENDIO HISTORICO EN 12 LECCIONES)
Guedemann, Moritz *see*
– DAS JUDENTHUM
– RELIGIONSGESCHICHTE-STUDIEN
Gueenaga de Silva, Rosario *see* RELACION DE PERO LOPEZ. VISION DE UN CONQUISTADOR DEL SIGLO 16
GUEFT UE SENID / Bey, Mehmet Ata – Istanbul: Mihran Matbaasi, 1304 [1887] – $30.00 – us MEDOC [470]
Guel, Conde de (Marques de Comillas) *see* APUNTES DE RECUERDOS
GUELADIO HAM BODEDIO : HEROS DE LA POULAGOU A TRAVERS DEUX RECITS EPIQUES PEULS / Wane, Animata – 1980 – us Res Libr [944]
GUELDENE AEPFEL IN SILBERBEN SCHAELEN / Pfeffel, J A – O-1254 1. 1746 – 9 – ne IDC [760]
GUELDENE ROSE, D.I. EINFAELTIGE BESCHREIBUNG DES ALLERGROESSESTEN VON.. – Hamburg, 1705 – 1 – us U.W. Library [800]
Guelich van Berch, Heindrik *see*
– ANTWORDT GESCHREUEN OP EIN BRIEFF, DIE EIN DOEPER IN VRIESZLANDT, GESANDT HAT, AN MARCO
– EIN VERSAMLUNG ODER ZAMENFUEGUNG, ETLICHER EINHEILIGER SPRUECH. NACH DER ORTHNUNG DES A. B. C. BETREFFENDE
GUELNIHAL – Dersaadet, [1875] – $45.00 – us MEDOC [470]
Guelzow, Erich *see*
– ERNST MORITZ ARNDT IN SCHWEDEN
– ERNST MORITZ ARNDTS BRIEFE AN EINE FREUNDIN
Guembel-Seiling, Max *see*
– BRUDER LUSTIG
– GEVATTER TOD
– DAS GLUECKSKIND
– DIE KLUGE BAUERNTOCHTER
– MARIENKIND
– DAS TAPFERE SCHNEIDERLEIN
– DER TREUE JOHANNES
– DAS WASSER DES LEBENS
– DIE ZERTANZTEN SCHUHE
Guemes, Gontrande *see* ASI SEGESTO LA DICTADURA
GUEMRUEK NIZAMNAME-I UMUMIYESI – Dersaadet [Istanbul]: Mahmud bey Matbaasi, 1309 [1893] – 9 – $35.00 – us MEDOC [380]
GUEMRUEK SIYASETIMIZIN ESASLARI – [Istanbul]: Tuerk Ocaklari Merkez Heyeti Matbaasi, 1928 – 9 – $20.00 – us MEDOC [380]
GUENAYDIN : TAGESZEITUNG FUER TUERKEN IN EUROPA – Frankfurt Main, DE. 1 Sep 1978-31 Aug 1979 – 3r – 1 – gw Mikrofilm [072]
Guenduez, Aka *see* YARIM TUERKLER
Guenee, A *see*
– HISTOIRE NATURELLE DES INSECTES
– TABLEAUX SYNOPTIQUES DES LEPIDOPTERES D'EUROPE
GUENES – Istanbul: Matbaa-i Ebuezziya, Vatan Matbaasi, 1927 – 9 – $80.00 – us MEDOC [956]
GUENSER ZEITUNG – Guens (Koeszeg), Hungary. 6 Jan 1929-1938 – 3r – 1 – gw Mikrofilm [072]
Guentekin, Resat Nuri *see* GIZLI EL
Guenter, H *see* DIE HABSBURGER-LIGA 1625-1635
GUENTER UND CHRISTIANE : ROMAN / Ball, Kurt Herwarth – 1. Aufl. Berlin: Buchverlag Der Morgen, 1964 – 1r – 1 – us U.W. Library [820]
Guentersberg, Christian Carl *see* DER FERTIG ORGELSPIELER, ODER CASUALMAGAZIN FUER ALLE VORKOMMENDE FAELLE IM ORGELSPIELE
Guenther, A C L *see* THE FISHES OF ZANZIBAR
Guenther, A C LG *see*
– CATALOGUE OF THE FISHES IN THE BRITISH MUSEUM
– AN INTRODUCTION TO THE STUDY OF FISHES
– REPTILES AND FISHES OF THE SOUTH SEA ISLANDS
– THE REPTILES OF BRITISH INDIA
Guenther, Agnes *see* VON DER HEXE DIE EINE HEILIGE WAR
Guenther, Carl *see* HEINRICH ZSCHOKKES JUGEND- UND BILDUNGSJAHRE (BIS 1798)
Guenther, Johann Christian *see*
– GEDICHTE
– SAEMTLICHE WERKE
Guenther, Johannes von *see* SONETTENGARTEN
Guenther, Kurt Martin *see* DIE ENTWICKLUNG DER NOVELLISTISCHEN KOMPOSITIONSTECHNIK KLEISTS BIS ZUR MEISTERSCHAFT
Guenther, Oskar *see* DAS VERHAELTNIS DER ETHIK THOMAS HILL GREENS ZU DERJENIGEN KANTS
Guenther, W W *see* BEGRIFF UND BEDEUTUNG DER GEBIETSHOHEIT
Guentter, Otto *see*
– FRIEDRICH SCHILLER, SEIN LEBEN UND SEINE DICHTUNGEN
– GESAMMELTE DICHTUNGEN
Guenzburg, M A *see*
– AVI'EZER
– DEVIR
GUENZBURGER ZEITUNG – Guenzburg, West Germany. 1978- – ca 9r per yr – 1 – gw Mikrofilm [072]
Guenzig, E *see* HA-ESHKOL
LA GUEPE – Montreal, Canada. 18 dec 1857-30 nov 1867 – 1r – 1 – Can$55.00 – cn Can Microfilming [072]
LES GUEPES – Montreal, Canada. 23 jul-13 aut 1870 – 1r – 1 – Can$25.00 – cn Can Microfilming [072]
Guepin, Ange *see* NANTES AU XIXE SIECLE. STATISTIQUE TOPOGRAPHIQUE, INDUSTRIELLE ET MORALE: HYGIENE PHYSIQUE ET MORALE
Gueranger, Prosper *see*
– L'ANNEE LITURGIQUE
– DE LA MONARCHIE PONTIFICALE A PROPOS DU LIVRE DE MGR. L'EVEQUE DE SURA
– DEFENCE OF THE ROMAN CHURCH AGAINST FATHER GRATRY
Guerard, Albert Leon *see*
– FRENCH PROPHETS OF YESTERDAY
– FRENCH PROPHETS OF YESTERDAY; A STUDY OF RELIGIOUS THOUGHT UNDER THE SECOND EMPIRE
Guerard, H *see* DE L'ASSISTANCE JUDICIAIRE DES ETRANGERS EN FRANCE
Gueraud, Armand *see*
– DOCUMENTS RECUEILLIS POUR REMANIER LE RECUEIL DE CHANTS POPULAIRES DU COMTE NANTAIS..., T.1-5
– NOTICE SUR HUET DE COETLISAN
– RECUEIL DE CHANTS POPULAIRES DU COMTE NANTAIS ET DU BAS-POITOU, T.1-3
Guericke, H E F *see* GESAMMTGESCHICHTE DES NEUEN TESTAMENTS ODER NEUTESTAMENTLICHE ISAGOGIK
Guericke, Henry E F *see* A MANUAL OF CHURCH HISTORY
GUERILLA – v. 1-4. 1970-73 – 1 – 155.00 – cn McLaren [073]
GUERILLASKRIEG : VERSPRENGTE LIEDER – Belle-Vue bei Konstanz: Verlags- und Sortiments-Buchhandlung, 1845 – 1r – 1 – us U.W. Library [810]
Guerin, Eugenie de *see* JOURNAL OF EUGENIE DE GUERIN
Guerin, M *see* RERUM NOVARUM: HOW TO ABOLISH POVERTY: HOW POVERTY WAS ABOLISHED
Guerini, Francesco *see* SONATE A VIOLINO CON VIOLA DI GAMBA O CEMBALO
Guerin-Meneville, Felix Edouard *see*
– GENERA DES INSECTES
– ICONOGRAPHIE DU REGNE ANIMAL DE G. CUVIER; OU, REPRESENTATION D'APRES NATURE DE L'UNE DES ESPECES LES PLUS REMARQUABLES ET SOUVENT NON ENCORE FIGUREES, DE CHAQUE GENRE D'ANI-MAUX
– SPECIES ET ICONOGRAPHIE GENERIQUE DES ANIMAUX ARTICULES
GUERINO DETTO IL MESCHINO; STORIA DELLE GRANDI IMPRESE E VITTORIE DE LUI RIPORTATE CONTRO I TURCHI DURANTE IL REGNO DI CARLO MAGNO.. / Barberino, Andrea da – Milano: Bietti, 1910. 566p – 1 – us U.W. Library [830]
GUERINO IL MESCHINO; ROMANZO CAVALLERESCO DI ANDREA DA BARBERINO,.. / Barberino, Andrea da – Milano: Bertieri e Vanzetti, 1923 – 1 – us U.W. Library [830]
Guerinot, A *see* REPERTOIRE D'EPIGRAPHIE JAINA PRECEDE D'UNE ESQUISSE DE L'HISTOIRE DU JAINISME D'APRES LES INSCRIPTIONS
Guerlach, le pere M *see* CHEZ LES SAUVAGES BAHNARS
Guernsey, Alfred Hudson *see* HARPER'S PICTORIAL HISTORY OF THE GREAT REBELLION
Guernsey, Alice M *see* UNDER OUR FLAG: A STUDY OF NATIONAL CONDITIONS IN AMERICA FROM THE STANDPOINT OF WOMAN'S HOME MISSION WORK

GUERNSEY BREEDER'S JOURNAL – (v127-. 1971-. 5,6. v135-. 1975-. 9) – 1- 1910- – 1 – us UMI [636]
GUERNSEY JEFFERSONIAN – (Weekly Democratic newspaper) – Washington, OH. jan 3, 1844-may 8, 1869 – 2r – 1 – us Western Res [071]
Guernsey, Rocellus Sheridan *see* A KEY TO STORY'S EQUITY JURISPRUDENCE, CONTAINING OVER EIGHT HUNDRED QUESTIONS
Guerra, Arthur *see* THE EFFECT OF SODIUM CITRATE INGESTION ON 1600 METER RUNNING PERFORMANCE
Guerra Camacho, Mercedes *see* EL COLERA MORBO EN BADAJOZ EN 1883
GUERRA CIVIL. INVENTARIO DE LA DOCUMENTACION DE LA GENERALITAT DE CATALUNA – 1989 – 9 – sp Cultura [355]
GUERRA DE EXTREMADURA Y SITIOS DE BADAJOZ (1706) / Silva, Alejandro de – Badajoz: Tip.Euc. A.Arqueros, 1945 – 1 – sp Bibl Santa Ana [350]
Guerra, Felipe Leon *see*
- NOTAS A LAS ANTIGUEDADES DE EXTREMADURA
- NOTAS A LAS ANTIGUEDADES E EXTREMADURA DE JOSE VIU

GUERRA FISICA, PROEZAS MEDICALES, HAZANAS DE LA IGNORANCIA... – (On same reel: various authors) – [16–] – us Res Libr [946]
Guerra Guerra, Arcadio *see*
- APUNTES BIBLIOGRAFICOS DE LA PRENSA PERIODICA DE LA BAJA EXTREMADURA. 1 Y 2
- EL BADAJOZ DEL SIGLO 16
- CARTA DE PRIVILEGIO DE LOS REYES CATOLICOS A LA CIUDAD DE BADAJOZ, FECHADA EN EL CAMPAMENTO REAL "SOBRE TORO" EL DIA 21 DE JULIO DE 1475
- CARTAS A LOPEZ PRUDENCIO
- DE HISTORIA. RELACIONES DE BADAJOZ CON LA CORTE Y CON DON MANUEL GODOY DURANTE EL VALIMIENTO DE ESTE
- FESTEJOS EN HONOR DEL PRINCIPE DE LA PAZ HABIDOS EN BADAJOZ EN 1807
- INSTITUTO MILITAR PESTOLOZZIANO DE MADRID, OBRA DEL EXTREMENO MANUEL GODOY
- LA MINERIA EN LA BAJA EXTREMADURA EN LA PRIMERA MITAD DEL SIGLO 29
- PRECIOS Y SALARIOS EN BADAJOZ DURANTE EL BIENIO 1775-76

Guerra Hontiveros, Marcelino *see*
- APUNTES...VILLA DE GATA
- NARRACIONES DE UN TROVADOR

LA GUERRA NACIONAL ESPANOLA ANTE LA MORAL Y EL DERECHO / Menendez-Reigada, Ignacio G – Bilbao, 1937? Fiche W 1044. (Blodgett Collection of Spanish Civil War Pamphlets) – 9 – us H.U. College Libr [946]
Guerra, P *see* IL DIRITTO D'ALBINAGGIO...
GUERRA PHISICA, PROEZAS MEDICALES O HAZANAS DE LA IGNORANCIA [4TH QUARTER OF 17TH CENT] – Madrid, Biblioteca Nacional [19–] – us Res Libr [946]
GUERRA SANTA: EL SENTIDO CATOLICO DE LA GUERRA ESPANOLA. BURGOS, 1938 / Castro Albarran, A de – Burgos: Razon y Fe, 1938 – 1 – sp Bibl Santa Ana [946]
GUERRA Y MARINA, EPOCA DE CARLOS 1 DE ESPANA... / Alvarez, C – Valladolid, 1949 – 9 – sp Cultura [920]
Guerrant, Edward Owings *see* THE GALAX GATHERERS
Guerrant, Grace *see* THE GALAX GATHERERS
GUERRAS CIVILES DEL PERU / Cieza de Leon, Pedro de – Madrid – 1 – sp Bibl Santa Ana [972]
GUERRAS DE RETAGUARDIA / Juez, Antonio – Badajoz: Tip.Espanola, 1937 – 1 – sp Bibl Santa Ana [946]
GUERRAS PIRATICAS DE FILIPINAS / Barrantes Moreno, Vicente – 1878 – 9 – 1.50f – sp Bibl Santa Ana [950]
LA GUERRE / Carred, Henri – Paris: Imp E Bautruche, 1848 – us Res Libr [944]
LA GUERRE AERIENNE ILLUSTREE – devenu: La Vie aerienne illustree. no. 1-163. Paris. 16 nov 1916-25 dec 1919 – 1 – fr A.C.R.P.P. [073]
LA GUERRE ANGLO-BOER : HISTOIRE ET RECITS D'APRES DES DOCUMENTS OFFICIELS / Rosny, J H – Paris: Editions de la Revue Blanche, 1902 – 1 – us Res Libr [960]
LA GUERRE AU DAHOMEY, 1888-1893 : D'APRES LES DOCUMENTS OFFICIELS / Aublet, Edouard Edmond – Paris: Berger-Levrault, 1894 – 1 – us Res Libr [960]
LA GUERRE DE CRIMEE – The beginning of authentic military journalism. Photographs. 1 reel. (Collections of the Department of Prints and Photographs) – 1 – 50.00 – fr Bibl Nationale [900]
LA GUERRE DE KONGO-WARA 1928-1931. UN CHAPITRE DE LA RESISTANCE ANTI-COLONIALE EN AFRIQUE EQUATORIALE / Nzabakomada, R – 9 – F100.00 – fr Ethnologie [960]
LA GUERRE DE MONTAGNE (NAVARRE 1834-35 ET KABYLIE 1841-47): LES DOMINATIONS FRANCAISES-SYRIE, CANADA, INDE, MOREE, EGYPTE, PLATA / Ducuing, Fr – Paris: L. Hachette, 1868. 04296. (Pre-1900 Canadiana) – 9 – cn C.I.H.M. [971]
LA GUERRE D'EUROPE / Champagne, Philias – Nashua, NH: Philias Champagne, 1914. SEM105P910 – 1mf – 9 – Can$2.25 – cn Bibl Nat [940]
GUERRE D'INDEPENDENCE: QUELS SONT LES NATIONAUX – Madrid, 193? Fiche W933. (Blodgett Collection of Spanish Civil War Pamphlets) – 9 – us H.U. College Libr [946]
LA GUERRE DU DAHOMEY : JOURNAL DE CAMPAGNE DUN SOUS-LIEUTENANT D'INFANTERIE DE MARINE / Morienval, Henri – Paris: A Hatier, [1893?] ed illus – 1 – us Res Libr [960]
LA GUERRE ET LA CONDITION PRIVEE DE LA FEMME / Isore, Andre – Paris: de Boccard, 1919. xi,511p. (Les Femmes Collection) – 6mf – 9 – $15.00 – fr Bibl Nationale [305]
LA GUERRE ET LA PAIX / Chossat, R P M – Paris, Barcelona, 1918 – 3mf – 1 – ILM-4087/1 – ne IDC [327]
LA GUERRE ET LA SOCIETE, STRATEGIE TACTIQUE ET POLITIQUE / Iung, Theodore – Paris. Charpentier. 1890. 316p. (Strategy of War Series) – 9 – fr Hachette [355]
"GUERRE ET PAIX" DE TOLSTOI AU POINT DE VUE MILITAIRE / Dragomirov, M I – Paris. L. Boudoin. 1896. 106p. (Strategy of War Series) – 9 – fr Hachette [355]
GUERRE ET RELIGION / La Souchere, Elena de – Paris, 1938? Fiche W934. (Blodgett Collection of Spanish Civil War Pamphlets) – 9 – us H.U. College Libr [946]
GUERRE OU PAIX EN ORIENT / Barrault, Emile – Paris, Desessart, 1836, 167 p. Les Saint-Simoniens, 1825-1834. 6969 – 9 – fr Hachette [335]
LA GUERRE SOCIALE – Red. en chef Gustave Herve. 19 dec 1906-15. Hebd. puis quot. a partir du 6 aout 1914. devenu: La Victoire. 1916. Paris. dec 1906-18 – 1 – fr A.C.R.P.P. [073]
Guerrero *see* RICARDO WAGNER, EL HOMBRE I EL ARTISTA
Guerrero, Alonso *see*
- ABISMO...Y DISCURSO...VIRGEN MARIA
- NORTE Y GUIA PARA EL CAMINO DEL CIELO

Guerrero, E *see*
- BEITIA, EUGENIO. APOSTOLADO DE LOS SEGLARES 2ND EDICION. MADRID, 1939
- MUCHACHAS EN FLOR. MADRID, 1946

Guerrero, Eduardo Garcia *see* RICARDO WAGNER, EL HOMBRE I EL ARTISTA
Guerrero, F *see* HISPANIAE SCHOLA MUSICA SACRA/OPERA VARIA [SAECAL 15, 16, 17 ET 18]...
Guerrero, J *see* SOL DE LA MEDICINA QUE ALUMBRA A LOS QUE IGNORAN LA VERDADERA DOCTRINA...
Guerrero. Mexico (State) *see* ...PERIODICO OFICIAL DEL GOBIERNO DEL ESTADO DE GUERRERO
Guerrero Meza, Hector Emilio *see* DEBEN DEROGARSE LOS ESCRITOS DE REPLICA, DUPLICA Y EXTRACTO DE LITIS DEL CODIGO DE PROCEDIMIENTOS CIVILES DEL ESTADO DE LA BAJA CALIFORNIA
Guerrero, Pedro *see* CONSTITUCIONES SYNODALES...GRANADA
Guerrero, Placido *see* TENTATIVA...LECCION DE DON VICENTE GARCIA DE LA HUERTA
LES GUERRES D'AFRIQUE DEPUIS LA CONQUETE D'ALGER PAR LES FRANCAIS JUSQU'A ET COMPRIS L'EXPEDITION DE KABYLIE EN 1858 / Ladimir, Jules – Paris: B Renault, 1859 – 1 – us Res Libr [960]
LES GUERRES D'IDIOME ET DE NATIONALITE / Bourgoing, P de – Paris, 1849 – 2mf – 9 – ILM-2722/1 – ne IDC [327]
GUERRIERS ET SORCIERS EN SOMALIE / Lippmann, Alphonse – [Paris]: Hatchette, [1953] – 1 – us Res Libr [306]
GUERRILLA AND COUNTERGUERRILLA WARFARE IN RUSSIA DURING WORLD WAR 2 / U.S. Army. Office of the Chief of Military History – 1963 – 1 – $20.00 – us L of C Photodup [947]
THE GUERRILLA RESISTANCE MOVEMENT IN THE PHILIPPINES / U.S. Army. Far East Command – 1948. 2v – 1 – 21.00 – us L of C Photodup [950]
Guerro, Alonso *see* (NATURAL DE FUENTE DE CANTOS) EN NOTAS DE BIBLIOGRAFIA FRANCISCANA
Guerry, Andre-Michel *see* ESSAI SUR LA STATISTIQUE MORALE DE LA FRANCE PRECEDE D'UN RAPPORT A L'ACADEMIE DES SCIENCES PAR MM. LACROIX, SILVESTRE ET GIRARD
Guerry, E *see* RECHERCHES SUR LA PERSONNALITE INTERNATIONALE DE L'INDIVIDU
Guertler N *see* HISTORIA TEMPLARIORUM
Guery, Ch. *see* ANTIQUES CEREMONIES DANS L'ABBAYE DE SAINT-EVROULT
Guesalaga, A *see* DERECHO DIPLOMATICO Y...
Guesde, Jules *see*
- DES LOIS PROTECTRICES DU TRAVAIL, CE QU'ELLES SONT, CE QU'ELLES DEVRAIENT ETRE
- EN GARDE CONTRE LES CONTREFACONS, LES MIRAGES ET LA FAUSSE MONNAIE DES REFORMES BOURGEOISES
- LE PARTI SOCIALISTE ET LA CONFEDERATION DU TRAVAIL
- LE SOCIALISME AU JOUR LE JOUR

GUESSES AT THE RIDDLE OF EXISTENCE AND OTHER ESSAYS ON KINDRED SUBJECTS / Smith, Goldwin – New York: Macmillan, 1898. 1 fiche – 9 – us A.T.L.A. [240]
Guest, Ann Hutchinson *see* ADVANCED LABANOTATION
Guesten, R *see* PROBLEMS OF ECONOMIC GROWTH AND PLANNING: THE SUDAN EXAMPLE; SOME ASPECTS AND IMPLICATIONS OF THE CURRENT TEN YEAR PLAN
Guestlings *see* THE WHITE AND BLACK BOOKS OF THE CINQUE PORTS
Gueterbock, K *see* BYZANZ UND PERSIEN IN IHREN DIPLOMATISCH-VOELKERRECHTLICHEN BEZIEHUNGEN IM ZEITALTER JUSTINIANS
GUETLIGE ZEUGNISSE UEBER DER JUENGSTE MATTHESONISCH-MUSICALISCHE KERN-SCHRIFT / Aristoxen der Juengere – Hamburg. 1738. BP-631 1 – 9 – ne IDC [780]
Guettee, Abbe *see* THE PAPACY
Guettee, Wladimir *see* EXPOSITION DE LA DOCTRINE DE L'EGLISE CATHOLIQUE ORTHODOXE
Guettler, Felix *see* WORDSWORTH'S POLITISCHE ENTWICKLUNG
Guettler, Wilhelm *see* DIE RELIGIOESE KINDERERZIEHUNG IM DEUTSCHEN REICHE
Gueudeville, Nicolas *see*
- CRITIQUE GENERALE DES AVENTURES DE TELEMAQUE
- IDEE D'UNE REPUBLIQUE HEUREUSE, OU L'UTOPIE DE THOMAS MORUS. CONTENANT LE PLAN D'UNE REPUBLIQUE DONT LES LOIS, LES USAGES ET LES COUTUMES TENDENT UNIQUEMENT A RENDRE HEUREUSES LES SOCIETES QUI LES SUIVRONT

Gueunier, N J *see* LES MONUMENTS FUNERAIRES ET COMMEMORATIFS DE BOIS SCULPTE BETSILEO (MADAGASCAR)
Gueusquin, M F *see* TLALOC (CELUI QUI FAIT GERMER) ET SES SUBORDONNES LES TLALOQUE
Guevara, Antonio *see* EPISTOLAS FAMILIARES
Guevara, Juan Francisco *see* ARGENTINA Y SU SOMBRA
Guevara, Tomas *see* HISTORIA DE LA CIVILIZACION DE ARAUCANIA
Gueye, Lamine *see* ETAPES ET PERSPECTIVES DE L'UNION FRANCAISE
Guffroy, Armand B J *see* LE TOCSIN, SUR LA PERMANENCE DE LA GARDE NATIONALE
Guffroy, J *see* BIBLIOGRAPHIE CRITIQUE ET ETAT DES CONNAISSANCES SUR LA PATAGONIE ARGENTINE
Guggenheim, P *see*
- L'IMPOSITION DES SUCCESSIONS EN DROIT INTERNATIONAL...
- DER VOELKERBUND...

Gugl, Matthaeus *see* FUNDAMENTA PARTITURAE IN COMPENDIO DATA. DAS 1ST: KURTZER UND GRUENDLICHER UNTERRICHT, DEN GENERAL-BASS, ODER PARTITUR, NACH DENEN REGLEN RECHT UND WOHL SCHLAGEN ZU LEHRNEN..
Gugler, Julius *see*
- DRAMATISCHES
- DER STERN DES WESTENS

Gugliehmi, P *see* [LA SPOSA FIDELE] ROBERT UND KALLISTE. EIN OPERETTE IN 3 AUFZUGEN. NACH DEM INHALT UND KOMPOSITION DER SPOSA FELEL VON CHIARI...
Gugliemi, P *see* [LA BELLA PESCATRICE] AL SUON SOAVE
Guglieri, A *see* DOCUMENTOS DE LA COMPANIA DE JESUS EN EL ARCHIVO HISTORICO NACIONAL
Guglieri Navarro, A *see* MADRID. ARCHIVO HISTORICO NACIONAL. SECCION DE SIGILOGRAFIA. CATALOGO DE SELLOS. 1-3
GUGONG BOWUYUAN YUANKAN = JOURNAL OF THE PALACE MUSEUM – (In Chinese, with Table of Contents in English in each issue) – 21p – 9 – $4.00f – cc Microforms [060]
Gugy, Augustus *see* FACTS DISCLOSED IN SOME UNREPORTED CASES: PUBLISHED FOR THE PUBLIC GOOD/BY A VICTIM
Guhl, Ernst *see* KUENSTLERBRIEFE UEBERSETZT UND ERLAEUTERT VON DR. ERNST GUHL. ZWEITE UMGEARBEITETE UND SEHR VERMEHRTE AUFLAGE VON DR. ADOLF ROSENBERG
O GUIA : ORGAO DE PROPAGANDA ESPIRITA – Manaus, Amazonas. 13 Dez 1905-Mar 1908; Jan-15 Out 1910 – 1,5,6 – bl Biblioteca [072]
GUIA ARTISTICA, MERCANTIL E INDUSTRIAL DE CACERES... – Caceres: Imp. Santos Floriano Glez, s.a. – 1 – sp Bibl Santa Ana [338]
GUIA COMERCIAL DE FERIAS Y FIESTAS MAYO, 1945 / Caceres. Ayuntamiento – Caceres: Imp. Garcia Floriano – sp Bibl Santa Ana [390]
GUIA COMERCIAL LITERARIA, MAYO 1913 – Caceres: Tip. El Noticiero, S.A. – 1 – sp Bibl Santa Ana [440]
GUIA DE BIBLIOGRAFIA HISTORICA PORTUGUESA / Academia Portuhuesa da Historia – Madrid: Archivo Ibero Americano, 1960 – 1 – sp Bibl Santa Ana [946]
GUIA DE CACERES Y SU PROVINCIA / Rosa Roque, Julio – Caceres: Tip. El Noticiero, 1951 – 1 – sp Bibl Santa Ana [946]
GUIA DE CASTELLANIZACION ORAL PARA INDIGENAS TZELTALES / Castro, Carlo A – San Cristobal L.C. (Chiapas): Instituto nacional indigenista, 1956 – 1 – F50.29 – fr Armell [305]
GUIA DE ESPECTACULOS. FERIA Y FIESTAS AGOSTO 1974 / Empresa Ber-Maq – Valencia de Alcantara: Tip. Avila, 1974 – 1 – sp Bibl Santa Ana [390]
GUIA DE ESPECTACULOS FERIAS Y FIESTAS, 1975 – Valencia de Alcantara: Tip. Avila, 1975 – 1 – sp Bibl Santa Ana [390]
GUIA DE FILIPINAS PARA [...] – (Issues for 1879, 1884 filmed with: Guia de forasteros en las Islas Filipinas para el ano [...] 1862-1865) – Manila, 1879, 1884, 1885, 1886, 1889-97,1898 – us Res Libr [950]
GUIA DE FORASTEROS EN FILIPINAS : PARA EL ANO DE [...] – (Issues for 1859, 1861 1879, 1884 filmed with: Guia de forasteros en las Islas Filipinas para el ano [...] 1854-57; Issues for 1862-65 filmed with: Guia de Filipinas para [...] 1879, 1884) – Manila: Imprenta de los Amigos del Pais, a cargo de M Sanchez, [1858-] 1859, 1861-65 – us Res Libr [950]
GUIA DE FORASTEROS EN FILIPINAS, PARA EL ANO DE [...] – Manila: Imprenta de los Amigos del Pais, a cargo de M Sanchez, 1858, 1860 – us Res Libr [950]
GUIA DE FORASTEROS EN LAS ISLAS FILIPINAS PARA EL ANO [...] – Manila: Imprenta de D Miguel Sanchez, [-1857]. 1851 – 1r – 1 – us Res Libr [980]
GUIA DE FORESTEROS EN LAS ISLAS FILIPINAS PARA EL ANO... – Manila: Imprenta de D Miguel Sanchez, 1842-50; 1852; 1854-57 – 1 – us Res Libr [950]

GUIA DE FUENTES PARA LA HISTORIA DE AFRICA SUBSAHARIANA – Madrid, 1987 – 9 – sp Cultura [960]
GUIA DE FUENTES PARA LA HISTORIA DE ASIA EN ESPANA – Madrid, 1987 – 9 – sp Cultura [950]
GUIA DE FUENTES PARA LA HISTORIA DE IBEROAMERICA CONSERVADAS EN ESPANA, TOMO 1 – Madrid, 1966-1969 – 2mf – 9 – sp Cultura [972]
GUIA DE LA CIUDAD DE PLASENCIA (CACERES) POR UN PLACENTINO – Plasencia: Imprenta Placentina, Ano 1. 1905 – 1 – sp Bibl Santa Ana [946]
GUIA DE LA CIUDAD DE PLASENCIA (CACERES) POR...ANO 1906 / Rosado, Joaquin – Plasencia: Farmacia de Rosado, s.a. – sp Bibl Santa Ana [946]
GUIA DE LOS ARCHIVOS DE MADRID – Madrid, 1952 – 9 – sp Cultura [020]
GUIA DE MERIDA / Almagro Basch, Martin – 5th ed corregida y aumentada con los ultimos hallazgos. Valencia: Direccion General de Bellas Artes, 1972 – 1 – sp Bibl Santa Ana [910]
GUIA DE MERIDA / Almagro Basch, Martin – 7th ed corregida y aumentada con los ultimos hallazgos. Valencia: Direccion General del Patrimonio Artistico y Cultural, 1977 – 1 – sp Bibl Santa Ana [910]
GUIA DE TRUJILLO / Acedo, Federico – Madrid: Artistica, 1925 – 1 – sp Bibl Santa Ana [946]
GUIA DE VILLAFRANCA DE LOS BARROS / Bogeat y Asuar, Antonio – Villafranca de los Barros, 1919 – 1 – sp Bibl Santa Ana [946]
GUIA DEL ARCHIVO DE LA CORONA DE ARAGON / Martinez Fernando, J E – Madrid, 1958 – 9 – sp Cultura [946]
GUIA DEL ARCHIVO FRANCISCANO DE LA BIBLIOTECA NACIONAL DE MEXICO / Rio, I de – Mexico: UNAM, Instituto de Investigaciones Bibliograficas. v1. 1975 – 7mf – 9 – ne IDC [240]
GUIA DEL ARCHIVO HISTORICO NACIONAL / Sanchez Belda, L – Madrid, 1958 – 9 – sp Cultura [946]
GUIA DEL ESPECTADOR / Publicidad Cos – (Seria A, num.2 abril, 1948) – Caceres: Tip. El Noticiero, 1948 – 1 – sp Bibl Santa Ana [946]
GUIA DEL FORASTERO – Caceres.1899 – 9 – 1.50f – sp Bibl Santa Ana [072]
GUIA DEPORTIVA DE CACERES 1975-76 – Caceres: Delegacion Provincial de Educacion Fisica y Deportes. Imp. Extremadura, 1976 – 1 – sp Bibl Santa Ana [790]
GUIA GENERAL...BADAJOZ / Sanchez Arjona y Sanchez Arjona, Francisco – 1881 – 9 – 1.50f – sp Bibl Santa Ana [946]
GUIA HIGIENICA Y MEDICA DEL MAESTRO / Delvaille, C – Badajoz: La Minerva Extremena, 1894 – 1 – sp Bibl Santa Ana [610]
GUIA HISTORIA Y DESCRIPTIVA DE LOS ARCHIVOS, BIBLIOTECAS Y MUSEOS ARQUEOLOGICOS DE ESPANA – Madrid, 1921 – 9 – sp Cultura [946]
GUIA OFICIAL / Philippines – 1834-98 – 1 – us Res Libr [324]
GUIA OFICIAL DE FILIPINAS / Philippines – 1879-97 – 1 – us Res Libr [950]
GUIA OFICIAL DE LAS FERIAS Y FIESTAS DE MIAJADAS, AGOSTO 1971 / Miajadas. Ayuntamiento – Caceres: Imp. T. Rodriguez, 1971 and 1974 – 1 – sp Bibl Santa Ana [910]
GUIA OFICIAL DEL ILUSTRE COLEGIO NOTARIAL DE CACERES. ANO DE 1936 – (Tambien anos 1940, 1941, 1943, 1944, 1945, 1946, 1947, 1948, 1949, 1950, 1951, 1952, 1953, 1954, 1956, 1957, 1958, 1959, 1961, 1962, 1963, 1970) – Caceres: Edit. Extremadura, 1936 – sp Bibl Santa Ana [946]
GUIA PARA ANALISIS ANALOGICO DE "LA RAZON DE ME VIDA" DE EVA PERON / Cantarella, Adelina – Buenos Aires: Editores Libreria Perlado, 1954 – 1 – CSUXAGN1149-B – us Hoover Inst Photo [320]
GUIA PARA EL TRABAJADOR ESPANOL EN FRANCIA, 1977 / Portalin Garcia, A – Caceres: Imp. Garcilaso, 1977 – 1 – sp Bibl Santa Ana [331]
Guia. Plasencia *see* MUY NOBLE, MUY LEAL Y MUY BENEFICA
GUIA POPULAR-CALLEJERA E HISTORICO-TURISTICA DE LLERENA LA LLANA Y SANTIAGUISTA – Badajoz: Imp. INCA, 1965 – sp Bibl Santa Ana [946]
GUIA TURISTICA DE PLASENCIA / Plasencia. Guia – Plasencia: Sanguino, Impresor, 1961 – 1 – sp Bibl Santa Ana [910]
GUIANA GRAPHIC – Georgetown, Guyana. Guyana Graphic. -d. 7 Oct 1951-28 June 1953; 1 Jan 1959-9 Feb 1961; 14 Jan 1963-1 April 1966; 1 Oct 1970-Dec 1972. 37 reels – 1 – uk British Libr Newspaper [072]
IL GUIBA ESPLORATO / Bottego, Vittorio – Rome, 1895 – 1 – us Res Libr [910]
IL GUIBA ESPORATO : SOTTO GLI AUSPICI DELLA SOCIETA GEOGRAFICA ITALIANA / Bottego, Vittorio – Roma, E Loescher, 1895 – us Res Libr [945]
Guibal, R *see* PEUT-ON FERMER LE CANAL DE SUEZ?
Guibert, Archdeacon of Toulouse *see* LEBEN DES HEILIGEN PAPSTES LEO 9
Guibert de Tournai *see* TRACTATUS DE PACE AUCTORE FR. GILBERTO DE TORNACO
Guibert, J *see*
- EL CARACTER. DEFINICION, IMPORTANCIA, IDEAL, ORIGENES...
- LA PRIMAVERA DE LA VIDA

Guibert, J A H de *see* ELOGE DU MARECHAL DE CATINAT
Guicciardi *see* RELATION HISTORIQUE DE LA REVOLUTION DU ROYAUME D'ITALIE EN 1814
Guicciardini, Francesco *see* HISTOIRE DES GUERRES D'ITALIE, 1490-1534
Guicciardini, L *see* ACCOUNT OF THE ANCIENT FLEMISH SCHOOL OF PAINTING
Guiccioli, Teresa *see* LORD BYRON JUGE PAR LES TEMOINS DE SA VIE
Guichardus, T *see* ORATIO HABITA AB ELOQUENTISSIMO VIRO. F. THOMA GUICHARDO RHODIO
Guichenon *see* HISTOIRE DE LA SOUVERAINETE DES DOMBES
Guichenon, Samuel *see*
- HISTOIRE DE BRESSE ET DE BUGEY CONTENANT CE QUI S'Y EST PASSE DE MEMORABLES SOUS LES ROMAINS
- HISTOIRE GENEALOGIQUE DE LA ROYALE MAISON DE SAVOYE

Guichenot, A *see* HISTOIRE NATURELLE DES REPTILES ET DES POISSONS
LA GUIDA ALLA MUSICA VOCALE. OP. 2 / Danby, John – c. 1800 – 9 – us Sibley [780]
GUIDA ARMONICA O DIZIONARIO ARMONICO, BEING A SURE GUIDE TO HARMONY AND MODULATION. OPERA X / Geminiani, Francesco – (A supplement to the Guida Armonica, with examples shewing it's use in composition.) ca.1742 – 9 – us Sibley [780]
GUIDANCE AND CONTROL – (Suppl to v40, Advances) – 1979 – 2mf – 9 – $10.00 – 0-87703-128-2 – us Univelt [629]
GUIDANCE AND CONTROL – (Suppl to v45, Advances) – 1981 – 5mf – 9 – $15.00 – 0-87703-156-8 – us Univelt [629]
GUIDANCE AND CONTROL – (Suppl to v48, Advances) – 1982 – 1mf – 9 – $10.00 – 0-87703-180-0 – us Univelt [629]
GUIDANCE AND CONTROL – (Suppl to v51, Advances) – 1983 – 2mf – 9 – $10.00 – 0-87703-214-9 – us Univelt [629]
GUIDANCE AND CONTROL – (Suppl to v57, Advances) – 1985 – 3mf – 9 – $15.00 – 0-87703-213-0 – us Univelt [629]
GUIDANCE AND CONTROL – (Suppl to v61, Advances) – 1986 – 3mf – 9 – $15.00 – 0-87703-259-9 – us Univelt [629]
GUIDANCE AND CONTROL – (Suppl to v66, Advances) – 1988 – 2mf – 9 – $10.00 – 0-87703-290-4 – us Univelt [629]
GUIDANCE AND CONTROL – (Suppl to v78, Advances) – 1992 – 3mf – 9 – $20.00 – 0-87703-355-2 – us Univelt [629]
GUIDANCE AND CONTROL – (Suppl v55, Advances) – 1984 – 4mf – 9 – $15.00 – 0-87703-201-7 – us Univelt [629]
GUIDANCE AND CONTROL 1993 – (Suppl to v81, Advances) – 1993 – 3mf – $20.00 – 0-87703-367-6 – us Univelt [629]
GUIDANCE AND CONTROL CONFERENCE – 1978 – 9mf – 9 – $20.00 – 0-87703-179-7 – us Univelt [629]
GUIDANCE AND COUNSELLING – (v10 1994/95 Can$29.00y) – Toronto. v1-10. 1985/86-1994/95 – 9 – Can$20.00y – cn Micromedia [150]
GUIDANCE & COUNSELLING – v1- . 1985- – 1,5,6,9 – us UMI [073]
GUIDANCE INDEX *see* ANNUAL GUIDANCE INDEX
GUIDE – Alliance, NE. -w. Nov. 1893-Jan. 1898 – 1 – us NE Hist [071]
GUIDE – (Also known as: Downtown Shopping Guide) – Fresno, CA. 1932-46; 1969-78 – 72r – 1 – $3,600.00 – B02257 – us Library Micro [071]
GUIDE – Brotherhood Commission publication. Oct 1966-67 – 1 – 7.63 – us Baptist [240]
GUIDE : A MONTHLY JOURNAL DEVOTED TO LEGAL NEWS AND PUBLIC AFFAIRS – v1-4. 1892-95 – 1 – $40.00 – us Hein [073]
LE GUIDE = THE GUIDE – Cowansville, Canada. 29 jan 1974-v4 n46. 22 nov 1977 – 2r – 1 – Can$60.00r – cn Can Microfilming [072]
THE GUIDE – (Also known as: Shipping Guide) – San Francisco, CA. 1906-66; May 1970-Aug 1971; May-Aug 1972 – 72r – 1 – $3,600.00 – B02819 – us Library Micro [623]
THE GUIDE – Battleford, Sask: Indian Industrial School, [1892-189- or 19–] – 9 – cn C.I.H.M. [370]
THE GUIDE *see* SHIPPING GUIDE
GUIDE AND CHECK LIST OF COUNTY GOVERNMENTAL ORGANIZATION & COUNTY RECORD SYSTEM, PAST & PRESENT OF KENTUCKY COUNTIES / Kentucky – 2 fiches. F-0505 – 9 – us A.G.L.L. [323]
GUIDE AND TRIBUNE; TRIBUNE – Fremont. Neb. 1883- – 1 – us UMI [071]
LE GUIDE COMMERCIAL POUR LA VILLE DE DETROIT ET SES ENVIRONS: CONTENANT L'HISTOIRE DE DETROIT, MONTREAL ET QUEBEC: AVEC LES NOMS DE LEURS FONDATEURS / Bedard, J Alphonse – Detroit: C. M. Rousseau, 1881. 04066. (Pre-1900 Canadiana) – 9 – cn C.I.H.M. [971]
LE GUIDE DE CEUX QUI VEULENT BATIR / Le Camus de Mezieres, Nicolas – Paris. 1786. 2v. in 8 fol. (Architecture Series) – 9 – fr Hachette [720]
GUIDE DE LA CONVERSATION EN QUATRE LANGUES: FRANCAIS-VOLOF-ANGLAIS-SERER – St-Joseph de Ngasobil, Imprimerie de la Mission. 1880 – 9 – 10.00 – fr Orientalistes [440]
GUIDE DE L'ACHETEUR – Quebec, Canada. nov 1924-dec 1927 – 1r – 1 – Can$25.00 – cn Can Microfilming [073]
LE GUIDE DE L'ACHETEUR = THE BUYER'S GUIDE – Quebec, Canada. 1 oct 1881 – 1r – 1 – Can$25.00 – cn Can Microfilming [380]
GUIDE DE L'ACHETEUR ECONOME DE LA RIVE SUD – Levis. v- n-. 14 jul 1934-1 mar 1935 – 1r – 1 – Can$30.00 – cn Can Microfilming [338]
LE GUIDE DE L'EST – Ste-Anne des Monts, Canada. 4 jul 1974 – 1r – 1 – Can$25.00 – cn Can Microfilming [072]
GUIDE DE L'INDUSTRIEL DESIRANT S'ETABLIR AU MAROC / Morocco. Ministere du Commerce – 1961. BNE-3078 1 – 9 – ne IDC [380]
GUIDE DE L'INDUSTRIEL; RESUMES DES ETUDES DE BRANCHES / Algeria. Caisse d'Equipement pour le Developpement de l'Algerie – 1962. BNE-8616 1 – 9 – ne IDC [330]
LE GUIDE DE MONTREAL-NORD = THE MONTREAL NORTH GUIDE – (Cont: Le Montreal-Nord. Becomes: the Montreal North Guide de Montreal-Nord 11 avr 1962-24 dec 1975) – Montreal, Canada. jan 1957-1 avr 1962 – 16r – 1 – Can$60.00r – cn Can Microfilming [073]
LE GUIDE DE MONTREAL-NORD / THE MONTREAL NORTH GUIDE *see* LE MONTREAL-NORD
GUIDE DE NOEL – Quebec, Canada. n3-17. 25 dec 1908-1922 – 1r – 1 – Can$25.00 – cn Can Microfilming [240]
LE GUIDE DES AMOUREUX ET DES GENS DU MONDE : L'AMOUR, LA COUR, LE MARRIAGE.. – Montreal: C.O. Beauchemin, 1898.05126.(Pre-1900 Canadiana) – 9 – cn C.I.H.M. [360]
LE GUIDE DU COLON DANS L'OUEST DU CANADA:.. – Compagnie de Chemin de Fer du Pacifique Canadien, 1893?.03417. (Pre-1900 Canadiana) – 9 – cn C.I.H.M. [971]
LE GUIDE DU COLON FRANCAIS AU CANADA – Paris: Impr. de l'Oeuvre de Saint-Paul, 1885. 05128. (Pre-1900 Canadiana) – 9 – cn C.I.H.M. [971]
LE GUIDE DU COLON, PROVINCE DE QUEBEC / Quebec (Province). Departement des Terres de la Couronne – Levis: Mercier & cie, 1877-1944. SEM105P618 – 36mf – 9 – Can$81.00 – cn Bibl Nat [300]
LE GUIDE DU CONCERT; HEBDOMADAIRE MUSICAL ILLUSTRE – v. 1-32. 1910-52 – 1 – 220.00 – us L of C Photodup [780]
GUIDE DU DIPLOMATE GUINEEN – Conakry: Imprimerie Nationale "Patrice Lumumba", 1979 – us Res Libr [980]
GUIDE DU JEUNE PIANISTE / Eschmann, Johann Carl (1826-82); ed by Dussault, J D – Lotbiniere, 1886. SEM105P11 – 2mf – 9 – Can$4.25 – cn Bibl Nat [780]
GUIDE DU PELERIN A SAINTE-ANNE DE BEAUPRE – Montreal: C O Beauchemin & fils, libraires-imprimeurs, 1900. SEM105P1741 – 1mf – 9 – Can$2.25 – cn Bibl Nat [240]
GUIDE DU VOYAGEUR A NANTES ET AUX ENVIRONS... / Etiennez, Hippolyte – Nantes: Petitpas, 1860 – fr Armell [910]
GUIDE DU VOYAGEUR EN ABYSSINIE / Afevork, G J – Rome, Paris, 1908 – 3mf – 9 – ne IDC [910]
GUIDE FOR INDUSTRIAL INVESTMENTS IN SAUDI ARABIA, 1392 A.H. (1972 A.D.) / Saudi Arabia. Industrial Studies and Development Centre – Ed. 2. Riyadh, 1972 – 9 – ne IDC [338]
GUIDE FOR INSTRUCTORS IN ORGANIZING AND CONDUCTING AGRICULTURAL ENGINEERING TRAINING COURSES – 1975 – 100p – it F.A.O. [631]
A GUIDE FOR NOTARIES PUBLIC AND COMMISSIONERS. / Barber, Gershom Morse – 3d ed. Cleveland 1894. 151 p. LL-6 – 1 – us L of C Photodup [340]
GUIDE FOR PLANNING PULP AND PAPER ENTERPRISES – 1977 – 379p – it F.A.O. [670]
GUIDE FOR THE COLLECTION OF TRADITIONAL MUSICAL INSTRUMENTS / Doumon, Genevieve & Arom, Simha – 1981 – 108p – 9 – 92-3-101846-9 – fr UNESCO [780]
GUIDE FOR THE DETERMINATION OF FISHES / Schuster, W H – SE 10,720 1. 1949 – 9 – ne IDC [590]
A GUIDE FOR THE GUESTS OF HOTEL ROBERVAL TO THE LAKE ST JOHN AND ITS TRIBUTARY WATERS – Montreal: S.L. Swett, 18–?. 03301. (Pre-1900 Canadiana) – 9 – cn C.I.H.M. [910]
GUIDE FOR TRAINING IN THE FORMULATION OF AGRICULTURAL RURAL INVESTMENT PROJECTS – 1986 – 583p – it F.A.O. [332]
GUIDE ILLUSTRE DE LA CHAMBRE DES COMMUNES DU CANADA: CONTENANT LES PORTRAITS PHOTOGRAPHIQUES DE SON EXCELLENCE LE GOUVERNEUR GENERAL.. – Ottawa: F. Campeau, 1875. 02143. (Pre-1900 Canadiana) – 9 – cn C.I.H.M. [971]
GUIDE ILLUSTRE DE MONTREAL ET DE SES INSTITUTIONS CATHOLIQUES AVEC PROGRAMME DE LA ST JEAN BAPTISTE POUR 1884 / Giroux, Henri – (Montreal: Gazette), 1884. 03443. (Pre-1900 Canadiana) – 9 – cn C.I.H.M. [240]
GUIDE INDISPENSABLE AU PEUPLE: CONTENANT D'ADRESSE SIC DES PRINCIPALES MAISONS DE COMMERCE, LISTE DE MEMBRES DU CONSEIL DE VILLE ET DES COMITES... TELEGRAPHE D'ALARMES, NOMS DES SOCIETES ET LEURS OFFICIERS, ETC., ETC / Beauchamp, Joseph – Quebec: J. Beauchamp, 1892. 03036. (Pre-1900 Canadiana) – 9 – cn C.I.H.M. [971]
GUIDE INTERNATIONAL DES ARCHIVES – Bibliotheque des Annales Institutorum, v4. Europe, Paris, Roma. 1934-35. BR-9828 1 – 9 – ne IDC [025]
GUIDE MUSICAL – Bruxelles. v1-59. 1855-1913. Lacking: 1867-1892, v. 17-38. – 387mf – 9 – ne IDC [073]
LE GUIDE MUSICAL. REVUE INTERNATIONALE DE LA MUSIQUE ET DES THEATRES LYRIQUES – v. 1-61, no. 38-40. 1855-1917 – 1 – 362.00 – us L of C Photodup [780]
GUIDE OF SCIENTISTS IN INDONESIA / Organisatie voor Natuurwetenschappelijk Onderzoek in Indonesie – SE-10,283 1. 3rd ed 1952 – 9 – ne IDC [500]

THE GUIDE OR COMPANION TO THE NEW ARMY LIST / Dunlevie, Horace G – s.l.: s.n., 1881 (Ottawa: Daily Citizen). 04285. (Pre-1900 Canadiana) – 9 – cn C.I.H.M. [971]

GUIDE PARLEMENTAIRE HISTORIQUE DE LA PROVINCE DE QUEBEC, 1792 A 1902 / Desjardins, Joseph – Quebec, 1902. SEM105P960 – 5mf – 9 – Can$11.25 – cn Bibl Nat [971]

GUIDE POUR L'APPLICATION DES LOIS SOCIALES / Indochina. French – Saigon: Impr. de l'Union, 1936. 45p. LL-10007 – 1 – us L of C Photodup [340]

GUIDE POUR L'USAGE DES CARTES DES VENTS ET DES COURANTS DU GOLFE DE GUINEE / Capello, de Brito – Traduction du portugais. Paris, Imprimerie administrative de P. Dupont. 1862 – 9 – 5.00 – fr Orientalistes [910]

GUIDE PRACTIQUE DES AGENTS POLITIQUES... / Garcia de la Vega, D de – Bruxelles, Paris, 1873 – 8mf – 1 – ILM-994/1 – ne IDC [327]

GUIDE PRATIQUE DES OPERATIONS DE LA BANQUE INDUSTRIELLE / Syria. Industrial Bank in the Syrian region – BNE-9706 1 – 9 – ne IDC [332]

GUIDE PRATIQUE POUR LE CHOIX DES PROFESSIONS FEMININES / Bureau, Helene – Paris: Colin, 1921. vii,140p. (Les Femmes Collection) – 2mf – 9 – $6.00 – fr Bibl Nationale [331]

GUIDE ROCK SIGNAL – Guide Rock, NE. -w. Feb 1883-Dec 1884; Jan 1886-Mar 1889; May-Dec 1889; Jan-Dec 1892; Mar 1896; Dec 1896-Aug 1919; Oct 1919-Apr 1957 – 1 – us NE Hist [071]

GUIDE ROCK WEEKLY NEWSLETTER – Guide Rock, NE. Feb 1906-May 1907 – 1 – us NE Hist [071]

LE GUIDE SANITAIRE – Montreal, Canada. nov 1874 – 1r – 1 – Can$25.00 – cn Can Microfilming [072]

GUIDE TO ARCHIVES AND MANUSCRIPTS AT HARVARD AND RADCLIFFE / Harvard and Radcliffe – 1990. 3,800 descriptive entries – 17mf – 9 – £140.00 – 0-89887-081-X – uk Chadwyck [090]

GUIDE TO BIBLE INTERPRETATION / Samson, George Whitefield – New York: Edward O. Jenkins, 1886. 1 fiche – 9 – us A.T.L.A. [240]

GUIDE TO CAPTURED GERMAN DOCUMENTS / Germany – Maxwell Airforce Base, Alabama, Dec 1952 and Suppl. National Archives, Washington DC, 1959. 1 roll. T1183 – 1 – us Nat'l Archives [943]

GUIDE TO CODEX MAXIMUM LIMITS FOR PESTICIDE RESIDUES – 1978 – 209p – it F.A.O. [640]

GUIDE TO COLLECTIONS OF MANUSCRIPTS RELATING TO AUSTRALIA / National Library of Australia – (Suppls A$10.00 ea: 1990 5mf. 1992 4mf. 1993 4mf. 1995) – 24mf – 9 – A$25.00 set – at Nat'l Libr [090]

A GUIDE TO COMMISSIONERS IN CHANCERY. / Matthews, James Muscoe – 2nd ed. Richmond, VA: Randolph and English, 1871. 254p. LL-912 – 1 – us L of C Photodup [340]

A GUIDE TO CONDITION SCORING OF ZEBU CATTLE = GRILLE DE NOTATION DE L'ETAT D'ENGRAISSEMENT DES BOVINS ZEBUS / Nicholson, M J & Butterworth, MH – 1986 – 9 – $5.00 – 92-9053-144-4 – et ILRI [636]

GUIDE TO CURRENT OFFICIAL STATISTICS. / India. Office of the Economic Advisor – (Filmed with: India: Imperial Record Dept List of the Heads of Administrations in India and of the India Office in England) – Delhi: Manager of Publ, [1945-49] – 1 – us Res Libr [950]

GUIDE TO EXTENSION TRAINING / Oakley, P & Garforth, C – 1985 – 144p – it F.A.O. [370]

A GUIDE TO FEDERAL AGENCY RULEMAKING / Administrative Conference of the U.S. (ACUS) – 1st ed 1983. Washington: GPO, 1983 (all publ) – 4mf – 9 – $6.00 – LLMC 94-336A – us L.L.M.C. [340]

A GUIDE TO FEDERAL AGENCY RULEMAKING / Administrative Conference of the U.S. (ACUS) – 2nd ed 1991. Washington: GPO, 1991 (all publ) – 5mf – 9 – $7.50 – LLMC 94-336B – us L.L.M.C. [340]

GUIDE TO FESTSCHRIFTEN / New York Public Library. Research Libraries – v1-2, The Retrospective Festschrift Collection: Materials Cataloged through 1971.-1977.-5900 cards 1 reel.-ISBN: 0-8161-1353-X – 1 – $170.00 – uk Hall [020]

GUIDE TO FOREST SEED HANDLING : WITH SPECIAL REFERENCE TO THE TROPICS – 1985 – 394p – it F.A.O. [634]

GUIDE TO INDONESIA / ed by Ch'en, Lu-wei – In Chinese. SE-4874 1. 4 v. in 1. 1962 – 9 – ne IDC [950]

A GUIDE TO MAGISTRATES AND CONSTABLES. / Pollard, John Garland – Richmond, Va.: Waddey, 1906. LL-1336 – 1 – us L of C Photodup [340]

A GUIDE TO MAGISTRATES, WITH PRACTICAL FORMS FOR THE DISCHARGE OF THEIR DUTIES OUT OF COURT / Mayo, Joseph – (Ibid. Richmond: Goode, 1892. 711p. LL-965) – 2d ed. Richmond: Morris, 1860. 726p. LL-291 – 1 – us L of C Photodup [340]

GUIDE TO MARINE INSURANCE : BEING A HANDBOOK ON THE LAW AND PRACTICE OF MARINE INSURANCE WITH SPECIAL REFERENCE TO POLICIES ON GOODS / Keate, Henry – London: Pitman & Sons, (post 1919?) – 3mf – 9 – $4.50 – LLMC 92-120 – us L.L.M.C. [360]

GUIDE TO MATERIALS FOR AMERICAN HISTORY IN RUSSIAN ARCHIVES / Golder, F A – Washington, DC, 1917-37.2v. R-10,674/1 – 9 – ne IDC [975]

GUIDE TO MICROFILMS IN THE CAPE ARCHIVES DEPOT, CAPE TOWN – 5th ed. Pretoria: State Archives Service, January 1993 – 1,5 – R3.00 – 0-7970-2736-X – sa State Archives [025]

GUIDE TO MICROFILMS IN THE NATAL ARCHIVES DEPOT, PIETERMARITZBURG – 3rd ed. Pretoria: State Archives Service, October 1990 – 1,5 – R1.10 – 0-7970-2210-4 – sa State Archives [025]

A GUIDE TO NEGRO PERIODICAL LITERATURE / ed by Marshall, A P – Winston-Salem. v1-4. 1941-46 – 1r – 1 – us Ross [975]

GUIDE TO NEGRO PERIODICAL LITERATURE – Jefferson City, Missouri. v. 1-4. Feb 1941-Feb 1943; Jan-Sept 1946 – 1 – us NY Public [305]

GUIDE TO PACIFIC ARCHIVES / Hutchinson, Fabian – Carlton South, Vic: Past Papers, 1990- – 1mf – A$10.00 – at Hutchinson [980]

GUIDE TO PUBLIC VITAL STATISTICS RECORDS IN GEORGIA / Georgia – 1941. 2 fiches.F-0623 – 9 – us A.G.L.L. [978]

A GUIDE TO PUNJAB GOVERNMENT REPORTS AND STATISTICS / Fazal, Cyril P K – Lahore, The Civil and Military Gazette, 1939 – us Res Libr [324]

THE GUIDE TO QUEBEC / Chambers, Edward Thomas Davies – Quebec Morning Chronicle. 1895. 00548. (Pre-1900 Canadiana) – 9 – cn C.I.H.M. [574]

A GUIDE TO RAWLINSON C745-747 (BODLEIAN LIBRARY, OXFORD) : "CORRESPONDANCE FROM THE OUTFORTS TO CAPE COAST CASTLE, 1681-1699" – (Filmed with Royal African Co of England Correspondence) – Madison. University of Wisconsin, 1972 – us Res Libr [960]

A GUIDE TO READING THE HEBREW TEXT : FOR THE USE OF BEGINNERS / Vibbert, William H – Andover: Warren F Draper, 1872 – 1mf – 9 – 0-8370-9328-7 – 1986-3328 – us A.T.L.A. [270]

A GUIDE TO RECORDS RELATING TO GHANA IN REPOSITORIES IN THE U.K. EXCLUDING THE PUBLIC RECORD OFFICE / Agyei, Samuel Kwasi – plus printed Guide – 7mf – 9 – £30.00 – uk Altair [324]

GUIDE TO SCIENTISTS IN INDONESIA / Organisatie voor Natuurwetenschappelijk Onderzoek in Indonesie – SE-12,027 1. 1949 – 9 – ne IDC [500]

GUIDE TO SELECTED LEGAL SOURCES OF MAINLAND CHINA / Hsia, Tao-tai – Washington: Library of Congress, 1967. 357p. LL-10036 – 1 – us L of C Photodup [340]

GUIDE TO SPECIFICATIONS FOR GENERAL NOTICES, GENERAL ANALYTICAL TECHNIQUES, IDENTIFICATION TESTS, TEST SOLUTIONS AND OTHER REFERENCE MATERIALS – 1991 – 322p – it F.A.O. [630]

GUIDE TO SPECIFICATIONS FOR GENERAL NOTICES, GENERAL METHODS, IDENTIFICATION TESTS SOLUTIONS AND OTHER REFERENCE MATERIALS : JOINT F.A.O./W.H.O. EXPERT COMMITTEE ON FOOD ADDITIVES – rev ed 1983 – 325p – it F.A.O. [640]

GUIDE TO THE ADMINISTRATION OF THE HOUSING ACTS, 1923 AND 1924 / Aldridge, Henry R – London, 1924. First supplement to Aldridge: The National Housing Manual, 1923 – 1 – £35.00r – uk Altair [941]

A GUIDE TO THE ARCHIVES AND RECORDS OF PROTESTANT CHRISTIAN MISSIONS FROM THE BRITISH ISLES TO CHINA 1796-1914 / Marchant, LR – Nedlands, Western Australia – 2mf – 9 – ne IDC [240]

GUIDE TO THE ARCHIVES OF INTERNATIONAL ORGANIZATIONS. PART 1 : THE UNITED NATIONS SYSTEM – 1984 – 279p – 9 – 92-3-102090-0 – fr UNESCO [020]

GUIDE TO THE CALIBRATION OF SOIL TESTS FOR FERTILIZER RECOMMENDATIONS – 1977 – 78p – it F.A.O. [631]

A GUIDE TO THE CHURCHES AND MISSIONS IN THE CITY OF NEW YORK / New York. (City) – 1877 – 9 – $50.00 – us Presbyterian [240]

GUIDE TO THE CITY OF QUEBEC: DESCRIPTIVE AND ILLUSTRATED WITH MAP – Quebec: F. Carrel, 1899.05129.(Pre-1900 Canadiana) – 9 – cn C.I.H.M. [971]

A GUIDE TO THE ENGLISH TONGUE / Dyche, Thomas – 1707. 159p. (English Linguistics Series 1500-1800) – 9 – us UMI [420]

GUIDE TO THE FISHING AND HUNTING RESORTS IN THE VICINITY OF THE GRAND TRUNK RAILWAY OF CANADA: CONTAINING PARTICULARS OF FISH, GAME, HOTELS.. – Montreal: J. Lovell, 1889. 03158. (Pre-1900 Canadiana) – 9 – cn C.I.H.M. [910]

A GUIDE TO THE GOLDEN CITY / Campbell, R – Toronto: Imrie & Graham, 1890. 00395. (Pre-1900 Canadiana) – 9 – cn C.I.H.M. [971]

GUIDE TO THE HEBREW PRESS / Kressel, G – Zug 1977. BJ-1-1 – 9 – ne IDC [072]

GUIDE TO THE HYDROLOGY OF CARBONATE ROCKS – 1984 – 345p – 9 – 92-3-102206-7 – fr UNESCO [550]

GUIDE TO THE INDEX OF EARLY SOUTHERN ARTISTS AND ARTISANS / Museum of Early Southern Decorative Arts – 36mf – 9 – $190.00 – us UPA [740]

GUIDE TO THE INDEX OF EARLY SOUTHERN ARTISTS AND ARTISANS / Museum of Early Southern Decorative Arts – Guide to a collection of information on the lives and working habits of Southern artists and artisans before 1821. Printed explanatory booklet (110p) – 36mf – 9 – $102.00 – us MESDA [740]

GUIDE TO THE INFORMATION ACTIVITIES IN EUROPEAN DEVELOPMENT NETWORKS – 1991 – 9 – 92-3-102737-9 – fr UNESCO [380]

A GUIDE TO THE IRAN'S 5TH PLAN / Iran – Kayhan research associates. Teheran. 1975. BD-1858 1 – 9 – ne IDC [338]

A GUIDE TO THE LAKE ST JOHN AND ITS TRIBUTARY WATERS – Montreal: J. Lovell, 18–?. 03542. (Pre-1900 Canadiana) – 9 – cn C.I.H.M. [910]

A GUIDE TO THE LAW AND LEGAL LITERATURE OF ARGENTINA, 1917-1946 / Clagett, Helen Lord – New York: Gordon Press, 1979 – 1 – CSUXADJ9179-B – us Hoover Inst Photo [340]

GUIDE TO THE LEGAL PROFESSION / Maxwell, Maurice W – 4th ed. London: Sweet and Maxwell, 1994 – 2mf – 9 – $3.00 – LLMC 91-068 – us L.L.M.C. [340]

GUIDE TO THE LITERATURE OF BOTANY : A CLASSIFIELD SELECTION OF BOTANICAL WORKS, INCLUDING NEARLY 6,000 TITLES NOT GIVEN IN PRITZEL "THESAURUS" / Jackson, BD – London, 1881 – 14mf – ne IDC [580]

GUIDE TO THE LITERATURE OF BOTANY; A CLASSIFIED SELECTION OF BOTANICAL WORKS, INCLUDING NEARLY 6,000 TITLES NOT GIVEN IN PRITZEL "THESAURUS" / Jackson, BD – London. 1881. B-1535 2 – 8 – ne IDC [580]

GUIDE TO THE MANUSCRIPT MATERIALS FOR THE HISTORY OF THE UNITED STATES TO 1783 IN THE BRITISH MUSEUM, MINOR LONDON ARCHIVES AND THE LIBRARIES OF OXFORD AND CAMBRIDGE / Andrews, Charles & Davenport, Frances G – 1 – uk Microform Academic [975]

GUIDE TO THE MANUSCRIPT MATERIALS FOR THE HISTORY OF THE UNITED STATES TO 1793, IN THE BRITISH MUSEUM, IN MINOR LONDON ARCHIVES, AND IN THE LIBRARIES OF OXFORD AND CAMBRIDGE / Andrews, Charles & Davenport, Frances G – Washington, D.C.: Carnegie Institution of Washington, 1908. (Carnegie Institution of Washington publication; no. 90) – 2mf – us A.T.L.A. [976]

GUIDE TO THE MATERIALS FOR AMERICAN HISTORY TO 1783 IN THE PUBLIC RECORD OFFICE, LONDON / Andrews, Charles – 1 – uk Microform Academic [975]

GUIDE TO THE MATERIALS FOR AMERICAN HISTORY, TO 1783, IN THE PUBLIC RECORD OFFICE OF GREAT BRITAIN / Andrews, Charles – Washington, D.C.: Carnegie Institution of Washington, 1912-1914 (Carnegie Institution of Washington publication; no. 90A. Papers of the Department of Historical Research.) – 2mf – us A.T.L.A. [975]

GUIDE TO THE MATERIALS IN LONDON ARCHIVES FOR THE HISTORY OF THE UNITED STATES SINCE 1783 / Paullin, CO & Paxon, FL – p. v. 1914, BRRAM – 1 – uk Microform Academic [025]

GUIDE TO THE NAVAL ACADEMY OF REPUBLIC OF INDONESIA / Indonesia. Akademi Angkatan Laut, Surabaja – SE-5529 1. 1962, 1963 – 9 – ne IDC [355]

A GUIDE TO THE PUBLIC RECORDS OF SOUTHERN RHODESIA, UNDER THE REGIME OF THE BRITISH SOUTH AFRICA COMPANY, 1890-1923 – Cape Town, The Archives in association with Longmans, Green, 1956 – us Res Libr [960]

GUIDE TO THE RECORDS OF PACIFIC MISSIONS IN BRITISH INSTITUTIONS / Hutchinson, Fabian – Carlton South, Vic: Past Papers, 1990- – 2mf – A$10.00 – at Hutchinson [240]

GUIDE TO THE RECORDS OF THE GUNTUR DISTRICT, 1795-1835 / Madras. (India: State). Record Office – Madras: Printed by the Superintendent, Govt. Press, 1934 – 1 – us U.W. Library [950]

GUIDE TO THE RECORDS OF THE MASULIPATAM DISTRICT, 1682 TO 1835 / Madras. (India: State). Record Office – Madras: Printed by the Superintendent, Govt. Press, 1935 – 1 – us U.W. Library [950]

GUIDE TO THE RECORDS OF THE NELLORE DISTRICT, 1801 TO 1835 / Madras. (India: State). Record Office – Madras: Printed by the Superintendent, Govt. Press, 1934 – 1 – us U.W. Library [950]

GUIDE TO THE RECORDS OF THE TINNEVELLY DISTRICT, 1796 TO 1835 / Madras. (India: State). Record Office – Madras: Printed by the Superintendent, Govt. Press, 1934 – 1 – us U.W. Library [950]

A GUIDE TO THE RELIGIONS OF AMERICA; THE FAMOUS LOOK MAGAZINE SERIES ON RELIGION, PLUS FACTS, FIGURES, TABLES, CHARTS, ARTICLES. / Look – 1952-55. Ed. by Leo Rosten. New York: Simon and Schuster, 1955. xiii,282p – 1 – us U.W. Library [240]

GUIDE TO THE SOURCES IN THE NETHERLANDS CONCERNING THE HISTORY OF ASIA AND OCEANIA, 1796-1949 / ed by Jacquet, F G P – Fasc. 1-7. Leiden. 1973-74. A collection of mainly unpublished inventories of archive materials in Dutch archives. The printed guide accompanies the microfiche collection. BSE-12.103 1 – 220mf – 9 – ne IDC [950]

A GUIDE TO THE STUDY OF CHURCH HISTORY / McGlothlin, William Joseph – New York: Hodder & Stoughton, G.H. Doran, c1914 – 1mf – us A.T.L.A. [240]

GUIDE TO THE STUDY OF FISHES / Jordan, D S – Z-2117 2. 2v. 1905 – 8 – ne IDC [590]

A GUIDE TO THE STUDY OF THE NEW TESTAMENT (CCC96) / Ch'eng, Chih-i – (In Chinese) – Hong Kong: Council on Christian Literature for Overseas Chinese, 1954 – 1r – 1 – 1984-B500 – us A.T.L.A. [220]

A GUIDE TO THE STUDY OF THE OLD TESTAMENT (CCC216) / Li, Yung-fang – (In Chinese) – Hong Kong: Council on Christian Literature for Overseas Chinese, 1954 – 1r – 1 – 1984-B500 – us A.T.L.A. [220]

A GUIDE TO THE STUDY OF THEOLOGY: ADAPTED...TO THE OXFORD HONOUR SCHOOL / Woods, Francis Henry – Oxford: James Thornton, 1880. 1 fiche – 9 – us A.T.L.A. [240]

GUIDE TO THE UNIVERSITY OF ILLINOIS ARCHIVES / Brichford, Maynard & Maher, William – 3mf + 10p – 9 – $10.00 – us Univ Ill Libr [020]
GUIDE TO UNPUBLISHED MATERIALS OF THE HOLOCAUST PERIOD / Bauer, Yehuda – Jerusalem, 1975. 413p v3 – 9 – 8.00 – is I.T.T.I. [025]
A GUIDE-BOOK TO THE POETIC AND DRAMATIC WORKS OF ROBERT BROWNING / Cooke, George Willis – Boston: c1919. 16 plus 451p. With: Hume: With Helps to the Study of Berkeley by T.H. Huxley. 1 reel. 1290 – 1 – us U.W. Library [420]
GUIDELINE SENTENCING : FJC IN-COURT EDUCATIONAL PROGRAM ON GUIDELINE SENTENCING ORIENTATION FOR U.S. DISTRICT AND CIRCUIT JUDGES, U.S. MAGISTRATES, U.S. PROBATION OFFICERS, SUPPORTING STAFF AND FEDERAL PUBLIC DEFENDERS – Washington: FJC, Oct 1987 – 6mf – 9 – $9.00 – LLMC 95-389 – us L.L.M.C. [340]
GUIDELINE SENTENCING : AN OUTLINE OF APPELLATE CASE LAW ON SELECTED ISSUES / Wood, Jefri & Sheehey, Diane – Washington: FJC, Sept 1994 – 3mf – 9 – $4.50 – LLMC 95-390 – us L.L.M.C. [340]
GUIDELINES : LAND EVALUATION FOR EXTENSIVE GRAZING – 1991 – 170p – it F.A.O. [636]
GUIDELINES – Saskatoon. v15-29. 1980-94 – 9 – Can$20.00y – cn Micromedia [073]
GUIDELINES FOR AGRICULTURAL TRAINING CURRICULA IN AFRICA – 1982 – 213p – it F.A.O. [640]
GUIDELINES FOR CAN MANUFACTURERS AND FOOD CANNERS – 1986 – 88p – it F.A.O. [650]
GUIDELINES FOR DAIRY ACCOUNTING – 1980 – 39p – it F.A.O. [650]
GUIDELINES FOR DESIGNING AND EVALUATING SURFACE IRRIGATION SYSTEMS – 1989 – 148p – it F.A.O. [631]
GUIDELINES FOR DESIGNING DEVELOPMENT PROJECTS TO BENEFIT THE RURAL POOR – 1986 – 140p – it F.A.O. [360]
GUIDELINES FOR ECONOMIC APPRAISAL OF WATERSHED MANAGEMENT PROJECTS – 1987 – 152p – it F.A.O. [330]
GUIDELINES FOR FOREST POLICY FORMULATION – 1987 – 91p – it F.A.O. [634]
GUIDELINES FOR FORESTRY INFORMATION PROCESSING – 1986 – 145p – it F.A.O. [650]
GUIDELINES FOR IMPROVING JUROR UTILIZATION IN U.S. DISTRICT COURTS – Washington: FJC, Oct 1972 – 1mf – 9 – $1.50 – LLMC 95-820 – us L.L.M.C. [340]
GUIDELINES FOR INTEGRATED CONTROL OF COTTON PESTS – 1984 – 199p – it F.A.O. [660]
GUIDELINES FOR INTEGRATED CONTROL OF MAIZE PESTS – 1979 – 98p – it F.A.O. [660]
GUIDELINES FOR INTEGRATED CONTROL OF RICE INSECT PESTS – 1979 – 123p – it F.A.O. [660]
GUIDELINES FOR MONITORING THE IMPACT OF STRUCTURAL ADJUSTMENT PROGRAMMES ON THE AGRICULTURAL SECTOR – 1990 – 83p – it F.A.O. [338]
GUIDELINES FOR PRESCRIBING UPPER BODY EXERCISE FOLLOWING OPEN HEART SURGERY / Huenerbein, Heidi A – University of Wisconsin-La Crosse, 1995 – 1mf – 9 – PH 1497 – us Microform Publ [617]
GUIDELINES FOR SEED EXCHANGE AND PLANT INTRODUCTION IN TROPICAL CROPS – 1986 – 216p – it F.A.O. [631]
GUIDELINES FOR SLAUGHTERING, MEAT CUTTING AND FURTHER PROCESSING – 1991 – 179p – it F.A.O. [660]
GUIDELINES FOR SOIL PROFILE DESCRIPTION – 2nd ed 1977 – 69p – it F.A.O. [631]
GUIDELINES FOR SOIL SURVEY AND LAND EVALUATION IN ECOLOGICAL RESEARCH / Breimer, R F et al – 1986 – 9 – 92-3-102366-7 – fr UNESCO [630]
GUIDELINES FOR STATISTICAL MONITORING – 1985 – 91p – it F.A.O. [639]
GUIDELINES FOR THE COMPUTATION OF SELECTED STATISTICAL INDICATORS – 1986 – 78p – it F.A.O. [300]
GUIDELINES FOR THE CONTROL OF SOIL DEGRADATION. F.A.O./UNEP – 1983 – 43p – it F.A.O. [631]
GUIDELINES FOR THE ESTABLISHMENT, OPERATION AND MANAGEMENT OF CEREAL BANKS – 1992 – 93p – it F.A.O. [660]
GUIDELINES FOR THE NATIONAL ROLLING PLAN (1990-1992) / Nigeria. Planning Office 1500 Lagos, 1990 – 2mf – 9 – ne IDC [338]
GUIDELINES FOR THE PROMOTION OF ENVIRONMENTAL MANAGEMENT OF COASTAL AQUACULTURE DEVELOPMENT – 1992 – 127p – it F.A.O. [650]
GUIDELINES FOR THE THIRD NATIONAL DEVELOPMENT PLAN 1975-1980 / Nigeria. Central Planning Office. Ministry of Economic Development and Reconstruction – BD-1811 1 – 9 – ne IDC [338]
GUIDELINES FOR WATERSHED MANAGEMENT – 1978 repr 1986 – 306p – it F.A.O. [550]
GUIDELINES: LAND EVALUATION FOR IRRIGATED AGRICULTURE – 1985 – 243p – it F.A.O. [631]
GUIDELINES: LAND EVALUATION FOR RAINFED AGRICULTURE – 1984 – 249p – it F.A.O. [631]
GUIDELINES ON THE STUDY OF SEAWATER INTRUSION INTO RIVERS / ed by Tuin, H van der – 1991 – 138p – 9 – 92-3-102765-4 – fr UNESCO [550]
GUIDES AND GUARDS IN CHARACTER-BUILDING / Payne, Charles Henry – New York: Phillips & Hunt, 1883.1 fiche – 9 – us A.T.L.A. [240]
GUIDES TO GERMAN RECORDS FILMED AT ALEXANDRIA, VA / National Archives Trust Fund Board. Washington, D.C – 4rolls. T733. (World War II Collection of Seized Enemy Records) – 1 – us Nat'l Archives [943]
GUIDES TO GERMAN RECORDS MICROFILMED AT ALEXANDRIA / U.S. National Archives and Records Service – 4rolls. T733. (World War II Collection of Seized Enemy Records) – 1 – us Nat'l Archives [324]
GUIDES TO RECORDS OF THE ITALIAN ARMED FORCES / U.S. National Archives and Records Service – 1roll. T94 – 1 – us Nat'l Archives [324]
Guidi, I *see* PROVERBI, STROFE E RACCONTI ABISSINI
Guidi, Ignazio *see* VOCABULARIO AMARICO-ITALIANO
Guidiccioni, L *see* BREVE RACCONTO DELLA TRANSPORTATIONE DEL CORPO DI PAPA PAOLO V. DALLA BASILICA DI S. PIETRO A'QUELLA DI S. MARIA MAGGIORE
THE GUIDING EYE, OR, THE HOLY SPIRIT'S GUIDANCE OF THE BELIEVER / Carman, Albert – Toronto: W. Briggs, 1899. 00929. (Pre-1900 Canadiana) – 9 – cn C.I.H.M. [240]
GUIDO AND LITA : A TALE OF THE RIVIERA / Argyll, John Douglas Sutherland Campbell, Duke of – New York: Macmillan, 1875. 03999. (Pre-1900 Canadiana) – 9 – cn C.I.H.M. [830]
Guido (Chauliac, Gui de) *see* THE QUESTYONARY OF CYRURGYENS
Guido de Columnis *see* HISTORIA DESTRUCTIONIS TROIAE
GUIDO FISCHER (1877-1959) : MATERIALIEN ZU EINER BIOGRAPHIE / Wolf, Manfred – 1995 – 2mf – 9 – DM80.00 – 3-8267-2237-X – gw Hänsel [610]
Guido Pastorino, Juan *see* REFORMA AGRARIA Y REFORMA POLITICA
Guido y Spano, Carlos *see* AUTOBIOGRAFIA Y SELECCION DE POESIAS
Guidon, N *see*
- L'ABRI CHAPADA DOS CRUZES, SITE DE LA VARIETE SERRA DA CAPIVARA ET DE STYLE SERRA DO TAPUIO, SUD-EST DU PIAUI, BRESIL
- ABRI TOCA DO PINGA DO BOI, SITE TYPIQUE DE LA VARIETE SERRA BRANCA, STYLE VARZEA GRANDE, BRESIL
- ABRIS PEINTS DE LA SERRA BRANCA ET DE LA SERRA NOVA, REGION DE VARZEA GRANDE, ETAT DU PIAUI, BRESIL
- ABRIS PEINTS DE LA SERRA DO CAPIVARA, REGION DE VARZEA GRANDE, ETAT DU PIAUI, BRESIL
- LES ABRIS TOCAS DO BAIXAO DO PERNA 1 ET 2, SITES DU STYLE VARZEA GRANDE, SUD-EST DU PIAUI, BRESIL
- PEINTURES RUPESTRES DE VARZEA GRANDE, PIAUI, BRESIL, NO. 2

Guidon, N et al *see* DEUX ABRIS DECORES DE LA SERRA NOVA, REGION DE SAO RAIMUNDO NONATO, ETAT DU PIAUI, BRESIL
Guidon, N. et al *see* UN ABRI DECORE DE LA SERRA NOVA, REGION DE SAO RAIMUNDO NONATO, ETAT DU PIAUI, BRESIL
Guignard, Ph *see* MONUMENTS PRIMITIFS DE LA RAEGLE CISTERCIENNE
Guignard, Ph. *see* MONUMENTS PRIMITIFS DE LA REGLE CISTERCIENNE
Guignebert, Charles *see*
- L'EVOLUTION DES DOGMES
- THE JEWISH WORLD IN THE TIME OF JESUS
- MODERNISME ET TRADITION CATHOLIQUE EN FRANCE

GUIGNOL ET LA REVOLUTION DANS L'EGLISE ROMAINE : M. VEUILLOT ET SON PARTI CONDAMNES PAR LES ARCHEVAEQUES ET EVAEQUES DE PARIS, TOURS, VIVIERS, ORLEANS, MARSEILLE, VERDUN, CHARTRES, MOULINS, ETC / Michaud, Eugene – Paris: Sandoz et Fischbacher, 1872 – 1mf – 9 – 0-8370-8772-4 – 1986-2772 – us A.T.L.A. [944]
EL GUIJO, BELALCAZAR Y CAPILLA. NUEVAS INSCRIPCIONES ROMANAS / Fita, Fidel – Madrid: Fortanet, 1912. B.R.A.H. 61. pp. 221-233 – 1 – sp Bibl Santa Ana [946]
Guilbault, George *see* L'OBSERVATEUR
Guilbault, Germaine *see* BIBLIOGRAPHIE ANALYTIQUE DE L'OEUVRE DE SON EXCELLENCE REV'ME MGR NAPOLEON-ALEXANDRE LABRIE, C.J.M.,....
Guilbault, Renee *see* BIBLIOGRAPHIE ANALYTIQUE DE L'OEUVRE DE BERTRAND VAC
Guilbert de Pixerecourt *see*
- LES RUINES DE BABYLONE OU GIAGGAR ET ZAIDA
- TEKELI OU LE SIEGE DE MONTGATZ
- VICTOR OU L'ENFANT DE LA FORET

GUILD NOTES – NY City, NY. 1981-1982 – 1r – 1 – $50.00 – R04924 – us Library Micro [071]
GUILD PRACTITIONER – (With its predecessor: National Lawyers Guild Quarterly v1-3 1937-40) – v1-47. 1940-90 – 1,5,6 – $360.00 – us Hein [073]
Guild, Reuben A *see* CHAPLAIN SMITH AND THE BAPTISTS
GUILDEROY / Ouida – British Fiction Archive: Unit 3 – 9 – uk Bell [830]
Guildhall Library, London *see*
- THE EXTEL RECORDS. ARCHIVES OF THE EXCHANGES TELEGRAPH CO. LTD.
- JANSON, COBB, PEARSON AND CO SOLICITORS. ARCHIVES
- LAND TAX COMISSIONERS FOR THE CITY OF LONDON
- RECORDS RELATING TO AUSTRALIA
- SUN INSURANCE FIRE POLICY REGISTERS AND THE ROYAL EXCHANGE ASSURANCE RECORDS

THE GUILDHALL LIBRARY, LONDON. CATALOGUES – (With printed guides) – 10r – £440.00 – uk World [941]
Guilford, Linda Thayer *see* PAPERS, MS 484
Guilhiermoz, P *see* ESSAI SUR L'ORIGINE DE LA NOBLESSE EN FRANCE AU MOYEN AGE
Guilhot, J *see* LE REGIME FISCAL DES VALEURS MOBILIERES...
Guillain, Charles *see*
- EXPLORATION DE LA COTE ORIENTALE D'AFRIQUE
- VOYAGE A LA COTE ORIENTALE D'AFRIQUE

Guillain, M *see* DOCUMENTS SUR L'HISTOIRE, LA GEOGRAPHIE ET LE COMMERCE DE L'AFRIQUE ORIENTALE
Guillamas, Manuel de *see* DE LAS ORDENES MILITARES DE CALATRAVA, ALCANTARA Y MONTESA
Guillaneuf, R *see* LA PRESSE EN COTE-D'IVOIRE: LA COLONISATION, L'AUBE DE LA DECOLONISATION (1906-1952)
Guillard, Achille *see* ELEMENTS DE STATISTIQUE HUMAINE OU DEMOGRAPHIE COMPAREE.
Guillard et Le Moine *see* MILTIADE A MARATHON
Guillaume *see*
- L'ESCAUT DEPUIS 1830
- LE MARIAGE...ET LA CONFERENCE DE LA HAYE

Guillaume, Alfred *see* PROPHECY AND DIVINATION AMONG THE HEBREWS AND OTHER SEMITES
Guillaume, C *see* LE PROTESTANTISME JUGE ET CONDAMNE PAR LES PROTESTANTS:..
GUILLAUME D'AUVERGNE, EVEQUE DE PARIS (1228-1249) : SA VIE ET DES OUVRAGES / Valois, Noel – Paris: A. Picard, 1880 – 1mf – us A.T.L.A. [240]
Guillaume, Gal A *see* LES BERBERES MAROCAINS ET LA PACIFICATION DE L'ATLAS CENTRAL
Guillaume, J M *see* ELOGE DE J.J. ROUSSEAU, CITOYEN DE GENEVE
GUILLAUME LE CONQUERANT, DUC DE NORMANDIE / Coffin-Roney & Clement – French Theatre Series. Paris. Fages, an XII. 1804 – 9 – fr Hachette [820]
Guillaumet, Edouard *see*
- LE SOUDAN EN 1894
- LE SOUDAN EN 1894: LA VERITE SUR TOMBOUCTOU; L'ESCLAVAGE AU SOUDAN

Guillaumin, Emile *see*
- AU PAYS DES CH'TITS GAS.
- THE LIFE OF A SIMPLE MAN
- LA PEINE AUX CHAUMIERES

Guillaumont-Jeanneney, S *see* POLITIQUE MONETAIRE ET CROISSANCE ECONOMIQUE EN FRANCE, 1950-1966
Guillaumot, C A *see* REMARQUES SUR UN LIVRE INTITULE OBSERVATIONS SUR L'ARCHITECTURE
Guillemaut, Lucien *see* NOTES ET REMARQUES SUR LA BRESSE LOUHANNAISE: ESQUISSE D'UNE TOPOGRAPHIE PHYSIOLOGIQUE ET MEDICALE DE L'ARRONDISSEMENT DE LOUHANS
Guillemeau, J *see* THE FRENCH CHIRURGERYE
Guillemin, Amedee *see* THE WORLD OF COMETS
Guillemin, J *see* COOPERATION ET INTERVENTION, LA POLITIQUE MILITAIRE DE LA FRANCE EN AFRIQUE NOIRE FRANCOPHONE ET A MADAGASCAR
Guillemin, J B A *see*
- ARCHIVES DE BOTANIQUE
- ICONES LITHOGRAPHICAE PLANTARUM AUSTRALASIAE RAIORUM

Guillemin, J B A et al *see* FLORAE SENEGAMBIAE TENTAMEN
Guillemin, Julien *see* DE LA PROTECTION DES ENFANTS DU PREMIER AGE
Guillemin, Michel P *see* OCCUPATIONAL HYGIENE
Guillen, Abraham *see*
- LA CONSPIRACION DE LA OLIGARQUIA
- LA OLIGARQUIA EN LA CRISIS DE LA ECONOMIA ARGENTINA

Guillen, Julio F *see*
- EL PRIMER VIAJE DE CRISTOBAL COLON. MADRID, 1942
- LOS TENIENTES DE NAVIO JORGE JUAN Y SANTACILIA Y ANTONIO DE ULLOA Y DE LA TORRE G.Y. LA MEDICION DEL MERIDIANO...

Guillen y Flores, Agustin *see*
- BREVES-GEOGRAFIA ASTRONOMICA
- DISCURSO...APERTURA DE CURSO SOBRE LA IMPORTANCIA DEL CATOLICISMO

Guillet de Saint-George, Georges *see*
- ATHENES ANCIENNE ET NOUVELLE ET L'ESTAT PRESENT DE L'EMPIRE DES TURCS, CONTENANT LA VIE DU SULTAN MAHOMET 4; LE MINISTRE DE COPROGLI, ACHMET PACHA, GRAND VIZIR AVEC LE PLAN DE LA VILLE D'ATHENES, PAR LE SR. DE LA GUILLETIERE
- LACEDEMONE ANCIENNE ET NOUVELLE: OU L'ON VOIT LES MOEURS ET LES COUTUMES DES GRECS MODERNES, DES MAHOMETANS, ET DES JUIFS DU PAYS
- LETTRES ECRITES SUR UNE DISSERTATION D'UN VOYAGE DE GRECE; PUBLIE PAR MR. SPON AVEC DES REMARQUES SELON LES NOUVELLES DECOUVERTES DE L'ANTIQUAIRE

Guillet, Didace *see* CINQUANTENAIRE DES OBLATS DE MARIE IMMACULEE EN CANADA: FETES JUBILAIRES LES 7, 8 ET 9 DECEMBRE 1891
Guillet, Joseph E *see* PROPALLADIA AND OTHER WORKS...
Guilleux, Charles *see* JOURNAL DE ROUTE D'UN CAPORAL DE TIRAILLEURS DE LA MISSION SAHARIENNE, 1898-1900
Guillevin, M *see* VOYAGE DANS DAHOMEY
Guilloreau, L *see* LES MEMOIRES DU R. P. DOM BERNARD AUDEBERT
Guillot, L *see* LA CONDITION JURIDIQUE DE LA FEMME MARIEE...
Guilloteaux, Erique *see* MADAGASCAR ET LA COTE DES SOMALIS SAINTE-MARIE ET LES SEYCHELLES
LA GUILLOTINE – Paris: Bonaventure et Ducessois, mar 1848 – us Res Libr [072]
THE GUILT OF SLAVERY AND THE CRIME OF SLAVEHOLDING / Cheever, George Barrell – Boston: J.P. Jewett, 1860 – 2mf – us A.T.L.A. [360]

Guimera, Angel *see* LA ARANYA
Guimet, Emile *see*
- PROMENADES JAPONAISES
- PROMENADES JAPONAISES, TOKIO-NIKKO
Guimier, J M *see* ETUDE MONOGRAPHIQUE DE LA COMMUNE DE CHERISY (EURE-ET-LOIR)
Guimond, E-L *see* LE LUTIN
Guindon, Arthur *see* LES TROIS COMBATS DU LONG-SAULT
Guinea *see* PLAN TRIENNAL DE DEVELOPPEMENT ECONOMIQUE ET SOCIAL DE LA REPUBLIQUE DE GUINEE
GUINEA EQUATORIAL ANEXO AL PLAN DE DESARROLLO / Guinea. Equatorial. Spain. Comisaria del Plan de Desarrollo Economico y Social – Madrid. 1964. BD-176 1 – 9 – ne IDC [338]
Guinea. Equatorial. Spain. Comisaria del Plan de Desarrollo Economico y Social *see* GUINEA EQUATORIAL ANEXO AL PLAN DE DESARROLLO
LA GUINEA ESPANOLA / Santa Isabel Misioneros Hijos del Immaculado – Corazon de Maria. v1-65 n1-1620. apr 1903-1967; Index v1-37 1903-40 – 1 – us Res Libr [073]
Guinea. French *see* JOURNAL OFFICIEL
Guinea. French. Laws, Statutes, etc *see* CODE PENAL
Guinea. Ministere du Plan *see* PLAN SEPTENNAL 1964-1970
GUINEA TIMES – Accra: Star Pub Co, apr 3-jun 13 1958 – us Res Libr [072]
Guinea-Bissau *see* BOLETIM OFICIAL
GUINEA-BISSAU (FORMERLY PORTUGUESE GUINEA) : ANUARIO ESTATISTICO 1947-1958 / Guinea-Bissau (formerly Portuguese Guinea). Reparticao Provincial dos Servicos de Economia e Estatistica Geral – (Coll title: African Official Statistical Serials, 1867-1982) – 19mf – 9 – £160.00 – uk Chadwyck [960]
Guinea-Bissau (formerly Portuguese Guinea). Reparticao Provincial dos Servicos de Economia e Estatistica Geral *see* GUINEA-BISSAU (FORMERLY PORTUGUESE GUINEA)
EN GUINEE – Paris: H Le Soudier, 1895 – 1 – us Res Libr [960]
LA GUINEE / Rouget, Fernand – Corbeil, France: Impr typ E Crete, 1906 – 1 – us Res Libr [960]
LA GUINEE FRANCAISE : RACES, RELIGIONS, COUTUMES, PRODUCTION, COMMERCE / Arcin, Andre – Paris: A Challamel, 1907 – 1 – us Res Libr [960]
LA GUINEE FRANCAISE, CONAKRY ET RIVIERES DU SUD : ETUDE ECONOMIQUE ET COMMERCIALE SUIVIE DE NOTES NOTES SUR LA GUINEE PORTUGAISE / Aspe-Fleurimont, Lucien Auguste – Paris: A Challamel, 1900 – 1 – us Res Libr [910]
GUINEE, PERSPECTIVES NOUVELLES – Conakry. n30-46. aug 1973-may 1975 – us Res Libr [980]
LA GUINEE SUPERIEURE ET SES MISSIONS : ETUDE GEOGRAPHIQUE, SOCIALE ET RELIGIEUSE DES CONTREES EVANGELISEES PAR LES MISSIONAIRES DE LA SOCIETE DES MISSIONS AFRICAINES DE LYON / Teilhard de Chardin, J – 3. ed. Keerlez-Maastricht, [1888] – 1 – us Res Libr [960]
Guiness, Lucy Evangeline *see* IN THE FAR EAST
Guiney, Louise Imogene *see* HURRELL FROUDE
Guinguene, Pierre-Louis *see* LETTRES SUR LES CONFESSIONS DE J.J. ROUSSEAU
Guinn, J M *see*
- HISTORICAL AND BIOGRAPHICAL RECORD OF SOUTHERN CALIFORNIA
- HISTORY OF CALIFORNIA AND AN EXTENDED HISTORY OF ITS SOUTHERN COAST COUNTIES
- HISTORY OF THE STATE OF CALIFORNIA AND BIOGRAPHICAL RECORD OF COAST COUNTIES
- HISTORY OF THE STATE OF CALIFORNIA AND BIOGRAPHICAL RECORD OF OAKLAND AND ENVIRONS
- HISTORY OF THE STATE OF CALIFORNIA AND BIOGRAPHICAL RECORD OF SAN JOAQUIN VALLEY
- HISTORY OF THE STATE OF CALIFORNIA AND BIOGRAPHICAL RECORD OF SANTA CRUZ, SAN BENITO, MONTEREY AND SAN LUIS OBISPO COUNTIES
- HISTORY OF THE STATE OF CALIFORNIA AND BIOGRAPHICAL RECORD OF THE SACRAMENTO VALLEY
Guinnes, H Grattan *see* THE NEW WORLD OF CENTRAL AFRICA
Guinness, Geraldine M *see* THE STORY OF THE CHINA INLAND MISSION
Guins, George Constantine *see* SIBIR, SOIUZNIKII KOLCHAK
GUION DE CONFERENCIAS PRONUNCIADAS EN EL AULA DE CULTURA DE LA CAJA DE AHORROS Y MONTE DE PIEDAD DE PLASENCIA. ABRIL-MAYO 1971 / Caja de Ahorros y Monte de Piedad – Caceres: Caja de Ahorros de Plasencia, 1972 – 1 – sp Bibl Santa Ana [946]
GUION DE FERIAS Y FIESTAS. AGOSTO 1959 / Jaraiz de la Vera. Ayuntamiento – Jaraiz de la era: Imp. La erata, 1959 – 1 – sp Bibl Santa Ana [390]
GUION DE FESTEJOS DE CUACOS DE LA VERA. SEPTIEMBRE DE 1954 – Imprenta la Verata, 1954 – 1 – sp Bibl Santa Ana [390]
Guion, Willie K *see* FAMILIAL PATTERNS OF VO(2MAX) AND PHYSICAL ACTIVITY LEVELS
Guiral, Leon *see* LE CONGO FRANCAIS DU GABON A BRAZZAVILLE
Guiraud, Jean *see*
- CARTULAIRE DE NOTRE DAME DE PROUILLE
- L'EGLISE ROMAINE ET LES ORIGINES DE LA RENAISSANCE
- L'ETAT PONTIFICAL APRES LE GRAND SCHISME
- QUESTIONS D'HISTOIRE ET D'ARCHEOLOGIE CHRETIENNE
- SAINT DOMINIC
Guiraudou, R *see* LA PREUVE DE LA NATIONALITE D'ORIGINE
Guire, Juliette de *see* BIBLIOGRAPHIE ANALYTIQUE DE L'OEUVRE DE MONSIEUR CHARLES-MARIE BOISSONNAULT, HISTORIEN, POETE ET CRITIQUE
GUISBOROUGH EXCHANGE – Guisborough, England. -w. 23 Feb, 25 Oct 1872; 23 April 1874-27 July 1878. 3 reels – 1 – uk British Libr Newspaper [072]
Guise, Jacques de *see* CHRONIQUES DES COMTES DE HAINAULT
GUISUANYAN XUEBAO – Journal of the Chinese Silicate Society. In Chinese but English abstracts to the main articles. F p66 – 9 – 4.00f – cc Microforms [073]
GUITARRA ESPANOLA, Y VANDOLA, EN DOS MANERAS DE GUITARRA, CASTELLANA / Amat, Juan Carlos – 17-? – 9 – us Sibley [780]
LA GUITARRE ROYALLE / Corbett, F – Paris, 1671. BP-782/1 – 9 – ne IDC [780]
Guiton, Jean *see*
- FROM EQUIVALENCE OF DEGREES TO EVALUATION OF COMPETENCE
- RECOGNITION OF STUDIES AND COMPETENCE
Guizhou and Yunnan Province. China *see*
- JIAJING PU'AN ZHOU ZHI, APPROX. 1537
- JIAJING SINAN FU ZHI, 1537
- JIAJING XUNDIAN FU ZHI, 1550
GUIZHOU RIBAO – China. Guizhou Daily. 1985-. M-D94 – 1 – $55.00r – cc Microforms [072]
GUIZHOU XINHAI GEMING ZILIAO XUANBIAN – Selected Materials on the Revolution of 1911 in Guizhou. Comp. by the Institute of History, Guizhou Academy of Social Science. 6 fiches. F H112 – 9 – $27.00 – cc Microforms [950]
GUIZOT DEMASQUE : REFUTATION DE SES DERNIERS ECRITS, SA REPUTATION USURPEE ET SA PROFESSION DE FOI / Stephanopoli-Comnene, M N – Paris [1848?] – us Res Libr [920]
Guizot, Francois *see* SAINT LOUIS AND THE THIRTEENTH CENTURY
Guizot, M Francois *see*
- MEDITATIONS SUR L'ESSENCE DE LA RELIGION CHRETIENNE
- MEDITATIONS SUR L'ETAT ACTUEL DE LA RELIGION CHRETIENNE
- A POPULAR HISTORY OF FRANCE, FROM THE EARLIEST TIMES
GUJARAT – Ahmedabad, India. 1963-65 – 2r – 1 – us L of C Photodup [072]
THE GUJARAT GOVERNMENT GAZETTE / Gujarat. India – Admedabad. 5 May 1960-66. For earlier file see: Bombay. Bombay Government Gazette – 1 – us NY Public [950]
Gujarat. India *see* THE GUJARAT GOVERNMENT GAZETTE
Gujarat Research Society *see* JOURNAL OF THE GUJERAT RESEARCH SOCIETY
GUJARAT SAMACHAR – Bombay, India. 1958 – 2r – 1 – us L of C Photodup [072]
GUJARATA SAMACARA – Ahmedabad, India. Mar 1966-1992 – 1 – 143r – us L of C Photodup [072]
GUJI MULU – Catalog of Ancient Books. Comp. by the Acquisition Library of the National Publication Administrative Bureau. 6 fiches. F J4 – 9 – $42.00 – cc Microforms [070]
GUJI ZHENGLI BIANMU – Ancient Books Collated and Catalogued. Comp. by the Board for the Revising and Publishing of Ancient Books. 2 fiches. F J5 – 9 – $9.00 – cc Microforms [070]
Gul', R *see* GEORGII IVANOV
Gulak, A *see* SEFER ZIKKARON LE-ASHER GULAK VELI-SHEMU'EL KLEIN
Gulberlet, C *see* PHILOSOPHISCHES JAHRBUCH
HET GULDEN CABINET VAN DE EDELE VRYE SCHILDERCONST ONTSLOTEN DOOR DEN LANCK GHEWENSCHTEN VREDE TUSSCHEN DE TWEE MACHTIGHE CROONEN VAN SPAIGNIEN EN VRANCKRYK / Bie, C de – Antwerpen. 1662. BO-146 1 – 9 – ne IDC [700]
DEN GULDEN SONNEN WYSER OFT HOROLOGIE VAN DE PASSIE ONS HEEREN IESU CHRISTI / T'sogart, Aigidius – Brussel, 1626 – 9mf – 8 – Dfl32.00 – ne Slangenburg [240]
GULDEN SPIEGEL, OFTE OPWECKINGE TOT CHRISTELIJCKE DEUGHDEN : AF-GEBEELT IN TWEE DEELEN; WAER IN VERTOONT WERT, DE SCHADELIJCKHEYT DER SONDEN, MITSGADERS DE GOFTHEYT ENDE WELDADEN GODTS OVER DEN BOETVAERDIGEN / Mayvogel, J C – Amsterdam, 1659 – 6mf – 9 – O-3120/1 – ne IDC [760]
DEN GULDEN WINCKEL DER KONSTLIEVENDE NEDERLANDERS GESTOFFEERT MET VEEL TREFFELYCKE HISTORISCHE, PHILOSOPHISCHE, POETISCHE MORALE ENDE SCHRIFTUERLIJCKE LEERINGEN : GECIERT MET SCHOONE KUNST PLATEN OFT BEELDENISSEN. VERMAKELYCK EN STICHTELIJCK VOOR ALLE STATEN VAN MENSCHEN / Vondel, J van den – 1st ed. Amsterdam, [1613] – 2mf – 9 – O-3195/1 – ne IDC [760]
DIE GULDIN ARCH DAREIN DER KERN VNND DIE BESTEN HAUPTSPRUECH DER HEYLIGEN SCHRIFFT / Franck von Woerd, S – Augspurg, H. Steyner. 1538. BME-80 1 – 9 – ne IDC [240]
Gulenkov, S *see* PROTIV RELIGII ZA SOTSIALIZM VO VTORI PYATILETKE
GULF COAST BAPTIST – Houston, TX. 1952-53 – 1 – 37.80 – us A.B.H.S. [071]
GULF COAST OIL AND GAS WORLD *see*
- HART'S OIL AND GAS WORLD
- PACIFIC OIL AND GAS WORLD
GULF COAST OIL REPORTER – v3-4. 1983-85 – 1,5,6,9 – us UMI [660]
GULF COAST OIL WORLD – v4-. 1985- – 1,5,6,9 – us UMI [660]
GULF COAST PROGRESS – Louis. Miss. 1893-1895; 1898-1915 – 1 – us UMI [071]
GULF COAST TIMES – Ocean Springs. Miss. 1951-1953 – 1 – us UMI [071]
Gulf, Colorado and Santa Fe Railway Company *see* RECORDS
GULF COUNTY BREEZE – Wewahitchka. Fl. -w. 1946-75 – 1 – us P.K. Yonge [071]
GULGONG ARGUS – 1875-1876. GA1 – 1r – 1 – at Corangamite [072]
GULGONG EVENING ARGUS – 1874-1875. GEA1-2 – 2r – 1 – at Corangamite [072]
GUL-I ZARD – (Sal-i 1, shumarah-i 1-24 (27 Sha'ban 1336-10 Shavval 1337[7 May 1918-July 1919]). Sal-i 2, shumarah-i 1-25 (24 Shavval 1337-1 Rabi' al-sani 1339[23 July 1919-13 December 1920]). Sal-i 3, shumarah-i 1-44 (1 Zu'l Qa'dah-25 Shavval) missing issue 28. Sal-i 4, shumarah-i 1-31 (3 Zu'l Qa'dah-19 Zu'l Qa'dah)) – Tehran – 1 reel – 1 – $140.00 – us MEDOC [950]
Gulick, Luther Halsey *see* PHYSICAL EDUCATION BY MUSCULAR EXERCISE
Gulielmus, Archbishop of Tyre *see* HISTOIRE DE LA GVERRE SAINCTE, DITE PROPREMENT, LA FRANCIADE ORIENTALE, ...
GULISTAN OU LE HULLA DE SAMARCANDE : OPERA EN TROIS ACTES / Dalayrac, N – Paris: Erard, 1805 – 1 – us Sibley [780]
Gulland, J A *see* MANUAL OF METHODS FOR FISH STOCK ASSESSMENT, PART 1
Gulledge, Tracey P *see* THE REPRODUCIBILITY OF LOW TESTOSTERONE IN ENDURANCE TRAINED MALES
GUM BRANCH CHURCH. GUM BRANCH, SOUTH CAROLINA : CHURCH RECORDS – 1796-Mar 1963 – 1 – 19.20 – us Baptist [240]
Gumbart, A S *see* MAKING THE MOST OF ONESELF
Gumbel, Hermann *see* DEUTSCHE SONDERRENAISSANCE IN DEUTSCHER PROSA
Gumilev, Nikolai Sepanovich *see*
- CHUZHOE NEBO
- DITIA ALLAKHA
- FARFOROVYI PAVIL'ON
- GIL'GAMESH
- GONDLA
- IZBRANNOE
- K SINEI ZVEZDE
- KOLCHAN
- KOSTER
- MIK. AFRIKANSKAIA POEMA
- OGNENNYI STOLP
- OTRAVLENNAIA TUNIKA I DRUGIE NEIZDANNYE PROIZVEDENIIA POD. RED. G.P. STURVE. IZD. IMENI CHEKHOVA
- PIS'MA O RUSSKOI POEZII
- ROMANTICHESKIE TSVETY
- SHATER
- SOBRANIE SOCHINENII V CHETYREKH TOMAKH
- STICHOTVORENIIA
- TEN' OT PAL'MY
- ZHEMCHUGA
Gumileva, A *see* NIKOLAI SEPANOVICH GUMILEV
GUMILEVE / Ivanov, G O – Sovremennye Zapiski. 1931. BH-3662 2 – 8 – ne IDC [460]
Gumilla, Jose *see* EL ORINOCO...ILUSTRADO
Gummere, Amelia Mott *see*
- THE QUAKER IN THE FORUM
- WITCHCRAFT AND QUAKERISM
GUMMI-ZEITUNG – (See also: Die Celluloid-Industrie, Berlin) – Berlin, Dresden. oct 1892-sep 1932 – 35r – 1 – uk British Libr Newspaper [670]
GUMMI-ZEITUNG, BERLIN *see* DIE CELLULOID-INDUSTRIE
Gumpelzhaimer, Adam *see*
- COMPENDIUM MUSICAE LATINO-GERMANICUM
- COMPENDIUM MUSICAE LATINO-GERMANICUM....NUNC EDITIONE HAC DECIMA..
- COMPENDIUM MUSICAE LATINO-GERMANICUM....NUNC EDITIONE HAC NONA..
- SACRORUM CONCENTUUM OCTONIS VOCIBUS MODULANDORUM...LIBER PRIMUS-SECUNDUS
Gumppenberg, Hanns, Freiherr von *see* DER MESSIAS
GUN CONTROL, A LIBERTARIAN PARTY POSITION PAPER / Feder, Donald A – No.7 – 9 – 1.00f – at Libertarian Micro [335]
Gunatilleke, Godfrey *see* MIGRATION TO THE ARAB WORLD
Gunawan, Kartono *see* POPULATION GROWTH AND ITS CONTROL, FOOD REQUIREMENTS AND FOOD PRODUCTION
GUN-BAO – (Library has holdings (incomplete) from between Apr. 6, 1929 and July 24, 1932) – Kharbin: "Gun-bao", 1926- – 1 – CSUX87-S36 – us Hoover Inst Photo [947]
Gunby *see* GUNBY'S CIRCUIT COURT OF APPEALS REPORTS
GUNBY'S CIRCUIT COURT OF APPEALS REPORTS / Gunby – (A Pre-NRS title) – 1v. 1885 – 2mf – 9 – $3.00 – LLMC 84-144 – us L.L.M.C. [340]
GUNDAGAI INDEPENDENT – Sep 7 1898-Dec 30 1918 – 9 – at Pascoe [072]
Gundelfinger, Friedrich *see* GOETHE IM GESPRAECH
Gundert, Hermann *see* DIE EVANGELISCHE MISSION
GUNDISSALINUS' DE DIVISIONE PHILOSOPHIAE : BGPHMA 4/2-3 / Baur, L – Muenster, 1903 – 7mf – 9 – ne Slangenburg [240]
Gundogan, Nese *see* MARKETING EFFECTIVENESS AND PROMOTIONAL STRATEGIES IN NATIONAL COLLEGIATE ATHLETIC ASSOCIATION DIVISION 1 BASKETBALL PROGRAMS
Gundolf, Ernst *see* NIETZSCHE ALS RICHTER UNSRER ZEIT
Gundolf, Friedrich *see*
- HEINRICH VON KLEIST
- MARTIN OPITZ
- REDE ZU GOETHES HUNDERTSTEM TODESTAG

GUNETHICS, OR, THE ETHICAL STATUS OF WOMAN / Brown, W Kennedy – 1887 – 9 – us A.T.L.A. [170]
GUNHILD DIE REITERIN / Wustmann, Erich – (Includes bibliographical references) – Reutlingen: Ensslin & Laiblin, [1939] – 1r – 1 – us U.W. Library [890]
Gunkel, Hermann *see*
- AUSGEWAEHLTE PSALMEN
- ELIAS, JAHVE, UND BAAL
- GENESIS
- LEGENDS OF GENESIS
- DIE WIRKUNGEN DES HEILIGEN GEISTES

Gunkel, Richard *see* GEORG BUECHNER UND DER DANDYSMUS
Gunn, B *see* STUDIES IN EGYPTIAN SYNTAX
Gunn, Harry C *see* NAPA COUNTY
Gunn, J M *see* HISTORY OF THE STATE OF CALIFORNIA AND BIOGRAPHICAL RECORD OF COAST COUNTIES
Gunn, John *see* AN HISTORICAL ENQUIRY RESPECTING THE PERFORMANCE ON THE HARP IN THE HIGHLANDS OF SCOTLAND.
Gunne, A Evelyn *see* THE SPIRIT OF THE NORTH AND OTHER POEMS
GUNNEDAH ADVERTISER – Jan 3 1898-Dec 30 1907 – 9 – at Pascoe [072]
GUNNEDAH COURIER – Jan 15 1901-Dec 18 1901 – 9 – at Pascoe [072]
Gunnerus, J E *see* FLORA NORVEGICA
Gunning, J H *see*
- DE GODSPRAKEN VAN AMOS
- VAN BIBEL NAAR JERUZALEM: DE GODSPRAKEN VAN SIONS LIJDEN EN HEERLIJKHEID (JESAJA 40-66)

Gunning, Mary J *see* MAXIMAL OXYGEN CONSUMPTION AND BODY COMPOSITION CHARACTERISTICS OF TRAINED MALE AND FEMALE RUNNERS
Gunning, Mary Jo *see* SURVEY OF AQUATIC PROGRAMS AND AQUATIC FACILITY ACCESSIBILITY FEATURES AVAILABLE TO AND UTILIZED BY PHYSICALLY HANDICAPPED STUDENTS AT FOUR-YEAR PENNSYLVANIA COLLEGES AND UNIVERSITIES
GUNPOWDER BAPTIST CHURCH. MIDDLETOWN, MARYLAND : CHURCH RECORDS – 1806-Sep 1966 – 1 – 34.11 – us Baptist [240]
Gunsaulus, Frank Wakeley *see*
- THE MINISTER AND THE SPIRITUAL LIFE
- TRANSFIGURATION OF CHRIST

Gunsteren, W F van *see* MOLECULAR SIMULATION
Gunstone, W D *see*
- COMPANION TO THE MINUTES OF CONFERENCE

Gunther, A C L G *see* THE REPTILES OF BRITISH INDIA
Gunther, Ernst A W *see* DIE DEUTSCHE HELDENSAGE DES MITTELALTERS
Gunther, John *see* THE SPANISH CIVIL WAR
Gunther, Max *see* THE WEEKENDERS
Guntli, Lucie *see* GOETHEZEIT UND KATHOLIZISMUS IM WERK IDA HAHN-HAHNS
GUNTON'S MAGAZINE – N.Y. v. 1-24. 1891-1903 – 1,5,6 – us Princeton Micro [800]
Gunung Agung, n.v. Djakarta *see* SEKEDAR TENTANG BIBLIOGRAFI NASIONAL, DENGAN TAMBAHAN TEKS BAHASA INGGERIS: SOME NOTES ON CURRENT NATIONAL BIBLIOGRAPHICAL AND OTHER DOCUMENTAL ACTIVITIES IN INDONESIA
Gunzburg, Nico *see* FIGHT CRIME, HELP THE DELINQUENTS AND LOVE HUMANITY
GUNZO, EPISTOLA AD AUGIENSES UND ANSELM VON BESATE (MGH QUELLEN..: 2.BD) : RHETORIMACHIA – 1958 – Dfl19.00 – ne Slangenburg [240]
GUO MING XIN BAO – China. 1917-24 – 9 – 5320.00 – cc Globe [072]
GUOGONG TANPAN WENXIAN ZILIAO XUANJI, 7.1945-3.1947 – A Selection of Materials on the Peace Talks Between the Nationalist and Communist Parties, Jul 1945-Mar 1947. Comp. by the Plum Garden Villa Memorial Hall, Nanjing. 6 fiches. F 42 – 9 – 12.00 – cc Microforms [950]
GUOJI JINGMAO XIAOXI – China. International Trade News. Three issues per week. 1986-. M-D105 – 1 – $40.00r – cc Microforms [072]
GUOJI SHANGBAO – China. International Business. Two issues per week. 1986-. M-D104 – 1 – $34.00r – cc Microforms [072]
GUOMIN – The National. May-Jun 1913. 3 fiches. F C33 – 9 – $25.00 – cc Microforms [073]
GUOWEN ZHOUBAO = NATIONAL NEWS WEEKLY – 1924-1937 – 23r – $1,035.00 – cc Microforms [950]
GUOXUE CONGKAN – Journal of National Culture. Feb-Jun 1911. 7 fiches. F C32 – 9 – $31.50 – cc Microforms [073]
Gup, Marc L *see* CONQUERING ANXIETY IN GRADE SCHOOL AGED SWIMMERS THROUGH THE USE OF IMAGINATIVE PLAY
THE GUPTA EMPIRE / Mookerji, Radha Kumud – 3rd ed. rev. Bombay: Hind Kitabs, 1959.174p. illus – 1 – us U.W. Library [950]
Gupta, M P *see* HINDI PUSTAKA-SAHITYA, 1867-1942
Gurevich, Aleksandr V *see* STARYI FOL'KLOR PRIBAIKAL'IA
Gurevich, Boris *see* ZASHCHISHCHAITE SVOBODU ROSSII
Gurian, W *see* DE STRIJD OM DE KERK IN HET DERDE RIJK
Gurian, Waldemar *see* EL BOLCHEVISMO... TRAD. DE EMILIO M. MARTINEZ AMADOR. BARCELONA, 1932
GURJUSTAN – Tbilisi, USSR. Nov 15-Dec 27 1990-Jan 5-Dec 21 1991 – 1r – 1 – us L of C Photodup [072]
Gurko-Kriazhin, Vladimir Aleksandrovich *see* DVA KRASNYKH GODA, NOI ABR 1917 G.-NOI ABR 1919 G
Gurland, J *see*
- GRUND-ZATSE DES EUROPAEISCHEN SEE-RECHTS
- LE-KOROT HA-GEZEIROT BE-YISRA'-EL

Gurland, J H *see* KURZE BESCHREIBUNG DER MATHEMATISCHEN, ASTRONOMISCHEN UND ASTROLOGISCHEN HEBRAEISCHEN HANDSCHRIFTEN DER FIRKOWITSCH'SCHEN SAMMLUNG IN DER KAISERLICHEN OEFFENTLICHEN BIBLIOTHEK ZU ST PETERSBURG
Gurley, Ralph R *see* LIFE OF JEHUDI ASHMUN WITH AN APPENDIX CONTAINING A BRIEF SKETCH OF THE LIFE OF REV. LOTT CARY
Gurlitt, Cornelius *see* KUNST UND KUENSTLER AM VORABEND DER REFORMATION
Gurlt, E *see* BIOGRAPHISCHES LEXIKON DER HERVORRAGENDEN AERZTE ALLER ZEITEN UND VOELKER
Gurney, Jane Tritton *see* A JOURNEY TO CANADA
Gurney, Joseph John *see*
- A LETTER TO THE FOLLOWERS OF ELIAS HICKS
- MEMOIRS OF JOSEPH JOHN GURNEY
- PUSEYISM TRACED TO ITS ROOT

Gurney, R *see* THE BRITISH FRESHWATER COPEPODA
Gurney, T *see*
- THE NATURE AND FITNESS OF THINGS
- PERSEVERANCE
- POEMS ON VARIOUS OCCASIONS:...

Gurney-Salter, Emma *see* FRANCISCAN LEGENDS IN ITALIAN ART: PICTURES IN ITALIAN CHURCHES AND GALLERIES
Gurnhill, James *see* ENGLISH RETRACED, OR, REMARKS, CRITICAL AND PHILOLOGICAL
Guro, E *see*
- NEBESNYE VERBLIUZHATA
- SHARMANKA PIESY, STIKHI, PROZA

Gurovich, I *see* ZAPISKI EMIGRANTA
Guru Dutt, K *see* PRINCIPLES OF HINDU ASTROLOGY: OR, THE BOOK OF FATE
Gusakov, A G *see* ZHELEZNODOROZHNOE PRAVO PO ZAKONODATEL' STVU SSSR
Guseinov, Ragim *see* OCHERKI REVOLIUTSIONNOGO DVIZHENIIA V AZERBAIDZHANE
GUSEL'KI-IAROVCHATY – Tambov, 1907-09 (monthly) – 8mf – 9 – us Ross [780]
Gusev, A M *see* SISTEMATICHESKII I KHRONOLOGICHESKII KATALOG BIBLIOTEKI BIBLIOFILA I BIBLIOGRAFA IA.F. BEREZINA-SHCHIRIAEVA. 1. RUSSKIIA KNIGI
Gusev, Sergiei Ivanovich *see* UROKI GRAZHDANKSOI VOINY
GUSHENGWU XUEBAO – Acta Palaeontologica Sinica. In Chinese but English abstracts to the main articles. F p49 – 9 – $3.50f – cc Microforms [073]
Gushiken, Thomas *see* THE EFFECTS OF LEISURE EDUCATION ON LIFE SATISFACTION AND LEISURE SATISFACTION AMONG JAPANESE AMERICAN OLDER ADULTS
GUSHU TONGMIN YICHENG JUYAO – A Selective Catalog of Ancient Books with Different Titles. Comp. by Zhang Xueyan. 4 fiches. F J6 – 9 – $18.00 – cc Microforms [070]
GUSII BRIDEWEALTH LAW AND CUSTOM / Mayer, Philip – Cape Town, Oxford UP, 1950 – us Res Libr [390]
Gusman, B *see* STO POETOV
Gusovius, Paul *see* DER LANDKREIS SAMLAND
Gussone, G *see*
- ENUMERATIO PLANTARUM VASCULARIUM IN INSULA INARIME
- FLORAE SICULAE PRODROMUS
- FLORAE SICULAE SYNOPSIS
- INDEX SEMINUM ANNI 1825-1826 QUAE AB HORTO REGIO BOCCADIFALCO
- PLANTAE RARIORES, QUAS IN ITINERE PER ORAS JONII AC ADRIATICI
- SICULAE PRODROMUS

Gustafson, R P *see* THE ROLE OF DIET AND EXERCISE IN WEIGHT CONTROL IN OBESE WOMEN
GUSTAV ADOLF IN DEUTSCHLAND, 1630-1632 / Egelhaaf, Gottlob – Halle: Verein fuer Reformationsgeschichte, 1901. ([Schriften des Vereins fuer Reformationsgeschichte; Bd. 68]) – 1mf – us A.T.L.A. [240]
GUSTAV FREYTAG UND DAS JUNGE DEUTSCHLAND / Mayrhofer, Otto – (Includes bibliographical references) – Marburg a.L.: N G Elwert, 1907 – 1 – us U.W. Library [430]
GUSTAV FREYTAG-GALERIE : NACH DEN ORIGINALGEMAELDEN UND CARTONS DER ERSTEN MEISTER DER NEUZEIT – Jubilaeums-Ausgabe. Leipzig: E Schloemp, [1887] – 1 – us U.W. Library [750]
GUSTAV FREYTAGS ROMANTECHNIK / Ulrich, Paul – (Includes bibliographical references (3rd prelim. leaf)) – Marburg a.L.: N G Elwert, 1907 – 1r – 1 – us U.W. Library [430]
GUSTAV FRIEDRICH WILHELM GROSSMANN : EIN BEITRAG ZUR DEUTSCHEN LITTERATUR-UND THEATERGESCHICHTE DES 18. JAHRHUNDERTS / Wolter, Joseph – (Includes bibliographical references) – Koeln: W Hoster, 1901 – 1r – 1 – us U.W. Library [430]
GUSTAV KUEHNE : SEIN LEBENSBILD UND BRIEFWECHSEL MIT ZEITGENOSSEN / ed by Pierson, Edgar – Dresden: E Pierson, [1889?] – 1 – us U.W. Library [860]
GUSTAV SCHWAB'S LEBEN / Schwab, Christoph Theodor – Freiburg i.B.: J C B Mohr (Paul Siebeck), 1883 – 1r – 1 – us U.W. Library [920]
GUSTAV STRUVE ALS POLITISCHER SCHRIFTSTELLER UND REVOLUTIONAER / Peiser, Juergen – Frankfurt a.M., 1973 – 4mf – 9 – DM90.00 – 3-89349-715-3 – gw Hänsel [460]
GUSTAV WALTER HEINEMANN PAMPHLET COLLECTION – 1954-1971 – 1 reel – 1 – CSUXANS2503-B – us Hoover Inst Photo [320]
GUSTAVE DE MOLINARI AND THE ANTI-ETATISTE LIBERAL TRADITION / Hart, David M – 1979. 2 fiches (24x) – 9 – 1.00f – at Libertarian Micro [320]
GUSTAVE MOREAU / Reunion des musees nationaux. Paris – 1961. 48 illus. 2 fiches – 9 – fr Réunion [700]
GUSTINE STANDARD – Gustin, CA. 1912- – 10+ r – 1 – $500.00 ($50.00y) – B02283 – us Library Micro [071]
GUTACHTEN VON GEISTLICHEN DER DIOECES GRIMMA UEBER DIE VORGESCHLAGENE VERDRAENGUNG DER VOLLSTAENDIGEN BIBEL AUS UNSERN VOLKSSCHULEN / Steglich, Friedrich August William – (Includes bibliographical references) – Leipzig: J C Hinrichs, 1869 – 1mf – 9 – 0-8370-8551-9 – 1986-2551 – us A.T.L.A. [370]
GUTACHTEN...BETREFFEND DIE BESTEUERUNG VON ERBSCHAFTEN IN DER SCHWEIZ DOMIZILIERTER RUSSEN / Burckhardt, W – [Bern, 1912] – 1mf – 1 – ILM-3788/1 – ne IDC [327]
GUTE MENSCHEN UND IHRE GESCHICHTEN : NOVELLEN / Sacher-Masoch, Leopold, Ritter von – Leipzig: E J Guenther, 1874 – 1r – 1 – us U.W. Library [830]
DIE GUTEN CHRISTEN : SCHAUSPIEL IN EINEM AKT / Telmann, Fritz – Leipzig: H Seemann, 1902 – 1r – 1 – us U.W. Library [820]
DER GUTEN FRAUEN ALLERSCHOENSTER KRAN : UND ANDERE HEITERE GESCHICHTEN / Presber, Rudolf – Berlin: P Neff, 1935 – 1r – 1 – us U.W. Library [830]
GUTENBERG – Berlin, may 13 1848-51 – 1 – Dist. gw Mikrofilm – gw Misc Inst [072]
GUTENBERG : PERIODICO NOTICIOSO E LITTERARIO – Manaos, Amazonas. 15 Nov 1891; Maio, 1 Jul 1892 – 1,5,6 – bl Biblioteca [072]
Guthe, Hermann *see*
- DE FOEDERIS NOTIONE JEREMIANA
- FRAGMENTE EINER LEDERHANDSCHRIFT ENTHALTEND MOSE'S LETZTE REDE AN DIE KINDER ISRAEL MITGETHEILT UND GEPRUEFT
- JESAIA
- DAS ZUKUNFTSBILD DES JESAIA

GUTHLAC ROLL – 1200. British Museum, Harley Ms. Roll 6 – 14 – uk Microform Academic [240]
GUTHRIAN – Guthrie Center. Iowa. -w. 1951- – 1 – us UMI [071]
Guthrie, C J *see* THE HISTORY OF THE REFORMATION OF RELIGION WITHIN THE REALM OF SCOTLAND
Guthrie, Ernst Graham *see* THE SIGNIFICANCE OF THE PERSONALITY OF CHRIST FOR THE MINISTER OF TODAY
Guthrie, Harold W *see* A STUDY OF SKILLED LABOR IN INDONESIA
Guthrie, James *see* OUR SHAM DEMOCRACY OR THE MAJORITY VOTE RACKET
Guthrie, James H *see* DIARY
Guthrie, Jas M *see* CAMPFIRES OF THE AFRO-AMERICANS
Guthrie, John *see* HEROES OF FAITH AS DELINEATED IN HEBREWS
Guthrie, Thomas *see*
- GOSPEL IN EZEKIEL: ILLUSTRATED IN A SERIES OF DISCOURSES
- PARABLES: READ IN THE LIGHT OF THE PRESENT DAY
- STUDIES OF CHARACTER FROM THE OLD TESTAMENT

GUTI LIXUE XUEBAO – Acta Mechanica Solida Sinica. In Chinese but English abstracts to the main articles. F p114 – 9 – $4.50f – cc Microforms [073]
Gutierres, Carlos *see* FRAY BARTOLOME DE LAS CASAS, SUS TIEMPOS Y SU APOSISLADO
Gutierrez Alonso, Paulino *see* THBY RN EL ESTUDIO DE LA BAJA ATMOSFERA EN UN NUCLEO URBANO
Gutierrez, C *see* MADRID. ARCHIVO HISTORICO NATIONAL. SECCION DE ORDENES MILITARES. GUIA DE LA SECCION DE ORDENES MILITARES
Gutierrez Carrasco, Octavio *see* LA FEDERACION INTERAMERICANA DE ABOGADOS; MEMORIA DE PRUEBA PARA OPTAR AL GRADO DE LICENCIADO EN LA FACULTAD DE CIENCIAS JURIDICAS Y SOCIALES DE LA UNIVERSIDAD DE CHILE
Gutierrez Coronel, Diego *see* HISTORIA DEL ORIGEN DEL CONDADO Y REINO DE CASTILLA
Gutierrez Cunado, Antolin *see* A VARIAS TINTAS
Gutierrez de Arevalo, P *see* PRACTICA DE BOTICARIOS
Gutierrez de Los Rios, G *see* NOTICIA GENERAL PARA LA ESTIMACION DE LAS ARTES...
Gutierrez de Santa Clara, Pedro *see* HISTORIA DE LAS GUERRAS CIVILES DEL PERU (1544-1548) Y DE OTROS SUCESOS DE LAS INDIAS
Gutierrez del Arroyo, C *see* MADRID. ARCHIVO HISTORICO NACIONAL. SECCION DE UNIVERSIDADES. LA SECCION DE UNIVERSIDADES
Gutierrez Gomez, Diego *see* DISLEXIAS
Gutierrez, Guillermo *see* PENETRACION IMPERIALISTA EN LA ARGENTINA
Gutierrez, J L *see* FEBRIOLOGIAE LECTIONES PINCIANAE, APRENDIX AD FEBRILOGIAM, DOLORIS DIAGNOSIM...
Gutierrez, Juan *see*
- CANONICARUM QUAESTIONUM
- CANONICARUM UTRUSQUE FORI LIBER PRIMUS
- CONSILIA
- CONSILIORUM SIVE RESPONSORUM
- DECISIONES S. ROTAE ROMANAE. OPERA OMNIA
- IURISCONSULTI PRAECLARISSIMI
- PRACTICARUM QUAESTIONUM
- PRACTICARUM...REAGIAS HISPANIAE
- PRACTICARUM...TRACTATUS DE BABELLIS
- PRAXIS CRIMINALIS CIVILIS Y CANONICA
- REPETITIONES ET ALLEGATIONES...IURIS
- REPETITIONES SEX QUATORDECIN... ALLEGATIONES
- TRACTATUS DE IURAMENTO CONFIRMATORIO

- TRACTATUS NOVUS DE TUTELIS CURIS MINORUM
- TRACTATUS...JURAMENTO

Gutierrez Lasanta, Francisco *see* DONOSO CORTES, EL PROFETA DE LA HISPANIDAD

Gutierrez, M *see* NUEVAS CONSIDERACIONES SOBRE LA LIBERTAD ABSOLUTA DE COMERCIO Y PUERTOS FRANCOS...

Gutierrez Macias, Valeriano *see*
- EL 1 CONGRESO NACIONAL DE BRUJOLOGIA EN SAN SEBASTIAN
- ALTA EXTREMADURA
- BREVE ENSAYO SOBRE LOS NOMBRES GENTILICIOS USADO EN LA ALTA EXTREMADURA
- EL CICERONE DEL PUEBLO
- COMARCAS NATURALES DE LA ALTA EXTREMADURA. LA JARA CACERENA
- COPLAS DEL BAILE DEL PANDERO
- LA EGREGIA FIGURA DE CARLOS DE YUSTE. (LAS POSTRIMERIAS DE SU VIDA Y SU MUERTE EJEMPLAR)
- EN VILLANUEVA DE LA SIERRA TUVO SU ORIGEN LA "FIESTA DEL ARBOL"
- FIGURAS ILUSTRES
- GERIFALTES EXTREMENOS. ANGEL MARINA, EL JUGLAR DE LA VIRGEN MORENA
- LIGERO APUNTE DE LA LOCALIDAD CACERENA DE PESCUEZA
- POR LA GEOGRAFIA CACERENA
- POR LA GEOGRAFIA CACERENA. (BANOS DE MONTEMAYOR)
- POR LA GEOGRAFIA CACERENA (FIESTAS POPULARES)
- VILLANUEVA DE LA VERA. FIESTAS DE PERO PALO, 1965

Gutierrez Marin, C *see* PASTOR J. JEZEQUEL VISITS REPUBLICAN SPAIN

Gutierrez, Miguel *see* ALBORES.ENSAYOS

Gutierrez Utrera, Benigno *see* COPIA DE LA PROTESTA...CONGRESO...ELECCION DE CORIA

Gutirrrez, Solano *see* ENSAYO BIOLOGICO SOBRE HERNANDO CORTES. TOMO 1. OAXACA, 1933

Gutjahr, F S *see* DIE GLAUBWUERDIGKEIT DES IRENAEISCHEN ZEUGNISSES UEBER DIE ABFASSUNG DES VIERTEN KANONISCHEN EVANGELIUMS

Gutkind, A E *see* A LINGUISTIC BIBLIOGRAPHY OF EAST AFRICA

Gutman, Anatolii *see* ROSSIIA I BOLSHEVIZM

Gutmann, F *see* DIE INTERNATIONALEN VERTRAEGE UEBER DIE NORDSEEFISCHEREI

GUTMANNS REISEN / Raabe, Wilhelm Karl – Berlin: Otto Janke, 1892 – 1r – 1 – us U.W. Library [830]

Gutmundsson, Einar *see* SKOTLANDS RIMUR

Gutscher, H *see* ERKLARUNG DER PROPHETEN NAHUM UND ZEPHANJA

GUTTEMBERG : ORGAO DA ASSOCIACAO TYPOGRAPHICA DE SOCORROS MUTUOS – Maceio, Alagoas. 13 Fev-Jul, Set-Nov 1881; Abr, Out, Nov 1883; Abr 1884; Jan 1885-Dez 1887; Fev, Maio 1888; Jun, Dez 1889; Jan, Mar, Jun 1892; Set-Nov 1894; Mar-Maio, Set-Dez 1895; Jan-Dez 1896; Mar-Abr, Jul, Set-Dez 1897; Jan-Dez 1899; Jul 1900; Jan 1904; Jan 1905-1 Dez 1911 – 1,5,6 – bl Biblioteca [072]

Guttman, M *see* BIBLIOGRAPHIE DER SCHRIFTEN WILHELM BACHERS NEBST EINEM HEBRAEISCHEN SACH- UND ORTSNAMENREGISTER

Guttmann, J *see*
- DER EINFLUSS DER MAIMONIDISCHEN PHILOSOPHIE AUF DAS CHRISTLICHE ABENDLAND
- FESTSCHRIFT
- MOSES BEN MAIMON, SEIN LEBEN, SEINE WERKE UND SEIN EINFLUSS
- DIE PHILOSOPHIE DES SALOMON IBN GABIROL
- DIE RELIGIONSPHILOSOPHIE DES SAADIA
- DIE SCHOLASTIK DES 13
- DAS VERHAELTNISS DES THOMAS VON AQUINO ZUM JUDENTHUM UND ZUR JUEDISCHEN LITTERATUR

Guttmann, L *see* VERANTWORTUNG CASPAR TAUBERS, DER ZU WIEN VERPRANT IST WORDEN

Guttzeit, Johannes *see* DER KREIS JOHANNISBURG

Gutwillig, Mike *see* EN VILLE

Gutzkow, Karl *see*
- BOERNE'S LEBEN
- RUECKBLICKE AUF MEIN LEBEN
- EINE SHAKESPEAREFEIER AN DER ILM

GUTZKOW-FUNDE : BEITRAEGE ZUR LITERATUR- UND KULTURGESCHICHTE DES 19. JAHRHUNDERTS / Houben, Heinrich Hubert – Berlin, 1901. x/568p – 4mf – 9 – DM98.00 – 3-89349-205-4 – gw Hänsel [430]

GUTZKOWS DRAMATURGISCHE TAETIGKEIT AM DRESDENER HOFTHEATER : UNTER BESONDERER BERUECKSICHTIGUNG SEINER BUEHNENBEARBEITUNGEN / Baumgard, Otto Wilhelm Gustav – (Includes bibliographical references) – Bonn: Rhenania-Verlag, 1915 – 1 – us U.W. Library [430]

GUTZKOWS THEORIE DES ROMANS IN SEINEM ROMAN "HOHENSCHWANGAU" / Koch, Johannes Guenther – (Includes bibliographical references) – Forst (Lausitz): Buch- und Steindruckerei E Hoene, 1936 – 1r – 1 – us U.W. Library [430]

Gutzlaff, Karl Friedrich August *see*
- CHINESE CHRISTIAN MONOGRAPH (CCC134)
- CONCERNING THE TRUE RELIGION (CCC131)
- CONSCIENCE (CCC137)
- CONSOLATIONS OF THE TRUE RELIGION (CCC132)
- DOCTRINE OF SALVATION IN THE CHINESE LANGUAGE (CCC136)
- PERFECT MAN'S MODEL (CCC135)
- WORLD OF JESUS (CCC133)

Gutzlaff, KF A *see* CHINESE MEDICAL MISSION

Gutzschhahn, Uwe-Michael *see* YOUNG POETS OF GERMANY

GUWAINI'S BERICHT UEBER DIE BEKEHRUNG DER UIGUREN / Marquart, J – SPAW 1912. BU-601 2 – 8 – ne IDC [460]

Guy, Basil *see* THE FRENCH IMAGE OF CHINA BEFORE AND AFTER VOLTAIRE

GUY DE MAUPASSANT A TRAVES DE LA CORRESPONDENCIA DE GUSTAVO FLAUBERT / Segura, Enrique – Madrid, 1950. Sep. de Cuadernos de Literatura, fasc. 19-21 – sp Bibl Santa Ana [946]

GUY LAVIOLETTE (MICHEL-HENRI GINGRAS), EN RELIGION, LE REVEREND FRERE ACHILLE DES FRERES DE L'INSTRUCTION CHRETIENNE, AUTEUR DE "GLOIRES NATIONALES" : BIBLIOGRAPHIE ANALYTIQUE / Marie-Stella, Soeur – 1954. SEM105P4 – 2mf – 9 – cn Bibl Nat [240]

GUY LIVINGSTONE, OR, "THOROUGH" / Lawrence, George Alfred – London: John W. Parker, 1857 – 1 roll – 1 – 1-55879-698-3 – uk Libr Preservation [999]

Guy, PLO *see* NEW LIGHT FROM ARMAGEDDON

GUYANA : STATISTICAL ABSTRACT OF GUYANA 1970-1974 / Guyana. Statistical Bureau – (1972, 1973 not available. Coll title: Latin American and Caribbean Official Statistical Serials, 1821-1982) – 12mf – 9 – £100.00 – uk Chadwyck [972]

Guyana *see* DEVELOPMENT PROGRAMME, 1966-1972

GUYANA HUMAN RIGHTS ASSOCIATION (GHRA) – Georgetown. 105 docs. 1980-1992 – 16mf – 9 – ne IDC [320]

Guyana. Ministry of Economic Development *see* DRAFT SECOND DEVELOPMENT PLAN, 1972-1976

Guyana. Ministry of Education and Social Development *see* TOWARDS NEW GOALS FOR SECONDARY EDUCATION IN THE COOPERATIVE REPUBLIC OF GUYANA

Guyana. Ministry of Higher Education *see* ANNUAL REPORT 1982

GUYANA STAR – Georgetown. Guyana. -d. 2 Mar-23 Apr 1966. (1 reel) – 1 – uk British Libr Newspaper [072]

Guyana. Statistical Bureau *see* GUYANA

GUYANE : ANNUAIRE STATISTIQUE DE LA GUYANE 1947/52-1961/70 / France. Institut National de la Statistique et des Etudes Economiques – (1947-52; 1957-59; 1961-70 not available. Coll title: Latin American and Caribbean Official Statistical Serials, 1821-1982) – 2mf – 9 – £17.00 – uk Chadwyck [972]

Guy-Grand, V J *see* DICTIONNAIRE FRANCAIS-VOLOF

Guy-Grand, VJ *see* DICTIONNAIRE FRANCAIS-VOLOF

Guyon, Claude Marie *see* HISTOIRE DES AMAZONES ANCIENNES ET MODERNES

Guyon, Louis *see* MONTFERRAND

Guyot, Arnold *see*
- CREATION
- CREATION, OR, THE BIBLICAL COSMOSGONY IN THE LIGHT OF MODERN SCIENCE

Guyot, Henri *see* L'INFINITE DIVINE DEPUIS PHILON LE JUIF JUSQU'A PLOTIN

Guyot, Yves *see*
- ECONOMIC PREJUDICES
- QUESNAY ET LA PHYSIOCRATIE

GUYS HOSPITAL REPORTS – 1957-58 – 7 – uk Microform Academic [610]

Guyton de Morveau, Louis-Bernard *see* MEMOIRE SUR L'EDUCATION PUBLIQUE, AVEC LE PROSPECTUS D'UN COLLEGE, SUIVANT LES PRINCIPES DE CET OUVRAGE

Guyton, Louis Marie *see* TOPOGRAPHIE ET STATISTIQUE MEDICALES DE LA VILLE ET DE LA COMMUNE D'AUTUN

GUZARISH'HA-YI BASTANSHINASI – Tehran. Sal-i 1-4 (Shahrivar 1329-Isfand 1338 [Aug/Sep 1950-Feb/Mar 1960]) – 3r – 1 – $175.00 – us MEDOC [950]

Guzman Gundian, Lucila *see* EL DIVORCIO, ESTUDIO DE LEGISLACION COMPARADA: ESPANA Y SUDAMERICA

Guzman, S V *see* EL DERECHO DE CONQUISTA...

Guzman y Martinez, Jesus *see*
- NUEVA SELECCION DE LECTURAS FRANCESAS
- PAGINAS ORTOGRAFICAS

G.V. PLEKHANOV PAMPHLET COLLECTION – 1924-1956 – 1 – CSUXANS1232-B – us Hoover Inst Photo [331]

Gvazzini, S *see* TRACTATVS DE PACE, TREVGA, VERBO DATO ALICVI PRINCIPE...

LA GVERRA FATTA DA CHRISTIANI CONTRA BARBARI PER LA RICVPERATIO... / Accoldi, B – Vinegia, 1549 – 3mf – 9 – H-8281/1 – ne IDC [956]

GWALIA – Bangor, Wales. -w. Aug 1881-1898. Lacking 1883, 1897. 14 reels – 1 – uk British Libr Newspaper [072]

Gwalior. India (State). Archaeological Department *see* ANNUAL ADMINISTRATION REPORT FOR THE YEARS 1940/41

Gwatkin, Henry Melvill *see*
- THE ARIAN CONTROVERSY
- THE CHURCH, PAST AND PRESENT
- EARLY CHURCH HISTORY TO A.D. 313
- STUDIES OF ARIANISM

Y GWEITHIWR – Aberdare, Wales. Sep 1858-Jun 1860 – 61ft – 1 – uk British Libr Newspaper [072]

Y GWEITHIWR CYMREIG – Aberdare, Wales. Jan 1885-Sep 1889 – 4r – 1 – uk British Libr Newspaper [072]

Gwekoh, Sol H *see* DISTINGUISHED 100: THE BOOK OF EMINENT ALUMNI OF THE UNIVERSITY OF THE PHILIPPINES

GWELO TIMES – Rhodesia. -w. 12 Jul 1901-17 Dec 1915. (5 reels) – 1 – uk British Libr Newspaper [072]

GWENDOLYN BENNETT PAPERS : FROM THE HOLDINGS OF THE SCHOMBURG CENTER FOR RESEARCH IN BLACK CULTURE, MANUSCRIPTS, ARCHIVES AND RARE BOOKS DIVISION: THE NEW YORK PUBLIC LIBRARY, ASTOR, LENOX AND TILDEN FOUNDATIONS – (Guide which covers all coll under "Literature and the Arts" sold separately for $20.00 D3305.G6) – 1995 – 2r – 1 – $170.00 – D3305P19 – Dist. us Scholarly Res – us L of C Photodup [420]

GWIAZDA – Toledo, Ohio. 1888-89 – 2r – 1 – $32.50r – us Archival [071]

GWIAZDA ZACHODU – Omaha, NE. -w. Feb 1918-Jun 1945 – 1 – us NE Hist [071]

GWIAZDA ZACHODU = WESTERN STAR – Omaha: [Gwiazda Zachodu Pub Co], [-1945]. dec 14 1917-1918 – 1r – 1 – us Res Libr [071]

Gwilt, Joseph *see* AN ENCYCLOPEDIA OF ARCHITECTURE, HISTORICAL, THEORETICAL AND PRACTICAL...

GWINNETT CHURCHES; A COMPLETE HISTORY OF EVERY CHURCH IN GWINNETT COUNTY, GEORGIA, WITH SHORT BIOGRAPHICAL SKETCHES OF ITS MINISTERS / Flanigan, J C – 1911. 7 fiches.F-0734 – 9 – us A.G.L.L. [920]

Gwo, Yun-Han *see* INDIGENOUS PREACHING IN CHINA WITH A FOCAL CRITIQUE ON JOHN SUNG

Gwoh, C Y *see* THE ROAD TO MATURE MANHOOD (CCC209)

Y GWRON CYMREIG – Carmarthen, Wales. Jan 1852-Sep 1860 – 3 1/2r – 1 – uk British Libr Newspaper [072]

Gwynn, John *see* ON A SYRIAC MS. BELONGING TO THE COLLECTION OF ARCHBISHOP USSHER

Gwynne, George John *see* A COMMENTARY, CRITICAL, EXEGETICAL, AND DOCTRINAL, ON ST. PAUL'S EPISTLE TO THE GALATIANS

Gwynne, Walker *see* THE CHRISTIAN YEAR

DIE GWYNN'SCHEN CAJUS- UND HIPPOLYTUS-FRAGMENTE (T.U.U. 1-6/3C) / Harnack, Adolf von – Leipzig, 1890 – 1mf – 9 – ne Slangenburg [240]

Gyarmathy, S *see* AFFINITAS LINGUAE HUNGARICAE CUM LINGUIS FENNICAE ORIGINIS GRAMMATICE DEMONSTRATA

GYERNVILLE TIMES – Santa Rosa. Calif. 1901-1909 – 1 – us UMI [071]

GYGES UND SEIN RING : EIN TRAGOEDIE IN FUENF AKTEN / Hebbel, Friedrich – (Includes bibliographical references) – Leipzig: Hesse & Becker, [19–?] – 1r – 1 – us U.W. Library [820]

Gyles, John *see* MEMORIES OF ODD ADVENTURES, STRANGE DELIVERANCES, ETC. IN THE CAPTIVITY OF JOHN GILES, ESQ., COMMANDER OF THE GARRISON OF SAINT GEORGE RIVER, IN THE DISTRICT OF MAINE

Gyllenhall, L *see* INSECTA SVECICA...CLASSIS I. COLEOPTERA SIVE ELEUTERATA

Gyllensten, Lars Johan Wictor *see* DIARIUM SPIRITUALE. ROMAN OM EN ROEST

O GYMNASIANO : ORGAM DOS ALUMNOS DO GYMNASIO AMAZONENSE – Manaus, Amazonas. 4 Maio-Jun 1910; Fev-Mar, Jul 1911; Jul-Ago 1921; Set 1922; Out-8 Dez 1925 – 1,5,6 – bl Biblioteca [072]

O GYMNASIO : HUMORISTICO E LITTERARIO – Manaos, Amazonas. 12 Jan-Mar, Maio, 5-21 Set 1907 – 1,5,6 – bl Biblioteca [072]

DAS GYMNASIUM MARIENWERDER : VON DER DOMSCHULE ZUR OBERSCHULE / Duehring, Hans – (Includes bibliographical references and index) – Wuerzburg: Holzner Verlag, 1964 – 1r – 1 – us U.W. Library [370]

GYMPIE MINER – Australia. 4 Sep 1889-23 Nov 1891. -w – 2r – 1 – uk British Libr Newspaper [622]

DER GYNAEKOLOGE – v. 1-13. 1968-80 – 1,5,9 – 956.00 – us UMI [618]

GYNANDROPSIS GYNANDRA (L.) BRIQ., A TROPICAL LEAFY VEGETABLE : ITS CULTIVATION AND UTILIZATION – 1991 – 46p – it F.A.O. [631]

GYNECOLOGIC AND OBSTETRIC INVESTIGATION – v6-. 1975- – 1,5,9 – us UMI [073]

The Gypsy Lore Society *see* JOURNAL OF THE GYPSY LORE SOCIETY, 1888-1973

Gyrowetz, Adalbert *see*
- DEUX SONATES POUR LE PIANOFORTE AVEC D'UN VIOLON OU FLUTE ET VIOLONCELLE
- NOTTURNO, NO 7, POUR LE PIANOFORTE AVEC ACCOMP. D'UN VIOLON ET VIOLONCELLE
- QUATUORS, SIX, 3E LIVRE
- QUATUORS, SIX, OP. 1
- QUATUORS, TROIS, POUR DEUX VIOLONS, ALTO ET BASSE, OEUVRE 17
- SIX QUATUORS CONCERTANTS POUR DEUX VIOLONS, ALTO ET BASSE...4E LIVRE DU QUATUORS, OUEVRE 17 1ER PARTIE
- TRE QUARTETTI PER DUE VIOLINI, VIOLA E VIOLONCELLO
- TROIS GRANDS QUATUORS CONCERTANS POUR DEUX VIOLONS, ALTO ET VIOLONCELLO...OP. 42
- TROIS QUATUORS POUR FLUTE, VIOLON, ALTO, ET BASSE, OP. 20
- TROIS SONATES POUR LE PIANOFORTE AVEC ACCOMPAGNEMENT D'UN VIOLON OU FLUTE ET VIOLONCELLE
- TROIS SONATES POUR PIANO-FORTE AVEC ACCOMPAGNEMENT DE VIOLON OU FLUTE ET VIOLONCELLE

Gysi, Fritz *see* RICHARD WAGNER UND DIE SCHWEIZ

GZEYRES TAKH = MONOGRAPH – (In Yiddish) – Vilnius, LT. 1938 – 1r – 1 – $25.00 – cn Can Microfilming [072]

Gzowski, Casimir Stanislaus *see* REPORT ON THE ACCOMMODATION FOR RAILWAYS ON THE WATER FRONT OF THE CITY OF TORONTO..

H AND S : HEARING AND SPEECH ACTION – (Cont: Hearing & Speech News. Cont by: Hearing & Speech Action) – Silver Spring. v43-45 jan 1975-aug 1977 1,5; v44-45 jan 1976-aug 1977 9 – 1,5,9 – D2140.01 – us UMI [073]

H. BLACKSTONE'S REPORTS : REPORTS OF CASES ARGUED AND DETRMINED IN THE COURTS OF COMMON PLEAS AND EXCHEQUER CHAMBER...1788-1791 / Blackstone, Henry – London: Whieldon & Butterworth. v1-2. 1791-96 (all publ) – 15mf – 9 – $22.50 – LLMC 95-271 – us L.L.M.C. [324]

H. BULLINGER AND THE ZURICH REFORMATION – Ed. by F. Buesser. Indexes, catalogs, bibliographies, reader. App. 90 titles per year – 9 – ne IDC [240]

H, E *see* SCRIPTURE PROOF FOR SINGING OF SCRIPTURE PSALMS, HYMNS, AND SPIRITUAL

H G C *see* EL CENTINELA DE ISRAEL

H. HEINE'S 'BUCH DER LIEDER' UND SEIN VERHAELTNIS ZUM DEUTSCHEN VOLKSLIED / Goetze, Robert – (Includes bibliographical references) – Halle: E Karras, 1895 – 1r – 1 – us U.W. Library [430]

H. REUTERDAHLS TEOLOGISKA ASKADNING : MED SAERSKILD HAENSYN TILL HANS STAELLNING TILL SCHLEIERMACHER / Aulen, Gustaf – Uppsala: W. Schultz, [1907] – 1mf – us A.T.L.A. [240]

H S Feng *see* THE JESUS I KNOW (CCC313)

HA DE NUESTRA SRA. DE GUADALUPE / Malagon, Joan – Salamanca: Imp. Cossio, 1672 – 1 – sp Bibl Santa Ana [946]

HA LEKACH – Rotterdam, 1910-1912. v1-2 – 6mf – 9 – J-261-38/1 – ne IDC [943]

HA MIZRACHI – Toronto, CN, 1932 – 1r – 1 – Can$25.00 – cn Can Microfilming [072]

Ha, Su-Guen *see* THEMENBEHANDLUNG IM FREMDSPRACHENUNTERRICHTLICHEN DISKURS

Ha Tinh Province's Military Service Commission *see* LUAT NGHIA VU QUAN SU

HA TINH TAN VAN – no. 6-24. Hue. 1929-juil 1930 – 1 – fr A.C.R.P.P. [073]

HA-ACH = THE BROTHER – (In Hebrew) – Lubavitch, RU. v3 no32-no5673 1913 – 1r – 1 – $25.00 – cn Can Microfilming [072]

Haack, Ernst *see* CHRISTENTUM UND KULTUR

Haag, Daniel *see* RIGHT TO EDUCATION

Haag Emile *see* LA FRANCE PROTESTANTE

Haag, Eugene *see* LA FRANCE PROTESTANTE

Haag, EugeneHaag, Emile *see* LA FRANCE PROTESTANTE

DIE HAAGER UEBEREINKUNFT VOM 12. JUNI 1902... / Hauser, E – Basel, 1909 – 1mf – 1 – ILM-3520/1 – ne IDC [327]

HA-AHDUT – v. 1-6. Jerusalem. 1910-15. Lacking: 1913, v. 4. BJ-91-7 1 – 9 – ne IDC [073]

HA-ALIYYOT HA-RISHONOT SHEL HA-HASIDIM LE-EREZ-YISRA'EL / Halpern, I – Jerusalem. 1947. BJ-27-24 1 – 9 – ne IDC [360]

HA'AM – (Vol. 1, no. 1 (Apr. 1972)-v. 2, no. 7 (Mar. 1973); v. 2, no. 10 (May 1973)-v. 7, no 5 (18 Apr. 1978); v. 8, no. 5 (1 May 1979); v. 9, no. 3 (17 Jan. 1980); v. 10, no. 2 (18 Nov. 1980)-v 10, no 6 (June 1981); v. 11, no. 3 (Dec. 1981); v. 11, no. 7 (Apr. 1982); v. 11, no. 9 (June 1982); v. 12, no. 1 (Oct. 1982)-Feb. 1985; Feb. 1989-Mar. 1989) – Los Angeles, California – 1 – us A.J.P.C. [978]

HA-'AM – New York. 1908 – 1 – us A.J.P.C. [073]

HA-AM – Moscow, 1916-1918 – 16mf – 9 – J-291-27/1 – ne IDC [072]

Ha-Am, Ahad *see* HA-SHILO'AH

HA'AMOED – 's-Gravenhage, 1931-1939. v1-8 – 91mf – 9 – J-261-33/1 – ne IDC [073]

Haan, Wilhelm *see* SAECHSISCHES SCHRIFTSTELLER-LEXICON

HAAPARANNANLEHTI – Haparanda, Sweden. 1882-1923 – 1 – sw Kungliga [072]

HAAPSALU BAPTISTI KOGUDUA: EESTI BAPTISMI SUNNIPAIK = HAAPSALU BAPTIST CHURCH: ESTONIAN BAPTIST BIRTHPLACE – (One part of a two-part item) – Keilas, Estonia: "Kulwaja" trukk, 1934 – 1r – 1 – $6.04 – us Baptist [240]

Haar, Bernard ter *see* ORATIO DE HISTORICA RELIGIONIS CHRISTIANAE INDOLE

Haarbeck, J *see* DIE STIFTSHUETTE

Haarbleicher, M M *see* AUS DER GESCHICHTE DER DEUTSCH-ISRAELITISCHEN GEMEINDE IN HAMBURG

HA'ARETZ – Tel Aviv. Israel. 1970- – 1 – us UMI [072]

HA-ARETZ – Israel, 1979- – 9 – $490.00y – us Ross [072]

HA-ARETZ = THE LAND – (In Hebrew. Weekly) – Jerusalem, IS. v30 no8729. 16 May 1948 (Birth of Israel Issue) – 1r – 1 – $25.00 – cn Can Microfilming [072]

HAARETZ – Jerusalem. 1919-69. BJ-91-95 3 – 1 – ne IDC [072]

Haarlem, W M van *see* EARLY PHOTOGRAPHS FROM EGYPT 1880-1910

Haas, J H de *see* MATERNAL AND CHILD HEALTH SURVEY IN INDONESIA (JAVA, BALI AND SUMATRA)

Haase, B *see* DER DEUTSCH-POLNISCHE STAATSVERTRAG...

Haase, Felix *see*
- BEGRIFF UND AUFGABE DER DOGMENGESCHICHTE
- DIE KOPTISCHEN QUELLEN ZUM KONZIL VON NICAEA
- LITERARKRITISCHE UNTERSUCHUNG ZUR ORIENTALISCH-APOKRYPHEN EVANGELIEN LITERATUR
- LITERARKRITISCHE UNTERSUCHUNGEN ZUR ORIENTALISCH-APOKRYPHEN EVANGELIENLITERATUR
- ZUR BARDESANISCHEN GNOSIS (T.U.U. 3-34/4)

Haase, Henning *see* DIE SUBJEKTIVE DIAGNOSTISCHE VALENZ VON INTELLIGENZTESTS

HA-ASIF / ed by Sokolow, N – v. 1-6. Warsaw. 1884-93. BJ-422-23 1 – 9 – ne IDC [470]

HA'ATIED – Amsterdam, 1935-1936. Nos. 3-8 – 2mf – 9 – J-261-34/1 – ne IDC [943]

Habana, Jose Gutierrez de la Concha y de Irigoyen *see* MEMORIAS SOBRE EL ESTADO POLITICO, GOBIERNO Y ADMINISTRACION DE LA ISLA DE CUBA

HABARI – (Nairobi; in English and native languages). v3-10, 1924-31 – 1 – us Res Libr [960]

HABARI ZA LEO – Dar-es-Salaam, Tanzania. -w. 21 May 1948-24 Feb 1956. Imperfect. 1 reel – 1 – uk British Libr Newspaper [072]

HABEAS CORPUS CASE RECORDS,1820-63, OF THE CIRCUIT COURT FOR THE DISTRICT OF COLUMBIA / U.S. District Courts. District of Columbia – 2rolls – 1 – M434 – us Nat'l Archives [324]

HABEAS CORPUS, THE LAW OF WAR, AND CONFISCATION / Nicholas, Samuel Smith – Louisville: Bradley & Gilbert, 1862. 29p. LL-1371 – 1 – us L of C Photodup [340]

Habela Patino, Eugenio *see*
- APENDICE A LA...SALIDA DE DON QUIXOTE
- EL TENIENTE APOLOGISTA UNIVERSAL

HABEN : DRAMA IN 14 BILDERN / Hay, Gyula – Berlin: B Henschel, 1947 – 1r – 1 – us U.W. Library [820]

HABEN WIR DEN AECHTEN SCHRIFTTEXT DER EVANGELISTEN UND APOSTEL? / Tischendorf, G von – Leipzig, 1873 – 1mf – 8 – ne Slangenburg [220]

HA-B'ER – and supplement ha-Dli. Pietrokov. v. 1-15. 1923-1938 – 1 – us NY Public [073]

HABER – Samsun. Mueduer-i Mes'ul: Emin Refik; Idare Mueduerue: Ibrahim Naci; Sermuharriri: Aziz Samih. No. 83 (28 Tesrinievvel 1341 [1925]) – 9 – $20.00 – us MEDOC [956]

Haber, Aliza *see* POPULATION AND BUILDING IN ISRAEL 1948-1973

HABER ANASI – Trabzon. Sahib-i Imtiyaz: Mehmed Tevfik; Mueduerue: Mustafa Sirri. No. 6 (5 Mart 1325 [1909]) – 9 – $20.00 – us MEDOC [956]

Habert, G *see* LA VIE DU CARDINAL DE BERULLE

Habertus, I Apxiepatikon *see* LIBER PONTIFICALIS ECCLESIAE GRAECAE

Habetna, K *see* COMPLEX VARIABLES

Habig, Jean-Marie *see* ENSEIGNEMENT MEDICO-SOCIAL POUR COLONIAUX

HABITABEC – Montreal. v1 no 1 23 Avril 1976-. SEM35P326 – 41r – 1 – cn Bibl Nat [072]

HABITABEC (EDITION DE QUEBEC) – Ste-Foy. v1 no 1 21 Sept 1984-. SEM35P327 – 8r – 1 – Can$450.00 – cn Bibl Nat [072]

HABITABEC (EDITION D'OTTAWA) – Ottawa. v1 no 1 Janv. 31st 1986-. SEM35P328 – 5r – 1 – Can$205.00 – cn Bibl Nat [072]

THE HABITANT – Pointe-au-Pic, Murray Bay. jul 1907-v14 n2. 15 aut 1922 – 1r – 1 – Can$35.00 – cn Can Microfilming [072]

THE HABITANT: AND OTHER FRENCH-CANADIAN POEMS / Drummond, William Henry – With an introduction by Louis Frechette: and with illustrations by Frederick Simpson Coburn. Toronto: Musson Book Co., 1897. 02777. (Pre-1900 Canadiana) – 9 – cn C.I.H.M. [810]

HABITAT – (Ceased v27 1984) – Ottawa. v1-27. 1958-84 – 9 – Can$20.00y – cn Micromedia [073]

HABITAT : U.N. CONFERENCE ON HUMAN SETTLEMENTS, VANCOUVER, CANADA / United Nations – 1976 – E/F.8 E.210 F.110 R.85 S.148 – 9 (A/CONF.70/) – us U.N. Pubs [307]

HABITAT INTERNATIONAL – v1- 1976- – 5,6,9 – us UMI [574]

LES HABITATIONS OUVRIERES / Roulliet, Antony – Paris. 1889. (La Condition Ouvriere. Part Two.) – 9 – 5.00 – fr Bibl Nationale [360]

LES HABITATIONS OUVRIERES DANS LES GRANDS CENTRES INDUSTRIELS ET PLUS PARTICULIEREMENT DANS LA REGION DU NORD / Dumont, A A – (Condition of 19th C. French working class series). 1905 – 9 – fr Hachette [360]

LES HABITATIONS OUVRIERES ET LES CONSTRUCTIONS CIVILES / Foucher de Careil, Louis A – Paris. 1873. (La Condition Ouvriere. Part Two.) – 9 – 5.00 – fr Bibl Nationale [360]

HABITI ANTICHI, ET MODERNI DI TUTTO IL MONDO / Vecellio, C – Venetia, 1589 – 12mf – 9 – H-8403/1 – ne IDC [945]

HABITS AND CUSTOMS OF THE INU OF THE WESTERN SHORE AND POINT BARROW / Ray, P H – BN 368 2. 1885 – 8 – ne IDC [306]

HABL AL-MATIN – Calcutta. Sal-i 8, shumarah-i 1-24 (13 Jumada al-Sani 1318 – 4 Zu al-Hijjah 1318 [8 October 1900-25 March 1901]) – 1 reel – 1 – $325.00 – us MEDOC [950]

HABLA EL CAUDILLO / Franco, Francisco – Burgos, 1938. Fiche W 891. (Blodgett Collection of Spanish Civil War Pamphlets) – 9 – us H.U. College Libr [946]

HABNAME-'I VEYSI – Istanbul, 1293 – 1mf – 9 – $6.00 – us MEDOC [949]

HA-BOKEOR = THE MORNING LIGHT – (In Hebrew) – Lemberg, UA. v3 no2 Nov 1877; v7 no- Sep 1880 – 1r – 1 – $30.00 – cn Can Microfilming [072]

HA-BOKER = THE MORNING LIGHT – (In Hebrew. Daily) – Tel-Aviv, IS. v14 no3817. 16 May 1948 (Birth of Israel Issue) – 1r – 1 – $25.00 – cn Can Microfilming [072]

HA-BOKER – Tel Aviv. 1935-65. Available: 1960-65. BJ-91-8 3 – 1 – ne IDC [470]

HA-BOKER LAYELADIM = THE MORNING FOR CHILDREN – (In Hebrew) – Tel-Aviv, IS. v5 no37. 16 May 1948 – 1r – 1 – $25.00 – cn Can Microfilming [072]

HA-BOKER OR = MORNING LIGHT – (In Hebrew) – Lwow & Warsaw, PL. v3 no1 Oct 1877-Sep 1880 – 1r – 1 – $30.00 – cn Can Microfilming [072]

HABONEH – (Missing 1935(1-2)) – Amsterdam, 1935(1-8) – 1mf – 9 – J-261-35/1 – ne IDC [943]

LA HABRA STAR – La Habra, CA. 1916-94 – 15r – 1 – $750.00 – R02332 – us Library Micro [071]

DIE HABSBURGER-LIGA 1625-1635 / Guenter, H – Berlin, 1908 – 6mf – 9 – ne IDC [943]

Hache, Patricia *see* BIO-BIBLIOGRAPHIE ANALYTIQUE DE ME MARIE-LOUIS BEAULIEU, AVOCAT A QUEBEC

Hachenburger, M *see* DE LA NATURE JURIDIQUE DU PROTECTORAT...

HACIA ALLA Y PARA ACA : UNA ESTADA INDIOS MOCOBIAS / Paucke, P Florian – Buenos-Aires: Tucuman, 1942. 4v – fr Armell [305]

HACIA ALLA Y PARA ACA... / Bayle, Constantino – Madrid: Missionalia Hispanica, 1949 – 1 – sp Bibl Santa Ana [240]

HACIA ALLA Y PARA ACA... / Pancke, Florian – Madrid: Missionalia Hispanica, 1949 – 1 – sp Bibl Santa Ana [240]

HACIA DONDE VA CHILE : POR EL PAN, LA TIERRA, LA PAZ Y LA LIBERTAD DE CHILE / Contreras Labarca, Carlos – [Montivideo: Imp "Central", 1943?] – 1 – us Res Libr [335]

HACIA LA GNOSIS / Roso de Luna, Mario – Madrid: Editorial Pueyo, 1921 – 1 – sp Bibl Santa Ana [240]

HACIA LA REALIZACION DE UNA DEMOCRACIA RESPONSABLE / Bambill, Benjamin A M – Buenos Aires: G. Kraft, [1953] – 1 – CSUXADH2083-B – us Hoover Inst Photo [320]

HACIA LA UNION DE LOS PUEBLOS LATINOS / Becerro de Bengoa, Ricardo – Caceres: Delegacion de Ex-Combatientes de la Alta Extremadura, S.A. – 1 – sp Bibl Santa Ana [946]

HACIA LAS RUTAS NUEVAS / Juez Nieto, Antonio – Badajoz: Dip. Provincial, 1938 – 1 – sp Bibl Santa Ana [946]

HACIA UN MAYOR Y MEJOR CONOCIMIENTO DE LA VERDADERA SITUACION ECONOMICA ARGENTINA : [DISCURSOS Y DECLARACIONES DEL MINISTRO DE HACIENDA DE LA NACION, Y PRESIDENTE DEL CONSEJO ECONOMICO NACIONAL DURANTE SU PERMANENCIA... EXTRAORDINARIA DEL CONSEJO INTERAMERICANO ECONOMICO Y SOCIAL DE LA ORGANIZACION DE LOS ESTADOS AMERICANOS / Cereijo, Ramon Antonio – Buenos Aires], 1950 – 1 – CSUXADQ3404-B – us Hoover Inst Photo [330]

HACIA UN MEJOR CONOCIMIENTO HISTORICO CIENTIFICO DE EXTREMADURA / Ramirez Ramirez, Enrique – Badajoz: Imp. Diputacion Provincial, 1974 – sp Bibl Santa Ana [946]

HACIA UNA ESPANA SIN GANADO? / Mendoza Ruiz, Manuel – Madrid: Obra Sindical de Colonizacion, 1965 – 1 – sp Bibl Santa Ana [946]

HACIA UNA ORDENACION GANADERA / Mendoza Ruiz, Manuel – Madrid: Obra Sindical de Colonizacion, 1965 – 1 – sp Bibl Santa Ana [946]

HACIVAD – Istanbul. 1 sene, nu. 1-2 13. Se'ban 1326-15 Se'ban 1326 (27 Agustos 1324-30 Agusto 1324 [9 Eyluel 1908-12 Eyluel 1908]) – 1mf – 9 – $20.00 – us MEDOC [949]

HACK *see* EL-HACK

Hack, Mary Pryor *see*
- CHRISTIAN WOMANHOOD
- CONSECRATED WOMEN

Hacke, H C *see* EENIGE OPMERKINGEN OVER HET POLITIETOEZICHT OP ZEE, IN VERBAND MET DE ZEEVISCHERIJ-CONVENTIE VAN 6 MEI 1882

HACKEBEILS ILLUSTRIERTE ZEITUNG – (Cont by: Neue Illustrierte Zeitung, 1931 n41) – Berlin, 1931-dec 20 1934 – 5r – 1 – Dist. gw Mikrofilm – gw Misc Inst [072]

HACKEBEILS ILLUSTRIERTE ZEITUNG *see* NEUE ILLUSTRIERTE ZEITUNG

Hackel, E *see* MONOGRAPHIA FESTUCARUM EUROPEARUM

Hackenberg, Fritz *see* ELISE VON HOHENHAUSEN

HACKENSACK RECORD – Hackensack, N.J. 1901- – 1 – us UMI [071]

Hackenschmidt, Karl *see* DER CHRISTLICHE GLAUBE IN ACHT BUECHERN

Hacker, Colleen M *see* MORAL JUDGMENT AND THE PERCEIVED LEGITIMACY OF INJURIOUS ACTS AMONG COLLEGIATE ATHLETES

Hacker, J *see* DIE MESSE IN DEN DEUTSCHEN DIOEZESAN-GESANG- UND GEBETBUECHERN

Hackett, Horatio Balch *see*
- CHRISTIAN MEMORIALS OF THE WAR, OR, SCENES AND INCIDENTS ILLUSTRATIVE OF RELIGIOUS FAITH AND PRINCIPLE, PATRIOTISM AND BRAVERY IN OUR ARMY
- A COMMENTARY ON THE ACTS OF THE APOSTLES

Hackett, J *see* A HISTORY OF THE ORTHODOX CHURCH OF CYPRUS

Hacki, Michael O Cist. *see* SERMONES CAPITULARES

Hackmann, Heinrich Friedrich *see* DIE ZUKUNFTSERWARTUNG DES JESAIA

Hackmann, Oskar *see*
- DIE POLYPHEMSAGE IN DER VOLKSUEBERLIEFERUNG
- SAGOR, REFERATSAMLING

HACKNEY AND KINGSLAND GAZETTE – London. -w. 1869-1909. (39 reels) – 1 – uk British Libr Newspaper [072]

Hackney, Anthony C *see*
- INFLUENCE OF DIET AND THE MENSTRUAL CYCLE ON LACTATE CONCENTRATION DURING INCREASING EXERCISE INTENSITIES
- THE INFLUENCE OF THE MENSTRUAL CYCLE AND DIET ON METABOLISM DURING REST AND EXERCISE
- THE RELATIONSHIP BETWEEN BLOOD TESTOSTERONE LEVELS AND BODY COMPOSITION IN PHYSICALLY ACTIVE, YOUNG ADULT MEN
- REPRODUCTIVE ENDOCRINE RESPONSE FOLLOWING ANAEROBIC AND AEROBIC EXERCISE

HACKNEY EXPRESS & SHOREDITCH OBSERVER. (SHOREDITCH OBSERVER) – London. 1886-1913.-w. 16 reels – 1 – uk British Libr Newspaper [072]

Hackwood, Frederick William *see*
- CHRIST LORE
- DRAGONS AND DRAGON SLAYERS

Hackworth, G H *see* DIGEST OF INTERNATIONAL LAW

Hackworth, Green Haywood *see* DIGEST OF INTERNATIONAL LAW
Ha-Cohen, I *see* BO'AZ VE-RUT
Ha-Cohen, S *see*
- AMAL VE-TIRSAH
- MATTA'EI KEDEM
HADA BUENA ARGENTINA – [Buenos Aires?: s.n., 195-?] – 1 – CSUXAJA7299-B – us Hoover Inst Photo [972]
HADASHIM GAM YESHANIM / Silberbush, D I – Cracow. 1888. BJ-422-101 1 – 9 – ne IDC [470]
HADASSAH BULLETIN – Cincinnati. Ohio. 1931-62 – 1 – us A.J.P.C. [071]
HADASSAH MAGAZINE – (New York). 1920-33. 1956-67 – 1 – us A.J.P.C. [073]
HADASSAH P & B BULLETIN – Cincinnati. Ohio. 1947-62 – 1 – us A.J.P.C. [071]
Hadat, D *see* DICTIONARY ENGLISH-INDONESIA
Hadd, James *see* HISTORY OF FAYETTE COUNTY, PENNSYLVANIA
Haddan, Arthur West *see*
- APOSTOLICAL SUCCESSION IN THE CHURCH OF ENGLAND
- COUNCILS AND ECCLESIASTICAL DOCUMENTS RELATING TO GREAT BRITAIN AND IRELAND
Hadden, James *see* A HISTORY OF FAYETTE COUNTY
Hadden, James Cuthbert *see* THOMAS CAMPBELL
HADDINGTON (DUNBAR AND HADDINGTON), 1820 : BRITISH ISLES CENSUS DIRECTORIES PROJECT, VOL 65 – 1mf – 9 – A$9.00 – at Vine [941]
HADDINGTONSHIRE, 1837 : BRITISH ISLES CENSUS DIRECTORIES PROJECT, SCOTLAND. VOL 40 – 1mf – 9 – A$9.00 – at Vine [941]
HADDOCK BAPTIST CHURCH. HADDOCK, GEORGIA : CHURCH RECORDS – (1,053p) – 1943-1990 – 1 reel – 1 – $47.39 – us Baptist [240]
Haddock, John A *see* THE GROWTH OF A CENTURY OF THE COUNTY OF JEFFERSON 1793-1894
Haddon, Eileen *see* COLLECTION OF SOUTHERN RHODESIA ARCHIVES, MANUSCRIPTS AND DOCUMENTS
HA-DEBORAH – (New York). 1911-12 – 1 – us A.J.P.C. [073]
Haden, T H *see* DIARIES, 1896-1946
HA-DEREKH – Tel Aviv. 1951-65. BJ-91-11 1 – 9 – ne IDC [335]
HA-DEROR – The swallow. (New York). 1911 – 1 – us A.J.P.C. [073]
HADERSLEV STIFTSBOG – (Lacks: 1970, 1973) – 1966-83; 1987-92 – Inquire – 1 – ATLA S0575 – us A.T.L.A. [073]
Hadewijch *see* STROPHISCHE GEDICHTEN
HADEWIJCH'S STROPHISCHE GEDICHTEN : EEN STUDIE VAN DE MINNE IN HET KADER DER 12DE EN 13DE EEUWSE MYSTIEK EN PROFANE MINNELYRIEK / De Paepe, N – Gent, 1967 – 8mf – 8 – ne Slangenburg [290]
HADIKAT UEL-SU'ADA / Fuzuli – [Istanbul]: Izzet Efendinin Matbaasi, 1289 [1872] – $85.00 – us MEDOC [470]
Hadiwijono, Harun *see* MAN IN THE PRESENT JAVANESE MYSTICISM
Hadiwijoto, S *see* PEMIMPIN SEMBAHJANG
HADLEIGH WEEKLY NEWS – Hadleigh, England. -w. 1978-81. 8 reels – 1 – uk British Libr Newspaper [072]
Hadley, George *see*
- GRAMMATICAL REMARKS ON THE PRACTICAL AND VULGAR DIALECT OF THE INDOSTAN LANGUAGE
- INTRODUCTORY GRAMMATICAL REMARKS ON THE PERSIAN LANGUAGE
Hadley, George P *see* HISTORY OF THE TOWN OF GOFFSTOWN 1733-1920
Hadley, H *see*
- SYMPHONY NO. 1, OP. 25, IN F
- SYMPHONY NO. 2, OP. 30, IN F MINOR
Hadley, James *see* INTRODUCTION TO ROMAN LAW, IN TWELVE ACADEMICAL LECTURES
Hadley, M *see* REPRODUCTIVE ECOLOGY OF TROPICAL FOREST PLANTS
Hadley, Samuel Hopkins *see* DOWN IN WATER STREET: A STORY OF SIXTEEN YEARS...IN WATER STREET MISSION
Hadley-Allen Family *see* PAPERS
Hadlich, Heinrich *see* DIE IDEE DES GESETZES IN DER PRAKTISCHEN VERNUNFT
HA-DOAR – (New York). 1921-50 – 1 – us A.J.P.C. [073]
HA-DOAR – New York. Daily v. 1-3. Nov 1921-Oct 19 1923 – 1 – us NY Public [071]
HA-DOR – Cracow. 1901, 1904. BJ-291-22 1 – 9 – ne IDC [956]
Hadorn, W *see* DAS TAUSENDJAEHRIGE REICH
Haeckel, Ernst Heinrich Philipp August *see*
- MONISM AS CONNECTING RELIGION AND SCIENCE; THE CONFESSION OF FAITH OF A MAN OF SCIENCE
- DIE RADIOLARIEN
HAECKEL'S MONISM FALSE : AN EXAMINATION OF THE RIDDLE OF THE UNIVERSE, THE WONDERS OF LIFE, THE CONFESSION OF FAITH OF A MAN OF SCIENCE BY PROFESSOR HAECKEL... / Ballard, Frank – London: Charles H. Kelly, [1905?] – 2mf – us A.T.L.A. [110]
Haefele, H F *see* NOTKERI BALBULI GESTA KAROLI MAGNI IMP. (MGH 6: 12.BD)
Haeften, Benedictus van *see*
- BENEDICTUS ILLUSTRATUS SIVE DISQUISITIONUM MONASTICARUM. LIBRI 12
- DE HEYR-BAENE DES CRUYS, WAER-LANGHS ALLE SOORTEN VAN MENSCHEN WORDEN GHEWESEN, ENDE SEKERLIJCK GHELEERT, OM DOOR DE CRUYCEN VAN ALDERHANDE LIJDEN OFT TEGHENSPOEDT VAN DESE BEDROEFDE TIJDELIJCKE WERELDT,...
- S. BENEDICTUS ILLUSTRATUS SIVE DISQUISITIONUM MONASTICARUM LIBRI 12
- SCHOLA CORDIS SIVE AVERSI A DEO CORDIS AD EUMDEM REDUCTIO, ET INSTRUCTIO
Haege, Christine *see* SOZIALPOLITISCHE LOESUNGSKONZEPTE ZUR ABSICHERUNG DES RISIKOS DER PFLEGEBEDUERFTIGKEIT
Haegele, Sigurd *see* GRUNDFRAGEN DER MOTOLOGIE
Haeger, W *see* DIE VOLLSTRECKUNG VON URTEILEN UND SCHIEDSSPRUECHEN...
HAELSINGEKURIREN – Soederhamn, 1949-60 – 9 – sw Kungliga [072]
HAELSINGEKURIREN FREDAG – Soederhamn, 1993-94 – 9 – sw Kungliga [072]
HA-EMET – New York. The truth. 1894 – 1 – us A.J.P.C. [073]
HA-EMET VE-HA-SHALOM EHAVU / Klein, S W – Frankfurt a.M. 1861. BJ-32-6 1 – 9 – ne IDC [270]
HA-EMETH – New York. v. 1-2 no. 10. July 1894-June 1895 – 1 – us NY Public [071]
HAEMODYNAMISCHE UND METABOLISCHE REAKTIONEN IM TENNISSPORT - UNTER BERUECKSICHTIGUNG DES HOEHEREN LEBENSALTERS / Masuhr, Andreas – 1994 – 3mf – DM98.00 – 3-8267-2079-2 – gw Hänsel [790]
HAEMOPHILIA – Oxford. v1-3. 1995-97+ – 1,5,9 – D21725 – us UMI [616]
HAEMORRHAGIC SEPTICAEMIA – 1982 – 58p – it F.A.O. [630]
HAEMOSTASIS – v4-. 1975- – 1,5,9 – us UMI [073]
HA-EMUNAH HA-RAMAH MICROFORM / Ibn Daud, Abraham ben David, Halevi – Yerushalayim, c1966. 104p. Hebrew trans. by Solomon Ibn Labi. 104p – 1 – us U.W. Library [100]
HAENDEL OPERAS FOR SOLO RECORDER – 26mf – 9 – MS-c – ne IDC [780]
Haenel, Karl *see* NIGERIEN, AM NIL DER SCHWARZEN
Haenicke, Diether H *see* THE CHALLENGE OF GERMAN LITERATURE
Haenisch, E *see* MONGGO HAN SAI DA SEKIYEN
Haensel, Anette *see* AKTIVES ZUHOEREN UND BEHALTEN
Haensel-Hohenhausen, Markus *see*
- DIE DEUTSCHSPRACHIGEN FREIMAURER-ZEITSCHRIFTEN DES 18. UND 19. JAHRHUNDERTS
- ELISE VON HOHENHAUSEN, GEB. VON OCHS (1789-1857)
- DIE FRUEHE DEUTSCHSPRACHIGE OSCAR-WILDE-REZEPTION (1893-1906)
- SAEMTLICHE AUFSAETZE UND MISZELLEN
HAERETICORUM CATALOGUS / Schluesselburg, C – Francofortii [Frankfort]. v1-6. 1601-1611. v7-13. 1599 – 85mf – 9 – ne IDC [240]
Haering, Theodor *see*
- DIE LEBENSFRAGE DER SYSTEMATISCHEN THEOLOGIE DIE LEBENSFRAGE DES CHRISTLICHEN GLAUBENS
- UEBER DAS BLEIBENDE IM GLAUBEN AN CHRISTUS
- ZUR VERSOEHNUNGSLEHRE
HAERNOSANDSPOSTEN – Harnosand, Sweden. 1842-1951 – 108r – 1 – sw Kungliga [072]
HA-ESHKOL / ed by Fox, J S & Guenzig, E – v. 1-7. Cracow. 1898-1913. BJ-422-24 1 – 9 – ne IDC [470]
HA'ETGAR – Berkeley, Calif. v1, no. 1; v1, no. 3-v 2, no. 3; v3, no. 2; v4, no. 2; v6, no. 1; v6, no. 3; v7, no. 1; v7, no. 3; v8, no. 1-v8, no. 2. [Nov. 1978-Winter 1986] – us A.J.P.C. [270]
HA-'ETH – Lemberg. no. 1-20. Jan 31-Mar 17 1907 – 1 – us NY Public [072]
Haetzer, L *see*
- ACTA ODER GESCHICHT WIE ES VFF DEM GESPRECH IN ZUERICH ERGANGEN IST
- ALLE PROPHETEN NACH HEBRAISCHER SPRACH VERTEUETSCHT
- ALLE PROPHETENN NACH HEBRIESCHER SPRACH VERDEUETSCHT
- DEN GETRUEWEN VND VSSERWELTEN BRUEDERN VND SCHWOESTERN IN CHRISTO JHESU, WUENSCHT L. HAETZER ERLOESUNG
- JUDICIUM DEI ET SPONSI NOSTRI, QUID CUM IMAGINIBUS, SEU SIMULACHRIS AGENDUM SIT, ETC
- VON DEN EUENGELISCHEN ZECHEN, VND VON DER CHRISTEN RED. AUSZ HAILIGER GESCHRIFFT
- AIN VRTAYL GOTTES VNSERS EEGEMAHELS, WIE MAN SICH MIT ALLEN GOETZEN UND BILDNUSSEN HALTEN SOLL
HAEUSLICHE ALTENPFLEGE : ERFAHRUNGEN MIT DEN LEISTUNGEN FUER SCHWERPFLEGEBEDUERFTIGE NACH DEM GESUNDHEITSREFORMGESETZ 1988 / Mayer, Renate – 1994 – 2mf – 9 – DM80.00 – 3-8267-2062-8 – gw Hänsel [360]
Haevernick, Heinr. A C *see* DR. HEINR. ANDR. CHRI HAEVERNICKS VORLESUNGEN UEBER DIE THEOLOGIE DES A.T
Haevernick, Heinrich Andreas Christoph *see* VORLESUNGEN UEBER DIE THEOLOGIE DES ALTEN TESTAMENTS
Hafen *see* HISTORY OF COLORADO
Hafen, Hans *see* STUDIEN ZUR GESCHICHTE DER DEUTSCHEN PROSA IM 18. JAHRHUNDERT
Hafenrefferus, M *see* DISPUTATIO, CONTRA ANABAPTISTAS, DE REGNO CHRISTI, DEF. IOH. HONOLD
Haffner, Karl *see* BEKANNTE UND UNBEKANNTE GROSSEN: SKIZZEN UND NOVELLETTEN AUS DER KUNST-UND THEATERWELT
Hafner, Gotthilf *see* DEUTSCHE DICHTUNG
HAFTA – Istanbul, 1881-1882 – $40.00 – us MEDOC [956]
HAFTARAH / Rabinovitz, A S – Tel-Aviv. 1925. BJ-422-69 1 – 9 – ne IDC [470]
DIE HAFTUNG BEI WECHSELFAELSCHUNGEN / Reissig, Helmut – Leipzig, 1936 – 1mf – DM48.00 – 3-8267-3006-2 – gw Hänsel [340]
DIE HAFTUNG DES HERRSCHENDEN UNTERNEHMENS FUR VERBINDLICHKEITEN DER ABHANGIGEN GESELLSCHAFT BEI EINEM MULTINATIONALEN UNTERNEHMEN / Langen, Albrecht – Bonn o.J – 1 – DM30.00 – gw Mikro Press [943]
DIE HAFTUNG DES KOMMANDITISTEN IM VERGLEICH MIT DER HAFTUNG DES KOMPLEMENTARS AUF GRUNDLAGE DES FRANZOSISCHEN, SCHWEIZERISCHEN UND DEUTSCHEN HANDELSRECHTES / Furrer, Reinhold – Luzern: Burkhardt, 1902. 256p. LL-4072 – 1 – us L of C Photodup [340]
HAGAGA – Nass River, B.C.: J.B. McCullagh, [1893-1910?] – 9 – cn C.I.H.M. [240]
A HAGAI KET BEKEKONFERENCIA CIMU ERTEKEZESE,... / Eoettevenyi, N O – Budapest, n.d. – 2mf – 1 – ILM-4098/1 – ne IDC [327]
HA-GALIL / ed by Rabinovitz, A Z – v. 1. Tiberias. 1919. BJ-422-25 1 – 9 – ne IDC [470]
HA-GAN / ed by Rabinovich, L – 2v. St. Petersburg. 1897. BJ-422-26 1 – 9 – ne IDC [470]
Hagan, R M et al *see* SUCCESSFUL IRRIGATION
HAGANAH SPEAKS – (v2, no1, (30 Jan. 1948)-v2, No24, (21 Jan. 1949); Continues: Americans for Haganah; Continued by: Israel Speaks) – New York, N.Y. – us A.J.P.C. [270]
HA-GAT / ed by Rabinovich, L – St. Petersburg. 1897. BJ-422-27 1 – 9 – ne IDC [470]
HAGEDORN UND DIE ERZAEHLUNG IN REIMVERSEN / Eigenbrodt, Wolrad – (Includes bibliographical references) – Berlin: Weidmann, 1884 – 1r – 1 – us U.W. Library [430]
Hagel, K *see* DAS LARCENY ACT, 1916
Hageman *see* HISTORY OF BURLINGTON AND MERCER COUNTIES
Hageman, Samuel Miller *see* ST. PAUL
Hagen, C G *see* TENTAMEN HISTORIAE LICHENUM ET PRAESERTIM PRUSSICORUM
Hagen, H A *see* BIBLIOTHECA ENTOMOLOGICA: DIE LITERATUR UEBER DAS GANZE GEBIET DER ENTOMOLOGIE BIS ZUM JAHRE 1862
Hagenbach, J J *see*
- MORMOLYCE, NOVUM COLEOPTERORUM GENUS
- SYMBOLA FAUNAE INSECTORUM HELVETIAE
Hagenbach, K R *see*
- GERMAN RATIONALISM
- A HISTORY OF CHRISTIAN DOCTRINES
- HISTORY OF THE CHURCH IN THE EIGHTEENTH AND NINETEENTH CENTURIES
- HISTORY OF THE REFORMATION IN GERMANY AND SWITZERLAND CHIEFLY
- JOHANN OEKOLAMPAD UND OSWALD MYCONIUS, DIE REFORMATOREN BASELS
HAGENER KREISBLATT – (Title change: Hagener Zeitung, 1 Jan 1864) – Hagen, Germany. 1872. Nos.1-150 – 1 – gw Mikrofilm [072]
HAGENER VOLKSZEITUNG – (Title change: Westfaelische Post, 11 Mar 1881; Westfaelisches Tageblatt, 10 Mar 1894) – Hagen, Germany. 30 Aug 1874-28 Jun 1934. No.172-253 (incomplete) – 1 – gw Mikrofilm [072]
HAGENER ZEITUNG *see* HAGENER KREISBLATT
Hagenguth, Edith *see* HARTMANNS IWEIN
Hager, Joseph *see* AN EXPLANATION OF THE ELEMENTARY CHARACTERS OF THE CHINESE
HAGERS-TOWN GAZETTE – Hagerstown. Md. 1809-1814 – 1,3 – us Readex [071]
HAGGADAH SHEL PESAH – Venice. 1609. BJ-43-20 1 – 9 – ne IDC [956]
HAGGAHOT YERUSHALMI / Elijah, Gaon of Vilna – Koenigsberg, 1858 – 1mf – 9 – ne IDC [270]
HAGGAI AND ZECHARIAH : WITH NOTES AND INTRODUCTION / Barnes, William Emery – (Includes bibliographical references and indexes) – Cambridge: University Press, 1917 – 1mf – 9 – 0-8370-6085-0 – 1986-0085 – us A.T.L.A. [220]
Haggard, Fred P *see* THE JUDSON CENTENNIAL, 1814-1914
Haggard, Henry Rider *see* ALLAN QUATERMAIN
Haggard, John *see* REPORTS OF CASES...IN THE CONSISTORY COURT OF LONDON: CONTAINING THE JUDGMENTS OF SIR WILLIAM SCOTT
Haggis, Sheila M et al *see* EDUCATION FOR ALL
Hagglund, B C *see* THE REBEL POET
Hagiz, M *see*
- PARASHAT ELLEH MASEI
- SEFAT EMET
The Hagley Museum and Library *see* TRADE CATALOGS
Hagner, Alexander Burton *see* ADDRESS ON THE LIFE AND CHARACTER OF WILLIAM CRANCH, DELIVERED JANUARY 10TH, 1907, BY ALEXANDER B. HAGNER AT THE REQUEST OF THE BAR ASSOCIATION OF THE DISTRICT OF COLUMBIA
Hagood, L M *see* THE COLORED MAN IN THE METHODIST EPISCOPAL CHURCH
HA-GORAL VE-HA-YERUSHAH / Weisbrem, I – Warsaw. BJ-422-95 1 – 9 – ne IDC [470]
HA-GOREN – Berdichev. Berlin, etc. 1897-1928. BJ-291-19 1 – 9 – ne IDC [270]
'HA-GRA' VE-TALMIDAV BE-YISHUV EREZ-YISRA'EL / Rivlin, J J – (Sefer ha-GRA). v. 2. Jerusalem. 1954. BJ-27-42 1 – 9 – ne IDC [270]
THE HAGUE, 1940-1945 – ca 4,000 photographs – 9 – ne IDC [770]
Hague, Dyson *see* WAYS TO WIN
The Hague. General State Archives *see* IMAGES OF EAST AND WEST
Hague, George *see* THE BANKING OF CANADA AS CONNECTED WITH ITS TRADE AND COMMERCE:...31ST MARCH 1897
Hague, John *see* CANADA FOR CANADIANS: A ROYALIST ROLAND FOR THE ANNEXATIONIST OLIVER

THE HAGUE RULES 1921 EXPLAINED / Cole, S D – Ed 2. London, 1922 – 2mf – 1 – ILM-3878/1 – ne IDC [327]
THE HAGUE RULES EXPLAINED... / Cole, S D – London, 1924 – 2mf – 1 – ILM-3709/1 – ne IDC [327]
DE HAGUE RULES IN DE BRUSSELSCHE CONVENTIE 1924 / Blusse van Oud-Alblas, A – Leiden, 1929 – 4mf – 9 – ILM-3346/1 – ne IDC [327]
HA-HAYYAL HA-IVRI – 1941-46. Lacking: 1943-46, v. 3 (9-end; 11-end). BJ-91-13 1 – 9 – ne IDC [072]
HA-HAYYIM HA-KALKALIYYIM BI-ZEFAT U-VI-SEVIVOTEHA / Kenaani, J – v. 6. Ziyyon. 1934. BJ-27-11 1 – 9 – ne IDC [956]
Hahn, Aaron *see* HISTORY OF THE ARGUMENTS FOR THE EXISTENCE OF GOD
Hahn, August *see* DAS EVANGELIUM MARCIONS IN SEINER URSPRUENGLICHEN GESTALT
Hahn, Augustus *see* BARDESANES GNOSTICUS SYRORUM PRIMUS HYMNOLOGUS
Hahn, C W *see*
- MONOGRAPHIE DER SPINNEN
- ORNITHOLOGISCHER ATLAS... DER AUSSEREUROPAEISCHEN VOEGEL

Hahn, CW *see* DIE ARACHNIDEN. GETREU NACH DER NATUR
Hahn, G G *see* DAS PERSONALSTATUT UND DIE GESCHAEFTSFAEHIGKEIT...
Hahn, G L *see* DIE LEHRE VON DEN SAKRAMENTEN IN IHRER GESCHICHTLICHEN ENTWICKELUNG INNERHALB DER ABENDLAENDISCHEN KIRCHE BIS ZUM CONCIL VOM TRIENT
Hahn, Heinrich August *see* VORLESUNGEN UEBER DIE THEOLOGIE DES ALTEN TESTAMENTS
Hahn, Johann Georg von *see* MYTHOLOGISCHE PARALLELEN
Hahn, Ludwig Ernst *see* FUERST BISMARCK: SEIN POLITISCHES LEBEN UND WIRKEN
Hahn, S *see* THOMAS BRADWARDINUS U. SEINE LEHRE V. D. MENSCHL. WILLENSFREIHEIT
Hahn, Traugott *see* IST DIE FORDERUNG EINES MODERNEN CHRISTENTUMS UND EINER MODERNEN THEOLOGIE BERECHTIGT?
Hahn, Werner *see* GESCHICHTE DER POETISCHEN LITTERATUR DER DEUTSCHEN
Hahn, Wilhelm *see* DER BERGARBEITERSTREIK VOM MAI 1889 IM RHEINISCH-WESTFALISCHEN INDUSTRIEGEBIET UNTER BESONDERER BERUECKSICHTIGUNG DER STELLUNG KAISER WILHELM 2. UND FURST
HA-HOKER – Ed. by Fuchs. Cracow. 1891-93; Vienna. 1894. BJ-100-162 1 – 9 – ne IDC [956]
HAHR: HISPANIC AMERICAN HISTORICAL REVIEW – v62-. 1982- – 1,5,6,9 – us UMI [073]
HAI CH'AO YIN – Sea tide echo, a Buddhist journal. 18 v. 1920-37. Lacking: v. 5 (3-7, 12) 1924; v. 6 (8) 1925; v. 7 (3-end) 1926; v. 9 (12) 1928; v. 10 (2, 12-end) 1929; v. 11 (3, 5, 12) 1930; v. 12 (2, 10) 1931. BCH-253 2 – 8 – ne IDC [290]
HAI CHUN TSA CHIH – Magazine of the Ministry of the Navy. Nanking, Chungking. 1928-42. Available: v5 (1-3, 8, 11, 12) 1932-33; v7 (5-8) 1934-35; v9 (2) 1936; v15 (6) 1942). BCH-1071 1 – 9 – ne IDC [355]
HAI SUI AN-CHUAN – Legal decisions. 1606. BCH-944 2 – 8 – ne IDC [340]
HA-IBRI – New York. 1916-21 – 1 – us A.J.P.C. [071]
HAI-CH'ENG HSIEN-CHIH – 1762, 24, 1. BCH-571 2 – 8 – ne IDC [950]
Haidemenakis, E D *see*
- GROWTH AND CHARACTERIZATION OF ELECTRONIC MATERIALS
- MAGNETISM

Haig, T *see* DIVERTIMENTOS, A SECOND SET OF THREE, FOR THE PIANOFORTE CONSISTING OF MARCHES, SCOTTISH [SIC] AIRS FOR SLOW MOVEMENTS, AND ORIGINAL GERMAN WALTZES WITH AN ACCOMP. FOR TAMBOURINO AND TRIANGLE AD LIB, OP. 18
Haigh, Arthur Elam *see* THE ATTIC THEATRE
Haight, Canniff *see*
- BEFORE THE COMING OF THE LOYALISTS
- COMING OF THE LOYALISTS
- A GENEALOGICAL NARRATIVE OF THE DANIEL HAIGHT FAMILY

Haight, Theron W *see* MEMOIRS OF WAUKESHA COUNTY
HAIGLER NEWS – Haigler, NE. -w. Aug 1909-Jul 1910; Dec 1910; Aug 1918-Sept 1954 – 1 – us NE Hist [071]
Hail, A D *see* JAPAN AND ITS RESCUE
Haile, Martin *see* JAMES FRANCIS EDWARD, THE OLD CHEVALIER
HAILE-SELASSIE'S GOVERNMENT – London: Longmans, 1968 – us Res Libr [960]
Hailey, Genevieve *see* CALIFORNIA ART RESEARCH
Hailey, O L *see*
- HISTORY OF THE BAPTISTS OF TENNESSEE
- J.R. GRAVES
- THE THREE PROPHETIC DAYS OF MATTHEW 12:40 OR JESUS AND JONAS

Haiman, Miecislaus *see* POLISH PIONEERS OF VIRGINIA AND KENTUCKY
Haimbaugh, Frank D *see* HISTORY OF DELAWARE COUNTY
Haime, J *see*
- DESCRIPTION DES ANIMAUX FOSSILES DU GROUPE NUMMULITIQUE DE L'INDE
- A MONOGRAPH OF THE BRITISH FOSSIL CORALS

Hain, H H *see* HISTORY OF PERRY COUNTY
Hain, L *see* REPERTORIUM BIBLIOGRAPHICUM
Hainan Mission. (Pres. Ch. in the U.S.A.) *see* RECORDS, 1893-1923
HAINAN NEWSLETTER / American Presbyterian Mission – (all publ ?). Sep 1912-Christmas 1949 – 1 reel – 1 – $140.00 – us UPA [240]
HAINAN RIBAO – (1984-88, 1r/y; 1989- , 2r/y) – Hainan Daily. 1984-. M D68 – 1 – $55.00r – cc Microforms [072]
HAINAN RIBAO = HAIWAI BAN – (Hainan Daily, Overseas Edition) – 1992- – $55.00r – cc Microforms [950]
Haines, C R *see* CHRISTIANITY AND ISLAM IN SPAIN, A.D. 756-1031
Haines, Elijah Middlebrook *see*
- LAWS OF WISCONSIN CONCERNING THE ORGANIZATION AND GOVERNMENT OF TOWNS, AND THE POWERS AND DUTIES OF TOWN OFFICERS AND BOARDS OF SUPERVISORS.
- A PRACTICAL TREATISE ON THE POWERS AND DUTIES OF JUSTICES OF THE PEACE.

HAINES RECORD – Haines, OR. -w. 20 Nov 1925-23 Oct 1931. 2 rolls – 1 – us U.O. Library [071]
HAINES RECORD THE COURIER – Haines OR. Oct 30 1931-May 5 1932 – 1 – us U.O. Library [071]
HAIRBREADTH ESCAPES OF MAJOR MENDAX: HIS PERILOUS ENCOUNTERS, STARTLING ADVENTURES, AND DARING EXPLOITS WITH INDIANS, CANNIBALS, WILD BEASTS, SERPENTS, BALLONS, GEYSERS, ETC., ETC., ALL OVER THE WORLD, IN THE BOWELS OF THE EARTH, AND ABOVE THE CLOUDS : A PERSONAL NARRATIVE / Crofton, Francis Blake – With spirited illustrations by Bennett. Halifax: A. MacKinlay, 1889. 02128. (Pre-1900 Canadiana) – 9 – cn C.I.H.M. [971]
HAIRENIK – Boston, MA. -w. 18 July 1946-30 Dec 1954. 4 reels – 1 – uk British Libr Newspaper [071]
Hairston, Samuel W *see* ANSWERS TO VIRGINIA BAR EXAMINATIONS
HA'ISCHA – Amsterdam, 1929-1940. v1-12 – 72mf – 9 – J-261-36/1 – ne IDC [943]
HAITI – Port-au-Prince: [s.n.], feb 19, 1916 – 1 sheet – 9 – us Res Libr [972]
Haiti *see*
- BUDGET DE CAPITAL PROGRAMME DE DEVELOPEMENT ECONOMIQUE, 1 OCT 1951-30 SEP 1956
- LE MONITEUR HAITIEN
- LE MONITEUR JORNAL OFICIAL
- LE MONITEUR: JOURNAL OFFICIEL

HAITI COMMERCIALE, INDUSTRIELLE ET AGRICOLE – Port-au-Prince: Frederick Morin. 1ere annee, n4-n37. 6 juil 1917-16 fevr 1918 – 3 sheet – 9 – us Res Libr [330]
Haiti. Conseil National de Developpement et de Planification *see*
- BASES ET PRIORITES DES PROGRAMMES SECTORIELS. PERIODE QUINQUENNALE 1971-76
- PLAN D'ACTION ECONOMIQUE ET SOCIAL 1970-1971
- PLAN D'ACTION ECONOMIQUE ET SOCIALE, 1968-1969
- PLAN FINANCIER DES PROGRAMMES DE DEVELOPPEMENT 1969-1970
- PLAN FINANCIER DES PROGRAMMES DE DEVELOPPEMENT 1971-72

HAITI DEMOCRATIQUE – Port-au-Prince: D Fignole. 1ere annee, n1-n91. 31 mai-30 dec 1953 – 7 sheets – 9 – us Res Libr [320]
HAITI ILLUSTREE – Port-au-Prince: J Chenet. 1ere annee n7-3eme annee n48. 28 mai 1890-3 dec 1892 – 4 sheets – 9 – us Res Libr [072]
HAITI INTEGRALE – Port-au-Prince: [s.n.]. v1 n1 11-12. aug 18, sep 18-23 1915 – 1 sheet – 9 – us Res Libr [072]
HAITI JOURNAL – Port-au-Prince. Haiti. 1930-35, 1937, 1942-43 – 1 – us UMI [072]
HAITI LITTERAIRE AND SOCIALE – Port-au-Prince: F Marcelin. 1ere annee n1-7e annee n142. 20 janv 1905-5 juil 1911 – 50 sheets – 9 – us Res Libr [072]
HAITI LITTERAIRE ET SCIENTIFIQUE – Port-au-Prince: E. LaForest, 5 janv 1912-5 juil 1913 – 16 sheets – 9 – us Res Libr [072]
L'HAITIEN – Gonaives: Bureau de l'imp du journal, sep 1876-oct-1878 – 3 sheets – 9 – us Res Libr [072]
HAITI-RENCONTRES – Lille: [s.n.], n1-n3. oct/dec 1958-aout 1959 – 2 sheets – 9 – us Res Libr [072]
HA-IVRI – v. 1-11. Berlin. New York. 1910-21. BJ-91-18 1 – 9 – ne IDC [073]
HAIYANG DIZHI YANJIU – Marine Geological Research. In Chinese but English abstracts to the main articles. F p126 – 9 – 4.00f – cc Microforms [073]
HAIYANG KEXUE – Journal of Marine Science. 1981-. F P230 – 9 – $4.50f – cc Microforms [073]
HAIYANG SHUICHAN YANJIU – Marine Fisheries Research. 1981-. F P236 – 9 – $4.50f – cc Microforms [073]
HAIYANG XUEBAO – Acta Oceanologica Sinica. In Chinese but English abstracts to the main articles. F p124 – 9 – 4.00f – cc Microforms [073]
HAIYANG YU HUZHAO – Oceanologia et Limnologia Sinica. In Chinese but English abstracts to the main articles. F p125 – 9 – 4.00f – cc Microforms [073]
HAIYANG YUYE – Marine Fisheries. 1981-. F P239 – 9 – $4.50f – cc Microforms [073]
HAJARDEEN – Amsterdam, 1935 – 1mf – 9 – J-261-37/1 – ne IDC [943]
HA-JARDEN – New York, NY. 1923-24 – 1 – us A.J.P.C. [073]
HAJDU-BIHARI NAPLO – Debrecen, Hungary. 1962-Jun 1991 – 65r – 1 – us L of C Photodup [072]
Haje, C F *see* LES ORIGINES DE LA CROIX-ROUGE
Haji Khalifah *see* THE HISTORY OF THE MARITIME WARS OF THE TURKS
Hajnal, H *see*
- THE DANUBE;...
- LE DROIT DU DANUBE INTERNATIONAL

HAJNT – (Missing: 1924(7-12); 1933(1-6); 1937(4-6)) – Warsaw, Odessa, 1908-1937 – 58r – 1 – J-92-24/3 – ne IDC [072]
HA-KARMEL / ed by Fuhn, S J – (1865 v5(21) has not been published) – Vilna, 1860-1880 – 115mf – 9 – ne IDC [270]
HA-KEDEM – v. 1-3. 1907-09. BJ-100-183 1 – 9 – ne IDC [073]
HAKEKAT HIDUP; SUATU TAFSIRAN / Sastroamidjojo, Achmad Seno – SE 4843 1. 1963 – 9 – ne IDC [950]
HA-KEREM – Warsaw. 1887. BJ-291-13 1 – 9 – ne IDC [940]
Hakes *see* LAND MARKS OF STUEBEN COUNTY
HAKIMIYET-I MILLIYE – Ankara: Vilayet Matbaasi, Hakimiyet-i Milliye Matbaasi, 1920-1928 – 9 – $20.00 – us MEDOC [956]
HAKLUYT SOCIETY – S.1. London, 1847-1899; S.2. Glasgow, 1903-1940. v1-85 – 1,270mf – 9 – H-771c/2 – ne IDC [360]
Hakluyt Society *see* EXTRA SERIES
HAKLUYT SOCIETY PUBLICATIONS, 1847-1954 – 1,484mf – 9 – $3,370.00 – us UPA [910]
HA-KOACH – College Park, Maryland, v1, no. 4 (Feb./Mar. 1976)-v1, no. 5 (Apr. 1976); v2, no. 2 (Nov. 1976)-v3, no. 3 (Feb. 1978 – us A.J.P.C. [270]
HAKOL – Stanford, CA. 1979-80 – 1 – us A.J.P.C. [071]
HAKRIAH VEHAKDUSHAH = TEXT AND HOLINESS – (In Yiddish and English) – Brooklyn, NY. v4 no 45. 1940-1944 – 1r – Can$30.00 – cn Can Microfilming [071]
Halac, Ricardo *see* LOPEZ REGA
Halacsy, Eyon *see* CONSPECTUS FLORA GRAECAE
Haladjian, B *see* DES PERSONNES MORALES ETRANGERES...
HALALI! : GESCHICHTELN AUS DEN BERGREVIEREN / Achleitner, Arthur – 5.-10. Aufl. Berlin: Hermann Seemann Nachfolger, [1896?] – 1r – 1 – us U.W. Library [830]
HALAMANTISH – Umdurman: [s.n.], jun 1-22 1988-jun 1989 (weekly suppl) – us Res Libr [072]
HALB MAER, HALB MEHR : ERZAEHLUNGEN, SKIZZEN UND REIME / Raabe, Wilhelm Karl – 3. Aufl. Berlin: G Grote, 1921 – 1 – us U.W. Library [800]
Halbe, Max *see*
- FRAU MESECK
- JUGEND
- DER STROM

EIN HALBES JAHRHUNDERT : ERINNERUNGEN UND AUFZEICHNUNGEN / Schack, Adolf Friedrich von – Stuttgart: Deutsche Verlags-Anstalt, 1888 – 1r – 1 – us U.W. Library [920]
Halbherr, B *see* BLENCO SISTEMATICO DEI COLEOTTERI FINORA RACCOLTI NELLA VALLE LAGARINA
HALBSOUVERAENITAET / Boghitchevitch, M – Berlin, 1901 – 1mf – 9 – ILM-1929/1 – ne IDC [327]
HALBSOUVERAENITAET / Boghitchevitch, M – Berlin, 1903 – 3mf – 9 – ILM-1930/1 – ne IDC [327]
HALCYON ITINERARY : AND TRUE MILLENNIUM MESSENGER – Marietta. v1-6 aug 1807-jan 1808 – 1 – D3580 – us UMI [240]
HALCYON LUMINARY : AND THEOLOGICAL REPOSITORY – New York. v1-2. 1812-13 – 1 – D3837 – us UMI [240]
Haldane, Robert *see* ADDRESS TO THE PUBLIC CONCERNING POLITICAL OPINIONS, AND PLANS LATELY ADOPTED TO PROMOTE RELIGION IN SCOTLAND
Haldane Society *see* LAW REFORM NOW: A PROGRAMME FOR THE NEXT THREE YEARS.
HALDEMAN-JULIUS – Girard. Kan. -w. 1922-29 – 1 – us UMI [071]
Haldeman-Julius, Emanuel *see*
- AN AGNOSTIC LOOKS AT LIFE; CHALLENGES OF A MILITANT PEN
- FREE SPEECH AND FREE THOUGHT IN AMERICA

Halder, Franz *see* THE PRIVATE WAR JOURNAL OF GENERALOBERST FRANZ HALDER, CHIEF OF THE GENERAL STAFF OF THE SUPREME COMMAND OF THE GERMAN ARMY, 14 AUGUST 1939 TO 24 SEPTEMBER 1942
Halderman-Julius, M *see* CLARENCE DARROW'S TWO GREAT TRIALS
HALDIMAND ADVOCATE – Cayuga, Mr1881-1933De – 12r – 1 – cn Preston [971]
THE HALDIMAND DEANERY MAGAZINE – (Cont by: The Church Monthly and the Haldimand Deanery Magazine) – [Dunnville, Ont?: s.n. 1899] – 9 – cn C.I.H.M. [240]
THE HALDIMAND DEANERY MAGAZINE – (Cont: The Church Monthly and the Haldimand Deanery Magazine) – Dunnville, Ont.: [s.n. 1901-1902] – 9 – cn C.I.H.M. [240]
THE HALDIMAND DEANERY MAGAZINE *see* THE CHURCH MONTHLY AND THE HALDIMAND DEANERY MAGAZINE
Haldimand, Frederick *see* PAPERS AND CORRESPONDENCE
Hale, Bruce D *see* THE EFFECTS OF INTERNAL AND EXTERNAL IMAGERY ON MUSCULAR AND OCULAR CONCOMITANTS
Hale, Donna C *see* WOMEN AND CRIMINAL JUSTICE
Hale, E E *see* JOSEPH TUCKERMAN ON THE ELEVATION OF THE POOR
Hale, Edward *see*
- THE PSYCHOLOGICAL ELEMENTS OF RELIGIOUS FAITH
- THEISM AND THE CHRISTIAN FAITH

Hale, Edward Everett *see*
- A FAMILY FLIGHT OVER EGYPT AND SYRIA
- JAMES FREEMAN CLARKE
- WORKS

Hale, Sarah *see* DIARIES OF MISS SARAH HALE, MISSIONARY FOR MANY YEARS TO MEXICO
Hale, William Benjamin *see* HANDBOOK ON THE LAW OF DAMAGES
Hale, William Pillsbury *see* CHRIST VERSUS CHRISTIANITY
Halensis, Alexander *see*
- IN 12 ARISTOTELIS METAPH.
- IN 12 ARISTOTELIS METAPH

HALEOM = THE DAY – New York City, NY. v5 no 5. 1906 – 1r – Can$25.00 – cn Can Microfilming [071]
Hales, Alexander de *see* GLOSSA IN QUATTUOR LIBROS SENTENTIARUM
HALESWORTH TIMES – England. 1978-81. -w. 8 reels – 1 – uk British Libr Newspaper [072]
Halet, Efendi *see* DIVAN
HA-LEVANON – Ed. by N. Bruell. Jerusalem. Paris. Mainz. London. 1863-87. Incomplete. BJ-100-166 1 – 9 – ne IDC [072]
Halevy, Joseph *see* MELANGES D'EPIGRAPHIE ET D'ARCHEOLOGIE SEMITIQUES
Halevy, S *see* HA-SEFARIM HA-IVRIYYIM SHE-NIDPESU BI-YERUSHALAYIM
HALF A CENTURY IN CHINA : RECOLLECTIONS AND OBSERVATIONS / Moule, Arthur Evans – London, New York: Hodder and Stoughton, [1911?] – 1mf – us A.T.L.A. [950]
A HALF CENTURY AMONG THE SIAMESE AND THE LAO : AN AUTOBIOGRAPHY / McGilvary, Daniel – New York: F.H. Revell, c1912 – 2mf – us A.T.L.A. [950]
HALF CENTURY MESSAGES TO PASTORS AND PEOPLE / Huntington, DeWitt C – c1905 – 9 – us A.T.L.A. [240]
HALF MOON BAY NEWS – Half Moon Bay, CA. 1922-1934 – 5r – 1 – $250.00 – C03235 – us Library Micro [071]
HALF MOON BAY REVIEW AND PESCADERO PEBBLE – Half Moon Bay, CA. 1939- – 56+ r – 1 – $2,800.00 ($150.00y) – C02284 – us Library Micro [071]
HALF OUR FUTURE: REPORT OF THE CENTRAL ADVISORY COUNCIL FOR ENGLAND / Great Britain. Central Advisory Committee for England – Newsom Report. 1963 – 9 – uk Microform Academic [324]
HALF TRUTHS AND THE TRUTH...UNBELIEF...IN RELATION TO...THE CHRISTIAN SYSTEM / Manning, Jacob Merrill – Boston: Lee & Shepard, 1872. 1 fiche – 9 – us A.T.L.A. [240]
HALF-CENTURY MAGAZINE – 1-18 2+1 (all publ). 1916-1925 – 1 reel – 1 – $90.00 – us UPA [305]
HALF-CENTURY MAGAZINE – New York. v1-18. aug 1916-feb 1925 – 1 – D7444 – us UMI [073]
A HALF-CENTURY OF THE UNITARIAN CONTROVERSY : WITH PARTICULAR REFERENCE TO ITS ORIGIN, ITS COURSE, AND ITS PROMINENT SUBJECTS AMONG THE CONGREGATIONALISTS OF MASSACHUSETTS: WITH AN APPENDIX / Ellis, George E – Boston: Crosby, Nichols, 1857 – 1mf – us A.T.L.A. [240]
Halfhide, J J *see*
- NEGERENGELSCH-HOLLANDSCH WOORDENBOEK
- VERZAMELING VAN ALLE MEEST BEKENDE NEGERENGELSCHE SPREEKWOORDEN MET UITGEZOCHT HOLLANDSCH, ENGELSCH EN DUITSCH MORAAL

HALF-HOURS WITH THE MINOR PROPHETS AND THE LAMENTATIONS / Wiles, Joseph Pitt – London:Morgan and Scott, [1908?] – 1mf – 9 – 0-8370-5848-1 – 1985-3848 – us A.T.L.A. [220]
Halfmann, Jost *see* PARADIGMENWECHSEL IN DER THEORIE DER WISSENSCHAFT
HALF-YEARLY STATISTICAL SUMMARY 1975-1986 (MARCH) / Hong Kong. Education Department – Hong Kong – 13mf – 9 – DE-145/1 – ne IDC [370]
Halhed, Nathaniel Brassey *see* A GRAMMAR OF THE BENGAL LANGUAGE
Haliburton, R G *see* THE MEN OF THE NORTH AND THEIR PLACE IN HISTORY
Haliburton, Robert Grant *see* INTERCOLONIAL TRADE: OUR ONLY SAFEGUARD AGAINST DISUNION
Halid *see* DIVAN
HALIFAT IGGAROT BEIN HA-KEHILLAH HA-ASHKENAZIT BI-YERUSHALAYIM VE-RABBI DAVID OPPENHEIM / Benayahu, M – v. 3. Yerushalayim. 1950. BJ-27-69 1 – 9 – ne IDC [956]
HALIFAX 1703-1902 – (Mf 1-7: Town Records 1734-98. Mf 4: Publishments 1773-97. Mf 5: Births & Marrs 1707-1810. Mf 6: Vital Records 1703-1811. Mf 8-14: Town Records 1798-1826. Mf 11-12: Marrs & Intentions 1798-1828. Mf 13: Births by Family 1775-1842. Mf 15-21: Town Records 1827-55. Mf 21-22: Intentions & Marrs 1828-55. Mf 23-24: Town Records 1828-55. Mf 25-35: Town Records 1853-75. Mf 36-48: Town Records 1875-1908. Mf 49-50: Birth Index 1842-1957. Mf 50-51: Marr Index 1841-1963. Mf 52: Death Index 1841-1963. Mf 53: Deaths 1841-99. Mf 54: Marriages 1841-1904. Mf 55-56: Births 1842-1902) – (mf ed 1992) – 56mf – 9 – 0-87623-152-0 – us Holbrook [920]
HALIFAX AND DOMINION REAL ESTATE REGISTER – (Cont: Halifax and Provincial Real Estate Register) – Halifax, N.S.: J. Naylor, Feb 1878- – 9 – cn C.I.H.M. [333]
HALIFAX AND DOMINION REAL ESTATE REGISTER *see* HALIFAX AND PROVINCIAL REAL ESTATE REGISTER
HALIFAX AND PROVINCIAL REAL ESTATE REGISTER – (Cont: Subscribers Real Estate Directory; Cont by: Halifax and Dominion Real Estate Register) – Halifax, N.S.: J Naylor, [1877?-1878?] – 9 – cn C.I.H.M. [333]
HALIFAX AND PROVINCIAL REAL ESTATE REGISTER *see*
- HALIFAX AND DOMINION REAL ESTATE REGISTER
- SUBSCRIBERS REAL ESTATE DIRECTORY

Halifax. Archives (Earl). Garrowby *see* THE HICKLETON PAPERS
HALIFAX BAPTIST CHURCH. VERMONT : CHURCH RECORDS – 1784-1791 – 1 – 5.00 – us Baptist [240]
Halifax Central Library. Archives *see* THE FAWCETT AND LISTER PAPERS
Halifax, Charles Lindley Wood *see* LORD HALIFAX'S GHOST BOOK; A COLLECTION OF STORIES OF HAUNTED HOUSES, APPARITIONS AND SUPERNATURAL OCCURRENCES
HALIFAX CITIZEN – Canada. The Citizen The Citizen and Evening Chronicle. 20 Dec 1864; Feb 1871-Jan 1888. 36 1 2 reels – 1 – uk British Libr Newspaper [072]
HALIFAX CITIZEN – Halifax, Canada. 1863-77 – 16r – 1 – $1,040.00 – cn Library Assoc [971]
HALIFAX COMET – England, 1893-Aug 1904 – 14r – 1 – uk British Libr Newspaper [072]
HALIFAX DAILY COURIER AND GUARDIAN – England.1897-9 Jun 1898; 1899-1967. -d. 276 reels – 1 – uk British Libr Newspaper [072]
HALIFAX EVENING REPORTER – Halifax, Canada. 1860-79 – 27r – 1 – $1,755.00 – cn Library Assoc [971]
HALIFAX GAZETTE / Nova Scotia – 1752-1800 – 10r – 1 – $650.00 – cn Library Assoc [971]
HALIFAX GAZETTE – South Boston. Va. -w. 1923- – 1 – us UMI [071]
HALIFAX GUARDIAN – England. -w. 1832-43. (6 reels) – 1 – uk British Libr Newspaper [072]
THE HALIFAX GUARDIAN *see* OUR LOCAL PORTFOLIO
HALIFAX & HUDDERSFIELD EXPRESS – England.Feb 1831-1840.-w. 4 reels – 1 – uk British Libr Newspaper [072]
HALIFAX LOCAL OPINION *see* HALIFAX COMET
HALIFAX MEETING: SEPT 16-17, 1885 / American Institute of Mining Engineers – Halifax, N.S., 1885. 00788. (Pre-1900 Canadiana) – 9 – cn C.I.H.M. [622]
HALIFAX MERCURY – England.24 May 1890-5 Jan 1895. -w. 4 1/s reels – 1 – uk British Libr Newspaper [072]
THE HALIFAX MONTHLY MAGAZINE – [Halifax, N.S.? : s.n. 1830-1833] – 9 – cn C.I.H.M. [971]
HALIFAX OBSERVER – England.9 Aug 1884-1887. -w. 3 reels – 1 – uk British Libr Newspaper [072]
THE HALIFAX PHILATELIC MAGAZINE – Halifax, N.S.: Muirhead and Van Malder, [1897?) – 9 – cn C.I.H.M. [760]
THE HALIFAX PHILATELIST – Halifax, N.S.: Halifax Philatelic Co, [1887?-1889] – 9 – cn C.I.H.M. [760]
HALIFAX RAILWAY AND PUBLIC WORKS / Canada. Gouverneur general – s.l: Printed by Lovell & Gibson, 1849. SEM105P122 – 1mf – 9 – Can$2.25 – cn Bibl Nat [380]
HALIFAX TIMES – England.16 Aug-25 Jul sic 1873; 5 Sept 1873; Jun 1889-Jan 1895. -w. 5 1/2 reels – 1 – uk British Libr Newspaper [072]
Halifax, Viscount *see* LEO 13 AND ANGLICAN ORDERS
Halife, Mehmet *see* TARIH-I GILMANI
Halim, Barli *see* THE ROLE AND FUNCTIONS OF THE COOPERATIVE ORGANIZATIONS IN MARKETING OF RICE IN CALIFORNIA
Halim Giray, Sultan *see* DIVAN
Halim, K *see* PALAWIDJA
HALK – Adana. Sahibi ve Sermuharriri: Mehmed Rasim. No. 107 (11 Kanunisani 1340 [1924]) – 9 – $20.00 – us MEDOC [956]
HALK BILGISI MECMUASI – (Nesreden: Halk Bilgisi Dernegi Umumi Merkezi. Mueduerue: Ziyaeddin Fahri Findikoglu. No. 1 (1928)) – Ankara: Iktisat Matbassi, 1928 – 3mf – 9 – $75.00 – us MEDOC [949]
HALK OVOZI – Dushanbe, USSR. Sept 10 1991-Dec 30 1992 – 1r – 1 – us L of C Photodup [072]
Halkett, John *see* PRECIS TOUCHANT LA COLONIE DU LORD SELKIRK SUR LA RIVIERE ROUGE
Halkin, J *see* RECEUIL DES CHARTES DE L'ABBAYE DE STAVELOT-MALMEDY
Halkin, Joseph *see* LES ABABUA (CONGO BELGE)
Hall *see* HISTORY OF LEAVENWORTH COUNTY
Hall, Arthur D *see* A LIFE OF THE POPE (LEO THE THIRTEENTH)
Hall, C F *see* NARRATIVE OF THE SECOND ARCTIC EXPEDITION
Hall, C J *see* LIGHT FROM THE EAST, OR THE WITNESS OF THE MONUMENTS
Hall, C L *see* BIOGRAPHICAL MANUAL OF THE MEMBERS AND OFFICERS OF THE 20TH LEGISLATURE OF NEBRASKA
Hall, Charles Cuthbert *see*
- CHRIST AND THE EASTERN SOUL
- CHRISTIAN BELIEF INTERPRETED BY CHRISTIAN EXPERIENCE
- THE GOSPEL OF THE DIVINE SACRIFICE
- PROGRESS IN RELIGIOUS AND MORAL EDUCATION
- THE UNIVERSAL ELEMENTS OF THE CHRISTIAN RELIGION

Hall, Charles Winslow *see* TWICE TAKEN: AN HISTORICAL ROMANCE OF THE MARITIME BRITISH PROVINCES
Hall, Cyrus *see* DIARY
Hall, D W *see* HANDLING AND STORAGE OF FOOD GRAINS IN TROPICAL AND SUBTROPICAL AREAS
Hall, David A *see* CLARKE AND HALL'S CASES IN CONTESTED ELECTIONS IN CONGRESS, 1789-1834
Hall, Edward Hepple *see* LANDS OF PLENTY: BRITISH NORTH AMERICA FOR HEALTH, SPORT AND PROFIT: A BOOK FOR ALL TRAVELLERS AND SETTLERS
Hall, Elizabeth R *see* MORAL DEVELOPMENT LEVELS OF ATHLETES IN SPORT SPECIFIC AND GENERAL SOCIAL SITUATIONS
Hall, Florence Marion Howe *see* GOOD FORM FOR ALL OCCASIONS; A MANUAL OF MANNERS, DRESS AND ENTERTAINMENT FOR BOTH MEN AND WOMEN
Hall, Frank *see* HISTORY OF COLORADO
Hall, Frederic *see*
- THE HISTORY OF SAN JOSE AND SURROUNDINGS
- LAWS OF ALASKA PERTAINING TO CIVIL GOVERNMENT, MINES, AND LAND

Hall, Frederick Lee *see* LEGAL RESEARCH IN THE SOUTH PACIFIC
Hall, Gayle C *see* LEGAL RELATIONSHIP OF STUDENT TEACHERS TO PUBLIC INSTITUTIONS OF HIGHER EDUCATION AND PUBLIC SCHOOLS
Hall, H *see* RED BOOK OF THE EXCHEQUER (RS99)
Hall, H R *see* THE 11TH DYNASTY TEMPLE AT DEIR EL-BAHARI (MEES VOL 32)
Hall, H S *see* STANDARDIZED PILOT MILK PLANTS
Hall, J *see*
- HALL'S CIRCUITS AND MINISTERS
- MEMORIALS OF WESLEYAN METHODIST MINISTERS

Hall, J Eugene *see* MAKING A WILL, BY WHOM, WHEN AND HOW; KINDS OF WILLS, WHY AND WHY NOT, AND IF NOT; SPECIMENS
Hall, J H *see* BIOGRAPHY OF GOSPEL SONG AND HYMN WRITERS
Hall, Jeffery C *see* JOURNAL OF NEUROGENETICS
Hall, John *see*
- FORTY YEARS' FAMILIAR LETTERS OF JAMES W. ALEXANDER, D.D.
- PARADOXES
- SERMONS

Hall, John Smythe *see*
- DISCOURS PRONONCE A LA SALLE WINDSOR, MONTREAL, LE 16 FEVRIER 1892, SUR LES AFFAIRES FINANCIERES DE LA PROVINCE ET CRITIQUE DE L'ADMINISTRATION MERCIER
- SPEECH DELIVERED ...BEFORE THE LEGISLATIVE ASSEMBLY...PROVINCE OF QUEBEC, ON 4TH AND 5TH DECEMBER 1894 ON THE LOAN OF 27,632,647 FRANCS (3 PER CENT BONDS AT 77 FOR 60 YEARS)

Hall, Joseph *see* CHRIST MYSTICAL
Hall, K L *see* SIMPLE SUGGESTION ON CLUBS AND OTHER WORK WITH BOYS (CCC138)
Hall, Kermit *see* RECORDS OF THE WICKERSHAM COMMISSION ON LAW OBSERVANCE AND ENFORCEMENT, PART 1
Hall, Livingston *see* THE LIVINGSTON HALL PAPERS
Hall, Mitchel *see* JOHNSON COUNTY, KENTUCKY, A HISTORY OF THE COUNTRY AND GENEALOGY OF ITS PEOPLE UP TO 1927
Hall, Nick Vine *see*
- BRITISH ISLES CENSUS DIRECTORIES PROJECT
- SHIPS PICTURES INDEX 1491-1991

Hall, Peter *see* FRAGMENTA LITURGICA
Hall, Prescott Farnsworth *see*
- THE MASSACHUSETTS LAW OF LANDLORD AND TENANT. INCLUDING THE CASES IN VOL. 170 OF THE REPORTS, AND THE LEGISLATION OF 1898
- REFERENCE LIST OF WILLS CONSTRUED BY THE SUPREME JUDICIAL COURT OF MASSACHUSETTS (INCLUDING THE CASES IN QUINCY AND FROM VOL. 1 TO VOL. 165 OF THE MASSACHUSETTS REPORTS)

Hall, R *see*
- A FRIENDLY ADDRESS TO THE METHODISTS
- A KEY TO THE BIRDS OF AUSTRALIA

HALL RADIO REPORT – v.1-6. 1975-80. Superseded by yRadio news – 1 – us UMI [073]
Hall, Robert *see* ONE DAY'S COURTSHIP : THE HERALDS OF FAME
Hall, Teri-Christine R *see* TRAINING AMENORRHEA IN COLLEGE ATHLETES
Hall, Thomas Bond *see* THE INFRINGEMENT OF PATENTS FOR INVENTIONS, NOT DESIGNS, WITH SOLE REFERENCE TO THE OPINIONS OF THE SUPREME COURT OF THE UNITED STATES
Hall, Thomas Cuming *see*
- HISTORY OF ETHICS WITHIN ORGANIZED CHRISTIANITY
- JOHN HALL, PASTOR AND PREACHER
- RELIGION AND LIFE
- THE SOCIAL MEANING OF MODERN RELIGIOUS MOVEMENTS IN ENGLAND

Hall, W E *see*
- THE RIGHTS AND DUTIES OF NEUTRALS
- A TREATISE ON INTERNATIONAL LAW...
- A TREATISE ON THE FOREIGN POWERS...

Hall, W, Jr *see* PURITANS IN THE BALKANS
Hallam, A *see*
- CLASSIC LITERATURE ON INVERTEBRATE PALAEONTOLOGY
- HISTORICAL BIOLOGY

Hallam, Arthur Henry *see* REMAINS, IN VERSE AND PROSE, OF ARTHUR HALLAM
Hallam, Frank *see*
- THE BREATH OF GOD
- BREATH OF GOD: A SKETCH...OF THE DOCTRINE OF INSPIRATION

Hallam, Henry *see*
- INTRODUCTION TO THE LITERATURE OF EUROPE
- VIEW OF THE STATE OF EUROPE DURING THE MIDDLE AGES

Hallam, J *see* JOURNAL, 1829-1835
Hallam, John *see* A BRIEF STATEMENT OF MUNICIPAL TAX EXEMPTIONS IN TORONTO FROM 1869 TO 1890
HALLAM PROGRESS – Hallam, NE. -w. Oct 1907-Sept 1908 – 1 – us NE Hist [071]
HALLAND – Halmstad, Sweden. 1882-1901 – 26r – 1 – sw Kungliga [072]
HALLANDING – Varberg, Sweden. 1888-89 – 1 reel – 1 – sw Kungliga [072]
HALLANDS FOLKBLAD – Halmstad, Sweden. 1916-43 – 108r – 1 – sw Kungliga [072]
HALLANDS LANS TIDNING – Halmstad, Sweden. 1837-51 – 3r – 1 – sw Kungliga [072]
HALLANDS NYHETER – Falkenberg, Sweden. 1919-78 – 310r – 1 – sw Kungliga [072]
HALLANDS NYHETER – Falkenberg, Sweden. 1979- – 1 – sw Kungliga [072]
HALLANDS TIDNING – Falkenberg, Sweden. 1889-96 – 2r – 1 – sw Kungliga [072]
HALLANDSPOSTEN – Halmstad, Sweden. 1850-56 – 2r – 1 – sw Kungliga [072]
HALLANDSPOSTEN – Halmstad, Sweden. 1857- – 136r – 1 – sw Kungliga [072]

HALLAZGO DE LA NECROPOLIS JUDAICA DE LA CIUDAD DE TERUEL / Floriano Cumbreno, Antonio C – Madrid: Tip. Arch. y Biblioteca y Museos, 1926 – 1 – sp Bibl Santa Ana [946]
HALLAZGO DE VEINTIOCHO CANCIONES POPULARES DE EXTREMADURA, RECOGIDAS EN LOS ANOS 1884-85 / Gil Garcia, Bonifacio – Badajoz: Diputacion Provincial, 1946 – 1 – sp Bibl Santa Ana [946]
HALLAZGO Y DESCRIPCION DE UNA AUTOBIOGRAFIA DEL PRIMER OBISPO DE MAINAS, DON FRAY HIPOLITO SANCHEZ RANGEL / Quecedo, Francisco – Madrid: Archivo Ibero Americano, 1932 – 1 – sp Bibl Santa Ana [240]
Hallberg, C W *see* THE SUEZ CANAL
Hallberg, L Eugene *see* WIELAND
Halle, Adam de la *see*
- LE JEU DE ROBIN ET MARION
- OEUVRES COMPLETES DU TROUVERE ADAM DE LA HALLE

Halle, J S *see* DIE KUNST DES ORGELBAUES, THEORETISCH UND PRAKTISCH BESCHRIEBEN
Halleck, H W *see* INTERNATIONAL LAW;...
Hallenbeck, Edwin Forrest *see* THE PASSION FOR MEN: A PLEA FOR ENDEAVOR IN SOUL WINNING
Haller, Albrecht von *see*
- DIE ALPEN
- BIBLIOTHECA ANATOMICA
- BIBLIOTHECA BOTANICA
- DE ALLII GENERE NATURALI LIBELLUS
- ENUMERATIO METHODICA STIRPIUM HELVETIAE INDIGENARUM
- ENUMERATIO PLANTARUM HORTI REGII ET AGRI GOTTINGENSIS AUCTA ET EMENDATA
- ENUMERATIO STIRPIUM QUAE IN HELVETIA RARIORES PROVENIUNT
- HISTORIA STIRPIUM INDIGENARUM HELVETIAE INCHOATA
- LETTRES DE FEU: M. DE HALLER CONTRE M. DE VOLTAIRE
- OPUSCULA SUA BOTANICA PRIUS EDITA RECENSUIT, RETRACTAVIT, AUXIT
- PHYSIOLOGY; BEING A COURSE OF LECTURES UPON THE VISCERAL ANATOMY AND VITAL ECONOMY OF HUMAN BODIES

HALLER ALS PHILOSOPH : EIN VERSUCH / Jenny, Heinrich Ernst – (Includes bibliographical references) – Basel: Basler Druck- und Verlags-Anstalt, 1902 – 1r – 1 – us U.W. Library [430]
Haller, Benedictus *see* TRACTATUS DE SPIRITU DEI
Haller Gillmer, Beverly von *see* EXPERIMENTS AND DEMONSTRATIONS IN PSYCHOLOGY
Haller, Johannes *see*
- DEUTSCHLAND UND RUSSLAND
- DIE QUELLEN ZUR GESCHICHTE DER ENTSTEHUNG DES KIRCHENSTAATES
- WARUM UND WOFUER WIR KAEMPFEN

HALLER MERKUR FUER DAS OBERAMT GAILDORF *see* HALLISCHES WOCHENBLATT
Haller, Paul *see* 'S JURAMAREILI
HALLER TAGBLATT *see* HALLISCHES WOCHENBLATT
Haller, W *see* IOVIANUS
Halleux, Jean *see* LA PHILOSOPHIE CONDAMNEE
Hallez, D-G *see* PLANS D'INSTRUCTIONS SUR LES SACREMENTS D'APRES LE CATECHISME DU CONCILE DE TRENTE
Halliday, Nancy *see* THE EFFECTS OF CONTEXTUAL INTERFERENCE AND THREE LEVELS OF DIFFICULTY ON THE ACQUISITION, RETENTION, AND TRANSFER OF HOCKEY STRIKING SKILLS BY SECOND GRADE CHILDREN
Halliday, Samuel B *see* THE LOST AND FOUND, OR, LIFE AMONG THE POOR
Halliday, William Reginald *see* THE PAGAN BACKGROUND OF EARLY CHRISTIANITY
Hallien, John *see* BIOGRAPHICAL AND PICTORIAL HISTORY OF ARKANSAS
Hallier, H J G *see* INDONESISCHE ACANTHACEEN
Hallier, L *see* UNTERSUCHUNGEN UEBER DIE EDESSENISCHE CHRONIK (T.U.U. 1-9/1A)
Hallifax, S *see* SAINT PAUL'S DOCTRINE OF JUSTIFICATION BY FAITH EXPLAINED IN THREE DISCOURSES PREACHED BEFORE THE UNIVERSITY OF CAMBRIDGE IN THE YEAR 1760
HALLISCHE BZW. DEUTSCHE JAHRBUCHER – Leipzig, Germany. 1838-1842 – 3r – 1 – gw Mikrofilm [943]
HALLISCHE BZW. DEUTSCHE JAHRBUECHER – Leipzig, 1838-42 – 3r – 1 – DM225.00 – gw Mikro Press [943]
HALLISCHE KINO-ZEITUNG – Halle/Saale. jul 25, 1919-dec 7, 1923 – 3r – 1 – gw Mikrofilm [790]
HALLISCHES TAGEBLATT – Halle, Germany. -d. 1856-88. 52 reels – 1 – uk British Libr Newspaper [072]
HALLISCHES WOCHENBLATT – (Title changes: Haller Merkur fuer das Oberamt Gaildorf; Schwaebischer Hausfreund; Haller Tagblatt) – Schwaebisch Hall, West Germany. 1978- – ca 7r per yr – 1 – gw Mikrofilm [072]
Halliwell, Barry *see* FREE RADICAL RESEARCH
Halliwell-Phillipps, James Orchard *see* AN HISTORICAL SKETCH OF THE PROVINCIAL DIALECTS OF ENGLAND
Hallmann, Georg *see* DAS INDIVIDUALITAETSPROBLEM BEI FRIEDRICH HEBBEL
Hallmann, Jayne E *see* THE EFFECT OF THE EDUCATION OF THIRD WORLD WOMEN ON FAMILY HEALTH
HALLOWED SONGS / Phillips, Philip – Rev. ed. 1871 – 1 – 11.48 – us Baptist [240]
Hallowell, Anna Davis *see* JAMES AND LUCRETIA MOTT: LIFE AND LETTERS
Hallowell, Benjamin *see* THE YOUNG FRIEND'S MANUAL
HALLOWELL FREE PRESS – Picton, Canada. 1830-34 – 2r – 1 – $136.00 – cn Library Assoc [971]
Hallowell, Richard P *see* THE QUAKER INVASION OF MASSACHUSETTS
HALLOWING OF CRITICISM: NINE SERMONS ON ELIJAH / Cheyne, Thomas Kelly – London: Hodder & Stoughton, 1888. 1 fiche – 9 – us A.T.L.A. [240]
HALL'S CIRCUITS AND MINISTERS : AN ALPHABETICAL LIST OF THE CIRCUITS IN GREAT BRITAIN...FROM 1765 TO 1912 / Hall, J; ed by Hartley, T G – London, [1912]. xix, [4], 609p – 7mf – 9 – ne IDC [240]
HALL'S CIRCUITS AND MINISTERS : AN ALPHABETICAL LIST OF THE CIRCUITS IN GREAT BRITAIN...FROM 1913 TO 1923 / Hall, J; ed by Hartley, T G – London, [1925]. [3], 94p – 2mf – 9 – ne IDC [240]
THE HALLS GRAPHIC – Halls. Tenn. 1961- – 1 – us UMI [071]
Hallum, John *see* BIOGRAPHICAL & PICTORIAL HISTORY
Hallwich, H *see* WALLENSTEIN'S ENDE
Halm, C *see*
- SALVIANI PRESBYTERI MASSILIENSIS LIBRI QUI SUPERSUNT (MGH1: 1.BD. 1.TEIL)
- VICTORIS VITENSIS HISTORIA PERSECUTIONIS AFRICANAE PROVINCIAE (MGH 1: 3. BD. 1. TEIL)

Halm, Carolus *see* RHERORS LATINI MINORES
Halm, Friedrich *see*
- DER FECHTER VON RAVENNA
- GRISELDIS
- DER SOHN DER WILDNISS

Halma, Nicolas B *see* DE L'EDUCATION
Halmel, Anton *see* DER ZWEITE KORINTHERBRIEF DES APOSTELS PAULUS
HALMSTADSBLADET – Halmstad, Sweden. 1853-82 – 13r – 1 – sw Kungliga [072]
HALOEAN POLITIK ISLAM / Kartosoewirjo, SM – Garoet, 1946. 42p – 1mf – 9 – ne IDC [260]
Haloun, G *see*
- SEIT WANN KANNTEN DIE CHINESEN DIE TOCHARER ODER INDOGERMANEN UEBERHAUPT
- ZUR UEE-TSI-FRAGE

Halper, B *see*
- POST-BIBLICAL HEBREW LITERATURE: AN ANTHOLOGY
- THE SCANSION OF MEDIAEVAL HEBREW POETRY

Halperin, David M *see* GLQ
Halperin, Leopoldo *see* EL PERONISMO
Halpern, I *see* HA-ALIYYOT HA-RISHONOT SHEL HA-HASIDIM LE-EREZ-YISRA'EL
Halphen, Louis *see*
- ETUDE SUR LES CHRONIQUES DES COMTES D'ANJOU ET DES SEIGNEURS D'AMBOIS
- ETUDES SUR L'ADMINISTRATION DE ROME AU MOYEN AGE (751-1252)

Halsey, A W et al *see* THE BELOVED
HALSEY ENTERPRISE – Halsey, OR. -w. 4 Jan 1917-17 Dec 1924; 10 Nov 1927 10 Jan 1929. – 1 – us U.O. Library [071]
Halsey, John J *see* HISTORY OF LAKE COUNTY
HALSEY JOURNAL – Halsey, OR. -w. 18 Aug 1932-3 Feb 1938. 1 roll – 1 – us U.O. Library [071]
Halsey, Leroy J *see* SCOTLAND'S INFLUENCE ON CIVILIZATION
HALSEY REVIEW – Halsey, OR. -w. 10 Feb 1938-13 Jun 1963. 6 rolls – 1 – us U.O. Library [071]
HALSINGEKURIREN – Soderhamn, Sweden. 1981- – 1 – sw Kungliga [072]
HALSINGLANDS TIDNING – Hudiksvall, Sweden. 1969 – 8r – 1 – sw Kungliga [072]
HALSINGLANDS TIDNING *see*
- HUDIKSVALLS TIDNING
- HUDIKSVALLSTIDNINGEN

Halsted, Caroline Amelia *see* LIFE OF MARGARET BEAUFORT...MOTHER OF KING HENRY THE SEVENTH
Halt, Marie Malezieux *see*
- L'ENFANCE DE SUZETTE: LIVRE DE LECTURE COURANTE A L'USAGE DES JEUNES FILLES
- LE MENAGE DE MME. SYLVAIN, LIVRE DE LECTURE COURANTE A L'USAGE DES JEUNES FILLES
- SUZETTE: LIVRE DE LECTURE COURANTE A L'USAGE DES JEUNES FILLES

HALTE-LA – Chicoutimi. 20 mar 1943-v1 n4. 28 mai 1943 – 1r – 1 – Can$35.00 – cn Can Microfilming [072]
Halten, A van *see* JOH. SEB. BACH
Halter, Eduard *see* DIE STRASSBURGER LITTERARISCHE "BESEGARD"
HALUMY – New York. N.Y. The nationlist. 1888-89 – 1 – us A.J.P.C. [071]
HALVVECKOTIDNINGEN SVENSKA FOLKET – Stockholm, 1910-11 – 9 – sw Kungliga [072]
HAM AND HIGH *see* HAMPSTEAD AND HIGHGATE EXPRESS
Ham, J G van *see* EERSTE BOEKJAAR DER INDISCHE PARTIJ 1912. SAMENGESTELD... ENZ
Ham, M G T van den *see* DEKRACHT VAN BUITENLANDSCHE VONNISSEN...
HAM RADIO – (Former titles: Ham Radio mar 1968-jan 1969. Ham Radio Magazine feb 1969-aug 1988) – Greenville. v1-23. mar 1968-jun 1990 1; v4-23 jan 1971-jun 1990 5; v7 1974. v9-23 jan 1976-jun 1990 9 – 1,5,9 – D3076 – us UMI [380]
HAM RADIO *see* HAM RADIO
HAM RADIO HORIZONS – Greenville. v1-4. mar 1977-dec 1980 1,5,9; v3 1979* 1; v4 1980* 9 – 1,5,9 – D11238 – us UMI [790]
HAM RADIO HORIZONS *see* HAM RADIO MAGAZINE
HAM RADIO MAGAZINE – (Includes: Ham Radio Horizons, 1977-80) – 1968-90 – over 350mf – $225.00 – us Buckmaster [621]
HAM RADIO MAGAZINE *see* HAM RADIO
HA-MA'AGAL / Katzenelson, I – Warsaw. 1911. BJ-422-35 1 – 9 – ne IDC [470]
HA-MABBIT – Der Beobachter. nr. 1-17. Vienna. 1878. BJ-291-7 1 – 9 – ne IDC [999]
HA-MABBIT – Ed. by P. Smolenskin. 17 nrs. Vienna. 1878. BJ-422-28 1 – 9 – ne IDC [072]
HA-MABBIT LE-YISRAEL – Ed. by P. Smolenskin. Vienna. 1878. BJ-422-29 1 – 9 – ne IDC [072]
HA-MAGGID – Lublin. 1623-27. BJ-43-21 1 – 9 – ne IDC [947]
HA-MAGGID – (v36 nos 24-50 1892 not publ. From the 1890s the name varies: Ha-Maggid, He-Hadash, Ha-Maggid le-Yisrael, Ha-Shavu'a) – Lyck, Berlin, Cracow, 1856-1903 – 523mf – 9 – J-92-2/1 – ne IDC [072]
HA-MAGGID LE-YISRAEL *see* HA-MAGGID
HAMAGID = THE PREACHER – (Hebrew weekly) – Krakow, PL. v- no28 23 Jul 1899-v- no24 20 Jun 1902 – 1r – 1 – $25.00 – cn Can Microfilming [072]
HAMAGID = PREACHER – (In Hebrew) – Lyck, DE. v5 no27 10 Jul 1861-v22 no40 9 Oct 1878 – 1r – 1 – $50.00 – cn Can Microfilming [072]
Hamaker, H J *see* AARD EN DOEL VAN...
HAMAKKOR – Middletown, CT. May 1980-May 1984 – 1 – us A.J.P.C. [071]
HAMAN KLOPER – London, UK. Purim 1930 – 1 – uk British Libr Newspaper [072]
Hamann, Hermann Emil *see* WIELANDS BILDUNGSIDEAL
Hamann, Johann Georg *see*
- SCHRIFTEN UND BRIEFE
- SIBYLLINISCHE BLAETTER DES MAGUS

HA-MA'OR – Berlin. Tel-Aviv. 1933-39. BJ-100-168 1 – 9 – ne IDC [072]
HA-MASHKIF = OBSERVER – (In Hebrew) – Tel Aviv, IS. v10 no2809. 16 May 1948 (Birth of Israel Issue) – 1r – 1 – $25.00 – cn Can Microfilming [072]
Hamberger, Julius *see* GOTT UND SEINE OFFENBARUNGEN IN NATUR UND GESCHICHTE
Hamberger, Wolfgang *see* MOTIVE UND WIRKUNGEN DES KOMMUNALWAHLSYSTEMS IN BADEN-WUERTTEMBERG
Hambis, L *see* NOTE SUR LES TUYUYUN
Hamburg *see*
- JAHRESBERICHTE DER VERWAITUNGSBEHOSDEN
- VERHANDLUNGEN ZWISCHEN SENAT UND BURGERSCHAFT

THE HAMBURG ITEM – Hamburg, PA. -w 1973 – 13 – $25.00r – us I.M.R. [071]
Hamburg. Laws, statutes, etc *see* HAMBURGISCHES GESETZ-UND VERORDNUNGSBLATT
HAMBURG: PAMPHLET COLLECTION – 1938 – 1 reel – 1 – CSUXANS9185-B – us Hoover Inst Photo [943]
HAMBURG UND DIE ANTILLEN : EIN SEEROMAN / Smidt, Heinrich – Hamburg: Hammerich & Lesser, [1944] – 1r – 1 – us U.W. Library [830]
HAMBURG-ALTONAER ILLUSTRIRTE ZEITUNG – Hamburg, Germany. 1864-69 (incomplete) – 1r – 1 – gw Mikrofilm [072]
HAMBURG-ALTONAER VOLKSBLATT – (Title changes: Gerichtszeitung, 10 Nov 1878; Buergerzeitung, 17 Apr 1881; Hamburger Echo, 2 Oct 1887; Hamburger Echo am Abend, 1 Jan 1964; Hamburger Abend echo, 1 Oct 1964; Abendecho, 21 Jul 1966) – Hamburg, Germany. 4 Oct 1887-Jun 1888; 1892-Sep 1925; 1926-3 Mar 1933; 1946-1949 – 100r – 1 – gw Mikrofilm [072]
Hamburg.Burgerschaft *see*
- PROTOKOLLE UND AUSSCHUSS-BERICHTE
- STENOGRAPHISCHE BERICHTE UEBER DIE SITZUNGEN DER BURGERSCHAFT ZU HAMBURG

HAMBURGER ABENDBLATT – Hamburg: Axel Springer & Soba, 1953-1955; 1956-aug 1977; sep 1977-1980 – 1 – us Res Libr [072]
HAMBURGER ABENDBLATT – Hamburg. jul 1-dec 31, 1953. apr 6-may 6, aug 19-sep 26, 1960 – 1 – gw Mikrofilm [072]
HAMBURGER ABENDBLATT – Hamburg, West Germany. 1958-10 Jun 1970 – 216r – 1 – gw Mikrofilm [072]
HAMBURGER ABENDECHO – (Also known as: Hamburger Echo am Abend) – Hamburg, Germany. 1946-Jun 1953; 1962-66 – 39r – 1 – us L of C Photodup [072]
HAMBURGER ABENDECHO *see* HAMBURG-ALTONAER VOLKSBLATT
HAMBURGER ANZEIGER – Hamburg. Nov. 2 1932; July 10 1937-Aug 31 1939. Incomplete – 1 – us NY Public [943]
DER HAMBURGER BEOBACHTER *see* DER HAMBURGER BEOBACHTER UND DAS ARCHIV WISSENSCHAFT UND KUENSTE
DER HAMBURGER BEOBACHTER UND DAS ARCHIV WISSENSCHAFT UND KUENSTE – (Title changes: Morgenzeitung, 31 Mar 1852; Der Hamburger Beobachter, 14 Apr 1852) – Hamburg, Germany. 25 Jul 1849-29 Dec 1852 – 2r – 1 – gw Mikrofilm [072]
HAMBURGER ECHO – 1892-1933 – Cumul – 1 – DM6,800.00 – sz Infoprint [072]
HAMBURGER ECHO – Germany. -d. 3 Apr 1946-19 Jul 1951. (12 reels) – 1 – uk British Libr Newspaper [072]
HAMBURGER ECHO – Hamburg, 1887-88; 1892-1925; 1926-33 – 97r – 1 – DM7,275.00 – gw Mikro Press [072]
HAMBURGER ECHO *see* HAMBURG-ALTONAER VOLKSBLATT
HAMBURGER ECHO AM ABEND *see*
- HAMBURG-ALTONAER VOLKSBLATT
- HAMBURGER ABENDECHO

Hamburger, Franz *see* LEHRER ZWISCHEN KAISER UND FUEHRER
HAMBURGER FREMDENBLATT – Hamburg, Germany. 3 Jan 1872-30 Nov 1936, 44.-108.Jg. (incomplete) – 289r – 1 – gw Mikrofilm [072]
HAMBURGER FREMDENBLATT – Hamburg. sep 1-oct 31, 1954 – 1 – gw Mikrofilm [072]
HAMBURGER FREMDEN-BLATT – Hamburg: Gustav Diedrich and Co, apr-jun 1932 – us Res Libr [072]
HAMBURGER GARTEN- UND BLUMENZEITUNG *see* NEUE ALLGEMEINE DEUTSCHE GARTEN- UND BLUMENZEITUNG
Hamburger Gewerkschaftskartell *see* BERICHT

HAMBURGER GRUNDEIGENTUEMER-ZEITUNG – Hamburg, Germany. 1929-30 – 1r – 1 – gw Mikrofilm [072]
HAMBURGER ILLUSTRIERTE ZEITUNG – Hamburg, Germany. 1919-44 – 26r – 1 – gw Mikrofilm [072]
Hamburger, M *see* ASIEN
HAMBURGER MORGENPOST – (1976-79 21r DM1,575.00) – Hamburg, 1949-71 – 85r – 1 – DM6,375.00 – gw Mikro Press [072]
HAMBURGER MORGENPOST – Hamburg, West Germany. 1990- – ca 10r per yr – 1 – gw Mikrofilm [072]
HAMBURGER NACHRICHTEN – Germany. 24 Aug 1914-31 Dec 1918; 1 Apr 1934-9 Mar 1939.-d. 106 reels – 1 – uk British Libr Newspaper [072]
HAMBURGER NACHRICHTEN – Hamburg, Germany. Dec 1899-Jun 1910; 1912-Jun 1913; Aug 1917-1919 – 115r – 1 – us L of C Photodup [072]
HAMBURGER NACHRICHTEN-BLATT – Hamburg, 1945-1946 – 1r – 1 – DM75.00 – gw Mikro Press [072]
HAMBURGER NACHRICHTEN-BLATT *see* HAMBURGER NACHRICHTEN-BLATT DER MILITAERREGIERUNG
HAMBURGER NACHRICHTEN-BLATT DER MILITAERREGIERUNG – (Title change: Hamburger Nachrichten-Blatt, 30 Nov 1945) – Hamburg, West Germany. 9 May 1945-28 Mar 1946 – 1r – 1 – gw Mikrofilm [072]
Hamburger Stiftung fuer Sozialgeschichte des 20. Jahrhunderts *see* DER "NUERNBERGER AERZTEPROZESS" 1946/47
HAMBURGER TAGEBLATT – Germany. 10 March 1939-30 May 1940. 7 reels – 1 – uk British Libr Newspaper [072]
Hamburger, Victor *see* SEALSFIELD-POSTL
HAMBURGER VOLKSZEITUNG *see* TRIBUENE DER DEMOKRATIE
HAMBURGISCHE ABEND-ZEITUNG *see* PRIVILIGIRTE LISTE DER BOERSENHALLE
HAMBURGISCHE ADDRESS-COMTOIR-NACHRICHTEN *see* KAYSERLICH-PRIVILEGIRTE HAMBURGISCHE NEUE ZEITUNG
HAMBURGISCHE ARBEITERZEITUNG – Hamburg, Germany. 1919-20 – 1 – gw Mikrofilm [072]
HAMBURGISCHE BOERSEN-HALLE *see* PRIVILIGIRTE LISTE DER BOERSENHALLE
HAMBURGISCHE NEUE ZEITUNG *see* KAYSERLICH-PRIVILEGIRTE HAMBURGISCHE NEUE ZEITUNG
HAMBURGISCHE STAATS-NEUIGKEITEN – Hamburg, Germany. 4 Jan-6 Mai 1752 – 1 – gw Mikrofilm [072]
HAMBURGISCHER CORRESPONDENT *see* STAATS- UND GELEHRTE ZEITUNG DES HOLLSTEINISCHEN UNPARTHEYISCHEN CORRESPONDENTEN
HAMBURGISCHER UNPARTHEYISCHER CORRESPONDENT / ed by Welke, Martin – Schiffbeck, 1721-30 und Hamburg, 1731-1800. Hildesheim, 1977-88 – 1000mf – 9 – DM7,500.00 diazo DM9,000.00 silver – gw Olms [943]
HAMBURGISCHES GESETZ-UND VERORDNUNGSBLATT / Hamburg. Laws, statutes, etc – Hamburg. 1961-1968 – 1 – us NY Public [340]
HAMBURGISCHES MAGAZIN, ODER GESAMMLETE SCHRIFTEN, AUS DER NATURFORSCHUNG UND DEN ANGENEHMEN WISSENSCHAFTEN UBERHAUPT – 1747-63.v1-13; v14-36.Also: Dreyfaches Universalregister und Repertorium. Hamburg and Leipzig, 1767 – 3 – us Readex [500]
HA-MEAGED – Rotterdam, 1938-1941. v1-4 – 10mf – 9 – J-261-39/1 – ne IDC [943]
HA-ME'AMMER / ed by Luncz, A M – Jerusalem v. 1-3. 1905-20. BJ-100-172 1 – 9 – ne IDC [072]
HA-ME'ASSEF – Jerusalem. 1896-1915. Lacking: 1915. BJ-100-170 1 – 9 – ne IDC [073]
HA-ME'ASSEF – Koenigsberg. Berlin. Breslau. Altona. Dessau. 1784-1810. Not published in 1787, 1791-93, 1798-1808. BJ-100-169 1 – 9 – ne IDC [470]
HA-MEASSEPH – (New York). 1881 – 1 – us A.J.P.C. [073]
Hamed, A et al *see* INTERNATIONAL JOURNAL OF COMPUTATIONAL FLUID DYNAMICS
Hamel, Andre *see* BIBLIOGRAPHIE SUR LE SCOUTISME CATHOLIQUE DANS LA PROVINCE DE QUEBEC
Hamel, Anton Gerard van *see* PROEVE EENER KRITIEK VAN DE LEER DER GODDELIJKE VOORZIENIGHEID
Hamel, F H *see* INTERNATIONAL LAW IN CONNEXION WITH...
Hamel, J M *see* THE EFFECTS OF SELF-TALK ON BATTING PERFORMANCE
Hamel, Marcel *see*
- LA NATION
- LA RUMEUR DU PORTAGE

Hamel, Philippe *see* LE TRUST DE L'ELECTRICITE, MENACE POUR LA SECURITE SOCIALE
Hamel, Thomas Etienne *see* COURS D'ELOQUENCE PARLEE D'APRES DELSARTE
Hamelink, Cees J *see* NEW INTERNATIONAL ECONOMIC ORDER
HAMELITZ = THE DEFENDER – (In Hebrew) – Odessa, UA. v? no? 1863/1864-v43 no146 13 Jul 1903 – 1r – 1 – $40.00 – cn Can Microfilming [072]
HA-MELIZ – Odessa, 1860-1904 – 18r – 1 – us Ross [270]
HA-MELIZ – Odessa, St Petersburg. v. 1-44 no. 18. 1860-Jan 30 1904. Incomplete – 1 – us NY Public [305]
Hamelle, Paul *see* HOMMES ET CHOSES D'OUTRE-MER
HA-MENAHEL – (New York). 1920 – 1 – us A.J.P.C. [800]
Hamengku, Buwono 9 *see* ADDRESS AT THE LIPI-NAS WORKSHOP ON FOOD IN DJAKARTA ON MAY 27 TO JUNE 1, 1968
DER HAMER = THE HAMMER – Montreal, CN. v1 no 12. 1916 – 1r – 1 – Can$25.00 – cn Can Microfilming [072]
HAMER CREEK BAPTIST CHURCH. MONTGOMERY ASSOCIATION. NORTH CAROLINA : CHURCH RECORDS – 1862-82 – 1 – 6.39 – us Baptist [240]
Hamer, Fannie Lou *see* FANNIE LOU HAMER PAPERS, 1917-77
Hamer, Philip M *see* HISTORY OF TENNESSEE
Hamersly, Lewis R *see* THE RECORDS OF LIVING OFFICERS OF THE U.S. NAVY AND MARINE CORPS
Hamesse, J *see* THESAURUS LIBRORUM SENTENTIARUM PETRI LOMBARDI
Hamet, Ismael *see* CHRONIQUES DE LA MAURITANIE SENEGALAISE
HAMEVAKER – Los Angeles, CA.1982-84 – 1 – us A.J.P.C. [071]
HA-MEVASER = JOURNAL HEBRAIQUE – (In Hebrew) – Istanbul, TU. v1 no50. 1914 – 1r – 1 – $25.00 – cn Can Microfilming [072]
Hamid 2, Sultan *see* SPEECH BROADCAST BY THE CHAIRMAN OF THE B.F.O. ON FEB. 27, 1949
Hamid, Abduelhak *see*
- DIVANELIKLERIM
- ESBER

Hamid, Ismail *see* HISTOIRE DU MAGHREB
Hamid, V Ahmet *see* KURUN-I CEDIDE VE NAVOLYON'UN SUKUNTUNA KADAR ASR-I HAZIR MEBADISI
Hamidoun, Mokhtar ould *see* CATALOGUE PROVISOIRE DES MANUSCRIPTS MAURITANIENS EN LANGUE ARABE PRESERVES EN MAURITANIE
Hamidullah, Muhammad et al *see* ISLAM, PHILOSOPHY AND SCIENCE
HA-MIFNEH BE-MA'AMADAH SHEL YERUSHALAYIM BA-MEAH HA-19 / ed by Hirschberg, H Z – Yad Y.Y. Rivlin. 1964. BJ-27-33 1 – 9 – ne IDC [956]
Hamilton *see* A STANDARD HISTORY OF JASPER AND NEWTON COUNTIES
HAMILTON 1714-1897 – (Mf 1: Birth Index 1781-1875. Mf 2: Marriage Index 1781-1875. Mf 3-4: Intentions Index 1781-1861. Mf 5: Death Index 1781-1875. Mf 6: Births, Deaths, Intentions 1750-1832. Mf 7-8: B,M,D 1844-60. Mf 9-10: Deaths 1859-96. Mf 11: Marriages 1860-96. Mf 12-13: Births 1859-97. Mf 14: Rebellion Records 1861-65. Mf 15-21: Death Index 1771-1941. Mf 17-21: Deaths 1771-1941. Mf 22-25: Marriages & Index 1714-1941. Mf 26-29: Births & Index 1755-1941) – (mf ed 1989) – 29mf – 9 – 0-87623-097-4 – us Holbrook [920]
HAMILTON 1750-1849 – (Mf 1T: Intentions 1795-1812; Deaths 1784-1832; Births 1750-1812; Intentions & Marriages 1812-38. Mf 2T: Intentions & Marriages 1838-49; Out-of-Town Marriages 1794-99; Births & Deaths 1812-48. Mf 3T: Deaths 1815-20; Births 1844-49. Mf 4T: Marriages & Deaths 1844-49) – (mf ed 1996) – 4mf – 9 – 0-87623-260-8 – us Holbrook [920]
Hamilton, Adelbert *see* THE INTERSTATE COMMERCE LAW
HAMILTON ADVERTISER – 1 – £42.00r – uk Scot News [072]
HAMILTON ADVERTISER – Scotland. 1862-75; 1898-99.-w. 6 reels – 1 – uk British Libr Newspaper [072]
Hamilton, Alexander *see*
- THE FEDERALIST AND OTHER CONSTITUTIONAL PAPERS
- PAPERS

Hamilton, Alexander et al *see* THE FEDERALIST
Hamilton, Andrew *see* STATUTORY REVISION OF THE LAWS OF NEW YORK AFFECTING MISCELLANEOUS CORPORATIONS, ENACTED IN 1892.
Hamilton, Charles *see* SKETCHES OF LIFE AND SPORT IN SOUTH-EASTERN AFRICA
HAMILTON CITY DIRECTORY – Hamilton, 1853-1935 – 28r – 1 – cn Preston [971]
Hamilton, Clayton *see* REPRESENTATIVE PLAYS, BY HENRY ARTHUR JONES
HAMILTON COUNTY DEMOCRAT – Aurora, NE. -w. Sep. 1895-Aug. 1896 – 1 – us NE Hist [071]
HAMILTON COUNTY LEDGER – Noblesville. Ind. 1889-1893; 1897-1909 – 1 – us UMI [071]
HAMILTON COUNTY REGISTER – Aurora, NE. -w. except -sw. 1922-1923. Dec. 1890-Dec. 1891; Nov. 1892-Mar. 1929 – 1 – us NE Hist [071]
HAMILTON COUNTY REGISTER – Aurora. Neb. 1891-1929 – 1 – us UMI [071]
HAMILTON COUNTY REGISTER – Noblesville. Ind. 1869-1871 – 1 – us UMI [071]
HAMILTON COUNTY TIMES – Noblesville. Ind. 1907-1909 – 1 – us UMI [071]
HAMILTON DAILY DEMOCRAT : DAILY DEMOCRATIC NEWSPAPER – Hamilton, OH, 11-16 Aug 1887 – 1r – 1 – us Western Res [071]
HAMILTON DAILY HERALD : DAILY DEMOCRATIC NEWSPAPER – Hamilton, OH, 28 Oct 1885 – 1r – 1 – us Western Res [071]
HAMILTON DAILY NEWS : DAILY REPUBLICAN NEWSPAPER – (Scattered issues) – Hamilton, OH, 27 Apr 1880-17 May 1893 – 1r – 1 – us Western Res [071]
HAMILTON DAILY NEWS – Hamilton, OH, 18 Apr 1921 – 1 reel – 1 – us Western Res [071]
HAMILTON DAILY REPUBLICAN : DAILY REPUBLICAN NEWSPAPER – Hamilton, OH. 17 May 1892 – 1r – 1 – us Western Res [071]
HAMILTON EVENING SUN : DAILY DEMOCRATIC NEWSPAPER – Hamilton, OH. 28-29 May 1903 – 1r – 1 – us Western Res [071]
Hamilton, F *see*
- COMMENTARY ON THE HERBARIUM AMBOINENSE
- A COMMENTARY ON THE HORTUS MALABARICUS

HAMILTON FREEMAN – Webster City. Iowa. 1857-1882 – 1 – us UMI [071]
Hamilton, Gail *see* A WASHINGTON BIBLE-CLASS
HAMILTON GAZETTE – Hamilton, Canada. 1852-55 – 3r – 1 – $204.00 – cn Library Assoc [971]
HAMILTON HERALD AND LANARKSHIRE WEEKLY NEWS – Scotland, UK. 3 Mar 1888-1900. -w. 12 reels – 1 – uk British Libr Newspaper [072]
HAMILTON HERALD & LANARKSHIRE WEEKLY NEWS – England.3 Mar 1888-Jun 1905. -w. 17 reels – 1 – uk British Libr Newspaper [072]
HAMILTON INTELLIGENCER : WEEKLY REPUBLICAN NEWSPAPER – Hamilton, OH, 1 Jan 1857-9 Jan 1862 – 2r – 1 – us Western Res [071]
Hamilton, J A de C *see* THE ANGLO-EGYPTIAN SUDAN FROM WITHIN
Hamilton, J Taylor *see*
- A HISTORY OF THE MISSIONS OF THE MORAVIAN CHURCH DURING THE EIGHTEENTH AND NINETEENTH CENTURIES
- TWENTY YEARS OF PIONEER MISSIONS IN NYASALAND

Hamilton, James *see*
- A MEMOIR OF RICHARD WILLIAMS, SURGEON
- THE PEARL OF PARABLES
- PEARL OF PARABLES: NOTES ON LUKE 15, 11-32

Hamilton, James Cleland *see* JOHN BROWN IN CANADA: A MONOGRAPH
HAMILTON JOURNAL – (Cont by: Kanada-Kurier, Winnipeg) – Pickering, Ont., Canada. 1972-76; 1978-5 Sep 1980 – 1 – gw Mikrofilm [072]
Hamilton, Kenneth *see*
- RECORDS OF THE NATIONAL NEGRO BUSINESS LEAGUE, PART 1
- RECORDS OF THE NATIONAL NEGRO BUSINESS LEAGUE, PART 2

Hamilton, N E S A *see* DE GESTIS PONTIFICUM ANGLORUM LIBRI QUINQUE (RS52)
Hamilton, Oscar B *see* HISTORY OF JERSEY COUNTY
HAMILTON PHYSIOG – Hamilton [Ont: s.n. 1858-18-?] – 9 – cn C.I.H.M. [072]
Hamilton, Pierce Stevens *see* THE FEAST OF SAINT ANNE AND OTHER POEMS
Hamilton. Presbytery (Pres. Ch. in the U.S.A. New School) *see* MINUTES, 1846-1870
Hamilton Public Library (Ont.) *see* QUARTERLY BULLETIN
Hamilton, Richard Vesey *see* NAVAL ADMINISTRATION
HAMILTON SPECTATOR DEATH NOTICES – 1859-1890 – 1mf – 9 – at Corangamite [920]
THE HAMILTON SUN – Hamilton. Ohio. 1905-1906 – 1 – us UMI [071]
Hamilton, T F *see* AMERICAN NEGLIGENCE CASES
HAMILTON TELEGRAPH : WEEKLY DEMOCRATIC NEWSPAPER – Hamilton, OH: 11 Aug 1853-31 Dec 1857 – 3r – 1 – us Western Res [071]
HAMILTON TELEGRAPH : WEEKLY DEMOCRATIC NEWSPAPER – Hamilton, OH. 18 Nov 1847-2 May 1850 – 2r – 1 – us Western Res [071]
HAMILTON TELEGRAPH : WEEKLY REPUBLICAN NEWSPAPER – Hamilton, OH. 13 June-21 Oct 1861. June 16, 1864. – 1r – 1 – us Western Res [071]
HAMILTON, THE BIRMINGHAM OF CANADA – Hamilton: The Times Printing Co., 1892.00925.(Pre-1900 Canadiana) – 9 – cn C.I.H.M. [971]
Hamilton, Theodore Frank *see*
- HAMILTON'S CYCLOPEDIA OF NEGLIGENCE CASES
- HAMILTON'S NEW YORK NEGLIGENCE CASES CLASSIFIED.

Hamilton Thompson, A *see*
- ENGLISH MONASTERIES
- THE GROUND PLAN OF THE ENGLISH PARISH CHURCH
- MILITARY ARCHITECTURE IN ENGLAND DURING THE MIDDLE AGES

HAMILTON TIMES – Hamilton, Canada. 1858-68 – 16r – 1 – $1,040.00 – cn Library Assoc [971]
HAMILTON TRUE TELEGRAPH : WEEKLY DEMOCRATIC NEWSPAPER – Hamilton, OH. 30 Oct 1862-20 Oct 1864 – 1r – 1 – us Western Res [071]
Hamilton, W *see* PRODROMUS PLANTARUM INDIAE OCCIDENTALIS
Hamilton, Wallace *see* CHRISTOPHER AND GAY: A PARTISAN'S VIEW OF THE GREENWICH VILLAGE HOMOSEXUAL SCENE
Hamilton, Walter *see* THE AESTHETIC MOVEMENT IN ENGLAND
HAMILTON WEEKLY SUN : WEEKLY DEMOCRATIC NEWSPAPER – Hamilton, OH. 18 July 1902 – 1r – 1 – us Western Res [071]
THE HAMILTON WEEKLY SUN – Hamilton. Ohio. 1903-1906 – 1 – us UMI [071]
HAMILTON WEEKLY TELEGRAPH : WEEKLY DEMOCRATIC NEWSPAPER – Hamilton, OH. 25 Sept 1851-4 Aug 1853 – 1r – 1 – us Western Res [071]
Hamilton, William *see* THE NAVIGATION LAWS AS THEY AFFECT THE MANNING OF THE NAVY
Hamilton, William Wistar *see* SANE EVANGELISM
HAMILTON'S CYCLOPEDIA OF NEGLIGENCE CASES / Hamilton, Theodore Frank – New York, Baker, Voorhis, 1904. 1083 p. LL-763 – 1 – us L of C Photodup [340]
HAMILTON'S NEW YORK NEGLIGENCE CASES CLASSIFIED. / Hamilton, Theodore Frank – (Supplement. Albany, Bender, 1899. 88 p. LL-864. 1899 annual. Albany, Bender, 1900. 179 p. LL-864) – New York, Remick, Schilling, 1898. 470 p. LL-864 – 1 – us L of C Photodup [340]
HAMISHAH HUMSHEI TORAH. HA-HAFTAROT. VE-HAMESH MEGILLOT – Basle. 1583. BJ-43-23 1 – 9 – ne IDC [270]

HAMISHAH HUMSHEI TORAH. HA-HAFTAROT. VE-HAMESH MEGILLOT – Basle. 1603. BJ-43-24 1 – 9 – ne IDC [270]
HAMISHAH HUMSHEI TORAH. HA-HAFTAROT. VE-HAMESH MEGILLOT – Cremona. 1560. BJ-43-22 1 – 9 – ne IDC [270]
HAMISHAH HUMSHEI TORAH. HA-HAFTAROT. VE-HAMESH MEGILLOT – Prague. 1610. BJ-43-25 1 – 9 – ne IDC [270]
HAMISHAH HUMSHEI TORAH IM HAMESH MEGILLOT. GAM HA-HAFTAROT – Augsburg. 1544. BJ-43-26 1 – 9 – ne IDC [270]
HAMISHAH HUMSHEI TORAH IM HAMESH MEGILLOT VEHA-HAFTAROT – Constance. 1544. BJ-43-27 1 – 9 – ne IDC [270]
HAMISHAH HUMSHEI TORAH. MEGILLOT. VE-HAFTAROT – Hanau. 1617. BJ-43-28 1 – 9 – ne IDC [270]
AL HA-MISHMAR – Tel Aviv. 1943-76. BJ-91-1 1 – 9 – ne IDC [470]
AL HAMISHMAR = RISE OF ISRAEL/THE DAILY GUARDIAN – (In Hebrew. Daily) – Tel-Aviv, IS. v6 no1459. 16 May 1948 – 1r – 1 – $25.00 – cn Can Microfilming [072]
HA-MITZPA – (New York). 1910-11 – 1 – us A.J.P.C. [071]
HA-MITZPEH = THE WATCHTOWER – (In Hebrew. Weekly) – Krakow, PL. no5 30 Jan 1914-no19 8 May 1914 – 1r – 1 – $25.00 – cn Can Microfilming [072]
HA-MIZPEH – (Missing: 1919-1920 v15-16) – Cracow, Poland. v1-11. 1904-1914; v14-17. 1917-1921 – 4r – 1 – J-91-22/3 – ne IDC [072]
HAMKA : A BIBLIOGRAPHY OF THE WORKS OF PROF. DR. HAJI ABDUL MALIK KARIM ABDULLAH / Mohamed bin Abas – 1983 – A$10.00 – 0-86758-072-0 – at BISA [013]
HAMLET STUDIES – New Delhi, India. v1-4. 1979-82 – 1 – $75.00 – us OmniSys [420]
Hamlin, Charles *see*
– DIARY
– THE INSOLVENT LAW, OF MAINE.
Hamlin, Charles S *see*
– THE ACTS TO REGULATE COMMERCE
– ICC ACTS INDEXED AND DIGESTED
Hamlin, Cyrus *see* MY LIFE AND TIMES
HAMLINE JOURNAL OF PUBLIC LAW *see* HAMLINE JOURNAL OF PUBLIC LAW AND POLICY
HAMLINE JOURNAL OF PUBLIC LAW AND POLICY – (v1-5 1980-84 on reel $75.00. v6-16 1985-95 on mf $147.00. Title varies: v1-2 1980-81 as Journal of Minnesota Public Law. v3-6 1982-85 as Hamline Journal of Public Law) – v1-16. 1980-95 – 5,6,9 – $222.00 set – us Hein [340]
HAMLINE LAW REVIEW – (v1-7 1978-84 on reel $75.00. v8-18 1985-95 on mf $153.00) – v1-18. 1978-95 – 5,6,9 – $228.00 set – us Hein [340]
Hamlyn, Raul *see* CORTES AND THE CONQUEST OF MEXICO
Hamm, Katherine *see* TULARE COUNTY SCHOOL
Hamm, Tracy M *see* MARATHON PERFORMANCE TIME IN RELATION TO AGE, PHYSICAL CHARACTERISTICS, PREVIOUS RUNNING EXPERIENCE, AND VARIOUS TRAINING INDICES OF FEMALE DISTANCE RUNNERS
Hammann, Otto *see* DER NEUE KURS; ERINNEERUNGEN VON OTTO HAMMANN
Hammel, Patricia A *see* CHANGES IN CLINICAL STUDENTS' PERCEPTIONS OF DEVELOPMENTAL PHYSICAL EDUCATION AND EFFECTIVE TEACHING
HAMMER AND STEEL NEWSLETTER – Boston. feb 1962-oct 1967. jan 1968-oct 1973 1; jan 1971-oct 1973 5 – 1,5 – D3259 – us UMI [670]
Hammer, Anton *see* DIE ERKENNTNISTHEORETISCHE BEDEUTUNG DES GEFUEHLSMAESSIGEN ERFASSENS BEI SCHLEICHERMEIER
Hammer, Bonaventure *see* MARY, HELP OF CHRISTIANS
THE HAMMER FOR THE STONE / Cary, W – M 325. 1581 – 9 – ne IDC [610]
Hammer, Franz *see* HERMANN STEHR UND DAS JUNGE DEUTSCHLAND
Hammer, Friedrich *see* DIE IDEE DER PERSOENLICHKEIT BEI PAUL HEYSE
Hammer, Julius *see* AUF STILLEN WEGEN
Hammer, Klaus *see* BEITRAEGE ZUR LITERATURGESCHICHTE UND – METHODOLOGIE
Hammerich, Frederik *see* ST. BIRGITTA
Hammerich, L L et al *see* INTERVENTIONS AT THE KLEINSCHMIDT CENTENNIAL
Hammer-Purgstall, Josef von *see*
– FUNDGRUBEN DES ORIENTS
– KHLESL'S, DES CARDINALS, DIRECTORS DES GEHEIMEN CABINETES KAISERS MATHIAS, LEBEN
HAMMERSCHLAEGE : EINE AUSWAHL / Lersch, Heinrich; ed by Fronemann, Wilhelm – Koeln: H Schaffstein, 1933 – 1r – 1 – us U.W. Library [800]
Hammerschlag, Meta *see* FRAUEN-ZUKUNFT, 1.1910-3.1913 (HQ, 21)
Hammerschmidt, A *see* MUSIKALISCHER ANDACT
Hammerschmidt, Andreas *see* MUSICALISCHES GESPRAECHE UBER DIE EUANGELIA, MIT 4, 5, 6 UND 7 STIMMEN NEBENST DA BASSO CONTINUO
Hammerschmidt, Ferdinand *see* GOETHE UND DER KATHOLIZISMUS
HAMMERSMITH AND FULHAM TIMES – (Also known as: Hammersmith, Fulham and Chiswick Times) – Jan-Jun 1990; Jul 6-Dec 21 1990; 1991-Jun 1992; Jul 3-Dec 1992; Jan 8-Jun 25 1993; Jul 1993-96; Jan 10-Jun 27 1997 – 12 1/2r – 1 – uk British Libr Newspaper [072]
HAMMERSMITH, FULHAM AND CHISWICK TIMES *see* HAMMERSMITH AND FULHAM TIMES
HAMMERSMITH FULHAM AND SHEPHERD'S BUSH GAZETTE *see* SHEPHERDS BUSH GAZETTE ETC
HAMMERSMITH SOCIALIST RECORD – London, UK. 1891-93. -irr. 4 feet – 1 – uk British Libr Newspaper [072]
Hammerstein, Ludwig von *see*
– DAS CHRISTENTUM
– DIE GEGNER "EDGARS"
Hammock, James W *see* EVALUATING AND RESHAPING A MODEL OF CHURCH RENEWAL AT THE FIRST BAPTIST CHURCH OF LONGWOOD, FLORIDA
Hammon, Louis Lougee *see*
– THE GENERAL PRINCIPLES OF THE LAW OF CONTRACT
– A TREATISE ON CHATTEL MORTGAGES FOR ILLINOIS
Hammon, Ulrich *see* DIE WIRTSCHAFTSDEMOKRATIE IM SINNE DER FREIEN GEWERKSCHAFTEN
Hammond, Barbara *see* THE VILLAGE LABOURER, 1760-1832
Hammond, Brean S *see* BRITISH JOURNAL FOR EIGHTEENTH-CENTURY STUDIES
Hammond, C E *see* LITURGIES, EASTERN AND WESTERN
Hammond, Charles Edward *see* OUTLINES OF TEXTUAL CRITICISM APPLIED TO THE NEW TESTAMENT
Hammond, Edward Payson *see* THE CONVERSION OF CHILDREN
HAMMOND FIRST SOUTHERN BAPTIST CHURCH. HAMMOND, INDIANA : CHURCH RECORDS – 1934-37 – 1 – 5.00 – us Baptist [240]
Hammond, H *see* THE WHOLE DUTY OF MAN
Hammond, J A *see* ESSAI DE RECHERCHE EN LINGUISTIQUE CONSTRASTIVE SUR LE SYNTAGME NOMINAL EN AKAN ET EN FRANCAIS
Hammond, James H *see* PAPERS
Hammond, John Lawrence *see* THE VILLAGE LABOURER, 1760-1832
Hammond, L M *see* HISTORY OF MADISON COUNTY
Hammond, OT *see* DIARY
Hammond, William Gardiner *see*
– SYNOPSIS OF LECTURES DELIVERED IN THE LAW DEPARTMENT OF IOWA STATE UNIVERSITY, ON EQUITY JURISPRUDENCE, AS ADMINISTERED IN THE SAME COURTS WITH COMMON LAW
– SYNOPSIS OF LECTURES DELIVERED IN THE LAW DEPARTMENT OF IOWA STATE UNIVERSITY, ON THE LAW OF REAL PROPERTY
Hammurabi, King of Babylonia *see* THE CODES OF HAMMURABI AND MOSES, WITH COPIOUS COMMENTS, INDEX, AND BIBLE REFERENCES
HAMMURABI'S GESETZ : BAND 4: UEBERSETZTE URKUNDEN, ERLAEUTERUNGEN / Kohler, J & Ungnad, A – Leipzig, 1910 – 3mf – 8 – ne Slangenburg [340]
HAMMURABI'S GESETZ : BAND 5: UEBERSETZTE URKUNDEN VERWALTUNGSREGISTER. INVENTARE, ERLAEUTERUNGEN / Kohler, J & Ungnad, A – Leipzig, 1911 – 4mf – 8 – ne Slangenburg [340]
HAMMURABI'S GESETZ : BAND 6: UEBERSETZTE URKUNDEN MIT RECHTSERLAEUTERUNGEN / Koschaker, P & Ungnad, A – Leipzig, 1923 – 6mf – 8 – ne Slangenburg [340]
HAMMURABI'S GESETZ / ed by Kohler, F J et al – Leipzig, 1904-1923 – 31mf – 8 – ne Slangenburg [220]
HA-MODI'A – Jerusalem. 1950- Agudat Israel. Suppl. for children, 1952-59. Available: 1960-76. BJ-91-24 3 – 1; Sfr2725.00; Sfr200.00 (y) – ne IDC [270]
HA-MODI'A – Poltava. Ukraine. 1910-14. Available: 1910-1911 12. Several pages missing. BJ-291-18 1 – 9 – ne IDC [270]
HAMODIA – [Israel], 1965- – 9 – $210.00y – us Ross [072]
Hamon, Louis *see* DE L'EXERCISE DE LA MEDICINE EN PROVINCE AU XIXE SIECLE
THE HAMOND NAVAL PAPERS, 1766-1825 – (With printed guide. Originally published by the University of Virginia Library) – Printed guide. 3 rolls. Originally published by the University of Virginia Library – 3r – 1 – $255.00 – D3181 – us Scholarly Res [355]
Hamonville, J C L T d' *see* CATALOGUE DES OISEAUZ D'EUROPE
HAMPA AFRO-CUBANA. LOS NEGROS BRUJOS (APUNTES PARA UN ESTUDIO DE ETNOLOGIA CRIMINAL) / Ortiz, Fernando – Madrid: Editorial-America, 1917?. 406p. illus – 1 – us U.W. Library [360]
HAMPDEN 1878-1895 – (Mf 1-2: Birth Index 1878-1986. Mf 3-4: Marriage Index 1878-1986. Mf 5-6: Death Index 1878-1986. Mf 7: Births 1878-95. Mf 8: Marriages 1878-95. Mf 9: Deaths 1878-95) – (mf ed 1987) – 9mf – 9 – 0-87623-042-7 – us Holbrook [920]
HAMPDEN AND HAMPSHIRE COUNTIES BUSINESS DIRECTORY AND REGISTER 1871/72 – Boston, 1870. Massachusetts Reel 5. (The Cox Library Collection) – 5 – us Americana [978]
HAMPDEN GUARDIAN – 1871-1877. 1873 lost. HG1-5 – 5r – 1 – at Corangamite [072]
Hampden, Maine. First Baptist Church *see* RECORDS
Hampden, R D *see* THE SCHOLASTIC PHILOSOPHY CONSIDERED IN ITS RELATION TO CHRISTIAN THEOLOGY
HAMPDEN SHIRE COUNCIL MINUTE BOOKS – 1859-1992. Bk.3 lost. SOH1-26 – 32r – 1 – at Corangamite [910]
HAMPDEN SHIRE COUNCIL RATE BOOKS – 1870-1936/93. Bks. 27;28;51 – 36r – 1 – at Corangamite [910]
Hampe, Th *see* NUERNBERGER RATSVERLAESSE UEBER KUNST UND KUENSTLER IM ZEITALTER DER SPAETGOTIK UND RENAISSANCE (1449)1474-1618 (1633)
Hampel, Beate *see* PREVOSTS "MANON LESCAUT" IN DEUTSCHEN UEBERSETZUNGEN DES 18., 19. UND 20. JAHRHUNDERTS
HAMPI RUINS, DESCRIBED AND ILLUSTRATED / Longhurst, A H – Madras. 1917. BI-1053 2 – 8 – ne IDC [930]
HAMPSHIRE ADVERTISER. (HAMPSHIRE ADVERTISER & INDEPENDENT) – Southampton, England. Jan 1901-Nov 1940.-w. 54 reels – 1 – uk British Libr Newspaper [072]
HAMPSHIRE BUSINESS GAZETTE *see* BASINGSTOKE AND HAMPSHIRE BUSINESS GAZETTE
HAMPSHIRE CHRONICLE – Southampton, Winchester, England. 1772-1983; 1986- – 229+ r – 1 – uk British Libr Newspaper [072]
HAMPSHIRE (EXC ISLE OF WIGHT), 1844 : BRITISH ISLES CENSUS DIRECTORIES PROJECT, ENGLAND – at Vine [941]
HAMPSHIRE (EXC ISLE OF WIGHT), 1852 : BRITISH ISLES CENSUS DIRECTORIES PROJECT, ENGLAND – at Vine [941]
HAMPSHIRE (EXC ISLE OF WIGHT), 1859 : BRITISH ISLES CENSUS DIRECTORIES PROJECT, ENGLAND. VOL 21 – 4mf – 9 – A$27.00 – at Vine [941]
HAMPSHIRE (EXC ISLE OF WIGHT), 1875 : BRITISH ISLES CENSUS DIRECTORIES PROJECT, ENGLAND. VOL 102 – 7mf – 9 – A$45.00 – at Vine [941]
HAMPSHIRE (INC ISLE OF WIGHT), 1823 : BRITISH ISLES CENSUS DIRECTORIES PROJECT, ENGLAND. VOL 219 – 1mf – 9 – A$9.00 – at Vine [941]
HAMPSHIRE (INC ISLE OF WIGHT), 1830 : BRITISH ISLES CENSUS DIRECTORIES PROJECT, ENGLAND. VOL 71 – 1mf – 9 – A$9.00 – at Vine [941]
HAMPSHIRE (INC ISLE OF WIGHT), 1867 : BRITISH ISLES CENSUS DIRECTORIES PROJECT, ENGLAND. VOL 89 – 7mf – 9 – A$45.00 – at Vine [941]
HAMPSHIRE (INC ISLE OF WIGHT), 1878 : BRITISH ISLES CENSUS DIRECTORIES PROJECT, ENGLAND. VOL 35 – 10mf – 9 – A$63.00 – at Vine [941]
HAMPSHIRE (INC ISLE OF WIGHT), 1895 : BRITISH ISLES CENSUS DIRECTORIES PROJECT, ENGLAND. VOL 43 – 12mf – 9 – A$75.00 – at Vine [941]
HAMPSHIRE INDEPENDENT – Southampton, England. Jan 1853-Jul 1923 – 68r – 1 – uk British Libr Newspaper [072]
HAMPSHIRE OBSERVER AND BASINGSTOKE NEWS – Basingstoke, England. 1911 – !R – 1 – uk British Libr Newspaper [072]
HAMPSHIRE (PORTSMOUTH, WINCHESTER, SOUTHAMPTON), 1805 : BRITISH ISLES CENSUS DIRECTORIES PROJECT, ENGLAND. VOL 185 – 1mf – 9 – A$9.00 – at Vine [941]
HAMPSHIRE RECORD SOCIETY – (Coll title: Publications of the English Record Societies, 1835-1972...) – v1-12. 1889-97 – 56mf – 9 – £410.00 – uk Chadwyck [941]
HAMPSHIRE RECORD SOCIETY – (Missing: v12) – v1-12. 1889-1897 – 94mf – 9 – H-825/2 – ne IDC [941]
HAMPSHIRE REVIEW – Romney. West Virginia. 1884-1969 – 1 – us UMI [071]
HAMPSHIRE TELEGRAPH AND NAVAL CHRONICLE – Portsmouth, England. 1911 – 1r – 1 – uk British Libr Newspaper [072]
HAMPSHIRE TELEGRAPH AND SUSSEX CHRONICLE – Portsmouth, England. 1874; 1897-98. -w. 3 reels – 1 – uk British Libr Newspaper [072]
Hampson, J *see* MEMOIRS OF THE LATE REV. JOHN WESLEY, A.M., WITH A REVIEW OF HIS LIFE AND WRITINGS AND A HISTORY OF METHODISM FROM ITS COMMENCEMENT IN 1729 TO THE PRESENT TIME
HAMPSTEAD AND HIGHGATE EXPRESS – (Also known as: Ham and High) – 1874; 1888; 1892; 1900-93; Jan-Jun 1994 (Ham and High ed); Jul 1994-Jun 1997 – 198 3/4r – 1 – uk British Libr Newspaper [072]
HAMPSTEAD AND HIGHGATE EXPRESS – London. -w. 1950-81. (62 reels) – 1 – uk British Libr Newspaper [072]
HAMPTON FIRST BAPTIST CHURCH. HAMPTON, SOUTH CAROLINA : CHURCH RECORDS – 1908-10, 1915-20, 1922-31, 1939-41, 1955-67. Board of Deacons. Church records. 1948-72 – 1 – 35.10 – us Baptist [240]
HAMPTON HERALD – Hampton, NE. -w. Feb 1884-Jan 1886 – 1 – us NE Hist [071]
Hampton, Iowa. First Baptist Church *see* MINUTES
HAMPTON LEDGER – Hampton, NE. -w. Jun 1937-Feb 1938 – 1 – us NE Hist [071]
HAMPTON MAGAZINE – New York. v1-28. apr 1898-may 1912* – 1 – D5659 – us UMI [073]
Hampton Normal and Agricultural Institute *see* SOUTHERN WORKMAN
HAMPTON PARK BAPTIST CHURCH. CHARLESTON COUNTY. SOUTH CAROLINA : CHURCH RECORDS – 1915-May 1942; Dec 1949-Apr 1970. Deacons' Minutes, May 1942-Apr 1950. Membership rolls and historical sketch. 934p – 1 – 42.03 – us Baptist [240]
HAMPTON ROADS BUSINESS CONTACT – Norfolk. v11-16. 1987-92* 1; v17-18 1993-94*. V19-21 1995-97+ 1,5,9 – 1,5,9 – D18187 – us UMI [380]
HAMPTON TIMES – Hampton, NE. -w. Oct-Dec 1891; Apr 1895; Nov 1895-Feb 1896; May 1896-Aug 1897 – 1 – us NE Hist [071]
HAMPTON UNIVERSITY NEWSPAPER CLIPPING FILE – (With printed name and subject index £105.00) – 790mf – 9 – £3,730.00 – uk Chadwyck [975]
Han, Dong H *see* COCAINE AND EXCERCISE
Han, K N et al *see* MINERAL PROCESSING AND TECHNICAL REVIEWS
HAN KO XIN WEN BAO – China. 1917-24 – 9 – 6495.00 – cc Globe [072]
HAN SIDO NOMBRADOS...EN PLASENCIA D. VICENTE PAREDES... / Fita, Fidel – Madrid: Est. Tip. Fortanet, 1897. B.R.A.H. 31, 1897, pp. 352 – sp Bibl Santa Ana [946]

Hanani, Y *see* TENU'AT HA-HASKALAH BE-EREZ-YISRA'EL BA-ME'AH HA-19
Hanau, S Z *see* ZOHAR HA-TEVAH
HANAUER ANZEIGER *see* WOCHENBLATT
HANAUER KREISBLATT *see* WOCHENBLATT
HANAUER NEUE EUROPAEISCHE ZEITUNG *see* EUROPAEISCHE ZEITUNG
HANAUER NEUE ZEITUNG *see* EUROPAEISCHE ZEITUNG
HANAUER WOCHENBLATT *see* WOCHENBLATT
HANAUER ZEITUNG – Hanau, Germany. 1 Jul-31 Dec 1943 – 1 – gw Mikrofilm [072]
HANAUER ZEITUNG *see* EUROPAEISCHE ZEITUNG
HANAUISCHES MAGAZIN.: MONATSBLAETTER FUER HEIMATKUNDE – Hanau. Jahrg. 4-18; 1925-39. Ceased with v. 18. Superseded in 1949 by Neues Magazin fur hanauische Geschichte. Film Mas C 336 – 1 – us H.U. Library [073]
Hanbury, D *see* HISTOIRE DES DROGUES D'ORIGINE VEGETALE
Hanbury, D T *see* THROUGH THE BARREN GROUND OF NORTH-EASTERN CANADA TO THE ARCTIC COAST
Hanbury. Staffordshire *see* PARISH REGISTERS
Hanciau, G *see* YAN' DARGENT, PEINTRE ET DESSINATEUR BRETON
HANCOCK 1767-1896 – (Mf 1-2: Vital Records 1767-1832. Mf 3-4: Vital Records 1832-44. Mf 5-7: Town Records 1776-1801. Mf 8-14: Town Records 1801-35. Mf 15-24: Town Records 1835-73. Mf 25-26: Vital Records 1843-77. Mf 27: Births 1878-96. Mf 28: Marriages 1878-97. Mf 29: Deaths 1872-1900) – (mf ed 1990) – 29mf – 9 – 0-87623-112-1 – us Holbrook [920]
Hancock, A *see*
- BRITISH NUCLIBRANCHIATE MOLLUSCA
- COMMUNICATION PLANNING FOR DEVELOPMENT
- A MONOGRAPH OF BRITISH NUCLIBRANCHIATE MOLLUSCA

Hancock, Alan *see*
- COMMUNICATION PLANNING REVISITED
- TECHNOLOGY TRANSFER AND COMMUNICATION

HANCOCK COUNTY COURIER – New Cumberland. West Virginia. -w. 1907-20, 1922-65 – 1 – us UMI [071]
HANCOCK COUNTY HERALD – McComb, Ohio. 1888-1960 – 22r – 1 – $32.50r – us Archival [071]
HANCOCK COUNTY NEWS-DEMOCRAT – Findlay, Ohio. 1933 – 1r – 1 – $32.50r – us Archival [071]
Hancock County. Ohio. Auditor *see*
- MILITIA ROLLS
- TAX LISTS

Hancock County. Ohio. Bethlehem United Methodist Church *see* RECORDS
Hancock County. Ohio. Biglick Township. Board of Education *see*
- ANNUAL FINANCIAL REPORTS
- ANNUAL REPORTS
- COUNTY AUDITORS' FUND RECORDS
- ENUMERATIONS OF YOUTH
- MINUTES
- MISCELLANEOUS BOARD RECORDS
- SCHOOL FUND ACCOUNT RECORDS
- SCHOOL REGISTERS, DISTRICT NO. 2
- SCHOOLHOUSE BLUEPRINTS
- SUB-DISTRICT DIRECTORS MINUTES
- TEACHERS' APPLICATION LETTERS
- TEACHERS' CERTIFICATES
- TEACHERS' CONTRACTS
- TEACHERS' MONTHLY TERM REPORTS
- TEACHERS' REPORT TO TWP. CLERK
- TEACHERS' SERVICE VERIFICATION

Hancock County. Ohio. Biglick Township. Board of Health *see* MINUTES
Hancock County, Ohio. Biglick Township. Board of Trustees *see*
- PETITIONS FOR ROAD IMPROVEMENT
- TAX LEVIES
- UNION CEMETERY RECORD

Hancock County. Ohio. Biglick Township. Board of Trustees *see*
- DITCH JOURNALS
- DITCH PLATS AND SURVEYS
- MINUTES

Hancock County. Ohio. Biglick Township. Township Clerk *see*
- ACCOUNT RECORDS
- ANNUAL APPROPRIATION RECORDS
- ANNUAL BUDGETS
- ANNUAL FINANCIAL REPORTS
- ANNUAL INVENTORIES
- APPROPRIATIONS LEDGERS
- APPROPRIATIONS RESOLUTIONS
- AUDIT REPORTS
- BUDGETS
- CASH JOURNAL AND APPROPRIATIONS
- CASH JOURNALS
- CERTIFICATES OF ELECTION
- CHATTEL MORTGAGE RECORDS
- DESCRIPTION OF STRAYS
- FINANCIAL REPORTS
- MISCELLANEOUS RECORD
- OFFICIALS' BONDS
- POLL BOOKS AND TALLY SHEETS
- POLL BOOKS/TALLY SHEETS
- REAL ESTATE APPRAISEMENTS
- RECEIPTS JOURNAL
- RECORD OF OFFICERS BONDS
- ROAD ACCOUNT RECORD
- SALARIES/CONTRACTS/LABOR REC.
- STATEMENT OF SCHOOL FUNDS
- STATEMENT OF TOWNSHIP FUNDS
- TOWNSHIP HALL PLANS

Hancock County, Ohio. Cass Township. Board of Education *see* MINUTES
Hancock County, Ohio. Cass Township. Township Clerk *see*
- CASH BOOK
- RECORD BOOK
- TRUSTEES MINUTES

Hancock County. Ohio. Common Pleas. Civil Division *see*
- NATURALIZATION RECORDS
- NATURALIZATIONS, ALIENS
- NATURALIZATIONS, DECLARATIONS
- NATURALIZATIONS, MINORS
- NATURALIZATIONS, SOLDIERS
- QUADRENNIAL ENUMERATIONS

Hancock County, Ohio. Eagle Township. Board of Education *see* CLASS REGISTER, FELLERS SCHOOL
Hancock County. Ohio. Eagle Township. Board of Trustees *see* MINUTES
Hancock County, Ohio. Engineer *see* CEMETERY PLAT MAPS
Hancock County. Ohio. Findlay, City Board of Cemetery Trustees *see* MAPLE GROVE BURIAL RECORDS
Hancock County. Ohio. Marion Township. Board of Education *see* SCHOOL REGISTERS
Hancock County. Ohio. Marion Township. Board of Trustees *see*
- CHATTEL MORTGAGES
- DITCH RECORD
- ELM GROVE CEMETERY RECORD
- ENUMERATIONS OF YOUTH
- MINUTES
- RECORD BOOK
- ROAD ABSTRACTS AND SURVEY RECORD
- ROAD TAX RECORD

Hancock County. Ohio. Probate Court *see*
- EXECUTOR'S BONDS AND APPOINTMENTS
- EXECUTOR'S BONDS AND LETTERS
- INVENTORY AND SALES BILLS
- RECORDS OF MINISTERS' LICENSES
- REGISTER OF PATENTS

Hancock County. Ohio. Treasurer *see*
- CASH BOOKS, MILITARY ORDERS
- TAX DUPLICATES

HANCOCK COURIER – Findlay, Ohio. 1851-95; 1907-14 – 16r – 1 – $32.50r – us Archival [071]
HANCOCK EAGLE – Nauvoo, Ill. v. 1 no. 2-21. Apr 10-Aug 28 1846. Incomplete – 1 – us NY Public [071]
HANCOCK FAMILY PAPERS, 1728-1830 – Massachusetts Historical Society – 2r – 1 – $150.00 – us UMI [920]
Hancock, H B *see* THE DELAWARE LOYALISTS
HANCOCK JEFFERSONIAN – Findlay, Ohio. 1857-70 – 6r – 1 – $32.50r – us Archival [071]
HANCOCK JOURNAL – Findlay, Ohio. 1850-52 – 1r – 1 – $32.50r – us Archival [071]
HAND – (Cont by: Journal of Hand Surgery – Journal of the British Society for Surgery of the Hand) – Edinburgh. v1-13. mar 1969-81* 1; v14-15 1982-oct 1983 1,5,9; v14 1982* 5 – 1 – D13428 – us UMI [617]
HAND AND TEALE'S SPECTACULAR DRAMA OF THE RELIEF OF LUCKNOW: AN ORIGINAL, OUTDOOR, MILITARY SPECTACLE.. / Hand, Thomas William – 1895?. 05353. (Pre-1900 Canadiana) – 9 – cn C.I.H.M. [820]
HAND BOOK OF CHICAGO BIOGRAPHY / Flinn, John J – Chicago: Standard Guide Co., 1893. Illinois Reel 19. (The Cox Library Collection) – 5 – us Americana [978]
HAND BOOK OF SOIL CONSERVATION FOR CCC CAMP SCS-5, SLIGO, PA – Sligo, PA: [s.n.], 1935-40 – us Res Libr [630]
HAND BOOK OF THE CEYLON NATIONAL CONGRESS, 1919-1928 / ed by Bandaranaike, S W R D – Colombo: H W Cave & Co, 1928 – 1 – us Res Libr [950]
HAND CLINICS – Philadelphia. v1-13. 1985-97+ 1,5,9; v1 1985*. v5-7 1989-91* 5 – 1,5,9 – D14732 – us UMI [617]
DIE HAND GOTTES / Winnig, August – Berlin: M Warneck, 1940 – 1 – us U.W. Library [890]
Hand, J E *see* IDEALS OF SCIENCE AND FAITH
Hand, Julia *see* DIARY
THE HAND OF GOD IN AMERICAN HISTORY : A STUDY OF NATIONAL POLITICS / Thompson, Robert Ellis – New York: T.Y. Crowell, 1902 – 1mf – us A.T.L.A. [240]
Hand, Thomas William *see* HAND AND TEALE'S SPECTACULAR DRAMA OF THE RELIEF OF LUCKNOW: AN ORIGINAL, OUTDOOR, MILITARY SPECTACLE..
HAND- UND ADRESSBUCH DER DEUTSCHEN ARCHIVE IM GEBIETE DES DEUTSCHEN REICHES, LUXEMBURGS, OESTERREICH-UNGARNS, DER RUSSISCHEN OSTSEEPROVINZEN UND DER DEUTSCHEN SCHWEIZ : PT. 1: HANDBUCH / Burkhardt, C A H – Leipzig, 1887 – 3mf – 9 – ne IDC [943]
HANDBALL – (Former title: Ace 1950-may 1971) – Skokie. v21-47. 1971-97+ 1; v24-47. 1974-97+ 5; v25-47. 1975-97+ 9 – 1,5,9 – D9816 – us UMI [790]
HANDBOEK VOOR CULTUUR- EN HANDELSONDERNEMINGEN IN NEDERLANDSCH-INDIE – Amsterdam, 1888. v1 – 9mf – 9 – ne IDC [306]
HANDBOEK VOOR DE FLORA VAN JAVA / Backer, C A – Batavia, 1924-1928 – 7mf – 9 – ne IDC [580]
HANDBOEK VOOR DE GESCHIEDENIS DER JODEN / Sluys, D E & Hoofien, J – v. 3. Amsterdam. 1873. BJ-262-80 1 – 9 – ne IDC [949]
HANDBOK I INTERNATIONELL RAETT FOER MARINEN – Stockholm, 1911 – 2mf – 1 – ILM-2431/1 – ne IDC [327]
HANDBOK I SKANDINAVIENS FLORA / Hartman, C J – Stockholm. 1820. B-6101 2 – 8 – ne IDC [580]
HANDBOK I SKANDINAVIENS FLORA INNEFATTANDE SVERIGES OCH NORGES VAXTER, TILL OCH MED MOSSORNA / Hartman, C J – ed. 10. Stockholm. 1870-71. B-105 – 8 – ne IDC [580]
HANDBOK I SKANDINAVIENS HAFSALGFLORA / Kjellman, F R – I. Fucoideae. Stockholm. 1890. B-5249 2 – 8 – ne IDC [580]
HANDBOOK / Amateur Basketball Association – 1975-76 – 9 – us UMI [073]
HANDBOOK ALMANAC FOR THE PACIFIC STATES – West Coast, 1864 – 1r – 1 – $50.00 – B06080 – us Library Micro [978]
HANDBOOK ALMANAC FOR THE PACIFIC STATES: AN OFFICIAL REGISTER AND BUSINESS DIRECTORY...CALIFORNIA AND OREGON; THE TERRITORIES...WASHINGTON, NEVADA AND UTAH;...COLONIES OF BRITISH COLUMBIA AND VANCOUVER / ed by Knight, William H – San Francisco: H.H. Bancroft & Co., 1863. California Reel 27. (The Cox Library Collection) – 5 – us Americana [978]
HANDBOOK AND INCIDENTS OF FOREIGN MISSIONS OF THE PRESBYTERIAN CHURCH, USA / Rankin, William – Newark, NJ: W H Shorts, 1893 – 1mf – 9 – 0-8370-6603-4 – 1986-0603 – us A.T.L.A. [240]
HANDBOOK AND INDEX TO THE MINUTES OF THE CONFERENCE : SHOWING THE GROWTH AND DEVELOPMENT OF THE WESLEYAN METHODIST CONSTITUTION FROM THE FIRST CONFERENCE, 1744 TO 1890 / Wansbrough, C E – London, 1890 – 4mf – 9 – ne IDC [240]
HANDBOOK AND PROCEEDINGS OF THE ANNUAL CONVENTION / National American Woman Suffrage Association – 16th, 25th-48th, 50th-51st. 1884, 1893-1916, 1919-20 – 1 – 59.00 – us L of C Photodup [977]
HANDBOOK FOR CANOEING COUNCILLORS / Deming, Eleanor – 1926. 20p. illus – 1 – us U.W. Library [790]
HANDBOOK FOR FEDERAL JUDGES' SECRETARIES – Washington: FJC, rev Dec 1983 – 2mf – 9 – $3.00 – LLMC 95-807 – us L.L.M.C. [340]
HANDBOOK FOR FEDERAL JUDGES' SECRETARIES – Washington: FJC, rev Sept 1985 – 2mf – 9 – $3.00 – LLMC 95-808 – us L.L.M.C. [340]
HANDBOOK FOR INFORMATION SYSTEMS AND SERVICES / Atherton, Pauline – 2nd ed 1980 – 259p – 9 – 92-3-101457-9 – fr UNESCO [000]
A HANDBOOK FOR MAGISTRATES, IN RELATION TO SUMMARY CONVICTIONS AND ORDERS AND INDICTABLE OFFENCES / McGuire, Thomas Horace – Toronto, Carswell, 1890. 92 p. LL-2321 – 1 – us L of C Photodup [340]
A HANDBOOK FOR NOTARIES PUBLIC AND COMMISSIONERS OF DEEDS OF NEW YORK. / Skinner, Joseph Osmun – 2d ed. Albany: Bender, 1927. 388p. LL-442 – 1 – us L of C Photodup [340]
HANDBOOK FOR SPEAKERS / Capricorn Africa Society – (Filmed with: Capricorn Africa Society Papers) – Salisbury: [s.n.], 1955 – us Res Libr [960]
HAND-BOOK FOR THE CITY OF MONTREAL AND ITS ENVIRONS: PREPARED FOR THE AMERICAN ASSOCIATION FOR THE ADVANCEMENT OF SCIENCE...AUGUST 1882 – Montreal, 1882. 02421. (Pre-1900 Canadiana) – 9 – cn C.I.H.M. [971]
HANDBOOK FOR THE CITY OF MONTREAL AND ITS ENVIRONS: WITH A PLAN OF THE CITY AND A GEOLOGICAL MAP OF THE SURROUNDING COUNTRY / Dawson, Samuel Edward – Montreal: Dawson Bros., 1882. 03776. (Pre-1900 Canadiana) – 9 – cn C.I.H.M. [971]
HAND-BOOK FOR THE DOMINION OF CANADA: PREPARED FOR THE MEETING OF THE BRITISH ASSOCIATION FOR THE ADVANCEMENT OF SCIENCE, AT MONTREAL, 1884 / Dawson, Samuel Edward – Montreal: Dawson, 1884. 02613. (Pre-1900 Canadiana) – 9 – cn C.I.H.M. [971]
A HANDBOOK FOR THE METHODIST NEW CONNEXION : CONTAINING INFORMATION OF ITS DOCTRINES, MINISTERS, CHURCHES, INSTITUTIONS, LEGAL RELATIONS, ETC. / Townsend, W J – London, 1899. 115p – 2mf – 9 – ne IDC [060]
HANDBOOK FOR THE STUDY OF EGYPTIAN TOPOGRAPHICAL LISTS / Simons, J – 1937 – 9 – $10.00 – us I.R.C. [930]
A HANDBOOK FOR TRAVELLERS ON THE CONTINENT: BEING A GUIDE.. / Murray, John – Index map. 5th ed. cor. and augm. London: J. Murray, 1845. xxxviii,574p. illus. fold. map, tables – 1 – us U.W. Library [910]
HANDBOOK OF AFRICAN LIVESTOCK STATISTICS / ILCA – 1993 – 9 – Free – 92-9053-247-5 – et ILRI [636]
HANDBOOK OF AMERICAN INDIAN LANGUAGES / Boas, Franz – BN 238 2. 1911-1922 – 8 – ne IDC [490]
HANDBOOK OF AMERICAN INDIANS NORTH OF MEXICO / ed by Hodge, Frederick W – (Bull. of Amer. Ethnol. v. 30, pt. 1-2). Washington. 1907-10. BN-237 2 – 8 – ne IDC [305]
HANDBOOK OF AMERICAN INDIANS: NORTH OF MEXICO / Hodge, Frederick W – Washington, DC: GPO, 1912. 2 Pts. Arizona Reel 3. (The Cox Library Collection) – 5 – us Americana [978]
HANDBOOK OF ARTISANAL BOATBUILDING – 1975 – 131p – it F.A.O. [623]
HAND-BOOK OF BENGAL MISSIONS, IN CONNEXION WITH THE CHURCH OF ENGLAND / Long, James – Together with an account of general educational efforts in north India. 1848 – 1 – us A.T.L.A. [240]
HANDBOOK OF BLACK ORGANIZATIONS – Durban, Black Community Programmes, 1973 – us Res Libr [360]
A HANDBOOK OF BRITISH BIRDS / Harting, J E – London, 1872. xxiv,198p. Z/1793/2 – 8 – ne IDC [590]
HANDBOOK OF BRITISH EAST AFRICA : INCLUDING ZANZIBAR, UGANDA, AND THE TERRITORY OF THE IMPERIAL BRITISH EAST AFRICA COMPANY – London: Printed for H M Stationery Office by Harrison, 1893 – 1 – us Res Libr [960]
A HANDBOOK OF BRITISH FERNS / Moore, T – London, 1848. 156, pp. B-7233 1 – 9 – ne IDC [580]
HANDBOOK OF BRITISH FUNGI, WITH DESCRIPTION OF ALL THE SPECIES / Cooke, M C – Ed. 2. London. 1883-90 – 8 – ne IDC [580]

HANDBOOK OF BRITISH MOSSES: COMPRISING ALL THAT ARE KNOWN TO BE NATIVES OF THE BRITISH ISLES / Berkeley, M J – London, 1863. xxxvi,324p. 24 pls. B-8123/1 – 9 – ne IDC [580]

HAND-BOOK OF CANADA – Publ. for local executive of British Association for the Advancement of Science. 1897. 02833. (Pre-1900 Canadiana) – 9 – cn C.I.H.M. [971]

HAND-BOOK OF CANADIAN METHODISM : BEING AN ALPHABETICAL ARRANGEMENT OF ALL THE MINISTERS AND PREACHERS WHOSE NAMES HAVE APPEARED IN CONNECTION WITH CANADIAN METHODISM... / Cornish, George H – Toronto: Wesleyan Printing Establishment, 1867 – 1mf – us A.T.L.A. [240]

A HANDBOOK OF CHEMICAL ENGINEERING / Davis, George Edward – Manchester, 1901-02. 2v. in 1. Illus – 1 – us U.W. Library [600]

A HAND-BOOK OF CHIKARANGA : OR THE LANGUAGE OF MASHONALAND / Springer, Helen Emily (Chapman) – (Filmed with the author's transl fr the Bible and her hymn) – Cincinnati: Printed by Jennings & Graham for the Methodist Episcopal Mission, Rhodesia, [1905] – 1 – us Res Libr [490]

HANDBOOK OF CHRISTIAN EVIDENCES / Stewart, Alexander Morris – New York: A.D.F. Randolph, 1895.1 fiche – 9 – us A.T.L.A. [240]

HANDBOOK OF COMMERCIAL TREATIES AND C., BETWEEN GREAT BRITAIN AND FOREIGN POWERS / ed by Bernhardt, G de – London, 1912 – 13mf – 9 – ILM-2725/1 – ne IDC [337]

HANDBOOK OF COMMERCIAL TREATIES AND C., BETWEEN GREAT BRITAIN AND FOREIGN POWERS – Ed 3. London, 1924 – 11mf – 1 – ILM-2726/1 – ne IDC [327]

A HANDBOOK OF CONGREGATIONALISM / Dexter, Henry Martyn – Boston: Congregational Publishing Society, c1880 – 1mf – us A.T.L.A. [240]

HANDBOOK OF EQUITY / McClintock, Henry Lacey – St. Paul, West, 1936. 421 p. LL-359 – 1 – us L of C Photodup [340]

HANDBOOK OF FLOWER POLLINATION / Knuth, P E O W – 3v. Oxford. 1906-09. B-5078 2 – 8 – ne IDC [580]

A HANDBOOK OF FOREIGN MISSIONS : CONTAINING AN ACCOUNT OF THE PRINCIPAL PROTESTANT MISSIONARY SOCIETIES IN GREAT BRITAIN – (Includes index) – London: Religious Tract Society, 1888 – 1mf – 9 – 0-8370-6511-9 – 1986-0511 – us A.T.L.A. [240]

HANDBOOK OF FORMS AND PRACTICE IN BANKRUPTCY / Menin, Abraham Isaac – New York: Industries Publishing Co., 1930. 370p. LL-1562 – 1 – us L of C Photodup [340]

HANDBOOK OF GEOLOGY: FOR THE USE OF CANADIAN STUDENTS / Dawson, John William – Montreal: Dawson, 1889. 02622. (Pre-1900 Canadiana) – 9 – cn C.I.H.M. [550]

HANDBOOK OF GREEK AND LATIN PALAEOGRAPHY / Thompson, E M – 2nd ed. London, 1894. B-335 2 – 8 – ne IDC [410]

HANDBOOK OF HINDU NAMES / Shanta – Calcutta: ARNICA International, 1969 – us Res Libr [490]

HANDBOOK OF INFORMATION OF THE GENERAL CONFERENCE OF THE MENNONITE CHURCH OF N.A. – 1947-48 (complete) – 1r – 1 – ATLA 1993-S007 – us A.T.L.A. [240]

HANDBOOK OF INTERNATIONAL LAW / Glenn, E F – St Paul, 1895 – 6mf – 1 – ILM-180/1 – ne IDC [327]

HANDBOOK OF INTERNATIONAL SOCIOMETRY – (Merged with: Group Psychotherapy and Psychodrama; to form: Group Psychotherapy, Psychodrama and Sociometry. Former titles: International Journal of Sociometry sep 1956. International Journal of Sociometry and Sociatry) – Beacon. v1-6 1956-72*. v7 1973 – 1 – D6906 – us UMI [150]

▶**A HANDBOOK OF IOWA** / Ashton & Crosby & Jarnagin – The Commission, Publisher, 1893.Iowa Reel 44. (The Cox Library Collection) – 5 – us Americana [978]

HAND-BOOK OF LUTHERANISM / Roth, J D – (Includes index) – 2nd ed. Utica, NY: Young Lutheran Co, 1891 – 2mf – 9 – 0-8370-8858-5 – 1986-2858 – us A.T.L.A. [240]

HANDBOOK OF NATIONAL ACCOUNTS FOR AFRICA; 04, THE NATIONAL ACCOUNTS OF SUDAN FOR 1960/1961, ADJUSTED TO CONFORM TO THE INTERMEDIATE SYSTEM OF NATIONAL ACCOUNTS / United Nations. Economic Commission for Africa – 1965. BNE-7694 1 – 9 – ne IDC [336]

HAND-BOOK OF NEWFOUNDLAND: CONTAINING AN ACCOUNT OF ITS AGRICULTURAL AND MINERAL LANDS, ITS FORESTS, AND OTHER NATURAL RESOURCES / Harvey, Moses – Boston: Doyle and Whittle, 1886.05518.(Pre-1900 Canadiana) – 9 – cn C.I.H.M. [971]

HANDBOOK OF PSYCHOLOGICAL LITERATURE / Louttit, Chauncey McKinley – Bloomington, IN: The Principia Press, 1932. viii,273p – 1 – us U.W. Library [150]

HANDBOOK OF REVIVALS : FOR THE USE OF WINNERS OF SOULS / Fish, Henry Clay – (Includes index) – Boston: James H. Earle, 1879, c1874 – 1mf – 9 – 0-8370-6183-0 – 1986-0183 – us A.T.L.A. [240]

HANDBOOK OF RURAL TECHNOLOGY FOR THE PROCESSING OF ANIMAL BY-PRODUCTS – 1989 – 160p – it F.A.O. [631]

HANDBOOK OF SOVIET LUNAR AND PLANETARY EXPLORATION – (v47 1979, Science and Technology) – 1979 – 9 – $25.00 – us Univelt [550]

HANDBOOK OF STATISTICAL METHODS FOR DEMOGRAPHERS / Jaffe, A J – 1977 – 1,5,9 – us Gordon [310]

A HANDBOOK OF SUGGESTIONS ON THE TEACHING OF GEOGRAPHY / Scarfe, N V – UNESCO – 7 – uk Microform Academic [910]

HANDBOOK OF THE BROMELIACEAE / Baker, J G – London, 1889 – XI, 243p – 8 – ne IDC [580]

A HANDBOOK OF THE COLEOPTERA...OF GREAT BRITAIN AND IRELAND / Cox, H E – London, 1874. 2v. Z-1150/2 – 8 – ne IDC [590]

HANDBOOK OF THE CONVOCATIONS, OR, PROVINCIAL SYNODS OF THE CHURCH OF ENGLAND / Joyce, James Wayland – London: Rivingtons, 1887 – 1mf – us A.T.L.A. [240]

HANDBOOK OF THE DIVINE LITURGY : A BRIEF STUDY OF THE HISTORICAL DEVELOPMENT OF THE MASS / Clarke, Charles Cowley – London: Kegan Paul, Trench, Truebner, 1910 – 1mf – us A.T.L.A. [240]

A HANDBOOK OF THE EPISTLE OF ST PAUL TO THE ROMANS: BASED ON THE REVISED VERSION AND THE REVISER'S TEXT: FOR THE USE OF STUDENTS AND BIBLE CLASSES / Burwash, Nathaniel – Toronto: W. Briggs, 1887. 00359. (Pre-1900 Canadiana) – 9 – cn C.I.H.M. [240]

HANDBOOK OF THE FERNS OF BRITISH INDIA, CEYLON AND MALAYA PENINSULAR / Beddome, R H – 1892 – 7 – uk Microform Academic [580]

HANDBOOK OF THE FERNS OF BRITISH INDIA, CEYLON AND THE MALAY PENINSULA / Beddome, R H – Calcutta. 1883; Supplement. Calcutta. 1892. B-5086 2 – 8 – ne IDC [580]

HANDBOOK OF THE FERNS OF KAFFRARIA / Sim, T R – Aberdeen, 1891. 62 pp., 66 pls. B-5162 2 – 8 – ne IDC [580]

A HANDBOOK OF THE GENERAL CONVENTION OF THE PROTESTANT EPISCOPAL CHURCH : GIVING ITS HISTORY AND CONSTITUTION, 1785-1880 / Perry, William Stevens – New York: T. Whittaker, 1881 – 1mf – us A.T.L.A. [240]

HAND-BOOK OF THE INDIAN FLORA / Drury, H – 3v. Madras, London. 1864-69. B-7312 1 – 9 – ne IDC [580]

HANDBOOK OF THE LAW OF EVIDENCE / McKelvey, John Jay – (2nd ed. St. Paul, West, 1907. 540p. LL-1277) – St. Paul, West, 1898. 468 p. LL-1482 – 1 – us L of C Photodup [340]

A HANDBOOK OF THE LAW OF PROTE COMPILED FROM DECISIONS OF AMERICAN AND ENGLISH COURTS / Williamson, Edward Hand – Philadelphia, 1889. 173 p. LL-1553 – 1 – us L of C Photodup [340]

HANDBOOK OF THE LAW OF TRUSTS / Bogert, George Gleason – 2d ed. St. Paul, West, 1942. 738 p. LL-298 – 1 – us L of C Photodup [340]

A HANDBOOK OF THE MENDE LANGUAGE / Sumner, A T – Freetown: Govt Printing Office, 1917 – 1 – us Res Libr [490]

HANDBOOK OF THE NEW YORK STATE REFORMATORY AT ELMIRA : INCLUDES...AN ABSTRACT OF LAWS RELATING TO THE REFORMATORY / Allen, Fred C – Elmira: The Summary Press, 1916 – 4mf – 9 – $6.00 – LLMC 92-141 – us L.L.M.C. [340]

HANDBOOK OF THE NEW ZEALAND FLORA / Hooker, J D – 7718 1. 1864-1867 – 9 – ne IDC [580]

A HANDBOOK OF THE ROMISH CONTROVERSY : BEING A REFUTATION IN DETAIL OF THE CREED OF POPE PIUS THE FOURTH, ON THE GROUNDS OF SCRIPTURE AND REASON / Stanford, Charles Stuart – Dublin: [s.n.], 1852 (Dublin: George Drought) – 1mf – 9 – 0-8370-8473-3 – 1986-2473 – us A.T.L.A. [240]

A HANDBOOK OF THE SHERBO LANGUAGE / Sumner, A T – London: Publ by the Crown Agents for the Colonies, for the Govt of Sierra Leone, 1921 – 1 – us Res Libr [490]

A HANDBOOK OF THE TEMNE LANGUAGE / Sumner, A T – Freetown: Govt Printing Office, 1922 – 1 – us Res Libr [490]

HAND-BOOK OF THE UNITED METHODIST FREE CHURCHES : COMPRISING AN ACCOUNT OF THEIR ORIGIN, DOCTRINES, INSTITUTIONS AND POLITY; COPY OF THE CONSTITUTION...FROM 1836 TO 1886 / Boyden, W & Askew, E – 2nd ed. London, 1887. xii/269p – 3mf – 9 – ne IDC [240]

HAND-BOOK OF THE UNITED METHODIST FREE CHURCHES : FREE METHODIST MANUAL...FROM 1836 TO 1898 / Boyden, W & Askew, E; ed by Askew, E – 3rd ed. London, 1899. xvi/415p – 5mf – 9 – ne IDC [240]

HANDBOOK OF TREATIES, ... COMMERCE AND NAVIGATION BETWEEN GREAT BRITAIN AND FOREIGN POWERS, ... 1907 / ed by Bernhardt, G de – London, 1908 – 13mf – 9 – ILM-2724/1 – ne IDC [327]

THE HANDBOOK OF UGANDA / Wallis, Henry Richard – 2nd ed. London: Publ for the Govt of the Uganda Protectorate by the Crown Agents for the Colonies, 1920 – 1 – us Res Libr [960]

HANDBOOK OF UNIVERSITY EXTENSION; WITH AN INTRODUCTION BY E.J. JAMES / James, George Francis – 2nd ed. enl. Philadelphia: American Society for the Extension of University Teaching, 1893. 19+425p – 1 – us U.W. Library [370]

HANDBOOK OF ZOOLOGY: WITH EXAMPLES FROM CANADIAN SPECIES, RECENT AND FOSSIL: PART 1 – INVERTEBRATA / Dawson, John William – Montreal: Dawson, 1870. 02623. (Pre-1900 Canadiana) – 9 – cn C.I.H.M. [971]

HANDBOOK ON AMERICAN MINING LAW / Costigan, George Purcell – St. Paul, West, 1908. 765 p. LL-238 – 1 – us L of C Photodup [340]

HANDBOOK ON HUMAN NUTRITIONAL REQUIREMENTS – 2nd printing – 66p – it F.A.O. [612]

HANDBOOK ON JURY USE IN THE FEDERAL COURTS / George, Jody et al – Washington: GPO, 1989 – 2mf – 9 – $3.00 – LLMC 95-345 – us L.L.M.C. [340]

HANDBOOK ON JUTE – 1983 – 237p – it F.A.O. [634]

HANDBOOK ON PASTORAL THEOLOGY (CCC244) / McNeur, George H – (In Chinese) – Hong Kong: Bible Book and Tract Depot for Council on Christian Literature for Overseas Chinese, 1953 – 1r – 1 – 1984-6583 – us A.T.L.A. [240]

HANDBOOK ON THE CONSTRUCTION AND INTERPRETATION OF THE LAWS. / Black, Henry Campbell – St Paul, West, 1896. 499 p. LL-853 – 1 – us L of C Photodup [340]

HANDBOOK ON THE LAW OF DAMAGES / Hale, William Benjamin – 2d ed. St. Paul, West, 1912. 632 p. LL-390 – 1 – us L of C Photodup [340]

HANDBOOK ON THE LAW OF DAMAGES / McCormick, Charles Tilford – St. Paul, West, 1935. 811 p. LL-345 – 1 – us L of C Photodup [340]

HANDBOOK ON THE LAW OF PARTNERSHIP, INCLUDING LIMITED PARTNERSHIPS / Gilmore, Eugene Allen – St. Paul: West, 1911. 721p. LL-575 – 1 – us L of C Photodup [340]

HANDBOOK ON THE LAW OF PERSONS AND DOMESTIC RELATIONS. 2D ED / Tiffany, Walter Checkley – St. Paul, West, 1909. 656 p. LL-1248 – 1 – us L of C Photodup [340]

HANDBOOK ON THE ORGANISATIONS DEALING WITH RURAL DEVELOPMENT IN THE BOMBAY STATE – (Filmed with: Pakistan Press Yearbook) – [s.l: s.n.], 1954 – 1 – us Res Libr [950]

A HANDBOOK ON TRAINING PARALEGALS : PHILIPPINES SEMINAR – 1989 – sz I.C.J.

HANDBOOK TO A COLLECTION OF THE MINERALS OF THE BRITISH ISLES:...FROM THE LUDLAM COLLECTION.. / London. Museum of Practical Geology – By F.R. Rudler. London: Wyman & Sons, 1905. 241p. Includes index – 1 – us U.W. Library [550]

HANDBOOK TO ARIZONA / Hinton, Richard J – San Francisco: Payot, Upham and Co., New York: American News Co., 1878. Arizona Reel 2. (The Cox Library Collection) – 5 – us Americana [978]

HAND-BOOK TO BRITISH COLUMBIA – Victoria, B.C.: Begg and Hoare, Aug/Sept 1894- – 9 – cn C.I.H.M. [910]

HANDBOOK TO KING SOLOMON'S TEMPLE : CONTAINING AN EXPLANATORY KEY AND AN ACCOUNT OF THE BUILDING OF THE MODEL NOW ON EXHIBITION IN THIS CITY – New York: C A Alvord, 1860 – 1mf – 9 – 0-8370-3462-0 – 1985-1462 – us A.T.L.A. [720]

A HANDBOOK TO OLD TESTAMENT HEBREW : CONTAINING AN ELEMENTARY GRAMMAR OF THE LANGUAGE: WITH READING LESSONS, NOTES ON MANY SCRIPTURE PASSAGES AND COPIOUS EXERCISES / ed by Green, Samuel Gosnell – (Includes indexes) – New York: Fleming H Revell; London: Religious Tract Society, [1901] – 1mf – 9 – 0-8370-9148-9 – 1986-3148 – us A.T.L.A. [470]

HANDBOOK TO THE BIBLE...DERIVED FROM ANCIENT MONUMENTS AND MODERN EXPLORATION / Conder, Francis R – London: Longmans, Green, 1890. 1 fiche – 9 – us A.T.L.A. [240]

HANDBOOK TO THE BIRDS OF AUSTRALIA / Gould, J – London, 1865. 2v. Z/1780/2 – 8 – ne IDC [590]

A HANDBOOK TO THE BIRDS OF GREAT BRITAIN / Sharpe, R B – Z 1930. 4 v. 1894-1897 – 9 – ne IDC [590]

A HANDBOOK TO THE BIRDS OF TASMANIA / Littler, F M – Z 1841. 1910 – 9 – ne IDC [590]

A HAND-BOOK TO THE ENGLISH PRE-MUTINY RECORDS IN THE GOVERNMENT RECORD ROOMS OF THE UNITED PROVINCES OF AGRA AND OUDH / Deward, D – Allahabad. 1920. BI-336 2 – 8 – ne IDC [350]

HANDBOOK TO THE FLORA OF CEYLON / Trimen, H A & Hooker, J D – Contains descriptions of all the species of flowering plants indigenous to the island and notes on their history, distribution and uses. pts. 1-5 in 5 v. London. 1893-1900. Plates in illustration of a Handbook to the flora of Ceylon. 4 v. London. 1893-98. B-486 2 – 8 – ne IDC [580]

A HAND-BOOK TO THE ORDER LEPIDOPTERA / Kirby, W F – London, 1894-97.5v. Z-1398/2 – 8 – ne IDC [590]

HAND-BOOK TO THE PUBLIC RECORDS / Great Britain. Public Record Office – By F.S. Thomas, Secretary of the Public Record Office. London, 1853. lxii, 482p. fold. col. pl – 1 – us U.W. Library [324]

A HANDBOOK TO THE RECORDS OF THE GOVERNMENT OF INDIA IN THE IMPERIAL RECORD DEPARTMENT, 1748-1859 / India. Imperial Record Department – Calcutta. 1925. Index. BI-311 2 – 8 – ne IDC [324]

A HANDBOOK TO THE WORKS OF WILLIAM SHAKESPEARE / Luce, Morton – London: G. Bell and Sons, 1924, c1906. x,463p. 1 reel.1246 – 1 – us U.W. Library [420]

HANDBOOKS TO THE BIRDS OF THE BOMBAY PRESIDENCY / Barnes, H E – Calcutta. 1885. BZ-261 2 – 8 – ne IDC [590]

HANDBUCH BEY DEM GENERALBASSE UND DER COMPOSITION / Marpurg, Friedrich Wilhelm – 3v. 1755-60. Contains also: ANHANG ZUM HANDBUCHE – 9 – us Sibley [780]

HANDBUCH BEY DEM GENERALBASSE UND DER COMPOSITION / Marpurg, Friedrich Wilhelm – P 710. 1755 – 9 – ne IDC [780]

HANDBUCH DER AESTHETIK / Heusinger, J H G – P 318. 1797 – 9 – ne IDC [700]

HANDBUCH DER ALLGEMEINEN MYKOLOGIE / Bonorden, H F – Stuttgart. 1851. B-5037 2 – 8 – ne IDC [580]

HANDBUCH DER ALTTESTAMENTLICHEN THEOLOGIE / Dillmann, August – (Includes indexes) – Leipzig: S Hirzel, 1895 – 2mf – 9 – 0-8370-2917-1 – 1985-0917 – us A.T.L.A. [220]

HANDBUCH DER ARCHITEKTUR – Unter Mitwirkung von Fachgenossen hrsg. von Josef Durm, Hermann Ende, Eduard Schmitt und Heinrich Wagner. Darmstadt, A. Bergstraesser, 1883-1939. Film Mas C 690 – 1 – us H.U. Library [720]

HANDBUCH DER BIOLOGISCHEN ARBEITSMETHODEN – Series 1-13. All pub – 1,5,6 – us Princeton Micro [574]

HANDBUCH DER BOTANISCHEN TERMINOLOGIE UND SYSTEMKUNDE / Bischoff, G W – Nuernberg. 3v. 1833-1844 – 47mf – ne IDC [580]

HANDBUCH DER BUECHERKUNDE FUER DIE AELTERE MEDICIN ZUR KENNTNISS DER GRIECHISCHEN,... / Choulant, J L – Leipzig, 1828 – 4mf – 9 – ne IDC [610]

HANDBUCH DER CHRISTLICHEN KIRCHEN- UND DOGMEN-GESCHICHTE / Ebrard, Johannes Heinrich August 4v. 1865-1867 – 1 – us A.T.L.A. [240]

HANDBUCH DER CONCHYLIOLOGIE UND MALACOZOOLOGIE / Philippi, R A – 2502 2. 1853 – 8 – ne IDC [590]

HANDBUCH DER DEUTSCHEN LITERATURGESCHICHTE / Bernt, Alois – (Includes index) – Reichenberg in Boehmen: Gebrueder Stiepel Gesellschaft m.b.H., 1928 – 1r – 1 – us U.W. Library [430]

HANDBUCH DER DUALA-SPRACHE / Christaller, Th. – Basel: Verlag der Missionsbuchh, 1892 – us Res Libr [410]

HANDBUCH DER EBRAEISCHEN MYTHOLOGIE : SAGE UND GLAUBE DER ALTEN EBRAER IN IHREM ZUSAMMENHANG MIT DEN RELIGIOESEN ANSCHAUUNGEN ANDERER SEMITEN... / Schultze, Martin – (Includes bibliographical references & index) – Nordhausen: Ferd Foerstemann, 1876 – 1mf – 9 – 0-8370-5165-7 – 1985-3165 – us A.T.L.A. [270]

HANDBUCH DER ENTOMOLOGIE / Burmeister, C H C – 2437 2. 5 v. 1832-1847 – 8 – ne IDC [590]

HANDBUCH DER FRAUENBEWEGUNG (HQ 26) / ed by Lange, Helene & Baeumer, Gertrud – Berlin. 5 Teile. 1901-06 (mf ed 1996) – 24mf – 9 – DM220.00 – 3-89131-138-9 – gw Fischer [305]

HANDBUCH DER HISTORISCH-GEOGRAPHISCHEN PATHOLOGIE / Hirsch, A – M 251. 2 v. 1860-64 – 9 – ne IDC [610]

HANDBUCH DER INTERNATIONALEN NACHLASSBEHANDLUNG ... / Boehm, F – 2nd ed. Augsburg, 1895 – 7mf – 9 – ILM-3785/1 – ne IDC [327]

HANDBUCH DER INTERNATIONALEN NACHLASSBEHANDLUNG ... / Boehm, F – Augsburg, 1881 – 9mf – 9 – ILM-3784/1 – ne IDC [327]

HANDBUCH DER MEDICINISCH-PHARMACEUTISCHEN BOTANIK... / Schleiden, M J – Leipzig, 1852-1857. 2v – 11mf – 9 – ne IDC [615]

HANDBUCH DER MISSIONSGESCHICHTE UND MISSIONSGEOGRAPHIE / Blumhardt, Johann Christoph – (Includes indexes) – 3., ganz neue Ausg. Calw: Vereinsbuchh; Stuttgart: J F Steinkopf. 2v. 1863 – 4mf – 9 – 0-8370-7287-5 – 1986-1287 – us A.T.L.A. [240]

HANDBUCH DER MUSIKALISCHEN LITERATUR ODER ALLGEMEINES SYSTEMATISCH-GEORDNETES VERZEICHNISS DER IN DEUTSCHLAND UND IN DEN ANGRENZENDEN LAENDERN GEDRUCKTEN MUSIKALIEN AUCH MUSIKALISCHEN SCHRIFTEN UND ABBILDUNGEN MIT ANZEIGE DER VERLEGER UND PREISE / Whistling, Carl Friedrich; ed by Hofmeister, A – 3rd ed v 1-10. Leipzig. 1845-93 – 9$71.00 – ne IDC [780]

HANDBUCH DER MUSIK-LITERATUR / ed by Hofmeister, A – Quinquennial cumulations. v1-19. pt1. 1817/29-1934/40 – 1 – us Schnase [780]

HANDBUCH DER NATURGESCHICHTE ALLER VOGEL DEUTSCHLANDS / Brehm, C L – Z-362 2. 1831 – 8 – ne IDC [590]

HANDBUCH DER PETRE FAKTENKUNDE / Quenstedt, F A von – 2541 2. Ed. 3. 1882-1885 – 8 – ne IDC [550]

HANDBUCH DER PFINGSTBEWEGUNG / Hollenweger, Walter J – 3v. in 10 pts. (3 reels) – 1 – us A.T.L.A. [240]

HANDBUCH DER PFLANZER KRANKHEITEN / Soraurer, P C H – Berlin, 1874. 406 pp., 16 pls. B-7488 1 – 9 – ne IDC [580]

HANDBUCH DES ORGANISTEN / Schneider, Friedrich – Halberstadt. 1830. 4v – 1 – 23.00 – us L of C Photodup [780]

HANDBUCH FUER BUECHERFREUNDE UND BIBLIOTHEKARE / Lawaetz, Heinrich Wilhelm – Halle. 11v. 1788-94 (mf ed 1992) – 42mf – DM460.00 – 3-89131-056-0 – gw Fischer [020]

HANDBUCH FUER DAS DEUTSCHE REICH / Germany. Reichsministerium des Innern – Berlin. 1877, 1879-1881, 1883-1914, 1918, 1922, 1922-23, 1926, 1932, 1936. Film Mas C 729 – 1 – us H.U. Library [943]

HANDBUCH ZUR DEUTSCHEN LITERARTURGESCHICHTE / Petry, Karl – (Includes bibliographical references and index) – Koeln: B Pick, 1949 – 1r – 1 – us U.W. Library [430]

HANDBUCH ZUR ERKENNUNG DER NUTZBARSTEN AM HAEUFTIGSTEN VORKOMMENDEN GEWAECHSE / Link, J H F – 3v. Berlin. 1829-33. B-5244 2 – 8 – ne IDC [580]

HANDBUECHER UND LEXIKA ZUR MILITAERGESCHICHTE : MILITAERHISTORISCHE NACHSCHLAGWERKE AUS DEM 19. UND FRUEHEN 20. JAHRHUNDERT – (mf ed 1997) – 198mf (1:24) – 9 – diazo DM4,000.00 silver DM4,600.00 – 3-598-33870-8 – silver ISBN: 3-598-33871-6 – gw Saur [355]

HANDE – (Cikaran: Feridun Fahri, Sahib-i Imtiyaz: Sedat Simavi, Mueduerue: Yakup Aziz. Nos. 2, 3, 14 (28 Temmuz-20 Tesriniewel 1332[1916])) – Istanbul: Karabet Matbaasi, 1916-1917 – 1mf – 9 – $12.00 – us MEDOC [949]

HANDE – (Mueduerue: Hueseyin Nazmi, Sermuharriri: Cevdet Ma'suki. No. 3 (5 Nisan 1326[1910])) – Istanbul Ahmed Saki Bey Matbaasi, 1910 – 1mf – 9 – $12.00 – us MEDOC [949]

HANDEL (DER GANTZE) VND GESCHICHT, VON DER STAT MUENSTER IN WESTPHALEN GELEGEN, WIE ES ERGANGEN IST, IN EINER KURTZEN SUMMA BEGRIFFEN – Nuernberg, H. Guldenmundt. 1535. BME-158 1 – 9 – ne IDC [943]

Handel, George Frederic *see*
- ACIS AND GALATEA AND ALEXANDER'E FEA VOLS 1 AND 4 FROM THE VOCAL WORKS OF HANDEL, WITH A SEPARATE ACCOMPANYMENT ARRANGED FOR THE ORGAN OR PIANOFORTE BY DR. JOHN CLARK
- AYLESFORD MANUSCRIPTS
- MANUSCRIPTS AND SKETCHES
- A NEW EDITION OF SIX CONCERTOS, FOR THE HARPSICHORD OR ORGAN
- SAMSON, AN ORATORIO, THE WORDS TAKEN FROM MILTON
- A SECOND SET OF SIX CONCERTOS FOR THE HARPSICHORD OR ORGAN [ARRANGEMENT VON 6 CONCERTI GROSSI AUS OP. 6]
- SIX CONCERTOS FOR THE HARPSICHORD OR ORGAN...OP. 4
- TE DEUM
- WERKE

HANDEL OG SAMFAERDSEL I OLDTIDEN – 1943 – 1 – us I.U. Libraries [390]

HANDEL ZAGRANICZNY – Warsaw. v1-20 1955-75*. v21-25 1976-80. v26-39 1981-94*. v40-42 1995-97+ – 1 – D6254 – us UMI [073]

DIE HANDELINGE VANDER OPENBAERDER DISPUTACIE, DIE GHEHOUDEN IS. TE STRAESBURCH, TEGHEN MELCHIOR HOFFMAN, DOOR DIE PREDICANTEN DERSELUER STADT / Butzer, M – Enz. Anno. 1533. Z. pl. en j. BME-124 1 – 9 – ne IDC [240]

HANDELINGEN / Netherlands. Parliament – Verbatim reports of the two houses of Parliament. Available from 1945- – 9 – ne Sdu MICRO [324]

HANDELINGEN VAN DE KERKERAAD DER NEDERL. GEMEENTE TE KEULEN, 1571-1591 (DE WERKEN..1,3) – Utrecht, 1881 – Dfl28.00 – ne Slangenburg [240]

HANDELINGEN VAN DEN VOLKSRAAD, 1918-1939/1942 – Batavia. 1929-43. – 2944mf – 9 – ne IDC [950]

Handel-Mazzetti, H *see* SYMBOLAE SINICAE

HANDELS- UND GEWERBE-ZEITUNG – Sombor, Yugoslavia. 1939-40 – 1r – 1 – us L of C Photodup [949]

HANDELSBLATT – 1946-1994 – 10 times per yr – 1 – DM500.00 – sz Infoprint [072]

HANDELSBLATT – (1967-78 70r DM5,250.00. 1979-84 45r DM3,375.00. 1985-91 63r DM4,725.00. 1992-94 30r DM2,250.00.) – Duesseldorf, 1946-66 – 62r – 1 – DM4,650.00 (DM600.00 subsc 1995) – gw Mikro Press [072]

HANDELSBLATT – Duesseldorf, 1946- – 10r per y – 1 – inquire – us Ross [072]

HANDELSBLATT – Duesseldorf. 1979- – 22310.00y; CPC; 9 – gw Alpha Com [072]

HANDELSBLATT – Duesseldorf, Germany. -d. 16 May 1946-15 July 1949; 4 Jan-30 Dec 1950; 22 Jan 1951-31 Dec 1957; 1 April 1964-31 Dec 1968. 92 reels – 1 – uk British Libr Newspaper [072]

HANDELSBLATT : WIRTSCHAFTS-UND FINANZZEITUNG – Duesseldorf, West Germany. 16 May 1946-1992 – 250r – 1 – gw Mikrofilm [380]

HANDELSGESCHICHTE DER JUDEN DES ALTERTUMS / Herzfeld, L – Ed. 2. Brunswick. 1894. In Hebrew. BJ-32-61 1 – 9 – ne IDC [930]

Handelsman, M *see* NAPOLEON ET LA POLOGNE, 1806-1807

DAS HANDELSMUSEUM / Oesterreichisches Handelsmuseum – Vienna. v20-40 1905-1925. Incomplete – 1 – us NY Public [060]

DIE HANDELSPOLITIK BULGARIENS / Abadjief, C – Berlin, 1909 – 1mf – 9 – ILM-985/1 – ne IDC [340]

DIE HANDELSPOLITIK POLENS SEIT ERLANGUNG DER SELBSTAENDIGKEIT BIS ZUM ABLAUF DER GENFER KONVENTION AM 15. JUNI 1925 / Braeutigam, Harald – Berlin, 1926 – 2mf – 9 – DM62.00 – 3-89349-328-X – gw Hänsel [327]

HANDELSPOLITISCHE BESTREBUNGEN ENGLANDS... / Baicoiano, C J – Muenchen, Berlin, 1913 – 1mf – 9 – ILM-1857/1 – ne IDC [340]

HANDELSWOCHE – Berlin, 1958-90 – 20r – 1 – Dist. gw Mikrofilm – gw Misc Inst [380]

HANDELSZEITUNG *see* SCHWABISCHER MERKUR

DAS HANDGRANATENKOEPFL : BILDER UND GESCHICHTEN VON DER EISMEERFRONT / Weinberger, Andreas – Muenchen: F Eher, 1944 – 1r – 1 – us U.W. Library [943]

DAS HANDGRANATENKOEPFL : BILDER UND GESCHICHTEN VON DER EISMEERFRONT / Weinberger, Andreas – Muenchen: F Eher, 1944 – 1 – us U.W. Library [830]

HANDICRAFT-HOBBY INDEX – v1- 1980-. Annotated index to current do-it-yourself periodical information. Bi-monthly, 6 times a year. Cumulating issues – 9 – $78.00y – us MELSA [640]

HANDING OVER NOTES / Wilson, J B – Swaziland: [s.n.], 1965 – us Res Libr [960]

HANDKOMMENTAR ZUM ALTEN TESTAMENT *see* DAS BUCH JEREMIA

Handl, Jacob *see* MUSICI OPERIS, HARMONIARUM QUATUOR, QUINQUE, SEX, OCTO, ET PLURIUM VOCUM

HANDLEIDING DER PATROLOGIE / Benvenutus V Venraai – 's-Hertogenbosch, 1912 – 8mf – 8 – ne Slangenburg [240]

HANDLEIDING TOT DE KENNIS DER FLORA VAN NEDERLANDSCH INDIE / Boerlage, J G – Leiden, 1890-1900. 3v – 22mf – 9 – ne IDC [580]

HANDLEIDING TOT DE KERKGESCHIEDVORSCHING EN KERKGESCHIEDSCHRIJVING / Acquoy, J G R – 's-Gravenhage: Nijhoff, 1910 – 1mf – us A.T.L.A. [240]

HANDLEITUNG ZUR VARIATION / Niedt, Friedrich E – 1706 – 9 – us Sibley [780]

Handler, Milton *see* CASES AND MATERIALS ON THE LAW OF VENDOR AND PURCHASE

HANDLEY CROSS : OR, MR. JORROCKS'S HUNT... / Surtees, Robert Smith – London: Bradbury and Evans, 1854 – 1 roll – 1 – 1-55879-331-3 – uk Libr Preservation [830]

HANDLING AND SHIPPING – (V14 n10-12 also called [New series] v5 n10 and v6 n11-12. Cont by Handling & Shipping Management. Former titles: Flow Quarterly jan 1952-sep 1954. Material Handling Illustrated oct 1954-aug/sep 1960. Handling and Shipping Illustrated oct/nov 1960-dec 1960/jan 1961) – Cleveland. v1-7 1952-jan 1958*. v8-14 win 1959-dec 1965. n7-19 1966-sep 1978 1; n12-19. 1971-sep 1978 5; n18-19. 1977-sep 1978 9 – 1,5,9 – D1401 – us UMI [380]

HANDLING AND SHIPPING *see* HANDLING AND SHIPPING MANAGEMENT

HANDLING AND SHIPPING ILLUSTRATED *see* HANDLING AND SHIPPING

HANDLING AND SHIPPING MANAGEMENT – (Cont: Handling and Shipping. Cont by: Transportation and Distribution) – Cleveland. n19-28. oct 1978-aug 1987 – 1,5,9 – D1401.01 – us UMI [380]

HANDLING AND SHIPPING MANAGEMENT *see* HANDLING AND SHIPPING

HANDLING AND STORAGE OF FOOD GRAINS IN TROPICAL AND SUBTROPICAL AREAS / Hall, D W – 2nd printing 1975 – 350p – it F.A.O. [630]

HANDLING, GRADING AND DISPOSAL OF WOOL – 1983 – 109p – it F.A.O. [636]

THE HANDLING OF PRISONERS OF WAR DURING THE KOREAN WAR / U.S. Army. Army, Pacific – 1960 – 1 – 20.00 – us L of C Photodup [950]

HANDLINGAR / Svenska Vetenskapsakademien, Stockholm – 1739-1812. v. 1-40; Series 2, v. 1-33 – 3 – us Readex [500]

HANDLIST OF BAPTISMAL REGISTERS HELD AT THE RECORD OFFICE OF THE REGISTRAR GENERAL BY WILLIAM LEARY / Leary, William – [1979] – 1mf – 9 – ne IDC [240]

HANDLIST OF HARTLEY-VICTORIA COLLEGE COLLECTION / Lloyd, Gareth – (Coll title: The People Called Methodists, Phase 1: Reference Tools) – Manchester, 1991 – 1mf – 9 – MP-608/1 – ne IDC [240]

HANDLIST OF MARRIAGE REGISTERS OF THE METHODIST CHURCH HELD AT LOCAL RECORD OFFICES / Leary, William – 1979 – 1mf – 9 – ne IDC [240]

HANDLIST OF THE DISTRICT MINUTES – Manchester: John Rylands University Library, Methodist Archives – 1mf – ne IDC [240]

A HANDLIST OF THE JAMAICA FERNS AND THEIR ALLIES / Jenman, G S – Demerara. 1881. B-7202 1 – 9 – ne IDC [580]

HANDLUNG ODER ACTA GEHALTNER DISPUTATION VND GESPRAECH ZU ZOFFINGEN INN BERNNER BIET MIT DEN WIDERTOEUFFERN / ed by Bullinger, H – Zuerich, 1532 – 4mf – 9 – PBU-692/1 – ne IDC [240]

DER HANDLUNGSSPIELRAUM DER ZENTRALBANK VON GRIECHENLAND UND SEIN EINFLUSS AUF DAS INFLATIONSNIVEAU DER GRIECHISCHEN VOLKSWIRTSCHAFT / Troullidis, Thomas – 1993 – 2mf – 9 – DM80.00 – 3-89349-788-9 – gw Hänsel [332]

THE HANDMAIDEN OF THE LORD, OR, WAYSIDE SKETCHES / Cooke, Sarah A Bass – 1899 – 9 – us A.T.L.A. [240]

Handmann *see* UEBERBLICK UEBER DES GEBIET DER EV.-LUTHER. MISSION IM TAMULENLANDE

Handmann, R *see* DAS HEBRAER-EVANGELIUM (T.U.U. 1-5/3)

HANDRAIL ASSISTED VERSUS NONHANDRAIL ASSISTED STAIRMASTER GAUNTLET ERGOMETRY / Gerhards, Marty D & Butts, Nancy Kay – 1991 – 1mf – $4.00 – us Microform Publ [613]

HANDRAIL SUPPORT VERSUS FREE ARM WING TREADMILL FITNESS TEST / Dremsa, Catherine J & Hunter, Gary – 1986 – 1mf – 9 – $4.00 – us Microform Publ [612]

HANDS – (Incorporated within: Crafts Plus, 1988) – Markham. v1-7. 1980-1987/88 – 9 – Can$20.00y – cn Micromedia [740]

HANDS *see* CRAFTS PLUS

HANDS TO SAVE THE SOIL – Washington, DC: USGPO, [1938?] – us Res Libr [630]

Hands, William *see* A PRACTICAL TREATISE ON FINES AND RECOVERIES IN THE COURT OF COMMON PLEAS; WITH PRECEDENTS

Handschin, Charles Hart *see*
- EKKEHARD
- DIE STEINKLOPFER

HANDSCHRIFT H. – (Werken van Hendrik Mande, Jan van Ruusbroec, Meister Eckhart, etc.) – 4 GEDATEERD 1588. BIBL. ST. ADELBERTSABDIJ, EGMOND – 18mf – 8 – ne Slangenburg [290]

DIE HANDSCHRIFTEN, AUSGABEN UND UEBERSETZUNGEN VON IAMBLICHOS DE MYSTERIIS : EINE KRITISCH-HISTORISCHE STUDIE (T.U.U. 5-62) / Sicherl, M – Berlin, 1957 – 5mf – 9 – ne Slangenburg [240]

DIE HANDSCHRIFTEN DER UNIVERSITAETSBIBLIOTHEK MUENCHEN : GESAMTEDITION DER DEUTSCHEN MITTELALTERLICHEN, DER LATEINISCHEN MITTELALTERLICHEN UND DER MUSIKHANDSCHRIFTEN – 1995 – 2,926mf – 9 – DM48,000.00 – 3-89131-200-8 – gw Fischer [090]

HANDSCHRIFTLICHE BRIEFE / Radek, Karl – 1 – DM40.00 – gw Mikro Press [400]

DIE HANDSCHRIFTLICHE UEBERLIEFERUNG DER SOGENANNTEN HISTORIA TRIPARTITA DES EPIPHANIUS-CASSIDOR (T.U.U. 5-59) / Jacob, W – Berlin, 1954 – 4mf – 9 – ne Slangenburg [240]

DIE HANDSCHRIFTLICHE UEBERLIEFERUNG DER ZACHARIAS- UND JOHANNES-APOKRYPHEN (T.U.U. 2-26/3A) / Berendts, Alexander – Leipzig, 1904 – 2mf – 9 – ne Slangenburg [240]

DIE HANDSCHRIFTLICHE UEBERLIEFERUNG DES EPIPHANIUS (T.U.U. 3-36/2) / Holl, Karl – Leipzig, 1910 – 2mf – 9 – ne Slangenburg [240]

THE HANDSOME HUMES / Black, William – British Fiction Archive: Unit 4 – 9 – uk Bell [830]

HANDS-ON ELECTRONICS – (Cont: Radio-electronics Special Projects. Cont by: Popular Electronics) – New York. v2-6. sum 1984-jan 1989 – 1,5,9 – D14798.01 – us UMI [380]

HANDSWORTH HERALD & NORTH BIRMINGHAM NEWS – England.1896. -w. 1 reel – 1 – uk British Libr Newspaper [072]

HANDSWORTH NEWS – England.13 Oct 1888-1895; 11 Apr-12 Dec 1896; 1897-1899. -w. 11 reels – 1 – uk British Libr Newspaper [072]

HANDT BOECXKEN: INHOLDENDE VELE GODLIJCKE TROUHERTIGHE VADERLIJCKE VERMANINGHEN VNDE LEERINGEN / Joris, David – BME-380 1 – 9 – ne IDC [240]

HANDT-BOECXKEN DER CHRISTELIJCKE GEDICHTEN... / Biens, C P – 2nd ed. C.P.B. Hoorn, 1635 – 3mf – 9 – ne IDC [700]

HANDWEAVER AND CRAFTSMAN – New York. v1-24 apr 1950-aug 1973. v26 jan-oct 1975 1; v22-24 win 1971-aug 1973. v26 jan-oct 1975 5 – 1,5 – D1427 – us UMI [640]

HANDWERK UND GEWERBE – (Cont by: Der Juedische Handwerker, oct 1925) – Berlin, jan, may, aug-oct 1915; jan-mar, jun-sep, nov 1916; oct 1925; jun 1930; apr 1933; oct 1934; jun 1935; feb 1936-37; sep 1938 – 1 – Dist. gw Mikrofilm – gw Misc Inst [072]

HANDWERK UND GEWERBE *see* DER JUEDISCHE HANDWERKER

DER HANDWERKER – Budweis, 1933-35 – 1 – Inquire at Mikrofilmarchiv for details – gw Misc Inst [072]

DER HANDWERKER – Budweis (Ceske Budejovice), Czechoslovakia. 1933-35 – 1 – gw Mikrofilm [072]

HANDWORTERBUCH DES DEUTSCHEN MAERCHENS – 1930-33, 34-40 – 1 – us I.U. Libraries [390]

HANDWRITTEN DIARIES / Taylor, George Baxton – 2400p – 1 – 84.00 – us Baptist [240]

HANDY ANDY : A TALE OF IRISH LIFE / Lover, Samuel – London: Frederick Lover and Richard Groombridge, 1842 – 1 roll – 1 – 1-55879-440-9 – uk Libr Preservation [830]

A HANDY DIGEST OF WESLEYAN RULES AND USAGES : CONTAINING THE LAWS AND REGULATIONS OF THE WESLEYAN-METHODIST CONNEXION / Povah, C – London, 1883 – 2mf – 9 – ne IDC [240]

Haner, Janet A S *see* DETERMINING TYPES AND TYPAL PROFILES OF ADULT AMATEUR THEATRE PARTICIPANTS THROUGH Q-TECHNIQUE

HANFORD CITY DIRECTORIES – Kings Co, CA. 1906; 1917; 1920; 1926; 1930; 1939; 1943 – 7r – 1 – $350.00 – D047 – us Library Micro [910]

HANFORD JOURNAL – (Also known as: Morning Journal) – Hanford, CA. 1891-1907; 1908-15; 1917-55 – 173r – 1 BC02285 – $8,650.00 – us Library Micro [071]

HANFORD SENTINEL – Hanford, CA. 1901- – 334+ r – 1 BC02286 – $16,700.00 ($400.00y) – us Library Micro [071]

HANGING LOOSE – Brooklyn. v1-16 1966-71*. v17-63 sum 1972-1993. v64-69 1993-94*. v70-78 1995-97+ 1; v21-31 win 1973-fal 1977*. v32-35 spr 1978-spr 1979. v36-69 fal 1979-1994*. v70-78 1995-97+ 5; v21-24 win 1973-win 1975. v25-48 sum 1975-fal 1985*. v49-63 spr 1986-93. v64-69 1993-94*. v70-78 1995-97+ 9 – 1,5,9 – D7624 – us UMI [073]

HANGKONG XUEBAO – Acta Aeronautica et Astronautica Sinica. In Chinese but English abstracts to the main articles. F p80 – 9 – $4.50f – cc Microforms [073]

HANGMAN – (Includes Special Comics No. 1) – Issue Nos. 2-4 Winter 1942-Fall 1942 – 4mf – 15 – $25.75 – us Comics [760]

HANGMAN – Issue Nos. 5-8 Winter 42-Fall 43 – 4mf – 15 – $25.75 – us Comics [760]

HANGYORE SINMUN – Seoul, Korea. May 15 1988-Dec 1990 – 10r – 1 – us L of C Photodup [072]

HANGZHOU DAXUE XUEBAO – (Zhexue Shehui Kexue Ban). Journal of Hangzhou University, Philosophy & Social Science. In Chinese but Table of Contents in English in each issue. F p206 – 9 – $4.50f – cc Microforms [073]

HANGZHOU DAXUE XUEBAO – Ziran Kexue Ban. Journal of Hangzhou University, National Science. In Chinese but English abstracts to the main articles. F p185 – 9 – $4.50f – cc Microforms [073]

HANGZHOU RIBAO – Hangzhou Daily. 1985-. M D84 – 1 – $55.00r – cc Microforms [072]

Hanhart, J *see* CONRAD GESSNER

HAN-HSUEEH / Centre Franco-Chinois d'Etudes Sinologiques de Pekin – Han-Hiue. Bulletin. v. 1-3. Peking. 1944-49. (lacking: v.3). BCH-254 2 – 8 – ne IDC [073]

HA-NIDDAHAT / Shaikevich, N M – Vilna. 1886. BJ-422-81 1 – 9 – ne IDC [470]

Hanim, Nigar *see* EFSUS

HANINGE ALLEHANDA – Vasterhaninge, Sweden. 1977-81 – 1 – sw Kungliga [072]

HANJIE XUEBAO – Transactions of the China Welding Institution. In Chinese but English abstracts to the main articles. F p142 – 9 – $4.50f – cc Microforms [073]

Hankamer, Paul *see* SPIEL DER MAECHTE

Hanke, Lewis *see*
- CUERPO DE DOCUMENTOS DEL SIGLO 16 SOBRE LOS DERECHOS DE ESPANA EN LAS INDIAS Y LAS FILIPINAS DESCUBIERTOS Y CONTADOS POR...
- CUERPO DE DOCUMENTOS DEL SIGLO 17 SOBRE LOS DERECHOS DE ESPANA EN LAS INDIAS Y LAS FILIPINAS, DESCUBIERTOS Y ANOTADOS POR LEWIS HANKE...MEXICO, 1943
- THE FIRST SOCIAL EXPERIMENTS IN AMERICA. A STUDY IN THE DEVELOPMENT OF SPANISH INDIAN POLICY...CAMBRIDGE (USA), 1935
- THE SPANISH STRUGGLE FOR JUSTICIE IN THEIR CONQUEST OF AMERICA...

Hankins, Col *see* DAKOTA LAND; OR, THE BEAUTY OF ST PAUL

HANKOU MINGUO RIBAO – Hankou, China. (The Republican Daily). Jan-Sept 1927. M B4 – 2r – 1 – $100.00 – cc Microforms [950]

Hanley, Keith *see* NINETEENTH-CENTURY CONTEXTS

Hanley, S *see*
- CONCHOLOGIA INDICA
- THE CONCHOLOGICAL MISCELLANY
- A HISTORY OF BRITISH MOLLUSCA AND THEIR SHELLS
- IPSA LINNAEI CONCHYLIA

Hanley, Thomas O'Brien *see* THE CHARLES CARROLL PAPERS

Hanmer, Lee Franklin *see* RECREATION LEGISLATION

Hanna, Charles Augustus *see*
- HISTORICAL COLLECTIONS OF HARRISON COUNTY
- THE SCOTCH-IRISH, OR, THE SCOT IN NORTH BRITAIN, NORTH IRELAND, AND NORTH AMERICA

Hanna, Hazel E B *see* HAZEL E.B. HANNA PAPERS

Hanna, William *see*
- FORTY DAYS AFTER OUR LORD'S RESURRECTION
- LAST DAY OF OUR LORD'S PASSION
- THE WARS OF THE HUGUENOTS
- WYCLIFFE AND THE HUGUENOTS

Hannaford, Phebe Ann Coffin *see* DAUGHTERS OF AMERICA, OR, WOMEN OF THE CENTURY

Hannah, J M *see* THE USE OF OXYGEN CONSUMPTION AND BLOOD LACTATE MEASURES IN TRAINING FOR PEAK CHAMPIONSHIP SWIMMING PERFORMANCE

Hannah, John *see* RELATIONS BETWEEN THE DIVINE AND HUMAN ELEMENTS IN HOLY SCRIPTURE: EIGHT LECTURES

Hannam, Susan E *see* SMOKELESS TOBACCO USE AMONG BIG TEN WRESTLERS AND FACTORS ASSOCIATED WITH USE

Hannay, James *see*
- THE LIFE AND TIMES OF SIR LEONARD TILLEY: BEING A POLITICAL HISTORY OF NEW BRUNSWICK FOR THE PAST SEVENTY YEARS
- THE STORY OF ACADIA

Hanne, Johann Wilhelm *see* DER GEIST DES CHRISTENTHUMS:...PROTESTANTISCHE BRIEFE

HANNELE : A DREAM POEM / Hauptmann, Gerhart – New York: Doubleday, Page, 1908 – 1r – 1 – us U.W. Library [810]

LE HANNETON – Illustre, satirique et litteraire. Paraissant le jeudi. Red. en chef Victor Azar. Paris. nov 1862-juil 1868 – 1 – fr A.C.R.P.P. [073]

LE HANNETON – Journal des toques. Dir.-red. en chef Le Guillois. Premiere annee, no.1. Paris. aout 1876 – 1 – fr A.C.R.P.P. [073]

HANNOEVERISCHE POLITISCHE NACHRICHTEN – Hannover, Germany. 1793-99 – 6r – 1 – gw Mikrofilm [072]

Hannon, John *see* THE DEVIL'S PARABLES

HANNOVERSCHE ALLGEMEINE ZEITUNG – Hannover, West Germany. 1971- – ca 10r per yr – 1 – gw Mikrofilm [072]

HANNOVERSCHE ALLGEMEINE ZEITUNG *see* SUEDHANNOVERSCHER ANZEIGER

HANNOVERSCHE GESCHICHTSBLAETTER – Hannover. v. 1-20, 23-32; 1898-1929. Film Mas C 436 – 1 – us H.U. Library [073]

HANNOVERSCHE LANDESBLAETTER – Hannover, Germany. 27 Nov 1845-46; 5 Jan-31 Mar 1847; 18 Jan 1848 – 1 – gw Mikrofilm [072]

HANNOVERSCHE NEUESTE NACHRICHTEN : AUSGABE SUEDHANNOVER – Goettingen. jul 3, 1946-aug 23, 1949 – 2r – 1 – gw Mikrofilm [072]

HANNOVERSCHE PRESSE – (Bereichsausgabe) – Goettingen. jul 19, 1946-aug 30, 1949 – 2r – 1 – gw Mikrofilm [072]

HANNOVERSCHE PRESSE – (Neue Hannoversche Presse 1946-73) – Hannover, 1971- – 163r – 1 – DM12,225.00 – gw Mikro Press [072]

HANNOVERSCHE PRESSE – (Title changes: Neue Hannoversche Presse, 22 Apr 1971; Neue Presse, 2 Jun 1981) – Hannover, Germany. 1979- – ca 9r per yr – 1 – gw Mikrofilm [072]

HANNOVERSCHE VOLKSSTIMME : AUSGABE SUEDHANNOVER – (Cont by: Niedersaechsische Volksstimme, dec 3, 1948?) – Goettingen. aug 16, 1946-oct 14, 1947. jan 16, 1948-nov 10, 1949 – 2r – 1 – gw Mikrofilm [072]

HANNOVERSCHE ZEITUNG – (Cont by: Neue Hannoversche Zeitung, jan 1, 1858) – Hannover, 1832 – 1 – gw Mikrofilm [943]

HANNOVERSCHE ZEITUNG – (Title change: Neue Hannoversche Zeitung) – Hannover, Germany. 1832-1883 – 76r – 1 – gw Mikrofilm [072]

HANNOVERSCHE ZEITUNG *see*
- NIEDERSAECHSISCHE BEOBACHTER
- NIEDERSAECHSISCHE TAGESZEITUNG
- NIEDERSAECHSISCHER BEOBACHTER

HANNOVERSCHER ANZEIGER – Hannover. jul 1, 1893-jun 25, 1914. 1915-feb 27, 1943 – 191r – 1 – gw Mikrofilm [072]

HANNOVERSCHER COURIER – (Cont by: Hannoverscher Kurier, aug 16, 1914) – Hannover. 1872-aug 31, 1944 – 328r – 1 – gw Mikrofilm [072]

HANNOVERSCHER KURIER – Hanover, Germany. -d. 1 Sept 1916-12 Aug 1919. Imperfect. 12 1 2 reels – 1 – uk British Libr Newspaper [072]

HANNOVERSCHES WOCHENBLATT FUER HANDEL UND GEWERBE – Hannover. jan 2, 1869-dec 23, 1876 – 2r – 1 – gw Mikrofilm [380]

Hanoi. Institute d'Archeologie. Comite des Sciences Sociales du Viet-Nam *see* KHAO CO HOC

HANOI MOI – [Ha-noi: s.n, jan 31 1968-1982; jul-dec 1986] – 1 – us Res Libr [072]

Hanoteau, A *see* ESSAI DE GRAMMAIRE DE LA LANGUE TAMACHEK

Hanoteau, Gal Adolphe *see* LA KABYLIE ET LES COUTUMES KABYLES

Hanoum, Leila *see* LE HAREM IMPERIAL ET LES SULTANES AU 19E SIECLE...

HANOVER 1712-1895 – (Mf 1-2: Vital Records 1725-1813. Mf 2-4: Town Records 1757-1837. Mf 4-5: Vital Records 1741-1815. Mf 5-6: Town Records 1746-1811. Mf 7-13: Town Records 1727-1802. Mf 10,13: Vital Records 1712-84. Mf 14-24: Town Meetings 1802-57. Mf 25-26: Births 1727-1857. Mf 26: Marriages 1728-1857. Mf 27: Deaths & Intentions 1728-1857. Mf 28: Vitals Index 1727-1857. Mf 29: Births 1769-1846. Mf 30: Marrs & Deaths 1814-44. Mf 31: Vital Records 1844-57. Mf 32: Rebellion Records 1861-65. Mf 33-35: Militia 1840-1907. Mf 36-39: Intentions 1815-89. Mf 40: Intentions 1897-1905. Mf 41-43: Births 1843-95. Mf 43-45: Marriages 1727-1895. Mf 45-47: Deaths 1857-95) – (mf ed 1992) – 47mf – 9 – 0-87623-153-9 – us Holbrook [920]

HANOVER POST – (1897-1991.-89r) – Hanover, 1993 – 3r – 1 – cn Preston [971]

Hanrahan, Susan N *see* TAMPON LABELING AND ITS EFFECT ON FEMALE ADOLESCENTS' KNOWLEDGE OF TAMPON ABSORBENCY, KNOWLEDGE OF TOXIC SHOCK SYNDROME AND TAMPON USAGE PATTERNS

HANS AUGUST VOWINCKEL, DER DICHTER UND SOLDAT : EIN EHRENBUCH / Vowinckel, Hans August; ed by Vowinckel, Renate – Stuttgart: J Engelhorn, 1942 – 1r – 1 – us U.W. Library [430]

HANS DIETRICH GENSCHER: PAMPHLET COLLECTION – 1970-1973 – 1 reel – 1 – CSUXANS3217-B – us Hoover Inst Photo [320]

HANS FOLZ : AUSWAHL BEARBEITET VON INGEBORG SPRIEWALD / Spriewald, Ingeborg – (Includes bibliographical references) – Berlin: Akademie-Verlag, 1960 – 1r – 1 – us U.W. Library [430]

HANS GLOBKE PAMPHLET COLLECTION – 1961?-19?? – 1 reel – 1 – CSUXANR9525-B – us Hoover Inst Photo [320]

HANS HEINER ROSELIEB'S EWIGER SONNTAG / Schotte, Heinrich – Kempten: J Koesel & F Pustet, 1921 – 1r – 1 – us U.W. Library [830]

HANS LUTHER PAMPHLET COLLECTION – 1931 – 1 – CSUXANR3435-B – us Hoover Inst Photo [320]

HANS NIELSEN HAUGE OG HANS SAMTID : ET TIDSBILLEDE FRA OMKRING AAR 1800 / Bang, A C – Kristiania: Gyldendalske Boghandel Nordisk Forlag, 1910 – 2mf – us A.T.L.A. [240]

HANS ROTHFELS : EIN HISTORIKER ZWISCHEN KAISERREICH UND NATIONALSOZIALISMUS / Petters, Karl Olaf – 1995 – 2mf – 9 – DM80.00 – 3-8267-2198-5 – gw Hänsel [943]

HANS SACHS AND GOETHE : A STUDY IN METER / Burchinal, Mary Cacy – (Includes bibliographical references (p.[50]-52)) – Goettingen: Vandenhoeck & Ruprecht; Baltimore: Johns Hopkins Press, 1912 – 1 – us U.W. Library [430]

HANS SACHS UND DIE REFORMATION / Kawerau, Waldemar – Halle: Verein fuer Reformationsgeschichte, 1889. ([Schriften des Vereins fuer Reformationsgeschichte; Bd. 26]) – 1mf – us A.T.L.A. [240]

HANS SACHS UND GOETHE : 1. [UND] 2. TEIL / Wahl, Georg – (Includes bibliographical references) – Coblenz: H L Scheid, 1892 – 1r – 1 – us U.W. Library [430]

DAS HANS THOMA-BUCH : FREUNDESGABE ZU DES MEISTERS 80. GEBURTSTAGE / ed by Friedrich, Karl Josef – Leipzig: E Seemann, 1919 – 1r – 1 – us U.W. Library [750]

HANSA – Hamburg, Germany. -w. 16 Sept 1916-9 Aug 1919. 5 reels – 1 – uk British Libr Newspaper [072]

HANSARD PARLIAMENTARY DEBATES : HOUSE OF COMMONS AND HOUSE OF LORDS – (Final version. Available for every session from 1984/85) – 1984/85- – 9 – enquire for price details – uk Chadwyck [324]

HANSA-THEATER : ARTISTISCHE NACHRICHTEN – (Incl suppl) – Hamburg. aug 1896-sep 1897. feb-mar 1898. aug 1899-oct 1914. jan 1915 – 2r – 1 – gw Mikrofilm [790]

Hansen, Adolfph *see* GOETHES LEIPZIGER KRANKHEIT UND "DON SASSAFRAS"

Hansen, E C *see* DE DANSKE GJODNINGSSVAMPE

Hansen, G von *see* DIE SAMMLUNGEN INLAENDISCHER ALTERTUEMER UND ANDERER AUF DIE BALTISCHEN PROVINZEN BEZUEGLICHEN GEGENSTAENDE DES ESTLAENDISCHEN PROVINZIAL-MUSEUMS

Hansen, Gary F *see*
- PERCEPTIONS OF AGENCIES THAT MARKET COLLEGIATE EMBLEMATIC MERCHANDISE TOWARD SELECTED FACTORS RELATED TO ROYALTY INCOME
- A STUDY OF ATTITUDES TOWARD HIGH SCHOOL ACADEMICS REPORTED BY CURRENT FOOTBALL PLAYERS ENROLLING AT SELECTED BIG TEN CONFERENCE UNIVERSITIES FROM 1985 THROUGH 1989

Hansen, Maurice G *see* THE REFORMED CHURCH IN THE NETHERLANDS

Hansen, R *see* DER DAVID-JORITEN-PROZESS IN TOENNING 1642

Hanserd Knollys Society for the Publication of the Works of Early English and other Baptist Writers *see*
- PUBLICATIONS

HANSERD KNOLLYS SOCIETY MATERIALS / Baptist Missionary Society. Archives. London – Minutes, Journal and Correspondence, 1844-58. 540p – 1 – $18.90 – us Baptist [240]

HANSERECESSE : 2. ABTEILUNG / ed by Ropp, Goswin von der – Leipzig, 1876-92. Hildesheim, 1991 – 53mf – 9 – DM450,00 diazo DM500,00 silver – gw Olms [943]

HANSERECESSE : 3. ABTEILUNG / ed by Schaefer, Dietrich & Techen, Friedrich – Leipzig, 1881-1913 – 80mf – 9 – subsc: DM560.00 diazo DM640.00 silver – gw Olms [943]

HANSERECESSE – Luebeck, Abt. 1. Die Recesse und andere Akten der Hansetage, 1256-1430; Muenchen, 1870-1897. v1-8 – 142mf – 9 – 2407/2 – ne IDC [943]

HANS-GEORG GADAMER : EEN FILOSOFIE VAN HET INTERPRETEREN / Vandenbuclke, J – Brugge, 1973 – 5mf – 8 – ne Slangenburg [140]

Hansgirg, A *see* PHYSIOLOGISCHE UND ALGOLOGISCHE STUDIEN

HANSON 1779-1849 – (Mf 1T: Marriage Intentions 1820-21; Births 1779-1847. Mf 2T: Deaths 1810-42; Marriages 1820-36; Births 1818-20. Mf 3T: Births 1843-49, 1827-47. Mf 4T: Marriages & Deaths 1843-49) – (mf ed 1996) – 9 – 0-87623-261-6 – us Holbrook [920]

HANSON 1820-1900 – (Mf 1-3: Index to Births 1820-1970. Mf 4-6: Index to Marriages 1820-1970. Mf 7-9: Index to Deaths 1820-1970. Mf 10-11: Marriages 1852-91. Mf 11-13: Births 1852-91. Mf 13-15: Deaths 1852-91. Mf 16: Births 1892-1900. Mf 17: Marriages 1892-1900. Mf 18: Deaths 1892-1901) – (mf ed 1992) – 18mf – 9 – 0-87623-146-6 – us Holbrook [920]

Hanson, Kenneth C *see* THE HYMNOLOGY AND THE HYMNALS OF THE RESTORATION MOVEMENT

HANSON'S LATIN AMERICAN LETTER – Ithaca. n1555-1606 jan-dec 1975. n1764-1866 jan 1979-dec 1980 1; n1764-1815 jan-dec 1979*. n1816-1866 jan-dec 1980 5; n1764-1866 jan 1979-dec 1980* 9 – 1,5,9 – D9319 – us UMI [073]

Hanssens, J M *see* AMALARII EPISCOPI OPERA

Hanstein, Penelope *see* DISCIPLINE-BASED DANCE EDUCATION

Hantboecxken, ofte *see* CONCORDANCIE, DAT IS

HANTBOECXKEN, OFTE: CONCORDANCIE, DAT IS: DE GHELIJCKLUYDENDE PLAETSEN, DER HEYLIGER SCHRIFT, BY EEN VERGADERT – 1576. BME-337 1 – 9 – ne IDC [240]

Hanthaler, Chrysostomus *see* QUINQUAGENA SYMBOLORUM HEROICA IN...SANCTAE REGULAE BENEDICTI

HANTHAWADDY – Rangoon, Burma. 9 Apr 1950-1951; 1959-Apr 1968 – 37r – 1 – us L of C Photodup [072]

Hantke, Friedrich *see* BIOLOGISCHE VERFAHREN DES PFLANZENSCHUTZES IM ZIERPFLANZENBAU, GEZEIGT AM BEISPIEL DES EINSATZES VON RAUBMILBEN (PHYTOSEIULUS PERSIMILIS ATHIAS-HENRIOT)

HANTKENINA IN THE NANGGULAN AREA AND COLLECTION OF SMALLER FORAMINIFERA / Indonesia. Geological Survey. (Paleontology Section) – SE-6257 1. 1960 – 9 – ne IDC [560]

HANTS & BERKS GAZETTE. (BASINGSTOKE GAZETTE) – Basingstoke, England. 1878-1975 (missing 1897, 1913).-w. 109 reels – 1 – uk British Libr Newspaper [072]

Hanway, Mary Ann *see* ELLINOR; OR, THE WORLD AS IT IS

Hanyevi Sefik, Efendi *see* DIVANCE

HANYU FANGYAN CIHUI – Dictionary of Chinese Dialects. Comp. by the Department of Chinese Language and Literature, Beijing University. 6 fiches. F J33 – 9 – $4.00f – cc Microforms [480]

HANYU PINYIN BAO *see* YUYAN WENZI BAO

HANYU PINYIN XIAOBAO – China. Tabloid of Chinese Phonetic Spelling. 1983-. M D39 – 1 reel/y – 1 – $23.00r – cc Microforms [480]

HA-OLAM – Cologne, Vilna, Odessa, London, Berlin, Jersualem, 1907-1914, 1919-1950 – 834mf – 9 – J-91-25/1 – ne IDC [072]

HA-OLAM, 1907-1950 – Central Hebrew-language publication of the World Zionist Organization – 1 – us Primary [270]

'HA'OR' : HET LICHT, ORGAAN VOOR LIBERALE JODEN IN NEDERLAND – Amsterdam. v1 (1-7). 1937 – 1mf – 9 – ne IDC [073]

HA-OR – New York, N.Y., 1981; v12, no. 5 (27 Oct. 1982); v12, no. 9 (9 Feb. 1983)-v12, no. 10 (23 Feb. 1983); v12, no. 12 (23 Mar. 1983); v13, no. 7 (14 Dec. 1983)-v13, no. 8 (7 Feb. 1984); v13, no. 10-v13, no. 11; v13, no. 13 (1 May 1984) – us A.J.P.C. [270]

HA-OR – New York, N.Y., v1, no. 2 (28 Mar. 1972); v1, no. 4 (9 May 1972); v2, no. 2 (30 Nov. 1972)-v2., no. 3 (19 Dec. 1972); v2, no. 5 (7 Mar. 1973)-v8, no. 1 (7 Aug. 1978); v8, no. 10 (28 Feb. 1979); v9, no. 2 (4 Oct. 1979)-v9, no. 3 (18 Oct. 1973); v9, no. 8 (14 Feb. 1980)-v9, no. 9 (28 Feb. 1980); v9, no. 11 (17 Apr. 1980)-v10, no. 8 (25 Feb. 1981); v11, no. 1 (3 Aug. 1981); v11, no. 3 (22 Oct. 1981)-v11, no. 5 (18 Nov.) – us A.J.P.C. [270]

HA-OZAR / Fuenn, S J – Lexicon of Biblical and Mishnaic Hebrew, with explanations in Hebrew, German in Hebrew characters, and Russian, letters sh-t by S. P. Rabinowitz. 4 v. ed. Warsaw. 1912-13. BJ-412-6 1 – 9 – ne IDC [470]

HA-OZAR : LEXICON OF BIBLICAL AND MISHNAIC HEBREW, WITH EXPLANATIONS IN HEBREW, GERMAN IN HEBREW CHARACTERS, AND RUSSIAN, LETTERS SH-T BY S.P. RABINOWITZ / Fuenn, S J – Warsaw. 4v. 1912-1913 – 44mf – ne IDC [220]

HAPARANDABLADET – Haparanda, Sweden. 1882-1923; 1975- – 1 – sw Kungliga [072]

HAPARANDABLADET – Haparanda, Sweden. 1924-27; 1953-55 – 10r – 1 – sw Kungliga [072]

Hapde, Augustin *see* CELESTE ET FALDONI OU LES AMANTS DE LYON

Hapde, Augustin et al *see* L'HOMME DU DESTIN

HA-PEDAGOG – Cracow. 1903-04. BJ-291-24 1 – 9 – ne IDC [270]

HA-PELES – v. 1-5. Poltava. Berlin. 1900-04. BJ-291-17 1 – 9 – ne IDC [470]

AL HA-PEREK / Rabinovitz, A S – Warsaw. 1887. BJ-422-67 1 – 9 – ne IDC [470]

Hapgood, George *see* SOLITAIRE AND PATIENCE; SEVENTY GAMES TO TEST THE CARD PLAYER'S SKILL AND MAKE A LONELY HOUR PASS QUICKLY

Hapgood, Powers *see* IN NON-UNION MINES: THE DIARY OF A COAL DIGGER IN CENTRAL PENNSYLVANIA, AUGUST-SEPTEMBER 1921

HAPISGOH – Chicago. The Summit. 1888-99 – 1 – us A.J.P.C. [071]

HA-PISOGOH – The Summit. (New York), 1888-99 – 1 – us A.J.P.C. [071]

Happart, G *see* DICTIONARY OF THE FAVORLANG DIALECT OF THE FORMOSAN LANGUAGE

Happel, Eberhard G *see* GROESSTE DENKWUERDIGKEITEN DER WELT ODER SOGENANNTE RELATIONES CURIOSAE

Happel, Julius *see* DER EID IM ALTEN TESTAMENT

Happel, Otto *see* DAS BUCH DES PROPHETEN HABACKUK

Happer, Andrew P *see* A VISIT TO PEKING

Happy Childhood Staff *see*
- THE CHILDREN'S BIBLE (CCC141)
- CHINESE CHRISTIAN MONOGRAPH, VOLS 3-5 (CCC140)
- EVENING DRUM (CCC144)
- HAPPY CHRISTMAS STORIES (CCC142)
- HAPPY STORIES (CCC143)

HAPPY CHRISTMAS STORIES (CCC142) / ed by Happy Childhood Staff – (In Chinese) – Hong Kong: Council on Christian Literature for Overseas Chinese, 1953 – 1r – 1 – 1984-B500 – us A.T.L.A. [240]

HAPPY DAYS – (Cont by: Playmate) – Toronto: Methodist Book and Pub. House, [1886?-1906] – 9 – cn C.I.H.M. [240]

HAPPY DAYS – (Library has: v.1, no.1-v.2, no.15, 17-20, 22-40, 43-v.3, no.32, 34-v.6, no.31; May 1933-Dec. 1938) – Washington, D.C.: The Happy Days Publishing Co., 1933-1942. 10v – 1 – CSUX87-S127 – us Hoover Inst Photo [978]

HAPPY DAYS – Los Angeles, CA. 1933-1934 – 1r – 1 – $50.00 – R03294 – us Library Micro [071]

HAPPY DAYS CCC DIRECTORY – Washington, DC: Happy Days Pub Co, 1940 – us Roc Libr [030]

HAPPY HOME AND PARLOR MAGAZINE – Boston. v1-10. 1855-59. jan-jan 1860* – 1 – D4821 – us UMI [640]

HAPPY STORIES (CCC143) / ed by Happy Childhood Staff – (In Chinese) – Hong Kong: Council on Christian Literature for Overseas Chinese, 1953 – 1r – 1 – 1984-B500 – us A.T.L.A. [240]

HAQAYIQ – (Sal-i 1, shumarah-'i 3-5 (8 Rabi'al-Sani 1325-9 Jumada al-Sani 1325[8 Mar 1907-7 Jul 1901])) – Baku, 1907- – 1 reel – 1 – $25.00 – us MEDOC [950]

Haqq, Abdul *see* MA-AASAMIRU-L-UMARA

Haque, I et al *see*
- BIBLIOGRAPHY ON SOILS, FERTILIZERS, PLANT NUTRITION AND GENERAL AGRONOMY IN ETHIOPIA
- CONTRIBUTION POTENTIELLE DES LEGUMINEUSES FOURRAGERES AUX SYSTEMES AGRAIRES DE L'AFRIQUE AU SUD DU SAHARA
- POTENTIAL OF FORAGE LEGUMES IN FARMING SYSTEMS OF SUB-SAHARAN AFRICA

HARABONY – New York. N.Y. 1912 – 1 – us A.J.P.C. [071]

Harahap, Elisa Sutan *see* KAMOES INDONESIA

Harahap, M *see* PEMBUKTIAN

Harahap, P *see* NIPPON DI MASA PERANG ! KESAN RINGKAS JANG DIDAPAT SELAMA TOEROET DALAM SEKAWAN OETOESAN DJAWA MELAWAT KE NIPPON, 2603

HARAR : FORSCHUNGSREISE NACH DEN SOMAL- UND GALLA-LAENDERN OST-AFRIKAS, AUSGEFUEHRT VON DR KAMMEL VON HARDEGGER UND PROF DR PAULITSCHKE – (Nebst Beitraegen von Gunther Ritter von Beck, L Ganglbauer und Heinrich Wichmann) – Leipzig: Brockhaus, 1888 – 1 – us Res Libr [910]

HARB MECMU'ASI – Vols. 1-3, nos. 1-27 (1334) – 13mf – 9 – $52.50 – us MEDOC [949]

Harbaugh, Henry *see*
- THE FATHERS OF THE GERMAN REFORMED CHURCH IN EUROPE AND AMERICA
- THE LIFE OF REV. MICHAEL SCHLATTER

Harbaugh, Linn *see* LIFE OF THE REV. HENRY HARBAUGH, D.D.

Harbaugh, Thomas C *see* CENTENNIAL HISTORY OF TROY, PIQUA AND MIAMI COUNTY AND REPRESENTATIVE CITIZENS

Harben, H *see* A DICTIONARY OF LONDON

HARBIN GONGYE DAXUE XUEBAO – Journal of Harbin University of Technology. In Chinese but English abstracts to the main articles. F p180 – 9 – 4.00f – cc Microforms [073]

HARBIN RIBAO – Harbin Daily. 1983-. M D41 – 1 reel/y – 1 – $55.00r – cc Microforms [072]

HARBIN SEVK VE IDARESI / Der Goltz Pasa – Istanbul: Sirket-i Mertebiye Matbaasi, 1315 [1897] – $95.00 – us MEDOC [956]

HARBINGER : DEVOTED TO SOCIAL AND POLITICAL PROGRESS – New York. v1-8. jun 1845-feb 1849 – 1 – D4376 – us UMI [073]

THE HARBINGER – Montreal: Printed for the Committee by J Lovell, [1842-1843] – 9 – cn C.I.H.M. [240]

THE HARBINGER: NEW YORK (DEVOTED TO SOCIAL AND POLITICAL PROGRESS) – v. 1-5. 1845-1847 – 1 – us Princeton Micro [073]

HARBINGER OF LIGHT – 1870-1954 – 22r – 1 – at Corangamite [072]

HARBINGER OF PEACE – v1-3. 1828-31 – 11mf – 9 – $55.00 – us UPA [320]

HARBINGER OF THE MISSISSIPPI VALLEY – Frankfort. v1. mar-apr 1832 – 1 – D4582 – us UMI [073]

HARBIYE VE IHTIYAT ZABIT MEKTEBLERI TALIMAN – Istanbul: Harbiye Mektebi Matbaasi, 1928 – $27.00 – us MEDOC [956]

HARBORNE AND WEST BIRMINGHAM NEWS – England.1894; 1900-02.-w. 4 reels – 1 – uk British Libr Newspaper [072]

HARBOROUGH MAIL *see* MARKET HARBOROUGH ADVERTISER

Harbour Commissioners of Montreal *see* EXTRACTS FROM THE MINUTES...AND OTHER DOCUMENTS WITH REFERENCE TO HYDRAULIC LOTS ON MILL STREET

Harbour Commissioners of Montreal. Commission of Engineers *see* REPORT ON A GENERAL SCHEME OF IMPROVEMENTS FOR THE HARBOUR

HARBOUR GRACE STANDARD – Harbour Grace, Canada. 1863-73 – 2r – 1 – $136.00 – cn Library Assoc [971]

Harbour, SK *see* HEART RATE RESPONSES OF COLLEGIATE FEMALE VOLLEYBALL PLAYERS DURING COMPETITION

Harbrecht, Hugo *see*
- PHILIPP VON ZESEN ALS SPRACHREINIGER

HARBURGER ANZEIGEN UND NACHRICHTEN *see* HARBURGER ANZEIGER

HARBURGER ANZEIGER – (Title change: Harburger Anzeigen und Nachrichten, 21 Sep 1949) – Hamburg-Harburg, West Germany. 1976- – ca 6r per yr – 1 – gw Mikrofilm [072]

Harburger, H *see*
- DER STRAFRECHTLICHE BEGRIFF INLAND...

Harcourt, Francis V *see* HINTS TO YOUNG OFFICERS ON THE PRINCIPLES OF MILITARY LAW

Harcourt, Guy M *see* BANKING AND COMMERCIAL GUIDE

[Harcourt, W G G Y V] *see*
- ADDITIONAL LETTERS BY HISTORICUS ON SOME QUESTIONS OF INTERNATIONAL LAW
- LETTERS BY HISTORICUS ON SOME QUESTIONS OF INTERNATIONAL LAW

HARD CASH : A MATTER-OF-FACT ROMANCE / Reade, Charles L – London: Sampson Low, Son, & Marston, 1863 – 2 rolls – 1 – 1-55879-222-8 – uk Libr Preservation [830]

HARD CASH / Reade, Charles L – British Fiction Archive: Unit 2 – 9 – uk Bell [830]

HARD SAYINGS : A SELECTION OF MEDITATIONS AND STUDIES / Tyrrell, George – London; New York: Longmans, Green, 1910 – 2mf – 9 – 0-8370-8626-4 – 1986-2626 – us A.T.L.A. [240]

HARD TIMES – Washington, DC. 1969-70 – 1r – 1 – $50.00 – R05502 – us Library Micro [071]

THE HARD WHEAT BELT – Brandon, Man: Western Publ Co, v1 no 1 (Feb 1898)- – 9 – cn C.I.H.M. [910]

HARDCOPY – (Absorbed by: Digital News) – Brea. v1-7 1981-87*. v8 jan-jun 1988 1; v6-7 1986-87. v8 jan-jun 1988* 5; v3-5 apr 1983-dec 1985*. v6-8 jan 1986-jun 1988 9 – 1,5,9 – D15032 – us UMI [000]

Hardeland, A *see*
- DAJACKSCH-DEUTSCHES WOERTERBUCH
- VERSUCH EINER GRAMMATIK DER DAJACKSCHEN SPRACHE

Harden *see* EARLY LIFE AND TIMES IN BOONE COUNTY

Harden, J M *see* THE ANAPHORAS OF THE ETHIOPIC LITURGY

HARDEN MURRUMBURRAH EXPRESS – May 17 1917-Nov 4 1918; Jan 17 1929-Dec 31 1951 – 9 – at Pascoe [072]

Harden, William *see* A HISTORY OF SAVANNAH AND SOUTH GEORGIA

Hardenberg, Friedrich von *see* EIN KLEINSTAATLICHER MINISTER DES ACHTZEHNTEN JAHRHUNDERTS

Harderwijk, I van *see* BIJDRAGE TOT DE KENNIS DER SCHRIFTEN VAN DAVID JORIS

Hardesty, W S *see* REPRESENTATIVE CITIZENS OF PAULDING COUNTY

Hardgrave, Wakefield *see* THE QUESTION OF A DOMINION PROHIBITORY LAW: CONSIDERED IN ITS FINANCIAL, MORAL AND RELIGIOUS ASPECTS

Hardin *see*
- GENEALOGICAL AND PERSONAL HISTORY OF FAYETTE COUNTY
- HISTORY OF HERKIMER COUNTY

Hardin, Bayless E *see* SCOTT'S PAPERS: KENTUCKY COURT & OTHER RECORDS,

HARDIN COUNTY DEMOCRAT – Kenton, Ohio. 1875-85 – 3r – 1 – $32.50r – us Archival [071]

Hardin County. Ohio. Board of County Commissioners *see*
- COMMISSIONERS' JOURNALS
- INDEX TO JOURNALS

Hardin County. Ohio. Courthouse Building Commission *see* JOURNAL

Hardin County. Ohio. Kenton. City Safety Service Director *see* CEMETERY DEED RECORDS

Hardin County. Ohio. Pleasant Township. Board of Trustees *see* MILITARY RELIEF JOURNAL

Hardin County, Ohio. Probate Court *see*
- BIRTH RECORDS
- DEATH RECORDS
- GENERAL INDEX TO BIRTHS/DEATHS
- JOURNALS

Hardin County. Ohio. St. Paul's Evangelical Lutheran Church *see* CHURCH RECORDS

HARDIN COUNTY TIMES – Iowa Falls. Iowa. -w. 1972- – 1 – us UMI [071]

HARDIN INTELLIGENCER – Kenton, Ohio. 1844 – 1r – 1 – $32.50r – us Archival [071]

Harding, AKW *see* FACTORS INFLUENCING FAMILY USE OF HEALTH CARE SERVICES IN TAMIL NADU (INDIA) VILLAGES

Harding, C G *see* THE REPUBLICAN:...

Harding, H *see* MUSICAL ORNAMENTS, SIMPLY EXPLAINED WITH NUMEROUS EXAMPLES FROM THE WORKS OF J.S. BACH, HANDEL, CLEMENTI, CZERNY ET AL

Harding, Warren G *see*
- PAPERS
- THE WARREN G. HARDING PAPERS

Hardinge, Emma *see* MODERN AMERICAN SPIRITUALISM

HARDING'S DUBLIN IMPARTIAL NEWSLETTER – Ireland, 21,25 Jul-1 Aug 1724 – 6ft – 1 – uk British Libr Newspaper [072]

HARDING'S WEEKLY IMPARTIAL NEWSLETTER – Ireland, 23,30 Mar, 4,7 May, 1,4,8 Jun, 6 Jul, 6 Aug 1723 – 8ft – 1 – uk British Libr Newspaper [072]

Hardjowirogo, Raden *see* HISTORY OF THE WAYANG PURWA

Hardman, William *see* LIGHTS AND SHADOWS OF CHURCH HISTORY

HARDMAN'S BAPTIST CHURCH. DEKALB COUNTY. GEORGIA : CHURCH RECORDS – 1825-55 – 1 – 9.00 – us Baptist [240]

HARDNESS REDUCERS IN DRILLING : A PHYSICO-CHEMICAL METHOD OF FACILITATING THE MECHANICAL DESTRUCTION OF ROCKS DURING DRILLING – Melbourne: Council for Scientific & Industrial Research, 1948 – 1 – us Res Libr [600]

HARDSCRABBLE OR THE FALL OF CHICAGO : A TALE OF INDIAN WARFARE / Richardson, John – New York: Pollard and Moss, 1888. SEM16P261 – 1r – 5 – Can$9.00 – cn Bibl Nat [830]

HARDSCRABBLE, OR, THE FALL OF CHICAGO. / Richardson, John – New-York: Pollard & Moss, 1888. SEM105P79 – 2mf – 9 – Can$4.50 – cn Bibl Nat [830]

Hardt, Ernst *see* KOENIG SALOMO

Hardt, H von der *see* RERUM CONCILII OECUMENCI CONSTANTIENSIS

Harduin, AX. *see* REMARQUES DIVERSES SUR LA PRONONCIATION ET L'ORTHOGRAPHE

Harduinus, Johannes *see*
- ACTA CONCILIORUM ET EPISTOLAE DECRETALES AC CONSTITUTIONES
- ACTA CONCILIORUM ET EPISTOLAE DECRETALES AC CONSTITUTIONES SUMMORUM PONTIFICUM

HARDWARE – (Cont by: Canadian Hardware and Metal Merchant) – Toronto: J.B. McLean, [1888?-189-?] – 9 – cn C.I.H.M. [680]

HARDWARE AGE – (Cont: Chilton's Hardware Age. Cont by: Chilton's Hardware Age) – Radnor. v218-220. dec 1981-dec 1983 – 1,5,9 – D946.01 – us UMI [670]

HARDWARE AGE – v10- 1894- – 1,5,6,9 – us UMI [670]

HARDWARE AGE HOME IMPROVEMENT MARKET – (Cont: Hardware Age Home Improvement Marketplace) – Radnor. v232-234. jul 1995-dec 1997+ – 1,5,9 – D946.04 – us UMI [073]

HARDWARE AGE HOME IMPROVEMENT MARKET *see* HARDWARE AGE HOME IMPROVEMENT MARKETPLACE

HARDWARE AGE HOME IMPROVEMENT MARKETPLACE – (Cont: Chilton's Hardware Age. Cont by: Hardware Age Home Improvement Market) – Radnor. v231-232. aug 1994-jun 1995 – 1,5,9 – D946.03 – us UMI [073]

HARDWARE AGE HOME IMPROVEMENT MARKETPLACE *see* HARDWARE AGE HOME IMPROVEMENT MARKET

HARDWARE AND METAL – 1888-14 May 1904 – 1 – us UMI [670]

HARDWARE AND METAL – 1905-3 Nov 1945 – 1 – us UMI [670]

HARDWARE AND METAL AND APPLIANCE DEALER – v70, no.16-v72, no.1. Aug 1958-Jan 1960 – 1 – us UMI [680]

HARDWARE AND METAL AND CANADIAN MACHINIST – 21 May 1904-21 Jan 1905 – 1 – us UMI [670]

HARDWARE AND METAL AND ELECTRICAL DEALER – v57, no.23-v70, no.15. 17 Nov 1945-26 Jul 1958 – 1 – us UMI [680]

HARDWARE MERCHANDISING – (v100-106 1988-94 Can$28.00y 9) – Willowdale. v1-106. 1888-1994 – 5,9 – Price varies – cn Micromedia [380]

HARDWARE MERCHANDISING – v72, no.2. Feb 1960-Sept 1984 – 1 – us UMI [380]

HARDWARE MERCHANDISING, BUILDING SUPPLY DEALER – Aug 1985- – 1,5,6,9 – us UMI [680]

HARDWARE WORLD – Radnor. v53-60. 1956-jun 1963 – 1 – D943 – us UMI [670]

HARDWICK 1670-1849 – (Mf 1T-6T: Births 1717-1840. Mf 1T-2T,4T: Publishments 1743-90. Mf 1T-4T: Marriages 1746-88. Mf 2T-3T,6T: Deaths 1746-1833. Mf 6T-7T,9T: Marriages 1788-1844. Mf 7T-10T: Publishments 1790-1849. Mf 10T: Deaths 1834-43; Births 1800-51; Out-of-Town Marriages 1670-1799. Mf 11T: Births 1843-49. Mf 12T: Marriages & Deaths 1844-49) – (mf ed 1996) – 12mf – 9 – 0-87623-262-4 – us Holbrook [920]

HARDWICK 1735-1895 – (Mf 1-4: Town & Vital Records 1730-50. Mf 5-15: Town & Vital Records 1734-1802. Mf 16-24: Town & Vital Records 1789-1833. Mf 25-31: Vital Records 1832-51. Mf 32-41: Miscellaneous Records 1851-88. Mf 42-43: B,M,D 1843-56. Mf 44-52: B,M,D 1852-95) – (mf ed 1987) – 52mf – 9 – 0-87623-038-9 – us Holbrook [920]

Hardwick, C *see* HISTORIA MONASTERII S. AUGUSTINI CANTUARIENSIS BY THOMAS OF ELMHAM, FORMERLY MONK AND TREASURER OF THAT FOUNDATION (RS8)

Hardwick, Charles *see*
- CHRIST AND OTHER MASTERS
- A HISTORY OF THE CHRISTIAN CHURCH DURING THE REFORMATION
- A HISTORY OF THE CHRISTIAN CHURCH, MIDDLE AGE

HARDWICKE'S SCIENCE-GOSSIP: AN ILLUSTRATED MEDIUM OF INTERCHANGE AND GOSSIP FOR STUDENTS AND LOVERS OF NATURE – London, 1866-93 – 3 – us Readex [500]

Hardy *see* HISTORICAL REVIEW OF SOUTHEAST TEXAS

Hardy, A S *see* LIFE AND LETTERS OF JOSEPH HARDY NEESIMA

HARDY COUNTY NEWS – Moorefield. West Virginia. 1897-1902; 1932-1942 – 1 – us UMI [071]

Hardy E L C P *see* RECUEIL DES CRONIQUES ET ANCHIENNES ISTORIES DE LA GRANT BRETAGNE (RS39)

Hardy, E L C P *see* A COLLECTION OF CHRONICLES AND ANCIENT HISTORIES OF GREAT BRITAIN (RS40)

Hardy, Ed *see* L'ECHO MUSICAL

Hardy, Edward John *see* MR. THOMAS ATKINS

Hardy, Edwin Noah *see* THE CHURCHES AND EDUCATED MEN

Hardy, Ernest George *see* CHRISTIANITY AND THE ROMAN GOVERNMENT: A STUDY IN IMPERIAL ADMINISTRATION

HARDY FERNS: HOW I COLLECTED AND CULTIVATED THEM / Bellairs, N – London. 1865. B-7160 1 – 9 – ne IDC [580]

Hardy, George *see*
- MONOPOLY AND THE INDIVIDUAL
- SOCIETY IN CONFLICT
- THE WAY OUT FROM THE DOOM OF THF WELFARE SOCIETY

Hardy, H *see* RECUEIL DES CRONIQUES ET ANCHIENNES ISTORIES DE LA GRANT BRETAGNE (RS39)

HARDY HERALD – Hardy, NE. -w. Dec 1892; Jan 1896-May 1898, scattered issues missing; Sept 1898-Sept 1927; Mar 1931-Nov 1947; Sept 1948-Sept 1957 – 1 – us NE Hist [071]

Hardy, John *see* DOCUMENTS ILLUSTRATIVE OF ENGLISH CHURCH HISTORY

Hardy, Mary Anne Duffus *see* THROUGH CITIES AND PRAIRIE LANDS: SKETCHES OF AN AMERICAN TOUR

Hardy, MG Le *see* ETUDE SUR LA BARONNIE ET L'ABBAYE D'AUNAY-SUR-ODON

Hardy, Nathaniel *see* FIRST GENERAL EPISTLE OF ST JOHN THE APOSTLE

Hardy, R *see* A LETTER FROM A CLERGYMAN TO ONE OF HIS PARISHIONERS WHO WAS INCLINED TO TURN METHODIST;...

Hardy, T D *see*
- DESCRIPTIVE CATALOGUE OF MATERIALS RELATING TO THE HISTORY OF GREAT BRITAIN AND IRELAND TO THE END OF THE REIGN OF HENRY 7 (RS26)
- LESTORIE DES ENGLES SOLUM LA TRANSLACION MAISTRE GEFFREI GAIMAR (RS91)
- REGISTRUM PALATINUM DUNELMENSE (RS62)
- SYLLABUS OF THE DOCUMENTS..."RYMER'S FOEDERA"

Hardy, Thomas *see*
- FAR FROM THE MADDING CROWD
- A GROUP OF NOBLE DAMES...
- LATE LYRICS AND EARLIER
- LIFE'S LITTLE IRONIES
- MOMENTS OF VISION AND MISCELLANEOUS VERSES
- ORIGINAL MANUSCRIPTS AND PAPERS
- POEMS OF THE PAST AND THE PRESENT
- SATIRES OF CIRCUMSTANCE
- SELECT POEMS OF WILLIAM BARNES
- TESS OF THE D'URBERVILLES
- THE THREE WAYFARERS
- TIME'S LAUGHINGSTOCKS AND OTHER VERSES
- WESSEX POEMS AND OTHER VERSES

Hardy, W *see* A COLLECTION OF CHRONICLES AND ANCIENT HISTORIES OF GREAT BRITAIN (RS40)

Hare, Augustus John Cuthbert *see*
- BIOGRAPHICAL SKETCHES; BEING MEMORIALS OF ARTHUR PENRHYN STANLEY... HENRY ALFORD...MRS. DUNCAN STEWART, ETC
- CITIES OF SOUTHERN ITALY & SICILY

Hare, Christopher pseud *see* A QUEEN OF QUEENS AND THE MAKING OF SPAIN

Hare, George Emlen *see* VISIONS AND NARRATIVES OF THE OLD TESTAMENT

Hare, J I C *see* SMITH'S LEADING CASES

Hare, John Innes Clark *see* AMERICAN LEADING CASES: BEING SELECT DECISIONS OF AMERICAN COURTS, IN SEVERAL DEPARTMENTS OF LAW; WITH ESPECIAL REFERENCE TO MERCANTILE LAW

Hare, Julius Charles *see*
- THE VICTORY OF FAITH
- VINDICATION OF LUTHER AGAINST HIS RECENT ENGLISH ASSAILANTS...
- VINDICATION OF LUTHER AGAINST HIS RECENT ENGLISH ASSAILANTS

Hare, Thomas *see* HARE'S REPORTS

Harel, M M *see* VOLTAIRE

LE HAREM IMPERIAL ET LES SULTANES AU 19E SIECLE... / Hanoum, Leila – 6e ed. Paris: Calmann-Levy, 1925 – 1 – F163.19 – fr Armell [306]

Haren, Willem van *see* ODE SUR LA VIE HUMAINE

Harendt, Norbert *see* GEOMETRISCHE ZUORDNUNG SEQUENTIELLER ROENTGENBILDER MIT HILFE DREHUNGS- UND MASSTABSINVARIANTER BILDMUSTER-MERKMALE

HARE'S REPORTS : REPORTS OF CASES ADJUDGED IN THE HIGH COURT OF CHANCERY / Hare, Thomas – (v11 contains a general index to the whole series and "A Historical Preface") – v1-11. 1841-53. London: A Maxwell & Son/W Maxwell, 1843-58 (all publ) – 86mf – 9 – $129.00 – LLMC 95-286 – us L.L.M.C. [324]

HARFIELD AND BISHOPSTON RECORDER – Bristol, England. 1899-Jan 1931 – 12r – 1 – uk British Libr Newspaper [072]

HARFLERIMIZIN MUEDAFAASI / Bey, Alican Serif – Yeni Matbaa, 1926 – $14.00 – us MEDOC [470]

HARFORD BUSINESS LEDGER – Aberdeen. 1989-94*. 1995-97+ – 1,5,9 – D18582 – us UMI [380]

Harford, Mrs. Keister *see* WOMAN'S POSITION IN THE CHURCH

Hargrave, Francis *see* JURIDICAL ARGUMENTS AND COLLECTIONS

Hargrove, R K *see* WOMAN'S WORK IN THE CHURCH

HARIAN KAMI – Djakarta, Indonesia. Jul 1966-Jan 21 1974 – 12r – 1 – us L of C Photodup [072]

HARICIYYE NEZARETI SALNAMESI – 1302 [1885] – 8mf – 9 – $140.00 – us MEDOC [949]

HARIJAN – Poona. 1933-56. Lacking: v. 1 (1-13, 15-52); v. 2 (1-15, 18-24, 26-31, 37, 43-44, 47-52); v. 3 (1, 3-52); v. 4-6; v. 7 (1-30, 37); v. 8 (1, 12-52); v. 9 (31-52); v. 10 (4, 30-31, 33, 35, 40, 45, 48); v. 11 (6, 16, 19-52); v. 12-19. BI-121 2 – 75mf – 8 – ne IDC [073]

HARINA RAKJAT – Djakarta. Indonesia. -d. 1952-65 – 1 – us UMI [071]

Harinegnies, Michael *see* LA SOURCE

Haringer, Michael *see* VITA DEL BEATO CLEMENTE MA. HOFBAUER

Hariot, P A *see* ATLAS DES ALGUES MARINES...

Hariri *see* MAKAMAT

Harjati *see* DJAKARTA GUIDE; A YEAR-ROUND VACATION CITY

HARJEDALEN – Sveg, Sweden. 1944-78 – 30r – 1 – sw Kungliga [072]

HARJEDALEN – Sveg, Sweden. 1979- – 1 – sw Kungliga [072]

Hark, Joseph Maximillian *see* UNITY OF TRUTH IN CHRISTIANITY AND EVOLUTION

Harkavy, A *see*
- CATALOG DER HEBRAEISCHEN BIBELHANDSCHRIFTEN DER KAISERLICHEN OEFFENTLICHEN BIBLIOTHEK IN ST PETERSBURG
- NEUAUFGEFUNDENE HEBRAEISCHE BIBELHANDSCHRIFTEN
- OPISANIE RUKOPISEI SAMARITIANSKOGO PIATIKNIZHNIIA KHRANIASHCHIKHSIA V IMPERATORSKOI PUBLICHNOI BIBLIOTEKE
- ZIKKARON LE-AVRAHAM ELIYYAHU FESTSCHRIFT. A. HARKAVY

DIE HARKE – Nienburg, feb 11-dec 14 1882; jan 1-sep 23 1884; aug 22-dec 17 1885; 1886-may 31 1941; 1950-76 – 181r – 1 – gw Mikrofilm [631]

Harker, Oliver Albert *see* THREE NEEDED REFORMS IN CRIMINAL PROCEDURE: AN ADDRESS BEFORE THE ILLINOIS STATES ATTORNEYS' ASSOCIATION AT CHICAGO, DECEMBER 28TH, 1915

Harkey, Simeon W *see* THE CHURCH'S BEST STATE, OR, CONSTANT REVIVALS OF RELIGION

Harkness, Edward S *see* COLLECTION(MEXICAN AND PERUVIAN DOCUMENTS)

Harkness, Effie *see* EXCERPTS FROM HER DIARIES RELATING TO HER SERVICE WITH THE METHODIST OVERSEAS MISSION IN THE SOLOMON ISLANDS

HARLAN COUNTY DEMOCRAT – Republican City, NE. -w. Jul 1895-May 1898; Dec 1898-Jun 1902 – 1 – us NE Hist [071]

HARLAN COUNTY JOURNAL – Alma, NE. -w. Aug. 1897-Sep. 1907. Incomplete; Sep. 1907-Jan. 1915; Feb. 1920-Dec. 1921; Jan. 1924- – 1 – us NE Hist [071]

HARLAN COUNTY JOURNAL – Alma. Neb. 1897-1960 – 1 – us UMI [071]

HARLAN COUNTY JOURNAL – Alma, Nebraska, 1904-1944 weekly – 1 – $35.00r – us NE Hist [071]

Harlan, Edgar R *see* PEOPLE OF IOWA

Harlan, Henry David *see* SYLLABUS OF THE HON. HENRY D. HARLAN'S LECTURES ON THE LAW OF DOMESTIC RELATIONS

THE HARLEIAN MISCELLANY – 4 reels – 1 – $175.00 – us Trans-Media [323]

Harleian Society. London *see* PUBLICATIONS

HARLEM HEIGHTS DAILY CITIZEN – New York. Oct. 18, 1933-Jan. 24, 1934 – 1 – us NY Public [071]
HARLEM QUARTERLY – Nos. 1-4 (all publ). 1949-1950 – 2mf – 9 – $55.00 – us UPA [975]
Harlen, Wynne *see* UNESCO SOURCEBOOK FOR SCIENCE IN THE PRIMARY SCHOOL
HARLEQUIN : A JOURNAL OF THE DRAMA – London. v1-9. may-jul 1829 – 1 – D5562 – us UMI [820]
HARLEQUIN SORCERER, SELECTIONS, ARR. HARPSICHORD, VIOLIN ETC. / Arne, T A – London: John Walsh, 1752 – 1 – us Sibley [780]
Harless, Adolf von *see* DAS VERHAELTNISS DES CHRISTENTHUMS ZU CULTUR- UND LEBENSFRAGEN DER GEGENWART
Harless, G C Adolf von *see* SYSTEM OF CHRISTIAN ETHICS
Harley, Lee C *see* WRITINGS
Harlow, Rex *see* OKLAHOMA LEADERS
Harlow, William Sturtevant *see*
- DUTIES OF SHERIFFS AND CONSTABLES, AS DEFINED BY THE LAWS, AND INTERPRETED BY THE SUPREME COURT, OF THE STATE OF CALIFORNIA
- DUTIES OF SHERIFFS AND CONSTABLES PARTICULARLY UNDER THE PRACTICE IN CALIFORNIA, AND THE PACIFIC STATES AND TERRITORIES

Harman, Edward George *see* THE COUNTESSE OF PEMBROKE'S ARCADIA, EXAMINED AND DISCUSSED
Harman, J *see* THE CROOKED DISCIPLE'S REMARKS UPON THE BLIND GUIDE'S METHOD OF PREACHING FOR SOME YEARS,...
Harmand, J *see* LICHENS DE FRANCE. CATALOGUE SYSTEMATIQUE ET DESCRIPTIF, EPINAL-PARIS, 1905
Harmar, John *see* PRAXIS GRAMMATICA
Harmelin-Vivien, M *see* ICHTYOFAUNE DES RECIFS CORALLIENS DE TULEAR, MADAGASCAR: ECOLOGIE ET RELATIONS TROPHIQUES
Harmer, Peter A P *see* PATERNALISM AND SPECIAL OLYMPICS
Harmon, Ada D *see* GLEN ELLY – THE STORY OF AN OLD TOWN
Harmon, Ada D, Compiler *see* GLEN ELLY – THE STORY OF AN OLD TOWN
HARMONIA – Rivista italiana di Musica. v. 1-2. 1913-1914 – 1 – us Schnase [780]
HARMONIA BIBLICA / Walther, Michael – 1696 – 1 – us A.T.L.A. [240]
HARMONIA CANTIONUM ECCLESIASTICARUM. / Calvisius, S – 1597 – 9 – us Sibley [780]
HARMONIA LINGUARUM : THE ORIGIN, HISTORY AND COMPARISON OF LANGUAGES IN EUROPEAN PHILOLOGY FROM 1500 TO 1800 / ed by Droixhe, D – (Individual titles available. Also listed separately) – 498mf – 9 – ne IDC [400]
HARMONIA LINGUARUM QUATUOR CARDINALIUM; HEBRAICAE, GRAECAE, LATINAE ET GERMANICAE / Cruciger, G – Francoforti, 1616 – 14mf – 9 – ne IDC [470]
THE HARMONICON – 1r – 1 – $480.00 – us UMI [780]
HARMONICS OR THE PHILOSOPHY OF MUSICAL SOUNDS / Smith, R – Ed. 2. London. 1759. BP-759 1 – 9 – ne IDC [780]
HARMONICS, OR THE PHILOSOPHY OF MUSICAL SOUNDS.. / Smith, Robert – Second edition.... 1759 – 2 – us Sibley [780]
HARMONIE – Recueil litteraire publiant les oeuvres des jeunes ecrivains de langue francaise. Dir. Eugene Bure. no. 1-11. oct 1891-aout 1892. devenu: Philosophie libertaire. Harmonie. Revue sociale et litteraire. no. 12-20. sept 1892-mai 1893. Marseille – 1 – fr A.C.R.P.P. [800]
L'HARMONIE PRATIQUE.. / Roussier, Pierre-Joseph – 1775 – 9 – us Sibley [780]
HARMONIE UNIVERSELLE / Mersenne, Marin – 1636-37 – 9 – us Sibley [780]
HARMONIE UNIVERSELLE, CONTENANT LA THEORIE ET LA PRATIQUE DE LA MUSIQUE / Mersenne, Marin – P 724. 1636 – 9 – ne IDC [780]
HARMONIELEHRE / Swobada, A – Wien: [F C Beck], 1828- – 1 – us Sibley [780]
HARMONIEN / Kuehnhold, Marianne – New-York: C Schmidt, 1869 – 1r – 1 – us U.W. Library [810]
HARMONIESYSTEM IN DUALER ENTWICKLUNG / Oettingen, A J – Leipzig: W Glaser, 1860 – 1 – us Sibley [780]
HARMONISCHE SEELEN LUST MUSICALISCHER GOENNER UND FREUNDE / Kauffmann, Georg F – 1733 – 9 – us Sibley [780]
DIE HARMONISTIK IM EVANGELIENTEXT IN CODEX CANTABRIGIENSIS (T.U.U. 3-36/1A) / Vogels, H J – Leipzig, 1910 – 2mf – 9 – ne Slangenburg [240]
HARMONOLOGIA MUSICA ODER KURTZE ANLEITUNG ZUR MUSICALISCHEN COMPOSITION / Werckmeister, A – 1702 – 9 – us Sibley [780]
HARMONOLOGIA MUSICA, ODER KURTZE ANLEITUNG ZUR MUSICALISCHEN COMPOSITION / Werckmeister, A – Franckfurth. Leipzig. 1702. BP-511 1 – 9 – ne IDC [780]
HARMONY / ed by Founder of Divine Science Organization – San Francisco, CA. v6-8. Oct 1893-Sept 1896 – 1r – 1 – $50.00 – B02815b – us Library Micro [071]
HARMONY – v1-5. Oct 1894-Apr 1900 – 1 – 400.00 – us Opus [073]
HARMONY BAPTIST CHURCH. CUSSETA, NORTH CAROLINA : CHURCH RECORDS – 1840-69 – 1 – 10.26 – us Baptist [240]
HARMONY GROVE BAPTIST CHURCH. LINCOLN COUNTY. MISSOURI (EXTINCT) : CHURCH RECORDS – 1880-1912. 288p – 1 – 12.96 – us Baptist [240]
A HARMONY OF SAMUEL, KINGS AND CHRONICLES / Crockett, William D – Baker. 1957 – 9 – $12.00 – us I.R.C. [220]
THE HARMONY OF SCRIPTURE : SHOWING THE ONENESS BETWEEN THE OLD AND NEW TESTAMENT / ed by Fearnley, Thomas – London: W Poole, 1878 – 1mf – 9 – 0-8370-9143-8 – 1986-3143 – us A.T.L.A. [220]
A HARMONY OF THE GOSPELS / Robertson, A T – 1950 – 9 – $12.00 – us I.R.C. [240]
HARMONY OF THE GOSPELS (CCC234) / Luce, H W – (In Chinese) – Shanghai: Mission Publ Co, [1902] – 1r – 1 – 1984-6573 – us A.T.L.A. [220]
HARMONY OF THE LIFE OF ST PAUL ACCORDING TO THE ACTS...AND THE PAULINE EPISTLES / Goodwin, Frank J – New York: American Tract Society, 1895 – 9 – us A.T.L.A. [240]
HARMONY OF THE OLD AND NEW COVENANTS – London: Frederic Norgate, 1881. 1 fiche – 9 – us A.T.L.A. [240]
THE HARMONY OF THE REFORMED CONFESSIONS AS RELATED TO THE PRESENT STATE OF EVANGELICAL THEOLOGY : AN ESSAY DELIVERED BEFORE THE GENERAL PRESBYTERIAN COUNCIL AT EDINBURGH, JULY 4, 1877 / Schaff, Philip – New York: Dodd, Mead, 1877 – 1mf – 9 – 0-8370-8786-4 – 1986-2786 – us A.T.L.A. [240]
Harmony Society *see* RECORDS
THE HARMONY SOCIETY AT ECONOMY, PENNA / Williams, Aaron – 1866 – 1 – us A.T.L.A. [240]
HARMONY SOCIETY RECORDS, 1786-1951 / Pennsylvania Historical and Museum Commission – (With printed guide. Subgroups available: Business File: Economy Oil Company 7r $560.00. General File 2r $160.00) – 311r – 1 – $26,435.00 coll $85.00r – D3293 – us Penn Hist [360]
Harms, Craig A *see*
- INADEQUATE HYPERVENTILATION AS A DETERMINANT OF EXERCISE INDUCED HYPOXEMIA
- INFLUENCE OF BODY FAT MASS ON EXCESS POST-EXERCISE OXYGEN CONSUMPTION

Harms, H *see* GENERA SIPHONOGAMARUM
Harms, Theodor *see* DAS HOHELIED
Harms, Wolfgang *see* DER KAMPF MIT DEM FREUND ODER VERWANDTEN IN DER DEUTSCHEN LITERATUR BIS UM 1300
Harmssen, G W *see* REPARATIONEN, SOZIALPRODUKT, LEBENSSTANDARD; VERSUCH EINER WIRTSCHAFTSBILANZ
Harn, Edith Muriel *see* WIELAND'S NEUER AMADIS
Harnack, Adolf von *see*
- DIE ACTEN DES KARPUS, DES PAPYLUS UND DER AGATHONIKE (T.U.U. 1-3/4B)
- THE ACTS OF THE APOSTLES
- DIE ALTERCATIO SIMONIS JUDAEI ET THEOPHILI CHRISTIANI UND DIE ACTA ARCHELAI UND DAS DIATERSSARON TATIANS (T.U.U. 1-1/3)
- ANALECTA ZUR AELTESTEN GESCHICHTE DES CHRISTENTUMS IN ROM (T.U.U. 2-28/2B)
- DER ANGEBLICHE EVANGELIENKOMMENTAR DES THEOPHILIUS VON ANTIOCHIEN (T.U.U. 1-1/4B)
- ANTWORT AUF DIE STREITSCHRIFT D. CREMERS, ZUM KAMPF UM DAS APOSTOLIKUM
- DIE APOSTELGESCHICHTE
- THE APOSTLES' CREED
- EINE BISHER NICHT ERKANNTE SCHRIFT DES PAPSTES SIXTUS 2 (T.U.U. 1-13/1A)
- EINE BISHER NICHT ERKANNTE SCHRIFT NOVATIANS (T.U.U. 1-13/4B)
- BRUCHSTUECKE DES EVANGELIUMS UND DER APOKALYPSE DES PETRUS (T.U.U. 1-9/2)
- CHRISTENTUM UND DIE GESCHICHTE
- CHRISTIANITY AND HISTORY
- DE APELLIS GNOSI MONARCHICA
- DIODOR VAN TARSUS
- DREI WENIG BEACHTETE CYPRIANISCHE SCHRIFTEN UND DIE "ACTA PAULI" (T.U.U. 2-19/3B)
- DAS EDICT DES ANTONIUS PIUS (T.U.U. 1-13/4A)
- DIE ENTSTEHUNG DES NEUEN TESTAMENTS UND DIE WICHTIGSTEN FOLGEN DER NEUEN SCHOEPFUNG
- DAS EVANGELIENFRAGMENT VON FAJJUM (T.U.U. 1-5/4B)
- DER GEFAELSCHTE BRIEF DES BISCHOFS THEONAS AN DEN OBERKAMMERHERRN LUCIAN (T.U.U. 2-24/3C)
- DIE GRIECHISCHE UEBERSETZUNG DES APOLOGETICUS TERTULLIAN'S (T.U.U. 1-8/4A)
- DIE GWYNN'SCHEN CAJUS UND HIPPOLYTUS-FRAGMENTE (T.U.U. 1-6/3C)
- DIE HYPOTIPOSEN DES THEOGNOST (T.U.U. 2-24/3B)
- IST DIE REDE DES PAULUS IN ATHEN EIN URSPRUENGLICHER BESTANDTEIL DER APOSTELGESCHICHTE (T.U.U. 3-39/1A)
- JUDENTUM UND JUDENCHRISTENTUM IM JUSTINS DIALOG MIT TRYPHO (T.U.U. 3-39/1B)
- EIN JUEDISCH-CHRISTLICHES PSALMBUCH AUS DEM ERSTEN JAHRHUNDERT (T.U.U. 3-35/4)
- DER KETZER-KATALOG DES BISCHOFS MARUTA VON MAIPHERKAT (T.U.U. 2-19/1B)
- DER KIRCHENGESCHICHTLICHE ERTRAG DER EXEGETISCHEN ARBEITEN DES ORIGENES
- KRITIK DES NEUEN TESTAMENTS VON EINEM GRIECHISCHEN PHILOSOPHEN DES 3. JAHRHUNDERTS (T.U.U. 3-37/4)
- DAS LEBEN CYPRIANS VON PONTIUS
- DIE LEHRE DER ZWOELF APOSTEL (T.U.U. 1-2/1.2.)
- LUKAS DER ARZT DER VERFASSER DES DRITTEN EVANGELIUMS UND DER APOSTELGESCHICHTE
- MARCION
- MEDICINISCHES AUS DER AELTESTEN KIRCHENGESCHICHTE (T.U.U. 1-8/4B)
- MILITIA CHRISTI
- DAS MOENCHTUM, SEINE IDEALE UND SEINE GESCHICHTE
- MONASTICISM
- NEUE STUDIEN ZU MARCION (T.U.U. 3-44/4)
- DAS NEUE TESTAMENT UM DAS JAHR 200
- NEUE UNTERSUCHUNGEN ZUR APOSTELGESCHICHTE UND ZUR ABFASSUNGSZEIT DER SYNOPTISCHEN EVANGELIEN
- NEW TESTAMENT STUDIES. 1: LUKE THE PHYSICIAN
- PATRISTISCHE MISCELLEN (T.U.U. 2-20/3B)
- DIE PFAFF'SCHEN IRENAEUS-FRAGMENTE ALS FAELSCHUNGEN PFAFFS NACHGEWIESEN
- DIE PFAFF'SCHEN IRENAEUS-FRAGMENTE ALS FAELSCHUNGEN PFAFFS (T.U.U. 2-20/3A)
- DER PSEUDOCYPRIANISCHE TRACTAT DE ALEATORBUS (T.U.U. 1-5/1)
- DER PSEUDOCYPRIANISCHE TRAKTAT DE SINGULARITATE CLERICORUM
- DIE QUELLEN DER SOGENANNTEN APOSTOLISCHEN KIRCHENORDNUNG (T.U.U. 1-2/5)
- DER SCHOLIEN-KOMMENTAR DAS ORIGENES ZUR APOKALYPSE JOHANNIS (T.U.U. 3-38/3)
- SIEBEN NEUE BRUCHSTUECKE DER SYLLOGISMEN DES APELLES (T.U.U. 1-6/3B)
- DIE TERMINOLOGIE DER WIEDERGEBURT UND VERWANDTER ERLEBNISSE IN DER AELTESTEN KIRCHE (T.U.U. 3-42/3B)
- UEBER DAS GNOSTISCHE BUCH PISTIS-SOPHIA; BROD UND WASSER, DIE EUCHARISTISCHEN ELEMENTE BEI JUSTIN
- UEBER DAS GNOSTISCHE BUCH PISTIS-SOPHIA. BROT UND WASSER
- UEBER DEN DRITTEN JOHANNESBRIEF (T.U.U. 1-15/3B)
- UEBER VERLORENE BRIEFE UND ACTENSTUECKE DIE SICH AUS DER CYPRIANISCHEN BRIEFSAMMLUNG ERMITTELN LASSEN (T.U.U. 2-23/2A)
- DIE UEBERLIEFERUNG DER GRIECHISCHEN APOLOGETEN (T.U.U. 1-1/1.2.)
- DER VORWURF DES ATHEISMUS IN DEN DREI ERSTEN JAHRHUNDERTEN (T.U.U. 2-28/4A)
- DAS WESEN DES CHRISTENTUMS
- WHAT IS CHRISTIANITY?: SIXTEEN LECTURES
- DIE ZEIT DES IGNATIUS UND DIE CHRONOLOGIE DER ANTIOCHENISCHEN BISCHOEFE BIS TYRANNUS
- ZUR ABERCIUS-INSCHRIFT (T.U.U. 1-12/4B)
- ZUR QUELLENKRITIK DER GESCHICHTE DES GNOSTICISMUS
- ZUR UEBERLIEFERUNGSGESCHICHTE DER ALTCHRISTLICHEN LITTERATUR (T.U.U. 1-12/1B)

Harnack, T *see*
- DIE KIRCHE, IHR AMT, IHR REGIMENT
- LUTHERS THEOLOGIE
- PRAKTISCHE THEOLOGIE

HARNEY COUNTY AMERICAN – Burns, OR. -w. 13 Dec 1935-27 Mar 1942. 2 rolls – 1 – us U.O. Library [071]
Harney, Richard J *see* HISTORY OF WINNEBAGO COUNTY
HARNEY TIMES – Harney OR. July 29 1893 – 1 – us U.O. Library [071]
HARNEY VALLEY ITEMS – Burns, OR. -w. 16 Feb 1887-26 Dec 1903. 1 roll – 1 – us U.O. Library [071]
Harnier, J A von *see* DIE STELLUNG AEGYPTENS SEIT 1922
Harnisch, Kaethe *see* DEUTSCHE MALERERZAEHLUNGEN
Harnsberger, R Scott et al *see* POPULAR CULTURE IN LIBRARIES
HAROLD : A DRAMA / Tennyson, Alfred, Lord – London: H.S. King, 1877 – 1 roll – 1 – 1-55879-556-1 – uk Libr Preservation [820]
Harold, B de *see* CATALOGUS COLEOPTERORUM HUCUSQUE DESCRIPTORUM SYNONYMICUS ET SYSTEMATICUS
THE HAROLD JANTZ COLLECTION OF GERMAN BAROQUE LITERATURE – From late 1500s to early 1700s – 1 – us Primary [800]
HAROLD THE DAUNTLESS : A POEM IN SIX CANTOS / Scott, Walter – London: Longman, Hurst, Rees, Orme, and Brown; Edinburgh: Archibald Constable, 1817 – 1 roll – 1 – 1-55879-664-9 – uk Libr Preservation [810]
HARP – Montreal. v1 2 5 7. 1874-82 – 5 – Can$100.00 – cn Micromedia [073]
THE HARP – Dublin, Ireland.1908-Jun 1910 – 1 – ie Microforms [072]
THE HARP – Ireland.24 Mar-7 Jul 1917 – 1 – ie Microforms [072]
THE HARP – Montreal, Canada. mai 1874-v6 n12. oct 1881 – 2r – 1 – Can$40.00r – cn Can Microfilming [073]
THE HARP OF ISRAEL: TO MEET THE LOUD ECHO IN THE WILDS OF AMERICA / Livermore, Harriet – 1835 – 9 – us A.T.L.A. [240]
HARPE DAVIDS – Rotterdam, 1932. v1(1-6) – 1mf – 9 – J-261-41/1 – ne IDC [943]
Harpell, J J *see* THE INSTRUCTOR
HARPENDEN ADVERTISER – Harpenden, England. 1976- – 86+ r – 1 – uk British Libr Newspaper [072]
HARPER, ALEXANDER, FAMILY PAPERS MS 3231 – (Letters, financial accounts, business files, legal documents, military records, and other documents related to the business and personal interest of the Harper family, early settlers of Ashtabula County, Ohio) – Ashtabula, 1755-1935 – 24r – 1 – us Western Res [920]
Harper, Andrew *see*
- THE BOOK OF DEUTERONOMY
- THE SONG OF SOLOMON

Harper, B *see* POST-BIBLICAL HEBREW LITERATURE, AN ANTHOLOGY
HARPER COUNTY TIMES – Harper. Kan. -w. 1878-85 – 1 – us UMI [071]
Harper, Elizabeth *see* DELAYED ONSET MUSCLE SORENESS AND DAMAGE IN RELATION TO ELECTROMYOGRAPHIC ACTIVITY DURING CONCENTRIC AND ECCENTRIC CONTRACTION

Harper, F A *see*
- LIBERTY- A PATH TO ITS RECOVERY
- WHY WAGES RISE

Harper, Frances Ellen Watkins *see* SELECTED WORKS
Harper, J Wilson *see* CHRISTIAN ETHICS AND SOCIAL PROGRESS
Harper, John Murdoch *see*
- CHAMPLAIN'S TOMB
- THE HISTORY OF NEW BRUNSWICK AND THE OTHER MARITIME PROVINCES
- THE HISTORY OF THE MARITIME PROVINCES

Harper, Robert Francis *see* ASSYRIAN AND BABYLONIAN LITERATURE
Harper, Robert Goodloe *see* THE ROBERT GOODLOE HARPER PAPERS
Harper, Samuel Northrup *see* CIVIC TRAINING IN SOVIET RUSSIA
Harper, William Rainey *see*
- ELEMENTS OF HEBREW SYNTAX BY AN INDUCTIVE METHOD
- INTRODUCTORY HEBREW METHOD AND MANUAL
- OLD TESTAMENT AND SEMITIC STUDIES IN MEMORY OF W.R. HARPER
- PRIESTLY ELEMENT IN THE OLD TESTAMENT
- THE PROPHETIC ELEMENT IN THE OLD TESTAMENT
- THE STORIES OF GENESIS
- THE UTTERANCES OF AMOS

HARPER'S – (v. 234- 1967- 5,6. v. 240- 1970- 9) – v. 1- 1850- – 1 – us UMI [073]
HARPER'S – (With cum index v1-70 1850-85 1. Absorbed: International Monthly Magazine of Literature, Science, and Art 1852. Former titles: harper's New Monthly Magazine jun 1850-nov 1900. Harper's Monthly Magazine dec 1900-may 1939. Harper's Magazine jun 1939-aug 1976) – New York. v1-295. jun 1850-dec 1997+ 1,9; v234-295 jan 1967-dec 1997+ 5 – 1,5,9 – D52 – us UMI [073]
HARPER'S BAZAAR – v1- 1868- – 1,5,6,9 – us UMI [073]
HARPER'S CASES IN EQUITY / South Carolina. Supreme Court – (A Pre-NRS title) – 1v. 1824 (all publ) – 3mf – 9 – $4.50 – LLMC 94-027 – us L.L.M.C. [340]
HARPER'S LAW REPORTS / South Carolina. Supreme Court – (A Pre-NRS title) – 1v. 1823-1831 (all publ) – 7mf – 9 – $10.50 – LLMC 94-015 – us L.L.M.C. [340]
HARPER'S MAGAZINE – v. 1-138. 1850-1919 – 1,5,6 – us Princeton Micro [073]
HARPER'S MAGAZINE *see* HARPER'S
HARPER'S MONTHLY MAGAZINE *see* HARPER'S
HARPER'S NEW MONTHLY MAGAZINE *see* HARPER'S
HARPER'S PICTORIAL HISTORY OF THE GREAT REBELLION / Guernsey, Alfred Hudson & Alden, Henry M – 2v. 1866-68 – 1r – 1 – us Ross [976]
HARPER'S PICTORIAL HISTORY OF THE WAR WITH SPAIN : WITH AN INTRODUCTION BY MAJOR-GENERAL NELSON A MILES – (Also: Harper's History of the War in the Philippines, ed by Marrion Wilcox) – 1899-1900 – 1r – 1 – us Ross [977]
HARPER'S WEEKLY – 1-62. 1857-1916 – 1 – us UMI [073]
HARPER'S WEEKLY – A Journal of Civilization. New York. v. 1-62. 1857-May 13 1916 and Index 1857-1887 – 1 – us NY Public [073]
HARPER'S WEEKLY – New York. v1-62. 1857-1916; index 1857-87 – 50r – 1 – us Ross [071]
HARPER'S WEEKLY – New York. v64-65. jan 1975-sep 1976 – 1 – D10344 – us UMI [073]
HARPER'S WEEKLY – v. 1-62. 1857-1916 – 1 – us Princeton Micro [073]
HARPER'S WEEKLY JOURNAL OF CIVILIZATION – v1-62. 1857-1916 – 9 – 1300.00 – us Opus [073]
L'HARRACH – Organe politique, economique, litteraire, scientifique, industriel, agricole et financier. no. 1-12. Alger. oct 1921-janv 1922 – 1 – fr A.C.R.P.P. [073]
Harrah, Charles Clark *see* THE ROAD
Harrelson, Gary L *see* PREDICTORS OF SUCCESS ON THE NATIONAL ATHLETIC TRAINERS ASSOCIATION CERTIFICATION EXAMINATION
HARRIMAN HERALD – Sparks, NV. Feb-Mar 1904 – 1r – 1 – $50.00 – U04747 – us Library Micro [071]
Harrington, E *see* STATISTICS OF THE MANUFACTURES AND COMMERCE OF LAKE MEMPHREMAGOG
Harrington, Grant W *see* ANNALS OF BROWN COUNTY
Harrington, J B *see* CEREAL BREEDING PROCEDURES
HARRIS AND GILL'S LAW REPORTS / Maryland. Court of Appeals – (A Pre-NRS title) – v1-2. 1826-29 (all publ) – 12mf – 9 – $18.00 – LLMC 84-148 – us L.L.M.C. [340]
HARRIS AND JOHNSON'S LAW REPORTS / Maryland. Court of Appeals – (A Pre-NRS title) – v1-7. 1800-1826 (all publ) – 48mf – 9 – $72.00 – LLMC 90-301 – us L.L.M.C. [340]
HARRIS AND MCHENRY'S LAW REPORTS / Maryland. Court of Appeals – (A Pre-NRS title) – v1-4. 1658-1799 (all publ) – 8mf – 9 – $36.00 – LLMC 84-146 – us L.L.M.C. [340]
Harris, Arthur Merton *see* LETTERS TO A YOUNG LAWYER
Harris, Arthur Travers *see* BOMBER OFFENSIVE
Harris, Carrie Jenkins *see*
- CYRIL WHYMAN'S MISTAKE
- MR. PERKINS OF NOVA SCOTIA, OR, THE EUROPEAN ADVENTURES OF A WOULD-BE ARISTOCRAT
- A ROMANTIC ROMANCE

Harris, Charles L *see* HARRIS' PUBLIC LAND GUIDE
Harris, Edward *see* UNITED EMPIRE LOYALISTS
Harris, George Emrick *see* A TREATISE ON THE LAW OF IDENTIFICATION, A SEPARATE BRANCH OF THE LAW OF EVIDENCE
Harris, J Henry *see* ROBERT RAIKES
Harris, J R *see*
- THE APOLOGY OF ARISTIDES ON BEHALF OF THE CHRISTIANS, FROM A SYRIAC MS
- A STUDY OF CODEX BEZAE

Harris, J Rendel *see*
- HERMAS IN ARCADIA
- UNION WITH GOD

Harris, James *see*
- HERMES, OR A PHILOSOPHICAL INQUIRY CONCERNING UNIVERSAL GRAMMAR
- HERMES OU RECHERCHES PHILOSOPHIQUES SUR LA GRAMMAIRE UNIVERSELLE
- HERMES:OR, A PHILOSOPHICAL INQUIRY CONCERNING LANGUAGE AND UNIVERSAL GRAMMAR
- PHILOLOGICAL INQUIRIES

Harris, James Bowmar *see* A DIGEST OF MISSISSIPPI RAILWAY DECISIONS FROM VOL. 1 TO AND INCLUDING VOL. 71, MISSISSIPPI REPORTS
Harris, James E *see* AN X-RAY ATLAS OF THE ROYAL MUMMIES
Harris, James Rendel *see*
- BIBLICAL FRAGMENTS FROM MOUNT SINAI
- THE CODEX SANGALLENSIS
- THE DIATESSARON OF TATIAN: A PRELIMINARY STUDY
- FURTHER RESEARCHES INTO THE HISTORY OF THE FERRAR-GROUP
- MEMORANDA SACRA
- ON THE ORIGIN OF THE FERRAR-GROUP
- THE ORIGIN OF THE LEICESTER CODEX OF THE NEW TESTAMENT

Harris, Johanna L *see* THE DEVELOPMENT OF COMPETENCY GUIDELINES FOR RIDING INSTRUCTORS AND EQUESTRIAN COACHES
Harris, John *see* BRITANNIA; OR, THE MORAL CLAIMS OF SEAMEN STATED
Harris, John Andrews *see*
- THE CALVINISTIC DOCTRINE OF ELECTION AND REPROBATION NO PART OF ST PAUL'S TEACHINGS
- PRINCIPLES OF AGNOSTICISM APPLIED TO EVIDENCES OF CHRISTIANITY

Harris, John Reese *see* INDUSTRIAL ENTREPRENEURSHIP IN NIGERIA
Harris, John T *see* WEST VIRGINIA LEGISLATIVE HANDBOOK AND MANUAL AND OFFICIAL REGISTER
Harris, Joseph S *see* AUTOBIOGRAPHY
Harris, Kenneth E *see* INDEX TO THE JOURNALS OF THE CONTINENTAL CONGRESS, 1774-1789
Harris, M *see* THE ENGLISH LEPIDOPTERA: OR, THE AURELIAN'S POCKET COMPANION
Harris, Malcolm H *see* HISTORY OF LOUISA COUNTY
Harris, Marjorie M *see* BASIC SWIMMING ANALYZED
Harris, Mattie Anstice *see* GLOSSARY OF THE WEST SAXON GOSPELS
Harris, Michael B *see* VITAMIN E SUPPLEMENTATION, DELAYED-ONSET MUSCULAR SORENESS, MUSCLE TISSUE DAMAGE AND LIPID PEROXIDATION
Harris, N *see* PROCEEDINGS AND ORDINANCES OF THE PRIVY COUNCIL OF ENGLAND
Harris, P G *see* SOKOTO PROVINCIAL GAZETTEER
Harris, Phil *see* REPORTING SOUTHERN AFRICA
HARRIS' PUBLIC LAND GUIDE : A COMPILATION OF PUBLIC LAND LAWS AND DEPARTMENTAL REGS. AS OF JULY 1, 1911 / Harris, Charles L – Chicago: Peterson, 1912 – 8mf – 9 – $12.00 – LLMC 82-101-7 – us L.L.M.C. [340]
Harris, Robert Jennings *see* THE JUDICIAL POWER OF THE UNITED STATES
Harris, Samuel *see* THE MAXIM FOR THE TIMES
Harris, Shane T *see* THE EFFECT OF ULTRASOUND ON TEMPERATURE RISE IN THE PREHEATED TRICEPS SURAE MUSCLE GROUP
Harris, Thomas *see* MODERN ENTRIES, ADAPTED TO THE AMERICAN COURTS OF JUSTICE.
Harris, Thomas Lake *see* TRUTH AND LIFE IN JESUS
Harris, W *see* DE MORBIS ACUTIS INFANTUM
Harris, William Richard *see* THE CATHOLIC CHURCH IN THE NIAGARA PENINSULA, 1626-1895
Harris, William Torrey *see* CONCORD LECTURES ON PHILOSOPHY
Harris, Z S *see*
- DEVELOPMENT OF THE CANAANITE DIALECTS
- GRAMMAR OF THE PHOENECIAN LANGUAGE

HARRISBURG BULLETIN – Harrisburg, OR. -w. 1 Aug 1901-3 Sep 1914; 6 Nov 1925-. – 1 – us U.O. Library [071]
HARRISBURG BULLETIN AND COMMONWEALTH – Harrisburg OR. Jan 4 1917-Oct 29 1925 – 1 – us U.O. Library [071]
HARRISBURG CHRONICLE – Harrisburg, PA., 1836 – 13 – $25.00r – us I.M.R. [071]
HARRISBURG COURIER – Harrisburg, PA. 1903-42. 27 rolls – 13 – $25.00r – us I.M.R. [071]
HARRISBURG DAILY TELEGRAPH – Harrisburg, PA., 1866-1915 – 13 – $25.00r – us I.M.R. [071]
HARRISBURG GUIDE – Harrisburg, PA. -w 1948 – 13 – $25.00r – us I.M.R. [071]
HARRISBURG HOME NEWS – Harrisburg, PA. -w 1948-1949 – 13 – $25.00r – us I.M.R. [071]
HARRISBURG INDEPENDENT PRESS – Harrisburg, PA. 1972-1975 – 2r – 1 – $100.00 – R04991 – us Library Micro [071]
HARRISBURG STAR INDEPENDENT – Harrisburg, PA., 1877-1976 – 13 – $25.00r – us I.M.R. [071]
HARRISBURG TELEGRAPH – Harrisburg, PA., 1866-1902 – 13 – $25.00r – us I.M.R. [071]
HARRISBURG WEEKLY TELEGRAPH – Harrisburg, PA., 1944-1948 – 13 – $25.00r – us I.M.R. [071]
HARRISMITH NEWS (CHRONICLE) – Harrismith, South Africa. 1899-1901 – 1 – sa State Libr [072]
Harrison *see* SURNAMES OF THE UNITED KINGDOM
Harrison, A H W et al *see* THE METHODIST CHURCH 1090 ITS ORIGIN, DIVISIONS AND REUNION
Harrison, Alexander James *see*
- ASCENT OF FAITH, OR, THE GROUNDS OF CERTAINTY IN SCIENCE AND RELIGION
- CHURCH IN RELATION TO SCEPTICS: A CONVERSATIONAL GUIDE TO EVIDENTIAL WORK
- PROBLEMS OF CHRISTIANITY AND SCEPTICISM: LESSONS FROM TWENTY YEARS EXPERIENCE

HARRISON AND HODGIN'S UPPER CANADA MUNICIPAL REPORTS / Ontario. Canada – 1v. 1845-52 (all publ) – 9mf – 9 – $13.50 – LLMC 81-060 – us L.L.M.C. [340]
Harrison, Benjamin *see* PAPERS
Harrison, Cynthia *see*
- CREATING THE FEDERAL JUDICIAL SYSTEM
- THE FEDERAL APPELLATE JUDICIARY IN THE 21ST CENTURY
- WOMEN IN NATIONAL POLITICS

Harrison, F *see* ON JURISPRUDENCE...
Harrison, Frederic *see*
- THE NATURE AND REALITY OF RELIGION: A CONTROVERSY BETWEEN...HARRISON AND...SPENCER
- THE RELIGION OF INHUMANITY
- TENNYSON, RUSKIN, MILL AND OTHER LITERARY ESTIMATES

HARRISON GRAY OTIS PAPERS, 1691-1870 / Otis, Harrison G – Massachusetts Historical Society – 11r – 1 – $845.00 – us UMI [920]
Harrison, Mrs J W *see*
- A.M. MACKAY
- THE STORY OF THE LIFE OF MACKAY OF UGANDA

Harrison, Maine.Harrison Baptist Church *see* RECORDS
Harrison, Maria E G *see* THE BIOMECHANICAL EFFECTS OF PROLOTHERAPY ON TRAUMATIZED ACHILLES TENDONS OF MALE RATS
HARRISON PRESS-JOURNAL – Harrison, NE. -w. Sept 1888-Jan 1905 – 1 – us NE Hist [071]
Harrison, Ralph *see* INSTITUTES OF ENGLISH GRAMMAR
Harrison, Robert *see* OUTLINES OF GERMAN LITERATURE
HARRISON SUN – Harrison, NE. -w. May 1900 to date – 1 – us NE Hist [071]
Harrison, Susie Frances *see* PINE, ROSE AND FLEUR DE LIS
Harrison, W *see* MINUTES OF VOYAGE, 1830-1
Harrison, W P *see* THE GOSPEL AMONG THE SLAVES
Harrison, William *see* HARRISON'S DESCRIPTION OF ENGLAND IN SHAKESPERE'S YOUTH
Harrison, William Henry *see* PAPERS
HARRISON-BUNDY FILES RELATING TO THE DEVELOPMENT OF THE ATOMIC BOMB, 1942-1946 / U.S. Office of the Chief of Engineers – RG 77. M1108. 9 rolls – 1 – us Nat'l Archives [355]
HARRISON'S DESCRIPTION OF ENGLAND IN SHAKESPERE'S YOUTH / Harrison, William – 2nd and 3rd books of his description of Britaine and England. Ed. from first 2 eds. of Holinshed's Chronicle...1577, 1587, by Frederick J. Furnivall. London: Chatto & Windus, 1908. 427p – 1 – us U.W. Library [941]
HARRISON'S REPORTS : A MOTION-PICTURE REVIEWING SERVICE BY A FORMER EXHIBITOR – New York. v1-44. 1919-62 – 7r – 1 – us Ross [790]
Harrisse, Henry *see*
- BIBLIOTHECA VETUSTISSIMA
- DECOUVERTE ET EVOLUTION CARTOGRAPHIQUE DE TERRE NEUVE ET DES PAYS CIRCONVOISINS 1497-1501-1769: ESSAIS..
- GASPAR CORTE-REAL: LA DATE EXACTE DE SA DERNIERE EXPEDITION AU NOUVEAU MONDE: D'APRES DEUX DOCUMENTS INEDITS..
- JEAN ET SEBASTIEN CABOT: LEUR ORIGINE ET LEURS VOYAGES, ETUDE D'HISTOIRE CRITIQUE; SUIVIE D'UNE CARTOGRAPHIE, D'UNE BIBLIOGRAPHIE ET D'UNE CHRONOLOGIE DES VOYAGES...1497 A 1550..
- JOHN CABOT, THE DISCOVERER OF NORTH AMERICA AND SEBASTIAN, HIS SON: A CHAPTER OF THE MARITIME HISTORY OF ENGLAND UNDER THE TUDORS, 1496-1557

Harrisson, Thomas Harnett *see* THE PEOPLES OF SARAWAK
HARROGATE FIRST BAPTIST CHURCH. HARROGATE, TENNESSEE : CHURCH RECORDS – 1946-76 – 1 – 37.44 – us Baptist [240]
Harrouff, George *see* ACCOUNT BOOKS AND MISCELLANEOUS PAPERS
HARROW GAZETTE – London. -m. Apr 1867-Dec 1870. (40 ft) – 1 – uk British Libr Newspaper [072]
HARROW MIDWEEK – London, UK. 1980-82. -w. 4 1/2 reels – 1 – uk British Libr Newspaper [072]
HARROW NEWS – London. -w. 24 Apr 1925-19 Feb 1926. (1 reel) – 1 – uk British Libr Newspaper [072]
HARROW OBSERVER *see* WEALDSTONE HARROW AND WEMBLEY OBSERVER
HARROW PRESS – (Harrow and Wealdstone Press). London. -w. 28 Oct 1892-16 Jul 1897. (4 reels) – 1 – uk British Libr Newspaper [072]

HARROW & WEALDSTONE NEWS – London, England. -w. 1 May 1907-27 July 1910. 1 reel – 1 – uk British Libr Newspaper [072]
HARROWING OF HELL = DAS ALTENGLISCHEN SPIEL VON CHRISTI HOLLENFAHRT / ed by Mall, E – Wuerzburg. 187-? – 1 – us Res Libr [820]
HARROWSMITH – (1985- . 5,6,9) – v1- . 1976- – 1 – us UMI [630]
HARROWSMITH – (Cont by: Harrowsmith Country Life at v19 no 3 1994/95) – Camden East. v1-19. 1976/77-1994/95 – 9 – Can$28.00y – cn Micromedia [073]
HARROWSMITH *see* HARROWSMITH COUNTRY LIFE
HARROWSMITH COUNTRY LIFE – (Cont: Harrowsmith at v19 no 3 1994) – v19. 1994/95 – 9 – Can$28.00y – cn Micromedia [073]
Harroy, Jean-Paul *see* AFRIQUE, TERRE QUI MEURT
HARRY BRIDGES COLLECTION : PAMPHLETS, CLIPPINGS, LETTERS – San Francisco Public Library – 1r – 1 – $50.00 – B40301 – us Library Micro [920]
HARRY HEATHCOTE OF GANGOIL : A TALE OF AUSTRALIAN BUSH LIFE / Trollope, Anthony – London: S. Low, Marston, Low, & Searle, 1874 – 1 roll – 1 – 1-55879-705-X – uk Libr Preservation [830]
Harry, Myriam *see*
- RADAME
- RANAVALO ET SON AMANT BLANC
- ROUTES MALGACHES

THE HARRY S. TRUMAN ORAL HISTORIES COLLECTION – (With printed guide) – 627mf – 9 – $4,485.00 – 1-55655-215-7 – us UPA [975]
HARRYDAPOSTEN – Harryda, Sweden. 1984- – 1 – sw Kungliga [072]
Harsha, David A *see*
- THE CHRISTIAN'S PRESENT FOR ALL SEASONS, CONTAINING DEVOTIONAL THOUGHTS OF EMINENT DIVINES FROM JOSEPH HALL TO WILLIAM JAY
- THE HEAVENLY TOKEN
- LIFE OF PHILIP DODDRIDGE, D.D.; WITH NOTICES OF SOME OF HIS CONTEMPORARIES AND SPECIMENS OF HIS STYLE
- LIFE OF REV. GEORGE WHITEFIELD
- LIFE OF THE REV. JAMES HERVEY
- NOTED LIVING ALBANIANS AND STATE OFFICIALS
- WANDERINGS OF A PILGRIM

Harsha, William J *see* STORY OF IOWA
Harsha, William Justin *see* SABBATH-DAY JOURNEYS
Harshberger, J W *see* THE BOTANISTS OF PHILADELPHIA AND THEIR WORK
Hart, Albert Bushnell *see*
- SALMON PORTLAND CHASE
- SLAVERY AND ABOLITION, 1831-1841

Hart, Amos Winfield *see* DIGEST OF DECISIONS OF LAW AND PRACTICE IN THE PATENT OFFICE AND THE UNITED STATES AND STATE COURTS IN PATENTS, TRADE-MARKS, COPYRIGHTS, AND LABELS
THE HART AND THE WATER-BROOKS: A PRACTICAL EXPOSITION OF THE 42ND PSALM / Macduff, John Ross – New York: Robert Carter, 1860. 1 fiche – 9 – us A.T.L.A. [240]
Hart, Burdett *see* BIBLICAL EPOCHS
Hart, David M *see* GUSTAVE DE MOLINARI AND THE ANTI-ETATISTE LIBERAL TRADITION
Hart, E I *see* WAKE UP! MONTREAL!
Hart, Elizabeth A *see* THE EFFECT OF PLANNED EXERCISE AS A DISINHIBITOR OF DIETARY RESTRAINT
Hart, G H C *see* DE VOLKSRAAD ALS KRISTALLISATOR VAN HET "INDISCHE BEWUSTZIJN"
Hart, Gerald Ephraim *see* THE QUEBEC ACT, 1774
Hart, H A *see* POINTERS BEING A BRIEF DIGEST OF DEBT, INTEREST, USURY, MORTGAGE AND FORECLOSURE, WITH COMMENTS AND CHAPTER ON EQUITY
Hart, H C *see* COL. H. C. HART'S NEW AND IMPROVED INSTRUCTOR FOR THE DRUM
Hart, Hans-Ulrich *see* WERTSYSTEME VON ENGLISCHLEHRERN
Hart, Hastings Hornell *see* JUVENILE COURT LAWS IN THE UNITED STATES
Hart, Heinrich *see* PETER HILLE
Hart, James Morgan *see* GERMAN UNIVERSITIES
Hart, James W T *see* THE AUTOBIOGRAPHY OF JUDAS ISCARIOT
Hart, John *see* AN ORTHOGRAPHIE, CONTEYNING THE DUE ORDER AND REASON
Hart, Joseph Kinmont *see* A CRITICAL STUDY OF CURRENT THEORIES OF MORAL EDUCATION
Hart, Julius *see* SEHNSUCHT
Hart, Normand *see* MONTREAL-METROPOLITAIN
Hart, Oliver *see* A FRAGMENT OF THE OLIVER HART DIARY, AUG. 4, 1754-OCT. 27, 1754
Hart, W H *see*
- CARTULARIUM MONASTERII DE RAMESEIA (RS79)
- HISTORIA ET CARTULARIUM MONSTERII S. PETRI CLOUCESTRIAE (RS33)
- INDEX EXPURGATORIOUS ANGLICANUS

Hart, William H *see* HISTORY OF SAC COUNTY
DAS HARTE GESCHLECHT : ROMAN / Vesper, Will – Hamburg: Hanseatische Verlagsanstalt, c1931 – 1r – 1 – us U.W. Library [830]
Hartert, E J O *see* DIE VOEGEL DER PALAEARKTISCHEN FAUNA
Hartford County. Connecticut *see*
- CEMETERY RECORDS IN WINDSOR, CT
- GLASTONBURY FOR TWO HUNDRED YEARS: A CENTENNIAL DISCOURSE
- SOME EARLY RECORDS OF & RELATING TO THE TOWN OF WINDSOR, CT

HARTFORD COURANT – (Former titles: Daily Courant 1837-39. Hartford Daily Courant 1840-87) – Hartford, CT. 1837-1997+ – 1 – D60152 – us UMI [071]
THE HARTFORD COURANT – Hartford, Conn. 1937- – 1 – us UMI [071]
HARTFORD DAILY COURANT *see* HARTFORD COURANT
HARTFORD SEMINARY RECORD : ISSUED UNDER THE AUSPICES OF THE FACULTY OF HARTFORD THEOLOGICAL SEMINARY – Hartford. v1-23. oct 1890-oct 1913 – 1 – D2897 – us UMI [220]
HARTFORD STUDIES IN LITERATURE – (Cont by: Studies in Literature) – West Hartford. v1-9. 1969-77 1; v4-9 1972-77 5; v6 1974*. v7 1975. v9 1977 9 – 1,5,9 – D6358 – us UMI [410]
HARTFORD TIMES – Genealogical columns, 1957-67, with surname index – 9 – $75.00 – us Godfrey [920]
Harth, Helene *see* DICHTUNG UND ARETE
Hartig, T *see* VOLLSTAENDIGE NATURGESCHICHTE DER FORSTLICHEN CULTURPFLANZEN DEUTSCHLANDS
Harting, J E *see* A HANDBOOK OF BRITISH BIRDS
Harting, P *see* MONOGRAPHIE DES MARATTIACEES
HARTINGTON HERALD – Hartington, NE. -w. Jun-Oct 1892, scattered issues missing; Mar 1894; May 1895-Jun 1899; Aug 1899-Jun 1905; Nov 1908-Jan 1944 – 1 – us NE Hist [071]
Hartland, Edwin Sidney *see* RITUAL AND BELIEF: STUDIES IN THE HISTORY OF RELIGION
HARTLAND FOREST / Bray, Anna Eliza – British Fiction Archive: Unit 2 – 9 – uk Bell [830]
Hartland Sunday School (Hartland Township, Huron County, Ohio) *see* RECORDS
Hartlaub, C JG *see* SYSTEM DER ORNITHOLOGIE WESTAFRICAS
Hartleben, Otto Erich *see*
- DIE ERZIEHUNG ZUR EHE, EINE SATIRE
- DER FROSCH

Hartleben, Selma *see* "MEI ERICH"
HARTLEPOOL GAZETTEER OF SHIPPING & COMMERCE – Hartlepool, England. -w. 2 Nov 1850-1 Feb 1851. 11 ft – 1 – uk British Libr Newspaper [072]
Hartley, Cecil B *see*
- THE GENTLEMEN'S BOOK OF ETIQUETTE; AND MANUEL OF POLITENESS.
- THE THREE MRS. JUDSONS: THE CELEBRATED FEMALE MISSIONARIES

Hartley, David *see*
- THE HARTLEY RUSSELL PAPERS
- OBSERVATIONS ON MAN

Hartley, H A S *see* CLASSICAL TRANSLATIONS
Hartley, Keith *see* DEFENCE AND PEACE ECONOMICS
Hartley, R *see* POIA
THE HARTLEY RUSSELL PAPERS / Hartley, David – 1761-88. Bekshire Record Office. BRRAM – 1 – uk Microform Academic [920]
Hartley, T G *see*
- HALL'S CIRCUITS AND MINISTERS

Hartlib, Samuel *see* THE TRUE AND READIE WAY TO LEARNE THE LATINE TONGUE
Hartlich, C *see* DIE URSPRUNG DES MYTHOSBEGRIFFES IN DER MODERNEN BIBELWISSENSCHAFT
Hartman, C J *see*
- HANDBOK I SKANDINAVIENS FLORA
- HANDBOK I SKANDINAVIENS FLORA INNEFATTANDE SVERIGES OCH NORGES VAXTER, TILL OCH MED MOSSORNA

Hartman, Edward R *see* SOCIALISM VERSUS CHRISTIANITY
Hartman, Greta B *see* THE ACCURACY OF HEART RATE AS AN INDICATOR OF METABOLIC RATE WHILE PERFORMING STEP AEROBICS
Hartman, H *see* THE COMPARISON BETWEEN AN AQUATIC RUNNING PROGRAM VERSUS A HARD SURFACE RUNNING PROGRAM ON AEROBIC CAPACITY AND BODY COMPOSITION
Hartmann, A *see* INSTITUTIONEN DES PRAKTISCHEN VOELKERRECHTS IN FRIEDENSZEITEN...
Hartmann, A T *see* DIE HEBRAEERIN AM PUTZTISCHE UND ALS BRAUT
Hartmann, Adolf *see* DIE STRAFRECHTSPFLEGE IN AMERIKA
Hartmann, Christ. *see* ANNALES HEREMI DEIPARAE MATRIS MONASTERII IN HELVETIA
Hartmann, David *see* DAS BUCH RUTH IN DER MIDRASCH-LITTERATUR
Hartmann, Eduard von *see*
- DAS JUDENTHUM IN GEGENWART UND ZUKUNFT
- DIE KRISIS DES CHRISTENTHUMS IN DER MODERNEN THEOLOGIE
- PHAENOMENOLOGIE DES SITTLICHEN BEWUSSTSEINS: PROLEGOMENA ZU JEDER KUNFTIGEN ETHIK
- PHILOSOPHY OF THE UNCONSCIOUS.
- DIE RELIGION DES GEISTES

Hartmann, Ernst of Osterode *see*
- GESCHICHTE DER STADT HOHENSTEIN IN OSTPREUSSEN
- GESCHICHTE DER STADT LIEBEMUEHL
- DER KREIS OSTERODE (OSTPR.)

Hartmann, Franz *see* THE LIFE OF JEHOSHUA, THE PROPHET OF NAZARETH
Hartmann, G *see*
- INTERNATIONALE GELDSCHULDEN
- DIE VOELKERRECHTLICHE ANERKENNUNG DER STAATEN

Hartmann, Hartwig *see* NECHEB UND NECHBET
Hartmann, Horst et al *see* WERKINTERPRETATIONEN ZUR DEUTSCHEN LITERATUR
Hartmann, I Z *see* ORATIO DE PACE FUTURA...
Hartmann, J *see* UHLANDS TAGEBUCH 1810-1820
Hartmann, J M *see* DE POTENTATU
Hartmann, Julius *see*
- HUMANITAET UND RELIGION
- JOHANN BRENZ
- JOHANNES BRENZ

Hartmann, L *see* DAS GESETZ UEBER DIE PRESSE VOM 12. MAI 1851, AUS DER ENTSTEHUNGSGESCHICHTE, DER RECHTSLEHRE UND DER ENTSCHEIDUNGEN DES KOENIGLICHEN OBER-TRIBUNALS ERLAUTERT.
Hartmann, Markus *see*
- STUDIEN ZUR METABOLISIERUNG UND ZUM INTRAZELLULAEREN WIRKMECHANISMUS TUMORRAFFINER RUTHENIUM(III)KOMPLEXE
- VERGLEICHENDE UNTERSUCHUNGEN UEBER STABILITAET UND SUBSTITUTIONSVERHALTEN TUMORHEMMENDER RUTHENIUM(III)KOMPLEXE IN PHYSIOLOGISCHEM BLUTPUFFER

Hartmann, Max *see* LUDWIG ACHIM VON ARNIM ALS DRAMATIKER
Hartmann, Philipp *see* REPERTORIUM RITUUM
Hartmann, Sabine *see* HOERSCHWELLENBESTIMMUNGEN BEI NEUGEBORENEN RISIKOKINDERN
HARTMANNS IWEIN : RECHTSARGUMENTATION UND BILDSPRACHE / Hagenguth, Edith – Heidelberg, 1969 – 3mf – 9 – DM76.00 – 3-89349-753-6 – gw Hänsel [430]
HARTMUTH VON KRONBERG : EINE CHARAKTERSTUDIE AUS DER REFORMATIONSZEIT / Bogler, Wilhelm – Halle: Verein fuer Reformationsgeschichte; 14. Jahrg., Schrift 57 – 1mf – us A.T.L.A. [240]
Hartney, Edward P *see* MANUAL SHOWING THE PRIVATE BILL PRACTICE OF THE PARLIAMENT OF CANADA
HART'S OIL AND GAS WORLD – (Cont in pt: Gulf Coast Oil and Gas World. Midcontinent Oil and Gas World. Pacific Oil and Gas World. And: Southwest Oil and Gas World) – Denver. v86-89. 1994-97+ – 1,5,9 – D20694 – us UMI [550]
HART'S OIL AND GAS WORLD *see* PACIFIC OIL AND GAS WORLD
Hartshorne, Francis Cope *see* THE RAILROADS AND THE COMMERCE CLAUSE
HARTSVILLE FIRST BAPTIST CHURCH. HARTSVILLE, SOUTH CAROLINA : CHURCH RECORDS – 1910-49. (Historical Report, 1954-72) – 1 – 18.68 – us Baptist [240]
Hartung, Ernst *see*
- ALLES UM LIEBE
- DAS GROSSE LEBEN
- VOM TAETIGEN LEBEN

Hartung, K *see* DER PROPHET AMOS: NACH DEM GRUNDTEXTE
Hartungen, Hartmut von *see* DER DICHTER SIEGFRIED LIPINER (1856-1911)
Hartwell, Steven *see* ALTERNATIVE DISPUTE RESOLUTION IN A BANKRUPTCY COURT
Hartwick *see* PIONEERS AND BUSINESSMEN OF TODAY
Hartz, Erich von *see* ODRUN
Hartzler, Jonas Smucker *see* MENNONITE CHURCH HISTORY
HARVARD 1723-1849 – (Mf 1T-3T: Births & Deaths 1723-66. Mf 1T-4T: Marriages 1732-1804. Mf 1T-5T: Publishments 1732-96. Mf 4T 5T: Births 1753-1020. Mf 5T-6T: Deaths A-W 1750-1819. Mf 6T: Out-of-Town Marriages 1732-99. Mf 6T-10T: Intentions 1796-1849. Mf 7T-9T: Marriages 1794-1845. Mf 9T-10T: Births A-Y 1777-1849. Mf 10T: Deaths A-W 1785-1843. Mf 11T: Vital Records 1844-49) – (mf ed 1996) – 11mf – 9 – 0-87623-263-2 – us Holbrook [920]
HARVARD 1723-1900 – (Mf 1-5: Vitals Indexed 1723-1848. Mf 6-11: Town Records 1732-1804. Mf 9-11: Marriages 1732-66. Mf 10-11,21,42: Deaths 1732-1849. Mf 9-11, 20: Births 1726-1820. Mf 12-21: Town Records 1765-1834. Mf 15: Marriages 1766-1805. Mf 18-20: Intentions 1766-95. Mf 22-38: Town Records 1782-1843. Mf 34-35: Intent/Marriages 1825-48. Mf 37-38,40-41: Births 1777-1850. Mf 43-52: Town Records 1819-68. Mf 51-52,63-64: Militia 1840-90. Mf 52,65: Out-of-Town Marriages 1732-98. Mf 52: Perkins Family 1765-1880. Mf 52,64: Dog Licenses 1862-76. Mf 53-64: Mortgage/Misc 1838-93. Mf 66-87: Church Records 1733-1909. Mf 88-90: Military 1822-65. Mf 91-104: Paupers 1832-1909. Mf 105: Voters 1877-84. Mf 106-110: Intentions 1848-1906. Mf 110-113: Vital Record Indexes 1841-1900. Mf 114-119: Vitals 1841-1900) – (mf ed 1997) – 119mf – 9 – 0-87623-390-6 – us Holbrook [920]
HARVARD ADVOCATE – (Suspended sep 1943-dec 1946. Former title: Advocate may 11, 1866-mar 1869) – Cambridge. v1-101 1866-1967*. v102-120 mar 1968-may 1987. v122-127 nov 1987-sum 1993. v128 fal 1993-spr 1994*. v129-132 sum 1994-sum 1998+ 1; v104-107 apr 1970-win 1974. v109-110 fal 1975-may 1977. v111 nov 1977-may 1978*. v112 dec 1978-may 1979. v113-116 nov 1979-nov 1982*. v117 mar 1983-dec 1984. v118-120 dec 1984-may 1987*. v122-129 nov 1987-spr 1995*. v130-132 fal 1995-sum 1998+ 5; v109 fal 1975-may 1976*. v110 oct 1976-may 1977. v111 nov 1977-may 1978*. v112-114 dec 1978-may 1981. v115 dec 1981-sum 1982*. v116-120 nov 1982-may 1987. v122-127 nov 1987-sum 1993. v128 fal 1993-spr 1994*. v129-132 sum 1994-sum 1998+ 9 – 1,5,9 – D3379 – us UMI [340]
Harvard African Expedition *see* THE AFRICAN REPUBLIC OF LIBERIA AND THE BELGIAN CONGO
Harvard and Radcliffe *see* GUIDE TO ARCHIVES AND MANUSCRIPTS AT HARVARD AND RADCLIFFE
HARVARD ANNUAL LEGAL BIBLIOGRAPHY, 1961-1981 : FULL CUMULATION / Harvard University. Law Library – 340mf – 9 – $825.00 – LLMC 83-100 – us L.L.M.C. [340]
HARVARD ARCHITECTURE REVIEW – Cambridge. v1-4. 1980-83* – 1 – D12321 – us UMI [720]
HARVARD BLACKLETTER JOURNAL – (Title varies: v1-2 1983-85 as The Blackletter Journal. v3-10 1986-93 as Harvard Blackletter Journal) – v1-12. 1984-95 – 9 – $100.00 set – us Hein [340]

HARVARD BLACKLETTER JOURNAL *see* HARVARD BLACKLETTER JOURNAL
HARVARD BUSINESS REPORTS – Cambridge. v1-11. 1926-32 – 5 – D6405 – us UMI [650]
HARVARD BUSINESS REVIEW – 1983-84 – 1 – us UMI [073]
HARVARD BUSINESS REVIEW – (With cum index for v16-25 1937-47) – Boston. v1-75. oct 1922-dec 1997+ 1; v45-75 1967-97+ 5; v38-75. 1960-97+ 9 – 1,5,9 – D634 – us UMI [650]
HARVARD CIVIL RIGHTS-CIVIL LIBERTIES LAW REVIEW – (v1-19 1966-84 on reel or mf $286.00. v20-30 1985-95 on mf $149.00) – v1-30. 1966-95 – 5,6,9 – $435.00 set – us Hein [321]
HARVARD CIVIL RIGHTS-CIVIL LIBERTIES LAW REVIEW – (With cum index for v1-7 1966-72 1) – Cambridge. v1-32. spr 1966-sum 1997+ 1; v10-32. win 1975-sum 1997+ 5; v11-32. win 1976-sum 1997+ 9 – 1,5,9 – D10519 – us UMI [340]
HARVARD CLASS REPORTS, 1833-1975 : FOR THE CLASSES OF 1833-1900 – (With printed index £105.00) – 1,088mf – 9 – £4,015.00 – uk Chadwyck [370]
Harvard College. Library *see*
– THE BLODGETT COLLECTION OF SPANISH CIVIL WAR PAMPHLETS
– DISTRIBUTABLE UNION CATALOG
HARVARD COURIER – Harvard, NE. -w. Jun 1892; Aug 1892; Oct 1895-Apr 1903; Jun 1903-Dec 1976 – 1 – us NE Hist [071]
HARVARD DIVINITY BULLETIN / Harvard University – v1-30. ns: v1-3; v1-22. 1935-93 (complete) – 7r – 1 – ATLA S0332 – us A.T.L.A. [240]
HARVARD EDUCATIONAL REVIEW – (Former title: Harvard Teachers Record feb 1931-oct 1936) – Cambridge. v1-35 1931-65*. v36-67 win 1966-win 1997+ 1; v38-67. win 1968-win 1997+ 5; v41-44 feb 1971-nov 1974. v54-67 feb 1984-win 1997+ 9 – 1,5,9 – D2267 – us UMI [370]
HARVARD ENVIRONMENTAL LAW REVIEW – (v1-8 1976-84 on reel $130.00. v9-20 1985-96 on mf $264.00) – v1-20. 1976-96 – 5,6,9 – $394.00 set – us Hein [340]
HARVARD EXCAVATIONS AT SAMARIA / Reisner, George A – Harvard. 1924. 2v – 9 – $21.00 – us I.R.C. [930]
HARVARD GRADUATES' MAGAZINE – (With cum index for v1-20 1892-1911) – Boston. v1-42. oct 1892-jun 1934 – 1 – D2898 – us UMI [073]
HARVARD HUMAN RIGHTS JOURNAL – (Title varies: v1-2 1988-89 as Harvard Human Rights Yearbook) – v1-8. 1988-95 – 9 – $100.00 set – us Hein [340]
HARVARD HUMAN RIGHTS YEARBOOK *see* HARVARD HUMAN RIGHTS JOURNAL
HARVARD INTERNATIONAL LAW CLUB BULLETIN *see* HARVARD INTERNATIONAL LAW JOURNAL
HARVARD INTERNATIONAL LAW CLUB JOURNAL *see* HARVARD INTERNATIONAL LAW JOURNAL
HARVARD INTERNATIONAL LAW JOURNAL – (With cum index for v1-10 1959-1969 1. Former titles: Alumni Bulletin of the Harvard International Law Club feb 1959-spr 1960. Harvard International Law Club Bulletin dec 1961-apr 1962. Harvard International Law Club Journal dec 1962-spr 1966) – Cambridge. v1-38. fal 1959-spr 1997+ 1; v13-38. win 1972-spr 1997+ 5; v17-38 win 1976-spr 1997+ 9 – 1,5,9 – D7400 – us UMI [340]
HARVARD INTERNATIONAL REVIEW – Cambridge. v1-14. feb 1979-1992* 1; v15-17 fal 1992-fal 1995*. v18-20 win 1995-fal 1998+ 1,5,9 – 1,5,9 – D20313 – us UMI [073]
HARVARD JOURNAL OF ASIATIC STUDIES – Cambridge, Mass. v1-26. 1936-66/67 – 229mf – 8 – ne IDC [073]
HARVARD JOURNAL OF ASIATIC STUDIES – (With cum index for v21-25 dec 1958-dec 66 1) – Cambridge. v1-57. 1936-97+ 1; v31-57 1971-97+ 5; v36-57 1976-97+ 9 – 1,5,9 – D2338 – us UMI [950]
HARVARD JOURNAL OF LAW AND PUBLIC POLICY – (v1-7 1978-84 on reel $78.00. v8-18 1985-95 on mf $272.00) – v1-18. 1978-95 – 5,6,9 – $350.00 set – us Hein [340]
HARVARD JOURNAL OF LAW AND TECHNOLOGY – v1-8. 1988-95 – 9 – $95.00 set – us Hein [340]
HARVARD JOURNAL ON LEGISLATION – Cambridge. v1-12. jan 1964-jun 1975 1; v9-12. nov 1971-jun 1975 5 – 1,5 – D1951 – us UMI [340]
HARVARD JOURNAL ON LEGISLATION – v1-32. 1964-95 – 1,5,6 – $585.00 – us Hein [073]
HARVARD LAMPOON – Cambridge. v1-170. feb 1876-1981* 1; v171-181 may 1981-91. v182 1992*. v183 1993-feb 1994. v184 1994-feb 1995*. v185-187 mar 1995-98+ 1,9; v171-184 may 1981-feb 1995*. v185-187 mar 1995-98+ 5 – 1,5,9 – D12895 – us UMI [073]
HARVARD LAW RECORD – Cambridge, MA. 1946-72 – 1 – 69.00 – us L of C Photodup [073]
HARVARD LAW RECORD – (v1-89 1946-90 on reel $595.00. v90-101 1990-95 on mf $238.00) – v1-101. 1946-1995 – 9 – $833.00 set – us Hein [340]
HARVARD LAW REVIEW – Cambridge. v1-111. apr 1887-jun 1998+ 1; v82-111. nov 1968-jun 1998+ 5; v90-111 nov 1976-jun 1998+ 9 – 1,5,9 – D753 – us UMI [340]
HARVARD LAW REVIEW – (More vols will be added as copyright expires) – v1-33. 1889-1919/20 – 241mf – 9 – $361.00 – LLMC 84-477 – us L.L.M.C. [073]
HARVARD LAW REVIEW – v1-109. 1887-1996 – 1,5,6,9 – $3,645.00 – us Hein [073]
Harvard Law School *see*
– RESEARCH IN INTERNATIONAL LAW
THE HARVARD LAW SCHOOL : STAGE 1 – 1643mf – 9 – H-1775-1778/1 – ne IDC [340]
THE HARVARD LAW SCHOOL ADDENDA : STAGE 6 – 567mf – 9 – H-1925-1929/1 – ne IDC [340]
HARVARD LECTURES ON THE REVIVAL OF LEARNING / Sandys, Edwin – Cambridge: University Press, 1905 – 1mf – us A.T.L.A. [240]
HARVARD LEGAL COMMENTARY – Papers from the Harvard Law School 2nd-year writing program. v1-9. 1964-72 – 34mf – 9 – $51.00 – LLMC 84-478 – us L.L.M.C. [073]
HARVARD LIBRARY BULLETIN – (Publication suspended 1961-66) – Cambridge. v1-36. win 1947-fal 1988 1; v23-36. jan 1975-fal 1988 5; v24-36. jan 1976-fal 1988 9; n1-4 spr 1990-win 1994. n5 win-fal 1994*. n6-8 win 1995-fal 1997+ 1,5,9 – 1,5,9 – D10303 – us UMI [020]
HARVARD LYCEUM – Cambridge. v1. jul 1810-mar 1811 – 1 – D3816 – us UMI [978]
HARVARD MONTHLY – Cambridge. v1-63. 1885-apr 1917* – 1 – D2899 – us UMI [073]
HARVARD REGISTER – Cambridge. v1-12. mar 1827-feb 1828 – 1 – D3749 – us UMI [073]
HARVARD REGISTER : AN ILLUSTRATED MONTHLY – Cambridge. v1-3. jan 1880-jul 1881 – 1 – D3872 – us UMI [073]
HARVARD REVIEW – Cambridge. v1-4. fal 1962-2qr 1968 1; v4. sum 1966-2qr 1968* 5,9 – 1,5,9 – D1680 – us UMI [073]
HARVARD TEACHERS RECORD *see* HARVARD EDUCATIONAL REVIEW
HARVARD THEOLOGICAL REVIEW – 1(1908)-39(1946) – 268mf – 9 – Dfl839.00 – ne Slangenburg [073]
HARVARD THEOLOGICAL REVIEW – v1-14. 1908-21 (complete) – 4r – 1 – ATLA S0004 – us A.T.L.A. [073]
THE HARVARD THEOLOGICAL REVIEW – Cambridge. v1-39. 1908-1946 – 268mf – 9 – ne IDC [240]
HARVARD UNION CATALOG – 1993 – ca 2376mf (1:48) – 9 – DM19,800.00 – 3-598-41223-1 – gw Saur [010]
Harvard University *see*
– CONTRIBUTIONS FROM THE PHYSICAL LABORATORIES
– HARVARD DIVINITY BULLETIN
– HEBREW BOOKS FROM THE HARVARD COLLEGE LIBRARY
Harvard University. Arnold Arboretum *see* JOURNAL
Harvard University. Baker Library *see* AUTHOR-TITLE CATALOG
Harvard University. Center for Italian Renaissance Studies at Villa I Tat *see* CATALOGUES OF THE BERENSON LIBRARY
Harvard University. Dumbarton Oaks Research Library. Washington, DC *see* DICTIONARY CATALOGUE OF THE BYZANTINE COLLECTION
HARVARD UNIVERSITY. FINE ARTS LIBRARY *see* CARD CATALOGS OF THE HARVARD UNIVERSITY FINE ARTS LIBRARY 1895-1981
Harvard University. Fogg Art Museum. Library *see* CATALOG OF THE HARVARD UNIVERSITY FINE ARTS LIBRARY
Harvard University. Graduate School of Business Administration. Baker Library *see*
– AUTHOR-TITLE AND SUBJECT CATALOGS OF THE BAKER LIBRARY. 1971
– SUBJECT CATALOG
Harvard University. Graduate School of Design. Frances Loeb Library *see*
– CATALOGUE OF THE LIBRARY
– CATALOGUE OF THE LIBRARY OF THE GRADUATE SCHOOL OF DESIGN
Harvard University. Gray Herbarium Library *see* GRAY HERBARIUM INDEX
Harvard University. Harvard-Yenching Library *see* CATALOG OF PROTESTANT MISSIONARY WORKS IN CHINESE
Harvard University Herbaria *see* ORCHID HERBARIUM OF OAKES AMES BOTANICAL MUSEUM
Harvard University. Houghton Library *see*
– BULLETIN
– INVENTORIES OF THE HOUGHTON MANUCRIPT COLLECTION
Harvard University. Law Library *see* HARVARD ANNUAL LEGAL BIBLIOGRAPHY, 1961-1981
HARVARD UNIVERSITY. LAW SCHOOL LIBRARY *see* CARD CATALOGS OF THE HARVARD LAW SCHOOL LIBRARY 1817-1981
Harvard University. Law School Library *see*
– COLLECTION OF STATE DOCUMENTS
– NIHONSI KANKEI SHIRYO
Harvard University. Library *see* DISTRIBUTABLE UNION CATALOG
THE HARVARD UNIVERSITY LIBRARY : A DOCUMENTARY HISTORY – Includes reports, letters, library regulations, charging records, proceedings, catalogues, inventories and list of prohibited books. Printed – 420 fiches – 9 – $2,390.00 – us UPA [020]
Harvard University. Museum of Comparative Zoology *see* CATALOGUE OF THE LIBRARY OF THE MUSEUM OF COMPARATIVE ZOOLOGY
Harvard University. Museum of Comparative Zoology. Library *see* CATALOG
HARVARD UNIVERSITY. MUSIC LIBRARY *see* CARD CATALOG OF THE HARVARD UNIVERSITY MUSIC LIBRARY TO 1985
Harvard University. Peabody Museum of Archaeology and Ethnology. Tozzer Library *see*
– AUTHOR AND SUBJECT CATALOGS
– AUTHOR/SUBJECT CATALOGUES
HARVARD UNIVERSITY – PROGRAM ON PUBLIC CONCEPTIONS OF SCIENCE : NEWSLETTER OF THE PROGRAM ON PUBLIC CONCEPTIONS OF SCIENCE – (Cont by: Newsletter on Science, Technology and Human Values) – Cambridge. v1-16. oct 1972-jun 1976* – 1 – D12326 – us UMI [073]
Harvard University. Widener Library *see* CATALOG OF THE ARABIC COLLECTION, HARVARD UNIVERSITY
HARVARD WOMEN'S LAW JOURNAL – (v1-7 1978-85 on reel $75.00. v8-19 1985-96 on mf $150.00) – v1-19. 1978-96 – 5,6,9 – $229.00 set – us Hein [340]
HARVARDIANA – Cambridge. v1-4. 1835-jul 1838 – 1 – D4377 – us UMI [978]
HARVEST / Ward, Mary Augusta – British Fiction Archive: Unit 2 – 9 – uk Bell [830]
HARVEST BELLS, 1882, 1884, 1887 / Penn, WE – 1 – 86.52 – us Baptist [240]
THE HARVESTER – 1936-83.annual – 1 – uk World [073]
HARVESTER, FOR GATHERING THE RIPENED CROPS ON EVERY HOMESTEAD: LEAVING THE UNRIPE TO MATURE / Merchant – Boston: William White, 1868. 1 fiche – 9 – us A.T.L.A. [240]
HARVESTING ANTS AND TRAPDOOR SPIDERS / Moggridge, J T – Z-2187 2. 1873-74 – 8 – ne IDC [590]
HARVESTING OCEAN ENERGY / Wick, Gerald L et al – 1981 – 173p – 9 – 92-3-101873-6 – fr UNESCO [333]
HARVESTING OF KRILL – 1978 – 82p – it F.A.O. [631]
Harvey, A Edward *see* MARTIN BUCKER IN ENGLAND
Harvey, Alfred *see* ENGLISH CHURCH FURNITURE
Harvey, Annie J *see* CHRONICLES OF AN OLD INN
Harvey, Arthur *see*
– CHAMPLAIN'S AMERICAN EXPERIENCES IN 1613
– THE DISCOVERY OF LAKE SUPERIOR: A STUDY FROM THE JESUITS JOURNALS
– HARVEY'S GUIDE TO PATENTS
Harvey, Charles Thompson *see* PAPERS
Harvey County. Kansas. District Court *see* RECORDS OF CASES
HARVEY COUNTY NEWS – Newton. Kan. 1875-77 – 1 – us UMI [071]
Harvey, Edwin R *see* CULTURAL POLICY IN ARGENTINA
Harvey, G *see*
– THE CONCLAVE OF PHYSICIANS
– A DISCOURSE OF THE PLAGUE
Harvey, Jacob *see* LETTERS, 1812-46
Harvey, Jean-Charles *see* LE JOUR
Harvey, Leonise *see* BIBLIOGRAPHIE ANALYTIQUE DES ILES-DE-LA-MADELEINE
Harvey, Moses *see*
– HAND-BOOK OF NEWFOUNDLAND: CONTAINING AN ACCOUNT OF ITS AGRICULTURAL AND MINERAL LANDS, ITS FORESTS, AND OTHER NATURAL RESOURCES
– NEWFOUNDLAND IN 1897: BEING QUEEN VICTORIA'S DIAMOND JUBILEE YEAR AND THE FOUR HUNDREDTH ANNIVERSARY OF THE DISCOVERY OF THE ISLAND BY JOHN CABOT
– NEWFOUNDLAND IN 1900: A TREATISE OF THE GEOGRAPHY, NATURAL RESOURCES AND HISTORY OF THE ISLAND...FINELY ILLUSTRATED WITH MAPS AND HALF-TONE ENGRAVINGS
Harvey, Oscar J *see* A HISTORY OF WILKES-BARRE, LUZERNE COUNTY AND WYOMING VALLEY
Harvey, Peter *see* REMINISCENCES OF DANIEL WEBSTER
Harvey Pirie, J H *see* SCOTTISH NATIONAL ANTARCTIC EXPEDITION, 1902-1904. DEEP SEA DEPOSITS
Harvey, Richard S *see*
– RIGHTS OF THE MINORITY STOCKHOLDER
– RIGHTS OF THE MINORITY STOCKHOLDER AND OF THE RAILWAY SECURITY HOLDER
Harvey, W *see*
– EXERCITATIO ANATOMICA DE MOTU CORDIS ET SANGUINIS IN ANIMALIBUS
– EXERCITATIONES DE GENERATIONE ANIMALIUM
Harvey, W H *see*
– ALGAE ANTARCTICA
– THE GENERA OF SOUTH AFRICAN PLANTS
– THESAURUS CAPENSIS
Harvey, William *see* LA CIRCULATION DU SANG. DES MOUVEMENTS DU COEUR CHEZ L'HOMME ET CHEZ LES ANIMAUX, DEUX REPONSES A RIOLAN
Harvey, William Patrick *see*
– SHALL WOMAN PREACH?
Harvey, Zola Emile *see*
– PROBLEMS AND SOLUTIONS IN EQUITY.
– PROBLEMS AND SOLUTIONS IN PERSONAL PROPERTY.
– PROBLEMS AND SOLUTIONS IN TORTS.
Harvey-Jellie, W Raymond *see* LE THEATRE CLASSIQUE EN ANGLETERRE, DANS L'AGE DE JOHN DRYDEN
Harvey-Jellie, Wallace Raymond *see* CHRONICLES
THE HARVEYS / Kingsley, Henry – British Fiction Archive: Unit 2 – 9 – uk Bell [830]
HARVEY'S GUIDE TO PATENTS / Harvey, Arthur – Ottawa: A.S. Woodburn, 1885. 05252. (Pre-1900 Canadiana) – 9 – cn C.I.H.M. [340]
HARWICH 1673-1895 – (Mf 1-4: B,M,D 1673-1752. Mf 5-8: Vital Records 1698-1790. Mf 9-14: B,M,D 1731-94. Mf 15-20: Vital Records 1731-94. Mf 21-23: Births & Deaths 1760-1842. Mf 24-36: Vital Records & Index 1796-1845. Mf 37-42: Marriage Intentions 1808-49. Mf 43-45: Births 1811-50. Mf 46-51: Vitals Records 1697-1849. Mf 52-54: Births & Deaths 1765-1840. Mf 55-56: B,M,D 1843-49. Mf 57-62: Births & Index 1848-95. Mf 63-69: Marriages & Index 1848-89. Mf 70-74: Deaths & Index 1848-95) – (mf ed 1987) – 74mf – 9 – 0-931248-95-7 – us Holbrook [920]
HARWICH AND MANNINGTREE STANDARD – England.1977. -d. 2 reels – 1 – uk British Libr Newspaper [072]
Harwood, Edwin *see* BUECHER DER KOENIGE

HARYANA GOVERNMENT GAZETTE / Haryana. India – Chandigarh. Part 1-3. Suppl. and index. Nov. 8-Dec. 27, 1966 – 1 – us NY Public [950]
Haryana. India *see* HARYANA GOVERNMENT GAZETTE
HARZ MOUNTAINS: PAMPHLET COLLECTION – 1926?-1928? – 1 reel – 1 – CSUXANS6079-B – us Hoover Inst Photo [943]
HARZ-KURIER – (Suppl. Bad Lauterberger Zeitung) – Herzberg i. Harz, West Germany. 1977- – ca 7r per yr – 1 – gw Mikrofilm [072]
HARZREISE / Heine, Heinrich; ed by Buchheim, C A – 3rd rev ed. Oxford: Clarendon Press, 1900 – 1 – us U.W. Library [830]
Harz-Verein fuer Geschichte und Altertumskunde *see* ZEITSCHRIFT
HAS OUDE BEEN WORSE GOVERNED BY ITS NATIVE PRINCES THAN OUR INDIAN TERRITORIES BY LEADENHALL STREET? / Lewin, Malcolm – (Filmed with: A historical sketch of Fyzabad Tehsil/P Carnegy) – London: J Ridgeway, 1857. Lucknow, 1870 – us Res Libr [950]
HASAHAR = CONFERENCE OF THE ORGANIZATION – (In Hebrew) – Rzeszow, PL. 1908 – 1r – 1 – $25.00 – cn Can Microfilming [072]
Hasan, Abul *see* BOOK IN MULTILINGUAL COUNTRIES
Hasan, BMZ *see* BIBLIOGRAPHY OF INDO-MOSLEM HISTORY
Hasbrouck, Jacob L *see* HISTORY OF MCLEAN COUNTY
Hase, C *see* HISTORIA SCRIPTORESQUE ALII AD RES BYZANTINAS PERTINENTES (CBH 39)
Hase, Carl Alfred *see* HERZOG ALBRECHT VON PREUSSEN UND SEIN HOFPREDIGER
Hase, Karl *see* LIFE OF JESUS: A MANUAL FOR ACADEMIC STUDY
Hase, Karl Alfred von *see*
- DIE BEDEUTUNG DES GESCHICHTLICHEN IN DER RELIGION
- SEBASTIAN FRANCK VON WOERD, DER SCHWARMGEIST

HASEFARDI HARSANGIER – (Missing: 1938. v1(1-2)) – 's-Gravenhage, 1938-1940 – 2mf – 9 – J-261-42/1 – ne IDC [943]
HA-SEFARIM HA-IVRIYYIM SHE-NIDPESU BI-YERUSHALAYIM / Halevy, S – Jersualem, 1963 – 6mf – ne IDC [470]
Hase-Koehler, Else von *see* URSULA SCHREIBT INS FELD
Hasenclever, Walter *see*
- JENSEITS
- DER JUENGLING

HA-SENEGOR – The Defender. (New York), 1890-91 – us A.J.P.C. [071]
HA-SHAHAR / ed by Smolenskin, P – Vienna. v1-12. 1868-84 – 9 – BJ-422-30 1 – ne IDC [073]
HA-SHAVU'A *see* HA-MAGGID
Hashem, O *see* MARXISME DAN AGAMA
HA-SHILO'AH / ed by Ha-Am, Ahad & Klausner, J G – Berlin. Cracow, etc. 1896-1926. BJ-422-31 1 – 9 – ne IDC [470]
Hashim, Talal J *see* A HEALTH KNOWLEDGE TEST FOR MALE COLLEGE FRESHMEN IN SAUDI ARABIA
HASHKAFA = OUTLOOK – (In Hebrew. Twice weekly) – Jerusalem, IS. v8 no54. Apr 1908 – 1r – 1 – $25.00 – cn Can Microfilming [072]
HA-SHOMER = THE GUARD – (In Hebrew) – Vienna, AU. May 1918-Jan 1919 – 1r – 1 – $25.00 – cn Can Microfilming [072]
HA-SHOMER : THE GUARD – (In Hebrew and Polish) – Lwow, PL. v2 no1. Sep 1919 – 1r – 1 – $25.00 – cn Can Microfilming [072]
HASHOMER HATZAIR = THE YOUNG GUARDIAN – (In Yiddish) – Munich, DE. v2 no-. 25 Nov 1948 (50th Jubilee Issue) – 1r – 1 – $25.00 – cn Can Microfilming [072]
Hasibuan, Sayuti *see* THE PALM-OIL INDUSTRY ON THE EAST COAST OF SUMATRA
Hasimi *see* DIVANCE
HASJALSJEELETH – 's-Gravenhage, 1939-1940 – 3mf – 9 – J-261-43/1 – ne IDC [943]
HASKALAH MEDUMMAH / Piurko, A M – Warsaw. 1887. BJ-422-65 1 – 9 – ne IDC [470]
Haskell, T H *see* HASKELL'S JUDGEMENTS OF THE HONORABLE EDWARD FOX FOR THE MAINE DISTRICT AND FIRST CIRCUIT, 1866-1881
HASKELL'S JUDGEMENTS OF THE HONORABLE EDWARD FOX FOR THE MAINE DISTRICT AND FIRST CIRCUIT, 1866-1881 / Haskell, T H – (Sometimes known as: Fox's Decisions) – Portland: Fessenden. v1-2. 1887 – 14mf – 9 – $21.00 – LLMC 81-482 – us L.L.M.C. [340]
Haskins, Dan D *see* SPECIALIZED LEADERSHIP TRAINING IN THE TENNESSEE TECH BAPTIST STUDENT UNION EXECUTIVE COUNCIL
Haskins, O *see* A COLLECTION OF ANCIENT TUNES, STEP SHUFFLING AND QUICK. FROM VARIOUS AUTHERS [!] AND CHURCHES OF BELIEVERS, BOTH FAR AND NEAR, AND HEREIN TRANSCRIBED FOR THE PURPOSE OF RETAINING THEM
Haskins,Ohio. Haskins Federated Church *see* RECORDS
Hasler, K *see* DAS EHELICHE GUETERRECHT...
HASLINGTON CHRONICLE & RAMSBOTTOM TIMES – Haslington, Ramsbottom, England. -w. 1 June 1867-30 Dec 1871. 1 1 2 reels – 1 – uk British Libr Newspaper [072]
Hasmet *see* DIVAN
Hasmosuwignjo *see* EXTENSION SELF-SUPPORTING RICE PROGRAM
HA-SOKER – Budapest. 1933-38. BJ-100-173 1 – 9 – ne IDC [072]
Hass, Hans-Egon *see* HEINRICH HEINE
Hassan, Abdulkadir *see* IS MUHAMMAD A TRUE PROPHET?
Hassan, Fuad *see* IDENTITAS NASIONAL
Hassard, Albert Richard *see* CANADIAN CONSTITUTIONAL HISTORY AND LAW
Hassaurek, Friedrich *see*
- GEDICHTE
- THE SECRET OF THE ANDES: A ROMANCE

Hasse, J A *see*
- ATTILIO REGOLO [DRAMMA PER MUSICA SI] SIG. GIO. ADOLFO HASSE [LA POESIA E DEL SIG. ABBATE PIETRO METASTASIO
- HYMNUS AMBROSIANUS SIVE TE DEUM LAUDAMUS. A QUATRO VOCI, 2 VIOLINI, VIOLA, OBOI, CORNI, TROMBE, TIMPANI ET ORGANO
- MISERERE, C. MINOR
- SOLIMANO
- TWELVE CONCERTOS IN SIX PARTS FOR A GERMAN FLUTE, TWO VIOLINS, A TENOR, WITH A THOROUGH BASS...OPERA TERZA
- VENETIAN BALLADS COMPOS'D BY SIGR. HASSE AND ALL THE CELEBRATED ITALIAN MASTERS

Hasse, Johann Adolf *see* ALCIDE AL BRIVO
Hasse, R *see* DIE BERGARBEITER-VERHAELTNISSE IN GROSSBRITANNIEN
Hasselquist, F *see* ITER PALAESTINUM, ELLER RESA TIL HELIGA LANDET FOERRAETTAD FRAN AR 1749 TIL 1752, MED BEKRIFTNINGAR, ROEN, ANMAERKNINGAR, OEFVER DE MAERKVAERDIGASTE NATURALIER
Hasselt, A L van *see* BIJDRAGEN TOT DE KENNIS DER FLORA VAN MIDDEN SUMATRA
Hasselt, J L van *see* GEDENBOEK VAN EEN VIJF-EN-TWINTIGJARIG ZENDELINGSLEVEN OP NIEUW-GUINEA (1862-1887)
Hasselt, Vincent B Van *see* JOURNAL OF CHILD AND ADOLESCENT SUBSTANCE ABUSE
Hassencamp, Robert *see* NEUE BRIEFE CHR. MART. WIELANDS
Hassenstein, Georg *see* LUDWIG UHLAND
Hassert, Kurt *see* DIE ERFORSCHUNG AFRIKAS.
Hasskarl, Gottlieb Christopher Henry *see* EVOLUTION, AS TAUGHT IN THE BIBLE
Hasskarl, J K *see*
- CATALOGUS PLANTARUM IN HORTO BOTANICO BOGORIENSI CULTARUM ALTER
- COMMELINACEAE INDICAE,...
- FILICES JAVANICAE SEU OBSERVATIONES BOTANICAE,...
- HORTI MALABARICI RHEEDEANI CLAVIS LOCUPLETISSIMA
- HORTUS BOGORIENSIS DESCRIPTUS...
- NEUER SCHLUESSEL ZU RUMPH'S HERBARIUM AMBOINENSE...
- PLANTAE JAVANICAE RARIORES...
- DE PLANTEN, DOOR DEN HEER NORONHA,...OPGESPOORD,...

Hassler, C D *see* EVAGATORIUM IN TERRAE SANCTAE, ARABIAE ET EGYPTI PEREGRINATIONEM
Hassler, H L *see* MISSAE QUATERNIS, 5. 6. ET 7 VOCIBUS...
Hassler, Hans Leo *see* PSALMEN UND CHRISTLICHE GESAENGE MIT VIER STIMMEN AUF DE MELODIEN FUGENWEISS COMPONIRT
HASTA LLEGAR A DIOS / Mejias, Lola – Zaragoza: Tip. Aragonesa, 1964 – 1 – sp Bibl Santa Ana [946]
Hastenpflug, Fritz *see* DAS DIMINUTIV IN DER DEUTSCHEN ORIGINALLITERATUR DES 12. UND 13. JAHRHUNDERTS
Hastie, Peter A *see* TASK ACCOUNT ABILITY IN SCHOOL PHYSICAL EDUCATION AND SPORTS SETTINGS
Hastie, W *see* OUTLINES OF THE SCIENCE OF JURISPRUDENCE
Hastie, William *see* THEOLOGY AS SCIENCE: AND ITS PRESENT POSITION AND PROSPECTS IN THE REFORMED CHURCH
Hastie, William H *see* THE WILLIAM H. HASTIE PAPERS
HASTINGS AND ST LEONARDS CHRONICLE – England.1849-52; 1858; 1884; 1892; 1896; 1898-1900. -w. 11 reels – 1 – uk British Libr Newspaper [072]
HASTINGS AND ST LEONARDS NEWS – Hastings, England. 1848-1900. -w. 24 1/4 reels. Missing: 1850; 1854; 1860; 1863-64; 1882; 1884-86; 1889; 1891-94; 1897 – 1 – uk British Libr Newspaper [072]
Hastings, Bessie *see* PUBLISHED MANUSCRIPTS
HASTINGS CHRONICLE – Hastings, Canada. 1861-64 – 1r – 1 – $68.00 – cn Library Assoc [971]
HASTINGS COLLEGE OF LAW : LIBRARY SHELF LIST – Dec 1983 – 6r – 5 – $300.00 – B50523 – us Library Micro [370]
HASTINGS COMMUNICATIONS AND ENTERTAINMENT LAW JOURNAL (COMM/ENT) – (v1-7 1977-85 on reel $112.00. v8-17 1985-95 on mf $208.00. Title varies: v1-5 1977-83 as COMM/ENT: A Journal of Communications and Entertainment Law. v6-10 1983-88 as COMM/ENT: Hastings Journal of Communications and Entertainment Law) – Hastings College of Law. v1-17. 1977-95 – 5,6,9 – $320.00 – us Hein [340]
HASTINGS CONSTITUTIONAL LAW QUARTERLY – (v1-12 1974-85 on reel $200.00. v13-22 1985-95 on mf $195.00) – v1-22. 1974-95 – 5,6,9 – $395.00 set – us Hein [323]
HASTINGS DAILY NEBRASKAN – Hastings, NE. Aug 1891-Dec 1894 – 1 – us NE Hist [071]
HASTINGS DAILY REPUBLICAN – Hastings, NE. May 1892; Oct 1895-May 1898; Jan 1899-Sept 1915 – 1 – us NE Hist [071]
HASTINGS DAILY TRIBUNE – Hastings, NE. Oct 1905-Sept 1906; May 1907-Mar 1908; Oct 1908 to date – 1 – us NE Hist [071]
HASTINGS EVENING RECORD – Hastings, NE. -d. Sept 1897-Jun 1898; Jan 1899-Nov 1900 – 1 – us NE Hist [071]
Hastings, Frederick *see*
- THE BACKGROUND OF SACRED STORY
- OBSCURE CHARACTERS AND MINOR LIGHTS OF SCRIPTURE

HASTINGS GAZETTE-JOURNAL – Hastings, NE. -w. Dec 1875; Dec 1876; May 1879-Nov 1882; Jan-Dec 1884; Dec 1885-Dec 1887 – 1 – us NE Hist [071]
Hastings, Horace Lorenzo *see*
- ARE THERE CORRUPTIONS IN THE NEW TESTAMENT
- ATHEISM AND ARITHMETIC
- A SQUARE TALK TO YOUNG MEN ABOUT THE INSPIRATION OF THE BIBLE

HASTINGS INTERNATIONAL AND COMPARATIVE LAW REVIEW – v1-18. 1977-95 – 1,5,6 – $270.00 – us Hein [073]
Hastings, James *see* SUB CORONA
HASTINGS JOURNAL – Hastings, NE. -w. Nov 1895-Jun 1899; Sept 1899-Dec 1900; May 1901-Mar 1902; May-Oct 1902 – 1 – us NE Hist [071]
HASTINGS LAW JOURNAL – (v1-36 1949-85 on reel or mf $706.00. v37-46 1985-95 on mf $256.00) – v1-46. 1949-95 – 5,6,9 – $962.00 set – us Hein [340]
Hastings, Robert J *see*
- PUBLISHED MANUSCRIPTS
- STEWARDSHIP DEVELOPMENT MATERIALS

Hastings, Thomas *see*
- THE HISTORY OF FORTY CHOIRS
- MUSICA SACRE
- PSALMIST OR CHOIR MELODIES

HASTINGS TRIBUNE – Hastings, NE. -w. Jun 1892-Feb 1893, scattered issues missing; Nov 1894-Sept 1895; Dec 1896-Oct 1914; Dec 1914-Aug 1917 – 1 – us NE Hist [071]
Hastings, Truman *see* LAW FOR THE MASSES: FOR EVERY-DAY USE
HASTINGS WEEKLY NEBRASKAN – Hastings, NE. (-sw. 1876-83). Mar 1878-Dec 1889, scattered issues missing; Sept 1891-Dec 1892; Feb 1893-Mar 1895 – 1 – us NE Hist [071]
Haswell, J P *see*
- AN ALPHABETICAL ARRANGEMENT OF ALL THE WESLEYAN-METHODIST MINISTERS, MISSIONARIES AND PREACHERS ON TRIAL, IN CONNEXION WITH THE BRITISH AND IRISH CONFERENCES
- AN ALPHABETICAL ARRANGEMENT OF ALL THE WESLEYAN-METHODIST MINISTERS, MISSIONARIES AND PREACHERS ON TRIAL IN CONNEXION WITH THE BRITISH AND IRISH CONFERENCES OR WITH THE AFFILIATED CONFERENCES
- AN ALPHABETICAL ARRANGEMENT OF ALL THE WESLEYAN-METHODIST MINISTERS, MISSIONARIES AND PREACHERS ON TRIAL IN CONNEXION WITH THE BRITISH AND IRISH CONFERENCES;...FROM THE COMMENCEMENT OF THEIR ITINERANCY TO...1846
- AN ALPHABETICAL ARRANGEMENT OF ALL THE WESLEYAN-METHODIST MINISTERS, MISSIONARIES AND PREACHERS ON TRIAL IN CONNEXION WITH THE BRITISH AND IRISH CONFERENCES;...FROM THE COMMENCEMENT OF THEIR ITINERANCY TO...1852

HAT DER DRITTE EVANGELIST DEN KANONISCHEN MATTHAEUS BENUTZT? / Simons, Eduard – Bonn: Carl Georgi, 1880.1 fiche – 9 – us A.T.L.A. [240]
HAT JESUS DAS PAPSTTUM GESTIFTET? : EINE DOGMENGESCHICHTLICHE UNTERSUCHUNG / Schnitzer, Joseph – Augsburg: Lampart, 1910 – 1mf – us A.T.L.A. [240]
HAT JESUS WUNDER GETAN?: EINE BIBLISCHE WIDERLEGUNG KIRCHLICHEN ABERGLAUBENS / Soltau, Wilhelm – Leipzig: Dieterich, 1903. 1 fiche – 9 – us A.T.L.A. [240]
HAT RICHARD WAGNER EINE SCHULE HINTERLASSEN? / Seidl, Arthur – (Includes bibliographical references) – Kiel: Lipsius und Tischer, 1892 – 1r – 1 – us U.W. Library [780]
HATASKORI JOGSZABALYOK ES HATASKORI HATAROZATOK TARA. – Budapest. On film: v1-9; 1909-17. LL-0249 – 1 – us L of C Photodup [340]
HATCH / Wisconsin. College of Agriculture. Dept. of Poultry Science – Sep 30, 1953-Jul 1969, v.1-1 to v.6-10 – 1,5 – us Spaulding [630]
HATCH ACT DECISIONS : POLITICAL ACTIVITIES CASES OF THE U.S. CIVIL SERVICE COMMISSION / Irwin, James W – (Pt 1-A text on principles and cases. Pt 2-A casebook on commission decisions) – Washington: GPO, 1949 – 4mf – 9 – $6.00 – LLMC 84-110 – us L.L.M.C. [340]
Hatch, Azel Farnsworth *see* STATUTES AND CONSTITUTIONAL PROVISIONS OF THE STATES AND TERRITORIES OF THE UNITED STATES AND THE STATUTES OF ENGLAND ON LIBEL AND SLANDER.
Hatch, E *see* CONCORDANCE TO THE SEPTUAGINT AND THE OTHER GREEK VERSIONS OF THE OLD TESTAMENT
Hatch, Edwin *see*
- GRIECHENTUM UND CHRISTENTUM
- THE INFLUENCES OF GREEK IDEAS AND USAGES UPON THE CHRISTIAN CHURCH
- AN INTRODUCTORY LECTURE ON THE STUDY OF ECCLESIASTICAL HISTORY
- THE ORGANISATION OF THE EARLY CHRISTIAN CHURCHES

HATCHERY AND FEED *see* FARM SUPPLIER
HATCHERY TRIBUNE *see* FARM SUPPLIER
HATCHIAH – Chicago. Regeneration. 1899-1900 – 1 – us A.J.P.C. [071]
Hateau, G *see* PANORAMA DE LA LITTERATURE BULGARE CONTEMPORAINE
HA-TEHIYYAH – Ed. by S. Sachs. 2 v. Berlin. 1850, 1856. BJ-100-161 1 – 9 – ne IDC [072]
HA-TEKUFAH – Moscow. Warsaw. Berlin. Tel Aviv. New York. 1918-50. Available; 1918-23, v. 1-19. BJ-91-28 1 – 9 – ne IDC [470]

HATEM UEL-ENBIYA / Ileri, Celal Nuri – Istanbul: Yeni Osmanli Matbaa ve Kitaphanesi, 1332 [1916] – $75.00 – us MEDOC [470]
Hatfield, Bradley D *see* CENTRAL AND AUTONOMIC NERVOUS SYSTEM ACTIVITY DURING SELF-PACED MOTOR PERFORMANCE: A STUDY OF THE ACTIVATION CONSTRUCT IN MARKSMEN
Hatfield, Edwin F *see* HISTORY OF ELIZABETH, INCLUDING AN EARLY HISTORY OF UNION COUNTY
Hathaway, Grace *see* FATE RIDES A TORTOISE; A BIOGRAPHY OF ELLEN SPENCER MUSSEY
Hathaway, Lillie Vinal *see* GERMAN LITERATURE OF THE MID-NINETEENTH CENTURY IN ENGLAND AND AMERICA
HATIKVA – Buenos Aires, Argentina. -f. 15 July-15 Nov 1948; 1 May 1949-27 June, Oct 1958. Imperfect. 3 reels – 1 – uk British Libr Newspaper [072]
HATIKVAH – New York, NY, v1, no. 1(Dec. 1971)-v2, no. 1 (20 Dec. 1972); v3, no. 1 (Nov. 1973)-v3, no. 2 (Jan. 1974); v3, no. 4 (15 Apr. 1974)-v5, no. 4 (May 1976); v6, no. 2 (June 1977)-v7, no. 2 (Jan. 1978); v9, no. 2 (Mar. 1980)-v10, no. 1 (Nov. 1980); v11, no. 1 (Jan. 1982)-v15, no. 3 (Dec. 1985); v15, no. 5 (May 1986)-v16, no. 1 (Nov. 1986); v16, no. 3 (Mar. 1987) – us A.J.P.C. [270]
HATIKWAH – Amsterdam, 1916-1930. v1-13 – 21mf – 9 – J-261-44/1 – ne IDC [943]
Hatings, Horace Lorenzo *see* SQUARE TALK TO YOUNG MEN ABOUT THE INSPIRATION OF THE BIBLE
HATIRAT-I NIYAZI / Resneli, Niyazi Bey – Istanbul: Sabah Matbaasi, 1326 [1910] – 9 – $65.00 – us MEDOC [956]
HA-TOR – Jerusalem. 1920-36. BJ-91-29 1 – 9 – ne IDC [470]
HA-TOREN – New York, NY. 1913-21 – 1 – us A.J.P.C. [073]
HATS'I HAMAR / Mankowni, N L – 1914 – 9 – $15.00 – us Scholars' Facs [490]
HATS'I HAMAR / Mankowni, N L – 1962 – 9 – $15.00 – us Scholars' Facs [490]
HATSOFE – New York. N.Y. 1872 – 1 – us A.J.P.C. [071]
Hatt, G *see*
- ARKTISKE SKINDDRAGTER I EURASIEN OG AMERIKA
- KYST-OG INDLANDSKULTUR I DET ARKTISKE
- MOCCASINS AND THEIR RELATION TO ARCTIC FOOTWEAR

HATT GIEGEN HATT : NIEDERDEUTSCHES BAUERNDRAMA IN 3 AUFZUEGEN / Wagenfeld, Karl – Hamburg: R Hermes, 1917 [c1916] – 1r – 1 – us U.W. Library [820]
Hatta, M *see* BEBERAPA FASAL EKONOMI. DJALAN KE EKONOMI DAN KOOPERASI
Hatta, Mohammad *see*
- THE CO-OPERATIVE MOVEMENT AS AN INSTITUTION FOR TEACHING AUTO-ACTIVITY AND A HIGH ECONOMIC CHARACTER
- THE CO-OPERATIVE MOVEMENT IN INDONESIA
- DEMOKRASI KITA
- EKONOMI KITA
- HOW FAR HAVE WE GOT?
- INDONESIAN AIMS AND IDEALS. A PERSONAL MESSAGE TO MY OLD COMRADES WHEREVER THEY MAY BE

Hattersley, Allan Frederick *see* LATER ANNALS OF NATAL
Hattery, Lowell H *see*
- TECHNOLOGICAL CHANGE IN PRINTING AND PUBLISHING
- TECHNOLOGY AND COPYRIGHT: SOURCES AND SELECTED MATERIALS
- TECHNOLOGY & COPYRIGHT: RESOURCES ON LAW, PRACTICE, OPINION

Hattery, Thomas H *see* WESTERN MARYLAND: A PROFILE
Hattler, Franz *see*
- CHRISTROSEN IM MARIENGARTEN
- DAS GNADENBILD DER MATER TER ADMIRABILIS VON INGOLSTADT IN BAYERN

Hatton, Christopher *see* BLAZON OF ARMS
Hatton, Joseph *see*
- HENRY IRVING'S IMPRESSIONS OF AMERICA: NARRATED IN A SERIES OF SKETCHES, CHRONICLES AND CONVERSATIONS
- THE LYCEUM "FAUST"
- NEWFOUNDLAND, THE OLDEST BRITISH COLONY: ITS HISTORY, ITS PRESENT CONDITION, AND ITS PROSPECTS IN THE FUTURE

HATZFELDER VOLKSBLATT – Hatzfeld (Jimbolia), Rumaenien. 30 Nov 1924-1932 – 2r – 1 – gw Mikrofilm [949]
HATZFELDER ZEITUNG – Hatzfeld (Jimbolia), Rumaenien. 10 Okt 1920-10 Dec 1939 – 5r – 1 – gw Mikrofilm [949]
HA-TZOFE – Israel, 1979- – 9 – $210.00y – us Ross [072]
Hauber, A *see* URKUNDENBUCH DES KLOSTERS HELIGENKREUZTAL
Haubrich, Stefan *see* KREBS DURCH NIEDERFREQUENTE MAGNETFELDER?
Hauch, Johannes Carsten *see* SAGA OM THORVALD VIDFORLE ELLER DEN VIDTBEREISTE
Hauck, Albert *see*
- DIE ENTSTEHUNG DER BISCHOEFLICHEN FUERSTENMACHT
- REALENCYCLOPAEDIE FUER PROTESTANTISCHE THEOLOGIE UND KIRCHE
- DIE TRENNUNG VON KIRCHE UND STAAT

Hauck, Gerhard *see* DIE POLITISCHEN FUEHRUNGSSCHICHTEN IN DEN NEUEN STAATEN SCHWARZ-AFRIKAS
HAUDESCHE ZEITUNG *see* BERLINISCHE NACHRICHTEN VON STAATS- UND GELEHRTEN SACHEN
Hauet, D *see* LA FORMATION PROFESSIONELLE PAR SES PROPRES MOYENS DANS LES PAYS EN VOIE DE DEVELOPPEMENT
Hauff, Reinhard von *see* NIETZSCHES STELLUNG ZUR CHRISTLICHEN DEMUT
Hauff, Wilhelm *see*
- AN CARABHAN
- CUENTOS
- DER WOLLMARKT

HAUFFS "MEMOIREN DES SATAN" : TEILDRUCK / Sommermeyer, Edwin – (Includes bibliographical references) – Berlin: E. Eberling, [1930] – 1r – 1 – us U.W. Library [430]
Haug, Karl *see* DIE AUTORITAET DER HLG. SCHRIFT UND DIE KRITIK
Haug, Rhea C *see* DEVELOPMENT AND VALIDATION OF A MAXIMAL TESTING PROTOCOL FOR THE NORDICTRACK CROSS-COUNTRY SKI SIMULATOR
Hauksbee, F *see* A COURSE OF MECHANICAL, OPTICAL HYDROSTATICAL AND PNEUMATICAL EXPERIMENTS...
Haule, James M *see* CONCORDANCES TO THE NOVELS OF VIRGINIA WOOLF
Haultain, Theodore Arnold *see*
- VERSICULI
- THE WAR IN THE SOUDAN: AND THE CAUSES WHICH LEAD TO IT: WITH SHORT BIOGRAPHICAL SKETCHES OF THE PRINCIPAL PERSONAGES ENGAGED

Haumant, E *see* LA CULTURE FRANCAISE EN RUSSIE (1700-1900)
Haunold, C *see* INSTITUTIONUM THEOLOGICARUM...
THE HAUNTED MAN AND THE GHOST'S BARGAIN : A FANCY FOR CHRISTMAS-TIME / Dickens, Charles – London: Bradbury & Evans, 1848 – 1 roll – 1 – 1-55879-302-X – uk Libr Preservation [830]
THE HAUNTED TOWER: A COMIC OPERA IN THREE ACTS. / Storace, Stephen – (Vocal score). 1789 – 9 – us Sibley [780]
Haupers, Clement B *see* PAPERS
Haupt, Erich *see*
- DIE ESCHATOLOGISCHEN AUSSAGEN JESU IN DEN SYNOPTISCHEN EVANGELIEN
- FIRST EPISTLE OF ST JOHN

Haupt, Georges *see* FRENCH SOCIALIST CONGRESSES
Haupt, Herman *see*
- DIE DEUTSCHE BIBELUEBERSETZUNG DES MITTELALTERLICHEN WALDENSER IN DEM CODEX TEPLENSIS UND DER ERSTEN GEDRUCKTEN DEUTSCHEN BIBEL NACHGEWIESEN
- DER WALDENSISCHE URSPRUNG DES CODEX TEPLENSIS UND DER VORLUTHERISCHEN DEUTSCHEN BIBELDRUCKE

Haupt, Moritz et al *see*
- ZEITSCHRIFT FUER DEUTSCHES ALTERTUM UND DEUTSCHE LITERATUR

Haupt, P *see*
- BEITRAEGE ZUR ASSYRIOLOGIE UND VERGLEICHENDEN SEMITISCHEN SPRACHWISSENSCHAFT
- ORIENTAL STUDIES

Haupt, Paul *see*
- BIBLISCHE LIEBESLIEDER
- BOOK OF ECCLESIASTES: A NEW METRICAL TRANSLATION
- SUMERISCHE STUDIEN

HAUPTERGEBNISSE DER AMTLICHEN LOHNERHEBUNG IN DER SCHUHINDUSTRIE – Statistisches Reichsamt. 1929. 13p. (Serial publications of German trade unions in the Memorial Library, University of Wisconsin-Madison.) – 1 – us U.W. Library [310]
Hauptman, M *see* DIE LEHRE VON DER HARMONIK, MIT BEIGEFUSTAN NOTEBEISPIELEN
DER HAUPTMANN / Grote, Hans Henning, Freiherr – Oldenburg: G Stalling, 1937, c1932 – 1r – 1 – us U.W. Library [830]
Hauptmann, Carl *see*
- DIE ARMSELIGEN BESENBINDER
- KRIEG
- UNSERE WIRKLICHKEIT
- WALDLEUTE

Hauptmann, Gerhart *see*
- BAHNWAERTER THIEL
- COLLEGE CRAMPTON
- THE COMING OF PEACE
- DOROTHEA ANGERMANN
- GOETHE
- GRISELDA
- HANNELE
- DIE HOCHZEIT AUF BUCHENHORST
- INDIPOHDI
- NEUE GEDICHTE
- DIE SPITZHACKE
- THE SUNKEN BELL.
- VELAND
- THE WEAVERS; A DRAMA OF THE FORTIES

HAUPTMANN-STUDIEN; UNTERSUCHUNGEN UEBER LEBEN UND SCHAFFEN GERHART HAUPTMANNS / Voigt, Felix Alfred – Breslau: Maruschke & Berendt, 1936- – 1 – us U.W. Library [430]
DAS HAUPTPROBLEM DER EVANGELIENFRAGE UND DER WEG ZU SEINER LOESUNG : EINE AKADEMISCHE VORLESUNG / Ewald, Paul – Leipzig:J C Hinrichs, 1890 – 1mf – 9 – 0-8370-3088-9 – 1985-1088 – us A.T.L.A. [220]
DIE HAUPTPROBLEME DER LEBEN-JESU-FORSCHUNG / Schmiedel, Otto – (Includes bibliographical references) – 2. verb verm Aufl. Tuebingen: J C B Mohr (Paul Siebeck), 1906 – 1mf – 9 – 0-8370-9741-X – 1986-3741 – us A.T.L.A. [240]
DIE HAUPTWERKE DER DEUTSCHEN LITERATUR IN ZUSAMMENHANGE MIT IHRER GATTUNG / Nagel, Siegfried Robert – (Includes index) – Wien: F Deuticke, 1904 – 1r – 1 – us U.W. Library [430]
Haureau, A B *see*
- GALLIA CHRISTIANA (GC)
- PROVINCIA TURONENSIS (GC 14)
- PROVINCIA VESUNTIONENSIS (GC 15)
- PROVINCIA VIENNENSIS (GC 16)

Haureau, B *see*
- BERNARD DELICIEUX ET L'INQUISITION ALBIGEOISE (1300-1320)
- HISTOIRE DE LA PHILOSOPHIE SCOLASTIQUE
- LES OEUVRES DE HUGUES DE SAINT-VICTOR
- DES POEMES LATINS ATTRIBUES A SAINT BERNARD
- SINGULARITES HISTORIQUES ET LITTERAIRES

Haureau, Barthelemy *see* GALLIA CHRISTIANA IN PROVINCIAS ECCLESIASTICAS DISTRIBUTA
HAUS DER KUNST CATALOGUE – (Individual titles not listed separately) – Munich, 1949-1975 – 64 catalogues on 158mf – 9 – £995.00 – uk Chadwyck [700]
DAS HAUS DES DR. PRADE : ROMAN / Wilke, Karl – Leipzig: Koehler & Amelang, c1930 – 1r – 1 – us U.W. Library [830]
DAS HAUS MIT DEN DREI TUEREN / Schaefer, Wilhelm – Muenchen: G Mueller, c1931 – 1r – 1 – us U.W. Library [830]
HAUS UND SIEDLUNG IM WANDEL DER JAHRTAUSENDE / Helbok, Adolf – 1937 – 1 – us I.U. Libraries [390]
HAUSA NEWSPAPERS : ASSEMBLED AND FILMED IN UNIVERSITY OF WISCONSIN, MEMORIAL LIBRARY – Madison: Memorial Library [for Cooperative Africana Microform Project] 1981? – us Res Libr [072]
DER HAUSBALL : EINE ERZAEHLUNG: 1781 – Wien: C Konegen, 1883 – 1 – us U.W. Library [830]
Hauser, E *see* DIE HAAGER UEBEREINKUNFT VOM 12. JUNI 1902...
Hauser, Henri *see*
- ETUDES SUR LA REFORME FRANCAISE
- HISTOIRE D'UNE GREVE AU XVIE SIECLE
- LE PRINCIPE DES NATIONALITES...
- TRAVAILLEURS ET MARCHANDS DANS L'ANCIENNE FRANCE

Haushofer, Albrecht *see* MOABITER SONETTE
Hausmann, F *see* REICHSKANZLEI UND HOFKALLE UNTER HEINRICH 5 UND KONRAD 3 (MGH SCHRIFTEN..: 14.BD)
DAS HAUSPERSONAL – Berlin, 1913-14 – 1 – Dist. gw Mikrofilm – gw Misc Inst [640]
Hausrath, Adolf *see*
- ALEANDER UND LUTHER AUF DEM REICHSTAGE ZU WORMS
- JESUS UND DIE NEUTESTAMENTLICHEN SCHRIFTSTELLER
- KLEINE SCHRIFTEN RELIGIONS-GESCHICHTLICHEN INHALTS
- MARTIN LUTHERS ROMFAHRT
- NEUTESTAMENTLICHE, ZEITGESCHICHTE
- DER VIER-CAPITEL-BRIEF DES PAULUS AN DIE KORINTHER

Hausrath, Adolrf *see* JESUS UND DIE NEUTESTAMENTLICHE SCHRIFTSTELLER
HAUSS APOTECK ZU YEDEN LEIBS GEBRESTEN, FUER DEN GEMAINEN MANN, VND DAS ARM LANDUOLCK / Brunschwig, Hieronymus – Augspurg, 1539 – 1 – us U.W. Library [615]
Haussleiter, Johannes *see* ZWEI APOSTOLISCHE ZEUGEN FUER DAS JOHANNES EVANGELIUM
Haussmann, Johannes *see* UNTERSUCHUNGEN UEBER SPRACHE UND STIL DES JUNGEN HERDER
Haussonville, O d' *see* HISTOIRE DE LA POLITIQUE EXTERIEURE...1830-48
HAUT LES FOURCHES – Journal des jeunesses paysannes. no. 5-6. Paris. juil-aout 1936 – 1 – fr A.C.R.P.P. [073]
HAUT SENEGAL NIGER / Delafosse, Maurice – Paris, Emile Larose. 1912 – 9 – 35.00 – fr Orientalistes [960]
DER HAUTARZT – v. 1-31. 1950-80 – 1,5,9 – 2906.00 – us UMI [073]
Haut-Canada. Parliament. House of Assembly *see* PROCEEDING HAD IN THE LEGISLATURE OF UPPER CANADA DURING THE YEARS 1831-2...
Haut-Canada. Parliament. House of Assembly. Select Committee Appointed to Report on the State of the Province *see* REPORT FROM THE SELECT COMMITTEE OF THE HOUSE OF ASSEMBLY OF UPPER CANADA, APPOINTED TO REPORT ON THE STATE OF THE PROVINCE
Haut-Canada. Parliament. Legislative Council *see* PROCEEDINGS OF THE LEGISLATIVE COUNCIL OF UPPER CANADA, ON THE BILL SENT UP FROM THE HOUSE OF ASSEMBLY ENTITLED, AN ACT TO AMEND THE JURY LAWS OF THIS PROVINCE
Haut-Canada. Parliament. Legislative Council. Select Committee on the State of the Province *see* REPORT FROM THE SELECT COMMITTEE OF THE LEGISLATIVE COUNCIL OF UPPER CANADA ON THE STATE OF THE PROVINCE
Hautcoeur, E *see*
- CARTULAIRE DE L'ABBAYE DE FLINES
- LA LITURGIE CAMBRESIENNE AU 18E SIECLE ET LE PROJET DE BREVIAIRE POUR TOUS LES DIOCESES DES PAYS-BAS

LA HAUTE MARNE ANCIENNE ET MODERNE / Jolibois – Chaumont, 1858 – 2mf – 9 – F60.00 – fr F.F.G. [944]
LA HAUTE SCIENCE – Revue documentaire de la tradition esoterique et du symbolisme religieux. Dir. F. Deschamps. Paris. 1893-janv 1895 – 1 – fr A.C.R.P.P. [073]
Hautecœur, Jean-Paul *see*
- ALPHA 94
- CURRENT RESEARCH IN LITERACY

Hautefeuille, L B *see*
- DES DROITS ET DES DEVOIRS...
- HISTOIRE DES ORIGINES,...
- QUESTIONS DE DROIT MARITIME...

Hautefeuille, Laurent B *see* PLAN DE COLONISATION DES POSSESSIONS FRANCAISES DANS L'AFRIQUE OCCIDENTALE, AU MOYEN DE LA CIVILISATION DES NEGRES INDIGENES
LE HAUT-PARLEUR / ed by Bouchard, T D & Michaud, Yves – St-Hyacinthe, Canada. 1 jan 1950-15 aut 1953 – 1r – 1 – Can$55.00 – cn Can Microfilming [072]
Hautsch, E *see* DIE EVANGLIENZITATE DES ORIGENES (T.U.U. 3-34/2A)
LE HAUT-SENEGAL ET NIGER – Corbeil, France: E Crete, 1906 – 1 – us Res Libr [960]
HAUT-SENEGAL-NIGER (SOUDAN FRANCAIS) / Delafosse, Maurice – (v.1: Le Pays, les Peuples, les Langues. v.2: L'Histoire. v.3: Les Civilisations) – 3v. BA-401 1. 1912 – 9 – ne IDC [960]

Hava, J *see* ARAB-ENGLISH DICTIONARY

Havard, Henry *see*
- L'ART ET LE COMFORT DANS LA VIE MODERNE.
- THE DEAD CITIES OF THE ZUYDER ZEE: A VOYAGE TO THE PICTURESQUE SIDE OF HOLLAND

Havard, Louis *see* LA MAISON SALUBRE ET LA MAISON INSALUBRE.

HAVAZZELET, JERUSALEM 4TH – Nisan. BJ-27-205 1 – 9 – ne IDC [947]

HAVE A GOOD TIME; POCKET MANUAL FOR PRACTICAL INDONESIAN / Siagian, Gajus – SE 4195 1. 1962 – 9 – ne IDC [490]

HAVE THE SACRED WRITERS ANYWHERE ASSERTED THAT THE SIN OR RIGHTEOUSNESS OF ONE IS IMPUTED TO ANOTHER? / Stuart, Moses – The Biblical Repository and Quarterly Observer, v7,no.22, 22 Apr 1836, p241-330 – 9 – us A.T.L.A. [240]

HAVE WE A REVOLUTION FROM GOD...SMITH'S ARTICLE, BIBLE, IN ENCYCLOPAEDIA BRITANNICA, 9TH ED – London: Bible Witness & Review, 1878. 1 fiche – 9 – us A.T.L.A. [240]

HAVE WE ANY "WORD OF GOD"? / Seeley, Robert Benton – London: S W Partridge, 1864? – 1mf – 9 – 0-8370-5214-9 – 1985-3214 – us A.T.L.A. [220]

HAVEKUNST – v.1-49. 1923-68. Superseded by Landskap – 1 – us UMI [740]

HAVELLAENDISCHES ECHO – (Bereichsausgabe der Spandauer Zeitung) – Berlin, jan-mar 1933 – 1r – 1 – Dist. gw Mikrofilm – gw Misc Inst [943]

HAVELOCK ELLIS: A BIOGRAPHICAL AND CRITICAL SURVEY / Goldberg, Isaac – New York: Simon & Schuster, 1926 – 1 – us U.W. Library [920]

HAVELOCK POST – Havelock, NE. -w. Jan 1918-Apr 1925 – 1 – us NE Hist [071]

Havelock, R G *see* SOLVING EDUCATIONAL PROBLEMS

Haverford College. Pennsylvania *see* QUAKER NECROLOGY

HAVERHILL 1641-1849 – (Mf 1T: Vital Records 1641-64. Mf 1T-2T: Family Vital Records 1642-1779. Mf 3T-10T: Vital Records 1701-1849. Mf 10T: Deaths 1809-42. Mf 10T-13T: Vital Records 1780-1849. Mf 13T-14T: Births 1844-49. Mf 14T-15T: Marriages 1844-49. Mf 15T-16T: Deaths 1844-49. Mf 16T-19T: Intentions 1782-1849) – (mf ed 1996) – 19mf – 9 – 0-87623-264-0 – us Holbrook [920]

HAVERHILL ECHO *see* THE ECHO

Haverhill, Massachusetts *see* MISCELLANEOUS EARLY NEWSPAPERS

Havers, C *see* OSTEOLOGIA NOVA

Havers, G R *see* VOLTAIRE'S CATALOGUE OF HIS LIBRARY AT FERNEY

Havestadt, J *see* DIE STAATSANGEHO-ERIGKEIT DER JURISTISCHEN PERSONEN...

Havet, Ernest *see* LA MODERNITE DES PROPHETES

Haviland, Charles Tappan *see* THE GENERAL CORPORATION LAW, THE STOCK CORPORATION LAW, THE TRANSPORTATION CORPORATIONS LAW, AND THE BUSINESS CORPORATION LAW, OF THE STATE OF NEW YORK.

Haviland, Frank Wood *see* SCIENCE

Haviland, Laura Smith *see* A WOMAN'S LIFE-WORK: LABORS AND EXPERIENCES OF LAURA S. HAVILAND

HAVING MY WAY / Read, Leonard E – 1974. 192p. Together with: Castles In the Air. 1975. 190p.; Then Truth Will Out. 1971. 188p. 1 fiche (36x) – 9 – 1.00f – at Libertarian Micro [320]

LE HAVRE – Perce, Canada. 12 oct 1977-26 dec 1990 – 14r – 1 – Can$70.00r – cn Can Microfilming [072]

HAWAII : SESSION LAWS OF AMERICAN STATES AND TERRITORIES – 1901-95 – 9 – $680.00 set – us Hein [340]

Hawaii *see*
- ATTORNEY GENERAL OPINIONS
- ATTORNEYS' ETHICS COLLECTION
- REPORTS AND OPINIONS (A-G)
- REPORTS, PRE-NRS

HAWAII APPELLATE REPORTS / Hawaii. Intermediate Court of Appeals – (No Pre-NRS vols. v9-10 ends official state set) – v1-8. 1980-91 – 80mf – 9 – $120.00 – LLMC 82-998 – us L.L.M.C. [340]

HAWAII APPELLATE REPORTS *see*
- ATTORNEY GENERAL OPINIONS
- ATTORNEYS' ETHICS COLLECTION
- COMPILED STATUTES
- HOUSE JOURNALS
- SENATE JOURNALS
- SESSION LAWS
- UNIVERSITY OF HAWAII LAW REVIEW

HAWAII ATTORNEY GENERAL REPORTS AND OPINIONS – (6 1845-1963 $70.00. 9 1961-1994 $152.50) – 1845-1994 – 6,9 – $222.50set – us Hein [340]

HAWAII BAPTIST – Honolulu. Aug 1947-1991 – 1 – $156.32 – us Baptist [240]

HAWAII BAR JOURNAL – (Merged with: Hawaii Bar News) – v1-23. 1963-1991 (all publ) – 9 – $95.00 set – us Hein [340]

HAWAII BAR JOURNAL (NS) – (Titles varies: v1- 1992 as Hawaii Bar News) – v1-27. 1991-94 – 9 – $295.00set – us Hein [340]

HAWAII BAR NEWS *see*
- HAWAII BAR JOURNAL
- HAWAII BAR JOURNAL (NS)

HAWAII BUSINESS *see* HAWAII BUSINESS AND INDUSTRY

HAWAII BUSINESS AND INDUSTRY – (Cont: Hawaii Industry. Cont by: Hawaii Business) – Honolulu. v8-14. jul 1962-oct 1968* – 1 – D17867.02 – us UMI [650]

HAWAII BUSINESS AND INDUSTRY *see* HAWAII INDUSTRY

HAWAII ENGINEER – (Cont by: Hawaii Industry) – Honolulu. v1-2. jul 1955-jun 1957* – 1 – D17867 – us UMI [620]

HAWAII ENGINEER *see* HAWAII INDUSTRY

HAWAII FARM AND HOME – Honolulu. v13. 1950 – 1 – D389 – us UMI [640]

HAWAII INDUSTRY – (Cont: Hawaii Engineer. Cont by: Hawaii Business and Industry) – Honolulu. v3-7. jul 1957-jun 1962* – 1 – D17867.01 – us UMI [620]

HAWAII INDUSTRY *see*
- HAWAII BUSINESS AND INDUSTRY
- HAWAII ENGINEER

Hawaii. Intermediate Court of Appeals *see* HAWAII APPELLATE REPORTS

HAWAII JEWISH NEWS – Honolulu, HI. 1977-85 – 1 – us A.J.P.C. [071]

Hawaii. Laws, Statutes, etc *see* PATENT LAWS OF THE REPUBLIC OF HAWAII, AND RULES OF PRACTICE IN THE PATENT OFFICE

Hawaii Legislature *see*
- COMPILED STATUTES
- HOUSE JOURNALS
- SENATE JOURNALS
- SESSION LAWS

HAWAII LIBRARY ASSOCIATION JOURNAL *see* HLA JOURNAL

HAWAII MEDICAL JOURNAL – (Former titles: Hawaii Medical Journal sep 1941-aug 1946. Hawaii Medical Journal and Inter-island Nurses' Bulletin sep/oct 1946-jan/feb 1962) – Honolulu. v1-56. sep 1941-dec 1997+ 1; v30-52 1971-93. v53 1994*. v54-56 1995-97+ 5; v33-56. 1974-97+ 9 – 1,5,9 – D332 – us UMI [610]

HAWAII MEDICAL JOURNAL *see* HAWAII MEDICAL JOURNAL

HAWAII MEDICAL JOURNAL AND INTER-ISLAND NURSES' BULLETIN *see* HAWAII MEDICAL JOURNAL

HAWAII REVISED STATUTES – 1905-Nov 1990 update – 9 – $575.00 set – us Hein [340]

HAWAII SUPREME COURT REPORTS – (Includes 4v of the US District Court for the Territory of Hawaii. v75 ends official state set. Pre-NRS run: v1-43 1847-1961 419mf $616.00) – v1-4; v1-74. 1847-1993. Including the 4v of the U.S. – 657mf – 9 – $985.00 – LLMC 77-101 – us L.L.M.C. [340]

HAWAII SUPREME COURT REPORTS *see*
- EDING'S DIGEST OF HAWAII SUPREME COURT DEC
- THAYER'S DIGEST OF HAWAII SUPREME COURT DEC

HAWAIIAN ENTOMOLOGICAL SOCIETY : PROCEEDINGS – Honolulu. v1-21. dec 1904-sep 1974 – 1 – D8703 – us UMI [590]

HAWAIIAN MISSION CHILDREN'S SOCIETY : ANNUAL REPORT – v1-132. 1853-1991 (complete) – Inquire – 1 – ATLA S0684 – us A.T.L.A. [073]

HAWAIIAN SHELL NEWS – 1952- – 1; 1974-5,6; 1975- 9 – us UMI [590]

Hawaiian/Pacific Collection of the Uni of Hawaii Library *see*
- MATERIALS ON THE COMPACT OF FREE ASSOCIATION FOR MICRONESIA, PALAU AND THE MARSHALLS

Haweis, Hugh Reginald *see*
- THE BROAD CHURCH
- THE CONQUERING CROSS (THE CHURCH)
- CURRENT COIN
- THE DEAD PULPIT
- SERMONS

Hawes, Granville Parker *see* THE LAW RELATING TO GENERAL VOLUNTARY ASSIGNMENTS FOR THE BENEFIT OF CREDITORS, AS PROVIDED FOR THE STATUTE OF 1860, AS AMENDED

Hawes, Joel *see* A LOOKING GLASS FOR LADIES

Hawes, W *see* AN EXAMINATION OF THE REV. MR. JOHN WESLEY'S 'PRIMITIVE PHYSIC', SHEWING THAT A GREAT NUMBER OF THE PRESCRIPTIONS THEREIN CONTAINED ARE FOUNDED ON IGNORANCE OF THE MEDICAL ART AND OF THE POWER AND OPERATION OF MEDICINES,...

HAWICK NEWS – 1 – £42.00r – uk Scot News [072]

Hawker, George *see*
- AN ENGLISHWOMAN'S TWENTY-FIVE YEARS IN TROPICAL AFRICA
- THE LIFE OF GEORGE GRENFELL

Hawker, Robert Stephen *see* THE POETICAL WORKS OF ROBERT STEPHEN HAWKER...

HAWKE'S BAY HERALD – Napier. New Zealand. -d. Jan 1885-Dec 1886. (4 reels) – 1 – uk British Libr Newspaper [072]

Hawkes, E W *see*
- THE DANCE FESTIVALS OF THE ALASKAN ESKIMO
- THE "INVITING-IN" FEAST OF THE ALASKAN ESKIMO
- THE LABRADOR ESKIMO

HAWKESBURY ADVOCATE – Windsor, Oct 6 1899-Dec 7 1900 – 9 – at Pascoe [072]

HAWKESBURY CHRONICLE AND FARMERS ADVOCATE – Windsor, Nov 26 1881-May 26 1888 – 9 – at Pascoe [072]

HAWKESBURY COURIER – Windsor, Jul 11 1844-Nov 5 1846 – 9 – at Pascoe [072]

HAWKESBURY HERALD – Windsor, May 1 1902-Jun 24 1904 – 9 – at Pascoe [072]

HAWK-EYE – Burlington. Iowa. 1843-1851; 1853- – 1 – us UMI [071]

HAWK-EYE – Eugene, OR. -w. 31 Jul 1873-20 Jun 1874. 1 roll – 1 – us U.O. Library [071]

HAWKEYE – Adin, CA. 6 Sept 1978 – 1r – 1 – $50.00 – B02002 – us Library Micro [071]

HAWKEYE – Burlington. Iowa. and Iowa Patriot. 1840-41 – 1 – us UMI [071]

HAWKEYE RECORD – Mount Vernon. Iowa. 1924-1957 – 1 – us UMI [071]

Hawkins *see* ARISE, O LORD

Hawkins, Everett D *see*
- CASES IN BUSINESS ADMINISTRATION; PERISTIWA-PERISTIWA PERUSAHAAN
- CONSUMER FINANCES IN THE REGION OF JOGJAKARTA; PRELIMINARY REPORT ON RESEARCH CONDUCTED IN AUGUST, 1959
- LABOR PROBLEMS IN A NEWLY INDEPENDENT COUNTRY: THE CASE OF INDONESIA

Hawkins, J *see*
- A GENERAL HISTORY OF THE SCIENCE AND PRACTICE OF MUSIC

Hawkins, John Caesar *see* HORAE SYNOPTICAE

Hawkins, Joshua *see* SIN AND ITS PENALTY

Hawkins, Margaret C *see* UTILIZATION OF HEALTH CARE PROFESSIONALS IN SELECTED INDUSTRIAL SETTINGS

HAWKINSVILLE FIRST BAPTIST CHURCH. HAWKINSVILLE, GEORGIA : CHURCH RECORDS – 1839-1958 – 1 – 72.72 – us Baptist [240]

Hawkridge, David *see* ORGANIZING EDUCATIONAL BROADCASTING

Hawks, Francis L *see*
- AURICULAR CONFESSION IN THE PROTESTANT EPISCOPAL CHURCH
- DOCUMENTARY HISTORY OF THE PROTESTANT EPISCOPAL CHURCH IN THE UNITED STATES OF AMERICA. SOUTH CAROLINA
- A NARRATIVE OF EVENTS CONNECTED WITH THE RISE AND PROGRESS OF THE PROTESTANT EPISCOPAL CHURCH IN MARYLAND
- A NARRATIVE OF EVENTS CONNECTED WITH THE RISE AND PROGRESS OF THE PROTESTANT EPISCOPAL CHURCH IN VIRGINIA

HAWLEY 1727-1892 – (Mf 1-4: Births/Deaths & Index 1727-1846. Mf 5: Marriages 1795-1846. Mf 6-12: Town Records 1792-1819. Mf 12-13: Births 1729-1826. Mf 13-14: Town Minutes 1826-44. Mf 15: Civil War Records 1861-65. Mf 16: Birth Index 1844-91. Mf 17-18: Marriage Index 1844-91. Mf 19: Marriage Intentions Index. Mf 20: Death Index 1844-91. Mf 21: B,M,D 1844-58. Mf 22-23: Births 1859-91. Mf 24-25: Marriages 1859-92. Mf 26-27: Deaths 1859-91) – (mf ed 1989) – 27mf – 9 – 0-87623-095-8 – us Holbrook [920]

Hawley, Charles *see* EARLY CHAPTERS OF CAYUGA HISTORY: JESUIT MISSIONS IN GOI-O-GOUEN, 1656-1684: ALSO...THE SULPITIAN MISSION AMONG THE EMIGRANT CAYUGAS...1668

Hawley, Charles Anthony *see* OUTLINES, DEFINITIONS, MAXIMS, QUOTATIONS, AND PROBLEMS IN ELEMENTARY LAW

Hawley, James H *see*
- HISTORY OF IDAHO
- HISTORY OF IDAHO, THE GEM OF THE MOUNTAINS

Hawley, John Gardner *see*
- INTER-STATE EXTRADITION
- A TREATISE ON THE LAW OF REAL PROPERTY

Hawley, Thomas De Riemer *see* INFALLIBLE LOGIC, A VISIBLE AND AUTOMATIC SYSTEM OF REASONING

Haworth, A H *see*
- LEPIDOPTERA BRITTANICA, 1803-(1828)
- SAXIFRAGEARUM ENUMERATIO. ACCEDUNT REVISIONES PLANTARUM SUCCULENTARUM
- SUPPLEMENTUM PLANTARUM SUCCULENTARUM
- SYNOPSIS PLANTARUM SUCCULENTARUM

Haworth, Charles B *see* CONGRESS AND THE COURTS

Haworth Press *see* ACQUISITIONS LIBRARIAN

HAWTHORN AND LAVENDER : WITH OTHER VERSES / Henley, William Ernest – New York: Harper, 1901 – 1 roll – 1 – 1-55879-833-1 – uk Libr Preservation [810]

HAWTHORNE FIRST BAPTIST CHURCH (FORMERLY: PLEASANT GROVE BAPTIST CHURCH). HAWTHORNE, FLORIDA : CHURCH RECORDS – 1853-1959 – 1 – 49.86 – us Baptist [240]

Hawthorne, James Boardman *see* PAUL AND THE WOMEN: AND OTHER DISCOURSES

Hawthorne, Nathaniel *see* GRANDFATHER'S CHAIR & BIOGRAPHICAL STORIES

Haxthausen, August von *see* ETUDES SUR LA SITUATION INTERIEURE, LA VIE NATIONALE ET LES INSTITUTIONS DE LA RUSSIE

HAY AGOROT / Weisbrem, I – Warsaw. 1888. BJ-422-96 1 – 9 – ne IDC [305]

HAY ANY WORKE FOR COOPER / Marprelate, Martin – Being A Reply To The "Admonition to the people of England." 1845 – 1 – us A.T.L.A. [240]

Hay, Charles A *see* MEMOIRS OF REV. JACOB GOERING, REV. GEORGE LOCHMAN, D.D., AND REV. BENJAMIN KURTZ, D.D., LL. D.

Hay du Chastelet, Paul *see* RECUEIL DE DIVERSES PIECES POUR SERVIR A L'HISTOIRE

Hay, Gustavus *see* THE LAW OF RAILWAY ACCIDENTS IN MASSACHUSETTS

Hay, Gyula *see* HABEN

Hay, John *see*
- CASTILIAN DAYS
- PAPERS

Hay, John Charles Dalrymple *see*
- ASHANTI AND THE GOLD COAST
- LINES FROM MY LOG-BOOKS

HAY QUE EVITAR SER TAN BRUTO COMO EL SOLDADO CANUTO, PERIPECIAS Y DESDICHAS DE UN MAL SOLDADO – 2nd ed. n.p. 1937? Fiche W 937. (Blodgett Collection of Spanish Civil War Pamphlets) – 9 – us H.U. College Libr [946]

HAY SPRINGS ENTERPRISE – Hay Springs, NE. -w. Feb 1893-Nov 1898, scattered issues missing; Apr 1901-Jan 1902, scattered issues missing; Sept 1904-Jan 1905; Aug 1908-Jun 1915 – 1 – us NE Hist [071]

HAY SPRINGS NEWS – Hay Springs, NE. -w. Jul 1915-Mar 1968 – 1 – us NE Hist [071]

HAYAL – Istanbul: Mehmet Rauf, ed. 1.-5. sene, nos. 1-368 (18 Tesriniewel 1289-18 Hariran 1293 [Oct 1873-June 1877]) – 26mf – 9 – $200.00 – us MEDOC [949]

Hayashi, Carl T *see* ACHIEVEMENT MOTIVATION AMONG ANGLO-AMERICAN AND HAWAIIAN PHYSICAL-ACTIVITY PARTICIPANTS

Hayashi, CT *see* A CROSS-CULTURAL ANALYSIS OF ACHIEVEMENT MOTIVATION IN ANGLO AMERICAN AND JAPANESE MARATHON RUNNERS

HAYAT – Adana. Sahibi: Muecavirzade Mustafa Emin; Basmuharriri: Ramazanzade Mehmed Kemal. No. 2 (27 Mart 1334 [1918]) – 9 – 20.00 – us MEDOC [956]
HAYAT – New Delhi, India. 1965 – 1r – 1 – us L of C Photodup [072]
Hayatt, Alice Nelson *see* AN ACCOUNT OF THE LIFE OF DR. WILLIAM AUGUSTUS CARLETON
Haycock, Ronald G *see* IMAGE OF THE INDIAN
Hayden, A S *see* EARLY HISTORY OF THE DISCIPLES IN THE WESTERN RESERVE, OHIO
Hayden, Chester *see* AN APPENDIX TO COWEN'S TREATISE ON THE CIVIL JURISDICTION OF JUSTICES OF THE PEACE IN THE STATE OF NEW YORK.
HAYDEN, FERDINAND V., PAPERS, MS 3154 – 1846-1865 – 1 reel – 1 – us Western Res [920]
Hayden, Ferdinand Vandeveer *see* NORTH AMERICA
Hayden, H H *see* A SKETCH OF THE GEOGRAPHY AND GEOLOGY OF THE HIMALAYA MOUNTAINS AND TIBET
Hayden, Hand *see* GENEALOGICAL AND FAMILY HISTORY OF WYOMING AND LACKAWANNA VALLEYS
Hayden, M P *see* THE BIBLE AND WOMAN: A CRITICAL AND COMPREHENSIVE EXAMINATION OF THE TEACHING OF THE SCRIPTURES CONCERNING THE POSITION AND SPHERE OF WOMAN
Hayden, R *see* THE SENATE AND TREATIES 1789-1817
Hayden, Samuel Augustus *see* THE COMPLETE CONSPIRACY TRIAL BOOK
Haydn, Hiram Collins *see* AMERICAN HEROES ON MISSION FIELDS
Haydn, Joseph *see*
- A 5TH SET OF SONATAS FOR PIANOFORTE OR HARPSICHORD. H. 16, NOS. 33, 34, 43
- CANZONETTA IN A PER UNA VOCE COL CEMBALO....AUTOGRAPH MS. PHILEMON UND BAUCIS
- CANZONETTA IN A-MAJOR PER UNA VOCE COL CEMBALO...
- CREATION
- A FAVORITE QUINETETTO FOR 2 VIOLINS, TWO TENORS, AND A BASS
- QUARTETS, STRINGS, H. 3: 31-36 [NOS. 32-37, OP. 20]
- QUARTETS, STRINGS, H. 3: 47-49 [NOS. 48-50, NOS. 4-6] OP. 29 LIBRO 2
- QUARTETS, STRINGS, H. 3: 69-71. TROIS QUATOURS POUR DEUX VIOLONS, ALTO ET VIOLONCELLE, OEUVRE 71...
- QUARTETS, STRINGS, H. 3: 75-77 [NOS. 76-78, OP. 76, NOS. 1-3]
- QUARTETS, STRINGS, H. 3: 78-80 [NOS. 79-81, OP. 76, NO. 4-6]
- QUARTETS, STRINGS, SELECTIONS
- DIE SCHOPFUNG. CREATION, AN ORATORIO, ARRANGED AS A QUARTET
- A SECOND SET OF SIX GRAND QUARTETTOS, OP. 16
- DIE SIEBEN WORTE DES ERLOSERS AM KREUTZ... STRING QUARTET VERSION. H. 20:1B, OP. 31
- SYMPHONY NO. 76 IN E-FLAT MAJOR ARR. FOR FORTEPIANO, 2 VIOLINS, ALTO AND BASSE
- SYMPHONY NO. 94, "THE SURPRISE" ANDANTE PER CLAVICEMBALO & PIANOFORTE

DIE HAYDN-DRUCKE DER HOBOKEN-SAMMLUNG MUSIKALISCHER ERST- UND FRUEHDRUCKE / Oesterreichische Nationalbibliothek Wien. Musiksammlung – Hildesheim, 1989 – 1219mf – 9 – DM11,000.00 diazo DM12,800.00 silver – gw Olms [780]
THE HAYDOCK PAPERS : A GLIMPSE INTO ENGLISH CATHOLIC LIFE UNDER THE SHADE OF PERSECUTION AND IN THE DAWN OF FREEDOM / Gillow, Joseph – London; New York: Burns & Oates, 1888 – 1mf – us A.T.L.A. [240]
Haydon, Edwin Scott *see* NOTES OF SELECTED DECISIONS OF HER MAJESTY'S HIGH COURT IN UGANDA, ON CASES ORIGINATING FROM THE BUGANDA COURTS, 1940-1958
Haydon, F S *see* EULOGIUM (HISTORIARUM SIVE TEMPORIS) (RS9)
Hay-Edward, C M *see* A HISTORY OF CLIFFORD'S INN
HA-YEHUDIM BE-EREZ HA-ZEVI – v. 5. Luah Yerushalayim. 1901. BJ-27-234 1 – 9 – ne IDC [956]
HA-YEHUDIM BI-YERUSHALAYIM BA-ME'AH HA-18 / Shochat, A – v. 1. Ziyyon. 1936. BJ-27-23 1 – 9 – ne IDC [956]
Hayek, A *see* PRODROMUS FLORAE PENINSULAE BALCANICAE
Hayek, F A *see* JUSTICE, SOCIALISM AND DEMOCRACY
AL HA-YERUSHALMI / Lieberman, S – Jerusalem. 1929. BJ-32-17 1 – 9 – ne IDC [270]
HA-YERUSHALMI KI-FESHUTO / Lieberman, S – Jerusalem. 1934. BJ-32-21 1 – 9 – ne IDC [270]
Hayes, A Wallace *see* COMMENTS ON TOXICOLOGY
HAYES COUNTY TIMES – Hayes Center, NE. -w. Jul, Nov 1892; Oct 1895-Feb 1896; Apr 1896-Nov 1898; Apr 1901-Oct 1902, scattered issues missing – 1 – us NE Hist [071]
Hayes, Dom B *see* THE VIA VITAE OF ST BENEDICT
Hayes, Everand A *see* A PLAIN TREATISE ON THE LAW OF MARRIAGE AND DIVORCE
Hayes, Isaac Israel *see*
- THE OPEN POLAR SEA
- THE OPEN POLAR SEA: A NARRATIVE OF A VOYAGE OF DISCOVERY TOWARDS THE NORTH POLE IN THE SCHOONER UNITED STATES

Hayes, John William *see* TERENCE VINCENT POWDERLY PAPERS, 1864-1937; THE JOHN WILLIAM HAYES PAPERS, 1880-1921
Hayes, Lyman S *see* HISTORY OF THE TOWN OF ROCKINGHAM
Hayes, Max S *see* PAPERS
Hayes, Richard J *see*
- MANUSCRIPT SOURCES OF THE HISTORY OF IRISH CIVILIZATION
- SOURCES FOR THE HISTORY OF IRISH CIVILIZATION, ARTICLES IN IRISH PERIODICALS

Hayes, Rutherford B *see* THE PAPERS OF RUTHERFORD BIRCHARD HAYES
Hayes, S P *see* SOME APPLICATIONS OF BEHAVIOURAL RESEARCH
Hayes, Thomas J *see* JOURNAL OF MARKETING FOR HIGHER EDUCATION
Hayes, W *see* PORTRAITS OF RARE AND CURIOUS BIRDS
Hayes, W M *see*
- CHURCH HISTORY (CCC145)
- EXPOSITORY LIFE OF CHRIST (CCC146)
- SYSTEMATIC THEOLOGY (CCC147)

Hayes, Walter M *see* MANUSCRIPT LISTINGS FOR THE AUTHORED WORKS OF THE PALAEOLOGAN PERIOD
Hayes, William C *see* THE BURIAL CHAMBER OF THE TREASURER SOBK-MOSE
Haygood, Atticus Greene *see*
- THE MAN OF GALILEE
- THE NEGRO IN THE CHRISTIAN PULPIT, OR, THE TWO CHARACTERS AND TWO DISTINIES
- PLEAS FOR PROGRESS

Haygood, Benjamin Iverson *see* A TRAINING PROGRAM FOR VOLUNTEER LEADERS AT THE FIRST BAPTIST CHURCH, ALMA, GEORGIA
HAYKAKAN MATENAGITUT'IWN : BIBLIOGRAPHIE ARMENIENNE / [Zarphanalian, G] – Venice, 1883 – 8mf – 9 – ne IDC [947]
Hayler, Guy *see* THE MASTER METHOD: AN ENQUIRY INTO THE LIQUOR PROBLEM IN AMERICA
Hayley, William *see* POEMS AND PLAYS
Hayne, FG *see* GETREUE DARSTELLUNG UND BESCHREIBUNG DER IN DER ARZNEYKUNDE GEBRAEUCHLICHEN GEWAECHSE
Hayne, MH E *see* THE PIONEERS OF THE KLONDYKE: BEING AN ACCOUNT OF TWO YEARS POLICE SERVICE ON THE YUKON
Hayne, Robert Y *see* PUBLICATIONS
HAYNES' BAPTIST CYCLOPAEDIA / Haynes, Thomas Wilson – 1848. v.1, Aa-Fo. 330p – 1 – $11.55 – us Baptist [240]
Haynes, Dudley C *see* CENTENNIAL EDITION OF THE BAPTIST DENOMINATION
Haynes, Edmund Sidney Pollck *see* RELIGIOUS PERSECUTION
Haynes, Edmund Sidney Pollock *see* RELIGIOUS PERSECUTION; A STUDY IN POLITICAL PSYCHOLOGY
Haynes, T H *see* TERRITORIAL WATERS AND OCEAN FISHERY RIGHTS
Haynes, Thomas Wilson *see* HAYNES' BAPTIST CYCLOPAEDIA
Haynes, William Casper *see* PAPERS
HAYNT – New York. v. 1-52. Jan 1-Feb 21 1920 – 1 – us NY Public [071]
HAYNT = TO-DAY – (In Yiddish. Includes the Court Report on the Bellis Case) – Warsaw, PL. no66 [16 Mar 1912-9 Feb 1914] no34; 14 Oct 1938 no235A – 1 – $50.00 – cn Can Microfilming [072]
HAYNT = TO-DAY – New York City, NY. v1 no 14 and 29. 1920 – 1r – Can$25.00 – cn Can Microfilming [071]
HA-YOM = THE DAY – (Hebrew daily) – Warsaw, PL. no14 Jan 1925-no 397 9 May 1926 – 1r – 1 – $40.00 – cn Can Microfilming [072]
HA-YOM – (Missing: Several numbers) – Spb., 1886-1888 – 2r – 1 – J-291-5/3 – ne IDC [072]
HA-YOM – (See also: Ha-Zefirah) – Warsaw, 1925-1926 – 2r – 1 – J-291-32-3 – ne IDC [072]
HA-YOM – St Petersburg. v1-2. 1886-1887 – 1 – us NY Public [072]
HA-YOM – St Petersburg. v1-2. 1886-87 – 2r – 1 – us Ross [072]
HA-YOM – Tel Aviv, 1966-69 – 1 – BJ-91-42 3 – ne IDC [072]
HA-YOM *see* HA-ZEFIRAH
HA-YONAH – Ed. by S. Sachs. Berlin. 1851. (various dates given e.g. 1848, 1860). BJ-100-164 1 – 9 – ne IDC [470]
HAYRENIK – Boston: Hairenik Association, Inc, nov 1916-38 – 45r – 1 – us Res Libr [072]
Hays, Brooks *see* PAPERS WHILE PRESIDENT OF SOUTHERN BAPTIST CONVENTION
Hays, George P *see* MAY WOMEN SPEAK? A BIBLE STUDY BY A PRESBYTERIAN MINISTER
Hays, J *see* THE CORRELATION OF THE PRE-KARROO SUCCESSION IN NORTHERN RHODESIA WITH THAT OF ADJACENT TERRITORIES
Hays. Kansas. Police Court *see* DOCKETS
HAYSLIP, JOHN, PAPERS, MS 2944 – 1801-1882 – 1 reel – 1 – us Western Res [340]
HAYWARD AND SAN LEANDRO CITY DIRECTORIES – Alameda Co, CA. 1925-1926; 1931-1934; 1938; 1940; 1946-1948 – 6r – 1 – $300.00 – D004 – us Library Micro [910]
Hayward, Edward F *see* LYMAN BEECHER
Hayward, Edward Farwell *see* ECCE SPIRITUS
HAYWARD JOURNAL – Hayward, CA. 1971-72 – 1r – 1 – $50.00 – B02289 – us Library Micro [071]
Hayward, Mildred *see* LIGHT BREAKING THROUGH
Haywood, H L *see* A STORY OF THE LIFE AND TIMES OF JACQUES DE MOLAY
HAYWOOD HILLS BAPTIST CHURCH. NASHVILLE, TENNESSEE : CHURCH RECORDS – (1,792p) – Sept 1959-1989 – 2r – 1 – $71.68 – us Baptist [240]
Haywood, William Dudley *see* EVIDENCE AND CROSS EXAMINATION OF WILLIAM D. HAYWOOD IN THE CASE OF THE U.S.A. VS. WM. D. HAYWOOD, ET. AL
HAYYEI OLAM – Freiburg. 1583. BJ-43-29 1 – 9 – ne IDC [470]
Hazairin *see* HUKUM ISLAM DAN MASJARAKAT
Hazanas y La Rua, Joaquin *see* LA IMPRENTA EN SEVILLA. NOTICIAS INEDITAS DESDE LA INTRODUCCION DEL ARTE TIPOGRAFICO EN ESTA CIUDAD HASTA EL SIGLO 29. VOL 1. SEVILLA, 1945
Hazard, Caroline *see*
- THE NARRAGANSETT FRIEND'S MEETING IN THE 18TH CENTURY
- SOME IDEALS IN THE EDUCATION OF WOMEN

Hazard, Rowland Gibson *see* FREEDOM OF MIND IN WILLING
HAZARDOUS SUBSTANCE RESOURCE BOOK – 39mf – 9 – us UMI [660]
HAZARDS, POLLUTION AND LEGISLATION IN THE COATINGS FIELD – London. v1-3 1981-83*. v4-5 1984-85 – 1,5,9 – D49474 – us UMI [680]
HAZARD'S REGISTER OF PENNSYLVANIA : DEVOTED TO THE PRESERVATION OF FACTS AND DOCUMENTS, AND EVERY KIND OF USEFUL INFORMATION RESPECTING THE STATE OF PENNSYLVANIA – (Former title: Register of Pennsylvania: Devoted to the Preservation of Facts and Documents, and every other kind of Useful Information Respecting the State of Pennsylvania jan 5, 1828-jun 25, 1831) – Philadelphia. 1-16. 1828-35 – 1 – D3987 – us UMI [978]
HAZARD'S REGISTER OF PENNSYLVANIA – Philadelphia. v1-16. 1828-36 (all publ) – 80mf – 9 – $120.00 – LLMC 82-926 – us L.L.M.C. [073]
Hazavehei, Seyyed M M *see* THE EFFECTS OF 6-WEEK AND 12-WEEK REHABILITATION PROGRAMS ON THE DEPRESSION LEVEL OF CARDIAC PATIENTS
HA-ZEFIRAH – (1874-1875 in Berlin; from 1886 a daily and 1917-1919 a weekly. In 1925-1926 published under the name Ha-Yom. Missing: several issues) – Warsaw (Berlin). v1-32, 36-51. 1862, 1874-1905, 1910-1921, 1926-1928, 1931 – 39r – 1 – J-291-4/3 – ne IDC [072]
HA-ZEFIRAH *see* HA-YOM
HAZEFIRAH = THE WATCHTOWER – (Hebrew daily) – Warsaw, PL. v26 no12 Jan 1899-v67 no187 13 Aug 1928 – 1r – 1 – $35.00 – cn Can Microfilming [072]
HAZEL E.B. HANNA PAPERS / Hanna, Hazel E B – 1911-19 – 1 – $100.00 – us Presbyterian [920]
HAZEL GROVE & DISTRICT POSTMAN – Hazel Grove, England. The Postman: Hazel Grove & District. -w. 24 Feb 1900-8 March 1902. 1 reel – 1 – uk British Libr Newspaper [072]
Hazelhurst, Mississippi *see* MISCELLANEOUS EARLY NEWSPAPERS
Hazelius, Ernest L *see* HISTORY OF THE AMERICAN LUTHERAN CHURCH
Hazeltine, F A *see* A YEAR OF SOUTH AMERICAN TRAVEL
Hazeltine, Gilbert W *see* THE EARLY HISTORY OF THE TOWN OF ELLICOTT
Hazeltine, H D *see* THE LAW OF THE AIR
Hazelwood, Hetty *see* A GARLAND GATHERED AT MORN: A COLLECTION OF SHORT POEMS
HA-ZEMAN – St Petersburg, Vilna, 1903-14 – 9r – 1 – us Ross [072]
HA-ZEMAN – St Petersburg, Wilna. 1903-July 31 1914 – 1 – us NY Public [072]
Hazik, Efendi *see* DIVAN
HAZIM BEY YAHUT HEDER / Naci, Muallim – Matbaa-i Aramiyan, 1298 [1881] – $20.00 – us MEDOC [470]
HAZINE-I EVRAK – (Nos. 1 (1 Mayis 1297[1881])-20, 22, 26, II. sene, nos. 1-15 (15 Kanunisani 1298-30 Nisan 1299[1882-1883])) – Istanbul: Mihran Matbaasi, 1881-? – 6mf – 9 – $125.00 – us MEDOC [949]
HAZINE-I FUENUN – (Sahib-i Imtiyaz: Doktor Cerrahiyan[Cerahizade], Mueduer-i Mes'ul: Kirkor Faik. Nos. 1-52 (3 Temmuz 1308-23 Temmuz 1310[1892-1894])) – Istanbul: Alem Matbaasi, Ahmed Ihsan ve Suerekasi Matbaasi, Akin Matbaasi, 1892-1896 – 7mf – 9 – $150.00 – us MEDOC [949]
HAZINE-I FUENUN – Vols. 1-4 (1311-1314) – 26mf – 9 – $130.00 – us MEDOC [949]
HAZIT HA-AM – Jerusalem, 1932-1934 – 2r – 1 – J-91-35-3 – ne IDC [072]
HAZLEHURST FIRST BAPTIST CHURCH. HAZLEHURST, MISSISSIPPI : CHURCH RECORDS – Mar 1870-1988. 4910p – 1 – 220.95 – us Baptist [240]
HAZLEHURST FIRST BAPTIST CHURCH. HAZLEHURST, MISSISSIPPI : CHURCH RECORDS – Oct 1950-1988. Lacking: 1967 – 1 – 68.27 – us Baptist [240]
Hazlitt, Henry *see* INSTEAD OF WHAT?
Hazlitt, William *see*
- CRITICISMS ON ART
- LECTURES ON THE ENGLISH POETS
- POLITICAL ESSAYS
- THE SPIRIT OF THE AGE
- THE TABLE TALK OF MARTIN LUTHER
- TABLE-TALK
- A VIEW OF THE ENGLISH STAGE

Hazlitt, William Carew *see*
- LAMB AND HAZLITT
- THE LAMBS

HA-ZMAN = TIME – (In Hebrew) – Vilnius, LT. no2 15 Dec 1904-no61 13 Mar 1914 – 1r – 1 – $25.00 – cn Can Microfilming [072]
HAZMON (THE TIME) – New York. N.Y. 1895-96 – 1 – us A.J.P.C. [071]
HAZOB LE-MO'ED / Mandelstamm, B – Vienna. 1878. BJ-290-10 1 – 9 – ne IDC [470]
HA-ZOFE = THE SENTINEL – (In Hebrew. Daily) – Tel Aviv, IS. v11 no23. 23 Sep 1949 – 1r – 1 – $25.00 – cn Can Microfilming [072]
HAZOFE = THE OBSERVER – (Hebrew daily) – Warsaw, PL. v1 no30 Feb 1903-v3 no628 Feb 1905 – 1r – 1 – $25.00 – cn Can Microfilming [072]

HA-ZOFEH – Jerusalem. 1937- Available: 1960-76. BJ-91-36 3 – 9 – ne IDC [072]

HA-ZOFEH – London. v. 1-3 no. 10. Mar 2 1894-Dec 6 1895 – 1 – us NY Public [072]

HA-ZOFEH – Warsaw. v. 1-4 no. 11. Jan 6 1903-Feb 27 1906 – 1 – us NY Public [072]

HA-ZOFEH – Warsaw. v1-3. 1903-1905 – 3r – 1 – J-291-20/3 – ne IDC [072]

HAZOFEH – Warsaw. n1-692; ns: v1-10. 1903-06 – 4r – 1 – us Ross [072]

HA-ZOFEH AL DARKHEI HA-MISHNAH / Auerbach, Berthold – Frankfurt a. Main. 1861. Lacking: p. 3-14. BJ-32-3 1 – 9 – ne IDC [900]

HA-ZOFEH LE-HOKHMAT YISRA'EL – v. 1-15. Budapest. 1911-15, 1921-31. BJ-100-176 1 – 9 – ne IDC [270]

HAZZARD AND WARBURTON'S PRINCE EDWARD ISLAND CASES / Prince Edward Island. Canada – v1-2. 1850-82 (all publ) – 12mf – 9 – $18.00 – LLMC 81-061 – us L.L.M.C. [340]

Hazzard, George *see* HAZZARD'S HISTORY OF HENRY COUNTY

HAZZARD'S HISTORY OF HENRY COUNTY / Hazzard, George – Military ed. 1822-1906. New Castle: 1906. Vols. 1-2. Indiana Reel 15. (The Cox Library Collection) – 5 – us Americana [978]

H.C. Cooper, Jr. & Co *see* HISTORY OF HOUSTON COUNTY

HCP AND M: HEALTH CARE PLANNING AND MARKETING – v1- 1981- – 1,5,6,9 – us UMI [610]

HE ARCHAIOTERA GNOSTE MORPHE TOON LEITOURGIOON,... / Mooraeitis, D – Bas., Chrys., 1957 – 1mf – 8 – Dfl6.00 – ne Slangenburg [240]

HE DESCENDED INTO HELL, OR, AN INTERPRETATION BASED ON REASON AND SCRIPTURE / Henderson, W – Pembroke, Ont.: Observer, 1868. 05541. (Pre-1900 Canadiana) – 9 – cn C.I.H.M. [240]

HE GUIQING DENG SHUZHA – Letters of He Guiqing and Others. Comp. by the Suzhou Museum. 4 fiches. F H96 – 9 – $18.00 – cc Microforms [950]

HE JISHU – Nuclear Techniques. In Chinese but English abstracts to the main articles. F p122 – 9 – $4.50f – cc Microforms [073]

He, Qin *see* EVALUATION OF STRETCH LOAD CAPACITY AND UTILIZATION OF STORED ELASTIC ENERGY IN LEG EXTENSOR MUSCLES DURING VERTICAL JUMPS

HE TENIDO SUJETA LA PALABRA ENTRE LOS DIENTES / Cayetano Rosado, Moises – Barcelona: Graficas Cromotip, 1972 – 1 – sp Bibl Santa Ana [946]

HEA SONUM JA EESTI BAPTISTI KOGUDUSED / Kaups, Richard – The Good News and the Estonian Baptist Congregations. 1974. 150p – 1 – 6.00 – us Baptist [240]

HEAD AND NECK – (Cont: Head and Neck Surgery) – New York. v11-19. 1989-97+ 1,9; v11-12 1989-90*. v13-19 1991-97+ 5 – 1 – D12710.01 – us UMI [617]

HEAD AND NECK *see* HEAD AND NECK SURGERY

HEAD AND NECK SURGERY – (Cont by: Head and Neck) – New York. v1-10. sep 1978-aug 1988 1,9; v1-2 sep 1978-aug 1980*. v3-9 sep 1980-aug 1987. v10 sep 1987-aug 1988* 5 – 1,5,9 – D12710 – us UMI [617]

HEAD AND NECK SURGERY *see* HEAD AND NECK

Head, Francis Bond *see*
- CANADA: COPIES OR EXTRACTS OF DESPATCHES FROM SIR F. B. HEAD, BART., K.C.H. ON THE SUBJECT OF CANADA
- THE ROYAL ENGINEER

HEAD, HEART, HEALTH AND HANDS IN VIRGINIA / Virginia. Polytechnic Institute. Extension Division – v1-52 May 1918-69 – 1,5 – us Spaulding [630]

HEAD QUARTERS – Fredericton, Canada. 1844-68 – 6r – 1 – $390.00 – cn Library Assoc [971]

HEADACHE – West Deptford. v1-37. apr 1961-dec 1997+ 1; v10-14 apr 1970-jan 1975. v16-37 mar 1976-dec 1997+ 5; v16-37. mar 1976-dec 1997+ 9 – 1,5,9 – D2336 – us UMI [616]

Headicar, B M *see* CATALOGUE OF THE BOOKS,... IN THE EDWARD FRY LIBRARY OF INTERNATIONAL LAW

Headlam, Arthur C *see* HISTORY, AUTHORITY AND THEOLOGY

Headlam, Cecil *see* THE INNS OF COURT

Headlam, Stewart D *see* THE SOCIALIST'S CHURCH

Headley, J T *see* LUTHER AND CROMWELL

Headley, JT *see* THE CHAPLAINS AND CLERGY OF THE REVOLUTION

Headley, P C *see* EVANGELISTS IN THE CHURCH

Headley, Russel *see*
- HISTORY OF ORANGE COUNTY
- THE NEW YORK CRIMINAL JUSTICE

HEADLIGHT – Prentiss. Miss. 1941-1950 – 1 – us UMI [071]

HEADLIGHT – Stromsburg, NE. -w. Oct 1885-Dec 1890; Feb 1891-Nov 1892; Jan 1893 to date – 1 – us NE Hist [071]

HEADLIGHT – Stromsburg. Neb. 1885- – 1 – us UMI [071]

HEADLIGHT – Terry. Miss. 1936-1966 – 1 – us UMI [071]

HEADLIGHT-HERALD – Tillamook, OR. -w. 1 Jan 1953 – 13 may 1971; 31 June 1971-. – 1 – us U.O. Library [071]

HEADLINE BOOKS *see* HEADLINE SERIES

HEADLINE SERIES – (Former title: Headline Books 1935-may 1943) – New York. v1-315. 1935-fal 1997+ 1; v199-218 feb 1970-dec 1973. v224-297 feb 1975-fal 1991. v299-315+ 5; v234-315. feb 1977-fal 1997 9; v301-306 win 1993-fal 1994* 1,5,9 – 1,5,9 – D1555 – us UMI [073]

HEADQUARTERS RECORDS / Arizona. Fort Verde – 1866-91. 11 rolls. M1076 – 1 – us Nat'l Archives [324]

HEADQUARTERS RECORDS / Kansas. Fort Dodge – 1866-82. 25 rolls. M989 – 1 – us Nat'l Archives [324]

HEADQUARTERS RECORDS / Kansas. Fort Scott – 1869-73. 2 rolls. M1077 – 1 – us Nat'l Archives [324]

HEADQUARTERS RECORDS / New Mexico. Fort Cummings – 1863-73, 1880-84. 8 rolls. M1081 – 1 – us Nat'l Archives [324]

HEADQUARTERS RECORDS / Texas. Fort Stockton – 1876-86. 8 rolls. M1189 – 1 – us Nat'l Archives [324]

HEADQUARTERS RECORDS OF FORT GIBSON, INDIAN TERRITORY, 1830-1857 – 6r – 1 – M1466 – us Nat'l Archives [355]

HEADQUARTERS RECORDS OF FORT SUMNER, NEW MEXICO, 1862-1869 – 5r – 1 – M1512 – us Nat'l Archives [355]

HEADQUARTERS RECORDS OF THE DISTRICT OF THE PECOS, 1878-1881 – 5r – 1 – M1381 – us Nat'l Archives [355]

HEADS OF FAMILIES AT THE FIRST CENSUS OF THE UNITED STATES TAKEN IN THE YEAR 1790, CONNECTICUT – 1908. Indexed. 5 fiches. F-0076 – 9 – us A.G.L.L. [920]

HEADS OF HEBREW GRAMMAR : CONTAINING ALL THE PRINCIPLES NEEDED BY A LEARNER / Tregelles, Samuel Prideaux – London: Samuel Bagster, [1852?] – 1mf – 9 – 0-8370-9275-2 – 1986-3275 – us A.T.L.A. [470]

HEADWAY – Apr/May 1920-Oct 1945 – 69mf – 9 – $275.00 – us UPA [320]

HEALDSBURG ENTERPRISE – (Also known as: Sonoma County Tribune between 1873-94) – Healdsburg, CA. 1873-79; 1888-90; 1893-94; 1902-07; 1913-27 – 6r – 1 – $585.00 – B02292a – us Library Micro [071]

THE HEALDSBURG TRIBUNE – Healdsburg, CA. 1888-1901; 1902-27; 1945- – 90+ r – 1 BC02292 – $4,500.00 ($90.00y) – us Library Micro [071]

Healey, Antonette DiPaolo *see* A MICROFICHE CONCORDANCE TO OLD ENGLISH

THE HEALING OF THE NATIONS : A TREATISE ON MEDICAL MISSIONS: STATEMENT AND APPEAL / Williamson, John Rutter – New York: Student Volunteer Movement for Foreign Missions, 1899 – 1mf – 9 – 0-8370-6719-7 – 1986-0719 – us A.T.L.A. [610]

HEALING SPRINGS BAPTIST CHURCH. BARNWEL COUNTY, SOUTH CAROLINA : CHURCH RECORDS – Feb. 1822-Oct. 1954 (scattered), Feb.-May 1955 – 1r – 1 – $20.88 – us Baptist [240]

HEAL'S CATALOGUES 1850-1950 / Victoria and Albert Museum. London. Archive of Art and Design – 95mf – 9 – $401.00 – 0-907696-23-6 – uk Emmett [740]

HEALTH – Chicago. v19-23. sep 1973-jun 1978 1; v20 sep 1974-aug 1975. v22-23 sep 1976-jun 1978 5 – 1,5 – D7778 – us UMI [613]

HEALTH – (Formed by the union of: In Health; and: Health) – San Francisco. v6-11. feb 1992-dec 97+ – 1,5,9 – D18476.02 – us UMI [613]

HEALTH : A HOME MAGAZINE DEVOTED TO PHYSICAL CULTURE AND OUT-DOOR LIFE – (Former titles: Water-cure Journal dec 1, 1845-apr 1848. Water-cure Journal and Herald of Reforms may 1848-dec 1858. Water-cure Journal and Herald of Health, Devoted to Physiology, Hydropathy and the Laws of Life jan 1859-jun 1861. Water-cure Journal, a Guide to Health jul 1861-jun 1862. Hygienic Teacher and Water-cure Journal jul 1862-dec 1862. Herald of Health 1863-92. Journal of Hygiene and Herald of Health jan 1893-sep 1898. Omega oct 1898-aug 1900) – New York. v1-34 dec 1845-dec 1862. v35-64 1863-1914* – 1 – D4583 – us UMI [613]

HEALTH – (Merged with: In Health. To form: Health. Cont: Family Health) – New York. v13-23. jul 1981-aug 1991 – 1,5,9 – D10761.01 – us UMI [613]

HEALTH *see*
- FAMILY HEALTH
- HEALTH

HEALTH AFFAIRS – Chevy Chase. v1-4. win 1981-win 1985* 1; v5-16. spr 1986-win 1997+ 1,5,9 – 1,5,9 – D14601 – us UMI [613]

HEALTH ALLIANCE ALERT – Washington. v9 1994*. v10-12 1995-97+ – 1,5,9 – D21691 – us UMI [613]

HEALTH AND HYGIENE – London. jul 1977-dec 1979*. v1-4 1980-83*. v5-11 1984-90. v12-15 1991-94*. v16-18 1995-97+ 1; v1-15 1980-94*. v16-18 1995-97+ 5; V1-7 1980-86*. v8-11 1987-90. v12-15 1991-94*. v16-18 1995-97+ 9 – 1,5,9 – D15528 – us UMI [613]

HEALTH AND PERSONAL SOCIAL SERVICES STATISTICS FOR ENGLAND : WITH SUMMARY TABLES FOR GREAT BRITAIN 1973-1977 – (Coll title: British Government Publications...1801-1977, Health and Public Welfare) – 13mf – 9 (£1,080.00 health and public welfare set of 171mf) – uk Chadwyck [360]

HEALTH AND PERSONAL SOCIAL SERVICES STATISTICS FOR ENGLAND AND WALES : WITH SUMMARY TABLES FOR GREAT BRITAIN 1969-1972 – (Coll title: British Government Publications...1801-1977, Health and Public Welfare) – 8mf – 9 (£1,080.00 health and public welfare set of 171mf) – uk Chadwyck [360]

HEALTH AND PERSONAL SOCIAL SERVICES STATISTICS FOR WALES 1974-1977 – (Coll title: British Government Publications...1801-1977, Health and Public Welfare) – 8mf – 9 (£1,080.00 health and public welfare set of 171mf) – uk Chadwyck [360]

HEALTH AND REHABILITATIVE LIBRARY SERVICES – (Cont by: American Library Association, Health and Rehabilitative Library Services Division: Journal) – Chicago. v1. mar-oct 1975 1,5; v1. mar-oct 1975* 9 – 1,5,9 – D11123 – us UMI [020]

HEALTH AND SAFETY AT WORK – v. 1-. 1978- – 1,5,6,9 – us UMI [380]

HEALTH AND SAFETY, MINES AND QUARRIES 1851-1965 – (1852, 1853, 1919 and 1920 not publ. Coll title: British Government Publications...1801-1977, Minerals) – 20r – 1 (£1,890.00 minerals set of 36r) – uk Chadwyck [360]

HEALTH AND SOCIAL CARE IN THE COMMUNITY – Oxford. v1-5. 1993-97+ 1,9; v1-2 1993-94*. v3-5 1995-97+ 5 – 1,5,9 – D19662 – us UMI [613]

HEALTH AND SOCIAL SERVICE JOURNAL – (Cont by: Health Service Journal) – London. v89-93 1979-83*. v94-96 jan 1984-feb1986 1, v94 1984*. v95-96 jan 1985-feb 1986 5; v94-96 jan 1984-feb 1986 9 – 1,5,9 – D14165.05 – us UMI [613]

HEALTH AND SOCIAL WORK – Silver Spring. v1-22. 1976-97+ – 1,5,9 – D11628 – us UMI [613]

HEALTH AND THE INNER LIFE : AN ANALYTICAL AND HISTORICAL STUDY OF SPIRITUAL HEALING THEORIES : WITH AN ACCOUNT OF THE LIFE AND TEACHINGS OF P.P. QUIMBY / Dresser, Horatio W – New York: G.P. Putnam, 1906. (The Inner life series) – 1mf – us A.T.L.A. [200]

HEALTH ASPECTS OF PESTICIDES ABSTRACT BULLETIN – (v1-2 1966-67 are experimental issues entitled Health Aspects of Pesticides Literature Bulletin. Publication began renumbering with v1 1968. Cont by: Pesticides Abstracts) – Washington. v1-4 1968-71*. v5-6 1972-73 1; Literature Bulletin v1-2 sep 1966-67. v1-6. 1968-73 5 – 1,5 – D6497 – us UMI [613]

HEALTH ASPECTS OF PESTICIDES LITERATURE BULLETIN *see* HEALTH ASPECTS OF PESTICIDES ABSTRACT BULLETIN

HEALTH ATTITUDES AND THEIR RELATION TO COMPLIANCE AND MEASURED CHOLESTEROL LEVELS / Donovan, Carolyn M – 1988 – 122p 2mf – 9 – $8.00 – us Microform Publ [614]

HEALTH BEHAVIORS AND ATTITUDES OF SELECTED NIGERIAN AND AMERICAN UNIVERSITY STUDENTS / Igbani, B & Maduabuchi, A – 1989 – 118p 2mf – 9 – $8.00 – us Microform Publ [370]

HEALTH BELIEFS, HEALTH VALUES, AND PREVENTIVE HEALTH PROMOTION ACTIVITIES OF AFRICAN- AND EURO-AMERICAN WOMEN : A COMPARATIVE STUDY / Herring, Rosa P & Kaplan, Leah E – 1992 – 3mf – $12.00 – us Microform Publ [613]

HEALTH CARE – (Cont: Hospital Administration in Canada at v21 1979. Ceased v33 no 2 1991. v21-27 Can$28.00y. v27-33 Can$20.00y) – Don Mills. v21-33. 1979-1991 – 9 – Price varies – cn Micromedia [360]

HEALTH CARE – (Former titles: Hospital Administration and Construction jun 1959-jun 1961. Hospital Administration in Canada jul 1961-sep 1978. Health Care in Canada oct 1978-jul 1979) – Don Mills. v1-20 1959-78*. v21-33 1979-91 – 9 – D35075 – us UMI [613]

HEALTH CARE – (Research materials from Parklawn Health Library, Rockville, MD, Parklawn Health Library, Hyattsville, MD, and National Health Planning Information Center, Hyattsville, MD. Base collection 3044mf $8300; 1979 update 502mf $1375; 1980 update 524mf $1375) – 4070mf complete collection – 9 – $11,050.00 – us UMI [610]

HEALTH CARE *see* HOSPITAL ADMINISTRATION IN CANADA

HEALTH CARE BILLER – Hales Corners. 1992-94* 1; 1995-97+ 1,5,9 – 1,5,9 – D24941 – us UMI [613]

HEALTH CARE COLLECTOR – Hales Corners. 1987-94* 1; 1995-97+ 1,5,9 – 1,5,9 – D21438 – us UMI [613]

HEALTH CARE EDUCATION – (Cont: In-service Training and Education) – New York. v6-7. 1977-79* 1; v8-10. feb 1979-nov 1981 1,5,9 – 1,5,9 – D12090.01 – us UMI [613]

HEALTH CARE FINANCING REVIEW – Washington. v1-7. sum 1979-86* 1; v8-19. fal 1986-sum 1998+ 1,9; v8-9 fal 1986-sum 1988. v10-13 fal 1988-sum 1992*. v14-19 fal 1992-sum 1998+ 5 – 1,5,9 – D15729 – us UMI [650]

HEALTH CARE FOR WOMEN INTERNATIONAL – (Cont: Issues in Health Care of Women) – Washington. v5-18. 1984-97+ – 1,5,9 – D14242.01 – us UMI [618]

HEALTH CARE IN CANADA *see* HEALTH CARE

HEALTH CARE MANAGEMENT – Philadelphia. 1994*. 1995-97+ – 1,5,9 – D21685 – us UMI [650]

HEALTH CARE MANAGEMENT REVIEW – Gaithersburg. v1-22. win 1976-fal 1997+ – 1,5,9 – D12679 – us UMI [650]

HEALTH CARE ON THE INTERNET : A JOURNAL OF METHODS AND APPLICATIONS / ed by Delozier, Eric P – v1 n1. 1997- – 1,9 – $85.00 in US $119.00 outside hardcopy subsc – us Haworth [360]

HEALTH CARE REGISTRAR – (Cont by: Health Care Registration) – Hales Corners. 1991-94* – 1 – D24946 – us UMI [310]

HEALTH CARE REGISTRAR *see* HEALTH CARE REGISTRATION

HEALTH CARE REGISTRATION – (Cont: Health Care Registrar) – Hales Corners. 1994* 1; 1995-98 1,5,9 – 1,5,9 – D24946.01 – us UMI [310]

HEALTH CARE REGISTRATION *see* HEALTH CARE REGISTRAR

THE HEALTH CARE SUPERVISOR – v1- 1982- – 1,5,6,9 – us UMI [610]

HEALTH CONSEQUENCES OF SMOKING: CUMULATIVE INDEX / U. S. Surgeon General – 15vs. 1964-82. With cumulative index in fiche and book form. Bound index only (50.00 plus 2.45 P&H) – 9 – 195.00 and 4.50 P&H – us Info Resources [613]

HEALTH EDUCATION MONOGRAPHS *see* HEALTH EDUCATION QUARTERLY

HEALTH EDUCATION QUARTERLY – (Cont: Health Education Monographs) – New York. v7-24. spr 1980-win 1997+ – 1,5,9 – D7933.01 – us UMI [370]
HEALTH EDUCATION RESEARCH – Oxford. v1-12. mar 1986-dec 1997+ 1,9; v1-9 mar 1986-dec 1994*. v10-12 1995-97+ 5 – 1,5,9 – D16451 – us UMI [370]
HEALTH EDUCATION RESOURCES – Chicago. v1-2. 1971-72*. v3-4. feb 1973-oct 1974 – 1 – D9679 – us UMI [370]
HEALTH FACILITIES MANAGEMENT – Chicago. v1 sep-dec 1988*. v2 1989. v3 1990*. v4 1991. v5 1992*. v6-10 1993-97+ 1,9; v1-7 sep 1988-94*. v8-10 1995-97+ 5 – 1,5,9 – D17724 – us UMI [650]
HEALTH INDUSTRY TODAY – (Cont: Surgical Business) – Union. v46-54 1983-91. v55 1992*. v56-60 1993-97+ 1,9; v46 1983*. v47-54 1984-91. v55 1992*. v56-60 1993-97+ 5 – 1,5,9 – D9918.01 – us UMI [680]
HEALTH INSURANCE AND EFFICIENT HEALTH SERVICE DELIVERY / Doman, Andrew S – 1986, 20p – 9 – 1.00f – at Libertarian Micro [360]
THE HEALTH JOURNAL – (Cont: Canada Health Journal (Ottawa, Ont: 1890)) – [Ottawa: Health Journal, 1888-1889] – 9 – cn C.I.H.M. [614]
THE HEALTH JOURNAL *see*
- CANADA HEALTH JOURNAL
- THE CANADA HEALTH JOURNAL

HEALTH KNOWLEDGE COMPETENCIES AND ESSENTIAL HEALTH SKILLS OF ENTRY LEVEL COLLEGE FRESHMEN ENROLLED IN OREGON'S RESEARCH UNIVERSITIES / Beeson, Luana J & Smith, Margaret M – 1992 – 2mf – 9 – $8.00 – us Microform Publ [613]
A HEALTH KNOWLEDGE TEST FOR MALE COLLEGE FRESHMEN IN SAUDI ARABIA / Hashim, Talal J – 1988 – 213p 3mf – 9 – $12.00 – us Microform Publ [370]
HEALTH LABORATORY SCIENCE – Washington. v1-15. 1964-oct 78 1; v8-10 1971-oct 1973. v12-15 1975-oct 1978 5; v14-15 1977-oct 1978 9 – 1,5,9 – D5964 – us UMI [619]
HEALTH LAWYER (ABA) – v1-7. 1982-95 – 9 – $50.00 set – us Hein [340]
HEALTH LEGISLATION AND REGULATION – (Former titles: Washington Report on Health Legislation jan 29, 1975-83. Washington Report on Health Legislation and Regulation aug 31, 1983-sep 3, 1986) – Washington. v12-19. 1986-93* 1; v20 1994*. v21-23 1995-97+ 1,5,9 – 1,5,9 – D17750 – us UMI [340]
HEALTH LETTER – Washington. v1-7. mar 1985-91* 1; v8-10 1992-94*. v11-13 1995-97+ 1,5,9 – 1,5,9 – D19997 – us UMI [613]
HEALTH LIBRARIES REVIEW – Oxford. v1-14. mar 1984-dec 1997+ 1,9; v1-6 mar 1984-dec 1989*. v7-14 mar 1990-dec 1997+ 5 – 1,5,9 – D15547 – us UMI [020]
HEALTH MANAGEMENT TECHNOLOGY – (Cont: Computers in Healthcare) – Overland Park. v15-18. 1994-97+ – 1,5,9 – D12663.02 – us UMI [650]
HEALTH MANPOWER MANAGEMENT – (Cont: Health Services Manpower Review) – Keele. v14-16. sep 1988-90* 1; v17-20 1991-94*. v21 1995 1,5,9 – 1,5,9 – D18910.01 – us UMI [650]
HEALTH MARKETING QUARTERLY – New York. v1-14. fal 1983-1998+ – 1,9 – D51021 – us UMI [650]
HEALTH MARKETING QUARTERLY / ed by Winston, William J – v1- 1983- – 1, 9 ($325.00 in US $455.00 outside hardcopy subsc) – us Haworth [610]
HEALTH MATRIX – (Cont by: Health Matrix) – Cleveland. v1-5. win 1983-win 1988* – 1 – D16158 – us UMI [610]
HEALTH MATRIX – (Health Matrix) – Cleveland. v1-4 spr 1991-sum 1994*. v5-7 spr 1995-sum 1997+ – 1,5,9 – D18794 – us UMI [610]
HEALTH MATRIX : JOURNAL OF LAW-MEDICINE – Case Western Reserve University. v1-5. 1991-95 – 9 – $76.00 set – us Hein [340]
HEALTH MATRIX *see*
- HEALTH MATRIX

HEALTH NEWS – (Index 1983-87; 1989) – Toronto. v1-13. 1983-95 – 9 – Can$20.00y – cn Micromedia [613]
HEALTH NEWS – Toronto. v1-10. feb 1983-92* 1; v11-12 1993-94*. v13-15 1995-97+ 1,5,9 – 1,5,9 – D19336 – us UMI [610]
HEALTH PERSPECTIVES – v1-4. Apr 1973-1977. Continued by: Consumer Health Perspectives – 1 – us UMI [073]
HEALTH PHYSICS : THE RADIATION PROTECTION JOURNAL – v62-71. 1992-1996 – 1,5,6,9 – $106.00r – us Williams [613]
HEALTH PHYSICS – v.1-. 1958- – 5,6,9 – us UMI [530]
HEALTH POLICY QUARTERLY – 1980-Fall,Winter 1982 – 1,5,6,9 – us UMI [073]
HEALTH PRACTITIONER – v1-2. 1977-78. Continued by: Health Practitioner, Physician Assistant – 1 – us UMI [073]
HEALTH PRACTITIONER, PHYSICIAN ASSISTANT – v2-3. 1978-79. Continued by: Physician Assistant, Health Practitioner – 1 – us UMI [073]
HEALTH PROGRESS / The Catholic Health Association of the United States – v65, no.8-. Sept 1984- – 1,5,6,9 – us UMI [616]
HEALTH RELATED MOTIVATIONAL DETERMINANTS AMONG PARTICIPANTS IN A WORKSITE WEIGHT MANAGEMENT INTERVENTION / Melichar, G A – 1990 – 2mf – 9 – $8.00 – us Microform Publ [150]
HEALTH SCIENCES SERIALS / U.S. Department of Health and Human Services – Quarterly. Citations listed represent The Nat'l. Library of Medicine's SERLINE database – 9 – $19.00y in US $23.75 outside – S-N 717-012-00000-3. Sub-list ID-HSS – us Gov't Printing [610]
HEALTH SERVICE JOURNAL *see* HEALTH AND SOCIAL SERVICE JOURNAL
HEALTH SERVICES MANPOWER REVIEW *see* HEALTH MANPOWER MANAGEMENT
HEALTH SERVICES REPORTS – (v. 80-89 1965-74. 5,6. v. 85-89 1970-74. 9) – v. 1-89. 1878-1974 – 1 – us UMI [610]
HEALTH VALUES *see* AMERICAN JOURNAL OF HEALTH BEHAVIOR
HEALTH VALUES; ACHIEVING HIGH LEVEL WELLNESS – (v.3 .1979 5,6,9) – v.1. 1977 – 1 – us UMI [073]
HEALTHCARE FINANCIAL MANAGEMENT – Journal of the Healthcare Financial Management Association. v36-. 1982- – 1,5,6,9 – us UMI [073]
HEALTH-RELATED FITNESS IN AND AMONG YOUTH / Lamb, Jennifer A – 1994 – 1mf – $4.00 – us Microform Publ [612]
HEALTH-RELATED FITNESS LEVELS IN BAHAMIAN ELEMENTARY SCHOOL AGE CHILDREN / Rowe, Daivd A & Mahar, Matthew T – 1992 – 3mf – $12.00 – us Microform Publ [612]
HEALTHSHARING – (Publ delay between v11 and 12) – Toronto. v1- 1979/80- – 9 – Can$20.00y – cn Micromedia [613]
Healy, Patrick J *see* THE VALERIAN PERSECUTION
Heanley, R M *see* A MEMOIR OF EDWARD STEERE, D.D., LL.D.
Heard, Albert F *see* THE RUSSIAN CHURCH AND RUSSIAN DISSENT
Heard, Franklin Fiske *see*
- A CONCISE TREATISE ON THE PRINCIPLES OF EQUITY PLEADING
- A CONCISE TREATISE ON THE PRINCIPLES OF EQUITY PLEADING.
- CURIOSITIES OF THE LAW REPORTERS
- ODDITIES OF THE LAW
- PRECEDENTS OF EQUITY PLEADINGS
- THE PRINCIPLES OF PLEADING IN CIVIL ACTIONS
- A TREATISE ADAPTED TO THE LAW AND PRACTICE OF THE SUPERIOR COURTS, AND OF TRIAL JUSTICES, DISTRICT, POLICE, AND MUNICIPAL COURTS, IN CRIMINAL CASES

Heard, J B *see*
- ALEXANDRIAN AND CARTHAGINIAN THEOLOGY CONTRASTED
- THE HISTORY OF THE EXTINCTION OF PAGANISM IN THE ROMAN EMPIRE VIEWED IN RELATION TO THE EVIDENCES OF CHRISTIANITY

Heard, John Bickford *see* OLD AND NEW THEOLOGY
HEARING AND SPEECH ACTION *see* H AND S
HEARING AND SPEECH NEWS *see* H AND S
HEARING INSTRUMENTS – v35-. 1984- – 1,5,6,9 – us UMI [073]
HEARING ON BILLS TO CONTINUE THE CIVIL GOVERNMENT FOR THE TTPI AND TO PROVIDE EX GRATIA PAYMENT TO THE PEOPLE OF BIKINI ATOLL IN THE MARSHALL ISLANDS : HEARING BEFORE THE HOUSE COMMITTEE... / U.S. Congress – mar 24 1975. Washington: GPO, 1975 (mf ed) – 1mf – 9 – $1.50 – LLMC 82-100F Title 111 – us L.L.M.C. [980]
HEARING ON H.R. 4689 TO AMEND THE U.C.M.J. : BEFORE THE MILITARY PERSONNEL AND COMPENSATION SUBCOMMITTEE OF THE COMMITTEE ON ARMED SERVICES – House of Rep. 97th Congress, 1st session, Oct 14 1981. Washington: GPO, 1981 – 2mf – 9 – $3.00 – LLMC 96-088 – us L.L.M.C. [340]
HEARING ON THE IMPLEMENTATION OF THE COMPACT OF FREE ASSOCIATION ACT IN THE MARSHALL ISLANDS AND THE FEDERATED STATES OF MICRONESIA : HELD BEFORE THE SUBCOMMITTEE ON INSULAR AND INTERNATIONAL AFFAIRS, 100TH CONG, 1ST SESS, NOV 19, 1987 / U.S. Congress. House Committee on Interior and Insular Affairs – Washington: GPO, 1989 – 5mf – 9 – $7.50 – LLMC 82-100F, Title 108 – us L.L.M.C. [980]
HEARING ON THE MICRONESIAN COMPACT : HELD BEFORE THE SUBCOMMITTEE ON IMMIGRATION, REFUGEES AND INTERNATIONAL LAW, OF THE HOUSE COMMITTEE ON THE JUDICIARY, 99TH CONG, 1ST SESS, JUL 18, 1985 / U.S. Congress – Washington: GPO, 1985 – 1mf – 9 – $1.50 – LLMC 82-100F, Title 107 – us L.L.M.C. [980]
HEARING RESEARCH – v1-16. 1978-84 – 1,5,6,13 – sz Elsevier [073]
HEARINGS / U.S. Congress. House. Select Committee Investigating Race Riots in East St. Louis in 1917 – RG 233. 7 rolls – 1 – M1167 – us Nat'l Archives [324]
HEARINGS / U.S. Nuclear Regulatory Commission – (Jan 1975-Aug 1979: ISBN 0-89093-281-6. $3,850.00; Supplements, Sept-Dec 1979: ISBN 0-89093-282-4. $580.00; Jan-Dec 1980: ISBN 0-89093-565-3. $965.00; Jan-Dec 1981: ISBN 0-89093-566-1. $860.00; Jan-Dec 1982: ISBN 0-89093-567-X. $965.00) – 1975-1982. With printed guides – 1 – $6,860.00 set – us UPA [355]
HEARINGS / U.S. President. Commission on the Assassination of President Kennedy (Warren Commission) – v. 1-26. 1964 – 1 – us Princeton Micro [324]
HEARINGS AND REPORTS / U.S. President's Commission on the Assassination of President Kennedy – 1,9 – us UMI [977]
HEARINGS BEFORE AND SPECIAL REPORTS MADE BY COMMITTEE ON ARMED SERVICES OF THE HOUSE OF REPRESENTATIVES ON SUBJECTS AFFECTING THE NAVAL AND MILITARY ESTABLISHMENTS, 1974. / U.S. Congress. House. Committee on Armed Services – Washington, Govt. Print. Off., 1975. 42p. LL-2345 – 1 – us L of C Photodup [340]
HEARINGS BEFORE THE COMMITTEE ON ARMED SERVICES, HOUSE OF REPRESENTATIVES, 98TH CONGRESS, IST SESSION, NOVEMBER 15 1983 : FULL COMMITTEE CONSIDERATION OF S. 974 (AS AMENDED) TO AMEND (UCMJ) TO IMPROVE THE QUALITY AND EFFICIENCY OF THE MILITARY JUSTICE SYSTEM, TO REVISE THE LAWS CONCERNING REVIEW OF COURTS-MARTIAL... – Washington: GPO, 1983 – 1mf – 9 – $1.50 – LLMC 96-085 – us L.L.M.C. [340]
HEARINGS BEFORE THE COMMITTEE ON ARMED SERVICES, HOUSE OF REPRESENTATIVES, MILITARY PERSONNEL AND COMPENSATION SUBCOMMITTEE, 98TH CONGRESS, 1ST SESSION, NOVEMBER 9 1983 ON S. 974 : TO AMEND (UCMJ) TO IMPROVE THE QUALITY AND EFFICIENCY OF THE MILITARY JUSTICE SYSTEM, TO REVISE THE LAWS CONCERNING REVIEW OF COURTS-MARTIAL... – Washington: GPO, 1983 – 1mf – 9 – $1.50 – LLMC 96-086 – us L.L.M.C. [340]
HEARINGS IN TRUK, PONAPE AND THE MARSHALL ISLANDS, JUL 1973 / Joint Committee on Future Status [TTPI (U.S.)] Eastern Districts Subcommittee – (Various pagination) – n.p, nov 1973 – 5mf – 9 – $7.50 – LLMC 82-100F, Title 49 – us L.L.M.C. [323]
HEARINGS IN YAP, PALAU AND THE MARIANAS, JUL 1973 / Joint Committee on Future Status [TTPI (U.S.)] Western Districts Subcommittee – (Various pagination) – n.p, nov 1973 – 4mf – 9 – $6.00 – LLMC 82-100F, Title 50 – us L.L.M.C. [323]
HEARINGS OF THE GENERAL BOARD OF THE U.S. NAVY, 1917-50 / U.S. Navy. General Board – 1983 – 15r – 1 – $1,275.00 – S1655 – Co-publ with the U.S. Naval Historical Center – us Scholarly Res [355]
HEARINGS ON THE COMPACT OF FREE ASSOCIATION (MICRONESIA-WIDE) : HELD BEFORE THE SUBCOMMITTEE ON PUBLIC LANDS AND NATIONAL PARKS, HSE.COMM ON INTERIOR AND INSULAR AFFAIRS, 98TH CONG, 2ND SESS, APR 27-DEC 12, 1984 / U.S. Congress – Washington: GPO. 8pts. 1984-85 – 29mf – 9 – $43.50 – LLMC 82-100F, Title 109 – us L.L.M.C. [980]
HEARINGS ON THE COMPACT OF FREE ASSOCIATION (MICRONESIA-WIDE) : HELD BEFORE THE SUBCOMMITTEE ON PUBLIC LANDS, HSE.COMM ON INTERIOR AND INSULAR AFFAIRS, 99TH CONG, 1ST SESS, MAR 7-MAY 20, 1985 / U.S. Congress – Washington: GPO. 4pts. 1986 – 14mf – 9 – $21.00 – LLMC 82-100F, Title 110 – us L.L.M.C. [980]
HEARINGS...THAT THE SENATE...FAVORS THE RECOGNITION OF THE PRESENT SOVIET GOVERNMENT... – Washington, 1924 – 6mf – 1 – ILM-1791/1 – ne IDC [327]
Hearn Academy. Board of Trustees. (Cave Spring, Georgia) *see* PROCEEDINGS
Hearn, G *see* THE SEVEN CITIES OF DELHI
Hearn, William E *see* THE THEORY OF LEGAL DUTIES AND RIGHTS
Hearne, S *see* A JOURNEY FROM PRINCE OF WALES'S FORT IN HUDSON'S BAY, TO THE NORTHERN OCEAN
HEARST'S INTERNATIONAL COMBINED WITH COSMOPOLITAN – v1-26. 1901-14 – 1 – us Princeton Micro [073]
HEART AND LUNG – (v.4- 1975- 9) – v.1-1972- – 1,5,6 – us UMI [073]
THE "HEART AT WORK" PROGRAM : FACTORS ASSOCIATED WITH MAINTENANCE AT THE WORKSITE / Frank, Laura B – 1994 – 1mf – $4.00 – us Microform Publ [613]
HEART MOUNTAIN SENTINEL – Heart Mountain, WY. 1942-43, 1945 – 1 – 24.00 – us Oregon Hist [071]
HEART MOUNTAIN SENTINEL *see* NEWSPAPERS PUBLISHED IN INTERNMENT CAMPS
THE HEART OF AFRICA : THREE YEARS' TRAVELS AND ADVENTURES IN THE UNEXPLORED REGIONS OF CENTRAL AFRICA, FROM 1868-1871 / Schweinfurth, Georg A – London. 2v. 1873 – 1r – 1 – us Ross [910]
THE HEART OF AFRICA: THREE YEARS TRAVELS AND ADVENTURES / Schweinfurth, Georg A – 2v. London. 1873. BA-169 2 – 8 – ne IDC [910]
HEART OF EUROPE / Cram, Ralph Adams – New York: Scribner, 1915 – 1mf – us A.T.L.A. [240]
THE HEART OF THE GOSPEL: A POPULAR EXPOSITION OF THE ATONEMENT / Campbell, James Mann – New York: Fleming H. Revell, 1907. 1 fiche – 9 – us A.T.L.A. [240]
THE HEART OF THE NATION / Dunne, Edward F – Chicago: Lewis Publ. Co., 1933. Vol. 1. Illinois Reel 2; Vols. 2-5. Illinois Reel 3. (The Cox Library Collection) – 5 – us Americana [978]
HEART RATE RESPONSES OF COLLEGIATE FEMALE VOLLEYBALL PLAYERS DURING COMPETITION / Harbour, SK – 1991 – 2mf – 9 – $8.00 – us Microform Publ [612]
THE HEART RATES OF ELEMENTARY CHILDREN DURING PHYSICAL EDUCATION CLASSES / Burton, Catherine J – Ball State University, 1996 – 1mf – 9 – PH 1489 – us Microform Publ [612]
HEART SONGS / Blewett, Jean – Toronto: G. Morang, 1897. 00143. (Pre-1900 Canadiana) – 9 – cn C.I.H.M. [830]
HEART TRANSPLANTATION/INTERNATIONAL SOCIETY FOR HEART TRANSPLANTATION – v1-3. 1981-84 – 1 – us UMI [617]
A HEART-BROKEN CORONER AND OTHER WONDERS / Belding, Albert Martin – 1895. 06158. (Pre-1900 Canadiana) – 9 – cn C.I.H.M. [830]
HEARTH AND HOME – New York, 1869 – 1r – 1 – us Ross [073]

HEARTH & HOME – New York. 26 Dec 1868-25 Dec 1875.-w. 8 reels – 1 – uk British Libr Newspaper [073]

THE HEARTHSTONE : ILLUSTRE / ed by Desbarats, George – Montreal, Canada. v3 n1. 6 jan 1872-v3 n52. 28 dec 1872 – 1r – 1 – Can$30.00 – cn Can Microfilming [073]

HEARTLAND EVENING NEWS *see* MIDLAND DAILY TRIBUNE

HEARTLAND NEWS – El Cajon, CA. 1950-52 – 1r – 1 – $50.00 – C02194 – us Library Micro [071]

HEARTLAND NEWS – El Cajon. Calif. 1950-1952 – 1 – us UMI [071]

HEARTS OF MEN / Fielding-Hall, Harold – New York: Macmillan, 1901. 1 fiche – 9 – us A.T.L.A. [240]

HEAT AND FLUID FLOW – (v6-. 1976-. 5,6,9) – v. 1-. 1971- – 1 – us UMI [621]

HEAT RECOVERY SYSTEMS AND CHP – v1-1981- – 5,6,9 – us UMI [621]

HEAT TRANSFER: JAPANESE RESEARCH – (v13-. 1984-. 5,6,9) – v1-. 1972- – 1 – us UMI [073]

HEAT TRANSFER: SOVIET RESEARCH – (v16-. 1984-. 5,6,9) – v1-. 1969- – 1 – us UMI [073]

HEATH 1737-1849 – (Mf 1T: Marriages 1804-40; Intentions 1805-25. Mf 2T: Intentions 1825-37. Mf 2T-5T: Births & Deaths 1737-1848. Mf 5T-6T: Marriages 1835-42, 1849. Mf 5T: Intentions 1838-49; Deaths 1833-37. Mf 6T: Births 1837-49; Out-of-Town Marriages 1790-98; Deaths 1844-49) – (mf ed 1996) – 6mf – 9 – 0-87623-265-9 – us Holbrook [920]

HEATH 1763-1899 – (Mf 1-6: B,M,D 1763-1844. Mf 7-8: Births 1844-99. Mf 8-9: Marriages 1790-1900. Mf 9-10: Deaths 1844-1900. Mf 11: Birth Index 1844-1900. Mf 12: Marriage Intentions Index 1844-1900. Mf 13: Marriage Index 1844-1900. Mf 14: Death Index 1844-1900. Mf 15-19: Church Records 1785-1889. Mf 20-21: Church Records 1805-56. Mf 22: Soldiers 1863; Overseer of Poor 1901-04) – (mf ed 1987) – 22mf – 9 – 0-87623-049-4 – us Holbrook [920]

Heath, Peter S *see* AN INDIVIDUALIZED SELF-CONTROL APPROACH TO WEIGHT REDUCTION

Heath, Richard *see*
- ANABAPTISM
- ANABAPTISM FROM ITS RISE AT ZWICKAU TO ITS FALL AT MUNSTER
- THE CAPTIVE CITY OF GOD, OR, THE CHURCHES SEEN IN THE LIGHT OF THE DEMOCRATIC IDEAL
- EDGAR QUINET
- THE REFORMATION IN FRANCE FROM THE DAWN OF REFORM TO THE REVOCATION OF THE EDICT OF NANTES
- THE REFORMATION IN FRANCE FROM THE REVOCATION OF THE EDICT OF NANTES TO THE INCORPORATION OF THE REFORMED CHURCHES INTO THE STATE
- SOCIAL DEMOCRACY, DOES IT MEAN DARKNESS OR LIGHT?

Heath, Sidney *see* PILGRIM LIFE IN THE MIDDLE AGES

HEATH SPRINGS BAPTIST CHURCH. HEATH SPRINGS, SOUTH CAROLINA : CHURCH RECORDS – 1889-1942. Scattered records, 1932-42 – 1 – 20.25 – us Baptist [240]

Heath, William *see* WILLIAM HEATH PAPERS, 1774-1872

THE HEATHEN HEART : AN ACCOUNT OF THE RECEPTION OF THE GOSPEL AMONG THE CHINESE OF FORMOSA / Moody, Campbell N – Edinburgh: Oliphant, Anderson & Ferrier, 1907 – 1mf – us A.T.L.A. [240]

HEATHEN HELPERS – 1882-89; The Baptist Basket. 1888 (also Southern Baptist Convention Directory, May 1880) – 1 – 23.87 – us Baptist [240]

THE HEATHER BEETLE / Cameron, A E et al – 1944 – 7 – uk Microform Academic [590]

HEATH'S BOOK OF BEAUTY – 1833-49 – 68mf – 9 – £500.00 – uk Chadwyck [800]

Heath-Stubbs, J *see* THE WATER WHEEL OF LOVE

HE-ATID – Warsaw. 1925-35. BJ-91-38 1 – 9 – ne IDC [956]

HEATID = FUTURE – (In Hebrew) – Warsaw, PL. v1 no1 23 Jan-no2 30 Jan 1925 – 1r – 1 – $25.00 – cn Can Microfilming [072]

HEATING AND AIR CONDITIONING JOURNAL – v43 no 508- Apr 1974- – 1,5,6,9 – us UMI [620]

HEATING, PIPING AND AIR CONDITIONING – 1- 1929- – 1,5,6,9 – us UMI [620]

Heaton, Sydney Lewell *see* ONTARIO DIVORCE LAW NOTEBOOK

Heaton, William James *see*
- THE BIBLE OF THE REFORMATION
- OUR OWN ENGLISH BIBLE

Heatwole, Cornelius Jacob *see* A HISTORY OF EDUCATION IN VIRGINIA

HE-AVAR – Petrograd. 1918. BJ-291-30 1 – 9 – ne IDC [900]

HEAVENER FIRST BAPTIST CHURCH. HEAVENER, OKLAHOMA : CHURCH RECORDS – 1912-80 – 1 – 73.84 – us Baptist [240]

HEAVENLY FATHER: LECTURES ON MODERN ATHEISM / Naville, Ernest – Boston: William V. Spencer, 1867. 1 fiche – 9 – us A.T.L.A. [240]

THE HEAVENLY TOKEN / Harsha, David A – 1857 – 9 – us A.T.L.A. [240]

HEAVENLY WIND = TIEN FENG – (In Chinese) – nos 83-631. 1947-63 (complete) – 5r – 1 – ATLA S0317 – us A.T.L.A. [073]

HEAVY CONSTRUCTION NEWS – 1957- – 1,5,6,9 – us UMI [690]

HEAVY CONSTRUCTION NEWS – Toronto. v1-38. 1957-94 – 9 – Can$28.00y – cn Micromedia [690]

HEBBEL : DAS DRAMA AN DER WENDE DER ZEIT / Scholz, Wilhelm von – 3. Aufl. Stuttgart, Berlin: Deutsche Verlags-Anstalt, c1922 – 1r – 1 – us U.W. Library [430]

HEBBEL / Wehner, Josef Magnus – Stuttgart: J G Cotta, 1938 – 1r – 1 – us U.W. Library [430]

HEBBEL ALS DICHTER DER FRAU / Engel-Mitscherlich, Hilde – Dresden: W Baensch, 1909 – 1r – 1 – us U.W. Library [430]

HEBBEL ALS LYRIKER / Moeller, Hans – (Includes bibliographical references) – [S.l.: s.n.], 1908 (Cuxhaven: Gedruckt bei C Rauschenplat) – 1r – 1 – us U.W. Library [430]

HEBBEL ALS NOVELLIST / Ebhardt, Rolf – (Includes bibliographical references) – Berlin: Weidmann, 1916 – 1r – 1 – us U.W. Library [430]

HEBBEL AND THE DREAM / Schueler, Herbert – (Includes bibliographical references) – New York: [s.n.], 1941 – 1r – 1 – us U.W. Library [430]

Hebbel, Friedrich *see*
- ERZAEHLUNGEN UND NOVELLEN
- FRIEDRICH HEBBELS DEMETRIUS
- GYGES UND SEIN RING
- HEBBEL PROSISTA
- HEBBELS WERKE
- JULIA

HEBBEL PROSISTA : AUTOBIOGRAFIA, IDEARIO, DEL DRAMA / Hebbel, Friedrich; ed by Icaza, Francisco A de – Madrid: [Impr. de J. Pueyo], 1919 – 1r – 1 – us U.W. Library [830]

HEBBEL UND DAS RELIGIOESE PROBLEM DER GEGENWART / Horneffer, Ernst – Jena: E Diederichs, 1907 – 1r – 1 – us U.W. Library [430]

HEBBEL UND DAS WIENER THEATER SEINER ZEIT / Kindermann, Heinz – Wien: W Frick, 1943 – 1r – 1 – us U.W. Library [430]

HEBBEL UND DIE MUSIK / Nagler, Alois Maria – (Includes bibliographical references) – Koeln: J P Bachem, 1928 – 1r – 1 – us U.W. Library [430]

HEBBEL UND DIE PHILOSOPHIE SEINER ZEIT / Waetzoldt, Wilhelm – (Includes bibliographical references) – [S.l.: s.n.], 1903 (Graefenhainichen: Druck von W Hecker) – 1r – us U.W. Library [430]

HEBBELPROBLEME : STUDIEN / Walzel, Oskar Franz – Leipzig: H Haessel, 1909 – 1r – 1 – us U.W. Library [430]

HEBBELS DITHMARSCHENFRAGMENT : ANORDNUNG / Bender, Heinrich – (Includes bibliographical references) – Bonn: P Rost, 1914 – 1r – 1 – us U.W. Library [430]

HEBBELS FRAUENGESTALTEN / Kreisler, Emil – Wien: Verlag der k. k. Franz Joseph-Realschule, 1907 – 1r – 1 – us U.W. Library [430]

HEBBELS HERODES UND MARIAMNE : VORTRAG / Bornstein, Paul – Hamburg: L Voss, 1904 – 1r – 1 – us U.W. Library [430]

HEBBELS JUDITH UND MARIA MAGDALENA IM URTEIL SEINER ZEITGENOSSEN / Beer, Oskar – (Includes bibliographical references) – [S.l.: s.n. 19–?] (Naumburg a.S.: Druck von G Paetz) – 1r – 1 – us U.W. Library [430]

HEBBELS LYRIK UND EPIK IM RAHMEN SEINES LEBENS : EINE ANREGUNG ZU HEBBELSTUDIEN UND HEBBELSTUNDEN / Schnass, Franz – (Includes bibliographical references) – Prag: A Haase, 1921 – 1r – 1 – us U.W. Library [430]

HEBBELS THEORIE UND KRITIK POETISCHER MUSTER : MIT BESONDERER RUECKSICHT AUF DIE ENTWICKLUNG SEINER LYRIK UNTER UHLANDS EINFLUSS / Herke, Karl – (Includes bibliographical references) – Berlin: H Lonys, 1913 – 1r – 1 – us U.W. Library [430]

HEBBELS WERKE / Hebbel, Friedrich; ed by Zeiss, Karl – (Includes bibliographical references) – Leipzig: Bibliographisches Institut. 4v. [1899?] – 1 – us U.W. Library [800]

DER HEBBELVEREIN IN HEIDELBERG : DIE GESCHICHTE EINER LITERARISCHEN GESELLSCHAFT – EIN RUECKBLICK AUF SEINE TAETIGKEIT VON 1902-1908 / Stahl, Ernst Leopold – Heidelberg: C Winter, 1911 – 1r – 1 – us U.W. Library [430]

Hebberd, Stephen Southric *see*
- HISTORY OF WISCONSIN UNDER THE DOMINION OF FRANCE
- SECRET OF CHRISTIANITY

Hebden, John *see* SIX CONCERTOS...OPERA 2

HEBDO COURRIER DE LAVAL *see* COURRIER DE LAVAL

HEBDO DE L'EST / ed by Morin, Pierre – Montreal-Est. v1 n2. 6 nov 1968-v1 n7. 11 dec 1968 – 1r – 1 – Can$25.00 – cn Can Microfilming [072]

L'HEBDO DE PORTNEUF *see* L'ECHO DE PORTNEUF-PRESSE

L'HEBDO DE SAINT-LEONARD – Ville St-Leonard, Canada. 29 mai 1970-v1 n12. 17 dec 1970 – 1r – 1 – Can$30.00 – cn Can Microfilming [072]

L'HEBDO DE SHERBROOKE – Sherbrooke, Canada. v1 n4. 5 oct 1966-17 jan 1968 – 1r – 1 – Can$50.00 – cn Can Microfilming [072]

HEBDO DE TROIS-RIVIERES – Trois-Rivieres. v1 n1. 11 aut 1971; v2 n31. 21 mar 1973 – 1r – 1 – Can$25.00 – cn Can Microfilming [072]

HEBDO DU CAP – (Cont: Le Journal du Cap) – Cap-de-la-Madeleine, 11 aut 1971-30 oct 1974 – 4r – 1 – Can$75.00 – cn Can Microfilming [072]

HEBDO DU CAP *see*
- HEBDO DU CAP-DE-LA-MADELEIME
- LE JOURNAL DU CAP

HEBDO DU CAP-DE-LA-MADELEIME – (Cont: Hebdo du Cap) – Cap-de-la-Madeleine, 7 nov 1974-29 dec 1980 – 9r – 1 – Can$75.00 – cn Can Microfilming [072]

HEBDO DU CAP-DE-LA-MADELEINE *see* LE JOURNAL DU CAP

L'HEBDO DU SAINT-MAURICE *see* L'ECHO DU SAINT-MAURICE

HEBDO JOURNAL – Trois-Rivieres, Canada. v1 n16. 12 fev 1964-v2 n25. 21 avr 1965 – 1r – 1 – Can$50.00 – cn Can Microfilming [072]

HEBDO QUEBEC – Quebec, 15 dec 1971-v1 n5. 16 jan 1972 – 1r – 1 – Can$25.00 – cn Can Microfilming [072]

L'HEBDOMADAIRE – Levis, Canada. 16 fev 1882-3 sep 1913 – 1r – 1 – Can$35.00 – cn Can Microfilming [072]

L'HEBDOMADAIRE – Levis, Canada. v1 n4. 16 fev 1939-v1 n34. 14 sep 1939 – 1r – 1 – Can$40.00 – cn Can Microfilming [072]

L'HEBDOMADAIRE DU TEMPS NOUVEAU – Dirige par les RR.PP. Dominicains. Lyon. dec 1940-aout 1941, sept 1944 – 1 – fr A.C.R.P.P. [073]

HEBDOMICILE – Hull: F Laferriere, 1986-. SEM35P296 – 1r – 1 – Can$34.00 – cn Bibl Nat [072]

HEBDO-SPORTS – Port-au-Prince: Federation de football. v1 n1-8,10-15,17-22,24-28 jan-feb, mar 11-apr 11, apr 25-jun 6, jun 20-jul 1951; v2 n1-28 feb-aug 1952; v3 n1-7 nov 6-dec 19/26 1952; v2 n8-26 jan-may 1953 – 11r – 1 – us Res Libr [072]

Hebei Province. China *see*
- HONGZHI BAODING JUN ZHI, APPROX. 1505
- HONGZHI YIZHOU ZHI, 1502
- JIAJING BAZHOU ZHI, 1548
- JIAJING GUANGPING FU ZHI, 1550
- JIAJING HEJIAN FU ZHI, 1540
- JIAJING LONGQING ZHI, 1535
- JIAJING XIONGCHENG, 1533
- LONGQING ZHAOZHOU ZHI, 1566
- ZHENGDE DAMING FU ZHI, APPROX. 1521

HEBEI RIBAO – Hebei Daily. 1983-. M D42 – 1 reel/y – 1 – $55.00r – cc Microforms [072]

Hebel, Johann Peter *see* ALLEMANNISCHE GEDICHTE

HEBEL UND KLEIST ALS MEISTER DER ANEKDOTE / Staehlin, Friedrich – (Includes bibliographical references) – Berlin: M Matthiesen, 1940 – 1 – us U.W. Library [430]

Heber, R *see* NARRATIVE OF A JOURNEY THROUGH THE UPPER PROVINCES OF INDIA

Heber, Reginald *see* THE POETICAL WORKS OF REGINALD HEBER, LORD BISHOP OF CALCUTTA

HEBERCI – Stockholm, Sweden. Isvicdegi Dini-Medini Tuerk-Islam Oyusmasi Karsisinda Vakitli Reviste Cigarilaridir. No. 1 (Dec 1952) – 9 – $20.00 – us MEDOC [956]

Heberden, William *see* COMMENTARIES ON THE HISTORY AND CURE OF DISEASE

Hebert, Charles *see* THE LORD'S SUPPER

Hebert, J et al *see* CITE LIBRE

Hebert, Jacques et al *see* VRAI

Hebert, Marcel *see* L'EVOLUTION DE LA FOI CATHOLIQUE

HEBO HUB – Hebo OR. June 1926 – 1 – us U.O. Library [071]

DER HEBRAEERBRIEF IN ZEITGESCHICHTLICHER BELEUCHTUNG (T.U.U. 3-35/3) / Weiss, Bernhard – Leipzig, 1910 – 2mf – 9 – ne Slangenburg [240]

DIE HEBRAEERIN AM PUTZTISCHE UND ALS BRAUT / Hartmann, A T – Amsterdam. 3v. 1809-1810 – 14mf – ne IDC [220]

HEBRAEISCHE BIBLIOGRAPHIE, BLAETTER FUER NEUERE UND AELTERE LITERATUR DES JUDENTHUMS... / ed by Steinschneider, M – (Missing: 1864-1865, v7-8; 1869-1871, v9-11) – 32mf – ne IDC [270]

HEBRAEISCHE ELEMENTARGRAMMATIK : EINE ZUR EINFUEHRUNG IN DAS STUDIUM DER GRAMMATISCHEN WERKE EWALDS UND BOETTCHERS BESTIMMTE VORSCHULE / Grundt, Friedrich Immanuel – Leipzig: Ferdinand Hirt, 1875 – 1mf – 9 – 0-8370-9238-8 – 1986-3238 – us A.T.L.A. [470]

DIE HEBRAEISCHE ELIAS-APOKALYPSE UND IHR STELLUNG IN DER APOKALYPTISCHEN LITTERATUR / Buttenweiser, M – Leipzig: Eduard Pfeiffer, 1897. 1 fiche – 9 – us A.T.L.A. [240]

HEBRAEISCHE GRAMMATIK FUER DEN UNTERRICHT MIT UEBUNGSSTUECKEN UND WOERTERVERZEICHNISSEN / Koenig, Eduard – Leipzig: J C Hinrichs, 1908 – 1mf – 9 – 0-8370-9482-8 – 1986-3482 – us A.T.L.A. [470]

DIE HEBRAEISCHE PRAEPOSITION LAMED / Giesebrecht, Friedrich – (Includes bibliographical references) – Halle (Saale): Max Niemeyer, 1876 – 1mf – 9 – 0-8370-9147-0 – 1986-3147 – us A.T.L.A. [470]

HEBRAEISCHE SCHRIFTGESTALTUNG IN DEUTSCHLAND VON DER JAHRHUNDERTWENDE BIS ZUM AUSBRUCH DES ZWEITEN WELTKRIEGES UNTER BESONDERER BERUECKSICHTIGUNG DER "FRANK-RUEHL"-LETTERN / Tamari, Ittai Joseph – 1995 – 7mf – 9 – DM130.00 – 3-8267-2262-0 – gw Hänsel [470]

DIE HEBRAEISCHE SPRACHWISSENSCHAFT VOM 10. BIS ZUM 16. JAHRHUNDERT : MIT EINEM EINLEITENDEN ABSCHNITTE UEBER DIE MASSORA JAHRHUNDERT / Bacher, Wilhelm – (Includes bibliographies & index of authors) – Trier: Sigmund Mayer, 1892 – 1mf – 9 – 0-8370-2537-0 – 1985-0537 – us A.T.L.A. [470]

DIE HEBRAEISCHEN HANDSCHRIFTEN DER K. HOF- UND STAATSBIBLIOTHEK IN MUENCHEN, BESCHRIEBEN... / Steinschneider, M – Muenchen, 1875 – 3mf – ne IDC [470]

DIE HEBRAEISCHEN HANDSCHRIFTEN DER K. HOF- UND STAATSBIBLIOTHEK IN MUENCHEN, BESCHRIEBEN... / Steinschneider, M – Muenchen, 1895 – 3mf – ne IDC [470]

DIE HEBRAEISCHEN TRADITIONEN IN DEN WERKEN DES HIERONYMUS / Rahmer, M – 2pts. Pt. 1: Die "Quaestiones in Genesin". Pt. 2: Die Commentarii zu den zwoelf kleinen Propheten. Breslau. Berlin. 1861-1902. BJ-32-56 1 – 9 – ne IDC [270]

DIE HEBRAEISCHEN UEBERSETZUNGEN DES MITTELALTERS UND DIE JUDEN ALS DOLMETSCHER, EIN BEITRAG ZUR LITERATURGESCHICHTE DES MITTELALTERS... / Steinschneider, M – Berlin. 2v. 1893 – 12mf – ne IDC [470]

HEBRAEISCHES FAMILIENRECHT IN VORPROPHETISCHER ZEIT / Rauh, Sigismund – Berlin: Gustav Schade, 1907 – 1mf – 9 – 0-8370-4844-3 – 1985-2844 – us A.T.L.A. [220]

HEBRAEISCHES SCHULBUCH / Hollenberg, Wilhelm Adolf – 4. Aufl. Berlin: Weidmann, 1880 – 1mf – 9 – 0-8370-9248-5 – 1986-3248 – us A.T.L.A. [470]

DEM HEBRAEISCH-PHOENIZISCHEN SPRACHZWEIGE ANGEHOERIGE LEHNWOERTER IN HIEROGLYPHISCHEN UND HIERATISCHEN TEXTEN / Bondi, J H – Leipzig. 1886. BNE-476 1 – 9 – ne IDC [930]

DAS HEBRAER-EVANGELIUM (T.U.U. 1-5/3) / Handmann, R – Leipzig, 1888 – 3mf – 9 – ne Slangenburg [240]

HEBRAIC AND YIDDISH CATALOG / U.S. Library of Congress – 39,000 entries – 1 – 320.00 – us L of C Photodup [010]

HEBRAICA – (Cont. as: AMERICAN JOURNAL OF SEMITIC LANGUAGES AND LITERATURES. Chicago. 1895-1941.) – Chicago. v1-11. 1884-95. Lacking: 1908. v25 – 343mf – 8 – ne IDC [470]

HEBRAICA *see*
- THE AMERICAN JOURNAL OF SEMITIC LANGUAGES AND LITERATURES
- JEWISH MESSENGER
- AMERICAN JOURNAL OF SEMITIC LANGUAGES AND LITERATURES

HEBRAICA ET RABBINICA / Pinczower, E & Porges, N – (Available: pt 1(A-F); pt 2(G-M)) – Leipzig, 1931-1932 – 3mf – ne IDC [270]

HEBREW – (San Francisco). 1864-87 – 1 – us A.J.P.C. [071]

THE HEBREW – New York. N.Y. 1892-1902 – 1 – us A.J.P.C. [071]

THE HEBREW – San Francisco, CA. 1864-1906 (incomplete) – 7r – 1 – $350.00 – B02820 – us Library Micro [071]

HEBREW ABSTRACTS – v1-16. 1954-75 – 1 – us UMI [270]

THE HEBREW AMERICAN – New York. N.Y. 1894-95 – 1 – us A.J.P.C. [071]

HEBREW AND JUDEO-ARABIC MSS. IN THE COLLECTIONS OF THE USSR / Katsh, A I – Moscow, 1962. v1, p421-429. BR-10,667/1 – 9 – ne IDC [090]

HEBREW AND JUDEO-ARABIC MSS IN THE COLLECTIONS OF THE USSR. M., 1962 = TRUDY DVADTSAT'-PIATOGO MEZHDUNARODNOGO KONGRASSA VOSTOKOVEDOV / Katsh, A I – Moskva 9-16 avgusta 1960 g. v1 (p. 421-429) – 1mf – ne IDC [470]

HEBREW ANNUAL REVIEW – (1985-. 5,6,9) – 1977- – 1 – us UMI [270]

HEBREW BOOKS FROM THE HARVARD COLLEGE LIBRARY / ed by Berlin, Charles – (Part 1. Rabbinical Works. 8647 fiches. (1:24). Part 2. Secular Works. 2900 fiches. Includes printed index) – 1990-1992 – 11,453mf – 9 – diazo DM56,400.00 (silver DM61,800.00 ISBN: 3-598-41200-2) – 3-598-41160-X – gw Saur [020]

Hebrew Butcher Workers' Union *see* BUTCHER WORKER

HEBREW CHARACTERISTICS: MISCELLANEOUS PAPERS – New York: American Jewish Publ. Soc., 1875. 1 fiche – 9 – us A.T.L.A. [270]

HEBREW CHARTS : CONTAINING THE ELEMENTS OF THE LANGUAGE / Irish, William Norman – Albany, NY: Weed, Parsons, 1872, c1871 – 1mf – 9 – 0-8370-9289-2 – 1986-3289 – us A.T.L.A. [470]

A HEBREW CHRESTOMATHY, OR, LESSONS IN READING AND WRITING HEBREW / Green, William Henry – (Notes in English; text in Hebrew) – New York: John Wiley, 1866, c1863 – 1mf – 9 – 0-8370-9473-9 – 1986-3473 – us A.T.L.A. [470]

HEBREW FAIR JOURNAL – Washington, D.C. 1886-96 – 1 – us A.J.P.C. [071]

HEBREW FEASTS IN THEIR RELATION TO...HYPOTHESES CONCERNING THE PENTATEUCH / Green, William Henry – London: James Nisbet, 1886. 1 fiche – 9 – us A.T.L.A. [270]

HEBREW FOR SELF-INSTRUCTION : BY WHICH, WITH THREE MONTHS' STUDY, THE STUDENT WILL BE ABLE TO READ THE HEBREW BIBLE AND UNDERSTAND ITS GRAMMATICAL STRUCTURE / Wheeler, H M – London: Simpkin, Marshall, 1850 – 1mf – 9 – 0-8370-9347-3 – 1986-3347 – us A.T.L.A. [470]

A HEBREW GRAMMAR / Lowe, William Henry – London: Hodder and Stoughton, 1887 – 1mf – 9 – 0-8370-9166-7 – 1986-3166 – us A.T.L.A. [470]

HEBREW GRAMMAR / Gesenius, H – 1910 – 9 – $21.00 – us I.R.C. [470]

HEBREW INSCRIPTIONS, FROM THE VALLEYS BETWEEN EGYPT AND MOUNT SINAI : IN THEIR ORIGINAL CHARACTERS, WITH TRANSLATIONS AND AN ALPHABET / Sharpe, Samuel – (Includes index to Hebrew and Aramaic words) – London: John Russell Smith, 1875 – 1mf – 9 – 0-8370-8620-5 – 1986-2620 – us A.T.L.A. [470]

HEBREW LEADER – New York. N.Y. 1867-70 – 1 – us A.J.P.C. [071]

HEBREW LITERATURE: COMPRISING TALMUDIC TREATISES, HEBREW MELODIES AND THE KABBALAH UNVEILED – New York: Colonial Press, 1901. 1 fiche – 9 – us A.T.L.A. [270]

THE HEBREW LITERATURE OF WISDOM IN THE LIGHT OF TO-DAY : A SYNTHESIS / Genung, John Franklin – Boston: Houghton Mifflin, 1906 – 1mf – 9 – 0-8370-9780-0 – 1986-3780 – us A.T.L.A. [220]

THE HEBREW LITERATURE OF WISDOM IN THE LIGHT OF TO-DAY; A SYNTHESIS / Genung, John Franklin – Boston, New York: Houghton, Mifflin and Company, 1906. xviii,408p – 1 – us U.W. Library [270]

HEBREW OBSERVER – London. 1853-54.-w. 1men reels – 1 – uk British Libr Newspaper [290]

HEBREW OBSERVER : WEEKLY JEWISH NEWSPAPER – Cleveland, OH. 1889-1898 – 1r – 1 – us Western Res [071]

THE HEBREW OBSERVER – Grand Rapids. Mich. 1942-55 – 1 – us A.J.P.C. [071]

THE HEBREW, OR, THE CHURCH WITH HER SURROUNDINGS : AS THEY TOGETHER APPEARED, THE THIRD OF A CENTURY AGO, TO A SUBORDINATE OFFICIAL – (Includes appendix) – New York: Holman, 1863 – 1mf – 9 – 0-8370-4512-6 – 1985-2512 – us A.T.L.A. [240]

HEBREW POETRY: SUNDAY AFTERNOON LECTURES / Dick, Robert P – Greensboro: C.F. Thomas, 1883. 1 fiche – 9 – us A.T.L.A. [470]

HEBREW PROPHET / Batten, Loring Woart – New York: Macmillan, 1905. 1 fiche – 9 – us A.T.L.A. [240]

THE HEBREW PROPHETS / Ottley, Robert Lawrence – New York: Edwin S. Gorham, 1905.1 fiche – 9 – us A.T.L.A. [240]

THE HEBREW PUCK – (New York). 1894-96 – 1 – us A.J.P.C. [071]

HEBREW RELIGION TO THE ESTABLISHMENT OF JUDAISM UNDER EZRA / Addis, William Edward – (Includes chronological tables. Includes index) – London: Williams & Norgate; New York: G P Putnam, 1906 – 1mf – 9 – 0-8370-2049-2 – 1985-0049 – us A.T.L.A. [270]

THE HEBREW RENAISSANCE – (New York). 1913 – 1 – us A.J.P.C. [071]

HEBREW SATIRE / Chotzner, J – London. 1911. BJ-421-16 – 9 – ne IDC [470]

HEBREW STANDARD – New York. N.Y. 1893-1922 – 1 – us A.J.P.C. [071]

THE HEBREW STUDENT'S COMMENTARY ON ZECHARIAH : HEBREW AND 70 WITH EXCURSUS ON SYLLABLE-DIVIDING, METHEG, INITIAL DAGESH, AND SIMAN RAPHEH / Lowe, William Henry – London:Macmillan, 1882 – 1mf – 9 – 0-8370-4186-4 – 1985-2186 – us A.T.L.A. [220]

HEBREW STUDIES – (1985-. 5,6,9) – v17-. 1976- – 1 – us UMI [270]

HEBREW SYNTAX / Davidson, Andrew Bruce – (Includes index) – Edinburgh: T & T Clark, 1894 – 1mf – 9 – 0-8370-9221-3 – 1986-3221 – us A.T.L.A. [470]

HEBREW TENSES / Driver, Samuel Rolles – 1898 – 9 – $12.00 – us I.R.C. [470]

THE HEBREW TEXT OF THE BOOK OF ECCLESIASTICUS / ed by Levi, Israel – Leiden: E J Brill, 1904 – 1mf – 9 – 0-8370-9399-6 – 1986-3399 – us A.T.L.A. [220]

HEBREW TITLES : 1964-1971 – 1972 – 6r – 1 – $200.00 – us A.J.P.C. [470]

HEBREW TITLES : 1972-1982 – 1984 – 82mf – 9 – $360.00 – us A.J.P.C. [470]

HEBREW TITLES : 1983-1989 – in prep – us A.J.P.C. [470]

HEBREW TWINS: A VINDICATION OF GOD'S WAYS WITH JACOB AND ESAU / Cox, Samuel – New York: Whittaker, 1894. 1 fiche – 9 – us A.T.L.A. [240]

Hebrew Union College *see* HEBREW UNION COLLEGE ANNUAL

HEBREW UNION COLLEGE ANNUAL – (Cincinnati). 1924-66 – 1 – us A.J.P.C. [370]

HEBREW UNION COLLEGE ANNUAL / Hebrew Union College – v1- . 1924- – 1,5,6,9 – us UMI [073]

Hebrew Union College. Jewish Institute of Religion. Klau Library *see* DICTIONARY CATALOG

Hebrew Union College-Jewish Institute of Religion. Cincinnati *see* DICTIONARY CATALOG OF THE KLAU LIBRARY

HEBREW UNION COLLEGE-JEWISH INSTITUTE OF RELIGION. FYI – (Cincinnati, Ohio) Feb. 27, 1978-Oct. 1988 – us A.J.P.C. [270]

THE HEBREW UTOPIA : A STUDY OF MESSIANIC PROPHECY / Adeney, Walter Frederic – London: Hodder & Stoughton, 1879 – 1mf – 9 – 0-8370-2051-4 – 1985-0051 – us A.T.L.A. [240]

HEBREW UTOPIA: A STUDY OF MESSIANIC PROPHECY / Adeney, Walter Frederic – London: Hodder & Stoughton, 1879. 1 fiche – 9 – us A.T.L.A. [240]

THE HEBREW VERB : A SERIES OF TABULAR STUDIES / Carrier, Augustus Stiles – Chicago: Max Stern, 1891 – 1mf – 9 – 0-8370-9212-4 – 1986-3212 – us A.T.L.A. [470]

HEBREW WATCHMAN – Memphis, TN. 1979-84 – 1 – us A.J.P.C. [071]

HEBREW WATCHWORD – (Philadelphia). 1896-98 – 1 – us A.J.P.C. [071]

THE HEBREW WORD – (In Russian) – v5? no3. 17 Jan 1919 – 1r – 1 – $25.00 – cn Can Microfilming [072]

Hebrew Writer's Association *see* MOZNAYIM

THE HEBREW-CHARACTER TITLE CATALOG OF THE JEWISH DIVISION / New York Public Library. Research Libraries – 1981. 52,167 cards. 4 reels. ISBN 0-8161-1443-9 – 1 – $550.00 – uk Hall [270]

HEBREWS : INTRODUCTION, AUTHORIZED VERSION, REVISED VERSION, WITH NOTES AND INDEX / ed by Peake, Arthur Samuel – Edinburgh: T C & E C Jack, [19–] – 1mf – 9 – 0-8370-6831-2 – 1986-0831 – us A.T.L.A. [220]

HEBRON BAPTIST CHURCH (FORMERLY: TINKER CREEK BAPTIST CHURCH). UNION COUNTY. SOUTH CAROLINA : CHURCH RECORDS – 1867-87, Oct 1937 and Jan 1938. History book. 1806-1958 – 1 – 5.00 – us Baptist [240]

HEBRON BAPTIST CHURCH. GASTON COUNTY. NORTH CAROLINA : CHURCH RECORDS – 1838-1922 – 1 – 7.74 – us Baptist [240]

HEBRON CHAMPION – Hebron, NE. -w. Jan-Jul 1896, scattered issues missing; Feb-Dec 1897; Mar 1898-May 1913; Jan 1914-Jan 1916 – 1 – us NE Hist [071]

HEBRON JOURNAL – Hebron, NE. -w. Feb 1871-Apr 1874, scattered issues missing; Apr 1875-Dec 1923; Jan 1926-Feb 1944 – 1 – us NE Hist [071]

HEBRON JOURNAL-REGISTER – Hebron, NE. -w. (-sw 1919-20). Jul 1892-Jul 1893, scattered issues missing; Nov 1893-Nov 1894; Aug 1895-Dec 1923; Feb 1924 to date – 1 – us NE Hist [071]

Hebron, New Hampshire. Hebron Baptist Church *see* RECORDS

HEBRON REPUBLICAN – Hebron, NE. -w. Nov 1895-Feb 1896; May 1896-May 1898; Jan 1899-Dec 1900 – 1 – us NE Hist [071]

HEC FORUM – New York. v1-2. 1989-90* 1; v3-9. 1991-97+ 1,5,9; v3-6 1991-94* 5 – 1,5,9 – D18621 – us UMI [073]

Hecart, G A J *see* DICTIONNAIRE ROUCHI-FRANCAIS

HECHALUTZ = PIONER – (In Yiddish) – Brzesc, PL. (-) 18 May 1926 – 1r – 1 – $25.00 – cn Can Microfilming [072]

LOS HECHOS – Panama City, Panama. 7 Jun-13 Jul 1912 – 1r – 1 – us L of C Photodup [072]

Hecht, Georg *see* GOETHES BRIEFWECHSEL MIT THOMAS CARLYLE

Hechtenberg, Klara *see* DAS FREMDWORT BEI GRIMMELSHAUSEN

Heck, J C *see*
- THE ART OF FINGERING
- THE ART OF PLAYING THOROUGH BASS WITH CORRECTNESS ACCORDING TO THE TRUE PRINCIPLES OF COMPOSITION
- A COMPLETE SYSTEM OF HARMONY
- SHORT AND FUNDAMENTAL INSTRUCTIONS FOR LEARNING THOROUGH BASS

Heckel, E M *see* LES PLANTES MEDICINALES ET TOXIQUES DE LA GUYANE FRANCAISE

Heckel, Hans *see* DAS DON JUAN-PROBLEM IN DER NEUEREN DICHTUNG

Hecker, Friedrich *see* REDEN UND VORLESUNGEN

Hecker, Isaac Thomas *see*
- ASPIRATIONS OF NATURE
- THE CHURCH AND THE AGE
- QUESTIONS OF THE SOUL

Hecker, Max *see* WILHELM MEISTERS WANDERJAHRE

Heckford, Sarah *see* A LADY TRAVELER IN THE TRANSVAAL

Heckman, George C *see* AN ADDRESS ON WOMAN'S WORK IN THE CHURCH

Heckrath, Goswin *see* ZUR ROLLE DER SORPTION BEIM VERHALTEN VON HERBIZIDEN IM BODEN

Hecquard, Hyacinthe *see* VOYAGE SUR LA COTE ET DANS L'INTERIEUR DE L'AFRIQUE OCCIDENTALE

Hecquard, Louis Hyacinthe *see* VOYAGE SUR LA COTE ET DANS L'INTERIEUR DE L'AFRIQUE OCCIDENTALE

HECTOR / Luce de Lancival – (French Theatre Series). Paris. J. Chaumerot. 1809 – 9 – fr Hachette [820]

Hector Chaussier *see* LA VIELLEUSE DU BOULEVARD

HECTOR ESTUDIOS DE HISTORIA COLONIAL VENEZOLANA... / Garcia, Huecos – Burgos: Razon y Fe, 1939 – 1 – sp Bibl Santa Ana [972]

Hector, J *see* FISHES OF NEW ZEALAND

HED HAAM = NATION – (In Hebrew. Weekly) – Jerusalem, IS. v3 no7(87). Nov 1926 – 1r – 1 – $25.00 – cn Can Microfilming [072]

HED HA-MIZRAH – v. 1-8. Jerusalem. 1942-51. BJ-91-39 1 – 9 – ne IDC [270]

HED HANDAR = YOUTH ECHO – (In Hebrew) – Warsaw, PL. v1 no1. Feb-May 1924 – 1r – 1 – $30.00 – cn Can Microfilming [072]

HED HAZMAN = TIME – (In Hebrew) – Vilnius, LT. no54 16 Mar 1908; no188 25 Aug 1908 – 1r – 1 – $25.00 – cn Can Microfilming [072]

HED LITA – Kovno. 1-2, no. 21. 1924-1925 – 1 – us NY Public [072]

HED LITA = "LIETUVOS AIDAS" – (In Yiddish) – Kaunas, LT. v1 no6 1924-v2 no4(29) 1925 – 1r – 1 – $25.00 – cn Can Microfilming [072]

Hedemann, Justus W *see* VOLKSGESETZBUCH. GRUNDREGEL UND BUCH I

HEDEMORA TIDNING – Hedemora, Sweden. 1864-80 – 5r – 1 – sw Kungliga [072]

Heden, C G *see* APPLIED MICROBIOLOGY

DE HEDENDAEGSCHE LANG-TONGE AF-GEBEELD IN TWAELF ZINNE-BEELDEN... / Pauwels, Jan Anton Frans – Antwerpen, 1774 – 9mf – 9 – ne IDC [700]

Hederer, Edgar *see* FRIEDRICH VON HARDENBERGS "CHRISTENHEIT ODER EUROPA"

Hederich, Benjamin *see* HEDERICHS WOERTERBUECHER

HEDERICHS WOERTERBUECHER : LATEINISCH-DEUTSCHE, DEUTSCH-LATEINISCHE UND GRIECHISCH-LATEINISCHE, LATEINISCH-GRIECHISCHE / Hederich, Benjamin – (mit einem Einleitungsband von Franz Josef Hausmann: "Altsprachliche Lexikographie im Zeitalter des Barock. Die Woerterbuecher des Benjamin Hederich (1675-1748)") – 1675-1748 (mf ed 1988) – 66mf – 9 – DM650.00 – 3-89131-032-3 – gw Fischer [040]

Hedge, Frederic Henry *see*
- HOURS WITH GERMAN CLASSICS
- MARTIN LUTHER
- THE PRIMEVAL WORLD OF HEBREW TRADITION
- REASON IN RELIGION
- RECENT INQUIRIES IN THEOLOGY BY EMINENT ENGLISH CHURCHMEN, BEING "ESSAYS AND REVIEWS."
- WAYS OF THE SPIRIT

HEDIYE-YI SAL – 1312-13 [1894-95] – 4mf – 9 – $36.75 – us MEDOC [949]

Hedley *see* CHAUTAUQUA COUNTY AND ITS PEOPLE

Hedley, James *see* CANADA AND HER COMMERCE: FROM THE TIME OF THE FIRST SETTLERS TO THAT OF THE REPRESENTATIVE MEN OF TODAY..

Hedrich, Franz *see* ALFRED MEISSNER - FRANZ HEDRICH

Hedwig, J *see*
- DESCRIPTIO ET ADUMBRATIO MICROSCOPICOANALYTICA MUSCORUM FRONDOSORUM
- FILICUM GENERA ET SPECIES
- FUNDAMENTUM HISTORIAE NATURALIS MUSCORUM FRONDOSORUM
- SPECIES MUSCORUM FRONDOSORUM

Hedwig, R A *see*
- GENERA PLANTARUM SECUNDUM CHARACTERES DIFFERENTIALES AD MIRBELLI EDITIONEM
- OBSERVATIONUM BOTANICARUM FASCICULUS PRIMUS

HEDWIGIA – Dresden, 1852-1940. v1-79 – 644mf – 9 – 107c/2 – ne IDC [943]

Heer, Oswald *see*
- FAUNA COLEOPTERORUM HELVETICA
- FLORA FOSSILIS ARCTICA
- FLORA FOSSILIS HELVETIAE
- MIOCENA BALTISCHE FLORA
- OBSERVATIONES ENTOMOLOLGICAE
- DIE URWELT DER SCHWEIZ

HEER UND HEIMAT – Berlin, 1917 – 1 – Dist. gw Mikrofilm – gw Misc Inst [943]

Heerbrand, J *see*
- ACTA DES COLLOQUIJ, ZWISCHEN DEN WUERTENBERGISCHEN THEOLOGEN VND D. IOANNE PISTORIO, ZU BADEN GEHALTEN...
- COMPENDIUM THEOLOGIE, METHODI QVAESTIONIBVS TRACTATVM

Heerbrandt, Gustav *see* GEDICHTE IN SCHWAEBISCHER MUNDART

Heeren, Arnold Hermann Ludwig *see* HISTORICAL RESEARCHES INTO THE POLITICS, INTERCOURSE, AND TRADE OF THE PRINCIPAL NATIONS OF ANTIQUITY

Heeren, H J *see* PROPOSALS FOR SOME URGENT FUTURE SOCIOLOGICAL STUDIES IN INDONESIA

Heeresarchiv. Potsdam *see* AN EXHIBIT OF GERMAN MILITARY DOCUMENTS..., 1679-1935

Heering, Hans *see* IDEE UND WIRKLICHKEIT BEI HANNS JOHST

Heers, Alois *see* DAS LEBEN FRIEDRICH VON MATTHISSONS

Heertje, H *see* DE DIAMANTBEWERKERS VAN AMSTERDAM

Hefele, C J *see*
- GESCHICHTE DER EINFUEHRUNG DES CHRISTENTUMS IM SUEDWESTLICHEN DEUTSCHLAND
- HISTOIRE DES CONCILES
- HISTOIRE DES CONCILES D'APRAES LES DOCUMENTS ORIGINAUX

Hefele, Carl Joseph *see* BEITRAEGE ZUR KIRCHENGESCHICHTE, ARCHAEOLOGIE UND LITURGIK

Hefele, Herman *see* DAS GESETZ DER FORM

Hefele, Karl Joseph von *see* THE LIFE OF CARDINAL XIMENEZ

Heffter, A G *see* LE DROIT INTERNATIONAL...

Heffter, H W *see* DAS EUROPAEISCHE VOELKERRECHT...

HEFT MECLIS / Ali, Mustafa – Dersaadet: Ikdam Matbaasi, 1316 [1900] – $16.00 – us MEDOC [956]

HEFTEN = LITTERATURE AND ART NOTEBOOKS : FAR LITERATUR UN KUNST – (In Yiddish) – Lodz, PL. no1. 1919 – 1r – 1 – $25.00 – cn Can Microfilming [072]

HEFTN – Montreal, CN, 1936-1937 – 1r – 1 – Can$25.00 – cn Can Microfilming [072]

HEFTN = NOTEBOOKS – Montreal & Toronto, CN. no 1. 1929 – 1r – 1 – Can$25.00 – cn Can Microfilming [072]

HEFT'N FAR LITERATUR KULTUR UN KRITIK = LITTERARY NOTEBOOK FOR LITERATURE, CULTURE AND CRITICISM – (In Yiddish) – Regensburg, DE. no1. Jun/Jul 1947 – 1r – 1 – $25.00 – cn Can Microfilming [072]

Hegeler, Wilhelm *see* KLEIST

EL HEGELISMO JURIDICO ESPANOL / Elias de Tejada Spinola, Francisco – Madrid: Revista de Derecho Privado, 1944 – sp Bibl Santa Ana [340]

EL HEGELISMO JURIDICO ESPANOL. MADRID, 1944 / Truyol Serra, A & Elias de Tejada, F – Madrid: Razon y Fe, 1946 – 1 – sp Bibl Santa Ana [340]

HEGELS DIALEKTISCHE ONTOLOGIE UND DIE THOMISTISCHE ANALEKTIK / Lakebrink, B – Koeln, 1955 – 9mf – 8 – ne Slangenburg [110]

HEGEL'S PHILOSOPHY OF THE STATE AND OF HISTORY / Morris, George Sylvester – Chicago: Griggs, 1887. 306p – 1 – us U.W. Library [900]

LA HEGEMONIA ARGENTINA EN EL PARAGUAY : EL DECALOGO DEL GRAL. PERON, DESAPRETAR A LAS AMARRAS DE LA DEPENDENCIA? / Gaona, Francisco – Buenos Aires: [edicion del autor, 1954] – 1 – CSUXAHZ3339-B – us Hoover Inst Photo [320]

Hegermann, H *see* DIE VORSTELLUNG VOM SCHOEPFUNGSMITTLER IM HELLENISTISCHEN JUDENTUM UND URCHRISTENTUM (T.U.U. 5-82)

Hegewisch, D H *see* UEBER DIE NEUTRALITAET BEY DEM GEGENWAERTIGEN KRIEGE

Hegglin, P *see* DER BENEDIKTINISCHE ABT

Hegler, A *see* PRINZIPIEN DES INTERNATIONALEN STRAFRECHTS

Hegler, Alfred *see*
- BEITRAEGE ZUR GESCHICHTE DER MYSTIK IN DER REFORMATIONSZEIT
- GEIST UND SCHRIFT BEI SEBASTIAN FRANCK
- JOHANNES BRENZ UND DIE REFORMATION IN HERZOGTUM WIRTEMBERG [SIC]
- SEBASTIAN FRANCKS LATEINISCHE PARAPHRASE DER DEUTSCHEN THEOLOGIE

HEGYONEI HA MAGGID / Gordon, D – (Ha-Maggid, Lyck, 1st Heshvan 5624). 1864. BJ-27-214 1 – 9 – ne IDC [956]

HE-HADASH *see* HA-MAGGID

HE-HALUTZ – Lemberg etc. v. 1-13. 1852-1889 – 1 – us NY Public [073]

HE-HALUZ – Lemberg, etc. 1852-89. BJ-91-41 1 – 9 – ne IDC [956]

HE-HALUZ : WISSENSCHAFTLICHE ABHANDLUNGEN UEBER JUDISCHE GESCHICHTE, LITERATUR – v1-13. 1852-89 – 1r – 1 – us Ross [270]

HE-HAVER = THE COMRADE – (In Hebrew) – Vilnius, LT. v1 no62. 26 Mar 1908 – 1r – 1 – $25.00 – cn Can Microfilming [072]

Hehn, Johannes *see*
- SIEBENZAHL UND SABBAT BEI DEN BABYLONIERN UND IM ALTEN TESTAMENT
- SUENDE UND ERLOESUNG

Hehn, Victor *see*
- GEDANKEN UEBER GOETHE
- THE WANDERINGS OF PLANTS AND ANIMALS FROM THEIR FIRST HOME

HE-HUAXUE YU FANGSHE HUAXUE – Journal of Nuclear & Radio-Chemistry. In Chinese but English abstracts to the main articles. F p123 – 9 – $4.50f – cc Microforms [073]

Heidborn, A *see* MANUEL DE DROIT PUBLIC ET ADMINISTRATIF DE L'EMPIRE OTTOMAN

Heidecker, H *see* UEBER DIE BEDEUTUNG DER)) 660, 661 DER DEUTSCHEN C P O...

DAS HEIDEDORF / Stifter, Adalbert – 2. Aufl. München: Georg W Dietrich, [19–?] – 1r – 1 – us U.W. Library [830]

Heidegger, M *see*
- DIE KATEGORIEN- U. BEDEUTUNGSLEHRE DES DUNS SCOTUS
- DIE SELBSTBEHAUPTUNG DER DEUTSCHEN UNIVERSITAET
- THEOLOGIE U. PHILOSOPHIE ALS MANUSKRIPT VERVIELFAELTIGT

Heidegger, Martin *see*
- HOELDERLIN UND DAS WESEN DER DICHTUNG
- HOELDERLINS HYMNE "WIE WENN AM FEIERTAGE..."

Heidel, Alexander *see* THE BABYLONIAN GENESIS, THE STORY OF CREATION

Heidelbach, Paul *see* DIE NEUEN ARGONAUTEN

HEIDELBERG ALS STOFF UND MOTIV DER DEUTSCHEN DICHTUNG / Goldschmit, Rudolf K – (Includes bibliographical references and index) – Berlin: W de Gruyter & Co, 1929 – 2r – 1 – us U.W. Library [430]

HEIDELBERG CATECHISM – Indonesian. SE-4990 1. 1964 – 9 – ne IDC [240]

THE HEIDELBERG CATECHISM : HISTORICAL AND DOCTRINAL STUDIES / Richards, George W – Philadelphia: Publication and Sunday School Board of the Reformed Church in the United States, 1913 – 1mf – us A.T.L.A. [240]

THE HEIDELBERG CATECHISM IN ITS NEWEST LIGHT / Good, James I – Philadelphia: Publication and Sunday School Board of the Reformed Church in the United States, 1914 – 1mf – us A.T.L.A. [240]

HEIDELBERG: PAMPHLET COLLECTION – 19?? – 1 – CSUXANS9187-B – us Hoover Inst Photo [943]

HEIDELBERGER GENERAL-ANZEIGER – (Cont by: Heidelberger Tageblatt, jan 3, 1884. Tageblatt, may 25, 1949. Heidelberger Tageblatt, jun 1, 1951) – Heidelberg. may 25, 1949-82 – 1 – gw Mikrofilm [072]

HEIDELBERGER JOURNAL *see* HEIDELBERGER WOCHENBLATT

DER HEIDELBERGER KATECHISMUS : ZUM 350JAEHRIGEN GEDAECHTNIS SEINER ENTSTEHUNG / Lang, August – Leipzig: Verein fuer Reformationsgeschichte, 1913. (Schriften des Vereins fuer Reformationsgeschichte; Jahrg. 31, 1. Stueck, Nr. 113) – 1mf – us A.T.L.A. [240]

HEIDELBERGER RUNDSCHAU – (Cont by: Communale, 1984) – Heidelberg. nov 20, 1975-sep 29, 1988 – 6r – 1 – gw Mikrofilm [072]

HEIDELBERGER TAGEBLAETTER *see* HEIDELBERGER WOCHENBLATT

HEIDELBERGER TAGEBLATT *see* HEIDELBERGER GENERAL-ANZEIGER

HEIDELBERGER WOCHENBLAETTER *see* HEIDELBERGER WOCHENBLATT

HEIDELBERGER WOCHENBLATT – (Cont by: Heidelberger Wochenblaetter, jan 3, 1831. Heidelberger Tageblaetter, jan 1, 1840. Heidelberger Journal, jul 1, 1842) – Heidelberg. 1844-45 – 3r – 1 – gw Mikrofilm [943]

HEIDELBERGER WOCHENBLATT – (Title changes: Heidelberger Wochenblaetter, 3 Jan 1831; Heidelberger Tageblaetter, 1 Jan 1840; Heidelberger Journal, 1 Jul 1842) – Heidelberg, Germany. 1848-49 – 3r – 1 – gw Mikrofilm [072]

Heidemann *see* UEBER LESSING'S EMILIA GALOTTI

DIE HEIDEN VON KUMMEROW : ROMAN / Welk, Ehm – Berlin: Deutscher Verlag, c1937 – 1r – 1 – us U.W. Library [830]

Heidenheim, W *see* DAREKHEI NO'AM

HEIDENHEIMER ZEITUNG – (Suppl. Suedwest-Presse, Ulm) – Heidenheim a.d. Brenz, West Germany. 1977- – ca 7r per yr – 1 – gw Mikrofilm [072]

DAS HEIDENROESLEIN / Joseph, Eugen – (Includes bibliographical references) – Berlin: Gebrueder Paetel, 1897 – 1r – 1 – us U.W. Library [430]

HEIDI : A STORY FOR CHILDREN AND THOSE WHO LOVE CHILDREN... / Spyri, Johanna – Boston: Cupples, Upham, & Co., 1885, [c1884] – 1 roll – 1 – 1-55879-982-6 – uk Libr Preservation [830]

Heigel, K T *see* DAS TAGEBUCH KAISER KARL'S 7. AUS DER ZEIT DES OESTERREICHISCHEN ERBFOLGEKRIEGS

Heigenmooser, J *see* EREMITENSCHULE IN ALTBAYERN

HEIGHTS BAPTIST CHURCH. AIKEN COUNTY. SOUTH CAROLINA : CHURCH RECORDS – Sept 1966-1983. 395p – 1 – 17.78 – us Baptist [240]

Heighway, Osborn W Trenery *see* LEILA ADA, THE JEWISH CONVERT

Heijk, H *see* DIE STAATSZUGEHOERIGKEIT DER SCHIFFE...1935

HEIKE MONOGATARI – 1ere partie. Traducteur by Turettini. Geneve. 1871 – 9 – 5.00 – fr Orientalistes [950]

Heikel, I A *see* KRITISCHE BEITRAEGE ZU DEN CONSTANTIN-SCHRIFTEN DES EUSEBIUS (T.U.U. 3-36/4)

Heil, DP *see* THE EFFECT OF SEAT-TUBE ANGLE VARIATION ON CARDIORESPIRATORY RESPONSES DURING SUBMAXIMAL BICYCLING

Heilborn, P *see* DAS VOELKERRECHTLICHE PROTEKTORAT

Heilbron, Carl H *see* HISTORY OF SAN DIEGO COUNTY

HEILBRONN: PAMPHLET COLLECTION – 1961 – 1 – CSUXANS9189-B – us Hoover Inst Photo [943]

HEILBRONNER STIMME – (Abweichende Seiten der Bezirksausgaben Eppinger Zeitung & Hohenloher Zeitung) – Heilbronn, West Germany. 1968- – ca 10r per yr – 1 – gw Mikrofilm [072]

Heilesen, SB *see* MODERN CHINESE PICTORIAL ART 1949-1979

HEILIG GEBRUIK DES ORGELS.. / Francken, Aegidius – 1734 – 9 – us Sibley [780]

HEILIG, MIT ZWEY CHOEREN UND EINER ARIETTE ZUR EINLEITUNG... / Bach, C P E – Hamburg: Im Verlag des Autors; Leipzig: aus der Breitkopfischen Buchdruckerey, 1779 – 1 – us Sibley [780]

Heilig, Otto *see* ALLEMANNISCHE GEDICHTE

DER HEILIGE ALFONS VON LIGUORI : DER KIRCHENLEHRER UND APOLOGET DES 18. JAHRHUNDERTS / Meffert, Franz – Mainz: F. Kirchheim, 1901 – 1mf – us A.T.L.A. [240]

DAS HEILIGE BAND : ROMAN / Planner-Petelin, Rose – Hamburg: Hanseatische Verlagsanstalt, c1942 – 1r – 1 – us U.W. Library [830]

DIE HEILIGE BISCHOFSWEIHE IN DER KATHOLISCHEN KIRCHE : NACH DEM ROEMISCHEN PONTIFICAL LATEINISCH UND DEUTSCH. NEBST EINER ERLAEUTERUNG DER WEIHECEREMONIEN UND DER AUSZEICHNUNGEN DES BISCHOFS – Eichstaett, Muenchen, 2nd ed 1879 – 1mf – 9 – DM48.00 – 3-89349-356-5 – gw Hänsel [240]

DER HEILIGE BORN : BLAETTER AUS DEM BILDERBUCHE DES SECHZEHNTEN JAHRHUNDERTS / Raabe, Wilhelm Karl – 2. verbess. Aufl. Berlin: Otto Janke, 1891 – 1r – 1 – us U.W. Library [830]

DER HEILIGE GEIST IN DER HEILSVERKUENDIGUNG DES PAULUS : EINE BIBLISCH-THEOLOGISCHE UNTERSUCHUNG / Gloel, Johannes – (Includes index) – Halles a.S: Max Niemeyer, 1888 – 1mf – 9 – 0-8370-3314-4 – 1985-1314 – us A.T.L.A. [220]

DER HEILIGE GEORG IN DER GRIECHISCHEN UEBERLIEFERUNG (ABAW.PPH 25/3) / Krumbacher, K – Muenchen, 1911 – Dfl35.00 – ne Slangenburg [240]

DER HEILIGE HASS : EXOTISCHER ROMAN / Voss, Richard – Berlin: P Francke, [1940?] – 1r – 1 – us U.W. Library [830]

DER HEILIGE KRIEG IM ALTEN ISRAEL / Schwally, Friedrich – Leipzig: Dieterich, 1901. 1 fiche – 9 – us A.T.L.A. [240]

DIE HEILIGE MISSION : MIT ALLEN IHREN PREDIGTEN, ANREDEN UND FEIERLICHKEITEN / Weninger, Francis Xavier – Cincinnati: [s.n.], 1885 – 2mf – 9 – 0-8370-6791-X – 1986-0791 – us A.T.L.A. [240]

HEILIGE NACHT : EINE WEIHNACHTSLEGENDE / Thoma, Ludwig – Muenchen; A Langen, 1930 – 1r – 1 – us U.W. Library [810]

HEILIGE PETRUS IN ROM UND ROM OHNE PETRUM = ROME AND THE POPES / Brandes, Karl – (In English) – New York: Benziger, 1868, c1867 – 1mf – 9 – 0-8370-6651-4 – 1986-0651 – us A.T.L.A. [240]

DIE HEILIGE PFLICHT : DREI ERZAEHLUNGEN / Jessen, Paul – Darmstadt: L Kichler, 1942 – 1r – 1 – us U.W. Library [830]

HEILIGE SCHRIFT UND KRITIK / Volck, Wilhelm – Erlangen: A. Deichert, 1897. 1 fiche. 8370-5654-3 – 9 – us A.T.L.A. [240]

DAS HEILIGE SCHRIFTWERK KOHELET IM LICHTE DER GESCHICHTE : NEUE FORSCHUNG UEBER ECCLESIASTES NEBST TEXT, UEBERSETZUNG UND KOMMENTAR / Leimdoerfer, David – (Text in German and HebreW Introduction and commentary in German) – Hamburg: G Fritzsche, 1892 – 1mf – 9 – 0-8370-4088-4 – 1985-2088 – us A.T.L.A. [220]

DIE HEILIGE STADT / Neumann, B – Hamburg. 1877. BJ-27-49 1 – 9 – ne IDC [910]

DER HEILIGE STUHL : EINE ZEITGEMAESSE, HISTORISCH-PHILOSOPHISCHE BETRACHTUNG / Goerres, Guido – Regensburg, 1838 – 1mf – DM48.00 – 3-8267-3080-1 – gw Hänsel [240]

DER HEILIGE STUHL UND DIE HEIRAT DER PRINZESSIN ELISABETH VON BAYERN MIT DEM KRONPRINZEN FRIEDRICH WILHELM VON PREUSSEN : NACH AKTEN DES VATIKANISCHEN GEHEIMARCHIVS / Bastgen, Hubert – Freiburg i.B., 1930. v/89p – DM50.00 – 3-89349-191-0 – gw Hänsel [240]

DER HEILIGEN KIND / Clausen, Ernst Alexander – Hamburg-Grossborstel: Verlag der Deutschen Dichter-Gedaechtnis-Stiftung, 1918 – 1 – us U.W. Library [890]

HEILIGES FEUER : EIN FAHRTENBUCH / Vershofen, Wilhelm – Leipzig: P List, c1936 – 1r – 1 – us U.W. Library [920]

DAS HEILIGKEITS-GESETZ, LEV. 17-26 : EINE HISTORISCH-KRITISCHE UNTERSUCHUNG / Baentsch, Bruno – Erfurt: Hugo Guether, 1893 – 1mf – 9 – 0-8370-2152-9 – 1985-0152 – us A.T.L.A. [220]

HEILIGTUM UND OPFERSTAETTEN IN DEN GESETZEN DES PENTATEUCH / Engelkemper, Wilhelm – Paderborn: F. Schoeningh, 1908. 1 fiche – 9 – us A.T.L.A. [240]
Heilman, Paula S *see* PHYSIOLOGICAL RESPONSES OBTAINED DURING EXERCISE ON THE STAIRMASTER GAUNTLET WITH AND WITHOUT THE USE OF HANDS
Heilmann, G *see* THE ORIGIN OF BIRDS
HEILONGJIANG RIBAO – Heilongjiang, China. -d. In Chinese. Current Subscription. Annual Delivery. 1981- , 1r/y. M D22 – 1 – $55.00r – cc Microforms [072]
HEILPAEDAGOGISCHE MOEGLICHKEITEN DER MUSIK IN DER SONDERPAEDAGOGIK / Drobnitzky-Eickhoff, Barbara – 1991 – 107p – 9 – DM98.00 – 3-89349-426-X – gw Hänsel [370]
DIE HEILPFLANZEN DER VERSCHIEDENEN VOELKER UND ZEITEN / Dragendorff, Georg – Stuttgart: Verlag von Ferdinand Enke, 1898. vi,884p – 1 – us U.W. Library [615]
Heilprin, Angelo *see*
- ALASKA AND THE KLONDIKE: A JOURNEY TO THE NEW ELDORADO...OBSERVATIONS ON THE PHYSICAL HISTORY AND GEOLOGY OF THE GOLD REGIONS
- THE ARCTIC PROBLEM: AND NARRATIVE OF THE PEARY RELIEF EXPEDITION OF THE ACADEMY OF NATURAL SCIENCES OF PHILADELPHIA

HEILSAME LEERE ENDE NUTTE ONDERWYSINGE VAN ENEN GODVRUCHTIGEN MAN SIJN KYNDER / Joriaen Ketel – (Geschreuen den 26 Junij Anno 1544). Een nye Liet. BME-168 1 – 9 – ne IDC [240]
DER HEILS-BOTE – v3-20. 1900-17 (gaps) – 1r – 1 – ATLA 1994-S036 – us A.T.L.A. [073]
HEILSTHATSACHEN UND GLAUBENSERFAHRUNG / Lemme, Ludwig – (Includes bibliographical references) – Heidelberg: Carl Winter, 1895 – 1mf – 9 – 0-8370-4318-2 – 1985-2318 – us A.T.L.A. [240]
HEI-LUNG-CHIANG JIH-PAO – Harbin, Heilungkiang, China. Heilungkiang Daily. 1956-65. 16 reels – 1 – 442.00 – us Chinese Res [072]
Heim, C *see* UNTERSUCHUNGEN UEBER FARNPROTHALLIEN
Heim, Karl *see* LEITFADEN DER DOGMATIK
DIE HEIMAT – Windhoek, South West Africa. 1927-75 – 1 – sa State Libr [072]
HEIMAT – Backa Palanka, Yugoslavia. Mar-Dec 1939 – 1r – 1 – us L of C Photodup [949]
HEIMAT – Deutsch Palanka (Backa Palanka), Jugoslawien. 6 Jan-28 Dez 1940 – 1r – 1 – gw Mikrofilm [949]
HEIMAT : DEUTSCHES WOCHENBLATT – Czernowitz (Cernauti), Rumaenien. 1 Jan 1927-6 Sep 1931 – 2r – 1 – gw Mikrofilm [949]
DIE HEIMAT DES VIERTEN EVANGELIUMS / Zurhellen, Otto – Tuebingen: J.C.B. Mohr, 1909. 1 fiche – 9 – us A.T.L.A. [240]
HEIMAT TAGBLATT – Saaz (Zatec), Czechoslovakia. 23 Mai 1928-31 Mai 1934 – 3r – 1 – gw Mikrofilm [072]
DER HEIMATDIENST – Berlin, 1928-32 – 2r – 1 – Dist. gw Mikrofilm – gw Misc Inst [072]
DER HEIMATDIENST – Berlin, aug 1 1920-26, jan-mar 1933 – 1 – Dist. gw Mikrofilm – gw Misc Inst [072]
DIE HEIMATH UND DER URSPRUNG DES CULTIVIRTEN MELONENBAUMES / Solms-Laubach, H M C L F – Carica papaya L. (Botanische Zeitung, 1889, v. 47, p. 709-720, 725-734, 741-749, 757-767, 773-781, 789-798). B-1589 2 – 8 – ne IDC [580]
HEIMATNACHRICHTEN AUS DEM KREIS ALTOETTING *see* AMTLICHE MITTEILUNGEN
HEIMAT-ZEITUNG DES KREISES GROSS-GERAU – Gross-Gerau, Germany. 1978- – ca 8r per yr – 1 – gw Mikrofilm [072]
Heimb, TheopH *see* BERNARDUS GUTOLFI MONACHI
Heimbucher, Max *see* DIE PAPSTWAHLEN UNTER DEN KAROLINGERN
Heimburg, W *see*
- KLOSTER WENDHUSEN; URSULA
- UNTER DER LINDE

Heimer, E H *see* STUDIER I INTERNATIONELL FOERMYNDERSKAPSTRAETT
Heimerl, A *see* DIE ARTEN, UNTERARTEN, VARIETAETEN UND HYBRIDEN DER SECTION PTARMICA DES GENUS ACHILLEA
HEIMGEKEHRT : SCHAUSPIEL IN DREI AKTEN / Wildermann, Ferdinand – Rheine: A Rieke, 1894 – 1r – 1 – us U.W. Library [820]
DER HEIMKEHRENDE GATTE UND SEIN WEIB IN DER WELTLITTERATUR : LITTERARHISTORISCHE ABHANDLUNG / Splettstoesser, W – 1995 – 1mf – 9 – DM48.00 – 3-8267-3131-X – gw Hänsel [410]
DER HEIMKEHRER – Goeppingen-Bad Godesberg, West Germany. Sep 1951-74 – 1 – gw Mikrofilm [072]
Heimlich, F *see* DIE HOHEITSVERHAELTNISSE AM BODENSEE
DER HEIMLICHE KOENIG : EINE DRAMATISCHE DICHTUNG IN FUENF AUFZUEGEN / Griese, Friedrich – Berlin: Theaterverlag A Langen/G Mueller, 1939 – 1r – 1 – us U.W. Library [810]
DAS HEIMLICHE LEUCHTEN / Menzel, Roderich – Berlin: R Moelich, [1943?] – 1r – 1 – us U.W. Library [880]
DIE HEIMLICHE NOT : ERZAEHLUNG / Witzany, Rudolf – Jena: E Diederichs, 1941, c1939 – 1r – 1 – us U.W. Library [830]
HEIMSKRINGLA – (In Icelandic) – Canada, 1886-1959 – 24r – 1 – cn Commonwealth Micro [072]
DIE HEIMSTAETTER : EIN DEUTSCHES SCHICKSAL IN KANADA / Goetz, Karl – Leipzig: P Reclam, 1944 – 1r – 1 – us U.W. Library [830]
Hein, Erica J *see* THE EFFECTS OF AN INDUCED INTERNAL AND EXTERNAL ATTENTIONAL FOCUS UPON UPPER BODY STRENGTH
Hein, Michael S *see* A SWIMMING PROTOCOL FOR DETERMINATION OF INDIVIDUAL ANAEROBIC THRESHOLD
HEIN WIECK : EINE STALL- UND SCHEUNENGESCHICHTE / Kroeger, Timm – Hamburg: A Janssen, 1905 – 1r – 1 – us U.W. Library [830]
HEINE : EIN LESEBUCH FUER UNSERE ZEIT / ed by Victor, Walther – (Includes bibliographical references) – Weimar: Volksverlag, 1956 – 1 – us U.W. Library [430]
Heine, Carl *see* DER UNGLUECKSEELIGE TODES-FALL CAROLI 12.
Heine, Gerhard *see*
- ERNST MORITZ ARNDT
- DER MANN DER NACH SYRAKUS SPAZIERENGING
- DAS VERHAELTNIS AESTHETIK ZUR ETHIK BEI SCHILLER

Heine, Heinrich *see*
- CUADROS DE VIAJE
- FLORENTINISCHE NAECHTE
- GERMANIIA
- HARZREISE
- HEINRICH HEINE'S BUCH DER LIEDER
- HEINRICH HEINES SAEMTLICHE WERKE
- LETZTE GEDICHTE UND GEDANKEN
- MEMORIAS
- NEUE HEINE-FUNDE
- THE NORTH SEA
- POEMES ET LEGENDES
- THE POEMS OF HEINE, COMPLETE
- RELIGION AND PHILOSOPHY IN GERMANY: A FRAGMENT
- SAEMTLICHE WERKE IN ZWOELF BAENDEN
- SELECTIONS FROM HEINE'S POEMS

HEINE UND DUESSELDORF : NEUE BEITRAEGE ZU EINER HEINE-BIOGRAPHIE / Moos, Eugen – (Includes bibliographical references) – Duesseldorf: Schmitz & Olbertz, 1909 – 1r – 1 – us U.W. Library [920]
Heineck, I G *see* PRAELECTIONES ACADEMICAE IN HUGONIS GROTII DE IURE BELLI ET PACIS LIBROS III
Heineck, J G *see* A METHODICAL SYSTEM OF UNIVERSAL LAW
Heinecke, Regina *see* TUHFAT AL-WUZARA
Heinecken, KH V *see*
- DICTIONNAIRE DES ARTISTES, DONT NOUS AVONS DES ESTAMPES
- DICTIONNAIRE DES ARTISTES, DONT NOUS AVONS DES ESTAMPES...
- NACHRICHTEN VON KUENSTLERN UND KUNST-SACHEN
- NEUE NACHRICHTEN VON KUENSTLERN UND KUNSTSACHEN

Heinemann, F *see* POSEIDONIOS METAPHYSISCHE SCHRIFTEN
Heinemann, Franz *see* DER RICHTER UND DIE RECHTSPFLEGE IN DER DEUTSCHEN VERGANGENHEIT
Heinemann, H *see* SHYLOCK UND NATHAN
Heinemann, I *see* DIE LEHRE VON DER ZWECKBESTIMMUNG DES MENSCHEN IM GRIECHISCH-ROEMISCHEN ALTERTUM UND IM JUEDISCHEN MITTELALTER
Heinemann, K *see* AUSGEWAEHLTE DICHTUNGEN
Heinemann, Karl *see*
- DIE DEUTSCHE DICHTUNG
- GOETHE
- KLOPSTOCKS LEBEN UND WERKE / WIELANDS LEBEN UND WERKE

Heinemann, Lothar *see* MODELLBILDUNG VON MEHRWICKLUNGSTRANSFORMATOREN BEI QUASI-STATIONAEREN FELDSTAERKEVERTEILUNGEN
Heinemann, O v. *see* ZUR ERINNERUNG AN GOTTHOLD EPHRAIM LESSING
Heinen, Mechthild *see* BERNHARD PANKOK
Heiner, Steven W *see* COMPARISON OF RISK FACTORS FOR CORONARY HEART DISEASE IN SEDENTARY AND PHYSICALLY ACTIVE COLLEGE STUDENTS
HEINES CHARAKTER UND DIE MODERNE SEELE : EINE STUDIE MIT NEUEN BRIEFEN UND DEM BISHER VERSCHOLLENEN JUGENDGEDICHT "DEUTSCHLAND 1815" / Kaufmann, Max – (Includes bibliographical references) – Zuerich: A Mueller, 1902 – 1r – 1 – us U.W. Library [430]
HEINES GEBURTSTAG / Franzos, Karl Emil – Berlin: Concordia Deutsche Verlags-Anstalt, 1900 – 1r – 1 – us U.W. Library [920]
HEINES LIEBESLEBEN / Kaufmann, Max – Zuerich: A Mueller, [1897] – 1r – 1 – us U.W. Library [920]
Heinichen, J D *see*
- DER GENERAL-BASS IN DER COMPOSITION
- NEU ERFUNDENE UND GRUENDLICHE ANWEISUNG WIE EIN MUSIKLIEBENDER AUSS GEWISSE VORTHEILHAFFTIGE ART KOENNE BIS ZU VOLKOMMENER ERLERNUNG
- NUE ERFUMDESE UND GRUNDLICHE ANWEISUNG...

Heinichen, Johann David *see* NEU ERFUNDENE UND GRUENDLICHE ANWEISUNG
Heinig, Kurt *see* DIE FINANZSKANDALE DES KAISERREICHS
Heinold, William D *see* HELPING RESPONSES IN AMBIGUOUS AND UNAMBIGUOUS EMERGENCIES AS A FUNCTION OF TRAINING IN FIRST AID
Heinrich, Anthony Philipp *see* THE DAWNING OF MUSIC IN KENTUCKY, OR THE PLEASURES OF HARMONY IN THE SOLITUDE OF NATURE
HEINRICH AUS ANDERNACH / Unruh, Fritz von – Frankfurt am Main: Frankfurter Societaets-Druckerei, Abt. Buchverlag, 1925 – 1r – 1 – us U.W. Library [430]
HEINRICH BULLINGER, DER NACHFOLGER ZWINGLIS / Schulthess-Rechberg, Gustav von – Halle a.d.S.: Verein fuer Reformationsgeschichte, 1904 (Schriften des Vereins fuer Reformationsgeschichte; 22. Jahrg., Schrift 82) – 1mf – us A.T.L.A. [240]
HEINRICH FEDERER. SEINE PERSOENLICHKEIT UND SEINE KUNSTFORM / Birnbach, Franz Bernhard – Bad Godesberg, 1935 – 1 – DM30.00 – gw Mikro Press [920]
HEINRICH HEINE : AUS SEINEM LEBEN UND AUS SEINER ZEIT / Karpeles, Gustav – Leipzig: A Titze, 1899 – 1r – 1 – us U.W. Library [920]
HEINRICH HEINE / Holzamer, Wilhelm – Berlin: Schuster and Loeffler, [19–?] – 1r – 1 – us U.W. Library [430]
HEINRICH HEINE : EIN LEBENS- UND ZEITBILD / Wendel, Hermann – (Includes index) – Dresden: Kaden, [1916?] – 1 – us U.W. Library [430]
HEINRICH HEINE : SEIN LEBEN, SEIN CHARATKER UND SEINE WERKE / Keiter, Heinrich – (Includes bibliographical references) – Koeln: J P Bachem, 1891 – 1 – us U.W. Library [920]
HEINRICH HEINE : EIN VORTRAG / Hass, Hans-Egon – Bonn: H Bouvier, 1949 – 1 – us U.W. Library [430]
HEINRICH HEINE ALS DICHTER DES JUDENTUMS : EIN VERSUCH / Plotke, Georg J – Dresden: C Reissner, 1913 – 1r – 1 – us U.W. Library [430]
HEINRICH HEINE ALS STUDENT / Scheuer, Oskar Franz – (Includes bibliographical references) – Bonn: A Ahn, 1922 – 1r – 1 – us U.W. Library [920]
HEINRICH HEINE UND DAS DEUTSCHE VOLKSLIED : EINE KRITISCHE UNTERSUCHUNG NACH DEM STOFFGEBIETE DER HEINE'SCHEN LYRIK / Greinz, Rudolf – Neuwied a. Rhein: A Schupp, [1894?] – 1r – 1 – us U.W. Library [430]
HEINRICH HEINE'S AN ESSAY, READ BEFORE THE MONDAY CLUB, MAY 21ST, 1883 / Kendig, Abby E G – Chicago, 1884. 14p – 1 – us U.W. Library [430]
HEINRICH HEINES AUFFASSUNGEN VON DER GESCHICHTE UND DER REVOLUTION ALS IMPULSGEBENDEN ELEMENTEN DES FRANZOESISCHEN EXILS (1831-1848) / Starke, Matthias – 1992 – 291p – 9 – DM98.00 – 3-89349-552-5 – gw Hänsel [943]
HEINRICH HEINES BEZIEHUNGEN ZU E.T.A. HOFFMANN / Siebert, Wilhelm – (Includes bibliographical references) – Marburg a.L.: N G Elwert, 1908 – 1r – 1 – us U.W. Library [430]
HEINRICH HEINE'S BIOGRAPHIE / Karpeles, Gustav – Hamburg: Hoffmann und Campe, 1885 – 1r – 1 – us U.W. Library [920]
HEINRICH HEINE'S BUCH DER LIEDER : VERVOLLSTAENDIGT HERAUSGEGEBEN / Heine, Heinrich; ed by Lachmann, Otto F – [3. Aufl.]. Leipzig: P Reclam jun., [1839?] – 1 – us U.W. Library [810]
HEINRICH HEINE'S LETZTE TAGE : ERINNERUNGEN / Selden, Camilla – Jena: H Costenoble, 1884 – 1 – us U.W. Library [920]
HEINRICH HEINE'S LIFE TOLD IN HIS OWN WORDS / ed by Karpeles, Gustav – New York: H Holt, 1893 – 1 – us U.W. Library [920]
HEINRICH HEINES RELIGIOESE ENTWICKLUNG BIS ZUM ABSCHLUSS SEINER UNIVERSITAETSJAHRE / Puetzfeld, Carl – (Includes bibliographical references) – Berlin: G Grote, 1912 – 1r – 1 – us U.W. Library [430]
HEINRICH HEINES SAEMTLICHE WERKE = WORKS / Heine, Heinrich; ed by Walzel, Oskar – (Includes bibliographical references and index) – Leipzig: Insel-Verlag, 1910-1915 – 1 – us U.W. Library [800]
HEINRICH HEINES VERHAELTNIS ZUR BILDENDEN KUNST / Hessel, Karl Robert Heinrich – (Includes bibliographical references) – Marburg a.L: N G Elwert, 1931 – 1r – 1 – us U.W. Library [700]
HEINRICH HEINE'S VERHAELTNIS ZUR RELIGION / Kalischer, Alfred Christlieb – Dresden: F Oehlmann, 1890 – 1r – 1 – us U.W. Library [240]
Heinrich, Julius *see* DIE ENTSTEHUNG DES NEUEN TESTAMENTS
HEINRICH LOEST UEBER E.T.A. HOFFMANN : 15. AUGUST 1823 / Loest, H W; ed by Mueller, Hans von – (Includes bibliographical references) – Koeln: P Gehly, 1922 – 1r – 1 – us U.W. Library [430]
HEINRICH LUBKE: PAMPHLET COLLECTION – 1965?-1966 – 1 reel – 1 – CSUXANS3219-B – us Hoover Inst Photo [320]
HEINRICH SEIDEL UND DER DEUTSCHE HUMOR : EINE LITTERARISCHE WUERDIGUNG / Biese, Alfred – (Includes bibliographical references) – Stuttgart: A G Liebeskind, [19–?] – 1 – us U.W. Library [430]
HEINRICH V, DER FRIEDFERTIGE : HERZOG VON MECKLENBURG, 1503-1552 / Schnell, H – Halle: Verein fuer Reformationsgeschichte, 1902. (Schriften des Vereins fuer Reformationsgeschichte; 19. Jahrg., Schrift 72) – 1mf – us A.T.L.A. [240]
HEINRICH V. KLEIST : EINE STUDIE / Eloesser, Arthur – Berlin o.J.. – 1mf – DM48.00 – 3-8267-3016-X – gw Hänsel [430]
HEINRICH V. KLEIST – KANT UND WIELAND / Luther, Bernhard; ed by Wieland-Museum – (Includes bibliographical references) – Biberach-Riss: Wieland Museum, 1933 – 1r – 1 – us U.W. Library [430]
HEINRICH VON KLEIST / Ayrault, Roger – (Includes bibliographical references) – Paris: Librairie Nizet et Bastard, 1934 – 1 – us U.W. Library [430]
HEINRICH VON KLEIST / Brahm, Otto – (Includes bibliographical references) – Berlin: Allgemeiner Verein fuer Deutsche Literatur, 1884 – 1r – 1 – us U.W. Library [920]

HEINRICH VON KLEIST : DARSTELLUNG DES PROBLEMS / Hellmann, Hanna – (Includes bibliographical references) – Heidelberg: C Winter, 1911 – 1r – 1 – us U.W. Library [430]
HEINRICH VON KLEIST : DER DICHTER DES PREUSSENTUMS / Fischer, Max – Stuttgart: J G Cotta, 1916 – 1r – 1 – us U.W. Library [430]
HEINRICH VON KLEIST / Graef, Hermann – Leipzig: Verlag fuer Literatur, Kunst und Musik, 1906 – 1r – 1 – us U.W. Library [920]
HEINRICH VON KLEIST / Gundolf, Friedrich – Berlin: G Bondi, 1922 – 1 – us U.W. Library [430]
HEINRICH VON KLEIST / Kiesgen, Laurenz – Leipzig: P Reclam, [1915?] – 1r – 1 – us U.W. Library [920]
HEINRICH VON KLEIST / Kuhn-Foelix, August – Murnau: U Riemerschmidt, c1948 – 1r – 1 – us U.W. Library [920]
HEINRICH VON KLEIST : LEHRJAHRE 1799-1801 / Howe, George M – (Includes bibliographical references) – [S.l.]: Modern Language Association of America, 1926 – 1 – us U.W. Library [920]
HEINRICH VON KLEIST : DAS PROBLEM SEINES LEBENS UND SEINER DICHTUNG; EIN VERSUCH / Hellmann, Hanna – (Includes bibliographical references) – Heidelberg: C Winter, 1908 – 1r – 1 – us U.W. Library [430]
HEINRICH VON KLEIST : EINE REDE / Bertram, Ernst – Bonn: F Cohen, 1925 – 1r – 1 – us U.W. Library [430]
HEINRICH VON KLEIST : "ROBERT GUISKARD" – EIN BEITRAG ZUR INSZENIERUNG DES FRAGMENTES / Birk, Karl – Prag: J G Calve, 1911 – 1r – 1 – us U.W. Library [430]
HEINRICH VON KLEIST / Schmidt, Erich – Leipzig, Wien: Bibliographisches Institut, [19–?] – 1r – 1 – us U.W. Library [920]
HEINRICH VON KLEIST : SEINE SPRACHE UND SEIN STIL / Minde-Pouet, Georg – (Includes bibliographical references) – Weimar: E Felber, 1897 – 1 – us U.W. Library [430]
HEINRICH VON KLEIST : DER ZERBROCHENE KRUG – EIN BEITRAG ZUR INSZENIERUNG DES LUSTSPIELES / Birk, Karl – (Includes bibliographical references) – Prag: C Bellmann, 1910 – 1r – 1 – us U.W. Library [430]
HEINRICH VON KLEIST ALS MENSCH UND DICHTER : NACH NEUEN QUELLENFORSCHUNGEN / Rahmer, Sigismund – (Includes bibliographical references and index) – Berlin: G Reimer, 1909 – 1 – us U.W. Library [430]
HEINRICH VON KLEIST IN SEINEN BRIEFEN : EINE CHARAKTERISTIK SEINES LEBENS UND SCHAFFENS / ed by Schur, Ernst – Charlottenburg: Schiller-Buchhandlung, [1911?] – 1 – us U.W. Library [920]
HEINRICH VON KLEIST IN SEINEN BRIEFEN : EIN VORTRAG, GEHALTEN AM 24. OKTOBER 1898 IM HISTORISCH-PHILOSOPHISCHEN VEREIN ZU HEIDELBERG / Warkentin, Roderich – Heidelberg: C Winter, 1900 – 1r – 1 – us U.W. Library [430]
HEINRICH VON KLEIST UND DAS DEUTSCHE THEATER / Kuehn, Walter – (Includes bibliographical references) – Muenchen: H Sachs-Verlag, 1912 – 1r – 1 – us U.W. Library [430]
HEINRICH VON KLEIST UND DIE FRAUEN / Kohut, Adolf – Hamburg: Verlagsgesellschaft Hamburg, 1911 – 1r – 1 – us U.W. Library [430]
HEINRICH VON KLEIST UND DIE KANTISCHE PHILOSOPHIE / Cassirer, Ernst – Berlin: Reuther & Reichard, 1919 – 1r – 1 – us U.W. Library [430]
HEINRICH VON KLEISTS GEHEIMNIS / Finger, Richard – Berlin: Puttkammer & Muehlbrecht, 1913 – 1r – 1 – us U.W. Library [430]
HEINRICH VON KLEISTS KUNST : VORTRAGE GEHALTEN ZUR FEIER DER 150. WIEDERKEHR VON KLEISTS GEBURTSTAG / Walzel, Oskar Franz – Bonn: L Rohrscheid, 1928 – 1r – 1 – us U.W. Library [430]
HEINRICH VON KLEISTS REISE NACH WUERZBURG / Morris, Max – (Includes excerpts from Kleist's letters to his sister and his fiancee) – Berlin: C Skopnik 1899 – 1r – 1 – us U.W. Library [430]
HEINRICH VON KLEISTS TRAGISCHER UNTERGANG / Servaes, Franz – Berlin: E Runge, [1900?] – 1r – 1 – us U.W. Library [430]
HEINRICH VON ZUETPHEN / Iken, J Friedrich – Halle: Verein fuer Reformationsgeschichte, 1886. ([Schriften des Vereins fuer Reformationsgeschichte; Bd.12]) – 1mf – us A.T.L.A. [240]
HEINRICH WINCKEL UND DIE REFORMATION IM SUEDLICHEN NIEDERSACHSEN / Jacobs, E – Halle: Verein fuer Reformationsgeschichte; 13. Jahrg., Schrift 53) 8250 240 – 1mf – us A.T.L.A. [943]
HEINRICH ZSCHOKKE : EIN BIOGRAPHISCHER UMRISS / Zschokke, Emil – 1r – 1 – us U.W. Library [943]
HEINRICH ZSCHOKKES JUGEND- UND BILDUNGSJAHRE (BIS 1798) : EIN BEITRAG ZU SEINER LEBENSGESCHICHTE / Guenther, Carl – (Includes bibliographical references) – Aarau: H R Sauerlaender, 1918 – 1r – 1 – us U.W. Library [430]
HEINRICH ZSCHOKKE'S NOVELLEN / Zschokke, Heinrich – Berlin, Wien, 18- . 10 v. in 5. Vols. 8-10 have title: Humoristische Novellen. Film Mas 8591 – us H.U. Library [830]
Heinrici, Carl Friedrich Georg *see*
- DIE BERGPREDIGT (MATTH. 5-7, LUK. 6, 20-49)
- DUERFEN WIR NOCH CHRISTEN BLEIBEN?
- GRIECHISCH-BYZANTINISCHE GESPRAECHSBUECHER UND VERWANDTES AUS SAMMELHANDSCHRIFTEN
- DER LEIPZIGER PAPYRUSFRAGMENTE DER PSALMEN
- THEOLOGIE UND RELIGIONSWISSENSCHAFT
- THEOLOGISCHE ENCYKLOPAEDIE

HEINRICI CHRONICON LIVONIAE (MGH 7: 31.BD) – 1874 – Dfl22.00 – ne Slangenburg [240]
HEIN'S BAR JOURNAL MICROFICHE SERVICE – (Inception-1969 $13,500.00 set. 1970-74 $2,950.00 set. 1975-79 $3,250.00 set. 1980-84 $4,250.00 set. 1985-95 $1,150.00v) – Inception-1995 – 9 – $33,000.00 set (1996 subsc $1,225.00) – us Hein [340]
HEIN'S EARLY FEDERAL LAWS COLLECTION – Installments 1-3 – 9 – $3,250.00 set – us Hein [340]
HEIN'S LEGAL THESES AND DISSERTATIONS MICROFICHE PROJECT – Instalment 1-4 thru Spring 1996 – 9 – $6,495.00 set – us Hein [340]
Heins, Otto *see* JOHANN RIST UND DAS NIEDERDEUTSCHE DRAMA DES 17. JAHRHUNDERTS
HEIN'S STATE BAR EXAMINATIONS – (Updated semi-annually) – 1985-1995 no 1 update – 9 – $1,100.00 set – 0-89941-632-2 – us Hein [340]
HEIN'S UNITED STATES TREATIES AND OTHER INTERNATIONAL AGREEMENTS – (1988-94 files complete. 1957-1987 additional files to follow. Index provided) – 1957-95 no 32 – 9 – $3,850.00 set – us Hein [327]
HEINSBERGER VOLKSZEITUNG – (Suppl. Aachener Volkszeitung) – Heinsberg, Germany. 1992- – 7r per yr – 1 – gw Mikrofilm [072]
HEINSE UND HOELDERLIN / Reuss, Theodor – Stuttgart: J F Steinkopf, 1906 – 1r – 1 – us U.W. Library [920]
HEINSES STELLUNG ZUR BILDENDEN KUNST UND IHRER AESTHETIK / Jessen, Karl Detlev – (Includes bibliographical references) – Berlin: Mayer & Mueller, 1901 – 1r – 1 – us U.W. Library [430]
Heinsius, D *see*
- AFBEELDINGEN VAN MINNE
- EMBLEMATA AMATORIA
- LOF-SANCK VAN IESUS CHRISTUS DEN EENIGEN ENDE EEUWIGEN SONE GODES
- NEDERDUYTSCHE POEMATA
- QUAERIS QUID SIT AMOR, QUID AMARE, CUPIDINIS ET QUID CASTRA SEQUI? CHARTAM HANC INSPICE, DOCTUS ERIS

Heinsius, Wilhelm *see*
- ALLGEMEINES BUCHER-LEXICON
- ALLGEMEINES BUECHERLEXIKON ODER VOLLSTAENDIGES VERZEICHNIS ALLER VON 1700 BIS ENDE 1892 ERSCHIENENEN BUECHER

HEINT – New York. 1, no. 1-52. Jan. 1-Feb. 21, 1920 – 1 – us NY Public [071]
HEINTIGE NAIS – Kaunas, 1940 – 2r – 1 – $150.00 – us Ross [072]
Heintze, W *see* DER KLEMENSROMAN UND SEINE GRIECHISCHEN QUELLEN (T.U.U. 3-40/2)
Heintzelman, Samuel *see* JOURNALS
Heinz, Margarete *see* UEBER DAS POLITISCHE BEWUSSTSEIN VON FRAUEN IN DER BUNDESREPUBLIK
HEINZ VON WOLFENBUETTEL : EIN ZEITBILD AUS DEM JAHRHUNDERT DER REFORMATION / Koldewey, Friedrich – Halle: Verein fuer Reformationsgeschichte, 1883 – 1mf – us A.T.L.A. [240]
Heinze, F K M *see* EHESCHEIDUNG FRANZOESISCHER UND BELGISCHER STAATSANGEHOERIGER IN DEUTSCHLAND
Heinze, Hermann *see*
- AUFGABEN AUS "MARIA STUART"
- AUFGABEN AUS WALLENSTEIN

Heinzel, Richard *see* GESCHICHTE DER NIEDERFRAENKISCHEN GESCHAEFTSSPRACHE
Heinzen, Karl Peter *see* DER TEUTSCHE EDITOREN-KONGRESS ZU CINCINNATI
THE HEIRESS OF MYRTLE GROVE: AN ENGLISH TALE FOUNDED ON FACTS / Brooks, Annie Elston – By a Montreal lady, A. E. B. Montreal: J. Lovell, 1870. 00288. (Pre-1900 Canadiana) – 9 – cn C.I.H.M. [830]
Heise, Christoph Ulrich *see* DIE GESETZESSAMMLUNG (ULOZENIE) VON 1649 UND IHRE AUSWIRKUNGEN AUF DIE KIRCHE IN DER AERA NIKONS
Heiseler, Henry von *see*
- PETER UND ALEXEJ
- WAWAS ENDE

Heiser, Robert F *see* THE ARCHAEOLOGY OF THE NAPA, CALIFORNIA REGION
Heisler, Daniel Yost *see* LIFE PICTURES OF THE PRODIGAL SON
Heiss, Willard *see* ABSTRACTS OF THE RECORDS OF THE SOCIETY OF FRIENDS IN INDIANA
Heissig, W *see* BOLUR ERIKE "EINE KETTE AUS BERGKRISTALLEN", EINE MONGOLISCHE CHRONIK DER KIENLUNG-ZEIT, VON RASIPUNGSUY (1774-1775) LITERATURHISTORISCH UNTERSUCHT
Heister, L *see*
- DESCRIPTIO NOVI GENERIS PLANTAE
- SYSTEMA PLANTARUM GENERALE EX FRUCTIFICATIONE

Heisterbach, Caesarius *see* DIALOGUS MIRACULORUM
Heit, Philip *see*
- DEATH EDUCATION AND DEATH ANXIETY IN STUDENT NURSE AIDES
- AN HIV EDUCATION NEEDS ASSESSMENT OF SELECTED TEACHER MEMBERS OF THE AMERICAN SCHOOL HEALTH ASSOCIATION AND THE AMERICAN HOME ECONOMICS ASSOCIATION

HEITERE GESCHICHTEN / Sealsfield, Charles – Prag: Volk und Reich Verlag, c1944 – 1r – 1 – us U.W. Library [830]
HEITERER GUCKKASTEN / Prochaska, Bruno – 4. Aufl. Berlin: C Stephenson, c1941 – 1r – 1 – us U.W. Library [830]
HEITERES UND WEITERES : KLEINE GESCHICHTEN / Wolzogen, Ernst von – 4. Aufl. Berlin: F Fontane, [190-?] – 1 – us U.W. Library [830]
Heitman, Francis B *see*
- HISTORICAL REGISTER AND DICTIONARY OF THE UNITED STATES ARMY, FROM ITS ORGANIZATION, SEPTEMBER 29, 1789, TO MARCH 2, 1903
- HISTORICAL REGISTER OF OFFICERS OF THE CONTINENTAL ARMY DURING THE WAR OF THE REVOLUTION APRIL 1775 TO DECEMBER 1783

Heitmann, Felix *see* ZUR ERZAEHLUNGSKUNST DER ANNETTE VON DROSTE-HUELSHOFF
Heitz, Frederic Charles *see* L'ALSACE EN 1789: TABLEAU DES DIVISIONS TERRITORIALES ET DES DIFFERENTES SEIGNEURIES D'ALSACE
DER HEIZER : EIN FRAGMENT / Kafka, Franz – Leipzig: K Wolff, 1913 – 1r – 1 – us U.W. Library [830]
HEJ – Helsingborg, 1968-69 – 1r – 1 – sw Kungliga [073]
HEKATE, 1823 / ed by Kotzebue, August von – 1823 (mf ed 1997) – 9mf – 9 – DM180.00 – 3-89131-236-9 – gw Fischer [305]
THE HEKATOMPATHIA, OR PASSIONATE CENTURIE OF LOVE / Watson, Thomas – 1582 – 9 – 10.00 – us Scholars' Facs [810]
HEKO – Dar es Salaam: Heko Publ, n3. dec 1985- – us Res Libr [072]
HEKS – 1977-93 (complete) – 2r – 1 – ATLA S0775 – us A.T.L.A. [073]
HEKSERIJ BIJ DE BALUBA VAN KASAI / Caeneghem, E P R van – [Bruxelles, 1955] – 1 – us Res Libr [960]
Hektoen, Ludvig *see* AN AMERICAN TEXT-BOOK OF PATHOLOGY
HELA VECKAN – Jonkoping, Sweden. 1982-87 – 1 – sw Kungliga [072]
HELBECK OF BANNISDALE / Ward, Mary Augusta – British Fiction Archive: Unit 2 – 9 – uk Bell [830]
Helbing, Robert *see* GRAMMATIK DER SEPTUAGINTA
Helbok, Adolf *see* HAUS UND SIEDLUNG IM WANDEL DER JAHRTAUSENDE
Helbronner, Horace *see* LE POUVOIR JUDICIAIRE AUX ETATS-UNIS; SON ORGANISATION ET SES ATTRIBUTIONS
Held, Georg *see* THEORIE DER MERKANTILRECHNUNG
HELD IN HOSTAGE / Ouida – British Fiction Archive: Unit 3 – 9 – uk Bell [830]
HELD OHNE NAMEN: EIN SCHICKSAL / Hepner, Gerda – Tubingen: R. Wunderlich, 1932 – 1 – us U.W. Library [900]
HELDEN TO HUS / Lau, Fritz – Hamburg: M Glogau, 1918 – 1r – 1 – us U.W. Library [830]
DIE HELDENBRAUT : EIN GEDICHT AUS DEM AMERIKANISCHEN BEFREIUNGS-KRIEGE / Alpers, Wilhelm – New York: Willmer & Rogers, 1876 – 1r – 1 – us U.W. Library [810]
HELDENDICHTUNG, GEISTLICHENDICHTUNG, RITTERDICHTUNG / Schneider, Hermann – (Includes bibliographical references and index) – Heidelberg: C Winter, 1925 – 1r – 1 – us U.W. Library [430]
HELDENTOD: STUDIEN ZUR VERGLEICHENDEN PSYCHOLOGIE / Spitta, Heinrich – Tuebingen: Kloeres, 1915. 32p – 1 – us U.W. Library [940]
HELD'S VOLKSVERTRETER – Berlin, 1846-47 – 1 – Dist. gw Mikrofilm – gw Misc Inst [072]
Helena, Ohio. Shiloh United Methodist Church *see* RECORDS
HELENA OU LES MIQUELETS / Saint-Cyr, Reveroni & Foignet – French Theatre Series. Paris. Toubon, an III. 1794 – 9 – fr Hachette [820]
Helene de la Presentation, Soeur *see* BIBLIOGRAPHIE DE LA CROISADE EUCHARISTIQUE, MOUVEMENT D'"ACTION CATHOLIQUE DES ENFANTS" (PIE 12)
HELFERICH PETER STURZ : NEBST EINER ABHANDLUNG UEBER DIE SCHLESWIGISCHEN LITERATURBRIEFE MIT BENUETZUNG HANDSCHRIFTLICHER QUELLEN / Koch, Max – (Includes bibliographical references and index) – Muenchen: Christian Kaiser, 1879 – 1r – 1 – us U.W. Library [430]
Helfferich, Adolf *see* JOHANN KARL PASSAVANT. EIN CHRISTLICHES CHARAKTERBILD
Helfferich, Karl Theodor *see* DER WELTKRIEG
HELGA : SCHAUSPIEL IN FUENF AKTEN / Hopfen, Hans – Berlin: Gebrueder Paetel, 1892 – 1r – 1 – us U.W. Library [820]
Helgans, R M *see* THE ROLE OF AEROBIC FITNESS AND SOCIAL SUPPORT IN REACTIVITY TO PSYCHOLOGICAL STRESS
HELIANTHUS / Ouida – British Fiction Archive: Unit 3 – 9 – uk Bell [830]
Helianus, L *see* LUDOUICI HELIANI VERCELLENSIS CHRSITANISSIMI FRANCO REGIS SENATORIS
Helie, Arthur *see* THESE POUR LA LICENCE
HELIKA: MEMOIRE D'UN VIEUX MAITRE D'ECOLE / Deguise, Charles – Montreal: E. Senecal, 1872. 02703. (Pre-1900 Canadiana) – 9 – cn C.I.H.M. [971]
Helinadus of Froidmont *see* LES VERS DE LA MORT
Helinant, Moine de Froidmont *see* LES VERS DE LA MORT
HELIX ADVOCATE – Helix OR. Sep 27 1912 – 1 – us U.O. Library [071]
HELIX HERALD – Helix, OR. -w. 25 May 1906-14 Jun 1907. 1 roll – 1 – us U.O. Library [071]
HELIX VIEW POINT – Helix OR. Jan 10 1929-Dec 14 1939 – 1 – us U.O. Library [071]
Helke, Fritz *see*
- FEHDE UM BRANDENBURG
- DIE GROSSE STUNDE
- PREUSSISCHE REBELLION
- DER SOLDAT AUF DEM THRON

HELL UPON EARTH, OR, THE TOWN IN AN UPROAR:. – London, 1729. 62p – 1 – us U.W. Library [941]

HELLAS : A LYRICAL DRAMA / Shelley, Percy Bysshe; ed by Wise, Thomas J – London: Published for the Shelley Society by Reeves and Turner, 2nd ed 1886 (London: Richard Clay & Sons) – 1 roll – 1 – 1-55879-280-5 – uk Libr Preservation [820]
HELLAS UND ROM / Forbiger, Albert – Populaere Darstellung des oeffentlichen und haeuslichen Lebens der Griechen und Roemer. Leipzig, Fucs, 1876. 2 v. in 6. Film Mas 9161 – 1 – us H.U. Library [900]
DER HELLASBOTE – Berlin, 1923-24 n8 – 1r – 1 – Dist. gw Mikrofilm – gw Misc Inst [072]
Hellen, Eduard von der *see*
- GOETHES BRIEFE
- SCHILLERS SAEMTLICHE WERKE
HELLENIC FREE PRESS – (In Greek) – Canada, 1967-Mar 1982 – 15r – 1 – cn Commonwealth Micro [072]
HELLENIC HERALD – (Greek language) – Sydney, Nov 16 1926-Dec 31 1959 – 9 – at Pascoe [072]
HELLENIC NEWS – (In Greek and English) – New York, 1963-72 – 2r – 1 – $170.00 – D3369 – us Scholarly Res [071]
HELLENIKON AIMA – Athens. Greece. -d. 12 Jan 1946-6 Jun 1947. (Imperfect). (2 reels) – 1 – uk British Libr Newspaper [949]
HELLENIKOS TYPOS = SALONIKI-GREEK PRESS – Chicago: Greek Press Pub Co, jan 16, 1941-42; 1946-74 – us Res Libr [071]
HELLENISM IN ENGLAND : A SHORT HISTORY OF THE GREEK PEOPLE IN THIS COUNTRY FROM THE EARLIEST TIMES TO THE PRESENT DAY: WITH SEVENTEEN ILLUSTRATIONS / Dowling, Theodore Edward & Fletcher, Edwin W – London: Faith Press; Milwaukee: Young Churchman, 1915 – 1mf – us A.T.L.A. [305]
HELLENISMUS UND CHRISTENTHUM, ODER, DIE GEISTIGE REAKTION DES ANTIKEN HEIDENTHUMS GEGEN DAS CHRISTENTHUM : MIT BESONDERER RUECKSICHT AUF DIE CHRISTENFEINDLICHE LITERATUR DES KLASSISCHEN ALTERTHUMS SO WIE AUCH DER GEGENWART / Kellner, Heinrich – Koeln: M. DuMont-Schauberg, 1866 – 2mf – us A.T.L.A. [230]
HELLENISMUS UND JUDENTUM IM NEUTESTAMENTLICHEN ZEITALTER / Krueger, Paul – Leipzig: J.C. Hinrichs, 1908. 1 fiche – 9 – us A.T.L.A. [930]
Heller, A A *see* MUEHLENBERGIA
Heller, B *see*
- BIBLIOGRAPHIE DE [SES] OUEVRES
- FESTSCHRIFT
Heller, F X. *see* FLORA WIRCEBURGENSIS
Heller, H *see* DIE SOUVERAENITAET
DAS HELLER MAGAZIN – Leipzig, Germany. Okt 1833-8 Nov 1834; 1835-42; 1844 – 1 – gw Mikrofilm [072]
Heller, R *see* NEW TRENDS IN BIOLOGY TEACHING
Heller, S *see* DIE ECHTEN HEBRAEISCHEN MELODIEN
DAS HELLER-BLATT – (Also known as: Magazin zur Verbreitung gemeinnuetziger Kenntnisse) – Breslau (Wroclaw), Germany. 1834. (1 Jg.) – 1r – 1 – gw Mikrofilm [073]
DAS HELLER-BLATT : ODER: MAGAZIN ZUR VERBREITUNG GEMEINNUETZIGER KENNTNISSE – Breslau, 1834-38 – 1 – Inquire at Mikrofilmarchiv for details – gw Misc Inst [072]
HELLES ABENDLIED : AUSGEWAEHLTE GEDICHTE / Hohlbaum, Robert – Muenchen: A Langen/G Mueller, c1941 – 1r – 1 – us U.W. Library [810]
Hellinghaus, Otto *see*
- BRIEFE FRIEDRICH LEOPOLDS GRAFEN ZU STOLBERG UND DER SEINIGEN AN JOHANN HEINRICH VOSS
- FRIEDRICH LEOPOLDS GRAFEN ZU STOLBERG ERSTE GATTIN AGNES GEB. VON WITZLEBEN
Helliwell, Arthur Llewellyn *see* A TREATISE ON STOCK AND STOCKHOLDERS, COVERING WATERED STOCK, TRUSTS, CONSOLIDATIONS AND HOLDING COMPANIES
Hellman, S *see* PSEUDO-CYPRIANUS DE 12 ABUSIVES SAECULI (T.U.U. 3-34/1A)
Hellmann, E *see* ROOIYARD SOCIOLOGICAL SURVEY OF AN URBAN NATIVE SLUM YARD
Hellmann, Hanna *see*
- HEINRICH VON KLEIST
Hellner, J *see* OM GILTIGHETEN AF UTOMLANDS INGANGNA AEKTENSKAP
Hellot, Jean *see* L'ART DE LA TEINTURE DES LAINES ET DES ETOFFES DE LAINE EN GRAND ET PETIT TEINT, AVEC UNE INSTRUCTION SUR LES DEBOUILLIS
Hellowell, S G *see* A HISTORY OF CRAGG VALE, YORKSHIRE
HELLWEGER ANZEIGER – Unna, West Germany. 1 Sept 1992- – 7r per yr – 1 – gw Mikrofilm [072]
Hellwig, Elsa *see* MORPHOLOGISCHER IDEALISMUS UND NEUE LYRIKDEUTUNG
Helm, Thomas B *see* HISTORY OF CASS COUNTY
Helme, J *see* A SPECIMEN OF PREACHING, AS PRACTISED AMONGST THE PEOPLE CALLED METHODISTS
Helmholtz, Hermann Ludwig Ferdinand von *see* UEBER GOETHE'S NATURWISSENSCHAFTLICHE ARBEITEN
Helmly, Ruth C *see* UTILIZATION OF VISUAL CUES BY SKILLED AND UNSKILLED BASKETBALL PLAYERS
HELMONDI PRESBYTERI BOZOVIENSIS CRONICA SLAVORUM (MGH 7: 32.BD) – 1909 – Dfl22.00 – ne Slangenburg [240]
Helmreich, E C *see* THE DIPLOMACY OF THE BALKAN WARS 1912-1913
Helms, O et al *see* DANSK ORNITHOLOGISK FORENINGS TIDSSKRIFT
HELMUT KOHL: PAMPHLET COLLECTION – 1975-1985 – 1 reel – 1 – CSUXANS3635-B – us Hoover Inst Photo [320]
HELMUT SCHMIDT: PAMPHLET COLLECTION – 1972-1980 – 1 reel – 1 – CSUXANS3628-B – us Hoover Inst Photo [320]
Helmy, S *see* TOWARDS THE FULL UTILIZATION OF THE WATERS OF THE NILE; PAST, PRESENT AND FUTURE POLICY
HELP FOR SOCIAL SCIENTISTS : A NEW KIND OF REFERENCE PROCESS / Riggs, Fred W – 1986 – 48p – 9 – 92-3-102414-0 – fr UNESCO [300]
Helper, Hinton Rowan *see* A SELECTION OF WORKS BY AND ABOUT H.R. HELPER
HELPING HAND – (Title varies: v1-24 as Macedonian. v25-30 as Macedonian and Record. v31-35 no 1 as Macedonian and Helping Hand) – v1-72. 1842-1914 (complete) – 5r – 1 – ATLA R0124 – us A.T.L.A. [073]
HELPING HIMSELF: OR, GRANT THORNTON'S AMBITION / Alger, Horatio – Philadelphia: Winston, c1886. 320p – 1 – us U.W. Library [830]
HELPING PARENTS FACILITATE THE RELIGIOUS EDUCATION OF PRESCHOOL CHILDREN IN THE HOME / Overman, David Gene – 1981 – 1 – 5.00 – us Baptist [240]
HELPING RESPONSES IN AMBIGUOUS AND UNAMBIGUOUS EMERGENCIES AS A FUNCTION OF TRAINING IN FIRST AID / Heinold, William D – 1982 – 2mf – 9 – $8.00 – us Microform Publ [610]
Helps, Arthur *see*
- FRIENDS IN COUNCIL
- THE SPANISH CONQUEST IN AMERICA AND ITS RELATION TO THE HISTORY OF SLAVERY AND TO THE GOVERNMENT OF COLONIES
HELPS BY THE WAY – Toronto: T.J. Hamilton, [1873?-1874?] – 9 – cn C.I.H.M. [210]
"HELPS BY THE WAY" SERIES OF LEAFLETS FOR LETTERS – Toronto: [s.n. 18–] – 9 – cn C.I.H.M. [210]
Helps, E A *see* PERSONAL WORK FOR CHRIST AND SOME EXPERIENCES
HELPS FOR SUDDAIN ACCIDENTS / Bradwell, S – M-312. 1633 – 9 – ne IDC [615]
Helps, Sir Arthur *see* THE LIFE OF LAS CASAS, "THE APOSTLE OF THE INDIES"
HELROL HETRE – (Filmed consecutively with: Magyar hirlap) – Detroit: Magyar Hirlap], feb 17 1918-aug 1 1919 – us Res Libr [071]
HELSINGBORGS DAGBLAD – Helsingborg, Sweden. 1884-1978 – 605r – 1 – sw Kungliga [072]
HELSINGBORGS DAGBLAD – (Klippans Dagblad 1979-84) – Helsingborg, Sweden. 1979- – 1 – sw Kungliga [072]
HELSINGBORGSPOSTEN SKANE-HALLAND – Helsingborg, Sweden. 1900-30 – 105r – 1 – sw Kungliga [072]
HELSINGEN – Soederhamn, 1994- – 9 – sw Kungliga [072]
HELSINGOR STIFTSBOG – 1978-84 (complete) – 1r – 1 – ATLA S0651 – us A.T.L.A. [073]
Helsinki University. Slavic Department *see* RUSSIAN OLD (SIC) CATALOG
HELSTON HAYLE AND THE LIZARD LEADER – (Discontinued) – Apr 9, Jun 4-Dec 24 1988; 1989-Jun 1990; Jul 7-Dec 22 1990; 1991-92; Jan 9-Jun 26, Jul 3-Dec 25 1993; Jan 8-Jun 25, Jul 2-Dec 24 1994; Jan-Dec 23 1995 – 10r – 1 – uk British Libr Newspaper [072]
HELSTON PACKET – England.21 Nov 1969-25 Dec 1970. -w. 1 reel – 1 – uk British Libr Newspaper [072]
Helton, J *see* REASONS FOR QUITTING THE METHODIST SOCIETY, BEING A DEFENCE OF BARCLAY'S 'APOLOGY', IN ANSWER TO A PRINTED LETTER TO A PERSON JOINED WITH THE PEOPLE CALLED QUAKERS;...
Helton, Peter *see* INSTRUCTIONS TO JURIES AND DECLARATIONS OF LAW
Helveg, Ludvig *see* DE DANSKE DOMKAPITLER
HELVETICA CHIMICA ACTA – Basel. v50-59,no.8. 1967-76. Lacking: 1974, v57,no.1; 1976, v59 (9). BH-578/1 – 9 – ne IDC [073]
HELVETICA CHIMICA ACTA – v1-38. 1918-55 – 1,5,6 – us Princeton Micro [540]
HELVETICA PHYSICA ACTA – Basel. 1940-48.v1-21.109/2 – 8 – ne IDC [073]
HELVETICA PHYSICA ACTA – v1-28. 1928-55 – 1,5,6 – us Princeton Micro [530]
Helvetius, Claude-Adrien *see*
- LES PROGRES DE LA RAISON, DANS LA RECHERCHE DU VRAI
- LE VRAI SENS DU SYSTEME DE LA NATURE
Helwig, Werner *see* RAUBFISCHER IN HELLAS
Helwys, Thomas *see*
- A DECLARATION OF FAITH OF THE ENGLISH PEOPLE
- A SHORT DECLARATION OF THE MYSTERY OF INIQUITY
Hely, V *see* ETUDE SUR LE DROIT DE LA GUERRE DE GROTIUS
Heman, Friedrich *see* DIE RELIGIOESE WELTSTELLUNG DES JUEDISCHEN VOLKES
Hemans, Felicia *see* THE BREAKING WAVES DASHED HIGH
Hemans, Felicia Dorothea Browne *see* THE POETICAL WORKS OF MRS. FELICIA HEMANS...
HEMATOLOGICAL ONCOLOGY – 1983- – 1,5,6,9 – us UMI [610]
HEMATOLOGY REVIEWS AND COMMUNICATIONS / ed by Roath, Stuart – 9,5,1 – us Harwood [616]
HEMEL HEMPSTEAD GAZETTE – Hemel Hempstead, England. 1980-81 – 7r – 1 – uk British Libr Newspaper [072]
HEMEL HEMPSTEAD GAZETTE AND WEST HERTS ADVERTISER – (Also known as: The Gazette (Hemel Hempstead)) – 1869; 1877; 1879; 1889; 1891; Feb-Mar 1945; 1950; Jan 4-Apr 18, May 16-Aug 29, Sep 5-Dec 19 1980; 1981-90; Jul 4 1991-96 – 77 3/4r – 1 – uk British Libr Newspaper [072]
Hemenway, Abbie M *see*
- INDEX TO CONTENTS OF THE VERMONT HISTORICAL GAZETTEER
- VERMONT HISTORICAL GAZETTEER
HEMET NEWS – Hemet, CA. 1899- – 267+ r – 1 RC02294 – $13,350.00 ($360.00y) – us Library Micro [071]
HEMET WEEK – Hemet, CA. 1990-1992 – 1r – 1 – $50.00 – R04031 – us Library Micro [071]
HEMINGFORD GUIDE – Alliance. Neb. 1892-1898 – 1 – us UMI [071]
HEMINGWAY AND MCDONALD'S REPORTS / Mississippi. Supreme Court – (A Pre-NRS title) – v1-2. 1881-1887 (all publ) – 17mf – 9 – $25.50 – LLMC 90-303 – us L.L.M.C. [340]
Hemingway, Ernest *see* THE SNOWS OF KILIMANJARO
HEMINGWAY FIRST BAPTIST CHURCH. HEMINGWAY, SOUTH CAROLINA : CHURCH RECORDS – 1926-28, 1941-54 – 1 – 5.00 – us Baptist [240]
HEMINGWAY REVIEW – v.1-. 1981- – 1,5,6,9 – us UMI [420]
HEMIPTERA AFRICANA / ed by Stal, C – Holmiae, 1864-1866 – 4v – 8 – ne IDC [590]
THE HEMIPTERA HETEROPTERA OF THE BRITISH ISLANDS / Saunders, E – London, 1892. vi,350p. 32 pls.Z-1592/2 – 8 – ne IDC [590]
HEMIPTERA SVECIAE / Fallen, C F – London, 1829. viii, 186p. Z-1237 2 – 8 – ne IDC [590]
THE HEMIPTERA-HOMOPTERA (CICADINA AND PSYLLINA) OF THE BRITISH ISLANDS... / Edwards, J – London, 1896 – xii/271p, 30pls – 8 – ne IDC [590]
HEMLANDET – Chicago. Ill. (Printed in Swedish). 1855-1914 – 1 – us UMI [071]
HEMLANDSVAENNEN – Stockholm, Sweden. 1894 July – Sept. – 1 – sw Kungliga [072]
Hemmerich, Karl *see* GERHART HAUPTMANNS VELAND
Hemmersbach, H *see* DEMAND STUDY FOR THE TEXTILE AND CLOTHING INDUSTRY IN LIBYA, A GENERAL OUTLINE
Hemmes, E *see*
- RICHARD WAGNERS "PARSIFAL"
- RICHARD WAGNERS PARSIFAL
Hemmet, C *see* DOUZE EVENTAILS DE BONZE SIAMOIS. ANALYSE ET DESCRIPTION
Hemmingsen, Neils *see* THE PREACHER, OR METHODE OF PREACHING
HEMOGLOBIN – (v8-. 1984-. 5,6,9) – v1-. 1976- – 1 – us UMI [073]
Hemon, Louis *see* MARIA CHAPDELAINE
Hemony, P *see* DE ON-NOODSAKELIJKHEID EN ONDIENSTIGHEID VAN CIS EN DIS IN DE BASSEN DER KLOKKEN, VERTOONT UYT VERSCHEYDE ADVYSEN VAN ERVAREN ORGANISTEN ENDE KLOKKENSPEELDERS BIJ EEN VERSAMELT
Hemphill, Charles Robert *see* THE VALIDITY AND BEARING OF THE TESTIMONY OF CHRIST AND HIS APOSTLES
Hemphill, J C *see* MEN OF MARK IN SOUTH CAROLINA
Hemphill, Samuel *see* HISTORY OF THE REVISED VERSION OF THE NEW TESTAMENT
Hempstead, Fay *see*
- HISTORICAL REVIEW OF ARKANSAS
- A PICTORIAL HISTORY OF ARKANSAS FROM EARLIEST TIME TO THE YEAR 1890
Hempstead, SH *see* HEMPSTEAD'S REPORTS OF CASES IN THE ARKANSAS DISTRICT AND CIRCUIT COURTS, 1836-1856
HEMPSTEAD'S REPORTS OF CASES IN THE ARKANSAS DISTRICT AND CIRCUIT COURTS, 1836-1856 / Hempstead, SH – Boston: Little-Brown. 1v. 1856 (all publ) – 9mf – 9 – $13.50 – LLMC 81-454 – us L.L.M.C. [340]
Hemrich, Guenter *see* ENTWICKLUNGSTENDENZEN IN DER LANDWIRTSCHAFTLICHEN PRODUKTION NACH DER EINFUEHRUNG MODERNER REISTECHNOLOGIE
Hemsley, W B *see* BOTANY OF CENTRAL AMERICA. BIOLOGIA CENTRALI-AMERICANA
HENAN MINGUO RIBAO – (The Republican Daily, Henan Province Ed.). China. M B6. Dec 1931-Apr 1932, Oct 1937, Feb 1938-Apr 1944 – 8r – 1 – $360.00 – cc Microforms [072]
Henan Province. China *see*
- HONGZHI YANSHI XIAN ZHI, 1504
- JIAJING CHANGYUAN XIAN ZHI, 1541
- JIAJING DENGZHOU ZHI, 1564
- JIAJING GUANGSHAN XIAN ZHI, 1556
- JIAJING GUSHI XIAN ZHI, 1542
- JIAJING KAIZHOU ZHI, 1534
- JIAJING LANYANG XIAN ZHI, 1546
- JIAJING LUSHAN XIAN ZHI, 1552
- JIAJING NEIHUANG XIAN ZHI,1537
- JIAJING WEISHI XIAN ZHI, 1548
- JIAJING XIANGCHENG XIAN ZHI, 1551
- JIAJING XIAYI XIAN ZHI, 1548
- JIAJING XUZHOU ZHI, 1541
- JIAJING YANLING ZHI, 1535
- JIAJING ZHANGDE FU ZHI, 1523
- ZHENGDE RUZHOU ZHI, 1506
- ZHENGDE XINXIANG XIAN ZHI, 1506
HENAN RIBAO – China. Henan Daily. 1986- . M-D27 – 1 reel/y – 1 – $55.00r – cc Microforms [072]
HENAN SHI DA XUEBAO – (1979-81 $4.50f; 1982-84 $3.50f) – Shehui Kexue Ban. Henan Teacher's University Journal, Social Sciences. In Chinese but Table of Contents in English in each issue. F p219 – 9 – cc Microforms [073]
Henao Davila, Fernando *see* ESTUDIO DE UN METODO ANALITICO PARA VALORACION CUANTITATIVA CONJUNTA DE LOS ACIDOS ORGANICOS EN VINOS DE TIERRA DE BARROS
Henao y Munoz, Manuel *see*
- CRONICA...BADAJOZ
- EL DRAMA DE LA VIDA
- EL LIBRO DEL PUEBLO
Henckell, Karl *see* HUNDERT GEDICHTE
Henckens, R P *see* SAINTE CHRISTINE L'ADMIRABLE DE SAINT-TROND

Hendel, Klaus *see* QUALITATIVE UND QUANTITATIVE UNTERSUCHUNGEN DER DYNAMIK VON MEHRKOERPERSYSTEMEN MITTELS STOERUNGSGLEICHUNGEN UND 1. INTEGRALEN
Henderson, Alexander *see*
- EARLY PIONEER FAMILIES OF VICTORIA AND RIVERINA
- SERMONS, PRAYERS, AND PULPIT ADDRESSES

Henderson, Charles Richmond *see*
- THE DEVELOPMENT OF DOCTRINE IN THE EPISTLES
- INTRODUCTION TO THE STUDY OF THE DEPENDENT, DEFECTIVE, AND DELINQUENT CLASSES
- MODERN METHODS OF CHARITY
- SOCIAL DUTIES FROM THE CHRISTIAN POINT OF VIEW
- SOCIAL ELEMENTS
- SOCIAL PROGRAMMES IN THE WEST
- SOCIAL SETTLEMENTS

HENDERSON, CLIFFORD, PAPERS, MS 4309 – 1928-1939 – 14r – 1 – us Western Res [790]
HENDERSON, DR. JOHN M., PAPERS, MS 533 – (Account book, correspondence, election tickets, resolutions, bylaws, minutes, essays, petitons and legal documents of this medical doctor, an early settler of Lake Co and founder of Willoughby Medical School) – Willoughby, Lake, OH. 1810-92 – 1r – 1 – us Western Res [920]
Henderson, Ebenezer *see*
- THE BOOK OF THE PROPHET EZEKIEL
- THE BOOK OF THE PROPHET JEREMIAH AND THAT OF THE LAMENTATIONS

Henderson, G C *see* THE POSITION OF FOREIGN CORPORATIONS IN AMERICAN CONSTITUTIONAL LAW
Henderson, George *see* LADY NAIRNE AND HER SONGS
Henderson, Henry F *see*
- CALVIN IN HIS LETTERS
- THE DREAM OF DANTE
- ERSKINE OF LINLATHEN
- THE RELIGIOUS CONTROVERSIES OF SCOTLAND

HENDERSON HOME NEWS – Henderson, NV. 1951-1955; 1956-1977 – 67+ r – 1 – $3,350.00 ($140.00y) – N04587 – us Library Micro [071]
Henderson, J *see* MEMORIALS OF JAMES HENDERSON..., MEDICAL MISSIONARY TO CHINA
Henderson, J B *see* A MONOGRAPH OF THE EAST AMERICAN SCAPHOPOD MOLLUSKS
Henderson, J Duff *see* ALVIRA ALIAS OREA
Henderson, James Max *see*
- QUESTIONS AND ANSWERS WITH PROBLEMS AND ILLUSTRATIVE MATTER ON CONFLICT OF LAWS.
- QUESTIONS AND ANSWERS WITH PROBLEMS AND ILLUSTRATIVE MATTER ON THE LAW OF DOMESTIC RELATIONS
- QUESTIONS AND ANSWERS WITH PROBLEMS AND ILLUSTRATIVE MATTER ON THE LAW OF EQUITY.
- QUESTIONS AND ANSWERS WITH PROBLEMS AND ILLUSTRATIVE MATTER ON THE LAW OF SALES.

Henderson, Leonard *see* RELATIONS AMONG FIGS, FIG WASPS AND SILVEREYES ON HERON ISLAND
HENDERSON MEMORIAL BAPTIST CHURCH. HOPKINSVILLE, KENTUCKY : CHURCH RECORDS – 1965-Jan 1986 – 1 – 18.77 – us Baptist [240]
HENDERSON NEWS – Henderson, NE. -w. Nov 1952 to date – 1 – us NE Hist [071]
Henderson, Robert B *see* THE CANADIAN LAW OF PARTNERSHIP
Henderson, Samuel *see* RECORDS OF SAMUEL HENDERSON AND E. B. TEAGUE
HENDERSON SHOPPING NEWS – Henderson, NV. 1947; 1948 – 2r – 1 – $100.00 – U04845 – us Library Micro [071]
Henderson, Thomas F *see* THE POETRY OF ROBERT BURNS
Henderson, W *see*
- HE DESCENDED INTO HELL, OR, AN INTERPRETATION BASED ON REASON AND SCRIPTURE
- LIBER PONTIFICALIS CHR. BAINBRIDGE ARCHIEPISCOPI EBORACENSIS
- MANUALE ET PROCESSIONALE AD USUM INSIGNIS ECCLESIAE EBORACENSIS
- MISSALE AD USUM INSIGNIS ECCLESIAE EBORANCENSIS
- MISSALE AD USUM PERCELEBRIS ECCLESIAE HERFORDENSIS
- PROCESSIONALE AD USUM INSIGNIS AC PRAECLARAE ECCLESIAE SARUM

Henderson, W P M *see* DURBAN
Henderson, William *see* NOTES ON THE FOLK-LORE OF THE NORTHERN COUNTIES OF ENGLAND AND THE BORDERS
Henderson, William Graham *see* A CONCISE SUMMARY OF THE LAW OF LIBEL AS IT AFFECTS THE PRESS
HENDERSON'S BRITISH COLUMBIA GAZETTEER AND DIRECTORY AND MINING COMPANIES : WITH WHICH IS CONSOLIDATED THE WILLIAM'S B.C. DIRECTORY FOR 1900-1901, COMPRISING COMPLETE ALPHABETICAL DIRECTORES OF THE CITIES AND COMPLETE BUSINESS DIRECTORY – Vancouver: Henderson Publishing Co, 1901 – 1r – 1 – cn U.B.C. Preserve [910]
HENDERSON'S BRITISH COLUMBIA GAZETTEER AND DIRECTORY FOR 1901 : COMPRISING COMPLETE ALPHABETICAL DIRECTORIES OF THE CITIES, AND A CLASSIFIED BUSINESS DIRECTORY – Vancouver: Henderson Publishing Co, 1901 – 1r – 1 – cn U.B.C. Preserve [910]
HENDERSON'S BRITISH COLUMBIA GAZETTEER AND DIRECTORY FOR 1902 : COMPRISING COMPLETE ALPHABETICAL DIRECTORIES OF THE CITIES AND A CLASSIFIED BUSINESS DIRECTORY – Vancouver: Henderson Publishing Co, 1902 – 1r – 1 – cn U.B.C. Preserve [910]
HENDERSON'S BRITISH COLUMBIA GAZETTEER AND DIRECTORY FOR 1903 : COMPRISING COMPLETE ALPHABETICAL DIRECTORIES OF THE CITIES, AND A CLASSIFIED BUSINESS DIRECTORY – Vancouver: Henderson Publishing Co, 1903 – 1r – 1 – cn U.B.C. Preserve [971]
HENDERSON'S BRITISH COLUMBIA GAZETTEER AND DIRECTORY FOR 1904 : COMPRISING COMPLETE ALPHABETICAL DIRECTORIES OF THE CITIES, AND A CLASSIFIED BUSINESS DIRECTORY – Vancouver: Henderson Publishing Co, 1904 – 1r – 1 – cn U.B.C. Preserve [910]
HENDERSON'S BRITISH COLUMBIA GAZETTEER AND DIRECTORY FOR 1905 : INCLUDING CONDENSED BUSINESS DIRECTORIES OF THE CITIES OF VANCOUVER AND VICTORIA AND A COMPLETE CLASSIFIED BUSINESS DIRECTORY – Vancouver: Henderson Publishing Co, 1905 – 1r – 1 – cn U.B.C. Preserve [910]
HENDERSON'S BRITISH COLUMBIA GAZETTEER AND DIRECTORY FOR 1910 : INCLUDING CONDENSED BUSINESS DIRECTORIES OF THE CITIES OF VANCOUVER AND VICTORIA AND A COMPLETE CLASSIFIED BUSINESS DIRECTORY – Vancouver: Henderson Publishing Co, 1910 – 2r – 1 – cn U.B.C. Preserve [971]
HENDERSON'S CITY OF VANCOUVER AND NORTH VANCOUVER DIRECTORY 1909 : COMPRISING AN IMPROVED STREET AND AVENUE GUIDE,... – Vancouver: Henderson Publishing Co, 1909 – 1r – 1 – cn U.B.C. Preserve [910]
HENDERSON'S CITY OF VANCOUVER AND NORTH VANCOUVER DIRECTORY 1910 : COMPRISING AN IMPROVED STREET AND AVENUE GUIDE,... – Vancouver: Henderson Publishing Co, 1910 – 2r – 1 – cn U.B.C. Preserve [910]
HENDERSON'S CITY OF VANCOUVER DIRECTORY : COMPRISING AN IMPROVED STREET AND AVENUE GUIDE,... – Vancouver: Henderson Publishing Co, 1905 – 1r – 1 – cn U.B.C. Preserve [910]
HENDERSON'S CITY OF VANCOUVER DIRECTORY : COMPRISING AN IMPROVED STREET AND AVENUE GUIDE,... – Vancouver: Henderson Publishing Co, 1906 – 1r – 1 – cn U.B.C. Preserve [910]
HENDERSON'S CITY OF VANCOUVER DIRECTORY : COMPRISING AN IMPROVED STREET AND AVENUE GUIDE,... – Vancouver: Henderson Publishing Co, 1907 – 1r – 1 – cn U.B.C. Preserve [910]
HENDERSON'S CITY OF VANCOUVER DIRECTORY : COMPRISING AN IMPROVED STREET AND AVENUE GUIDE,... – Vancouver: Henderson Publishing Co, 1908 – 1r – 1 – cn U.B.C. Preserve [910]
HENDERSON'S GREATER VANCOUVER CITY DIRECTORY, 1914 : EMBRACING THE AREA OF GREATER VANCOUVER, COVERING THE CITY PROPER, NORTH VANCOUVER, WEST VANCOUVER, SOUTH VANCOUVER, POINT GREY AND NEW WESTMINSTER,... – Vancouver: Henderson Publishing Co, 1914 – 2r – 1 – cn U.B.C. Preserve [910]
HENDERSON'S GREATER VANCOUVER CITY DIRECTORY, 1915 : EMBRACING THE AREA OF GREATER VANCOUVER, COVERING THE CITY PROPER, NORTH VANCOUVER, WEST VANCOUVER, SOUTH VANCOUVER AND POINT GREY,... – Vancouver: Henderson Publishing Co, 1915 – 1r – 1 – cn U.B.C. Preserve [910]
HENDERSON'S GREATER VANCOUVER CITY DIRECTORY, 1916 : EMBRACING THE AREA OF GREATER VANCOUVER, COVERING THE CITY PROPER, NORTH VANCOUVER, WEST VANCOUVER, SOUTH VANCOUVER AND POINT GREY,... – Vancouver: Henderson Publishing Co, 1916 – 1r – 1 – cn U.B.C. Preserve [910]
HENDERSON'S GREATER VANCOUVER CITY DIRECTORY, 1917 : EMBRACING THE AREA OF GREATER VANCOUVER, COVERING THE CITY PROPER, NORTH VANCOUVER, WEST VANCOUVER, SOUTH VANCOUVER AND POINT GREY, COMPRISING A COMPLETE STREET AND AVENUE DIRECTORY OF THE CITY... – Vancouver: Henderson Publishing Co, 1917 – 1r – 1 – cn U.B.C. Preserve [910]
HENDERSON'S GREATER VANCOUVER CITY DIRECTORY, 1918 : EMBRACING THE AREA OF GREATER VANCOUVER, COVERING THE CITY PROPER, NORTH VANCOUVER, WEST VANCOUVER, SOUTH VANCOUVER AND POINT GREY, COMPRISING A COMPLETE STREET AND AVENUE DIRECTORY OF THE CITY... – Vancouver: Henderson Publishing Co, 1918 – 1r – 1 – cn U.B.C. Preserve [910]
HENDERSON'S GREATER VANCOUVER CITY DIRECTORY, 1919 : EMBRACING THE AREA OF GREATER VANCOUVER, COVERING THE CITY PROPER, NORTH VANCOUVER, WEST VANCOUVER, SOUTH VANCOUVER AND POINT GREY, COMPRISING A COMPLETE STREET AND AVENUE DIRECTORY OF THE CITY... – Vancouver: Henderson Publishing Co, 1919 – 1r – 1 – cn U.B.C. Preserve [910]
HENDERSON'S GREATER VANCOUVER CITY DIRECTORY FOR 1913 : EMBRACING THE AREA OF GREATER VANCOUVER, COVERING THE CITY PROPER, NORTH VANCOUVER, POINT GREY, SOUTH VANCOUVER, NEW WESTMINSTER AND FRASER VALLEY DISTRICT,... – Vancouver: Henderson Publishing Co, 1913 – 2r – 1 – cn U.B.C. Preserve [910]
HENDERSON'S GREATER VANCOUVER, NEW WESTMINSTER AND FRASER VALLEY DIRECTORY, 1911 : COMPRISING AN IMPROVED STREET AND AVENUE GUIDE,... – Vancouver: Henderson Publishing Co, 1911 – 2r – 1 – cn U.B.C. Preserve [910]
HENDERSON'S GREATER VANCOUVER, NEW WESTMINSTER AND FRASER VALLEY DIRECTORY, 1912 : COMPRISING AN IMPROVED STREET AND AVENUE GUIDE,... – Vancouver: Henderson Publishing Co, 1912 – 2r – 1 – cn U.B.C. Preserve [910]
HENDERSON'S GREATER VICTORIA CITY AND VANCOUVER ISLAND GAZETTEER AND DIRECTORY 1910-1911 : INCLUDING A COMPLETE CLASSIFIED BUSINESS DIRECTORY – Victoria, BC: Henderson Publishing Co, 1911 – 1r – 1 – cn U.B.C. Preserve [910]
HENDERSON'S GREATER VICTORIA CITY DIRECTORY, 1917 : COMPRISING A COMPLETE STREET AND AVENUE DIRECTORY OF THE CITY,... – Victoria, B.C.: Henderson Publishing Co, 1917 – 1r – 1 – cn U.B.C. Preserve [910]
HENDERSON'S GREATER VICTORIA CITY DIRECTORY, 1918 : COMPRISING A COMPLETE STREET AND AVENUE DIRECTORY OF THE CITY,... – Victoria, B.C.: Henderson Publishing Co, 1918 – 1r – 1 – cn U.B.C. Preserve [910]
HENDERSON'S GREATER VICTORIA CITY DIRECTORY AND VANCOUVER ISLAND GAZETTEER, 1912 : INCLUDING A COMPLETE BUSINESS DIRECTORY – Victoria, BC: Henderson Publishing Co, 1912 – 1r – 1 – cn U.B.C. Preserve [910]
HENDERSON'S GREATER VICTORIA CITY DIRECTORY AND VANCOUVER ISLAND GAZETTEER, 1913 : INCLUDING A COMPLETE CLASSIFIED BUSINESS DIRECTORY – Victoria, BC: Henderson Publishing Co, 1913 – 1r – 1 – cn U.B.C. Preserve [910]
HENDERSON'S GREATER VICTORIA CITY DIRECTORY AND VANCOUVER ISLAND GAZETTEER, 1914 : INCLUDING A COMPLETE CLASSIFIED BUSINESS DIRECTORY – Victoria: Henderson Publishing Co, 1914 – 1r – 1 – cn U.B.C. Preserve [910]
HENDERSON'S GREATER VICTORIA CITY DIRECTORY AND VANCOUVER ISLAND GAZETTEER, 1915 : INCLUDING A COMPLETE CLASSIFIED BUSINESS DIRECTORY – Victoria, B.C.: Henderson Publishing Co, 1915 – 1r – 1 – cn U.B.C. Preserve [910]
HENDERSON'S KAMLOOPS CITY DIRECTORY FOR 1914 : COMPRISING A STREET AND AVENUE DIRECTORY OF THE CITY, AN ALPHABETICALLY ARRANGED LIST OF BUSINESS FIRMS AND COMPANIES, PROFESSIONAL MEN AND PRIVATE CITIZENS, AND A COMPLETE CLASSIFIED BUSINESS DIRECTORY – Vancouver: Henderson Directory Co, 1914 – 1r – 1 – cn U.B.C. Preserve [910]
HENDERSON'S PRINCE RUPERT CITY DIRECTORY, 1910-1911 : COMPRISING AN ALPHABETICALLY ARRANGED LIST OF BUSINESS FIRMS AND COMPANIES, PROFESSIONAL MEN AND PRIVATE CITIZENS, AND A CLASSIFIED BUSINESS DIRECTORY,... – Vancouver: Henderson Publishing Co, 1910 – 1r – 1 – cn U.B.C. Preserve [910]
HENDERSON'S PRINCE RUPERT CITY DIRECTORY FOR 1913 : COMPRISING STREET DIRECTORY OF THE CITY, AN ALPHABETICALLY ARRANGED LIST OF BUSINESS FIRMS AND COMPANIES, PROFESSIONAL MEN AND PRIVATE CITIZENS, AND A CLASSIFIED BUSINESS DIRECTORY – Vancouver: Henderson Publishing Co, 1913 – 1r – 1 – cn U.B.C. Preserve [910]
HENDERSON'S PRINCE RUPERT CITY DIRECTORY FOR 1914 : COMPRISING AN ALPHABETICALLY ARRANGED LIST OF BUSINESS FIRMS AND COMPANIES, PROFESSIONAL MEN AND PRIVATE CITIZENS,... – Vancouver: Henderson Publishing Co, 1914 – 1r – 1 – cn U.B.C. Preserve [910]
HENDON AND FINCHLEY TIMES *see* HENDON TIMES
HENDON COURIER – London, England. 10 Feb 1887-Dec 1897 – 10r – 1 – uk British Libr Newspaper [072]
HENDON HEALTH BOOKS AND SANITARY INSPECTORS JOURNAL 1900-52 – 1 – uk Microform Academic [610]
HENDON RATE BOOKS, 1837-90 – 1 – uk Microform Academic [941]
HENDON TIMES – London, Oct 1876-94;: 1898-Nov 1964; 1966- – 218+ r – 1 – uk British Libr Newspaper [072]
HENDON-EDGWARE INDEPENDENT – London, UK. 9 Apr 1983 – 2r – 1 – uk British Libr Newspaper [072]
HENDRICK GOLTZIUS ALS MALER, 1600-1617 / Hirschmann, O – O 518 – 9 – ne IDC [750]
Hendrickson, Thomas L *see* THE PHYSIOLOGICAL RESPONSES TO WALKING WITH AND WITHOUT POWER POLES(TM) ON TREADMILL EXERCISE
Hendrickson, William R *see* THE EFFECTS OF RECOVERY TIME ON THROWING VELOCITY AND ACCURACY OF COLLEGE BASEBALL PITCHERS
HENDRIK MANDE, BIJDRAGE TOT DE KENNIS DER NOORD-NEDERLANDSCHE MYSTIEK / Visser, G – 's-Gravenhage, 1899 – 4mf – 8 – ne Slangenburg [290]
Hendriks, Lawrence *see* THE LONDON CHARTERHOUSE, ITS MONKS AND ITS MARTYRS.
Hendrix, Eugene Russell *see* THE RELIGION OF THE INCARNATION DELIVERED BEFORE THE VANDERBILT UNIVERSITY
HENDRY COUNTY NEWS – La Belle. Fl. -w. 1938-41, 1945-72. Name change: Caloosa Belle. 1972- – 1 – us P.K. Yonge [071]
HENEPIN LAWYER – (Lacking: v1-8. v43 no 6. v47. Updates planned) – v1-48. 1932-78 – 85mf – 9 – $127.00 – LLMC 84-479 – us L.L.M.C. [073]
Henfrey, A *see* BOTANICAL AND PHYSIOLOGICAL MEMOIRS
Hengard-Lapalice, Ovide Michel *see* HISTOIRE DE LA SEIGNEURIE MASSUE ET DE LA PAROISSE DE SAINT-AIME
Hengel, Wessel Albertus van *see* DE TESTAMENTEN DER TWAALF PATRIARCHEN

HENGFENG SHACHANG DE FASHENG FAZHAN YU GAIZHAO (SHANGHAI ZIBENZHUYI DIANXING QIYE SHILIAO) – Historical Materials on Typical Bourgeois Enterprises in Shanghai: The Rise, Development and Transformation of the Hengfeng Cotton Mill. Comp. by the Institute of Economics, Shanghai Academy of Social Sciences. 2 fiches. F H173 – 9 – 4.00f – cc Microforms [330]
HENGST MAESTOSO AUSTRIA : LIEBESGESCHICHTE ZWEIER MENSCHEN UND EINES EDLEN PFERDES / Lehmann, Arthur Heinz – Dresden: W Heyne, 1939 – 1r – 1 – us U.W. Library [830]
Henke, E LT *see* SCHLEIERMACHER UND DIE UNION
Henke, Ernst Ludwig Theodor *see*
- DR. E.L.TH. HENKE'S NACHGELASSENE VORLESUNGEN UEBER LITURGIK UND HOMILETIK
- JAKOB FRIEDRICH FRIES
- THEOLOGORUM SAXONICORUM CONSENSUS REPETITUS FIDEI VERE LUTHERANAE

Henke, Frederick Goodrich *see* A STUDY IN THE PSYCHOLOGY OF RITUALISM
Henke, Heinz-Werner *see* MESSUNG DER DESINTEGRATIONSLEISTUNG DES HOLMIUM-YAG-LASERS IN HINBLICK AUF DEN EINSATZ IN DER LITHOTRIPSIE
HENLEY AND SOUTH OXFORDSHIRE STANDARD *see* HENLEY FREE PRESS
HENLEY CHRONICLE *see* HENLEY CHRONICLE AND SOUTH OXFORDSHIRE GAZETTE
HENLEY CHRONICLE AND SOUTH OXFORDSHIRE GAZETTE – Henley, South Oxfordshire, England. 1904-11 – 7r – 1 – uk British Libr Newspaper [072]
HENLEY FREE PRESS – (1886, 1889, 1890 imperfect) – England, 21 Feb 1885-17 Jul 1886; Jan 1889- – 106+ r – 1 – uk British Libr Newspaper [072]
Henley, John *see* THE COMPLEAT LINGUIST
Henley, Robert Henley Eden *see*
- A COMPENDIUM OF THE LAW AND PRACTICE OF INJUNCTIONS, AND OF INTERLOCUTORY ORDERS IN THE NATURE OF INJUNCTIONS
- A TREATISE ON THE LAW OF INJUNCTIONS

HENLEY STANDARD *see* HENLEY FREE PRESS
Henley, William Ernest *see*
- A BOOK OF VERSES
- HAWTHORN AND LAVENDER
- LONDON VOLUNTARIES
- THE POETRY OF ROBERT BURNS
- VIEWS AND REVIEWS

Henne am Rhyn, Otto *see* ANTI-ZARATHUSTRA
Henneberger, August *see* BRIEFE VON JOHANN PETER UZ AN EINEN FREUND
Hennecke, E *see* DEI APOLOGIE DES ARISTIDES (T.U.U. 1-4/3)
Hennecke, Edgar *see*
- ALTCHRISTLICHE MALEREI UND ALTKIRCHLICHE LITERATUR
- DIE APOLOGIE DES ARISTIDES

Henneguy, LF *see* LES INSECTES: MORPHOLOGIE, REPRODUCTION, EMBRYOGENIE
HENNEPIN LAWYER – v9-64. 1940-95 – 9 – $355.00 set – us Hein [340]
Hennepin, Louis *see* VOYAGE CURIEUX DU R. P. LOUIS HENNEPIN
Hennequin, Amedee *see* DE L'ORGANISATION DE LA STATISTIQUE DU TRAVAIL ET DU PLACEMENT DES OUVRIERS
Hennessey *see* BENCH AND BAR OF ILLINOIS - 1920
Hennessy, Joseph Patrick *see* A LEADING CASE AS TO HOTEL-KEEPERS AND GUESTS; A SUMMARIZED OPINION WITH DECISION OF THE COURT OF APPEALS OF THE STATE OF NEW YORK
Hennessy, W M *see*
- ANNALS OF LOCH CE (RS54)
- CHRONICON SCOTORUM (RS46)

Hennesy, William M *see* ANNALS OF ULSTER OTHERWISE ANNALS OF SENAT
Hennig, M *see* QUELLENBUCH ZUR GESCHICHTE DER INNEREN MISSION
Henniker, Florence *see* IN SCARLET AND GREY
Henning *see* HISTORY OF SCHUYLKILL COUNTY
Henning, Hans *see* DIE DEUTSCHE LITERATUR
Henning, M *see* D. JOHANNES HINRICH WICHERNS LEBENSWERK IN SEINER BEDEUTUNG FUER DAS DEUTSCHE VOLK
Henning, W B *see* SOGDICA
Hennings, A *see* GEGENWAERTIGER ZUSTAND DER BESITZUNGEN DER EUROPAEER IN OSTINDIEN
Henningsen, Charles-Frederick *see* REVELATIONS SUR LA RUSSIE OU L'EMPEREUR NICOLAS ET SON EMPIRE EN 1844, PAR UN RESIDENT ANGLAIS
Henningsen, Emanuel *see* FRA LAALAND: NY FORTAELLINGER
HENOCH – 1979-87 (complete) – 4r – 1 – ATLA S0788 – us A.T.L.A. [073]
HENRI BANCAL, DEPUTE A LA CONVENTION, A ANACHARSIS CLOOTZ, SON COLLEGUE / Bancal Des Issarts, Jean Henri – Paris. Imprimerie du Cercle Social. 1793 – 9 – fr Hachette [321]
HENRI BATE DE MALINES : SPECULUM DIVINORUM ET QUORUNDAM NATURALIUM / Wallerand, G – (Etude critique et texte inedit) – 1931 – 9mf – 8 – ne Slangenburg [100]
HENRI DE GAND : ESSAY SUR LES TENDANCES DE SA METAPHYSIQUE / Paulus, J – Paris, 1938 – 11mf – 8 – ne Slangenburg [110]
HENRI DOMINIQUE LACORDAIRE : A BIOGRAPHICAL SKETCH / Lear, H L Sidney – London: Rivingtons, 1882 – 1mf – us A.T.L.A. [240]
Henri, Ernst *see* HITLER OVER RUSSIA?
HENRI HEINE : L'HOMME ET L'OEUVRE / Bianquis, Genevieve – (Includes bibliographical references) – Paris: Boivin, c1948 – 1 – us U.W. Library [430]
HENRI MICHAUX / Reunion des musees nationaux. Paris – 1965. 12 illus. 1 fiche – 9 – fr Réunion [700]
[HENRI PETAIN PAMPHLET COLLECTION] – 1940-1980 – 1 reel – 1 – CSUXANQ4904-B – us Hoover Inst Photo [320]
LA HENRIADE / Chateau-Lyon, PL d'Aquin de – Avec la reponse de M. B.2121 a chacune des principales objections. et plusieurs autres morceaux curieux relatifs a Voltaire. Berlin. Paris. J. Fr. Bastien. 1780. XXIV – 9 – fr Hachette [920]
Henrich, Manuel *see* ICONOGRAFIA DE LAS EDITIONES DEL QUIJOTE DE MIGUEL CERVANTES SAAVEDRA
Henrich, Timothy W *see* INFLUENCE OF REACTIVE HYPEREMIA IN MUSCLE DURING EXERCISE
Henrichs, Norbert *see* BRIEFE DEUTSCHER PHILOSOPHEN (1750-1850)
HENRICI BARYPHONI PLEJADES MUSICAE QUAE FUNDAMENTA MUSICAE THEORETICAE EX PRINCIPIIS MATHEMATICIS QUA / Baryphonus, H – P-153. 1630 – 9 – ne IDC [780]
Henrici de Blaneforde *see* CHRONICA ET ANNALES 1259-1296, 1307-1324, 1392-1406 (CHRONIA..3)
HENRICI DE BRACTON DE LEGIBUS ET CONSUETUDINES ANGLIAE LIBRI QUINQUE IN VARIOS TRACTATUS DISTINCTI (RS70) / Henry de Bracton; ed by Twiss, Travers – (v1 1878 Dfl49.00. v2 1879 v3 1880 v4 1881 Dfl46.00v. v5 1882 Dfl39.00. v6 1883 Dfl42.00) – ne Slangenburg [240]
HENRICI HUNTENDUNIENSIS HISTORIA ANGLORUM (RS74) = THE HISTORY OF THE ENGLISH BY HENRY, ARCHDEACON OF HUNTINGDON : FROM B C 55 TO A D 1154. IN EIGHT BOOKS / Henry Of Huntingdon; ed by Arnold, T – 1879 – Dfl30.00 – ne Slangenburg [941]
Henrick Alewijnsz *see*
- VEEL SCHOONE GRONDIGE LEERINGEN WT DES HEEREN WOORT

HENRICO HERALD – Richmond. Va. -w. 1939-46, 1956- – 1 – us UMI [071]
Henricus A Gandovo *see* SUMMA THEOLOGICA
Henricus, Magister Gorichem *see* TEXTUS SENTENTIALE PETRI LOMBARDI CUM CONCLUSIONIBUS MAGISTRI HENRICI GORICHEM
Henries, A Doris B *see*
- LIBERIAN EDUCATION
- WRITINGS OF A. DORIS B. HENRIES

Henriet, MO *see* COMMUNAUTE VILLAGEOISE ET HABITAT RURAL A GOZO
HENRIK IBSEN, EIN ERLEBNIS DER DEUTSCHEN / Thalmann, Marianne – (Includes bibliographical references) – Marburg a.L.: N G Elwert, 1928 – 1r – 1 – us U.W. Library [430]
HENRIK IBSENS EINFLUSS AUF HERMANN SUDERMANN / Juergensen, Hans – [Lausanne: s.n. 1903] – 1r – 1 – us U.W. Library [410]
HENRIK STEFFENS : EIN LEBENSBILD / Petersen, Richard – Gotha: F A Perthes, 1884 – 1r – 1 – us U.W. Library [920]
HENRIK STEFFENS ROMANE : EIN BEITRAG ZUR GESCHICHTE DES HISTORISCHEN ROMANS / Karsen, Fritz – (Includes bibliographical references) – Leipzig: Quelle & Meyer, 1908 – 1 – us U.W. Library [430]
Henrion, C *see* LA NATION ET LE DROIT DES GENS
Henriot, Constant *see* LES ORDRES RELIGIEUX AU POINT DE VUE SOCIAL: LECTURE...AU CERCLE VILLE-MARIE DE MONTREAL
Henriquez, Chrysostomus *see*
- FASCICULUS SANCTORUM ORDINIS CISTERCIENSIS
- MENOLOGIUM CISTERCIENSIS
- PHOENIX REVIVISCENS. LIBRI 2
- QUINQUE PRUDENTES VIRGINES
- REGULA, CONSTITUTIONES ET PRIVILEGIA ORDINIS CISTERCIENSIS

HENRY 8 / Pollard, AF – London, New York: Longmans, Green, 1905 – 2mf – us A.T.L.A. [941]
HENRY 8 AND THE ENGLISH MONASTERIES : AN ATTEMPT TO ILLUSTRATE THE HISTORY OF THEIR SUPPRESSION / Gasquet, Francis Aidan – London: John Hodges, 1888-1889. (The Catholic standard library) – 3mf – us A.T.L.A. [944]
Henry 8, King *see* ASSERTIO SEPTEM SACRAMENTORUM, OR, DEFENCE OF THE SEVEN SACRAMENTS
HENRY A. WALLACE PAPERS / Wallace, Henry Agard – 69r – 1 – $5025.00 – us UMI [920]
HENRY ADAMS PAPERS, 1843-1938 / Adams, Henry – Massachusetts Historical Society – 36r – 1 – $2715.00 – us UMI [920]
HENRY BANKES'S TREATISE ON LITHOGRAPHY / Bankes, Henry – London: Printing Historical Society. 1976. Reprinted from the 1813 and 1816 editions. 1 reel – 1 – us U.W. Library [760]
HENRY BARROW, SEPARATIST (1550?-1593), AND THE EXILED CHURCH OF AMSTERDAM (1593-1622) / Powicke, F J – London: J. Clarke, 1900 – 1mf – us A.T.L.A. [320]
HENRY BAZELY : THE OXFORD EVANGELIST: A MEMOIR / Hicks, E L – London: Macmillan, 1886 – 1mf – us A.T.L.A. [240]
Henry, Benjamin Couch *see*
- THE CROSS AND THE DRAGON
- LING-NAM

HENRY BRADSHAW SOCIETY – London. v1-94. 1891-1963 – 445mf – 9 – Dfl1,568.00 – ne IDC [941]
HENRY BRADSHAW SOCIETY, VOL 1 *see* MISSALE AD USUM ECCLESIAE WESTMONASTERIENSIS. FASC. 1
HENRY BRADSHAW SOCIETY, VOL 2 *see* THE MANNER OF CORONATION OF KING CHARLES 1 OF ENGLAND AT WESTMINISTER, 2 FEBR. 1626
HENRY BRADSHAW SOCIETY, VOL 3 *see* THE MARTILOGE IN ENGLYSSHE AFTER THE USE OF THE CHURCH OF SALISBURY AND AS IT REDDE IN SYON. WITH ADDICYONS
HENRY BRADSHAW SOCIETY, VOL 4 *see* THE ANTIPHONARY OF BANGOR
HENRY BRADSHAW SOCIETY, VOL 6 *see* OFFICIUM ECCLESIASTICUM ABBATUM SECUNDUM USUM EVESHAMENSIS MONASTERII
HENRY BRADSHAW SOCIETY, VOL 7 *see* THE TRACTS OF CLEMENT MAYDESTON WITH THE REMAINS OF CAXTON'S ORDINALE
HENRY BRADSHAW SOCIETY, VOL 8 *see* THE WINCHESTER TROPER, FROM MSS OF THE 10TH AND 11TH CENTURIES, WITH OTHER DOC. ILL. THE HISTORY OF TROPES IN ENGLAND AND FRANCE
HENRY BRADSHAW SOCIETY, VOL 9 *see* THE MARTYROLOGY OF GORMAN
HENRY BRADSHAW SOCIETY, VOL 10 *see* THE ANTIPHONARY OF BANGOR: PART 2
HENRY BRADSHAW SOCIETY, VOL 11 *see* THE MISSAL OF ROBERT OF JUMIEGES
HENRY BRADSHAW SOCIETY, VOL 12 *see* MISSALE AD USUM ECCLESIAE WESTMONASTERIENSIS: FAC. 3
HENRY BRADSHAW SOCIETY, VOL 13 AND 14 *see* THE IRISH LIBER HYMNORUM
HENRY BRADSHAW SOCIETY, VOL 15 *see* THE ROSSLYN MISSAL
HENRY BRADSHAW SOCIETY, VOL 16 *see* CORONATION BOOK OF CHARLES 5 OF FRANCE
HENRY BRADSHAW SOCIETY, VOL 17 *see* MISSALE ROMANUM MEDIOLANI 1474, VOL 1
HENRY BRADSHAW SOCIETY, VOL 18 *see* THE PROCESSIONAL OF THE NUNS OF CHESTER
HENRY BRADSHAW SOCIETY, VOL 19 *see* THREE CORONATION ORDERS
HENRY BRADSHAW SOCIETY, VOL 20 AND 22 *see* ORDINALE SARUM SIVE DIRECCTORIUM SACERDOTUM LIBER
HENRY BRADSHAW SOCIETY, VOL 21 *see* FACSIMILES OF HORAE DE B.M.V. 11TH CENTURY
HENRY BRADSHAW SOCIETY, VOL 23 *see* CUSTOMARY OF THE BENEDICTINE MONASTERIES OF ST AUGUSTINE, CANTERBURY AND ST PETER, WESTMINSTER, VOL 1
HENRY BRADSHAW SOCIETY, VOL 24 *see* THE BENEDICTIONAL OF ARCHBISHOP ROBERT
HENRY BRADSHAW SOCIETY, VOL 25 *see* THE CLERC'S BOOK OF 1549
HENRY BRADSHAW SOCIETY, VOL 26 *see* THE HEREFORD BREVIARY, VOL. 1
HENRY BRADSHAW SOCIETY, VOL 28 *see* CUSTOMARY OF THE BENEDICTINE MONASTERIES OF ST AUGUSTINE, CANTERBURY AND ST PETER, WESTMINSTER, VOL. 2
HENRY BRADSHAW SOCIETY, VOL 33 *see* MISSALE ROMANUM MEDIOLANI 1474, VOL 2
Henry, Caroline Vinton *see* PERSONAL REMINISCENCES OF CARDINAL NEWMAN
HENRY CLAY / Schurz, Carl – Boston & NY: Houghton, Mifflin & Co. 2v. 1899 – 11mf – 9 – $16.50 – LLMC 96-026 – us L.L.M.C. [975]
THE HENRY CLAY FAMILY PAPERS – 23r – 1 – $805.00 – Dist. us Scholarly Res – us L of C Photodup [975]
HENRY CLOETE IN NATAL, 1843-1855 / Flanagan, Brigid – Durban, 1946 – us Res Libr [920]
HENRY COUNTY JOURNAL – Bassett. Va. -w. 1947-54, 1956- – 1 – us UMI [071]
Henry County. Ohio. Auditor *see* ENUMERATIONS OF DEAF, DUMB, ETC
Henry County. Ohio. Board of County Commissioners *see*
- COMMISSIONERS' JOURNALS
- INDEX TO JOURNALS
- JOURNALS, COUNTY HOME

Henry County. Ohio. Common Pleas. Civil Division *see*
- COMPLETE RECORDS
- INDEX TO COMPLETE RECORDS
- INDEX TO JOURNALS
- JOURNALS
- NATURALIZATION RECORDS
- NATURALIZATIONS, DECLARATIONS

Henry County. Ohio. District Court *see*
- CHANCERY RECORDS
- COMPLETE RECORDS
- JOURNALS

Henry County. Ohio. Recorder *see*
- CEMETERY DEED RECORDS
- CORPORATION RECORDS
- DEED RECORDS
- INDEX TO MISCELLANEOUS RECORDS
- INDEX TO MORTGAGE RECORDS
- MORTGAGE RECORDS
- SOLDIERS' DISCHARGE RECORDS
- SOLDIERS' GRAVE RECORDS

Henry County. Ohio. Supreme Court *see*
- COMPLETE RECORDS
- JOURNALS

HENRY COUNTY REVIEW – Holgate, Ohio. 1894-1982 – 32r – 1 – $32.50r – us Archival [071]
HENRY COUNTY SIGNAL – Napoleon, Ohio. 1881-1973 – 85r – 1 – $32.50r – us Archival [071]
HENRY CRABB ROBINSON DIARIES, TRAVEL JOURNALS AND REMINISCENCES 1790-1867 / Dr. Williams's Library – 11r – 1 – £450.00 – 1-897955-19-7 – uk Academic [090]
Henry de Bracton *see* HENRICI DE BRACTON DE LEGIBUS ET CONSUETUDINES ANGLIAE LIBRI QUINQUE IN VARIOS TRACTATUS DISTINCTI (RS70)
HENRY DE MARSAN'S NEW COMIC AND SENTIMENTAL SINGERS JOURNAL – New York, 1868-82 – 1 – £60.00 – uk Chadwyck [780]
HENRY DE POMEROY / Bray, Anna Eliza – British Fiction Archive: Unit 2 – 9 – uk Bell [830]
HENRY DISPATCH – Henry, NE. -w. Nov 1920-Sept 1921 – 1 – us NE Hist [071]

THE HENRY DREYFUSS ARCHIVE : DRAWINGS, DESIGNS AND DOCUMENTS / The Henry Dreyfuss Archive. New York – (Leading American industrial designer of 20th C. Over 6,000 reproductions. Fully indexed) – 100mf – 9 – $575.00 – 0-907006-58-2 – uk Mindata [740]
The Henry Dreyfuss Archive. New York *see* THE HENRY DREYFUSS ARCHIVE
HENRY DUNBAR: THE STORY OF AN OUTCAST / Braddon, Mary Elizabeth – British Fiction Archive: Unit 5 – 9 – uk Bell [830]
HENRY E. SHEFFIELD ACCOUNT BOOK *see* SHEFFIELD, HENRY E., ACCOUNT BOOK
HENRY FOTHERGILL CHORLEY : AUTOBIOGRAPHY, MEMOIR, AND LETTERS / Hewlett, Henry Gay – London: Richard Bentley and Son, 1873 – 1 roll – 1 – 1-55879-159-0 – uk Libr Preservation [920]
Henry, G W *see* SHOUTING, GENUINE AND SPURIOUS
Henry, George Adams *see* THE PROBATE LAW AND PRACTICE AND THE LAWS OF SUCCESSION OF THE STATE OF INDIANA.
HENRY HART MILMAN, D.D. : DEAN OF ST. PAUL'S: A BIOGRAPHICAL SKETCH / Milman, Arthur – London: J. Murray, 1900 – 1mf – us A.T.L.A. [240]
Henry, Hugh Thomas *see* POEMS, CHARADES, INSCRIPTIONS OF POPE LEO 13
HENRY IRVING, ACTOR AND MANAGER : A CRITICAL STUDY / Archer, William – London: Field & Tuer, Ye Leadenhalle Presse, E.C.; Simpkin, Marshall; Hamilton, Adams, [1883?] – 1 roll – 1 – 1-55879-952-4 – uk Libr Preservation [790]
HENRY IRVING'S IMPRESSIONS OF AMERICA: NARRATED IN A SERIES OF SKETCHES, CHRONICLES AND CONVERSATIONS / Hatton, Joseph – Boston: J.R. Osgood, 1884. 05513. (Pre-1900 Canadiana) – 9 – cn C.I.H.M. [970]
[HENRY IV] OUVERTURE ET ENTR'ACTE D'. ARR. CLAVECIN OU LE PIANO-FORTE AVEC ACCOMPAGNEMANET DE VIOLON PAR M. CESAR / Martini, J -P – (Piano part only) – Paris: boyer, 179- – 1 – us Sibley [780]
HENRY J. BOLLERS FORTEPIANO BOOK / Bollers, H J – 1815 – 9 – us Sibley [780]
Henry, Jos *see* L'AME D'UN PEUPLE AFRICAIN, LES BAMABARA, LEUR VIE PSYCHIQUE, ETHIQUE, SOCIALE, RELIGIEUSE
Henry Knighton *see* CHRONICON HENRICI KNIGHTON, VEL CNITTHON, MONACHI LEYCESTRENSIS (RS92)
HENRY KNOX PAPERS, 1719-1825 / Knox, Henry – New England Historic Genealogical Society; Massachusetts Historical Society – 55r – 1 – $4150.00 – us UMI [920]
HENRY LAURENS PAPERS / Laurens, Henri – (1747-1792) – 13r – 1 – $1405.00 – us UMI [920]
HENRY M. WHEELER – Collection of glass photographic plates – 1 reel – 1 – us UMI [920]
HENRY M. WHEELER COLLECTION OF GLASS PHOTOGRAPHIC PLATES – (Photographs of historic sites, monuments, and historic buildings in Massachusetts) – Massachusetts Historical Society – 1r – 1 – $85.00 – us UMI [720]
Henry, Marc *see* BEYOND THE RHINE: MEMORIES OF ART AND LIFE IN GERMANY BEFORE THE WAR
HENRY MARTYN / Bell, Charles Dent – New York: A C Armstrong, 1881 – 1mf – 9 – 0-8370-6564-X – 1986-0564 – us A.T.L.A. [920]
HENRY MARTYN : HIS LIFE AND LABOURS, CAMBRIDGE-INDIA-PERSIA / Page, Jesse – New York: Fleming H Revell, [189-?] – 1mf – 9 – 0-8370-6292-6 – 1985-0292 – us A.T.L.A. [920]
HENRY MARTYN : SAINT AND SCHOLAR: FIRST MODERN MISSIONARY TO THE MOHAMMEDANS 1781-1812 / Smith, George Adam – New York: F.H. Revell, [1892?] – 2mf – us A.T.L.A. [240]
HENRY MELCHIOR MUHLENBERG : PATRIARCH OF THE LUTHERAN CHURCH IN AMERICA / Frick, William K – Philadelphia: Lutheran Publication Society, c1902. (Lutheran handbook series) – 1mf – us A.T.L.A. [240]
HENRY MESSENGER – Henry, NE. -w. Jan-Jul 1920 – 1 – us NE Hist [071]
Henry, N *see* LES GOUVERNEMENTS DE FAIT...
Henry Of Huntingdon *see* HENRICI HUNTENDUNIENSIS HISTORIA ANGLORUM (RS74)
HENRY OF NAVARRE AND THE HUGUENOTS IN FRANCE / Willert, P F – New York: Putnam, 1893 – 2mf – us A.T.L.A. [944]
Henry, Paul-Marc *see* POVERTY, PROGRESS AND DEVELOPMENT
HENRY ROWE SCHOOLCRAFT PAPERS – L110023 – 69r – 1 – $2,415.00 – 1167-6 – us L of C Photodup [305]
HENRY SATER / Maclay, Walker – 1690-1754. Sater Genealogy. 1897. Historical sketch of Sater Baptist Church, 1742-1917 – 1 – 8.26 – us Baptist [920]
Henry Taylor and Co *see*
- COMPENDIUM OF HISTORY AND BIOGRAPHY OF CASS COUNTY
- COMPENDIUM OF HISTORY AND BIOGRAPHY OF LINN COUNTY
- COMPENDIUM OF HISTORY AND BIOGRAPHY OF THE CITY OF DETROIT AND WAYNE COUNTY
- GENERAL HISTORY OF MACON COUNTY
- GENERAL HISTORY OF SHELBY COUNTY

Henry the Minstrel *see* THE ACTIS AND DEIDIS OF SCHIR WILLIAM WALLACE
HENRY THE THIRD AND THE CHURCH : A STUDY OF HIS ECCLESIASTICAL POLICY AND OF THE RELATIONS BETWEEN ENGLAND AND ROME / Gasquet, Abbot – London: G. Bell, 1905 – 2mf – us A.T.L.A. [240]
HENRY VANDERBURGH PAPERS, MS 132 / Vanderburgh, Henry – 1777-1808. 1 reel – 1 – us Western Res [920]
Henry, Victor *see* A SHORT COMPARATIVE GRAMMAR OF ENGLISH AND GERMAN AS TRACED BACK TO THEIR COMMON ORIGIN AND CONTRASTED WITH THE CLASSICAL LANGUAGES
HENRY WARD BEECHER / Abbott, Lyman – Boston: Houghton, Mifflin, 1903 – 2mf – us A.T.L.A. [240]
HENRY WARD BEECHER : THE SHAKESPEARE OF THE PULPIT / Barrows, John Henry – New York: Funk & Wagnalls, 1893 – 2mf – us A.T.L.A. [240]
HENRY WHEATON, 1785-1848 / Baker, E F – Philadelphia, 1937 – 5mf – 9 – ILM-337/1 – ne IDC [340]
Henry, William Wirt *see* ADDRESS OF THE PRESIDENT, HON. WILLIAM WIRT HENRY, DELIVERED AT THE NINTH ANNUAL MEETING, HELD AT THE HOT SPRINGS OF VIRGINIA, AUGUST 3, 4 AND 5, 1897
Henschel, A W E Th *see* JANUS
Henschenius, G *see* ACTA SANCTORUM
Hensel, Sebastian *see* DIE FAMILIE MENDELSSOHN 1729-1847
Henselt, A *see* TRIO IN A MOLL FUER PIANOFORTE, VIOLINE UND VIOLONCELLO, OP. 24
Henshaw, Julia Wilmotte *see* HYPNOTIZED?, OR, THE EXPERIMENT OF SIR HUGH GALBRAITH: A ROMANCE
Henslow, George *see*
- CHRISTIAN BELIEFS RECONSIDERED IN THE LIGHT OF MODERN THOUGHT
- PRESENT-DAY RATIONALISM CRITICALLY EXAMINED
- THE VULGATE

Henslow, George et al *see* CHRISTIAN APOLOGETICS
Henson, H Hensley *see*
- CHURCH PROBLEMS
- CROSS-BENCH VIEWS OF CURRENT CHURCH QUESTIONS
- GODLY UNION AND CONCORD
- THE LIBERTY OF PROPHESYING
- LIGHT AND LEAVEN
- MORAL DISCIPLINE IN THE CHRISTIAN CHURCH
- THE NATIONAL CHURCH
- NOTES OF MY MINISTRY
- NOTES ON POPULAR RATIONALISM
- PREACHING TO THE TIMES
- PURITANISM IN ENGLAND
- THE RELATION OF THE CHURCH OF ENGLAND TO THE OTHER REFORMED CHURCHES
- THE ROAD TO UNITY
- SINCERITY AND SUBSCRIPTION
- WAR-TIME SERMONS
- WESTMINSTER SERMONS

Henson, Hensley *see*
- APOSTOLIC CHRISTIANITY
- THE CREED IN THE PULPIT
- ECCLESIASTICA
- THE ISSUE OF KIKUYO
- REUNION AND INTERCOMMUNION
- STUDIES IN ENGLISH RELIGION IN THE SEVENTEENTH CENTURY

Henson, P S *see* MANUSCRIPTS OF 19 SERMONS DELIVERED AT FIRST BAPTIST CHURCH, CHICAGO, 1891
Hentisberus, Gulielmus *see* TRACTATUS GULIELMI HENTISBERI DE SENSU COPOSITO ET DIVISO
Hentsch, G F *see* EPITOME ENTOMOLOGIAE SYSTEMATICAE SECUNDUM FABRICIUM
Hentschel, Ute *see* SPRACHE, ERKENNTNIS UND HANDLUNG – "SPRACHINHALTSFORSCHUNG" UND "SPRACHPRAGMATIK" ALS EINANDER ERGAENZENDE WISSENSCHAFTEN
HENTY OBSERVER – Feb 21 1914-Aug 10 1917 – 9 – at Pascoe [072]
Hentz, John P *see* HISTORY OF THE LUTHERAN VERSION OF THE BIBLE
Henze, Wilhelm *see*
- ECK SEGGE MAN BLOSS
- IS DUET 'NE WELT!
- SAU SUIHSTE IUT!
- TAU'N LUSTIGEN STEEBEL
- WAT SEI ALLES MAKET!

Henzen, Wilhelm *see* MARTIN LUTHER
HEORTOLOGY : A HISTORY OF THE CHRISTIAN FESTIVALS FROM THEIR ORIGIN TO THE PRESENT DAY / Kellner, Karl Adam Heinrich – London: K. Paul, Trench, Truebner, 1908. (The International Catholic library; v7) – 2mf – us A.T.L.A. [240]
HEORTOLOGY SIC; A HISTORY OF THE CHRISTIAN FESTIVALS FROM THEIR ORIGIN TO THE PRESENT DAY / Kellner, Karl Adam Heinrich – Tr. from 2nd German ed. London: K. Paul, Trench, Truebner, 1908. xviii,466p – 1 – us U.W. Library [240]
DIE HEPATICAE DER FLORA VON BUITENZORG... / Schiffner, V – Leiden, 1900 – 3mf – 9 – 12,473/1 – ne IDC [580]
HEPATICAE EUROPAE / Dumortier, B C J – Jungermannieae Europae post semisculum recensitae, adjunctis Hepaticis. Bruxelles, Lipsiae. 1874. B-952 2 – 8 – ne IDC [580]
HEPATICOLOGIA GERMANICA / Huebener, J W P – Mannheim. 1834. B-2327 2 – 8 – ne IDC [580]
DIE HEPATISCHE DURCHBLUTUNG BEI HYPERTHERMIE : UNTERSUCHUNGEN IM UEBERWAERMUNGSBAD / Utsch, Sabine – Frankfurt a.M., 1984 – 1mf – 9 – DM48.00 – 3-89349-657-2 – gw Hänsel [616]
HEPATITIS C BEI HAEMODIALYSEPATIENTEN : EINE EINJAEHRIGE VERLAUFSSTUDIE AN HAEMODIALYSEPATIENTEN, NIERENTRANSPLANTIERTEN PATIENTEN UND DEM PERSONAL EINER DIALYSEKLINIK IN WUPPERTAL / Bock, Ulrich Manfred – 1995 – 1mf – 9 – DM60.00 – 3-8267-2145-4 – gw Hänsel [616]
HEPATO-GASTROENTEROLOGY *see* ACTA HEPATO-GASTROENTEROLOGICA
Hepner, Gerda *see* HELD OHNE NAMEN: EIN SCHICKSAL
Hepp, F *see* THEORIE GENERALE...
Hepp, Michael *see* SOZIALSTRATEGIEN DER DEUTSCHEN ARBEITSFRONT
Hepp, P *see* MIKROSKOPISCHE ABBILDUNGEN UND BESCHREIBUNGEN DER SPOREN DER EUROPAEISCHEN LICHENEN
Heppe, H *see*
- THE REFORMERS OF ENGLAND AND GERMANY IN THE SEXTEENTH CENTURY
- DAS SCHULWESEN DES MITTELALTERS UND DESSEN REFORM IM SECHSZEHNTEN JAHRHUNDERT

Heppe, Heinrich *see*
- DIE CONFESSIONELLE ENTWICKLUNG DER ALTPROTESTANTISCHEN KIRCHE DEUTSCHLANDS
- DIE ENTSTEHUNG UND FORTBILDUNG DES LUTHERTUMS UND DIE KIRCHLICHEN BEKENNTNISSCHRIFTEN DESSELBEN VON 1548-76
- GESCHICHTE DER QUIETISTISCHEN MYSTIK IN DER KATHOLISCHEN KIRCHE
- GESCHICHTE DES PIETISMUS UND DER MYSTIK IN DER REFORMIERTEN KIRCHE
- DIE PRESBYTERIALE SYNODALVERFASSUNG DER EVANGELISCHEN KIRCHE IN NORDDEUTSCHLAND
- THEODOR BEZA
- URSPRUNG UND GESCHICHTE DER BEZEICHNUNGEN "REFORMIERTE" UND "LUTHERISCHE" KIRCHE

Heppe, Robert A *see* THE KINEMATIC VARIABLES RELATED TO THE EFFICIENCY OF THROWING
Hepple, Alexander *see* PAPERS, 1937-1964
Heppner, A *see* AUS VERGANGENHEIT UND GEGENWART DER JUDEN. IN DEN POSENER LANDEN
HEPPNER GAZETTE – Heppner, OR. -w,-sw. 22 Jun 1883-28 Feb 1901. 4 rolls – 1 – us U.O. Library [071]
HEPPNER GAZETTE-TIMES – Heppner, OR. Incl. Heppner Gazette. -w, sw. 1901-51 – 1 – 384.00 – us Oregon Hist [071]
HEPPNER GAZETTE-TIMES – Heppner, OR. -w. 5 Jul 1951-. – 1 – us U.O. Library [071]
HEPPNER HERALD – Heppner, OR. -sw. 2 May 1914-15 Apr 1924. 2 rolls – 1 – us U.O. Library [071]
HEPPNER TIMES – Heppner, OR. -w. 26 Nov 1903-8 Dec 1904. 1 roll – 1 – us U.O. Library [071]
HEPTACHORDUM DANICUM SEU NOVA SOLSISATIO IN QUA MUSICAE PRACTICAE USUS / Corvinus, J M – Hafniae. 1646. BP-226 1 – 9 – ne IDC [780]
THE HEPTAMERON; OR TALES AND NOVELS OF MARGUERITE, QUEEN OF NAVARRE / Marguerite, Queen of Navarre – Trans. by Arthur Machen, with an introd.London: G. Routledge & Sons, New York: E.P. Dutton, 1911. xx,392p – 1 – us U.W. Library [830]
Heptonstall. Yorkshire *see* PARISH REGISTERS
HER CONVICT / Braddon, Mary Elizabeth – British Fiction Archive: Unit 5 – 9 – uk Bell [830]
HER HUSBAND IS DEAD. SHE MUST SAVE HER CHILDREN – NY, n.d. Fiche W 938. (Blodgett Collection of Spanish Civil War Pamphlets) – 9 – us H.U. College Libr [946]
HERACLITO : JORNAL SISUDO E SEMANAL – Rio de Janeiro, 8 Sep-26 Dec 1867 – 1,5,6 – bl Biblioteca [072]
HERACLIUS, VON DEN FARBEN UND KUNSTEN DER ROEMER / Ilg, Albert – O 517d. 1873 – 9 – ne IDC [930]
HERALD – Ada. Ohio. -w. 1949-60 – 1 – us UMI [071]
HERALD – Alliance. Neb. 1895-1922 – 1 – us UMI [071]
HERALD – and pred. Ainsworth. Neb. 1892-1901 – 1 – us UMI [071]
HERALD – and Pred. Circleville. Ohio. 1919- – 1 – us UMI [071]
HERALD – Anderson. Ind. 1952- – 1 – us UMI [071]
HERALD – Ashton. Neb. 1925-1934 – 1 – us UMI [071]
HERALD – Augusta. Ga. 1939- – 1 – us UMI [071]
HERALD – Aurora. Ill. 1871-86 – 1 – us UMI [071]
HERALD – Austin. Minn. 1896-1911; 1950- – 1 – us UMI [071]
HERALD – Azusa. Calif. 1928- – 1 – us UMI [071]
HERALD – Baltimore. Md. 1790-1804; 1875-1904 – 1 – us UMI [071]
HERALD – Barberton. Ohio. 1928-1932; 1934 – 1 – us UMI [071]
HERALD – Bayonne. N.J. and Greensville Register. 1869-1915 – 1 – us UMI [071]
HERALD – Bellingham. Wash. -d. 1904- – 1 – us UMI [071]
HERALD – Big Spring. Tex. 1921- – 1 – us UMI [071]
HERALD – Billings. Mont. 1882-1885; 1947-1951 – 1 – us UMI [071]
HERALD – Biloxi. Miss. -w. 1888-98 – 1 – us UMI [071]
HERALD – Bloomington. Iowa. 1841-1848 – 1 – us UMI [071]
HERALD – Boston. Mass. Morning. 1848-1858; 1860-1865; 1866-1869; 1870-1873; 1879; 1881-1936; 1939-1967 – 1 – us UMI [071]
HERALD – Bristol. Conn. 1888-1901 – 1 – us UMI [071]
HERALD – Cairo. Ill. 1915-16 – 1 – us UMI [071]
HERALD – Caliente. Nev. -w. 1949- – 1 – us UMI [071]
HERALD – Caliente, NV. 1928-68 – 20r – 1 – $1,000.00 – U04430 – us Library Micro [071]
HERALD – Cambridge. Ohio. 1901-1904 – 1 – us UMI [071]
HERALD – Carpinteria. Calif. -w. 1954-67 – 1 – us UMI [071]
HERALD – Charlottetown, Canada. 1864-71 – 2r – 1 – $136.00 – cn Library Assoc [971]
HERALD – Chetopa. Kan. 1876-1878 – 1 – us UMI [071]
HERALD – Cimarron. Kan. and Kansas Sod House. 1885-86 – 1 – us UMI [071]

HERALD – Cincinnati. Ohio. -w. 1961- – 1 – us UMI [071]

HERALD – Clearfield. Pa. 1912-1913 – 1 – us UMI [071]

HERALD – Clinton. Iowa. 1856-1868; 1870-1891; 1895; 1897; 1898-1899; 1900; 1901-1907 – 1 – us UMI [071]

HERALD – Clyde Park. Mont. 1910-1924 – 1 – us UMI [071]

HERALD – Coffee Creek. Mont. 1915-1923 – 1 – us UMI [071]

HERALD – Colusa, CA. 1916-32 – 18r – 1 – $810.00 – B02133 – us Library Micro [071]

HERALD – Crab Orchard. Neb. 1892-1936 – 1 – us UMI [071]

HERALD – Cranston. R.I. -w. 1936- – 1 – us UMI [071]

HERALD – Dayton. Ohio. 1878-1908; 1909-49 – 1 – us UMI [071]

HERALD – Dayton. Or. 1893-1906 – 1 – us UMI [071]

HERALD – Decatur. Ill. 1899-1907 – 1 – us UMI [071]

HERALD – Delphos. Ohio. 1869-70; 1894- – 1 – us UMI [071]

HERALD – Denison. Tex. 1875- – 1 – us UMI [071]

HERALD – Dillon. S.C. 1904-1939 – 1 – us UMI [071]

HERALD – Dixon. Ill. -w. 1868-69 – 1 – us UMI [071]

HERALD – Dunsmuir, CA. 1897-98 – 1r – 1 – $50.00 – B02185 – us Library Micro [071]

HERALD – Durham. N.C. 1901- – 1 – us UMI [071]

HERALD – Elk Creek. Neb. 1895-1910 – 1 – us UMI [071]

HERALD – Eureka, CA. Jan-May 1905; 1907-13. 3 rolls – 27r – 1 – $1,350.00 – B02216 – us Library Micro [071]

HERALD – Eureka. Kan. 1868-77 – 1 – us UMI [071]

HERALD – Everett. Wash. 1915, 1921- – 1 – us UMI [071]

HERALD – Everett. Wash. -w. 1892-96 – 1 – us UMI [071]

HERALD – Fairborn. Ohio. 1950- – 1 – us UMI [071]

HERALD – Fairfax. Va. 1923-30; 1935-45; 1950- – 1 – us UMI [071]

HERALD – Fairfield. Neb. 1895-1907 – 1 – us UMI [071]

HERALD – Fallon. Mont. 1916-1920 – 1 – us UMI [071]

HERALD – Farmville. Va. 1933-1944; 1967- – 1 – us UMI [071]

HERALD – Fincastle. Va. 1935-45; 1950- – 1 – us UMI [071]

HERALD – Florence. Kansas. 1876-1891 – 1 – us UMI [071]

HERALD – Fort Lauderdale. Fl. -w. 1919-23 – 1 – us UMI [071]

HERALD – Fort Scott. Kan. 1878-1885 – 1 – us UMI [071]

HERALD – Fromberg. Mont. 1954-1956 – 1 – us UMI [071]

HERALD – Galt. Calif. -w. 1912-66 – 1 – us UMI [071]

HERALD – Garden City. Kan. -w. 1883-1920 – 1 – us UMI [071]

HERALD – Geneva. Ind. 1894-1924; 1927-1940; 1942-1970 – 1 – us UMI [071]

HERALD – Gridley. Calif. -w. 1943-56 – 1 – us UMI [071]

HERALD – Hagerstown. Md. and Torchlight. 1891-95 – 1 – us UMI [071]

HERALD – Hagerstown. Md. and Torchlight. -W. 1865-1906 – 1 – us UMI [071]

HERALD – Halton Hills, 1916-1991 – 90r – 1 – cn Preston [971]

HERALD – Hamilton, 1907-1925 – 68r – 1 – cn Preston [971]

HERALD – Harare (Salisbury), Zimbabwe (Rhodesia). 1 Jan 1927- . Formerly 'Rhodesian Herald' – 441r – 1 – sa Microfile [960]

HERALD – Harper Woods. Mich. 1962- – 1 – us UMI [071]

HERALD – Harvard. Ill. 1887-1944; 1947-1966 – 1 – us UMI [071]

HERALD – Harvard. Ill. and Independent. 1937-44 – 1 – us UMI [071]

HERALD – Harvard. Ill. standard edition. -w. 1893-1966 – 1 – us UMI [071]

HERALD – Harvard. Ill. -w. 1888-92, 1967- – 1 – us UMI [071]

HERALD – Hebron. Ill. -w. 1960-67 – 1 – us UMI [071]

HERALD – Hillsboro. Kansas. 1886-1889 – 1 – us UMI [071]

HERALD – Hornsilver, NV. May-Sep 1908 – 1r – 1 – $50.00 – U04588 – us Library Micro [071]

HERALD – Hudson. Ohio. 1921-29 – 1 – us UMI [071]

HERALD – Huntington. Ind. 1891-1929 – 1 – us UMI [071]

HERALD – Huntington. West Virginia. 1903-1908 – 1 – us UMI [071]

HERALD – (July 1789-1990. 1795-7 and 1799 missing. 926r £27,000.00 set. £33.00r) – 24r per yr – 1 – £650.00y – uk Herald [072]

HERALD – Juniata. Neb. 1877-1917 – 1 – us UMI [071]

HERALD – Kearney. Neb. 1865 – 1 – us UMI [071]

HERALD – Kingston-upon-Thames, England. 1985 – 1 1/2r – 1 – uk British Libr Newspaper [072]

HERALD – Kiowa. Kan. 1884-1890 – 1 – us UMI [071]

HERALD – Lakin. Kan. 1881-1884 – 1 – us UMI [071]

HERALD – Leavenworth. Kan. -w. 1854-57 – 1 – us UMI [071]

HERALD – Lincoln. Neb. -w. 1890-1936 – 1 – us UMI [071]

HERALD – Lockridge. Iowa. 1909-1915 – 1 – us UMI [071]

HERALD – Mansfield. Ohio. -w. 1857-83 – 1 – us UMI [071]

HERALD – Marshfield. Wis. -w. 1911-27 – 1 – us UMI [071]

HERALD – Martinsburg. West Virginia. 1881-1913 – 1 – us UMI [071]

HERALD – Marysville, CA. 1850-58 – 5r – 1 – $250.00 – C02432 – us Library Micro [071]

HERALD – Marysville. Calif. -w. 1850-58 – 1 – us UMI [071]

HERALD – Merced, CA. 1867-1868 – 1r – 1 – $50.00 – B05042 – us Library Micro [071]

HERALD – Merrill. Wis. 1956-1968 – 1 – us UMI [071]

HERALD – Metropolis. Ill. 1906-1908; 1911-1917 – 1 – us UMI [071]

HERALD – Middletown. Ohio. -w. 1853-54 – 1 – us UMI [071]

HERALD – Milwaukee. Wis. -d. 1897-1929 – 1 – us UMI [071]

HERALD – Missoula. Mont. 1906-1911 – 1 – us UMI [071]

HERALD – Montgomery. West Virginia. 1951-1966 – 1 – us UMI [071]

HERALD – Montreal, 1874-1957 – 443r – 1 – cn Preston [971]

HERALD – Morris. Ill. 1957- – 1 – us UMI [071]

HERALD – Muncie. Ind. 1892-1905 – 1 – us UMI [071]

HERALD – Muscatine. Iowa. 1841-1848 – 1 – us UMI [071]

HERALD – Narragansett. R.I. 1876-1898 – 1 – us UMI [071]

HERALD – Neihart. Mont. 1891-1892 – 1 – us UMI [071]

HERALD – Newport. R.I. 1787-1790; 1892-1944 – 1 – us UMI [071]

HERALD – Olathe. Kan. -w. 1891-93 – 1 – us UMI [071]

HERALD – Omaha. Neb. 1867-69; 1871; 1873-1889 – 1 – us UMI [071]

HERALD – Omaha. Neb. -w. 1866-88 – 1 – us UMI [071]

HERALD – Ontonagon. Mich. 1894-1896 – 1 – us UMI [071]

HERALD – Ottawa. Kan. 1896- – 1 – us UMI [071]

HERALD – Ottawa. Kan. -w. 1889-1915 – 1 – us UMI [071]

HERALD – Overton. Neb. 1902-1915; 1918-1938 – 1 – us UMI [071]

HERALD – Palmetto, NV. 1906 (scattered issues) – 1r – 1 – $50.00 – U04638 – us Library Micro [071]

HERALD – Park Ridge. Ill. 1889-1922; 1929-1935; 1937-1949 – 1 – us UMI [071]

HERALD – Pasco. Wash. -w. 1918-47 – 1 – us UMI [071]

HERALD – Pascoag. R.I. 1892-1918 – 1 – us UMI [071]

HERALD – Pascoag. R.I. and Burrillville News Gazette. 1895-99 – 1 – us UMI [071]

HERALD – Passaic. N.J. 1902-1932 – 1 – us UMI [071]

HERALD – Phoenix. Ariz. 1879-99 – 1 – us UMI [071]

HERALD – Plainview. N.Y. -w. 1956-64 – 1 – us UMI [071]

HERALD – Plattsmouth. Neb. -w, sw. 1891-1912 – 1 – us UMI [071]

HERALD – Plentywood. Mont. 1958-1959; 1966- – 1 – us UMI [071]

HERALD – Port Gibson. Miss. and Correspondent. 1821-51 – 1 – us UMI [071]

HERALD – Port Huron. Mich. 1900-10 – 1 – us UMI [071]

HERALD – Portage. Mich. -w. 1958- – 1 – us UMI [071]

HERALD – Portland OR. Dec 23 1932 – 1 – us U.O. Library [071]

HERALD – Portsmouth. N.H. 1874-1875; 1885; 1898- – 1 – us UMI [071]

HERALD – Providence. R.I. 1879-1883; 1886-1887 – 1 – us UMI [071]

HERALD – Pullman. Wash. -w. 1888-1905, 1906- – 1 – us UMI [071]

HERALD – Rhyolite, NV. 1905-07; 1909-12 – 6r – 1 – $300.00 – U04731 – us Library Micro [071]

HERALD – Rutland. Vt. -w. 1792-1907 – 1 – us UMI [071]

HERALD – Saginaw. Mich. -w. 1880-82, 1889 – 1 – us UMI [071]

HERALD – Salem. West Virginia. -w. 1936- – 1 – us UMI [071]

HERALD – San Jose, CA. 1876-81; 1882-89; 1890-96; 1897-1900 – 32r – 1 – $1,600.00 – B02879 – us Library Micro [071]

HERALD – Sanford. Fl. 1918-22, May 1946-1980 – 1 – us P.K. Yonge [071]

HERALD – Sanford. N.C. 1931- – 1 – us UMI [071]

HERALD – Sharon. Pa. 1878- – 1 – us UMI [071]

HERALD – Sharpsburg. Pa. 1896-1968; 1972-1973 – 1 – us UMI [071]

HERALD – Shickley. Neb. 1895-1924 – 1 – us UMI [071]

HERALD – Sidney. Mont. 1966- – 1 – us UMI [071]

HERALD – Sikeston. Mo. 1916-1960 – 1 – us UMI [071]

HERALD – Southbridge. Mass. 1902-1929 – 1 – us UMI [071]

HERALD – Spartanburg. S.C. 1894-1903; 1950- – 1 – us UMI [071]

HERALD – St. Joseph. Mich. 1868-1872; 1874-1889 – 1 – us UMI [071]

HERALD – St. Joseph. Mo. 1865-1900 – 1 – us UMI [071]

HERALD – St. Joseph. Mo. -w. 1890, 1894-99 – 1 – us UMI [071]

HERALD – Steubenville. Ohio. -w. 1815-1916 – 1 – us UMI [071]

HERALD – Suffolk. Va. -w. 1900-01, 1925-26 – 1 – us UMI [071]

HERALD – Tacoma. Wash. -w. 1877-80, 1891-98, 1905-11, 1914-32 – 1 – us UMI [071]

HERALD – Three Forks. Mont. 1958-1959; 1966-1967 – 1 – us UMI [071]

HERALD – Three Rivers. Mich. 1881-1883 – 1 – us UMI [071]

HERALD – Titusville. Pa. 1865- – 1 – us UMI [071]

HERALD – Torrance. Calif. -w. 1960-64 – 1 – us UMI [071]

HERALD – Turners Falls. Mass. 1940-42 – 1 – us UMI [071]

HERALD – Tyrone. Pa. 1910-15; 1952- – 1 – us UMI [071]

HERALD – Vicksburg. Miss. 1906-1910; 1915-1925; 1946-1957 – 1 – us UMI [071]

HERALD – Wellsburg. West Virginia. -w. 1850-65, 1903-08 – 1 – us UMI [071]

HERALD – West Union. West Virginia. -w. 1959- – 1 – us UMI [071]

HERALD – Westerly. R.I. 1899-1901 – 1 – us UMI [071]

HERALD – Wheatland, CA. 1934-1935 – 1r – 1 – $45.00 – B03099 – us Library Micro [071]

HERALD – Wilmington. N.C. -w. 1851-53, 1857-58 – 1 – us UMI [071]

HERALD – Woodbury. N.J. and Gloucester FarmerAND Columbia Herald. 1819-24 – 1 – us UMI [071]

HERALD – Wyandotte. Kan. 1872-1910 – 1 – us UMI [071]

HERALD – Wyandotte. Mich. -bw. 1938-62 – 1 – us UMI [071]

HERALD – Wyandotte. Mich. -w. 1881, 1886-92, 1895-43 – 1 – us UMI [071]

HERALD – Yakima. Wash. -w. 1889-1905 – 1 – us UMI [071]

HERALD – Yazoo City. Miss. 1902-1937; 1945-1953 – 1 – us UMI [071]

HERALD – Yonkers. N.Y. 1891-1932 – 1 – us UMI [071]

HERALD *see* WELWYN GARDEN CITY HERALD AND POST

THE HERALD – Brockway. Mont. 1929-1930 – 1 – us UMI [071]

THE HERALD – (Cont. by: The Herald) – Livermore, CA. 1986-1987 – 18r – 1 – $900.00 – B03611 – us Library Micro [071]

THE HERALD – (Cont: The Fonetic Herald) – Toronto: [s.n. 1886-1913?] – 9 – cn C.I.H.M. [971]

THE HERALD – Franklin. West Virginia. 1930-1932 – 1 – us UMI [071]

THE HERALD – Freemantle, Australia. Feb 1867-Jul 1886 – 12r – 1 – uk British Libr Newspaper [072]

THE HERALD – Montreal. v143 n244. 6 aut 1954-7 jun 1957 – 1r – 1 – Can$50.00 – cn Can Microfilming [072]

THE HERALD – New Castle, PA., 1920-1923 – 13 – $25.00r – us I.M.R. [071]

THE HERALD – Piedmont. West Virginia. -w. 1890-1966 – 1 – us UMI [071]

THE HERALD – Punta Gorda. Fl. 1970- – 1 – us UMI [071]

THE HERALD – Rosco, CA. 1936-1938 – 1r – 1 – $50.00 – C03419 – us Library Micro [071]

THE HERALD – Salisbury [Harare, Zimbabwe]: Rhodesian Print & Pub Co, [aug 15, 1978-] – 1 – us Res Libr [072]

THE HERALD *see*
- DAILY HERALD
- THE FONETIC HERALD
- THE HERALD
- RICHMOND HERALD

THE HERALD – Blantyre: Midas Print & Pub, feb 16-jun 13, 29-jul 14 1994 – 1r – 1 – us Res Libr [071]

HERALD ADVOCATE – Wauchula. Fl. -w. 1955- – 1 – us P.K. Yonge [071]

HERALD AMERICAN – Compton. Calif. -w. 1960-62, 1963- – 1 – us UMI [071]

HERALD AMERICAN – Los Altos, CA. 1955-1956 – 6r – 1 – $300.00 – H04023 – us Library Micro [071]

THE HERALD AMERICAN – Compton, CA. 1960-72 – 67r – 1 – $3,350.00 – C02134 – us Library Micro [071]

HERALD AND CENTRAL NEVADAN – Battle Mountain, NV. 1907-11 – 1r – 1 – $50.00 – U04408 – us Library Micro [071]

HERALD AND MIRROR – Carlisle, PA., 1881 – 13 – $25.00r – us I.M.R. [071]

HERALD AND NEWS – Klamath Falls, OR. -d. 1 Jun 1942-. – 1 – us U.O. Library [071]

HERALD AND PLACER TIMES; SACRAMENTO TRANSCRIPT – Sacramento, CA. – 1 – $50.00 – B06007 – us Library Micro [071]

HERALD COURIER – Bristol. Va. and Sunday. 1952- – 1 – us UMI [071]

Y HERALD CYMRAEG – (Lacking: 1912) – Caernarvon, Wales. May 1855-Dec 1916 – 1 – uk British Libr Newspaper [072]

HERALD, DAILY REVIEW – Decatur. Ill. and Sunday Herald and Review. 1931- Filmed together – 1 – us UMI [071]

HERALD DISPATCH – Decatur. Ill. -sw. 1895-99 – 1 – us UMI [071]

HERALD DISPATCH – Decatur. Ill. -w. 1891-95 – 1 – us UMI [071]

HERALD DISPATCH – Huntington. West Virginia. 1909- – 1 – us UMI [071]

HERALD ENTERPRISE – (Also known as: News-Bulletin, Shipping News) – Bellflower, CA. 1926-1959 (Scats) – 42r – 1 – $2,100.00 – H03151 – us Library Micro [071]

HERALD EXAMINER – Los Angeles, CA.1951- – 1 – us UMI [071]

HERALD EXPRESS – Aurora. Ill. -sw. 1894-97, 1899-1901 – 1 – us UMI [071]

HERALD EXPRESS – Aurora. Ill. -w. 1887-92 – 1 – us UMI [071]

HERALD EXPRESS – Los Angeles, CA. 1945-1960 – 196r – 1 – $9,800,00 – C02384 – us Library Micro [071]

HERALD EXPRESS – Los Angeles. Calif. 1951-1959 – 1 – us UMI [071]

HERALD EXTRA – Wells, NV. 1906 – 1r – 1 – $50.00 – U04807 – us Library Micro [071]

THE HERALD; GAZETTE FOR THE COUNTRY – New York. N.Y. -bw. 1794-95 – 1 – us UMI [071]

HERALD MISCELLANY AND ADVERTISER *see* HERALD UNIVERSAL AND MISCELLANY

HERALD NEWS – (Also known as: Livermore Herald. Cont by: Tri-Valley Herald and News) – Livermore, CA. 1896-1904; 1906-07; 1909-13; 1915-72 – 84r – 1 – $4,200.00 – B02350 – us Library Micro [071]
HERALD NEWS – and Pred. Fontana. Calif. 1956-1958; 1965-1968 – 1 – us UMI [071]
HERALD NEWS – Joliet. Ill. 1940- – 1 – us UMI [071]
HERALD NEWS – Passaic. N.J. 1932- – 1 – us UMI [071]
HERALD NEWS – Providence. R.I. 1947-1948 – 1 – us UMI [071]
HERALD NEWS – Punta Gorda. Florida. 1974-. See also: Charlotte Herald – 1 – us UMI [071]
THE HERALD NEWS – Fontana, CA. 1958 – 2r – 1 – $100.00 – B03596 – us Library Micro [071]
HERALD OF FREEDOM – Concord. N.H. 1842-44 – 1 – us UMI [071]
HERALD OF FREEDOM – Hagerstown. Md. and Torchlight. 1839-59 – 1 – us UMI [071]
HERALD OF FREEDOM – Wilmington. Ohio. 1852-1854 – 1 – us UMI [071]
THE HERALD OF FREEDOM – Boston. Mass. 1788-1791. The Argus. 1791-1793. Sold as one unit – 3 – us Readex [071]
HERALD OF GOSPEL LIBERTY – Portsmouth. N.H. 1808-10, 1814-16; Herald of Gospel Liberty: Portland. ME. 1810-1811; Herald of Gospel Liberty: Philadelphia. PA. 1811-1814. Sold as one unit – 3 – us Readex [071]
HERALD OF GRACE – v2-7. May 1942-1947 (complete) – 1r – 1 – ATLA S0542 – us A.T.L.A. [073]
HERALD OF HEALTH *see* HEALTH
HERALD OF HOLINESS – (Some pgs missing) – v1-73. 17 Apr 1912-1984 – 60r – 1 – ATLA S0166 – us A.T.L.A. [073]
HERALD OF LIFE – (Lacking: v20-26) – v1-104. 1863-82; 1889-1966 – 26r – 1 – ATLA S0328 – us A.T.L.A. [073]
HERALD OF LIFE AND THE COMING KINGDOM – v. 5. 1867-1882 – 1 – us UMI [240]
HERALD OF PROGRESS – Gateshead, England. -w. 16 July 1880-25 July 1884. 3 reels – 1 – uk British Libr Newspaper [072]
HERALD OF PROGRESS – London. 1846 – 1 – uk Microform Academic [073]
HERALD OF REVOLT – London, England. -m. Dec 1910-May 1914. 33 ft – 1 – uk British Libr Newspaper [072]
HERALD OF REVOLT : ORGAN OF THE COMING SOCIAL REVOLUTION – v1-4. no. 5 (all publ). 1910-1914 – 1 reel – 1 – $65.00 – us UPA [335]
HERALD OF THE FUTURE – Manchester. 1839-40 – 1 – uk Microform Academic [073]
HERALD OF THE KINGDOM AND AGE TO COME – v. 9. 1859-1861 – 1 – us UMI [240]
HERALD OF THE MORNING – (Missing: some issues and pgs) – v1-7 nos 1-2. Mar 1897-Mar, Apr 1903 – 1r – 1 – ATLA S0220 – us A.T.L.A. [073]
HERALD OF THE RIGHTS OF INDUSTRY – Manchester. 1834 – 1 – uk Microform Academic [073]
HERALD OF THE VALLEY – Fincastle. Va. 1820-1823 – 1 – us UMI [071]
THE HERALD OF TRUTH – Saint John, N.B.: Friends of Truth, [1843-18–] – 9 – cn C.I.H.M. [210]
THE HERALD OF TRUTH – v1-45. 1864-1908 (complete) – 12r – 1 – ATLA 1991-S002 – us A.T.L.A. [073]
HERALD PRESS – Huntington. Ind. 1929- – 1 – us UMI [071]
HERALD PRESS – Palestine. Tex. 1942- – 1 – us UMI [071]
HERALD PRESS – St. Joseph. Mich. 1916-1965 – 1 – us UMI [071]
HERALD PROGRESS – Ashland. Va. -w. 1919- – 1 – us UMI [071]
HERALD RECORDER – (Cont: Arroyo Grande Valley Herald Recorder) – Arroyo Grande, CA. 1940-1950 – 5r – 1 – $250.00 – B03144 – us Library Micro [071]
Herald. (Ship) *see* THE BOTANY OF THE VOYAGE OF H.M.S. HERALD. 1845-51
HERALD STATESMAN – Yonkers. N.Y. 1932- – 1 – us UMI [071]
HERALD TABLOID EDITION – Harvard. Ill. -w. 1964-66 – 1 – us UMI [071]
HERALD TO THE TRADES' ADVOCATE AND CO-OPERATIVE JOURNAL – 1-36 with Appendix (all publ). 1820-31 – 7mf – 9 – $65.00 – us UPA [335]
HERALD TRAVELER – Boston. Mass. 1967- – 1 – us UMI [071]
HERALD TRIBUNE – 1985-1995 – 3r per y – 5,6 – Sfr1,176.00 – sz Infoprint [975]
HERALD TRIBUNE – New York. N.Y. European Edition. 1944- – 1 – us UMI [071]
HERALD TRIBUNE – Sarasota. Fl. 1926- – 1 – us UMI [071]
HERALD TRIBUNE "BOOKS INDEX" – New York. N.Y. 1924-1959 – 1 – us UMI [071]
HERALD UNIVERSAL AND MISCELLANY – (Includes: Herald Miscellany and Advertiser 26 nov 1789-18 nov 1790f. Index) – Quebec, 24 nov 1788-9 nov 1789f – 1r – 1 – Can$40.00 – cn Can Microfilming [072]
HERALD WEEKLY – Stratford, 1867-1897 – 7r – 1 – cn Preston [971]
HERALD-DISPATCH – Utica. N.Y. 1898-1922 – 1 – us UMI [071]
HERALDIC AND GENEALOGICAL MANUSCRIPTS, 16TH-17TH CENTURIES / Lambeth Palace Library – 4r – 1, 14 – £305.00 – 1-897955-54-5 – uk Academic [090]
HERALDIC MANUSCRIPTS CA 1300-CA 1800 / Society of Antiquaries of London – 9r – 1, 14 – £690.00 – 1-897955-64-2 – uk Academic [090]
HERALDICA DE EXTREMADURA / Sanchez Mateos, Dorita – Salamanca: Imp. Varona, s.a. – 1 – sp Bibl Santa Ana [946]
HERALDICA GENERAL Y FUENTES DE LAS ARMAS DE ESPANA / Vincente Cascante, Ignacio – Barcelona: Salvat, 1956 – 1 – us U.W. Library [920]
HERALD-LEADER – Menominee. Mich. 1950- – 1 – us UMI [071]
HERALD-MESSENGER – Crookston, NE. -w. Sep. 1913-Nov. 1920; Jan. 1921; Mar. 1921-Jul. 1921 – 1 – us NE Hist [071]
HERALD-NEWS – Wolf Point. Mont. 1948-1954; 1956-1959; 1966- – 1 – us UMI [071]
O HERALDO – Panjim, India. Jun 1975-1980 – 11r – 1 – us L of C Photodup [072]
EL HERALDO CATOLICO – (In Spanish) – Sacramento, CA. 1979 – 8+ r – 1 – $400.00 ($50.00y) – B03644 – us Library Micro [071]
EL HERALDO DE CACERES – Caceres, 1898 – 5 – sp Bibl Santa Ana [072]
HERALDO DE CACERES – Caceres, 1893. 1 numero – 5 – sp Bibl Santa Ana [073]
EL HERALDO DE LA REVOLUCION – Malalos: [s.n.], sep 29-dec 1898-jan 1899 – us Res Libr [072]
EL HERALDO DE MEXICO – Los Angeles: C F Marburg y Cia, dec 1917-mar 1923 – 18r – 1 – us Res Libr [072]
HERALDO DE PARIS – Dir. Luis Bonafoux. no. 1-69. Paris. oct 1900-mai 1904. mq no. 7, 53 – 1 – fr A.C.R.P.P. [073]
HERALDO FILIPINO – Malolos: [s.n.] jan 26-mar 23 1899 – us Res Libr [072]
HERALD-OBSERVER – Belle Glade, Florida. -w. Sept 29, 1979- – 1 – us P.K. Yonge [071]
HERALDOS DEL REY – 1927. 164p – 1 – 5.74 – us Baptist [240]
HERALD-REPUBLIC – Yakima. Wash. 1968- – 1 – us UMI [071]
HERALDS OF REVOLT; STUDIES IN MODERN LITERATURE AND DOGMA / Barry, William Francis – London: Hodder & Stoughton, 1904. xv,383p – 1 – us U.W. Library [000]
HERALDS OF SALVATION : BEING BRIEF MEMORIAL SKETCHES OF WESLEYAN MISSIONARIES WHO HAVE DIED IN THE WORK SINCE THE COMMENCEMENT OF THE ENTERPRISE / Moister, William – London, 1878. [8], 316p – 4mf – 9 – ne IDC [240]
HERALD-SENTINEL – Shickley, NE. -w. Oct 1895-Oct 1902; Mar 1908-Dec 1919; May 1920-Jan 1925 – 1 – us NE Hist [071]
HERALD-STAR – Steubenville. Ohio. 1847-1910; 1914- – 1 – us UMI [071]
HERALD-TIMES REPORTER – Manitowoc. Wis. 1960- – 1 – us UMI [071]
HERALD-TIMES-CITIZEN – Port Colborne, 1898-1929 – 13r – 1 – cn Preston [971]
HERALD-TRIBUNE – New York. N.Y. 1924-1966 – 1 – us UMI [071]
HERALD-WHIG – Quincy. Ill. 1946- – 1 – us UMI [071]
HERAPATH'S RAILWAY MAGAZINE – London, England. Herapath's Railway & Commercial Journal – Herapath's Railway Journal. See: Railway Magazine – 1 – uk British Libr Newspaper [073]
Heras, H *see*
– BEGINNINGS OF VIJAYANAGARA HISTORY
– THE CONVERSION POLICY OF THE JESUIT IN INDIA. BOMBAY, 1933
Heraud, John Abraham *see*
– THE DESCENT INTO HELL
– THE JUDGEMENT OF THE FLOOD
Herault de Sechelles, Marie-Jean *see* VOYAGE A MONTBAR CONTENANT DES DETAILS TRES INTERESSANTS SUR LE CARACTERE, LA PERSONNE ET LES ECRITS DE BUFFON...
LE HERAULT DE STE-ADELE : INDEPENDANT – Ste-Adele, Canada. 19 jun 1959-2 oct 1959 – 1r – 1 – Can$40.00 – cn Can Microfilming [072]
Herault, G *see*
– L'AIZI. ESQUISSE PHONOLOGIQUE ET ENQUETE LEXICALE
– ETUDE PHONETIQUE ET SYNTAXIQUE DU FRANCAIS D'ELEVES DE COURS PRPARATOIRE DE LA REGION D'ABIDJAN
Herault, L *see* MARIAGE ET FIANCAILLES DANS LE HAUT-BOCAGE VENDEEN (XXE SIECLE): LES MARIES DE CHAMBRETAUD
DE HERAUT – Amsterdam, 1877-1945 – 22r – 9 – ne IDC [943]
LE HERAUT D'ARMES – Art, theatre, litterature. no. 1-31. Paris. avr-dec 1869. suite de: Le Fouet voir a ce titre – 1 – fr A.C.R.P.P. [073]
AN HERBAL – 1525 – 9 – $10.00 – us Scholars' Facs [615]
HERBAL / Bodleian Library – From Bodleian Ms 130 (12th century) – 14 – uk Microform Academic [760]
HERBAL *see* AN HERBAL
THE HERBAL / Turner, W – M 413. 1568 – 9 – ne IDC [580]
THE HERBALL OR GENERAL HISTORIE OF PLANTES / Gerarde, J – M 252. 1597 – 9 – ne IDC [580]
HERBAR : ARZNEIBUCH 'MACER' / Breidenbach, Bernhard von & Baierland, Ortolf von – c50p + 7 color mf – DM650.00 – 3-89219-013-5 – gw Lengenfelder [090]
HERBARIUM / Bertoloni, A – (Including index on microfiche) – Bologna – 52mf – 9 – 748/2 – ne IDC [580]
HERBARIUM / Candolle, A P de – Geneve, Stockholm. 1962. – 2,842mf – 8 – ne IDC [580]
HERBARIUM / Ceylon – (Including the collection of Stadhouder and Index) – Zug. 1968. – 6mf – 8 – ne IDC [580]
HERBARIUM / Desfontaines, R L – (Includes index on microfiche) – Paris – 103mf – 9 – 5043/2 + 6210/2 – ne IDC [580]
HERBARIUM / Forsskal, P – Copenhagen – 138mf – 9 – 2200/2 – ne IDC [580]
HERBARIUM / Humboldt, Alexander von & Bonpland, A J A & Kunth, CS – Paris. – 172mf – 8 – ne IDC [580]
HERBARIUM / Isert, P E & Thonning, P – Copenhagen – 112mf – 9 – 2203/2 – ne IDC [580]
HERBARIUM / Jussieu, A H L de – (Includes index) – Paris – 1,293mf – 8 – ne IDC [580]
HERBARIUM / Lamarck, J B A P M de – Paris – 771mf – 9 – 6207/2 – ne IDC [580]
HERBARIUM / Linnaeus, Carl – (Includes a reprint of the book by Spencer Savage: A catalogue of the Linnaean Herbarium London, 1945. xv, 225p) – (Linn. Soc.). London – 870mf – 9 – 177/2 – ne IDC [580]
HERBARIUM / Linnaeus, Carl – (Including index on microfiche) – (Nat. Mus.). Stockholm – 421mf – 9 – 5075/2 – ne IDC [580]
HERBARIUM / Loureiro, J de – (Includes index on microfiche) – Paris – 5mf – 9 – 6212/2 – ne IDC [580]
HERBARIUM / Michaux, A – Paris – 145mf – 9 – 6211/2 – ne IDC [580]
HERBARIUM : ORGAN ZUR FOERDERUNG DES AUSTAUSCHES WISSENSCHAFTLICHER EXSICCATENSAMMLUNGEN – Leipzig, 1908-1932. Nos. 1-86 – 11mf – 9 – 8633/1 – ne IDC [580]
HERBARIUM / Rauwolff, L – Leiden. – 38mf – 9 – ne IDC [580]
HERBARIUM / Reichenbach, Heinrich G L – Vienna – 265mf – 9 – 8802/1 – ne IDC [580]
HERBARIUM / Rottboll, C F – Copenhagen. – 19mf – 8 – ne IDC [580]
HERBARIUM / Rousseau, Jean-Jacques & Aublet, J B C F – Paris – 41mf – 9 – 6213/2 – ne IDC [580]
HERBARIUM / Smith, J E – London. – 1,011mf – 8 – ne IDC [580]
HERBARIUM / Thunberg, C P – (Includes index on microfiche by C.P. Thunberg) – Uppsala – 1,161mf – 9 – 1036/2 + 5184/2 – ne IDC [580]
HERBARIUM / Tournefort, Joseph Pitton de – Paris – 360mf – 9 – 6208/2 – ne IDC [580]
HERBARIUM / Vahl, M – Copenhagen – 80mf – 9 – 2201/2 – ne IDC [580]
HERBARIUM / Wallich, N – (Includes the Wallich catalogue on microfiche) – Kew – 911mf – 9 – 7394/1 – ne IDC [580]
HERBARIUM / Willdenow, C L – (Includes index on microfiche and the printed book by P. Hiepko: Herbarium Willdenow. Alphabetical Index. Zug, 1972. xvii, 138p) – Berlin – 1,522mf – 9 – 7440/1 + 7740/1 – ne IDC [580]
HERBARIUM AMBOINENSE,... / Rumphius, G E – Amsterdam, 1741-55.-6v – 105mf – 9 – 292/1 – ne IDC [580]
HERBARIUM AUSTRALE SEU CATALOGUS PLANTARUM EXSICCATARUM / Forster, J G A – Gottingae. 1797. B-03 2 – 8 – ne IDC [580]
HERBARIUM BLACKWELLIANUM. VERMEHRTES UND VERBESSERTES BLACKWELLISCHES KRAEUTER-BUCH / Trew, C J – v. 1-6. Norimbergae. 1750-73. B-5776 1 – 9 – ne IDC [580]
HERBARIUM FLORAE AEGYPTIACAE / Sieber, F W – Vindobonae, 1820, 4 pp. B-1285 2 – 8 – ne IDC [580]
HERBARIUM HORTUS SICCUS / Burser, Joachim – Uppsala. 24v. (1583-1639) – 185mf – 8 – ne IDC [580]
HERBARIUM OF CEYLON PLANTS / Hermann, P – Leiden – 9mf – 9 – ne IDC [580]
HERBARIUM PEDEMONTANUM, AUGUSTAE TAURINORUM, 1833-1837 / Colla, L A – 8v. B-5367 2 – 8 – ne IDC [580]
HERBARIUM RAFINESQUANUM / Rafinesque-Schmaltz, Constantine S – Philadelphia. 1833. B-5653 1 – 9 – ne IDC [580]
Herbart, Johann Friedrich *see* HERBART'S ABC OF SENSE-PERCEPTION, AND MINOR PEDAGOGICAL WORKS
HERBART'S ABC OF SENSE-PERCEPTION, AND MINOR PEDAGOGICAL WORKS / Herbart, Johann Friedrich – Tr., with introd., notes and commentary by William J. Eckoff. New York: D. Appleton and company, 1896.xxxi,288p. 2 tab. (International Education Series, v36) – 1 – us U.W. Library [370]
Herbelot de Molainville, B d' *see*
– BIBLIOTHEQUE ORIENTALE, OU DICTIONNAIRE UNIVERSEL,...
Herber, J G *see* ABHANDLUNG UEBER DEN URSPRUNG DER SPRACHE
Herbert, A P *see* MISLEADING CASES IN THE COMMON LAW
Herbert, Charles *see* WHEREFORE, O GOD?
Herbert, Claude Jacques *see* ESSAI SUR LA POLICE GENERALE DES GRAINS, SUR LEURS PRIX ET SUR LES EFFETS DE L'AGRICULTURE
Herbert, Hilary A *see* PAPERS
[HERBERT HUPKA: PAMPHLET COLLECTION] – 1971 – 1 reel – 1 – CSUXANS3218-B – us Hoover Inst Photo [320]
HERBERT J WEISS COLLECTION ON THE BELGIAN CONGO, 1947-62 – Palo Alto: Stanford University, [19–?] – 13r – 1 – us Res Libr [960]
HERBERT SPENCER AND SCIENTIFIC EDUCATION = HERBERT SPENCER ET L'EDUCATION SCIENTIFIQUE / Compayre, Gabriel – (In English) – New York: Thomas Y Crowell, 1907 – 1mf – 9 – 0-8370-7617-X – 1986-1617 – us A.T.L.A. [370]
Herbert, W *see* AN APPENDIX (TO THE BOTANICAL REGISTER) CONTAINING A TREATISE ON BULBOUS ROOTS
Herbert, William *see* ANTIQUITIES OF THE INNS OF COURT AND CHANCERY
HERBIER GENERALE DE L'AMATEUR / ed by Loiseleur-Deslongchamps, J L A & Lemaire, C A – Paris. 5v. 1839-50. – 56mf – 8 – ne IDC [580]
Herbin, John Frederic *see* CANADA, AND OTHER POEMS

L'Herbon de Lussats *see* STATISTIQUE ADMINISTRATIVE ET MEDICALE DE L'ASILE PUBLIC DES ALIENEES DE LILLE, POUR LES ANNEES 1847 A 1851: RAPPORT? MR. LE PREFET DE DEPART. DU NORD

HERBORDI DIALOGUS DE VITA OTTONIS EPSICOPI BABENBERGENSIS (MGH 7: 33.BD) – 1868 – Dfl19.00 – ne Slangenburg [240]

HERBORISATIONS AU LEVANT / Barbey, C & Barbey, W – Lausanne. 1882. B-7377 1 – 9 – ne IDC [580]

Herbouville, Charles J F d' *see* STATISTIQUE DU DEPARTEMENT DES DEUX-NETHES

Herbst, Adolf *see* UEBER DIE VON SEBASTIAN MUENSTER UND JEAN DU TILLET...EVANGELIUMS MATTHAEI

Herbst, J FW *see* NATURSYSTEM UNGEFLUEGELTEN INSEKTEN

Herbst, Johannes A *see*
- ARTE PRATTICA ET POETICA
- MUSICA MODERNA PRATTICA
- MUSICA POETICA, SIVE COMPENDIUM MELOPOETICUM
- MUSICA POETICA, SIVE COMPENDIUM MELOPOETICUM, DAS IST: EINE KURZE ANLEITUNG. HARMONIAM. COMPONIREN UND MACHEN SOLL
- MUSICA PRACTICA SIVE INSTRUCTIO PRO SYMPHONIACIS

Herbst, Wilhelm *see*
- JOHANN HEINRICH VOSS
- WILHELM HERBSTS HILFSBUCH FUER DIE DEUTSCHE LITTERATURGESCHIHTE

HERBSTGESANG : NEUE GEDICHTE / Miegel, Agnes – Jena: E Diederichs, c1933 – 1r – 1 – us U.W. Library [810]

Herchner, Hans *see* DIE CYROPAEDIE IN WIELANDS WERKEN

HERCVLANA, IN LINGVA VENETIANA, NELLA VITTORIA DELL' ARMATA CHRISTIANA CONTRA TURCHI / Maganza, G B – Venetia, 1571 – 1mf – 9 – H-8314/1 – ne IDC [956]

Herd, David *see* THE ANCIENT AND MODERN SCOTS SONGS, HEROIC BALLADS, AND C.

HERDABREF TILL PRAESTERSKAPET OCH FOERSAMLINGARNA I UPPSALA AERKESTIFT / Soederblom, Nathan – Uppsala: F.C. Askerberg, [1914?] – 1mf – us A.T.L.A. [240]

Herden, Editha Martina *see* VOM EXPRESSIONISMUS ZUM "SOZIALISTISCHEN REALISMUS"

HERDENKING STICHTING BOEDI OETOMO, 1908-20 MEI-1918 : JAVAANSCHE KUNSTAVOND...GEHOUDEN DOOR IN NEDERLAND VERBLIJVENDE JAVANEN – 's-Gravenhage 1918 – 1mf – 9 – ne IDC [943]

HERDER : EIN LESEBUCH FUER UNSERE ZEIT / ed by Dobbek, Wilhelm – (Includes bibliographical references and indexes) – Weimar: Volksverlag, 1955 – 1 – us U.W. Library [430]

HERDER ALS DEUTSCHER : EIN LITERARHISTORISCHER BEITRAG ZUR ENTWICKLUNG DER DEUTSCHEN NATIONALIDEE / Goeken, Walther – Stuttgart: W Kohlhammer, 1926 – 1r – 1 – us U.W. Library [430]

HERDER CORRESPONDENCE – New York City, NY. 1963-68 – 1r – 1 – $50.00 – R04910 – us Library Micro [071]

Herder, Ferdinand Gottfried von *see* AUS HERDERS NACHLASS

Herder, Johann Gottfried *see*
- AUS HERDERS NACHLASS
- AUSWAHL
- HERDER'S BRIEFWECHSEL MIT NICOLAI
- HERDERS SAEMMTLICHE WERKE
- VOM GEIST DER HEBRAEISCHEN POESIE

HERDER, NOVALIS UND KLEIST : STUDIEN UEBER DIE ENTWICKLUNG DES TODESPROBLEMS IN DENKEN UND DICHTEN VOM STURM UND DRANG ZUR ROMANTIK / Unger, Rudolf – (Includes bibliographical references) – Frankfurt am Main: M Diesterweg, 1922 – 1 – us U.W. Library [430]

HERDER PRECURSEUR DE DARWIN? : HISTOIRE D'UN MYTHE / Rouche, Max – (Includes bibliographical references) – Paris: Societe d'edition Les belles lettres, 1940 – 1r – 1 – us U.W. Library [430]

HERDER UND COLERIDGE / Moore, Joachim Michael – Bern, 1951 – 1mf – DM48.00 – 3-8267-3032-1 – gw Hänsel [140]

HERDER UND DIE DEUTSCHE KULTURANSCHAUUNG / Bran, Friedrich Alexander – (Includes bibliographical references (p. 107-110)) – Berlin: Junker und Duennhaupt, 1932 – 1r – 1 – us U.W. Library [430]

HERDERBUCH : REISEJOURNAL; SHAKESPEARE; OSSIAN; AUS DEN HOMER (HOMER EIN GUENSTLING DER ZEIT; HOMER U OSSIAN): IN AUSWAHL / ed by Loeber, J – (Includes bibliographical references) – 4. Aufl. Leipzig: L Ehlermann, [between 1900 and 1915?] – 1 – us U.W. Library [920]

HERDER'S BRIEFWECHSEL MIT NICOLAI : IM ORIGINALTEXT / Herder, Johann Gottfried; ed by Hoffmann, Otto – (Includes bibliographical references) – Berlin: Nicolai (R Stricker), 1887 – 1r – 1 – us U.W. Library [920]

HERDER'S CID : NACH DEN BESTEN QUELLEN REVIDIRTE AUSGABE / ed by Wollheim da Fonseca – Berlin: G Hempel, [1869?] – 1r – 1 – us U.W. Library [830]

HERDER'S CONCEPTION OF "DAS VOLK" / Simpson, Georgiana Rose – (Includes bibliographical references) – Private ed. Chicago, IL: Distributed by the University of Chicago Libraries, 1921 – 1r – 1 – us U.W. Library [430]

HERDERS DRAMATISCHE DICHTUNGEN : MIT BENUTZUNG UNGEDRUCKTER QUELLEN / Treutler, Amand – Stuttgart: Metzler, 1915 – 1r – 1 – us U.W. Library [430]

HERDERS "GOTT" / Hoffart, Elizabeth – (Includes bibliographical references) – Halle a.d.S.: M Niemeyer, 1918 – 1r – 1 – us U.W. Library [430]

HERDERS SAEMMTLICHE WERKE / Herder, Johann Gottfried; ed by Suphan, Bernhard – (Includes bibliographical references and indexes) – Berlin: Weidmann. 33v. 1877-1913 – 1 – us U.W. Library [800]

HERDERS THEORETISCHE STELLUNG ZUM DRAMA / Koschmieder, Arthur – (Includes bibliographical references) – Stuttgart: J B Metzler, 1913 – 1r – 1 – us U.W. Library [430]

HERDER-STUDIEN : UNTERSUCHUNGEN ZU HERDERS KRITISCHEM STIL UND ZU SEINEN LITERATURKRITISCHEN GRUNDEINSICHTEN / Kohlschmidt, Werner – (Includes bibliographical references) – Berlin: Junker und Duennhaupt, 1929 – 1r – 1 – us U.W. Library [430]

Herdman, W A *see* REPORT TO THE GOVERNMENT OF CEYLON ON THE PEARL OYSTER FISHERIES OF THE GULF OF MANAAR WITH SUPPLEMENTARY REPORTS ON THE MARINE BIOLOGY OF CEYLON

Herdon, Dallas T *see* CENTENNIAL HISTORY OF ARKANSAS

Herdt, Ludwig *see* IMMANENZ UND GESCHICHTE

Herdt, Ursula *see* DIE VERFASSUNGSTHEORIE KARL V. ROTTECKS

HERE AND NOW – Tuscon, AZ. 26 Jan 1979 – 1 – us A.J.P.C. [071]

HERE AND NOW; A CANADIAN QUARTERLY MAGAZINE OF LITERATURE AND ART – 1947-49 – 1 – 60.00 – cn McLaren [073]

HERE AND THERE IN THE GREEK NEW TESTAMENT / Potwin, Lemuel Stoughton – Chicago: Fleming H. Revell, 1898. 1 fiche – 9 – us A.T.L.A. [240]

Heredia, Jose Felix *see* LA CONSAGRACION DE LA REPUBLICA DEL ECUADOR AL SAGRADO CORAZON DE JESUS. QUITO, 1935

HEREDITAS : GENETIST ARKIV – Lund 1920-1941, v. 1-27 – 201mf – 8 – ne IDC [073]

HEREDITAS – v. 1- 1920- – 1. ; 5,6. ; 9 – apply; v.64-; v.85- – us UMI [575]

HEREDITE ET ALCOOLISME, ETUDE PSYCHOLOGIQUE ET CLINIQUE SUR LES DEGENERES BUVEURS ET LES FAMILLES D'IVROGNES / Legrain, Paul Maurice – Avec une preface de M. le docteur Magnan. v. v. (French Precursors of Psychiatry Series). Paris. O. Doin. 1889 – 9 – fr Hachette [616]

HEREDITY – (An International Journal of Genetics.) v. 1-23. 1947-1968 – 1,5,6 – us Princeton Micro [575]

HEREDITY: AN INTERNATIONAL JOURNAL OF GENETICS – (1982-. 1,5,6,9) – v1-. 1947- – 1 – us UMI [575]

HEREDITY, WITH PRELUDES ON CURRENT EVENTS / Cook, Joseph – Boston: Houghton, Mifflin, 1882, c1879 – 1mf – us A.T.L.A. [240]

THE HEREFORD BREVIARY, VOL. 1 / Frere, Walter H & Brown, L E G – 1904 – 8mf – 8 – Dfl30.00 – ne Slangenburg [240]

THE HEREFORD BREVIARY, VOL. 2 / Frere, Walter H & Brown, L E G – 1911 – 7mf – 8 – ne Slangenburg [240]

THE HEREFORD BREVIARY, VOL. 3 / Frere, Walter H & Brown, L E G – 1914 – 5mf – 8 – ne Slangenburg [240]

Hereford. England. Diocese *see* REGISTERS OF THE BISHOPS, 1275-1535 AND

HEREFORD JOURNAL – Hereford. Previously known as British Chronicle or Pugh's Hereford Journal – 1 – uk Microform Academic [072]

HEREFORD MID-WEEK TIMES AND BULLETIN – Hereford. 1964-69 – 1 – uk Microform Academic [072]

HEREFORDSHIRE, 1822 : BRITISH ISLES CENSUS DIRECTORIES PROJECT, ENGLAND – (In prep) – at Vine [941]

HEREFORDSHIRE, 1830 : BRITISH ISLES CENSUS DIRECTORIES PROJECT, ENGLAND – at Vine [941]

HEREFORDSHIRE, 1835 : BRITISH ISLES CENSUS DIRECTORIES PROJECT ENGLAND, VOL 55 – 1mf – 9 – A$9.00 – at Vine [941]

HEREFORDSHIRE, 1842 : BRITISH ISLES CENSUS DIRECTORIES PROJECT, ENGLAND – (In prep) – at Vine [941]

HEREFORDSHIRE, 1844 : BRITISH ISLES CENSUS DIRECTORIES PROJECT, ENGLAND – at Vine [941]

HEREFORDSHIRE, 1850 : BRITISH ISLES CENSUS DIRECTORIES PROJECT, ENGLAND – at Vine [941]

HEREFORDSHIRE, 1858 : BRITISH ISLES CENSUS DIRECTORIES PROJECT, ENGLAND – at Vine [941]

HEREFORDSHIRE, 1863 : BRITISH ISLES CENSUS DIRECTORIES PROJECT, ENGLAND – (In prep) – at Vine [941]

HEREFORDSHIRE, 1885 : BRITISH ISLES CENSUS DIRECTORIES PROJECT, ENGLAND – (In prep) – at Vine [941]

HEREFORDSHIRE, 1909 : BRITISH ISLES CENSUS DIRECTORIES PROJECT, ENGLAND – at Vine [941]

HEREFORDSHIRE, 1917 : BRITISH ISLES CENSUS DIRECTORIES PROJECT, ENGLAND – at Vine [941]

HEREFORDSHIRE, 1926 : BRITISH ISLES CENSUS DIRECTORIES PROJECT, ENGLAND – at Vine [941]

HEREFORDSHIRE (HEREFORD, ROSS AND LEDBURY), 1847 : BRITISH ISLES CENSUS DIRECTORIES PROJECT, ENGLAND – at Vine [941]

HEREJIAS Y SUPERTICIONES EN LA NUEVA ESPANA. LOS HETERODOXOS EN MEJICO / Jimenez Rueda, Julio – Madrid: Missionalia Hispanica, 1948 – 1 – sp Bibl Santa Ana [390]

Herera, Antonio de *see* HISTORIA GENERAL DE LOS HECHOS DE LOS CASTELLANOS EN LAS ISLAS Y TIERRA-FIRME DE EL MAR OCEANO

HERESGAST : EINE ERZAEHLUNG AUS GERMANISCHER VORZEIT / Auerswald, Annmarie von – Dresden: Meinhold, 1940 – 1r – 1 – us U.W. Library [830]

L'HERESIE A LA CHARITE-SUR-LOIRE ET LES DEBUTS DE L'INQUISITION MONASTIQUE DANS LA FRANCE DU NORD AU 13E SIECLE / Chenone, E – Paris, 1917 – Dfl6.00 – ne Slangenburg [240]

HERESIES OF SEA POWER / Jane, Frederick T – 1906 – 9 – uk Libr Preservation [355]

THE HERESY OF THE FREE SPIRIT IN THE LATER MIDDLE AGES / Lerner, R E – Los Angeles, 1972 – Dfl28.00 – ne Slangenburg [240]

HERETIQUES ET REVOLUTIONNAIRES / Dide, Auguste – Paris, Charavay, 1886 – 1mf – us A.T.L.A. [240]

Herford, Brooke *see*
- SERMONS OF COURAGE AND CHEER
- THE SMALL END OF GREAT PROBLEMS
- THE STORY OF RELIGION IN ENGLAND
- TRAVERS MADGE

Herford, Charles Harold *see* GOETHE

HERFORDER KREISBLATT – Herford, Germany. 1 Jun 1992- – 7r per yr – 1 – gw Mikrofilm [072]

Hergenroether, Joseph *see* CATHOLIC CHURCH AND CHRISTIAN STATE

Herguijuela. Ayuntamiento *see* FIESTAS PATRONALES EN HONOR DE SAN BARTOLOME

Heribaud, J *see* LES DIATOMEES D'AUVERGNE

Hericourt, Pierre *see* ARMS FOR RED SPAIN

Hericurt, Pierre *see* ARMES FOR RED SPAIN

Herinco, F *see* MANUEL GENERAL DES PLANTES, ARBRES, ARBUSTES

Hering, Hermann *see*
- DOKTOR POMERANUS, JOHANNES BUGENHAGEN
- DIE MYSTIK LUTHERS

Hering, J *see* PHENOMENOLOGIE ET PHILOSOPHIE RELIGIEUSE

Hering, Robert *see* SPINOZA IM JUNGEN GOETHE

HERIR EN LA SOMBRA / Hurtado y Nunez de Arce, G – 1866 – 9 – 1.50f – sp Bibl Santa Ana [830]

Herissant, LT *see* PRINCIPES DE STYLE

HERITAGE – Khartoum, Sudan. Nov 5 1984-Nov 7 1988 – 1r – 1 – us L of C Photodup [072]

HERITAGE – Los Angeles. Calif. 1960-67 – 1 – us A.J.P.C. [071]

THE HERITAGE – (Library has: v.3,no.15-v.4,no.19,21-29,31-v.5,no.19,21-v.6,no.23,25-26,30-v.7,no.10; Nov.1966-Oct.1970) – New York: The Heritage Press, 196?- – 1 – CSUX86-S172 – us Hoover Inst Photo [978]

HERITAGE CANADA – (Cont by: Canadian Heritage, 1979/80) – Ottawa. v1-5. 1974-79 – 9 – Can$20.00y – cn Micromedia [971]

HERITAGE CANADA 1979/80 *see* CANADIAN HERITAGE

L'HERITAGE DE BEHANZIN / Mimande, Paul – Paris, Perrin et Cie. 1898 – 9 – 10.00 – fr Orientalistes [960]

THE HERITAGE OF THE REFORMATION / Pauck, Wilhelm – Glencoe, 2nd ed 1961 – 7mf – 8 – ne Slangenburg [240]

THE HERITAGE OF THE REFORMATION GLENCOE / Pauck, Wilhelm – 2nd ed 1961 – 7mf – 8 – ne Slangenburg [240]

HERITAGE SOUTHWEST JEWISH PRESS – Los Angeles, CA. 1959- – 25+ r – 1 – $1,250.00 ($50.00y) – C02385 – us Library Micro [071]

HERITAGE SOUTHWEST JEWISH PRESS – Sacramento. Calif. 1965- – 1 – us UMI [071]

Herites, Frantisek *see* SEBRANE SPISY

L'Heritier de Brutelle, C L Cornus *see*
- GERANIOLOGIA, SEU ERODII, PELARGONII, GERANII, MONSONIAE ET GRIELI HISTORIA ICONIBUS ILLUSTRATA
- SERTUM ANGLICUM, SEU PLANTAE RARIORES
- SPECIMEN BOTANICUM SISTENS DESCRIPTIONES ET ICONES
- STIRPES NOVAE AUT MINUS COGNITAE

Herke, Karl *see* HEBBELS THEORIE UND KRITIK POETISCHER MUSTER

Herkenne, Heinrich *see* DE VETERIS LATINAE ECCLESIASTICI CAPITIBUS I-XLIII

Herkless, John *see*
- THE EARLY CHRISTIAN MARTYRS AND THEIR PERSECUTIONS
- FRANCIS AND DOMINIC AND THE MENDICANT ORDERS
- RICHARD CAMERON

Herlitz, G *see* JUEDISCHES LEXICON

Herloßsohn, C *see* DAMEN-CONVERSATIONS-LEXIKON (HQ 13)

HERMA NABI : THE ETHIOPIC VERSION OF PASTOR HERMAE / Schodde, Georghe Henry – Leipzig: F.A. Brockhaus, 1876 – 1mf – us A.T.L.A. [240]

HERM'AELOGIUM: OR, AN ESSAY AT THE RATIONALITY OF THE ART OF SPEAKING / Jones, Bassett – 1659. 113p. (English Linguistics Series 1500-1800) – 9 – us UMI [420]

HERMAN CYCLONE – Herman, NE. -w. Apr 1906-Apr 1907 – 1 – us NE Hist [071]

Herman, N *see*
- EIN MANDAT ETC
- EYN MANDAT JESU CHRISTI
- EIN MANDAT JESU CHRISTI. AUS DEM ORIGINALI, MIT PRAEFATION AN TAG GEGEBEN DURCH C. PAWLER
- AIN MANDAT JHESU CHRISTI
- EYN MANDAT JHESU CHRISTI, AN ALLE SEYNE GETREWEN
- AIN NEUEW MANDAT JESU CHRISTI
- EIN NEW MANDAT JESU CHRISTI
- EIN NEW MANDAT JHESU CHRISTI

HERMAN NEWS – Herman, NE. -w. Dec 1892; Mar-Jun 1894, scattered issues missing; Aug 1894-Jan 1895 – 1 – us NE Hist [071]

HERMAN RECORD – Herman, NE. -w. Jan 1920-Dec 1923; Jan 1926-Nov 1946 – 1 – us NE Hist [071]

Herman von Wied, Abp. of Cologne *see* SIMPLE AND RELIGIOUS CONSULTATION..

HERMAN WEEKLY REVIEW – Herman, NE. Sept 1896-Jan 1898 – 1 – us NE Hist [071]

LE HERMANDAD – Pueblo. Colo. 1896-1906 – 1 – us UMI [071]

LA HERMANDAD DE ALFERECES Y EL DESTINO DE ESPANA / Becerro de Bengoa, Ricardo – Caceres: Imprenta Moderna, 1962 – 1 – sp Bibl Santa Ana [946]

Hermandad de Donates de Sangre *see* BOLETIN INFORMATIVO EXTRAORDINARIO

HERMANDAD DEL SANTO SEPULCRO. ESTATUTOS POR LOS QUE HA DE REGIRSE.. – Caceres: Imprenta Moderna, 1960 – sp Bibl Santa Ana [946]

Hermandad Sindical *see* ORDENANZAS DE LA (TIPO)

Hermandad Sindical de Labradores y Ganaderos *see*
- REGLAMENTO
- ROMERIA DE SAN ISIDRO. EN VENTA E CULEBRIN

HERMANN – London, England. Deutsches Wochenblatt aus London. -w. 1859-67. 3 reels – 1 – uk British Libr Newspaper [072]

Hermann, A *see* TRACTATUS THEOLOGICI IN PRIMUM SENTENTIARUM LIBRUM...

HERMANN AND DOROTHEA / Goethe, Johann Wolfgang von – Muenchen: F Bruckmann, [1874?] – 1r – 1 – us U.W. Library [820]

[HERMANN AXEN: PAMPHLET COLLECTION] – 1968-1989 – 1 reel – 1 – CSUXANS5574-B – us Hoover Inst Photo [320]

Hermann, Binger *see* THE LOUISIANA PURCHASE AND OUR TITLE WEST OF THE ROCKY MOUNTAINS: WITH A REVIEW OF ANNEXATION BY THE UNITED STATES

[HERMANN EHLERS PAMPHLET COLLECTION] – 1975-1977 – 1 reel – 1 – CSUXANS2495-B – us Hoover Inst Photo [320]

HERMANN FLAYDERS AUSGEWAEHLTE WERKE / ed by Bebermeyer, Gustav – (Latin text with an introduction in German) – Leipzig: K W Hiersemann, 1925 – 1 – us U.W. Library [890]

Hermann, Francis *see* PHYSICIAN'S RECORDS: NEW RIEGEL, OHIO

Hermann, Fritz H *see* DIE VERFASSUNG DER HESSEN-DARMSTAEDTISCHEN LANDSTAENDE AM AUSGANG DES 18. JAHRHUNDERTS

HERMANN GOERING ALBUMS / U.S. Library of Congress. Prints and Photographs Division – 47 albums (13,500 images) from 1914-18 and 1933-42. 7 reels. P&P3128 – 1 – 23.00r – us L of C Photodup [080]

HERMANN HESSE UND GOTTFRIED KELLER : EINE STUDIE / Buehner, Karl Hans – Stuttgart: U Bonz, 1927 – 1r – 1 – us U.W. Library [430]

Hermann, Karl Freidrich *see* LEHRBUCH DER GRIECHISCHEN ANTIQUITAETEN

HERMANN KURZ' SAEMTLICHE WERKE / Kurz, Hermann; ed by Fischer, Hermann – Leipzig: M Hesse's Verlag. 12v in 3. [19–?] – 1 – us U.W. Library [800]

HERMANN LINGG UND SEINE LYRISCHE DICHTUNG / Knote, Walter – (Includes bibliographical references) – Wuerzburg: R Mayr, 1936 – 1 – us U.W. Library [430]

HERMANN LOENS : SEIN LEBEN UND WIRKEN / Deimann, Wilhelm – (Includes bibliographical references) – Dortmund: Lensing, 1922 – 1r – 1 – us U.W. Library [920]

HERMANN LOENS : EIN SOLDATISCHES VERMAECHTNIS / Deimann, Wilhelm – Berlin-Dahlem: Ahnenerbe-Stiftung Verlag, c1939 – 1r – 1 – us U.W. Library [430]

Hermann, P *see* HERBARIUM OF CEYLON PLANTS

HERMANN SAMUEL REIMARUS UND JOHANN CHRISTIAN EDELMANN / Moenckeberg, Carl – 1867 – 1 – us A.T.L.A. [240]

HERMANN SIEBECK'S RELIGIONSPHILOSOPHIE DARGESTELLT UND BEURTEILT / Geisler, Victor – Berlin: Leopold Eber, 1908 – 9 – us A.T.L.A. [240]

HERMANN STARK : DEUTSCHES LEBEN / Redewitz, Oskar von – 3. Aufl. Stuttgart: J G Cotta, 1879 – 1r – 1 – us U.W. Library [920]

HERMANN STEHR : DIE GESCHICHTE EINES LEBENS UND SEINES WERKES IN 5 KAPITELN / ed by Koehler, Willibald – Schweidnitz: L Heege, 1927 – 1r – 1 – us U.W. Library [430]

HERMANN STEHR, SCHLESIER, DEUTSCHER, EUROPAEER : EIN GEDENKBUCH ZUM 100. GEBURTSTAG DES DICHTERS / ed by Richter, Fritz – (Includes bibliographical references) – Wuerzburg: Holzner, 1964 – 1 – us U.W. Library [430]

HERMANN STEHR UND DAS JUNGE DEUTSCHLAND : BEKENNTNIS ZUM 75. GEBURTSTAG DES DICHTERS / ed by Hammer, Franz – Eisenach: E Roeth, 1939 – 1r – 1 – us U.W. Library [430]

HERMANN SUDERMANN : EINE KRITISCHE STUDIE / Kawerau, Waldemar – 2. Aufl. Leipzig: B Elischer, [1897?] – 1r – 1 – us U.W. Library [430]

HERMANN UND DOROTHEA / Goethe, Johann Wolfgang von – Muenchen: F Bruckmann, [1874?] – 1 – us U.W. Library [830]

HERMANN UND DOROTHEA = HERMANN UND DOROTHEA / Goethe, Johann Wolfgang von – Philadelphia: J B Lippincott, 1889 – 1r – 1 – us U.W. Library [820]

[HERMANN VON UNNA] OVERTURE; ARRANGED FOR PIANO / Vogler, Georg Joseph – Mainz: Schott, 180- – 1 – us Sibley [780]

DIE HERMANNSSCHLACHT : EIN DRAMA IN FUENF AUFZUEGEN / Kleist, Heinrich von – (Includes bibliographical references) – Wien: K Graeser, [18–?] – 1r – 1 – us U.W. Library [820]

HERMANNSTAEDTER ZEITUNG *see* DIE WOCHE

Hermannus, P *see* MUSAEUM ZEYLANICUM, SIVE CATALOGUS PLANTARUM, IN ZEYLANA SPONTE NASCENTIUM

HERMANNUS QUONDAM JUDAEUS (MGH QUELLEN..: 4.BD) : OPUSCULUM DE CONVERSIONE SUA – 1963 – Dfl13.00 – ne Slangenburg [240]

LOS HERMANOS DEL DESTINO (LOS PIZARROS Y LA CONQUISTA DEL PERU) / Birney, Hoffman – Buenos Aires: Editorial Juventud Argentina, S.A., 1946 – sp Bibl Santa Ana [350]

HERMAS IN ARCADIA : AND OTHER ESSAYS / Harris, J Rendel – Cambridge: University Press; New York: Macmillan [distributor], 1896 – 1mf – us A.T.L.A. [240]

HERMATHENA – v. 1-. 1873- – 1; 1975- 5,6,9 – us UMI [073]

Hermbstadt, Sigismund Friedrich *see* SYSTEMATISCHER GRUNDRIS DER ALLGEMEINEN EXPERIMENTAL-CHEMIE ZUM GEBRAUCH SEINER VORLESUNGER ENTWORFEN

Hermelink, Heinrich *see*
- BUENDNIS UND BEKENNTNIS 1529/1530
- REFORMATION UND GEGENREFORMATION

HERMEN : ESSAYS UND ETUDIEN / Spiero, Heinrich – (Includes bibliographical references) – Leipzig: H. Finck, 1912 – 1r – 1 – us U.W. Library [430]

HERMENEUTICAE BIBLICAE GENERALIS PRINCIPIA RATIONALIA CHRISTIANA ET CATHOLICA: SELECTIS EXEMPLIS ILLUSTRATA / Ranolder, Joannes – Ed 2. Budae [Budapest]: C R Scient Universitatis, 1859 – 1mf – 9 – 0-8370-6934-3 – 1986-0934 – us A.T.L.A. [220]

THE HERMENEUTICAL PROBLEM OF YAHWEH WAR IN THE BOOK OF JOSHUA 1-12 / Dobayashi, Yoichi – 1981 – 1 – 5.00 – us Baptist [240]

HERMENEUTICS OF THE NEW TESTAMENT / Immer, Albert – Andover: Warren F. Draper, 1877.1 fiche – 9 – us A.T.L.A. [240]

HERMENEUTIK DES NEUEN TESTAMENTES / Immer, Albert – (Includes index) – Wittenberg: Herman Koelling, 1873 – 1mf – 9 – 0-8370-3722-0 – 1985-1722 – us A.T.L.A. [220]

HERMES : APRIL 4 1938-SEPTEMBER 13 1962 – 1995 – us NE Hist [370]

HERMES – Hugoton. Kan. 1887-1889 – 1 – us UMI [071]

HERMES : ZEITSCHRIFT FUER KLASSISCHE PHILOLOGIE – Berlin, 1866-1940. v1-75 – 793mf – 9 – 115c/2 – ne IDC [430]

HERMES : ZEITSCHRIFT FUER KLASSISCHE PHILOLOGIE – v1-36 – 45mf – 9 – subsc: DM390.00 – gw Olms [450]

Hermes, Georg *see* POSTITIVE EINLEITUNG

HERMES MERCURIUS TRISMEGISTUS, HIS DIVINE PYMANDER, IN SEVENTEEN BOOKS. TOGETHER WITH HIS SECOND BOOK, CALLED ASCLEPIUS / Hermes Trismegistus – London, 1657 – 1 – us U.W. Library [920]

Hermes, Neil *see* COMPARATIVE STUDY OF SOME METHODS OF CENSUSING BIRDS

HERMES, OR A PHILOSOPHICAL INQUIRY CONCERNING UNIVERSAL GRAMMAR / Harris, James – (Linguistic series). 1801 – 9 – fr Hachette [400]

HERMES OU RECHERCHES PHILOSOPHIQUES SUR LA GRAMMAIRE UNIVERSELLE / Harris, James – 9 – fr I.C.S. [400]

Hermes Trismegistus *see*
- DEVX LIVRES, L'VN DE LA PUISSANCE & SAPIENCE DE DIEU, L'AUTRE DE LA VOLONTE DE DIEU
- HERMES MERCURIUS TRISMEGISTUS, HIS DIVINE PYMANDER, IN SEVENTEEN BOOKS. TOGETHER WITH HIS SECOND BOOK, CALLED ASCLEPIUS

HERMES UNMASKED / Browne, Thomas Gunter – 1795. 135p. (English Linguistics Series 1500-1800) – 9 – us UMI [400]

HERMES:OR, A PHILOSOPHICAL INQUIRY CONCERNING LANGUAGE AND UNIVERSAL GRAMMAR / Harris, James – 1751. 478p. (English Linguistics Series 1500-1800) – 9 – us UMI [400]

Hermet, G *see* EMIGRANTS SAISONNIERS ESPAGNOLS EN FRANCE

HERMETISCHER ROSENKRANTZ, DAS IST, VIER SCHOENE, AUSERLESENE CHYMISCHE TRACTAETLEIN.. – 1747. Comp. by David Herlitz. 1 reel. 1205 – 1 – us U.W. Library [540]

L'HERMINE – Journal de la Bretagne et de la Vendee. Nantes. 1837-39, 1842-48, juil 1849-6 nov 1850 – 1 – fr A.C.R.P.P. [073]

HERMISTON HERALD – Hermiston, OR. -w. 3 Apr 1915-. – 1 – us U.O. Library [071]

HERMITAGE BAPTIST CHURCH. KERSHAW COUNTY. SOUTH CAROLINA : CHURCH RECORDS – 1920-23, 1943-51, 1957-72 – 1 – 14.58 – us Baptist [240]

THE HERMITS / Kingsley, Charles – 1868 – 1 – us A.T.L.A. [240]

THE HERMITS AND ANCHORITIES OF ENGLAND / Clay, Rotha Mary – London: Methuen, 1914 – 1mf – us A.T.L.A. [240]

Hermogenes *see* APOCALYPSIS SPAGYRICA ET PHILOSOPHICA

HERMOSA *see* SOUTH BAY DAILY BREEZE

HERMOSA BEACH REVIEW – Hermosa Beach, CA. 1913-1950; 1956-1973; 1976-1979 – 34r – 1 – $1,700.00 – H03241 – us Library Micro [071]

Hermoso, Eugenio *see* COMETA

Hermsen, Hugo *see* DIE WIEDERTAEUFER ZU MUENSTER IN DER DEUTSCHEN DICHTUNG

Hernadez, Marcial *see* HERNANDEZ MARCIAL

HERNAN CENTENO. EL TRAVIESO, SENOR DEL CASTILLO DE RAPAPELO EN SIERRA DE GATA / Velo Nieto, Gervasio – Badajoz: Dip. Prov., 1958 – sp Bibl Santa Ana [946]

HERNAN CORTES / Cortes, Hernando – (1869 ed.1.50f; 9) – 1868 – 9 – 1.50f – sp Bibl Santa Ana [946]

HERNAN CORTES / Justiniano Arribas, Juan – 1887 – 9 – 1.50f – sp Bibl Santa Ana [946]

Hernan Cortes *see* CARTAS DE RELACION DE LA CONQUISTA DE MEJICO

HERNAN CORTES EN EXTREMADURA : VISION HISTORICO-LITERARIA DEL PRECONQUIS TADOR / Reynolds, Winton A – Madrid: Castalia, 1966 – 1 – sp Bibl Santa Ana [972]

HERNAN CORTES, LETTERS FROM MEXICO / Cortes, Hernando – New York: A.R. Pagden, 1971 – sp Bibl Santa Ana [350]

HERNAN CORTES. LIBERTADOR DEL INDIO / Trueba, Alfonso – Mexico: Editorial Cempeador, 2nd ed 1954. Col.F: y episodios de la Hª de Majico no 6 – sp Bibl Santa Ana [350]

Hernandez, Amado V *see* ISANG DIPANG LANGIT

Hernandez Andres, J M *see* CATALOGO DE UNA SERIE MISCELANEA PROCEDENTE DEL CONVENTO DE SAN ANTONIO DEL PRADO Y COLEGIOS JESUITICOS...

Hernandez Cardenal, Garcia *see* CONSIDERACIONES SOBRE LO QUE SIGNIFICA...CRISTIANO

Hernandez de Soto, Sergio *see*
- CUENTOS POPULARES...EXTREMADURA
- JUEGOS INFANTILES DE EXTREMADURA

Hernandez Diaz, Erasmo *see* BANOS DE MONTEMAYOR. PUERTA DE EXTREMADURA. APUNTES 1971

Hernandez Diaz, Jose *see* EXPEDICION DEL ADELANTADO HERNANDO DE SOTO A LA FLORIDA

Hernandez, F *see* OPERA CUM EDITA TUM INEDITA

Hernandez, Felix *see* ALCAZABA OF MERIDA. EARLY MUSLIM ARCHITECTURE

Hernandez Gil, Antonio *see* METODOLOGIA DEL DERECHO (ORDENACION CRITICA DE LAS PRINCIPALES DIRECCIONES METODOLOGICAS). MADRID, 1945

Hernandez Gil, Fernando *see* TUTELA Y DIGNIFICACION DEL TRABAJO

Hernandez, Jesus *see*
- ATRAS LOS INVASORES
- EL PARTIDO COMUNISTA ANTES, DURANTE Y DESPUES DE LA CRISIS DEL GOBIERNO LARGO CABALLERO

HERNANDEZ MARCIAL : OBRAS COMPLETAS... / Hernadez, Marcial; ed by Bayle, Constantino – Madrid: Razon y Fe, 1940 – 1 – sp Bibl Santa Ana [440]

Hernandez, Mariano *see* ORTOGRAFIA ESPANOLA. COLEGIO DE SAN JOSE, VILLAFRANCA (BADAJOZ)

Hernandez Pacheco, E et al *see* EL SAHARA ESPANOL

Hernandez Pacheco, Eduardo *see*
- EXTREMADURA Y LOS EXTREMENOS
- FISIOGRAFIA DEL GUADIANA
- PINTURAS PREHISTORICAS Y DOLMENES DE LA REGION DE ALBURQUERQUE
- LAS TIERRAS NEGRAS DEL EXTREMO SUR DE ESPANA Y SUS YACIMIENTOS POLEOLITICOS

Hernandez Pacheco, Francisco *see*
- DISCURSO LEIDO EN LA APERTURA DEL CURSO ACADEMICO 1943-44
- RASGOS FISIOGRAFICOS Y GEOLOGICOS DEL TERRITORIO DE IFNI Y RASGOS FISIOGRAFICOS Y GEOLOGICOS DEL SAHARA

Hernandez Valbuena, Ramiro *see* LA LUZ DEL VATICANO

Hernandez y Herrero, Joaquin *see* CARTA PASTORAL...QUENTA CURA

HERNANDO CORTES / Corona Baratech, Carlos E – Madrid: Publicaciones Espanolas, 1959 Temas Espanoles, no 57 (2nd ed.) – sp Bibl Santa Ana [920]

HERNANDO CORTES / Corraliza, Jose V – Badajoz: Imp. de la Dip. Provincial, 1965. Sep. REE – sp Bibl Santa Ana [250]

HERNANDO CORTES / Justiniano Arribas, Juan – 1877 – 9 – 1.50f – sp Bibl Santa Ana [946]

HERNANDO CORTES / Madariaga, Salvador – Buenos Aires: Editorial Sudamericana, 1945 – 1 – sp Bibl Santa Ana [350]

HERNANDO CORTES / Piron, Alexo – 1776 – 9 – 1.50f – sp Bibl Santa Ana [946]

HERNANDO CORTES / Ramirez, Alfonso Francisco – Mexico: D.F., 1950 – sp Bibl Santa Ana [920]

HERNANDO CORTES / Sandoval, M de – Glorias de Espana. Madrid: Laultima moda, 1898 – 1 – sp Bibl Santa Ana [920]

HERNANDO CORTES / Torres, Luis de – 1830 – 9 – 1.50f – sp Bibl Santa Ana [946]

HERNANDO CORTES AND THE MARQUESADO IN MORELOS, 1522-1547 / Riley, G Michael – Alburquerque: University of New Mexico Press, 1973 – sp Bibl Santa Ana [920]

HERNANDO CORTES. CONQUEROR OF MEXICO / Madariaga, Salvador – London: Hodder-Stoughton, 1942 – 1 – sp Bibl Santa Ana [350]

HERNANDO CORTES (CONQUISTADOR DE MEJICO) / Torres, Luis de – Madrid: Biblioteca Nueva, 2nd ed 1942 – sp Bibl Santa Ana [350]

HERNANDO CORTES, ESTAMPAS DE SU VIDA / Margarinos, Santiago – Madrid, 1947 – 1 – sp Bibl Santa Ana [910]

HERNANDO CORTES (ESTUDIO DE UN CARACTER) / Polavieja, Marques de – Toledo, Imprenta y Libreria de la Viuda e hijos de I, Pelaez, 1909 – 1 – sp Bibl Santa Ana [920]

HERNANDO CORTES (ESTUDIO DE UN CARACTER) POR EL TENIENTE GENERAL MARQUES DE POLARIEGA / Altolaguirre, Angel de – Madrid: Fortanet, 1909. B.R.A.H. 55, pp. 506-514 – sp Bibl Santa Ana [920]

HERNANDO CORTES, EXEQUIAS, ALMONEDA E INVENTARIO DE SUS BIENES / Muro Orejon, Antonio – Sevilla: Escuela de Estudios Hispano-Americanos, 1958. Sep. – sp Bibl Santa Ana [946]

HERNANDO CORTES. LIBERTADOR DEL INDIO / Trueba, Alfonso – Mexico: Editorial Jus, 3rd ed 1958 – sp Bibl Santa Ana [350]

HERNANDO CORTES O LA CONQUISTA DE MEJICO / Escofet, Jose – Barcelona: S.A. Ig. S. Barral Hermanos, 1925. Col. Los Grandes Esploradores espanoles. vol 3 – sp Bibl Santa Ana [972]
HERNANDO CORTES Y EL DERECHOS INTERNACIONAL EN EL SIGLO 16 / Esquivel Obregon, Toribio – Mexico: Editorial Polis, 1939 – sp Bibl Santa Ana [920]
HERNANDO CORTES Y FRANCISCO PIZARRO / Gonzalez Ruiz, Nicolas – Barcelona: Editorial Cervantes, 1952 – sp Bibl Santa Ana [350]
HERNANDO CORTES Y SUS PARIENTES LOS JUAREZ / Ramos-Olivera, Antonio – Mexico: Cia. General de Ediciones, S.A., 1972 – sp Bibl Santa Ana [320]
HERNANDO DE SOTO / Villanueva y Canedo, Luis – 1892 – 9 – 1.50f – sp Bibl Santa Ana [920]
HERNANDO DE SOTO, PALADIN DE FLORIDA Y DESCUBRIDOR DEL MISSISIPI / Munoz de San Pedro, Miguel – Madrid: Novelas y cuentos, 1954 – 1 – sp Bibl Santa Ana [910]
Herndon, Richard *see* MEN OF PROGRESS: BIOGRAPHICAL SKETCHES AND PORTRAITS OF LEADERS IN BUSINESS AND PROFESSIONAL LIFE IN AND OF THE STATE OF MAINE
HERNE BAY PRESS – (Missing: Jan-Jun 1898) – England, 1883-1975 – 88r – 1 – uk British Libr Newspaper [072]
HERNOESANDSPOSTEN HALFVECKOUPPLAGEN – Haernoesand, Sweden. 1909-10 – sw Kungliga [072]
THE HERO IN HEMINGWAY: A STUDY IN DEVELOPMENT / Dahiya, Bhim S – Chandigarh: Bahri Publications, 1978. xv,225p. Includ. index and bibliog. With: Letters of two queens. Bathhurst, Hon. A.B – 1 – us U.W. Library [420]
THE HERO OF ESTHONIA AND OTHER STUDIES IN THE ROMANTIC LITERATURE OF THAT COUNTRY / Kirby, William Forsell – Comp. from Esthonian and German sources.London: J.C. Nimmo, 1895. 2v. ill. map – 1 – us U.W. Library [460]
Heroard, Jean *see* JOURNAL...SUR L'ENFANCE ET LA JEUNESSE DE LOUIS XIII (1601-1628)
Herod, G *see* BIOGRAPHICAL SKETCHES OF SOME OF THOSE PREACHERS WHOSE LABOURS CONTRIBUTED TO THE ORIGINATION AND EARLY EXTENSION OF THE PRIMITIVE METHODIST CONNEXION
HERODINDE : PRELUDE [DE ACTE 3] POUR ORCHESTRE / Massenet, J – Paris: Heugel & Cie, [1899] – 1 – us Sibley [780]
Herodotus *see*
- HISTORIAE
- THE HISTORY OF HERODOTUS. A NEW ENGLISH VERSION

THE HERODS / Farrar, Frederic William – New York: E R Herrick, [1898] – 1mf – 9 – 0-8370-9697-9 – 1986-3697 – us A.T.L.A. [930]
EL HEROE SERAFICO DE SAN PEDRO DE ALCANTARA / Camberos de Yegros, Fernando – 1723 – 9 – $1.50f – sp Bibl Santa Ana [830]
HEROES DAY AND THE INDONESIAN REVOLUTION / Ruslan, Abdulgani – SE 4891 1. 1964 – 9 – ne IDC [320]
HEROES EXTREMENOS : ALVARO DE SANDE / Munoz Carrero, Pedro – Caceres: Tipografia Extremadura, 1923 – 1 – sp Bibl Santa Ana [946]
HEROES: NARRACIONES PARA SOLDADOS / Arendt, Erich – Barcelona, 1938? Fiche W 725. (Blodgett Collection of Spanish Civil War Pamphlets) – 9 – us H.U. College Libr [946]
HEROES OF BOHEMIA : HUSS, JEROME AND ZISCA / Mears, John W – Philadelphia: Presbyterian Board of Publication, c1879 – 1mf – us A.T.L.A. [240]
HEROES OF FAITH : LECTURES ON THE ELEVENTH CHAPTER OF THE EPISTLE TO THE HEBREWS / Vaughan, Charles John – London: Macmillan, 1876 – 1mf – 9 – 0-8370-5622-5 – 1985-3622 – us A.T.L.A. [220]
HEROES OF FAITH AS DELINEATED IN HEBREWS / Guthrie, John – Glasgow: John S. Marr, 1878. 1 fiche – 9 – us A.T.L.A. [240]
HEROES OF FAITH: LECTURES ON THE 11TH CHAPTER...EPISTLES TO THE HEBREWS / Vaughan, Charles John – London: Macmillan, 1876.1 fiche – 9 – us A.T.L.A. [240]
HEROES OF HEBREW HISTORY / Wilberforce, Samuel – London: Daldy, Isbister, 1879. 1 fiche – 9 – us A.T.L.A. [270]
HEROES OF ISRAEL : A TEACHER'S MANUAL TO BE USED IN CONNECTION WITH THE STUDENT'S TEXTBOOK / Soares, Theodore Gerald – (Includes bibliographies) – Chicago, IL: University of Chicago Press; New York: Baker & Taylor [distributor], 1910 – 1mf – 9 – 0-8370-9419-4 – 1986-3419 – us A.T.L.A. [220]
HEROES OF SAN JACINTO / Dixon & Kemp – Houston: Anson Jones Press, 1932. Texas Reel 13. (The Cox Library Collection) – 5 – us Americana [978]
HEROES OF THE CROSS IN AMERICA / Shelton, Don Odell – (Includes index) – New York City: Literature Dept, Presbyterian Home Missions, 1904 – 1mf – 9 – 0-8370-6515-1 – 1986-0515 – us A.T.L.A. [920]
HEROES OF THE MIDDLE WEST: THE FRENCH / Catherwood, Mary Hartwell – Boston: Ginn, 1900. 00700. (Pre-1900 Canadiana) – 9 – cn C.I.H.M. [971]
HEROES OF THE MISSION FIELD : LINKS IN THE STORY OF MISSIONARY WORK FROM THE EARLIEST AGES TO THE CLOSE OF THE EIGHTEENTH CENTURY / Walsh, William Pakenham – New York: Laymen's Missionary Movement, [1879] – 1mf – 9 – 0-8370-6786-3 – 1986-0786 – us A.T.L.A. [920]
HEROES OF THE SADDLE BAGS, A HISTORY OF CHRISTIAN DENOMINATION IN THE REPUBLIC OF TEXAS / Smith, Jesse Guy – 1951 – 1 – 8.75 – us Baptist [240]
HEROES OF THE SOUTH SEAS / Banks, Martha Burr – New York: American Tract Society, c1896 – 1mf – 9 – 0-8370-6006-0 – 1986-0006 – us A.T.L.A. [240]
HEROGLYFIC / Jones, Rowland – 1768. 89p. (English Linguistics Series 1500-1800) – 9 – us UMI [400]
THE HEROIC AGE / Chadwick, H M – H-1171 2. 1912 – 8 – ne IDC [930]
AN HEROIC BISHOP : THE LIFE-STORY OF FRENCH OF LAHORE / Stock, Eugene – London: Hodder and Stoughton, 1913 – 1mf – us A.T.L.A. [240]
HEROIC IDYLS : WITH ADDITIONAL POEMS / Landor, Walter Savage – London: T. Cautley Newby, 1863 – 1 roll – 1 – 1-55879-863-3 – uk Libr Preservation [810]
HEROIC MEN : THE DEATH ROLL OF THE PRIMITIVE METHODIST MINISTRY, BEING SKETCHES OF THE MINISTERS WHO HAVE DIED BETWEEN THE CONFERENCES OF 1888-1889,... / Brownson, W J, et al – London, [1889] – 4mf – 9 – ne IDC [240]
A HEROIC PRIEST : MEMOIR OF JOSEPH FRANCIS BROPHY, D.D.: APOSTLE OF CONEY ISLAND / Boyton, Paul (Mrs) – [S.l.]: George C Tilyou and Paul Boyton, 1910 – 1mf – 9 – 0-8370-6967-X – 1986-0967 – us A.T.L.A. [920]
HEROICA M. CLAUDI PARADINI, BELLIIOCENSIS CANONICI, ET D. GABRIELIS SYMEONIS, SYMBOLAT / Paradin, Claude & Simeoni, G – Antwerpen, 1563 – 4mf – 9 – ne IDC [700]
HEROIDES / Ovid – 28p + 5 color mf – DM520.00 – 3-89219-001-1 – gw Lengenfelder [090]
HEROIDES / Ovid – 14th cent. Holkham ms. 319. Holkham Hall, Norfolk, England – 1 – uk Microform Academic [760]
A HEROINE OF CHARITY AND A QUEEN BY RIGHT DIVINE / O'Meara, Kathleen – London: Burns & Oates, [1891] – 1mf – 9 – 0-8370-6927-0 – 1986-0927 – us A.T.L.A. [920]
HEROINES OF THE MISSION FIELD: BIOGRAPHICAL SKETCHES OF FEMALE MISSIONARIES WHO HAVE LABORED IN VARIOUS LANDS AMONG THE HEATHEN / Pitman, Emma Raymond – 1881 – 9 – us A.T.L.A. [920]
HEROINES OF THE MISSIONARY ENTERPRISE / Eddy, Daniel Clarke – 1850 – 9 – us A.T.L.A. [240]
OS HEROIS DE COARO E PIRAPO / Bayle, Constantino & Jaeger, Luis Gonzaga – Madrid: Razon y Fe, 1943 – 1 – sp Bibl Santa Ana [946]
DER HEROLD – Detroit. 1898-1918 (incomplete) – 16r – 1 – gw Mikrofilm [071]
DER HEROLD – Grand Island, NE. -w. 16 Sep 1886-16 Jun 1892. In German – 1 – us NE Hist [071]
HEROLD – Providence. R.I. -w. (German Language). 1879-83, 1886-87 – 1 – us UMI [071]
HEROLD DER WAHRHEIT – Elkhart, IN. v1-45. 1912-56 (complete) – 14r – 1 – ATLA 1993-S016 – us A.T.L.A. [073]
HEROLD DER WAHRHEIT – (Lacking: v37) – Chicago, IL. v1-38. 1864-1901 – 10r – 1 – ATLA 1992-S002 – us A.T.L.A. [073]
Herold, H W *see* LEBENSVERSICHERUNGEN BEI FEINDLAENDISCHEN GESELLSCHAFTEN
Herold, Reinhold *see* GESCHICHTE DER REFORMATION IN DER GRAFSCHAFT OETTINGEN, 1522-1569
HEROLOGUES OU CHANTS DES POETES ROIS ET L'HOMME RENOUVELE, RECIT MORAL EN VERS / Lemercier, Nepomucene – Paris: Renouard, 1804. 143p. 2 fiches.(Literature Collection) – 9 – 6.00 – fr Bibl Nationale [810]
Heron, James *see*
- THE CELTIC CHURCH IN IRELAND
- THE CHURCH OF THE SUB-APOSTOLIC AGE
- A SHORT HISTORY OF PURITANISM

LE HEROS DE LA MONONGAHELA: ESQUISSE HISTORIQUE / Beaujeu, Monongahela de – Montreal: Desaulniers, 1892. 03031. (Pre-1900 Canadiana) – 9 – cn C.I.H.M. [971]
HERPETOLOGICA – (v.36 .1980 5,6,9) – v.1 1936 – 1 – us UMI [073]
HERPETOLOGISCHE MISCELLEN / Boettger, O – Z-116 2. 1889 – 8 – ne IDC [590]
LE HERPEUR, M.L'ORATOIR DE FRANCE... / ed by Bayle, Constantino – Madrid: Razon y Fe, 1926 – 1 – sp Bibl Santa Ana [944]
DER HERR GEVATTER VON DER STRASSE : GENREBILD IN EINEM AUFZUGE / Langer, Anton – Wien: A Landvogt, 1868 – 1 – us U.W. Library [820]
HERR HEINRICH : DIE SAGA VOM ERSTEN DEUTSCHEN REICH / Vater, Fritz – 3. Aufl. Muenchen: F Eher, 1943 – 1r – 1 – us U.W. Library [943]
HERR UND HUND : IDYLLE / Mann, Thomas – 11.-16. Aufl. Berlin: S Fischer, 1929 – 1r – us U.W. Library [830]
HERREN OHNE HEER : ROMAN DES BALTISCHEN DEUTSCHTUMS / Vegesack, Siegfried von – Berlin: Universitas, c1934 – 1r – 1 – us U.W. Library [830]
HERREN (VONN DES) NACHTMAL, DER PAPISTEN MESSEN – 1526. BME-32 1 – 9 – ne IDC [240]
Herrera, Antonio de *see*
- DESCRIPCION DE LAS INDIAS OCCIDENTALES...
- DESCRIPCIONES DE INDIAS OCCIDENTALES
- HISTORIA GENERAL DE LOS HECHOS DE LOS CASTELLANOS EN LAS ISLAS Y TIERRA FIRME DEL MAR OCEANO
- HISTORIA GENERAL DE LOS HECHOS DE LOS CASTELLANOS EN LAS ISLAS Y TIERRA-FIRME DE EL MAR OCEANO
- HISTORIA GENERAL DE LOS HECHOS DE LOS CASTELLANOS EN LAS ISLAS Y TIERRAFIRME DEL MAR OCEANO
- HISTORIA GENERAL DE LOS HECHOS DE LOS CASTELLANOS EN LAS ISLAS Y TIERRA-FIRME DEL MAR OCEANO
- HISTORIA GENERAL DE LOS HECHOS DE LOS CASTELLANOS EN LAS ISLAS Y TIERRAFIRME DEL MAR OCEANO
- HISTORIA GENERAL...CASTELLANOS...OCEANO
- HISTORIA...CASTELLANOS EN LAS ISLAS... OCEANO
- HISTORIA...INDIAS OCCIDENTALES

Herrera, Benardino *see* MEMORIAS HISTORIAS...CARLOTA JOAQUINA Y DONA MARIANA VICTORIAS
Herrera, Bonifacio *see* PANEGIRICO...SANTA OLALLA
Herrera Carrasco, F *see* SATISFACCION PUBLICA DE UNA...CALUMNIA SOBRE LA CONSTITUCION PLEURISTICO CATHARRAL... DE AIG
Herrera, G *see* OBRA DE AGRICULTURA COMPILADA DE DIVERSOS AUTORES
Herrera Maldonado, Francisco *see* DIALOGOS MORALES DE LUCIANO
Herrera Oria, P Enrique *see* HISTORIA DE LA RECONQUISTA DE ESPANA CONTADA A LA JUVENTUD
Herrera, Philip *see* ENERGY
Herrero Alvarado, Antonio *see* HUELLAS JUVENILES
Herrero, Antonio Maria *see* CARTA DE DON...EN QUE DEMUESTRA QUAN INACCESIBLES HAN SIDO LOS ESFUERZOS DE D. BERNARDO ARAYO PARA DEFENDER QUE NO QUE PHTISIS PULMONAR...
Herrero, Leandro *see*
- EL MONGE DEL MONASTERIO DE YUSTE (ULTIMOS DIAS DEL EMPERADOR CARLOS 5)
- EL MONJE DEL MONASTERIO DE YUSTE

Herrero Mediavilla, Victor *see*
- AFRICAN BIOGRAPHICAL ARCHIVE (AFBA)
- ARCHIVO BIOGRAFICO DE ESPANA, PORTUGAL E IBEROAMERICA 1960-1995

Herrero, Miguel *see* PEDRO ALVARADO, 4TH CENTENARIO DE LA MUERTE DE...1541-1941
Herrero Picado, Manuel F *see* REEMPLAZO DEL EJERCITO Y MILICIAS
Herrero-Mediavilla, Victor *see* ARCHIVO BIOGRAFICO DE ESPANA, PORTUGAL E IBEROAMERICA (ABEPI 1)
Herreruela. Ayuntamiento *see* GRANDES FIESTAS EN HONOR DE SAN JUAN BAUTISTA, 1974
Herrgott, M *see* VETUS DISCIPLINA MONASTICA
DER HERRGOTTSMANTEL : KULTURBILD AUS DEM BAYRISCH-BOEMISCHEN WALDGEBIRGE / Schmidt, Maximilian – Berlin: Hermann Hillger, [189-?] – 1r – 1 – us U.W. Library [910]
Herrich-Schaeffer, G A W *see*
- NOMENCLATOR ENTOMOLOGICUS
- SAMMLUNG NEUER, ODER WENIG BEKANNTER, AUSSEREUROPAEISCHER SCHMETTERLINGEN

HERRICK AND DOXSEE'S PROBATE LAW AND PRACTICE OF THE STATE OF IOWA. / Iowa. Laws, Statutes, etc – 2d ed. Chicago: Callaghan, 1898. 892p. LL-87 – 1 – us L of C Photodup [340]
Herrick, C L *see* THE GEOLOGY OF THE ALBUQUERQUE SHEET
Herrick, George F *see* CHRISTIAN AND MOHAMMEDAN
Herrick, Henry Martyn *see*
- KINGDOM OF GOD IN THE WRITINGS OF THE FATHERS
- THE KINGDOM OF GOD IN THE WRITINGS OF THE FATHERS

HERRICK, MYRON T. PAPERS, MS 2925 – (Correspondence, speeches, articles, memoirs, clippings, memoranda, notes, deeds, reports, diaries and engagement books of this Cleveland born businessman, banker, politician, and diplomat) – 1827-1941 – 49r – 1 – us Western Res [920]
Herridge, William Thomas *see*
- ANNIVERSARY SERMON, 1889: PREACHED...IN ST ANDREW'S CHURCH, SUNDAY EVENING, DEC 1ST
- CHRISTIANITY IN ITS RELATION TO THE STATE AND THE CHURCH: TWO SERMONS PREACHED IN ST ANDREW'S CHURCH, OTTAWA, ON APRIL 7TH AND APRIL 14TH 1889
- A SERMON PREACHED IN ST ANDREW'S CHURCH, OTTAWA, TO STRATHCONA'S HORSE PREVIOUS TO THEIR DEPARTURE FOR SERVICE IN SOUTH AFRICA, ON SUNDAY, THE 11TH MARCH, 1900

Herries, John *see* THE ELEMENTS OF SPEECH
Herrig, Hans *see* LUTHER
Herrig, L *see* ARCHIV FUER DAS STUDIUM DER NEUEREN SPRACHEN
Herrin Daily Journal *see* SOUVENIR PROGRAM OF WILLIAMSON COUNTY CENTENNIAL (AUGUST 26-SEPTEMBER 1, 1929)
HERRIN UND SKLAVE NACH SACHER MASOCH / Esau – Berlin, (Privattyposkript ca. 1910) – 1mf – DM48.00 – 3-8267-3017-8 – gw Hänsel [430]
Herring, Frances Elizabeth *see* CANADIAN CAMP LIFE
Herring, G *see* THE PEOPLE OF THE POLAR NORTH
Herring, Hubert Clinton *see* SPAIN, BATTLEGROUND OF DEMOCRACY
HERRING, NAN TRAMMELL AND JAMES ALEXANDER = MISSIONARIES TO CHINA : CORRESPONDENCE. 1929-1964 – Furman University Library, Greenville, SC Baptist History Collection – 1r – 1 – $37.76 – us Baptist [240]
Herring, Rosa P *see* HEALTH BELIEFS, HEALTH VALUES, AND PREVENTIVE HEALTH PROMOTION ACTIVITIES OF AFRICAN- AND EURO-AMERICAN WOMEN

DIE HERRLICHKEIT GOTTES : EINE BIBLISCH-THEOLOGISCHE UNTERSUCHUNG AUSGEDEHNT UEBER DAS ALTE TESTAMENT, DIE TARGUME, APOKRYPHEN, APOKALYPSEN UND DAS NEUE TESTAMENT / Gall, August, Frieherr von – (Includes bibliographical references) – Giessen: J Ricker, 1900 – 1mf – 9 – 0-8370-3225-3 – 1985-1225 – us A.T.L.A. [220]

Herrmann, A *see* DAS LAND DER DEIDE UND TIBET IM LICHTE DER ANTIKE

Herrmann, Christian *see* DIE WELTANSCHAUUNG GERHART HAUPTMANNS IN SEINEN WERKEN

Herrmann, E *see* DIPLOMATISCHE CORRESPONDENZEN AUS DER REVOLUTIONSZEIT 1791-1797

Herrmann, Emil Alfred *see*
- DER GESTIEFELTE KATER – DAS ROTKAEPPCHEN
- DAS GOTTES KIND

Herrmann, Helene *see* STUDIEN ZU HEINES ROMANZERO

Herrmann, Johannes *see* DIE IDEE DER SUEHNE IM ALTEN TESTAMENT

Herrmann, Peter *see* GESELLSCHAFT UND ORGANISATION

HERRMANN UND ULRIKE : EIN ROMAN / Wezel, Johann Karl; ed by Maassen, Carl Georg von – (Includes bibliographical references) – Muenchen: Georg Mueller, 1919 – 1r – 1 – us U.W. Library [830]

HERRN FIGULLAS SCHAUFENSTER : HEITERE GESCHICHTEN / Menzel, Herybert – 2. Aufl. Hamburg: Hanseatische Verlagsanstalt, 1942 – 1r – 1 – us U.W. Library [830]

HERRN PROF. GELLERTS GEISTLICHE ODEN UND LIEDER / Bach, C P E – 1758 – 9 – us Sibley [780]

HERRN SCHELLBOGEN'S ABENTEUER : EIN STUECKLEIN AUS DEM ALTEN BERLIN / Rodenberg, Julius – Berlin: Gebrueder Paetel, 1890 – 1r – 1 – us U.W. Library [430]

Herron, George D *see* A PLEA FOR THE GOSPEL

HERRSCHAFTSZEICHEN UND STAATSYMBOLIK (MGH SCHRIFTEN..: 13.BD) : BEITRAEGE ZU IHRER GESCHICHTE VOM 3. BIS ZUM 16. JAHRHUNDERT / Schramm, P E – 3 Bde. 1954-1956 – Dfl102.00 – ne Slangenburg [240]

Herschel, John FW *see* PHYSICAL GEOGRAPHY OF THE GLOBE

Herschel, Sir John *see*
- LETTERS AND PAPERS OF SIR JOHN HERSCHEL

Herse, Wilhelm *see* DIE GOETHEZEIT IN DEUTSCHLAND

Hersekli Arif Hikmet, Beg *see* DIVAN

HERSFELDER ZEITUNG – Bad Hersfeld, West Germany. 1969- – ca 10r per yr – 1 – gw Mikrofilm [072]

Hershaw, L M *see* THE HORIZON: A JOURNAL OF THE COLOR LINE

HERSHEY CITIZEN – Hershey, NE. -w. May 1941-Apr 1942 – 1 – us NE Hist [071]

HERSHEY ENTERPRISE – Hershey, NE. -w. Jan 1947-Jul 1963 – 1 – us NE Hist [071]

HERSHEY REVIEW – Hershey, NE. -w. May 1896-Apr 1897 – 1 – us NE Hist [071]

HERSHEY TIMES – Hershey, NE. -w. (-sw 1936). May 1914-Jun 1919; Jul-Nov 1919, scattered issues missing; Jan 1920-Jan 1938 – 1 – us NE Hist [071]

HERSTELLUNG UND SPEKTROSKOPISCHE CHARAKTERISIERUNG MATRIX-ISOLIERTER SILBERCLUSTER / Bauer, Martin – 1992 – 129p – DM98.00 – 3-89349-532-0 – gw Hänsel [540]

HERSTORY – (Herstory 1, 1956-1971. Supplementary Set 1, update -1973. Supplementary Set 2, update -1974. With guide) – 1991 – 90r – 1 – $7,650.00 – D3280 – us Scholarly Res [305]

Hertel, J W *see*
- SAMMLUNG MUSIKALISCHER SCHRIFTEN, GROESSTENTHEILS AUS DEM WERKEN DER ITALIAENER UND FRANZOSEN UEBERSETZT
- SAMMLUNG MUSIKALISCHER SCHRIFTEN, GROESSTENTHEILS AUS DEN WERKEN DER ITALIAENER UND FRANZOSEN UEBERSETZT,...

HERTFORD AND WARE PATRIOT *see* WARE PATRIOT

HERTFORD COUNTY HERALD – Ahoskie. N.C. -w. 1914- – 1 – us UMI [071]

HERTFORDSHIRE, 1823 : BRITISH ISLES CENSUS DIRECTORIES PROJECT, ENGLAND. VOL 211 – 1mf – 9 – A$9.00 – at Vine [941]

HERTFORDSHIRE, 1839 : BRITISH ISLES CENSUS DIRECTORIES PROJECT, ENGLAND. VOL 14 – 2mf – 9 – A$15.00 – at Vine [941]

HERTFORDSHIRE, 1846 : BRITISH ISLES CENSUS DIRECTORIES PROJECT, ENGLAND – at Vine [941]

HERTFORDSHIRE, 1855 : BRITISH ISLES CENSUS DIRECTORIES PROJECT, ENGLAND. VOL 250 – 9mf – 9 – A$57.00 – at Vine [941]

HERTFORDSHIRE, 1862 : BRITISH ISLES CENSUS DIRECTORIES PROJECT, ENGLAND – (In prep) – at Vine [941]

HERTFORDSHIRE, 1864 : BRITISH ISLES CENSUS DIRECTORIES PROJECT, ENGLAND – at Vine [941]

HERTFORDSHIRE, 1874 : BRITISH ISLES CENSUS DIRECTORIES PROJECT, ENGLAND – at Vine [941]

HERTFORDSHIRE, 1886 : BRITISH ISLES CENSUS DIRECTORIES PROJECT, ENGLAND – at Vine [941]

HERTFORDSHIRE, 1899 : BRITISH ISLES CENSUS DIRECTORIES PROJECT, ENGLAND – at Vine [941]

HERTFORDSHIRE, 1908 : BRITISH ISLES CENSUS DIRECTORIES PROJECT, ENGLAND – at Vine [941]

HERTFORDSHIRE EXPRESS *see* HITCHIN AND ROYSTON EXPRESS

HERTFORDSHIRE MERCURY – Hertford, England. Nov 1834-35; 1844-47; 1868-75; 1077-89; 1897; 1913, 1916-18, 1950; Nov 1963-Apr 1967; 1980- – 112+ r – 1 – uk British Libr Newspaper [072]

HERTFORDSHIRE MERCURY – Hoddesdon ed. Hertford, England. Nov 1963-Sep 1974 – 30r – 1 – uk British Libr Newspaper [072]

Hertlein, Eduard *see* DER DANIEL DER ROEMERZEIT

Hertling, Georg Freiherr von *see*
- AUGUSTIN
- DAS PRINCIP DES KATHOLICISMUS UND DIE WISSENSCHAFT

Hertling, Georg von *see* ALBERTUS MAGNUS

Hertogenbosch, Ioannes Evangelista van 'S *see*
- HET EEUWIGH LEVEN
- HET RIJCK GODTS INDER ZIELEN OFT BINNEN U-LIEDEN

HERTS ADVERTISER – St Albans, England. 1858-95; 1897-1907; 1970-Sep 1971; 1977- – 121+ r – 1 – uk British Libr Newspaper [072]

HERTS AND CAMBS REPORTER AND ROYSTON CROW – England, Sep 1876-77; 1883; 1889; 1950; 1980- – 39+ r – 1 – uk British Libr Newspaper [072]

HERTS AND ESSEX OBSERVER (SAFFRON WALDEN EDN) *see* SAFFRON WALDEN AND DISTRICT OBSERVER

Hertslet, Charles John Belcher *see* THE LAW RELATING TO MASTER AND SERVANT.

Hertslet, E *see*
- THE MAP OF EUROPE BY TREATY...
- RECOLLECTIONS OF THE OLD FOREIGN OFFICE

HERTSLET'S COMMERCIAL TREATIES – 1827-1925. 14 reels – 1 – $850.00 – us Trans-Media [340]

HERTSLET'S COMMERCIAL TREATIES – (Indices included) – London. v1-30. 1840-1924. – 382mf – 9 – ne IDC [380]

HERTSPIEGHEL / Spieghel, H L – 1694. O$762 – 9 – ne IDC [760]

HERTSPIEGHEL / Spieghel, H L – O 763. 1723 – 9 – ne IDC [760]

Herttell, Thomas *see* THE DEMURRER: OR, PROOFS OF ERROR IN THE DECISION OF THE SUPREME COURT OF THE STATE OF NEW YORK, REQUIRING FAITH IN PARTICULAR RELIGIOUS DOCTRINES AS A LEGAL QUALIFICATION OF WITNESSES.

Hertz, Eduard *see* VOLTAIRE UND DIE FRANZOSISCHE STRAFRECHTSPFLEGE IM ACHTZEHNTEN JAHRHUNDERT

Hertz, Gottfried Wilhelm *see* NATUR UND GEIST IN GOETHES FAUST

Hertz, Wilhelm *see* DIE NIBELUNGENSAGE

Hertzka, Theodor *see*
- FREELAND A SOCIAL ANTICIPATION
- A VISIT TO FREELAND OR THE NEW PARADISE REGAINED

Hertzler, Arthur Emanuel *see* PAPERS

HERTZOG AND THE SOUTH AFRICAN NATIONALIST PARTY / Lovell, Colin Rhys – Madison 1947 – us Res Libr [960]

HERTZOG-ANNALE – Pretoria, Suid Afrikaanse Akademie vir Wetenskap en Kuns. v1-17, n21. jun 1952-1968 – us Res Libr [960]

HERUT – Tel Aviv. 1948-65. Cont. by Ha-Yom. Available: 1949-65. BJ-91-42 3 – 1 – ne IDC [956]

HERUT U.S.A – New York, NY. 1981 – 1 – us A.J.P.C. [071]

HERVARIUM AUSTRALE GOTTINGAE / Forster, G – 1797 – 1 – uk Microform Academic [580]

Hervas. Ayuntamiento *see*
- FERIAS Y FIESTAS, 1954
- FERIAS Y FIESTAS 1961
- FERIAS Y FIESTAS 1964
- FERIAS Y FIESTAS. HERVAS, 1962
- FERIAS Y FIESTAS HERVAS 1971
- FERIAS Y FIETAS 1963

HERVAS (CACERES) / Junta Provincial de Turismo – (Fotos Javier y Grediol) – Vitoria: Tip. Fournier, s.a. – 1 – sp Bibl Santa Ana [338]

Hervas Y Panduro, Lorenzo *see* CATALOGO DELLE LINGUE CONOSCIUTE E NOTIZIA DELLA LORO AFFINITA E DIVERSITA

Hervas y Panduro, Lorenzo *see*
- CATALOGO DE LAS LENGUAS. TOMO 1
- CATALOGO DE LAS LENGUAS. TOMO 2
- CATALOGO DE LAS LENGUAS. TOMO 3
- CATALOGO DE LAS LENGUAS. TOMO 4
- CATALOGO DE LAS LENGUAS. TOMO 5
- CATALOGO DE LAS LENGUAS. TOMO 6
- CATALOGO DELLE LINGUE CONOSCIUTE E NOTIZIA DELLA LORO AFFINATA, E DIVERSITA
- HISTORIA DE LA VIDA DEL HOMBRE. TOMO I
- HISTORIA DE LA VIDA DEL HOMBRE. TOMO 2
- HISTORIA DE LA VIDA DEL HOMBRE. TOMO 3
- HISTORIA DE LA VIDA DEL HOMBRE. TOMO 4
- HISTORIA DE LA VIDA DEL HOMBRE. TOMO 5
- HISTORIA DE LA VIDA DEL HOMBRE. TOMO 6
- HISTORIA DE LA VIDA DEL HOMBRE. TOMO 7
- EL HOMBRE FISICO. TOMO 1
- EL HOMBRE FISICO. TOMO 2
- VIAGE ESTATICO AL MUNDO PLANETARIO. TOMO 1
- VIAGE ESTATICO AL MUNDO PLANETARIO. TOMO 2
- VIAGE ESTATICO AL MUNDO PLANETARIO. TOMO 3
- VIAGE ESTATICO AL MUNDO PLANETARIO. TOMO 4

Hervey, A B *see* CATALOGUE OF NORTH AMERICAN MUSCI

Hervey, Arthur Charles *see*
- THE AUTHENTICITY OF THE GOSPEL OF ST LUKE
- THE PENTATEUCH

Hervey, George Winfred *see* MANUAL OF REVIVALS

Hervey, James *see* ELEVEN LETTERS FROM THE LATE REV. MR. HERVEY TO THE REV. MR. JOHN WESLEY, CONTAINING AN ANSWER TO THAT GENTLEMAN'S 'REMARKS ON THERON AND ASPASIO'...

Hervieux, J-A *see* LE NORD

HERVORMD NEDERLAND : H.N. MAGAZINE – (Some issues lacking) – v25-49. 1969-93 – 36r – 1 – ATLA S0274 – us A.T.L.A. [240]

DER HERVORMER – v38-42; v51-68; v70; v75-83. 1947-Aug 1950; 1960-79; 1984-1990/91 (complete) – 8r – 1 – ATLA S0792 – us A.T.L.A. [073]

DE HERVORMING IN SPANJE : IN DE ZESTIENDE EEUW / Lennep, M F van – Haarlem: De Erven Loosjes, 1901 – 2mf – us A.T.L.A. [240]

HERWARTH WALDEN UND DIE EUROPAEISCHE AVANTGARDE / Berlin. Staatliche Museen – 1961 – 9 – $9.80 – uk Chadwyck [700]

HERWEGH ALS UEBERSETZER / Kilian, Werner – Stuttgart: Metzler, 1914 – 1r – 1 – us U.W. Library [430]

Herwig, Rachel Monika *see* DIE JUEDISCHE FRAU ALS MUTTER

Herxheimer, S *see* A KEY TO THE EXERCISES OF THE NEW METHOD OF LEARNING THE HEBREW LANGUAGE

HERZ IN BOEHMEN : GEDICHTE / Hoeller, Franz – 2. Aufl. Prag: Volk und Reich Verlag, 1943 – 1r – 1 – us U.W. Library [810]

Herzberg, I *see* AUS VERGANGENHEIT UND GEGENWART DER JUDEN. IN DEN POSENER LANDEN

Herzberger, FW *see* PILGERKLAENGE

Herzen, Aleksandr I *see*
- DE L'AUTRE RIVE
- DU DEVELOPPEMENT DES IDEES REVOLUTIONNAIRES EN RUSSIE PAR A. ISCANDER
- LETTRES DE FRANCE ET D'ITALIE (1847-1852)
- LE MONDE RUSSE ET LA REVOLUTION, MEMOIRES
- NOUVELLE PHASE DE LA LITTERATURE RUSSE
- LE PEUPLE RUSSE ET LE SOCIALISME

HERZENSERGIESSUNGEN EINES KUNSTLIEBENDEN KLOSTERBRUDERS / Wackenroder, Wilhelm Heinrich; ed by Jessen, Karl Detlev – Leipzig: E Diederichs, 1904 – 1r – 1 – us U.W. Library [430]

HERZENSERGIESSUNGEN EINES KUNSTLIEBENDEN KLOSTERBRUDERS / Wackenroder, Wilhelm Heinrich – Leipzig: E Diederichs, 1904 – 1 – us U.W. Library [830]

Herzfeld, G *see* THE OLD ENGLISH MARTYROLOGY

Herzfeld, Hans *see* JOHANNES VON MIQUEL. SEIN ANTEIL AM AUSBAU DES DEUTSCHEN REICHES BIS ZUR JAHRHUNDERTWENDE

Herzfeld, L *see* HANDELSGESCHICHTE DER JUDEN DES ALTERTUMS

Herzfeld, Levi *see* EINBLICKE IN DAS SPRACHLICHE DER SEMITISCHEN URZEIT BETREFFEND DIE ENTSTEHUNGSWEISE DER MEISTEN HEBRAEISCHEN WORTSTAEMME

Herzig, Thomas *see* STRUKTURANALYSE AB INITIO SCHWACH STREUENDEN KRISTALLEN MIT SYNCHROTRONSTRAHLUNG

Herzl, T *see*
- BERICHTE AUS PARIS AN DIE "NEUE FREIE PRESSE" IN WIEN, 1891-1895
- BRIEFE

HERZL VE-HA-YISHUV HA-YASHAN BI-YERUSHALAYIM / Malachi, E R – (Ha-Do'ar). New York. 1957. BJ-27-46 1 – 9 – ne IDC [956]

HERZL-BUND-BLAETTER – Berlin, 1913-18 (incomplete) – 1r – 1 – Dist. gw Mikrofilm – gw Misc Inst [072]

HERZL-BUND-BLAETTER – Berlin. v1-40. 1913-18. Incomplete. 1 reel. B98 (Leo Baeck Institute. German-Jewish Periodicals, Pt 2) – 1 – $60.00 – us UPA [270]

DIE HERZMARKE : DRAMA IN ZWEI TEILEN / Langmann, Philipp – Stuttgart: J Cotta, [1902] – 1r – 1 – us U.W. Library [820]

Herzog, A *see* REPORTS ON CLINICAL SIGNIFICANCE OF CATALASE

HERZOG ALBRECHT VON PREUSSEN ALS REFORMATORISCHE PERSOENLICHKEIT / Tschackert, Paul – Halle: Verein fuer Reformationsgeschichte, 1894. ([Schriften des Vereins fuer Reformationsgeschichte; Bd. 45]) – 1mf – us A.T.L.A. [240]

HERZOG ALBRECHT VON PREUSSEN UND SEIN HOFPREDIGER : EINE KOENIGSBERGER TRAGOEDIE AUS DEM ZEITALTER DER REFORMATION / Hase, Carl Alfred – Leipzig: Breitkopf und Haertel, 1879 – 1mf – us A.T.L.A. [240]

Herzog, Johann J *see*
- ABRISS DER GESAMTEN KIRCHENGESCHICHTE
- DIE ROMANISCHEN WALDENSER

Herzog, Johannes *see* DER BEGRIFF DER BEKEHRUNG

Herzog, Karl *see* GESCHICHTE DER DEUTSCHEN NATIONAL-LITTERATUR MIT PROBEN DER DEUTSCHEN DICHTKUNST UND BEREDSAMKEIT

HERZOG KARL AUGUST UND GOETHE / Wachsmuth, Wilhelm – Leipzig: Xenien-Verlag, 1911 – 1r – 1 – us U.W. Library [430]

Herzog, Peter *see* JOHANNES VON MUELLER UND DIE FRANZOESISCHE LITERATUR

Herzog, Rudolph *see* DIE SCHLESISCHEN MUSENALMANACHE VON 1773-1823

DER HERZOG UND DAS GENIE : FRIEDRICH SCHILLERS JUGENDJAHRE / Mueller, Ernst – (Includes index) – Stuttgart: W Kohlhammer, c1955 – 1r – 1 – us U.W. Library [920]

Herzog, Werner *see* MYSTIK UND LYRIK BEI NOVALIS

DAS HERZOGSPAAR FERDINAND UND JULIE VON ANHALT-KOETHEN, DIE ANFAENGE DER KATHOLISCHEN PFARREI KOETHEN UND DER HEILIGE STUHL / Bastgen, Hubert – Paderborn, 1937 – 80p – 9 – DM48.00 – 3-89349-252-6 – gw Hänsel [240]

HERZTAETIGKEIT UND EEG-NEGATIVIERUNG IN ERWARTUNG BEDROHLICHER INFORMATIONEN : EIN DIFFERENTIELLER PSYCHOPHYSIOLOGISCHER BEITRAG ZUR AUFMERKSAMKEITSREGULATION / Felinger, Martina – 1993 – 2mf – 9 – DM98.00 – 3-89349-634-3 – gw Hänsel [150]
Hes, Else *see* CHARLOTTE BIRCH-PFEIFFER ALS DRAMATIKERIN
Hesbert, R J *see*
- ANTIPHONALE MISSARUM SEXTUPLEX
- CORPUS ANTIPHONALIUM OFFICII

Heselman, George J *see* DIGEST OF THE DECISIONS...IN CASES RELATED TO PUBLIC LANDS
Hesius, G *see* EMBLEMATA SACRA DE FIDE, SPE, CHARITATE
Hesman, Gerrit *see*
- CHRISTELYKE AANDACHTEN OF VLAMMENDE ZIEL-ZUCHTEN, EENER GODVREESENDE ZIELE, MET EEN GODDELIJK ANTWOORD DAAR OP PASSENDE
- CUPIDOOS MENGELWERKEN OF MINNESPIEGEL DER DEUGDEN, BESTAANDE UIT STIGHTELYKE ZINNEBEELDEN

HESPERIAN – Gainesville. Tex. 1888-97; 1904-07 – 1 – us UMI [071]
HESPERIAN – Gainesville. Tex. -w. 1890-96 – 1 – us UMI [071]
HESPERIAN – Portland, OR. 9 Sept 1883-17 May 1884. 1 roll – 1 – us U.O. Library [071]
DIE "HESPERIDINE" IN DEN ACHAENEN DER KOMPOSITEN / Gorschboth, P – Repert. sp. nov., Beih. Dahlem bei Berlin, 1927 – 2mf – 9 – ne IDC [615]
HESPERIIDAE INDICAE / Watson, E Y – 7321 2. 1891 – 8 – ne IDC [580]
HESPERIS : ARCHIVES BERBERES ET... – Paris. v1-28. 1921-41. – 277mf – 8 – ne IDC [073]
HESPEROS – (In Greek) – Leipzig, Germany. May-Oct 1888 – 4r – 1 – uk British Libr Newspaper [072]
Hess, Adolf *see* CHRISTIAN WEISES HISTORISCHE DRAMEN UND IHRE QUELLEN
Hess, J *see*
- DISPOSITIEN DER MERKWAARDIGSTE KERK-ORGELEN, WELKEN IN DE ZEVEN VEREEENIGDE PROVINCIEN ALS MEDE IN DUYTSLAND EN ELDERS AANGETROFFEN WORDEN
- OVER DE VEREISCHTEN IN EENEN ORGANIST

Hess, M *see* ROM UND JERUSALEM DIE LETZTE NATIONALITAETENFRAGE
Hess, Moses *see* DIE LETZTEN PHILOSOPHEN
Hesse *see* STAATS ANZEIGER. WIESBADEN. 1959-1968
Hesse, Friedrich Hermann *see*
- DIE ENTSTEHUNG DER NEUTESTAMENTLICHEN HIRTENBRIEFE
- DER TERMINISTISCHE STREIT

Hesse, Hermann *see*
- AUSGEWAEHLTE GEDICHTE
- DER BLUETENZWEIG
- NEUE GEDICHTE
- DIE NUERNBERGER REISE
- WANDERUNG

Hesse, Johann H *see* KURZE, DOCH HINLAENGLICHE ANWEISUNG ZUM GENERAL-BASSE
Hesse, Johannes *see* VOM GEGENSGANG DER BIBEL DURCH DIE HEIDENWELT
Hesse, O *see* DIE FLECHTENSTOFFE
Hesse. Statistisches Landesamt *see* HESSISCHE MONATSZAHLEN
Hessel, Karl *see* DEUTSCHE KOLONISATION IN OSTAFRIKA.
Hessel, Karl Robert Heinrich *see* HEINRICH HEINES VERHAELTNIS ZUR BILDENDEN KUNST
Hesselbarth, Hermann *see* DREI PSYCHOLOGISCHE FRAGEN ZUR SPANISCHEN THRONKANDIDATUR LEOPOLDS VON HOHENZOLLERN, MIT GEHEIMDEPESCHEN BISMARCKS
Hesselman, Bengt *see* HUVUDLINJER I NORDISK SPRAKHISTORIA
[HESSEN FOUNDATION FOR PEACE AND CONFLICT RESEARCH PAMPHLET COLLECTION] – 1972 – 1 – CSUXAMJ3094-B – us Hoover Inst Photo [327]
Hessen, Jozef van *see* NIKOLAUS LENAU UND DAS JUNGE DEUTSCHLAND
Hessen, Moritz von *see* LEXICUM FRANTZOESISCH UND TEUTSCH (AEL, ABT 2;14)
HESSEN-DARMSTAEDTISCHE PRIVILEGIRTE LANDES-ZEITUNG – (Title changes: Grossherzoglich Hessische Landzeitung, 19 Aug 1806; Grossherzoglich Hessische Zeitung, 2 Jul 1808; Darmstaedter Zeitung, 22 Mar 1848) – Darmstadt, Germany. 1848-1849 – 4r – 1 – gw Mikrofilm [072]
HESSEN-KURIER – Friedberg. 1948 n3, 6, 8 – 1 – gw Mikrofilm [073]
Hessey, James Augustus *see* MORAL DIFFICULTIES CONNECTED WITH THE BIBLE
Hesshusen, T *see*
- ANTIDOTVM CONTRA IMPIVM ET BLASPHEMVM DOGMA MATTHIAE FLACII ILLYRICI,...
- BEKENDTNIS DOCTORIS TILEMANNI HESHVSII VON DER PERSOENLICHEN VND IN ALLE EWIGKEIT VNZERTRENLICHEN VEREINIGUNG BEYDER NATUREN IN JHESU CHRISTO...
- DE DVABVS NATVRIS IN CHRISTO, EARVMQVE VNIONE HYPOSTATICA TRACTATVS
- EXAMEN THEOLOGICVM, COMPLECTENS PRAECIPVA CAPITA DOCTRINAE CHRISTIANAE, DE QVIBVS INTERROGATI...
- EXPLICATIO EPISTOLAE PAVLI AD GALATAS
- EXPLICATIO EPISTOLAE PAVLI AD ROMANOS
- EXPLICATIO PRIORIS EPISTOLAE PAVLI AD CORINTHIOS
- EXPLICATIO PSALMI CX. IN QVA DOCTRINA DE SPIRITUALI REGNO...
- EXPLICATIO SECVNDAE EPISTOLAE PAVLI AD CORINTHIOS
- POSTILLA DAS IST AUSSLEGUNG DER EUANGELIEN AUFF ALLE FEST VND APOSTEL TAGE DURCHS GANTZE JAR

HESSIAN DOCUMENTS OF THE AMERICAN REVOLUTION, 1776-1783 / Lidgerwood Collection of Morristown National Historical Park – 1989 – 364mf – 9 – $1650.00 Export $1980.00 – 0-8161-1748-9 – uk Hall [025]
HESSISCHE ALLGEMEINE (HNA) – (Title change: Fritzlar-Homberger Allgemeine, 26 Jun 1991) – Fritzlar, West Germany. 1977- – ca 8r per yr – 1 – gw Mikrofilm [072]
HESSISCHE ALLGEMEINE (HNA) *see* HESSISCHE NACHRICHTEN
DER HESSISCHE BAUER *see* DEUTSCHE VOLKSWACHT
HESSISCHE BLAETTER FUER BOLKSKUNDE – Leipzig etc. Bd. 1-24; 1902-25. Film Mas C 642 – 1 – us H.U. Library [073]
HESSISCHE HEIMAT – Friedberg. may 10, 1950-dec 24, 1960 – 1 – gw Mikrofilm [073]
HESSISCHE MONATSZAHLEN / Hesse. Statistisches Landesamt – Feb 1947-Dec 1955. Jan-Jun 1948, Jul-Dec 1950 wanting – 1 – 122.00 – us L of C Photodup [943]
HESSISCHE NACHRICHTEN – Kassel, 1945-49 – 4r – 1 – DM300.00 – gw Mikro Press [072]
HESSISCHE NACHRICHTEN – Kassel, Germany. 26 Sep 1945-30 Jun 1951 – 12r – 1 – uk British Libr Newspaper [072]
HESSISCHE NACHRICHTEN – (Title change: Hessische Allgemeine (HNA), 28 Apr 1959) – Kassel, West Germany. 1968- – ca 12r per yr – 1 – gw Mikrofilm [072]
HESSISCHE POST / ed by Die Amerikanische Armee – 28 Apr-22 Sep 1945 – 1r – 1 – DM75.00 – gw Mikro Press [072]
HESSISCHE POST / ed by Die Amerikanische Armee – Kassel, West Germany. 28 Apr-22 Sept 1945 – 1r – 1 – gw Mikrofilm [072]
DER HESSISCHE VOLKSFREUND – Marburg, Germany. 22 Mar 1848-29 Jun 1853 – 2r – 1 – gw Mikrofilm [072]
HESSISCHE/NIEDERSAECHSISCHE ALLGEMEINE – (Bereichsausgabe der Hessischen/Niedersaechsischen Allgemeinen, Kassel. Nur Regionalseite "Suedniedersachsen" bzw "Kreis Goettingen") – Goettingen. 1975-92 – 6r – 1 – gw Mikrofilm [072]
Hessling, T von *see* DIE PERLMUSCHELN UND IHRE PERLEN
HESTER THRALE-PIOZZI, SAMUEL JOHNSON AND LITERARY SOCIETY, 1755-1821 – Thrale-Piozzi and related manuscripts from the John Rylands University Library Manchester. Part 1: Letters to and from Hester Thrale-Piozzi; Part 2: Inventories, Journals and Writings of Thrale-Piozzi, Williams family correspondence and Samuel Johnson's papers – 1 – us Primary [090]
HESTIA – Athenai, Greece, 1973-81 – 1 – us Res Libr [949]
HESTIA – Athens, Greece. 4 Jan 1876-2 Jul 1895 – 19r – 1 – uk British Libr Newspaper [949]
HESTIA EIKONOGRAPHEMENE *see* HESTIA
HETCHERY TRIBUNE AND FEED RETAILER *see* FARM SUPPLIER
HETEROCYCLES – v. 1-. 1973- – apply; v,1; v.7- 1978- 5,6,9 – us UMI [540]
HETERODOX LONDON, OR, PHASES OF FREE THOUGHT IN THE METROPOLIS / Davies, Charles Maurice – London: Tinsley, 1874 – 2mf – us A.T.L.A. [240]
Hetherington, Clark W *see* SCHOOL PROGRAM IN PHYSICAL EDUCATION
Hetherington, W M *see* HISTORY OF THE CHURCH OF SCOTLAND
Hetherwick, Alexander *see* A PRACTICAL HANDBOOK OF THE NYANJA LANGUAGE
HETHITISCHE STAATSVERTRAEGE : EIN BEITRAG ZU IHRER JURISTISCHEN WERTUNG / Koresec, V – Leipzig, 1931 – 3mf – 8 – ne Slangenburg [490]
HETI HIREK – London, UK. 1 Feb-20 Dec 1957 – 1 – uk British Libr Newspaper [072]
Hettinger, Franz *see* DIE "KRISE DES CHRISTENTUMS"
Hettner, Alfred *see* GEOGRAPHISCHE ZEITSCHRIFT
HETTY WESLEY / Quiller-Couch, Arthur Thomas – London, New York: Harper and Brothers, 1903 – 1 roll – 1 – 1-55879-511-1 – uk Libr Preservation [890]
Hetu, Jean *see* LE COURRIER DE TERREBONNE
Heubach, Helga *see* DIE FASERPFLANZE HANF
Heucher, J H von *see*
- INDEX PLANTARUM HORTI... VITEMBERGENSIS...
- NOVI PROVENTUS HORTI MEDICI...

Heufler, L R von *see* ASPLENII SPECIES EUROPAEAE
Heuglin, M Th. von *see*
- ORNITHOLOGIE NORDOST-AFRIKA'S
- REISE IN DAS GEBIET DES WEISSEN NIL, IN DEN JAHREN 1862-1864
- REISE IN NORDOST AFRIKA: NEBST ZOOLOGISCHEN SKIZZEN
- REISE NACH ABESSINIEN, IN DEN JAHREN 1861 UND 1862
- SYSTEMATISCHE UEBERSICHT DER VOEGEL NORD OST AFRIKA S

Heukenkamp, Marianne *see* DEN ‚WILLEN ZUM IDEAL' INS LEBEN SELBST VERWANDELN
Heun, Hans Georg *see* SHAKESPEARE IN DEUTSCHEN UEBERSETZUNGEN
Heupel, WE *see* DE SIZILISCHE GROSSHOF UNTER KAISER FRIEDRICH 2 (MGH SCHRIFTEN..: 4.BD)
Heurck, H F van *see*
- PRODROME DE LA FLORE DES ALGUES MARINES DES ILES ANGLO-NORMANDES ET DES COTES NORD-OUEST DE LA FRANCE
- SYNOPSIS DES DIATOMEES DE BELGIQUE

L'HEURE – Journal republicain du soir. Paris. janv-juin 1917 – 1 – fr A.C.R.P.P. [073]
UNE HEURE DE MARIAGE : COMEDIE EN UN ACTE ET EN PROSE / Dalayrac, N – (Score) – Pleyel, 1804 – 1 – us Sibley [780]
L'HEURE ESPAGNOL. TRIO SUR L'OPERA... : EDITION POUR PIANO, FLUTE ET VIOLONCELLE AVEC CONTRABASSE ET CLARINNETE AD LIBITUM / Ravel, M & Moulton, H – Paris: Durand & Fils, 1912 – 1 – us Sibley [780]
HEURES A L'USAGE DE REIMS, EN LATIN – Paris: J. du Pre, 1495 – fr Armell [910]
HEURES ROMAINES, CONTENANT LES OFFICES DE LA SAINTE VIERGE ET DES MORTS – 2e ed. Quebec: Jean Neilson, 1812. SEM16P30 – 1r – 5 – Can$9.00 – cn Bibl Nat [240]
HEURES ROMAINES, CONTENANT LES OFFICES DE LA SAINTE VIERGE ET DES MORTS – Quebec: Jean Neilson, 1795. SEM16P93 – 1r – 5 – Can$9.00 – cn Bibl Nat [240]
L'HEUREUSE NATION, OU RELATIONS DU GOUVERNEMENT DES FELICIENS, PEOPLE SOUVERAINEMENT LIBRE SOUS L'EMPIRE ABSOLU DE SES LOIS / Le Mercier de la Riviere – (Utopias in the Enlightment series). 1792 – 9 – fr Hachette [300]
L'HEUREUX NAUFRAGE OU L'ON TROUVE UNE IDEE DE LEGISLATION CONFORME A L'HUMANITE, A LA NATURE, AU BIEN PUBLIC / Serane, Philippe – (Utopias of the Enlightenment series). 1789 – 9 – fr Hachette [190]
L'HEUREUZ DEPIT : COMEDIE LIRIQUE EN UN ACTE, EN VERS / Chapelle, P – (Full Score) – Paris: Deslaurier, 177- – 1 – us Sibley [780]
Heuschele, Otto *see*
- DIE FUERSTIN
- DIE GENERALIN
- LEONORE
- DIE WANDLUNG

Heuschkel, Walter *see* UNTERSUCHUNGEN UEBER RAMLERS UND LESSINGS BEARBEITUNG VON SINNGEDICHTEN LOGANS
Heuschling, Xavier *see* COUP-D'OEIL SUR LA NOUVELLE ORGANISATION DE LA STATISTIQUE GENERALE EN FRANCE, ET LES ORGANISATIONS ANTERIEURES
Heuser, Ralph *see* METHODIK DER FLOW-OF-FUNDS-RECHNUNG FUER PROGNOSEN DES MONETAEREN SEKTORS IN ENTWICKLUNGSLAENDERN
Heusinger, J H G *see* HANDBUCH DER AESTHETIK
Heusner, William *see* THE EFFECTS OF EXERCISE TRAINING AND SEVERE CALORIC RESTRICTION ON LEAN-BODY MASS IN THE OBESE
Heuss, Theodor *see* ZWISCHEN GESTERN UND MORGEN
Heussen, H F van *see* BATAVIA SACRA OF KERKELIJKE HISTORIE EN OUDHEDEN
Heussen, J van *see* OUDHEDEN EN GESTICHTEN
Heussi, Karl *see*
- JOHANN LORENZ MOSHEIM
- UNTERSUCHUNGEN ZU NILUS DEM ASKETEN (T.U.U. 3-42/2)
- DER URSPRUNG DES MOENCHTUMS

HEUTE UND MORGEN : WOCHENSCHRIFT FUER POLITIK, WIRTSCHAFT UND KULTUR – Sevres-Paris-Vanves. Sept 1934-Oct 1936 – 2r – 1 – gw Mikrofilm [072]
HEUTE UND MORGEN *see* CHUG. KREIS DER BUECHERFREUNDE
HEUTE UND MORGEN. AUJOURD'HUI ET DEMAIN – Wochenschrift fuer Politiek, Wirtschaft und Kultur. Herausgegeben von Wolf Franck. Sevres, Paris puis Vanves. sept 1934-oct 1936 – 1 – fr A.C.R.P.P. [073]
HEUTE UND MORGEN/ANITFASCHISTISCHE REVUE *see* CHUG. KREIS DER BUECHERFREUNDE
DER HEUTIGE STAND DER ROEMISCHEN RECHTSWISSENSCHAFT; ERREICHTES UND ERSTREBTES / Wenger, Leopold – Munchen, Beck, 1927. 113 p. LL-4016 – 1 – us L of C Photodup [340]
Heutz, N M *see* THE SPIDERS OF THE UNITED STATES
Heveningham, William *see* STATE PAPERS AND FAMILY DOCUMENTS/COMMONPLACE BOOK
HEVES ETTIM / Nazim, Nabizade – Istanbul: Mihran Matbaasi, 1302 [1885] – $20.00 – us MEDOC [470]
Hevesi, Lajos *see*
- BLAUE FERNEN
- DER ZERBROCHENE FRANZ

HEVRA – (In English) – Montreal, CN. v2 no 2. 1972-1973 – 1r – 1 – Can$25.00 – cn Can Microfilming [072]
Hewes, John *see*
- FLORILOGIUM PHRASICON
- A PERFECT SURVEY OF THE ENGLISH TONGUE

Hewison, James King *see*
- THE COVENANTERS
- THE RUNIC ROODS OF RUTHWELL AND BEWCASTLE

Hewit, Augustine Francis *see*
- PROBLEMS OF THE AGE
- TEACHING OF ST JOHN THE APOSTLE TO THE CHURCHES OF ASIA AND THE WORLD

Hewitson, W C *see* DESCRIPTIONS OF NEW INDIAN LEPIDOPTEROUS INSECTS
Hewitt, James *see*
- THE BATTLE OF TRENTON
- THREE SONATAS FOR THE PIANO FORTE, OPUS 5
- YANKEE DOODLE WITH VARIATIONS

Hewitt, John *see* HISTORY AND TOPOGRAPHY OF THE PARISH OF WAKEFIELD AND ITS ENVIRONS
Hewlett, H G *see* LIBER QUI DICITUR FLORES HISTORIARUM AB A. D. 1154 ANNOQUE HENRICI ANGLORUM REGIS SECUNDI PRIMO (RS84)
Hewlett, Henry Gay *see* HENRY FOTHERGILL CHORLEY
Hewson, W *see* EXPERIMENTAL INQUIRIES

Hewstone Burotto, Luis *see* LA FUERZA MAYOR EN EL DERECHO MERCANTIL.

HEXACHORDUM APOLLINIS SEX ARIAS.. / Pachelbel, Johann – 1699 – 9 – us Sibley [780]

DER HEXAMETER BEI KLOPSTOCK UND VOSS / Linckenheld, Emil – (Includes bibliographical references (p. 9-10)) – Strassburg i.E.: C J Goeller, 1906 – 1r – 1 – us U.W. Library [430]

THE HEXATEUCH ACCORDING TO THE REVISED VERSION – Arranged by members of the Society of Historical Theology, Oxford. Ed. with introd., notes, marginal references and synoptical tables by J. Estlin Carpenter and G. Harford-Battersby. London, New York: Longmans, Green and Co., 1900. 2v – 1 – us U.W. Library [240]

DER HEXENHAMMER : DIE MITTELALTERLICHE HISTORIE VON DER FOLTERUNG DES MEDICUS JOHANN WEYER / ed by Juhn, Kurt – New York City: F Krause, 1944 – 1 – us U.W. Library [943]

HEXENWAHN UND HEXENPROZESS : VORNEHMLICH IM 16. JAHRHUNDERT / Paulus, Nikolaus – (Includes bibliographical references and index) – Freiburg i.B.: Herder, 1910 – 1mf – 9 – 0-8370-7415-0 – 1986-1415 – us A.T.L.A. [230]

Hey, Friedrich Oskar *see* DER TRAUMGLAUBE DER ANTIKE: EIN HISTORISCHER VERSUCH

Heyd, Guenther *see* GOETHE ALS MENSCH UND DEUTSCHER

Heyd, U *see*
- DAHIR-AL'UMAR SHALLIT HA-GALIL
- TE'UDOT TURKIYYOT AL YEHUDEI ZEFAT BA-MEAH HA-16
- YEHUDEI EREZ-YISRA'EL BE-SOF HA-ME'AH HA-17

Heydecker, Edward Le Moyne *see*
- COMMENTARY ON MECHANIC'S LIEN LAW FOR THE STATE OF NEW YORK; CHAPTER XLIX OF THE GENERAL LAWS.
- THE WAR REVENUE LAW OF 1898

Heyden, J van der *see* THE LOUVAIN AMERICAN COLLEGE, 1857-1907

Heyden, S *see* DE ARTE CANENDI

Heydenreich, G H *see* LEPIDOPTERORUM EUROPAEORUM CATALOGUS METHODICUS

Heydon, John *see* THE ENGLISH PHYSITIANS GUIDE OR A HOLYGUIDE; LEADING THE WAY TO KNOW ALL THINGS, PAST, PRESENT & TO COME

Heyl, Lewis *see* STATUTES OF THE UNITED STATES RELATING TO REVENUE, COMMERCE, NAVIGATION, AND THE CURRENCY

HET HEYLICH HERTE VER-EERT AEN ALLE GODT-VRUGHTIGHE HERTEN VOOR EEN NIEU-IAER / Poirters, Adrianus – Antwerpen, 1660 – 3mf – 9 – ne IDC [700]

HEYLIGH HOF VANDEN KEYSER THEODOSIUS VERCIERT MET SINEBEELDEN, RYMDICHTEN, EN SEDELEERINGEN / Poirters, Adrianus – Ieperen, Antwerpen, 1696 – 4mf – 9 – O-3150/1 – ne IDC [760]

Heylyn, Peter *see* HISTORIA QUINQU-ARTICULARIS..

Heym, Georg *see* DER EWIGE TAG

Heymer, Juergen *see* DIAGNOSE DES TECHNISCHEN ZUSTANDES UND DES INNENRAUMZUSTANDES VON GASLEITUNGEN UNTER DER BEDINGUNG UNVOLLSTAENDIGER INFORMATION

HEYMISH = AT HOME – (In Yiddish) – Berlin, DE. no1. Mar 1924 – 1r – 1 – $25.00 – cn Can Microfilming [072]

Heymowski, Adam *see* CATALOGUE PROVISOIRE DES MANUSCRIPTS MAURITANIENS EN LANGUE ARABE PRESERVES EN MAURITANIE

Heynen, J D *see* DEVELOPMENT AND EDUCATION IN THE MWANZA DISTRICT (TANZANIA)

Heynen, Walter *see* DAS BUCH DEUTSCHER BRIEFE

Heynhold, G *see* NOMENCLATOR BOTANICUS HORTENSIS

Heynicke, Kurt *see* KAMPF UM PREUSSEN

Heyns, Maria *see* BLOEMHOF DER DOORLUCHTIGE VOORBEELDEN

Heyns, P *see* ESBATIMENT MORAL, DES ANIMAUX

Heyns, Z *see* EMBLEMATA. EMBLEMES CHRESTIENES ET MORALES

DE HEYR-BAENE DES CRUYS, WAER-LANGHS ALLE SOORTEN VAN MENSCHEN WORDEN GHEWESEN, ENDE SEKERLIJCK GHELEERT, OM DOOR DE CRUYCEN VAN ALDERHANDE LIJDEN OFT TEGHENSPOEDT VAN DESE BEDROEFDE TIJDELIJCKE WERELDT,... / Haeften, Benedictus van – 1st ed. Brugge, 1667 – 5mf – 9 – O-3076/1 – ne IDC [760]

HEYSE AND HIS PREDECESSORS IN THE THEORY OF THE NOVELLE / Mitchell, Robert McBurney – Frankfurt a.M.: J Baer, 1915 – 1r – 1 – us U.W. Library [430]

Heyse, Paul *see*
- ABENTEUER EINES BLAUSTRUEMPFCHENS
- ANDREA DELFIN
- AUS DEN VORBERGEN
- DAS MAEDCHEN VON TREPPI
- MEDEA
- NOVELLEN
- NOVELLENSCHATZ DES AUSLANDES
- DER SALAMANDER
- VETTER GABRIEL

Heyse, Theodore *see*
- BIBLIOGRAPHIE DU CONGO BELGE ET DU RUANDA-URUNDI
- DOCUMENTATION GENERALE SUR LE CONGO ET LE RUANDA-URUNDI, 1953-1955
- INDEX BIBLIOGRAPHIQUE COLONIAL
- LE REGIME DU TRAVAIL AU CONGO BELGE.
- LE REGIME DU TRAVAIL AU CONGO BELGE

Heyse, Ulrich *see* KARTENSPIEL

HEYTESBURY REFORMER – 1897-1918 – 7r – 1 – at Corangamite [072]

HEYTHROP JOURNAL : A QUARTERLY REVIEW OF PHILOSOPHY AND THEOLOGY – (1985-5,6,9) – v1- 1960- – 1 – us UMI [100]

Heyward, DuBose *see* "PORGY" DRAFTS

HEYWOOD ADVERTISER – Heywood, England. 1865-67; 1960-74. 18 reels – 1 – uk British Libr Newspaper [072]

Heywood, Oliver *see* THE REVEREND OLIVER HEYWOOD, B.A. 1630-1702

HEYWOOD SHIRE MINUTES – 1988-1994 – 6r – 5 – at Corangamite [910]

Heywood, Thomas *see*
- AN APOLOGY FOR ACTORS (1612) BY THOMAS HEYWOOD, BOUND WITH A REFUTATION OF THE APOLOGY FOR ACTORS (1615) BY I.G
- A MEMOIR OF SIR BENJAMIN HEYWOOD, BARONET. WITH TWO CHAPTERS OF DOMESTIC LIFE AND LETTERS, 1840-65

Heywood, William S *see* AUTOBIOGRAPHY OF ADIN BALLOU, 1803-1890

Hezekia, Moses ben *see* ZUR LOESUNG DER JUDENFRAGE DURCH DIE JUDEN: EIN JUEDISCHER OSTERABEND

H.F. Kett and Co *see*
- HISTORY OF CARROLL COUNTY
- HISTORY OF HENRY COUNTY (ITS TAX-PAYERS AND VOTERS)
- HISTORY OF JO DAVIESS COUNTY
- HISTORY OF OGLE COUNTY
- HISTORY OF WINNEBAGO COUNTY
- PAST AND PRESENT OF BOONE COUNTY, ILLINOIS
- PAST AND PRESENT OF LA SALLE COUNTY
- PAST AND PRESENT OF ROCK ISLAND COUNTY
- THE VOTERS AND TAXPAYERS OF BUREAU COUNTY, ILLINOIS

HGR : HOME GOODS RETAILING – (Cont: Home Goods Retailing. Cont by: Home Goods Retailing) – Toronto. v21-35 jan 1975-jan 1989* – 1 – D15481.01 – us UMI [640]

H.H. Hill and Co *see*
- HISTORY OF LEE COUNTY
- HISTORY OF MERCER AND HENDERSON COUNTIES
- HISTORY OF WABASHA COUNTY AND WINONA COUNTY
- HISTORY OF WINONA AND OLMSTED COUNTIES
- HISTORY OF WINONA COUNTY
- HISTORY OF WINONA, OLMSTED AND DODGE COUNTIES

HI DESERT STAR – Yucca Valley, CA. 1957- – 114+ r – 1 – $5,700.00 ($360.00y) – R03131 – us Library Micro [071]

HI FI-STEREO BUYERS' GUIDE – 1975- – 1 – us UMI [073]

HIAPANIA SIC – London, UK. 1912-1 Aug 1915; 1 Nov 1915-27 Jun 1916. -m. 2 reels – 1 – uk British Libr Newspaper [072]

Hiatt, James M *see* THE VOTER'S TEXT BOOK

HIBBAT ZIYYON / Horowitz, H – Jerusalem. 1844. BJ-27-52 1 – 9 – ne IDC [956]

HIBBERT JOURNAL – v. 1-66. 1902-1968 – 1,5,6 – us Princeton Micro [240]

Hibbert-Ware, G *see* CHRISTIAN MISSIONS IN THE TELUGU COUNTRY

HIBBUREI LEKET – Lublin. 1612. Cowley. BJ-43-31 1 – 9 – ne IDC [956]

THE HIBERNIAN – Dublin, Ireland.26 Jun 1915-22 Apr 1916 – 1 – ie Microforms [072]

THE HIBERNIAN – Ireland, 26 June-22 April 1916 – 1 – ie Microforms [941]

HIBERNIAN CHRONICLE – Ireland.1769-1801. 11 reels – 1 – ie Microforms [072]

HIBERNIAN JOURNAL – Dublin. Ireland. -sw. 1807-08. (2 reels) – 1 – uk British Libr Newspaper [072]

HIBERNIAN JOURNAL – Ireland.1771-1801. 14 reels – 1 – ie Microforms [072]

HIBERNIAN MAGAZINE, OR, COMPENDIUM OF ENTERTAINING KNOWLEDGE *see* WALKER'S HIBERNIAN MAGAZINE

Hibernicus, Thomas *see* FLORES OMNIUM DOCTORUM ILLUSTRIUM...

THE HIBERNO-ARGENTINE REVIEW : A CATHOLIC WEEKLY – Buenos Aires: Hiberno-Argentine Review, v1 n33-v5 n216 dec 7 1906-jun 1910; v13 ns: n33 64,68-69,71,73-74,76-77,79-102 jan 9, aug 13, sep 10-17, oct 1, 15-22, nov 5-12 1920; nov 26 1920-may 6 1921; v17 ns: n218-278 aug 1923-jun 1924 – 6r – 1 – us Res Libr [072]

HIC! / Tevfik, Neyzen – Istanbul: Mahmud Bey Matbaasi, 1919 – $17.00 – us MEDOC [470]

Hick, Barbara A *see* FRESHMAN ELIGIBILITY IN INTERCOLLEGIATE ATHLETICS

Hickathrift, Thomas *see* THE HISTORY OF THOMAS HICKATHRIFT

Hickenlooper, Frank *see* AN ILLUSTRATED HISTORY OF MONROE COUNTY

Hickes, G *see* INSTITUTIONES GRAMMATICAE ANGLOSAXONICAE...

Hickes, George *see*
- GRAMMATICA ANGLO-SAXONICA EX HICKESIANO
- INSTITUTIONES GRAMMATICAE ANGLO-SAXONICAE, ET MOESO-GOTHICAE
- LINGUARUM VETT

Hickey, David *see* WILLIAM AND MARY: A TALE OF THE SIEGE OF LOUISBURG, 1745

Hickey, Kathleen P *see* A COMPARISON OF DIVISION IA FOOTBALL PLAYERS' GRADES IN SEASON AND OUT OF SEASON

Hickey, W *see* THE CONSTITUTION OF THE UNITED STATES

HICKEY'S BENGAL GAZETTE – Calcutta, India. -w. July 1780-March 1782. 1 reel – 1 – uk British Libr Newspaper [072]

THE HICKLETON PAPERS / Halifax. Archives (Earl). Garrowby – Index. 1800-85 – 1 – uk Microform Academic [941]

HICKMAN BAPTIST CHURCH. HICKMAN, TENNESSEE : CHURCH RECORDS – Sept 1828-Dec 1980 – 1 – 49.14 – us Baptist [240]

HICKMAN BAPTIST CHURCH. TENNESSEE : CHURCH RECORDS – Sep 1828-Dec 1980. Lacks Nov 1851-Aug 1870. 1092p – 1 – 49.14 – us Baptist [240]

HICKMAN ENTERPRISE – Hickman, NE. -w. May 1891-Apr 1893; Jun 1893-Mar 1952; Jun-Jul 1973 – 1 – us NE Hist [071]

Hickman, James Thomas *see* CRISIS ON THE HIGH PLAINS: A STUDY OF AMARILLO BAPTISTS, 1920 TO 1940

Hickok, Laurens P *see* HUMANITY IMMORTAL, OR, MAN TRIED, FALLEN, AND REDEEMED

Hickok, Laurens Perseus *see* CREATOR AND CREATION

HICKORY COVE BAPTIST CHURCH. ROGERSVILLE, TENNESSEE : CHURCH RECORDS – 1820-1948 – 1 – 41.22 – us Baptist [240]

HICKORY GROVE BAPTIST CHURCH. LAWNES COUNTY. FORT DEPOSIT, ALABAMA : CHURCH RECORDS – 1844-56 – 1 – 7.29 – us Baptist [240]

Hicks, E L *see* HENRY BAZELY

Hicks, E W *see* HISTORY OF KENDALL COUNTY

Hicks, Edward *see* TRACES OF GREEK PHILOSOPHY AND ROMAN LAW IN THE NEW TESTAMENT

Hicks, Frederick Charles *see* AIDS TO THE STUDY AND USE OF LAW BOOKS: A SELECTED LIST, CLASSIFIED AND ANNOTATED, OF PUBLICATIONS RELATING TO LAW LITERATURE, LAW STUDY AND LEGAL ETHICS

Hicks, Lewis Ezra *see* A CRITIQUE OF DESIGN-ARGUMENTS

Hicks, R D *see* STOIC AND EPICUREAN

Hicks, Wesley Jones *see* THE TENNESSEE MANUAL OF CHANCERY PRACTICE

Hicks-Judd Co *see* THE SAN FRANCISCO BLOCK BOOK

HICKSVILLE NEWS / Hicksville, Ohio – 1885-1887 – 2r – 1 – $32.50r – us Archival [071]

Hicksville, Ohio *see* HICKSVILLE NEWS

HICKY'S BENGAL GAZETTE OR CALCUTTA ADVERTISER – India. 1780-82 – 1 – uk Microform Academic [072]

Hidalgo de Aguero, B *see* TESORO DE LA VERDADERA CIRUGIA...

Hidalgo, Diego *see* UN NOTARIO ESPANOL EN RUSIA

Hidalgo, Juan Francisco *see* APUNTE DESCRIPTIVO DE LA SERENA

Hidalgo. Mexico (State) *see* PERIODICO OFICIAL DEL GOBIERNO DEL ESTADO DE HIDALGO

HIDALGUIA EXTREMENA / Munoz Gallardo, Juan Antonio – (Familia Morales-Arce: Condes de Torre-Arce, Condes de Casa Ayala). Badajoz: Imprenta Diputacion Provincial, 1976 – 1 – sp Bibl Santa Ana [946]

THE HIDDEN HAND / Southworth, Emma Dorothy Eliza Nevitte – New York: Grosset & Dunlap, (1920?). 487p – 1 – us U.W. Library [830]

A HIDDEN JEWEL : SHORT SKETCH OF THE LIFE AND WORK OF REV. JOHN ALEXANDER FREY AS HE IS KNOWN TO THE WRITER FOR THIRTY YEARS / Kweetin, John – New York, 1920. Publ. No. 6299 c. One of five items on a reel – 1 – us Baptist [240]

HIDDEN RESOURCES – Portland OR. Dec 6 1898 – 1 – us U.O. Library [071]

HIDDEN WORD: THIRTY DEVOTIONAL STUDIES OF THE PARABLES OF OUR LORD / Dover, Thomas Birkett – New York: James Pott, 1887. 1 fiche – 9 – us A.T.L.A. [240]

HIDES AND SKINS IMPROVEMENT IN DEVELOPING COUNTRIES – 1986 – 138p – it F.A.O. [660]

HIDES, SKINS AND LEATHER DEVELOPMENT AND TRAINING PROJECT. FINAL REPORT / Sudan. FAO – 1969 – 9 – ne IDC [338]

HIDROCILO PAREDES / Paredes Guillen, Vicente – 1891 – 9 – 1.50f – sp Bibl Santa Ana [946]

Hidroelectrica Espanola *see*
- CURSO DE INSTRUCTORES EN HIGIENE Y SEGURIDAD DEL TRABAJO
- CURSO DE INSTRUCTORES EN HIGIENE Y SEGURIDAD DEL TRABAJO. 199TH CURSO DE MONITORES DE H.E. GABRIEL Y GALAN. CACERES, JULIO 1977
- PROGRAMA DEL CURSO...FORMACION PARA MIEMBROS DE COMITE DE SEGURIDAD...Y VIGILANTES DE SEGURIDAD DE LA OBRA DEL SALTO DE CEDILLO (CACERES)

Hidroelectrica Espanola, S.A. *see* SALTO DE CEDILLO. SERVICIO DE MEDICINA Y SEGURIDAD DE H.E. 122ND CURSO DE FORMACION DE MONITORES DE SEGURIDAD

HIDUP KATOLIK – Djakarta. Incomplete. SE-368 1. 1947-1971 – 9 – ne IDC [240]

Hiecke, Katharina *see*
- EXZITONENTRANSFER IN SEMIMAGNETISCHEN CDTE/CDMNTE-DOPPEL-QUANTENGRABENSTRUKTUREN
- UNTERSUCHUNGEN ZUM EXZITONENTRANSFER IN ASYMMETRISCHEN CDTE/(CD,MN)TE-DOPPELGRABENSTRUKTUREN

Hiep Nguyen Duc *see* VIETNAMESE COLLECTION OF THE ANU LIBRARY

HIER ET AUJOURD'HUI, OU, L'OPPOSITION ET LE POUVOIR: CONSIDERATIONS SUR LA POLITIQUE CANADIENNE: SUIVIES DU TRAITE...ENTRE LE CANADA ET LES ETATS-UNIS – 1874. 02573. (Pre-1900 Canadiana) – 9 – cn C.I.H.M. [971]

HIER IN SPANIEN – Benisa, jul 21 1978- (incomplete) – 1 – Dist. gw Mikrofilm – gw Misc Inst [072]

HIERARCHIES / Dionysius of Halicarnassus – 1759. Transcript – 1 – uk Microform Academic [240]

THE HIERARCHY OF THE CATHOLIC CHURCH IN THE U.S / Shea, John Dawson Gilmary – 1886 – 1 – us A.T.L.A. [240]

HIERATIC PAPYRI FROM KAHU AND GUROB / ed by Griffith, F L – H-240 2. 1898 – 8 – ne IDC [490]

HIERATISCHE PALAEOGRAPHIE. DIE AEGYPTISCHE BUCHSCHRIFT IN IHRER ENTWICKLUNG VON DER FUENFTEN DYNASTIE BIS ZUR ROEMISCHEN KAISERZEIT / Moeller, G – 3v. Leipzig, 1909-12. BNE-453 1 – 9 – ne IDC [410]
HIERATISCHE PAPYRUS AUS DEN KOENIGLICHEN MUSEEN ZU BERLIN – (I. Rituale fuer den Kultus des Amon..., 1901; II. Hymnen an verschiedene Goetter..., 1905; III. Schriftstuecke der VI. Dynastie..., 1911) – 18mf – 9 – H-390/2 – ne IDC [090]
HIERATISCHE UND HIERATISCH-DEMOTISCHE TEXTE DER SAMMLUNG AEGYPTISCHER ALTERTHUEMER DES ALLERHOECHSTEN KAISERHAUSES / Bergmann, E – Vienna, 1886. BNE-377 1 – 9 – ne IDC [470]
HIEROCLIS SYNECDEMUS ET NOTOTIAE GRAECAE EPISCOPATUUM : ACCEDUNT NILI DOXAPATRII NOTITIA PATRIARCHATUUM ET LOCORUM NOMINA IMMUTATA – (Texts in Greek with Latin translation. Includes index) – Berolini: In aedibus Friderici Nicolai, 1866 – 1mf – 9 – 0-8370-8605-1 – 1986-2605 – us A.T.L.A. [240]
HIEROGLYPHICA; ANDERS, EMBLEMATA SACRA / Groenewegen, H – O-822. 1693 – 9 – ne IDC [760]
HIEROGLYPHICA OF MERK BEELDEN DER OUDE VOLKEREN / Hooghe, Romein de – O-298. 1735 – 9 – ne IDC [410]
HIEROGLYPHICA, PER BER NARDINUM TREBATIUM VICENTINUM DE GRAECIS TRANSLATA / Horus Apollo – O 848. 1518 – 9 – ne IDC [760]
HIEROGLYPHISCH-DEMOTISCHES WOERTERBUCH / Brugsch, H – Leipzig. 7v. 1867-1882 – 58mf – ne IDC [450]
HIERONYMI MAGII DE TINTINNABULIS LIBE POSTUMUS : FRANCISUS SWEERTIRUS F. ANTWERP. NOTIS ILLSTRABAT / Magii, G – Hanovi: Typis Wechelianis, apud C Marnium & heredes I Aubrii, 1608 – 1 – us Sibley [780]
HIERONYMI TRAGI, DE STIRPIVM, MAXIME EARVM QVAE IN GERMANIA NOSTRA NASCVNTUR, USITATIS NOMENCLATURIS, PROPRIJSQ DIFFERENTIJS, NEQ NON TEMPERATURIS AC FACULTATIBUS, COMMENTARIORUM LIBRI TRES / Bock, Hieronymus – Argentorati, Excudebat V. Rihelius, 1552 – 1 – us U.W. Library [943]
Hieronymus *see* CONTRA RUFINUM
HIERONYMUS EMSER : EIN LEBENSBILD AUS DER REFORMATIONSGESCHICHTE / Kawerau, Gustav – Halle: Verein fuer Reformationsgeschichte, 1898. (Schriften des Vereins fuer Reformationsgeschichte; 15. Jahrg., Schrift 61) – 1mf – us A.T.L.A. [240]
Hieronymus, G *see* POLYPODIORUM ASPLENIORUM SPECIES NOVAE ET NON SATIS NOVAE AND OTHER ITEMS
HIERONYMUS LIBER DE VIRIS INLUSTRIBUS : GENNADIUS LIBER DE VIRIS INLUSTRIBUS (T.U.U. 1-14/1A) / Richardson, E C – Leipzig, 1896 – 3mf – 9 – ne Slangenburg [240]
Hieronymus, Saint *see*
– EPISTOLAE
– EXTRACTS
– OMNIUM OPERUM DIUI EUSEBII HIERONYMI STRIDONENSIS
– SUGGESTIONS ON THE TEACHING OF HISTORY
HIERRO – Bilbao, Spain. -d. 11 Feb 1943-26 May 1945. Imperfect. 8 reels – 1 – uk British Libr Newspaper [072]
HIFZ AL-SIHHAH – Sal-i 1, shumarah-i 3-9 (Rabi' al-Lani 1324-Shavval 1324 [May 1906-November 1906]) – 1 reel – 1 – $75.00 – us MEDOC [950]
HIGGAYON BE-KHINNOR / Almanzi, J – Vienna. 1839. BJ-422-3 1 – 9 – ne IDC [470]
HIGGIN'S COURT OF CIVIL APPEALS REPORTS / Tennessee. Supreme Court – (A Pre-NRS title) – v1-8. 1911-1919 (all publ) – 64mf – 9 – $96.00 – LLMC 91-041 – us L.L.M.C. [340]
Higgins, George Henry *see* PROCEDURE ACT OF 1887, AND SECTION FIVE OF ACT OF MARCH 21ST, 1806.
Higgins, Godfrey *see* ANACALYPSIS
Higgins, John F *see* ILLINOIS POLITICAL DIRECTORY – 1899
Higgins, Katherine *see* PUBLICATIONS FILED BY NEW MEXICO STATE AGENCIES WITH THE NEW MEXICO STATE LIBRARY
Higgins, Kathleen L *see* VALIDITY AND OBJECTIVITY OF A RATING SCALE FOR THE OVERHEAD AND FOREARM VOLLEYBALL PASS
Higgins, Thomas Alfred *see* THE LIFE OF JOHN MOCKETT CRAMP, D.D., 1796-1881, LATE PRESIDENT OF ACADIA COLLEGE..
Higginson, T W *see*
– POEMS
Higginson, Thomas *see* THE POETICAL WORKS OF THOMAS HIGGINSON
Higginson, Thomas Wentworth *see*
– CONTEMPORARIES
– PAPERS
– SELECTED WORKS
– WOMEN IN CHRISTIAN CIVILIZATION
HIGGINSVILLE FIRST BAPTIST CHURCH. HIGGINSVILLE, MISSOURI : CHURCH RECORDS – 1910-64 – 1 – 40.64 – us Baptist [240]
HIGH CALLING: MEDITATIONS ON ST PAUL'S LETTER TO THE PHILIPPIANS / Jowett, John Henry – New York: Fleming H. Revell, 1909. 1 fiche – 9 – us A.T.L.A. [240]
HIGH CHURCH EPISCOPACY : ITS ORIGIN, CHARACTERISTICS AND FRUITS / Annan, William – (Includes bibliographical references) – Pittsburgh: R S Davis: Presbyterian Book Store [distributor], 1874 – 1mf – 9 – 0-8370-8643-4 – 1986-2643 – us A.T.L.A. [240]
HIGH COMMISSIONER'S GAZETTE / Great Britain. High Commissioner for Aden – Mar 1963-2 Apr 1965 – 1 – us NY Public [956]
High Council of Sufism *see* AL-TASAWWUF AL-ISLAMI
HIGH DESERT ADVOCATE – Wendover, NV. 1993 – 2+ r – 1 – $100.00 ($90.00y) – U04903 – us Library Micro [071]
THE HIGH DUTCH MINERVA – anon. 1680. 213p. (English Linguistics Series 1500-1800) – 9 – us UMI [430]
HIGH ENERGY CHEMISTRY – v1-27. 1967-93 – 1,5 – $80.00v – us UMI [540]
HIGH FIDELITY/MUSICAL AMERICA – (v. 18-1968- 5,6. v. 20- 1970- 9) – v. 1- 1951- – 1 – us UMI [780]
HIGH GRADE NEWS – New Pine Creek OR. May 4 1912 – 1 – us U.O. Library [071]
HIGH HILL BAPTIST CHURCH. DARLINGTON, SOUTH CAROLINA : CHURCH RECORDS – Feb 1886-1955, 1960-1980 – 1 – $45.14 – us Baptist [240]
HIGH HILLS OF SANTEE BAPTIST CHURCH. SUMTER COUNTY. SOUTH CAROLINA : CHURCH RECORDS – (Includes Membership Rolls, Bulletins, etc, 1949-1975. 461p) – 1948-1984 – 1 reel – 1 – $20.75 – us Baptist [240]
High, James Lambert *see*
– A TREATISE ON EXTRAORDINARY LEGAL REMEDIES, EMBRACING MANDAMUS, QUO WARRANTO AND PROHIBITION
– A TREATISE ON THE LAW OF INJUNCTIONS, AS ADMINISTERED IN THE COURTS OF THE UNITED STATES AND ENGLAND
THE HIGH JUMP AS PERFORMED BY THE 1979 UNITED STATES OUTDOOR FEMALE RECORD HOLDER: A BIOMECHANICAL ANALYSIS / Kimura, Iris F – 1981 – 1mf – 9 – $4.00 – us Microform Publ [790]
HIGH LIGHTS AND FLIGHTS IN NEW GUINEA...ACCOUNT OF THE DISCOVERY AND DEVELOPMENT OF THE MOROBE GOLDFIELDS / Rhys, Lloyd – London: Hodder and Stoughton, 1942. 252p. illus. Maps. Plates. Bibliography – 1 – us U.W. Library [980]
HIGH PEAK REPORTER *see* ASHTON WEEKLY REPORTER AND STALYBRIDGE AND DUKINFIELD CHRONICLE
HIGH PERFORMANCE – (1985- . 5,6,9) – v1- . 1978- – 1 – us UMI [073]
HIGH PERFORMANCE POLYMERS / ed by Wilson, D – UK: 10P Publishing Ltd., 1993.- v5 – 1,5,6,9 – £123.00 – uk I.O.P. [621]
HIGH PRESSURE RESEARCH : AN INTERNATIONAL JOURNAL / ed by Besson, J M – 1,5,9 – us Gordon [530]
HIGH PRIESTHOOD AND SACRIFICE: AN EXPOSITION OF THE EPISTLE TO THE HEBREWS / DuBose, William Porcher – New York: Longmans, Green, 1908.1 fiche – 9 – us A.T.L.A. [240]
HIGH RIVER TIMES – Alberta, CN. Dec 1905- – 1r per yr – 1 – Can$57.00r – cn Commonwealth Micro [072]
HIGH SCHOOL BEHAVIORAL SCIENCE – (See also: Behavioral and Social Science Teacher) – v3-5. 1975-77 – 1,5,6,9 – us UMI [370]
HIGH SCHOOL ENTERPRISE – Eureka, NV. 21 Nov 1896 – 1r – 1 – $50.00 – U04512 – us Library Micro [071]
HIGH SCHOOL JOURNAL – (v.55- 1971- 5,6. v.59- 1975- 9) – v.1- 1918- – 1 – us UMI [073]
THE HIGH SCHOOL JOURNAL – Orillia [Ont]: High School Literary Society, [1889?-19–] – 9 – cn C.I.H.M. [370]
THE HIGH SCHOOL MONTHLY – New Glasgow, N.S.: Students of the New Glasgow High School, v1 no 1 (Dec 1890)- – 9 – cn C.I.H.M. [370]
HIGH SCHOOL MONTHLY (NEW GLASGOW, N.S.) *see* THE SCHOLARS' MONTHLY
HIGH SCHOOLS AND SEX EDUCATION / U.S. Public Health Service. Surgeon General; ed by Gruenberg, Benjamin C in collaboration with U.S Bureau – Manual GPO, 1922. vii,98p. 1236 – 1r – 1 – us U.W. Library [613]
HIGH SHOALS BAPTIST CHURCH. LAMAR COUNTY. GEORGIA : CHURCH RECORDS – (942p) – 1837-Feb 1990 – 1 reel – 1 – $42.39 – us Baptist [240]
HIGH SIERRA TIMES – Incline Village, NV. 1976-1978 – 1r – 1 – $50.00 – N03706 – us Library Micro [071]
HIGH TECHNOLOGY – 1980 – 1,5,6,9 – us UMI [073]
HIGH TECHNOLOGY LAW JOURNAL – University of California at Berkeley. v1-10. 1986-95 – 9 – $264.00 set – us Hein [340]
HIGH TECHNOLOGY LAW JOURNAL – v1- . 1986- – 1,5,6,9 – us UMI [073]
HIGH TEMPERATURE – v1-31. 1963-93 – 1,5 – $80.00v – us UMI [530]
THE HIGH VIEW – (Also known as: Low Down) – Fallon, NV. 1926-1927 – 1r – 1 – $50.00 – U04528 – us Library Micro [071]
Highbaugh, Irma *see* THE CHRISTIAN FAMILY IN CHANGING EAST ASIA (CCC246)
THE HIGHER CHRISTIAN EDUCATION / Dwight, Benjamin W – (Includes index) – New York: A S Barnes & Burr, 1859 – 1mf – 9 – 0-8370-7628-5 – 1986-1628 – us A.T.L.A. [370]
THE HIGHER CRITICISM : FOUR PAPERS / Driver, Samuel Rolles – new ed. New York: Hodder and Stoughton, 1912 – 1mf – 9 – 0-8370-9379-1 – 1986-3379 – us A.T.L.A. [220]
THE HIGHER CRITICISM CROSS-EXAMINED: AN APPEAL AND A WARNING / Storey, Frederick Davis – Philadelphia: Griffith & Row, 1905. 1 fiche – 9 – us A.T.L.A. [240]
HIGHER CRITICISM OF THE HEXATEUCH – New York: Scribner's, 1893. 1 fiche – 9 – us A.T.L.A. [240]
HIGHER CRITICISM OF THE PENTATEUCH / Green, William Henry – New York: Charles Scribner, 1906 – 9 – us A.T.L.A. [220]
THE HIGHER CRITICISM...VERDICT OF THE MONUMENTS / Sayce, Archibald Henry – London: S.P.C.K., 1894. 575p. 2 fiches – 9 – us A.T.L.A. [240]
HIGHER EDUCATION – v1-13. 1972-84 – 1,5,6,13 – sz Elsevier [073]
HIGHER EDUCATION *see* AMERICAN EDUCATION
HIGHER EDUCATION ABSTRACTS – v20-. Fall 1984- – 1,5,6,9 – us UMI [073]
HIGHER EDUCATION BULLETIN – (v5-6. 1976-78. 5,6,9) – v. 3-6. 1974-78 – 1 – us UMI [370]
HIGHER EDUCATION DAILY – (v4-. 1976-. 9) – v. 1-. 1973- – 1,5,6 – us UMI [370]
HIGHER EDUCATION, ENROLMENT AND OUTPUT 1968-1977 / Ceylon. Ministry of Planning and Economic Affairs – Colombo, 1968 – 1mf – 9 – DE-586/1 – ne IDC [370]
HIGHER EDUCATION IN INDONESIA / U.S. Operations Mission to Indonesia – Reports by Raymond B. Allen. SE 4972 1. 1960 – 9 – ne IDC [324]
THE HIGHER EDUCATION OF WOMEN, IN CONNECTION WITH MCGILL UNIVERSITY / Dawson, John William – s.l.: s.n., 1884?. 02624. (Pre-1900 Canadiana) – 9 – cn C.I.H.M. [370]
HIGHER EDUCATION OF WOMEN IN EUROPE = FRAUENBILDUNG / Lange, Helene – (In English) – New York: D Appleton, 1897, c1890 – 1mf – 9 – 0-8370-7642-0 – 1986-1642 – us A.T.L.A. [370]
HIGHER EDUCATION: REPORT OF THE COMMITTEE APPOINTED BY THE PRIME MINISTER / Great Britain. Committee on Higher Education – 1962-63. Cmd. 2154 (1-13) – 9 – uk Microform Academic [324]
HIGHER EDUCATION REVIEW – Croydon. v1-1968- 1, v7- 1974- 5,6; v8-. 1975- 9 – us UMI [370]
HIGHER EDUCATION REVIEW: A BULLETIN OF THE ASSOCIATION FOR THE STUDY OF HIGHER EDUCATION – v1. 1977-78. Continued by: Review of Higher Education – 1 – us UMI [073]
THE HIGHER LAW IN ITS RELATIONS TO CIVIL GOVERNMENT : WITH PARTICULAR REFERENCE TO SLAVERY AND THE FUGITIVE SLAVE LAW / Hosmer, William – Auburn: Derby & Miller, 1852 – 1mf – us A.T.L.A. [320]
THE HIGHER LIFE DOCTRINE OF SANCTIFICATION: TRIED BY THE WORD OF GOD / Boardman, Henry Augustus – Philadelphia: Presb. Bd. of Pub., 1877. 1 fiche – 9 – us A.T.L.A. [240]
HIGHER TECHNOLOGICAL EDUCATION: REPORT OF THE COMMITTEE APPOINTED BY THE MINISTER ON.. / Great Britain. Committee on Higher Technological Education – Percy Report. 1945 – 9 – uk Microform Academic [324]
THE HIGHEST CRITICS VS THE HIGHER CRITICS / Munhall, Leander Whitcomb – New York: Fleming H Revell, c1892 – 1mf – 9 – 0-8370-4541-X – 1985-2541 – us A.T.L.A. [220]
HIGHLAND BAPTIST CHURCH (FORMERLY: SECOND STREET BAPTIST). SHELBYVILLE, KENTUCKY : CHURCH RECORDS – 1949-70 – 1 – 25.47 – us Baptist [240]
HIGHLAND BAPTIST CHURCH. METAIRIE, LOUISIANA : CHURCH RECORDS – 1953-75 – 1 – 27.72 – us Baptist [240]
HIGHLAND BOTE – Highland, IL: P Voegele, [mar 31 1860-65] – 1 – us Res Libr [071]
HIGHLAND BOTE UND SCHUETZEN-ZEITUNG – Highland, IL: T Gruaz, [jan 12 1866-mar 12 1869] – 1 – us Res Libr [071]
Highland Cemetery, Geary County, KS *see* INTERMENT RECORD NO. 1-4051
HIGHLAND COURIER – Newburgh. N.Y. 1846-1848 – 1 – us UMI [071]
HIGHLAND COUSINS: A NOVEL / Black, William – British Fiction Archive: Unit 4 – 9 – uk Bell [830]
HIGHLAND DEMOCRAT – Peekskill. N.Y. 1871-1887 – 1 – us UMI [071]
HIGHLAND EAGLE – Peekskill. N.Y. 1851-1858 – 1 – us UMI [071]
Highland. Kansas. Highland Presbyterian Church *see* RECORDS
HIGHLAND NEWS – 1 – £42.00r – uk Scot News [072]
HIGHLAND PARK NEWS-HERALD AND JOURNAL – Los Angeles. Calif. -bw. 1906- – 1 – us UMI [071]
HIGHLAND RECORDER – Monterey. Va. 1950- – 1 – us UMI [071]
HIGHLAND UNION – Highland, Madison Co, IL: G Rutz & J S Hoerner, oct 22 1868-sep 9 1910 – 1 – us Res Libr [071]
Highland University *see* RECORDS
THE HIGHLANDER – Riverside, CA: UC Riverside, 1972-93 – 21r – 1 – $1,050.00 – R02717 – us Library Micro [370]
HIGHLANDER PRESS COURIER – Covina, CA. 1981-1986 – 6r – 1 – $300.00 – RH03191 – us Library Micro [071]
HIGHLANDS COUNTY NEWS – Sebring. Fl. May 1948-59 – 1 – us P.K. Yonge [071]
HIGH-LEVEL MANPOWER REQUIREMENTS AND RESOURCES, 1968-1972 / Seal, J B – 1967. BNE-7683 1 – 9 – ne IDC [331]
HIGHLIGHTS OF AGRICULTURAL RESEARCH / Alabama. Agricultural Experiment Station – v. 1-20. 1954-73 – 1,5,6 – us Spaulding [630]
HIGHLIGHTS OF AGRICULTURAL RESEARCH / Auburn University. Agricultural Experiment Station – No.1-29.1954-82. 1 reel – 1, 5 – us Spaulding [630]
HIGHLIGHTS OF THE FIFTH FOUR-YEAR ECONOMIC DEVELOPMENT PLAN OF THE REPUBLIC OF CHINA / China. Republic – March. 1969. BD-1570 1 – 9 – ne IDC [338]
HIGHLIGHTS OF THE SECOND FOUR-YEAR PLAN FOR THE ECONOMIC DEVELOPMENT IN TAIWAN / China. People's Republic. Economic Stabilization Board – Taipei. 1957. BD-137 1 – 9 – ne IDC [338]
HIGH-SPEED SURFACE CRAFT *see* FAST FERRY INTERNATIONAL

HIGHVIEW BAPTIST CHURCH. LOUISVILLE, KENTUCKY : CHURCH RECORDS – Sep 1947-Jul 1979 – 1 – 35.01 – us Baptist [240]

HIGHWAY – (Lacks: Aug 1946. Cont: Kimberley and Kuruman Diocesan Magazine) – v8-10. 1946-49 – 1r – 1 – ATLA S0727A – us A.T.L.A. [073]

HIGHWAY *see* KIMBERLY AND KURUMAN DIOCESAN MAGAZINE

HIGHWAY AND HEAVY CONSTRUCTION – v119- 1976- – 1,5,6,9 – us UMI [625]

HIGHWAY DESIGN AND CONSTRUCTION – 1934-1973 – 1 – us UMI [625]

HIGHWAY DEVELOPMENT PLAN FOR UNITED ARAB REPUBLIC, NORTHERN REGION – 1961. BNE-9746 1 – 9 – ne IDC [338]

HIGHWAY ENGINEER – v24-30 no 7 1977-Jul 1983 – 1,5,6,9 – us UMI [625]

A HIGHWAY IN THE DESERT : A HISTORY OF SOUTHERN BAPTIST WORK IN ARIZONA / Maxwell, C B – 1 – $5.00 – us Baptist [240]

HIGHWAYS AND PUBLIC WORKS – v46- 1978- – 1,5,6,9 – us UMI [625]

HIGHWAYS AND ROAD CONSTRUCTION – 1974-1976 – 1,5,6,9 – us UMI [625]

HIGHWAYS AND ROAD CONSTRUCTION INTERNATIONAL – v44-45 1976-1978 – 1,5,6,9 – us UMI [625]

HIGHWAYS AND TRANSPORTATION: JOURNAL OF THE INSTITUTION OF HIGHWAYS AND TRANSPORTATION & HTTA – v30 no 8-9- Aug-Sept 1983- – 1,5,6,9 – us UMI [625]

HIGIENE ANTICOLERICA RAZONADA / LO – 1885 – 9 – 1.50f – sp Bibl Santa Ana [610]

HIGIENE Y PROFILAXIS EN EL MEDIO RURAL / Juarez, Ernesto – Caceres: Imp. Garcia Floriano, 1951 – sp Bibl Santa Ana [610]

Higley, Mary *see* ELMER FERN COPE PAPERS

Higley, Mary S *see*
- PAPERS

Higuera La Real.Spain.Ayuntamiento *see* ORDENANZAS MUNICIPALES

UNA HIJA DE MARIA (MARIA PEREZ DE GUZMAN Y SANJUAN) / Gomez Bravo, Vicente – Villafranca de los Barros; Colegio de San Jose (Imp. Bolanos), 1940 – 1 – sp Bibl Santa Ana [240]

EL HIJO DEL PUEBLO – Manzanillo: Imp el Comercio de la viuda de A Martin. v1 n2-10. may 24-jul 19 1885 – 1 sheet – 9 – us Res Libr [072]

LOS HIJOD DEL MAR / Diaz Maciaz, Jose – 1889 – 9 – 1.50f – sp Bibl Santa Ana [830]

LOS HIJOS AMERICANOS DE LOS PIZARROS DE LA CONQUISTA / Cuneo-Vidal, Romulo – Madrid: Tip. Rev. de Arch. Bibliot. y Museos, 1925 – 1 – sp Bibl Santa Ana [060]

LOS HIJOS DE LA FORTUNA. NOVELA ORIGINAL DE COSTUMBRES ESPANOLAS / Rivera, Luis; ed by Gonzalez, J de M – Madrid, 1855 – 1 – sp Bibl Santa Ana [830]

LOS HIJOS DE LUTERO ENTRE LOS HIJOS DEL SOL / Bayle, Constantino – Madrid: Razon y Fe, 1930 – 1 – sp Bibl Santa Ana [240]

Hijos de Reus *see* FUERO DE USAGRE (SIGLO 18)

HIJOS ILUSTRES DE EXTREMADURA / Velo Nieto, Gervasio – Badajoz: Imprenta Diputacion Provincial, 1971 – sp Bibl Santa Ana [946]

Hijosa del Valle, Gregorio *see* CUADERNO DE LENGUAJE CURSO 2-1. OTONO

HIKAJAT PANDJI SEMIRANG, MENOEROET NASKAH LAMA : DIHIASI DENGAN 11 BOEAH GAMBAR – Tjetakan 6. Djakarta, Balai Poestaka, 2602. 157p – 39-40mf – 9 – ne IDC [950]

HIKMA *see* AL-HIKMA

HIKMAH – Djakarta. Incomplete. SE-369 1. 1948-1960 – 9 – ne IDC [073]

HIKMAT – (Vol. 8, no. 7-8 (271-272), 16-17 (280-281), 19 (283) (20 Rabi al-awwal 1317-20 Rajab 1317[28 Jul 1899-24 Nov 1899])) – Cairo – 1 reel – 1 – $50.00 – us MEDOC [950]

Hikmet Arif, Seyhuelislam *see* DIVAN

HILAL – Istanbul. Turkey. -d. In French. 5 Sep 1917-27 Sep, 26 Oct 1918. (Imperfect). (2 reels) – 1 – uk British Libr Newspaper [949]

Hilarius Pictaviensis *see* DE TRINITATE

HILARIUS VON POITIERS : EINE MONOGRAPHIE / Reinkens, Joseph Hubert – Schaffhausen: Fr. Hurter, 1864 – 1mf – us A.T.L.A. [240]

Hilbck, A *see* ZUM BERGARBEITERAUSSTAND IM RUHRREVIER

Hilbert, Carey A *see* COMPARISON OF RESTING METABOLIC RATE AND EXCESS POST-EXERCISE OXYGEN CONSUMPTION IN NORMAL AND LOW CALORIE DIETING FEMALES

Hildebrand, Alexander *see* FRAUENLOBS STREITGEDICHT ZWISCHEN MINNE UND WELT

HILDEBRAND AND HIS TIMES / Stephens, William Richard Wood – London, New York: Longmans, Green, 1914.xvi,230p. map. Includes index – 1 – us U.W. Library [240]

Hildebrand, E *see* WALLENSTEIN UND SEINE VERBINDUNGEN MIT DEN SCHWEDEN

Hildebrand, P OF M Cap. *see* DE KAPUCIJNEN IN DE NEDERLANDEN EN HET PRINSBISDOM LUIK

Hildebrand, Ulrich *see* DIE BILANZRECHTLICHEN BESCHLUESSE DER GROSSEN SENATE VON RFH UND BFH

Hildebrand, Wolfgang *see* MAGIA NATURALIS: DAS IST KUNST UND WUNDERBUCH DARRINE BEGRIFFEN WUNDERBAHRE SECRETA

Hildebrandt, Kurt *see* WAGNER UND NIETZSCHE

Hildegarde, H *see* VOORSPELLINGEN VAN DE H. HILDEGARDE OMTRENT DE BELGISCHE OMWENTELING

HILDESHEIMER ALLGEMEINE ZEITUNG – Hildesheim, West Germany. 1977- – ca 6r per yr – 1 – gw Mikrofilm [072]

Hildesheimer, I *see* SHAY LE-MOREH. JUBELSCHRIFT. ISRAEL HILDESHEIMER

HILDESHEIMER RELATIONS-COURIER – (Title changes: Luedemannsche Zeitung, 1751; Privilegirte Hildesheimische Zeitung, 1775) – Hildesheim, Germany. 1706-17, (incomplete); 1719, (incomplete); 1721, (incomplete); 1726-27, (incomplete); 1748-52; 1754-93, (incomplete); 1795-1801, (incomplete); 1809 – 27r – 1 – gw Mikrofilm [072]

HILDESHEIMER RELATIONS-COURIER *see* HILDESHEIMER ALLGEMEINE ZEITUNG

HILDRETH TELESCOPE – Hildreth, NE. -w. Dec 1892; Nov 1895-Nov 1942; Jul 1943-Sept 1961 – 1 – us NE Hist [071]

HILF = RELIEF : BULLETIN...CONFERENCE UNIVERSELLE JUIVE DE SECOURS – (In Yiddish) – Paris, FR. Jan 1921-v1 no3 25 Sep 1921 – 1r – 1 – $25.00 – cn Can Microfilming [072]

DIE HILFE : ZEITSCHRIFT FUER POLITIK, LITERATUR UND KUNST – Berlin, 1894-1941 – 30r – 1 – Dist. gw Mikrofilm – gw Misc Inst [073]

DIE HILFE : ZEITSCHRIFT FUER POLITIK, LITERATUR UND KUNST – Berlin, dec 2 1894-jun 17 1944 – 30r – 1 – DM2,250.00 – gw Mikro Press [073]

HILFE, DIE NICHT ANKOMMT : DER ZIELGRUPPENBEZUG BEI DER FOERDERUNG VON ENTWICKLUNGSBANKEN ALS DEFIZITBEREICH DEUTSCHER ENTWICKLUNGSPOLITIK / Graef, Peter Leo – 1995 – 2mf – 9 – DM80.00 – 3-8267-2208-6 – gw Hänsel [332]

Hilgenfeld, A *see*
- ACTA APOSTOLORUM
- DIE APOSTOLISCHEN VAETER
- BARDESANES, DER LETZTE GNOSTIKER
- HISTORISCH-KRITISCHE EINLEITUNG IN DAS NEUE TESTAMENT
- ZEITSCHRIFT FUER WISSENSCHAFTLICHE THEOLOGIE

Hilgenfeld, Adolf *see* DER KANON UND DIE KRITIK DES NEUEN TESTAMENTS IN IHRER GESCHICHTLICHEN AUSBILDUNG UND GESTALTUNG

HI-LINE ENTERPRISE – Curtis, NE. -w. May 1892; Jul 1895-Dec. 1895; Apr. 1896-May 1898; Jan. 1899-Jan. 1901; Apr. 1901-Oct. 1902; Jan. 1918- – 1 – us NE Hist [071]

HI-LINE HERALD – Havre. Mont. 1966- – 1 – us UMI [071]

Hill, A P *see* MRS. HILL'S NEW COOK BOOK

Hill City, Kansas *see* MISCELLANEOUS EARLY NEWSPAPERS

HILL CREST / Flewellyn, Julia Colliton – Toronto: Cooper, 1894. 03166. (Pre-1900 Canadiana) – 9 – cn C.I.H.M. [971]

Hill, D H *see* PESTE DES PETITS RUMINANTS (PPR) IN SHEEP AND GOATS

Hill, Don Gleason *see* THE RECORDS OF BIRTHS, MARRIAGES, AND DEATHS IN THE TOWN OF DEDHAM

Hill, E B *see* MOONLIGHT, FOR PIANO, OP. 8 NO. 1

Hill, Edward Judson *see*
- THE CHANCERY JURISDICTION AND PRACTICE, ACCORDING TO STATUTES AND DECISIONS IN THE STATE OF ILLINOIS, FROM THE EARLIEST PERIOD TO 1873
- THE COMMON LAW JURISDICTION AND PRACTICE, ACCORDING TO STATUTES AND DECISIONS IN THE STATE OF ILLINOIS, FROM THE EARLIEST PERIOD TO 1872
- THE PROBATE JURISDICTION AND PRACTICE IN THE COUNTY COURTS, ACCORDING TO THE STATUTES AND DECISIONS IN THE STATE OF ILLINOIS.
- THE PROBATE JURISDICTION AND PRACTICE IN THE COURTS OF THE STATE OF ILLINOIS.

HILL FARM FACTS.FORESTRY / Louisiana State University. Agricultural Experiment Station. North Louisiana Hill Farm Experiment Station – No.9-10.Jul-Aug 1974. 1 reel – 1,5 – us Spaulding [634]

Hill, Geoffry *see* ENGLISH DIOCESES

Hill, George Canning *see*
- HOMESPUN: OR, FIVE AND TWENTY YEARS AGO
- OUR PARISH; OR, PEN PAINTINGS OF VILLAGE LIFE

Hill, George W *see* HISTORY OF ASHLAND COUNTY

Hill, J *see*
- THE BRITISH HERBAL
- EDEN
- THE VEGETABLE SYSTEM

Hill, J Stanley *see* THE EFFECT OF THE EDUCATION OF THIRD WORLD WOMEN ON FAMILY HEALTH

Hill, John *see*
- THE FAMILY PRACTICE OF PHYSIC
- A REVIEW OF THE WORKS OF THE ROYAL SOCIETY OF LONDON

Hill, John B *see* PRESBYTERY OF KANSAS CITY, 1821-1901

Hill, John Ward *see* A MANUAL OF THE LAW OF FIXTURES

Hill, Kate Alexander *see* CORRESPONDENCE

Hill, Larry B *see* THE OMBUDSMAN

Hill, Larry T *see* TIME MOTION ANALYSIS OF THE SKATING CHARACTERISTICS OF PROFESSIONAL ICE HOCKEY PLAYERS

Hill, Luther B *see* HISTORY OF THE STATE OF OKLAHOMA

Hill, Merritt B *see* THE LAWS OF THE UNITED STATES RELATING TO PATENTS AND TRADEMARKS.

Hill, N N *see*
- HISTORY OF COSHOCTON COUNTY
- HISTORY OF KNOX COUNTY ITS PAST AND PRESENT
- HISTORY OF LICKING COUNTY ITS PAST AND PRESENT

Hill, Richard *see*
- AN ANSWER TO SOME CAPITAL ERRORS CONTAINED IN MINUTES OF SOME LATE CONVERSATIONS BETWEEN THE REV. MR. WESLEY AND OTHERS PRINTED AT BRISTOL, 1770, BY JOHN WESLEY, M.A.,...
- A CONVERSATION BETWEEN RICHARD HILL, ESQ., THE REV. MR. MADAN AND FATHER WALSH,...HELD...JULY 13, 1771,...
- AN EVENING CONVERSATION BETWEEN FOUR VERY GOOD OLD LADIES OVER A COMFORTABLE GAME AT QUADRILLE
- THE FINISHING STROKE, CONTAINING SOME STRICTURES ON THE REV. MR. FLETCHER'S PAMPHLET ENTITLED 'LOGICA GENEVENSIS
- FIVE LETTERS TO THE REVEREND MR. F— —R RELATIVE TO HIS 'VINDICATION' OF THE MINUTES OF THE REVEREND MR. JOHN WESLEY,...
- FRIENDLY REMARKS OCCASIONED BY THE SPIRIT AND DOCTRINES CONTAINED IN THE REV. MR FLETCHER'S 'VINDICATION', AND MORE PARTICULARLY IN HIS 'SECOND CHECK TO ANTINOMIANISM';...
- GOLIATH SLAIN, BEING A REPLY TO THE REVEREND DR. NOWELL'S ANSWER TO 'PIETAS OXONIENSIS',...
- THE GOSPEL-SHOP
- AN IMPORTANT CASE ARGUED, IN THREE DIALOGUES BETWEEN DR. OPIUM, GALLIO AND DISCIPULUS,...
- IMPOSTURE DETECTED AND THE DEAD VINDICATED, IN A LETTER TO A FRIEND,...
- A LASH AT ENTHUSIASM, IN A DIALOGUE FOUNDED UPON REAL FACTS BETWEEN MRS. CLINKER AND MISS MARTHA STEADY
- A LETTER OF ADVICE FROM A FATHER TO HIS SON, JUST ENTERING INTO HOLY ORDERS
- LOGICA WESLEIENSIS
- PIETAS OXONIENSIS
- THREE LETTERS...TO THE REV. J. FLETCHER, VICAR OF MADELEY, IN THE YEAR 1773, SETTING FORTH MR. HILL'S REASONS FOR DECLINING ANY FURTHER CONTROVERSY RELATIVE TO MR. WESLEY'S PRINCIPLES

Hill, Rowley *see* THE TITLES OF OUR LORD

Hill, Shuldham SC *see* HUDSON'S BAY AND ITS RESOURCES: WITH FEASIBILITY OF STOCKING THE BAY WITH BEHRING SEA FUR-SEAL: A LECTURE...27TH NOVEMBER 1894

Hill, Thomas *see* A STATEMENT OF THE NATURAL SOURCES OF THEOLOGY

Hill, W *see*
- AN ALPHABETICAL AND CHRONOLOGICAL ARRANGEMENT OF THE WESLEYAN METHODIST MINISTERS AND PREACHERS ON TRIAL IN CONNEXION WITH THE BRITISH AND IRISH CONFERENCES; ...FROM THE COMMENCEMENT OF THEIR ITINERANCY TO...1900; ...
- AN ALPHABETICAL AND CHRONOLOGICAL ARRANGEMENT OF THE WESLEYAN METHODIST MINISTERS AND PREACHERS ON TRIAL IN CONNEXION WITH THE BRITISH AND IRISH CONFERENCES; ...FROM THE COMMENCEMENT OF THEIR ITINERANCY TO...1912; ...
- AN ALPHABETICAL AND CHRONOLOGICAL ARRANGEMENT OF THE WESLEYAN METHODIST MINISTERS AND PREACHERS ON TRIAL IN CONNEXION WITH THE BRITISH AND IRISH CONFERENCES; ...FROM THE COMMENCEMENT OF THEIR ITINERANCY TO...1916; ...
- ALPHABETICAL AND CHRONOLOGICAL ARRANGEMENTS OF THE WESLEYAN METHODIST MINISTERS AND PROBATIONERS IN CONNEXION WITH THE BRITISH AND IRISH CONFERENCES; ...FROM THE COMMENCEMENT OF THEIR ITINERANCY TO...1922
- AN ALPHABETICAL ARRANGEMENT
- AN ALPHABETICAL ARRANGEMENT OF ALL THE WESLEYAN METHODIST MINISTERS AND PREACHERS ON TRIAL IN CONNEXION WITH THE BRITISH AND IRISH CONFERENCES; ...FROM THE COMMENCEMENT OF THEIR ITINERANCY TO...1892; ...
- AN ALPHABETICAL ARRANGEMENT OF ALL THE WESLEYAN METHODIST MINISTERS AND PREACHERS ON TRIAL IN CONNEXION WITH THE BRITISH AND IRISH CONFERENCES; ...FROM THE COMMENCEMENT OF THEIR ITINERANCY TO...1896; ...
- AN ALPHABETICAL ARRANGEMENT OF ALL THE WESLEYAN METHODIST PREACHERS AND MISSIONARIES, WHO ARE NOW TRAVELLING IN GREAT-BRITAIN AND IN DISTANT PARTS OF THE GLOBE,...
- AN ALPHABETICAL ARRANGEMENT OF ALL THE WESLEYAN-METHODIST MINISTERS, AND PREACHERS ON TRIAL, IN CONNECTION WITH THE BRITISH AND IRISH CONFERENCES
- AN ALPHABETICAL ARRANGEMENT OF ALL THE WESLEYAN-METHODIST MINISTERS, AND PREACHERS ON TRIAL, IN CONNECTION WITH THE BRITISH AND IRISH CONFERENCES;
- AN ALPHABETICAL ARRANGEMENT OF ALL THE WESLEYAN-METHODIST MINISTERS AND PREACHERS ON TRIAL, IN CONNECTION WITH THE BRITISH AND IRISH CONFERENCES
- AN ALPHABETICAL ARRANGEMENT OF ALL THE WESLEYAN-METHODIST MINISTERS, MISSIONARIES AND PREACHERS ON TRIAL, IN CONNEXION WITH THE BRITISH AND IRISH CONFERENCES
- AN ALPHABETICAL ARRANGEMENT OF ALL THE WESLEYAN-METHODIST MINISTERS, MISSIONARIES AND PREACHERS ON TRIAL IN CONNEXION WITH THE BRITISH AND IRISH CONFERENCES OR WITH THE AFFILIATED CONFERENCES
- AN ALPHABETICAL ARRANGEMENT OF ALL THE WESLEYAN-METHODIST MINISTERS, MISSIONARIES AND PREACHERS ON TRIAL IN CONNEXION WITH THE BRITISH AND IRISH CONFERENCES;...FROM THE COMMENCEMENT OF THEIR ITINERANCY TO...1846
- AN ALPHABETICAL ARRANGEMENT OF ALL THE WESLEYAN-METHODIST MINISTERS, MISSIONARIES AND PREACHERS ON TRIAL IN CONNEXION WITH THE BRITISH AND IRISH CONFERENCES;...FROM THE

COMMENCEMENT OF THEIR ITINERANCY TO...1852
- AN ALPHABETICAL ARRANGEMENT OF ALL THE WESLEYAN-METHODIST PREACHERS AND MISSIONARIES IN CONNEXION WITH THE BRITISH AND IRISH CONFERENCES;... FROM THE COMMENCEMENT OF THEIR ITINERANCY TO...1837
- AN ALPHABETICAL ARRANGEMENT OF ALL THE WESLEYAN-METHODIST PREACHERS AND MISSIONARIES IN CONNEXION WITH THE BRITISH AND IRISH CONFERENCES;... FROM THE COMMENCEMENT OF THEIR ITINERANCY TO...1840
- AN ALPHABETICAL ARRANGEMENT OF ALL THE WESLEYAN-METHODIST PREACHERS AND MISSIONARIES, WHO ARE NOW TRAVELLING IN GREAT-BRITAIN AND IN DISTANT PARTS OF THE GLOBE,...
- AN ALPHABETICAL ARRANGEMENT OF ALL THE WESLEYAN-METHODIST PREACHERS AND MISSIONARIES WHO ARE NOW TRAVELLING, OR ARE LOCATED, IN GREAT BRITAIN, AND IN DISTANT PARTS OF THE GLOBE,...

Hill, W Alfred *see* THE POETICAL WORKS OF THOMAS CAMPBELL

Hill, William *see* HISTORY OF THE RISE, PROGRESS, GENIUS, AND CHARACTER OF AMERICAN PRESBYTERIANISM

Hill, William Bancroft *see* THE PRESENT PROBLEMS OF NEW TESTAMENT STUDY

THE HILL-ADAMSON ALBUMS / National Portrait Gallery. London – 1843-48. With printed index – 14 – £95.00 – uk World [700]

Hillard, Gustav *see* SPIEL MIT DER WIRKLICHKEIT

Hillary, W *see* OBSERVATIONS ON THE CHANGES OF THE AIR AND THE CONCOMITANT EPIDEMICAL DISEASES IN THE ISLAND OF BARBADOS

Hillary, William *see* AN APPEAL TO THE BRITISH NATION, ON THE HUMANITY AND POLICY OF FORMING A NATIONAL INSTITUTION, FOR THE PRESERVATION OF LIVES AND PROPERTY FROM SHIPWRECK

HILLCREST BAPTIST CHURCH. LAURENS COUNTY. SOUTH CAROLINA : CHURCH RECORDS – 1955-72 – 1 – 11.48 – us Baptist [240]

Hille, Curt *see* DIE DEUTSCHE KOMOEDIE UNTER DER EINWIRKUNG DES ARISTOPHANES

HILLEBIEGEL / Watzlik, Hans – Regensburg: G Bosse, [194-?] – 1r – 1 – us U.W. Library [430]

Hillekamps, Karl Heinz *see* TRANSICION DE ESTADOS A NACIONES EN LATINO-AMERICA

HILLEL? – Seattle, WA. 22 Jan 1941. Continued by: Hillel World – 1 – us A.J.P.C. [071]

HILLEL BANNER – Bloomington, IN.Nov-Dec 1941; May 1944 – 1 – us A.J.P.C. [071]

HILLEL BEACON – Oxford, Ohio. 17 Nov 1941 – 1 – us A.J.P.C. [071]

HILLEL HERALD – Evanston, IL. Nov 1946 – 1 – us A.J.P.C. [071]

HILLEL HERALD – New Brunswick, NJ. 25 May 1946; Nov-Dec 1946 – 1 – us A.J.P.C. [071]

HILLEL NEWS – New York, NY. 8 Dec 1947; Hanukkah 1948 – 1 – us A.J.P.C. [071]

HILLEL OBSERVER – New York, NY. 23 Oct-27 Nov 1946; Dec 1947 – 1 – us A.J.P.C. [071]

HILLEL POST – Durham, NC. June 1944; Aug-Dec 1944; Feb 1945 – 1 – us A.J.P.C. [071]

HILLEL RECORD – Detroit, MI. Feb 1948 – 1 – us A.J.P.C. [071]

HILLEL REVIEW – Madison, WI. 5 Oct 1929-30 Oct 1960. Many issues missing – 1 – us A.J.P.C. [071]

HILLEL SCRIBE – New York, NY. 19 Feb 1941-20 Dec 1945. Many issues missing. Continues: Hillel Scroll (New York) – 1 – us A.J.P.C. [071]

HILLEL SCROLL – Bangor, ME. Feb 1948 – 1 – us A.J.P.C. [071]

HILLEL SCROLL – Columbus, OH. 28 Oct 1937-27 May 1953. Many issues missing – 1 – us A.J.P.C. [071]

HILLEL SCROLL – New York, NY. 12 Nov 1940. Continued by: Hillel Scribe – 1 – us A.J.P.C. [071]

HILLEL SHOFAR – University, AL. May 1944 – 1 – us A.J.P.C. [071]

HILLEL STAR – Montreal, Quebec, Canada. 1982-84 – 1 – us A.J.P.C. [072]

HILLELIFE – Evanston, IL. Dec 1935-Jan 1936 – 1 – us A.J.P.C. [071]

HILLELITES – Madison, WI. 28 Oct 1943, 10 Feb-30 Mar 1944. Continues: You Name It – 1 – us A.J.P.C. [071]

Hiller, Francis Hemperley *see* JUVENILE COURT LAWS OF THE UNITED STATES

Hiller, H Croft *see* DID CHRIST CLAIM TO BE SON OF GOD?

Hiller, J *see* LEBENSBESCHREIBUNGEN BERUEHMTER MUSIKGELEHRTEN UND TONKUENSTLER...

Hiller, Johann Adam *see*
- LEBENSBESCHREIBUNGEN BERUEHMTER MUSIKGELEHRTEN UND TONKUENSTLER, NEUERER ZEIT. 1. THEIL
- LEBENSBESCHREIBUNGEN BERUEHMTER MUSIKGELEHRTEN UND TONKUENSTLZR
- DER LUSTIGE SCHUSTER, ODER DER TEUFEL IST LOS, ZWEYTER THEIL
- NACHRICHT VON DER AUFFUEHRUNG DES HAENDELSCHEN MESSIAS, IN DER DOMKIRCHE ZU BERLIN
- UEBER DIE MUSIK UND DEREN WIRKUNGEN, MIT ANMERKUNGEN. HERAUSGEGEBEN VON JOHANN HILLER
- DIE VERWANDELTEN WEIBER, ODER DER TEUFEL IST LOS, ERSTER THEIL
- WOECHENTLICHE NACHRICHTEN UND ANMERKUNGEN DIE MUSIK BETREFFEND

Hiller, Louise *see* GEMUETHS-SCHAETZE

Hillern, Wilhelmine von *see* AUS EIGENER KRAFT

Hillert, Freimut *see*
- ROUTENOPTIMIERUNG MIT GREEDY-ALGORITHMEN
- TOURENOPTIMIERUNG IM HANDEL

Hillesden *see* HILLESDEN, BUCKS, TERRARS HOUSEKEEPING ACCOUNTS, SERVANTS BOOKS AND HOUSEHOLD ACCOUNTS OF

HILLESDEN, BUCKS, TERRARS HOUSEKEEPING ACCOUNTS, SERVANTS BOOKS AND HOUSEHOLD ACCOUNTS OF / Hillesden – 1657-1869 – 1 – uk Microform Academic [640]

Hilliard, Francis *see*
- AMERICAN LAW
- THE AMERICAN LAW OF REAL PROPERTY
- THE ELEMENTS OF LAW: BEING A COMPREHENSIVE SUMMARY OF AMERICAN CIVIL JURISPRUDENCE
- THE LAW OF INJUNCTIONS
- THE LAW OF MORTGAGES, OF REAL AND PERSONAL PROPERTY
- THE LAW OF REMEDIES FOR TORTS, OR PRIVATE WRONGS
- THE LAW OF SALES OF PERSONAL PROPERTY
- THE LAW OF TORTS OR PRIVATE WRONGS

Hilliard-D'Auberteuil, Michel Rene de *see* MISS MCCREA

Hillier, George *see* NARRATIVE OF THE ATTEMPTED ESCAPES OF KING CHARLES 1ST FROM CARISBROOK CASTLE, AND OF HIS DETENTION IN THE ISLE OF WIGHT FROM NOVEMBER 1647, TO THE SEIZURE OF HIS PERSON BY THE ARMY AT NEWPORT, IN NOVEMBER 1648

Hilliger, Benno *see* DIE WAHL PIUS' 5 ZUM PAPSTE

Hillquist, Morris *see* MORRIS HILLQUIT PAPERS

HILL-ROSEDALE TOPICS – Toronto. 1923-26 – 1 – 95.00 – cn McLaren [971]

Hills, Aaron Merritt *see* HOLINESS AND POWER

HILL'S CASES IN EQUITY / South Carolina. Supreme Court – (A Pre-NRS title) – v1-2. 1833-1837 (all publ) – 14mf – 9 – $21.00 – LLMC 94-030 – us L.L.M.C. [340]

HILL'S LAW REPORTS / South Carolina. Supreme Court – (A Pre-NRS title) – v1-3. 1833-1837 (all publ) – 18mf – 9 – $27.00 – LLMC 94-017 – us L.L.M.C. [340]

HILLS LIFE IN NEW SOUTH WALES – Sydney, 1832-33 – 1r – 1 – A$31.00 silver A$27.00 vesicular – at Pascoe [073]

HILLSBORO ARGUS – Hillsboro, OR. -w. 26 Jul 1894-. – 1 – us U.O. Library [071]

HILLSBORO INDEPENDENT – Hillsboro, OR. -w. 1893-1931 – 1 – 312.00 – us Oregon Hist [071]

HILLSBORO INDEPENDENT – Hillsboro, OR. -w. 8 Feb, 12 July 1901. – 1 – us U.O. Library [071]

HILLSDALE BAPTIST CHURCH. HARTSVILLE, TENNESSEE : CHURCH RECORDS – 1892-1953 – 1 – 34.02 – us Baptist [240]

THE HILLSIDE JOURNAL OF CLINICAL PSYCHIATRY – (v6-. 1984-. 5,6,9) – v1-. 1979- – 1 – us UMI [616]

HILLSTON NEWS – 1882-1883. HS1 – 1r – 1 – at Corangamite [072]

HILLSTON SPECTATOR – Jan 5 1901-Dec 25 1903; Jan 5 1933-Dec 18 1952 – 9 – at Pascoe [072]

HILLTOP MIRROR – Berkeley, CA. 1944-1946; 1948-1949; 1956-1957 – 3r – 1 – $150.00 – B06013 – us Library Micro [071]

THE HILLYARS AND THE BURTONS / Kingsley, Henry – British Fiction Archive: Unit 2 – 9 – uk Bell [830]

Hillyer, Curtis *see* CODE OF LAW, PRACTICE AND FORMS FOR JUSTICES' AND OTHER INFERIOR COURTS IN THE WESTERN STATES

Hilmi, Tueccarzade Ibrahim *see* MEMALIK-I OSMANIYE CEP ATLASI

Hilpert, Walter *see* JOHANN GEORG HAMANN ALS KRITIKER DER DEUTSCHEN LITERATUR

Hilprecht, H V *see* OLD BABYLONIAN INSCRIPTIONS CHIEFLY FROM NIPPUR

Hilprecht, Hermann Vollrat *see*
- ASSYRIACA
- THE EARLIEST VERSION OF THE BABYLONIAN DELUGE STORY AND THE TEMPLE LIBRARY OF NIPPUR

HILPRECHT'S FRAGMENT OF THE BABYLONIAN DELUGE STORY : BABYLONIAN EXPEDITION OF THE UNIVERSITY OF PENNSYLVANIA, SERIES D, VOLUME V, FASC. I / Barton, George A – (In English and Akkadian. Includes bibliographical references) – [S.l.: s.n.], 1910 – 1mf – 9 – 0-8370-7605-6 – 1986-1605 – us A.T.L.A. [930]

Hils, Hans-Peter *see* FECHTBUCH

Hilsendager, Sarah A *see* A SURVEY ANALYSIS OF DANCE WELLNESSRELATED CURRICULA IN AMERICAN HIGHER EDUCATION

Hiltebrandt, G A *see* NEU-EROEFFNETER ANMUTHIGER BILDERSCHATZ

Hilton, W *see* DE RECLUSIS/SPECULUM HUMANAE SALVATIONIS

Hilts, Joseph Henry *see* AMONG THE FOREST TREES, OR, HOW THE BUSHMAN FAMILY GOT THEIR HOMES: BEING A BOOK OF FACTS AND INCIDENTS OF PIONEER LIFE IN UPPER CANADA..

HILVANES Y ZURZIDOS. LO QUE SE LLAMA PERDER EL TIEMPO. ENSAYOS POETICOS / Bachiller Cantaclaro – Madrid: Imp. Luz y Vida, 1935 – 1 – sp Bibl Santa Ana [810]

HIMACHAL PRADESH GAZETTE / Himachal Pradesh. India – Simla. 1962-1966 – 1 – us NY Public [950]

Himachal Pradesh. India *see* HIMACHAL PRADESH GAZETTE

HIMENEA. TESTO, INTRODUZIONE E NOTE DI ANNAMARIA GALLINA / Torres Naharro, Bartolome – Milano: Edit. Cisalpino, (1961) – sp Bibl Santa Ana [946]

Himioben, Heinrich *see* DIE SCHOENHEIT DER KATHOLISCHEN KIRCHE

HIMMA KATSINA – (Filmed with: Zaruma and other Hausa newspapers) – Zaria, Nigeria: [Gaskiya Corp. n66-88. jan-oct 9 1958] – 1 – us Res Libr [960]

Himmel, F H *see*
- TROIS SONATES POUR LE PIANOFORTE AVEC ACCOMP. DE VIOLON ET VIOLONCELLE, NO. 3
- TROIS SONATES POUR LE PIANOFORTE AVEC ACCOMP. DE VIOLON ET VIOLONCELLE, NO. 11
- TROIS SONATES POUR LE PIANOFORTE AVEC ACCOMP. DE VIOLON ET VIOLONCELLE, OP. 16 NO. 3

Himmel, Paul *see* UNTERSUCHUNG UEBER DIE ENTWICKLUNG UND DEN STAND DER BETRIEBSVERHAELTNISSE EINES SCHLESISCHEN RITTERGUTES

DER HIMMEL UND SEINE WUNDER : EINE ARCHAEOLOGISCHE STUDIE NACH ALTEN JUEDISCHEN MYTHOGRAFIEN / Bergel, Joseph – Leipzig: Wilhelm Friedrich, 1881 – 1mf – 9 – 0-8370-2282-7 – 1985-0282 – us A.T.L.A. [460]

Himmelheber, H *see*
- DIE DAN, EIN BAUERNVOLK IM WESTAFRIKANISCHEN URWALD: ERGEBNIS DREIER VOELKERKUNDLICHER EXP. 1949/50, 1952/53, 1955/56
- ESKIMOKUENSTLER

Himmelheber, U *see* DIE DAN, EIN BAUERNVOLK IM WESTAFRIKANISCHEN URWALD: ERGEBNIS DREIER VOELKERKUNDLICHER EXP. 1949/50, 1952/53, 1955/56

Himmler, Gebhard *see*
- ZUR SPRACHE DES AEGIDIUS ALBERTINUS

Himmlisch, J F *see* PANTHEVM SIVE ANATOMIA ET SYMPHONIA PAPATVS,...

HIMMLISCHE LANDSCHAFT / Schickele, Rene – 1.-5. Aufl. Berlin: S Fischer, 1933, [c1932] – 1r – 1 – us U.W. Library [890]

DER HIMMLISCHE ZECHER : AUSGEWAEHLTE GEDICHTE / Mombert, Alfred – Berlin: Schuster & Loeffler, 1909 – 1r – 1 – us U.W. Library [810]

HIMPUNAN ISTILAH DAN KIASAN BAHASA INGGERIS, ARTI DAN TUDJUANNJA / Mokhtar Muhydin, H – SE-4546 1. 1957 – 9 – ne IDC [950]

HIMPUNAN KULIAH-KULIAH PENGANTAR ILMU EKONOMI; JANG DIKULIAHKAN PADA FAKULTAS HUKUM DAN PENGETAHUAN MASJARAKAT UNIVERSITAS INDONESIA DI DJAKARTA / Marsudi, Djojodipuro – SE-5101 1. 1963 – 9 – ne IDC [338]

HIMPUNAN MAHASISWA ISLAM. DIKTAT KUMPULAN TENTANG: – 9 – ne IDC [300]

HIMPUNAN SURAT – SURAT KEPUTUSAN / PERATURAN DAERAH KABUPATEN BOJOLALI TAHUN DINAS ... DAN UNTUK LANDASAN PEDOMAN KERDJA DALAM TAHUN DINAS... / Bojolali, Indonesia (Kabupaten) – Bojolali. v1-10. 1968-1969/1970 – 12mf – 9 – SE-1361/1 – ne IDC [380]

Himsworth, Sheila J *see* SURVEY OF METHODIST RECORDS [...CONNEXIONAL COMMITTEES, RESIDENTIAL SCHOOLS AND COLLEGES,...

Hinchliff, P *see* THE SOUTH AFRICAN LITURGY

HINCKLEY NEWS – England.5 Oct 1861-1871; 6 Jan, 6 Apr-Dec 1872; 18 Apr-26 Dec 1874; Jan-10 Dec 1892. -w. 25 1/2 reels – 1 – uk British Libr Newspaper [072]

HINCKLEY TIMES – Hinckley, England. 1889; 1985 – 38+ r – 1 – uk British Libr Newspaper [072]

HINCKLEY TIMES AND LUTTERWORTH NEWS ETC *see* LUTTERWORTH NEWS ETC

Hincks, Edward *see* ON THE POLYPHONY OF THE ASSYRIO-BABYLONIAN CUNEIFORM WRITING

Hincks, Francis *see*
- MONTREAL WEEKLY PILOT
- THE PILOT

Hincks, Sir Francis *see*
- RELIGIOUS ENDOWMENTS IN CANADA: THE CLERGY RESERVE AND RECTORY QUESTIONS: A CHAPTER OF CANADIAN HISTORY
- REMINISCENCES OF HIS PUBLIC LIFE
- SIR FRANCIS HINCKS' BUDGET SPEECH, FRIDAY, MARCH 10, 1871

HINCMARUS DE ORDINE PALATII (MGH LEGES 4: 3.BD) – 1894 – Dfl6.00 – ne Slangenburg [240]

Hind, Henry Youle *see*
- BRITISH NORTH AMERICA: REPORTS OF PROGRESS TOGETHER WITH A PRELIMINARY AND GENERAL REPORT, ON THE ASSINNIBOINE AND SASKATCHEWAN EXPLORING EXPEDITION
- NORTHWEST TERRITORY
- TERRITOIRE DU NORD-QUEST

Hinde, G J *see* A MONOGRAPH OF THE BRITISH FOSSIL SPONGES

Hinder, E M *see* LIFE AND LABOUR IN SHANGHAI. A DECADE OF LABOUR AND SOCIAL ADMINISTRATION IN INTERNATIONAL SETTLEMENT

Hinderer, Anna Martin *see* SEVENTEEN YEARS IN THE YORUBA COUNTRY. MEMORIALS OF ANNA HINDERER

HINDI MILAP – Hyderabad, India. 7 Sept 1953-1954 – 3r – 1 – us L of C Photodup [072]

HINDI PUNCH – Bombay. v1-49. 1907-31 – 1,479mf – 8 – ne IDC [073]

HINDI PUSTAKA-SAHITYA, 1867-1942 / Gupta, M P – Isvi. Ilahabada. 1945. BI-342 2 – 8 – ne IDC [490]

Hindlip, Charles Allsopp *see* BRITISH EAST AFRICA

THE HINDOOS AS THEY ARE / Bose, S C – London, Calcutta. 1881. B-615 2 – 8 – ne IDC [280]

Hindos, Jose de *see* BEETHOVEN. SUGESTIONES

Hindret, J *see* L'ART DE BIEN PRONONCER

Hinds, Allen *see* A GARNER OF SAINTS

Hinds, Asher C *see*
- HIND'S PARLIAMENTARY PRECEDENTS OF THE HOUSE OF REPRESENTATIVES
- HIND'S PRECEDENTS OF THE HOUSE OF REPRESENTATIVES
- HINDS' PRECEDENTS OF THE HOUSE OF REPRESENTATIVES OF THE UNITED STATES.

- PARLIAMENTARY PROCEDURES OF THE HOUSE OF REPRESENTATIVES OF THE U.S

HINDS COUNTY GAZETTE – Raymond. Miss. 1854-1918; 1922-1924; 1936- – 1 – us UMI [071]

HIND'S PARLIAMENTARY PRECEDENTS OF THE HOUSE OF REPRESENTATIVES / Hinds, Asher C – Washington: GPO, 1898 (all publ) – 4mf – 9 – $14.00 – LLMC 84-103 – us L.L.M.C. [340]

HIND'S PRECEDENTS OF THE HOUSE OF REPRESENTATIVES / Hinds, Asher C – Washington: GPO. 8v. 1907-08 (all publ) – 29mf – 9 – $43.50 – LLMC 84-104 – us L.L.M.C. [323]

HINDS' PRECEDENTS OF THE HOUSE OF REPRESENTATIVES OF THE UNITED STATES. / Hinds, Asher C – Washington: GPO, 1907-08. 8v. LL-1235 – 1 – us L of C Photodup [340]

Hinds, R B *see* ZOOLOGY OF THE VOYAGE OF H.M.S. SULPHUR, 1836-1842

Hinds, William Alfred *see* AMERICAN COMMUNITIES AND CO-OPERATIVE COLONIES

THE HINDU – Madras. India. 1951- – 1 – us UMI [072]

THE HINDU : ILLUSTRATED SUNDAY EDITION – Madras: K Gopalan, 1936-41 – us Res Libr [072]

THE HINDU – Madras, India: K Gopalan, [1942-]. mar-may 1945; jan-jul 1947; feb 28 1954, 1950-1975, 1976-1983 (weekly ed) – us Res Libr [072]

HINDU CASTES AND SECTS / Bhattacharya, J N – Calcutta, 1896. 623 pp. BI-329 2 – 8 – ne IDC [305]

THE HINDU (DAILY EDITION) – Madras, India: K Gopalan, [dec 5 1929-dec 1936]; mar-may 1945; jan-jul 1947; 1956-60; jan 1961-mar 1969; apr 1969-dec 1975; 1976-83 – 1 – us Res Libr [072]

HINDU MISSIONARY – (Lacking some pgs. Some original pgs damaged) – v1-7. 1917-24 – 1r – 1 – ATLA S0715 – us A.T.L.A. [073]

HINDU ORGAN – (Also known as: Intu Catanam) – Jaffna, Sri Lanka. 1899-31 Mar 1974 – 13r – 1 – us L of C Photodup [072]

HINDU OUTLOOK – New Delhi. [v2 n44-v5 n43 jan 11 1939-jan 11 1941 1r. jan 26 1941-sep 1957 r2-5] – 5r – 1 – us Res Libr [950]

HINDU OUTLOOK – New Delhi. v2 n44-v5 n43. jan 1939-jan 1941 – 1r – 1 – us Res Libr [072]

HINDU WEEKLY REVIEW – Madras, India. 10 Aug 1953-Aug 1968 – 11r – 1 – us L of C Photodup [073]

HINDUBANI – Bankura. v1 n1-22 oct 1947-sep 1948; v6-7 dec 1952-sep 1954; v10-15 n23 oct 1956-sep 1962; v23 n1-21 oct 1969-oct 1970 – 5r – 1 – us Res Libr [072]

HINDUSTAN – Madras, India. Mar 1947-18 Dec 1949 – 2r – 1 – us L of C Photodup [072]

HINDUSTAN REVIEW – (Missing: 1897-1900, v1-2; 1903, v7(3, 4); 1907, v15 (90, 91, 93); 1907, v16(96, 98-100); 1908, v17(101); 1916, v34(199,205)) – Allahabad, 1897-1928. v1-51 – 454mf – 9 – I-112/2 – ne IDC [950]

HINDUSTAN TIMES – New Delhi, II. 1984 – 1r – $50.00 – R63615 – us Library Micro [072]

HINDUSTAN TIMES – New Delhi, India. 1952-55; 1960-Oct 1995 – 296r – 1 – us L of C Photodup [072]

HINDUSTANA AND HINDVASI – New Delhi, India. 6 Sept 1946-1953; 1961-Jul 1987 – 136r – 1 – us L of C Photodup [072]

HINDUSTANU = HINDUSTAN SINDHI DAILY – Bombay, India. 1962-Jun 1977; 1978-93 – 79r – 1 – us L of C Photodup [072]

HINDUSTHAN STANDARD – Calcutta, India. Apr 1944-Jun 1982 – 150r – 1 – us L of C Photodup [072]

HINDVASI – Bombay, India. 1962-64 – 3r – 1 – us L of C Photodup [072]

Hine, Charles Cole *see* LAWS OF THE SEVERAL STATES IN REGARD TO INSURANCE COMPANIES FROM OTHER STATES AND COUNTRIES

Hine, Edward *see* FORTY-SEVEN IDENTIFICATIONS OF THE LOST BRITISH NATION AND THE U.W. WITH THE TEN LOST TRIBES

Hines, Harvey Kimball *see*
- AN ILLUSTRATED HISTORY OF THE STATE OF OREGON
- MISSIONARY HISTORY OF THE PACIFIC NORTHWEST
- STATE OF WASHINGTON

Hingeston, C *see* CHRONICLE OF ENGLAND (RS1)

Hingeston, F C *see*
- LIBER DE ILLUSTRIBUS HENRICIS (RS7)
- ROYAL AND HISTORICAL LETTERS DURING THE REIGN OF HENRY THE FOURTH, KING OF ENGLAND AND OF FRANCE, AND LORD OF IRELAND (RS18)

HINGHAM 1635-1900 – (Mf 1-2: Vital Records 1635-1780. Mf 3: Out-of-Town Marriages 1657-1799. Mf 4-5: First Settlers 1635-50. Mf 6-11: Town Records 1635-1700. Mf 12-18: Land Records 1635-77. Mf 19-21: Proprietors 1720-69. Mf 22: Valuation in 1749. Mf 23: Town Records 1642-51. Mf 24-36: Selectmen Books 1661-1859. Mf 37-40: Mortgages 1825-46. Mf 41-80: Town Records 1635-1858. Mf 81-91: Town Meetings 1819-66. Mf 92-94: Rebellion Record 1861-66. Mf 95-96: Out-of-Town Deaths 1844-90. Mf 97-100: Intentions 1700-1823. Mf 100-106: Intentions 1853-97. Mf 107-131: Births 1635-1880. Mf 132-155: Marriages 1635-1880. Mf 156-174: Deaths 1635-1880. Mf 175-188: B,M,D Index 1645-1900. Mf 189-208: Vital Records 1635-1835. Mf 209-215: Vital Records 1790-1848. Mf 216-219: Vital Records 1844-55. Mf 220-225: Vital Records 1847-69. Mf 226-230: Vital Records 1865-80. Mf 231-234: Deaths 1877-1900. Mf 235-236: Marriages 1878-1900. Mf 237-238: Births 1880-99) – (mf ed 1990) – 238mf – 9 – 0-87623-116-4 – us Holbrook [920]

Hingham, Massachusetts. Hingham Baptist Church *see* RECORDS

Hinkel, John Vincent *see* THE COMMUNIST NETWORK

Hinkhouse, John Frederick *see* THE BELOVED

Hinkley, Edward Otis *see* THE LAW OF ATTACHMENTS IN MARYLAND

Hinkley, Edyth *see* A STRUGGLE FOR A SOUL AND OTHER STORIES OF LIFE AND WORK IN SOUTH INDIA

Hinkovic, Henrik *see* LES CROATES SOUS LE JOUG MAGYAR

Hinloopen Labberton, C van *see* THE WAYANG OR SHADOW PLAY AS GIVEN IN JAVA

Hinojois, Marques de *see* EPIGRAFIA ROMANA Y VISIGOTICA DE MONTEMOLIN

Hinojosa del Valle, Gregorio *see*
- CUADERNO DE LENGUAJE. CURSO NO 2. PT. 2
- LENGUAJE. CURSO SEGUNDO

Hinrichs, I Ch *see* ENSTEHUNG, FORTGANG UN IETZIGE BESCHAFFENHEIT DER RUSSISCHEN IAGDMUSIK

Hinschius, Paul *see* DIE PAEPSTLICHE UNFEHLBARKEIT UND DAS VATIKANISCHE KONCIL

HINSDALE 1784-1849 – (Mf 1T: Intentions & Marriages 1804-43; Births & Deaths 1784-1851. Mf 2T: Births & Deaths 1791-1844; Intentions & Marriages 1814-50. Mf 3T: B,M,D 1844-49) – (mf ed 1996) – 3mf – 9 – 0-87623-266-7 – us Holbrook [920]

HINSDALE 1860-1893 – (Mf 1: Births 1860-79. Mf 2: Births 1879-93; Marriages 1860-69. Mf 3: Marriages 1870-89. Mf 4: Marriages 1890-93; Deaths 1860-76. Mf 5: Deaths 1876-90. Mf 6: Deaths 1890-93) – (mf ed 1983) – 6mf – 9 – 0-931248-43-4 – us Holbrook [920]

Hinsdale, New Hampshire.North Hinsdale Baptist Church *see* RECORDS

Hinson, BT *see* MARKERS OF MUSCLE DAMAGE FOLLOWING PROLONGED SWIMMING, CYCLING, AND RUNNING AND A TRIATHLON COMPETITION

Hinson, William G *see*
- DIARY
- PAPERS OF WILLIAM G. HINSON

Hintenlang, Hubert *see* UNTERSUCHUNGEN ZU DEN HOMER-APORIEN DES ARISTOTELES

HINTER DER MASKE : SUDERMAN UND HAUPTMANN IN DEN DRAMEN JOHANNES, DIE DREI REHERFEDERN, SCHLUC UND JAU / Gimmerthal, Armin – (Includes index) – Berlin: C A Schwetschke, 1901 – 1 – us U.W. Library [790]

HINTERLAENDER ANZEIGER – Biedenkopf, Germany. 1983- – ca 78r per yr – 1 – gw Mikrofilm [072]

HINTERLAENDER ANZEIGER – (Incl suppl. Cont: Anzeige-Blatt fuer den Kreis Biedenkopf und Bezirk Voehl, -1848; Der Hinterlaender Bote [...], -1868; Kreisblatt, -1876. Today Bereichsausgabe der Wetzlarer Neuen Zeitung.) – Biedenkopf, jan 9-dec 25 1841, 1843, 1846, 1847, 1849, 1851, 1854, 1855, 1861, 1865-69 (many issues missing), 1872-75, 1877-1943, aug 1 1949-oct 24 1969, 1983- – 1 – Inquire at Mikrofilmarchiv for details – gw Misc Inst [943]

DER HINTERLAENDER BOTE [...] *see* HINTERLAENDER ANZEIGER

HINTERLASSENE WERKE UEBER KREIG UND KRIEGFUEHRUNG / Clausewitz, Carl von – Berlin. F. Duemmler. 1832-37. 10 v. (Strategy of War Series) – 9 – fr Hachette [355]

Hinton, Edward Wilcox *see* CASES ON THE LAW OF EVIDENCE, SELECTED FROM DECISIONS OF ENGLISH AND AMERICAN COURTS

Hinton, Richard J *see* HANDBOOK TO ARIZONA

HINTS AND EXPEDIENTS: A POCKET BOOK FOR YOUNG TEACHERS / Boyle, David – Toronto: Crip Print. and Pub. Co., 1892. 00227. (Pre-1900 Canadiana) – 9 – cn C.I.H.M. [370]

HINTS FOR SOME IMPROVEMENTS IN THE AUTHORIZED VERSION OF THE NEW TESTAMENT / Scholefield, James – (Includes index) – 4th ed. Cambridge: Deighton, Bell; London: Bell and Daldy, 1857 – 1mf – 9 – 0-8370-9269-8 – 1986-3269 – us A.T.L.A. [220]

HINTS FOR TOMORROW'S POULTRYMEN / Virginia. Polytechnic Institute. Extension Division – 1952-Nov 1964 – 1,5 – us Spaulding [636]

HINTS FROM A LAWYER: OR, LEGAL ADVICE TO MEN AND WOMEN. / Spencer, Edgar A – New York, Putnam, 1888. 227 p. LL-1244 – 1 – us L of C Photodup [340]

HINTS ON BIBLE STUDY / Trumbull, Henry Clay et al – Philadelphia: John D. Wattles, 1898. 1 fiche – 9 – us A.T.L.A. [240]

HINTS ON OLD TESTAMENT THEOLOGY / Duff, Archibald – (Includes index) – London: Adam & Charles Black, 1908 – 1mf – 9 – 0-8370-2987-2 – 1985-0987 – us A.T.L.A. [220]

HINTS ON PREACHING (CCC91) = CH'UAN TAO I YU / Ch'en, Chin-yung – (In Chinese) – Shanghai: Christian Literature Society, 1930 – 1r – 1 – 1984-B500 – us A.T.L.A. [240]

HINTS ON THE FORMATION OF RELIGIOUS OPINIONS : ADDRESSED ESPECIALLY TO YOUNG MEN AND WOMEN OF CHRISTIAN EDUCATION / Palmer, Ray – New York: Anson D F Randolph, 1867 – 1mf – 9 – 0-8370-4661-0 – 1985-2661 – us A.T.L.A. [210]

HINTS RESPECTING COMMENTARIES UPON THE SCRIPTURES / Stuart, Moses – The Biblical Repository, v3,no.9, Jan 1833, p130-185 – 9 – us A.T.L.A. [240]

HINTS TO YOUNG OFFICERS ON THE PRINCIPLES OF MILITARY LAW : AND ON THE PRACTICE OF COURTS-MARTIAL / Harcourt, Francis V – London: W Houghton, 1833 – 2mf – 9 – $3.00 – LLMC 89-030 – us L.L.M.C. [340]

HINTS TOWARDS THE FORMATION OF A MORE COMPREHENSIVE THEORY OF LIFE / Coleridge, Samuel Taylor; ed by Watson, Seth B – London: John Churchill, 1848 – 1 roll – 1 – 1-55879-295-3 – uk Libr Preservation [100]

Hintze, Carl Ernst *see* DIE ENDLOSE STRASSE

Hintze, F *see* DIE BERLINER HANDSCHRIFT DER SAHIDISCHEN APOSTELGESCHICHTE (T.U.U. 5-109)

Hinz, J *see* GRAMMAR AND VOCABULARY OF THE ESKIMO LANGUAGE

Hinz, W *see* EIN ORIENTALISCHES HANDELSUNTERNEHMEN IM 15. JAHRHUNDERT

HIOB FUER DIE DRITTE AUFLAGE NACH L. HIRZEL UND J. OLSHAUSEN / Dillmann, August – (Includes bibliographical references) – 3. Aufl. Leipzig: S Hirzel, 1869 – 1mf – 9 – 0-8370-3550-3 – 1985-1550 – us A.T.L.A. [220]

HIOB, ODER, DIE VIER SPIEGEL : GEDICHTE / Wolfskehl, Karl – Hamburg: Claassen Verlag, vorm. Claassen & Goverts, c1950 – 1r – 1 – us U.W. Library [810]

HIP : THE JAZZ RECORD DIGEST – v1-5, no. 5; n.s. v1-10, no. 6 (all publ). Sept 1962-Jan 1967; Mar 1967-Dec 1971 (Jazz Periodicals) – 1 reel – 1 – $140.00 – us UPA [780]

HIPI; MADJALAH EKONOMI – (Lacking: 1946, V.2(1)) – Djakarta, 1945-1946 – 6mf – 9 – ne IDC [330]

HIPOLITO RUIZ LOPEZ, 1754-1815 AND JOSE ANTONIO PAVON Y JIMENEZ, 1754-1844 / Royal Botanical Garden, Madrid – 302mf – 9 – ne IDC [580]

HIPPARCHUS BITHYNIUS – In Arati et Eudoxi Phaenomena Commentariorum. German. 1894. Ed. by Karl Manitius – 1 – us U.W. Library [520]

HIPPOCRATICAS THESES EX LIBRIS APHOR, PROGNOSTIC. Y VICT.... / Morera, J M – Valencia, 1745 – 1mf – 9 – sp Cultura [610]

HIPPOLYTOS' CAPITEL GEGEN DIE MAGIER : REFUT. HAER. 4 28-42 (T.U.U. 3-39/2) / Ganschinietz, R – Leipzig, 1913 – 2mf – 9 – ne Slangenburg [240]

HIPPOLYTS DANIELCOMMENTAR (T.U.U. 3-38/1B) / Diobouniotis, C – Leipzig, 1911 – 1mf – 9 – ne Slangenburg [240]

HIPPOLYTS KOMMENTAR ZUM HOHENLIED AUF GRUND VON N. MARRS AUSGABE DES GRUSINISCHEN TEXTES (T.U.U.2-23/2C) / Bonwetsch, G N – Leipzig, 1902 – 2mf – 9 – ne Slangenburg [240]

HIPPOLYTS SCHRIFT UEBER DIE SEGNUNGEN JAKOBS (T.U.U. 3-38/1A) / Dlabounlotls, C & Beis, N – Leipzig, 1911 – 1mf – 9 – ne Slangenburg [240]

HIPPOLYTSSTUDIEN (T.U.U. 2-16/4) / Achelis, Hans – Leipzig, 1897 – 4mf – 9 – ne Slangenburg [240]

HIPPOLYTUS AND HIS AGE, OR, THE BEGINNINGS AND PROSPECTS OF CHRISTIANTY / Bunsen, Christian Charles Josias – London: Longman, Brown, Green, and Longmans, 1854. (Christianity and mankind. Historical section / by Christian Charles Josias Bunsen; v1-2) – 3mf – us A.T.L.A. [240]

HIPPOLYTUS UND DIE ROEMISCHEN ZEITGENOSSEN, ODER, DIE PHILOSOPHUMENA UND DIE VERWANDTEN SCHRIFTEN NACH URSPRUNG, COMPOSITION UND QUELLEN / Volkmar, Gustav – Zuerich: E. Kiesling, 1855 – 1mf – us A.T.L.A. [240]

HIPPOLYTUS VON ROM IN SEINER STELLUNG ZU STAAT UND WELT : NEUE FUNDE UND FORSCHUNGEN ZUR GESCHICHTE VON STAAT UND KIRCHE IN DER ROEMISCHEN KAISERZEIT / Neumann, Karl Johannes – Leipzig: Veit & Comp., 1902 – 1mf – us A.T.L.A. [240]

Hipps, Richard Sherrill *see* AN INVESTIGATION OF THE ETHICAL DILEMMAS IN THE PRACTICE OF EUTHANASIA

Hiral, Ange-Marie *see* LE LIS REFLEURI

Hirato, K *see* SENDJINKOEN DAN TENTERA SOEKARELA. (TERKOEMPOEL OLEH K. HIRATO, A.O.)

Hiriartia, J de *see* LE CAS DES CATHOLIQUES BASQUES

HIRMONDO – Budapest, Hungary. Nov. 1859-Oct 1860.-m. 20 ft – 1 – uk British Libr Newspaper [072]

Hirsch, A *see* HANDBUCH DER HISTORISCH-GEOGRAPHISCHEN PATHOLOGIE

Hirsch, Emil Gustav *see* PAUL, THE APOSTLE OF HEATHEN JUDAISM, OR, CHRISTIANITY

Hirsch, Etienne *see* EMPLOYMENT AND INCOME POLICIES FOR IRAN

Hirsch, Franz *see* GESCHICHTE DER DEUTSCHEN LITTERATUR VON IHREN ANFAENGEN BIS AUF DIE NEUESTE ZEIT

Hirsch, Hermann *see* DER WEISSE MANTEL FAELLT

Hirsch, Max *see* THE FISCAL SUPERSTITION (H. OPPOSES PROTECTIONISM)

Hirsch, S A *see* A BOOK OF ESSAYS

Hirsch, Samson Raphael *see* NEUNZEHN BRIEFE UEBER JUDENTHUM

Hirsch, Samuel Abraham *see* THE GREEK GRAMMAR OF ROGER BACON AND A FRAGMENT OF HIS HEBREW GRAMMAR

Hirschbein, P *see* MAHAZOT

Hirschberg, H Z *see*
- DAPPIM AL HALUKKAT HOVOT HA-YEHUDIM BI-YERUSHALAYIM BA-MEAH HA-18
- HA-MIFNEH BE-MA'AMADAH SHEL YERUSHALAYIM BA-MEAH HA-19

Hirschberg, J *see* GESCHICHTE DER AUGENHEILKUNDE

Hirsche, K *see* PROLEGOMENA ZU EINER NEUEN AUSGABE DER IMITATIO CHRISTI NACH DEM AUTOGRAPH DES THOMAS VON KEMPEN
Hirschfeld, Georg *see* THE MOTHERS
Hirschfeld, H *see* NEW RESEARCHES INTO THE COMPOSITION AND EXEGESIS OF THE QORAN
Hirschfeld, Magnus *see* ZEITSCHRIFT FUER SEXUALWISSENSCHAFT, 1908 (HQ 27)
Hirschfelder, Jacob Mair *see* THE IMMORTALITY OF THE SOUL: BEING A CRITICAL INVESTIGATION OF THE DOCTRINE...AS SET FORTH IN THE OLD TESTAMENT
Hirschl, Andrew Jackson *see* THE LAW OF FRATERNITIES AND SOCIETIES...WITH SPECIAL REFERENCE TO THEIR INSURANCE FEATURE
Hirschl, Samuel D *see* BUSINESS LAW
Hirschmann, O *see* HENDRICK GOLTZIUS ALS MALER, 1600-1617
Hirschstein, Hans *see* DIE FRANZOESISCHE REVOLUTION IM DEUTSCHEN DRAMA UND EPOS NACH 1815
Hirscht, Arthur *see* DIE APOKALYPSE UND IHRE NEUESTE KRITIK
Hirsch-Weber, Wolfgang *see* LATEINAMERIKA
Hirson, Denis *see* SOUTH AFRICAN SHORT STORIES FROM 1945 TO THE PRESENT
Hirst, Thomas Archer *see* NATURAL KNOWLEDGE IN SOCIAL CONTEXT: THE JOURNALS OF THOMAS ARCHER HIRST
DER HIRT DES HERMAS / Zahn, Theodor – (Includes bibliographical references) – Gotha: Friedrich Andreas Perthes, 1868 – 2mf – 9 – 0-8370-9675-8 – 1986-3675 – us A.T.L.A. [920]
HIRTENNOVELLE / Wiechert, Ernst Emil – Muenchen: K Desch, c1945 – 1r – 1 – us U.W. Library [830]
HIRTH ANNIVERSARY VOLUME / Hirth, Friedrich – (Asia Major introductory volume). London. 1923. Illus. BU-293 2 – 8 – ne IDC [920]
Hirth, Friedrich *see*
- AUS FRIEDRICHS HEBBELS KORRESPONDENZ
- FESTSCHRIFT FUER FRIEDRICH HIRTH ZU SEINEM 75 GEBURTSTAG 16 APRIL 1920
- HIRTH ANNIVERSARY VOLUME

Hirzel, Ludwig *see*
- ALBRECHT HALLERS TAGEBUECHER SEINER REISEN NACH DEUTSCHLAND, HOLLAND UND ENGLAND
- GESCHICHTE DER GELEHRTHEIT
- WIELAND UND MARTIN UND REGULA KUENZLI

Hirzel, R *see* DER NAME
HIS DARLING SIN / Braddon, Mary Elizabeth – British Fiction Archive: Unit 5 – 9 – uk Bell [830]
HIS DISCOURS OF VOYAGES INTO Y^E EASTE AND WEST INDIES / Linschoten, J H van – (Books 1-3 are dated 1598. Deals briefly with China; more on Macao, Canton and the southern and eastern sea routes. Uneven mixture of fact and medieval storytelling. Cf. Kammerer, La decouverte 156-197 on the rutter for the China coasts) – London. 4v. [1598] – 11mf – 9 – H-8431/1 – ne IDC [910]
HIS GRANDMOTHERS – 1877?. 05635. (Pre-1900 Canadiana) – 9 – cn C.I.H.M. [830]
HIS HONOUR AND A LADY / Duncan, Sara Jeannette – By Mrs. Everard Cotes. Toronto: G. Rose, 1896. 05293. (Pre-1900 Canadiana) – 9 – cn C.I.H.M. [830]
HIS HOUSE IN ORDER : A COMEDY IN FOUR ACTS / Pinero, Arthur Wing – London: W. Heinemann, 1907 [c1906] – 1 roll – 1 – 1-55879-406-9 – uk Libr Preservation [870]
HIS MAJESTY'S GOVERNMENT GAZETTE / Malaysia – 1957-67 – 22r – 1 – us Ross [324]
His Majesty's Theatre. Montreal *see* MME. SARAH BERNHARDT
HIS MICROLOGVS / Ornithoparcus, Andrea – or Introdvction: Containing the Art of Singing. London. 1609. BP-734 1 – 9 – ne IDC [780]
HIS SUNDAY SCHOOLS AND HIS FRIENDS / Raikes, Robert – 336p – 1 – 11.76 – us Baptist [240]
HIS TRIUMPHANT CHARIOT OF ANTIMONY / Basil, V – M 302. 1678 – 9 – ne IDC [840]
HIS WRITINGS / Wheelwright, John – (Also: A Memoir by Charles H. Bell. 1876) – 1 – $50.00 – us Presbyterian [240]
Hislop, Alexander *see* THE TWO BABYLONS
Hispalensis, Isidorus episcopus *see* DE ECCLESIASTICIS OFFICIIS
HISPANIA – v. 1- 1918- – 1. ; 5,6. ; 9 – apply; v.52-; v.58- – us UMI [073]
HISPANIA – v. 22-46. 1939-1963 – 1 – us Princeton Micro [946]
HISPANIAE SCHOLA MUSICA SACRA/OPERA VARIA [SAECAL 15, 16, 17 ET 18]... / Morales, C & Guerrero, F – (Other composers: A. Cabezon, J.G. Perez) – Barcelona: J B Pujol, 1894-98 – 1 – us Sibley [780]
HISPANIARUM REGINE. POEMAS GUADALUPENSES / Corredor Garcia, Antonio (OF M) – Sevilla: Editorial San Antonio, 1950 – 1 – sp Bibl Santa Ana [440]
HISPANIC AMERICAN HISTORICAL REVIEW – v. 1-23. 1918-1943 – 1 – us Princeton Micro [946]
THE HISPANIC COLLECTION – 14r – 1 – $490.00 – Dist. us Scholarly Res – us L of C Photodup [975]
HISPANIC CULTURE SERIES – 575r – 1 – $35,900.00 $1,200.00y – us OmniSys [946]
HISPANIC JOURNAL OF BEHAVIORAL SCIENCES – v.1. 1979 – 1,5,6,9 – us UMI [073]
HISPANIC REVIEW – v1- 1933- – 1,5,6,9 – us UMI [440]
Hispanic Society of America. New York *see* CATALOGUE OF THE LIBRARY OF THE HISPANIC SOCIETY OF AMERICA
HISPANICAE ADVOCATIONIS / Gentili, A – Amstelredami, 1661 – 4mf – 1 – ILM-1022/1 – ne IDC [327]
HISPANIC-AMERICAN HISTORICAL REVIEW – (v.49-61. 1969-81. 5,6. v.55-61. 1975-81. 9) – v.37-61. 1957-81 – 1 – us UMI [073]
Hispanicus *see* BADAJOZ
EL HISPANO-AMAZONENSE – Manaos, Amazonas. 17 Maio 1918-Ago 1920; Jan 1921-30 Set 1922 – 1,5,6 – bl Biblioteca [072]
EL HISPANO-AMERICANISMO / Berenguer, F – Habana, 1919 – 3mf – 9 – ILM-4071/1 – ne IDC [327]
HISTAMINE IN MARINE PRODUCTS : PRODUCTION BY BACTERIA, MEASUREMENT AND PREDICTION OF FORMATION – 1985 – 67p – it F.A.O. [574]
HISTOCHEMICAL JOURNAL – (1983-. 5,6,9) – v1-. 1968- – 1 – us UMI [073]
HISTOCHEMIE – HISTOCHEMISTRY. HISTOCHIMIE *see* ZEITSCHRIFT FUER ZELLFORSCHUNG UND MIKROSKOPISCHE ANATOMIE
HISTOCHEMISTRY – v. 1-70. 1958-80 – 1,5,9 – 12,863.00 – us UMI [073]
HISTOIE DE L'ACADEMIE ROYALE DES SCIENCES ET DES BELLES-LETTRES DE BERLIN. ANNEE 1745-1769 – Berlin, 1746-1769. v1-25 – 296mf – 9 – H-413/2 – ne IDC [060]
L'HISTOIRE – (Cont by: Journal L'Histoire 6 fev-17 jul 1962. Cont by: Le Progres de la Mauricle 21 aut 1962-26 avr 1966) – Shawinigan, Canada. 19 mar 1959-23 jan 1962 – 1r – 1 – Can$55.00 – cn Can Microfilming [072]
HISTOIRE : AVEC LES MEMOIRES / Akademie der Wissenschaften. Berlin – 25v. 1745-69 – 1 – us Schnase [500]
HISTOIRE ABREGEE DES INSECTES QUI SE TROUVENT AUX ENVIRONS DE PARIS... / Geoffroy, E L – Paris, [1799-1800] – 2vols – 8 – ne IDC [590]
HISTOIRE ABREGEE DES PLANTES DES PYRENEES / Lapeyrouse, P P de – Toulouse. 1813; suppl. Toulouse. 1818. B-6006 2 – 8 – ne IDC [580]
HISTOIRE ABREGEE DU JANSENISME ET REMARQUES SUR L'ORDONNANCE DE M. L'ARCHEVEQUE DE PARIS / Louail-Fouillou-de Joncoux – Cologne, 1698 – 3mf – 8 – Dfl13.00 – ne Slangenburg [240]
HISTOIRE ADMIRABLE ET VERITABLE DES CHOSES ADVENUES A L'ENDROIT D'UNE RELIGIEUSE / Buisseret, Francois – Paris. 1586 – 9 – fr Hachette [360]
HISTOIRE ANCIENNE DE L'AFRIQUE DU NORD / Gsell, S – A 624. 8 v. 1913-1928 – 8 – ne IDC [960]
HISTOIRE ANCIENNE DE L'AFRIQUE DU NORD / Gsell, Stephane – Paris. 1920-28. 8v – 1 – us Res Libr [960]
HISTOIRE ANCIENNE DU CANON DU N. TEST / Lagrange, Marie Joseph – 1933 – 4mf – 8 – ne Slangenburg [220]
HISTOIRE ANECDOTIQUE ET RAISONNEE DU THEATRE ITALIEN / Jullien, Jean-Auguste – 1770. 7v – 9 – us Sibley [780]
HISTOIRE AUTHENTIQUE... / Capefigue, J B H R – Paris, 1847 – 4mf – 1 – ILM-361/1 – ne IDC [327]
HISTOIRE BIOGRAPHIQUE ILLUSTREE DE NOS DEPUTES / Xau, Fernand-Arthur-Pierre – Paris: Duclaux fils, 1877 – fr Armell [920]
HISTOIRE CHIMIQUE ET PHYSIOLOGIQUE D'UNE BOUCHEE DE PAIN: CONFERENCE FAITE A L'UNION CATHOLIQUE DE MONTREAL, LE 27 AVRIL 1890 / Carrier, Joseph C – Montreal?, 1890. 00475. (Pre-1900 Canadiana) – 9 – cn C.I.H.M. [971]
HISTOIRE CHRONOLOGIQUE DE LA NOUVELLE FRANCE, 1504-1632 / Le Tac, Sixte – Paris: Fischbacher, 1888. SEM35P71 – 1r – 1 – Can$15.00 – cn Bibl Nat [971]
HISTOIRE CIVILE, POLITIQUE ET RELIGIEUSE DE LA VILLE ET DU COMTE DE NANTES... / Travers, Nicolas – Nantes: Forest, 1836-1841. 3t – 2r – 1 – F869.10 – fr Armell [910]
HISTOIRE COMPLETE DES VOYAGES ET DECOUVERTES EN AFRIQUE. ACCOMPAGNEE D'UN PRECIS GEOGRAPHIQUE SUR CE CONTINENT / Leyden, John & Murray, Hugh – Traducation de l'anglais. Paris, Arthus Bertrand. 1821 – 9 – $47.00 – fr Orientalistes [910]
HISTOIRE CONTENANT VNE SOMMAIRE DESCRIPTION DES GENEALOGIES, ALLIANCES, ET GESTES DE TOUS LES PRINCES ET GRANS SEIGNEURS / Lusignano, S di – Paris, 1579 – 2mf – 9 – H-8353/1 – ne IDC [920]
HISTOIRE CRITIQUE DE LA LITTERATURE PROPHETIQUE DES HEBREUZ / Bruston, Charles – Paris: Librairie Fischbacher, 1881. 1 fiche – 9 – us A.T.L.A. [220]
HISTOIRE CRITIQUE DE MANICHEE ET DU MANICHEISME / Beausobre, M de – Amsterdam. v1-2. 1734-1739 – Dfl137.00 – ne Slangenburg [290]
HISTOIRE CRITIQUE DE NICOLAS FLAMEL ET DE PERENELLE SA FEMME; ON Y A JOINT LE TESTAMENT DE PERENELLE & PLUSIEURS AUTRES PIECES INTERESSANTES / Villain, Etienne Francois – Paris, 1761 – 1 – us U.W. Library [944]
HISTOIRE CRITIQUE DES DOCTRINES DE L'EDUCATION EN FRANCE DEPUIS LE SEIZIEME SIECLE / Compayre, Gabriel – Paris: Hachette, 1904. 2v. 10 fiches. (Education Collection) – 9 – 25.00 – fr Bibl Nationale [370]
HISTOIRE CRITIQUE DES DOCTRINES DE L'EDUCATION EN FRANCE DEPUIS LE XVIE SIECLE / Compayre, Gabriel – 1879 – 9 – fr I.C.S. [370]
HISTOIRE CRITIQUE DES LIVRES DE L'ANCIEN TESTAMENT = THORA EN DE HISTORISCHE BOEKEN DES OUDEN VERBANDS : TOME PREMIER, LES LIVRES HISTORIQUES / Kuenen, Abraham – (Includes bibliographical references) – Paris: Michel Levy, 1866 – 2mf – 9 – 0-8370-9801-7 – 1986-3801 – us A.T.L.A. [220]
HISTOIRE CRITIQUE DU CATHOLICISME LIBERAL EN FRANCE : JUSQU'AU PONTIFICAT DE LEON 13: COMPLEMENT DE TOUTES LES HISTOIRES DE L'EGLISE / Fevre, Justin Louis Pierre – (Includes bibliographical references) – Saint-Dizier: G Saint-Aubin et Thevenot, 1897 – 2mf – 9 – 0-8370-8571-3 – 1986-2571 – us A.T.L.A. [240]
HISTOIRE CRITIQUE DU VIEUX TESTAMENT / Richard, Simon – Rotterdam, 1685 – 21mf – 8 – ne Slangenburg [220]
HISTOIRE CRITIQUE DU VIEUX TESTAMENT / Simon, R – Paris, 1680 – 7mf – 9 – CA-150/1 – ne IDC [240]
L'HISTOIRE DAHOMEENNE DE LA FIN DU XIXE SIECLE A TRAVERS LES TEXTES – Port Novo, 195? (Etudes Dahomeennes, n.9) – 1 – us Res Libr [960]
HISTOIRE D'ALGER SOUS LA DOMINATION TURQUE / Grammont, Henri Delmas de – Paris, 1887. 16 + 420p – 1 – us U.W. Library [956]
HISTOIRE DE BLONDINE, DE BONNE-BICHE ET DE BEAU-MINON / Segur, Sophie, Comtesse de – Quebec: Louis-Alexandre Belisle, editeur, [1942?] (Quebec: la Semaine commerciale). SEM105P1269 – 1mf – 9 – Can$2.25 – cn Bibl Nat [971]
HISTOIRE DE BRESSE ET DE BUGEY CONTENANT CE QUI S'Y EST PASSE DE MEMORABLES SOUS LES ROMAINS / Guichenon, Samuel – Lyon: Jean Antoine Huguetan et Marc Ant. Ravaud, 1650. SEM35P156 – 1r – 1 – Can$51.00 – cn Bibl Nat [944]
HISTOIRE DE CENT MILLE PIANOS ET D'UNE SALLE DE CONCERT... / Comettant, O – Paris: Fischbacher, 1890 – 1 – us Sibley [780]
HISTOIRE DE CHRISTOPHE COLOMB. – Montreal: Librarie Saint Joseph, Cadieux & Derome, 1883. SEM105P78 – 2mf – 9 – Can$4.50 – cn Bibl Nat [910]
HISTOIRE DE CINQUANTE ANS (1791-1841): ANNALES PARLEMENTAIRES ET POLITIQUES DU BAS CANADA DEPUIS LA CONSTITUTION JUSQU'A L'UNION / Bedard, Theophile Pierre – Quebec, L. Brousseau, 1869. 03308. (Pre-1900 Canadiana) – 9 – cn C.I.H.M. [971]
HISTOIRE DE GEORGES CASTRIOT, SVRNOMME SCANDERBEG, ROY D'ALBANIE. CONTENANT SES ILLUSTRES FAICTS, D'ARMES, ET MEMORABLES VICTOIRES A L'ENCONTRE DES TURCS / Lavardin, J de – Paris, 1598 – 11mf – 9 – H-8398/1 – ne IDC [956]
HISTOIRE DE JESUS-CHRIST OU, ANALYSE RAISONNEE DES EVANGILES / Holbach, Paul-Thiry d' – (D'Holbach series). 1770 – 9 – fr Hachette [240]
HISTOIRE DE LA BANQUE NATIONALE / Bechard, Auguste – St. Roch de Quebec, Laberge & Gingras, 1878. 00903. (Pre-1900 Canadiana) – 9 – cn C.I.H.M. [336]
HISTOIRE DE LA BELGIQUE SOUS LE REGNE DE MARIE-THERESE / Bruyne, Philippe Charles Antoine de – Namur. 1861. 201p. (Historical Studies Series) – 9 – 9.00 – fr Bibl Nationale [900]
HISTOIRE DE LA BIBLE ET DE L'EXEGESE BIBLIQUE JUSQU'A NOS JOURS / Wogue, L – (Includes bibliographical references and index) – Paris: Imprimerie nationale, 1881 – 1mf – 9 – 0-8370-7356-1 – 1986-1356 – us A.T.L.A. [220]
HISTOIRE DE LA BULGARIE DEPUIS LES ORIGINES JUSQU' A NOS JOURS, 485-1913 / Songeon, R P – Paris. 1913. BR-3913 2 – 8 – ne IDC [949]
HISTOIRE DE LA CIVILISATION CONTEMPORAINE / Seignobos, Charles – Paris: Masson et Cie., 1890. 424p. Includes bibliographies – 1 – us U.W. Library [000]
HISTOIRE DE LA CLARTE FRANCAISE, SES ORIGINES, SON EVOLUTION, SA VALEUR / Mornet, Daniel – Paris: Payot, 1929 – 1 – us U.W. Library [440]
HISTOIRE DE LA CLASSE OUVRIERE EN FRANCE DE LA REVOLUTION A NOS JOURS; LA CONDITION MATERIELLE DES TRAVAILLEURS, LES SALAIRES ET LE COUT DE LA VIE / Louis, Paul – Paris: M. Riviere, 1927.412p – 1 – us U.W. Library [944]
HISTOIRE DE LA CONDITION CIVILE... / Demangeat, C – Paris, 1844 – 5mf – 1 – ILM-499/1 – ne IDC [327]
HISTOIRE DE LA CONGREGATION DE SAINT-MAUR / Martene, Dom E – (Ed. Charvin). Tables (1612-1747). 1954 – Dfl13.00 – ne Slangenburg [240]
HISTOIRE DE LA CONGREGATION DE SAINT-MAUR / Martene, Dom E – (Ed. Charvin). Tome 1 (1612-1630).). 1928 – Dfl28.00 – ne Slangenburg [240]
HISTOIRE DE LA CONGREGATION DE SAINT-MAUR / Martene, Dom E – (Ed. Charvin). Tome 2 (1630-1641). 1929 – Dfl28.00 – ne Slangenburg [240]
HISTOIRE DE LA CONGREGATION DE SAINT-MAUR / Martene, Dom E – (Ed. Charvin). Tome 3 (1645-1655). 1929 – Dfl25.00 – ne Slangenburg [240]
HISTOIRE DE LA CONGREGATION DE SAINT-MAUR / Martene, Dom E – (Ed. Charvin). Tome 4 (1656-1667). 1930 – Dfl22.00 – ne Slangenburg [240]
HISTOIRE DE LA CONGREGATION DE SAINT-MAUR / Martene, Dom E – (Ed. Charvin). Tome 6 (1681-1687). 1937 – Dfl22.00 – ne Slangenburg [240]
HISTOIRE DE LA CONGREGATION DE SAINT-MAUR / Martene, Dom E – (Ed. Charvin). Tome 7 (1688-1700). 1937 – Dfl22.00 – ne Slangenburg [240]
HISTOIRE DE LA CONGREGATION DE SAINT-MAUR / Martene, Dom E – (Ed. Charvin). Tome 8 (1701-1712). 1942 – Dfl22.00 – ne Slangenburg [240]
HISTOIRE DE LA CONGREGATION DE SAINT-MAUR / Martene, Dom E – (Ed. Charvin). Tome 9 (1713-1747). 1943 – Dfl30.00 – ne Slangenburg [240]

HISTOIRE DE LA CONGREGATION DE SAINT-MAUR / Martene, E – (Ed. Charvin). Tome 5 (1668-1680). 1930 – Dfl25.00 – ne Slangenburg [240]

HISTOIRE DE LA CONQUE'TE DES ISLES MOLUQUES... / Leonardo y Argensola, B J – (Missing: v2; v3) – Amsterdam. 3v. 1706 – 5mf – 9 – ne IDC [950]

L'HISTOIRE DE LA DECADENCE DE L'EMPIRE GREC, ET ESTABLISSEMENT DE CELVY DES TURCS; ... / Chalcocondylas, Laonici – Paris, 1584 – 9mf – 9 – H-8362/1 – ne IDC [956]

HISTOIRE DE LA FAMILLE COURTEMANCHE, 1663-1895 / Courtemanche, Joseph Israel – Montreal: Cie d'imprimerie commerciale, 1895. 03618. (Pre-1900 Canadiana) – 9 – cn C.I.H.M. [971]

HISTOIRE DE LA FILLE MALEFICIEE DE COURSON / Lange – Lisieux. 1717 – 9 – fr Hachette [360]

HISTOIRE DE LA FLORIDE / Laudonniere, R – Paris. 1853. B-188 2 – 8 – ne IDC [580]

HISTOIRE DE LA GUADELOUPE / Lacour, Auguste – 4v. 1856-60 – 1r – 1 – us Ross [330]

HISTOIRE DE LA GUERRE AU DAHOMEY / Barbou, Alfred – Paris. 1893. 154p. (Historical Studies Series) – 9 – 6.00 – fr Bibl Nationale [900]

HISTOIRE DE LA GVERRE QUI C'EST PASSEE, ENTRE LES VENITIENS ET LA SAINCTE LIGUE, CONTRE LES TURCS, POUR L'ISLE DE CYPRE, ES ANNEES 1570, 1571 ET 1572 / Bizari, P – Paris, 1573 – 4mf – 9 – H-8338/1 – ne IDC [956]

HISTOIRE DE LA GVERRE SAINCTE, DITE PROPREMENT, LA FRANCIADE ORIENTALE, ... / Gulielmus, Archbishop of Tyre – Paris, 1573 – 14mf – 9 – H-8340/1 – ne IDC [956]

HISTOIRE DE LA JUSTICE CRIMINELLE. / Allard, Alberic – Gran, 1868. 525 p. LL-4061 – 1 – us L of C Photodup [340]

HISTOIRE DE LA LANGUE FRANCAISE / Littre, E – 1863 – 9 – fr I.C.S. [440]

HISTOIRE DE LA LITTERATURE ALLEMANDE / Zink, Georges... et al – (Includes bibliographical references and indexes) – [Paris]: Aubier, 1970 – 1r – 1 – us U.W. Library [430]

HISTOIRE DE LA LITTERATURE CONTEMPORAINE EN RUSSIE / Courriere, C – (Russia – 19th C. series). 1875 – 9 – fr Hachette [460]

HISTOIRE DE LA LITTERATURE FEMININE EN FRANCE / Larnac, Jean – Paris: Editions Kra, (1929). 296p – 1 – us U.W. Library [440]

HISTOIRE DE LA LITTERATURE HINDOUI ET HINDOUSTANI / Garcin de Tassy – 1839-47 – 1 – uk Microform Academic [490]

HISTOIRE DE LA LITTERATURE HINDOUI ET HINDOUSTANI / Tassy, M Garcin de – Paris: Printed under the auspices of the Oriental Translation Committee of Great Britain and Ireland, 1839-47 – us Res Libr [490]

HISTOIRE DE LA LITTERATURE HINDOUIE ET HINDOUSTANI / Tassy, M Garcin de – 2nd rev cor aug ed. Paris: A Labitte, 1870-71 – us Res Libr [490]

HISTOIRE DE LA LITTERATURE HONGROISE / Horvath, C & Kardos, A & Endroedi, A – Trans. by J. Kont. Budapest, etc. 1900. BR-5349 2 – 8 – ne IDC [460]

HISTOIRE DE LA MEDECINE JAPONAISE MODERNE / Briot, Alain – 1974 – 9 – fr Orientalistes [610]

HISTOIRE DE LA MILICE CANADIENNE-FRANCAISE, 1760-1897 / Sulte, Benjamin – Montreal: Desbarats, 1897. SEM35P142 – 1r – 1 – Can$15.00 – cn Bibl Nat [971]

HISTOIRE DE LA MUSIQUE ET DE SES EFFETS / Bonnet, J – 1715 – 9 – us Sibley [780]

HISTOIRE DE LA MUSIQUE ET DE SES EFFETS / Bonnet, J – 4v. 1726 – 9 – us Sibley [780]

HISTOIRE DE LA MUSIQUE, ET DE SES EFFETS / Bonnet, J – 1725. P 645 – 9 – ne IDC [780]

HISTOIRE DE LA NAVIGATION DE J.H. DE LINSCOT ET DE SON VOYAGE DES INDES ORIENTALES, A QUOI SONT AJOUTEES QUELQUES AUTRES DESCRIPTIONS TANT DU PAYS DE GUINEE ET AUTRES COTES D'ETHIOPIE, QUE DES NAVIGATIONS DES HOLLANDAIS VERS LE NORD / Linschoten, J H van – (African Library). 1610 – 9 – fr Hachette [910]

HISTOIRE DE LA NOUVELLE ESPAGNE / Diaz del Castillo, Bernal – 1878 – 9 – 1.50f – sp Bibl Santa Ana [972]

HISTOIRE DE LA NOUVELLE FRANCE CONTENANT LES NAVIGATIONS, DECOURVERTES, ET HABITATIONS FAITES PAR LES FRANCOIS ES INDES OCCIDENTAL ET NOUVELLE FRANCE.. / Lescarbot, Marc – Paris: Chez Jean Milot, 1609. SEM105P287 – 10mf – 9 – Can$22.50 – cn Bibl Nat [971]

HISTOIRE DE LA NOUVELLE-FRANCE / Lescarbot, Marc – Paris, France. 1v. 1618 – 1r – 1 – cn Can Microfilming [971]

HISTOIRE DE LA PHILOSOPHIE EN BELGIQUE / Wulf, M de – Bruxelles, Paris, 1910 – 11mf – 8 – ne Slangenburg [100]

HISTOIRE DE LA PHILOSOPHIE HERMETIQUE : ACCOMPAGNEE D'UN CATALOGUE RAISONNE DES ECRIVAINS DE CETTE SCIENCE / Lenglet Du Fresnoy, Nicolas – Paris, 1744 – 1 – us U.W. Library [190]

HISTOIRE DE LA PHILOSOPHIE SCOLASTIQUE / Haureau, B – Paris: Durand et Pedone-Lauriel, 1872-1880 – 4mf – us A.T.L.A. [100]

HISTOIRE DE LA PHILOSOPHIE SCOLASTIQUE / Haureau, B – (Tome premier.-18mf; Tome second.-9mf) – 8 – ne Slangenburg [150]

HISTOIRE DE LA PHILOSOPHIE SCOLASTIQUE DANS LES PAYS-BAS ET LA PRINCIAPAUTE DE LIEGE / Wulf, M de – 1893 – 7mf – 8 – ne Slangenburg [100]

HISTOIRE DE LA POLITIQUE EXTERIEURE... 1830-48 / Haussonville, O d' – Paris. 2v. 1850 – 9mf – 1 – ILM-3620/1 – ne IDC [327]

HISTOIRE DE LA POSSESSION DE LA MERE JEANNE DES ANGES..., SUPERIEURE DES RELIGIEUSES URSULINES DE LOUDUN / Loudun, Ursulines – 17th cent. 3v – 1 – F239.10 – fr Armell [240]

HISTOIRE DE LA PRAGMATIQUE SANCTION DE BOURGES SOUS CHARLES 7 / Valois, Noel – Paris: A. Picard, 1906 – 1 – us U.W. Library [944]

HISTOIRE DE LA PRAGMATIQUE SANCTION DE BOURGES SOUS CHARLES 7 / Valois, Noel – Paris: A. Picard, 1906 – 2mf – us A.T.L.A. [240]

HISTOIRE DE LA PRINCESSE ROSETTE / Segur, Sophie, Comtesse de – Quebec: Louis-Alexandre Belisle, editeur, [1942?] (Quebec: Imp. la Semaine commerciale). SEM105P1292 – 1mf – 9 – Can$2.25 – cn Bibl Nat [971]

HISTOIRE DE LA PROVINCE ECCLESIASTIQUE D'OTTAWA ET DE LA COLONISATION DANS LA VALLEE DE L'OTTAWA / Alexis, OFM – Ottawa: Imp. d'Ottawa, 1897. SEM105P295 – 13mf – 9 – Can$26.00 – cn Bibl Nat [240]

HISTOIRE DE LA PROVINCE ECCLESIASTIQUE D'OTTAWA ET DE LA COLONISATION DANS LA VALLEE DE L'OTTAWA. V2 / Barbezieux, Alexis de – (v1. 1897. 03592) – 1897?. 03593. (Pre-1900 Canadiana) – 9 – cn C.I.H.M. [240]

HISTOIRE DE LA REFORMATION ET DU REFUGE DANS LE PAYS DE NEUCHATEL / Godet, Frederic Louis – 1859 – 9 – us A.T.L.A. [240]

HISTOIRE DE LA RELIGION CHRETIENNE AU JAPON DEPUIS 1598 A 1651 / Pages, Leon – Paris, Charles Douniot. 1869 et 1870 – 9 – 35.00 – fr Orientalistes [240]

HISTOIRE DE LA REPUBLIQUE DES ETATS-UNIS DEPUIS L'ETABLISSEMENT DES PREMIERES COLONIES JUSQU'A L'ELECTION DU PRESIDENT LINCOLN (1620-1860) / Astie, J F – Paris: Grassart, 1865 – 3mf – us A.T.L.A. [975]

HISTOIRE DE LA RESTAURATION / Viel-Castel, Louis de – Paris: Michel Levy freres, 1860-78. 20v – 1 – us U.W. Library [944]

HISTOIRE DE LA RESTAURATION DU PROTESTANTISME EN FRANCE AU 18E SIECLE : ANTOINE COURT / Hugues, Edmond – Paris: Grassart, 1875 – 3mf – us A.T.L.A. [240]

HISTOIRE DE LA REVOLUTION RUSSE – Preparee sous direction de Maxime Gorki, V. Molotov, K. Vorochilov, Serge Kirov, A Jdanov et J. Staline. Paris: Editions sociales, 1946 – 1 – us U.W. Library [947]

HISTOIRE DE LA SEIGNEURIE DE ST-OURS / Couillard-Despres, Azarie – Montreal: Imprimerie de l'Institution des sourds-muets. 2v. 1915-1917. SEM105P1495 – 10mf – 9 – Can$22.50 – cn Bibl Nat [971]

HISTOIRE DE LA SEIGNEURIE MASSUE ET DE LA PAROISSE DE SAINT-AIME / Hengard-Lapalice, Ovide Michel – [Quebec (Province): s.n.], 1930. SEM105P1650 – 5mf – 9 – Can$11.25 – cn Bibl Nat [971]

HISTOIRE DE LA SOUVERAINETE DES DOMBES / Guichenon – 2nd ed. Lyon, 1874. 2v – 3mf – 9 – F90.00 – fr F.F.G. [944]

HISTOIRE DE LA TOLERANCE RELIGIEUSE : EVOLUTION D'UN PRINCIPE SOCIAL / Matagrin, Amedee – Paris: Fischbacher, 1905 – 2mf – us A.T.L.A. [320]

HISTOIRE DE LA VIE ET DES OUVRAGES DE VOLTAIRE / Paillet de Warcy, L – Suivis des jugements qu'ont portes de cet homme celebre divers auteurs estimes. Paris. Mme Dufriche. 1824 – 9 – fr Hachette [920]

HISTOIRE DE LA VIE ET MOEURS DE MARIE TESSONNIERE... / La Riviere, L de – Lyon, 1650 – 7mf – 9 – CA-172/1 – ne IDC [240]

HISTOIRE DE LA VILLE DE KHOTAN / Remusat, A – Paris. 1820. BU-616 2 – 8 – ne IDC [950]

HISTOIRE DE LA VILLE ET DE TOUT LE DIOCESE DE PARIS / Lebeuf, Jean – Paris: Prault pere, 1754-58. SEM16P347 – 2r – 5 – Can$58.00 – cn Bibl Nat [910]

HISTOIRE DE LA ZOOLOGIE DEPUIS L'ANTIQUITE JUSQU'AU XIXE SIECLE / Carus, Victor – Paris: J. Bailliere, 1880. viii,623p. Histoire des Sciences XVIIe-XIXe Siecles. 7930 – 9 – fr Hachette [590]

HISTOIRE DE L'ABBAYE DE SAINT-GERMAIN-DES-PREZ / Bouillard, Dom J, OSB – Paris, 1724 – Dfl91.00 – ne Slangenburg [240]

HISTOIRE DE L'ABBAYE ROYALE DE SAINT-DENYS EN FRANCE / Felibien, Dom M OSB – Paris, 1706 – Dfl137.00 – ne Slangenburg [240]

HISTOIRE DE L'ABBAYE ROYALE ET DE L'ORDRE DES CHANOINES REGULIERS DE ST VICTOR DE PARIS / Bonnard, F – Paris, 1907 – 22mf – 8 – Dfl77.00 – ne Slangenburg [240]

HISTOIRE DE L'ABBEYE SAINTE-CROIX DE BORDEAUX : ARCHIVES DE LA FRANCE MONASTIQUE 9 / Chauliac, A – 1910 – 9mf – 8 – Dfl32.00 – ne Slangenburg [240]

HISTOIRE DE L'ACADEMIE / Akademie der Wissenschaften. Berlin; ed by Formey – 1752 – 1 – us Schnase [500]

HISTOIRE DE L'ACADEMIE ROYALE DES SCIENCES. AVEC LES MEMOIRES DE MATHEMATIQUE ET DE PHYSIQUE – Paris, 2nd ed 1699-1790 – 1,261mf – 9 – 468/2 – ne IDC [510]

HISTOIRE DE L'ACADEMIE ROYALE DES SCIENCES. DEPUIS 1666 JUSQU'A 1699 – Paris, 1729-1734. v1-2 – 15mf – 9 – 466/2 – ne IDC [060]

HISTOIRE DE L'ACADEMIE ROYALE DES SCIENCES ET DES BELLES-LETTRES DE BERLIN / Akademie der Wissenschaften. Berlin – 1745-1769 – 3 – us Readex [500]

HISTOIRE DE L'ACADEMIE ROYALE DES SCIENCES...AVEC LES MEMOIRES DE MATHEMATIQUE & DE PHYSIQUE...TIRES DES REGISTRES DE CETTE ACADEMIE / Academie des Sciences. Paris – 1699-1790 – 3 – us Readex [500]

HISTOIRE DE L'AGRICULTURE A L'ERE INDUSTRIELLE / Noilhan, Henri – Paris. 1965. (La Condition Ouvriere. Part Two.) – 9 – 22.50 – fr Bibl Nationale [360]

HISTOIRE DE L'ALCHIMIE: 19E SIECLE: NICHOLAS FLAMEL / Poisson, Albert – Paris, 1893 (Science Collection) – xii/222p 3mf – 9 – $8.00 – fr Bibl Nationale [190]

HISTOIRE DE L'ANNEE 1865 / Le Hir, Jean Louis – Paris. "La Revue Mensuelle". 1866. 264p. (Historical Studies Series) – 9 – 9.00 – fr Bibl Nationale [900]

HISTOIRE DE L'ASIE CENTRALE / Boukhari, Mir A K – Texte persan, traduction francaise par Ch. Schefer. 1876 – 9 – fr Orientalistes [950]

HISTOIRE DE L'EDITION BENEDICTINE DE SAINT AUGUSTIN / Ingold, A M P – Paris: A. Picard, 1903 – 1mf – us A.T.L.A. [240]

HISTOIRE DE L'EGLISE D'ALEXANDRIE : DEPUIS SAINT MARC JUSQU'A NOS JOURS / Macaire, Georges – Le Caire [Cairo]: Imprimerie Generale, 1894 – 1mf – 9 – 0-8370-7646-3 – 1986-1646 – us A.T.L.A. [240]

HISTOIRE DE L'EGLISE D'ALEXANDRIE / Vansleb, J M; ed by Marc, S – Paris, 1677 – 5mf – 8 – Dfl22.00 – ne Slangenburg [944]

HISTOIRE DE L'EGLISE DE COREE : PRECEDEE D'UNE INTRODUCTION SUR L'HISTOIRE, LES INSTITUTIONS, LA LANGUE, LES MOEURS ET COUTUMES COREENNES... / Dallet, C – Paris: V. Palme, 1874 – 3mf – us A.T.L.A. [240]

HISTOIRE DE L'EGLISE DEPUIS LES ORIGINES JUSQUA NOS JOURS / ed by Fliche, A & Martin, V – (Vols also listed individually. Vol no given in brackets with title) – Paris. v1-21. 1934-1964 – Dfl1,001.00 set – ne Slangenburg [240]

HISTOIRE DE L'EGLISE DEPUIS LES ORIGINES JUSQUA NOS JOURS *see*
– LA CHRETIENTE ROMAINE, 1198-1274 (10)
– LA CRISE RELIGIEUSE DU 16E SIECLE (16)
– LA CRISE REVOLUTIONNAIRE, 1789-1846 (20)
– DE LA FIN DU 2E SIECLE A LA PAIX CONSTANTINIENNE (2)
– DE LA MORT DE THEODOSE A L'ELECTION DE GREGOIRE LE GRAND (4)
– DE LA PAIX CONSTANTINIENNE A LA MORT DE THEODOSE (3)
– DU PREMIER CONCILE DU LATRAN A L'AVENEMENT D'INNOCENT 3, 1123-1198 (9)
– L'EGLISE A L'EPOQUE DU CONCILE DE TRENTE (17)
– L'EGLISE AU POUVOIR DES LAIQUES, 888-1057 (7)
– L'EGLISE AU TEMPS DU GRAND SCHISME ET DE LA CRISE CONCILIAIRE, 1378-1449 (14)
– L'EGLISE ET LA RENAISSANCE, 1449-1517 (15)
– L'EGLISE PRIMITIVE (1)
– L'EPOQUE CAROLINGIENNE (6)
– GREGOIRE LE GRAND
– INSTITUTIONS ECCLESIASTIQUES DE LA CHRETIENTE MEDIEVALE (12)
– LES LUTTES POLITIQUES ET DOCTRINALES AUX 17E ET 18E SIECLES (19)
– LE MOUVEMENT DOCTRINALE DU 19E AU 14E SIECLE (13)
– LE PONTIFICAT DE PIE 19, 1846-1878 (21)
– LA REFORME GREGORIENNE ET LA RECONQUETE CHRETIENNE, 1057-1123 (8)
– LA RESTAURATION CATHOLIQUE, 1563-1648 (18)

HISTOIRE DE L'EGLISE VAUDOISE : DEPUIS SON ORIGINE ET DES VAUDOIS DU PIEMONT JUSQU'A NOS JOURS... / Monastier, Antoine – Lausanne: G. Bridel, 1847 – 2mf – us A.T.L.A. [240]

HISTOIRE DE L'EMPIRE DE CONSTANTINOPLE SOUS LES EMPEREURS FRANCOIS (CBH 26) / Villehardouin, Geoffroy de – Venise, 1729 – Dfl67.00 – ne Slangenburg [930]

HISTOIRE DE L'ESCLAVAGE PENDANT LES DEUX DERNIERES ANNEES / Schoelcher, Victor – (Slave Trade and Abolitionism in France series). 1847 – 9 – fr Hachette [305]

HISTOIRE DE L'ETABLISSEMENT, DES PROGRES ET DE LA DECADENCE DU CHRISTIANISME DANS L'EMPIRE DU JAPON / Charlevoix, Francois Xavier de – Rouen: J. J. Le Boullenger. 1715 – 9 – 35.00 – fr Orientalistes [240]

HISTOIRE DE L'ETABLISSEMENT DES PROTESTANTS FRANCAIS EN SUEDE / Puaux, Frank – Paris: G. Fischbacher; Stockholm: E. Giron, 1891 – 1mf – us A.T.L.A. [948]

HISTOIRE DE L'ETHIOPIE ORIENTALE COMPOSEE EN PORTUGAIS / Santos, Jean Dos – (African Library series). 1684 – 9 – fr Hachette [960]

HISTOIRE DE L'ETHIOPIE ORIENTALE...TRADUIT EN FRANCOIS PAR...GAETAN CHARPY / Santos Joao dos – Paris. 1684 – 1 – us Res Libr [960]

HISTOIRE DE L'HOTEL-DIEU DE QUEBEC / Casgrain, Henri-Raymond – Quebec: L. Brousseau, 1878. 00646. (Pre-1900 Canadiana) – 9 – cn C.I.H.M. [971]

HISTOIRE DE L'IMPRIMERIE ET DE LA LIBRAIRIE A MONTAUBAN: BIBLIOGRAPHIE MONTALBANAISE / Forestie, Emerand – Montauban: Imp. E. Forestie, 1898. 5 fiches. (Miscellaneous Selections) – 9 – 12.00 – fr Bibl Nationale [070]

HISTOIRE DE L'INSURRECTION DU CANADA / Papineau, Louis Joseph – Burlington, VT: Ludger Duvernay, 1839. SEM105P872 – 1mf – 9 – Can$2.25 – cn Bibl Nat [971]

HISTOIRE DE LOANGO ET D'AUTRES ROYAUMES D'AFRIQUE, REDIGEE D'APRES LES MEMOIRES DES PREFETS APOSTOLIQUES DE LA MISSION FRANCAISE / Proyart, Abbe – Paris. 1776. BA-135 2 – 8 – ne IDC [240]

HISTOIRE DE LOANGO, KARONGO ET AUTRES ROYAUMES D'AFRIQUE / Proyart, Lievin-Bonaventure – Paris, Berton. 1776 – 9 – 12.50 – fr Orientalistes [960]

HISTOIRE DE L'OPERA BOUFFON. POUR SERVIR A L'HISTOIRE DES THEATRES DE PARIS / Contant d'Orville, Andre Guillaume – Premiere-Seconde Partie. 1768 – 9 – us Sibley [780]

HISTOIRE DE L'OUEST CANADIEN DE 1822 A 1869 : EPOQUE DES TROUBLES / Dugas, Georges – Montreal, 1906. SEM105P525 – 2mf – 9 – Can$4.50 – cn Bibl Nat [971]

HISTOIRE DE LOUIS LE JUSTE, 13E DU NOM, ROI DE FRANCE ET DE NAVARRE / Dupleix, Scipion – Paris: Cl. Sonnius, 1635 – fr Armell [944]

HISTOIRE DE LOUIS-PHILIPPE-JOSEPH, DUC D'ORLEANS / Orleans, Duc d'... – Paris, 1842 – 7mf – ne IDC [944]

HISTOIRE DE MAGDELAINE BAVENT, RELIGIEUSE DU MONASTERE DE SAINT LOUIS DE LOUVIERS / Desmarets, P – Paris. 1652 – 9 – fr Hachette [360]

HISTOIRE DE MARTHE BROSSIER PRETENDUE POSSEDEE TIREE DU LATIN / Thou, Jacques A de – Rouen. 1652 – 9 – fr Hachette [360]

HISTOIRE DE MME. DUCHESNE: RELIGIEUSE DE LA SOCIETE DU SACRE-COEUR DE JESUS ET FONDATRICE DES PREMIERES MAISONS DE CETTE SOCIETE EN AMERIQUE / Baunard, Louis – Paris: Poussielgue, 1878. 04308. (Pre-1900 Canadiana) – 9 – cn C.I.H.M. [240]

HISTOIRE DE NOTRE DAME DE LOURDES / Gros, L; ed by Bayle, Constantino – Madrid: Razon y Fe, 1928 – 9 – sp Bibl Santa Ana [240]

HISTOIRE DE PHOTIUS, PATRIARCHE DE CONSTANTINOPLE / Jager, Abbe – Louvain, 1845 – 8mf – 8 – Dfl30.00 – ne Slangenburg [240]

HISTOIRE DE REGNE DU KHEDIVE ISMAIL. L'EMPIRE AFRICAIN. TOME 3, LE ET 2E PARTIES / Douin, Georges – Cairo. 1936-39 – 1 – us Res Libr [960]

HISTOIRE DE SAINT AUGUSTIN : SA VIE, SES OEUVRES, SON SIECLE, INFLUENCE DE SON GENTE / Poujoulat, M – Paris, A. Vaton, 1852 – 3mf – us A.T.L.A. [240]

HISTOIRE DE SAINT FRANCOIS D'ASSISE = HISTORY OF S. FRANCIS OF ASSISI / Le Monnier, Leon – London: Kegan Paul, Trench, Truebner, 1894 – 2mf – 9 – 0-8370-7080-5 – 1986-1080 – us A.T.L.A. [920]

HISTOIRE DE TIMUR-BEC, CONNU SOUS LE NOM DU GRAND TAMERLAN, EMPEREUR DES MONGOLS ET TARTARES / Croix, P de la – 4v. Delft. 1723. BU-734 1 – 9 – ne IDC [920]

HISTOIRE DE TROIS OUVRIERS FRANCAIS: RICHARD LENOIR, ABRAHAM LOUIS BREGUET, MICHEL BREZIN / Ernouf, Alfred Auguste – 2nd ed. Paris: Librairie Hachette, 1873. 263p. Includes bibliog. references – 1 – us U.W. Library [330]

HISTOIRE DES AMAZONES ANCIENNES ET MODERNES / Guyon, Claude Marie – Paris: Villette, 1740. 2v. (Les Femmes Collection) – 6mf – 9 – $15.00 – fr Bibl Nationale [305]

HISTOIRE DES ARBRES FORESTIERS DE L'AMEA1RIQUE SEPTENTRIONALE / Michaux, Francois Andre – Paris, 1810-1813. 3 vols. B-6066 1 – 9 – ne IDC [580]

HISTOIRE DES ARTS / Monier, P – O-986 1. 1698 – 9 – ne IDC [700]

HISTOIRE DES ASSEMBLEES POLITIQUES DES REFORMES DE FRANCE, 1573-1622 / Anquez, L – H-376 2. 1859 – 8 – ne IDC [944]

HISTOIRE DES CHAMPIGNONS COMESTIBLES ET VENENEUX / Roques, J – 6307 2. 1841 – 8 – ne IDC [580]

HISTOIRE DES CHAMPIGNONS COMESTIBLES ET VENENEUX / Roques, J – Paris. 1832. B-7336 2 – 8 – ne IDC [580]

HISTOIRE DES CHEA4NES DE L'AMEA1RIQUE / Michaux, A – Paris, 1801. B-6065 1 – 9 – ne IDC [580]

HISTOIRE DES CHEVALLIERS HOSPITALIERS DE S JEAN DE JERUZALEM / Vertot, R A de – Paris. Tom. 1-4. 1726 – Dfl172.00 – ne Slangenburg [240]

HISTOIRE DES CHOSES PLUS MEMORABLES ADVENUES TANT EZ INDES ORIENTALES, QUE AUTRES PAIS DE LA DESCOUVERTE DES PORTUGAIS, EN L'ESTABLISSEMENT ET PROGREZ DE LA FOY CHRESTIENNE, ET CATHOLIQUE... / Jarric, P du – Bordeaux, 1608-1614, 3v – 8mf – 9 – ne IDC [950]

HISTOIRE DES CLASSES OUVRIERES EN FRANCE DEPUIS LA CONQUETE DE LA GAULE JUSQU'A NOS JOURS / Cellier, Florent de – (Condition of 19th Century French working class series). 1859 – 9 – fr Hachette [360]

HISTOIRE DES CONCILES / ed by Hefele, C J & Leclercq, H – Paris, 1907-1911. 10v – 145mf – 9 – H-2984/1 – ne IDC [060]

HISTOIRE DES CONCILES D'APRAES LES DOCUMENTS ORIGINAUX / Hefele, C J & Leclercq, H – Paris. Tom 1-11. 1907-1952 – Dfl879.00 – ne Slangenburg [240]

HISTOIRE DES CONFERVES D'EAU DOUCE / Vaucher, J P – Geneve. 1803. B-6413 – 9 – ne IDC [580]

HISTOIRE DES COQUILLES TERRESTRES ET FLUVIATILES QUI VIVENT AUX ENVIRONS DE PARIS / Brard, C P – Paris, Geneve, 1815 – 23, 239, 17 [1]p, 10pls – 8 – ne IDC [590]

HISTOIRE DES DIFFERENS PEUPLES DU MONDE. / Contant d'Orville, Andre Guillaume – Paris, 1770-71. v.4, Africa – 1 – us Res Libr [960]

HISTOIRE DES DIFFERENTS PEUPLE DU MONDE, CONTENANT LES CEREMONIES RELIGIEUSES ET CIVILES, L'ORIGINE DES RELIGIONS, LEURS SECTES ET SUPERSTITIONS ET LES MOEURS ET USAGES DE CHAQUE NATION / Contant d'Orville, Andre Guillaume – (African Library series). 1770 – 9 – fr Hachette [306]

HISTOIRE DES DROGUES D'ORIGINE VEGETALE / Flueckiger, F A & Hanbury, D – Paris, 1878. 2v – 16mf – 9 – ne IDC [615]

HISTOIRE DES EDITS DE PACIFICATION ET DES MOYENS QUE LES PRETENDUS REFORMEZ ONT EMPLOYE POUR LES OBTENIR... / Soulier, P – Paris, 1682 – 6mf – 9 – CA-108/1 – ne IDC [240]

HISTOIRE DES EMPEREURS ET DES AUTRES PRINCES QUI ONT REGNE DURANT LES SIX PREMIERS SIECLES DE L'EGLISE / Lenain De Tillemont, LS – Bruxelles. Tom 1-6. 1733 – Dfl319.00 – ne Slangenburg [941]

HISTOIRE DES ENFANTS ABANDONNES ET DELAISSES / Lallemand, Leon – Paris. 1885. (La Condition Ouvriere. Part Two.) – 9 – 22.50 – fr Bibl Nationale [360]

HISTOIRE DES ENFANTS TROUVES, NOUVELLE EDITION REVUE ET AUGMENTEE / Terme, J F & Monfalcon, J B – Condition of 19th C. French working class series. 1840 – 9 – fr Hachette [305]

HISTOIRE DES ETATS UNIS DEPUIS LES PREMIERS ETABLISSEMENTS JUSQU'A NOS JOURS / Clapin, Sylvia – Montreal: C. Beauchemin, 1900. 03197. (Pre-1900 Canadiana) – 9 – cn C.I.H.M. [975]

HISTOIRE DES FRANCS, TEXTES DE MANUSCRITS DE CORBIE ET DE BRUXELLES / Gregory, Saint, Bishop of Tours – Nouv. ed. par Rene Poupardin. Paris: A. Picard, 1913. xxx/501p – 1 – us U.W. Library [944]

HISTOIRE DES GUERRES D'ITALIE, 1490-1534 / Guicciardini, Francesco – London: P. et I. Vaillant, 1738.3v. (Strategy of War Series) – 9 – fr Hachette [355]

HISTOIRE DES GUERRES ... TRAITE DE WESTPHALIE, ... / Bougeant – Paris. 3v. 1744 – 21mf – 9 – ILM-989/1 – ne IDC [327]

L'HISTOIRE DES GVERRES FAICTES PAR LES CHRESTIENS CONTRE LES TVRCS, SOVS LA CONDUICTE DE GODEFROY DE BOUILLON, DUC DE LORRAINE, POUR LE RECOUUREMENT DE LA TERRE SAINCTE / Aubert, Georges – Paris, 1559 – 2mf – 9 – H-8293/1 – ne IDC [956]

HISTOIRE DES IDEES MESSIANIQUES : DEPUIS ALEXANDRE JUSQU'A L'EMPEREUR HADRIEN / Vernes, Maurice – (Includes bibliographical references) – Paris: Sandoz et Fischbacher, 1874 – 1mf – 9 – 0-8370-6439-2 – 1986-0439 – us A.T.L.A. [270]

HISTOIRE DES INCAS, ROIS DU PEROU / Garcilaso de la Vega (el Inca) – Paris: Prault fils, 1744. SEM16P238 – 1r – 5 – Can$12.00 – cn Bibl Nat [972]

HISTOIRE DES INSECTES NUISIBLES A L'HOMME, AUX BESTIAUX / Buchoz, P J – Paris, 1781. Z-1107/2 – 8 – ne IDC [590]

HISTOIRE DES INSTITUTIONS DE CHARITE DE BIENFAISANCE ET D'EDUCATION DU CANADA: DEPUIS LEUR FONDATION JUSQU'A NOS JOURS / Drapeau, Stanislas – Ottawa?: s.n., 1877 (Ottawa: Impr. du Foyer domestique). 02761. (Pre-1900 Canadiana) – 9 – cn C.I.H.M. [971]

HISTOIRE DES KOSAQUES, PRECEDEE D'UNE INTRODUCTION, OU COUP D'OEIL SUR LES PEUPLES QUI ONT HABITE LE PAYS DES KOSAQUES, AVANT L'INVASION DES TARTARES / Lesur – (Russia – 19th C. series). 1814 – 9 – fr Hachette [947]

HISTOIRE DES LICHENS / Delise, D F – Genre Sticta. Paris-Caen. 1822-25. B-480 2 – 8 – ne IDC [580]

HISTOIRE DES MAITRES GENERAUX DE L'ORDRE DES FRERES PRECHEURS / Mortier, D A OP – Paris. v1-8. 1903-1920 – Dfl420.00 – ne Slangenburg [240]

HISTOIRE DES METAMORPHOSES DE QUELQUES COLEOPTERES EXOTIQUES / Candeze, E C A – Liege, 1861. 86p. 6 pls. Z-1119/2 – 8 – ne IDC [590]

HISTOIRE DES MONSTRES DEPUIS L'ANTIQUITE JUSQU'A NOS JOURS / Martin, Ernest – Paris, Reinwald, 1880, 415 p. Histoire des Sciences XVIIe-XIXe Siecles. 7929 – 9 – fr Hachette [612]

HISTOIRE DES ORIGINES,... / Hautefeuille, L B – Paris, 1869 – 6mf – 1 – ILM-190/1 – ne IDC [327]

HISTOIRE DES OUVRAGES DES SAVANS, PAR B.. – Basnages de Beauval. Rotterdam. sept 1687-juin 1709 (I-XXV) – 1 – fr A.C.R.P.P. [073]

HISTOIRE DES PATRIARCHES D'ALEXANDRIE DEPUIS LA MORT DE L'EMPEREUR ANASTASE JUSQU'A LA RECONCILIATION DES EGLISES JACOBITES (518-616) / Maspero, J – Paris, 1923 – 7mf – 8 – Dfl28.00 – ne Slangenburg [240]

HISTOIRE DES PERSECUTIONS DE L'EGLISE, LA POLEMIQUE PAIENNE A LA FIN DU IIE SIECLE / Aube, Benjamin – Paris: Didier, 1878 – 2mf – us A.T.L.A. [240]

HISTOIRE DES PLANTES / Baillon, H E – 13 v. Paris. 1866-95. B-735 2 – 8 – ne IDC [580]

HISTOIRE DES PLANTES DE DAUPHINE / Villars, D – 3v. Grenoble. 1786-89. B-702 2 – 8 – ne IDC [580]

HISTOIRE DES PLANTES DE LA GUIANE FRANCAISE / Aublet, J B C F – Londres. Paris. 1775. B-5449 2 – 8 – ne IDC [580]

HISTOIRE DES PLANTES LES PLUS REMARQUABLES DU BRESIL / Saint-Hilaire, A F C P de – Paris. 1824-26. B-5157 2 – 8 – ne IDC [580]

HISTOIRE DES PLANTES MEDICINALES,... / Bulliard, J BF – Paris, 1808 – 5mf – 9 – ne IDC [615]

HISTOIRE DES POPULATIONS DE MADAGASCAR / Dandouau, Andre & Chapus, G-S – Paris: Larose, 1952 – 1 – us Res Libr [301]

HISTOIRE DES POPULATIONS DU SOUDAN CENTRAL / Urvoy, Y – 1936. BA-352 2 – 8 – ne IDC [956]

HISTOIRE DES POPULATIONS DU SOUDAN CENTRAL (COLONIE DU NIGER) / Urvoy, Y – Paris: Larose, 1936 – us Res Libr [960]

L'HISTOIRE DES QUATRE DERNIERES ANNEES – 1891?. 03675. (Pre-1900 Canadiana) – 9 – cn C.I.H.M. [971]

HISTOIRE DES RAPPORTS DE L'EGLISE ET DE L'ETAT EN FRANCE DE 1789 A 1870 / Debidour, Antonin – Paris: F. Alcan, 1898 – 2mf – us A.T.L.A. [240]

HISTOIRE DES REFUGIES HUGUENOTS EN AMERIQUE / Baird, Charles Washington – Toulouse: Societe des livres religieux, 1886. 04083. (Pre-1900 Canadiana) – 9 – cn C.I.H.M. [240]

HISTOIRE DES RELATIONS DE LA CHINE AVEC L'ANNAM-VIETNAM DU XIVE AU XIXE SIECLE / Deveria, G – 1880 – 9 – fr Orientalistes [950]

HISTOIRE DES ROIS : TRADUCTION DU TANTARAN'NY ANDRIANA DU R P CALLET / Chapus, G S & Ratsimba, Emmanuel – Tananarive, Academie malgache, 1953-58 – us Res Libr [960]

HISTOIRE DES SCIENCES: 17-18 SIECLES – Ed. by R. Taton.48 titles – 9 – fr Hachette [500]

HISTOIRE DES SEVARAMBES, PEUPLES QUI HABITENT UNE PARTIE DU TROISIEME CONTINENT COMMUNEMENT APPELE LA TERRE AUSTRALE: CONTENANT UN COMPTE EXACT DU GOUVERNEMENT DES MOEURS, DE LA RELIGION ET DU LANGAGE DE CETTE NATION / Vairasse D'Allais, Denis – (Utopias in the Enlightenment series). 1677 – 9 – fr Hachette [980]

HISTOIRE DES SULTANS MAMLOUKS DE L'EGYPTE / Maqrizi – 1837-42 – 1 – uk Microform Academic [900]

HISTOIRE DES SYNODES NATIONAUX DES EGLISES REFORMEES DE FRANCE / Felice, G de – Paris: Grassart, 1864 – 1mf – us A.T.L.A. [240]

HISTOIRE DES TAIRATIREE DU NIT-PON GWAI-SI – Extrait de l'Atsume Gusa. Traducteur by Francois Turrettini. Traduction du chinois. Geneve, H. Georg. 1874-75 – 9 – 5.00 – fr Orientalistes [950]

HISTOIRE DES VAUDOIS : INTRODUCTION / Comba, E – Paris: Fischbacher; Florence: Claudienne, 1898 – 1mf – us A.T.L.A. [240]

HISTOIRE DES VEGETAUX FOSSILES / Brongniart, A T – 1828 and 1837 – 7 – uk Microform Academic [560]

HISTOIRE DES VEGETAUX RECUEILLIS DANS LES ISLES AUSTRALES D'AFRIQUE / Du Petit-Thouars, L M A A – Paris. 1806. B-6127 2 – 8 – ne IDC [580]

HISTOIRE DES VEGETAUX RECUEILLIS SUR LES ISLES DE FRANCE, LA REUNION (BOURBON) ET MADAGASCAR / Du Petit-Thouars, L M A A – Paris. 1804. B-5213 2 – 8 – ne IDC [580]

HISTOIRE DOCUMENTAIRE DE LA CONGREGATION DES MISSIONNAIRES...OTAWA, 1963 / Carriere, Gaston – Madrid: Graf. Calleja, 1966 – 1 – sp Bibl Santa Ana [240]

HISTOIRE DU BIENHEUREUX PIERRE CLAVER DE LA COMPAGNIE DE JESUS : APOTRE DES NEGRES DE CARTHAGENE ET DES INDES-OCCIDENTALES / Daurignac, J M S – Lyon: J B Pelagaud, 1854 – 2mf – 9 – 0-8370-6895-9 – 1986-0895 – us A.T.L.A. [920]

HISTOIRE DU BREVIAIRE DE ROUEN / Colette, A – Rouen, 1902 – 6mf – 8 – Dfl25.00 – ne Slangenburg [240]

HISTOIRE DU BREVIAIRE ROMAIN = HISTORY OF THE ROMAN BREVIARY / Batiffol, Pierre – (In English. Includes appendix and index) – London; New York: Longmans, Green, 1898 – 1mf – 9 – 0-8370-7282-4 – 1986-1282 – us A.T.L.A. [240]

HISTOIRE DU CALVINISME / Maimbourg, L – Ed 3. Paris. 2v. 1682 – 10mf – 9 – CA-102/1 – ne IDC [240]

HISTOIRE DU CALVINISME, CONTENANT SA NAISSANCE... / Soulier, P – Paris, 1686 – 8mf – 9 – CA-151/1 – ne IDC [240]

HISTOIRE DU CANADA, 1841 A 1867 / Royal, Joseph – Montreal: Beauchemin, 1909. SEM16P288 – 1r – 5 – Can$9.00 – cn Bibl Nat [971]

HISTOIRE DU CANADA A L'USAGE DES MAISONS D'EDUCATION / Laverdiere, C-H – Quebec: des Presses d'Augustin Cote, Editeur, 1873 [i.e. 1874] – 3mf – 9 – Can$6.75 – cn Bibl Nat [971]

HISTOIRE DU CANADA: COURS ELEMENTAIRE / Christian Brothers – Montreal, c1883. 03256. (Pre-1900 Canadiana) – 9 – cn C.I.H.M. [370]

HISTOIRE DU CANON DE L'ANCIEN TESTAMENT DANS L'EGLISE GRECQUE ET L'EGLISE RUSSE / Jugie, Martin – Paris: G. Beauchesne, 1909 (Etudes de theologie orientale; 1) – 1mf – us A.T.L.A. [240]

HISTOIRE DU CHRISTIANISME DANS LE MONDE PAIEN : LES MISSIONS EN ASIE / Gindraux, Jules – (Includes index) – Geneve: J-H Jeheber, [1908?] – 1mf – 9 – 0-8370-6498-8 – 1986-0498 – us A.T.L.A. [240]

HISTOIRE DU CIEL: CONSIDEREE SELON LES IDEES DES POETES, DES PHILOSOPHES ET DE MOISE / Pluche, Antoine – Paris: Vve. Estienne, 1739 (Philosophy Collection) – 2v 10mf – 9 – $25.00 – fr Bibl Nationale [240]

HISTOIRE DU CONCILE DE TRENTE / Baguenault de Puchesse, M Fernand – (Includes bibliographical references) – Paris: Victor Palme, 1870 – 1mf – 9 – 0-8370-8320-6 – 1986-2320 – us A.T.L.A. [240]

HISTOIRE DU CONCILE DE TRENTE / P A L LA VICINI, S – Paris. Tom 1-3. 1844 – Dfl147.00 – ne Slangenburg [240]
HISTOIRE DU CONCILE DE TRENTE / Pallavicini, S – Paris. Tomes 1-3. 1844 – 42mf – 8 – Dfl147.00 – ne Slangenburg [240]
HISTOIRE DU CULTE DE SIN EN BABYLONIE ET EN ASSYRIE / Combe, E – Paris. 1908. BNE-409 1 – 9 – ne IDC [290]
HISTOIRE DU CURE SANTA CRUZ. PARIS, 1928 / Bernoville, Gactan La Croix de Sang; ed by Bayle, Constantino – Madrid: Razon y Fe, 1928 – 9 – sp Bibl Santa Ana [946]
HISTOIRE DU DOGME DE LA DIVINITE DE JESU-CHRIST / Reville, Albert – (Includes bibliographical references) – 2e rev augm ed. Paris: Germer Bailliere, 1876 – 1mf – 9 – 0-8370-3998-3 – 1985-1998 – us A.T.L.A. [240]
HISTOIRE DU DOGME DE LA PAPAUTE : DES ORIGINES A LA FIN DU QUATRIEME SIECLE / Turmel, Joseph – Paris: A. Picard, [1908?] – 2mf – us A.T.L.A. [240]
HISTOIRE DU DOGME DU PECHE ORIGINEL / Turmel, Joseph – Macon: Protat, 1904 – 1mf – us A.T.L.A. [240]
HISTOIRE DU DROIT FLUVIAL CONVENTIONNEL / Engelhardt, E – Paris, 1889 – 2mf – 1 – ILM-1849/1 – ne IDC [327]
HISTOIRE DU LUTHERANISME / Maimbourg, L – Paris, 1680 – 7mf – 9 – CA-103/1 – ne IDC [240]
HISTOIRE DU MAGHREB : COURS PROFESSE A L'INSTITUT DES HAUTES ETUDES MAROCAINES / Hamid, Ismail – Paris: E Laroux, 1923 – 1 – us Res Libr [960]
HISTOIRE DU MATERIALISME ET CRITIQUE DE SON IMPORTANCE A NOTRE EPOQUE / Lange, Friedrich Albert – Paris: Schleicher, 1910-11. 2v.11 fiches. (Political Science Collection) – 9 – 27.00 – fr Bibl Nationale [140]
HISTOIRE DU MONTREAL / Dollier de Casson, Francois – Montreal: des presses a vapeur de "La Minerve", 1868 [i.e. 1869]. SEM105P1528 – 4mf – 9 – Can$9.00 – cn Bibl Nat [910]
HISTOIRE DU MONTREAL, 1640-1672 / Dollier de Casson, Francois – Montreal: Eusebe Senecal, 1871 [i.e. 1927]. SEM105P1529 – 2mf – 9 – Can$4.50 – cn Bibl Nat [910]
HISTOIRE DU NAUFRAGE ET DE LA CAPTIVITE DE M. DE BRISSON / Brisson – Geneve, Barde, Manget et Cie. 1790 – 9 – 5.00 – fr Orientalistes [960]
HISTOIRE DU NAUFRAGE ET DE LA CAPTIVITE DE M. DE BRISSON, OFFICIER DE L'ADMINISTRATION DES COLONIES; AVEC LA DESCRIPTION DES DESERTS D'AFRIQUE, DEPUIS LE SENEGAL JUSQU'AU MAROC / Brisson, PR de – (African Library series). 1789 – 9 – fr Hachette [960]
L'HISTOIRE DU NOUVEAU-MONDE OU DESCRIPTION DES INDES OCCIDENTALES / Laet, Jean de – Leyden: Bonaventure and Abraham Elseviers, 1640. SEM35P69 – 1r – 1 – Can$31.00 – cn Bibl Nat [910]
HISTOIRE DU PANTHEISME POPULAIRE AU MOYEN AGE ET AU SEIZIEME SIECLE : SUIVIE DE PIECES INEDITIES CONCERNANT LES FRERES DU LIBRE ESPRIT, MAITRE ECKHART, LES LIBERTINS SPIRITUELS, ETC. / Jundt, Auguste – Paris: Sandoz et Fischbacher, 1875 – 1mf – us A.T.L.A. [290]
HISTOIRE DU PEAGE DE L'ESCAUT / Grandgaignage, E – Anvers, 1868 – 2mf – 1 – ILM-2288/1 – ne IDC [327]
HISTOIRE DU REGNE DU KHEDIVE ISMAIL : L'EMPIRE AFRICAIN: TOME 3, 2 I.E. PARTIES / Douin, Georges – Caire: Imp de l'Institut francais d'archeologie orientale du Caire pour la Soc royale de geographie d'Egypte, 1936-39 – 1r – 1 – us Res Libr [930]
HISTOIRE DU ROYAUME HOVA : SES ORIGINES JUSQU'A SA FIN / Malzac, V – Tananarive [Malagasy Rep]: Imprimerie Catholique, 1930 – 1 – us Res Libr [960]
HISTOIRE DU SENEGAL DU XVE SIECLE A 1870 / Cultru, P – Paris. 1910. BA-299 2 – 8 – ne IDC [900]
HISTOIRE DU SENTIMENT RELIGIEUX EN FRANCE / Bremond, A – 126mf – 8 – ne Slangenburg [200]
HISTOIRE DU SULTAN DJELAL-EDDIN MANKOBIRTI, PRINCE DU KHAREZM / Houdas, O – v. 1-2. 1891, 1895. BU-796 2 – 8 – ne IDC [920]
HISTOIRE DU THEATRE DE L'ACADEMIE ROYALE DE MUSIQUE / Durey de Noinville, J -B – 2nd ed. Premiere-Seconde Partie. 1757 – 9 – us Sibley [780]
HISTOIRE DU THEATRE DE L'OPERA COMIQUE / Jullien, Jean-Auguste – 1769. 2v – 9 – us Sibley [780]
HISTOIRE DU THEATRE DE L'OPERA EN FRANCE DEPUIS L'ETABLISSEMENT DE L'ACADEMIE ROYALE DE MUSIQUE, JUSQU'A PRESENT. EN DEUX PARTIES / Durey de Noinville, J -B – Premiere-Seconde Partie. 1753 – 9 – us Sibley [780]
HISTOIRE DU THEATRE DE L'OPERA EN FRANCE DEPUIS L'ETABLISSEMENT DE L'ACADEMIE ROYALW DE MUSIQUE JUSQU'A PRESENT / Durey de Noinville, J -B – P 252. 1753 – 9 – ne IDC [780]
L'HISTOIRE DU VAILLANT PIERRE DE PROVENCE ET DE LA BELLE MAGUELONNE... – Nantes: Mercier, [17..?] – 1 – F50.00 – fr Armell [944]
HISTOIRE D'UN DESSINATEUR: COMMENT ON APPREND A DESSINER / Viollet-Le-Duc, Eugene Emmanuel – Paris: Hetzel, 1903. 268p. 3 fiches. (Art) – 9 – $8.00 – fr Bibl Nationale [740]
HISTOIRE D'UN PAYSAN, 1789 / Erckmann, Emile – Paris. 1868. (La Condition Ouvriere. Part Two.) – 9 – 10.00 – fr Bibl Nationale [360]
HISTOIRE D'UNE DAME CHRETIENNE DE LA CHINE,... / [Couplet, P] – Paris, 1688 – 2mf – 9 – ne IDC [950]
HISTOIRE D'UNE DETENTION DE TRENTE-NEUF ANS... / Saint-Aulaire, Yrieix Beaupoil de – Amsterdam: [s.n.], 1787 – 1 – F64.52 – fr Armell [944]
HISTOIRE D'UNE GREVE AU XVIE SIECLE / Hauser, Henri – Paris. 1894. (La Condition Ouvriere. Part Two.) – 9 – 2.50 – fr Bibl Nationale [360]
HISTOIRE D'UNE JEUNE REVEUSE DE QUARANTE ANS – Montreal: (s.n.), 1893. SEM105P72 – 1mf – 9 – Can$2.25 – cn Bibl Nat [971]
HISTOIRE ELECTORALE DE BANYULS-SUR-MER : 1945-1989 / Razouls, Claude – F50.00 – fr Ethnologie [320]
HISTOIRE ELEMENTAIRE ET CRITIQUE DE JESUS / Peyrat, Alphonse – Paris: Michel Levy Freres, 1864.1 fiche – 9 – us A.T.L.A. [240]
HISTOIRE ET ABREGE DES OUVRAGES LATINS, ITALIENS ET FRANCOIS, POUR ET CONTRE LA COMEDIE ET L'OPERA / Lalouette, Le P A – 1697 – 9 – us Sibley [780]
HISTOIRE ET AVENTURES DE FORTUNATUS, AVEC SA BOURSE ET SON CHAPEAU(...) – Nantes: Mercier, [18..?] – fr Armell [944]
HISTOIRE ET CARTULAIRE DE L'ABBAYE DEMALBUISSON / Dutilleux, A & Depoin, J – Pontoise, 1882 – Dfl60.00 – ne Slangenburg [240]
HISTOIRE ET DESCRIPTION GENERALE DE LA NOUVELLE FRANC / Charlevoix, Francois Xavier de – Paris, France. 1744 – 1r – 1 – cn Can Microfilming [971]
HISTOIRE ET DESCRIPTION GENERALE DE LA NOUVELLE FRANCE / Charlevoix, Francois Xavier de – 52 2. 1744 – 8 – ne IDC [944]
HISTOIRE ET GEOGRAPHIE DE MADAGASCAR / Escamps, Henri d' – Nouv. ed. Paris: Firmin-Didot, 1884 – 1 – us Res Libr [960]
HISTOIRE ET INFLUENCE DES EGLISES WALLONNES DANS LES PAYS-BAS / Poujol, D F – 1902 – 1 – us A.T.L.A. [240]
HISTOIRE ET ORIGINE DES FOULAHS OU FELLANS / Eichthal, Gustave d' – Paris, Vve Dondey-Dupre. 1841 – 9 – 10.00 – fr Orientalistes [960]
HISTOIRE ET STATISTIQUES DES INSTITUTIONS CATHOLIQUES DE MONTREAL / Giroux, Henri – (Montreal: Presses a vapeur de la Minerve), 1869. 03444. (Pre-1900 Canadiana) – 9 – cn C.I.H.M. [240]
HISTOIRE GENEALOGIQUE DE LA MAISON DE BEAUVAU ET DE SES ALLIANCES / Chevillard, Jacques – 18th c. – fr Armell [920]
HISTOIRE GENEALOGIQUE DE LA MAISON DE BETHUNE / Duchesne, Andre – Paris, 1639 – 11mf – 9 – F330.00 – fr F.F.G. [920]
HISTOIRE GENEALOGIQUE DE LA MAISON DE MONTMORENCY / Duchesne, Andre – Paris, 1624 – 13mf – 9 – F390.00 – fr F.F.G. [920]
HISTOIRE GENEALOGIQUE DE LA MAISON DE QUATREBARBES OU LA PLUS PART DE SES ALLIANCES SONT REPRESENTEES... – S.d. after 1843 – fr Armell [920]
HISTOIRE GENEALOGIQUE DE LA MAISON DU BELLAY... / Trincant, Louis – 18th c. – fr Armell [920]
HISTOIRE GENEALOGIQUE DE LA ROYALE MAISON DE SAVOYE / Guichenon, Samuel – Lyon: Chez Guillaume Barbier, 1660. SEM35P190 – 1r – 1 – Can$55.00 – cn Bibl Nat [920]
HISTOIRE GENEALOGIQUE DE PLUSIEURS MAISONS ILLUSTRES DE BRETAGNE / Augustinus du Paz – Paris, 1619 – 12mf – 9 – F360.00 – fr F.F.G. [920]
HISTOIRE GENEALOGIQUE DE PLUSIEURS MAISONS ILLUSTRES DE BRETAGNE... AVEC L'HISTOIRE CHRONOLOGIQUE DES EVESQUES DE TOUS LES DIOCESES DE BRETAGNE... / Du Paz, Augustin – Paris: N. Buon, 1620 – 1 – F527.59 – fr Armell [920]
HISTOIRE GENEALOGIQUE DU MUSEE DES CROISADES / Boudin, Amedee – Paris, 1858-68. 4v, 7 pts – 4mf – 9 – F120.00 – fr F.F.G. [920]
HISTOIRE GENERAL DU JANSENISME / Gerberon, Dom Gabriel – Amsterdam: J L de Lorme. v1-5. 1701 – 35mf – 8 – Dfl88.00 – ne Slangenburg [240]
HISTOIRE GENERALE CRITIQUE ET PHILOLOGIQUE DE LA MUSIQUE / Blainville, Charles-H de – P-170. 1767 – 9 – ne IDC [780]
HISTOIRE GENERALE, CRITIQUE ET PHILOLOGIQUE DE LA MUSIQUE / Blainville, Charles-H de – 1767 – 9 – us Sibley [780]
HISTOIRE GENERALE DE LA DIPLOMATIE EUROPEENNE / Combes, F – Paris, 1856 – 5mf – 1 – ILM-1792/1 – ne IDC [327]
HISTOIRE GENERALE DE NORMANDIE CONTENANT LES CHOSES MEMORABLES ADVENUES DEPUIS LES PREMIERES COURSES DES NORMANDS PAYENS, TANT EN FRANCE QU'AUX AUTRE PAYS / Du Moulin, Gabriel – Rouen: Chez Jean Osmont, 1631. SEM105P383 – 8mf – 9 – Can$18.00 – cn Bibl Nat [944]
HISTOIRE GENERALE DES AUTEURS SACRES ET ECCLESIASTIQUES / Ceillier, R – Paris, 1860-1869. 17v – 320mf – 8 – ne Slangenburg [240]
HISTOIRE GENERALE DES INSECTES / Swammerdam, Jan – Z 205 2. 1685 – 8 – ne IDC [590]
HISTOIRE GENERALE DU MOUVEMENT JANSENISTE DEPUIS SES ORIGINES JUSQU'A NOS JOURS / Gazier, Augustin Louis – Paris: E. Champion, 1922. 2v – 1 – us U.W. Library [240]
HISTOIRE GENERALE ET ICONOGRAPHIE DES LEPIDOPTERES ET DES CHENILLES DE L'AMERIQUE SEPTENTRIONALE / Boisduval, J B A D de & Leconte, J L – Paris, 1833. v1. 228p. 78 pls. Z-1083/2 – 8 – ne IDC [590]
HISTOIRE GENERALE ET SYSTEME COMPARE DES LANGUES SEMITIQUES. PREMI ERE PARTIE, HISTOIRE GENERALE DES LANGUES SEMITIQUES / Renan, Ernest – (Includes bibliographical references) – 3e rev augm ed. Paris: L'Imprimerie imperiale, 1863 – 2mf – 9 – 0-8370-8936-0 – 1986-2936 – us A.T.L.A. [470]
HISTOIRE HORRIBLE ET ESPOUVANTABLE DE CE QUI S'EST FAIT ET PASSE AU FAUX-BOURG S. MARCEL – Arras – 9 – fr Hachette [360]
HISTOIRE ILLUSTREE DES MONNAIES ET JETONS DU CANADA: DONNANT L'HISTOIRE, LA GRAVURE = ILLUSTRATED HISTORY OF COINS AND TOKENS RELATING TO CANADA: GIVING ILLUSTRATIONS WITH THE HISTORY / Breton, Pierre Napoleon – Montreal: Breton, 1894. 00242. (Pre-1900 Canadiana) – 9 – cn C.I.H.M. [730]
HISTOIRE LAPIDAIRE DU CHATEAU DE NANTES / Jeulin, Paul – Rennes: Imp. du Nouvelliste, 1925 – fr Armell [910]
HISTOIRE LITERAIRE DE LA FRANCE / Religieux Benedictins de la Congregation de S. Maur – Paris. Tomes 1-37. 1733 ss – 744mf – 9 – Dfl2,604.00 – ne Slangenburg [440]
HISTOIRE LITTERAIRE DE L'AFRIQUE CHRETIENNE DEPUIS LES ORIGINES JUSQU'A L'INVASION ARABE / Monceaux, P – Paris. Tome 4-6. 1912-1923 – 27mf – 8 – ne Slangenburg [240]
HISTOIRE LITTERAIRE DE L'EDUCATION MORALE ET RELIGIEUSE EN FRANCE ET DANS LA SUISSE ROMANDE / Burnier, L – (Includes bibliographical references and indexes) – Lausanne: Georges Bridel. 2v. 1864 – 4mf – 9 – 0-8370-7609-9 – 1986-1609 – us A.T.L.A. [240]
HISTOIRE LITTERAIRE DE L'EUROPE CONTENANT L'EXTRAIT DES MEILLEURS LIVRES – La Haye. 1726-27 (I-VI) – 1 – fr A.C.R.P.P. [410]
HISTOIRE LITTERAIRE ET PHILOSOPHIQUE DE VOLTAIRE / Durdent, R J – Paris. A. Emery. 1818. III – 9 – fr Hachette [440]
HISTOIRE MALACOLOGIQUE DU LAC BALATON EN HONGRIE / Servain, G – Z 787 2. 1881 – 8 – ne IDC [574]
HISTOIRE MEMORABLE ET ESPOUVANTABLE, ARRIVEE EN CHASTEAU DE BISSESTRE PRES DE PARIS – Paris. 1623 – 9 – fr Hachette [360]
HISTOIRE METALLIQUE DE LA REVOLUTION FRANCAISE, OU RECUEIL DES MEDAILLES ET MONNAIES (...) / Millin, Aubin-L – Paris: Imp. imperiale, 1806 – fr Armell [944]
HISTOIRE NATURELLE, CIVILE, ET ECCLESIASTIQUE DE L'EMPIRE DU JAPON / Kaempfer, Engelbert – La Haye: P. Gosse et J. Neaumme. 1729 – 9 – 25.00 – fr Orientalistes [950]
HISTOIRE NATURELLE DE LA PAROLE / Court de Gebelin, A – 1776 – 9 – fr I.C.S. [400]
HISTOIRE NATURELLE DE LA PAROLE OU ORIGINE DU LANGAGE, DE L'ECRITURE ET DE LA GRAMMAIRE UNIVERSELLE / Court de Gebelin, A – (Linguistics series). 1772 – 9 – fr Hachette [400]
HISTOIRE NATURELLE DES ANIMAUX SANS VERTEBRES / ed by Lamarck, J B A P M de – Paris, Ed.2. 1835-1845. 11v – 115mf – 9 – ne IDC [590]
HISTOIRE NATURELLE DES ARAIGNEES (ARANEIDES) / Simon, E – Paris. 1864. BZ-2243 1 – 9 – ne IDC [590]
HISTOIRE NATURELLE DES ARANEIDES / Walckenaer, C A – Z 2213 2. 1806 – 8 – ne IDC [590]
HISTOIRE NATURELLE DES EQUISETUM DE FRANCE / Duval-Jouve, J – Paris. 1864. B-5488 2 – 8 – ne IDC [580]
HISTOIRE NATURELLE DES ILES CANARIES / Webb, P B & Berthelot, S – 3v. Paris. 1835-50. Lacking: v. 2, pt. 1; v. 3, pt. 2. B-2690 2 – 8 – ne IDC [500]
HISTOIRE NATURELLE DES INSECTES QUI / Blanchard, C E – Paris, 1845. 2v. Z-1070/2 – 8 – ne IDC [590]
HISTOIRE NATURELLE DES INSECTES / Boisduval, J B A D de & Guenee, A – Paris, 1836-58. v1,5-10. Atlas. v2-4 never issued. Z-1081/2 – 8 – ne IDC [590]
HISTOIRE NATURELLE DES INSECTES, HEMIPTERES / Amyot, Charles Jean Baptiste & Audinet-Serville, J G – Paris: Roret, 1843. xxvi,675p. 12 f. de pl. 8 fiches.(Science Collection) – 9 – 20.00 – fr Bibl Nationale [590]
HISTOIRE NATURELLE DES LEPIDOPTERES. 1885-1886 / Marbille, P – From: Grandidier, A. Histoire physique v. 18-19. B-5936-J 2 – 8 – ne IDC [590]
HISTOIRE NATURELLE DES LEPIDOPTERES, OU PAPILLONS DE FRANCE / Godart, J B – Paris, 1820-1821-1840.11vols. Suppl. Paris, 1832-42.v1-4 – 8 – ne IDC [590]
HISTOIRE NATURELLE DES MOLLUSQUE TERRESTRES ET D'EAU DOUCE QUI VIVENT EN FRANCE / Dupuy, D – Z-508 2. 1847-52 – 8 – ne IDC [590]
HISTOIRE NATURELLE DES MOLLUSQUES PTEROPODES / Rang, PKS L & Souleyet, FLA – Z 739 2. 1852 – 8 – ne IDC [590]
HISTOIRE NATURELLE DES MOLLUSQUES TERRESTRES ET FLUVIATILES DE LA FRANCE. / Draparnaud, Jacques PR – Paris: Plassan et Montpellier, Renaud, c1804. viii,164p. 2 fiches. (Science Collection) – 9 – 6.00 – fr Bibl Nationale [574]
HISTOIRE NATURELLE DES OISEAUX D'AFRIQUE / Levaillant, Francois – 5180 2. 6 v. 1799-1808 – 8 – ne IDC [590]
HISTOIRE NATURELLE DES OISEAUX DE PARADIS / Lesson, R P – Z 1833. 1834-1835 – 9 – ne IDC [590]

HISTOIRE NATURELLE DES PERROQUETS / Levaillant, Francois – 2101 2. 2 v. 1801-1805. v. 3: 1837-1838 – 8 – ne IDC [590]
HISTOIRE NATURELLE DES PLANTES / Baillon, H E – v. 33-36. 1886-97. From: Grandidier, A. Histoire physique. v. 33-36. B-5936Q 2 – 8 – ne IDC [580]
HISTOIRE NATURELLE DES PLANTES / Drake del Castillo, E – 1902 – 8 – ne IDC [580]
HISTOIRE NATURELLE DES POISSONS / ed by Cuvier, Georges & Valenciennes, A – Paris. 22 v. 1828-1849 – 205mf – 8 – ne IDC [590]
HISTOIRE NATURELLE DES PRINCIPALES PRODUCTIONS DE L'EUROPE MERIDIONALE ET PARTICULIEREMENT DE CELLES DES ENVIRONS DE NICE ET DES ALPES MARITIMES / Risso, J A – 5v. Paris. 1826-28. BZ-317 2 – 8 – ne IDC [580]
HISTOIRE NATURELLE DES REPTILES ET DES POISSONS / Guichenot, A – 2676 2. Zoology, v. 3. 1850 – 8 – ne IDC [590]
HISTOIRE NATURELLE DES VEAGEA1TAUX / Spach, E – Paris, 1834-1848. v. 1-15. B-5576 1 – 9 – 63.00 – ne IDC [580]
HISTOIRE NATURELLE DU SENEGAL AVEC LA RELATION ABREGEE D'UN VOYAGE FAIT EN CE PAYS PENDANT LES ANNEES 1749,-50,-51,-52 ET-53 / Adanson, Michel – (African Library series). 1757 – 9 – fr Hachette [910]
HISTOIRE NATURELLE DU SENEGAL (COQUILLAGE) / Adanson, Michel – 1335 2. 1757 – 8 – ne IDC [574]
HISTOIRE NATURELLE D'UNE PARTIE D'OISEAUX NOUVEAUX ET RARES DE L'AMERIQUE ET DES INDES / Levaillant, Francois – v. 1. Paris. 1801-02. BZ-306 2 – 8 – ne IDC [590]
HISTOIRE NATURELLE ET ICONOGRAPHIE DES INSECTES COLEOPTERES / Castelnau, FL de & Gory, H L – Paris, Londres, 1837-41. 4v text. 4v atlas. Z-1128/2 – 8 – ne IDC [590]
HISTOIRE NATURELLE ET MEDICALE DE LA FAMILLE DES VALERIANEES / Dufresne, P – Montpellier. 1811 – 8 – ne IDC [580]
HISTOIRE NATURELLE ET MEDICALE DES CASSES,... / Colladon, LT F – Montpellier, 1816 – 4mf – 9 – ne IDC [615]
HISTOIRE NATURELLE ET MEDICALE DES RENONCULES,... / Biria, J A J – Montpellier, 1811 – 1mf – 9 – ne IDC [615]
HISTOIRE NATURELLE ET MEDICALE D'IPECACUANHA... / Richard, Achille – Paris, 1820 – 1mf – 9 – ne IDC [610]
HISTOIRE NATURELLE GENERALE ET PARTICULIERE / ed by Buffon, Georges L L – (Supplement. 1774-89. 7v.) – Paris. 37v. 1749-1804. – 594mf – 8 – ne IDC [500]
HISTOIRE NATURELLE, GENERALE ET PARTICULIERE DES REPTILES / Daudin, F M – v. 1-8. 1802-05. BZ-2242 1 – 9 – ne IDC [590]
HISTOIRE NATURELLE MEDICALE ET ECONOMIQUE DES SOLANUM,... / Dunal, M F – Paris, 1813 – 6mf – 9 – ne IDC [615]
HISTOIRE NOUVELLE, MERVEILLEUSE ET ESPOUVANTABLE, D'UN JEUNE HOMME D'AIX EN PROVENCE – Paris. 1614 – 9 – fr Hachette [360]
HISTOIRE OU POLICE DU ROYAUME DE GALA / Brancas-Villeneuve, Andre Francois de – (Utopias in the Enlightenment series). 1754 – 9 – fr Hachette [830]
HISTOIRE PARTICULIERE DES PLANTES ORCHIDEES RECUEILLIES SUR LES TROIS ISLES D'AFRIQUE, DE FRANCE, DE BOURBON ET DE MADAGASCAR / Du Petit-Thouars, L M A A – Paris. 1822. B-5380 2 – 8 – ne IDC [580]
HISTOIRE PARTICULIERE DU NAN-TCHAO / Sainson, Camille – 1904 – 9 – fr Orientalistes [950]
HISTOIRE PHILOSOPHIQUE DE L'HOMME / Millot, Claude-Francois-Xavier – (D'Holbach series). 1766 – 9 – fr Hachette [190]
HISTOIRE PHILOSOPHIQUE, LITTERAIRE, ECONOMIQUE DES PLANTES DE L'EUROPE / Poiret, J L M – 7v. Paris. 1825-29. B-5643 2 – 8 – ne IDC [580]
HISTOIRE PHYSIQUE ET POLITIQUE DE L'ILE DE CUBA / Sagra, R de la – 2v. Paris. 1842-43. v. 1: Histoire physique et politique. v. 2: Agriculture, commerce, revenus et appendice. B-5707A 2 – 8 – ne IDC [972]
HISTOIRE PHYSIQUE, NATURELLE ET POLITIQUE DE MADAGASCAR / ed by Grandidier, Alfred – Paris. 1898-1905. – 421mf – 8 – ne IDC [500]
HISTOIRE PHYSIQUE, POLITIQUE ET NATURELLE DE L'ILE DE CUBA / ed by Sagra, R de la – Paris. 12v. 1838-57. – 113mf – 8 – ne IDC [972]
HISTOIRE PITTORESQUE D'UNE FAMILLE DE PALESTINE. AKKINAI AU PAYS DE JESUS. PARIS, 1933 / Miramar, Aloys – Madrid: Razon y Fe, 1934 – 1 – sp Bibl Santa Ana [920]
HISTOIRE POETIQUE DU QUINZIEME SIECLE.. / Champion, Pierre – Paris: E. Champion, 1923. 2v. 60pl. With: Masters in Modern German Literature by O.E. Lessing: The Little Whaler by F. Gerstacker; Introduction to Roman Law by J. Hadley; The Meditations of Marcus Aurelius Antoninus. 1 reel. 1261 – 1 – us U.W. Library [440]
HISTOIRE POLITIQUE DE LA SECURITE SOCIALE FRANCAISE, 1945-1952 / Galant, H C – F50.00 – fr Ethnologie [320]
HISTOIRE POLITIQUE ET RELIGIEUSE DE L'ARMENIE / Tournebize, F – Paris: A. Picard, [1900?] – 2mf – us A.T.L.A. [949]
HISTOIRE POPULAIRE DE MONTREAL DEPUIS SON ORIGINE JUSQU'A NOS JOURS / Leblond de Brumath, A – 3e ed. rev. et Augm. Montreal: Librairie Beauchemin Limitee, 1926 – 4mf – 9 – Can$9.00 – cn Bibl Nat [971]
HISTOIRE POPULAIRE DU CANADA, D'APRES LES DOCUMENTS FRANCAIS ET AMERICAINS / Baudoncourt, Jacques de – Paris: Bloud & Barral, 1886? 03502. (Pre-1900 Canadiana) – 9 – cn C.I.H.M. [971]
HISTOIRE PRODIGIEUSE D'UN GENTILHOMME AUQUEL LE DIABLE S'EST APPARU – Paris. 1613 – 9 – fr Hachette [360]
HISTOIRE PRODIGIEUSE NOUVELLEMENT ARRIVEE A PARIS D'UNE JEUNE FILLE AGITEE D'UN ESPRIT FANTASTIQUE ET INVISIBLE – Paris. 1625 – 9 – fr Hachette [360]
HISTOIRE PRODIGIEUSES ET ESPOUVANTABLE DE PLUS DE DEUX CENS 50 SORCIERS ET CORCIERES EMMENEZ POUR LEUR ESTRE FAIT ET PARFAIT LEUR PROCEZ AU PARLEMENT DE THOLOZE – Paris. 1649 – 9 – fr Hachette [360]
HISTOIRE RURALE DU COMTE DE DAMMARTIN-EN-GOELE AU DEBUT DE LA RENAISSANCE. RECHERCHES SUR LA RECONSTRUCTION APRES LA GUERRE DE CENT ANS / Du Roizel-Marlier, M C – 9 – fr Hachette [944]
HISTOIRE SOCIALISTE – v. 1-13. 1901-08 – 1 – 93.00 – us L of C Photodup [335]
HISTOIRE STATISTIQUE DE LA POPULATION FRANCAISE / Chervin, Arthur – Paris, extr. de la "Revue Scientifique," 1889, 64 p. 1 fiche. (Statistics Series: Demography) – 9 – 6.00 – fr Bibl Nationale [310]
HISTOIRE TERRITORIALE DU DEPARTEMENT DE RHONE-ET-LOIRE / Bernard, Auguste Joseph – Lyon, impr. A. Vingtrinier, 1865. 180 p. 2 fiches. (Statistics Series: Topography) – 9 – 6.00 – fr Bibl Nationale [944]
HISTOIRE UNIVERSELLE / Daron, E Acoghih de – Traduit de l'armenien par E. Dulaurier. 1883, 1887 – 9 – fr Orientalistes [900]
HISTOIRE UNIVERSELLE DES INDES ORIENTALES ET OCCIDENTALES / Wytfliet, Cornelius – Douay: Francois Fabri, 1605. SEM105P880 – 3mf – 9 – Can$6.75 – cn Bibl Nat [900]
HISTOIRE VERITABLE ET NATURELLE DES MOEURS ET PRODUCTIONS DU PAYS DE LA NOUVELLE-FRANCE, VULGAIREMENT DITE LE CANADA / Boucher, Pierre – Paris: chez Florentin Lambert, 1664. SEM16P6 – 1r – 5 – Can$9.00 – cn Bibl Nat [971]
HISTOIRE VERITABLE ET NATURELLE DES MOEURS & PRODUCTIONS DU PAYS DE LA NOUVELLE FRANCE, VULGAIREMENT DITE LE CANADA / Boucher, Pierre – Paris: Florentin Lambert, 1664. 00001. (Pre-1900 Canadiana) – 9 – cn C.I.H.M. [971]
HISTOIRE VERITABLE ET PRODIGIEUSE SUR LA VIE, MORT ET PUNITION D'UN HOMME QUI A ESTE CONDAMNE PAR ARREST A ESTRE PENDU ESTRANGLE, PUIS BRUSLE / Ameron, Jean d' – Paris. 1627 – 9 – fr Hachette [360]
HISTOIRE...DI TVTTI I FATTI DEGNI DI MEMORIA NEL MONDO SVCCESSI DELL' ANNO M.D.24 / Guazzo, M – Vinegia, 1546 – 8mf – 9 – H-8277/1 – ne IDC [956]
HISTOIRES DES BOURSES DU TRAVAIL / Pelloutier, Fernand L E – Paris. 1902. (La Condition Ouvriere. Part Two.) – 9 – 7.50 – fr Bibl Nationale [360]
HISTOIRES ESPOUVANTABLES DE DEUX MAGICIENS QUI ONT ESTE ESTRANGLEZ PAR LE DIABLE DANS PARIS LA SEPMAINE SAINCTE – Paris. 1615 – 9 – fr Hachette [360]
HISTOIRES GALANTES ET MELANCOLIQUES / Theuriet, Andre – Paris: E. Flammarion, 1904. 198p. 4 fiches. (Literature Collection) – 9 – 10.00 – fr Bibl Nationale [830]
DES HISTOIRES ORIENTALES ET PRINCIPALEMENT DES TURKES OU TURCHIKES ET SCHITIQUES OU TARTARESQUES ET AULTRES QUI EN SONT DESCENDUES, ... / Postel, G – Paris, 1575 – 6mf – 9 – H-8347/1 – ne IDC [956]
HISTOIRES SOMALIES : LA MALICE DES PRIMITIFS / Duchenet, Edouard – Paris: Larose, 1936 – 1 – us Res Libr [960]
HISTOIRES VERITABLES ARRIVEES EN LA PERSONNE DE DEUX BOURGEOIS DE LA VILLE DE CHARLEVILLE – Charleville. 1637 – 9 – fr Hachette [360]
HISTOIRES VRAIES – Montreal: les Ed. Histoires vraies, ca 1943?-57. SEM16P332 – 4r – 5 – Can$107.00 – cn Bibl Nat [073]
HISTOIRE...SVR LES CHOSES FAICTES ET AUENUES DE SON TEMPS EN TOUTES LES PARTIES DU MONDE / Giovio, P – Paris. 2v. 1581 – 22mf – 9 – H-8359/1 – ne IDC [956]
HISTOLOGY : NOTES FOR STUDENTS OF ANIMAL HUSBANDRY – 1972 – 109p – it F.A.O. [636]
HISTOLOGY OF BRITISH MOSSES / Trotter, L B C & Else, J – 1964 – 14 – uk Microform Academic [580]
HISTORI DESS SACRAMENTSTREITS... / Chemnitz, Martin – N.p., 1591 – 8mf – 9 – ne IDC [240]
HISTORI DESS SACRAMENTSTREITS DARINNEN KLAERLICH AUSSGEFUEHRET WIRDT WIE DIESE ZWYTRACHT ENTSTANDEN BISS AUFF VNSERE ZEIT CONTINUIRET... / Kirchner, T – N.p., 1591 – 8mf – ne IDC [240]
HISTORIA : IOELIS: CHRONOGRAPHIA COMPENDIARIA. IOANNIS CANANI: NARRATIO DE BELLO CP (CBH 14) / Acropolitae, Georgii; ed by Allatius, L – Parisiis, 1651 – Dfl67.00 – ne Slangenburg [930]
HISTORIA – Lima, Peru. v. 1-3 no. 10. Mar Apr 1943-Apr July 1945 – 1 – us NY Public [900]
HISTORIA : REVISTA PERUANA DE CULTURA – Lima. v1-3. 1943-45 – 1r – 1 – us Ross [073]
HISTORIA; A MAGAZINE OF LOCAL HISTORY – Norwell, Mass. v. 1. (1-6). Nov. 1898-Oct. 1899 – 1 – us NY Public [073]
HISTORIA ABBATIAE CASSINENSIS / Gattula, Erasmus, OSB – Venetiis. v1-3. 1733 – Dfl238.00 – ne Slangenburg [240]
HISTORIA AETHIOPICA : SIVE BREVIS ET SUCCINCTA DESCRIPTIO REGNI HABESSINORUM,... / Ludolfi, Iobi (alias Leutholf) – Francofurti ad Moenum (Frankfurt a. Main): prostat apud J D Zunner, 1681 – 1 – us Res Libr [960]
HISTORIA AMARANTHORUM / Willdenow, C L – Turici. 1790. B-5813 2 – 8 – ne IDC [580]
HISTORIA ANGLICANA (A.D. 449-1298) (RS16) : NECNON EJUSDEM LIBER DE ARCHIEPISCOPIS ET EPISCOPIS ANGLIAE / Bartholomeus de Cotton; ed by Luard, H R – 1859 – Dfl35.00 – ne Slangenburg [240]
HISTORIA ANGLICANA (CHRONIA..1) / Thomas Walsingham – v1-2. 1863 – Dfl63.00 – ne Slangenburg [240]
HISTORIA ANGLORUM, SIVE, UT VULGO DICITUR, HISTORIA MINOR (RS44) : ITEM, EJUSDEM ABREVIATIO CHRONICORUM ANGLIAE / Matthaei Parisiensis; ed by Madden, F – (v1 1866 Dfl35.00. v2 1866 Dfl32.00. v3 1869 Dfl39.00) – ne Slangenburg [941]
HISTORIA ANIMALIUM. LIBRI 1 DE QUADRUPEDIBUS VIVIPARIS... / Gesner, C – Tiguria, 1551 – 12mf – 9 – sp Cultura [590]
HISTORIA ANIMALIUM. LIBRI 2 DE QUADRUPEDIBUS VIVIPARIS... / Gesner, C – Tiguria, 1551 – 2mf – 9 – sp Cultura [590]
HISTORIA ANIMALIUM. LIBRI 3 DE DE AVIUM NATURA... / Gesner, C – Tiguria, 1551 – 9mf – 9 – sp Cultura [590]
HISTORIA ANIMALIUM. LIBRI 4 DE PISCIUM ET AQUATILIUM... / Gesner, C – Tiguria, 1558 – 14mf – 9 – sp Cultura [590]
HISTORIA ANIMALIUM. LIBRI 5 DE SERPENTIUM NATURA... / Gesner, C – Tiguria, 1587 – 2mf – 9 – sp Cultura [590]
HISTORIA AVGVSTANAE CONFESSIONIS,... / Chytraeus, D – 8mf – 9 – ne IDC [240]
HISTORIA BELLI PERSICI, GESTI INTER MVRATHEM 3 : TVRCARVM, ET MEHEMETEM HODABENDE, PERSARUM REGEM, ... / Porsius, H – Francofvrti. 2pts. 1583 – 3mf – 9 – H-8418/1 – ne IDC [956]
HISTORIA BIBLIOGRAFICA DE LA MEDICINA ESPANOLA / Fernandez Morejon, Antonio – 1852 – 9 – 1.50f – sp Bibl Santa Ana [610]
HISTORIA BIBLIOTHECAE ROMANORUM PONTIFICUM / Ehrle, F S J – Tom 1 (Et Unicus). Romae, 1890 – Dfl123.00 – ne Slangenburg [240]
HISTORIA BRITONUM / Nennius, Abbott of Bangor – 1 – uk Microform Academic [941]
HISTORIA BYZANTINA (CBH 15) / Nepotis, Ducae Michaelis; ed by Bullialdus, IsM – Parisiis, 1649 – Dfl49.00 – ne Slangenburg [930]
HISTORIA BYZANTINA (CSHB 21) : REC. ET INTERPRETE ITALO ADDITO SUPPL. IMM. BEKKERUS / Nepotis, Michaelis Ducae – Bonnae, 1834 – Dfl42.00 – ne Slangenburg [930]
HISTORIA BYZANTINA DUPLICI COMMENTARIO ILLUSTRATA (CBH 25,1) : TOM. 1: FAMILIAE AUGUSTAE BYZANTINAE / ed by Cange, C du – Venetiis, 1729 – Dfl49.00 – ne Slangenburg [930]
HISTORIA BYZANTINA DUPLICI COMMENTARIO ILLUSTRATA (CBH 25,2) : TOM. 2: CONSTANTINOPOLIS CHRISTIANA / ed by Cange, C du – Venetiis, 1729 – Dfl49.00 – ne Slangenburg [930]
HISTORIA (CBH 13) / Acominati, Nicetae; ed by Fabrotus, C A – Parisiis, 1647 – Dfl81.00 – ne Slangenburg [930]
HISTORIA CHRONICA : PARS ALTERA. DE IMPERATORIBUS CHRISTIANIS (CBH 30,4) / Malalae, Joannis Antiocheni; ed by Hodius, H – Venetiis, 1733 – Dfl32.00 – ne Slangenburg [240]
HISTORIA CHRONICA (CBH 30,3) : PARS PRIMA / Malalae, Joannis Antiocheni; ed by Hodius, H – Venetiis, 1733 – Dfl30.00 – ne Slangenburg [240]
HISTORIA COMICA DE TRUJILLO DESDE LOS TIEMPOS MAS REMOTOS HASTA EL FINAL DEL SIGLO 18 / Ramons Sanguino, Joaquin – Trujillo: Establecimiento Tipografico La Minerva, 1913 – 1 – sp Bibl Santa Ana [946]
HISTORIA COMPOSTELLANA – 1988 – 14mf – 9 – Bf1,975.00 – 2-503-63702-7 – be Brepols [240]
HISTORIA CONTROVERSIARUM DE RITIBUS SINICIS / Pray, G – Pestini Budae ac Cassoviae, 1789 – 3mf – 9 – HTM-230/1 – ne IDC [240]
HISTORIA CRITICA DE LA REVOLUCION DEL 43 : PROGRAMA CONSTRUCTIVO PARA EL MANANA / Ghioldi, Americo – [Buenos Aires], 1950 – 1 – CSUXAHZ6318-B – us Hoover Inst Photo [320]
HISTORIA CRITICA DE LOS SISTEMAS FILOSOFICOS... / Nieto y Serrano, M – Madrid, 1898 – 9mf – 9 – sp Cultura [100]
HISTORIA (CSHB 23) / Choniatae, Nicetae; ed by Bekkeri, Imm – Bonnae, 1835 – Dfl60.00 – ne Slangenburg [930]
HISTORIA (CSHB 48) / Attaliotae, Michaelis; ed by Bekkerus, Imm – Bonnae, 1853 – Dfl25.00 – ne Slangenburg [930]
HISTORIA DA LITTERATURA BRAZILEIRA / Romero, Sylvio – (3rd ed., aug., with preface by Nelson Romero. Rio de Janeiro: J. Olympio, 1943.5v) – Rio de Janeiro: B.L. Garnier, 1888. 2v – 1 – us U.W. Library [440]
HISTORIA DA REVOLUCAO PORTUGUEZE DE 1880 / Arriaga, Pablo Jose de – 1887-89. 4v. (Historical Studies Series) – 9 – 96.00 – fr Bibl Nationale [900]
HISTORIA DAS MISSIOES DO PADROADO PORTUGES DE ORIENTE / Silva Rego, Antonio da – Madrid: Missionalia Hispanica, 1949 – 1 – sp Bibl Santa Ana [910]

HISTORIA DAVIDIS GEORGI EJUSQUE ASSECLARUM / Zeidtler, C G & Martius, J G – Lipsiae. 1701. BME-419 1 – 9 – ne IDC [240]

HISTORIA DE A CUERDA GRANADINA CONTADA POR ALGUNOS DE SUS NUDOS, APUNTES PARA LA MISMA RECOPILADOS POR... / Cascales Munoz, Jose – Madrid: Tipografia de la Revista de Archivos, 1926 – 1 – sp Bibl Santa Ana [946]

HISTORIA DE ALBURQUERQUE / Duarte Insua, Lino – Badajoz: Tip. Libr. enc. Arqueros, 1929 – 1 – sp Bibl Santa Ana [946]

HISTORIA DE AMERICA ESPANOLA 1920-1925 / Bayle, Constantino – Madrid: Razon y Fe, 1926 – 1 – sp Bibl Santa Ana [972]

HISTORIA DE BADAJOZ / Suarez de Figueroa, Diego – Capitulo 35-36. 1732 – 1 – sp Bibl Santa Ana [946]

HISTORIA DE CACERES Y SU PATRONA / Buxoyo, Simon Benito – Caceres: Public. Dep. Prov. Seminarios FET y JONS, 1952 – 1 – sp Bibl Santa Ana [946]

HISTORIA DE COSAS DEL ORIENTE PRIMERA Y SEGUNDA PARTE. CONTIENE VNA DESCRIPCION GENERAL DE LOS REYNOS DE ASSIA CON LAS COSAS MAS NOTABLES DELLOS / Centeno, A – Cordoua, 1595 – 4mf – 9 – H-8427/1 – ne IDC [950]

HISTORIA DE ESPANA DIRIGIDA POR...TOMOS 5, 14 Y 18, MADRID, 1965-1966 / Menendez Pidal, Ramon – Madrid: Graf. Calleja, 1968 – 1 – sp Bibl Santa Ana [946]

HISTORIA DE EXPEDITIONE FRIDERICI IMPERATORIS ET QUIDAM ALII RERUM GESTARUM FONTES EIUSDEM EXPEDITIONIS (MGH 6: 5.BD) / ed by Chroust, A – 1928 – Dfl25.00 – ne Slangenburg [240]

HISTORIA DE FAMILIAS CUBANAS / Santa Cruz y Mallen, Francisco Xavier de – La Habana: Editorial Hercules, 1940-(86). (v1-8) – 1 – us U.W. Library [920]

HISTORIA DE FRAY GERUNDIO DE CAMPAZAS. TOMO 1 / Isla, Jose Francisco – 1758 – 1mf – 9 – Pta1,000.00 – 84-7848-246-6 – sp Pentalfa [240]

HISTORIA DE FRAY GERUNDIO DE CAMPAZAS. TOMO 2 / Isla, Jose Francisco – 1770 – 1mf – 9 – Pta1,000.00 – 84-7848-247-4 – sp Pentalfa [240]

HISTORIA DE GENTIBUS SEPTENTRIONALIBUS / Magnus Gothus, O – Romae. 1555. Index. BN-308 2 – 8 – ne IDC [910]

HISTORIA DE GIBRALTAR / Lopez de Ayala, Ignacio – 1782 – 2mf – 9 – Pta1,500.00 – 84-7848-198-2 – sp Pentalfa [946]

HISTORIA DE GUATEMALA / Fuentes y Guzman, Francisco A – 1882-83.2v – 9 – 1.50f – sp Bibl Santa Ana [972]

HISTORIA DE ISLA DE CUBA / Pezuela y Lobo, Jacobo de la – Madrid. 4v. 1868-78 – 1 – 23.00r – us L of C Photodup [972]

HISTORIA DE LA ANTIQUISIMA E ILUSTRE VILLA DE FREGENAL / Martin Moreno, Rafael – Sevilla: Imp. Alvarez, 1960 – sp Bibl Santa Ana [946]

HISTORIA DE LA CIUDAD DE BADAJOZ... : EXTRACTADAS DEL DOCTOR... / Suarez de Figueroa, Diego – Badajoz: Imprenta de Vicente Rodriguez, 1916 – 1 – sp Bibl Santa Ana [946]

HISTORIA DE LA CIUDAD Y CORTE DE LEON Y DE SUS REYES / Risco, Manuel – 1792 – 2mf – 9 – Pta1,500.00 – 84-7848-110-9 – sp Pentalfa [946]

HISTORIA DE LA CIVILIZACION DE ARAUCANIA / Guevara, Tomas – (T.1: 1898; T.2: 1902; T.3: Los Araucanos: la republica. 1902; T.4: Psicologia del pueblo araucano. 1908; T.5: Folklore araucano... 1911; T.6: Los Araucanos en la revolucion... 1910; T.7: Las Ultimas familias; costumbres araucanas. 1913; T.8: La Mentalidad araucana. 1916; T.9: La Etnolojia araucana... 1920; T.10: Historia de la justicia araucana. 1922) – Santiago de Chile: Cervantes – 1 – F2,532.11 – fr Armell [972]

HISTORIA DE LA COMPOSICION DEL CUERPO HUMANO / Valverde de Hamusco, J – Roma, 1556 – 6mf – 9 – sp Cultura [612]

HISTORIA DE LA COMQUISTA DE MEXICO... TOMO 3 / Solis, Antonio de – (Tambien Tomo 2, 1843) – Barcelona: Consortes Sierra, Oliver y Marti, 1789 – 1 – sp Bibl Santa Ana [972]

HISTORIA DE LA CONQUISTA DE LA PROVINCIA DE ITZA... / Villagutierre Soto-Mayor, Juan de – Guatemala, 1933; Madrid: Razon y Fe, 1934 – 1 – sp Bibl Santa Ana [972]

HISTORIA DE LA CONQUISTA DE MEJICO / Solis Rivadeneyra, Antonio de – (v2-3. 1789. v1-2. 1780. v1-3. 1791. 1732. 1704. 1684. 1756) – v1. 1843 – 9 – 1.50f – sp Bibl Santa Ana [972]

HISTORIA DE LA CONQUISTA DE MEXICO / Lopez de Gomara, Francisco – Mexico: Editorial Pedro Robleda, 1943.-v1 – sp Bibl Santa Ana [972]

HISTORIA DE LA CONQUISTA DE MEXICO / Solis, Antonio de – Barcelona: Lucas de Bezaras y Urrutia, 1756 – 1 – sp Bibl Santa Ana [972]

HISTORIA DE LA CONQUISTA DE MEXICO / Solis, Antonio de – Madrid: Antonio de Sancha, Tomo 1. 1783 – 1 – sp Bibl Santa Ana [972]

HISTORIA DE LA CONQUISTA DE MEXICO / Solis, Antonio de – Madrid: Antonio de Sancha, Tomo 2. 1784 – 1 – sp Bibl Santa Ana [972]

HISTORIA DE LA CONQUISTA DE MEXICO / Solis, Antonio de – Madrid: Bernardino Peralta, 1732 – 1 – sp Bibl Santa Ana [972]

HISTORIA DE LA CONQUISTA DE MEXICO / Solis, Antonio de – Madrid: Manuel Martin, Tomo 1. 1780 – 1 – sp Bibl Santa Ana [350]

HISTORIA DE LA CONQUISTA DE MEXICO / Solis, Antonio de – Madrid: Manuel Martin, Tomo 2, 1780 – 1 – sp Bibl Santa Ana [350]

HISTORIA DE LA CONQUISTA DE MEXICO / Solis Rivadeneira, Antonio de – Madrid: Juan de San Martin, 1756 – 1 – sp Bibl Santa Ana [972]

HISTORIA DE LA CONQUISTA DE MEXICO. TOMO 2 / Solis, Antonio de – Barcelona: Consortes Sierra, Oliver y Marti, 1789 – 1 – sp Bibl Santa Ana [972]

HISTORIA DE LA CONQUISTA DE NUEVA ESPANA / Diaz del Castillo, Bernal – 1632 – 9 – 1.50f – sp Bibl Santa Ana [972]

HISTORIA DE LA CONQUISTA DEL PERU... INCAS / Prescott, Guillermo H – 1853 – 9 – 1.50f – sp Bibl Santa Ana [972]

HISTORIA DE LA CONQUISTA, POBLACION U PROGRESOS DE LA MERICA SEPTENTRIONAL, CONOCIDA CON EL NOMBRE DE NUEVA ESPANA / Solis Rivadeneyra, Antonio de – 9 – sp Bibl Santa Ana [946]

HISTORIA DE LA "CUERDA GRANADINA", CONTADA POR ALGUNOS DE SUS...MADRID, 1926 / Munoz, Jose; ed by Valle, A Cascales – Madrid: Razon y Fe, 1928 – 9 – sp Bibl Santa Ana [946]

HISTORIA DE LA DIOCESIS DE SIGUENZA Y DE SUS OBISPOS, POR TORIBIO MINGUELLA Y ARNEDO / T'Serclaes, Duque de – Madrid: Fortanet, 1912. B.R.A.H. 61, pp. 154-152 – sp Bibl Santa Ana [240]

HISTORIA DE LA DISPUTA QUE SOBRE LA ENFERMEDAD QUE QUITO LA VIDA A MANUEL RODRIGUEZ... / Lopez de Araujo, B – Madrid, 1756 – 1mf – 9 – sp Cultura [616]

HISTORIA DE LA DOMINACION ESPANOLA EN MEJICO / Orozco y Berra, Manuel – Madrid: Razon y Fe, 1944 – 1 – sp Bibl Santa Ana [320]

HISTORIA DE LA EPIDEMIA DE CALENTURAS BENIGNAS...EN SEVILLA / Nieto de Pina, C – Sevilla, 1784 – 1mf – 9 – sp Cultura [614]

HISTORIA DE LA EPIDEMIA...DE BARBASTRO EN EL ANO DE 1748... / Ased y Latorre, A – Zaragoza, SA – 2mf – 9 – sp Cultura [614]

HISTORIA DE LA FILOSOFIA Y DE LAS CIENCIAS / Frutos Cortes, Eugenio – Zaragoza: Editora Libreria General, 1965 – sp Bibl Santa Ana [100]

HISTORIA DE LA FLORIDA / Lasso de la Vega, Garcia – 1605 – 9 – 1.50f – sp Bibl Santa Ana [978]

HISTORIA DE LA FUNDACION DE GRANADA, HOY GRANADILLA – Caceres: Imp. Garcilasso, 1974 – 1 – sp Bibl Santa Ana [910]

HISTORIA DE LA FUNDACION DEL CONVENTO DE RELIGIOSAS CARMELITAS DE BADAJOZ / Mateos, Francisco – Badajoz: Tip.Arqueros, Tomo 1. 1930 – 1 – sp Bibl Santa Ana [240]

HISTORIA DE LA GOBERNACION DEL TUCUMAN (SIGLO 16). BUENOS AIRES, 1928 / Lizondo Borda, Manuel – Madrid: Razon y Fe, 1929 – 1 – sp Bibl Santa Ana [320]

HISTORIA DE LA HISTORIOGRAFIA ESPANOLA. TOMO 1. HASTA LA PUBLICACION DE LA CRONICA DE OCAMPO. TOMO 2 DE OCAMPO A SOLIS. MADRID, 1941, 1944 / Sanchez Alonso, B – Madrid: Razon y Fe, 1946 – 1 – sp Bibl Santa Ana [946]

HISTORIA DE LA IMAGEN DE NUESTRA SENORA DE LA FUENTE SANTA EXCELSA PATRONA DE ZORITA / Fernandez Sanchez, Teodoro – Caceres: Tip. Extremadura, 1972 – 1 – sp Bibl Santa Ana [240]

HISTORIA DE LA ISLA Y CATEDRAL DE CUBA / Morell de Santa Cruz, Pedro Agustin – La Habana, 1929; Madrid: Razon y Fe, 1931 – 1 – sp Bibl Santa Ana [972]

HISTORIA DE LA MEDICINA EN MEXICO. MEXICO, 1934 / Ocaranza, Fernando – Madrid: Razon y Fe, 1935 – 1 – sp Bibl Santa Ana [610]

HISTORIA DE LA MILICIA ESPANOLA / Marin Mendoza, Joaquin – 1776 – 2mf – 9 – Pta1,500.00 – 84-7848-316-0 – sp Pentalfa [350]

HISTORIA DE LA NUEVA ESPANA / Aguilar, Fray Francisco de – Mexico: Ediciones Botas, 1938 – sp Bibl Santa Ana [946]

HISTORIA DE LA NUEVA ESPANA / Zorita, Alonso de – Madrid: Libreria General de Victoriano Suarez, 1909. v1 – 1 – sp Bibl Santa Ana [946]

HISTORIA DE LA PROVINCIA DE SAN ANTONIO DEL NUEVO REINO DE GRANADA. CARACAS, 1930 / Zamora, Alonso de – Madrid: Razon y Fe, 1930 – 1 – sp Bibl Santa Ana [946]

HISTORIA DE LA PROVINCIA DE SAN VICENTE DE CHIAPA Y GUATEMALA, DE LA ORDEN DE PREDICACDORES. TOMO 1. GUATEMALA, 1929 / Ximenez, Francisco – Madrid: Razon y Fe, 1930 – 1 – sp Bibl Santa Ana [240]

HISTORIA DE LA PROVINCIA DE SAN VICENTE DE CHIAPA Y GUATEMALA DE LA ORDEN DE PREDICADORES...TOMO 3 / Ximenez, Francisco – Guatemala, 1931; Madrid: Razon y Fe, 1932 – 1 – sp Bibl Santa Ana [972]

HISTORIA DE LA PUBLICACION MONUMENTA HISTORICA SOCIETATIS JESU / Gomez Rodeles, Cecilio – Madrid: Imprenta del Asilo de huerfanos del S. C. de Jesus, 1913 – 1mf – us A.T.L.A. [240]

HISTORIA DE LA REAL Y GENERAL JUNTA DE COMERCIO, MONEDA Y MINAS... / Larruga y Boneta, E – Madrid, 1789 – 246mf – 9 – sp Cultura [380]

HISTORIA DE LA RECONQUISTA DE ESPANA CONTADA A LA JUVENTUD / Herrera Oria, P Enrique – Madrid. 1943 – 1 – us Res Libr [946]

HISTORIA DE LA REPUBLICA DE EL SALVADOR... / Bayle, Constantino – Madrid: Razon y Fe, 1928 – 9 – sp Bibl Santa Ana [972]

HISTORIA DE LA SERAFICA PROVINCIA DE CATALUNA POR EL R.P... / Sanahuja, Pedro de – Madrid: Arch. Ibero Americano, 1961 – 1 – sp Bibl Santa Ana [946]

HISTORIA DE LA VIDA DEL HOMBRE. TOMO 1 / Hervas y Panduro, Lorenzo – 1789 – 1mf – 9 – Pta1,000.00 – 84-85422-81-3 – sp Pentalfa [920]

HISTORIA DE LA VIDA DEL HOMBRE. TOMO 2 / Hervas y Panduro, Lorenzo – 1789 – 2mf – 9 – Pta1,500.00 – 84-85422-82-1 – sp Pentalfa [920]

HISTORIA DE LA VIDA DEL HOMBRE. TOMO 3 / Hervas y Panduro, Lorenzo – 1794 – 1mf – 9 – Pta1,000.00 – 84-85422-83-X – sp Pentalfa [920]

HISTORIA DE LA VIDA DEL HOMBRE. TOMO 4 / Hervas y Panduro, Lorenzo – 1796 – 1mf – 9 – Pta1,000.00 – 84-85422-84-8 – sp Pentalfa [920]

HISTORIA DE LA VIDA DEL HOMBRE. TOMO 5 / Hervas y Panduro, Lorenzo – 1798 – 1mf – 9 – Pta1,000.00 – 84-85422-85-6 – sp Pentalfa [920]

HISTORIA DE LA VIDA DEL HOMBRE. TOMO 6 / Hervas y Panduro, Lorenzo – 1798 – 2mf – 9 – Pta1,500.00 – 84-85422-86-4 – sp Pentalfa [920]

HISTORIA DE LA VIDA DEL HOMBRE. TOMO 7 / Hervas y Panduro, Lorenzo – 1799 – 2mf – 9 – Pta1,500.00 – 84-85422-87-2 – sp Pentalfa [920]

HISTORIA DE LA VIDA Y MARTIRIO DE LA SANTA EULALIA DE MERIDA / Quiros y Benavides, Felipe Bernardo – Madrid: Francisco Sanz, 1672 – 1 – sp Bibl Santa Ana [240]

HISTORIA DE LA...NUEVA ESPANA / Diaz del Castillo, Bernal – 1795-96.4v – 9 – 1.50f – sp Bibl Santa Ana [972]

HISTORIA DE LAS COSAS MAS NOTABLES DEL GRAN REYNO DE CHINA / Gonzales de Mendoza, Juan – Madrid: Missionalia Hispanica, 1945 – 1 – sp Bibl Santa Ana [950]

HISTORIA DE LAS GUERRAS CIVILES DEL PERU (1544-1548) Y DE OTROS SUCESOS DE LAS INDIAS / Gutierrez de Santa Clara, Pedro – Madrid: Victoriano Suarez, 1929 – 1 – sp Bibl Santa Ana [972]

HISTORIA DE LAS LEYES / Colombia. Laws, Statutes, etc – Bogota. On film: 1925-33. LL-062 – 1 – us L of C Photodup [340]

HISTORIA DE LAS MISIONES / Unanue, H & Sobrevida, M – Madrid: Graf. Calleja, 1966 – 1 – sp Bibl Santa Ana [240]

HISTORIA DE LAS MISIONES FRANCISCANAS : 1619-1921 / Izaguirre, Fray Bernardino – Madrid: Razon y Fe, 1927 – 1 – sp Bibl Santa Ana [240]

HISTORIA DE LAS REVOLUCIONES DE HUNGARIA / Brenner, D A I – 1687-89 – 1 – uk Microform Academic [943]

HISTORIA DE LAS VIDAS Y MILAGROS DE NUESTRO BEATO P. FR. PEDRO DE ALCANTARA / Cogolludo, Francisco de – 1664 – 9 – $1.50f – sp Bibl Santa Ana [240]

HISTORIA DE LAS VIRTUDES Y PROPIEDADES DEL TABACO Y DE LOS MODOS DE TOMARSE... / Castro, J – Cordoba, 1620 – 3mf – 9 – sp Cultura [630]

HISTORIA DE LAS YERVAS Y PLANTAS... / Jarava, J – Amberes, 1557 – 9mf – 9 – sp Cultura [630]

HISTORIA DE LOS ESTABLECIMIENTOS ULTRAMARINOS. TOMO 1 / Lujan Suarez, Pedro de – 1784 – 2mf – 9 – Pta1,500.00 – 84-7848-257-1 – sp Pentalfa [946]

HISTORIA DE LOS ESTABLECIMIENTOS ULTRAMARINOS. TOMO 2 / Lujan Suarez, Pedro de – 1785 – 2mf – 9 – Pta1,500.00 – 84-7848-258-X – sp Pentalfa [946]

HISTORIA DE LOS ESTABLECIMIENTOS ULTRAMARINOS. TOMO 3 / Lujan Suarez, Pedro de – 1786 – 2mf – 9 – Pta1,500.00 – 84-7848-259-8 – sp Pentalfa [946]

HISTORIA DE LOS ESTABLECIMIENTOS ULTRAMARINOS. TOMO 4 / Lujan Suarez, Pedro de – 1788 – 2mf – 9 – Pta1,500.00 – 84-7848-260-1 – sp Pentalfa [946]

HISTORIA DE LOS ESTABLECIMIENTOS ULTRAMARINOS. TOMO 5 / Lujan Suarez, Pedro de – 1790 – 2mf – 9 – Pta1,500.00 – 84-7848-261-X – sp Pentalfa [946]

HISTORIA DE LOS GRUPOS Y PARTIDOS POLITICOS DE LA REPUBLICA ARGENTINA DESDE 1810 A 1983 / Garcia, Cesar Reinaldo – Buenos Aires, Argentina: Sainte-Claire Editora, 1983 – 1 – CSUXAHZ5256-B – us Hoover Inst Photo [320]

HISTORIA DE LOS LIMITES DEL PERU / Angulo y Puente-Arnao, J – Ed 2. Lima, 1927 – 5mf – 9 – ILM-2539/1 – ne IDC [340]

HISTORIA DE LOS ORACULOS / Fontenelle – Merida: Imprenta de Manuel Galvan, 1868 – 1 – sp Bibl Santa Ana [946]

HISTORIA DE LOS REYES CATOLICOS / Bernaldez, Andres – Sevilla: Imp. de Jose Maria Geofrin, Tomo 1. 1869 – 1 – sp Bibl Santa Ana [240]

HISTORIA DE LOS...DON FERNANDO Y.. / Bernaldez, Andres – 1856. 2 tomas – 9 – 1.50f – sp Bibl Santa Ana [946]

HISTORIA DE MEJICO...HERNANDO CORTES / Lopez de Gomara, Francisco – 1554 – 9 – $1.50f – sp Bibl Santa Ana [972]

HISTORIA DE MEXICO, DE FRANCISCO BENEGAS GALVAN / Bayle, Constantino – Madrid: Razon y Fe, 1924 – 1 – sp Bibl Santa Ana [972]

HISTORIA DE MONTSERRAT / Alboreda, A M – Monasterio de Montserrat, 1931; Madrid: Razon y Fe, 1933 – 1 – sp Bibl Santa Ana [946]

HISTORIA DE NUESTRA SENORA DE GUADALUPE... / Rubio German, Francisco; ed by Bayle, Constantino – Madrid: Razon y Fe, 1928 – 9 – sp Bibl Santa Ana [972]
HISTORIA DE NUEVA ESPANA...Y NOTAS DEL ILMO. D.F.A. LORENZANA.. / Cortes, Hernando – 1770 – 9 – 1.50f – sp Bibl Santa Ana [972]
HISTORIA DE PERU / Cappa, Ricardo S J – (1886 ed. 1887 ed) – 1885 – 9 – 1.50f – sp Bibl Santa Ana [972]
HISTORIA DE PERU : LIBROS 1,2,3 / Cappa, Ricardo S J – Lima: Prince, 1885, 1886, 1887 – 1 – F296.97 – fr Armell [972]
HISTORIA DE PERU...AUSTRIACA / Lorente, Sebastian – 1863 – 9 – 1.50f – sp Bibl Santa Ana [972]
HISTORIA DE PIEDRA ESCRITA / San Jose, Francisco de – 1751 – 9 – 1.50f – sp Bibl Santa Ana [946]
HISTORIA DE POLONIA / Brandenburger, C L & Laubert, M – Barcelona, 1932; Madrid: Razon y Fe, 1934 – 1 – sp Bibl Santa Ana [946]
HISTORIA DE SANTA MARIA DE LA VICTORIA / Tena Fernandez, Juan; ed by Rodrigo, Sanchez – Serradilla, 1930 – 1 – sp Bibl Santa Ana [240]
A HISTORIA DE SAO PAULO ENSINADA PELA BIOGRAPHIA DOS SAUS VULTOS MAIS NOTAVEIS / Amaral, Tancredo do – Rio de Janeiro: Alves, 1895. 351p. ports. Bibliog. footnotes – 1 – us U.W. Library [920]
HISTORIA DE TALAVERA LA REAL / Diaz Perez, Nicolas – (1879 ed.1.50f; 9) – 1885 – 9 – 1.50f – sp Bibl Santa Ana [946]
HISTORIA DE TALAVERA LA REAL / Diaz y Perez, Nicolas – Madrid: Imp. Manuel Gines Hernandez, 2nd ed. 1879 – 1 – sp Bibl Santa Ana [946]
HISTORIA DE TALAVERA LA REAL... / Diaz Perez, Nicolas – Madrid: Imp. J. Antonio Garcia, 1875 – 1 – sp Bibl Santa Ana [946]
HISTORIA DE TEODOSIO EL GRANDE. TOMO 1 / Flechier – 1783 – 1mf – 9 – Pta1,000.00 – 84-7848-241-5 – sp Pentalfa [946]
HISTORIA DE TEODOSIO EL GRANDE. TOMO 2 / Flechier – 1783 – 1mf – 9 – Pta1,000.00 – 84-7848-242-3 – sp Pentalfa [946]
HISTORIA DE UNA GRAN LEY : EL SINDICALISMO NACIONAL Y LA LEY DE ASOCIACIONES PROFESIONALES / Allende, Alfredo E – Buenos Aires: Ediciones Aray u, [1963] – 1 – CSUXAHZ2795-B – us Hoover Inst Photo [972]
HISTORIA DE UNA MANCHA DE TINTA (EL MANUSCRITO DE LONGO) / Courier, Pablo Luis – Valencia: Editorial Castalia, 1948 – sp Bibl Santa Ana [946]
HISTORIA DE VITIS ROMANORUM PONTIFICUM (CBH 19,2) / Anastasius Bibliothecaris; ed by Fabrotus, C A – Parisiis, 1649 – Dfl53.00 – ne Slangenburg [240]
HISTORIA DEGLI IMPERATORI GRECI / Nicetas, A C – Venetia, 1562 – 7mf – 9 – H-8301/1 – ne IDC [956]
HISTORIA DEL ALMIRANTE DON CRISTOBAL COLON. TOMO 1 / Colon, Hernando – Madrid, 1932 – 1 – sp Bibl Santa Ana [910]
HISTORIA DEL ARTE HISPANOAMERICANO. TOMO 1. BARCELONA, 1945 / Angulo, D – Madrid: Razon y Fe, 1946 – 1 – sp Bibl Santa Ana [700]
HISTORIA DEL COMERCIO MUNDIAL... / Schmidt, M G – Madrid: Razon y Fe, 1927 – 1 – sp Bibl Santa Ana [380]
HISTORIA DEL CULTO Y SAN TUARIO DE NUESTRA SENORA DE LA MONTANA PATRONA DE CACERES / Orti Belmonte, Miguel Angel – Caceres: Dip.Prov. Caceres, Tomo 1. 1949 – 1 – sp Bibl Santa Ana [240]
HISTORIA DEL CULTO Y SANTUARIO DE NUESTRA SENORA DE LA MONTANA / Orti Belmonte, Miguel Angel – Coleccion de Estudios Extremenos. Caceres Diput Prov. de Caceres, Tomo 2. 1950 – 1 – sp Bibl Santa Ana [240]
HISTORIA DEL DESCUBRIMIENTO DE TUCUMAN, SEGUIDA DE INVESTIGACIONES HISTORICAS / Jaimes Freyre, Ricardo – Universidad de Tucuman. Buenos Aires: Impr. de Coni hermanos, 1916. 312p – 1 – us U.W. Library [972]
HISTORIA DEL GREMIALISMO ARGENTINO – [Buenos Aires?: Servicio International de Publicaciones Argentinas, 1953?] – 1 – CSUXADH6509-B – us Hoover Inst Photo [972]
HISTORIA DEL HOMBRE QUE TUVO EL MUNDO EN LA MANO : JOHANN WOLFGANG VON GOETHE / Nelken, Margarita – Mexico: Ediciones de la Secretaria de Educacion Publica, 1943 – 1r – 1 – us U.W. Library [430]
HISTORIA DEL MAGNANIMO, ET VALOROSO SIGNOR GEORGIO CASTRIOTO, DETTO SCANDERBEGO, DIGNISSIMO PRINCIPE DE GLI ALBANI / Barletius, M – Venetia, 1580 – 9mf – 9 – H-8354/1 – ne IDC [945]
HISTORIA DEL MONASTERIO (SIECLE 19) / Montes, San Pedro de – Astorga – 1r – 5,6 – sp Cultura [240]
HISTORIA DEL MONESTARIO DE YUSTE / G Maria de Alboraya, Domingo de – Madrid: Suc.de Rivadeneira, 1906 – 1 – sp Bibl Santa Ana [240]
HISTORIA DEL MOVIMIENTO SINDICAL / Iscaro, Rubens – Buenos Aires: Editorial Fundamentos, 1973 – 9 – us Hoover Inst Photo [972]
HISTORIA DEL ORIGEN DEL CONDADO Y REINO DE CASTILLA / Gutierrez Coronel, Diego – 1785 – 1mf – 9 – Pta1,000.00 – 84-7848-030-7 – sp Pentalfa [946]
HISTORIA DEL PERIODISMO EN FREGENAL DE LA SIERRA / Real, Enrique – 1897 – 9 – 1.50f – sp Bibl Santa Ana [440]
HISTORIA DEL PERONISMO Y DE LOS ORIGENES DEL MOVIMIENTO NACIONAL – Buenos Aires: Editorial Latitud Sur, [1974?- – 1 – CSUXADQ7384-B – us Hoover Inst Photo [320]
HISTORIA DEL PERU / Lorente, Sebastian – 1861 – 9 – 1.50f – sp Bibl Santa Ana [972]
HISTORIA DEL PUEBLO DE ALANGE / Diaz y Perez, Nicolas – Badajoz: Imp. Artes Graficas, 1930 – 1 – sp Bibl Santa Ana [946]
HISTORIA DEL REAL MONASTERIO DE SAHAGUN / Escalona, Romualdo – 1782 – 5mf – 9 – Pta3,000.00 – 84-7848-229-6 – sp Pentalfa [240]
HISTORIA DEL REGRESO / Barrau, Miguel Angel – Buenos Aires: [Fa-Va-Ro], 1973 – 1 – CSUXAHZ2584-B – us Hoover Inst Photo [972]
HISTORIA DEL REINO DE BADAJOZ DURANTE LA DOMINACION MUSULMANA / Martinez Martinez, Matias Ramon – Badajoz: Tip. y Libr. de A. Arqueros, 1904 – 1 – sp Bibl Santa Ana [946]
HISTORIA DEL REINO DE BADAJOZ DURANTE LA DOMINACION MUSULMANA. NOTICIA / Martinez Martinez, Matias Ramon – Madrid: Fortant, 1905. B.R.A.H. XLVII, pp. 406-407 – sp Bibl Santa Ana [946]
HISTORIA DEL SANTISIMO CRISTO DE LA VICTORIA QUE SE VENERA EN LA VILLA DE SERRADILLA (CACERES) / Cantera, Eugenio – Monachil: Tip. Santa Rita, 1922 – sp Bibl Santa Ana [240]
HISTORIA DEL SINDICALISMO : LOS OBREROS, LA ECONOMIA, LA POLITICA / Abella Blasco, Mario – [Buenos Aires], A. Pena Lilio, [1967] – 1 – CSUXAHZ3570-B – us Hoover Inst Photo [330]
HISTORIA DEL TRASLADO DEL COLEGIO DE ARTILLERIA DE BADAJOZ / Lanuza, Francisco de – Segovia: Imp. Gabel, 1952 – 1 – sp Bibl Santa Ana [355]
HISTORIA DEL TROTSKISMO ARGENTINO, 1929-1960 / Coggiola, Osvaldo – Buenos Aires: Centro Editor de America Latina, c1985 – 1 – CSUXAHZ6194-B – us Hoover Inst Photo [320]
HISTORIA DELA COMPANIA DE JESUS NO BRASIL... / Leite, Serafin – Burgos: Razon y Fe, 1939 – 1 – sp Bibl Santa Ana [972]
HISTORIA DELA CONQUISTA DE MEXICO / Lopez de Gomara, Francisco – Editorial Pedro Robledo, 1943 – sp Bibl Santa Ana [972]
HISTORIA DELAS COSAS MAS NOTABLES, RITOS Y COSTUMBRES, DEL GRAN REYNO DELA CHINA,... / Gonzalez de Mendoza, J – Roma, 1585 – 5mf – 9 – H-8420/1 – ne IDC [950]
LA HISTORIA DELL' IMPRESA DI TRIPOLI DI BARBARIA, ... / Ulloa, Antonio de – Venevia, 1566 – 3mf – 9 – H-8305/1 – ne IDC [960]
HISTORIA DELL' INDIE ORIENTALI, ... / Lopes de Castanheda, F – (History of Portuguese discoveries and colonization. It contains a good deal on Portuguese contacts with China) – Venetia. 2v. 1577-1578 – 20mf – 9 – H-8351/1 – ne IDC [946]
HISTORIA DELLA GVERRA FRA TVRCHI, ET PERSIANI / Minadoi, GT – Venetia, 1588 – 5mf – 9 – H-8371/1 – ne IDC [956]
HISTORIA DER BELEGERUNG VND EROBERUNG DER STATT MUENSTER ANNO 1535 – 1535. BME-159 1 – 9 – ne IDC [240]
HISTORIA DER PASSION VNSERS LIEBEN HERRN VND HEILANDS JESU / Chemnitz, Martin – N.p., 1590 – 8mf – 9 – ne IDC [240]
HISTORIA DESTRUCTIONIS TROIAE / Guido de Columnis – With an introd. to the text tradition and the iconography by Hugo Buchthal – 3 color mf & text (40p) – hb – DM410.00 – 3-89219-003-8 – gw Lengenfelder [930]
L'HISTORIA DI CASA ORSINA / Sansovino, F – O 1030 1. 1565 – 9 – ne IDC [945]
L'HISTORIA DI CASA ORSINA... / Sansovino, F – Venetia, 1565 – 9 – ne IDC [720]
HISTORIA DI ZIGHET, ISPVGNATA DA SVLIMAN, RE DE' TVRCHI, L'ANNO 1566 – Venetia, 1570 – 1mf – 9 – H-8169/1 – ne IDC [956]
HISTORIA DISPVTATIONIS SEV POTIVS COLLOQVII INTER IACOBVM COLERVM ET MATHIAM FLACIVM ILLYRICVM DE PECCATO ORIGINIS,... / Coler, J – Berlini, 1585 – 2mf – 9 – ne IDC [240]
HISTORIA DO FANATISMO RELIGIOSO NO CEARA / Montenegro, Abelardo Fernando – Fortaleza: A. Batista Fontenele, 1959. 76p. Inc. bibliog. references. 1 reel. 1188 – 1 – us U.W. Library [240]
HISTORIA DOCUMENTADA DE LA VIDA Y GLORIOSA MUERTE DE LOS PADRES ROQUE GONZALEZ DE SANTA CRUZ, ALONSO RODRIGUEZ Y JUAN DEL CASTILLO...BUENOS AIRES, 1929 / Blanco, Jose Maria – Madrid: Razon y Fe, 1930 – 1 – sp Bibl Santa Ana [240]
HISTORIA ECCLESIAE ULTRAJECTINAE / Hoynck Van Papendrecht, C P – Mechlinae, 1725 – Dfl70.00 – ne Slangenburg [240]
HISTORIA ECCLESIASTICA SIVE CHRONOGRAPHIA TRIPERTITA (CBH 19,1) / Anastasius Bibliothecaris; ed by Fabrotus, C A – Parisiis, 1649 – Dfl42.00 – ne Slangenburg [240]
HISTORIA ECLESIASTICA DE CUYO. TOMO 1. MILANO, 1931 / Verdaguer, Jose A – Madrid: Razon y Fe, 1935 – 1 – sp Bibl Santa Ana [240]
HISTORIA ECLESIASTICA DE LA CIUDAD Y OBISPADO DE BADAJOZ : PRIMERA PARTE / Solano de Figueroa y Altamirano, Juan – Badajoz, 1929; Madrid: Razon y Fe, 1931 – 1 – sp Bibl Santa Ana [240]
HISTORIA ECLESIASTICA DE LA CIUDAD Y OBISPADO DE BADAJOZ. CONTINUACION DE LA DE SOLANO DE FIGUEROA – Badajoz: Tip. Vda. de A. Arqueros, Tomo 2. 1945. Publ. de la Caja Rural de Badajoz – 1 – sp Bibl Santa Ana [240]
HISTORIA ECLESIASTICA INDIANA / Mendieta, Geronimo – (Tomo II.1870. 1.50f; 9) – Tomo I. 1870 – 9 – 1.50f – sp Bibl Santa Ana [240]
HISTORIA ET CARTULARIUM MONSTERII S. PETRI CLOUCESTRIAE (RS33) / ed by Hart, W H – (v1 1863 Dfl32.00. v2 1865 Dfl25.00. v3 1867 Dfl35.00) – ne Slangenburg [240]
HISTORIA, ETC / Diaconus, Paulus – 15th cent. Holkham mss. 459, 121, 451, 647. 11th cent., ms. 419. Holkham Hall, Norfolk, England – 1 – uk Microform Academic [760]
HISTORIA FATAL : ASANAS DE LA IGNORANCIA, GUERRA FISICA, PROESAS MEDICALES SACADAS A LAS DEL CONOSIMIENTO POR UN ENFERMO [...] – (Filmed with: Valle y Caviedes, J Guerra fisica, proezas medicales, hazanas de la ignorancia) – [1690?] – us Res Libr [946]
HISTORIA FILICUM / Smith, J – 1875 – 7 – uk Microform Academic [580]
HISTORIA FILICUM / Smith, J – London, 1875. 429 pp., 30 pls. B-5164 2 – 8 – ne IDC [580]
HISTORIA FUCORUM / Gmelin, S G – Petropoli. 1768. B-5106 2 – 8 – ne IDC [580]
HISTORIA GENERAL DE CHILE / Barros Arana, Diego – Santiago, 1884-1902. 16 v – 1 – 80.00 – us L of C Photodup [972]
HISTORIA GENERAL DE FILIPINAS. NAVAS DEL VALLE. CATALOGO DE MONUMENTOS REFERENTES A ISLAS FILIPINAS... / Pastells, Pablo – Madrid: Razon y Fe, v8. 1935 – 1 – sp Bibl Santa Ana [950]
HISTORIA GENERAL DE FILIPINAS, POR DON JOSE MONTERO Y VIDAL. INFORME / Barrantes Moreno, Vicente – Madrid: Fortanet, 1887. B.R.A.H. XI, pp. 340-344 – sp Bibl Santa Ana [950]
HISTORIA GENERAL DE LA YNDIA ORIENTAL / San Roman de Ribadeneyra, A – Valladolid, 1603 – 15mf – 9 – ne IDC [950]
HISTORIA GENERAL DE LAS INDIAS OCCIDENTALES, Y PARTICULAR DE LA GOBERNACION DE CHIAPA Y GUATEMALA TOMO 1 Y 2 / Remesal, Antonio – Guatemala, 2nd ed 1932; Madrid: Razon y Fe, 1934 – 1 – sp Bibl Santa Ana [972]
HISTORIA GENERAL DE LOS HECHOS DE LOS CASTELLANOS EN LAS ISLAS Y TIERRA FIRME DEL MAR OCEANO / Herrera, Antonio de – Madrid: Real Academia de la Historia, 1935.-v3 – 1 – sp Bibl Santa Ana [946]
HISTORIA GENERAL DE LOS HECHOS DE LOS CASTELLANOS EN LAS ISLAS Y TIERRA-FIRME DE EL MAR OCEANO / Herera, Antonio de – Asuncion de Paraguay, Editorial, 1945.-v3 – 1 – sp Bibl Santa Ana [946]
HISTORIA GENERAL DE LOS HECHOS DE LOS CASTELLANOS EN LAS ISLAS Y TIERRA-FIRME DE EL MAR OCEANO / Herrera, Antonio de – Buenos Aires: Editorial Guarania, 1945 – 1 – sp Bibl Santa Ana [946]
HISTORIA GENERAL DE LOS HECHOS DE LOS CASTELLANOS EN LAS ISLAS Y TIERRA-FIRME DEL MAR OCEANO / Herrera, Antonio de – Buenos Aires: Talleres Graficos Continental La valle, 1944.-v1 – 1 – sp Bibl Santa Ana [946]
HISTORIA GENERAL DE LOS HECHOS DE LOS CASTELLANOS EN LAS ISLAS Y TIERRAFIRME DEL MAR OCEANO / Herrera, Antonio de – Madrid: Real Academia de la Historia, 1936.-v5 – 1 – sp Bibl Santa Ana [946]
HISTORIA GENERAL DE LOS HECHOS DE LOS CASTELLANOS EN LAS ISLAS Y TIERRAFIRME DEL MAR OCEANO / Herrera, Antonio de – Madrid: Real Acedemia de la Historia, 1936.-v4 – 1 – sp Bibl Santa Ana [946]
HISTORIA GENERAL DEL DERECHO ESPANOL / Chapado Garcia, Eusebio Maria – Valladolid: Montero, 1900. 971p. LL-8005 – 1 – us L of C Photodup [340]
HISTORIA GENERAL DEL PERU / Murua, Martin, Fray – Madrid: Imp. Gongora, Libro 2. 1964 – 1 – sp Bibl Santa Ana [972]
HISTORIA GENERAL DEL PERU / Murua, Martin, Fray – Madrid: Imp. Gongora, Tomo 1. 1962 – 1 – sp Bibl Santa Ana [972]
HISTORIA GENERAL...CASTELLANOS... OCEANO / Herrera, Antonio de – (Decada Tercera. 1726. 1.50f; 9. Decada Quarta. 1736. 1.50f; BSA; 9. Decada Quinta. 1728. 1.50f; BSA; 9) – 1726. Decada segunda – 9 – 1.50f – sp Bibl Santa Ana [972]
HISTORIA GERAL DAS GUERRAS ANGOLANAS, 1680 / ed by Delgado, Jose Matias – [Lisboa]: Agencia Geral das Colonias, Divisao de Publicacaoes e Bibliteca, 1940-42 – 1 – us Res Libr [960]
HISTORIA HUNGARORUM ECCLESIASTICA : INDE AB EXORDIO NOVI TESTAMENTI AD NOSTRA USQUE TEMPORA EX MONUMENTIS PARTIM EDITIS, PARTIM VERO INEDITIS, FIDE DIGNIS / Bod, Petri; ed by Rauwenhoff, L W E – Lugduni-Batavorum: E.J. Brill, 1888-1890 – 4mf – us A.T.L.A. [240]
HISTORIA JACOBITARUM / Abudacnus, Jos. – Lugd. Batavorum, 1740 – Dfl22.00 – ne Slangenburg [240]
HISTORIA JUDAICA : A JOURNAL OF STUDIES IN JEWISH HISTORY – (Index v1-20) – New York. v1-23. 1938-61 – 85mf – 9 – ne IDC [270]
HISTORIA KHALIFATUS OMARI 2, JAZIDI 2 ET HISCHAMI / ed by Goeje, M J de – Lugduni Batavorum, 1865 – Dfl9.00 – ne Slangenburg [260]

HISTORIA LEPIDOPTERORUM AGI BONONIENSIS / Bertoloni, G - Bononiae, 1844 -49. 212p. (Novi Comment. Accad. Sci. Instit. Bonon., v.7-9). Z-1064 2 - 8 - ne IDC [590]
HISTORIA LIBERAL DEL JUEGO DEL AXEDREZ / Osuna Lara, Antonio J - Badajoz: Imprenta Diputacion Provincial, 1965 - sp Bibl Santa Ana [920]
HISTORIA LITERARIA DE ESPANA. TOMO 1 / Rodriguez Mohedano, P & Rodriguez Mohedano R - 1766 - 2mf - 9 - Pta1,500.00 - 84-7848-151-6 - sp Pentalfa [440]
HISTORIA LITERARIA DE ESPANA. TOMO 2 PARTE 1 / Rodriguez Mohedano, P & Rodriguez Mohedano R - 1768 - 1mf - 9 - Pta1,000.00 - 84-7848-152-4 - sp Pentalfa [440]
HISTORIA LITERARIA DE ESPANA. TOMO 2 PARTE 2 / Rodriguez Mohedano, P & Rodriguez Mohedano R - 1768 - 1mf - 9 - Pta1,000.00 - 84-7848-153-2 - sp Pentalfa [440]
HISTORIA LITERARIA DE ESPANA. TOMO 3 / Rodriguez Mohedano, P & Rodriguez Mohedano R - 1770 - 2mf - 9 - Pta1,500.00 - 84-7848-154-0 - sp Pentalfa [440]
HISTORIA LITERARIA DE ESPANA. TOMO 4 / Rodriguez Mohedano, P & Rodriguez Mohedano R - 1772 - 2mf - 9 - Pta1,500.00 - 84-7848-155-9 - sp Pentalfa [440]
HISTORIA LITERARIA DE ESPANA. TOMO 5 / Rodriguez Mohedano, P & Rodriguez Mohedano R - 1777 - 2mf - 9 - Pta1,500.00 - 84-7848-156-7 - sp Pentalfa [440]
HISTORIA LITERARIA DE ESPANA. TOMO 6 / Rodriguez Mohedano, P & Rodriguez Mohedano R - 1780 - 2mf - 9 - Pta1,500.00 - 84-7848-157-5 - sp Pentalfa [440]
HISTORIA LITERARIA DE ESPANA. TOMO 7 / Rodriguez Mohedano, P & Rodriguez Mohedano R - 1781 - 1mf - 9 - Pta1,000.00 - 84-7848-158-3 - sp Pentalfa [440]
HISTORIA LITERARIA DE ESPANA. TOMO 8 / Rodriguez Mohedano, P & Rodriguez Mohedano R - 1781 - 2mf - 9 - Pta1,500.00 - 84-7848-159-1 - sp Pentalfa [440]
HISTORIA LITERARIA DE ESPANA. TOMO 9 / Rodriguez Mohedano, P & Rodriguez Mohedano R - 1785 - 1mf - 9 - Pta1,000.00 - 84-7848-160-5 - sp Pentalfa [440]
LA HISTORIA MILITAR DE ESPANA / Barado, Francisco - 1893 - 9 - 1.50f - sp Bibl Santa Ana [946]
HISTORIA MILITAR DO BRASIL / Barroso, Gustavo - Sao Paulo, 1935 - 6mf - 8 - ne Slangenburg [355]
HISTORIA MISSIONORUM ORDINIS FRATRUM MINORIS 3. AMERICA SEPTENTRIONALIS. ROMA, 1968 / Barrado Manzano, Arcangel - Madrid: Graf. Calleja, 1969 - 1 - sp Bibl Santa Ana [975]
HISTORIA MISSIONUM ORDINIS FRATUM MINORUM 1. ASIA-CENTRO ORIENTALIS ET OCEANIA. ROMA, 1967 / Barrado Manzano, Arcangel - (Tambien Africa) - Madrid: Graf. Calleja, 1967 - 1 - sp Bibl Santa Ana [240]
HISTORIA MOLLUSCORUM SVECIAE TERRESTRIUM ET FLUVIATILIUM BREVITER DELINEATA / Nilsson, S - Z-685 2. 1822 - 8 - ne IDC [590]
HISTORIA MONACHORUM UND HISTORIA LAUSIACA / Reitzenstein, R - Goettingen, 1916 - Dfl22.00 - ne Slangenburg [240]
HISTORIA MONASTERII AMORBACENSIS ORD. S. BENEDICTI / Gropp, I OSB - Francofurti, 1736 - Dfl74.00 - ne Slangenburg [240]
HISTORIA MONASTERII S. AUGUSTINI CANTUARIENSIS BY THOMAS OF ELMHAM, FORMERLY MONK AND TREASURER OF THAT FOUNDATION (RS8) / Thomas Of Elmham; ed by Hardwick, C - 1858 - Dfl35.00 - ne Slangenburg [240]
HISTORIA MOSCHI, AD NORMAM ACADEMIAE NATURAE CURIOSORUM CONSCRIPTA / Schroeckius, Lucas Luc. - Augustae Vindelicorum (Augsburg), Theophilus Goebel, 1682. 12, 224, 5 p. Film Mas 8913 - 1 - us H.U. Library [500]
HISTORIA MUSCORUM / Dillen, J J - Edinburgh. 1811. B-6488 2 - 8 - ne IDC [580]
HISTORIA MUSCORUM / Dillen, J J - Oxonii. 1741 - 8 - ne IDC [580]
HISTORIA MUSCORUM: A GENERAL HISTORY OF LAND AND WATER / Dillen, J J - London. 1768. B-6487 2 - 8 - ne IDC [580]
HISTORIA MUSCORUM FRONDOSORUM / Voit, J G W - Norimbergae. 1812. B-5321 2 - 8 - ne IDC [580]
HISTORIA MUSICA / Bontempi, G A A - 1695 - 9 - us Sibley [780]
HISTORIA MVSICA, NELLA QUALE SI HA PIENA COGNITIONE DELLA TEORICA, E DELLA PRATICA ANTICA DELLA MVSICA HARMONICA / Bontempi, G A A - Pervgia. 1695. BP-646 1 - 9 - ne IDC [780]
HISTORIA NATURAL Y MEDICA DE ASTURIAS / Casal Julian, Gaspar - 1762 - 2mf - 9 - Pta1,500.00 - 84-7848-226-1 - sp Pentalfa [610]
HISTORIA NATURAL Y MEDICA DEL PRINCIPADO DE ASTURIAS / Casal, G - Madrid, 1762 - 8mf - 9 - sp Cultura [610]
HISTORIA NATURAL Y MORAL DE LAS AVES - SL, SA - 9mf - 9 - sp Cultura [500]
HISTORIA NATURALIS / Pliny - 1476. Holkham ms. 394. Holkham Hall, Norfolk, England - 14 - uk Microform Academic [760]
HISTORIA NATURALIS PALMARUM / Martius, Friedrich Philipp von - Leipzig, 1831-ca 1850 - 2r - 1 - $125.00 - us Universal [580]
HISTORIA NATURALIS PALMARUM / Martius, Karl Friedrich Philipp von - Lipsiae, 1823-1853. 350 pp., 445 pls. B-5443 2 - 8 - ne IDC [580]
HISTORIA NATURALIS RANARUM NOSTRATIUM / Roesel von Rosenhof, A J - 2138 2. 1758 - 9 - ne IDC [580]
HISTORIA NOVA, NELLA QVALE SI CONTENGONO TUTTI I SUCCESSI DELLA GUERRA TURCHESCA, LA CONGIURA DEL DUCA DE NORTSOLCH CONTRA LA REGINA D'INGHILTERRA; ... / Manolesso, E M - Padoua, 1572 - 3mf - 9 - H-8330/1 - ne IDC [956]
HISTORIA PATRIARCHARUM ALEXANDRINORUM JACOBIUARUM / Renaudot, E - Parisiis, 1713 - Dfl74.00 - ne Slangenburg [240]
HISTORIA PEREGRINA DE UN INCA ANDALUZ / ed by Bayle, Constantino - Madrid: Razon y Fe, 1927 - 1 - sp Bibl Santa Ana [910]
HISTORIA PISCIUM / Gouan, A - Z-2110 2. 1770 - 8 - ne IDC [580]
HISTORIA PISCIUM LIBRI QUATUOR / Willughby, F - 2593. 1686 - 9 - ne IDC [580]
HISTORIA PLANTARUM / Ray, J - 3v. London. 1686-1704. BM-390 2 - 8 - ne IDC [580]
HISTORIA PLANTARUM IN PALATINATU ELECTORALI / Pollich, J A - 3v. Mannheim. 1776-77. B-7133 1 - 9 - ne IDC [580]
HISTORIA PLANTARUM RARIORUM / Martyn, J - Londini, 1728. 52 pp., 50 pls. B-6056 1 - 9 - ne IDC [580]
HISTORIA PLANTARUM UNIVERSALIS / Bauhin, J & Cherler, J H - 3v. Ebroduni. Yverdon. 1650-51. B-7385 1 - 9 - ne IDC [580]
HISTORIA POLITICA DEL MOVIMIENTO OBRERO ARGENTINO (1944-1985) / Ceballos, Ernesto S - Capital Federal, Buenos Aires, Argentina: Ediciones de Mar Dulce, c1985 - 1 - CSUXADJ0049-B - us Hoover Inst Photo [320]
HISTORIA POLITICA ET PATRIARCHICA (CSHB 47) : CONSTANTINOPOLEOS EPIROTICA / ed by Bekkerus, Imm - Bonnae, 1849 - Dfl25.00 - ne Slangenburg [930]
HISTORIA QUINQU-ARTICULARIS.. / Heylyn, Peter - 1660 - 1 - us A.T.L.A. [400]
HISTORIA REI LITERARIAE O.S.B. / Ziegelbauer, M; ed by Legipontius, O - (v1 31mf; v2 26mf; v3 30mf; v4 32mf) - Augustae Vindelicorum. v1-4. 1754 - 9 - Dfl417.00 - ne Slangenburg [240]
HISTORIA RERUM A MICHAELE PALAEOLOGO (CBH 28,1) / Pachymeris, Georgii; ed by Possinus, P - Romae, 1666 - Dfl95.00 - ne Slangenburg [240]
HISTORIA RERUM AB ANDRONICO SENIORE (CBH 28,2) / Pachymeris, Georgii; ed by Possinus, P - Romae, 1669 - Dfl102.00 - ne Slangenburg [240]
HISTORIA RERUM ANGLICARUM, BK 5 (CHRONICLES..2) : ANNALES FURNESIENSES (1199-1298), A CONTINUATION OF WILLIAM OF NEWBURGH'S HISTORY TO 1298 - ETIENNE DE ROUEN, DRACO NORMANNICUS / William Of Newburg - 1885 - Dfl32.00 - ne Slangenburg [240]
HISTORIA RERUM ANGLICARUM, BKS 1-4 (CHRONICLES..1) / William Of Newburg - 1884 - Dfl30.00 - ne Slangenburg [240]
HISTORIA RERVM IN ORIENTE GESTARVM AB EXORDIO MVNDI ET ORBE CONDITO AD NOSTRA HAEC VSQVE TEMPORA - Francofvrti ad Moenvm, 1587 - 12mf - 9 - H-8220/1 - ne IDC [956]
HISTORIA SALICUM ICONIBUS ILLUSTRATA / Hoffmann, G F - 2v. Leipzig. 1785-91. B-5954 2 - 8 - ne IDC [580]
HISTORIA SCRIPTORESQUE ALII AD RES BYZANTINAS PERTINENTES (CBH 39) : PARISIIS, 1819 / Diaconi, Leonis; ed by Hase, C - Dfl53.00 - ne Slangenburg [220]
HISTORIA SECRETA DEL GABINETE DE NAPOLEON (ANNO 1811) / Goldsmith, Lewis - Santiago - 1r - 5,6 - sp Cultura [944]
HISTORIA SIVE NOTITIA EPISCOPATUS DAVENTRIENSIS / Lindeborn, J - Coloniae Agrippinae, 1670 - Dfl35.00 - ne Slangenburg [240]
HISTORIA SIVE SYNOPSIS METHODICA CONCHYLIORUM / Lister, M - Recensuit et indice. Z-216 2. 1823 - 8 - ne IDC [580]
HISTORIA SOCIAL DE CHILE / Amunategui Solar, Domingo - Madrid: Razon y Fe, 1934 - 1 - sp Bibl Santa Ana [972]
HISTORIA STIRPIUM INDIGENARUM HELVETIAE INCHOATA / Haller, Albrecht von - 3v. Bernae. 1768. B-5946 2 - 8 - ne IDC [580]
HISTORIA TEMPLARIORUM / Guertler N - Ed. 2a. Amstelaedami, 1703 - Dfl74.00 - ne Slangenburg [240]
HISTORIA THEOLOGICA-CRITICA DE VITA : ATQUE DOCTRINA SANCTORUM PATRUM / Lumper, G - Pars 1-13. Augustae Vindelicorum, 1783-1799 - 157mf - 8 - ne Slangenburg [240]
HISTORIA UNIVERSAL...GUADALUPE / San Jose, Francisco de - 1743 - 9 - 1.50f - sp Bibl Santa Ana [972]
HISTORIA UNIVERSITATIS PARISIENSIS / Bulaeus (du Boulay), Caesar Egassius - Parisiis. v1-6. 1665-1673 - 219mf - 8 - Dfl767.00 - ne Slangenburg [240]
HISTORIA UTRIUSQUE BELLI DACICI A TRAIANO CAESARE GESTI...QUAE IN COLUMNA EIUSDEM ROMAE VISUNTUR / Ciacono, A - Romae, 1616. BO-1082 1 - 9 - ne IDC [930]
HISTORIA VERDADERA DE LA CONQUISTA DE LA NUEVA ESPANA / Bayle, Constantino & Diaz del Castillo, Bernal - Madrid: Razon y Fe, 1944.-3v - 1 - sp Bibl Santa Ana [946]
HISTORIA VERDADERA DE LA CONQUISTA DE LA NUEVA ESPANA / Diaz del Castillo, Bernal - Madrid: Espasa-Calpe, S.A., 1928.-v1 - 1 - sp Bibl Santa Ana [946]
HISTORIA VERDADERA DE LA CONQUISTA DE LA NUEVA ESPANA / Diaz del Castillo, Bernal - Mexico: Editorial Pedro Robledo, 1944.-v2 - sp Bibl Santa Ana [946]
HISTORIA VERDADERA DE LA CONQUISTA DE LA NUEVA ESPANA / Diaz del Castillo, Bernal - Mexico: oficina Tipografica de la Secretaria de Fomento, 1904.-v1 - sp Bibl Santa Ana [946]
HISTORIA VERDADERA DE LA CONQUISTA DE LA NUEVA ESPANA / Diaz del Castillo, Bernal - Mexico: Porrua, 1969 - 1 - sp Bibl Santa Ana [946]
HISTORIA VERDADERA DE LA CONQUISTA DE LA NUEVA ESPANA... / Diaz del Castillo, Bernal - Madrid: Espasa-Calpe, 1928.-v2 - sp Bibl Santa Ana [946]
HISTORIA VERDADERA DE LA CONQUISTA DE LA NUEVA ESPANA... / Diaz del Castillo, Bernal - Madrid: Imprenta Talleres de Silverio Aquirre, 1940 - sp Bibl Santa Ana [946]
HISTORIA VERDADERA DE LA CONQUISTA DE LA NUEVA ESPANA. UNICA EDICION HECHA SEGUN EL CODICE AUTOGRAFO / Diaz del Castillo, Bernal - Mexico: Oficina Tip. de la Secretaria de Fomento, 1904.-v2 - sp Bibl Santa Ana [946]
HISTORIA VERDADERA DE LA CONQUISTA DE NUEVA ESPANA / Diaz del Castillo, Bernal - Mexico: Editorial Pedro Robledo, 1944.-v1 - sp Bibl Santa Ana [946]
LA HISTORIA, VERDADERA ENSENANZA EN LOS CAMINOS DE LA RURA DE ESPANA / Munoz Gallardo, Juan Antonio - Badajoz: Imp. de la Diputacion Prov., 1974. Sep. Rev. Estu. Extremenos - 1 - sp Bibl Santa Ana [946]
HISTORIA VITAE, DOCTRINAE, AC RERUM GESTARUM DAVIDIS GEORGII HAERESIARCHAE / Blesdijk, Nicolaas M van - Ed. by J. Revius. Daventriae, N. Costius. 1642. BME-391 1 - 9 - ne IDC [240]
HISTORIA VNIVERSALE DELL' ORIGINE, ET IMPERIO DE' TVRCHI, ... / Sansovino, F - Venetia, 1573 - 11mf - 9 - H-8341/1 - ne IDC [956]
HISTORIA VON DAVID GEOERGEN, EINEM HEILLOSEN MANN VND GOTTESLAESTERLICHEN ERTZ-KETZER / Stolterfoht, J - Luebeck, M. Janovius. 1635. BME-413 1 - 9 - ne IDC [240]
HISTORIA VON DES BERUFFENEN ERTZ-KAETZERS DAVID JORIS ODER GEORGI, LEHR UND LEBEN - 1713. BME-418 1 - 9 - ne IDC [240]
HISTORIA WESTFALIA : OPUS POSTHUMUM / Schaten, N S J - Neuhussi, 1690 - Dfl102.00 - ne Slangenburg [240]
HISTORIA Y SOCIEDAD - Mexico City, MX. 1974-1978 - 3r - $150.00 - R04222 - us Library Micro [320]
HISTORIA...CASTELLANOS EN LAS ISLAS... OCEANO / Herrera, Antonio de - (Decada Primera. 1601. 1.50f; 9. Decada Segunda. 1601. 1.50f; BSA; 9. Decada Tercera. 1601. 1.50f; BSA; 9. Decada Quarta. 1601. 1.50f; BSA; 9. Decada Quinta. 1728. 1.50f; BSA; 9. Decada Sesta. 1736. 1.50f; BSA; 9. Decada Septima. 1730. 1.50f; BSA; 9) - 1736 - 9 - 1.50f - sp Bibl Santa Ana [972]
HISTORIA...COMARCA DE LA SERENA...CABEZA DEL BUEY / Perez Jimenez, Nicolas - 1889 - 9 - 1.50f - sp Bibl Santa Ana [946]
HISTORIA...CRUZ DEL CASAR DE PALOMERO / Martin Santivanez, Romualdo - 1870 - 9 - 1.50f - sp Bibl Santa Ana [946]
HISTORIA...DE LA ESCANDALOSA NEGOCIACION DEL TRATADO DEL CANAL DE PANAMA / Bunau-Varilla, P - Panama, 1930 - 2mf - 1 - ILM-2437/1 - ne IDC [327]
HISTORIA...DE LOS ANGELES / Guadelupe, Andres - 1662 - 9 - 1.50f - sp Bibl Santa Ana [240]
HISTORIA...DE MEDELLIN / Solano de Figueroa y Altamirano, Juan - 1650 - 9 - 1.50f - sp Bibl Santa Ana [946]
HISTORIA...DEL CASTANAR...BEJAR / Yague, Francisco - 1795 - 9 - 1.50f - sp Bibl Santa Ana [946]
UN HISTORIADOR MODERNO DE LA TIERRA DE LA SERENA (D. NICOLAS PEREZ JIMENEZ) / Barrantes Moreno, Vicente - Madrid: Fortanet, 1890. B.R.A.H. 17, pp. 481-492 - sp Bibl Santa Ana [946]
HISTORIAE / Herodotus - 15th cent. Holkham ms. 440. Holkham Hall, Norfolk, England - 1 - uk Microform Academic [900]
HISTORIAE / Orosius - 1370. Holkham ms. 370. Holkham Hall, Norfolk, England - 1 - uk Microform Academic [760]
HISTORIAE AEVI SALICI (MGH 5: 11.BD) - 1854 - Dfl67.00 - ne Slangenburg [240]
HISTORIAE AEVI SALICI (MGH 5: 12.BD) - 1856 - Dfl88.00 - ne Slangenburg [240]
HISTORIAE ANIMALIUM / Gesner, C - 5v. 1551-87. B-8316 1 - 9 - ne IDC [590]
HISTORIAE AVIUM PRODROMUS / Klein, J T - Z 1816. 1750 - 9 - ne IDC [590]
HISTORIAE COELESTIS BRITANNICAE.. / Flamsteed, John - Londini: Typis H. Meere, 1725 - 1 - us U.W. Library [520]
HISTORIAE DE BELLO NVPER VENETIS A SELIMO 2. TVRCARVM IMPERATORE ILLATO, LIBER VNVS, EX ITALICO SERMONE IN LATINUM CONUERSUS, ... / Contarini, G P - Basileae, 1573 - 2mf - 9 - H-8339/1 - ne IDC [956]
HISTORIAE DE REBUS HISPANIAE LIBRI TRIGINTA. ACCENDUNT JOSEPHI EMMANUELIS MINIANAE.. / Mariana, Juan de - 1733. SEM35P228 - 1r - 1 - Can$63.00 - cn Bibl Nat [946]

HISTORIAE FRANCORUM SCRIPTORES COAETANEI / Duchesne, Andre – Lutetiae Parisiorum, 1636-49. SEM35P265 – 3r – 1 – Can$155.00 – cn Bibl Nat [944]

HISTORIAE GENUENSIUM LIBRI 12 / Foglietta, U – Genvae, 1585 – 12mf – 9 – H-8419/1 – ne IDC [956]

HISTORIAE HUSITARUM / Cochlaeus, J – S Victor, 1549 – 16mf – 8 – Dfl56.00 – ne Slangenburg [240]

HISTORIAE INSECTORUM LIBELLUS QUI EST DE SCORPIONE / Gesner, C – Tiguria, 1587 – 1mf – 9 – sp Cultura [590]

HISTORIAE LIBRI TRES, AB AUTORE INNUMERIS LOCIS EMENDATI ATQUE EXPOLITI. IN QVIBVS SARRACENORUM, TURCARUM, ALIARUMQUE; GENITUM ORIGINES ET RES PER ANNOS SEPTIN GENTOS GESTAE, CONTINENTUR / Curio, C A – Basileae, 1568 – 6mf – 9 – H-8308/1 – ne IDC [956]

HISTORIAE LIBRI X ET LIBER DE VELITATIONE BELLICA NICEPHORI AUGUSTI E REC. CAR. BEN. HASII (CSHB 5) : ADDITA EJUSDEM VERSIONE ATQUE ANNOTATIONIBUS AB IPSO RECOGNITIS. ACCEDUNT THEODOSII ACROASES, DE CRETA CAPTA E REC. FR. JACOBSII ET LUITPRANDI, LEGATIO CUM ALIIS LIBELLIS, QUI NICEPHORI PHOCAE / Caloensis. Leonis Diaconi – lo. Tzimiscis Historiam Illustrant. Bonnae, 1828 – Dfl42.00 – ne Slangenburg [240]

HISTORIAE MUSCORUM HEPATICORUM PRODROMUS / Schwaegrichen, C F – Lipsiae. 1814. B-2329 2 – 8 – ne IDC [580]

HISTORIAE MUSCORUM HEPATICORUM PRODROMUS / Weber, F – Kiliae. 1815. B-2330 2 – 8 – ne IDC [580]

HISTORIAE MVSVLMANAE TVRCORVM, DE MONVMENTIS IPSORVM EXSCRIPTAE, LIBRI 18 / Leunclavius, J – Francofvrti, 1591 – 10mf – 9 – H-8376/1 – ne IDC [956]

HISTORIAE SIVE SYNOPSIS METHODICAE CONCHYLIORUM / Lister, M – Z-215 2. 4 v. 1685-1688 – 8 – ne IDC [590]

HISTORIA...ESPANA...BADAJOZ / Romero Morera, Joaquin – 1878 – 9 – 1.50f – sp Bibl Santa Ana [946]

HISTORIA...FRAMONTANOS CELTIVEROS / Paredes Guillen, Vicente – 1888 – 9 – 1.50f – sp Bibl Santa Ana [946]

HISTORIA...GUADALUPE / Gabriel de Talavera, Fray – 1597 – 9 – 1.50f – sp Bibl Santa Ana [946]

HISTORIA...GUADALUPE / Malagon, Joan – 1672 – 9 – 1.50f – sp Bibl Santa Ana [972]

HISTORIA...GUADALUPE / Talavera, Fr. Gabriel – 1597 – 9 – 1.50f – sp Bibl Santa Ana [972]

HISTORIA...INDIANA / Mendieta, Geronimo – 1870 – 9 – 1.50f – sp Bibl Santa Ana [978]

HISTORIA...INDIAS OCCIDENTALES / Herrera, Antonio de – (Tomo II.1728. 1.50f; 9. Tomo IV.1728. 1.50f; BSA; 9) – Tomo I. 1728 – 9 – 1.50f – sp Bibl Santa Ana [972]

HISTORIA...INDIAS...MAR OCEANO / Fernandez de Oviedo Valdes, Gonzalo – 1851-53, 1865. 4v – 9 – 1.50f – sp Bibl Santa Ana [972]

HISTORIA...INDIE...OCCIDENTALI / Lopez de Gomara, Francisco – 1564 – 9 – 1.50f – sp Bibl Santa Ana [972]

HISTORIA...JAPON / Orfanel, Jacinto – 1633 – 9 – 1.50f – sp Bibl Santa Ana [950]

HISTORIAL DE FISTAS Y DONATIVOS, INDICE DE CABALLEROS Y REGLAMENTO DE UNIFORMIDAD DE LA REAL MAESTRANZA DE CABALLERIA DE SEVILLA, POR DON PEDRO LEON Y MANJON / T'Serclaes, Duque de – Madrid: Fortanet, 1910. B.R.A.H. 56, 1910, pp. 437-439 – sp Bibl Santa Ana [390]

HISTORIAL GENEALOGICO DEL LIBERTADOR / Sucre, Luis Alberto – Caracas, 2nd ed 1930; Madrid: Razon y Fe, 1932 – 1 – sp Bibl Santa Ana [920]

HISTORIALE DESCRIPTION DE L'AFRIQUE, TIERCE PARTIE DU MONDE, CONTENANT SES ROYAUMES, REGIONS, VILLES, CITEZ / Leon L'Africain, Hasan ibm Mohammed al-Wassan al-Fasi (dit Jean) – Anvers, Christophle Plantin. 1556 – 9 – 25.00 – fr Orientalistes [960]

HISTORIALE DESCRIPTION DE L'ETHIOPIE CONTENANT LA VRAIE RELATION DES TERRES ET PAYS DU GRAND ROI ET EMPEREUR PRETE-IAN, L'ASSIETTE DE SES ROYAUMES ET PROVINCES, LEURS COUTUMES, LOIS ET RELIGION / Alvarez, Francois – (African Library series). 1558 – 9 – fr Hachette [960]

HISTORIAM NOVARUM LEGUM DE FLUMINUM COMMUNIUM NAVIGATIONE / Bergh, I L C van den – Lugduni Batavorum, 1835 – 2mf – 9 – ILM-1071/1 – ne IDC [327]

HISTORIA...MEJICO...HERNANDO CORTES / Prescott, Guillermo H – (v1-3. 1847 ed. 1.50f; 9. v4. 1850 ed. 1.50f; BSA; 9) – v1-2. 1844 – 9 – 1.50f – sp Bibl Santa Ana [972]

HISTORIA...MEJICO...NUEVA ESPANA / Solis Rivadeneyra, Antonio de – (1851. 1.50f; 9. 1843. 1.50f; BSA; 9. 1885. 1.50f; BSA; 9) – 1766 – 9 – 1.50f – sp Bibl Santa Ana [972]

HISTORIA...MERIDA / Moreno de Vargas, Bernabe – (1892 ed.1.50f; 9) – 1633 – 9 – 1.50f – sp Bibl Santa Ana [946]

HISTORIA...MONTACHEZ / Lozano Rubio, Tirso – 1894 – 9 – 1.50f – sp Bibl Santa Ana [900]

HISTORIAN – Springfield OR. Apr 20 27 1966 – 1 – us U.O. Library [071]

HISTORIAN; A JOURNAL OF HISTORY – v. 1- 1938- – 1. ; 5,6. ; 9 – apply; v.33-; v.39- – us UMI [900]

HISTORIANS IN TROPICAL AFRICA : PROCEEDINGS OF THE LEVERHULME INTER-COLLEGAITE HISTORY CONFERENCE, SEPTEMBER 1930 – Salisbury, Southern Rhodesia: The College, 1962 – us Res Libr [960]

THE HISTORIANS OF THE CHURCH OF YORK AND ITS ARCHBISHOPS (RS71) / ed by Raine, J – (v1 1879 Dfl39.00. v2 1886 Dfl35.00. v3 1894 Dfl30.00) – ne Slangenburg [240]

HISTORIA...PERU...INCAS / Lasso de la Vega, Garcia – (Tomo XIII. 1801. 1.50f; 9) – Tomos I-XII. 1800 – 9 – 1.50f – sp Bibl Santa Ana [972]

HISTORIARUM INDICARUM LIBRI 16 / Maffei, G P – Coloniae Agrippinae, 1589 – 16mf – 9 – ne IDC [950]

HISTORIARUM LIBRI 4 (CBH 17) / Cantacuzeni, Ioannis; ed by Pontanus, J – Parisiis, 1645 – Dfl175.00 – ne Slangenburg [240]

HISTORIARUM LIBRI 5 (CSHB 1) : CUM VERSIONE LATINA ET ANNOTATIONIBUS B. VULCANI. B.G. NIEBUHRIUS GRAECA RECENSUIT. ACCEDUNT AGATHIAE EPIGRAMMATA / Myrinaei, Agathiae – Bonnae, 1828 – Dfl308.00 – ne Slangenburg [240]

HISTORIARUM LIBRI 8 (CBH 2,1) / Simocattae, Theophylacti; ed by Pontanus, J – Parisiis, 1648 – Dfl46.00 – ne Slangenburg [240]

HISTORIARUM LIBRI 8 (CSHB 22) : GENESIUS, REC. C. LACHMANNUS / Simocattae, Theophylacti; ed by Bekkerus, Imm – Bonnae, 1834 – Dfl39.00 – ne Slangenburg [240]

HISTORIARUM LIBRI DECEM DE REBUS TURCICIS (CBH 16) / Chalcocondylae, Laonici – Parisiis, 1650 – Dfl81.00 – ne Slangenburg [240]

HISTORIARUM QUAE SUPERSUNT (CSHB 14) : ACCEDUNT ECLOGAE PHOTII EX OLYMPIODORO, CANDIDO, NONNOSO ET THEOPHANE, ET PROCOPII SOPHISTAE PANEGYRICUS, GRAECE ET LATINE, PRISCIANI PANEGYRICUS, ANNOTATIONES H. VALESII, LABBEI ET VILLOISONIS, ET INDICES CLASSENI / Dexippi et al; ed by Bekkeri, Imm & Niebuhrii, B G – Bonnae, 1829 – Dfl42.00 – ne Slangenburg [240]

HISTORIARUM SUI TEMPORIS AB ANNO DOMINI 1543 USQUE AD ANNUM 1607 LIBRI 138 / Thuanus, Iac. Aug. – Francofurti. Tomus 1-4. 1625-1628 – 167mf – 8 – ne Slangenburg [240]

HISTORIARUM SUI TEMPORIS LIBRI 8 (CBH 3,1) / Caesariensis, Procopii; ed by Maltret, C L – Parisiis, 1662 – Dfl102.00 – ne Slangenburg [930]

HISTORIAS DE MERIDA / Madrazo, Pedro de – Madrid: Tip. Fortanet, 1895 – 1 – sp Bibl Santa Ana [946]

LAS HISTORIAS DEL ORIGEN DE LAS INDIAS DE ESTA PROVINCIA DE GUATEMALA / ed by Bayle, Constantino – Madrid: Razon y Fe, 1926 – 1 – sp Bibl Santa Ana [972]

HISTORIAS DEL PERONISMO / ed by Real, J C Martini et al – Buenos Aires: Corregidor, 1973 – 1 – CSUXAJA8025-B – us Hoover Inst Photo [320]

HISTORIAS INFANTILES – 1960. 100p – 1 – $5.00 – us Baptist [240]

LAS HISTORIAS Y LOS HISTORIADORES DE SEVILLA / Perez de Guzman, Juan – 1892 – 9 – $1.50f – sp Bibl Santa Ana [946]

HISTORIAS...MERIDA / Fernandez y Perez, Gregorio – (1857 ed.1.50f; 9) – 1893 – 9 – 1.50f – sp Bibl Santa Ana [946]

HISTORIC AMERICAN BUILDINGS SURVEY / U.S. Library of Congress – Collection of measured drawings for 50 states, Puerto Rico, Virgin Islands, Canal Zone, and District of Columbia. 1933-74 – 1 – 1,160.00 – us L of C Photodup [978]

HISTORIC AMERICAN BUILDINGS SURVEY / Washington, DC. Library of Congress. Prints and Photographs Division – (Coll consists of photos, text & drawings describing nearly 35,000 historically significant sites and structures. Pts also listed separately. Also available by state) – 2pts – 4287mf – 9 – £13,620.00 coll – uk Chadwyck [720]

HISTORIC AMERICAN BUILDINGS SURVEY, PT 1 : 1933-1979 – (Describes 20,000 sites and structures. Contains 45,000 photographs) – 1567mf – 9 – £5,390.00 – uk Chadwyck [720]

HISTORIC AMERICAN BUILDINGS SURVEY, PT 2 : 1980-1988 – (Lists 13,000 additional sites and structures, and all measured architectural drawings for pt1 as well as pt2) – 2720mf – 9 – £9,460.00 – uk Chadwyck [720]

HISTORIC AMERICAN ENGINEERING RECORD (HAER) / National Park Service et al – (Contains over 24,000 photographs and more than 20,000 pages documenting 1,827 structures throughout America) – 870mf – 9 – £3,310.00 – uk Chadwyck [620]

HISTORIC AND MUNICIPAL DOCUMENTS, IRELAND, A.D. 1172-1320 (RS53) : FROM THE ARCHIVES OF THE CITY OF DUBLIN, ETC / ed by Gilbert, John Th – 1870 – Dfl39.00 – ne Slangenburg [941]

HISTORIC ASPECTS OF THE...ARGUMENT CONCERNING THE BEING...OF GOD: FOUR LECTURES / Cazenove, John Gibson – London: Macmillan, 1886.1 fiche – 9 – us A.T.L.A. [240]

HISTORIC BUILDINGS IN BRITAIN : ENGLAND, SCOTLAND AND WALES / Great Britain. Royal Commissions on Ancient and Historical Monuments and Constructions – (England 179mf £1,130; Scotland 102mf £640; Wales 52mf £380. Inventories are available by country and by certain counties and cities within each country. Also listed individually) – 333mf – 9 – £1,470.00 – uk Chadwyck [720]

HISTORIC BUILDINGS IN BRITAIN. INVENTORY : ENGLAND / Great Britain. Royal Commissions on Ancient and Historical Monuments and Constructions – (Buckinghamshire 14mf £117.00. Cambridgeshire 10mf £84.00. City of Cambridge 13mf £110.00. Dorset 33mf £280.00. Essex 24mf £200.00. Herefordshire 18mf £150.00. Hertfordshire 1910 5mf £42.00. Huntingdonshire 1926 6mf £50.00. London 25mf £210.00. Middlesex 1937 5mf £42.00; City of Oxford 1939 6mf £50.00. Westmoreland 1936 6mf £50.00. City of York 14mf £120.00) – 179mf – 9 – £1,130.00 – uk Chadwyck [930]

HISTORIC BUILDINGS IN BRITAIN. INVENTORY : SCOTLAND / Great Britain. Royal Commissions on Ancient and Historical Monuments and Constructions – (Argyll 11mf £92.00. County of Berwick 1915 (revised issue) 4mf £34.00. Caithness 1911 4mf £34.00. County of Dumfries 5mf £42.00. East Lothian 1924 4mf £34.00. City of Edinburgh 1951 6mf £50.00. Fife, Kinross and Clackmannan 1933 7mf £60.00. Galloway 10mf £84.00. Midlothian and West Lothian 1929 5mf £42.00. Orkney and Shetland 11mf £92.00. Outer Hebrides, Skye and the Small Isles 1928 5mf £42.00. Peeblesshire 7mf £60.00. Roxburghshire 8mf £67.00. Selkirkshire 1957 3mf £25.00. Stirlingshire 9mf £75.00. Sutherland 1911 3mf £25.00.) – 102mf – 9 – £640.00 – uk Chadwyck [930]

HISTORIC CANADIAN GROUND: THE LA SALLE HOMESTEAD OF 1666 AND OTHER OLD LANDMARKS OF FRENCH CANADA ON THE LOWER LACHINE ROAD / Fraser, John – By the author of Canadian pen and ink sketches. Montreal?: s.n., 1892 (Montreal: Witness). 03178. (Pre-1900 Canadiana) – 9 – cn C.I.H.M. [971]

HISTORIC CITY OF NARA : AN ARCHAEOLOGICAL APPROACH / Tsuboi, Kiyotari & Tanaka, Migaku – 1992 – 150p – 9 – 92-3-102627-5 – Co-published with the Centre for East Asian Cultural Studies, Tokyo – fr UNESCO [930]

HISTORIC CITY OF TAXILA / Dani, Ahmad Hasan – 1987 – 9 – 92-3-102361-6 – Co-publication with the Centre for East Asian Cultural Studies. The Centre has exclusive sales rights in Japan. Unesco has exlusive sales rights in the UK and USA – fr UNESCO [910]

HISTORIC CRIMES AND CRIMINALS / Finger, Charles Joseph – Girard, Kansas: Halderman-Julius Company, (c1922) – 1 – us U.W. Library [360]

THE HISTORIC EPISCOPATE : AN ESSAY ON THE FOUR ARTICLES OF CHURCH UNITY PROPOSED BY THE AMERICAN HOUSE OF BISHOPS AND THE LAMBETH CONFERENCE / Shields, Charles Woodruff – New York: Scribner, 1894 – 1mf – us A.T.L.A. [240]

THE HISTORIC EPISCOPATE / Thompson, Robert Ellis – Philadelphia: Westminster, 1910 – 1mf – us A.T.L.A. [240]

THE HISTORIC EVIDENCE OF THE AUTHORSHIP AND TRANSMISSION OF THE BOOKS OF THE NEW TESTAMENT : A LECTURE / Tregelles, Samuel Prideaux – 2nd ed. London:Samuel Bagster, 1881 – 1mf – 9 – 0-8370-5567-9 – 1985-3567 – us A.T.L.A. [220]

THE HISTORIC EXODUS / Toffteen, Olof Alfred – Chicago: University of Chicago Press, 1909. 1 fiche – 9 – us A.T.L.A. [240]

HISTORIC FAMILIES OF KENTUCKY – By Thomas Marshall Green, 1964. Orig. publ. 1889. Indexed. 5 fiches. F-1095 – 9 – us A.G.L.L. [920]

THE HISTORIC GARRISON AT ANNAPOLIS ROYAL: SOME OF ITS EARLY HISTORY AS TOLD BY ANDREW GILMORE: THE LAST BRITISH SOLDIER THAT STOOD SENTRY ON THE OLD GARRISON GATE / Gilmore, Andrew – (Annapolis N.S.: Spectator, 1894. 05571. (Pre-1900 Canadiana) – 9 – cn C.I.H.M. [971]

THE HISTORIC GARRISON AT ANNAPOLIS ROYAL: SOME OF ITS EARLY HISTORY AS TOLD BY ONE OF ITS DEFENDERS / Gilmore, Andrew – Comp. by J. Herbert Runciman. (Annapolis, N.S.: W. Banks, 1886). 05572.(Pre-1900 Canadiana) – 9 – cn C.I.H.M. [971]

HISTORIC HOMES AND INSTITUTIONS AND GENEALOGICAL AND PERSON MEMOIRS OF WORCESTER COUNTY / Crane, Ellery B; ed by Crane, Ellery B – New York, Lewis Publ. Co., 1907. Vols. 1-2, Massachusetts Reel 7; Vols. 3-4, Massachusetts Reel 8. (The Cox Library Collection) – 5 – us Americana [978]

HISTORIC MANUAL OF THE REFORMED CHURCH IN THE UNITED STATES / Dubbs, Joseph Henry – Lancaster, Pa.: [s.n.], 1885 (Lancaster: Inquirer) – 1mf – us A.T.L.A. [240]

HISTORIC MORGAN AND CLASSIC JACKSONVILLE / Eames, Charles M – Historical and biographical sketches. Jacksonville: Daily Journal Steam Job Printing, 1885. Illinois Reel 47. (The Cox Library Collection) – 5 – us Americana [978]

HISTORIC ORIGIN OF THE BIBLE / Bissell, Edwin Cone – New York: A.D.F. Randolph, 1899.1 fiche – 9 – us A.T.L.A. [220]

HISTORIC PROOF OF THE DOCTRINAL CALVINISM OF THE CHURCH OF ENGLAND,... : 1. A BRIEF ACCOUNT OF SOME EMINENT PERSONS FAMOUS FOR THEIR ADOPTION OF THAT SYSTEM,...2. AN INCIDENTAL REVIEW OF THE RISE AND PROGRESS OF ARMINIANISM IN ENGLAND,... / Toplady, Augustus Montague – London, 1774.-2v – 9mf – 9 – MP-493/1 – ne IDC [240]

HISTORIC QUEBEC – Chateau Frontenac Co., 1894. 00585. (Pre-1900 Canadiana) – 9 – cn C.I.H.M. [971]

Historic Record Co *see*
- HISTORY OF CONTRA COSTA COUNTY
- HISTORY OF FRESNO COUNTY
- HISTORY OF SAN JOAQUIN COUNTY
- HISTORY OF SANTA CLARA COUNTY

- HISTORY OF SOLANO AND NAPA COUNTIES
- HISTORY OF TULARE AND KINGS COUNTIES, CALIFORNIA
- HISTORY OF YUBA AND SUTTER COUNTIES
- SAN LUIS OBISPO COUNTY AND ENVIRONS

HISTORIC SKETCHES OF FREE METHODISM / Kirsop, J – London, 1885. 113p – 2mf – 9 – ne IDC [240]

HISTORIC SOCIETY OF LANCASHIRE AND CHESHIRE – (Coll title: Publications of the English Record Societies, 1835-1972...) – v1-124. 1848-1972 – 423mf – 9 – £2,220.00 – uk Chadwyck [941]

HISTORIC STUDIES IN VAUD, BERNE, AND SAVOY; FROM ROMAN TIMES TO VOLTAIRE, ROUSSEAU, AND GIBBON / Read, John Meredith – With illus. London: Chatto & Windus, 1897. 2v.31 plates – 1 – us U.W. Library [900]

HISTORIC VIEW OF THE NEW TESTAMENT / Gardner, Percy – London: A.&C. Black, 1901. 1 fiche – 9 – us A.T.L.A. [240]

HISTORICA MONUMENTA ORDINIS S. HIERONYMI CONGREGATIONIS B. PETRI DE PISIS / Sajanello, J -B – Ed. 2a. Venetiis. v1-3. 1758-1762 – Dfl284.00 – ne Slangenburg [240]

HISTORICA NARRATIO PROFECTIONIS ET INAUGURATIONIS SERENISSIMORUM / Bochius, I – Antverpiae, 1602. BO-161 1 – 9 – ne IDC [760]

HISTORICAE RELATIONIS CONTINVATIO / Francus, I – N.p., 1593 – 2mf – 9 – H-8377/1 ne IDC [956]

A HISTORICAL ACCOUNT OF CHRIST CHURCH, BOSTON: AN ADDRESS, DELIVERED ON THE ONE HUNDRED AND FIFTIETH ANNIVERSARY OF THE OPENING OF THE CHURCH, DECEMBER 29TH, 1873 / Burroughs, Henry – Boston: A. Williams, 1874. 02008. (Pre-1900 Canadiana) – 9 – cn C.I.H.M. [978]

HISTORICAL ACCOUNT OF SOME OF THE MORE IMPORTANT VERSIONS AND EDITIONS OF THE BIBLE / Darling, Charles William – New York, 1894. 173p – 1 – us U.W. Library [240]

AN HISTORICAL ACCOUNT OF THE BRITISH ARMY AND OF THE LAW MILITARY... / Samuel, E – London, William Clowes, 1816 – 8mf – 9 – $12.00 – LLMC 89-022 – us L.L.M.C. [340]

AN HISTORICAL ACCOUNT OF THE RISE AND DEVELOPMENT OF PRESBYTERIANISM IN SCOTLAND / Burleigh, Lord Balfour of – Cambridge: University Press; New York: G.P. Putnam [distributor], 1911. (The Cambridge manuals of science and literature) – 1mf – us A.T.L.A. [240]

HISTORICAL ACCOUNT OF THE WORK OF THE AMERICAN COMMITTEE OF REVISION OF THE AUTHORIZED ENGLISH VERSION OF THE BIBLE : PREPARED FROM THE DOCUMENTS AND CORRESPONDENCE OF THE COMMITTEE / American Revision Committee – NY: Charles Scribner, 1885 – 1mf – 9 – 0-8370-2088-3 – 1985-0088 – us A.T.L.A. [220]

HISTORICAL AND BIOGRAPHICAL ALBUM OF THE CHIPPEWA VALLEY / Forrester, George – Chicago: A. Warner Publisher, 1891-1892. Wisconsin Reel 4. (The Cox Library Collection) – 5 – us Americana [978]

HISTORICAL AND BIOGRAPHICAL ANNALS OF BERKS COUNTY / Montgomery, Morton L – Chicago, J. H. Beers and Co., 1909. Vols. 1-2, Pennsylvania Reel 11. (The Cox Library Collection) – 5 – us Americana [978]

HISTORICAL AND BIOGRAPHICAL RECORD OF BLACK HAWK COUNTY / Inter-State Publishing Co – Chicago, 1886. Iowa Reel 6. The Cox Library Collection – 5 – us Americana [978]

HISTORICAL AND BIOGRAPHICAL RECORD OF DOUGLAS COUNTY / Gresham, J – Logansport: Wilson, Humphreys and Co., 1900. Illinois Reel 23. (The Cox Library Collection) – 5 – us Americana [978]

HISTORICAL AND BIOGRAPHICAL RECORD OF HOWARD AND TIPTON COUNTIES / Blanchard, Charles – Chicago: F. A. Battey and Co., 1883. Indiana Reel 16. (The Cox Library Collection) – 5 – us Americana [978]

HISTORICAL AND BIOGRAPHICAL RECORD OF LENAWEE COUNTY / Whitney & Bonner, Richard I – Adrian: Willard Stearns, 1880. Michigan Reel 16. (The Cox Library Collection) – 5 – us Americana [978]

HISTORICAL AND BIOGRAPHICAL RECORD OF MONMOUTH AND WARREN COUNTIES / Robinson, Luther E – Chicago: Munsell Publ. Co., 1927. Vols. 1-2. Illinois Reel 59. (The Cox Library Collection) – 5 – us Americana [978]

HISTORICAL AND BIOGRAPHICAL RECORD OF SOUTHERN CALIFORNIA / Guinn, J M – Chicago: Chapman Publ. Co., 1902. California Reel 7. (The Cox Library Collection) – 5 – us Americana [978]

HISTORICAL AND BIOGRAPHICAL RECORD OF THE CATTLE INDUSTRY AND THE CATTLEMEN OF TEXAS AND ADJACENT TERRITORY / Cox, James – 1 – 13.82 – us Baptist [920]

HISTORICAL AND BIOGRAPHICAL SKETCHES, KENTUCKY, 1882-1888 – With particular coverage of Bourbon, Christian, Fayette, Harrison, Scott, Todd and Trigg Counties, with an index of many more by Bailey F. Davis. Perrin ed – 1 – 195.23 – us Baptist [240]

HISTORICAL AND BIOGRAPHICAL STATISTICAL RECORD OF GRATIOT COUNTY / Tucker, Willard D – Saginaw: Seeman and Peters, 1913. Michigan Reel 11. (The cox Library Collection) – 5 – us Americana [978]

HISTORICAL AND BIOGRAPHICAL WORKS / Strype, John – 24 v. 1812-24 – 1 – us A.T.L.A. [240]

HISTORICAL AND CONTEMPORARY REVIEW OF BENCH AND BAR IN CALIFORNIA. MARCH, 1926 / The Recorder. San Francisco – San Francisco, The Recorder 1926. 61p. LL-1681 – 1 – us L of C Photodup [340]

HISTORICAL AND DESCRIPTIVE ACCOUNT OF THE ISLAND OF CAPE BRETON: AND OF ITS MEMORIALS OF THE FRENCH REGIME: WITH BIBLIOGRAPHICAL, HISTORICAL AND CRITICAL NOTES / Bourinot, John George – Montreal: W. Foster Brown, 1892. 00191. (Pre-1900 Canadiana) – 9 – cn C.I.H.M. [971]

AN HISTORICAL AND DESCRIPTIVE ACCOUNT OF THE KACHARI TRIBES IN THE NORTH CACHAR HILLS / Soppitt, C A – Shillong. 1885. (Reprinted 1901). BSE-73 2 – 8 – ne IDC [950]

HISTORICAL AND DESCRIPTIVE SKETCHBOOK OF NAPA, SONOMA, LAKE AND MENDOCINO / Menefee, C A – Napa City: Reporter Publ. House, 1873. California Reel 20. (The Cox Library Collection) – 5 – us Americana [978]

AN HISTORICAL AND GEOGRAPHICAL MEMOIR OF THE NORTH-AMERICAN CONTINENT, ITS NATIONS AND TRIBES / Gordon, James B – Dublin: Printed for John Jones, 1820. SEM35P65 – 1r – 1 – Can$18.00 – cn Bibl Nat [970]

THE HISTORICAL AND RELIGIOUS VALUE OF THE FOURTH GOSPEL / Scott, Ernest Findlay – Boston: Pilgrim Press, 1909. 1 fiche – 9 – us A.T.L.A. [240]

HISTORICAL AND SOCIOCULTURAL RELATIONS BETWEEN BLACK AFRICA AND THE ARAB WORLD FROM 1935 TO THE PRESENT – 1984 – 9 – 92-3-102161-3 – fr UNESCO [960]

HISTORICAL ATLAS AND CHRONOLOGY OF THE LIFE OF JESUS CHRIST : A TEXT BOOK AND COMPANION TO A HARMONY OF THE GOSPELS / Hodge, Richard Morse – Wytheville, VA:D.A. St. Clair Press, 1899 – 1mf – 9 – 0-8370-3609-7 – 1985-1609 – us A.T.L.A. [220]

HISTORICAL BIOLOGY : AN INTERNATIONAL JOURNAL OF PALEOBIOLOGY / ed by Buffetaut, E & Hallam, A – 9,5,1 – us Harwood [560]

THE HISTORICAL BOOKS OF THE HOLY SCRIPTURES : JUDGES, RUTH, 1 AND 2... / Jamieson, Robert – (With critical and explanatory commentary) – Philadelphia: William S & Alfred Martien, 1860 – 1mf – 9 – 0-8370-3764-6 – 1985-1764 – us A.T.L.A. [220]

HISTORICAL BULLETIN – v1-5. n.d. F-0017 to F-0021 – 9 – us A.G.L.L. [978]

HISTORICAL CATALOG AND HISTORY / Georgetown College – 1829-1920 – 1 – 8.33 – us Baptist [240]

THE HISTORICAL CHARACTER OF ST. JOHN'S GOSPEL : THREE LECTURES / Robinson, Joseph Armitage – London; New York: Longmans, Green, 1908 – 1mf – 9 – 0-8370-7330-8 – 1986-1330 – us A.T.L.A. [220]

AN HISTORICAL CHART OF GERMAN LITERATURE FOR USE IN SCHOOLS AND COLLEGES / Greene, Nelson Lewis – Chicago, Ill.: Educational Screen, c1923 – 1 – us U.W. Library [430]

THE HISTORICAL COLLECTION OF A CITIZEN OF LONDON IN THE FIFTEENTH CENTURY / ed by Gairdner, James – H-1313 2.. 1876 – 8 – ne IDC [941]

HISTORICAL COLLECTIONS / Essex Institute – v1- 1859- 1; v107- 5,6; v113- 9 – us UMI [920]

HISTORICAL COLLECTIONS / Essex Institute. Salem, Mass – v1-92. 1859-1956 – 1,5,6 – 22555.00 – us Princeton Micro [975]

HISTORICAL COLLECTIONS OF GEORGIA:...FACTS, TRADITIONS, BIOGRAPHICAL SKETCHES, ANECDOTES, ETC / White, George – 1854. Biog. and hist. sketches.Indexed. 12 fiches. F-0637 – 9 – us A.G.L.L. [920]

HISTORICAL COLLECTIONS OF GEORGIA:...FACTS, TRADITIONS, BIOGRAPHICAL SKETCHES, ANECDOTES, ETC / White, George – 1854. Indexed. 12 fiches. F-0637 – 9 – us A.G.L.L. [978]

HISTORICAL COLLECTIONS OF HARRISON COUNTY / Hanna, Charles Augustus – New York: Privately Printed, 1900. Ohio Reel 38. (The Cox Library Collection) – 5 – us Americana [978]

HISTORICAL COLLECTIONS OF OHIO / Howe, Henry – An Encyclopedia of the State. Norwalk: State of Ohio, Laning Printing Co., 1896. Vols. 1-2. Ohio Reel 1. (The Cox Library Collection) – 5 – us Americana [978]

HISTORICAL COLLECTIONS OF SOUTH DAKOTA / South Dakota. State Department of History – Pierre, 1922. South Dakota Reel 3. (The Cox Library Collection) – 5 – us Americana [978]

HISTORICAL COLLECTIONS OF THE GEORGIA CHAPTERS / Daughters of the American Revolution – 9 – us A.G.L.L. [920]

HISTORICAL COLLECTIONS OF THE MAHONING VALLEY / Mahoning Valley Historical Society – Biographical sketches. Youngstown: 1876. Mississippi Reel 8. (The Cox Library Collection) – 5 – us Americana [978]

HISTORICAL COLLECTIONS OF THE MAHONING VALLEY / Mahoning Valley Historical Society – Youngstown: 1876. Ohio Reel 46. (The Cox Library Collection) – 5 – us Americana [978]

HISTORICAL COLLECTIONS OF THE STATE OF NEW YORK / Barber & Howe – Facts, traditions, biographical sketches, anecdotes, etc. New York, S. Tuttle, 1842. New York Reel 1. (The Cox Library Collection) – 5 – us Americana [978]

HISTORICAL COLLECTIONS RELATING TO THE AMERICAN COLONIAL CHURCH / Perry, William Stevens – 5v – 1 – us A.T.L.A. [240]

HISTORICAL COLLECTIONS–RELATING TO THE HISTORY AND ANTIQUITIES OF EVERY TOWN IN MASSACHUSETTS / Barber, John W – Worcester, Dorr, Howland and Co., 1840. Massachusetts Reel 1. (The Cox Library Collection) – 5 – us Americana [978]

A HISTORICAL COMMENTARY ON ST. PAUL'S EPISTLE TO THE GALATIANS / Ramsay, William Mitchell – New York: G P Putnam, 1900 – 2mf – 9 – 0-8370-9812-2 – 1986-3812 – us A.T.L.A. [220]

THE HISTORICAL CONNECTION OF THE JEWISH PEOPLE WITH PALESTINE / Jewish Agency for Palestine – Jerusalem, 1936 – 1mf – 9 – ILM-2743/1 – ne IDC [956]

HISTORICAL DATA OF THE NATIONAL ASSEMBLY FROM 1938-1947 / China – (Kuo-min tsan-cheng-hui shih-liao). 1962.674p. 1 reel – 1 – 32.50 – ch Transmission [950]

THE HISTORICAL DELUGE : IN ITS RELATION TO SCIENTIFIC DISCOVERY AND TO PRESENT QUESTIONS / Dawson, John William – (Includes an appendix) – New York:Fleming H. Revell, [1895] – 1mf – 9 – 0-8370-2852-3 – 1985-0852 – us A.T.L.A. [220]

HISTORICAL DICTIONARY OF GUATEMALA BY... / Moore, Richard E – Madrid: Graf. Calleja, 1968 – 1 – sp Bibl Santa Ana [972]

Historical Directory Publishing Co
see SOUVENIR OF SETTLEMENT AND PROGRESS OF WILL COUNTY

AN HISTORICAL DISCOURSE ON THE CIVIL AND RELIGIOUS AFFAIRS OF THE COLONY OF RHODE-ISLAND / Callender, John – 1838 – 1 – 9.66 – us Baptist [240]

A HISTORICAL DOCUMENTATION, AN INSTRUCTIONAL MANUAL AND AN ANNOTATED BIBLIOGRAPHY OF SELECTED FOLK DANCES OF PUERTO RICO / Figueroa-Cruz, Blas E & Jacobson, Phyllis C – 1990 – 4mf – $16.00 – us Microform Publ [790]

HISTORICAL DOCUMENTS / Literary and Historical Society of Quebec – Series 19. 1838-1915 – 1 – cn Precision [025]

HISTORICAL DOCUMENTS ADVOCATING CHRISTIAN UNION : EPOCH-MAKING STATEMENTS BY LEADERS AMONG THE DISCIPLES OF CHRIST FOR THE RESTORATION OF THE CHRISTIANITY OF THE NEW TESTAMENT: ITS DOCTRINES, ITS ORDINANCES, AND ITS FRUITS / Young, Charles Alexander – Chicago: Christian Century, 1904 – 1mf – us A.T.L.A. [240]

HISTORICAL DOCUMENTS AND MANUSCRIPTS / Centre for East Asian Cultural Studies for Unesco – (Burma. 114 reels. Cambodia. 72 reels. India. 189 reels. Malaysia and Singapore. 366 reels. Nepal. 25 reels. Philippines. 196 reels) – Catalogues describing the reels on each country available from the Centre – 1 – ja CEACS [950]

HISTORICAL ENCYCLOPEDIA OF ILLINOIS / Bateman et al – Chicago: Munsell Publ. Co., 1925. Vols. 1-2. Illinois Reel 6. (The Cox Library Collection) – 5 – us Americana [978]

HISTORICAL ENCYCLOPEDIA OF ILLINOIS AND HISTORY OF CASS COUNTY / Bateman et al – Chicago: Munsell Publ. Co., 1915. Illinois Reel 14. (The Cox Library Collection) – 5 – us Americana [978]

HISTORICAL ENCYCLOPEDIA OF ILLINOIS AND HISTORY OF CHRISTIAN COUNTY / Fowkes, Henry L – Chicago: Munsell Publ. Co., 1918. Vols. 1-2. Illinois Reel 15. (The Cox Library Collection) – 5 – us Americana [978]

HISTORICAL ENCYCLOPEDIA OF ILLINOIS AND HISTORY OF CLARK COUNTY / Bell, H C – Chicago: Middle West Publ. Co., 1907. Illinois Reel 15. (The Cox Library Collection) – 5 – us Americana [978]

HISTORICAL ENCYCLOPEDIA OF ILLINOIS AND HISTORY OF EVANSTON / Hurd & Sheppard – Chicago: Munsell Publ. Co., 1906. Vols. 1-2. Illinois Reel 20. (The Cox Library Collection) – 5 – us Americana [978]

HISTORICAL ENCYCLOPEDIA OF ILLINOIS AND HISTORY OF KANE COUNTY / Wilcox, John S – Chicago: Munsell Publ. Co., 1904. Illinois Reel 32. (The Cox Library Collection) – 5 – us Americana [978]

HISTORICAL ENCYCLOPEDIA OF ILLINOIS AND HISTORY OF KENDALL COUNTY / Munsell Publishing Co – Chicago, 1914. Vols. I and II. (Illinois Reel 33). (The Cox Library Collection) – 5 – us Americana [978]

HISTORICAL ENCYCLOPEDIA OF ILLINOIS AND HISTORY OF ROCK ISLAND COUNTY / Bateman, N & Selby, P – Chicago: Munsell Publ. Co., 1914. Illinois Reel 51. (The Cox Library Collection) – 5 – us Americana [978]

HISTORICAL ENCYCLOPEDIA OF ILLINOIS AND HISTORY OF SANGAMON COUNTY / Munsell Publishing Co – Chicago, 1912. Vols. 1-3 (Illinois Reel 54). (The Cox Library Collection) – 5 – us Americana [978]

HISTORICAL ENCYCLOPEDIA OF ILLINOIS AND HISTORY OF ST CLAIR COUNTY / Munsell Publishing Co – Chicago, 1907. Vols. I and II. (Illinois Reel 52). (The Cox Library Collection) – 5 – us Americana [978]

HISTORICAL ENCYCLOPEDIA OF ILLINOIS AND HISTORY OF WARREN COUNTY / Bateman, N & Selby P – Chicago: Munsell Publ. Co., 1903. Illinois Reel 59. (The Cox Library Collection) – 5 – us Americana [978]

HISTORICAL ENCYCLOPEDIA OF ILLINOIS AND KNOX COUNTY / Munsell Publishing Co – Chicago, 1899. (Illinois Reel 34). (The Cox Library Collection) – 5 – us Americana [978]

AN HISTORICAL ENQUIRY CONCERNING THE ATTEMPT TO RAISE A REGIMENT OF SLAVES BY RHODE ISLAND DURING THE WAR OF THE REVOLUTION : WITH SEVERAL TABLES PREPARED BY JEREMIAH OLNEY / Rider, Sidney S – (Filmed with: [Baird, H C] Washington u. Jackson uber die Neger als Soldaten) – Providence: S S Rider, 1880 – us Res Libr [976]

AN HISTORICAL ENQUIRY RESPECTING THE PERFORMANCE ON THE HARP IN THE HIGHLANDS OF SCOTLAND. / Gunn, John – 1807 – 9 – us Sibley [780]

AN HISTORICAL ESSAY ON THE MAGNA CHARTA OF KING JOHN. / Thomson, Richard – London, Major, 1829. 612 p. LL-130 – 1 – us L of C Photodup [340]

HISTORICAL ESSAYS / Lightfoot, Joseph B – London; New York: Macmillan, 1895 – 1mf – us A.T.L.A. [240]

HISTORICAL ESSAYS AND REVIEWS / Creighton, Mandell – London; New York: Longmans, Green, 1902 – 1mf – us A.T.L.A. [900]

HISTORICAL EVIDENCE / George, H B – Oxford: Clarendon Press, 1909 – 1mf – us A.T.L.A. [240]

THE HISTORICAL EVIDENCE FOR THE RESURRECTION OF JESUS CHRIST / Lake, Kirsopp – New York: G.P. Putnam, 1907. 1 fiche – 9 – us A.T.L.A. [240]

HISTORICAL EVIDENCES OF THE NEW TESTAMENT / Maclear, George Frederick et al – (Includes bibliographical references) – New York: American Tract Society, [1895?] – 1mf – 9 – 0-8370-3594-5 – 1985-1594 – us A.T.L.A. [220]

THE HISTORICAL EVIDENCES OF THE TRUTH OF THE SCRIPTURE RECORDS, STATED ANEW, WITH SPECIAL REFERENCE TO THE DOUBTS AND DISCOVERIES OF MODERN TIMES / Rawlinson, George – 1873. Eight Oxford lectures, 1859. From the London ed, 1873 – 1 – us U.W. Library [240]

AN HISTORICAL EXPOSITION OF THE BOOK OF DANIEL THE PROPHET / Rule, William Harris – London: Seeley, Jackson & Halliday, 1869 – 1mf – 9 – 0-8370-4995-4 – 1985-2995 – us A.T.L.A. [220]

HISTORICAL FILES OF THE AMERICAN EXPEDITIONARY FORCES IN SIBERIA / U.S. Army – 1918-20. 11 rolls. M917 – 1 – us Nat'l Archives [324]

HISTORICAL FILES OF THE AMERICAN EXPEDITIONARY FORCES, NORTH RUSSIA / U.S. Army – 1918-19. 2 rolls. M924 – 1 – us Nat'l Archives [324]

HISTORICAL GAZETTEER AND BIOGRAPHICAL MEMORIAL OF CATTARAUGUS COUNTY / Adams, William – Syracuse: Lyman, Horton and Co., 1893. New York Reel 9. (The Cox Library Collection) – 5 – us Americana [978]

HISTORICAL GAZETTEER OF LONDON BEFORE THE GREAT FIRE / Keene, Derek – Part 1: Cheapside – 9 – £690.00 – uk Chadwyck [310]

HISTORICAL GENEALOGY OF THE LAWRENCE FAMILY, 1635-1858 / Lawrence, Thomas – 1858 – 1 – $50.00 – us Presbyterian [920]

AN HISTORICAL, GEOGRAPHICAL, AND PHILOSOPHICAL VIEW OF THE CHINESE EMPIRE;... / Winterbotham, W – London, 1795 – 7mf – 9 – ne IDC [950]

A HISTORICAL GEOGRAPHY OF THE HOLY LANDS / Smith, George Adam – 1894 – 9 – $27.00 – us I.R.C. [910]

HISTORICAL GEOLOGY OF THE ANTILLEAN CARIBBEAN REGION / Schuchert, C – 2422 2. 1935 – 8 – ne IDC [550]

HISTORICAL HAND-BOOK OF REFORMED CHURCH IN THE UNITED STATES / Good, James I – Philadelphia: Heidelberg, 1901 – 1mf – us A.T.L.A. [240]

HISTORICAL INFORMATION RELATING TO MILITARY POSTS AND OTHER INSTALLATIONS. CA. 1700-1900 / U.S. War Department. Adjutant General's Office – 8rolls. M661 – 1 – us Nat'l Archives [324]

HISTORICAL INSCRIPTIONS OF GUJARAT (FROM ANCIENT TIMES TO THE END OF THE VAGHELA DYNASTY) / ed by Acharya Girjashankar Vallabhaji – 3pts. Bombay. 1933, 1935, 1942. BI-789 2 – 8 – ne IDC [410]

THE HISTORICAL INSCRIPTIONS OF SOUTHERN INDIA / Sewell, R – (Madras University Hist. Series, v). Madras, 1932. BI-792 2 – 8 – ne IDC [410]

AN HISTORICAL INTRODUCTION TO MODERN PSYCHOLOGY / Murphy, Gardner – With suppl. by Heinrich Kluever.New York: Harcourt Brace & Co., 1938. 1932. xx,471p. 4th ed – 1 – us U.W. Library [150]

AN HISTORICAL INTRODUCTION TO THE MARPRELATE TRACTS : A CHAPTER IN THE EVOLUTION OF RELIGIOUS AND CIVIL LIBERTY IN ENGLAND / Pierce, William – London: A. Constable, 1908 – 1mf – us A.T.L.A. [941]

THE HISTORICAL JESUS OF NAZARETH / Schlesinger, Max – New York: Charles P Somerby, 1876 – 1mf – 9 – 0-8370-5093-6 – 1985-3093 – us A.T.L.A. [240]

HISTORICAL JOURNAL / University of Birmingham – H798. v1-9. 1947-1964 – 9 – ne IDC [073]

HISTORICAL JOURNAL – v1- 1958- – 1,5,6,9 – us UMI [900]

HISTORICAL JOURNAL OF FILM, RADIO AND TELEVISION – 1981- 13v. Impact of mass communications on the political and social history of the 20th century – 9 – £188.50 – 0143-9685 – uk Carfax [320]

HISTORICAL JOURNAL OF MASSACHUSETTS – (1981-. 1,5,6,9) – v8-. 1980- – 1 – us UMI [073]

AN HISTORICAL JOURNAL OF THE CAMPAIGNS IN NORTH-AMERICA FOR THE YEARS 1757, 1758, 1759 AND 1760 / Knox, John – London, 1769. SEM105P884 – 10mf – 9 – Can$22.50 – cn Bibl Nat [971]

HISTORICAL JOURNAL OF WESTERN MASSACHUSETTS – v1-8. 1972-80 – 1 – us UMI [073]

HISTORICAL JURISPRUDENCE : AN INTRODUCTION TO THE SYSTEMATIC STUDY OF THE DEVELOPMENT OF LAW / Lee, Guy C – New York: The Macmillan Co, 1900 – 6mf – 9 – $9.00 – LLMC 95-152 – us L.L.M.C. [340]

HISTORICAL LECTURES AND ADDRESSES / Creighton, Mandell; ed by Creighton, Louise – London; New York: Longmans, Green,1903 – 1mf – us A.T.L.A. [240]

HISTORICAL LECTURES AND ESSAYS / Kingsley, Charles – London: Macmillan, 1880 – 1mf – us A.T.L.A. [240]

HISTORICAL LECTURES ON THE LIFE OF OUR LORD JESUS CHRIST / Ellicott, Charles J – Boston: Gould & Lincoln, 1862. 1 fiche – 9 – us A.T.L.A. [240]

THE HISTORICAL, LITERARY, THEOLOGICAL, AND MISCELLANEOUS REPOSITORY *see* THE NOVA-SCOTIA AND NEW-BRUNSWICK MAGAZINE, OR, THE HISTORICAL, LITERARY, THEOLOGICAL, AND MISCELLANEOUS REPOSITORY

Historical Manuscripts Commission *see* MANUSCRIPTS OF THE HOUSE OF LORDS, 1678-1693

HISTORICAL MATERIALS / Georgia Baptist Associations – 1 – 5.00 – us Baptist [240]

HISTORICAL MATERIALS ON BAPTISTS AND OTHER EVANGELICALS IN SOVIET RUSSIA AND OTHER EASTERN EUROPEAN COUNTRIES – (Books and booklets by Evangelical, Orthodox and Soviet authors. 21,116p. Union Congresses and other Union materials. 791p. Historical Papers. 616p. Theses. 1037p. Periodicals. 92,020p) – 1 – us Baptist [240]

HISTORICAL MEMORIALS OF WESTMINSTER ABBEY / Stanley, Arthur Penrhyn – First American from the sixth London ed, with author's final revisions. New York: Anson D.F. Randolph, 1887. 3v. illus – 1 – us U.W. Library [941]

HISTORICAL MICROFICHE SERIES (1990). ANNUAL SUPPLEMENT / ed by Australian Bureau of Statistics – ca 800mf – 9 – A$2,100.00; A$1,950.00 after subsc – at Statistics [980]

HISTORICAL MICROFICHE SERIES (1901-84) / ed by Australian Bureau of Statistics – over 10,000mf – 9 – A$16,000 set – at Statistics [980]

HISTORICAL MICROFICHE SERIES (1986-1989). UPDATES / ed by Australian Bureau of Statistics – ca 3750mf – 9 – A$9,950.00; A$9,200.00 after subsc – at Statistics [980]

HISTORICAL MICROFICHE SERIES, GROUP 1 – GENERAL : SUBGROUP 11, CATALOGUES AND GUIDES – 84mf – 9 – at Statistics [980]

HISTORICAL MICROFICHE SERIES, GROUP 1 – GENERAL : SUBGROUPS 12, WORK MANUALS/CLASSIFICATIONS – 227mf – 9 – at Statistics [980]

HISTORICAL MICROFICHE SERIES, GROUP 1 – GENERAL : SUBGROUPS 13, PRINCIPAL AND MULTI-SUBJECT PUBLICATIONS – 2170mf – 9 – at Statistics [980]

HISTORICAL MICROFICHE SERIES, GROUP 2 – CENSUS OF POPULATION AND HOUSING – 777mf – 9 – at Statistics [980]

HISTORICAL MICROFICHE SERIES, GROUP 3 – ESTIMATES OF POPULATION, POPULATION PROJECTIONS, VITAL STATISTICS, MIGRATION : SUBGROUPS 31, GENERAL DEMOGRAPHY – 235mf – 9 – at Statistics [304]

HISTORICAL MICROFICHE SERIES, GROUP 3 – ESTIMATES OF POPULATION, POPULATION PROJECTIONS, VITAL STATISTICS, MIGRATION : SUBGROUPS 32, POPULATION TRENDS – (Population Estimates and Counts, Population Projections) – 66mf – 9 – at Statistics [304]

HISTORICAL MICROFICHE SERIES, GROUP 3 – ESTIMATES OF POPULATION, POPULATION PROJECTIONS, VITAL STATISTICS, MIGRATION : SUBGROUPS 33, VITAL STATISTICS – (Births, Deaths, Life Tables, Marriages and Divorces) – 99mf – 9 – at Statistics [304]

HISTORICAL MICROFICHE SERIES, GROUP 3, ESTIMATES OF POPULATION, POPULATION PROJECTIONS, VITAL STATISTICS, MIGRATION : SUBGROUPS 34, MIGRATION – (Overseas Arrivals and Departures, Internal Migration) – 89mf – 9 – at Statistics [304]

HISTORICAL MICROFICHE SERIES, GROUP 4 – EDUCATION HEALTH, WELFARE; JUSTICE AND OTHER SOCIAL : SUBGROUPS 41, GENERAL SOCIAL STATISTICS – 50mf – 9 – at Statistics [300]

HISTORICAL MICROFICHE SERIES, GROUP 4 – EDUCATION HEALTH, WELFARE; JUSTICE AND OTHER SOCIAL : SUBGROUPS 42, EDUCATION – (Primary, Secondary and Tertiary) – 109mf – 9 – at Statistics [370]

HISTORICAL MICROFICHE SERIES, GROUP 4 – EDUCATION HEALTH, WELFARE; JUSTICE AND OTHER SOCIAL : SUBGROUPS 43, HEALTH AND HOSPITALS – (Hospitals and Nursing Homes, Mental Hospitals and Psychiatric Centres, Medical and Hospital Benefits, Nutrition and Australian Diet, Morbidity) – 96mf – 9 – at Statistics [360]

HISTORICAL MICROFICHE SERIES, GROUP 4 – EDUCATION HEALTH, WELFARE; JUSTICE AND OTHER SOCIAL : SUBGROUPS 44, WELFARE AND SOCIAL SERVICES – (Children's Services, Adoptions, Ex-Service Personnel, Their Widows and Children; Related Welfare Services) – 25mf – 9 – at Statistics [360]

HISTORICAL MICROFICHE SERIES, GROUP 4 – EDUCATION HEALTH, WELFARE; JUSTICE AND OTHER SOCIAL : SUBGROUPS 45, JUSTICE AND OTHER SOCIAL – (Selected Crimes, Criminal Courts, Prisons, Public Justice; Language Usage, Recreation, Personal and Other Services) – 4mf – 9 – at Statistics [360]

HISTORICAL MICROFICHE SERIES, GROUP 5 – NATIONAL ACCOUNTS, BALANCE OF PAYMENTS AND FOREIGN INVESTMENT, FOREIGN TRADE, PUBLIC FINANCE, PRIVATE FINANCE : SUBGROUPS 53, BALANCE OF PAYMENTS AND FOREIGN INVESTMENT – (Australia's International Economic Transactions Grouped into Goods, Services, Transfers and Capital Items, Flows and Levels of Foreign Investment in Australia, Australian Investment Abroad and Related Income Flows) – 136mf – 9 – at Statistics [337]

HISTORICAL MICROFICHE SERIES, GROUP 5 – NATIONAL ACCOUNTS, BALANCE OF PAYMENTS AND FOREIGN INVESTMENT, FOREIGN TRADE, PUBLIC FINANCE, PRIVATE FINANCE : SUBGROUPS 54, FOREIGN TRADE – (Exports and Imports by Country and Commodity, Import Orders Outstanding and Import Clearances for Motor Vehicles) – 1730mf – 9 – at Statistics [380]

HISTORICAL MICROFICHE SERIES, GROUP 5 – NATIONAL ACCOUNTS, BALANCE OF PAYMENTS AND FOREIGN INVESTMENT, FOREIGN TRADE, PUBLIC FINANCE, PRIVATE FINANCE : SUBGROUPS 55, PUBLIC FINANCE – (Expenditure and Receipts by Economic Categories at Federal State and Local Government Levels, Public Corporations, Taxation, Public Authority Superannuation Schemes) – 237mf – 9 – at Statistics [336]

HISTORICAL MICROFICHE SERIES, GROUP 5 – NATIONAL ACCOUNTS, BALANCE OF PAYMENTS AND FOREIGN INVESTMENT, FOREIGN TRADE, PUBLIC FINANCE, PRIVATE FINANCE : SUBGROUPS 56, PRIVATE FINANCE – (Money and Banking, Cooperative Savings and Lending Organisations, Financial Corporations, Friendly Societies, Unit Trusts and Mutual Funds, Capital Expenditure and Capital Raisings by Private Enterprises, Instalment Credit, Stocks Owned by Private Enterprise) – 502mf – 9 – at Statistics [332]

HISTORICAL MICROFICHE SERIES, GROUP 5 – NATIONAL ACCOUNTS, BALANCE OF PAYMENTS AND FOREIGN INVESTMENT, FOREIGN, TRADE, PUBLIC FINANCE, PRIVATE FINANCE : SUBGROUPS 51, GENERAL FINANCE – 1mf – 9 – at Statistics [330]

HISTORICAL MICROFICHE SERIES, GROUP 5 – NATIONAL ACCOUNTS, BALANCE OF PAYMENTS AND FOREIGN INVESTMENT, FOREIGN, TRADE, PUBLIC FINANCE, PRIVATE FINANCE : SUBGROUPS 52, NATIONAL ACCOUNTS – (National Income and Expenditure, Gross Domestic Product, Input-Output Tables) – 231mf – 9 – at Statistics [339]

HISTORICAL MICROFICHE SERIES, GROUP 6 – LABOUR FORCE, EMPLOYMENT CONDITIONS, PRICES, CONSUMER INCOME AND EXPENDITURE : SUBGROUPS 61, GENERAL LABOUR – 170mf – 9 – at Statistics [331]

HISTORICAL MICROFICHE SERIES, GROUP 6 – LABOUR FORCE, EMPLOYMENT CONDITIONS, PRICES, CONSUMER INCOME AND EXPENDITURE : SUBGROUPS 62, LABOUR FORCE – (Characteristics and Employment Experience of the Labour Force, Labour Turnover and Mobility, Job Vacancies, Multiple Job Holders, Unemployment, School Leavers) – 281mf – 9 – at Statistics [331]

HISTORICAL MICROFICHE SERIES, GROUP 6 – LABOUR FORCE, EMPLOYMENT CONDITIONS, PRICES, CONSUMER INCOME AND EXPENDITURE : SUBGROUPS 63, EARNINGS, HOURS AND EMPLOYMENT CONDITIONS – (Rates of Wages and Hours of Work, Weekly and Hourly Earnings, Award Rates of Pay, Incidence of Industrial Awards, Annual Leave, Frequency of Pay, Superannuation Cover, Industrial Disputes, Industrial Accidents and Workers Compensation, Trade Unions) – 205mf – 9 – at Statistics [331]

HISTORICAL MICROFICHE SERIES, GROUP 6 – LABOUR FORCE, EMPLOYMENT CONDITIONS, PRICES, CONSUMER INCOME AND EXPENDITURE : SUBGROUPS 64, PRICES – (Retail Prices, Consumer Price Index, Export and Import Price Indexes and Other Price Indexes) – 171mf – 9 – at Statistics [338]

HISTORICAL MICROFICHE SERIES, GROUP 6 – LABOUR FORCE, EMPLOYMENT CONDITIONS, PRICES, CONSUMER INCOME AND EXPENDITURE : SUBGROUPS 65, CONSUMER INCOME AND EXPENDITURE – (Income of Individuals and Families, Income Earners and Income Recipients, Expenditure of Households) – 42mf – 9 – at Statistics [338]

HISTORICAL MICROFICHE SERIES, GROUP 7 – AGRICULTURE, FORESTRY AND FISHING : SUBGROUPS 71, GENERAL AGRICULTURE – 135mf – 9 – at Statistics [630]

HISTORICAL MICROFICHE SERIES, GROUP 7 – AGRICULTURE, FORESTRY AND FISHING : SUBGROUPS 72, LIVESTOCK AND LIVESTOCK PRODUCTS – (Number and Types of Livestock, Livestock Slaughtered and Meat Produced, Whole Milk Production, Poultry Industry, Wool Production and Shearing, Bees and Natural Honey) – 184mf – 9 – at Statistics [636]

HISTORICAL MICROFICHE SERIES, GROUP 7 – AGRICULTURE, FORESTRY AND FISHING : SUBGROUPS 73, CROPS AND PASTURES – (Cereals, Vegetables, Fruit Growing and Vineyards, Horticultural Plants, Crops for Industrial Purposes (Sugar Cane, Tobacco, Hops, Mushrooms)) – 96mf – 9 – at Statistics [631]

HISTORICAL MICROFICHE SERIES, GROUP 7 – AGRICULTURE, FORESTRY AND FISHING : SUBGROUPS 74, AGRICULTURAL IMPROVEMENTS AND PRACTICES – (Farm Machinery, Irrigation, Usage of Fertilisers, Aerial Top-Dressing and Seeding) – 32mf – 9 – at Statistics [630]

HISTORICAL MICROFICHE SERIES, GROUP 7 – AGRICULTURE, FORESTRY AND FISHING : SUBGROUPS 75, VALUE OF AGRICULTURAL PRODUCTION AND FINANCIAL STATISTICS – 41mf – 9 – at Statistics [338]

HISTORICAL MICROFICHE SERIES, GROUP 7 - AGRICULTURE, FORESTRY AND FISHING : SUBGROUPS 76, FISHING AND FORESTRY - 20mf - 9 - at Statistics [639]

HISTORICAL MICROFICHE SERIES, GROUP 8 - MANUFACTURING, MINING, INTERNAL TRADE, BUILDING AND CONSTRUCTION : SUBGROUPS 81, GENERAL INDUSTRY - 150mf - 9 - at Statistics [338]

HISTORICAL MICROFICHE SERIES, GROUP 8 - MANUFACTURING, MINING, INTERNAL TRADE, BUILDING AND CONSTRUCTION : SUBGROUPS 82, MANUFACTURING ESTABLISHMENTS AND ELECTRICITY AND GAS ESTABLISHMENTS: STRUCTURAL DATA - 256mf - 9 - at Statistics [670]

HISTORICAL MICROFICHE SERIES, GROUP 8 - MANUFACTURING, MINING, INTERNAL TRADE, BUILDING AND CONSTRUCTION : SUBGROUPS 83, MANUFACTURING ESTABLISHMENTS: PRODUCTION OF COMMODITIES - (Food, Beverages and Tobacco, Textiles and Textile Products, Wearing Apparel and Leather Products, Building Materials and Fittings, Household Appliances and Furnishings, Machinery, Transport Equipment and Accessories, Paper Products and Printing, Chemicals, Steel Wire and Wire Products, Non-Ferrous Rolled, etc. Products) - 874mf - 9 - at Statistics [338]

HISTORICAL MICROFICHE SERIES, GROUP 8 - MANUFACTURING, MINING, INTERNAL TRADE, BUILDING AND CONSTRUCTION : SUBGROUPS 85, INTERNAL TRADE: MERCHANDISING - (Retail and Wholesale Sales of Commodities; Stocks, Deliveries, Receipts and Sales of Agricultural and Construction Machinery) - 94mf - 9 - at Statistics [338]

HISTORICAL MICROFICHE SERIES, GROUP 8 - MANUFACTURING, MINING, INTERNAL TRADE, BUILDING AND CONSTRUCTION : SUBGROUPS 86, INTERNAL TRADE: SERVICE ESTABLISHMENTS - (Retail and Wholesale Establishments and Details of Their Operations, Tourist Accommodation Establishments (Hotels, Motels, Caravan Parks) and Details of Their Operations) - 113mf - 9 - at Statistics [338]

HISTORICAL MICROFICHE SERIES, GROUP 8 - MANUFACTURING, MINING, INTERNAL TRADE, BUILDING AND CONSTRUCTION : SUBGROUPS 87, BUILDING AND CONSTRUCTION - (Approvals, Commencements and Completions of Residential and Non-Residential Buildings: Type, Number and Value of Dwellings; Construction Other Than Buildings (Roadwork, Heavy Industrial Facilities, Dams, etc.)) - 156mf - 9 - at Statistics [690]

HISTORICAL MICROFICHE SERIES, GROUP 8 - MANUFACTURING, MINING, INTERNAL, TRADE, BUILDING AND CONSTRUCTION : SUBGROUPS 84, MINING - (Mining Establishments and Details of their Operations, Productions of Minerals and Mineral Products, Exploration of Minerals and Petroleum) - 246mf - 9 - at Statistics [622]

HISTORICAL MICROFICHE SERIES, GROUP 9 - TRANSPORT AND COMMUNICATION : SUBGROUPS 91, GENERAL TRANSPORT AND COMMUNICATION - 61mf - 9 - at Statistics [380]

HISTORICAL MICROFICHE SERIES, GROUP 9 - TRANSPORT AND COMMUNICATION : SUBGROUPS 92, TRANSPORT SERVICES AND TRANSPORT FACILITIES - (Bus, Rail and Air Transport; Overseas Shipping, Method of Travel by Commuters, Parking Lots, Length of Roads Open to Traffic) - 103mf - 9 - at Statistics [380]

HISTORICAL MICROFICHE SERIES, GROUP 9 - TRANSPORT AND COMMUNICATION : SUBGROUPS 93, STOCK OF MOTOR VEHICLES - (Registrations and Types of New Motor Vehicles, Number and Type of Motor Vehicles on Register) - 209mf - 9 - at Statistics [380]

HISTORICAL MICROFICHE SERIES, GROUP 9 - TRANSPORT AND COMMUNICATION : SUBGROUPS 94, MOTOR VEHICLE ACCIDENTS - (Injuries and Fatalities, Type of Motor Vehicle and Road Users Involved, Features of Roadways, Time and Day of Occurrence) - 37mf - 9 - at Statistics [360]

HISTORICAL MONOGRAPH: PRISONER OF WAR OPERATIONS DIVISION, OFFICE OF THE PROVOST MARSHAL GENERAL / U.S. Prisoner of War Operations Division - v. 1-4. 1945-46 - 1 - 93.00 - us L of C Photodup [360]

THE HISTORICAL NEW TESTAMENT : BEING THE LITERATURE OF THE NEW TESTAMENT ARRANGED IN THE ORDER OF ITS LITERARY GROWTH AND ACCORDING TO THE DATES OF THE DOCUMENTS: A NEW TRANSLATION / ed by Moffatt, James - (Includes bibliographical references and indexes) - Edinburgh: T & T Clark, 1901 - 2mf - 9 - 0-8370-9404-6 - 1986-3404 - us A.T.L.A. [220]

HISTORICAL NEWSPAPERS FROM WESTERN UKRAINE - (Mainly cover the period between 1930s and the early 1940s) - L'viv: Stefanyk Library - 15 titles 26r - 1 - $2,100.00 coll $90.00r - us Ross [072]

HISTORICAL NOTE: WOMAN'S WORK IN THE CHURCH / Charteris, Archibald Hamilton - (The Presbyterian review, v. 9, April 1888, p. 285-292) - 9 - us A.T.L.A. [240]

HISTORICAL NOTES / DeSaussure, Wilmot Gibbes - ca.1885-ca.1897. 5 fiches - 9 - us South Carolina Historical [976]

HISTORICAL NOTES ON CERTAIN EMIRATES AND TRIBES : PRINTED BY ORDER OF HIS EXCELLENCY, THE GOVERNOR / ed by Burdon, J A - London: Waterlow, 1909 - 1 - us Res Libr [960]

HISTORICAL NOTES ON EDUCATION IN ANTIGUA 1837-1984 / Antigua and Barbuda. Archives Committee - 1mf - 9 - DE-509/1 - ne IDC [370]

HISTORICAL NOTES ON ENGLISH CATHOLIC MISSIONS / Kelly, Bernard William - London: Kegan Paul, Trench, Truebner; St Louis, MO: Herder, 1907 - 2mf - 9 - 0-8370-7162-3 - 1986-1162 - us A.T.L.A. [240]

HISTORICAL NOTES ON THE EMPLOYMENT OF NEGROES IN THE AMERICAN ARMY OF THE REVOLUTION / Moore, George H - (Filmed with: [Baird, H C,] Washington u. Jackson uber die Neger als Soldaten) - New York: C T Evans, 1862 - us Res Libr [976]

HISTORICAL NOTES ON THE TRACTARIAN MOVEMENT, A.D. 1833-1845 / Oakeley, Frederick - London: Longman, Green, Longman, Roberts & Green, 1865 - 1mf - us A.T.L.A. [240]

HISTORICAL NOTICE OF PENAL LAWS AGAINST CATHOLICS... / Madden, Richard Robert - London: Thomas Richardson & Son, 1865 - 3mf - 9 - $4.50 - LLMC 91-089 - us L.L.M.C. [340]

HISTORICAL NOTICE OF PENAL LAWS AGAINST ROMAN CATHOLICS : THEIR OPERATION AND RELAXATION DURING THE PAST CENTURY, OF PATRIAL MEASURES OF RELIEF IN 1779, 1782,... / Madden, Richard Robert - London: T. Richardson, 1865 - 1mf - us A.T.L.A. [240]

HISTORICAL PAPERS AND LETTERS FROM THE NORTHERN REGISTERS (RS61) / ed by Raine, J - 1873 - Dfl32.00 - ne Slangenburg [941]

HISTORICAL PAPERS ON SHELTER ISLAND / Mallmann, Jacob E - 1899 - 1 - $50.00 - us Presbyterian [240]

HISTORICAL PHOTOGRAPHS OF THE MIDDLE EAST / ed by Grant, Gillian - (Includes a printed guide) - 190mf - 9 - ne IDC [770]

AN HISTORICAL, POLITICAL AND STATISTICAL ACCOUNT OF CEYLON AND ITS DEPENDENCIES / Pridham, C - 2v. London. 1849. BI-981 2 - 8 - ne IDC [950]

AN HISTORICAL PRESENTATION OF AUGUSTINISM AND PELAGIANISM : FROM THE ORIGINAL SOURCES / Wiggers, G F - Andover: Gould, Newman & Saxton, 1840 - 1mf - us A.T.L.A. [240]

HISTORICAL PRINTS IN THE BRITISH MUSEUM / British Museum. Department of Prints and Drawings - (Over 10,000 prints arr. in chronological order of event or scene depicted. Fully captioned and with museum accession number) - 204mf - 9 - $995.00 - 0-907006-49-3 - uk Mindata [760]

HISTORICAL PROJECT, E-5-E-5C / U.S. Army. Signal Corps - Washington, D.C.. 1946. 4 v. illus., charts, maps, photos. By Pauline M. Oakes - 1 - 24.00 - us L of C Photodup [977]

Historical Publishing Co *see*
- FRANKLIN COUNTY AT THE BEGINNING OF THE 20TH CENTURY
- HISTORY OF CEDAR COUNTY
- HISTORY OF THE BENCH AND BAR OF OREGON

HISTORICAL RECORD AND SOUVENIR / Los Angeles County Pioneer Society - Los Angeles: Times-Mirror Press, 1923. California Reel 17. The Cox Library Collection - 5 - us Americana [978]

AN HISTORICAL RECORD OF THE LIGHT HORSE VOLUNTEERS OF LONDON AND WESTMINSTER : WITH THE MUSTER ROLLS FROM THE FIRST FORMATION OF THE REGIMENT, 1779 TO THE RELODGEMENT OF THE STANDARDS IN THE TOWER 1829 / Collyer, James N - London: Wright, MDCCCXLIII [1843] - 1 - us U.W. Library [355]

HISTORICAL RECORDS AND STUDIES THOMAS F. MECHAN / Bayle, Constantino - New York, 1932; Madrid: Razon y Fe, 1933 - 1 - sp Bibl Santa Ana [900]

HISTORICAL RECORDS AND STUDIES...NEW YORK, CATHOLIC HISTORICAL SOCIETY. 1929 / Bayle, Constantino - Madrid: Razon y Fe, 1930 - 1 - sp Bibl Santa Ana [240]

HISTORICAL RECORDS OF EARLY CANADA / Lawrence Lande Collection - 1981 - 1 - cn Micromedia [971]

HISTORICAL RECORDS OF HILLSBOROUGH COUNTY, TAMPA, FLORIDA / Burns, A W - Compiled from the U.S. Census 1830-1870. Washington, DC. Florida Reel 1. (The Cox Library Collection) - 5 - us Americana [978]

HISTORICAL RECORDS OF MARE ISLAND NAVAL SHIPYARD VALLEJO, CALIFORNIA - (Detailed index available) - 1854-1961 - 1750mf - 9 - $1,750.00 - B40160 - us Library Micro [978]

THE HISTORICAL RECORDS OF THE HIGH AUTHORITY OF THE EUROPEAN COAL AND STEEL COMMUNITY, PART 1 : 1952-1956 / Commission of the European Communities - (Indexes v1 £40.00. v2+3 £68.00. Inventories 1952+1953 £27.00) - Cambridge - 9,883mf - 9 - £9,895.00 diazo £14,000.00 silver - uk Chadwyck [940]

THE HISTORICAL RECORDS OF THE HIGH AUTHORITY OF THE EUROPEAN COAL AND STEEL COMMUNITY, PART 2 : 1957-1961 / Commission of the European Communities - (With printed indexes and inventories. Inquire for prices) - 15,660mf - 9 - £15,690.00 diazo £22,250.00 silver - uk Chadwyck [940]

HISTORICAL RECORDS OF THE NEW BRUNSWICK REGIMENT, CANADIAN ARTILLERY - Comp. by John B.M. Baxter. St. John, N.B.: Officers of the Corps, 1896. 02997. (Pre-1900 Canadiana) - 9 - cn C.I.H.M. [971]

HISTORICAL REFERENCE BOOK / Whitman, Benjamin - Erie, S. B. Nelson, Publ., 1896. Pennsylvania Reel 21. (The Cox Library Collection) - 5 - us Americana [978]

HISTORICAL REGISTER AND DICTIONARY OF THE UNITED STATES ARMY, FROM ITS ORGANIZATION, SEPTEMBER 29, 1789, TO MARCH 2, 1903 / Heitman, Francis B - Washington: Government Printing Office, 1903. v1-2. Military Books, reel 3. (Cox Library Collection) - 5 - us Americana [355]

HISTORICAL REGISTER OF OFFICERS OF THE CONTINENTAL ARMY DURING THE WAR OF THE REVOLUTION APRIL 1775 TO DECEMBER 1783 / Heitman, Francis B - Washington, DC: The Rare Book Shop Publ. Co., Inc., 1914. Military Books, reel 2. (Cox Library Collection) - 5 - us Americana [920]

HISTORICAL RELATIONS ACROSS THE INDIAN OCEAN : REPORTS AND PAPERS OF THE MEETING OF EXPERTS ORGANIZED BY UNESCO, MAURITIUS, 1974 - 1980 - 9 - 92-3-101740-3 - fr UNESCO [960]

HISTORICAL REPORTS OF THE STATE ACTING ASSISTANT PROVOST MARSHALS GENERAL AND DISTRICT PROVOST MARSHALS, 1865 / U.S. Provost Marshal General's Bureau - RG 110. M1163. 5 rolls - 1 - us Nat'l Archives [976]

HISTORICAL RESEARCH : AN OUTLINE OF THEORY AND PRACTICE / Vincent, John Martin - New York: H. Holt, 1911 - 1mf - us A.T.L.A. [900]

[HISTORICAL RESEARCH SOURCES IN ISTANBUL PAMPHLET COLLECTION] - 1952 - 1 - CSUXANR0519-B - us Hoover Inst Photo [949]

HISTORICAL RESEARCHES IN WESTERN PENNSYLVANIA, PRINCIPALLY CATHOLIC *see* AMERICAN CATHOLIC HISTORICAL RESEARCHES

HISTORICAL RESEARCHES INTO THE POLITICS, INTERCOURSE, AND TRADE OF THE PRINCIPAL NATIONS OF ANTIQUITY / Heeren, Arnold Hermann Ludwig - London. 4v. 1846 - 1r - 1 - us Ross [930]

HISTORICAL REVIEW OF ARKANSAS / Hempstead, Fay - (Chicago:Lewis Publ. Co., 1911) Vol. 1-3. Arkansas Reel 1. (The Cox Library Collection) - 5 - us Americana [978]

HISTORICAL REVIEW OF CHICAGO AND COOK COUNTY / Waterman, A N - Chicago: Lewis Publ. Co., 1908. Vols. 1-3. Illinois Reel 18. (The Cox Library Collection) - 5 - us Americana [978]

HISTORICAL REVIEW OF E.I.F.A.C. ACTIVITIES - 1981 - 42p - it F.A.O. [060]

HISTORICAL REVIEW OF LOGAN COUNTY / Kennedy, Robert P - Biographical sketches. Chicago: S. J. Clarke Publ. Co., 1903. Ohio Reel 43. (The Cox Library Collection) - 5 - us Americana [978]

HISTORICAL REVIEW OF SOUTHEAST TEXAS / Hardy & Roberts - Chicago: Lewis Publ. Co., 1910. 2v. Texas Reel 9. (The Cox Library Collection) - 5 - us Americana [978]

HISTORICAL SCENES FROM THE OLD JESUIT MISSIONS / Kip, William Ingraham - New York: Anson D.F. Randolph, c1875 - 1mf - us A.T.L.A. [240]

Historical Science Society *see* REKISHIGAKU KENKYU

HISTORICAL SKETCH OF EVANGELICAL REFORMED CHURCH, FREDERICK, MARYLAND / Eschbach, E R - 1894 - 1 - $50.00 - us Presbyterian [240]

A HISTORICAL SKETCH OF FYZABAD TEHSIL *see* BENGAL TENANCY BILL

A HISTORICAL SKETCH OF JOHNSON COUNTY, INDIANA / Banta, D D - 1881. Indiana Reel 17. (The Cox Library Collection) - 5 - us Americana [978]

AN HISTORICAL SKETCH OF LOS ANGELES COUNTY CALIFORNIA - Los Angeles: O W Smith, 1936. California Reel 17. (The Cox Library Collection) - 5 - us Americana [978]

HISTORICAL SKETCH OF MONTREAL: THE STORY OF ITS FOUNDATION - 1891?. 05638. (Pre-1900 Canadiana) - 9 - cn C.I.H.M. [971]

HISTORICAL SKETCH OF PRESBYTERIANISM WITHIN THE BOUNDS OF THE SYNOD OF CENTRAL NEW YORK / Fowler, Philemon H - 1877 - 1 - us A.T.L.A. [240]

HISTORICAL SKETCH OF PROTESTANT MISSIONS IN SIAM, 1828-1928 / ed by McFarland, George Bradley - 1928 - 1 - us A.T.L.A. [240]

HISTORICAL SKETCH OF PROTESTANT MISSIONS IN SIAM, 1828-1928 / McFarland, George Bradley - Bankok: Bankok Times Press, 1928 - 1r - 1 - $50.00 - us Presbyterian [240]

HISTORICAL SKETCH OF SAGUENAY / Committee of Writers - Quebec: Printed by Leger Brousseau, 1883. SEM105P375 - 1mf - 9 - Can$2.25 - cn Bibl Nat [910]

HISTORICAL SKETCH OF THE BARTON LODGE NO.6, G.R.C., A.F. AND A.M - Compiled by authority of the Lodge. Hamilton Ont.: G. E. Mason, 1895. 03242. (Pre-1900 Canadiana) - 9 - cn C.I.H.M. [971]

HISTORICAL SKETCH OF THE GRANDE LIGNE MISSION / Ayer, Albert Azro - 1898. 05846. (Pre-1900 Canadiana) - 9 - cn C.I.H.M. [971]

HISTORICAL SKETCH OF THE MISSION OF THE GENERAL COUNCIL OF THE EVANGELICAL LUTHERAN CHURCH, AMONG THE TELUGUS OF INDIA / Trabert, George Henry - Philadelphia: Jas B Rodgers, 1890 - 1mf - 9 - 0-8370-6428-7 - 1986-0428 - us A.T.L.A. [240]

HISTORICAL SKETCH OF THE MISSION TO THE NESTORIANS / Perkins, Justin - New York: John A. Gray, 1862 - 1mf - us A.T.L.A. [240]

AN HISTORICAL SKETCH OF THE OLD VILLAGE OF NEW LISBON, OHIO - Lisbon: George T. Farrell, Printer, 1903. Ohio Reel 22.(The Cox Library Collection) - 5 - us Americana [978]

AN HISTORICAL SKETCH OF THE PROVINCIAL DIALECTS OF ENGLAND / Halliwell-Phillipps, James Orchard - Albany: J. Munsell, 1863. 126p - 1 - us U.W. Library [420]

HISTORICAL SKETCH OF THE RISE, PROGRESS, AND DECLINE OF THE REFORMATION IN POLAND : AND OF THE INFLUENCE WHICH THE SCRIPTURAL DOCTRINES HAVE EXERCISED ON THAT COUNTRY IN LITERARY, MORAL, AND POLITICAL RESPECTS / Krasinski, Valerian – London: Printed for the author: Murray [distributor], 1838-1940 – 3mf – us A.T.L.A. [943]

HISTORICAL SKETCH... SYNOD OF CENTRAL NEW YORK / Fowler, Philemon H – 1877 – 1 – $50.00 – us Presbyterian [240]

HISTORICAL SKETCHES AND REMINISCENCES OF MADISON COUNTY / Forkner & Dyson – Logansport: Wilson, Humphreys and Co., 1897. Indiana Reel 20. (The Cox Library Collection) – 5 – us Americana [978]

HISTORICAL SKETCHES FOR JURISDICTIONAL AND SUBJECT HEADINGS USED FOR THE LETTERS RECEIVED BY THE OFFICE OF INDIAN AFFAIRS, 1824-80 / U.S. National Archives and Records Service – 1r – 1 – T1105 – us Nat'l Archives [324]

HISTORICAL SKETCHES OF FRANKLIN COUNTY / Seaver, Fredrick J – Short biographies. Albany, J. B. Lyon Co., 1918. New York Reel 15. (The Cox Library Collection) – 5 – us Americana [978]

HISTORICAL SKETCHES OF IOWA BAPTISTS / Burdette Co – Burlington: 1886. Iowa Reel 2. (The Cox Library Collection) – 5 – us Americana [978]

HISTORICAL SKETCHES OF OLD VINCENNES / Smith, Hubbard M – Vincennes: 1902. Indiana Reel 17. (The Cox Library Collection) – 5 – us Americana [978]

HISTORICAL SKETCHES OF POCAHONTAS COUNTY / Price, William T – Marlinton, Price Brothers Publishing, 1901. West Virginia Reel 5. (The Cox Library Collection) – 5 – us Americana [978]

HISTORICAL SKETCHES OF THE COUNTY OF ELGIN – St. Thomas, Ont.: The Elgin Historical and Scientific Institute, 1895. 05232.(Pre-1900 Canadiana) – 9 – cn C.I.H.M. [971]

HISTORICAL SKETCHES OF THE SOUTH OF INDIA, IN AN ATTEMPT TO TRACE THE HISTORY OF MYSOOR.. / Wilks, Mark – 2nd ed. Madras: Hurst, 1869. 2v. fold. map – 1 – us U.W. Library [950]

HISTORICAL SKETCHES OF WOMEN'S MISSIONARY SOCIETIES IN AMERICA AND ENGLAND / Daggett, L H – c1883 – 9 – us A.T.L.A. [240]

HISTORICAL SKETCHES OF...MISSIONS UNDER...PRESBYTERIAN CHURCH USA – (Includes bibliographies) – Philadelphia: Women's Foreign Missionary Society, 1897 – 1mf – 9 – 0-8370-6315-9 – 1985-0315 – us A.T.L.A. [240]

Historical Society of Geauga County *see* PIONEER AND GENERAL HISTORY OF GEAUGA COUNTY

HISTORICAL STUDIES IN PHILOSOPHY / Boutroux, Emile – London: Macmillan, 1912 – 1mf – us A.T.L.A. [100]

HISTORICAL STUDIES IN THE PHYSICAL AND BIOLOGICAL SCIENCES: HSPS – v16- . 1986- – 1,5,6,9 – us UMI [530]

HISTORICAL STUDIES IN THE PHYSICAL SCIENCES – (1985- . 5,6,9) – v1-15. 1969-85 – 1 – us UMI [530]

HISTORICAL STUDIES SERIES / Bibliotheque Nationale – 41 titles (available separately). In French, German, Spanish, Portuguese – 9 – approx. 675.00 – fr Bibl Nationale [900]

HISTORICAL STUDY OF THE ACTS AND THE EPISTLES (CCC235) / Luce, H W – (In Chinese) – [S.l: s.n. 3v. 1903] – 1r – 1 – 1984-6574 – us A.T.L.A. [220]

HISTORICAL SUMMARIES OF ADMINISTRATION MEASURES IN THE SEVERAL BRANCHES OF PUBLIC BUSINESS ADMINISTERED IN THE DEPARTMENT OF REVENUE AND AGRICULTURE, DRAWN UP IN 1896 – Calcutta: Office of the Superintendent of Govt Printing India, 1897 – 1 – us Res Libr [950]

AN HISTORICAL SURVEY OF BLACK BAPTIST HYMNODY IN AMERICA / Barker, George Stanley – 1981 – 1 – 5.20 – us Baptist [240]

AN HISTORICAL SURVEY OF THE FIRST PRESBYTERIAN CHURCH, CALDWELL, N.J / Berry, Charles T – 1871 – 1 – us A.T.L.A. [240]

HISTORICAL TRACTS AND DOCUMENTS, STATE PAPERS, ETC / Holkham Hall. Norfolk. England – 1562-82. Holkham Ms 678 – 1 – uk Microform Academic [941]

HISTORICAL TRIALS RELEVANT TO TODAY'S ISSUES – Transcripts of over 100 British and American trials, most from the 18th and 19th cents. Slavery, impeachment, libel, treason, piracy, mutiny, murder, kidnapping and divorce. 652 fiches – 9 – $1,940.00 – us UPA [340]

AN HISTORICAL VIEW OF THE PHILIPPINE ISLANDS / Martinez de Zuniga, J – Manila, 1966 – 3mf – 9 – ne IDC [950]

A HISTORICAL VINDICATION OF THE ABROGATION OF THE PLAN OF UNION BY THE PRESBYTERIAN CHURCH IN THE UNITED STATES OF AMERICA / Brown, Isaac V – Philadelphia: Wm. S. & Alfred Martien, 1855, c1854 – 1mf – us A.T.L.A. [240]

HISTORICAL WORK / Screven, William – From collect. of Maine Historical Society, 1629, 1663-69, 1783-87, 1820-37. 202p – 1 – 7.07 – us Baptist [978]

THE HISTORICAL WORK OF MASTER RALPH DE DICETO, DEAN OF LONDON (RS68) = RADULPHI DE DICETO DECANI LUNDONIENSIS, OPERA HISTORICA / Ralph De Diceto; ed by Stubbs, W – (v1 1876 Dfl35.00. v2 1876 Dfl30.00) – ne Slangenburg [941]

HISTORICAL WORKS, THE CHRONICLE OF THE REIGNS OF STEPHEN, HENRY 2 AND RICHARD 1 (RS73) : BY GERVASE, THE MONK OF CANTERBURY / Gervase Of Canterbury; ed by Stubbs, W – v1 1879 v2 1880 – Dfl42.00 – ne Slangenburg [941]

A HISTORICAL-ETHNOGRAPHIC ACCOUNT OF A CANADIAN WOMAN IN SPORT, 1920-1938 : THE STORY OF MARGARET (BELL) GIBSON / Laubman, Katherine M & Schrodt, P Barbara – 1991 – 3mf – 9 – $12.00 – us Microform Publ [790]

HISTORICI GERMANIAE SAEC. 12 (MGH 5: 21.BD) – 1869 – Dfl60.00 – ne Slangenburg [240]

HISTORICI GERMANIAE SAEC. 12 (MGH 5: 22.BD) – 1872 – Dfl53.00 – ne Slangenburg [240]

AN HISTORICO-CRITICAL INQUIRY INTO THE ORIGIN AND COMPOSITION OF THE HEXATEUCH / Kuenen, Abraham – London: Macmillan, 1886.1 fiche – 9 – us A.T.L.A. [220]

HISTORICO-CRITICO-MEDICO-PRACTICA EN QUE SE ESTABLECE EL AGUA POR REMEDIO UNIVERSAL DE LAS DEOLENCIAS : HISTORICO-CRITICO-MEDICO-PRACTICA EN QUE SE ESTABLECE EL AGUA POR REMEDIO / Perez, V – Madrid, 1753 – 2mf – 9 – sp Cultura [615]

HISTORICO-IURIDICA DE MODERNO USU CONSTITUTIONIS PACIS PUBLICAE ... / Behrens, C E – Giessae, 1750 – 1mf – 9 – ILM-941/1 – ne IDC [327]

HISTORIE DE LA PAROISSE DE SAINTE-ANNE DES PLAINES, ERIGEE SOUS MGR HUBERT, EVEQUE DE QUEBEC, EN L'ANNEE 1787 / Dugas, Georges – Montreal: Granger Freres, 1900. 05193. (Pre-1900 Canadiana) – 9 – cn C.I.H.M. [971]

LE HISTORIE DELLE INDIE ORIENTALI / Maffei, G P – Venetia, 1589 – 10mf – 9 – H-8412/1 – ne IDC [950]

HISTORIE DER WEISZHEIT UND THORHEIT ZUSAMMENGETRAGEN VON CHR. THOMAS – Th. I-III. Halle, Chr. Salfelden. 1693. BME-415 1 – 9 – ne IDC [240]

A HISTORIE OF IRELAND / Campion, Edmund – C.1571 – 9 – 10.00 – us Scholars' Facs [941]

HISTORIE OFTE BESCHRIJVING VAN 'T UTRECHTSCHE BISDOM – Leiden. v1-3. 1719 – Dfl112.00 – ne Slangenburg [240]

LE HISTORIE VINITIANE DI MARCO ANTONIO SABELLICO, ... / Coccius, M A – Vinegia, 1554 – 6mf – 9 – H-8287/1 – ne IDC [945]

HISTORIE VOM HERZOG HERPIN – ca 40p + 7 color mf – DM650.00 – 3-89219-017-8 – gw Lengenfelder [440]

HISTORIE VON GROENLAND / Cranz, D – BN 178 2. v. 1-3. 1770 – 8 – ne IDC [948]

DIE "HISTORIE VON VIER KAUFMAENNERN" UND DEREN DRAMATISCHE BEARBEITUNGEN IN DER DEUTSCHEN LITERATUR DES 16. UND 17. JAHRHUNDERTS / Mechel, Kurt – Halle, 1914 – 1mf – DM 48.00 – 3-8267-3097-6 – gw Hänsel [430]

HISTORIE...CONTENENO LE GVERRE DI MAHOMETTO IMPERATORE DE TURCHI / Guazzo, M – Venetia, 1545 – 1mf – 9 – H-8275/1 – ne IDC [956]

HISTORIEN DER ALDEN E / ed by Gerhard, Wilhelm – (Includes bibliographical references and index) – Leipzig: K W Hiersemann, 1927 – 1 – us U.W. Library [830]

HISTORIENBIBEL – 30p + 9 color mf – DM540.00 – 3-89219-006-2 – gw Lengenfelder [220]

HISTORIES OF CIVIL WAR GENERALS – v. 1-50. 1888. Duke Cigarette miniature volumes – 7 – 41.00 – us L of C Photodup [976]

HISTORIESE STUDIES – Pretoria. South Africa. 1939-49 – 1 – sa State Libr [072]

HISTORIESE STUDIES – University of Pretoria. v.1-9, 1939-49 – 1 – us Res Libr [960]

HISTORIKAI MELETAI / Papadopoulos, Chrysostomou – En Ierosolumois: Ek tou typographeiou tou Hierou Koinou tou Panagiou Taphou, 1906 – 1mf – us A.T.L.A. [240]

[HISTORIOGRAPHY OF CZECHOSLOVAKIA PAMPHLET COLLECTION] – 1968 – 1 – CSUXANL4459-B – us Hoover Inst Photo [947]

HISTORIOGRAPHY OF SOUTHERN AFRICA – 1980 – 112p – 9 – 92-3-101775-6 – fr UNESCO [960]

[HISTORIOGRAPHY OF THE RUSSIAN REVOLUTION PAMPHLET COLLECTION] – 1987 – 1 – CSUXANS8451-B – us Hoover Inst Photo [947]

HISTORIOGRAPHY OF THE SOVIET UNION PAMPHLET COLLECTION – 1923-1983 – 1 reel – 1 – CSUXANR3691-B – us Hoover Inst Photo [947]

HISTORIOGRAPHY OF TURKEY PAMPHLET COLLECTION – 1952-1967 – 1 – CSUXANQ7481-B – us Hoover Inst Photo [949]

HISTORIOGRAPHY OF WORLD WAR 2 PAMPHLET COLLECTION – 1941-1945 – 1 reel – 1 – CSUXANM6451-B – us Hoover Inst Photo [355]

HISTORIQUE DE LA TRAITE ET DU DROIT DE VISITE / Jollivet, Th. M Ad – (Slave Trade and Abolitionism in France series). 1841 – 9 – fr Hachette [360]

HISTORIQUE DE L'ECOLE SOCIETAIRE FONDEE PAR CHARLES FOURIER SUIVI D'UN RESUME DE LA DOCTRINE FOURIERISTE ET DU SOMMAIRE DU GERANTISME ELUCIDE / Alhaiza, Adolphe – Paris: La Renovation, 1894. 152p. 2 fiches. (Political Science Collection) – 9 – 6.00 – fr Bibl Nationale [335]

HISTORIQUE DES JOURNAUX D'OTTAWA / Audet, Francis Joseph – Ottawa: A. Bureau, 1896. 00058. (Pre-1900 Canadiana) – 9 – cn C.I.H.M. [971]

HISTORIQUE DU CERCLE ET RAPPORT GENERAL DU SECRETAIRE POUR L'ANNEE 1886-87 / Cercle Ville-Marie. Montreal, Canada – 1887. SEM105P814 – 1mf – 9 – Can$2.25 – cn Bibl Nat [971]

HISTORIQUE DU CERCLE LOUIS 16TH : 1760-1907 / Lisle du Dreneuc, Pitre de – Nantes: Dugas, 1907 – fr Armell [944]

HISTORIQUE DU SAGUENAY / Un Comite de Collaborateurs – Quebec: Imp. Leger Brousseau, 1883. SEM105P376 – 1mf – 9 – Can$2.25 – cn Bibl Nat [971]

HISTORIQUE DU SAGUENAY: SOUVENIR DE L'EXCURSION DE LA PRESSE D'ONTARIO ET DE QUEBEC A CHICOUTIMI, AU GRAND-BRULE ET A ST ALPHONSE, LE 9 AOUT 1883 / Comite de Collaborateurs – Quebec?, 1883. 05640. (Pre-1900 Canadiana) – 9 – cn C.I.H.M. [971]

HISTORISCH ODER MYTHISCH? : BEITRAEGE ZUR BEANTWORTUNG DER GEGENWAERTIGEN LEBENSFRAGE DER THEOLOGIE / Ullmann, C – Hamburg: F. Perthes, 1838 – 1mf – us A.T.L.A. [240]

HISTORISCH WOORDENBOEK VAN ZUIDWESTELIJK CELEBES, DOOR A. LIGTVOET, C1880 – 2v. KITLV,H 606bl-II. BSD-104/1 mf. 1-5 – 9 – ne IDC [950]

HISTORISCH-BIOGRAPHISCHE STUDIEN / Ranke, Leopold von – Leipzig: Duncker & Humblot, 1877 – 2mf – us A.T.L.A. [240]

HISTORISCH-BIOGRAPHISCHE URKUNDEN DES MITTLEREN REICHES / Sethe, K – (Urkunden des Agyptischen Altertums, Herausgegeben von Georg Steindorff. Siebente Abteilung heft 1). Leipzig. 1935. BNE-399 1 – 9 – ne IDC [930]

HISTORISCH-BIOGRAPHISCHES LEXICON DER TONKUENSTLER / Gerber, E L – Erster-Zweyter Theil. 1790-92 – 9 – us Sibley [780]

HISTORISCH-BIOGRAPHISCHES LEXICON DER TONKUENSTLER, WELCHES NACHRICHTEN VON DEM LEBEN UND WERKEN MUSKALISCHER SCHRIFTSTELLER, BERUEMTER COMPONISTEN, SAENGER... / Gerber, E L – Leipzig: Breitkopf, 1790-1792 – 27mf – ne IDC [780]

HISTORISCH-COMPARATIVE SYNTAX DER HEBRAEISCHEN SPRACHE / Koenig, F E – Leipzig. 1897. BJ-412-11 1 – 9 – ne IDC [470]

HISTORISCH-CRITISCHE BIJDRAGEN / Scholten, Johannes Henricus – Leiden: S.C. van Doesburgh, 1882. 1 fiche – 9 – us A.T.L.A. [240]

HISTORISCHE ARBEITEN VORNEHMLICH ZUR REFORMATIONSZEIT / Cornelius, C A – Leipzig: Duncker & Humblot, 1899 – 2mf – us A.T.L.A. [240]

HISTORISCHE BESCHREIBUNG DER EDELEN SING- UND KLING-KUN. / Printz, Wolfgang C – 1690 – 9 – us Sibley [780]

HISTORISCHE BESCHREIBUNG DER EDELEN SING-UND KLING-KUNST VON WOLFGANG CASPAR PRINTZEN / Printz, Wolfgang C – Dresden. 1690. BP-437 1 – 9 – ne IDC [780]

HISTORISCHE BESCHREIBUNG DES GANTZEN STREITS ZWISCHEN D. HUNNEN VND D. HUBERN VON DER GNADENWAHL WIE DERSELBIGE ENTSPRUNGEN VND BISS DAHER ZUGENOMEN HABE... / Huber, S – [Oberursel], 1597 – 2mf – ne IDC [240]

HISTORISCHE BESCHRYVING DER STADT AMSTERDAM: WAER IN DE VOORNAEMITE GEICHIEDENIFFEN.. / Dapper, O – Amsterdam: J. van Meurs, 1663 – 1 – us U.W. Library [949]

DIE HISTORISCHE ENTWICKLUNG DER INTERDEPENDENZ VON ATMUNG UND HERZ-KREISLAUFSYSTEM UND DER EINFLUß DER ATMUNG AUF DIE HERZZEITINTERVALLE UNTER BESONDERER BERUECKSICHTIGUNG DER KOERPERPOSITION / Geider, Stefan – 1994 – 1mf – DM60.00 – 3-8267-2030-X – gw Hänsel [611]

HISTORISCHE ERKLAERUNG DES ZWEITEN TEILS DES JESAIA, CAPITEL 40 BIS CAPITEL 66 / Ley, Julius – Marburg: N.G. Elwert, 1893. 1 fiche – 9 – us A.T.L.A. [240]

Historische Gesellschaft fuer die Provenz Posen *see* ZEITSCHRIFT

Historische Gesellschaft zu Berlin *see*
- JAHRESBERICHTE DER GESCHICHTSWISSENSCHAFT
- MITTEILUNGEN AUS DER HISTORISCHEN LITTERATUR

DER HISTORISCHE HANS KOHLHASE UND HEINRICH VON KLEIST'S MICHAEL KOHLHAAS / Burkhardt, C A H – (Includes bibliographical footnotes) – Leipzig: Vogel, 1864 – 1r – 1 – us U.W. Library [430]

HISTORISCHE NACHRICHT VON DEM AKADEMISCHEN WUERDEN IN DER MUSIK UND OEFFENTLICHEN MUSIKALISCHEN AKADEMIEN UND GESELLSCHAFTEN / Oelrichs, J C C – Berlin. 1752. BP-733 1 – 9 – ne IDC [780]

HISTORISCHE NACHRICHTEN UND POLITISCHE BETRACHTUNGEN UEBER DIE FRANZOESISCHE REVOLUTION – Berlin, 1792-97, 1802-03 – 1 – Dist. gw Mikrofilm – gw Misc Inst [943]

HISTORISCHE QUELLEN ZUR FRAUENBEWEGUNG UND GESCHLECHTERPROBLEMATIK *see*
- DER ABOLITIONIST, 1. 1902 – 32. 1933 (HQ 28)
- ALLGEMEINER FRAUENKALENDER, 1.1885-2.1886 DIE FRAUENBESTREBUNGEN UNSERER ZEIT, 3.1887 (HQ, 17)
- ARCHIV FUER FRAUENKUNDE UND EUGENIK, 1914. ARCHIV FUER FRAUENKUNDE UND EUGENETIK, 1915-1923. ARCHIV FUER FRAUENKUNDE UND KONSTITUTIONSFORSCHUNG, 1924-1933 (HQ, 19)
- BIBLIOGRAPHISCHE MITTEILUNGEN UEBER DIE RECHTSSTELLUNG DER FRAU IM DEUTSCHEN REICH UND IN OESTERREICH (HQ 2)
- DAMEN-CONVERSATIONS-LEXIKON (HQ 13)
- DIE FRAU (HQ 1)
- DIE FRAU IM STAAT (HQ 9)
- FRAUENANWALT, 1. 1870/71 – 6. 1875/76; DEUTSCHER FRAUENANWALT, 1878-81 (HQ 29)

- FRAUENBERUF (HQ, 18)
- DIE FRAUENBEWEGUNG (HQ 10)
- FRAUENBILDUNG, 1. 1902-22. 1923 (HQ 23)
- FRAUENTASCHENBUCH (HQ, 22)
- FRAUEN-ZUKUNFT, 1.1910-3.1913 (HQ, 21)
- FREYA
- GESCHLECHT UND GESELLSCHAFT (HQ 3)
- HANDBUCH DER FRAUENBEWEGUNG (HQ 26)
- ILLUSTRIERTES KONVERSATIONS-LEXIKON DER FRAU (HQ 12)
- JAHRBUCH FUER SEXUELLE ZWISCHENSTUFEN 1.1899-23.1923 (HQ, 20)
- MITTEILUNGEN DES DEUTSCH-EVANGELISCHEN FRAUENBUNDES, 1. 1900/01 - 4. 1903/04; EVANGELISCHE FRAUENZEITUNG, 5. 1904/05 - 42. 1940/41 (HQ 25)
- MUTTERSCHUTZ (HQ 5)
- DIE NEUE GENERATION (HQ 6)
- NUTZBARES, GALANTES UND CURIOESES FRAUENZIMMER-LEXIKON...(HQ 14)
- SEXUAL-PROBLEME (HQ 7)
- SEXUALREFORM (HQ 4)
- ZEITSCHRIFT FUER SEXUALWISSENSCHAFT, 1908 (HQ 27)
- ZEITSCHRIFT FUER SEXUALWISSENSCHAFT (HQ 8)

HISTORISCHE REMARQUES UEBER DIE NEUESTEN SACHEN IN EUROPA – Hamburg, Germany. 1701-03 – 3r – 1 – gw Mikrofilm [072]

HISTORISCHE ZEITSCHRIFT – Muenchen, 1859-1930. v1-141 – 1,474mf – 9 – H-576/2 – ne IDC [943]

HISTORISCHE ZEITSCHRIFT – v1-100. 1859-1908 – 18r – 1 – $1,300.00 – us OmniSys [073]

HISTORISCHER BERICHT, VON DEM ZU REGENSBURGK UNLANGST GEHALTENEN COLLOQVIO, ZWISCHEN DEN THEOLOGEN AUGSBURGISCHER CONFESSION VND DEN PAPISTEN / Hunnius, A – Wittenberg, 1602 – 1mf – ne IDC [240]

Historischer Verein. Bamberg *see* BERICHT

HISTORISCHER VEREIN DER PFALZ – Mitteilungen des Historischen Vereins der Pfalz.v1-. 1870-.-irr. 1870-1932; annual, 1953- – 1 – us U.W. Library [943]

Historischer Verein. Dillingen *see* JAHRBUCH

Historischer Verein fuer die Graftschaft Ravensberg zu Bielefeld *see* JAHRESBERICHT

Historischer Verein. Niederbayern *see* VERHANDLUNGEN

Historischer Verein. Niedersachsen, Hannover *see* ZEITSCHRIFT

Historischer Verein. Oberpfalz and Regensburg *see* VERHANDLUNGEN

Historischer Verein von Unterfranken und Aschaffenburg. Wuerzburg *see* ARCHIV DES HISTORISCHEN VEREINS VON UNTERFRANKEN UND ASCHAFFENBURG

HISTORISCHES GEOGRAPHISCHES LEXIKON VON DER SCHWEIZ ODER VOLLSTAENDIGE BESCHREIBUNG ALLER IN DER GANZEN SCHWEIZERISCHEN EIDGENOSSENSCHAFT UND DEN DERSELBEN ZUGEWANDTEN ORTEN LIEGENDEN STAEDTE (AEL, ABT 1;29) – Ulm. 2 bde. 1796 (mf ed 1995) – 8mf – 9 – DM180.00 – 3-89131-207-5 – gw Fischer [059]

HISTORISCHES JAHRBUCH : GOERRES-GESELLSCHAFT ZUR PFLEGE DER WISSENSCHAFT IM KATHOLISCHEN DEUTSCHLAND – Bonn, 1880-1941. v1-61. 1914, Index v1-34 – 887mf – 9 – H-628c/2 – ne IDC [060]

HISTORISCHES JAHRBUCH DER GOERRES-GESELLSCHAFT – 14(1893)-20(1899); 22(1901)-26(1905); 49(1929)- 58(1938) – 314mf – 9 – Dfl1,099.00 – ne Slangenburg [073]

HISTORISCH-KRITISCHE AUSGABE / Deutsche National-Literatur – 163v. 1882-99 – 1 – $645.00 – us L of C Photodup [430]

HISTORISCH-KRITISCHE BEYTRAEGE ZUR AUFNAHME DER MUSIK / Marpurg, Friedrich Wilhelm – 1754-78.5v – 9 – us Sibley [780]

HISTORISCH-KRITISCHE BEYTRAEGE ZUR AUFNAHME DER MUSIK / Marpurg, Friedrich Wilhelm – P 712. 5 v. 1754-1760 – 9 – ne IDC [780]

HISTORISCH-KRITISCHE EINLEITUNG IN DAS NEUE TESTAMENT / Hilgenfeld, A – Leipzig, 1875 – 14mf – 8 – ne Slangenburg [220]

HISTORISCH-POLITISCHE BLAETTER FUER DAS KATHOLISCHE DEUTSCHLAND – Muenchen. Bd. 67-171; 1871-1923. Reel 36 includes Register zu Bd. 1-130. Succeeded by Gelbe Hefte. Film Mas C 282 – 1 – us H.U. Library [073]

HISTORISCH-POLITISCHE SCHRIFTEN DES DIETRICH VON NIEHEIM (MGH 10: 5.BD) : 1. STUECK: VIRIDARIUM IMPERATORUM ET REGUM ROMANORUM – 1956 – Dfl19.00 – ne Slangenburg [240]

HISTORISCH-THEORETISCH UND PRAKTISCHE UNTERSUCHUNG DES INSTRUMENTS DER LAUTEN / Baron, E G – Nuernberg, Ruediger. 1727. BP-151 1 – 9 – ne IDC [780]

HISTORISK AFHANDLING OM MUSIK OCH INSTRUMENTER SAERDELES OM ORGWERKS INRAETTNINGEN I ALLMAENHET, JEMTE KORT BESKRIFNING OEFWER-ORGWERKEN I SWERIGE / Huelphers, A – Westeras. 1773. BP-329 1 – 9 – ne IDC [780]

DER HISTORISMUS UND SEINE UEBERWINDUNG: FUENF VORTRAEGE / Troeltsch, Ernst – Berlin: R. Heise, 1924 – xii/108p – 1 – us U.W. Library [190]

HISTORY / Comanche County. Kansas. Union Church Edifice Society – 1879 – 1 – us KS Hist [978]

HISTORY / Greensburg. Kansas. Greensburg Town Company – 1884-88 – 1 – us KS Hist [978]

HISTORY / Jantzen Family – 1744-1947 – 1 – us KS Hist [978]

HISTORY / Nielson, Jens Christian – 1853-1915[?], In Danish – 1 – us KS Hist [920]

HISTORY / Nielson, Jens Christian – 1853-[1915?], In English – 1 – us KS Hist [920]

HISTORY – n.s. v. 1-50, nos. 1-170. London. 1916-65 – 9 – 24300.00; 4.00v – uk Dawson [900]

HISTORY – orig. s. v. 1-4. London. 1912-15 – 9 – 2416.00; 4.00v – uk Dawson [900]

HISTORY : THE QUARTERLY JOURNAL OF THE HISTORICAL ASSOCIATION – N.S. London, 1916-1941. v1-26 – 168mf – 9 – H-786c/2 – ne IDC [060]

HISTORY – v. 1-11. 1972-83 – 1. – apply; v.1-11 1972-83. 5,6,9 – us UMI [900]

HISTORY / Villani, Giovanni & Villani, Matteo – 15th cent. Holkham ms. 552. Holkham Hall, Norfolk, England – 1 – uk Microform Academic [025]

HISTORY. / Lowndes County.Georgia – 1825-1941. 6 fiches. F-0944 – 9 – us A.G.L.L. [920]

HISTORY AND ANNALS OF HEBREW PRINTING IN THE FIFTEENTH AND SIXTEENTH CENTURIES / Marx, Moses – (A list of the contents is available on request: Most of the reels are available separately) – 13r – 1 – $650.00 – us A.J.P.C. [680]

HISTORY AND ANTHROPOLOGY / ed by Humphrey, C et al – 1,5,9 – us Harwood [900]

HISTORY AND ANTIQUITIES OF LONDON, WESTMINSTER, SOUTHWARK AND PARTS ADJACENT / Allen, Thomas – 5v. 1837. London – 1 – 26.00 – us L of C Photodup [941]

HISTORY AND ANTIQUITIES OF THE BOROUGH OF NEW WINDSOR / Windsor Castle. Royal Archives – 1 – uk Microform Academic [025]

HISTORY AND ANTIQUITIES OF THE COUNTY OF CUMBERLAND / Hutchinson, William – 7 – uk Microform Academic [941]

HISTORY AND ANTIQUITIES OF THE COUNTY OF LEICESTER / Nichols, John – 7 – uk Microform Academic [941]

HISTORY AND ANTIQUITIES OF THE EXCHEQUER OF THE KINGS OF ENGLAND / Madox, Thomas – H-1189 2. 1711. Index, 1741 – 8 – ne IDC [941]

THE HISTORY AND ART OF GLASS : INDEX OF PERIODICAL ARTICLES, 1980-1982 / Corning Museum of Glass – 1984. 4320 entries on 1 reel – 1 – $90.00 export $105.00 – 0-8161-1482-X – uk Hall [660]

THE HISTORY AND ART OF GLASS: INDEX OF PERIODICAL LITERATURE / Corning Museum of Glass – (1980-82.-1984.-4320 entries 1 reel. $100.00 ISBN: 0-8161-1482-X) – 1956-79.-1982.-16,000 entries 1 reel, ISBN: 0-8161-1409-9; or 25mf ISBN: 0-8161-1741-1 – 1,9 – $100.00 – uk Hall [740]

HISTORY AND AUTOBIOGRAPHICAL SKETCHES OF MADISON COUNTY, ARKANSAS – 1968. Part of: History of Arkansas. Orig. publ., 1889.Indexed. 3 fiches. F-1294 – 9 – us A.G.L.L. [978]

HISTORY AND BELIEFS OF THE MAJOR RELIGIONS / Scholl, Warren – Girard, KS: Haldeman-Julius, 1924. 64p – 1 – us U.W. Library [230]

HISTORY AND BIOGRAPHICAL GAZETTEER OF MONTREAL TO THE YEAR 1892 / Borthwick, John Douglas – Montreal: J. Lovell, 1892. 00850. (Pre-1900 Canadiana) – 9 – cn C.I.H.M. [971]

HISTORY AND BIOGRAPHICAL REMINISCENCES OF DENTON COUNTY / ed by Bates, F – Denton: McNitzky Print. Co., 1918. Texas Reel 11. (The Cox Library Collection) – 5 – us Americana [978]

HISTORY AND BIOGRAPHY OF WASHINGTON COUNTY AND THE TOWN OF QUEENSBURY / Gresham Publishing Co – New York, 1894. New York Reel 37. (The Cox Library Collection) – 5 – us Americana [978]

HISTORY AND CHARACTER OF AMERICAN REVIVALS OF RELIGION / Colton, Calvin – London: F. Westley and A.H. Davids, 1832 – 1mf – us A.T.L.A. [240]

THE HISTORY AND DESCRIPTION OF AFRICA / Africanus, L – Trans. by J. Pory. Ed. by R. Brown. 3 v. London. 1896. BA-333 2 – 8 – ne IDC [960]

A HISTORY AND DESCRIPTION OF MODERN WINE / Redding, Cyrus – 3rd ed. with add. and correc. London: H.G. Bohn, 1851.viii,440p. illus – 1 – us U.W. Library [640]

A HISTORY AND DESCRIPTION OF ROMAN POLITICAL INSTITUTIONS / ed by Abbott, Frank F – 3rd ed. Boston: Ginn & Co, 1911 – 5mf – 9 – $7.50 – LLMC 92-241 – us L.L.M.C. [340]

HISTORY AND DIGEST OF THE INTERNATIONAL ARBITRATIONS TO WHICH THE UNITED STATES HAS BEEN A PARTY / Moore, John Bassett – 6v in 5bks + 1 mf binder – 9 – $480.00 set – 0-89941-915-1 – us Hein [340]

HISTORY AND DIRECTORY OF KENT COUNTY, MICHIGAN / Dillenback & Leavitt – Grand Rapids: Daily Eagle Steam Printing House, 1870. Michigan Reel 15. (The Cox Library Collection) – 5 – us Americana [978]

HISTORY AND GEOGRAPHY OF TEXAS AS TOLD IN COUNTY NAMES / Fulmore, Z T – Texas State Historical Association, 1915. Texas Reel 13. (The Cox Library Collection) – 5 – us Americana [978]

HISTORY AND HISTORIANS IN THE NINETEENTH CENTURY / Gooch, G P – London; New York: Longmans, Green, 1913 – 2mf – us A.T.L.A. [900]

THE HISTORY AND LIFE OF THE REVEREND DOCTOR JOHN TAULER OF STRASBOURG; WITH TWENTY-FIVE OF HIS SERMONS (TEMP. 1340) / Tauler, Johannes – Trans. by Susanna Winkworth. Preface by Rev. Charles Kingsley. London: Smith, Elder, and comp., 1857.xl,415p – 1 – us U.W. Library [920]

HISTORY AND OUTLINE OF LAWS RELATING TO VESSEL INSPECTION / Arzt, Frederick Karl – Washington, 1940-. 106 p. LL-392 – 1 – us L of C Photodup [340]

THE HISTORY AND PRESENT CONSTITUTION OF THE SHERIFF COURTS OF SCOTLAND; A LETTER TO WILLIAM STIRLING / Robertson, Robert – Glasgow: Maclehose, 1863. 35p. LL-2287 – 1 – us L of C Photodup [340]

THE HISTORY AND PRESENT STATE OF ELECTRICITY, WITH ORIGINAL EXPERIMENTS / Priestley, Joseph – 1 – uk Microform Academic [620]

HISTORY AND PROBLEMS OF ORGANIZED LABOR / Carlton, Frank T – New York, Chicago: D C Heath & Co, 1920 – 6mf – 9 – $9.00 – LLMC 92-221 – us L.L.M.C. [331]

THE HISTORY AND RECORDS OF THE CONFERENCE : TOGETHER WITH ADDRESSES DELIVERED AT THE EVENING MEETINGS / World Missionary Conference 1910 Edinburgh, Scotland – (Includes index) – Edinburgh: Oliphant, Anderson & Ferrier; New York: Fleming H Revell, [1910?] – 1mf – 9 – 0-8370-6546-1 – 1986-0546 – us A.T.L.A. [240]

HISTORY AND REMINISCENCES OF DOUGHERTY COUNTY, GEORGIA – Comp. by members of Thronateeska Chapter Daughters of American Revolution. 1924. Biog. and hist. sketches. 7 fiches. F-0668 – 9 – us A.G.L.L. [920]

HISTORY AND REMINISCENCES OF LOS ANGELES CITY AND COUNTY / Spalding, William A – Los Angeles: J.R. Finnell and Sons, n.d.3v. California Reel 17. (The Cox Library Collection) – 5 – us Americana [978]

HISTORY AND REPOSITORY OF PULPIT ELOQUENCE, DECEASED DIVINES / Fish, Henry Clay – (Containing The Masterspieces Of Bossuet...[et al.]: With Discourses From Chrysostom...[et al.]: Also Sixty Other Celebrated Sermons...: The Whole Arranged In Their Proper Order, And Accompanied With Historical Sketches Of Preaching In The Different Countries Represented : And Biographical And Critical Notices Of The Several Preachers And Their Discourses) – New York: M.W. Dodd, 1856 – 3mf – us A.T.L.A. [240]

HISTORY AND SOCIAL SCIENCE TEACHER – (See also: Canadian Journal of History and Social Science) – v10-. 1974- – 1. – apply; v.13- 1977- 5,6,9 – us UMI [900]

HISTORY AND SOCIAL SCIENCE TEACHER – (v22-25 1986/87-1989/90 Can$20.00y 9. Cont: Canadian Journal of History and Social Science, 1974/75. Cont by: Canadian Social Studies at v26 no 1 1991) – Toronto. v10-25. 1974/75-1989/90 – 5,9 – Price varies – cn Micromedia [370]

HISTORY AND SOCIAL SCIENCE TEACHER *see*
- CANADIAN JOURNAL OF HISTORY AND SOCIAL SCIENCE
- CANADIAN SOCIAL STUDIES

HISTORY AND TECHNOLOGY / ed by Krige, J – 1983- – 1,5,9 – us Harwood [073]

HISTORY AND THEOLOGY IN THE FOURTH GOSPEL / Martyn, James L – 1968 – 1 – us A.T.L.A. [240]

HISTORY AND THEORY – 1- 1960- – 1. ; 5,6. ; 9 – apply; v.10-; v.15- – us UMI [900]

HISTORY AND TOPOGRAPHY OF THE PARISH OF WAKEFIELD AND ITS ENVIRONS / Hewitt, John – 1862 – 9 – uk Microform Academic [941]

THE HISTORY AND USE OF HYMNS AND HYMN-TUNES / Breed, David R – Chicago: Fleming H. Revell, 1903 – 1mf – us A.T.L.A. [780]

HISTORY, AUTHORITY AND THEOLOGY / Headlam, Arthur C – London: J. Murray, 1909 – 1mf – us A.T.L.A. [240]

HISTORY BRANCH OFFICE OF JUDGE ADVOCATE GENERAL WITH THE U.S. FORCES EUROPEAN THEATER, 18 JULY, 1942-1 NOVEMBER, 1945 / U.S. European Theater. Office of the Judge Advocate General – v. 1-2. 1945 – 1 – 27.00 – us L of C Photodup [340]

THE HISTORY, CIVIL AND COMMERCIAL, OF THE BRITISH WEST INDIES WITH A CONTINUATION TO THE PRESENT TIME / Edwards, Bryan – Philadelphia. 5v. 1806-19 – 1r – 1 – us Ross [972]

"HISTORY IN THE MAKING" – New York. N.Y. 1945-51 – 1 – us UMI [071]

HISTORY IN THE MAKING – San Bernardino, CA. 1951-64 – 2r – 1 – $100.00 – R02765 – us Library Micro [071]

HISTORY, JURISDICTION, AND PRACTICE OF THE COURT OF CLAIMS OF THE UNITED STATES / Richardson, William Adams – Washington: Govt. Print. Off., 1882. 20p. LL-1221 – 1 – us L of C Photodup [340]

HISTORY NOTES *see* VIRGINIA MAGAZINE OF HISTORY AND BIOGRAPHY

THE HISTORY OF A COLORADO REAL ESTATE MORTGAGE. / Webber, Henry William – Denver, Chain & Hardy, 1895. 154 p. LL-1554 – 1 – us L of C Photodup [340]

THE HISTORY OF A FAMOUS COURT HOUSE LOCATED AT CARLINVILLE, ILLINOIS / Brown, William Barrick – Carlinville, Carlinville Democrat, 1934 54 p. LL-1234 – 1 – us L of C Photodup [340]

HISTORY OF A LAWSUIT / Caruthers, Abraham – 3d ed. Cincinnati: Clarke, 1888. 688p. LL-739 – 1 – us L of C Photodup [340]

HISTORY OF A SIX WEEKS' TOUR THROUGH A PART OF FRANCE, SWITZERLAND, GERMANY AND HOLLAND... / Shelley, Mary Wollstonecraft – London, 1817 – 1 roll – 1 – 1-55879-659-2 – uk Libr Preservation [910]

THE HISTORY OF A SUIT AT LAW, ACCORDING TO THE PRACTICE OF THIS STATE / Conner, James – Charleston, S.C., Courtenay, 1857. 72 p. LL-2286 – 1 – us L of C Photodup [340]

HISTORY OF A SUIT IN EQUITY, AS PROSECUTED AND DEFENDED IN THE VIRGINIA STATE COURTS. / Sands, Alexander Hamilton – 2d ed. Richmond: Randolph & English, 1882. 760, lxp. LL-1337 – 1 – us L of C Photodup [340]

THE HISTORY OF A TITLE / Crocker, Uriel Haskell – Boston, The Massachusetts Title Insurance Company, 1885. 24 p. LL-540 – 1 – us L of C Photodup [340]

HISTORY OF A ZOOLOGICAL TEMPERANCE CONVENTION : HELD IN CENTRAL AFRICA IN 1847 / Hitchcock, Edward – Boston: Nathaniel Noyes, 1855 – 2mf – 9 – $3.00 – LLMC 91-092 – us L.L.M.C. [360]

HISTORY OF ABEOKUTA / Ajisafe, Ajayi Kolawole – [2nd ed]. Bungay, Suffolk: Clay, 1924 – 1 – us Res Libr [960]

HISTORY OF ADAIR COUNTY / Violette, E M – Reminiscences and biographical sketches.Denslow History Co., 1911. Missouri Reel 8. (The Cox Library Collection) – 5 – us Americana [978]

HISTORY OF ADAIR, SULLIVAN, PUTNAM AND SCHUYLER COUNTIES – Chicago, 1888. Missouri Reel 7.(The Cox Library Collection) – 5 – us Americana [978]

HISTORY OF ADAMS COUNTY – Biographical sketches. Chicago, 1885. Ohio Reel 12. (The Cox Library Collection) – 5 – us Americana [978]

HISTORY OF ADAMS COUNTY / Evans & Strivers – Earliest settlement to present time. West Union: E.B. Strivers, 1900. Ohio Reel 11. (The Cox Library Collection) – 5 – us Americana [978]

THE HISTORY OF ADAMS COUNTY, ILLINOIS / Murray & Williamson C W & Phelps – Chicago: 1879. Illinois Reel 11. (The Cox Library Collection) – 5 – us Americana [978]

HISTORY OF ADDISON COUNTY / Smith, H P – Syracuse, D. Mason and Co., 1886. Vermont Reel 6. (The Cox Library Collection) – 5 – us Americana [978]

A HISTORY OF AGRICULTURE AND PRICES IN ENGLAND : FROM THE YEAR AFTER THE OXFORD PARLIAMENT (1259) TO THE COMMENCEMENT OF THE CONTINENTAL WAR (1793) / Rogers, J E T – Oxford, 1866-1902. 7v – 96mf – 9 – H-1266/2 – ne IDC [630]

HISTORY OF ALAMEDA COUNTY / M.W. Wood, Publisher – Oakland, 1883. California Reel 9. The Cox Library Collection – 5 – us Americana [978]

HISTORY OF ALAMEDA COUNTY / Wood, W M – Alameda Co, CA. 1964 – 1r – 1 – $50.00 – B40204 – us Library Micro [978]

HISTORY OF ALAMEDA COUNTY, CALIFORNIA – Chicago, 1928. v2. California Reel 10. The Cox Library Collection – 5 – us Americana [978]

HISTORY OF ALBANIA PAMPHLET COLLECTION – 1913-1945 – 1 reel – 1 – CSUXANQ7730-B – us Hoover Inst Photo [947]

HISTORY OF ALEXANDER COUNTY, UNION AND PULASKI COUNTIES / Perrin, William Henry – Chicago: O. L. Baskin and Co., 1883. Illinois Reel 12. (The Cox Library Collection) – 5 – us Americana [978]

A HISTORY OF ALL RELIGIONS : AS DIVIDED INTO PAGANISM, MAHOMETANISM, JUDAISM AND CHRISTIANITY... / Benedict, David – Providence: J. Miller, printer, 1824 – 1mf – us A.T.L.A. [230]

HISTORY OF ALLEGAN AND BARRY COUNTIES / D.W. Ensign and Company – Historical and biographical sketches. Philadelphia, 1880. Michigan Reel 4. The Cox Library Collection – 5 – us Americana [978]

HISTORY OF ALLEGANY COUNTY – L. R. Titsworth and Co., 1923. Vols. 1-2. Maryland Reel 2. (The Cox Library Collection) – 5 – us Americana [978]

HISTORY OF ALLEGHENY COUNTY / A. Warner and Co – Chicago, 1889. Pennsylvania Reel 7. The Cox Library Collection – 5 – us Americana [978]

HISTORY OF ALLEN AND WOODSON COUNTIES / Duncan & Scott – Iola Register Printers and Binders, 1901. Kansas Reel 6. (The Cox Library Collection) – 5 – us Americana [978]

HISTORY OF ALLEN COUNTY / Miller, Charles C – Chicago: Richmond and Arnold, 1906. Ohio Reel 12. (The Cox Library Collection) – 5 – us Americana [978]

THE HISTORY OF ALLIED FORCE HEADQUARTERS, 1942-1945 / U.S. Army – 1r – 1 – $85.00 – S1683 – us Scholarly Res [355]

HISTORY OF ALSACE-LORRAINE PAMPHLET COLLECTION – 1898-1945 – 4r – 1 – CSUXANR9461-B – us Hoover Inst Photo [944]

A HISTORY OF AMERICAN BAPTIST MISSIONS IN ASIA, AFRICA, EUROPE AND NORTH AMERICA : UNDER THE CARE OF THE AMERICAN BAPTIST MISSIONARY UNION / Gammell, William – Boston: Gould & Lincoln, 1854 – 1mf – 9 – 0-8370-6049-4 – 1986-0049 – us A.T.L.A. [240]

A HISTORY OF AMERICAN CHRISTIANITY / Bacon, Leonard – New York: Christian Literature, 1897. (The American church history series; v.13) – 1mf – us A.T.L.A. [240]

A HISTORY OF AMERICAN CURRENCY. / Sumner, William Graham – 1884. 400p. 1 fiche (29x) – 9 – 1.00f – at Libertarian Micro [320]

THE HISTORY OF AMERICAN MUSIC / Elson, Louis C – New York: Macmillan, 1904. (The history of American art) – 1mf – us A.T.L.A. [780]

A HISTORY OF AMERICAN PRIVATEERS / Maclay, Edgar Stanton – 1900 – 9 – 20.00 – uk Libr Preservation [975]

A HISTORY OF AMERICAN REVIVALS / Beardsley, Frank Grenville – New York: American Tract Society, c1912 – 1mf – us A.T.L.A. [240]

THE HISTORY OF AMERICAN SLAVERY AND METHODISM FROM 1780 TO 1849; AND, HISTORY OF THE WESLEYAN METHODIST CONNECTION OF AMERICA / Matlack, Lucius C – New York: [s.n.], 1849 – 1mf – us A.T.L.A. [240]

A HISTORY OF ANCIENT GEOGRAPHY / Tozer, Henry Fanshawe – Cambridge: University Press, 1897 – 1mf – us A.T.L.A. [910]

HISTORY OF ANCIENT WINDHAM, CONNECTICUT / Windham.Connecticut – Part 1 (A-Bil) by William L. Weaver, 1864. Item A. Includes index. SW16-0225 – 5 – us A.G.L.L. [920]

HISTORY OF ANCIENT WINDSOR, CONNECTICUT / Windsor.Connecticut – By Henry R. Stiles, M.D., 1850. Item F.Includes index. SW16-0227 – 5 – us A.G.L.L. [920]

A HISTORY OF AND BIOGRAPHICAL CYCLOPEDIA OF BUTLER COUNTY / Western Biographical Publishing Co – Cincinnati, 1882. Ohio Reel 16.(The Cox Library Collection) – 5 – us Americana [978]

HISTORY OF AND DIRECTORY OF YATES COUNTY / Cleveland, Stafford C – Penn Yan: S. C. Cleveland, 1873. New York Reel 39. (The Cox Library Collection) – 5 – us Americana [978]

HISTORY OF ANIMALS : BEING THE FOURTH VOLUME OF ELEMENTS OF USEFUL KNOWLEDGE / Webster, Noah – 1812 – 1r – 1 – us Ross [636]

HISTORY OF ANKOLE / Morris, Henry Francis – Nairobi, East African Literature Bureau, 1962 – us Res Libr [960]

A HISTORY OF ANTELOPE COUNTY, NEBRASKA 1868-1883 / Leach, A J – Chicago: R.R. Donnelley and Sons Co., 1909. Nebraska Reel 5. (The Cox Library Collection) – 5 – us Americana [978]

A HISTORY OF ANTI-PEDOBAPTISM : FROM THE RISE OF PEDOBAPTISM TO A.D. 1609 / Newman, Albert Henry – Philadelphia: American Baptist Publication Society, 1897, c1896 – 1mf – us A.T.L.A. [240]

HISTORY OF ANTI-PEDOBAPTISM / Newman, Albert Henry – 1896. 430p – 1 – 15.05 – us Baptist [240]

A HISTORY OF ARABIC LITERATURE / Huart, Clement – London: W. Heinemann, 1903 (Short histories of the literatures of the world; 11) – 2mf – us A.T.L.A. [470]

HISTORY OF ARCHIVES ADMINISTRATION : A SELECT BIBLIOGRAPHY / ed by Evans, Frank B – 1979 – 255p – 9 – 92-3-101646-6 – fr UNESCO [020]

HISTORY OF ARIZONA / Farish, Thomas Edwin – Phoenix: Filmer Brothers Electrotype Co., 1915. 4v. Arizona Reel 1. (The Cox Library Collection) – 5 – us Americana [978]

HISTORY OF ARIZONA / Sloan & Adams – Phoenix: Record Publ. Co., 1930.v1, Arizona Reel 1. v2-4, Arizona Reel 2. (The Cox Library Collection) – 5 – us Americana [978]

HISTORY OF ARMSTRONG COUNTY / Smith, Robert W – Chicago: Waterman, Watkins and Co., 1883. Pennsylvania Reel 9. (The Cox Library Collection) – 5 – us Americana [978]

HISTORY OF ASHLAND COUNTY / Baughman, A J – Biographical sketches of prominent citizens. Chicago: S.J. Clarke Publ. Co., 1909. Ohio Reel 13. (The Cox Library Collection) – 5 – us Americana [978]

HISTORY OF ASHLAND COUNTY / Hill, George W – Biographical sketches. Philadelphia: Williams Brothers, 1880. Ohio Reel 13. (The Cox Library Collection) – 5 – us Americana [978]

HISTORY OF ASHTABULA COUNTY – Biographical sketches. Philadelphia, 1878. Ohio Reel 13. (The Cox Library Collection) – 5 – us Americana [978]

HISTORY OF ASHTABULA COUNTY / Large, Moina W – Indianapolis: Historical Publ. Co., 1924. 2v. Ohio Reel 14. (The Cox Library Collection) – 5 – us Americana [978]

HISTORY OF ASSURBANIPAL / Ashurbanipal, King of Assyria – (In English and Akkadian) – London: Williams and Norgate, 1871 – 1mf – 9 – 0-8370-8562-4 – 1986-2562 – us A.T.L.A. [470]

HISTORY OF ATCHISON COUNTY / Ingalls, Sheffield – Lawrence: Standard Publ. Co., 1916. Kansas Reel 6. (The Cox Library Collection) – 5 – us Americana [978]

HISTORY OF ATHENS COUNTY / Walker, Charles M – Cincinnati: Robert Clarke and Co., 1869.Ohio Reel 14. (The Cox Library Collection) – 5 – us Americana [978]

HISTORY OF AUDRAIN COUNTY / National Historical Co – St. Louis, 1884.Missouri Reel 8. (The Cox Library Collection) – 5 – us Americana [978]

A HISTORY OF AURICULAR CONFESSION AND INDULGENCES IN THE LATIN CHURCH / Lea, Henry Charles – London. v1-3. 1896 – 30mf – 8 – Dfl105.00 – ne Slangenburg [240]

HISTORY OF BALTIMORE CITY AND COUNTY / Scharf, Thomas J – Philadelphia, Louis H. Everts, 1881. Maryland Reel 3. (The Cox Library Collection) – 5 – us Americana [978]

HISTORY OF BALTIMORE, MARYLAND FROM ITS FOUNDING AS A TOWN TO THE CURRENT YEAR–1729-1898 / Nelson, S B – 1898. Maryland Reel 3. (The Cox Library Collection) – 5 – us Americana [978]

HISTORY OF BANAT PAMPHLET COLLECTION – 1918-1924 – 1 reel – 1 – CSUXANL5798-B – us Hoover Inst Photo [947]

THE HISTORY OF BAPTISM / Robinson, Robert – reprinted from the original London edition of 1790, with introduction and notes by J.R. Graves. Nashville: Southwestern Baptist Publ. Hse., 1860. Pub. No. 6380 – 1 – $35.60 – us Baptist [240]

HISTORY OF BAPTIST INDIAN MISSIONS / McCoy, Isaac – 1840 – 1 – 21.91 – us Baptist [240]

A HISTORY OF BAPTISTS IN NIGERIA 1849-1935 WITH APPROPRIATE PROJECTIONS INTO LATER YEARS / Roberson, Cecil F – 1986 – 1 – 16.56 – us Baptist [240]

HISTORY OF BAPTISTS IN NORTH CAROLINA / Williams, Charles – 1901 – 1 – 9.45 – us Baptist [240]

HISTORY OF BAPTISTS OF LOUISIANA / Christian, John T – (260p) – Shreveport: Executive Beard, Louisiana Baptist Convention, 1923 – 1 reel – 1 – $10.40 – us Baptist [240]

HISTORY OF BARNARD / Newton, William M – With family genealogies. Vermont Historical Society, 1928. Vols. 1-2. Vermont Reel 11. (The Cox Library Collection) – 5 – us Americana [920]

HISTORY OF BARNSTABLE COUNTY MASSACHUSETTS – New York, 1890. Massachusetts Reel 2. (The Cox Library Collection) – 5 – us Americana [978]

HISTORY OF BARRON COUNTY / Newton & Wedge – Minneapolis: H. C. Cooper, Jr. and Co., 1922. Wisconsin Reel 6. (The Cox Library Collection) – 5 – us Americana [978]

HISTORY OF BARTHOLOMEW COUNTY / Brant, Fuller and Co – Historical and biographical sketches. Madison: 1888. Indiana Reel 5. (The Cox Library Collection) – 5 – us Americana [978]

HISTORY OF BATES COUNTY / Atkeson, W O – Topeka: Historical Publ. Co., 1918. Missouri Reel 9. (The Cox Library Collection) – 5 – us Americana [978]

HISTORY OF BAY COUNTY AND REPRESENTATIVE CITIZENS / Gansser, Augustus H – Chicago: Richmond and Arnold, 1905. Michigan Reel 5. (The Cox Library Collection) – 5 – us Americana [920]

HISTORY OF BEAVER COUNTY / A. Warner and Co – Philadelphia, 1888. Pennsylvania Reel 9. The Cox Library Collection – 5 – us Americana [978]

HISTORY OF BEAVER COUNTY CENTENNIAL CELEBRATION / Bausman, Joseph H – New York, Knickerbocker Press, 1904. Vols. 1-2, Pennsylvania Reel 10. (The Cox Library Collection) – 5 – us Americana [978]

HISTORY OF BEAVER CREEK BAPTIST CHURCH / Thompson, Mrs. J Frank – us Baptist [240]

HISTORY OF BEDFORD AND SOMERSET COUNTIES / Koontz, William H – New York, Lewis Publ. Co., 1906. Vols. 1-3, Pennsylvania Reel 10. (The Cox Library Collection) – 5 – us Americana [978]

HISTORY OF BELL COUNTY / Tyler, George W – San Antonio: Naylor Co., 1936. Texas Reel 10. (The Cox Library Collection) – 5 – us Americana [978]

HISTORY OF BELMONT AND JEFFERSON COUNTIES / Caldwell, J A – Wheeling: Historical Publ. Co., 1880. Ohio Reel 15. (The Cox Library Collection) – 5 – us Americana [978]

HISTORY OF BENTON COUNTY – Chicago: 1878. Iowa Reel 6. (The Cox Library Collection) – 5 – us Americana [978]

HISTORY OF BENTON, WASHINGTON, CARROLL, MADISON, CRAWFORD, FRANKLIN AND SEBASTIAN COUNTIES, ARKANSAS – Chicago: 1889. Arkansas Reel 3. (The Cox Library Collection) – 5 – us Americana [978]

HISTORY OF BERGEN COUNTY 1630-1923 / Westervelt, Frances A – Historical and biographical. New York, Lewis Historical Publ. Co., 1923. Vols. 1-3. New Jersey Reel 1. (The Cox Library Collection) – 5 – us Americana [978]

HISTORY OF BERKLEY COUNTY / Evans, Willis F – 1928. West Virginia Reel 3. (The Cox Library Collection) – 5 – us Americana [978]

HISTORY OF BERKS COUNTY / Montgomery, Morton L – Philadelphia: Everts, Peck and Richards, 1886. Pennsylvania Reel 11. (The Cox Library Collection) – 5 – us Americana [978]

HISTORY OF BERKSHIRE COUNTY / J.H. Beers and Co – New York, 1885. Massachusetts Reel 2. The Cox Library Collection – 5 – us Americana [978]

HISTORY OF BERLIN–1945 TO THE PRESENT: PAMPHLET COLLECTION – 1948-1988 – 3r – 1 – CSUXANS9151-B – us Hoover Inst Photo [943]

HISTORY OF BERLIN–1917-1945: PAMPHLET COLLECTION – 1957 – 1 – CSUXANS9144-B – us Hoover Inst Photo [943]

HISTORY OF BERRIEN AND VAN BUREN COUNTIES / D.W. Ensign and Company – Biographical sketches. Philadelphia, 1880. Michigan Reel 5. The Cox Library Collection – 5 – us Americana [978]

A HISTORY OF BETHLEHEM BAPTIST ASSOCIATION / Kellie, E I – 1851-96. 62p – 1 – 5.00 – us Baptist [240]

HISTORY OF BINGHAMPTON AND BROOME COUNTIES / Seward, William F – Historical and biographical. New York, Lewis Historical Publ. Co., 1924. Vol. 1. New York Reel 8; Vols. 2-3. New York Reel 9. (The Cox Library Collection) – 5 – us Americana [978]

HISTORY OF BLACK HAWK COUNTY AND REPRESENTATIVE CITIZENS / Van Metre, Isaian – (Chicago: Biographical Publ. Co., 1904). Iowa Reel 6. (The Cox Library Collection) – 5 – us Americana [978]

A HISTORY OF BLAIR COUNTY / Davis & Shenk – Harrisburg, National Historical Asso., 1931. Vols. 1-2, Pennsylvania Reel 12. (The Cox Library Collection) – 5 – us Americana [978]

A HISTORY OF BOHEMIAN LITERATURE / Luetzow, Franz H H V von – London: W. Heinemann, 1907. (Short histories of the literatures of the world) – 2mf – us A.T.L.A. [460]

HISTORY OF BOND AND MONTGOMERY COUNTIES / Perrin, William Henry – Chicago: O. L. Baskin and Co., 1882. Illinois Reel 12. (The Cox Library Collection) – 5 – us Americana [978]

HISTORY OF BOONE COUNTY – Biographical sketches. St. Louis, 1882.Missouri Reel 9. (The Cox Library Collection) – 5 – us Americana [978]

HISTORY OF BOONE COUNTY / Crist, L M – Biographical and genealogical sketches. Indianapolis: A. W. Bowen and Co., 1914. Vols. 1-2. Indiana Reel 6. (The Cox Library Collection) – 5 – us Americana [978]

THE HISTORY OF BOONE COUNTY AND ITS CITIES AND TOWNS / Union Historical Co – Des Moines: Birdsall, Williams and Co., 1880. Iowa Reel 7. (The Cox Library Collection) – 5 – us Americana [978]

HISTORY OF BOURBON COUNTY, KANSAS TO THE CLOSE OF 1865 – By T.F. Robley. 1894. Item N. Includes synoptical index. 210p. SW16-0171 – 5 – us A.G.L.L. [920]

HISTORY OF BOURBON, SCOTT, HARRISON AND NICHOLAS COUNTIES / Perrin, William Henry – Chicago: O.L. Baskin and Co., 1882. Kentucky Reel 6. (The Cox Library Collection) – 5 – us Americana [978]

HISTORY OF BOURBON, SCOTT, HARRISON & NICHOLAS COUNTIES, KENTUCKY – Ed. by William Henry Perrin, 1968. Hist. and biog. sketches. Orig. publ. 1882. 13 fiches. F-0460 – 9 – us A.G.L.L. [920]

HISTORY OF BRADFORD / McKeen, Silas – Includes genealogical sketches. Montpelier, J. D. Clark and Son, 1875. Vermont Reel 7. (The Cox Library Collection) – 5 – us Americana [978]

HISTORY OF BRADFORD COUNTY / Bradsby, H C – Biographical sketches. Chicago, S. B. Nelson and Co., 1891. Pennsylvania Reel 12. (The Cox Library Collection) – 5 – us Americana [978]

THE HISTORY OF BRAINTREE, VERMONT / Bass, H Royce – Rutland: Tuttle and Co., State Printers, 1883. Vermont Reel 7. (The Cox Library Collection) – 5 – us Americana [978]

HISTORY OF BRANCH COUNTY / Everts & Abbott – Biographical sketches. Philadelphia, 1879. Michigan Reel 6. (The Cox Library Collection) – 5 – us Americana [978]

HISTORY OF BREMER COUNTY / Grawe, J F – (Chicago: S. J. Clarke Publ. Co., 1914). Vol. 1-2. Iowa Reel 7. (The Cox Library Collection) – 5 – us Americana [978]

HISTORY OF BRITISH AMERICA: FOR THE USE OF SCHOOLS / Calkin, John Burgess – Halifax, N.S.: A. & W. Mckinlay, 1882. 00382. (Pre-1900 Canadiana) – 9 – cn C.I.H.M. [971]

A HISTORY OF BRITISH BIRDS / Beilby, R – v. 1; Land birds. 2070 2. 1797 – 8 – ne IDC [590]

A HISTORY OF BRITISH BIRDS / Morris, F O – Z 1862. 6 v. Ed. 4. 1895-1896 – 9 – ne IDC [590]

A HISTORY OF BRITISH BIRDS / ed by Seebohm, H – London, 1882-1885. 3vols, Atlas – 8 – ne IDC [590]

A HISTORY OF BRITISH BIRDS, INDIGENOUS AND MIGRATORY / MacGillivray, W – 2104 2. 5 v. 1837-1852 – 8 – ne IDC [590]

A HISTORY OF BRITISH DIPLOMACY AT THE COURT OF THE PESHWAS, 1786-1818 : BASED ON ENGLISH RECORDS OF MAHRATTA HISTORY / Choksey, Rustom Dinshaw – Poona: R.D. Choksey, 1951. iii,xix,399p – 1 – us U.W. Library [950]

A HISTORY OF BRITISH FERNS AND ALLIED PLANTS / Newman, E – ed. 2. London, 1844. 424 pp. B-5303 2 – 8 – ne IDC [580]

A HISTORY OF BRITISH FISHES / Yarrell, W – Z 2140 2. 2 v. plus suppl. 1835-1836. 1839 – 8 – ne IDC [590]

A HISTORY OF BRITISH MOLLUSCA AND THEIR SHELLS / Forbes, E A & Hanley, S – Z-532 2. 4 v. 1848-1853 – 8 – ne IDC [590]

HISTORY OF BRITISH RELATIONS WITH ZANZIBAR, 1800-86 / Lewis, O T – Cardiff, 1936 – us Res Libr [960]

HISTORY OF BROOME COUNTY / Smith, H P – Biographical sketches. Syracuse, D. Mason and Co., 1885. New York Reel 8. (The Cox Library Collection) – 5 – us Americana [978]

HISTORY OF BROWN COUNTY – Chicago, 1883. Ohio Reel 16. The Cox Library Collection – 5 – us Americana [978]

HISTORY OF BROWN COUNTY / Ruley, A N – 1930. Kansas Reel 7. (The Cox Library Collection) – 5 – us Americana [978]

HISTORY OF BROWN COUNTY PAST AND PRESENT – Chicago, 1913. Wisconsin Reel 6. The Cox Library Collection – 5 – us Americana [978]

HISTORY OF BROWN UNIVERSITY, 1764-1914 / Bronson, Walter C – 1 – 19.74 – us Baptist [240]

HISTORY OF BRULE'S DISCOVERIES AND EXPLORATIONS, 1610-26: BEING A NARRATIVE OF THE DISCOVERY BY STEPHEN BRULE OF LAKES HURON, ONTARIO AND SUPERIOR, AND OF HIS EXPLORATIONS...OF PENNSYLVANIA AND WESTERN NEW YORK: ALSO OF THE PROVINCE OF ONTARIO / Butterfield, Consul Willshire – Cleveland, Ohio: Helman-Taylor, 1898. 00368. (Pre-1900 Canadiana) – 9 – cn C.I.H.M. [910]

HISTORY OF BUCHANAN COUNTY / Union Historical Co – Biographical sketches. St. Joseph, 1881. Missouri Reel 10. (The Cox Library Collection) – 5 – us Americana [978]

HISTORY OF BUCHANAN COUNTY AND ITS PEOPLE – Chicago, 1914. Iowa Reel 7. The Cox Library Collection – 5 – us Americana [978]

HISTORY OF BUCHANAN COUNTY AND ST JOSEPH / History Publishing Co – Platte Purchase to 1915, biographical sketches. St. Joseph, 1915. Missouri Reel 11. (The Cox Library Collection) – 5 – us Americana [978]

HISTORY OF BUCHANAN COUNTY AND THE CITY OF ST JOSEPH / Rutt, Chris L – 1826-1904. Chicago: Biographical Publ. Co., 1904. Missouri Reel 10. (The Cox Library Collection) – 5 – us Americana [978]

HISTORY OF BUCKS COUNTY / Battle, J H – Philadelphia, A. Warner and Co., 1887. Pennsylvania Reel 13. (The Cox Library Collection) – 5 – us Americana [978]

HISTORY OF BUCKS COUNTY / Davis, William W – New York, Lewis Publ. Co., 1905. Vols. 1-2, Pennsylvania Reel 13; Vol. 3, Pennsylvania Reel 14. (The Cox Library Collection) – 5 – us Americana [978]

HISTORY OF BUFFALO COUNTY AND ITS PEOPLE / Bassett, Samuel C – Chicago: S.J. Clarke Publ. Co., 1916. 2v. Nebraska Reel 6. (The Cox Library Collection) – 5 – us Americana [978]

HISTORY OF BUFFALO COUNTY, WISCONSIN / Kessinger, L – Alma: 1888. Wisconsin Reel 6. (The Cox Library Collection) – 5 – us Americana [978]

HISTORY OF BULGARIA PAMPHLET COLLECTION – 1881?-1978 – 1 reel – 1 – CSUXANL7434-B – us Hoover Inst Photo [947]

A HISTORY OF BUNCOMBE COUNTY / Sondley, F A – Asheville, Advocate Printing Co., 1930. Vols. 1-2. North Carolina Reel 1. (The Cox Library Collection) – 5 – us Americana [978]

HISTORY OF BUREAU COUNTY / Bradsby, H C – Chicago: World Publ. Co., 1885. Illinois Reel 13. (The Cox Library Collection) – 5 – us Americana [978]

HISTORY OF BURLINGTON AND MERCER COUNTIES / Woodward & Hageman – Biographical sketches. Philadelphia, Everts and Peck, 1883. New Jersey Reel 1. (The Cox Library Collection) – 5 – us Americana [978]

HISTORY OF BURMA INCLUDING BURMA PROPER, PEGU, TAUNGU, TENASSERIM, AND ARAKAN / Phayre, A P – London, 1883 – 4mf – 9 – ne IDC [950]

HISTORY OF BURT COUNTY 1803-1929 / Ludi Printing Co – Wahoo, n.d. Nebraska Reel 6. (The Cox Library Collection) – 5 – us Americana [978]

HISTORY OF BUTLER AND BREMER COUNTIES – Springfield: 1883. Iowa Reel 8. (The Cox Library Collection) – 5 – us Americana [978]

HISTORY OF BUTLER COUNTY / R.C. Brown and Co – 1895. Pennsylvania Reel 14. The Cox Library Collection – 5 – us Americana [978]

HISTORY OF BUTTE COUNTY / Mansfield, George C – Butte Co, CA. 1918 – 1r – 1 – $50.00 – B40206 – us Library Micro [978]

HISTORY OF BUTTE COUNTY / Wells, Harry L – Butte Co, CA. 1882 – 1r – 1 – $50.00 – B40209 – us Library Micro [978]

HISTORY OF BUTTE COUNTY, CALIFORNIA / Mansfield, George C – Los Angeles: Historic Record Co., 1918. California Reel 11. (The Cox Library Collection) – 5 – us Americana [978]

HISTORY OF BUTTE COUNTY, OROVILLE, CALIFORNIA / McGee, Joseph F – Butte Co, CA. 1956 – 1r – 1 – $50.00 – B40208 – us Library Micro [978]

HISTORY OF CALDWELL AND LIVINGSTON COUNTIES / National Historical Co – St. Louis, 1886.Missouri Reel 11. (The Cox Library Collection) – 5 – us Americana [978]

HISTORY OF CALHOUN COUNTY / Gardner, Washington – Chicago: Lewis Publishing Company, 1913. 2v. Michigan Reel 7. The Cox Library Collection – 5 – us Americana [978]

HISTORY OF CALIFORNIA / Irvine, Leigh – Its people and resources. Chicago: Lewis Publ. Co., 1905. v1, California Reel 2. v2, California Reel 3. (The Cox Library Collection) – 5 – us Americana [978]

HISTORY OF CALIFORNIA AND AN EXTENDED HISTORY OF ITS SOUTHERN COAST COUNTIES / Guinn, J M – Los Angeles: Historic Record Co., 1907. v1, California Reel 7. v2, California Reel 8. (The Cox Library Collection) – 5 – us Americana [978]

HISTORY OF CALLAWAY COUNTY / National Historical Co – St. Louis, 1884.Missouri Reel 11. (The Cox Library Collection) – 5 – us Americana [978]

HISTORY OF CAMBRIA COUNTY / Storey, Henry W – Genealogical memoirs. New York, Lewis Publ. Co., 1907. Vols. 1-3, Pennsylvania Reel 15. (The Cox Library Collection) – 5 – us Americana [978]

A HISTORY OF CANADA FOR THE USE OF SCHOOLS / Archer, Andrew – London: T. Nelson: Saint John, N.B.: J. & A. McMillan, 1875. 02474. (Pre-1900 Canadiana) – 9 – cn C.I.H.M. [971]

HISTORY OF CAPE MAY COUNTY / Stevens, Lewis T – Cape May City, 1897. New Jersey Reel 2. (The Cox Library Collection) – 5 – us Americana [978]

HISTORY OF CARBON COUNTY / Brenckman, Fred – Biographical sketches. Harrisburg: James J. Nungesser, 1913. Pennsylvania Reel 15. (The Cox Library Collection) – 5 – us Americana [978]

HISTORY OF CAROLINE COUNTY / Wingfield, Marshall – Richmond, Trevvet Christian and Co., 1924. Virginia Reel 2. (The Cox Library Collection) – 5 – us Americana [978]

HISTORY OF CARROLL AND HARRISON COUNTIES / Eckley & Perry – Chicago: Lewis Publ. Co., 1921. 2v. Ohio Reel 17. (The Cox Library Collection) – 5 – us Americana [978]

HISTORY OF CARROLL COUNTY / H.F. Kett and Co – Chicago, 1878. Illinois Reel 13. The Cox Library Collection – 5 – us Americana [978]

HISTORY OF CARROLL COUNTY / Maclean, Paul – (Chicago: S. J. Clarke Publ. Co., 1912). Vols. 1-2. Iowa Reel 8. (The Cox Library Collection) – 5 – us Americana [978]

HISTORY OF CARROLL COUNTY, ARKANSAS / Braswell, O Klute – 1889. History of its towns from Indian occupation to Jan 1889, plus biog. sketches. 2 fiches. F-0014 – 9 – us A.G.L.L. [978]

HISTORY OF CASS AND BATES COUNTIES / National Historical Co – Biographical sketches. St. Joseph, 1883. Missouri Reel 12. (The Cox Library Collection) – 5 – us Americana [978]

HISTORY OF CASS COUNTY / Glenn, Allen – Topeka: Historical Publ. Co., 1917. Missouri Reel 12. (The Cox Library Collection) – 5 – us Americana [978]

HISTORY OF CASS COUNTY / Helm, Thomas B – Historical and biographical sketches., Chicago: Brant and Fuller, 1886. Indiana Reel 7. (The Cox Library Collection) – 5 – us Americana [978]

HISTORY OF CASS COUNTY / Perrin, William Henry – Chicago: O. L. Baskin and Co., 1882. Illinois Reel 13. (The Cox Library Collection) – 5 – us Americana [978]

HISTORY OF CASS COUNTY / Powell, Jehu Z – Chicago: Lewis Publ. Co., 1913. Vols. 1-2. Indiana Reel 7. (The Cox Library Collection) – 5 – us Americana [978]

HISTORY OF CASS COUNTY – Springfield: 1884. Iowa Reel 9. (The Cox Library Collection) – 5 – us Americana [978]

HISTORY OF CASS COUNTY FROM 1825 TO 1875 / Rogers, Howard S – Cassopolis: W.H. Mansfield, Vigilant Book and Job Print, 1875. Michigan Reel 8. (The Cox Library Collection) – 5 – us Americana [978]

A HISTORY OF CAVALRY FROM THE EARLIEST TIMES, WITH LESSONS FOR THE FUTURE / Denison, George Taylor – 2nd ed. London: Macmillan and Co. Ltd., 1913. xxxi,468p. maps, plans – 1 – us U.W. Library [355]

HISTORY OF CAYUGA COUNTY, 1789 / Storke, Yda A – Biographical sketches. Syracuse, D. Mason and Co., 1879. New York Reel 9. (The Cox Library Collection) – 5 – us Americana [978]

HISTORY OF CEDAR COUNTY – Chicago: 1878. Iowa Reel 9. (The Cox Library Collection) – 5 – us Americana [978]

HISTORY OF CEDAR COUNTY / Historical Publishing Co – Cedar Rapids. Vols. 1-2. Iowa Reel 9. (The Cox Library Collection) – 5 – us Americana [978]

HISTORY OF CENTRAL AND WESTERN TEXAS / Paddock, BB – Chicago: Lewis Publ. Co., 1911. 2v. Texas Reel 9. (The Cox Library Collection) – 5 – us Americana [978]

HISTORY OF CENTRE AND CLINTON COUNTIES / Linn, John Blair – Philadelphia: Louis H. Everts, 1883. Pennsylvania Reel 16. (The Cox Library Collection) – 5 – us Americana [978]

HISTORY OF CEYLON – Peradeniya: University of Ceylon Press Board. v1. [1959-] – us Res Libr [950]

THE HISTORY OF CEYLON FROM THE EARLIEST PERIOD TO THE YEAR 1815 / Philalethes (Pseud. of R. Fellowes) – 1817 – 9 – ne IDC [950]

THE HISTORY OF CHAMPAIGN AND LOGAN COUNTIES FROM THEIR FIRST SETTLEMENT / Antrim, Joshua – Bellefontaine: Press Printing Co., 1872.Ohio Reel 17. (The Cox Library Collection) – 5 – us Americana [978]

HISTORY OF CHAMPAIGN COUNTY – Chicago, 1881. Ohio Reel 18. The Cox Library Collection – 5 – us Americana [978]

HISTORY OF CHAMPAIGN COUNTY / Middleton, Evan P – Biographical Sketches. Indianapolis: B.F. Bowen and Co., 1917. v1. Ohio Reel 18. v2, Ohio Reel 19. (The Cox Library Collection) – 5 – us Americana [978]

HISTORY OF CHARITON AND HOWARD COUNTIES / Smith, T Berry & Gehrig, Pearl S – Topeka: Historical Publ. Co., 1923. Missouri Reel 12. (The Cox Library Collection) – 5 – us Americana [978]

HISTORY OF CHARLESTON AND KANAWHA COUNTY / Laidley, W S – Chicago, Richmond-Arnold Publishing Co. West Virginia Reel 3. (The Cox Library Collection) – 5 – us Americana [978]

A HISTORY OF CHARLESTON ASSOCIATION OF BAPTIST CHURCHES IN THE STATE OF SOUTH CAROLINA / Furman, Wood – 244p – 1 – 8.54 – us Baptist [240]

HISTORY OF CHAUTAUQUA COUNTY / Young, Andrew W – Biographical sketches from the earliest time to the present. Buffalo: Matthews and Warren, 1874. New York Reel 10. (The Cox Library Collection) – 5 – us Americana [978]

HISTORY OF CHENANGO AND MADISON COUNTIES / Smith, James H – Biographical sketches. Syracuse, D. Mason and Co., 1880. New York Reel 12. (The Cox Library Collection) – 5 – us Americana [978]

HISTORY OF CHEROKEE COUNTY / McCulla, Thomas – (Chicago: S. J. Clarke Publ. Co., 1914). Vols. 1-2. Iowa Reel 10. (The Cox Library Collection) – 5 – us Americana [978]

HISTORY OF CHEROKEE COUNTY AND REPRESENTATIVE CITIZENS / Allison, Nathaniel T – Chicago: Biographical Publ. Co., 1904. Kansas Reel 7. (The Cox Library Collection) – 5 – us Americana [978]

HISTORY OF CHESHIRE AND SULLIVAN COUNTIES / Hurd, D Hamilton – Philadelphia, J. W. Lewis, 1886. New Hampshire Reel 3. (The Cox Library Collection) – 5 – us Americana [978]

HISTORY OF CHICAGO / Andreas, A T – Chicago: 1884-86. Vols. 1-2. Illinois Reel 17. (The Cox Library Collection) – 5 – us Americana [978]

HISTORY OF CHICKASAW AND HOWARD COUNTIES / Alexander, W E – (Decorah: Western Publ. Co., 1883). Iowa Reel 10. (The Cox Library Collection) – 5 – us Americana [978]

HISTORY OF CHITTENDEN COUNTY / Rann, W S – Illustrations and biographical sketches. Syracuse, D. Mason and Co., 1886. Vermont Reel 7. (The Cox Library Collection) – 5 – us Americana [978]

A HISTORY OF CHRISTIAN COUNTY / Mechan, Charles M – Nashville: Marshall and Bruce Co., 1930.Kentucky Reel 6. (The Cox Library Collection) – 5 – us Americana [978]

A HISTORY OF CHRISTIAN DOCTRINE / Shedd, William Greenough Thayer – New York: Scribner, 1863 – 3mf – us A.T.L.A. [240]

HISTORY OF CHRISTIAN DOCTRINE / Fisher, George Park – (Includes bibliographical references and index) – New York: Charles Scribner, 1908, c1896 – 2mf – 9 – 0-8370-6328-0 – 1986-0328 – us A.T.L.A. [240]

A HISTORY OF CHRISTIAN DOCTRINES / Hagenbach, K R – Edinburgh: T.& T. Clark; New York: Scribner and Welford [distributor], 1880-1881. (Clark's foreign theological library ; new ser., v1, 3, 8) – 4mf – us A.T.L.A. [240]

HISTORY OF CHRISTIAN ETHICS BEFORE THE REFORMATION / Luthardt, Christoph Ernst – Edinburgh: T. & T. Clark, 1889. xxxii,388p. 1 fiche – 9 – us A.T.L.A. [240]

A HISTORY OF CHRISTIAN MISSIONS DURING THE MIDDLE AGES / Maclear, George Frederick – (Includes bibliographical references & index) – Cambridge: Macmillan, 1863 – 2mf – 9 – 0-8370-6214-4 – 1986-0214 – us A.T.L.A. [240]

THE HISTORY OF CHRISTIAN PREACHING / Pattison, Thomas Harwood – Philadelphia: American Baptist Publication Society, 1903 – 2mf – us A.T.L.A. [240]

A HISTORY OF CHRISTIAN THOUGHT (CCC261) / P'eng, Peter – (In Chinese) – Hong Kong: Bible Book and Tract Depot for Council on Christian Literature for Overseas Chinese, 1953 – 1r – 1 – 1984-6600 – us A.T.L.A. [240]

THE HISTORY OF CHRISTIANITY : CONSISTING OF THE LIFE AND TEACHINGS OF JESUS OF NAZARETH, THE ADVENTURES OF PAUL AND THE APOSTLES AND THE MOST INTERESTING EVENTS IN THE PROGRESS OF CHRISTIANITY, FROM THE EARLIEST PERIOD TO THE PRESENT TIME / Abbott, John Stevens Cabot & Mallalieu, W F – Cleveland, Ohio: American Publ, (1877) – 2mf – us A.T.L.A. [240]

THE HISTORY OF CHRISTIANITY : FROM THE BIRTH OF CHRIST TO THE ABOLITION OF PAGANISM IN THE ROMAN EMPIRE / Milman, Henry Hart – London: John Murray, 1840 – 3 rolls – 1 – 1-55879-066-7 – uk Libr Preservation [240]

HISTORY OF CHRISTIANITY IN CHINA (CCC307) = CHUNG-KUO CHI TU CHIAO SHIH KANG / Wang, Chih-hsin – (In Chinese) – Shanghai: Association Press of China, 1940 – 1r – 1 – 1984-6646 – us A.T.L.A. [240]

A HISTORY OF CHRISTIANITY IN JAPAN : PROTESTANT MISSIONS / Cary, Otis – (Includes bibliographical references and indexes) – New York: Fleming H Revell, c1909 – 1mf – 9 – 0-8370-6654-9 – 1986-0654 – us A.T.L.A. [240]

A HISTORY OF CHRISTIANITY IN JAPAN : ROMAN CATHOLIC AND GREEK ORTHODOX MISSIONS / Cary, Otis – (Includes bibliographical references and index) – New York: Fleming H Revell, c1909 – 1mf – 9 – 0-8370-6655-7 – 1986-0655 – us A.T.L.A. [240]

HISTORY OF CHRISTIANITY IN THE HOLY LAND – 13,431mf – 9 – ne IDC [240]

A HISTORY OF CHRISTIAN-LATIN POETRY FROM THE BEGINNINGS TO THE CLOSE OF THE M.A / Raby, F J E – Oxford, 1953 – Dfl39.00 – ne Slangenburg [240]

HISTORY OF CINCINNATI AND HAMILTON COUNTY / S.B. Nelson and Company – Cincinnati, 1894. Ohio Reel 36. The Cox Library Collection – 5 – us Americana [978]

HISTORY OF CINCINNATI, OHIO / Ford, H A & Ford, K B – Cleveland: L. A. Williams and Co., 1881. Ohio Reel 36. (The Cox Library Collection) – 5 – us Americana [978]

HISTORY OF CISCO BAPTIST ASSOCIATION IN TEXAS / Brannon, J D – 1955. 480p – 1 – 16.80 – us Baptist [240]

HISTORY OF CITY OF KENOSHA AND KENOSHA COUNTY / Lyman, Frank H – Chicago: S. J. Clarke Publ. Co., 1916. Vols. 1-2. Wisconsin Reel 13. (The Cox Library Collection) – 5 – us Americana [978]

HISTORY OF CIVILIZATIONS OF CENTRAL ASIA / ed by Dani, Ahmad Hassan & Masson, V M – 2v – 9 – fr UNESCO [930]

HISTORY OF CLARK COUNTY – Chicago, 1881. Ohio Reel 19. The Cox Library Collection – 5 – us Americana [978]

HISTORY OF CLAY AND PLATTE COUNTIES / National Historical Co – St. Louis, 1885.Missouri Reel 13. (The Cox Library Collection) – 5 – us Americana [978]

HISTORY OF CLAY COUNTY / Woodson, W H – Topeka: Historical Publ. Co., 1920. Missouri Reel 13. (The Cox Library Collection) – 5 – us Americana [978]

HISTORY OF CLAY COUNTY TO 1909 / Steele, James E – (Chicago: S. J. Clarke Publ. Co., 1909). Iowa Reel 10. (The Cox Library Collection) – 5 – us Americana [978]

HISTORY OF CLAYTON COUNTY / Inter-State Publishing Co – Chicago, 1882. Iowa Reel 11. The Cox Library Collection – 5 – us Americana [978]

HISTORY OF CLAYTON COUNTY / Price, Realto E – (Chicago: Robert O. Law Co., 1916). Vols. 1-2. Iowa Reel 11. (The Cox Library Collection) – 5 – us Americana [978]

HISTORY OF CLEAR CREEK AND BOULDER VALLEYS / O.L. Baskin and Co – Chicago, 1880. Colorado reel 4. Cox Library Collection – 5 – us Americana [978]

HISTORY OF CLEAR CREEK BAPTIST CHURCH, KENTUCKY / Taylor, John – 1830 – 1 – 5.00 – us Baptist [240]

HISTORY OF CLERMONT AND BROWN COUNTIES / Williams, Byron – Milford: Hobart Publ. Co., 1913.v1, Ohio Reel 20. v2, Ohio Reel 21. (The Cox Library Collection) – 5 – us Americana [978]

HISTORY OF CLERMONT COUNTY / Bancroft, R J – Biographical sketches. Philadelphia: Louis H. Everts, 1880. Ohio Reel 21. (The Cox Library Collection) – 5 – us Americana [978]

HISTORY OF CLEVELAND / Orth, Samuel P – Chicago: S.J. Clarke Publ. Co., 1910. v1, Ohio Reel 25.v2-3, Ohio Reel 26. (The Cox Library Collection) – 5 – us Americana [978]

HISTORY OF CLEVELAND AND ITS ENVIRONS / Avery, Elroy M – Chicago: Lewis Publ. Co., 1918. v1, Ohio Reel 26. v2-3, Ohio Reel 27. (The Cox Library Collection) – 5 – us Americana [978]

A HISTORY OF CLIFFORD'S INN : WITH A CHAPTER ON PRESENT OWNERS / Hay-Edward, C M – London: T W Laurie, 1912 – 3mf – 9 – $4.50 – LLMC 84-293 – us L.L.M.C. [941]

HISTORY OF CLINCH COUNTY / J.W. Burke and Co – Macon, 1916. Georgia Reel 3. The Cox Library Collection – 5 – us Americana [978]

HISTORY OF CLINTON AND CLADWELL COUNTIES / Johnson, Carrie P & McGlumphy, W H S – Topeka: Historical Publ. Co., 1923. Missouri Reel 14. (The Cox Library Collection) – 5 – us Americana [978]

HISTORY OF CLINTON AND FRANKLIN COUNTIES / J.W. Lewis Publishing Co – Biographical sketches. Philadelphia, 1880. New York Reel 12. The Cox Library Collection – 5 – us Americana [978]

HISTORY OF CLINTON COUNTY / Brown, Albert J – Biographical Sketches. Indianapolis: B.F. Bowen and Co., 1915. Ohio Reel 22. (The Cox Library Collection) – 5 – us Americana [978]

HISTORY OF CLINTON COUNTY – Chicago: 1879. Iowa Reel 11. (The Cox Library Collection) – 5 – us Americana [978]

HISTORY OF CLINTON COUNTY – Chicago, 1882. Ohio Reel 21. The Cox Library Collection – 5 – us Americana [978]

HISTORY OF CLINTON COUNTY / Claybaugh, Joseph – Historical and genealogical sketches. Indianapolis: A. W. Bowen and Co., 1913. Indiana Reel 8. (The Cox Library Collection) – 5 – us Americana [978]

HISTORY OF CLINTON COUNTY / Inter-State Publishing Co – Historical and biographical sketches. Chicago, 1886. Indiana Reel 8. The Cox Library Collection – 5 – us Americana [978]

HISTORY OF CLINTON COUNTY / National Historical Co – St. Joseph, 1881. Missouri Reel 13. (The Cox Library Collection) – 5 – us Americana [978]

HISTORY OF COLE, MONITEAU, MORGAN, BENTON, MILLER, MARIES AND OSAGE COUNTIES – Biographical appendix. Chicago, 1889. Missouri Reel 14. (The Cox Library Collection) – 5 – us Americana [978]

HISTORY OF COLES COUNTY – Chicago, 1879. Illinois Reel 16. The Cox Library Collection – 5 – us Americana [978]

HISTORY OF COLGATE BAPTIST CHURCH, BALTIMORE, MARYLAND, 19 OCT 1945-NOV 1961 – 1 – 6.89 – us Baptist [240]

A HISTORY OF COLONIZATION ON THE WESTERN COAST OF AFRICA / Alexander, Archibald – Philadelphia: William S. Martien, 1849 – 2mf – us A.T.L.A. [960]

HISTORY OF COLORADO / Baker & Hafen – (v3-5. Colorado reel 2) – Denver: Linderman Co., 1927. v1-2. Colorado reel 1. (Cox Library Collection) – 5 – us Americana [978]

HISTORY OF COLORADO / Hall, Frank – Chicago: Blakely Print. Co., 1889. v1-4.Colorado Reel 1. (Cox Library Collection) – 5 – us Americana [978]

HISTORY OF COLUMBIA AND MONTEUR COUNTIES / Battle, J H – Chicago, A. Warner and Co., 1887. Pennsylvania Reel 16. (The Cox Library Collection) – 5 – us Americana [978]

HISTORY OF COLUMBIA COUNTY – Biographical sketches. Philadelphia, 1878. New York Reel 12. (The Cox Library Collection) – 5 – us Americana [978]

HISTORY OF COLUMBIA COUNTY – Chicago: 1880. Wisconsin Reel 7. (The Cox Library Collection) – 5 – us Americana [978]

HISTORY OF COLUMBIA COUNTY / Jones, J E – Chicago: Lewis Publ. Co., 1914. Vols. 1-2. Wisconsin Reel 7. (The Cox Library Collection) – 5 – us Americana [978]

HISTORY OF COLUMBIA RIVER VALLEY / Lockley, Fred – Chicago: S.J. Clarke Publ. Co., 1928. v1-3. Oregon reel 4. (Cox Library Collection) – 5 – us Americana [978]

HISTORY OF COLUMBIANA COUNTY / D.W. Ensign and Company – Biographical sketches. Philadelphia, 1879. Ohio Reel 22. The Cox Library Collection – 5 – us Americana [978]

HISTORY OF COLUMBIANA COUNTY AND REPRESENTATIVE CITIZENS / McCord, William B – Chicago: Biographical Publ. Co., 1905. Ohio Reel 23. (The Cox Library Collection) – 5 – us Americana [978]

HISTORY OF COMPTON COUNTY: AND SKETCHES OF THE EASTERN TOWNSHIPS, DISTRICT OF ST FRANCIS, AND SHERBROOKE COUNTY / Channell, Leonard Stewart – Supplemented with the records of four hundred families, two hundred illustrations of buildings and leading citizens in the county. Cookshire, Quebec: L. Channell, 1896. 00558. (Pre-1900 Canadiana) – 9 – cn C.I.H.M. [971]

HISTORY OF CONCORD ASSOCIATION, KENTUCKY – 1821-1906 – 1 – 5.00 – us Baptist [240]

A HISTORY OF CONFERENCES : AND OTHER PROCEEDINGS CONNECTED WITH THE REVISION OF THE BOOK OF COMMON PRAYER FROM THE YEAR 1558 TO THE YEAR 1690 / Cardwell, Edward – Oxford: University Press, 1849 – 2mf – us A.T.L.A. [240]

A HISTORY OF CONFERENCES AND OTHER PROCEEDINGS...REVISION OF THE BOOK OF COMMON PRAYER / Cardwell, Edward – 1558-1690. 2nd ed. Oxford: University Press, 1841. xiii, 464p. With: Krushenie by N.A. Lappo Danilevskaia – 1r – 1 – us U.W. Library [240]

A HISTORY OF CONGREGATIONAL INDEPENDENCY IN SCOTLAND / Ross, James – Glasgow: J. MacLehose, 1900 – 1mf – us A.T.L.A. [240]

HISTORY OF CONGREGATIONS OF THE PRESBYTERIAN CHURCH IN IRELAND AND BIOGRAPHICAL NOTICES OF EMINENT PRESBYTERIAN MINISTERS AND LAYMEN / Reid, James Seaton; ed by Killen, W D – Belfast: J. Cleeland; Edinburgh: J. Gemmell, 1886 – 1mf – us A.T.L.A. [240]

THE HISTORY OF CONNECTICUT FROM THE FIRST SETTLEMENT OF THE COLONY TO THE ADOPTION OF THE PRESENT CONSTITUTION – Vol.2 by G.H. Hollister, 1855. V133-0001 – 1 – us A.G.L.L. [920]

HISTORY OF CONTRA COSTA COUNTY / Fraser, J P Munro – Contra Costa, CA. 1882 – 1r – 1 – $50.00 – B40213 – us Library Micro [978]

HISTORY OF CONTRA COSTA COUNTY / Historic Record Co – Los Angeles, 1926. California Reel 12. (The Cox Library Collection) – 5 – us Americana [978]

HISTORY OF COOK COUNTY / Andreas, A T – Chicago: 1884. Illinois Reel 16. (The Cox Library Collection) – 5 – us Americana [978]

HISTORY OF COOPER COUNTY / Johnson, W F – Topeka: Historical Publ. Co., 1919. Missouri Reel 15. (The Cox Library Collection) – 5 – us Americana [978]

HISTORY OF CORN MILLING / Bennet, R & Elton, J – 4v. H-1348 2. 1898-1904 – 8 – ne IDC [660]

HISTORY OF CORSICA PAMPHLET COLLECTION – 1943-1976 – 1 reel – 1 – CSUXANQ7761-B – us Hoover Inst Photo [945]

HISTORY OF CORTLAND COUNTY / Smith, H P – Syracuse, D. Mason and Co., 1885. New York Reel 13. (The Cox Library Collection) – 5 – us Americana [978]

HISTORY OF COSHOCTON COUNTY / Hill, N N – Newark: A.A. Graham and Co., 1881. Ohio Reel 23. (The Cox Library Collection) – 5 – us Americana [978]

HISTORY OF COUNTY OF ALBANY, 1609-1886; HISTORY OF COUNTY OF SCHENECTADY, 1662-1886 – New York, 1886. New York Reel 7. The Cox Library Collection – 5 – us Americana [978]

A HISTORY OF CRAGG VALE, YORKSHIRE / Hellowell, S G – 1959 – 1 – uk Microform Academic [941]

HISTORY OF CRAWFORD AND CLARK COUNTIES / Perrin, William Henry – Chicago: O. L. Baskin and Co., 1883. Illinois Reel 21. (The Cox Library Collection) – 5 – us Americana [978]

HISTORY OF CRAWFORD AND RICHLAND COUNTIES – Springfield: 1884. Wisconsin Reel 8. (The Cox Library Collection) – 5 – us Americana [978]

A HISTORY OF CRAWFORD COUNTY / Pleasant, Hazen Hayes – Greenfield: Wm. Mitchell Printing Co., 1926. Indiana Reel 8. (The Cox Library Collection) – 5 – us Americana [978]

HISTORY OF CRAWFORD COUNTY / Baskin and Battey Historical Publishing Co – Chicago, 1881. Ohio Reel 24. The Cox Library Collection – 5 – us Americana [978]

HISTORY OF CRAWFORD COUNTY – Chicago, 1885. Pennsylvania Reel 17. (The Cox Library Collection) – 5 – us Americana [978]

HISTORY OF CRAWFORD COUNTY AND REPRESENTATIVE CITIZENS / Hopley, John E – Chicago: Richmond-Arnold Publ. Co., n.d.Ohio Reel 24. (The Cox Library Collection) – 5 – us Americana [978]

A HISTORY OF CREEDS AND CONFESSIONS OF FAITH IN CHRISTENDOM AND BEYOND : WITH HISTORICAL TABLES / Curtis, William A – Edinburgh: T.& T. Clark; New York: Scribner [distributor], 1911 – 2mf – us A.T.L.A. [200]

HISTORY OF CUMBERLAND AND ADAMS COUNTIES / Warner, Beers and Co – Chicago, 1886. Pennsylvania Reel 17. (The Cox Library Collection) – 5 – us Americana [978]

HISTORY OF CUMBERLAND CO., PA – 1886 – 9 – $13.00 – us Godfrey [978]

HISTORY OF CUMBERLAND COUNTY, MAINE / Everts & Peck – Biographical sketches. Philadelphia, 1880. Maine Reel 3. (The Cox Library Collection) – 5 – us Americana [978]

HISTORY OF CYPRUS PAMPHLET COLLECTION – 1957-1969 – 1 reel – 1 – CSUXANR0405-B – us Hoover Inst Photo [949]

HISTORY OF CZECHOSLOVAKIA AFTER 1945 PAMPHLET COLLECTION – 1946-1973 – 1 reel – 1 – CSUXANL4873-B – us Hoover Inst Photo [947]

HISTORY OF CZECHOSLOVAKIA FROM 1918 TO 1938 PAMPHLET COLLECTION – 1918-1953 – 3r – 1 – CSUXANL4497-B – us Hoover Inst Photo [947]

HISTORY OF CZECHOSLOVAKIA FROM 1938 TO 1945 PAMPHLET COLLECTION – 1939-1950 – 2r – 1 – CSUXANL4867-B – us Hoover Inst Photo [947]

HISTORY OF CZECHS (BOHEMIANS) IN NEBRASKA / Rosicky, Rose – Omaha: Czech Historical Society of Nebraska, 1929. Nebraska Reel 4. (The Cox Library Collection) – 5 – us Americana [978]

THE HISTORY OF DAHOMEY / Dalzel, A – London. 1793. BA-301 2 – 8 – ne IDC [960]

HISTORY OF DAKOTA AND GOODHUE COUNTIES / Curtiss-Wedge, Franklyn – Chicago: H.C. Cooper, Jr. and Co., 1910.2v. Minnesota Reel 5.(The Cox Library Collection) – 5 – us Americana [978]

HISTORY OF DAKOTA COUNTY AND THE CITY OF HASTINGS / Neill, Edward D – Minneapolis: North Star Publ. Co., 1881.Minnesota Reel 4. (The Cox Library Collection) – 5 – us Americana [978]

HISTORY OF DAKOTA TERRITORY, SOUTH DAKOTA, ITS HISTORY AND ITS PEOPLE / Kingsburg, G W & Smith, G M – Chicago: S.J. Clarke Publ. Co., 1915. v1, South Dakota Reel 1. v2-4, South Dakota Reel 2. v5, South Dakota Reel 3.(The Cox Library Collection) – 5 – us Americana [978]

HISTORY OF DANE COUNTY – Chicago: 1880. Wisconsin Reel 8. (The Cox Library Collection) – 5 – us Americana [978]

HISTORY OF DANE COUNTY / Western Historical Co – Biographical and genealogical. Madison: 1906. Wisconsin Reel 9. (The Cox Library Collection) – 5 – us Americana [978]

HISTORY OF DANE COUNTY / William J. Park and Co – Madison, 1877. Wisconsin Reel 8. The Cox Library Collection – 5 – us Americana [978]

HISTORY OF DARKE COUNTY – Chicago, 1880. Ohio Reel 27. The Cox Library Collection – 5 – us Americana [978]

HISTORY OF DARKE COUNTY / Hobart Publishing Co – From its earliest settlement to the present time with biographical sketches. Milford, 1914. 2v.Ohio Reel 28. (The Cox Library Collection) – 5 – us Americana [978]

HISTORY OF DAUPHIN AND LEBANON COUNTIES / Egle, William Henry – Genealogical and biographical. Philadelphia: Everts and Peck, 1883. Pennsylvania Reel 18. (The Cox Library Collection) – 5 – us Americana [978]

HISTORY OF DAUPHIN COUNTY / Kelker, Luther R – Genealogical memoirs. New York, Lewis Publ. Co., 1907. Vols. 1-3, Pennsylvania Reel 19. (The Cox Library Collection) – 5 – us Americana [978]

HISTORY OF DAVENPORT AND SCOTT COUNTY / Downer, Harry E – Chicago: S.J. Clarke Publ. Co., 1910. v1, Iowa Reel 38.v2, Iowa Reel 39. (The Cox Library Collection) – 5 – us Americana [978]

THE HISTORY OF DAVID GRIEVE / Ward, Mary Augusta – British Fiction Archive: Unit 2 – 9 – uk Bell [830]

HISTORY OF DAVIDSON COUNTY / Clayton, W Woodford – Illustrations and biographical sketches. Philadelphia: J. W. Lewis and Co., 1880. Tennessee Reel 2. (The Cox Library Collection) – 5 – us Americana [978]

HISTORY OF DAVIESS AND GENTRY COUNTIES / Leopard, J C et al – Topeka: Historical Publ. Co., 1922. Missouri Reel 15. (The Cox Library Collection) – 5 – us Americana [978]

HISTORY OF DAVIESS COUNTY / Birdsall & Dean – Biographical sketches. Kansas City, 1882. Missouri Reel 15. (The Cox Library Collection) – 5 – us Americana [978]

HISTORY OF DAVIS COUNTY / State Historical Co – Des Moines: 1882. Iowa Reel 12. (The Cox Library Collection) – 5 – us Americana [978]

HISTORY OF DAYTON AND MONTGOMERY COUNTY / Drury, A W – Chicago: S. J. Clarke Publ. Co., 1909. Vols. 1-2. Ohio Reel 50. (The Cox Library Collection) – 5 – us Americana [978]

HISTORY OF DE WITT COUNTY – Philadelphia, 1882. Illinois. The Cox Library Collection – 22r – 5 – us Americana [978]

HISTORY OF DE WITT COUNTY / Pioneer Publishing Co – Chicago, 1910. Vs.1 and 2. Illinois Reel 23. (The Cox Library Collection) – 5 – us Americana [978]

HISTORY OF DEARBORN AND OHIO COUNTIES / F.E. Weakley and Co – Historical and biographical sketches. Chicago, 1885. Indiana Reel 9. The Cox Library Collection – 5 – us Americana [978]

HISTORY OF DEERFIELD / Reichelt, Marie W – Glenview Press, 1928. Illinois Reel 36. (The Cox Library Collection) – 5 – us Americana [978]

HISTORY OF DEFIANCE COUNTY – Historical and biographical. Chicago, 1883. Ohio Reel 28. (The Cox Library Collection) – 5 – us Americana [978]

HISTORY OF DEKALB COUNTY / B.F. Bowen and Co – Biographical sketches of representative citizens and genealogical records of old families. Indianapolis, 1914. Indiana Reel 9. The Cox Library Collection – 5 – us Americana [920]

HISTORY OF DEKALB COUNTY / Inter-State Publishing Co – Historical and biographical sketches. Chicago, 1885. Indiana Reel 9. The Cox Library Collection – 5 – us Americana [978]

HISTORY OF DELAWARE 1609-1888 / Scharf, Thomas J – Philadelphia, L. J. Richards and Co., 1888. Vols. 1-2. Delaware Reel 1. (The Cox Library Collection) – 5 – us Americana [978]

HISTORY OF DELAWARE COUNTY / Ashmead, Henry G – Philadelphia, L. H. Everts and Co., 1884. Pennsylvania Reel 19. (The Cox Library Collection) – 5 – us Americana [978]

HISTORY OF DELAWARE COUNTY – Chicago: 1878. Iowa Reel 12. (The Cox Library Collection) – 5 – us Americana [978]

HISTORY OF DELAWARE COUNTY / Haimbaugh, Frank D – Indianapolis: Historical Publ. Co., 1924. Vols. 1-2. Indiana Reel 10. (The Cox Library Collection) – 5 – us Americana [978]

HISTORY OF DELAWARE COUNTY / O.L. Baskin and Co – Chicago, 1880. Ohio Reel 28. The Cox Library Collection – 5 – us Americana [978]

HISTORY OF DELAWARE COUNTY / Smith, George Adam – Philadelphia, Henry G. Ashmead, 1862. Pennsylvania Reel 19. (The Cox Library Collection) – 5 – us Americana [978]

HISTORY OF DELAWARE COUNTY AND ITS PEOPLE / Jordan, John W – New York, Lewis HIstorical Publ. Co., 1914. Vols. 1-3, Pennsylvania Reel 20. (The Cox Library Collection) – 5 – us Americana [978]

HISTORY OF DELAWARE COUNTY AND ITS PEOPLE / Merry, John F – Chicago: S. J. Clarke Publ. Co., 1914. Vols. 1-2. Iowa Reel 13. (The Cox Library Collection) – 5 – us Americana [978]

HISTORY OF DES MOINES AND ITS PEOPLE / Antrobus, Augustine M – Chicago: S. J. Clarke Publ. Co., 1915. Vols. 1-2. Iowa Reel 14. (The Cox Library Collection) – 5 – us Americana [978]

HISTORY OF DES MOINES COUNTY – Chicago: 1879. Iowa Reel 13. (The Cox Library Collection) – 5 – us Americana [978]

THE HISTORY OF DEVONSHIRE / Polwhele, R – H 1118 2. 3 v. 1797-1806 – 8 – ne IDC [941]

A HISTORY OF DICKINSON COUNTY, IOWA / Smith, R A – Des Moines: The Kenyon Printing Mfg. Co., 1912. Iowa Reel 14. (The Cox Library Collection) – 5 – us Americana [978]

THE HISTORY OF DISSENTERS: FROM THE REVOLUTION TO THE YEAR 1808 / Bogue, David – 2nd ed. London: F. Westley and A.H. Davis, 1833. 2v. Includes index – 1 – us U.W. Library [240]

HISTORY OF DODGE AND WASHINGTON COUNTIES / Buss & Osterman & Blair – Chicago: American Historical Society, 1921. 2v.Nebraska Reel 7. (The Cox Library Collection) – 5 – us Americana [978]

HISTORY OF DODGE COUNTY – Chicago: 1880. Wisconsin Reel 10. (The Cox Library Collection) – 5 – us Americana [978]

HISTORY OF DOOR COUNTY / Martin, Charles I – Sturgeon Bay: Expositor Job Print., 1881. Wisconsin Reel 10. (The Cox Library Collection) – 5 – us Americana [978]

HISTORY OF DU PAGE COUNTY / Blanchard, Rufus – Chicago: O. L. Baskin and Co., 1882. Illinois Reel 23. (The Cox Library Collection) – 5 – us Americana [978]

HISTORY OF DUBUQUE COUNTY – Chicago: 1880. Iowa Reel 15. (The Cox Library Collection) – 5 – us Americana [978]

HISTORY OF DUBUQUE COUNTY / Goodspeed, W A & Goodspeed, K C – Goodspeed Historical Asso., 1911. Iowa Reel 15. (The Cox Library Collection) – 5 – us Americana [978]

HISTORY OF DULUTH AND ST LOUIS COUNTY PAST AND PRESENT / Woodbridge & Pardee – Chicago: C.F. Cooper and Co., 1910. 2v.Minnesota Reel 13. (The Cox Library Collection) – 5 – us Americana [978]

HISTORY OF DWIGHT / Dustin & Wassell – 1853-1894. Illinois Reel 40. (The Cox Library Collection) – 5 – us Americana [978]

A HISTORY OF EARLY BAPTIST MISSIONS AMONG THE FIVE CIVILIZED TRIBES / Moffitt, James W – 1946 – 1 – 7.28 – us Baptist [240]

HISTORY OF EARLY CHRISTIAN ART / Cutts, Edward L – London: S.P.C.K.; New York: E.& J. Young, 1893. (Side-lights of church history) – 1mf – us A.T.L.A. [240]

HISTORY OF EARLY CHRISTIAN LITERATURE IN THE FIRST THREE CENTURIES / Krueger, Gustav – New York: Macmillan, 1897 – 1mf – us A.T.L.A. [240]

HISTORY OF EASTERN EUROPE PAMPHLET COLLECTION – 1944-1952 – 1 reel – 1 – CSUXANL7359-B – us Hoover Inst Photo [947]

HISTORY OF EASTLAND COUNTY / Langston, George – Dallas: A.D. Aldridge and Co., 1904. Texas Reel 11. (The Cox Library Collection) – 5 – us Americana [978]

HISTORY OF EASTON / Condit, Uzal W – George W. West. Vols. 1-2. Pennsylvania Reel 34. (The Cox Library Collection) – 5 – us Americana [978]

HISTORY OF ECONOMIC THOUGHT. NEWSLETTER – 1968- – 1; 1975- 5,6,9 – us UMI [330]

HISTORY OF ECONOMICS SERIES – (Units available separately: Thomas Robert Malthus collection $8905 – Malthus monographs $4780 + Malthus preliminaries $4590; John Stuart Mill collection $4590; David Ricardo collection $5205 – Early Writings and Letters $1630 + References to Ricardo's Writing and Correspondence $2580 + Sources $1405; Adam Smith collection $9875; Royal Statistical Society collection $580) – 10,507mf – 9 – $24,700.00 complete collection – us UMI [330]

HISTORY OF EDGECOMBE COUNTY / Turner & Bridgers – Raleigh: Edwards and Broughton Printing Co., 1920. North Carolina Reel 1. (The Cox Library Collection) – 5 – us Americana [978]

HISTORY OF EDGEFIELD COUNTY / Chapman, John A – From earliest settlement to 1897. Newberry, Elbert H. Aull, 1897. South Carolina Reel 2. (The Cox Library Collection) – 5 – us Americana [978]

HISTORY OF EDUCATION – (Subject breakouts available) – Filmed from the holdings of the Milbank Memorial Library, Teachers College, Columbia University – 9 – us Primary [370]

A HISTORY OF EDUCATION BEFORE THE MIDDLE AGES / Graves, Frank Pierrepont – New York: Macmillan, 1909 – 1mf – us A.T.L.A. [370]

A HISTORY OF EDUCATION DURING THE MIDDLE AGES : AND THE TRANSITION TO MODERN TIMES / Graves, Frank Pierrepont – New York: Macmillan, 1910 – 1mf – us A.T.L.A. [370]

HISTORY OF EDUCATION IN DELAWARE / Powell, Lyman P – (U.S. Bureau of Education Circular of Information no. 3). 1893 – 1 – $50.00 – us Presbyterian [370]

A HISTORY OF EDUCATION IN MODERN TIMES / Graves, Frank Pierrepont – New York: Macmillan, 1913 – 1mf – us A.T.L.A. [370]

A HISTORY OF EDUCATION IN VIRGINIA / Heatwole, Cornelius Jacob – New York: Macmillan, 1916. xviii,382p – 1 – us U.W. Library [370]

HISTORY OF EDUCATION QUARTERLY – v. 1-. 1961- – 1. – apply; v.14-6; v.15- 1975- 9 – us UMI [370]

History of Education Society *see* BULLETIN

HISTORY OF EDUCATION TODAY / Leon, Antoine – 1985 – 117p – 9 – 92-3-102271-7 – fr UNESCO [370]

HISTORY OF EFFINGHAM COUNTY / Perrin, William Henry – Chicago: O. L. Baskin and Co., 1883. Illinois Reel 24. (The Cox Library Collection) – 5 – us Americana [978]

A HISTORY OF EGYPT / Zaidan, Jurji – Cairo, 1889 – 1 – us NY Public [960]

HISTORY OF EGYPT / Zaidan, Jurji – 1889 – 1r – 1 – us Ross [960]

HISTORY OF EGYPT, CHALDEA, SYRIA, BABYLONIA, AND ASSYRIA / Maspero, Gaston; ed by Sayce, A H – London. 9v. 1903 – 2r – 1 – us Ross [930]

HISTORY OF EGYPT FROM 330 B.C. TO THE PRESENT TIME / Rappoport, Angelo Solomon – London. 3v. 1904 – 1r – 1 – us Ross [960]

HISTORY OF ELECTIONS IN THE AMERICAN COLONIES / Bishop, Cortlandt Field – v3. 1893 – 1r – 1 – us Ross [975]

HISTORY OF ELIZABETH, INCLUDING AN EARLY HISTORY OF UNION COUNTY / Hatfield, Edwin F – New York, Carlton and Lanahan, Publishers, 1868. New Jersey Reel 6. (The Cox Library Collection) – 5 – us Americana [978]

HISTORY OF ELKHART COUNTY – Chicago, 1881. Indiana Reel 11. The Cox Library Collection – 5 – us Americana [978]

HISTORY OF ELLIS COUNTY BAPTIST ASSOCIATION / Brooks, A D – 1907. 200p – 1 – 7.00 – us Baptist [240]

THE HISTORY OF EMILY MONTAGUE / Brooke, Frances – London: J Dodsley. 4v. 1769. SEM16P114 – 1r – 5 – Can$9.00 – cn Bibl Nat [920]

HISTORY OF EMMETT AND DICKINSON COUNTIES / Pioneer Publishing Co – Chicago: 1917. Vols. 1-2. Iowa Reel 15. (The Cox Library Collection) – 5 – us Americana [978]

HISTORY OF ENGLAND, A.D. 1800-1815; BEING AN INTRODUCTION TO THE HISTORY OF THE PEACE / Martineau, Harriett – London: G. Bell and Sons, 1878. xii,548p – 1 – us U.W. Library [941]

A HISTORY OF ENGLAND AND GREATER BRITAIN / Cross, Arthur Lyon – New York: Macmillan, 1914 – 3mf – us A.T.L.A. [941]

HISTORY OF ENGLAND DURING THE REIGNS OF KING WILLIAM, QUEEN ANNE, AND KING GEORGE 1 / Ralph, James – 1978 – 1r – 1 – $85.00 – S1855 – us Scholarly Res [941]

THE HISTORY OF ENGLAND FROM THE INVASION OF JULIUS CAESAR TO THE ABDICATION OF JAMES THE SECOND, 1688 / Hume, David – New ed. with the author's last corrections and improvements. New York: Harper & Bros., 1859-64. 6v – 1 – us U.W. Library [941]

THE HISTORY OF ENGLAND IN RHYME / Adams, Robert Chamblet – Boston: D. Lothrop, c1880. 00876. (Pre-1900 Canadiana) – 9 – cn C.I.H.M. [941]

THE HISTORY OF ENGLISH DEMOCRATIC IDEAS IN THE SEVENTEENTH CENTURY / Gooch, G P – Cambridge: University Press; New York: Macmillan [distributor], 1898 (Cambridge historical essays; no. 10) – 1mf – us A.T.L.A. [320]

THE HISTORY OF ENGLISH GLASS PAINTING / Drake, N M – H-1349 2. 1912 – 8 – ne IDC [740]

THE HISTORY OF ENGLISH LAW BEFORE THE TIME OF EDWARD I / Pollock, F & Maitland, F W – H 1178 2. 2 v. Ed. 2. 1898 – 8 – ne IDC [340]

HISTORY OF ENGLISH NONCONFORMITY FROM WICLIF TO THE CLOSE OF THE NINETEENTH CENTURY / Clark, Henry W – London: Chapman and Hall, 1911 – 3mf – us A.T.L.A. [240]

THE HISTORY OF ENGLISH RATIONALISM IN THE NINETEENTH CENTURY / Benn, Alfred William – London, New-York: Longmans, Green, 1906 – 3mf – us A.T.L.A. [140]

HISTORY OF ENGLISH THOUGHT IN THE EIGHTEENTH CENTURY / Stephen, Leslie – New York: Putnam, 1876 – 1 roll – 1 – 1-55879-236-8 – uk Libr Preservation [190]

A HISTORY OF ENGLISH UTILITARIANISM / Albee, Ernest – London: Sonnenschein, 1902 – 1mf – us A.T.L.A. [140]

HISTORY OF EPIRUS PAMPHLET COLLECTION – 1919?-1946 – 1 reel – 1 – CSUXANL5812-B – us Hoover Inst Photo [949]

HISTORY OF ERIE COUNTY / Aldrich, Lewis C – Biographical sketches. Syracuse: D. Mason and Co., 1889. Ohio Reel 29. (The Cox Library Collection) – 5 – us Americana [978]

HISTORY OF ERIE COUNTY – Chicago, 1884. Pennsylvania Reel 20. (The Cox Library Collection) – 5 – us Americana [978]

HISTORY OF ERIE COUNTY / Peeke, Hewson L – Chronicle of people with family lineage and memoirs. Chicago: Lewis Publ. Co., 1916. 2v. Ohio Reel 29. (The Cox Library Collection) – 5 – us Americana [978]

HISTORY OF ERIE COUNTY / Reed, John E – Indianapolis: Historical Publ. Co., 1925. Vols. 1-2. Pennsylvania Reel 21. (The Cox Library Collection) – 5 – us Americana [978]

HISTORY OF ESSEX AND HUDSON COUNTIES / Shaw, William H – Philadelphia, Everts and Peck, 1884. Vols. 1-2. New Jersey Reel 2. (The Cox Library Collection) – 5 – us Americana [978]

HISTORY OF ESSEX COUNTY / Hurd, D Hamilton – Philadelphia, J. W. Lewis and Co., 1888. Vol. 1, Massachusetts Reel 3; Vol. 2, Massachusetts Reel 4. (The Cox Library Collection) – 5 – us Americana [978]

HISTORY OF ESSEX COUNTY / Smith, H P – Biographical sketches. Syracuse, D. Mason and Co., 1885. New York Reel 15. (The Cox Library Collection) – 5 – us Americana [978]

HISTORY OF ETHICS WITHIN ORGANIZED CHRISTIANITY / Hall, Thomas Cuming – (Includes bibliographical references and index) – New York: Charles Scribner, 1910 – 2mf – 9 – 0-8370-6062-1 – 1986-0062 – us A.T.L.A. [170]

HISTORY OF EUROPEAN IDEAS – v1- 1980- – 5,6,9 – us UMI [940]

HISTORY OF FAIRFIELD AND PERRY COUNTIES / Graham, A A – Chicago: W.H. Beers and Co., 1883. Ohio Reel 30. (The Cox Library Collection) – 5 – us Americana [978]

HISTORY OF FAIRFIELD COUNTY / Hurd, D Hamilton – Philadelphia, J. W. Lewis and Co., 1881. Connecticut Reel 3. (The Cox Library Collection) – 5 – us Americana [978]

HISTORY OF FAIRFIELD COUNTY AND REPRESENTATIVE CITIZENS / Miller, Charles C – Chicago: Richmond-Arnold Publ. Co., 1912. Ohio Reel 30.(The Cox Library Collection) – 5 – us Americana [978]

THE HISTORY OF FARIBAULT COUNTY / Kiester, J A – From the first settlement to the close of 1879. Minneapolis: Harrison and Smith, 1896. Minnesota Reel 5. (The Cox Library Collection) – 5 – us Americana [978]

A HISTORY OF FAYETTE COUNTY / Hadden, James – History of Uniontown, the County Seat. 1913. Pennsylvania Reel 23. (The Cox Library Collection) – 5 – us Americana [978]

HISTORY OF FAYETTE COUNTY / Barrows, Frederick I – Biographical sketches. Indianapolis: B. F. Bowen and Co., 1917. Indiana Reel 12. (The Cox Library Collection) – 5 – us Americana [978]

HISTORY OF FAYETTE COUNTY / B.F. Bowen and Co – Biographical sketches. Indianapolis, 1914. Ohio Reel 31. The Cox Library Collection – 5 – us Americana [978]

HISTORY OF FAYETTE COUNTY / Dills, R S – Dayton: Odell and Mayer Publ. Co., 1881.Ohio Reel 31. (The Cox Library Collection) – 5 – us Americana [978]

HISTORY OF FAYETTE COUNTY / Ellis, Franklin – Biographical sketches. Philadelphia: L. H. Everts and Co., 1882. Pennsylvania Reel 22. (The Cox Library Collection) – 5 – us Americana [978]

HISTORY OF FAYETTE COUNTY / Peter, Robert – Chicago: O.L. Baskin and Co., 1882. Kentucky Reel 6. (The Cox Library Collection) – 5 – us Americana [978]

HISTORY OF FAYETTE COUNTY / Peters & Carden, Allen D – Charleston, Jarrett Printing Co., 1926. West Virginia Reel 3. (The Cox Library Collection) – 5 – us Americana [978]

HISTORY OF FAYETTE COUNTY, PENNSYLVANIA / Jordan, John W & Hadd, James – (Genealogical and Personal History of Fayette County Pennsylvania) – Fayette, PA. New York: Lewis Historical Publ Co. v1-3. 1912 – 1r – 1 – us Western Res [920]

HISTORY OF FILMORE COUNTY / Curtiss-Wedge, Franklyn – Chicago: H.C. Cooper & Co., 1912. 2v. Minnesota Reel 6. (The Cox Library Collection) – 5 – us Americana [978]

HISTORY OF FILMORE COUNTY / Neill, Edward D – Sioux Massacre of 1862 and State Education. Minneapolis: Minnesota Historical Co., 1892. Minnesota Reel 6. (The Cox (Library Collection) – 5 – us Americana [978]

HISTORY OF FINNEY COUNTY / Finney County Historical Society – 1950. Kansas Reel 8. (The Cox Library Collection) – 5 – us Americana [978]

HISTORY OF FIRST BAPTIST CHURCH, LEITCHFIELD, KENTUCKY, SESQUICENTENNIAL / McBeath, William H – 1804-1954. 39p – 1 – 5.00 – us Baptist [240]

HISTORY OF FIRST BAPTIST CHURCH, WILLIAM LAKE, BRITISH COLUMBIA, CANADA / Janzen, D M – 1967-72 – 1 – $5.00 – us Baptist [240]

HISTORY OF FLOYD COUNTY / Inter-State Publishing Co – Chicago, 1882. Iowa Reel 17. The Cox Library Collection – 5 – us Americana [978]

HISTORY OF FOND DU LAC COUNTY – Chicago. Wisconsin Reel 10. (The Cox Library Collection) – 5 – us Americana [978]

HISTORY OF FORD COUNTY TO 1908 / Gardner, E A – Chicago: S. J. Clarke Publ. Co., 1908. Vols. 1-2. Illinois Reel 24. (The Cox Library Collection) – 5 – us Americana [978]

HISTORY OF FORT WAYNE AND TOWNSHIPS OF ALLEN COUNTY / Robert O. Law Co – Chicago, 1917. Indiana Reel 4. The Cox Library Collection – 5 – us Americana [978]

THE HISTORY OF FORTY CHOIRS / Hastings, Thomas – New York: Mason, 1854, c1853 – 1mf – us A.T.L.A. [780]

HISTORY OF FOUNTAIN COUNTY / Beckwith, H W – Chicago: H. H. Hill and N. Iddings, 1881. Indiana Reel 12. (The Cox Library Collection) – 5 – us Americana [978]

THE HISTORY OF FRANCE / Godwin, Parke – v1., Ancient Gaul. New York: Harper, 1860. xxiv,495p. No more publ – 1 – us U.W. Library [944]

HISTORY OF FRANCESTOWN – From its earliest settlement to January 1, 1891, with genealogical records of the families. Nashua, 1895. Published by the Town. New Hampshire Reel 5. (The Cox Library Collection) – 5 – us Americana [978]

HISTORY OF FRANKLIN AND PICKAWAY COUNTIES – Biographical sketches. Philadelphia, 1880. Ohio Reel 32. (The Cox Library Collection) – 5 – us Americana [978]

HISTORY OF FRANKLIN ASSOCIATION (ILLINOIS) OF UNITED BAPTISTS / Throgmorton, W P – 1880 – 1 – 10.78 – us Baptist [240]

HISTORY OF FRANKLIN COUNTY – Chicago, 1887. Pennsylvania Reel 23. (The Cox Library Collection) – 5 – us Americana [978]

HISTORY OF FRANKLIN COUNTY / Reifel, August – Historical and biographical sketches. Indianapolis: B. F. Bowen and Co., 1915. Indiana Reel 12. (The Cox Library Collection) – 5 – us Americana [978]

HISTORY OF FRANKLIN COUNTY AND CERRO CORDO COUNTY – Springfield: 1883. Iowa Reel 17. (The Cox Library Collection) – 5 – us Americana [978]

HISTORY OF FRANKLIN, JEFFERSON, WASHINGTON, CRAWFORD AND GASCONADE COUNTIES – Biographical appendix. Chicago, 1888. Missouri Reel 16. (The Cox Library Collection) – 5 – us Americana [978]

HISTORY OF FREEBORN COUNTY / Curtiss-Wedge, Franklyn – Chicago: H.C. Cooper and Co., 1911. Minnesota Reel 7. (The Cox Library Collection) – 5 – us Americana [978]

HISTORY OF FREEBORN COUNTY / Neill, Edward D – Sioux Massacre of 1862 and State Education. Minneapolis: Minnesota Historical Co., 1882. Minnesota Reel 6. (The Cox Library Collection) – 5 – us Americana [978]

A HISTORY OF FREEDOM OF THOUGHT / Bury, J B – New York: Henry Holt; London: Williams and Norgate, c1913. (Home University Library of Modern Knowledge, v69.) – 1mf – us A.T.L.A. [100]

THE HISTORY OF FREEMASONRY : ITS LEGENDS AND TRADITIONS, ITS CHRONOLOGICAL HISTORY. THE HISTORY OF THE SYMBOLISM OF FREEMASONRY: THE ANCIENT ACCEPTED SCOTTISH RITE AND THE ROYAL ORDER OF SCOTLAND / Mackey, Albert Gallatin & Singleton, William R – New York; London: The Masonic History Co, 1906, c1898 – us Res Libr [360]

HISTORY OF FREMONT COUNTY / Iowa Historical and Biographical Co – Des Moines: 1881. Iowa Reel 17. (The Cox Library Collection) – 5 – us Americana [978]

HISTORY OF FRESNO COUNTY – Fresno Co, CA: Elliot & Co Publ, 1881 – 1r – 1 – $50.00 – B40217 – us Library Micro [978]

HISTORY OF FRESNO COUNTY / Historic Record Co – Los Angeles, 1919. 2v. California Reel 12. (The Cox Library Collection) – 5 – us Americana [978]

HISTORY OF FRESNO COUNTY AND THE SAN JOAQUIN VALLEY / Winchell, Lilbourne Alsip – Fresno Co, CA. 1933 – 1r – 1 – $50.00 – B40218 – us Library Micro [978]

HISTORY OF FULTON COUNTY – Chicago and Peoria, 1879. Illinois Reel 25. The Cox Library Collection – 5 – us Americana [978]

HISTORY OF FULTON COUNTY / Frothingham, Washington – Syracuse, D. Mason and Co., 1892. New York Reel 16. (The Cox Library Collection) – 5 – us Americana [978]

HISTORY OF GAGE COUNTY / Dobbs, Hugh J – Lincoln: Western Publishing and Eng. Co., 1918. Nebraska Reel 9. (The Cox Library Collection) – 5 – us Americana [978]

HISTORY OF GALLITON, SALINE, HAMILTON, FRANKLIN AND WILLIAMSON COUNTIES – Chicago, 1887. Illinois Reel 25. (The Cox Library Collection) – 5 – us Americana [978]

HISTORY OF GENESEE COUNTY / Wood, Edwin O – Indianapolis: Federal Publ. Co., 1916. Vols. 1-2. Michigan Reel 9. (The Cox Library Collection) – 5 – us Americana [978]

HISTORY OF GENTRY AND WORTH COUNTIES / National Historical Co – St. Joseph, 1882. Missouri Reel 16. (The Cox Library Collection) – 5 – us Americana [978]

HISTORY OF GEOGRAPHY / Keltie, Sir John Scott & Howarth, OJ R – Illus. and maps. New York, London: G.P. Putnam, 1913. vii,208p – 1 – us U.W. Library [910]

HISTORY OF GEORGIA / Howell, Clark – 4v, 1926. F-0101/F-0104 – 9 – us A.G.L.L. [978]

HISTORY OF GEORGIA / Howell, Clark – Atlanta, S. J. Clarke Publ. Co., 1926. Vols. 1-4. Georgia Reel 1. (The Cox Library Collection) – 5 – us Americana [978]

THE HISTORY OF GEORGIA / Jones, Charles C, Jr – 1883. Aboriginal & colonial epochs. 10 fiches.F-0100 – 9 – us A.G.L.L. [978]

A HISTORY OF GEORGIA, FROM ITS DISCOVERY BY EUROPEANS TO THE ADOPTION OF THE PRESENT CONSTITUTION IN 1798 / Stevens, William Bacon – 2v, 1847, 1859. 16 fiches. F-0097/0098 – 9 – us A.G.L.L. [978]

A HISTORY OF GERMAN LITERATURE = GESCHICHTE DER DEUTSCHEN LITTERATUR / Scherer, Wilhelm; ed by Mueller, Max – (Includes bibliographical references and index) – Oxford: Clarendon Press, 1886 – 1r – 1 – us U.W. Library [430]

A HISTORY OF GERMAN LITERATURE / Robertson, John George – (Includes bibliographical references and index) – 3rd rev enl ed. Edinburgh: W Blackwood, 1959 – 1r – 1 – us U.W. Library [430]

A HISTORY OF GERMAN LITERATURE / Robertson, John George – (Includes bibliographical references and index) – New York: G P Putnam's Sons Ltd; Edinburgh: W Blackwood and Sons Ltd, [1931] – 1r – 1 – us U.W. Library [430]

HISTORY OF GERMAN THEOLOGY IN THE NINETEENTH CENTURY / Lichtenberger, Frederic – Edinburgh: T. & T. Clark, 1889 – 2mf – us A.T.L.A. [240]

HISTORY OF GIBSON COUNTY / Stormont, Gil. R – Her people, industries, and institutions. Indianapolis: B. F. Bowen and Co., 1914. Indiana Reel 13. (The Cox Library Collection) – 5 – us Americana [978]

HISTORY OF GLASS / Corning Museum of Glass – 1817 images – 15 – $1,755.00 set – 0-88354-077-0 – us UPA [740]

A HISTORY OF GLASS IN JAPAN / Blair, Dorothy – 1973. 479p., 240 illus., maps, plates. 10 fiches Fiche no. 972 – 9 – $15.00 – us Corning Mus [740]

A HISTORY OF GLOUCESTERSHIRE / Wantner – 1714 – 1 – uk Microform Academic [941]

HISTORY OF GOODHUE COUNTY / Wood, Alley and Co – Biographical sketches. Red Wing, 1878. Minnesota Reel 7. (The Cox Library Collection) – 5 – us Americana [978]

A HISTORY OF GOTHIC ART IN ENGLAND / Prior, E S – H 1294 2. 1900 – 8 – ne IDC [941]

THE HISTORY OF GRADED EXERCISE TESTING IN CARDIAC REHABILITATION / Bickum, Bonnie D – 1992 – 2mf – $8.00 – us Microform Publ [615]

HISTORY OF GRAND RAPIDS AND ITS INDUSTRIES / Goss, Dwight – Chicago: C. F. Cooper and Co., 1906. Michigan Reel 16. (The Cox Library Collection) – 5 – us Americana [978]

HISTORY OF GRAND RAPIDS AND KENT COUNTY. FROM THE FIRST SETTLEMENT TO THE PRESENT TIME / Fisher, Ernest B – Robert O. Law and Co., 1918. Vols. 1-2. Michigan Reel 16. (The Cox Library Collection) – 5 – us Americana [978]

HISTORY OF GRANT COUNTY – Chicago: 1881. Wisconsin Reel 11. (The Cox Library Collection) – 5 – us Americana [978]

HISTORY OF GREECE AFTER 1945 PAMPHLET COLLECTION – 1948-1953 – 1 reel – 1 – CSUXANL6488-B – us Hoover Inst Photo [949]

HISTORY OF GREECE FROM 1939 TO 1945 PAMPHLET COLLECTION – 1942-1950 – 1 reel – 1 – CSUXANL6495-B – us Hoover Inst Photo [949]

THE HISTORY OF GREECE FROM ITS COMMENCEMENT TO THE CLOSE OF THE INDEPENDENCE OF THE GREEK NATION / Holm, Adolf – Tr. from the German by Frederick Clarke.London, New York: Macmillan, 1894-98. 4v – 1 – us U.W. Library [930]

HISTORY OF GREECE PAMPHLET COLLECTION – 1822-1988 – 2r – 1 – CSUXANL6472-B – us Hoover Inst Photo [949]

A HISTORY OF GREELEY AND THE UNION COLONY OF COLORADO / Boyd, David – Greeley: The Greeley Tribune Press, 1890. Colorado reel 4. (Cox Library Collection) – 5 – us Americana [978]

HISTORY OF GREEN COUNTY – Springfield: 1884. Wisconsin Reel 12. (The Cox Library Collection) – 5 – us Americana [978]

HISTORY OF GREEN COUNTY, WISCONSIN / Bingham, Helen M – Milwaukee: Burdick and Armitage, 1877. Wisconsin Reel 11. (The Cox Library Collection) – 5 – us Americana [978]

HISTORY OF GREENE AND JERSEY COUNTIES – Springfield, 1885. Illinois Reel 26. (The Cox Library Collection) – 5 – us Americana [978]

HISTORY OF GREENE AND SULLIVAN COUNTIES – Biographical sketches. Chicago, 1884. Indiana Reel 13. (The Cox Library Collection) – 5 – us Americana [978]

HISTORY OF GREENE COUNTY / Bates, Samuel P – Chicago, Nelson Rishforth and Co., 1888. Pennsylvania Reel 23. (The Cox Library Collection) – 5 – us Americana [978]

HISTORY OF GREENE COUNTY / Dills, R S – Dayton: Odell and Mayer Publ., 1881. Ohio Reel 34. (The Cox Library Collection) – 5 – us Americana [978]

HISTORY OF GREENE COUNTY / Donnelly & Gassette & Loyd – Chicago: 1879. Illinois Reel 25. (The Cox Library Collection) – 5 – us Americana [978]

HISTORY OF GREENE COUNTY / J.B. Beers and Co – New York, 1884. New York Reel 16. The Cox Library Collection – 5 – us Americana [978]

HISTORY OF GREENE COUNTY / Robinson, George F – Chicago: S. J. Clarke Publ. Co., 1902. Ohio Rel 35. (The Cox Library Collection) – 5 – us Americana [978]

HISTORY OF GREENE COUNTY – St. Louis, 1883.Missouri Reel 16. (The Cox Library Collection) – 5 – us Americana [978]

HISTORY OF GRUNDY COUNTY / Birdsall & Dean – Kansas City, 1881. Missouri Reel 17. (The Cox Library Collection) – 5 – us Americana [978]

HISTORY OF GRUNDY COUNTY / Ford, James E – Trenton: News Publ. Co., 1908. Missouri Reel 18. (The Cox Library Collection) – 5 – us Americana [978]

HISTORY OF GRUNDY COUNTY / O.L. Baskin and Co – Chicago, 1882. Illinois Reel 26. The Cox Library Collection – 5 – us Americana [978]

HISTORY OF GUERNSEY COUNTY / Sarchet, Cyrus P B – Indianapolis: B. F. Bowen and Co., 1911. Vols. 1-2. Ohio Reel 35. (The Cox Library Collection) – 5 – us Americana [978]

A HISTORY OF GUJARAT / Mir Abu Turab Vali – Tarikh i Gujaraa8t. Calcutta, 1909. BI-766 2 – 8 – ne IDC [950]

HISTORY OF GUTHRIE AND ADAIR COUNTIES – Springfield: 1884. Iowa Reel 18. (The Cox Library Collection) – 5 – us Americana [978]

THE HISTORY OF GUTTA-PERCHA WILLIE: THE WORKING GENIUS / MacDonald, George – Eight page illus. by Arthur Hughes. New ed. London: Blackie, 1901. 212p. illus – 1 – us U.W. Library [830]

HISTORY OF GWINNETT COUNTY 1818-1943 / Flanigan, J C – Hopeville, Tyler and Co., 1943. Georgia Reel 3. (The Cox Library Collection) – 5 – us Americana [978]

HISTORY OF HALIFAX COUNTY / Allen, W C – Boston, Cornhill Co., 1918. North Carolina Reel 1. (The Cox Library Collection) – 5 – us Americana [978]

HISTORY OF HALL COUNTY / Buechler & Barr & Stough – Lincoln: Western Publ. and Eng. Co., 1920. Nebraska Reel 10. (The Cox Library Collection) – 5 – us Americana [978]

HISTORY OF HAMILTON AND CLAY COUNTIES / Burr & Buck – Chicago: S.J. Clarke Publ. Co., 1921. 2v. Nebraska Reel 9. (The Cox Library Collection) – 5 – us Americana [978]

HISTORY OF HAMILTON COUNTY / Ford, H A & Ford, K B – Biographical sketches. L. A. Williams and Co., 1881. Ohio Reel 36. (The Cox Library Collection) – 5 – us Americana [978]

HISTORY OF HAMILTON COUNTY AND CHATTANOOGA / Armstrong, Zella – Chattanooga: Lookout Publ. Co., 1931. Vols. 1-2. Tennessee Reel 2. (The Cox Library Collection) – 5 – us Americana [978]

HISTORY OF HAMILTON COUNTY BAPTIST CHURCH LIBRARY ORGANIZATION, CHATTANOOGA, TENNESSEE – 1951-71 – 1 – 5.00 – us Baptist [240]

HISTORY OF HAMPSHIRE COUNTY / Maxwell & Swisher – Morganstown, A. Brown Boughner Printer, 1897. West Virginia Reel 3. (The Cox Library Collection) – 5 – us Americana [978]

HISTORY OF HANCOCK COUNTY / Beardsley, D B – From earliest settlement to the present time with biographical sketches. Springfield: Republic Printing Co., 1881. Ohio Reel 37. (The Cox Library Collection) – 5 – us Americana [978]

HISTORY OF HANCOCK COUNTY – Chicago: 1886. Ohio Reel 37. (The Cox Library Collection) – 5 – us Americana [978]

HISTORY OF HANCOCK COUNTY / Gregg, Thomas – Chicago: Charles C. Chapman and Co., 1880. Illinois Reel 26. (The Cox Library Collection) – 5 – us Americana [978]

HISTORY OF HANCOCK COUNTY / Richman, George J – Biographical sketches. Indianapolis: Federal Publ. Co., Inc., 1916. Indiana Reel 14. (The Cox Library Collection) – 5 – us Americana [978]

HISTORY OF HANOVER TOWNSHIP / Plumb, Henry B – Including Sugar Notch, Ashley and Nantecoke Boroughs and a history of Wyoming Valley. Wilkes-Barre, Robert Baur, Printer, 1885. Pennsylvania Reel 29. (The Cox Library Collection) – 5 – us Americana [978]

HISTORY OF HARDIN COUNTY – Chicago: 1883. Ohio Reel 38. (The Cox Library Collection) – 5 – us Americana [978]

HISTORY OF HARDIN COUNTY – Springfield: 1883. Iowa Reel 19. (The Cox Library Collection) – 5 – us Americana [978]

HISTORY OF HARRISON AND CARROLL COUNTIES / J.H. Beers and Co – Biographical sketches. Chicago, 1891. Ohio Reel 39. The Cox Library Collection – 5 – us Americana [978]

HISTORY OF HARRISON COUNTY / National Publishing Co – Chicago: 1891. Iowa Reel 19. (The Cox Library Collection) – 5 – us Americana [978]

HISTORY OF HARRISON COUNTY / Wanamaker, George W – Topeka: Historical Publ. Co., 1921. Missouri Reel 18. (The Cox Library Collection) – 5 – us Americana [978]

HISTORY OF HARRISON COUNTY, IOWA / Smith, Joe H – Des Moines: Iowa Printing Co., 1888. Iowa Reel 19. (The Cox Library Collection) – 5 – us Americana [978]

HISTORY OF HARRISON COUTNY / Hunt, Herbert & Clark – Indianapolis: B. F. Bowen and Co., 1915. Iowa Reel 20. (The Cox Library Collection) – 5 – us Americana [978]

HISTORY OF HARTFORD COUNTY 1608-1812 / Preston – Baltimore, 1901. Maryland Reel 3. (The Cox Library Collection) – 5 – us Americana [978]

HISTORY OF HARTFORD, JULY 4, 1761-APRIL 4, 1889 / Tucker, William H – Burlington, Free Press Association, 1889. Vermont Reel 10. (The Cox Library Collection) – 5 – us Americana [978]

HISTORY OF HENDRICKS COUNTY / B.F. Bowen and Co – Biographical sketches of representative citizens and genealogical records of many old families. Indianapolis, 1914. Indiana Reel 14. The Cox Library Collection – 5 – us Americana [978]

HISTORY OF HENDRICKS COUNTY / Inter-State Publishing Co – Biographical sketches. Chicago, 1885. Indiana Reel 14. The Cox Library Collection – 5 – us Americana [978]

HISTORY OF HENNEPIN COUNTY AND THE CITY OF MINNEAPOLIS / Neill, Edward D – Minneapolis: North Star Publ. Co., 1881.Minnesota Reel 7. (The Cox Library Collection) – 5 – us Americana [978]

HISTORY OF HENRY AND FULTON COUNTIES / Aldrich, Lewis C – Syracuse: D. Mason and Co., 1888. Ohio Reel 39. (The Cox Library Collection) – 5 – us Americana [978]

HISTORY OF HENRY AND ST CLAIR COUNTIES / National Historical Co – St. Joseph, 1883. Missouri Reel 18. (The Cox Library Collection) – 5 – us Americana [978]

HISTORY OF HENRY COUNTY – Chicago: 1879. Iowa Reel 20. (The Cox Library Collection) – 5 – us Americana [978]

HISTORY OF HENRY COUNTY / Inter-State Publishing Co – Biographical sketches. Chicago, 1884. Indiana Reel 15. The Cox Library Collection – 5 – us Americana [978]

HISTORY OF HENRY COUNTY / Kinner, J L – Chicago: Pioneer Publ. Co., 1910. Vols. 1-2. Illinois Reel 28. (The Cox Library Collection) – 5 – us Americana [978]

HISTORY OF HENRY COUNTY / Lamkin, Uel W – Topeka: Historical Publ. Co., 1919. Missouri Reel 19. (The Cox Library Collection) – 5 – us Americana [978]

HISTORY OF HENRY COUNTY (ITS TAX-PAYERS AND VOTERS) / H.F. Kett and Co – Chicago, 1877. Illinois Reel 27. The Cox Library Collection – 5 – us Americana [978]

THE HISTORY OF HENRY ESMOND, ESQ. : A COLONEL IN THE SERVICE OF HER MAJESTY QUEEN ANNE / Esmond, Henry & Thackeray, William Makepeace – London: Smith, Elder, & Co., 1858 – 1 roll – 1 – 1-55879-718-1 – uk Libr Preservation [350]

HISTORY OF HERKIMER COUNTY / F.W. Beers and Co – New York, 1879. New York Reel 17. The Cox Library Collection – 5 – us Americana [978]

HISTORY OF HERKIMER COUNTY / Hardin & Willard – Syracuse: D. Mason and Co., 1893. New York Reel 17. (The Cox Library Collection) – 5 – us Americana [978]

A HISTORY OF HERKIMER COUNTY, INCLUDING THE UPPER MOHAWK VALLEY / Benton, Nathaniel S – Albany: J. Munsell, 1856. New York Reel 16. (The Cox Library Collection) – 5 – us Americana [978]

THE HISTORY OF HERODOTUS. A NEW ENGLISH VERSION / Herodotus – By George Rawlinson assisted by Col. Sir Henry Rawlinson and Sir J.G. Wilkinson. New York: D. Appleton & Co., 1859-60. 4v.ill. plates. fold. maps. plans – 1 – us U.W. Library [930]

HISTORY OF HICKORY, POLK, CEDAR, DADE AND BARTON COUNTIES – Biographical appendix. Chicago, 1889. Missouri Reel 19. (The Cox Library Collection) – 5 – us Americana [978]

HISTORY OF HILLSBORO COUNTY / Hurd, D Hamilton – Philadelphia, J. W. Lewis and Co., 1885. New Hampshire Reel 4. (The Cox Library Collection) – 5 – us Americana [978]

HISTORY OF HILLSBOROUGH, 1735-1921 / Browne, George W – (Vol. 1. History and Description. (New Hampshire Reel 5). 5. Vol. 2. Genealogy. (New Hampshire Reel 6). 5) – Manchester, John B. Clarke Co., Printers, 1921. 2 Vols. (The Cox Library Collection) – 5 – us Americana [978]

HISTORY OF HOCKING VALLEY / Inter-State Publishing Co – Biographical sketches. Chicago, 1883. Mississippi Reel 8. The Cox Library Collection – 5 – us Americana [978]

HISTORY OF HOLLYWOOD / Palmer, Edwin O – Hollywood: Arthur H. Cawston, 1937. 2v.California Reel 18. (The Cox Library Collection) – 5 – us Americana [978]

HISTORY OF HOLT AND ATCHISON COUNTIES / National Historical Co – Biographical sketches. St. Joseph, 1882. Missouri Reel 19. (The Cox Library Collection) – 5 – us Americana [978]

HISTORY OF HOLT COUNTY FROM THE TIME OF PLATTE PURCHASE TO THE END OF YEAR 1916 / History Publishing Co – St. Joseph, n.d.Missouri Reel 19. (The Cox Library Collection) – 5 – us Americana [978]

HISTORY OF HOMEOPATHY AND ITS INSTITUTIONS IN AMERICA; THEIR FOUNDERS, BENEFACTORS, FACULTIES, OFFICERS, HOSPITALS.. / King, William Harvey – New York, Chicago: The Lewis Publishing Company, 1905. 4v. illus, plates, ports – 1 – us U.W. Library [610]

HISTORY OF HOPEWALL CHURCH / Lathan, Robert – 1879 – 9 – $50.00 – us Presbyterian [240]

HISTORY OF HOUSTON COUNTY / H.C. Cooper, Jr. & Co – Winona, 1919. Minnesota Reel 8. The Cox Library Collection – 5 – us Americana [978]

HISTORY OF HOWARD AND COOPER COUNTIES / National Historical Co – St. Louis, 1883.Missouri Reel 20. (The Cox Library Collection) – 5 – us Americana [978]

HISTORY OF HUMANITY, VOL. 1 : PREHISTORY AND THE BEGINNINGS OF CIVILIZATION / Laet, S J De – 750p – 9 – 92-3-102810-3 – fr UNESCO [900]

HISTORY OF HUMBOLDT COUNTY / Irvine, Leigh – Los Angeles: Historic Record Co., 1915. California Reel 13. (The Cox Library Collection – 5 – us Americana [978]

HISTORY OF HUNGARY FROM 1918 TO 1945 PAMPHLET COLLECTION – 1919-1940 – 1 reel – 1 – CSUXANL5768-B – us Hoover Inst Photo [947]

HISTORY OF HUNGARY FROM 1945 TO 1989 PAMPHLET COLLECTION – 1945-1957 – 1 reel – 1 – CSUXANL5772-B – us Hoover Inst Photo [947]

HISTORY OF HUNGARY PAMPHLET COLLECTION – 1907-1962 – 2r – 1 – CSUXANL5761-B – us Hoover Inst Photo [947]

HISTORY OF HUNTINGTON COUNTY / Brant, Fuller and Co – Historical and biographical sketches. Chicago: 1887. Indiana Reel 16. (The Cox Library Collection) – 5 – us Americana [978]

HISTORY OF HURON COUNTY / Baughman, A J – Biographical sketches. Chicago: S. J. Clarke Publ. Co., 1909. Vols. 1-2. Ohio Reel 40. (The Cox Library Collection) – 5 – us Americana [978]

THE HISTORY OF HYDUR NAIK/THE HISTORY OF THE REIGN OF TIPU SULTAN / Husain Ali, Kirmani – 1842, 1844 – 1 – uk Microform Academic [900]

HISTORY OF IDAHO / Franch, Hiram – Chicago: Lewis Publ. Co., 1914. v1-3. Idaho reel 1. (Cox Library Collection) – 5 – us Americana [978]

HISTORY OF IDAHO / Hawley, James H – Chicago: S.J. Clarke Publ. Co., 1920. v1-3. Idaho reel 2. (Cox Library Collection) – 5 – us Americana [978]

HISTORY OF IDAHO; A NARRATIVE ACCOUNT OF ITS HISTORICAL PROGRESS, ITS PEOPLE, AND ITS PRINCIPAL INTERESTS – 3v, by Hiram T. French, 1914. Biog. and hist. sketches.Indexed. V145-0001 – 5 – us A.G.L.L. [920]

HISTORY OF IDAHO, THE GEM OF THE MOUNTAINS / ed by Hawley, James H – 3v, 1920. Biog. and hist. sketches. Indexed. V145-0002 – 5 – us A.G.L.L. [920]

HISTORY OF IDEAS IN EUROPE – (Based on Shelf List of the Union Theological Seminary in New York City, covering aspects of religious and idealogical struggle in Europe during 16th century) – 2,261mf – 9 – $6,300.00 – us OmniSys [240]

HISTORY OF ILLINOIS 1673-1873 / Stuve, Bernard et al – Springfield: Illinois Journal Co., 1874. Illinois Reel 1. (The Cox Library Collection) – 5 – us Americana [978]

HISTORY OF ILLINOIS 1814-1847 / Ford, Thomas – Chicago: S. C. Griggs and Co., 1854. Illinois Reel 1. (The Cox Library Collection) – 5 – us Americana [978]

HISTORY OF ILLINOIS: ACCOMPANY SIC AN HISTORICAL MAP OF THE STATE / Blanchard, Rufus – Chicago: National School Furnishing Co., 1883. 00878. (Pre-1900 Canadiana) – 9 – cn C.I.H.M. [978]

HISTORY OF ILLINOIS AND HER PEOPLE / Smith, George W – Chicago: American Historical Society, 1927. Vol. 1. Illinois Reel 1; Vols. 2-6. Illinois Reel 2. (The Cox Library Collection) – 5 – us Americana [978]

HISTORY OF IMPERIAL COUNTY / Farr, FC – Berkeley: Elms and Franks, 1918.California Reel 13. (The Cox Library Collection) – 5 – us Americana [978]

A HISTORY OF INDIAN MISSIONS OF THE PACIFIC COAST : OREGON, WASHINGTON, IDAHO / Eells, Myron – (Includes bibliographical references) – Philadelphia: American Sunday-School Union, c1882 – 1mf – 9 – 0-8370-6181-4 – 1986-0181 – us A.T.L.A. [240]

HISTORY OF INDIANA / Brant and Fuller and Company – Special edition for Marshall County. Madison, 1890. 2v. Indiana Reel 22. (The Cox Library Collection) – 5 – us Americana [978]

HISTORY OF INDONESIA'S NATIONAL MOVEMENT / Indonesia – SE-2667 1. 1949 – 9 – ne IDC [950]

THE HISTORY OF INTELLIGENCE ACTIVITIES UNDER GENERAL DOUGLAS MACARTHUR, 1942-1950 / Supreme Command for the Allied Powers – 1984 – 8r – 1 – $680.00 – S1657 – us Scholarly Res [355]

THE HISTORY OF INTERCOLLEGIATE SWIMMING AT THE COLLEGE OF WILLIAM AND MARY (1928-1987) / Lanchantin, Margaret M – 1989 – 107p 2mf – 9 – $8.00 – us Microform Publ [370]

HISTORY OF IONIA AND MONTCALM COUNTIES / Schenck, John L – Biographical sketches. Philadelphia: D. W. Ensign and Co., 1881. Michigan Reel 13. (The Cox Library Collection) – 5 – us Americana [978]

HISTORY OF IONIA COUNTY / Branch, E E – Biographical sketches. Indianapolis: B. F. Bowen and Co., 1916. Vols. 1-2. Michigan Reel 13. (The Cox Library Collection) – 5 – us Americana [978]

HISTORY OF IOWA AND DIRECTORY OF JACKSON COUNTY – 1907. Iowa Reel 22. (The Cox Library Collection) – 5 – us Americana [978]

A HISTORY OF IOWA BAPTIST SCHOOLS / Abernethy, Alonzo – (Includes index) – Osage, IA: A Abernethy, 1907 – 1mf – 9 – 0-8370-8640-X – 1986-2640 – us A.T.L.A. [370]

HISTORY OF IOWA COUNTY / Union Historical Co – Des Moines: 1881. Iowa Reel 21. (The Cox Library Collection) – 5 – us Americana [978]

HISTORY OF IRA, VERMONT / Peck, S L – Rutland: The Tuttle Co., 1926. Vermont Reel 8. (The Cox Library Collection) – 5 – us Americana [978]

HISTORY OF IROQUOIS COUNTY / Beckwith, H W – Chicago: H. H. Hill and Co., 1880. Illinois Reel 28. (The Cox Library Collection) – 5 – us Americana [978]
HISTORY OF IRWIN COUNTY / Clements, J B – 1932. Georgia Reel 3. (The Cox Library Collection) – 5 – us Americana [978]
HISTORY OF JACKSON COUNTY – Chicago: 1879. Iowa Reel 21. (The Cox Library Collection) – 5 – us Americana [978]
HISTORY OF JACKSON COUNTY / Ellis, James W – Chicago: S. J. Clarke Publ. Co., 1910. Vol. 1, Iowa Reel 21; Vol. 2, Iowa Reel 22. (The Cox Library Collection) – 5 – us Americana [978]
HISTORY OF JACKSON COUNTY / Inter-State Publishing Co – Biographical sketches. Chicago, 1881. Michigan Reel 14. The Cox Library Collection – 5 – us Americana [978]
HISTORY OF JACKSON COUNTY / Union Historical Co – Kansas City, 1881. Missouri Reel 20. (The Cox Library Collection) – 5 – us Americana [978]
HISTORY OF JACKSON COUNTY, OHIO / Williams, D W – Jackson: 1900. Ohio Reel 40. (The Cox Library Collection) – 5 – us Americana [978]
THE HISTORY OF JAMAICA : OR, GENERAL SURVEY OF THE ANCIENT AND MODERN STATE OF THAT ISLAND: WITH REFLECTIONS ON ITS SITUATION, SETTLEMENTS, INHABITANTS, CLIMATE, PRODUCTS, COMMERCE, LAWS, AND GOVERNMENT / Long, Edward – London. 3v. 1774 – 1r – 1 – us Ross [972]
HISTORY OF JASPER COUNTY – Chicago: 1878. Iowa Reel 22. (The Cox Library Collection) – 5 – us Americana [978]
HISTORY OF JASPER COUNTY / Mills and Co – History of Carthage and Joplin, also biographical sketches. Des Moines, 1883. Missouri Reel 21. (The Cox Library Collection) – 5 – us Americana [978]
THE HISTORY OF JAVA / Raffles, T S – London. 2v. 1817 – 15mf – 9 – ne IDC [950]
HISTORY OF JAY COUNTY INCLUDING WORLD WAR RECORD / Jay, Milton – Indianapolis: Historical Publ. Co., 1922. Vols. 1-2. Indiana Reel 17. (The Cox Library Collection) – 5 – us Americana [978]
HISTORY OF JEFFERSON COUNTY – Chicago: 1879. Iowa Reel 23. (The Cox Library Collection) – 5 – us Americana [978]
HISTORY OF JEFFERSON COUNTY – Chicago. Wisconsin Reel 12. (The Cox Library Collection) – 5 – us Americana [978]
HISTORY OF JEFFERSON COUNTY / L.H. Everts and Co – Biographical sketches. Philadelphia, 1878. New York Reel 17. The Cox Library Collection – 5 – us Americana [978]
HISTORY OF JEFFERSON COUNTY / Perrin, William Henry – Chicago: Globe Publ. Co., 1883. Illinois Reel 29. (The Cox Library Collection) – 5 – us Americana [978]
HISTORY OF JEFFERSON COUNTY / Scott, Kate M – Syracuse, D. Mason and Co., 1888. Pennsylvania Reel 24. (The Cox Library Collection) – 5 – us Americana [978]
HISTORY OF JERAULD COUNTY / Dunnam, N J – Earliest settlement to 1 Jan 1909. Wassington Springs, 1909. South Dakota Reel 5.(The Cox Library Collection) – 5 – us Americana [978]
HISTORY OF JEROME TOWNSHIP, UNION COUNTY / Curry, W L – Columbus: 1913. Ohio Reel 64. (The Cox Library Collection) – 5 – us Americana [978]
HISTORY OF JERSEY COUNTY / Hamilton, Oscar B – Chicago: Munsell Publ. Co., 1919. Illinois Reel 29. (The Cox Library Collection) – 5 – us Americana [978]
HISTORY OF JERSEYVILLE 1822-1901 / Cooper, M M – Jerseyville Republican Print., 1901. Illinois Reel 29. (The Cox Library Collection) – 5 – us Americana [978]
A HISTORY OF JESSAMINE COUNTY / Young, Bennett H – Louisville: Courier Journal Job Printing, 1898. Kentucky Reel 7. (The Cox Library Collection) – 5 – us Americana [978]
HISTORY OF JEWELL COUNTY, KANSAS, WITH A FULL ACCOUNT OF THE EARLY SETTLEMENTS & INDIAN ATROCITIES COMMITTED WITHIN ITS BORDERS – By M. Winsor, et al. 1878. Incomplete.V30-0018 – 1 – us A.G.L.L. [920]
HISTORY OF JO DAVIESS COUNTY / H.F. Kett and Co – Chicago, 1878. Illinois Reel 29. The Cox Library Collection – 5 – us Americana [978]
HISTORY OF JOHNSON COUNTY / Blair, Ed – Lawrence: Standard Publ. Co., 1915. Kansas Reel 8. (The Cox Library Collection) – 5 – us Americana [978]
HISTORY OF JOHNSON COUNTY / Brant, Fuller and Co – Historical and biographical sketches. Chicago: 1888. Indiana Reel 17. (The Cox Library Collection) – 5 – us Americana [978]
HISTORY OF JOHNSON COUNTY / Cockrell, Ewing – Topeka: Historical Publ. Co., 1918. Missouri Reel 22. (The Cox Library Collection) – 5 – us Americana [978]
HISTORY OF JOHNSON COUNTY 1836-1882 – Iowa City: 1883. Iowa Reel 23. (The Cox Library Collection) – 5 – us Americana [978]
HISTORY OF JOHNSON COUNTY, ARKANSAS / Langford, Ella Molloy – 1921. Item F. 210p. SW16-0126 – 5 – us A.G.L.L. [978]
A HISTORY OF JOHNSON COUNTY, ILLINOIS / Chapman, PT – The Herrin News, 1925. Illinois Reel 30. (The Cox Library Collection) – 5 – us Americana [978]
HISTORY OF JONES COUNTY – Chicago: 1879. Iowa Reel 24. (The Cox Library Collection) – 5 – us Americana [978]
THE HISTORY OF JOSHUA...AND THE CUSTOMS OF THE TIMES IN WHICH HE LIVED / Smith, Thornley – New York: A.D.F. Randolph, 187?. 1 fiche – 9 – us A.T.L.A. [240]
HISTORY OF JOURNALISM IN THE PHILIPPINE ISLANDS / Valenzuela, Jesus Z – With introd. by Teodoro M. Kalaw, Willard Grosvenor Bleyer, Farael Palma. Manila: J.Z. Valenzuela, 1933. xiv,217p. illus., bibliog – 1 – us U.W. Library [070]
HISTORY OF KANE COUNTY / Joslyn, R W & Joslyn, F W – Historical and biographical sketches. Chicago: Pioneer Publ. Co., 1908. Vols. 1-2. Illinois Reel 32. (The Cox Library Collection) – 5 – us Americana [978]
A HISTORY OF KANSAS – By Noble L. Prentis. 1899. 7 fiches. F-0738 – 9 – us A.G.L.L. [920]
HISTORY OF KANSAS / Connelley, William Elsey – Chicago: American Historical Society, Inc., 1928. v1-2, Kansas Reel 3. v3-5, Kansas Reel 4. (The Cox Library Collection) – 5 – us Americana [978]
HISTORY OF KATSINA / Daniel, F de F – (Filmed with: Sokoto Provincial Gazetteer by P G Harris) – [s.l: s.n, 1940?] – 1 – us Res Libr [960]
HISTORY OF KENDALL COUNTY / Hicks, E W – Aurora: Knickerbocker and Hodder, 1877. Illinois Reel 33. (The Cox Library Collection) – 5 – us Americana [978]
HISTORY OF KENT COUNTY – Biographical sketches. Chicago, 1881. Michigan Reel 15. The Cox Library Collection – 5 – us Americana [978]
A HISTORY OF KENTUCKY – By Elizabeth Shelby Kenkead, 1896. Item A. Includes index. SW16-0223 – 5 – us A.G.L.L. [978]
HISTORY OF KENTUCKY / Connelley, William Elsey & Coulter, E M – Chicago: American Historical Society, 1922. v1-3. Kentucky Reel 2; v4-5, Kentucky Reel 3.(The Cox Library Collection) – 5 – us Americana [978]
HISTORY OF KENTUCKY / Lewis & Collins – Louisville: John P. Morton and Co., 1924. 2v. Kentucky Reel 3.(The Cox Library Collection) – 5 – us Americana [978]
A HISTORY OF KENTUCKY AND KENTUCKIANS / Johnson, E Polk – Chicago: The Lewis Publishing Co., 1912.v1-2, Kentucky Reel 1; v3, Kentucky Reel 2. (The Cox Library Collection) – 5 – us Americana [920]
A HISTORY OF KENTUCKY BAPTISTS / Spencer, J H – Cincinnati, 1886. 2v. Kentucky Reel 4.(The Cox Library Collection) – 5 – us Americana [978]
A HISTORY OF KENTUCKY BAPTISTS FROM 1769 TO 1885 – 2v, by J.H. Spencer. 1886. More than 1600 biog. sketches. Indexed. 24 fiches. F-0162/0163 – 9 – us A.G.L.L. [920]
HISTORY OF KENTUCKY IN FIVE VOLUMES – v1, by William Elsey Connelley, et al. 1922. Hist. & biog. sketches. Indexed. 11 fiches. F-0499 – 9 – us A.G.L.L. [920]
HISTORY OF KENTUCKY, V2: BY THE LATE LEWIS COLLINS / Collins, Lewis – Rev., enl. fourfold and brought down to the year 1874. 1966. Indexed. 15 fiches. F-1074 – 9 – us A.G.L.L. [978]
HISTORY OF KEOKUK COUNTY – Des Moines: 1880. Iowa Reel 24. (The Cox Library Collection) – 5 – us Americana [978]
HISTORY OF KERN COUNTY / Miller, Thelma B – Chicago: S.J. Clarke Publ. Co., 1929. 2v. California Reel 14. (The Cox Library Collection) – 5 – us Americana [978]
HISTORY OF KERN COUNTY / Morgan, Wallace – Los Angeles: Historic Record Co., 1914. California Reel 13. (The Cox Library Collection) – 5 – us Americana [978]
HISTORY OF KING AND QUEEN COUNTY / Bagby, Alfred – Washington, Neale Publishing Co., 1908. Virginia Reel 3. (The Cox Library Collection) – 5 – us Americana [978]
A HISTORY OF KING'S CHAPEL IN BOSTON : THE FIRST EPISCOPAL CHURCH IN NEW ENGLAND: COMPRISING NOTICES OF THE INTRODUCTION OF EPISCOPACY INTO THE NORTHERN COLONIES / Greenwood, FWP – Boston: Carter, Hendee, 1833 – 1mf – us A.T.L.A. [240]
HISTORY OF KINGS COUNTY AND BROOKLYN 1683-1884 / ed by Stiler, Henry R – New York, W. W. Munsell and Co., 1884. Vols. 1-2. New York Reel 19. (The Cox Library Collection) – 5 – us Americana [978]
HISTORY OF KNOX COUNTY – Chicago, 1878. Illinois Reel 33. The Cox Library Collection – 5 – us Americana [978]
HISTORY OF KNOX COUNTY / Perry, A J – Historical and biographical sketches. Chicago: S. J. Clarke Publ. Co., 1912. Vols. 1-2. Illinois Reel 35. (The Cox Library Collection) – 5 – us Americana [978]
HISTORY OF KNOX COUNTY ITS PAST AND PRESENT / Hill, N N – Mt. Vernon: A. A. Graham and Co., 1881. Ohio Reel 41. (The Cox Library Collection) – 5 – us Americana [978]
A HISTORY OF KNOX COUNTY, OHIO 1779-1862 / Norton, A Banning – Includes sketch of Kenyon College. Columbus: Richard Nevins, Printer, 1862. Ohio Reel 41. (The Cox Library Collection) – 5 – us Americana [978]
HISTORY OF KOSSUTH AND HUMBOLDT COUNTIES – Springfield: 1884. Iowa Reel 25. (The Cox Library Collection) – 5 – us Americana [978]
HISTORY OF KOSSUTH, HANCOCK, AND WINNEBAGO COUNTIES – Springfield: 1884. Iowa Reel 25. (The Cox Library Collection) – 5 – us Americana [978]
HISTORY OF LA CROSSE COUNTY – Chicago: 1881. Wisconsin Reel 13. (The Cox Library Collection) – 5 – us Americana [978]
HISTORY OF LA SALLE COUNTY / Baldwin, Elmer – Chicago: Rand, McNally & Co., 1877. Illinois Reel 36. (The Cox Library Collection) – 5 – us Americana [978]
HISTORY OF LA SALLE COUNTY / Hoffman, W J – Historical and biographical sketches. Chicago: S. J. Clarke Publ. Co., 1906. Illinois Reel 37. (The Cox Library Collection) – 5 – us Americana [978]
HISTORY OF LA SALLE COUNTY / Inter-State Publishing Co – Historical and biographical sketches. Vol 1, Illinois Reel 36 and Vol 2, Illinois Reel 37. The Cox Library Collection – 5 – us Americana [978]
HISTORY OF LABETTE COUNTY / Case, Nelson – Topeka: Crane and Co.,Publ., 1893. Kansas Reel 8. (The Cox Library Collection) – 5 – us Americana [978]
HISTORY OF LACLEDE, CAMDEN, DALLAS, WEBSTER, WRIGHT, TEXAS, PULASKI, PHELPS AND DENT COUNTIES – Chicago, 1899. Missouri Reel 22. (The Cox Library Collection) – 5 – us Americana [978]
HISTORY OF LAFAYETTE COUNTY – Chicago: 1881. Wisconsin Reel 14. (The Cox Library Collection) – 5 – us Americana [978]
HISTORY OF LAFAYETTE COUNTY / Missouri Historical Co – St. Louis, 1881.Missouri Reel 22. (The Cox Library Collection) – 5 – us Americana [978]
HISTORY OF LAKE COUNTY / Halsey, John J – Chicago: Harmegnies and Howell, 1912. Illinois Reel 36. (The Cox Library Collection) – 5 – us Americana [978]
HISTORY OF LANCASTER CO., PA / Rupp, Israel – 1844 – 9 – $7.00 – us Godfrey [978]
HISTORY OF LANCASTER COUNTY / Ellis & Evans – Biographical sketches. Philadelphia, Everts and Peck. 1883. Pennsylvania Reel 26. (The Cox Library Collection) – 5 – us Americana [978]
HISTORY OF LANGLADE COUNTY / Dessureau, Robert M – Biographical sketches. Antigo: Berner Brothers Publ. Co., 1922. Wisconsin Reel 14. (The Cox Library Collection) – 5 – us Americana [978]
HISTORY OF LAPEER COUNTY – Biographical sketches. Chicago, 1884. Michigan Reel 16. The Cox Library Collection – 5 – us Americana [978]
HISTORY OF LAPORTE COUNTY – Historical and biographical sketches. Chicago, 1880. Indiana Reel 19. The Cox Library Collection – 5 – us Americana [920]
HISTORY OF LARIMER COUNTY / Watrons, Ansil – Fort Collins: Courier Printing and Publ. Co., 1911. Colorado reel 4. (Cox Library Collection) – 5 – us Americana [978]
HISTORY OF LAWRENCE AND MONROE COUNTIES / B.F. Bowen and Co – Indianapolis, 1914. Indiana Reel 20. The Cox Library Collection – 5 – us Americana [978]
HISTORY OF LAWRENCE, ORANGE AND WASHINGTON COUNTIES – Historical and biographical sketches. Chicago: 1884. Indiana Reel 19. (The Cox Library Collection) – 5 – us Americana [978]
HISTORY OF LEAVENWORTH COUNTY / Hall & Hunt, Herbert – Topeka: Historical Publ. Co., 1921. Kansas Reel 9. (The Cox Library Collection) – 5 – us Americana [978]
HISTORY OF LEE COUNTY – Chicago: 1879. Iowa Reel 25. (The Cox Library Collection) – 5 – us Americana [978]
HISTORY OF LEE COUNTY / H.H. Hill and Co – Historical and biographical. Chicago, 1881. Illinois Reel 38. The Cox Library Collection – 5 – us Americana [978]
HISTORY OF LEE COUNTY / Stevens, Frank E – Chicago: S. J. Clarke Publ. Co., 1914. Vols. 1-2. Illinois Reel 39. (The Cox Library Collection) – 5 – us Americana [978]
HISTORY OF LEHIGH AND CARBON COUNTIES / Matthews & Hungerford – Philadelphia, Everts and Richards. 1884. Pennsylvania Reel 28. (The Cox Library Collection) – 5 – us Americana [978]
HISTORY OF LEHIGH COUNTY / Roberts, Charles R – Biographical and genealogical records. Allentown, Lehigh Valley Publishing Co., 1914. Vol. 1. Pennsylvania Reel 28; Vols. 2-3. Pennsylvania Reel 29. (The Cox Library Collection) – 5 – us Americana [978]
HISTORY OF LEWIS, CLARK, KNOX AND SCOTLAND COUNTIES – Chicago, 1887. Missouri Reel 23. (The Cox Library Collection) – 5 – us Americana [978]
HISTORY OF LEWIS COUNTY / Hough, Franklin B – Beginning settlement to present. Albany: Munsell and Rowland, 1860. New York Reel 20. (The Cox Library Collection) – 5 – us Americana [978]
HISTORY OF LEWIS COUNTY / Hough, Franklin B – Biographical sketches. Syracuse, D. Mason and Co., 1883. New York Reel 20. (The Cox Library Collection) – 5 – us Americana [978]
HISTORY OF LEXINGTON BAPTIST CHURCH, OGLETHORPE COUNTY, GEORGIA, 1847-1974 / Brooks, Gladys C – 1 – 5.00 – us Baptist [240]
HISTORY OF LIBERTY / Eliot, Samuel – Boston. 4v. 1854 – 1r – 1 – us Ross [975]
HISTORY OF LICKING COUNTY ITS PAST AND PRESENT / Hill, N N – Newark: A. A. Graham and Co., 1881. Ohio Reel 42. (The Cox Library Collection) – 5 – us Americana [978]
HISTORY OF LIECHTENSTEIN PAMPHLET COLLECTION – 19??-1970 – 1 reel – 1 – CSUXANQ3130-B – us Hoover Inst Photo [943]
HISTORY OF LINCOLN, ONEIDA AND VILAS COUNTIES / McVean & Jones – Minneapolis: H. C. Cooper and Co., 1924. Wisconsin Reel 14. (The Cox Library Collection) – 5 – us Americana [978]
HISTORY OF LINN COUNTY / Birdsall & Dean – Kansas City, 1882. Missouri Reel 24. (The Cox Library Collection) – 5 – us Americana [978]
HISTORY OF LINN COUNTY – Chicago: 1878. Iowa Reel 26. (The Cox Library Collection) – 5 – us Americana [978]

HISTORY OF LINN COUNTY / Mitchall, William A – Kansas City, 1928. Kansas Reel 9. (The Cox Library Collection) – 5 – us Americana [978]

HISTORY OF LIVINGSTON COUNTY / D. Mason and Co – Biographical sketches. Syracuse, 1881. New York Reel 21. The Cox Library Collection – 5 – us Americana [978]

HISTORY OF LIVINGSTON COUNTY / Doty, Lockwood L – Geneseo, Edward E. Doty, 1876. New York Reel 2l. (The Cox Library Collection) – 5 – us Americana [978]

HISTORY OF LIVINGSTON COUNTY – Historical and biographical sketches. Chicago, 1878. Illinois Reel 39. The Cox Library Collection – 5 – us Americana [978]

HISTORY OF LIVINGSTON COUNTY. BIOGRAPHICAL SKETCHES / Everts & Abbott – Philadelphia: 1880. Michigan Reel 18. (The Cox Library Collection) – 5 – us Americana [978]

A HISTORY OF LLOYD'S FROM THE FOUNDING OF LLOYD'S COFFEE HOUSE TO THE PRESENT DAY / Wright, Charles & Fayle, C Ernest – London: Macmillan & Co, 1928 – 7mf – 9 – $10.50 – LLMC 92-183 – us L.L.M.C. [360]

HISTORY OF LOGAN COUNTY / Donnelly, Loyd and Co – Historical and biographical sketches. Chicago, 1878. (Illinois Reel 40). (The Cox Library Collection) – 5 – us Americana [978]

HISTORY OF LOGAN COUNTY / Inter-State Publishing Co – Historical and biographical sketches. Chicago, 1886. Illinois Reel 40. The Cox Library Collection – 5 – us Americana [978]

HISTORY OF LOGAN COUNTY AND OHIO – 1880. Ohio Reel 43. (The Cox Library Collection) – 5 – us Americana [978]

HISTORY OF LONDON, 19TH AND 20TH CENTURIES, PAMPHLET COLLECTION – 1906-1910 – 1 reel – 1 – CSUXANP3065-B – us Hoover Inst Photo [941]

HISTORY OF LONG ISLAND / Ross, Peter – Kings, Nassau and Suffolk Counties. New York, Lewis Publ. Co., 1902. Vols. 1-2. New York Reel 20. (The Cox Library Collection) – 5 – us Americana [978]

HISTORY OF LONG ISLAND'S MATTITUCK / Craven, Charles E – 1906. New York Reel 34. (The Cox Library Collection) – 5 – us Americana [978]

HISTORY OF LORAIN COUNTY – Biographical sketches. Philadelphia: 1879. Ohio Reel 43. (The Cox Library Collection) – 5 – us Americana [978]

THE HISTORY OF LORD SEATON'S REGIMENT, THE 52ND LIGHT INFANTRY AT THE BATTLE OF WATERLOO; TOGETHER WITH VARIOUS INCIDENTS CONNECTED WITH THAT REGIMENT.. / Leeke, William – London: Hatchard and Co., 1866. 2v – 1 – us U.W. Library [941]

HISTORY OF LOS ANGELES COUNTY / McGroarty, John S – Chicago: American Historical Society, 1923. 3v.California Reel 15. (The Cox Library Collection) – 5 – us Americana [978]

HISTORY OF LOUISA COUNTY / Harris, Malcolm H – Richmond, Dietz Press, 1936. Virginia Reel 3. (The Cox Library Collection) – 5 – us Americana [978]

HISTORY OF LOWER SCIOTO VALLEY / Inter-State Publishing Co – Chicago: 1884. Ohio Reel 11. (The Cox Library Collection) – 5 – us Americana [978]

HISTORY OF LUSATIA: PAMPHLET COLLECTION – 1949 – 1 – CSUXANS6087-B – us Hoover Inst Photo [943]

A HISTORY OF LUTHERAN MISSIONS / Laury, Preston A – (Includes indexes) – 2nd rev ed. Reading, PA: Pilger Publ House, c1905 – 1mf – 9 – 0-8370-6205-5 – 1986-0205 – us A.T.L.A. [240]

HISTORY OF LUZERNE COUNTY / Bradsby, H C – Biographical sketches. Chicago, S. B. Nelson and Co., 1893. Pennsylvania Reel 30. (The Cox Library Collection) – 5 – us Americana [978]

HISTORY OF LUZERNE, LACKAWANNA AND WYOMING COUNTIES – New York, 1880. Pennsylvania Reel 29. The Cox Library Collection – 5 – us Americana [978]

HISTORY OF LYCOMING COUNTY / Meginnes, John F – Chicago, Brown, Runk and Co., 1892. Pennsylvania Reel 31. (The Cox Library Collection) – 5 – us Americana [978]

HISTORY OF MACOMB COUNTY / M.A. Leeson and Co – Chicago, 1882. Michigan Reel 18. The Cox Library Collection – 5 – us Americana [978]

HISTORY OF MACOUPIN COUNTY / Brink, McDonough and Co – Biographical sketches. Philadelphia, 1879. Illinois Reel 41. The Cox Library Collection – 5 – us Americana [978]

HISTORY OF MADAGASCAR...THE PROGRESS OF THE CHRISTIAN MISSION ESTABLISHED IN 1818, AND AN AUTHENTIC ACCOUNT OF THE...MARTYRDOM OF THE NATIVE CHRISTIANS / Ellis, William – London: Fisher, 1838. 2v. illus. plates, map, table – 1 – us U.W. Library [240]

HISTORY OF MADISON COUNTY – Biographical Sketches. Edwardsville, 1882. Illinois. The Cox Library Collection – 42r – 5 – us Americana [978]

HISTORY OF MADISON COUNTY / Bryan, Chester E – Biographical sketches. Indianapolis: B. F. Bowen and Co., 1915. Ohio Reel 46. (The Cox Library Collection) – 5 – us Americana [978]

HISTORY OF MADISON COUNTY – Chicago, 1883. Ohio Reel 46. The Cox Library Collection – 5 – us Americana [978]

HISTORY OF MADISON COUNTY / Hammond, L M – Syracuse: Truair, Smith and Co., 1872. New York Reel 21. (The Cox Library Collection) – 5 – us Americana [978]

HISTORY OF MADISON COUNTY / Union Historical Co – Des Moines: 1879. Iowa Reel 27. (The Cox Library Collection) – 5 – us Americana [978]

HISTORY OF MADISON COUNTY AND ITS PEOPLE / Mueller, Herman A – Chicago: S. J. Clarke Publ. Co., 1915: Vols. 1-2. Iowa Reel 27. (The Cox Library Collection) – 5 – us Americana [978]

HISTORY OF MADISON COUNTY ARKANSAS WITH AUTOBIOGRAPHICAL SKETCHES – 1889. Item T. Added index by Hilda Chance, 1968. SW16-0142 – 5 – us A.G.L.L. [978]

HISTORY OF MADISON TOWNSHIP, INCLUDING GROVEPORT AND CANAL WINCHESTER, FRANKLIN COUNTY, OHIO / Barrios, George F – Canal Winchester, 1902. Ohio Reel 33. (The Cox Library Collection) – 5 – us Americana [978]

HISTORY OF MAHASKA COUNTY / Union Historical Co – Des Moines: 1878. Iowa Reel 28. (The Cox Library Collection) – 5 – us Americana [978]

HISTORY OF MAHONING BAPTIST ASSOCIATION / Smith, M A M – 1820-30 – 1 – 8.05 – us Baptist [240]

HISTORY OF MAJOR JOHN MONTGOMERY WHO CAME FROM IRELAND ABOUT 1720 OR '24 / Montgomery, John – 1 – $50.00 – us Presbyterian [240]

HISTORY OF MANISTEE, MASON AND OCEANA COUNTIES – Biographical sketches. Chicago, 1882. Michigan Reel 18. The Cox Library Collection – 5 – us Americana [978]

HISTORY OF MARIE ANTOINETTE / Abbott, John Stevens Cabot – New York: Harper & Bros., 1872. 322p – 1 – us U.W. Library [920]

HISTORY OF MARIETTA AND WASHINGTON COUNTY / Andrews, Martin R – Chicago: Biographical Publ. Co., 1902. Ohio Reel 66. (The Cox Library Collection) – 5 – us Americana [978]

HISTORY OF MARIN COUNTY / Munro-Fraser, J P – Marin Co, CA. 1880 – 1r – 1 – $50.00 – B40228 – us Library Micro [978]

AN HISTORY OF MARINE ARCHITECTURE OF ALL NATIONS / Charnock, John – 3v. 1800-02 – 9 – $100.00 – uk Libr Preservation [623]

HISTORY OF MARION COUNTY / Leggett, Conaway and Co – Chicago: 1883. Ohio Reel 47. (The Cox Library Collection) – 5 – us Americana [978]

HISTORY OF MARION COUNTY / Sellers, W W – Columbia, R. L. Byran Company, 1902. South Carolina Reel 2. (The Cox Library Collection) – 5 – us Americana [978]

HISTORY OF MARION COUNTY / Union Historical Co – Des Moines: 1881. Iowa Reel 28. (The Cox Library Collection) – 5 – us Americana [978]

HISTORY OF MARION COUNTY AND INDIANAPOLIS / Sulgrove, B R – Philadelphia: L.H. Everts and Co., 1884.Indiana Reel 21. (The Cox Library Collection) – 5 – us Americana [978]

HISTORY OF MARION COUNTY AND REPRESENTATIVE CITIZENS / Jacoby, J Wilbur – Chicago: Biographical Publ. Co., 1907. Ohio Reel 48. (The Cox Library Collection) – 5 – us Americana [978]

HISTORY OF MARSHALL COUNTY – Chicago: 1878. Iowa Reel 28. (The Cox Library Collection) – 5 – us Americana [978]

HISTORY OF MARSHALL COUNTY / Forter, E Emma – Indianapolis: B.F. Bowen and Co., 1917. Kansas Reel 10.(The Cox Library Collection) – 5 – us Americana [978]

THE HISTORY OF MARY, QUEEN OF SCOTS / Mignet, F A – 7th ed. London: R. Bentley and son, 1887. xii,466p. Trans. by Andrew Scoble – 1 – us U.W. Library [920]

HISTORY OF MARYLAND / McSherry, James – Baltimore, Baltimore Book Co., 1904. Maryland Reel 1. (The Cox Library Collection) – 5 – us Americana [978]

HISTORY OF MASSAC COUNTY / Page, O J – Historical and biographical sketches. Metropolis: 1900. Illinois Reel 42. (The Cox Library Collection) – 5 – us Americana [978]

THE HISTORY OF MASSACHUSETTS / Barry, John S – Vols. 1-3. Boston, Phillips, Sampson and Co., 1855-57. Massachusetts Reel 1. (The Cox Library Collection) – 5 – us Americana [978]

HISTORY OF MCDONOUGH COUNTY / Lusk, D W – Historical and biographical. Springfield: S. J. Clarke Publ. Co., 1878. Illinois Reel 43. (The Cox Library Collection) – 5 – us Americana [978]

HISTORY OF MCDONOUGH COUNTY – Springfield, 1885. (Illinois Reel 43). (The Cox Library Collection) – 5 – us Americana [978]

HISTORY OF MCHENRY COUNTY / Inter-State Publishing Co – Historical and biographical sketches. Chicago, 1885. Illinois Reel 43. The Cox Library Collection – 5 – us Americana [978]

HISTORY OF MCHENRY COUNTY / Munsell Publishing Co – Chicago, 1922. Vols. I (Illinois Reel 43) and II (Illinois Reel 44). (The Cox Library Collection) – 5 – us Americana [978]

HISTORY OF MCKEAN, ELK, CAMERON AND POTTER COUNTIES / J.H. Beers and Co – Chicago, 1890. Pennsylvania Reel 3l. The Cox Library Collection – 5 – us Americana [978]

HISTORY OF MCLEAN COUNTY – Chicago, 1879. Illinois Reel 44. The Cox Library Collection – 5 – us Americana [978]

HISTORY OF MCLEAN COUNTY / Hasbrouck, Jacob L – Indianapolis: Historical Publ. Co., 1924. Vols. 1-2. Illinois Reel 45. (The Cox Library Collection – 5 – us Americana [978]

HISTORY OF MCLEOD COUNTY / Curtiss-Wedge, Franklyn – Winona: H.C. Cooper, Jr. & Co., 1917. Minnesota Reel 9.(The Cox Library Collection) – 5 – us Americana [978]

HISTORY OF MECKLENBURG COUNTY AND THE CITY OF CHARLOTTE 1749-1903 / Tompkins, D A – Charlotte: Observer Printing House, 1903. Vol. 1. Narrative, and Vol. 2. Appendix (North Carolina Reel 2). (The Cox Library Collection) – 5 – us Americana [978]

HISTORY OF MEDICINE – 9 – ne IDC [610]

HISTORY OF MEDINA COUNTY / Baskin and Battey Historical Publishing Co – Chicago: 1881. Ohio Reel 48. The Cox Library Collection – 5 – us Americana [978]

HISTORY OF MENARD AND MASON COUNTIES / O.L. Baskin and Co – Historical and biographical sketches. Chicago, 1879. Illinois Reel 46. The Cox Library Collection – 5 – us Americana [978]

HISTORY OF MERCED COUNTY / Outcalt, John – Los Angeles: Historic Record Co., 1925. California Reel 20. (The Cox Library Collection) – 5 – us Americana [978]

HISTORY OF MERCER AND HENDERSON COUNTIES / H.H. Hill and Co – Chicago, 1882. Illinois Reel 46. The Cox Library Collection – 5 – us Americana [978]

HISTORY OF MERCER COUNTY / Brown, Runk and Co – Chicago, 1888. Pennsylvania Reel 32. (The Cox Library Collection) – 5 – us Americana [978]

HISTORY OF MERCER COUNTY AND REPRESENTATIVE CITIZENS / Scranton, S S – Chicago: Biographical Publ. Co., 1907. Ohio Reel 48. The Cox Library Collection – 5 – us Americana [978]

HISTORY OF MERRIMACK AND BELKNAP COUNTIES / Hurd, D Hamilton – Philadelphia, J. W. Lewis and Co., 1885. New Hampshire Reel 6. (The Cox Library Collection) – 5 – us Americana [978]

A HISTORY OF METHODISM : COMPRISING A VIEW OF THE RISE OF THIS REVIVAL OF SPIRITUAL RELIGION IN THE FIRST HALF OF THE EIGHTEENTH CENTURY, AND OF THE PRINCIPAL AGENTS BY WHOM IT WAS PROMOTED IN EUROPE AND AMERICA... / McTyeire, Holland N – Nashville, Tenn.: Publishing House of the Methodist Episcopal Church, South, 1898, c1884 – 2mf – us A.T.L.A. [240]

A HISTORY OF METHODISM, CHIEFLY FOR THE USE OF STUDENTS / Gregory, J R – London, 1911. 2v, viii/320p; viii/328p – 8mf – 9 – ne IDC [240]

THE HISTORY OF METHODISM IN CANADA : WITH AN ACCOUNT OF THE RISE AND PROGRESS OF THE WORK OF GOD AMONG THE CANADIAN INDIAN TRIBES / Playter, George F – Toronto: A. Green, 1862 – 1mf – us A.T.L.A. [240]

HISTORY OF METHODISM IN IRELAND / Crookshank, C H – Belfast, 1885-1888. 3v: xvi/480p; xi/480p; xi/544p – 18mf – 9 – ne IDC [240]

A HISTORY OF METHODISM IN KENTUCKY – v1 (1935), 1783-1820; v2 (1936), 1820-1846. By W.E. Arnold. Indexed. 12 fiches. F-0165 and F-0164 – 9 – us A.G.L.L. [240]

THE HISTORY OF METHODISM...BRITISH METHODISM : WITH THE ASSISTANCE OF THOMAS EDWIN BRIGDEN / Hurst, John F – New York, 1902. 3v, 1478p – 18mf – 9 – ne IDC [240]

A HISTORY OF METHODISTS IN THE UNITED STATES / Buckley, James Monroe – New York: Christian Literature, 1896. (The American church history series; v5) – 2mf – us A.T.L.A. [240]

HISTORY OF MIAMI COUNTY / Bodurtha, Arthur L – Chicago: Lewis Publ. Co., 1914. 2v. Indiana Reel 22. (The Cox Library Collection) – 5 – us Americana [978]

HISTORY OF MIAMI COUNTY – Chicago, 1880. Ohio Reel 48. The Cox Library Collection – 5 – us Americana [978]

HISTORY OF MICHIGAN / Moore, Charles – Chicago: Lewis Publishing Co., 1915. 4v. Michigan Reel 1. (The Cox Library Collection) – 5 – us Americana [978]

A HISTORY OF MIDDLE NEW RIVER SETTLEMENTS AND CONTIGUOUS TERRITORY / Johnston, David E – Huntington, Standard Printing and Publishing Company, 1906. Virginia Reel 5. (The Cox Library Collection) – 5 – us Americana [978]

HISTORY OF MIDDLESEX COUNTY / Hurd, D Hamilton – Biographical sketches. Philadelphia, J. W. Lewis and Co., 1890. Vols. 1-2, Massachusetts Reel 5; Vol. 3, Massachusetts Reel 6. (The Cox Library Collection) – 5 – us Americana [978]

HISTORY OF MIDDLESEX COUNTY 1664-1920 / Wall & Pickersgill – New York, Lewis Historical Publ. Co, 1921. Vols. 1-2. New Jersey Reel 4; Vol. 3. New Jersey Reel 5. (The Cox Library Collection) – 5 – us Americana [978]

HISTORY OF MILITARY GOVERNMENT TRAINING / U.S. Office of the Provost Marshal General – v. 1-4. 1945? – 1 – 109.00 – us L of C Photodup [370]

HISTORY OF MILLS COUNTY / State Historical Co – Des Moines: 1881. Iowa Reel 29. (The Cox Library Collection) – 5 – us Americana [978]

THE HISTORY OF MILTON, MASS. 1640 TO 1887 / ed by Teele, A K – Boston: Rockwell and Churchill, Printers, 1887. Massachusetts Reel 8A. (The Cox Library Collection) – 5 – us Americana [978]

HISTORY OF MILWAUKEE / Western Historical Co – Biographical sketches. Chicago: 1881. Wisconsin Reel 15. (The Cox Library Collection) – 5 – us Americana [978]

HISTORY OF MILWAUKEE COUNTY AND CITY / Conard, Howard L – Chicago: American Biographical Publ. Co., 1895. Vols. 1-2. Wisconsin Reel 15. (The Cox Library Collection) – 5 – us Americana [978]

HISTORY OF MINNEAPOLIS THE GATEWAY TO THE NORTHWEST / Shutter, Marion Daniel – Chicago: S.J. Clarke Publ. Co., 1923. v1, Minnesota Reel 7. v2-3, Minnesota Reel 8. (The Cox Library Collection) – 5 – us Americana [978]

HISTORY OF MINNEHAHA COUNTY / Bailey, Dana R – Sioux Falls: Brown and Saenger, 1899. South Dakota Reel 5. (The Cox Library Collection) – 5 – us Americana [978]

A HISTORY OF MISSIONS IN INDIA / Richter, Julius – Trans. by Sydney H. Moore. Edinburgh: Cliphant, (1908).8+469p – 1 – us U.W. Library [240]

HISTORY OF MISSISSIPPI: THE HEART OF THE SOUTH / Rowland, Dunbar – Counties Adams to Yazoo. Jackson: S. J. Clarke Publ. Co., 1925. Vols. 1-2. Mississippi Reel 1. (The Cox Library Collection) – 5 – us Americana [978]

A HISTORY OF MISSOURI AND MISSOURIANS / Shoemaker, Floyd C – Columbia: Lucas Brothers, 1927. Missouri Reel 2. (The Cox Library Collection) – 5 – us Americana [978]

HISTORY OF MITCHELL AND WORTH COUNTIES / Clyde & Dwelle – Chicago: S. J. Clarke Publ. Co., 1918. Vols. 1-2. Iowa Reel 30. (The Cox Library Collection) – 5 – us Americana [978]

HISTORY OF MITCHELL AND WORTH COUNTIES – Springfield: 1884. Iowa Reel 29. (The Cox Library Collection) – 5 – us Americana [978]

THE HISTORY OF MODERN ENTHUSIASM FROM THE REFORMATION TO THE PRESENT TIMES / Evans, T – London, 2nd ed 1757 – 3mf – 9 – MP-359/1 – ne IDC [240]

HISTORY OF MODERN MACEDONIA PAMPHLET COLLECTION – 1904-1970 – 2r – 1 – CSUXANQ8175-B – us Hoover Inst Photo [949]

HISTORY OF MONMOUTH COUNTY / Ellis, Franklin – Philadelphia, R. T. Peck and Co., 1885. New Jersey Reel 5. (The Cox Library Collection) – 5 – us Americana [978]

THE HISTORY OF MONMOUTH COUNTY 1664-1920 – New York, 1922. Vols. 1-3. New Jersey Reel 5. (The Cox Library Collection) – 5 – us Americana [978]

HISTORY OF MONONGALIA COUNTY / Wiley, Samuel T – Kingwood, Preston Publishing Co., 1883. West Virginia Reel 4. (The Cox Library Collection) – 5 – us Americana [978]

HISTORY OF MONROE COUNTY / Morton, Oren F – Staunton, McClure Publishing Co., 1916. West Virginia Reel 4. (The Cox Library Collection) – 5 – us Americana [978]

HISTORY OF MONROE COUNTY – Philadelphia, 1877. New York Reel 22. (The Cox Library Collection) – 5 – us Americana [978]

HISTORY OF MONROE COUNTY / Wing, Talcott E – New York: Munsell and Co., 1890. Michigan Reel 19. (The Cox Library Collection) – 5 – us Americana [978]

HISTORY OF MONROE COUNTY AND SHELBY COUNTY / National Historical Co – St. Louis, 1884.Missouri Reel 25. (The Cox Library Collection) – 5 – us Americana [978]

HISTORY OF MONROE COUNTY PAST AND PRESENT / Richards, Randolph A – Chicago: C. E. Cooper and Co., 1912. Wisconsin Reel 16. (The Cox Library Collection) – 5 – us Americana [978]

HISTORY OF MONTANA / Sanders, Helen F – (v3. Montana reel 2) – Chicago: Lewis Publ. Co., 1913. v1-2. Montana reel 1. (Cox Library Collection) – 5 – us Americana [978]

HISTORY OF MONTANA FROM 1739 TO 1885 – Chicago, 1885. Montana reel 1. (Cox Library Collection) – 5 – us Americana [978]

HISTORY OF MONTENEGRO FROM 1918 TO 1945 – 1918?-1920? – 1 reel – 1 – CSUXANL7471-B – us Hoover Inst Photo [947]

HISTORY OF MONTEREY AND SANTA CRUZ COUNTIES / Watkins, Robin G – Monterey Co, CA. 1925 – 1r – 1 – $50.00 – B40235 – us Library Micro [978]

HISTORY OF MONTEREY AND SANTA CRUZ COUNTIES / Watkins, Robin G – Santa Cruz Co, 1925 – 1r – 1 – $50.00 – B40263 – us Library Micro [978]

HISTORY OF MONTGOMERY AND FULTON COUNTIES / F.W. Beers and Co – New York, 1878. New York Reel 23. The Cox Library Collection – 5 – us Americana [978]

HISTORY OF MONTGOMERY COUNTY / A.W. Bowen and Co – Personal sketches. Chicago, n.d. 2v. Indiana Reel 23. The Cox Library Collection – 5 – us Americana [978]

HISTORY OF MONTGOMERY COUNTY / Bean, Theodore W – Philadelphia, Everts and Peck, 1884. Pennsylvania Reel 32. (The Cox Library Collection) – 5 – us Americana [978]

HISTORY OF MONTGOMERY COUNTY / Beckwith, H W – Historical notes of the Wabash Valley. Chicago: H.H. Hill and N. Iddings Publs., 1881. Indiana Reel 22. (The Cox Library Collection) – 5 – us Americana [978]

HISTORY OF MONTGOMERY COUNTY – Chicago, 1882. Ohio Reel 49. The Cox Library Collection – 5 – us Americana [978]

HISTORY OF MONTGOMERY COUNTY / Frothington, Washington – Syracuse, D. Mason and Co., 1892. New York Reel 23. (The Cox Library Collection) – 5 – us Americana [978]

HISTORY OF MONTGOMERY COUNTY / Iowa Historical and Biographical Co – Des Moines: 1881. Iowa Reel 30. (The Cox Library Collection) – 5 – us Americana [978]

HISTORY OF MONTREAL: INCLUDING THE STREETS OF MONTREAL, THEIR ORIGIN AND HISTORY / Borthwick, John Douglas – Montreal: D. Gallagher, 1897. 02839. (Pre-1900 Canadiana) – 9 – cn C.I.H.M. [971]

HISTORY OF MORGAN COUNTY / Robertson, Charles – Biographical sketches. Chicago: L. H. Watkins and Co., 1886. Ohio Reel 51. (The Cox Library Collection) – 5 – us Americana [978]

HISTORY OF MORGAN COUNTY ITS PAST AND PRESENT / Donnelly, Loyd and Co – Chicago, 1878. Illinois Reel 46. The Cox Library Collection – 5 – us Americana [978]

HISTORY OF MORRIS COUNTY, NEW JERSEY – Biographical and genealogical. Chicago, 1899. Vols. 1-2. New Jersey Reel 6. (The Cox Library Collection) – 5 – us Americana [978]

HISTORY OF MORROW COUNTY / Baughman, A J & Bartlett – Chicago: Lewis Publ. Co., 1911. Vols. 1-2. Ohio Reel 51. (The Cox Library Collection) – 5 – us Americana [978]

HISTORY OF MORROW COUNTY / O.L. Baskin and Co – Chicago: 1880. Ohio Reel 51. The Cox Library Collection – 5 – us Americana [978]

HISTORY OF MOWER COUNTY / Curtiss-Wedge, Franklyn – Chicago: H.C. Cooper, Jr. & Co., 1911. Minnesota Reel 9. (The Cox Library Collection) – 5 – us Americana [978]

HISTORY OF MOWER COUNTY / Inter-State Historical Co – Biographical sketches. Mankato: Free Press Publ. House, 1884. Minnesota Reel 9. (The Cox Library Collection) – 5 – us Americana [978]

A HISTORY OF MUHLENBERG COUNTY / Rothert, Otto A – Louisville: John P. Morton and Co., 1913. Kentucky Reel 8. (The Cox Library Collection) – 5 – us Americana [978]

HISTORY OF MURRAY, IOWA, 1868-1968 – Index by Lester Saffell Jr., et al. Item F. Includes index. 200p. SW16-0106 – 5 – us A.G.L.L. [920]

HISTORY OF MUSCATINE COUNTY / Richman, Irving B – Chicago: S. J. Clarke Publ. Co., 1911. Vols. 1-2. Iowa Reel 31. (The Cox Library Collection) – 5 – us Americana [978]

HISTORY OF MUSIC – Based on holdings of the Houghton, Loeb and Widener Libraries at Harvard University – 1 – us Primary [780]

A HISTORY OF MUSIC IN NEW ENGLAND : WITH BIOGRAPHICAL SKETCHES OF REFORMERS AND PSALMISTS / Hood, George – Boston: Wilkins, Carter, 1846 – 1mf – us A.T.L.A. [780]

THE HISTORY OF MUSICAL INSTRUMENTS : MANUALS, TUTORS AND METHODS – (Pt 1: Instrumental tutors from the Bate Collection of Musical Instruments, Oxford, and Bate's private library. Pt 2: Instrumental tutors from the Fetis Collection at Bibliotheque Royal Albert ler, Brussells) – 1 – us Primary [780]

HISTORY OF MUSKEGON AND OTTAWA COUNTIES – Biographical sketches. Chicago, 1882. Michigan Reel 19. The Cox Library Collection – 5 – us Americana [978]

HISTORY OF MUSLIM EDUCATION / Shalaby, Ahmad – Karachi: Indus Publications, 1979 – us Res Libr [370]

HISTORY OF MY RELIGIOUS OPINIONS / Newman, John Henry – London: Longman, Green, Longman, Roberts, and Green, 1865 – 1 roll – 1 – 1-55879-381-X – uk Libr Preservation [240]

HISTORY OF MY RELIGIOUS OPINIONS / Newman, John Henry – London: Longman, Green, Longman, Roberts, and Green, 1865 – 1mf – us A.T.L.A. [240]

HISTORY OF NAPA AND LAKE COUNTIES / Slocum, Bowen & Co – San Francisco, 1881. California Reel 21. (The Cox Library Collection) – 5 – us Americana [978]

THE HISTORY OF NAPA AND LAKE COUNTIES – Napa Co, 1881 – 1r – 1 – $50.00 – B40238 – us Library Micro [978]

HISTORY OF NAPA COUNTY / Enquirer Print – Oakland, 1901. California Reel 21. (The Cox Library Collection) – 5 – us Americana [978]

HISTORY OF NAPA COUNTY / Wallace, W F – 1r – 1 – $50.00 – B40237 – us Library Micro [978]

HISTORY OF NATRONA COUNTY 1888-1922 / Mokler, Alfred J – Chicago: R.R. Donnelley and Sons, 1923. Wyoming reel 3.(Cox Library Collection) – 5 – us Americana [978]

HISTORY OF NEBRASKA / Johnson, Harrison – Omaha: Herald Printing House, 1880. Nebraska Reel 1. (The Cox Library Collection) – 5 – us Americana [978]

HISTORY OF NEGRO RACE IN AMERICA FROM 1619 TO 1880 / Williams, George Washington – Negroes as slaves, as soldiers, and as citizens; together with a preliminary consideration of the unity of the human family, an historical sketch of Africa, and an account of the Negro governments of Sierra Leone and Liberia. 2 v. 1883 – 1 – us A.T.L.A. [975]

HISTORY OF NEMAHA COUNTY / Dindas, J H – Auburn, 1902. Nebraska Reel 11.(The Cox Library Collection) – 5 – us Americana [978]

HISTORY OF NEOSHA AND WILSON COUNTIES / Duncan, L Wallace – Fort Scott: Monitor Printing Co., 1902. Kansas Reel 10.(The Cox Library Collection) – 5 – us Americana [978]

HISTORY OF NEVADA, 1881 – Oakland, 1881. Nevada reel 1. (Cox Library Collection) – 5 – us Americana [978]

HISTORY OF NEVADA COUNTY – Nevada Co, CA: Thompson & West, 1880 – 1r – 1 – $50.00 – B40248 – us Library Micro [978]

HISTORY OF NEVADA COUNTY / Thompson & West – Oakland, 1880. California Reel 21. (The Cox Library Collection) – 5 – us Americana [978]

THE HISTORY OF NEW BRUNSWICK AND THE OTHER MARITIME PROVINCES / Harper, John Murdoch – Saint John, N.B.: J. & A. McMillan, 1876. 05369. (Pre-1900 Canadiana) – 9 – cn C.I.H.M. [971]

A HISTORY OF NEW BRUNSWICK GEOLOGY / Ells, Robert Wheelock – Montreal: Gazette Printing Co., 1887. 02910. (Pre-1900 Canadiana) – 9 – cn C.I.H.M. [550]

A HISTORY OF NEW ENGLAND / Backus, Isaac – 2v. 1871. With this is filmed: Drisko, Ralph Chandler, A New Index of Backus – 1 – us A.T.L.A. [970]

A HISTORY OF NEW ENGLAND THEOLOGY / Boardman, George Nye – New York: A.D.F. Randolph, 1899 – 1mf – us A.T.L.A. [240]

A HISTORY OF NEW ENGLAND WITH PARTICULAR REFERENCE TO THE DENOMINATION OF CHRISTIANS CALLED BAPTISTS / Backus, Isaac – (v1. 578p. 20.23; 1. v2. 454p. 15.89; SBC; 1. v3. 340p. 11.90; SBC; 1) – v1-3, 1777, 1784, 1796. 1372p – 1 – 48.02 – us Baptist [240]

HISTORY OF NEW HAMPSHIRE / McClintock, John N – Boston, B. B. Russell, 1889. New Hampshire Reel 1. (The Cox Library Collection) – 5 – us Americana [978]

HISTORY OF NEW HAVEN COUNTY / Rockey, J L – New York, W. W. Preston and Company, 1892. Vols. 1-2. Connecticut Reel 5. (The Cox Library Collection) – 5 – us Americana [978]

THE HISTORY OF NEW IPSWICH / Gould & Lincoln – Boston, 1852. New Hampshire Reel 4. (The Cox Library Collection) – 5 – us Americana [978]

HISTORY OF NEW LONDON COUNTY / Hurd, D Hamilton – Philadelphia, J. W. Lewis and Co., 1882. Connecticut Reel 6. (The Cox Library Collection) – 5 – us Americana [978]

A HISTORY OF NEW MEXICO / Coan, Charles F – (v3. New Mexico reel 3) – Chicago: American Historical Society, 1925. v1-2. New Mexico reel 2. (Cox Library Collection) – 5 – us Americana [978]

HISTORY OF NEW MEXICO / Pacific States Publishing Co – Los Angeles, 1907. New Mexico reel 1. (Cox Library Collection) – 5 – us Americana [978]

HISTORY OF NEWBURY / Wells, Frederic P – Genealogical records of many families. St. Johnsbury, Caledonian Co., 1902. Vemont Reel 8. (The Cox Library Collection) – 5 – us Americana [978]

THE HISTORY OF NEWPORT 1766-1878 / Wheeler, Edmund – Concord, Republican Press Asso., 1879. New Hampshire Reel 7. (The Cox Library Collection) – 5 – us Americana [978]

HISTORY OF NEWTON, LAWRENCE, BARRY AND MCDONALD COUNTIES – Biographical appendix. Chicago, 1888. Missouri Reel 26. (The Cox Library Collection) – 5 – us Americana [978]

HISTORY OF NICOLLET AND LE SUEUR COUNTIES / Gresham, William G – Indianapolis: B.F. Bowen and Co., 1916. 2v. Minnesota Reel 10.(The Cox Library Collection) – 5 – us Americana [978]

HISTORY OF NOBLE COUNTY / L.H. Watkins and Co – Biographical sketches. Chicago, 1887. Ohio Reel 52. The Cox Library Collection – 5 – us Americana [978]

A HISTORY OF NORFOLK / Rye, Walter – London: E. Stock, 1885. viii,316p. illus – 1 – us U.W. Library [941]

HISTORY OF NORFOLK COUNTY / J.W. Lewis Publishing Co – History and biography. Philadelphia, 1884. Massachusetts Reel 6. The Cox Library Collection – 5 – us Americana [978]

HISTORY OF NORFOLK COUNTY / Stewart, William H – Chicago, Biographical Publishing Co., 1902. Virginia Reel 3. (The Cox Library Collection) – 5 – us Americana [978]

HISTORY OF NORTH AMERICAN PINNIPEDS: A MONOGRAPH OF THE WALRUSES, SEA-LIONS, SEA-BEARS AND SEALS OF NORTH AMERICA / Allen, Joel Asaph – Washington: GPO, 1880. 02388. (Pre-1900 Canadiana) – 9 – cn C.I.H.M. [590]

HISTORY OF NORTH CENTRAL OHIO / Duff, William A – Indianapolis: Historical Publ. Co., 1931. Vols. 1-2. Mississippi Reel 6; Vol. 3. Mississippi Reel 7. (The Cox Library Collection) – 5 – us Americana [978]

HISTORY OF NORTH IDAHO – Including Nez Perces, Idaho, Latah, Kootenai, and Shoshone counties. 1903. Idaho reel 3. (Cox Library Collection) – 5 – us Americana [978]

HISTORY OF NORTHAMPTON COUNTY AND THE GRAND VALLEY OF THE LEHIGH / American Historical Society – New York, 1920. Vols. 1-3. Pennsylvania Reel 34. (The Cox Library Collection) – 5 – us Americana [978]

HISTORY OF NORTHEASTERN MISSOURI / Williams, Walter – Chicago: Lewis Publ. Co., 1913. v1, Missouri Reel 4. v2-3, Missouri Reel 5. (The Cox Library Collection) – 5 – us Americana [978]

HISTORY OF NORTHERN IRELAND PAMPHLET COLLECTION – 1922-1991 – 1 reel – 1 – CSUXANQ2038-B – us Hoover Inst Photo [941]

A HISTORY OF NORTHERN PENINSULA OF MICHIGAN AND ITS PEOPLE / Sawyer, Alvah L – Chicago: Lewis Publishing Co., 1911. v1, Michigan Reel 2; v2-3, Michigan Reel 3. (The Cox Library Collection) – 5 – us Americana [978]

HISTORY OF NORTHERN WISCONSIN – Chicago: 1881. Wisconsin Reel 3. (The Cox Library Collection) – 5 – us Americana [978]

HISTORY OF NORTHUMBERLAND COUNTY / Bell, Herbert C – Chicago, Brown, Runk and Co., 1891. Pennsylvania Reel 33. (The Cox Library Collection) – 5 – us Americana [978]

HISTORY OF NORTHWEST MISSOURI / Williams, Walter – Chicago: Lewis Publ. Co., 1915. v1, Missouri Reel 6. v2-3, Missouri Reel 7. (The Cox Library Collection) – 5 – us Americana [978]

A HISTORY OF NORTHWEST OHIO / Winter, Nevin O – Chicago: Lewis Publ. Co., 1917. Vol. 1. Mississippi Reel 4; Vols. 2-3. Mississippi Reel 5. (The Cox Library Collection) – 5 – us Americana [978]

A HISTORY OF NORWAY FROM THE EARLIEST TIMES / Boyesen, Hjalmar Hjorth – London: T.F. Unwin, c1900. xxxi,572p. ill. 1 fold. map. With new chapter on the recent history of Norway by C.F. Keary – 1 – us U.W. Library [948]

HISTORY OF NURSING – (Pt 1 Adelaide Nutting Historical Nursing Collection, 1550 monographs 15th-20th centuries 3776mf $10,340; Pt 2 Archives of the Dept of Nursing Education, Teachers College, Columbia University, 85,000 items 1899-present 4309mf $16,385; Supplement to Pt 2 Archives, Papers of Eleanor C. Lambertsen and Eugenia K. Spalding 1274mf $3425. Cataloging available) – 9,359mf – 9 – $32,025.00 complete collection – us UMI [610]

HISTORY OF OAKLAND COUNTY / L.H. Everts and Co – Philadelphia, 1877. Michigan Reel 19. The Cox Library Collection – 5 – us Americana [978]

HISTORY OF O'BRIEN COUNTY / Perkins, D A W – Sioux Falls: Brown & Saenger, Printers, 1897. Iowa Reel 31. (The Cox Library Collection) – 5 – us Americana [978]

HISTORY OF OGLE COUNTY / H.F. Kett and Co – Chicago, 1878. Illinois Reel 47. The Cox Library Collection – 5 – us Americana [978]

HISTORY OF OLD VINCENNES AND KNOX COUNTY – Historical and biographical sketches. Chicago, 1911. v1-2. Indiana Reel 17. The Cox Library Collection – 5 – us Americana [978]

HISTORY OF OLMSTED COUNTY / Leonard, Hon. Joseph – Biographical sketches of pioneers, citizens, etc. Chicago: Goodspeed Historical Association, 1910. Minnesota Reel 10. (The Cox Library Collection) – 5 – us Americana [978]

HISTORY OF ONEIDA COUNTY / Everts & Fariss – Biographical sketches. Philadelphia, 1878. New York Reel 24. (The Cox Library Collection) – 5 – us Americana [978]

HISTORY OF ONEIDA COUNTY 1700 TO PRESENT / Cookinham, Henry J – Chicago, S. J. Clarke Publ. Co., 1912. Vols. 1-2. New York Reel 25. (The Cox Library Collection) – 5 – us Americana [978]

HISTORY OF ONONDAGA COUNTY / Clayton, W Woodford – Biographical sketches. Syracuse, D. Mason and Co., 1878. New York Reel 26. (The Cox Library Collection) – 5 – us Americana [978]

HISTORY OF ONTARIO COUNTY / Conover & Aldrich – Syracuse, D. Mason and Co., 1893. New York Reel 28. (The Cox Library Collection) – 5 – us Americana [978]

HISTORY OF ONTARIO COUNTY AND ITS PEOPLE / Milliken, Charles F – Genealogical and biographical. New York, Lewis Historical Publ. Co., 1911. Vols. 1-2. New York Reel 28. (The Cox Library Collection) – 5 – us Americana [978]

HISTORY OF ORANGE COUNTY / Armor, Samuel – (1911 ed.California Reel 22) – Los Angeles: Historic Record Co., 1921. California Reel 22. (The Cox Library Collection) – 5 – us Americana [978]

HISTORY OF ORANGE COUNTY – Biographical sketches. Philadelphia: Everts and Peck, 1881. New York Reel 28. (The Cox Library Collection) – 5 – us Americana [978]

HISTORY OF ORANGE COUNTY / Headley, Russel – Middletown: Van Dusen and Elmes, 1908. New York Reel 29. (The Cox Library Collection) – 5 – us Americana [978]

HISTORY OF ORANGE COUNTY / Pleasants, J E – Los Angeles: J.R. Finnell & Sons Publ. Co., 1931. California Reel 22. (The Cox Library Collection) – 5 – us Americana [978]

HISTORY OF ORANGEBURG COUNTY / Salley, A S – Orangeburg, R. Lewis Berry, 1898. South Carolina Reel 3. (The Cox Library Collection) – 5 – us Americana [978]

A HISTORY OF OREGON, 1792-1849 / Gray, W H – 1870. Orgeon reel 1. (Cox Library Collection) – 5 – us Americana [978]

HISTORY OF ORISSA, FROM THE EARLIEST TIMES TO THE BRITISH PERIOD / Banerji, Rakhal Das – Calcutta: R. Chatterjee, 1930-31. 2v. plates, maps – 1 – us U.W. Library [950]

THE HISTORY OF ORLANDO FURIOSO, 1594.. / Greene, Robert – London: Printed for the Malone Society by H. Hart at the Oxford University Press, 1907. x,60p. With facsimile of the original. 1 reel. 1249 – 1 – us U.W. Library [810]

HISTORY OF OSWEGO COUNTY / L.H. Everts and Co – Philadelphia, 1877. New York Reel 29. The Cox Library Collection – 5 – us Americana [978]

A HISTORY OF OUR FIRM; SOME ACCOUNT OF THE FIRM OF POLLOK, GILMOUR AND CO., AND ITS OFF-SHOOTS AND CONNECTIONS / Rankin, John – Liverpool: University Press of Liverpool, 1908. 365p – 1 – us U.W. Library [380]

HISTORY OF PAGE COUNTY / Kershaw, W L – Chicago: S. J. Clarke Publ. Co., 1909. Vols. 1-2. Iowa Reel 32. (The Cox Library Collection) – 5 – us Americana [978]

THE HISTORY OF PAINTING IN ITALY FROM PERIOD OF THE REVIVAL OF THE FINE ARTS TO THE END OF THE EIGHTEENTH CENTURY / Lanzi, L – Trans. by T. Roscoe. O-981 1. 6 v. Lacking: v. 2, v. 5, v. 6. 1828 – 9 – ne IDC [750]

THE HISTORY OF PAINTING, SCULPTURE, ARCHITECTURE, GRAVING; AND OF THOSE WHO HAVE EXCELL'D IN THEM / Monier, P – O-985 1. 1699 – 9 – ne IDC [920]

HISTORY OF PALO ALTO COUNTY, IOWA / McCarty, Dwight G – Cedar Rapids: The Torch Press, 1910. Iowa Reel 32. (The Cox Library Collection) – 5 – us Americana [978]

A HISTORY OF PANTOMIME / Broadbent, R J – London: Simpkin, Marshall, Hamilton, Kent, 1901 – 1 roll – 1 – 1-55879-907-9 – uk Libr Preservation [790]

HISTORY OF PASADENA AND THE SAN GABRIEL VALLEY / Carew, Harold D – Chicago: S.J. Clarke Publ. Co., 1930. v1, California Reel 18. v2-3, California Reel 19. (The Cox Library Collection) – 5 – us Americana [978]

THE HISTORY OF PASUNDAN / Kusmen, Karhiwikarta – 1964 – 9 – SE-5094 1 – ne IDC [960]

HISTORY OF PATRICK AND HENRY COUNTIES / Pedigo, Virginia G & Lewis, G – Roanoke: Stone Printing and Manufacturing Co., 1933. Virginia Reel 4. The Cox Library Collection – 5 – us Americana [978]

HISTORY OF PEMBROKE, NEW HAMPSHIRE 1730-1895 / Carter & Fowler – Historical. Concord, Republican Press Asso., 1895. New Hampshire Reel 7. (The Cox Library Collection) – 5 – us Americana [978]

HISTORY OF PENDLETON COUNTY / Martin, Orem F – Franklin, 1910. West Virginia Reel 5. The Cox Library Collection – 5 – us Americana [978]

HISTORY OF PENOBSCOT COUNTY / Williams, Chase and Co – Cleveland, 1882. Maine Reel 4. (The Cox Library Collection) – 5 – us Americana [978]

HISTORY OF PEORIA COUNTY / Johnson and Co – Chicago, 1880. (Illinois Reel 48). (The Cox Library Collection) – 5 – us Americana [978]

HISTORY OF PERRY COUNTY / De La Hunt, Thomas J – Indianapolis: W.K. Stewart Co., 1916. Indiana Reel 23. (The Cox Library Collection) – 5 – us Americana [978]

HISTORY OF PERRY COUNTY / Hain, H H – Harrisburg, Hain Moore Co., 1922. Pennsylvania Reel 35. (The Cox Library Collection) – 5 – us Americana [978]

HISTORY OF PERRY COUNTY, OHIO / Martzolff, Clement L – New Lexington: Ward and Weiland, 1902. Ohio Reel 53. (The Cox Library Collection) – 5 – us Americana [978]

THE HISTORY OF PERSIA, FROM THE MOST EARLY PERIOD TO THE PRESENT TIME; CONTAINING AN ACCOUNT OF THE RELIGION, GOVERNMENT, USAGES, AND CHARACTER OF THE INHABITANTS OF THAT KINGDOM / Malcolm, John – New rev. ed. London: Murray, 1829. 2v – 1 – us U.W. Library [956]

HISTORY OF PETERBOROUGH COUNTY, ONTARIO / Roginson, G B – Illus. Toronto, 1884. Canada reel 5. (Cox Library Collection) – 5 – us Americana [971]

HISTORY OF PETTIS COUNTY / North, F A – 1882. Missouri Reel 26.(The Cox Library Collection) – 5 – us Americana [978]

HISTORY OF PHILADELPHIA, 1609-1884 – Philadelphia, L. H. Everts and Co., 1884. Vols. 1-3. Pennsylvania Reel 35. (The Cox Library Collection) – 5 – us Americana [978]

HISTORY OF PHOTOGRAPHY – Collection of monographs and serials 1830-early 1900's – 1 – us Primary [770]

THE HISTORY OF PHYSICK / Leclerc, D – Trans. by Drake and Baden. M 375. 1699 – 9 – ne IDC [530]

HISTORY OF PIATT COUNTY / Piatt, Emma C – Biographical sketches. Chicago: Shepard and Johsnon, 1883. Illinois Reel 49. (The Cox Library Collection) – 5 – us Americana [978]

HISTORY OF PICKAWAY COUNTY AND REPRESENTATIVE CITIZENS / Van Cleaf, Aaron R – Chicago: Biographical Publ. Co., 1906. Ohio Reel 53. (The Cox Library Collection) – 5 – us Americana [978]

THE HISTORY OF PICKWICK : AN ACCOUNT OF ITS CHARACTERS, LOCALITIES, ALLUSIONS, AND ILLUSTRATIONS, WITH A BIBLIOGRAPHY / Fitzgerald, Percy Hetherington – London: Chapman and Hall, 1891 – 1 roll – 1 – 1-55879-874-9 – uk Libr Preservation [420]

HISTORY OF PIERCE COUNTY / Bonney, W P – (v2-3. Washington reel 4) – Chicago: Pioneer Hist. Co., 1927. v1. Washington reel 3. (Cox Library Collection) – 5 – us Americana [978]

HISTORY OF PIKE COUNTY – Historical and biographical sketches. Chicago, 1880. Illinois Reel 49. The Cox Library Collection – 5 – us Americana [978]

HISTORY OF PIKE COUNTY / Mills and Co – Des Moines, 1883. Missouri Reel 27. (The Cox Library Collection) – 5 – us Americana [978]

HISTORY OF PLACER AND NEVADA COUNTIES / Lardner, W B & Brock, M J – Nevada Co, 1924 – 1 – B40249 – us Library Micro [978]

HISTORY OF PLATTE PRESBYTERY / Clark, Walter H – 1910 – 1 – $50.00 – us Presbyterian [240]

HISTORY OF PLEASANTS COUNTY / Pemberton, Robert L – St. Marys, Oracle Press, 1929. West Virginia Reel 5. (The Cox Library Collection) – 5 – us Americana [978]

HISTORY OF PLYMOUTH / Hurd, D Hamilton – Philadelphia, J. W. Lewis and Co., 1884. Massachusetts Reel 7. (The Cox Library Collection) – 5 – us Americana [978]

HISTORY OF PLYMOUTH PLANTATION 1620-1647 / Bradford, William – Boston: Published for the Massachusetts Historical Society by Houghton Mifflin, 1912 – 3mf – us A.T.L.A. [971]

HISTORY OF POINT ANO NUEVO, SAN MATEO COUNTY / Stanyer, F M – 1r – 1 – $50.00 – B40260 – us Library Micro [978]

HISTORY OF POLAND FROM 1864 TO 1918 PAMPHLET COLLECTION – 1912-1917? – 1 reel – 1 – CSUXANL6699-B – us Hoover Inst Photo [947]

HISTORY OF POLAND FROM 1918 TO 1945 PAMPHLET COLLECTION – 1919-1949 – 2r – 1 – CSUXANL6726-B – us Hoover Inst Photo [947]

HISTORY OF POLAND PAMPHLET COLLECTION – 1915?-1958? – 4r – 1 – CSUXANL6655-B – us Hoover Inst Photo [947]

HISTORY OF POLITICAL CONVENTIONS IN CALIFORNIA / Davis, Winfield J – 1893 – 1r – 1 – $50.00 – B50528 – us Library Micro [978]

A HISTORY OF POLITICAL THEORIES FROM LUTHER TO MONTESQUIEU / Dunning, William A – New York, London: Macmillan Co, 1919 – 5mf – 9 – $7.50 – LLMC 92-139 – us L.L.M.C. [320]

HISTORY OF POLK COUNTY / Union Historical Co – Des Moines: 1880. Iowa Reel 33. (The Cox Library Collection) – 5 – us Americana [978]

HISTORY OF PORTAGE COUNTY – Chicago: 1885. Ohio Reel 53. (The Cox Library Collection) – 5 – us Americana [978]

HISTORY OF PORTER COUNTY – Chicago, 1912. 2v. Indiana Reel 24. (The Cox Library Collection) – 5 – us Americana [978]

HISTORY OF PORTLAND / Scott, H W – Syracuse: D. Mason and Co., 1890. Oregon reel 5. (Cox Library Collection) – 5 – us Americana [978]

HISTORY OF POSEY COUNTY – Historical and biographical sketches. Chicago, 1886. Indiana Reel 24. (The Cox Library Collection) – 5 – us Americana [920]

HISTORY OF POTTAWATAMIE COUNTY / Field, Homer H & Reed, Joseph R – Chicago: S.J. Clarke Publ. Co., 1907. Vol 1, Iowa Reel 35; Vol 2, Iowa Reel 36. The Cox Library Collection – 5 – us Americana [978]

HISTORY OF POTTAWATTAMIE COUNTY / O.L. Baskin and Co – Chicago: 1883. Iowa Reel 35. The Cox Library Collection – 5 – us Americana [978]

HISTORY OF POWESHIEK COUNTY / Union Historical Co – Des Moines: 1880. Iowa Reel 36. (The Cox Library Collection) – 5 – us Americana [978]

HISTORY OF POWESHIEK COUNTY, IOWA / Parker, L F – Chicago: S. J. Clarke Publ. Co., 1911. Vols. 1-2. Iowa Reel 36. (The Cox Library Collection) – 5 – us Americana [978]

HISTORY OF PRAGUE PAMPHLET COLLECTION – 1965-1969 – 1 reel – 1 – CSUXANL5554-B – us Hoover Inst Photo [947]

A HISTORY OF PREACHING : FROM THE APOSTOLIC FATHERS TO THE GREAT REFORMERS A.D. 70-1572 / Dargan, Edwin Charles – New York: A.C. Armstrong, 1905-1912 – 3mf – us A.T.L.A. [240]

HISTORY OF PREBLE COUNTY / H.Z. Williams and Brothers – Biographical sketches. Philadelphia, 1881. Ohio Reel 54. The Cox Library Collection – 5 – us Americana [978]

HISTORY OF PREBLE COUNTY / Lowry, R E – Indianapolis: B. F. Bowen and Co., 1915. Ohio Reel 54. (The Cox Library Collection) – 5 – us Americana [978]

A HISTORY OF PRESBYTERIANISM IN NEW ENGLAND / Blaikie, Alexander – 1882 – 1 – us A.T.L.A. [240]

HISTORY OF PRESTON COUNTY / Morton, Oren F – Kingwood, Journal Publishing Co., 1914. Vols. 1-2. West Virginia Reel 5. (The Cox Library Collection) – 5 – us Americana [978]

HISTORY OF PRIMITIVE BAPTISTS IN TEXAS, OKLAHOMA AND INDIAN TERRITORY / Newman, J S – 1906. v.1. 338p – 1 – 11.83 – us Baptist [240]

HISTORY OF PROCEDURE IN ENGLAND FROM THE NORMAN CONQUEST; THE NORMAN PERIOD 1066-1204 / Bigelow, Melville M – H-1212 2. 1880 – 8 – ne IDC [941]

THE HISTORY OF PROTESTANT MISSIONS IN INDIA : FROM THEIR COMMENCEMENT IN 1706-1881 / Sherring, Matthew Atmore – (Includes appendixes) – new rev ed. London: Religious Tract Society, 1884 – 2mf – 9 – 0-8370-6516-X – 1986-0516 – us A.T.L.A. [240]

THE HISTORY OF PROTESTANT MISSIONS IN INDIA FROM THEIR COMMENCEMENT IN 1706 TO 1881 / Sherring, Matthew Atmore – New ed., rev. and...to date. London: Religious Tract Soc., 1884. xv,463p. tables, 4 fold. maps – 1 – us U.W. Library [240]

HISTORY OF PROTESTANT THEOLOGY = GESCHICHTE DER PROTESTANTISCHEN THEOLOGIE : PARTICULARLY IN GERMANY: VIEWED ACCORDING TO ITS FUNDAMENTAL MOVEMENT AND IN CONNECTION WITH THE RELIGIOUS, MORAL, AND INTELLECTUAL LIFE / Dorner, Isaak August – (Includes index) – Edinburgh: T & T Clark. 2v. 1871 – 4mf – 9 – 0-8370-8663-9 – 1986-2663 – us A.T.L.A. [240]

HISTORY OF PROVO / Jensen, J Marinus – Provo, 1924. Utah reel 4. (Cox Library Collection) – 5 – us Americana [978]

HISTORY OF PSYCHOLOGY : A SKETCH AND AN INTERPRETATION / Baldwin, James Mark – New York: G.P. Putnam, 1913 – 1mf – us A.T.L.A. [150]

THE HISTORY OF PUBLIC EDUCATION IN BRITISH COLUMBIA : A MICROFILM COLLECTION – Vancouver, BC: University of British Columbia Library, Facilities and Preservation Office, 1993 – 111r – 1 – Can$60.00r – cn U.B.C. Preserve [370]

A HISTORY OF PUBLIC EDUCATION IN RHODE ISLAND, FROM 1636 TO 1876 / ed by Stockwell, Thomas B – Providence: Providence Press Co., 1876. 458p – 1 – us U.W. Library [370]

HISTORY OF PUTMAN COUNTY / Kinder, George D – Indianapolis: B. F. Bowen and Co., 1915. Ohio Reel 55. (The Cox Library Collection) – 5 – us Americana [978]

HISTORY OF QUINCY AND ITS MEN OF MARK / Redmond, Pat H – Quincy: Heirs and Russell, 1869. Illinois Reel 11. (The Cox Library Collection) – 5 – us Americana [978]

HISTORY OF RACINE AND KENOSHA COUNTIES – Chicago: 1879. Wisconsin Reel 17. (The Cox Library Collection) – 5 – us Americana [978]

HISTORY OF RANDOLPH AND MACON COUNTIES / National Historical Co – St.Louis, 1884. Missouri Reel 27. (The Cox Library Collection) – 5 – us Americana [978]

HISTORY OF RANDOLPH COUNTY / Tucker, E – Chicago: A.L. Kingman, 1882. Indiana Reel 25. (The Cox Library Collection) – us Americana [978]

HISTORY OF RANDOLPH COUNTY, ARKANSAS / Dalton, Lawrence – 6 fiches. F-0047 – 9 – us A.G.L.L. [978]

THE HISTORY OF RANDOLPH COUNTY, WEST VIRGINIA / Maxwell, Hu – Morgantown, The Acme Publishing Co., 1898. Virginia Reel 4. (The Cox Library Collection) – 5 – us Americana [978]

HISTORY OF RANDOLPH, MONROE AND PERRY COUNTIES / J.L. McDonough and Co – Biographical sketches. Philadelphia, 1883. Illinois Reel 50. The Cox Library Collection – 5 – us Americana [978]

HISTORY OF RATIONALISM : EMBRACING A SURVEY OF THE PRESENT STATE OF PROTESTANT THEOLOGY / Hurst, John F – New York: Scribner, Armstrong, c1865 – 2mf – us A.T.L.A. [240]

THE HISTORY OF REDDING, CONNECTICUT / Todd, Charles B – New York, The John A. Gray Press, 1880. Connecticut Reel 3. (The Cox Library Collection) – 5 – us Americana [978]

THE HISTORY OF REDWOOD COUNTY / Curtiss-Wedge, Franklyn – Chicago: H.C. Cooper, Jr. and Co., 1916.2v. Minnesota Reel 12. (The Cox Library Collection) – 5 – us Americana [978]

HISTORY OF RELIGIONS – Chicago.v1-26.1961-87 – 1,5,6 – us Princeton Micro [200]

HISTORY OF RELIGIONS – (v. 17- 1977- 9) – v. 1- 1961- – 1. ; 5,6 – apply; v.11- – us UMI [200]

THE HISTORY OF RELIGIOSITY IN LATIN AMERICA, 1880-1970 : CIDOC COLLECTION / ed by Borremans, Valentina & Illich, Ivan – 576 serials – 9 – ne IDC [200]

HISTORY OF RELIGIOUS ORDERS : A COMPENDIOUS AND POPULAR SKETCH OF THE RISE AND PROGRESS OF THE PRINCIPAL MONASTIC, CANONICAL, MILITARY, MENDICANT, AND CLERICAL ORDERS AND CONGREGATIONS OF THE EASTERN AND WESTERN CHURCHES / Currier, Charles Warren – (Includes bibliographical references and index) – New York: Murphy & McCarthy, 1895, c1894 – 2mf – 9 – 0-8370-7132-1 – 1986-1132 – us A.T.L.A. [240]

HISTORY OF RENO COUNTY / Ploughe, Sheridon – Indianapolis: B.F. Bowen and Co., 1917. v1, Kansas Reel 10. v2, Kansas Reel 11. (The Cox Library Collection) – 5 – us Americana [978]

HISTORY OF RENSSELAER COUNTY / Sylvester, Nathaniel B – Biographical sketches. Philadelphia: Everts and Peck, 1880. New York Reel 31. (The Cox Library Collection) – 5 – us Americana [978]

HISTORY OF RENVILLE COUNTY / Curtiss-Wedge, Franklyn – Chicago: H.C. Cooper and Co., 1916. 2v.Minnesota Reel 12. (The Cox Library Collection) – 5 – us Americana [978]

HISTORY OF REPUBLIC COUNTY / Savage, I O – Beloit: Jones and Chubbic Art Printers, 1901. Kansas Reel 11. (The Cox Library Collection) – 5 – us Americana [978]

HISTORY OF RESISTANCE IN NAMIBIA / Katjavivi, Peter H – 1988 – xxxii/152p – 9 – 92-3-102511-2 – Co-production James Curry, London (rights UK); OAU, Interafrican Cultural Fund, Addis Ababa (rights Africa); UNESCO – fr UNESCO [320]

HISTORY OF RHON: PAMPHLET COLLECTION – 193? – 1 – CSUXANS8667-B – us Hoover Inst Photo [943]

HISTORY OF RICE COUNTY / Neill, Edward D – Sioux Massacre of 1862 and State Education. Minneapolis: Minnesota Historical Co., 1882. Minnesota Reel 12. (The Cox Library Collection) – 5 – us Americana [978]

HISTORY OF RICE COUNTY AND STEELE COUNTY / Curtiss-Wedge, Franklyn – Chicago: H.C. Cooper and Co., 1910. 2v.Minnesota Reel 13. (The Cox Library Collection) – 5 – us Americana [978]

HISTORY OF RICHLAND COUNTY / Baughman, A J – Chicago: S. J. Clarke Publ. Co., 1908. Vols. 1-2. Ohio Reel 56. (The Cox Library Collection) – 5 – us Americana [978]

HISTORY OF RICHLAND COUNTY ITS PAST AND PRESENT / Graham, A A – Mansfield: A. A. Graham and Co., 1807-1880. Ohio Reel 55. (The Cox Library Collection) – 5 – us Americana [978]

HISTORY OF RITCHIE COUNTY / Lowther, MK – Wheeling, 1911. Missouri Reel 28. (The Cox Library Collection) – 5 – us Americana [978]

HISTORY OF RIVERSIDE COUNTY / Holmes, Elmer W – Los Angeles: Historic Record Co., 1912. California Reel 23. (The Cox Library Collection) – 5 – us Americana [978]

HISTORY OF ROANE COUNTY / Bishop, William H – Spencer, 1927. West Virginia Reel 5. (The Cox Library Collection) – 5 – us Americana [978]

HISTORY OF ROCK COUNTY – Chicago: 1879. Wisconsin Reel 17. (The Cox Library Collection) – 5 – us Americana [978]

HISTORY OF ROCKBRIDGE COUNTY / Morton, Oren F – Staunton, McClure Co., 1920. Virginia Reel 4. (The Cox Library Collection) – 5 – us Americana [978]

HISTORY OF ROCKFORD AND WINNEBAGO COUNTY / Church, Charles A – Rockford: W. P. Lamb, Publ., 1900. Illinois Reel 63. (The Cox Library Collection) – 5 – us Americana [978]

HISTORY OF ROCKINGHAM COUNTY / Wayland, John W – Dayton, Ruebush-Elkins Co., 1912. Virginia Reel 4. (The Cox Library Collection) – 5 – us Americana [978]

HISTORY OF ROMAN PRIVATE LAW / Clark, E C – Cambridge: The University Press. pts 1-3 in 4 bks. 1906-19 – 18mf – 9 – $27.00 – LLMC 95-181 – us L.L.M.C. [340]

HISTORY OF ROMANIA FROM 1914 TO 1944 PAMPHLET COLLECTION – 1917?-1973 – 1 reel – 1 – CSUXANQ4815-B – us Hoover Inst Photo [947]

HISTORY OF ROMANIA PAMPHLET COLLECTION – 1916-1939 – 1 reel – 1 – CSUXANL8138-B – us Hoover Inst Photo [947]

A HISTORY OF ROME. AMPLY ILLUSTRATED WITH MAPS, PLANS, AND ENGRAVINGS / Leighton, Robert Fowler – New York: Clark & Maynard, 1879.xxviii,515p. illus. maps – 1 – us U.W. Library [900]

A HISTORY OF ROME AND FLOYD COUNTY (GEORGIA), INCLUDING NUMEROUS INCIDENTS OF MORE THAN LOCAL INTEREST, 1540-1922 – v1, by George Magruder Battey, 1922. Biog. and hist. sketches. 10 fiches. F-0727 – 9 – us A.G.L.L. [978]

HISTORY OF ROSS AND HIGHLAND COUNTIES – Biographical sketches. Cleveland: 1880. Ohio Reel 56. (The Cox Library Collection) – 5 – us Americana [978]

HISTORY OF ROYALTON / Lovejoy, Evelyn M Wood – With family genealogies. Burlington, Published by The Town and the Royalton Woman's Club, 1911. Vermont Reel 11. (The Cox Library Collection) – 5 – us Americana [920]

HISTORY OF RUSH COUNTY / Brant, Fuller and Co – Historical and Biographical sketches. Chicago, 1888. Indiana Reel 25. (The Cox Library Collection) – 5 – us Americana [978]

HISTORY OF RUSSELL CREEK ASSOCIATION OF BAPTISTS IN KENTUCKY – 1954 – 1 – 5.00 – us Baptist [240]

HISTORY OF RUSSIA DURING THE 19TH CENTURY PAMPHLET COLLECTION – 1896-1946 – 1 reel – 1 – CSUXANS1273-B – us Hoover Inst Photo [947]

HISTORY OF RUSSIA DURING THE REIGN OF NICHOLAS 2 PAMPHLET COLLECTION – 1905-1915 – 1 reel – 1 – CSUXANS7933-B – us Hoover Inst Photo [947]

HISTORY OF RUSSIA, FROM EARLIEST TIMES TO THE RISE OF COMMERCIAL CAPITALISM / Pokrovskii, Mikhail N – Trans. and ed. by J.D. Clarkson and M.R.M. Griffiths. New York: International Publishers, c1931. xvi,383p. maps – 1 – us U.W. Library [947]

HISTORY OF RUSSIA PAMPHLET COLLECTION – 1854-1956 – 1 reel – 1 – CSUXANR3700-B – us Hoover Inst Photo [947]

HISTORY OF RUSSIAN NOBILITY : (BOOKS AND PERIODICALS ON MICROFICHE) FROM THE NATIONAL LIBRARY OF RUSSIA, ST PETERSBURG – (Coll covers the period from the late 18th century to the 1910s) – 14 titles 213mf – 9 – $990.00 coll – us Ross [920]

HISTORY OF RUTLAND COUNTY – Illustrations and biographical sketches. Syracuse, D. Mason and Co., 1886. Vemont Reel 8. (The Cox Library Collection) – 5 – us Americana [978]

HISTORY OF SAC COUNTY / Hart, William H – Indianapolis: B. F. Bowen and Co., 1914. Iowa Reel 37. (The Cox Library Collection) – 5 – us Americana [978]

HISTORY OF SACERDOTAL CELIBACY IN THE CHRISTIAN CHURCH / Lea, Henry Charles – London: Williams and Norgate, 1907 – 3mf – us A.T.L.A. [240]

HISTORY OF SACRAMENTO COUNTY / Reed, G Walter – Los Angeles: Historic Record Co., 1923. California Reel 24. (The Cox Library Collection) – 5 – us Americana [978]

HISTORY OF SACRAMENTO COUNTY / Willis, William – Los Angeles: Historic Record Co., 1913. California Reel 24. (The Cox Library Collection) – 5 – us Americana [978]

HISTORY OF SAGINAW COUNTY – Chicago, 1881. Michigan Reel 20. The Cox Library Collection – 5 – us Americana [978]

HISTORY OF SAGINAW COUNTY / Mills, James C – Historical, commercial and biographical. Saginaw: Seemann and Peter Publ., 1918. Vols. 1-2. Michigan Reel 20. (The Cox Library Collection) – 5 – us Americana [978]

HISTORY OF ST. CLAIR COUNTY / Brink, McDonough and Co – Historical and biographical. Philadelphia, 1881. Illinois Reel 51. The Cox Library Collection – 5 – us Americana [978]

THE HISTORY OF ST. DOMINIC : FOUNDER OF THE FRIARS PREACHERS / Drane, Augusta Theodosia – London, New York: Longmans, Green, 1891 – 2mf – us A.T.L.A. [240]

HISTORY OF ST. EDMUNDS COLLEGE, OLD HALL / Ward, Bernard – London: K. Paul, Trench, Truebner, 1893 – 1mf – us A.T.L.A. [370]

HISTORY OF ST. JOSEPH COUNTY – Chicago, 1880. Indiana Reel 26. The Cox Library Collection – 5 – us Americana [978]

HISTORY OF ST. LAWRENCE COUNTY / L.H. Everts and Co – Biographical sketches. Philadelphia, 1878. New York Reel 32. The Cox Library Collection – 5 – us Americana [978]

HISTORY OF SALINE COUNTY / Missouri Historical Co – Biographical sketches. St. Louis, 1881.Missouri Reel 32. (The Cox Library Collection) – 5 – us Americana [978]

HISTORY OF SALT LAKE CITY AND ITS FOUNDERS / Tullidge, Edward W – Salt Lake City, 1850. Utah reel 4. (Cox Library Collection) – 5 – us Americana [978]

HISTORY OF SAN BERNARDINO AND RIVERSIDE COUNTIES / Brown & Boyd – Western Historical Assoc., 1922. 3v. California Reel 25. The Cox Library Collection – 5 – us Americana [978]

HISTORY OF SAN DIEGO 1542-1908 / Smythe, William E – San Diego: History Co., 1908. v1, Old Town; v2, Modern City. California Reel 25. (The Cox Library Collection) – 5 – us Americana [978]

HISTORY OF SAN DIEGO AND IMPERIAL COUNTIES – Chicago, 1913. 2v. California Reel 26. The Cox Library Collection – 5 – us Americana [978]

HISTORY OF SAN DIEGO COUNTY / Black, Samuel – Chicago: S.J. Clarke Publ. Co., 1913. v1, California Reel 25. v2, California Reel 26. (The Cox Library Collection) – 5 – us Americana [978]

HISTORY OF SAN DIEGO COUNTY / Heilbron, Carl H – San Diego: San Diego Press Club, 1936. California Reel 27. (The Cox Library Collection) – 5 – us Americana [978]

HISTORY OF SAN FRANCISCO / Byington & Lewis – San Francisco: S.J. Clarke Publ. Co., 1931. v1-2, California Reel 28. v3, California Reel 29. (The Cox Library Collection) – 5 – us Americana [978]

HISTORY OF SAN JOAQUIN COUNTY / Historic Record Co – Los Angeles, 1923. California Reel 30. (The Cox Library Collection) – 5 – us Americana [978]

THE HISTORY OF SAN JOSE AND SURROUNDINGS / Hall, Frederic – San Francisco: A.L. Bancroft & Co., 1871. California Reel 32. (The Cox Library Collection) – 5 – us Americana [978]

HISTORY OF SAN MATEO COUNTY / Allen, B F – San Mateo Co, CA. 1883 – 1r – 1 – $50.00 – B40257 – us Library Micro [978]

HISTORY OF SANDY CREEK BAPTIST ASSOCIATION, NORTH CAROLINA / Teague, H A – 1858-1958 – 1 – 6.72 – us Baptist [240]

HISTORY OF SANDY RUN BAPTIST CHURCH, HAMPTON, S.C – 1903-64 – 1 – 5.00 – us Baptist [240]

HISTORY OF SANGAMON COUNTY / Inter-State Publishing Co – Historical and biographical sketches. Chicago, 1881. Illinois Reel 53. The Cox Library Collection – 5 – us Americana [978]

HISTORY OF SANPETE AND EMERY COUNTIES / Lever, W H – Ogden, 1898. Utah reel 4. (Cox Library Collection) – 5 – us Americana [978]

HISTORY OF SANTA BARBARA COUNTY / Phillips, Michael J – San Francisco: S.J. Clarke Publ. Co., 1927. 2v.California Reel 31. (The Cox Library Collection) – 5 – us Americana [978]

HISTORY OF SANTA CLARA COUNTY / Historic Record Co – Los Angeles, 1922. California Reel 32. (The Cox Library Collection) – 5 – us Americana [978]

HISTORY OF SANTA CLARA COUNTY / Sawyer, Eugene T – Santa Clara Co, CA. 1922 – 1r – 1 – $50.00 – B40261 – us Library Micro [978]

HISTORY OF SARATOGA COUNTY / Sylvester, Nathaniel B – Philadelphia: Everts and Ensign, 1878. New York Reel 32. (The Cox Library Collection) – 5 – us Americana [978]

HISTORY OF SARATOGA COUNTY / Sylvester, Nathaniel B et al – Biographical sketches. New York, Gresham Publ. Co., 1893. New York Reel 32. (The Cox Library Collection) – 5 – us Americana [978]

HISTORY OF SAUK COUNTY / Butterfield, Consul Willshire – Chicago: Western Historical Co., 1880. Wisconsin Reel 19. (The Cox Library Collection) – 5 – us Americana [978]

A HISTORY OF SAVANNAH AND SOUTH GEORGIA / Harden, William – 1913. 10 fiches. F-0726 – 9 – us A.G.L.L. [978]

A HISTORY OF SCANDINAVIAN FISHES / Fries, BF & Ekstroem, CV & Sundevall, C – Z-2103 2. 2v. Ed. 2. 1893-1895 – 8 – ne IDC [590]

HISTORY OF SCHLEY COUNTY GEORGIA / Williams, Mrs H J – 1 fiche. F-0733 – 9 – us A.G.L.L. [978]

HISTORY OF SCHOHARIE COUNTY / Roscoe, William E – Biographical sketches. Syracuse, D. Mason and Co., 1882. New York Reel 33. (The Cox Library Collection) – 5 – us Americana [978]

HISTORY OF SCHUYLKILL COUNTY – Biographical sketches. New York, 1881. Pennsylvania Reel 37. The Cox Library Collection – 5 – us Americana [978]

HISTORY OF SCHUYLKILL COUNTY / Schalck & Henning – State Historical Association, 1907. Vols. 1-2. Pennsylvania Reel 37. (The Cox Library Collection) – 5 – us Americana [978]

HISTORY OF SCIENCE AND TECHNOLOGY – (Series One: The Papers of Sir Hans Sloane, 1660-1753 from the British Library London; Part 1: Science and Society, 1660-1773. Part 2: Voyages of Discovery,1492-1750. 20r.$2,500.00. Part 3: Voyages of Discovery, 1492-1750. 20r.$2,500.00. Series Two: The Papers of Sir Joseph Banks, 1743-1820. Part 1: Correspondence and Papers Relating to Voyages of Discovery, 1740-1805, from the British Library, London. $2,300.00. Part 2: Papers Relating to

Voyages of Discovery, 1760-1800, from the British Library, London. 16r. $2,100.00) – Marlborough: Adam Matthew Publications, 1991 – 17r – 1 – $2,350.00 – uk Matthew [500]

HISTORY OF SCIENCE IN FRANCE: 17TH-19TH CENTURIES / ed by Taton, Rene – 48 titles. Available individually – 9 – fr Hachette [500]

THE HISTORY OF SCIENCE, INDUSTRY AND MEDICINE : A PICTORIAL RECORD OF THE SCIENCE MUSEUM. LONDON – (The 17,000 captioned photographs are grouped by subject into 135 categories) – Bath, England: Mindata Ltd., May 1994 – 294mf – 9 – $1,800.00 – 1-900853-35-3 – uk Mindata [500]

A HISTORY OF SCIOTO COUNTY AND SOUTHERN OHIO PIONEER RECORD / Evans, Nelson W – Portsmouth, 1903. Ohio Reel 58. (The Cox Library Collection) – 5 – us Americana [978]

THE HISTORY OF SCOTISH POETRY / Irving, David; ed by Carlyle, John Aitken – Edinburgh: Edmonston and Douglas, 1861 – 1 roll – 1 – 1-55879-617-7 – uk Libr Preservation [420]

HISTORY OF SCOTT COUNTY / Inter-State Publishing Co – Chicago, 1882. Iowa Reel 38. The Cox Library Collection – 5 – us Americana [978]

HISTORY OF SCRANTON / Hitchcock, Frederick L – New York, Lewis Historical Publishing Co., 1914. Pennsylvania Reel 26. (The Cox Library Collection) – 5 – us Americana [978]

HISTORY OF SEATTLE / Bagley, Clarence B – Chicago: S.J. Clarke Publ. Co., v1-3. Washington reel 3. (Cox Library Collection) – 5 – us Americana [978]

HISTORY OF SEATTLE / Grant, James F – New York: American Publ. Co., 1891. Washington reel 3. (Cox Library Collection) – 5 – us Americana [978]

"HISTORY OF SEIBERT AND BOESE FAMILIES." / Seibert, Grant – 1 – us KS Hist [920]

HISTORY OF SENECA COUNTY – Chicago: 1886. Ohio Reel 57. (The Cox Library Collection) – 5 – us Americana [978]

HISTORY OF SENECA COUNTY FROM THE CLOSE OF THE REVOLUTIONARY WAR TO JULY, 1880 / Lang, W – Biographical sketches. Springfield: Transcript Printing Co., 1880. Ohio Reel 57. (The Cox Library Collection) – 5 – us Americana [978]

HISTORY OF SERBIA PAMPHLET COLLECTION – 1915-1971 – 1 reel – 1 – CSUXANQ5661-B – us Hoover Inst Photo [947]

THE HISTORY OF SERVIA AND THE SERVIAN REVOLUTION : WITH A SKETCH OF THE INSURRECTION IN BOSNIA / Ranke, Leopold von – London: H.G. Bohn, 1853 – 2mf – us A.T.L.A. [949]

HISTORY OF SEWARD COUNTY, NEBRASKA / Cox, W W – Lincoln: State Journal Co., Printers, 1888. Nebraska Reel 12. (The Cox Library Collection) – 5 – us Americana [978]

HISTORY OF SHANGHAI / Couling, S – 2v. Shanghai. 1923. Lacking: v. 1, 1923. BCH-941 2 – 8 – ne IDC [950]

HISTORY OF SHAWNEE COUNTY AND REPRESENTATIVE CITIZENS / James, King L – Chicago: Richmond and Arnold, 1905. Kansas Reel 12. (The Cox Library Collection) – 5 – us Americana [978]

HISTORY OF SHEBOYGAN COUNTY / Franklin Publishing Co – Sheboygan: 1898. Wisconsin Reel 19. (The Cox Library Collection) – 5 – us Americana [978]

HISTORY OF SHELBY COUNTY / Brant, Fuller and Co – Historical and biographical sketches. Chicago, 1887. Indiana Reel 26. (The Cox Library Collection) – 5 – us Americana [978]

HISTORY OF SHELBY COUNTY AND REPRESENTATIVE CITIZENS / Hitchcock, A B C – Chicago: Richmond-Arnold Publ. Co., 1913. Ohio Reel 58. (The Cox Library Collection) – 5 – us Americana [978]

HISTORY OF SHENANDOAH COUNTY / Wayland, John W – Strasburg, Shenandoah Publishing Co., 1927. Virginia Reel 5. (The Cox Library Collection) – 5 – us Americana [978]

HISTORY OF SHEYBOYGAN COUNTY / Zillier, Carl – Chicago: S. J. Clarke Publ. Co., 1912. Vols. 1-2. Wisconsin Reel 19. (The Cox Library Collection) – 5 – us Americana [978]

HISTORY OF SHOAL CREEK ASSOCIATION, MISSOURI WITH HISTORY OF HER CHURCHES AND BIOGRAPHIES OF MINISTERS / Largen, T L – 1908 – 1 – 6.93 – us Baptist [240]

HISTORY OF SINO-JAPANESE WAR / U.S. Office of the Chief of Military History – 1967 – 1 – 29.00 – us L of C Photodup [950]

A HISTORY OF SLAVERY IN CUBA, 1511 TO 1868 / Aimes, Hubert Hillary Suffern – New York and London: G.P. Putnam's Sons, 1907. xi,298p – 1 – us U.W. Library [972]

HISTORY OF SLOVAKIA PAMPHLET COLLECTION – 1910-1956 – 1 reel – 1 – CSUXANL5645-B – us Hoover Inst Photo [947]

HISTORY OF SLOVENIA PAMPHLET COLLECTION – 1941 – 1 reel – 1 – CSUXANQ7335-B – us Hoover Inst Photo [947]

HISTORY OF SNOHOMISH COUNTY / Whitfield, William – Seattle: Pioneer Hist. Publ. Co., 1926. v1-2. Washington reel 5. (Cox Library Collection) – 5 – us Americana [978]

HISTORY OF SOCIALISM ON MICROFICHE – (A Data MATE 895A microfiche reader is given free to purchasers of the complete collection) – Gld57,800.00 0010058212mf – ne IDC [320]

HISTORY OF SOLANO AND NAPA COUNTIES – Chicago, 1926. California Reel 33. The Cox Library Collection – 5 – us Americana [978]

HISTORY OF SOLANO AND NAPA COUNTIES / Historic Record Co – Los Angeles, 1912. California Reel 33. (The Cox Library Collection) – 5 – us Americana [978]

HISTORY OF SOLANO AND NAPA COUNTIES, CALIFORNIA / Gregory, Tom – (Includes biographical sketches) – Napa Co, 1912 – 1r – 1 – $50.00 – B40239 – us Library Micro [978]

HISTORY OF SOLANO COUNTY / Munro-Fraser, J P – Solano Co, CA. 1879 – 1r – 1 – $50.00 – B40273 – us Library Micro [978]

HISTORY OF SOLANO COUNTY / Wood, Alley and Co – East Oakland, 1879. California Reel 33. (The Cox Library Collection) – 5 – us Americana [978]

HISTORY OF SOLDIERS' AND SAILORS' MONUMENT / Gleason, William J – Cleveland, Ohio: The Monument Commissioners, 1894 – 1 reel – 1 – us Western Res [355]

HISTORY OF SONOMA COUNTY / Alley, Bowen & Co – San Francisco, 1880. California Reel 33. (The Cox Library Collection) – 5 – us Americana [978]

HISTORY OF SONOMA COUNTY – Chicago, 1889. California Reel 34. (The Cox Library Collection) – 5 – us Americana [978]

HISTORY OF SONOMA COUNTY – Chicago, 1926. California Reel 34. The Cox Library Collection – 5 – us Americana [978]

HISTORY OF SONOMA COUNTY / Finlay, Ernest L – Santa Rosa: Press Democrat Publ. Co., 1937. California Reel 35.(The Cox Library Collection) – 5 – us Americana [978]

HISTORY OF SONOMA COUNTY / Gregory, Tom – Los Angeles: Historic Record Co., 1911. California Reel 34. (The Cox Library Collection) – 5 – us Americana [978]

HISTORY OF SOUTH CAROLINA / Snowden, Gilbert T – New York, Lewis Publishing Co., 1920. Vols. 1-5. South Carolina Reel 1. (The Cox Library Collection) – 5 – us Americana [978]

HISTORY OF SOUTH DAKOTA / Robinson, Doane – Indianapolis: B.F. Bowen and Co., 1904. 2v. South Dakota Reel 1. (The Cox Library Collection) – 5 – us Americana [978]

HISTORY OF SOUTHEAST MISSOURI / Douglas, Robert S – Chicago: Lewis Publ. Co., 1912. 2v. Missouri Reel 6. (The Cox Library Collection) – 5 – us Americana [978]

HISTORY OF SOUTHEAST MISSOURI – Ste. Genevieve, St. Francois, Perry, Cape Girardeau, Bollinger, Madison, New Madrid, Pemiscot, Dunklin, Scott, Mississippi, Stodard, Butler, Wayne and Iron. Chicago, 1888. Missouri Reel 5. (The Cox Library Collection) – 5 – us Americana [978]

HISTORY OF SOUTHEASTERN OHIO AND THE MUSKINGUM VALLEY 1788-1928 – Chicago, 1928. v1-3. Mississippi Reel 7. The Cox Library Collection – 5 – us Americana [978]

HISTORY OF SOUTHERN BAPTISTS, 1684-1918 / Riley, B F – 1057p – 1 – 36.99 – us Baptist [240]

A HISTORY OF SOUTHWESTERN WISCONSIN AND OLD CRAWFORD COUNTY / Gregory, John G – Chicago: S. J. Clarke Publ. Co., 1932. Vols. 1-4. Wisconsin Reel 5. (The Cox Library Collection) – 5 – us Americana [978]

HISTORY OF SRI VIJAYA / Nilakanta Sastri, K A – (Sir W. Meyer lectures, 1946-1947). Madras. 1949. BSE-811 1 – 3mf – 9 – ne IDC [950]

HISTORY OF ST CLAIR COUNTY / A.T. Andreas and Co – Chicago: 1883. Michigan Reel 21. (The Cox Library Collection) – 5 – us Americana [978]

HISTORY OF ST LOUIS CITY AND COUNTY / Scharf, Thomas J – Biographical sketches. Philadelphia: Louis H. Everts and Co., 1883. 2v. Missouri Reel 29.(The Cox Library Collection) – 5 – us Americana [978]

HISTORY OF ST PAUL / Andrews, C C – Biographical sketches of pioneers and prominent men. Syracuse: D. Mason and Co., 1890.Minnesota Reel 11. (The Cox Library Collection) – 5 – us Americana [978]

HISTORY OF ST PETERSBURG, FLORIDA / Grismer, Karl H – Historical and biographical. 1 roll – 1 – 20.00 – uk Libr Preservation [978]

HISTORY OF ST. VINCENT DE PAUL = HISTOIRE DE SAINT-VINCENT DE PAUL : FOUNDER OF THE CONGREGATION OF THE MISSION (VINCENTIANS) AND OF THE SISTERS OF CHARITY / Bougaud, Emile – London; New York: Longmans, Green, 1908 – 1mf – 9 – 0-8370-6965-3 – 1986-0965 – us A.T.L.A. [920]

HISTORY OF STANISLAUS COUNTY – Stanislaus Co, CA: Elliot, 1880 – 1r – 1 – $50.00 – B40278 – us Library Micro [978]

HISTORY OF STANISLAUS COUNTY / Tinkham, George H – Los Angeles: Historic Record Co., 1921. California Reel 35. (The Cox Library Collection) – 5 – us Americana [978]

HISTORY OF STARK COUNTY / Blue, Herbert T O – Chicago: S. J. Clarke Publ. Co., 1928. Vols. 1-3. Ohio Reel 60. (The Cox Library Collection) – 5 – us Americana [978]

HISTORY OF STARK COUNTY / Perrin, William Henry – Chicago: Baskin and Battey Historical Publ. Co., 1881. Ohio Reel 59. (The Cox Library Collection) – 5 – us Americana [978]

HISTORY OF STATE OF RHODE ISLAND AND PROVIDENCE PLANTATIONS / Bicknell, Thomas W – Historical and biographical. American Historical Society, Inc., 1920. Vols. 1-5. Rhode Island Reel 1. (The Cox Library Collection) – 5 – us Americana [978]

HISTORY OF STEARNS COUNTY / Mitchell, William Bell – Chicago: H.C. Cooper, Jr. and Co., 1915.v1, Minnesota Reel 14.v2, Minnesota Reel 15. (The Cox Library Collection) – 5 – us Americana [978]

HISTORY OF STEELE AND WASECA COUNTIES – An album of history and biography. Chicago, 1887. Minnesota Reel 15. (The Cox Library Collection) – 5 – us Americana [978]

HISTORY OF STEPHENSON COUNTY – Chicago, 1880. (Illinois Reel 55). (The Cox Library Collection) – 5 – us Americana [978]

HISTORY OF STEPHENSON COUNTY / Fulwider, Addison L – Biographical Sketches. Chicago: S. J. Clarke Publ. Co., 1910. Vols. 1-2. Illinois Reel 56. (The Cox Library Collection) – 5 – us Americana [978]

HISTORY OF STORY COUNTY / Allen, William G – Des Moines: Iowa Printing Co., 1887. Iowa Reel 39. (The Cox Library Collection) – 5 – us Americana [978]

HISTORY OF STORY COUNTY / Payne, WO – Chicago: S.J. Clarke Publ. Co., 1911. 2v. Iowa Reel 39. (The Cox Library Collection) – 5 – us Americana [978]

HISTORY OF SULLIVAN COUNTY / Quinlan & Beebe & Morgans – Biographical sketches. Liberty, W. T. Morgans and Co., 1873. New York Reel 34. (The Cox Library Collection) – 5 – us Americana [978]

THE HISTORY OF SUMATRA / Marsden, W – Ed. 3. London, 1811 – 6mf – 9 – ne IDC [950]

HISTORY OF SUMMERS COUNTY / Miller, James H – Hinton, 1908. West Virginia Reel 6. (The Cox Library Collection) – 5 – us Americana [978]

HISTORY OF SUMMIT COUNTY / Perrin, William Henry – Chicago: Baskin and Battey Historical Publ. Co., 1881. Ohio Reel 60. (The Cox Library Collection) – 5 – us Americana [978]

THE HISTORY OF SUNDAY SCHOOLS AND OF RELIGIOUS EDUCATION FROM THE EARLIEST TIMES / Pray, Lewis G – Boston: Crosby and Nichols, 1847 – 1mf – us A.T.L.A. [240]

HISTORY OF SURRY COUNTY OR ANNALS OF NORTHWEST NORTH CAROLINA / Hollingsworth, J G – 1935. North Carolina Reel 2. (The Cox Library Collection) – 5 – us Americana [978]

HISTORY OF SUSQUEHANNA AND JUNIATA VALLEYS / Everts & Peck & Richards – Philadelphia, 1886. Vols. 1-2, Pennsylvania Reel 3. (The Cox Library Collection) – 5 – us Americana [978]

HISTORY OF SWEETWATER VALLEY / Lenoir, W B – Richmond: Presbyterian Committee of Publications, 1916. Tennessee Reel 2. (The Cox Library Collection) – 5 – us Americana [978]

HISTORY OF TAMA COUNTY / Caldwell, J R – Chicago: Lewis Publ. Co., 1910. Iowa Reel 40. (The Cox Library Collection) – 5 – us Americana [978]

HISTORY OF TAMA COUNTY – Springfield, 1883. Iowa Reel 40. (The Cox Library Collection) – 5 – us Americana [978]

HISTORY OF TAYLOR COUNTY / State Historical Co – Des Moines, 1881. Iowa Reel 40.(The Cox Library Collection) – 5 – us Americana [978]

HISTORY OF TAZEWELL COUNTY AND THE SOUTHWEST VIRGINIA / Pendleton, William C – Richmond, W. C. Hill Publishing Co., 1920. Virginia Reel 5. (The Cox Library Collection) – 5 – us Americana [978]

A HISTORY OF TEN BAPTIST CHURCHES, KENTUCKY-VIRGINIA / Taylor, John – A journal of the author's life for more than fifty years. 1770-1818 – 1 – 10.50 – us Baptist [240]

HISTORY OF TENNESSEE / Hamer, Philip M – New York: American Historical Society, 1933. Vols. 1-4. Tennessee Reel 1. (The Cox Library Collection) – 5 – us Americana [978]

HISTORY OF TEXAS / Brown, John Henry – From 1685 to 1892. St. Louis: L.E. Daniell Publ., n.d. 2v. Texas Reel 1. (The Cox Library Collection) – 5 – us Americana [978]

A HISTORY OF TEXAS AND TEXANS / Johnson, Frank W – New York and Chicago: American Historical Society, 1916.v1-4, Texas Reel 2. v5, Texas Reel 3. (The Cox Library Collection) – 5 – us Americana [978]

HISTORY OF TEXAS BAPTISTS / Carroll, J M – Dallas: Baptist Standard Publ. Co., 1923. Texas Reel 6.(The Cox Library Collection) – 5 – us Americana [978]

HISTORY OF TEXAS TOGETHER WITH A BIOGRAPHICAL HISTORY OF MILAM, WILLIAMSON, BASTROP, TRAVIS, LEE AND BURLESON COUNTIES – Chicago, 1893. Texas Reel 12. (The Cox Library Collection) – 5 – us Americana [978]

A HISTORY OF THAI EDUCATION / Thailand. Ministry of Education – Bangkok, 1976 – 2mf – 9 – DE-287/1 – ne IDC [370]

HISTORY OF THE 10TH ROYALS AND OF THE ROYAL GRENADIERS, FROM THE FORMATION OF THE REGIMENT UNTIL 1896 / Champion, Thomas Edward – Toronto: Hunter, Rose Co., 1896. 00552. (Pre-1900 Canadiana) – 9 – cn C.I.H.M. [971]

A HISTORY OF THE ABYSSINIAN EXPEDITION / Markham, Clements R – (With a chapter containing an account of the mission and captivity of Mr Rassam and his companions, by Lieutenant W F Prideaux) – London: Macmillan & Co, 1869 – 1 – us Res Libr [960]

HISTORY OF THE AFGHANS / Nimat Allah – 1829 and 1836 – 1 – uk Microform Academic [950]

HISTORY OF THE AFRICAN METHODIST EPISCOPAL CHURCH / Payne, Daniel Alexander; ed by Smith, C S – Nashville, 1891 – 1r – 1 – us Ross [240]

A HISTORY OF THE ALABAMA AGRICULTURAL EXPERIMENT STATION, 1883-1983. 1985. 1 REEL / Auburn University. Agricultural Experiment Station – 1, 5 – us Spaulding [630]

THE HISTORY OF THE ALMOHADES / Al Marrekoshi, Abdo-'L-Wahid; ed by Dozy, R – 2nd ed. Leyden, 1881 – Dfl25.00 – ne Slangenburg [260]

HISTORY OF THE AMERICAN BIBLE SOCIETY : REVISED, AND BROUGHT DOWN TO THE PRESENT TIME / Strickland, William Peter – New York: Harper, 1856 – 2mf – 9 – 0-8370-6704-9 – 1986-0704 – us A.T.L.A. [220]

HISTORY OF THE AMERICAN COLONY IN LIBERIA, 1821-1823 / Ashmun, Jehudi – 1 – 7.21 – us Baptist [960]

HISTORY OF THE AMERICAN LUTHERAN CHURCH : FROM ITS COMMENCEMENT IN THE YEAR OF OUR LORD 1685 TO THE YEAR 1842 / Hazelius, Ernest L – Zanesville, Ohio: Edwin C. Church, 1846 – 1mf – us A.T.L.A. [240]

A HISTORY OF THE AMERICAN SUNDAY-SCHOOL UNION / Rice, Edwin Wilbur – Philadelphia: American Sunday-School Union, 1899 – 1mf – us A.T.L.A. [240]

A HISTORY OF THE ANABAPTISTS IN SWITZERLAND / Burrage, Henry S – Philadelphia: American Baptist Publication Society, c1882 – 1mf – us A.T.L.A. [949]

HISTORY OF THE ANCIENT CHAPEL OF STRETFORD / Crofton, H T – 1 – uk Microform Academic [920]

HISTORY OF THE ANDOVER THEOLOGICAL SEMINARY / Woods, Leonard – Boston: J.R. Osgood, 1885 – 2mf – us A.T.L.A. [370]

A HISTORY OF THE ARABS IN THE SUDAN / Macmichael, H A – 2v. Cambridge. 1922. BA-339 2 – 8 – ne IDC [956]

A HISTORY OF THE ARCHITECTURE OF THE ABBEY CHURCH OF ST ALBAN; WITH SPECIAL REFERENCE TO THE NORMAN STRUCTURE / Buckler, John Chessell – London: Longman, Brown, Green, and Longmans, 1847. x,168p. illus. Plans, plates – 1 – us U.W. Library [720]

HISTORY OF THE ARGUMENTS FOR THE EXISTENCE OF GOD / Hahn, Aaron – (Includes bibliographical references) – Cincinnati: Bloch, 1885 – 1mf – 9 – 0-8370-3448-5 – 1985-1448 – us A.T.L.A. [210]

HISTORY OF THE ARKANSAS VALLEY, COLORADO / O.L. Baskin and Co – Chicago, 1881. Colorado reel 3. Cox Library Collection – 5 – us Americana [978]

HISTORY OF THE ASSOCIATE REFORMED SYNOD OF THE SOUTH : TO WHICH IS PREFIXED A HISTORY OF THE ASSOCIATE PRESBYTERIAN AND REFORMED PRESBYTERIAN CHURCHES / Lathan, Robert – Harrisburg, Pa.: Published for the author, 1882 – 1mf – us A.T.L.A. [240]

A HISTORY OF THE ATTEMPTS TO ESTABLISH THE PROTESTANT REFORMATION IN IRELAND : AND THE SUCCESSFUL RESISTANCE OF THAT PEOPLE (TIME, 1540-1830) / McGee, Thomas D'Arcy – Boston: Patrick Donahoe, 1853, c1852 – 1mf – 9 – 0-8370-7168-2 – 1986-1168 – us A.T.L.A. [240]

THE HISTORY OF THE AUGSBURG CONFESSION : FROM ITS ORIGIN TILL THE ADOPTION OF THE FORMULA OF CONCORD / Stuckenberg, John Henry Wilburn – Philadelphia: Lutheran Publication Society, c1897 – 1mf – us A.T.L.A. [240]

HISTORY OF THE BALKANS PAMPHLET COLLECTION – 1914-1954 – 1 reel – 1 – CSUXANL7344-B – us Hoover Inst Photo [947]

A HISTORY OF THE BAPTIST AT IREDELL, TEXAS / Tidwell, D D – 78p – 1 – 5.00 – us Baptist [240]

HISTORY OF THE BAPTIST CHURCHES COMPOSING THE STURBRIDGE ASSOCIATION FROM THEIR ORIGIN TO 1843 / Committee of the Sturbridge Association – New York: J.R. Bigelow, 1844 – 1 – 5.00 – us Baptist [240]

A HISTORY OF THE BAPTIST CHURCHES IN THE UNITED STATES / Newman, Albert Henry – New York: Christian Literature, 1894. (The American church history series; v2) – 2mf – us A.T.L.A. [240]

HISTORY OF THE BAPTIST DENOMINATION IN GEORGIA – 1881. Biog. compendium & portrait gallery of Baptist ministers & other GA Baptists. 13 fiches. F-0091 – 9 – us A.G.L.L. [920]

HISTORY OF THE BAPTIST MISSION AT ISHOKUN, OYO / Roberson, Cecil F – 1826-1925 – 1 – us Baptist [950]

HISTORY OF THE BAPTIST MISSIONARY ASSOCIATION OF TEXAS / Parks, W H – n.d. 136p – 1 – 5.00 – us Baptist [240]

A HISTORY OF THE BAPTISTS : TRACED BY THEIR VITAL PRINCIPLES AND PRACTICES FROM THE TIME OF OUR LORD AND SAVIOUR JESUS CHRIST TO THE YEAR 1886 / Armitage, Thomas – New York: Bryan, Taylor, 1887, c1886 – 3mf – us A.T.L.A. [240]

HISTORY OF THE BAPTISTS IN ALABAMA / Holcombe, Hosea – 1840 – 1 – 13.58 – us Baptist [240]

HISTORY OF THE BAPTISTS IN MAINE / Burrage, Henry S – Portland, Me.: Marks Printing House, Printers, 1904 – 2mf – us A.T.L.A. [240]

A HISTORY OF THE BAPTISTS IN NEW ENGLAND / Burrage, Henry S – Philadelphia: American Baptist Publication Society, 1894. (Baptist history series; 1) – 1mf – us A.T.L.A. [240]

A HISTORY OF THE BAPTISTS IN THE MIDDLE STATES / Vedder, Henry Clay – Philadelphia: American Baptist Publication Society, 1898 – 1mf – us A.T.L.A. [305]

A HISTORY OF THE BAPTISTS IN THE SOUTHERN STATES EAST OF THE MISSISSIPPI / Riley, B F – Philadelphia: American Baptist Publication Society, 1898 – 1mf – us A.T.L.A. [240]

A HISTORY OF THE BAPTISTS IN THE WESTERN STATES EAST OF THE MISSISSIPPI / Smith, J A – 1896 – 1 – 14.70 – us Baptist [240]

A HISTORY OF THE BAPTISTS IN THE WESTERN STATES EAST OF THE MISSISSIPPI / Smith, Justin A – Philadelphia: American Baptist Publ. Society, 1896 – 1mf – us A.T.L.A. [305]

A HISTORY OF THE BAPTISTS OF HILL COUNTY, TEXAS / Daniel, J C – 1907 – 1 – 5.00 – us Baptist [240]

HISTORY OF THE BAPTISTS OF SOUTH CAROLINA, 1683-1937 – Ms. Brief unpublished history by W.C. Allen. 565p – 1 – 19.77 – us Baptist [240]

HISTORY OF THE BAPTISTS OF TENNESSEE / Hailey, O L – 448p – 1 – 15.68 – us Baptist [240]

HISTORY OF THE BATTLE OF BUNKER'S (BREED'S) HILL, ON JUNE 17, 1775: FROM AUTHENTIC SOURCES IN PRINT AND MANUSCRIPT / Ellis, George E – Boston: Lockwood, Brooks, 1875. 02907. (Pre-1900 Canadiana) – 9 – cn C.I.H.M. [971]

HISTORY OF THE BATTLE OF LAKE ERIE AND MISCELLANEOUS PAPERS / Bancroft, George – Also: LIFE AND WRITINGS OF GEORGE BANCROFT by Oliver Dyer. New York: R. Bonner, 1891. 03328. (Pre-1900 Canadiana) – 9 – cn C.I.H.M. [971]

A HISTORY OF THE BAUSHI / Chimba, Barnabas – rev ed. Cape Town, Oxford UP,1949 – us Res Libr [960]

HISTORY OF THE BENCH AND BAR / Stevens, Hiram F – Minneapolis-St. Paul: Legal Publ. & Engineering Co., 1904. 2v. Minnesota Reel 2. (The Cox Library Collection) – 5 – us Americana [978]

HISTORY OF THE BENCH AND BAR OF CALIFORNIA / Bates, J C – San Francisco: Bench & Bar Publ. Co., 1912. California Reel 3. (The Cox Library Collection) – 5 – us Americana [978]

HISTORY OF THE BENCH AND BAR OF CALIFORNIA / Shuck, Oscar T – Los Angeles: Commercial Printing House, 1901. California Reel 3. (The Cox Library Collection) – 5 – us Americana [978]

HISTORY OF THE BENCH AND BAR OF OREGON / Historical Publishing Co – Portland, 1910. Oregon reel 2. (Cox Library Collection) – 5 – us Americana [978]

HISTORY OF THE BENCH AND BAR OF WISCONSIN / Berryman, John R – Chicago: H. C. Cooper, Jr. and Co., 1898. Vol. 1. Wisconsin Reel 2. Vol. 2. Wisconsin Reel 3. (The Cox Library Collection) – 5 – us Americana [978]

A HISTORY OF THE BETHEL BAPTIST ASSOCIATION IN KENTUCKY, 1807-1944 / Masters, Frank M – 1 – 23.73 – us Baptist [240]

HISTORY OF THE BIBLE: ARRANGED FOR USE AS A TEXT-BOOK / Mutch, William James – New Haven: W.J. Mutch, 1901. 1 fiche – 9 – us A.T.L.A. [240]

HISTORY OF THE BIG SPRING PRESBYTERIAN CHURCH, NEWVILLE, PA., 1737-1898 / Swope, Gilbert E – 1898 – 1 – $50.00 – us Presbyterian [240]

A HISTORY OF THE BIRDS OF CEYLON / Legge, W V – 2099 2. 1878-1880 – 8 – ne IDC [590]

A HISTORY OF THE BIRDS OF EUROPE / Bree, C R – 4v. Z-361 2. 1859-1863 – 8 – ne IDC [590]

A HISTORY OF THE BIRDS OF EUROPE / Dresser, H E – Z-2067 2. 9 v. plus Supp. 1871-1890 – 9 – ne IDC [590]

HISTORY OF THE BOSTON NAVY YARD, 1797-1874 / U.S. Navy. Office of Naval Records and Library – 1roll. M118. Printed guide – 1 – us Nat'l Archives [355]

THE HISTORY OF THE BRITISH AND FOREIGN BIBLE SOCIETY : FROM ITS INSTITUTION IN 1804, TO THE CLOSE OF ITS JUBILEE IN 1854 / Browne, George – (Includes appendixes) – London: Bagster. 2v. 1859 – 4mf – 9 – 0-8370-6167-9 – 1986-0167 – us A.T.L.A. [220]

THE HISTORY OF THE BRITISH COLONIES IN THE WEST INDIES / Edwards, Bryan – London. 2v. 1793-94 – 1r – 1 – $60.00r – us Ross [972]

HISTORY OF THE BROOKS ARTILLERY / Prince, Albert Happoldt – 1898. 2 fiches – 9 – us South Carolina Historical [975]

HISTORY OF THE CANON OF THE HOLY SCRIPTURES IN THE CHRISTIAN CHURCH = HISTOIRE DU CANON DES SAINTES-ECRITURES DANS L'EGLISE CHRETIENNE / Reuss, Eduard – (Includes bibliographical references and index) – 2nd ed. Edinburgh:R W Hunter, 1891 – 1mf – 9 – 0-8370-4882-6 – 1985-2882 – us A.T.L.A. [220]

HISTORY OF THE CASE OF PROFESSOR W. ROBERTSON SMITH / Moncreiff, Henry Wellwood – 1879 – 9 – us A.T.L.A. [240]

HISTORY OF THE CATHOLIC CHURCH IN SCOTLAND : FROM THE INTRODUCTION OF CHRISTIANITY TO THE PRESENT DAY / Bellesheim, Alphons – Edingburgh: William Blackwood, 1887-1890 – 5mf – us A.T.L.A. [240]

HISTORY OF THE CATHOLIC CHURCH IN THE NINETEENTH CENTURY (1789-1908) / MacCaffrey, James – Dublin: M.H. Gill; St. Louis, Mo.: B. Herder, 1910 – 3mf – us A.T.L.A. [240]

HISTORY OF THE CATHOLIC MISSIONS AMONG THE INDIAN TRIBES OF THE UNITED STATES, 1529-1854 / Shea, John Dawson Gilmary – (Includes index) – New York: P J Kenedy, c1854 – 2mf – 9 – 0-8370-6375-2 – 1986-0375 – us A.T.L.A. [240]

HISTORY OF THE CHARLESTON ASSOCIATION OF BAPTIST CHURCHES IN SOUTH CAROLINA – 1683-1802 – 1 – 8.61 – us Baptist [240]

HISTORY OF THE CHARLESTON LIBRARY SOCIETY / Porcher, Elizabeth L – Typescript for illus. pamphlet – 1mf – 9 – us South Carolina Historical [020]

HISTORY OF THE CHEMUNG BAPTIST ASSOCIATION / Smiley, Thomas – 1796-1829 – 1 – us Baptist [240]

A HISTORY OF THE CHESHIRE COUNTY UNION OF CONGREGATIONAL CHURCHES / Powicke, Frederick J – Manchester: T. Griffiths, 1907 – 1mf – us A.T.L.A. [240]

HISTORY OF THE CHINA THEATER / U.S. Army, China Theater – 1946 – 1 – 34.00 – us L of C Photodup [950]

A HISTORY OF THE CHOIR AND MUSIC OF TRINITY CHURCH, NEW YORK, FROM ITS ORGANIZATION TO THE YEAR 1897 / Messiter, A H – New York: E.S. Gorham, 1906 – 1mf – us A.T.L.A. [780]

HISTORY OF THE CHRISTIAN CHURCH / Fisher, George Park – New York: Scribner, 1890, c1887 – 2mf – us A.T.L.A. [240]

A HISTORY OF THE CHRISTIAN CHURCH DURING THE FIRST SIX CENTURIES / Cheetham, S – London; New York: Macmillan, 1894 – 2mf – us A.T.L.A. [240]

A HISTORY OF THE CHRISTIAN CHURCH DURING THE REFORMATION / Hardwick, Charles – London: Macmillan, 1880 – 1mf – us A.T.L.A. [240]

HISTORY OF THE CHRISTIAN CHURCH, FROM ITS ORIGIN TO THE PRESENT TIME...INCLUDING A HISTORY OF THE CUMBERLAND PRESBYTERIAN CHURCH.. / Smith, James – 1835 – 1 – us A.T.L.A. [240]

A HISTORY OF THE CHRISTIAN CHURCH IN THE APOSTOLIC TIMES / Thiersch, Heinrich Wilhelm Josias – London: Thomas Bosworth, 1883. 1 fiche – 9 – us A.T.L.A. [240]

A HISTORY OF THE CHRISTIAN CHURCH, MIDDLE AGE / Hardwick, Charles – London: Macmillan, 1872 – 2mf – us A.T.L.A. [240]

A HISTORY OF THE CHRISTIAN CHURCH SINCE THE REFORMATION / Cheetham, S – London: Macmillan, 1907 – 1mf – us A.T.L.A. [240]

THE HISTORY OF THE CHRISTIAN MISSIONS OF THE SIXTEENTH, SEVENTEENTH, EIGHTEENTH, AND NINETEENTH CENTURIES : CONTAINING ACCOUNTS OF THE PROPAGATION OF CHRISTIANITY BY THE VARIOUS MISSIONARY SOCIETIES... / Brown, William – (Includes bibliographical references and index) – 3rd enl ed. London: Thomas Baker, 1864 – 6mf – 9 – 0-8370-6567-4 – 1986-0567 – us A.T.L.A. [240]

A HISTORY OF THE CHURCH : FROM THE EDICT OF MILAN, A.D. 313, TO THE COUNCIL CHALCEDON, A.D. 451 / Bright, William – Oxford: J.H. and Jas. Parker, 1860 – 2mf – us A.T.L.A. [240]

HISTORY OF THE CHURCH AND STATE IN NORWAY : FROM THE TENTH TO THE SIXTEENTH CENTURY / Willson, Thomas B – Westminster: A. Constable, 1903 – 1mf – us A.T.L.A. [948]

THE HISTORY OF THE CHURCH AND STATE OF SCOTLAND FROM THE ACCESSION OF K. CHARLES 1, TO THE RESTORATION OF K. CHARLES 2 / Stevenson, Andrew – 1753-57 – 3v – 2 – us A.T.L.A. [240]

HISTORY OF THE CHURCH FROM OUR LORD'S INCARNATION / Eusebius – 1709 – 1 – uk Microform Academic [240]

HISTORY OF THE CHURCH IN EASTERN CANADA AND NEWFOUNDLAND / Langtry, John – London: S.P.C.K.; New York: Society's agents [distributor], 1892 (Colonial church histories) – 1mf – us A.T.L.A. [240]

A HISTORY OF THE CHURCH IN SCOTLAND : FROM THE EARLIEST TIMES DOWN TO THE PRESENT DAY / MacPherson, John – Paisley: Alexander Gardner, 1901 – 2mf – us A.T.L.A. [240]

HISTORY OF THE CHURCH IN THE EIGHTEENTH AND NINETEENTH CENTURIES / Hagenbach, K R – New York: C. Scribner, 1869 – 3mf – us A.T.L.A. [240]

A HISTORY OF THE CHURCH IN VENEZUELA. CHAPEL HILL, 1933 / Watters, Mary – Madrid: Razon y Fe, 1935 – 1 – sp Bibl Santa Ana [240]

THE HISTORY OF THE CHURCH MISSIONARY SOCIETY, ITS ENVIRONMENT, ITS MEN AND ITS WORK / Stock, Eugene – London: Church Missionary Society, 1899-1916. illus., ports., 3 fold. maps. 4v – 1 – us U.W. Library [920]

THE HISTORY OF THE CHURCH OF ENGLAND IN THE COLONIES AND FOREIGN DEPENDENCIES OF THE BRITISH EMPIRE / Anderson, James – London: Rivingtons, 1856 – 5mf – us A.T.L.A. [240]

HISTORY OF THE CHURCH OF IRELAND, FROM THE EARLIEST TIMES TO THE PRESENT DAY / ed by Phillips, Walter Alison – London: Oxford University Press, H. Milford, 1933-34. 3v. Comp. under the auspices of the General Synod of the Church of Ireland. 1 reel. 1304 – 1 – us U.W. Library [240]

THE HISTORY OF THE CHURCH OF ROME : TO THE END OF THE EPISCOPATE OF DAMASUS, A.D. 384 / Shepherd, Edward John – (Includes index) – London: Longman, Brown, Green, and Longmans, 1851 – 2mf – 9 – 0-8370-8945-X – 1986-2945 – us A.T.L.A. [240]

A HISTORY OF THE CHURCH OF RUSSIA / Mouravieff, AN – Oxford: J.H. Parker, 1842 – 2mf – us A.T.L.A. [240]

HISTORY OF THE CHURCH OF SCOTLAND : FROM THE INTRODUCTION OF CHRISTIANITY TO THE PERIOD OF THE DISRUPTION, MAY 18,1843... / Hetherington, W M – Edinburgh: J. Johnstone, 1848 – 3mf – us A.T.L.A. [240]

HISTORY OF THE CHURCH OF SCOTLAND DURING THE COMMONWEALTH / Beattie, James – 1842 – 1 – us A.T.L.A. [240]

HISTORY OF THE CHURCH OF THE UNITED BRETHREN IN CHRIST / Berger, Daniel – Dayton, Ohio: United Brethren Pub. House, 1897 – 2mf – us A.T.L.A. [240]

HISTORY OF THE CHURCHES OF BOONE'S CREEK BAPTIST ASSOCIATION OF KENTUCKY, 1780-1923 / Conkwright, S J – 1 – 6.86 – us Baptist [240]

THE HISTORY OF THE CINEMA, 1895-1940 / ed by Short, Kenneth et al – (With printed guide and index. Guide only £120 Cataloguing on Marc tapes in US MArc format £440) – 3,574mf – 9 – £11,245.00 – uk Chadwyck [790]

HISTORY OF THE CITY OF BUFFALO AND ERIE COUNTY / Smith, H P – Biographical sketches. Syracuse, D. Mason and Co., 1884. Vols. 1-2. New York Reel 14. (The Cox Library Collection) – 5 – us Americana [978]

HISTORY OF THE CITY OF CAIRO / Lansden, John M – Chicago: R. R. Donnelley and Sons Co., 1910. Illinois Reel 12. (The Cox Library Collection) – 5 – us Americana [978]

HISTORY OF THE CITY OF CHICAGO / Inter-Ocean Publishing Co – Chicago, 1900. Illinois Reel 18. The Cox Library Collection – 5 – us Americana [978]

HISTORY OF THE CITY OF DENVER AND ARAPAHOE COUNTY AND COLORADO / O.L. Baskin and Co – Chicago, 1880. Colorado reel 4. Cox Library Collection – 5 – us Americana [978]

HISTORY OF THE CITY OF OMAHA AND SOUTH OMAHA / Savage & Bell & Butterfield, Consul Willshire – Chicago: Munsell and Co., 1894. Nebraska Reel 7. (The Cox Library Collection) – 5 – us Americana [978]

A HISTORY OF THE CITY OF ST PAUL AND OF THE COUNTY OF RAMSEY / Williams, J Fletcher – St.Paul: Publ. by the Society, 1876. Minnesota Reel 10.(The Cox Library Collection) – 5 – us Americana [978]

HISTORY OF THE CITY OF ST PAUL AND RAMSEY COUNTY / Neill, Edward D – Minneapolis: North Star Publ. Co., 1881.Minnesota Reel 11. (The Cox Library Collection) – 5 – us Americana [978]

HISTORY OF THE CITY OF TOLEDO AND LUCAS COUNTY / Waggone, Clark – Toledo: Munsell and Co., 1888. Ohio Reel 44. (The Cox Library Collection) – 5 – us Americana [978]

A HISTORY OF THE CITY OF VINCENNES / Cauthorn, Henry S – Terre Haute: Margaret C. Cauthorn, 1902. Indiana Reel 17. (The Cox Library Collection) – 5 – us Americana [978]

A HISTORY OF THE CITY OF VINCENNES, FROM 1702 TO 1901 / Indiana – By Henry S. Cauthorn. 1901. 4 fiches. F-0295 – 9 – us A.G.L.L. [978]

A HISTORY OF THE COLONIZATION OF AFRICA BY ALIEN RACES / Johnston, Sir Harry Hamilton – Cambridge: University Press; New York: G.P.Putnam [distributor], 1913 (Cambridge historical series; [24]) – 2mf – us A.T.L.A. [960]

HISTORY OF THE COLONY OF SIERRA LEONE, WESTERN AFRICA / Crooks, John Joseph – (With maps and appendices) – Dublin: Browne & Nolan, 1903 – 1 – us Res Libr [960]

THE HISTORY OF THE COLORED METHODIST EPISCOPAL CHURCH IN AMERICA : COMPRISING ITS ORGANIZATION, SUBSEQUENT DEVELOPMENT, AND PRESENT STATUS / Phillips, Charles H – Jackson, TN, 1900 – 1r – 1 – us Ross [240]

HISTORY OF THE COMMERCE AND TOWN OF LIVERPOOL, AND OF THE RISE OF THE MANUFACTURING INDUSTRY IN THE ADJOINING COUNTIES / Baines, Thomas – London: Longman, Brown, Green, and Longmans, 1852. xvi,844p. 3 fold. plans – 1 – us U.W. Library [380]

HISTORY OF THE COMMONWEALTH AND PROTECTORATE, 1649-1656 / Gardiner, Samuel R – London; New York: Longmans, Green, 1903 – 4mf – us A.T.L.A. [941]

HISTORY OF THE COMMONWEALTH OF FLORENCE, FROM THE EARLIEST INDEPENDENCE OF THE COMMUNE TO THE FALL OF THE REPUBLIC IN 1531 / Trollope, Thomas Adolphus – London, 1865. 4v – 1 – us U.W. Library [945]

HISTORY OF THE CONDEMNATION OF THE PATRIARCH NICON : BY A PLENARY COUNCIL OF THE ORTHODOX CATHOLIC EASTERN CHURCH HELD AT MOSCOW A.D. 1666-67 / Ligarides, Paisius – (Includes bibliographical references) – London: Truebner, 1873 – 2mf – 9 – 0-8370-7562-9 – 1986-1562 – us A.T.L.A. [240]

HISTORY OF THE CONFLICT BETWEEN RELIGION AND SCIENCE / Draper, John William – 8th ed. New York: D. Appleton and Co., 1878. xxii,373p – 1 – us U.W. Library [240]

HISTORY OF THE CONFLICT BETWEEN RELIGION AND SCIENCE / Draper, John William – New York: D. Appleton, 1875, c1874. (The International scientific series; v12) – 1mf – us A.T.L.A. [240]

HISTORY OF THE CONGREGATIONAL ASSOCIATION OF OREGON AND WASHINGTON TERRITORY, THE HOME MISSIONARY SOCIETY OF OREGON AND ADJOINING TERRITORIES, AND THE NORTHWESTERN ASSOCIATION OF CONGREGATIONAL MINISTERS / Eells, M – Portland, Oregon: Himes, 1881 – 1mf – us A.T.L.A. [240]

HISTORY OF THE CONGREGATIONAL CHURCHES IN THE BERKS, SOUTH OXON AND SOUTH BUCKS ASSOCIATION : WITH NOTES ON THE EARLIER NONCONFORMIST HISTORY OF THE DISTRICT / Summers, W H – London: Publication Dept.; Newbury: W.J. Blacket, 1905 – 1mf – us A.T.L.A. [240]

A HISTORY OF THE CONGREGATIONAL CHURCHES IN THE UNITED STATES / Walker, Williston – New York: Christian Literature, 1894. (The American church history series; v3) – 2mf – us A.T.L.A. [240]

HISTORY OF THE CONNECTICUT VALLEY IN MASSACHUSETTS / Everts, Louis H – Philadelphia, 1879. Vol. 1, Massachusetts Reel 1; Vol. 2, Massachusetts Reel 2. (The Cox Library Collection) – 5 – us Americana [978]

HISTORY OF THE CONSTITUTIONS OF IOWA / Shambaugh, Benjamin Franklin – Des Moines: Historical Department of Iowa, 1902. 352p. LL-1613 – 1 – us L of C Photodup [340]

A HISTORY OF THE CONVOCATION OF THE CHURCH OF ENGLAND : FROM THE EARLIEST PERIOD TO THE YEAR 1742 / Lathbury, Thomas – London: J. Leslie, 1853 – 2mf – us A.T.L.A. [240]

HISTORY OF THE CORPORATION OF BIRMINGHAM; WITH A SKETCH OF THE EARLIER GOVERNMENT OF THE TOWN / Bunce, John Thackray – Birmingham: Cornish Brothers, 1878-1957.6v – 1 – us U.W. Library [941]

A HISTORY OF THE COUNCIL OF TRENT / Buckley, Theodore Alois – London: George Routledge, 1852. 549p. 2 fiches – 9 – us A.T.L.A. [240]

HISTORY OF THE COUNCIL OF TRENT / Bungener, Laurence Louis Felix – Ed. from the 2nd London ed., with summary of the acts of the Council, by John M'Clintock. New York: Harper, 1855. xlii,546p – 1 – us U.W. Library [240]

HISTORY OF THE COUNTIES OF WOODBURY AND PLYMOUTH / A. Warner and Co – Chicago, 1890-91. Iowa Reel 43. The Cox Library Collection – 5 – us Americana [978]

HISTORY OF THE COUNTY OF ANNAPOLIS / Calnek, William Arthur – Including Old Port Royal and Acadia. Toronto, Montreal, Halifax, London: William Briggs, 1897. Canada reel 6. (Cox Library Collection) – 5 – us Americana [971]

HISTORY OF THE COUNTY OF HUDSON / Winfield, Charles B – New York, Kennard and Hay Stationery Mfg. and Printing, 1874. New Jersey Reel 3. (The Cox Library Collection) – 5 – us Americana [978]

HISTORY OF THE COUNTY OF MIDDLESEX, CANADA / W.A. and C.L. Goodspeed, Publishers – From the earliest time to the present. Toronto, London, 1889. Canada reel 5. Cox Library Collection – 5 – us Americana [971]

HISTORY OF THE COUNTY OF MIDDLESEX, CANADA: FROM THE EARLIEST TIME TO THE PRESENT:.. – Toronto: Goodspeed, 1889. 05642. (Pre-1900 Canadiana) – 9 – cn C.I.H.M. [971]

HISTORY OF THE COUNTY OF MONTGOMERY / Merritt, W W – From earliest days to 1906. Red Oak: Express Publ. Co., 1906. Iowa Reel 30. (The Cox Library Collection) – 5 – us Americana [978]

HISTORY OF THE COUNTY OF ORANGE / Ruttenbur, Edward M – 1875 – 1 – $50.00 – us Presbyterian [978]

A HISTORY OF THE COUNTY OF YARMOUTH, NOVA SCOTIA / Campbell, John Roy – Saint John, N.B.: J. & A. McMillan, 1876. 00389. (Pre-1900 Canadiana) – 9 – cn C.I.H.M. [971]

THE HISTORY OF THE COURT OF THE KING OF CHINA / Baudier, M – London, 1862 – 2mf – 9 – ne IDC [950]

A HISTORY OF THE CRUSADES / Runciman, St – Cambridge, 1951 – Dfl28.00 – ne Slangenburg [240]

HISTORY OF THE CUMBERLAND PRESBYTERIAN CHURCH / McDonnold, B W – Nashville, Tenn.: Board of Publication of Cumberland Presbyterian Church, 1888 – 2mf – us A.T.L.A. [240]

HISTORY OF THE DEACONESS MOVEMENT IN THE CHRISTIAN CHURCH / Golder, Christian – c.1903 – 9 – us A.T.L.A. [240]

HISTORY OF THE DENTON COUNTY BAPTIST ASSOCIATION AND THE SIXTY CHURCHES ORGANIZED WITHIN ITS JURISDICTION / Rayzor, James Newton – 1936 – 1 – 9.52 – us Baptist [240]

HISTORY OF THE DEPARTMENT OF JUSTICE (1963-69) / U.S. Department of Justice – 1980 (Presidential Documents Series) – 1 – $580.00 – 0-89093-360-X – us UPA [340]

A HISTORY OF THE DISCIPLES OF CHRIST, THE SOCIETY OF FRIENDS, THE UNITED BRETHREN IN CHRIST AND THE EVANGELICAL ASSOCIATION / Tyler, B B et al – New York: Christian Literature, 1894. (The American church history series; v12) – 2mf – us A.T.L.A. [240]

A HISTORY OF THE DOCTRINE OF THE HOLY EUCHARIST / Stone, Darwell – H 348 2. 2 v. 1909 – 8 – ne IDC [240]

A HISTORY OF THE DOCTRINE OF THE HOLY EUCHARIST / Stone, Darwell – London, New York: Longmans, Green, 1909 – 3mf – us A.T.L.A. [240]

THE HISTORY OF THE DOMINION OF CANADA / Clement, William Henry Pope – Toronto: W. Briggs, 1897. 00683. (Pre-1900 Canadiana) – 9 – cn C.I.H.M. [971]

HISTORY OF THE DONATISTS : WITH NOTES / Benedict, David – Pawtucket, R.I.: Printed for Maria M. Benedict by Nickerson, Sibley, 1875 – 1mf – us A.T.L.A. [240]

HISTORY OF THE DUTCH EAST INDIES / Shen, Chuen – In Chinese. SE 6420 1. 1954 – 9 – ne IDC [950]

HISTORY OF THE EARLY KINGS OF PERSIA / Mir Khwand – 1832 – 1 – uk Microform Academic [900]

THE HISTORY OF THE EARLY PURITANS : FROM THE REFORMATION TO THE OPENING OF THE CIVIL WAR IN 1642 / Marsden, J B – London: Hamilton, Adams, 1860 – 2mf – us A.T.L.A. [941]

THE HISTORY OF THE EARLY PURITANS: FROM THE REFORMATION TO THE OPENING OF THE CIVIL WAR IN 1642 / Marsden, John Buxton – London: Hamilton, Adams, & Co., 1850. xv,426p – 1 – us U.W. Library [240]

HISTORY OF THE EARLY SETTLERS OF SANGAMON COUNTY / Power, John C – Springfield: Edwin A. Wilson, 1876. Illinois Reel 52. (The Cox Library Collection) – 5 – us Americana [978]

HISTORY OF THE EASTERN CHURCH (CCC262) / Plopper, C H – (In Chinese) – Hong Kong: Bible Book and Tract Depot for Council on Christian Literature for Overseas Chinese, 1954 – 1r – 1 – 1984-6601 – us A.T.L.A. [240]

A HISTORY OF THE EASTERN DEFENSE COMMAND / Brook, William M – New York, Raleigh. 1945. 4v. maps, charts – 1 reel – 1 – $24.00 – us L of C Photodup [977]

A HISTORY OF THE EASTERN ROMAN EMPIRE FROM THE FALL OF IRENE TO THE ACCESSION OF BASIL I. (A.D. 802-867) / Bury, J B – London; New York: Macmillan, 1912 – 2mf – us A.T.L.A. [930]

HISTORY OF THE EGYPTIAN RELIGION / Tiele, Cornelius Petrus – Trans. from the Dutch by James Ballingal. Boston: Houghton, Mifflin, 1882. xxiii,230p – 1 – us U.W. Library [290]

HISTORY OF THE ELKHORN VALLEY / Scoville, C H – Historical and biographical sketches. Omaha: National Publ. Co., 1892. Nebraska Reel 9. (The Cox Library Collection) – 5 – us Americana [978]

HISTORY OF THE ENGLISH BIBLE / Ayers, S G – New York: Ketcham, 1898.1 fiche – 9 – us A.T.L.A. [240]

THE HISTORY OF THE ENGLISH BIBLE / Moulton, William Fiddian – London: Cassell Petter, 1878. 1 fiche – 9 – us A.T.L.A. [240]

THE HISTORY OF THE ENGLISH BIBLE / Pattison, Thomas Harwood – (Includes index) – Philadelphia: American Baptist Publ Society, 1894 – 1mf – 9 – 0-8370-4676-9 – 1985-2676 – us A.T.L.A. [220]

THE HISTORY OF THE ENGLISH CHURCH AND PEOPLE IN SOUTH AFRICA / Wirgman, A Theodore – London, New York: Longmans, Green, 1895 – 1mf – us A.T.L.A. [240]

A HISTORY OF THE ENGLISH CHURCH DURING THE CIVIL WARS AND UNDER THE COMMONWEALTH, 1640-1660 / Shaw, William Arthur – London, New York: Longmans, Green, 1900 – 3mf – us A.T.L.A. [240]

A HISTORY OF THE ENGLISH CHURCH IN NEW ZEALAND / Purchas, H T – Christchurch, N.Z.: Simpson & Williams, 1914 – 1mf – us A.T.L.A. [240]

A HISTORY OF THE ENGLISH EPISCOPACY FROM THE PERIOD OF THE LONG PARLIAMENT TO THE ACT OF UNIFORMITY : WITH NOTICES OF THE RELIGIOUS PARTIES OF THE TIME, AND A REVIEW OF ECCLESIASTICAL AFFAIRS IN ENGLAND FROM THE REFORMATION / Lathbury, Thomas – London: J.W. Parker, 1836 – 1mf – us A.T.L.A. [240]

THE HISTORY OF THE ENGLISH LANGUAGE / Emerson, Oliver Farrar – New York: Macmillan, 1894 – 1 roll – 1 – 1-55879-583-9 – uk Libr Preservation [420]

THE HISTORY OF THE ENGLISH LANGUAGE / Peyton, V J – 1771. 38p. (English Linguistics Series 1500-1800) – 9 – us UMI [420]

THE HISTORY OF THE ENGLISH REVOLUTION / Dahlmann, FC – London: Longman, Brown, Green and Longmans, 1844 – 1mf – us A.T.L.A. [941]

HISTORY OF THE ENGLISH SETTLERS IN EDWARDS COUNTY / Flower, George – Chicago: Fergus Printing Co., 1882. Illinois Reel 23. (The Cox Library Collection) – 5 – us Americana [978]

HISTORY OF THE ENTERTAINMENT BRANCH, SPECIAL SERVICES DIVISION / U.S. Army. Army Service Forces. Special Services Division – 1 – 39.00 – us L of C Photodup [790]

A HISTORY OF THE EVANGELICAL LUTHERAN CHURCH IN THE UNITED STATES / Jacobs, Henry Eyster – New York: Christian Literature, 1893. (The American church history series; v4) – 2mf – us A.T.L.A. [240]

A HISTORY OF THE EVANGELICAL PARTY IN THE CHURCH OF ENGLAND / Balleine, G R – London, New York: Longmans, Green, 1908 – us A.T.L.A. [240]

THE HISTORY OF THE EXTINCTION OF PAGANISM IN THE ROMAN EMPIRE VIEWED IN RELATION TO THE EVIDENCES OF CHRISTIANITY : BEING THE ESSAY WHICH OBTAINED THE HULSEAN PRIZE FOR 1851 / Heard, J B – Cambridge: Macmillan; London: George Bell, 1852 – 1mf – us A.T.L.A. [930]

A HISTORY OF THE FALL OF THE ROMAN EMPIRE...A VIEW OF THE INVASION & SETTLEMENT OF THE BARBARIANS / Sismondi, Jean Charles Leonard Simonde de – London: Longman, Rees, Orme, Brown, Green & Longman, 1834. 2v – 1 – us U.W. Library [900]

HISTORY OF THE FEDERAL TRADE COMMISSION (1963-69) / U.S. Federal Trade Commission – 1980. (Presidential Documents Series) – 1 – $210.00 – 0-89093-361-8 – us UPA [380]

HISTORY OF THE FIRE LANDS / Williams, W W – Comprising Huron and Erie Counties. 1879. Ohio Reel 40. (The Cox Library Collection) – 5 – us Americana [978]

A HISTORY OF THE FIRST BAPTIST CHURCH *see* MISCELLANEOUS BOOKS AND PAMPHLETS

A HISTORY OF THE FIRST BAPTIST CHURCH, ELDORADO, TEXAS, 1 SEP 1901-31 AUG 1957 / Hoover, L M – 1 00 $5.00 – us Baptist [240]

HISTORY OF THE FIRST BAPTIST CHURCH IN PROVIDENCE. PROVIDENCE, RHODE ISLAND : CHURCH RECORDS – 1639-1877 – 1 – 5.00 – us Baptist [240]

HISTORY OF THE FIRST BAPTIST CHURCH OF CHRIST AT MACON (MACON, GA), 1826-1968 / Batts, H Lewis – 1968-69.5 fiches. F-0943 – 9 – us A.G.L.L. [240]

A HISTORY OF THE FIRST BULGARIAN EMPIRE / Runciman, S – London. 1930. BR-3910 2 – 8 – ne IDC [949]

HISTORY OF THE FIRST CHURCH IN HARTFORD, 1633-1883 / Walker, George Leon – Hartford: Brown & Gross, 1884 – 2mf – us A.T.L.A. [240]

HISTORY OF THE FIRST WEST INDIA REGIMENT / Ellis, Alfred Burdon – London: Chapman and Hall, 1885. xii,366p. Maps, plan, col. front. With: Griechisches Erbe by F. Klatt. 1 reel. 1293 – 1 – us U.W. Library [355]

A HISTORY OF THE FISHES OF MADEIRA / Lowe, R T – Z-2120 2. 1843-1860 – 8 – ne IDC [590]

A HISTORY OF THE FISHES OF THE BRITISH ISLANDS / Couch, J – London, 1862-1865. 4v – 39mf – 9 – ne IDC [590]

THE HISTORY OF THE FIVE INDIAN NATIONS OF CANADA / Colden, C – BN 166 2. 1747 – 8 – ne IDC [305]

A HISTORY OF THE FOOCHOW YMCA (CCC348) – (In Chinese) – [s.l: s.n, 19–] – 1r – 1 – 1984-6687 – us A.T.L.A. [360]

A HISTORY OF THE FOREIGN MISSIONARY WORK OF THE PROTESTANT EPISCOPAL CHURCH / Denison, S D – New York: Foreign Committee of the Board of Missions, 1871 – 1mf – us A.T.L.A. [240]

HISTORY OF THE FORMATION OF THE CONSTITUTION : OF THE UNITED STATES OF AMERICA / Bancroft, George – 3rd ed. New York: D Appleton & Co. 2v. 1883 – 12mf – 9 – $18.00 – LLMC 90-365 – us L.L.M.C. [323]

A HISTORY OF THE FOSSIL INSECTS IN THE SECONDARY ROCKS OF ENGLAND... / Brodie, P B – London, 1845 – XVIII, 130p, 11pls – 8 – ne IDC [560]

THE HISTORY OF THE FREEWILL BAPTISTS FOR HALF A CENTURY / Stewart, I D – Dover: Freewill Baptist Print. Establishment, 1862, c1861 – 2mf – us A.T.L.A. [240]

THE HISTORY OF THE GENERAL CONFERENCE OF THE MENNONITES OF NORTH AMERICA / Krehbiel, H P – [S.l.]: H.P. Krehbiel, 1898; (St. Louis, Mo.: A. Wiebusch) – 2mf – us A.T.L.A. [240]

HISTORY OF THE GENERAL HEADQUARTERS REGULATING SYSTEM, 2 NOV 1943-31 AUG 1945 / U.S. Army. Forces in the Southwest Pacific – 1946 – 1 – 18.00 – us L of C Photodup [950]

HISTORY OF THE GENERAL PUBLIC HOSPITAL IN THE CITY OF SAINT JOHN, N.B / Bayard, William – 1896. 02223. (Pre-1900 Canadiana) – 9 – cn C.I.H.M. [610]

HISTORY OF THE GEORGIA BAPTIST ASSOCIATION / Robinson, R L – 1928. Hist. and biog. sketches.4 fiches. F-0093 – 9 – us A.G.L.L. [920]

HISTORY OF THE GERMAN BAPTIST BRETHREN CHURCH / Falkenstein, George N – Lancaster, Pa.: New Era, 1901 – 1mf – us A.T.L.A. [240]

A HISTORY OF THE GERMAN BAPTIST BRETHREN IN EUROPE AND AMERICA / Brumbaugh, Martin Grove – Mount Morris, Ill.: Brethren Publishing House, 1899 – 2mf – us A.T.L.A. [240]

A HISTORY OF THE GERMAN LANGUAGE / Super, Charles William – Columbus, O: Hann & Adair, 1893.x,316p – 1 – us U.W. Library [430]

HISTORY OF THE GIRTYS: A CONCISE ACCOUNT OF THE GIRTY BROTHERS, THOMAS, SIMON, JAMES AND GEORGE, AND OF THEIR HALF-BROTHER JOHN TURNER : ALSO OF THE PART TAKEN BY THEM IN LORD DUNSMORE'S WAR, IN THE WESTERN BORDER WAR OF THE REVOLUTION, AND IN THE INDIAN WAR OF 1790-95. / Butterfield, Consul Willshire – Cincinnati, OH: R. Clarke, 1890. 00370. (Pre-1900 Canadiana) – 9 – cn C.I.H.M. [920]

HISTORY OF THE GOLD COAST AND ASANTE, BASED ON TRADITIONS AND HISTORICAL FACTS : COMPRISING A PERIOD OF MORE THAN THREE CENTURIES FROM ABOUT 1500 TO 1860 / Reindorf, Carl Christian – Basel: Printed for the author [by] Missionbuchhandlung, 1895 – 1 – us Res Libr [960]

A HISTORY OF THE GOTHIC REVIVAL : AN ATTEMPT TO SHOW HOW THE TASTE FOR MEDIAEVAL ARCHITECTURE, WHICH LINGERED IN ENGLAND DURING THE TWO LAST CENTURIES, HAS SINCE BEEN ENCOURAGED AND DEVELOPED / Eastlake, Charles L – London: Longmans, Green; New York: Scribner, Welford, 1872 – 2mf – us A.T.L.A. [720]

THE HISTORY OF THE GREAT BOER TREK AND THE ORIGINS OF SOUTH AFRICAN REPUBLICS / Cloete, Henry; ed by Brodrick-Cloete, W – London: Murray, 1899 – 1 – us Res Libr [960]

HISTORY OF THE GREAT CIVIL WAR, 1642-1649 / Gardiner, Samuel R – London: Longmans, Green, 1893 – 4mf – us A.T.L.A. [940]

HISTORY OF THE GREAT FIRE IN SAINT JOHN, JUNE 20 AND 21, 1877 / Conwell, Russell H – Boston: B. B. Russell; Saint John, N. B.: Jones & Morrison; Toronto: Might & Taylor, 1877. 00109. (Pre-1900 Canadiana) – 9 – cn C.I.H.M. [971]

THE HISTORY OF THE GREAT IRISH FAMINE OF 1847, WITH NOTICES OF EARLIER IRISH FAMINES / O'Rourke, John – 3rd ed. Dublin: J. Duffy, 1902.xxiv,559p – 1 – us U.W. Library [941]

HISTORY OF THE GREAT KANAUHA VALLEY / Brant, Fuller and Co – Madison, 1891. Vols. 1-2. West Virginia Reel 2. (The Cox Library Collection) – 5 – us Americana [978]

HISTORY OF THE GREAT LAKES / J.H. Beers and Co – Chicago, 1899. v1-2. Illinois Reel 4. The Cox Library Collection – 5 – us Americana [978]

HISTORY OF THE GREAT PATRIOTIC WAR OF THE SOVIET UNION, 1941-1945 – v1-3. 1960-61 – 1 – $65.00 – us L of C Photodup [947]

THE HISTORY OF THE GREAT PATRIOTIC WAR OF THE SOVIET UNION, 1941-1945 : OFFICIAL SOVIET HISTORY OF WORLD WAR 2 / ed by Pospelov, Poitr N – 1985 – 7r – 1 – $595.00 – S1656 – Co-publ with the U.S. Army Center of Military History and the Foreign Technology Division, Air Force Systems Command – us Scholarly Res [947]

HISTORY OF THE GREAT SECESSION FROM THE METHODIST EPISCOPAL CHURCH IN THE YEARS 1845 : EVENTUATING IN THE ORGANIZATION OF THE NEW CHURCH, ENTITLED THE "METHODIST EPISCOPAL CHURCH, SOUTH" / Elliott, Charles – Cincinnati: Swormstedt & Poe for the Methodist Episcopal Church, 1855, c1854 – 2mf – us A.T.L.A. [240]

HISTORY OF THE HALIFAX VOLUNTEER BATTALION AND VOLUNTEER COMPANIES, 1859-1887 / Egan, Thomas J – Halifax, N.S.: A. & W. Mackinlay, 1888. 02889. (Pre-1900 Canadiana) – 9 – cn C.I.H.M. [971]

HISTORY OF THE HARBOR DISTRICT OF LOS ANGELES / Ludwig, Ella A – Historic Record Co., Inc., n.d. California Reel 17. (The Cox Library Collection) – 5 – us Americana [978]

A HISTORY OF THE HEBREW MONARCHY: FROM THE ADMINISTRATION OF SAMUEL TO THE BABYLONIAN CAPTIVITY / Newman, Francis – 2nd ed. 1853 – 9 – us A.T.L.A. [270]

A HISTORY OF THE HIGH OPERATION FOR THE STONE / Carpue, J C – M-87. 1819 – 9 – ne IDC [610]

THE HISTORY OF THE HIGHER CRITICISM OF THE NEW TESTAMENT / Nash, Henry Sylvester – New York: Macmillan, 1901. 1 fiche – 9 – us A.T.L.A. [240]

A HISTORY OF THE HOLY EUCHARIST IN GREAT BRITAIN / Bridgett, T E – London: Burns & Oates; St. Louis, Mo.: Herder, 1908 – 1mf – us A.T.L.A. [240]

THE HISTORY OF THE HOLY, MILITARY, SOVEREIGN ORDER OF ST. JOHN OF JERUSALEM : OR KNIGHTS HOSPITALLERS, KNIGHTS TEMPLARS, KNIGHTS OF RHODES, KNIGHTS OF MALTA / Taaffe, John – London: Hope, 1852 – 4mf – us A.T.L.A. [240]

HISTORY OF THE HUDSON RIVER VALLEY (RIVER OF DESTINY) / Greene, Nelson – Chicago, 1931. Vols. 1-5. New York Reel 6. (The Cox Library Collection) – 5 – us Americana [978]

HISTORY OF THE HUGUENOT EMIGRATION TO AMERICA / Baird, Charles Washington – 2v. New York: Dodd, Mead, c1885. 07409, 07410.(Pre-1900 Canadiana) – 9 – cn C.I.H.M. [240]

A HISTORY OF THE HUGUENOTS OF THE DISPERSION : AT THE RECALL OF THE EDICT OF NANTES / Poole, Reginald Lane – London: Macmillan, 1880 – 1mf – us A.T.L.A. [305]

A HISTORY OF THE ICONOCLASTIC CONTROVERSY / Martin, Edward James – London, (1930). 282p. map. The Church Historical Society, Publications, New Series – 1 – us U.W. Library [240]

HISTORY OF THE ILLINOIS RIVER VALLEY / Conger, John L – Chicago: S. J. Clarke Publ. Co., 1932. Vol. 1. Illinois Reel 4; Vols. 2-3. Illinois Reel 5. (The Cox Library Collection) – 5 – us Americana [978]

THE HISTORY OF THE INDEPENDENT OR CONGREGATIONAL CHURCH IN CHARLESTON, S.C / Ramsay, David – 1815 – 1 – $50.00 – us Presbyterian [240]

HISTORY OF THE INDIAN ARCHIPELAGO / Crawfurd, J – Edinburgh. 3v. 1820 – 20mf – 9 – ne IDC [950]

HISTORY OF THE INDONESIAN PUBLISHERS' ASSOCIATION : INTRODUCTION / Hutauruk, Marulam – SE-6656 1. 1968 – 9 – ne IDC [070]

HISTORY OF THE INQUISITION: FROM ITS ESTABLISHMENT IN THE TWELFTH CENTURY TO ITS EXTINCTION IN THE NINETEENTH / Rule, William Harris – London: Hamilton, Adams; New York: Scribner, Welford, 1874. 2v. illus – 1 – us U.W. Library [240]

A HISTORY OF THE INQUISITION OF THE MIDDLE AGES / Lea, Henry Charles – New York. v1-3. 1922 – 33mf – 8 – Dfl116.00 – ne Slangenburg [240]

HISTORY OF THE INTELLECTUAL DEVELOPMENT OF EUROPE / Draper, John William – New York: Harper, 1876 – 3mf – us A.T.L.A. [900]

A HISTORY OF THE INTERPRETATION OF ROMANS 14:1-15:13, 1845-1980 / Lamkin, Thomas Elwood – 1982 – 1 – 5.00 – us Baptist [240]

A HISTORY OF THE IRISH PRESBYTERIANS / Latimer, William Thomas – Belfast: J. Cleeland, W. Mullan, 1902 – 2mf – us A.T.L.A. [240]

THE HISTORY OF THE ISLAND OF ANTIGUA : ONE OF THE LEEWARD CARIBBEES IN THE WEST INDIES, FROM THE FIRST SETTLEMENT IN 1635 TO THE PRESENT TIME / Oliver, Vere Langford – London. 3v. 1894-99 – 2r – 1 – us Ross [972]

A HISTORY OF THE ISLAND OF CAPE BRETON: WITH SOME ACCOUNT OF THE DISCOVERY AND SETTLEMENT ON CANADA, NOVA SCOTIA AND NEWFOUNDLAND / Brown, Richard FGS – London: Sampson, Low, Son and Marston, 1869. 00314. (Pre-1900 Canadiana) – 9 – cn C.I.H.M. [971]

THE HISTORY OF THE JEWISH CHURCH / Stanley, Arthur Penrhyn – 3v. 1879 – 9 – us A.T.L.A. [270]

HISTORY OF THE JEWS FROM THE EARLIEST PERIOD DOWN TO MODERN TIMES / Milman, Henry Hart – 3rd ed. 1863 – 9 – us A.T.L.A. [270]

A HISTORY OF THE JEWS IN ENGLAND / Hyamson, Albert Montefiore – With portraits and 2 maps. London: Chatto & Windus, 1908. xx,364p – 1 – us U.W. Library [941]

HISTORY OF THE JEWS IN RUSSIA AND POLAND / Dubnov, S M – Philadelphia. 3v. 1916-20. BR-4955 2 – 8 – ne IDC [305]

HISTORY OF THE KARAITE JEWS / Rule, William Harris – London: Longmans, Green, 1870 – 1mf – 9 – 0-8370-4996-2 – 1985-2996 – us A.T.L.A. [270]

HISTORY OF THE KINETOGRAPH, KINETOSCOPE AND KINETOPHONOGRAPH / Dickson, William K L – N.Y, 1895(?). SEM16P235 – 1r – 5 – Can$9.00 – cn Bibl Nat [770]

HISTORY OF THE KINGDOM OF SIAM AND OF THE REVOLUTIONS THAT HAVE CAUSED THE OVERTHROW OF THE EMPIRE, UP TO A.D. 1770 / Turpin, M – Bangkok, 1908 – 3mf – 9 – ne IDC [950]

THE HISTORY OF THE LAST FOUR YEARS – 1891?. 03691. (Pre-1900 Canadiana) – 9 – cn C.I.H.M. [971]

THE HISTORY OF THE LAST QUARTER-CENTURY IN THE UNITED STATES, 1870-1895 / Andrews, Elisha Benjamin – New York. v1-2.1896 – 1r – 1 – us Ross [976]

A HISTORY OF THE LATER ROMAN EMPIRE : FROM ARCADIUS TO IRENE (395 A.D. TO 800 A.D.) / Bury, J B – London; New York: Macmillan, 1889 – 3mf – us A.T.L.A. [930]

A HISTORY OF THE LAW, THE COURTS, AND THE LAWYERS OF MAINE, FROM ITS FIRST COLONIZATION TO THE EARLY PART OF THE PRESENT CENTURY / Willis, William – Portland, Bailey & Noyes, 1863. 712 p. LL-1546 – 1 – us L of C Photodup [340]

HISTORY OF THE LEMEN FAMILY OF ILLINOIS, VIRGINIA, AND ELSEWHERE, 1656-1898 / Lemen, Frank B – 1 – 23.66 – us Baptist [240]

THE HISTORY OF THE LITIGATION AND LEGISLATION RESPECTING PRESBYTERIAN CHAPELS AND CHARITIES IN ENGLAND AND IRELAND BETWEEN 1861 AND 1849 / James, T S – London: H Adams; Birmingham: Hudson, 1867 – 3mf – us A.T.L.A. [340]

THE HISTORY OF THE LONDON MISSIONARY SOCIETY / Lovett, Richard – 2v. 1795-1895 – 1 – us A.T.L.A. [240]

THE HISTORY OF THE LONDON SOCIETY FOR PROMOTING CHRISTIANITY AMONGST THE JEWS : FROM 1809 TO 1908 / Gidney, William Thomas – (Includes bibliographical references and index) – London: Society for Promoting Christianity Amongst the Jews, 1908 – 2mf – 9 – 0-8370-6052-4 – 1986-0052 – us A.T.L.A. [230]

HISTORY OF THE LOST STATE OF FRANKLIN / Williams, Samuel C – New York: The Press of the Pioneers, 1933. Tennessee Reel 1. (The Cox Library Collection) – 5 – us Americana [978]

HISTORY OF THE LUTHERAN VERSION OF THE BIBLE / Hentz, John P – Columbus, OH: F J Heer, 1910 – 1mf – 9 – 0-8370-9156-X – 1986-3156 – us A.T.L.A. [220]

THE HISTORY OF THE MARITIME PROVINCES / Harper, John Murdoch – Saint John, N.B.: J. McMillan, 1876. 05370. (Pre-1900 Canadiana) – 9 – cn C.I.H.M. [971]

THE HISTORY OF THE MARITIME WARS OF THE TURKS / Haji Khalifah – 1831 – 1 – uk Microform Academic [900]

HISTORY OF THE MAUMEE RIVER BASIN / Slocum, Charles Elihu – Historical and biographical from Basin to counties. Indianapolis: Bowen and Slocum. Vols. 1-2. Indiana Reel 4, Vol. 3. Indiana Reel 5. (The Cox Library Collection) – 5 – us Americana [978]

HISTORY OF THE MAUMEE VALLEY / Knapp, H S – Toledo: Blade Mammouth Printing and Publ. House, 1872. Ohio Reel 9. (The Cox Library Collection) – 5 – us Americana [978]

THE HISTORY OF THE MELANESIAN MISSION / Armstrong, E S – London: Isbister, 1900 – 1mf – us A.T.L.A. [240]

A HISTORY OF THE METHODIST CHURCH, SOUTH, THE UNITED PRESBYTERIAN CHURCH, THE CUMBERLAND PERSBYTERIAN CHURCH, AND THE PRESBYTERIAN CHURCH, SOUTH, IN THE UNITED STATES / Alexander, Gross – New York: Christian Literature, 1894. (The American church history series; v11) – 2mf – us A.T.L.A. [240]

HISTORY OF THE METHODIST CHURCH WITHIN THE TERRITORIES EMBRACED IN THE LATE CONFERENCE OF EASTERN BRITISH AMERICA : INCLUDING NOVA SCOTIA, NEW BRUNSWICK, PRINCE EDWARD ISLAND, AND BERMUDA / Smith, T Watson – Halifax, N.S.: Methodist Book Room, 1877-[1809?] – 3mf – us A.T.L.A. [240]

HISTORY OF THE METHODIST EPISCOPAL CHURCH IN CANADA / Webster, Thomas – Hamilton: Canada Christian Advocate, 1870 – 1mf – us A.T.L.A. [240]

A HISTORY OF THE MIDDLE DISTRICT BAPTIST ASSOCIATION / Moore, L W – 1 – 5.00 – us Baptist [240]

HISTORY OF THE MILITARY INTELLIGENCE DIVISION, 7 DECEMBER 1941-2 SEPTEMBER 1945 / U.S. War Department. General Staff. G-2 Division – 1 – 25.00 – us L of C Photodup [355]

HISTORY OF THE MILITARY INTELLIGENCE DIVISION, DEPARTMENT OF THE ARMY GENERAL STAFF / U.S. Army – By Bruce W. Bidwell. 1959-61 – 7 – 41.00 – us L of C Photodup [970]

HISTORY OF THE MINNESOTA VALLEY / Neill, Edward D – Sioux Massacre history. Minneapolis: North Star Publ. Co., 1882. Minnesota Reel 3. (The Cox Library Collection) – 5 – us Americana [978]

HISTORY OF THE MISSION OF THE AMERICAN BOARD OF COMMISSIONERS FOR FOREIGN MISSIONS TO THE SANDWICH ISLANDS / Anderson, Rufus – (Includes index) – rev ed. Boston Congregational Pub Board, 1874 – 1mf – 9 – 0-8370-6560-7 – 1986-0560 – us A.T.L.A. [240]

A HISTORY OF THE MISSIONS IN JAPAN AND PARAGUAY / Caddell, Cecilia Mary – New York: D & J Sadlier, [1856] – 1mf – 9 – 0-8370-7049-X – 1986-1049 – us A.T.L.A. [240]

HISTORY OF THE MISSIONS OF THE AMERICAN BOARD OF COMMISSIONERS FOR FOREIGN MISSIONS IN INDIA / Anderson, Rufus – (Includes bibliographical references, list of publ and index) – Boston: Congregational Publ Society, 1875, c1874 – 2mf – 9 – 0-8370-6001-X – 1986-0001 – us A.T.L.A. [240]

HISTORY OF THE MISSIONS OF THE AMERICAN BOARD OF COMMISSIONERS FOR FOREIGN MISSIONS TO THE ORIENTAL CHURCHES / Anderson, Rufus – Boston: Congregational Publishing Society, 1872 – 3mf – us A.T.L.A. [240]

HISTORY OF THE MISSIONS OF THE METHODIST EPISCOPAL CHURCH : FROM THE ORGANIZATION OF THE MISSIONARY SOCIETY TO THE PRESENT TIME / Strickland, William Peter – Cincinnati: L. Swormstedt & J.H. Power, 1850, c1849 – 1mf – us A.T.L.A. [240]

A HISTORY OF THE MISSIONS OF THE MORAVIAN CHURCH DURING THE EIGHTEENTH AND NINETEENTH CENTURIES / Hamilton, J Taylor – Bethlehem, Pa.: Times, 1901 – 1mf – us A.T.L.A. [240]

HISTORY OF THE MIT RADAR SCHOOL IN RELATION TO ARMY TRAINING FROM JUNE 23, 1941 TO JUNE 30, 1945 / McIlroy, Malcom S & Zimmerman, Henry J – 1945. 63 p. 1 reel – 1 – 16.00 – us L of C Photodup [621]

A HISTORY OF THE MODES OF CHRISTIAN BAPTISM : FROM HOLY SCRIPTURE, THE COUNCILS ECUMENICAL AND PROVINCIAL, THE FATHERS, THE SCHOOLMEN, AND THE RUBRICS OF THE WHOLE CHURCH EAST AND WEST... / Chrystal, James – Philadelphia: Lindsay and Blakiston, 1861 – 1mf – us A.T.L.A. [240]

A HISTORY OF THE MOHAMMEDAN DYNASTIES IN SPAIN / Maqqari – 1 – uk Microform Academic [946]

HISTORY OF THE MONTREAL PRISON FROM A. D. 1784 TO A. D. 1886 / Borthwick, John Douglas – Montreal: Periard, 1886. 00186. (Pre-1900 Canadiana) – 9 – cn C.I.H.M. [971]

A HISTORY OF THE MORAVIAN CHURCH / Hutton, Joseph Edmund – London: Moravian Publication Office, 1909 – 2mf – us A.T.L.A. [240]

A HISTORY OF THE MORAVIAN CHURCH / Hutton, Joseph Edmund – London: Moravian Publication Office, 1909. 520p – 1 – us U.W. Library [240]

HISTORY OF THE MUNICIPALITIES OF HUDSON COUNTY / Van Winkle, Daniel – Historical and biographical. New York, Lewis Historical Publ. Co., 1924. Vols. 1-2. New Jersey Reel 3; Vol. 3. New Jersey Reel 4. (The Cox Library Collection) – 5 – us Americana [978]

A HISTORY OF THE NATIONAL CEMETERY IN FAYETTEVILLE, ARKANSAS; CEMETERY LISTS OF FAYETTEVILLE, ARKANSAS; THE SOUTHERN MEMORIAL ASSOCIATION – From Publications of the Washington County Historical Society, v1, 1956. 3 fiches. F-0049 – 9 – us A.G.L.L. [978]

THE HISTORY OF THE NEGRO BAPTISTS IN MISSISSIPPI / Thompson, Patrick – 1898 – 1 – us A.T.L.A. [240]

A HISTORY OF THE NEGRO TROOPS IN THE WAR OF THE REBELLION, 1861-1865 109=PRECEDED BY A REVIEW OF THE MILITARY SERVICES OF NEGROES IN ANCIENT AND MODERN TIMES / Williams, George W – (Filmed with: [Baird, H C] Washington und Jackson uber die Neger als Soldaten) – New York: Harper, 1888 – us Res Libr [976]

A HISTORY OF THE NEW SCHOOL : AND OF THE QUESTIONS INVOLVED IN THE DISRUPTION OF THE PRESBYTERIAN CHURCH IN 1838 / Baird, Samuel J – Philadelphia: Claxton, Remses & Haffelfinger, 1868 – 2mf – us A.T.L.A. [240]

THE HISTORY OF THE NEW TESTAMENT CANON IN THE SYRIAN CHURCH / Bewer, Julius A – 1900 – 1 – us A.T.L.A. [240]

A HISTORY OF THE NORTH AMERICAN BIRDS / Baird, Spencer Fullerton & Brewer, T M & Ridgway, R – 3v. Z339. 1875 – 8 – ne IDC [590]

A HISTORY OF THE NORWEGIANS OF ILLINOIS / Strand, A E – Chicago: John Anderson Publ. Co., 1905. Illinois Reel 9. (The Cox Library Collection) – 5 – us Americana [978]

THE HISTORY OF THE NOVEL IN ENGLAND / Lovett, Robert Morss & Hughes, Helen Sard – Boston, New York: Houghton, Mifflin Co., c1932 – 1 – us U.W. Library [420]

HISTORY OF THE OCCUPATION OF KOREA, AUG 1945-MAY 1978 *see* HISTORY OF THE UNITED STATES ARMED FORCES IN KOREA, AUG 1945-MAY 1948

HISTORY OF THE OFFICE OF CENSORSHIP / U.S. Office of Censorship – An original microform collection of archival records declassified in 1971, providing an authoritative history of the Office of Censorship from 1941 to 1945 – 1 – $295.00 – 0-89093-101-1 – us UPA [324]

HISTORY OF THE OHIO FALLS CITIES AND THEIR COUNTIES / L.A. Williams and Co – Cleveland, 1882. 2v. Kentucky Reel 5. The Cox Library Collection – 5 – us Americana [978]

HISTORY OF THE OHIO FALLS CITIES & THEIR COUNTIES – v1, 1968. Orig. publ. 1882. Hist. and biog. Sketches. 13 fiches. F-1066 – 9 – us A.G.L.L. [978]

HISTORY OF THE OLD COVENANT / Kurtz, Johann Heinrich – 3v. 1859 – 1 – us A.T.L.A. [240]

HISTORY OF THE ORDERS OF KNIGHTHOOD / Nicolas, H – H-1264 2. 4v. 1841-1842 – 8 – ne IDC [920]

HISTORY OF THE ORIGIN AND DEVELOPMENT AND CONDITION OF MISSIONS AMONG THE SHERBRO AND MENDI TRIBES IN WESTERN AFRICA / Flickinger, Daniel Kumler & McKee, William – Dayton, OH: United Brethren Pub House, 1885 – 1 – us Res Libr [240]

HISTORY OF THE ORIGIN, FORMATION AND ADOPTION OF THE CONSTITUTION OF THE UNITED STATES : WITH NOTICES OF ITS PRINCIPAL FRAMERS / Curtis, George Ticknor – New York: Harper & Bros. 2v. 1854-58 – 13mf – 9 – $19.50 – LLMC 90-366 – us L.L.M.C. [323]

A HISTORY OF THE ORIGIN OF THE DOCTRINE OF THE TRINITY IN THE CHRISTIAN CHURCH / Stannus, Hugh Hutton – (Includes bibliographical references) – London: Christian Life : Williams and Norgate, 1882 – 1mf – 9 – 0-8370-5542-3 – 1985-3542 – us A.T.L.A. [240]

HISTORY OF THE ORPHAN BRIGADE / Thompson, Ed Porter – Louisville: Lewis N. Thompson, 1898. Kentucky Reel 1. (The Cox Library Collection) – 5 – us Americana [978]

HISTORY OF THE ORTHODOX CHURCH IN AUSTRIA-HUNGARY / Dampier, Margaret G – London: Published for the Eastern Church Association [by] Rivingtons, 1905 – 1mf – us A.T.L.A. [240]

A HISTORY OF THE ORTHODOX CHURCH OF CYPRUS : FROM THE COMING OF THE APOSTLES PAUL AND BARNABAS TO THE COMMENCEMENT OF THE BRITISH OCCUPATION (A.D. 45-A.D. 1878)... / Hackett, J – London: Methuen, 1901 – 2mf – us A.T.L.A. [240]

HISTORY OF THE OTTAWA AND CHIPPEWA INDIANS OF MICHIGAN: A GRAMMAR ON THEIR LANGUAGE, AND PERSONAL AND FAMILY HISTORY OF THE AUTHOR / Blackbird, Andrew J – Ypsilanti, Mich.: Ypsilanti Job Print House. 1887. 00429. (Pre-1900 Canadiana) – 9 – cn C.I.H.M. [978]

HISTORY OF THE PACIFIC NORTHWEST AND CANADIAN NORTHWEST – (Out-of-print and rare documents emphasized) – 1 – us Primary [971]

HISTORY OF THE PACIFIC NORTHWEST: WASHINGTON AND OREGON / North Pacific History Co – Portland, 1889. v1-2. Oregon reel 3. (Cox Library Collection) – 5 – us Americana [978]

HISTORY OF THE PACIFIC STATES-NORTH AMERICA / Bancroft, Hubert Howe – Arizona & New Mexico 1530-1888. San Francisco: History Co. Publs., 1888. Arizona Reel 2.(The Cox Library Collection) – 5 – us Americana [978]

THE HISTORY OF THE PASSION AND RESURRECTION OF OUR LORD / Steinmeyer, Franz Ludwig – Edinburgh: T. & T. Clark, 1879. 1 fiche – 9 – us A.T.L.A. [240]

THE HISTORY OF THE PENAL LAWS ENACTED AGAINST ROMAN CATHOLICS : THE OPERATION AND RESULTS OF THAT SYSTEM OF LEGALIZED PLUNDER, PERSECUTION, AND PROSCRIPTION ORIGINATING IN RAPACITY AND FRAUDULENT DESIGNS ... / Madden, Richard Robert – London: Thomas Richardson, 1847 – 1mf – us A.T.L.A. [941]

A HISTORY OF THE PEOPLE OF IOWA / Cole, Cyrenus – (Cedar Rapids: The Torch Press, 1921). Iowa Reel 1. (The Cox Library Collection) – 5 – us Americana [978]

A HISTORY OF THE PEOPLE OF THE UNITED STATES / McMaster, John B – 1883-1913 – 1 – 145.00 – us L of C Photodup [975]

HISTORY OF THE PHILIPPINE INSURRECTION AGAINST THE U.S., 1899-1903, AND DOCUMENTS RELATING TO THE WAR DEPT. PROJECT FOR PUBLISHING THE HISTORY / U.S. War Department. Adjutant General's Office – 9rolls. M719. Printed guide – 1 – us Nat'l Archives [324]

HISTORY OF THE PHILOSOPHY OF MIND : EMBRACING THE OPINIONS OF ALL WRITERS ON MENTAL SCIENCE FROM THE EARLIEST PERIOD TO THE PRESENT TIME / Blakey, Robert – London: Longman, Brown, Green and Longmans, 1850 – 6mf – us A.T.L.A. [100]

THE HISTORY OF THE PIRATES...MISSON, BOWEN, KIDD, TEW, HALSEY, WHITE, CONDENT, BELLAMY, AND THEIR SEVERAL CREWS – Hartford: H. Benton, 1829, c1825. 283p – 1 – us U.W. Library [972]

A HISTORY OF THE PLYMOUTH BRETHREN / Neatby, William Blair – London: Hodder and Stoughton, 1902 – 1mf – us A.T.L.A. [240]

A HISTORY OF THE PRESBYTERIAN CHURCH IN GEORGIA / Stacy, James – 1912. Hist. and biog. sketches.7 fiches. F-0094 – 9 – us A.G.L.L. [920]

HISTORY OF THE PRESBYTERIAN CHURCH IN GEORGIA / Stacy, James – 1 – $50.00 – us Presbyterian [240]

HISTORY OF THE PRESBYTERIAN CHURCH IN IRELAND; FOR READERS ON THIS SIDE OF THE ATLANTIC / Cleland, William – Toronto: Hart & Co., 1890. 00681. (Pre-1900 Canadiana) – 9 – cn C.I.H.M. [240]

HISTORY OF THE PRESBYTERIAN CHURCH IN SALINE CO., MO. *see* AMERICAN PRESBYTERIANA 1

HISTORY OF THE PRESBYTERIAN CHURCH IN SOUTH CAROLINA / Howe, George – 1883 – 1 – $50.00 – us Presbyterian [240]

HISTORY OF THE PRESBYTERIAN CHURCH IN THE DOMINION OF CANADA : FROM THE EARLIEST TIMES TO 1834 : WITH A CHRONOLOGICAL TABLE OF EVENTS TO THE PRESENT TIME, AND MAP / Gregg, William – Toronto: Presbyterian Printing and Publishing Company, 1885 – 2mf – us A.T.L.A. [240]

HISTORY OF THE PRESBYTERIAN CHURCH IN THE STATE OF KENTUCKY : WITH A PRELIMINARY SKETCH OF THE CHURCHES IN THE VALLEY OF VIRGINIA / Davidson, Robert – New York: R. Carter, 1847 – 2mf – us A.T.L.A. [240]

HISTORY OF THE PRESBYTERIAN CHURCH IN THE UNITED STATES OF AMERICA / Gillett, Ezra Hall – 1864 – 1 – us A.T.L.A. [240]

HISTORY OF THE PRESBYTERIAN CHURCH IN THE UNITED STATES OF AMERICA / Gillett, Ezra Hall – Rev. ed., 1873 – 1 – us A.T.L.A. [240]

A HISTORY OF THE PRESBYTERIAN CHURCHES IN THE UNITED STATES / Thompson, Robert Ellis – New York: Christian Literature, 1895. (The American church history series; v6) – 2mf – us A.T.L.A. [240]

THE HISTORY OF THE PRESBYTERIAN CONTROVERSY, WITH EARLY SKETCHES OF PRESBYTERIANISM / Woods, Henry – Louisville: Printed by N.H. White, 1843.viii,(9)-204p – 1 – us U.W. Library [240]

HISTORY OF THE PRESBYTERIANS IN ENGLAND : THEIR RISE, DECLINE AND REVIVAL / Drysdale, Alexander Hutton – London: Publication Committee of the Presbyterian Church of England, 1889 – 2mf – us A.T.L.A. [240]

HISTORY OF THE PRESBYTERY OF ERIE / Eaton, Samuel J M – 1868 – 1 – $50.00 – us Presbyterian [240]

A HISTORY OF THE PRIMITIVE BAPTISTS IN THE WESTERN DISTRICTS OF TENNESSEE AND KENTUCKY / Edgar, Lewis M – 1828-80 – 1 – 6.51 – us Baptist [240]

HISTORY OF THE PRIMITIVE METHODIST CHURCH / Kendall, H B – London, 1919. vii/177p – 2mf – 9 – ne IDC [240]

THE HISTORY OF THE PRIMITIVE METHODIST CONNEXION FROM ITS ORIGIN TO THE CONFERENCE OF 1859 / Petty, J – London, 1860. x/464p – 6mf – 9 – ne IDC [240]

THE HISTORY OF THE PRIMITIVE METHODIST CONNEXION, FROM ITS ORIGIN TO THE CONFERENCE OF 1860, THE FIRST JUBILEE YEAR OF THE CONNEXION / Petty, J; ed by MacPherson, J – London, 1880. xv/662p – 8mf – 9 – ne IDC [240]

HISTORY OF THE PROGRESS AND SUPPRESSION OF THE REFORMATION IN ITALY IN THE SIXTEENTH CENTURY : INCLUDING A SKETCH OF THE HISTORY OF THE REFORMATION IN THE GRISONS / M'Crie, Thomas – Edinburgh: William Blackwood, 1856 (The works of Thomas M'Crie; v. 3a) – 1mf – us A.T.L.A. [240]

A HISTORY OF THE PROTESTANT EPISCOPAL CHURCH IN THE UNITED STATES / Tiffany, Charles C – New York: Christian Literature, 1895. (The American church history series; v7) – 2mf – us A.T.L.A. [240]

A HISTORY OF THE PROTESTANT REFORMATION IN ENGLAND AND IRELAND / Cobbett, William – (Includes bibliographical references) – new ed. New York: Benziger, 1896 – 1mf – 9 – 0-8370-7374-X – 1986-1374 – us A.T.L.A. [240]

HISTORY OF THE PROTESTANTS OF FRANCE : FROM THE COMMENCEMENT OF THE REFORMATION TO THE PRESENT TIME / Felice, G de – London: Routledge, 1853 – 2mf – us A.T.L.A. [240]

HISTORY OF THE PUGET SOUND COUNTRY / Prosser, William Farrand – Chicago: Lewis Publ. Co., 1903. v1-2. Washington reel 1. (Cox Library Collection) – 5 – us Americana [978]

HISTORY OF THE QUEBEC DIRECTORY SINCE ITS FIRST ISSUE IN 1844 UP TO THE PRESENT DAY / Cherrier, A Benjamin – Quebec: Dawson, 1879. 02988. (Pre-1900 Canadiana) – 9 – cn C.I.H.M. [073]

HISTORY OF THE RECENT AGRICULTURAL POLICY OF THE UNITED STATES / Malin, James C – undated – 1 – us KS Hist [630]

HISTORY OF THE RED RIVER VALLEY PAST AND PRESENT / C.F. Cooper and Co – Chicago, 1909. 2v. Minnesota Reel 4. The Cox Library Collection – 5 – us Americana [978]

HISTORY OF THE REFORMATION IN ENGLAND / Perry, George G – London, New York: Longmans, Green, 1911 – 1mf – us A.T.L.A. [941]

HISTORY OF THE REFORMATION IN GERMANY / Ranke, Leopold von; ed by Johnson, Robert A – Trans. by Sarah Austin. London: G. Routledge; New York: E.P. Dutton, 1905. xxiv,792p – 1 – us U.W. Library [240]

HISTORY OF THE REFORMATION IN GERMANY AND SWITZERLAND CHIEFLY / Hagenbach, K R – Edinburgh: T.& T. Clark, 1878-1879. (Clark's foreign theological library; new ser., v59, 62) – 1mf – us A.T.L.A. [240]

HISTORY OF THE REFORMATION IN SWITZERLAND / Ruchat, Abraham – London: W.E. Painter, 1845 – 1mf – us A.T.L.A. [949]

THE HISTORY OF THE REFORMATION OF RELIGION WITHIN THE REALM OF SCOTLAND / Knox, John; ed by Guthrie, C J – London: A. and C. Black, 1898 – 1mf – us A.T.L.A. [240]

THE HISTORY OF THE REFORMED CHURCH, DUTCH, THE REFORMED CHURCH, GERMAN, AND THE MORAVIAN CHURCH IN THE UNITED STATES / Corwin, E T et al – New York: Christian Literature, 1895, c1894. (The American church history series; v8) – 2mf – us A.T.L.A. [240]

HISTORY OF THE REFORMED CHURCH IN THE U.S. IN THE NINETEENTH CENTURY / Good, James I – New York: Board of Publication of the Reformed Church in America, 1911 – 2mf – us A.T.L.A. [240]

HISTORY OF THE REFORMED CHURCH OF GERMANY, 1620-1890 / Good, James Isaac – (Includes index) – Reading, PA: Daniel Miller, 1894 – 2mf – 9 – 0-8370-4706-4 – 1985-2706 – us A.T.L.A. [240]

HISTORY OF THE REFORMED PRESBYTERIAN CHURCH / Glasgow, W. Melanchthon – 1888 – 1 – $50.00 – us Presbyterian [240]

HISTORY OF THE REFORMED PRESBYTERIAN CHURCH IN AMERICA : WITH SKETCHES OF ALL HER MINISTRY, CONGREGATIONS, MISSIONS, INSTITUTIONS, PUBLICATIONS, ETC., AND EMBELLISHED WITH OVER FIFTY PORTRAITS AND ENGRAVINGS / Glasgow, William Melancthon – Baltimore: Hill & Harvey, 1888 – 2mf – us A.T.L.A. [240]

HISTORY OF THE REGULAR BAPTISTS / Coffey, Achilles – 1877 – 1 – 6.30 – us Baptist [240]

THE HISTORY OF THE REIGN OF TIPU SULTAN.. / Husain Ali, Kirmani – Trans. from an original Persian ms...by Col. W. Miles. London, Printed for the Oriental Translation Fund of Great Britain and Ireland; Paris: Sold by Wm. H. Allen. 1844. xv,291p – 1 – us U.W. Library [956]

HISTORY OF THE REIGNS OF LOUIS XVIII AND CHARLES X / Crowe, Eyre Evans – London: R. Bentley, 1854. 2v – 1 – us U.W. Library [944]

THE HISTORY OF THE RELIGION OF ISRAEL : AN OLD TESTAMENT PRIMER / Toy, Crawford Howell – (Includes bibliographies and index) – Boston: Unitarian Sunday-School Society, 1910, c1882 – 1mf – 9 – 0-8370-9321-X – 1986-3321 – us A.T.L.A. [270]

HISTORY OF THE RELIGIOUS SOCIETY OF FRIENDS... / Janney, Samuel M – Philadelphia: T.E. Zell, 1867, c1859-c1867 – 5mf – us A.T.L.A. [240]

HISTORY OF THE RENSSELAER POLYTECHNIC INSTITUTE, 1824-1894 / Ricketts, Palmer Chamberlain – New York: J. Wiley & Sons, 1895.x,193p. illus – 1 – us U.W. Library [370]

HISTORY OF THE REVEREND MOTHER SACRED HEART OF JESUS : NEE TEZENAS OF MONTCEL, SECOND SUPERIOR-GENERAL OF THE CONGREGATION OF THE SISTERS OF ST. JOSEPH OF LYONS / Rivaux, Jean Joseph, Abbe – Montreal: Messenger Press, 1910 – 1mf – 9 – 0-8370-6937-8 – 1986-0937 – us A.T.L.A. [920]

HISTORY OF THE REVISED VERSION OF THE NEW TESTAMENT / Hemphill, Samuel – London: Eliot Stock, 1906. 1 fiche – 9 – us A.T.L.A. [240]

HISTORY OF THE REVISIONS OF THE DISCIPLINE OF THE METHODIST EPISCOPAL CHURCH / Sherman, David – 1874 – 1 – us A.T.L.A. [240]

HISTORY OF THE RHINELAND: PAMPHLET COLLECTION – 1915-1944 – 3r – 1 – CSUXANS8664-B – us Hoover Inst Photo [943]

HISTORY OF THE RISE AND FALL OF THE SLAVE POWER IN AMERICA / Wilson, Henry – 3v. 1872-77 – 1r – 1 – us Ross [976]

THE HISTORY OF THE RISE AND PROGRESS OF POETRY THROUGH IT'S SEVERAL SPECIES / Brown, J – Newcastle, 1764 – 3mf – 9 – ne IDC [420]

HISTORY OF THE RISE AND PROGRESS OF THE ALTON RIOTS, CULMINATING IN THE DEATH OF REV. ELIJAH P. LOVEJOY, 7 NOV 1837 / Tanner, Henry – 1838 – 1 – $50.00 – us Presbyterian [920]

HISTORY OF THE RISE AND PROGRESS OF THE BAPTISTS IN VIRGINIA / Semple, R B – 1810 – 1 – 16.45 – us Baptist [240]

THE HISTORY OF THE RISE, INCREASE, AND PROGRESS OF THE CHRISTIAN PEOPLE CALLED QUAKERS / Sewel, W – London, 1722 – Dfl91.00 – ne Slangenburg [240]

HISTORY OF THE RISE OF THE HUGUENOTS OF FRANCE / Baird, Henry Martyn – New York: Scribner, 1896, c1879 – 3mf – us A.T.L.A. [240]

HISTORY OF THE RISE, PROGRESS, GENIUS, AND CHARACTER OF AMERICAN PRESBYTERIANISM : TOGETHER WITH A REVIEW OF "THE CONSTITUTIONAL HISTORY OF THE PRESBYTERIAN CHURCH IN THE UNITED STATES OF AMERICA, BY CHAS. HODGE, D.D...." / Hill, William – Washington City: J. Gideon, Jr., 1839 – 1mf – us A.T.L.A. [240]

HISTORY OF THE ROCK PRESBYTERIAN CHURCH IN CECIL CO., MD / Johns, J H – 1872 – 1 – $50.00 – us Presbyterian [240]

HISTORY OF THE ROCKY SPRING CHURCH / Wylie, Samuel S et al – 1895 – 1 – $50.00 – us Presbyterian [240]

A HISTORY OF THE ROMAN CATHOLIC CHURCH IN THE UNITED STATES / O'Gorman, Thomas – New York: Christian Literature, 1895. (The american church series; v9) – 2mf – us A.T.L.A. [240]

THE HISTORY OF THE ROYAL-SOCIETY / Spratt, T – M 408. 1667 – 9 – ne IDC [941]

HISTORY OF THE RUHR: PAMPHLET COLLECTION – 1920-1949 – 2r – 1 – CSUXANS8670-B – us Hoover Inst Photo [943]

HISTORY OF THE SAAR VALLEY: PAMPHLET COLLECTION – 1919-1955 – 2r – 1 – CSUXANS8671-B – us Hoover Inst Photo [943]

HISTORY OF THE SABBATH AND FIRST DAY OF THE WEEK / Andrews, J N & Conradi, LR – Washington, D.C.: Review and Herald, c1912 – 2mf – us A.T.L.A. [240]

HISTORY OF THE SACRAMENTO VALLEY / Wooldridge, J W – Chicago: Pioneer Historical Publ. Co., 1931. v1-2, California Reel 5. v3, California Reel 6.(The Cox Library Collection) – 5 – us Americana [978]

THE HISTORY OF THE SACRAMENTO VALLEY / Woolridge, J W – Sacramento Co, CA. v1-3. 1931 – 1r – 1 – $50.00 – B40253 – us Library Micro [978]

HISTORY OF THE SAN FERNANDO VALLEY / Keffer, Frank M – Glendale: Stillman Printing Co., 1934. California Reel 19. (The Cox Library Collection) – 5 – us Americana [978]

A HISTORY OF THE SANDY CREEK BAPTIST ASSN., NORTH CAROLINA, FROM ITS ORGANIZATION, 1758-1858 / Purefoy, George W – 1 – 12.00 – us Baptist [240]

A HISTORY OF THE SCOTCH PRESBYTERIAN CHURCH, ST GABRIEL STREET, MONTREAL / Campbell, Robert, 1835-1921 – Montreal: W. Drysdale, 1887. 00397. (Pre-1900 Canadiana) – 9 – cn C.I.H.M. [240]

HISTORY OF THE SCOTTISH EPISCOPAL CHURCH : FROM THE REVOLUTION TO THE PRESENT TIME / Lawson, John Parker – Edinburgh: Gallie and Bayley, 1843 – 2mf – us A.T.L.A. [240]

HISTORY OF THE SECOND EMPIRE IN FRANCE PAMPHLET COLLECTION – 1869-1928 – 1 reel – 1 – CSUXANQ4880-B – us Hoover Inst Photo [944]

HISTORY OF THE SEPARATE BAPTIST CHURCH, WITH A NARRATIVE OF OTHER DENOMINATIONS / Scott, Morgan – 1901 – 1 – 11.48 – us Baptist [240]

HISTORY OF THE SETTLEMENT OF UPPER CANADA (ONTARIO): WITH SPECIAL REFERENCE TO THE BAY QUINTE / Canniff, William – Toronto: Dudley & Burns, 1869. 00468. (Pre-1900 Canadiana) – 9 – cn C.I.H.M. [971]

HISTORY OF THE SEVENTH DAY BAPTISTS, 1802-1865 / Bailey, James – 1 – 11.27 – us Baptist [240]

HISTORY OF THE SHAFTSBURY BAPTIST ASSOCIATION, VERMONT, 1781-1853 / Wright, Stevens – 1 – 16.66 – us Baptist [240]

HISTORY OF THE SIGNAL CORPS DEVELOPMENT OF U.S. ARMY RADAR EQUIPMENT / U.S. Army. Signal Corps – 1943, 1945. 3 v. illus., charts, maps, photos. Pts. 2 and 3 prepared by Capt. Harry M. Davis. 1 reel – 1 – 22.00 – us L of C Photodup [621]

A HISTORY OF THE SO-CALLED JANSENIST CHURCH OF HOLLAND : WITH A SKETCH OF ITS EARLIER ANNALS, AND SOME ACCOUNT OF THE BROTHERS OF THE COMMON LIFE / Neale, John Mason – Oxford: J.H. and J. Parker, 1858 – 1mf – us A.T.L.A. [240]

HISTORY OF THE SOMBANSI RAJ AND THE ESTATE OF PARTABGARH IN OUDH / Tholal, Pundit Bishambhar Nath – (Filmed with: Carnegy, P A historical sketch of Fyzabad Tehsil. Lucknot, 1870) – Cawnpore, 1900 – us Res Libr [950]

HISTORY OF THE SOMONAUK UNITED PRESBYTERIAN CHURCH / Patten & Graham – Chicago: 1928. Illinois Reel 22. (The Cox Library Collection) – 5 – us Americana [978]

HISTORY OF THE SOUTH CAROLINA COLLEGE, FROM ITS INCORPORATION, DEC. 19, 1801 TO DEC. 19, 1865, INCLUDING SKETCHES OF ITS PRESIDENTS AND PROFESSORS / Laborde, Maximilian – 2nd ed. Charleston: Walker Evans & Cogswell, Printers, 1874. xliii, 596p. With appendix and prefaced by a life of the author – 1 – us U.W. Library [370]

A HISTORY OF THE SPIDERS OF GREAT BRITAIN AND IRELAND / Blackwall, J – 1861 and 1864 – 1. 84.00; ; 7 – uk Microform Academic [590]

A HISTORY OF THE SPIDERS OF GREAT BRITAIN AND IRELAND / Blackwall, J – 2v. Z-2162 2. 1860-1864 – 8 – ne IDC [590]

THE HISTORY OF THE SQUARES OF LONDON, TOPOGRAPHICAL & HISTORICAL / Chancellor, E Beresford – London: K. Paul, Trench, Trubner & Co., 1907. xvii,420p. illus – 1 – us U.W. Library [941]

HISTORY OF THE STATE OF CALIFORNIA AND BIOGRAPHICAL RECORD OF COAST COUNTIES / Guinn, J M – Chicago: Chapman Publ. Co., 1904. California Reel 4. (The Cox Library Collection) – 5 – us Americana [978]

HISTORY OF THE STATE OF CALIFORNIA AND BIOGRAPHICAL RECORD OF COAST COUNTIES / Gunn, J M – CA, 1904 – 1r – 1 – $50.00 – B40203 – us Library Micro [978]

HISTORY OF THE STATE OF CALIFORNIA AND BIOGRAPHICAL RECORD OF OAKLAND AND ENVIRONS / Guinn, J M – Los Angeles: Historic Record Co., 1907. 2v. California Reel 11. (The Cox Library Collection) – 5 – us Americana [978]

HISTORY OF THE STATE OF CALIFORNIA AND BIOGRAPHICAL RECORD OF SAN JOAQUIN VALLEY / Guinn, J M – Chicago: Chapman Publ. Co., 1905. California Reel 5. (The Cox Library Collection) – 5 – us Americana [978]

HISTORY OF THE STATE OF CALIFORNIA AND BIOGRAPHICAL RECORD OF SANTA CRUZ, SAN BENITO, MONTEREY AND SAN LUIS OBISPO COUNTIES / Guinn, J M – Chicago: Chapman Publ. Co., 1903. California Reel 8. (The Cox Library Collection) – 5 – us Americana [978]

HISTORY OF THE STATE OF CALIFORNIA AND BIOGRAPHICAL RECORD OF THE SACRAMENTO VALLEY / Guinn, J M – Chicago: Chapman Publ. Co., 1906. California Reel 4. (The Cox Library Collection) – 5 – us Americana [978]

THE HISTORY OF THE STATE OF GEORGIA FROM 1850 TO 1881 – 1881. Biog. and hist. sketches.12 fiches. F-0099 – 9 – us A.G.L.L. [978]

HISTORY OF THE STATE OF KANSAS / Andreas, A T – Chicago, 1883. Kansas Reel 4. (The Cox Library Collection) – 5 – us Americana [978]

HISTORY OF THE STATE OF NEBRASKA – Chicago, 1882. Nebraska Reel 1.(The Cox Library Collection) – 5 – us Americana [978]

HISTORY OF THE STATE OF OKLAHOMA / Hill, Luther B – Chicago: Lewis Publ. Co., 1908. 2v. Oklahoma Reel 1. (The Cox Library Collection) – 5 – us Americana [978]

A HISTORY OF THE STATE OF OKLAHOMA AND ITS PEOPLE – New York: Lewis Historical Publ. Co., 1929. 3v.Oklahoma Reel 1. (The Cox Library Collection) – 5 – us Americana [978]

A HISTORY OF THE STRUGGLE FOR SLAVERY EXTENSION OR RESTRICTION IN THE UNITED STATES : FROM THE DECLARATION OF INDEPENDENCE TO THE PRESENT DAY / Greeley, Horace – New York, 1856 – 1r – 1 – us Ross [976]

HISTORY OF THE STUDY OF THEOLOGY / Briggs, Charles Augustus; ed by Briggs, Emilie Grace – London: Duckworth, 1916 – 1mf – us A.T.L.A. [240]

HISTORY OF THE SUPREME COURT OF THE TERRITORY AND STATE OF WASHINGTON. / Reinhart, Caleb S – n.p., 193?. 148p. LL-1353 – 1 – us L of C Photodup [340]

THE HISTORY OF THE SWEDES / Geijer, Eric Gustave – London: Whittaker, [1845?] – 4mf – us A.T.L.A. [948]

HISTORY OF THE SWEDES OF ILLINOIS / Olson & Engberg – Chicago: Engberg-Holmberg Publ. Co., 1908. Illinois Reel 10. (The Cox Library Collection) – 5 – us Americana [978]

HISTORY OF THE SWEDISH BAPTISTS IN SWEDEN AND AMERICA : BEING AN ACCOUNT OF THE ORIGIN, PROGRESS AND RESULTS OF THAT MISSIONARY WORK DURING THE LAST HALF OF THE NINETEENTH CENTURY / Schroeder, Gustavus W – Greater New York: G. Schroeder, 1898 – 1mf – us A.T.L.A. [305]

HISTORY OF THE SWISS REFORMED CHURCH SINCE THE REFORMATION / Good, James I – Philadelphia: Publication and Sunday School Board of the Reformed Church in the United States, 1913 – 2mf – us A.T.L.A. [240]

A HISTORY OF THE TEMPLE OF JERUSALEM / Jalal-al-Din, al Suyuti – 1836 – 1 – uk Microform Academic [240]

HISTORY OF THE TERRITORY OF WISCONSIN / Strong, Moses M – Madison: Democrat Printing Co., 1885. Wisconsin Reel 1. (The Cox Library Collection) – 5 – us Americana [978]

A HISTORY OF THE TEXTUAL CRITICISM OF THE NEW TESTAMENT / Vincent, Marvin Richardson – New York: Macmillan, 1899. 1 fiche – 9 – us A.T.L.A. [240]

A HISTORY OF THE THEOLOGY OF THE DISCIPLES OF CHRIST / Kirk, Hiram van – St. Louis: Christian Publishing Co., 1907 – 1mf – us A.T.L.A. [240]

HISTORY OF THE THIRD REPUBLIC IN FRANCE–1870 TO 1940–PAMPHLET COLLECTION – 1???-1984 – 1 reel – 1 – CSUXANQ4891-B – us Hoover Inst Photo [944]

HISTORY OF THE THIRTY YEARS' WAR / Gindely, Anton – New York: Putnam, 1884 – 3mf – us A.T.L.A. [949]

HISTORY OF THE THIRTY YEARS' WAR, COMPLETE: HISTORY OF THE REVOLT OF THE NETHERLANDS, TO THE CONFEDERACY OF THE GUEUX / Schiller, Friedrich von – Trans. from the German by Rev. A.J.W. Morrison. London: Bell and Daldy, 1873. vii,519p – 1 – us U.W. Library [943]

HISTORY OF THE TOWN OF CANTERBURY 1727-1912 / Lyford, James O – (Vol. 1. Narrative. (New Hampshire Reel 6). 5. Vol. 2. Genealogy. (New Hampshire Reel 7). 5) – Concord, Rumford Press, 1912. 2 Vols. (The Cox Library Collection) – 5 – us Americana [978]

HISTORY OF THE TOWN OF CORNISH / Child, William H – With genealogical record. Concord, Rumford Press, 1910. Vol. 1 (Narrative) and Vol. 2 (Genealogy), New Hampshire Reel 8. (The Cox Library Collection) – 5 – us Americana [978]

HISTORY OF THE TOWN OF GOFFSTOWN 1733-1920 / Hadley, George P – (Vol. 1. Narrative. 5. Vol. 2. Genealogy. 5) – Concord. Published by the Town, 1922. New Hampshire Reel 5. (The Cox Library Collection) – 5 – us Americana [978]

HISTORY OF THE TOWN OF HAMPTON FALLS 1640-1900 / Brown, Warren – Manchester, John B. Clarke Co., 1900. New Hampshire Reel 7. (The Cox Library Collection) – 5 – us Americana [978]

HISTORY OF THE TOWN OF HOLLIS / Worcester, Samuel T – From its first settlement to 1879. Nashua, Press of O. C. Moore, 1879. New Hampshire Reel 4. (The Cox Library Collection) – 5 – us Americana [978]

THE HISTORY OF THE TOWN OF LITCHFIELD, CONNECTICUT, 1720-1920 / Litchfield County. Connecticut – By Alain C. White, 1920.11 fiches. F-0084 – 9 – us A.G.L.L. [920]

HISTORY OF THE TOWN OF MAMARONECK IN THE COUNTY OF WESTCHESTER AND STATE OF NEW YORK / De Lancey, Edward Floyd – New York: s.n., 1886. 04218. (Pre-1900 Canadiana) – 9 – cn C.I.H.M. [971]

HISTORY OF THE TOWN OF PITTSFORD / Caverly, A M – Biographical sketches and family records. Rutland: Tuttle and Co., 1872. Vermont Reel 8. (The Cox Library Collection) – 5 – us Americana [978]

HISTORY OF THE TOWN OF RINDGE 1736-1874 / Stearns, Ezra Scollay – With genealogical register. Boston, George H. Ellis, 1875. New Hampshire Reel 2. (The Cox Library Collection) – 5 – us Americana [978]

HISTORY OF THE TOWN OF ROCKINGHAM / Hayes, Lyman S – Including the villages of Bellows Falls, Saxtons River, Rockingham, Cambridgeport, and Bartonsville. Bellows Falls, published by the town, 1907. Vermont Reel 9. (The Cox Library Collection) – 5 – us Americana [978]

HISTORY OF THE TOWN OF SPRINGFIELD / Hubbard & Dartt – Genealogical record. Boston, George H. Walker and Co., 1895. Vermont Reel 10. (The Cox Library Collection) – 5 – us Americana [978]

HISTORY OF THE TOWN OF WAITSFIELD / Jones, Matt B – With family genealogies. Boston, George E. Littlefield, 1909. Vermont Reel 9. (The Cox Library Collection) – 5 – us Americana [978]

HISTORY OF THE TOWN OF WILTON / Livermore & Putman – With genealogical register. Lowell: Marden and Rowell, Printers, 1888. New Hampshire Reel 4. (The Cox Library Collection) – 5 – us Americana [978]

A HISTORY OF THE TOWNSHIPS OF BYBERRY AND MORELAND IN PHILADELPHIA / Martindale – 1904. Pennsylvania Reel 36. (The Cox Library Collection) – 5 – us Americana [978]

HISTORY OF THE TRANQUEBAR MISSION : WORKED OUT FROM THE ORIGINAL PAPERS / Fenger, J Ferd – Tranquebar: Evangelical Lutheran Mission Press, 1863 – 1mf – 9 – 0-8370-7137-2 – 1986-1137 – us A.T.L.A. [240]

HISTORY OF THE TRINIDAD SECTOR AND BASE COMMAND / U.S. Army. Caribbean Defense Command. Historical Section – Lt. Robert A. Johnston and Cap't. James C. Shoultz, Jr. Port-of-Spain. 1945-47. 5v. illus., charts, maps, photos – 1 reel – 1 – $32.00 – us L of C Photodup [355]

THE HISTORY OF THE UNION BANK OF SCOTLAND / Rait, Robert Sangster – Glasgow, J. Smith, 1930 – 1 – us U.W. Library [941]

A HISTORY OF THE UNITARIANS AND THE UNIVERSALISTS IN THE UNITED STATES / Allen, Joseph Henry & Eddy, Richard – New York: Christian Literature, 1894. (The American church history series; v10) – 2mf – us A.T.L.A. [240]

HISTORY OF THE UNITED STATES ARMED FORCES IN KOREA, AUG 1945-MAY 1948 / U.S. Army. Office of the Chief of Military History – v1-4. 1948 – 1 – $87.00 – us L of C Photodup [977]

HISTORY OF THE UNITED STATES FOOD ADMINISTRATION / Mullendore, William C – 1917-19. 1941. 399p – 1 – 35.00r – us Hoover Inst Photo [977]

HISTORY OF THE UNITED STATES MARINE CORPS / U.S. Marine Corps. Historical Division – Edwin N. McClellan. Washington, D.C. 1925-1934. 2 v – 1 – us NY Public [355]

THE HISTORY OF THE UNIVERSITY OF DUBLIN : FROM ITS FOUNDATION TO THE END OF THE EIGHTEENTH CENTURY: WITH AN APPENDIX OF ORIGINAL DOCUMENTS WHICH, FOR THE MOST PART, ARE PRESERVED IN THE COLLEGE / Stubbs, John William – Dublin: Hodges, Figgis; London: Longmans, Green, 1889 – 1mf – us A.T.L.A. [370]

HISTORY OF THE UPPER MISSISSIPPI VALLEY / Neill, Edward D – Outlines of the history of Minnesota and state education. Minneapolis: Minnesota Historical Co., 1881. Minnesota Reel 3. (The Cox Library Collection) – 5 – us Americana [978]

HISTORY OF THE UPPER OHIO VALLEY – Madison: 1891. Vols. 1-2. Mississippi Reel 8. (The Cox Library Collection) – 5 – us Americana [978]

HISTORY OF THE UPPER OHIO VALLEY – With historical account of Columbiana County. Madison, 1891. 2v. Ohio Reel 22. (The Cox Library Collection) – 5 – us Americana [978]

HISTORY OF THE U.S. ARMY MILITARY GOVERNMENT IN KOREA, SEP 1945-30 JUN 1946 / Korea. (Territory under U.S. Occupation, 1945-). Military Governor – v. 1-4. 1946-47 – 1 – 38.00 – us L of C Photodup [950]

HISTORY OF THE U.S. STRATEGIC BOMBING SURVEY(EUROPEAN). 1944-45. V. 1-2. 1946 / U.S. War Department. Office of the Administrative Assistant – 7 – 41.00 – us L of C Photodup [943]

HISTORY OF THE U.S. STRATEGIC BOMBING SURVEY(PACIFIC). 1945-46. V. 1-2. 1946 / U.S. War Department. Office of the Administrative Assistant – 1 – 26.00 – us L of C Photodup [950]

A HISTORY OF THE USE OF INCENSE IN THE DIVINE WORSHIP / Atchley, F – London, 1909 – 9mf – 8 – Dfl32.00 – ne Slangenburg [200]

HISTORY OF THE VIETNAM WAR / ed by Pike, Douglas – (Unit 1 Grand Strategy and General Assessment of the War $3415; Unit 2 General History of the Vietnam War $3715; Unit 3 Topical History of the Vietnam War $3450; Unit 4 Political Settlement Efforts; Unit 5 National Liberation Front (Viet Cong); Unit 6 Democratic Republic of Vietnam (North Vietnam) Unit 7 Republic of Vietnam (South Vietnam); Unit 8 Indochina; Unit 9 Asian Region During the Vietnam War; Unit 10 Chronology of the Vietnam War) – 1 – $30,000 complete collection – us UMI [950]

HISTORY OF THE WALDENSES OF ITALY : FROM THEIR ORIGIN TO THE REFORMATION / Comba, Emilio – London: Truslove & Shirley, 1889 – 1mf – us A.T.L.A. [240]

HISTORY OF THE WAR BETWEEN GERMANY AND FRANCE, WITH BIOGRAPHICAL SKETCHES OF THE PRINCIPAL PERSONAGES. / McCabe, James Dabney – Philadelphia, 1871. 815p. illus. fold. maps – 1 – us U.W. Library [944]

HISTORY OF THE WAR DEPARTMENT, 1879 / Ingersoll – Military Books reel 4. (Cox Library Collection) – 5 – us Americana [975]

HISTORY OF THE WAR IN SOUTH AFRICA, 1899-1902 / Maurice, John Frederick – London. 4v. 1906-10 – 2r – 1 – us Ross [960]

HISTORY OF THE WAYANG PURWA / Hardjowirogo, Raden – SE-6933 1. 1958 – 9 – ne IDC [950]

HISTORY OF THE WELSH BAPTISTS, FROM THE YEAR 1763 TO THE YEAR 1770 / Davis, J – 1 – 7.42 – us Baptist [240]

HISTORY OF THE WESLEYAN METHODIST CHURCH OF SOUTH AFRICA / Whiteside, Joseph – London: E. Stock, 1906. 479p. ill. Includes index – 1 – us U.W. Library [240]

HISTORY OF THE WEST AFRICA MISSION / Nassau, Robert Hamill – 1919 – 1 – $100.00 – us Presbyterian [240]

A HISTORY OF THE WEST INDIES... / Coke, Thomas – Liverpool. 3v. 1808-11 – 1r – 1 – us Ross [972]

HISTORY OF THE WESTERN RESERVE / Upton, Harriet Taylor – Chicago: Lewis Publ. Co., 1910. Vol. 1. Mississippi Reel 5; Vols. 2-3. Mississippi Reel 6. (The Cox Library Collection) – 5 – us Americana [978]

HISTORY OF THE WILLAMETTE VALLEY – Chicago, 1927. v2. Oregon Reel 6; v3. Oregon Reel 7. The Cox Library Collection – 5 – us Americana [978]

HISTORY OF THE WOMAN'S TEMPERANCE CRUSADE / Wittenmyer, Annie Turner – 1882 – 9 – us A.T.L.A. [240]

THE HISTORY OF THE WOMEN'S CLUB MOVEMENT IN AMERICA / Croly, Jane Cunningham – New York: H.G. Allen & Co., c1898. illus – 1 – us U.W. Library [305]

A HISTORY OF THE YEAR: WITH ESPECIAL REFERENCE TO CANADIAN AFFAIRS – Toronto: Mail Print. Co., 1894. 05644. (Pre-1900 Canadiana) – 9 – cn C.I.H.M. [971]

HISTORY OF THE YOUNG MEN'S CHRISTIAN ASSOCIATION. VOLUME 1, THE FOUNDING OF THE ASSOCIATION, 1844-1855 / Doggett, L L – New York: International Committee of Young Men's Christian Associations, 1896 – 1mf – us A.T.L.A. [240]

THE HISTORY OF THOMAS HICKATHRIFT / Hickathrift, Thomas – 1885 – 1 – us I.U. Libraries [390]

HISTORY OF THRACE PAMPHLET COLLECTION – 1919-1922 – 1 reel – 1 – CSUXANL5818-B – us Hoover Inst Photo [947]

HISTORY OF TIOGA, CHEMUNG, TOMPKINS, AND SCHUYLER COUNTIES – Biographical sketches. Philadelphia, 1879. New York Reel 34. (The Cox Library Collection) – 5 – us Americana [978]

HISTORY OF TIOGA COUNTY / R.C. Brown and Co – 1897. Pennsylvania Reel 39. The Cox Library Collection – 5 – us Americana [978]

A HISTORY OF TRAVAILLE INTO VIRGINIA / ed by Major, R H – Hakluyt Society. 1610-12 – 7 – uk Microform Academic [910]

HISTORY OF TRIAL BY JURY / Forsyth, William – 2d ed. New York: Cockcroft, 1878. 388p. LL-112 – 1 – us L of C Photodup [340]

HISTORY OF TRINIDAD 1838 – In Trinidad Almanac and Pocket Register for 1840 – 1 reel – 1 – $68.00 – cn Library Assoc [972]

HISTORY OF TRINIDAD WITH TRINIDAD ALMANAC / Joseph, Edward L – 1840 – 1 – us UMI [972]

THE HISTORY OF TRINITY CHURCH & ITS FORERUNNERS: THORN CHAPEL, THORN SCHOOL & BAREKMAN'S CHAPEL – By June Barekman. Item L. 18p.SW16-0113 – 5 – us A.G.L.L. [240]

HISTORY OF TRUMBUL AND MAHONING COUNTIES / H.Z. Williams and Brothers – Biographical sketches. 1882. Vol 1, Ohio Reel 62; Vol 2, Ohio Reel 63. The Cox Library Collection – 5 – us Americana [978]

HISTORY OF TUCKER COUNTY / Maxwell, Hu – Biographical sketches. Kingwood, Preston Publishing Co., 1884. West Virginia Reel 6. (The Cox Library Collection) – 5 – us Americana [978]

HISTORY OF TUGALO BAPTIST ASSOCIATION, GEORGIA / Goode, J F – 1924 – 1 – 7.98 – us Baptist [240]

HISTORY OF TULARE AND KINGS COUNTIES, CALIFORNIA / Historic Record Co – Los Angeles, 1913. California Reel 36. (The Cox Library Collection) – 5 – us Americana [978]

HISTORY OF TULARE COUNTY – Chicago, 1926. California Reel 36. The Cox Library Collection – 5 – us Americana [978]

HISTORY OF TURKEY DURING THE EARLY TWENTIETH CENTURY PAMPHLET COLLECTION – 1909-1922 – 1 reel – 1 – CSUXANQ7727-B – us Hoover Inst Photo [947]

HISTORY OF TURKEY FROM 1918 TO 1960 PAMPHLET COLLECTION – 1919-1958 – 2r – 1 – CSUXANQ7800-B – us Hoover Inst Photo [947]

HISTORY OF TURKEY PAMPHLET COLLECTION – 1912-1946 – 1 reel – 1 – CSUXANQ7710-B – us Hoover Inst Photo [947]

HISTORY OF TUSCARAWAS COUNTY – Chicago: 1884. Ohio Reel 63. (The Cox Library Collection) – 5 – us Americana [978]

THE HISTORY OF TYTHES / Selden, J – 1618 – 1 – 18.72 – us Baptist [240]

A HISTORY OF UGANDA LAND AND SURVEYS AND OF THE UGANDA LAND AND SURVEY DEPARTMENT / Thomas, Harold Beken & Spencer, A E – Entebbe: Uganda Govt Press, 1938 – 1 – us Res Libr [960]

HISTORY OF ULSTER COUNTY / Sylvester, Nathaniel B – Biographical sketches. Philadelphia: Everts and Peck, 1880. New York Reel 35. (The Cox Library Collection) – 5 – us Americana [978]

HISTORY OF UNION AND MIDDLESEX COUNTIES / Clayton, W Woodford – Biographical sketches. Philadelphia, Everts and Peck, 1882. New Jersey Reel 6. (The Cox Library Collection) – 5 – us Americana [978]

HISTORY OF UNION COUNTY / Ricord, F W – Newark, East Jersey History Co., 1897. New Jersey Reel 7. (The Cox Library Collection) – 5 – us Americana [978]

HISTORY OF UNION COUNTY ITS PEOPLE, INDUSTRIES AND INSTITUTIONS / Curry, W L – Indianapolis: B. F. Bowen and Co., 1915. Ohio Reel 64. (The Cox Library Collection) – 5 – us Americana [978]

A HISTORY OF UPPER CANADA COLLEGE, 1829-1892: WITH CONTRIBUTIONS BY OLD UPPER CANADA COLLEGE BOYS:.. – Comp. and ed. by Geo. Dickson & G. Mercer Adam. Toronto: Rowsell & Hutchison, 1893. 02659. (Pre-1900 Canadiana) – 9 – cn C.I.H.M. [971]

HISTORY OF UPPER MONONGAHELA VALLEY / Butcher, Bernard L – Genealogical and personal. New York, Lewis Historical Publishing Co., 1912. Vol. 1. West Virginia Reel 1; Vols. 2-3. West Virginia Reel 2. (The Cox Library Collection) – 5 – us Americana [978]

HISTORY OF UPSHUR COUNTY / Cutright, W B – 1907. West Virginia Reel 6. (The Cox Library Collection) – 5 – us Americana [978]

HISTORY OF UTAH 1540-1887 / Bancroft, Hubert Howe – San Francisco: History Co., 1890. Utah reel 1. (Cox Library Collection) – 5 – us Americana [978]

A HISTORY OF VAGRANTS AND VAGRANCY, AND BEGGARS AND BEGGING / Ribton-Turner, Charles James – London: Chapman and Hall, 1887. xx,720p. plates – 1 – us U.W. Library [300]

HISTORY OF VAN WERT AND MERCER COUNTIES / R. Sutton and Co – Biographical sketches. Wapakoneta, 1882. Ohio Reel 64. The Cox Library Collection – 5 – us Americana [978]

HISTORY OF VAN WERT COUNTY AND REPRESENTATIVE CITIZENS / Gilliland, Thaddeus S – Chicago: Richmond-Arnold Publ. Co., 1906. Ohio Reel 65. (The Cox Library Collection) – 5 – us Americana [978]

HISTORY OF VANDERBURGH COUNTY / Brant, Fuller and Co – Historical and biographical sketches. Chicago, 1889. Indiana Reel 28. (The Cox Library Collection) – 5 – us Americana [920]

HISTORY OF VARTAN / Elisaeus – 1830 – 1 – uk Microform Academic [900]

HISTORY OF VENANGO COUNTY PAST AND PRESENT / Brown, Runk and Co – Chicago, 1890. Pennsylvania Reel 40. (The Cox Library Collection) – 5 – us Americana [978]

HISTORY OF VENTURA COUNTY / Sheridan, Sol. N – Chicago: S.J. Clarke Co., 1926. 2v. California reel 36. (Cox Library Collection) – 5 – us Americana [978]

HISTORY OF VERMILION COUNTY / Beckwith, H W – Biographical sketches. Chicago: H. H. Hill and Co., 1879. Illinois Reel 57. (The Cox Library Collection) – 5 – us Americana [978]

HISTORY OF VERMILION COUNTY / Jones, Lottie E – Chicago: Pioneer Publ. Co., 1911. Vols. 1-2. Illinois Reel 58. (The Cox Library Collection) – 5 – us Americana [978]

HISTORY OF VERMILION COUNTY / Williams, Jack M – Indianapolis: Historical Publ. Co., 1930. Vols. 1-2. Illinois Reel 58. (The Cox Library Collection) – 5 – us Americana [978]

HISTORY OF VERMONT-THE GREEN MOUNTAIN STATE / Crockett, Walter H – New York, Century History Co., 1921. Vols. 1-5. Vermont Reel 1. (The Cox Library Collection) – 5 – us Americana [978]

HISTORY OF VERNON COUNTY / Brown and Co – St. Louis, 1887.Missouri Reel 32. (The Cox Library Collection) – 5 – us Americana [978]

HISTORY OF VERNON COUNTY – Springfield: 1884. Wisconsin Reel 20. (The Cox Library Collection) – 5 – us Americana [978]

HISTORY OF VERNON COUNTY PAST AND PRESENT / Johnson, J B – Chicago: C.F. Cooper and Co., 1911. 2v.Missouri Reel 32. (The Cox Library Collection) – 5 – us Americana [978]

HISTORY OF VIGO COUNTY WITH A BIOGRAPHICAL SELECTION / S.B. Nelson and Company – Chicago, 1891. Indiana Reel 28. The Cox Library Collection – 5 – us Americana [920]

THE HISTORY OF VOLLEYBALL IN THE UNITED STATES / Flanagan, Lance – University of Columbia, 1960 – 3mf – 9 – $13.00 – us Microform Publ [790]

HISTORY OF WABASHA COUNTY / Curtiss-Wedge, Franklyn – Winona: H.C. Cooper, Jr. and Co., 1920. Minnesota Reel 16. (The Cox Library Collection) – 5 – us Americana [978]

HISTORY OF WABASHA COUNTY AND WINONA COUNTY / H.H. Hill and Co – Chicago, 1884. Minnesota Reel 15. The Cox Library Collection – 5 – us Americana [978]

HISTORY OF WALKER COUNTY, GEORGIA / Sartain, James Alfred – v1, 1932. Indexed. 9 fiches. F-0600 – 9 – us A.G.L.L. [920]

HISTORY OF WALLA WALLA COUNTY / Lyman, W D – W.H. Lever, 1901. Washington reel 7. (Cox Library Collection) – 5 – us Americana [978]

HISTORY OF WALWORTH COUNTY / Beckwith, Albert C – Indianapolis: B. F. Bowen and Co., 1912. Vols. 1-2. Wisconsin Reel 20. (The Cox Library Collection) – 5 – us Americana [978]

HISTORY OF WALWORTH COUNTY – Chicago: 1882. Wisconsin Reel 21. (The Cox Library Collection) – 5 – us Americana [978]

HISTORY OF WAPELLO COUNTY – Chicago, 1878. Iowa Reel 40. (The Cox Library Collection) – 5 – us Americana [978]

HISTORY OF WAPELLO COUNTY / Waterman, Harrison L – Chicago: S.J. Clarke Publ. Co., 1914. 2v – 5 – us Americana [978]
HISTORY OF WARREN COUNTY – Biographical sketches. Syracuse, D. Mason and Co., 1887. Pennsylvania Reel 41. (The Cox Library Collection) – 5 – us Americana [978]
HISTORY OF WARREN COUNTY – Chicago, 1882. Ohio Reel 65. The Cox Library Collection – 5 – us Americana [978]
HISTORY OF WARREN COUNTY / Martin, W C – Chicago: S.J. Clarke Publ. Co., 1908. Iowa Reel 41. (The Cox Library Collection) – 5 – us Americana [978]
HISTORY OF WARREN COUNTY / Smith, H P – Biographical sketches. Syracuse, D. Mason and Co., 1885. New York Reel 36. (The Cox Library Collection) – 5 – us Americana [978]
HISTORY OF WARRICK, SPENCER AND PERRY COUNTIES – Historical and biographical sketches. Chicago, 1885. Indiana Reel 29. (The Cox Library Collection) – 5 – us Americana [978]
HISTORY OF WASHINGTON AND OZAUKEE COUNTIES – Chicago. Wisconsin Reel 21. (The Cox Library Collection) – 5 – us Americana [978]
HISTORY OF WASHINGTON COUNTY – Biographical sketches. Philadelphia, 1878. New York Reel 37. (The Cox Library Collection) – 5 – us Americana [978]
HISTORY OF WASHINGTON COUNTY / Burrell, Howard A – Chicago: S.J. Clarke Publ. Co., 1909. 2v. Iowa Reel 42. (The Cox Library Collection) – 5 – us Americana [978]
HISTORY OF WASHINGTON COUNTY / Crumrine, Boyd – Biographical sketches. Philadelphia, L. H. Everts and Co., 1882. Pennsylvania Reel 41. (The Cox Library Collection) – 5 – us Americana [978]
HISTORY OF WASHINGTON COUNTY / H.Z. Williams and Brothers – Biographical sketches. Philadelphia, 1881. Ohio Reel 65. The Cox Library Collection – 5 – us Americana [978]
HISTORY OF WASHINGTON COUNTY / Union Historical Co – Des Moines, 1880. Iowa Reel 41.(The Cox Library Collection) – 5 – us Americana [978]
HISTORY OF WASHINGTON COUNTY AND THE CROIX VALLEY / Neill, Edward D – Minneapolis: North Star Publ. Co., 1881.Minnesota Reel 16. (The Cox Library Collection) – 5 – us Americana [978]
HISTORY OF WASHTENAW COUNTY – Chicago, 1881. Michigan Reel 22. The Cox Library Collection – 5 – us Americana [978]
HISTORY OF WATERBURY / Lewis, Theodore G – Waterbury, Harry C. Whitehill, 1915. Vermont Reel 9. (The Cox Library Collection) – 5 – us Americana [978]
HISTORY OF WAUKESHA COUNTYK – Biographical section. Chicago: 1880. Wisconsin Reel 21. (The Cox Library Collection) – 5 – us Americana [978]
HISTORY OF WAYNE AND CLAY COUNTIES / Globe Publishing Co – Chicago, 1884. (Illinois Reel 59). (The Cox Library Collection) – 5 – us Americana [978]
HISTORY OF WAYNE COUNTY / B.F. Bowen and Co – Indianapolis, 1910. v1-2. Ohio Reel 67. The Cox Library Collection – 5 – us Americana [978]
HISTORY OF WAYNE COUNTY / Douglas, Ben – Indianapolis: Robert Douglas, Publisher, 1878. Ohio Reel 66. (The Cox Library Collection) – 5 – us Americana [978]
HISTORY OF WAYNE COUNTY / Inter-State Publishing Co – Historical and biographical sketches. Chicago, 1884. 2v. Indiana Reel 30. (The Cox Library Collection) – 5 – us Americana [920]
HISTORY OF WAYNE COUNTY / Young, Andrew W – Historical and biographical sketches. Cincinnati: Robert Clarke and Co., 1872. Indiana Reel 30. (The Cox Library Collection) – 5 – us Americana [920]
HISTORY OF WESLEYAN METHODISM / Smith, G – 2nd ed, revised [for V.1 only]. London, 1858-1861. 3v, xxiv/722p; xii/699p; xxiv/769p – 25mf – 9 – ne IDC [240]
HISTORY OF WESTCHESTER COUNTY – Earliest settlement to 1900. New York, New York History Co., 1900. New York Reel 37. (The Cox Library Collection) – 5 – us Americana [978]
HISTORY OF WESTCHESTER COUNTY / French, Alvah P – New York, Lewis Publishing Co, 1925. Vols. 1-4. New York Reel 38. (The Cox Library Collection) – 5 – us Americana [978]
HISTORY OF WESTERN NEBRASKA AND ITS PEOPLE / Shumway, Grant L – Lincoln: Western Publ. and Engraving Co., 1921. Nebraska Reel 4. (The Cox Library Collection) – 5 – us Americana [978]
HISTORY OF WESTERN OHIO AND AUGLAIZE COUNTY / Williamson, C W – Biographical sketches. Columbus: W.M. Linn and Sons, 1905. Ohio Reel 15. (The Cox Library Collection) – 5 – us Americana [978]
A HISTORY OF WESTERN TIBET, ONE OF THE UNKNOWN EMPIRES / Francke, August Hermann – London: Partridge, 1907 – 1 – us U.W. Library [950]
HISTORY OF WESTMORELAND COUNTY / Boucher, John N – New York, Lewis Publishing Co., 1906. Vol. 1. Pennsylvania Reel 42; Vols. 2-3. Pennsylvania Reel 43. (The Cox Library Collection) – 5 – us Americana [978]
HISTORY OF WHATCOM COUNTY / Roth, Lottie R – Seattle: Pioneer Historical Publ. Co., 1926. v1-2. Washington reel 7. (Cox Library Collection) – 5 – us Americana [978]
HISTORY OF WHEELING CITY AND REPRESENTATIVE CITIZENS / Cranmer, Gibson L – Chicago, Biographical Publishing Co., 1902. West Virginia Reel 4. (The Cox Library Collection) – 5 – us Americana [978]
HISTORY OF WHITE COUNTY / Inter-State Publishing Co – Chicago, 1884. Illinois Reel 60. The Cox Library Collection – 5 – us Americana [978]
HISTORY OF WHITESIDE COUNTY / Bent, Charles – Biographical sketches. Morrison, 1877. Illinois Reel 60. (The Cox Library Collection) – 5 – us Americana [978]
HISTORY OF WHITESIDE COUNTY / Davis, William W – Chicago: Pioneer Publ. Co., 1908. Vols. 1-2. Illinois Reel 61. (The Cox Library Collection) – 5 – us Americana [978]
HISTORY OF WHITMAN COUNTY / Lever, W H – 1901. Washington reel 7. (Cox Library Collection) – 5 – us Americana [978]
HISTORY OF WICHITA AND SEDGWICK COUNTIES / Bentley, OH – Chicago: C.F. Cooper and Co., 1910. 2v.Kansas Reel 12. (The Cox Library Collection) – 5 – us Americana [978]
A HISTORY OF WILKES-BARRE, LUZERNE COUNTY AND WYOMING VALLEY / Harvey, Oscar J – Wilkes-Barre, 1909. Vols. 1-2. Pennsylvania Reel 30. (The Cox Library Collection) – 5 – us Americana [978]
HISTORY OF WILL COUNTY – Biographical sketches. Chicago, 1878. Illinois Reel 61. The Cox Library Collection – 5 – us Americana [978]
HISTORY OF WILL COUNTY / Maue, August – Indianapolis: Historical Publ. Co., 1928. Vol. 1. Illinois Reel 62; Vol. 2. Illinois Reel 63. (The Cox Library Collection) – 5 – us Americana [978]
HISTORY OF WILLIAMSON COUNTY, ILLINOIS / Erwin, Milo – Herrin: The Herrin News, 1914. Illinois Reel 63. (The Cox Library Collection) – 5 – us Americana [978]
HISTORY OF WINDHAM COUNTY / Bayles, Richard M – New York: W. W. Preston and Co., 1889. Connecticut Reel 7. (The Cox Library Collection) – 5 – us Americana [978]
HISTORY OF WINDHAM COUNTY / Larned, Ellen D – Worcester, Charles Hamilton, 1874. Vols. 1-2. Connecticut Reel 7. (The Cox Library Collection) – 5 – us Americana [978]
HISTORY OF WINDSOR COUNTY / Aldrich & Holmes – With illustrations and biographical sketches. Syracuse, D. Mason and Co., 1891. Vermont Reel 10. (The Cox Library Collection) – 5 – us Americana [978]
HISTORY OF WINNEBAGO COUNTY / Harney, Richard J – Oshkosh: Allen and Hicks, 1880. Wisconsin Reel 22. (The Cox Library Collection) – 5 – us Americana [978]
HISTORY OF WINNEBAGO COUNTY / H.F. Kett and Co – Biographical sketches. Chicago, 1877. Illinois Reel 63. The Cox Library Collection – 5 – us Americana [978]
HISTORY OF WINNESHIEK AND ALLAMAKEE COUNTIES / Alexander, W E – Sioux City: Western Publ. Co., 1882. Iowa Reel 43. (The Cox Library Collection) – 5 – us Americana [978]
HISTORY OF WINONA AND OLMSTED COUNTIES / H.H. Hill and Co – Chicago, 1883. Minnesota Reel 17. The Cox Library Collection – 5 – us Americana [978]
HISTORY OF WINONA COUNTY / H.H. Hill and Co – Biographical matter. Chicago, 1883. Minnesota Reel 17. The Cox Library Collection – 5 – us Americana [978]
HISTORY OF WINONA, OLMSTED AND DODGE COUNTIES / H.H. Hill and Co – Chicago, 1884. Minnesota Reel 17. The Cox Library Collection – 5 – us Americana [978]
HISTORY OF WISCONSIN UNDER THE DOMINION OF FRANCE / Hebberd, Stephen Southric – Madison, WI: Midland Pub. Co., 1890. 05531. (Pre-1900 Canadiana) – 9 – cn C.I.H.M. [978]
THE HISTORY OF WITCHCRAFT AND DEMONOLOGY / Summers, Montague – New York: A.A. Knopf, 1926. xv,353p. (Half-title: The History of Civilization) – 1 – us U.W. Library [130]
A HISTORY OF WITCHCRAFT IN ENGLAND FROM 1558 TO 1718 / Notestein, Wallace – Washington: American Historical Association, 1911 – 2mf – us A.T.L.A. [130]
HISTORY OF WOMEN – A comprehensive collection based on the holdings of nine major libraries – 1 – us Primary [305]
HISTORY OF WOOD COUNTY / Jones & McVean – Minneapolis: H. C. Cooper and Co., 1923. Wisconsin Reel 22. (The Cox Library Collection) – 5 – us Americana [978]
HISTORY OF WYANDOT COUNTY / Leggett, Conaway and Co – Chicago: 1884. Ohio Reel 68. (The Cox Library Collection) – 5 – us Americana [978]
HISTORY OF WYANDOTTE, BUTTE COUNTY, CALIFORNIA / Dunstane, William – Butte Co, CA. 1884 – 1r – 1 – $50.00 – B40210 – us Library Micro [978]
HISTORY OF WYANDOTTE COUNTY / Morgan, PW – Chicago: Lewis Publ. Co., 1911. Kansas Reel 13.(The Cox Library Collection) – 5 – us Americana [978]
HISTORY OF WYOMING / Bartlett, IS – Chicago: S.J. Clarke Publ. Co., 1918. v1-3. Wyoming reel 1. (Cox Library Collection) – 5 – us Americana [978]
THE HISTORY OF WYOMING / Coutant, C G – Laramie: Chaplin, Spafford and Mathison, 1899. Wyoming reel 1. (Cox Library Collection) – 5 – us Americana [978]
HISTORY OF WYOMING COUNTY / F.W. Beers and Co – Biographical sketches. New York, 1880. New York Reel 39. The Cox Library Collection – 5 – us Americana [978]
HISTORY OF YATES COUNTY / Aldrich, Lewis C – Syracuse, D. Mason and Co., 1892. New York Reel 39. (The Cox Library Collection) – 5 – us Americana [978]
THE HISTORY OF YIDDISH LITERATURE IN THE NINETEENTH CENTURY / Wiener, Leo – New York: Charles Scribner, 1899. 1 fiche – 9 – us A.T.L.A. [470]
HISTORY OF YORK COUNTY / Gibson, John – F. A. Battey and Co., 1886. Pennsylvania Reel 43. (The Cox Library Collection) – 5 – us Americana [978]
HISTORY OF YORK COUNTY AND ITS PEOPLE / Sedgwick, T E – Chicago: S.J. Clarke Publ. Co., 1921. 2v. Nebraska Reel 13. (The Cox Library Collection) – 5 – us Americana [978]
HISTORY OF YUBA AND SUTTER COUNTIES / Historic Record Co – Los Angeles, 1924. Calif. reel 37. (Cox Library Collection) – 5 – us Americana [978]
THE HISTORY OF YUCATAN, FROM ITS DISCOVERY TO THE CLOSE OF THE SEVENTEENTH CENTURY / Fancourt, Charles Saint John – London: J. Murray, 1854.xvi,340p. fold. map – 1 – us U.W. Library [972]
HISTORY OF YUGOSLAVIA DURING THE AXIS OCCUPATION PAMPHLET COLLECTION – 1941-1969 – 1 reel – 1 – CSUXANQ7278-B – us Hoover Inst Photo [947]
HISTORY OF YUGOSLAVIA FROM 1918 TO 1945 PAMPHLET COLLECTION – 1919-1945 – 1 reel – 1 – CSUXANQ5784-B – us Hoover Inst Photo [947]
HISTORY OF YUGOSLAVIA FROM 1945 TO 1980 PAMPHLET COLLECTION – 1945-1975 – 1 reel – 1 – CSUXANQ7294-B – us Hoover Inst Photo [947]
HISTORY OF YUGOSLAVIA PAMPHLET COLLECTION – 1916-1955 – 1 reel – 1 – CSUXANQ5699-B – us Hoover Inst Photo [947]
History Publishing Co *see*
– HISTORY OF BUCHANAN COUNTY AND ST JOSEPH
– HISTORY OF HOLT COUNTY FROM THE TIME OF PLATTE PURCHASE TO THE END OF YEAR 1916
HISTORY TEACHER – v. 1- 1967- – 1. ; 5,6. ; 9 – apply; v.5-; v.9- – us UMI [900]
HISTORY THROUGH THE TIMES; A COLLECTION OF LEADING ARTICLES ON IMPORTANT EVENTS, 1800-1937.. / The Times. London – Selected by Sir James Marchant, K.B.E., with introd. by Geoffrey Dawson. London: Cassell and Co. Ltd., 1937 xi/619p – 1 – us U.W. Library [900]
HISTORY TODAY – (v. 19- 1969- 5,6. v. 25-1975- 9) – 1- 1951- – 1 – us UMI [900]
HISTORYCKE LISTY – (1992-98 1r per 2yrs) – Czech Republic, 1999- – 1r per y standing order – 1 – us Ross [072]
THE HISTORY...HERNANDO DE SOTO / Shipp, Barnard – 1881 – 9 – 1.50f – sp Bibl Santa Ana [910]
HIT LAB REPORTS – v.1-6. 1970-75. Superseded by HSRI Research (Highway Safety Research Institute) – 1 – us UMI [629]
HITAVADA – Bhopal, India. Jul-Sept 1966 – 1r – 1 – us L of C Photodup [072]
HITAVADA – Nagpur, India. Apr 1944-Jul 1994 – 214r – 1 – us L of C Photodup [072]
Hitchcock, A B C *see* HISTORY OF SHELBY COUNTY AND REPRESENTATIVE CITIZENS
Hitchcock, A S *see* THE GENERA OF GRASSES OF THE UNITED STATES
Hitchcock, Albert Wellman *see*
– THE PSYCHOLOGY OF JESUS
– PSYCHOLOGY OF JESUS: A STUDY OF THE DEVELOPMENT OF HIS SELF-CONSCIOUSNESS
HITCHCOCK COUNTY HERALD – Culbertson, NE. -w. Jan. 1903-Jan. 1904 – 1 – us NE Hist [071]
HITCHCOCK COUNTY NEWS – Trenton, NE. -w. Dec 1890-Nov 1891; Dec 1892; Nov 1894-Sept 1898; Apr 1899 to date – 1 – us NE Hist [071]
HITCHCOCK COUNTY NEWS – Trenton. Neb. 1891-1957 – 1 – us UMI [071]
HITCHCOCK COUNTY REPUBLICAN – Culbertson, NE. -w. Jan. 1888-Dec. 1888; Jul. 1890-Oct. 1890; Aug. 1895-Nov. 1895 – 1 – us NE Hist [071]
Hitchcock, Edward *see*
– HISTORY OF A ZOOLOGICAL TEMPERANCE CONVENTION
– THE POWER OF CHRISTIAN BENEVOLENCE: ILLUSTRATED IN THE LIFE AND LABORS OF MARY LYON
Hitchcock, Frederick L *see* HISTORY OF SCRANTON
Hitchcock, Loranus Eaton *see* POWERS AND DUTIES OF SHERIFFS, CONSTABLES, TAX COLLECTORS, AND OTHER OFFICERS IN THE NEW ENGLAND STATES
HITCHIN AND ROYSTON EXPRESS – (Also known as: Hertfordshire Express; Hitchin Gazette; The Gazette (Hitchin)) – Mar 12-Oct 8 1859; Oct 15 1859-Dec 27 1862; Jan 3 1863-Dec 30 1865; 1866-Mar 26 1870; May 2 1874; May 1875-77; 1879-80; 1950; 1980-87; Jan 8 1988-92; Jan 8-Jun 25, Jul 2-Dec 24 1993; Jul-Dec 23 1994; 1995-96 – 67 3/4r – 1 – uk British Libr Newspaper [072]
HITCHIN COMET – Luton, England. 1980- – 65+ r – 1 – uk British Libr Newspaper [072]
HITCHIN GAZETTE – England, 1980-81 – 8r – 1 – uk British Libr Newspaper [072]
HITCHIN GAZETTE *see* HITCHIN AND ROYSTON EXPRESS
Hitler, Adolf *see* SPEECH DELIVERED IN THE REICHSTAG, FEBRUARY 20TH, 1938..
HITLER OVER RUSSIA? : THE COMING FIGHT BETWEEN THE FASCIST AND SOCIALIST ARMIES / Henri, Ernst – Trans. by Michael Davidson. New York: Simon and Schuster, 1936. x,340p – 1r – 1 – us U.W. Library [940]
HITLER-JUGEND PAMPHLET COLLECTION – 19??-1982 – 1 reel – 1 – CSUXANS0349-B – us Hoover Inst Photo [320]

DER HITLERJUNGE QUEX : ROMAN / Schenzinger, Karl Aloys – Berlin: Zeitgeschichte-Verlag, W Andermann, c1932 – 1r – 1 – us U.W. Library [830]
HITLER'S FIRST FOES; A STUDY IN RELIGION AND POLITICS / Mason, John Brown – Minneapolis: Burgess Publishing Co., c1936. v,118p – 1 – us U.W. Library [320]
HITLER'S WAR / Irving, David – Selected Documents, Diaries, Interviews, etc. Index – 1 – uk Microform Academic [943]
HITYASHEVUT HA-MEKUBBAL RABBI AVRAHAM ROVIGO VA-HAVURATO BI-YERUSHALAYIM / Mann, J – v. 6. Ziyyon. Me'assef. 1934. BJ-27-21 1 – 9 – ne IDC [270]
Hitz, Alex M *see* AUTHENTIC LIST OF ALL LAND LOTTERY GRANTS MADE TO VETERANS OF THE REVOLUTIONARY WAR BY THE STATE OF GEORGIA
Hitzeroth, Carl *see* JOHANN HEERMANN (1585-1647)
Hitzig, Ferdinand *see*
- DAS BUCH HIOB UEBERSETZT UND AUSGELEGT
- DR. FERDINAND HITZIG'S VORLESUNGEN UEBER BIBLISCHE THEOLOGIE...DES ALTEN TESTAMENTS
- DAS HOHE LIED
- DER PROPHET EZECHIEL
- DER PROPHET JEREMIA
- VORLESUNGEN UEBER BIBLISCHE THEOLOGIE UND MESSIANISCHE WEISSAGUNGEN DES ALTEN TESTAMENTS
- DIE ZWOELF KLEINEN PROPHETEN

AN HIV EDUCATION NEEDS ASSESSMENT OF SELECTED TEACHER MEMBERS OF THE AMERICAN SCHOOL HEALTH ASSOCIATION AND THE AMERICAN HOME ECONOMICS ASSOCIATION / Kerr, Dianne L & Heit, Philip – 1992 – 2mf – 9 – $8.00 – us Microform Publ [613]
Hives, Frank *see* MOMO AND I
Hixson, Karen A *see* AN EPIDEMIOLOGIC INVESTIGATION OF THE RELATIONSHIP BETWEEN RELIGIOSITY, SELECTED HEALTH BEHAVIORS, AND BLOOD PRESSURE
HIYABAN – (Sahib-i Mecmua: Muestecabizade Ismet. Nos. 4-5 (3-18 Temmuz 1330[1914])) – Izmir: Kesisyan Matbaasi, 1914 – 1mf – 9 – $12.00 – us MEDOC [949]
HIZIRAGAZADE ARIF AGA'NIN MAHDUMU SAIT BEY DIVANI / Bey, Sait – $13.00 – us MEDOC [470]
HIZMET – Izmir, 1925-1928 – 9 – $20.00 – us MEDOC [956]
DIE HJ – DAS KAMPFBLATT DER HITLER-JUGEND – Berlin, 1935-39 n12 – 1 – Dist. gw Mikrofilm – gw Misc Inst [370]
Hjeimslev, L *see* OMKRING SPROGTEORIENS GRUNDLAEGGELSE
Hjelt, Arthur *see*
- DIE ALTSYRISCHE EVANGELIENUEBER-SETZUNG UND TATIANS DIATESSARON, BESONDERS IN IHREM GEGENSEITIGEN VERHAELTNIS
- DE JOHANNEISKA SMAABREFVENS URSPRUNG
- DE JOHANNEISKA SMABREFVENS URSPRUNG

HJO NYA TIDNING *see* HJO TIDNING
HJO TIDNING – Hjo, Sweden. 1979- – 1 – sw Kungliga [072]
HJO TIDNING – (Lordagsposten, 1849-50; Hjo Nya Tidning, 1851-60) – Hjo, Sweden. 1847-49 – 2r – 1 – sw Kungliga [072]
HJO WECKOTIDNING – Hjo, Sweden. 1859-66 – 2r – 1 – sw Kungliga [072]
DER HL. THOMAS VON AQUIN UEBER DAS UNFEHLBARE LEHRAMT DES PAPSTES / Leitner, Franz Xaver – (Includes bibliographical references) – Freiburg i.B.: Herder, 1872 – 1mf – 9 – 0-8370-8442-3 – 1986-2442 – us A.T.L.A. [240]
HLA JOURNAL – (Publication is believed to have ceased with v41 1984. Former titles: HLA Journal june 1944-sep 1945. Hawaii Library Association Journal dec 1945-fal 1964) – Honolulu. v1-41. jun 1944-84 1; v28-41. jun 1971-84 5; v32-34 dec 1975-77*. v35-41 1978-84 9 – 1,5,9 – D2192 – us UMI [020]
HLA JOURNAL *see* HLA JOURNAL
Hladik, C M et al *see*
- FOOD AND NUTRITION IN THE AFRICAN RAIN FOREST
- TROPICAL FORESTS, PEOPLE AND FOOD

Hladny, Ernst *see* HUGO VON HOFMANNSTHAL'S GRIECHENSTUECKE
HLAS – Cleveland, OH, 1912-1913 – 1 reel – 1 – us I.H.R.C. [978]
HLAS = VOICE – Cleveland, OH: John Pankuch Co, jan 5 1925-nov 1927 – 1 – us Res Libr [071]
HLAS DOMOVA – Melbourne, Australia. 18 Feb 1957-1 Sep 1969 (imperfect) – 2r – 1 – uk British Libr Newspaper [072]
HLAS L'UDU – Bratislava, Czechoslovakia. 1956-70 – 12r – 1 – us L of C Photodup [072]
HLAS L'UDU – Presov, Czechoslovakia. May-Oct 1946 – 1r – 1 – us L of C Photodup [072]
HLAS NITRIANSKEHO KRAJA – Nitra, Czechoslovakia. 1956-Mar 1960 – 3r – 1 – us L of C Photodup [072]
HLAS (WEEKLY EDITION) = VOICE – [Cleveland, OH]: John Pankuch Co, dec 1917-sep 1921 – 1 – us Res Libr [071]
HLASATEL – Chicago: [s.n.], jan 6-apr 23 1920; 1945-jul 1975 – us Res Libr [071]
Hlavaek, I *see* DAS URKUNDEN- UND KANZLEIWESEN DES BOEHMISCHEN UND ROEMISCHEN KOENIGS WENZEL (4.) 1376-1419 (MGH SCHRIFTEN..: 23.BD)
Hlawitschka, E *see* LOTHARINGIEN UND DAS REICH AN DER SCHWELLE DER DEUTSCHEN GESCHICHTE (MGH SCHRIFTEN..: 21.BD)
Hmae, Pasteur Apou *see* CORRESPONDANCE
HMS "CHALLENGER" EXPEDITION, 1878-1883. MOLLUSCABY / Waltson, R B – Z-852/2. – 8 – ne IDC [910]
HMS NORTHUMBERLAND LOGBOOK – (From the D.Z. Norton Napoleonic Collection, this vol is the logbook of the Royal Navy warship H.M.S. Northumberland. At this time the ship transported Napoleon Bonaparte to exile on St. Helena) – 1 Jun 1815-11 Aug 1815 – 1r – 1 – us Western Res [355]
HMSO'S COURT OF APPEAL JUDGEMENTS – (Text from 1951-1980) – 2,175mf – 9 – $4,200.00 set Diazo duplicate set $3,600.00 – 0-89111-022-4 – us UNIFO [340]
HMSO'S STATUTES IN FORCE : COMPLETE TEXT THROUGH DECEMBER 1990 – (Annual subscription for quarterly undate. $650.00; Diazo duplicate set. $2,550.00; Annual subscription for quarterly update (diazo). $500.00) – ca 829mf – 9 – $3,100.00 silver halide – 0-89111-016-X – us UNIFO [340]
Hnilicky, Martin *see* DRAMA V INDONEZII
HNO – v.1-29, 1947-81. ISSN: 0017-6192 – 1,5,6,9,13 – us UMI [617]
HO / University of Kentucky. Department of Horticulture – No.1-61.1972-83. 7 fiches – 9 – us Spaulding [630]
Ho, Alice *see* PENSION PLANS, 1936-1954
Ho, Chi Minh *see* TRACH NHIEM CUA NHAN DAN VA CAN BO, DOI VOI CHINH QUYEN CACH MANG
Ho, Ch'ing-ju *see* YOUTH AND VOCATION (CCC149)
Ho, David Chi-hsing *see* VICTORY OF LOVE (CCC148)
Ho, Shih-ming *see*
- CHRISTIAN FAITH AND LIFE (CCC150)
- CHRISTIANITY AND FILIAL PIETY (CCC151)
- CUP OF BLESSING (CCC152)
- EDUCATION OF LIFE (CCC153)
- FAITH IN PRACTICE (CCC155)
- THE KEY TO LIFE (CCC154)
- TWELVE TALKS ON CHRISTIANITY (CCC156)

Ho, Shou-liang *see* CATECHISM (CCC158)
Ho, Siew Liong *see* THE CATECHISM FOR THE METHODIST CHURCH MEMBERS (CCC157)
Ho, Winnie WY *see* FACTORIAL VALIDITY OF A TEACHER EFFECTIVENESS SCALE FOR THE TEACHER PREPARATION PROGRAM IN HONG KONG
Hoadly, George *see* THE CONSTITUTIONAL GUARANTEES OF THE RIGHT OF PROPERTY AS AFFECTED BY RECENT DECISIONS.
HOAM – New York. N.Y. 1916 – 1 – us A.J.P.C. [071]
HOAN CHAN TAN BAO – no. 1-7. Hue. janv-juil 1930. mq no. 2, 5 – 1 – fr A.C.R.P.P. [073]
Hoang, P *see* LE MARIAGE CHINOIS AU POINT DE VUE LEGALE
HOARD'S DAIRYMAN – (v. 124- 1979- 5,6,9) – v. 95- 1950- – 1 – us UMI [636]
Hoare, Edward Hatch *see* THE SCRIPTURE GROUND OF JUSTIFICATION
Hoare, Prince *see* THE ARTIST
Hobart *see* BIOGRAPHICAL REVIEW OF CALHOUN COUNTY
HOBART INDEX – Gary. Ind. and Commonwealth. 1934-38 – 1 – us UMI [071]
HOBART MERCURY – 1 – F3,413.00 – sz Infoprint [072]
Hobart Publishing Co *see*
- BIOGRAPHICAL REVIEW OF DES MOINES COUNTY
- BIOGRAPHICAL REVIEW OF HANCOCK COUNTY
- BIOGRAPHICAL REVIEW OF HENRY COUNTY
- HISTORY OF DARKE COUNTY

HOBART TOWN COURIER – Hobart, 1827-43 – 3r – 1 – A$118.00 silver A$101.00 – at Pascoe [072]
Hobbes, Thomas *see*
- THE METAPHYSICAL SYSTEM OF HOBBES AS CONTAINED IN TWELVE CHAPTERS FROM HIS ELEMENTS OF PHILOSOPHY CONCERNING BODY...AND HUMAN NATURE... AND LEVIATHAN
- TRACTS OF MR. THOMAS HOBBS, OF MALMSBURY CONTAINING: I. BEHEMOTH, THE HISTORY OF THE CAUSES OF THE CIVIL WARS OF ENGLAND FROM 1640 TO 1660
- TRIPOS IN THREE DISCOURSES
- A TRUE ECCLESIASTICAL HISTORY FROM MOSES TO THE TIME OF MARTIN LUTHER: IN VERSE

HOBBIES – (v74- 1969- 5,6 v75- 1970- 9) – v36- 1931- – 1 – us UMI [790]
HOBBS, NEW MEXICO. FIRST BAPTIST CHURCH – Church Records, 1936-1988. 1,806p – 1 – $81.27 – us Baptist [240]
Hoben, Allan *see* VIRGIN BIRTH
Hobfoll, Stevan E *see* ANXIETY, STRESS, AND COPING
HOBHOUSE LETTERS, 1722-55 / Isaac Hobhouse and Co – Bristol Central Library and Bristol Record Office. BRRAM – 1 – uk Microform Academic [025]
Hobhouse, LT *see* MORALS IN EVOLUTIONS
HOBO-QUEBEC : JOURNAL D'ECRITURES ET IMAGES – Montreal. nos 1-47. 1973-81. SEM35P261 – 1r – 1 – Can$42.00 – cn Bibl Nat [400]
Hobson, Alphonzo Augustus *see* THE DIATESSARON OF TATIAN AND THE SYNOPTIC PROBLEM
Hobson, B *see*
- A GENERAL REPORT OF THE HOSPITAL AT KUM-LE-FAU, IN CANTON
- SUBSTANCE OF AN ADDRESS...AT A MEETING OF THE FRIENDS OF THE CHINESE ASSOCIATION, IN AID OF THE MEDICAL MISSIONARY SOCIETY IN CHINA

Hobson, J A *see* RICHARD COBDEN – THE INTERNATIONAL MAN
HOBSON-JOBSON : A GLOSSARY OF COLLOQUIAL ANGLO-INDIAN WORDS AND PHRASES... / Yule, H & Burnell, A C – London, 1903 – 19mf – ne IDC [420]
HOBSON-JOBSON; A GLOSSARY OF COLLOQUIAL ANGLO-INDIAN WORDS AND PHRASES / Yule, H & Burnell, A C; ed by Crooke, W – London, 1903. 1021 pp. BI-358 2 – 8 – ne IDC [420]
Hoburg, Christiano *see*
- EMBLEMATA SACRA
- LEVENDIGE HERTS-THEOLOGIE, DAT ZIJN AENDACHTIGE BETRACHTINGEN, HOE JESUS IN DER GELOOVIGEN HERTEN WIL WOONEN, WERKEN EN LEVEN, EN HAAR WIL ZIJN ALLES IN ALLEN

Hoby, J *see* THE BAPTISTS IN AMERICA
DU HOC BAO – Bulletin bimensuel puis mensuel de la Societe d'encouragement aux etudes occidentales. Hue. 1er sept 1927-sept 1935 – 1 – fr A.C.R.P.P. [073]
HOC SINH – Hanoi. 1936, 1939-41 – 1 – fr A.C.R.P.P. [073]
HOC TAP : TAP CHI LY LUAN VA CHINH TRI CUA DANG LAO DONG VIET-NAM – Hanoi: [s.n. v9 n90-v22 n252. jul 1963-1976] – 17r – 1 – us Res Libr [072]
HOCA NASREDDIN – Istanbul, No. 1 (1908) – 1mf – 9 – $10.00 – us MEDOC [949]
HOC-BAO – Hanoi. sept 1922-aout 1923; sept 1925-juin 1929; sept 1936-juil/aout 1937, 1938-39 – 1 – fr A.C.R.P.P. [073]
Hocedez, E S J *see* RICHARD DE MIDDLETON
Hoch, Alexander *see* PAPST PIUS 10
Hoch, Horace Lind *see* SHAKESPEARE'S INFLUENCE UPON GRABBE
HOCH OESTERREICH : PATRIOTISCHES LIEDERSPIEL / Purschke, Marie Sidonie – Wien: Verlag des katholischen Waisen-Hilfsvereins, 1885 – 1r – 1 – us U.W. Library [780]
HOCHAUFLOESENDE ABSORPTION-SSPEKTROSKOPIE IM WEICHEN ROENTGENBEREICH AN AUSGEWAEHLTEN ATOMEN UND MOLEKUELEN / Remmers, Guido – 1992 – 135p – 9 – DM98.00 – 3-89349-604-1 – gw Hänsel [530]
HOCHAUFLOESENDE INTERFEROMETRISCHE MESSUNGEN IN DER ASTONOMIE MIT CCD-DETEKTOREN : DIE BEOBACHTUNG DER OBJEKTE ETA CARINAE, RED RECTANGLE UND BETEIGEUZE / Weghorn, Hans – 1994 – 2mf – 9 – DM80.00 – 3-89349-869-9 – gw Hänsel [520]
HOCHAUFLOESENDE PHOTOELEKTRONEN-SPEKTROSKOPISCHE UNTERSUCHUNGEN DES SUPRALEITENDEN ZUSTANDS VON BI2SR2CACU08+D(DELTA) / Simmons, C Thomas – (In englischer Sprache) – 1993 – 1mf – 9 – DM60.00 – 3-89349-736-6 – gw Hänsel [540]
Hochdoerfer, Richard *see* INTRODUCTORY STUDIES IN GERMAN LITERATURE
Hochdorf, Max *see* GOTTFRIED KELLER IM EUROPAEISCHEN GEDANKEN
Hocheimer, Lewis *see*
- A MANUAL OF CRIMINAL LAW, AS ESTABLISHED IN THE STATE OF MARYLAND
- A TREATISE ON THE LAW RELATING TO THE CUSTODY OF INFANTS, INCLUDING PRACTICE AND FORMS

HOCHFREQUENZTECHNIK UND ELEKTROAKUSTIK – v. 1-38. 1907-31. Formerly: Jahrbuch der Drahtlosen Telegraphie und Telephone – 1,5,6 – us Princeton Micro [621]
HOCHFREQUENZTECHNIK UND ELEKTROAKUSTIK – v31-55. 1907-31 – 1 – us Princeton Micro [621]
HO-CHOU CHIH – 1876; 1878, 16, 1. BCH-715 2 – 8 – ne IDC [950]
DAS HOCHSCHULWESEN – 1953-1989 – 604mf – 1 – DM3,442.80 – gw Mikro Press [370]
Hochstetter, E *see* STUDIEN ZUR METAPHYSIK UND ERKENNTNISLEHRE WILHELMS VON OCKHAM
DER HOCHVERRATSPROZESS GEGEN SINCLAI : EIN BEITRAG ZUM LEBEN HOELDERLINS / Kirchner, Werner – (Includes bibliographical references) – Marburg/Lahn: Simons, 1949 – 1r – 1 – us U.W. Library [430]
DER HOCHWACHTER – Cincinnati: Friedrich Hassaurek, jul 1845-jul 1846 – 1r – 1 – us Res Libr [071]
HOCHWASSER : NOVELLEN / Seidel, Ina – 3. Aufl. Berlin: E Fleischel, 1920 – 1r – 1 – us U.W. Library [830]
DIE HOCHZEIT AUF BUCHENHORST : ERZAEHLUNG / Hauptmann, Gerhart – Berlin: S Fischer, 1932 – 1 – us U.W. Library [830]
DIE HOCHZEIT DER FEINDE : ROMAN / Andres, Stefan Paul – Muenchen: R Piper, 1953, c1952 – 1r – 1 – us U.W. Library [830]
DIE HOCHZEIT DER SOBEIDE : DRAMATISCHES GEDICHT / Hofmannsthal, Hugo von – 2. Ausg. Berlin: S Fischer, 1909 – 1r – 1 – us U.W. Library [810]
HOCHZEITPREDIGTEN. VOM EHESTAND VND HAUSSWESEN... / Mathesius, Johannes – Nuernberg, 1584 – 4mf – ne IDC [240]
Hock, Erich *see* "DORT DRUEBEN IN WESTFALEN"
Hock, S *see* ANTON AUERSPERGS (ANASTASIUS GRUENS) POLITISCHE REDEN UND SCHRIFTEN
Hocken, T M *see* SETTLEMENT OF OTAGO
HOCKEY NEWS – Don Mills. v1-48. 1947-1994/95 – 1 – Can$130.00y – cn Micromedia [790]
Hocking, Joseph *see* SHALL ROME RECONQUER ENGLAND?
HOCKING SENTINEL – Logan. Ohio. 1845-1883 – 1 – us UMI [071]
Hockings, Paul *see* VISUAL ANTHROPOLOGY
Hocquenghem, Anne Marie *see*
- CODE POUR L'ANALYSE DES REPRESENTATIONS FIGURES SUR LES VASES MOCHICAS
- DOCUMENTS ICONOGRAPHIQUES SUR SAN ANDRES SAJCABAJA
- LES TEXTILES ET LE VETEMENT DANS LA CULTURE MOCHICA (PEROU)

Hodde, Jason P *see* REMODELING CHARACTERISTICS OF THE RABBIT ACHILLES TENDON COMPLEX FOLLOWING REPAIR WITH SMALL INTESTINAL SUBMUCOSA

Hodder, Edwin *see*
- CONQUESTS OF THE CROSS
- THE LIFE AND WORK OF THE SEVENTH EARL OF SHAFTESBURY, K.G.
- SIMON PETER
- SIMON PETER: HIS LIFE, TIMES AND FRIENDS

Hodder-Williams, J E *see* THE LIFE OF SIR GEORGE WILLIAMS
HODDESDON BROXBOURNE MERCURY *see* HODDESDON MERCURY
HODDESDON MERCURY – (Hoddesdon Broxbourne Mercury, 1986-) – England, 16 Sep 1983- – 68+ r – 1 – uk British Libr Newspaper [072]
HODDESDON MERCURY AND JOURNAL *see* HERTFORDSHIRE MERCURY
Hodell, Charles W *see* THE OLD YELLOW BOOK
DER HODESH – v. 1, no. 1-3. Jan.-Mar. 1921 – 1 – us NY Public [073]
Hodey, Le *see* JOURNAL DES ETATS GENERAUX
HODGE : SERIES OF NOTABLE BRITISH TRIALS – 359mf – 9 – us UMI [340]
Hodge, Archibald Alexander *see*
- THE ATONEMENT
- A COMMENTARY ON THE CONFESSION OF FAITH
- THE LIFE OF CHARLES HODGE, D.D.
- THE SYSTEM OF THEOLOGY CONTAINED IN THE WESTMINSTER SHORTER CATECHISM

Hodge, Caspar Wistar *see*
- GOSPEL HISTORY
- GOSPEL HISTORY: A SYLLABUS OF PROFESSOR C.W. HODGE'S GOSPEL HISTORY
- NEW TESTAMENT CRITICISM
- NEW TESTAMENT CRITICISM: LECTURES
- SYLLABUS OF LECTURES ON APOSTOLIC HISTORY AND LITERATURE

Hodge, Charles *see*
- THE CONSTITUTIONAL HISTORY OF THE PRESBYTERIAN CHURCH IN THE UNITED STATES OF AMERICA
- DISCUSSIONS IN CHURCH POLITY
- AN EXPOSITION OF THE FIRST EPISTLE TO THE CORINTHIANS
- EXPOSITION OF THE FIRST EPISTLE TO THE CORINTHIANS
- EXPOSITION OF THE SECOND EPISTLE TO THE CORINTHIANS
- AN EXPOSITION OF THE SECOND EPISTLE TO THE CORINTHIANS
- SERMONS

Hodge, Frederick W *see*
- HANDBOOK OF AMERICAN INDIANS: NORTH OF MEXICO
- HANDBOOK OF AMERICAN INDIANS NORTH OF MEXICO

Hodge, Richard Morse *see* HISTORICAL ATLAS AND CHRONOLOGY OF THE LIFE OF JESUS CHRIST
HODGE SERIES OF NOTABLE TRIALS – (Pt 1 Notable British Trials 1586-1953 $1335; Pt 2 War Crimes Trials $170. Originally published London: William Hodge and Co., 1905-53) – 359mf – 9 – $1505.00 complete collection – us UMI [340]
Hodge, William L *see* THE LAW OF ATTACHMENT IN MARYLAND
Hodgeman County. Kansas. St. Michael's Evangelical Lutheran Church *see* RECORDS
HODGENVILLE FIRST BAPTIST CHURCH. HODGENVILLE, KENTUCKY : CHURCH RECORDS – 1838-57, 1878-1966 – 1 – 82.17 – us Baptist [240]
Hodges, Ann M *see* SONGS..
Hodges Brothers. Olathe, Kansas *see* LEDGERS, DAY BOOKS
Hodges, Donald Clark *see* ARGENTINA, 1943-1976
Hodges, George *see*
- THE EPISCOPAL CHURCH
- THREE HUNDRED YEARS OF THE EPISCOPAL CHURCH IN AMERICA

Hodges, Henry G *see* THE DOCTRINE OF INTERVENTION
Hodges, James *see* CONSTRUCTION OF THE GREAT VICTORIA BRIDGE IN CANADA
Hodges, Richard *see*
- THE ENGLISH PRIMROSE
- MOST PLAIN DIRECTIONS FOR TRUE WRITING

HODGIN'S CANADA ELECTION CASES / Ontario. Canada – 1v. 1871-78 (all publ) – 9mf – 9 – $13.50 – LLMC 81-046 – us L.L.M.C. [340]
Hodgins, J George *see* THE ACTS RELATING TO COMMON SCHOOLS AND ALSO SEPARATE SCHOOLS IN ONTARIO:..
Hodgkin *see* PEN PICTURES OF REPRESENTATIVE MEN OF OREGON
Hodgkin, Thomas *see*
- THE DYNASTY OF THEODOSIUS, OR, EIGHTY YEARS' STRUGGLE WITH THE BARBARIANS
- GEORGE FOX
- ITALY AND HER INVADERS 376-814
- THEODORIC THE GOTH

Hodgkins, Louise Manning *see* VIA CHRISTI
Hodgson, James Muscutt *see* THELOGIA (SIC) PECTORIS
Hodgson, MGS *see* THE ORDER OF ASSASSINS
Hodgson, Phyllis *see* THE CLOUD OF UNKNOWING AND THE BOOK OF PRIVY COUNSELLING
Hodgson, S *see* SHORT ACCOUNT, 1772-1792
Hodius, H *see*
- HISTORIA CHRONICA
- HISTORIA CHRONICA (CBH 30,3)

DER HODSCHA NASREDDIN / ed by Wesselski, Albert – 2v, complete. 1911. Humorous anecdotes about Nasreddin Hoca, a legendary character – 1 – us I.U. Libraries [390]
Hodson, Arnold Wienholt *see* AN ELEMENTARY AND PRACTICAL GRAMMAR OF THE GALLA OR OROMO LANGUAGE
Hodson, T C *see*
- CENSUS ETHNOGRAPHY, 1901-1931
- THE PRIMITIVE CULTURE OF INDIA

Hodson, V C P *see* LIST OF OFFICERS OF THE BENGAL ARMY, 1758-1834
Hodson, William Stephen Raikes *see* TWELVE YEARS OF A SOLDIER'S LIFE IN INDIA: BEING EXTRACTS FROM THE LETTERS OF THE LATE MAJOR W.S.R. HODSON.
HOE, R. AND COMPANY *see* RECORDS
HOE WIJ MOGELIJK ZULLEN SLAGEN IN DE NIEUWE NEDERLANDSCHE VOLKSPLANTING IN NIEUW-GUINEA / Versluis, W – (Orig. text dated 10 Sept. 1944). SE 5284 1. 1948 – 9 – ne IDC [025]
Hoechheimer, S *see* UEBER MOSES MENDELSSOHNS TOD
HOECHSTER KREISBLATT : BA DER FRANKFURTER NEUEN PRESSE – Frankfurt-Main, DE. 1978- – ca 7r per yr – 1 – gw Mikrofilm [072]
HOECHSTER STADTRUNDSCHAU : BA DER FRANKFURTER RUNDSCHAU, AUSGABE LAND 2 – Frankfurt/Main, DE. Nov 1972-Dec 1974 – 1 – gw Mikrofilm [072]
Hoeck, F *see* BEITRAEGE ZUR MORPHOLOGIE, GRUPPIERUNG UND GEOGRAPHISCHEN VERBREITUNG DER VALERIANACEEN
Hoecker, Gustav *see* HOFFART UND DEMUT
Hoecker, R *see* DAS LEHRGEDICHT DES KAREL VAN MANDER
Hoedemaker, Philippus J *see* DE MOZAISCHE OORSPRONG VAN DE WETTEN IN DE BOEKEN EXODUS, LEVITICUS EN NUMERI
Hoedemaker, Philippus Jacobus *see*
- DE MOZAEISCHE OORSPRONG VAN DE WETTEN IN DE BOEKEN EXODUS, LEVITICUS EN NUMERI
- MOZAISCHE OORSPRONG VAN DE WETTEN IN DE BOEKEN EXODUS, LEVITICUS EN NUMERI

Hoefer, Edmund *see* GOETHE UND CHARLOTTE V. STEIN
Hoefer, F de *see* NOUVELLE BIOGRAPHIE GENERALE DEPUIS LE TEMPS LES PLUS RECULES JUSQU'A NOS JOURS
Hoefer, Ferdinand *see* AFRIQUE AUSTRALE, EMPIRE DU MAROC
HOEFER INTELLIGENZ-BLATT *see* NEUES HOEFER INTELLIGENZ-BLATT
HOEFER INTELLIGENZ-ZEITUNG *see* NEUES HOEFER INTELLIGENZ-BLATT
Hoefer, Karl-Heinz *see*
- DEUTUNGEN UND BEKENNTNISSE
- KLEINE LITERARTURFIBEL

HOEFER WOCHEN-BLATT *see* NEUES HOEFER INTELLIGENZ-BLATT
Hoeffner, Johannes *see*
- FRAU RAT
- GOETHE UND DAS WEIMARER HOFTHEATER

Hoefig, Willi *see* THE DISSIDENT PRESS OF REVOLUTIONARY IRAN
DER HOEFISCH-GALANTE ROMAN DES 17. JAHRHUNDERTS BEI EBERHARD WERNER HAPPEL / Lock, Gerhard – (Includes bibliographical references) – Wuerzburg: K Triltsch, 1939 – 1r – 1 – us U.W. Library [430]
Hoefler, C *see* DIE AVIGNONESISCHEN PAEPSTE, IHRE MACHTFUELLE UND IHR UNTERGANG
Hoefler, Constantin Ritter von *see* BONIFATIUS, DER APOSTEL DER DEUTSCHEN, UND DIE SLAVENAPOSTEL, KONSTANTINOS (CYRILLUS) UND METHODIOS
Hoefler, Karl Adolf Constantin, Ritter von *see*
- DIE DEUTSCHEN PAEPSTE
- MAGISTER JOHANNES HUS UND DER ABZUG DER DEUTSCHEN PROFESSOREN UND STUDENTEN AUS PRAG, 1409

Hoefling, J W *see* GRUNDSAETZE EVANGELISCH-LUTHERISCHER KIRCHENVERFASSUNG
HOEGANAES TIDNING – Hoeganaes, 1889-1924 – 9 – sw Kungliga [072]
HOEHERE STAATSSCHULE IN CUXHAVEN *see* WIELANDS VERHAELTNIS ZU LUCIAN
DIE HOEHEREN CRYPTOGAMEN PREUSSENS. EIN BEITRAG ZUR FLORA DER PROVINZ KOENIGSBERG 1858 / Klinggraeff, H von – B-7303 1 – 9 – ne IDC [580]
Hoehlbaum, K *see* DAS BUCH WEINSBERG, BD 2 1552-1577 (PGRG 3)
HOEI-LAN-KI (HISTOIRE DU CERCLE DE CRAIE) / Li Hsing-Tao – 1832 – 1 – uk Microform Academic [950]
Hoekstra, Sytze *see* BRONNEN EN GRONDSLAGEN VAN HET GODSDIENSTIG GELOOF
HOELDERLIN : CHOIX DE TEXTES / Hoelderlin, Friedrich; ed by Leonhard, Rudolf & Rovini, Robert – (Includes bibliographical references) – [Paris]: P Seghers, [1953] – 1 – us U.W. Library [800]
HOELDERLIN : FELDAUSWAHL / ed by Beissner, Friedrich – [Stuttgart]: Cotta, [1943] – 1r – 1 – us U.W. Library [430]
HOELDERLIN / Przywara, Erich – Nuernberg: Glock und Lutz, 1949 – 1r – 1 – us U.W. Library [430]
HOELDERLIN, FRIEDRICH : BEITRAGE ZU SEINEM 200. GEBURTSTAG / ed by Bundessekretariat des Deutschen Kulturbundes, Sektor Publikationen – (Includes bibliographical references) – Berlin: Deutscher Kulturbund, 1970 – 1 – us U.W. Library [430]
Hoelderlin, Friedrich *see*
- AUSGEWAEHLTE WERKE
- GESAMMELTE WERKE
- GESANG DES DEUTSCHEN
- HOELDERLIN
- HOELDERLINS GESAMMELTE DICHTUNGEN
- POEMS
- DER TOD DES EMPEDOKLES
- VOM HEILIGEN REICH DER DEUTSCHEN
- WERKE

HOELDERLIN UND CHRISTUS / Winklhofer, Alois – Nuernberg: Glock und Lutz, 1946 – 1r – 1 – us U.W. Library [430]
HOELDERLIN UND DAS DEUTSCHE THEATER / Kindermann, Heinz – Wien: W Frick, 1943 – 1 – us U.W. Library [840]
HOELDERLIN UND DAS WESEN DER DICHTUNG / Heidegger, Martin – Muenchen: A Langen/G Mueller, c1937 – 1r – 1 – us U.W. Library [430]
HOELDERLIN UND DIE PHILOSOPHIE / Hoffmeister, Johannes – 2. durchgesehene Aufl. Leipzig: F Meiner, 1944 – 1r – 1 – us U.W. Library [100]
HOELDERLIN UND DIE PHILOSOPHIE / Hoffmeister, Johannes – (Includes bibliographical references) – 1. Aufl. Leipzig: F Meiner, 1944 – 1r – 1 – us U.W. Library [430]
HOELDERLIN UND DIE PHILOSOPHIE / Hoffmeister, Johannes – Leipzig, 1942 – 2mf – DM62.00 – 3-8267-3014-3 – gw Hänsel [100]
HOELDERLIN UND DIE SCHWEIZ / ed by Boehm, Wilhelm – (Includes bibliographical references) – Frauenfeld/Leipzig: Huber, c1935 – 1 – us U.W. Library [920]
HOELDERLINS BEGEGNUNG MIT GOETHE UND SCHILLER / Fahrner, Rudolf – (Includes bibliographical references) – Marburg a.L.: N G Elwert, 1925 – 1r – 1 – us U.W. Library [430]
HOELDERLINS CHRISTLICHES ERBE / Wocke, Helmut – (Includes bibliographical references) – Muenchen: Leibniz, 1949 – 1 – us U.W. Library [430]
HOELDERLINS DEUTUNG DES "OEDIPUS" UND DER "ANTIGONE" : DIE "ANMERKUNGEN" IM RAHMEN DER KLASSISCHEN UND ROMANTISCHEN DEUTUNGEN DES ANTIK-TRAGISCHEN / Schrader, Hans – (Includes bibliographical references) – Bonn a. Rh.: L Roehrscheid, 1933 – 1r – 1 – us U.W. Library [450]
HOELDERLINS GESAMMELTE DICHTUNGEN : NEUE DURCHGESEHENE UND VERMEHRTE AUSG. MIT BIOGRAPHISCHER EINLEITUNG / Hoelderlin, Friedrich; ed by Litzmann, Berthold – (Icnludes bibliographical references) – Stuttgart: J G Cotta'sche Buchhandlung Nachfolger. 2v. [1895?] – 1 – us U.W. Library [800]
HOELDERLINS HYMNE "WIE WENN AM FEIERTAGE..." / Heidegger, Martin – Halle a.d.S.: M Niemeyer, [1941?] – 1r – 1 – us U.W. Library [780]
HOELDERLINS STUDIENJAHRE IM TUEBINGER STIFT / Betzendoerfer, Walter – (Includes bibliographical references) – Heilbronn: E Salzer, 1922 – 1r – 1 – us U.W. Library [920]
Hoelemann, Hermann Gustav *see* DIE REDEN DES SATAN IN DER HEILIGEN SCHRIFT
DIE HOELLE – Chemnitz, Germany. 1925-26, (incomplete) – 1 – gw Mikrofilm [072]
Hoeller, Franz *see*
- BOEHMISCHES WANDERBUCH
- HERZ IN BOEHMEN

DIE HOELLISCHE TRINITAET : ROMAN AUS DEN JAHREN DER VOLLENDUNG DES MEISTERS MATHIS NITHART, DER FAELSCHLICH MATTHIAS GRUENEWALD GENANNT WURDE / Weismantel, Leo – (Includes bibliographical references) – Muenchen: K Alber, 1943 – 1 – us U.W. Library [830]
Hoellrigl, Franz *see* DIE FREIFRAUEN
Hoelscher, Eberhard *see* LEBEN, MEYNUNGEN UND THATEN VON HIERONIMUS JOBS DEM KANDIDATEN, UND WIE ER SICH WEILAND VIEL RUHM ERWARB AUCH ENDLICH ALS NACHTSWAECHTER ZU SULZBURG STARB
Hoelscher, Gustav *see*
- KANONISCH UND APOKRYPH
- DIE QUELLEN DES JOSEPHUS FUER DIE ZEIT VOM EXIL BIS ZUM JUEDISCHEN KRIEGE

Hoelscher, U *see* DAS GRABDENKMAL DES KOENIGS CHEPHREN
Hoeltje, Georg *see* ZEITLICHE UND BEGRIFFLICHE ABGRENZUNG DER SPAETGOTIK INNERHALB DER ARCHITEKTUR VON DEUTSCHLAND, FRANKREICH, UND ENGLAND
Hoenegg, M Hoe von *see*
- CALVINISTARUM VERA, VIVA ET GENUINA DESCRIPTIO
- GRUENDLICHE ABLEINUNG FUENFFZIG STATLICHER AUSSERLESENER VND IN ALLE EWIGE EWIGKEIT UNERWEISSLICHER CALVINISCHER ERTZ- VND HAUPTLUEGEN...
- GRUENDLICHE, SUMMARISCHE, APOSTOLISCHE AUSFUEHRUNG, DER GANTZEN REINEN CATHOLISCHEN EVANGELISCHEN LEHRE...IN FUNFFZIG PREDIGTEN VERFASSET
- GRUENDLICHER BERICHT, AUFF DIE VON DEN CALVINISTEN EINGEGEBENE KLAEGLICHE SUPPLIKATION, DARINNEN DIE HIMMELSCHE GOETTLICHE WAHRHEIT,...

Hoenes, Christian *see* LUDWIG UHLAND
Hoenig, Johannes *see* FERDINAND GREGOROVIUS ALS DICHTER
Hoeniger, R *see* KOELNER SCHREINSURKUNDEN DES 12. JAHRHUNDERT (PGRG 1)
HOENNE-ZEITUNG – Balve, jan 5 1957-jun 28 1958, jul 5 1958-60 – 1 – Dist. gw Mikrofilm – gw Misc Inst [072]
Hoensbroech, Paul, Graf von *see* DAS PAPSTTHUM IN SEINER SOZIAL-KULTURELLEN WIRKSAMKEIT
HOER MIT MIR – NEUE FUNKSTUNDE *see*
- OSTDEUTSCHE ILLUSTRIERTE FUNKSTUNDE

HOER ZU – Hamburg. dec 15, 1946-jun 30, 1956. dec 14, 1991-96 – 45r – 1 – gw Mikrofilm [790]
HOEREN UND FERNSEHEN *see* WESTFUNK
HOEREN UND SEHEN *see* WESTFUNK
Hoermann, G *see* STUDIEN UEBER DIE PROTOPLASMASTROEMUNG BEI DEN CHARACEEN
Hoerner, Herbert von *see*
- DER GROSSE BAUM
- DIE LETZTE KUGEL
- DIE WELLE

HOERNERKLANG DER FRUEHE / Zerkaulen, Heinrich – 3. Aufl. Leipzig: E Huyke, [1943?] – 1 – us U.W. Library [830]
HOERSCHWELLENBESTIMMUNGEN BEI NEUGEBORENEN RISIKOKINDERN : EINE PROSPEKTIVE VERLAUFSSTUDIE / Hartmann, Sabine – 1993 – 1mf – 9 – DM60.00 – 3-89349-800-1 – gw Hänsel [618]

Hoeser, Conrad *see* BRIEFWECHSEL ZWISCHEN JOSEPH VICTOR VON SCHEFFEL UND PAUL HEYSE
Hoestermann, Emilie *see* BEITRAEGE ZUR TECHNIK IN HEBBELS TAGEBUCH
Hoet, G *see* CATALOGUS OF NAAMLIJST VAN SCHILDERIJEN...
Hoetzl, Petrus *see* IST DOELLINGER HAERETIKER?
Hoetzsch, Otto *see* RUSSLAND; EINE EINFUEHRUNG AUF GRUND SEINER GESCHICHTE VOM JAPANISCHEN BIS ZUM WELTKRIEG
Hoevell, G W W C van *see* VOCABULARIUM VAN VREEMDE WOORDEN, VOORKOMENDE IN HET AMBONSCH-MALEISCH, BENEVENS KORTE OPMERKINGEN OVER DIT LOCAAL-MALEISCH EN VERDER EENIGE AMBONSCHE SPREEKWOORDEN, EIGENAARDIGE UITDRUKKINGEN EN GEZEGDEN TE AMBON GEBRUIKELIJK
Hoeven, A van der *see* LAMBERT TEN KATE
Hoeven, v.d. *see* TIJDSCHRIFT VOOR NATUURLIJKE GESCHIEDENIS EN PHYSIOLOGIE
Hoeynck, F A *see* GESCHICHTE DER KIRCHLICHEN LITURGIE DES BISTHUMS AUGSBURG
DER HOF AM BRINK : ERZAEHLUNG AUS DEM DREISSIGJAEHRIGEN KRIEGE / Strauss und Torney, Lulu von – Jena: E Diederichs, 1935 – 1r – 1 – us U.W. Library [830]
Hofberg, Herman *see* SWEDISH FOLK-LORE
HOFER ANZEIGER *see* NEUES HOEFER INTELLIGENZ-BLATT
HOFER ANZEIGER. FRANKENPOST *see* NEUES HOEFER INTELLIGENZ-BLATT
Hofer, Hans *see* WELTANSCHAUUNGEN IN VERGANGENHEIT UND GEGENWART
Hofer, Klara *see*
- FRUEHLING EINES DEUTSCHEN MENSCHEN
- GOETHES EHE

Hofer, Paul J *see*
- THE CONSEQUENCES OF MANDATORY MINIMUM PRISON TERMS
- HOME CONFINEMENT

HOFER TAG-BLATT *see* NEUES HOEFER INTELLIGENZ-BLATT
Hoffart, Elizabeth *see* HERDERS "GOTT"
HOFFART UND DEMUT : ERZAEHLUNG AUS DER ZEIT MARIA THERESIAS / Hoecker, Gustav – Stuttgart: Gebrueder Kroener, [18–?] – 1 – us U.W. Library [830]
Hoffding, Harald *see* OM NOGLE RELIGIONSFILOSOFISKE ARBEJDER FRA DEN NYESTE TID
Hoffer, A *see* NEDERDUYTSCHE POEMATA
Hoffer, Johann *see* ICONES CATECHESEOS ET VIRTUTUM AC VITIORUM ILLUSTRATAE NUMERIS: ITEM HISTORIA PASSIONIS DOMINI NOSTRI JESU CHRISTI EFFIGIATA
Hoffert, Troy A *see* PEAK TORQUE RELIABILITY OF BIODEX B-2000 ISOKINETIC DYNAMOMETER DURING CONCENTRIC LOADING OF BACK FLEXORS AND EXTENSORS
Hoffman *see* LE BRIGAND
Hoffman, Carl von *see* JUNGLE GODS
Hoffman, David *see*
- AN ADDRESS TO STUDENTS OF LAW IN THE UNITED STATES. (CIRCULAR)
- A LECTURE; BEING THE THIRD OF A SERIES OF LECTURES, INTRODUCTORY TO A COURSE OF LECTURES NOW DELIVERING IN THE UNIVERSITY OF MARYLAND

Hoffman, Diana M *see* THE EFFECTS OF VISUAL IMAGERY ABILITY COMBINED WITH VISUAL MENTAL PRACTICE TECHNIQUES UPON MOTOR PERFORMANCE
Hoffman, E *see* DAS KONVERSENINSTITUT DES CISTERZIENSERORDENS
Hoffman, Frank Sargent *see*
- THE SPHERE OF RELIGION
- SPHERE OF RELIGION: A CONSIDERATION OF ITS NATURE AND OF ITS INFLUENCE

Hoffman, Frederick Lewis *see* THE OHIO SUPREME COURT REPORTS REDUCED TO QUESTIONS AND ANSWERS.
Hoffman, H A *see* QUATUORS, 3, POUR DEUX VIOLONS, ALTO ET VIOLONCELLE, OEUVRE 7
Hoffman, J L *see* VERSUCH EINER GESCHICHTE DER MAHLERISCHEN HARMONIE UEBERHAUPT UND DER FARBENHARMONIE INSBESONDERE
Hoffman, M *see* WEYSSAGUNG AUSZ HEILIGER GOTLICHER GESCHRIFFT
Hoffman, Marilyn A *see* COMPARISON OF TWO INSTRUMENTS FOR NEEDS ASSESSMENT AND EVALUATION OF AN EMPLOYEE HEALTH PROMOTION PROGRAM
Hoffman, Murray *see*
- ECCLESIASTICAL LAW IN THE STATE OF NEW YORK
- A TREATISE ON THE LAW OF THE PROTESTANT EPISCOPAL CHURCH IN THE U.S.

Hoffman, Ogden *see*
- HOFFMAN'S REPORTS OF CASES IN THE DISTRICT COURT FOR NORTHERN CALIFORNIA, 1853-1858
- REPORT OF THE LAND CASES, JUNE 1853-JUNE 1858

Hoffman, Publius V *see* INDIANA ADDENDUM TO GREEN'S PLEADING AND PRACTICE
Hoffman, W J *see* HISTORY OF LA SALLE COUNTY
Hoffmann *see* LYSISTRATA OU LES ATHENIENNES
Hoffmann, Andreas Gottlieb *see* THE PRINCIPLES OF SYRIAC GRAMMAR
Hoffmann, C *see* PLANZEN-ATLAS NACH DEM LINNE'SCHEN SYSTEM...
Hoffmann, David *see*
- ANTWORT AUFF D. CHRISTOPHORI PEZELII PREDIGERS ZU BREMEN FALSCH GEBRAUCHTE GRUENDE:...
- APOLOGIA DANIELIS HOFMANNI, MISSA AD THEODORVM BEZAM QUA TO RETON IN VERBIS COENAE SACRAE:...
- AVREA ET VERE THEOLOGICA COMMENTATIO D. DANIELIS HOFMANNI...
- CHRISTLICHE PREDIGT AUS DEM 48. CAPITTEL ESAIAE VON DEN GROSSEN WOLTHATEN GOTTES...
- EPISTOLAE REVERENDI,...DANIELIS HOFFMANNI...DE LIBRO CONCORDIAE,...
- HOMILIARVM EVANGELICARVM NOTAE BREVES
- LE-DAVID ZEVI. FESTSCHRIFT. DAVID HOFFMANN
- ORTHODOXA DE EXORCISMO A QVIBVSDAM ECCLESIIS AVGVSTANAM CONFESSIONEM AMPLECTENTIBUS IN BAPTISMI ADMINISTRATIONE...
- SCHULCHAN-URUCH UND DIE RABBINEN UEBER DAS VERHAELTNISS DER JUDEN ZU ANDERSGLAEUBIGEN
- VON DER MODERATION UND MESSIGUNG HERRN PHILLIPI MELANTHONIS IN DEM BETRUEBTEM LANGWIRIGEM STREITE VOM HEILIGEN ABENDMAHL
- ZUR EINLEITUNG IN DIE HALACHISCHEN MIDRASCHIM

Hoffmann, Ernst Theordor Amadeus *see*
- DAS FRAEULEIN VON SCUDERI
- DER GOLDNE TOPF
- LEBENS-ANSICHTEN DES KATERS MURR
- MEISTER MARTIN DER KUEFNER UND SEINE GESELLEN
- DER SANDMANN

Hoffmann, G F *see*
- COMMENTATIO DE VARIO LICHENUM USU
- DARSTELLUNG UND KRITIK DER VON HERDER GEGEBENEN ERGAENZUNG UND FORTBILDUNG DER ANSICHTEN LESSINGS IN SEINEM LAOKOON
- DESCRIPTIO ET ADUMBRATIO PLANTARUM E CLASSE CRYPTOGAMICA LINNAEI QUAE LICHENS DICUNTUR
- DEUTSCHLANDS FLORA ODER BOTANISCHES TASCHENBUCH FUER 1800 (1804)
- DEUTSCHLANDS FLORA ODER BOTANISCHES TASCHENBUCH FUER DAS JAHR 1791 UND FUER DAS JAHR 1795
- ENUMERATIO LICHENUM ICONIBUS ET DESCRIPTIONIBUS ILLUSTRATA
- GENERA PLANTARUM UMBELLIFERARUM
- GRUNDLAGEN, STILE, GESTALTEN DER DEUTSCHEN LITERATUR
- HISTORIA SALICUM ICONIBUS ILLUSTRATA
- HORTUS MOSQUENSIS

Hoffmann, Georg *see* UEBER EINIGE PHOENIZISCHE INSCHRIFTEN
Hoffmann, H *see*
- GOTTESFRIEDE UND TREUGA DEI (MGH SCHRIFTEN..: 20.BD)
- INDEX FUNGORUM

Hoffmann, Heinrich *see*
- DIE MONDZUEGLER
- UEBER DIE BETEUERUNGEN IN SHAKESPEARE'S DRAMEN

HOFFMANN LE FANTASTIQUE / Mistler, Jean – (Includes bibliographical references) – Paris: Albin Michel, c1950 – 1 – us U.W. Library [430]
Hoffmann, Leopold Alois *see* WIENER ZEITSCHRIFT 1792-1793
(Hoffmann, M) *see* DIALOGUS U. GRUENDL. BERICHTUNG GEHALTENER DISPUTATION ZU HOLSTEIN VOM NACHTMAL
Hoffmann, M *see*
- DER DIALOG BEI DEN CHRISTLICHEN SCHRIFTSTELLERN DER ERSTEN VIER JAHRHUNDERTE (T.U.U. 5-96)
- DIE EEDELE HOGHE ENDE TROOSTLIKE SENDEBRIEF, DEN DIE HEYLIGE APOSTEL PAULUS TO DEN ROMEREN GESCREUEN HEEFT, VERCLAERT ENDE. WTGELECHT

Hoffmann, Michael *see* STIL UND STILZUG IM KOMMUNIKATEN KONTEXT
Hoffmann, Norbert *see* MENORAH, JARHON MESEWAJER LEBET HA-JEHUDI
Hoffmann, O *see* COMPOSITAE
Hoffmann, Otto *see* HERDER'S BRIEFWECHSEL MIT NICOLAI
Hoffmann, S *see* ORGANISATIONS INTERNATIONALES ET POUVOIRS POLITIQUES DES ETATS
HOFFMANN VON FALLERSLEBEN ALS VORKAEMPFER UND ERFORSCHER DER NIEDERLAENDISCH-VLAEMISCHEN LITERATUR / Berneisen, Ewald – (Includes bibliographical references) – Muenster i.W.: Der Westfale, 1914 – 1r – 1 – us U.W. Library [430]
Hoffmann von Fallersleben, August Heinrich *see*
- ALLEMANNISCHE LIEDER
- DEUTSCHE GASSENLIEDER
- DEUTSCHE SALONLIEDER
- FRAENZCHENS LIEDER
- SPITZKUGELN
- STREIFLICHTER

HOFFMANN VON FALLERSLEBEN UND JOHANNA KAPP : BEGEGNUNG IN HEIDELBERG / Derwein, Herbert – (Includes bibliographical references) – 2. Aufl. [Fallersleben?]: Hoffmann von Fallersleben-Gesellschaft, [1956?] – 1r – 1 – us U.W. Library [920]
HOFFMANN VON FALLERSLEBEN UND SEIN DEUTSCHES VATERLAND / Gerstenberg, Heinrich – (Includes selected verse) – Berlin: F Fontane, 1890 – 1r – 1 – us U.W. Library [430]
HOFFMANN VON FALLERSLEBENS "TEXANISCHE LIEDER" / Goebel, Julius – S.l.: s.n., 1919? – 1r – 1 – us U.W. Library [430]
Hoffmann, Wilhelm *see* PROPHECIES OF OUR LORD AND HIS APOSTLES: A SERIES OF DISCOURSES
HOFFMANN'S CATHOLIC DIRECTORY, ALMANAC AND CLERGY LIST – QUARTERLY, FOR THE YEAR OF OUR LORD... – (Includes suppls) – Milwaukee: Hoffmann Brothers, 1889, 1891-1896 – 7r – 1 – $40.00r – us U.N.D. Archives [240]
HOFFMANN'S CATHOLIC DIRECTORY, ALMANAC, AND CLERGY LIST – QUARTERLY, FOR THE YEAR OF OUR LORD... – (Includes suppls) – Milwaukee: M H Wiltzius and Co., 1897-1899 – 3r – 1 – $40.00r – us U.N.D. Archives [240]
Hoffmannsegg, J C von *see*
- FLORE PORTUGAISE
- VERZEICHNISS DER PFLANZENKULTUREN IN DEN GRAEFL. HOFFMANNSEGGISCHEN GAERTEN ZU DRESDEN UND RAMMENAU

HOFFMAN'S CHANCERY APPEALS REPORTS / New York. (State) – (A Pre-NRS title) – 1v. 1839-40 (all publ) – 7mf – 9 – $10.50 – LLMC 80-002 – us L.L.M.C. [340]
Hoffmans, J *see*
- ETUDE SUR LES MANUSCRITS DES QUODLIBETS
- LE HUITIEME QUODLIBET DE GODEFROID DE FONTAINES
- LES QUODLIBET CINQ, SIX ET SEPT DE GODEFROID DE FONTAINES
- LES QUODLIBETS ONZE ET DOUZE DE GODEFROID DE FONTAINES

HOFFMAN'S REPORTS OF CASES IN THE DISTRICT COURT FOR NORTHERN CALIFORNIA, 1853-1858 / Hoffman, Ogden – San Francisco: Hubert. 1v. 1862 (all publ) – 7mf – 9 – $10.50 – LLMC 81-455 – us L.L.M.C. [340]
Hoffmeister, Franz A *see*
- CONCERTO, [7E] POUR LA FLUTE. [OP. 22?]
- QUATUOR POUR LE CLAVECIN OU PIANO FORTE
- QUATUOR POUR LE CLAVECIN, OU PIANO-FORTE AVEC VIOLIN, VIOLA ET VIOLONCELLE
- SONATAS, HARPSICHORD, FLUTE AND VIOLONCELLO, OP. 4
- TROIS QUATUORS CONCERTANT POUR FLUTE, VIOLON, ALTO, ET VIOLONCELLE..
- TROIS TRIOS POUR DEUX VIOLONS ET BASSE, OEUVRE 37.
- TROIS TRIOS PROGRESSIVE POUR DEUX VIOLONS ET VIOLONCELL, [OP. 28], LIV. 2
- TROIS TRIOS PROGRESSIVE POUR DEUX VIOLONS ET VIOLONCELLO, LIV. 1

Hoffmeister, Johannes *see*
- HOELDERLIN UND DIE PHILOSOPHIE

Hoffmeister, Karl *see*
- SCHILLERS SAEMMTLICHE WERKE IN ZWOELF BAENDEN
- SUPPLEMENTE ZU SCHILLERS WERKEN AUS SEINEM NACHLASS

Hoffstad, Olaf Alfred *see* NORSK FLORA
DIE HOFKAPELLE DER DEUTSCHEN KOENIGE (MGH SCHRIFTEN..: 16.BD. 1.TEIL) : GRUNDLEGUNG. DIE KAROLINGISCHE HOFKAPELLE / Fleckenstein, J – 1959 – Dfl25.00 – ne Slangenburg [240]
DIE HOFKAPELLE IM RAHMEN DER OTTONISCH-SALISCHEN REICHSKIRCHE (MGH SCHRIFTEN..: 16.BD. 2.TEIL) – 1966 – Dfl28.00 – ne Slangenburg [240]
Hofmann, Adelheid *see* LITERATURSOZIOLOGISCHE UNTERSUCHUNGEN ZU DER WESTSAECHSISCHEN STADT SCHNEEBERG AN DER WENDE VOM 17. ZUM 18. JAHRHUNDERT
Hofmann, Bernd *see* BEITRAG ZUR BESTIMMUNG DER PARAMETER UND ZUR DETEKTION DER STRUKTUR VON ZWEIPHASENSTROEMUNGEN MITTELS ULTRASCHALL
Hofmann, Carl *see* PRAKTISCHES HANDBUCH DER PAPIER-FABRIKATION
Hofmann, Ernst *see* DIE STELLUNG DER KONSTANZER BISCHOEFE ZU PAPST UND KAISER WAEHREND DES INVESTITURSTREITS
Hofmann, Georg *see* PREDIGTEN
Hofmann, Hans-Otto *see* DIE VERMOEGENSRECHTLICHEN BEZIEHUNGEN DER EHEGATTEN NACH DEM RECHTE DES BAYERISCHEN STAMMES IN NEUERER ZEIT
Hofmann, Johann von *see* ENCYCLOPAEDIE DER THEOLOGIE
Hofmann, Juergen *see* STRUKTUR, UMFELDBEDINGUNGEN UND MOTIVATIONEN BEI SCHUELERHANDBALLMANNSCHAFTEN (C, D-, E-JUGEND) DES KREISES BERGSTRASSE
Hofmann, Karl *see* A PRACTICAL TREATISE ON THE MANUFACTURE OF PAPER IN ALL ITS BRANCHES
Hofmann, Thomas *see* KINDGERECHTE BESTIMMUNG DER TRANSEPITHELIALEN POTENTIALDIFFERENZ AM RESPIRATORISCHEN EPITHEL DER NASE
Hofmannsthal, Hugo von *see*
- ARIADNE AUF NAXOS
- ELEKTRA
- DAS GESPRAECH UEBER GEDICHT
- GESTERN
- DIE HOCHZEIT DER SOBEIDE
- DAS SCHRIFTTUM ALS GEISTIGER RAUM DER NATION
- DER TOD DES TIZIAN
- DER WEISSE FAECHER

(Hofmeister, A) *see* ZUR GESCHICHTE DER WIEDERTAEUFER IN ROSTOCK
Hofmeister, A *see*
- CHRONICA MATHIAE DE NUWENBURG (MGH 6: 4.BD)
- HANDBUCH DER MUSIKALISCHEN LITERATUR ODER ALLGEMEINES SYSTEMATISCH-GEORDNETES VERZEICHNISS DER IN DEUTSCHLAND UND IN DEN ANGRENZENDEN LAENDERN GEDRUCKTEN MUSIKALIEN AUCH MUSIKALISCHEN SCHRIFTEN UND ABBILDUNGEN MIT ANZEIGE DER VERLEGER UND PREISE
- HANDBUCH DER MUSIK-LITERATUR

Hofmeister, F D *see* VERZEICHNISS DER IM JAHRE 1904-1922 ERSCHIENENEN MUSIKALIEN, AUCH MUSIKALISCHEN SCHRIFTEN UND ABBILDUNGEN MIT ANZEIGE DER VERLEGER UND PREISE
Hofmeister, W F B *see*
- DIE ENTSTEHUNG DES EMBRYO DER PHANEROGAMEN. EINE REIHE MIKROSKOPISCHER UNTERSUCHUNGEN
- NEUE BEITRAEGE ZUR KENNTNISS DER EMBRYOBILDUNG DER PHANEROGAMEN
- ON THE GERMINATION, DEVELOPMENT AND FRUCTIFICATION OF THE HIGHER CRYPTOGAMIA AND ON THE FRUCTIFICATION OF THE CONIFERAE
- VERGLEICHENDE UNTERSUCHUNGEN DER KEIMUNG, ENTFALTUNG UND FRUCHTBILDUNG HOEHEREN KRYPTOGAMEN

Hofmiller, Josef *see* EINKEHR BEI JOSEF HOFMILLER
DI HOFNUNG – 1-41. 15 Sep-10 Nov 1907 – 1 – us NY Public [072]

DIE HOFSCHRANZEN DES DICHTERFUERSTEN : DER GOETHECULT UND DESSEN TEMPELDIENER: ZUM ERSTEN MALE AKTENMAESSIG VON DER HUMORISTISCHEN SEITE BETRACHTET / Brunner, Sebastian – (Includes bibliographical references) – Wuerzburg, Wien: L Woerl, 1889 – 1r – 1 – us U.W. Library [430]
Hofstadt, Ulrich H E *see* DIE SCHMERZZEICHNUNG ("PATIENT PAIN DRAWING") ALS SCREENING-METHODE FUER LUMBAGO-ISCHIALGIE-SYNDROM-PATIENTEN
Hofstede de Groot, Cornelis *see* ARNOLD HOUBRAKEN UND SEINE "GROOTE SCHOUBURGH."O 518A. 1893
Hofstede de Groot, Cornelius *see* DIE URKUNDEN UEBER REMBRANDT (1575-1721)
Hofstede de Groot, P *see* BASILIDES AM AUSGANGE DES APOSTOLISCHEN ZEITALTERS ALS ERSTER ZEUGE FUER ALTER UND AUTORITAET NEUTESTAMENTLICHER SCHRIFTEN
Hofstede de Groot, Petrus *see* DIE GROENINGER THEOLOGEN
Hofstede, Petrus *see* BRIEF AAN DEN HOOGGELEERDEN HEER..
Hofstee, E W *see* RURAL SOCIOLOGY IN ACTION
Hofsteede, W M F *see* DECISION-MAKING PROCESSES IN FOUR WEST JAVANESE VILLAGES
HOFSTRA ENVIRONMENTAL LAW DIGEST – v1-9. 1984-92 – 9 – $65.00 set – us Hein [340]
HOFSTRA LABOR LAW FORUM *see* HOFSTRA LABOR LAW JOURNAL
HOFSTRA LABOR LAW JOURNAL – (Title varies: v1 1983 as Hofstra Labor Law Forum) – v1-13. 1983-96 – 9 – $161.00 set – us Hein [340]
HOFSTRA LAW REVIEW – v1-23. 1973-95 – 9 – $519.00 set – us Hein [340]
HOFSTRA PROPERTY LAW JOURNAL – (Supersedes: International Property Investment Journal) – v1-6. 1987-93 (all publ) – 9 – $63.00 set – us Hein [340]
HOFZEITUNG *see* BERLINISCHE NACHRICHTEN VON STAATS- UND GELEHRTEN SACHEN
Hogan, Benedict *see* PLAIN TALK
HOGANAS TIDNING *see* NORDVASTRA SKANES TIDNINGAR ENGELHOLMS TIDNING
HOGANAS TIDNING ORESUNDSPOSTEN *see*
- NORDVASTRA SKANES TIDNINGAR ENGELHOLMS TIDNING
- NORDVASTRA SKANES TIDNINGAR ENGELHOLMS TIDNING OCH KLIPPANS TIDNING

EL HOGAR CRISTIANO – 1957. 212p – 1 – 7.42 – us Baptist [240]
EL HOGAR DE LA EMPLEADA / Fundacion Ayuda Social Maria Eva Duarte de Peron – [Buenos Aires?]: Fundacion Eva Peron, [195-?] – 1 – CSUXAGP9647-B – us Hoover Inst Photo [320]
Hogar Extremeno de Zaragoza *see* FIESTAS PATRONALES SEPTIEMBRE-OCTUBRE, 1977
Hogar Extremeno en Paris. Paris *see* MEMORIA, ANO 1976
HOGARES DE TRANSITO / Fundacion Ayuda Social Maria Eva Duarte de Peron – [Buenos Aires?: Fundacion Eva Peron, 195-?] – 1 – CSUXADH4534-B – us Hoover Inst Photo [380]
Hogben, Thomas *see*
- GOD'S PLAN FOR SOUL-WINNING
- MY WITNESSES

Hoge, Dean R *see* DIVISION IN THE PROTESTANT HOUSE
Hogg, Charles Edgar *see*
- EQUITY PROCEDURE, EMBODYING THE PRINCIPLES OF PLEADING AND PRACTICE APPLICABLE TO COURTS OF EQUITY...IN VIRGINIA AND WEST VIRGINIA..
- PLEADING AND FORMS...NOW IN USE IN THE STATE OF WEST VIRGINIA

Hogg, James *see*
- TALES AND SKETCHES. BY THE ETTRICK SHEPHERD. INCLUDING THE BROWNIE OF BODSBECK, WINTER EVENING TALES, SHEPHERD'S CALENDAR...
- THE THREE PERILS OF WOMAN

HOGLANDET – Jonkoping, Sweden. 1981-86 – 1 – sw Kungliga [072]
DER HOHE BEFEHL : OPFERGANG UND BEKENNTNIS DES WERNER VOSS / Welk, Ehm – Berlin: Im Deutschen Verlag, 1939 – 1r – 1 – us U.W. Library [830]
DAS HOHE LIED : DIE KLAGLIEDER / Hitzig, Ferdinand – (Includes bibliographical references) – Leipzig:S Hirzel, 1855 – 1mf – 9 – 0-8370-3568-6 – 1985-1568 – us A.T.L.A. [780]
DIE HOHEITSVERHAELTNISSE AM BODENSEE / Heimlich, F – Konstanz, 1930 – 2mf – 1 – ILM-2320/1 – ne IDC [327]
DAS HOHELIED : AUF GRUND ARABISCHER UND ANDERER PARALLELEN / Jacob, Georg – (Includes bibliographical references) – Berlin: Mayer & Mueller, 1902 – 1mf – 9 – 0-8370-3744-1 – 1985-1744 – us A.T.L.A. [220]
DAS HOHELIED : AUS DEM HEBRAEISCHEN ORIGINALTEXT INS DEUTSCHE UEBERTRAGEN: WIE AUCH SPRACHLICH UND SACHLICH ERLAEUTERT UND MIT EINER UMFASSENDEN EINLEITUNG / Kaempf, Saul Isaac – (Includes index) – 3. neurev. verm. Ausg. Prag: Heinr. Mercy, 1884 – 1mf – 9 – 0-8370-3827-8 – 1985-1827 – us A.T.L.A. [220]
DAS HOHELIED / Delitzsch, Franz – Leipzig: Doerffling und Franke, 1851 – 1mf – 9 – 0-8370-9375-9 – 1986-3375 – us A.T.L.A. [220]
DAS HOHELIED : KURZ ERKLAERT / Harms, Theodor – Hermannsburg: Missionshausdruckerei, 1870 – 1mf – 9 – 0-8370-3476-0 – 1985-1476 – us A.T.L.A. [220]
DAS HOHELIED: INHALTLICH UND SPACHLICH ERLAEUTERT / Feilchenfeld, Wolf – Breslau: Wilhelm Koebner, 1893. 1 fiche – 9 – us A.T.L.A. [240]
DAS HOHELIED NEU UEBERSETZT UND AESTHETISCHSITTLICH BEURTEILT / Thilo, Martin – Bonne, Marcus, 1921. 3, 48 p. Film Mas 9142 – 1 – us H.U. Library [780]
DAS HOHELIED SALOMOS : EINE BIBLISCHE WEISSAGUNG AUF DAS MODERNE BABEL / Jaeger, Adolf – Berlin: Hermann Walther, 1903 – 1mf – 9 – 0-8370-3755-7 – 1985-1755 – us A.T.L.A. [220]
DAS HOHELIED SALOMO'S BEI DEN JUEDISCHEN ERKLAERERN DES MITTELALTERS : NEBST EINEM ANHANGE, ERKLAERUNGSPROBEN AUS HANDSCHRIFTEN / Salfeld, Siegmund – (Includes bibliographical references, index of authors) – Berlin: Julius Benzian, 1879 – 1mf – 9 – 0-8370-5026-X – 1985-3026 – us A.T.L.A. [220]
Hohenacker, R F *see* ENUMERATIO PLANTARUM QUAS IN ITINERE PER PROVINCIAM TALYSCH COLLEGIT
Hohenberg, F *see* CIVITATES ORBIS TERRARVM
Hohenfellner, R Markus *see* EXPERIMENTELLE UND KLINISCHE UNTERSUCHUNGEN ZUR THERAPIE VON NEUROGENEN BLASENFUNKTIONSSTOERUNGEN
HOHENLOHER TAGBLATT : BA DER SUEDWEST-PRESSE ULM – Gerabronn, Germany. 1983- – ca 8r per yr – 1 – gw Mikrofilm [072]
HOHENLOHER ZEITUNG : BA DER HEILBRONNER STIMME (SINCE 1 JUL 1974) – Oehringen, West Germany. 1968- – ca 9r per yr – 1 – gw Mikrofilm [072]
HOHENLOHER ZEITUNG *see* HEILBRONNER STIMME
Hohenlohe-Waldenburg-Schillingsfuerst, Alexander Fuerst von *see* LICHTBLICKE UND ERLEBNISSE AUS DER WELT UND DEM PRIESTERLEBEN
HOHENSALZAER ZEITUNG – Hohensalza (Inowroclaw), Poland. 1940-Jun 1943; Oct-Dec 1943 – 1 – gw Mikrofilm [943]
HOHENSCHOENHAUSENER LOKALBLATT – Berlin, 1937-40 – 4r – 1 – Dist. gw Mikrofilm – gw Misc Inst [943]
HOHENZOLLERISCHE ZEITUNG : BA DER SUEDWEST-PRESSE – Hechingen, Germany. 1987-89 – 18r – 1 – gw Mikrofilm [072]
Hohenzollerischer Geschichtverein *see* MITTEILUNGEN
DER HOHENZOLLERN WELTGESCHICHTLICHER BERUF *see* DER BURGGRAF VON NUERNBERG, ODER, DER HOHENZOLLERN WELTGESCHICHTLICHER BERUF
Hohes, Pauline B *see* CENTENNIAL HISTORY OF ANDERSON COUNTY
Hohlbau, Robert *see* GRILLPARZER
Hohlbaum, Robert *see*
- BALLADEN VOM GEIST
- FRONT DER HERZEN
- DER FRUEHLINGSWALZER
- GETRENNT MARSCHIEREN
- HELLES ABENDLIED
- MEIN LEBEN
- STUNDE DER STERNE
- SYMPHONIE IN DREI SAETZEN
- UNSTERBLICHE
- WINTERBRAUTNACHT

Hohler, Thomas Beaumont *see* DIPLOMATIC PETREL
Hohlfeld, A R *see*
- THE GOETHE CENTENARY AT THE UNIVERSITY OF WISCONSIN
- ZUM IRDISCHEN AUSGANG VON GOETHES FAUSTDICHTUNG

Hohn, Hermann *see* VOCATIONS
Hohnel, Ludwig, Ritter von *see* DISCOVERY OF LAKES RUDOLF AND STEFANIE
Hohoff, Kaplan *see* CHRISTENTHUM UND SOCIALISMUS
HOI VA DAP VE HOP-DONG KINH TE = QUESTIONS AND ANSWERS ON ECONOMIC CONTRACTS / Civil law sub-group of the Legal Studies group of the National Scientific Committee – 1964 – 1mf – 9 SEL-123/1 – ne IDC [340]
Hoinkes, Carl *see* CHRISTIAN UND DIE KATALOGE
Hoisington, William A, Jr *see* TAXPAYER REVOLT IN FRANCE: THE NATIONAL TAXPAYERS' FEDERATION
HOJA PARROQUIAL DE CORIA-CACERES – (Suplemento al Boletin Oficial del Obispado) – Caceres, 1951-1978 – 5 – sp Bibl Santa Ana [073]
HOJAS DE ARBOL CAIDAS / Cordero, Juan Luis – Caceres: Tip. El Noticiero, 1954 – sp Bibl Santa Ana [946]
Hojvat, Carlos *see* GEOGRAFIA ECONOMICO-SOCIAL ARGENTINA
Hok Hoi Association Library. Hong Kong *see* CATALOGUE
HOKI BUNRUI TAIZEN = COLLECTION OF LAWS, REGULATIONS AND ORDINANCES OF JAPAN FROM MEIJI RESTORATION TO THE MEIJI CONSTITUTION (1868-1899) / ed by Board of Documents, Cabinet of Japan – 1st ser. 69v; 2nd ser. 16v 52,380p. Tokyo. 1889-1894 – 30r – 1 – Y324,000.00 – ja Yushodo [340]
HOKUBEI MAINICHI – San Francisco, CA. 1962- – 63+ r – 1 – $3,150.00 ($135.00y) – C02821 – us Library Micro [071]
HOKUBIE MANICHI – San Francisco. Calif. (NAD). 1962- – 1 – us UMI [071]
HOKURIKU CHUUNICHI SHIMBUN – Japan, 1960-78 – 422r – 1 – inquire – us Ross [072]
HOKURIKU CHUUNICHI SHIMBUN – November 1960-December 1994 – 806r – 1 – Y8,204,000 – ja Japan Micro [950]
Holaind, Rene I *see* NATURAL LAW AND LEGAL PRACTICE
Holand, Patricia *see* THE PAPERS OF ELIZABETH CADY STANTON AND SUSAN B. ANTHONY
OS HOLANDESES NO BRASIL / Netscher, P M – Sao Paulo, 1942 – 6mf – 8 – ne Slangenburg [972]
HOLBACH AND HIS FRIENDS ANTICLERICAL THOUGHT IN FRANCE: 1760-1789 / ed by Vercruysse, Jeroom – 70 titles – 9 – fr Hachette [944]
HOLBACH ET SES AMIS, 1760-1789 – (Abauzit, Firmin. Barbeu-Dubourg, Jacques. Bonafous, Louis-Abel de. Borde, Charles. Boulanger, Nicolas A. Burigny, Jean-Levesque de. Castilhon, Jean-Louis. Cloots, Jean-Baptiste. Collins, Anthony. Du Laurens, Henri-Joseph. Dumarsais, Cesar-Chesneau. Freret, Nicolas. Helvetius, Claude-Adrien. Holbach, Paul-Thiry d'. Meister, Jacques-Henri. Millot, Claude-Francois-Xavier. Mirabaud, Jean-Baptiste de. Morellet, Andre. Orobio, Isaac. Toland, John. Van Haren, Willem. Woolston, Thomas) – (series). In French. Titles also available individually; enquire. Following authors from this Series are also listed individually – 9 – fr Hachette [240]
Holbach, Paul-Thiry d' *see*
- L'ABBE ET LE RABBIN
- ARRET RENDU A L'AMPHITHEATRE DE L'OPERA, SUR LA PLAINTE DU MILIEU DU PARTERRE, INTERVENANT DANS LA QUERELLE DES DEUX COINS
- LE BON SENS OU IDEES NATURELLES OPPOSEES AUX IDEES SURNATURELLES
- LE CHRISTIANISME DEVOILE
- LA CONTAGION SACREE OU HISTOIRE NATURELLE DE LA SUPERSTITION
- ELEMENTS DE LA MORALE UNIVERSELLE OU CATECHISME DE LA NATURE
- ESSAI SUR L'ART DE RAMPER, A L'USAGE DES COURTISANS
- ESSAI SUR LES PREJUGES, OU, DE L'INFLUENCE DES OPINION SUR LES MOEURS ET SUR LE BONHEUR DES HOMMES
- ETHOCRATIE OU LE GOUVERNEMENT FONDE SUR LA MORALE
- HISTOIRE DE JESUS-CHRIST OU, ANALYSE RAISONNEE DES EVANGILES
- LETTRE A UNE DAME D'UN CERTAIN AGE, SUR L'ETAT PRESENT DE L'OPERA
- LETTRES A EUGENIE OU PRESERVATIF CONTRE LES PREJUGES
- LE MILITAIRE PHILOSOPHE OU DIFFICULTES SUR LA RELIGION PROPOSEES AU R.P. MALEBRANCHE, PRETRE DE L'ORATOIRE
- LA MORALE UNIVERSELLE OU LES DEVOIRS DE L'HOMME FONDES SUR SA NATURE
- LA POLITIQUE NATURELLE. OU DISCOURS SUR LES VRAIS PRINCIPES DU GOUVERNEMENT
- SYSTEME DE LA NATURE, OU DES LOIS DU MONDE PHYSIQUE ET DU MONDE MORAL
- SYSTEME SOCIAL. OU PRINCIPES NATURELS DE LA MORAL ET DE LA POLITIQUE. AVEC UN EXAMEN DE L'INFLUENCE DU GOUVERNEMENT SUR LES MOEURS
- TABLEAU DES SAINTS, OU EXAMEN DE L'ESPRIT, DE LA CONDUITE, DES MAXIMES ET DU MERITE DES PERSONNAGES QUE LE CHRISTIANISME REVERE ET PROPOSE POUR MODELE
- THEOLOGIE PORTATIVE OU DICTIONNAIRE ABREGE DE LA RELIGION CHRETIENNE

Holbein, H 2 *see* ICONES HISTORICUM VETERIS TESTAMENTI
Holboll, C P *see* ORNITHOLOGISCHER BEITRAG ZUR FAUNA GROENLANDS
HOLBROOK 1872-1900 – (Mf 1: Death Index 1872-1900+ A-G. Mf 2: Death Index 1872-1900+ G-O. Mf Death Index 1872-1900+ O-Z. Mf 4: Marriage Index 1872-1900+ A-C. Mf 5: Marriage Index 1872-1900+ D-H. Mf 6: Marriage Index 1872-1900+ H-M. Mf 7: Marriage Index 1872-1900+ M-S. Mf 8: Marriage Index 1872-1900+ S-Z. Mf 9: Birth Index 1872-1900+ A-D. Mf 10: Birth Index 1872-1900+ D-J. Mf 11: Birth Index 1872-1900+ J-O. Mf 12: Birth Index 1872-1900+ P-W. Mf 13: Birth Index 1872-1900+ W-Z. Mf 14: Births 1872-81. Mf 15: Births 1881-90. Mf 16: Births 1890-1900. Mf 17: Marriages 1872-90. Mf 18: Marriages 1890-1900. Mf 19: Deaths 1872-95. Mf 20: Deaths 1895-1904) – (mf ed 1994) – 20mf – 9 – 0-87623-188-1 – us Holbrook [920]
Holbrook, Edwin M *see* MANUAL OF LAWS RELATING TO PRIVATE CLAIMS AGAINST THE STATE OF NEW YORK..
HOLBROOK HERALD – Holbrook, NE. -w. Oct-Dec 1895; Feb 1896-May 1898; Jul 1898-Mar 1899 – 1 – us NE Hist [071]
Holbrook, J E *see*
- ICHTHYOLOGY OF SOUTH CAROLINA
- NORTH AMERICAN HERPETOLOGY

Holbrook, Jay Mack *see*
- BIBLIOGRAPHY OF MASSACHUSETTS VITAL RECORDS 1620-1905
- FAMILY STRUCTURE IN 17TH-CENTURY WINDSOR, CONNECTICUT
- TOPICAL INDEX TO MAYFLOWER DESCENDANT 1620-1937

Holbrook, Jos. P *see* WORSHIP IN SONG
Holbrook, Martin Luther *see* HOW TO STRENGTHEN THE MEMORY; OR, NATURAL AND SCIENTIFIC METHODS OF NEVER FORGETTING
HOLBROOK OBSERVER – Holbrook, NE. -w. Apr 1908-Sept 1918; Jan 1918 to date – 1 – us NE Hist [071]
Holcomb Family *see* LETTERS
Holcomb, Helen Harriet *see* MEN OF MIGHT IN INDIA MISSIONS
Holcomb, T L *see* PAPERS WHILE EXECUTIVE SECRETARY OF THE SUNDAY SCHOOL BOARD, JUNE 1935-MAY 1945
Holcombe, Hosea *see* HISTORY OF THE BAPTISTS IN ALABAMA
Holcombe, Robert A *see* THE EFFECTS OF AUDITORY BIOFEEDBACK ON THE ACCURACY OF THE TENNIS VOLLEY
Holcroft, T *see* THE DESERTED DAUGHTER
HOLDEN 1739-1849 – (Mf 1T-5T: Births 1739-1844. Mf 1T-3T: Marriages & Deaths 1742-94. Mf 2T-3T: Intentions 1782-92. Mf 5T-6T: Publishments 1840-49. Mf 6T-7T: Deaths 1771-1844. Mf 7T-10T: Publishments 1803-40. Mf 10T-11T: Marriages 1792-1845. Mf 11T-12T: Births 1843-49. Mf 12T-13T: Marriages 1844-49. Mf 13T: Deaths 1844-49;

Out-of-Town Marriages 1743-99. Mf 13T-14T: Births A-W 1720-1847. Mf 14T: Vital Records A-W 1742-1852) – (mf ed 1996) – 14mf – 9 – 0-87623-267-5 – us Holbrook [920]
Holden, Edith *see* BLYDEN OF LIBERIA
Holden, Oliver *see*
- AMERICAN HARMONY: CONTAINING A VARIETY OF AIRS SUITABLE FOR DIVINE WORSHIP, ON THANKSGIVINGS, ORDINATIONS, CHRISTMAS, FASTS, FUNERALS AND OTHER OCCASIONS
- SACRED DIRGES, HYMNS, AND ANTHEMS, COMMEMORATIVE OF THE DEATH OF GENERAL GEORGE WASHINGTON, THE GUARDIAN OF HIS COUNTRY AND THE FRIEND OF MAN

Holder, Charles Frederick *see*
- CHARLES DARWIN
- THE QUAKERS IN GREAT BRITAIN AND AMERICA

Holder, W *see* A TREATISE OF THE NATURAL GROUND AND PRINCIPLES OF HARMONY
Holder, William *see* ELEMENTS OF SPEECH
Holder-Egger, O *see* MONUMENTA GERMANIAE HISTORICA (MGH)
HOLDING COMPANIES ACT OF 1935 RELEASES / U.S. Securities and Exchange Commission – nos 1-17865. 12 Feb 1935-26 Jan 1973 (all publ) – 818mf – 9 – $1,227.00 – LLMC 84-356 – us L.L.M.C. [340]
HOLDING COMPANY ACT OF 1935. SEP 1935-JAN 1973 / U.S. Securities and Exchange Commission – 9 – us UMI [336]
HOLDINGS / Kansas State Historical Society, Manuscripts Department – 1854-1985 – 1 – us KS Hist [978]
Holdnak, Andrew *see* THE IMPACTS OF MARINE DEBRIS, WEATHER CONDITIONS, AND UNEXPECTED EVENTS ON RECREATIONAL BOATER SATISFACTION ON THE DELAWARE INLAND BAYS
HOLDREGE DAILY CITIZEN – Holdrege, NE. (-tw 1932-36; -d 1936 to date). Dec 1887; Jan-May 1889; Jul 1889-Dec 1893; Jan 1895 to date – 1 – us NE Hist [071]
HOLDREGE PROGRESS – Holdrege, NE. -w. (-sw 1933). Oct 1895-Dec 1897; Nov 1898-Feb 1904; Dec 1904-Apr 1943 – 1 – us NE Hist [071]
HOLDREGE REPUBLICAN – Holdrege, NE. -w. Sept 1884-Jul 1886 – 1 – us NE Hist [071]
Holdren, John *see* ENERGY
Hole, Charles *see*
- THE EARLY HISTORY OF THE CHURCH MISSIONARY SOCIETY FOR AFRICA AND THE EAST TO THE END OF A.D. 1814
- EARLY MISSIONS TO AND WITHIN THE BRITISH ISLANDS

Hole, Hugh Marshall *see* THE MAKING OF RHODESIA
HOLGATE BAPTIST CHURCH. PORTLAND, OREGON : CHURCH RECORDS – Feb1954-Jun 1973 – 1 – 10.13 – us Baptist [240]
Holgate.Ohio. Holgate United Methodist Church *see* RECORDS
Holgate.Ohio. St. John's Lutheran Church *see* RECORDS
HOLIDAY – (v45-58. 1969-77. 5,6. v27-58. 1960-77. 9) – v1-58. 1946-77 – 1 – us UMI [910]
THE HOLIDAY ADVERTISER – St John, N.B.: W.A. Barnes, [1880?] – 9 – cn C.I.H.M. [971]
HOLIDAYS OF THE FRENCH CANADIANS / Bender, Prosper – 1888? 00118. (Pre-1900 Canadiana) – 9 – cn C.I.H.M. [305]
HOLINESS AND POWER : FOR THE CHURCH AND THE MINISTRY / Hills, Aaron Merritt – (Includes index) – Cincinnati, OH: M W Knapp, 1897 – 1mf – 9 – 0-8370-4877-X – 1985-2877 – us A.T.L.A. [240]
HOLINESS: AS UNDERSTOOD BY THE WRITERS OF THE BIBLE / Beet, Joseph Agar – New York: Phillips & Hunt, 1889.1 fiche – 9 – us A.T.L.A. [240]
THE HOLINESS EVANGEL – v1-3. Sept 1906-Jan 1910 (complete) – 1r – 1 – ATLA S0416 – us A.T.L.A. [240]
HOLINESS LAYMAN – 1910; 1917-25 (complete) – 1r – 1 – ATLA S0417 – us A.T.L.A. [240]
HOLINESS SYMBOLIC AND REAL / Beet, Joseph Agar – 1910 – 9 – us A.T.L.A. [240]
Holinshed, R *see* THE WHOLE VOLUME OF CHRONICLES CONTAINING THE CHRONICLES OF ENGLAND, THE CHRONICLES OF SCOTLAND, THE CHRONICLES OF IRELAND
HOLISSO ANUMPA TOSHOLI – An English and Choctaw Definer. 1852 – 1 – 9.10 – us Baptist [490]
A HOLISTIC ANALYSIS OF STRESS WITH IMPLICATIONS FOR STRESS MANAGEMENT AS A FUNCTION OF PASTORAL COUNSELING / Gray, Edward A – 1981 – 1 – 6.80 – us Baptist [240]
HOLISTIC HEALTH REVIEW – 1978-80 – 1,5,6,9 – us UMI [073]
HOLISTIC NURSING PRACTICE – v1- . 1986- – 1,5,6,9 – us UMI [073]
Holker, John *see* PAPERS
HOLKHAM DEEDS / Holkham Hall. Norfolk. England – 1100-1459 – 1 – uk Microform Academic [025]
HOLKHAM ESTATE PAPERS / Holkham Hall. Norfolk. England – 1779-1833 – 1 – uk Microform Academic [332]
HOLKHAM ESTATES, FARM PREMISES AND COTTAGES / Holkham Hall. Norfolk. England – 1856 – 1 – uk Microform Academic [332]
HOLKHAM GENERAL ESTATE DEEDS / Holkham Hall. Norfolk. England – 1579-1641 – 1 – uk Microform Academic [332]
Holkham Hall. Norfolk, England *see* CASTLEACRE ROLLS
Holkham Hall. Norfolk. England *see*
- ACCOUNTS
- AUDIT BOOKS
- BIBLE PICTURE BOOK
- CASTLEACRE ROLLS
- CATALOGUE
- COUNTRY ACCOUNTS
- COURT ROLLS
- CRONICA DI PISA. ETC
- DOMESTIC ACCOUNTS
- FIFTEENTH CENTURY HOLKHAM MANUSCRIPT
- HISTORICAL TRACTS AND DOCUMENTS, STATE PAPERS, ETC
- HOLKHAM DEEDS
- HOLKHAM ESTATE PAPERS
- HOLKHAM ESTATES, FARM PREMISES AND COTTAGES
- HOLKHAM GENERAL ESTATE DEEDS
- HOLKHAM HOME FARM ACCOUNTS
- HOLKHAM LETTER BOOKS OF FRANCIS BLAIKIE, AGENT TO "COKE OF NORFOLK." 1816-37
- HOLKHAM MS 137
- HOLKHAM MS 311
- HOLKHAM MSS. 306, 407, AND 408
- HOLKHAM OFFICE CASH ACCOUNTS
- ILLUMINATED MSS. FROM THE LIBRARY OF THE EARL OF LEICESTER
- INVENTORY AND VALUATION
- INVENTORY OF THE CONTENTS OF HOLKHAM HALL
- LECTIONARIUM EVANGELIORUM
- MAGNA CHARTA AND STATUTA
- MANUSCRIPTS: ALIENATED ESTATES; HILLESDEN AND FARNHAM ROYAL, BUCKS
- MEDIEVAL BACKGROUND
- OFFICES OF MOST CHARGES APPERTAINING UNTO A CAMP
- PLANS OF HOLKHAM
- POLITICAL AND SATYRICAL POEMS
- STATUTA ENDING 1330; REGISTRUM BREVIUM, ETC.; STATUTA FROM 1344-1388; NATURA BREVIUM; BREVIA PLACITATA ETC.; TENURES, NATURA BREVIUM, ETC
- TERRIERS, DEEDS, PARTICULARS, ETC
- TREASURES OF HOLKHAM HALL LIBRARY

HOLKHAM HOME FARM ACCOUNTS / Holkham Hall. Norfolk. England – 1814-22 – 1 – uk Microform Academic [941]
HOLKHAM LETTER BOOKS OF FRANCIS BLAIKIE, AGENT TO "COKE OF NORFOLK." 1816-37 / Holkham Hall. Norfolk. England – 1 – uk Microform Academic [650]
HOLKHAM MS 137 / Holkham Hall. Norfolk. England – 1 – uk Microform Academic [340]
HOLKHAM MS 311 / Holkham Hall. Norfolk. England – 1 – uk Microform Academic [340]
HOLKHAM MSS. 306, 407, AND 408 / Holkham Hall. Norfolk. England – 1 – uk Microform Academic [025]
HOLKHAM OFFICE CASH ACCOUNTS / Holkham Hall. Norfolk. England – 1808-44 – 1 – uk Microform Academic [650]
DIE HOLK'SCHEN JAEGER / Pueltz, Wilhelm – Muenchen: Deutscher Volksverlag, 1943 – 1r – 1 – us U.W. Library [830]
Holl, Karl *see*
- AMPHILOCHIUS VON IKONIUM
- ENTHUSIASMUS UND BUSSGEWALT BEIM GRIECHISCHEN MOENCHTUM
- FRAGMENTE VORNICAENISCHER KIRCHENVAETER AUS DEN SACRA PARALLELA (T.U.U. 2-20/2)
- DIE GEISTLICHEN UEBUNGEN DES IGNATIUS VON LOYOLA
- DIE HANDSCHRIFTLICHE UEBERLIEFERUNG DES EPIPHANIUS (T.U.U. 3-36/2)
- JOHANNES CALVIN
- LUTHER UND DAS LANDESHERRLICHE KIRCHENREGIMENT
- DER MODERNISMUS
- DIE SACRA PARALLELA DES JOHANNES DAMASCENUS (T.U.U. 2-16/1)

HOLLAENDISCHE ZEITUNG – Amsterdam, jan 4-dec 30 1785 – 1 – Dist. gw Mikrofilm – gw Misc Inst [949]
HOLLAND 1771-1890 – (Mf 1-2,4: Marriages/ Intentions 1771-1824. Mf 1-4: Births & Deaths 1767-1840. Mf 2-4: Church Members 1784-1834. Mf 5-6: Bargains & Sales 1834-40. Mf 6-7: Births 1837-84. Mf 7-8: Marriages 1844-80. Mf 9: Deaths 1876-90; Marriages 1882-93; Births 1885-90. Mf 10: B,M,D 1781-1861) – (mf ed 1984) – 10mf – 9 – 0-931248-62-0 – us Holbrook [920]
HOLLAND COLLECTION *see* HOLOGRAPH, COPY AND PRINTED PLAYS.
Holland, Emily *see* EMILY HOLLAND PAPERS AT CORNELL UNIVERSITY
Holland, Frederic May *see* OUR CLERGYWOMEN
Holland, Henri *see* LETTRE A MESSIEURS LES DISCIPLES DE SAINT-SIMON SUR QUELQUES POINTS DE LEUR DOCTRINE
Holland, Henry Scott *see*
- THE APOSTOLIC FATHERS
- A BUNDLE OF MEMORIES
- OPTIMISM OF BUTLER'S ANALOGY
- THE OPTIMISM OF BUTLER'S 'ANALOGY' DELIVERED IN THE SHELDONIAN THEATRE, JUNE 13 1908
- PERSONAL STUDIES

Holland, J Read *see* INDONESIAN LIVING CONDITIONS REPORT
Holland, Josiah Gilbert *see* GOLD-FOIL
Holland Land Company. Philadelphia, PA *see* ARCHIVES....,1789-1869
Holland, Patricia *see* THE COLLECTED CORRESPONDENCE OF LYDIA MARIA CHILD, 1817-1880
Holland, Rupert Sargent *see* BUILDERS OF UNITED ITALY
Holland, Thomas E *see*
- THE ELEMENTS OF JURISPRUDENCE

Holland, Wilhelm Ludwig *see*
- UHLANDS GEDICHTE UND DRAMEN
- ZU LUDWIG UHLANDS GEDAECHTNIS

Hollander, Nancy *see*
- LA MUJER
- WOMEN, SLAVES OF HISTORY OR HISTORY OF SLAVES

Hollander, Richard *see* VIDEO DEMOCRACY: THE VOTE-FROM-HOME REVOLUTION
HOLLANDIA – London, UK. 6 Nov 1897-30 Dec 1899 – 1 – uk British Libr Newspaper [072]
DE HOLLANDSCHE AFRIKANEN EN HUNNE REPUBLIEK IN ZUID-AFRIKA / Stuart, Jacobus – (Filmed with: Souvenir of the Union of South Africa) – Amsterdam: G W Tielkemeijer, 1854 – 1 – us Res Libr [960]
Hollandsche maatschappij der wetenschappen, Haarlem *see* NATUURKUNDIGE VERHANDELINGEN VAN DE HOLLANDSCHE MAATSCHAPPIJ DER WETENSCHAPPEN TE HAARLEM
Holle, G von *see* FARNFLORA DER GEGEND VON HANNOVER
Holle, Paul *see* DE LA SENEGAMBIE FRANCAISE
Hollebeke, L van *see* LISSEWEGHE, SON EGLISE ET SON ABBAYE
Hollenberg, Wilhelm Adolf *see* HEBRAEISCHES SCHULBUCH
Hollenweger, Walter J *see* HANDBUCH DER PFINGSTBEWEGUNG
Holler, P *see*
- AN ENGLISH-TELUGU SCIENTIFIC DICTIONARY
- A SMALL ENGLISH-TELUGU DICTIONARY
- A TELUGU-ENGLISH CLASSICAL DICTIONARY
- VOCABULARY TO THE TELUGU BIBLE

Holley, Frances C *see* ONCE THEIR HOME OR OUR LEGACY FROM THE DAHKOTAHS
Holley, Marietta *see*
- JOSIAH ALLEN'S WIFE AS A P.A. AND P. I. SAMENTHA AT THE CENTENNIAL.
- SAMANTHA AMONG THE BRETHREN

Holley, Robert P *see* RESOURCE SHARING AND INFORMATION NETWORKS
Hollibaugh, E F *see* BIOGRAPHICAL HISTORY CLOUD COUNTY
Holliday, Cyrus Kurtz *see*
- LETTERS AND CLIPPINGS
- PAPERS

Holliday, Fernandes C *see* A BIBLE HAND-BOOK, THEOLOGICALLY ARRANGED
Holliday, Frederic C *see* INDIANA METHODISM; BEING AN ACCOUNT OF THE INTRODUCTION, PROGRESS AND PRESENT POSITION OF METHODISM IN THE STATE ... WITH SKETCHES OF THE PRINCIPAL METHODIST EDUCATORS IN THE STATE DOWN TO 1872
Holliday, Omar *see* 700 YEARS OF HOLLIDAYS
Holliman, Susan C *see* EFFECTS OF THE MENSTRUAL CYCLE PHASES ON THE ENERGY INTAKE AND EXPENDITURE IN PHYSICALLY ACTIVE AND INACTIVE WOMEN
Hollin, Clive et al *see* PSYCHOLOGY, CRIME, AND LAW
Hollinger, William C *see* THE NATIONAL INCOME OF INDONESIA, 1951-1952: A CRITICAL COMMENTARY OF THE NEUMARK ESTIMATES
Hollingsworth, J G *see* HISTORY OF SURRY COUNTY OR ANNALS OF NORTHWEST NORTH CAROLINA
HOLLIN'S LIEBELEBEN : EIN ROMAN / Arnim, Ludwig Achim, Freiherr von – (Added t.p. of Goettingen 1802 ed) – Freiburg: J C B Mohr, 1883 – 1r – 1 – us U.W. Library [830]
Hollis, New Hampshire. Hollis Baptist Church *see* RECORDS
HOLLISTER ADVANCE – Hollister, CA. 1919-56; 1981; 1983 – 18r – 1 BC02296 – $900.00 – us Library Micro [071]
Hollister, G W *see*
- SIN AND SALVATION (CCC160)
- UNDERSTANDING THE BIBLE (CCC159)
- WHY FEAR EVOLUTION? (CCC161)

Hollister, Paul *see* PAPERWEIGHTS: FLOWERS WHICH CLOTHE THE MEADOWS
HOLLISTON 1720-1849 – (Mf 1T-2T: Births 1720-55. Mf 3T: Births 1776-98. Mf 4T: Births 1799-1824. Mf 5T: Births 1825-44. Mf 6T-7T: Marriages 1729-1843. Mf 7T: Intentions 1767-68. Mf 7T-9T: Deaths 1725-1844. Mf 9T-11T: Publishments 1766-1849. Mf 11T-13T: Births 1843-49, 1807-39. Mf 13T-14T: Marriages 1843-49. Mf 14T: Deaths 1843-49, 1842) – (mf ed 1996) – 14mf – 9 – 0-87623-268-3 – us Holbrook [920]
Hollmann, Georg *see*
- JEWISH RELIGION IN THE TIME OF JESUS
- URCHRISTENTUM IN KORINTH: EINE RELIGIONS- UND KULTURGESCHICHTLICHE STUDIE

Hollon, D Leslie *see* THE MEANING OF SANCTIFICATION IN TWENTIETH CENTURY SOUTHERN BAPTIST THOUGHT
HOLLOWAY AND HORNSEY PRESS *see* HOLLOWAY PRESS
HOLLOWAY AND ISLINGTON JOURNAL – London, 1971-74 – 7r – 1 – uk British Libr Newspaper [072]
HOLLOWAY PRESS – (North Metropolitan and Holloway Press. Holloway Press and Hornsey Press. Holloway and Hornsey Press. Islington and Holloway Press. North London Press) – London, 1872-1971 – 72r – 1 – uk British Libr Newspaper [072]
HOLLOWAY PRESS AND HORNSEY PRESS *see* HOLLOWAY PRESS
HOLLOWAYS BAPTIST CHURCH. LIBERTY ASSOCIATION. DAVIDSON COUNTY. NORTH CAROLINA : CHURCH RECORDS – 1832-1927 – 1 – 29.25 – us Baptist [240]
Hollrung, M *see* JAHRESBERICHT UEBER NEUERUNGEN UND LEISTUNGEN AUF DEM GEBIET DES PFLANZENSCHUTZES
Holly, James Theodore *see* A VINDICATION OF THE CAPACITY OF THE NEGRO RACE FOR SELF-GOVERNMENT, AND CIVILIZED PROGRESS, AS DEMONSTRATED BY HISTORICAL EVENTS OF THE HAYTIAN REVOLUTION
HOLLY LEAVES – Hollywood, CA. 1918-1924 – 11r – 1 – $550.00 – R03245 – us Library Micro [071]
HOLLY SPRINGS BAPTIST CHURCH. PICKENS COUNTY. SOUTH CAROLINA : CHURCH RECORDS – 1839-1954. 702p – 1 – 31.59 – us Baptist [240]
HOLLY SPRINGS BAPTIST CHURCH. SPARTANBURG COUNTY. SOUTH CAROLINA : CHURCH RECORDS – 1834-1866, 1910-19, 1926-73; 754p – 1 – 33.93 – us Baptist [240]

Holly Springs, Mississippi *see* MISCELLANEOUS EARLY NEWSPAPERS
HOLLYWOOD CITIZEN NEWS – 1911-57.Chronicles of the birth and life of the Golden Era of Hollywood. 398 rolls.Individual rolls available – 1 – 11,950.00 – uk Libr Preservation [071]
HOLLYWOOD CITIZEN NEWS – Hollywood, CA. 1903-1957 – 442r – 1 – $22,100.00 – R03243 – us Library Micro [071]
HOLLYWOOD DIRECTORIES – Los Angeles Co, CA. 1906; 1928 – 2r – 1 – $100.00 – D053 – us Library Micro [790]
HOLLYWOOD PRESS – Salem OR. Feb 10 1928-Dec 9 1932 – 1 – us U.O. Library [071]
HOLLYWOOD REPORTER – Hollywood, CA. 1976-80 – 17r – 1 – $850.00 – R02299 – us Library Micro [071]
THE HOLLYWOOD REPORTER : TODAY'S FILM NEWS TODAY – Hollywood. v18-66. 1935-41 – 11r – 1 – us Ross [071]
HOLLYWOOD RIVIERA TRIBUNE *see* PALOS VERDES NEWS AND ROLLING HILLS HERALD
HOLLYWOOD STAR – Salem OR. Feb 10 1939 – 1 – us U.O. Library [071]
Holm, Adolf *see*
- GESCHICHTE SICILIENS IM ALTERTHUM
- GRIECHISCHE GESCHICHTE VON IHREM URSPRUNGE BIS ZUM UNTERGANGE DER SELBSTAENDIGKEIT DES GRIECHISCHEN VOLKES
- THE HISTORY OF GREECE FROM ITS COMMENCEMENT TO THE CLOSE OF THE INDEPENDENCE OF THE GREEK NATION

Holm, G *see*
- BIDRAG TIL KJENDSKABET OM ESKIMOERNES HERKOMST
- DEN DABSKE KONEBAADS-EXPEDITION TIL GRONLANDS OSTKUST
- ETHNOLOGISK SKIZZE AF ANGMAGSALIKERNE
- SAGN OG FORTAELLINGER FRA ANGMAGSALIK

Holm, Norbert *see* SOLDAT UND KAEMPFER
Holman, Charles *see* DIARY
Holman, James *see* VOYAGE ROUND THE WORLD
Holman, Sharon S *see* A SYLLABUS OF THE AMERICAN SOCIAL DANCE SILVER LEVEL TECHNIQUE
Holmberg, H J *see* ETHNOGRAPHISCHE SKIZZEN UEBER DIE VOELKER DES RUSSISCHEN AMERIKA
Holmboe, J *see*
- LIST OF PLANTS FROM ARMENIA AND TREBIZOND
- NOGLE UGRAESPLANTERS INDVANDRING I NORGE

Holme, LR *see* THE EXTINCTION OF THE CHRISTIAN CHURCHES IN NORTH AFRICA
Holme, Randle *see* THE ACADEMY OF ARMORY
Holmes *see* HISTORY OF WINDSOR COUNTY
Holmes, Calvin Pratt *see* PROBATE LAW AND PRACTICE OF THE STATE OF IOWA..
HOLMES COUNTY ADVERTISER – Bonifay. Fl. -w. May 1936-1941, 1948- – 1 – us P.K. Yonge [071]
HOLMES COUNTY HERALD – Lexington. Miss. 1959-1966 – 1 – us UMI [071]
HOLMES COUNTY, OHIO, CEMETERY RECORDS : AND RICHARDH. DICKINSON; HOLMES COUNTY, OHIO, CEMETERY RECORDS / Dickinson, Marguerite – Millersburg, OH: s.p., 1970 – 1r – 1 – us Western Res [920]
Holmes, Daniel B *see* LETTERS
Holmes, E E *see* VISITATION CHARGES DELIVERED TO THE CLERGY AND CHURCHWARDENS OF THE DIOCESES OF CHESTER AND OXFORD
Holmes, Edmund Gore Alexander *see* CREED OF CHRIST
Holmes, Elmer W *see* HISTORY OF RIVERSIDE COUNTY
Holmes, Henry S *see* DIARY
Holmes, J S *see* HOLMES' REPORTS OF CASES IN THE FIRST CIRCUIT, 1870-1875
Holmes, ML *see* THE ANALYSIS OF ENROLLMENT PATTERNS AND STUDENT PROVILE CHARACTERISTICS AT A SMALL RURAL NEW ENGLAND UNIVERSITY 1978-1988
Holmes, Oliver Wendell, Jr *see*
- COLLECTED LEGAL PAPERS
- MECHANISM IN THOUGHT AND MORALS
- THE OLIVER WENDELL HOLMES, JR. PAPERS
- SOME TABLE TALK OF MR. JUSTICE HOLMES AND "THE MRS."...WITH CHRISTMAS GREETINGS FROM RICHARD WALDEN HALE

Holmes, Patricia A *see* PERSONALITY TYPES OF NCAA AND NAIA MALE AND FEMALE ADMINISTRATORS
HOLMES' REPORTS OF CASES IN THE FIRST CIRCUIT, 1870-1875 / Holmes, J S – Boston: Little-Brown. 1v. 1877 (all publ) – 6mf – 9 – $9.00 – LLMC 81-456 – us L.L.M.C. [340]
Holmes, Richard J *see* A COMPARISON OF HEMODYNAMIC RESPONSES TO ARM AND LEG EXERCISE OF THE SAME INTENSITIES
Holmes, Robert R *see*
- MAIN GROUP CHEMISTRY NEWS
- PHOSPHORUS AND SULFER AND THE RELATED ELEMENTS

Holmes, T Scott *see* THE ORIGIN AND DEVELOPMENT OF THE CHRISTIAN CHURCH IN GAUL DURING THE FIRST SIX CENTURIES OF THE CHRISTIAN ERA
Holmested, George Smith *see* THE MECHANICS' LIEN ACTS; BEING THE REVISED STATUTE OF ONTARIO, CHAPTER 120, AND 41 VICTORIAE, CHAPTER 17, WITH ANNOTATIONS
Holmoe, Thomas A *see* THE SELECTION AND USE OF TEAM CAPTAINS IN COLLEGE FOOTBALL
HOLOCAUST / Israel. Yad Vashem. Remembrance Authority – Jerusalem, 1975. 79 p. Illus – 9 – 2.00 – is I.T.T.I. [324]
HOLOGRAPH, COPY AND PRINTED PLAYS. / Vega, Lope de – Formerly in the Holland Collection, now at Melbury House, Dorset – 1 – uk Microform Academic [790]
HOLOPHOTE : CRITICO E NOTICIOSO – Maceio-AL, Brazil. 8 Nov 1896-9 Ago 1897 – 1 – bl Biblioteca [072]
HOLOPHOTE : HUMORISTICO – Penedo-AL, Brazil. 6 Jul, Nov 1902-25 Jan 1903 – 1 – bl Biblioteca [072]
O HOLOPHOTE : JORNAL HUMORISTICO E CRITICO – Manaos, Amazonas. 30 Jul, Out, 31 Dez 1905 – 1,5,6 – bl Biblioteca [072]
HOLOS UKRAINY – Kyiv: Verkhovna Rada Ukrainy, 1991- – 3mf per year – 9 – $229.95y – us East View [320]
HOLOS VOSTOCHNOI TSERKVY = VOICE OF THE EASTERN CHURCH – Perth Amboy, NJ: Vestal Publ Co, v1 n1-v5 n35. nov 1941-apr 1945 – 1 – us Res Libr [073]
Holoway, Ron *see* MUSIC EFFECTS ON THE ACQUISITION OF A MOTOR SKILL
Holscher, Kurt Heimart *see* FEINDE DES VOLKES
Holst, G *see* THE AMERICAN RONDO
Holst, Herman E von *see*
- CONSTITUTIONAL HISTORY OF THE UNITED STATES
- JOHN C. CALHOUN

Holstein, Hugo *see* DIE REFORMATION IM SPIEGELBILDE DER DRAMATISCHEN LITERATUR DES SECHZEHNTEN JAHRHUNDERTS
HOLSTEIN REPORTER – Holstein, NE. -w. Feb-Nov 1925 – 1 – us NE Hist [071]
HOLSTEINISCHER COURIER – Neumuenster, Germany. 1969- – ca 6r per yr – 1 – gw Mikrofilm [072]
Holsten, C *see* ZUM EVANGELIUM DES PAULUS UND DES PETRUS
Holsten, Carl *see*
- DIE DREI URSPRUENGLICHEN, NOCH UNGESCHRIEBENEN EVANGELIEN
- IST DIE THEOLOGIE WISSENSCHAFT?
- DIE SYNOPTISCHEN EVANGELIEN NACH DER FORM IHRES INHALTES

Holsten, Earl J *see* ZUM EVANGELIUM DES PAULUS UND DES PETRUS; ALTES UND NEUES
Holstenius, L *see* CODEX REGULARUM
HOLT AND GREGSON PAPERS 1778-1830 / Liverpool. City Libraries – BRRAM – 1 – uk Microform Academic [025]
HOLT CO. INDEPENDENT – O'Neill. Neb. 1893-1963 – 1 – us UMI [071]
HOLT COUNTY BANNER – O'Neill, NE. -w. Apr 1882; Jun 1882; Jan 1883-Feb 1884 – 1 – us NE Hist [071]
HOLT COUNTY REPUBLICAN – Atkinson, NE. -w. Aug. 1899-Jul. 1900 – 1 – us NE Hist [071]
HOLT COUNTY REPUBLICAN – Atkinson. Neb. 1899-1900 – 1 – us UMI [071]
Holt, Francis Ludlow *see* THE LAW OF LIBEL: IN WHICH IS CONTAINED A GENERAL HISTORY OF THIS LAW IN THE ANCIENT CODES.
Holt Hutton, Richard *see*
- BIOGRAPHICAL STUDIES
- ECONOMIC STUDIES

HOLTEI ALS DRAMATIKER / Moschner, Alfred – (Includes bibliographical references) – Breslau: F Hirt, 1911 – 1 – us U.W. Library [430]
Holtei, Karl von *see*
- BRIEFE AN LUDWIG TIECK
- ERZAEHLENDE SCHRIFTEN
- GOETHE UND SEIN SOHN
- SCHLESISCHE GEDICHTE

Holth, Sverre *see* MEDITATIONS ON THE LORD'S PRAYER (CCC162)
Holthaus, Arno *see* DIE KONTROVERSE UM DIE TRANSFERPROBLEMATIK 1924-1929
Holthaus, Thomas *see* PHAENOMENOLOGIE DES UNGLUECKS
Holthouse, Henry James *see* A NEW LAW DICTIONARY
Holthusen, Hans Egon *see* DIE WELT OHNE TRANSZENDENZ
HOLTVILLE TRIBUNE – Holtville, CA. 1923-26 – 2r – 1 – $100.00 – R02300 – us Library Micro [071]
Holtz, Kurt *see*
- 1 SAMUEL 1-7, 1
- I SAMUEL 1-7:1

Holtz, T *see*
- DIE CHRISTOLOGIE DER APOKALYPSE DES JOHANNES (T.U.U. 5-85)
- UNTERSUCHUNGEN UEBER DIE ALTTESTAMENTLICHEN ZITATE BEI LUKAS (T.U.U. 5-104)

Holtzendorff, Franz von *see*
- REPUBLIKANISCHE LIEDER
- ZEITGLOSSEN DES GESUNDEN MENSCHENVERSTANDES

Holtzhauser, Helmut *see* ARBEITERBEWEGUNG UND KLASSIK
Holtzman, Wayne H *see* IMPACT OF EDUCATIONAL TELEVISION ON YOUNG CHILDREN
Holtzmann, Adolf *see* GERMANISCHE ALTERTHUEMER. MIT TEXT, UEBERSETZUNG UND ERKLAERUNG VON TACITUS GERMANIA
Holtzmann, Heinrich Julius *see* KRITIK DER EPHESER- UND KOLOSSERBRIEFE
Holtzmann, Joseph *see* DIE PESCHITTA ZUM BUCHE DER WEISHEIT: EINE KRITISCH-EXEGETISCHE STUDIE
Holtzmann, Oskar *see*
- DER CHRISTLICHE GOTTESGLAUBE: SEINE VORGESCHICHTE UN URGESCHICHTE
- DAS JOHANNESEVANGELIUM
- LEBEN JESU
- NEUTESTAMENTLICHE ZEITGESCHICHTE
- WAR JESUS EKSTATIKER?: EINE UNTERSUCHUNG ZUM LEBEN JESU

Holtzmann, R *see* THIETMARI MERSEBURGENSIS EPISCOPI CHRONICON (MGH 6: 9.BD)
Holtzmann, W *see* KOENIG HEINRICH 1 UND DIE HEILIGE LANZE
Holub, E *see*
- BEITRAEGE ZUR ORNITHOLOGIE SUEDAFRIKAS
- VON DER CAPSTADT INS LAND DER MASCHUKULUMBE

Holum, E *see* SIEBEN JAHRE IN SUED-AFRIKA
THE HOLY CATECHISM OF NICOLAS BULGARIS / Bulgaris, Nicolas; ed by Bromage, Richard Raikes – (Includes indexes) – London: J Masters; New York: J Pott, 1893 – 1mf – 9 – 0-8370-7532-7 – 1986-1532 – us A.T.L.A. [240]
THE HOLY GHOST DISPENSATION / Clark, Dougan – Chicago: Publishing Association of Friends, 1892, c1891 – 1mf – us A.T.L.A. [240]
HOLY GHOST GREEK CATHOLIC CHURCH : MARRIAGE RECORDS – Cleveland, OH, 1909-1967 – 1r – 1 – us I.H.R.C. [920]
THE HOLY LAND AND THE BIBLE / Geikie, John Cunningham – 2v. 1888 – 1 – us A.T.L.A. [240]
A HOLY LIFE AND HOW TO LIVE IT / Macgregor, George Hogarth Carnaby – New York: Fleming H Revell, c1897 – 1mf – 9 – 0-8370-7238-7 – 1986-1238 – us A.T.L.A. [240]
HOLY ORDERS / Corelli, Marie – British Fiction Archive: Unit 1 – 9 – uk Bell [830]
THE HOLY QURAN REMOLDS MANKIND / Sukarno, Pres. Indonesia – SE 6245 1. Speech on occasion of the Nuzulul Quran at State Palace, on March 6, 1961 – 9 – ne IDC [324]
THE HOLY ROMAN EMPIRE / Bryce, James – New York: Macmillan, 1904 – 2mf – us A.T.L.A. [900]
THE HOLY SPIRIT: HIS PERSONALITY, DIVINITY, OFFICE AND AGENCY, IN THE REGENERATION AND SANCTIFICATION OF MAN / Dewar, Daniel – 1847 – 1 – us A.T.L.A. [240]
THE HOLY SPIRIT IN MISSIONS : SIX LECTURES / Gordon, Adoniram Judson – (Includes bibliographical references and index) – New York: Fleming H Revell, c1893 – 1mf – 9 – 0-8370-6054-0 – 1986-0054 – us A.T.L.A. [240]
THE HOLY SPIRIT IN THE NEW TESTAMENT : A STUDY OF PRIMITIVE CHRISTIAN TEACHING / Swete, Henry Barclay – (Includes bibliographical references and indexes) – London: Macmillan, 1909 – 1mf – 9 – 0-8370-9424-0 – 1986-3424 – us A.T.L.A. [220]
THE HOLY SPIRIT IN THE NEW TESTAMENT SCRIPTURES / Scofield, William Campbell – Chicago:Fleming H. Revell, c1896 – 1mf – 9 – 0-8370-5188-6 – 1985-3188 – us A.T.L.A. [220]
HOLY SPRINGS BAPTIST CHURCH. RALEIGH ASSOCIATION. WAKE COUNTY. NORTH CAROLINA : CHURCH RECORDS – 1822-1918 – 1 – 65.79 – us Baptist [240]
HOLY TRINITY MINORIES / London. Guildhall Library. Parish Registers – 1563-1713. Mss. 9238-45 – 1 – uk Microform Academic [920]
THE HOLY WAR IN TRIPOLI / Abbott, George F – London: E Arnold, 1912 – 1 – us Res Libr [960]
THE HOLY WOMEN OF OLD: SEVENTEEN LESSONS / Smith, Mary Ann – Edinburgh: John Anderson, 1897. 1 fiche – 9 – us A.T.L.A. [240]
HOLY WRIT AND MODERN THOUGHT : A REVIEW OF TIMES AND TEACHERS / Coxe, Arthur Cleveland – New York:E.P. Dutton, 1892 – 1mf – 9 – 0-8370-2766-7 – 1985-0766 – us A.T.L.A. [220]
THE HOLY YEAR OF JUBILEE : AN ACCOUNT OF THE HISTORY AND CEREMONIAL OF THE ROMAN JUBILEE / Thurston, Herbert – London: Sands, 1900 – mf – us A.T.L.A. [240]
Holyoake, George Jacob *see* ENGLISH SECULARISM: A CONFESSION OF BELIEF
HOLYOAKE PAPERS / Bishopsgate Institute. London – 1835-1906 – 1 – uk Microform Academic [360]
HOLYOAKE PAPERS: INDEX / Bishopsgate Institute. London – 1 – uk Microform Academic [360]
HOLYOKE 1850-1895 – (Mf 1-5: Births 1850-70. Mf 6-11: Births 1871-82. Mf 12-16: Births 1882-87. Mf 17-21: Births 1887-91. Mf 22-26: Births 1891-95. Mf 27-32: Birth Index 1850-86. Mf 33-37: Birth Index 1887-95. Mf 38-42: Marriages 1850-72. Mf 43-47: Marriages 1872-81. Mf 48-53: Marriages 1881-87. Mf 54-55: Marriages 1887-89. Mf 56-64: Marriages 1889-96. Mf 65-70: Marriage Index 1850-91. Mf 71-75: Marriage Index 1892-1906. Mf 76-79: Deaths 1850-71. Mf 80-84: Deaths 1871-84. Mf 85-89: Deaths 1884-92. Mf 90-94: Deaths 1892-98. Mf 95-99: Death Index 1850-91. Mf 100-103: Death Index 1892-1902) – (mf ed 1986) – 103mf – 9 – 0-87623-026-5 – us Holbrook [920]
Holyoke, Samuel *see*
- THE INSTRUMENTAL ASSISTANT

HOLZ ALS ROH- UND WERKSTOFF – v. 9-38. 1951-80 – 1,5,9 – 2925.00 – us UMI [073]
Holz, Arno *see*
- DIE KUNST, IHR WESEN UND IHRE GESETZE
- SOCIALARISTOKRATEN

Holzamer, Wilhelm *see*
- CONRAD FERDINAND MEYER
- HEINRICH HEINE

Holzapfel, Karl Maria *see* EINER BAUT EINEN DOM
Holzapfel, Otto *see* STUDIEN ZUR FORMELHAFTIGKEIT DER MITTELALTERLICHEN DAENISCHEN VOLKSBALLADE
HOLZARBEITER FRAUENBLATT – Berlin, Germany. Nov-Dez 1914, Okt 1919-Aug 1923 – 1 – gw Mikrofilm [072]
HOLZARBEITER-ZEITUNG – Hamburg, DE. 1893-1933 – 13r – 1 – gw Mikrofilm [072]
HOLZARBEITER-ZEITUNG – v15, no.25. 1907. (Serial publications of German trade unions in the Memorial Library, University of Wisconsin-Madison.) – 1 – us U.W. Library [331]

Holzhey, Carl *see*
- DIE INSPIRATION DER HL. SCHRIFT IN DER ANSCHAUUNG DES MITTELALTERS
- DER NEUENTDECKTE CODEX SYRUS SINAITICUS

Holzinger, H *see* EINLEITUNG IN DEN HEXATEUCH

Holzinger, Heinrich *see*
- DAS BUCH JOSUA
- EXODUS ERKLAERT
- GENESIS
- NUMERI

Holzinger, Regina *see* DUX-GONG

Holzmann, Michael *see* LUDWIG BOERNE

HOMAGE OF EMINENT PERSONS TO THE BOOK / Bailey, Samuel Wordswoth – New York: [s.n.], 1869, [Boston: Rand, Avery & Frye] – 1mf – 9 – 0-8370-2157-X – 1985-0157 – us A.T.L.A. [220]

Homans, Isaac Smith *see*
- THE COMMERCIAL LAWS OF THE STATES: A SUMMARY OF THE LAWS RELATING TO ARREST ASSIGNMENTS ATTACHMENT...&C
- THE NATIONAL BANK ACT.

EL HOMBRE ANTE EL HOMBRE / Caba, Pedro – Badajoz: Imp. de la Dip. Provincial, 1969. Sep. de la Revista de Estudios Extremenos – 1 – sp Bibl Santa Ana [946]

EL HOMBRE CONTRA LA NATURALEZA / Caba, Pedro – sp Bibl Santa Ana [946]

UN HOMBRE DE ESTADO / Lopez de Ayala, Adelardo – 1851 – 9 – 1.50f – sp Bibl Santa Ana [820]

EL HOMBRE FISICO. TOMO 1 / Hervas y Panduro, Lorenzo – 1800 – 2mf – 9 – Pta1,500.00 – 84-7848-026-9 – sp Pentalfa [946]

EL HOMBRE FISICO. TOMO 2 / Hervas y Panduro, Lorenzo – 1800 – 2mf – 9 – Pta1,500.00 – 84-7848-027-7 – sp Pentalfa [946]

HOMBRE. GRABADOS DE FRANCISCO MATEOS / Alvarez Lencero, Luis – Madrid: Trilce, 1961 – 1 – sp Bibl Santa Ana [700]

HOMBRE, MARXISMO Y CRISTIANISMO / Aduriz, Joaquin – Buenos Aires: Editorial Heroica, 1961 – 1 – CSUXAGP9753-B – us Hoover Inst Photo [335]

EL HOMBRE QUE PERDIO SU SOMBRA / Chamisso, Adelbert von – (Spanish translation of Peter Schlemihls wundersame Geschichte. Includes bibliographical references) – 2nd ed. Santiago de Chile: Empresa Editora Zig-Zag, 1966 – 1 – us U.W. Library [830]

HOMBRES DE LA ARGENTINA : DICCIONARIO BIOGRAFICO CONTEMPORANEO – Buenos Aires: Veritas, 2nd ed 1946 – 1 – CSUXADJ1356-B – us Hoover Inst Photo [920]

LOS HOMBRES DE PERON : EL PERONISMO RENOVADOR – Buenos Aires: Puntosur 1987 – 9 – us Hoover Inst Photo [972]

HOMBRES NUEVOS Y NUEVOS CUADROS; INFORME PRONUNCIADO EN LA QUINTA SESION DE LA CONFERENCIA EL DIA 16 DE ENERO / Medrano, Trifon – Valencia, 1937. Fiche W 1041. (Blodgett Collection of Spanish Civil War Pamphlets) – 9 – us H.U. College Libr [946]

HOMBRES Y PROBLEMAS ARGENTINOS / Repetto, Nicolas – Buenos Aires: Editorial La Vanguardia, 1944 [i.e. 1945] – 1 – CSUXADJ1478-B – us Hoover Inst Photo [972]

HOME – 1981- – 1,5,6,9 – us UMI [740]

HOME ALLIANCE – Woodland, CA. 1896-1929 – 17r – 1 – $850.00 – C03695 – us Library Micro [071]

HOME AND AUTO *see* AFTERMARKET BUSINESS

HOME AND FARM CONVENIENCES / Alabama. Polytechnic Institute. Extension Service – Nos 1-17 – 1mf – 9 – us Spaulding [630]

HOME AND FOREIGN FIELDS *see* PERIODICALS

HOME AND FOREIGN JOURNAL *see* PERIODICALS

THE HOME AND FOREIGN RECORD / Presbyterian Church in the U.S.A. – Philadelphia, Pa. v1-11. 1850-1867 – 4r – 1 – $200.00 – us Presbyterian [240]

THE HOME AND FOREIGN RECORD FOR THE CANADA PRESBYTERIAN CHURCH *see* THE PRESBYTERIAN RECORD FOR THE DOMINION OF CANADA

THE HOME AND FOREIGN RECORD OF THE CANADA PRESBYTERIAN CHURCH – (Cont by: Presbyterian Record for the Dominion of Canada) – Toronto: W.C. Chewett, [1861-1875] – 9 – cn C.I.H.M. [240]

THE HOME AND FOREIGN RECORD OF THE PRESBYTERIAN CHURCH OF THE LOWER PROVINCES OF BRITISH NORTH AMERICA – (Cont by: The Presbyterian Record for the Dominion of Canada) – Halifax, N.S.: J Barnes, [1861-1875] – 9 – cn C.I.H.M. [240]

THE HOME AND FOREIGN RECORD OF THE PRESBYTERIAN CHURCH OF THE LOWER PROVINCES OF BRITISH NORTH AMERICA *see* MISSIONARY REGISTER OF THE PRESBYTERIAN CHURCH OF NOVA-SCOTIA

HOME AND GARDEN BULLETINS / U.S. Department of Agriculture – Nos. 1-245. 266 fiches – 9 – $340.00 – us Updata [630]

HOME AND SCHOOL – Toronto: W Briggs, [1883?-189- or 19–] – 9 – cn C.I.H.M. [370]

HOME AND YOUTH – (Cont: Our Home) – Toronto: Home and Youth Pub. Co, [1897-19–] – 9 – cn C.I.H.M. [370]

HOME AND YOUTH *see* OUR HOME

Home Authors (sic) *see* TWENTIETH CENTURY HISTORY AND BIOGRAPHICAL RECORD OF CRAWFORD COUNTY

THE HOME BASE OF MISSIONS : WITH SUPPLEMENT, PRESENTATION AND DISCUSSION OF THE REPORT IN THE CONFERENCE ON 23RD JUNE 1910 – (Includes indexes) – Edinburgh: Publ for the World Missionary Conference by Oliphant, Anderson & Ferrier; New York: Fleming H Revell, [1910?] – 2mf – 9 – 0-8370-0470-7 – 1986-0476 – us A.T.L.A. [240]

HOME BULLETIN – Hampton. Va. 1885-1891 – 1 – us UMI [071]

HOME BULLETIN – Newport News. Va. 1884-86 – 1 – us UMI [071]

HOME CENTER MAGAZINE – v1227- 1899- – 1,5,6,9 – us UMI [640]

HOME CIRCLE LEADER – Toronto: Home Circle Print and Pub, v1 no1(Oct. 1889)- – 9 – cn C.I.H.M. [360]

HOME COMPANION – Findlay, Ohio. 1855-57 – 1r – 1 – $32.50r – us Archival [071]

HOME CONFINEMENT : AN EVOLVING SANCTION IN THE FEDERAL CRIMINAL JUSTICE SYSTEM / Hofer, Paul J & Meierhoefer, Barbara S – Washington: FJC, 1987 – 1mf – 9 – $1.50 – LLMC 95-356 – us L.L.M.C. [340]

HOME COURT ADVANTAGE IN MEN'S AND WOMEN'S BIG TEN INTERCOLLEGIATE BASKETBALL / Stoklosa, S M – 1991 – 1mf – 9 – $4.00 – us Microform Publ [150]

HOME DEMONSTRATION SERIES / Auburn University. Extension Service – 1930-39 – 1,5,6 – us Spaulding [630]

HOME DEPARTMENT MAGAZINE – 1914-46. (Better Home. 1935-46) – 1 – $309.19 – us Baptist [640]

HOME ECONOMICS BULLETIN / Iowa State University. Cooperative Extension Service in Agriculture and Home Economics – No 1-115 1915/16-1928 – 1r – 1,5 – us Spaulding [640]

HOME ECONOMICS CIRCULAR / Iowa State University. Cooperative Extension Service in Agriculture and Home Economics – 1912-25 – 1r – 1,5 – us Spaulding [640]

HOME ECONOMICS PAMPHLET / South Dakota. State University. Agricultural Experiment Station – Nos 1-7 1943-47 – 1,5,6 – us Spaulding [640]

HOME ECONOMICS RESEARCH DEPARTMENTAL SERIES / Alabama. Agricultural Experiment Station – v. 1-2. 1963-64 – 1,5,6 – us Spaulding [630]

HOME ECONOMICS RESEARCH JOURNAL – (v3- 1974- 5,6 v4- 1975- 9) – v1- 1972- – 1 – us UMI [640]

HOME ECONOMICS RESEARCH JOURNAL *see* FAMILY AND CONSUMER SCIENCES RESEARCH JOURNAL

HOME ECONOMICS SERIES / North Carolina State University. Agricultural Extension Service – Nos 126-265 – 1,5 – us Spaulding [640]

HOME ECONOMICS SERIES / North Carolina. State University. Raleigh. Agricultural Extension Service – v1-125 Sep 1963-69 – 1,5 – us Spaulding [640]

HOME EVANGELIST *see* HOME MISSION HERALD

Home, F *see*
- ENQUIRY INTO THE NATURE, CAUSE AND CURE OF THE CROUP
- MEDICAL FACTS AND EXPERIMENTS

L'HOME FRANC – ou Journal tout noubel en patois. no. 1. Toulouse. fevr 1791 – 1 – fr A.C.R.P.P. [073]

HOME FRONT NEWS – San Mateo, CA. 1944-46 – 1r – 1 – $50.00 – B02917 – us Library Micro [071]

HOME FURNISHINGS – New York, 1950- – 1 – $330.00y – us Fairchild Micro [740]

HOME GARDEN'S NATURAL GARDENING MAGAZINE *see* FAMILY HANDYMAN

HOME GOODS RETAILING – v1-20. 1955-74 – 1 – us UMI [650]

HOME GOODS RETAILING – (v34 1988 filmed under the title HGR: Home Goods Retailing. Ceased v36 1990. v1-31 1955-85 Can$550.00) – Toronto. v1-36. 1955-90 – 5 – Can$50.00y – cn Micromedia [380]

HOME GOODS RETAILING *see* HGR

HOME HEALTH CARE SERVICES QUARTERLY / ed by Simmons, W June – v1- 1979- – 1, 9 ($265.00 in US $371.00 outside hardcopy subsc) – us Haworth [610]

HOME HEALTHCARE NURSE – (1986- . 5,6,9) – v1- . 1983- – 1 – us UMI [073]

HOME IMPROVEMENT CONTRACTOR – (v31-1979- 5,6,9) – v29- 1977- – 1 – us UMI [640]

HOME IMPROVEMENTS – v21-28 1969-76. Continued by: Home Improvement Contractor – 1 – us UMI [640]

HOME INTELLIGENCE REPORTS, 1940-1944 / Great Britain. Home Office – The British people and World War II – 1 – us Primary [941]

HOME JOURNAL – Baldwyn. Miss. 1915-1918; 1936-1940 – 1 – us UMI [071]

HOME JOURNAL – Lafayette. Ind. 1896-1904 – 1 – us UMI [071]

HOME JOURNAL – Oakland, CA. 1870-1874 – 1r – 1 – $50.00 – C03624 – us Library Micro [073]

THE HOME JOURNAL – Toronto: [s.n. 1861-] – 9 – cn C.I.H.M. [073]

THE HOME JOURNAL NEWS – New York. N.Y – 1 – us NY Public [071]

Home Journal Steam Printing *see* RECORDS OF OLDEN TIMES. FIFTY YEARS ON THE PRAIRIES

HOME KNOWLEDGE MONTHLY REVIEW – Toronto: Belden Bros, [1890?-18– or 19–] – 9 – cn C.I.H.M. [073]

HOME LIFE – (Successor to Better Home). 1947-61 – 1 – $144.97 – us Baptist [640]

HOME LYRICS, A BOOK OF POEMS / Battersby, Hannah S – Toronto: Hunter, Rose & Co., 1887. 06082. (Pre-1900 Canadiana) – 9 – cn C.I.H.M. [810]

HOME MISSION HERALD – Atlanta, Ga. v1-4. 1908-1911 – 1r – 1 – $50.00 – us Presbyterian [240]

HOME MISSION HERALD – (Suspended: Apr 1866-72. Title varies) – v1-17. 1849-66; v41-42. 1873-74 (complete) – 1r – 1 – ATLA R0118 – us A.T.L.A. [240]

HOME MISSION HEROES : A SERIES OF SKETCHES – (Includes bibliographies) – New York City: Literature Dept, Presbyterian Home Missions, 1904 – 1mf – 9 – 0-8370-6782-0 – 1986-0782 – us A.T.L.A. [920]

THE HOME MISSION JOURNAL – Saint John, N.B.: Committee of the Home Mission Board of New Brunswick, [1898-1904] – 9 – cn C.I.H.M. [240]

HOME MISSION MONTHLY – v1-38. 1886-1924 – 1 – $250.00 – us Presbyterian [240]

HOME MISSION MONTHLY, 1886-1924 – 5r – 1 – $425.00 – D3328 – Co-publ with the Presbyterian Historical Society, Dept of History, Presbyterian Church (U.S.A.) 1995 – us Scholarly Res [240]

HOME MISSION RECORD *see* HOME MISSION HERALD

THE HOME MISSION TASK : ITS FUNDAMENTAL CHARACTER, MAGNITUDE AND PRESENT URGENCY / ed by Masters, Victor I – Atlanta: Home Mission Board of the Southern Baptist Convention, 1912 – 1mf – us A.T.L.A. [240]

HOME MISSIONS : A SERMON IN BEHALF OF THE AMERICAN HOME MISSIONARY SOCIETY / Barnes, Albert – New York: Printed for the American Home Missionary Society by W. Osborn, 1849 – 1mf – us A.T.L.A. [240]

HOME MISSIONS IN ACTION / Allen, Edith H – New York: Revell, c1915. (Interdemoninational home mission study course) – 1mf – us A.T.L.A. [240]

HOME NEWS – Henderson. Nev. -w. 1958- – 1 – us UMI [071]

HOME NEWS – New Brunswick. N.J. 1903- – 1 – us UMI [071]

HOME NEWS – Richmond. Va. 1958-1960 – 1 – us UMI [071]

Home of Hebrew Orphans *see* RECORD OF THE HOME OF HEBREW ORPHANS

THE HOME OF THE WOLVERENE AND BEAVER, OR, FUR-HUNTING IN THE WILDS OF CANADA / Eden, Charles Henry – London: Society for Promoting Christian Knowledge. 1876?. 02877. (Pre-1900 Canadiana) – 9 – cn C.I.H.M. [971]

HOME OFFICE COMPUTING *see* FAMILY AND HOME OFFICE COMPUTING

HOME OFFICE PAPERS AND RECORDS: ORDER AND AUTHORITY IN ENGLAND, SERIES 1 / Great Britain. Public Record Office – (Part 1: 1782-92. PRO Class HO 42, Boxes 1-23. Part 2: 1793-97. PRO Class HO 42, Boxes 24-41. Part 3: 1798-1802. PRO Class HO 42, Boxes 42-66. Part 4: 1803-09. PRO Class HO 42, Boxes 67-99. Part 5: 1810-12. PRO Class HO 42, Boxes 100-131. Part 6: 1813-15. PRO Class HO 42, Boxes 132-147. Part 7: 1816-17. PRO Class HO 42, Boxes 148-172. Part 8: 1818-Aug 1819. PRO Class HO 42, Boxes 173-193. Part 9: Sept 1819-20. PRO Class HO 42, Boxes 194-218) – PRO Class HO 42, 1782-1820 – 1 – us Primary [941]

HOME RECORD – David City, NE. -w. Jan. 1902-Apr. 1903 – 1 – us NE Hist [071]

HOME RULE – Madras, India 29 Oct 1967-27 Jan 1971 – 4r – 1 – us L of C Photodup [072]

HOME RULE FOR IRELAND: EXTRACT OF A SPEECH MADE BEFORE THE LEGISLATIVE ASSEMBLY OF THE PROVINCE OF QUEBEC, ON THE 16TH OF APRIL, 1886 / Flynn, Edmund James – Quebec: s.n., 1886?. 03118. (Pre-1900 Canadiana) – 9 – cn C.I.H.M. [971]

HOME SAFETY REVIEW *see* FAMILY SAFETY

HOME SHOP MACHINIST – (1984-. 5,6,9) – v1-. 1982- – 1 – us UMI [621]

HOME STAR – Harrisburg, PA. -w 1949-1964 – 13 – $25.00r – us I.M.R. [071]

HOME STUDY – v1 Feb 1896-Jan 1897 – 1 – us Res Libr [370]

HOME STUDY LEAFLET – St John, N.B.: T.F. Fotheringham, [1894-189- or 19–] – 9 – cn C.I.H.M. [240]

THE HOME STUDY QUARTERLY – (Merger of: The Home Study Quarterly for Senior Scholars and the Home Department. Merger of: The Home Study Quarterly for Intermediate Scholars) – [Toronto: Published under authority of the General Assembly, 1898-19–] – 9 – cn C.I.H.M. [240]

THE HOME STUDY QUARTERLY *see* THE HOME STUDY QUARTERLY FOR SENIOR SCHOLARS AND THE HOME DEPARTMENT

THE HOME STUDY QUARTERLY FOR INTERMEDIATE SCHOLARS – [S.1.: s.n. 1895?-1898?] – 9 – cn C.I.H.M. [240]

THE HOME STUDY QUARTERLY FOR INTERMEDIATE SCHOLARS *see*
- THE HOME STUDY QUARTERLY
- THE HOME STUDY QUARTERLY FOR SENIOR SCHOLARS AND THE HOME DEPARTMENT

THE HOME STUDY QUARTERLY FOR SENIOR SCHOLARS AND THE HOME DEPARTMENT – (Merged with: The Home Study Quarterly for Intermediate Scholars. Merged to become: The Home Study Quarterly) – [S.1.: s.n. 1895-1898] – 9 – cn C.I.H.M. [240]

THE HOME STUDY QUARTERLY FOR SENIOR SCHOLARS AND THE HOME DEPARTMENT *see* THE HOME STUDY QUARTERLY

HOME TEXTILES TODAY – 1985-. -biw – 1 – us UMI [073]

HOME TOWN NEWS – Selma, CA. 1942-45 – 1r – 1 – $50.00 – B02989 – us Library Micro [071]

HOME WEEKLY – Alma. Kan. 1881-1883 – 1 – us UMI [071]

HOME WEEKLY – Eskridge. Kan. 1884-1888 – 1 – us UMI [071]

HOME WORK BULLETIN / National Council of the Y.M.C.A – (Cont by: National Council of the Y.M.C.A. Bulletin) – v1-5. 1926-31 (incomplete) – 1r – 1 – us A.T.L.A. [073]

HOME WORK BULLETIN *see* NATIONAL COUNCIL OF THE Y.M.C.A

THE HOMEFINDER – (New York). 1922-33, 1941-57 – 1 – us A.J.P.C. [720]

HOMELIES POPULAIRES SUR LES EVANGILES DE CHAQUE DIMANCHE DE L'ANNEE / Lobry, J-B – (Includes bibliographical references) – 5e ed. Paris: Louis Vives, 1885 – 2mf – 9 – 0-8370-7476-2 – 1986-1476 – us A.T.L.A. [240]
HOMELINKS – London, UK. 1898-1900. -irr. 24 feet – 1 – uk British Libr Newspaper [072]
HOMELY TALKS / Pearse, Mark Guy – 1881 – 9 – us A.T.L.A. [240]
O HOMEM DE COR – (Cont by: O Mulato, ou O Homem de Cor) – Rio de Janeiro, 14-28 Sep 1833 – 1,5,6 – bl Biblioteca [072]
O HOMEM DE COR *see* O MULATO, OU O HOMEM DE COR
O HOMEM DO POVO – Rio de Janeiro, 26 Feb-12 Nov 1840 – 1,5,6 – bl Biblioteca [072]
O HOMEM E A AMERICA : JORNAL DA SOCIEDADE DEFENSORA DA LIBERDADE E INDEPENDENCIA NACIONAL DO RIO DE JANEIRO – Rio de Janeiro, 11 Nov-Dec 1831; Jan-Mar, May-Oct 1832; Feb-2 Mar 1833 – 1,5,6 – bl Biblioteca [072]
HOMEMAKER / National Extension Homemakers Council – (1986- 1,5,6) – 1977- – 9 – us UMI [640]
HOMEMAKER'S MAGAZINE – (Microfiche available to v22 1987 only) – Vancouver. v1-22. 1965-87 – 9 – Can$28.00y – cn Micromedia [640]
HOMENAGEM A MEMORIA DE CARLOS GOMES – [s.l.] Sem Data – 1,5,6 – bl Biblioteca [072]
HOMENAGEM AO CONSOLIDADOR DA REPUBLICA MARECHAL FLORIANO PEIXOTO – [s.l.] Jun 1903 – 1,5,6 – bl Biblioteca [072]
HOMENAGEM DA CONGREGACAO DO GYMNASIO AMAZONENSE E ESCOLA NORMAL – Manaos, Amazonas. 30 Jul 1899 – 1,5,6 – bl Biblioteca [072]
HOMENAJE A EUGENIO HERMOSO / Academia de Bellas Artes de San Fernando – Madrid: Blass, S.A. Tipografia, 1964 – 1 – sp Bibl Santa Ana [946]
HOMENAJE A HERNANDO CORTES EN MEJICO / Pereyra, Carlos – Madrid: Revista de Indias, 1941 – 1 – sp Bibl Santa Ana [920]
HOMENAJE A NUESTROS MAYORES – Caceres: Imp. Linea 21, 1979 – 1 – sp Bibl Santa Ana [946]
HOMENAJE AL MAESTRO DON..., CABALLERO DE LA ORDEN DE ALFONSO 10TH EL SABIO SEPTIEMBRE, 1958 / Cruz Rebosa, Maximo – Caceres: Tip. La Minerva, 1958 – 1 – sp Bibl Santa Ana [946]
HOMENAJE DE ALCUESCAR AL ACADEMICO DE LAS REALES ACADEMIAS DE LA LENGUA ESPANOLA Y SEVILLANA DE BUENOS LETRAS DON RAFAEL GARCIA-PLATA DE OSMA, 22 DE MARZO DE 1953 – Caceres: Tip. El Noticiero – sp Bibl Santa Ana [370]
HOMENAJE DE GRATITUD A DR. EZEQUIEL FERNANDEZ SANTANA / Fernandez Santana, Ezequiel – Madrid: Tipografia Artistica, S.A. – 1 – sp Bibl Santa Ana [946]
HOMENAJE. POESIAS DEDICADAS A LA EXIMIA POETISA EVA CERVANTES EN OCASION DE SUS ONOMASTICAS Y OTROS VARIOS MOTIVOS / Sanchez-Arjona, Vicente – Sevilla: Imp. Alvarez, 1960 – 1 – sp Bibl Santa Ana [810]
HOMENAJE POSTUMO AL EXCELENTISIMO SENOR PRESIDENTE DE LA NACION TENIENTE GENERAL DON JUAN D. PERON / Congreso de la Nacion – Buenos Aires: El Congreso, 1974 – 1 – CSUXAHZ6853-B – us Hoover Inst Photo [320]
HOMENAJE QUE LOS MEDICOS DE MERIDA RINDEN AL QUE FUE UNO DE SUS MAS ILUSTRES COMPANEROS : JOSE FERNANDEZ DOMINGUEZ – Badajoz: Manuel Huerta Esteve, 1968 – 1 – sp Bibl Santa Ana [946]
HOMEOSTASIS IN HEALTH AND DISEASE – 1,5,69 – us UMI [612]
HOMEOWNERS HOW TO – (v.4 .1979 5,6,9) – v.1 .1976 – 1 – us UMI [073]
HOMER FREE PRESS – Homer, NE. -w. Aug 1906-Apr 1910 – 1 – us NE Hist [071]
HOMER HERALD – Homer, NE. -w. Apr 1897-Jun 1898 – 1 – us NE Hist [071]
HOMER IN DER FRUEHCHRISTLICHEN LITERATUR BIS JUSTININ (T.U.U. 5-105) / Glockmann, G – Berlin, 1968 – 4mf – 9 – ne Slangenburg [240]
HOMER PATRIOT – Homer, NE. -w. Aug 1896-Mar 1897 – 1 – us NE Hist [071]
Homer, William Bradford *see* WRITINGS
HOMES AND HAUNTS OF THE MOST EMINENT BRITISH POETS / Howitt, William – London: R. Bentley, 1847 – 2 rolls – 1 – 1-55879-974-5 – uk Libr Preservation [420]
THE HOMES OF OUR ANCESTORS IN STONINGTON, CONNECTICUT / New London County. Connecticut – By Grace Denison Wheeler, 1903. Item O.Mostly history, includes index.286p. SW16-0107 – 5 – us A.G.L.L. [978]
HOMESPUN: OR, FIVE AND TWENTY YEARS AGO / Hill, George Canning – By Thomas Lackland (pseud). New York: Hurd and Houghton, 1867. viii, (9),346p. Title vignette. Verse and prose. 1 reel. 1291 – 1 – us U.W. Library [810]
HOMESTEAD NEWSLEADER – Homestead. Fl. 1923-26, 1928-69 – 1 – us P.K. Yonge [071]
HOME-TALKS / Noyes, John Humphrey; ed by Alfred Barron & Miller, George Noyes – v. 1. 1875 – 1 – us A.T.L.A. [240]
HOMEWOOD FLOSSMOOR STAR – Chicago Heights. Ill. -w. 1941-48, 1959- – 1 – us UMI [071]
A HOMILETIC COMMENTARY ON THE BOOK OF ECCLESIASTES / Leale, Thomas Henry – London: Richard Dickinson, 1877.1 fiche – 9 – us A.T.L.A. [240]
THE HOMILETIC MONTHLY – (Cont by: The Homeletic Review) – Toronto: W Briggs, [1876?-1884] – 9 – cn C.I.H.M. [240]
THE HOMILETIC MONTHLY *see* THE HOMILETIC REVIEW
THE HOMILETIC REVIEW – (Cont: The Homiletic Monthly) – Toronto: W Briggs, [1885?-189- or 19–] – 9 – cn C.I.H.M. [240]
THE HOMILETIC REVIEW *see* THE HOMILETIC MONTHLY
HOMILETICS / Hoppin, James Mason – 4th ed., Rev. 1893 – 1 – us A.T.L.A. [240]
HOMILETICS (CCC243) = HSUAN TAO HSUEH / McNeur, George H – (In Chinese) – Hong Kong: Bible Book and Tract Depot for Council on Christian Literature for Overseas Chinese, 1953 – 1r – 1 – 1984-6582 – us A.T.L.A. [240]
HOMILETISCHE MONATSHEFTE – 1948-91 (complete) – Inquire – 1 – ATLA S0345 – us A.T.L.A. [073]
HOMILIA A...SAN JUAN CRISOSTOMO / Franco y Lozano, Francisco – 1883 – 9 – $1.50f – sp Bibl Santa Ana [240]
HOMILIAE / Caesarii Heisterbasensis; ed by Coppenstein, Ioan – Coloniae, 1615 – 21mf – 8 – Dfl74.00 – ne Slangenburg [240]
HOMILIAE CATECHISTICAE QVADRAGIN TA, IN QUIBUS PRAECIPUA TOTIUS CHRISTIANAE RELIGIONIS CAPITA COM PENDIOSE... / Huberinus, Caspar – Frankfurt a.M.: Christian Egenolph, [Jan. 1554]. [G.F.: 21.7] – 4mf – 9 – HUB-50/1 – ne IDC [240]
HOMILIAE (CODICE UNCIAL, SIECLE 6-7) / Gregorio, San – Barcelona – 1r – 5,6 – sp Cultura [240]
HOMILIAE MATHESII. DAS IST: AUSSLEGUNG... DER ERSTEN UND ANDERN EPISTELN...AN DIE CORINTHIER / Mathesius, Johannes – Leipzig, 1590 – 12mf – ne IDC [240]
HOMILIAE PER CIRCULUM ANNI / Autissiodorensis, Heiricus – 1994 – 26mf – 9 – Bf4,500.00 – 2-503-64162-8 – be Brepols [450]
HOMILIAE QVI SVNT SERMONES HABITI DE IIS, QVAE IN CHRISTIANIS ECCLESIIS LEGVNTVR... / Camerarius, J – Lipsiae, [1573] – 5mf – 9 – ne IDC [240]
HOMILIAE SEU SERMONES / Clichtove, J – Coloniae, 1550 – 13mf – 9 – CA-85/1 – ne IDC [240]
DAS HOMILIARIUM KARLS DES GROSSEN AUF SEINE URSPRUENGLICHEN GESTALT HIN UNTERSUCHT / Wiegand, F – (SGTK 1 Band, 2 Heft) – Leipzig, 1897 – 2mf – 8 – Dfl9.00 – ne Slangenburg [240]
HOMILIARUM SACRARUM IN PERICOPAS EVANGELIORUM DOMINICALIUM... / Gerhard, J – Jenae, 1634-1640. 3v – 46mf – ne IDC [240]
HOMILIARVM EVANGELICARVM NOTAE BREVES / Hoffmann, David – Magdebvrgi, 1600 – 2mf – ne IDC [240]
HOMILIES OF SCIENCE / Carus, Paul – Chicago: Open Court, 1897. 1 fiche – 9 – us A.T.L.A. [240]
HOMILJARIUM – Floriacense Mss. Orleans, Bibl. Mun. 154 – 7mf – 8 – ne Slangenburg [240]
HOMIN UKRAINY – (In Ukrainian) – Canada, 1948- – 1 – cn Commonwealth Micro [072]
HOMMAGE A ARISTIDE MAILLOL, 1861-1944. CENTENAIRE DE SA NAISSANCE / Reunion des musees nationaux. Paris – 1961. 40 illus. 2 fiches – 9 – fr Réunion [730]
HOMMAGE A CEZANNE / Reunion des musees nationaux. Paris – 1954. 32 illus. 1 fiche – 9 – fr Réunion [700]
HOMMAGE A COROT / Reunion des Musees Nationaux. Paris – 1975 – 9 – fr Réunion [760]
HOMMAGE A CORREGE. DESSINS DU MAITRE, DE SES ELEVES ET DES ARTISTES QUI ONT SUBI SON INFLUENCE / Reunion des musees nationaux. Paris – 1934. 1 illus. 1 fiche – 9 – fr Réunion [740]
HOMMAGE A KWAME N'KRUMAH – Conakry: Imprimerie Nationale "Patrice Lumumba", 1972 – us Res Libr [920]
HOMMAGE A MAFORY BANGOURA / Toure, Ahmed Sekou – Conakry, R G: Parti-Etat de Guinee, 1976 – us Res Libr [920]
L'HOMME – St Helier, England. 30 Nov 1853-31 Oct 1855 – 49ft – 1 – uk British Libr Newspaper [072]
L'HOMME DE COULEUR / Verdier, Cardinal et al – Paris: Plon, 1939 – 1 – us Res Libr [300]
L'HOMME DU DESTIN / Hapde, Augustin et al – French Theatre Series. Paris. Barba. 1810 – 9 – fr Hachette [820]
L'HOMME DU PEUPLE – Lyon: Impr de Mme veuve Ayne, Aug 24, 1849 – us Res Libr [072]
L'HOMME ENCHAINE – Paris. Continued as L'Homme Libre. Jan. 1, 1915-Nov. 17, 1917. Missing: scattered issues – 1 – 35.00r – us Hoover Inst Photo [072]
L'HOMME ENCHAINE – Paris. Journal quot. du matin. Red. en chef, G. Clemenceau. 8 oct 1914-17 nov 1917, 21-23 sept 1939 – 1 – fr A.C.R.P.P. [072]
HOMME ET LA SOCIETE – Paris. 1966-68. BH-1803 1 – 9 – ne IDC [300]
L'HOMME ET LE MONDE A TRAVERS LES PROVERBES TOGOLAIS DE LANGUE EVE / Agudze-Vioka, B – 9 – F160.00 – fr Ethnologie [490]
L'HOMME LIBRE – Brussels, Apr 1891-Dec 1892 – 1r – 1 – uk British Libr Newspaper [072]
L'HOMME LIBRE – Dir. Louis Blanc. Paris. 27 oct 1876-3 mai 1877 – 1 – fr A.C.R.P.P. [073]
L'HOMME LIBRE – Ni Dieu, ni maitre. Dir. Edouard Vaillant. no. 1-70. Paris. 21 juin-29 aout 1888 – 1 – fr A.C.R.P.P. [073]
L'HOMME LIBRE – Paris, France. 18 Nov 1917-12 Aug 1919 (imperfect) – 3r – 1 – uk British Libr Newspaper [072]
L'HOMME LIBRE – Paris. Nov. 18, 1917-Dec. 31, 1918. Missing: scattered issues – 1 – 35.00r – us Hoover Inst Photo [072]
L'HOMME LIBRE – Paris. Red. en chef, G. Clemenceau. 5 mai 1913-nov 1917, 1918-10 oct 1939, 10 mai 1943, 25 mai 1951-24 juil 1953 – 1 – fr A.C.R.P.P. [073]
L'HOMME LIBRE – Quebec, Canada. v1 n2. 30 dec 1922-v3 n37. 24 jul 1926 – 1r – 1 – Can$35.00 – cn Can Microfilming [072]
L'HOMME LIBRE *see* L'IDEE OUVRIERE
L'HOMME LIBRE – Gonaives: Impr de "L'homme libre". 1ere annee n23-3eme annee n15. 5 sep 1878-23 fevr 1881 – 2 sheets – 9 – us Res Libr [072]
L'HOMME NOUVEAU – Brazzaville, Congo, mar 1960-63 – 4r – 1 – us Res Libr [072]
L'HOMME NOUVEAU – ou LE MESSAGER DU BONHEUR. Lyon, Durval, 1833. Prospectus, s. d., no. 1 (14 juillet)-no. 4 (aout 1833), 4 et 16 p. Les Saint-Simoniens, 1825-1834. 6930 – 9 – fr Hachette [335]
L'HOMME NOUVEAU – Revue mensuelle. no. 1-35. 1934-avr 1937. devenu: Idees et peuples. L'Homme nouveau. Paris. juil 1938 – 1 – fr A.C.R.P.P. [073]
L'HOMME NOUVEAU – (Issues filmed with: Bartlett, Robert E: Collection of African newspapers) – Brazzaville jun 25 1960 – us Res Libr [072]
UN HOMME PAREIL AUX AUTRES: ROMAN / Maran, Rene – Paris: A. Michel, 1962 – 1 – us U.W. Library [830]
L'HOMME QUI RIT JAUNE / Arnaud, Robert – Paris: A Michel, [c1926] – 1 – us Res Libr [960]
L'HOMME REEL – Revue mensuelle du syndicalisme et de l'humanisme. Paris. 1934-sept 1938 – 1 – fr A.C.R.P.P. [073]
L'HOMME SAUVAGE. HISTOIRE TRADUITE PAR M. MERCIER / Mercier, Louis-Sebastien – (Utopias in the Enlightenment series) – 9 – fr Hachette [830]
Hommel, F *see* ETHNOLOGIE UND GEOGRAPHIE DES ALTEN ORIENTS
HOMMES DE L'OUARSENIS / Vignet-Zunz, J – Une communaute rurale en Algerie – 9 – F100.00 – fr Ethnologie [306]
LES HOMMES DE PROMETHEE / Colardeau, Charles Pierre – Amsterdam and Paris: Le Jay, 1775. 38p.1 fiche. (Literature Collection) – 9 – 6.00 – fr Bibl Nationale [440]
LES HOMMES DU JOUR – puis Annales politiques, sociales, litteraires et artistiques. Paris. 1908-23 – 1 – fr A.C.R.P.P. [073]
HOMMES ET CHOSES D'OUTRE-MER / Hamelle, Paul – Paris: Fischbacher, 1899. 05347. (Pre-1900 Canadiana) – 9 – cn C.I.H.M. [971]
LES HOMMES ET LES ACTES DE L'INSURRECTION DE PARIS DEVANT LA PSYCHOLOGIE MORBIDE. LETTRES A M. LE DOCTEUR MOREAU DE TOURS / Laborde, Jean B V – (French Precursors of Psychiatry Series). Paris. Germer Bailliere. 1872 – 9 – fr Hachette [150]
LES HOMMES ET LEURS TRAVAUX DANS LES PAYS DE LA MOYENNE GARONNE. / Deffontaines, Pierre – Lille. 1932. (La Condition Ouvriere. Part Two.) – 9 – 15.00 – fr Bibl Nationale [360]
DIE HOMOCENTRISCHEN SPHAEREN DES EXODUS DES KALLIPPUS UND DES ARISTOTELES / Schiaparelli, Giovani Virginio – 7 – uk Microform Academic [180]
A HOMOEOPATHIA : PERIODICO DAS DOCTRINAS MEDICAS E SCIENCIAS ACCESSORIAS – Rio de Janeiro, 28 Jul-4 Aug 1850 – 1,5,6 – bl Biblioteca [072]
Homolka, Walter *see* EIN DEM UNTERGANG NAHER ARAMAEER WAR MEIN VATER... DAS "KLEINE GESCHICHTLICHE CREDO" UND SEINE WIRKUNGSGESCHICHTE IM MIDRASCH DER PESSACH-HAGGADA
HOMONYME WURZELN IM SYRISCHEN : EIN BEITRAG ZUR SEMITISCHEN LEXICOGRAPHIE / Schulthess, Friedrich – (Includes bibliographical references and index) – Berlin: Reuther & Reichard, 1900 – 1mf – 9 – 0-8370-8866-6 – 1986-2866 – us A.T.L.A. [470]
DES HOMONYMES FRANCAIS / Philipon-de-la-Madelaine – 3e ed. 1806 – 9 – fr I.C.S. [440]
HOMOPTEREN-FAUNA VON CEYLON / Melichar, L – Berlin. 1903. BZ-1468 2 – 8 – ne IDC [590]
THE HON. ALEXANDER MACKENZIE: HIS LIFE AND TIMES / Buckingham, William & Ross, George W – Fifth ed. Toronto: Rose, 1892. 03821. (Pre-1900 Canadiana) – 9 – cn C.I.H.M. [920]
L'HON. J. A. CHAPLEAU, RETOUR D'EUROPE: DEMONSTRATION ENTHOUSIASTE: ADDRESSE DE BIENVENUE: DISCOURS EN REPONSE: AVANT TOUT SOYONS CANADIENS: NOTRE POSITION, NOS DEVOIRS, MONTREAL 24 AVRIL 1889 / Chapleau, Joseph Adolphe – 1889? 00615. (Pre-1900 Canadiana) – 9 – cn C.I.H.M. [971]
HON. J. A. CHAPLEAU: WELCOMED AT MONTREAL ON HIS RETURN FROM EUROPE, 24TH APRIL, 1889, HIS ADDRESS IN REPLY: THE POLITICAL POSITION AND RESPONSIBILITIES OF CANADIANS / Chapleau, Joseph Adolphe – 1889? 02862. (Pre-1900 Canadiana) – 9 – cn C.I.H.M. [971]
HO-NAN HSIANG-SHIH LU – List of successful candidates in the imperial examination in Honan province. Scattered years 1759-1903. 1 reel – 1 – 24.00 – us Chinese Res [950]
Honckeny, G A *see* SYNOPSIS PLANTARUM GERMANIAE
HONDERD CHRISTELIJKE ZINNEBEELDEN NAAR GEORGETTE DE MONTENAY, DOOR ANNA ROEMERS VISSCHER : UITGEGEVEN NAAR HET OORSPRONKELIJK HANDSCHRIFT DOOR A.D. SCHINKEL. MET EEN FAC-SIMILE. NIET IN DEN HANDEL. GEDRUKT HONDERDVIJFENTWINTIG EXEMPLAREN / Montenay, G de – [Den Haag], 1854 – 2mf – 9 – O-3246/1 – ne IDC [760]

HONDURAS : ANUARIO ESTADISTICO 1952-1969 / Honduras. Direccion General de Estadistica y Censos – (1969 not available. Coll title: Latin American and Caribbean Official Statistical Serials, 1821-1982) – 66mf – 9 – £485.00 – uk Chadwyck [972]

Honduras *see*
- LA GACETA DIARIO OFICIAL

HONDURAS, 1930-45 / U.S. Department of State – (See also series listing) – 42 reels with printed guide. Series: Confidential U.S. Diplomatic Post Records: Central America and the Caribbean – 1 – $4,620.00 – us UPA [972]

HONDURAS AQUACULTURE DEVELOPMENT PROJECT / International Center for Aquaculture – Mar 1976. 1 reel – 1, 5 – us Spaulding [639]

Honduras. British *see*
- BELIZEAN SEVEN YEAR DEVELOPMENT PLAN, 1964-1970
- DEVELOPMENT PLAN, 1964-1970
- DEVELOPMENT PLAN, PART 3 (1955-60)
- REVIEW OF PROGRESS IN THE DEVELOPMENT AND WELFARE OF THE COLONY OF BRITISH HONDURAS DURING THE PERIOD 1948-1954

Honduras. Consejo Nacional de Economia *see*
- PLAN NACIONAL DE DESARROLLO ECONOMICO Y SOCIAL DE HONDURAS, 1965-1969
- PROGRAMA CUATRIENAL DE INVERSIONES PUBLICAS, 1962-1965
- PROGRAMA NACIONAL DE DESARROLLO ECONOMICO Y SOCIAL DE HONDURAS, 1965-69 VERSION PRELIMINAR

Honduras. Direccion General de Estadistica y Censos *see*
- COMERCIO EXTERIOR
- HONDURAS
- INVESTIGACION INDUSTRIAL
- POBLACION Y VIVIENDA

Honduras. Inter-American Economic and Social Council *see* EVALUACION DEL PLAN NAC. DE INV. PUB. 1963-1964 DE HONDURAS

Honduras. Laws, Statutes, etc *see* CODIGO DE PROCEDIMIENTOS ADMINISTRATIVOS

Hone, William *see*
- FACETIAE AND MISCELLANIES
- SIXTY CURIOUS AND AUTHENTIC NARRATIVES AND ANECDOTES RESPECTING EXTRAORDINARY CHARACTERS

HONEA PATH FIRST BAPTIST CHURCH. HONEA PATH, SOUTH CAROLINA : CHURCH RECORDS – May 1869-Jul 1955 – 1 – 48.42 – us Baptist [240]

THE HONEST INJUN – Victoria, B.C.: D Falconer, [1897] – 9 – cn C.I.H.M. [420]

HONESTY – Dublin, Ireland.1925-31 – 1 – ie Microforms [072]

HONESTY – Ireland.16 Oct-22 Apr 1916 – 1 – ie Microforms [072]

HONEY GROVE FIRST BAPTIST CHURCH. HONEY GROVE, TEXAS : CHURCH RECORDS – 1847-73. Includes Church history. 1884-1912 – 1 – 12.69 – us Baptist [240]

Honey, Michael J *see* THE IMPACT OF INTERSCHOLASTIC ATHLETICS ON ACADEMIC PERFORMANCE

HONEYBEE DISEASES AND ENEMIES IN ASIA : A PRACTICAL GUIDE – 1987 – 59p – it F.A.O. [636]

HONEYBEE MITES AND THEIR CONTROL : A SELECTED ANNOTATED BIBLIOGRAPHY – 1986 – 149p – it F.A.O. [660]

Honeyman, Abraham Van Doren *see*
- DIRECTORY OF THE MEMBERS OF THE BAR IN PRACTICE IN NEW JERSEY.
- A TREATISE ON THE JURISDICTION OF CIVIL AND CRIMINAL PROCEEDINGS IN THE COURT FOR THE TRIAL OF SMALL CAUSES IN NEW JERSEY

HONEYWELL INDEPENDENT USERS MONTHLY – 1984- – 1,5,6,9 – us UMI [510]

Hong Kong *see*
- THE DEVELOPMENT OF SECONDARY AND TERTIARY EDUCATION
- EDUCATION ORDINANCE, CHAPTER 279, 1964
- EDUCATION POLICY APRIL 1965
- EDUCATION REGULATIONS 1971
- A PERSPECTIVE ON EDUCATION IN HONG KONG
- PRIMARY EDUCATION AND PRE-PRIMARY SERVICES 1981
- REPORT OF THE FULTON COMMISSION 1963
- REPORT OF THE WORKING PARTY SET UP TO REVIEW THE SECONDARY SCHOOL PLACES ALLOCATION SYSTEM 5TH JANUARY 1981
- SECONDARY EDUCATION IN HONG KONG DURING THE NEXT DECADE

Hong Kong. Board of Education *see* REPORT ON THE PROPOSED EXPANSION OF SECONDARY SCHOOL EDUCATION IN HONG KONG OVER THE NEXT DECADE

Hong Kong. Chinese Language Committee *see*
- THE FIRST REPORT...
- THE FOURTH (AND FINAL) REPORT...
- THE SECOND REPORT...
- THE THIRD REPORT...

Hong Kong. Committee on Vocational Training *see* REPORT ON THE SURVEY ON EMPLOYERS' ASSESSMENT OF VOCATIONAL TRAINING AND PRE-VOCATIONAL AND SECONDARY MODERN EDUCATION, CONDUCTED IN AUGUST 1976

THE HONG KONG DAILY PRESS – Hong Kong: [H L Murrow, jul 1870-sep 30 1941] – 166r – 1 – us Res Libr [072]

Hong Kong. Education Commission *see* REPORT 1963

Hong Kong. Education Department *see*
- ADULT EDUCATION SECTION
- ANNUAL SUMMARY 1975/76-1989/90
- BRIEF ACCOUNT OF THE EDUCATIONAL SYSTEM WITH STATISTICAL SUMMARY 1972; 1976
- THE DEVELOPMENT OF SENIOR SECONDARY AND TERTIARY EDUCATION
- HALF-YEARLY STATISTICAL SUMMARY 1975-1986 (MARCH)
- INFORMATION SHEET
- INFORMATION SHEET ON SECONDARY EDUCATION 1975-1976
- INFORMATION SHEET ON SPECIAL EDUCATION
- INFORMATION SHEET ON THE ADVISORY INSPECTORATE
- LIST OF SCHOOLS HAVING LOWER / UPPER FORM 6 LEADING TO THE ADVANCED LEVEL EXAMINATION OF THE UNIVERSITY OF HONG KONG

Hong Kong. Education Department. Science Subject Section *see* REPORT ON FIRST YEAR TRIAL OF THE INTEGRATED SCIENCE PROJECT 1973-1974

THE HONG KONG EDUCATION SYSTEM / Hong Kong. Government Secretariat – Hong Kong, 1981 – 5mf – 9 – DE-151/1 – ne IDC [370]

Hong Kong. Educational Department *see* INFORMATION SHEET ON PRIMARY EDUCATION

HONG KONG GOVERNMENT GAZETTE – v100-112. 1958-70 – 34r – 1 – us Ross [324]

Hong Kong. Government Secretariat *see* THE HONG KONG EDUCATION SYSTEM

Hong Kong. Governor in Council *see* EDUCATION (AMENDMENT) REGULATIONS 1974

Hong Kong. Industrial Training Advisory Committe *see* REPORT OF THE WORKING PARTY ON PRE-VOCATIONAL EDUCATION OF THE FUNCTIONAL COMMITTEE ON VOCATIONAL TRAINING JANUARY 1970

Hong Kong. Industrial Training Advisory Committee *see* FINAL REPORT ... MARCH 1971

HONG KONG LAW REPORTS / Hong Kong. Supreme Court – 40v. 1905-56 – 1,9 – $99.00 – at Butterworths [340]

Hong Kong. Laws, Statutes, etc *see*
- THE COMPANIES ORDINANCE OF HONGKONG, BEING NO. 1 OF 1865.
- ORDINANCE NO. 13 OF 1873. SPECIAL EDITION OF "THE HONGKONG CODE OF CIVIL PROCEDURE,".

Hong Kong. Legislative Council *see* STATEMENT ON GOVERNMENT'S POLICY ON THE REORGANIZATION OF THE STRUCTURE OF PRIMARY AND SECONDARY EDUCATION

HONG KONG NATURALIST – 1930-41 – 1 – uk Microform Academic [574]

Hong Kong. Polytechnic Planning Committee *see* FINAL REPORT ... JULY 1971

HONG KONG PRESS SUMMARIES *see*
- CURRENT BACKGROUND
- EXTRACTS FROM CHINA MAINLAND PUBLICATIONS
- INDEX TO SURVEY OF CHINA MAINLAND PRESS, SELECTIONS FROM CHINA MAINLAND MAGAZINES AND CURRENT BACKGROUND
- REVIEW OF HONGKONG CHINESE PRESS
- SELECTIONS FROM CHINA MAINLAND MAGAZINES
- SUPPLEMENT TO SELECTIONS OF CHINA MAINLAND MAGAZINES
- SUPPLEMENT TO SURVEY OF CHINA MAINLAND PRESS
- SURVEY OF CHINA MAINLAND PRESS

Hong Kong. Special Committee on Higher Education *see*
- INTERIM REPORT 1966
- SECOND INTERIM REPORT 1968

HONG KONG STANDARD – (In English. Yrly reel count varies) – 1949- – 1 – inquire – us Ross [072]

Hong Kong. Supreme Court *see* HONG KONG LAW REPORTS

THE HONG KONG TIMES : DAILY ADVERTISER AND SHIPPING GAZETTE – Hong Kong: Printed and published by William Curtis, may 1873-apr 29, 1876 – 8r – 1 – us Res Libr [072]

Hong Kong. University and Politechnic Grants Committee *see* SPECIAL REPORT OCTOBER 1965 – JUNE 1976

Hong Kong. University and Polytechnic Grants Committee *see* NOTES ON PROCEDURES

Hong Kong University Press *see* JOURNAL OF ORIENTAL STUDIES

HONG KONG WEEKLY PRESS – Hong Kong. 1895-1909 – 1 – uk Microform Academic [072]

HONG QI – China. News daily of the Central Committee of the Communist Party. Mar 1931-Mar 1934.54 ill. DL4f – 9 – 220.00 – cc Globe [072]

HONG QI – Published within the party. Nov 1928-2 Aug 1930. 32 ill. DL9f – 9 – 130.00 – cc Globe [073]

HONG QI *see* HUNG CH'I

HONG QI ZHOU KAN – Published within the party. 15 Aug 1930-1931. 11 ill. DL3f – 9 – 55.00 – cc Globe [073]

HONG SE ZHONG HUA – China. Central Committee newspaper. Dec 1931-Jan 1937.27 ill. DL1f – 9 – 110.00 – cc Globe [072]

HONG SE ZHONG HUA – China. Special edition from Jan-Feb 1934. 1 ill. DL2f – 9 – 30.00 – cc Globe [072]

Hong-Joe, Christina M *see* DISCIPLINE-BASED DANCE EDUCATION

HONGKONG : LATE CANTON, REGISTER – (Filmed with: Canton register, 1841-jun 10 1843; jun 20-dec 26 1843) – Hongkong: J Slade, 1843 – us Res Libr [072]

HONGKONG MERCURY AND SHIPPING GAZETTE – Hongkong: G M Bain, jun 1-dec 4 1866 – 1r – 1 – us Res Libr [072]

THE HONGKONG NEWS – [Hong Kong: Hongkong News, feb-jul 1943; dec 29 1943-jan 22 1944; may 21-aug 17 1945 – us Res Libr [072]

THE HONGKONG REGISTER / ed by Cairns, John – (Filmed consecutively with: General price current, mercantile register and shipping list jan 3-aug 22 1845. Issue for mar 23 1858, nov 24 1860 filmed with: Hongkong Register, and Daily Advertiser jan 2 1844-dec 25 1855; jan 5-mar 30 1858 ; apr 6-dec 28 1858; mar 23 1858) – Victoria: publ by John Cairns, 1844- – us Res Libr [072]

THE HONGKONG REGISTER, AND DAILY ADVERTISER – (Filmed with: Hongkong Register) – Victoria: [s.n.], mar 23 1858, nov 24 1860 – us Res Libr [072]

HONGKONG SUNDAY HERALD – Hong Kong: David Christian Wilson, 1929-jun 1941 – 17r – 1 – us Res Libr [072]

HONGKONG TELEGRAPH – (Issues for oct 1-14 1946 filmed with: Hongkong Telegraph (1881)) – Victoria, HK: F B Franklin, 1946-51 – 1 – us Res Libr [072]

THE HONGKONG TELEGRAPH – (Issues for aug 6-sep 30 1941 filmed with Hongkong telegraph (Victoria, Hong Kong: 1946)) – Victoria, Hongkong: Robert Fraser-Smith, [oct 1-14 1946]. jun 16 1881-sep 1941 – us Res Libr [072]

HONGKONG TIGER STANDARD – Hongkong: Star Newspaper Enterprises, mar 1949-mar 1952; oct 1954-1961 – 1 – us Res Libr [072]

HONGQI – Red Flag. In Chinese. F p1 – 9 – $4.50f – cc Microforms [073]

HONGQI RIBAO – Red Flag Daily. 1930-31. 1 reel. M/B 28 – 1 – $55.00 – cc Microforms [072]

LA HONGRIE – Paris: N Chaix, jul 1848 – us Res Libr [072]

LA HONGRIE CALVINISTE / Doumergue, Emile – Toulouse: Societe d'edition de Toulouse, [1912?] – 1mf – us A.T.L.A. [240]

LA HONGRIE LITTERAIRE ET SCIENTIFIQUE / Kont, J – Paris. 1896. BR-5394 2 – 8 – ne IDC [490]

HONGZHI BAODING JUN ZHI, APPROX. 1505 / Hebei Province. China – Records of Baoding Prefecture in the reign of Hongzhi. 25 vols. Comp. by Zhao Yin and Xu Gui. F A4. (Rare Local Records in Chinese...1420-1507) – 9 – $54.00 – cc Microforms [950]

HONGZHI HUANGZHOU FU ZHI, 1560 / Hubei Province. China – Records of Huangzhou Prefecture during the reign of Hongzhi. 10 vols. Comp. by Luo Xizhe. F A80. (Rare Local Records in Chinese...1420-1507) – 9 – $45.00 – cc Microforms [950]

HONGZHI HUIZHOU FU ZHI, 1502 – Records of Huizhou Prefecture in the reign of Hongzhi. 12 vols. Comp. by Wang Shunmin. F A28. (Rare Local REcords in Chinese...1420-1507) – 9 – $81.00 – cc Microforms [950]

HONGZHI JURONG XIAN ZHI, 1496 / Jiangsu Province. China – Records of Jurong County in the reign of Hongzhi. 12 vols. Comp. by Cheng Wen. F A14. (Rare Local Records in Chinese...1420-1507) – 9 – $40.50 – cc Microforms [950]

HONGZHI YANSHI XIAN ZHI, 1504 / Henan Province. China – Records of Yanshi County in the reign of Hongzhi. 4 vols. Comp. by Wei Jin. F A79. (Rare Local Records in Chinese...1420-1507) – 9 – $13.50 – cc Microforms [950]

HONGZHI YANSHI XIAN ZHI, 1504 / Yanshi County. China – Records...in the Reign of Hongzhi 4v. Comp. by Wei Jin. 3 fiches. F/A79 – 9 – $13.50 – cc Microforms [950]

HONGZHI YIZHOU ZHI, 1502 / Hebei Province. China – Records of Yizhou in the reign of Hongzhi. 20 vols. Comp. by Dai Xian. F A8. (Rare Local Records in Chinese...1420-1507) – 9 – $27.00 – cc Microforms [950]

Honiara. Catholic Archdiocese *see* ARCHIVES

Honich, T C *see* EEN GRONDELIJCKE VERCLARINGHE: VAN DEN ECHTELIJCKEN STAET. IN TWEE GHESPRAKEN GHESTELT

Honigsheim, Paul *see* DIE STAATS- UND SOZIAL-LEHREN DER FRANZOESISCHEN JANSENISTEN IM 17. JAHRHUNDERT

Honka, Rita J M *see* BODY THERAPY REPATTERNING AND THE NEUROMOTOR SYSTEM

HONNEFER VOLKSZEITUNG – Bad Honnef, jan 5 1889-93. jul 3 1894-jun 30 1910. 1911-jun 28 1912. 1913-jun 30 1942. oct 1 1949-77 – 95r – 1 – gw Mikrofilm [072]

Honnell, T C *see* LETTERS

L'HONNETE CRIMINEL OU L'INNOCENCE RECONNUE / Fenouillot, Falbaire De – (French Theatre Series). Amsterdam, et Paris, Merlin. 1767 – 9 – fr Hachette [820]

HONNETE EL EPHANT *see* CHESTNY I SLON L'HONNETE EL EPHANT

HONOR AWARDS FOR ARCHITECTURE – (Mf available for missing yrs 1987, 1990, 1991. Microfilm indexes available for 1984-86, 1988-89. A paper index is available for 1987) – 1981-86, 1988-89, 1992-94, 1996-97 – 87r – 1 – $6,960.00 – us Ross [720]

HONOR AWARDS FOR INTERIORS – (Also available in mf) – 1992-97 – 17r – 1 – $1,360.00 – us Ross [720]

HONOR AWARDS FOR URBAN DESIGN – 1992-97 – 10r – 1 – $800.00 – us Ross [720]

HONOR EDGEWORTH, OR, OTTAWA'S PRESENT TENSE – Ottawa: A. Woodburn, 1882. 00556. (Pre-1900 Canadiana) – 9 – cn C.I.H.M. [830]

HONOR ROLL OF SHAWNEE COUNTY – World War 1. Jefferson City, n.d. Kansas Reel 12. The Cox Library Collection – 5 – us Americana [978]

HONOR ROLL OF VETERANS BURIED IN ILLINOIS : UNKNOWN WARS / Illinois. Military Records – Alpha card file by veterans' names. Z129-0020 to 0029 – 1 – us A.G.L.L. [920]

HONOR ROLL OF VETERANS BURIED IN ILLINOIS : WARS FROM 1774-1898 / Illinois. Military Records – Alpha card file by veterans' names. Z129-0001 to 0020 – 1 – us A.G.L.L. [920]

HONOR ROLL OF VETERANS BURIED IN ILLINOIS: PEACETIME BURIALS / Illinois. Military Records – Alpha card file by veterans' names. Z129-0029 to 0031 – 1 – us A.G.L.L. [920]
HONOR ROLL OF VETERANS OF THE ARMED FORCES...BURIED IN THE STATE OF ILLINOIS PRIOR TO JULY 1, 1955 / Illinois. Military Records – V128-0001 to V128-0006 – 1 – us A.G.L.L. [920]
HONOR Y PATRIA / Leon Gutierrez, Florencio – 1900 – 9 – 1.50f – sp Bibl Santa Ana [810]
L'HONORABLE A.-N. MORIN / Bechard, Auguste – Quebec, 1885. SEM105P53 – 3mf – 9 – Can$6.75 – cn Bibl Nat [920]
A L'HONORABLE CHARLES FITZPATRICK / Beaubien, Louis – Quebec, 1898? 03039. (Pre-1900 Canadiana) – 9 – cn C.I.H.M. [971]
L'HONORABLE F.-A. QUESNEL / Cherrier, Come Seraphin – Montreal: J. Chapleau, 1878. 00599. (Pre-1900 Canadiana) – 9 – cn C.I.H.M. [920]
L'HONORABLE J.A. CHAPLEAU : SA BIOGRAPHIE – Montreal: Eusebe Senecal et fils, 1887. SEM105P296 – 6mf – 9 – Can$13.50 – cn Bibl Nat [920]
L'HONORABLE LS. JOSEPH PAPINEAU / David, Laurent Olivier – Montreal: s.n., 1872 (Montreal: G. Desbarats). 02515. (Pre-1900 Canadiana) – 9 – cn C.I.H.M. [971]
L'HONORABLE MAURICE TELLIER : BIO-BIBLIOGRAPHIE / Payette, Ange-Albert – 1960. SEM105P4 – 656mf – 9 – Can$1,476.00 – cn Bibl Nat [920]
HONORE DE BALZAC, HIS LIFE AND WRITINGS / Sandars, Mary Frances – New York: Dodd, Mead & Co., 1905. xvii,377p – 1 – us U.W. Library [920]
Honorio, Cirilo S *see* TAGUMPAY NG MANGGAGAWA
A HONOSSAQ A BUENTETOE JOGBAN / Doleschall, A – Budapest, 1901 – 3mf – 1 – ILM-2409/1 – ne IDC [327]
THE HONOURABLE GUEST (CCC89) / Ch'en, Chu – (In Chinese) – 1st ed. Hong Kong: Council on Christian Literature for Overseas Chinese, 1953 – 1r – 1 – 1984-B500 – us A.T.L.A. [820]
HONPO SHOGYO KAIGISHO SHIRYO = HISTORICAL DOCUMENTS OF THE CHAMBER OF COMMERCE OF JAPAN / Chamber of Commerce of Japan – Monthly and annual reports of Chambers of Commerce. Northeastern area: 15 chs. of commerce; southwestern area: 22 chs. of commerce; Proceedings of the Chamber of Commerce Assoc., Tokyo. 1890-1927 – 176r – 1 – Y1,743,000.00 – ja Yushodo [380]
HONRA DO BRASIL DESAFRONTADA DE INSULTOS DA ASTREA EXPADAXINA – Rio de Janeiro, 8 Apr-20 Aug 1828 – 1,5,6 – bl Biblioteca [072]
LA HONRADA / Picon, Jacinto O – 1890 – 9 – 1.50f – sp Bibl Santa Ana [830]
Honved, A *see* SKETCHES OF THE HUNGARIAN EMIGRATION INTO TURKEY
Honyman, Robert *see* DIARY
Hood, E Lyman *see* THE NATIONAL COUNCIL OF CONGREGATIONAL CHURCHES OF THE UNITED STATES
Hood, Edmund Lyman *see* THE NEW WEST EDUCATION COMMISSION, 1880-93
Hood, Edwin Paxton *see*
– CHRISTMAS EVANS
– THE GREAT REVIVAL OF THE EIGHTEENTH CENTURY
– ISAAC WATTS
– THE THRONE OF ELOQUENCE: GREAT PREACHERS, ANCIENT AND MODERN
– THE VILLAGES OF THE BIBLE
Hood, George *see* A HISTORY OF MUSIC IN NEW ENGLAND
Hood, J W *see* ONE HUNDRED YEARS OF THE AFRICAN METHODIST EPISCOPAL ZION CHURCH, OR, THE CENTENNIAL OF AFRICAN METHODISM
Hood, Paxton *see* OLIVER CROMWELL
HOOD RIVER BREEZE – Hood River OR. Nov 1913 – 1 – us U.O. Library [071]
HOOD RIVER COUNTY SUN – Hood River, OR. -d. 5 Jan 1938-13 May 1949 – 1 – us U.O. Library [071]
HOOD RIVER DAILY SUN – Hood River OR. May 16 1949-Aug 5 1952 – 1 – us U.O. Library [071]
HOOD RIVER GLACIER – Hood River, OR. -w. 1889-1933 – 1 – 377.00 – us Oregon Hist [071]
HOOD RIVER NEWS – Hood River, OR. -w. 10 Feb 1909-24 Nov 1909, 1 roll; 2 Jan 1953-. – 1 – us U.O. Library [071]
HOOD RIVER NEWS – Hood River, OR. -w. 1909-53 – 1 – 480.00 – us Oregon Hist [071]
HOOD RIVER NEWSLETTER – Hood River, OR. -w. 7 Oct 1905-21 Oct 1908. 1 roll – 1 – us U.O. Library [071]
Hood, Thomas *see*
– ODES AND ADDRESSES TO GREAT PEOPLE
– THE PLEA OF THE MIDSUMMER FAIRIES
Hoofien, J *see* HANDBOEK VOOR DE GESCHIEDENIS DER JODEN
Hooft, P C *see* EMBLEMATA AMATORIA
HOOFT-SOMMA VNDE GRONT VAN 'TGENE WY WT DIE LEERE DAVID IORIS HEBBEN CONNEN VERSTAEN / Blesdijk, Nicolaas M van – Int Jaer 1547. 1607. BME-388 1 – 9 – ne IDC [240]
Hoog, Simone *see* LA DYNASTIE DES BOURBONS
Hooge, N C *see* EFFECTS OF RATIONAL BEHAVIOR TRAINING ON ATTITUDES OF REHABILITATION SUPPORT PERSONNEL
Hoogers, J *see* THEORIE ET PRATIQUE DE LA PIETE FILIALE CHEZ LES CHINOIS
Hoogerwerf, A *see* DE AVIFAUNA VAN TJIBODAS EN OMGEVING, INCLUSIEF HET NATUURMONUMENT TJIBODAS-GN. GEDE, WEST-JAVA
Hoogh, D. van der *see* GRONDSLAG VAN HET VOCAAL MUZYK
Hooghe, Romein de *see*
– CARTES MARINES A L'USAGE DES ARMEES DU ROY DE LA GRANDE BRETAGNE.
– HIEROGLYPHICA OF MERK BEELDEN DER OUDE VOLKEREN
Hoogstraten, Francois van *see*
– DE SCHOOLE DER WERELD, GEOPENT IN 140. VLIEGENDE BEDENKINGEN OP VEERLERHANDE VOORVALLENDE GEZICHTEN EN ZAEKEN
– HET VOORHOF DER ZIELE
Hoogstraten, J van *see*
– STAAT- EN ZEDEKUNDIGE ZINNEPRENTEN, OF LEERZAME FABELEN
– ZEGEPRAAL DER GODDELYKE LIEFDE, VERTOONT IN ZEVEN EN VEERTIG ZIEL OPWEKKENDE ZINNEBEELDEN
Hoogstraten, Samuel van *see* INLEYDING TOT DE HOOGE SCHOOLE DER SCHILDERKONST
Hook, Alfred J *see* AMERICAN NEGLIGENCE DIGEST
Hook, James *see*
– THE ASCENSION: A SACRED ORATORIO
– CONCERTO PER IL ORGANO O CEMBALO
– SKETCHES OF VOCAL AND INSTRUMENTAL MUSIC
Hook, Theodore Edward *see* JACK BRAG
Hooke, Robert *see*
– MICROGRAPHIA
Hooke, SH *see*
– THE LABYRINTH
– MYTH AND RITUAL
HOOKER COUNTY TRIBUNE – Mullen, NE. -w.Sept-Dec 1902; Oct 1903-Jul 1925 (incomplete); 1926- – 1 – us NE Hist [071]
Hooker, Edward William *see* MEMOIR OF MRS. SARAH L. HUNTINGTON SMITH: LATE OF THE AMERICAN MISSION IN SYRIA
Hooker, Isabella B *see* PAPERS AND CORRESPONDENCE
Hooker, J D *see*
– ALGAE ANTARCTICA
– ENUMERATIO PLANTARUM ZEYLANICAE. ASSISTED. J. D. HOOKER
– FLORA INDICA
– FLORA OF BRITISH INDIA
– GENERA PLANTARUM
– HANDBOOK OF THE NEW ZEALAND FLORA
– HANDBOOK TO THE FLORA OF CEYLON
– ILLUSTRATIONS OF HIMALAYAN PLANTS
Hooker, JD *see*
– THE RHODODENDRONS OF SIKKIM-HIMALAYA
– THE RODODENDRONS OF SIKKIM-HIMALAYA
Hooker, John *see* THE BIBLE AND WOMAN SUFFRAGE
Hooker, Thomas *see* REDEMPTION: THREE SERMONS 1637-1656
Hooker, W J *see*
– BOTANICAL MISCELLANY
– THE BOTANY OF CAPTAIN BEECHEY'S VOYAGE
– THE BRITISH FERNS
– THE BRITISH FLORA COMPRISING THE PHAENOGAMOUS OR FLOWERING PLANTS AND THE FERNS
– BRITISH JUNGERMANNIAE: BEING A HISTORY AND DESCRIPTION WITH COLOURED FIGURES OF EACH SPECIES OF THE GENUS
– A CENTURY OF FERNS
– COMPANION TO THE BOTANICAL MAGAZINE
– EXOTIC FLORA, CONTAINING FIGURES AND DESCRIPTIONS OF EXOTIC PLANTS
– FILICES EXOTICAE; OR COLOURED FIGURES AND DESCRIPTIONS OF EXOTIC FERNS, CHIEFLY OF SUCH AS ARE CULTIVATED IN THE ROYAL GARDENS OF KEW
– FLORA BOREALI-AMERICANA
– FLORA SCOTICA
– GARDEN FERNS
– GENERA FILICUM
– ICONES FILICUM
– ICONES PLANTARUM
– JOURNAL OF BOTANY
– JOURNAL OF BOTANY AND KEW GARDEN MISCELLANY
– LONDON JOURNAL OF B0TANY
– LONDON JOURNAL OF BOTANY
– MUSCI EXOTICI, CONTAINING FIGURES AND DESCRIPTIONS OF NEW OR LITTLE KNOWN FOREIGN MOSSES
– MUSCI NEPALENSES
– MUSCOLOGIA BRITANNICA
– PLANTAE CRYPTOGAMICAE, QUAS IN PLAGA ORBIS NOVI AEQUINOCTIALI COLLEGERUNT A. DE HUMBOLDT ET A. BONPLAND
– A SECOND CENTURY OF FERNS
– SPECIES FILICUM
– SYNOPSIS FILICUM
Hookes, Ellis *see* INSTRUCTIONS FOR RIGHT SPELLING
Hoole, Charles *see*
– THE LATINE GRAMMAR
– A NEW DISCOVERY OF THE OLD ART OF TEACHING SCHOOLE
Hoole, Elijah *see* MADRAS, MYSORE, AND THE SOUTH OF INDIA, OR, A PERSONAL NARRATIVE OF A MISSION TO THOSE COUNTRIES FROM MDCCCXX TO MDCCCXXVII.
Hoonacker, Albin van *see* DE RERUM CREATIONE EX NIHILO
HOOPER SENTINEL – Hooper, NE. -w. Apr 1892; Dec 1892; Oct 1895-Jan 1904; Aug 1908 to date – 1 – us NE Hist [071]
Hooper, William Hope *see* LETTERS
Hooper, Wynnard *see* THE INFLUENCE OF STATE BORROWING ON COMMERCIAL CRISES
Hoopes, Darlington *see* THE SOCIALIST PARTY OF THE UNITED STATES
HOOSIER FOLKLORE – Hoosier Folklore Society: Indianapolis. -q. v5, no.1-v9, no.4. Mar 1946-Dec 1950. 1 reel – 1 – us I.U. Libraries [390]
HOOSIER FOLKLORE BULLETIN – Hoosier Folklore Society: Indianapolis. v1, no.1-v4, no.4. Jun 1942-Dec 1945. -irr. -q. 1 reel – 1 – us I.U. Libraries [390]
HOOSIER MOSAICS / Thompson, Maurice – 1875 – 9 – $15.00 – us Scholars' Facs [830]
Hoover, Herbert *see* PROCLAMATIONS AND EXECUTIVE ORDERS
Hoover Institution *see*
– CATALOG OF THE CHINESE COLLECTION
– CATALOG OF THE JAPANESE COLLECTION
– CATALOG OF THE WESTERN LANGUAGES COLLECTION
– CATALOG OF THE WESTERN LANGUAGES COLLECTION: SERIALS AND NEWSPAPERS
– CHINESE COMMUNIST PERIODICALS AND NEWSPAPERS
Hoover, L M *see* A HISTORY OF THE FIRST BAPTIST CHURCH, ELDORADO, TEXAS, 1 SEP 1901-31 AUG 1957
Hoover Library. Stanford University *see* SELECTED PERSIAN TITLES FROM PERSIAN COLLECTION
THE HOPE – (Philadelphia) – 1 – us A.J.P.C. [071]
Hope, Anne Fulton *see*
– THE FIRST DIVORCE OF HENRY 8
– FRANCISCAN MARTYRS IN ENGLAND
– THE LIFE OF S. THOMAS A BECKET OF CANTERBURY
Hope, Anthony *see* THE PRISONER OF ZENDA
Hope, Eva *see* LIFE OF GENERAL GORDON
HOPE FOR THE FUTURE / M'Bow, Amadou-Mahtar – 1984 – 292p – 9 – 92-3-102221-0 – fr UNESCO [303]
Hope, FW *see*
– A CATALOGUE OF HEMIPTERA IN THE COLLECTION OF...F.W. HOPE
– A CATALOGUE OF THE LUCANOID COLEOPTERA IN THE COLLECTION OF...F.W. HOPE
– THE COLEOPTERIST'S MANUAL. CONTAINING LAMELLICORN INSECTS BY LINNEUS AND FABRICIUS
Hope, J *see* A TREATISE ON THE DISEASES OF THE HEART AND GREAT VESSELS
Hope, John *see* PAPERS OF JOHN AND LUGENIA BURNS HOPE
Hope, Lugenia (Burns) *see* PAPERS OF JOHN AND LUGENIA BURNS HOPE
HOPE STANDARD – British Columbia, CN. Apr 1968- – 1r per y – 1 – Can$57.00r – cn Commonwealth Micro [072]
Hope, W H ST John *see* INVENTORIES OF CHRISTCHURCH, CANTERBURY
HOPEDALE COMMUNITY COLLECTION, 1821-1938 – 6r – 1 – $445.00 – us UMI [240]
HOPEFUL BAPTIST CHURCH. WAYNESBORO, GEORGIA : CHURCH RECORDS – (264p) – 1814-1870 – 1 reel – 1 – $11.88 – us Baptist [240]
HO-PEI JIH-PAO – Paoting, Hopeh. Aug 1, 1949-. Scattered issues missing. 5 reels – 1 – 87.50 – us Chinese Res [072]
HOPES AND FEARS FOR ART : FIVE LECTURES DELIVERED IN BIRMINGHAM, LONDON AND NOTTINGHAM, 1878-1881 / Morris, William – London: Ellis & White, 1882 – 1 roll – 1 – 1-55879-399-2 – uk Libr Preservation [700]
HOPETOUN COURIER – 1921-1960. HC1-11 – 14r – 1 – at Corangamite [072]
HOPEWELL BAPTIST CHURCH. ANDERSON COUNTY. SOUTH CAROLINA : CHURCH RECORDS – 1868-90, 1963-88. 1619p – 1 – $72.86 – us Baptist [240]
HOPEWELL BAPTIST CHURCH. ARLINGTON, KENTUCKY : CHURCH RECORDS – Sept 1881 – Jan 1975. Incomplete – 1 – 35.82 – us Baptist [240]
HOPEWELL BAPTIST CHURCH. BETHEL ASSOCIATION. SOUTH CAROLINA : CHURCH RECORDS – 1813-37 – 1 – 18.00 – us Baptist [240]
HOPEWELL BAPTIST CHURCH. HENRY COUNTY. KENTUCKY : CHURCH RECORDS – 1836-1961 – 1 – 12.78 – us Baptist [240]
HOPEWELL BAPTIST CHURCH. ROBERTSON COUNTY. SPRINGFIELD, TENNESSEE : CHURCH RECORDS – 1846-1964 – 1 – 38.34 – us Baptist [240]
HOPEWELL FIRST BAPTIST CHURCH. HOPEWELL, VIRGINIA : CHURCH RECORDS – 1915-68 – 1 – 58.23 – us Baptist [240]
HOPEWELL FRIENDS HISTORY OF FREDERICK COUNTY / Wayland, John W – Strasburg, Shenandoah Publishing Co., 1936. Virginia Reel 3. (The Cox Library Collection) – 5 – us Americana [978]
HOPEWELL NEWS – Va. 1958- – 1 – us UMI [071]
HOPEWELL TELEPHONE – Hopewell, PA., 1891-1898 – 13 – $25.00r – us I.M.R. [071]
Hopfen, H J *see*
– FARM IMPLEMENTS FOR ARID AND TROPICAL REGIONS
– SMALL FARM IMPLEMENTS
Hopfen, Hans *see*
– GEDICHTE
– DIE GESCHICHTEN DES MAJORS
– HELGA
– KLEINE LEUTE
– MEIN ERSTES ABENTEUER UND ANDERE GESCHICHTEN
HOPI ACTION NEWS – 1966-68. (American Indian Periodicals in the Princeton University Library). 1 reel – 1 – $65.00 – us UPA [305]
HOPITAL DU SACRE-COEUR : 25: CARTIERVILLE – Montreal: Hopital du Sacre-Coeur, impression 1951 [Quebec (Province)]. SEM105P1960 – 1mf – 9 – Can$2.25 – cn Bibl Nat [360]
LES HOPITAUX MODERNES AU XIXE SIECLE / Tollet, Casimir – Paris, 1894. Fol., xi, 334 p., fig., pl. (Architecture Series) – 9 – fr Hachette [720]
Hopkins, Alphonso Alva *see* GERALDINE: A SOUVENIR OF THE ST LAWRENCE
HOPKIN'S CHANCERY APPEALS REPORTS / New York. (State) – (A Pre-NRS title) – 1v. 1823-26 (all publ) – 7mf – 9 – $10.50 – LLMC 80-024 – us L.L.M.C. [340]

HOPKINS' COMMITTEE REPORT : REPORT TO THE U.S. SECRETARY OF THE NAVY BY THE COMMITTEE TO STUDY THE NAVAL ADMINISTRATION OF GUAM AND AMERICAN SAMOA – 1947 – 2mf – 9 – $3.00 – LLMC 82-100C Title 10 – us L.L.M.C. [327]
Hopkins, Daniel C *see* TRUE CAUSE OF ALL CONTENTION, STRIFE, AND CIVIL WAR IN CHRISTIAN COMMUNITIES
Hopkins, Earl Palmer *see* PROBLEMS AND QUIZ ON CRIMINAL PROCEDURE
Hopkins, Henry W *see*
- ATLAS OF THE CITY AND ISLAND OF MONTREAL
- ATLAS OF THE TOWN OF SAINT JOHNS AND SOREL
- ATLAS OF THE TOWN OF SOREL AND COUNTY OF RICHELIEU, PROVINCE OF QUEBEC

Hopkins, Joe R *see* THE EFFECTS OF HIP POSITION AND ANGULAR VELOCITY ON QUADRICEPS AND HAMSTRING ECCENTRIC PEAK TORQUE
Hopkins, John Abel *see* LA ESTRUCTURA ECONOMICA Y EL DESARROLLO INDUSTRIAL DE LA REPUBLICA ARGENTINA
Hopkins, John Henry *see*
- A CANDID EXAMINATION OF THE QUESTION WHETHER THE POPE OF ROME IS THE GREAT ANTICHRIST OF SCRIPTURE
- THE LAW OF RITUALISM
- A SPIRITUAL, ECCLESIASTICAL AND HISTORICAL VIEW OF SLAVERY
- TRANSACTIONS OF THE NEW-YORK ECCLESIOLOGICAL SOCIETY

Hopkins, Mark *see*
- EVIDENCES OF CHRISTIANITY: LECTURES BEFORE THE LOWELL INSTITUTE
- MODERN SKEPTICISM IN ITS RELATIONS TO YOUNG MEN
- THE SCRIPTURAL IDEA OF MAN

Hopkins, Ruth A *see* EFFECTS OF AGE AND ETHANOL ON THERMOREGULATORY RESPONSES OF MEN TO A COLD AIR STRESS
Hopkins, T M *see* SPOTS ON THE SUN, OR, THE PLUMB-LINE PAPERS
Hopkins, Theodore Weld *see* THE DOCTRINE OF INSPIRATION
Hopkins, Thomas D *see* FEDERAL USER FEES
Hopkinson, Alfred *see* THE FACULTY OF LAWS, AND THE IDEA OF LAW
Hopkinson, Francis *see* FRANCIS HOPKINSON: HIS BOOK
Hopkinson, J *see* THE BRITISH FRESHWATER RHIZOPODA AND HELIOZOA
HOPKINSVILLE FIRST BAPTIST CHURCH. HOPKINSVILLE, KENTUCKY : CHURCH RECORDS – 1818-1904, 1961-1971. Membership/Contribution Records 1913-1956; Deacon Minutes 1923-1979. Formerly: New Providence Baptist Church; includes 66th anniversary minutes, Bethel Bapt. Assn., 1890; 4229p – 1 – $190.31 – us Baptist [240]
HOPKINTON 1705-1849 – (Mf 1T-3T: Births 1705-96. Mf 2T-3T: Intentions 1737-95; Marriages 1726-95. Mf 3T: Deaths 1728-91. Mf 4T-6T: Births & Deaths 1752-1839. Mf 6T-7T: Intentions 1795-1835. Mf 7T-9T: Marriages 1793-1844. Mf 9T-11T: Intentions 1835-49. Mf 11T-12T: Births & Deaths 1812-47. Mf 13T-15T: Vital Records 1844-49. Mf 15T: Marriages 1720-99; Births 1774-92) – (mf ed 1996) – 15mf – 9 – 0-87623-269-1 – us Holbrook [920]
Hopley, John E *see* HISTORY OF CRAWFORD COUNTY AND REPRESENTATIVE CITIZENS
Hopp, Ernst Otto *see* TRANSATLANTISCHE STIMMEN
Hoppe, Alfred *see* DIE STAATSAUFFASSUNG HEINRICH VON KLEISTS
Hoppe, D H *see*
- BOTANISCHE ZEITUNG
- BOTANISCHES TASCHENBUCH FUER DIE ANFAENGER DIESER WISSENSCHAFT UND DER APOTHEKERKUNST
- FLORA ODER ALLGEMEINE BOTANISCHE ZEITUNG

Hoppe, DH *see*
- ENUMERATIO INSECTORUM ELYTRATORUM CIRCA ERLANGAM INDIGENARUM
- TAGEBUCH EINER REISE NACH DEN KUESTEN DES ADRIATISCHEN MEERES UND DEN GEBIRGEN VON KRAIN, VORZUEGLICH IN BOTANISCHER UND ENTOMOLOGISCHER HINSICHT

Hoppe, Ingeborg Marei *see* DIE FREUNDIN
Hoppe, Karl *see* DER JUNGE WIELAND
Hoppe, R *see* ARCHIV DER MATHEMATIK UND PHYSIK
Hoppenbrouwers, H *see* LA PLUS ANCIENNE VERSION LATINE DE LA VIE DE ST ANTOINE
Hopper, R P *see* OLD-TIME PRIMITIVE METHODISM IN CANADA, 1829-1884
Hoppers, W H ML *see* STRUCTURE AND SOCIAL CONTEXT OF NON-FORMAL TRAINING IN LUSAKA
HOPPE-SEYLER'S ZEITSCHRIFT FUER PHYSIOLOGISCHE CHEMIE – v1-301. 1877-1955 – 1,5,6 – us Princeton Micro [540]
HOPPE-SEYLER'S ZEITSCHRIFT FUER PHYSIOLOGISCHE CHEMIE – (v352-365, no.12.1971-84. 5,6. v357-365, no.12.1976-84. 9) – v1-365, no.12. 1877-1984 – 1 – us UMI [073]
Hoppin, James Mason *see* HOMILETICS
Hopwood, Charles H *see* MIDDLE TEMPLE RECORDS
Hopwood, D *see* MIDDLE EAST AND ISLAM: A BIBLIOGRAPHICAL INTRODUCTION
Hopwood, Derek *see* MIDDLE EAST/NORTH AFRICA DEVELOPMENT DOCUMENTS
HORA – Athens, Greece. -d. 9 June 1876-31 Dec 1889. Imperfect. 26 reels – 1 – uk British Libr Newspaper [949]
HORA ARGENTINA Y TEMAS ANALITICOS RACIONLISTAS / Barrio, Inocencio – Buenos Aires, 1954 – 1 – CSUXADJ1303-B – us Hoover Inst Photo [972]
HORA CRUCIAL EN LA ARGENTINA / Juarez, Carlos Arturo – 1a ed. Buenos Aires, Argentina: Pena Lillo Editor, 1982 – 9 – us Hoover Inst Photo [972]
LA HORA DE LA UNIDAD / Montes, Eugenio – Burgos, 1937. Fiche W 1058. (Blodgett Collection of Spanish Civil War Pamphlets) – 9 – us H.U. College Libr [946]
LA HORA DECISIVA / Goni Moreno, Jose Maria – Buenos Aires, 1966 – 1 – CSUXAHZ7363-B – us Hoover Inst Photo [972]
Hora, Tomio *see* CHOHATSU BUKKEN ICHIRANHYO
HORACE GREELY PAPERS, 1831-1873 : FROM THE HOLDINGS OF THE RARE BOOKS AND MANUSCRIPTS DIVISION CENTER FOR THE HUMANITIES, THE NY. PUBLIC LIBRARY, ASTOR, LENOX, AND TILDEN FOUNDATIONS – (With Guide) – 1997 – ca 6r – 1 – ca $510.00 – S3359 – us Scholarly Res [975]
THE HORACE MAIN BOND PAPERS, PART 1 : BOND FAMILY PAPERS, 1892-1971 : GENERAL CORRESPONDENCE, 1926- 1972 – 9 – $860.00 – 1-55655-081-2 – us UPA [975]
THE HORACE MANN BOND PAPERS, PART 2 : SUBJECT FILES, 1926-1971 – 9 – $3,455.00 – 1-55655-082-0 – us UPA [975]
THE HORACE MANN BOND PAPERS, PART 3 : INSTITUTIONAL FILES, 1919-1972 – 9 – $3,650.00 – 1-55655-083-9 – us UPA [975]
THE HORACE MANN BOND PAPERS, PART 4 : RESEARCH FILES; 1910-1971 AND WRITINGS, 1926-1972 – 9 – $1,440.00 – 1-55655-084-7 – us UPA [975]
Horace Mann-Lincoln Institute *see* RESEARCH BULLETIN
HORACKER : ERZAEHLUNG / Raabe, Wilhelm Karl – Berlin: Aufbau-Verlag, 1956 – 1r – 1 – us U.W. Library [830]
HORACKER / Raabe, Wilhelm Karl – 4. Aufl. Berlin: G Grote, 1891 – 1 – us U.W. Library [830]
HORAE = BOOK OF HOURS / Clare College. Cambridge – (French). 15th century. Ms KK 3.2 – 1 – uk Microform Academic [240]
HORAE ENTOMOLOGICAE / Charpentier, T von – Wratislaviae, 1825. xvi,255p. 9pls. Z-1132/2 – 8 – ne IDC [590]
HORAE HEBRAICAE / Crawford, Francis J – (In English and Hebrew) – London: Williams & Norgate, 1868 – 1mf – 9 – 0-8370-9217-5 – 1986-3217 – us A.T.L.A. [470]
HORAE PETRINAE : OR, STUDIES IN THE LIFE OF ST PETER / Howson, John Saul – (Includes appendixes) – [London]: Religious Tract Society, [ca 1883] – 1mf – 9 – 0-8370-3682-8 – 1985-1682 – us A.T.L.A. [920]
HORAE PHYSICAE BEROLINENSIS / Nees von Esenbeck, C G D – Bonn, 1820, 123 pp., 27 pls. B-6094 1 – 9 – ne IDC [580]
HORAE SABBATICAE : REPRINT OF ARTICLES CONTRIBUTED TO THE SATURDAY REVIEW / Stephen, James Fitzjames – London, New York: Macmillan, 1892 – 2 rolls – 1 – 1-55879-230-9 – uk Libr Preservation [340]
HORAE SYNOPTICAE : CONTRIBUTIONS TO THE STUDY OF THE SYNOPTIC PROBLEM / Hawkins, John Caesar – (Includes appendixes) – 2nd rev ed. Oxford, Clarendon Press, 1909 – 1mf – 9 – 0-8370-3539-2 – 1985-1539 – us A.T.L.A. [220]
Horaninow, P *see* DIE PILZE IN MEDIZINISCH-POLIZEILICHER BEZIEHUNG
HORARIO E ITINERARIO DE LAS PROCESIONES DE SEMANA SANTA...1962 / Junta de Cofradias de Penitencia – Badajoz: Imp. Dip. Provincial, 1962 – 1 – sp Bibl Santa Ana [946]
HORARIUM BMV – Doornik, ca. 1480 – 2mf – 8 – Dfl9.00 – ne Slangenburg [240]
HORAS DIFICILES : SEPTIEMBRE 1955-1962 / Guardo, Ricardo C – Buenos Aires, 1963 – 1 – CSUXAHZ7408-B – us Hoover Inst Photo [972]
HORATIO GATES PAPERS – 1726-1828. Massachusetts Historical Society – 20r – 1 – us UMI [920]
HORATIO GATES PAPERS, 1726-1828 / Gates, Horatio – 20r – 1 – $1375.00 – us UMI [976]
Horatius *see* OPERA
Horder, W Garrett *see* THE TREASURY OF AMERICAN SACRED SONG
Hore, A H *see*
- THE CHURCH IN ENGLAND
- EIGHTEEN CENTURIES OF THE ORTHODOX GREEK CHURCH

Hore, Rafael *see* CONTESTACION... EXTREMADURA POR EL AVISO
HOREB BAPTIST CHURCH. NIMROD HALL, VIRGINIA : CHURCH RECORDS – 30 Apr 1876-1945 – 1 – 7.29 – us Baptist [240]
HOREI ZENSHO = STATUTES AT LARGE OF JAPAN: OFFICIAL EDITION OF THE COMPLETE STATUTES OF THE JAPANESE EMPIRE, 1868-1945 – Edited by the Cabinet Secretariat, yearly for 1868-85 and monthly for 1886-1945. With general and author and subject indexes in 2v for 1868-85 and yearly index from 1886 – 235r – 1 – Y2,157,000.00 – ja Yushodo [340]
DIE HOREN : EINE MONATSSCHRIFT / ed by Schiller, Friedrich von – Tuebingen, 1795-97. Hildesheim, 1977 – 69mf – 9 – DM580.00 diazo DM680.00 silver – gw Olms [430]
Horenstein, Bonnie *see* THE USE OF OCLC IN ACADEMIC LIBRARIES IN NEW YORK STATE. A REPORT OF A SURVEY. ED 244-637
HOREV – v. 1-15. New York. 1934-60. BJ-100-163 1 – 9 – ne IDC [270]
Horine, M C *see* PRACTICAL REFLECTIONS ON THE BOOK OF RUTH
O HORISONTE : ORGAO LITTERARIO E NOTICIOSO – Maceio, Alagoas. 4 Maio, Jul-13 Dez 1891 – 1,5,6 – bl Biblioteca [072]
THE HORITES / Campbell, John – 18?? 00377. (Pre-1900 Canadiana) – 9 – cn C.I.H.M. [900]
HORITSU SHIMBU, 1900-1934 = LEGAL NEWS – (In Japanese) – 91r – 1 – $3,185.00 in US $40.00r outside – L9400079 – us L of C Photodup [950]
L'HORIZON – (Also: L'Appel 1 sep 1945-v3 n24 22 avr 1948; v25 n25 15 avr 1970) – Sillery, Canada. 12 jul-23 aut 1945 – 1r – 1 – Can$30.00 – cn Can Microfilming [072]
HORIZON – London. v. 1-20. 1940-Jan 1950 – 1 – us NY Public [073]
HORIZON – London. v1-20. 1940-50 – 3r – 1 – us Ross [073]
HORIZON – Montreal, Canada. Mar 9 1987-Dec 5 1988; Jan 9 1989-Dec 23 1991 – 2r – 1 – us L of C Photodup [072]
HORIZON – (v. 11- 1969- 5,6. v. 12- 1970- 9) – v. 1- 1958- – 1 – us UMI [073]
HORIZON – v.1-. 1980-. Publ. by WIL (Women for Individual Liberty), Brisbane, Australia – 9 – 1.00f – at Libertarian Micro [320]
HORIZON *see* PRS JOURNAL
HORIZON 1980 : UNE ETUDE SUR L'EVOLUTION DE L'ECONOMIE DU QUEBEC DE 1946 A 1968 ET SUR SES PERSPECTIVES D'AVENIR / Lebel, Gilles – Quebec: Ministere de l'industrie et du commerce, 1970. SEM35P72 – 1r – 1 – Can$15.00 – cn Bibl Nat [339]
THE HORIZON: A JOURNAL OF THE COLOR LINE / ed by DuBois, W E B & Murray, F H M & Hershaw, L M – v1, no. 1-v6, no. 2. Jan 1907-Jul 1910. Washington, D.C.; Alexandra, Va. Not published from Jan-Oct 1909. No. 77-1 – 1 reel – 1 – $20.00 – us Partington [073]
HORIZON (WIL) – Jul 1980 – Jul 1982. To be contd. 1 fiche (29x) – 9 – 1.00f – at Libertarian Micro [320]
HORIZON, WOMEN FOR INDIVIDUAL LIBERTY / ed by Maxwell, Joclyn – 1fiche (29x) – 9 – 1.00f – at Libertarian Micro [320]
HORIZONS – The Marxist Quarterly – 9 – 45.75 – cn McLaren [971]
HORIZONS – (v.7 .1980 5,6,9) – v.1. 1974 – 1 – us UMI [073]
HORIZONS *see* LE MAURICIEN
HORIZONS IN BIBLICAL THEOLOGY – (1985-. 5,6,9) – v1-. 1979- – 1 – us UMI [240]
HORIZONT – 1968-1989 – 1,534mf – 1 – DM8,743.80 – gw Mikro Press [320]
HORIZONT : SOZIALISTISCHE WOCHENZEITUNG FUER INTERNATIONALE POLITIK UND WIRTSCHAFT – Berlin, nov 1968-89 – 24r – 1 – Dist. gw Mikrofilm – gw Misc Inst [072]
O HORIZONTE : PERIODICO HUMORISTICO – LITERARIO E NOTICIOSO – Pao d'Assucar, Alagoas. 24 Ago 1882 – 1,5,6 – bl Biblioteca [072]
HORIZONTE DE LA METAFISICA ARISTOTELICA / Gomez Nogales, Salvador – Madrid: Imp. del Colegio Maximus, 1955 – 9 – sp Bibl Santa Ana [180]
LA HORMESINDA. TRAGEDIA / Fernandez de Moratin, Nicolas – s.a. – 1mf – 9 – Pta1,000.00 – 84-7848-230-X – sp Pentalfa [820]
HORMONE RESEARCH – v6-. 1975- – 1,5,9 – us UMI [616]
HORMONES IN ANIMAL PRODUCTION – 1982 – 62p – it F.A.O. [636]
Hormuzaki, C von *see* UNTERSUCHUNGEN UEBER DIE LEPIDOPTERENFAUNA DER BUCOVINA
HORN BOOK MAGAZINE – (v. 45- 1969- 5,6. v. 46- 1970- 9) – v. 1- 1924- – 1 – us UMI [830]
Horn, Ernst *see* OEFFENTLICHE RECHENSCHAFT UEBER MEINE ZWOELFJAEHRIGE DIENSTFUEHRUNG ALS ZWEITER ARZT DES KOENIGL. CHARITE-KRANKENHAUSES ZU BERLIN NEBST ERFAHRUNGEN UEBER KRANKENHAEUSER UND IRRENANSTALTEN
Horn, Ewald *see* BIBLIOGRAPHIE DER DEUTSCHEN UNIVERSITAETEN. SYSTEMATISCH GEORDNETES VERZEICHNIS DER BIS ENDE 1899 GEDRUCKTEN BUECHER UND AUFSAETZE UEBER DAS DEUTSCHE UNIVERSITAETSWESEN
Horn, Franz *see* GESCHICHTE UND KRITIK DER DEUTSCHEN POESIE UND BEREDSAMKEIT
Horn, J E *see* BANKFREIHEIT
THE HORN OF AFRICA / Silberman, Leo – (Includes bibliography and index) – Chicago, 1969 – us Res Libr [960]
HORNBOOK AND NUTSHELL SERIES – St Paul: West Pub Co, 1921-Sept 1993 – 9 – $1,450.00 set – us Hein [340]
HORNCASTLE AND MID-LINCS STANDARD *see* HORNCASTLE STANDARD
HORNCASTLE NEWS ETC – Sep 5-Dec 25 1886; 1887-95; Jan 9-Nov 27 1897; 1898-1996 – 94 1/2r – 9 – uk British Libr Newspaper [072]
HORNCASTLE STANDARD – (Also known as: Lincolnshire Standard (Horncastle Edn); Horncastle and Mid-Lincs Standard) – Jul 1912-14; Jan 2-Jun 26 1915; Jul, Dec 1928; 1929-30; Jul 1931-34; 1986-Sep 1991; Oct 4-Dec 26 1991; Jan-Jun 25 1993; Jul 1993-96 – 53r – 9 – uk British Libr Newspaper [072]
Horne, Bernardino C *see* POLITICA AGRARIA Y REGULACION ECONOMICA
Horne, C Silvester *see*
- NONCONFORMITY IN THE 19TH CENTURY
- A POPULAR HISTORY OF THE FREE CHURCHES

Horne, Charles S *see* THE STORY OF THE L.M.S., 1795-1895
Horne, Herman Harrell *see* FREE WILL AND HUMAN RESPONSIBILITY
Horne, Richard H *see* ORION
Horne, William *see* REASON AND REVELATION
Hornedo, A M *see* UNA FAMILIA DE INGENIOS, LOS RAMIREZ DE PRADO
Hornedo, R M *see* ENTRAMBASAGUAS, JOAQUIN DE. LA BIBLIOTECA EN RAMIREZ DE PRADO. MADRID, 1943
Horneffer, Ernst *see* HEBBEL UND DAS RELIGIOESE PROBLEM DER GEGENWART

Hornemann, Friedrich K *see*
- AFRICAN RESEARCHES
- VOYAGE DANS L'AFRIQUE SEPTENTRIONALE, DEPUIS LE CAIRE JUSQU'A MOURZOUK, CAPITALE DU ROYAUME DE FEZZAN
- VOYAGES DANS L'INTERIEUR DE L'AFRIQUE PENDANT LES ANNEES 1797, 1798

Hornemann, J W *see*
- FORSOG TIL DANSK OKONOMISK PLANTELAERE
- HORTUS REGIUS BOTANICUS HAFNIENSIS, IN USUM TIRONUM ET BOTANOPHILORUM

Horner, Francis Asbury *see* CRIMINAL FORMS FOR THE STATE OF INDIANA, COMPLETE UNDER THE CRIMINAL STATUTES OF THE STATE DOWN TO 1903
Horner, G *see* THE SERVICE FOR THE CONSECRATION OF A CHURCH AND ALTAR ACCORDING TO THE COPTIC RITE
Horner, J *see* THE STATUES OF THE APOSTLES OR CANONES ECCLESIASTICI
Horney, Julie *see* OBSERVATION AND STUDY IN THE FEDERAL DISTRICT COURTS
DIE HORNISSE : ZEITUNG FUER HESSISCHE BIEDERMAENNER – Kassel, Germany. Aug 1848-Dec 1850 – 1r – 1 – gw Mikrofilm [072]
Hornovhos. Ayuntamiento *see* ORDENANZAS MUNICIPALES
Horn-Sauder, Erdmute *see* PRESSEARCHIV ZUR GESCHICHTE DEUTSCHLANDS SOWIE ZUR INTERNATIONALEN POLITIK VON 1949-60
HORNSBY ADVOCATE – (1944-95 40r) – Sydney, 1923-931 – 4r – 1 – at Pascoe [072]
Hornschuch, C F *see*
- DE VOITIA ET SYSTYLIO
- SYLLOGE PLANTARUM NOVARUM ITEMQUE MINUS COGNITARUM

Hornschuch, CF *see* BRYOLOGIA GERMANICA
Hornschuch, F *see* TAGEBUCH EINER REISE NACH DEN KUESTEN DES ADRIATISCHEN MEERES UND DEN GEBIRGEN VON KRAIN, VORZUEGLICH IN BOTANISCHER UND ENTOMOLOGISCHER HINSICHT
Horodezky, S A *see* EDER HA-YEKAR
Horodyski, B *see* PODRECZNIK PALEOGRAFII RUSKIEJ
HOROLOGICAL JOURNAL – 1943-50 – 1 – uk Microform Academic [520]
Horovitz, S *see* DIE PSYCHOLOGIE BEI DEN JUEDISCHEN RELIGIONSPHILOSOPHEN DES MITTELALTERS VON SAADJA BIS MAIMUNI
Horowicz, Alejandro *see* LOS CUATRO PERONISMOS
Horowitz, H *see* HIBBAT ZIYYON
Horozco y Covarruvias, Juan de *see* EMBLEMAS MORALES
HORRIBLES CRUELDADES DE LOS CONQUISTADORES DE MEXICO... / Bustamante, Carlo M de – Mexico: Valdes, 1829 – 1 – F74.96 – fr Armell [972]
HORRY HERALD – Conway. S.C. 1887-1954 – 1 – us UMI [071]
THE HORRY NEWS – Conway. S.C. 1871-1877 – 1 – us UMI [071]
Horsburgh, J Heywood *see* "DO NOT SAY"
Horsch, John *see* MENNO SIMONS, HIS LIFE, LABORS, AND TEACHINGS
HORSE CAVE BAPTIST CHURCH. KENTUCKY : CHURCH RECORDS – 1868-1968 – 1 – 101.25 – us Baptist [240]
HORSE SHORT COURSE PROCEEDINGS / Texas A & M University. Department of Animal Science – 1965-82.14 fiches – 9 – us Spaulding [636]
HORSED – Hamar [ie Mogadishu]: Society for Somali Language and Literature, n1-23 1967-1968 – us Res Libr [470]
HORSELESS AGE – New York. v2-3, 21. 1896-99, 1908 – 1r – 1 – us Ross [380]
THE HORSELESS AGE – New York: Horseless Age Co, 1895-1918. v12 n1-26 jul-dec 1903; v33 n13-25 apr-jun 24 1914 – us Res Libr [071]
HORSES AND OTHER ANIMALS / Royal Library. Windsor Castle – (117 drawings, 115 details. Fully indexed) – 1986 – 6 colour mf – 15 – $205.00 – 0-907716-14-8 – uk Mindata [740]
Horsfield, T *see*
- A CATALOGUE OF THE BIRDS IN THE MUSEUM OF THE HONORABLE EAST INDIA COMPANY
- A CATALOGUE OF THE LEPIDOPTEROUS INSECTS IN THE MUSEUM OF THE HONOURABLE EAST INDIA COMPANY
- MAP OF THE ISLAND OF JAVA,...

HORSHAM ADVERTISER. (WEST SUSSEX TIMES.-WEST SUSSEX COUNTY TIMES) – Horsham, England. -w. Nov 1871-1900; 1962-69; 1973-83.79 reels – 1 – uk British Libr Newspaper [072]
HORSHAM TIMES – 1921-1930 – 20mf – 9 – at Corangamite [980]
HORSHAM TIMES – 1931-1959 – 42r – 1 – at Corangamite [980]
Horsley, J *see* BRITANNIA ROMANA
Horst, Cornelius van der *see* DAS LACHEN DES SERGEANTEN WASSENAAR
Horst, Karl August *see* ICH UND GNADE
Horst, L *see* LEVITICUS 17-26 UND HEZEKIEL
Horsthemke, Johannes *see* MELCHIOR VON DIEPENBROCK ALS UEBERSETZER SPANISCHER DICHTUNGEN
Horstmann, Christina *see* DIE LITERARHISTORISCHE GESELLSCHAFT BONN IM ERSTEN DRITTEL DES 20. JAHRHUNDERTS
Hort, A F *see* THE GOSPEL ACCORDING TO MARK
Hort, Arthur *see* THE GOSPEL ACCORDING TO ST. MARK
Hort, Fenton John Anthony *see*
- THE APOCALYPSE OF ST. JOHN, 1-3
- THE APOCALYPSE OF ST. JOHN 1-3
- THE EPISTLE OF ST. JAMES
- THE EPISTLE OF ST JAMES I 1-IV.7
- THE FIRST EPISTLE OF ST PETER 1. 1-2. 17
- THE FIRST EPISTLE OF ST PETER, I.1-II.17
- LIFE AND LETTERS OF FENTON JOHN ANTHONY HORT
- PROLEGOMENA TO ST. PAUL'S EPISTLES TO THE ROMANS AND THE EPHESIANS
- PROLEGOMENA TO ST PAUL'S EPISTLES TO THE ROMANS AND THE EPHESIANS
- VILLAGE SERMONS
- VILLAGE SERMONS IN OUTLINE

Hort, Fenton John Antony *see* JUDAISTIC CHRISTIANITY
Horten, M *see* DAS BUCH DER RINGSTEINE FARABIS
Hortensius, L *see* TVMVLTVVM ANABAPTISTARVM LIBER VNVS
HORTENSIUS THE ADVOCATE : AN HISTORICAL ESSAY ON THE OFFICE AND DUTIES OF AN ADVOCATE / Forsyth, William – Jersey City: N J Frederick D Linn & Co, 1882 – 5mf – 9 – $7.50 – LLMC 95-159 – us L.L.M.C. [340]
HORTI ELTHAMENSIS PLANTARUM RARIORUM ICONES ET NOMIA / Dillen, J J – 2v. Lugduni Batavorum. 1774 – 8 – ne IDC [580]
HORTI MALABARICI RHEEDEANI CLAVIS LOCUPLETISSIMA / Hasskarl, J K – Dresden. 1867. B-5700 2 – 3mf – 8 – ne IDC [580]
HORTI MEDICI AMSTELODAMENSIS RARIORUM TAM ORIENTALIS, QUAM OCCIDENTALIS INDIAE / Commelin, J – 2v. Amstelodami. 1697-1701. B-5325 2 – 8 – ne IDC [580]
HORTI UPSALIENSIS PLANTAE CULTAE 1780-1800 / Thunberg, C P – Upsaliae. 1803-11. B-1337 2 – 8 – ne IDC [580]
HORTICULTURAL JOURNAL *see* NEW ENGLAND FARMER AND HORTICULTURAL JOURNAL, 1822-1846
HORTICULTURAL MARKETING : A RESOURCE AND TRAINING MANUAL FOR EXTENSION OFFICERS – 1991 – 125p – it F.A.O. [650]
HORTICULTURAL PROGRESS REPORT / Louisiana State University. Agricultural Experiment Station. North Louisiana Experiment Station, Calhoun – 1969-78.No.1-5. 1 reel – 1,5 – us Spaulding [580]
HORTICULTURE : A SELECTED BIBLIOGRAPHY – 1976 – 56p – it F.A.O. [634]
HORTICULTURE – (v. 47- 1969- 5,6. v. 48- 1970- 9) – 1- 1904- – 1 – us UMI [631]
HORTICULTURE LEAFLET / Clemson University. Agricultural Extension Division – No.11-51. 1970-82. 1 reel – 1,5 – us Spaulding [580]
HORTICULTURE PAMPHLET / South Dakota. State University. Agricultural Experiment Station – nos.1-52. 1943-50 – 1,5,6 – us Spaulding [580]
HORTICULTURE PROGRESS REPORT / Nebraska. College of Agriculture – n.1-79. 1938-69 – 1,5 – us Spaulding [580]
HORTICULTURE SERIES / Auburn University. Agricultural Experiment Station – No.1-28.1960-82. 1 reel – 1, 5 – us Spaulding [580]
Horton, Mary B *see* A BRIEF EXPOSITION OF GOSPEL DIFFERENCES GIVEN ACCORDING TO THE DIVINE LAW OF PROGRESSIVE INSTRUCTION

Horton, Robert Forman *see*
- THE BIBLE
- THE BOOK OF PROVERBS
- THE CARTOONS OF ST. MARK
- ENGLAND'S DANGER
- INSPIRATION AND THE BIBLE
- THE PASTORAL EPISTLES
- PASTORAL EPISTLES: TIMOTHY AND TITUS
- REVELATION AND THE BIBLE: AN ATTEMPT AT RECONSTRUCTION
- SHALL ROME RECONQUER ENGLAND?
- THE TEACHING OF JESUS
- THIS DO
- WOMEN OF THE OLD TESTAMENT

Horton, Walter M *see* GOD (CCC163)
HORTULUS ANIMAE : DAT IS, DER SIELEN BOGAERT – Antwerpen, 1606 – 9mf – 8 – ne Slangenburg [240]
HORTULUS CHELICUS / Walther, Johann J – (Score). 1694 – 9 – us Sibley [780]
HORTULUS MUSICES PRACTICE OMIBUS DIVINO GREGORIANI COCENTUS / Burchard, U – P 186. 1514 – 9 – ne IDC [780]
HORTUS BENGALENSIS / Roxburgh, W – Serampore. 1814. B-5696 2 – 8 – ne IDC [580]
HORTUS BEROLINENSIS SIVE ICONES ET DESCRIPTIONES PLANTARUM RARIORUM / Willdenow, C L – 2v. Berolini. 1803-1806-16. B-234 2 – 8 – ne IDC [580]
HORTUS BOGORIENSIS DESCRIPTUS... / Hasskarl, J K – Amstelodami, Bonnae, 1858. Pt. 1 – 5mf – 9 – ne IDC [580]
HORTUS BOTANICUS R. ACADEMIAE MONACENSIS, SEU HORTI BOTANICI, QUI MONACHII FLORET, HISTORIA BREVITER ENARRATA, ET PRAESENS CONDITIO DESCRIPTA / Martius, Karl Friedrich Philipp von – Monachii, 1825. 28 pp., 2 pls. B-6144 2 – 8 – ne IDC [580]
HORTUS BOTANICUS VINDOBONENSIS SEU PLANTARUM RARIORUM / Jacquin, N J von – 3v. Vindobonae. 1770-76. B-409 2 – 8 – ne IDC [580]
HORTUS BRITANNICUS / Sweet, R – 1020. 1826-1827 – 9 – ne IDC [580]
HORTUS BRITANNICUS / Sweet, R – 1274. Ed. 3. 1839 – 9 – ne IDC [580]
HORTUS BRITANNICUS / Sweet, R – ed. 2. London, 1830. 622 pp. B-1135 2 – 8 – ne IDC [580]
HORTUS BRITANNICUS. A CATALOGUE OF ALL THE PLANTS INDIGENOUS, CULTIVATED IN OR INTRODUCED TO BRITAIN / Loudon, J C – London, 1832. 602 pp., second additional suppl. 1839, p. 602-742. B-5563 2 – 8 – ne IDC [580]
HORTUS CANTABRIGIENSIS / Donn, J – Ed. 13. London. 1845. B-5527 2 – 8 – ne IDC [580]
HORTUS CLIFFORTIANUS / Linnaeus, Carl – Amstelaedami. 1737. B-167 2 – 8 – ne IDC [580]
HORTUS COLLINSONIANUS / Dillwyn, L W – An account of the plants cultivated by the late Peter Collinson. Swansea. 1843 – 8 – ne IDC [580]
HORTUS ELTHAMENSIS / Dillen, J J – London. 1732. B-654 2 – 8 – ne IDC [580]
HORTUS FLUMINENSIS / Barbosa Rodriques, Joao – Rio de Janeiro. 1893-94. B-5313 2 – 8 – ne IDC [580]
HORTUS GOTTINGENSIS SEU PLANTAE NOVAE ET RARIORES HORTI REGII BOTANICI GOTTINGENSIS DESCRIPTAE ET ICONIBUS ILLUSTRATAE / Schrader, H A – Goettingae. 1809. B-5205 2 – 8 – ne IDC [580]
HORTUS HERRENHUSANUS, SEU PLANTAE RARIORES QUAE IN HORTO REGIO HERRENHUSANO / Wendland, J C – Hannoverae. 1798-1801. B-767 2 – 8 – ne IDC [580]
HORTUS INCLUSUS : MESSAGES FROM THE WOOD TO THE GARDEN, SENT IN HAPPY DAYS TO THE SISTER LADIES OF THE THWAITE, CONISTON... / Ruskin, John – Orpington, Kent: G. Allen, 1887 – 1 roll – 1 – 1-55879-492-1 – uk Libr Preservation [860]
HORTUS INDICUS MALABARICUS / Rheede Tot Drakestein, H A van – 12 v. Amsterdam. 1678-1703. B-8304 1 – 9 – ne IDC [580]
HORTUS JAMAICENSIS / Lunan, J – Jamaica, 1814. v. 1. 538 pp. v. 2, 402 pp. B-5256 2 – 8 – ne IDC [580]
HORTUS KEWENSIS / Aiton, W – 3v. London. 1789. B-430 2 – 8 – ne IDC [580]
HORTUS KEWENSIS / Aiton, W – Ed. 2. 5 v. London. 1810-13. B-431 2 – 8 – ne IDC [580]

HORTUS MEDICUS / Sutherland, J – M 409. 1683 – 9 – ne IDC [610]
HORTUS MOSQUENSIS / Hoffmann, G F – M. 1808. B-5955 2 – 8 – ne IDC [580]
HORTUS NITIDISSIMUS / Trew, C J – 3v. Nuernberg. 1750-86. B-5775 1 – 9 – ne IDC [580]
HORTUS REGIUS BOTANICUS BEROLINENSIS / Link, J H F – 2v. Berolini. 1827-33. B-5567 2 – 8 – ne IDC [580]
HORTUS REGIUS BOTANICUS HAFNIENSIS, IN USUM TIRONUM ET BOTANOPHILORUM / Hornemann, J W – 2v. Hafniae. 1813-15. B-5204 2 – 8 – ne IDC [580]
HORTUS REGIUS MONSPELIENSIS / Gouan, A – Lyon. 1762. B-812 2 – 8 – ne IDC [580]
HORTUS REGIUS MONSPELIENSIS / Magnol, P – Monspelii, 1697. 209 pp., 21 pls. B-5586 2 – 8 – ne IDC [580]
HORTUS SUBURBANUS CALCUTTENSIS / Voigt, J O – Calcutta. 1845. B-354 2 – 8 – ne IDC [580]
HORTUS SUBURBANUS LONDINENSIS: OR A CATALOGUE OF PLANTS / Sweet, R – 5759. 1818 – 9 – ne IDC [580]
HORTUS UPSALIENSIS / Linnaeus, Carl – Stockholmiae. 1748. B-568 2 – 8 – ne IDC [580]
Horup, Ellen *see* SPAIN, THE BATTLEFIELD OF CAPITALISM
Horus Apollo *see*
- DE SACRIS NOTIS ET SCULPTURIS LIBRI DUO
- HIEROGLYPHICA, PER BER NARDINUM TREBATIUM VICENTINUM DE GRAECIS TRANSLATA
- ORI APOLLINIS NILIACI, DE SACRIS NOTIS

Horvath, C *see* HISTOIRE DE LA LITTERATURE HONGROISE
Horvath, M *see* HUSZONOET EV MAGYARORSZAG TOERTENELMEBOEL 1823-TOL 1848-IG
HORVOT YERUSHALAYIM / ed by Rivlin, E – Jerusalem. 1928. BJ-27-14 1 – 9 – ne IDC [270]
Horwitz, R *see* COMMUNICATION REVIEW
Horwood, A J *see*
- YEAR BOOKS OF THE REIGN OF KING EDWARD 1 (RS31A)
- YEAR BOOKS OF THE REIGN OF KING EDWARD 3 (RS31B)

HORYZONTY – No.1-180, 1956-71 – 1 – us I.U. Libraries [073]
Hosa Library. Nagoya. Japan *see* OZAKI KYUYA COLLECTION
HOSEA : WITH NOTES AND INTRODUCTION / Cheyne, Thomas Kelly – (Includes bibliographical references and indexes) – Cambridge: University Press, 1884 – 1mf – 9 – 0-8370-6808-8 – 1986-0808 – us A.T.L.A. [220]
HOSEAS ILLUSTRATUS CHALDAICA JONATHANIS VERSIONE AND CELEBRIUM RABBINORUM RASCHI ABEN-ESRAE ET KIMCHI COMMENTARIIS – Goettingae, 1775 – 4mf – 8 – ne Slangenburg [270]
DIE HOSEN DES DOKTORS IM NONNENKLOSTER : EIN WELTLICHES LIED, ENTHALTEND DAS ABENTHEYERLICHE FATUM / Schmidt, Johann – Muenchen: Bibliographisch-artistisches Institut, [1920?] – 1r – 1 – us U.W. Library [810]
Hosius, Stanislaus *see*
- DE ORIGINE HAERESIVM NOSTRI TEMPORIS
- OPERA

Hoskier, H C *see* THE COMPLETE COMMENTARY OF OECUMENIUS ON THE APOCALYPSE
HOSKINS HEADLIGHT – Hoskins, NE. -w. Aug 1908-Oct 1909; Dec 1911-Jun 1923 – 1 – us NE Hist [071]
Hoskyns, Ed *see* THE FOURTH GOSPEL
Hosmer, James Kendall *see* A SHORT HISTORY OF GERMAN LITERATURE
Hosmer, William *see*
- THE HIGHER LAW IN ITS RELATIONS TO CIVIL GOVERNMENT
- SLAVERY AND THE CHURCH

LA HOSPEDERIA REAL DE GUADALUPE / Pescador del Hoyo, Maria del Carmen – Badajoz: Imp. Diputacion Provincial, 1965 – sp Bibl Santa Ana [946]
LA HOSPEDERIA REAL DE GUADALUPE 2 / Pescador del Hoyo, Maria del Carmen – Badajoz: Imp. Diputacion Provincial, 1968 – sp Bibl Santa Ana [946]
HOSPICE -JEAN DE DIEU, ASILE DE LA LONGUE-POINTE / Bellay, A – Montreal: Arbour & Laperie, 1892. 00108. (Pre-1900 Canadiana) – 9 – cn C.I.H.M. [610]

THE HOSPICE JOURNAL : THE OFFICIAL JOURNAL OF THE NATIONAL HOSPICE ORGANIZATION / ed by Infeld, Donna Lind – v1- 1985- – 1, 9 ($200.00 in US $280.00 outside hardcopy subsc) – us Haworth [360]
HOSPITAL ACCOUNTING – v.1-22. 1946-68. Superseded by Hospital Financial Management – 1 – us UMI [650]
HOSPITAL ADMINISTRATION AND CONSTRUCTION *see* HEALTH CARE
HOSPITAL ADMINISTRATION IN CANADA – (Cont by: Health Care at v21 1979) – Don Mills. v1-20. 1959-78 – 9 – Can$28.00y – cn Micromedia [350]
HOSPITAL ADMINISTRATION IN CANADA *see* HEALTH CARE
HOSPITAL ADMINISTRATION OF CANADA *see* HEALTH CARE
HOSPITAL AND COMMUNITY PSYCHIATRY – 1- 1950- – 1,5,6,9 – apply; v.22- – us UMI [616]
HOSPITAL FINANCIAL MANAGEMENT – (v.34-. 1980$ 5,6,9) – v.22-. 1968- – 1 – us UMI [380]
HOSPITAL FORMULARY – v19-. Dec 1984- – 1,5,6,9 – us UMI [616]
DAS HOSPITAL IN JERUSALEM – (Allgemeine Zeitung des Judentums). 1843. BJ-27-238 1 – 9 – ne IDC [956]
HOSPITAL INFECTION CONTROL – (v.6$.1979 5,6,9) – v.1. 1974 – 1 – us UMI [073]
L'Hospital, J E *see* APOLOGIE DE VOLTAIRE
HOSPITAL LITERATURE INDEX – (1982-. 1,5,6,9) – v13-. 1957- – 1 – us UMI [610]
HOSPITAL MANAGED CARE AND DIRECT CONTRACTING *see* ALLAN FINE'S TRENDS IN INTEGRATED HEALTH CARE
HOSPITAL MANAGEMENT – 1-112. 1916-71 – 1 – us UMI [650]
HOSPITAL MATERIAL MANAGEMENT QUARTERLY – v.1. 1979 – 1,5,6,9 – us UMI [073]
HOSPITAL MEDICAL STAFF – v1-14, no.2. 1972-Feb 1985 – 1,5,6,9 – us UMI [610]
L'Hospital, Michel de *see* MEMOIRE ADRESSE A CHARLES 10
HOSPITAL PEER REVIEW – (v.4 .1979 5,6,9) – v.1. 1976 – 1 – us UMI [073]
HOSPITAL PERIODICAL LITERATURE INDEX – v11-13. 1955-57 – 1 – us UMI [610]
HOSPITAL PHARMACIST – v.1-21. 1948-68. Superseded by yCanadian Journal of Hospital Pharmacy – 1 – us UMI [610]
HOSPITAL PROGRESS – 1- 1920- – 1. ; 5,6. ; 9 – apply; v.51-; v.57- – us UMI [610]
HOSPITAL PROGRESS – (v51-64. 1970-84. 5,6. v57-65, no.7. 1976-Jul-Aug 1984. 9) – v1-65, no.7. May 1920-Jul-Aug 1984 – 1 – us UMI [610]
THE HOSPITAL REPORTS OF THE MEDICAL MISSIONARY SOCIETY IN CHINA FOR THE YEAR 1839 – [Canton], 1840 – 1mf – 9 – ne IDC [617]
HOSPITAL RISK MANAGEMENT – v.1. 1979 – 1,5,6,9 – us UMI [073]
HOSPITAL SATURDAY NEWS – Katoomba, Apr 19 1930 – 9 – at Pascoe [072]
HOSPITAL TOPICS – 1- 1922- – 1. ; 5,6. ; 9 – apply; v.49-; v.54- – us UMI [610]
HOSPITAL TRANSCRIPT *see* NEW SOUTH (BEAUFORT, SOUTH CAROLINA), MARCH 7, 1895
HOSPITAL TRUSTEE – (v.3 .1979 5,6,9) – v.1. 1977 – 1 – us UMI [073]
L'HOSPITALITE – (Microform available to v15 no 13 1991 only) – Toronto. v14- 1990- – 9 – Can$20.00y – cn Micromedia [610]
HOSPITALITY: FOOD AND LODGING – v1-15 1962-76 – 1,5,6,9 – us UMI [640]
HOSPITALITY: LODGING – v1-32 1949-76 – 1,5,6,9 – us UMI [640]
HOSPITALITY: RESTAURANT – (See also: American Restaurant Hospitality; American Restaurant Magazine; Restaurant Hospitality) – v52-60 1968-76 – 1 – us UMI [640]
AN HOSPITALL FOR THE DISEASED / C, T – London, [1580] – 1mf – 9 – ne IDC [610]
HOSPITALS – 1- 1927- – 1. ; 5,6,9 – apply; v.44- – us UMI [610]
HOSPITALS – Journal of the American Hospital Association. Chicago, v34-40. 1960-66. Lacking: 1963, v37. M-18/2 – 8 – ne IDC [073]
HOSPITALS DURING WORLD WAR 1 PAMPHLET COLLECTION – 1915-1920 – 2r – 1 – CSUXANL3578-B – us Hoover Inst Photo [610]
HOSPODAR – Omaha, NE. -m. 15 Mar 1891-15 Dec 1961. In Czech – 1 – us NE Hist [071]
HOSPODARSKE NOVIGNY – 1990 – 4r – 1 – Sfr480.00 – sz Infoprint [332]
HOSPODARSKE NOVIGNY – (Standing order available from De 1994 +. 6r per year. Sfr675.00y) – De 1991 a 1993 – 6r – 1 – Sfr720.00 – sz Infoprint [332]
HOSPODARSKE NOVINY – (1990 4r $340; 1991-98 6r per y $480y) – Czech Republic, 1999- – 6r per y – $480.00 standing order – us Ross [072]
HOSPODARSKE ZAZNAMY – London, UK. 25 Mar, 18 Aug, 22 Sept, 29 Dec 1943 – 1 – uk British Libr Newspaper [072]
Hossbach, Th *see* VORLESUNGEN UEBER DIE APOKALYPSE
HOST DO DOMU – v1-6, 9-17. 1954-59, 1962-70 – 1 – us I.U. Libraries [073]
Host, N T *see*
– FLORA AUSTRIACA
– ICONES ET DESCRIPTIONES GRAMINUM AUSTRIACORUM
– SALIX
– SYNOPSIS PLANTARUM IN AUSTRIA PROVINCIISQUE ADJACENTIBUS SPONTE CRESCENTIUM
HOSTAGES TO FORTUNE / Braddon, Mary Elizabeth – British Fiction Archive: Unit 5 – 9 – uk Bell [830]
Hoste, C H et al *see*
– LE BETAIL TRYPANOTOLERANT D'AFRIQUE OCCIDENTALE ET CENTRALE
– TRYPANOTOLERANT LIVESTOCK IN WEST AND CENTRAL AFRICA
Hoste, William *see* MEMOIRS AND LETTERS OF CAPT. SIR W.H
Hosten, Henry *see* ANTIQUITIES FROM SAN THOME AND..
HOSTILITY AND CORONARY RISK FACTORS AMONG NATIVE AMERICANS AND CAUCASIANS / Cofrancesco, Lisa – 1993 – 2mf – $8.00 – us Microform Publ [616]
Hot Club of Chicago *see* JAZZ SESSION
HOT CO CO – v1-. 1983- – 1,5,6,9 – us UMI [073]
Hot Record Society *see* HRS SOCIETY RAG
HOT ROD MAGAZINE – 1- 1948- – 1. ; 5,6,9 – apply; v.24- – us UMI [073]
HOT ROD...ANNUAL – (1986-. 1,5,6) – 1982- – 9 – us UMI [790]
HOT WORDS AND HAIR TRIGGERS / Fitzsimmons, Mabel Trott – 1938. 8 fiches – 9 – us South Carolina Historical [978]
HOTAM TOKHNIT / Polak, GI & Luzzatto, SD – (Contains, inter alia, Abraham Bedersi's vHa-Herev vha-Mithappekhet with detailed commentary). Amsterdam. 1865. BJ-421-74 1 – 9 – ne IDC [470]
Hotchkiss, Jedediah *see* PAPERS
HOTEL – New York: Hotel Workers of New York, 1967-71 – 1r – 1 – us Ross [331]
HOTEL AND MOTEL MANAGEMENT – v199-. Dec 1984- – 1,5,6,9 – us UMI [650]
HOTEL AND RESTAURANT *see* CANADIAN HOTEL AND RESTAURANT
L'HOTEL DE RAMBOUILLET: CONFERENCE FAITE A L'UNIVERSITE LAVAL / Bourassa, Gustave – Montreal: C. Beauchemin, 1897. 00204. (Pre-1900 Canadiana) – 9 – cn C.I.H.M. [971]
L'Hotel Drouot *see* GAZETTE
HOTEL GUEST REGISTERS, 1922-38; 1965-66 / Ridgecrest. North Carolina. Ridgecrest Baptist Assembly – 9746p – 1 – 341.11 – us Baptist [240]
HOTEL REGISTER / Neodesha House. Neodesha, Kansas – 1871-74 – 1 – us KS Hist [978]
Hotel-Dieu de Montreal. Archives *see* ANNALES DE SOEUR MORIN (1697-1730)
L'HOTEL-DIEU DE QUEBEC, 1639-1900 : NOTICES HISTORIQUES ET DEPOUILLEMENT DES REGISTRES, 2E PARTIE, 1759-1900 / Sainte-Leonie, Soeur – 1964. SEM105P4 – 656mf – 9 – Can$1,476.00 – cn Bibl Nat [360]
Hotel-Dieu. Nantes *see* REGLEMENS DE L'HOTEL-DIEU DE NANTES
HOTELS AND RESTAURANTS INTERNATIONAL – (1984- 5,6,9) – v16-1982- – 1 – us UMI [640]
HOTLINER – v.1 .1980 – 1,5,6,9 – us UMI [073]
Hotten, J C *see* ORIGINAL LISTS OF AMERICAN EMIGRANTS, 1600-1700
LES HOTTETERRE, CELEBRES JOUERS ET FACTEURS DE FLUTES, HAUTBOIS, BASSONS ET MUSETTES DES 17E ET 18E SIECLES; NOUVELLES RECERCES PAR N. MAUGER / Mauger, Nicolas – Paris: Fischbacher, 1912 – 1 – us Sibley [780]
LES HOTTETERRE ET LES CHEDEVILLES CELEBRES JOUERS ET FRACTEURS DE FLUTES, HAUTBOIS, BASSOONS ET MUSETTES DES 17E ET 18E SIECLES, AVEC PORTRAITS ET FAC-SIMILES / Thoinan, Ern – Paris: E Sagot, 1894 – 1 – us Sibley [780]
Hotteterre, J *see*
– METHODE POUR LA MUSETTE
– PRINCIPES DE LA FLUTE TRAVERSIERE
Hottinger, J J *see* THE LIFE AND TIMES OF ULRIC ZWINGLI
Hotzel, Curt *see* DER UNVERBLUEMTE AMOR
Houben, Heinrich Hubert *see*
– DAMALS IN WEIMAR
– GUTZKOW-FUNDE
– STUDIEN UEBER DIE DRAMEN CARL GUTZKOWS
Houbotte, E *see* DES SOCIETES ANONYMES EN DROIT INTERNATIONAL PRIVE
Houbraken, Arnold *see*
– DICHTKUNDIGE BESPIEGELINGEN OP 57 GEPASTE IN KOPER GEBRAGTE ZINNEBEELDEN
– DE GROOTE SCHOUBURGH DER NEDERLANTSCHE KONSTSCHILDERS EN SCHILDERESSEN...
– STICHTELYKE ZINNEBEELDEN GEPAST OP DEUGDEN EN ONDEUGDEN, IN 57 TAFEREELEN VERTOOND
Houck, Louis *see* A TREATISE ON THE LAW OF NAVIGABLE RIVERS
Houdas, O *see* HISTOIRE DU SULTAN DJELAL-EDDIN MANKOBIRTI, PRINCE DU KHAREZM
Houde, Marguerite A *see* BIBLIOGRAPHIE ANALYTIQUE DE L'OEUVRE DE M. AVILA BEDARD, I.F.M.F., SOUSMINISTRE DES TERRES ET FORETS DANS LE CABINET PROVINCIAL
Houdeau. S *see* L'ESSENCE D'UN CONTE
Houdini, Harry *see* SCRAPBOOKS
Houdmon, A *see* SECRETS POUR TEINDRE LA SOYE, LE FIL, LA LENNE, LE BOIS, L'OR ET L'YVOIRE...
Houdoy, Jules *see* LA FILATURE DE COTON DANS LE NORD DE LA FRANCE
Houerou, H N Le *see* BROWSE IN AFRICA
Hough, Franklin B *see*
– AMERICAN CONSTITUTIONS
– THE COUNTY OF HIGHLAND
– HISTORY OF LEWIS COUNTY
Hough, Granville W *see* TECHNOLOGY DIFFUSION
Hough, Samuel *see* BORN OF WATER AND SPIRIT
Hough, W *see* AN ESKIMO STRIKE-A-LIGHT FROM CAPE BATHURST
Hough, William *see*
– MILITARY LAW AUTHORITIES
– THE PRACTICE OF COURTS-MARTIAL
– THE PRACTICE OF COURTS-MARTIAL AND OTHER MILITARY COURTS
HOUGH'S VICE ADMIRALTY REPORTS / New York. (State) – 1v. 1715-88 (all publ) – 4mf – 9 – $6.00 – LLMC 80-006 – us L.L.M.C. [340]
Houghton, Louise *see* FROM OLIVET TO PATMOS: THE FIRST CHRISTIAN CENTURY IN PICTURE AND STORY
Houghton, Louise Seymour *see* ANTIPAS, SON OF CHUZA
Houghton, Richard Monckton Milnes *see* MONOGRAPHS PERSONAL AND SOCIAL
Houghton, Ross C *see* JOHN THE BAPTIST
Houghton, W *see* BRITISH FRESH-WATER FISHES
Houlbert, C *see* LES COLEOPTERES D'EUROPE: FRANCE ET REGIONS VOISINES
Houle, Alphonse *see* BIBLIOGRAPHIE
Houle, Hector *see* LA VOIX METROPOLITAINE
Houle, R *see* BIO-BIBLIOGRAPHIE DE FEU SON EMINENCE LE CARDINAL JEAN-MARIE-RODRIGUE VILLENEUVE, OBLAT DE MARIE IMMACULEE, ARCHEVEQUE DE QUEBEC
Houlee, J-B *see* LE COURRIER CANADIEN
HOUMOH – New York. N.Y. 1915 – 1 – us A.J.P.C. [071]
HOUND AND HORN – Portland, Maine. v. 1-7. Sept 1927-Sept 1934. Incomplete – 1 – us NY Public [073]
HOUND AND HORN – v1-7. 1927-34 – 2r – 1 – us Ross [790]
THE HOUND OF THE BASKERVILLES / Doyle, Arthur Conan – In Indonesian – 9 – ne IDC [830]
DER HOUPME LOMBACH : BERNDEUTSCHE NOVELLE / Tavel, Rudolf von – 7. Aufl. Bern: A Francke, 1931 – 1r – 1 – us U.W. Library [830]
HOUR / American Council Against Nazi Propaganda – 1-153 (all publ). 1939-1943 – 9mf – 9 – $60.00 – us UPA [900]
THE HOUR – London. 24 Mar -Dec 1874. -f. 10mqn reels – 1 – uk British Libr Newspaper [072]
THE HOUR – Norwalk. Conn. 1970- – 1 – us UMI [071]
HOURS IN A LIBRARY / Stephen, Leslie – London: Smith, Elder, Duckworth, 1907 – 2 rolls – 1 – 1-55879-983-4 – uk Libr Preservation [190]
HOURS OF EXERCISE IN THE ALPS / Tyndall, John – London: Longmans, Green, and Co., 1871 – 1 roll – 1 – 1-55879-801-3 – uk Libr Preservation [910]
HOURS OF IDLENESS : A SERIES OF POEMS, ORIGINAL AND TRANSLATED / Byron, George Gordon Byron – Newark: Printed and sold by S. and J. Ridge..., 1807 – 1 roll – 1 – 1-55879-296-1 – uk Libr Preservation [810]
HOURS WITH A SCEPTIC / Faunce, Daniel Webster – Philadelphia: American Baptist Publishing Society. 1 fiche – 9 – us A.T.L.A. [240]
HOURS WITH GERMAN CLASSICS / Hedge, Frederic Henry – Boston: Roberts Brothers, 1886 – 1r – 1 – us U.W. Library [430]
HOUSE AND GARDEN – (v. 135- 1969- 5,6; v. 137- 1970- 9) – 1- 1901- – 1 – us UMI [073]
HOUSE AND HEARTH / Spofford, Harriet Prescott – New York: Dodd, Mead and Co, 1891 – us Res Libr [071]
HOUSE AND HOME – (v35-52. 1969-77. 5,6. v49-52. 1976-77. 9) – v1-52. 1952-77.Continued by: Housing – 1 – us UMI [720]
HOUSE AND SENATE BILLS AND RESOLUTIONS / U.S. Congress – (1ST-6TH. 1789-1801. $258.00. 7th-36th. 1801-61. $1,854.00. 37th-46th. 1861-81. $2,815.00. 47th-56th. 1881-1901. $9,793.00. 57th-65th. 1901-19. $12,298.00. 66th-72nd. 1919-33. $8,835.00. 92nd. 1971-72. $6,397.00) – 1 – us L of C Photodup [324]
HOUSE BEAUTIFUL'S COLONIAL HOMES – (v.5. 1979. 5,6,9) – v1-5. 1975-79. Continued by: Colonial Homes – 1 – us UMI [720]
HOUSE JOURNALS / Michigan Legislature – (Lacking: 1868 reg sess. 1892 spec sess. 1899 ext sess. 1900 2nd ext sess. 1944 ext sess. 1954 2nd ext sess. Updates planned) – 1835-1979 – 2425mf – 9 – $3,638.00 – LLMC 79-438H – us L.L.M.C. [340]
HOUSE JOURNALS : TERRITORIAL LEGISLATURE TO DATE / Hawaii Legislature – (Add vols after 1994 planned) – 1901-94 – 1290mf – 9 – $1,935.00 – LLMC 77-105 – us L.L.M.C. [323]
HOUSE JOURNALS 1966-79 : 2ND REG SESS OF THE CONGRESS OF MICRONESIA TO THE SESS OF THE INTERIM CONGRESS OF THE FEDERATED STATES OF MICRONESIA (1978-79) / Congress of Micronesia – n.p, n.d. – 123mf – 9 – $184.00 – LLMC 82-100F, Title 31 – us L.L.M.C. [323]
HOUSE OF ASSEMBLY : JOURNALS / Tasmania. Australia. Parliament – 1856-83 – 15r – 1 – A$482.00 silver A$415.00 vesicular – at Pascoe [073]
HOUSE OF CHIEFS DEBATES – (Issues for 1956-1958 filmed with its Western House of Chiefs debates 1953) – Ibadan: Govt Printer. 4th-6th sessions. 1956-1958 – 1r – 1 – us Res Libr [323]
THE HOUSE OF CHIMHAM / Work, Edgar Whitaker – New York: American Tract Society, 1909. 1 fiche – 9 – us A.T.L.A. [240]
HOUSE OF COMMONS PARLIAMENTARY PAPERS, 1801-1900 / ed by Cockton, Peter – (Individual vols available: 1-49mf £8; 50-99mf £7; 100-249mf £6; 250+ mf £5; Subject catalogue £1,250) – 46,196mf – 9 – £45,500.00 coll – uk Chadwyck [324]
HOUSE OF COMMONS PARLIAMENTARY PAPERS, 1801-1900 *see*
– APPENDICES TO VOTES AND PROCEEDINGS, 1817-1890 AND REPORTS OF THE SELECT COMMITTEES ON PUBLIC PETITIONS, 1833-1900
– DIVISION LISTS, 1836-1909
HOUSE OF COMMONS PARLIAMENTARY PAPERS, 1901-1974/1975 *see*
– HOUSE OF COMMONS PARLIAMENTARY PAPERS, 1901-21

- HOUSE OF COMMONS PARLIAMENTARY PAPERS 1922-1944/45
- HOUSE OF COMMONS PARLIAMENTARY PAPERS, 1945/1946- 1960/1961
- HOUSE OF COMMONS PARLIAMENTARY PAPERS, 1961/1962- 1974/1975

HOUSE OF COMMONS PARLIAMENTARY PAPERS, 1901-21 – 17,944mf – 9 – £29,500.00 coll – uk Chadwyck [324]

HOUSE OF COMMONS PARLIAMENTARY PAPERS 1922-1944/45 – 5962mf – 9 – £19,600.00 – uk Chadwyck [324]

HOUSE OF COMMONS PARLIAMENTARY PAPERS, 1945/1946- 1960/1961 – 5806mf – 9 – £19,600.00 – uk Chadwyck [324]

HOUSE OF COMMONS PARLIAMENTARY PAPERS, 1961/1962- 1974/1975 – 6686mf – 9 – £19,600.00 – uk Chadwyck [324]

HOUSE OF COMMONS PARLIAMENTARY PAPERS, 1975/1976- *see*
- HOUSE OF COMMONS PARLIAMENTARY PAPERS, 1975/1976-1993/1994
- HOUSE OF COMMONS PARLIAMENTARY PAPERS, 1975/1976-1994/1995
- HOUSE OF COMMONS PARLIAMENTARY PAPERS, 1975/1976-1995/1996
- HOUSE OF COMMONS PARLIAMENTARY PAPERS, 1975/1976-1996/1997
- HOUSE OF COMMONS PARLIAMENTARY PAPERS, 1975/1976-1997/1998

HOUSE OF COMMONS PARLIAMENTARY PAPERS, 1975/1976-1993/1994 – (From 1987/88, price includes free index on computer output mf. Commmand papers are available separately from 1979) – 18,726mf – 9 – £27,650.00 coll – uk Chadwyck [324]

HOUSE OF COMMONS PARLIAMENTARY PAPERS, 1975/1976-1994/1995 – (Price includes free index on CD-Rom and also on computer output mf) – 9 – £1,560.00 coll – uk Chadwyck [324]

HOUSE OF COMMONS PARLIAMENTARY PAPERS, 1975/1976-1995/1996 – (Price includes free index on CD-Rom and also on computer output mf) – 9 – £1,590.00 – uk Chadwyck [324]

HOUSE OF COMMONS PARLIAMENTARY PAPERS, 1975/1976-1996/1997 – 9 – £1,660.00 – uk Chadwyck [324]

HOUSE OF COMMONS PARLIAMENTARY PAPERS, 1975/1976-1997/1998 – 9 – £1,725.00 – uk Chadwyck [324]

THE HOUSE OF EDWARD WINSLOW / Pratt, Walter E – 1949 – 1 – $5.00 – us Baptist [240]

HOUSE OF HABSBURG PAMPHLET COLLECTION – 1943-1945 – 1 reel – 1 – CSUXANQ2259-B – us Hoover Inst Photo [920]

THE HOUSE OF HALLIWELL / Wood, Ellen – British Fiction Archive: Unit 1 – 9 – uk Bell [830]

HOUSE OF LORDS CASES (CLARK AND FINNELLY) : CASES ON APPEAL AND WRITS OF ERROR, CLAIMS OF PEERAGE, AND DIVORCES DURING THE SESSIONS OF 1847-1866 / Clark, Charles & Finnelly, W – v1-11. 1847-66. London: Spettigue & Farance/Butterworth, 1849-66 (all publ) – 109mf – 9 – $163.00 – LLMC 95-284 – us L.L.M.C. [324]

HOUSE OF LORDS PARLIAMENTARY PAPERS – (1984/85-1986/87 in a single sequence, and 1987/88- in two series, Bills and Papers) – 1984/85- – 9 – uk Chadwyck [324]

THE HOUSE OF THE LORD : A STUDY OF HOLY SANCTUARIES, ANCIENT AND MODERN / Talmage, James Edward – Salt Lake City, Utah: Deseret News, 1912 – 1mf – us A.T.L.A. [240]

THE HOUSE OF WORTH FASHION DESIGNS : 1899-1929 / Victoria and Albert Museum. London – (Photographic documentation of over 7,000 designs, grouped by type in chronological order) – 150mf – 9 – $645.00 – 0-907006-98-1 – uk Mindata [740]

A HOUSE PARTY / Ouida – British Fiction Archive: Unit 3 – 9 – uk Bell [830]

HOUSE REPORT APPROVING THE COMPACT OF FREE ASSOCIATION WITH THE MARSHALL ISLANDS AND THE FEDERATED STATES OF MICRONESIA, AND APPROVING CONDITIONALLY THE COMPACT OF FREE ASSOCIATION WITH PALAU : HSE.REPT N99-188, 99TH CONG, 1ST SESS, JUL 1, 1985 / U.S. Congress. House Committee on Foreign Affairs – Washington: GPO. 4pts. 1985 – 10mf – 9 – $15.00 – LLMC 82-100F, Title 21 – us L.L.M.C. [980]

HOUSEHOLD ACCOUNTBOOK. 1797-98 / Macartney, G M – 3mf – 9 – sa SA Libr [640]

HOUSEHOLD ACCOUNTS AND EXPENSES OF EDWARD 5, RICHARD 3, HENRY 7 AND JAMES 1 / Great Britain – (From the Archives of the Marquess of Bath) – 1 – uk Microform Academic [324]

HOUSEHOLD ACCOUNTS AND EXPENSES OF HENRY 6 (1452-3), THE THIRD EARL OF STAFFORD (1370-2), THE THIRD DUKE OF BUCKINGHAM (1506), WILLIAM MALVERN, ABBOT OF ST PETER'S GLOUCESTER (1524-5) AND FRANCES DEVEREUX (1641-2) / Great Britain – From the Archives of the Marquess of Bath – 1 – uk Microform Academic [324]

HOUSEHOLD ACCOUNTS AND EXPENSES OF THE EARL OF WARWICK, (1420-1), DUKE OF RICHMOND (1527-8), DUKE OF BUCKINGHAM (1506-7) AND EDWARD SEYMOUR (1538-41) 15TH/16TH / Great Britain – From the Archives of the Marquess of Bath – 1 – uk Microform Academic [324]

THE HOUSE-HOLD BUDGET SURVEY IN THE GEZIRA-MANAGIL AREA / Sudan. Dept. of Statistics – 1965. BNE-7616 1 – 9 – ne IDC [310]

THE HOUSEHOLD COMPANION – Toronto: J.E. Bryant, v1 no 1(Sept 1891)- – 9 – cn C.I.H.M. [640]

THE HOUSEHOLD JOURNAL – Montreal: [s.n. 1878-18– or 19–] – 9 – cn C.I.H.M. [640]

THE HOUSEHOLD LIBRARY OF EXPOSITION *see* THE TEMPTATION OF CHRIST

THE HOUSEHOLD LIFE – Toronto: T.H. Churchill, [1884-18–?] – 9 – cn C.I.H.M. [615]

HOUSEHOLD MAGAZINE – West Bromwich. England. -w. 10 Mar-9 Jun 1888. (11 ft) – 1 – uk British Libr Newspaper [073]

HOUSEWARES – 1983- – 1,5,6,9 – us UMI [640]

HOUSING – v53-62 1978-82. Continues: House and Home – 1,5,6,9 – us UMI [720]

HOUSING AND PEOPLE – (Ceased v8 1977/78. v1-7 1970-1976/77 Can$75.00. v8 1977/78 Can$50.00) – Ottawa. v1-8. 1970-77/78 – 5 – cn Micromedia [360]

HOUSING AND PLANNING NEWS BULLETIN / National Housing and Town Planning Council. London, England – 1940-47. With printed Finding List – 1 – £35.00r – uk Altair [710]

HOUSING AND PLANNING REFERENCE – (1977-. 9) – 1948-76 – 9 – us UMI [360]

HOUSING AND TRANSPORTATION OF THE HANDICAPPED : LAWS, LEGISLATIVE HISTORIES AND ADMINISTRATIVE DOCUMENTS / ed by Reams, Bernard D Jr – Over 250 documents – 9 – $1,675.00 set – 0-89941-247-5 – us Hein [340]

HOUSING AND URBAN AFFAIRS (HUD) – (Base collection 1965-76 $8010; updates 1977-80 $1375 ea) – 4071mf – 9 – $13,510.00 – us UMI [360]

HOUSING, BUILDING AND PLANNING COMMITTEE / UN Economic Commission for Europe (ECE) – 1947-89 – E/F.154 E.1705 F.1607 R.1407 – 9 – us U.N. Pubs [340]

HOUSING IN LIBYA / Libya. Ministry of Planning and Development. Doxiadis Associates – v. 2. Problems, Policies, Programmes. (Document DOX-LIB-A 17 (22-4-64). Prepared for the Government of the Kingdom of Libya. BNE-1102 1 – 9 – ne IDC [360]

HOUSING IN LIBYA / Libya. Ministry of Planning and Documentation. Doxiadis Associates – v. 1. Existing conditions (Document DOX-LIBA 17 (22-4-64). Prepared for the Government of the Kingdom of Libya. BNE-1101 1 – 9 – ne IDC [360]

HOUSING ONTARIO – (Cont: Ontario Housing. Cont by: Community Ontario. v21-24 Can$100.00. v25-26no2 Can$50.00) – Toronto. v21-26. 1977-82 – 5 – Price varies – cn Micromedia [360]

HOUSING ONTARIO *see*
- COMMUNITY ONTARIO
- ONTARIO HOUSING

HOUSING STATISTICS / U.S. Housing and Home Finance Agency – v. 1-22. 1948-1969 – 1,5,6 – us Princeton Micro [323]

HOUSING STUDIES – 1995, Vol 10 – £101.00 – uk Carfax [360]

Housman, Alfred Edward *see* A SHROPSHIRE LAD

HOUSTON BAR BULLETIN – (Lacking: 1959) – 1945-64 (all publ) – 7mf – 9 – $31.50 – LLMC 84-481 – us L.L.M.C. [073]

HOUSTON BAR JOURNAL – v1 nos 1-10. 1930-31 (all publ) – 2mf – 9 – $3.00 – LLMC 84-480 – us L.L.M.C. [073]

HOUSTON BUSINESS JOURNAL – 1971- – 1 – us UMI [650]

HOUSTON EAGLE – Dothan. Ala. 1903-05 – 1 – us UMI [071]

HOUSTON JOURNAL OF INTERNATIONAL LAW – v1-18. 1918-96 – 9 – $225.00set – us Hein [340]

Houston, Martha Lou *see* REPRINT OF OFFICIAL REGISTER OF LAND LOTTERY OF GEORGIA

HOUSTON POST – Houston, TX 1880- – 1 – us UMI [071]

HOUSTON POST INDEX – Houston. Texas. 1880$ – 1 – us UMI [071]

Houston, Rab *see* RECORDS OF A SCOTTISH VILLAGE

HOUSTON'S CRIMINAL REPORTS – Delaware. 1v. 1856-79 (all publ) – 7mf – 9 – $10.50 – LLMC 84-129 – us L.L.M.C. [340]

Houtin, Albert *see*
- L'AMERICANISME
- LA CRISE DU CLERGE
- EVAEQUES ET DIOCESES. DEUXI EME SERIE
- UN PRAETRE MARIE
- LA QUESTION BIBLIQUE CHEZ LES CATHOLIQUES DE FRANCE AU 19E SIECLE

Houtsma, M Th *see* IBN-WASHIH QUI DICITUR AL-JA'QUBI

Houtsma, M Th. *see* ZUR GESCHICHTE DER SELGUQEN VON KERMAN

Houtte, L van *see* SEED CATALOGUE

Houttuyn, M *see*
- NATUURLIJKE HISTORIE OF UITVOERIGE BESCHRIJVING DER DIEREN, PLANTEN EN MINERAALEN,...
- NEDERLANDSCHE VOGELEN; VOLGENS HUNNE HUISHOUDING, AERT EN EIGENSCHAPPEN BESCHREEVEN

HOU-ZEE : ORGAAN VAN DEN KRING NOORD SUMATRA DER NATIONAAL SOCIALISTISCHE BEWEGING – Medan 1935-1938. Nos. 9-73 – 17mf – 9 – ne IDC [073]

Hovey, Alvah *see*
- BIBLICAL ESCHATOLOGY
- A COMMENTARY ON THE ACTS OF THE APOSTLES
- GOD WITH US, OR, THE PERSON AND WORK OF CHRIST
- A MEMOIR OF THE LIFE AND TIMES OF THE REV. ISAAC BACKUS, A.M
- THE MIRACLES OF CHRIST
- RELIGION AND THE STATE

HOW ARE THE MIGHTY FALLEN: A SERMON PREACHED ON THE DEATH OF GENERAL JAMES A. GARFIELD, LATE PRESIDENT OF THE UNITED STATES, IN TRINITY CHURCH, SAINT JOHN, ON SUNDAY, SEPTEMBER 25, 1881 / Brigstocke, Frederick Hervey John – St. John, N. B.: J. & A. McMillan, 1881. 00866. (Pre-1900 Canadiana) – 9 – cn C.I.H.M. [975]

HOW CANADA IS GOVERNED: A SHORT ACCOUNT OF ITS EXECUTIVE, LEGISLATIVE, JUDICIAL AND MUNICIPAL INSTITUTIONS: WITH AN HISTORICAL OUTLINE OF THEIR ORIGIN AND DEVELOPMENT / Bourinot, John George – Toronto: Copp, Clark, 1895. 00193. (Pre-1900 Canadiana) – 9 – cn C.I.H.M. [971]

HOW CHILDREN MAY BE BROUGHT TO CHRIST / Dayton, A C – 1859 – 1 – 5.00 – us Baptist [240]

HOW DID THE SATELLITES HAPPEN – A study of the Soveit seizure of eastern Europe, by a student of affairs. Preface by Hector McNeil. London: Batchworth Press, (1952).304p – 1 – us U.W. Library [947]

HOW DOES THE DEATH OF CHRIST SAVE US? : OR, THE ETHICAL ENERGY OF THE CROSS / Mabie, Henry Clay – Philadelphia: American Baptist Publ Society, c1908 – 1mf – 9 – 0-8370-4283-6 – 1985-2283 – us A.T.L.A. [230]

HOW FAR HAVE WE GOT? / Hatta, Mohammad – (Radio address on occasion of IVth Cooperatives Day, 12th July, 1954). SE-10,473 1 – 9 – ne IDC [334]

HOW FAR METHODISM CONDUCES TO THE INTERESTS OF CHRISTIANITY AND THE WELFARE OF SOCIETY,... / Clapham, S – Leeds, [1794] – 1mf – 9 – MP-584/1 – ne IDC [240]

How, Frederick Douglas *see*
- ARCHBISHOP MACLAGAN
- BISHOP JOHN SELWYN
- WILLIAM CONYNGHAM PLUNKET

HOW GOD INSPIRED THE BIBLE: THOUGHTS FOR THE PRESENT DISQUIET / Smyth, John Paterson – Dublin: Eason, 1892. 1 fiche – 9 – us A.T.L.A. [240]

HOW I CROSSED AFRICA / Pinto, S – Trans. by A. Elwes. 2 v. London. 1881. BA-173 2 – 8 – ne IDC [910]

HOW I ONCE FELT: SONGS OF LOVE AND TRAVEL / Currie, George Graham – Montreal?: s.n., 1893 (Montreal: J. Lovell). 02244. (Pre-1900 Canadiana) – 9 – cn C.I.H.M. [971]

HOW LEISURE BELIEFS RELATE TO ATTITUDES TOWARD THE NORMALIZATION PRINCIPLE AS PERCEIVED BY SERVICE PROVIDERS FOR PEOPLE WITH MENTAL RETARDATION / Neumayer, Robert J & Lundegren, Herberta M – 1993 – 2mf – 9 – $8.00 – us Microform Publ [150]

HOW LONG CAN CAPITALISM SURVIVE? / Acharya, M P T – 1951. 3p – 9 – 1.00f – at Libertarian Micro [320]

HOW MUCH IS LEFT OF THE OLD DOCTRINES? / Gladden, Washington – 1899 – 9 – us A.T.L.A. [240]

HOW MUSSOLINI PROVOKED THE SPANISH CIVIL WAR – Documentary evidence. London, 1938. Fiche W948. (Blodgett Collection of Spanish Civil War Pamphlets) – 9 – us H.U. College Libr [946]

HOW NOT TO MAKE PEACE / Stead, W T – 1343 2.. 1900 – 8 – ne IDC [320]

HOW SHALL WE CONFORM TO THE LITURGY OF THE CHURCH OF ENGLAND? / Robertson, James Craigie – London: J. Murray, 1869 – 1mf – us A.T.L.A. [240]

HOW SHOULD YOU SAY IT IN INDONESIAN? SHORT GUIDE FOR FOREIGNERS / Indonesia. Kementerian Penerangan – SE-2868 1. 1956? – 9 – ne IDC [490]

HOW THE BIBLE WAS MADE / Wood, Ezra Morgan – Cincinnati: Walden and Stowe; New York: Phillips & Hunt, 1884 – 1mf – 9 – 0-8370-9350-3 – 1986-3350 – us A.T.L.A. [220]

"HOW THE CHEROKEE ACQUIRED AND DISPOSED OF THE OUTLET [OKLAHOMA]" / Chapman, Berlin B – undated, Concerns tribal history and federal land policy – 1 – us KS Hist [305]

HOW THE CODEX WAS FOUND : A NARRATIVE OF TWO VISITS TO SINAI FROM MRS. LEWIS'S JOURNALS, 1892-93 / Gibson, Margaret Dunlop – Cambridge: Macmillan and Bowes, 1893 – 1mf – 9 – 0-8370-9255-8 – 1986-3255 – us A.T.L.A. [220]

HOW THE GERMAN FLEET SHELLED ALMERIA – London, 1937? Fiche W949. (Blodgett Collection of Spanish Civil War Pamphlets) – 9 – us H.U. College Libr [946]

HOW THE PEASANT LIVED IN SPAIN / Spain. Embajada. United States – Washington, DC, 193? Fiche W1180. (Blodgett Collection of Spanish Civil War Pamphlets) – 9 – us H.U. College Libr [946]

HOW TO ANSWER OBJECTIONS TO REVEALED RELIGION / Whately, Elizabeth Jane – New York: American Tract Society, 1880. 1 fiche – 9 – us A.T.L.A. [240]

HOW TO BE YOUR OWN LAWYER – New York: Richardson, 1885. 507p. LL-1696 – 1 – us L of C Photodup [340]

HOW TO BRING MEN TO CHRIST / Torrey, Reuben Archer – New York: Fleming H Revell, 1910 – 1mf – 9 – 0-8370-6426-0 – 1986-0426 – us A.T.L.A. [240]

HOW TO COMMEND CHRISTIANITY TO THE CHINESE (CCC165) / Hsieh, En-kuang – (In Chinese) – Shanghai: Christian Literature Society, 1917 – 1r – 1 – 1984-B500 – us A.T.L.A. [240]

HOW TO DOUBLE THE WEALTH OF CANADA: IMPERIAL FEDERATION, CONTINENTAL UNION / Ewen, T E – s.l.: s.n., 1893 (Belleville, Ont.: "Daily Ontario"). 02079. (Pre-1900 Canadiana) – 9 – cn C.I.H.M. [971]

HOW TO ECONOMIZE ON CANNED FOODS, A MANUAL ON HOME CANNING AND PRESERVING / School of Living – 1 fiche (29x) – 9 – $1.00f – at Libertarian Micro [320]

HOW TO END INFLATION / Cook, John C – n.d., 2p – 9 – 1.00f – at Libertarian Micro [332]

HOW TO GET ON / Feeney, Bernard – 4th ed. New York: Benziger, c1891 – 1mf – 9 – 0-8370-6116-4 – 1986-0016 – us A.T.L.A. [170]

HOW TO GET STRONG AND HOW TO STAY SO / Blaikie, William – 1879 – 5mf – 9 – $15.00 – us Microform Publ [790]

HOW TO INVEST IN MOROCCO: STATEMENT OF THE GENERAL REGULATIONS REGARDING THE INVESTMENTS OF CAPITAL; ENCOURAGEMENT MEASURES DESTINED TO PROMOTE THESE INVESTMENTS / Morocco. Banque Marocaine du Commerce Exterieur – 1962. Dec 1974. BNE-3006 1 – 9 – ne IDC [332]

HOW TO MAKE ABSTRACTS OF TITLE AND SEARCHES / Foye, Edward M – Erie, PA: Dispatch, Printing and Engraving Co., 1896. 32p. LL-280 – 1 – us L of C Photodup [340]

HOW TO MAKE AND SET FADS (FISH AGGREGATING DEVICES) – 1989 – 68p – it F.A.O. [639]

HOW TO PLAY FOOTBALL / ed by Camp, Walter Chauncey – New York, c1914.95p – 1 – us U.W. Library [790]

HOW TO PLAY GOLF / Vardon, Harry – Philadelphia: G.W. Jacobs, 1912?. 187p. Includes index – 1 – us U.W. Library [790]

HOW TO PREPARE SERMONS AND GOSPEL ADDRESSES / Evans, William – In Indonesian. SE-5063 1. 1963 – 9 – ne IDC [240]

HOW TO READ CHARACTER / Emberson, Frederick C – Montreal: Dawson Bros., 1883. 04263. (Pre-1900 Canadiana) – 9 – cn C.I.H.M. [971]

HOW TO READ JOSEPHUS / Auchincloss, William Stuart – New York: D van Nostrand, 1906 – 1mf – 9 – 0-8370-2128-6 – 1985-0128 – us A.T.L.A. [240]

HOW TO READ THE BIBLE: HINTS FOR S-S TEACHERS AND OTHER BIBLE STUDENTS / Adeney, Walter Frederic – New York: Thomas Whittaker, 1897. 1 fiche – 9 – us A.T.L.A. [220]

HOW TO REASON: A LECTURE DELIVERED BEFORE THE YOUNG MEN'S ASSOCIATION OF ZION CHURCH, AND PUBLLISHED AT THEIR REQUEST, 2ND NOVEMBER, 1871 / Chapman, Charles – Montreal: F. Grafton, 1871. 00616. (Pre-1900 Canadiana) – 9 – cn C.I.H.M. [240]

HOW TO REPAIR VIOLINS AND OTHER MUSICAL INSTRUMENTS... / Common, A – London: W Reeves, 1909 – 1 – us Sibley [780]

HOW TO STRENGTHEN THE MEMORY; OR, NATURAL AND SCIENTIFIC METHODS OF NEVER FORGETTING / Holbrook, Martin Luther – New York: M.L. Holbrook & Co., (c1886). 152p – 1 – us U.W. Library [150]

HOW TO STUDY BOTANY / Burgess, Thomas Joseph Workman – 1888? 00892. (Pre-1900 Canadiana) – 9 – cn C.I.H.M. [580]

HOW TO STUDY THE ENGLISH BIBLE / Girdlestone, Robert B – New York: Fleming H. Revell, (1894) – 9 – us A.T.L.A. [240]

HOW TO STUDY THE LIFE OF CHRIST : A HANDBOOK FOR SUNDAY-SCHOOL TEACHERS AND OTHER BIBLE STUDENTS / Butler, Alford Augustus – New York: Thomas Whittaker, c1901 – 1mf – 9 – 0-8370-2555-9 – 1985-0555 – us A.T.L.A. [240]

HOW TO STUDY THE NEW TESTAMENT: THE EPISTLES (FIRST SECTION) / Alford, Henry – London: Strahan, 1868. 1 fiche – 9 – us A.T.L.A. [220]

HOW TO STUDY THE NEW TESTAMENT: THE GOSPELS: THE ACTS OF THE APOSTLES / Alford, Henry – London: Alexander Strahan, 1865.1 fiche – 9 – us A.T.L.A. [220]

HOW TO SUCCEED : A BOOK FOR THE YOUNG / Lister, J B – Philadelphia: American Baptist Publ Society, [18–?] – 1mf – 9 – 0-8370-9293-0 – 1986-3293 – us A.T.L.A. [240]

HOW TO SUCCESSFULLY KEEP R&D PROJECTS ON TRACK / Szakonyi, Robert – 1988. ISBN: 0-912338-26-1 – 9 – 14.00 – us Lomond [650]

HOW TO TEACH SWIMMING AND DIVING / Cureton, Thomas Kirk – New York: Association Press, 1934. illus., tables, diagrs – 1 – us U.W. Library [370]

HOW TO THINK ABOUT WAR AND PEACE / Adler, Mortimer Jerome – New York: Simon and Schuster, c1944. xxiii,307p – 1 – us U.W. Library [320]

HOW TO WIN SOULS / Willing, Jennie Fowler – Chicago: Christian Witness, 1909 – 1mf – 9 – 0-8370-6465-1 – 1986-0465 – us A.T.L.A. [240]

HOW TO WRITE THE HISTORY OF A PARISH : AN OUTLINE GUIDE TO TOPOGRAPHICAL RECORDS, MANUSCRITS, AND BOOKS / Cox, John Charles – London: George Allen, 1909 – 1mf – us A.T.L.A. [910]

HOW TWO DOCUMENTS MAY BE FOUND IN ONE: A MONOGRAPH IN CONNECTION WITH THE HIGHER CRITICISM / Carmichael, James – Montreal: Gazette, 1895. 00502. (Pre-1900 Canadiana) – 9 – cn C.I.H.M. [240]

HOW WE ARE GOVERNED / Fraser, George A – Toronto: Educational Publishing Co., c1899. 03176. (Pre-1900 Canadiana) – 9 – cn C.I.H.M. [971]

HOW WE FIND RELICS / Riggs, CW – Chicago, IL: W.B. Conkey Co., 1893 – 1 reel – 1 – us Western Res [930]

HOW WE LIVED THEN, 1914-1918: A SKETCH OF SOCIAL AND DOMESTIC LIFE IN ENGLAND DURING THE WAR / Peel, Dorothy Constance Bayliff – London: John Lane, 1929. xiv,235p. plates, facsims – 1 – us U.W. Library [941]

How, William W *see* NEW TESTAMENT OF OUR LORD AND SAVIOUR JESUS CHRIST ACCORDING TO THE AUTHORIZED VERSION

Howald, Johann *see* GESCHICHTE DER DEUTSCHEN LITERATUR

HOWARD A. KESTER PAPERS, 1923-1972 / Kester, Howard A – 14r – 1 – $1015.00 – us UMI [977]

HOWARD COUNTY HERALD – St. Paul, NE. -w. Jun 1892; Nov 1893-Feb 1971 – 1 – us NE Hist [071]

Howard, Eric C *see* A SURVEY OF THE DESIRED EDUCATIONAL PREPARATION AND EMPLOYMENT MARKET FOR HIGH SCHOOL ATHLETIC TRAINERS IN METROPOLITAN WASHINGTON, DC AS PERCEIVED BY HIGH SCHOOL ATHLETIC DIRECTORS

Howard, George Broadley *see* THE CHRISTIANS OF ST THOMAS AND THEIR LITURGIES

Howard, H N *see* THE BALKAN CONFERENCES AND THE BALKAN ENTENTE, 1930-1935

Howard, James Henri *see* THE PONCA TRIBE

Howard, John R *see*
- BIBLE STUDIES
- PATRIOTIC ADDRESSES

HOWARD JOURNAL OF CRIMINAL JUSTICE – v23-. Feb 1984- – 1,5,6,9 – us UMI [340]

HOWARD JOURNAL OF PENOLOGY AND CRIME PREVENTION – (v20-22, no.3. 1981-83. 5,6,9) – v11, no.4-v22, no.3. 1965-83 – 1 – us UMI [360]

THE HOWARD JOURNAL OF PENOLOGY AND CRIME PREVENTION – v. 1-15. 1921-76. Index available separately – us Primary [360]

HOWARD LAW JOURNAL – (v1-27 1955-84 on reel $380.00. v28-38 1985-95 on mf $235.00) – v1-38. 1955-95 – 5,6,9 – $615.00 set – us Hein [340]

HOWARD LEAGUE FOR PENAL REFORM. GREAT BRITAIN. ARCHIVES *see* THE HOWARD JOURNAL OF PENOLOGY AND CRIME PREVENTION

Howard League for Penal Reform. Great Britain. Archives *see* CRIME, CRIMINOLOGY AND CIVIL LIBERTIES, SERIES ONE

HOWARD MEDICAL NEWS / Howard University. School of Medicine – Washington, D.C. v. 1, no. 7; v. 2, no. 3, 5-6, 8, 10; v. 3, no. 1-5, 7-8; v. 4, no. 1, 3-4, 6-10; v. 5, no. 5. 1925-1929 – 1 – us NY Public [610]

Howard, Overton *see* THE LIFE OF THE LAW, OR, UNIVERSAL PRINCIPLES OF LAW

Howard, Philip E *see*
- THE LIFE STORY OF HENRY CLAY TRUMBULL
- THEIR CALL TO SERVICE

Howard, Richard A *see* CHARLES WRIGHT IN CUBA, 1856-1867

HOWARD SCROLL : SOCIAL JUSTICE REVIEW – v1-2. 1993-94 – 9 – $25.00 set – us Hein [340]

HOWARD SHUMAN, SENATE SERVICE 1955-1982 : AIDE TO SENATORS PAUL DOUGLAS AND WILLIAM PROXMIRE – 7mf – 9 – $35.00 – us Scholarly Res [320]

Howard, T E *see* ST. JOSEPH COUNTY, INDIANA

Howard University. School of Medicine *see* HOWARD MEDICAL NEWS

HOWARD'S APPEAL CASES : UNREPORTED – New York. 1v. 1847-48 (all publ) – 9mf – 9 – $13.50 – LLMC 80-010 – us L.L.M.C. [340]

HOWARD'S PRACTICE REPORTS / New York. (State) – 1st series: v1-67. 1844-84; ns: v1-3. 1884-86 (all publ) – 489mf – 9 – $733.00 – LLMC 78-102 – us L.L.M.C. [340]

Howarth, Margery D *see* REPORT AND RECOMMENDATIONS; ATLAS OF INDONESIAN RESOURCES

Howarth, OJ R *see* HISTORY OF GEOGRAPHY

Howat, G R *see* WORLD NUTRITION AND NUTRITION EDUCATION

Howat, Kenneth J *see* THE EFFECT OF HALF-TIME WARM-UP PROCEDURES UPON INJURIES TO HIGH SCHOOL VARSITY FOOTBALL PLAYERS

Howat, William F *see* A STANDARD HISTORY OF LAKE COUNTY AND THE CALUMET REGION

Howdell, W *see* RELIGION PRODUCTIVE OF JOY AND CONSISTENT WITH POLITENESS

Howden. Yorkshire *see* PARISH REGISTERS

Howe *see* HISTORICAL COLLECTIONS OF THE STATE OF NEW YORK

Howe, Daniel Wait *see*
- THE LAWS AND COURTS OF NORTHWEST AND INDIANA TERRITORIES
- THE PURITAN REPUBLIC
- THE PURITAN REPUBLIC OF THE MASSACHUSETTS BAY IN NEW ENGLAND

Howe, Elias *see*
- (FIRST PART OF THE) MUSICIAN'S COMPANION
- HOWE'S NEW CORNET INSTRUCTOR; CONTAINING FULL AND COMPLETE RULES, EXERCISES, AND INSTRUCTIONS TO ENABLE THE LEARNER TO PLAY THIS FAVORITE INSTRUMENT, WITHOUT A MASTER
- LEVIATHAN COLLECTION OF INSTRUMENTAL MUSIC
- (THIRD PART OF THE) MUSICIAN'S COMPANION
- YOUNG AMERICA'S COLLECTION OF INSTRUMENTAL MUSIC

Howe, Frank Clifford *see* ALL EXAMINATION QUESTIONS USED FOR TWELVE YEARS, IN THE REGULAR COURSES IN COLUMBIAN UNIVERSITY.

Howe, George *see*
- A DISCOURSE ON THEOLOGICAL EDUCATION
- HISTORY OF THE PRESBYTERIAN CHURCH IN SOUTH CAROLINA

Howe, George M *see* HEINRICH VON KLEIST

Howe, Henry *see* HISTORICAL COLLECTIONS OF OHIO

Howe, Julia Ward *see* MARGARET FULLER (MARCHESA OSSOLI)

Howe, Laura G *see* THE RESEARCH AND DEVELOPMENT OF MULTIMEDIA LEISURE-LEARNING PACKAGES FOR THE RURAL ELDERLY

Howe, M A De Wolfe *see*
- MEMOIRS OF THE LIFE AND SERVICES OF THE RT. REV. ALONZO POTTER, D.D., LL.D.
- THE MEMORY OF LINCOLN; POEMS SELECTED WITH AN INTROD

Howell, Charles Boynton *see* THE CHURCH AND THE CIVIL LAW

Howell, Clark *see*
- HISTORY OF GEORGIA

Howell, David B *see* THE CHRISTOLOGY OF PAUL'S OPPONENTS IN SECOND CORINTHIANS AND ITS RELATIONSHIP TO THEIR CONCEPT OF APOSTLESHIP

Howell, Edward Beach *see* MONTANA MINERS' CODE.

Howell, George *see* SELECTED PAPERS

Howell, Gerald Emmett *see* A STUDY OF AUTHORITY FROM A THEOLOGICAL PERSPECTIVE AND ITS IMPLICATIONS FOR BUCK RUN BAPTIST CHURCH

Howell, Joseph Morton *see* EGYPT'S PAST, PRESENT AND FUTURE

Howell, M S *see* GRAMMAR OF THE CLASSICAL ARABIC LANGUAGE

Howell, Robert Boyte C *see*
- AN ADDRESS DELIVERED BEFORE THE UNIVERSITY OF NASHVILLE, 1839
- COLLECTION, MANUSCRIPTS AND BOOKS
- THE EARLY BAPTISTS OF VIRGINIA
- MANUSCRIPT NOTES OF SERMONS, 1838-1957
- MEMORIAL OF FIRST BAPTIST CHURCH, NASHVILLE, TENN., 1820-63

Howell, T B *see* ENGLISH STATE TRIALS, 1163-1858

Howell, T J *see* ENGLISH STATE TRIALS, 1163-1858

Howell, Williamson S *see* THE UNITED STATES AND FRANCE

Howells, G *see* CHEMISTRY AND ECOLOGY

HOWELLS JOURNAL – Howells, NE. -w. Nov 1892-Oct 1902, scattered issues missing; Jan 1908 to date – 1 – us NE Hist [071]

HOWELL'S NISI PRIUS CASES – Michigan. 1v. 1868-84 (all publ) – 5mf – 9 – $7.50 – LLMC 81-304 – us L.L.M.C. [340]

HOWELL'S STATE TRIALS *see* COBBETT'S STATE TRIALS / HOWELL'S STATE TRIALS

Howells, William Cooper *see* RECOLLECTIONS OF LIFE IN OHIO FROM 1813 TO 1840

Howells, William Dean *see*
- LETTERS OF AN ALTRURIAN TRAVELLER
- PREFACES TO CONTEMPORARIES
- TUSCAN CITIES

HOWE'S NEW CORNET INSTRUCTOR; CONTAINING FULL AND COMPLETE RULES, EXERCISES, AND INSTRUCTIONS TO ENABLE THE LEARNER TO PLAY THIS FAVORITE INSTRUMENT, WITHOUT A MASTER / Howe, Elias – With a large collection of popular polkas, schottisches, waltzes, quicksteps, marches, quadrilles, &c. Boston: Elias Howe, 1860. MUSIC 1989, Item 2 – 1 – us L of C Photodup [780]

HOWFF BURIAL GROUND: MONUMENTAL INSCRIPTIONS WITH INDEX / Dundee, Scotland – 1 – uk Microform Academic [920]

HOWGRAVE'S STAMFORD MERCURY LINCOLN *see* STAMFORD MERCURY

Howie, John *see* THE SCOTS WORTHIES

Howison, George H *see* THE FUNCTION OF UNIVERSITIES IN RELIGION

Howitt, A W *see* NATIVE TRIBES OF SOUTH EAST AUSTRALIA

Howitt, William *see* HOMES AND HAUNTS OF THE MOST EMINENT BRITISH POETS

Howland, Charles R *see* "HOWLAND'S DIGEST"

Howland, Emily *see* EMILY HOWLAND PAPERS

Howland, F *see* BLATCHFORD AND HOWLAND'S REPORTS OF CASES IN THE SOUTHERN DISTRICT COURT OF NEW YORK, 1827-1837

Howland, John D *see* A MANUAL FOR EXECUTORS, ADMINISTRATORS AND GUARDIANS, EMBRACING ALL THE STATUTES IN FORCE IN THE STATE OF INDIANA RELATING TO THE SETTLEMENT OF DECENDENTS' ESTATES.

Howland, William *see* JOHN HOWLAND: A MAYFLOWER PILGRIM

"HOWLAND'S DIGEST" / Howland, Charles R – 3 sep 1862-31 jan 1912 (mf ed Washington: GPO, 1912) – 12mf – 9 – $18.00 – LLMC 84-229 – us L.L.M.C. [340]

Howlet, F M *see* INDIAN INSECT LIFE

Howlett, R *see*
- CHRONICLES OF THE REIGNS OF STEPHEN, HENRY 2 AND RICHARD 1 (RS82)
- MONUMENTA FRANCISCANA (RS4)

Howley, J P *see* THE BEOTHUCKS OR RED INDIANS

Howley, Michael Francis *see* ECCLESIASTICAL HISTORY OF NEWFOUNDLAND

Howorth, Henry H *see*
- SAINT AUGUSTINE OF CANTERBURY
- SAINT GREGORY THE GREAT

Howse, Joseph *see* A GRAMMAR OF THE CREE LANGUAGE

Howson, John Saul *see*
- THE COMPANIONS OF ST PAUL
- THE EVIDENTIAL VALUE OF THE ACTS OF THE APOSTLES
- HORAE PETRINAE
- MEDITATIONS ON THE MIRACLES OF CHRIST

HOY – 5Jul 1941-24 Dec 1949. nos. 228-670. nos. 473, 475-478, 480-488, 567-575, 615, 627, 631-632, and 659 wanting – 1 – 579.00 – us L of C Photodup [073]

HOY – Badajoz, 1933-1936 – 5 – sp Bibl Santa Ana [073]

HOY EL PERONISMO *see* ARGENTINA

Hoyem, OJ *see* NEW ELLER BYNES (OG BUVIK) EN BYGDEBESKRIVELSE

Hoyer, Richard *see* MENSCHENSCHICKSALE

Hoyle, J *see* A COMPLETE DICTIONARY OF MUSIC

Hoynck Van Papendrecht, C P *see* HISTORIA ECCLESIAE ULTRAJECTINAE

Hoyos Sainz, Luis de *see* LA RAZA EXTREMENA

Hoyt, James T *see* THE COLLECTION LAWS, SPECIAL, EXEMPTION, PROPERTY, BANKING, AND INTEREST LAWS, OF ILLINOIS, INDIANA, MICHIGAN, IOWA, WISCONSIN AND MINNESOTA.

Hozumi, Nobushige *see* ANCESTOR-WORSHIP AND JAPANESE LAW

HPB SURGERY : A WORLD JOURNAL OF HEPATIC, PANCREATIC AND BILIARY SURGERY / ed by Puntis, Malcolm – 9,5,1 – us Harwood [617]

HR : HUMAN RESOURCES PLANNING – (v.4-. 1981-. 5,6,9) – v.1-. 1978- – 1 – us UMI [305]

HRAF PROBABILITY SAMPLE PROGRAM-PART A / Human Relations Area Files – (Part B. 1984. 40 cultural files available in 6 modules. 2050.00 each; 9) – 1980. 60 cultural files constituting a worldwide sample. Available in 7 modules – 9 – 2050.00 each – us H.R.A.F. [306]

HRAF TOPICAL PROGRAM / Human Relations Area Files – (Hunting and Gathering Societies.3990.00; 9. Pastoral Societies. 3325.00; HRA; 9. Historical Societies. 3325.00; HRA; 9) – 1984 – 9 – Apply – us H.R.A.F. [306]

Hrdlicka, A *see*
- ANTHROPOLOGICAL SURVEY IN ALASKA, 1928-1929
- CONTRIBUTIONS TO THE ANTHROPOLOGY OF THE CENTRAL AND SMITH SOUND ESKIMO

HRI OBSERVATIONS – (No issues publ in 1989 or 1990. Publ available to 1992 only. Nos 1-11 1974-76 Can$20.00. Nos 12-13 1976 Can$20.00) – Toronto. nos 1-35. 1974-92 – 9 – Can$20.00y – cn Micromedia [073]

HRLSD JOURNAL – v.2-3. 1976-78 – 1,5,6,9 – us UMI [073]

HRLSD JOURNAL / American Library Association. Health and Rehabilitative Library Services Division – (Ceased publ. Cont: American Library Association. Health and Rehabilitative Library Services Division. Journal) – Springfield. v2-3. Fal 1976-Spr 1978 – 1,5,9 – D11123.02 – us UMI [020]

HRN. B.H. BROCKES...VERTEUTSCHTER BETHLEHEMITISCHER KINDER-MORD DES RITTERS MARINO. / Marino, Giambattista – 3rd ed. Hamburg: J.C. Kissner, 1727. illus. Trans. of La Strage degli Innocenti with original text on facing pages – 1 – us U.W. Library [430]

HROMADSKE KHARCHUVANNIA UKRAINY 1933 R : PIDSUMKY PEREPISU / Upravlinii a narodno-hospodarskoho obliku USSR – Kharkiv: Narodne hospodarstvo ta oblik, 1934 – 1 – CSUX91-B992 – us Hoover Inst Photo [947]

HROTSVITHAE OPERA (MGH 7: 34.BD) – 1902 – Dfl35.00 – ne Slangenburg [240]

HRS SOCIETY RAG / Hot Record Society – nos. 1-11(?) (all publ). Jul 1938-Mar 1941. (Jazz Periodicals) – 1 reel – 1 – $60.00 – us UPA [780]

Hruschka, Alois *see* UEBER DEUTSCHE ORTSNAMEN

Hrushevskyi, Mykhailo *see*
- NATSIONALNYI VOPROSI AVTONOMIIA
- OSVOBOZHDENIE ROSSII I UKRAINSKII VOPROS
- UKRAJINA A RUSKO

HRVATSKA = CROATIA – Calumet: Croatian Print Co, dec 14 1917-aug 15 1924 – 3r – 1 – us Res Libr [072]

HRVATSKA GRUDA – Buenos Aires, Argentina. -m. Oct 1959-Dec 1975. 3 reels – 1 – uk British Libr Newspaper [072]

HRVATSKA SMOTRA – Zagreb, Croatia. v3-12. 1935-1944 – 1 – us I.U. Libraries [073]

HRVATSKA SMOTRA ZA KNJIZEVNOST, UMJETNOST I DRUSTVENI ZIVOT – v1-2. 1933-1934 – 1 – us I.U. Libraries [073]

HRVATSKA SMOTRA ZA POLITIKU, KNJIZEVNOST, ZNANOST, UMJETNOST I KRITIKU – v1-4. 1906-1908 – 1 – us I.U. Libraries [073]

HRVATSKA STRAZA ZA KRSCANSKU PROSYJETU – v2, 4-7. 1904, 1906-1909 – 1 – us I.U. Libraries [073]

HRVATSKA ZASTAVA – Chicago, IL, Aug. 3, 1905-Oct. 30, 1917 – 5r – 1 – us I.H.R.C. [975]

HRVATSKI DNEVNIK – Zagreb. Yugoslavia. -d. 16 Apr 1939-29 Mar 1941. (17 reels) – 1 – uk British Libr Newspaper [949]

HRVATSKI GLASNIK – Allegheny, PA, Dec. 12, 1908-Sep. 13, 1919 – 3r – 1 – us I.H.R.C. [071]

HRVATSKI GLASNIK = CROATIAN HERALD – Allegheny: Hrvatsko novinarsko drustvo, [1908-]. dec 1917-sep 1 1921 – us Res Libr [072]

HRVATSKI LIST AND DANICA HRVATSKA – New York, Jan. 20, 1922-Dec. 29, 1928; Jan. 2, 1930-Dec. 30, 1941 – 15r – 1 – us I.H.R.C. [975]

HRVATSKI NAROD – Zagreb. Yugoslavia. -d. 2 Jan 1942-4 Jul 1944, 31 Dec 1944-22 Mar 1945. (Very imperfect). (10 reels) – 1 – uk British Libr Newspaper [949]

HRVATSKI NAROD – Zagreb, Yugoslavia: Hrvastski narod, oct 1941-feb 1 1945 – 12r – 1 – us Res Libr [072]

HRVATSKO KOLO – Zagreb, Croatia, 1905. 1929-43 – 1 – us I.U. Libraries [073]

HRVATSKO KOLO – Zagreb, Croatia, 1948. v1-7, 1948-55 – 1 – us I.U. Libraries [073]

Hrynchenko, BD *see* SLOVAR' UKRAINSKOGO IAZYKA

H.S. Crocker Co *see* SANTA CRUZ COUNTY

H.S. KNISPEL COLLECTION OF CLIPPINGS RELATED TO THE LINDBERGH BABY KIDNAPPING – Most of the clippings are from St. Paul, MN newspapers. 1r, including filmed inventory – 1 – $30.00r – us M.H.S. [360]

HSEIH CHIN *see* MARCHING IN HARMONY

Hsia, Ching-Lin *see* STUDIES IN CHINESE DIPLOMATIC HISTORY

Hsia, Tao-tai *see* GUIDE TO SELECTED LEGAL SOURCES OF MAINLAND CHINA

HSIA-ERH KUAN-CHEN – Hongkong. v4 n3. 1856 – 8 – BCH-789 2 – ne IDC [920]

HSIA-MEN CHIH – 1832; 1839, 16. BCH-568 2 – 8 – ne IDC [950]

HSIANG KANG CHI TU CHIAO HUI SHIH (CCC228) / Liu, Yueh-sheng – (In Chinese) – [s.l: s.n, 1941] – 1r – 1 – 1984-B500 – us A.T.L.A. [240]

HSIAO CHING TONG KAO (CCC295) / Tsan, Ju-kun – (In Chinese) – [s.l: s.n, 1937] – 1r – 1 – 1984-6634 – us A.T.L.A. [240]

Hsieh, En-kuang *see* HOW TO COMMEND CHRISTIANITY TO THE CHINESE (CCC165)

Hsieh, Fu-ya *see*
- CHI-TU-CHIAO YU CHUNG-KUO (CCC168)
- CHRISTIANITY AND MODERN THOUGHT (CCC166)
- THE COMMON GROUND OF CONFUCIANISM, TAOISM AND CHINESE BUDDHISM (CCC169)
- A FAITH FOR A NEW AGE (CCC170)
- PHILOSOPHY OF RELIGION (CCC171)
- PRINCIPLES OF THE YOUNG MEN'S CHRISTIAN ASSOCIATION (CCC167)

Hsieh, Hung-lai *see*
- THE CHARACTER OF JESUS (CCC175)
- CHRISTIANITY AND SCIENCE (CCC173)
- LIVES OF PROMINENT CHINESE PASTORS (CCC174)
- REASONS FOR CHRISTIAN FAITH (CCC172)

Hsieh, Shou-ling *see* VICTORIOUS LIVING (CCC177)

Hsieh, Sung-kao *see*
- CHINESE CHRISTIAN MONOGRAPH (CCC180)
- NEW TESTAMENT CHARACTERS (CCC181)
- PEOPLE'S STORIES (CCC178)
- A PREACHER'S BOOK OF RELIGIOUS EDUCATION (CCC182)
- A SHORT LIFE OF D L MOODY (CCC184)
- A SHORT LIFE OF SPURGEON (CCC185)
- A SHORT STUDY OF EDUCATION IN THE CHRISTIAN HOME
- A SHORT STUDY OF RELIGIONS (CCC183)
- SHORT TERM READERS FOR ILLITERATE CHURCH MEMBERS (CCC186)

HSIEN-TAI – Les Contemporains. v. 1-6. Shanghai. 1932-35. Lacking: v. 6 (1, 3) 1935. BCH-256 2 – 8 – ne IDC [073]

HSIEN-TAI CHIH-NA CHIH CHI-LU – Newspaper clippings. 1924-32 – 1 – 35.00r – us Hoover Inst Photo [072]

HSIEN-TAI FO-HSUEH – Contemporary Buddhism. Peking. 1957-63. Lacking: v. 1-7, 1957; v. 1-12, 1960. BCH-910 2 – 8 – ne IDC [290]

HSIEN-TAI P'ING-LUN – (Contemporary Review). v. 1-8. Peking, Shanghai. 1924-28. BCH-257 2 – 8 – ne IDC [073]

HSIEN-TAI SHIH-LIAO – Shanghai. A collection of articles dealing with the political and historical development of contemporary China. 1934-1935. (2970 3122) – 1 – 35.00r – us Hoover Inst Photo [950]

HSI-KUO CHIN-SHIH HUI-PIEN – Shanghai. 1873-74; 1876-77 – 8 – BCH-788 2 – ne IDC [920]

HSIN CHUNG-HUA = NEW CHINA MAGAZINE – 1933-51. (Semi-monthly 1933-37, monthly 1943-45; semi-monthly 1946-51). Shanghai. "Hsin chung-hua tsung-mu". Peking. 1933-49. Available: 1933-36; n.s., v. 2 (1-6) 1944; v. 3 (1-10) 1945. BCH-262 1 – 9 – ne IDC [073]

HSIN KUAN-CH'A – New Observer. Peking. 1951-59. Lacking: v. 1, v. 3 (10-12) 1951; v. 2, 4, 6-10, 12, 18, 23, 1952; v. 1-10, 19, 1953; v. 17, 21, 1954. BCH-913 2 – 8 – ne IDC [073]

HSIN SHENG-MING = THE NEW LIFE – Shanghai. v1-3. Jan 1928-Dec 1930 (complete) – 4r – 1 – $102.00 – us Chinese Res [073]

HSIN SHENG-MING – New Life. v. 1-3 (12). Shanghai. 1928-30. monthly. Available: v. 1, v. 2 (1-2, 4-12). BCH-266 2 – 8 – ne IDC [073]

HSIN UYEH HUA PAO – Hanoi. North Vietnam. 1961-1964 – 1 – us UMI [072]

HSIN YUEH HUA PAO = BAO TAN VIET HOA – Hanoi: Yueh-nan Hua chiao lien ho tsung hui, jul 1967-sep 2 1976 – 16r – 1 – us Res Libr [072]

HSIN YUEH HUA PAO – Hanoi, Vietnam. Jan 1-31 1958; Oct 3-Dec 3 1964; Jan 1965-Oct 28 1967 – 6r – 1 – us L of C Photodup [072]

HSIN-CH'AO – Renaissance. v. 1 (1-5), v. 2 (1-5), v. 3 (1-2). Peking. 1919-21. monthly. BCH-259 2 – 8 – ne IDC [073]

HSIN-CHIANG JIH-PAO – Urumchi, Sinkiang, China. Sinkiang Daily. Jan 1948-Dec 1965. 26 reels – 1 – 632.00 – us Chinese Res [072]

HSING HSIEN JIH PAO – Bangkok. Thailand – 1 – us UMI [072]

HSING HSIEN JIH PAO – Bangkok, Thailand. 1960-1989 – 214r – 1 – us L of C Photodup [072]

HSING T'AI WAN PAO – Bangkok. Thailand. 1950- – 1 – us UMI [072]

HSING-HUA FU-CHIH – 1871. 54. 1503. BCH-559 2 – 8 – ne IDC [950]

HSIN-HAI KO-MING – Documents on 1911 revolution. 8 v. 1957. Lacking: v. 1, v. 8, 1957. BCH-954 2 – 8 – ne IDC [950]

HSIN-HUA JIH-PAO – Hankow and Chungking. 1938-46 – 1 – 198.00 – us Chinese Res [072]

HSINHUA NEWS AGENCY – Daily News Release. Hongkong. 1957-1964. Missing: scattered issues – 1 – 35.00r – us Hoover Inst Photo [072]

HSIN-HUA YUEH-PAO – New China Monthly. Peking. 1949-55. Cont. as: Hsin Hua pan yueh k'an. New China Fortnightly. Peking. 1956-64. Lacking: v. 3 (5) 1951; v. 21-24, 1959-60. BCH-912 2 – 8 – ne IDC [073]

HSIN-HUI HSIEN-CHIH – 1840, 14. BCH-596 2 – 8 – ne IDC [950]

HSIN-HUI HSIEN-CHIH – 1871, 10. BCH-597 2 – 8 – ne IDC [950]

HSIN-MIN TS'UNG-PAO – New Citizen Magazine. v. 25, 27-48. Tokyo. 1904-05. fortnightly. BCH-264 2 – 8 – ne IDC [073]

HSIN-WEN T'IEN-TI – Hong Kong. (Newsdom). Sinwen Tienti Weekly. Jan. 1945-Dec. 1970. (9200 0714) – 1 – 35.00r – us Hoover Inst Photo [950]

HSIN-YA-HSI-YA YUEH-K'AN – New Asia Monthly. v. 1-13. Shanghai. 1930-37. Lacking: v. 13 (3-6) 1937. BCH-790 2 – 8 – ne IDC [073]

HSIN-YUEH – Crescent Moon. v. 1-4 (7). Shanghai. 1928-32. BCH-268 2 – 8 – ne IDC [073]

HSI-TSANG JIH-PAO – Lhasa, Tibet. Apr 22, 1956-. Scattered issues missing. 5 reels – 1 – 87.50 – us Chinese Res [072]

HSIU YANG WEI TI (CCC342) / Wu, Yung-chuan – (In Chinese) – [s.l: s.n, 1950] – 1r – 1 – 1984-6681 – us A.T.L.A. [240]

Hsiu, Yao-ch'un *see* CHINESE CHRISTIAN MONOGRAPH (CCC187)

HSI-WANG – (Lacking: Pt2) – (Hope), 1937 – 8 – BCH-969 2 – ne IDC [920]

HSRI RESEARCH – (Highway Safety Research Institute. v.6-7. 1975-77. Superseded by H S R I Research Review – 1 – us UMI [380]

HSRI RESEARCH REVIEW – (v.10-. 1979- 5,6,9) – (Highway Safety Research Institute). v.7-. 1977- – 1 – us UMI [380]

H.S.T.C. HOOTER *see* THE LUMBERJACK

Hsu, C H *see* NINETY YEARS' HISTORY OF THE PRESBYTERIAN CHURCH IN NORTH FORMOSA (CCC188)

Hsu, Ch'ien *see* CHRISTIAN SALVATION OF CHINA (CCC189)

Hsu, Pi-chang *see* MY EXPERIENCE IN RURAL WORK (CCC190)

Hsu, Sung-shih *see*
- BIBLE AND FILIAL PIETY (CCC194)
- THE CHINESE NATION THROUGH THE EYES OF JESUS (CCC196)
- THE CHRISTIAN AWAKENING OF FAITH (CCC195)
- CHRISTIANITY AND CHINESE CULTURE (CCC192)
- JESUS THROUGH THE EYES OF THE CHINESE NATION (CCC193)

Hsu, Ti-shan *see* TAO CHIAO SHIH, VOL 1 (CCC197)

Hsu, Tsung-che *see* TRACTATUS DE DEO UNO ET TRINO (CCC198)

Hsuan-Tsang *see*
- MEMOIRES SUR LES CONTREES OCCIDENTALES
- SI-YU-KI

HSUEH HENG – The critical review. v. 1-79. Shanghai. 1922-33. monthly. BCH-270 2 – 8 – ne IDC [073]

HSUEH JEN (CCC74) / Chao, Tzu-ch'en – (In Chinese) – [1936] – 1r – 1 – 1984-B500 – us A.T.L.A. [240]

HSUEH LIN – Forest of Learning. v. 1-10. Shanghai. 1940-41. BCH-272 2 – 8 – ne IDC [000]

HSUEH-HSI – Study. v. 1-7. Peking. 1952-58. BCH-914 2 – 8 – ne IDC [370]

HSUEH-SHU SHIH-CHIEH – Scholarly World.Shanghai, 1935-37. -m. 2v. Lacking: 1935, v1(2). BCH-273/1 – 9 – ne IDC [073]

HSUN-CHOU FU-CHIH – 1874, 38, 1. BCH-653 2 – 8 – ne IDC [950]

HSUN-T'IEN HSIANG-SHIH LU – List of successful candidates in the imperial examination in Hsun-t'ien province. Scattered years 1714-1903. 3 reels – 1 – 90.00 – us Chinese Res [950]

Hu, I-ku *see* THE YOUTHS' BOOK-READING MOVEMENT (CCC199)

Hu, M *see* EFFECTS OF SENSORY BALANCE TRAINING IN OLDER ADULTS

Hu, Shih *see* THE DEVELOPMENT OF THE LOGICAL METHOD IN ANCIENT CHINA

HUA CH'IAO TSAI YIN-NI. (OVERSEAS CHINESE IN INDONESIA) / Chung, Kuang-hsing – SE-3042 1. 1959 – 9 – ne IDC [950]

HUA NIEN *see* GOOD YEARS

HUA ZHONG RI BAO – China. 1947-48 – 9 – 350.00 – cc Globe [072]

HUA-CHOU-CHIH – 1888, 1890, 12. BCH-630 2 – 8 – ne IDC [950]

HUADONG FANGZHI GONGXUEYUAN XUEBAO – Journal of the East China Textile Institute. 1981-. F 33 – 9 – 4.00f – cc Microforms [073]

HUADONG HUAGONG XUEYUAN XUEBAO – Journal of East China Institute of Chemical Technology. 1979-. F P238 – 9 – $4.50f – cc Microforms [073]

HUA-DONG SHIFAN DAXUE XUEBAO – Zhexue Shehui Kexue Ban. Journal of Eastern China Normal University, Philosophy and Social Science. In Chinese but Table of Contents in English in each issue. F p204 – 9 – $4.50f – cc Microforms [073]

HUAGONG JINZHAN – Chemical Industry & Engineering Progress. 1985.F/P 296 – 9 – $4.50f – cc Microforms [073]

HUA-HSI HSIEH-HO TA-HSUEEH CHUNG-KUO WEN-HUA YEN-CHIU-SO CHI-K'AN – Studia Serica. v. 1-9. Chengtu. 1940-50. (lacking: v. 1(2, p. 1-118)). BCH-274 2 – 8 – ne IDC [073]

HUA-HSIEN CHIH – 1687. 1866, 4. BCH-600 2 – 8 – ne IDC [950]

HUANG JUEZI ZOUSHU XU NAIJI ZOUYI HEKAN (ZHONGGUO JINDAISHI ZILIAO CONGSHU) – Historical Materials of Modern China Series: Combined issue of Huang Juezi's and Xu Naiji's Memorials to the Emperor. Comp. by Qi Sihe. 3 fiches. F H188 – 9 – $21.00 – cc Microforms [950]

Huang, Samuel K *see* ABIDING KNOWLEDGE OF CHRISTIAN TRUTH (CCC202)

HUANG-MING-WEN-HAI = HISTORICAL BIOGRAPHY COMPILED ON THE AUTHORITY OF INSCRIPTIONS AND EPITAPHS IN THE MING DYNASTY, MEDIEVAL CHINA / ed by Kanda, Kiichiro – 175v in 170. In custody of the Hosokawa family – 24reels – 1 – Y240,000.00 – ja Yushodo [920]

HUANGPU JUNXIAO SHILIAO, 1924-27 – Historical Materials of the Huangpu Military Academy, 1924-27. Comp. by the Guangdong Museum of Revolutionary History. 7 fiches. F H194 – 9 – $31.50 – cc Microforms [355]

HUA-NIEN – (Youth). 6 v. Shanghai. 1932-37. weekly. Lacking: v. 1 (19) 1932; v. 2 (17-?) 1933; v. 3 (1-19) (21-40) (42-?) 1934; 1935; 1936; 1937. BCH-275 1 – 9 – ne IDC [073]

HUANJING BAOHU – Environmental Protection. 1983-84. F/P 264 – 9 – 4.00f – cc Microforms [073]

HUANJING HUAXUE – Environmental Chemistry.1982-83. F/P 263 – 9 – $4.50f – cc Microforms [073]

HUANJING KEXUE XUEBAO – Acta Scientiae Circumstantiae. In Chinese but English abstracts to the main articles. F p99 – 9 – $4.50f – cc Microforms [073]

Huard, Charles *see* NOS AMIS LES QUEBECQUOIS

Huard, Victor Amedee *see* LA VIE ET L'OEUVRE DE L'ABBE PROVANCHER

Huart, A *see* LA LIBRE PAROLE

Huart, Clement *see* A HISTORY OF ARABIC LITERATURE

Huart, V Alphonse *see* MONSEIGNEUR DOMINIQUE RACINE, PREMIER EVEQUE DE CHICOUTIMI.

Huarte de San Juan, Juan *see* EXAMEN DE INGENIOS: THE EXAMINATION OF MENS WITS

HUASHENG BAO – China. Voice of China. -w. 1983-. M D36 – 1 reel/y – 1 – $28.00r – cc Microforms [072]

HUA-TUNG CHENG-FA HSUEH-PAO – (East China Journal of Politics and Law). Shanghai. n.1-3, Jun-Dec 1956. FA-HSUEH. (Legal Studies). Shanghai. 1957-Sep 1958. 1957: 1 missing – 1 – 13.85 – us Chinese Res [950]

HUA-TZU JIH-PAO – Hong Kong. 1895-1940 – 1 – 1238.00 – us Chinese Res [072]

HUA-WEN YUEH-K'AN – (Chinese Language Monthly). v. 1 (1-6), v. 2 (1). Chengtu. 1941-42. BCH-791 2 – 8 – ne IDC [480]

HUAXUE SHIJI – Chemical Reagents. 1983-. F P257 – 9 – $4.50f – cc Microforms [073]

HUAXUE SHIJIE – Chemical World. 1983-84. F/P 298 – 9 – $4.50f – cc Microforms [073]

HUAXUE XUEBAO – Acta Chimica Sinica. In Chinese but English abstracts to the main articles. F p35 – 9 – $4.50f – cc Microforms [073]

HUA-YANG HSIEN-CHIH – 1816, 44, 1. Available: pt. 1-20, BCH-693 2 – 8 – ne IDC [950]

HUAZHONG GONGXUEYUAN XUEBAO – Journal of Huazhong Institute of Technology. In Chinese but English abstracts to the main articles. F p195 – 9 – $4.50f – cc Microforms [073]

HUA-ZHONG SHI YUAN XUEBAO – (1980 $4.50f; 1979, 1981-82 $3.50f) – Zhexue Shehui Kexue Ban. Journal of Teacher's College of Central China, Philosophy and Social Science. In Chinese but Table of Contents in English in each issue. F p225 – 9 – cc Microforms [073]

HUB – Centralia. Wash. 1913-1919 – 1 – us UMI [071]

HUB – Kearney. Neb. 1889- – 1 – us UMI [071]

Hubback (Brown), Edith Charlotte *see* JANE AUSTEN'S SAILOR BROTHERS: BEING THE ADVENTURES OF SIR FRANCIS AUSTEN, G.C.B., ADMIRAL OF THE FLEET, AND REAR-ADMIRAL CHARLES AUSTEN

Hubback, John Henry *see* JANE AUSTEN'S SAILOR BROTHERS: BEING THE ADVENTURES OF SIR FRANCIS AUSTEN, G.C.B., ADMIRAL OF THE FLEET, AND REAR-ADMIRAL CHARLES AUSTEN

Hubball, Harry T *see* THE IMPACT OF AN ADULT HEALTH EDUCATION PROGRAM ON EXERCISE SELF-EFFICACY AND PARTICIPATION IN LEISURE-TIME PHYSICAL ACTIVITY

Hubbard *see* HISTORY OF THE TOWN OF SPRINGFIELD

HUBBARD ENTERPRISE – Hubbard, OR. -w. 1917-35 – 1 – 144.00 – us Oregon Hist [071]

HUBBARD ENTERPRISE : WEEKLY INDEPENDANT NEWSPAPER – Hubbard, OH. 6 Feb 1913-18 Oct 1917 – 2r – 1 – us Western Res [071]

Hubbard, Ethel Daniels *see* UNDER MARCHING ORDERS: A STORY OF MARY PORTER GAMEWELL

Hubbard, G *see* DE L'ORGANISATION DES SOCIETES DE PREVOYANCES OU DE SECOURS MUTUEL

HUBBARD HERALD – Hubbard, OR. -w. 8 Aug 1912-20 Feb 1913. 1 roll – 1 – us U.O. Library [071]

HUBBARDSTON 1746-1849 – (Mf 1T-4T: Births & Deaths 1746-1853. Mf 1T-2T: Marriages 1770-93. Mf 4T-7T: Marriages & Intentions 1802-49. Mf 7T-8T: Births 1822-44. Mf 8T: Marriages 1798-1802; Births 1843-49. Mf 9T: Births & Deaths 1793-1843; Marriages, Deaths 1843-49) – (mf ed 1996) – 9mf – 9 – 0-87623-270-5 – us Holbrook [920]

HUBBARDSTON 1747-1900 – (Mf 1,3,7: Vitals 1747-1803. Mf 1-7: Town Records 1767-95. Mf 8-11: Births, Deaths 1771-1853. Mf 11-15: Marriages 1798-1886. Mf 15: Births & Deaths 1825-1844. Mf 16-18: Births, Deaths 1749-1853. Mf 19-21: Marriages 1798-1844. Mf 22-41: Town Records 1795-1838. Mf 41: Church Members 1821-35. Mf 42-61: Town Records 1838-76. Mf 62-64: Accounts 1829-50. Mf 65-67: Paupers 1820-74. Mf 68-76: Valuations 1836-55. Mf 77-80: Town Orders 1831-63. Mf 81-82: Rebellion 1861-65. Mf 83-84: Veterans Aid 1884-1945. Mf 85-86: Town Farm 1868-85. Mf 87-124: Mortgages 1832-1905. Mf 125-126: Birth Index 1848-1914. Mf 126-127: Marr Index 1848 1914. Mf 127-128: Death Index 1848-1914. Mf 129-131: Births 1843-1901. Mf 130: Marriages 1843-51. Mf 130-131: Deaths 1843-59. Mf 132-133: Marriages 1852-1904. Mf 134-136: Deaths 1860-1905) – (mf ed 1994) – 136mf – 9 – 0-87623-186-5 – us Holbrook [920]

Hubbell, Levi *see* TRIAL OF IMPEACHMENT OF LEVI HUBBELL, JUDGE OF THE SECOND JUDICIAL CIRCUIT, BY THE SENATE OF THE STATE OF WISCONSIN, JUNE 1853

HUBBELL STANDARD – Hubbell, NE. -w. Feb-Sep 1900, scattered issues missing; Aug 1902-Jan 1918; Apr 1918-Dec 1922 – 1 – us NE Hist [071]

HUBEI GEMING SHILU GUAN WUCHANG QIYI DANGAN ZILIAO XUANBIAN (SHANG JUAN) – A Selection of Materials on the Wuchang Uprising in the holdings of the Hubei Revolutionary Archives. v1. Comp. by the Institute of Modern History, Chinese Academy of Social Sciences. 5 fiches. F H106 – 9 – $22.50 – cc Microforms [950]

HUBEI KAICAI MEITIE ZONGJU JINGMEN KUANGWU ZONGJU: SHEN XUANHUAI DANGAN ZILIAO XUANJI ZHI ER – Selection of Archival Materials in the Possession of Shen Xuanhuai, Part II: Hubei General Bureau of Coal and Iron Mining. Jingman Bureau of Mines. Comp. by Chen Xulu, etc. 7 fiches. F H170 – 9 – $27.00 – cc Microforms [622]

Hubei Province. China *see*
- HONGZHI HUANGZHOU FU ZHI, 1560
- JIAJING HANYANG FU ZHI, 1546
- JIAJING MIANYANG ZHI, 1531
- JIAJING QIZHOU ZHI, 1529
- JIAJING YINGSHAN XIAN ZHI, 1540
- ZHENGDE GUANGHUA XIAN ZHI, 1515

HUBEI RIBAO = HUBEI DAILY – China. 1984-. M/D67 – 1 reel/y – 1 – $55.00r – cc Microforms [072]

Hubel, Henni *see* "BELAUSCHT!"

Huber, A *see* INDONESIE

Huber, J C *see* BIBLIOGRAPHIE DER KLINISCHEN ENTOMOLOGIE

Huber, Johannes *see*
- DER JESUITEN-ORDEN
- JOHANNES SCOTUS ERIGENA
- DIE PHILOSOPHIE DER KIRCHENVAETER

Huber, M *see* NOTICES GENERALES DES GRAVEURS

Huber, S *see*
- AUSLEGUNG DES 129TH PSALMEN DAUIDS AUFF GEGENWERTIGEN ZUSTAND DER KIRCHEN ZU WITTENBERG...
- BESTENDIGE BEKANTNUS D. SAMUEL HUBERS. OB GOTT DURCH SEINEN LIEBEN SON JESUM CHRISTUM NUR ALLEIN ETLICH WENIG MENSCHEN ORDER ZUMAL ALLE MENSCHEN...VOM TODE ALLESAMPT ERLOE..HABE
- BESTENDIGE ENTDECKUNG DES CALUINISCHEN GEISTS WELCHER SICH VNTERSTEHE DAS LEIDEN JHESU CHRISTI FUER VNSERE SUENDE ZU VERLAEUGNEN VND AUFFZUHEBEN
- CHRISTLICHE PREDIGTEN. VBER EN CXXIX. PSALM DAUIDS. DARINNE ANGEZEIGET WIRD WIE DIE CALUINISCHE SCHWERMER DER KIRCH ZU WITTENBERG VNND IM GANTZEN CHURKREISS SEYEN MIT JHREM HEILLOSEN PFLUG...
- CLANGORES TUBAE ADVERSVS THEODORVM BEZAM. VT PRIUSQUAM IN ALTERUM EXSPIRAT SECVLVM, HVC RESPICIAT UND PERPENDAT,...
- CONFVTATIO BREVIS LIBRI, SUB ALIENO NOMINE EDITI, DE CONTROVERSIA INTER THEOLOGOS VVITTEBERGENSES,...
- DEMONSTRATIO FALLACIARUM JOHANNIS CALVINI, IN DOCTRINA DE COENA DOMINI QVIBVS VSVS EST IN LIBRO INSTITUTIONIS CHRISTIANAE, AND EX QUO SUUM CALVINISMUM IN OMNEM EGURGITAVIT CHRISTIANUM ORBEM
- DISPVTATIO SECVNDA CONTRA CALVINISTAS, AND PRAESERTIM SYNOPSIN KIMEDONCIJ...
- DISPVTATIO TERTIA CONTRA CALVINISTAS. QVOD FACIANT DEVM AVTOREM PECCATI...
- DREY SCHRIFFTEN: 1. PROTESTATION SAMUEL HUBERS DOCTOR VND PROFESSORS DER H. SCHRIFFT ZU WITTEMBERG
- DIE EWIGE VNND EINIGE GRUNDFESTE AUFF WELCHEM DER SELIGMACHENDE GLAUBE STEHEN VND VERHARREN MUSS
- HISTORISCHE BESCHREIBUNG DES GANTZEN STREITS ZWISCHEN D. HUNNEN VND D. HUBERN VON DER GNADENWAHL WIE DERSELBIGE ENTSPRUNGEN VND BISS DAHER ZUGENOMEN HABE...
- KURTZE ANLEYTUNGE VNND NACHRICHTUNGE WIE MAN D. EGIDIUM HUNNEN VND D. LUCAM OSIANDERN SAMPT JREM ANHANG EXAMINIEREN...
- KURTZE ERJNNERUNG VON GEGENWERTIGEM ZWEYTRACHT VBER DIE LEHRE VON DER GNADEN WAHL...
- NOTWENDIGE ENDECKUNG WIE D. LUCAS OSIANDER IN SEINER PREDIGT VON DER GNADEN-WAHL DIE VERZWEYFFELTE CALUINISCHE LERE VERSTECKT MIT FUERSATZ DIESELBIGE IN DIE REINE CHRISTLICHE KIRCHEN IN WUERTEMBERG...
- PROTESTATION SAMUEL HUBERS PROFESSORN DER H. SCHRIFFT ZU WITTEMBERG. WIDER JOHAN WILHELM STUCK ZU ZUERICH D. JOHANN JACOB GRYNEUM ZU BASEL VND JOHAN JETZLERN (WELCHER SICH SEITHERO HAT GRATIANUM SERLEYU TAUFFENM LASSEN) ZU SCHAFFHAUSEN...
- RETTUNG DES SPRUCHS ROM. 8. DENN WELCHE ER ZUUOR VERSEHEN HAT DIE HAT ER AUCH VERORDNET DAS SIE GLEICH SEIN SOLTEN DEM EBENBILD SEINES SONS,...
- RETTUNG MEINER ALLEZEIT BESTENDIGEN BEKANTNUS VON DER GNADENWAHL DARINNEN AUFF DISMAL HINDAN GESETZT ALLER NEBENSTREITTEN ALLES VND ALLEIN WAS ZUM HAUPTSTREIT GEHOERIG...ERKLERET WIRD...
- SENDBRIEFF AN DIE...BURGERMEISTER VND RHAT DER LOEBLICHEN STATT ZUERICH. DARJNNEN SIE ERJNNERT...WERDEN WAS JRE KICHENDIENER VNTER DEM SCHEIN EINER ANTWORT AUFF D. PHILIPPI NICOLAI BUCH FUER SEIN WERCK WIDER JESUM CHRISTUM...
- THESES, CHRISTVM IESVM ESSE MORTVVM PRO PECCATIS TOTIVS GENERIS HVMANI...
- VON DER CALUINISCHEN PREDICANTEN SCHWINDELGEIST VNND DEM GERECHTEN GERICHT GOTTES VBER DISE SECT
- VON H. SCHRIFFT. 2. VON DER CHRISTLICHEN KIRCHEN. 3. VON DER BAEPTISCHEN KIRCHEN. 4. VON D. LUTHERS PERSON. 5. VON HANS PISTORIJ PERSON VND SEINEM SCHRECKLICHEM ANBLJCK

Huber, Siegfried *see* PIZARRO ET SES FRERES. CONQUERANTS DE L'EMPIRE DES INCAS

Huber, Thomas *see* STUDIEN ZUR THEORIE DES UEBERSETZENS IM ZEITALTER DER DEUTSCHEN AUFKLAERUNG, 1730-1770

Huber, Walther *see* GOTTFRIED KELLER UND DIE FRAUEN

Huberich, C H *see* THE POLITICAL AND LEGISLATIVE HISTORY OF LIBERIA

Huberinus, Caspar *see*
- [BUECHLEIN DER HAUSZUCHT]
- DER CATECHISMUS MIT VIEL SCHOENEN SPRUECHEN DER HEILIGEN SCHRIFFT GEGRUENDET...
- DER CATECHISMUS. MIT VIL SCHOENEN SPRUECHEN VN HISTORIEN DER HAILIGE SCHRIFFT GEGRUENDET...
- ETLICH SCHLUSRED VOM GNADEN BUNDT CHRISTI DAS IST VOM TAUFF VND VOM KINDER GLAUBEN
- ETLICHE TROSTSPRUECH FUER DIE BLOEDEN SCHWACHEN GEWISSEN...
- ETLICHE TROSTSPRUECHE FUER DIE BLOEDEN VND SCHWACHEN GEWISSEN...
- HOMILIAE CATECHISTICAE QVADRAGIN TA, IN QUIBUS PRAECIPUA TOTIUS CHRISTIANAE RELIGIONIS CAPITA COM PENDIOSE...
- IMAGINES DE MORTE, ET EPIGRAMATA,...
- DER KLAINE CATECHISMUS
- EIN KURTZER AUSZUG AUSS DER HEYLIGEN SCHRIFFT DARINNEN ANGEZEYGT WIRD WIE EIN BETRUEBT MENSCH BEGRIFFEN IN GROSSER ANGST VNND NOTH SCHREYT ZU GOTT VMB HILFF...
- AIN KURTZER AUSZZUG AUSS DER HAYLIGEN SCHRIFFT...
- MANCHERLEY FORM ZU PREDIGEN VON DEN FUERNEMBSTEN STUECKEN SO IN DER CHRISTLICHEN KIRCHEN TEGLICH GELERT VND GETRIEBEN SOLLEN WERDEN
- OPERA OMNIA
- POSTILLA DEUDSCH VBER ALLE FEST VND GEMEINE FEYERTAG DER HEYLIGEN DURCHS GANTZE IAR / KURTZE VND NUTZLICHE AUSSLEGUNG
- POSTILLA TEUETSCH VBER ALLE SONTAEGLICHE EUANGELIEN VOM ADUENT BISS AUF OSTERN / KURTZE...
- SEELEN ARSTEDYE VOR DE GESUNDEN VND KRANCKEN...
- SEUENTICH SLUYTREDENEN VAN DER RECHTER HANT GODS EN DER MACHT CHRISTI
- SIBENDTZIG SCHLUSSRED DAS BEIDE TEIL DES SACRAMENTS ALLEN GLEUEBIGE CHRISTEN GEREICHET SOLL WERDEN
- SIBENTZIG SCHLUSSREDE DAS BEYDE THEYL DES SACRAMENTES ALLEN GLAUBIGEN CHRISTEN GEREYCHET SOLL WERDEN
- SIBENZIG SCHLUSRED ODDER PUNCTEN VON DER RECHTEN HAND GOTTES VND DER GEWALT CHRISTI
- SIBENZIG SCHLUSREDE ODDER PUNCTE VON DER RECHTEN HANDT GOTTES VND DER GEWALT CHRISTJ. ZU TROSTE DENEN DIE SICH IN DER ZWINGELISCHEN SACHE NICHT BERICHTEN KOENEN RC
- SIMOLACHRI, HISTORIE, E FIGVRE DE LA MORTE
- SPIEGEL DER HAUSSUCHT. IESUS SYRACH GENAND...
- SPIEGEL DER HAUSSUCHT. IESUS SYRACH GENANDT...
- SPIEGEL DER HAUSTZUCHT, IHESUS SYRACH GENANT...
- DAS STREIT BUECHLIN
- DER TODTENDANTZ DURCH ALLE STENDE VNND GESCHLECHT DER MENSCHEN...
- AIN TRERVE WARNUNG VOR DER KUENFFTIGEN STRAFF GOTTES
- AIN TROESTLICHE SERMO VON DER VRSTENDT CHRISTI...
- TROESTUNG AUSS GOETTLICHER SCHRIFFT...
- TROSTUNG AUSS GOETTLICHER GESCHRIFFT
- VAM TORN VNDE DER GUEDICHEIT GADES
- VIERTZIG KURTZE PREDIG VBER DEN GANTZEN CATECHISMUM
- VIERTZIG KURTZE PREDIG VBER DEN GANTZEN CATECHISMUM...
- VOM CHRISTLICHEN RITTER
- VOM WAREN ERKENDTNUSS GOTTES. VON NEWEM UEBERLESEN, FLEISSIG CORRIGIERT VNND GEBESSERT
- VOM ZORN VND DER GUETE GOTTES
- VOM ZORN VND DER GUETTE GOTTES
- VON BOESEN FALSCHEN ZUNGEN
- WARZU DAS HAILIGE CREUETZ NUTZ VNND GUT SEY
- WARZU DAS HAYLIGE CREUETZ NUTZ VND GUT SEY
- WIE AIN BETRUEBTER MENSCH RUEFFT ZU GOTT VMB HILFF VND WIE DER GAYST GOTTES JN TROESTET
- WIE MAN DIE KRANCKEN TROESTEN SOLL
- ZEHENERLEY KURTZE FORM ZU PREDIGEN

Huberman, A M *see* SOLVING EDUCATIONAL PROBLEMS

Hubert, F *see* DIE STRASZBURGER LITURGISCHEN ORDNUNGEN IM ZEITALTER DER REFORMATION

Hubert, Lucien *see* UNE POLITIQUE COLONIALE

HUBERT ROBERT. 2E CENTENAIRE DE SA NAISSANCE / Reunion des musees nationaux. Paris – 1933. 24 illus. 2 fiches – 9 – fr Réunion [700]
Hubert-Valleroux, P *see* LES ASSOCIATIONS COOPERATIVES EN FRANCE ET A L'ETRANGER
Huberty, A *see* NEU METHOD – MESSIGE VIOL D'AMOUR STUECKE AUS ALLEN THOENEN, OHNE VERSYUEMUNG, THEILS MIT BASSE, THEILS ALLEINE, AUCH MIT AUSGESUCHTEN ARIETTEN VERMUESCHT AM ENDE DES BUCHS...
HUBLI GAZETTE – Hubli, India. 29 Oct 1944-29 Dec 1946 – 1r – 1 – us L of C Photodup [072]
Hubmaier, Balthasar *see*
- WRITINGS
Hubner, Joseph A de *see* PROMENADE AUTOUR DU MONDE
HUBUNGAN ANTARA INTENSITY DAN DJARAK EPICENTER / Supomo – Also bound in: Seismic zones in Indonesia,BY R. Sutadi. SE 6682 1. 1962 – 9 – ne IDC [500]
HUBUNGAN DIPONEGORO-SENTOT / Sukanto, Bustaman – SE 4899 1. 1959 – 9 – ne IDC [950]
HUBUNGAN INDONESIA DENGAN INDUSTRI MINJAK DUNIA / Standard-Vacuum Oil Company – SE 3589 1. 1958 – 9 – ne IDC [660]
Huch, Friedrich *see*
- GESCHWISTER
- TRAEUME
Huch, Ricarda *see*
- ALTE UND NEUE GEDICHTE
- BLUETHEZEIT DER ROMANTIK
- GEDICHTE
- DAS JUDENGRAB – AUS BIMBOS SEELENWANDERUNGEN
- NATUR UND GEIST ALS DIE WURZELN DES LEBENS UND DER KUNST
Huch, Rudolf *see* MEIN LEBEN
Huchet, Albert *see* CHARTIER ANCIEN DE MONTMORIGNY
Huckel, Oliver *see* MELODY OF GOD'S LOVE
HUCKNALL AND BULWEL DISPATCH – 1979-Jun 1996 – 33r – 9 – uk British Libr Newspaper [072]
HUCKNALL MORNING STAR AND ADVERTISER – (Rushcliffe Advertiser: 16 Mar 1888-27 Dec 1895; 10 Apr-25 Dec 1896; 7 Jan 1898-9 Apr 1909. 19 1/2r) – England, 1888-1911; 4 Jan 1912-28 Mar 1913 – 22r – 1 – uk British Libr Newspaper [072]
HUD *see* HOUSING AND URBAN AFFAIRS (HUD)
HUD NEWSLETTER – v3-13 no 13. 1972-29 Mar 1982 – 1,5,6,9 – us UMI [620]
Hudail. (Tribe) *see* POEMS OF THE HUZAILIS
HUDAVENDIGAR – (No.s 423 (11 Haziran 1873), 3156 (26 Subat 1341[1925])) – Bursa: Matbaa-yi Vilayet, 1896-? – 1mf – 9 – $10.00 – us MEDOC [949]
Hudaya, M A M *see* SARINAH IAN SARINO
Hudayi 'Aziz Mahmud, Efendi *see* DIVAN
HUDDERSFIELD AND HOLMFIRTH EXAMINER – England. Sep 1851-Dec 1856.-w. 5 reels – 1 – uk British Libr Newspaper [072]
HUDDERSFIELD BORO' ADVERTISER. (BORO ADVERTISER) – England. 3 Jan 1913-27 Apr 1917; 8 Dec 1922-16 Jan 1943.-w. 11 reels – 1 – uk British Libr Newspaper [072]
HUDDERSFIELD ECHO – England.2 Oct 1886-1887. -w. 1/2 reel – 1 – uk British Libr Newspaper [072]
Huddersfield. Yorkshire *see* PARISH REGISTERS
Huddilston, John Homer *see* ESSENTIALS OF NEW TESTAMENT GREEK
HUDDINGEPOSTEN – Stockholm, Sweden. 1979-82 – 1 – sw Kungliga [072]
Huder, Karin *see* METHANREFORMIERUNG MIT CO2 BEI ENERGIEEINKOPPLUNG DURCH DIREKTBESTRAHLUNG DES KATALYSATORS
Hudgings, William Franklyn *see* WHAT EVERYBODY SHOULD KNOW ABOUT THE LAWS OF MARRIAGE AND DIVORCE...ALSO THE DIVORCE LAWS OF MEXICO, CUBA, CANADA, ENGLAND, AND FRANCE
HUDIKSVALLS TIDNING – Hudiksvall, Sweden. 1986- – 1 – sw Kungliga [072]
HUDIKSVALLSPOSTEN – Hudiksvall, Soderhamn, Sweden. 1864-1954 – 1 – sw Kungliga [072]
HUDIKSVALLSTIDNINGEN – (Halsinglands Tidning 1971-78) – Hudiksvall, Sweden. 1909-43, 1969-78 – 154r – 1 – sw Kungliga [072]
HUDIKSVALLSTIDNINGEN – Hudiksvall, Sweden. 1979-86. Halsinglands Tidning – 1 – sw Kungliga [072]
HUDIKSWALLS WECKOBLAD – Hudiksvall, Sweden. 1845-59, 1861-64 – 1 – sw Kungliga [072]
HUDSON 1866-1900 – (Mf 1: Births 1866-76. Mf 2: Births 1876-86. Mf 3: Births 1886-91. Mf 4: Marriages 1866-77. Mf 5: Marriages 1877-87. Mf 6: Marriages 1888-91. Mf 7: Deaths 1866-82. Mf 8: Deaths 1883-91. Mf 9: Births 1892-98. Mf 10: Births 1899-1900. Mf 11: Marriages 1892-1900. Mf 12: Deaths 1892-98. Mf 13: Deaths 1899-1906) – (mf ed 1993) – 13mf – 9 – 0-87623-174-1 – us Holbrook [920]
Hudson, Alfred B *see* TELANG: A MA'ANJAN DAJAK VILLAGE OF CENTRAL KALIMANTAN
HUDSON BAY COMPANY : PAPERS PRESENTED BY COMMAND OF HER MAJESTY...TO ASCERTAIN THE LEGALITY OF THE POWERS IN RESPECT TO TERRITORY, TRADE, TAXATION AND GOVERNMENT,... / Grande-Bretagne. Colonial Office – [s.l.]: the House of Commons, 1850. SEM105P425 – 1mf – 9 – Can$2.25 – cn Bibl Nat [971]
HUDSON BAY: PROPOSED UTILIZATION OF ITS LAND AND WATER RESOURCES: A NEW COLONY, A RAILWAY TO REACH IT / Baillairge, Charles – 1895? 00057. (Pre-1900 Canadiana) – 9 – cn C.I.H.M. [971]
Hudson, C T *see* THE ROTIFERA; OR WHEELANIMALCULES
HUDSON, DAVID, FAMILY PAPERS, MS 3893 – (Personal journals of David Hudson, 1799-1801, and David Hudson, Jr., 1820-1836. David Hudson, Sr., was the founder of the town of Hudson, Summit Co., Ohio) – Hudson, Summit, OH. 1799-1836 – 1r – 1 – us Western Res [920]
HUDSON DISPATCH – Union City. N.J. 1900- – 1 – us UMI [071]
Hudson, G V *see* AN ELEMENTARY MANUAL OF NEW ZEALAND ENTOMOLOGY
THE HUDSON HIGHLANDS – New York: Printed for Henry Cranston, 1883. 03623. (Pre-1900 Canadiana) – 9 – cn C.I.H.M. [978]
Hudson, New Hampshire. Hudson Baptist Church *see* RECORDS
Hudson, Ohio *see* MISCELLANEOUS EARLY NEWSPAPERS
HUDSON, OHIO, TAXES, MS V.F.O. – (True copy of resident proprietors lists for the District of Hudson, June 29 1801) – 1801 – 1r – 1 – us Western Res [978]
HUDSON REVIEW – 1- 1948- – 1. ; 5,6. ; 9 – apply; v.21-; v.29- – us UMI [073]
Hudson, Sanford Amos *see* LAW FOR THE CLERGY: A COMPILATION OF THE STATUTES OF THE STATES OF ILLINOIS, INDIANA, IOWA, MICHIGAN, MINNESOTA, OHIO, AND WISCONSIN.
Hudson, Thomson Jay *see* THE DIVINE PEDIGREE OF MAN
Hudson, W *see*
- FLORA ANGELICA
- FLORA ANGLICA
Hudson, W H *see* ARGENTINE ORNITHOLOGY
Hudson, William Henry *see*
- A SHEPHERD'S LIFE
- STUDIES IN INTERPRETATION
HUDSON'S BAY / Ballantyne, Robert Michael – BN-112 2. 1848 – 8 – ne IDC [971]
HUDSON'S BAY AND ITS RESOURCES: WITH FEASIBILITY OF STOCKING THE BAY WITH BEHRING SEA FUR-SEAL: A LECTURE...27TH NOVEMBER 1894 / Hill, Shuldham SC – Quebec: T.J. Moore, 1895. 05619. (Pre-1900 Canadiana) – 9 – cn C.I.H.M. [971]
HUDSON'S BAY COMPANY : PAPERS PRESENTED BY COMMAND OF HER MAJESTY.. – s.l: House of Commons, 1850. SEM105P425 – 1mf – 9 – Can$2.25 – cn Bibl Nat [971]
Hudson's Bay Company *see* COPY OF MEMORIAL AND PETITION FROM INHABITANTS OF THE RED RIVER SETTLEMENT,...
Hue, A M *see* LICHENES. EXTRA-EUROPAEI A PLURIBUS COLLECTORIBUS AD MUSEUM PARISIENSE MISSI
HUE AND CRY : THE STORY OF HENRY AND JOHN FIELDING AND THEIR BOW STREET RUNNERS / Pringle, Patrick – England: William Morrow & Co, n.d. – 3mf – 9 – $4.50 – LLMC 96-052 – us L.L.M.C. [360]
Hue, Otto *see* UNSERE TAKTIK BEIM GENERALSTREIK
Huebener, J W P *see*
- HEPATICOLOGIA GERMANICA
- MUSCOLOGIA GERMANICA
Huebler, Franz *see* MILTON UND KLOPSTOCK
HUEBNER / Sanguino y Michel, Juan – Caceres: Tip. Enc. y Lib. Jimenez, 1901 – 1 – sp Bibl Santa Ana [946]
Huebner, E *see* IL PONTE D'ALCANTARA
Huebner, Emilio *see*
- CACERES EN TIEMPO DE LOS ROMANOS
- CORPUS INSCRIPTIONUM LATINARUM
- INSCRIPCIONES ROMANAS DE MERIDA
- INSCRIPCIONES ROMANAS SEPULCRALES DE IBAHERNANDO
- SITUACION DE LA ANTIGUA NORBA
Huebner, Friedrich Markus *see*
- DIE ZIERDE DER GEISTLICHEN HOCHZEIT, UN DIE KLEINEREN SCHRIFTEN
- DIE ZIERDE DER GEISTLICHEN HOCHZEIT, UND DIE KLEINEREN SCHRIFTEN
Huebner, J *see* SAMMLUNG EUROPAEISCHER SCHMETTERLINGE
Huebner, Solomon S *see* PROPERTY INSURANCE
Hueffer, H *see* QUELLEN ZUR GESCHICHTE DES ZEITALTERS DER FRANZOESISCHEN REVOLUTION
DIE HUEGELMUEHLE : ROMAN IN FUENF BUECHERN / Gjellerup, Karl – Leipzig: Quelle & Meyer, 1920 – 1r – 1 – us U.W. Library [830]
LA HUELGA / Diaz Maciaz, Jose – 1897 – 9 – 1.50f – sp Bibl Santa Ana [830]
HUELLAS JUVENILES / Herrero Alvarado, Antonio – Sevilla: Editorial Catolica Espanola, S.A., 1956 – 1 – sp Bibl Santa Ana [946]
Huelphers, A *see* HISTORISK AFHANDLING OM MUSIK OCH INSTRUMENTER SAERDELES OM ORGWERKS INRAETTNINGEN I ALLMAENHET, JEMTE KORT BESKRIFNING OEFWER-ORGWERKEN I SWERIGE
Huenefeld, Guenther, Freiherr von *see* VOM EWIGEN KAMPF
Hueneke, Heinrich *see* EXPERIMENTELLE UNTERSUCHUNG ZUM PROBLEM DES ZUSAMMENHANGS ZWISCHEN ERFRAGTEM UND BEOBACHTETEM VERHALTEN
Huenerbein, Heidi A *see* GUIDELINES FOR PRESCRIBING UPPER BODY EXERCISE FOLLOWING OPEN HEART SURGERY
Huennerkopf, Richard *see* BEITRAEGE ZUR DESKRIPTIVEN POETIK IN DEN MITTELHOCHDEUTSCHEN VOLKSEPEN UND IN DER THIDREKSSAGA
HUER FIKIR – Izmit. Mueduer-i Mes'ul: Kilicoglu Hakki. Nos. 16 (25 Nisan 1924), 85 (21 Eyluel 1925) – 9 – $20.00 – us MEDOC [956]
HUER MARKOPASA – (Last title in the Markopasa set, published in Istanbul by Aziz Nesin) – n.s., vol. 1, nos. 1-5 (1950) – 2mf – 9 – $21.00 – us MEDOC [949]
HUER MARKOPASA – Vol. 1, nos 1-19 (1949) – 2mf – 9 – $21.00 – us MEDOC [949]
HUERRIYET – London. Muharriri ve Nasiri: Civanpir, 1895-1897 – 9 – $25.00 – us MEDOC [956]
HUERRIYET : TAGESZEITUNG FUER TUERKISCHE ARBEITNEHMER IN EUROPA – Neu-Isenburg, Germany. 1 Sept 1978- – ca 6r per yr – 1 – gw Mikrofilm [072]
HUERRIYET VE ITILAF NASIL DOGDU, NASIL OLDU? / Nur, Riza – Dersaadet: Aksam Matbaasi, 1335 [1919] – $20.00 – us MEDOC [470]
Huerta de Animas *see*
- ESTATUTOS DEL CENTRO JUVENIL NUESTRA SENORA DEL ROSARIO DE HUERTA DE ANIMAS
- FIESTAS PATRONALES EN HONOR DE LA SANTISIMA VIRGEN DEL ROSARIO
- FIESTAS PATRONALES EN HONOR DE LA VIRGEN DEL ROSARIO. 1973
Huerta, J *see* DE PROBLEMAS FILOSOFICOS...
Huerta Vega, Fco. M and Alii *see* COLECCION DE DISERTACIONES
Huertas y Barrero, Francisco *see*
- CONFERENCIAS SOBRE LA PLUROTONIA
- LA EPIDEMIA DE VIRUELA
HUESN VE ASK / Dede, Galib – Kostantiniye: Matbaa-i Ebuezziya, 1304 [1887] – $65.00 – us MEDOC [470]
Huet de Coetlizan, Jean-Baptiste *see*
- RECHERCHES ECONOMIQUES. SUR LE DEPARTEMENT DE LA LOIRE-INFERIEURE
- STATISTIQUE DU DEPARTEMENT DE LA LOIRE-INFERIEURE
HUET, EVEQUE D'AVRANCHES, OU, LE SCEPTICISME THEOLOGIQUE / Bartholmess, Christian – Paris: Marc Ducloux, 1850 – 1mf – us A.T.L.A. [240]
DER HUETER DER SCHWELLE : VON WEISHEIT UND LIEBE IN DER GEISTESWELT / Novalis; ed by Bonsels, Waldemar – 3. Aufl. Muenchen: Muenchner Buchverlag, 1943 – 1r – 1 – us U.W. Library [830]
DER HUETER ISRAELS : KRIEGSNOVELLEN AUS DER HEIMAT / Pauls, Eilhard Erich – Leipzig: G Schloessmann, 1915 – 1r – 1 – us U.W. Library [830]
Huettenberger, Peter *see* NICHTLIMITIERTE KOMPONENTEN IM ABGAS VON OTTOMOTOREN
Huf, Stefan *see* ALTERN IN DER ARBEITSGESELLSCHAFT
Hufeland, C W *see* JOURNAL DER PRACTISCHEN ARZNEYKUNDE UND WUNDARZNEYKUNST 1. 1795-98. 1844
Hufeland, CW *see* ENCYCLOPAEDISCHES WOERTERBUCH DER MEDICINISCHEN WISSENSCHAFTEN (AEL, ABT 3;13)
Huffcut, Ernest Wilson *see*
- AMERICAN CASES ON CONTRACT.
- CASES ON THE LAW OF AGENCY, INCLUDING THE LAW OF PRINCIPAL AND AGENT AND THE LAW OF MASTER AND SERVANT
- PRINCIPLES OF THE ENGLISH LAW OF CONTRACT AND OF AGENCY
Huffcut, Wilson *see* THE ELEMENTS OF BUSINESS LAW
Hug, Bernhard *see* ENTWICKLUNG EINES KOMBINIERTEN LASER-ELEKTRODEN-KATHETERS ZUR AV-KNOTEN-KOAGULATION BEI TACHYKARDEN RHYTHMUSSTOERUNGEN
Hug, Gall Joseph *see* DIE CHRISTLICHE FAMILIE
DIE HUGENOTTENKIRCHE – v17-45. 1964-92 (complete) – Inquire – 1 – ATLA S0467 – us A.T.L.A. [073]
Huggenberger, Alfred *see* DEM BOLLME SI BOES WUCHE
Huggon, Jim *see* SPEAKERS' CORNER
THE HUGH HUNT COLLECTION – (With printed guide) – 83mf – 9 – $266.00 – 1-869934-32-6 – uk Emmett [790]
HUGH SMYTHE PAPERS : FROM THE HOLDINGS OF THE SCHOMBURG CENTER FOR RESEARCH IN BLACK CULTURE, MANUSCRIPTS, ARCHIVES AND RARE BOOKS DIVISION: THE NEW YORK PUBLIC LIBRARY, ASTOR, LENOX AND TILDEN FOUNDATIONS – (Guide which covers all coll under "International Affairs" sold separately for $20.00 D3305.G5) – 1995 – 6r – 1 – $510.00 – D3305P15 – Dist. us Scholarly Res – us L of C Photodup [320]
Hughes, A *see*
- THE BEC MISSAL
- THE PORTIFORIUM OF ST WULSTAN
Hughes, Barry G *see*
- RAPID BIMANUAL MOVEMENT: EFFECTS OF DIRECTION CHANGES ON COORDINATION
- THE REPRESENTATION AND REPRODUCTION OF TWO-DIMENSIONAL MOVEMENT PATTERNS
Hughes, Charles Evans *see* MR. HUGHES' ATTITUDE TOWARD THE NEGRO
Hughes, Dorothea Price *see* THE LIFE OF HUGH PRICE HUGHES
Hughes, E R *see* CHINESE CHRISTIAN MONOGRAPH (CCC203)
Hughes, Edwin Holt *see* THE TEACHING OF CITIZENSHIP
Hughes, George *see* FRAGRANT MEMORIES OF THE TUESDAY MEETING: AND THE GUIDE TO HOLINESS,AND THEIR FIFTY YEARS' WORK FOR JESUS
Hughes, Griffith *see* THE NATURAL HISTORY OF BARBADOS
Hughes, Helen Sard *see* THE HISTORY OF THE NOVEL IN ENGLAND
Hughes, Hugh J *see* LIFE OF HOWELL HARRIS, THE WELSH REFORMER
Hughes, J C *see* DE LAGARDES AUSGABE DER ARABISCHEN UEBERSETZUNG DES PENTATEUCHS
Hughes, J E *see* EIGHTEEN YEARS ON LAKE BANGWEULU
Hughes, John *see* CONTROVERSY BETWEEN REV. MESSRS. HUGHES AND BRECKENRIDGE
Hughes, Kevin P *see* INFLUENCE OF CONCEPTUALLY BASED PHYSICAL EDUCATION ON STUDENT ATTITUDES TOWARD PHYSICAL ACTIVITY

HUGHES' KEY TO THE REVELATION : PARAGRAPHED WITH PROPER HEADINGS AND ILLUSTRATIVE DIAGRAMS AND AN ADDRESS ON THE APOSTOLATE OF THE REVELATION – [Holland, MI: J S Hughes], c1906 – 1mf – 9 – 0-8370-3687-9 – 1985-1687 – us A.T.L.A. [220]
Hughes, Langston *see* SIMPLE STAKES A CLAIM
Hughes, Nicholas Collin *see* GENESIS AND GEOLOGY: THE HARMONY OF THE SCRIPTURAL AND GEOLOGICAL RECORDS
Hughes, R M *see* THE DUTIES OF JUDGE ADVOCATES...
Hughes, R O *see* COMMUNITY CIVICS
Hughes, R W *see* HUGHES' REPORTS OF CASES IN THE FOURTH CIRCUIT, 1792-1883
HUGHES' REPORTS OF CASES IN THE FOURTH CIRCUIT, 1792-1883 / Hughes, R W – Washington/New York: Morrison/ Banks. v1-5. 1877-83 (all publ) – 36mf – 9 – $54.00 – LLMC 81-457 – us L.L.M.C. [340]
Hughes, T *see* THE FRIENDSHIP OF BOOKS AND OTHER LECTURES
Hughes, Thomas *see*
- JAMES FRASER, SECOND BISHOP OF MANCHESTER
- THE MANLINESS OF CHRIST

Hughes, Thomas P *see* AMERICAN ANCESTRY
Hughes, Thomas Welburn *see*
- CASES ON THE LAW OF EVIDENCE.
- AN ILLUSTRATED TREATISE ON THE LAW OF EVIDENCE
- SPRAGUE'S ILLUSTRATIVE CASES UPON THE LAW OF EVIDENCE

Hughes, William Taylor *see*
- EQUITY, ITS PRINCIPLES IN PROCEDURE, CODES AND PRACTICE ACTS.
- PROCEDURE, ITS THEORY AND PRACTICE

HUGHESVILLE MAIL – Hughsville, PA. -w 1900-1912 – 13 – $25.00r – us I.M.R. [071]
Hugi, Franz Joseph *see* UEBER DAS WESEN DER GLETSCHER: UND, WINTERREISE IN DAS EISMEER
HUGIDEO : EINE ALTE GESCHICHTE / Scheffel, Joseph Viktor von – 5. Aufl. Stuttgart: A Bonz, 1887 – 1r – 1 – us U.W. Library [830]
Hugle, Richard Friedrich *see* ZUR BUEHNENTECHNIK ADOLPH MUELLNERS
HUGO DE GROOT EN ZIJN RECHTSPHILOSOPHIE / Bertens, H – Tilburg, 1906 – 2mf – 9 – ILM-633/1 – ne IDC [327]
HUGO DE GROOT EN ZIJN RECHTSPHILOSPHIE / Bertens, H – Tilburg, 1906 – 2mf – ne IDC [340]
HUGO DE GROOTEN ZIJN GESLACHT / Oyen, A A Vorsterman van – Amsterdam, 1883 – 1mf – ne IDC [270]
HUGO GROTIUS... / Vreeland, H – New York, 1917 – 3mf – 9 – ILM-696/1 – ne IDC [270]
HUGO GROTIUS: VON DER FREIHEIT DES MEERES / ed by Boschan, R – Leipzig, 1919 – 1mf – 9 – ILM-2554/1 – ne IDC [327]
Hugo, H *see*
- L'AME AMANTE DE SON DIEU, REPRESENTEE DANS LES EMBLEMES DE HERMANNUS HUGO SUR SES PIEUX DESIRS
- GODDELYCKE WENSCHEN VERLICHT MET SINNEBEELDEN EN VIERIGE UYTSPRAKEN DER OUT-VADERS
- GODDELYCKEWENSCHEN. TRANS. BY J. DE HARDUYN. O 640. 1629
- DE GODLIEVENDE ZIEL VERTOONT IN ZINNEBEELDEN
- PIA DESIDERIA EMBLEMATIS, ELEGIIS ET AFFECTIBUS
- PIA DESIDERIA EMBLEMATIS ELEGIIS ET AFFECTIBUS SS. PATRUM
- PIA DESIDERIA. LIB. 3. AD URBANUM 8
- PIA DESIDERIA TRIBUS LIBRIS COMPREHENSA

Hugo, L C *see* LA VIE DE S. NORBERT, ARCHEVEQUE DE MAGDEBOURG ET FONDATEUR DE L'ORDRE DES CHANOINES PREMONTREZ
Hugo, Lud. *see*
- SACRAE ANTIQUITATIS MONUMENTA
- SACRI ET CANONICI ORDINIS PRAEMONSTRATENSIS ANNALES

Hugo, Victor *see* SELECTIONS, CHIEFLY LYRICAL, FROM THE POETICAL WORKS.
HUGO VON HOFMANNSTHAL : EINE LITERARISCHE STUDIE / Sulger-Gebing, Emil – (Includes bibliographical references. "Anhang. Chronologisches Verzeichnis der Dichtungen und Aufsatz Hugo von Hofmannsthals") – Leipzig: M Hesse, 1905 – 1r – 1 – us U.W. Library [430]
HUGO VON HOFMANNSTHAL'S GRIECHENSTUECKE : 1 [UND] 2 / Hladny, Ernst – (Includes bibliographical references) – Leoben: Im Verlag des k. k. Staatsgymnasiums in Leoben, 1910 – 1r – 1 – us U.W. Library [430]
HUGO VON HOFMANNSTHALS MYTHOLOGISCHE OPER "DIE AEGYPTISCHE HELENA" / Lenz, Eva-Maria – Frankfurt a.M., 1972 – 2mf – 9 – DM62.00 – 3-89349-743-9 – gw Hänsel [430]
HUGO VON HOFMANNSTHALS NACHGELASSENES LUSTSPIELFRAGMENT "DIE RHETORENSCHULE" ODER "TIMON DER REDNER" : LITERARISCHE UND HISTORISCHE HINTERGRUENDE / Fackert, Juergen – Frankfurt a.M., 1972 – 1mf – 9 – DM48.00 – 3-89349-665-3 – gw Hänsel [430]
Hugolin, Pere *see*
- ECHOS HEROI-COMIQUES DU NAUFRAGE DES ANGLAIS SUR L'ISLE-AUX-OEUFS EN 1711
- VICTOIRES ET CHANSONS

Hugolinus, B *see* THESAURUS ANTIQUITATUM SACRARUM
HUGONIS GROTII DE JURE BELLI AC PACIS LIBRI 3... / Groot, Hugo de – Parisii: apud N. Buon, 1625 – fr Armell [949]
Huguenot Society of South Carolina *see* TRANSACTIONS
THE HUGUENOTS AND HENRY OF NAVARRE / Baird, Henry Martyn – New York: Scribner, 1886 – 3mf – us A.T.L.A. [944]
THE HUGUENOTS AND THE REVOCATION OF THE EDICT OF NANTES / Baird, Henry Martyn – New York: Scribner, 1895 – 3mf – us A.T.L.A. [240]
THE HUGUENOTS; OR, REFORMED FRENCH CHURCH / Foote, William Henry – 1870 – 1 – us A.T.L.A. [240]
THE HUGUEONOTS / Punshon, William Moreley – 6th ed. London: James Nisbet, 1872. 76p – 1 – us U.W. Library [944]
Hugues, Clovis *see* POESIES CHOISIES
Hugues, Edmond *see*
- HISTOIRE DE LA RESTAURATION DU PROTESTANTISME EN FRANCE AU 18E SIECLE
- LEIBNIZ ET BOSSUET

Huguet, Jean A *see* TABLEAU DE SITUATION DU DEPARTEMENT DE L'ALLIER
Hui, Sai C *see* COMPARISON OF ACUTE HEART RATE AND BLOOD PRESSURE RESPONSES AMONG ISOMETRIC, ISOTONIC, AND ISOKINETIC EXERCISE
HUI-AN HSIEN HSU-CHIH – 1934-1833. 12. BCH-563 2 – 8 – ne IDC [950]
HUI-AN HSIEN-CHIH – 1936, 1803. 36, 1. BCH-562 2 – 8 – ne IDC [950]
HUI-CHOU FU-CHIH – 1687, 20, 1. BCH-606 2 – 8 – ne IDC [950]
Huidekoper, Frederic *see*
- INDIRECT TESTIMONY OF HISTORY TO THE GENUINENESS OF THE GOSPELS
- JUDAISM AT ROME

DE HUIDIGE STAND VAN HET NATIONALISME : VOORDRACHT GEHOUDEN OP DE INDONESISCHE CONFERENTIE TE HARDENBROEK, DEN 17EN APRIL 1929 – Neder-Langbroek, 1929 – 1mf – 9 – ne IDC [950]
Huigens, C *see* GHEBRUIK, EN ONGHEBRUIK VAN 'T ORGHEL, IN DE KERKEN DER VEREENIGHDE NEDERLANDEN
Huiginn, E J V *see* THE GRAVES OF MYLES STANDISH AND OTHER PILGRIMS
HUIPILS TZOTZILS ET LEURS DECORS / Lugnier, S – 9 – F30.00 – fr Ethnologie [306]
HET HUISELIK EN MAA SCHAPPELIK LEVEN VAN DE ZUID-AFRIKANER IN DE EERSTE HELFT DER 18DE EEUW / Dominicus, Foort Cornelius – Gravenhage, 1919 – 1 – us Res Libr [960]
HET HUISELIK EN MAATSCHAPPELIK LEVEN VAN SE ZUID-AFRIKANER IN DE EERSTE HELFT DER 18DE EEUW / Dominicus, F C – s Gravenhage, M Nijhoff, 1919 – us Res Libr [960]
DIE HUISGENOOT – Cape Town, South Africa. 1 May 1916-29 Dec 1950. 123 reels – 1, 16 diazo available at reduced price – sa SA Libr [073]
HUIT MOIS A MADAGASCAR / Rolland, J B – Marseille: T Samat, 1890 – 1 – us Res Libr [960]
HUIT MOIS AU CONGO / Maitrejean, Auguste – [Paris: Tolra, c1926, 1929] – 1 – us Res Libr [960]
HUIT MORCEAUX CHARACTERISTIQUES, OP. 36. CAHIER 1-3 / Moszkowski, M – Breslau: Hainauer, 186- – 1 – us Sibley [780]
HUIT SONATES A 2 FLUTES TRAVERSIERES ET BASSE, OP. 5 / Campioni, C – (Parts) – Paris: Vendome, ca 1770 – 1 – us Sibley [780]
LE HUITIEME QUODLIBET DE GODEFROID DE FONTAINES / Hoffmans, J – 1924 – 14mf – 8 – ne Slangenburg [100]
HUI-T'UNG HSIEN-CHIH – 1820, 10. BCH-639 2 – 8 – ne IDC [950]
HUKUM – Djakarta. Incomplete. SE-645 1. 1947-1958 – 9 – ne IDC [073]
HUKUM ATJARA PIDANA DI INDONESIA / Wirjono, Prodjodikoro – SE 4232 1. 1962 – 9 – ne IDC [950]
HUKUM DAN MASJARAKT – (Irregular) – Djakarta, 1960(1-6) – 5mf – 9 – SE-646/1 – ne IDC [950]
HUKUM ISLAM DAN MASJARAKAT / Hazairin – SE-4989 1. 1963 – 9 – ne IDC [950]
HUKUM LAUT BAGI INDONESIA / Wirjono, Prodjodikoro – SE 4696 1. 1963 – 9 – ne IDC [950]
HUKUM NIKAH, THALAK RUDJU' (N.T.R.) KU M. SA'ID / Said, M – In Sundanese, Partly in Arabic. SE 5437 1. 1960? – 9 – ne IDC [270]
HUKUM PEMBUKTIAN / Subekti – SE 5201 1. 1964 – 9 – ne IDC [950]
HUKUM PERDATA TENTANG PERSETUDJUAN2 TERTENTU / Wirjono, Prodjodikoro – SE 3967 1. 1959 – 9 – ne IDC [950]
Hul, Dick van den *see*
- DANCE COLLECTION
- EUROPEAN MUSICAL INSTRUMENTS ON PRINTS AND DRAWINGS
- FRENCH OPERA SCORES
- KEYBOARD MUSIC
- MUSIC FOR SOLO INSTRUMENT AND ENSEMBLE
- OPERA COLLECTION
- PORTRAITS OF COMPOSERS AND MUSICIANS

HULASATUE'L-EFKAR – (Nos. 3-66 (13 Haziran-25 Agustos 1289[1873])) – Istanbul: Sahib-i Imtiyaz: Antuvan, Umur-i Tahiriyye: Luefti, 1873-1874 – 5mf – 9 – $75.00 – us MEDOC [949]
Hulbert, Henry Woodward *see* THE CHURCH AND HER CHILDREN
Hulbert, J Jr *see* THE COMPLETE FIFER'S MUSEUM
HULDA A. REES: THE PENTECOSTAL PROPHETESS / Rees, Byron Johnson – 1898 – 9 – us A.T.L.A. [240]
HULDE ALBUM / Vanderheyden, J F – Leuven, 1970 – Dfl22.00 – ne Slangenburg [240]
HULDREICH ZWINGLI UND SEIN REFORMATIONSWERK : ZUM VIERHUNDERTJAEHRIGEN GEBURTSTAGE ZWINGLIS / Staehelin, Rudolf – Halle: Verein fuer Reformationsgeschichte, 1883. ([Schriften des Vereins fuer Reformationsgeschichte; Bd. 3]) – 1mf – us A.T.L.A. [240]
HULL 1630-1849 – (Mf 1T: Intentions & Marriages 1686-1843; Births & Deaths 1630-1734. Mf 2T: Births 1731-1843; Marriages 1808-43; Deaths 1693-1844. Mf 3T: Vital Records 1833-49) – (mf ed 1996) – 3mf – 9 – 0-87623-271-3 – us Holbrook [920]
HULL 1630-1900 – (Mf 1-2: Land Grants 1657-1841. Mf 3: B,D,M 1630-1757; Intents & Marriages 1696-1843. Mf 4: Births & Deaths 1693-1749, 1771-1863; Town Records 1666-1734+; Deaths 1691, 1749-66. Mf 5-9: Town Records 1675-1788. Mf 10-11: Births 1842-92. Mf 11-13: Marriages 1843-92. Mf 13-16: Deaths 1843-1905. Mf 17: Marriages 1892-1900. Mf 18: Births 1892-1900)) – (mf ed 1990) – 18mf – 9 – 0-87623-117-2 – us Holbrook [920]
THE HULL ADVERTISER – Hull, Canada. v1 n51. 13 fev 1874 – 1r – 1 – Can$20.00 – cn Can Microfilming [072]
Hull, Augustus Longstreet *see* ANNALS OF ATHENS, GEORGIA, 1801-1901
Hull. Central Library *see* WHALING LOG BOOKS: EARLY 19TH
Hull, Cordell *see* THE MEMOIRS OF CORDELL HULL
Hull, David William *see* THE RIVERSIDE PREACHERS: MODELS FOR PREACHING PEACE
Hull, Hannah Clothier *see* THE PAPERS OF HANNAH CLOTHIER HULL, 1889-1958
Hull, John ST *see* CENSUS OF IOWA FOR 1836-1880
HULL MATIN : QUOTIDIEN – Hull, Canada. 7 sep 1965-v1 n25. 5 oct 1965 – 1r – 1 – Can$40.00 – cn Can Microfilming [072]
HULL PACKET – England. -w. 29 Jan 1793; 7 Jan 1800-Dec 1886 (Wanting 1802, 1820-22, 1824, 1825) (1880-88 imperfect). (71 reels) – 1 – uk British Libr Newspaper [072]
HULL'S CRUCIBLE – Boston, MA, 1 Jan 1874-10 Nov 1877 – 1 reel – 1 – us Western Res [071]
Hulme, Edward Maslin *see* THE RENAISSANCE, THE PROTESTANT REVOLUTION AND THE CATHOLIC REFORMATION IN CONTINENTAL EUROPE
Huloet, Richard *see* ABCEDARIUM ANGLICO LATINUM
Hulshof, Abraham *see* GESCHIEDENIS VAN DE DOOPSGEZINDEN TE STRAATSBURG VAN 1525 TO 1557
Hulshof, Franz *see* ALBAN STOLZ IN SEINER ENTWICKLUNG ALS SCHRIFTSTELLER
Hulsius, B *see*
- EMBLEMATA SACRA. S.L.1631
- DEN ONDERGANCK DES ROOMSCHEN ARENTS

Hulsius, Levinus *see*
- DICTIONAIRE FRANCOIS ALLEMAND ET ALLEMAND FRANCOIS; DICTIONARIUM TEUTSCH FRANTZOESISCH UND FRANTZOESISCH TEUTSCH (AEL, ABT.5;5)
- DICTIONARIUM TEUTSCH-ITALIAENISCH UND ITALIAENISCH-TEUTSCH (AEL, ABT.2;7)
- DICTIONNAIRE FRANCOIS-ALEMAND ET ALEMAND-FRANCOIS

Hulstaert, G *see*
- LE MARIAGE DES NKUNDO
- LES SANCTIONS COUTUMIERE CONTRE L'ADULTERE CHEZ LES NKUNDO

Hultin, M *see* SKILL DEVELOPMENT FOR SELF RELIANCE
HULTSCHINER ZEITUNG – Hultschin (Hlucin), Czechoslovakia. 30 Apr-21 Dec 1938 – 1r – 1 – gw Mikrofilm [072]
Hultzch, E *see* THE MEGHADUTA KALIDASA
THE HUM OF THE COLLEGE – [Sackville, N.S.]: Mt Allison Ladies' College Rhetoric Class, [1894?-189- or 1900] – 9 – cn C.I.H.M. [370]
HUMAN AND PEOPLES' RIGHTS IN AFRICA AND THE AFRICAN CHARTER (1985 NAIROBI SEMINAR) – 1986 – sz I.C.J. [320]
HUMAN AWARENESS PROGRAMME (HAP) – Grant Park. 150 docs. 1982-1990 – 121mf – 9 – ne IDC [320]
HUMAN BEHAVIOR – v. 1-8. 1972-79 – 1,5,6,9 – us UMI [150]
HUMAN BIOLOGY – (v. 37- 1965- 5,6. v. 42- 1970- 9) – v. 1- 1929- – 1 – us UMI [611]
HUMAN COMMUNICATION RESEARCH – v. 1- 1974- – 1. ; 5,6,9 – apply; v.3- – us UMI [150]
HUMAN DEVELOPMENT – v1-. 1958- – 1,5,9 – us UMI [073]
HUMAN ECOLOGY – v1-22. 1972-94 – 1,5 – $80.00v – us UMI [304]
HUMAN ELEMENT IN THE INSPIRATION OF THE SACRED SCRIPTURES / Curtis, Thomas F – New York: D. Appleton, 1867. 1 fiche – 9 – us A.T.L.A. [240]
HUMAN EVENTS : A WEEKLY ANALYSIS FOR THE AMERICAN CITIZEN – Washington, DC. v1-19, 27-30. 1944-62, 1967-70 – 237mf – 9 – $5.00f – us Ross [073]
HUMAN EXPERIMENTATION : FEDERAL LAWS, LEGISLATIVE HISTORIES, REGULATIONS AND RELATED DOCUMENTS / ed by Reams, Bernard D & Gray, Carol – (Binder + current index $125.00; Release 1.-9. $375.00; Release 2.-9. $375.00; Release 1.-1. $250.00; Release 2.-1. $250.00) – 6r with 1 looseleaf binder or 150mf with 1 looseleaf binder – 1,9 – us Trans-Media [340]
Human Factors Society. Annual Meeting *see* PROCEEDINGS
HUMAN GENETICS – v. 1-57. 1964-80 – 1,5,9 – 12,264.00 – us UMI [073]
HUMAN HEREDITY – v25-. 1975- – 1,5,9 – us UMI [573]
HUMAN IMMUNOLOGY – v1-11. 1980-84 – 1,5,6,13 – sz Elsevier [073]

HUMAN INFLUENCES IN AFRICAN PASTURELAND ENVIRONMENTS, WITH SPECIAL REFERENCE TO THE ARID AND SEMIARID PASTORAL REGIONS OF EASTERN AFRICA – 1980 – 102p – it F.A.O. [630]
HUMAN LEARNING – 1982- – 1,5,6,9 – us UMI [370]
HUMAN LIFE – Boston. v. 1-13 no. 5. Apr 1905-Aug 1911 – 1 – us NY Public [073]
HUMAN LIFE – Boston. v1-13. 1905-11 – 1r – 1 – us Ross [073]
HUMAN LIFE : A POEM / Rogers, Samuel – London: J. Murray, 1819 – 1 roll – 1 – 1-55879-342-9 – uk Libr Preservation [810]
HUMAN LIFE REVIEW – (v.5 .1979 5,6,9) – v.1. 1975- – 1 – us UMI [073]
HUMAN MOSAIC – (v.13 .1979 5,6,9) – v.1. 1966 – 1 – us UMI [073]
THE HUMAN MOTOR / Amar, Jules – 1920 – 10mf – 9 – $30.00 – us Microform Publ [600]
HUMAN NEEDS AND SATISFACTIONS : A GLOBAL SURVEY – 2r – 1 – $170.00 – S1857 – us Scholarly Res [150]
HUMAN NUTRITION IN TROPICAL AFRICA / Latham, M C – rev ed 1980 – 268p – it F.A.O. [640]
HUMAN ORGANIZATION – v. 1-. 1941- – 1. – apply; v.37- 1978- 5,6,9 – us UMI [300]
HUMAN PHYSIOLOGY – v1-19. 1975-93 – 1,5 – $80.00v – us UMI [612]
HUMAN POPULATION PROBLEMS IN THE BIOSPHERE : SOME RESEARCH STRATEGIES AND DESIGNS / ed by Baker, Paul – 1977 – 82p – 9 – 92-3-101482-X – fr UNESCO [304]
HUMAN PROGRESS THROUGH MISSIONS / Barton, James Levi – New York: Fleming H. Revell, c1912 – 1mf – us A.T.L.A. [240]
HUMAN RELATIONS – (v27-47 1974-94 $150.00v) – v1-26. 1948-73 – 1,5 – $60.00v – us UMI [300]
Human Relations Area Files *see*
- AREA STUDIES PROGRAM
- COMPLETE ARCHIVE PROGRAM
- CULTURAL DIVERSITY PROGRAM
- CULTURAL TYPES PROGRAM
- HRAF PROBABILITY SAMPLE PROGRAM-PART A
- HRAF TOPICAL PROGRAM
- TRADITIONAL CULTURES OF THE WORLD PROGRAM

HUMAN RESOURCE – (Ceased v7 no 3 1991) – Don Mills. v1-7. 1983-1990/91 – 9 – Can$20.00y – cn Micromedia [333]
HUMAN RESOURCE DEVELOPMENT IN INDONESIA; PROBLEMS, POLICIES, PROGRAMS / U.S. AID Mission to Indonesia. Employment and Manpower Advisor – SE 11,235 1. 1964 – 9 – ne IDC [331]
HUMAN RESOURCE MANAGEMENT – v1-23. 1961-84 – 1,5,6 – us Princeton Micro [650]
HUMAN RESOURCES AND THE APPLICATION OF SCIENCE AND TECHNOLOGY IN THE DEVELOPING AREAS / Sadarjun, Siswomartojo – SE 5613 1. 1962 – 9 – ne IDC [500]
HUMAN RESPONSE TO FROST HAZARDS IN THE ORCHARD INDUSTRY : OKANAGAN VALLEY, BRITISH COLUMBIA / Boyer, Jeanette C – 1977 – 207p – 9 – $7.00 set – cn Geography [631]
HUMAN RIGHTS – Portland OR. Nov 1934 – 1 – us U.O. Library [071]
HUMAN RIGHTS : QUESTIONS AND ANSWERS – 2nd rev ed 1990 – 9 – 92-3-102509-0 – fr UNESCO [320]
HUMAN RIGHTS (ABA) – v1-19. 1970-1992 – 9 – $125.00 set – us Hein [340]
HUMAN RIGHTS (ABA) – v1-20. 1970-93 – 1,5,6 – $225.00 – us Hein [073]
HUMAN RIGHTS ADVOCACY IN THE PHILIPPINES – 1985 – sz I.C.J. [320]
HUMAN RIGHTS AND MENTAL PATIENTS IN JAPAN – 1986 – sz I.C.J. [350]
HUMAN RIGHTS AND SCIENTIFIC AND TECHNOLOGICAL DEVELOPMENT / ed by Weeramantry, C G – 9 – $14.00 – 92-808-0731-5 – ja U.N. Univ [320]
HUMAN RIGHTS BULLETINS : NOS.9 – 35 / United Nations. Commission on Human Rights – 1973-1982 – E.40 F.41 R.22 S.38 – 9 – us U.N. Pubs [320]
HUMAN RIGHTS COMMISSION – Johannesburg. 47 docs. 1988-1990 – 20mf – 9 – ne IDC [320]
HUMAN RIGHTS COMMISSION – Johannesburg. 75 docs. 1988-1991 – 37mf – 9 – ne IDC [320]
HUMAN RIGHTS DOCUMENTS 1991 – (Includes detailed, printed guide. Individual titles available, also listed separately) – 1,195mf – 9 – ne IDC [320]
HUMAN RIGHTS, EUROPEAN POLITICS, AND THE HELSINKI ACCORD : THE DOCUMENTARY EVOLUTION OF THE CONFERENCE ON SECURITY AND CO-OPERATION IN EUROPE 1973-1975 / Kavass, Igor I & Granier, Jacqueline P & Dominick, Mary F – 7v – 9 – $100.00 – us Hein [320]
HUMAN RIGHTS IN A WORLD FEDERATION / Breitner, Thomas C – 1967, 5 sections – 9 – 1.00f – at Libertarian Micro [335]
HUMAN RIGHTS IN GHANA – 1985 – sz I.C.J. [320]
HUMAN RIGHTS IN GUATEMALA – 1979 – sz I.C.J. [320]
HUMAN RIGHTS IN NICARAGUA : YESTERDAY AND TODAY – 1980 – sz I.C.J. [320]
HUMAN RIGHTS IN SURINAME – 1983 – sz I.C.J. [320]
HUMAN RIGHTS IN URBAN AREAS – 1983 – 9 – 92-3-101983-X – fr UNESCO [320]
HUMAN RIGHTS INTERNET / ed by Wiseberg, Laurie – (Includes printed guide. Suppl 1989-90 doc 65-73 24mf Dfl216.00. Suppl 1991 doc 74-75 6mf Dfl54.00) – Cambridge. 1980-91 – 12,309mf – 9 – ne IDC [320]
HUMAN RIGHTS NETWORK – London. 58 docs. 1979-1990 – 25mf – 9 – ne IDC [320]
HUMAN RIGHTS QUARTERLY – (Separate parts available. Includes printed guide) – Baltimore. 52 docs. 1979-91 – 88mf – 9 – ne IDC [340]
HUMAN RIGHTS REVIEW – Monrovia: [s.n.], jun 1993-nov/dec 1994 – 1r – 1 – us Res Libr [073]
HUMAN RIGHTS, THE HELSINKI ACCORDS AND THE UNITED STATES : SELECTED EXECUTIVE AND CONGRESSIONAL DOCUMENTS / ed by Kavass, Igor I & Granier, Jacquelin P – Series 1-3 in 9bks – 9 – $198.00 set – 0-89941-466-4 – us Hein [324]
HUMAN RIGHTS WATCH – (Formerly the Watch Committees) – New York, Washington DC. 75 docs. 1984-1991 – 62mf – 9 – ne IDC [320]
HUMAN SERVICES IN THE RURAL ENVIRONMENT – v.1-3. 1976-78 – 1,5,6,9 – us UMI [073]
HUMAN SOCIETY : ITS PROVIDENTIAL STRUCTURE, RELATIONS, AND OFFICES / Huntington, Frederic Dan – (Includes bibliographical references) – New York:Robert Carter, 1860, c1859 – 1mf – 9 – 0-8370-4509-6 – 1985-2509 – us A.T.L.A. [230]
HUMAN SYSTEMS MANAGEMENT – v1-4. 1980-84 – 1,5,6,13 – sz Elsevier [650]
HUMAN TORCH – Issue Nos. 11-15 Spring 1943-Spring 1944 – 5mf – 15 – $31,95 – us Comics [760]
HUMAN TORCH – Issue Nos. 16-20 Fall 1944-Fall 1945 – 5mf – 15 – $31,95 – us Comics [760]
HUMAN TORCH – Issue Nos. 21-25 Winter 45-46-Winter 46-47 – 5mf – 15 – $31,95 – us Comics [760]
HUMAN TORCH – Issue Nos. 6-10 Winter 1942-Winter 1942-43 – 5mf – 15 – $31,95 – us Comics [760]
HUMAN TORCH – (No. 1 not published, two issues of No. 5) – Issue Nos. + 2-5 Fall 1940-Fall 1941 – 5mf – 15 – $31,95 – us Comics [760]
HUMAN TOXICOLOGY – v1-. 1981- – 1,5,6,9 – us UMI [073]
THE HUMAN TRAGEDY / Austin, Alfred – Edinburgh, London: Macmillan, 1876 – 1 roll – 1 – 1-55879-397-6 – uk Libr Preservation [820]
HUMAN TRAITS OF CHARACTER: IN RHYME / Crouter, John Wesley – London, Ont.: s.n., 1885 (London, Ont.: Free Press Print. Co.). 02225. (Pre-1900 Canadiana) – 9 – cn C.I.H.M. [810]
HUMANISM IN 16TH CENTURY ZURICH / ed by Buesser, F – 1994 in 2 installments – 731mf – 9 – ne IDC [700]
HUMANISM IN POLAND PAMPHLET COLLECTION – 1968 – 1 – CSUXANR0938-B – us Hoover Inst Photo [140]
EL HUMANISMO JUSTICIALISTA EN LA ERA TECNOTRONICA / Figuerola, Francisco Jose – Buenos Aires: Ediciones Tematica, 1983 – 1 – CSUXAJB7807-B – us Hoover Inst Photo [360]
EL HUMANISMO Y LA MORAL DE JUAN PABLO SARTRE (CRITICA) / Frutos Cortes, Eugenio – sp Bibl Santa Ana [120]
DER HUMANIST – 1973-91 (complete) – 7r – 1 – ATLA S0752 – us A.T.L.A. [240]
HUMANIST – v1- 1941 1; v31 5,6; v35 9 – us UMI [140]
HUMANITAET UND HUMANISMUS. ERSTER THEIL : GRUNDZUEGE EINER KULTURGESCHICHTE / Weiss, Albert Maria – (Includes bibliographical references) – Freiburg i.B.; St Louis, MO: Herder, 1879 – 3mf – 9 – 0-8370-7352-9 – 1986-1352 – us A.T.L.A. [230]
HUMANITAET UND RELIGION : EINE VON DER GESELLSCHAFT ZUR VERTHEIDIGUNG DER CHRISTLICHEN RELIGION GEKROENTE PREISSCHRIFT / Hartmann, Julius – Leiden: E J Brill, 1873 – 1mf – 9 – 0-8370-3511-2 – 1985-1511 – us A.T.L.A. [200]
L'HUMANITAIRE – Organe de la science sociale. no. 1-2. Paris. juil-aout 1841 – 1 – fr A.C.R.P.P. [073]
HUMANITAS – Berlin, jan 11 1962-89 – 13r – 1 – Dist. gw Mikrofilm – gw Misc Inst [072]
HUMANITAS INTERNATIONAL – Menlo Park. 40 docs. 1980-1990 – 8mf – 9 – ne IDC [320]
LA HUMANITAT – Montpelier and Paris. France. -w. 6 Jun 1946-25 Dec 1948, 17 Feb 1949-Mar 1952. (33 ft) – 1 – uk British Libr Newspaper [072]
L'HUMANITE – 1988- – 3r per y – 5 – inquire – us Ross [072]
L'HUMANITE / Communist Party. France – Paris, 1904-14, 1917, 1920, 1936-44, 1951-55, 1966-77, 1978-90 – 1 – $35.00r – us Hoover Inst Photo [335]
L'HUMANITE : JOURNAL SOCIALISTE QUOTIDIEN – Paris: Fond. J Jaures, 1904-1914 – 1 – fr A.C.R.P.P. [072]
L'HUMANITE – Paris: Imprimerie des arts et manufactures, 1949-55; 1956-69 – us Res Libr [072]
HUMANITE – 1904-1994 – 1 – sz Infoprint [072]
HUMANITE – 1988-1995 – 3r per y – 5,6 – Sfr1,123.00 – sz Infoprint [944]
HUMANITE – 1995 – 1 – F5,500.00 – sz Infoprint [072]
L'HUMANITE-DIMANCHE / Communist Party. France – Paris. oct 1948-1993 – 1 – fr A.C.R.P.P. [073]
HUMANITIES – v.1. 1980 – 1 – us UMI [073]
HUMANITIES COLLECTIONS / ed by Kinder, Robin – v1 n1. 1997- – 1,9 – $65.00 in US $91.00 outside hardcopy subsc – us Haworth [073]
HUMANITIES JOURNAL – v. 1-. 1967- – 1. – apply; v.9- 1975- 5,6,9 – us UMI [000]
HUMANITY : ITS DESTINY AND THE MEANS TO ATTAIN IT: A SERIES OF DISCOURSES / Denifle, Heinrich – Ratisbon, New York: Fr. Pustet, 1909 – 1mf – us A.T.L.A. [240]
THE HUMANITY, BENEVOLENCE AND CHARITY LEGISLATION OF THE PENTATEUCH AND THE TALMUD / Fluegel, Maurice – Baltimore: H. Fluegel, 1908. 1 fiche – 9 – us A.T.L.A. [220]
HUMANITY IMMORTAL, OR, MAN TRIED, FALLEN, AND REDEEMED / Hickok, Laurens P – Boston: Lee and Shepard, 1872 – 1mf – us A.T.L.A. [240]
HUMANITY'S GAIN FROM UNBELIEF / Bradlaugh, Charles – 1929. 1 fiche (24x) – 9 – 1.00f – at Libertarian Micro [320]
HUMANIZING CITY LIFE – (See also: Doing It) – n. 9. 1978 – 1,5,6,9 – us UMI [300]
HUMANIZING PUBLIC ORGANIZATIONS / Golembiewski, Robert – 1985. 377p. ISBN-0-912338-44-X – 9 – 16.50 – us Lomond [323]
HUMAYTHAENSE – Rio Madeira/Humaytha, Amazonas. 3 Set 1891; Ago-Nov 1892; Mar 1893; Jan-Abr, Jun-Out 1894; Mar, Maio, Jul-Ago 1895; Jan-Abr, Jul-Out 1897; Mar, Dez 1898; Mar, Maio, Jul 1899; Mar, Jul 1900; Jan, Jun-Jul 1902; Jan-Fev, Jun, Ago-Nov 1903; 1904; Jan-Maio, Ago, Dez 1905; Ago, Out-Dez 1906; Jan-Out, Dez 1907; Jan-Mar, Maio Dez 1908; Jan-Dez 1909; Jan-Maio, Ago-Dez 1910; Fev-Mar 1911; Out 1916-22 Jul 1917 – 1,5,6 – bl Biblioteca [072]
Humbert, Aime *see* LE JAPON ILLUSTRE
Humbert, J *see* NOUVEAU GLOSSAIRE GENEVOIS
Humbertclaude, P *see* LA DOCTRINE ASCETIQUE DE SAINT BASILE DE CESAREE
A HUMBLE OVERTURE FOR METHODIST UNIFICATION IN THE DOMINION OF CANADA / Carroll, John – Toronto: J. Carroll, 18?? 00145. (Pre-1900 Canadiana) – 9 – cn C.I.H.M. [240]
Humboldt, Alejandro de *see* ENSAYO POLITICO SOBRE EL REINO DE LA NUEVA ESPANA
Humboldt, Alexander von *see*
- BRIEFE VON ALEXANDER VON HUMBOLDT AN VARNHAGEN VON ENSE AUS DEN JAHREN 1827 BIS 1858
- DE DISTRIBUTIONE GEOGRAPHICA PLANTARUM
- ESSAI SUR LA GEOGRAPHIE DES PLANTES
- FLORAE FIBERGENSIS SPECIMEN
- HERBARIUM
- HUMBOLDT CENTENNIAL. BOUND NEWSPAPER CLIPPINGS CONCERNING THE PROCEEDINGS IN VARIOUS CITIES IN THE UNITED STATES
- HUMBOLDT-PERLEN
- KOSMOS. ENTWURF EINER PHYSISCHEN WELTBESCHREIBUNG
- LETTRES AMERICAINES: 1798-1807
- POLITICAL ESSAY ON THE KINGDOM OF NEW SPAIN
- SYNOPSIS PLANTARUM, QUAS IN ITINERE AD PLAGAM AEQUINOCTIALEM ORBIS NOVI
- VOYAGE AUX REGIONS EQUINOCTIALES DU NOUVEAU CONTINENT
- VOYAGE AUX REGIONS EQUINOXIALES DU NOUVEAU CONTINENT
- VOYAGE AUX REGIONS EQUINOXIALES DU NOUVEAU CONTINENT, FAIT DANS LES ANNEES 1799-1804

Humboldt, Alexander von et al *see* VOYAGE AUX REGIONS EQUINOCTIALES DU NOUVEAU CONTINENT, FAIT EN 1799-1804
HUMBOLDT BAY REGION, 1850-1895 : A STUDY IN AMERICAN COLONIZATION OF CALIFORNIA / Coy, Owen C – Eureka, CA: California Hist Assn – 1r – 1 – $50.00 – B40221 – us Library Micro [978]
HUMBOLDT BEACON AND FORTUNA ADVANCE – Fortuna, CA. 1907- – 63+ r – 1 – $3,150.00 ($120.00y) – C02246 – us Library Micro [071]
HUMBOLDT BEACON AND FORTUNA ADVANCE – Fortuna. Calif. -w. 1948-67 – 1 – us UMI [071]
HUMBOLDT CENTENNIAL. BOUND NEWSPAPER CLIPPINGS CONCERNING THE PROCEEDINGS IN VARIOUS CITIES IN THE UNITED STATES / Humboldt, Alexander von – 1869. 2v – 1 – us U.W. Library [574]
HUMBOLDT COUNTY – 1908-33; 1992- – 28+ r – 1 – $1,400.00 – P00036 – us Library Micro [910]
HUMBOLDT COUNTY BULLETIN – Winnemucca. Nev. 1962-1964 – 1 – us UMI [071]
HUMBOLDT COUNTY BULLETIN – Winnemucca, NV. 1961-1972 – 10r – 1 – $500.00 – N04812 – us Library Micro [071]
HUMBOLDT COUNTY INCLUDING EUREKA – Humboldt Co, CA. 1895-1896; 1926-1950 – 16r – 1 – $800.00 – D039 – us Library Micro [978]
HUMBOLDT DAILY STANDARD *see* HUMBOLDT STANDARD
HUMBOLDT ENTERPRISE – Humboldt, NE. -w. Feb-Aug 1887, scattered issues missing; Jan 1888-Jul 1889; May-Jul 1892, scattered issues missing; Oct 1895-Jun 1905 – 1 – us NE Hist [071]
HUMBOLDT INDEPENDENT – (Also known as: Independent and Sun) – Rio Dell, CA. 1967-1970 – 2r – 1 – $100.00 – B02701 – us Library Micro [071]
HUMBOLDT INDEPENDENT NEWS *see* NORTH COAST RIPSAW; RANK AND FILE REPORTER; HUMBOLDT INDEPENDENT NEWS
HUMBOLDT INDEPENDENT (RIO DELL) – Eureka, CA. May 1967-1970 – 2r – 1 – $100.00 – B02212 – us Library Micro [071]
HUMBOLDT, LAKE, MARIN, MENDOCINO, NAPA, SOLANO, SONOMA AND YOLO COUNTIES – Humboldt Co, CA. 1884-1886 – 3r – 1 – $150.00 – D038 – us Library Micro [978]
HUMBOLDT, LAKE, MARIN, MENDOCINO, NAPA, SOLANO, SONOMA AND YOLO COUNTIES – Lake Co, CA. 1884-1886 – 3r – 1 – $150.00 – D038 – us Library Micro [978]
HUMBOLDT, LAKE, MARIN, MENDOCINO, NAPA, SOLANO, SONOMA AND YOLO COUNTIES – Marin Co, CA. 1884-1886 – 3r – 1 – $150.00 – D038 – us Library Micro [978]

HUMBOLDT, LAKE, MARIN, MENDOCINO, NAPA, SOLANO, SONOMA AND YOLO COUNTIES – Mendocino Co, CA. 1884-1886 – 3r – 1 – $150.00 – D038 – us Library Micro [978]
HUMBOLDT, LAKE, MARIN, MENDOCINO, NAPA, SOLANO, SONOMA AND YOLO COUNTIES – Solano Co, CA. 1884-1886 – 3r – 1 – $150.00 – D038 – us Library Micro [978]
HUMBOLDT, LAKE, MARIN, MENDOCINO, NAPA, SOLANO, SONOMA AND YOLO COUNTIES – Sonoma Co, CA. 1884-1886 – 3r – 1 – $150.00 – D038 – us Library Micro [978]
HUMBOLDT, LAKE, MARIN, MENDOCINO, NAPA, SOLANO, SONOMA AND YOLO COUNTIES – Yolo Co, CA. 1884-1886 – 3r – 1 – $150.00 – D038 – us Library Micro [978]
HUMBOLDT LIFE AND TIMES – Eureka, CA. Oct 1976-1980 – 3r – 1 – $135.00 – B02218 – us Library Micro [071]
HUMBOLDT NATIONAL – Winnemucca, NV. Aug-Oct 1869 – 1r – 1 – $50.00 – U04813 – us Library Micro [071]
HUMBOLDT NEWS – Humboldt, NE. -w. May 1897-Dec 1900; Apr 1901-Jan 1902; Mar-Sep 1902; Mar 1908-Jan 1923 – 1 – us NE Hist [071]
HUMBOLDT REGISTER – Unionville, NV. 1866-70; Jan-Nov 1876 – 2r – 1 – $100.00 – U04776 – us Library Micro [071]
HUMBOLDT REGISTER – Winnemucca, NV. 1866-70; 28 Jan, 11 Nov 1876 – 2r – 1 – $100.00 – U04814 – us Library Micro [071]
HUMBOLDT SEMI-WEEKLY STANDARD – Eureka, CA. 1899-1905 – 3r – 1 – $135.00 – B02220 – us Library Micro [071]
HUMBOLDT STANDARD – (Also known as: Humboldt Daily Standard) – Eureka, CA. 1884-1939; 1948-51 – 144r – 1 BC02219 – $7,200.00 – us Library Micro [071]
HUMBOLDT STANDARD – Eureka. Calif. 1952-1967 – 1 – us UMI [071]
HUMBOLDT STANDARD – Humboldt, NE. -w. Oct 1884-Aug 1888; Jun 1892; Oct 1893-Sep 1898; Jan 1899-Dec 1900; Apr 1901-Aug 1902; Mar 1908 to date – 1 – us NE Hist [071]
HUMBOLDT STANDARD – Winnemucca, NV. Feb-Sep 1903 – 1r – 1 – $50.00 – U04815 – us Library Micro [071]
HUMBOLDT STAR – Winnemucca. Nev. 1949- – 1 – us UMI [071]
HUMBOLDT STAR *see* STAR
HUMBOLDT SUN – Winnemucca, NV. 1972 – 32+ r – 1 – $1,600.00 ($90.00y) – U04816 – us Library Micro [071]
HUMBOLDT TIMES – Eureka. Calif. 1950-1967 – 1 – us UMI [071]
THE HUMBOLDT TIMES – Eureka, CA. 1854-1908 – 12r – 1 – $600.00 – B02221 – us Library Micro [071]
HUMBOLDT WEEKLY STANDARD – Eureka, CA. 1888-98 – 2r – 1 – $100.00 – B02222 – us Library Micro [071]
Humboldt, Wilhelm, Freiherr von *see*
- ANSICHTEN UEBER AESTHETIK UND LITERATUR
- THE LIMITS OF THE EFFECTIVENESS OF THE STATE
- DER STAAT, IDEEN ZU EINEM VERSUCH DIE GRENZEN DER WIRKSAMKEIT DES STAATES ZU BESTIMMEN

HUMBOLDT-PERLEN : EIN DEMANTKRANZ AUS ALEXANDER VON HUMBOLDT'S LEBEN UND SCHRIFTEN – NEBST EINER CHRONOLOGISCHEN UEBERSICHT SEINES LEBENS, EINEM VERZEICHNIS SEINER ZAHLREICHEN WERKE UND EINEM PORTRAET A. V. HUMBOLDT'S NACH DEM VON IHM SELBST ENTWORFENEN SPIEGELBILDE / Humboldt, Alexander von – Leipzig: E Wartig, 1869 – 1r – 1 – us U.W. Library [920]
HUMBOLDTY, LAKE, MARIN, MENDOCINO, NAPA, SOLANO, SONOMA AND YOLO COUNTIES – Napa Co, CA. 1884-1886 – 3r – 1 – $150.00 – D038 – us Library Micro [978]
HUMBUG – Melbourne, 1869-70 – 1r – 1 – A$31.00 silver A$27.00 vesicular – at Pascoe [072]
HUME / Huxley, Thomas Henry – New York: Harper & Brothers, 1879. vi,206p. (English Men of Letters) – 1 – us U.W. Library [920]
Hume, A O *see*
- MY SCRAP BOOK OR ROUGH NOTES ON INDIAN OOLOGY AND ORNITHOLOGY
- THE NESTS AND EGGS OF INDIAN BIRDS

Hume, Alexander *see* GRAMMATICA NOVA IN USUM JUVENTUTIS SCOTICAE
Hume, Allan O *see*
- THE GAME BIRDS OF INDIA, BURMA AND CEYLON
- THE GAME BIRDS OF INDIA, BURMAH AND CEYLON

Hume, David *see* THE HISTORY OF ENGLAND FROM THE INVASION OF JULIUS CAESAR TO THE ABDICATION OF JAMES THE SECOND, 1688
Hume, Robert Allen *see* MISSIONS FROM THE MODERN VIEW
Hume, Rolando *see* SUBLEVACION EN CURUZ U CUATIA
HUME STUDIES – London. v1-19. 1975-93 – 9 – Can$20.00y – cn Micromedia [073]
HUME, WITH HELPS TO THE STUDY OF BERKELEY : ESSAYS / Huxley, Thomas Henry – New York: D. Appleton and Company, 1896 – 319p. 1r – 1 – us U.W. Library [190]
Humes, Thomas W *see* THE LOYAL MOUNTAINEERS OF TENNESSEE
DIE HUMMEL : WOCHENBLATT FUER EINWANDERER – New York. Mar-Apr 1851 – 1r – 1 – gw Mikrofilm [071]
HUMMELSTOWN SUN – Hummelstown, PA. -w 1895-1959 – 13 – $25.00r – us I.M.R. [071]
HUMMER – Holmesville, NE. -w. Apr 1902-Jan 1903 – 1 – us NE Hist [071]
HUMMING BIRD : A MONTHLY SCIENTIFIC, ARTISTIC, AND INDUSTRIAL REVIEW – London, 1891-1894. v1-4 – 14mf – 9 – Z-2020/2 – ne IDC [500]
HUMOR E IRONIA EN LA OBRA DE THEOPHILE GAUTIER / Fernandez Sanchez, Ma Carmen – 2mf – 9 – Pta1,500.00 – 84-85422-77-5 – sp Pentalfa [440]
HUMORADAS / Sanchez-Arjona, Vicente – Sevilla: Graficas Sevillanas, 1951 – 1 – sp Bibl Santa Ana [810]
HUMORBUCH : DEUTSCHE DICHTER AUS FUENF JAHRHUNDERTEN / ed by Riess, Richard – Muenchen: G Mueller, 1918 – 1 – us U.W. Library [870]
HUMORESKEN / Stinde, Julius – Berlin: Freund & Jeckel, 1892 – 1r – 1 – us U.W. Library [870]
HUMORESQUE DE CONCERT, OP. 14, CAHIER 1, [A L'ANTIQUE] / Paderewski, Ignace Jan – Berlin: Bote & Book, 188- – 1 – us Sibley [780]
HUMORESQUE DE CONCERT, OP. 14, CAHIER 2, ["MODERNE"] / Paderewski, Ignace Jan – Berlin: Bote & Book, 188- – 1 – us Sibley [780]
HUMORISMOS Y SATIRAS / Moreno Torrado, Luis – Merida: Imprenta y Estereotipia de Corchero y Compania, 1902 – 1 – sp Bibl Santa Ana [810]
HUMORISTISCHE GEDICHTE / Knortz, Karl – 2. verb. Aufl. Glarus: J Vogel, 1889 – 1r – 1 – us U.W. Library [810]
HUMOROUS PHASES OF THE LAW / Browne, Irving – San Francisco: Sumner Whitney & Co, 1876 – 3mf – 9 – $4.50 – LLMC 95-163 – us L.L.M.C. [870]
THE HUMOUROUS SIDE OF CANADIAN HISTORY / Bengough, John Wilson – Read before the Canadian Club of New York. New York, 1877. 02317. (Pre-1900 Canadiana) – 9 – cn C.I.H.M. [971]
THE HUMOURS AND CONVERSATIONS OF THE TOWN – 1693 – 9 – 10.00 – us Scholars' Facs [390]
Humphrey, C et al *see* HISTORY AND ANTHROPOLOGY
HUMPHREY DEMOCRAT – Humphrey, NE. -w. Mar-Nov 1888; May 1889-Feb 1890; Jun 1892; Feb 1893 to date – 1 – us NE Hist [071]
HUMPHREY DUKE OF GLOUCESTER. A BIOGRAPHY / Vickers, K H – H 1340 2. 1907 – 8 – ne IDC [920]
Humphrey, George C *see* RIGHTEOUSNESS OF GOD A REDEMPTIVE QUALITY: A STUDY IN BIBLICAL THEOLOGY
Humphrey, George Magoffin *see* PAPERS, MS 3132
Humphrey, Heman *see* REVIVAL SKETCHES AND MANUAL
Humphrey, Henry M *see* DUPLA DEFESA, RESPOSTA AO PAMPHLETO
Humphrey, John *see* NO DISTANT MILLENNIUM
Humphrey, Simon James *see* ESHCOL
Humphrey, William *see*
- CONSCIENCE AND LAW
- THE ONE MEDIATOR

Humphreys, A E *see* THE EPISTLES TO TIMOTHY AND TITUS
Humphreys, Charles *see* A COMPENDIUM OF THE COMMON LAW IN FORCE IN KENTUCKY
Humphreys, Christmas *see* STUDIES IN ZEN
Humphreys, John F *see* WOMAN'S WORK IN THE CHURCH
Humphreys, Mary Gay *see* MISSIONARY EXPLORERS AMONG THE AMERICAN INDIANS
Humpshire, Barry *see* WORKING WITH BRAILLE
HUNAGRIAN STUDIES REVIEW *see* CANADIAN AMERICAN REVIEW OF HUNGARIAN STUDIES
HUNAN DAXUE XUEBAO – Journal of Hunan University. In prep. F/P 303 – 9 – 4.00f – cc Microforms [073]
HU-NAN HSIANG-SHIH LU – List of successful candidates in the imperial examination in Hunan province: 1888, 1903. 1 reel – 1 – 12.00 – us Chinese Res [950]
HUNAN MINBAO = HUNAN PEOPLE'S DAILY – Nov 1926-May 1927 – 1 reel – $35.00 – cc Microforms [950]
Hunan Province. China *see*
- JIAJING CHANGDE FU ZHI, 1526
- JIAJING HENGZHOU FU ZHI, 1536
- LONGQING YUEZHOU FU ZHI, 1572
- WANLI CHENZHOU ZHI, 1576
- WANLI CILI XIAN ZHI, 1573

HUNAN RIBAO = HUNAN DAILY – China. 1983- . M/D83 – 1 – $55.00r – cc Microforms [072]
HU-NAN SHIH-YEH TSA-CHIH – Hunan. (Industrial magazine of Hunan Province). 1922, nos. 55-57, 59, 61-62; 1923, nos. 64-67, 69-71. (439.25 3433) – 1 – 35.00r – us Hoover Inst Photo [330]
HUNAN YIXUEYUAN XUEBAO – Bulletin of Hunan Medical College. In Chinese but English abstracts to the main articles. F p165 – 9 – 4.00f – cc Microforms [073]
HUNDERT GEDICHTE : AUSWAHL DES VERFASSERS – MIT EINER SELBSTBIOGRAPHIE DES DICHTERS / Henckell, Karl – (Includes bibliographical references) – Leipzig: Hesse & Becker, [1914?] – 1r – 1 – us U.W. Library [810]
HUNDERT GEISTLICHE MELODIEN EVANGELISCHEN LIEDER / Reusner, Esaias – 1676 – 9 – us Sibley [780]
HUNDERT VND DREISSIG GEMEYNER FRAGESTUECKE FUER DIE IUNGEN KINDER YNN DER DEUDSCHEN MEYDLIN SCHULE ZU EYSSLEBEN / Johannes Agricola aus Eisleben – [Wittemberg, 1528] – 1mf – ne IDC [240]
THE HUNDRED BOSTON ORATORS APPOINTED BY THE MUNICIPAL AUTHORITIES AND OTHER PUBLIC BODIES, FROM 1770 TO 1852. / Loring, James Spear – 2nd ed. enl. Boston: J.P. Jewett, 1853.viii,720p – 1 – us U.W. Library [978]
A HUNDRED YEARS OF MISSIONS : OR, THE STORY OF PROGRESS SINCE CAREY'S BEGINNING / Leonard Delavan Levant – (Includes index) – New York: Funk & Wagnalls, 1895 – 1mf – 9 – 0-8370-6678-6 – 1986-0678 – us A.T.L.A. [240]
A HUNDRED YEARS WORK FOR CHILDREN, 1803-1903 / Groser, William H – A sketch of the history and operation of Sunday School Union from its formation in 1803 to its centenary in 1903 – 1 – 8.96 – us Baptist [240]
Huneker, James *see*
- ICONOCLASTS
- INTIMATE LETTERS OF JAMES GIBBONS HUNEKER, COLLECTED AND EDITED BY JOSEPHINE HUNEKER

HUNG CH'I – (In Chinese) – 1958-71 – 5r – 1 – $175.00 in US $40.00r outside – L9300044 – Dist. us Scholarly Res – us L of C Photodup [950]
HUNG CHI – Peking, CC. 1976-1984 – 6r – $300.00 – R63598 – us Library Micro [072]
Hung ch'i *see* PEOPLE OF INDONESIA, UNITE AND FIGHT TO OVERTHROW THE FASCIST REGIME
HUNG TSA-CHIH – The Scarlet Magazine. 1922-24. BCH-977 2 – 8 – ne IDC [073]
HUNGARIAN ACADEMY OF SCIENCES PAMPHLET COLLECTION – 1979? – 1 – CSUXANL1844-B – us Hoover Inst Photo [500]
HUNGARIAN ALMANACS PAMPHLET COLLECTION – 1935-1936 – 1 reel – 1 – CSUXANL5659-B – us Hoover Inst Photo [947]
HUNGARIAN CHURCH PRESS – v20-42. 1968-90 (complete) – 7r – 1 – ATLA S0845 – us A.T.L.A. [073]
HUNGARIAN EVANGELICAL REFORMED CONVENTUS ARCHIVES – Budapest, Hungary. ca 1904-1915 – us I.H.R.C. [240]
HUNGARIAN HISTORY, 1918 TO 1945, PAMPHLET COLLECTION – 1939? – 1 – CSUXANQ3134-B – us Hoover Inst Photo [947]
HUNGARIAN NATIONALISM PAMPHLET COLLECTION – 1969 – 1 – CSUXANL5786-B – us Hoover Inst Photo [320]
THE HUNGARIAN PEACE NEGOTIATIONS / Hungary. Versailles Peace Conference Delegation – Documentary record of Hungary's activities before, during and after World War I – 1 – $95.00 – 0-89093-022-8 – us UPA [940]
HUNGARIAN PRESS SUMMARY – Budapest, Hungary. Feb 1949-1987 – 85r – 1 – us L of C Photodup [073]
HUNGARIAN REFORMED CHURCH, CLEVELAND, OHIO – 1890-1944 – us I.H.R.C. [240]
HUNGARIAN REVIEW – 1955- – 1. 1976-; ; 56,9 – us UMI [073]
HUNGARIAN REVOLUTION OF 1956 PAMPHLET COLLECTION – 1956-1960 – 1 reel – 1 – CSUXANL5790-B – us Hoover Inst Photo [947]
HUNGARIAN STUDIES REVIEW – (Cont: Canadian-American Review of Hungarian Studies at v11 1984. Publ delay at v18 1991) – Toronto. v11-21. 1984-94 – 9 – Can$20.00y – cn Micromedia [943]
HUNGARIAN STUDIES REVIEW: HSR – (1983-. 1,5,6,9) – v8-. 1981- – 1 – us UMI [073]
HUNGARIAN TERRITORIAL QUESTIONS AFTER WORLD WAR 1 PAMPHLET COLLECTION – 1919 – 1 – CSUXANR0898-B – us Hoover Inst Photo [320]
THE HUNGARIAN THREE YEAR PLAN / Hungary – (Hungarian Bulletin). Budapest. 1947. BD-639 1 – 9 – ne IDC [943]
HUNGARIAN UPRISING, 1956 / Irving, David – 1 – uk Microform Academic [943]
HUNGARIANS IN ROMANIA PAMPHLET COLLECTION – 1972-1987 – 1 reel – 1 – CSUXANL8126-B – us Hoover Inst Photo [305]
HUNGARIANS IN TRANSYLVANIA PAMPHLET COLLECTION – 1927 – 1 – CSUXANQ5254-B – us Hoover Inst Photo [305]
HUNGARY = STATISTICAL YEARBOOK OF HUNGARY 1872-1965 : STATISZTIKAI EVKOENYV / Hungary. Statisztikai Hivatal – (Coll title: European Official Statistical Serials, 1841-1984) – 472mf – 9 – £2,480.00 – uk Chadwyck [947]
Hungary *see*
- THE FIVE-YEAR PLAN OF THE HUNGARIAN PEOPLE'S REPUBLIC
- THE HUNGARIAN THREE YEAR PLAN

HUNGARY AND ITS PEOPLE. / Felbermann, Lajos – 2nd ed. with suppl. London: Griffith Farran, 1893. illus. map – 1 – us U.W. Library [943]
Hungary. Az Oteves Tervvel a Szocializmus Fele *see* TORVENY A MAGYAR NEPKOZTARSASAG ELSO OTEVES NEPGAZDASAGI TERVEROL
Hungary. Courts *see*
- DONTVENYTAR
- UJ DONTVENYTAR.

Hungary. FAO National Committee *see* INFORMATION BULLETIN
Hungary. Itelotablak *see* A KIRALYI ITELOTABLAK FELULVIZSGALATI TANACSAINAK ELVI JELENTOSEGU HATAROZATAI.
Hungary. Kozponti Statisztikai Hivatal *see*
- MAGYAR ORZAG TISZTI CIM-ES NEVTARA
- STATISZTIKAI SZEMLE
- UNGARISCHES STATISTISCHES JAHRBUCH

Hungary. Kuria *see*
- FELSOBIROSAGAINK ELVI HATAROZATAI
- MAGANJOGI DONTVENYTAR.
- POLGARIJOGI HATAROZATOK TARA, A KIR. KURIANAK HIVATALOS KIADVANYA.

Hungary. Kuria. Felulvizsgalati tanacs *see* A MAGYAR KIR. CURIA FELULVIZSGALATI TANACSA ALTAL A SOMMAS ELJARASROL SZOLO TORVENY (1893: XVIII. TCZ.) ALAPJAN HOZOTT HATAROZATOKNAK GYUJTEMENYE.

Hungary. Laws, Statutes, etc *see*
- AZ 1948. I.E. EZERKILENCSZAZNEGYVENNYOLCADIK EVI AMNESZTIA.
- AZ IGAZOLO ELJARASOK ZSEBKONYVE
- AZ UJ NEPBIROSAGI TORVENY (1947: 34. T.-C.) EGYSEGES SZERKEZETBEN A HATALYOS NEPBIROSAGI RENDELETEKKEL
- A BUNVADI PERRENDTARTAS ZSEBKONYVE, KIEGESZITVE AZ UJABB BUNVADI ELJARASI SZABALYOKKAL; IRTAK EDVI ILLES KAROLY ES VARGHA FERENC
- TORVENYJAVASLAT A KOZIGAZGATAS ES AZ ONKORMANYZAT RENDEZERSEROL A VARMEGYEKBEN

Hungary. Magyar Kozlony *see* A MAGYAR NEPKOZTARSASAG HIVATALOS LAPJA

Hungary. Magyar Statisztikai Evkonyv *see* STATISTISCHES JAHRBUCH

Hungary. Nemzetgyueles *see* IROMANYOK

Hungary. Orszaggyules. Felsohaz *see* IROMANYOK

Hungary. Statisztikai Hivatal *see* HUNGARY

Hungary. Versailles Peace Conference Delegation *see* THE HUNGARIAN PEACE NEGOTIATIONS

Hungary.Orszaggyules. Kepviselohaz *see* NAPLO

Hungary.Statisztikai Evkonyv *see* MAGYAR STATISZTIKAI EVKONYV

Hungate, Jesse Avery *see* THE ORDINATION OF WOMEN TO THE PASTORATE IN BAPTIST CHURCHES

HUNG-CH'I – Red Flag. Peking. 1958-69. Available: v. 1-14, 1958; v. 1-13, 1959-65; v. 1-15, 1966; v. 1-16, 1967; v. 1-5, 1968; v. 1-8, 1969 and suppl. 1964. BCH-915 2 – 8 – ne IDC [950]

HUNG-CH'I P'IAO-P'IAO – Red Banners. v. 1-11. 1957-59. BCH-842 2 – 8 – ne IDC [335]

Hunger, Bertolt *see* ZUM BEGRIFF DER KAUSALITAET IN DER KRIEGSURSACHENFORSCHUNG

Hunger, J *see* BECHERWAHRSAGUNG BEI DEN BABYLONIERN

Hunger, Johannes *see* BECHERWAHRSAGUNG BEI DEN BABYLONIERN

Hungerford *see* HISTORY OF LEHIGH AND CARBON COUNTIES

HUNG-MEI KUEI – (Red Roses; A literary Magazine). 1924-28. Lacking: v. 4 (37-?) 1928. BCH-958 2 – 8 – ne IDC [480]

HUNGRY HORSE NEWS – Columbia Falls. Mont. 1949-1954; 1966; 1967 – 1 – us UMI [071]

HUNG-YA HSIEN-CHIH – 1813, 25, 1. BCH-759 2 – 8 – ne IDC [950]

HUNNINGTU JI JIANZHU GOUJIAN – Concrete and Structural Members. 1982-. F P234 – 9 – $4.50f – cc Microforms [690]

Hunnius, A *see*
- ARTICVLVS DE LIBERO ARBITRIO, SEV HVMANI ARBITRII VIRIBVS, EX SCRIPTVRAE
- ARTICVLVS DE PERSONA CHRISTI: DVARVM IN EA NATVRARVM VNIONE HYPOSTATICA...
- ASSERTIO SANAE ET ORTHODOXAE DOCTRINAE DE PERSONA ET MAIESTATE DOMINI NOSTRI IESV CHRISTI,...
- CALVINVS IVDAIZANS, HOC EST: IVDAICAE GLOSSAE ET CORRVPTELE, QVIBVS IOHANNES CALVINVS ILLUSTRISSIMA...
- CATECHISMUS ODER KINDERLEHR VON DEN FUERNEMMEN HAEUPTPUNCTEN CHRISTLICHER RELIGION ALS DA SIND:...
- DE AETERNA PRAEDESTINATIONE FILIORVM DEI AD SALVTEM PROPOSITIONES THEOLOGICAE:...
- DE PRAEDESTINATIONE SALUANDORUM, AND HUIC OPPOSITA REPROBATIONE DAMNANDORUM, DISPUTATIO...
- HISTORISCHER BERICHT, VON DEM ZU REGENSBURGK UNLANGST GEHALTENEN COLLOQVIO, ZWISCHEN DEN THEOLOGEN AUGSBURGISCHER CONFESSION VND DEN PAPISTEN
- KURTZER VND NUETZLICHER BERICHT VON DEM HEILSAMEN VND CHRISTLICHEM BUCH FORMULAE CONCORDIAE...
- METHODVS CONCIONANDI PRAECEPTIS ET EXEMPLIS DOMINICALIVM QVORVNDAM...
- POSTILLA ODER AVSSLEGUNG DER EPISTELN VND EUANGELIEN AUFF ALLE SONTAG FEST VND FEYERTAGE DURCH DAS GANTZE JAHR
- WARHAFFTER GRUENDTLICHER BERICHT VON RECHTER ORDENLICHER WAHL VNND BERUFF DER EUANGELISCHEN PREDIGER...

Hunolt, Franz *see* THE CHRISTIAN STATE OF LIFE

HUN'S SUPREME COURT REPORTS / New York. (State). Supreme Court – v1-92. 1874-95 (all publ) – 961mf – 9 – $1,141.00 – LLMC 80-007 – us L.L.M.C. [340]

HUNSRUECKER ZEITUNG – Simmern, Germany. 1 Jun 1983- – ca 7r per yr – 1 – gw Mikrofilm [072]

Hunt, Brian R *see* ESTIMATION OF VO(2MAX) FROM A SUBMAXIMAL 1-MILE TRACK JOG FOR RELATIVELY FIT TEENAGE INDIVIDUALS

Hunt, Galliard *see* THE DEBATES IN THE FEDERAL CONVENTION OF 1789

Hunt, George Laird *see* TEN MAKERS OF MODERN PROTESTANT THOUGHT: SCHWEITZER, RAUSCHENBUSCH, TEMPLE, KIERKEGAARD, BARTH, BRUNNER, NIEBUHR, TILLICH, BULTMANN, BUBER

Hunt, Herbert *see*
- HISTORY OF HARRISON COUTNY
- HISTORY OF LEAVENWORTH COUNTY
- TACOMA: ITS HISTORY AND ITS BUILDERS
- WASHINGTON WEST OF THE CASCADES

Hunt, Horace Washington *see* LANDLORD AND TENANT LAWS OF TEXAS

Hunt, J *see* BRITISH ORNITHOLOGY

Hunt, J E *see* CRAMMER'S FIRST LITANY 1544 AND MERBECKE'S BOOK OF COMMON PRAYER NOTED 1550

Hunt, J R E *see* LUTHERAN HOME MISSIONS

Hunt, John *see*
- AN ESSAY ON PANTHEISM
- PANTHEISM AND CHRISTIANITY
- RELIGIOUS THOUGHT IN ENGLAND, FROM THE REFORMATION TO THE END OF LAST CENTURY
- RELIGIOUS THOUGHT IN ENGLAND IN THE NINETEENTH CENTURY

Hunt, John Eddy *see* THE ACKNOWLEDGMENT OF DEEDS, CONTAINING ALL THE STATUTES, TERRITORIAL AND STATE, OF ILLINOIS.

Hunt, L E *see* EFFECTS OF PERCEIVED QUALITY OF LIFE BETWEEN CORONARY ARTERY BYPASS GRAFT AND HEART TRANSPLANTATION PATIENTS WITH REGARD TO CARDIAC REHABILITATION

Hunt, Leigh *see*
- CRITICAL ESSAYS ON THE PERFORMERS OF THE LONDON THEATRES, INCLUDING GENERAL OBSERVATIONS ON THE PRACTISE AND GENIUS OF THE STAGE
- A JAR OF HONEY FROM MOUNT HYBLA
- TALES BY LEIGH HUNT

Hunt, Rockwell A *see* CALIFORNIA AND CALIFORNIANS

Hunt, Thomas *see* LIBELLUS ORTHOGRAPHICUS

Hunt, William *see*
- THE ENGLISH CHURCH FROM ITS FOUNDATION TO THE NORMAN CONQUEST (597-1066)
- THE ENGLISH CHURCH IN THE MIDDLE AGES

Hunter, David Gilbert *see* PENNSYLVANIA ORPHANS' COURT COMMON PLACE BOOK

Hunter, Elmo B *see* THE JUDICIAL CONFERENCE AND ITS COMMITTEE ON COURT ADMINISTRATION

Hunter, Fannie McDowell *see* WOMEN PREACHERS

Hunter, Gary *see* HANDRAIL SUPPORT VERSUS FREE ARM WING TREADMILL FITNESS TEST

Hunter, J *see*
- THE NATURAL HISTORY OF THE HUMAN TEETH
- TREATISE ON THE BLOOD, INFLAMMATION AND GUNSHOT WOUNDS
- A TREATISE ON THE VENEREAL DISEASE
- THE WORKS OF JOHN HUNTER

Hunter, J Marvin *see* PIONEER HISTORY OF BANDERA COUNTY

Hunter, M *see* THE STUDY OF AFRICAN SOCIETY

Hunter, P B *see* THE EFFECTS OF RUNNING WITH A FUNCTIONAL KNEE BRACE ON LOWER EXTREMITY JOINT MOMENTS OF FORCE IN ANTERIOR CRUCIATE LIGAMENT INJURED SUBJECTS

Hunter, Peter Hay *see* THE STORY OF DANIEL

Hunter, Robert Mercer Taliaferro *see* THE PAPERS OF R.M.T. HUNTER, 1817-1887

Hunter, W D *see* LETTERS RECEIVED BY THE BUREAU OF ENTOMOLOGY FROM W.D. HUNTER

Hunter, W Patison *see* NARRATIVE OF THE LATE EXPEDITION TO SYRIA, UNDER THE COMMAND OF ADMIRAL THE HON. SIR ROBERT STOPFORD

Hunter, W W *see* THE IMPERIAL GAZETTEER

Hunter, William S, Jr *see* HUNTER'S PANORAMIC GUIDE FROM NIAGARA FALLS TO QUEBEC

Hunter, William Wilson *see*
- BOMBAY, 1885 TO 1890: A STUDY IN INDIAN ADMINISTRATION
- THE IMPERIAL GAZETTEER
- LIFE OF THE EARL OF MAYO, FOURTH VICEROY OF INDIA

HUNTER'S PANORAMIC GUIDE FROM NIAGARA FALLS TO QUEBEC / Hunter, William S, Jr – Montreal: Publ by Hunter & Pickup, 1860. SEM105P87 – 1mf – 9 – Can$2.25 – cn Bibl Nat [910]

HUNTER'S TORRENS CASES / Canada. General – 1v. 1865-93 (all publ) – 7mf – 9 – $11.50 – LLMC 81-012 – us L.L.M.C. [340]

HUNTING AND HUNTED IN THE BELGIAN CONGO / Cooper, Reginald Davey; ed by Johnston, R Keigh – London: Smith, 1914. 263p. ill – 1 – us U.W. Library [639]

HUNTING DONSHIRE POST *see* HUNTS HERALD AND POST

HUNTING FOR GOLD: REMINISENCES (SIC) OF PERSONAL EXPERIENCE AND RESEARCH IN THE EARLY DAYS OF THE PACIFIC COAST FROM ALASKA TO PANAMA / Downie, William – San Francisco, Cal.: Calif. Pub. Co., 1893. 02753. (Pre-1900 Canadiana) – 9 – cn C.I.H.M. [971]

THE HUNTING OF THE SNARK : AN AGONY IN EIGHT FITS / Carroll, Lewis – New York: Macmillan, 1899 – 2mf – 9 – $3.00 – LLMC 91-014 – us L.L.M.C. [810]

HUNTING SKETCHES: REPRINTED FROM THE "PALL MALL GAZETTE" / Trollope, Anthony – London: Chapman and Hall, 1865 – 1 roll – 1 – 1-55879-814-5 – uk Libr Preservation [940]

THE HUNTINGDON ADVOCATE – Huntingdon, Canada. v2 n26. 26 jun 1884-v3 n50. 24 dec 1885 – 1r – 1 – Can$50.00 – cn Can Microfilming [072]

HUNTINGDON GAZETTE – Huntingdon, PA. -w 1806-1835 – 13 – $25.00r – us I.M.R. [071]

THE HUNTINGDON HERALD – Huntingdon, Canada. v1 n15. 19 aut 1859-v3 n44. 7 mar 1862 – 1r – 1 – Can$35.00 – cn Can Microfilming [072]

THE HUNTINGDON JOURNAL – Huntingdon, Canada. v1 n6. 20 jun 1862-v9 n2. 30 jun 1870 – 1r – 1 – Can$35.00 – cn Can Microfilming [072]

THE HUNTINGDON NEWS – Huntingdon, Canada. 28 sep 1866-v1 n31. 3 mai 1867 – 1r – 1 – Can$35.00 – cn Can Microfilming [072]

Huntingdon. Presbytery *see* MINUTES, 1795-1895

HUNTINGDON TONN CRIER *see* ST IVES AND HUNTINGDON TOWN CRIER

HUNTINGDONSHIRE, 1823 : BRITISH ISLES CENSUS DIRECTORIES PROJECT, ENGLAND. VOL 220 – 1mf – 9 – A$9.00 – at Vine [941]

HUNTINGDONSHIRE, 1830 : BRITISH ISLES CENSUS DIRECTORIES PROJECT, ENGLAND. VOL 218 – 1mf – 9 – A$9.00 – at Vine [941]

HUNTINGDONSHIRE, 1839 : BRITISH ISLES CENSUS DIRECTORIES PROJECT, ENGLAND. VOL 17 – 2mf – 9 – A$15.00 – at Vine [941]

HUNTINGDONSHIRE, 1850 : BRITISH ISLES CENSUS DIRECTORIES PROJECT, ENGLAND. VOL 84 – 2mf – 9 – A$15.00 – at Vine [941]

HUNTINGDONSHIRE, 1854 : BRITISH ISLES CENSUS DIRECTORIES PROJECT, ENGLAND – at Vine [941]

HUNTINGDONSHIRE, 1864 : BRITISH ISLES CENSUS DIRECTORIES PROJECT, ENGLAND. VOL 120 – 2mf – 9 – A$15.00 – at Vine [941]

HUNTINGDONSHIRE, 1877 : BRITISH ISLES CENSUS DIRECTORIES PROJECT, ENGLAND – at Vine [941]

HUNTINGDONSHIRE, 1898 : BRITISH ISLES CENSUS DIRECTORIES PROJECT, ENGLAND. VOL 68 – 3mf – 9 – A$21.00 – at Vine [941]

Huntingford, Edward *see* THE APOCALYPSE

Huntington, Arria *see* MEMOIR AND LETTERS OF FREDERIC DAN HUNTINGTON, FIRST BISHOP OF CENTRAL NEW YORK

HUNTINGTON BEACH – 1938; 1948 – 2r – 1 – $100.00 – P00037 – us Library Micro [910]

HUNTINGTON BEACH CITY DIRECTORY – Orange Co., CA. 1949 – 1r – 1 – $50.00 – D073 – us Library Micro [910]

HUNTINGTON BEACH DAILY PILOT – Huntington Beach, CA. 1966 (Scats); 1968 – 15r – 1 – $750.00 – H03248 – us Library Micro [071]

HUNTINGTON BEACH INDEPENDENT – Huntington Beach, CA. 1965 – 29+ r – 1 – $1,450.00 – H04043 – us Library Micro [071]

HUNTINGTON BEACH NEWS – Huntington Beach, CA. 1905-1968; 1969-1982 – 48r – 1 – $2,400.00 – H04014 – us Library Micro [071]

Huntington, Collis P *see* COLLIS P. HUNTINGTON PAPERS, 1856-1901

Huntington, DeWitt C *see*
- HALF CENTURY MESSAGES TO PASTORS AND PEOPLE
- IS THE LORD AMONG US?
- SIN AND HOLINESS OR WHAT IT IS TO BE HOLY

Huntington, Ezra Abel *see* NOTES ON THE EPISTLE TO THE HEBREWS

Huntington, Frederic Dan *see*
- CHRIST IN THE CHRISTIAN YEAR AND IN THE LIFE OF MAN
- ELIM: OR, HYMNS OF HOLY REFRESHMENT
- THE FITNESS OF CHRISTIANITY TO MAN
- HUMAN SOCIETY
- LESSONS ON THE PARABLES OF THE SAVIOUR
- PERSONAL RELIGIOUS LIFE IN THE MINISTRY AND IN MINISTERING WOMEN
- SERMONS FOR THE PEOPLE

Huntington, George *see* THE CHURCH'S WORK IN OUR LARGE TOWNS

HUNTINGTON HERALD – Huntington, OR. -w. 7 Jan 1905-29 Dec 1906. 1 roll – 1 – us U.O. Library [071]

HUNTINGTON LIBRARY QUARTERLY – v.1-1937- – 1. ; 5,6. ; 9 – apply; v.34-; v.40- – us UMI [020]

Huntington, Mark W *see* PREDICTORS OF SUCCESS ON THE HUMAN ANATOMY-RELATED PORTIONS OF THE NATIONAL ATHLETIC TRAINERS' ASSOCIATION CERTIFICATION EXAMINATION

HUNTINGTON PARK SIGNAL – Huntington Park, CA. 1925-1983 – 451r – 1 – $22,550.00 – H04016 – us Library Micro [071]

Huntington, Samuel *see*
- LETTERS, MS 3947
- PAPERS

Huntington, Susan L *see*
- BUDDHIST AND HINDU ART OF EASTERN INDIA AND BANGLADESH

Huntington, Susan L et al *see* SOUTH ASIAN ART PHOTOGRAPH COLLECTION

Huntington, W *see* THE FUNERAL OF ARMINIANISM, DELIVERED IN SUBSTANCE AT PROVIDENCE CHAPEL ON SUNDAY MORNING, MARCH 13, 1791

Huntington, William Reed *see*
- THE CHURCH-IDEA
- THE FOUR THEORIES OF VISIBLE CHURCH UNITY
- A NATIONAL CHURCH
- THE PEACE OF THE CHURCH
- PSYCHE
- THE TALISMAN OF UNITY

Huntley, Edward L *see* ED. L. HUNTLEY'S PANEGYRIC ON THE JEWS

Huntley, Elizabeth A *see* THE EFFECTS OF A TEN-WEEK STEP AEROBIC TRAINING PROGRAM ON THE BODY COMPOSITION OF COLLEGE-AGED WOMEN

Huntley, Henry Veel *see* SEVEN YEARS' SERVICE ON THE SAVLE COAST OF WESTERN AFRICA

HUNTRESS *see* PAUL PRY

HUNTS HERALD AND POST – (Also known as: Hunts Post; Hunting Donshire Post) – Nov 18 1893-96; Apr 24-Dec 25 1897; 1898-99; 1986-Feb 1989; Mar 2-Apr 27 1989; May-Jun 1989; Jul 6 1989-92; Jan 7 1993-Oct 1996; Nov 6-Dec 18 1996 – 57 1/2r – 9 – uk British Libr Newspaper [072]

HUNT'S MERCHANTS MAGAZINE YEARBOOK – New York. 1v. 1871 – 24mf – 9 – $7.50 – LLMC 84-482 – us L.L.M.C. [340]

HUNTS POST *see* HUNTS HERALD AND POST

HUNTSMAN'S ECHO – Wood River Center, NE. -w. Jun 1860-Aug 1861, scattered issues missing – 1 – us NE Hist [071]

HUNTSVILLE FIRST BAPTIST CHURCH. HUNTSVILLE, MISSOURI : CHURCH RECORDS – 1837-1963 – 1 – 67.95 – us Baptist [240]

HUNTSVILLE NEWS – Huntsville, Ala. 1968- – 1 – us UMI [071]
HUNTSVILLE TIMES – Huntsville, Ala. 1928- – 1 – us UMI [071]
Huntz, Jack *see* SPOTLIGHT ON SPAIN
Hunziker, Rudolf *see*
– ERLEBNISSE EINES SCHULDENBAUERS
– DER GELDSTAG
– JAKOBS, DES HANDWERKSGESELLEN WANDERUNGEN DURCH DIE SCHWEIZ
– KALENDERGESCHICHTEN
– SAEMTLICHE WERKE IN 24 BAENDEN
– DIE WASSERNOT IM EMMENTAL; DIE ARMENNOT; EINES SCHWEIZERS WORT
– WIE ULI DER KNECHT GLUECKLICH WIRD
Hunzinger, A W *see*
– DAS FURCHTMOTIV IN DER KATHOLISCHEN BUSSLEHRE VON AUGUSTIN BIS PETRUS LOMBARDUS
– DAS FURCHTPROBLEM IN DER KATHOLISCHEN LEHRE VON AUGUSTIN BIS LUTHER
– LUTHERS NEUPLATONISMUS IN DER PSALMENVORLESUNG VON 1513-1516
Huonder, Anton *see*
– DER CHINESISCHE RITENSTREIT
– DER EINHEIMISCHE KLERUS IN DEN HEIDENLAENDERN
Huot, M-G *see* QUEBEC 9
Hupay De Fuveau, Joseph-Alexandre-Victor d' *see* REGLEMENT D'EDUCATION NATIONALE MIS SOUS LES AUSPICES DE BERNARDIN DE SAINT-PIERRE
HU-PEI HSIANG-SHIH LU – List of successful candidates in the imperial examination in Hupeh province: 1879, 1885, 1900, 1901. 1 reel – 1 – 12.00 – us Chinese Res [950]
Huppert, Thomas C *see* THE PAPERS OF CARLOS MONTEZUMA, M.D
HUR SOZ – Izmit: Muduru Selehattin Telser, jan 1951-sep 1953 – 3r – 1 – us Res Libr [072]
HUR SOZ – Lefkosa, Kibris: Hur soz, dec 1949-sep-dec 1954 – 3r – 1 – us Res Libr [072]
Hurd *see*
– HISTORICAL ENCYCLOPEDIA OF ILLINOIS AND HISTORY OF EVANSTON
– NEW UNIVERSAL HISTORY OF THE RELIGIOUS RIGHTS, CEREMONIES AND CUSTOMS OF THE WHOLE WORLD
Hurd, D Hamilton *see*
– HISTORY OF CHESHIRE AND SULLIVAN COUNTIES
– HISTORY OF ESSEX COUNTY
– HISTORY OF FAIRFIELD COUNTY
– HISTORY OF HILLSBORO COUNTY
– HISTORY OF MERRIMACK AND BELKNAP COUNTIES
– HISTORY OF MIDDLESEX COUNTY
– HISTORY OF NEW LONDON COUNTY
– HISTORY OF PLYMOUTH
Hurd, F H *see* EARNEST MEN
Hurd, John *see* GENEALOGICAL RECORDS OF HANOVER, NEW HAMPSHIRE
Hurd, John C *see* THE LAW OF FREEDOM AND BONDAGE IN THE UNITED STATES
Hureau, J C *see*
– CHECKLIST OF THE FISHES OF THE NORTH-EASTERN ATLANTIC AND OF THE MEDITERRANEAN (CLOFNAM)
– FAO SPECIES INDENTIFICATION SHEETS FOR FISHERY PURPOSES
HURI : PERIODICO LITTERARIO E NOTICIOSO RIO NEGRO – Sam Joaquim, Amazonas. 15 Jun 1904 – 1,5,6 – bl Biblioteca [072]
Hurlbut, Henry H *see* CHICAGO ANTIQUITIES
Huron County. Ohio. Auditor *see*
– INSOLVENTS' OATHS
– SCHOOL LAND RECORDS
– TAX LISTS
Huron County. Ohio. Board of County Commissioners *see* TOWNSHIP INCORPORATION RECORDS
Huron County. Ohio. Board of Education *see* BOARD OF EXAMINERS' MINUTES
Huron County. Ohio. Children's Services Board *see* MATRONS' MONTHLY REPORTS
Huron County. Ohio. Clerk of Courts *see*
– JUSTICES' OATHS/MAYORS' CERTIFS
– NOTARIES' COMMISSIONS RECORDS
Huron County. Ohio. Common Pleas. Civil Division *see*
– APPEARANCE DOCKETS
– CHANCERY RECORDS
– COMPLETE RECORDS
– GENERAL INDEXES
– JOURNALS
– LICENSE RECORDS
Huron County. Ohio. County Home *see*
– BIRTH RECORDS
– DEATH RECORDS
– INDENTURE RECORDS
– MINUTES
– PAUPERISM STATISTICS
– REGISTERS
Huron County. Ohio. District Court *see*
– CHANCERY RECORDS
– JOURNAL
Huron County. Ohio. Engineer *see* FREE TURNPIKE RECORD
Huron. County, Ohio. New London, Village Village Clerk *see* BURIAL TRANSIT PERMITS
Huron County. Ohio. Plymouth, Village. Cemetery Trustees *see*
– CEMETERY DEED ACCOUNT RECORD
– CEMETERY DEED RECORDS
Huron County. Ohio. Plymouth. Village. Cemetery Trustees. *see* MINUTES
Huron County. Ohio. Probate Court *see*
– CRIMINAL DOCKET
– CRIMINAL RECORDS
– MENTALLY ILL PERSONS RECORDS
Huron County. Ohio. Recorder *see*
– DEED RECORDS, FIRELANDS
– LAND SURVEYS
– PLAT MAPS
Huron County. Ohio. Supreme Court *see*
– CHANCERY RECORDS
– COMPLETE RECORDS
– JOURNALS
– TRIAL DOCKETS
Huron County. Ohio. Treasurer *see* TAX DUPLICATES
HURON EXPOSITER – Seaforth, Canada. 1869-1920 – 33r – 1 – $2,145.00 – cn Library Assoc [971]
HURON NEWS – Ontario, CN. 1896-11 – 16r – 1 – cn Commonwealth Micro [072]
Huron. Presbytery (Pres. Ch. in the USA) *see* MINUTES
HURON REFLECTOR – Norwalk. Ohio. -w. 1830-53 – 1 – us UMI [071]
HURRAH OU LA REVOLUTION PAR LES COSAQUES / Coeurderoy, Ernest – (Russia – 19th C. series). 1854 – 9 – fr Hachette [947]
HURRELL FROUDE : MEMORANDA AND COMMENTS / Guiney, Louise Imogene – London: Methuen, 1904 – 2mf – us A.T.L.A. [240]
HURRICANE BAPTIST CHURCH. CLINTON, SOUTH CAROLINA : CHURCH RECORDS – 1949-62 – 1 – 29.52 – us Baptist [240]
HURRICANE BAPTIST CHURCH. LAURENS COUNTY. SOUTH CAROLINA : CHURCH RECORDS – 1893-1949, 1962-72 – 1 – 29.03 – us Baptist [240]
THE HURRICANE BREEZE – Hurricane. West Virginia. -w. 1936- – 1 – us UMI [071]
HURRICANE CREEK BAPTIST CHURCH. STEWART COUNTY. TENNESSEE : CHURCH RECORDS – 1949-68 – 1 – 36.27 – us Baptist [240]
HURRISH : A STUDY / Lawless, Emily – British Fiction Archive: Unit 4 – 9 – uk Bell [830]
HURRIYET – (Yrly reel count varies) – 1980- – 1 – inquire – us Ross [072]
Hurst, John F *see*
– THE HISTORY OF METHODISM...BRITISH METHODISM
– HISTORY OF RATIONALISM
– INDIKA
– LITERATURE OF THEOLOGY
– MARTYRS TO THE TRACT CAUSE
– OUR THEOLOGICAL CENTURY
– OUTLINE OF BIBLE HISTORY
– SHORT HISTORY OF THE EARLY CHURCH
– SHORT HISTORY OF THE MEDIAEVAL CHURCH
Hurst, Samuel Need *see* A COMPLETE POPULAR ENCYCLOPEDIA OF VIRGINIA LAW AND FORMS AND BUSINESS GUIDE OR HOW-BOOK FOR THE BUSINESSMAN AND CITIZEN.
Hurtado, Antonio *see*
– EL ARGUMENTO DE UN DRAMA
– BARBA AZUL. OPERA
– EL BUSTO DE ELISA
– UNA CANCION DE AMOR
– EL COLLAR DE LESCOT
– LA COMEDIA DE LA VIDA
– CORTE Y CORTIJO
– COSAS DEL MUNDO
– EN EL CUARTO DE MI MUJER
– ENTRE EL DEBER Y EL DERECHO
– EL FACEDOR DE UN ENTUERTO...AGRAVIOS
– INTRIGA Y AMOR
– EL MATRIMONIO SECRETO
– LA MAYA
– EL MEDICO DE CAMARA
– LA NIETA DEL ZAPATERO
– EL ROMANCERO DE LA PRINCESA
– EN LA SOMBRA
– SUENOS Y REALIDADES
– EL TOISON (SIC) ROTO
– VERY WELL
– LA VIRGEN DE LA MONTANA
– LA VOZ DEL CORAZON
Hurtado de Mendoza, Luis *see* CORTES DE LA MUERTE
Hurtado de Mendoza, M *see* TRATADO HISTORICO Y FISIOLOGICO...SOBRE LA GENERACION, EL HOMBRE Y LA MUJER
Hurtado de Mendoza, Publio *see*
– ALONSO GOLFIN. LEYENDA
– AMOR Y MARTIRIO
– LA BATALLA DE ZALACA. EPISODIO HISTORICO-EXTREMENO
– CASTILLOS, TORRES Y CASAS FUERTES DE LA PROVINCIA DE CACERES
– EL CINTURON DE AFRODITA
– DISPUTATIONES DE UNIVERSA PHILOSOPHIA
– EXTREMADURA EN TOLEDO. IMPRESIONES DE TURISTA
– EL IDOLO ROTO (REALIDADES DE OTROS DIAS)
– INDIANOS CACERENOS
– LA PARROQUIA DE SAN MATEOS DE CACERES Y SUS AGREGADOS
– SUPERSTICIONES EXTREMENAS. PROLOGO DE URBANO GONZALEZ SERRANO
– TRIBUNALES Y ABOGADOS CACERENOS
Hurtado Munoz de Lucas, Vicente *see* PARTICIPACION POLITICA POPULAR. (GUIONES PARA UN CURSILLO MONOGRAFICO)
Hurtado y Nunez de Arce, G *see*
– HERIR EN LA SOMBRA
– LA JOTA ARAGONESA
– EL LAUREL DE LA ZUBIA
Hurter, H *see*
– NOMENCLATOR LITERARIUS RECENTIORIS THEOLOGIAE CATHOLICAE
– NOMENCLATOR LITERARIUS RECENTIORIS THEOLOGIAE CATHOLICAE, 1109-1899.
– NOMENCLATOR LITRARIUS THEOLOGIAE CATHOLICAE
Hurtubise, Cheryl L *see* COMPARISON OF WAIST TO HIP RATIO MEASUREMENTS IN RELATION TO CARDIOVASCULAR RISK FACTORS IN HEALTHY MENOPAUSAL WOMEN
Hurwicz, Elias *see* DIE ORIENTPOLITIK DER 3. INTERNATIONALE
HUS DAHLEN : ERZAEHLUNG IN MUENSTERLAENDISCHER MUNDART / Wibbelt, Augustin – 4. Aufl. Essen: Fredebeul & Koenen, 1920 – 1r – 1 – us U.W. Library [390]
Husain Ali, Kirmani *see*
– THE HISTORY OF HYDUR NAIK/THE HISTORY OF THE REIGN OF TIPU SULTAN
– THE HISTORY OF THE REIGN OF TIPU SULTAN..
Husain ibn 'abd (Abu 'Ali) *see* AL-QANUN FI AL-TIBB. A SYSTEM OF MEDICINE, AND OTHER WORKS
Husband, Charles *see* RICHER VISION
Husbandman *see* MONEY AND THE MONEY QUESTION IN CANADA: AND SOME CONSIDERATIONS ARISING THEREFROM
HUSBANDRY AND HEALTH OF THE DOMESTIC BUFFALO / ed by Cockrill, W R – 2nd printing 1976 – 993p – it F.A.O. [636]
Husch, B *see* PLANNING A FOREST INVENTORY
Husein, Kartasasmita *see* ECONOMIC PROBLEMS OF INDUSTRY AND MINING
Husenbeth, F C *see* NOTICES OF THE ENGLISH COLLEGES AND CONVENTS ESTABLISHED ON THE CONTINENT AFTER THE DISSOLUTION OF RELIGIOUS HOUSES IN ENGLAND
Huseyin, Husameddin *see* AMASYA TARIHI
HU-SHIH COLLECTANEA – (v1 The Narration of Knowledge; v2 Research; v3 Personages; v4 Annual Genealogy; v5 History; v6 Politics; v7 Preface; v8 Miscellany; v9 Diary; v10 Letter; v11 Poetry; v12 Translation; v13 Speech) – (Hu-Shih hsuan-chi). Celebrated philosopher, educator and diplomat. Selections from his mss. Comp. by Wen-Shing Shu-Tien. Taipei, 1966. 13v. 3300p. 3 reels – 1 – $141.00 – ch Transmission [180]
HUSKISSON PAPERS / British Library – 1 – uk World [941]
Husnot, T *see* MUSCOLOGIA GALLICA
Huss, John *see*
– DE ECCLESIA
– THE LETTERS OF JOHN HUS
Hussein, Kartasasmita *see* PETUNDJUK SINGKAT TENTANG "SUMBANGAN WADJIB ISTIMEWA 1962 ATAS BANGUNAN" (S.W.I. BANGUNAN); DILENGKAPI DENGAN TEKS PERATURAN DAN PENDJELASANNJA, SERTA BENTUK2 PORMULIR PELAKSANAAN
Hussey, Arthur *see* NOTES ON THE CHURCHES IN THE COUNTIES OF KENT, SUSSEX AND SURREY, MENTIONED IN DOMESDAY BOOK, AND THOSE OF MORE RECENT DATE
Hussey de Burgh, U H *see*
– THE LANDOWNERS OF IRELAND
– LANDOWNERS OF IRELAND 1878
Hussey, T J *see* ILLUSTRATIONS OF BRITISH MYCOLOGY
THE HUSSITE WARS / Luetzow, Franz H H V von – London: J.M. Dent; New York: E.P. Dutton, 1914 – 1mf – us A.T.L.A. [240]
LES HUSSITES OU LE SIEGE DE NAUMBOURG / Duval, Alexandre & Duval, Mehul – French Theatre Series. Paris. Vente, an XII. 1804 – 9 – fr Hachette [820]
Husson, Armand *see* LES CONSOMMATIONS DE PARIS
Husson, Pere Camille *see* LOIS PRINCIPALES DU MOUVEMENT DE LA POPULATION DANS LA VILLE ET DANS L'ARRONDISSEMENT DE TOUL: STATISTIQUE MEDICALE ET HYGIENE
Hust, Gerhard *see* UNTERSUCHUNGEN ZU CLAUDIO MONTEVERDIS MESSKOMPOSITIONEN
HUSTING ROLLS OF DEEDS AND WILLS 1252-1485 / ed by Martin, G H – (With printed guide £26.00) – 30r – 1 – £2010.00 – uk Chadwyck [941]
Huston, Charles *see* AN ESSAY ON THE HISTORY AND NATURE OF ORIGINAL TITLES TO LAND IN THE PROVINCE AND STATE OF PENNSYLVANIA
Huston, J *see* L'ARTISAN
HUSUMER NACHRICHTEN – Husum, West Germany. 1977- – ca 7r per yr – 1 – gw Mikrofilm [072]
HUSZONOET EV MAGYARORSZAG TOERTENELMEBOEL 1823-TOL 1848-IG / Horvath, M – Ed. 2, rev. and enl. 3 v. Budapest. 1886. BR-5285 2 – 8 – ne IDC [943]
Hutagalung, Wasinton *see* TAROMBO-MARGA NI SUKU BATAK
HUTAN-REBOISASI MEMPERTINGGI KEMAKMURAN / Supardi – SE 4216 1. 1954 – 9 – ne IDC [950]
Hutauruk, Bulan *see* A BIBLIOGRAPHY ON OIL PALM "ELAEIS GUINEENSIS JACQUIN"; ITS AGRONOMY, BOTANY, BREEDING AND SELECTION, DISEASES AND PESTS
Hutauruk, Marulam *see* HISTORY OF THE INDONESIAN PUBLISHERS' ASSOCIATION
Hutcheson, F *see*
– AN ESSAY ON THE NATURE AND CONDUCT OF THE PASSIONS AND AFFECTIONS WITH ILLUSTRATIONS ON THE MORAL SENSE
– A SYSTEM OF MORAL PHILOSOPHY...PUBLISHED BY HIS SON...TO WHICH IS PREFIXED SOME ACCOUNT OF THE LIFE, WRITINGS AND CHARACTER OF THE AUTHOR BY W. LEECHMAN
HUTCHINGS CALIFORNIA MAGAZINE – San Francisco, CA. Jul 1856-Apr 1861 – 3r – 1 – $150.00 – B02822 – us Library Micro [073]
Hutchings, William Henry *see* THE MYSTERY OF THE TEMPTATION
Hutchins, Harry Burns *see* ILLUSTRATIVE CASES ON EQUITY JURISPRUDENCE
Hutchins, Stephen C *see* CIVIL LIST AND CONSTITUTIONAL HISTORY OF THE COLONY AND STATE OF NEW YORK
Hutchinson, E W *see* ADVENTURES IN SIAM IN THE 17TH CENTURY
Hutchinson, Fabian *see*
– GUIDE TO PACIFIC ARCHIVES
– GUIDE TO THE RECORDS OF PACIFIC MISSIONS IN BRITISH INSTITUTIONS
Hutchinson, John *see* A CATALOGUE OF NOTABLE MIDDLE TEMPLE TEMPLARS
Hutchinson, Louisa *see* IN TENTS IN TRANSVAAL
Hutchinson, T J *see* NARRATIVE OF THE NIGER, TSADDA AND BINUE EXPLORATION
Hutchinson, William *see*
– HISTORY AND ANTIQUITIES OF THE COUNTY OF CUMBERLAND
– A TREATISE ON PRACTICAL SEAMANSHIP
Hutchinson, Woods *see* THE GOSPEL ACCORDING TO DARWIN
Hutchison, Eloise P *see* OUT OF THE PAST, A TALE OF TWO MODERN CITIES, SHREVEPORT-LITTLE ROCK

Hutchison, J *see* THE ANCIENT EAST
Hutchison, John *see*
- LECTURES CHIEFLY EXPOSITORY ON ST PAUL'S EPISTLE TO THE PHILIPPIANS
- LECTURES CHIEFLY EXPOSITORY ON ST PAUL'S FIRST AND SECOND EPISTLES TO THE THESSALONIANS
- OUR LORD'S SIGNS IN ST JOHN'S GOSPEL

Huth, E *see* CLAVIS RIVINIANA, SCHLUESSEL ZU DEN KUPFERWERKEN DES A. Q. RIVINUS
THE HUTH LIBRARY : CATALOGUE OF THE PRINTED BOOKS, MANUSCRIPTS, AUTOGRAPH LETTERS, AND ENGRAVINGS, COLLECTED BY HENRY HUTH – London. 5v. 1880 – 22mf – subsc: DM160.00 – gw Olms [020]
Huther, Johann Eduard *see* CRITICAL AND EXEGETICAL HANDBOOK TO THE GENERAL EPISTLES OF PETER AND JUDE
Hutin, P *see* LA VIE QUOTIDIENNE D'UNE COOPERATIVE DE TRAVAIL AGRICOLE FAMILIALE VENDEE
Huttman, Maude Aline *see* THE ESTABLISHMENT OF CHRISTIANITY AND THE PROSCRIPTION OF PAGANISM
Hutton, A W *see* THE MORAL ARGUMENT AGAINST COMPULSORY VACCINATION
Hutton, Arthur Wollaston *see*
- THE ANGLICAN MINISTRY
- CARDINAL MANNING

Hutton Buscel. Yorkshire *see* PARISH REGISTERS
Hutton, Charles F *see* UNCONSCIOUS TESTIMONY
Hutton, FW *see* FISHES OF NEW ZEALAND
Hutton, G H *see* AN EARLY VICTORIAN RAILWAY STATION
Hutton, J *see*
- MISSIONARY LIFE IN THE SOUTHERN SEAS
- THEORY OF THE EARTH, WITH PROOFS AND ILLUSTRATIONS

Hutton, Joseph Edmund *see*
- A HISTORY OF THE MORAVIAN CHURCH

Hutton, Richard Holt *see*
- CARDINAL NEWMAN
- ESSAYS ON SOME OF THE MODERN GUIDES OF ENGLISH THOUGHT IN MATTERS OF FAITH
- THE INCARNATION AND PRINCIPLES OF EVIDENCE

Hutton, S K *see* AMONG THE ESKIMOS OF LABRADOR
Hutton, W *see* A VOYAGE TO AFRICA
Hutton Wandsley. (Long Marston). Yorkshire *see* PARISH REGISTERS
Hutton, William *see* A VOYAGE TO AFRICA; INCLUDING A NARRATIVE OF AN EMBASSY TO ONE OF THE INTERIOR KINGDOMS.
Hutton, William Holden *see*
- THE AGE OF REVOLUTION
- THE CHURCH AND THE BARBARIANS
- THE CHURCH OF THE SIXTH CENTURY
- THE ENGLISH CHURCH FROM THE ACCESSION OF CHARLES
- THE INFLUENCE OF CHRISTIANITY UPON NATIONAL CHARACTER ILLUSTRATED BY THE LIVES AND LEGENDS OF THE ENGLISH SAINTS
- SIR THOMAS MORE
- THOMAS BECKET
- WILLIAM LAUD

Hutzinger, O *see* TOXICOLOGICAL AND ENVIRONMENTAL CHEMISTRY REVIEWS
Hutzli, Walther *see* JEREMIAS GOTTHELF
HU'U THANH – Hanoi. fevr 1922-sept 1924 – 1 – fr A.C.R.P.P. [073]
Huvala, J M *see* DER PAHLAVI TEXT
Huvelin, Paul L *see* ESSAI HISTORIQUE SUR LE DROIT DES MARCHES ET DES FOIRES
HUVUDLINJER I NORDISK SPRAKHISTORIA / Hesselman, Bengt – 1948-53 – 1 – us I.U. Libraries [390]
HUWELIJKEN VAN NEDERLANDERS IN HET BUITENLAND... / ed by Kisch, I & Beekers, L M – Ed 5. Alphen aan den Rijn, 1935 – 9 – 3mf – ILM-3607/1 – ne IDC [327]
Huxham, J *see* AN ESSAY ON FEVERS
Huxley, J *see* THE CONSERVATION OF WILD LIFE AND NATURAL HABITATS IN CENTRAL AND EAST AFRICA
Huxley, J S *see* AFRICA VIEW
Huxley, T H *see* ON THE CLASSIFICATION OF BIRDS
Huxley, Thomas *see* THE OCEANIC HYDROZOS: A DESCRIPTION OF THE CALYCOPHORIDAE AND PHYSOPHORIDAE
Huxley, Thomas Henry *see*
- HUME
- HUME, WITH HELPS TO THE STUDY OF BERKELEY
- SCIENCE AND CHRISTIAN TRADITION: ESSAYS
- SCIENCE AND HEBREW TRADITION

Huygen, J *see* DE BEGINSELEN VAN GODS KONINKRYK IN DEN MENSCH
Huygen, Jan *see*
- STICHTELYKE RYMEN OP VERSCHEIDE STOFFEN, IN TWEE DEELEN
- STICHTELYKE RYMEN OP VERSCHEIDEN STOFFEN, WAAR VAN ONTRENT DE HELFT NOOIT VOOR-DEESEN GEDRUKT ZIJN

Huygen P *see* DE BEGINSELEN VAN GODS KONINKRYK IN DEN MENSCH
Huygen, P *see* DE BEGINSELEN VAN GODS KONINGKRYK IN DEN MENSCH
Huysmans, Joris Karl *see*
- A REBOURS
- CENTAINS: G. MOREAU, DEGAS, CHERET, WHISTLER, ROPS
- CROQUIS PARISIENS: A VAU L'EAU; UN OFLEMME
- TROIS PRIMITIFS: LES GRUNEWALD DU MUSEE DE COLMAR, LE MAITRE DE FLEMMALLE ET LA FLORENTINE DU MUSEE DE FRANCFORT SUR LE MAIN

Huysmans, Joris-K *see* LA SORCELLERIE EN POITOU
HUZMA SAFA / Safa, Ismail – Istanbul: Alem Matbaasi, 1308 [1891] – $50.00 – us MEDOC [470]
Huzni *see* DIVAN
H.V. KLEISTS WERKE : KRITISCH DURCHGESEHENE UND ERLAEUTERTE GESAMTAUSGABE / Kleist, Heinrich von; ed by Schmidt, Erich – (Includes bibliographical references and index) – Leipzig: Bibliographisches Institut. 5v. [1905?] – 1 – us U.W. Library [800]
HVAD CHRISTUS DOMMER OM OFFICIEL CHRISTENDOM / Kierkegaard, Soren – Kjobenhavn: C.A. Reitzel, 1855 – 1mf – us A.T.L.A. [190]
HVAD HAR HANDT? – Lulea, Sweden. 1856-62 – 1 reel – 1 – sw Kungliga [072]
HVAD HAR HANDT? – Umea, Sweden. 1847 – 1 reel – 1 – sw Kungliga [072]
HVAD NYTT? – Skaenninge, Sweden. 1911-12 – 1 – sw Kungliga [072]
Hwa Kang et al *see* CHINESE CULTURE
Hwai River Comm *see* TAO HUAI WEI YUAN HUI PAN NIEN K'AN
HWOMELY RHYMES : A SECOND COLLECTION OF POEMS IN THE DORSET DIALECT / Barnes, William – London: J.R. Smith, 1859 – 1 roll – 1 – 1-55879-552-9 – uk Libr Preservation [810]
Hyamson, A *see* THE BRITISH CONSULATE IN JERUSALEM IN RELATION TO THE JEWS IN PALESTINE
Hyamson, Albert Montefiore *see* A HISTORY OF THE JEWS IN ENGLAND
Hyannis, Massachusetts. First Baptist Church and Society *see* RECORDS
Hyatt, A *see* PHYLOGENY OF AN ACQUIRED CHARACTERISTIC
HYATT ON TRIALS: A TREATISE ON THE TRIAL OF CIVIL AND CRIMINAL CASES IN STATE AND FEDERAL COURTS. / Hyatt, William Harvey – San Francisco: Bender-Moss Co., 1924. 2v. LL-542 – 1 – us L of C Photodup [340]
Hyatt, Thaddeus *see*
- CORRESPONDENCE AND PAPERS
- THADDEUS HYATT PAPERS

Hyatt, William Harvey *see* HYATT ON TRIALS: A TREATISE ON THE TRIAL OF CIVIL AND CRIMINAL CASES IN STATE AND FEDERAL COURTS.
Hybaeum, Mel *see* A STUDY OF THE PEOPLE OF MIDDLETOWN OF SICILIAN EXTRACTION
HYBRID SEED PRODUCTION OF SELECTED CEREAL OIL AND VEGETABLE CROPS – 1987 – 371p – it F.A.O. [631]
Hyckel, Georg *see* GESCHICHTE UND BESIEDLUNG DES RATIBORER LANDES
Hyde, A B *see* THE STORY OF METHODISM THROUGHOUT THE WORLD, FROM THE BEGINNING TO THE PRESENT TIME;...
Hyde, A M *see* A DIPLOMATIC HISTORY OF BULGARIA, 1870-1886
Hyde, Douglas *see* BESIDE THE FIRE
Hyde, John *see* THE GLORY AND DIVINITY OF THE HOLY BIBLE AND ITS SPIRITUAL SENSE
HYDE PARK 1868-1892 – (Mf 1: Births 1868-75. Mf 2: Births 1875-83. Mf 3: Births 1883-89. Mf 4: Births 1889-91. Mf 5: Marriages 1868-77. Mf 6: Marriages 1878-85. Mf 7: Marriages 1885-90. Mf 8: Marriages 1891-92. Mf 9: Deaths 1868-79. Mf 10: Deaths 1879-89. Mf 11: Deaths 1890-92. Mf 12-13: Index 1868-89) – (mf ed 1988) – 13mf – 9 – 0-931248-87-6 – us Holbrook [920]
HYDE PARK HERALD – Chicago. Ill. -w. 1961- – 1 – us UMI [071]
Hyde, Thomas Alexander *see* CHRIST THE ORATOR
Hyde, William *see* ENCYCLOPEDIA OF THE HISTORY OF ST LOUIS
Hyde, William De Witt *see* OUTLINES OF SOCIAL THEOLOGY
Hyde, William de Witt *see* JESUS' WAY
HYDERABAD – Hyderabad. pt3. 1901 – us Res Libr [310]
HYDERABAD ARCHAEOLOGICAL SERIES – Calcutta. Nos.1-19. 1915-56. Lacking: 1935 (11); 1953 (17). – 50mf – 8 – ne IDC [930]
Hyderabad. India. Department of Statistics and Census *see* VILLAGE LIST OF DISTRICT NO 9, KARIMNAGAR
Hyderabad. India. (State). Superintendent of Census Operations *see* CODES OF CENSUS PROCEDURES FOR THE HYDERABAD ASSIGNED DISTRICTS
HYDRAULICS AND PNEUMATICS – 1- 1948- – 1,5,6,9 – us UMI [627]
EN HYDRAVION AU-DESSUS DU CONTINENT NOIR / Bernard, Marc – Paris: B Grasset, 1927 – 1 – us Res Libr [550]
HYDROBIOLOGICAL RESEARCH – (v20-. 1984-. 5,6,9) – v5-. 1969- – 1 – us UMI [574]
HYDROCARBON PROCESSING – International ed. 1- 1922- – 1. ; 5,6. ; 9 – apply; v.44-; v.54- – us UMI [660]
HYDROCARBON PROCESSING – v29-41 1950-62 – 1,5,6 – us Princeton Micro [660]
HYDRODYNAMISCHE KENNGROESSEN VON GLEITLAGERN MIT UNTERBROCHENER RINGNUT UND IHRE ANWENDUNG BEI DER BERECHNUNG DYNAMISCH BEANSPRUCHTER RADIALGLEITLAGER / Reischke, Gerhard – 1994 – 2mf – DM80.00 – 3-8267-2009-1 – gw Hänsel [627]
HYDROGRAPHIE, CONTENANT LA THEORIE ET LA PRATIQUE DE TOUTES LES PARTIES DE LA NAVIGATION / Fournier, Georges – Paris: Chez Michel Soly, 1643. SEM105P280 – 10mf – 9 – Can$22.50 – cn Bibl Nat [623]
HYDROLOGICAL ASPECTS OF DROUGHT / Beran, M A & Rodier, J A – 1985 – 149p – 9 – 92-3-102288-1 – fr UNESCO [550]
HYDROLOGICAL TECHNIQUES FOR UPSTREAM CONSERVATION – 1979 – 145p – it F.A.O. [550]
HYDROLOGY AND WATER RESOURCES OF SMALL ISLANDS : A PRACTICAL GUIDE / ed by Falkland, A – 1992 – xiii/435p – 9 – 92-3-102753-0 – fr UNESCO [550]
HYDROMETALLURGY – v1-13. 1975-84 – 1,5,6,13 – sz Elsevier [660]
HYDROTECHNICAL CONSTRUCTION – 1967-. GIDROTEKNICHESKOE STROITEL 'STOVO. Eng. Trans – 1,5,6,9 – us UMI [627]
HYDROTECHNICAL CONSTRUCTION – v15-28. 1981-94 – 1,5 – $100.00v – us UMI [600]
HYGIE – v1-. 1982- – 1,5,6,9 – us UMI [073]
HYGIEINA / Bright, T – M 314. 1582 – 9 – ne IDC [610]
L'HYGIENE A PARIS. L'HABITATION DU PAUVRE / Du Mesnil, O – (Condition of 19th C. French working class series). 1890 – 9 – fr Hachette [360]
L'HYGIENE DANS L'EDUCATION: CONFERENCE FAITE DEVANT L'UNION CATHOLIQUE DE MONTREAL, LE 15 MARS 1891 / Desroches, J Israel – s.l.: s.n., 1891?. 02669. (Pre-1900 Canadiana) – 9 – cn C.I.H.M. [971]
L'HYGIENE DU PAYSAN. / Boell, E – Angers. 1896. (La Condition Ouvriere. Part Two.) – 9 – 7.50 – fr Bibl Nationale [360]
HYGIENE ET ASSAINEMENT DES VILLES / Fonssagrives, J B – Paris. 1874. (La Condition Ouvriere. Part Two.) – 9 – 15.00 – fr Bibl Nationale [360]
HYGIENE ET MEDICINE SCOLAIRE ET UNIVERSITAIRE – 1947- – 1; 1978- 5,6,9 – us UMI [610]
HYGIENE INFANTILE ET MODERNE / Auvard, Aldred & Pingat, Henri – Paris, H. Rongier, 1889. 76 p. 1 fiche. (Statistics: Medical Studies Series) – 9 – 6.00 – fr Bibl Nationale [310]
HYGIENE PUBLIQUE OU MEMOIRES SUR LES QUESTIONS LES PLUS IMPORTANTES DE L'HYGIENE APPLIQUEE AUX PROFESSIONS ET AUX TRAVAUX D'UTILITE PUBLIQUE / Parent-Duchatelet, A J B – (Condition of 19th C. French working class series). 1836 – 9 – fr Hachette [610]
HYGIENE SOCIALE CONTRE LE PAUPERISME / Coste, Adolphe – (Condition of 19th C. French working class series). 1882 – 9 – fr Hachette [360]
HYGIENIC TEACHER AND WATER-CURE JOURNAL *see* HEALTH
Hylan, John P *see* PUBLIC WORSHIP
HYLAS ET TEMIRE / Bossi, C – (From Collection "Dances & Marches") – London: R Birchall, 180- – 1 – us Sibley [780]
Hymans, Louis Salomon *see* LE DIABLE A BRUXELLES
HYMENOMYCETEN AUS SUDBAYERN, 1879-1897 / Britzelmayr, M – (Jahresber. der Naturhist. Vereins Augsburg, nr. 28). Augsburg. 1885. B-5096 2 – 8 – ne IDC [580]
DES HYMENOMYCETES / Patouillard, N – 1900 – 7 – uk Microform Academic [580]
HYMENOMYCETES BRITANNICI / Stevenson, J – British Fungi (Hymenomycetes). 2 v. Edinburgh, London. 1886. B-6319 2 – 8 – ne IDC [580]
HYMENOMYCETES EUROPAEI / Fries, E M – 1874 – 7 – uk Microform Academic [580]
HYMENOMYCETES EUROPAEI / Fries, E M – Upsaliae. 1874. B-5381 2 – 8 – ne IDC [580]
HYMENOPHYLLACEAE / Presl, K B – Eine botanische Abhandlung. Prag. 1843. (Abhandl. K. Boehm. Ges. Wissensch. v. 3. Prag. 1845). B-7247 1 – 9 – ne IDC [580]
HYMENOPHYLLACEAE JAVANICAE;... / Bosch, R B van den – Amsterdam, 1861 – 2mf – 9 – ne IDC [580]
HYMENOPHYLLUM / Copeland, E B – 1937 – 7 – uk Microform Academic [580]
THE HYMENOPTERA ACULEATA OF THE BRITISH ISLANDS / Saunders, E – London, 1896. xii,391p.54 pls. Z-1593/2 – 8 – ne IDC [590]
HYMENOPTERA EUROPAEA PRAECIPUE BOREALIA / Dahlbom, A G – Lund, Berolini, 1843-53.2v. Z-1171/2 – 8 – ne IDC [590]
HYMENOPTERA SCANDINAVIAE / Thomson, C G – 1874 – 7 – uk Microform Academic [590]
DIE HYMENOPTEREN MITTELEUROPAS / Schmiedeknecht, H L O – Jena, 1907. vii,804p. Z-1612/2 – 8 – ne IDC [590]
HYMENOPTEROLOGISCHES STUDIEN / Foerster, A – Aachen, 1850-56.2pts. Z/1250/2 – 8 – ne IDC [590]
Hymer, Julian B *see* "AS I REMEMBER KANSAS CITY FROM MY BOYHOOD AND ITS TOWNHOOD DAYS."
HYMN – (1986- . 5,6,9) – v1- . 1949- – 1 – us UMI [073]
HYMN AND TUNE COLLECTION FROM LIBRARY OF EDMOND D. KEITH – (Includes: The Divine Companion, or, David's Harp New Tunes. 4th Ed. Fawcett, John. Hymns...of Public Worship and Private Devotions. Leeds. 1782. Gould, Nathanial D. Church Music in America. Boston. 1852. Hammond, William. Psalms, Hymns and Spiritual Songs. London. 1765) – 1 – $251.02 – us Baptist [780]
HYMN BOOK – (Methodist). Published by the General Conference of the Methodist Episcopal Church vca.1847 (Title page is missing) – 1 – $26.81 – us Baptist [780]
HYMN BOOK: THE NEW CASKET – Charleston. 1869 – 1 – $12.32 – us Baptist [780]
HYMN BOOKS – (Includes: Bradbury, William B. and Sanders, Charles W. The Young Choir... New York. 1841; Bradbury, William B. Bradbury's Golden Chain of Sabbath School Melodies. New York. 1861. Dobwell, John. A New Selection of Seven Hundred Evangelistical Hymns. Morristown, NJ. 1815. Edson, William J. and Reed, Ephraim. Musical Monitor. Ithaca, NY. 1825) – 1 – $81.48 – us Baptist [780]
THE HYMN OF THE SOUL, CONTAINED IN THE SYRIAC ACTS OF ST THOMAS / ed by Bevan, Anthony Ashley – 1897 – 1mf – 9 – ne Slangenburg [220]

HYMNARIUM QUOTIDIANUM B.M.V. : EX HYMNIS MEDII AEVI COMPARATUM – (In Latin and French. Includes indexes) – Parisiis: P Lethielleux; Neo Eboraci [New York]: F Pustet, [1892?] – 2mf – 9 – 0-8370-8854-2 – 1986-2854 – us A.T.L.A. [240]

HYMNE AU SOLEIL – (D'Holbach series). 1769 – 9 – fr Hachette [810]

L'HYMNE DES COMBATS / Bonneville, Nicolas de – Hommage aux armees de la Republique. Paris. Imprimerie-Librairie du Cercle Social. 1797 – 9 – fr Hachette [321]

HYMNEN AN DAS DIADEM DER PHARAONEN / Erman, A – (Abhandlungen der Koenig. Preuss. Akademie der Wissenschaften). Berlin. 1911. BNE-462 1 – 9 – ne IDC [290]

HYMNEN UND GEBETE AN NEBO / Pinckert, J – (Leipziger semitistische studien. v. 3, pt. 4. Leipzig. 1920). Leipzig. 1920. BNE-20,114 1 – 9 – ne IDC [290]

THE HYMNES AND SONGS OF THE CHURCH, DIVIDED INTO TWO PARTS:...CANONICALL HYMNES...THE SECOND PART...SPIRITUALL SONGS.. / Wither, George – Trans. and composed by G.W. London: Printed by the assignes of George Wither, 1623. 68p. With music, by Orlando Gibbons, to some of the hymnes – 1 – us U.W. Library [240]

HYMNES LATINES ET HYMNAIRES / Baudot, Jules – Paris: Bloud and Gay, 1914 – 1mf – us A.T.L.A. [780]

HYMNI ECCLESIAE; PARS 1: E BREVIARIO PARISIENSI, PARS 2: E BREVIARIIS ROMANO, SARISBURIENSI, ABORACENSI, ET ALIUNDE / ed by Newman, John Henry – Londini: A. Macmillan, 1865. xiv,406p – 1 – us U.W. Library [240]

HYMNI ECCLESIASTICI, PRAESERTIM QUI AMBROSIANI DICUNTUR. – Coloniae, 1556. Includes index – 1 – us U.W. Library [240]

HYMNI ET SAECULA / Arias Montano, Benito – 1593 – 9 – 1.50f – sp Bibl Santa Ana [240]

HYMNI ET SECULA / Arias Montano, Benito – Antuerpiae: Officina. Plantiniana, 1593 – sp Bibl Santa Ana [240]

HYMNI ET SERMONES / Ephraemi Syri; ed by Lamy, Thomas Josephus – 1 1882 15mf; 2 1886 14mf; 3 1889 18mf; 4 1906 16mf – 8 – ne Slangenburg [240]

HYMNI SACRI IN USUM LUDI ILLUSTRIS AD FONTES SALUTARES MELODIIS & NUMERIS COMPOSTI & COLLECTTI A JOHANNE NESERO, MUSICAE IN EODEM LUDO MODERATORE / Neser, J – Curiae Variscorum (i.e. stadt-am-hof) ex officina Matthaee Pfeilschmidii, anno Christi MDCXII [1612] – 1 – us Sibley [780]

HYMNODIA HISPANICA / Arevalo, Faustino – 1786 – 9 – 1.50f – sp Bibl Santa Ana [780]

HYMNOGRAPHIE DE L'EGLISE GRECQUE : DISSERTATION ACCOMPAGNEE DES OFFICES DU 16 JANVIER, DES 29 ET 30 JUIN EN L'HONNEUR DE S. PIERRE ET DES APOTRES / Pitra, J B – Rome: Imprimerie de la Civilta cattolica, 1867 – 3mf – us A.T.L.A. [780]

THE HYMNOLOGY AND THE HYMNALS OF THE RESTORATION MOVEMENT / Hanson, Kenneth C – Thesis. 1951 – 1 – 12.56 – us Baptist [240]

HYMNOR[UM] ET THRENDORIARVM SANCTAE CRVCIS IN SALVTAREM PASSIONIS IESU CHRI.. / Besler, Samuel – Wratislaviae [i.e. Wroclaw] ex officina typographica Georgi Bauman, [Published by the author], [1613] – 1 – us Sibley [780]

HYMNOR'(UM] ET THRENODIARVM SANCTAE CRVCIS IN DEVOTAM PASSIONIS IESU CHRISTI DEI... / Besler, Samuel – Wratislaviae [i.e. Breslau] ex officina typographica Georgi Bauman. Published by the author, [1611] – 1 – us Sibley [780]

HYMNS / Bowring, John – 1825 – 1 – $50.00 – us Presbyterian [780]

HYMNS : THEIR HISTORY AND DEVELOPMENT IN THE GREEK AND LATIN CHURCHES, GERMANY AND GREAT BRITAIN / Selborne, Roundell Palmer, Earl of – London: A. and C. Black, 1892 – 1mf – us A.T.L.A. [780]

HYMNS ANCIENT AND MODERN / Monk, William H – 1869 – 1 – 10.92 – us Baptist [240]

HYMNS ANCIENT AND MODERN FOR USE IN THE SERVICES OF THE CHURCH WITH ACCOMPANYING TUNES – (Historical Edition with notes) – London, 1909 – 27mf – 8 – Dfl95.00 – ne Slangenburg [780]

HYMNS AND ANTHEMS ADAPTED FOR JEWISH WORSHIP : SELECTED AND ARRANGED BY GUSTAV GOTTHEIL / Gottheil, Gustav – (Includes index of first lines) – NY: G P Putnam, 1887, c1886 – 1mf – 9 – 0-8370-3349-7 – 1985-1349 – us A.T.L.A. [780]

HYMNS AND PSALMS – (Starting from opposite cover) – Manuscript, 1804 – 1 – us Sibley [780]

HYMNS AND SPIRITUAL SONGS / Dupuy, Starke – Ed. and rev. by John M. Peck. 1843 – 1 – 14.07 – us Baptist [240]

HYMNS AND SPIRITUAL SONGS – Newport. 1766 – 1 – 6.65 – us Baptist [240]

HYMNS FOR THE PEOPLE (CCC75) / Chao, Tzu-ch'en – (In Chinese) – Shanghai: Christian Literature Society, 1931 – 1r – 1 – 1984-B500 – us A.T.L.A. [240]

HYMNS OF PRAISE / ed by Underwood, Horace Grant – (In Korean language) – Yokohama, Japan, 1894 – 1r – 1 – $50.00 – us Presbyterian [240]

HYMNS OF THE ATHARVA-VEDA / ed by Mueller, Friedrich Max – (Translated by M. Bloomfield) – 1897 – 14mf – 8 – ne Slangenburg [280]

HYMNS, PSALMS AND SPIRITUAL SONGS / Graves, Absalom – 1825 – 1 – 14.63 – us Baptist [240]

HYMNUS AMBROSIANUS SIVE TE DEUM LAUDAMUS. A QUATRO VOCI, 2 VIOLINI, VIOLA, OBOI, CORNI, TROMBE, TIMPANI ET ORGANO / Hasse, J A – (Manuscript) – 180- – 1 – us Sibley [780]

HYMN-WRITERS OF THE NINETEENTH CENTURY : WITH SELECTIONS AND BIOGRAPHICAL NOTICES / Leask, G A – London: E. Stock, 1902 – 1mf – us A.T.L.A. [780]

HYMODY OF THE 16TH CENTURY ANABAPTISTS / Duerksen, Rosella R – 1956. Sacred Music thesis – 1 – 11.48 – us Baptist [240]

Hyndman, B et al *see* AUTOMEDICA

Hyner, Gerald G *see* PSYCHOSOCIAL FACTORS IN THE DEVELOPMENT OF BREAST CANCER

HYPERTENSION – v.1. 1979 – 1,5,6,9 – us UMI [073]

HYPNOTISM / Moll, Albert – 4th ed. rev. and enl. London, 1898. 448p. (Contemporary Science Series) – 1 – us U.W. Library [615]

HYPNOTISM AND SPIRITISM = IPNOTISMO E SPIRITISMO : A CRITICAL AND MEDICAL STUDY / Lapponi, Giuseppe – (In English. Includes index) – New York: Longmans, Green, 1907 – 1mf – 9 – 0-8370-6993-9 – 1986-0993 – us A.T.L.A. [130]

HYPNOTISM AND SUGGESTION IN THERAPEUTICS, EDUCATION, AND REFORM / Mason, Rufus Osgood – New York: H. Holt, 1901.344p – 1 – us U.W. Library [150]

L'HYPNOTISME ET LES RELIGIONS, OU, LA FIN DU MERVEILLEUX / Skepto – Paris: Octave Doin, 1888. 1 fiche – 9 – us A.T.L.A. [150]

HYPNOTISME, SUGGESTION, PSYCHOTHERAPIE. ETUDES NOUVELLES. V. V. V / Bernheim, Hippolyte – (French Precursors of Psychiatry Series). Paris. O. Doin. 1891 – 9 – fr Hachette [150]

HYPNOTIZED?, OR, THE EXPERIMENT OF SIR HUGH GALBRAITH: A ROMANCE / Henshaw, Julia Wilmotte – Toronto: Ontario Pub. Co., 1898.05545.(Pre-1900 Canadiana) – 9 – cn C.I.H.M. [830]

HYPOMNEMATA MUSICA, ODER MUSIKALISCHES MEMORIAL/WELCHES BESTEHT IN KURTZER ERINNERUNG DESSEN / Werckmeister, A – Qvedlinburg. 1697. BP-774 1 – 9 – ne IDC [780]

HYPOMNEMATUM MUSICAE POETICAE / Burmeister, J – P 187. 1599 – 9 – ne IDC [780]

DIE HYPOTIPOSEN DES THEOGNOST (T.U.U. 2-24/3B) / Harnack, Adolf von – Leipzig, 1903 – 1mf – 9 – ne Slangenburg [240]

Hyvernat, Henri *see*
– LES ACTES DES MARTYRS DE L'EGYPTE
– NOTICES SUR L'HISTOIRE ANCIENNE DE L'ARMENIE ET LES INSCRIPTIONS CUNEIFORMES DU BASSIN DE VAN
– PETITE INTRODUCTION A L'ETUDE DE LA MASSORE

H.Z. Williams and Brothers *see*
– HISTORY OF PREBLE COUNTY
– HISTORY OF TRUMBUL AND MAHONING COUNTIES
– HISTORY OF WASHINGTON COUNTY

I A R (Institute of Administrative Research) *see* RESEARCH BULLETIN

I ACCUSE / Bartlett, Vernon – London, 1937. Fiche W 748. (Blodgett Collection of Spanish Civil War Pamphlets) – 9 – us H.U. College Libr [946]

I ACCUSE FRANCE – High Wycombe, 1936? Fiche W951. (Blodgett Collection of Spanish Civil War Pamphlets) – 9 – us H.U. College Libr [946]

I ALTA – (Includes c.1: 1894:Jan.11, 20, Apr.24, Aug.10, 20, Sept. 10, Oct.1-5; 1894:Oct.18-28; 1895:Nov.23, Dec.9; 1896:Jan.3-6, Mar.3, 24, June 2, July 2, 17, Sept.26) – I Alta: [s.n.], 1893 – 1 – CSUXADP5002-S – us Hoover Inst Photo [947]

I AM CAPTURED (CCC81) = WO PEI TAI CHU LE / Chao, Tzu-ch'en – (In Chinese) – Shanghai: Association Press of China, 1950 – 1r – 1 – 1984-B500 – us A.T.L.A. [240]

THE I. AND N. REPORTER / U.S. Immigration and Naturalization Service – (Cont by: The I.N.S. Reporter) – v1-25 no 1. Jul 1952-Summer 1976 (all publ) – 25mf – 9 – $37.50 – LLMC 81-505 – us L.L.M.C. [324]

THE I. AND N. REPORTER *see*
– THE I.N.S. REPORTER
– MONTHLY REVIEW OF THE IMMIGRATION AND NATURALIZATION SERVICE

I AND P : ISRAEL AND PALESTINE POLITICAL REPORT – v85-. 1981- – 1,5,6,9 – us UMI [073]

I APONII A NA RUSSKOM DALNEM VOSTOKE : KROVAVAI A EPOPEI A I APONSKO I INTERVENTSII / Communist International. Executive Committee – Moskva: Izdatelskoe otd-nie T S.K.R.K.P., 1922 – 1 – CSUX88-B5837 – us Hoover Inst Photo [320]

I ASLI / ORGAN NARKOMZDRAVA R.S.F.S.R. – (Library has: 1933, no.2) – Moskva: Gos. med. izd-vo (Medgiz), 1933-1934. 2v – 1 – CSUX89-S903 – us Hoover Inst Photo [947]

I AUGI – (Yrly reel count varies) – [Greece], 1989- – 1 – inquire – us Ross [072]

I BELIEVE IN GOD THE FATHER ALMIGHTY / Barrows, John Henry – Chicago:Fleming H. Revell, c1892 – 1mf – 9 – 0-8370-2548-6 – 1985-0548 – us A.T.L.A. [210]

I CATALOGO DE LA BIBLIOTECA CIRCULANTE A UTILIZAR POR LOS ASEGURADOS Y BENEFICIARIOS INTERNADOS EN ESTE CENTRO SANITARIO, CONSTA DE UN TOTAL DE SEISCIENTOS VOLUMENES / Ministerio de Trabajo – Badajoz: Tip. Barrena, 1962 – 1 – sp Bibl Santa Ana [020]

I CHING – Unorthodox Classics. v. 1-36. Shanghai. 1936-37. Lacking: v. 36, 1937. BCH-276 2 – 8 – ne IDC [280]

I COMMENTARI I DELLE GVERRE FATTO CO' TURCHI DA D. GIOVANNI D'AVSTRIA, ... / Carocciolo, F – Fiorenza, 1581 – 2mf – 9 – H-8358/1 – ne IDC [956]

I COMMENTARI...DELL' ORIGINE DE PRINCIPI TURCHI, ET DE' CONSTUMI DI QUELLA NATIONE / Spandugino, T – Fiorenza, 1551 – 3mf – 9 – H-8283/1 – ne IDC [956]

I CONTRATTI DIFFERENZIALI... / Diena, G – Milano, 1910 – 1mf – 1 – ILM-3260/1 – ne IDC [327]

I CROSSED THE PLAINS IN THE '50'S / Carpenter, James C – 1 – us KS Hist [978]

I DIECI LIBRI DE L'ARCHITETTURA / Alberti, L B – O-1033. 1546 – 9 – ne IDC [720]

I DIRITTO REALI CONSIDERATI NEL DIRITTO INTERNAZIONALE PRIVATO / Diena, G – Torino, 1895 – 5mf – 1 – ILM-3563/1 – ne IDC [327]

I DISCORSI. SOPRA L'IMPRESE / Palazzi, Giovanni Andrea – O-387. 1575 – 9 – ne IDC [760]

I FIORI DEI TRE COMPAGNI...MILANO, 1967 / Cambell, Jacques – Madrid: Graf. Calleja, 1967 – 1 – sp Bibl Santa Ana [946]

I JORNADAS DE PROMOCION DEL DEPORTE LABORAL / Obra Sindical de Educacion y Descanso – Caceres: T. Extremadura, 1975 – 1 – sp Bibl Santa Ana [370]

I JORNADAS FRUTICOLAS DE EXTREMADURA – Don Benito: Graficas Sanchez Trejo, 1969 – 1 – sp Bibl Santa Ana [630]

I KATHEMERINI – (Yrly reel count varies) – [Greece], 1987- – 1 – inquire – us Ross [072]

I MARMI / Doni, A F – BD-1004 1. 1552 – 9 – ne IDC [720]

I MICETI DELL' AGRO BRESCIANO / Venturi, Adolfo – Brescia. 1845-60. B-896 2 – 8 – ne IDC [580]

I MOLLUSCHI DEI TERRENI TERZIARI DEL PIEMONTE E DELLA LIGURIA / ed by Bellardi, L & Sacco, F – Torino. 30pts. 1872-1904 – 152mf – 9 – ne IDC [945]

I. MOSKOVSKOE ARKHEOLOGICHESKOE OBSHCHESTVO V PERVOE PIATIDESIATILETIE EGO SUZHCHESTVOVANIIA (1864-1914 GG.) – Tom. II; I. Biograficheskii slovar' chlenov obshchestva. 2. Spisok trudov chlenov obshchestva. M. 1915. BR-5905 2 – 8 – ne IDC [930]

I NOSTRI ERRORI, TREDICI ANNI IN ERITREA – Torino. 1898 – 1 – us Res Libr [960]

I NOSTRI PROTESTANTI / Comba, Emilio – Firenze: Claudiana, 1895-1897 – 3mf – us A.T.L.A. [240]

I NUOVI ORIZZONTI DELLA SCIENZA... / Fiore, P – Napoli, 1909 – 1mf – 1 – ILM-2116/1 – ne IDC [327]

I PLATONICI ITALIANI / Semprini, Giovanni – Milano: Edizioni Athena, 1926 – 119p – 1 – us U.W. Library [180]

I POSSEDIMENTE ITALIANI IN AFRICA (LIBIA, ERITREA, SOMALIA) / Stefanini, Giuseppe – Firenze. 1929 – 1 – us Res Libr [960]

I PRIMI INFLUSSI DI DANTE, DEL PETRARCA, E DEL BOCCACCIO SULLA LETTERATURA SPAGNUOLA, CON APPENDICE DI DOCUMENTI INEDITI.. / Sanvisenti, Bernardo – Milano: U. Hoepli, 1902.xvi,463p – 1 – us U.W. Library [440]

I PRIMO FASTI DELLA MUSICA ITALIANA A PARIGI: 1645-1662 / Ademollo, Alessandro – Milan: Ricordi, 1884. 113,vip. 2 fiches. (Music Collection) – 9 – 6.00 – fr Bibl Nationale [780]

I QUATTRO LIBRI DELL' ARCHITETTURA / Palladio, Andrea – O-388. 1570 – 9 – ne IDC [720]

I QUATTRO PRIMI LIBRI DI ARCHITETTURA / Cataneo, P – O-1008 1. 1554 – 9 – ne IDC [720]

I SAMUEL 1-7:1 : TEXT- UND QUELLEN-KRITISCH UNTERSUCHT / Holtz, Kurt – Leipzig: W. Drugulin, 1904. 1 fiche – 9 – us A.T.L.A. [220]

I SEARCH FOR TRUTH IN RUSSIA / Citrine, Walter McLennan – Popular ed. rev.London: G. Routledge & sons, 1938. x,420p. map – 1 – us U.W. Library [947]

I TIPOGRAFI EBREI DI SONCINO, STUDII BIBLIOGRAFICI / Sacchi, F – Cremona, 1877 – 1mf – ne IDC [470]

I TRINDARIDI : DRAMME PER MUSICA IN CINQUE ATTI / Traetta, T – (Orchestral score) – Ms copy, 176- – 1 – us Sibley [780]

I TRION FI FESTE, ET LIVREE FATTE DALLI SIGNORI CONSERVATORI, ET POPOLO ROMANO, ET DA TUTTE LE ARTI DI ROMA, ... / Colonna, M A – Venetia, 1571 – 1mf – 9 – H-8155/1 – ne IDC [945]

I UNY I PROLETARI I : ORGAN PETERBURGSKOGO GORODSKOGO I GUBERNSKOGO KOMITETOV ROSSI ISKOGO KOMMUNISTICHESKOGO SOI UZA MOLODEZHI – (Library has: 1919, no. 18/19) – Petrograd: Peterburgski i komitet Rossi iskogo kommunisticheskogo soi uza molodezhi, 1917-1936. 20v – 1 – CSUX89-S942 – us Hoover Inst Photo [941]

I Uridicheski i otdel Vestnika pute i soobshcheniia *see* VOPROSY TRANSPORTNOGO PRAVA

I UZHNAI A GAZETA – (c.1: 1917:Oct.21-22. Nov.9, 15) – Kiev: "I Uzhnai a kopi e ika", 19uu – 1 – CSUXAKG5960-S – us Hoover Inst Photo [947]

I UZHNOE SLOVO – (Includes c.1: 1919:Dec.9, 24) – Odessa: "Russkai a kultura", 1919 – 1 – CSUXANR4509-S – us Hoover Inst Photo [947]

I VIAGGI DI NICOLO DE CONTI. / Bellemo, Vincenzo – Milan: A. Brigota, 1883.336p. illus., map. 4 fiches.(Literature Collection) – 9 – 10.00 – fr Bibl Nationale [920]

I WANT THE EARTH, PLUS FIVE PERCENT – Anonymous. Social Credit Pamphlet. Reproduced as the starting point for a discussion with David Taylor. 21p – 9 – 1.00f – at Libertarian Micro [335]

I WAS A FRANCO SOLDIER / MacKee, Seumas – London, 1938. Fiche W1011. (Blodgett Collection of Spanish Civil War Pamphlets) – 9 – us H.U. College Libr [946]

I WAS DEFEATED / Kodama, Yoshio – Transl. from the Japanese. (Tokyo?): R. Booth and T. Fukuda, (1951). 223p – 1 – us U.W. Library [950]

IA. GUMILEV / Levinson, A – Sovremennye Zapiski. 1922. BR-3673 2 – 8 – ne IDC [460]

Iacob Iansen Kist en Hans De Ries *see* NOOTWENDIGE VERANTWOORDINGE DER VERDRUCTER WAERHEYT

IACP LAW ENFORCEMENT LEGISLATION AND LITIGATION REPORT – (International Association of Chiefs of Police). 1970-1976 – 1 – us UMI [073]

Iagich, V *see*
- CODEX MARIANUS GLAGOLITICUS. QUATTUOR EVANGELIORUM VERSIONIS PALAEOSLOVENICAE
- ISTORIIA SLAVIANSKOI FILOLOGII
- VOPROS O RUNAKH U SLAVIAN. GRECHESKOE PIS'MO IX-X STOLETII.

IAK PRYISHLO V ROSII DO REVOLIUTSII / Danko, Mykola & Trotskyi, M – Viden: Nakladom Soi uza vyzvolenni a Ukrainy, 1917 – 1 – CSUX89-B1628 – us Hoover Inst Photo [947]

Iakhontov, A N *see* OPISANIE PUSHKINSKAGO MUZEIA IMP

Iakhontov, P V *see*
- KAK ORGANIZOVAT' KREDITNUIU RABOTU V PROMYSLOVOI KOOPERATSII
- PROMYSLOVOE KREDITNOE TOVARISHCHESTVO

Iakhontov, SD *see* BIBLIOGRAFICHESKII SLOVAR' PISATELEI, UCHENYKH I KHUDOZHNIKOV UROZHENTSEV (PREIMUSHCHESTVENNO) RIAZANSKOI GUBERNII

Iakobson, R *see* NOVEISHAIA RUSSKAIA POEZIIA

IAKOR' – Antologiia zarubezhnoi (emigrantskoi) poezii. Pod red. Adamovicha i Kantora. Berlin-Petropolis. 1936. BR-3317 2 – 8 – ne IDC [460]

IAKOV MIKHAILOVICH SVERDLOV, EGO ZHIZN I DEIATELNOST : K DESIATILETNEI GODOVSHCHINE EGO SMERTI 16 MARTA 1919–16 MARTA 1929 / Gaisinskii, Mikhail Grigorevich – Moskva: Gos. izd-vo, 1929 – 1 – CSUX88-B7539 – us Hoover Inst Photo [947]

Iakovlev, A I *see* ZA ULUCHSHENIE KOOPERATIVNYKH KADROV

Iakovlev, A V *see*
- MELKII ZEMEL'NYI KREDIT V ROSSII
- SEL'SKIE SSUDNYE TOVARICHESTVA

Iakovlev, I A *see* GOD SLUZHBY "SOTSIALISTOV" KAPITALISTAM

Iakovleva, V K *see* IAZYK IORUBA

Iakushkin, E I *see* OBYCHNOE PRAVO

Iakushkin, V E *see* RUSSKAIA PECHAT' I TSENZURA V PROSHLOM I NASTOIASHCHEM

IAKUTSKAIA KOOPERATSIIA – (Missing: 1921 n2-3. 1922/23 n8-9) – Iakutsk, 1921-24 n1 – 4mf – 9 – COR-710/1 – ne IDC [334]

Ianantuoni, Domingo Rafael *see* EL PLAN QUINQUENAL EXPLICADO A LOS NINOS

IANIDA MIANI SENENSIS AD LEONEM 10. PONT. MAX. DE EXPEDITIONE IN TURCAS ELEGEIA, CU ARGUTISSIMIS / Damianus, J – Basileae, 1515 – 2mf – 9 – H-8227/1 – ne IDC [956]

Iankova, Z *see* IZMENENIIA STRUKTURY SOTSIALNYKH ROLEI ZHENSHCHIN V RAZVITOM SOTSIALISTICHESKOM OBSHCHESTVE I MODEL SEMI

Ianovskii, A D *see* NAPOLEON – SA FAMILLE – SON ENTOURAGE

Ianzhul, I I *see*
- IZ VOSPOMINANII I PEREPISKI FABRICHNAGO INSPEKTORA PERVAGO PRIZYVA
- VOSPOMINANIIA O PEREZHITOM I VIDENNOM V 1864-1909 GG

IAPI OAYE, THE WORD CARRIER = THE WORD CARRIER – (In English, 1884-1937. 29 fiches. $125.00) – 1871-1939. In Dakota language. (American Indian Periodicals in the Princeton University Library).57 fiches – 9 – $230.00 – us UPA [305]

IAPONSKAIA INTERVENTSIIA 1918-1922 GG. V DOKUMENTAKH / ed by Mintz, I I – Moscow, 1934 – 1 – $35.00r – us Hoover Inst Photo [947]

IAR'. STIKHI LIRICHESKIE I LIROEPICHESKIE / Gorodetskii, S – Spb. 1907. BR-1126 2 – 8 – ne IDC [460]

IAROSLAVSKII LITERATURNYI SBORNIK – v. 1-2. Iaroslval'. 1849-50. BR-3204 2 – 8 – ne IDC [073]

IARYI GOD / Sologub, F – Razskazy. M. 1911. BR-862 2 – 8 – ne IDC [460]

Iashchenko, A *see* RUSSKAIA BIBLIOGRAFIIA PO ISTORII DREVNEI FILOSOFII

Iasinskii, I I *see* ROMAN MOEI ZHIZNI

IASNAIA POLIANA – no. 1-2. Moscou. janv-fevr 1862 – 1 – fr A.C.R.P.P. [073]

IASNAIA POLIANA – Zhurnal pedagogicheskii. v. 1-2. M. 1862. B-1497 2 – 8 – ne IDC [073]

IASWR BUDDHIST SANSKRIT MANUSCRIPTS : FROM NEPAL – (Complete set of the IASWR Buddhist Sanskrit Manuscripts.- 1,185mf. $3400.00; Catalog of Titles.-1mf. $1.00; Alphabetical title list.- 1mf. $1.00; Descriptive Catalog, Part 1.-6mf. $6.00; Descriptive Catalog, Part 2.-9mf. $9.00; Descriptive Catalog, Part 3.-2mf. $2.00; Recently compiled Supplemental Manuscripts.- 314mf. $900.00; Supplemental Descriptive Catalog.-1mf. $1.00) – us I.A.S.W.R. [280]

Iatsevich, Andrei Grigor'evich *see* KREPOSTNOI PETERBURG PUSHKINSKOGO VREMENI

Iatsimirskii, A I *see* BIBLIOGRAFICHESKII OBZOR APOKRIFOV V IUZHNOSLAVIANSKOI I RUSSKOI PIS'MENNOSTI (SPISKI PAMIATNIKOV)

Iatsmirskii, A I *see* SLAVIANSKIIA I RUSSKIIA RUKOPISI RUMYNSKIKH BIBLIOTEK

IAZYK IORUBA / Iakovleva, V K – Moskva: Izd-vo vostochnoi lit-ry, 1963 – us Res Libr [072]

IAZYK PUSHKINA / Vinogradov, V V – M., 1935 – 8mf – 9 – 1171/2 – ne IDC [460]

IAZYK ULOZHENIIA 1649 GODA / Chernykh, P Ia – Moscow, 1953. BR-10,320/1 – 9 – ne IDC [947]

Iazykov, D D *see*
- NOVYE MATERIALY DLIA ISTORII RUSSKOI DUKHOVNOI LITERATURY
- OBZOR ZHIZNI I TRUDOV RUSSKIKH PISATELEI I PISATEL'NITS

Ibanez, F *see* TOPOGRAFIA HIPOCRATICA O DESCRIPCION DE LA EPIDEMIA DE CALENTURAS TERCIANAS INTERMITENTES MALIGNAS...EN LA ALCARRIA DEIDE 1784

Ibarguren, Carlos *see*
- DISCURSOS A LOS VASCOS DE AMERICA
- EL PAISAJE Y EL ALMA ARGENTINA
- LA REFORMA CONSTITUCIONAL, SUS FUNDAMENTOS Y SU ESTRUCTURA

Ibarguren, Federico *see* ORIGENES DEL NACIONALISMO ARGENTINO

Ibarra y Berge, Javier de *see*
- DE CALIFORNIA A ALASKA. MADRID, 1945
- EL MORO VIZCAINO (JOSE MARIA DE MURGA). MADRID, 1944

Ibarrola, Jose *see*
- EL ASESINATO DEL REGATO DE LOS AVELLANOS
- LITERATURA SUBLIME E HISTORIA GLORIOSA Y TRAGICA. COPIADA LA PRIMERA Y RELATADA LA SEGUNDA EN ARTICULOS

Ibarruri, Dolores *see*
- EJERCITO POPULAR UNIDO, EJERCITO DE LA VICTORIA
- LA ESPANA FRANQUISTA, SATELITE DE HITLER
- FOR THE INDEPENDENCE OF SPAIN, FOR LIBERTY, FOR THE REPUBLIC, UNION OF ALL SPANIARDS
- NO HAY MAS POSIBILIDAD DE GOBERNAR NI DE VICTORIA QUE A TRAVES DEL FRENTE POPULAR
- UN PLENO HISTORICO
- POR LA INDEPENDENCIA DE ESPANA, POR LA LIBERTAD, POR LA REPUBLICA

Ibbotson, H *see* THE FERNS OF YORK

Ibel, Rudolf *see* DON CARLOS

IBERGANG = TRANSITION – (Yiddish in Latin characters) – Munich, DE. no39 23 Sep 1947-no43 2 Nov 1947 – 1r – 1 – $25.00 – cn Can Microfilming [072]

IBERIA FIRST BAPTIST CHURCH. IBERIA, MISSOURI : CHURCH RECORDS – 1877-1968 – 1 – 59.31 – us Baptist [240]

D'IBERVILLE, OU, LE JEAN-BART CANADIEN ET LA BAIE D'HUDSON – Montreal: s.n., 1868. 02655. (Pre-1900 Canadiana) – 9 – cn C.I.H.M. [971]

O IBIRACI : ORGAO DA PREFEITURA MUNICIPAL – Ibiraci, 7 Sep, Nov 1933; Dec 1934; Jan-Mar, Aug-Oct 1935; Apr-Aug, Nov-Dec 1936; Jan-May 1937; Jan-Jun, Sep-Nov 1938; Apr-Jun, Sep 1939; Feb, May-Jun, Nov 1940; Jan-Feb, Apr-Jun, Aug-Sep, Nov-Dec 1941; Jan, 8 Mar 1942 – 1,5,6 – bl Biblioteca [072]

IBIS : A JOURNAL OF GENERAL ORNITHOLOGY / ed by Sclater, P L et al – London, 1859-1942. v1-84 – 1,125mf – 9 – Z-244c/2 – ne IDC [590]

IBITEEKEREZO: HISTORICAL NARRATIVES FROM RWANDA / Vansina, Jan – A collection of texts and translations – 1 – us Res Libr [960]

O IBITI-RUI – Cidade do Serro, 1 Jul-1 Aug 1918 – 1,5,6 – bl Biblioteca [072]

IBM COMPATIBLES PLUS – 1984- – 1,5,6,9 – us UMI [510]

IBM JOURNAL OF RESEARCH AND DEVELOPMENT – Armonk. v1-39 jan 1957-nov 1995 1; v10-39 jan 1966-nov 1995 5; v14-39 jan 1970-nov 1995 9; v40-41 jan 1996-nov 1997+ 1,5,9 – 1,5,9 – D1525 – us UMI [073]

Ibn Abidin, Muhammad ibn Muhammad Amin *see* QURRAT 'UYUN AL-AKHYAR

Ibn al Fayyumi, Nathanael *see* THE BUSTAN AL-UKUL

Ibn Al-Arabi *see* TARJUMAN AL-ASHWAQ

Ibn Batutah *see* TRAVELS

Ibn Daud, Abraham ben David, Halevi *see* HA-EMUNAH HA-RAMAH MICROFORM

Ibn Habib, M *see* DAREKHEI NO'AM

IBN KHALDUN'S PHILOSOPHY OF HISTORY: A STUDY IN THE PHILOSOPHIC FOUNDATION OF THE SCIENCE OF CULTURE / Mahdi, Muhsin – London: G. Allen and Unwin, 1957. Bibliography.325p – 1 – us U.W. Library [180]

Ibn Khallikan *see* BIOGRAPHICAL DICTIONARY

Ibn Malik *see* ALFIYYA (QUINTESSENCE DE LA GRAMMAIRE ARABE)

ibn Pakuda, Bahya ben Joseph *see* THE DUTIES OF THE HEART

Ibn Yaoish, Abu al-Baqa Yaoish ibn Ali *see* DE ENUNTIATIONIBUS RELATIVIS SEMITICIS. PARS PRIOR, PRAEMISSO IBN JAOI SI IN ZAMACH SARII, DE PRONOMINIBUS RELATIVIS LOCUM COMMENTARIO, DE ENUNTIATIONIBUS RELATIVIS ARABICIS AGENS

Ibn-al-Balkhi *see* DESCRIPTION OF THE PROVINCE OF FARS IN PERSIA

Ibn-Badroun *see*
- COMENTAIRE...POEME...IBN ABDOUN
- COMMENTAIRE HISTORIQUE SUR LE POEME D'IBN-ABDOEN

Ibn-Omar El-Tounsy, Cheyky M *see* VOYAGE AU OUADAY

IBN-WASHIH QUI DICITUR AL-JA'QUBI : HISTORIAE / ed by Houtsma, M Th – (Pars 1: Historiam ante-Islamicam continens Dfl30.00. Pars 2: Historiam Islamicam continens Dfl39.00) – Lugduni Batavorum, 1883 – ne Slangenburg [260]

IBO IA–BOLSHEVIK!! / Britan, Iliia – Berlin: [s.n.], 1924 – 1 – CSUX88-B5853 – us Hoover Inst Photo [947]

IBON – Manila. 175 docs. 1980-1991 – 52mf – 9 – ne IDC [320]

Ibrahim, Hanna et al *see*
- AL-ASWAR

IBRI – Dordrecht, 1869. v1 – 1mf – 9 – J-261-45/1 – ne IDC [073]

IBRI ANOCHI = I AM A JEW – (Hebrew weekly) – Brody, UA. v21 no19 19 Jun 1885; v21 no22 14 Aug 1885 – 1r 1610 $25.00 – 1 – cn Can Microfilming [072]

Ibsen, Henrik *see* LETTERS..

THE ICA AGRICULTURAL ASSISTANCE PROGRAM IN INDONESIA,BY LAWRENCE A. BEERY. SE 5340/1. 1959 / U.S. Operations Mission to Indonesia – 9 – ne IDC [630]

ICA ASSISTED PROJECTS WITHIN TRAVELING DISTANCE OF DJAKARTA / U.S. Operations Mission to Indonesia – SE 3306 1. 1960 – 9 – ne IDC [630]

ICA COMMUNICAE / Auburn University. Agricultural Experiment Station – No.2-5. 1979-82. 1 reel – 1, 5 – us Spaulding [630]

ICA-KURIREN – Vasteras, Sweden. 1942-78 – 55r – 1 – sw Kungliga [073]

ICAO (INTERNATIONAL CIVIL AVIATION ORGANISATION) – Printed index. Updated every 60 days – 6,9 – us Info Handling [380]

ICARIA : A CHAPTER IN THE HISTORY OF COMMUNISM / Shaw, Albert – New York: Putnam, 1884 – 1mf – us A.T.L.A. [335]

Icaza, Francisco A de *see* HEBBEL PROSISTA

ICC ACTIVITIES : 1889-1937 / U.S. Interstate Commerce Commission – (Vol covering 1937-62 believed to exist) – Washington: GPO. 1v. 1937 – 3mf – 9 – $4.50 – LLMC 81-230 – us L.L.M.C. [324]

ICC ACTS INDEXED AND DIGESTED : THE ACTS TO REGULATE COMMERCE / Hamlin, Charles S – Boston: Little-Brown, 1907 – 5mf – 9 – $7.50 – LLMC 80-525 – us L.L.M.C. [324]

I.C.C. PRACTITIONERS' JOURNAL *see* TRANSPORTATION PRACTITIONERS' JOURNAL

ICC PRACTITIONERS' JOURNAL *see* JOURNAL OF TRANSPORTATION LAW, LOGISTICS AND POLICY

ICE RECORD – Philadelphia. v. 1-2. 1900-1901. Incomplete – 1 – us NY Public [073]

ICE TRADE JOURNAL – Philadelphia: Thos E Cahill. r1: v1-8 oct 1877-jul 1885; r2-3: v9 n6-v23 n8 1886-mar 1900 – 1 – us Res Libr [380]

Iceland. Organization for European Economic Cooperation *see*
- INTERIM REPORT ON THE EUROPEAN RECOVERY PROGRAMME
- REPORT TO THE ECONOMIC COOPERATION ADMINISTRATION ON THE 1949/50 PROGRAMME

ICELANDIC SAGAS AND OTHER HISTORICAL DOCUMENTS RELATING TO THE SETTLEMENTS AND DESCENTS OF THE NORTHMEN ON THE BRITISH ISLES (RS88) / ed by Vigfusson, G – (v1,2 1887 Dfl32.00v. v3,4 1894 Dfl35.00v) – ne Slangenburg [941]

I.C.F.C. *see* REPORT OF THE 4TH SESSION OF THE COMMITTEE FOR THE DEVELOPMENT AND MANAGEMENT OF FISHERIES IN THE BAY OF BENGAL

"ICH" : LIEDESKUNST / Wolff-Cassel, Louis – 4., erw. Aufl. Dresden: E Pierson, 1901 – 1 – us U.W. Library [430]

ICH BIN KEIN INTELLEKTUELLER : EIN HEITERES BUCH / Weiss-Ferdl – Muenchen: P Hugendubel, 1941 – 1r – 1 – us U.W. Library [870]

ICH GLAUBE! : BEKENNTNISSE / Johst, Hanns – Muenchen: A Langen/G Mueller, 1928 – 1r – us U.W. Library [240]

ICH HABE MICH RASIEREN LASSEN : EIN DRAMATISCHER SCHERZ / Schiller, Friedrich von; ed by Kuenzel, Carl – Leipzig: Englische Kunst-Anstalt von A H Payne, [1862?] – 1r – 1 – us U.W. Library [870]

ICH UND GNADE : EINE STUDIE UEBER FRIEDRICH SCHLEGELS BEKEHRUNG / Horst, Karl August – (Includes bibliographical references) – Freiburg: Verlag Herder, 1951 – 1r – 1 – us U.W. Library [190]

I-Ching, 635-713. I-Ching *see* RECORD OF THE BUDDHIST RELIGION AS PRACTICED IN INDIA AND THE MALAY ARCHIPELAGO

ICHNOS : AN INTERNATIONAL JOURNAL FOR PLANT AND ANIMAL TRACES / ed by Pemberton, S George & Pickerill, Ronald K – 9,5,1 – us Harwood [560]

ICHTHYOLOGIE OU HISTOIRE GENERALE ET PARTICULIERE DES POISSONS / ed by Bloch, M E – Berlin, 1785-1797. 12v – 114mf – 9 – 2121/2 – ne IDC [590]

ICHTHYOLOGY OF SOUTH CAROLINA / Holbrook, J E – Z-252 2. 1860 – 9 – ne IDC [590]

ICHTISAR AKAR-AKAR MARXISME DAN FASCISME / Nasution, Muchtar – SE-3604 1. 1946? – 9 – ne IDC [335]

ICHTISAR HUKUM PERDATA DAN HUKUM DAGANG / Tirtodiningrat, R M T – SE 4224 1. 1963 – 9 – ne IDC [950]

ICHTISAR ILMU TAUHID / Abdulmuin, M Taib T – SE-5770 1. 196- – 9 – ne IDC [950]

ICHTISAR ISI PERS DALAM DOEA MINGGOE TEROETAMA PERS DI INDONESIA – (Lacking: 1946, V.1(2)) – Pematang Siantar, Djabatan Penerangan Dalam Negeri. July, 1946(1-3) – 2mf – 9 – ne IDC [950]

ICHTISAR ISI PERS DALAM SAMINGGOE TEROETAMA PERS DI INDONESIA – (Lacking: 1946, V.1(10-12, p269-344, 16-17, p401-434)) – Djakarta, 1946 – 7mf – 9 – ne IDC [950]

ICHTISAR RINGKAS TENTANG RIWAJAT SOSIAL-EKONOMIS INDONESIA / Sunaria, R M – SE 5277 1. 1945 – 9 – ne IDC [330]

ICHTISAR SEDJARAH INDONESIA, OENTOEK SEKOLAH MENENGAH / Siahaan, L – (Microfiche No 161) – Bandoeng: Poestaka Ksatrian, (2604) – 1mf – 9 – SE-2002/1 – ne IDC [950]

ICHTYOFAUNE DES RECIFS CORALLIENS DE TULEAR, MADAGASCAR: ECOLOGIE ET RELATIONS TROPHIQUES / Harmelin-Vivien, M – Marseille. 1979. iv/165p. 115p. annexes – 9 – F160.00 – fr Ethnologie [590]

ICHTYOFAUNE DES SECTEURS INDIEN OCCIDENTAL ET ATLANTIQUE ORIENTAL DE L'OCEAN AUSTRAL: BIOGEOGRAPHIE, CYCLES BIOLOGIQUES ET DYNAMIQUE DES POPULATIONS / Duhamel, Georges – 9 – F150.00 – fr Ethnologie [574]

ICHUD – (In Polish) – Warsaw, PL. v2 no6 15 May 1946-v2 no8 20 Jun 1946 – 1r – 1 – $25.00 – cn Can Microfilming [072]

ICHUD – (In Yiddish) – Lodz, PL. v1 no2(18). Feb/Mar 1947 – 1r – 1 – $25.00 – cn Can Microfilming [072]

ICI LONDRES – London, UK. Bulletin hebdomadaire des services europeens de la BBC. 21 Feb 1948-1 Nov 1957 – 1 – uk British Libr Newspaper [072]

ICI MONTREAL – Montreal. n94. 27 mar 1954-5 aut 1966 – 1r – 1 – Can$40.00 – cn Can Microfilming [072]

ICI RADIO-CANADA – (Cont: La Semaine a Radio-Canada) – Montreal, Canada. 1 avr 1967-1 aut 1975 – 7r – 1 – Can$60.00r – cn Can Microfilming [072]

ICI RADIO-CANADA *see* LA SEMAINE A RADIO-CANADA

ICICLE – Dalhousie [N.B: s.n. 1885?-18–?] – 9 – cn C.I.H.M. [971]

Iciek, X.A *see* POLACY W AMERYCE

THE ICILA DANCE, OLD STYLE : A STUDY IN AFRICAN MUSIC AND DANCE OF THE LALA TRIBE OF NORTHERN RHODESIA 101=JONES, A M+KOMBE, L – Roodepoort, Longmans, Green for African Music Society, 1952 – us Res Libr [790]

ICJ PLEADINGS, BARCELONA TRACTION / United Nations. International Court of Justice – Vols 1-10 – E/F.129 – 9 – us U.N. Pubs [340]

ICJ PLEADINGS/MEMOIRES / United Nations. International Court of Justice – E/F.974 – 9 – us U.N. Pubs [340]

ICJ YEARBOOK / United Nations. International Court of Justice – (1947-1989. Yearbook. E.187; 1947-1987. Annuaire. F.185) – 9 – us U.N. Pubs [340]

ICL TODAY – v1-. 1986- – 1,5,6,9 – us UMI [510]

ICMAL-I NETAYIC YAHUT MUTIRA-I FUNUN-I IDADIYE / Feyzi, Emin – Istanbul: Karabet Matbaasi, 1309 [1892] – $75.00 – us MEDOC [956]

ICOGRAPHIC – n. 12-. 1978- – 5,6,9 – us UMI [070]

ICON REGIA MONARCHAE SINARUM... 1699 / Bouvet, J – N.p., n.d. – 2mf – 9 – ne IDC [950]

ICONES AD FLORAM EUROPAE NOVO FUNDAMENTO INSTAURANDAM SPECTANTES / Jordan, A & Fourreau, P J – Parisiis. 1866-70. B-5980 2 – 8 – ne IDC [580]

ICONES AROIDEARUM / Schott, H W – Vindobonae. 1857. B-1031 2 – 8 – ne IDC [580]

ICONES AVIUM / Gould, J – London, 1837-38.2pts. 18pls. Z/1771/2 – 8 – ne IDC [590]

ICONES CARPOLOGICAE / Ralph, T S – London. 1849. B-5149 2 – 8 – ne IDC [580]

ICONES CATECHESEOS ET VIRTUTUM AC VITIORUM ILLUSTRATAE NUMERIS: ITEM HISTORIA PASSIONIS DOMINI NOSTRI JESU CHRISTI EFFIGIATA / Hoffer, Johann – Wittenburg. 1558. (Religion series) – 9 – 3.00 – fr Bibl Nationale [240]

ICONES ET DESCRIPTIO FUNGORUM QUORUNDAM SINGULARIUM / Schaeffer, J C – Ratisbonae. 1761. B-5712 2 – 8 – ne IDC [580]

ICONES ET DESCRIPTIONES FUNGORUM MINUS COGNITORUM / Persoon, C H – Lipsiae. 1798-1800. B-6296 2 – 8 – ne IDC [580]

ICONES ET DESCRIPTIONES GRAMINUM AUSTRIACORUM / Host, N T – 4v. Vindobonae. 1801-09. B-704 2 – 8 – ne IDC [580]

ICONES ET DESCRIPTIONES NOVARUM ET MINUS COGNITARUM STIRPIUM / Lehmann, J G C – Hamburgi. 1821-24. B-6013 2 – 8 – ne IDC [580]

ICONES ET DESCRIPTIONES PLANTARUM MINUS COGNITARUM / Schreber, J C D von – Decas unica. Halae. 1766. B-7132 1 – 9 – ne IDC [580]

ICONES ET DESCRIPTIONES PLANTARUM NOVARUM CRITICARUM ET RARIORUM EUROPAE AUSTRO-OCCIDENTALIS PRAECIPUE HISPANIAE / Willkomm, H M – 2v. Lipsiae. 1852-1856-62. B-5580 2 – 8 – ne IDC [580]

ICONES ET DESCRIPTIONES PLANTARUM, QUAE AUT SPONTE IN HISPANIA... / Cavanilles, A J – Matriti. 6v. 1791-1801 – 40mf – 98 – ne IDC [580]

ICONES EUPHORBIARUM, OU FIGURES DE CENT VING-DEUX ESPECES / Boissier, E P – Paris. 1866. B-5440 2 – 8 – ne IDC [580]

ICONES FILICUM / Hooker, W J & Greville, R K – 2v. London. 1827-29-1831-32. B-5088 2 – 8 – ne IDC [580]

ICONES FLORAE GERMANICAE ET HELVETICAE. DEUTSCHLANDS FLORA / ed by Reichenbach, Heinrich G L – Leipzig. 25v. 1834-1914 – 189mf – 8 – ne IDC [580]

ICONES FUCORUM / Esper, E J C – 1797-1802 – 7 – uk Microform Academic [580]

ICONES FUCORUM. ABBILDUNGEN DER TANGE / Esper, E J C – Nuernborg. 1797-1808. B-61 2 – 8 – ne IDC [580]

ICONES FUNGORUM HUCUSQUE COGNITORUM / Corda, A C – 1837-54 – 1 – uk Microform Academic [580]

ICONES FUNGORUM HUCUSQUE COGNITORUM / Corda, A C – Abbildungen der Pilze und Schwaemme. 6 v. Pragae. 1837-54 – 8 – ne IDC [580]

ICONES FUNGORUM JAVANICORUM / Penzig, A J O & Saccardo, P A – Leiden. 1904. B-6293 2 – 8 – ne IDC [580]

ICONES HEPATICARUM / ed by Geissler, Patricia – 165mf – 9 – ne IDC [580]

ICONES HEPATICARUM / ed by Stephani, F – Zug, 1985 – 166mf – 9 – 13256/1 – ne IDC [580]

ICONES HISTORICUM VETERIS TESTAMENTI / Holbein, H 2 – O-1035 1. 1547 – 9 – ne IDC [760]

ICONES HISTORIQUES DES LEPIDOPTERES NOUVEAUX OU PEU CONNUS / Boisduval, J B A D de – Paris, 1832-34. 2v. Z-1076/2 – 8 – ne IDC [590]

ICONES ILLUSTRATIONI PLANTARUM AMERICANARUM / Vahl, M – Kjobenhavn. 1798-99. B-5786 2 – 8 – ne IDC [580]

ICONES INSECTORUM PRAESERTIM ROSSIAE SIBIRIAEQUE PECULIARIUM / Pallas, Peter Simon – Erlangae, 1781. viii,104p. 8 pls. BZ-1525/2 – 8 – ne IDC [590]

ICONES JAPONICORUM INSECTORUM / Nawa, Y – Gifu, 1904, v1. BZ-1498/2 – 8 – ne IDC [590]

ICONES LITHOGRAPHICAE PLANTARUM AUSTRALASIAE RAIORUM / Guillemin, J B A – Parisiis. 1827. B-6456 2 – 8 – ne IDC [580]

ICONES LIVIANAE / Amman, J – O-1014 1. 1572 – 9 – ne IDC [450]

ICONES MUSCORUM / Sullivant, W S – London, 1864. 216 pp., 129 pls. B-620 2 – 8 – ne IDC [580]

ICONES MUSCORUM, SUPPLEMENT / Sullivant, W S – London, 1874. 109 pp., 81 pls. B-621 2 – 8 – ne IDC [580]

ICONES ORNITHOPTERORUM / Rippon, R H F – 2481 2. 2 v. 1890-1914 – 8 – ne IDC [760]

ICONES PICTAE PLANTARUM RARIORUM / Smith, J E – Londini, 1790 -1793. Fasc. 1-3. B-5258 2 – 8 – ne IDC [580]

ICONES PICTAE RARIORUM FUNGORUM / Persoon, C H – Paris. 1803-08. B-5034 2 – 8 – ne IDC [580]

ICONES PLANTARUM / ed by Hooker, W J – London. 30 v. 1836-1913 – 136mf – 8 – ne IDC [580]

ICONES PLANTARUM ASIATICARUM / Griffith, W – 4v. Calcutta. 1847-54. B-94 2 – 8 – ne IDC [580]

ICONES PLANTARUM GALLIAE RARIORUM NEMPE INCERTARUM AUT NONDUM DELINEATARUM / Candolle, A P de – Parisiis. 1808. B-5872 2 – 8 – ne IDC [580]

ICONES PLANTARUM INCOGNITARUM QUAS IN INDIA OCCIDENTALI / Swartz, O P – Erlangae, 1794. 8 pp., 13 pls. Fasc. 1. B-5758 2 – 8 – ne IDC [580]

ICONES PLANTARUM INDIAE ORIENTALIS / Wight, R – or FIGURES OF Indian plants. 6 v. Madras. 1840-53. Including: Cleghorn, H. E. C. General index of the plants described and figured in Dr. Wight's work. London. 1921. B-1051 2 – 8 – ne IDC [580]

ICONES PLANTARUM JAPONICARUM / Thunberg, C P – Upsaliae. 1794-1805. B-5767 2 – 8 – ne IDC [580]

ICONES PLANTARUM KOISIKAVENSES / Matsumura, J – Tokyo, 1911-1915. 2 vols. B-7380 1 – 9 – ne IDC [580]

ICONES PLANTARUM NOVARUM VEL IMPERFECTE COGNITARUM FLORAM ROSSICAM / Ledebour, CF von – Riga. 5v. 1829-1834 – 41mf – 9 – ne IDC [580]

ICONES PLANTARUM RARIORUM / Jacquin, N J von – 3v. Vindobonae. 1781-1793-95. B-128 2 – 8 – ne IDC [580]

ICONES PLANTARUM RARIORUM / Voorhelm Schneevoogt, G – Haerlem. 1793-95. B-5721 2 – 8 – ne IDC [580]

ICONES PLANTARUM RARIORUM HORTI REGII BOTANICI BEROLINENSIS / Link, J H F & Klotsch, J F & Otto, CF – 2v. Berlin. 1841-44. B-6037 2 – 8 – ne IDC [580]

ICONES PLANTARUM RARIORUM HORTI REGII BOTANICI BEROLINENSIS / Link, J H F & Otto, CF – Abbildungen neuer und seltener Gewaechse. pars 1. Berlin. 1828-31. B-6036 2 – 8 – ne IDC [580]

ICONES PLANTARUM SELECTARUM HORTI REGII BOTANICI BEROLINENSIS / Link, J H F & Otto, CF – Abbildungen auserlesener Gewaechse. Berlin. 1820-28. B-6035 1 – 9 – ne IDC [580]

ICONES PLANTARUM SYRIAE RARIORUM / Labillardiere, J J H de – Lutetiae Parisiorum. 1791-1812. B-5996 2 – 8 – ne IDC [580]

ICONES RERUM NATURALIUM QUAS IN ITINERE ORIENTALI DEPINGI CURAVIT P. FOSKAL / Forsskal, P – Havnaie. 1776. B-6433 2 – 8 – ne IDC [580]

ICONES SELECTAE HORTI THENENSIS / Wildeman, E de – 6v. Bruxelles. 1899-1909. B-7378 1 – 8 – ne IDC [580]

ICONES SELECTAE HYMENOMYCETUM FENNIAE / Karsten, P A – Helsingforsiae. 1883-89. B-5098 2 – 8 – ne IDC [580]

ICONES SELECTAE HYMENOMYCETUM HUNGARIAE PER S. SCHULZER ET C. KALCHBRENNER OBSERVATORIUM ET DELINEATORUM / Kalchbrenner, C – 4pts. Pestini. 1873-77. B-6278 2 – 8 – ne IDC [580]

ICONES SELECTAE PLANTARUM / Delessert, B – 5v. Paris. 1820-46. B-655 2 – 8 – ne IDC [580]

ICONES SELECTAE PLANTARUM / Kaempfer, Engelbert – Londini. 1791. B-1123 2 – 8 – ne IDC [580]

ICONES SELECTAE PLANTARUM CRYPTOGAMICARUM QUAS IN ITINERE PER BRASILIAM ANNIS 1817-1820 INSTITUTO COLLEGIT ET DESCRIPSIT / Martius, Karl Friedrich Philipp von – Monachii, 1828-1834. 138 pp., 76 pls. B-5400B 2 – 8 – ne IDC [580]

ICONES SYMBOLICAE VITAE ET MORTIS B. JOSAPHAT MARTYRIS ARCHIEPISCOPI POLOCENSIS EXPRESSAE... / Mlodzianowski, A – Vilnae, 1675 – 2mf – 9 – ne IDC [700]

ICONOCLASTS : A BOOK OF DRAMATISTS: IBSEN, STRINDBERG, BECQUE, HAUPTMANN, SUDERMANN, HERVIEU, GORKY, DUSE AND D'ANNUNZIO, MAETERLINCK AND BERNARD SHAW / Huneker, James – New York: Charles Scribner's, 1905 – 1 roll – 1 – 1-55879-404-2 – uk Libr Preservation [410]

ICONOGRAFIA DE BENITO ARIAS MONTANO / Doetsch, Carlos – Madrid: Tip. Blass, 1927 – 1 – sp Bibl Santa Ana [946]

ICONOGRAFIA DE BENITO ARIAS MONTANO POR CARLOS DOETSCH / Fernandez de Castro, Eduardo Felipe – Malaga: Revista Espanola de Estudios Biblicos, 1928 – 1 – sp Bibl Santa Ana [946]

ICONOGRAFIA DE LAS EDITIONES DEL QUIJOTE DE MIGUEL CERVANTES SAAVEDRA / Henrich, Manuel – Barcelona. 1905. 3v – 1 – $23.00 – us L of C Photodup [760]

ICONOGRAFIA ESPANOLA DE CONTEMPORANEOS. COLECCION DE SEMBLANZAS – Madrid: Tip. Frances, 1908 – 1 – sp Bibl Santa Ana [946]

ICONOGRAPHIA BOTANICA / Reichenbach, Heinrich G L – Lipsiae. 1823-32. B-5571 – 8 – ne IDC [580]

ICONOGRAPHIA BOTANICA EXOTICA / Reichenbach, Heinrich G L – 3v. Lipsiae. 1824-, 1827-30. B-5662 2 – 8 – ne IDC [580]

ICONOGRAPHIA GENERUM PLANTARUM / Endlicher, S L – Vindobonae. 1837, 1838-41. B-5922 2 – 8 – ne IDC [580]

ICONOGRAPHIA PHYCOLOGICA ADRIATICA / Zanardini, G A M – 3v. Venezia. 1860-76. B-5274 2 – 8 – ne IDC [580]

ICONOGRAPHIA PHYCOLOGICA SEU PHYCEARUM NOVARUM ET RARIORUM / Areschoug, J E – Gothoburgi. 1847. B-6341 2 – 8 – ne IDC [580]

ICONOGRAPHIE CALVINIENNE : OUVRAGE DEDIE A L'UNIVERSITE DE GEN'EVE / Doumergue, Emile – Lausanne: G. Bridel, 1909 – 1mf – us A.T.L.A. [700]

ICONOGRAPHIE DES PERROQUETS / Souance, C de – Paris, 1857 – 6mf – ne IDC [590]

ICONOGRAPHIE DES PERROQUETS / Souance, C de – Z 1933. 1857 – 9 – ne IDC [760]

ICONOGRAPHIE DU REGNE ANIMAL DE G. CUVIER; OU, REPRESENTATION D'APRES NATURE DE L'UNE DES ESPECES LES PLUS REMARQUABLES ET SOUVENT NON ENCORE FIGUREES, DE CHAQUE GENRE D'ANI-MAUX / Guerin-Meneville, Felix Edouard – Paris, 1829-1844 – 1 – us U.W. Library [590]

ICONOGRAPHIE VAN HUGO GROTIUS / Beresteyn, E A van – 's-Gravenhage, 1929 – 3mf – 9 – ILM-888/1 – ne IDC [327]

ICONOGRAPHIE ZOOPHYTOLOGIQUE / Michelin, J L H – Z-152 2. 1840-1847 – 8 – ne IDC [760]

ICONOGRAPHY OF AUSTRALIAN SALSOLACEOUS PLANTS / Mueller, Ferdinand Jakob Heinrich von – Decas 1-9. Melbourne. 1889-91. B-8056 1 – 9 – ne IDC [580]

ICONOGRAPHY OF AUSTRALIAN SPECIES OF ACACIA AND COGNATE GENERA / Mueller, Ferdinand Jakob Heinrich von – Melbourne, 1887-1888. Decade 1-13. B-7492 1 – 9 – ne IDC [580]

ICONOGRAPHY OF CANDOLLEACEOUS PLANTS / Mueller, Ferdinand Jakob Heinrich von – Melbourne. 1 Dec 1892. B-8058 1 – 9 – ne IDC [580]

ICONOLOGIA DEL CAVALIERE / Ripa, Cesare – O 413 1. 5 v. 1764-1767 – 9 – ne IDC [760]

ICONOLOGIA DEORU, ODER ABBILDUNG DER GOETTER... / Sandrart, J von – Nuernberg, 1680 – 9 – ne IDC [700]

ICONOLOGIA, OF BEELDESPRAECK / Ripa, Cesare – O 832. c.1656 – 9 – ne IDC [760]

ICONOLOGIA, OF UYTBEELDINGHE DES VERSTANTS. UYT HET ITALIAENS VERTAELT DOOR D. P. PERS / Ripa, Cesare – O 734. 1644 – 9 – ne IDC [760]

ICONOLOGIE, OU, EXPLICATION NOUVELLE DE PLUSIEURS IMAGES / Ripa, Cesare – O 1266 1. 1644 – 9 – ne IDC [760]

ICONOLOGY, OR EMBLEMATIC FIGURES EXPLAINED / Pinnock, William Henry – O 869. 1830 – 9 – ne IDC [760]

ICONOTHECAE BOTANICAE. CATALOGUS ILLUSTRATUS HORTI BERGIANI STOCKHOLMIENSIS / Wittrock, V B – Stockholm. v3 (2-3). 1903 – 11mf – ne IDC [580]

ICONUM BOTANICARUM INDEX LOCUPLETISSIMUS / Pritzel, G A – 2v. Berlin. 1855-66. B-683 2 – 8 – ne IDC [580]

ICOR – Montreal, CN. v1 no 1. 1933 – 1r – 1 – Can$25.00 – cn Can Microfilming [072]

ICOR, ASSOCIATION FOR JEWISH COLONIZATION IN THE SOVIET UNION – Toronto, Ont., Canada. 1934-36 – 1 – us A.J.P.C. [072]

ICOR BULLETIN – Toronto, CN, 1934-1937 – 1r – 1 – Can$25.00 – cn Can Microfilming [072]

ICTIHAD – Istanbul, Sene 1-28, nos. 1-358 (Eyluel 1904-Kanunieveel 1932) – 68mf – 9 – $500.00 – us MEDOC [949]

ICTIMAIYYAT MECMUASI – (Yayimliyan: Dar'uel-Fuenun Ictimaiyat Dar'uel-Mesaisi. Muedueruе: Necmeddin Sadak. Nos. 1-3, 5 (Nisan-Agustos 1917)) – Istanbul: Matbaa-i Amire, 1917 – 4mf – 9 – $90.00 – us MEDOC [949]

ID – (Cont: Misiones Extranjeras del Clero secular espanol) – 1941-50 (incomplete) – 1r – 1 – ATLA S0705A – us A.T.L.A. [073]

ID / University of Kentucky. Cooperative Extension Service – No.1-58.1972-83. 14 fiches – 9 – us Spaulding [630]

ID *see* MISIONES EXTRANJERAS DEL CLERO SECULAR ESPANOL

IDA AJU MARUTI, PRAWAN BALI; GAMBAR KENTARDJO – In Javanese. SE-5220 1. 1964 – 9 – ne IDC [950]

IDA COUNTY PIONEER RECORD – Ida Grove. Iowa. -w. 1951- – 1 – us UMI [071]

IDA OU QUE DEVIENDRA-T-ELLE / Radet – (French Theatre Series). Paris. Barba, an X. 1802 – 9 – fr Hachette [820]

IDADE D'OURO DO BRAZIL – Bahia, Brazil. 14 May 1811-Dec 1812 – 1 – bl Biblioteca [072]

IDAHO : OFFICIAL CODE – Charlottesville: Michie Co, 1949-Mar 1996 update – 9 – $1,655.00 set – us Hein [340]

IDAHO : SESSION LAWS OF AMERICAN STATES AND TERRITORIES – 1863-1996 – 9 – $1,027.50 set – us Hein [340]

Idaho *see*
– REPORTS AND OPINIONS (A-G)
– REPORTS, POST-NRS
– REPORTS, PRE-NRS

IDAHO ATTORNEY GENERAL REPORTS AND OPINIONS – (6 1893-1978 $70.00. 9 1979-1994 $197.50) – 1893-1994 – 6,9 – $267.50 set – us Hein [340]

Idaho. Dept. of Immigration, Labor and Statistics *see* STATE LABOR REPORTS

IDAHO ENCYCLOPEDIA / U. S. Works Progress Administration. Federal Writers' Project – Caldwell: Caxton Printers, Ltd., 1938. Idaho reel 3. (Cox Library Collection) – 5 – us Americana [978]

THE IDAHO ENCYCLOPEDIA – Comp. by the Federal Writers' Project of the WPA, Vardis Fisher, Dir. 1938. Indexed. V145-0003 – 5 – us A.G.L.L. [920]

IDAHO FARMER – Jun 1914-Jun 1971 – 1 – us UMI [630]

IDAHO FARMER-STOCKMAN – v89,no.13-v102. Jul 1971-1979 – 1 – us UMI [636]

IDAHO FARMER-STOCKMAN. INLAND EDITION – (1985- . 5,6,9) – v97- . 1980- – 1 – us UMI [630]

IDAHO FARMER-STOCKMAN. INTERNATIONAL EDITION – (1985- . 5,6,9) – v97- . 1980- – 1 – us UMI [636]

IDAHO, HER GOLD FIELDS AND THE ROUTE TO THEM: A HANDBOOK FOR EMIGRANTS / Fisk, James L – Overlander's guidebook written by the expedition leader. 99p. 1863. 1r – 1 – $5.00 – us M.H.S. [978]

IDAHO LAW JOURNAL – Idaho School of Law. v1-3. 1931-33 – 13mf – 9 – $19.50 – LLMC 84-483 – us L.L.M.C. [073]

IDAHO LAW REVIEW – (v1-20 1964-84 and index on reel $168.00. v21-31 1985-95 on mf $221.00. Includes a 15-yr index) – v1-31. 1964-95 – 5,6,9 – $389.00 set – us Hein [340]

IDAHO MAPS : CITIES AND TOWNS – 1884-1907. 475 maps. 49 towns. Sanborn Company Fire Insurance Maps – 1 – $63.00r – us Shkurkin [910]

IDAHO MISSIONARY BAPTIST FLAG – 1946-Aug 1973 – 1 – 44.87 – us Baptist [240]

Idaho. State Bar Association *see* PROCEEDINGS

IDAHO STATE BAR JOURNAL *see* ADVOCATE (IDAHO STATE BAR JOURNAL)

IDAHO STATE BAR REPORTS OF PROCEEDINGS – (Lacking: v8,9,38) – v1-1. 1921-23. v1-44. 1925-70 (all publ) – 37mf – 9 – $100.00 – LLMC 84-484 – us L.L.M.C. [073]

Idaho. Supreme Court *see*
– CUMMINS' TERRITORY REPORTS
– IDAHO SUPREME COURT REPORTS

IDAHO SUPREME COURT REPORTS / Idaho. Supreme Court – (Pre-NRS: v1 1886-83 3mf $13.50. Updates planned) – v1-32. 1866-1918/20 – 72mf – 9 – $552.00 – LLMC 84-131 – us L.L.M.C. [340]

IDAHO SUPREME COURT REPORTS *see* CUMMINS' TERRITORY REPORTS

Idaho. (Territory). Laws, Statutes, etc *see* THE COMPILED AND REVISED LAWS OF THE TERRITORY OF IDAHO.

IDALIA / Ouida – British Fiction Archive: Unit 3 – 9 – uk Bell [830]

[IDALIDE] AH CHE NEL PETTO LO SENTO / Paisiello & Mazzinghi – London: Goulding/ Skillern, 1791 – 1 – us Sibley [780]

IDDINGS' TERM REPORTS / Ohio. Dayton – 1v. 1899-1900 (all publ) – 2mf – 9 – $3.00 – LLMC 84-185 – us L.L.M.C. [324]

Ide inai a gruppa Vpered *see* SOVREMENNOE POLOZHENIE I ZADACHI PARTII

L'IDEA – Brooklyn, NY. 1923-1925 – us I.H.R.C. [073]

A IDEA : ORGAM DO CLUB DOS ESTUDANTES – Curitiba, 1 Oct 1888-14 Jul 1889 – 1,5,6 – bl Biblioteca [072]

A IDEA – Penedo, Alagoas. 17 Mar-16 Abr 1885 – 1,5,6 – bl Biblioteca [072]

IDEA : JOURNAL OF LAW AND TECHNOLOGY – (v1-25 1957-85 on reel $329.00. v26-35 1985-95 on mf $259.00. Title varies: v1-7 1957-64 as Patent, Trademark and Copyright Journal of Research and Educations. v8-15 1964-72 as Patent, Trademark and Copyright Journal of Research Education. v16-18 no 1 1973-76 as IDEA: The PTC Journal of Research and Education) – v1-35. 1957-95 – 5,6,9 – $588.00 set – us Hein [340]

IDEA *see* IDEA

LA IDEA – Badajoz, 1890 – 5 – sp Bibl Santa Ana [073]

LE IDEA – v21-32. 1937-49 (complete) – 1r – 1 – ATLA S0666A – us A.T.L.A. [073]

THE IDEA AND REALITY OF REVELATION AND TYPICAL FORMS OF CHRISTIANITY : TWO LECTURES / Wendt, Hans Hinrich – London: Philip Green, 1904 – 1mf – 9 – 0-8370-5786-8 – 1985-3786 – us A.T.L.A. [240]

L'IDEA DE PITTORI, SCULTORI, ET ARCHITETTI / Zuccaro, F – O 470 1. 1607 – 9 – ne IDC [700]

IDEA DE UN PERFECTO PRELADO DISCURRIDA A LA ELECCION DE MINISTRO PROVINCIAL... / Romera de la Torre, Francisco – 1 – sp Bibl Santa Ana [946]

IDEA DE UN PRINCIPE POLITICO CHRISTIANO REPRESENTADA EN CIEN EMPRESAS / Saavedra, Faxardo D de – O 739. 1655 – 9 – ne IDC [240]

IDEA DE UN PRINCIPE POLITICO CHRISTIANO, REPRESENTADA EN CIEN EMPRESAS / Saavedra, Faxardo D de – Amsterdam, 1659 – 11mf – 9 – O-3257/1 – ne IDC [760]

IDEA DEL TEATRO DE ORTEGA Y GASSET / Frutos Cortes, Eugenio – sp Bibl Santa Ana [790]

IDEA DEL TEMPIO DELLA PITTURA / Lomazzo, G P – O-1002 1. 1590 – 9 – ne IDC [760]

L'IDEA DELLI UNIVERSAE ARCHITECTURE DIVISA IN 10. LIBRI / Scamozzi, V – O 426. 1615 – 9 – ne IDC [720]

L'IDEA NAZIONALE – Roma: Casa Editrice Nazionale, mar 1 1911-dec 27 1925 – 1 – us Res Libr [072]

L'IDEA NAZIONALE – Rome, 11 Oct 1914-1 Apr 1915; 28 Dec 1915-27 Dec 1925 (1914 imperfect) – 28r – 1 – uk British Libr Newspaper [072]

IDEA OF GOD AS AFFECTED BY MODERN KNOWLEDGE – Boston: Houghton, Mifflin, 1887 – 1mf – 9 – us A.T.L.A. [240]

THE IDEA OF GOD IN RELATION TO THEOLOGY / Read, Eliphalet Allison – (Includes bibliographical references) – Chicago: Uni of Chicago Press, 1900 – 1mf – 9 – 0-8370-5607-1 – 1985-3607 – us A.T.L.A. [240]

THE IDEA OF THE HOLY / Otto, Rudolf – 1923 – 9 – $10.00 – us I.R.C. [210]

AN IDEA OF THE PERFECTION OF PAINTING / Freart, Roland – O-1187 1. 1668 – 9 – ne IDC [750]

IDEA POLITICA VERI CHRISTIANI, SIVE ARS OBLIVIONIS / Luzon de Millares, A – O 679. 1665 – 9 – ne IDC [240]

LA IDEA TRADICIONAL. DESTINO DE ESPANA POR / Becerro de Bengoa, Ricardo – Caceres: Tip. Garcia Floriano, 1945 – 1 – sp Bibl Santa Ana [946]

O IDEAL – Manaos, Amazonas. 17 Out 1905-9 Jun 1906 – 1,5,6 – bl Biblioteca [072]

'IDEAL' AND OTHER POEMS / Cochrane, Hugh – Montreal: Waters Bros., 1890?. 00689. (Pre-1900 Canadiana) – 9 – cn C.I.H.M. [810]

IDEAL AND PROGRESS; ESSAYS / Ghose, Aurobindo – 2nd ed., rev. Calcutta: Arya Pub. House, 19??. 68p – 1 – us U.W. Library [950]

IDEAL CLUB – Manaos, Amazonas. Set 1904 – 1,5,6 – bl Biblioteca [072]

IDEAL DE FAMILIA...MEMORIA / Soler Arques, Carlos – 1887 – 9 – 1.50f – sp Bibl Santa Ana [920]

IDEAL DE LOS CONQUISTADORES / Corraliza, Jose V – San Lorenzo del Escorial, 1923 – 1 – sp Bibl Santa Ana [350]

L'IDEAL ESTHETIQUE : ESQUISSE D'UNE PHILOSOPHIE DE LA BEAUTE / Roussel-Despierres, Fr – Paris: Felix Alcan, 1904 – 1mf – 9 – 0-8370-6610-7 – 1986-0610 – us A.T.L.A. [110]

THE IDEAL LIFE: ADDRESSES HITHERTO UNPUBLISHED / Drummond, Henry – With memorial sketches by Ian Maclaren and W. Robertson Nicoll. Toronto: F. H. Revell, 1898. 02774. (Pre-1900 Canadiana) – 9 – cn C.I.H.M. [850]

THE IDEAL MAGAZINE / ed by Ryan, Dessins d'Alonzo – Montreal, Canada. oct 1906; v1 n2. nov 1906 – 1r – 1 – Can$25.00 – cn Can Microfilming [073]

L'IDEAL RELIGIEUX DES GRECS ET L'EVANGILE / Festugiere, A – Paris, 1932 – 7mf – 8 – ne Slangenburg [240]

L'IDEAL RELIGIEUX DES GRECS ET L'EVANGILE / Festugiere, A J – Paris, 1932 – Dfl28.00 – ne Slangenburg [240]

IDEAL UND LEBEN : NACH SCHILLER UND KANT / Thikoetter, Julius – Bremen: M Heinsius, 1892 – 1 – us U.W. Library [430]

DIE IDEALE DER SOCIALDEMOKRATIE UND DIE AUFGABE DES ZEITALTERS / Glogau, Gustav – (Includes bibliographical references) – Kiel: Lipsius und Tischer, 1891 – 1r – 1 – us U.W. Library [320]

DIE IDEAL-EHE – Berlin, Germany. 1927-29 – 1 – gw Mikrofilm [072]

IDEAL-EHE – Berlin, 1927-28 – 1 – Dist. gw Mikrofilm – gw Misc Inst [072]

IDEALES CULTURALES DE LA EDAD MEDIA. TOMO 4. LA VIDA MONASTICA / Vedel, Waldemar – Barcelona, 1931; Madrid: Razon y Fe, 1934 – 1 – sp Bibl Santa Ana [240]

IDEALES MISIONEROS DE LOS REYES CATOLICOS / Bayle, Constantino – (Order number B1822) – Madrid: Missionalia Hispanica, 1952 – 1 – sp Bibl Santa Ana [240]

IDEALES MISIONEROS DE LOS REYES CATOLICOS / Bayle, Constantino – (Order number B1823) – Madrid: Missionalia Hispanica, 1952 – 1 – sp Bibl Santa Ana [240]

IDEALIDAD / Sanchez-Arjona, Vicente – Sevilla: Imp. Carlos Acuna, 1954 – 1 – sp Bibl Santa Ana [810]

IDEALISM AND THEOLOGY : A STUDY OF PRESUPPOSITIONS / D'Arcy, Charles Frederick – London: Hodder and Stoughton, 1899 – us A.T.L.A. [240]

L'IDEALISMO DI GEORGIO, BERKELEY... / Olgiati, Francesco – Madrid: Razon y Fe, 1927 – 1 – sp Bibl Santa Ana [120]

O IDEALISTA : ORGAO INDEPENDENTE DO POVO PARA O POVO – Pocos de Caldas, 3 Feb 1963-7 Sep 1964 – 1,5,6 – bl Biblioteca [072]

THE IDEALISTIC REACTION AGAINST SCIENCE / Aliotta, Antonio – London: Macmillan, 1914 – 2mf – us A.T.L.A. [100]

IDEAL'NAIA ZHIZN' – Zhurnal. nr. 1-5. Spb. 1907. BR-4120 2 – 8 – ne IDC [073]

IDEALS OF SCIENCE AND FAITH : ESSAYS BY VARIOUS AUTHORS / ed by Hand, J E – (Includes bibliographical references and index) – New York: Longmans, Green; London: George Allen, 1904 – 1mf – 9 – 0-8370-5077-4 – 1985-3077 – us A.T.L.A. [210]

IDEALY KOOPERATSII / Posse, V A – M., 1911 – 1mf – 9 – COR-98/1 – ne IDC [334]

IDEARIO DE LA COLEGIO DE EGB Y FORMACION PROFESIONAL / Colegio Santiago y Santa Margarita. Sociedad Cooperativa – Caceres: Imp. Garcia Carrasco, 1979 – 1 – sp Bibl Santa Ana [060]

IDEARIO DE UN CENTRO EDUCATIVO JOSEFINO TRINITARIO – Caceres: Imp. Moderna, 1977 – sp Bibl Santa Ana [370]

IDEAS ACTUALES SOBRE LAS PLAGAS DE LANGOSTA / Moreno Marquez, Victor & Canizo Gomez, Jose del – Madrid: Direccion General de Agricultura. Secc. Plagas del campo y Fitopatologia. Servicio de lucha contra la langosta. Estacion de Fitopatologia Agricola, 1940 – 1 – sp Bibl Santa Ana [630]

IDEAS ARCHIVES NO. 1 / Solneman, K H Z – English ed.1980 and German Ed. 1949. For the establishment of a genuine market for new ideas and talents. 98p. 1 fiche (24x) – 9 – 1.00f – at Libertarian Micro [320]

IDEAS AS TO THE EFFECT OF HEAVY ORDNANCE DIRECTED AGAINST AND APPLIED BY SHIPS OF WAR / Simmons, Thomas Frederick – 1837 – 9 – uk Libr Preservation [355]

IDEAS FROM NATURE: TALKS WITH STUDENTS / Elder, William – Philadelphia: American Baptist Publ., 1898. 1 fiche – 9 – us A.T.L.A. [240]

IDEAS IN NATURE OVERLOOKED BY DR. TYNDALL...DR. TYNDALL'S BELFAST ADDRESS / McCosh, James – New York: Robert Carter, 1875. 1 fiche – 9 – us A.T.L.A. [240]

IDEAS POLITICAS DE ANGEL GANIVET / Elias de Tejada Spinola, Francisco – Madrid: Grafica Universal, 1939 – 1 – sp Bibl Santa Ana [320]

THE IDEAS THAT HAVE INFLUENCED CIVILIZATION, IN THE ORIGINAL DOCUMENTS / ed by Thatcher, Oliver Joseph – Milwaukee, Boston: Roberts-Manchester Publ., c1901. 10v. plates – 1 – us U.W. Library [000]

DIE IDEE DER LIEBE. LEONE EBREO / Pflaum, H – Zwei Abhandlungen zur Geschichte der Philosophie in der Renaissance. Tuebingen. 1926. BJ-33-34 1 – 9 – ne IDC [190]

DIE IDEE DER PERSOENLICHKEIT BEI PAUL HEYSE / Hammer, Friedrich – (Includes bibliographical references) – Dresden: Risse-Verlag, 1935 – 1r – 1 – us U.W. Library [430]

DIE IDEE DER SUEHNE IM ALTEN TESTAMENT : EINE UNTERSUCHUNG UEBER GEBRAUCH UND BEDEUTUNG DES WORTES KIPPER / Herrmann, Johannes – (Includes index) – Leipzig: J C Hinrichs, 1905 – 1mf – 9 – 0-8370-3571-6 – 1985-1571 – us A.T.L.A. [220]

DIE IDEE DES GESETZES IN DER PRAKTISCHEN VERNUNFT / Hadlich, Heinrich – Koenigsberg, 1938 – 1mf – 9 – DM48.00 – 3-89349-304-2 – gw Hänsel [160]

IDEE D'UN TABLEAU OU ETAT GENERAL DE LA FRANCE / Laboulinere, Pierre – (French Socialist Congresses Series). Tarbes. F. Lavigne. 1811 – 9 – fr Hachette [310]

IDEE D'UNE REPUBLIQUE HEUREUSE, OU L'UTOPIE DE THOMAS MORUS. CONTENANT LE PLAN D'UNE REPUBLIQUE DONT LES LOIS, LES USAGES ET LES COUTUMES TENDENT UNIQUEMENT A RENDRE HEUREUSES LES SOCIETES QUI LES SUIVRONT / More, Thomas & Gueudeville, Nicolas – (Utopias in the Enlightenment series). 1730 – 9 – fr Hachette [830]

IDEE ET ACTION – Revue, mensuelle du Mouvement socialiste et syndicaliste international. Dir. J. London. no. 1-9 10. Paris. juin 1936-avr mai 1937. suite de: Le Combat marxiste voir a ce titre – 1 – fr A.C.R.P.P. [073]

IDEE GENERALE DE LA CHINE : MEMOIRES CONCERNANT L'HISTOIRE, LES SCIENCES... DES CHINOIS... – Paris. v5. 1776-1783 – 2mf – 9 – ne IDC [960]

L'IDEE NOUVELLE = THE NEW IDEA – Worcester, MA. v1 n2. 3 jun 1869-v1 n9. 24 jul 1869 – 1r – 1 – Can$35.00 – cn Can Microfilming [071]

L'IDEE OUVRIERE / ed by Brady, Gerard – (Cont by: L'Homme Libre 7 aut 1937-15 mar 1960. Cont by: Journal Drummond, Drummondville 23 mar 1960-29 mar 1962. Cont by: L'Homme Libre 5 avr 1962-21 aut 1963) – St-Hyacinthe, Canada. 15 jun 1934-31 jul 1937 – 8r – 1 – Can$55.00r – cn Can Microfilming [072]

EINE IDEE UEBER DAS STUDIUM DER THEOLOGIE / De Wette, Wilhelm Martin Leberecht – Leipzig: T.O. Weigel, 1850 – 1mf – us A.T.L.A. [240]

IDEE UND WIRKLICHKEIT BEI HANNS JOHST / Heering, Hans – (Includes bibliographical references) – Berlin: Junker und Duennhaupt, 1938 – 1 – us U.W. Library [430]

IDEELLE KONTINENTALSPERRE / Lenard, Philipp Eduard Anton – Written in Aug 1914. Muenchen: F. Eher, 1940. 21p – 1 – us U.W. Library [940]

IDEEN ZU DER ORGANISATION DER TEUTSCHEN KIRCHE : EIN BEITRAG ZUM KUENFTIGEN KONKORDAT / Kopp, Georg Ludwig Karl – Frankfurt a.M., 1814 – 92p – 9 – DM48.00 – 3-89349-081-7 – gw Hänsel [240]

DER IDEENGEHALT VON RICHARD WAGNERS DRAMATISCHEN DICHTUNGEN : IM ZUSAMMENHANGE MIT SEINEM LEBEN UND SEINER WELTANSCHAUUNG, NEBST EINEM ANHANG: NIETZSCHE UND WAGNER / Drews, Arthur – (Includes bibliographical references) – Leipzig: E Pfeiffer, c1931 – 1 – us U.W. Library [780]

IDEES – Revue de la revolution nationale. no. 1-33. Vichy. nov 1941-juil 1944 – 1 – fr A.C.R.P.P. [073]

LES IDEES : REVUE / ed by Pelletier, Albert – Montreal, Canada. jan 1935-jun 1939 – 2r – 1 – Can$40.00r – cn Can Microfilming [073]

LES IDEES – v1-3 Jan 1935-36 – 1 – cn Precision [100]

IDEES PATRIOTIQUES, SUR LA METHODE ET L'IMPORTANCE D'UNE EDUCATION NATIONALE POUR ASSURER LE REGENERATION DE LA FRANCE / Varennes, Raymond de – Paris. Garnery. 1790 – 9 – fr Hachette [370]

LES IDEES PHILOSOPHIQUES ET RELIGIEUSES DE PHILON D'ALEXANDRIE / Brehier, Emile – 1908 – 1 – us A.T.L.A. [240]

IDEES SUR LA METEROLOGIE / Luc, Jean Andre de – Paris, 1787 – 1 – us U.W. Library [380]

A IDEIA : ORGAO LITTERARIO, NOTICIOSO E HUMORISTICO – Pao de Assucar-AL, Brazil. 17 Abr-19 Jun 1910 – 1 – bl Biblioteca [072]

IDENSHTATT-JUDENSHTAT = THE JEWISH STATE – (Monthly) – New York City, NY. v1 no 1 and 3. 1934 – 1r – Can$25.00 – cn Can Microfilming [071]

IDENTIDEX SYSTEM – Tablet-capsule identification system including street slang terminology and manufacturers' telephone numbers. Republished quarterly – 9 – us Micromedex [610]

IDENTIFICATION ANTHROPOMETRIQUE; INSTRUCTIONS SIGNALETIQUES / Bertillon, Alphonse – Melun, 1893. lxxxiv,148p. illus – 1 – us U.W. Library [573]

IDENTIFICATION OF BODY BUILT STEREOTYPES IN PREADOLESCENTS : RELATIONSHIP TO EATING DISORDERS / Steele, Kristy J – Purdue University, 1995 – 1mf – 9 – PSY 1902 – us Microform Publ [150]

THE IDENTIFICATION OF EMPLOYEE TYPES THROUGH Q-METHODOLOGY : A STUDY OF PART-TIME AND SEASONAL RECREATION AND PARKS EMPLOYEES / McDade, Susan E S – 1989 – 114p 2mf – 9 – $8.00 – us Microform Publ [790]

IDENTIFICATION OF PESTS AND DISEASES IN FIELD AND VEGETABLE CROPS / Israel. Ministry of Agriculture – By R. Shoham Ausher. CH. 1977. 56 p. illus – 9 – 2.00 – is I.T.T.I. [630]

THE IDENTIFICATION OF THE 144,000 OF REVELATION 7 / Moulton, George Ernest – 1982 – 1 – 5.68 – us Baptist [240]

THE IDENTIFICATION OF THE MINIMUM QUALIFICATIONS FOR TENNIS TEACHING PROFESSIONALS TO BE HIRED AT MANAGED TENNES FACILITIES IN THE UNITED STATES / Warrell, Theresa & Jackson, Michael W – 1992 – 2mf – 9 – $8.00 – us Microform Publ [790]

HET IDENTIFICEEREND KARAKTER DER POSSESSIEVE FLEXIE IN TALEN VAN NOORD-AMERIKA / Uhlenbeck, C C – (Versl. en Mededeel. K. Akad. van Wetensch). Amsterdam. 1916. BN-438 2 – 8 – ne IDC [490]

DIE IDENTIFIZIERUNG UND CHARAKTERISIERUNG CHOLINERGER UND NITREGER ENTERISCHER SCHALTKREISE IM MYENTERISCHEN PLEXUS DES MEERSCHWEINCHENMAGENS / Schaaf, Cornelia – 1995 – 2mf – 9 – DM80.00 – 3-8267-2236-1 – gw Hänsel [574]

IDENTITAS NASIONAL / Hassan, Fuad – SE-5826 1. 1965 – 9 – ne IDC [320]

IDENTITIES / ed by Schiller, Nina Glick – 9,5,1 – us Gordon [301]

IDEOLOGICHESKAIA BOR'BA V RUSSKOI PUBLITSISTIKE / Lur'e, Ia. S – Kontsa XV-nachala XVI v.M. L. 1960. BR-8094 2 – 8 – ne IDC [321]

L'IDEOLOGIE DU CONTE CHEZ LES BWA DU MALI / Dembele, P C – Etude ethnolinguistique – 9 – F220.00 – fr Ethnologie [390]

IDEOLOGY AND POLITICS OF THE AMERICAN BAPTIST CHURCHES IN 1900-1917 / Kislov, A A – 1969. Russian. 210p – 1 – 7.35 – us Baptist [240]

IDEOLOGY, TECHNOLOGY AND THE HISTORICAL AVANT GARDE / Knapp, Ferdinand M – 1995 – 1mf – 9 – DM60.00 – 3-8267-2209-4 – gw Hänsel [400]

IDH-HAR-HAQQ : OU MANIFESTATION DE LA VERITE / El-Hage Rahmat-Ullah Effendi de Dehli – (Traduit de l'Arabe revue par P. V. Carletti) – Paris. Tom 1-2. 1880 – Dfl63.00 – ne Slangenburg [260]

IDILIOS Y ELEGIAS / Moreno Torrado, Luis – 1890 – 9 – 1.50f – sp Bibl Santa Ana [810]

EL IDIOMA DE LA RAZON / Caracciolo, Luis Antonio – 1779 – 1mf – 9 – Pta1,000.00 – 84-7848-171-0 – sp Pentalfa [301]

EL IDIOMA DE LA RELIGION / Caracciolo, Luis Antonio – 1777 – 1mf – 9 – Pta1,000.00 – 84-7848-170-2 – sp Pentalfa [240]

THE IDISHE ARBETER SHTIME = THE JEWISH WORKERS' VOICE – New York, NY. v6 no 1 and 4. 1940 – 1r – Can$25.00 – cn Can Microfilming [071]

DI IDISHE AVTONOMIE UN DER NATSIONALER SEKRETARIAT IN UKRAYNE – Kiev. 1920. BJ-290-22 1 – 9 – ne IDC [947]

DI IDISHE BIHNE = THE JEWISH STAGE – New York City, NY. v1 no 1. 1909; v1 no 22. 1910 – 1r – Can$25.00 – cn Can Microfilming [071]

IDISHE BIZNESMAN FIRER = THE JEWISH MERCHANT & GUIDE – Los Angeles, CA.1927 – 1 – us A.J.P.C. [071]

IDISHE FOLK – London, UK. 2/9 Aug 1968- – 1 – uk British Libr Newspaper [072]

IDISHE FOLK – London, UK. 7 Sept 1934-1 Feb 1935 – 1 – uk British Libr Newspaper [072]

DI IDISHE GAS (EVREISKAIA ULITSA) – (Formerly: Sovetish Heymland 1961-91 1340mf $4,900) – Russia, 1996- – 16mf 4 issues per y – 9 – $80.00 standing order – us Ross [073]

DOS IDISHE LEBEN = JEWISH LIFE – (In Yiddish and English. Monthly) – London, GB. v1 no1 Mar-v1 no4 Jun 1923 – 1r – 1 – $25.00 – cn Can Microfilming [072]

IDISHE LEBEN (JEWISH LIFE) – London, UK. 1 Mar-Aug 1923 – 1 – uk British Libr Newspaper [072]

DI IDISHE MILKHOMES = WARS OF THE JEWS (JOSEPHUS FLAVIUS) : MONOGRAPH – Vilnius, LT. v2 1914; v1 1923 – 1r – 1 – $25.00 – cn Can Microfilming [072]

IDISHE POST UN EKSPRES (JEWISH POST AND EXPRESS) – London, UK. 8 Oct 1926-7 Aug 1935 – 1 – uk British Libr Newspaper [072]

IDISHE PRESSE – Los Angeles, CA.1935-36 – 1 – us A.J.P.C. [071]

IDISHE PRESSE (THE JEWISH PRESS) – London, UK. 3 Feb-17 Sept 1903 – 1 – uk British Libr Newspaper [072]

IDISHE SHPRIKHVERTER UN REDENSARTN / Bernstein, Ignatz – Ed. 2. Warsaw. 1908. BJ-290-29 1 – 9 – ne IDC [430]

DI IDISHE SHTIME *see* ZYDU BALSAS

IDISHE SHTIME – New York, NY. 1941-47 – 1 – us A.J.P.C. [071]

IDISHE SHTIME (THE JEWISH VOICE) – London, UK. 19 Nov-27 Dec 1916 – 1 – uk British Libr Newspaper [072]

DI IDISHE SHTIME (ZYDU BALSAS) = JEWISH VOICE – (In Yiddish) – Kaunas, LT. v- no- Jan 1931-v- no- 16 Sep 1935 – 1r – 1 – $25.00 – cn Can Microfilming [072]

IDISHE TAGEBLAT = THE JEWISH DAILY NEWS – New York City, NY. v26 no69, v39 no 134. 1910-1923 – 1r – Can$30.00 – cn Can Microfilming [071]

IDISHE TRIBUNE (THE JEWISH TRIBUNE) – London, UK. Mar 1938 – 1 – uk British Libr Newspaper [072]

DI IDISHE TSAYTUNG (EL DIARIO ISRAELITA) = JEWISH JOURNAL – (In Yiddish) – Buenos Aires, AG. v21 no6314 25 Aug 1935-v23 no7034 23 Dec 1937 – 2r – 1 – $50.00 – cn Can Microfilming [072]

IDISHE VELT = THE JEWISH WORLD – Toronto, CN. v2 no 44. 1932-1933 – 1r – 1 – Can$40.00 – cn Can Microfilming [072]

DI IDISHE VELT [MUNDO ISRAELITA] = JEWISH WORLD – (In Yiddish) – Buenos Aires, AG. v7 no3(no291) 21 Sep 1928-v7 no4(no292) 28 Sep 1928 – 1r – 1 – $25.00 – cn Can Microfilming [072]

DI IDISHE VOKH = THE JEWISH WEEK – New York City, NY. v3 no 5. 1958 – 1r – Can$25.00 – cn Can Microfilming [071]

DER IDISHER ADVOKAT – Capetown. v. 3-4, 6-9. Oct 19 1906-Sept 18 1908; Sept 30 1910-June 5 1914. Incomplete – 1 – us NY Public [072]

DER IDISHER ADWOKAT – Capetown. v3-9. 1906-14 – 1r – 1 – us Ross [072]

DER IDISHER ARBAYTER / Kirzhnitz, A – 4v. Moscow. 1925-28. Lacking: 1925, v. 1. BJ-290-20 1 – 9 – ne IDC [331]

DER IDISHER EKSPRES = THE JEWISH EXPRESS – Johannesburg, SA. v2 no 52, v5 no 50. 1935-1941 – 1r – 1 – Can$25.00 – cn Can Microfilming [072]

IDISHER EKSPRES (THE JEWISH EXPRESS) – London, UK. 6 Nov 1896-25 Dec 1924; 7 Jan-22 Sept 1926 – 1 – uk British Libr Newspaper [072]

DER IDISHER FOLK-LERER = THE JEWISH FOLK TEACHER – New York City, NY. v1, no 1. 1934 – 1r – Can$25.00 – cn Can Microfilming [071]

IDISHER FOLKSFRAYND = THE JEWISH PEOPLE'S FRIEND – (In Yiddish) – Pittsburg, PA. v36 no1764. 8 Jun 1923 – 1r – 1 – $25.00 – cn Can Microfilming [071]

IDISHER GEIST – New York, NY. 1910-14 – 1 – us A.J.P.C. [071]

IDISHER HANDELS-ZHURNAL – London, UK. May 1920-Mar 1922 – 1 – uk British Libr Newspaper [072]

IDISHER KEMFER = THE JEWISH FIGHTER – New York City, NY. v6 no 45(85), v12 no 5. 1917-1935 – 1r – Can$35.00 – cn Can Microfilming [071]

DER IDISHER KEMPFER = THE JEWISH FIGHTER – Montreal, CN, 1918 – 1r – 1 – Can$25.00 – cn Can Microfilming [072]

IDISHER KEMPFER – New York. v1-9. 1906-20 – 3r – 1 – us Ross [071]

IDISHER KURIER = THE DAILY/SUNDAY JEWISH COURIER – Chicago, IL. no 253. 1917-1938 (50th Ann. Issue) – 2r – Can$65.00 – cn Can Microfilming [071]

IDISHER LEBN ["ZYDY GYVENIMAS"] = JEWISH LIFE – (In Yiddish) – Kaunas, LT. v1 no6. Aug 1921 – 1r – 1 – $25.00 – cn Can Microfilming [072]

DER IDISHER LEGIONER = THE JEWISH LEGIONAIRE – New York City, NY. no 1 and 5. 1918 – 1r – Can$25.00 – cn Can Microfilming [071]

IDISHER MOMENT = THE JEWISH MOMENT – Los Angeles, CA.1941 – 1 – us A.J.P.C. [071]

IDISHER MONAT BUCH = ISRAEL'S MONTHLY MAGAZINE – New York, NY. 1900-02 – 1 – us A.J.P.C. [073]

DER IDISHER POYER [PEASANT] = JEWISH FARMER – (In Yiddish) – Buenos Aires, AG. no7. May 1930 – 1r – 1 – $25.00 – cn Can Microfilming [072]

DER IDISHER REKORD = THE JEWISH RECORD – Saint-Louis. v23 no 2162. 1937 – 1r – Can$25.00 – cn Can Microfilming [071]

IDISHER TREID YUNIONIST (THE JEWISH TRADE UNIONIST) – London, UK. 15 Jan-5 Feb 1892 – 1 – uk British Libr Newspaper [072]

IDISHER VECHENTLICHER ZHURNAL (THE JEWISH WEEKLY JOURNAL) – London, UK. 28 Nov 1906-17 Apr 1907 – 1 – uk British Libr Newspaper [072]

DER IDISHER VEKHTER = THE JEWISH GUARDIAN – (In Yiddish) – Cleveland, OH. v1 no59. 25 May 1923 – 1r – 1 – $25.00 – cn Can Microfilming [071]

DER IDISHER ZHURNAL = THE DAILY HEBREW JOURNAL – Toronto, CN. v21 no 7547, no 16,842. 1931-1962 – 8r – 1 – Can$65.00r – cn Can Microfilming [072]

IDISHER ZHURNAL – New York. v. 1-7. May 26 1899-Apr 20 1906 – 1 – us NY Public [071]

IDISHER ZHURNAL (THE JEWISH JOURNAL) – London, UK. 19 May 1905-3 Dec 1914 – 1 – uk British Libr Newspaper [072]

IDISHER ZSHURNAL = THE JEWISH JOURNAL – Boston, MA. 1922 – 1 – us A.J.P.C. [071]

IDISHER ZSHURNAL – New York. v1-7. 1899-1906 – 7r – 1 – us Ross [071]

IDISHES TAGEBLAT = JEWISH DAILY – (In Yiddish) – Warsaw, PL. no58. 24 Jul 1906 – 1r – 1 – $25.00 – cn Can Microfilming [072]

IDISHES TOGBLAT – (Missing: 1906(1,47,87,100-102,133-136); 1907(20,21,24,121,177,265,266,269)) – Warsaw. v1-2. 1906-1907 – 2r – 1 – J-92-21/3 – ne IDC [072]

IDISZE SZRIFTN – Warsaw. Poland. -m. Jan 1956-Jul 1968. (2 reels) – 1 – uk British Libr Newspaper [947]

IDLER – (Ceased no 38 1993) – Toronto. nos 1-38. 1985-93 – 9 – Can$20.00y – cn Micromedia [073]

IDOC – Rome, IT. 1977-1983 – 3r – $150.00 – R63574 – us Library Micro [072]

IDOC (International Documentation on the Contemporary Church) Documentation Service *see* BULLETIN

IDOC INTERNAZIONALE – (1986- . 5,6,9) – v1- . 1970- – 1 – us UMI [073]

L'IDOLATRIE HUGUENOTE FIGUREE AU PATRON DE LA VIEILLE PAYENNE... / Richeome, L – Lyon, 1608 – 9mf – 9 – CA-146/1 – ne IDC [240]

IDOLATRIES, OLD AND NEW : THEIR CAUSE AND CURE / Brown, James Baldwin – London: Jackson, Walford & Hodder, 1867 – 1mf – us A.T.L.A. [240]

IDOLINO : ERZAEHLUNG / Penzoldt, Ernst – 1. bis 3. Aufl. Berlin: S Fischer, c1935 – 1r – 1 – us U.W. Library [830]

EL IDOLO ROTO (REALIDADES DE OTROS DIAS) / Hurtado de Mendoza, Publio – Caceres: Tip., Enc. y Lib. de Jimenez, 1904 – 1 – sp Bibl Santa Ana [946]

IDOLS OF CLAY, A NOVEL / Smythies, Harriet Maria Gordon – London: Saunders, Otley, 1867. 3v – 1 – us U.W. Library [830]

IDOMENEE : TRAGEDIE EN MUSIQUE / Campra, A – (Skeleton score) – Paris: J B C Ballard, 1731 – 1 – us Sibley [780]

Idowu, A *see* REPORT OF A SURVEY OF THE UNIVERSAL PRIMARY EDUCATION SCHEME 1978

IDRAETSLIV – Oslo, Norway. Idrettsliv. -sw. 5 April 1923-30 June 1932. 16 reels – 1 – uk British Libr Newspaper [072]

IDRC, Ottawa *see* IDRC PROJECTS REPORTS

IDRC PROJECTS REPORTS / IDRC, Ottawa – complete holdings – Can$2.00f – cn I.D.R.C. [630]

Idries, Iskandar *see* TAFSIER MUCHTASOR

IDROES AND SITY NOERMA / Rih, Sjeh – SE 6759 1. v. 2 only. 1959? – 9 – ne IDC [950]

IDROTT OCH LEK – 1933 – 1 – us I.U. Libraries [390]

IDROTTSBLADET – Stockholm, Sodertalje, Sweden. 1910-88 – 1 – sw Kungliga [790]

IDUN – Stockholm, Sweden. 1888-89 – 1 – sw Kungliga [073]

IDUNA – Hamburg, Germany. 1831-34 – 1 – gw Mikrofilm [072]

IDYLLIA / Rue, Charles de la – O 665. 1672 – 9 – ne IDC [760]

IDYLLS ET CAPRICES / Colomer, B M – Fantaisies pour piano a 4 mains. c.1863 – 9 – us Sibley [780]

IDYLLS OF OUR ISLAND / Boa, Myrtle J – [Montreal ?: s.n., 1923 ?]. SEM105P1636 – 1mf – 9 – Can$2.25 – cn Bibl Nat [971]

IDYLLS OF THE KING / Tennyson, Alfred, Lord – London: Strahan, 1869 – 1 roll – 1 – 1-55879-396-8 – uk Libr Preservation [810]

IDYLLWILD TOWN CRIER – Idyllwild, CA. 1967-93 – 33R – 1 – $1,650.00 – R02301 – us Library Micro [071]

IEC (INTERNATIONAL ELECTROTECHNICAL COMMISSION) – Complete English-language collection of standards and recommendations. Printed index. Updated every 60 days – 6,9 – us Info Handling [621]

IEE PROCEEDINGS ON MICROFICHE – (Science, Measurement and Technology, 1980-; Electric Power Applications, 1980-; Generation, Transmission and Distribution, 1980-; Control Theory and Applications, 1980-; Computers and Digital Techniques, 1980-; Radar, Sonar and Navigation, 1980-; Circuits, Devices and Systems, 1980-; Microwaves, Antennas and Propagation, 1980-; Communications, Speech and Vision, 1980-; Optoelectronics, 1985-; Vision, Image and Signal Processing, 1993-) – uk INSPEC [621]
IEE PROCEEDINGS, PART A / Institution of Electrical Engineers – (Physical Science, Measurement and Instrumentation, Management and Educational Reviews) – v127- 1980- – 1,5,6 – us UMI [621]
IEE PROCEEDINGS, PART B / Institution of Electrical Engineers – (Electrical Power Applications) – v127- 1980- – 1,5,6 – us UMI [621]
IEE PROCEEDINGS, PART C / Institution of Electrical Engineers – (Generation Transmission and Distribution) – v127- 1980- – 1,5,6 – us UMI [621]
IEE PROCEEDINGS, PART D / Institution of Electrical Engineers – (Control Theory and Applications) – v127- 1980- – 1,5,6 – us UMI [621]
IEE PROCEEDINGS, PART E / Institution of Electrical Engineers – Computers and Digital Techniques. v127- 1980- – 1,5,6 – us UMI [621]
IEE PROCEEDINGS, PART F / Institution of Electrical Engineers – Communications, Radar, and Signal Processing. v127- 1980- – 1,5,6 – us UMI [621]
IEE PROCEEDINGS, PART G / Institution of Electrical Engineers – Electronic Circuits and Systems. v127- 1980- – 1,5,6 – us UMI [621]
IEE PROCEEDINGS, PART H / Institution of Electrical Engineers – Microwaves, Optics, and Antennas. v127- 1980- – 1,5,6 – us UMI [621]
IEE PROCEEDINGS, PART I / Institution of Electrical Engineers – Solid-state and Electron Devices. v127- 1980- – 1,5,6 – us UMI [621]
IEE PROCEEDINGS. PART J / Institution of Electrical Engineers – Optoelectronics. v132-. Feb 1985- – 1,5,6,9 – us UMI [621]
IEEE ANNALS OF THE HISTORY OF COMPUTING *see* ANNALS OF THE HISTORY OF COMPUTING
IEEE (INSTITUTE OF ELECTRICAL AND ELECTRONICS ENGINEERS) – Standards. Printed index. Updated every 60 days – 6,9 – us Info Handling [621]
IEEE PROCEEDINGS – 1913-77 – 1,5,6 – 2820.00 – us I.E.E.E. [621]
IEEE PROCEEDINGS – 1970-78 – 9 – 63.00y – us I.E.E.E. [621]
IEEE SPECTRUM – 1964-77 – 1,5,6 – 535.00 – us I.E.E.E. [621]
IEEE SPECTRUM – 1970-78 – 9 – 54.00y – us I.E.E.E. [621]
IEEE TRANSACTIONS – 1951-77 – 1,5,6 – 10,085.00 – us I.E.E.E. [621]
IEEE TRANSACTIONS – 1970-78 – 9 – 1252.00y – us I.E.E.E. [621]
Ienna, Tiziana M *see* THE ASTHMATIC ATHLETE
IERC BULLETIN – 1973-78. (American Indian Periodicals in the Princeton University Library). 7 fiches – 9 – $45.00 – us UPA [305]
IEROSOLYMITIKE BIBLIOTHEKE / Papadopoulos-Kerameoos, A – St. Petersburg. Tomus 1-5. 1891-1915 – 87mf – 8 – ne Slangenburg [240]
IERUSALIM I PALESTINA V RUSSKOI LITERATURE, NAUKE, ZHIVOPISI I PEREVODAKH (MATERIALY DLIA BIBLIOGRAFII) / Ponomareva, S – Spb. 1877. BR-7219 2 – 8 – ne IDC [956]
IERVSALEM, VETVSTISSIMA ILLA ET CELEBERRIMA TOTIVS MVNDI CIVITAS, EX SACRIS LITERIS ET APPROBATIS HISTORICIS AD UNGUEM DESCRIPTA / Reissner, A – Francofvtri, 1563 – 13mf – 9 – H-8302/1 – ne IDC [956]
IES (ILLUMINATING ENGINEERING SOCIETY) – Standards. Printed index. Updated every 60 days – 6,9 – us Info Handling [621]
IETS OVER AANVARINGEN IN VOL ZEE / Brouwer, A – Leiden, 1881 – 1mf – 1 – ILM-3395/1 – ne IDC [327]
IEVADS BALTU FILOLOG'IA / Endzelin, J – Riga. 78p. 1945 – 2mf – 9 – ne IDC [460]
I.F. STONE'S BI-WEEKLY – v. 1-19. 1953-71 – 1. ; 5,6 – apply; v.19 – us UMI [320]
IF YOU WANT TO SEARCH GOD, READ THE HOLY QUR'AN / Sukarno, Pres. Indonesia – Address at anniversary celebrations of Nuzulul Qur'an. SE 10,979 1. 1964 – 9 – ne IDC [324]
IFAC SYMPOSIA SERIES – 1993 – 5,6,9 – us UMI [380]
IFA-RUNDSCHAU – Berlin, 1930-31 – 1r – 1 – Dist. gw Mikrofilm – gw Misc Inst [072]
IFDA THIRD SYSTEM PROJECT PAPERS / International Foundation for Development Alternatives (IFDA), Nyon, Switzerland – (a: the complete set of IFDA Dossiers from January 1978 to August 1987; b: the complete set of supporting and background papers, in total 347 documents; Includes a printed guide and 2 plastic binders) – 283mf – 9 – ne IDC [307]
IFFLAND IN SEINEN SCHRIFTEN ALS KUENSTLER, LEHRER UND DIRECTOR DER BERLINER BUEHNE : ZUM GEDAECHTNIS SEINES 100JAEHRIGEN GEBURTSTAGES AM 19. APRIL 1859 – (Includes bibliographical references) – Berlin: Duncker und Humblot, 1859 – 1r – 1 – us U.W. Library [790]
IFI (INDUSTRIAL FASTENERS INSTITUTE) – Printed index. Updated every 60 days – 6,9 – us Info Handling [670]
IFPC *see* REPORT OF THE 21ST SESSION OF THE INDO-PACIFIC FISHERIES COMMISSION
IFRIQIYA – Ifriqia. no. 1, 3. Alger. 1919 – 1 – fr A.C.R.P.P. [073]
Ifwanga, WP *see* LES GENRES LITTERAIRES YAKA, REPUBLIQUE DU ZAIRE
IGAZSAG – Cluj, Romania. 1963-64; 1966-73; Jul 1975-76; 1978-80; 1982-84; 1987-89 – 25r – 1 – us L of C Photodup [949]
Igbani, B *see* HEALTH BEHAVIORS AND ATTITUDES OF SELECTED NIGERIAN AND AMERICAN UNIVERSITY STUDENTS
IGBO "WOMEN'S WAR" OF 1929 – Documents relating to the Aba riots in Eastern Nigeria – 9 – uk Microform Academic [960]
Igelmo Pinilia, Eulogio *see* ORG. SINDICAL-BADAJOZ. 4 CONSEJO ECONOMICO S. PROV. C. 15^{A} (FACTORES HUMANOS Y SOCIALES PRODUCTIVIDAD
IGERNES SCHULD : EIN KAMMERSPIEL IN VIER AKTEN / Pulver, Max – Leipzig: Insel-Verlag, 1918 – 1r – 1 – us U.W. Library [820]
IGGAROT / Gordon, J L – 2v. Warsaw. 1894-95. BJ-290-11 1 – 9 – ne IDC [940]
IGGERETH BAALE CHAJJIM / Landsberger, J – Darmstadt. 1882. BJ-421-81 1 – 9 – ne IDC [470]
IGGEROT HA-PEKIDIM VE-HA-AMARKALIM ME-AMSTERDAM / Rivlin, J J & Rivlin, B – 2pts. Jerusalem. 1965-70. BJ-27-6 1 – 9 – ne IDC [270]
IGGEROT RABBI SHEMUEL ABOHAB VE-RABBI MOSHEH ZAKKUT / Benayahu, M – v. 5. Yerushalayim. 1955. BJ-27-66 1 – 9 – ne IDC [900]
IGGROT DAVID FRISCHMANN / ed by Malachi, E R – New York. 1927. BJ-422-56 1 – 9 – ne IDC [920]
IGLESIA : NUEVA FRONTERA / Aradillas Agudo, Antonio – Madrid: Sociedad de Educacion Atenas, S.A., 1967 – 1 – sp Bibl Santa Ana [240]
Iglesia *see* CANTOS LITURGICOS
IGLESIA ANO 2000 / Aradillas Agudo, Antonio – Madrid: PPC, 1972 – 1 – sp Bibl Santa Ana [240]
IGLESIA DE LEON Y MONASTERIOS ANTIGUOS Y MODERNOS / Risco, Manuel – 1792 – 1mf – 9 – Pta1,000.00 – 84-7848-111-7 – sp Pentalfa [720]
LA IGLESIA DE SANTIAGO DE LOS CABALLEROS DE CACERES Y EL ESCULTOR ALONSO BERRUGUETE / Floriano Cumbreno, Antonio C – Caceres, S.L., 1918 – 1 – sp Bibl Santa Ana [240]
LA IGLESIA DE SANTIAGO DE LOS CABALLEROS. DESCRIPCION HISTORICO-ARTISTICA / Floriano Cumbreno, Antonio C – Caceres: Tip. de Santos Floriano y otros, 1915 – sp Bibl Santa Ana [720]
LA IGLESIA EN LA INDEPENDENCIA DEL URUGUAY / Sallaberry, Juan Faustino – Montevideo, Madrid: Razon y Fe, 1932 – 1 – sp Bibl Santa Ana [320]
LA IGLESIA EN TOLEDO... / Rivera Reno, Juan Francisco – Madrid: Graf. Calleja, 1967 – 1 – sp Bibl Santa Ana [946]
LA IGLESIA FILIPINA INDEPENDIENTE – Manila. Philippine Islands. -w. 11-26 Oct, 8 Nov 1903. (4 ft) – 1 – uk British Libr Newspaper [072]
IGLESIA PARROQUIAL DE SAN JOSE / Caceres. Parroquia de San Jose – Caceres: Tip. Extremadura, 1978 – sp Bibl Santa Ana [240]
Iglesia, Ramon *see* CRONISTA E HISTORIADORES DE LA CONQUISTA DE MEXICO, FONDO DE CULTURA ECONOMICA
IGLESIA Y JUSTICIALISMO : 1943-1955 / Chiesa, Carlos & Sosa, Enrique – Buenos Aires: Centro de Investigacion y Orientacion Social, 1983 – 1 – CSUXADQ7296-B – us Hoover Inst Photo [200]
LA IGLESIA Y LA EDUCACION POPULAR EN INDIAS / Bayle, Constantino – Madrid: Razon y Fe, 1932 – 1 – sp Bibl Santa Ana [370]
LA IGLESIA Y LA MASONERIA EN VENEZUELA... / Navarro, Nicolas E; ed by Bayle, Constantino – Madrid: Razon y Fe, 1928 – 9 – sp Bibl Santa Ana [290]
LA IGLESIA Y LA PATRIA. LA ACCION CATOLICA / Delgado Gomez, Enrique – Pamplona: Graficas Iruna, 1948 – sp Bibl Santa Ana [240]
IGLESIAS – Mexico: Centro Nacional de Comunicacion Social y Comision Evangelica Latinoamericana de Educacion Cristiana, 1983. ns: v1 n1/2-v9 n107. 1984-1992 – 4r – 1 – us Res Libr [240]
IGLESIAS BOMBARDEADAS POR LOS REBELES / Spain. Ministerio de Propaganda – Churches bombarded by the rebels. n.p., 1936. Fiche W956. (Blodgett Collection of Spanish Civil War Pamphlets) – 9 – us H.U. College Libr [946]
LAS IGLESIAS CRISTIANAS DE ORIENTE / Morillo Trivino, Santiago – Granada: Publicaciones OMDOC, 1946 – 1 – sp Bibl Santa Ana [240]
Iglesias de la Casa, Jose *see*
– POESIAS POSTUMAS. TOMO 1
– POESIAS POSTUMAS. TOMO 2
Iglesias, M *see* MEMORIAL SOBRE LAS ANALOGIAS Y DIFERENCIAS...ENTRE EL GARROTILLO...Y LA ANGINA...
IGLESIAS MOZARABES : ARTE ESPANOL DE LOS SIGLOS 9 A 11 / Gomez-Moreno, M – Madrid, 1919 – 25mf – 8 – Dfl88.00 – ne Slangenburg [946]
IGLULIK AND CARIBOU ESKIMO TEXTS / Rasmussen, Knud – 1930 – 8 – BN 364 2 – ne IDC [490]
IGNACE D'ANTIOCHE, SES EPITRES, SA VIE, SA THEOLOGIE : ETUDE CRITIQUE SUIVIE D'UNE TRADUCTION ANNOTEE / Bruston, Edouard – Paris: G. Fischbacher, 1897 – 1mf – us A.T.L.A. [240]
IGNACE JAN PADEREWSKI PAMPHLET COLLECTION – 1919-1932 – 1 reel – 1 – CSUXANL6741-B – us Hoover Inst Photo [920]
IGNACIO DE AZCUEDO... / Costa, Manuel G da – Madrid: Missionalia Hispanica, 1949 – 1 – sp Bibl Santa Ana [240]
Ignacio Diaz, Melchor *see* ELEMENTOS DE IDEOLOGIA Y GRAMATICA GENERAL-HISTORIA DE LA LOGICA
Ignacio, Rosendo *see* AKLAT NG PAGLULUTO
Ignat'ev, A I *see* PRAKTIKA ARBITRAZHNOI KOMISSII VSNKH SSSR I RSFSR
Ignatev, VI *see* NEKOTORYE FAKTY I ITOGI CHETYREKH LET GRAZHDANSKOI VOINY 1917-1921
Ignat'eva, G M et al *see* SELECTED TOPICS IN EMBRYOLOGY
IGNATIAN – Cleveland, OH, 8 Oct 1924-15 June 1925 – 1 reel – 1 – us Western Res [071]
THE IGNATIAN EPISTLES ENTIRELY SPURIOUS : A REPLY TO THE RIGHT REV. DR. LIGHTFOOT, BISHOP OF DURHAM / Killen, W D – Edinburgh: T.& T. Clark, 1886 – 1mf – us A.T.L.A. [240]
Ignatius of Loyola, Saint *see* EXERCITIA SPIRITUALIA
Ignatius, Saint *see*
– CORPUS IGNATIANUM: A COMPLETE COLLECTION OF THE IGNATIAN EPISTLES TRANSL. AND ANNOTATED BY WILLIAM CURETON
– EPISTLES OF SAINT IGNATIUS
IGNATIUS VON ANTIOCHIEN ALS CHRIST UND THEOLOGE (T.U.U. 1-12/3A) / Goltz, Eduard von der – Leipzig, 1894 – 4mf – 9 – ne Slangenburg [240]
IGNATIUS VON ANTIOCHIEN UND DIE PAULUSBRIEFE (T.U.U. 5-99) / Rathke, H – Berlin, 1967 – 2mf – 9 – ne Slangenburg [240]
IGNATIUS VON LOYOLA / Gothein, Eberhard – Halle: Verein fuer Reformationsgeschichte, 1885. ([Schriften des Vereins fuer Reformationsgeschichte; Bd. 11]) – 1mf – us A.T.L.A. [240]
IGNATIUS VON LOYOLA UND DER PROTESTANTISMUS / Goetz, Leopold Karl – Muenchen: J.F. Lehmann, 1901 – 1mf – us A.T.L.A. [240]
IGNATIUS VON LOYOLA UND DIE GEGENREFORMATION / Gothein, Eberhard – Halle: M. Niemeyer, 1895 – 2mf – us A.T.L.A. [240]
Ignatov, S S *see* E.T.A. HOFFMANN
Ignatovskii, I S *see* MEZHEVYE AKTY I UKRIEPLENIE VOTCHINNYKH PRAV NA NEDVIZHIMYIA IMIENIIA. V DVUKH CHASTIAKH. I. S. IGNATOVSKAGO
IGNAZ VON DOELLINGER : SEIN LEBEN AUF GRUND SEINES SCHRIFTLICHEN NACHLASSES / Friedrich, Johann – Muenchen: Beck, 1899-1901 – 5mf – us A.T.L.A. [240]
LA IGNORANCIA DEL DERECHO, CON UN AMPLIO ESTUDIO PRELIMINAR / Costa y Martinez, Joaquin – Buenos Aires, Editorial Partenon, 1945. 158p. LL-4093 – 1 – us L of C Photodup [340]
Ignotus *see*
– BUDUSHCHNOST RUSSKAGO TSARIA
– THE PIONEER
IGOR' SEVERIANIN I FUTURIZM / Khodasevich, V – Russkie vedomosti, 1914, issues from 29 Apr and 1 May. BR-3559 2 – 8 – ne IDC [700]
IGOSS GENERAL PLAN AND IMPLEMENTATION PROGRAMME 1977-1982 – 1977 – 36p – 9 – 92-3-101524-9 – fr UNESCO [060]
IGRA = THE PERFORMANCE – Moscow. n1-3. 1918 – 6mf – 9 – $50.00 – us Ross [790]
IGREJA 2001 / Aradillas Agudo, Antonio – Lisboa: Liber, 1975 – 1 – sp Bibl Santa Ana [946]
IGREJAS DE SAO PAULO : INTRODUCAO AO ESTUDO DOS TEMPLOS MAIS CARACTERISTICOS DE SAO PAOLO NAS SUAS RELACACOES COM A CRONICA DA CIDADE / Arroyo, Leonardo – Rio de Janeiro: Livraria Jose Olympio Editora, 1954 – 1 – us Res Libr [240]
IGREJAS, DESENVOLVIMENTO E PARTICIPACAO POPULAR : CONSULTA LATINO-AMERICANA SOBRE A "PARTICIPACAO DAS IGREJAS EM PROGRAMAS E PROJETOS DE DESENVOLVIMENTO," ITAICI, BRASIL, SETEMBRO DE 1980 – Rio de Janeiro: Contro Ecumenico de Documentacao e Informacao: Tempo e Presenca Editora, 1981 – us Res Libr [972]
LA IGUALDAD – Madrid, Spain. -d. 2 Jan 1872-30 Dec 1874. 3 reels – 1 – uk British Libr Newspaper [072]
Iguiniz, J B *see*
– BIBLIOGRAFIA BIOGRAFICA MEXICANA
– BIBLIOGRAFIA DE LOS ESCRITORES DE LA PROVINCIA MEXICANA DE LA COMPANIA DE JESUS, DESDE SU RESTAURACION EN 1816 HASTA NUESTROS DIAS
– DISQUISICIONES BIBLIOGRAFICAS: AUTORES, LIBROS, BIBLIOTECAS, ARTES GRAFICAS
Ihaza, Daniel E *see* FOREIGN TRADE OF NIGERIA
Ihering, Rudolf von *see*
– LAW AS A MEANS TO AN END
– THE STRUGGLE FOR LAW
IHI (ISHIKAWAJIMA-HARIMA HEAVY INDUSTRIES) ENGINEERING REVIEW – v1- 1968- – 1,5,6,9 – us UMI [620]
IHIA *see* EL-IHIA
Ihle, A *see* DAS ALTE KOENIGREICH KONGO
Ihme, Gertrud *see* DIE THEORETISCHEN AUFFASSUNGEN VOM ERFOLG DER VOLKSWIRTSCHAFT
Ihme, Heinrich *see* DER VOLKSBEGRIFF DER DEUTSCHEN VOLKSKUNDE IN SEINER GESCHICHTLICHEN ENTWICKLUNG
Ihmels, Ludwig *see* DIE CHRISTLICHE WAHRHEITSGEWISSHEIT
Ihne, Wilhelm *see* ROEMISCHE GESCHICHTE
I-HO-T'UAN – Documents on the Boxer Uprising. 4 v. 1953. BCH-952 2 – 8 – ne IDC [950]
I-HO-T'UAN TANG-AN SHIH-LIAO – Collection of documents on the Boxer Uprising. 2 v. 1959. BCH-951 2 – 8 – ne IDC [950]

IHR MITTEL : LUSTSPIEL IN VIER AUFZUEGEN / Reitler, Marzellin Adalbert – [Wien: J N Vernay, 188-?] – 1r – 1 – us U.W. Library [820]
Ihre, J *see* GLOSSARIUM SUIOGOTHICUM...
IHRER VIER : LEBEN UND ENDE EINIGER JUNGER MISSIONSKAUFLEUTE / Schneider, Hermann G – Herrnhut: Verlag der Missionsbuchhandlung, [1903?] – 1mf – us A.T.L.A. [240]
IHSAI YILLIK – [1928] – 5mf – 9 – $150.00 – us MEDOC [949]
Ihsan (Hamamizade) *see* DIVAN
Ihsan, Mustafa *see* POSTA REHBERI
II UL 1917 GODA / Ilin-Zhenevskii, Aleksandr Fedorovich – Moskva: Gos. izdvo, 1927 – 1 – CSUX88-B5454 – us Hoover Inst Photo [947]
IIC : INTERNATIONAL REVIEW OF INDUSTRIAL PROPERTY AND COPYRIGHT LAW – v1-27. 1970-96 – 1,5,6,13 – us V.C.H. [340]
IIE TRANSACTIONS *see* AIIE TRANSACTIONS
IISUS NEIZVESTNYI / Merezhkovskii, Dimitrii – v. 1-2 (2). Beograd. 1932. BR-766 2 – 8 – ne IDC [460]
Ijzermans, Jan *see* MUSIC AND DANCE IN SURINAM
IK BESCHULDIG... / Mangoenkoesomo, Tjipto – Soerakarta, 1915 – 1mf – 9 – ne IDC [950]
IKBAL – Trabzon, 1908-19? – 9 – $20.00 – us MEDOC [956]
L'IKDAM – Hebdomadaire de defense des interets musulmans nord-africains le sous-titre varie. Dir. S. Denden, H. Adjammar, Emir Khaled, etc. El-Biar. mars 1919-avr 1923, mars 1931-janv 1935. suite de: L' Islam voir a ce titre – 1 – fr A.C.R.P.P. [073]
L'IKDAM – Politique, litteraire, artistique. Organe de defense des interets des indigenes et des Musulmans francais algeriens.Dir., A. Haddou. No.1-4. Alger.fevr-mars 1925 – 1 – fr A.C.R.P.P. [073]
Ikels, Marion *see* DIE QUALITAET VON CONJOINT ANALYSEN
Iken, J Friedrich *see* HEINRICH VON ZUETPHEN
IKHWEZI LASE TRANSKEI – Umtata, South Africa. 1966-76. 1 reel.Title varies: Ikwezi – 1, 16 diazo available at reduced price – sa SA Libr [072]
IKHWEZI LOMSO – Queenstown: Ikhwezi Lomso, sep, nov 1958; feb, may 1959; feb 1960 – 1r – 1 – us Res Libr [072]
Iki, Mme. *see* ORIENTAL HAIR STYLES
IKINCI BES YIL 1968-1972, 1968 YILI PROGRAMI / Turkey. Devlet Planlama Teskilati – (Second development plan 1968-1972, 1968 annual program). Ankara. 1967. BD-1766 1 – 9 – ne IDC [338]
IKINCI BES YIL 1968-1972, 1969 YILI PROGRAMI / Turkey. Devlet Planlama Teskilati – (Second development plan 1968-1972, 1969 annual program). Ankara. 1969. BD-1767 1 – 9 – ne IDC [338]
IKINCI BES YIL 1968-1972, 1970 YILI PROGRAMI / Turkey. Devlet Planlama Teskilati – (Second development plan 1968-1972, 1970 annual program). Ankara. 1970. BD-1768 1 – 9 – ne IDC [338]
Ikoma, Toshiaki *see*
- JAPANESE TECHNOLOGY REVIEWS: SECTION A
- JAPANESE TECHNOLOGY REVIEWS: SECTION B
- JAPANESE TECHNOLOGY REVIEWS: SECTION E

Ikonnikov, V S *see*
- OPYT RUSSKOI ISTORIOGRAFII

IKONOGRAPHIE DER CHRISTLICHEN KUNST / Kuenstle, Karl – O-328. 2 v. 1926-1928 – 9 – ne IDC [240]
IKONOLOGISCHES WOERTERBUCH... / Prezel, L de – Gotha, 1759 – 5mf – ne IDC [700]
IKUF BLETER = I.K.U.F. LEAVES – (In Yiddish) – Bucarest, RM. v5 no1 18 Mar 1946-v7 no211 5 Dec 1952 – 1r – 1 – $50.00 – cn Can Microfilming [072]
ILA MADE EASY : LANGUAGE OF THE BAILA OF NORTHERN RHODESIA / Smith, Edwin William – Kasenga, NR [Zambia]: Book Room of the Baila-Batonga Mission, 1914 – 1 – us Res Libr [490]
ILAKECARI – Chunnakam, Sri Lanka. 1932-58 – 12r – 1 – us L of C Photodup [072]
ILANGA LASE NATAL – Durban, South Africa. 1903-1978 – 1 – sa State Libr [072]
Ilarii, Ieromonakh *see* OPISANIE SLAVIANSKIKH RUKOPISEI BIBLIOTEKI SVIATO-TROITSKOI SERGIEVOI LAVRY
THE ILA-SPEAKING PEOPLES OF NORTHERN RHODESIA / Smith, E W & Dale, A M – 2v. London. 1920. BA-372 2 – 8 – ne IDC [960]
ILAVELI NUEZHET UEL-MUENSEAT / Rifat, Ilaveli – [Istanbul]: Sirket Sahafiye Osmaniye Matbaasi, 1318 [1901] – $28.00 – us MEDOC [470]
Ilberg, J *see* NEUE JAHRBUECHER FUER DAS KLASSICHE ALTERTUM, GESCHICHTE UND DEUTSCHE LITERATUR UND FUER PAEDAGOGIK
Ilbert, Peregrine *see* BENGAL TENANCY BILL
ILCA *see*
- HANDBOOK OF AFRICAN LIVESTOCK STATISTICS
- LIVESTOCK PRODUCTION IN THE SUBHUMID ZONE OF WEST AFRICA
- LIVESTOCK SYSTEMS RESEARCH MANUAL
- MATHEMATICAL MODELLING OF LIVESTOCK PRODUCTION SYSTEMS
- PASTORAL SYSTEMS RESEARCH IN SUB-SAHARAN AFRICA.
- POTENTIAL FOR IMPACT

ILCA BULLETIN – (Ceased publication in December 1989; last issue no. 35) – Quarterly. 36-44p – et ILRI [630]
ILCA IN PRINT = PUBLICATIONS DU CIPEA : 1975-1988 / Atlaw, Amekalech & Sahlu, Marcos – 1989 – 9 – free – 92-9053-156-8 – et ILRI [630]
ILCA IN PRINT = PUBLICATIONS DU CIPEA : SUPPLEMENT 1 – 1990 – 9 – free – 92-9053-157-6 – et ILRI [630]
ILCA IN PRINT = PUBLICATIONS DU CIPEA : SUPPLEMENT 2 – 1991 – 9 – Free – 92-9053-219-X – et ILRI [630]
ILCAInstitut d'Economie Rurale du Mali *see* EVALUATION OF THE PRODUCTIVITIES OF MAURE AND PEUL CATTLE BREEDS AT THE SAHELIAN STATION, NIONO, MALI
L'ILE DE SABLE / Chevalier, Henri Emile – Paris: Levy, 1878. 00603. (Pre-1900 Canadiana) – 9 – cn C.I.H.M. [971]
L'ILE MYSTERIEUSE: LE SECRET DE L'ILE / Verne, Jules – 7th ed. Paris, 1875. 190p. 4 fiches. (Literature Collection) – 9 – 20.00 – fr Bibl Nationale [830]
L'ILE SONNANTE – Petite revue des lettres. no. 1-32. Paris. nov 1909-13 – 1 – fr A.C.R.P.P. [800]
ILEACH – 1 – £42.00r – uk Scot News [072]
ILERI – (Continues Suengue) – Manastir: Neyyir-i Hakikat Matbaasi. Sahib-i Imtiyaz ve Mueduer-i Mes'ul: Matli Ziya, 1911. No. 3 (22) (21 Temmuz 1327 [1911]) – 9 – $25.00 – us MEDOC [956]
Ileri, Celal Nuri *see* HATEM UEL-ENBIYA
LES ILES CANARIES: FLORE DE L'ARCHIPEL / Pitard, J & Proust, L – Paris. 1908. B-7404 1 – 9 – ne IDC [580]
LES ILES DE L'OCEAN INDIEN OCCIDENTAL ET LE BATEAU : COMMUNICATION DES HOMMES ET DES IDEES A TRAVERS LES ARCHIVES DE LA COMPAGNIE DES MESSAGERIES MARITIMES, 1840-1920 / Barret, D – Paris, 1982 – 477p – 9 – F130.00 – fr Ethnologie [306]
LES ILES FORTUNEES, OU LES AVENTURES DE BATHYLLE ET DE CLEOBULE, PAR M.M.D.C.A.S / Moutonnet de Clairfons, Julien-Jacques – (Utopias in the Enlightenment series). 1778 – 9 – fr Hachette [830]
ILES SAMOA : NOTES POUR SERVIR A UNE MONOGRAPHIE DE CET ARCHIPEL / Marques, A – Lisbon: Impr Nationale, 1899 – 3mf – 9 – $4.50 – LLMC 82-100C Title 27 – us L.L.M.C. [980]
LES ILES SAMOA OU DES NAVIGATEURS : LE CONFLICT ENTRE LES ETATS-UNIS ET L'ALLEMAGNE ET LA NOUVELLE CONFERENCE DE BERLIN / Lort-Serignam, Arthur M T (pseud Arthur de Ganniers) – Paris: Charles Bayle, 1889 – 1mf – 9 – $1.50 – LLMC 82-100C Title 25 – us L.L.M.C. [980]
ILESHA – AND BEYOND! : THE STORY OF THE WESLEY GUILD MEDICAL WORK IN WEST AFRICA / Souton, Arthur E – London: Cargate Press, [193-?] – 1 – us Res Libr [960]
ILFORD AND REDBRIDGE POST *see* REDBRIDGE POST
ILFORD LEADER – Sep-Oct 1994; Nov 2-Dec 14 1994; 1995-96 – 9 1/2r – 9 – uk British Libr Newspaper [072]
ILFORD RECORDER *see* REDBRIDGE RECORDER
ILFORD YELLOW ADVERTISER *see* YELLOW ADVERTISER (REDBRIDGE EDN)
ILFRACOMBE CHRONICLE – England.1872-24 Jun 1876. -w.4 1/2 reels – 1 – uk British Libr Newspaper [072]
ILFRACOMBE GAZETTE AND OBSERVER – England.1897-98; 1901; Jan-25 Oct 1912. -w. 4 reels – 1 – uk British Libr Newspaper [072]
Ilg, A *see* THEOPHILUS PRESBYTER SCHEDULA DIVERSARUM ARTIUM
Ilg, Albert *see*
- HERACLIUS, VON DEN FARBEN UND KUNSTEN DER ROEMER
- KUNST ODER TRACTAT DER MALEREI DES CENNINO CENNINI DA COLLE DI VALDELSA

Ilgen, Pedro *see*
- STECHAEPFEL
- TIEFGLUTH
- UNTER WESTLICHEN STERNEN
- WELT- UND GOTTESREICHSKLAENGE

Ilgenstein, Heinrich *see* WILHELM VON POLENZ
IL'IA MUROMETS I BOGATYRSTVO KIEVSKOE / Miller, OF – Spb., 1870 – 16mf – 9 – ne IDC [947]
IL'IA MUROMETS I BOGATYRSTVO KIEVSKOE / Miller, OF – Spb., 1870 – 16mf – 9 – 2196/2 – ne IDC [947]
ILIAMNA VOLCANO AND ITS BASEMENT / Juhle, Werner – 1957 – 1r – 1 – $50.00 – B70064 – us Library Micro [550]
IL'IAZD – Lidantlu fAram. Paris. 1923. Br-936 2 – 8 – ne IDC [460]
IL'IAZD – Voskhishchenie. Roman. Paris. 1930. BR-938 2 – 8 – ne IDC [460]
Ilichevskii *see* SKAZKA O BOLSHEVIKI E I IVANI E DURAKI E
THE ILIFF REVIEW – 1940-88 (complete) – 7r – 1 – ATLA S0582 – us A.T.L.A. [073]
Iliffe, J H *see* A SHORT GUIDE TO THE EXHIBITION OF THE PALESTINE ARCHAEOLOGICAL MUSEUM, ILLUSTRATING THE STONE AND BRONZE AGES IN PALESTINE
ILIM FEN FELSEFE TETEBBUATI MECMUASI – Ankara. Umur-i Tahririye Muedirí: Hakki Baha. Umur-i Edebiye Muedirir: Ahmed Edib. No. 1 (Haziran 1338 [1922]) – 9 – $30.00 – us MEDOC [956]
Ilimskii, D I *see*
- KOOPERATIVNYE SOIUZY V SIBIRI (1908-1918 GG.)
- SIBIRSKAIA KOOPERATSIIA I MOSKOVSKII NARODNYI BANK

Ilimskii, D I (D I Golenishchev-Kutuzov) *see* OCHERKI PO TEORII KOOPERATSII
Ilin, A A *see* TOPOGRADIIA KLADOV SEREBRIANYKH I ZOLOTYKH SLITKOV
Il'in, Valilii *see* O POKLONENII BOGO OTTSTU V" VUKHE I ISTINE
Ilin-Zhenevskii, Aleksandr Fedorovich *see* II UL 1917 GODA
Iliukhov, Nikolai Kirillovich *see* PARTIZANSKOE DVIZHENIE V PRIMORI 1918-1920 GG
ILK ADIM – Nigde, 1926-19? – 9 – $20.00 – us MEDOC [956]
ILKESTON ADVERTISER – 1889; Feb 27-Dec 18 1897; Mar 21-Dec 26 1913; 1986-Aug 1987; Sep 4-Dec 18 1987; 1988-Jun 1989; Jul 7-Dec 22 1989; Jan-Jun 1990; Jul 6-Dec 21 1990; 1991-96 – 26r – 9 – uk British Libr Newspaper [072]
ILKLEY GAZETTE – England. -w. 1869-84. (5 reels) – 1 – uk British Libr Newspaper [072]
ILKLEY RATE BOOKS – Yorkshire. 1936-51 – 1 – uk Microform Academic [941]
Ilkley. Yorkshire. England. Urban District Council *see* MINUTE BOOKS
ILLERTALBOTE : BA DER SUEDWEST-PRESSE – Dietenheim-Ulm, Germany. 1975- – 112r (1975-1990) – 1 – gw Mikrofilm [072]
L'ILLETTRE / ed by Levy-Beaulieu, Victor – Montreal, jan-oct 1970 – 1r – 1 – cn Can Microfilming [400]
Illgen, Christianus Fridericus *see* SYMBOLARUM AD VITAM ET DOCTRINAM LAELII SOCINI
Illich, Ivan *see* THE HISTORY OF RELIGIOSITY IN LATIN AMERICA, 1880-1970
ILLICIT DRUGS: MYTH AND REALITY / DuQuesne, Terence – LA pamphlet no.5, 12p – 9 – 1.00f – at Libertarian Micro [360]
ILLICIT TRAFFIC / United Nations. Commission on Narcotic Drugs – 1977-1982 – E.49 F.50 S.39 – 9 (E/IT) – us U.N. Pubs [360]
Illiger, K *see* MAGAZIN DER INSEKTENKUNDE
Illing, Robert *see* STUDIES OF THE ENGLISH METRICAL PSALTER AT THE TIME OF THE REFORMATION
Illingworth, J Richardson *see* DIVINE IMMANENCE:...ON THE SPIRITUAL SIGNIFICANCE OF MATTER
Illingworth, John Richardson *see*
- THE DOCTRINE OF THE TRINITY
- PERSONALITY, HUMAN AND DIVINE
- REASON AND REVELATION

ILLINOIS : SESSION LAWS OF AMERICAN STATES AND TERRITORIES – 1809-1994 – 9 – $2,943.00 set – us Hein [340]
ILLINOIS : WEST'S SMITH-HURD ILLINOIS COMPILED STATUTES ANNOTATED – St Paul: West Pub Co, 1934-Mar 1996 update – 9 – $5,311.00 set – us Hein [340]
Illinois *see*
- COUNTY RECORDS
- MATTHEWS AND BANGS' CIRCUIT COURT REPORTS
- RECORDS OF THE NATIONAL HOME FOR DISABLED SOLDIERS
- REPORTS AND OPINIONS (A-G)
- REPORTS, PRE-NRS
- STATE LABOR REPORTS
- STATE REPORTS, POST-NRS
- STATE WATER RESOURCES REPORTS
- VOTING REGISTERS

ILLINOIS ADVOCATE – (Filmed with: Illinois advocate and State register (Vandalia, IL)) – Edwardsville: S S Brooks, feb 1831-apr 1833 – us Res Libr [071]
ILLINOIS ADVOCATE – Vandalia: J Y Sawyer, apr 15 1835-mar 16 1836 – us Res Libr [071]
ILLINOIS ADVOCATE AND STATE REGISTER – (Filmed with: Illinois advocate (Edwardsville, Il)) – Vandalia: J Y Sawyer, apr 1833-apr 1835 – 3r – 1 – us Res Libr [071]
ILLINOIS AGRICULTURAL ECONOMICS / Illinois. Department of Agricultural Economics – n.1-9. 1961-69 – 1,5 – us Spaulding [630]
Illinois. Agricultural Experiment Station *see*
- BULLETIN
- DIXON SPRINGS SHEEPDAY: PROCEEDINGS: ROBBS
- ILLINOIS RESEARCH
- PROGRESS IN SOLVING FARM PROBLEMS OF ILLINOIS REPORT
- RESEARCH PROGRESS
- SOIL REPORT

Illinois. Appellate Court *see* ILLINOIS APPELLATE REPORTS
ILLINOIS APPELLATE REPORTS / Illinois. Appellate Court – (All vols are Pre-NRS. Vols after v215 are still in copyright and will be filmed as they become available) – v1-216. 1877-1920 – 1424mf – 9 – $2,136.00 – LLMC 80-803 – us L.L.M.C. [340]
ILLINOIS APPELLATE REPORTS *see* MATTHEWS AND BANGS' CIRCUIT COURT REPORTS
ILLINOIS ATTORNEY GENERAL REPORTS AND OPINIONS – (6 1872-1978 $490.00. 9 1979-1995 $103.00) – 1872-1995 – 6,9 – $593.00set – us Hein [340]
ILLINOIS BAPTIST – Springfield, Illinois: Illinois Baptist State Association, 1906-1991 – 1 – $1,542.72 – us Baptist [240]
ILLINOIS BAPTIST BULLETIN – Normal/Joliet, IL. Illinois Baptist State Convention. 1909-35. Incomplete. Single reels available – 1 – $121.05 – us A.B.H.S. [240]
ILLINOIS BAPTIST BULLETIN – Upper Alton, IL.Baptist General Assoc. of Illinois. 1892-98. Incomplete – 1 – $15.90 – us A.B.H.S. [240]
ILLINOIS BAPTIST NEWS/BAPTIST NEWS – Joliet/Springfield, IL. Illinois Baptist State Convention. 1935-70. Includes Chicago ed. Single reels available – 1 – 128.40 – us A.B.H.S. [071]
ILLINOIS BAR JOURNAL – (v1-72 1912-84 on reel or mf $835.00. v73-82 1984-94 on mf $186.00. Title varies: v1-20 no 1 1912-32 as Illinois State Bar Association Quarterly) – v1-82. 1912-94 – 5,6,9 – $1,021.00 set – us Hein [340]
ILLINOIS CAREER EDUCATION JOURNAL – v. 1-. 1943- – 1. – apply; v.34- 1977- 5,6,9 – us UMI [370]
ILLINOIS CATTLE FEEDERS DAYS / Illinois. Department of Animal Science – 1940-69 – 1,5 – us Spaulding [636]
Illinois. Census *see*
- 1820 FEDERAL CENSUS OF ILLINOIS
- EVALUATION FOR ACREAGE, LIVESTOCK AND CROPS, 1870
- EVALUATION OF ACREAGE, 1870
- FEDERAL AGRICULTURAL CENSUS, 1850
- FEDERAL AGRICULTURAL CENSUS, 1860
- FEDERAL AGRICULTURAL CENSUS, 1865

- FEDERAL AGRICULTURAL CENSUS, 1870
- FEDERAL AGRICULTURAL CENSUS, 1880
- FEDERAL CENSUS OF THE DEAF, DUMB, BLIND AND INSANE, 1855
- FEDERAL INDUSTRIAL AND SOCIAL STATISTICS, 1850
- FEDERAL INDUSTRIAL AND SOCIAL STATISTICS, 1870
- FEDERAL INDUSTRIAL CENSUS, 1860
- FEDERAL MANUFACTURERS CENSUS, 1880
- ILLINOIS CENSUS RETURNS, 1810 & 1818
- ILLINOIS CENSUS RETURNS, 1820
- INDUSTRY, 1870
- MORTALITY SCHEDULES, 1850
- MORTALITY SCHEDULES, 1860
- MORTALITY SCHEDULES, 1870
- MORTALITY SCHEDULES, 1880
- SOCIAL STATISTICS, 1870
- STATE CENSUS, 1825
- STATE CENSUS, 1830
- STATE CENSUS, 1835
- STATE CENSUS, 1840
- STATE CENSUS, 1845
- STATE CENSUS, 1855
- STATE CENSUS, 1865

ILLINOIS CENSUS RETURNS, 1810 & 1818 / Illinois. Census; ed by Norton, Margaret Cross – 1969. Orig. publ. 1935 as Collections of the Illinois State Historical Library, v24. Indexed. F-0838 – 6mf – 9 – us A.G.L.L. [310]

ILLINOIS CENSUS RETURNS, 1820 / Illinois. Census; ed by Norton, Margaret Cross – 1969. Orig. publ. 1934 as Collections of the Illinois State Historical Library, v26. Indexed. F-0840 – 8mf – 9 – us A.G.L.L. [310]

Illinois. College of Agriculture *see*
- AGRICULTURAL COMMUNICATIONS RESEARCH REPORT
- EXTENSION CIRCULARS
- SPECIAL PUBLICATION

Illinois. College of Agriculture. Extension Service *see* ILLINOIS TURFGRASS CONFERENCE PROCEEDINGS

Illinois. College of Agriculture. Extension Service in Agriculture and Home Economics *see*
- COMMUNICATIONS EVALUATION REPORT
- ILLINOIS CUSTOM SPRAY OPERATORS TRAINING SCHOOL

Illinois. Commerce Commission *see*
- ILLINOIS ELECTRIC UTILITIES: A COMPARATIVE STUDY OF ELECTRIC SALES STATISTICS
- ILLINOIS GAS UTILITIES: A COMPARATIVE STUDY OF GAS SALES STATISTICS
- REPORTS

Illinois. Consumer Credit Division *see* ANALYSIS OF REPORTS FILED BY CONSUMER FINANCE AND CONSUMER IN STALLMENT LOAN COMPANIES

Illinois. Cooperative Extension Service in Agriculture and Home Economics *see* CIRCULAR

ILLINOIS: COUNTY AND REGIONAL HISTORIES AND ATLASES – 1 – us Primary [978]

ILLINOIS COUNTY HISTORY INDEX (CARDS) – Z1-0001 to Z1-0088 – 5 – us A.G.L.L. [920]

Illinois County Records *see*
- CLASSIFICATION OF ILLINOIS HIGHWAYS
- SWAMPLAND RECORDS, 1852-1874

ILLINOIS CUSTOM SPRAY OPERATORS TRAINING SCHOOL / Illinois. College of Agriculture. Extension Service in Agriculture and Home Economics – Nos 1-27 1949-75 – 1,5 – us Spaulding [630]

Illinois. Department of Agricultural Economics *see*
- BULLETIN
- ILLINOIS AGRICULTURAL ECONOMICS
- ILLINOIS FARM ECONOMICS
- RESEARCH REPORTS AERR

Illinois. Department of Agronomy *see* AGRONOMY FACTS

Illinois. Department of Animal Science *see*
- ILLINOIS CATTLE FEEDERS DAYS
- ILLINOIS NUTRITION CONFERENCE PROCEEDINGS
- ILLINOIS SHEEP DAY: PAPERS

Illinois. Department of Forestry *see* FORESTRY NOTE

Illinois. Department of Insurance *see*
- REPORTS
- REPORTS BY THE DIRECTOR

Illinois. Department of Labor *see* REPORTS

Illinois. Department of Labor. Division of Statistics and Research *see* REPORTS ON COMPENSABLE WORK INJURIES IN ILLINOIS

Illinois. Department of Revenue *see* REPORTS

ILLINOIS EDUCATION – v. 1-61. 1913-72 – 1,; 5,6 – apply; v. 59-61. 1970-72. apply – us UMI [370]

ILLINOIS ELECTRIC UTILITIES: A COMPARATIVE STUDY OF ELECTRIC SALES STATISTICS / Illinois. Commerce Commission – 1933-79. 41 fiches. (Harvard Law School Library Collection.) – 9 – 1.50f – us H.U. Law [336]

ILLINOIS FARM ECONOMICS / Illinois. Department of Agricultural Economics – n.1-227. 1935-57 – 1,5 – us Spaulding [630]

ILLINOIS FREE TRADER – Ottawa. Ill. -w. 1840-78 – 1 – us UMI [071]

ILLINOIS GAS UTILITIES: A COMPARATIVE STUDY OF GAS SALES STATISTICS / Illinois. Commerce Commission – 1931-79. 44 fiches. (Harvard Law School Library Collection.) – 9 – 1.50f – us H.U. Law [336]

Illinois. General Assembly *see*
- FIRST GENERAL ASSEMBLY, 1ST SESSION, 1812, LEGISLATIVE COUNCIL JOURNAL
- FIRST GENERAL ASSEMBLY, 2ND SESSION, 1813
- ILLINOIS REPORTS OF THE 14TH & 15TH GENERAL ASSEMBLY, 1844-47
- SECOND GENERAL ASSEMBLY, 1ST SESSION, 1814

ILLINOIS: HISTORICAL AND STATISTICAL / Moses, John – Chicago: Fergus Printing Co., 1892. Illinois Reel 1. (The Cox Library Collection) – 5 – us Americana [978]

ILLINOIS HISTORICAL JOURNAL – v77, no.3-. Autumn 1984- – 1,5,6,9 – us UMI [073]

ILLINOIS INSURANCE – (v.10-1979- 5,6,9) – v.1. 1969 – 1 – us UMI [073]

ILLINOIS JOURNAL OF MATHEMATICS – Urbana. v1-28. 1957-84 – 5,9 – Dfl2,800.00; Dfl100.00v – ne Swets [510]

ILLINOIS LAW BULLETIN *see* ILLINOIS LAW QUARTERLY

THE ILLINOIS LAW OF VOLUNTARY ASSIGNMENTS FOR THE BENEFIT OF CREDITORS / Candlish, William James – Chicago: Callaghan, 1896. 222p. LL-659 – 1 – us L of C Photodup [340]

ILLINOIS LAW QUARTERLY – (Title varies: v1-2 as Illinois Law Bulletin. v3 as University of Illinois Law Bulletin) – Urbana. v1-6. 1917-24 – 1 – $40.00 – us Hein [073]

ILLINOIS LAW REVIEW – (More vols planned as copyright expires) – Northwestern University Law School. v1-6. 1906-12 – 42mf – 9 – $63.00 – LLMC 84-485 – us L.L.M.C. [073]

Illinois. Laws, Statutes, etc *see* PRIVATE AND GENERAL LAWS RELATING TO THE CHICAGO, BURLINGTON AND QUINCY RAILROAD, 1867

ILLINOIS LEGISLATIVE MANUAL FOR 30TH GENERAL ASSEMBLY-1877 AND 1878 / M.G. Tousley and Co – Springfield, 1877. Illinois Reel 8. The Cox Library Collection – 5 – us Americana [978]

ILLINOIS LIBRARIES – 1- 1919- – 1. ; 5,6. ; 9 – apply; v.51-; v.59- – us UMI [071]

Illinois. Military Records *see*
- BLACK HAWK WAR RECORDS, 1832
- HONOR ROLL OF VETERANS BURIED IN ILLINOIS
- HONOR ROLL OF VETERANS BURIED IN ILLINOIS: PEACETIME BURIALS
- HONOR ROLL OF VETERANS OF THE ARMED FORCES...BURIED IN THE STATE OF ILLINOIS PRIOR TO JULY 1, 1955
- MILITARY CENSUS, 1861-1862
- MILITARY CENSUS, 1862-1863
- REVOLUTIONARY SOLDIERS BURIED IN ILLINOIS

ILLINOIS MISCELLANEOUS RECORDS – V148-0004 – 1 – us A.G.L.L. [978]

ILLINOIS NUTRITION CONFERENCE PROCEEDINGS / Illinois. Department of Animal Science – n.2-10. 1954-62 – 1, 5 – us Spaulding [360]

Illinois. Office of Secretary of State. Securities Division *see* REPORTS

Illinois. Office of the Commissioner of Banks and Trust Companies *see* REPORTS

Illinois. Office of the Governor *see*
- EXECUTIVE RECORD, 1818-60
- EXECUTIVE REGISTER, 2ND SERIES

ILLINOIS POLITICAL DIRECTORY – 1899 / Higgins, John F – Chicago: 1899. Illinois Reel 8. (The Cox Library Collection) – 5 – us Americana [978]

ILLINOIS POLITICAL DIRECTORY AND SKETCHBOOK, 1898 WITH PORTRAITS OF PARTY LEADERS / Bodine and Co – Chicago, 1898. Illinois Reel 8. (The Cox Library Collection) – 5 – us Americana [978]

ILLINOIS PUBLIC DOMAIN LAND SALES – 1985 – 144mf – 9 – $25.00 – us IL Archives [333]

Illinois. Railroad and Warehouse Commission *see* REPORTS

ILLINOIS REPORTS OF THE 14TH & 15TH GENERAL ASSEMBLY, 1844-47 / Illinois. General Assembly – Collection of legis. reports concerning the Mormon War in Hancock Co. and misc. hand written documents. V148 – 1 – us A.G.L.L. [920]

ILLINOIS RESEARCH / Illinois. Agricultural Experiment Station – n.1-19. 1959-77 – 1, 5 – us Spaulding [630]

ILLINOIS SCHOOL RESEARCH – (See also: Illinois School Research and Development) – v1-12. 1964-1976 – 1 – us UMI [370]

ILLINOIS SCHOOL RESEARCH AND DEVELOPMENT – v. 13-. 1976- – 1,5,6,9 – us UMI [370]

Illinois. Second Presbytery (Associate Reformed Church) *see* MINUTES, 13 APRIL 1852-13 APRIL 1859

ILLINOIS SHEEP DAY: PAPERS / Illinois. Department of Animal Science – 1951-67 – 1, 5 – us Spaulding [636]

ILLINOIS STAATS-HEROLD – (Bound with Staats-Herold) – Chicago, apr 1932 – 1r – 1 – us Res Libr [071]

ILLINOIS STAATS-ZEITUNG – Chicago, IL: [Hoffgen, 1871-87; may 1888-1900] – 1 – us Res Libr [071]

Illinois. State Bar Association *see* PROCEEDINGS 1877-1939

ILLINOIS STATE BAR ASSOCIATION ANNUAL REPORTS – 1st to 63rd meetings. 1877-1939 (all publ) – 262mf – 9 – $393.00 – LLMC 84-486 – us L.L.M.C. [073]

ILLINOIS STATE BAR ASSOCIATION QUARTERLY *see* ILLINOIS BAR JOURNAL

ILLINOIS STATE CHRONICLE – Decatur. Ill. 1855-1861 – 1 – us UMI [071]

Illinois State Historical Society *see*
- PIERRE MENARD COLLECTION
- TRANSACTIONS FOR THE YEAR 1936

ILLINOIS STATE JOURNAL – Springfield. Ill. 1849-1879; 1921- – 1 – us UMI [071]

Illinois. State Public Utilities Commission *see* REPORTS

ILLINOIS STATE REGISTER – Springfield. Ill. 1849-1879; 1921- – 1 – us UMI [071]

Illinois. State Tax Commission *see* REPORTS

Illinois. Supreme Court *see* ILLINOIS SUPREME COURT REPORTS

ILLINOIS SUPREME COURT REPORTS / Illinois. Supreme Court – (Pre-NRS: v1-112 1819 827mf $1,240.00. Updates planned) – v1-293. 1819-1920 – 2282mf – 9 – $3,423.00 – LLMC 80-802 – us L.L.M.C. [340]

Illinois Territory *see* EXECUTIVE REGISTER

ILLINOIS TURFGRASS CONFERENCE PROCEEDINGS / Illinois. College of Agriculture. Extension Service – n.1-17. 1960-76 – 1,5 – us Spaulding [580]

ILLINOIS UNDERWRITER – (See also: Insurance Exchange Magazine) – v50-. 1978- – 1,5,6,9 – us UMI [336]

Illinois University *see* DESIGN BY MOTLEY

Illinois. University at Urbana-Champaign *see* DICTIONARY CATALOG OF THE APPLIED LIFE STUDIES LIBRARY

Illinois. University at Urbana-Champaign. Communications Library *see* CATALOG

ILLINOIS VALLEY COURIER – Cave City, OR. -w. 25 Apr 1935-30 May 1935. 1 roll – 1 – us U.O. Library [071]

ILLINOIS VALLEY NEWS – Cave City, OR. -w. 7 Mar 1935-11 Apr 1935. 1 roll – 1 – us U.O. Library [071]

ILLINOIS VALLEY NEWS – Cave Junction, OR. -w. 13 May 1937-. – 1 – us U.O. Library [071]

ILLINOIS WOCHENBLATT = ILLINOIS WEEKLY – Winona: Westlicher Harold Pub Co, oct 1920-oct 1921 – 1r – 1 – us Res Libr [071]

THE ILLITERATE POPULATION OF THAILAND 1957-1980 / Thailand. National Education Commission – c. 1974 – 1mf – 9 – DE-271/1 – ne IDC [370]

ILLIUSTRATSIIA – Ezhenedel'noe illiustrirovannoe izdanie. v. 1-12. Spb. 1858-63. BR-3382 2 – 8 – ne IDC [760]

ILLIUSTRIROVANNAIA GAZETA – Ezhenedel'nik. Spb. 1864-67. Lacking: 1864 (34-37). BR-3381 2 – 8 – ne IDC [073]

ILLIUSTRIROVANNAIA ROSSIIA – Titre francais: La Russie illustree. Paris. 1924-avr 1939 – 1 – fr A.C.R.P.P. [947]

ILLIUSTRIROVANNYI KATALOG T-VA "KUL'TURA" – Spb. 1907. BR-5680 2 – 8 – ne IDC [760]

ILLIUSTRIROVANNYI SEMEINYI LISTOK – Zhurnal zanimatel- nago i poleznago chteniia. Ezhenedel'nik. v. 1-8. Spb. 1859-63. Lacking: 1861 (5). BR-3212 2 – 8 – ne IDC [073]

Illiustrov, I *see* IURIDICHESKIE POSLOVITSY I POGOVORKI RUSSKOGO NARODA

ILLOGICAL GEOLOGY: THE WEAKEST POINT IN THE EVOLUTION THEORY / Price, George McCready – Los Angeles: Modern Heretic, 1906. 1 fiche – 9 – us A.T.L.A. [240]

LA ILLUMINATA DE TUTTI I TUONI DI CANTO FERMO.. / Aiguino da Brescia, Illuminato – 1562 – 9 – us Sibley [780]

ILLUMINATED MSS. FROM THE LIBRARY OF THE EARL OF LEICESTER / Holkham Hall. Norfolk. England – 1,14 – uk Microform Academic [760]

ILLUMINATING ENGINEERING – v1-50. 1906-55 – 1,5,6 – us Princeton Micro [660]

ILLUSION IN RELIGION / Abbott, Edwin Abbott – London: Francis Griffiths, [190-?] – 1mf – us A.T.L.A. [200]

A ILLUSTRACAO : PERIODICO CRITICO E NOTICIOSO – Jaragua, Alagoas. 30 Set 1891 – 1,5,6 – bl Biblioteca [072]

ILLUSTRACAO ANGLO-BRAZILEIRA – London, England. -irr. 13 Sept, 3 Nov 1870. 4 ft – 1 – uk British Libr Newspaper [072]

ILLUSTRATED ALBUM OF BIOGRAPHY OF RED RIVER VALLEY AND PARK REGIONS / Alden, Ogle & Co – Minnesota and North Dakota. Chicago, 1889. Minnesota Reel 3. (The Cox Library Collection) – 5 – us Americana [978]

ILLUSTRATED ALBUM OF BIOGRAPHY OF SOUTHWESTERN MINNESOTA / Occidental Publishing Co – Biographical sketches. Chicago, 1889. Minnesota Reel 3. (The Cox Library Collection) – 5 – us Americana [978]

ILLUSTRATED ALECTRICAL REVIEW *see* FACTORY

ILLUSTRATED AUSTRALIAN NEWS – Melbourne, Australia. -f. 1869-70; 1872; 1883-96. 4 reels – 1 – uk British Libr Newspaper [072]

ILLUSTRATED BERWICK JOURNAL – (Berwick Journal. 1856-73) – England. 16 Jun 1855-1873; 1881-1910; 1915; 1917 – 40r – 1 – uk British Libr Newspaper [072]

ILLUSTRATED BOOKS – 1839-1908 – 2r – 1 – us Ross [090]

ILLUSTRATED CATALOG OF PHOTOGRAPHIC EQUIPMENT AND MATERIALS FOR AMATEURS / Anthony and Co. – 1894, 1901. Reel 14 – 1 – $50.00 – us UPA [760]

ILLUSTRATED CATALOGUE OF INTERNATIONAL EXHIBITIONS – 1862. Vols. 1 & 2. BGM1-2 – 2r – 1 – at Corangamite [000]

AN ILLUSTRATED COMMENTARY ON THE ACTS OF THE APOSTLES : FOR FAMILY USE AND REFERENCE, AND FOR THE GREAT BODY OF CHRISTIAN WORKERS OF ALL DENOMINATIONS / Abbott, Lyman – New York: A S Barnes, 1878 – 1mf – 9 – 0-8370-2021-2 – 1985-0021 – us A.T.L.A. [220]

ILLUSTRATED COMMENTARY ON THE GOSPEL ACCORDING TO MATTHEW / Abbott, Lyman – New York: A.S. Barnes, 1875. 1 fiche – 9 – us A.T.L.A. [240]

AN ILLUSTRATED COMMENTARY ON THE GOSPEL ACCORDING TO ST. JOHN : FOR FAMILY USE AND REFERENCE, AND FOR THE GREAT BODY OF CHRISTIAN WORKERS OF ALL DENOMINATIONS / Abbott, Lyman – (Includes index) – New York: A S Barnes, 1879 – 1mf – 9 – 0-8370-2023-9 – 1985-0023 – us A.T.L.A. [220]

ILLUSTRATED COMMENTARY ON THE GOSPEL ACCORDING TO ST JOHN / Abbott, Lyman – New York: A.S. Barnes, 1879. 1 fiche – 9 – us A.T.L.A. [240]

ILLUSTRATED COMMENTARY ON THE GOSPEL OF LUKE / Abbott, Lyman – New York: A.S. Barnes, 1878. 1 fiche – 9 – us A.T.L.A. [240]

ILLUSTRATED COMMENTARY ON THE GOSPELS ACCORDING TO MARK AND LUKE / Abbott, Lyman – New York: A.S. Barnes, 1877. 1 fiche – 9 – us A.T.L.A. [240]

ILLUSTRATED DAILY NEWS – Los Angeles, CA. 1926-1927 – 20r – 1 – $1,000.00 – R03298 – us Library Micro [071]

ILLUSTRATED DESCRIPTION OF THISTLES / Mueller, Ferdinand Jakob Heinrich von – Melbourne. 1893. B-8060 1 – 9 – ne IDC [580]

ILLUSTRATED DRAMATIC & SPORTING NEWS – 1874-1964 – 1 – uk Manchester Libr [790]

ILLUSTRATED EXPLANATION OF THE COMMANDMENTS...OF GOD AND OF THE CHURCH / Rolfus, Hermann – New York: Benziger, 1897. 1 fiche – 9 – us A.T.L.A. [240]

AN ILLUSTRATED FLORA OF THE NORTHERN UNITED STATES, CANADA AND THE BRITISH POSSESSIONS / Britton, N L & Brown, A – 7514 2. 3 v. 1896-1898 – 9 – ne IDC [580]

ILLUSTRATED GLOSSARY OF RICE PROCESSING MACHINES – 1979 repr 1986 – 104p – it F.A.O. [631]

ILLUSTRATED HINDU – New Delhi, India. Oct 1942-Nov 1947 – 2r – 1 – us L of C Photodup [072]

ILLUSTRATED HISTORY AND BIOGRAPHICAL RECORD OF LENAWEE COUNTY / Knapp & Bonner, Richard I – Adrian: The Times Printing Co., 1903. Michigan Reel 17. (The Cox Library Collection) – 5 – us Americana [978]

AN ILLUSTRATED HISTORY OF CENTRAL OREGON / Western Historical Co – Spokane, 1905. Oregon reel 3. (Cox Library Collection) – 5 – us Americana [978]

ILLUSTRATED HISTORY OF KANDIYOHI COUNTY / St. Paul Pioneer Press – St. Paul, 1905. Minnesota Reel 8. (The Cox Library Collection) – 5 – us Americana [978]

ILLUSTRATED HISTORY OF KENNEBEC COUNTY / Kingsburg, G W & Deyo – New York, H. W. Blake and Co., 1892. Maine Reel 4. (The Cox Library Collection) – 5 – us Americana [978]

AN ILLUSTRATED HISTORY OF LINCOLN COUNTY AND HER PEOPLE / Bare & McDudd – Chicago: American Historical Society, 1920. 2v.Nebraska Reel 11. (The Cox Library Collection) – 5 – us Americana [978]

AN ILLUSTRATED HISTORY OF LOS ANGELES COUNTY, CALIFORNIA – Chicago, 1889. California Reel 14. (The Cox Library Collection) – 5 – us Americana [978]

ILLUSTRATED HISTORY OF LOWELL AND VICINITY / Courier-Citizen Co – Lowell, 1897. Massachusetts Reel 6. The Cox Library Collection – 5 – us Americana [978]

AN ILLUSTRATED HISTORY OF LYON COUNTY / Rose, Arthur P – Marshall: Northern History Publ. Co., 1912. Minnesota Reel 9. (The Cox Library Collection) – 5 – us Americana [978]

AN ILLUSTRATED HISTORY OF MONROE COUNTY / Hickenlooper, Frank – Kansas City: Hudson-Kimberly Pub. Co., 1896. Iowa Reel 30. (The Cox Library Collection) – 5 – us Americana [978]

AN ILLUSTRATED HISTORY OF NEW MEXICO – Chicago, 1895. New Mexico reel 1. (Cox Library Collection) – 5 – us Americana [978]

ILLUSTRATED HISTORY OF NEW MEXICO / Read, Benjamin M – Santa Fe: New Mexican Printing Co., 1912. New Mexico reel 2. (Cox Library Collection) – 5 – us Americana [978]

AN ILLUSTRATED HISTORY OF NORTH IDAHO, EMBRACING NEZ PERCES, IDAHO, LATAH, KOOTENAI, AND SHOSHONE COUNTIES – 1903. Biog. and hist. sketches.Indexed. V145-0003 – 5 – us A.G.L.L. [920]

ILLUSTRATED HISTORY OF SAN JOAQUIN COUNTY – Chicago, 1890. California Reel 30. (The Cox Library Collection) – 5 – us Americana [978]

AN ILLUSTRATED HISTORY OF SKAGIT AND SNOHOMISH COUNTIES / Inter-State Publishing Co – 1906. Washington Reel 5. The Cox Library Collection – 5 – us Americana [978]

AN ILLUSTRATED HISTORY OF SOUTHERN CALIFORNIA – Chicago, 1890. California Reel 6. (The Cox Library Collection) – 5 – us Americana [978]

AN ILLUSTRATED HISTORY OF SPOKANE COUNTY, STATE OF WASHINGTON / Edwards, Jonathan – W.H. Lever, 1900. Washington reel 6. (Cox Library Collection) – 5 – us Americana [978]

AN ILLUSTRATED HISTORY OF THE FLUTE, AND SKETCH OF THE SUCCESSIVE IMPROVEMENTS MADE IN THE FLUTE, AND A STATEMENT OF THE PRINCIPLES UPON WHICH FLUTES... / Badger, A – New York: Firth, Pond & Co, 1861 – 1 – us Sibley [780]

AN ILLUSTRATED HISTORY OF THE NEW WORLD: CONTAINING A GENERAL HISTORY OF ALL THE VARIOUS NATIONS, STATES AND REPUBLICS OF THE WESTERN CONTINENT...AND A COMPLETE HISTORY OF THE UNITED STATES TO THE PRESENT TIME. / ed by Denison, John Ledyard – Norwich, Conn.: H. Bill, 1868. 05412. (Pre-1900 Canadiana) – 9 – cn C.I.H.M. [971]

AN ILLUSTRATED HISTORY OF THE STATE OF IDAHO – 1899. Biog. and hist. sketches.Indexed. V145-0001 – 5 – us A.G.L.L. [920]

ILLUSTRATED HISTORY OF THE STATE OF IDAHO – Chicago, 1899. Idaho reel 1. (Cox Library Collection) – 5 – us Americana [978]

AN ILLUSTRATED HISTORY OF THE STATE OF OREGON / Hines, Harvey Kimball – Chicago: Lewis Publ. Co., 1893. Oregon reel 1. (Cox Library Collection) – 5 – us Americana [978]

ILLUSTRATED HISTORY OF THE STATE OF WISCONSIN / Tuttle, Charles R – Boston: B. B. Russell, 1875. Wiconsin Reel 1. (The Cox Library Collection) – 5 – us Americana [978]

AN ILLUSTRATED HISTORY OF YELLOW MEDICINE COUNTY / Rose, Arthur P – Marshall: Northern History Publ. Co., 1914. Minnesota Reel 17. (The Cox Library Collection) – 5 – us Americana [978]

ILLUSTRATED INDEX OF BRITISH SHELLS / Sowerby, G B – Z 800 2. 1859 – 8 – ne IDC [590]

AN ILLUSTRATED INTRODUCTION TO LAMARCK'S CONCHOLOGY / Crough, E A – 2494 2. 1826 – 8 – ne IDC [760]

ILLUSTRATED INVENTOR – London. 31 Oct 1857-10 Apr 1858.-w. 33 ft – 1 – uk British Libr Newspaper [072]

ILLUSTRATED JOURNAL / Scott, Minnie – 1902-1959, Scrapbook containing clippings, certificates, photographs, souvenirs, publications, and other items relating to her training and career as a nurse. Included are items from her service in England during World War I; her job as city health nurse in Lawrence, KS; her houses in Lecompton and Topeka, KS; and a brief chronology – 1 – us KS Hist [920]

ILLUSTRATED JOURNAL / Scott, Minnie – 1902-59 – 1 – us KS Hist [978]

THE ILLUSTRATED JOURNAL OF AGRICULTURE – Montreal: E Senecal, [1879-1897] – 9 – cn C.I.H.M. [630]

ILLUSTRATED LONDON NEWS – (1978-. 5,6,9) – v1-. 14 May 1842- – 1 – us UMI [073]

THE ILLUSTRATED MAGAZINE OF ART – 1853-54 – 20mf – 9 – £110.00 – uk Chadwyck [700]

ILLUSTRATED OUTDOOR NEWS – v1-7. May 1903-Sep 1906. n.s. v1, nos. 1-4 (all publ). Oct 1906-Jan 1907. (frequency varies; numbering irregular) – 3r – 1 – $380.00 – us UPA [970]

ILLUSTRATED OXFORDSHIRE TELEGRAPH – Bicester, England. Oxfordshire Telegraph – Oxfordshire, Buckinghamshire, and Northamptonshire Telegraph. -w. 29 Dec 1858-20 June 1894. Lacking 1872, 1874. 11 reels – 1 – uk British Libr Newspaper [072]

ILLUSTRATED POLICE BUDGET – London, UK. 1899. 1 reel – 1 – uk British Libr Newspaper [072]

ILLUSTRATED POLICE NEWS – London, UK. 1888, 1892.-w. 1 reel – 1 – uk British Libr Newspaper [072]

THE ILLUSTRATED POLICE NEWS – Parish of St Mary Le-Strand, London: George Purkess, jan 1870 – us Res Libr [071]

THE ILLUSTRATED POLICE NEWS AND SPORTING TIMES – Montreal, Canada. 4 jul-2 aut 1879 – 1r – 1 – Can$35.00 – cn Can Microfilming [072]

ILLUSTRATED POPULAR BIOGRAPHY OF CONNECTICUT / Spalding, J A – Hartford, 1891. Connecticut Reel 2. (The Cox Library Collection) – 5 – us Americana [978]

ILLUSTRATED QUEBEC: THE GIBRALTER AND TOURISTS' MECCA OF AMERICA UNDER FRENCH AND ENGLISH OCCUPANCY / Adam, Graeme Mercer – Introd. by Arthur G. Doughty and suppl. chaps. by J. M. Lemoine. Montreal: J.McConniff, c1891. 00772. (Pre-1900 Canadiana) – 9 – cn C.I.H.M. [971]

ILLUSTRATED RURAL INDUSTRIES AND COUNTRY PRODUCE MART – London, UK. Mar 1906. -irr – 1 – uk British Libr Newspaper [072]

ILLUSTRATED SAN FRANCISCO NEWS – San Francisco, CA. 1869 – 1r – 1 – $50.00 – C03481 – us Library Micro [071]

ILLUSTRATED SATURDAY READER – (Cont by: Saturday Reader (1867)) – Montreal: R Worthington, 1866-[1867] – 9 – cn C.I.H.M. [971]

ILLUSTRATED SATURDAY READER *see*
– THE SATURDAY READER

THE ILLUSTRATED SKETCH BOOK AND DIRECTORY OF JEFFERSON CITY AND COLE COUNTY / Johnston, J W – Jefferson City: Missouri Illustrated Sketch Book Co., n.d. Missouri Reel 14. (The Cox Library Collection) – 5 – us Americana [978]

ILLUSTRATED SPORTING AND DRAMATIC NEWS – London. -w. 28 Feb 1874-Dec 1890. (24 reels) – 1 – uk British Libr Newspaper [073]

ILLUSTRATED SPORTING NEWS – (Illustrated Sporting and Theatrical News). London. -w. Mar 1862-Mar 1870. (6 reels) – 1 – uk British Libr Newspaper [073]

ILLUSTRATED SUN – St. Augustine. Fl. 1949-50 – 1 – us UMI [071]

ILLUSTRATED SUTTON AND EPSOM MAIL – London, England. Sutton & Cheam Mail – Sutton Times & Cheam Mail. -w. 26 Oct 1922-6 Sept 1962. 44 reels – 1 – uk British Libr Newspaper [072]

ILLUSTRATED SYDNEY NEWS – Australia. -w. 1864-Dec 1875. Imperfect. 1 1 reels – 1 – uk British Libr Newspaper [072]

ILLUSTRATED SYDNEY NEWS – Australia. -w. June 1855; Jan 1882-July 1892. 4 reels – 1 – uk British Libr Newspaper [072]

ILLUSTRATED SYDNEY NEWS – Sydney, 1853-Jun 1855; Jul 1864-94 – 11r – 1 – A$345.00 silver A$297.00 vesicular – at Pascoe [072]

ILLUSTRATED TIMES – London. 9 Jun 1855-2 Mar 1872.-w. 16mqn reels – 1 – uk British Libr Newspaper [072]

ILLUSTRATED TORONTO: THE QUEEN CITY OF THE WEST / Adam, Graeme Mercer – Montreal: J. McConniff, c1891. 02390. (Pre-1900 Canadiana) – 9 – cn C.I.H.M. [910]

AN ILLUSTRATED TREATISE ON THE LAW OF EVIDENCE / Hughes, Thomas Welburn – 3d impression. Chicago: Callaghan, 1907. 678p. LL-1466 – 1 – us L of C Photodup [340]

ILLUSTRATED WEEKLY OF INDIA – Bombay, II. 1972-1985 – 21r – $1,050.00 – R63614 – us Library Micro [072]

ILLUSTRATED WEEKLY TELEGRAPH *see*
BRADFORD WEEKLY TELEGRAPH

ILLUSTRATED WITNESS : A PICTORIAL NEWSPAPER – Montreal. v3 n7. 13 fev 1908 – 1r – 1 – Can$25.00 – cn Can Microfilming [072]

ILLUSTRATIO SPECIERUM ACONITI GENERIS / Reichenbach, Heinrich G L – Lipsiae. 1823-27. B-1585 2 – 8 – ne IDC [580]

L'ILLUSTRATION – (Cont by: L'Illustration-Nouvelle) – Montreal, Canada. v1 n45. 25 aut 1930-25 fev 1936 – 12r – 1 – cn Can Microfilming [072]

L'ILLUSTRATION – Journal universel. Paris. 1866-67 – 1 – fr A.C.R.P.P. [073]

L'ILLUSTRATION : THE WEEKLY MAGAZINE, 1843-1944 – 280r – 1 – $18,000.00 – us Ross [320]

L'ILLUSTRATION *see* L'ILLUSTRATION-NOUVELLE

ILLUSTRATION CATALOG OF THE LIBRARY OF THE NEW YORK AKADEMY OF MEDICINE / New York Academy of Medicine – 1976. 5500 cards on 1 reel – 1 – $35.00 export $45.00 – 0-8161-1328-9 – uk Hall [610]

ILLUSTRATION CATALOG OF THE LIBRARY. THIRD EDITION REV. AND ENL / New York Academy of Medicine – 1976. 5500 cards. 1 reel. ISBN 0-8161-1328-9 – 1 – $40.00 – uk Hall [610]

ILLUSTRATION HORTICOLE – v. 1-43. Gand. 1854-96. B-7354 1 – 9 – ne IDC [760]

L'ILLUSTRATION INDUSTRIELLE : HEBDO – Montreal, Canada. 1 oct 1880 – 1r – 1 – Can$25.00 – cn Can Microfilming [380]

L'ILLUSTRATION MODERNE – (The covers are missing) – Mensuel, Saint-Etienne (Loire), nov. 1894-(?) 1897 (couv. manquantes) – 1r – 1 – F281,79 – fr Armell [073]

L'ILLUSTRATION POPULAIRE – Montreal: Imp. metropolitaine, v1 no 1(8 juin 1895)- – 9 – cn C.I.H.M. [971]

L'ILLUSTRATION POPULAIRE – v1-3. 1895-1897. SEM16P368 – 1r – 5 – Can$30.00 – cn Bibl Nat [073]

ILLUSTRATIONES ALGARUM / Postels, A & Ruprecht, F J – Petropoli. 1840. B-5283 2 – 8 – ne IDC [580]

ILLUSTRATIONES ET DESCRIPTIONES PLANTARUM NOVARUM SYRIAE ET TAURI OCCIDENTALIS / Fenzl, E – Stuttgart. 1843. B-658 2 – 8 – ne IDC [580]

ILLUSTRATIONES FLORAE ATLANTICAE / Cosson, E S C – 2v. Paris. 1882-97. B-5545 2 – 8 – ne IDC [760]

ILLUSTRATIONES FLORAE HISPANIAE INSULARUMQUE BALEARUM / Willkomm, H M – 2v. Stuttgart. 1881-92. B-5817 2 – 8 – ne IDC [580]

ILLUSTRATIONES FLORAE INSULARUM MARIS PACIFICI / Drake del Castillo, E – Paris. 1886-92 – 8 – ne IDC [760]

ILLUSTRATIONES FLORAE NOVAE HOLLANDIAE / Bauer, F L – London. 1806-13. B-5839 2 – 8 – ne IDC [580]

ILLUSTRATIONES PLANTARUM IMPERFECTE VEL NONDUM COGNITARUM / Pallas, Peter Simon – Lipsiae. 1803-06. B-5267 2 – 8 – ne IDC [580]

ILLUSTRATIONES PLANTARUM ORIENTALIUM / Jaubert, H F & Spach, E – 5v. Paris. 1842-57. B-814 2 – 8 – ne IDC [580]

L'ILLUSTRATION-NOUVELLE – (Cont: L'Illustration. Cont by: Montreal-Matin) – Montreal, Canada. 26 fev 1936-12 aut 1941 – 14r – 1 – cn Can Microfilming [072]

L'ILLUSTRATION-NOUVELLE *see*
– L'ILLUSTRATION
– MONTREAL-MATIN

ILLUSTRATIONS 63 – Munich, 1964-73 – 2r – 1 – £120.00 – uk Chadwyck [740]

ILLUSTRATIONS AND DESCRIPTIONS OF THE PLANTS WHICH COMPOSE THE NATURAL ORDER CAMELLIAE / Booth, W B – London. 1830-31. B-5857 2 – 8 – ne IDC [580]

LES ILLUSTRATIONS CANADIENNES: PREMIERE SERIE, 1494-1676 / Dupuy, Paul – Montreal: Cadieux & Derome, 1887. 02803 – 9 – cn C.I.H.M. [971]

ILLUSTRATIONS DE LA FLORE DE L'ARCHIPEL INDIEN... / Miquel, F A W – Amsterdam, Utrecht, Leipzig, 1871 – 2mf – 9 – ne IDC [580]

ILLUSTRATIONS D'ORCHIDEES DES INDES ORIENTALES NEERLANDAISES... / Vriese, W H de – La Haye, 1854-[1855] – 4mf – 9 – 5794/2 – ne IDC [580]

ILLUSTRATIONS OF BRITISH BIRDS / Meyer, H L – Z-1857 2. 4 v. Lacking: v. 2-4. 1835-1850 – 8 – ne IDC [590]

ILLUSTRATIONS OF BRITISH ENTOMOLOGY... / Stephens, J F – London, (1827-)1828-1835(-1845). 11vols, v1-4, Haustellata. v1-7, Mandibulata. Suppl., London, 1846. VI, [1], 32p, 15pls – 8 – ne IDC [590]

ILLUSTRATIONS OF BRITISH FUNGI (HYMENOMYCETES) TO SERVE AS AN ATLAS TO THE "HANDBOOK OF BRITISH FUNGI" / Cooke, M C – 8v. London. 1881-91. B-6258 2 – 8 – ne IDC [580]

ILLUSTRATIONS OF BRITISH MYCOLOGY / Hussey, T J – 2v. London. 1847-55. B-857 2 – 8 – ne IDC [580]

ILLUSTRATIONS OF BRITISH ORNITHOLOGY / Selby, P J – Z 1926. 1833 – 9 – ne IDC [590]

ILLUSTRATIONS OF HIMALAYAN PLANTS / Hooker, J D – London. 1855. B-5957 2 – 8 – ne IDC [580]

ILLUSTRATIONS OF INDIAN ORNITHOLOGY / Jerdon, T C – Z-275 2. 1847 – 8 – ne IDC [760]

ILLUSTRATIONS OF INDIAN ZOOLOGY(CHIEFLY FROM COLLECTION OF MAJOR-GENERAL HARDWICKE). Z-307/2. 1830-1834(-35) / Gray, J E – 8 – ne IDC [590]
ILLUSTRATIONS OF NAPA COUNTY WITH HISTORICAL SKETCH / Smith and Elliott – Napa Co, CA. 1878 – 1r – 1 – $50.00 – B40240 – us Library Micro [978]
ILLUSTRATIONS OF NATURAL HISTORY, WHEREIN ARE EXHIBITED...FIGURES OF EXOTIC INSECTS / Drury, D – London, 1770-82.3v. Z/1201/2 – 8 – ne IDC [590]
ILLUSTRATIONS OF ORNITHOLOGY / Jardine, W & Selby, P J – 2093 2. 4 v. 1826-1843 – 8 – ne IDC [760]
ILLUSTRATIONS OF SOUTH AMERICAN PLANTS / Miers, J – London, 1846-1857. 2 vols. B-5143 2 – 8 – ne IDC [580]
ILLUSTRATIONS OF THE AUTHOR OF WAVERLEY : BEING NOTICES AND ANECDOTES OF REAL CHARACTERS, SCENES, AND INCIDENTS, SUPPOSED TO BE DESCRIBED IN HIS WORKS / Chambers, Robert – Edinburgh: John Anderson, jun.; London: Simpkin and Marshall, 2nd ed 1825 – 1 roll – 1 – 1-55879-637-1 – uk Libr Preservation [420]
ILLUSTRATIONS OF THE BOTANY AND OTHER BRANCHES OF NATURAL HISTORY OF THE HIMALAYAN MOUNTAINS AND OF THE FLORA OF CASHMERE / Royle, J F – 695. 2 V. 1833-; 1839 40 – 9 – ne IDC [580]
ILLUSTRATIONS OF THE CONCHOLOGY OF GREAT BRITAIN AND IRELAND / Brown, T – Z-450 2. 1827 – 8 – ne IDC [590]
ILLUSTRATIONS OF THE FLOWERING PLANTS AND FERNS OF THE FALKLAND ISLANDS / Vallentin, E F – London. 1921. B-7273 2 – 8 – ne IDC [580]
ILLUSTRATIONS OF THE FOREST FLORA OF NORTH-WEST AND CENTRAL INDIA / Stewart, J L & Brandis, D – London. 1874. B-7320 1 – 9 – ne IDC [580]
ILLUSTRATIONS OF THE FOSSIL CONCHOLOGY OF GREAT BRITAIN AND IRELAND / Brown, T – G-103 2. 1849 – 8 – ne IDC [560]
ILLUSTRATIONS OF THE FUNGI OF OUR FIELDS AND WOODS / Price, S – London. 1864. S. 2. London. 1865. B-6302 2 – 8 – ne IDC [580]
ILLUSTRATIONS OF THE GENUS CAREX / Boott, F – 4v. London. 1858-67. B-1027 2 – 8 – ne IDC [580]
ILLUSTRATIONS OF THE HISTORICAL BALL: GIVEN BY THEIR EXCELLENCIES THE EARL AND COUNTESS OF ABERDEEN IN THE SENATE CHAMBER, OTTAWA, 17TH FEBRUARY, 1896 / Bourinot, John George – With a short historical introd. by J. G. Bourinot. Ottawa: J. Durie, 1896. 00195. (Pre-1900 Canadiana) – 9 – cn C.I.H.M. [971]
ILLUSTRATIONS OF THE HISTORY OF MEDIAEVAL THOUGHT : IN THE DEPARTMENTS OF THEOLOGY AND ECCLESIASTICAL POLITICS / Poole, Reginald Lane – London: Williams and Norgate, 1884 – 1mf – us A.T.L.A. [180]
ILLUSTRATIONS OF THE LOTUS OF THE ANCIENTS AND TAMARA OF INDIA / Duppa, R – 1 – uk Microform Academic [760]
THE ILLUSTRATIONS OF THE MAQAMAT / Grabar, Oleg – (196p accompanying text) – 1984 – 10mf – 9 – $48.00f – 0-226-69057-1 – us Chicago [750]
ILLUSTRATIONS OF UNIVERSAL PROGRESS : A SERIES OF DISCUSSIONS / Spencer, Herbert – New York: Appleton, 1881 – xxiv/439p – 1 – us U.W. Library [190]
ILLUSTRATIONS TO BLAIR'S THE GRAVE / Blake, William – 1 – uk Microform Academic [810]
ILLUSTRATIONS TO BUNYAN'S PILGRIM'S PROGRESS / Blake, William – 14 – uk Microform Academic [760]
ILLUSTRATIONS TO EDWARD YOUNG'S NIGHT THOUGHTS, FROM BRITISH MUSEUM, DEPT. OF PRINTS AND DRAWINGS / Blake, William – 14 – uk Microform Academic [740]
ILLUSTRATIVE CASES IN EQUITY / Pattee, William Sullivan – (3d ed. St. Paul: West, 1896. 157p. LL-1088) – 2d ed. St. Paul: West, 1893. 110p. LL-1099 – 1 – us L of C Photodup [340]
ILLUSTRATIVE CASES ON EQUITY JURISPRUDENCE / Hutchins, Harry Burns – 2d ed. St. Paul: West, 1904. 908p. LL-850 – 1 – us L of C Photodup [340]
ILLUSTRATIVE CASES ON PERSONAL RIGHTS AND THE DOMESTIC RELATIONS INCLUDING TEACHER AND PUPIL / Chadman, Charles Erehart – Chicago: American School of Law, 1907. 301p. LL-1605 – 1 – us L of C Photodup [340]
ILLUSTRATIVE CASES UPON THE LAW OF BILLS AND NOTES / Johnson, Elias Finley – St. Paul, West, 1895. 219 p. LL-440 – 1 – us L of C Photodup [340]
ILLUSTRATIVE RULES GOVERNING COMPLAINTS OF JUDICIAL MISCONDUCT AND DISABILITY : PREPARED BY A SPECIAL COMMITTEE OF THE CHIEF JUDGES OF THE U.S. COURTS OF APPEALS – Washington: FJC, 1986 – 1mf – 9 – $1.50 – LLMC 95-379 – us L.L.M.C. [340]
ILLUSTRAZIONE DI ALCUNE PIANTE DELLA GRECIA E DELLA ASIA MINORE / Visiani, R de – Venezia. 1842. B-718 2 – 8 – ne IDC [580]
ILLUSTRAZIONE ISTORICA DEL PALAZZO DELLA SIGNORIA / Rastrelli, M – BO 1050 1.1792 – 9 – ne IDC [700]
ILLUSTRAZIONE ISTORICA DEL PALAZZO DELLA SIGNORIA / Rastrelli, M – Firenze, 1792 – 9 – ne IDC [720]
ILLUSTRERET FOLKE-VISEBOG – 1873 – 1 – us I.U. Libraries [390]
ILLUSTRES DISQUISITIONES MORALES / Candidus, Vinc. OP – Venetiis. Tomi 1-4. 1639 – Romae. 1643. – 76mf – 8 – ne Slangenburg [240]
ILLUSTRIERTE BERLINER ZEITSCHRIFT – Berlin, 1951-sep 1953, 1954-sep 1963 – 1 – Dist. gw Mikrofilm – gw Misc Inst [072]
ILLUSTRIERTE FAMILIEN-ZEITUNG – Berlin, sep 21 1913-17 – 1 – Dist. gw Mikrofilm – gw Misc Inst [072]
DIE ILLUSTRIERTE FUER BREMEN – Bremen, apr 4-aug 8 1914 – 1r – 1 – Inquire at Mikrofilmarchiv for details – gw Misc Inst [072]
ILLUSTRIERTE GESCHICHTE DER DEUTSCHEN LITERATUR VON DEN AELTESTEN ZEITEN BIS ZUR GEGENWART / Salzer, Anselm – Muenchen: Allgemeine Verlags-Gesellschaft m.b.h., [1912] – 1 – us U.W. Library [430]
ILLUSTRIERTE GESCHICHTE DER DEUTSCHER LITERATUR VON DEN AELTESTEN ZEITEN BIS ZUR GEGENWART / Salzer, Anselm – (Includes bibliographical references and index) – 2., neu bearb. Aufl. Regensburg: J Habbel, 1926-1932 – 1 – us U.W. Library [430]
ILLUSTRIERTE GESCHICHTE DES DEUTSCHEN SCHRIFTTHUMS IN VOLKSTHUEMLICHER DARSTELLUNG / Leixner-Gruenberg, Otto von – (Includes bibliographical references and index) – Leipzig: O Spamer, 1880-1881 – 1r – 1 – us U.W. Library [430]
ILLUSTRIERTE GESCHICHTE DES PREUSSISCHEN HOFES, DES ADELS UND DER DIPLOMATIE VOM GROSSEN KURFUERSTEN BIS ZUM TODE KAISER WILHELMS 1 / Vehse, Eduard – Stuttgart, 1901 – xii/496p; viii/448p – 9 – DM148.00 – 3-89349-110-4 – gw Hänsel [320]
ILLUSTRIERTE KRIEGS-CHRONIK – Leipzig, 1871 – 1r – 1 – gw Mikrofilm [072]
ILLUSTRIERTE REICHSBANNER-ZEITUNG *see* ILLUSTRIERTE REPUBLIKANISCHE ZEITUNG
ILLUSTRIERTE REPUBLIKANISCHE ZEITUNG – (Cont: Illustrierte Reichsbanner-Zeitung) – Magdeburg/Berlin, jan 3 1925-mar 4 1933 – 6r – 1 – gw Mikrofilm [943]
ILLUSTRIERTE WESTDEUTSCHE WOCHENSCHAU – (Cont by: Die Wochenschau, 1911. Westdeutsche Illustrierte Zeitung, mar 1924. Die Wochenschau, sep 1926) – Duesseldorf. oct 2, 1909-oct 13, 1943 – 33r – 1 – gw Mikrofilm [072]
ILLUSTRIERTE ZEITUNG – Leipzig/Berlin, jul 1 1843-jun 29 1899. aug 3, aug 24 1899. jan 4 1900-sep 1944 – 124r – 1 – gw Mikrofilm [072]
ILLUSTRIERTER FILMKURIER – Wien, 1919-44 – 14r – 1 – gw Mikrofilm [790]
ILLUSTRIERTES KONVERSATIONS-LEXIKON DER FRAU (HQ 12) – Oldenburg, 1900 (mf ed 1993) – 20mf – 9 – DM290.00 – 3-89131-124-9 – gw Fischer [305]
ILLUSTRIERTES KREUZ-BLATT – Augsburg, 1868-70 (incomplete) – 1r – 1 – Dist. gw Mikrofilm – gw Misc Inst [072]
ILLUSTRIETER SONNTAG *see* DER GERADE WEG/ILLUSTRIERTER SONNTAG
ILLUSTRIOUS CHINESE CHRISTIANS : BIOGRAPHICAL SKETCHES / Bentley, William Preston – Cincinnati: Standard Publ, 1906 – 1mf – 9 – 0-8370-6016-8 – 1986-0016 – us A.T.L.A. [920]
ILLUSTRIOUS DAMES OF THE COURT OF THE VALOIS KINGS / Brantome, Pierre de Bourdeille – Trans. by Katharine Prescott Wormeley. Illus. with photogravures from the original paintings. New York: The Lamb Publ. Co., 1912 – 1 – us U.W. Library [920]
ILLUSTRIOUS LOCAL PREACHERS / ed by Whiteley, D – Bradford, 1891 – 4mf – 9 – ne IDC [240]
ILLUSTRIOUS LOCAL PREACHERS / ed by Whiteley, D – Bradford, 1891. 320p – 4mf – 9 – ne IDC [240]
ILLUSTRIRTE FOLKS SHTIME = PEOPLE'S VOICE ILLUSTRATED : SUPPLEMENT – (In Yiddish) – Lodz, PL. no1 no15 no54 no75 no79 no124 (no dates) – 1r – 1 – $35.00 – cn Can Microfilming [072]
DAS ILLUSTRIRTE JOURNAL – Leipzig, Germany. 1864-65 – 1 – gw Mikrofilm [072]
ILLUSTRIRTE JUGENDZEITUNG – Leipzig, Germany. 1846-47 (incomplete) – 1r – 1 – gw Mikrofilm [072]
ILLUSTRIRTE YOM-TOV-BLETER = ILLUSTRATED HOLIDAY NEWS – (In Yiddish) – Warsaw, PL. 1903 (Holiday folios, Hanuka) – 1r – 1 – $25.00 – cn Can Microfilming [072]
ILLUSTRIRTE ZEITUNG FUEER BLECHINDUSTRIE – Leipzig, Germany. -w. 1886-91; 1895-96; 1899-1900; 1903; 1907-09 – 25r – 1 – uk British Libr Newspaper [670]
ILLUSTRIRTE ZEITUNG FUER BUCHBINDEREI UND CARTONNAGEN FABRIKANTEN – Leipzig, Germany. Apr 1868-Dec 1874; 1895-1900; Jul 1901-Jun 1903.-f. 5 reels – 1 – uk British Libr Newspaper [073]
ILLUSTRIRTE ZEITUNG FUER DAS KATHOLISCHE DEUTSCHLAND – Leipzig, Germany. 1855 – 1 – gw Mikrofilm [072]
ILLUSTRIRTE ZEITUNG FUER DIE JUGEND – Leipzig, Germany. 1846-47 – 1r – 1 – gw Mikrofilm [072]
ILLUSTRIRTER DORFBARBIER – (Suppl to: Gartenlaube, Leipzig) – Leipzig. 1853; 1856; 1861 – 1r – 1 – gw Mikrofilm [072]
ILLUSTRIRTER KALENDER – Leipzig, Germany. 1846-50, 1855 – 1 – gw Mikrofilm [072]
ILLUSTRIRTES CONCHYLIENBUCH / Kobelt, W – 6217 2. 1880-1881 – 9 – ne IDC [760]
ILLUSTRIRTES FAMILIEN-JOURNAL – Leipzig, Germany. 1854 (incomplete); 1856; 1858 – 1 – gw Mikrofilm [072]
ILLUSTRIRTES PANORAMA – Berlin, 1861, 1862 (incomplete), 1865-66 – 1r – 1 – Dist. gw Mikrofilm – gw Misc Inst [072]
ILLUSTRIRTES UNTERHALTUNGSBLATT FUER DAS VOLK – Hamburg, Germany. 1887-88 – 1 – gw Mikrofilm [072]
ILLUSTRIUM JURIS TRACTATUUM / Valencia, Melchor de – Allobrogum: Fratrum de Tournes, 1753 – 1 – sp Bibl Santa Ana [340]
ILLUSTROWANY KURIER POLSKI – (Some issues missing) – Bydgoszcz, Poland. Oct 1945-Jan 1947; Jul 1950-Jun 1970 – 27r – 1 – us L of C Photodup [943]
GLI ILLVSTRI ET GLORIOSI GESTI, ET VITTORIOSE IMPRESSE, FATTE CONTRA TURCHI,... / Francus, D – Vinegia, 1584 – 2mf – 9 – H-8204/1 – ne IDC [956]
ILM VA JAMI'AH – (Sal-i 1, shumarah-'i 1-34 (1358-1363[1979-1984])) – Alexandria, Virg.: Persian Journal for Science and Society, 1979- – 2r – 1 – $250.00 – us MEDOC [500]
ILMIYYE SALNAMESI – 1334 [1916] – 8mf – 9 – $36.75 – us MEDOC [949]
ILMOE TOEMBOEH-TOEMBOEHAN. OENTOEK DIPAKAI DI SEKOLAH DJOEROE-OBAT (ASSISTANTAPOTHEKER) / Rasad, BZ – (Microfiche Nos 143-144) – Djakarta: Ika Daigaku Yakugakubu, 2605 – 2mf – 9 – SE-2002/1 – ne IDC [950]
ILMU BERGAUL / Nasution, M Yunan – SE-3087 1. 1960 – 9 – ne IDC [950]
ILMU BERUSAHA PRAKTIS UNTUK SEKOLAH TEHNIK 3 TAHUN / Wargosupono, S – ca 1962 – 9 – SE-4861 1 – ne IDC [370]
ILMU BUMI KABUPATEN 50 KOTA / Alamsjah, Z St – SE-4697 1. 1963 – 9 – ne IDC [950]
ILMU BUMI PROPINSI SUMATERA BARAT DENGAN RIWAJAT PENDEK MINANGKABAU / Maharadja, Habib Sutan – 1962 – 9 – SE-4680 1 – ne IDC [950]
ILMU DJIWA SOSIAL DAN SESEORANG, OLEH ADI NEGORO / Adinegoro, Djamaludin – Tjet. 2 Djakarta, Balai Pustaka, 1952. 100 p. 19 cm. SEM-14107-14108 – 9 – ne IDC [150]
ILMU MARXIS – (Title varies: Marxist Science) – Djakarta. 1957-1965. Lacking: 1957, v1(2-end); 1959, v3(1); 1960, v4(2,pg65 -129; 1961-63, v5-7 – 17mf – 9 – ne IDC [073]
ILMU TUMBUH-TUMBUHAN / Sanif, Sutan – SE 4566 1. 1950 – 9 – ne IDC [950]
ILMUTUSTRAAMATU SELETUS = AN EXPLANATION TO THE BOOK OF REVELATION / Kaups, Richard – Santa Barbara, CA: Autori, 178p.1971-72 – 1 – 7.12 – us Baptist [240]
ILO LEGISLATIVE SERIES (1919-1975) – 1,400mf – 9 – $3,200.00 – us UNIFO [331]
ILO PUBLICATIONS AND DOCUMENTS : TITLE LIST, 1919-1990 / International Labour Organisation – 9 – Sfr35.00 – 92-2-108074-9 – sz I.L.O. [331]
EL ILOCANO – Manila. Philippine Islands. -f. 28 Jun 1889-30 May 1890. (18 ft) – 1 – uk British Libr Newspaper [072]
Ilovaiskii, Vladimir *see* GOD PUTI
ILP NEWS – London. -m. Apr 1897-Dec 1903. (1 reel) – 1 – uk British Libr Newspaper [331]
ILSA JOURNAL OF INTERNATIONAL AND COMPARATIVE LAW – (Cont: Ilsa Journal of International Law) – v1-2. 1995-96 – 9 – $70.00set – us Hein [340]
ILSA JOURNAL OF INTERNATIONAL LAW – (Title varies: v1-10 1977-1986 as ASILS International Law Journal) – American Society of International Law Schools. v1-16. 1977-93 (all publ) – 5,6,9 – $105.00 set – us Hein [340]
ILSA JOURNAL OF INTERNATIONAL LAW *see* ILSA JOURNAL OF INTERNATIONAL AND COMPARATIVE LAW
Iltz, Johannes *see* DE VI ET USU PRAEPOSITIONUM EPI, META, PARA, PERI, PROS, HUPO APUD ARISTOPHANEM
ILUSTRACION APOLOGETICA / Feijoo Montenegro, Benito J – 1729 – 1mf – 9 – Pta1,000.00 – 84-7848-009-9 – sp Pentalfa [946]
EL ILUSTRISIMO FRAY HIPOLITO SANCHEZ RANGEL, PRIMER OBISPO DE MAYNAS / Bayle, Constantino & Quecedo, Francisco – Madrid: Razon y Fe, 1944 – 1 – sp Bibl Santa Ana [240]
ILUSTRISIMO SENOR DOCTOR JOSE ANTONIO PONTE. CARACAS, 1929 / Sosa Saa, Jose Thomas – Madrid: Razon y Fe, 1930 – 1 – sp Bibl Santa Ana [946]
Ilwof, Franz *see* DER PROTESTANTISMUS IN STEIERMARK, KAERNTEN UND KRAIN
IM ALTEN DEUTSCHLAND : ERINNERUNGEN EINES SECHZIGJAEHRIGEN / Litzmann, Berthold – (Includes bibliographical references) – Berlin: G Grote, 1923 – 1r – 1 – us U.W. Library [943]
IM ANFANG LIEGT DAS ENDE : GRILLPARZERS EPILOG AUF DIE GESCHICHTE / Schneider, Reinhold – Baden-Baden: H Buehler, 1946 – 1r – 1 – us U.W. Library [943]
IM BANN DER IRREDENTA : ROMAN / Samarow, Gregor – Stuttgart: Deutsche Verlags-Anstalt, 1889 – 1r – 1 – us U.W. Library [830]
IM BANNE DES SCHICKSALS : ZWEI HISTORISCHE ERZAEHLUNGEN AUS DER NORDOSTMARK / Wichert, Ernst – Bayreuth: Gauverlag Bayreuth, 1944 – 1r – 1 – us U.W. Library [830]
IM DEUTSCHEN REICH – Berlin, jul 1895-apr 1922 – 6r – 1 – Dist. gw Mikrofilm – gw Misc Inst [943]
IM DEUTSCHEN REICH – Berlin. v1-28. 1895-1922. Complete. 6 reels. B105 (Leo Baeck Institute. German-Jewish Periodicals, Pt 1) – 1 – $415.00 – us UPA [270]
IM DUNKLEN ERDTEIL : REISEN UND ERLEBNISSE STANLEYS, EMIN PASCHAS, ROHFS U. A., FUR DIE REIFERE JUGEND / Burmann, Karl – Leipzig, O Drewitz Nachf. [189-] – us Res Libr [910]
IM FAMILIEN-KREISE – (Milwaukee). 1880-81 – 1 – us A.J.P.C. [071]

IM FELDE GEGEN DIE HEREROS : ERLEBNISSE EINES MITKAMPFERS / Bulow, Franz von – Bremen: G A v Harlem, [1905?] – 1 – us Res Libr [960]

IM GRUENEN TANN : SCHWARZWALD-NOVELLEN / Achleitner, Arthur – Berlin: Verein der Buecherfreunde, Schall & Grund, [1897?] – 1r – 1 – us U.W. Library [830]

IM HERERO- UND HOTTENTOTTENLAND / Trautmann, O – Pretoria, State Library, 1979. Orig. publ., Oldenburg: Gerhard Stalling, 1913. (Microfiche Reprint Series, State Library, no.4). 4 fiche and printed booklet – 9 – sa State Libr [910]

IM HERZEN DER HAUSSALAENDER : REISE IM WESTLICHEN SUDAN NEBST BERICHT UEBER DEN VERLAUF DER DEUTSCHEN NIGER-BENUE EXPEDITION... / Staudinger, Paul – Berlin: Landsberger, 1889 – 1 – us Res Libr [960]

IM HIRTENHAUS : EINE OBERFRAENKISCHE DORFGESCHICHTE / Schaumberger, Heinrich – Leipzig: P Reclam, [1905?] – 1r – 1 – us U.W. Library [390]

IM HOCHLAND VON MITTEL-KAMERUN / Thorbecke, Franz – Hamburg: L Friedrichsen, 1914-51 – 1 – us Res Libr [960]

IM INNERN AFRIKAS / Wissmann, H von – Ed. 2. Leipzig. 1891. BA-174 2 – 8 – ne IDC [910]

IM JAHRE 38 / Tumler, Franz – Muenchen: A. Langen, G Mueller, 1939 – 1r – 1 – us U.W. Library [943]

"IM KAMPF UM DAS DRITTE REICH" / U.S. Library of Congress. Prints and Photographs Division – 23 vols. of news photographs (6000 images) from Sept 1936-Jun 1942. 4 reels. P&P2970 – 1 – 23.00r – us L of C Photodup [080]

IM KAMPF UM DIE WELTANSCHAUUNG : BEKENNTNISSE EINES THEOLOGEN / Wimmer, Richard – 10.-12. Aufl. Freiburg i.B.: J C B Mohr (Paul Siebeck), 1913 – 1mf – 9 – 0-8370-5869-4 – 1985-3869 – us A.T.L.A. [240]

IM KAMPF UM GOTT UND UM DAS EIGENE ICH : ERNSTHAFTE PLAUDEREIEN / Koenig, Karl – (Includes bibliographical references) – Freiburg i. B: Paul Waetze, 1901 – 1mf – 9 – 0-8370-3976-2 – 1985-1976 – us A.T.L.A. [240]

IM KREUZFEUER ZWEIER REVOLUTIONEN / Boehm, Wilhelm – Munich. 1924 – 1 – us Res Libr [943]

IM LANDE DER BIBEL – 1955-85 (complete) – 2r – 1 – ATLA S0791 – us A.T.L.A. [073]

IM LANDE JESU – 1938-41 (complete) – 1r – 1 – ATLA S0664B – us A.T.L.A. [073]

IM RAMPENLICHT – Berlin. n1 1919 – 1 – gw Mikrofilm [790]

IM REGIMENT : ROMAN / Osten, H von – Stuttgart: Deutsche Verlags-Anstalt, 1889 – 1r – 1 – us U.W. Library [830]

IM SCHATTEN DER EXZELLENZ : NOVELLE / Moeller, Karl von – Muenchen: F Eher, [194-?] – 1r – 1 – us U.W. Library [830]

IM SCHRITT DER JAHRHUNDERTE : GESCHICHTLICHE BILDER / Molo, Walter Ritter von – 7.-10. verm. Aufl. Muenchen: A Langen, c1918 – 1r – 1 – us U.W. Library [943]

IM SOMMER DANACH / Ball, Kurt Herwarth – Halle (Saale): Mitteldeutscher Verlag, 1966 – 1r – 1 – us U.W. Library [430]

IM STROM : ROMAN EINES LEBENS / Johann, A E – Berlin: Deutscher Verlag, c1942 – 1r – 1 – us U.W. Library [830]

DIE IM TAHKEMONI VORKOMMENDEN ANGABEN UEBER HARIZIS LEBEN / Albrecht, K – Studien und Reisen. Goettingen. 1890. BJ-421-70 1 – 9 – ne IDC [920]

IM UMKREIS VON VIER MEILEN / Rothenburg, Adelheid von – Halle: Julius Fricke, 1876 – 1r – 1 – us U.W. Library [830]

IM UMSTRITTENEN GEBIET : ROMAN / Janitschek, Ellinor – Berlin: Phoenix-Verlag C Siwinna, c1921 – 1r – 1 – us U.W. Library [830]

IM WEISSEN ROESSL : LUSTSPIEL IN DREI AUFZUEGEN / Blumenthal, Oskar – 2. Aufl. Charlottenburg: M Simson, c1898 – 1 – us U.W. Library [820]

IM ZWISCHENLAND : FUENF GESCHICHTEN AUS DEM SEELENLEBEN HALBWUECHSIGER MAEDCHEN / Andreas-Salome, Lou – Stuttgart: Cotta, 1911 – 1r – 1 – us U.W. Library [830]

IMADUDDIN / Alaydrus, Ali – SE-6198 1. 1964 – 9 – ne IDC [950]

L'IMAGE : EDITION: BELOEIL, MCMASTERVILLE, ST-HILAIRE, OTTERBURN PARK – Longueuil. v1 no 1 (27 Sept 1978). SEM105P1135 – 1mf – 9 – Can$2.25 – cn Bibl Nat [073]

L'IMAGE : EDITION: BOUCHERVILLE; ST-BASILE, ST-BRUNO, STE-JULIE, BELOEIL, MCMASTERVILLE, ST-HILAIRE, OTTERBURN PARK – Longueuil. v1 no 2 (4 Oct 1978)-. SEM105P1138 – 8mf – 9 – Can$18.00 – cn Bibl Nat [073]

L'IMAGE : EDITION: BOUCHERVILLE, ST-BRUNO, ST-BASILE, STE-JULIE – Longueuil. v1 no 1 (27 Sept 1978). SEM105P1136 – 1mf – 9 – Can$2.25 – cn Bibl Nat [073]

L'IMAGE : EDITION: BROSSARD, ST-HUBERT, GREENFIELD PARK, ST-LAMBERT, VILLE LEMOYNE – Longueuil. v1 no 10 (16 Mai 1979). SEM105P1137 – 2mf – 9 – Can$4.50 – cn Bibl Nat [073]

L'IMAGE – Paris, 1896-97 – 1r + 16 col slides – 1 – £120.00 – uk Chadwyck [700]

L'IMAGE – Revue litteraire et artistique ornee de figures sur bois. no. 1-17. Paris. sept 1894-nov 1899 – 1 – fr A.C.R.P.P. [073]

IMAGE AND VISION COMPUTING – v1-. 1983- – 1,5,6,9 – us UMI [073]

L'IMAGE DE LA RIVE SUD = SOUTH SHORE IMAGE – Longueuil. v1-3. 1978-80. SEM35P273 – 5r – 1 – Can$246.00 – cn Bibl Nat [073]

THE IMAGE OF GOD IN MAN ACCORDING TO CYRIL OF ALEXANDRIA / Burghardt, W J – 1957 – 4mf – 9 – ne Slangenburg [240]

IMAGE OF THE INDIAN / Haycock, Ronald G – 1971. The Canadian Indian as a Subject and a Concept in a Sampling of the Popular National Magazines Read in Canada 1900-1970 – vii/98p – $12.00 – 0-88920-083-1 – cn W.L.U. Press [307]

IMAGENES DE CHILE VIDA Y COSTUMBRES CHILENAS EN LOS SIGLOS 18 Y 19 A TRAVES DE... / Slas, Mariano Picon & Cruz, Guillermo Feliu – Madrid: Razon y Fe, 1940 – sp Bibl Santa Ana [306]

IMAGENES (VERSIONES POETICAS) ROSAS DEL TIEMPO ANTIGUO. MIES DE LOGRONO / Diez Canedo, Enrique – Paris: Sociedad de Ediciones Literarios y artisticos, Libreria Paul Ollendorff, S.A. – 1 – sp Bibl Santa Ana [810]

IMAGES – Toronto, Ontario. Mar 1980-Nov 1984. Many issues missing. Continued by: The Scribe (Jewish Students' Union-B'nai B'rith Hillel Foundation (University of Tronto) – 1 – us A.J.P.C. [072]

IMAGES DE LA FEMME DANS LES LITTERATURES ORALES ASHANTI ET FON / Dyja-Ruelland, S – 9 – F70.00 – fr Ethnologie [305]

IMAGES DE PARIS – Revue libre d'art et de litterature. Paris. oct 1919-mai juil 1926 – 1 – fr A.C.R.P.P. [073]

IMAGES ET SYMBOLES: ESSAIS SUR LE SYMBOLISME MAGICO-RELIGIEUX / Eliade, Mircea – (Paris): Gallimard, (1952). 238p – 1 – us U.W. Library [150]

IMAGES MALGACHES DU FOKONOLONA TRADITIONNEL / Perrin, R – 9 – fr Hachette [999]

IMAGES OF EAST AND WEST : MAPS, PLANS, VIEWS AND DRAWINGS FROM DUTCH COLONIAL ARCHIVES, 1583-1950 / The Hague. General State Archives – (Subsections availabe: Atlases Dfl7,750.00; Europe Dfl480.00; Africa Dfl570.00; Asia Dfl3,300.00; Australia Dfl40.00; N. America Dfl160.00; Caribbean Dfl670.00; S. America Dfl2,430.00) – Part 1: The Early Period, c. 1583-1814[1840]. Printed guide and inventories separately Dfl125.00 – 1,519mf – 9 – Dfl9,900.00 – ne MMF Publ [900]

IMAGES OF EAST AND WEST : MAPS, PLANS, VIEWS AND DRAWINGS FROM DUTCH COLONIAL ARCHIVES, 1583-1963 – Part 1: The Early Period, c. 1583-1814, 1840. 1519mf.Dfl9,900.00; Part 2: Collection of the Ministry of the Colonies, 1814-1963, 1993. 1929mf.Dfl12,500.00; Part 3: Collection of the Topographical Service (18th-20th Centuries), 1995; Part 4: Colonial Aquisitions, 1995; Guides and Inventories for parts 1 and 2 are available for Dfl250.00 each – 9 – ne MMF Publ [900]

IMAGES POPULAIRES DU MANS, DE CHARTRES ET D'ORLEANS / Reunion des musees nationaux. Paris – 1951. 1 fiche – 9 – fr Réunion [700]

DIE IMAGINAERE UND DIE REALE HEXE : ZWEI ERSCHEINUNGSFORMEN EINES SOZIALGESCHICHTLICHEN PHAENOMENS IN DER FRUEHEN NEUZEIT; UNTERSUCHUNGEN IN NORD- UND NORDWESTDEUTSCHLAND VOM 16. BIS ZUM 18. JAHRHUNDERT / Gailus-Doering, Sigrid – 1992 – 9 – DM98.00 – 3-89349-522-3 – gw Hänsel [943]

IMAGINARY PORTRAITS / Pater, Walter – London, New York: Macmillan and Co., 1887 – 1 roll – 1 – 1-55879-899-4 – uk Libr Preservation [420]

IMAGINES DE MORTE, ET EPIGRAMATA,... / Huberinus, Caspar – Lyon, J. & F. Frellon, 1542. [G.F.: 5.1] – 2mf – 9 – HUB-20/1 – ne IDC [240]

IMAGINES DEORUM / Cartari, V – O-1238 1. 1687 – 9 – ne IDC [760]

IMAGING ABSTRACTS – 1,5,69 – us UMI [000]

IMAGING SCIENCE – v1-. 1982- – 1,5,6,9 – us UMI [073]

IMAGINI DELLI DEI DE GLI ANTICHI / Cartari, V – O-1236 1. 1587 – 9 – ne IDC [760]

IMAGINI DELLI DEI DE GLI ANTICHI / Cartari, V – O-1237 1. 1647 – 9 – ne IDC [760]

IMAGO – Zeitschrift fuer Psychoanalytische Psychologie. Wien. 1912-37 (t. I-XXIII) – 1 – fr A.C.R.P.P. [073]

IMAN DAN ISLAM. (SERIE ISLAMOLOGIE) / Usman el Muhammady, T. M – SE 4582 1. 1963 – 9 – ne IDC [260]

IMANISHI COLLECTION OF ORIGINAL TEXTS ON KOREAN HISTORY – In The Tenri Central Library, Nara Pref., totaling 667 items, 1,532 parts – 154r – 1 – Y950,000.00 – ja Yushodo [950]

Imaz, Jose Luis de *see* LOS QUE MANDAN

Imbart de la Tour, Pierre *see*
- LES ELECTIONS EPISCOPALES DANS L'EGLISE DE FRANCE DU IXE AU XIIE SIECLE
- QUESTIONS D'HISTOIRE SOCIALE ET RELIGIEUSE

Imbault-Huart, C *see*
- LE PAYS DE HAMI OU KHAMIL
- RECUEIL DE DOCUMENTS SUR L'ASIE CENTRALE

IMBE-NO-HIRONARI'S KOGOSHUI, OR, GLEANINGS FROM ANCIENT STORIES / Inbe, Hironari – Trans. with introd. and notes by Genchi Kato and Hikoshiro Hoshino. Tokyo: Meiji Japan Society, 1924. ii,109p. Bibliog. and index in English and Japanese – 1 – us U.W. Library [950]

Imbert de la Platiere, S *see* GALERIE UNIVERSELLE DES HOMMES QUI SE SONT ILLUSTRES: VOLTAIRE

Imbert, Jean *see*
- ENCHIRIDION, OV, BRIEF RECVEIL DV DROICT ESCRIT: GARDE ET OBSERVE OV ABROGE EN FRANCE
- LA PRACTIQVE LVDICIAIRE: TANT CIVILE QVE CRIMINELLE, RECEVE ET OBSERUEE PAR TOUT DE ROYAUME DE FRANCE

Imbrie, William *see* THE CHURCH OF CHRIST IN JAPAN

Imbroeck, Thomas van *see* CONFESSIO

Imbusch, H *see* 25 JAHRE GEWERKVEREIN CHRISTLICHER BERGARBEITER

I-MEN HSIEN-CHIH – 1845; 1846, 14, 1. BCH-667 2 – 8 – ne IDC [950]

IMENOTTERI, NEUROTTERI, PSEUDO-NEUROTTERI, ORTOTTERI ET RINCHOTI ITALIANI / Griffini, A – Milani, 1897. Z/1313/2 – 8 – ne IDC [590]

Imes, Merle Graybill *see* "THE FLOOD-1903"

Imhoff, Alexander Jesse *see* THE LIFE OF REV. MORRIS OFFICER, A.M.

Imhoff, G W van *see* MEMOIR LEFT BY G.W. BARON VAN IMHOFF, GOVERNOR AND DIRECTOR OF CEYLON TO HIS SUCCESSOR W.M. BRUYNINK

Imhoff, L *see* VERSUCH EINER EINFUEHRUNG IN DAS STUDIUM DER KOLEOPTERN

IMIBONO YABOMDABU = BLACK OPINION – King William's Town, South Africa. 4 Oct 1985-30 May 1986. 1 reel – 1, 16 diazo available at reduced price – sa SA Libr [072]

IMIRCE, OU LA FILLE DE LA NATURE / DuLaurens, Henri J – Berlin: Impr. du Philosophe de Sans Souci, 1765. 378p. (Les Femmes Collection) – 4mf – 9 – $10.00 – fr Bibl Nationale [830]

L'IMITATEUR DE JESUS-CHRIST, OU LA VIE DU VENERABLE PERE ANTOINE YVAN / Gondon, G – Paris, 1662 – 7mf – 9 – CA-168/1 – ne IDC [240]

Imitatio Christi. Francais *see* IMITATION DE JESUS-CHRIST

L'IMITATION DE JESUS-CHRIST / Kempis, Thomas a – Quebec: Nouvelle Imprimerie, 1813. SEM16P21 – 1r – 5 – Can$12.00 – cn Bibl Nat [240]

IMITATION DE JESUS-CHRIST / Imitatio Christi. Francais – Quebec: J.P. Garneau, [entre 1914 et 1920]. SEM105P1646 – 5mf – 9 – Can$11.25 – cn Bibl Nat [240]

IMKANIYAT AL-TANMIYAH AL-ZIRAIYAH FI SINA / Sadiq, Fawziyah Mahmud – al-Kuwayt: Qism al-Jughrafiya bi-Jamiat al-Kuwayt wa-al-Jamiyah al- Jughrafiyah al-Kuwaytiyah, 1983 – us Res Libr [956]

Imlay, Gilbert *see* THE EMIGRANTS

THE IMMACULATE CONCEPTION = RESUME DE CONFERENCES SUR LE DOGMA L'IMMACULATE CONCEPTION : SUMMARY OF CONFERENCES / Vercruysse, Bruno – (In English) – Dublin: McGlashan & Gill, 1874 – 1mf – 9 – 0-8370-8395-8 – 1986-2395 – us A.T.L.A. [240]

L'IMMACULEE CONCEPTION : ETUDES SUR L'ORIGINE D'UN DOGME / Stap, A – (Includes bibliographical references and index) – Nouv ed. Paris: Librarie internationale; Bruxelles: Lacroix, Verboeckhoven, 1869 – 1mf – 9 – 0-8370-8386-9 – 1986-2386 – us A.T.L.A. [240]

THE IMMANENCE OF CHRIST IN MODERN LIFE / Swan, Frederick R – London: James Clarke, 1907 – 1mf – 9 – 0-8370-5551-2 – 1985-3551 – us A.T.L.A. [240]

THE IMMANENCE OF GOD / Bowne, Borden Parker – Boston: Houghton, Mifflin, 1905.1 fiche – 9 – us A.T.L.A. [240]

THE IMMANENCE OF GOD IN RABBINICAL LITERATURE / Abelson, J – London, 1912 – 7mf – 8 – ne Slangenburg [270]

IMMANENCIA Y TRASCENDENCIA DEL SER Y DEL CONOCER EN HEIDEGGER / Frutos Cortes, Eugenio – Madrid, 1950. Rev. Filosofia (Tomo 9, num. 33) del Instituto Luis Vives – sp Bibl Santa Ana [100]

IMMANENZ UND GESCHICHTE : ZUM BEGRIFF DER KREATIVITAET IN DER METAPHYSIK ALFRED N. WHITEHEADS / Herdt, Ludwig – Frankfurt a.M., 1975 – 1mf – DM48.00 – 3-89349-851-6 – gw Hänsel [110]

IMMANUEL : OR, THE MYSTERY OF THE INCARNATION OF THE SON OF GOD / Ussher, James – (Repr fr the editions of 1649 and 1677) – London: James Nisbet, 1862 – 1mf – 9 – 0-8370-5649-7 – 1985-3649 – us A.T.L.A. [210]

IMMANUEL BAPTIST CHURCH. EL PASO, TEXAS : CHURCH RECORDS – 1919-75. 1534p – 1 – $69.03 – us Baptist [240]

IMMANUEL BAPTIST CHURCH. FRANKFORT, KENTUCKY : CHURCH RECORDS – Sept 1961-Sept 1989; Membership rolls 1961-1991. 1,669p – 1 – $75.11 – us Baptist [240]

IMMANUEL BAPTIST CHURCH. HENDERSON, KENTUCKY : CHURCH RECORDS – 1914-87.6 reels – 1 – 409.73 – us Baptist [240]

IMMANUEL BAPTIST CHURCH. LEXINGTON, KENTUCKY : CHURCH RECORDS – 1909-13 – 1 – 7.11 – us Baptist [240]

IMMANUEL BAPTIST CHURCH. NASHVILLE, TENNESSEE : CHURCH RECORDS – v. 1-8. 1887-1980 – 1 – 319.86 – us Baptist [240]

IMMANUEL BAPTIST CHURCH. PADUCAH, KENTUCKY : CHURCH RECORDS – 1920-Oct 1964 – 1 – 6.93 – us Baptist [240]

IMMANUEL BAPTIST CHURCH. WICHITA, KANSAS : CHURCH RECORDS – 1914-61 – 1 – 45.99 – us Baptist [240]

IMMANUEL BAPTIST MESSENGER/TEMPLE ADVOCATE – Chicago.Immanuel Baptist Church. 1902-03, 1905-16. Incomplete. Single reels available – 1 – 134.10 – us A.B.H.S. [073]

IMMANUEL HA-ROMI / Tchernichowsky, S – Berlin. 1925. BJ-422-91 1 – 9 – ne IDC [470]

IMMANUEL KANT IN ENGLAND, 1793-1838 / Wellek, Rene – Princeton: Princeton University Press, 1931 – vii/317p – 1 – us U.W. Library [190]

IMMANUEL KANT'S CRITIQUE OF PURE REASON / Kant, Immanuel – In commemoration of the centenary of its first publ. Trans. by F. Max Mueller, introd. by Ludwig Noiré. London: Macmillan, 1881. 2v – 1 – us U.W. Library [190]

Immanuel Lutheran Church (Upper Sandusky, Ohio) *see*
- RECORDS

THE IMMEDIATE EFFECT OF CONCURRENT VISUAL FEEDBACK ON BEGINNING TARGETS ARCHERS / Trexler, James G – 1982 – 1mf – 9 – $4.00 – us Microform Publ [790]

IMMENSEE : MIT 23 HELIOGRAVUEREN NACH W. HASEMANN UND EDMUND KANOLDT / Storm, Theodor – 3. Aufl. Leipzig: C F Amelang, 1896 – 1r – 1 – us U.W. Library [430]

IMMENSEE; IM SONNENSCHEIN; EIN GRUENES BLATT; ABSEITS : NOVELLEN / Storm, Theodor – Stuttgart: Verlag Deutsche Volksbuecher, 1942 – 1r – 1 – us U.W. Library [830]

Immer, Albert *see*
- HERMENEUTICS OF THE NEW TESTAMENT
- HERMENEUTIK DES NEUEN TESTAMENTES

IMMER BEREIT FUER DIE VERTEIDIGUNG DER FREIHEIT DES VOLKES / Komitee der Antifaschistischen Widerstandskaempfer in der DDR – Berlin, 1956. Fiche W 957. (Blodgett Collection of Spanish Civil War Pamphlets) – 9 – us H.U. College Libr [946]

Immermann, Karl Leberecht *see*
- DER CARNAVAL UND DIE SOMNAMBUELE
- MUENCHHAUSEN
- DER OBERHOF
- DAS TRAUERSPIEL IN TYROL
- TRISTAN UND ISOLDE

IMMERMANNS ALEXIS : EINE LITERARHISTORISCHE UNTERSUCHUNG / Leffson, August – (Includes bibliographical references) – Gotha: F A Perthes, 1904 – 1r – 1 – us U.W. Library [430]

IMMERMANNS "TRISTAN UND ISOLDE" / Szymanzig, Max – (Includes bibliographical references) – Marburg a.L.: N G Elwert, 1911 – 1r – 1 – us U.W. Library [430]

IMMERSION ESSENTIAL TO CHRISTIAN BAPTISM / Broadus, John A – 76p – 1 – 5.00 – us Baptist [240]

THE IMMIGRANT / Colgate, Robert – (A genealogy of the New York Colgates and some associated lines, comp. by Truman Abbe and Hubert Howson. 1703-1910 – 1 – 20.09 – us Baptist [240]

THE IMMIGRANT IN AMERICA – (Available by individual ethnic group) – 1789-1929 – 1 – us Primary [970]

IMMIGRANT WORKERS IN EUROPE : THEIR LEGAL STATUS, A COMPARATIVE STUDY / Thomas, Eric-Jean – 1982 – 9 – 92-3-101867-1 – fr UNESCO [340]

IMMIGRANTS TO NEW ENGLAND – 1700-1775. Comp. by Ethel Stanwood Bolton, 1966. Orig. publ., 1931. Indexed. 4 fiches. F-0863 – 9 – us A.G.L.L. [978]

IMMIGRATION : SPECIAL STUDIES – (1969-82. 12r. ISBN: 0-89093-596-3. $1,320.00; 1982-85. 4r. ISBN: 0-89093-627-7. $440.00; 1985-88. 12r. ISBN: 1-55655-132-0. $1,320.00) – With printed guides – 1 – us UPA [323]

IMMIGRATION AND ABSORPTION 1970-1975 / Israel. Ministry of Immigrant Absorption – Jerusalem, 1975. 27 p. In cooperation with the World Zionist Organization, Aliyah Dept – 9 – 2.00 – is I.T.T.I. [324]

IMMIGRATION AND NATIONALITY : ADMINISTRATIVE DECISIONS UNDER THE IMMIGRATION AND NATIONALITY LAWS – (Contains opinions of the AG, the Board of Immigration Applications, the Commissioner of Immigration, and the INS) – v1-19. 1940-89 (all publ?) – 179mf – 9 – $269.00 – LLMC 80-900 – us L.L.M.C. [324]

IMMIGRATION AND NATIONALITY ACTS : LEGISLATIVE HISTORIES AND RELATED DOCUMENTS / ed by Trelles, Oscar M & Bailey, James F – (With index) – 15v in 16bks – 9 – $535.00 set – 0-89941-334-X – us Hein [340]

IMMIGRATION AND NATIONALITY ADMINISTRATIVE DECISIONS *see* IMMIGRATION AND NATURALIZATION SERVICE ANNUAL REPORTS

IMMIGRATION AND NATIONALITY LAWS AND REGULATIONS AS OF MARCH 1 1944 / U.S. Justice Department – (Includes suppl nos 1-3 1944-46 (all publ)) – Washington: GPO, 1944 – 17mf – 9 – $25.50 – LLMC 81-503 – us L.L.M.C. [340]

IMMIGRATION AND NATURALIZATION SERVICE ANNUAL REPORTS – 1955-82 – 50mf – 9 – $75.00 – LLMC 81-501 – us L.L.M.C. [324]

IMMIGRATION AND REFUGEE BOARD. DOCUMENTATION, INFORMATION, AND RESEARCH BRANCH. RESOURCE CENTRE = COMISSION DE L'IMMIGRATION ET DU STATUT DE REFUGIE. DIRECTION GENERALE DE LA DOCUMENTATION, DE L'IMMIGRATION ET DES RECHERCHES. CENTRE DE RESSOURCES. – Ottawa. 151 docs. 1988-1991 – 127mf – 9 – ne IDC [320]

IMMIGRATION COMMISSION : "DILLINGHAM COMMISSION" REPORTS / U.S. Immigration Commission – Washington: GPO. 41v. 1911 – 320mf – 9 – $480.00 – LLMC 81-510 – us L.L.M.C. [324]

L'IMMIGRATION EN FRANCHE-COMTE / Prost, Albert – Paris. 1929. (La Condition Ouvriere. Part Two.) – 9 – 5.00 – fr Bibl Nationale [360]

IMMIGRATION LAND SETTLEMENT AND DEVELOPMENT REPORT / Great Britain. Colonial Office. Palestine – London. Oct 1930. Cmd. 3687. BJ-28-74 1 – 9 – ne IDC [956]

THE IMMIGRATION PROBLEM / Jenks, Jeremiah W – New York: Funk & Wagnalls, 1912 c1911.xvi,496p. incl. tables – 1 – us U.W. Library [323]

THE IMMIGRATION PROBLEM: A STUDY OF AMERICAN IMMIGRATION CONDITIONS AND NEEDS / Jenks, Jeremiah W – 3rd. ed. rev. and enl. New York, London: Funk & Wagnalls, 1913. xxiii,551p. incl. tables – 1 – us U.W. Library [323]

IMMIGRATION TO ISRAEL 1976 / Israel. Prime Minister's Office. Ministry of Immigrant Absorption and the Jewish Agency, Aliya and Absorption Dept – Jerusalem, 1977. 11, 42, 10 p. (Special Series no. 547). Text also in Hebrew – 9 – 2.00 – is I.T.T.I. [324]

IMMIGRATION TO ISRAEL 1948-1972 / Israel. Prime Minister's Office – Part 2. Composition by period of Immigration. Jerusalem, 1975. 10, 44, 8 p. (Special Series no. 489). Text also in Hebrew. In cooperation with Ministry of Immigrant Absorption and the Jewish Agency, Aliya and Absorption Dept – 9 – 2.00 – is I.T.T.I. [324]

IMMIGRATION TODAY – New York, NY. 1973-85 – 3r – 1 – $150.00 – R04911 – us Library Micro [071]

L'IMMIGRATO – Victoria, 11 Nov 1895 – 1,5,6 – bl Biblioteca [072]

IMMIXTIO ET CONSECRATIO / Andrieu, M – Paris, 1924 – 5mf – 8 – Dfl22.00 – ne Slangenburg [240]

THE IMMORTAL HISTORY OF SOUTH AFRICA : THE ONLY TRUTHFUL, POLITICAL, COLONIAL...HISTORY...OF THE CAPE COLONY, NATAL, THE ORANGE FREE STATE, TRANSVAAL, AND SOUTH AFRICA / Boon, Martin James – London: W Reeves, 1885 – 1 – us Res Libr [960]

IMMORTALITY, AND OTHER ESSAYS / Everett, Charles Carroll – Boston: American Unitarian Association, 1902 – 1mf – us A.T.L.A. [240]

THE IMMORTALITY OF THE SOUL / Beet, Joseph Agar – 1901 – 9 – us A.T.L.A. [240]

THE IMMORTALITY OF THE SOUL / Mattison, Hiram – 1864 – 9 – us A.T.L.A. [240]

THE IMMORTALITY OF THE SOUL: BEING A CRITICAL INVESTIGATION OF THE DOCTRINE...AS SET FORTH IN THE OLD TESTAMENT / Hirschfelder, Jacob Mair – Toronto: Rowsell & Hutchison, 1876. 05633. (Pre-1900 Canadiana) – 9 – cn C.I.H.M. [240]

IMMORTELLEN HEINRICH HEINE'S / ed by Strodtmann, Adolf – New York: S Zickel, 1872 – 1 – us U.W. Library [430]

IMMUNE SYSTEM HERBALS, APPROACHES, FOLKLORE : A HOW TO FIND OR LECATE WORKBOOK / Lamp Light Press Staff – 1mf – 9 – $15.00 – 0-917593-28-6 – us Continnuus [619]

LES IMMUNITES DES CONSULS / Grand, A le – Beauvais, 1911 – 2mf – 1 – ILM-1039/1 – ne IDC [327]

IMMUNOGENETICS – v. 1-11. 1974-80 – 1,5,9 – 949.00 – us UMI [073]

IMMUNOLOGIC RESEARCH – v1-. 1982- – 1,5,9 – us UMI [073]

IMMUNOLOGICAL COMMUNICATIONS – (v13-. 1984-. 5,6,9) – v1-13. 1972-84 – 1 – us UMI [073]

IMMUNOLOGICAL INVESTIGATIONS – v14-. 1985- – 1,5,6,9 – us UMI [073]

IMMUNOLOGY ABSTRACTS – 9 – us C.S.A. [610]

IMMUNOLOGY LETTERS – v1-9. 1979-84 – 1,5,6,13 – sz Elsevier [073]

IMMUNOLOGY TODAY – v1-5. 1980-84 – 1,5,6,13 – sz Elsevier [073]

IMMUNOPHARMACOLOGY – v1-8. 1978-84 – 1,5,6,13 – sz Elsevier [073]

Imp. Mediko-Khirurgicheskoi Akademii. Saint Petersburg *see* SISTEMATICHESKII KATALOG BIBLIOTEK IMP. MEDIKOKHIRURGICHESKOI AKADEMII

THE IMP. VARIETY AND PICTURE HALL – Stoke-on-Trent, England. -w. 26 Feb 1913-8 Dec 1915. 2 reels – 1 – uk British Libr Newspaper [072]

Imp. Voenno-Meditsinsko Akademii. Library *see* SISTEMATICHESKII KNIZHNYI KATALOG BIBLIOTEKI IMP. VOENNO-MEDITSINSKOI AKADEMII

IMPACT – -irr. v.8, no.3, Jan. 1976- . Washington, D.C.: Student National Education Association, 1976-. Other title. Student Impact – 1 – us U.W. Library [073]

IMPACT – May 1944-71. Pub. by the Conservative Baptist Foreign Mission Society. Continues: News and Views, May 1944-46; Conservative Baptist, 1947-Aug 1965; Impact, Sept 1965-71. 2610p – 1 – 91.35 – us Baptist [240]

IMPACT – (Some original pgs damaged) – v29-40. 1972-May 1983 – 1r – 1 – ATLA S0451 – us A.T.L.A. [073]

IMPACT CHANGING TECHNOLOGICAL AND ECONOMIC FACTORS ON MARKETS FOR NATURAL INDUSTRIES FIBRES : CASE STUDIES ON JUTE, KENAF, SISAL AND ABACA – 1989 – 76p – it F.A.O. [338]

IMPACT DES POLITIQUES DES PRIX DU BETAIL SUR LA PRODUCTION DE VIANDE ET DE LAIT DANS CERTAINS PAYS DE L'AFRIQUE SUBSAHARIENNE / Williams, T O – 1993 – 9 – $15.00 – 92-9053-237-8 – et ILRI [338]

THE IMPACT OF AN ADULT HEALTH EDUCATION PROGRAM ON EXERCISE SELF-EFFICACY AND PARTICIPATION IN LEISURE-TIME PHYSICAL ACTIVITY / Hubball, Harry T – 1994 – 2mf – $8.00 – us Microform Publ [613]

IMPACT OF COMMUNICATION TECHNOLOGIES ON WOMEN / ed by Perez-Vitoria, Silvia – 1994 – 9 – 92-3-102833-2 – fr UNESCO [305]

IMPACT OF EDUCATIONAL TELEVISION ON YOUNG CHILDREN / ed by Holtzman, Wayne H & Reyes-Lagunes, Isabel – 1981 – 60p – 9 – 92-3-101792-6 – fr UNESCO [370]

THE IMPACT OF FOREIGN LOANS ON THE LIBERIAN FISCAL SYSTEM : AN ESSAY / Uzoaga, W Okefie – 1953 – us Res Libr [332]

THE IMPACT OF INTERSCHOLASTIC ATHLETICS ON ACADEMIC PERFORMANCE / Honey, Michael J – 1994 – 1mf – $4.00 – us Microform Publ [370]

IMPACT OF LIVESTOCK PRICING POLICIES ON MEAT AND MILK OUTPUT IN SELECTED SUB-SAHARAN AFRICAN COUNTRIES / Williams, T O – 1993 – 9 – $15.00 – 92-9053-236-X – et ILRI [338]

IMPACT OF MICROELECTRONICS AND INFORMATION TECHNOLOGY : CASE-STUDIES IN LATIN AMERICA / Rada, Juan F – 1982 – 9 – 92-3-102004-8 – fr UNESCO [303]

IMPACT OF NATIONAL GRAIN POLICIES ON WORLD GRAIN SUPLLIES AND PRICES – 1985 – 40p – it F.A.O. [338]

THE IMPACT OF PROJECT ADVENTURE ACTIVITIES ON SELF-PERCEPTION / France, Thaddeus J & Jensen, Barbara E – 1993 – 2mf – $8.00 – us Microform Publ [150]

IMPACT OF SCIENCE ON SOCIETY – 1- 1950- – 1. ; 5,6. ; 9 – apply; v.20-; v.25- – us UMI [303]

IMPACT OF STABILIZATION AND STRUCTURAL ADJUSTMENT POLICIES ON THE RURAL SECTOR : CASE STUDIES OF COTE D'IVOIRE, SENEGAL, LIBERIA, ZAMBIA AND MOROCCO – 1991 – 244p – it F.A.O. [630]

IMPACT OF STRUCTURAL ADJUSTMENT ON SMALLHOLDERS – 1992 – 91p – it F.A.O. [338]

THE IMPACT OF TECHNICAL COOPERATION BETWEEN SAUDI ARABIA AND THE UNITED NATIONS AND ITS SPECIALIZED AGENCIES / Saudi Arabia – 1966 – 9 – ne IDC [337]

IMPACT OF THE ACQUIRED IMMUNODEFICIENCY SYNDROME (AIDS) : KNOWLEDGE, ATTITUDES, AND BEHAVIORS OF EMERGENCY CARE PROVIDERS / Beaver, Kathryn L – 1989 – 54p 1mf – 9 – $4.00 – us Microform Publ [370]

THE IMPACT OF THE FEDERAL DRUG AFTERCARE PROGRAM / Eaglin, James B – Washington: FJC, 1986 – 2mf – 9 – $3.00 – LLMC 95-331 – us L.L.M.C. [340]

THE IMPACT OF THE LA CROSSE WELLNESS PROJECT ON THE HEALTH PROMOTION INVOLVEMENT OF COLLEGE STUDENTS RESIDING ON THE CAMPUS OF THE UNIVERSITY OF WISCONSIN-LA CROSSE / Burns, Julia A & Gilmore, Gary D – 1992 – 1mf – $4.00 – us Microform Publ [613]

THE IMPACT OF THE PATENT SYSTEM ON RESEARCH / Melman, Seymour – Washington: Govt. Print. Off., 1958. 62p. LL-2308 – 1 – us L of C Photodup [340]

THE IMPACT OF THERAPEUTIC HORSEBACK RIDING ON THE SELF-CONCEPT AND RIDING PERFORMANCE OF CHILDREN AND ADOLESCENTS WITH DISABILITIES / Stuler, Lesley R – 1993 – 1mf – $4.00 – us Microform Publ [150]

IMPACT OF URBANIZATION AND INDUSTRIALIZATION ON WATER RESOURCES PLANNING AND MANAGEMENT / Zuidema, Floris C – 1979 – 111p – 9 – 92-3-101624-5 – fr UNESCO [333]

THE IMPACT OF "WINNING WEIGHS" WEIGHT CONTROL PROGRAM ON PERCEIVED BODY IMAGE / Kaufmann, Barbara E & Pretasky, Barbara J – 1991 – 2mf – $8.00 – us Microform Publ [150]

THE IMPACT OF WORD PROCESSING AND ELECTRONIC MAIL ON U.S. COURTS OF APPEALS / Greenwood, J Michael & Farmer, Larry – Washington: FJC, Mar 1979 – 2mf – 9 – $3.00 – LLMC 95-817 – us L.L.M.C. [340]

IMPACTO. MEDITACIONES PARA MILITANTES / Aradillas Agudo, Antonio – Madrid: Ediciones Studium, 1964 – 1 – sp Bibl Santa Ana [946]

THE IMPACTS OF MARINE DEBRIS, WEATHER CONDITIONS, AND UNEXPECTED EVENTS ON RECREATIONAL BOATER SATISFACTION ON THE DELAWARE INLAND BAYS / Holdnak, Andrew & Graefe, Alan R – 1992 – 2mf – 9 – $8.00 – us Microform Publ [790]

IMPACTS OF PREIMPOUNDMENT CLEARING ON RESERVOIR ECOLOGY AND FISHERIES IN THE UNITED STATES AND CANADA – 1985 – 40p – it F.A.O. [636]

EL IMPARCIAL – Curacao. Netherlands West Indies. 1874-1875 – 1 – us UMI [072]

EL IMPARCIAL – Madrid. Spain. -d. 1 Jan 1870-22 May 1874, 1 Jan 1875-30 May 1933. (169 reels) – 1 – uk British Libr Newspaper [072]

IMPARCIAL – Manaos, Amazonas. 1 Fev-Mar, Maio-Jul, Set-30 Nov 1918 – 1,5,6 – bl Biblioteca [072]

O IMPARCIAL – Cidade de Uba, 31 Jul 1918; 3 Jul 1921 – 1,5,6 – bl Biblioteca [072]

O IMPARCIAL – Estancia, Brazil. 16 Mar 1870 – 1 – bl Biblioteca [072]

O IMPARCIAL – Manaos, Amazonas. 7 Mar-31 Jul 1897 – 1,5,6 – bl Biblioteca [072]

O IMPARCIAL – Nanuque, Brazil. Nov-Dec 1970; Jan, Jun, Auq-Oct 1971 – 1 – bl Biblioteca [072]

O IMPARCIAL : ORGAO DA ASSOCIACAO COMMERCIO E INDUSTRIA – Manaus, Amazonas. 3 Ago-21 Nov 1890 – 1,5,6 – bl Biblioteca [072]

O IMPARCIAL : PERIODICO LITTERARIO E NOTICIOSO – Pilar, Alagoas. 15 Abr, 30 Jun 1897 – 1,5,6 – bl Biblioteca [072]

O IMPARCIAL – Pouso Alegre, 7 Jul-Dec 1935; Jan-Mar, May-Dec 1936; Jan-Jun, 26 Dec 1937 – 1,5,6 – bl Biblioteca [072]

O IMPARCIAL – Rio Branco, Acre. 17 Set 1966; Ago-Set 1967; Fev, Ago-24 Nov 1968 – 1,5,6 – bl Biblioteca [072]

O IMPARCIAL – Rio de Janeiro, 13 Aug 1912-Aug 1916; Jan 1917-Feb 1942 – 1,5,6 – bl Biblioteca [072]

O IMPARCIAL – Rio Pomba, 7 Jan-Dec 1979 – 1,5,6 – bl Biblioteca [072]

O IMPARCIAL – Sao Luis, 27 May 1899 – 1,5,6 – bl Biblioteca [072]

O IMPARCIAL – Sacramento: Quaresma and Armas Co, sep 1917-jan 1922 – 3r – 1 – us Res Libr [071]

EL IMPARCIAL DE TEXAS – San Antonio, TX: El Imparcial de Texas, [dec 23 1917-mar 1921] – 1 – us Res Libr [071]
L'IMPARTIAL – Detroit, MI. v1 n1. 20 nov 1869 – 1r – 1 – Can$25.00 – cn Can Microfilming [071]
L'IMPARTIAL – Journal de Smyrne. Politique, commercial et litteraire. Constantinople. mai 1848-fevr 1852, aout 1889-juin 1890 – 1 – fr A.C.R.P.P. [073]
L'IMPARTIAL / ed by Malo, J-H – Montreal, Canada. 15 avr 1882 – 1r – 1 – Can$50.00 – cn Can Microfilming [072]
L'IMPARTIAL – Nashua, NH. v62 n43. 25 nov 1959; v67 n7. 19 mar 1964 – 1r – 1 – Can$25.00 – cn Can Microfilming [071]
L'IMPARTIAL / ed by Raymond, J-Moise & Jaumenne, N-D J – Laprairie, Canada. 2 nov 1834; 26 nov 1834-14 mai 1835 – 1r – 1 – Can$50.00 – cn Can Microfilming [072]
L'IMPARTIAL / ed by Rouillard, J B – Longueuil, Canada. 22 jan 1885-13 dec 1888 – 1r – 1 – Can$50.00 – cn Can Microfilming [072]
L'IMPARTIAL – Tignish, Canada. 1893-1915 – 9r – 1 – $585.00 – cn Library Assoc [971]
L'IMPARTIAL – Tignish, PEI. v6 n50. 20 jun 1907 – 1r – 1 – Can$25.00 – cn Can Microfilming [072]
L'IMPARTIAL – Vermillonville, LA. v2 n19. 6 mai 1843 – 1r – 1 – Can$25.00 – cn Can Microfilming [071]
L'IMPARTIAL – Paris: Impr Bonaventure et Ducessois, jun 1848 – us Res Libr [071]
THE IMPARTIAL – La Prairie [Quebec: s.n. 1834-1835?] – 9 – cn C.I.H.M. [971]
AN IMPARTIAL ACCOUNT OF A LATE DEBATE AT LYME IN THE COLONY OF CONNECTICUT / Buckley, John – 1729 – 1 – 7.14 – us Baptist [240]
AN IMPARTIAL ACCOUNT OF THE LATE DEBATE AT LYME IN THE COLONY OF CONNECTICUT / Bulkley, John – 1729. London. 204p – 1 – 7.14 – us Baptist [240]
IMPARTIAL DE LONDRES – London, UK. 21 Jun 1873 – 1 – uk British Libr Newspaper [072]
L'IMPARTIAL DE SAONE-ET-LOIRE – Journal republicain hebdomadaire puis bihebdomadaire. Dir. J. Fargues. Chalon-sur-Saone. fevr 1900-oct 1904 – 1 – fr A.C.R.P.P. [073]
L'IMPARTIAL FRANCAIS – Journal de critique politique, litteraire et sociale. Dir. Gaston Gremy. Paris. puis quot. 1925-1er mai 1928 – 1 – fr A.C.R.P.P. [073]
IMPARTIAL OBSERVER – Cooperstown, NY.1808-09. Also: Federalist, 1809-17; Freeman's Journal, 1817-20. Sold as one unit – 1,3 – us Readex [071]
IMPARTIAL OCCURRENCES, FOREIGN AND DOMESTICK – (Pue's Occurrences). Ireland. -sw. 26 Dec 1704-9 Feb 1706, 27 Jul 1714, 3 Jan-22 Dec 1719. (41 ft) – 1 – uk British Libr Newspaper [072]
IMPARTIAL REGISTER – Salem. Mass. 1800-1801. and Salem Register. 1802-1807. and Essex Register. 1807-1820 – 1,3 – us Readex [071]
IMPARTIAL REPORTER (ENNISKILLEN) – 1826-77; Jan 17-Dec 26 1878; Jan 2-Apr 29, Jun 19 1879-96; 1898-1918; Jan 9-Dec 25 1919; 1920-50; Jan-Dec 18 1986; 1987-Dec 21 1989; Jan-Dec 20 1990; 1991-Dec 23 1992; 1993-96 – 107 3/4r – 9 – uk British Libr Newspaper [072]
IMPEACHMENT: A MONOGRAPH ON THE IMPEACHMENT OF THE FEDERAL JUDICIARY / Brown, Wrisley – Washington Govt. Print. Off. 1914. 18 p. LL-613 – 1 – us L of C Photodup [340]
IMPEDANZSPEKTRONISCHE UNTERSUCHUNGEN ZUR ADSORPTIONSGESCHWINDIGKEIT AN POLY- UND MONOKRISTALLINEN PLATIN-ELEKTRODEN / Oelgeklaus, Rainer – 1995 – 2mf – 9 – DM80.00 – 3-8267-2180-2 – gw Hänsel [540]
IMPEDIMIENTOS DE MISIONEROS / Bayle, Constantino – Madrid: Missionalia Hispanica, 1947 – 1 – sp Bibl Santa Ana [240]
IMPERATOR NIKOLAI 2 I EGO TSARSTVOVANIE, 1894-1917 – Po materialiam sobrannym starym professorom. Nitstsa, 1928 – 1 – $35.00r – us Hoover Inst Photo [920]
IMPERATOR PAVEL I. ZIZN' I TSARSTVOVANIE / Shumigorskii, E S – Spb. 1907. BR-7906 2 – 8 – ne IDC [920]
IMPERATORII GRAMMATICI HISTORIARUM LIBRI SEX SEU DE REBUS GESTIS A JOANNE ET MANNUELE GOMMENSIS IMPP. CP. (CBH 11,1) / Cinnami, Joannis; ed by Cange, C du – Parisiis, 1670 – Dfl77.00 – ne Slangenburg [240]
Imperatorskaia akademiia nauk *see* MATERIALY DLIA BIOGRAFICHESKAGO SLOVARIA DIE ISTVITELNYKH CHLENOV IMPERATORSKO I AKADEMII NAUK
Imperatorskoe moskovskoe tekhnicheskoe uchilishche *see* RABOTY IMPERATORSKAGO MOSKOVSKAGO TEKHNICHESKAGO UCHILISHCHA NA OBORONU
IMPERATRITSA MARIIA FEDOROVNA (1759-1828) / Shumigorskii, E S – v. 1. Spb. 1892. BR-7904 2 – 8 – ne IDC [920]
IMPERIAL ACADEMY: PROCEEDINGS – v1-21 1926-45 – 1,5,6 – us Princeton Micro [540]
EL IMPERIAL COLEGIO DE INDIOS DE LA SANTA CRUZ DE TLALTELOCO. MEXICO, 1934 / Ocaranza, Fernando – Madrid: Razon y Fe, 1935 – 1 – sp Bibl Santa Ana [972]
IMPERIAL COLONIST : THE OFFICIAL ORGAN OF THE BRITISH WOMEN'S EMIGRATION ASSOCIATION AND THE SOUTH AFRICAN EXPANSION COMMITTEE – London, 1902-1927 – 68mf – 9 – W-19/1 – ne IDC [305]
IMPERIAL COUNTY – 1914-34; 1992-94 – 23r – 1 – $1,150.00 – P00038 – us Library Micro [910]
IMPERIAL COUNTY INCLUDING IMPERIAL VALLEY – Imperial Co, CA. 1908; 1911-1913; 1917-1918; 1926-1949; 1952 – 14r – 1 – $700.00 – D042 – us Library Micro [978]
Imperial Court of Protectorate of the New Guinea Company – Eastern Jurisdiction District Journal/Gerichts – Journal *see* [(COURT) DAILY REGISTER OF LETTERS RECEIVED], 1893-1897
IMPERIAL FEDERATION / Argyll, John Douglas Sutherland Campbell, Duke of – London: S. Sonnenschein, 1885. 03986. (Pre-1900 Canadiana) – 9 – cn C.I.H.M. [320]
IMPERIAL FEDERATION / Fenety, George Edward – Fredericton, N.B.: s.n., 1888? (Fredericton, N.B.: Queen's Printer). 03081. (Pre-1900 Canadiana) – 9 – cn C.I.H.M. [971]
IMPERIAL FEDERATION / Forster, William Edward – Ottawa: Government Printing Bureau, 1900. 05585. (Pre-1900 Canadiana) – 9 – cn C.I.H.M. [971]
IMPERIAL FEDERATION: A LECTURE DELIVERED...SEPTEMBER 13TH, 1889 / Grant, George Monro – Winnipeg: Manitoba Free Press, 1890. 05118. (Pre-1900 Canadiana) – 9 – cn C.I.H.M. [971]
IMPERIAL FEDERATION LEAGUE / Imperial Federation League – London: W.B. Whittingham, 1884?.02065.(Pre-1900 Canadiana) – 9 – cn C.I.H.M. [971]
Imperial Federation League *see*
– EXPRESSIONS OF OPINION ON IMPERIAL FEDERATION: BY PUBLIC MEN AT HOME IN THE COLONIES
– IMPERIAL FEDERATION LEAGUE
IMPERIAL FEDERATION: WELDING THE LINKS OF UNION / Ansell, David Abraham – Paper read before the Montreal branch of the Imperial Federation League in Canada, Tuesday, 23rd November 1886. Montreal, 1886. 02195. (Pre-1900 Canadiana) – 9 – cn C.I.H.M. [971]
THE IMPERIAL GAZETTEER / ed by Hunter, William Wilson – London. Ed.2. 14v. 1885-87. – 92mf – 9 – ne IDC [950]
THE IMPERIAL GAZETTEER / India – Calcutta. Provincial series. 19v. 1908-09. – 212mf – 8 – ne IDC [950]
THE IMPERIAL GAZETTEER / India; ed by Hunter, W W – London. 9v. 1881. – 58mf – 9 – ne IDC [950]
THE IMPERIAL GAZETTEER / India – Oxford. New ed. 26v. 1907-09. – 218mf – 8 – ne IDC [950]
THE IMPERIAL GAZETTEER OF INDIA : DISTRICT SERIES – (Includes printed guide) – 1822-1945. 1,221v. Text and Statistics – 5,111mf – 9 – 1601/2 – ne IDC [950]
Imperial Government of German New Guinea *see* CORRESPONDENCE FILES, SINGLE NUMBER SERIES, 1899-1911
IMPERIAL HISTORY / Great Britain. Colonial Office – British Colonial Records, 1889-1939; The Statesman and Friend of India, 194 1-1951 – 1 – us Primary [941]
THE IMPERIAL LEGISLATIVE COUNCIL MANUAL : INCLUDING THE GOVERNMENT OF INDIA ACT, 1915, THE RULES AND REGULATIONS FOR THE LEGISLATIVE COUNCIL OF THE GOVERNOR GENERAL, AND AN APPENDIX CONTAINING THE REPEALED INDIAN COUNCIL ACTS, 1861, 1892 AND 1909, AND GOVERNMENT OF INDIA ACT, 1912 – Delhi: Supt Govt Printer, India, 1916 – 1 – us Res Libr [950]
THE IMPERIAL LEGISLATIVE COUNCIL MANUAL *see* RULES OF BUSINESS
IMPERIAL NETWORK AND EXTERNAL DEPENDENCY : THE CASE OF ANGOLA / Minter, William M – Madison 1971 – us Res Libr [960]
IMPERIAL NIGHT HAWK – v1-2. 1923-24 – 1r – 1 – us Ross [073]
THE IMPERIAL NIGHT HAWK – Atlanta, Ga. v. 1-2 no. 34. Mar 28 1923-Nov 19 1924 – 1 – us NY Public [073]
Imperial Order of the Daughters of the Empire *see* ECHOES
IMPERIAL PRESS – Imperial, CA. 1902-06 (broken issues) – 1r – 1 – $50.00 – C02302 – us Library Micro [071]
Imperial Record Dept. India *see* AN ALPHABETICAL LIST OF THE FEASTS AND HOLIDAYS OF THE HINDUS AND MUHAMMADANS
IMPERIAL REPUBLICAN – Imperial, NE. -w. Aug-Dec 1899, scattered issues missing; Jun 1905; Apr 1908-Jun 1911; Aug 1911-Apr 1915, scattered issues missing; May 1919-Dec 1922; Aug 1923; Jan 1925 to date – 1 – us NE Hist [071]
Imperial Russian Historical Society *see* SBORNIK MATERIALOV, OTNOSIASCHIKHSIA DO ARKHIVNOI CHASTI V ROSSII
IMPERIAL STATUTES IN FORCE IN NEW SOUTH WALES... / Bignold, H B – (V1 contains chronological and alphabetical tables of all the imperial statutes and also of the Commonwealth and N.S.W. statutes dealing with the imperial statutes. v2-3 contain the text of all imperial statutes declared to be in force, and a selection of imperial statutes not authoritatively declared, but presumed to be in force, together with indexes and case references) – Sydney: The Law Book Company of Australasia. v1-3. 1913-14 – 18mf – 9 – $27.00 – LLMC 96-001 – us L.L.M.C. [323]
IMPERIAL UNITY AND THE DOMINIONS / Keith, Arthur Berriedale – Oxford: Clarendon Press, 1916. 626p – 1 – us U.W. Library [941]
IMPERIAL VALLEY PRESS – El Centro, CA. 1901- – 268+ r – 1 RC02196 – $13,400.00 ($390.00y) – us Library Micro [071]
IMPERIAL VALLEY PRESS – El Centro. Calif. 1901-1949- – 1 – us UMI [071]
Imperial War Museum. London *see* BRITISH 20TH CENTURY WAR ART
L'IMPERIALE. CANTATA FOR THE PARIS EXHIBITION... OP. 26 / Berlioz, H – 1855 – 1 – us Sibley [780]
IMPERIALISM AND NATIONALISM; A STUDY OF CONFLICT IN THE NEAR EA. / Page, Kirby – New York: George H. Doran Co., (c1925). vii,leaf,7-92p – 1 – us U.W. Library [321]
IMPERIALISM AND THE MANDATES SYSTEM / Gilchrist, H – New York, 1928 – 1mf – 1 – ILM-1916/1 – ne IDC [327]
THE IMPERIALISM OF JOHN MARSHALL: A STUDY IN EXPEDIENCY / Bryan, George – Boston, Stratford Co., 1924. 112 p. LL-1535 – 1 – us L of C Photodup [340]
IMPERIALISME DAN KAPITALISME SERTA IMPERIALISME DI INDONESIA / Sukarno, Pres. Indonesia – SE 4305 1. 1959 – 9 – ne IDC [025]
L'IMPERIALISME DU CAPITALISME FRANCAIS EN TUNISIE ET LE NATIONALISME TUNISIEN (1891-1914) / Sammut, C – 9 – F70.00 – fr Ethnologie [944]
IMPERIALISMO Y DESARROLLO ECONOMICO : LA ARGENTINA FRENTE A NUEVAS RELACIONES DE DEPENDENCIA / Esteban, Juan Carlos – Buenos Aires: Merayo Editor, 1972 – 1 – us Hoover Inst Photo [320]
LOS IMPERIALISMOS DE JUAN GINES DE SEPULVEDA EN SU : DEMOCRATES ALTER / Bayle, Constantino – Madrid: Missionalia Hispanica, 1948 – 1 – sp Bibl Santa Ana [320]
IMPERIALISTICHESKAIA VOINA K DESIATOI GODOVSHCHINE : MATERIALY DLIA RABOCHIKH, KRASNOARMEISKIKH I SHKOLNYKH KLUBOV – Leningrad: "Pribo i", 1924 – 1 – CSUX89-B6734 – us Hoover Inst Photo [355]
IMPERIALIZM I NAKOPLENIE KAPITALA : TEORETICHESKI I ETI UD / Bukharin, Nikolai Ivanovich – Izd. 2-e. Moskva: Gos. izd-vo, 1927 – 1 – CSUX89-B3117 – us Hoover Inst Photo [320]
IMPERIUM AND SACERDOTIUM ACCORDING TO ST BASIL THE GREAT / Reilly, G F – 1945 – 4mf – 9 – ne Slangenburg [240]
IMPERIUM ORIENTALE SIVE ANTIQUITATES CONSTANTINOPOLITANI (CBH 24,1) / Banduri, A – Venetiis. Tom. 1. 1729 – Dfl98.00 – ne Slangenburg [930]
IMPERIUM ORIENTALE SIVE ANTIQUITATES CONSTANTINOPOLITANI (CBH 24,2) / Banduri, A – Venetiis. Tome 2. 1729 – Dfl74.00 – ne Slangenburg [930]
IMPERSKAI A ROSSII A : ORGAN ROSSI ISKAGO SOTSIAL-NATSIONALISTICHESKAGO IMPERSKAGO DVIZHENII A – (Includes c.1: 1937:Jan./Feb.-1938:Apr., Sept., 1939:Jan.) – Paris: [Dvizhenie], 1937- – 1 – CSUXANR1624-S – us Hoover Inst Photo [947]
IMPETU, PASION Y FUGA / Caba, Ruben – Madrid: Ediciones Alfaguara, 1972 – 1 – sp Bibl Santa Ana [946]
L'IMPITOYABLE – Paris: Blondeau, sep 1848 – us Res Libr [072]
IMPLANT DENTISTRY – v1-5. 1992-1996 – 5r – 1,5,6,9 – $65.00r – us Williams [617]
IMPLEMENTATION AND ADMINISTRATION OF AGRICULTURAL PRICE POLICY IN ASIA – 1989 – 76p – it F.A.O. [650]
THE IMPLEMENTATION OF A PERENNIAL PROGRAM OF EVANGELISM / Jones, James Edward – 1982 – 1 – 7.28 – us Baptist [240]
IMPLEMENTATION OF FIVE YEAR PLAN-EVALUATION REPORT FOR 1949-1951 / Ethiopia. Planning Board – D-917 1. 1959 – 9 – ne IDC [338]
IMPLEMENTATION OF NATIONAL POLICY ON EDUCATION 1986 : A PROGRESS REPORT AS ON 30TH NOVEMBER 1988 / India. Department of Education – New Delhi, 1988 – 1mf – 9 – DE-612/1 – ne IDC [370]
IMPLEMENTATION REPORT ON THE FIRST FIVE YEAR PLAN / Syria. Ministry of Planning – 1960/61-1961/62, 1964-65. 1961-67. Lacking: 1966/67. BNE-9720 1 – 9 – ne IDC [338]
IMPLEMENTATION REPORT ON THE FOURTH STAGE PLAN, JAN-DEC 1964, OF THE FIRST FIVE YEARS DEVELOPMENT PLAN / Syria. Ministry of Planning – Damascus. 1965 – 9 – ne IDC [338]
IMPLEMENTATION REPORT ON THE THIRD STAGE PLAN, JUL 1962-DEC 1963 OF THE FIRST YEAR DEVELOPMENT PLAN / Syria. Ministry of Planning – Damascus. 1964. BD-652 1 – 9 – ne IDC [338]
THE IMPORT DUTIES ENQUIRY *see* THE REPORT ON THE CENSUS OF PRODUCTION 1907-1967
THE IMPORTANCE OF BEING EARNEST : A TRIVIAL COMEDY FOR SERIOUS PEOPLE... / Wilde, Oscar – London: L. Smithers, 1899, [c1898] – 1 roll – 1 – 1-55879-905-2 – uk Libr Preservation [820]
THE IMPORTANCE OF CANADA CONSIDERED IN TWO LETTERS TO A NOBLE LORD / Lee, Charles – London: printed for R and J Dodsley, 1761. SEM105P71 – 1mf – 9 – Can$2.25 – cn Bibl Nat [971]
THE IMPORTANCE OF CANADA CONSIDERED IN TWO LETTERS TO A NOBLE LORD / Lee, Charles – London: Printed for R and J Dodsley, 1761. SEM16P55 – 1r – 5 – Can$9.00 – cn Bibl Nat [971]
THE IMPORTANCE OF DEDAKPADI IN LIVESTOCK FEEDING IN INDONESIA / Lubis, Darul Asjhar – In Indonesian. SE-5734 1. 1958 – 9 – ne IDC [636]
THE IMPORTANCE OF HISTORIC RESEARCH FOR THE THEOLOGICAL STUDENT OF TO-DAY : AN ADDRESS / Scott, Hugh M – Chicago: Jameson & Morse, 1882 – 1mf – us A.T.L.A. [240]
THE IMPORTANCE OF TERTULLIAN IN THE DEVELOPMENT OF CHRISTIAN DOGMA / Morgan, James – London: K. Paul, Trench, Trubner, 1928. xviii,295p – 1 – us U.W. Library [240]
IMPORTANCE OF THE FORT STANTON EXPERIMENTAL RANCH AND ITS IMPACT ON RANGE LIVESTOCK INDUSTRY OF NEW MEXICO / New Mexico State University. College of Architecture and Home Economics – 2 Aug 1978. 1 reel – 1,5 – us Spaulding [636]

THE IMPORTANCE OF THE JEWS FOR THE PRESERVATION AND REVIVAL OF LEARNING DURING THE MIDDLE AGES / Schleiden, Matthias Jacob – London: Siegle, Hill, 1911 – us A.T.L.A. [940]

AN IMPORTANT CASE ARGUED, IN THREE DIALOGUES BETWEEN DR. OPIUM, GALLIO AND DISCIPULUS,... / Hill, Richard – London, 1788 – 1mf – 9 – MP-561/1 – ne IDC [240]

IMPORTANT DECREE ISSUED BY THE PRESIDENT OF THE CABINET / Azana, Manuel – Barcelona, 1937. Fiche W 741. (Blodgett Collection of Spanish Civil War Pamphlets) – 9 – us H.U. College Libr [946]

THE IMPORTANT DOCTRINES OF ORIGINAL SIN, JUSTIFICATION BY FAITH AND REGENERATION CLEARLY STATED FROM SCRIPTURE AND REASON, AND VINDICATED FROM THE MISREPRESENTATIONS OF THE METHODISTS;... / Whiston, T – [London], 1740 – 1mf – 9 – MP-273/1 – ne IDC [240]

IMPORTANT FEDERAL LAWS / Lapp, John A – Indianapolis: B F Bowen & Co, 1917 – 10mf – 9 – $15.00 – LLMC 94-204 – us L.L.M.C. [340]

IMPORTANT ISSUES UNDERLYING THE SECOND FIVE YEAR PLAN OF EDUCATION AND CONCLUSIONS ARRIVED AT AS A RESULT OF THE STUDIES / Pakistan. Planning Commission. Education and Training – 1959 – 1mf – 9 – DE-578/1 – ne IDC [370]

IMPORTANT PERIODICALS OF ITALIAN AND INTERNATIONAL SOCIALISM, 1868-1917 – (See also indiv. listings: L'Egalite; Bulletin de la Federation Jurassienne de l'Association Internationale des Travailleurs; La Plebe; Lotta di Classe; Prosvescenie; Cuore E Critica; Rivista Internazionale del Socialismo; Rivista Italiana des Socialismo) – 1 – $620.00 set – us UPA [335]

IMPORTANT RELIGIOUS TRUTHS / Doe, Walter P – Providence, RI: A Crawford Greene, 1883 – 1mf – 9 – 0-8370-2942-2 – 1985-0942 – us A.T.L.A. [240]

IMPORTANTE CUESTION DE DERECHO INTERNACIONAL... / Gonzalez, R – Mendoza, 1877 – 1mf – 1 – ILM-3856/1 – ne IDC [327]

IMPORTERS AND BREEDERS OF FRENCH COACH, PERCHERON AND ARABIAN HORSES: CATALOGUE FOR 1889-90 / The Company of the Haras National – (Montreal: Gazette), 1889. 04236. (Pre-1900 Canadiana) – 9 – cn C.I.H.M. [636]

IMPORT/EXPORT : INTERNATIONAL FLOW OF TELEVISION FICTION – 1990 – 94p – 9 – 92-3-102677-1 – fr UNESCO [380]

IMPORTS BY OIL COMPANIES, 1969-1970 / Libya. Technical Planning Body. Census and Statistical Department – BNE-1213 1 – 9 – ne IDC [380]

IMPOSICION SOBRE LA RENTA EN LA LEY DE REFORMA TRIBUTARIA DE 11-6-1964 / Aparicio Perez, Antonio – 3mf – 9 – Pta2,000.00 – 84-85422-24-4 – sp Pentalfa [304]

L'IMPOSITION DES MAINS ET LES RITES CONNEXES DANS LE NOUVEAU TESTAMENT ET DANS L'EGLISE ANCIENNE / Coppens, J – Paris, 1925 – 8mf – 8 – Dfl30.00 – ne Slangenburg [220]

L'IMPOSITION DES SUCCESSIONS EN DROIT INTERNATIONAL... / Guggenheim, P – Geneve, 1928 – 2mf – 1 – ILM-2957/1 – ne IDC [327]

DIE IMPOSSIBILIA DES SIGER VON BRABANT / Baeumker, C – Muenster, 1898 – 4mf – 8 – ne Slangenburg [100]

DIE IMPOSSIBILIA DES SIGER VON BRABANT : BGPHMA 2/6 / Baeumker, C – Muenster, 1898 – 4mf – 9 – ne Slangenburg [240]

IMPOST BOOKS OF THE COLLECTOR OF CUSTOMS AT PHILADELPHIA, 1789-1804 / U.S. Bureau of the Customs – 6rolls. T255 – 1 – us Nat'l Archives [324]

THE IMPOSTOR DETECTED : OR, THE COUNTERFEIT SAINT TURN'D INSIDE OUT,... / Kirkby, J – London, 1750 – 1mf – 9 – MP-338/1 – ne IDC [240]

IMPOSTURE DETECTED AND THE DEAD VINDICATED, IN A LETTER TO A FRIEND,... / Hill, Richard – London, 1777 – 1mf – 9 – MP-519/1 – ne IDC [240]

THE IMPOSTURE OF METHODISM DISPLAY'D : IN A LETTER TO THE INHABITANTS OF THE PARISH OF DEWSBURY,... / Bowman, W – London, 1740 – 1mf – 9 – MP-272/1 – ne IDC [240]

IMPRECOR (ENGLISH EDITION) *see* INPRECOR

THE IMPREGNABLE ROCK OF HOLY SCRIPTURE / Gladstone, William Ewart – rev enl ed. Philadelphia: John D Wattles, 1891, c1890 – 1mf – 9 – 0-8370-3306-3 – 1985-1306 – us A.T.L.A. [220]

A IMPRENSA : ORGAO DO PARTIDO REPUBLICANO CONSERVADOR DE ITACOATIARA – Itacoatiara, Amazonas. 21 Nov 1912-13 Abr 1913 – 1,5,6 – bl Biblioteca [072]

A IMPRENSA – Sao Luiz, 4 Jun 1857-29 Jan 1862 – 1,5,6 – bl Biblioteca [072]

A IMPRENSA – Visconde do Rio Branco, 15 Dec 1977; Jan, Apr, Jun-Dec 1978; Jan-Feb, 15 Apr 1979 – 1,5,6 – bl Biblioteca [072]

IMPRENSA CATHOLICA : PERIODICO RELIGIOSO – Maceio, Alagoas. 9 Nov 1873 – 1,5,6 – bl Biblioteca [072]

A IMPRENSA DE CUYABA : PERIODICO POLITICO, MERCANTIL E LITERARIO – Cuiaba, 31 Jul-Aug 1859; Jun-Sep 1860; Jan-Mar, Dec 1861; Dec 1862; Jan, Mar, Jul-Dec 1863; Jan 1864-Jan 1865 – 1,5,6 – bl Biblioteca [072]

IMPRENSA LIVRE – Curitiba, 6 Jun 1867 – 1,5,6 – bl Biblioteca [072]

IMPRENSA POPULAR – Rio de Janeiro, BL. 1951-1958 – 15r – $750.00 – R04175 – us Library Micro [320]

A IMPRENSA UNIDA – Manaos, Amazonas. 31 Maio 1888 – 1,5,6 – bl Biblioteca [072]

LA IMPRENTA EN SEVILLA. NOTICIAS INEDITAS DESDE LA INTRODUCCION DEL ARTE TIPOGRAFICO EN ESTA CIUDAD HASTA EL SIGLO 29. VOL 1. SEVILLA, 1945 / Hazanas y La Rua, Joaquin – Madrid: Razon y Fe, 1946 – 1 – sp Bibl Santa Ana [700]

LE IMPRESE ILLUSTRI CON ESPOSITIONI, ET DISCORSI / Ruscelli, Jeronimo – O 738. 1566 – 9 – ne IDC [760]

IMPRESE ILLUSTRI DI DIVERSI / Camilli, Camillo – O-188. 1586 – 9 – ne IDC [760]

IMPRESIONES DE UN VIAJE POR DON... DEDICADAS A LOS JOVENES ESTUDIANTES DE LAS ESCUELAS DEL AVE MARIA DE LA CIUDAD DE DON BENITO / Torre Isunza de Hita, Pedro – Cabra: Tip. Manuel Cordon, 1923 – sp Bibl Santa Ana [946]

IMPRESIONES INTIMAS / Spinola de Gironza, Araceli – Madrid: Graficas Nebrija, 1966 – 1 – sp Bibl Santa Ana [946]

LE IMPRESSE ILLUSTRI / Ruscelli, I – O 420 1. 1584 – 9 – ne IDC [760]

IMPRESSIONISM : SUBJECT COLLECTIONS – (Individual titles not listed separately) – 121 catalogues on 184mf – 9 – £1,160.00 – uk Chadwyck [700]

IMPRESSIONISM IN THE ARTS AND ITS INFLUENCE ON SELECTED DANCE WORKS / Collins, Sherry L – 1989 – 202p 3mf – 9 – $12.00 – us Microform Publ [790]

DER IMPRESSIONISMUS HOFMANNSTHALS ALS ZEITERSCHEINUNG : EINE STILKRITISCHE STUDIE / Berendsohn, Walter Arthur – Hamburg: W Gente, 1920 – 1r – 1 – us U.W. Library [430]

IMPRESSIONIST AND MODERN PAINTINGS, DRAWINGS AND SCULPTURE – (7,300 reproductions) – 122mf – 9 – $770.00 – 0-907006-82-5 – uk Mindata [750]

IMPRESSIONIST, MODERN AND CONTEMPORARY PAINTINGS, DRAWINGS AND SCULPTURE AND MODERN PRINTS – (6,000 images) – 58mf – 9 – $330.00 – 0-907006-13-2 – uk Mindata [700]

L'IMPRESSIONNISTE – Journal d'art. no. 1-4. Paris. avr 1877 – 1 – fr A.C.R.P.P. [073]

IMPRESSIONNISTES DE LA COLLECTION COURTAULD DE LONDRES. 1955. 92 ILLUS. 2 FICHES / Reunion des musees nationaux. Paris – 9 – fr Réunion [700]

(IMPRESSIONS) / France. Assemblee nationale. Senat – Paris. 1907 (no.244)-1940 (no.83). 38 reels – 1 – 23.00r – us L of C Photodup [944]

IMPRESSIONS / France. Assemblee nationale – Projets de lois, propositions, rapports, etc. Sessions 1946-1985/86 – 1 – fr A.C.R.P.P. [323]

IMPRESSIONS / France. Chambre des Deputes – Programmes electoraux, dits Barodets. IIle Republique, 3e-15e legislatures. 1882, 1886, 1890, 1894, 1899, 1903, 1907, 1910, 1914, 1920, 1925, 1928, 1933 – 1 – fr A.C.R.P.P. [323]

IMPRESSIONS / France. Senat – Projets de lois, propositions, rapports, etc. Sessions 1957/58-1985/86 – 1 – fr A.C.R.P.P. [323]

IMPRESSIONS AND EXPERIENCES OF THE WEST INDIES AND NORTH AMERICA IN 1849 / Baird, Robert – Philadelphia: Lea & Blanchard, 1850 – 1mf – us A.T.L.A. [970]

IMPRESSIONS AND OPINIONS / Moore, George – London: David Nutt, 1891 – 1 roll – 1 – 1-55879-477-8 – uk Libr Preservation [800]

IMPRESSIONS DE THEATRE / Lemaitre, Jules – Paris. 1889-1920. 11v – 1 – 23.00 – us L of C Photodup [790]

IMPRESSIONS D'ESPAGNE, 15 JOURS EN ESPAGNE REPUBLICAINE, 11-25 NOVEMBRE 1937 / Jezequel, Jules – Paris, 1937. Fiche W971. (Blodgett Collection of Spanish Civil War Pamphlets) – 9 – us H.U. College Libr [946]

IMPRESSIONS OF A CARELESS TRAVELER / Abbott, Lyman – New York: Outlook, 1908, c1907 – 1mf – us A.T.L.A. [240]

IMPRESSIONS OF FRANCO'S SPAIN / Rodriguez Vega, Jose – London, 1943. Fiche W1147. (Blodgett Collection of Spanish Civil War Pamphlets) – 9 – us H.U. College Libr [946]

IMPRESSIONS OF JAPANESE ARCHITECTURE AND THE ALLIED ARTS / Cram, Ralph Adams – New York: Baker & Taylor, 1905 – 1mf – us A.T.L.A. [720]

IMPRESSIONS OF THEOPHRASTUS SUCH / Eliot, George – Edinburgh: William Blackwood, 1879 – 1 roll – 1 – 1-55879-770-X – uk Libr Preservation [890]

L'IMPRIMERIE – Paris, France. 15 Jan 1900-31 Dec 1913 – 5r – 1 – uk British Libr Newspaper [073]

L'IMPRIMEUR – Montreal, Canada. v14 n9. jan 1950-v15 n11. mar 1952 – 1r – 1 – Can$25.00 – cn Can Microfilming [073]

THE IMPRINT – Toronto: Toronto Type Foundry, v1 no 1(May 1893)- – 9 – cn C.I.H.M. [680]

IMPROBATIO QUORUNDAM ARTICULORUM MARTINI LUTHERI... / Clichtove, J – Parisiis, 1533 – 2mf – 9 – CA-84/1 – ne IDC [240]

IMPROVE YOUR TAGALOG / Aspillera, Paraluman S – 2nd ed. Manila, Philippines: [sl: sn], 1958, c1957 – us Res Libr [490]

IMPROVED PRODUCTION SYSTEMS AS AN ALTERNATIVE TO SHIFTING CULTIVATION – 1984 – 215p – it F.A.O. [631]

IMPROVED RENDERINGS OF THOSE PASSAGES IN THE ENGLISH VERSION OF THE NEW TESTAMENT... / Craik, Henry – 2nd ed. London:Bagster, 1866 – 1mf – 9 – 0-8370-2768-3 – 1985-0768 – us A.T.L.A. [220]

IMPROVED USE OF PLANT NUTRIENTS – 1981 – 159p – it F.A.O. [630]

IMPROVED WEED MANAGEMENT IN THE NEAR EAST – 1987 – 243p – it F.A.O. [631]

IMPROVEMENT AND PRODUCTION OF MAIZE, SORGHUM AND MILLET – it F.A.O. [338]

THE IMPROVEMENT OF AGRICULTURE, AND THE ELEVATION IN THE SOCIAL SCALE OF BOTH HUSBANDMAN AND OPERATIVE / Anderson, James – Montreal: Printed by De Montigny & Company, 1858. SEM105P225 – 1mf – 9 – Can$2.25 – cn Bibl Nat [630]

THE IMPROVEMENT OF AGRICULTURE RESEARCH ESTABLISHMENTS IN INDONESIA / Sumintawikarta, Sadikin – 1962. SE 5662 1 – 9 – ne IDC [630]

IMPROVEMENT OF NUTRITIONAL QUALITY OF FOOD CROPS – 1981 – 96p – it F.A.O. [630]

IMPROVING AND EVALUATING THE CHILD'S WORSHIP AT THE FIRST BAPTIST CHURCH / Marcum, Billy Darrell – 1982 – 1 – 5.12 – us Baptist [240]

IMPROVING COLLEGE AND UNIVERSITY TEACHING – (v.19-30. 1971-82. 5,6. v.23-30. 1975-82. 9) – v.1-30. 1953-82 – 1 – us UMI [073]

IMPROVING THE FEDERAL COURT LIBRARY SYSTEM : REPORT AND RECOMMENDATIONS SUBMITTED TO THE JUDICIAL CONFERENCE OF THE U.S. BY THE BOARD OF THE FEDERAL JUDICIAL CENTER – Washington: FJC, Feb 1978 – 2mf – 9 – $3.00 – LLMC 95-821 – us L.L.M.C. [340]

IMPROVING WEED MANAGEMENT : PROCEEDINGS OF THE FAO/IWSS EXPERT CONSULTATION. ROME, 1982 – 1983 2nd print 1984 – 190p – it F.A.O. [631]

L'IMPROVISATION OU LA VIE EN ITALIE / Andersen, Hans Christian – Paris: Amyot, 1847. 2v.310;298p. 8 fiches. (Literature Collection) – 9 – 20.00 – fr Bibl Nationale [910]

IMPRSKI I KLICH = APPEL DE L'EMPIRE: ORGANE DE L'UNION IMPERIALE RUSSE : ORGAN ROSSI ISKAGO IMPERSKAGO SOI UZA – (Includes c.1: no.1 1932:June 25-no.28 (1936:July)) – Paris: Soi uz, 1932- – 1 – CSUXAHZ6226-S – us Hoover Inst Photo [947]

IMPULSE – 1993 – 9 – DM231.00 – gw IOS [943]

IMPULSE – (Cont by: M5V Magazine, 1991. No vol publ in 1983/84) – Toronto. v1-16. 1971/72-1990 – 9 – Can$20.00y – cn Micromedia [073]

IMPULSE *see* M5V MAGAZINE

IMRA. JOURNAL / Industrial Marketing Research Association – 1965- – 1; 1975-5,6,9 – us UMI [650]

IMRE NAGY PAMPHLET COLLECTION – 1958 – 1 – CSUXANL5756-B – us Hoover Inst Photo [920]

IMTIYAZAT VE MUKAVELAT – Istanbul Matbaa-i Osmaniye. Vols 1-7 (1884-1897) – 70mf – 9 – $750.00 – us MEDOC [949]

IMVAHO – Kigali: Impr scolaire, nov 1984-mar 1994 – 3r – 1 – us Res Libr [072]

IMVAHO NSHYA – Kigali: [s.n.], oct 19/25 1994-dec 26 1994/jan 1 1995; mar 13/19-apr 1995 – us Res Libr [072]

IMVO NELISO LOMSI *see* IMVO ZABANTSUNDU

IMVO NELISO LOMZI = NATIVE OPINION AND GUARDIAN – King William's Town: J Tengo-Jabavu, jan 1895-mar 1898 – us Res Libr [072]

IMVO ZABANTSUNDU – King William's Town, [South Africa]: J Tengo-Jabavu, nov 3 1884-dec 19 1894 – 1 – us Res Libr [072]

IMVO ZABANTSUNDU – (Title varies: Imvo Neliso Lomsi) – King William's Town, South Africa. 3 Nov 1884-26 Dec 1936 – 31r – 1, 16 diazo available at reduced price – sa SA Libr [072]

IMVO ZABANTSUNDU – King William's Town: Jabavu and Co, Ltd, mar 1912-oct 1961] – us Res Libr [072]

IMVO ZABANTSUNDU BASE AFRIKA = SOUTH AFRICAN NATIVE OPINION – King William's Town: Jabavu and Co, feb 1903-dec 1909 – us Res Libr [072]

IMVO ZABANTSUNDU BOMZANTSI AFRIKA = NATIVE OPINION OF SOUTH AFRICA – King William's Town: Jabavu and Co Ltd, dec 1909-feb 1912 – us Res Libr [072]

IMVO ZABANTSUNDU BOMZANTSI AFRIKA = SOUTH AFRICAN NATIVE OPINION – King William's Town: Jabavu and Co, oct 1902-jan 1903] – us Res Libr [072]

IMVO ZONTSUNDU, NELISO LOMZI = NATIVE OPINION – King William's Town: Jabavu and Bokwa, apr 1898-aug 1901] – us Res Libr [072]

IN : INDONESIE-NEDERLAND – Batavia, 1946-1947 – 5mf – 9 – SE-886/1 – ne IDC [950]

IN 4. PRIORA CAPITA EUANGELIJ SECUNDUM MATTHAEUM / Bugenhagen, J – VVittembergae, 1543 – 3mf – 9 – ne IDC [240]

IN 12 ARISTOTELIS METAPH. / Halensis, Alexander – Venetiis: de Karera, 1572 – 43mf – 8 – ne Slangenburg [110]

IN 12 LIBROS METAPHYSICAE ARISTOTELIS / Dominicus de Flandria – Agrippinae, 1621 – 55mf – 8 – ne Slangenburg [110]

IN 31 DAVIDIS PSALMOS / Arias Montano, Benito – 1605. Ed. Pedro de Valencia – 9 – 1.50f – sp Bibl Santa Ana [240]

IN A WINTER CITY / Ouida – British Fiction Archive: Unit 3 – 9 – uk Bell [830]

IN ACTA APOSTOLORUM COMMENTARIA / Lorinus, Ioan. – Lugduni, 1605 – 45mf – 8 – ne Slangenburg [220]

IN AID OF FAITH / Abbott, Lyman – New York: E.P. Dutton, 1886. 1 fiche – 9 – us A.T.L.A. [240]

IN ANATOMEN CORPORIS HUMANI... / Vassaevs, L – Venecia, 1549 – 4mf – 9 – sp Cultura [611]

IN AND OUT OF THE BARRIO: ADAPTED FROM BOOK TWO / Preiser, Rosa C – Manila, 1948. 316p. illus. (Philippine public school readers) – 1 – us U.W. Library [360]

IN- AND OUT-LETTERS, 1750-1815 / Wesley, Sarah – (Coll title: The People Called Methodists, Phase 2: Primary Sources 1738-1800) – 3mf – 9 – MP-663/1 – ne IDC [240]

IN- AND OUT-LETTERS, 1776-1826 / Wesley, Sally – (Coll title: The People Called Methodists, Phase 2: Primary Sources 1738-1800) – 2mf – 9 – MP-654/1 – ne IDC [240]

IN- AND OUT-LETTERS, 1780-1823 / Wesley, Sally – (Coll title: The People Called Methodists, Phase 2: Primary Sources 1738-1800) – 1mf – 9 – MP-655/1 – ne IDC [240]

IN- AND OUT-LETTERS, 1795-1799, RELATING TO THE FORMATION OF THE METHODIST NEW CONNEXION / Kilham, A – (Coll title: The People Called Methodists, Phase 3: Primary Sources, 1801-1850) – 39mf – 9 – MP-691/1 – ne IDC [240]

IN- AND OUT-LETTERS, 1820-1849 / Everett, J – (Coll title: The People Called Methodists, Phase 3: Primary Sources, 1801-1850) – 11mf – 9 – MP-674/1 – ne IDC [240]

IN APHORISMO ET LIBELLUM DE ALIMENTO HIPOCRATIS, COMMENTARIA / Valles de Covarrubias, F – Alcala de Henares, 1561 – 12mf – 9 – sp Cultura [610]

IN APOCALYPSIN COMMENTARIUS / Liebana, Beatus a – 41p + 9 color mf – DM660.00 – 3-89219-016-X – gw Lengenfelder [090]

IN ARTEM POETICAM HORATII / Sanchez de las Brozas, Francisco – 1591 – 9 – 1.50f – sp Bibl Santa Ana [450]

IN BUSINESS – 1986- – 1,5,6,9 – us UMI [380]

IN CAMP AND TEPEE : AN INDIAN MISSION STORY / Page, Elizabeth Merwin – New York: F.H. Revell, c1915 – 1mf – us A.T.L.A. [240]

IN CANTICUM CANTICORUM : IN LIBRUM PRIMUM REGUM / Gregorius Magnus – 1982 – 18mf – 9 – Bf1,650.00 – 2-503-61442-6 – be Brepols [240]

IN CANTICUM CANTICORUM EXPOSITIO / Apponius – 1986 – 13mf – 9 – Bf1,900.00 – 2-503-60192-8 – be Brepols [240]

IN CATABAPTISTARUM STROPHAS ELENCHUS / Zwingli, H – Tiguri, Chr. Froschouer. 1527. BME-88 1 – 9 – ne IDC [240]

IN CATHOLICAS BB. IACOBI ET IUDAE APOSTOLORUM EPISTOLAS COMMENTARII / Lorinus, Ioan. – Moguntiae, 1622 – 21mf – 8 – ne Slangenburg [220]

IN CATHOLICAS TRES B. JOANNIS, ET DUAS B. PETRI EPISTOLAS COMMENTARII / Lorinus, Ioan. – Lugduni, 1609 – 20mf – 8 – ne Slangenburg [220]

IN CHORDIS ET ORGANO (FASTES D'ORGANIERS) / Morin, Victor – Montreal, 1940. SEM105P783 – 1mf – 9 – Can$2.25 – cn Bibl Nat [971]

IN CHRIST JESUS : OR, THE SPHERE OF THE BELIEVER'S LIFE / Pierson, Arthur Tappan – New York: Funk & Wagnalls, 1898 – 1mf – 9 – 0-8370-4750-1 – 1985-2750 – us A.T.L.A. [220]

...IN CONNECTION WITH THE FUNERAL SERVICES OF ITS FIRST PRESIDENT, THE RT. HON. SIR JOHN S. D. THOMPSON – Ottawa: Catholic Truth Society of Ottawa, 1894. 03217. (Pre-1900 Canadiana) – 9 – cn C.I.H.M. [240]

IN D. THOMAE AQ. COMMENTARIA SUPER LIBROS POSTERIORUM ANALYTICORUM ARISTOTELIS / Dominicus de Flandria – 1600 – 9mf – 8 – ne Slangenburg [180]

IN DARKEST AFRICA : OR, THE QUEST, RESCUE AND RETREAT OF EMIN, GOVERNOR OF EQUATORIA / Stanley, Henry Morton – London. 2v. 1890 – 1r – 1 – us Ross [960]

IN DARKEST AFRICA / Stanley, Henry Morton – New York, 1890 – 1 – us Res Libr [960]

IN DARKEST ENGLAND AND THE WAY OUT / Booth, William – London; New York: International Headquarters of the Salvation Army, [1890?] – 1mf – us A.T.L.A. [240]

IN DEFENCE OF COMPANIES / Burrage, Robert – 1986, LA Economic Notes, No.9, 2p – 9 – 1.00f – at Libertarian Micro [335]

IN DEFENCE OF FREE MIGRATION / Ebeling, Richard – 1979, LA Libertarian Reprints, no.3, 2p – 9 – 1.00f – at Libertarian Micro [335]

IN DEFENCE OF THE FAITH / Oliver, Alexander – Edinburgh: Oliphant, Anderson, 1886. 1 fiche – 9 – us A.T.L.A. [240]

IN DEN BERGEN, DA LAUERT DER WILDSCHUETZ : ROMAN AUS DER ALPENWELT / Achleitner, Arthur – Berlin: Gebrueder Paetel, [191-?] – 1r – 1 – us U.W. Library [830]

IN DER NOTH LERNET MAN DIE FREUNDE KENNEN : EIN ORIGINALLUSTSPIEL IN UNGEBUNDENER REDE UND FUENF AUFZUEGEN / Bergobzoomer, Johann Baptist – [Wien?]: zu finden beym Logenmeister, 1777 – 1 – us U.W. Library [820]

DER IN DER RECHEN-UND MESSKUNST WOHLERFAHRNE ORGELBAUMEISTER/ WELCHER DIE BEHOERIGE WEITE UND LAENGE ALLER ORGEL PFEIFEN / Sorge, G A – 1773. BP-761 1 – 9 – ne IDC [780]

IN DER STILLE : GEDANKEN UND BETRACHTUNGEN / Korn, Karl – Berlin-Schildow: E Sicker, 1944 – 1r – 1 – us U.W. Library [840]

IN DER VERANDA : EINE DICHTERISCHE NACHLESE / Gruen, Anastasius – Berlin: G Grote, 1876 – 1 – us U.W. Library [810]

IN DEVTERONOMIVM MOSIS ENARRATIO... / Chytraeus, D – VVitebergae, 1575 – 9mf – 9 – ne IDC [240]

IN DIT TEGENWOORDIGHE BOECXKEN ZIJN VEEL SCHOONE ENDE LIEFLIJCKE BRIEUEN VAN EENEN GHENAEMT JACOB DE KEERSMAECKER / Keersmaecker, Jacob de – BME-183 1 – 9 – ne IDC [240]

IN DIT TEGENWOORDIGHE BOECXKEN ZIJN VEEL SCHOONE ENDE LIEFLIJCKE BRIEUEN, VAN EENEN GHENAEMT JACOB DE KEERSMAECKER / Keersmaecker, Jacob de – die. 1584. BME-184 1 – 9 – ne IDC [240]

IN DULCI IUBILO, NUN SINGET UND SEID FROH : EIN BEITRAG ZUR GESCHICHTE DER DEUTSCHEN POESIE / Fallersleben, Hoffmann von – Hannover, 1861 – 3mf – 8 – Dfl13.00 – ne Slangenburg [240]

IN EN OM DE CHINEESCHE KAMP / Moerman, J – Reel 4002. 1929 – 1 – ja CEACS [950]

IN- EN UITVOER – Amsterdam, Netherlands. -w. 3 Oct 1917-6 Aug 1919. Imperfect. 3 reels – 1 – uk British Libr Newspaper [949]

IN EPISTOLAM D. PAVLI AD ROMANOS SCRIPTAM COMMENTARIVS... / Corner, C – Heidelbergae, 1583 – 5mf – 9 – ne IDC [240]

IN EPISTOLAS B. PAULI COMMENTARII / Theodorus of Mopsuestia – The Latin version with the Greek fragments. With an introduction, notes and indices, by H. B. Swete. 2 v. 1880-82 – 1 – us A.T.L.A. [240]

IN EXODVM ENARRATIO,... / Chytraeus, D – Vitebergae, 1561 – 4mf – 9 – ne IDC [240]

IN FACT – 1-22 2+1 (all publ). 1940-1950 – 41mf – 9 – $235.00 – us UPA [335]

IN FAR LOCHABER / Black, William – British Fiction Archive: Unit 4 – 9 – uk Bell [830]

IN FOCUS AND MUSE NEWS – Fallon, NV. 1987 – 2+ r – 1 – $100.00 ($50.00y) – U04840 – us Library Micro [071]

IN FOEDVS ET VICTORIAM CONTRA TVRCAS / Gherardius, P – Venetiis, 1572 – 6mf – 9 – H-8327/1 – ne IDC [956]

IN GENESIN ENARRATIO,... / Chytraeus, D – Vitebergae, 1557 – 6mf – 9 – ne IDC [240]

IN GERANGL = DANS LA LUTTE – (In Yiddish) – Brussels, BE. no66(78) 18 Jul 1947; no67-68(79-80) 1 Aug 1947 – 1r – 1 – $25.00 – cn Can Microfilming [072]

IN GEVIRBL = WHIRLWIND – Toronto, CN. v1 no 2. 1930 – 1r – 1 – Can$25.00 – cn Can Microfilming [072]

IN HEALTH *see*
– HEALTH

IN HIGH PLACES / Braddon, Mary Elizabeth – British Fiction Archive: Unit 5 – 9 – uk Bell [830]

IN HISTORIAM CREATONIS MOSAICAM COMMENTATIO = ERLAEUTERUNGEN ZUR MOSAISCHEN SCHOEPFUNGS-GESCHICHTE / Pianciani, G B – (In German. Includes bibliographical references) – Regensburg: Friedrich Pustet, 1853 – 1mf – 9 – 0-8370-6930-0 – 1986-0930 – us A.T.L.A. [220]

IN HISTORIAM IUDICUM POPULI ISRAEL...COMMENTARIUS / Chytraeus, D – Francofurti ad Moenum, 1589 – 6mf – 9 – ne IDC [240]

IN IBIN OCIDI IN TERNARIUM... ANNOTATIONES / Sanchez de las Brozas, Francisco – 1598 – 9 – 1.50f – sp Bibl Santa Ana [450]

IN IEREMIAM PROPHETAM...COMMENTARIUM... / Bugenhagen, J – VVittembergiae, 1546 – 13mf – 9 – ne IDC [240]

IN INVESTIGANDA MONCHATUS ORIGINE... / Bornemann, F W B – Goettingen, 1885 – 3mf – 8 – Dfl13.00 – ne Slangenburg [240]

IN LEPER-LAND : BEING A RECORD OF MY TOUR OF 7,000 MILES AMONG INDIAN LEPERS: INCLUDING SOME NOTES ON MISSIONS... / Jackson, John – (Includes index of places) – London: Marshall, [1901?] – 1mf – 9 – 0-8370-6128-8 – 1986-0128 – us A.T.L.A. [240]

IN LEVITICVM,...COMPLECTEN... / Chytraeus, D – Vvitebergae, 1569 – 6mf – 9 – ne IDC [240]

IN LIBROS SENTENTIARUM COMMENTARIA / Estius, G – Duaci. Tomus 1-4. 1616 – 67mf – 8 – ne Slangenburg [240]

IN LIBRUM DUODECIM PROPHETARUM COMMENTARII / Ribera, F – Duaci, 1611 – 30mf – 8 – ne Slangenburg [220]

IN LIGHT TIMES – Las Vegas, NV. 1989 – 1+ r – 1 – $50.00 ($50.00y) – U04858 – us Library Micro [071]

IN LINGUAM GALLICAM ISAGOGE / Sylvius, Dit Jacques Dubois – 1531 – 9 – fr I.C.S. [450]

IN LONGFELLOWS PANTOFFELN : UND ANDERE GESCHICHTEN / Allen, Philip Schuyler – Goettingen: W F Kaestner, 1892 – 1r – 1 – us U.W. Library [830]

IN LUCULENTUM ET SACROSANCTUM EVENGELIUM...SECUNDUM LUCAM COMMENTARIORUM LIB. 9 / Bullinger, H – Tiguri, 1557 – 12mf – 8 – ne Slangenburg [240]

IN LUV UN LEE / Lau, Fritz – Hamburg: M Glogau, 1918 – 1r – 1 – us U.W. Library [830]

IN MAREMMA / Ouida – British Fiction Archive: Unit 3 – 9 – uk Bell [830]

IN MATHEO / Radbertus, Pascasius – 1984 – 38mf – 9 – Bf3,750.00 – 2-503-63562-8 – be Brepols [220]

IN MEMORIAM / Stimpson, Thomas Morrill – Essex Bar Assoc., Salem, Mass. n.p., 1899?. 23 p. LL-475 – 1 – us L of C Photodup [340]

IN MEMORIAM: A DISCOURSE OCCASIONED BY THE DEATH OF THE LATE A. W. LILLIE, ESQ., AND DELIVERED IN THE CONGREGATIONAL CHURCH, GUELPH, ON SABBATH EVENING, OCTOBER 18TH, 1868 / Clarke, William Fletcher – Guelph, Ont., 1869. 00677. (Pre-1900 Canadiana) – 9 – cn C.I.H.M. [920]

IN MEMORIAM BROADMAN HARTWELL CRUMPTON *see* MISCELLANEOUS BOOKS AND PAMPHLETS

IN MEMORIAM. CONSTANT GUILLOU / Philadelphia. Bar – Philadelphia: Stern, 1872. 25p. LL-1198 – 1 – us L of C Photodup [340]

IN MEMORIAM...AND OTHER GENEALOGICAL DATA ON THE FIELD FAMILY / Field, Samuel – 1 – $50.00 – us Presbyterian [920]

IN MEMORIAN : JERONIMO VYCENTE GOMES – [s.l.] Sem Data – 1,5,6 – bl Biblioteca [072]

IN MEMORY OF THE BRAVE MEN WHO MET THEIR DEATH WHILE IN THE DISCHARGE OF THEIR DUTIES AT THE ST URBAIN STREET FIRE ON SUNDAY, APRIL 29, 1877: AND WHOSE FUNERALS ARE TO TAKE PLACE THIS DAY / Crankshaw, James – Montreal: s.n., 1877. 00374. (Pre-1900 Canadiana) – 9 – cn C.I.H.M. [971]

IN MONSUN UND PORI / Wenig, Richard – Berlin: Safari Verlag, c1922. 161p. plates – 1 – us U.W. Library [940]

IN NATALITIAM MEMORIAM R. PATRIS D. MARTINI LVTHERI... / Cramer, D – VVitebergae, 1598 – 1mf – 9 – ne IDC [240]

IN NON-UNION MINES: THE DIARY OF A COAL DIGGER IN CENTRAL PENNSYLVANIA, AUGUST-SEPTEMBER 1921 / Hapgood, Powers – New York: Bureau of Industrial Research, 1922.48p – 1 – us U.W. Library [331]

IN NOVUM TESTAMENTUM ANNOTATIONES / Erasmus, Desiderius – Basileae, in officina Frobeniana, 1540 – 35mf – 8 – ne Slangenburg [220]

IN NVMEROS...ENARRATIO / Chytraeus, D – Vitebergae, 1572 – 6mf – 9 – ne IDC [240]

IN OMNES BEATI PAULI ET SEPTEM CATHOLICAS APOSTOLORUM EPISTOLAS COMMENTARIA / Estius, G – Parisiis, 1679 – 44mf – 8 – ne Slangenburg [220]

IN OMNES D. PAULI EPISTOLAS : ITEM IN CATHOLICAS COMMENTARII / Estius, Guilielmus – (Includes indexes) – Nova editio. Parisiis: Ludovico Vives. 3v. 1891 – 6mf – 9 – 0-8370-6662-X – 1986-0662 – us A.T.L.A. [220]

IN OMNES DIVI PAULI APOSTOLI, ET ALIAS SEPTEM CANONICAS EPISTOLAS...COMMENTARIA.. / Politus, Ambrosius C – 1566 – 1 – us A.T.L.A. [240]

IN ORATIONES QUASDAM CICERONIS ETC / Asconius – 14th and 15th cents. Holkham mss. 392, 367. Holkham Hall, Norfolk, England – 1 – uk Microform Academic [450]

IN OTHER WORDS / Moreno Izquierdo, Juan – 1882 – 9 – $1.50f – sp Bibl Santa Ana [190]

IN PRISON : BEING A REPORT BY KATE RICHARDS O'HARE TO THE PRESIDENT OF THE UNITED STATES AS TO THE CONDITIONS UNDER WHICH WOMEN FEDERAL PRISONERS ARE CONFINED IN THE MISSOURI STATE PENITENTIARY... / O'Hare, Kate Richards – (Filmed with materials relating to the author's pardon) – St Louis, MO: Publ by Frank P O'Hare, c1920 – 1 – us Res Libr [360]

IN PROPHETAM HOSEAM COMMENTARIUS / Tarnow, Johannes – 1646 – 1 – us A.T.L.A. [240]

IN PSALMOS (SIECLE 7) / Augustinus, St – Autun – 1r – 5,6 – sp Cultura [220]

IN PSALMVM 118TH...PRAELECTIONES,... / Chytraeus, D – Rostochii, 1590 – 1mf – 9 – ne IDC [240]

IN PURSUIT OF HAPPINESS / Tolstoy, Leo – Trans. by Mrs. Aline Delano. Boston: D. Lothrop Company, c1887 – 193p 1r – 1 – us U.W. Library [460]

IN QUATUOR SACRO-SANCTA IESU CHRISTI EVANGELIA. SCHOLIA / Gagneius, Ioan. – Parisiis, 1660 – Dfl46.00 – ne Slangenburg [220]

IN QUATUOR SACRO-SANCTA IESU CHRISTI EVANGELIA..SCHOLIA / Gagneius, Ioan. – Parisiis, 1660 – 13mf – 8 – ne Slangenburg [220]

IN QUEST OF A LAW OF RECOGNITION / Graham, M W – Berkeley, 1933 – 1mf – 1 – ILM-1675/1 – ne IDC [327]

IN QUEST OF LIGHT / Smith, Goldwin – New York: Macmillan, 1906 – 1mf – 9 – 0-8370-6383-3 – 1986-0383 – us A.T.L.A. [240]

IN RE: GERMANY – A critical bibliography of books and magazine articles on Germany. New York. Feb 1942-Mar 1944 – 1r – 1 – gw Mikrofilm [943]

IN REGULAM DIVI BENEDICTI COMMENTARIUS / Trithemius, J – Valencis, 1608 – 18mf – 8 – Dfl63.00 – ne Slangenburg [240]

IN REGULAM S. BENEDICTI EXPOSITIO / Bernardi Abbatis Casinensis – Monte Casino, 1894 – 11mf – 8 – Dfl39.00 – ne Slangenburg [240]

IN REGVM DVOS VLTIMOS LIBROS, ANNOTATIONES...POST SAMUELEM IAM PRIMU EMISSAE... / Bugenhagen, J – Norembergae, 1526 – 3mf – 9 – ne IDC [240]

IN REIH' UND GLIED : ROMAN / Spielhagen, Friedrich – Leipzig: L Staackmann, 1890 – 1r – 1 – us U.W. Library [830]

IN RELIEF OF DOUBT / Welsh, Robert Ethol – London: H.R. Allenson, 1902. 1 fiche – 9 – us A.T.L.A. [240]

IN REMEMBRANCE-ADDRESS ON OCCASION OF THE DEATH OF CHARLES GREELY LORING. / Bartol, Cyrus Augustus – Boston, The Society, 1867. 32 p. LL-470 – 1 – us L of C Photodup [340]

IN REVIEW : CANADIAN BOOKS FOR CHILDREN – 1967-74 – 1r – 1 – $68.00 – cn Library Assoc [420]

IN SACRAM BEATI JOHANNIS APOSTOLI APOCALIPSIN COMMENTARII / Ribera, F – Antverpiae, 1594 – 11mf – 8 – ne Slangenburg [220]

IN SACRO...HUOR EVANGELIA / Trejo, Gutierre – 1554 – 9 – 1.50f – sp Bibl Santa Ana [240]

IN SACROSANCTUM EVANGELIUM DOMINI NOSTRI IESU CHRISTI SEC. MARCUM COMMENTARIORUM LIB. 6 / Bullinger, H – Tiguri, 1554 – 5mf – 8 – ne Slangenburg [240]

IN SACROSANCTUM IESU CHRISTI..EVANGELIUM SECUNDUM IOANNEM ENARRATIONES / Ferus, Ioan. – Antverpiae, 1556 – 19mf – 8 – ne Slangenburg [220]

IN SACROSANCTUM IESU CHRISTI..EVANGELIUM SECUNDUM MATHEUM..ENARRATIONES / Ferus, Ioan. – Lugduni, 1609 – 11mf – 8 – ne Slangenburg [220]

IN SACROSANCTUM IOANNIS EVANGELIUM COMMENTARIE / Toletus, Franciscus – Coloniae Agrippinae, 1611 – 36mf – 8 – ne Slangenburg [240]

IN SACROSANCTUM JOANNIS EVANGELIUM COMMENTARII / Toledo, Francisco de – Romae. 2v. 1592 – 16mf – 9 – CA-74/1 – ne IDC [240]

IN SCARLET AND GREY : STORIES OF SOLDIERS AND OTHERS. BY FLORENCE HENNIKER AND THE SPECTRE OF THE REAL BY THOMAS HARDY AND FLORENCE HENNIKER / Henniker, Florence – Boston: Roberts, 1896 – 1 roll – 1 – 1-55879-393-3 – uk Libr Preservation [830]

IN SEARCH OF AN INDONESIAN IDENTITY / Ruslan, Abdulgani – SE 2590 1. 1960? – 9 – ne IDC [320]

IN SENTENTIAS THEOLOGICAS PETRI LOMBARDI COMMENTARIUM LIBRI QUATTUOR 1556 / Durandus de S Porciano – 34mf – 8 – ne Slangenburg [290]

IN SILK ATTIRE: A NOVEL / Black, William – British Fiction Archive: Unit 4 – 9 – uk Bell [830]

IN SITU – (v8-. 1984-. 5,6,9) – v1-. 1977- – 1 – us UMI [500]

IN SITU CONSERVATION OF LIVESTOCK AND POULTRY – 1992 – 119p – it F.A.O. [636]

IN SOMALIA : NOTE E IMPRESSIONI DI VIAGGIO / Stefanini, Giuseppi – Firenze: F Le Monnier, 1922 – 1 – us Res Libr [960]

IN SPAIN / Andersen, Hans Christian – Trans., Mrs. Bushby. London: R. Bentley, 1864. 306p – 1 – us U.W. Library [946]

IN SPAIN WITH THE INTERNATIONAL BRIGADE : A PERSONAL NARRATIVE / Bayle, Constantino – London, 1938; Burgos: Razon y Fe, 1938 – 1 – sp Bibl Santa Ana [355]

IN SPAIN WITH THE INTERNATIONAL BRIGADE, A PERSONAL NARRATIVE – London, 1938. Fiche W958. (Blodgett Collection of Spanish Civil War Pamphlets) – 9 – us H.U. College Libr [946]

IN SPIRITUS AUFBEWAHRT : HEITERE WIENER SKIZZEN / Poetzl, Eduard – Berlin: Carl Stephenson, [1942] – 1r – 1 – us U.W. Library [830]

IN SUPPORT OF THE RAISON D'ETRE : SOME ASPECTS OF THE POLITICAL GEOGRAPHY OF BOTSWANA / Knights, David B – Ypsilanti 1967 – us Res Libr [960]

IN TENTS IN TRANSVAAL / Hutchinson, Louisa – London: R Bentley, 1879 – 1 – us Res Libr [910]

IN THE BANQUETING HOUSE / Pearse, Mark Guy – 1902 – 9 – us A.T.L.A. [240]

IN THE CIRCUIT COURT OF APPEALS FOR THE EIGHTH CIRCUIT. DECEMBER TERM, 1909. NO.3150-NO.3163 UNITED STATES APPELLANT V. JAMES P. ALLEN ET AL. / U.S. Department of Justice – Washington, Govt. Print. Off., 1909 180 p. LL-2353 – 1 – us L of C Photodup [340]

IN THE CIRCUIT COURT OF APPEALS FOR THE EIGHTH CIRCUIT. DECEMBER TERM, 1909. NO.3161-3163; 3150-3160 UNITED STATES, APPELLANT V. WALTER P. NICHOLS. / U.S. Department of Justice – Washington, Govt. Print. Off., 1909 30 p. LL-2355 – 1 – us L of C Photodup [340]

IN THE DAYS OF LAGGAN PRESBYTERY, 1908 / Lecky, Alexander G – Also: The Laggan and its Presbyterianism, 1905; Ulster. General Synod, Records, 1691-1820, 1890, 1897, 1898 – 1 – $50.00 – us Presbyterian [240]

IN THE DAYS OF THE COMET / Wells, H G – London: Macmillan and Co., 1906 – 1 roll – 1 – uk Libr Preservation [830]

IN THE DAYS OF THE COUNCILS : A SKETCH OF THE LIFE AND TIMES OF BALDASSARE COSSA (AFTERWARD POPE JOHN THE TWENTY-THIRD) / Kitts, Eustace J – London: Constable, 1908 – 2mf – us A.T.L.A. [240]

IN THE DISPERSION – 1962-68. Superseded by Dispersion and Unity – 1 – us UMI [270]

IN THE EARLY DAYS : THE REMINISCENCES OF PIONEER LIFE ON THE SOUTH AFRICAN DIAMOND FIELDS / Angove, John – Kimberley: Handel House, 1910 – 1 – us Res Libr [960]

IN THE EXCHEQUER COURT OF CANADA:.. / Berlinguet, Francois Xavier – Ottawa?, 1876?. 02309. (Pre-1900 Canadiana) – 9 – cn C.I.H.M. [340]

IN THE FAR EAST : LETTERS FROM GERALDINE GUINNESS IN CHINA / Taylor, Howard (Mrs); ed by Guiness, Lucy Evangeline – London: Morgan & Scott; New York: Fleming H Revell, [1889?] – 1mf – 9 – 0-8370-6154-7 – 1986-0154 – us A.T.L.A. [920]

IN THE FOOTPRINTS OF CHARLES LAMB / Martin, Benjamin Ellis – London: R. Bentley and Son, 1891 – 1 roll – 1 – 1-55879-346-1 – uk Libr Preservation [420]

IN THE FOOTSTEPS OF CADILLAC / Burton, Clarence Monroe – Detroit?: Wolverine, 1899. 02006. (Pre-1900 Canadiana) – 9 – cn C.I.H.M. [910]

IN THE HEART OF BANTULAND : A RECORD OF TWENTY-NINE YEARS' PIONEERING IN CENTRAL AFRICA AMONG THE BANTU PEOPLES, WITH A DESCRIPTION OF THEIR HABITS, CUSTOMS, SECRET SOCIETIES AND LANGUAGES / Campbell, Dugald – London: Seeley, Service, 1922 – 1 – us Res Libr [306]

IN THE HOUSEHOLD OF FAITH / Smith, Charles Ernest – New York: Longmans, Green, 1896, c1895 – 1mf – 9 – 0-8370-8868-2 – 1986-2868 – us A.T.L.A. [230]

IN THE KING'S SERVICE / Watson, Charles Roger – Philadelphia, Pa.: Board of Foreign Missions of the United Presbyterian Church of N.A., c1905 – 1mf – us A.T.L.A. [240]

IN THE LAND OF THE OIL RIVERS : THE STORY OF THE QUA IBOE MISSION / M'Keown, Robert L – London: Marshall Bros, 1902 – us Res Libr [960]

IN THE LAND OF THE STRENUOUS LIFE / Klein, Felix – Chicago: A.C. McClurg, 1905 – 1mf – us A.T.L.A. [240]

IN THE MATTER OF EXXON CORPORATION ET AL : RECORDS OF THE FEDERAL TRADE COMMISSION'S CASE AGAINST THE MAJOR OIL COMPANIES / U.S. Federal Trade Commission – (Basic Collection, 1973-77: 23r ISBN: 0-89093-200-X. 1978. $2,215.00; Supplements, 1978-81: 9r ISBN: 0-89093-482-7. 1982. $860.00. With printed guides) – 1 – us UPA [380]

IN THE MIDST OF ALARMS / Barr, Robert – New York: F. Stokes Co., c1894. 03348. (Pre-1900 Canadiana) – 9 – cn C.I.H.M. [830]

IN THE NEW CAPITAL, OR, THE CITY OF OTTAWA IN 1999 / Galbraith, John – Toronto: Toronto News, 1897. 03283. (Pre-1900 Canadiana) – 9 – cn C.I.H.M. [971]

IN THE POWER OF THE SPIRIT : OR, CHRISTIAN EXPERIENCE IN THE LIGHT OF THE BIBLE / Boardman, William Edwin – Boston: Willard Tract Repository, 1875 – 1mf – 9 – 0-8370-2733-0 – 1985-0733 – us A.T.L.A. [240]

IN THE PUBLIC INTEREST – State University at Buffalo. v1-13. 1990-93 – 9 – $36.00 set – us Hein [340]

IN THE QUEEN'S BENCH: IN APPEAL FROM SUPERIOR COURT, MONTREAL: REVEREND ROBERT DOBIE, PETIONER-APPELLANT VS. BOARD FOR THE MANAGEMENT OF THE TEMPORALITIES FUND OF THE PRESBYTERIAN CHURCH OF CANADA... : APPELLANTS' FACTUM WITH APPENDIX / Dobie, Robert – Montreal: MacMasters, Hall & Greenshields, 1880. 02167. (Pre-1900 Canadiana) – 9 – cn C.I.H.M. [971]

IN THE SHADOW OF THE BUSH / Talbot, P A – London. 1912. BA-373 2 – 8 – ne IDC [960]

IN THE SUPERIOR COURT: THE REVEREND ROBERT DOBIE, PETITIONER, VS. BOARD FOR THE MANAGEMENT OF THE TEMPORALITIES' FUND OF CANADA, THE PRESBYTERIAN CHURCH OF CANADA, IN CONNECTION WITH THE CHURCH OF SCOTLAND. ET AL., RESPONDENTS / Dobie, Robert – Montreal?: s.n., 1878?. 02166. (Pre-1900 Canadiana) – 9 – cn C.I.H.M. [971]

IN THE SUPREME COURT OF SOUTH AFRICA (APPELLATE DIVISION) IN THE MATTER BETWEEN BENJAMIN POGRUND, APPELLANT, AND DR PERCY YUTAR, RESPONDENT – [s.l: s.n, 19–?] – 1 – us Res Libr [960]

IN THE TIGER JUNGLE:...MISSIONARY WORK AMONG THE TELUGUS OF INDIA / Chamberlain, Jacob – New York: Fleming H. Revell, 1896. 218p. 1 fiche – 9 – us A.T.L.A. [240]

IN THE VALLEY OF THE NILE : A SURVEY OF THE MISSIONARY MOVEMENT IN EGYPT / Watson, Charles Roger – New York: F.H. Revell, c1908 – 1mf – us A.T.L.A. [240]

IN THE VOLUME OF THE BOOK, OR, THE PROFIT AND PLEASURE OF BIBLE STUDY / Pentecost, George Frederick – New York: Ward & Drummond, 1880.1 fiche – 9 – us A.T.L.A. [240]

IN THEORY ONLY – v. 1-. 1975- – 1,5,6,9 – us UMI [780]

IN THESE TIMES – Chicago, IL. 1977-86 – 12r – 1 – $600.00 – R04301 – us Library Micro [071]

IN THESE TIMES – v.1. 1976 – 1 – us UMI [073]

IN TOBIAM. IN PROVERBIA. IN CANTICA CANTICORUM. IN HABACUC / Beda Venerabilis – 1983 – 13mf – 9 – Bf1,550.00 – 2-503-61194-X – be Brepols [240]

IN TREUE FEST : GESCHICHTLICHER ROMAN / Achleitner, Arthur – 2. durchges. Aufl. Leipzig: Hesse & Becker, [19–?] – 1r – 1 – us U.W. Library [830]

IN 12 ARISTOTELIS METAPH / Halensis, Alexander – Venetiis, de Karera, 1572 – 43mf – 9 – ne Slangenburg [240]

IN UNITY – Australia. v14-31. 1967-84 (complete) – 1r – 1 – ATLA S0809 – us A.T.L.A. [073]

IN VITRO – v1-20. 1965-84 – 1 – us UMI [576]

IN VITRO CELLULAR AND DEVELOPMENTAL BIOLOGY – v21-. 1985- – 1,5,6,9 – us UMI [576]

IN VIVO INSULIN ACTION ON WHOLE BODY AND INDIVIDUAL TISSUES IN OBESE SHHF/MCC-CP RATS WITH OR WITHOUT ACUTE EXERCISE / Gao, Jiaping & Sherman, William M – 1991 – 2mf – 9 – $8.00 – us Microform Publ [613]

IN ZULULAND WITH THE BRITISH THROUGHOUT THE WAR OF 1879 / Norris-Newman, Charles L – London: W H Allen, 1880 – 1 – us Res Libr [960]

INADEQUATE HYPERVENTILATION AS A DETERMINANT OF EXERCISE INDUCED HYPOXEMIA / Harms, Craig A – 1994 – 2mf – $8.00 – us Microform Publ [612]

INAINTE – Craiova, Romania. 1962-Jun 1980 – 26r – 1 – us L of C Photodup [949]

LA INAPRESABLE / Vera, Francisco – Madrid: Imp. Alrededor del Mundo, 1923 – 1 – sp Bibl Santa Ana [999]

INAUGURAL ADDRESS : DELIVERED TO THE UNIVERSITY OF ST. ANDREWS, FEB. 1ST 1867 / Mill, John Stuart – London: Longmans, Green, Reader, and Dyer, 1867 – 1 roll – 1 – 1-55879-883-8 – uk Libr Preservation [190]

INAUGURAL ADDRESS DELIVERED BEFORE KNOX COLLEGE METAPHYSICAL AND LITERARY SOCIETY ON THE EVENING OF FRIDAY, DECEMBER 1ST, 1871 / Armstrong, William Dunwoodie – Toronto: The Society, 1871? 00824. (Pre-1900 Canadiana) – 9 – cn C.I.H.M. [370]

AN INAUGURAL ADDRESS, "THREE CHANGES IN THEOLOGICAL INSTITUTIONS" / Boyce, James Petigru – 1856. South Carolina – 1 – 5.00 – us Baptist [240]

THE INAUGURAL ADDRESSES, ETC. DELIVERED AT THE OPENING OF THE LAW SCHOOL IN CONNECTION WITH DALHOUSIE UNIVERSITY, HALIFAX, NOVA SCOTIA...1883.. / Archibald, Adams George – Halifax: Nova Scotia Printing Co., 1884.02472.(Pre-1900 Canadiana) – 9 – cn C.I.H.M. [340]

INAUGURAL ADDRESSES OF PRESIDENTS / New Orleans Baptist Theological Seminary – 1927-59. 244p – 1 – 8.54 – us Baptist [240]

INAUGURAL DISCOURSE DELIVERED BEFORE THE UNIVERSITY IN CAMBRIDGE, 10 AUG 1819 / Norton, Andrews – 1819 – 9 – us A.T.L.A. [240]

AN INAUGURAL LECTURE / Bury, J B – Cambridge: University Press; New York: Macmillan [distributor], 1903 – 1mf – us A.T.L.A. [240]

INAUGURAL MEETING OF THE LOCAL COUNCIL OF WOMEN OF HALIFAX / Aberdeen and Temair, Ishbel Gordon – Address by Her Excellency the Countess of Aberdeen. August 24th, 1894. Halifax, N.S., Morning Herald. 1894. (Pre-1900 Canadiana) – 9 – cn C.I.H.M. [971]

INAUGURAL SPEECH ON STUDIUM GENERALE / Sardjito, K – Gadjah Mada University, Jogjakarta. SE 4469 1. 1959 – 9 – ne IDC [370]

INAYNEM – (Chicago). 1924-25 – 1 – us A.J.P.C. [071]

Inbar, Galit *see* THE POST-EXERCISE BLOOD PRESSURE RESPONSE TO ACUTE EXERCISE IN BORDERLINE HYPERTENSIVE WOMEN

Inbe, Hironari *see* IMBE-NO-HIRONARI'S KOGOSHUI, OR, GLEANINGS FROM ANCIENT STORIES

Inber, Vera Mikhailovna *see* SOLNECHNYI ZAIATS

INBREEDING AND OUTBREEDING; THEIR GENETIC AND SOCIOLOGICAL SIGNIFICANCE / East, Edward Murray – Philadelphia, London: J.B. Lippincott, c1919. 285p. illus., plates – 1 – us U.W. Library [576]

INC – v.1. 1979 – 1,5,6,9 – us UMI [073]

INCA CIVILIZATION – 1993 – 36p – 9 – 92-3-102684-4 – fr UNESCO [930]

Incantalupo, Patricia *see* THE PORTRAYAL OF WOMEN IN SPORT ADVERTISING IN TWO WOMEN'S FITNESS MAGAZINES

L'INCAPACITE DE LA FEMME MARIEE... / Aubry, E – Paris, 1933 – 4mf – 9 – ILM-3095/1 – ne IDC [340]

L'INCAPACITE DE LA FEMME MARIEE... / Aubry, E – Paris, 1933 – 4mf – 9 – ILM-3180/1 – ne IDC [340]

THE INCARNATE WORD : BEING THE FOURTH GOSPEL ELUCIDATED BY INTERPOLATION FOR POPULAR USE / Gill, William Hugh – Philadelphia: George W Jacobs, c 1900 – 1mf – 9 – 0-8370-3285-7 – 1985-1285 – us A.T.L.A. [220]

THE INCARNATION : A STUDY OF PHILIPPIANS 2. 5-11 / Gifford, Edwin Hamilton – (Includes bibliographical references) – New York: Dodd, Mead, 1897 – 1mf – 9 – 0-8370-3802-2 – 1985-1802 – us A.T.L.A. [220]

THE INCARNATION AND PRINCIPLES OF EVIDENCE / Hutton, Richard Holt – A THEOLOGICAL ESSAY. 1871 – 1 – us A.T.L.A. [240]

THE INCARNATION AND RECENT CRITICISM / Cooke, Richard Joseph – (Includes bibliographical references and index) – New York: Eaton & Mains; Cincinnati: Jennings & Graham, c1907 – 1mf – 9 – 0-8370-6039-7 – 1986-0039 – us A.T.L.A. [210]

INCARNATION OF THE LORD: A SERIES OF SERMONS / Briggs, Charles Augustus – New York: Scribner's, 1902. 1 fiche – 9 – us A.T.L.A. [240]

THE INCARNATION OF THE SON OF GOD; BEING THE BAMPTON LECTURES FOR THE YEAR 1891 / Gore, Charles – 1891 – 1 – us A.T.L.A. [240]

LES INCAS OU LA DESTRUCTION DE L'EMPIRE DU PEROU / Marmontel, M – Lyon: Bruyset, Tomo 2. 1817 – 1 – sp Bibl Santa Ana [972]

LES INCAS...EMPIRE DU PEROU / Marmontel, M – (Tomo II.1817. 1.50f; 9. Tomo III. 1817.1.50f; BSA; 9) – Tomo I. 1817 – 9 – 1.50f – sp Bibl Santa Ana [972]

INCENDIO DE CONVENTOS EN ESPANA Y SUPRESION DE COLEGIOS Y MISIONES ESPANOLAS EN ULTRAMAR / Alonso Getino, G – Madrid: Razon y Fe, 1932 – 1 – sp Bibl Santa Ana [240]

EL INCENDIO DE LA BIBLIOTECA / Bartholino, Tomas – Valencia: Editorial Castalia, 1949 – sp Bibl Santa Ana [020]

INCENTIVE MARKETING – v. 1-. 1905- – 1. – apply; v.143- 1977- 5,6,9 – us UMI [380]

INCENTIVE MOTIVATION, COMPETITIVE ORIENTATION AND GENDER IN COLLEGIATE ALPINE SKIERS / Chroni, Stiliani – 1994 – 2mf – $8.00 – us Microform Publ [150]

INCENTIVE MOTIVATION DIFFERENCES IN UNITED STATES MASTERS SWIMMERS / Mowrey, Rebecca J – 1989 – 173p 2mf – 9 – $8.00 – us Microform Publ [150]

INCENTIVE MOTIVATION OF FEMALE BASKETBALL PLAYERS ACROSS THREE AGE LEVELS / Drennan, Meredith L – Springfield College, 1994 – 2mf – 9 – $8.00 – PSY1843 – us Microform Publ [150]

INCENTIVES AND DISINCENTIVES FOR FARMERS IN DEVELOPING COUNTRIES – 1976 – 47p – it F.A.O. [338]

INCENTIVES FOR COMMUNITY INVOLVEMENT IN CONSERVATION PROGRAMMES – 1987 – 168p – it F.A.O. [360]

Inchambre, Diego de *see* NOTICIAS SOBRE LAS PROVINCIAS FRANCISCANAS DE CANARIAS. TENERIFE, 1966

THE INCHANTED FORREST / Geminiani, Francesco – An instrumental composition expressive of the same ideas as the poem of Tasso of that title. 1755 – 15 – us Sibley [780]

Inchaurre Aldape, Diego *see* COMPILACION DE ARTICULOS REFERENTES A LAS ORDENES...

Inchbald, Mrs. *see*
- EVERY ONE HAS HIS FAULT
- WIVES AS THEY WERE, AND MAIDS AS THEY ARE

THE INCIDENTAL BISHOP / Allen, Grant – London: C.A. Pearson, 1898. 05045. (Pre-1900 Canadiana) – 9 – cn C.I.H.M. [830]

INCIDENTAL ILLUSTRATIONS OF THE ECONOMY OF SALVATION: ITS DOCTRINES AND DUTIES / Palmer, Phoebe Worrell – 1855 – 9 – us A.T.L.A. [240]

LES INCIDENTS ET LES EXCEPTIONS DEVANT LES TRIBUNAUX MILITAIRES EN TEMPS DE PAIX ET AUX ARMEES / Pages, E L – Nouv. ed.. Baden-Baden: Regie autonome des publications officielles 1948. 246p. LL-4114 – 1 – us L of C Photodup [340]

INCIDENTS OF SOCIAL LIFE AMID THE EUROPEAN ALPS / Zschokke, Heinrich – New York: D Appleton & Co, 1844 – 1 – us U.W. Library [943]

LES INCIDENTS...DE LA GUERRE RUSSO-JAPONAISE... / Carre, H – Paris, n.d. – 2mf – 1 – ILM-926/1 – ne IDC [327]

INCIDER – v1-. 1983- – 1,5,6,9 – us UMI [073]

Inclan, M *see* REFLEXIONES SOBRE ADUANAS Y EFECTOS DE LA LEY PROHIVITIVA

DIE INCLUSEN IN DEUTSCHLAND VORNEHMLICH IN DER GEGEND DES NIEDERRHEINS UM DIE WENDE DES 12. UND 13. JAHRHUNDERTS / Basedow, A – Heidelberg, 1895 – 1mf – 8 – Dfl6.00 – ne Slangenburg [240]

THE INCOME TAX : A STUDY OF THE HISTORY, THEORY AND PRACTICE OF INCOME TAXATION AT HOME AND ABROAD / Seligman, Edwin R A – New York: Macmillan, 1914 – 8mf – 9 – $12.00 – LLMC 82-710 – us L.L.M.C. [336]

INCOME TAX ADMINISTRATION IN THE STATE OF ISRAEL / Anderson, Wayne F – Tel Aviv, 1956. LL-4195 – 1 – us L of C Photodup [336]

INCOME TAX APPEAL BOARD PRACTICE; A PRACTICAL TREATISE ON PROCEDURE BEFORE THE BOARD / Fordham, Reginald Sydney Walter – Montreal: CCH Canadian, 1953. 138p. LL-2334 – 1 – us L of C Photodup [340]

THE INCOMING MILLIONS / Grose, Howard B – New York: F.H. Revell, c1906. (Home mission study course; 4) – 1mf – us A.T.L.A. [240]

INCONGRUENCIAS LEGALES DE LAS FALTAS CONTRA LA PROPIEDAD DE CORCHERO Y COMPANIA / Carrasco Alvarez, Antonio – 1901. Imprenta. Corchero y Cia., Merida – sp Bibl Santa Ana [340]

INCONTROVERTIBLE FACTS REGARDING THE DESTRUCTION OF GUERNICA: SPEECH / Leizaola, Jesus Maria de – Washington, DC, 193? Fiche W994. (Blodgett Collection of Spanish Civil War Pamphlets) – 9 – us H.U. College Libr [946]

LA INCORPORACION DE LAS MASAS POPULARES A LA HISTORIA / Montseny, Frederica – Barcelona? 1937? Fiche W 1060. (Blodgett Collection of Spanish Civil War Pamphlets) – 9 – us H.U. College Libr [946]

...INCORPORATED 1882:... TO PROVIDE A CONVENIENT PLACE FOR SOCIAL AND BUSINESS PURPOSES / Albany Club – s.l., s.n., 1889?. (Toronto: Roswell & Hutchison). 04008. (Pre-1900 Canadiana) – 9 – cn C.I.H.M. [971]

INCORPORATED ACCOUNTANTS' JOURNAL *see* ACCOUNTANCY

INCORPORATING FORM SAMPLES OR INFORMATION FOR THE 50 STATES / Data Notes Staff – 1988 – 9 – $11.95 – us Continnuus [650]

INCORPORATING IN THE CAYMAN ISLANDS, UNITED KINGDOM, HONG KONG, DELAWARE AND OTHERS / Data Notes Staff – A How to Find or Locate Guide with some forms, 1989 – 9 – $19.95 – us Continnuus [380]

IN-COURT ORIENTATION PROGRAMS IN THE FEDERAL DISTRICT COURTS / Meierhoefer, Barbara S – Washington: FJC, Apr 1984 – 1mf – 9 – $1.50 – LLMC 95-837 – us L.L.M.C. [340]

THE INCREASE OF THE ISRAELITES IN EGYPT / Ashpitel, Francis – 1863 – 9 – us A.T.L.A. [240]

INCREASING VERTICAL JUMP : A COMPARISON BETWEEN TWO TRAINING PROGRAMS / Timmons, Scott A – Ball State University, 1996 – 1mf – 9 – PE 3675 – us Microform Publ [612]

L'INCUNABLE – Montreal: Bibliotheque nationale du Quebec. v18-20. 1984-1986. SEM16P359 – 3r – 5 – Can$24.00 – cn Bibl Nat [070]

INCUNABLES DESCONOCIDOS : ARS CONSTRUCTIONIS ORDINANDAE / Lopez Serrano, Mathilde – Madrid: CSIC, 1947. Sep. Sup. no 1 de Rev. Bibliografica y Documental (T.1, 1947, no 2, Abril-Junio) – 1 – sp Bibl Santa Ana [946]

INCUNABLES ESPANOLES : OBSIDIONIS RHODIE DESCRIPTO. DE GUILLERMO CROURSIN / Lopez Serrano, Mathilde – Madrid: CSIC, 1947. Sep. Sup. no 1 de Rev. Bibliografica y Documental (T.1, 1947, no 3 y 4. Julio-Diciembre) – 1 – sp Bibl Santa Ana [946]

INCUNABLES ESPANOLES DESCONOCIDOS : "DE MORIBUS" DE SENECA / Lopez Serrano, Mathilde – Madrid: CSIC, 1951. Sep. Rev. Bibliografica y Documental. (T.5, 1951, Fasciculos 1,2,3 y 4, Enero-Diciembre) – 1 – sp Bibl Santa Ana [946]

LES INCUNABLES ORIENTAUX... AU COMMENCEMENT DU 16 SIECLE / Schab, M – Paris, 1883 – 2mf – ne IDC [700]

INCUNABLES. RECUEIL DE 28 INCUNABLES CONSERVES A LA B.M. DE NANTES, RELIES ET MICROFILMES ENSEMBLE = SET OF 28 INCUNABULA KEPT BY THE PUBLIC LIBRARY OF NANTES, BOUND AND MICROFILMED TOGETHER – fr Armell [944]

INCUNABULA : THE PRINTING REVOLUTION IN EUROPE, 1455-1500 – (Comprehensive collection of the earliest printed books in Europe. Unit 1: Printing in Mainz before 1480. Unit 2: Classics in Translation. Unit 3: The Image of the World: Geography and Cosmography. Unit 4: Chronicles and Historiography Pt 1. Unit 5: Chronicles and Historiography Pt 2. Unit 6: The Image of the World: Travellers Tales. Unit 7: Printing in Italy Pt 1. Unit 8: Printing in Italy Pt 2. Unit 9: Printing in Italy Pt 3. Unit 10: Printing in Italy Pt 4. Units 11-15: Medical Pts 1-5. Units 16-17: Hebraica Pts 1-2) – Units 1-3 1992. Units 4-6 1993. Units 7-10 1994. Units 11-15 1995. Units 16-17 1996. Units 18-20 over the next few years – us Primary [090]

INCUNABULA MEDICA : A STUDY OF THE EARLIEST PRINTED MEDICAL BOOKS 1467-1480 / Osler, W – Oxford, 1923 – 7mf – ne IDC [610]

INCUNABULA SCIENTIFICA ET MEDICA / Klebs, A C – Bruges, 1938 – 7mf – ne IDC [610]

INDABA – Lovedale, South Africa. 1 Aug 1862-28 Feb 1865.1 reel – 1, 16 diazo available at reduced price – sa SA Libr [072]

INDAGACIONES SOBRE LA GEOGRAFIA / Aguirre, Manuel de – 1782 – 1mf – 9 – Pta1,000.00 – 84-7848-136-2 – sp Pentalfa [900]

INDAGATIONES MATHEMATICAE – v17-28. Amsterdam. 1955-66 – 5,9 – Dfl1,320.00; Dfl110.00v – ne Swets [510]

INDAGINI SU HEGEL, E SCHIARIMENTI FILOSOFICI / Croce, Benedetto – Bari: G. Laterza, 1952 – 1 – us U.W. Library [190]

O INDAYA – Dores do Indaya, 15 May 1898; Nov 1901; 28 Jan 1906 – 1,5,6 – bl Biblioteca [072]

INDE AB A. 911 USQUE AD A. 1197 (MGH LEGES 2D: 1.BD) – 1893 – Dfl67.00 – ne Slangenburg [240]

INDE AB A. 1198 USQUE AD A. 1272 (MGH LEGES 2D: 2.BD) – 1896 – Dfl63.00 – ne Slangenburg [240]

INDE AB A. 1273 USQUE AD A. 1298 (MGH LEGES 2D: 3.BD) – 1904-1906 – Dfl67.00 – ne Slangenburg [240]

INDE AB A. 1298 USQUE AD A. 1313 (MGH LEGES 2D: 4.BD) – 1906-1911 – Dfl147.00 – ne Slangenburg [240]

INDE AB A. 1313 USQUE AD A. 1324 (MGH LEGES 2D: 5.BD) – 1909-1913 – Dfl88.00 – ne Slangenburg [240]

INDE AB A. 1325 USQUE AD A. 1330 (MGH LEGES 2D: 6.BD) – 1914-1927 – Dfl74.00 – ne Slangenburg [240]

INDE AB A. 1345 USQUE AD A. 1348 (MGH LEGES 2D: 8.BD) – 1910-1926 – Dfl77.00 – ne Slangenburg [240]

INDENTURE RECORDS / Huron County. Ohio. County Home – 1850-1859 – 1r – 1 – $32.50r – us Archival [324]

INDENTURE RECORDS / Wood County. Ohio. County Home – 1870-1890 – 1r – 1 – $32.50r – us Archival [324]

INDENTURES / Van Wert County, Ohio. Van Wert, City. City Council – 1870-1893 – 1r – 1 – $32.50r – us Archival [324]

L'INDEPENDANCE – Chronique bimensuelle. no. 1-48. Paris. mars 1911-juil 1913 – 1 – fr A.C.R.P.P. [073]

L'INDEPENDANCE – Lowell, MA. v1 n4. 11 avr 1890-v1 n25. 19 sep 1890 – 1r – 1 – Can$35.00 – cn Can Microfilming [071]

L'INDEPENDANCE : ORGANE DES JEUNESSES PATRIOTES. NUMERO SPECIAL DEDIE A L'ABBE GROULX / ed by O'Leary, Walter-P – Montreal, Canada. 6 fev 1936 – 1r – 1 – Can$25.00 – cn Can Microfilming [360]

L'INDEPENDANCE : ORGANE OFFICIEL DU RASSEMBLEMENT POUR L'INDEPENDENCE NATIONALE – Montreal. v1-6. 1962-68. SEM35P23 – 1r – 1 – Can$41.00 – cn Bibl Nat [073]

L'INDEPENDANCE – Leopoldville: Patrice Lumumba, sep 1959-feb 1960 – us Res Libr [072]

INDEPENDANCE – Port-au-Prince: Imp. de "L'Action", sep 1954-dec 1956 – 24r – 1 – us Res Libr [072]

L'INDEPENDANCE BELGE – Brussels, 1850-1940 – 319r – 1 – uk British Libr Newspaper [072]

L'INDEPENDANCE BELGE – Bruxelles. 27 fevr-30 juin 1848, juil 1850-52, juil-dec 1865 – 1 – fr A.C.R.P.P. [949]

L'INDEPENDANCE CANADIENNE / ed by Lanctot, Mederic – Montreal, Canada. 15 fev 1868-25 avr 1868 – 1r – 1 – Can$31.25 – cn Can Microfilming [072]

L'INDEPENDANCE CANADIENNE – Montreal, Trois-Rivieres, Canada. 13 oct 1894-13 jun 1896 – 1 – Can$35.00 – cn Can Microfilming [072]

L'INDEPENDANCE DES MAGISTRATS, DES AVOCATS ET DES OFFICIERS MINISTERIELS EN REPUBLIQUE DE GUINEE – 1988 – sz I.C.J. [340]

L'INDEPENDANCE ECONOMIQUE DU CANADA FRANCAIS / Bouchette, Errol – Arthabaska: Impr. d'Arthabaskaville, 1906. SEM16P112 – 1r – 5 – Can$9.00 – cn Bibl Nat [330]

L'INDEPENDANCE FRANCAISE – (Filmed as pt of: Commune de Paris newspapers) – Paris: Impr Kugelmann, may 13-19 1871 – us Res Libr [072]

L'INDEPENDANCE MEDICALE : JOURNAL PANAMERICAIN DES SCIENCES MEDICALES FRANCAISES, DE PHARMACIE, ETC – Montreal, Canada. v2 n2 15 jun 1921; v2 n11. 15 mar 1922 – 1r – 1 – Can$30.00 – cn Can Microfilming [610]

L'INDEPENDANT / ed by Buies, Arthur – Montreal, Quebec, Canada. v1 n19. 29 sep 1870-v1 n45. 10 dec 1870 – 1r – 1 – Can$35.00 – cn Can Microfilming [072]

L'INDEPENDANT – Fall River, MA. v1n7. 8 mai 1885-v71 n13. 11 avr 1955 – 1r – 1 – Can$65.00 – cn Can Microfilming [071]

L'INDEPENDANT : FEUILLE DE COMMERCE, POLITIQUE ET LITTERAIRE – Rio de Janeiro, 21 Apr-24 Jun 1827 – 1,5,6 – bl Biblioteca [072]

L'INDEPENDANT – Quebec, Canada. v1 n2. 5 jul 1854; v1 n4. 12 jul 1854 – 1r – 1 – Can$25.00 – cn Can Microfilming [072]

L'INDEPENDANT – Windsor, Ontario. 25 mar 1892 – 1r – 1 – Can$25.00 – cn Can Microfilming [072]

L'INDEPENDANT – Port-au-Prince: Impr du Commerce. 1ere annee, n3-n6. 23 mai-13 juin 1877 – 1 sheet – 9 – us Res Libr [072]

INDEPENDANT – London, UK. 8 May-19 Jun 1830 – 1 – uk British Libr Newspaper [072]

L'INDEPENDANT DE CHATEAU-GONTIER : HEBDOMADAIRE REPUBLICAIN – (1 missing number) – Hebd., Chateau-Gontier (Mayenne), oct. 1944-aout 1968 (1 no. manquant) – 7r – 1 – F8,303.90 – fr Armell [072]

L'INDEPENDANT DE WOONSOCKET – Woonsocket. R.I. 1935-1942 – 1 – us UMI [071]

L'INDEPENDANT DES BOUCHES-DU-RHONE – Journal des interets democratiques, commerciaux, artistiques et litteraires. no. 2-3, 6-12. Marseille. mai-juin 1848 – 1 – fr A.C.R.P.P. [073]

L'INDEPENDANT DES PYRENEES – Journal republicain quotidien. Fond. Emile Garet. Pau. 1939-19 aout 1944 – 1 – fr A.C.R.P.P. [073]

L'INDEPENDANT DES PYRENEES ORIENTALES – Journal politique, litteraire, agricole, commercial et scientifique. no. 115. Perpignan. 3 fevr 1847. no. 222-272, fragm. 19 fevr-5 aout 1848 – 1 – fr A.C.R.P.P. [073]

L'INDEPENDANTISTE / ed by Roy, Raoul – Montreal, Canada. mar 1963-printemps v1 n3. 1968 – 1r – 1 – Can$25.00 – cn Can Microfilming [072]

INDEPENDENCE – Georgetown. Guyana. -w. 20 Feb 1960-22 Jul 1961. (1 reel) – 1 – uk British Libr Newspaper [072]

INDEPENDENCE – Maseru, Dept of Information and Broadcasting. oct 1-7, 1976 – us Res Libr [072]

L'INDEPENDENCE BELGE – [Brussels]: P Werll, jul 1938-may 9 1940 – 14r – 1 – us Res Libr [949]

THE INDEPENDENCE COUNTY CHRONICLE – v1-5, 1959-64. F-1085 to F-1089 – 9 – us A.G.L.L. [978]

INDEPENDENCE DEBATE : OFFICIAL REPORT, HANSARD, UNREVISED / Parliament of Basutoland, Senate – Maseru: The Senate, 1966 – us Res Libr [320]

INDEPENDENCE ENTERPRISE – Independence, OR. -w. 6 Dec 1894-29 Aug 1901; 15 Oct 1908-31 May 1913; 5 Jan 1917-26 June 1969. – 1 – us U.O. Library [071]

INDEPENDENCE ENTERPRISE AND MONMOUTH HERALD – Independence, OR. -w. 3 Jul 1969-31 Jul 1975. 5 rolls – 1 – us U.O. Library [071]

INDEPENDENCE ENTERPRISE AND WEST SIDE – Independence OR. May 29 1902-Dec 31 1903 – 1 – us U.O. Library [071]

Independence. Missouri. Calvary Baptist Church *see* SCRAPBOOK

INDEPENDENCE MONITOR – Independence, OR. -w. 1 Aug 1912-6 Jul 1918. 1 roll – 1 – us U.O. Library [071]

THE INDEPENDENCE OF THE HOLY SEE / Manning, Henry Edward – London: Henry S. King, 1877 – 1mf – us A.T.L.A. [240]

INDEPENDENCE TRADE FAIR, LIMBE, JUL 4-7, 1964 : NATURAL RESOURCES EXHIBIT – Zomba, Govt Press, 1964 – us Res Libr [380]

INDEPENDENCER – (v6 1977 Can$50.00 5. Ceased v6 1977) – Ottawa. v1-5. 1971-76 – 9,5 – Can$28.00 – cn Micromedia [073]

EL INDEPENDENCIA – Malabon: [s.n.], nov 22 1898 – us Res Libr [072]

LA INDEPENDENCIA – Malabon: Impr del Asilo de Malabon, sep-dec 1898-jan-mar 1899 – us Res Libr [072]

LA INDEPENDENCIA DE UN PUEBLO CON UN HIJO ILUSTRE FRAY PEDRO DE GODOY / Parron Fernandez, Felipe – Badajoz: Imprenta de la Diputacion Provincial, 1976 – sp Bibl Santa Ana [240]

INDEPENDENCIA POLITICA ARGENTINA; INDEPENDENCIA ECONOMICA ARGENTINA – [Buenos Aires?, 1947?] – 1 – CSUXAHZ5767-B – us Hoover Inst Photo [320]

INDEPENDENT – 1-121. 1848-1928 – 1 – us UMI [330]

INDEPENDENT – 1995 – 6 – sz Infoprint [072]

INDEPENDENT – (Also known as: Marin Independent Journal, Novato) – San Rafael, CA. 1927-48 – 88r – 1 – $4,400.00 – B02926 – us Library Micro [073]
INDEPENDENT – Anderson. S.C. 1944- – 1 – us UMI [071]
INDEPENDENT – Antelope. Mont. 1923-1924 – 1 – us UMI [071]
INDEPENDENT – Arlington, OR. -w. 12 Oct 1900-3 May 1901; 27 Feb 1913-17 Feb 1916. 2 rolls – 1 – us U.O. Library [071]
INDEPENDENT – Ashland. Ky. 1922- – 1 – us UMI [071]
INDEPENDENT – Atlanta. Ga. 1904-1928 – 1 – us UMI [071]
INDEPENDENT – Big Rapids. Mich. and Magnet. 1870-84 – 1 – us UMI [071]
INDEPENDENT – Birmingham. Ala. 1963-1969 – 1 – us UMI [071]
INDEPENDENT – Booneville. Miss. 1934-1935 – 1 – us UMI [071]
INDEPENDENT – Brookport. Ill. -w. 1966- – 1 – us UMI [071]
INDEPENDENT – Buckner. Kan. 1879-1881 – 1 – us UMI [071]
INDEPENDENT – Burlington. Kan. 1876-1907; 1910-1914 – 1 – us UMI [071]
INDEPENDENT – Carson City, NV. 1863-1864 – 1r – 1 – $50.00 – U04457 – us Library Micro [071]
INDEPENDENT – Chewelah. Wash. 1907-1908 – 1 – us UMI [071]
INDEPENDENT – Clovis. Calif. -w. 1941-56 – 1 – us UMI [071]
INDEPENDENT – Colon, Panama. 1904-1914 (incomplete) – 4r – 1 – us L of C Photodup [072]
INDEPENDENT – Edinboro. Pa. 1943-57 – 1 – us UMI [071]
INDEPENDENT – Elko. Nev. -w. 1949- – 1 – us UMI [071]
INDEPENDENT – Elko, NV. 1869-73; 1875-1914; 1923; 1929; 1911-42 (scats) – 13r – 1 – $650.00 – U04500 – us Library Micro [071]
INDEPENDENT – Elmore, Ohio. 1888-1900 – 4r – 1 – $32.50r – us Archival [071]
INDEPENDENT – Forsyth. Mont. 1923-1959; 1966- – 1 – us UMI [071]
INDEPENDENT – Georgetown, 1973-1978 – 14r – 1 – cn Preston [971]
INDEPENDENT – Gothenburg. Neb. 1892-1897 – 1 – us UMI [071]
INDEPENDENT – Grand Island. Neb. 1945- – 1 – us UMI [071]
INDEPENDENT – Harrison, NE. -w. Sept 1892-Jul 1893 – 1 – us NE Hist [071]
INDEPENDENT – Harvard. Ill. -w. 1867-1913 – 1 – us UMI [071]
INDEPENDENT – Havre. Mont. 1954-1957 – 1 – us UMI [071]
INDEPENDENT – Hawarden. Iowa. -w. 1951- – 1 – us UMI [071]
INDEPENDENT – Helena. Mont. 1874-1943 – 1 – us UMI [071]
INDEPENDENT – Hillsboro. Or. 1893-1931 – 1 – us UMI [071]
INDEPENDENT – Hillsboro OR. Sep 29 1882 + – 1 – us U.O. Library [071]
INDEPENDENT – Hudson. Ohio. 1897-1919 – 1 – us UMI [071]
INDEPENDENT – Huntingburg. Ind. 1937-1970 – 1 – us UMI [071]
INDEPENDENT – (Includes index. Also known as: County Independent; San Lorenzo Valley Sun) – Santa Cruz, CA. 1950-58; 1976-78 – 8r – 1 BC02957 – $400.00 – us Library Micro [071]
INDEPENDENT – Issaquah. Wash. 1900-1917 – 1 – us UMI [071]
INDEPENDENT – Katoomba, Mar 14 1930-Mar 5 1931 – 9 – at Pascoe [072]
INDEPENDENT – Libertyville. Ill. -w. 1916-29 – 1 – us UMI [071]
INDEPENDENT – Lincoln. Neb. 1889-1907 – 1 – us UMI [071]
INDEPENDENT – Long Beach. Calif. 1938- – 1 – us UMI [071]
INDEPENDENT – Los Angeles, CA. 1988 – 36+ r – 1 – $1,800.00 ($300.00y) – H04046 – us Library Micro [071]
INDEPENDENT – Martinsburg. West Virginia. 1874-1899 – 1 – us UMI [071]
INDEPENDENT – Mill Valley, CA. 1908-10 – 1r – 1 – $50.00 – B02458 – us Library Micro [071]
INDEPENDENT – Montrose. Pa. -w. 1955- – 1 – us UMI [071]
INDEPENDENT – New Cumberland. West Virginia. 1915-1964 – 1 – us UMI [071]
INDEPENDENT – New Platz. N.Y. 1869-1885 – 1 – us UMI [071]
INDEPENDENT – New York. n151-191. 1965-69 – 1r – 1 – us Ross [071]
INDEPENDENT – New York. N.Y. 1849-1928 – 1 – us UMI [071]
INDEPENDENT – Noblesville. Ind. 1878-1888 – 1 – us UMI [071]
INDEPENDENT – Okanogan. Wash. -w. 1907-55 – 1 – us UMI [071]
INDEPENDENT – Oskaloosa. Kan. -w. 1870-1900 – 1 – us UMI [071]
INDEPENDENT – Oswego. Kan. -w. 1872-76 – 1 – us UMI [071]
INDEPENDENT – Ottawa. Kan. and Journal. 1902-06 – 1 – us UMI [071]
INDEPENDENT – Pasadena. Calif. 1955-1960; 1961- – 1 – us UMI [071]
INDEPENDENT – Paulding, Ohio. 1859-63 – 1r – 1 – $32.50r – us Archival [071]
INDEPENDENT – Payne, Ohio, 1885-1885 – 1r – 1 – $32.50r – us Archival [978]
INDEPENDENT – Pittsburg. Calif. 1928-44 – 1 – us UMI [071]
INDEPENDENT – Portland OR. 2 issues ca 1932 – 1 – us U.O. Library [071]
INDEPENDENT – Raton. N.M. -w. 1884-89 – 1 – us UMI [071]
INDEPENDENT – Reno. Nev. 1956-58 – 1 – us UMI [071]
INDEPENDENT – Richmond. Calif. 1945-1949 – 1 – us UMI [071]
INDEPENDENT – Rising City. Neb. 1892-1930 – 1 – us UMI [071]
INDEPENDENT – Saco. Mont. 1958-1959; 1966- – 1 – us UMI [071]
INDEPENDENT – Santa Barbara. Calif. 1883-1913 – 1 – us UMI [071]
INDEPENDENT – Seward. Neb. and pred. 1892-1964 – 1 – us UMI [071]
INDEPENDENT – Shelton. Wash. 1930-1936 – 1 – us UMI [071]
INDEPENDENT – Sheperdstown. West Virginia. -w. 1934-58 – 1 – us UMI [071]
INDEPENDENT – Sutro, NV. 1875-76 – 1r – 1 – $50.00 – U04758 – us Library Micro [071]
INDEPENDENT – Tillamook OR. Dec 31 1902, Jan 7 Apr 18 1903 – 1 – us U.O. Library [071]
INDEPENDENT – Toronto, Canada. 1849-50 – 1 reel – 1 – $68.00 – cn Library Assoc [971]
INDEPENDENT – Union City. Pa. 1957-1969 – 1 – us UMI [071]
INDEPENDENT – Vancouver. Wash. -w. 1875-1910 – 1 – us UMI [071]
INDEPENDENT – Wahoo. Neb. 1876-1886 – 1 – us UMI [071]
INDEPENDENT : WEEKLY REPUBLICAN NEWSPAPER – Willoughby, OH. 11 Jan 1917-27 May 1920 – 3r – 1 – us Western Res [071]
INDEPENDENT – Weston. West Virginia. 1894-1968 – 1 – us UMI [071]
INDEPENDENT *see* CLARE INDEPENDENT ETC
THE INDEPENDENT – Broderick, CA. 1946-48 – 1r – 1 – $50.00 – C02080 – us Library Micro [071]
THE INDEPENDENT – Broderick. Calif. 1946-48 – 1 – us UMI [071]
THE INDEPENDENT – Castle Rock. Wash. -w. 1917-19 – 1 – us UMI [071]
THE INDEPENDENT – (Cont by: North East Bay Independent and Gazette) – Richmond, CA. 1910-78 – 124r – 1 – $6,200.00 – B02692 – us Library Micro [071]
THE INDEPENDENT – Fenton. Mich. 1935-1969 – 1 – us UMI [071]
THE INDEPENDENT – Freetown. Sierra Leone. -f. Dec 1874-May 1878. (1 reel) – 1 – uk British Libr Newspaper [072]
THE INDEPENDENT – Great Britain, Oct 1986- – 1 – us Primary [072]
THE INDEPENDENT – Lachute, Canada. 21 apr 1888-v4 n16. 26 sep 1891 – 1r – 1 – Can$30.00 – cn Can Microfilming [072]
THE INDEPENDENT – Livermore, CA. 1964-66; 1967-83; 1987- – 55+ r – 1 – $2,750.00 ($50.00y) – B02351 – us Library Micro [071]
THE INDEPENDENT – (Merged into Outlook and Independent, later New Outlook.) v. 49-121. 1897-1928 – 1,5,6 – us Princeton Micro [073]
THE INDEPENDENT – Nevada City, CA. Jul 1969-1978; 1981-Aug 1982 – 8r – 1 – $400.00 – B02514 – us Library Micro [071]
THE INDEPENDENT – Paso Robles, CA. 1894-95; 1964-65 – 2r – 1 – $100.00 – B02614 – us Library Micro [071]
THE INDEPENDENT – Quebec, Canada. v1 n3. 16 sep 1878 – 1r – 1 – Can$25.00 – cn Can Microfilming [072]
THE INDEPENDENT – Seoul. An exponent of Korean News. v. 1-3. 7 Apr 1896-1898 – 1 – us NY Public [072]
THE INDEPENDENT : STREET EDITION – Richmond, CA. 1976-Feb 1977 – 8r – 1 – $400.00 – B02693 – us Library Micro [071]
THE INDEPENDENT *see* THE DAILY INDEPENDENT
THE INDEPENDENT – Monrovia: [s.n.], nov 29 1954; mar 12 1955 – us Res Libr [072]
INDEPENDENT AGENT – (v.77-. 1979- 5,6,9) – v.66-. 1969-. Continues: American Agency Bulletin – 1 – us UMI [073]
INDEPENDENT AGENT *see* AMERICAN AGENCY BULLETIN
INDEPENDENT AMERICAN – Ballston Spa. N.Y. 1808-18 – 1,3 – us Readex [071]
INDEPENDENT AMERICAN – Georgetown. D.C. 1809-1811 – 1,3 – us Readex [071]
INDEPENDENT AMERICAN – New Orleans. La. 1964 – 1 – us UMI [071]
INDEPENDENT AND ADVERTISER – Huntington. West Virginia. 1873-1876 – 1 – us UMI [071]
INDEPENDENT AND JOURNAL – New York, NY. 1783-88 – 1,3 – us Readex [071]
INDEPENDENT AND N. SIMCOE FRELANCE – Collingwood, 1895-1896 – 1r – 1 – cn Preston [971]
INDEPENDENT AND SUN *see* HUMBOLDT INDEPENDENT
INDEPENDENT AND TRIBUNE – Clovis, CA. 1976- – 15+ r – 1 – $750.00 ($50.00y) – B02118 – us Library Micro [071]
INDEPENDENT CALISTOGIAN – Calistoga, CA. 1877-92; 1894-96 – 5r – 1 – $250.00 – B02089 – us Library Micro [071]
INDEPENDENT CHRONICLE – Boston. Mass. 1776-1820 – 3 – us Readex [071]
INDEPENDENT COAST OBSERVER – Gualala, CA. 1969 – 19+ r – 1 – $950.00 ($90.00y) – B03233 – us Library Micro [071]
INDEPENDENT DEMOCRAT – Elyria. Ohio. 1852-77 – 1 – us UMI [071]
INDEPENDENT DEMOCRAT – North Platte. Neb. and Independent Era. 1891-1905 – 1 – us UMI [071]
INDEPENDENT DEMOCRAT AND THE INDEPENDENT ERA – North Platte, NE. -w. (-sw 1899-1900). Mar 1891-Apr 1893, scattered issues missing; May 1893-Apr 1894; Aug-Sept 1894; Nov 1894-Nov 1895; Jan 1896-Sept 1898; Nov 1898-May 1900; Apr 1901-Mar 1902, scattered issues missing; Aug 1902-Jul 1905 – 1 – us NE Hist [071]
INDEPENDENT ENQUIRER – (Also known as: Oakland Enquirer) – Oakland, CA. 1885-1886 – 1r – 1 – $50.00 – C03364 – us Library Micro [071]
INDEPENDENT EXAMINER – Beaver Crossing, NE. -w. Mar. 1905-Nov. 1906 – 1 – us NE Hist [071]
THE INDEPENDENT FORESTER AND FORESTER'S HERALD – [London, Ont?]: Independent Order of Foresters, [1880-1930] – 9 – cn C.I.H.M. [630]
INDEPENDENT GAZETTEER – Philadelphia. Pa. 1782-1796 – 1,3 – us Readex [071]
INDEPENDENT HERALD – (Also known as: Morning Herald. Cont: Valley Herald) – Yuba City, CA. 1947-79 – 99r – 1 – $4,950.00 – B03126 – us Library Micro [071]
INDEPENDENT HERALD – Hinton. West Virginia. 1909-1919 – 1 – us UMI [071]
INDEPENDENT HERALD – Hinton. West Virginia. -w. 1903-52 – 1 – us UMI [071]
INDEPENDENT HERALD – Pineville. West Virginia. -w. 1941- – 1 – us UMI [071]
INDEPENDENT HERALD – Yuba City and Marysville. Calif. and Bi-County Farmer. -W. 1954- – 1 – us UMI [071]
THE INDEPENDENT HINDUSTAN – San Francisco: Hindustan Gadar Party. v1 n1-11. sep 1920-1921 – 1 – us Res Libr [950]
INDEPENDENT JEWISH PRESS SERVICE – New York. N.Y. 1941-47 – 1 – us A.J.P.C. [071]
Independent Labor League of America *see* WORKERS AGE
Independent Labour Party. Great Britain *see*
- ANNUAL REPORTS
- ARCHIVES OF THE INDEPENDENT LABOUR PARTY, SERIES 1
- ARCHIVES OF THE INDEPENDENT LABOUR PARTY, SERIES 2
- ARCHIVES OF THE INDEPENDENT LABOUR PARTY, SERIES 3
- ARCHIVES OF THE INDEPENDENT LABOUR PARTY, SERIES 4
- MINUTE BOOKS
- REPORTS, RESOLUTIONS AND SPECIAL NATIONAL CONFERENCE REPORTS, 1914-60
- WEEKLY NOTES FOR SPEAKERS

Independent Labour Party. Great Britain. *see* REPORT: 1893-1934
INDEPENDENT LEADER – Sacramento, CA. 1922-1932 – 5r – 1 – $250.00 – C03428 – us Library Micro [071]
THE INDEPENDENT LEDGER – Boston. Mass. 1778-1786 – 3 – us Readex [071]
INDEPENDENT MECHANIC – New York. -w. 6 Apr 1811-26 Sep 1812. (45 ft) – 1 – uk British Libr Newspaper [071]
INDEPENDENT MESSENGER – Emporia. Va. -w. 1957- – 1 – us UMI [071]
INDEPENDENT MESSENGER – Nevada City, CA. 1987 – 1r – 1 – $50.00 – B03621 – us Library Micro [071]
INDEPENDENT METHODIST ARCHIVES : INTRODUCTORY NOTES / Wigan. - Independent Methodist Bookroom – N.p. [1988] – 1mf – 9 – ne IDC [240]
INDEPENDENT NEWS – Oakwood, Ohio. 1913-15 – 1r – 1 – $32.50r – us Archival [071]
INDEPENDENT NEWS – Portland OR. Jan 22-Nov 3 1934 – 1 – us U.O. Library [071]
INDEPENDENT NEWS : WEEKLY NEWSPAPER – (Scattered issues) – New Richmond, OH, 2 Jan 1913-29 Jan 1914 – 1r – 1 – us Western Res [071]
INDEPENDENT OBSERVER – Conrad. Mont. 1956-1957; 1966-1967 – 1 – us UMI [071]
INDEPENDENT OBSERVER – Scottdale. Pa. 1882-1888; 1890-1909; 1911-1915; 1917-1918; 1920-1925 – 1 – us UMI [071]
INDEPENDENT ON SUNDAY – Great Britain, Jan 1990- – 1 – us Primary [072]
Independent Order of Good Templars, Grand Lodge of British Columbia *see* BC GOOD TEMPLAR
Independent Order of Good Templars. Grand Lodge of Manitoba and N.W.T. *see* THE MANITOBA GOOD TEMPLAR
INDEPENDENT PATRIOT – Jackson. Mo. 1820-1826 – 1 – us UMI [071]
INDEPENDENT POWER *see* ALTERNATIVE SOURCES OF ENERGY
INDEPENDENT PRESS – British West Indies. St. Lucia. 1843-1844 – 1 – us UMI [072]
INDEPENDENT PRESS – Wakeman, Ohio. 1875-1915 – 9r – 1 – $32.50r – us Archival [071]
INDEPENDENT RECORD – Helena. Mont. 1874-1936; 1943- – 1 – us UMI [071]
INDEPENDENT REGISTER – Libertyville. Ill. -w. 1930- – 1 – us UMI [071]
AN INDEPENDENT REPORT ON THE BELAU PLEBISCITE OF 1984 – Koror: Belau Pacific Center, nov 1984 – 1mf – 9 – $1.50 – LLMC 82-100G, Title 29 – us L.L.M.C. [323]
INDEPENDENT REPUBLICAN – Portland OR. May 12 19 1894 – 1 – us U.O. Library [071]
INDEPENDENT. (SAN LORENZO VALLEY SUN) – Santa Cruz. Calif. 1950-58 – 1 – us UMI [071]
Independent Socialist Party. Germany *see* FREIHEIT
Independent Television Authority. (Great Britain) *see* ANNUAL REPORT AND STATEMENT OF ACCOUNTS
INDEPENDENT TIMES AND COUNTY OF STANSTEAD ADVERTISER – Stanstead, Canada. v2 n2. 11 jan-v2 n40. 26 sep 1888 – 1r – 1 – Can$40.00 – cn Can Microfilming [072]
INDEPENDENT WHIG – London. 1808-11. (1811 imperfect). -w. 1 reels – 1 – uk British Libr Newspaper [072]
L'INDEPENDENTE – New York, NY. Oct 1924-Dec 1926 – 2r – 1 – us I.H.R.C. [073]
O INDEPENDENTE – Manhuassu, 10 Apr, Nov 1910; Apr 1911; Nov 1912; Feb 1913; Jul, Oct 1915; 19 Nov 1916 – 1,5,6 – bl Biblioteca [072]
O INDEPENDENTE : SEMANARIO POLITICO, LITTERARIO E DE INFORMACOES – Tres Coracoes, 27 Feb 1916 – 1,5,6 – bl Biblioteca [072]
O INDEPENDENTE – Hong Kong: E Ferreira, sep 1869-oct 1897* – 1r – 1 – us Res Libr [072]
INDEPENDENT/INDEPENDENT ON SUNDAY – Oct 1986-1987 – 1 – F6,679.00 – sz Infoprint [072]

INDEPENDENT/INDEPENDENT ON SUNDAY – Oct 1988-1994 – 1 – F6,941.00 – sz Infoprint [072]

INDEPENDENT/INDEPENDENT ON SUNDAY – Subscription – 1 – F7,771.00 – sz Infoprint [072]

INDEPENDENT-LEADER *see* SACRAMENTO TRIBUNE-PROGRESS

THE INDEPENDENT-REPORTER – Skowhegan: Independent-Reporter Co, 1913-51 – 24r – 1 – us Res Libr [072]

Indermaur, John *see* AN EPITOME OF LEADING COMMON LAW CASES; WITH SOME SHORT NOTES THEREON...SMITH'S LEADING CASES

Inderwick, Frederick Andrew *see* THE INTERREGNUM (A.D. 1648-1660); STUDIES OF THE COMMONWEALTH, LEGISLATIVE, SOCIAL, AND LEGAL

INDEX / Baptist Southern Convention – (1954-65. 5.00; 1) – 1845-1953 – 1 – 10.99 – us Baptist [240]

INDEX / Colorado Genealogist – v1-10, 1941-1949. 5 fiches. F-0945 – 9 – us A.G.L.L. [920]

INDEX / Defense Metals Information Center – 1952-71. By title, subject, author and report numbers – 1mf – 9 – 25.00 – us Updata [670]

INDEX – Greenwood. S.C. 1897-1918 – 1 – us UMI [071]

INDEX – Petersburg. Va. 1866-1873 – 1 – us UMI [071]

THE INDEX – A weekly journal devoted to the exposition of the mutual interests of Great Britain and the Confederate States of America. London. -w. May 1862-Aug 1865. (2 reels) – 1 – uk British Libr Newspaper [072]

THE INDEX / Bryant, Stratton and Odell's Business College – Toronto: [s.n. 1866-18– or 19–] – 9 – cn C.I.H.M. [650]

THE INDEX – Pittsburgh. Pa. 1900-1930 – 1 – us UMI [071]

THE INDEX – Uniontown. Pa. 1899-1927 – 1 – us UMI [071]

INDEX ALPHABETIQUE DES NOMS DE 3400 FAMILLES DE DOUZE ENFANTS VIVANTS / Dumais, A – Quebec: Departement des Terres, Mines et Pecheries: Departement des Terres et Forets, 1904-1906 – 4mf – 9 – Can$9.00 – cn Bibl Nat [304]

INDEX ALTER PLANTARUM, QUAE IN HORTO ACADEMICO LUGDUNO-BATAVO ALUNTUR / Boerhaave, H – Lugduni Batavorum. 2pts. 1727 – 23mf – ne IDC [580]

INDEX AND CATALOGUE / Moravian Archives. London – 1 – uk Microform Academic [240]

INDEX AND LEGISLATIVE HISTORY : UNIFORM CODE OF MILITARY JUSTICE, 1950 / U.S. Army Court of Military Appeals – 1950; 1985. n.p,n.d. – 34mf – 9 – $51.00 – LLMC 87-320A – us L.L.M.C. [324]

INDEX ANIMALIUM / Sherborn – 1758-1800 – 5 – uk Microform Academic [590]

INDEX APOLOGETICUS, SIVE, CLAVIS IUSTINI MARTYRIS OPERUM : ALIORUMQUE APOLOGETARUM PRISTINORUM / Goodspeed, Edgar J – Leipzig: J.C. Hinrichs, 1912 – 1mf – us A.T.L.A. [240]

INDEX BIBLIOGRAPHIQUE COLONIAL : CONGO BELGE ET RUANDA-URUNDI / ed by Heyse, Theodore – Bruxelles: Falk, [1937-40] – 1 – us Res Libr [960]

INDEX BOOKS, 1789-1928, AND MINUTES AND BENCH DOCKETS, 1789-1870 / U.S. District Courts. Southern District of Georgia – RG 21. 3 rolls – 1 – M1172 – us Nat'l Archives [340]

INDEX BRYOLOGICUS / Paris, E. G – Ed. 2. 5 v. Paris. 1903-06. B-1143 2 – 8 – ne IDC [580]

INDEX BY COUNTY TO PRIVATE LAND GRANT CASES / U.S. District Courts. California. Northern and Southern Districts – 1 roll – 1 – T1216 – us Nat'l Archives [340]

INDEX BY DISTRICT TO U.S.C.G. REPORTS OF ASSISTANCE, 1917-38 / U.S. Coast Guard – T919 – 19r – 5 – us Nat'l Archives [977]

INDEX BY FLOATING UNIT TO U.S.C.G. REPORTS OF ASSISTANCE, 1917-35 / U.S. Coast Guard – T921 – 5r – 5 – us Nat'l Archives [977]

INDEX BY STATION TO U.S.C.G. REPORTS OF ASSISTANCE, 1924-38 / U.S. Coast Guard – T920 – 9r – 5 – us Nat'l Archives [977]

INDEX CANONUM : THE GREEK TEXT, AN ENGLISH TRANSLATION AND A COMPLETE DIGEST OF THE ENTIRE CODE OF CANON LAW OF THE UNDIVIDED PRIMITIVE CHURCH / Fulton, John – New York: Thomas Whittaker, 1892,c1883 – 1mf – us A.T.L.A. [240]

INDEX CATALOG OF THE ARMY MEDICAL LIBRARY, 1880-1961 / U. S. Surgeon General – 3 – us Readex [610]

INDEX CATALOG OF THE LIBRARY OF THE SURGEON GENERAL'S OFFICE / U. S. Surgeon General – Series 1-5. 1880-1961 – 1,5,6 – us Princeton Micro [610]

INDEX CORPORIS HISTORICODIPLOMATICI LIVONIAE, ESTHONIAE, CURONIAE. KURZER AUSZUG AUS DERJEIGEN URKUNDEN-SAMMLUNG. FUER DIE GESCHICHTE UND DAS ALTE STAATSRECHT LIV-, EST-, UND KURLANDS / Napiersky, C E – 2v. Riga, Tartu. 1833-35. BR-9840 1 – 9 – ne IDC [947]

INDEX DECLARATIONS OF INTENT / Ottawa County. Ohio. Probate Court – n.d. – 1r – 1 – us Archival [324]

INDEX DER ANTIKEN KUNST UND ARCHITEKTUR = INDEX OF ANCIENT ART AND ARCHITECTURE. MONUMENTS OF GREEK AND ROMAN CULTURA L HERITAGE IN THE PHOTOGRAPHIC COLLECTION OF THE GERMAN ARCHAEOLOGOCAL INSTITUTE IN ROME : DENKMAELER DES GRIECHISCH-ROEMISCHEN ALTERTUMS IN DER PHOTOSAMMLUNG DES DEUT HEN ARCHAEOLOGISCHEN INSTITUTS IN ROM / ed by Deutsches Archaeologisches Institut. Rome – (Special Editions: Idealplastik. 1991. Fiches 1-279. DM2,100. ISBN 3-598-32084-1; Portraitplastik. 1991. Fiches 280-514. DM1,780. ISBN 3-598-32085-X; Sarkophage. 1991. Fiches 515-698. DM1,380. ISBN 3-598-32086-8; Reliefs. 1991. Fiches 699-889. DM1,480. ISBN 3-598-32087-6; Figuerliche Bauplastik. 1991. Fiches 890-1004. DM880. ISBN 3-598-32088-4; Architekturteile 1991. Fiches 1005-1031. DM200. ISBN 3-598-32089-2; Inschriften. 1991. Fiches 1032-1071. DM300. ISBN 3-598-32090-6; Stuck. 1991. Fiches 1072-1080. DM120. ISBN 3-598-32091-4; Malerei. 1991. Fiches 1081-1167. DM660. ISBN 3-598-32092-2; Mosaik. 1991. Fiches 1168-1211. DM360. ISBN 3-598-32093-0; Topographie. 1991. Fiches 1212-1551. DM2,500. ISBN 3-598-32094-9; Vasen. 1991. Fiches 1552-1764. DM1,600. ISBN 3-598-32095-7; Terrakotta. 1991. Fiches 1765-1854. DM700. ISBN 3-598-32096-5; Bronze/Unedle Metalle. 1991. Fiches 1855-1951. DM730. ISBN 3-598-32097-3; Kleinkunst. 1991. Fiches 1952-1994. DM330. ISBN 3-598-32098-1; Index and Commentary Volume. 1991. 420p. hb. DM38. Free for subscribers to the complete edition. ISBN 3-598-32083-3) – 1988-1990 – 2,714 fiches (1:24) – 9,17 – silver DM15,000.00 – 3-598-32070-1 – gw Saur [700]

INDEX DES CORPS PUBLICS ET INCORPORES ET DU DROIT PRIVE ET LOCAL.. / Baudouin, Philibert – Montreal: C.O. Beauchemin, 1897?. 06702. (Pre-1900 Canadiana) – 9 – cn C.I.H.M. [340]

INDEX DES DOCUMENTS MICROFICHES A MADAGASCAR – 1988 – 9 – $10.00 – 92-9053-213-0 – et ILRI [636]

INDEX DES DOCUMENTS MICROFICHES AU BENIN – 1986 – 9 – $9.50 – 92-9053-210-6 – et ILRI [636]

INDEX DES DOCUMENTS MICROFICHES AU BURKINA FASO – 1994 – 106p – 9 – $7.00 – 92-9053-516-4 – et ILRI [636]

INDEX DES DOCUMENTS MICROFICHES AU MALI – 1991 1610 $10.00 – 9 – 92-9053-226-2 – et ILRI [636]

INDEX DES DOCUMENTS MICROFICHES AU NIGER – 1987 – ix/149p – 9 – $16.00 – 92-9053-211-4 – et ILRI [636]

INDEX DES DOCUMENTS MICROFICHES AU RWANDA – 1984 – 9 – $6.00 – 92-9053-209-2 – et ILRI [636]

INDEX DES DOCUMENTS MICROFICHES AU SENEGAL – 1983 – 9 – $6.50 – 92-9053-206-8 – et ILRI [636]

INDEX DES DOCUMENTS MICROFICHES AU TOGO – 1987 – 9 – $7.50 – 92-9053-212-2 – et ILRI [636]

INDEX DES DOCUMENTS MICROFICHES AU ZAIRE – 1982 – 9 – $5.00 – 92-9053-205-X – et ILRI [636]

INDEX DES DOCUMENTS MICROFICHES PAR L'EQUIPE CIPEA/CRDI EN COTE D'IVOIRE – 1984 – 9 – $6.00 – 92-9053-208-4 – et ILRI [636]

INDEX DES NOMS SCIENTIFIQUES AVEC LEURS EQUIVALENTS MALGACHES / Boiteau, P – Dictionnaire des noms malgaches de vegetaux – 9 – F130.00 – fr Ethnologie [580]

INDEX DESMIDIACEARUM LOCUPLETISSIMUS / Nordstedt, C F O – Lundae, 1896. 310 pp. suppl. Berolini, 1908. 149 pp. B-6385 1 – 9 – ne IDC [580]

INDEX DU BULLETIN DES RECHERCHES HISTORIQUES / Roy, Antoine – Montreal: Archive nationales du Quebec: Bibliotheque nat. du Quebec, 1988 – 9mf – 9 – Can$45.00 (brochure + fiches) – cn Bibl Nat [971]

INDEX ENTOMOLOGICUS : OR, A COMPLETE ILLUSTRATED CATALOGUE... / Wood, W – London, 1839 – 7mf – ne IDC [590]

INDEX ENTOMOLOGICUS, SISTENS OMNES INSECTORUM SPECIES IN G.W.F. PANZERI FAUNA INSECTORUM GERMANICA DESCRIPTAS / Panzer, G W F – Norimbergae, 1813. viii,216p. Z-1530/2 – 8 – ne IDC [590]

INDEX EXPURGATORIOUS ANGLICANUS : OR A DESCRIPTIVE CATALOGUE OF THE PRINCIPAL BOOKS PRINTED OR PUBLISHED IN ENGLAND, WHICH HAVE BEEN SUPPRESSED OR BURNT BY THE COMMON HANGMAN, OR CENSURED, OR FOR WHICH THE AUTHORS, PRINTERS, OR PUBLISHERS HAVE BEEN PROSECUTED / Hart, W H – London: John Russell Smith, 1872 – 4mf – 9 – $6.00 – LLMC 92-105 – us L.L.M.C. [320]

INDEX FILICUM / Christensen, C F A – Hafniae. 1905; Suppl. 1906-1912. Hafniae. 1913; Suppl. 1913-1916. Hafniae. 1917; Suppl. 1917-1933. Hafniae. 1934. B-558 2 – 8 – ne IDC [580]

INDEX FILICUM / Christiansen, Carl – v. 1 and 2. 1753-1905 and 1906-12 – 7 – uk Microform Academic [580]

INDEX FILICUM: A SYNOPSIS, WITH CHARACTERS, OF THE GENERA AND AN ENUMERATION OF THE SPECIES OF FERNS WITH SYNONYMS, REFERENCES ETC / Moore, T – London, 1857. 372 pp., 78 pls. B-5490 2 – 8 – ne IDC [580]

INDEX FUNGORUM / Hoffmann, H – Lipsiae. 1863. B-5035 2 – 8 – ne IDC [580]

INDEX GENERAL DES STATUTS DE LA PROVINCE DE QUEBEC DE 1899 A 1928 INC / Quebec. (Province). Laws, Statutes, etc – Quebec: Les Editions Themis, 1928. 222p. LL-2385 – 1 – us L of C Photodup [340]

INDEX ICONOLOGICUS, 1250-1940 / ed by Langedijk, Karia – (Links art images with literary and historical backgrounds. 60,000 entries, alphabetical by keyword) – 400mf – 9 – us UMI [700]

AN INDEX IN TWO PARTS TO EVANGELICAL SECTARIANS IN MISSIONERSKOE OBZRENIE, 1896-1916 / Wardin, Albert – 42p – 1 – us Baptist [240]

INDEX INSCRIPTIONUM BIRMANICARUM / Burma – (Publications Arch. Dept., Burma, no. 1). Rangoon, 1900. 10p. BI-705 – 9 – ne IDC [410]

INDEX JOURNAL – (Cont by: The Californian, Salinas) – Salinas, CA. 1928-42 – 42r – 1 – $2,100.00 – B02753 – us Library Micro [071]

INDEX JOURNAL – Greenwood. S.C. 1919- – 1 – us UMI [071]

INDEX JOURNAL *see* DAILY INDEX

INDEX, KENTUCKY MORTALITY RECORDS FOR THE YEARS ENDING JUNE 1, 1850, 1860, 1870 – Comp. and typed by the State of Kentucky D.A.R., 194-. 5 fiches. F-1062 – 9 – us A.G.L.L. [920]

INDEX LIBRARY / British Record Society Ltd – (Coll title: Publications of the English Record Societies, 1835-1972) – v1-88. 1888-1976 – 387mf – 9 – £2,030.00 – uk Chadwyck [941]

INDEX LIBRORUM PROHIBITORUM – (Bibliography in various languages; introduction in Latin) – [Vatican-City]: Typis Polyglottis Vaticanis, 1948 – 2mf – 9 – 0-8370-6941-6 – 1986-0941 – us A.T.L.A. [012]

INDEX LIBRORUM PROHIBITORUM (1559) – (1980 reprint by the Houghton Library) – Romae: Ex Officina Saluiana, 15 Feb 1559 – 1mf – 9 – $1.50 – LLMC 91-056 – us L.L.M.C. [340]

INDEX LIBRORUM PROHIBITORUM (LEO 13) – Romae: S C de Propaganda Fide, 1831 – 5mf – 9 – $7.50 – LLMC 91-055 – us L.L.M.C. [340]

INDEX LINGUAE VETERIS SCYTHO-SCANDICAE SIVE GOTHICAE... / Verelius, O – Uppsala, 1691 – 4mf – ne IDC [430]

INDEX LONDINENSIS TO ILLUSTRATIONS OF FLOWERING PLANTS : FERNS AND FERN ALLIES... / ed by Stapf, O – Oxford. v1-6. 1929-1941. 2 Suppls – 151mf – ne IDC [580]

INDEX MATERIARUM QUAE IN SINGULIS... / Lopez de Tovar, Gregorio – Madrid: Juan Hefray, 1611 – 1 – sp Bibl Santa Ana [020]

INDEX MEDICUS – (Abridged.) v. 1-. 1970- – 1. – apply; v.3-6; v.6- 1975- 9 – us UMI [610]

INDEX MEDICUS – (Series 2, v. 1-18. 1903-1920. Series 3, v. 1-6. 1921-1927. 529.00; 1,5,6) – v. 1-21. 1879-1899 – us Princeton Micro [610]

INDEX MEDICUS – v1-21, 1879-99; ser.2,v1-18, 1903-20; ser.3,v1-6, 1921-27 – 1 – us UMI [610]

INDEX MOLLUSCORUM GROENLANDIAE / Moeller, H P C – Hafniae. 1842. BZ-660 2 – 8 – ne IDC [590]

INDEX MOLLUSCORUM LITORA / Loven, S L – Z-631 2. 1845 – 8 – ne IDC [590]

INDEX NEW ZEALAND *see* INNZ

INDEX OF ALL ESTATES IN PROBATE IN SAN FRANCISCO 1850-1888 / Thomas, P J – San Francisco. Calif. Reel 37. (Cox Library Collection) – 5 – us Americana [978]

THE INDEX OF AMERICAN DESIGN *see*
- ARCHITECTURE AND NATIVE ART (TIAM, PT 3)
- THE ART AND DESIGN OF UTOPIAN AND RELIGIOUS COMMUNITIES (TIAM, PT 2)
- CERAMICS AND GLASS (TIAM, PT 8)
- DOMESTIC UTENSILS (TIAM, PT 5)
- FURNITURE AND DECORATIVE ACCESSORIES (TIAM, PT 6)
- SILVER, COPPER, PEWTER AND TOLEWARE (TIAM, PT 9)
- TEXTILES, COSTUME AND JEWELRY (TIAM, PT 1)
- TOOLS, HARDWARE, FIREARMS AND VEHICLES (TIAM PT 4)
- TOYS AND MUSICAL INSTRUMENTS (TIAM, PT 10)
- WOOD CARVINGS AND WEATHERVANES (TIAM, PT 7)

THE INDEX OF AMERICAN DESIGN (TIAM) / Washington, DC. National Gallery of Art; ed by Tinkham, Sandra Shaffer – (Coll covers every aspect of the decorative, folk & popular arts. Coll is divided into 10pts wh are also listed separately. Each is accompanied by its own printed catalogue. Complete coll is also accompanied by a consolidated catalogue & manual on b/w mf ISBN: 0-914146-94-7 £70) – (mf ed 1978) – 10pts on 291mf – 15 – £5,130.00 coll – uk Chadwyck [740]

AN INDEX OF ANCESTORS AND ROLL OF MEMBERS OF THE SOCIETY.. / Society of Colonial Wars. General Assembly – The Honor Roll-Services of members... during the World War 1917-18. New York, 1922. Military Books reel 2. (Cox Library Collection) – 5 – us Americana [350]

INDEX OF ASTRANA MARINS' VIDA EJEMPLAR Y HEROICA DE MIGUEL DE CERVANTES SAAVEDRA / Emerson, Phyllis S – 1r – 1 – $73.00 – us OmniSys [440]

INDEX OF BIRTHS, DEATHS AND MARRIAGES REGISTERED IN THE NORTHERN TERRITORY FOR THE PERIODS 1870-1902 – 5mf – 9 – A$50.00 – item 27 – at G.S.N.T. [920]

INDEX OF BOATS MENTIONED IN NT NEWSPAPERS NOVEMBER 1873-DECEMBER 1914 – 9 – A$5.00 – 0-949124-55-9 – item 23 – at G.S.N.T. [920]

INDEX OF CBI-IBT, POA, AND A-P OPINIONS / U.S. Army. Judge Advocate General. Board of Review – Washington: JAG Office, Military Justice Div, 1952 – 2mf – 9 – $3.00 – LLMC 84-226 – us L.L.M.C. [340]

INDEX OF CONFERENCE PROCEEDINGS RECEIVED, 1964-1988 / British Library. Document Supply Centre – 25-year cumulation of the centre's conference collection – 9 – £130.00 (+ VAT UK); £134.00 overseas – uk British Libr Humanities [010]

INDEX OF CURRENT EVENTS – Montreal, Canada. v2 n12. 4 apr 1889 – 1r – 1 – Can$25.00 – cn Can Microfilming [072]

THE INDEX OF CURRENT EVENTS – Montreal: H. Dalby, [1888-1891] – 9 – cn C.I.H.M. [320]

INDEX OF CURRENT HOSPITAL LITERATURE – v1-10. 1945-54 – 1 – us UMI [610]

INDEX TO COMPILED SERVICE RECORDS OF REVOLUTIONARY WAR SOLDIERS WHO SERVED WITH THE AMERICAN ARMY IN CONNECTICUT MILITARY ORGANIZATIONS / U.S. War Department. Collection of Revolutionary War Records – M920 – 25r – 1 – us Nat'l Archives [324]

INDEX TO COMPILED SERVICE RECORDS OF REVOLUTIONARY WAR SOLDIERS WHO SERVED WITH THE AMERICAN ARMY IN GEORGIA MILITARY ORGANIZATIONS / U.S. War Department. Adjutant General's Office – M1051 – 1r – 1 – us Nat'l Archives [324]

INDEX TO COMPILED SERVICE RECORDS OF VOLUNTEER SOLDIERS WHO SERVED DURING INDIAN WARS AND DISTURBANCES, 1815-58 / U.S. War Department. Adjutant General's Office – M629. Printed guide – 42r – 5 – us Nat'l Archives [324]

INDEX TO COMPILED SERVICE RECORDS OF VOLUNTEER SOLDIERS WHO SERVED DURING THE CHEROKEE DISTURBANCES AND REMOVAL IN ORGANIZATIONS FROM THE STATE OF GEORGIA / U.S. War Department. Adjutant General's Office – M907 – 1r – 1 – us Nat'l Archives [920]

INDEX TO COMPILED SERVICE RECORDS OF VOLUNTEER SOLDIERS WHO SERVED DURING THE CHEROKEE DISTURBANCES AND REMOVAL IN ORGANIZATIONS FROM THE STATE OF TENNESSEE AND THE FIELD AND STAFF OF THE ARMY OF THE CHEROKEE NATION / U.S. War Department. Adjutant General's Office – M908 – 2r – 1 – us Nat'l Archives [920]

INDEX TO COMPILED SERVICE RECORDS OF VOLUNTEER SOLDIERS WHO SERVED DURING THE CHEROKEE DISTURBANCES AND REMOVALS IN ORGANIZATIONS FROM THE STATE OF NORTH CAROLINA / U.S. War Department. Adjutant General's Office – M256. Printed guide – 1r – 5 – us Nat'l Archives [324]

INDEX TO COMPILED SERVICE RECORDS OF VOLUNTEER SOLDIERS WHO SERVED DURING THE CHEROKEE REMOVAL IN ORGANIZATIONS FROM THE STATE OF ALABAMA / U.S. War Department. Adjutant General's Office – M243. Printed guide – 1r – 5 – us Nat'l Archives [324]

INDEX TO COMPILED SERVICE RECORDS OF VOLUNTEER SOLDIERS WHO SERVED DURING THE CREEK WAR IN ORGANIZATIONS FROM THE STATE OF ALABAMA / U.S. War Department. Adjutant General's Office – 2 reels. M244. Printed guide – 5 – us Nat'l Archives [324]

INDEX TO COMPILED SERVICE RECORDS OF VOLUNTEER SOLDIERS WHO SERVED DURING THE FLORIDA WAR IN ORGANIZATIONS FROM THE STATE OF ALABAMA / U.S. War Department. Adjutant General's Office – (Louisiana. 1 roll. M239. Printed guide) – M245. Printed guide – 1r – 5 – us Nat'l Archives [324]

INDEX TO COMPILED SERVICE RECORDS OF VOLUNTEER SOLDIERS WHO SERVED DURING THE MEXICAN WAR / U.S. War Department. Adjutant General's Office – M616. Printed guide – 41r – 5 – us Nat'l Archives [324]

INDEX TO COMPILED SERVICE RECORDS OF VOLUNTEER SOLDIERS WHO SERVED DURING THE PATRIOT WAR, 1838-39 / U.S. War Department. Adjutant General's Office – Michigan. 1 roll. M630. Printed guide. New York. 1 roll. M631. Printed guide – 5 – us Nat'l Archives [324]

INDEX TO COMPILED SERVICE RECORDS OF VOLUNTEER SOLDIERS WHO SERVED DURING THE PHILLIPPINE INSURRECTION / U.S. War Department. Adjutant General's Office – M872 – 24r – 1 – us Nat'l Archives [324]

INDEX TO COMPILED SERVICE RECORDS OF VOLUNTEER SOLDIERS WHO SERVED DURING THE REVOLUTIONARY WAR IN ORGANIZATIONS FROM THE STATE OF NORTH CAROLINA / U.S. War Department. Collection of Revolutionary War Records – M257. Printed guide – 2r – 5 – us Nat'l Archives [324]

INDEX TO COMPILED SERVICE RECORDS OF VOLUNTEER SOLDIERS WHO SERVED DURING THE WAR OF 1812 / U.S. War Department. Adjutant General's Office – M602 – 234r – 5 – us Nat'l Archives [324]

INDEX TO COMPILED SERVICE RECORDS OF VOLUNTEER SOLDIERS WHO SERVED DURING THE WAR OF 1812 IN ORGANIZATIONS FROM THE STATE OF: / U.S. War Department. Adjutant General's Office – Louisiana. 3 rolls. M229. Printed guide.. North Carolina. 5 rolls. M250. Printed guide. South Carolina. 7 rolls. M652. Printed guide – 5 – us Nat'l Archives [324]

INDEX TO COMPILED SOLDIERS WHO SERVED DURING THE WAR OF 1837-38 IN ORGANIZATIONS FROM THE STATE OF LOUISIANA / U.S. War Department. Adjutant General's Office – M241. Printed guide – 1r – 5 – us Nat'l Archives [324]

INDEX TO COMPILED SERVICE RECORDS OF VOLUNTEER SOLDIERS WHO SERVED DURING THE WAR WITH SPAIN IN ORGANIZATIONS FROM THE STATE OF: / U.S. War Department. Adjutant General's Office – Louisiana. 1 roll. M240. Printed guide. North Carolina. 2 rolls. M413. Printed guide – 5 – us Nat'l Archives [324]

INDEX TO COMPILED SERVICE RECORDS OF VOLUNTEER SOLDIERS WHO SERVED FROM 1784-1811 / U.S. War Department. Adjutant General's Office – M694. Printed guide – 9r – 5 – us Nat'l Archives [324]

INDEX TO COMPILED SERVICE RECORDS OF VOLUNTEER UNION SOLDIERS WHO SERVED DURING THE CIVIL WAR IN ORGANIZATIONS FROM THE STATE OF: / U.S. War Department. Adjutant General's Office – Alabama. 1 roll. M263. Printed guide. Arizona Territory. 1 roll. M532. Printed guide. Arkansas. 4 rolls. M383. Printed guide. California. 7 rolls. M533. Printed guide. Colorado Territory. 3 rolls. M534. Printed guide. Connecticut. 17 rolls. M535. Printed guide. Dakota Territory. 1 roll. M536. Printed guide. Delaware. 4 rolls. M537. Printed guide. District of Columbia. 3 rolls. M538. Printed guide. Florida. 1 roll. M264. Printed guide. Georgia, 1 roll. M385. Printed guide. Illinois. 101 rolls. M539. Printed guide. Indiana. 86 rolls. M540. Printed guide. Iowa. 29 rolls. M541. Printed guide. Kansas. 10 rolls. M542. Printed guide. Kentucky. 30 rolls. M386. Printed guide. Louisiana. 4 rolls. M387. Printed guide.. Maine. 23 rolls. M543. Printed guide. Maryland. 13 rolls. M388. Printed guide. Massachusetts. 44 rolls. M544. Printed guide. Michigan. 48 rolls. M545. Printed guide. Minnesota. 10 rolls. M546. Printed guide.. Mississippi. 1 roll. M389. Printed guide. Missouri. 54 rolls. M390. Printed guide. Nebraska. 2 rolls. M547. Printed guide. Nevada. 1 roll. M548. Printed guide. New Hampshire. 13 rolls. M549. Printed guide. New Jersey. 26 rolls. M550. Printed guide. New Mexico Territory. 4 rolls. M242. Printed guide. New York. 157 rolls. M551. Printed guide. North Carolina. 2 rolls. M391. Printed guide. Ohio. 122 rolls. M552. Printed guide. Oregon. 1 roll. M553. Printed guide. Pennsylvania. 136 rolls. M554. Printed guide. Rhode Island. 7 rolls. M555. Printed guide. Tennessee. 16 rolls. M392. Printed guide. Texas. 2 rolls. M393. Printed guide. Utah Territory. 1 roll. M556. Printed guide. Vermont. 14 rolls. M557. Printed guide. Virginia. 1 roll. M394. Printed guide. Washington Territory. 1 roll. M558. Printed guide. West Virginia. 13 rolls. M507. Printed guide. Wisconsin. 33 rolls. M559. Printed guide – 5 – us Nat'l Archives [324]

INDEX TO COMPILED SERVICE RECORDS OF VOLUNTEER UNION SOLDIERS WHO SERVED DURING THE CIVIL WAR IN THE VETERAN RESERVE CORPS / U.S. War Department. Adjutant General's Office – M636. Printed guide – 44r – 5 – us Nat'l Archives [324]

INDEX TO COMPILED SERVICE RECORDS OF VOLUNTEER UNION SOLDIERS WHO SERVED DURING THE CIVIL WAR WITH U.S. COLORED TROOPS / U.S. War Department. Adjutant General's Office – M589. Printed guide – 98r – 5 – us Nat'l Archives [324]

INDEX TO COMPLETE RECORDS / Henry County. Ohio. Common Pleas. Civil Division – 1r – 1 – $32.50r – us Archival [324]

INDEX TO CONTENTS OF THE VERMONT HISTORICAL GAZETTEER / Hemenway, Abbie M – Rutland, Tuttle Co., 1923. Vermont Reel 2. (The Cox Library Collection) – 5 – us Americana [978]

INDEX TO CRIMINAL RECORDS / Allen County. Ohio. Probate Court – 1853-1927 – 1r – 1 – $32.50r – us Archival [324]

INDEX TO DEATH RECORDS / Putnam County. Ohio. Probate Court – 1867-1920 – 1r – 1 – $32.50r – us Archival [324]

INDEX TO DEATH RECORDS / Putnam County. Ohio. Probate Court – 1867-1920 – 1r – 1 – $32.50r – us Archival [324]

INDEX TO DECLARATIONS OF INTENTION AND PETITIONS FOR NATURALIZATION / U.S. Circuit and District Courts. Pennsylvania – 1820-1906. M1208 – 3r – 1 – us Nat'l Archives [975]

INDEX TO DEED RECORDS, 1815-1817 / Indiana – Item T. Earliest recorded deeds for Knox County, IN. 24 mimeo. pages.SW16-0091 – 5 – us A.G.L.L. [920]

INDEX TO DOMINION STATUTE AMENDMENTS (1907-1921) / Canada. Laws, Statutes, etc – Toronto 1922? LL-2271 – 1 – us L of C Photodup [340]

INDEX TO DUCTH LANGUAGE INDONESIAN NEWSPAPERS *see* REGISTER OVER DE INDISCHE COURANTEN, 1810-1923

INDEX TO DUTCH-LANGUAGE INDONESIAN NEWSPAPERS, 1810-1923 – (The following papers have been indexed: Bataviasch Koloniale Courant, 1810-1811; Java Government Gazette, 1812-1816; Bataviasche Courant, 1816-1827; Javasche Courant, 1828-1923; Soerabaiasch Handelsblad, 1866-1923; Algemeen Dagblad van Nederlandsch Indie, 1873-1923; Bataviaasch Nieuwsblad, 1855-1923; Sumatra Post, 1898-1923) – 149mf – 9 – Dfl1,475.00 – ne MMF Publ [072]

INDEX TO EARLY TENNESSEE BAPTISTS / Taylor, O W – Comp. by A. Stan Rescoe. 70p – 1 – 5.00 – us Baptist [240]

INDEX TO EARLY WELLINGTON NEWSPAPERS 1839-1865 – (Includes guide) – 22mf – 9 – NZ$73.10 – nz Nat'l Libr [072]

INDEX TO EAST AFRICAN SERIES : PAMPHLET COLLETION – [Belfast]: Queen's Uni Dept of Photography, 1965 (mf ed) – 1 – us Res Libr [960]

INDEX TO EASTERN PROVINCES AND DOMINION STATUTE AMENDMENTS TO 1926. / Canada. Laws, Statutes, etc – Toronto: Garrett 1927? 122nos. LL-2313 – 1 – us L of C Photodup [340]

AN INDEX TO ENGLISH LANGUAGE KOREAN PERIODICAL LITERATURE – 1890-1940 – 1 – us UMI [010]

INDEX TO ESTATES / Van Wert County. Ohio. Probate Court – 1839-1933 – 1r – 1 – $32.50r – us Archival [324]

INDEX TO EVENTS RELATING TO INDIA AND THE EAST REFERRED TO IN "THE TIMES" BETWEEN THE YEARS 1850 AND 1889 INCLUSIVE / The Times. London – London, 1893. BI-345 2 – 8 – ne IDC [072]

INDEX TO FEDERAL BUREAU OF INVESTIGATION CLASS 61 – TREASON OR MISPRISION OF TREASON – 1921-1931 : RECORD GROUP 65 – 1992 – 15r – 1 – $345.00 set in US $30.00r outside – M1531 – us Nat'l Archives [360]

AN INDEX TO FIFTH CENSUS OF THE UNITED STATES, 1830 POPULATION SCHEDULES, TERRITORY OF ARKANSAS – Comp. by Bobbie Jones McLane. 1965. 2 fiches. F-0003 – 9 – us A.G.L.L. [304]

INDEX TO GENERAL CORRESPONDENCE..., 1890-1917 / U.S. War Department. Adjutant General's Office – 1269 rolls. M698. Printed guide – 1 – us Nat'l Archives [324]

INDEX TO GENERAL CORRESPONDENCE OF THE RECORD AND PENSION OFFICE, 1889-1920 / U.S. War Department. Adjutant General's Office – 385 rolls. M686. Printed guide – 5 – us Nat'l Archives [324]

INDEX TO GENERAL STATUTES OF CONNECTICUT, AND PUBLIC ACTS, FROM 1875 TO 1882 / Connecticut. Laws, Statutes, etc – Hartford, Case, Lockwood & Brainard, 1883. 191 p. LL-1619 – 1 – us L of C Photodup [340]

INDEX TO GREAT REGISTER OF ALAMEDA COUNTY – 1900. California Reel 10. (The Cox Library Collection) – 5 – us Americana [978]

INDEX TO HEALTH INFORMATION MICROFICHE LIBRARY – (Provides access to statistical and congressional publications on issues of public health. Printed index available in combination on an annual subscription basis) – 1988- – 9 – Apply for prices – us CIS [020]

INDEX TO HOOSIER FOLKLORE BULLETIN (1942-45) AND HOOSIER FOLKLORE (1946-50) / Posen, I Sheldon – 1973 – 1 – us I.U. Libraries [390]

AN INDEX TO ILLUSTRATIONS OF SHAKESPEARE'S PLAYS / Pressey, W Benfield – 3r – 1 – $55.00 set – us Dartmouth [420]

INDEX TO ILLUSTRATIONS OF SHAKESPEARE'S PLAYS / ed by Pressey, W Benfield – (17,000 index cards citing illustrative material, arranged by play, act, and scene) – 3r – 1 – $220.00 – us UMI [420]

INDEX TO INDIAN DECISIONS / U.S. Department of the Interior – (1st 2v entitled: "Digest of Indian Probate Law". Coverage now extends to all legal matters of Indians and Alaska natives. Updated index publ annually with 5yr cumulations. Add vols planned) – Office of Hearings and Appeals, 1972-94 – 14mf – 9 – $21.00 – LLMC 87-304 – us L.L.M.C. [324]

INDEX TO INDIAN WARS PENSION FILES, 1892-1926 / U. S. Veterans Administration – 12 rolls. T318 – 5 – us Nat'l Archives [324]

INDEX TO JOURNAL, BILLS / Allen County. Ohio. Board of County Commissioners – 1913-1926 – 1r – 1 – $32.50r – us Archival [324]

INDEX TO JOURNALS / Fulton County. Ohio. Board of County Commissioners – 1883-1919 – 2r – 1 – $32.50r – us Archival [324]

INDEX TO JOURNALS / Hardin County. Ohio. Board of County Commissioners – 4r – 1 – $32.50r – us Archival [324]

INDEX TO JOURNALS / Henry County. Ohio. Board of County Commissioners – 1881-1986 – 5r – 1 – $32.50r – us Archival [324]

INDEX TO JOURNALS / Henry County. Ohio. Common Pleas. Civil Division – 3r – 1 – $32.50r – us Archival [324]

INDEX TO JOURNALS / Ottawa County. Ohio. Board of County Commissioners – 1840-1894 – 2r – 1 – $32.50r – us Archival [324]

INDEX TO JOURNALS / Williams County. Ohio. Board of County Commissioners – 1873-1967 – 3r – 1 – $32.50r – us Archival [324]

INDEX TO JOURNALS / Wyandot County. Ohio. Board of County Commissioners – 1892-1952 – 2r – 1 – $32.50r – us Archival [324]

INDEX TO JOURNALS, BILLS / Van Wert County. Ohio. Board of County Commissioners – 1865-1964 – 2r – 1 – $32.50r – us Archival [324]

INDEX TO JOURNALS, INFIRMARY / Van Wert County. Ohio. Board of County Commissioners – 1930-1965 – 2r – 1 – $32.50r – us Archival [324]

INDEX TO LANGE'S COMMENTARY ON THE OLD TESTAMENT: 1. HEBREW. 2. TOPICAL / Pick, Bernhard – New York: Charles Scribner, 1882. vi/36p 1 fiche – 9 – us A.T.L.A. [240]

INDEX TO LATIN AMERICAN LEGISLATION, 1950-1961 / U.S. Library of Congress. Law Library – 1961.-30,900 entries 4 reels.-ISBN: 0-8161-1305-X – 1 – $215.00 – uk Hall [340]

INDEX TO LEARNED CHINESE PERIODICALS / Columbia University. East Asian Library – 1962.-4500 entries 1 reel.-ISBN: 0-8161-1407-2 – 1 – $85.00 – uk Hall [073]

AN INDEX TO LEGAL PERIODICAL LITERATURE – v. 1-6. Boston. 1888-1924; Indianapolis. 1933-37 – 1 – 52.00 – us L of C Photodup [340]

INDEX TO LETTERS RECEIVED BY THE COMMISSION TO THE FIVE CIVILIZED TRIBES, 1897-1913 – 23r – 1 – M1314 – us Nat'l Archives [350]

INDEX TO LIVESTOCK LITERATURE MICROFICHED IN BOTSWANA – 1985 – 9 – $16.00 – 92-9053-163-0 – et ILRI [636]

INDEX TO LIVESTOCK LITERATURE MICROFICHED IN ETHIOPIA – 1990 – 9 – $21.00 – 92-9053-220-3 – et ILRI [630]

INDEX TO LIVESTOCK LITERATURE MICROFICHED IN GHANA – 1982 – 9 – $6.50 – 92-9053-161-4 – et ILRI [636]

INDEX TO LIVESTOCK LITERATURE MICROFICHED IN KENYA – 1988. 1794 citations – 9 – $20.00 – 92-9053-166-5 – et ILRI [636]

INDEX TO LIVESTOCK LITERATURE MICROFICHED IN MALAWI – 1993 – 139p – 9 – $9.50 – 92-9053-250-5 – et ILRI [636]

INDEX TO LIVESTOCK LITERATURE MICROFICHED IN NIGERIA – 1992 – v/279p – 9 – $16.00 – 92-9053-224-6 – et ILRI [636]

INDEX TO LIVESTOCK LITERATURE MICROFICHED IN SUDAN – 1982 – 9 – $11.00 – 92-9053-159-2 – et ILRI [636]

INDEX TO LIVESTOCK LITERATURE MICROFICHED IN THE GAMBIA – 1994 – 57p – 9 – $4.00 – 92-9053-515-6 – et ILRI [636]

INDEX TO LIVESTOCK LITERATURE MICROFICHED IN UGANDA – 1992 – 9 – $6.00 – 92-9053-241-6 – et ILRI [636]

INDEX TO LIVESTOCK LITERATURE MICROFICHED IN ZAMBIA – 1982 – 9 – $5.00 – 92-9053-160-6 – et ILRI [636]

INDEX TO LIVESTOCK LITERATURE MICROFICHED IN ZIMBABWE (PARTS 1 AND 2) – 1986 – 9 – $21.00 – 92-9053-164-9 – et ILRI [636]

INDEX TO MANUSCRIPTS, EDINBURGH UNIVERSITY LIBRARY / Edinburgh University – 1964. 31,000 cards on 4 reels – 1 – $175.00 export $210.00 – 0-8161-1356-4 – uk Hall [090]

INDEX TO MANUSCRIPTS IN THE LIBRARY / Edinburgh University. Library – (First suppl., 1981.-13,325 cards 1 reel.-£130.00) – 1964.-31,000 cards.-ISBN: 0-8161-1356-4 – 4r – 1 – £190.00 – uk Hall [090]

INDEX TO MAPS IN BOOKS AND PERIODICALS / American Geographical Society. Library. New York. – (First suppl., 1971.-12,600 cards reels. $120.00 ISBN: 0-8161-1433-1; Second suppl., 1976.- 11,900 cards 1 reel. $120.00 ISBN: 0-8161-1416-1; Third Suppl., 1987.-14,200 cards 1 reel. $190.00 ISBN: 0-8161-1524-9) – 1968.- 164,000 cards 10 reels.-ISBN: 0-8161-1420-X – 1 – $1090.00 – uk Hall [910]

INDEX TO MARRIAGE RECORDS / Defiance County, Ohio. Probate Court – 1845-1885 – 1r – 1 – $32.50r – us Archival [324]

INDEX TO MEDICAL SOCIOECONOMIC LITERATURE, 1962-1970 / American Medical Association. Division of Library and Archival Services – (Available on microfilm by request) – 1980. 37,000 entries – 9 – $310.00 export $375.00 – uk Hall [610]

INDEX TO 'MEMORIAL TO THE JEWS DEPORTED FROM FRANCE' – 1mf – 9 – $2.50 – us A.G.L.L. [920]

INDEX TO MEXICAN WAR PENSION FILES, 1887-1926 / U. S. Veterans Administration – 14 rolls. T317 – 5 – us Nat'l Archives [324]

INDEX TO MISCELLANEOUS RECORDS / Henry County. Ohio. Recorder – 1r – 1 – $32.50r – us Archival [324]

INDEX TO MORTALITY SCHEDULES, 1880 – (Meri-Z. T655-0017) – A-Mere. T655-0016 – 1 – us A.G.L.L. [920]

INDEX TO MORTGAGE RECORDS / Henry County. Ohio. Recorder – 1847-1902 – 2r – 1 – $32.50r – us Archival [324]

INDEX TO NAME CHANGES IN THE PALESTINE GAZETTE – 6mf – 9 – $15.00 – us A.G.L.L. [920]

INDEX TO NAMES OF U.S. MARSHALS, 1789-1960 – T577-0001 – 1 – us A.G.L.L. [920]

INDEX TO NAMES OF U.S. MARSHALS, 1789-1960 / U.S. Department of Justice – 1 roll. T577 – 5 – us Nat'l Archives [340]

INDEX TO NATURALIZATION PETITIONS...1797-1956 / U.S. Circuit and District Courts. Maryland – RG 21. M1168. 25 rolls – 1 – us Nat'l Archives [324]

INDEX TO NATURALIZATION RECORD / Ottawa County. Ohio. Probate Court – 1910-1940s – 1r – 1 – $32.50r – us Archival [324]

INDEX TO NEW ENGLAND NATURALIZATION PETITIONS, 1791-1906 / U.S. Immigration and Naturalization Service – (Connecticut. M1299-001 to M1299-038. Rhode Island. M1299-039 to M1299-46. Maine, Massachusetts, New Hampshire. M1299-047 to M1299-117) – 1983. 117 reels – 1 – us A.G.L.L. [320]

INDEX TO NORTH AMERICAN FERNS / Broun, M – Orleans, 1938 – 4mf – ne IDC [580]

INDEX TO NORTH CAROLINA MARRIAGE BONDS, 1741-1868 / ed by North Carolina Division of Archives and History – Raleigh, N.C.: Division of Archives and History, 1977 – 88mf – 9 – $100.00 set – us NC Archives [920]

INDEX TO NORTHWEST MISSIONS MANUSCRIPTS / ed by Nute, Grace Lee – ca 1766-1926 – 5r – 5 – $150.00 $30.00r – us M.H.S. [240]

INDEX TO OBITUARIES AND DEATH NOTICES IN THE NEW ZEALAND MEDICAL JOURNAL 1886-FEBRUARY 1981 / ed by Jamieson, D G & Poland, Jocelyn – 1985 – 1mf – NZ$15.00 – nz Libr & Info [920]

INDEX TO OFFICERS' JACKETS, 1913-25 (OFFICERS DIRECTORY) / U.S. Navy. Bureau of Naval Personnel – 2rolls. T1102 – 1 – us Nat'l Archives [355]

INDEX TO OFFICIAL AND HISTORICAL ATLAS OF YUBA COUNTY, CALIFORNIA – Thompson & West, 1873 – 2r – 5,9 – $100.00 – B40148 – us Library Micro [978]

INDEX TO OFFICIAL PUBLISHED DOCUMENTS RELATING TO CUBA AND THE INSULAR POSSESSIONS OF THE U.S., 1876-1906 / U.S. Bureau of Insular Affairs – 3r – 1 – M24 – us Nat'l Archives [324]

INDEX TO PASSENGER LISTS OF VESSELS ARRIVING AT BALTIMORE, 1820-97 (FEDERAL PASSENGER LISTS) / U.S. Bureau of the Customs – 171 rolls. M327. Printed guide – 5 – us Nat'l Archives [324]

INDEX TO PASSENGER LISTS OF VESSELS ARRIVING AT BALTIMORE, 1833-66 / U.S. Bureau of the Customs – 22 rolls. M326. Printed guide – 5 – us Nat'l Archives [324]

INDEX TO PASSENGER LISTS OF VESSELS ARRIVING AT BALTIMORE, MARYLAND / U.S. Bureau of the Customs – 1833-66. 22 rolls. M326 – 5 – us Nat'l Archives [324]

INDEX TO PASSENGER LISTS OF VESSELS ARRIVING AT BOSTON, 1848-91 / U.S. Bureau of the Customs – 282 rolls. M265. Printed guide – 5 – us Nat'l Archives [324]

INDEX TO PASSENGER LISTS OF VESSELS ARRIVING AT BOSTON, JAN 1, 1902-JUNE 30, 1906 / U.S. Immigration and Naturalization Service – 11 rolls. T521 – 5 – us Nat'l Archives [324]

INDEX TO PASSENGER LISTS OF VESSELS ARRIVING AT BOSTON, MASSACHUSETTS / U.S. Bureau of the Customs – Jul 1, 1906 – Dec 31, 1920. 11 rolls. T617 – 1 – us Nat'l Archives [324]

INDEX TO PASSENGER LISTS OF VESSELS ARRIVING AT GALVESTON, TEXAS, 1896-1906 – 3r – 1 – M1357 – us Nat'l Archives [340]

INDEX TO PASSENGER LISTS OF VESSELS ARRIVING AT GALVESTON, TEXAS, 1906-1951 – 7r – 1 – M1358 – us Nat'l Archives [340]

INDEX TO PASSENGER LISTS OF VESSELS ARRIVING AT NEW ORLEANS, 1900-1952 / U.S. Immigration and Naturalization Service – RG 85. T618. 22 rolls – 1 – us Nat'l Archives [975]

INDEX TO PASSENGER LISTS OF VESSELS ARRIVING AT NEW ORLEANS BEFORE 1900 / U.S. Bureau of the Customs – 32 rolls. T527 – 5 – us Nat'l Archives [324]

INDEX TO PASSENGER LISTS OF VESSELS ARRIVING AT NEW YORK, 1820-46 / U.S. Bureau of the Customs – 103 rolls. M261. Printed guide – 5 – us Nat'l Archives [324]

INDEX TO PASSENGER LISTS OF VESSELS ARRIVING AT NEW YORK, JUNE 16, 1897-JUNE 30, 1902 / U.S. Immigration and Naturalization Service – 115 rolls. T519 – 5 – us Nat'l Archives [324]

INDEX TO PASSENGER LISTS OF VESSELS ARRIVING AT PHILADELPHIA, 1800-1906 / U.S. Bureau of the Customs – 151 rolls. M360. Printed guide – 5 – us Nat'l Archives [324]

INDEX TO PASSENGERS ARRIVING AT GULFPORT, AUGUST 27, 1904-AUGUST 28, 1954, AND AT PASCAGOULA, JULY 15, 1903-MAY 21, 1935 / U.S. Immigration and Naturalization Service – RG 85. T523. 1 roll – 1 – us Nat'l Archives [975]

INDEX TO PASSENGERS ARRIVING AT NEW BEFORD, JULY 1, 1902-NOVEMBER 18, 1954 / U.S. Immigration and Naturalization Service – RG 85. T522. 2 rolls – 1 – us Nat'l Archives [975]

INDEX TO PASSENGERS ARRIVING AT PORTLAND, MAINE, JANUARY 29, 1893-NOVEMBER 22, 1954 / U.S. Immigration and Naturalization Service – RG 85. T524. 1 roll – 1 – us Nat'l Archives [975]

INDEX TO PASSENGERS ARRIVING AT PROVIDENCE, RHODE ISLAND, JUNE 18, 1911-OCTOBER 5, 1954 / U.S. Immigration and Naturalization Service – RG 85. T518. 2 rolls – 1 – us Nat'l Archives [975]

INDEX TO PASSENGERS OF VESSELS ARRIVING AT PORTS IN ALABAMA, FLORIDA, GEORGIA, AND SOUTH CAROLINA / U.S. Bureau of the Customs – 1890-1924. 26 rolls. T517 – 1 – us Nat'l Archives [324]

INDEX TO PAY LEDGERS FOR THE NEW SOUTH WALES MILITARY FORCES INVOLVED IN THE BOER WAR, 1899-1902 – 15r – 1 – CRS B5206 – at Archives [920]

INDEX TO PERIODICAL ARTICLES, 1979-1989, IN THE LIBRARY OF THE ROYAL INSTITUTE OF INTERNATIONAL AFFAIRS / Royal Institute of International Affairs – (1950-1964.-1964.-31,500 cards available on microfilm by request.$250.00 export $300.00.-ISBN 0-8161-0711-4) – Boston: G.K. Hall & Co., 1990 – 30,000 cards on 47mf – 9 – $250.00 export $295.00 – 0-8161-1784-5 – uk Hall [327]

INDEX TO PERSONNEL FILES / Great Northern Railway Company. Personnel Dept – 4r – 5 – 30.00r – us M.H.S. [380]

INDEX TO PERSONNEL FILES / Northern Pacific Railway Company. Personnel Dep't – 3r – 5 – 30.00r – us M.H.S. [380]

INDEX TO PLANT DISTRIBUTION MAPS IN NORTH AMERICAN PERIODICALS THROUGH 1972 / Phillips, W Louis & Stuckey, Ronald L – (Available on microfilm by request) – 1976.-29,000 cards 1 reel – 1 – $115.00 export $140.00 – 0-8161-0009-8 – uk Hall [580]

INDEX TO PORTRAITS IN BOOKS / Royal College of Physicians – Suppl. to printed catalogue – 1 – uk Microform Academic [920]

INDEX TO PRESIDENTIAL PROCLAMATIONS, 1789-1947 / U.S. Congress – 2r – 1 – T279 – us Nat'l Archives [324]

INDEX TO PRINTED MAPS / California. University.Berkeley. Bancroft Library – 1964.-10,900 entries 1 reel.-ISBN: 0-8161-1550-8 – 1 – $85.00 – uk Hall [910]

INDEX TO PRIVATE LAND GRANT CASES / U.S. District Court. California. Northern District – 1853-1903. 1 roll – 1 – T1214 – us Nat'l Archives [340]

INDEX TO PRIVATE LAND GRANT CASES / U.S. District Court. California. Southern District – 1 roll – 1 – T1215 – us Nat'l Archives [340]

INDEX TO PROCEEDINGS OF THE ECONOMIC AND SOCIAL COUNCIL / United Nations – 14th – 63th Sess., 1952-1977; Years 1978-1989 – E.103 – 9 (ST/LIB/Ser.B/E.5-66) – us U.N. Pubs [330]

INDEX TO PROCEEDINGS OF THE GENERAL ASSEMBLY / United Nations – 5th – 43rd Sess., 1950-1989 – E.267 – 9 (ST/LIB/Ser.B/A.1-44) – us U.N. Pubs [324]

INDEX TO PROCEEDINGS OF THE SECURITY COUNCIL / United Nations – 19th – 44th Years, 1964-1989 – E.43 – 9 (ST/LIB/Ser.B/S.1-26) – us U.N. Pubs [324]

INDEX TO PROCEEDINGS OF THE TRUSTEESHIP COUNCIL / United Nations – 11th – 55th Sess., 1952-1988 – E.42 – 9 (ST/LIB/Ser.B/T.6-50) – us U.N. Pubs [324]

INDEX TO RAILWAY LEGISLATION OF THE DOMINION OF CANADA FROM 1867 TO 1897 INCLUSIVE – J.E.W. Currier, comp. Ottawa, 1898. 02247. (Pre-1900 Canadiana) – 9 – cn C.I.H.M. [340]

INDEX TO RECORD REVIEWS, 1978-1983, FIRST SUPPLEMENT / Myers, Kurtz – 1985 – 1 reel – 1 – $165.00 export $200.00 – 0-8161-0435-2 – uk Hall [780]

INDEX TO RECORDS AND MINUTES / Seneca County, Ohio. Tiffin, City. City Council – 1850-1968 – 1r – 1 – $32.50r – us Archival [324]

INDEX TO REFERENCE CARDS FOR WORK PROJECTS ADMINISTRATION PROJECT FILES / U. S. Work Projects Administration – (1935-37.79 rolls. T935. 1938. 15 rolls. T936. 1939-42. 19 rolls. T937) – 5 – us Nat'l Archives [324]

INDEX TO REGISTER OF ISSUE OF MEDALS AND CLASPS, 1903-1911 – 6r – 1 – CRS B5183 – at Archives [920]

INDEX TO REGULAR AND PRIMITIVE BAPTIST ASSOCIATIONS' ANNUALS / Baptist Associations – 1 – 25.00 – us Baptist [240]

INDEX TO RENDEZVOUS REPORTS, ARMED GUARD PERSONNEL – 1917-20. 3 rolls. T1101 – 1 – us Nat'l Archives [324]

INDEX TO RENDEZVOUS REPORTS, ARMED GUARD PERSONNEL, 1917-20 / U.S. Navy. Bureau of Naval Personnel – 3rolls. T1101 – 5 – us Nat'l Archives [355]

INDEX TO RENDEZVOUS REPORTS, BEFORE AND AFTER THE CIVIL WAR (1846-61; 1865-84) / U.S. Navy. Bureau of Naval Personnel – 32 rolls. T1098 – 5 – us Nat'l Archives [355]

INDEX TO RENDEZVOUS REPORTS, CIVIL WAR, 1861-65 / U.S. Navy. Bureau of Naval Personnel – 31 rolls. T1099 – 5 – us Nat'l Archives [355]

INDEX TO RENDEZVOUS REPORTS, NAVAL AUXILIARY SERVICE, 1846-84 / U.S. Navy. Bureau of Naval Personnel – 1roll. T1100 – 5 – us Nat'l Archives [355]

INDEX TO REPORTS OF SPECIES / Peck, C H – 7 – uk Microform Academic [580]

INDEX TO ROBERSON COLLECTION AT JENKINS MEMORIAL LIBRARY, FOREIGN MISSIONS BOARD, SBC, RICHMOND, VA / Roberson, Cecil F – 1984 – 1 – 8.46 – us Baptist [240]

INDEX TO RUSSIAN CONSULAR RECORDS – 7mf – 9 – $17.50 – us A.G.L.L. [338]

INDEX TO SAN FRANCISCO CITY LICENSES – San Francisco, 1850-56 – 2r – 1 – $100.00 – B40330 – us Library Micro [978]

INDEX TO SOUTH CAROLINA PLEADING AND PRACTICE FORMS / Taylor, Esten C – Spartanburg Galloway, 1936. 202 p. LL-632 – 1 – us L of C Photodup [340]

INDEX TO SURVEY OF CHINA MAINLAND PRESS, SELECTIONS FROM CHINA MAINLAND MAGAZINES AND CURRENT BACKGROUND / U.S. Consulate General. Hong Kong – 1 Nov 1950-72; 1973- – 1 – $254.00 – us L of C Photodup [950]

INDEX TO TELEGRAMS COLLECTED BY THE OFFICE OF THE SECRETARY...(UNBOUND), 1860-70 / U.S. War Department. Office of the Secretary – 20 rolls. M564. Printed guide – 5 – us Nat'l Archives [324]

INDEX TO THE 1860 FEDERAL CENSUS OF PLEASANT, UNION COUNTY, IOWA – By Lester F. Saffell Jr. et al. Item S.SW16-0100 – 5 – us A.G.L.L. [310]

INDEX TO THE 1870 FEDERAL CENSUS OF PLEASANT, UNION COUNTY, IOWA – By Lester F. Saffell Jr. et al. Item T.SW16-0100 – 5 – us A.G.L.L. [310]

INDEX TO THE ANAMOSA JOURNAL, CENTENNIAL ED – 1838-1938. Comp. by Lester Saffell. Item G. 32p. SW16-0160 – 5 – us A.G.L.L. [073]

INDEX TO THE ANNEXURES AND PRINTED PAPERS OF THE HOUSE OF ASSEMBLY... 1854-1897 / Cape of Good Hope. Parliament. House – Cape Town, 1899 – 1 – us Res Libr [960]

INDEX TO THE ARGUS 1855 – APRIL 1859 / Feely, J A – 4mf – 9 – A$36.00 – at State Libr Vic [980]

INDEX TO THE ARGUS 1846-1854 / Feely, J A – Library Council of Victoria, 1976 – 3mf – 9 – A$20.00 – at State Libr Vic [980]

AN INDEX TO THE ARKANSAS REPORTS, VOLS 1 TO 31 INCLUSIVE, AND HEMPSTEAD'S U.S. COURT REPORTS, ALSO ALL THE ARKANSAS CASES IN WOOLWORTH'S AND DILLON'S U.S.C.C. REPORTS / Brady, Charles B – St. Louis, Gilbert, 1878. 760 p. LL-2358 – 1 – us L of C Photodup [340]

INDEX TO THE BURLINGTON MAGAZINE 1903-1972 – Bath: Mindata, July 1996 – 16mf – 9 – $110.00 – 1-900853-55-8 – uk Mindata [700]

INDEX TO THE COMPILED SERVICE RECORDS OF VOLUNTEER SOLDIERS WHO SERVED IN THE CHEROKEE REMOVAL IN ORGANIZATIONS FROM THE STATE OF ALABAMA – Listed alpha. SW16-0181 – 5 – us A.G.L.L. [350]

INDEX TO THE CRIMINAL & PENAL STATUTES OF CANADA, AS AFFECTING THE PROVINCE OF QUEBEC. / Dubreuil, Joseph Fereol – Montreal, Beauchemin & Valois, 1877. 95 p. LL-2335 – 1 – us L of C Photodup [340]

INDEX TO THE ELEVENTH CENSUS OF THE UNITED STATES / U.S. Bureau of the Census – 1890. 2 rolls. M496. Covers the names appearing on the few surviving 1890 population schedules – 5 – us Nat'l Archives [324]

INDEX TO THE FEDERAL STATUTES, 1874-1931 / U. S. Laws, Statutes, etc – (Revision of the Scott/Beaman Index thru 1931 by Walter H. McClenon & Wilfred C. Gilbert. Washington: GPO, 1933?) – 15mf – 9 – $22.50 – LLMC 84-100B – us L.L.M.C. [324]

- ANNUAL REPORT ON THE WORKING OF THE RAJPUTANA MUSEUM, AJMER FOR THE YEAR ENDING 1930
- ANTIQUARIAN REMAINS IN HYDERABAD STATE
- ARCHAEOLOGICAL SURVEY
- ARCHAEOLOGICAL SURVEY OF INDIA
- ARCHAEOLOGICAL SURVEY OF MAYURABHANJA
- ARCHAEOLOGICAL SURVEY OF WESTERN INDIA
- BHARATA KA RAJAPATRA
- CATALOGUE OF BOOKS
- CATALOGUE OF BOOKS, REGISTERED IN THE PUNJAB
- CENSUS OF INDIA REPORTS
- CIVIL SERVICE EXAMINATIONS
- GAZETTE OF INDIA
- GOVERNMENT GAZETTE
- THE IMPERIAL GAZETTEER
- INDIAN ARCHIVES
- LAW REPORTS
- LIST OF ANCIENT MONUMENTS SELECTED FOR CONSERVATION IN THE MADRAS PRESIDENCY
- LIST OF ARCHITECTURAL AND ARCHAEOLOGICAL REMAINS IN COORG
- LIST OF PARLIAMENTARY COLLECTIONS IN INDIA, WITH INDEX
- LIST OF TOMBS AND MONUMENTS ERECTED IN MADRAS
- LISTS AND GUIDES TO OFFICIAL INDIAN PUBLICATIONS
- LISTS OF ANCIENT MONUMENTS IN BENGAL
- LISTS OF ANTIQUARIAN REMAINS IN HIS HIGHNESS THE NIZAM'S TERRITORIES
- LISTS OF CHRISTIAN TOMBS AND MONUMENTS OF ARCHAEOLOGICAL AND HISTORICAL INTEREST AND THEIR INSCRIPTIONS IN THE N.W. PROV. AND OUDH
- LISTS OF INSCRIPTIONS AND A SKETCH OF THE DYNASTIES OF SOUTHERN INDIA
- LISTS OF MONUMENTS
- LISTS OF STATUES, MONUMENTS, AND BUSTS ERECTED IN MADRAS IN HONOUR OF DISTINGUISHED SERVANTS OF THE STATE
- PAPERS RELATING TO THE ADMISSION OF NATIVES TO THE CIVIL SERVICE OF INDIA
- REVISED LIST OF ANCIENT MONUMENTS IN BENGAL
- REVISED LISTS OF ANTIQUARIAN REMAINS IN THE BOMBAY PRESIDENCY AND THE NAT. STATES OF BARODA, PALANPUR, RADHANPUR, KATHIAWAS, KACHI, KOLHAPUR, AND THE SOUTHERN MARATHA MINOR STATES
- SELECTION AND TRAINING OF INDIAN CANDIDATES FOR THE CIVIL SERVICE
- SELECTION OF PAPERS REGARDING THE HILL TRACTS BETWEEN ASSAM AND BURMAH
- SELECTIONS FROM THE RECORDS OF THE GOVERNMENT OF INDIA
- SIX-YEAR DEVELOPMENT PLAN OF THE UNION OF INDIA, 1951-57
- TRANSLATION OF REPORT ON THE GENERAL CENSUS OF THE POPULATION OF PORTUGUESE INDIA, TAKEN ON THE 17 FEB 1881

INDIA ALERT – Oak Park. 19 docs. 1986-1991 – 9mf – 9 – ne IDC [320]

INDIA: AN INDEX-CATALOGUE OF BIBLIOGRAPHICAL WORKS / Campbell, FBF – 1897 – 1 – uk Microform Academic [950]

INDIA AND CHRISTIAN OPPORTUNITY / Beach, Harlan Page – (Includes appendixes) – New York: Student Volunteer Movement for Foreign Missions, 1908, c1904 – 1mf – 9 – 0-8370-6645-X – 1986-0645 – us A.T.L.A. [240]

INDIA AND INDIA MISSIONS : INCLUDING SKETCHES OF THE GIGANTIC SYSTEM OF HINDUISM, BOTH IN THEORY AND PRACTICE... / Duff, Alexander – Edinburgh: J. Johnstone; London: Whittaker, 1840 – 2mf – us A.T.L.A. [240]

INDIA AND ITS NATIVE PRINCES / Rousselet, L – London, 1876. rev., ed 317 ills., 6 maps. BI-1133 1 – 9 – ne IDC [305]

INDIA AND MALAYSIA / Thoburn, James Mills – Cincinnati: Cranston & Curts; New York: Hunt & Eaton, 1892 – 2mf – us A.T.L.A. [240]

INDIA AND THE APOSTLE THOMAS : AN INQUIRY, WITH A CRITICAL ANALYSIS OF THE ACTA THOMAE / Medlycott, A E – London: David Nutt, 1905 – 1mf – us A.T.L.A. [240]

INDIA. ANDHRA PRADESH : REVIEW OF ECONOMIC TRENDS AND STATE PLAN 1985-1986 – Hyderabad, 1985 – 5mf – 9 – ne IDC [338]

INDIA. ANDHRA PRADESH : SURVEY OF ECONOMIC TRENDS AND STATE PLAN 1987-1988 – Hyderabad. v7. 1987 – 5mf – 9 – ne IDC [338]

India. Andhra Pradesh. Finance and Planning (Planning Wing) Department *see* REVIEW OF PROGRESS

India. Archaeological Department. Mysore *see* ANNUAL REPORT FOR THE YEARS 1886-1946

India. Archaeological Department of His Highness the Nizam's Dominions *see* ANNUAL REPORT OF THE INDIAN ARCHAEOLOGICAL DEPARTMENT

India. Archaeological Department. Travancore *see* ADMINISTRATION REPORT

India. Archaeological Survey *see*
- ANNUAL REPORT
- ANNUAL REPORT ON SOUTH INDIAN EPIGRAPHY, 1933/34-1944/45, 1955-1961
- ANNUAL REPORTS
- MEMOIRS OF THE ARCHAEOLOGICAL SOCIETY OF INDIA

India. Archaeological Survey Department. Southern Circle. Madras *see* ANNUAL REPORT, 1912/13-1920/21

India. Archaeological Survey of Western India *see* REPORT ON THE ARCHITECTURAL AND ARCHAEOLOGICAL REMAINS IN THE PROVINCE OF KACHH

India. Archaeological Survey. Southern Circle *see* PROGRESS REPORT OF THE ARCHAEOLOGICAL SURVEY DEPARTMENT, SOUTHERN CIRCLE, FOR THE YEAR...

India. Assam. Directorate of Elementary Education *see* ASSAM

India. Bihar. Education Department *see* FOURTH FIVE YEAR PLAN ON GENERAL EDUCATION 1969-1974

India. Census Commissioner *see* CENSUS COMMISSIONER'S NOTES ON CENSUS ARRANGEMENTS IN INDIVIDUAL PROVINCES AND STATES

India. Central Provinces *see* LIST OF CHIEFS AND LEADING FAMILIES

India Christian Mission *see* INDIAN CHRISTIAN MISSION

India. Commercial Intelligence Department *see*
- STATISTICAL ABSTRACT FOR BRITISH INDIA WITH STATISTICS, WHERE AVAILABLE RELATING TO CERTAIN INDIA STATES
- STATISTICAL ABSTRACT RELATING TO BRITISH INDIA
- STATISTICAL TABLES FOR BRITISH INDIA

India. Coorg. Lesigiative Council *see* DEBATES

INDIA CULTURES QUARTERLY – (Cont: India's Culture) – v2-5. 1942-45; v15-40. 1957-85 (incomplete) – 1r – 1 – ATLA S0757 – us A.T.L.A. [073]

India. Deccan Riots Commission *see* REPORT OF THE COMMITTEE ON THE RIOTS IN POONA AND AHMEDNAGAR

India. Department of Education *see*
- ANALYSIS OF BUDGETED EXPENDITURE ON EDUCATION 1980-1981 TO 1982-1983
- EXPENDITURE ON EDUCATION AS SHOWN IN CENTRAL AND STATE ANNUAL BUDGETS 1977/78-1979/80
- FOREIGN STUDENTS IN INDIAN UNIVERSITIES, INSTITUTIONS 1982-1983
- IMPLEMENTATION OF NATIONAL POLICY ON EDUCATION 1986
- PERFORMANCE BUDGET 1988/89-1990/91
- TRENDS OF EXPENDITURE ON EDUCATION 1968/69-1978/79

India. Dept. of Commercial Intelligence and Statistics *see* ACCOUNTS RELATING TO THE FOREIGN TRADE AND NAVIGATION OF INDIA

India. Directorate of Adult Education *see*
- LITERACY STATISTICS AT A GLANCE
- NATIONAL ADULT EDUCATION PROGRAMME

India. Famine Commission *see*
- REPORT

India. Famine Inquiry Commission *see* MORTALITY IN BENGAL IN 1943

INDIA GAZETTE – Calcutta, India. 1782-1788; 1822-1843 – 1 – uk Microform Academic [072]

INDIA GAZETTE – Calcutta, India. -w. 25 Nov 1780-28 Dec 1782. 1 reel – 1 – uk British Libr Newspaper [072]

INDIA GAZETTEERS / Scholberg, Henry – (The Imperial Gazetteer: 1907-1909 26 vols 218mf Dfl1,317.00; Provincial Series: 1908-1909 19 vols 212mf Dfl1,281.00; District Series: 1822-1945 1,221 vols 4,050mf Dfl24,309.00) – 9 – ne IDC [019]

India. Gujarat. Directorate of Education *see* FOURTH FIVE YEAR PLAN IN EDUCATION 1969/70-1973/74

INDIA. HISTORICAL DOCUMENTS AND MANUSCRIPTS *see* HISTORICAL DOCUMENTS AND MANUSCRIPTS

India. Home Department *see* PROPORTIONS OF EUROPEANS AND NATIVES IN THE PUBLIC SERVICE

India House Library *see* A SHORT CATALOGUE

India. Imperial Record Department *see*
- A HANDBOOK TO THE RECORDS OF THE GOVERNMENT OF INDIA IN THE IMPERIAL RECORD DEPARTMENT, 1748-1859
- LIST OF THE HEADS OF ADMINISTRATION IN INDIA AND OF THE INDIA OFFICE IN ENGLAND

India. Imperial Record Office *see*
- INDEX TO THE LAND REVENUE RECORDS, 1830-1859
- LIST OF FINANCE DEPARTMENT RECORDS IN THE IMPERIAL RECORD OFFICE, CALCUTTA, 1805-1908
- LIST OF FOREIGN DEPARTMENT RECORDS IN THE IMPERIAL RECORD OFFICE, CALCUTTA, 1756-1859
- LIST OF FOREIGN DEPARTMENT RECORDS IN THE IMPERIAL RECORD OFFICE, CALCUTTA, PART 3
- LIST OF HOME DEPARTMENT RECORDS IN THE IMPERIAL RECORD OFFICE, CALCUTTA, 1749-1892
- LIST OF MILITARY DEPARTMENT RECORDS IN THE IMPERIAL RECORD OFFICE, CALCUTTA
- LISTS OF PUBLIC WORKS DEPARTMENT RECORDS IN THE IMPERIAL RECORD OFFICE, CALCUTTA, 1880-1894
- PRESS LIST OF "MUTINY PAPERS", 1857
- PRESS LISTS OF THE PUBLIC DEPARTMENT RECORDS, 1748-1800

India. Intelligence Bureau *see* THE GHADR DIRECTORY

India. Intelligence Bureau. Home Department *see* TERRORISM IN INDIA, 1917-1936

India. Judicial and Administrative Department *see* STATISTICS OF BRITISH INDIA

India. Laws, Statutes, etc *see*
- THE INDIAN PENAL CODE, AS MODIFIED UP TO THE 1ST AUGUST 1890
- RULES OF BUSINESS

India. Legislative Council *see* PROCEEDINGS OF THE LEGISLATIVE COUNCIL OF INDIA 1854-61

India. Legislature. Legislative Assembly *see* MANUAL OF BUSINESS AND PROCEDURE.

India. Maharashtra. Ministry of Education *see* WHITE PAPER (DRAFT) OUTLINING THE EDUCATIONAL RECONSTRUCTION PROPOSED TO BE UNDERTAKEN DURING THE NEXT 15-20 YEARS, WITH SPECIAL REFERENCE TO THE NEW FOURTH FIVE YEAR PLAN (1969-1974)

INDIA, MALAYSIA, AND THE PHILIPPINES : A PRACTICAL STUDY IN MISSIONS / Oldham, W F – New York: Eaton & Mains; Cincinnati: Jennings & Graham, c1914 – 1mf – us A.T.L.A. [240]

India. Ministry of Education *see* DRAFT THIRD FIVE YEAR PLAN OF EDUCATION FOR CENTRAL AND CENTRALLY SPONSORED SCHEMES

India. Ministry of Education and Culture *see* PROGRESS OF EDUCATION OF SCHEDULED CASTES AND SCHEDULED TRIBES 1976-1977

India. Ministry of Education and Social Welfare *see* EDUCATIONAL DEVELOPMENTS IN INDIA 1971-1977

India. Ministry of Home Affairs. Office of the Registrar General *see* CENSUS OF INDIA

India. Ministry of Human Resource Development. Department of Education *see* ANNUAL REPORT 1987 (1)

India. Ministry of Information and Broadcasting *see* THIRD FIVE YEAR PLAN SUMMARY OF DRAFT OUTLINE

India. National Archives *see*
- CONFIDENTIAL PUBLICATIONS AND HOME POLITICAL FILES

India. National Congress *see*
- REPORTS AND PROCEEDINGS IN THE INDIAN NATIONAL CONGRESS
- YEARS OF FREEDOM

India. National Council of Educational Research and Training. Publication Department *see* VOCATIONALIZATION OF EDUCATION: PROFILE AND DIRECTIONS

India. National Institute of Educational Planning and Administration *see* EDUCATIONAL GROWTH IN INDIA

INDIA NEWS – London. 1949-61 – 1 – uk Microform Academic [072]

India Office Library. London *see* POPULAR INDIAN PAINTINGS IN THE INDIAN OFFICE LIBRARY

India. Office of the Economic Advisor *see* GUIDE TO CURRENT OFFICIAL STATISTICS.

INDIA OFFICE RECORDS: GUIDE, 1600-1858 / Foster, R – 1 – uk Microform Academic [950]

INDIA OFFICE RECORDS, HOME MISCELLANEOUS SERIES, 1600-1900 – 335r – 1 – $20,550.00 – us UMI [950]

India. Orissa. National Institute of Educational Planning and Administration *see* A SPECIAL STUDY OF ADMINISTRATION OF ELEMENTARY EDUCATION IN RELATION TO THE PROGRAMME OF UNIVERSALISATION IN ORISSA

India. Planning Commission *see*
- ANNUAL PLAN 1966-67
- ANNUAL PLAN 1967-68
- ANNUAL PLAN 1968-69
- ANNUAL PLAN 1969-70
- ANNUAL PLAN 1970-1971
- ANNUAL PLAN 1971-72
- ANNUAL PLAN 1972-73
- ANNUAL PLAN 1993/94
- APPRAISAL AND PROSPECTS OF THE SECOND FIVE YEAR PLAN
- DEVELOPMENT SCHEMES IN THE FIRST FIVE YEAR PLAN
- DRAFT FIFTH FIVE YEAR PLAN 1974-1979
- DRAFT FOURTH PLAN MATERIAL AND FINANCIAL BALANCES, 1964-65, 1970-71 AND 1975-76
- THE FIRST FIVE YEAR PLAN
- THE FIRST FIVE-YEAR PLAN A DRAFT OUTLINE
- FIVE YEAR PLAN PROGRESS REPORT FOR 1951-52 AND 1952-53
- FIVE YEAR PLAN PROGRESS REPORT FOR 1953-54
- FOURTH FIVE YEAR PLAN
- FOURTH FIVE YEAR PLAN 1969-1974
- FOURTH FIVE YEAR PLAN, 1969-74-DRAFT
- FOURTH FIVE YEAR PLAN A DRAFT OUTLINE
- MEMORANDUM ON THE FOURTH FIVE YEAR PLAN (1965/66-1970/71)
- NOTES ON PERSPECTIVE OF DEVELOPMENT, INDIA 1960-61 TO 1975-76
- PROGRAMMES OF INDUSTRIAL DEVELOPMENT, 1951-56
- PROGRAMMES OF INDUSTRIAL DEVELOPMENT, 1956-61
- PROGRAMMES OF INDUSTRIAL DEVELOPMENT, 1961-66
- PROGRESS OF THE PLAN A SHORT SURVEY OF THE WORKING OF THE FIVE YEAR PLAN FROM APR 1951 TO SEP 1953
- REAPPRAISAL OF THE SECOND FIVE YEAR PLAN A RESUME
- SECOND FIVE YEAR PLAN PROGRESS REPORT, 1958-59
- SECOND FIVE-YEAR PLAN
- SECOND FIVE-YEAR PLAN A DRAFT OUTLINE
- STATE DEVELOPMENT PLANS REVIEW OF PROGRESS
- THIRD FIVE YEAR PLAN
- THIRD FIVE YEAR PLAN A DRAFT OUTLINE

India. Planning Commission. Education Division *see* EDUCATIONAL DEVELOPMENT IN THE FOURTH PLAN 1969-1974

India. Preservation of National Monuments *see*
- AGRA AND GWALIOR
- BUILDINGS IN THE PUNJAB
- DELHI
- FORTRESS GWALIOR
- GOLDEN TEMPLE AT AMRITSAR, PUNJAB
- GRAECO-BUDDHIST SCULPTURES FROM YUSUFZAI
- GREAT BUDDHIST TOPE AT SANCHI
- GREAT TEMPLE TO SIVA AND HIS CONSORT AT MADURA
- MEYWAR, RAJPUTANA

- REPORTS OF THE COMMITTEE APPOINTED BY THE GOVERNMENT OF HYDERABAD STATE (NO. 594). PART 2: PRESERVATION AND MAINTENANCE OF THE CAVE-TEMPLES OF ELLORA
- TEMPLES AT TRICHINOPOLY
- TOMB OF JAHANGIR AT SHAHDARA NEAR LAHORE

INDIA QUARTERLY – New Delhi. v1.20. 1945-64. – 169mf – 8 – ne IDC [073]

India. Rajasthan. Directorate of Education *see* A DRAFT PAPER ON DEVELOPMENT PLANS FOR HIGHER EDUCATION IN RAJASTHAN 1968/69 TO 1985/86, WITH SPECIAL REFERENCE TO THE FOURTH FIVE YEAR PLAN

India. Rajasthan. Directorate of Primary and Secondary Education *see*
- A NOTE ON EDUCATIONAL DEVELOPMENT AND RELATED SCHEMES IN RAJASTHAN
- TWO DECADES OF EDUCATION IN RAJASTHAN 1950-1971

INDIA REGISTER – (Cont. as: INDIA OFFICE LIST. London. 1876-1947) – London. 1768-1876. – 2,842mf – 8 – ne IDC [950]

India. Secretary of State *see*
- CORRESPONDENCE BETWEEN THE SECRETARY OF STATE FOR INDIA AND THE VARIOUS LOCAL GOVERNMENTS
- SELECTIONS FROM DESPATCHES, ADDRESSED TO THE GOVERNMENT OF INDIA BY THE SECRETARY OF STATE IN COUNCIL, 1858-1936

India. Sikkim. Directorate of Education *see* SIKKIM EDUCATION NEWSLETTER

INDIA TODAY = INTERNATIONAL EDITION – New Delhi. v1-9 dec 1975-84*. v10-16 jan 1985-dec 1991. v17-19 jan 1992-dec 1994* 1. v20-22 jan 1995-dec 1997+ 1,5,9; v10-19 jan 1985-dec 1994* 5; v10-16 jan 1985-dec 1991. v17-19 jan 1992-dec 1994* 9 – 1,5,9 – D15068 – us UMI [073]

INDIA WEEKLY – London. v13 1977; v15 1979 – 1 – D8685 – us UMI [073]

India. West Bengal. International Institute for Educational Planning. Calcutta University, Department of Statistics *see* GRADUATE EMPLOYMENT AND HIGHER EDUCATION IN WEST BENGAL

THE INDIAN – Hagersville. v1. 1885-86 – 1 – 65.00 – cn McLaren [305]

THE INDIAN – Kuala Lumpur. Malaysia. -w. Dec 1935-Jun 1941. (6 reels) – 1 – uk British Libr Newspaper [072]

Indian Academy of Sciences *see*
- PROCEEDINGS: ANIMAL SCIENCES
- PROCEEDINGS: CHEMICAL SCIENCES
- PROCEEDINGS: EARTH AND PLANETARY SCIENCES
- PROCEEDINGS: MATHEMATICAL SCIENCES
- PROCEEDINGS: PLANT SCIENCES

THE INDIAN ADVANCE – Carson City, NV. Sep 1899; 1901-03 – 1r – 1 – $50.00 – U04458 – us Library Micro [071]

INDIAN ADVOCATE – 1846-55 – 1 – 10.71 – us Baptist [240]

INDIAN AFFAIRS / Association on American Indian Affairs – 1934-82.(American Indian Periodicals in the Princeton University Library). 8 fiches – 9 – $50.00 – us UPA [305]

INDIAN AFFAIRS – New York. 1949-71. v82-142 jan 1972-Spr 1998+ 1; v82-105 jan 1972-dec 1982. v106-107 may-oct 1984*. v108-142 feb 1985-Spr 1998+ 5; v88-142 apr 1975-Spr 1998+ 9 – 1,5,9 – D6669 – us UMI [073]

INDIAN AFFAIRS RECORD – New Delhi. v1-11. 1955-65. Lacking: v. 1 (1, 3-4); v. 7 (12); v. 9 (9-12); v. 10 (1-12). – 66mf – 8 – ne IDC [073]

INDIAN AND ESKIMO CHILDREN / U.S. Bureau of Indian Affairs – 1969 – 9 – $5.00f – us Ross [970]

INDIAN AND FOREIGN REVIEW – New Delhi. v1-25 oct 1963-may 1988 1; v16-25 oct 1978-may 1988 5,9 – 1,5,9 – D9913 – us UMI [073]

INDIAN ANNUAL REGISTER – (Missing: 1925. v1) – Calcutta, 1920-1947 – 782mf – 9 – I-110/2 – ne IDC [304]

INDIAN ANTIQUARY – Bombay, London, 1872-1933. v1-62. Index 1872-1921. v1-50. pt. I-III. S.3, 1964. v1 – 638mf – 9 – I-285/2 – ne IDC [930]

INDIAN ARCHITECTURAL DRAWINGS. P. I / Northwest Provinces and Oudh. India – Prepared by Edmond W. Smith. Allahabad. 1897. BI-694 2 – 8 – ne IDC [720]

INDIAN ARCHIVES – 1968-75. 5 fiches. (American Indian Periodicals in the Princeton University Library) – 9 – $45.00 – us UPA [305]

INDIAN ARCHIVES : QUARTERLY PUBLISHED BY THE GOVERNMENT OF INDIA / India – New Delhi. v1-16. 1947-66 – 59mf – 8 – ne IDC [324]

INDIAN ART SERIES / New Mexico Association of Indian Affairs – Nos.1-12, 1936. 1 fiche. (American Indian Periodicals in the Princeton University Library) – 9 – $45.00 – us UPA [700]

INDIAN BAPTIST – Calcutta, India.v1-5, 1882-86.Baptist Mission Press – 1 – 52.20 – us A.B.H.S. [073]

INDIAN CALENDARS / United Society for the Propagation of the Gospel – 1815-59 – 1 – uk Microform Academic [240]

INDIAN CENSUS ROLLS, 1884-1940 / U.S. Bureau of Indian Affairs – 692 rolls. M595. Printed guide – 1 – us Nat'l Archives [324]

Indian Chemical Society. Calcutta *see* JOURNAL

THE INDIAN CHIEF JOURNEYCAKE / Mitchell, S H – 1895 – 1 – 5.00 – us Baptist [240]

INDIAN CHRISTIAN MISSION : MISSIONARY NOTES / India Christian Mission – 1934-39 (complete) – 1r – 1 – ATLA S0725B – us A.T.L.A. [073]

THE INDIAN CHRISTIANS OF ST THOMAS: OTHERWISE CALLED THE SYRIAN CHRISTIANS OF MALABAR.. / Richards, William Joseph – London: Bemrose, 1908. 138p. ill – 1 – us U.W. Library [240]

THE INDIAN CHURCH MAGAZINE – v18-36. 1922-53 (complete) – 1r – 1 – ATLA S0522 – us A.T.L.A. [073]

INDIAN CLAIMS COMMISSION ANNUAL REPORTS / U.S. Department of the Interior – 1968-77 + Final Report for 1946-78 (all publ) – 13mf – 9 – $19.50 – LLMC 88-004 – us L.L.M.C. [340]

INDIAN CLAIMS COMMISSION DECISIONS – (Also included in LLMC's Native American Collection als Title 4105) – 1948-78. v1-43 (all publ) – 485mf – 9 – $727.00 – LLMC 80-510 – us L.L.M.C. [340]

INDIAN CLAIMS COMMISSION DECISIONS *see* INDIAN CLAIMS COMMISSION ANNUAL REPORTS

INDIAN CONSTITUTIONAL REFORMS, GOVERNMENT OF INDIA BILL – (Filmed with: India. Legislative Council: The Imperial Legislative Council; The Imperial Legislative Council Manual 1916) – [s.l: s.n.], 19– – 1 – us Res Libr [950]

THE INDIAN CRAFTSMAN / Coomaraswamy, Ananda Kentish – London: Probsthain & Co., 1909. Appendices – 1 – us U.W. Library [950]

INDIAN CREEK BAPTIST CHURCH. CAMPBELL COUNTY. JACKSBORO, TENNESSEE : CHURCH RECORDS – Apr 1833-Apr 1954. Lacking: Jul 1862-Jan 1886; 1911-28. Formerly Mt. Pleasant on Indian Creek – 1 – $42.03 – us Baptist [240]

THE INDIAN CRUSADER – 1969-76. (American Indian Periodicals in the Princeton University Library). 3 fiches – 9 – $45.00 – us UPA [305]

INDIAN DAILY NEWS – Calcutta, India. -d. Feb 1867-Dec 1889. 87 reels – 1 – uk British Libr Newspaper [072]

INDIAN ECONOMIC AND SOCIAL HISTORY REVIEW – New Delhi. v1-19 jul 1963-dec 1982 1; v13-19 jan 1976-dec 1982 5,9; v20-34 jan 1983-dec 1997+ 1,5,9 – 1,5,9 – D9323 – us UMI [300]

INDIAN ECONOMIC JOURNAL – (Vols 1-4 not available for filming) – Bombay. v5-45. jul 1957-jun 1998+ 1; v24-45 jul 1976-jun 1998+ 5,9 – 1,5,9 – D2345 – us UMI [330]

INDIAN ED – (Cont by: Canadian Journal of Native Education) – Edmonton, 1973-80* – 1,5,9 – D21906 – us UMI [370]

INDIAN EDUCATION – 1936-65. (American Indian Periodicals in the Princeton University Library). 37 fiches – 9 – $135.00 – us UPA [370]

INDIAN EDUCATION : A NATIONAL TRAGEDY, A NATIONAL CHALLENGE / U.S. Congress. Senate. Committee on Labor and Public Welfare – 1969 – 5mf – 9 – $5.00f – us Ross [370]

INDIAN EDUCATION NEWSLETTER – 1970-75. (American Indian Periodicals in the Princeton University Library). 5 fiches – 9 – $45.00 – us UPA [370]

THE INDIAN EDUCATOR – United Indians of All Tribes Foundation.-m,-bim,-irr,-m. Sept 1981- Jun-Jul 1985. Numbering irregular – 1 – us U.W. Library [073]

INDIAN ELECTION MANIFESTOS – 1967. Materials from 12 parties – 1 – us Res Libr [950]

INDIAN ELECTION RESULTS : NEWSPAPERS, MARCH 11-19 1971 – Charlottesville, NC: Alderman Library Photographic Services, 1971 – 1 – us Res Libr [950]

INDIAN ELECTION RESULTS, 1967 – Chicago: Uni of Chicago Lib, Dept of Photodup, [196-] – 3r – 1 – us Res Libr [950]

THE INDIAN EMPIRE REVIEW – [London: Indian Empire Society] v1-8. nov 1931-1939 – 1 – us Res Libr [950]

The Indian Empire Society *see* [PAMPHLETS]

AN INDIAN EPHEMERIS, A.D. 700 TO A.D. 1999 / Swamikannu Pillai, L D – Madras, 1922-1923. 7 vols. BI-588 2 – 8 – ne IDC [520]

INDIAN EVANGELICAL REVIEW : A JOURNAL OF MISSIONARY THOUGHT AND EFFORT – v1-29. Jul 1873-1903 (complete) – 14r – 1 – ATLA S0139 – us A.T.L.A. [073]

INDIAN EXPRESS – New Delhi, India. 1962-Jul 1995 – 194r – 1 – us L of C Photodup [072]

INDIAN FAMILY DEFENSE / Association on American Indian Affairs – 1974-79. (American Indian Periodicals in the Princeton University Library). 1 fiche – 9 – $45.00 – us UPA [305]

INDIAN FARMING – v. 1-. 1940- – 1. – apply; v.26- 1976- 5,6,9 – us UMI [630]

INDIAN FILMS AND FILM WORLD, 1976 / ed by Jayabharathi – Madras: Jwala, 1976 – us Res Libr [790]

INDIAN FOREST RECORDS – Calcutta, (New) Delhi. v1-20. 1908-34. – 175mf – 8 – ne IDC [634]

INDIAN FORESTER – (Missing: v74(6-7)) – Allahabad, Calcutta, 1875-1967. v1-93. Index 1875-1904. v1-30 – 1,414mf – 9 – I-531/2 – ne IDC [634]

INDIAN GEMS FOR THE MASTER'S GROWN : 1. INDIAN DEVOTEE AND HIS DISCIPLES: 2. FROM BONDAGE TO FREEDOM, OR, THE LIFE OF TULSI PAUL / Droese, Miss – London: Religious Tract Society, 1892 – 1mf – 9 – 0-8370-6734-0 – 1986-0734 – us A.T.L.A. [240]

INDIAN GEOGRAPHICAL JOURNAL – v. 1-40. 1926-65. Lacking: v. 10 (3); v. 20; v. 21; v. 26-v. 29 (1); v. 31; v. 32; v. 35-v. 38. – 159mf – 8 – ne IDC [910]

INDIAN HEMP: A SOCIAL MENACE / Johnson, Donald McIntosh – Foreword by H. Pullar-Strecker. London: C. Johnson, 1952. 112p. Bibliography – 1 – us U.W. Library [360]

INDIAN HERALD – Allahabad, India. -w. 28 April 1879-15 March 1882. 10 reels – 1 – uk British Libr Newspaper [072]

INDIAN HISTORIAN – San Francisco. v1-12. 1967-79 – 48mf – 9 – $5.00f – us Ross [970]

INDIAN HISTORICAL QUARTERLY – Calcutta, 1925-1961. v1-37 – 427mf – 9 – I-133/2 – ne IDC [950]

Indian Historical Records Commission *see* PROCEEDINGS OF THE INDIAN HISTORICAL RECORDS COMMISSION

Indian History Congress *see* PROCEEDINGS OF THE INDIAN HISTORY CONGRESS 1938-41, 1945-63

Indian Home Guards. First Regiment *see* DAY BOOK

INDIAN HOME RULE / Gandhi, Mahatma – Reprinted with new forward by the author. Madras: Ganesh & Co., 1919?. 136p – 1 – us U.W. Library [950]

INDIAN HORIZONS – (Former titles: Indo-Asian Culture (jul 1952-oct 1971)) – New Delhi. v1-46 jul 1952-1997+; cum index v1-10 jul 1952-pr 1961 1; v25-27 1976-78*. v28 1979. v29-35 1980-86*. v36 1987. v37-43 1988-94*. v44-46 1995-97+ 5; v24-46 1976-97+ 9 – 1,5,9 – D7460 – us UMI [073]

INDIAN IMAGES / Smithsonian Institution – 1970 – 9 – $5.00f – us Ross [970]

INDIAN INSECT LIFE / Maxwell-Lefroy, H & Howlet, F M – Z-283 2. 1909 – 8 – ne IDC [590]

INDIAN INSECT LIFE: A MANUAL OF THE INSECTS OF THE PLAINS / Lefroy, H M – 2156 2. 1909 – 8 – ne IDC [590]

INDIAN INSECT PESTS / Maxwell-Lefroy, H – Calcutta. 1906. BZ-282 2 – 8 – ne IDC [590]

Indian Institute of Public Opinion *see* QUARTERLY ECONOMIC REPORT

Indian Institute of Science *see* ANNUAL REPORT OF THE DIRECTOR TO THE COUNCIL

INDIAN JOURNAL OF ADULT EDUCATION – New Delhi. v1-35 1939-74*. v36-58 jan 1975-dec 1997+ 1; v36-37 jan 1975-dec 1976*. v38 1977. v39-55 jan 1978-dec 1994*. v56-58 1995-1997+ 5; v36 1975*; v37-58 jan 1976-dec 1997+ 9 – 1,5,9 – D10442 – us UMI [370]

INDIAN JOURNAL OF AGRICULTURAL SCIENCE – New Delhi. v1-44 1931-74* 1. v45-67 jan 1975-dec 1997+ 1,9; v45-57 jan 1975-dec 1987*. v58 1988. v59-64 jan 1989-dec 1994*. v65-67 1995-97+ 5 – 1,5,9 – D10654 – us UMI [630]

INDIAN JOURNAL OF ANIMAL SCIENCES – (Former title: Indian Journal of Veterinary Science and Animal Husbandry (mar 1931-68)) – New Delhi. v1-44 1931-74* 1. v45-67 jan 1975-dec 1997+ 1,9; v45-51 jan 1975-dec 1981*. v52 1982. v53-64 jan 1983-dec 1994*. v65-67 1995-97+ 5 – 1,5,9 – D10655 – us UMI [636]

INDIAN JOURNAL OF APPLIED PSYCHOLOGY – (Vols 10 & 12 (1973, 1975) not available for filming) – Madras. v1-9 jan 1964-jul 1972. v11-19 jan 1974-jul 1982. v20-31 jan 1983-jul 1994*. v32-34 jan 1995-jul 1997+ – 1 – D7275 – us UMI [150]

INDIAN JOURNAL OF CANCER – Bombay. v1-11 1963-74*. v12-17 mar 1975-dec 1980. v18-30 mar 1981-dec 1993*. . v31 mar-dec 1994*. v32-34 mar 1995-dec 1997+ – 1 – D10454 – us UMI [616]

INDIAN JOURNAL OF CHEMICAL TECHNOLOGY – (Cont in pt: Indian Journal Technology) – New Delhi. v1 jan-nov 1994*. v2-4 jan 1995-97+ – 1,5,9 – D20870 – us UMI [660]

INDIAN JOURNAL OF CHEMICAL TECHNOLOGY *see* INDIAN JOURNAL OF TECHNOLOGY

INDIAN JOURNAL OF DERMATOLOGY, VENEROLOGY AND LEPROLOGY – Vellore. v46. 1980 – 1,5,9 – D688.01 – us UMI [616]

INDIAN JOURNAL OF ECONOMICS – Allahabad. v1-31. 1916-51. Lacking: v. 19 (1); v. 25-30. – 324mf – 8 – ne IDC [330]

INDIAN JOURNAL OF ENGINEERING AND MATERIALS – (Cont in pt: Indian Journal of Technology) – New Delhi. v1 feb-dec 1994*. v2-4 feb 1995-dec 1997+ – 1,5,9 – D20871 – us UMI [620]

INDIAN JOURNAL OF ENGINEERING AND MATERIALS SCIENCE *see* INDIAN JOURNAL OF TECHNOLOGY

INDIAN JOURNAL OF EXPERIMENTAL PSYCHOLOGY – (Publ believed to have ceased with v8 n2 jul 1974) – Madras. v1-8 1967-74* – 1 – D7274 – us UMI [073]

INDIAN JOURNAL OF MEDICAL RESEARCH – v13-66. 1925-77 – 1,5,6 – us Princeton Micro [073]

INDIAN JOURNAL OF PEDIATRICS – New Delhi. v1-38 1933-71*. v39-64 jan 1972-dec 1997+ 1; v39 1972. v41 1974*. v42 1975. v43-46 1976-79*. v47-48 1981. v49-50 1982-83*. v51-52 1984-85. v53 1986*. v54 1987. v55-57 1988-90*. v58-64 1988-97+ 5; v41-64 1974-97+ 9 – 1,5,9 – D7252 – us UMI [618]

INDIAN JOURNAL OF PHARMACEUTICAL SCIENCES – (Cont: Indian Journal of Pharmacy) – Bombay. v45-55 jan 1983-dec 1993*. v40-44 mar 1978-dec 1982. v56 1994*. v56-59 jan 1995-dec 1997+ – 1 – D7397.01 – us UMI [615]

INDIAN JOURNAL OF PHARMACEUTICAL SCIENCES *see* INDIAN JOURNAL OF PHARMACY

INDIAN JOURNAL OF PHARMACY – (Cont by: Indian Journal of Pharmaceutical Sciences) – Bombay. v1-36 jan 1939-dec 1974*. v37-40 jan 1975-feb 1978 – 1 – D7397 – us UMI [615]

INDIAN JOURNAL OF PHARMACY *see* INDIAN JOURNAL OF PHARMACEUTICAL SCIENCES

INDIAN JOURNAL OF PHYSICS AND PROCEEDINGS OF THE INDIAN ASSOCIATION FOR THE CULTIVATION OF SCIENCE – v. 1-34. 1926-60 – 1 – us Princeton Micro [530]

INDIAN JOURNAL OF POLITICAL STUDIES – Jodhpur. v1-2 jan 1977-jul 1978 1,5,9* – 1,5,9 – D11294 – us UMI [320]

INDIAN JOURNAL OF POWER AND RIVER VALLEY DEVELOPMENT – (Vols 1-3 not available for filming) – Calcutta. v4-30 jun 1954-dec 1980 1; v28-29 jan 1978-dec 1979*. v30 1980 5; v28-30 jan 1978-dec 1980* 9 – 1,5,9 – D7286 – us UMI [333]

INDIAN JOURNAL OF PSYCHOLOGY – New Delhi. v1-48 1926-73*. v49-72 mar 1974-1997+ 1; v50-51 mar 1975-dec 1976. v52-69 mar 1977-1994*. v70-72 1995-97+ 5; v52-72 mar 1977-1997+ – 1,5,9 – D9106 – us UMI [150]

INDIAN JOURNAL OF SOCIAL WORK – Bombay. v1-58 jun 1940-oct 1997+. cum index v1-25 1940-65 1; v33-47 apr 1972-jan 1987. v48-55 apr 1987-oct 1994*. v56-58 jan 1995-oct 1997+ 5; v37-58 apr 1976-oct 1997+ 9 – 1,5,9 – D7019 – us UMI [360]

INDIAN JOURNAL OF TECHNOLOGY – (Split into: Indian Journal of Chemical Technology, and: Indian Journal of Engineering and Materials Science) – New Delhi. v1-31 jan 1963-dec 1993 1; v8-31 jan 1970-dec 1993 5; v14-31 jan 1976-dec 1993 9 – 1,5,9 – D3034 – us UMI [660]

INDIAN JOURNAL OF TECHNOLOGY *see*
- INDIAN JOURNAL OF CHEMICAL TECHNOLOGY
- INDIAN JOURNAL OF ENGINEERING AND MATERIALS

INDIAN JOURNAL OF VETERINARY SCIENCE AND ANIMAL HUSBANDRY *see* INDIAN JOURNAL OF ANIMAL SCIENCES

INDIAN LAW REPORTER – (v1-11 1974-84 on reel $468.00. v12-22 1985-95 on mf $681.00) – v1-22. 1974-95 – 5,6,9 – $1,149.00 set – us Hein [340]

INDIAN LAW RESOURCE CENTER – Washington DC. 60 docs. 1980-1991 – 20mf – 9 – ne IDC [340]

INDIAN LIBRARIAN – Jullundur City. v1-36 jun 1947-mar 1982 1; v31-35 jun 1976-mar 1981. v36 jun 1981-mar 1982* 5; v31-33 jun 1976-mar 1979. v34-35 jun 1979-mar 1981*. v36 jun 1981-mar 1982 9 – 1,5,9 – D1942 – us UMI [020]

INDIAN LINGUISTICS – v. 1-23. 1931-62. – 82mf – 8 – ne IDC [400]

INDIAN MAGAZINE *see* JOURNAL OF THE NATIONAL INDIAN ASSOCIATION

THE INDIAN MAGAZINE – (Cont by: Brant Agriculturist and Indian Magazine) – Ohsweken, Ont: [s.n. 1893-1897] – 9 – cn C.I.H.M. [630]

THE INDIAN MAGAZINE *see* BRANT AGRICULTURIST AND INDIAN MAGAZINE

INDIAN MANAGEMENT – New Delhi. v1-10 sep 1961-dec 1971. v11-33 jan 1972-dec 1994*. v34-36 jan 1995-dec 1997+ – 1 – D5973 – us UMI [650]

Indian Mathematical Society. Madras *see* JOURNAL

INDIAN MEDICINAL PLANTS / Kirtikar, KR & Basu, BD – 2pts. text, 4 pts. pls. Allahabad. 1918. B-7289 1 – 9 – ne IDC [580]

INDIAN MIRROR – Calcutta, India. -w. 1878-89. 22 reels – 1 – uk British Libr Newspaper [072]

INDIAN MISSIONARY – Oklahoma. 1884-91 – 1 – 30.80 – us Baptist [240]

INDIAN MISSIONARY MANUAL : HINTS TO YOUNG MISSIONARIES IN INDIA / Murdoch, John – (Includes appendix & index) – 4th rev enl ed. London: James Nisbet, 1895 – 2mf – 9 – 0-8370-6227-6 – 1986-0227 – us A.T.L.A. [240]

INDIAN MISSIONARY RECORD – (Cont by: Indian Record at v20 1957. v1-11 1938-48 Can$115.00. v12-19 1949-56 Can$115.00) – Winnipeg. v1-19. 1938-56 – 1 – cn Micromedia [240]

Indian Museum *see* MEMOIRS OF THE INDIAN MUSEUM

INDIAN MUSIC, SCIENTIFIC AND PRACTICAL : ITS ORIGIN, HISTORY AND DIVISIONS; WRITERS OF OLD AND MODERN TIMES; DESCRIPTION AND CLASSIFICATION OF RAGES AND RAGNIS, MEANINGS AND MEASURES OF TALS AND SURS; FORMS AND USES OF MUSICAL INSTRUMENTS / Prasad, N – Aligarh: Viddyasager, 1906 – 1 – us Sibley [780]

Indian Musicological Society *see* JOURNAL OF THE INDIAN MUSICOLOGICAL SOCIETY

INDIAN MYTHS, OR, LEGENDS, TRADITIONS, AND SYMBOLS OF THE ABORIGINES OF AMERICA: COMPARED WITH THOSE OF OTHER COUNTRIES INCLUDING HINDOSTAN, EGYPT, PERSIA, ASSYRIA, AND CHINA / Emerson, Ellen Russell – London: Truebner, 1884. 02914. (Pre-1900 Canadiana) – 9 – cn C.I.H.M. [971]

INDIAN NATION – Patna, India. Apr 1944-Nov 1989 – 145r – 1 – us L of C Photodup [072]

Indian National Congress *see* ELECTION MANIFESTO, 1967

Indian National Congress. All-India Congress Committee *see*
- FILES CONCERNING BENGAL, 1927-1947
- PAPERS, 1914-1920
- YEARS OF FREEDOM

INDIAN NEWS – (Ceased v23 no 3 1982) – Ottawa. v1-23. 1954-82 – 1 – Price varies – cn Micromedia [305]

INDIAN NEWS AND CHRONICLE OF EASTERN AFFAIRS – London, UK. 11 Jun 1840-6 Dec 1843; 1844-27 Jul 1858. -w – 1 – uk British Libr Newspaper [072]

AN INDIAN NEWS SHEET – London: Indian Empire Society. n1-37. apr 1940-oct 1949 – 1 – us Res Libr [950]

INDIAN NOTES AND QUERIES : INCLUDING PUNJAB NOTES AND QURIES, AND NORTH INDIAN NOTES AND QUERIES – Allahabad. v1-4. 1883-87; v. 1-5. 1891-96. – 35mf – 8 – ne IDC [073]

INDIAN OBSERVER – Calcutta. 1798. – 8mf – 8 – ne IDC [950]

INDIAN OBSERVER – Calcutta, India. -w. Feb 1871-May 1872. 2 reels – 1 – uk British Libr Newspaper [072]

INDIAN OCEAN FISHERY COMMISSION REPORT OF THE 3RD SESSION OF THE COMMITTEE FOR THE DEVELOPMENT AND MANAGEMENT OF FISHERIES IN THE BAY OF BENGAL : AND THE 9TH MEETING OF THE ADVISORY COMMITTEE FOR THE DEVELOPMENT OF SMALL-SCALE FISHERIES OF THE BAY OF BENGAL PROGRAMME. BANGKOK, 1985 – 1985 – 31p – it F.A.O. [639]

THE INDIAN OCEAN: POLITICAL AND STRATEGIC FUTURE: HEARINGS. / U.S. Congress. House. Committee on Foreign Affairs. Subcommittee on National Security Policy and Scientific Developments – Washington, Govt. Print. Off., 1971. 242 p. LL-2361 – 1 – us L of C Photodup [340]

INDIAN OPINION – Durban and Phoenix. South Africa. -w. Jun 1903-Dec 1916. (15 reels) – 1 – uk British Libr Newspaper [072]

INDIAN OPINION – Phoenix, Natal: International Printing Press, 1917-jun 1934; 1935; 1937-47; 1953-jun 1957 – 1 – us Res Libr [072]

INDIAN OPINION – Phoenix: International Printing Press, jan 8 1960-aug 4 1961 – us Res Libr [975]

THE INDIAN PENAL CODE, AS MODIFIED UP TO THE 1ST AUGUST 1890 / India. Laws, Statutes, etc – Calcutta: Superintendent of Government Printing, 1890. 203p. LL-996 – 1 – us L of C Photodup [340]

INDIAN PHILOSOPHICAL REVIEW – Baroda [etc]: Indian Philosophical Assoc. [v1 n2-v3] oct 1917-1920 – 1 – us Res Libr [100]

INDIAN PIGEONS AND DOVES / Baker, E C S – Z-257 2. 1913 – 8 – ne IDC [590]

INDIAN PIONEER – Kuala Lumpur. Malaysia. -w. Mar 1929-Aug 1930. (1 reel) – 1 – uk British Libr Newspaper [072]

INDIAN PIONEER PAPERS, 1860-1935 – 1019mf – 9 – $5.00f – us Ross [970]

INDIAN PLASTICS REVIEW – Calcutta. v19 1973* 1; v17-18 jan 1971-dec 1972 1,5,9 – 1,5,9 – D7880 – us UMI [660]

INDIAN POLITICAL SCIENCE REVIEW – New Delhi. v1-19 oct 1966-dec 1985 1; v9-19 jan 1975-dec 1985 5; v10-19 jan 1975-dec 1985 9 – 1,5,9 – D7474 – us UMI [320]

AN INDIAN PRIESTESS : THE LIFE OF CHUNDRA LELA / Lee, Ada – London: Morgan & Scott, [1912?] – 1mf – us A.T.L.A. [240]

THE INDIAN PRINCESS, OR LA BELLE SAVAGE / Bray, John – Philadelphia: George E. Blake 1808. MUSIC 464 – 1 – us L of C Photodup [780]

THE INDIAN PROBLEM IN KENYA / Maini, P L – London, 1944 – us Res Libr [305]

INDIAN PROGRESS – 1959-74. 6 fiches. (American Indian Periodicals in the Princeton University Library) – 9 – $45.00 – us UPA [305]

INDIAN PROSCRIBED TRACTS, 1907-1947 – Chicago, IL: Uni of Chicago Photodup Dept, [19–?] – 1 – us Res Libr [950]

INDIAN PUBLIC OPINION – Lahore, Pakistan. -w. March 1870-Feb 1877. c49 reels – 1 – uk British Libr Newspaper [072]

INDIAN PUBLIC OPINION AND PUNJAB TIMES – Lahore, India. -d. March 1870-Feb 1877. 60 reels – 1 – uk British Libr Newspaper [072]

INDIAN PULP AND PAPER – Calcutta. v27 jul 1972-jan 1973. v30 jun 1975-may 1976. v31-34 jun 1976-may 1980*. v35 jun 1980-may 1981 1; v30-32 jun 1975-jul 1978. v33-35 jun 1978-may 1981* 5; v30-32 jun 1975-jul 1978*. v33-35 jun 1978-may 1981 9 – 1,5,9 – D8172 – us UMI [670]

INDIAN RECORD – (v47-50 1984-87 Can$50.00y 5. Index 1938-86 Can$50.00 5. Cont: Indian Missionary Record at v20 1957. Ceased v50 1987) – Winnipeg. v20-46. 1957-1982/83 – 1 – Price varies – cn Micromedia [240]

INDIAN RECORD – Winnipeg. 1964-70. (American Indian Periodicals in the Princeton University Library). 7 fiches – 9 – $45.00 – us UPA [305]

INDIAN RECORD *see* INDIAN MISSIONARY RECORD

INDIAN RECORDER AND DIGEST – v9-21. 1963-75 – 1 – us UMI [073]

INDIAN RECORDS / United Society for the Propagation of the Gospel – 1751-1835. Series C/Ind. – 1 – uk Microform Academic [240]

INDIAN RECORDS / United Society for the Propagation of the Gospel – 1770-1900 – 1 – uk Microform Academic [240]

INDIAN RECORDS / United Society for the Propagation of the Gospel – 1840-61. Series E/PRE – 1 – uk Microform Academic [240]

INDIAN RECORDS / United Society for the Propagation of the Gospel – 1856-1900. Series E/V – 1 – uk Microform Academic [240]

INDIAN REVIEW – Madras. v1-54. 1900-53. Lacking: v. 38 (3) 1937; v. 39 (5) 1938; v. 41 (11) 1940; v. 42 (2, 6, 8-10) 1941; v. 43 (4) 1942; v. 43 (7-12) 1942; v. 44-48 1943-47; v. 49 (4-5, 9-12) 1948; v. 54 (1, 3) 1953. – 999mf – 8 – ne IDC [073]

Indian Rights Association *see*
- PAPERS
- PUBLICATIONS; 2ND SERIES. NO. 1-99. 1893-1915. (NOS. 19 AND 35 WANTING)

THE INDIAN RIGHTS ASSOCIATION, 1885-1901 – 1972 – 26r – 1 – $2,210.00 – S1858 – us Scholarly Res [360]

Indian Rights Association. Executive Committee *see* ANNUAL REPORTS

INDIAN RIGHTS ASSOCIATION PAPERS, 1864-1973 – (Series 1 Correspondence 1864-1968; Series 2 Organizational Records, 1882-1973; Series 3 Printed Matter 1830-1969; Series 4 Herbert Welsh Papers 1877-1934; Series 5 Photographs; Series 6 Council on Indian Affairs 1943-68) – 136r – 1 – $9810.00 – us UMI [323]

INDIAN RIVER NEWS – Sebastian. Fl. -w. 1959-1966 – 1 – us P.K. Yonge [071]

INDIAN SCHOOL JOURNAL – 1902-52. (American Indian Periodicals in the Princeton University Library). 226 fiches – 9 – $920.00 – us UPA [370]

INDIAN SCHOOL JOURNAL – Washington. v76 nov 1976-jun 1977*. v77-78 oct 1977-may 1979. v79 sep 1979-apr 1980* 1; v76-79 nov 1976-apr 1980 5; v76-77 nov 1976-may 1978*. v78-79 sep 1978-apr 1980 9 – 1,5,9 – D7424 – us UMI [370]

THE INDIAN SENTINEL – 1916-62. (American Indian Periodicals in the Princeton University Library). 93 fiches – 9 – $350.00 – us UPA [305]

INDIAN SENTINEL ANNUAL REPORTS – 1902-16. (American Indian Periodicals in the Princeton University Library). 7 fiches – 9 – $45.00 – us UPA [305]

INDIAN SNAKE POISONS, THEIR NATURE AND EFFECTS / Wall, A J – Z 297 2. 1883 – 8 – ne IDC [615]

INDIAN SNAKES / Nicholson, E – With descriptive catalogue of snakes found in India and the adjoining countries. Madras. 1870. BZ-285 2 – 8 – ne IDC [590]

INDIAN SOCIAL REFORMER – Madras. India. -w. 25 Dec 1898-26 Aug 1906. (4mqn reels) – 1 – uk British Libr Newspaper [072]

Indian Society of Oriental Art *see* JOURNAL OF THE INDIAN SOCIETY OF ORIENTAL ART

INDIAN SPECTATOR – Bombay, India. Indian Spectator & Voice of India. -w. 1886-1899. 10 reels – 1 – uk British Libr Newspaper [072]

INDIAN TERRITORY BAR ASSOCIATION REPORTS – 1st to 5th annual meetings. 1900-04 (all publ) – 5mf – 9 – $7.50 – LLMC 84-490 – us L.L.M.C. [073]

INDIAN TERRITORY REPORTS – (A Pre-NRS title) – v1-6. 1896-1907 (all publ) – 20mf – 9 – $90.00 – LLMC 84-132 – us L.L.M.C. [340]

Indian Territory. Synod (Pres. Ch. in the U.S.A.) *see* MINUTES, 1887-1906

INDIAN TREATIES AND SURRENDERS : FROM 1680 TO 1890 – Ottawa. 2v. 1891 – 10mf – 9 – ILM-2304/1 – ne IDC [327]

INDIAN TREES / Brandis, D – London. 1906. B-7305 2 – 8 – ne IDC [580]

INDIAN TRUTH – 1924-73. (American Indian Periodicals in the Princeton University Library). 38 fiches – 9 – $145.00 – us UPA [305]

INDIAN TRUTH – v1-260. 1924-84 – 59mf – 9 – $5.00f – us Ross [073]

INDIAN VALLEY RECORD – Greenville, CA. 1954-57; 1972; 1977 – 4r – 1 – $200.00 – B02279 – us Library Micro [071]

INDIAN VALLEY RECORD – Greenville. Calif. 1931-1953; 1960- – 1 – us UMI [071]

INDIAN VALLEY RECORD – Quincy, CA. 1954-57; 1972; 1977 – 4r – 1 – $200.00 – B02651 – us Library Micro [071]

INDIAN VIEWS – Durban, South Africa. 6 Jul 1934-26 Jun 1936. 4 reels – 1, 16 diazo available at reduced price – sa SA Libr [072]

INDIAN VIEWS – (S. Africa). 5 Jan 1945-1 Jul 1953 – 1 – 129.00 – us L of C Photodup [073]

INDIAN VOICE – 1969-81. 40 fiches. (American Indian Periodicals in the Princeton University Library) – 9 – $145.00 – us UPA [305]

INDIAN VOICES – 1963-68. (American Indian Periodicals in the Princeton University Library). 9 fiches – 9 – $50.00 – us UPA [305]

INDIAN WARS AND PIONEERS OF TEXAS / Brown, John Henry – Austin: L.E. Daniell Publ., n.d.Texas Reel 6. (The Cox Library Collection) – 5 – us Americana [978]

THE INDIAN WARS OF THE WEST AND FRONTIER ARMY LIFE, 1862-1898 : OFFICIAL HISTORIES AND PERSONAL NARRATIVES – (With printed guide) – 1996 – ca 750mf – 9 – ca $4,690.00 – 1-55655-598-9 – us UPA [977]

INDIAN WELLS VALLEY INDEPENDENT – Ridgecrest. Calif. 1955-1967 – 1 – us UMI [071]

INDIAN WITNESS – v24-88. 1895-1958 (complete) – 55r – 1 – ATLA S0027 – us A.T.L.A. [073]

INDIAN ZOOLOGY / Pennant, T – Z-286 2. 2nd ed. 1790 – 8 – ne IDC [590]

INDIANA : BURNS INDIANA STATUTES ANNOTATED – Charlottesville: Michie Co, 1977-Mar 1996 update – 9 – $2,575.50 set – us Hein [340]

INDIANA : COUNTY AND REGIONAL HISTORIES AND ATLASES – 1 – us Primary [978]

INDIANA : SESSION LAWS OF AMERICAN STATES AND TERRITORIES – 1801-1995 – 9 – $1,905.00 set – us Hein [340]

Indiana *see*
- COUNTY HISTORIES
- A HISTORY OF THE CITY OF VINCENNES, FROM 1702 TO 1901
- INDEX TO DEED RECORDS, 1815-1817
- OLD VINCENNES
- REGISTER OF NEGRO SLAVES & MASTERS
- REPORTS AND OPINIONS (A-G)
- REPORTS, POST-NRS
- REPORTS, PRE-NRS
- SOME EARLY ITEMS CONCERNING VINCENNES, INDIANA FROM THE YEAR OF 1783-1790
- STATE LABOR REPORTS

INDIANA ADDENDUM TO GREEN'S PLEADING AND PRACTICE / Hoffman, Publius V – St. Louis: Gilbert, 1881. 182p. LL-85 – 1 – us L of C Photodup [340]

INDIANA AMERICAN – Brookville. Ind. 1833-1853; 1855-1856; 1869-1871 – 1 – us UMI [071]

INDIANA AND INDIANANS / Dunn, Jacob Pratt – Chicago: American Historical Society, 1919. Vols. 1-5. Indiana Reel 1. (The Cox Library Collection) – 5 – us Americana [978]

Indiana. Appellate Court *see* INDIANA APPELLATE REPORTS

INDIANA APPELLATE REPORTS / Indiana. Appellate Court – (No Pre-NRS vols. Updates planned) – v1-67. 1890-1919 – 575mf – 9 – $862.00 – LLMC 80-805 – us L.L.M.C. [340]

INDIANA APPELLATE REPORTS *see* WILSON'S SUPERIOR COURT REPORTS

INDIANA ATTORNEY GENERAL REPORTS AND OPINIONS – (6 1891-1979 $385.00. 9 1979-1995 $92.00) – 1891-1995 – 6,9 – $477.50set – us Hein [340]

INDIANA BAPTIST – 1959-1991 – 1 – $460.24 – us Baptist [240]

INDIANA BAPTIST/BAPTIST OUTLOOK – Indianapolis, IN. 1886, 1894-96, 1898-1902. Single reels available – 1 – 142.85 – us A.B.H.S. [073]

INDIANA CENSUSES ON MICROFICHE – 9 – us A.G.L.L. [920]

INDIANA COUNTY GAZETTE – Indiana. Pa. 1890-1912 – 1 – us UMI [071]

INDIANA COUNTY: HER PEOPLE, PAST AND PRESENT / Stewart, J T – Genealogical and biographical records. Chicago, J. H. Beers and Co., 1913. Vols. 1-2, Pennsylvania Reel 24. (The Cox Library Collection) – 5 – us Americana [978]

INDIANA COUNTY HISTORIES – (V153. 1) – 929 titles. V140 – 5,9 – us A.G.L.L. [920]

INDIANA DEMOCRAT – Indiana, PA. -w 1896-1912 – 13 – $25.00r – us I.M.R. [071]

Indiana. Dept. of Insurance. Audit and Control *see* REPORTS OF THE AUDITOR

Indiana. Employment Security Board *see* EMPLOYMENT SECURITY IN INDIANA

INDIANA FOLKLORE – Journal of the Hoosier Folklore Society. semiann. v1, no.1-v12. 1968-80. 2 reels. Continued as: Newsletter. v13, no.1-2. 1980- – 1 – us I.U. Libraries [390]

INDIANA HERALD – Huntington. Ind. 1848-1864; 1867-1887 – 1 – us UMI [071]

INDIANA HERALD – Indianapolis. Ind. 1954- – 1 – us UMI [071]

Indiana Historical Records Survey *see* INVENTORY OF COUNTY ARCHIVES–NO. 2. ALLEN COUNTY (FORT WAYNE)

INDIANA INTERNATIONAL AND COMPARATIVE LAW REVIEW – v1-5. 1991-1995 – 9 – $50.00set – us Hein [340]

THE INDIANA JEWISH CHRONICLE – Indianapolis. Ind. 1945-50; 52-53. 1957-66 – 1 – us A.J.P.C. [071]

INDIANA JOURNAL – Indianapolis. Ind. -w, sw. 1831-34 – 1 – us UMI [071]

INDIANA LAW JOURNAL – (Lacking: 1898 nos 2+4. 1899 nos 2-3) – v1-3. 1898-99 (all publ) – 9 – LLMC 84-487 – us L.L.M.C. [073]

INDIANA LAW JOURNAL – v1-72. 1926-97 – 1,5,6,9 – $1,305.00 – us Hein [073]

INDIANA LAW MAGAZINE – Indianapolis. v1-5. 1883-85 – 1 – $40.00 – us Hein [073]

THE INDIANA LAW MAGAZINE – (Includes: The Corporation Digest and The Corporation Reporter) – v1-5. 1883-85 (all publ) – 29mf – 9 – $42.50 – LLMC 84-488 – us L.L.M.C. [073]

THE INDIANA LAW REPORTER – v1. 1881 (all publ) – 1mf – 9 – $4.50 – LLMC 84-489 – us L.L.M.C. [073]

INDIANA LAW REVIEW – v1-29. 1967-96 – 1,5,6 – $720.00 – us Hein [073]

INDIANA METHODISM; BEING AN ACCOUNT OF THE INTRODUCTION, PROGRESS AND PRESENT POSITION OF METHODISM IN THE STATE ... WITH SKETCHES OF THE PRINCIPAL METHODIST EDUCATORS IN THE STATE DOWN TO 1872 / Holliday, Frederic C – 1873 – 9 – us A.T.L.A. [240]

Indiana. Morgan Raid Commission *see* JOURNAL, MS 3506

INDIANA NEWSPAPER PROJECT – (Contains 1,000 Indiana newspapers) – Indianapolis: Indiana Historical Society – 16,000r – 1 – $15.00r – us I.H.S. [071]

INDIANA PROGRESS – Indiana, PA. -w 1903-1940; 1944-1945 – 13 – $25.00r – us I.M.R. [071]

INDIANA SOCIAL STUDIES QUARTERLY – (v30-. 1977-. 5,6,9) – v. 1-. 1945- – 1 – us UMI [073]

INDIANA STAATS-HEROLD – Hammond: Staats-Herold Pub Co, oct 1931-mar 5 1932 – 1r – 1 – us Res Libr [071]

Indiana. State Bar Association *see* PROCEEDINGS

INDIANA STATE BAR ASSOCIATION ANNUAL REPORTS – (Lacking: 1925) – 1st to 31st annual meetings. 1897-1927 (all publ) – 35mf – 9 – $52.50 – LLMC 84-491 – us L.L.M.C. [073]

Indiana. State Convention of Baptists *see* EXECUTIVE BOARD MINUTES

Indiana. Superior Court *see* WILSON'S SUPERIOR COURT REPORTS

Indiana. Supreme Court *see*
- BLACKFORD'S REPORTS
- INDIANA SUPREME COURT REPORTS
- SMITH'S REPORTS

INDIANA SUPREME COURT REPORTS / Indiana. Supreme Court – (Pre-NRS: v1-101 1848-84 714mf $1,071.00. Updates planned) – v1-188. 1848-1918/20 – 1424mf – 9 – $2,136.00 – LLMC 80-804 – us L.L.M.C. [340]

INDIANA SUPREME COURT REPORTS *see*
- BLACKFORD'S REPORTS
- SMITH'S REPORTS

Indiana. Territory *see* REPORTS, PRE-NRS

THE INDIANA TIMES – Indiana, PA. -w 1889-1912 – 13 – $25.00r – us I.M.R. [071]

INDIANA TODAY / ed by McCarty, C Walter – Indianapolis: Indiana Editor's Assoc., 1942. Indiana Reel 3. (The Cox Library Collection) – 5 – us Americana [978]

INDIANA UNIVERSITY 1820-90 / Wylie, Theophilus A – Biographical sketches of its Presidents, Professors and Graduates, and a list of its Students from 1820 to 1887. Indianapolis: Wm. B. Burford, 1890. Indiana Reel 3. (The Cox Library Collection) – 5 – us Americana [978]

Indiana University. Institute for Sex Research. Library *see* CATALOG OF PERIODICAL LITERATURE IN THE SOCIAL AND BEHAVIORAL SCIENCES SECTION, INCLUDING SUPPLEMENT TO MONOGRAPHS, 1973-75

INDIANA UNIVERSITY. SCHOOL OF EDUCATION. BULLETIN OF THE SCHOOL OF EDUCATION *see* VIEWPOINTS

Indiana. Vital Records *see* INDEXES TO BIRTH, DEATH, MARRIAGE, AND MISC. RECORDS..

INDIANA WEEKLY MESSENGER – Indiana. Pa. 1890-1892 – 1 – us UMI [071]

Indiana.Census *see* 1820 FEDERAL CENSUS FOR INDIANA

INDIANAPOLIS 500-MILE RACE HISTORY / ed by Clymer, Joseph Floyd – Deluxe ed. Los Angeles: Floyd Clymer, c1946. 320p. illus., tables, diagrs – 1 – us U.W. Library [790]

Indian-Eskimo Association of Canada *see* CASNP BULLETIN

INDIANIAN-REPUBLICAN – Warsaw. Ind. 1882-1894 – 1 – us UMI [071]

INDIANISCHE SAGEN VON DE NORD-PACIFISCHEN KUESTE AMERIKAS / Boas, Franz – Berlin: A. Asher, 1895. 02419. (Pre-1900 Canadiana) – 9 – cn C.I.H.M. [390]

INDIANISCHE SAGEN VON DER NORD-PACIFISCHEN KUESTE AMERIKAS / Boas, Franz – BN 142 2. 1895 – 8 – ne IDC [390]

INDIANOLA INDEPENDENT – Indianola, NE. -w. Nov 1900-Jan 1901; May 1901-Nov 1902; Apr 1903-May 1903 – 1 – us NE Hist [071]

INDIANOLA NEWS – Indianola, NE. -w. Mar 1950 to date – 1 – us NE Hist [071]

Indianola. Synod (Cum. Pres. Ch.Pres. Ch. in the U.S.A.) *see* MINUTES, 1898-1906

INDIANOS CACERENOS / Hurtado de Mendoza, Publio – 1892 – 9 – 1.50f – sp Bibl Santa Ana [946]

INDIANS / U.S. Government Printing Office – 1927-70 – 168mf – 9 – $5.00f – us Ross [324]

INDIANS AT WORK – 1933-40. (American Indian Periodicals in the Princeton University Library) – 9 – $350.00 – us UPA [305]

INDIANS, ESKIMOS AND ALEUTS OF ALASKA / U.S. Bureau of Indian Affairs – 1968 – 9 – $5.00f – us Ross [970]

INDIAN'S FRIEND – Philadelphia. v1-63. 1888-1951 – 3r – 1 – us Ross [970]

THE INDIAN'S FRIEND – v. 1-52. Mar 1888-Nov 1940 – 1 – 75.00 – us L of C Photodup [360]

THE INDIAN'S FRIEND / Women's National Indian Association – 1888-1951. (American Indian Periodicals in the Princeton University Library) – 55mf – 9 – $205.00 – us UPA [305]

INDIANS OF ARIZONA / U.S. Bureau of Indian Affairs – 1968 – 9 – $5.00f – us Ross [970]

INDIANS OF CALIFORNIA / U.S. Bureau of Indian Affairs – 1969 – 9 – $5.00f – us Ross [970]

INDIANS OF MONTANA AND WYOMING / U.S. Bureau of Indian Affairs – 1968 – 9 – $5.00f – us Ross [970]

INDIANS OF NEW MEXICO / U.S. Bureau of Indian Affairs – 1968 – 9 – $5.00f – us Ross [970]

INDIANS OF NORTH AMERICA / U.S. Bureau of Indian Affairs – 1760-1952 – 2r – 1 – us Ross [970]

INDIANS OF OKLAHOMA / U.S. Bureau of Indian Affairs – 1968 – 9 – $5.00f – us Ross [970]

INDIANS OF THE CENTRAL PLAINS / U.S. Bureau of Indian Affairs – 1968 – 9 – $5.00f – us Ross [970]

INDIANS OF THE DAKOTAS / U.S. Bureau of Indian Affairs – 1968 – 9 – $5.00f – us Ross [970]

INDIANS OF THE EASTERN SEABOARD / U.S. Bureau of Indian Affairs – 1967 – 9 – $5.00f – us Ross [970]

INDIANS OF THE GREAT LAKES AREA / U.S. Bureau of Indian Affairs – 1968 – 9 – $5.00f – us Ross [970]

INDIANS OF THE GULF COAST STATES / U.S. Bureau of Indian Affairs – 1968 – 9 – $5.00f – us Ross [970]

INDIANS OF THE LOWER PLATEAU / U.S. Bureau of Indian Affairs – 1968 – 9 – $5.00f – us Ross [970]

INDIANS OF THE NORTHWEST / U.S. Bureau of Indian Affairs – 1968 – 9 – $5.00f – us Ross [970]

INDIA'S CULTURE *see* INDIA CULTURES QUARTERLY

INDIA'S NORTH-EAST FRONTIER IN THE NINETEENTH CENTURY / Elwin, Verrier – London: Oxford University Press, 1959 – 1 – us U.W. Library [950]

INDIA'S PROBLEM, KRISHNA OR CHRIST / Jones, John Peter – (Includes statistical tables and index) – 4th ed. New York: Laymen's Missionary Movement, c1903 – 1mf – 9 – 0-8370-6670-0 – 1986-0670 – us A.T.L.A. [230]

INDIC MANUSCRIPT COLLECTION / University of Pennsylvania. Library – (Descriptive catalog by Stephan Levitt et al. 70 mf $70.00; With photocopy of first and last leaves 705mf $360.00; Set 1: Vedic Texts (Poleman nos 1-429) 513mf $270.00; Set 2: Upanisadic Texts (Poleman nos 430-805) 425mf $230.00; Set 3: Epic Texts (Poleman nos 806-1008) 374mf $200.00; Set 4: Purana (Poleman nos 1009-1624) 1049mf $560.00; Set 5: Miscellaneous Literature (Poleman nos 1625-2434) 600mf $325.00; Set 6: Grammar, Lexicons and Prosody (Poleman nos 2435-2813) 571mf $300.00; Set 7: Dharmasastra, Puja, Vyavahara, Artha and Nitisastra (Poleman nos 2814-3505) 986mf $530.00; Set 8: Philosophical Schools (General, Mimamsa, Samkhya, Yoga, etc.) (Poleman nos 3506-4667) 1639mf $880.00; Set 9: Jyotisa (Astrology, Astronomy, etc) (Poleman nos 4668-5285) 320mf $170.00; Set 10: Medicine (Poleman nos 5286-5349) 93 mf $50.00; Set 11: Architecture (Poleman nos 5350-5362) 62mf $60.00; Set 12: Jain, Buddhist and Vernacular Texts (Poleman nos 5363-7273) 536mf $300.00; Set 13: The University Museum Manuscripts (Museum nos 1-47) 285mf $155.00; Set 14: Descriptive catalog (language, title, author, category, no. of folios, no. of lines per folio, material, size, script, date, scribe, condition, donor, and comments) 3mf $3.00) – 3404 titles (almost entirely Hindu texts). 7255mf – 9 – $3,600.00 – us I.A.S.W.R. [280]

INDICACIONES DE FILOSOFIA Y PEDAGOGIA / Sama, J – 1893 – 9 – $1.50f – sp Bibl Santa Ana [190]

L'INDICATEUR – Montreal: G.P. Labat, v1 no 1(1 juin 1895)- – 9 – cn C.I.H.M. [971]

L'INDICATEUR DE LA REGION FLAMANDE – Hazebrouck, France. 1 Jan 1911-27 Sep 1914 – 2r – 1 – uk British Libr Newspaper [072]

L'INDICATEUR DE TOURCOING (ET DE ROUBAIX) : FEUILLE D'ANNONCES (...) – Hebd., Tourcoing (Nord), janv. 1840-nov. 1913 – 13r – 1 – F8,303.90 – fr Armell [073]

L'INDICATEUR NANTAIS OU NOUVELLES ETRENNES NANTAISES, POUR L'ANNEE BISSEXTILE 1792 CONTENANT UNE IDEE GENERALE DU MONDE... – Nantes: Uimar, an III – fr Armell [910]

INDICATEURS DE FRANCISATION DES ENTREPRISES : OBJECTIFS ET METHODES / Robert, Roger – Montreal: Bibliotheque nationale du Quebec, 1978. SEM105P3 – 3mf – 9 – Can$6.75 – cn Bibl Nat [440]

INDICATIONS OF THE SECOND BOOK OF MOSES CALLED EXODUS / Latch, Edward Biddle – Philadelphia: J.B. Lippincott, 1892. 1 fiche – 9 – us A.T.L.A. [240]

THE INDICATOR – Chicago, 1878- – 1 – £165.00 – uk Chadwyck [780]

THE INDICATOR – Pueblo. Colo. 1913-1948 – 1 – us UMI [071]

THE INDICATOR'S DIGEST OF INSURANCE DECISIONS – Detroit, Leavenworth, 1899. 661 p. LL-436 – 1 – us L of C Photodup [340]

INDICE ALFABETICO DEI RABBINI E SCRITTORI ISRAELITTI... IN ITALIA / Mortara, M – Padova, 1886 – 2mf – ne IDC [270]

INDICE DE INFORMES PEDIDOS POR EL GOBIERNO DE S.M. Y CUERPOS DEL ESTADO A LA REAL ACADEMIA DE LA HISTORIA, EVACUADOS POR ESTA – Madrid: Fortanet, 1900. B.R.A.H. 37, 1900, pp. 63-106 – sp Bibl Santa Ana [946]

INDICE DE K. REICHE: ESTUDIOS CRITICOS DE LA FLORE CHILENA / Munoz Pizarro, C – Chile, 1942. B-5182 2 – 8 – ne IDC [580]

INDICE DE LA BIBLIOTECA EXTREMENA.. / Barrantes Moreno, Vicente – 1881 – 9 – 1.50f – sp Bibl Santa Ana [020]

INDICE DE LA COLECCION DE HISTORIADORES Y DE DOCUMENTOS RELATIVOS A LA INDEPENDENCIA DE CHILE / Villalobos R, Sergio – Santiago: Universidad de Chile, Instituto Pedagogicao, Seminario de Historia de Chile, 1956. xi,108p – 1 – us U.W. Library [972]

INDICE DE LA COLECCION SALAZAR, TOMOS 20, 8-37. MADRID, 1961-1966 / Cuartero, Baltasar & Vargas Zuniga, Antonio; ed by Uribe, Angel – Madrid: Graf. Calleja, 1967 – 1 – sp Bibl Santa Ana [946]

INDICE DE LA REVISTA DE OCCIDENTE / Segura Covarsi, Enrique – Madrid: Instituto Miguel de Cervantes, 1952 – 1 – sp Bibl Santa Ana [946]

INDICE DE LAS LEYES Y GLOSAS DE LAS SIETE PARTIDAS / Lopez de Tovar, Gregorio – (1757) – 1789. Tomo III – 9 – 1.50f – sp Bibl Santa Ana [340]

INDICE DE LAS LEYES Y GLOSAS DE LAS SIETE PARTIDAS DEL REY DON ALFONSO EL SABIO, POR EL LICENCIADO GREGORIO LOPEZ / Lopez de Tovar, Gregorio – Madrid: Oficina de Benito Cerro, 1789.-v4 – 1 – sp Bibl Santa Ana [946]

INDICE DE LAS PRUEBAJ DE CABALLEROS DE LA ORDEN DE SANTIAGO / Vignau, V & Uragon, F de – Madrid, 1904 – 155mf – 9 – sp Cultura [025]

INDICE DE LOS DOCUMENTOS DE LA CATEDRAL – Zamora – 1r – 5,6 – sp Cultura [240]

INDICE DE LOS DOCUMENTOS QUE PRESENTO PARA INGRESAR EN EL REAL CUERPO...Y...ORDEN MILITAR DE MALTA... / Solar y Taboada, Antonio – Badajoz: Imprenta y Libreria La Minerva Extremena, 1927 – 1 – sp Bibl Santa Ana [355]

INDICE DE LOS DOCUMENTOS REFERENTES A LOS OBISPOS DE VENEZUELA (1532-1816) EXISTENTES EN EL ARCHIVO GENERAL DE INDIAS DE SEVILLA / Nectario Maria, H – Caracas: Univ. Andres Bello, Inst. de Inv. Historicas, 1975 – 4mf – 9 – ne IDC [972]

INDICE DE LOS LIBROS QUE CONTIENE... GASPAR DE MOLINA – 1749 – 9 – 1.50f – sp Bibl Santa Ana [020]

INDICE DE LOS PAPELES DE LA JUNTA CENTRAL SUPREMA GUBERNATIVA DEL REINO Y... / Carretas, J & Olavide, I – Madrid, 1904 – 2mf – 9 – sp Cultura [350]

INDICE DE LOS PRIVILEGIOS DE LA CIUDAD (ANNO 1655) / Toyuela, Nicolas Perez – Albarracin – 1r – 5,6 – sp Cultura [946]

INDICE DE PERSONAS NOBLES Y OTRAS DE CALIDAD... / Retana, WE – sp Bibl Santa Ana [920]

INDICE DE PERSONAS NOBLES Y OTRAS DE CALIDAD QUE HAN ESTADO EN FILIPINAS (1521-1898) / Retana, WE – Madrid: Fortanet, 1920. Edit. Reus 1921, 76 p. 485-502, 77 pp. 60-67 y 245-272, y 78, pp. 68-78 y 148-161. B.R.A.H. – sp Bibl Santa Ana [920]

INDICE DE RESUMENES ANALITICOS SOBRE EDUCACION EN AMERICA LATINA Y EL CARIBE / Chile. Centro de Investigacion y Desarrollo de la Educacion – (Missing: v1-2) – Santiago. 3v – 4mf – 9 – DE-653/1 – ne IDC [370]

INDICE DEL ARCHIVO PARROQUIAL DE ZACUALPAN DE AMILPAS / Zarandona, Aguilar et al – Mexico D.F.: Universidad Iberoamericana, 1978 – 2mf – 9 – ne IDC [972]

INDICE DEL TEATRO CRITICO DE FEIJOO / Faro Vasconcelos, D – 1752 – 1mf – 9 – Pta1,000.00 – 84-7848-024-2 – sp Pentalfa [440]

INDICE DO COMMERCIO – Manaos, Amazonas. 7 Ago 1890 – 1,5,6 – bl Biblioteca [072]

INDICE GENERAL ALFABETICO DE LAS OBRAS DE FEIJOO Y SARMIENTO / Santos, Jose – 1774 – 1mf – 9 – Pta1,000.00 – 84-7848-023-4 – sp Pentalfa [440]

INDICE – RESUMEN, ALFABETICO Y CRONOLOGICO DEL ARCHIVO GENERAL DE LA ARQUIDIOCESIS DE YUCATAN / Arrigunaga Peon, J de – Merida, Yuc. 1965 – 2mf – 9 – ne IDC [972]

INDICES BOTANICI ET MATERIAE MEDICAE, QUIBUS PLANTARUM GENERA / Monti, G L – Bononiae, 1753. B-6080 2 – 8 – ne IDC [580]

INDICES OP DE GEWONE RESOLUTIES VAN DE STATEN VAN HOLLAND, 1524-1795 = INDEXES TO THE PUBLIC RESOLUTIONS OF THE STATES OF HOLLAND, 1524-1795 / Netherlands. General State Archives – 142mf – 9 – DG1,430.00 silver – ne MMF Publ [949]

INDICES OP DE RESOLUTIES VAN DE GECOMMITTEERDE RADEN IN HET ZUIDERKWARTIER, 1621-1795 = INDEXES TO THE RESOLUTIONS OF THE GEOCOMMITTEERDE RADEN OF SOUTH HOLLAND (ZUIDERKWARTIER), 1621-1795 / Netherlands. General State Archives – 191mf – 9 – Dfl2175.00 silver – ne MMF Publ [949]

INDICES OP DE SECRETE RESOLUTIES VAN DE STATEN VAN HOLLAND, 1653-1795 = INDEXES TO THE SECRET RESOLUTIONS OF THE STATES OF HOLLAND, 1653-1795 / Netherlands. General State Archives – 22mf – 9 – Dfl220.00 silver – ne MMF Publ [949]

INDICES QVIDAM IONNIS BVGENHAGIJ POMERANI IN EUANGELIA... / Bugenhagen, J – Augsburg, 1525 – 1mf – 9 – ne IDC [240]

INDICTMENT IN THE CASE OF FORMER MEMBERS OF THE JAPANESE ARMED FORCES – [Moscow: s.n.], 1950 – 1 – CSUX91-B1087 – us Hoover Inst Photo [340]

INDIE : WEEKBLAD VOOR NEDERLAND EN KOLONIEN – Haarlem, 1917-1927. v1-11 – 261mf – 9 – ne IDC [072]

INDIE EN INDONESIE : KRANTEN EN KNIPSELS – 1946-1947 – 5mf – 9 – ne IDC [950]

INDIE IN DE NEDERLANDSCHE STUDENTENWERELD – 's-Gravenhage, 1918 – 1mf – 9 – ne IDC [370]

DE INDIEER – Zaltbommel, Netherlands. -w. 4 July 1850-25 Dec 1862. 6 reels – 1 – uk British Libr Newspaper [949]

INDIEN IN WORT UND BILD / Schlagintweit, E – Leipzig, 1880. 2 vols., ills. BI-1141 1 – 9 – ne IDC [950]

INDIER – Schiedam, 1913-1914. v1-2 – 13mf – 9 – ne IDC [950]

INDIESE VOLKSSCHOOL – Makassar, Malang, 1918-1919 – 5mf – 9 – ne IDC [370]

INDIFFERENTISM : OR, IS ONE RELIGION AS GOOD AS ANOTHER? / MacLaughlin, John – London: Burns & Oates; New York: Benziger, 1894 – 1mf – 9 – 0-8370-7085-6 – 1986-1085 – us A.T.L.A. [230]

OS INDIGENAS DO NORDESTE / Pinto, Estevao – Sao Paulo, 1935 – 5mf – 8 – ne Slangenburg [305]

LES INDIGENES D'A O F : LEUR CONDITION POLITIQUE ET ECONOMIQUE / Moreau, Paul Joseph – Paris: Editions Domat-Montchrestien, 1938 – 1 – us Res Libr [960]

INDIGENIZATION OF THE YMCA IN CHINA (CCC349) = CHUNG-HUA CHI TU CHIAO CHING WIE SHIH LUEH / Yu, Jeh-chang – (In Chinese) – Shanghai: Association Press of China, 1927 – 1r – 1 – 1984-6688 – us A.T.L.A. [360]

INDIGENOUS DRUGS INQUIRY : A REVIEW OF THE WORK / Chopra, Ram Nath – Simla: Liddell's Press, 1939 – 1 – us Res Libr [950]

INDIGENOUS FLOWERS OF THE HAWAIIAN ISLANDS : PAINTED IN WATER-COLOURS AND DESCRIBED BY MRS FRANCIS SINCLAIR, JR / Sinclair, Isabella – 1880 – 2mf – 15 – us Ross [580]

INDIGENOUS PREACHING IN CHINA WITH A FOCAL CRITIQUE ON JOHN SUNG / Gwo, Yun-Han – 1982 – 1 – $5.92 – us Baptist [240]

INDIGENT SOLDIERS' BURIAL RECS / Fulton County. Ohio. Board of County Commissioners – 1885-1892 – 1r – 1 – $32.50r – us Archival [324]

INDIGENT SOLDIERS' BURIALS / Putnam County. Ohio. Auditor – 1885-1912 – 1r – 1 – $32.50r – us Archival [324]

INDIGENUS FLOWERS OF THE HAWAIIAN ISLANDS : FORTY-FOUR PLATES, PAINTED IN WATER-COLOURS AND DESCRIBED BY MRS. FRANCIS SINCLAIR, JR. / Sinclair, Francis Isabella – 2mf – 15 – $65.00 – us Universal [580]

INDIKA : THE COUNTRY AND THE PEOPLE OF INDIA AND CEYLON / Hurst, John F – New York: Harper, 1891 – 2mf – us A.T.L.A. [950]

O INDIO : JORNAL INDEPENDENTE, LITTERARIO E NOTICIOSO – Palmeira dos Indios, Alagoas. 13 Fev 1921-7 Jan 1925 – 1,5,6 – bl Biblioteca [072]

O INDIO – Palmeira dos Indios, Brazil. Feb. 1921-Jan 1925 – 1 – bl Biblioteca [072]

EL INDIO LIBERAL – Madrid, Spain. 29 Apr-4 May 1820.-w. 4 ft – 1 – uk British Libr Newspaper [072]

L'INDIPENDENTE – New York, NY. -m. Oct 1924-1926. 2 reels, 35 feet – 1 – us I.H.R.C. [071]

L'INDIPENDENTE : ITALIAN JOURNAL – Syracuse: [s.n.], 1917-nov 22 1918 – 1r – us Res Libr [071]

INDIPENDENTE – 1991-1995 – 3r per y – 5,6 – Sfr962.00 – sz Infoprint [945]

L'INDIPENDENZA ITALIANA – Paris: Impr de Lange Levy et Comp, feb 27 1848 – us Res Libr [072]

INDIPOHDI : DRAMATISCHES GEDICHT / Hauptmann, Gerhart – Berlin: S Fischer, 1921 – 1r – 1 – us U.W. Library [810]

INDIRECT TESTIMONY OF HISTORY TO THE GENUINENESS OF THE GOSPELS / Huidekoper, Frederic – (Includes bibliographical references, appendix & indexes) – 5th ed. New York: David G Francis, 1886, c1879 – 1mf – 9 – 0-8370-3690-9 – 1985-1690 – us A.T.L.A. [220]

INDISCH PERSOVERZICHT VAN DE REGEERINGS VOORLICHTINGS DIENST – (Scattered Issues) – 7mf – 9 – ne IDC [950]

INDISCH TIJDSCHRIFT VAN HET RECHT; ORGAAN DER NEDERLANDSCH-INDISCHE JURISTEN-VEREENIGING. – Batavia. Publ. suspended from 1869 to 1874. Title varies. On film: v1-151; 1849-1940. Missing: v35-36; 1880-81. LL-0281 – 1 – us L of C Photodup [340]

INDISCHE (DE) MERCUUR – Orgaan voor Handel, Landbouw, Nijverheid en Mijnwezen in Nederlansch Oost-en West-Indie. Amsterdam. Jaargang. 8-63. 1885-Apr 1940 – 1 – us NY Public [330]

O DE INDISCHE GIDS – Batavia. 1879-1941 (and register 1879-1903). SE-20,113 – 8 – ne IDC [073]

INDISCHE GIDS – (Register 1879-1903. Includes a printed bibliography.) – Djakarta, 1879-1941. – 1172mf – 9 – ne IDC [330]

INDISCHE KUNST / Doehring, K – v. 1. Berlin. 1925. BI-1137 1 – 9 – ne IDC [700]

DE INDISCHE MERCUUR – Amsterdam, Netherlands. -w. Jan 1878-Dec 1881. 1 reel – 1 – uk British Libr Newspaper [949]

INDISCHE MISSIONSGESCHICHTE = A HISTORY OF MISSIONS IN INDIA / Richter, Julius – (In English. Includes bibliographical references and index) – Edinburgh: Oliphant Anderson & Ferrier, [1908?] – 2mf – 9 – 0-8370-6607-7 – 1986-0607 – us A.T.L.A. [240]

INDISCHE PALAESTE UND WOHNHAEUSER MIT BEITRAEGEN VON CONRAD PREUSSER UND FRIEDRICH WETZEL / Reuther, O – Berlin. 1925. BI-1051 2 – 8 – ne IDC [720]

INDISCHE STUDIEN : ZEITSCHRIFT FUER DIE KUNDE DES INDISCHEN ALTERTHUMS / ed by Weber, A – Berlin, Leipzig, 1850-1898. 18v – 104mf – 9 – I-1301/1 – ne IDC [930]

INDISCHE VRUCHTEN / Ochse, J J – Weltevreden, 1927. viii/330p. 141 figs. B-8124/1 – 4mf – 9 – ne IDC [950]

INDISCH-GENOOTCHAP – Naamlist der leden, 1904-1913 – 1mf – 9 – ne IDC [950]

THE INDIVIDUAL – Pueblo. Colo. 1896-1898 – 1 – us UMI [071]

THE INDIVIDUAL / ed by Swain, G W – (Brauchen Sie Einen Vormund?, by Mackay Gesellschaft. Staatssozialismus und Anarchismus, by Benj. R. Tucker) – Nos. I-III. Cont'd. 1 fiche (24x). Together with: – 9 – 1.00f – at Libertarian Micro [320]

INDIVIDUAL, CORPORATE AND FIRM NAMES / McAdam, David – New York, Diossy, 1894. 84 p. LL-531 – 1 – us L of C Photodup [340]

INDIVIDUAL EVANGELISM : CHRISTIAN WITNESSING AND WORK: THE CALL OF CHRIST TO THE LAITY / Beach, Charles Fisk – (Includes bibliographical references) – Philadelphia: Westminster Press, c1908 – 1mf – 9 – 0-8370-6012-5 – 1986-0012 – us A.T.L.A. [240]

INDIVIDUAL EVANGELISM (CCC241) / MacNaughtan, W – (In Chinese) – Shanghai: National Christian Council of China, 1930 – 1r – 1 – 1984-6580 – us A.T.L.A. [240]

INDIVIDUAL PSYCHOLOGIST – (Merged with: Journal of Individual Psychology to form: Individual Psychology) – Austin, 1964-81* – 1 – D13066 – us UMI [150]

INDIVIDUAL PSYCHOLOGIST *see*
- INDIVIDUAL PSYCHOLOGY
- JOURNAL OF INDIVIDUAL PSYCHOLOGY

INDIVIDUAL PSYCHOLOGY – (Formed by the union of: Journal of Individual Psychology, and: The Individual Psychologist) – Austin. v38-53. mar 1982-dec 1997+ – 1,5,9 – D7717.01 – us UMI [150]

INDIVIDUAL PSYCHOLOGY *see*
- INDIVIDUAL PSYCHOLOGIST
- JOURNAL OF INDIVIDUAL PSYCHOLOGY

INDIVIDUAL PSYCHOLOGY BULLETIN *see* JOURNAL OF INDIVIDUAL PSYCHOLOGY

INDIVIDUAL PSYCHOLOGY NEWS *see* JOURNAL OF INDIVIDUAL PSYCHOLOGY

INDIVIDUAL RIGHTS / Doorn, Robert J – 1979, 42 points – 9 – 1.00f – at Libertarian Micro [335]

INDIVIDUALISM, A SYSTEM OF POLITICS / Donisthorpe. Wordsworth – 1889. 399p. 1 fiche (29x) – 9 – 1.00f – at Libertarian Micro [320]

INDIVIDUALISM AND SOCIALISM / Ball, Sidney – 1898. Economic Review, 7p – 9 – 1.00f – at Libertarian Micro [335]

INDIVIDUALISM AND THE LAND QUESTION / Wilson, Roland K et al – 1912. 1 fiche (29x) – 9 – $1.00f – at Libertarian Micro [320]

DAS INDIVIDUALITAETSPROBLEM BEI FRIEDRICH HEBBEL / Hallmann, Georg – Leipzig: L Voss, 1920 – 1r – us U.W. Library [430]

INDIVIDUALITY AND INTIMACY IN PASTORAL MARITAL COUNSELING / O'Neill, James H – 1982 – 1 – 6.64 – us Baptist [240]

INDIVIDUALIZATSIIA ZEMLEVLADENIIA V ROSSII I EE POSLEDSTVIIA OTTISK IZ "VESTNIK SEL. KHOZ" 1914 G / Oganovskii, N P – M., 1914 – 2mf – 9 – COR-82/1 – ne IDC [334]

AN INDIVIDUALIZED SELF-CONTROL APPROACH TO WEIGHT REDUCTION / Heath, Peter S – 1982 – 1mf – 9 – $4.00 – us Microform Publ [610]

INDIVIDUELLE UND GESELLSCHAFTLICHE REPRAESENTATIONEN VON AIDS : EIN VERGLEICH ZWISCHEN BREMEN UND ROSTOCK / Paul, Doris & Schulz, Thomas – 1993 – 2mf – 9 – DM98.00 – 3-89349-654-8 – gw Hänsel [150]

INDO-ASIAN CULTURE *see* INDIAN HORIZONS

Indochina. French *see*
- BULLETIN ADMINISTRATIF
- BULLETIN OFFICIEL
- BULLETIN PERIODIQUE DES ACTES ADMINISTRATIFS
- CONG BAO
- GUIDE POUR L'APPLICATION DES LOIS SOCIALES
- JOURNAL OFFICIEL
- PREMIER RAPPORT DE LA SOUS-COMMISSION DE MODERNISATION DE L'INDOCHINE

Indochina. French. Commissariat *see*
- BULLETIN OFFICIEL

Indochina. French. Direction des douanes et regies *see* STATISTIQUE MENSUELLE DU COMMERCE EXTERIEUR DE L'INDOCHINE

Indochina. French. Laws, Statutes, etc *see*
- RECUEIL DES REGLEMENTS CONCERNANT L'ORGANISATION DES REGIES EN INDOCHINE
- REPERTOIRE CHRONOLOGIQUE ET ALPHABETIQUE DES LOIS, DECRETS, ARRETES MINISTERIELS PROMULGUES EN INDOCHINE DU 1 JANVIER 1926 AU 1 JANVIER 1935

INDOCHINA JOURNAL – Burlingame. 41 docs. 1980-1991 – 15mf – 9 – ne IDC [950]

INDOCHINA PROJECT – (Formerly Center for International Policy, Indochina Project) – Washington D.C. 88 docs. 1980-1990 – 12mf – 9 – ne IDC [320]

L'INDOCHINE – Journal quotidien de rapprochement franco-annamite. Red. A. Malraux, P. Monin. Saigon. juin-aout 1925 – 1 – fr A.C.R.P.P. [073]

L'INDOCHINE ENCHAINEE – Dir. A. Malraux et P. Monin. Ed. provisoire de: L' Indochine. no. 1-23. Saigon. 1925-fevr 1926 – 1 – fr A.C.R.P.P. [073]

THE INDO-CHINESE GLEANER – (Missing: 1819. v2(8)) – Malacca, 1818-1822. 3v – 11mf – 9 – HT-568/1 – ne IDC [950]

INDO-CHINESE PATRIOT – George Town and Singapore. Singapore. -w. Feb-Oct 1895, 20 Sep 1900-11 Dec 1901. (22 ft) – 1 – uk British Libr Newspaper [072]

INDOGERMANISCHE FORSCHUNGEN – (Zeitschrift fuer Indogermanische Sprach und altertumskunde). (Supplements known as: Anzeiger fuer Sprach und Altertumskunde). v. 1-37. 1891-1917 – 1,5,6 – us Princeton Micro [400]

INDOGERMANISCHE MYTHEN / Meyer, Elard Hugo – Berlin: Duemmler, 1883-87 – 1 – us U.W. Library [390]

INDOGERMANISCHE SPRACHWISSENSCHAFT / Krahe, Hans – Berlin: W. de Gruyter, 1943. 184p. diagrs – 1 – us U.W. Library [400]

INDO-IRANIAN JOURNAL – (v27-. 1984-. 5,6,9) – v1-. 1957- – 1 – us UMI [073]

INDO-IRANIAN STUDIES...IN HONOUR OF SHAMS-UL-ULLEMA DASTUR DARAB PESHOTAN SANJANA – London: K. Paul, Trench, Truebner & Co., 1925. viii,293p. front – 1 – us U.W. Library [490]

INDOLOGENBLAD – Leiden, 1909-1923 – 57mf – 9 – ne IDC [072]

'INDONE' DJOETEN – n.p. 2603 ? 249p – 43-45mf – 9 – ne IDC [999]

INDONESIA – Bangkok. 1949-1954. Lacking: 1949-53, v1-5(1-268); 1954, v6(271-75, 277-280 ,288) – 10mf – 9 – ne IDC [950]

INDONESIA – Djakarta, 1954-1959 – 26mf – 9 – SE-888/1 – ne IDC [950]

INDONESIA – Paris. SE-549 1. 1960 – 9 – ne IDC [073]

INDONESIA – v1- 1966- – 1,5,6,9 – us UMI [950]

Indonesia *see*
- AIDE-MEMOIRE FROM OBSERVERS OF REPUBLIC OF INDONESIA TO THE U.N. MALAYSIA MISSION IN SARAWAK AND SABAH
- ATLAS INDONESIA
- BALI, THE ISLE OF THE GODS
- BALI; WHERE, WHAT, WHEN, HOW
- BOGOR, CITY OF THREE MOUNTAINS AND THREE RIVERS
- BOGOR; ROAD TO ASIAN-AFRICAN SOLIDARITY
- CURRENT U.S. ECONOMIC ASSISTANCE TO INDONESIA
- THE DEMAK PROJECT
- DJAKARTA, INDONESIA'S NATIONAL CAPITAL
- EDUCATIONAL PROGRESS IN THE REPUBLIC OF INDONESIA
- HISTORY OF INDONESIA'S NATIONAL MOVEMENT
- INDONESIA, 20 YEARS NATIONHOOD,17 AUG. 1945-17 AUG. 1965
- INDONESIA DEVELOPS: REPELITA 5
- INVESTMENT: NEW POLICIES AND PROCEDURES ON INDONESIA'S FOREIGN CAPITAL INVESTMENT
- IRIAN BARAT DAERAH KITA
- KONSULAT
- NATIONAL MILITARY ACADEMY
- NEW IMPRESSIONS ON NEW NEIGHBOR PEOPLE
- OUTLINE OF THE INDONESIAN QUESTION

- POLA BIMBINGAN KEPARIWISA TAAN DAERAH CHUSUS IBUKOTA DJAKARTA
- POLA PEMBANGUNAN DAERAH BAGIAN
- POLA PEMBANGUNAN DAERAH KABUPATEN PURWOREDJO
- POLA PEMBANGUNAN PROPINSI DJAWA-TENGAH
- POLITICAL MANIFESTO OF THE GOVERNMENT OF THE REPUBLIC OF INDONESIA
- POSITION PAPER ON THE MALAYSIAN PROBLEM
- PRESS AND BROADCAST RELEASES ISSUED BY THE DEPARTMENT OF INFORMATION
- RENCANA PEMBANGUNAN LIMA TAHUN KEDUA 1974/75-1978/79
- RENTJANA INDUK DJAKARTA
- RENTJANA PEMBANGUNAN LIMA TAHUN
- RENTJANA PEMBANGUNAN LIMA TAHUN D.C.I
- SEDJARAH REVOLUSI INDONESIA; PERIODE REVOLUSI PHYSIK 1945-1950
- SELECTED DOCUMENTS; SOME ASPECTS CONCERNING PROGRESS; 7 PRINCIPLES OF THE INDONESIAN REVOLUTION
- STATISTICAL REPORT, YEAR: 1954, 1955, 1956, 1957, 1958
- TANAH AIR KITA: A PICTORIAL INTRODUCTION TO INDONESIA
- WEDDING CEREMONIALS
- WHY INDONESIA OPPOSES BRITISH-MADE MALAYSIA
- WORKBOOK FOR SECRETARIES AND TYPISTS IN ANY AGENCY OF THE GOVERNMENT

INDONESIA, 20 YEARS NATIONHOOD,17 AUG. 1945-17 AUG. 1965 / Indonesia – SE-11,538 1 – 9 – ne IDC [950]

INDONESIA AGRICULTURAL PROGRAM, 1951-1956 / U.S. Operations Mission to Indonesia – SE 11,631 1. 1957 – 9 – ne IDC [630]

Indonesia. Agriculture *see* PRESENT STATUS OF INDONESIAN AGRICULTURE

Indonesia. Akademi Angkatan Laut, Surabaja *see* GUIDE TO THE NAVAL ACADEMY OF REPUBLIC OF INDONESIA

Indonesia. Akademi Ilmu Pelajaran *see* DEVELOPING A MERCHANT MARINE OFFICER CORPS FOR INDONESIA

INDONESIA AND THE BANDUNG CONFERENCE / Indonesia. Bandung Conference – Boyd R. Compton.1955. SE-5801-1 – 9 – ne IDC [950]

INDONESIA AND THE INTERNATIONAL OLYMPIC COMMITTEE / Indonesian Olympic Committee – SE-3349 1. 1963 – 9 – ne IDC [950]

Indonesia. Angkatan Darat *see*
- THE CURRENT INDONESIAN NATIONAL ARMY'S ROLE IN THE REPUBLIC OF INDONESIA
- OKTOBER HARI PERINGATAN KESAKTIAN PANTJA SILA

INDONESIA: ANNUAL REPORT 1948 TO THE FOOD AND AGRICULTURE ORGANIZATION OF THE UNITED NATIONS / Dutch East Indies – SE-11,811 1. 1948 – 9 – ne IDC [630]

INDONESIA, AUG. 18, 1967. EXCHANGE OF NOTES BETWEEN AUSTRALIA AND INDONESIA, CONSTITUTING AN AGREEMENT FOR THE FURTHER EXTENSION OF THE OPERATION OF THE TRADE AGREEMENT OF 17 DEC. 1959 / Australia. Dept. of External Affairs, Treaties, etc – SE-6814 1. 1967 – 9 – ne IDC [950]

Indonesia: Bali *see* TOURS, WALKS, AND SIGHTS OF BALI; PRACTICAL GLIMPSES OF BALI FOR THE TOURIST

Indonesia. Bandung *see*
- BRIEF REPORT CONCERNING THE SITUATION OF THE MUNICIPALITY OF BANDUNG
- BUSINESS MANAGEMENT TRAINING
- CURRICULUM; UPPER DIVISION
- PEDOMAN KOTA BANDUNG

Indonesia. Bandung Conference *see* INDONESIA AND THE BANDUNG CONFERENCE

Indonesia. Bank Negara *see*
- LAPORAN
- REPORT
- STATUTE OF BANK NEGARA INDONESIA

Indonesia. Bank Pembangunan *see* INFORMATION FOLDERS

INDONESIA BERKIBAR – (Cont by: Indonesian Review) – New York: Indonesia League of America, July 1947 – 1mf – 9 – ne IDC [073]

Indonesia. Biro Perantjang Negara *see* BROAD OUTLINES OF THE FIVE-YEAR DEVELOPMENT PLAN, 1956-1960

Indonesia. Biro Perpustakaan *see* BIBLIOGRAFI NASIONAL INDONESIA, KUMULASI 1945-1963

Indonesia. Biro Pusat Statistik *see*
- EXPORT BY COMMODITY SPECIFIED BY THE MOST IMPORTANT COUNTRIES AND PORTS OF EXPORT
- THE FIRST AND SECOND DEMOGRAPHIC SURVEYS IN INDONESIA
- LIST OF COMMODITIES AND COUNTRIES FOR THE IMPORT AND EXPORT STATISTICS OF INDONESIA
- OUTLINE OF INFORMATION AVAILABLE AT THE CENTRAL OFFICE OF STATISTICS
- POPULATION CENSUS 1961
- POPULATION CENSUS 1961; THE RESULT OF HOUSEHOLD LISTING IN MARCH, 1961, ALL INDONESIA
- POPULATION INCREASE IN INDONESIA
- PRODUCTION OF PRINCIPAL FOODSTUFFS IN INDONESIA
- RUBBER: AREA, PRODUCTION, TRADE AND CONSUMPTION
- STATISTICAL ABSTRACTS
- STATISTICAL POCKET BOOK OF INDONESIA
- SUMMARY REPORT: MATERIALS USED AND PRODUCTION OF RUBBER REMILLING MILLS

INDONESIA CIRCLE – London. 1973-94* 1; 1995-97+ 1,5,9 – 1,5,9 – D22890 – us UMI [073]

Indonesia. Commercial Advisory Foundation *see* THE NEW IMPORT REGULATIONS AND LISTS OF COMMODITIES, 1960

Indonesia. Constitution *see*
- CONSTITUTION OF THE INDONESIAN REPUBLIC
- DEKRIT PRESIDEN, UNDANG-UNDANG DASAR 1945
- THE PROVISIONAL CONSTITUTION OF THE REPUBLIC OF INDONESIA
- UNDANG-UNDANG DASAR 1945 DAN PENDJELASAN
- UUD 1945 DAN MANIFESTO POLITIK REPUBLIK INDONESIA

Indonesia. Departemen Agama *see*
- THE DJAKARTA CHARTER; THE SPIRIT OF THE CONSTITUTION OF 1945
- THE FUNCTION OF THE DEPARTMENT OF RELIGIOUS AFFAIRS IN THE REPUBLIC OF INDONESIA
- MULIAKANLAH ASMA TUHAN
- THE STATE SHOULD BELIEVE IN GOD

Indonesia. Departemen Dalam Negeri *see* WEST IRIAN IMPLEMENTATION OF THE ACT OF FREE CHOICE, JULY 14-AUGUST 2, 1969

Indonesia. Departemen Kesedjahteraan Sosial *see* SELF-HELP AND MUTUAL-AID HOUSING

Indonesia. Departemen Luar Negeri *see*
- ADDRESS BY LEIMENA, ACTING FOREIGN MINISTER ON THE OCCASION OF UNITED NATIONS DAY
- COLONIAL PURPOSES IN WEST IRIAN; AN EXPOSE OF DUTCH INTENTIONS
- THE ERA OF CONFRONTATION
- THE MALAYSIA ISSUE; BACKGROUND AND DOCUMENTS

Indonesia. Departemen Pekerdjaan Umum dan Tenaga *see* PROGRESS REPORT FASE REHABILISASI TAHUN 1967; SUB-BIDANG PEKERDJAAN UMUM

Indonesia. Departemen Penerangan *see*
- THE BIRTH OF GANEFO
- DOCUMENTS RELATED TO KHRUSCHEV'S VISIT TO INDONESIA IN 1960
- DRAFT OF FIVE YEAR PLAN OF INDONESIA
- FIRST FIVE-YEAR DEVELOPMENT PLAN (1969/70-1973/74)
- GELORA KONFRONTASI MENGGANJANG MALAYSIA
- ORBA; A GUIDE TO THE NEW ORDER, GOVERNMENT POLICY
- PROGRAMME EKA DASA RUDRA. CENTENARY TEMPLE FESTIVAL AT PURA BESAKIH BALI, MARCH-APRIL 1963
- SIARAN ASIAN GAMES, AGUSTUS 1962
- SOLO REHABILITATION CENTRE
- SPECIAL ISSUE; REFERENCE EDITION
- THE WORLD CRUISE OF R.I. DEWARUTJI

Indonesia. Departemen Perindustrian Rakjat *see*
- INDUSTRIAL ESTATES
- A REPORT ON THE CENTRAL PRODUCTION PLANTS OF INDONESIA

Indonesia. Departemen Pertanian *see* PROGRAM FOR INCREASING PRODUCTION OF FOOD AND FOREST PRODUCTS FOR THE YEAR 1967

Indonesia. Department of Education and Culture. Office of Research and Development *see* THE USE OF INDIGENOUS CULTURE AS A MEDIUM FOR DEVELOPMENT

Indonesia. Department of Finance *see* A MODERN BUDGET SYSTEM FOR INDONESIA

Indonesia. Department of National Research *see* SELECTED LIST OF RESEARCH PROJECTS

Indonesia. Dept. of Education *see* WORKING THESES FOR DEVELOPING TECHNICAL EDUCATION IN INDONESIA

Indonesia. Dept. of National Research, Council for Sciences of Indonesia *see* INDEX OF INDONESIAN LEARNED PERIODICALS, 1964

INDONESIA DEVELOPS: REPELITA 5 : FIVE YEAR DEVELOPMENT PLAN 1989/90-1993/94 / Indonesia – Jakarta, [1991] – 3mf – 9 – ne IDC [338]

Indonesia. Dewan Perantjang Nasional *see*
- BROAD OUTLINES OF THE NATIONAL OVERALL DEVELOPMENT PLAN, 1961-1969
- EXCERPTS OF IMPORTANCE TO THE OIL INDUSTRY FROM THE DRAFT BASIC LAWS FOR THE OVERALL NATIONAL DEVELOPMENT; EIGHT YEAR PLAN: 1961-1969
- NATIONAL OVERALL DEVELOPMENT PLAN, 1961-1969; LIST OF PROJECTS

Indonesia. Dewan Perwakilan Rakjat *see* FRACTIONS AND SECTIONS IN THE HOUSE OF REPRESENTATIVES OF THE REPUBLIC OF INDONESIA, AND A SHORT BIOGRAPHY OF THE CHAIRMAN, VICE CHAIRMAN AND MEMBERS OF HOUSE OF REPRESENTATIVES OF REPUBLIC OF INDONESIA ON AUGUST 1, 1954

Indonesia. Dewan Tourisme *see* LIST OF HOTELS AND LODGEMENTS IN INDONESIA

Indonesia. Direktorat Film *see*
- DOKUMEN 1966-1968; LAPORAN UMUM PROGRAM KERDJA 1968
- LAMPIRAN

Indonesia. Direktorat Geologi *see* ENGLISH-INDONESIAN AND INDONESIAN-ENGLISH TERMS OF GEOLOGY AND RELATED SCIENCES

Indonesia. Djawatan Pendidikan Masjarakat *see*
- MASS EDUCATION IN INDONESIA
- REPORT OF THE MASS EDUCATION DEPARTMENT, INDONESIA

INDONESIA ECONOMIC BULLETIN – (Missing: 1970(141); 1971(163)) – Amsterdam, 1967-1970 – 20mf – 9 – SE-1699/1 – ne IDC [330]

Indonesia. English Language Materials Development Project (1962) *see* EXTRACTS FROM REPORT ON ENGLISH LANGUAGE MATERIALS DEVELOPMENT PROJECT CONFERENCES

INDONESIA FACES ITS ECONOMIC PROBLEMS / Sastroamidjojo, Ali – SE 3639 1. 1952? – 9 – ne IDC [338]

INDONESIA FACING PROBLEMS OF NEW LIFE AND REINTEGRATION / Supomo – SE 1193 1. 1959 – 9 – ne IDC [320]

Indonesia. Food Board *see* REPORT TO THE DIRECTOR OF LAND DEVELOPMENT REGARDING THE AGRICULTURE MECHANIZATION ASPECTS OF THE FOOD BOARD'S EXPANDED LAND DEVELOPMENT PROJECT,BY J.K. GARNER. SE-2495/1. 1959

Indonesia. Forest Service *see* THE TEAK FORESTS OF TJEPU; HISTORY OF THE MANAGEMENT AND ITS WORKING PLANS

INDONESIA, GENERAL INFORMATION AND TOURISM / Atmadi, Endang T – SE-3984 1. 1962? – 9 – ne IDC [950]

Indonesia. Geological Survey. (Paleontology Section) *see* HANTKENINA IN THE NANGGULAN AREA AND COLLECTION OF SMALLER FORAMINIFERA

Indonesia. Health Education Section, KMD, Bekasi *see* BETTER HEALTH FOR RURAL INDONESIA

INDONESIA IN BRIEF / Sukarno, Pres. Indonesia – SE 2047 1. 1954? – 9 – ne IDC [950]

INDONESIA IN PERSPECTIVE / Nazir, Datuk Pamontjak – SE-10,120 1. 1958? – 9 – ne IDC [950]

INDONESIA IN THE UNITED NATIONS / Sastroamidjojo, Ali – Speeches by Indonesian permanent representative to the UN. SE 10,612 1 – 9 – ne IDC [950]

Indonesia. Institute for the Research of Rice at Bogor *see* CULTIVATION, MANURING AND WATERING "SAWAH-RICE" (RICE GROWN IN FLOODED FIELDS)

Indonesia. Jogjakarta *see*
- BADAN TURISME. YOUR GUIDE IN JOGJAKARTA
- COME TO JOGJAKARTA
- CONSIDERATIONS PERTINENT TO A PROPOSED NEW STATISTICAL SERVICE FOR THE GOVERNMENT OF SPECIAL DISTRICT OF JOGJAKARTA
- MUSEUM 'SONO BUDOJO' (SIC)
- A SHORT GUIDE TO JOGJAKARTA
- SOME INFORMATION ABOUT GADJAH MADA UNIVERSITY

INDONESIA, KAMI SIAP / Sukarno, Pres. Indonesia – SE 6961 1. Speech 4 5 Oktober 1949 – 9 – ne IDC [324]

Indonesia. Kedutaan Besar. Egypt *see* THE CASE OF WEST IRIAN (WEST NEW GUINEA)

Indonesia. Kedutaan Besar. Great Britain *see*
- GENERAL ABDUL HARRIS NASUTION; BIOGRAPHICAL NOTE. PROGRESS IN EFFORTS TO RESTORE SECURITY IN INDONESIA
- THE PROBLEM OF MALAYSIA

Indonesia. Kedutaan Besar. U.S *see* THE GEOGRAPHY OF INDONESIA

Indonesia. Kementerian Luar Negeri *see*
- THE CASE OF WEST IRIAN (WEST NEW GUINEA); DISPUTE BETWEEN INDONESIA AND THE NETHERLANDS
- DIPLOMATIC AND CONSULAR LIST
- EXPLANATION OF GOVERNMENT OF REPUBLIC OF INDONESIA'S STATEMENT OF 4 AUG. 1956; INDONESIA'S DEBTS TO THE DUTCH
- LIST OF MATERIAL AND PERSONAL OUTRAGES AND INJURIES PERPETRATED AGAINST INDONESIANS BY DUTCH SOLDIERY IN THE CITY OF DJAKARTA (OCT.-DEC. 1945)
- THE QUESTION OF WEST IRIAN
- REPORT ON THE MILITARY SITUATION IN JAVA, SUMATRA, MADURA, AUG. 4-SEPT. 4, 1947

Indonesia. Kementerian Pekerdjaan Umum dan Tenaga *see*
- APPENDIX: SPECIFICATION FOR CONSTRUCTION OF DIVERSION TUNNEL AND COFFER-DAM
- COMPREHENSIVE REPORT ON KALI BRANTAS OVERALL PROJECT
- KALI KONTO PROJECT: SELOREDJO DAM AND POWER STATION
- PRELIMINARY REPORT ON KALI BRANTAS OVERALL PROJECT
- RIAM KANAN PROJECT: SPECIFICATION FOR PURCHASE, TRANSPORTATION AND ERECTION OF PENSTOCK AND ACCESSORIES

Indonesia. Kementerian Pendidikan *see*
- DEVELOPMENT OF EDUCATION IN INDONESIA
- STATISTICS ON SCHOOLS, PUPILS AND TEACHERS, 1957-58
- TEXTBOOK OF INDONESIAN

Indonesia. Kementerian Penerangan *see*
- AIMS IN THE PACIFIC
- ARTS AND CRAFTS IN INDONESIA
- DUA TOKOH ASIA-AFRIKA: DR. IR. HADJI SOEKARNO – DR. RAJENDRA PRASAD
- FOR THE ELECTION OF MEMBERS OF THE CONSTITUENT ASSEMBLY AND OF THE HOUSE OF REPRESENTATIVES
- HOW SHOULD YOU SAY IT IN INDONESIAN? SHORT GUIDE FOR FOREIGNERS
- INTERNATIONAL RECOGNITION OF SOVEREIGNTY
- KRONIK
- OUR TENGGER
- POLITICAL PARTIES, ARMED GROUPS, LABOUR UNIONS AND YOUTH ORGANIZATIONS IN INDONESIA
- SOEKARNO, PRESIDENT OF INDONESIA
- SPECIAL ISSUE
- SPECIAL RELEASE ON CURRENT INDONESIAN AFFAIRS
- TITO IN INDONESIA
- THE TRUTH ABOUT WEST IRIAN
- TWO TASKS OF ALLIED FORCES IN INDONESIA FULFILLED
- VOX POPULI
- WEST IRIAN LIBERATION CAMPAIGN

Indonesia. Kementerian Perekonomian *see* INDONESIAN ECONOMIC NEWS

Indonesia. Kementerian Pertanian *see*
- 5 YEAR PLAN OF AGRICULTURAL DEVELOPMENT IN INDONESIA; RESULTS OF INSPECTORS' CONFERENCE OF MINISTRY OF AGRICULTURE HELD IN DJAKARTA FROM APRIL 28, 1954 TILL MAY 5, 1954

- 5 YEAR PLAN; RESULTS OF CONFERENCE BETWEEN HEADS AND INSPECTORS OF MINISTRY OF AGRICULTURE, DJAKARTA, APR. 28-MAY 5, 1954
- THREE YEAR PLAN, DEPT. OF AGRICULTURE

Indonesia. Kementerian Sosial *see*
- OUTLINE OF THE TRANSMIGRATION DEPARTMENT IN INDONESIA
- TOWARDS SOCIAL WELFARE IN INDONESIA

Indonesia. Konsulat. San Francisco. Trade Section *see* REPUBLIC OF INDONESIA, ECONOMIC PROGRESS

INDONESIA LANGKAH PERTAMA KE OLYMPIADE 15 HELSINKI, 1952 / Stolk, C J – SE 4571 1. 1952 – 9 – ne IDC [790]

INDONESIA, LAPORAN SEBUAH PENANAM MODEL ASING / Caltex Pacific Oil Company – SE-2473 1. 1959 – 9 – ne IDC [380]

Indonesia. Laws, Statutes, etc *see*
- ACT OF THE INDONESIAN COUNCIL FOR THE SCIENCES
- DECREES CONCERNING THE STATE OF EMERGENCY
- FOR THE ELECTION OF MEMBERS OF THE CONSTITUENT ASSEMBLY AND OF THE HOUSE OF REPRESENTATIVES
- FOREIGN CAPITAL INVESTMENT REGULATIONS
- GOVERNMENT REGULATIONS ON MINING AND THE EXTRACTION OF OIL AND NATURAL GAS
- THE INDONESIAN COOPERATIVES, ACT NO. 79 YEAR 1958; GOVERNMENT REGULATION NO. 60 YEAR 1959; INSTRUCTION OF THE PRESIDENT, PRIME-MINISTER OF REPUBLIC OF INDONESIA NO. 2 YEAR 1960
- KUMPULAN PERATURAN-PERATURAN 17 APRIL 1964
- LAND-REFORM IN INDONESIA AND BASIC REGULATIONS GOVERNING THIS
- TARIFF BOOK OF THE NEW INDONESIAN CUSTOMS IMPORT DUTIES AND CLASSIFICATION OF IMPORT COMMODITIES IN GROUP 1,2,3

INDONESIA LEAVES THE UNITED NATIONS / Asian-African Conference. First Executive Command, 10th Anniversary – SE-11,173 1. 1965 – 9 – ne IDC [950]

Indonesia. Lembaga Ekonomi dan Kemasjarakatan Nasional *see*
- POPULATION STUDY AND DEMOGRAPHIC RESEARCH IN INDONESIA (RECOMMENDATIONS)
- REPORT OF NATIONAL ECONOMIC AND SOCIAL RESEARCH INSTITUTE, 1963
- REPORT ON THE NATIONAL ECONOMIC AND SOCIAL RESEARCH INSTITUTE

Indonesia. Library service *see* REPORT ON A SURVEY AND RECOMMENDATIONS FOR THE ESTABLISHMENT OF A NATIONAL LIBRARY SERVICE IN INDONESIA

Indonesia. London office *see* REVIEW OF THE BRITISH PRESS

Indonesia. Madjelis Permusjawaratan Rakjat Sementara *see* RINGKASAN KETETAPAN, NO. 1 DAN 2/MPRS/1960

INDONESIA MAGAZINE – (Missing: 1969(1); 1970(3)) – Djakarta, 1969-1971(1-16) – 34mf – 9 – SE-1697/1 – ne IDC [950]

Indonesia. Malino Conference, 1946 *see*
- CONFERENTIE? PERMOESJAWARATAN MALINO, 15-24 JULY 1946
- KESIMPOELAN2 DAN KEPOETOESAN2 MOETAMAR DI MALINO

INDONESIA: MEMORIES VAN OVERGAVE : RETROSPECTS FOR NEW OFFICIALS / General State Archives, The Hague – (With three card catalogues: Geographical by area; Geographical by feature; Author index. Includes four plastic binders4) – 815mf – 9 – ne IDC [950]

INDONESIA MERDEKA – Djakarta, Hokokai, Himpunan Kebaktian Rakjat, 2605. 4p – 276mf – 9 – ne IDC [950]

INDONESIA MERDEKA – (Lacking: 1946, V.1(5, 10-21?); 1947 V.2(1-5, 7)) – Pematangsiantar, 1946-1947 – 7mf – 9 – ne IDC [950]

Indonesia. Ministry of Basic Education and Culture. Dept. of Community Education *see* OUTLINE OF ANTI-ILLITERACY CAMPAIGN AND ITS FOLLOW-UP ACTIVITIES

Indonesia. Ministry of Education *see*
- COMMUNITY EDUCATION IN INDONESIA
- MEMORANDUM CONCERNING THE MINISTRY OF EDUCATION

Indonesia. Ministry of Health *see* SOME ASPECTS OF HEALTH PROTECTION TO LOCAL AREAS IN INDONESIA

Indonesia. National Income Committee *see* THE CONTRIBUTION TO THE NATIONAL INCOME OF INDONESIA, 1957 AND 1958, BY THE AGRICULTURE SECTOR

Indonesia. National Malaria Eradication Assessment Team *see* REPORT, DEC. 11, 1962

Indonesia. National Malaria Eradication Service *see* COMMUNITY SURVEY FOR RURAL AREAS OF THE SPECIAL DISTRICT, JOGJAKARTA

Indonesia. Office of Educational and Cultural Research and Development *see* THE EDUCATION SECTOR

Indonesia. Office of Educational Development *see* DEVELOPMENT OF NON-FORMAL EDUCATION IN INDONESIA

INDONESIA ON THE MARCH / Subandrio – Collected speeches while Ambassador to Court of St. James, 1950-1954. SE 2218 1. 2 v. 1959 – 9 – ne IDC [025]

INDONESIA ON THE MARCH / Subandrio – SE 4063 1. v. 1-2 only. v. 1: collected speeches while Ambassador to Court of St. James, 1950-1954. v. 2: collection of addresses as Foreign Minister – 9 – ne IDC [025]

Indonesia. Panitia Chusus Penjelidikan Pendidikan Tehnik *see* TECHNICAL REPORTS OF THE SPECIAL STUDY COMMITTEE ON TECHNICAL EDUCATION

Indonesia. Pemerintah Revolusioner Republik *see* SOME ASPECT OF THE FINANCIAL POLICY OF THE DJAKARTA GOVERNMENT, ITS IMPACTS AND ITS RELATIONS TO THE DEMANDS PUT FORWARD BY THE P.R.R.I

Indonesia. Permanent Mission to the United Nations *see*
- PEACE AND SECURITY OF THE DEVELOPING NATIONS
- STATEMENT OF HIS EXCELLENCY SUBANDRIO IN GENERAL ASSEMBLY OF UNITED NATIONS ON 9 OCT. 1961

INDONESIA: PERSPEKTIP DAN SARAN2 UNTUK BANTUAN EKONOMI AMERIKA SERIKAT KEPADA PRESIDEN / U.S. Economic Survey Team to Indonesia – SE 5021 1. 1962 – 9 – ne IDC [338]

INDONESIA, PILIHLAH DEMOKRASIMU JANG SEDJATI / Sukarno, Pres. Indonesia – SE 4207 1. Speech 28 Okt. 1956 – 9 – ne IDC [324]

INDONESIA PRE-INDEPENDENCE – 543 titles – 9 – ne IDC [950]

Indonesia. President. (Sukarno) *see*
- NEW REGULATION ON STATE OF EMERGENCY. PRESIDENT'S DECISION NO. 315/1959
- TEXT OF PRESIDENTIAL REGULATION NO. 10 OF 1959, UNDER WHICH ALIEN RETAILERS ARE BANNED IN RURAL AREA I

Indonesia. Progressive Indonesian Journalists *see* BEWARE: THE INDONESIAN FASCIST REGIME USES REACTIONARY JOURNALISTS TO DECEIVE PEOPLE AND TO SPLIT AFRO-ASIAN SOLIDARITY

INDONESIA RAYA – Djakarta. Indonesia. 1955-1958 – 1 – us UMI [072]

INDONESIA RAYA – Djakarta, Indonesia. Oct 1968-Jan 21 1974 – 14r – 1 – us L of C Photodup [072]

Indonesia. Religious groups *see* MESSAGE FROM THE TEAM OF CONSULTATION OF THE RELIGIOUS GROUPS IN INDONESIA

INDONESIA: RENTJANA INDUK DJAKARTA – D-1005 1. 1965-1985 – 9 – ne IDC [073]

Indonesia. Seminar Tenaga Atom, 1st *see* SEMINAR TENAGA ATOM INSTITUTE TECHNOLOGI BANDUNG 27/31 MARET 1962

INDONESIA SINGS OF AFRO-ASIA / Suradi, Bintang – SE 4488 1. 1962 – 9 – ne IDC [490]

INDONESIA: SOCIAL AND CULTURAL REVOLUTION / Alisjahbana, Sutan Takdir – SE-6843 1. 1966 – 9 – ne IDC [950]

INDONESIA: STATE TRADING AND PRIVATE ENTERPRISE / Panglaykim, J – SE-10,599 1. 1963? – 9 – ne IDC [380]

INDONESIA THROUGH FOREIGN EYES – (Missing: 1955(1-4, 6-...); 1956(1-2, 6-...); 1957, v2(1, 3-7)) – Djakarta, 1955-1958 – 6mf – 9 – SE-550/1 – ne IDC [950]

INDONESIA TIMES – Jakarta: Djamal Ali, S H, may 2 1974- – 1 – us Res Libr [072]

INDONESIA TO-DAY – (Missing: 1968. v2(3)) – London, 1964-1968 – 14mf – 9 – SE-551/1 – ne IDC [950]

INDONESIA UNDER FASCISM / Sumartono – SE 6172 1. 1967 – 9 – ne IDC [950]

Indonesia. Union of Democratic Control *see* CONTAINS NEWS ITEMS AND THE POLITICAL PROGRAMME OF THE INDONESIAN SOCIALIST PARTY

Indonesia. Venereal Disease Research Institute *see*
- A BRIEF SURVEY ABOUT THE SYPHILIS PROBLEM IN JAVA
- THE FIRST TWO YEARS DEVELOPMENT OF THE VENEREAL DISEASE RESEARCH INSTITUTE

INDONESIAN ABSTRACTS – Djakarta, 1958-1965. v1-7(4) – 17mf – 9 – SE-568/1 – ne IDC [950]

INDONESIAN ADVENTURE FOR CHRIST / Cleveland, Clyde C – SE-5342 1. 1965 – 9 – ne IDC [240]

INDONESIAN AFFAIRS – (Missing: 1951. v1(6)) – Djakarta, 1951-1954 – 33mf – 9 – SE-543/1 – ne IDC [320]

INDONESIAN AIMS AND IDEALS. A PERSONAL MESSAGE TO MY OLD COMRADES WHEREVER THEY MAY BE / Hatta, Mohammad – SE-11,886 1. 1945 – 9 – ne IDC [950]

INDONESIAN ARCHAEOLOGICAL PHOTOGRAPHS / Kern Institute, University of Leiden – (Includes an index on microfiche and plastic binder) – 282mf – 9 – ne IDC [770]

INDONESIAN ART / Asia Institute. New York – A loan exhibition from the Royal Indies Institute, Amsterdam. Jan 7-Feb 6, 1949. Albricht Art Gallery, Buffalo, NY. 211p. BSEM-426-429 1 – 9 – ne IDC [700]

INDONESIAN CHEMICAL NOMENCLATURE / Sutarman – Djakarta, Madjelis Ilmu Pengetahuan Indonesia. Council for Sciences of Indonesia [1957?] 35p. 25 cm. Translation of Intisati tatanama kimia anorganik dan kimia organik beserta kamus istilah – 9 – ne IDC [540]

THE INDONESIAN COMMUNIST PARTY / Darsono – SE-4663 1. 1957 – 9 – ne IDC [335]

THE INDONESIAN COOPERATIVES, ACT NO. 79 YEAR 1958; GOVERNMENT REGULATION NO. 60 YEAR 1959; INSTRUCTION OF THE PRESIDENT, PRIME-MINISTER OF REPUBLIC OF INDONESIA NO. 2 YEAR 1960 / Indonesia. Laws, Statutes, etc – SE-10,270 1. 1962? – 9 – ne IDC [340]

INDONESIAN CURRENT AFFAIRS TRANSLATION BULLETIN – (Cont by: Current Affairs Translations Bulletin) – Jakarta, 1975 1,5* – 1,5 – D9950 – us UMI [490]

INDONESIAN CURRENT AFFAIRS TRANSLATION BULLETIN *see* CURRENT AFFAIRS TRANSLATIONS BULLETIN

Indonesian Current Affairs Translation Service *see* BULLETIN

INDONESIAN CURRENT AFFAIRS TRANSLATION SERVICE. BULLETIN – Kebajoran Baru, 1968-1971 – 59mf – 9 – SE-1698/1 – ne IDC [320]

INDONESIAN DAILY NEWS – Surabaya, Indonesia. 1964; Jul 1965-Dec 1978 – 18r – 1 – us L of C Photodup [072]

INDONESIAN DOCUMENTATION AND INFORMATION CENTRE – Leiden. 38 docs. 1981-1991 – 30mf – 9 – ne IDC [360]

INDONESIAN ECONOMIC NEWS / Indonesia. Kementerian Perekonomian – Incomplete. SE-291 1. 1948-1955 – 9 – ne IDC [330]

INDONESIAN ECONOMIC REVIEW – Djakarta, 1968(May-Oct) – 7mf – 9 – SE-1700/1 – ne IDC [330]

THE INDONESIAN ECONOMY: FACING A NEW ERA? / Panglaykim, J – SE-11,564 1. 1966 – 9 – ne IDC [338]

AN INDONESIAN EXPERIENCE, ITS STATE TRADING CORPORATION / Panglaykim, J – SE-10,953 1. 1965 – 9 – ne IDC [380]

INDONESIAN EXPORTS; PERFORMANCE AND PROSPECTS, 1950-1970 / Panglaykim, J – SE-6037 1. 1967 – 9 – ne IDC [380]

INDONESIAN EXPORTS' TRENDS; GEOGRAPHIC ORIGIN / U.S. Embassy. Indonesia – SE 3855 1. 1963 – 9 – ne IDC [324]

INDONESIAN FACT BOOK – SE-10,581 1. 1965 – 9 – ne IDC [950]

INDONESIAN FOLK TALES – Selected and trans. by Mrs. Thio. SE-3851 1. 1962 – 9 – ne IDC [390]

INDONESIAN FOR TODAY; A PRACTICAL COURSE FOR ENGLISH-SPEAKING PEOPLE / ed by Schmidgall Tellings, Aluzius Eduard – SE 2419 1. 1957 – 9 – ne IDC [490]

INDONESIAN GOVERNMENT AND PRESS DURING GUIDED DEMOCRACY / Oey, Hong Lee – SE-662 1. 1971 – 9$6.00 – ne IDC [380]

INDONESIAN HERALD – Djakarta. Indonesia. 1961-1966 – 1 – us UMI [072]

INDONESIAN IMPRINTS 1942-1945 – (Selected from the checklist by Dr. John Echols and filmed from the Cornell Library Collection. BSE-2.002 1) – 1963 – 538mf – 9 – ne IDC [010]

INDONESIAN INFLUENCE ON JAVANESE / Supomo Pudjosudarmo – (Thesis). SE 6111 1. 1967 – 9 – ne IDC [490]

INDONESIAN INFORMATION – (Cont. as: Indonesian news. London, 1962-1968. v12-17. 1970. v1; Some vols missing) – London, 1950-1961. v1-11 – 54mf – 9 – SE-441/1 – ne IDC [950]

INDONESIAN INFORMATION / Information Department. Indonesian Office – London. 1947-49. Lacking: 1947/48, V.1-2(1-17); 1948, V.2(39-41, 48-49); 1948, V.3(43-45); 1949, V.4(2-3, 10, 14-22) – 20mf – 9 – ne IDC [950]

INDONESIAN INTENTIONS TOWARDS MALAYSIA / Malaysia. Dept. of Information – SE-10,823 1 – 9 – ne IDC [320]

INDONESIAN LANGUAGE PRESS SUMMARY – (Irregular publication; Missing: 1963(Jan-July 4, Aug 22-Sep 30, Nov 6-28, Nov 30-Dec 31). 1964-1965) – Djakarta, 1961-1965 – 39mf – 9 – SE-527/1 – ne IDC [950]

INDONESIAN LIFE – Jogjakarta. 1946-1947. Lacking: 1946, v1(1,2) – 2mf – 9 – ne IDC [306]

INDONESIAN LIVING CONDITIONS REPORT / Holland, J Read – SE-2037 1. 1957 – 9 – ne IDC [360]

INDONESIAN MONOGRAPHS / ed by Karni, R S – 1945-1973. – 9,856 titles – 9 – ne IDC [950]

INDONESIAN NATIONALIST MOVEMENT – (Peasant revolt 282mf Dfl1,692.00; Modern nationalism 316mf Dfl1,896.00) – 9 – ne IDC [320]

Indonesian Nationalist Movement *see*
- SELECTED MANUSCRIPT MATERIALS FROM THE DUTCH STATE ARCHIVES AND THE R.I.L.A. ON PEASANT MOVEMENT
- SELECTED PRINTED MATERIALS

INDONESIAN NEWS – (Some vols missing) – Stockholm, 1951-1968(Nov.) – 71mf – 9 – SE-443/1 – ne IDC [950]

INDONESIAN NEWS AND ECONOMIC BULLETIN *see* WEEKLY ECONOMIC REVIEW

INDONESIAN NEWS AND VIEWS – (Missing: 1967(14); 1968(7-?); 1969(Sept.-Dec.); 1970; 1971(1-2, 5-12); 1972(1)) – Washington, 1967-1972(9) – 16mf – 9 – SE-574/1 – ne IDC [950]

INDONESIAN NEWS BULLETIN – The Hague. Incomplete. SE-577 1. 1956-1957 – 9 – ne IDC [072]

INDONESIAN OBSERVER – Djakarta, Indonesia. 1959-Apr 1992 – 75r – 1 – us L of C Photodup [072]

Indonesian Olympic Committee *see*
- INDONESIA AND THE INTERNATIONAL OLYMPIC COMMITTEE
- L'INDONESIE ET LE COMITE OLYMPIQUE INTERNATIONAL

INDONESIAN PAMPHLET ON FREEDOM AND SELF-DETERMINATION – In Indonesian. SE-2875 1. 1945 – 9 – ne IDC [320]

INDONESIAN POPULAR MELODIES AND SIGHTSEEINGS / Mekar Bunga Indonesia – SE-3913 1. 1962 – 9 – ne IDC [950]

INDONESIAN PRESS REVIEW – (Some vols missing) – Djakarta, 1953-1955 – 130mf – 9 – SE-578/1 – ne IDC [950]

INDONESIAN PRESS REVIEW / U.S. Embassy. Indonesia – Djakarta, Indonesia: US Embassy, Sept 1965-30 Dec 1993 – 37r – 1 – us L of C Photodup [073]

THE INDONESIAN PROBLEM. FACTS AND FACTORS; WHAT HAPPENED SINCE THE END OF THE PACIFIC WAR / Dutch East Indies. Regeeringsvoorlichtings-Dienst – SE-11,836 1. 1947 – 9 – ne IDC [950]

INDONESIAN REVIEW – Djakarta, 1950 – 8mf – 9 – SE-894/1 – ne IDC [950]

INDONESIAN REVIEW – Djakarta, 1951. v1(1-5); 1954. v2(1) – 10mf – 9 – SE-1702/1 – ne IDC [950]

INDONESIAN REVIEW *see* INDONESIA BERKIBAR

INDONESIAN REVOLUTION AND THE IMMEDIATE TASKS OF THE COMMUNIST PARTY OF INDONESIA / Aidit, Dipa Nusantara – (in French). SE-5171 1. 1965 – 9 – ne IDC [335]

INDONESIAN SERIALS – 1945-1970 – 9 – ne IDC [010]
Indonesian Socialist Party *see* – PEDOMAN
INDONESIAN SOCIETY AND THE INDONESIAN REVOLUTION / Aidit, Dipa Nusantara – SE-6690 1. 1958 – 9 – ne IDC [335]
THE INDONESIAN SPECTATOR – (Missing: 1959(23-24)) – Djakarta, 1956/1957-1959 – 46mf – 9 – SE-376/1 – ne IDC [950]
INDONESIAN TRADE DIRECTORY – Peraturan import baru. SE-2511 1. 1956 – 9 – ne IDC [380]
Indonesian Trade-unions *see* CONSTITUTIONS OF INDONESIAN TRADE-UNIONS
INDONESIAN TRIBUNE – (Missing: 1966, v1(1); 1967, v1(4/5); 1970, v4(2-4)) – Tirana (Albania), 1966-1972. v1-6(1) – 22mf – 9 – SE-1704/1 – ne IDC [950]
THE INDONESIAN-ENGLISH DICTIONARY OF TERMINOLOGY / Lathief, Abdul Karim – Defined in English. SE-11,975 1. 1949 – 9 – ne IDC [490]
INDONESIAN-ENGLISH SUPPLEMENTAL WORD-LIST TO EXISTING DICTIONARIES / Schmidgall Tellings, Aluzius Eduard – SE-10,528 1. 1964 – 9 – ne IDC [490]
INDONESIAN-UNITED STATES COOPERATION FOR INDONESIAN ECONOMIC DEVELOPMENT / U.S. Agency for International Development – SE 10,995 1. 1961 – 9 – ne IDC [337]
INDONESIA'S NAHDATUL ULAMA MOVEMENT: FACTORS THAT LED TO ITS EMERGENCE AS A POLITICAL PARTY / Naim, Mochtar – SE-3169 1. 1961 – 9 – ne IDC [320]
INDONESIA'S NATIONAL LANGUAGE / Compton, Boyd – SE-4518 1. 1952 – 9 – ne IDC [480]
INDONESIA'S POLITICAL MANIFESTO 1959-1964 / Sukarno, Pres. Indonesia – SE 5452 1. 1964 – 9 – ne IDC [324]
INDONESIA'S VIEWS ON EN H BOMB TESTS / Sukarno, Pres. Indonesia – SE 1217 1. Speech at meeting against bomb tests, 12 June 1958 – 9 – ne IDC [324]
INDONESIE / Rutgers, S J & Huber, A – Amsterdam, 1937 – 3mf – 9 – SE-1286/1 – ne IDC [950]
INDONESIE BEVRIJD : MANIFEST VAN DE PERHIMPUNAN INDONESIA – Amsterdam, 1945 – 1mf – 9 – ne IDC [320]
INDONESIE CULTUREEL – (Missing: 1948(4, p. 49-64); 1949(1, p. 1-16)) – Batavia, 1948-1950 – 7mf – 9 – SE-658/1 – ne IDC [307]
L'INDONESIE ET LE COMITE OLYMPIQUE INTERNATIONAL / Indonesian Olympic Committee – SE-4710 1. 1963 – 9 – ne IDC [950]
INDONESIEN – (Missing: 1956, v1(1-6, 10); 1957, v2(2-4)) – Stockholm, 1956-1957 – 9mf – 9 – SE-552/1 – ne IDC [950]
INDONESISCH BULLETIN – (Missing: v1(1-3,7) 1950) – 's-Gravenhage, 1950-1957 – 100mf – 9 – SE-553/1 – ne IDC [950]
INDONESISCHE ACANTHACEEN / Hallier, H J G – Halle, 1897 – 2mf – 9 – ne IDC [580]
INDONESISCHE DOCUMENTATIE *see* INDONESISCH BULLETIN
INDONESISCHE VOORLICHTUNG *see* INDONESISCH BULLETIN
INDONEZIISKAIA LITERATURA; KRATKII OCHERK / Sikorskii, Vilen Vladimirovich – SE 5197 1. 1965 – 9 – ne IDC [800]
INDONEZIISKIE IAZYKI / Arakin, Vladimir D – SE-5486 1. 1965 – 9 – ne IDC [950]
INDOOR ENVIRONMENT – v2-. 1993- – us UMI [613]
INDOVELSE I CHRISTENDOM / Kierkegaard, Soren – Kjobenhavn: C.A. Reitzel, 1850 – 1mf – us A.T.L.A. [190]
INDOVELSE I CHRISTENDOM / Kierkegaard, Soren – Kjobenhavn: Forlagt af C.A. Reitels Bo og [sic] Arvinger, 1855 – 1mf – us A.T.L.A. [240]
INDRE MISSIONS TIDENDE – v104-140. 1957-93 (complete) – 34r – 1 – ATLA S0361 – us A.T.L.A. [240]
INDUCTIVE PREACHING: AN ANALYSIS OF CONTEMPORARY THEORY AND PRACTICE / Culpepper, James Edward – 1981 – 1 – 5.00 – us Baptist [240]
INDUCTIVE STUDIES IN THE TWELVE MINOR PROPHETS / White, Wilbert Webster – Chicago: Young Men's Era, 1893. 1 fiche. 8370-5823-6 – 9 – us A.T.L.A. [240]
DAS INDULGENZ-EDICT DES ROEMISCHEN BISCHOFS KALLIST (T.U.U. 1-11/3) / Rolffs, Ernst – Leipzig, 1893 – 3mf – 9 – ne Slangenburg [240]

INDUSTRI – Djakarta. Incomplete. SE-293 1. 1956-1962 – 9 – ne IDC [338]
INDUSTRIA / U.S.S.R. Moscow – no. 1-227. 1937-40 – 1 – 129.00 – us L of C Photodup [947]
INDUSTRIA BRITANICA – London, UK. Aug 1931-Jun 1965; Dec 1968- – 1 – uk British Libr Newspaper [072]
LA INDUSTRIA EN LA ARGENTINA / Argentina. Direccion General de Relaciones Culturales y Difusion – [Buenos Aires?, 1953?] – 1 – CSUXADJ7922-B – us Hoover Inst Photo [338]
INDUSTRIA Y CONCENTRACION ECONOMICA / Jorge, Eduardo F – [Buenos Aires]: Siglo Veintiuno Argentina Editores, [1971- – 1 – CSUXADJ1785-B – us Hoover Inst Photo [338]
O INDUSTRIAL – Rio Pomba, Brazil. Jun 1908 – 1 – bl Biblioteca [072]
INDUSTRIAL ACCIDENT REPORTS / New Jersey. Division of Workmen's Compensation – 1932-55. 12 fiches. (Harvard Law School Library Collection.) – 9 – 1.50f – us H.U. Law [610]
INDUSTRIAL ACCOUNTANT – (1975-. 5,6,9) – 1961- – 1 – us UMI [650]
INDUSTRIAL ADVOCATE – El Dorado. Kan. 1890-1915 – 1 – us UMI [071]
THE INDUSTRIAL ADVOCATE – Halifax, [N.S.]: Maritime Newspaper Col, [1884-1916] – 9 – cn C.I.H.M. [971]
INDUSTRIAL AGE – Caldwell. Kan. -w. 1887-89 – 1 – us UMI [330]
INDUSTRIAL AND COMMERCIAL INTEGRATION IN EUROPE – 1963-66. (Britain and Europe since 1945-1973 Update) – 9 – us Primary [338]
INDUSTRIAL AND ENGINEERING CHEMISTRY – v1-62. 1909-70 – 1,5,6 – us A.C.S. [660]
INDUSTRIAL AND ENGINEERING CHEMISTRY FUNDAMENTALS – v1-25. 1962-86 – 1,5,6,9 – us A.C.S. [660]
INDUSTRIAL AND ENGINEERING CHEMISTRY PROCESS DESIGN AND DEVELOPMENT – v1-25. 1962-86 – 1,5,6,9 – us A.C.S. [660]
INDUSTRIAL AND ENGINEERING CHEMISTRY PRODUCT RESEARCH AND DEVELOPMENT – v1-25. 1962-86 – 1,5,6,9 – us A.C.S. [660]
INDUSTRIAL AND ENGINEERING CHEMISTRY RESEARCH – v26- 1987- – 1,5,6,9 – us A.C.S. [660]
INDUSTRIAL AND LABOR RELATIONS FORUM – Cornell University. v1-15. 1969-81 (all publ) – 9 – $168.00 set – us Hein [340]
INDUSTRIAL AND LABOR RELATIONS REVIEW – v. 1-23. Ithaca. 1947-70. Lacking: v. 1, 1947; v. 18, 1965. BH-1797 1 – 9 – ne IDC [331]
INDUSTRIAL AND LABOR RELATIONS REVIEW – (v.24- 1970- 5,6. v.29- 1975- 9) – v.1- 1947- – 1 – us UMI [331]
THE INDUSTRIAL AND MINING PROGRAM UNDER TAIWAN'S THIRD FOUR-YEAR PLAN / China. Republic. Ministry of Economic Affairs. Industrial Planning and Coordination Group – Taipei, 1961. BD-433-1 – 9 – ne IDC [338]
INDUSTRIAL AUSTRALIAN *see* AUSTRALIAN MINING STANDARD
THE INDUSTRIAL BANK OF SUDAN, 17 NOV 1961 / Sudan. Industrial Bank – BNE-7650 – 9 – ne IDC [332]
THE INDUSTRIAL BANK OF SUDAN, 1962-1968: AN EXPERIMENT IN DEVELOPMENT BANKING / Saeed, O H – 1971. BNE-7682 1 – 9 – ne IDC [332]
THE INDUSTRIAL BANK, U.A.R / Egypt. Industrial Bank – 1963. BNE-4634 1 – 9 – ne IDC [332]
INDUSTRIAL BULLETIN – (1975-. 5,6,9) – 1942- – 1 – us UMI [600]
INDUSTRIAL CANADA – May 1966-Apr 1971 – 5r – 1 – cn Commonwealth Micro [073]
INDUSTRIAL CANADA – Toronto, Canada. Jan 1922-Jun Jul 1973.-m. 88 reels – 1 – uk British Libr Newspaper [338]
INDUSTRIAL CANADA – Toronto: W.S. Johnston, v1 no 1(Jan 1896)- – 9 – cn C.I.H.M. [338]
INDUSTRIAL CANADA – v1-71. June 1900-April 1971 – 1 – cn Precision [338]
INDUSTRIAL CATALOGS/PRODUCT COMPARISONS/PRODUCT-VENDOR SEGMENTS – 6,9 – us Info Handling [670]
INDUSTRIAL CHARCOAL MAKING – 1985 – 139p – it F.A.O. [660]
INDUSTRIAL CHEMICAL NEWS – v.1. 1980 – 1,5,6,9 – us UMI [540]
INDUSTRIAL CHEMISTRY BULLETIN – v1-. 1982- – 1,5,6,9 – us UMI [073]

INDUSTRIAL COOPERATION: THE STORY OF A PEACEFUL REVOLUTION / ed by Webb, Catherine – 1912. 309p. 1 fiche (29x) – 9 – 1.00f – at Libertarian Micro [320]
INDUSTRIAL DEMOCRACY / League for Industrial Democracy – 1-6 2+6. 1932-1938 – 18mf – 9 – $105.00 – us UPA [335]
INDUSTRIAL DEMOCRACY / McKenna, J M – Pamphlet. 1 fiche (29x) – 9 – 1.00f – at Libertarian Micro [320]
INDUSTRIAL DEMOCRACY, WORKERS' PARTICIPATION, WORKERS' CONTROL, CO-OWNERSHIP, EXTENSIVE PROFIT-SHARING, COOPERATIVE PRODUCTION, VOLUNTARY SOCIALISM OR EXTENDED CAPITALISM / Zube, John – A first Compilation in this series, mainly from: "Work and People". Together with: Drei Kernforderungen zur Vermoegensverteilung, by K. H. Z. Solneman. Total: 504p. 4 fiches (29x) – 9 – 1.00f – at Libertarian Micro [320]
INDUSTRIAL DESIGN – (v13-. 1966-. 5,6. v23-. 1976-. 9) – 1- 1954- – 1 – us UMI [760]
INDUSTRIAL DEVELOPMENT – (v139-153, no.6. 1970-Nov-Dec 1984. 5,6. v145-153, no.6. 1976-Nov-Dec 1984. 9) – v5-153, no.6. Feb 1884-Nov-Dec 1984 – 1 – us UMI [073]
INDUSTRIAL DEVELOPMENT AND SITE SELECTION HANDBOOK – v30-. Feb 1985- – 1,5,6,9 – us UMI [073]
INDUSTRIAL DISTRIBUTION – (v60-. 1970-. 5,6. v66-. 1976-. 9) – 6- 1916- – 1 – us UMI [330]
INDUSTRIAL DISTRIBUTOR NEWS – (v22-26,no.5. 1980-May 1984. 5,6,9) – v4-26,no.5. 1962-May 1984 – 1 – us UMI [073]
INDUSTRIAL ECONOMICS / Sadli, Mohammad – SE 10,965 1. 1959? – 9 – ne IDC [338]
INDUSTRIAL EDUCATION – (v. 57- 1968- 5,6. v. 59- 1970- 9) – v. 1- 1914- – 1 – us UMI [380]
INDUSTRIAL ENGINEER *see* FACTORY
INDUSTRIAL ENGINEERING *see* FACTORY
INDUSTRIAL ENTREPRENEURSHIP IN NIGERIA / Harris, John Reese – Evanston, 1967 – us Res Libr [338]
INDUSTRIAL EQUIPMENT NEWS – (v25-. 1976-. 5,6,9) – v. 1-. 1951- – 1 – us UMI [621]
INDUSTRIAL ESTATES / Indonesia. Departemen Perindustrian Rakjat – SE-4120 1. 1963? – 9 – ne IDC [324]
INDUSTRIAL FINISHING – (v52-. 1976-. 5,6,9) – v. 1- 1924- – 1 – us UMI [600]
INDUSTRIAL FINISHING AND SURFACE COATINGS – v22-28. 1970-76 – 1 – us UMI [073]
INDUSTRIAL GERONTOLOGY *see* AGING AND WORK
INDUSTRIAL HYGIENE *see* AMERICAN INDUSTRIAL HYGIENE ASSOCIATION JOURNAL
INDUSTRIAL INDIA – (1975-. 5,6,9) – 1950- – 1 – us UMI [380]
THE INDUSTRIAL JOURNAL – Bangor, ME: [The Journal Pub Co]. n262-1322. 1885-sep 1918 – 1 – us Res Libr [073]
INDUSTRIAL LABORATORY – v24-59. 1958-93 – 1,5 – $180.00v – us UMI [660]
INDUSTRIAL MAINTENANCE – 1942-53 – 1 – us UMI [073]
INDUSTRIAL MAINTENANCE AND PLANT OPERATION – 1954-Apr 1982 – 1 – us UMI [073]
INDUSTRIAL MAINTENANCE NEWS – 1940-41 – 1 – us UMI [073]
INDUSTRIAL MANAGEMENT – (1976-. 5,6,9) – 1970- – 1 – us UMI [650]
INDUSTRIAL MANAGEMENT – (Ceased v12 no 9 1988) – Oakville. v1-12. 1977-1988 – 9 – Can$28.00y – cn Micromedia [650]
INDUSTRIAL MARKETING – (v.50- 1965- 5,6. v.60- 1975- 9) – v.1- 1935- – 1 – us UMI [073]
INDUSTRIAL MARKETING MANAGEMENT – v1-13. 1972-84 – 1,5,6,13 – sz Elsevier [650]
Industrial Marketing Research Association *see* IMRA. JOURNAL
INDUSTRIAL MEDICINE *see* AMERICAN INDUSTRIAL HYGIENE ASSOCIATION JOURNAL
INDUSTRIAL METAL WORKING SHOPS / Development Projects Consulting Service (Indonesia) – SE-5345 1. 3v in 1. 1962 – 9 – ne IDC [670]
INDUSTRIAL MOBILISATION IN BRITAIN, 1915-1918 – History of the Ministry of Munitions with an introd. by Dr. Cameron Hazlehurst – 9 – us Primary [941]

THE INDUSTRIAL MUTUAL NEWS – Flint. Mich. 1923-1938 – 1 – us UMI [071]
INDUSTRIAL PHOTOGRAPHY – 1- 1952- – 1. ; 5,6. ; 9 – apply; v.19-; v.25- – us UMI [770]
INDUSTRIAL PIONEER / Industrial Workers of the World – Series 1: v1 (all publ). 1921-22. Series 2: v1-4 (all publ). 1923-26 – 31mf – 9 – $185.00 – us UPA [331]
INDUSTRIAL PLANTS DESERVING CULTURE IN THE COLONY OF VICTORIA / Mueller, Ferdinand Jakob Heinrich von – Ballarat. 1876. B-8061 1 – 9 – ne IDC [580]
INDUSTRIAL RELATIONS – A Journal of Economy and Society. v. 1-. 1961- – 1. – apply; v.14-6; v.15- 1976- 9 – us UMI [331]
INDUSTRIAL RELATIONS DIGEST *see* INDUSTRIAL RELATIONS LAW DIGEST
INDUSTRIAL RELATIONS LAW DIGEST – (Title varies: v1-5 as Industrial Relations Digest) – University of Michigan. v1-20. 1958-78 – 9 – $185.00 set – us Hein [340]
INDUSTRIAL RELATIONS LAW REPORTS – 1972- – 1; 1975- 5,6,9 – us UMI [331]
INDUSTRIAL RELATIONS REVIEW AND REPORT – 1971- – 1; 1975- 5,6,9 – us UMI [331]
INDUSTRIAL REVIEW – London. n429-593. 1869-73 – 1r – 1 – us Ross [338]
INDUSTRIAL REVOLUTION: A DOCUMENTARY HISTORY : SERIES ONE: THE BOULTON AND WATT ARCHIVE AND THE MATTHEW BOULTON PAPERS FROM BIRMINGHAM CENTRAL LIBRARY / ed by Goodison, Nicholas Sir & Tann, Jennifer – (Part 1: Lunar Society Correspondence. Part 2: Muirhead 1 – Notebooks + Papers of James Watt and Family, 12 reels. $1,500. Part 3: Engineering Drawings – Sun and Planet Type, ca 1775-1802, 8 reels. $950.00. Part 4: Matthew Boulton Correspondence (Subject Material: Albion Mill-Steam Engines), 23 reels. $2,700.00. Part 5: Engineering Drawings-Crank, Canal, Dock and Harbour, Mint, Blowing, Pumping and other Engines, ca 1775-1800, 5 reels. $600.00. Part 6: Muirhead 2-Notebooks and Papers of James Watt and Family. ca 33r.$3,900.00. Part 7: Matthew Boulton Correspondence (Subject material and individual Correspondence including Garbett, Rennie, Southern and Wilkinson) ca 20r.$2,400.00. Part 8: Muirhead 3-Notebooks and Papers of James Watt and Family. 28r.$2,950.00. Series Two: The Samuel Oldknow Papers and Josiah Wedgwood Correspondence from the John Rylands University Library of Manchester. in prep) – Marlborough: Adam Matthew Publications, 1993 – 17r – 1 – $2,100.00 – uk Matthew [330]
INDUSTRIAL SAFETY PRODUCTS NEWS – (v.14-. 1980- 5,6,9) – v.12-. 1978- – 1 – us UMI [610]
INDUSTRIAL SENSOR DIRECTORY – 1985- – 1 – us UMI [073]
INDUSTRIAL SOCIETY – London, 1918-93. Continued annually – 1 – £1,795.00 – uk World [380]
INDUSTRIAL SOLIDARITY – Chicago, 1909-31 – 7r – 1 – us Ross [331]
INDUSTRIAL SOLIDARITY / Industrial Workers of the World – Official Organ. Chicago etc. Dec 18 1909-1931. Incomplete – 1 – us NY Public [331]
INDUSTRIAL STATISTICS YEARBOOK / United Nations – (1982-1987, Vol 1. ST/ESA/STAT/Ser.P/21-26. E.74; 1982-1987, Vol 2. ST/ESA/STAT/Ser.P/21-26. E/F.92) – 9 – us U.N. Pubs [338]
INDUSTRIAL SUPERVISOR – v. 1-46. 1935-82 – 1. – apply; v.40-46. 1976-82. 5,6,9 – us UMI [650]
INDUSTRIAL SUPPLIER AND DISTRIBUTOR NEWS – v.1-3. 1959-61. Superseded by Industrial Distributor News – 1 – us UMI [073]
INDUSTRIAL SURVEY OF KUWAIT / Kuwait. Industrial and process engineering consultants. (Great Britain, London) – 2v. 1963. BNE-9016 1 – 9 – ne IDC [956]
INDUSTRIAL UNION – Williamsport, PA., 1891 – 13 – $25.00r – us I.M.R. [071]
INDUSTRIAL UNION BULLETIN / Industrial Workers of the World – 1-2 2+31 (all publ). 1907-09 – 1 reel – 1 – $115.00 – us UPA [331]
THE INDUSTRIAL UNION BULLETIN – Chicago. Mar. 2, 1907-Mar. 6, 1909 – 1 – us NY Public [073]

INDUSTRIAL UNION NEWS / Workers' International Industrial Union – Nos. 1-251 (all publ). 1912-24 – 1 reel – 1 – $115.00 – us UPA [331]
Industrial Union of Marine and Shipbuilding Workers *see* THE SHIPBUILDER
Industrial Union Party *see* INDUSTRIAL UNIONIST
INDUSTRIAL UNIONIST / Industrial Union Party – Series 1: v1-8, 2+3 (all publ). 1932-40. Series 2: nos. 1-4 (all publ). 1941. Series 3: nos. 1-6 (all publ). 1949-50 – 1 reel – 1 – $115.00 – us UPA [331]
INDUSTRIAL UNIONIST / Industrial Workers of the World – 1-2 (all publ). 1925-26 – 1 reel – 1 – $115.00 – us UPA [331]
INDUSTRIAL UNIONIST – Manchester. England. -m. Mar 1908-Jun 1909. (10 ft) – 1 – uk British Libr Newspaper [072]
INDUSTRIAL UNIONIST – Portland, OR. 1925 – 1 – 17.00 – us Oregon Hist [071]
INDUSTRIAL UNIONIST – Portland, OR. -w. 11 Apr 1925-7 Oct 1925. 1 roll – 1 – us U.O. Library [071]
INDUSTRIAL WATER AND WASTES – v. 1-9. 1955-64 – 1 – us UMI [628]
INDUSTRIAL WORKER – Chicago. v2-70. 1917-73 – 16r – 1 – us Ross [331]
INDUSTRIAL WORKER / Industrial Workers of the World – 1-5 2+21 (all publ). 1903-13 – 1 reel – 1 – $115.00 – us UPA [331]
INDUSTRIAL WORKER – London, England. -m. Nov 1913-Aug 1914; July-Nov 1916; Oct 1917. 7 ft – 1 – uk British Libr Newspaper [072]
INDUSTRIAL WORKER (SEATTLE, WASH.) – (Library has on microfilm May 5, 1917-Oct. 17, 1931; in original edition: July 26, 1933-Jan. 7, 1939 (many issues missing from both editions)) – Seattle, Wash.: Western Locals of the Industrial Workers of the World, 1916- – 1 – CSUX86-S109 – us Hoover Inst Photo [331]
Industrial Workers of the World *see*
- INDUSTRIAL PIONEER
- INDUSTRIAL SOLIDARITY
- INDUSTRIAL UNION BULLETIN
- INDUSTRIAL UNIONIST
- INDUSTRIAL WORKER
- ONE BIG UNION MONTHLY
- IL PROLETARIO

INDUSTRIAL WORLD AND NATIONAL ECONOMIST – (Cont by: Canadian Manufacturer and Industrial World) – Ottawa: Industrial World Pub. Co, [1880-1882] – 9 – cn C.I.H.M. [330]
INDUSTRIAL WORLD AND NATIONAL ECONOMIST *see* THE CANADIAN MANUFACTURER AND INDUSTRIAL WORLD
INDUSTRIALER ARBAYTER – Chicago, IL. 1919-20 – 1 – us A.J.P.C. [071]
THE INDUSTRIALIST – 1908-10 – 1 – 60.00 – uk World [331]
LA INDUSTRIALIZACION DE LA AGENTINA / Abarca, Mariano – Buenos Aires: Ministerio de agricultura de la nacion, Direccion general de industria, 1944 – 1 – CSUXAHZ5818-B – us Hoover Inst Photo [338]
LA INDUSTRIALIZACION DE LOS REGADIOS DE LA PROVINCIA DE CACERES : CONFERENCIA PRONUNCIADA...AYUNTAMIENTO DE CACERES... / Sanchez Torres, Clemente – Plasencia: Imprenta La Victoria, 1951 – 1 – sp Bibl Santa Ana [338]
INDUSTRIALIZATION OF SPACE – (Suppl to v36, Advances) – 1978 – 9mf – 9 – $15.00 – 0-87703-121-5 – us Univelt [338]
INDUSTRIAS CARNICAS / Aranguez Sanz, Bibiano – Madrid: Sociedad Veterinaria de Zootecnica, 1947. Sep. 1 Congreso Veterinario de Zootecnia. Madrid, 26 Octubre a 2 Noviembre. 1947 – 1 – sp Bibl Santa Ana [590]
INDUSTRIAS PALEOLITICAS EN EL TRAMO EXTREMENO DEL TAJO / Santonja Gomez, M & Queral, Maria A – Badajoz: Imp. Dipt. Provincial, 1975 – sp Bibl Santa Ana [946]
INDUSTRIAS RURALES / Fructuoso, Gonzalo – Caceres: Tip. El Noticiero, 1936 – 1 – sp Bibl Santa Ana [338]
INDUSTRIAS SANTIAGUINAS / Martinez, Mariano – Santiago de Chile: Imprenta y encuadernacion Barcelona, 1896 – 1 – us Res Libr [380]
L'INDUSTRIE – Joliette, Canada. 24 fev 1873-26 mar 1874 – 1r – 1 – Can$35.00 – cn Can Microfilming [072]
DIE INDUSTRIE AM NIEDERRHEIN BAND 2 / Thun, Alphons – Leipzig. 1879 – 1 – DM30.00 – gw Mikro Press [380]
DIE INDUSTRIE AM NIEDERRHEIN UND IHRE ARBEITER – Bd. II, Heft 2 u. 3. Leipzig 1879 – 1 – DM30.00 – gw Mikro Press [331]
L'INDUSTRIE DE LA CHAUSSURE AU MAROC / Taieb, M – Paris. 1961. BNE-3104 1 – 9 – ne IDC [338]
L'INDUSTRIE DES ARANEINA / Wagner, W – Z 2211 2. 1894 – 8 – ne IDC [590]
INDUSTRIE: DONNEES SUR L'INDUSTRIE ALGERIENNE, 1968, (1-3); 1968 (1-2) / Algeria. Direction Generale du Plan et des Etudes Economiques – BNE-8636 1 – 9 – ne IDC [338]
L'INDUSTRIE ELECTRIQUE – Paris, France. Jan 1892-Dec 1909 – 6r – 1 – uk British Libr Newspaper [073]
L'INDUSTRIE FRANCAISE – Paris. Organe de la defense du travail national. Dir., Edmond Rousset. mai 1877-82, 1884-89. mq: no.23 – 1 – fr A.C.R.P.P. [073]
LE INDUSTRIE, L'AGRICOLTURA, IL COMMERCIO – Turin, Italy. 1874-75.-f. 1 reel – 1 – uk British Libr Newspaper [338]
L'INDUSTRIE, L'ENERGIE ET LES MINES: COMPTES D'EXPLOITATION, EMPLOI, INVESTISSEMENTS / Morocco. Division du Plan et des Etudes Economiques – 1964-66. BNE-3044 1 – 9 – ne IDC [333]
L'INDUSTRIE OSSEUSE DE L'AURIGNACIEN / Prost-Leroy, C – Essai regional de classification Poitou-Charentes-Perigord – 9 – F160.00 – fr Ethnologie [930]
L'INDUSTRIE SUCRIERE AU MAROC / Morocco. Direction de l'Industrie – 1967. BNE-3033 1 – 9 – ne IDC [338]
INDUSTRIE- UND HANDELS-ZEITUNG – Berlin. jan 2-sep 30, 1922. apr 9, 1926-30 – 13r – 1 – gw Mikrofilm [380]
DIE INDUSTRIEANSIEDLUNG IN LUDWIGSHAFEN AM RHEIN BIS 1892 (CHEMIE UND METALLVERARBEITUNG) / Kube, Helga – Heidelberg, 1962 – 3mf – 9 – DM76.00 – 3-89349-366-2 – gw Hänsel [338]
INDUSTRIE-ANZEIGER – v1- 1879- – 1,5,6,9 – us UMI [380]
INDUSTRIEBAU – Leipzig, Germany. 1910-12, 1919-30 – 5r – 1 – gw Mikrofilm [072]
INDUSTRIEKURIER – Duesseldorf. Germany. -d. 31 Dec 1953-2 Oct 1968. (86 reels) – 1 – uk British Libr Newspaper [338]
L'INDUSTRIEL / ed by Dufresne, J-A – Shawinigan, Canada. v4 n46. 6 avr 1906-v12 n13. 28 aut 1914 – 1r – 1 – Can$45.00 – cn Can Microfilming [072]
L'INDUSTRIEL DE LOUVIERS – Echo du Neubourg. Louviers. 1930-39 – 1 – fr A.C.R.P.P. [073]
INDUSTRIES ET TECHNIQUES – 1989-1995 – 2r per y – 5,6 – Sfr909.00 – sz Infoprint [600]
INDUSTRIES ET TECHNIQUES – Le magazine de l'innovation technique puis de la productivite francaise. no. 1-246. Paris. mars 1959-73 – 1 – fr A.C.R.P.P. [073]
THE INDUSTRIES OF PHILADELPHIA / Blodget, Lorin – 1876 – 1 – us Res Libr [300]
INDUSTRIOUS MEN / Villamor, Ignacio – Manila: Oriental Commercial Co., 1932. xxiv,211p – 1 – us U.W. Library [920]
INDUSTRY – 1948-50; and Industry Illustrated. 1933-47 – 1 – uk Microform Academic [073]
INDUSTRY, 1870 / Illinois. Census – Adams-Coles County. V123-0014 – 1 – us A.G.L.L. [310]
INDUSTRY AND PROPERTY, A PLEA FOR TRUTH AND HONESTY IN ECONOMICS AND FOR LIBERTY AND JUSTICE IN SOCIAL REFORM / Brooks, George – 1893. 255p – 9 – 1.00f – at Libertarian Micro [335]
INDUSTRY AND STATE: MYTH AND REALITY / Botsford, David – LA Political Notes, No. 13, 2p – 9 – 1.00f – at Libertarian Micro [335]
INDUSTRY IN SOUTH AFRICA : A SURVEY OF OPPORTUNITIES FOR INDUSTRIAL EXPANSION – Cape Town: Unie-Volkspers, 1942 – 1 – us Res Libr [960]
INDUSTRY, INFORMATION, RESEARCH AND TECHNICAL REPORT / Texas A & M University. Agricultural Market Research and Development Center – 69/1-82/3. 1969-82. 58 fiches – 9 – us Spaulding [630]
INDUSTRY MART – (v4-11, no.4. 1975-Aug 1982. Apply; 9) – v1-11, no.4. 1972-Aug 1982 – 1,5,6 – us UMI [073]
INDUSTRY OF JORDAN; INCLUDING A CLASSIFIED DIRECTORY, INDUSTRIAL FIRMS AND PRODUCTS AND BASIC INFORMATION ABOUT JORDAN / Jordan. Chamber of Commerce and Industry – 1969. BNE-9750/1 – 9 – ne IDC [956]
INDUSTRY REFORM = KUNG-YEH KAI-TSAO – (In Chinese) – nos 8-10. 5 Jan 1926-no 18. Feb 1929 (incomplete) – 1r – 1 – ATLA S02960 – us A.T.L.A. [073]
INDUSTRY WEEK – (v. 160- 1967- 5,6. v. 166- 1970- 9) – 13- 1880- – 1 – us UMI [330]
"INDUZIERTE HYPERVOLAEMIE" UND "KONTROLLIERTE VOLUMENANPASSUNG", ZWEI NEUE METHODEN ZUR PROPHYLAXE UND THERAPIE DER AKUTEN TONISCHEN KREISLAUFINSUFFIZIENS / Kirchner, Erich – Marburg, 1965 – 3mf – DM76.00 – 3-8267-2040-7 – gw Hänsel [612]
THE INDWELLING CHRIST / Campbell, James Mannann – Chicago:Fleming H. Revell, c1895 – 1mf – 9 – 0-8370-3126-5 – 1985-1126 – us A.T.L.A. [210]
INDYOHESHA-BIRAYI / Kagame, P Alegisi – Kabgayi, [Ruwanda]: Les Editions Royales, 1949 – 1 – us Res Libr [960]
INEFFABILIS DEUS : THE BULL "INEFFABILIS" IN FOUR LANGUAGES, OR, THE IMMACULATE CONCEPTION OF THE MOST BLESSED VIRGIN MARY DEFINED / Pope Pius 9; ed by Bourke, Ulick Joseph – (In English, French, Irish and Latin) – Dublin: John Mullany, 1868 – 1mf – 9 – 0-8370-8410-5 – 1986-2410 – us A.T.L.A. [240]
INEFFICACIO, DOPO LA CONVENZIONE DELL'AJA DEL 1902... / Esperson, P – Genova, 1907 – 1mf – 1 – ILM-3668/1 – no IDC [327]
Ineichen, Alfred *see* WIE ANNE BAEBI JOWAEGER HAUSHALTET UND WIE ES IHM MIT DEM DOKTERN GEHT
INES DE CASTRO : TRAGEDIE / LaMotte, Antoine Houdar de – Seconde ed. A Paris: Chez G Dupuis, F Flahault, 1723. SEM105P1414 – 1mf – 9 – Can$2.25 – cn Bibl Nat [820]
[INES DE CASTRO] SELECTIONS / Bianchini, F – London: Lavenu, 1798 & 1805 – 1 – us Sibley [780]
INFACT MEDICAL SCHOOL INFORMATION SYSTEM – (Backfile $110.00) – Complete current catalogs of U.S. and Canadian medical schools on microfiche, with index guide. Current year. Updated three times per year – 9 – $210.00y – ISSN 0073-5639 – us Dataflow [370]
L'INFAILLIBILITE DU PAPE ET LE SYLLABUS : ETUDE HISTORIQUE ET THEOLOGIQUE / Viollet, Paul – Besancon: Jacquin; Paris: P Lethielleux, 1904 – 1mf – 9 – 0-8370-8396-6 – 1986-2396 – us A.T.L.A. [240]
DIE INFALLIBILITAET DES OBERHAUPTES DER KIRCHE UND DIE ZUSTIMMUNGSADRESSEN AN HERRN V. DOELLINGER, NAMENTLICH DIE MUENSTER'SCHE / Stoeckl, Albert – Muenster: Adolph Russell, 1870 – 1mf – 9 – 0-8370-8387-7 – 1986-2387 – us A.T.L.A. [240]
INFALLIBILITY : A PAPER / McNabb, Vincent – (Includes bibliographical references with appendix in Latin with English translation) – London; New York: Longmans, Green, 1905 – 1mf – 9 – 0-8370-8531-4 – 1986-2531 – us A.T.L.A. [240]
INFALLIBLE LOGIC, A VISIBLE AND AUTOMATIC SYSTEM OF REASONING / Hawley, Thomas De Riemer – Lansing: R. Smith, 1896 – xxviii/659p – 1 – us U.W. Library [160]
A INFANCIA : PUBLICACAO LITTERARIA E NOTICIOSA – DEDICADA A MOCIDADE ARTISTICA – Maceio, Alagoas. 14 Jul-1 Ago 1878 – 1,5,6 – bl Biblioteca [072]
INFANCY OF OUR LORD – (Ms Selden Supra 38) – 14 – uk Microform Academic [240]
INFANT BAPTISM: WHEN-WHERE-WHY INSTITUTED / Adams, Henry – Yarmouth, N.S.?: 1888. 06150. (Pre-1900 Canadiana) – 9 – cn C.I.H.M. [240]
INFANT MENTAL HEALTH JOURNAL – 1980 – 1,5,6,9 – us UMI [073]
INFANT SALVATION IN ITS RELATION TO INFANT DEPRAVITY, INFANT REGENERATION AND INFANT BAPTISM / Bomberger, John H A – Philadelphia: Lindsay & Blakiston, 1859 – 1mf – us A.T.L.A. [240]
INFANTAS LUNTANAS REINAS DE ESPANA E INFANTAS ESPANOLAS REINAS DE PORTUGAL / Lancastre-Laboreiro e Souza de Villalobos, Anna – Caceres: Imp. Moderna, 1931 – 1 – sp Bibl Santa Ana [946]
Infante, Modesto *see* PLUTARCO
INFANTERIE! : EIN GEDICHT GEWIDMET DEM VOLKE IN WAFFEN / Wildgans, Anton – (Numbered limited edition signed by the author) – Wien: H Heller, 1915 – 1r – 1 – us U.W. Library [810]
L'INFANTICIDE, ETUDE MORALE ET JURIDIQUE / Bouton, Rene – Paris. 1897. (La Condition Ouvriere. Part Two.) – 9 – 7.50 – fr Bibl Nationale [360]
INFANTRY – v. 1- 1930- – 1. ; 5,6. ; 9 – apply; v.61-; v.65- – us UMI [355]
INFARED INTERACTANCE : RELIABILITY AND VALIDITY IN DETERMINING BODY COMPOSITION / Durrett, M – 1991 – 1mf – 9 – $4.00 – us Microform Publ [790]
INFECTION – v.3-5. 1975-77 – 1,5,6 – 2235.00 – us Princeton Micro [610]
INFECTION AND IMMUNITY – v1-50. 1970-85 – 1,5,6 – us Princeton Micro [610]
INFECTION CONTROL – (1982-. 1,5,6,9) – v1-. 1980- – 1 – us UMI [616]
INFECTIOUS DISEASES IN CLINICAL PRACTICE – v1-5. 1992-1996 – 5r – 1,5,6,9 – $80.00r – us Williams [616]
Infeld, Donna Lind *see* THE HOSPICE JOURNAL
INFERTILITY – (v7-. 1984-. 5,6,9) – v1-. 1978- – 1 – us UMI [618]
THE INFIDEL: A STORY OF THE GREAT REVIVAL / Braddon, Mary Elizabeth – British Fiction Archive: Unit 5 – 9 – uk Bell [830]
INFIDEL OBJECTIONS TO THE SCRIPTURES / Whitmore, F B – New York: Thomas Nelson, 1884. 1 fiche – 9 – us A.T.L.A. [240]
INFIDELITY AMONG SOUTHERN BAPTISTS ENDORSED BY HIGHEST OFFICIALS / Norris, J Frank – n.d – 1 – 5.84 – us Baptist [240]
INFIDELITY DISARMED / Stephens, Edward – Toronto: Methodist Book Room, 1900. 1 fiche – 9 – us A.T.L.A. [240]
INFIDELITY DISSECTED : THE EVANGELICAL ALLIANCE PRIZE ESSAY ON INFIDELITY / Pearson, Thomas – (Includes bibliographical references) – Chicago: Geo. MacDonald, c1874 – 1mf – 9 – 0-8370-4690-4 – 1985-2690 – us A.T.L.A. [210]
INFIDELITY: ITS ASPECTS, CAUSES AND AGENCIES / Pearson, Thomas – New York: R. Carter & Bros., 1854. 620p. 'Being the prize essay of the British Organization of the Evangelical Alliance.' Bibliog. footnotes. With: Anthropologiia, by E.I. Petri – 1 – us U.W. Library [306]
INFIDELITY REFUTED BY INFIDELS / Sprecher, Samuel P – New York: Funk & Wagnalls, 1888 – 1mf – 9 – 0-8370-5348-X – 1985-3348 – us A.T.L.A. [240]
INFILTRACION JUSTICIALISTA EN AMERICA / Caridge, Alberto J – Montevideo: [S.n.], 1952 – 1 – CSUXADM8355-B – us Hoover Inst Photo [360]
THE INFINITE AFFECTION / Macfarland, Charles Stedman – 2nd ed. Boston: Pilgrim Press; London: James Clarke, 1907 – 1mf – 9 – 0-8370-4255-0 – 1985-2255 – us A.T.L.A. [240]
L'INFINITE DIVINE DEPUIS PHILON LE JUIF JUSQU'A PLOTIN : AVEC UNE INTRODUCTION SUR LE MAEME SUJET DANS LA PHILOSOPHIE GRECQUE AVANT PHILON LE JUIF / Guyot, Henri – Paris: Felix Alcan, 1906 – 1mf – 9 – 0-8370-9700-2 – 1986-3700 – us A.T.L.A. [180]
THE INFINITIVE IN POLYBIUS COMPARED WITH THE INFINITIVE IN BIBLICAL GREEK / Allen, Hamilton Ford – Chicago: University of Chicago Press, 1907 – 4mf – 9 – 0-8370-9280-9 – 1986-3280 – us A.T.L.A. [450]
INFIZIERBARKEIT VERSCHIEDENER ERYTHROZYTENPOPULATONEN MIT MALARIA / Stottmeister, Frank – 1994 – 2mf – DM80.00 – 3-89349-915-6 – gw Hänsel [574]
INFLAMMATION – v1-18. 1975-94 – 1,5 – $80.00v – us UMI [610]
INFLAMMATION RESEARCH *see* AGENTS AND ACTIONS
INFLATION IS COMING / Borsodi, Ralph – c1946. 1 fiche (29x) – 9 – 1.00f – at Libertarian Micro [320]

INFLUENCE – (Ceased v7 no 2 1987/88) – Toronto. v1-7. 1982/83-1987/88 – 9 – Can$20.00y – cn Micromedia [073]

INFLUENCE AND RESULTS OF WORLD WAR 1 PAMPHLET COLLECTION – 1916-19?? – 2r – 1 – CSUXAML7853-B – us Hoover Inst Photo [355]

L'INFLUENCE DE L'EMIGRATION DES CAMPAGNES SUR LA NATALITE FRANCAISE / Cannes, Henri – Reprod. d'un extrait de la Revue politique et parlementaire, 1895, p309-329. 1 fiche. (Statistics Series: Medical Studies) – 9 – 6.00 – fr Bibl Nationale [310]

INFLUENCE DES FACTEURS PHYSICO-CHIMIQUES DE L'ENVIRONNEMENT SUR LES ACTIVITES RESPIRATOIRES ET VENTILATOIRES D'UN ORGANISME INTERTIDAL: LE CRABE CARCINUS MAENAS (L.) / Duhamel-Jouve, A – 9 – F60.00 – fr Ethnologie [590]

DE L'INFLUENCE DES GRANDES COMMOTIONS POLITIQUES ET SOCIALES SUR LE DEVELOPPEMENT DES MALADIES MENTALES: MOUVEMENT DE L'ALIENATION MENTALE EN FRANCE PENDANT LES ANNEES 1869 A 1873 / Lunier, Jules Joseph Ludger – (French Precursors of Psychiatry Series). Paris. F. Savy. 1874 – 9 – fr Hachette [150]

INFLUENCE DES MACHINES SUR LA CLASSE OUVRIERE / Jousset, Edouard – Bordeaux. 1903. (La Condition Ouvriere. Part Two.) – 9 – 5.00 – fr Bibl Nationale [360]

INFLUENCE DES MEMBRES MASCULINS DE LA FAMILLE SUR L'ENFANT MUKONGO : ETUDE DESCRIPTIVE ET INTERPRETATIVE / Matota, H – Louvain, Belgium, Universite catholique, 1958 – us Res Libr [920]

L'INFLUENCE DES SYSTEMES ELECTORAUX SUR LA VIE POLITIQUE / Duverger, Maurice et al – F30.00 – fr Ethnologie [320]

THE INFLUENCE OF A GODLY LIFE: A SERMON PREACHED ON THE OCCASION OF THE DEATH OF THE LATE REV. A. WALLACE, A.B., HUNTINGDON, QUEBEC / Clarke, W C – (Montreal: J. Lovell), 1870. 00675. (Pre-1900 Canadiana) – 9 – cn C.I.H.M. [240]

INFLUENCE OF AGE AND CAFFEINE ON RESTING METABOLIC RATE, BLOOD PRESSURE, AND MOOD STATE IN YOUNGER AND OLDER INDIVIDUALS / Arciero, Paul J & Mahar, Matthew T – 1993 – 2mf – $8.00 – us Microform Publ [612]

THE INFLUENCE OF AGILITY ON THE MILE RUN AND PACER TESTS OF AEROBIC ENDURANCE IN FOURTH- AND FIFTH-GRADE SCHOOL CHILDREN / Dinschel, Kimberly M – 1994 – 1mf – $4.00 – us Microform Publ [612]

THE INFLUENCE OF ALCOHOL AND OTHER DRUGS ON FATIGUE : THE CROONIAN LECTURES DELIVERED AT THE ROYAL COLLEGE OF PHYSICIANS IN 1906 / Rivers, William Halse R – London: E Arnold, 1908 – 1 – us Res Libr [610]

THE INFLUENCE OF ANIMISM ON ISLAM; AN ACCOUNT OF POPULAR SUPERSTITIONS / Zwemer, Samuel Marinus – New York: The Macmillan Co., 1920. viii,2 leaves,246p. front., illus., plates. Bibliography p245-246 – 1 – us U.W. Library [260]

THE INFLUENCE OF ARISTOCRACIES ON THE REVOLUTIONS OF NATIONS; CONSIDERED IN RELATION TO THE PRESENT CIRCUMSTANCES OF THE BRITISH EMPIRE / Macintyre, James J – London: Fisher, son, & Co.,1843.16p,448p – 1 – us U.W. Library [320]

INFLUENCE OF BODY FAT MASS ON EXCESS POST-EXERCISE OXYGEN CONSUMPTION / Harms, Craig A & Cordain, Loren – 1990 – 1mf – 9 – $4.00 – us Microform Publ [612]

INFLUENCE OF CHRISTIANITY ON WAR / Bethune-Baker, James Franklin – Cambridge: Macmillan and Bowes, 1888 – 1mf – us A.T.L.A. [320]

THE INFLUENCE OF CHRISTIANITY UPON INTERNATIONAL LAW : THE HULSEAN PRIZE ESSAY IN THE UNIVERSITY OF CAMBRIDGE FOR THE YEAR 1854 / Kennedy, C M – Cambridge: Macmillan, 1856 – 1mf – us A.T.L.A. [240]

THE INFLUENCE OF CHRISTIANITY UPON NATIONAL CHARACTER ILLUSTRATED BY THE LIVES AND LEGENDS OF THE ENGLISH SAINTS : BEING THE BAMPTON LECUTRES / Hutton, William Holden – London: W. Gardner, Darton, [1903?] – 1mf – us A.T.L.A. [240]

THE INFLUENCE OF CHRISTIANITY UPON SOCIAL AND POLITICAL IDEAS / Carlyle, A J – London: A.R. Mowbray, [1911?] (Christian social union handbooks) – 1mf – us A.T.L.A. [303]

INFLUENCE OF CONCEPTUALLY BASED PHYSICAL EDUCATION ON STUDENT ATTITUDES TOWARD PHYSICAL ACTIVITY / Hughes, Kevin P – Springfield College, 1994 – 2mf – 9 – $8.00 – PE3601 – us Microform Publ [370]

THE INFLUENCE OF CRYOTHERAPY AND AIRCAST BRACING ON TOTAL BODY BALANCE AND PROPRIOCEPTION / Rivers, Debra A – 1994 – 1mf – $4.00 – us Microform Publ [617]

THE INFLUENCE OF DARWIN ON PHILOSOPHY, AND OTHER ESSAYS IN CONTEMPORARY THOUGHT / Dewey, John – New York: Henry Holt, 1910 – 1mf – us A.T.L.A. [100]

INFLUENCE OF DIET AND THE MENSTRUAL CYCLE ON LACTATE CONCENTRATION DURING INCREASING EXERCISE INTENSITIES / Berend, Julia Z & Hackney, Anthony C – 1992 – 2mf – 9 – $8.00 – us Microform Publ [613]

THE INFLUENCE OF ETHNICITY UPON THE POLITICAL BEHAVIOUR OF THE NEW YORK CITY ITALIAN-AMERICAN COMMUNITY SINCE WW2 / Montalto, Nicholas V – June 1969 – 1r – 1 – us I.H.R.C. [320]

THE INFLUENCE OF FITNESS-ORIENTED PHYSICAL ACTIVITY ON THE PHYSICAL SELF-PERCEPTION AND GLOBAL SELF-WORTH OF BOYS AND GIRLS / Fine, Deborah L & Jensen, Barbara E – 1993 – 2mf – $8.00 – us Microform Publ [150]

THE INFLUENCE OF GOAL SETTING ON EXERCISE ADHERENCE OF APPARENTLY HEALTHY ADULTS / Cobb, L E – 1991 – 2mf – 9 – $8.00 – us Microform Publ [150]

THE INFLUENCE OF GOAL SETTING ON INDIVIDUAL ENDURANCE SWIMMING PERFORMANCE / LaClair, Kirsten W & Mann, Betty J – 1993 – 2mf – $8.00 – us Microform Publ [150]

THE INFLUENCE OF HEALTH BEHAVIOR CONTRACTING ON INTERNAL LOCUS OF CONTROL / Flint, Matthew O – 1993 – 1mf – $4.00 – us Microform Publ [150]

INFLUENCE OF IN-SHOE ORTHOTICS ON LOWER EXTREMITY FUNCTION IN CYCLING / Joganich, T G – 1991 – 2mf – 9 – $8.00 – us Microform Publ [790]

THE INFLUENCE OF JEWISH COLONISATION ON ARAB DEVELOPMENT IN PALESTINE / Jewish Agency for Palestine. Jerusalem – Memorandum submitted in Mar 1946 to the Anglo-American Committee of Inquiry. 1947. BJ-28-147 1 – 9 – ne IDC [956]

INFLUENCE OF MENSTRUAL CYCLE PHASE AND ORAL CONTRACEPTIVE USE ON CARDIOVASCULAR REACTIVITY IN WOMEN WITH A PARENTAL HISTORY OF HYPERTENSION / Silvey, C M – 1991 – 1mf – 9 – $4.00 – us Microform Publ [612]

INFLUENCE OF MENTAL IMAGERY ON TENNIS SERVICE ACCURACY OF INTERMEDIATE LEVEL TENNIS PLAYERS / Choboy, Jon A & Murray, Mimi – 1992 – 1mf – $4.00 – us Microform Publ [150]

THE INFLUENCE OF MUSICAL PREFERENCE ON THE AFFECTIVE STATE, HEART RATE, AND PERCEIVED EXERTION RATINGS OF PARTICIPANTS IN AEROBIC DANCE/ EXERCISE CLASSES / Patton, N W – 1991 – 2mf – 9 – $8.00 – us Microform Publ [150]

THE INFLUENCE OF PARTICIPATION IN A SPORTS TRAINING PROGRAM ON THE SELF-CONCEPTS OF THE EDUCABLE MENTALLY RETARDED ATTENDING A ONE-WEEK SPECIAL OLYMPICS SPORTS CAMP / Edmiston, Paula A – 1982 – 2mf – 9 – $8.00 – us Microform Publ [790]

THE INFLUENCE OF PHYSICAL CONDITIONING AND DECONDITIONING UPON CARDIAC STRUCTURE OF MALES AND FEMALES / Al-Muhailani, Abdul-Rahman S – 1980 – 2mf – 9 – $8.00 – us Microform Publ [790]

THE INFLUENCE OF PHYSICAL CONDITIONING ON THE POST-MENOPAUSAL HOT FLASH / Krasnoff, Joanne B – Indiana University, 1995 – 1mf – 9 – $4.00 – PH1466 – us Microform Publ [612]

INFLUENCE OF POST-EXERCISE GLUCOSE INGESTION ON PLASMA POTASSIUM LEVELS AND ECG MEASUREMENTS / Reynolds, H – 1991 – 1mf – 9 – $4.00 – us Microform Publ [612]

INFLUENCE OF REACTIVE HYPEREMIA IN MUSCLE DURING EXERCISE / Henrich, Timothy W – 1988 – 152p 2mf – 9 – $8.00 – us Microform Publ [612]

INFLUENCE OF REINFORCERS ON MOTORIZED BICYCLE ON-TASK TIME OF PROFOUNDLY MENTALLY RETARDED ADOLESCENTS / Owlia, G – 1991 – 2mf – 9 – $8.00 – us Microform Publ [150]

INFLUENCE OF RELIGIOUS ELITES ON POLITICAL CULTURE AND COMMUNITY INTEGRATION IN KANO, NIGERIA / Paden, John N – Cambridge 1968 – us Res Libr [305]

THE INFLUENCE OF ROLE STATUS, SELF-EFFICACY AND SOCCER PERFORMANCE / Mandell, Ross A – 1994 – 2mf – $8.00 – us Microform Publ [150]

INFLUENCE OF RULES FOR RECOVERY OF ATTORNEYS' FEES ON SETTLEMENT OF CIVIL CASES / Shapard, J E – Washington: FJC, 1984 – 1mf – 9 – $1.50 – LLMC 95-319 – us L.L.M.C. [340]

THE INFLUENCE OF SCEPTICISM ON CHARACTER / Watkinson, William Lonsdale – London: Charles H. Kelly, 1898. 1 fiche – 9 – us A.T.L.A. [240]

THE INFLUENCE OF SEA POWER UPON THE FRENCH REVOLUTION AND EMPIRE, 1793-1815 / Mahan, Alfred Thayer – 2v 1892 – 9 – $60.00 – uk Libr Preservation [944]

THE INFLUENCE OF SITUATION CRITICALITY ON THE PERFORMANCE OF MALE COLLEGIATE BASKETBALL PLAYERS / Roberts, N A – 1989 – 1mf – 9 – $4.00 – us Microform Publ [150]

THE INFLUENCE OF STATE BORROWING ON COMMERCIAL CRISES / Hooper, Wynnard – 1fiche (29x) – 9 – 1.00f – at Libertarian Micro [320]

THE INFLUENCE OF THE APOSTLE PAUL ON THE DEVELOPMENT OF CHRISTIANITY / Pfleiderer, Otto – New York: Charles Scribner, 1885. 1 fiche – 9 – us A.T.L.A. [240]

THE INFLUENCE OF THE HOLY SPIRIT IN CONVERSION : A DEBATE BETWEEN ASA SLEETH AND J.W RANDALL: QUESTION, DO THE SCRIPTURES TEACH THE DIRECT INFLUENCE OF THE HOLY SPIRIT IN CONVERSION? / Sleeth, Asa – Cincinnati: Chase & Hall, 1876 – 1mf – 9 – 0-8370-5184-3 – 1985-3184 – us A.T.L.A. [220]

THE INFLUENCE OF THE HOME ENVIRONMENT ON THE MOTOR PERFORMANCE OF PRESCHOOL CHILDREN / Botha, Marika G – 1982 – 2mf – 9 – $8.00 – us Microform Publ [790]

THE INFLUENCE OF THE MENSTRUAL CYCLE AND DIET ON METABOLISM DURING REST AND EXERCISE / Brammeier, Michele R & Hackney, Anthony C – 1992 – 1mf – 9 – $4.00 – us Microform Publ [613]

THE INFLUENCE OF THE ROMAN LAW ON THE LAW OF ENGLAND / Scrutton, Thomas Edward – Cambridge: University Press, 1885. 199p. LL-125 – 1 – us L of C Photodup [340]

THE INFLUENCE OF THE SCOTTISH CHURCH IN CHRISTENDOM : BEING THE BAIRD LECTURE FOR 1895 / Cowan, Henry – London: Adam and Charles Black, 1896 – 1mf – us A.T.L.A. [240]

INFLUENCE OF THE SEPTUAGINT UPON THE PESHITTA PSALTER / Berg, J Frederic – Leipzig: W. Drugulin, 1895. 1 fiche – 9 – us A.T.L.A. [240]

THE INFLUENCE OF THE SEPTUAGINT UPON THE PESITTAA PSALTER / Berg, Joseph Frederic – (Includes a vita, appendixes and bibliography) – NY: [s.n.] 1895 (Leipzig: W Drugulin) – 1mf – 9 – 0-8370-2281-9 – 1985-0281 – us A.T.L.A. [220]

INFLUENCE OF THE STRENGTH SHOE AND THREE PLYOMETRIC DRILLS ON THE STRENGTH, VELOCITY, AND JUMPING ABILITY OF HIGH SCHOOL FOOTBALL PLAYERS / Ramsey, Jill K & Kimura, Iris F – 1992 – 1mf – 9 – $4.00 – us Microform Publ [612]

THE INFLUENCE OF WEALTH IN IMPERIAL ROME / Davis, William Stearns – New York: Macmillan, 1910 – 1mf – us A.T.L.A. [240]

THE INFLUENCES OF GREEK IDEAS AND USAGES UPON THE CHRISTIAN CHURCH / Hatch, Edwin – 1897 – 9 – us A.T.L.A. [240]

A INFLUENCIA AFRICANA NO PORTUGUES DO BRASIL / Mendonca, Renato – Sao Paulo, 1935 – 5mf – 8 – ne Slangenburg [972]

INFLUENCIA DE EXTREMADURA EN LA LITERATURA ESPANOLA / Diaz Perez, Nicolas – 1883 – 9 – 1.50f – sp Bibl Santa Ana [440]

INFLUENCIA DE LA MATEMATICA... CARRERAS / Leon Gutierrez, Florencio – 1898 – 9 – 1.50f – sp Bibl Santa Ana [510]

INFLUENCIA DEL MANANTIAL DE MARCO EN EL DESARROLLA MATERIAL DE CACERES / Castel, Joaquin – 1895, 1896 – 9 – $1.50f – sp Bibl Santa Ana [000]

INFLUENCING A BROADER UNDERSTANDING OF JAZZ DANCE / Giddins, Kevin J & Black, Catherine H – 1992 – 1mf – $4.00 – us Microform Publ [790]

INFLUENTIAL PHYSICAL EDUCATION BOOKS OF THE TWENTIETH CENTURY / VanClief, Elizabeth W – 1982 – 6mf – 9 – $24.00 – us Microform Publ [790]

INFO – Berlin, Germany.West Berlin: Homosexuelle Aktion, 1972- – 1 – us U.W. Library [073]

INFO – Djakarta. Indonesia. 1966-1968 – 1 – us UMI [072]

INFO AAU *see* AAU NEWS

INFO AAU / Amatour Athletic Union of the United States – (Cont: AAU News) – Indianapolis. v52-. 1981-* – 1,5,9 – D8556.01 – us UMI [790]

INFO CANADA – (Incorporates: I.T. Magazine at v19 no 3 1994) – v19- 1994- – 1 – Can$85.00y – cn Micromedia [000]

INFO-EXPLO – Rouyn-Noranda. v1 n1. 12 jul 1985-28 nov 1988 – 1r – 1 – Can$60.00 – cn Can Microfilming [072]

INFOLDINGS AND UNFOLDINGS OF THE DIVINE GENIUS, IN NATURE AND MAN / Pulsford, John – London: James Clarke, 1901. 1 fiche. 8370-4810-9 – 9 – us A.T.L.A. [240]

INFO-MATIN – 1994-1995 – 3 times per yr – 6 – F4,000.00 – sz Infoprint [072]

INFOPERSPECTIVES – 1984-. -m – 1 – us UMI [073]

INFOR – (1983-. 1,5,6,9) – v9-. 1971- – 1 – us UMI [000]

INFOR-BURUNDI : BULLETIN HEBDOMADAIRE D'INFORMATION DE L'OFFICE NATIONAL DE PRESSE DU BURUNDI – Usumbura: L'Office, n1-49. jan 6-dec 10, 1962; n53-98. jan-nov 25, 1963 – 1r – 1 – us Res Libr [072]

Inforcongo. 1ere Direction. Presse et relations publiques *see* BULLETIN DE PRESSE

INFORM : INFORMATION MONITOR – Colombo, Sri Lanka. 30 docs. 1988-1991 – 5mf – 9 – ne IDC [360]

INFORMA / Costa Rica. Direccion General de Estadistica y Censo – 1897, 1908-47 – 1 – 46.00 – us L of C Photodup [310]

INFORMACAO DO REINO DO CONGO, 1793-95 – Lisbon, Portugal: Biblioteca Nacional de Lisboa, 1970 – us Res Libr [960]

LA INFORMACION – Santiago, Chile. -m. March 1920-Nov 1922; Sept 1926-April 1930. 5 reels – 1 – uk British Libr Newspaper [072]

INFORMACION EN DERECHO...JUAN SANTOS CUENDA...LOS JUICIOS / Medinaceli, Duquesa de – 1877 – 9 – 1.50f – sp Bibl Santa Ana [340]

INFORMACION QUE DA AL PUBLICO EL DR. JOSE GOSSALBES...SOBRE LA ULTIMA ENFERMEDAD... / Gossalbes, Jose – Valencia, 1746 – 1mf – 9 – sp Cultura [610]

INFORMACION SOBRE EL LINAJE DE HERNANDO PIZARRO / Munoz de San Pedro, Miguel – Badajoz: Dip. Prov. de Badajoz, 1966. Sep. Rev. Est. Extremenos – 1 – sp Bibl Santa Ana [920]

INFORMACION Y CURACION DE LA PESTE EN ZARAGOZA Y PERSERVACION CONTRA LA PESTE... / Porcell, J – Zaragoza, 1565 – 5mf – 9 – sp Cultura [615]

INFORMACIONES – Madrid, 1940-55 – 1 – us Res Libr [072]

INFORMACIONES – Madrid, SP. 1978-1980 – 24r – $1,200.00 – R63582 – us Library Micro [072]

INFORMACIONES ARGENTINAS – (Includes c.1: no.8 1938:Sept., no.39 (1940:Jan.)-; no.42 1940:Apr., no.45 (1940:Sept.); no.47 1940:Oct.-no.50 (1940:Dec.); no.60 1942:Jan.-no.67 (1942:Oct.)) – 1 – CSUXAHZ3713-S – us Hoover Inst Photo [972]

INFORMACION...MARQUES DE PERALES / Perez Castro, Pedro A – 1796 – 9 – 1.50f – sp Bibl Santa Ana [920]

INFORMACIONS SISTEMATICA – Colonia del Valle, MX. 1976-1982 – 8r – $400.00 – R04213 – us Library Micro [072]

EL INFORMADOR – Berkeley, CA. 1967- – 1+ r – 1 – $50.00 – R03156 – us Library Micro [071]

O INFORMADOR – Manaos, Amazonas. 1 Jan 1918 – 1,5,6 – bl Biblioteca [072]

INFORMADOR GUERRILERO – Cuba, GT. 1982-1985 – 1r – $50.00 – R04211 – us Library Micro [072]

INFORMAL OPINIONS (A-G) / Pennsylvania – 1934-56; 1951-78 (1970 never published). 15 reels – 1 – $35.00r – us Trans-Media [340]

AN INFORMAL RECORD OF MISSIONARY SERVICE IN THE ISLAND OF TONGOA AND THE SHEPHERD ISLANDS, 1941-1947 / Miller, J Graham & Miller, Flora – 1r – at Pacific Mss [240]

INFORMAL SECTOR SERVICE CENTRE – Kathmandu. 3 docs. 1991 – 2mf – 9 – ne IDC [350]

INFORMAT SIONNO-SPRAVOCHNY I EZHENEDELNIK NARODNOGO KOMISSARIATA PO PROSVESHCHENII U *see* EZHENEDELNIK NARODNOGO KOMISSARIATA PO PROSVESHCHENII U

L'INFORMATEUR : CONSEIL INTERMUNICIPAL DE L'ILE JESUS – (Cont by: Informo 7 oct 1965) – Ville de Laval (Ste-Rose). Canada. dec 1964 – 1r – 1 – Can$25.00 – cn Can Microfilming [971]

L'INFORMATEUR HAITIEN – Port-au-Prince: Imp Aug A Heraux, jan 15-feb 22, feb 25-apr 30, may 3-jul 9, jul 11-aug 22, 25-30 1919 – 7 sheets – 9 – us Res Libr [072]

INFORMATIA BUCURESTIULUI – (Cont as: Libertatea as of 29 Dec 1989) – Bucharest, Romania. 1962-25 Aug 1990 – 40r – 1 – us L of C Photodup [949]

INFORMATIK – 1969-1989 – 195mf – 1 – DM1,111.50 – gw Mikro Press [000]

INFORMATIK – v. 16-25. 1969-1978 – 1. – apply; v.24-25 1977-1978 5,6,9 – us UMI [020]

INFORMATIK-SPEKTRUM – v.1-4, 1978-80. ISSN: 0170-6012 – 1,5,6,9,13 – 63.00v – us UMI [000]

L'INFORMATION – French West Indies. Martinique. 1941-1951; 1956-1962 – 1 – us UMI [072]

L'INFORMATION : HEBDOMADAIRE REGIONAL – Mont Joli, Canada. 27 jan 1971 – 1r – 1 – Can$25.00 – cn Can Microfilming [072]

L'INFORMATION : JOURNAL DE SAINTE-JULIE, DE SAINTE-AMABLE ET DE LA REGION – Ste. Julie. v1- 1975-. SEM35P215 – 1 – cn Bibl Nat [073]

L'INFORMATION – Montreal. v31 n32. 28 avr 1951-v33 n33. 9 mai 1953 – 1r – 1 – Can$40.00 – cn Can Microfilming [072]

L'INFORMATION – Politique, economique, financiere. Paris. 21 oct 1899-11 juin 1940, 19 juil 1941, 30 juin 1942, 1963-6 oct 1967 – 1 – fr A.C.R.P.P. [073]

L'INFORMATION – Cap-Haitien: [s.n.], jan 13 1934-dec 28 1935 – 7 sheets – 9 – us Res Libr [072]

INFORMATION – (Cont: Le Portage) – Le Portage, Canada. 5 jan 1972-24 dec 1975 – 4r – 1 – Can$60.00 – cn Can Microfilming [072]

INFORMATION / CRE (Conference des Recteurs Europeens) – v25- 1974- 1; v33- 5,6,9 – us UMI [370]

INFORMATION : AN ESSENTIAL FACTOR IN EDUCATIONAL PLANNING AND POLICY / ed by Psacharopoulos, George – 1980 – 303p – 9 – 92-3-101668-7 – fr UNESCO [370]

INFORMATION – St-Damase, Canada. mai 1974; v1 n7. nov 1974 – 1r – 1 – Can$25.00 – cn Can Microfilming [072]

INFORMATION : DER VERTRETER DES PV DER SPD – TYSKA SOCIALDEMOKRATISKA PARTIETS REPRESENTANT – (Also known as: Zur Information) – Stockholm, Sweden. Mar 1943-Sep 47 – 1r – 1 – gw Mikrofilm [072]

INFORMATION *see* LE PORTAGE

INFORMATION ABOUT NUSA TENGGARA TIMUR – 1961 – 9 – SE-3107 1 – ne IDC [950]

INFORMATION ABOUT THE FORESTS / Libya. Ministry of Agriculture and Livestock – Pamphlet nr.36. 1964. BNE-1031 1 – 9 – ne IDC [634]

INFORMATION AGE – v4-. 1982- – 1,5,6,9 – us UMI [000]

INFORMATION AND COMMENTS-SWAPO OF NAMIBIA – v6,no.2.Mar-Apr 1984. London: SWAPO. ill. -m. Absorbed by SWAPO Information Bulletin – 1 – us U.W. Library [073]

INFORMATION AND MANAGEMENT – v1-7. 1978-84 – 1,5,6,13 – sz Elsevier [650]

INFORMATION BULLETIN / Fundamental Baptist Fellowship – Dec 1946-72 – 1 – 61.32 – us Baptist [240]

INFORMATION BULLETIN / Hungary. FAO National Committee – Budapest. v. 1, no. 1-4, no. 4. 1 Mar 1947-Oct 1949 – 1 – us NY Public [330]

INFORMATION BULLETIN / Mississippi State University. Agricultural Experiment Station. Agricultural and Forestry Experiment Station – No.1-31.1978-82. 1 reel – 1,5 – us Spaulding [630]

INFORMATION BULLETIN / Soviet Antarctic Expedition – v4 irr – 1,5,6 – $30.00v – us A.G.U. [550]

INFORMATION BULLETIN / Spanish Committee in Defense of Democracy – Washington, DC, 1937. Fiche W1199. (Blodgett Collection of Spanish Civil War Pamphlets) – 9 – us H.U. College Libr [946]

INFORMATION BULLETIN / U.S. Library of Congress – Jan 1942-Dec 1977 – 1 – 556.00 – us L of C Photodup [324]

INFORMATION BULLETIN – v20-. 1982- – 1,5,6,9 – us UMI [000]

INFORMATION BULLETIN. / Partido Obrero de Unificacion Marxista. Spain – Barcelona, 1936? Fiche W1098. (Blodgett Collection of Spanish Civil War Pamphlets) – 9 – us H.U. College Libr [946]

INFORMATION BULLETIN OF THE SCIENCE COOPERATION OFFICE FOR SOUTHEAST ASIA – (Missing: Nos. 6-29) – Djakarta, Nos. 1-34 – 4mf – 9 – SE-977/1 – ne IDC [500]

INFORMATION CASE FILES / U.S. Circuit and District Courts. Pennsylvania – 1789-1843. Related Records, 1792-1918, of the U.S. District Court for the Eastern District of Pennsylvania. 10 rolls – 1 – M992 – us Nat'l Archives [324]

INFORMATION CENTRE FOR POLISH AFFAIRS – London. 277 docs. 1980-1991 – 153mf – 9 – ne IDC [947]

L'INFORMATION CENTRE-VILLE NEWS – Montreal, Canada. v1 n7. 29 aut 1973; v1 n19. 27 nov 1973 – 1r – 1 – Can$25.00 – cn Can Microfilming [072]

INFORMATION CIRCULARS / U.S. Bureau of Mines – Nos 6783-8750. 1934-77 – 1,5,6 – us Princeton Micro [622]

INFORMATION CIRCULARS AND VARIOUS SALES CODES (ONUG) / United Nations – 1946-1984 – E/F.236 E.258 F.184 R.75 S.9 – 9 – us U.N. Pubs [320]

INFORMATION CONTROL AND PROPAGANDA : RECORDS OF THE OFFICE OF WAR INFORMATION – Part 1: The Director's Central Files, 1942-45. 12 reels with printed guide – 1 – $1,150.00 – 0-89093-975-6 – us UPA [977]

INFORMATION CONTROL AND PROPAGANDA : RECORDS OF THE OFFICE OF WAR INFORMATION – Part 2: Office of Policy Coordination. Series A: Propaganda and Policy Directives for Overseas Programs, 1942-45. 15 reels with printed guide – 1 – $1,450.00 – 0-89093-976-4 – us UPA [380]

L'INFORMATION CO-OP – Ville de St-Leonard, Canada. 15 nov 1957-avr 1962 – 1r – 1 – Can$45.00 – cn Can Microfilming [072]

L'INFORMATION DE CHATEAUGUAY – Chateauguay, Canada. v1 n13. 23 mai 1956; v1 n16. 13 jun 1956 – 1r – 1 – Can$25.00 – cn Can Microfilming [072]

Information Department. Indonesian Office *see* INDONESIAN INFORMATION

L'INFORMATION "FEMINA-JOURNAL" – Montreal, Canada. 27 mai 1963-v1 n7. 8 jul 1963 – 1r – 1 – Can$25.00 – cn Can Microfilming [073]

INFORMATION FOLDERS / Indonesia. Bank Pembangunan – SE-5339 1 1964 – 9 – ne IDC [950]

INFORMATION FOR IMMIGRANTS, SETTLERS AND PURCHASERS OF PUBLIC LANDS, WITH MAPS.. / Canada. Ministere des Terres de la Couronne – (1863 ed. 1mf Can$2.00. SEM105P238) – Quebec: Printed by Hunter, Rose & Lemieux, 1862. SEM105P237 – 1mf – 9 – Can$2.25 – cn Bibl Nat [360]

INFORMATION GUIDE / New Hampshire. Cooperative Extension Service – v. 1-12. 1967-69 – 1,5,6 – us Spaulding [630]

INFORMATION HOTLINE – (See also: Information Part One: News/Sources/Profiles and Information News and Sources) – v8-. 1976- – 1,5,6,9 – us UMI [020]

INFORMATION LEAFLET / Georgia. Agricultural Experiment Station. Athens – v. 1-7. 1952-54 – 1,5,6 – us Spaulding [630]

INFORMATION LETTER / American Indian Press Association – (American Indian Periodicals in the Princeton University Library) – 1r – 1 – $45.00 – us UPA [305]

INFORMATION LETTER / National Canners Association – 1923-72 1; 1971-72 5,6 – us UMI [670]

L'INFORMATION LITTERAIRE – Paris. 1949-62 – 1 – fr A.C.R.P.P. [800]

INFORMATION MANAGEMENT – v17-. 1983- – 1,5,6,9 – us UMI [650]

INFORMATION MANAGEMENT *see* ADMINISTRATIVE MANAGEMENT

INFORMATION MANAGEMENT REVIEW – 1985- – 1,5,6,9 – us UMI [020]

L'INFORMATION MEDICALE ET PARAMEDICALE – Montreal. v1-32. 1948-72. SEM35P41 – 20r – 1 – Can$1,126.00 – cn Bibl Nat [610]

INFORMATION NEWS AND SOURCES – v. 6-7. 1974-1975 – 1,5,6 – us UMI [020]

INFORMATION ON INDONESIA : PERMANENT MISSION OF THE REPUBLIC OF INDONESIA TO THE UNITED NATIONS – (Missing: 1958(2-3, 5, 17); 1958-1959(19-94, 96, 100)) – New York, 1958-1959 – 10mf – 9 – SE-545/1 – ne IDC [950]

L'INFORMATION OUVRIERE ET SOCIALE. ACTION, SYNDICALE, ORGANISATION DU TRAVAIL EVOLUTION ECONOMIQUE – Paris. mars 1918-35 – 1 – fr A.C.R.P.P. [073]

INFORMATION PAPER : CENSUS 86 – AUSTRALIAN STANDARD GEOGRAPHICAL CLASSIFICATION (ASGC): GEOGRAPHICAL CODE LIST – 9 – at Statistics [304]

INFORMATION PAPERS – (Filmed with: League of Arab States document collection) – New York: Arab Information Center, 1955-66. n2-8 nov 1956-nov 1959; n10-13 jan-nov 1960; n15 1961; n17-19 sep-nov 1961; n22 jul 1964; n25 jan 1964 – 1r – 1 – us Res Libr [072]

INFORMATION PART ONE: NEWS/SOURCES/ PROFILES – v. 1-5. 1969-1973 – 1 – us UMI [020]

INFORMATION PRIVACY – v1-3. 1978-81 – 1 – us UMI [000]

INFORMATION PROCESSING AND MANAGEMENT – v1- 1963- – 5,6,9 – us UMI [000]

INFORMATION PROCESSING LETTERS – v1-19. 1971-84 – 1,5,6,13 – sz Elsevier [073]

INFORMATION RE: JAYNE'S HYMNAL BY MRS. R. T. STOWE OF WESTFIELD, N.J., PICTURES OF GRAVE AND HOME – 9p – 1 – us Baptist [240]

L'INFORMATION REGIONALE – Beauharnois, Ville de Lery, Canada. v10 n31. 4 jul 1962; v14 n38. 15 jun 1966-v31 n10. 24 jan 1973 – 9r – 1 – Can$70.00r – cn Can Microfilming [072]

INFORMATION RELATING TO MUNICIPAL LEGISLATION OF THE LIQUOR TRAFFIC: ALSO OF MUNICIPAL FRANCHISE FOR WOMEN / Craig, Maria G – s.l.: s.n., 1899?. 03621. (Pre-1900 Canadiana) – 9 – cn C.I.H.M. [971]

INFORMATION RELATIVE TO THE ASSESSMENT AND COLLECTION OF TAXES / Connecticut. Dept. of Revenue Services – 1907-78. 130 fiches. (Harvard Law School Library Collection.) – 9 – 1.50f – us H.U. Law [336]

INFORMATION RETRIEVAL AND LIBRARY AUTOMATION – v1-23. 1965-88.-m – 1 – $36.00y – us UMI [000]

L'INFORMATION REVOLUTIONNAIRE / Toure, Ahmed Sekou – [Conakry?: s.n., 1981?] – us Res Libr [320]

INFORMATION SCIENCE ABSTRACTS – (v19-29 1984 94 $160.00v) – v1-18. 1966-83 – 1,5 – $80.00v – us UMI [000]

INFORMATION SCIENCES – v1-34. 1969-84 – 1,5,6,13 – sz Elsevier [000]

INFORMATION SERIES / Connecticut. Agricultural Experiment Station. Storrs – v. 1-53. 1949-53 – 1,5,6 – us Spaulding [630]

INFORMATION SERVICE : CATHOLIC CHURCH. PONT. CONSILIUM AD CHRIST. UNITATEM FOVENDAM – 1989-93 (complete) – Inquire – 1 – ATLA S0916 – us A.T.L.A. [073]

INFORMATION SERVICE / International Committee of Coordination and Information to Aid Republican Spain – Paris, 1938. Fiche W966. (Blodgett Collection of Spanish Civil War Pamphlets) – 9 – us H.U. College Libr [946]

INFORMATION SERVICE – New York. v1-48. 1919-69 (complete) – 9r – 1 – ATLA S0028 – us A.T.L.A. [073]

INFORMATION SERVICES AND USE – v1-4. 1981-84 – 1,5,6,13 – sz Elsevier [073]

INFORMATION SERVICES ON RESEARCH IN PROGRESS : A WORLDWIDE INVENTORY / ed by Smithsonian Science Information Exchange, Inc. – 2nd ed 1982 – 330p – 9 – 92-3-102071-4 – fr UNESCO [020]

INFORMATION SHEET : EDUCATION FACILITIES FOR ENGLISH-SPEAKING CHILDREN / Hong Kong. Education Department – Hong Kong, 1975 – 1mf – 9 – DE-167/1 – ne IDC [370]

INFORMATION SHEET / Mississippi. Agricultural Experiment Station. State College – v. 1-1121. 1933-70 – 1,5,6 – us Spaulding [630]

INFORMATION SHEET / Mississippi State University. Agricultural Experiment Station – 1970-82.1122-1312. 1 reel – 1,5 – us Spaulding [630]

INFORMATION SHEET / Mississippi State University. Cooperative Extension Service – No.351-1100 – 1,5 – us Spaulding [630]

INFORMATION SHEET / Mississippi State University. Cooperative Extension Service – v. 201-390 – 1,5,6 – us Spaulding [630]

INFORMATION SHEET : TECHNICAL/ VOCATIONAL EDUCATION AND TRAINING IN HONG KONG / Hong Kong. Education Department – Hong Kong, 1975 – 1mf – 9 – DE-535/1 – ne IDC [370]

INFORMATION SHEET ON PRIMARY EDUCATION / Hong Kong. Educational Department – Hong Kong, 1975 – 1mf – 9 – DE-169/1 – ne IDC [370]

INFORMATION SHEET ON SECONDARY EDUCATION 1975-1976 / Hong Kong. Education Department – Hong Kong – 1mf – 9 – DE-170/1 – ne IDC [370]

INFORMATION SHEET ON SPECIAL EDUCATION / Hong Kong. Education Department – Hong Kong – 1mf – 9 – DE-171/1 – ne IDC [370]

INFORMATION SHEET ON THE ADVISORY INSPECTORATE / Hong Kong. Education Department – Hong Kong, 1975 – 1mf – 9 – DE-172/1 – ne IDC [370]

INFORMATION SOCIETY – v.1. 1981 – 1,5,6,9 – us UMI [000]

INFORMATION STORAGE AND RETRIEVAL *see* INFORMATION PROCESSING AND MANAGEMENT

INFORMATION SYSTEMS – (Incorporating: Database Technology) – v1- 1975- – 5,6,9 – us UMI [073]

INFORMATION SYSTEMS ON LATIN AMERICA – Berkeley, Ca. 1973-1980 – 16r – 1 – $800.00 – R03155 – us Library Micro [000]

INFORMATION TECHNOLOGY AND LIBRARIES – v.1-. 1982- – 1,5,6,9 – us UMI [020]

INFORMATION TECHNOLOGY IN HUMAN AFFAIRS – v. 1-. 1980- – 5,6,9 – us UMI [020]

INFORMATION TECHNOLOGY, RESEARCH AND DEVELOPMENT – 1982- – 1,5,6,9 – us UMI [000]

INFORMATION WORLD – 1978- – 1,5,6,9 – us UMI [020]

INFORMATIONEN ZUR JUDENFRAGE *see* WELT-DIENST

INFORMATIONS COOPERATIVES 1928-1968 / International Labour Organisation – 9 – Sfr275.00 – 92-2-206573-5 – sz I.L.O. [334]

INFORMATIONS (CRIMINAL AND QUO WARRANTO) MANDAMUS AND PROHIBITION / Shortt, John – 1st American ed. from the English ed. 1887. Boston: Edson, 1888. 771p. LL-1628 – 1 – us L of C Photodup [340]

INFORMATIONS INDONESIENNES – (Missing: 1950-1954, v1-5(1-14); 1954, v5(16); 1955, v6(1, 6, 10, 15-16); 1956, v7(16)) – Paris, 1950-1960 – 62mf – 9 – SE-554/1 – ne IDC [950]
INFORMATIONS MENSUELLES – Kinshasa nov 1969-jan 1970 – us Res Libr [072]
INFORMATIONS OFFICIELLES DE LA REPUBLIQUE DU CONGO / Congo – Publies par le Ministere de l'Information et du Tourisme a Leopoldville. 5v. 1964-66. – 41mf – 9 – ne IDC [960]
INFORMATIONS OUVRIERES / La Federation des Comites d'Alliance Ouvriere – (Suppl. mens. fevr 1964-juin; juil 1968. 1) – Paris, 1968-72. Pierre Lambert, Dir – 1 – fr A.C.R.P.P. [331]
LES INFORMATIONS POLITIQUES ET SOCIALES – (Filmed with: Bartlett, Robert E: Collection of African newspapers) – Paris jan 25, 1962 – us Res Libr [072]
INFORMATIONS PRECISES ET OFFICIELLES TOUCHANT L'ENREGISTREMENT ET L'IMPOT / Auger, Joseph Cyrille – Montreal: Whiteford & Theoret, 1895. 02447. (Pre-1900 Canadiana) – 9 – cn C.I.H.M. [971]
INFORMATIONSBLAETTER – Berlin, 1933-38 – 1r – 1 – Dist. gw Mikrofilm – gw Misc Inst [072]
INFORMATIONSBLAETTER : IM AUFTRAGE DES ZENTRAL-AUSSCHUSSES DER DEUTSCHEN JUDEN FUER HILFE UND AUFBAU – Berlin. v1-6. 1933-38. Complete. 1 reel. B106 (Leo Baeck Institute. German-Jewish Periodicals, Pt 2) – 1 – $75.00 – us UPA [270]
INFORMATIONSBLATT DER AUSLANDSVERTRETUNG DER DEUTSCHEN GEWERKSCHAFTEN : BEILAGE DES BULLETINS DES INTERNATIONALEN GEWERKSCHAFT – Paris, France. 16 Nov 1937-29 Aug 1939 – 1r – 1 – gw Mikrofilm [072]
INFORMATIONSBLATT DER FREIEN GEWERKSCHAFTEN – Hamburg, Schleswig-Holstein. 1946-49 – 1r – 1 – DM75.00 – gw Mikro Press [331]
INFORMATIONSBLATT DER FREIEN GEWERKSCHAFTEN – Hamburg, Schleswig-Holstein, West Germany. 19 Jun 1946-10 Dec 1949 – 1r – 1 – gw Mikrofilm [072]
INFORMATIONSBRIEF / ed by Arbeitsgemeinschaft deutscher, oesterreicherscher und tschechoslowakischer Sozialisten – Oslo, Norway. 22 Sept 1939-28 Mar 1940 – 1 – gw Mikrofilm [072]
INFORMATIONSBRIEF – (Publ in Rostock, 1925-26) – Berlin, 1925-38 – 1 – Dist. gw Mikrofilm – gw Misc Inst [073]
INFORMATIONSDIENST DER CDU *see* CDU-INFORMATIONSDIENST
INFORMATIONSDIENST DER CDU DEUTSCHLANDS *see* UNION IN DEUTSCHLAND
INFORMATIONSDIENST DER CDU/CSU *see* CDU-INFORMATIONSDIENST FUER DIE BRITISCHE ZONE
INFORMATIQUE ET BUREAUTIQUE : REVUE MENSUELLE – Montreal, avr 1980-mar 1992 – 4r – 1 – Can$60.00 – cn Can Microfilming [072]
INFORMATIQUE QUEBEC : MENSUEL – Quebec. 25 oct 1979-v1 n11. oct 1980 – 1r – 1 – Can$40.00 – cn Can Microfilming [072]
INFORMATIVO MUNICIPAL – Rio Branco, Acre. Out 1984; Abr, Jul, Set 1985 – 1,5,6 – bl Biblioteca [072]
INFORMATIVO VOZ DO CAMPO – Rio Branco, Acre. Mar 1985-Out 1986 – 1,5,6 – bl Biblioteca [072]
INFORMATSIONNY I BI ULLETEN : SOI UZ RUSSKIKHI [SIC] INVALIDOV V BOLGARII – (Includes c.1: no.8 1933:Jan.-no.11 (1933:Aug.)) – Sofiia: Soi uz, 19uu – 1 – CSUXAKG2008-S – us Hoover Inst Photo [947]
INFORMATSIONNY I BI ULLETEN OTDELA NARODNOGO OBRAZOVANII A MOSK. SOV. RAB., KR. I KRASN. DEP – (Includes c.1: no.8/9 1921:June 1/15, no.12/13 (1921:Aug.1/15)) – [Moskva: Otdel], 1921 – 1 – CSUXAKZ2537-S – us Hoover Inst Photo [947]
INFORMATSIONNY I BI ULLETEN SOI UZ RUSSKIKH INVALIDOV V BOLGARII *see* INFORMATSIONNY I BI ULLETEN
INFORMATSIONNYI LISTOK ZAGRANICHNOI ORGANIZATSII BUNDA : VSEOBSHCHII EVREISKII RABOCHII SOIUZ V LITVE, POL'SHE I ROSSII, (BUND) – (Missing: no 6) – Geneva. n1-11. 1911-1916 – 2mf – 9 – ne IDC [947]
INFORMAZYE BLETER FUN DER EMMIGRAZYE : BULLETIN D'INF. DE L'ASS'N D'EMIGRATION HICK JCA – (In Yiddish) – Paris, FR. Jan 1930 – 1r – 1 – $25.00 – cn Can Microfilming [072]
INFORME : COMISION INVESTIGADORA DE ACTIVIDADES ANTIARGENTINAS / Argentina. Congreso de la Nacion et al – (Includes c.1: no.1 1941:Aug. 29, no.4 (1941:Sept. 30); 1942:Sept., Dec.; 1943:Jan.) – Buenos Aires: Camara de Diputados de la Nacion, 1941- – 1 – CSUXAHZ5759-S – us Hoover Inst Photo [972]
INFORME / Ecuador. Ministerio de Gobierno – 1935 36-1943 – 1 – 23.00 – us L of C Photodup [324]
Informe *see* SOBRE INVENTARIO...DEL MUSEO DE BADAJOZ
INFORME [...] / Bolivia Ministerio de Guerra – La Paz: Impr de "El Comercio", 1886-87, 1889 – us Res Libr [072]
INFORME [...] / Bolivia Ministerio de Guerra – La Paz: Impr de la Union Americana, [-1881] – us Res Libr [072]
INFORME [...] / Bolivia Ministerio de Hacienda e Industria – La Paz: Impr de "El Nacional" de Isaac V Vila, 1891-96 – us Res Libr [072]
INFORME [...] / Bolivia Ministerio de Hacienda e Industria – Sucre: Impr Boliviana, 1886-88 – us Res Libr [072]
INFORME [...] / Bolivia Ministerio de Relaciones Exteriores y Culto – La Paz: Imp y Tip de "El Nacional", 1889-91 – us Res Libr [072]
INFORME [...] / Bolivia Ministerio de Relaciones Exteriores y Colonizacion – La Paz: Impr de "El Diario", 1885 – us Res Libr [072]
INFORME AJUSTADO AL NUNCIO POR PARTE DEL P. GENERAL (CACERES) EN EL PLEYTO CON LOS PADRES DIPUTADOS / Davila, Andres – s.l., s.i., s.a., 1642 – 1 – sp Bibl Santa Ana [946]
INFORME ANUAL DE INMIGRACION DE LA REPUBLICA ARGENTINA EN EL ANO 1875 – Buenos Aires, 1875 – 9mf – 9 – sp Cultura [972]
INFORME DE LA COMISION DE HACIENDA DIPUTACION...BADAJOZ – 1844 – 9 – 1.50f – sp Bibl Santa Ana [946]
INFORME DE LA COMISION, "ESTUDIO DE PRE-FACTIBILIDAD DE UN PROYECTO DE PROPOSITOS MULTIPLES PARA EL SERVICIO DE LA GRAN LIMA" / Peru. Instituto Nacional de Planificacion. Comission Coordinadora del sistema "Marcopomacocha" – 2v. Lima. 1965. BD-1844 1 – 9 – ne IDC [330]
INFORME DE LA OBRA TITULADA "ESTUDIO BIOGRAFICO DE ESPRONCEDA" POR JOSE CASCALES Y MUNOZ / Novo y Colson, Pedro de – Madrid: Fortanet, 1912. B.R.A.H. 60, pp. 426-428 – sp Bibl Santa Ana [946]
INFORME DE LABORES DE LA SECRETARIA DE RECURSOS HIDRAULICOS / Mexico Secretaria de Recursos Hidraulicos – Mexico: Talleres Graficos de la Nacion, 1946/47-1959/60 – 11r – 1 – us Res Libr [972]
INFORME DE LOS PERITOS...EXAMINAR LA CONTABILIDAD...FERROCARRIL MERIDA-SEVILLA – 1897 – 9 – 1.50f – sp Bibl Santa Ana [310]
INFORME DE LOS RESULTADOS DE LA ENCUESTA SOBRE LA SITUACION DEL COMERCIO, INDUSTRIA Y SERVICIOS / Camara Oficial de Comercio e Industria de Caceres – Caceres: Imp. Maygom, 1976 – 1 – sp Bibl Santa Ana [338]
INFORME DEL C PRESIDENTE DE LOS ESTADOS UNIDOS MEXICANOS AL H CONGRESO DE LA UNION. : PARTE CORRESPONDIENTE A LA SECRETARIA DE HACIENDA Y CREDITO PUBLICO, POR EL PERIODO DE [...] – Mexico, D F: la Secretaria, 1927/28-1928/29 – us Res Libr [972]
INFORME DEL DEPARTAMENTO NACIONAL DE AGRICULTURA / Argentina Departamento Nacioanl de Agricultura – Buenos Aires: Impr de "La Nacion", 1872-74 – 1r – 1 – us Res Libr [972]
INFORME DEL MINISTRO DE HACIENDA DE BOLIVIA AL CONGRESO ORDINARIO DE [...] / Bolivia Ministerio de Hacienda – La Paz: Impr de "El Nacional" de Isaac V Villa, 1885 – us Res Libr [972]
INFORME DEL MINISTRO DE HACIENDA E INDUSTRIA A LA ASAMBLEA ORDINARIA DE [...] / Bolivia Ministerio de Hacienda e Industria – Sucre: Impr de La Libertad, 1874 – us Res Libr [972]
INFORME DEL PLAN NACIONAL DE INTEGRACION DE LA POBLACION ABORIGEN. ENERO 1962-JUNIO 1963 / Peru. Ministerio de Trabajo y Asuntos Indigenas – Lima. 1963. BD-1842 1 – 9 – ne IDC [310]
INFORME DEL PRESIDENTE DEL CREDITO PUBLICO NACIONAL PEDRO AGOTE SOBRE LE DEUDO PUBLICA / Argentine Republic. Junta de Administracion del Credito Publico Nacional – Libro 1-4. 1881-87 – 1 – $46.00 – us L of C Photodup [336]
INFORME DEL SUPERINTENDENTE DE ESCUELAS DE CUBA : CON INCLUSION DE LOS RENDIDOS POR LOS SUPERINTENDENTES DE INSTRUCCION E INSPECTORES PEDAGOGICOS / Cuba. Superindendencia de Escuelas – Habana: Impr de Rambla y Bouza, [1903-] – us Res Libr [972]
INFORME DIRIGIDO AL HONORABLE SENOR PRESIDENTE DE LA REPUBLICA [...] POR EL SECRETARIO DE HACIENDA [...] SOBRE LOS TRABAJOS REALIZADOS POR EL DEPARTAMENTO DESDE EL [...] / Cuba. Secretaria de Hacienda – Habana: Montalvo y Cardenas, 1927/28 – us Res Libr [972]
INFORME ESTADISTICO GANADERO / Rubio Garcia, Jose – Badajoz: Junta Provincial de Fomento Pecuario, 1952 – 1 – sp Bibl Santa Ana [304]
INFORME LEGAL POR D. FRANCISCO DE ULLOA Y FLORES...CON D. FRANCISCO JAVIER ESCOBAR Y TORRES...Y DONA MARIA LUISA FLORES CHAVES...SOBRE LA PROPIEDAD DE LOS MAYORAZGOS QUE FUNDARON D. JUAN DE LA HINOJOSA Y DONA TERESA CALDERON... / Merino Ortiz, Tomas – 1 – sp Bibl Santa Ana [340]
INFORME POLITICO DEL GOBIERNO AL CONSEJO NACIONAL DEL MOVIMIENTO SOBRE POLITICA DE VIVIENDA, URBANISMO Y ARQUITECTURA / Martinez Sanchez-Arjona, Jose Maria – Madrid: Servicio Central de Publicaciones del Ministerio de la Vivienda, 1969 – sp Bibl Santa Ana [320]
INFORME PRELIMINAR SOBRE LA UNIFICACION DEL DERECHO RELATIVO AL CHEQUE / Alta Comision Internacional – Washington, 1918 – 1mf – 9 – ILM-3825/1 – ne IDC [340]
INFORME PRESENTADO A LA JUNTA DE AGRICULTURA, INDUSTRIA Y COMERCIO DE ESTA PROVINCIA ACERCA DE LAS BASES PARA LA FORMACION DE UN PROYECTO DE ENSENANZA AGRICOLA / Paredes Guillen, Ramon – Caceres: Tip. Bello Hermanos, Arnedo y Fernandez, s.a. 1871? – 1 – sp Bibl Santa Ana [630]
INFORME PRESENTADO AL CONGRESO ORDINARIO DE [...] / Bolivia Ministerio de la Guerra – La Paz: Impr de La Revolucion, 1893 – us Res Libr [972]
INFORME PRONUNCIADO POR DON...ACTUANDO COMO DEFENSOR EN LA VISTA SEGUIDA CONTRA URBANO CALVO SANCHEZ / Romero Carvajal, Jose Ignacio – Caceres: Tip. El Noticiero, 1949 – 1 – sp Bibl Santa Ana [946]
INFORME PRONUNCIADO POR...ACUSADOR PRIVADO...CONTRA VICENTE SANCHEZ PEREZ...POR ASESINATO, 1948 / Perez Cordoba, Luis – Caceres: Tip. El Noticiero, s.a. – 1 – sp Bibl Santa Ana [946]
INFORME QUE EL OFICIAL MAYOR ENCARGADO DEL MINISTERIO DE HACIENDA PRESENTA A LA ASAMBLEA NACIONAL ORDINARIA DE [...] / Bolivia. Ministerio de Hacienda – [Sucre?]: Impr del Estado a direccion de M Martinez, 1863 – us Res Libr [972]
INFORME QUE PRESENTA A LA LEGISLATURA ORDINARIA DE [...] / Bolivia. Ministerio de Hacienda y Estadistica – La Paz: El Ministerio, 1940 – us Res Libr [972]
INFORME RELATIVO A PARTE DE LA VIA ROMANA NUM. 25 DEL ITINERARIO DE ANTONINO / Blazquez, Antonio – Madrid: Fortanet, 1912. B.R.A.H. LX, pp. 306-317 – sp Bibl Santa Ana [946]
INFORME SOBRE : HISTORIA DE LA PIRATERIA MALAYO-MAHOMETANA EN MINDANAO, JOLO Y BORNEO, POR D. JOSE MONTERO Y VIDAL / Barrantes Moreno, Vicente – Madrid: Fortanet, 1892. B.R.A.H. 20, pp. 155-159 – sp Bibl Santa Ana [946]
INFORME SOBRE DECLARACION DE MONUMENTO NACIONAL DE PUENTE DE ALCANTARA / Blazquez, Antonio – Madrid: Tip. Revista de Arch. Bibliot. y Museos, 1924 – 1 – sp Bibl Santa Ana [946]
INFORME SOBRE EL CENSO DE CUBA, 1899 / U.S. War Department. Cuban Census Office – Washington: Impr. del Gobierno, 1900. 793p. tables, maps. diagrs – 1 – us U.W. Library [310]
INFORME SOBRE EL CENSO DE CUBA DE 1889 – Washington, 1900 – 17mf – 9 – sp Cultura [972]
INFORME SOBRE EL CONVENTO DE SAN BENITO DE ALCANTARA Y FALLECIMIENTO / Lamperez Romea, Vicente – Madrid: Ed. Reus, 1923. B.R.A.H. 82. pp. 191 y 193-194 – 1 – sp Bibl Santa Ana [946]
INFORME SOBRE EL LUGAR DE NACIMIENTO DE HERNANDO DE SOTO / Munoz de San Pedro, Miguel – Badajoz: Imprenta de Diputacion Prov., 1963. Sep. Revista de Estudios Extremenos – 1 – sp Bibl Santa Ana [910]
INFORME SOBRE EL RAMO DE HACIENDA Y CREDITO PUBLICO : DEL CUAL SE EXTRACTO EL QUE RINDIO EL C PRESIDENTE DE LA REPUBLICA AL H CONGRESO DE LA UNION EL DIA [...] / Mexico. Secretaria de Hacienda y Credito Publico – Mexico, D F: la Secretaria, 1934 – us Res Libr [972]
INFORME SOBRE JUEGOS, ESPECTACULOS Y DIVERSIONES PUBLICAS / Jovellanos, Melchor Gaspar de – 1812 – 1mf – 9 – Pta1,000.00 – 84-7848-122-2 – sp Pentalfa [946]
INFORME SOBRE LA CATALOGACION DE LA COLECCION NUMISMATICA DEL MUSEO DE CACERES / Floriano Cumbreno, Antonio C – Caceres: Imp. Santos Floriano Gonzalez, s.a. – 1 – sp Bibl Santa Ana [060]
INFORME SOBRE LA DECLARACION DE MONUMENTO NACIONAL DE LA IGLESIA. PARROQUIAL DE SANTA EULALIA DE ALAMIA / Monsalud, Marques de – 1 – sp Bibl Santa Ana [946]
INFORME SOBRE LA GUERRA CIVIL EN EL PAIS VASCO, DICIEMBRE, 1937 – Buenos Aires, 1938. Fiche W959. (Blodgett Collection of Spanish Civil War Pamphlets) – 9 – us H.U. College Libr [946]
INFORME SOBRE LA INSTITUCION DE LA CRUZ-INSIGNIA DE LA REAL MAESTRANZA DE CABALLERIA DE ZARAGOZA / Monsalud, Marques de – Madrid: Est. Tip. Fortanet, 1908. B.R.A.H.T.53, 1908, pp. 338-341 – 1 – sp Bibl Santa Ana [946]
INFORME (SOBRE) LETTRES INTIMES DE J.M. ALBERONI... / Barrantes Moreno, Vicente – Madrid: Tip. Fortanet, 1899 – sp Bibl Santa Ana [946]
INFORME SOBRE LEY AGRARIA / Jovellanos, Melchor Gaspar de – 1795 – 1mf – 9 – Pta1,000.00 – 84-7848-034-X – sp Pentalfa [630]
INFORME SOBRE LEY AGRARIA / Jovellanos, Melchor Gaspar de – 1820 – 1mf – 9 – Pta1,000.00 – 84-7848-125-7 – sp Pentalfa [630]
INFORME SOBREEL NACIMIENTO DE FRANCISCO PIZARRO / Munoz de San Pedro, Miguel – Badajoz: Imp. Diputacion Prov., 1970. Separata de la Rev. de Estudios Extremenos – 1 – sp Bibl Santa Ana [910]
UN INFORME, UNA OPINION Y UNA ORIENTACION / Martinez Barrio, Diego – Discurso pronunciado ante el microfono de union radio instalado en el teatro Olympia de Valencia, el 31 enero 1937. Valencia, 1937. Fiche W 1031. (Blodgett Collection of Spanish Civil War Pamphlets) – 9 – us H.U. College Libr [946]
INFORME...FERROCARRILES / Lorenzana y Molina, Manuel – 1869 – 9 – 1.50f – sp Bibl Santa Ana [380]
INFORME...GUADALUPE...FISCAL...A ABADIA ALVANEZA / Santos Calderon de la Barca, Bernardo – 1712 – 9 – 1.50f – sp Bibl Santa Ana [972]
INFORME...PROPIEDAD...JUAN DE HINOJOSA Y.. / Ulloa y Florez, Francisco, Ma – 1797 – 9 – 1.50f – sp Bibl Santa Ana [946]
INFORMER – Houston. Tex. -w. 1919- – 1 – us UMI [071]
INFORMER AND TEXAS FREEMAN – Houston, TX. 1964-67 – 3r – 1 – us Ross [071]
INFORME-RESUMEN LEIDO EN LA JUNTA GENERAL DE ACCIONISTAS DE LA SUCURSAL DEL BANCO DE ESPANA EN BADAJOZ EL...1908 – Badajoz: Tip. Lit. y Enc. de Uceda Hermanos, 1908 – sp Bibl Santa Ana [946]

INFORMES DE LOS CONSEJEROS LEGALES DEL PODER EJECUTIVO / Argentine Republic – Publicacion Oficial. 10v. 1890-1902 – 1 – 69.00 – us L of C Photodup [323]

INFORMO *see* L'INFORMATEUR

INFOSYSTEMS – v. 1- 1959- – 1,5,6,9 – us UMI [020]

INFO-TURK – Brussels. 146 docs. 1980-1991 – 38mf – 9 – ne IDC [320]

INFOWELT – 1986- – 1 – us UMI [020]

INFOWORLD – v.2-. 1980- – 1,5,6,9 – us UMI [020]

INFRARED PHYSICS – v1- 1961- – 5,6,9 – us UMI [073]

INFRARED SPECTRAL DATA : A "LIVING" COM-MICROFICHE COLLECTION OF REFERENCE DATA / ed by Passlack, M et al – 1986 – 96mf – 9 – DM1,450.00 – 3-527-26330-6 – gw V.C.H. [540]

INFRARED SYSTEMS: FOR DETECTION, DIRECTION-FINDING AND AUTOMATIC TRACKING OF MOVING OBJECTS / Kriksunov, L & Usol'tev, I F – 1,5,9 – us Gordon [530]

L'INFRASTRUCTURE SCOLAIRE EN COTE D'IVOIRE / Leblanc, C – (Africa series) – 9 – fr Hachette [370]

THE INFRINGEMENT OF PATENTS FOR INVENTIONS, NOT DESIGNS, WITH SOLE REFERENCE TO THE OPINIONS OF THE SUPREME COURT OF THE UNITED STATES / Hall, Thomas Bond – Cincinnati, Clarke, 1893. 275 p. LL-1508 – 1 – us L of C Photodup [340]

DIE INFUSIONSTHIERCHEN ALS VOLLKOMMENE ORGANISMEN / Ehrenberg, CG – Leipzig, 1838 – 38mf – 9 – ne IDC [574]

Ingalls, John James and Family *see* PAPERS

Ingalls, Sheffield *see* HISTORY OF ATCHISON COUNTY

Inge, William Ralph *see*
- THE PHILOSOPHY OF PLOTINUS
- SOCIETY IN ROME UNDER THE CAESARS
- STUDIES OF ENGLISH MYSTICS
- TRUTH AND FALSEHOOD IN RELIGION
- TYPES OF CHRISTIAN SAINTLINESS

INGENIERIA BRITANICO *see* COMERCIO ARGENTINO-BRITANICO

INGENIERO ESPANOL *see* INGENIERO Y FERRETERO ESPANOL Y SUD AMERICANO

INGENIERO INDUSTRIAL *see* ELECTRICAL TIMES E INGENIERO INDUSTRIAL

INGENIERO Y FERRETERO ESPANOL Y SUD AMERICANO – (Ingeniero Espanol Sept 1893-Nov 1905) – London, UK. 15 Jan 1887-Jul 1893 – 1 – uk British Libr Newspaper [072]

INGENIERO Y METALISTA – London, UK. Jan 1932 – 1 – uk British Libr Newspaper [072]

L'INGENIEUR – Montreal. v41-73. 1955-1987. SEM16P358 – 7r – 5 – Can$167.00 – cn Bibl Nat [620]

L'INGENIEUR (1988) : LE JOURNAL DE L'ECOLE POLYTECHNIQUE ET DE SES DIPLOMES – Montreal. v1 no 1 (Sept 1988)- . SEM35P332 – 1 – Can$17.00 – cn Bibl Nat [620]

INGENIEUR ARCHIV – v1-11 1930-40 – 1 – us Princeton Micro [620]

L'INGENIEUR FRANCAIS – Organe mensuel corporatif, economique, social et technique. no. 1-24. Paris. 15 avr 1926-janv fevr 1929. mq no. 7 – 1 – fr A.C.R.P.P. [073]

INGENIEUR INDUSTRIEL – London, UK. Apr 1915-Aug 1917 – 1 – uk British Libr Newspaper [072]

INGENIEUR UNIVERSEL – Manchester, UK. 13 Sept 1878-25 Feb 1881 – 1 – uk British Libr Newspaper [072]

INGENIEUR-ARCHIV – v16-49. 1947-80 – 1,5,9 – $3876.00 – us UMI [620]

Ingersoll *see* HISTORY OF THE WAR DEPARTMENT, 1879

Ingersoll, Mrs. Albert Converse *see* EARLY LAWS OF MISSOURI PERTAINING TO WOMEN

Ingersoll, Charles Jared *see* GENERAL JACKSON'S FINE

INGERSOLL CHRONICLE – Ontario Prov., Canada. -w. Aug 1854-Oct 1919 – 1 – cn Commonwealth Micro [072]

Ingersoll, LA *see* A MEMORIAL AND BIOGRAPHICAL HISTORY OF THE COAST COUNTIES OF CENTRAL CALIFORNIA

Ingersoll, Luther A *see*
- CENTURY HISTORY OF THE SANTA MONICA BAY CITIES
- INGERSOLL'S CENTURY ANNALS OF SAN BERNARDINO COUNTY

Ingersoll, Robert Green *see*
- COMPLETE LECTURES OF COL. R.G. INGERSOLL
- THE GODS AND OTHER LECTURES

Ingersoll, William Halsey *see* LOVE AND LAW IN RELIGION

INGERSOLL'S CENTURY ANNALS OF SAN BERNARDINO COUNTY / Ingersoll, Luther A – Los Angeles, 1904. California Reel 24. (The Cox Library Collection) – 5 – us Americana [978]

INGHAM COUNTY NEWS – Mason. Mich. -w. 1859-68 – 1 – us UMI [071]

Inglefield, E A *see* A SUMMER SEARCH FOR SIR JOHN FRANKLIN

Ingler, Francis Marion *see* QUIZ MANUAL ON PERSONAL PROPERTY

Inglesby, John Walker *see* PAPERS OF JOHN WALKER INGLESBY

INGLEWOOD ADVERTISER – 1921-1963 – 14 – 1 – at Corangamite [072]

INGLISH ORTHOGGRAPHY EPITTOMIZED / Elphinston, James – 1790. 156p. (English Linguistics Series 1500-1800) – 9 – us UMI [420]

Ingold, A M P *see* HISTOIRE DE L'EDITION BENEDICTINE DE SAINT AUGUSTIN

Ingpen, Arthur R *see* MASTER WORSLEY'S BOOK ON THE HISTORY AND CONSTITUTION OF THE MIDDLE TEMPLE

Ingraham, Joseph *see* JOURNALS, BRIGANTINE HOPE

Ingram, J Forsyth *see* NATALIA

Ingram, John H *see* THE PHILOSOPHY OF HANDWRITING, BY DON FELIX DE SALAMANCA (PSEUD.)... WITH 135 AUTOGRAPHS

Ingram, K E *see* SOURCES OF JAMAICAN HISTORY, 1655-1838

Ingram, T Dunbar *see* ENGLAND AND ROME

INGRAM'S INFOFICHE – Revised and issued weekly. Contains Major book promotions, Bestseller lists, New books at Ingram and Important book status – 9 – us Ingram [070]

INGRAM'S INVENTORY INFORMATION – Four classifications: Author, title, publisher and subject. Also includes inventory status. Weekly updates – 9 – us Ingram [070]

INGURTHA *see* EBBE UND FLUTH

INHALT ETLICHER HENDLEN. DIE EIN BURGERMEISTER, RADT ETC. DER STATT ZUERICH – 1525. BME-5 1 – 9 – ne IDC [340]

INHALT UND AUSLEGUNG DES HOHEN LIEDES : VORTRAG GEHALTEN IN DER LUEBECKISCHEN SCHILLERSTIFTUNG AM 2. MAERZ 1892 / Leverkuehn, A – Leipzig: Akademische Buchh (W Faber), 1892 – 1mf – 9 – 0-8370-4091-4 – 1985-2091 – us A.T.L.A. [220]

INHERITANCE TAX CALCULATIONS / Wolfe, Samuel Herbert – New York, Baker, Voorhis, 1905. 300 p. LL-1505 – 1 – us L of C Photodup [340]

INHERITANCE TAX RECORDS / Allen County. Ohio. Probate Court – 1920-1955 – 10r – 1 – $32.50r – us Archival [324]

INHERITANCE TAXATION; A TREATISE ON LEGACY SUCCESSION AND INHERITANCE TAXES UNDER THE LAWS OF ARKANSAS, CALIFORNIA, COLORADO. / Ross, Peter V – San Francisco: Bancroft-Whitney, 1912. 841p. LL-1176 – 1 – us L of C Photodup [340]

DE INHOUD DER OVEREENKOMSTEN IN HET INTERNATIONAAL PRIVAATRECHT / Testa, G M R – Amsterdam, 1886 – 3mf – 9 – ILM-2977/1 – ne IDC [327]

INIS ATOMINDEX – v1-11. 1970-80 – 1,5,6 – us Princeton Micro [530]

INITERA CONSTANTINOPOLITANVM ET AMASIANVM... / Gislenius, A – Antverpiae, 1581 – 2mf – 9 – H-8357/1 – ne IDC [956]

INITIA BIBLIOTHECAE MEDICOPRACTICAE ET CHIRUGICAE REALIS SIVE REPERTORII MEDICINAE PRACTICAE ET CHIRURGIAE / ed by Ploucquet, W G – Tubingae. v8. 1793-1797 – 95mf – ne IDC [617]

INITIA BIBLIOTHECAE MEDICOPRACTICAE ET CHIRUGICAE REALIS SIVE REPERTORII MEDICINAE PRACTICAE ET CHIRURGIAE / ed by Ploucquet, W G – Tubingae, 1793-1797. 8v – 95mf – 9 – ne IDC [617]

INITIA COMMENTARIORUM QUAESTIONUM ET TRACTATUUM LATINORUM IN ARISTOTELIS LIBROS DE ANIMA. SAECULIS XIII, XIV, XV EDITORUM : BIBLIOGRAPHY / Smet, A J – Leuven: Se Wulf Mansion-Centrum, 1963 – 105 leaves – 1 – us U.W. Library [180]

INITIA PATRUM, CONLEGIT AC LITTERARUM ORDINE DISPOSUIT / Vattaso, Marcus – Studi e Testi 16. v1 A-M – 18mf – 9 – ne Slangenburg [240]

INITIA PATRUM, CONLEGIT AC LITTERARUM ORDINE DISPOSUIT / Vattaso, Marcus – Studi e Testi 17. v2 N-Z – 17mf – 9 – ne Slangenburg [240]

THE INITIAL MANUSCRIPT OF THE WAR HISTORY OF THE NATIONAL REVOLUTIONARY ARMY / Chen-pu-lei – 1952, 6v., 3061p. 2 reels – 5 – 80.00 – ch Transmission [950]

L'INITIATION : REVUE PHILOSOPHIQUE DES HAUTES ETUDES – Paris, 1889-1912 – 5r – 1 – us Ross [370]

INITIATION A LA LANGUE DE L'ILE DES PINS, NOUVELLE-CALEDONIE / Dubois, M J – 9 – F30.00 – fr Ethnologie [490]

INITIATION A LA LANGUE DE MARE / Dubois, M J – 9 – F50.00 – fr Ethnologie [490]

THE INITIATION OF CRIMINAL PROSECUTIONS BY INDICTMENT OR INFORMATION / Moley, Raymond – Ann Arbor, 1931 431p. LL-573 – 1 – us L of C Photodup [340]

INITIATIVE *see* EINIGUNG

THE INITIATIVE, REFERENDUM AND RECALL. / American Academy of Political and Social Science – Philadelphia, 1912. 352 p. LL-231 – 1 – us L of C Photodup [340]

INITSIATIVA I IZOBRETATEL'NOST' – Zhurnal svobodnago tvorchestva. v. 1. Petrograd, Janvar'-Mart. 1917. BR-3213 2 – 8 – ne IDC [073]

INJURIES OF NERVES AND THEIR CONSEQUENCES / Mitchell, S W – M-114. 1872 – 9 – ne IDC [150]

INJUSTICE WITHIN THE LAW; A STUDY OF THE CASE OF THE DORSETSHIRE LABOURERS / Evatt, Herbert Vere – Sydney, Law Book Co. of Australasia 1937 136 p. LL-2260 – 1 – us L of C Photodup [340]

INKANYISO YASE NATAL – Pietermaritzburg, South Africa. 1889-96 – 1 – sa State Libr [072]

INKILAB. BITTIGI YERDE BASLAR – Ankara. Cumhuriyet, Milliyet ve Demokrasi Fikrinin Koeklesmesine Calisir Tuerk Gazetesidir. Mesul Mueduerue: Ali Suereyya. No. 16 (22 Agustos 1925) – 9 – $20.00 – us MEDOC [956]

INKILAP – Siyasi gazete. No. 3-6, 8-9, 11-13, 15 (1 Eyluel-13 Eyluel 1930) – 9 – $45.00 – us MEDOC [956]

Inkins, J *see* BAPTISTU ZIHNAS LIHDSEKTI

INKLE AND YARICO / Arnold, Samuel – A comic opera....Piano-vocal score. 1787? – 9 – us Sibley [780]

INKLE AND YARICO: AN OPERA, IN THREE ACTS.. / Colman, George – Libretto. 1825 – 9 – us Sibley [780]

INKRA : ORGAN DER BPO DER SED DES VEB INDUSTRIE- UND KRAFTWERKSROHRLEITUNGEN – Bitterfeld, 1964-90 – 5r – 1 – Inquire at Mikrofilmarchiv for details – gw Misc Inst [670]

INKULULEKO = FREEDOM – Johannesburg: Inkululeko. [n1-189] dec 1940-jun 1950 – 1 – us Res Libr [072]

INKULULEKO (FREEDOM) – 1939-45. Passive Register, 1946-48 (Johannesburg) – 1 – uk Microform Academic [960]

INKUNDLA YA BANTU = THE BANTU FORUM – Verulam, South Africa: Verulam Press. [n27-268] jun 1940-apr 29 1950 – 1 – us Res Libr [072]

INKUNDLA YA BANTU – Verulam. Natal. Jan 1944-Dec 1949; Jan-Nov 1951 – 1 – 35.00r – us Hoover Inst Photo [072]

INKUNDLA YA BANTU *see* THE TERRITORIAL MAGAZINE

DAS INLAND – Muenchen, DE. 1829-Jun 1831 – 6r – 1 – gw Mikrofilm [072]

INLAND AFRICA – 1917-82 – 1 – us UMI [290]

INLAND AQUACULTURE ENGINEERING : LECTURES PRESENTED AT THE ADCP INTER-REGIONAL TRAINING COURSE IN INLAND AQUACULTURE ENGINEERING. BUDAPEST, 1983 – 1984 – 596p – it F.A.O. [639]

INLAND ARCHITECT AND NEWS RECORD *see* AMERICAN ARCHITECT AND ARCHITECTURE

INLAND CALIFORNIA LABOR JOURNAL – San Bernardino, CA. Sept 1943-Dec 1947 – 1r – 1 – $50.00 – C02766 – us Library Micro [331]

INLAND CAPTURE FISHERIES OF THE USSR – 1990 – 149p – it F.A.O. [338]

INLAND EMPIRE – Hamilton, NV. 1869-1870 – 1r – 1 – $50.00 – U04574 – us Library Micro [071]

INLAND EMPIRE – Pendleton OR. Sep 23 1886 – 1 – us U.O. Library [071]

INLAND EMPIRE – San Bernardino, CA. 1984-1985 – 6r – 1 – $300.00 – R03454 – us Library Micro [071]

INLAND EMPIRE – The Dalles. OR. -w. 28 Dec 1878-24 May 1879. 1 roll – 1 – us U.O. Library [071]

INLAND EMPIRE DAILY CALIFORNIAN *see* DAILY CALIFORNIAN

INLAND EMPIRE MINER – Baker City, OR. -w. 13 Sept 1899-3 Jan 1906. 3 rolls. Incl. Sumpter Miner – 1 – us U.O. Library [071]

INLAND EMPIRE MINER – Baker, OR. 1905-06 – 1 – 24.00 – us Oregon Hist [071]

INLAND EMPIRE-NORTH – 1992-94 – 5r – 1 – $250.00 – P00039 – us Library Micro [910]

INLAND EMPIRE-SPANISH – 1992-94 – 3r – 1 – $150.00 – P00040 – us Library Micro [910]

INLAND FISHERIES IN MULTIPLE USE OF RESOURCES – 1985 – 171p – it F.A.O. [636]

INLAND FISHERIES OF AFRICA – 1979 – 76p – it F.A.O. [639]

INLAND FISHERIES OF EUROPE – 1990 – 484p – it F.A.O. [639]

INLAND HERALD – Spokane. Wash. 1910-1911 – 1 – us UMI [071]

INLAND PRINTER/AMERICAN LITHOGRAPHER – 1- 1883- – us UMI [760]

INLAND TRIBUNE – Great Bend. Kan. 1876-1887 – 1 – us UMI [071]

INLAND VALLEY TIMES – Claremont, CA. 1991 – 1r – 1 – $50.00 – R04015 – us Library Micro [071]

AN INLAND VOYAGE / Stevenson, Robert Louis – London: C. Kegan Paul, 1878 – 1 roll – 1 – 1-55879-601-0 – uk Libr Preservation [830]

INLAND WATERS OF LATIN AMERICA – 1979 – 179p – it F.A.O. [550]

THE INLANDER – 1915-27 (complete) – 1r – 1 – ATLA S0716B – us A.T.L.A. [073]

INLEIDING TOT DE MUZIEKKUNDE / Lustig, Johann Wilhelm – P 379. Ed. 2. 1771 – 9 – ne IDC [780]

IN-LETTERS, 1735-1787 / Wesley, Charles – (Coll title: The People Called Methodists, Phase 2: Primary Sources 1738-1800) – 2mf – 9 – MP-637/1 – ne IDC [240]

IN-LETTERS, 1737-1786 / Wesley, Charles – (Coll title: The People Called Methodists, Phase 2: Primary Sources 1738-1800) – 4mf – 9 – MP-638/1 – ne IDC [240]

IN-LETTERS, 1742-1788 / Wesley, Charles – (Coll title: The People Called Methodists, Phase 2: Primary Sources 1738-1800) – 2mf – 9 – MP-641/1 – ne IDC [240]

IN-LETTERS, 1749-1789 / Wesley, Sarah – (Coll title: The People Called Methodists, Phase 2: Primary Sources 1738-1800) – 1mf – 9 – MP-664/1 – ne IDC [240]

IN-LETTERS, 1749-1810 / Wesley, Sarah – (Coll title: The People Called Methodists, Phase 2: Primary Sources 1738-1800) – 1mf – 9 – MP-665/1 – ne IDC [240]

IN-LETTERS, 1752-1783 / Wesley, Charles – (Coll title: The People Called Methodists, Phase 2: Primary Sources 1738-1800) – 1mf – 9 – MP-642/1 – ne IDC [240]

IN-LETTERS, 1756-1812 / Wesley, Sarah – (Coll title: The People Called Methodists, Phase 2: Primary Sources 1738-1800) – 1mf – 9 – MP-666/1 – ne IDC [240]

IN-LETTERS, 1775-1820 / Wesley, Sally – (Coll title: The People Called Methodists, Phase 2: Primary Sources 1738-1800) – 2mf – 9 – MP-656/1 – ne IDC [240]

IN-LETTERS, 1776-1816 / Wesley, Sarah – (Coll title: The People Called Methodists, Phase 2: Primary Sources 1738-1800) – 1mf – 9 – MP-667/1 – ne IDC [240]

IN-LETTERS, 1780-1827 / Wesley, Sally – (Coll title: The People Called Methodists, Phase 2: Primary Sources 1738-1800) – 8mf – 9 – MP-657/1 – ne IDC [240]

IN-LETTERS, 1789-1828 / Wesley, Charles – (Coll title: The People Called Methodists, Phase 2: Primary Sources 1738-1800) – 1mf – 9 – MP-650/1 – ne IDC [240]

IN-LETTERS, 1836-1848, RELATING TO THE METHODIST NEW CONNEXION IN IRELAND / Cooke, W – (Coll title: The People Called Methodists, Phase 3: Primary Sources, 1801-1850) – 17mf – 9 – MP-690/1 – ne IDC [240]

IN-LETTERS FROM METHODIST PREACHERS ON RELIGIOUS EXPERIENCE, 1738-1788 / Wesley, Charles – (Coll title: The People Called Methodists, Phase 2: Primary Sources 1738-1800) – 13mf – 9 – MP-639/1 – ne IDC [240]
INLEYDING TOT DE HOOGE SCHOOLE DER SCHILDERKONST / Hoogstraten, Samuel van – O-301. 1678 – 9 – ne IDC [700]
INLEYDINGE TOT DE ALGEMEENE TEYKENKONST / Goeree, W – Amsterdam. 1697. BO-273 1 – 9 – ne IDC [700]
INLIEDIG TOT DE MUZYKKUNDE... / Lustig, Jacob Willem – Te Groningen, Gedruckt voor den auteur, by H Veehnerus, 1751 – 1 – us Sibley [780]
Inman, Henry *see* MILITARY RECORDS
THE INMAN LEADER – Inman, Holt County. Nebraska. 1914- . -w. Lacks scattered issues – 1 – us NE Hist [071]
INMAN NEWS – Inman, NE. -w. Sep 1894-Dec 1896, scattered issues missing; Jan 1897-Aug 1905; Nov 1905; Jul-Oct 1906; Jan-Jun 1907 – 1 – us NE Hist [071]
Inman, W G *see* PLANTING AND PROGRESS OF THE BAPTISTS' CAUSE IN TENNESSEE
INMERSION; EL ACTO DEL BAUTISMO CRISTIANO / Christian, Juan T – 1907. 200p – 1 – 7.00 – us Baptist [240]
EL INMIGRANTE EN LA ARGENTINA – [Buenos Aires?: Servicio Internacional de Publicaciones Argentinas, 1952] – 1 – CSUXADP7792-B – us Hoover Inst Photo [304]
THE INN ALBUM / Browning, Robert – London: Smith, Elder, 1875 – 1 roll – 1 – 1-55879-585-5 – uk Libr Preservation [890]
THE INNER AND MIDDLE TEMPLE : LEGAL, LITERARY AND HISTORIC ASSOCIATIONS / Bellot, Hugh Hale L – London: Methuen & Co, 1902 – 6mf – 9 – $9.00 – LLMC 84-274 – us L.L.M.C. [340]
THE INNER CHAMBER AND THE INNER LIFE / Murray, Andrew – New York: Fleming H Revell, c1905 – 1mf – 9 – 0-8370-5998-4 – 1985-3998 – us A.T.L.A. [240]
INNER CITY EXPRESS – West Covina, CA. 1977 – 11+ r – 1 – $550.00 ($50.00y) – R03571 – us Library Micro [071]
THE INNER KINGDOM – Cambridge: John Wilson, 1870 – 1mf – 9 – 0-8370-8923-9 – 1986-2923 – us A.T.L.A. [240]
THE INNER LIFE OF THE NAVY...TOGETHER WITH A DETAILED ACCOUNT OF THE SYSTEMS OF VICTUALLING AND UNIFORM IN VOGUE DURING THE LATTER PART OF THE NINETEENTH AND OPENING YEARS OF THE TWENTIETH CENTURY / Yexley, Lionel – 1908 – 9 – uk Libr Preservation [941]
THE INNER MISSION : FOUR ADDRESSES / Paton, J B – London: Wm. Isbister, 1888 – 1mf – us A.T.L.A. [240]
THE INNER MISSION : A HANDBOOK FOR CHRISTIAN WORKERS / Ohl, J F – Philadelphia: General Council Publication House, 1911 – 1mf – us A.T.L.A. [240]
INNER PASSAGES : A CHOREOGRAPHIC EXPLORATION OF THE EFFECTS OF ENTRAINMENT ON CHOREOGRAPHY / Miller, Rebecca D – 1993 – 1mf – $4.00 – us Microform Publ [790]
INNER ROME : POLITICAL, RELIGIOUS, AND SOCIAL / Butler, Clement Moore – Philadelphia: J.B. Lippincott, 1866, c1865 – 1mf – us A.T.L.A. [930]
INNER TEMPLE : MASTERS OF THE BENCH AND TEMPLE / Inner Temple. London. Library – (Covers: Masters of the Bench, 1450-1883; Masters of the Temple, 1540-1883) – London: Clowes & Sons, 1883 – 2mf – 9 – $3.00 – LLMC 84-298 – us L.L.M.C. [340]
Inner Temple. London. Library *see*
– ARCHIVES
– INNER TEMPLE
– MANUSCRIPTS AND EARLY PRINTED WORKS
DIE INNERE ENTWICKLUNG DES PELAGIANISMUS : EIN BEITRAG ZUR DOGMENGESCHICHTE / Klasen, Franz – Freiburg im Breisgau, St. Louis, Mo.: Herder, 1882 – 1mf – us A.T.L.A. [240]
DIE INNERE FRONT – Berlin, 1939-40 (incomplete) – 1 – Dist. gw Mikrofilm – gw Misc Inst [072]
INNERE GESCHICHTE DER ENTWICKLUNG DER DEUTSCHEN NATIONAL-LITTERATUR / Rinne, Karl-Friedrich; ed by Garber, Klaus – Leipzig. 2pts in 1v. 1842/43 – 10mf – 9 – subsc: DM80.00 diazo DM100.00 silver – gw Olms [430]
DIE INNERE MOTIVIERUNG IN GRABBES DRAMEN / Schoettler, Wilhelm – (Includes bibliographical references) – Berlin: Junker und Duennhaupt, 1931 – 1r – 1 – us U.W. Library [430]
INNERE RECHTSKRAFT IM ERBHOFRECHT / Roesner, Werner – Leipzig, 1938 – 1mf – DM48.00 – 3-8267-3004-6 – gw Hänsel [340]
DAS INNERE REICH – Muenchen, apr 1934-45 n1 – 5r – 1 – gw Mikrofilm [800]
INNERHALB ETTERS / Kurz, Hermann; ed by Kurz, Isolde – Tuebingen: Rainer Wunderlich (H Leins), [1926?] – 1 – us U.W. Library [830]
Innes, Alexander Taylor *see*
– CHURCH AND STATE
– JOHN KNOX
– THE LAW OF CREEDS IN SCOTLAND
– STUDIES IN SCOTTISH HISTORY
– TRIAL OF JESUS CHRIST
– THE TRIAL OF JESUS CHRIST
Innes, C A *see* MADRAS DISTRICT GAZETTEER
Innes, Mary C *see* A MEMOIR OF WILLIAM WOLSELEY
Innes, R F *see* FLAYING AND CURING OF HIDES AND SKINS AS A RURAL INDUSTRY
INNES REVIEW – 1950-58 – 1 – uk Microform Academic [073]
INNISFAIL FREE LANCE – Alberta. Canada. 1902-08 – 1 – cn Commonwealth Micro [07?]
INNISFAIL PROVINCE – Alberta, Mar 1906-Jan 1908; Jun, Aug, Nov 1921; 1922-1924 – 1 – cn Commonwealth Micro [072]
INNOCENT / Corelli, Marie – British Fiction Archive: Unit 1 – 9 – uk Bell [830]
INNOCENT 3: LES ROYAUTES VASSALES DU SAINTE-SIEGE / Luchaire, Achille – Paris. 1908. 279p (Historical Studies Series) – 9 – $9.00 – fr Bibl Nationale [900]
INNOCENT THE GREAT : AN ESSAY ON HIS LIFE AND TIMES / Pirie-Gordon, Charles Harry Clinton – London, New York: Longmans, Green, 1907 – 1mf – us A.T.L.A. [240]
INNOCENT THE GREAT, AN ESSAY ON HIS LIFE AND TIMES / Pirie-Gordon, Charles Harry Clinton – London, New York: Longmans, Green, 1907.xxiii,273p. maps. geneal – 1 – us U.W. Library [940]
LES INNOCENTES, OU LA SAGESSE DES FEMMES / Noailles, Anna Elizabeth de Brancovan – Paris: Fayard, 1923. 256p. (Les Femmes Collection) – 3mf – 9 – $8.00 – fr Bibl Nationale [305]
INNOVATION – (Ceased 1991) – Ottawa, 1989-1991 – 9 – Can$20.00y – cn Micromedia [600]
INNOVATION – Geneva, Switzerland. No.1- . 1975- . UNESCO International Bureau of Education. illus. -q. Cont. by: Educational Innovation and Information – 1 – us U.W. Library [370]
INNOVATION IN SOCIAL SCIENCES RESEARCH – 1987- 6v – 9 – £143.00 – 1012-8050 – uk Carfax [300]
INNOVATIONS FOR LARGE CLASSES : A GUIDE FOR TEACHERS AND ADMINISTRATORS / Valerien, Jean – 1991 – 77p – 9 – 92-3-102713-1 – fr UNESCO [370]
INNOVATIONS IN SCIENCE AND TECHNOLOGY EDUCATION / ed by Layton, David – 9 – fr UNESCO [370]
INNOVATIVE APPROACHES TO DEVELOPMENT PLANNING – 1988 – 266p – 9 – 92-3-102539-2 – fr UNESCO [307]
INNOVATIVE HIGHER EDUCATION *see* ALTERNATIVE HIGHER EDUCATION
INNOVATIVE METHODS IN TECHNOLOGICAL EDUCATION – 1990 – 182p – 9 – 92-3-102637-2 – fr UNESCO [370]
INNRE MISSION : VOLKSERZIEHUNG UND PROPHETENTHUM: DREI VORTRAEGE / Zezschwitz, Gerhard von – (Includes bibliographical references) – Frankfurt a.M.: Heyder & Zimmer, 1864 – 1mf – 9 – 0-8370-6079-6 – 1986-0079 – us A.T.L.A. [240]
THE INNS OF COURT / Headlam, Cecil – (Painted by Gordon Home) – London: A & C Black, 1909 – 4mf – 9 – $6.00 – LLMC 84-294 – us L.L.M.C. [340]
THE INNS OF COURT : AN HISTORICAL DESCRIPTION / Ringrose, Hyacinthe – Boston: Little-Brown, 1910 – 3mf – 9 – $4.50 – LLMC 84-313 – us L.L.M.C. [340]
THE INNS OF COURT AND CHANCERY / Loftie, William J – new ed. London: Seeley & Co, 1895 – 4mf – 9 – $6.00 – LLMC 84-304 – us L.L.M.C. [340]
Inns of Court. England. Council of Legal Education *see* COUNCIL OF LEGAL EDUCATION CALENDAR, 1901-1925/26
Inns of Court Students Union. London *see* GLIM
INNZ : INDEX NEW ZEALAND 1994 – (1993, 1994 Annual cumulation only. NZ$250.00; Five year cumulation, 1987-1991. NZ$375.00; Back issues 1987/88-92. NZ$120.00ea. Also avail. on CD-ROM) – 4 Cumulative issues – NZ$280.00y – nz Nat'l Libr [010]
INORGANIC AND NUCLEAR CHEMISTRY LETTERS – v.1-17. 1965-81 – 5,6,9 – us UMI [073]
INORGANIC CHEMISTRY – v1- 1962- – 1,5,6,9 – us A.C.S. [073]
INORGANIC MATERIALS – v1-29. 1965-93 – 1,5 – $180.00v – us UMI [540]
INORGANICA CHIMICA ACTA – Incorporating Chimica Acta Reviews. v1-95. 1967-84 – 1,5,6,13 – sz Elsevier [073]
INORODCHESKOE OBOZRENIE – Prilozhenie k zhurnalu "Pravoslavnyi sobesednik". Kazan'. 1912-17. BR-4121 2 – 8 – ne IDC [073]
INOSTRANNYA LITERATURA – Moscow. U.S.S.R. -m. 1968- – 1 – us UMI [072]
Inostrantsev, K *see* CHYN-NU I GUNNY
Inoue, Kowashi Viscount *see* GOIN BUNKO INOUE KOWASHI MONJO
Inoue, Tadashiro *see* INOUE TADASHIRO MONJO
INOUE TADASHIRO MONJO = INOUE TADASHIRO RECORDS / Inoue, Tadashiro – 168r – 1 – Y2,300,000t – ja Yushodo [950]
INPRECOR : CORRESPONDANCE DE PRESSE INTERNATIONALE. CORRESPONDANCE DE PRESSE INTERNATIONALE – [Ed. francaise]. Bruxelles, Belgique: [s.n.], 19uu – 1 – CSUXALM0092-S – us Hoover Inst Photo [943]
INPRECOR : INTERNATIONAL PRESS CORRESPONDENCE – Montreuil Cedex, France: [s.n.], 19uu – 1 – CSUXALM0078-S – us Hoover Inst Photo [943]
INPRECOR (EDITION FRANCAISE) *see* INPRECOR
INPUTS IN RESEARCH AND DEVELOPMENT IN ACADEMIC INSTITUTIONS 1970/71 / Israel. Prime Minister's Office – Jerusalem, 1975. 12; 53; 53 p. (Special Series no. 502). Text also in Hebrew. In cooperation with the National Council for Research and Development – 9 – 3.00 – is I.T.T.I. [324]
INQILAB VA AZADI – (Shumarah-'i 1-9 (11 Urdibihisht 1360-Payiz 1362[1 May 1981-Fall 1983])) – Detroit, Mich.: Anjuman-i Azadi, 1981-1983 – 1 reel – 1 – $25.00 – us MEDOC [950]
INQILAB-I ISLAMI – (Sal-i 1, shumarah-'i 1-sal-i 2, shumarah-'i 557 (29 Khurdad 1358-17 Khurdad 1360[19 Jun 1979-7 Jun 1981])) – Tehran, 1979-1980 – 1 reel – 1 – $350.00 – us MEDOC [950]
INQUESTS / Allen County. Ohio. Coroner – 1886-1927 – 2r – 1 – $32.50r – us Archival [324]
INQUIETUD / Liano, Manuela – Zafra: Industrias Tipograficas Extremenas, 1969 – 1 – sp Bibl Santa Ana [946]
INQUIRER – Brookville. Ind. 1824-1833 – 1 – us UMI [071]
INQUIRER – Galion. Ohio. 1878-1897; 1907-1909; 1910- – 1 – us UMI [071]
INQUIRER – Owensboro. Ky. 1890-1954 – 1 – us UMI [071]
INQUIRER – Philadelphia. Pa. 1861- – 1 – us UMI [071]
THE INQUIRER – Journal of the Unitarian Movement 1842-1992 continued annually 64 reels – £3,500.00 – uk World [240]
THE INQUIRER – (Lacking: v3 nos 19,29,30. Title varies: Christian Inquirer. Liberal Christian) – v1-32 no 34. 17 Oct 1846-27 Sep 1877 – 16r – 1 – ATLA S0154 – us A.T.L.A. [073]
THE INQUIRER – Lancaster. Pa. 1862-1885; 1887-1920 – 1 – us UMI [071]
THE INQUIRER – Perth, Australia. Jan 1864-Jun 1901.-w. 31 reels – 1 – uk British Libr Newspaper [072]
THE INQUIRER – (Yrly reel count varies) – 1842- – 1 – inquire – us Ross [073]
THE INQUIRER – Monrovia: New Era Publications, jan 15 1991-dec 30 1994 – 5r – 1 – us Res Libr [072]
THE INQUIRER AND THREE-RIVERS COMMERCIAL ADVERTISER *see* THE INQUIRER / THE INQUIRER AND THREE-RIVERS COMMERCIAL ADVERTISER
THE INQUIRER / THE INQUIRER AND THREE-RIVERS COMMERCIAL ADVERTISER – Trois-Rivieres, Canada. v4 n20. 12 aut 1857-v10 n4. 13 jun 1863 – 1r – 1 – Can$40.00 – cn Can Microfilming [072]
INQUIRIES ELEMENTARY AND HISTORICAL IN THE SCIENCE OF LAW / Reddie, James – London: Longman, Orme, Brown, Green & Longmans, 1840 – 3mf – 9 – $4.50 – LLMC 95-182 – us L.L.M.C. [340]
INQUIRY – (1981-. 1,5,6,9) – v1-. 1958- – 1 – us UMI [073]
'INQUIRY DOCUMENTS' (SPECIAL REPORTS AND STUDIES), 1917-1919 / U.S. Commission to Negotiate Peace. World War 1 – RG 256. M1107 – 47r – 1 – us Nat'l Archives [940]
AN INQUIRY INTO CAUSES AND CONSEQUENCES... / Baring, A – London, 1808 – 2mf – 9 – ILM-693/1 – ne IDC [340]
AN INQUIRY INTO THE ACCORDANCE OF WAR... / Dymond, J – Philadelphia, n.d. – 2mf – 1 – ILM-1227/1 – ne IDC [327]
AN INQUIRY INTO THE CAUSES AND EFFECTS OF THE VARIOLAE VACCINAE / Jenner, Edward – M 107. 1798 – 9 – ne IDC [610]
AN INQUIRY INTO THE CAUSES OF RESPIRATION ON THE MOTION OF THE BLOOD / Carson, J – Ed. 2. II-110 2. 1833 – 8 – ne IDC [610]
AN INQUIRY INTO THE JUSTICE AND EXPEDIENCY OF COMPLETING THE PUBLICATION OF THE AUTHENTIC RECORDS OF THE COLONY OF THE CAPE OF GOOD HOPE RELATIVE TO THE ABORIGINAL TRIBES / Moodie, Donald – Cape Town. 1841 – 1 – us Res Libr [960]
AN INQUIRY INTO THE NATURE OF OUR LORD'S KNOWLEDGE AS MAN / Swayne, William Shuckburgh – (Includes bibliographical references) – London, New York: Longmans, Green, 1891 – 1mf – 9 – 0-8370-5563-6 – 1985-3563 – us A.T.L.A. [210]
AN INQUIRY INTO THE PERCEIVED IDEALS HELD BY EXPERTS FOR REGIONAL TOURISM DEVELOPMENT IN THE STATE OF PENNSYLVANIA FOR THE YEAR 2000 / Wang, P C – 1991 – 3mf – 9 – $12.00 – us Microform Publ [338]
AN INQUIRY INTO THE PRINCIPLES OF CHURCH-AUTHORITY : OR, REASONS FOR RECALLING MY SUBSCRIPTION TO THE ROYAL SUPREMACY / Wilberforce, Robert Isaac – (Includes bibliographical references) – Baltimore: Hedian & O'Brien, 1855 – 1mf – 9 – 0-8370-6876-2 – 1986-0876 – us A.T.L.A. [240]
AN INQUIRY INTO THE PRINCIPLES OF POLITICAL OECONOMY : BEING AN ESSAY ON THE SCIENCE OF DOMESTIC POLICY IN FREE NATIONS / Steuart, J – London, 1767. 2v – 24mf – 9 – ne IDC [320]
AN INQUIRY INTO THE SOURCES OF CHARLES SEALSFIELD'S NOVEL MORTON, ODER, DIE GROSSE TOUR / Thompson, Garrett William – (Includes bibliographical references) – [S.l: s.n, 19–?] – 1r – 1 – us U.W. Library [400]
INQUIRY INTO THE SYMPTOMS AND CAUSES OF THE SYNCOPE ANGINOSA / Parry, C – London. 1799 – 9 – ne IDC [610]
LA INQUISICION EN GUADALUPE / Fita, Fidel – Madrid: Fortanet, 1893. B.R.A.H. 23, pp 283-344 – sp Bibl Santa Ana [972]
INQUISICION. OBSERVACIONES DE LA... AVISADOR DE BADAJOZ – 1884 – 9 – 1.50f – sp Bibl Santa Ana [946]
L'INQUISITEUR – Montreal, Canada. 5 sep 1935 – 1r – 1 – Can$25.00 – cn Can Microfilming [072]
THE INQUISITION : A CRITICAL AND HISTORICAL STUDY OF THE COERCIVE POWER OF THE CHURCH / Vacandard, E – New York: Langmans, Green, 1908, c1907 – 1mf – us A.T.L.A. [240]
THE INQUISITION IN THE SPANISH DEPENDENCIES : SICILY, NAPLES, SARDINIA, MILAN, THE CANARIES, MEXICO, PERU, NEW GRANADA / Lea, Henry Charles – New York: Macmillan, 1908 – 2mf – us A.T.L.A. [946]
INQUISITIONS – Organe du Groupe d'etudes pour la pheno menologie humaine. L. Aragon, R. Caillois, T. Tzara. no. 1. Paris. juin 1936 – 1 – fr A.C.R.P.P. [073]

THE I.N.S. REPORTER / U.S. Immigration and Naturalization Service – (Cont: The I. and N. Reporter) – v25 no 2-v35 no 2. summer 1976-winter 1986 – 17mf – 9 – $25.50 – LLMC 81-506 – us L.L.M.C. [324]

THE I.N.S. REPORTER *see* THE I. AND N. REPORTER

INS VOLLE MENSCHENLEBEN : NEUE ERZAEHLUNGEN / Steguweit, Heinz – Hamburg: Hanseatische Verlagsanstalt, 1942 – 1 – us U.W. Library [830]

INSANIYET – (Purchase with Istirak) – Istanbul, 1. sene, nos. 1-2 (13 (UEe'ban 1328-5 Agustos [20 UEe'ban 1326-12 Agustos 1326] [1910]) – 9 – us MEDOC [949]

DIE INSCHRIFT AUF DEM DENKMAL MESA'S KOENIGS VON MOAB : (9. VORCHR. JAHRH.): MIT EINEM ANHANG BETREFFEND DIE GRABSCHRIFT DES SID. KOENIGS ESCHMUNAZAR / Kaempf, Saul Isaac – Prag: F Tempsky, 1870 – 1mf – 9 – 0-8370-7395-2 – 1986-1395 – us A.T.L.A. [470]

DIE INSCHRIFT DES KOENIGS MESA VON MOAB : (9. JAHRHUNDERT VOR CHRISTUS) / Noeldeke, Theodor – (Includes bibliographical references) – Kiel: Schwers, 1870 – 1mf – 9 – 0-8370-7318-9 – 1986-1318 – us A.T.L.A. [470]

DIE INSCHRIFT ESCHMUNAZARS, KOENIGS DER SIDONIER / Schlottmann, Konstantin – (Includes bibliographical references) – Halle: Buchh des Waisenhauses, 1868 – 1mf – 9 – 0-8370-7423-1 – 1986-1423 – us A.T.L.A. [470]

INSCHRIFTEN VON NABUCHODONOSOR, KOENIG VON BABYLON (604-561 V. CHR.) – (Texts in Akkadian; Preface in German. Includes indexes) – Leipzig: Eduard Pfeiffer, 1889 – 1mf – 9 – 0-8370-9187-X – 1986-3187 – us A.T.L.A. [470]

INSCRIPCION ARABE EN TRUJILLO / Codera, Francisco – Madrid: Fortanet, 1914. B.R.A.H. lxiv/pp. 117-119 – 1 – sp Bibl Santa Ana [946]

INSCRIPCION HEMISFERICA DE SANTA CRUZ Y LAPIDA DE SOLANS DE CABANAS. NOTAS A UNA CARTA DE ROSO DE LUNA / Fita, Fidel – Madrid: Fortanet, 1902. B.R.A.H. 40. pp. 564-566 – 1 – sp Bibl Santa Ana [946]

INSCRIPCION ROMANA DE LA PARRA Y DE ALMENDRALEJO / Fita, Fidel – Madrid: Tip. de Fortanet, 1897 – sp Bibl Santa Ana [946]

INSCRIPCION ROMANA DE MERIDA / Fita, Fidel – Madrid: Tip. de Fortanet, 1898 – sp Bibl Santa Ana [946]

INSCRIPCION ROMANA DE RIOLOBOS / Fita, Fidel – Madrid: Tip. de Fortanet, 1896 – sp Bibl Santa Ana [946]

INSCRIPCION ROMANA DE TITULCIA / Roso de Luna, Mario – Madrid: Fortanet, 1918. B.R.A.H. 72, pp. 279-280 – sp Bibl Santa Ana [946]

INSCRIPCION ROMANA DE VALERA LA VIEJA, JUNTO A FREGENAL / Fita, Fidel – Madrid: Tip. Fortanet, 1901 – sp Bibl Santa Ana [946]

INSCRIPCION ROMANA INSIGNE DE CACERES / Sanguino y Michel, Juan – Madrid: Fortanet, 1913. B.R.A.H. 63, pp. 422-427 – sp Bibl Santa Ana [946]

INSCRIPCIONES CACERENAS INEDITAS / Corchon Garcia, Justo – Madrid: Imprenta y Editorial Maestre, 1955 – 1 – sp Bibl Santa Ana [946]

INSCRIPCIONES CONSTANTINIANAS DE MERIDA / Fita, Fidel – Madrid: Fortanet, 1913. B.R.A.H. lxii/pp. 576-580 – 1 – sp Bibl Santa Ana [946]

INSCRIPCIONES INEDITAS DE MERIDA, BADAJOZ, ALANJE, CANETE DE LAS TORRES Y VILCHES / Fita, Fidel – Madrid: Fortanet, 1912. B.R.A.H. 61. pp 511-524 – 1 – sp Bibl Santa Ana [946]

INSCRIPCIONES ROMANAS DE BURGUILLOS / Martinez Martinez, Matias Ramon – Madrid: Tip. Fortanet, 1898 – sp Bibl Santa Ana [946]

INSCRIPCIONES ROMANAS DE CACERES, UBEDA Y ALCALA DE HENARES / Fita, Fidel – Madrid: Fortanet, 1885. B.R.A.H. vii/ pp. 45-53 – 1 – sp Bibl Santa Ana [946]

INSCRIPCIONES ROMANAS DE MERIDA / Huebner, Emilio – Madrid: Tip. Fortanet, 1894 – 1 – sp Bibl Santa Ana [946]

INSCRIPCIONES ROMANAS DE MERIDA Y NAVA DE RICO MALILLO / Fita, Fidel – Madrid: Tip. Fortanet, 1900 – sp Bibl Santa Ana [946]

INSCRIPCIONES ROMANAS DE MERIDA Y REINA / Melida, Jose Ramon – Madrid: Tip. Fortanet, 1911. BRAH lviii/ pp. 187-196 – sp Bibl Santa Ana [946]

INSCRIPCIONES ROMANAS INEDITAS DE CACERES, BRANDOMIL, NARANCO Y LERIDA / Fita, Fidel – Madrid: Fortanet, 1885. B.R.A.H. vi/pp. 430-436 – 1 – sp Bibl Santa Ana [946]

INSCRIPCIONES ROMANAS INEDITAS DE TRUJILLO / Fita, Fidel – Madrid: Fortanet, 1917. B.R.A.H. lxviii/p. 163-170 – 1 – sp Bibl Santa Ana [946]

INSCRIPCIONES ROMANAS SEPULCRALES DE IBAHERNANDO / Huebner, Emilio – Caceres: Tip. Enc. y Lib. Jimenez, 1900 – 1 – sp Bibl Santa Ana [946]

INSCRIPCIONES VISIGOTICAS : ESTUDIOS HAGIOLOGICOS / Fita, Fidel – Madrid: Tip. Fortanet, 1897 – sp Bibl Santa Ana [946]

INSCRIPCION...SATURNINO PENITENTE / Salcedo, Coronel Garcia – 1890 – 9 – 1.50f – sp Bibl Santa Ana [440]

INSCRIPCION...SATURNINO...MERIDA / Perez de Guzman, Juan – 1890 – 9 – 1.50f – sp Bibl Santa Ana [440]

INSCRIPCION...SATURNINO...MERIDA / Salcedo, Coronel Garcia – 1890 – 9 – 1.50f – sp Bibl Santa Ana [440]

L'INSCRIPTION CHINOISE D'IDIQNTSAHRI / Pelliot, P – T'oung Pao, v24. 1926. BU-618 2 – 8 – ne IDC [410]

L'INSCRIPTION DE KASRINE, EN TUNISIE / Armieux, Louis Leon Cyrille – Toulouse, A. Chauvin, 1883. 12 p., illus. 1 fiche. (Statistics: Medical Studies Series) – 9 – 6.00 – fr Bibl Nationale [310]

L'INSCRIPTION DE QUIRINIUS ET LE RECENSEMENT DE S. LUC / Bour, R S – 1896 – 1 – us A.T.L.A. [240]

UNE INSCRIPTION FRAGMENTAIRE D'AUGUSTA EMERITA. EMERITA DE LUSITANIE A LA LUMIERE DES "HISTOIRES" DE TACITE / Le Roux, Patrick – 1 – sp Bibl Santa Ana [946]

INSCRIPTION HISTORIQUE DE PINODJEM 3 / Naville, E – Paris, 1883. BNE-20,004 1 – 9 – ne IDC [410]

INSCRIPTIONES ANTIQUAE ORAE SEPTENTRIONALIS PONTI EUXINI GRAECAE ET LATINAE / Latysev, V V – v. 1. Petropoli. 1885; v. 2. Petropoli. 1890; v. 3, not pub.; v. 4. Petropoli. 1901. BU-550 2 – 8 – ne IDC [930]

INSCRIPTIONES GRAECAE / ed by Kern, Otto – Bonnae, 1913. xxiiip. Bibliography – 1 – us U.W. Library [410]

INSCRIPTIONES GRAECAE ANTIQVISSIMAE / ed by Roehl – Berolini, 1882 – 7mf – 9 – 125/2 – ne IDC [930]

INSCRIPTIONES GRAECAE, SICILIAE ET ITALIAE / ed by Kaibel, Georg – H-326 2. 1890 – 8 – ne IDC [450]

INSCRIPTIONES LATINAE CHRISTIANAE VETERES / ed by Diehl, E – 3v – 43mf – 8 – ne Slangenburg [240]

INSCRIPTIONS IN THE HIERATIC AND DEMOTIC CHARACTER, FROM THE COLLECTIONS OF THE BRITISH MUSEUM / Birch, S – London, 1868. BNE-367 1 – 9 – ne IDC [410]

INSECT BIOCHEMISTRY AND MOLECULAR BIOLOGY – v1- 1971- – 5,6,9 – us UMI [540]

INSECT LIFE – Washington, 1888-1895. v1-7. Index – 63mf – 9 – Z-958/2 – ne IDC [590]

INSECT PARASITES OF OTHER INSECTS / Kerrich, G J – 1939 – 7 – uk Microform Academic [590]

INSECT SCIENCE AND ITS APPLICATIONS. THE INTERNATIONAL JOURNAL OF TROPICAL INSECT SCIENCE – v. 1-. 1980- – 5,6,9 – us UMI [590]

INSECTA : REVUE ILLUSTREE D'ENTOMOLOGIE – Rennes, 1911-1924 – 58mf – 9 – Z-959/2 – ne IDC [590]

INSECTA BRITANNICA: LEPIDOPTERA. TINEINA / ed by Stainton, H T – London, 1854 – VIII, 313p, 10pls – 8 – ne IDC [590]

INSECTA CAFFRARIA ANNIS 1838-45 A J.A. WAHLBERG COLLECTA...COLEOPTERA / Boheman, C H – Holmiae, 1848. 2 pts. Z-1074/2 – 8 – ne IDC [590]

INSECTA SVECICA...CLASSIS I. COLEOPTERA SIVE ELEUTERATA / Gyllenhall, L – Scaris, 1808-27.v1,4pts. Z/1322/2 – 8 – ne IDC [590]

LES INSECTES: MORPHOLOGIE, REPRODUCTION, EMBRYOGENIE / Henneguy, LF – Paris, 1904. Z/1339/2 – 8 – ne IDC [590]

LES INSECTES VESICANTS / Beauregard, H – Paris, 1890. xv,544p. 19 pls. Z-1053/2 – 8 – ne IDC [590]

INSECTICIDES AND APPLICATION EQUIPMENT FOR TSETSE CONTROL – 1977 – 80p – it F.A.O. [660]

INSECTOS NUEVOS O POCO CONOCIDOS DE LA FAUNA ESPANOLA / Perez Arcas, L – Madrid, 1865(-68). 3 pts., 86p.Z-1537/2 – 8 – ne IDC [590]

LES INSECTS PHOSPOHORESCENTS... / Gadeau de Kerville, H – Rouen, 1881 – 55p, 4pls – 8 – ne IDC [590]

INSECUTOR INSCITIAE MENSTRUUS : A MONTHLY JOURNAL OF ENTOMOLOGY... – Washington, 1913-1926. v1-14 – 58mf – 9 – Z-962/2 – ne IDC [590]

DIE INSEKTEN / Graber, V – Muenchen, 1877-79. 2v. Z/1299/2 – 8 – ne IDC [590]

DIE INSEKTEN IM BERNSTEIN / Berendt, G C – Danzig-Berlin, 1830. v1, 38p. Z-1056/2 – 8 – ne IDC [590]

DIE INSEL *see* DIE INSEL DER EINSAMEN

DIE INSEL DER EINSAMEN – (Cont by: Die Insel, 1923 n6. Das Freundschaftsblatt, 1925 n1) – Berlin, 1923-33 n11 – 1r – 1 – Dist. gw Mikrofilm – gw Misc Inst [072]

INSEL IM SEEWIND : SCHICKSALE VOR DEICH UND DUENE / Schreiner, Wilhelm – Stuttgart: J F Steinkopf, 1943 – 1r – 1 – us U.W. Library [430]

THE INSERVICE NEEDS OF SOUTH CAROLINA PUBLIC SCHOOL PHYSICAL EDUCATORS PROVIDING INSTRUCTION TO HANDICAPPED STUDENTS / White, C – 1989 – 2mf – 9 – $8.00 – us Microform Publ [790]

IN-SERVICE TRAINING AND EDUCATION – v.1-6. Nov 1972-77. Superseded by Health Care Education – 1 – us UMI [610]

IN-SERVICE TRAINING AND EDUCATION *see* HEALTH CARE EDUCATION

O INSETO : FOLHA DE MAIOR CIRCULACAO DO DEPARTAMENTO – Rio Branco, Acre. 20 Ago-26 Nov 1916 – 1,5,6 – bl Biblioteca [072]

GLI INSETTI: LORO ORGANIZZAZIONE SVILUPPO, ABITUDINI E RAPPORTI COLL'UOMO / Berlese, Adolf A – Milano, 1909-25.2v. Z-1063/2 – 8 – ne IDC [590]

INSIDE A SOVIET EMBASSY / Kaznacheev, Aleksandr IUr'evich – In Indonesian. SE-5184 1. 1962 – 9 – ne IDC [320]

INSIDE CANBERRA – Canberra, 1948-75 – 3r – 1 – A$124.00 silver A$107.00 vesicular – at Pascoe [072]

INSIDE DRUG LAW – v1-. Aug 1984- – 1,5,6,9 – us UMI [073]

INSIDE EDUCATION – (v59-69, no.4. Sept 1972-Spring-Summer 1983. 5,6. v62-69, no.4. Sept 1975-Spring-Summer 1983. 9) – v2-69, no.4. Mar 1915-Spring-Summer 1983 – 1 – us UMI [073]

INSIDE GERMANY REPORTS – Issued by the American Friends of German Freedom. New York. 15 Apr 1939-May 1944 – 1r – 1 – gw Mikrofilm [943]

INSIDE HISTORY OF FIRST BAPTIST CHURCH, FORT WORTH AND TEMPLE BAPTIST CHURCH, DETROIT: LIFE STORY OF J. F. NORRIS / Norris, J Frank – 1 – 12.35 – us Baptist [240]

INSIDE NAZI GERMANY – London. Oct 1939-Feb 1940 – 1r – 1 – gw Mikrofilm [073]

INSIDE NAZI GERMANY *see* GERMANY TO-DAY

INSIDE SPORTS – New York, NY. 1980- – 1 – us UMI [073]

INSIDE SPORTS – v.1 4. 1979 82 – 1,5,6,9 – us UMI [073]

INSIDE THE BAR AND OTHER OCCASIONAL POEMS / May, John Wilder – Portland, ME: Hoyt, Fogg & Donham, 1884 – 3mf – 9 – $4.50 – LLMC 91-004 – us L.L.M.C. [810]

INSIDE THE CUP OR MY 21 YEARS IN FORT WORTH / Norris, J Frank – n.d. 218p – 1 – 7.63 – us Baptist [240]

AN INSIDE VIEW OF THE VATICAN COUNCIL : IN THE SPEECH OF THE MOST REVEREND ARCHBISHOP KENRICK OF ST. LOUIS / ed by Bacon, Leonard Woolsey – New York: American Tract Society, [187-?] – 1mf – 9 – 0-8370-6674-3 – 1986-0674 – us A.T.L.A. [240]

INSIDER – Canadian Corporate Reports.- 1975 – 9 – cn Micromedia [650]

INSIDERS' CHRONICLE – 1978- – 1,5,6,9 – us UMI [380]

INSIDER'S REPORT – v1-5. 1973-Apr 1977 – 1 – us UMI [073]

INSIEME – 1991-1995 – 1r per y – 5,6 – Sfr401.00 – sz Infoprint [072]

INSIGHT – Fresno, CA. CSU Fresno: 1969 – 7+ r – 1 – $350.00 ($50.00y) – B07453 – us Library Micro [370]

INSIGHT – v1- . 1985- – 1,5,6,9 – us UMI [800]

INSIGNIA DEL...ALMIRANTE...PRINCIPE DE LA PAZ – 1807 – 9 – $1.50f – sp Bibl Santa Ana [920]

INSINJUR INDONESIA – Bandung. Incomplete. SE-895 1. 1954-1971 – 9 – ne IDC [073]

THE INSOLVENT ACT OF 1869: WITH TARIFF, NOTES, FORMS AND A FULL INDEX / Edgar, James David – Toronto: Copp, Clark, 1869. 05217. (Pre-1900 Canadiana) – 9 – cn C.I.H.M. [971]

THE INSOLVENT ACT OF 1875: WITH AN INTRODUCTORY CHAPTER, NOTES, FORMS, TARRIFS OF ONTARIO, QUEBEC AND NEW BRUNSWICK, AND A FULL INDEX / Edgar, James David – F. H. Chyrsler. Toronto: Copp, Clark, 1875. 02880. (Pre-1900 Canadiana) – 9 – cn C.I.H.M. [971]

THE INSOLVENT LAW, OF MAINE. / Hamlin, Charles – Portland, Loring, Short & Harmon, 1878. 162 p. LL-81 – 1 – us L of C Photodup [340]

INSOLVENTS' OATHS / Huron County. Ohio. Auditor – 1820-1834 – 1r – 1 – $32.50r – us Archival [324]

Inspeccion Provincial de Ensenanza Prima Ria *see* NORMAS Y CUESTIONARIOS PARA LAS CLASES ESPECIA LES DE ADULTOS

INSPECTION ET REGLEMENTATION CONCERNANT LA PREVENTION DES INCENDIES / Laurin, Fernand – Quebec: Ministere des Affaires Municipales, Direction Generale de la Prevention des Incendies, Service de la Prevention, 1981. SEM105P481 – 1mf – 9 – Can$2.25 – cn Bibl Nat [340]

INSPECTION REPORT / Purdue University. Agricultural Experiment Station – No.1-145. 1956-83 – 1,5 – us Spaulding [630]

INSPECTION REPORTS..., 1814-42 / U.S. Army. Inspector General – 3rolls. M624. Printed guide – 1 – us Nat'l Archives [324]

INSPECTION REPORTS AND RELATED RECORDS RECEIVED BY THE INSPECTION BRANCH IN THE CONFEDERATE ADJUTANT AND INSPECTOR GENERAL'S OFFICE – 18 rolls. M935 – 1 – us Nat'l Archives [324]

INSPECTION REPORTS OF PRISONERS OF WAR CAMPS, FLORENCE, ARIZONA, AND NAVAJO ORDNANCE DEPOT, FLAGSTAFF, ARIZONA, 1945 – Washington, DC, National Archives and Records Service, [19–] – us Res Libr [975]

INSPECTION REPORTS OF THE OFFICE OF THE INSPECTOR GENERAL / U.S. Office of the Inspector General – 1814-42. 3 rolls. M624 – 1 – us Nat'l Archives [324]

INSPECTOR – Dublin, Ireland.7 Sept-19 Oct 1850. -w. 16 feet – 1 – uk British Libr Newspaper [072]

INSPECTOR-GENERAL SIR JAMES RANALD MARTIN / Fayrer, Joseph – London: A D Innes, 1897 – us Res Libr [920]

INSPECTOR'S HANDBOOK OF THE PHONOGRAPH / Edison Phonograph Works – Orange, NJ. 1889 – 1r – 1 – us Ross [621]

INSPIRATION / Sanday, William – London: Longmans, Green, 1893. 464p. 2 fiches – 9 – us A.T.L.A. [240]

INSPIRATION: A CLERICAL SYMPOSIUM / Farrar, Archdeacon, et al – New York: Thomas Whittaker, 1885. 1 fiche – 9 – us A.T.L.A. [240]

THE INSPIRATION AND AUTHORITY OF THE BIBLE / Clifford, John – (Includes index) – 2nd rev enl ed. London: James Clarke, 1895 – 1mf – 9 – 0-8370-2688-1 – 1985-0688 – us A.T.L.A. [220]

INSPIRATION AND INERRANCY / Briggs, Charles Augustus – 1891 – 1 – us A.T.L.A. [240]

INSPIRATION AND INERRANCY : A HISTORY AND A DEFENSE / Smith, Henry – Cincinnati: R. Clarke, 1893, c1982 – 1mf – us A.T.L.A. [240]

INSPIRATION AND OTHER LECTURES / Rooke, Thomas George – Edinburgh: T.&T. Clark, 1893. 1 fiche – 9 – us A.T.L.A. [240]

INSPIRATION AND THE BIBLE : AN INQUIRY / Horton, Robert Forman – [2nd ed]. New York: E P Dutton, [c1888] – 1mf – 9 – 0-8370-3667-4 – 1985-1667 – us A.T.L.A. [220]

INSPIRATION CONSIDERED AS A TREND / Faunce, Daniel Webster – Philadelphia: American Baptist Publishing Society. 1 fiche – 9 – us A.T.L.A. [240]

DIE INSPIRATION DER HEILIGEN SCHRIFT UND IHRE BESTREITER / Rohnert, Wilhelm – Leipzig: Georg Boehme, 1889. 1 fiche – 9 – us A.T.L.A. [240]

DIE INSPIRATION DER HL. SCHRIFT IN DER ANSCHAUUNG DES MITTELALTERS / Holzhey, Carl – Muenchen: J.J. Lentner, 1895. 1 fiche – 9 – us A.T.L.A. [240]

INSPIRATION: ITS NATURE AND PROOFS / Smith, Robert – Edinburgh: MacNiven & Wallace, 1891. 1 fiche – 9 – us A.T.L.A. [240]

THE INSPIRATION OF HISTORY / Mulchahey, James – New York: Thomas Whittaker, 1896. 1 fiche. 8370-4537-1 – 9 – us A.T.L.A. [240]

THE INSPIRATION OF RESPONSIBILITY, AND OTHER PAPERS / Brent, Charles H – New York: Longmans, Green, 1915 – 1mf – us A.T.L.A. [240]

INSPIRATION OF THE HOLY SCRIPTURES / Jamieson, Robert – Edinburgh: William Blackwood, 1873. 1 fiche – 9 – us A.T.L.A. [240]

THE INSPIRATION OF THE HOLY SCRIPTURES / Pidge, John Bartholomew Gough – 1884. 1 fiche – 9 – us A.T.L.A. [240]

INSPIRATION OF THE NEW TESTAMENT / Browne, Walter Raleigh – London: C. Kegan Paul, 1880. 1 fiche – 9 – us A.T.L.A. [240]

THE INSPIRATION OF THE OLD TESTAMENT INDUCTIVELY CONSIDERED : THE SEVENTH CONGREGATIONAL UNION LECTURE / Cave, Alfred – (Includes bibliographical references) – 2nd ed. London: Congregational Union of England and Wales, 1888 – 2mf – 9 – 0-8370-9452-6 – 1986-3452 – us A.T.L.A. [220]

THE INSPIRATION OF THE SCRIPTURES / Patton, Francis Landey – Philadelphia: Presb. Bd. of Pub., 1869. 1 fiche – 9 – us A.T.L.A. [240]

INSPIRED THROUGH SUFFERING / Mears, David Otis – New York: Fleming H Revell, c1895 – 1mf – 9 – 0-8370-6334-5 – 1986-0334 – us A.T.L.A. [240]

THE INSPIRED WORD: A SERIES OF PAPERS...AT THE BIBLE-INSPIRATION CONFERENCE / Pierson, Arthur Tappan – New York: A.D.F. Randolph, 1888.1 fiche – 9 – us A.T.L.A. [240]

INSTABILITAETEN, BIFURKATIONEN UND CHAOS FUER EINEN DREIDIMENSIONALEN VAN DER POL OSZILLATOR / Suenner, Tobias – 1995 – 2mf – 9 – DM80.00 – 3-8267-2097-0 – gw Hänsel [530]

INSTABILITY IN TERMS OF TRADE OF PRIMARY COMMODITIES, 1900-1982 – 1987 – 238p – it F.A.O. [380]

L'INSTALLATION DES TUTSHOKWE DANS L'EMPIRE LUNDA 1850-1903 / N'Dua, Edouard – Leopoldville, Universite Lovanium de Kinshasa, 1971 – us Res Libr [960]

L'INSTANT – Revue franco-catalane d'art de litterature. Dir. J. Perez-Jorba. I, no. 1-7 8; II, no. 1-4. Paris, Barcelona. juil 1918-sept 1919 – 1 – fr A.C.R.P.P. [073]

INSTAURATIO MAGNA / Bacon, Francis – M-290 2. 1620 – 8 – ne IDC [500]

INSTEAD OF A BOOK / Tucker, B R – 1897. 526p. 2 fiches (24x) – 9 – 1.00f – at Libertarian Micro [320]

INSTEAD OF WHAT? / Hazlitt, Henry – 2fiches (24x) – 9 – 1.00f – at Libertarian Micro [320]

INSTERBURGER ZEITUNG – Insterburg, Germany. 1866 (incomplete) – 1 – gw Mikrofilm [072]

INSTIGATOR – North Bend OR. Dec 1912 – 1 – us U.O. Library [071]

INSTITUCION HARMONICA, O DOCTRINA MUSICAL, THEORICA, Y PRACTICA.. / Roel del Rio, Antonio V – 1748 – 9 – us Sibley [780]

INSTITUCIONES DEL DERECHO CIVIL DE CASTILLA / Jordan de Asso, Ignacio – 1805 – 2mf – 9 – Pta1,500.00 – 84-7848-193-1 – sp Pentalfa [350]

INSTITUCIONES POLITICAS / Bielfeld, Baron de – 1781 – 1mf – 9 – Pta1,000.00 – 84-7848-233-4 – sp Pentalfa [320]

INSTITUCIONES PRACTICAS DE LOS JUICIOS CIVILES / Canada, Conde de la – 1794 – 9 – 1.50f – sp Bibl Santa Ana [340]

INSTITUCIONES SOCIALES DE LA AMERICA ESPANOLA EN EL PERIODO COLONIAL. LA PLATA, 1934 / Ots, Jose Maria – Madrid: Razon y Fe, 1935 – 1 – sp Bibl Santa Ana [970]

INSTITUCION...IGLESIA / Nunez de Torres, Juan – 1618 – 9 – 1.50f – sp Bibl Santa Ana [240]

L'INSTITUT – (Cont: Journal des Etudiants) – Montreal, Canada. 7 mar 1841-22 mai 1841 – 1r – 1 – Can$25.00 – cn Can Microfilming [370]

Institut Bouddhique, Phnom-Penh *see* CAMBODIAN TIPITAKA

Institut Catholique. Paris. Bibliotheque *see* FONDS DES LIVRES DU XVIE SIECLE

L'INSTITUT DE RECHERCHE ET D'HISTOIRE DES TEXTES (I.R.H.T) – (Catalogue 1: Repertoire Bio-bibliographique des Auteurs Latins, Patristiques et Medievaux 492mf £1.700.00. Catalogue 2: Repertoire des Fins de Textes Latins Classiques et Medievaux 224mf £780.00. Catalogue 3: Repertoire d'Incipit de Sermons Latins Antiquite Tardive et Moyen Age 273mf £935.00) – 3 catalogues 989mf – 9 – £3,465.00 set – uk Chadwyck [450]

Institut de recherches scientifiques au Congo *see* BULLETIN

Institut des Etudes Augustiniennes. Paris *see* FICHIER AUGUSTINIEN-AUGUSTINE BIBLIOGRAPHY

L'INSTITUT DES FRERES DES ECOLES CHRETIENNES : SON ORIGINE, SON BUT ET SES OEUVRES / Caisse, Joseph Camille – Montreal: J. Chapleau, 1883. 00376. (Pre-1900 Canadiana) – 9 – cn C.I.H.M. [240]

Institut d'Ethnologie. Museum National d'Histoire Naturelle. Paris *see*
- ARCHIVES ET DOCUMENTS
- CHEFS D'OEUVRE DE L'AMERIQUE PRECOLOMBIENNE
- SPLENDEUR DES COSTUMES DU MONDE

L'Institut d'etudes et recherches balkaniques *see* BALCANIA

Institut Fourier *see* ANNALES

Institut Francais d'Afrique Noire *see*
- L'AGGLOMERATION DAKAROISE; QUELQUES ASPECTS SOCIOLOGIQUES ET DEMOGRAPHIQUES
- BULLETIN
- LA PRESQU'ILE DU CAP-VERT.

Institut francais de Damas *see* BULLETIN D'ETUDES ORIENTALES

Institut Francais d'Opinion Publique *see* BULLETIN D'INFORMATIONS

Institut fuer Sozialforschung *see* ZEITSCHRIFT FUER SOZIALFORSCHUNG

Institut fuer Weltwirtschaft. Bibliothek. Kiel *see*
- KATALOGE DER BIBLIOTHEK DES INSTITUTS FUER WELTWIRTSCHAFT

Institut fuer Weltwirtschaft. Kiel. Bibliothek *see*
- KATALOGE DER BIBLIOTHEK...: SACHKATALOG
- PERSONENKATALOG

Institut fuer Zeitgeschichte *see*
- KATALOGE DER BIBLIOTHEK DES INSTITUTS FUER ZEITGESCHICHTE

Institut fuer Zeitgeschichte Muenchen *see*
- AKTEN DER PARTEIKANZLEI DER NSDAP
- WIDERSTAND ALS "HOCHVERRAT" 1933-1945

Institut fuer Zeitgeschichte. Muenchen.Bibliothek *see* ALPHABETISCHER KATALOG

Institut General Psychologique. Paris *see* BULLETIN

Institut Indochinois pour l'Etude de l'Homme. Hanoi *see* BULLETINS ET TRAVAUX COMPTE RENDU DES SEANCES

INSTITUT INTERNATIONAL DE BIBLIOGRAPHIE. BULLETIN – (v17-18 never publ. Cont. as: Revue de la Documentation (Review of Documentation)) – The Hague. v1-16, 19. 1895/96-1914 – 5,9 – Dfl1,020.00; Dfl60.00v – ne Swets [010]

INSTITUT INTERNATIONAL DES DROITS DE L'HOMME = INTERNATIONAL INSTITUTE OF HUMAN RIGHTS – Strasbourg. 144 docs. 1980-1990 – 66mf – 9 – ne IDC [320]

Institut konkretnykh sotsialnykh issledovanii AN SSSR *see*
- DINAMIKA IZMENENIIA POLOZHENIIA ZHENSHCHINY I SEMIA

Institut konkretnykh sotsialnykh issledovanii SSSR *see* DINAMIKA IZMENENIIA POLOZHENIIA ZHENSHCHINY I SEMIA

Institut Lenina. Moscow *see* ZAPISKI

INSTITUT NATIONAL DE LA FORMATION PROFESSIONNELLE DES ADULTES RAPPORT / Algeria. ILO – 1970. BNE-8723 1 – 9 – ne IDC [324]

Institut National de Recherche et de Documentation *see* RECHERCHES AFRICAINES

Institut Pasteur. Paris *see*
- ANNALES
- ANNALES DE MICROBIOLOGIE
- ANNALES D'IMMUNOLOGIE
- BULLETIN

Institut po izucheniiu istorii i kul'tury S SS R *see* UKAZATEL' PERIODICHESKIKH IZDANII EMIGRATSII IZ ROSSII I SSSR ZA 1919-1952 GG

INSTITUT SEL'SKOKHOZIAISTVENNOI I PROMYSLOVOI KOOPERATSII V 1922-23 V AKADEMICHESKOM GODU – M., 1923 – 1mf – 9 – COR-249/1 – ne IDC [334]

Institut sovetskogo prava *see* SPUTNIK SOVETSKOGO IURISTA

Institut Technique du Batiment et des Travaux Public *see* ANNALES

Institut V I Lenina. Moscow *see* ZAPISKI

Instituta ekonomiki Komakademii, T Sentrosoi uza SSSR i R.S.F.S.R. i Narkomsnaba SSSR *see* SOVETSKAIA TORGOVLIA

THE INSTITUTE / American Law Institute. Philadelphia – 1927. 107 p. LL-2342 – 1 – us L of C Photodup [340]

THE INSTITUTE – Vancouver: Vancouver Young People's Methodist Institute, v1 no 1(Mar 1889)- – 9 – cn C.I.H.M. [240]

INSTITUTE ASSEMBLY HERALD – Chautauqua. N.Y. 1878-1905 – 1 – us UMI [071]

Institute d'estudis Catalans. Barcelona *see* BIBLIOTECA DE CATALUNYA

Institute for Great Lakes Research *see* PORTAGE LAKE AND LAKE SUPERIOR CANALS COLLECTION

INSTITUTE FOR PALESTINE STUDIES – Washington DC. 104 docs. 1980-1991 – 249mf – 9 – ne IDC [956]

Institute for Soviet and East European Studies. University of Amsterdam *see* THE SOVIET WORLD 1948-1989

INSTITUTE FOR THE STUDY OF THE U.S.S.R. – Munich, DE. 1967-1971 – 1r – $50.00 – R63569 – us Library Micro [072]

INSTITUTE FOR THE STUDY OF THE USSR – Germany, USSR. 1967-1971 – 1r – $50.00 – R63569 – us Library Micro [072]

Institute for the Study of the USSR *see* RESEARCH MATERIALS

THE INSTITUTE LEAFLET FOR CHURCH SUNDAY SCHOOLS – Toronto: Rowsell and Hutchison, [1881?-18– or 19–] – 9 – cn C.I.H.M. [240]

Institute of Actuaries *see* JOURNAL

INSTITUTE OF ADVANCED LEGAL STUDIES ANNUAL REPORTS – University of London. 1st to 36th. 1947-83 – 45mf – 9 – $202.00 – LLMC 84-583 – us L.L.M.C. [340]

Institute of Aerospace Studies. University of Toronto. Canada *see* COLLECTION

INSTITUTE OF BANKERS JOURNAL – v1-76. 1879-1955 – 1,5,6 – us Princeton Micro [336]

Institute of Chartered Accountants *see* COLLECTION OF RARE BOOKS ON ACCOUNTING AND RELATED SUBJECTS, 15TH-19TH CENTURIES

Institute of Chinese Economics, Yamaguchi College of Commerce, Japan *see* TOA KEIZAI KENKYU

Institute of Commonwealth Studies. University of London *see*
- COMMONWEALTH POLITICAL EPHEMERA: BAHAMAS AND THE CARIBBEAN
- TWENTIETH CENTURY POLITICAL EPHEMERA. PART 1, SOUTH AFRICA
- TWENTIETH CENTURY POLITICAL EPHEMERA. PART 2, CENTRAL AFRICA
- TWENTIETH CENTURY POLITICAL EPHEMERA: PART 3, EAST AFRICA
- TWENTIETH CENTURY POLITICAL EPHEMERA: PART 4, WEST AFRICA

Institute of Electrical Engineers *see* PROCEEDINGS

Institute of Historical Research *see*
- BULLETIN

Institute of History of the Spanish Civil War *see* BIBLIOGRAPHY OF THE SPANISH CIVIL WAR 1936-1939

Institute of Humanitarian Political Research and library of "Memorial" *see* ANTI-SEMITISM AND NATIONALISM AT THE END OF THE SOVIET ERA

INSTITUTE OF INDIAN STUDIES – University of South Dakota, 1956-81. (American Indian Periodicals in the Princeton University Library). 7 fiches – 9 – $45.00 – us UPA [305]

Institute of Marine Engineers *see* TRANSACTIONS

Institute of Metals *see*
- JOURNAL
- JOURNAL OF THE INSTITUTE OF METALS

Institute of Oceanographic Sciences. (Great Britain) *see* DISCOVERY REPORTS

INSTITUTE OF PACIFIC RELATIONS – AMERICAN COUNCIL: MEMORANDUM *see* FAR EASTERN SURVEY

The Institute of Paper Science & Technology, Inc *see* ABSTRACT BULLETIN

Institute of Petroleum *see*
- JOURNAL

Institute of Social Studies. The Hague *see* DEVELOPMENT AND CHANGE

Institute of Texan Cultures. Library *see*
- EARLY CZECH NEWSPAPERS OF TEXAS
- EARLY TEXAS NEWSPAPERS
- TRANSLATIONS OF STATISTICAL AND CENSUS REPORTS OF TEXAS, 1782-1836

Institute of Welding *see* TRANSACTIONS

INSTITUTE ON EMINENT DOMAIN (SOUTHWESTERN LEGAL FOUNDATION) : PROCEEDINGS – v1-9. 1959-68 – 1,5,6 – $90.00 – us Hein [340]

INSTITUTE ON ESTATE PLANNING UNIVERSITY OF MIAMI : ANNUAL PROCEEDINGS – v1-26. 1967-92 – 1,5,6 – $765.00 – us Hein [340]

INSTITUTE ON FEDERAL TAXATION (NEW YORK UNIVERSITY) : PROCEEDINGS – v1-50. 1942-92 – 1,5,6 – $2,160.00 – us Hein [336]

INSTITUTE ON LABOR SOUTHWESTERN LEGAL FOUNDATION. LABOR LAW DEVELOPMENTS : ANNUAL PROCEEDINGS – v11-39. 1964-92 – 1,5,6 – $315.00 – us Hein [340]

INSTITUTE ON OIL AND GAS LAW AND TAXATION. SOUTHWESTERN LEGAL FOUNDATION : ANNUAL PROCEEDINGS – v1-42. 1949-91 – 1,5,6 – $540.00 – us Hein [340]

INSTITUTE ON PLANNING AND ZONING (SOUTHWESTERN LEGAL FOUNDATION) : PROCEEDINGS – v1-8. 1960-69 – 1,5,6 – $45.00 – us Hein [340]

INSTITUTE ON PLANNING ZONING AND EMINENT DOMAIN (SOUTHWESTERN LEGAL FOUNDATION) : PROCEEDINGS – v1-22. 1971-92 – 1,5,6 – $225.00 – us Hein [340]

INSTITUTE ON PRIVATE INVESTMENTS AND INVESTORS ABROAD : SOUTHWESTERN LEGAL FOUNDATION – v1-36. 1959-93 – 1,5,6 – $360.00 – us Hein [073]

INSTITUTES OF COMMON AND STATUTE LAW / Minor, John Barbee – (4th ed. Richmond, 1891-. 2v. LL-860) – 2d ed. Richmond, 1876-95. 4v. in 6. LL-1432 – 1 – us L of C Photodup [340]

INSTITUTES OF ENGLISH GRAMMAR / Harrison, Ralph – 1777. 69p. (English Linguistics Series 1500-1800) – 9 – us UMI [420]

THE INSTITUTES OF LAW : A TREATISE ON THE PRINCIPLES OF JURISPRUDENCE / Lorimer, James – Edinburgh: T & T Clark, 1872 – 5mf – 9 – $7.50 – LLMC 95-175 – us L.L.M.C. [340]

INSTITUTES OF LEARNING TAKEN FROM ARISTOTLE, PLUTARCH, LONGINUS—AND MANY OTHER WRITERS BOTH ANCIENT AND MODERN / Manwaring, Edward – 1737. 83p. (English Linguistics Series 1500-1800) – 9 – us UMI [400]

INSTITUTES OF MUSSALMAN LAW, A TREATISE ON PERSONAL LAW ACCORDING TO THE HANAFITE SCHOOL, WITH REFERENCES TO ORIGINAL ARABIC SOURCES...1795 TO 1906 / Abdur Rahman, A F M – Calcutta: Thacker, Spink, 1907. lxi,532p – 1 – us U.W. Library [950]

INSTITUTES OF THE CHRISTIAN RELIGION / Calvin, Jean – Trans. by John Allen. 6th American ed. rev. and corr. Philadelphia: Presbyterian Board of Publication and Sabbath-School Work, 1921. 2v – 1 – us U.W. Library [240]

THE INSTITUTES OF VISHNU / ed by Mueller, Friedrich Max – (Translated by Julius Jolly) – 1880 – 7mf – 8 – ne Slangenburg [280]

L'INSTITUTEUR DES INSTITUTEURS. ST JEAN DE LA SALLE. PARIS, 1929 / Laudet, Fernand – Madrid: Razon y Fe, 1930 – 1 – sp Bibl Santa Ana [060]
L'INSTITUTEUR RURAL : REVUE D'EDUCATION – Port-au-Prince: Publiee par le Service national de la production agricole et de l'enseignement rural, [1939-]. v1 n1,3-4. 3rd qtr 1939, 1st-2nd qtr 1940 – 1r – 1 – us Res Libr [370]
LES INSTITUTEURS ET LE SYNDICALISME / Laurin, MT – Paris. 1908. (La Condition Ouvriere. Part Two.) – 9 – 2.50 – fr Bibl Nationale [360]
INSTITUTIO GALLICAE LINGUAE / Garnier, J – 1558 – 9 – fr I.C.S. [440]
INSTITUTIO GRAECAE GRAMMATICES COMPENDIARIA / Camden, William – 1595. 83p. (English Linguistics Series 1500-1800) – 9 – us UMI [450]
INSTITUTION CATHOLIQUE, OU EST DECLAREE ET CONFIRMEE LA VERITE DE LA FOY / Coton, P – Paris, 1612 – 13mf – 9 – CA-122/1 – ne IDC [240]
L'INSTITUTION DES SOURDS-MUETS DE MONTREAL (1848-1948) : BIBLIOGRAPHIE / Dufresne, Lise – 1964. SEM105P4 – 2mf – 9 – cn Bibl Nat [616]
THE INSTITUTION OF A YOUNG NOBLE MAN / Cleland, James – 1607 – 9 – $20.00 – us Scholars' Facs [370]
Institution of Chemical Engineers *see*
– TRANSACTIONS
Institution of Civil Engineers. London *see* MINUTES OF PROCEEDINGS
Institution of Diesel and Gas Turbine Engineers *see* TRANSACTIONS
Institution of Electrical Engineers *see*
– IEE PROCEEDINGS, PART A
– IEE PROCEEDINGS, PART B
– IEE PROCEEDINGS, PART C
– IEE PROCEEDINGS, PART D
– IEE PROCEEDINGS, PART E
– IEE PROCEEDINGS, PART F
– IEE PROCEEDINGS, PART G
– IEE PROCEEDINGS, PART H
– IEE PROCEEDINGS, PART I
– IEE PROCEEDINGS. PART J
Institution of Mechanical Engineers *see*
– JOURNAL AND PROCEEDINGS
– PROCEEDINGS
– PROCEEDINGS OF THE INSTITUTION OF MECHANICAL ENGINEERS
– PROCEEDINGS, PART B
– PROCEEDINGS, PART C
– PROCEEDINGS, PART D
Institution of Mechanical Engineers, London *see* LIBRARY CATALOGUE OF THE INSTITUTION OF MECHANICAL ENGINEERS
Institution of Mechanical Engineers. Railway Division *see* JOURNAL
Institution of Naval Architects *see* TRANSACTIONS
EINE INSTITUTION ZIEHT UM : THERAPEUTISCHE NACHSORGE VON DROGENABHAENGIGEN IN LAENDLICHER INSEL-IDYLLE UND SZENE-NAHER KUNST-UND MAERCHENSTADT / Weil, Thomas – 1995 – 2mf – 9 – DM80.00 – 3-8267-2163-2 – gw Hänsel [360]
INSTITUTIONAL ARRANGEMENTS FOR WATER MANAGEMENT : CANADIAN EXPERIENCES / ed by Mitchell, Bruce – 1975 – 285p – 9 – $7.00 set – cn Geography [350]
INSTITUTIONAL ASPECTS OF SHIFTING CULTIVATION IN AFRICA – 1984 – 177p – it F.A.O. [350]
INSTITUTIONAL CHANGES IN AGRICULTURAL PRODUCTS AND INPUT MARKETS AND THEIR IMPACT ON AGRICULTURAL PERFORMANCE – 1991 – 60p – it F.A.O. [338]
THE INSTITUTIONAL CHURCH : A PRIMER IN PASTORAL THEOLOGY / Judson, Edward – New York: Lentilhon, c1899. (Handbooks for practical workers in church and philanthropy) – 1mf – us A.T.L.A. [240]
INSTITUTIONAL DISTRIBUTION – (v16- 1980-5,6,9) – v1- 1965 – 1 – us UMI [380]
INSTITUTIONAL INVESTOR – 1976- – 1; 1978-5,6,9 – us UMI [332]
INSTITUTIONALIZATION OF A FARMING SYSTEMS APPROACH TO DEVELOPMENT – 1992 – 339p – it F.A.O. [630]
INSTITUTIONEN DES PRAKTISCHEN VOELKERRECHTS IN FRIEDENSZEITEN... / Hartmann, A – Hanover, 1878 – 4mf – 1 – ILM-184/1 – ne IDC [327]
INSTITUTIONES; DIGESTUM (BOOKS 40-50); NOVELLAE CONSTITUTIONES / Justinianus – 12th and 14th cents. Holkham mss. 207, 208, 209. Holkham Hall, Norfolk, England – 1 – uk Microform Academic [760]
INSTITUTIONES ENTOMOLOGICAE / Petagna, V – Neapoli, 1792. xii,718p. 10 pls. Z-1544/2 – 8 – ne IDC [590]
INSTITUTIONES GRAMMATICAE ANGLOSAXONICAE... / Hickes, G – Oxoniae, 1689 – 2mf – 9 – ne IDC [420]
INSTITUTIONES GRAMMATICAE ANGLO-SAXONICAE, ET MOESO-GOTHICAE / Hickes, George – 1689 392p. (English Linguistics Series 1500-1800) – 9 – us UMI [420]
INSTITUTIONES HISTORICO-PHYSICAE REGNI VEGETABILIS / Ludwig, C G – Lipsiae, 1757. 264 pp. B-6047 2 – 8 – ne IDC [580]
INSTITUTIONES. LINGUAE SYRIACAE, ASSYRIACAE / Caninius, (A Canini) – (Linguistics series). 1554 – 9 – fr Hachette [470]
INSTITUTIONES MEDICAE / Boerhaave, H – Ed. 5. M 40. 1734 – 9 – ne IDC [615]
INSTITUTIONES MUSICAE.. / Koesfelt, Coenraad Z van – 1743 – 9 – us Sibley [780]
INSTITUTIONES MUSICAE, OF KORTE ONDERWYZINGEN RAKENDE DE PRACTYK VAN DE MUZYK EN IN-ZONDERHEID VAN DEN GENERAALEN BAS OF BASSUS CONTINUUS, BENEVENS DE DAER UIT SPRUITENDE GRONDEN VAN DE COMPOSITIE, UITGEGEVEN DOOR EEN LIEFHEBBER VAN DEZE KUNST / Zumbag de Koesfelt, C – Te Leiden, by Gerard Potvliet. 1743. BP-530 1 – 9 – ne IDC [780]
INSTITUTIONES PHILOSOPHIAE MORALIS / Ferretti, Augustus – (Includes bibliographical references) – Romae: S C de Propaganda fide, 1893-1902 – 4mf – 9 – 0-8370-6182-2 – 1986-0182 – us A.T.L.A. [170]
INSTITUTIONES PHILOSOPHICAE AD USUM STUDIOSAE JUVENTUTIS / Demers, Jerome – Quebec, 1835. SEM16P130 – 1r – 5 – Can$9.00 – cn Bibl Nat [100]
INSTITUTIONES PROPAEDEUTICAE AD SACRAM THEOLOGIAM / Pesch, Christian – Freiburg i.B.: Herder, 1894. 1 fiche – 9 – us A.T.L.A. [240]
INSTITUTIONES QUE SU MAGESTAD MANDO HACER A VIS MERCADO PARA EL EXAMEN DE LOS ALGEBRISTAS / Mercado, L – Madrid, 1599 – 3mf – 9 – sp Cultura [500]
INSTITUTIONES REI HERBARIAE / Crantz, H J N von – 2v. Viennae. 1766. B-62 2 – 8 – ne IDC [580]
INSTITUTIONES REI HERBARIAE / Tournefort, Joseph Pitton de – 755. 3 V. Ed. 3. 1719 – 9 – ne IDC [580]
INSTITUTIONES REI HERBARIAE / Tournefort, Joseph Pitton de – Ed. 2. Parisiis. 1700. B-932 2 – 8 – ne IDC [580]
INSTITUTIONES THEOLOGICAE ANTIQUORUM PATRUM / Thomasius, J M – Romae. v1-3. 1769 – 43mf – 8 – ne Slangenburg [240]
LES INSTITUTIONS DE BIENFAISANCE, DE CHARITE ET DE PREVOYANCE A MARSEILLE / Camau, Emile – Marseille, n.d. (La Condition Ouvriere. Part Two.) – 9 – 10.00 – fr Bibl Nationale [360]
INSTITUTIONS DU... / Gerard de Reyneval, J M – Paris, 1803 – 6mf – 1 – ILM-185/1 – ne IDC [327]
INSTITUTIONS ECCLESIASTIQUES DE LA CHRETIENTE MEDIEVALE (12) – Paris, 1959 – Dfl56.00 – ne Slangenburg [240]
INSTITUTIONS ET COUTUMES CANAQUES / Rau, Eric – Paris: Larose, 1944 – 1 – F110.06 – fr Armell [306]
INSTITUTIONS OF LANGUAGE / Martin, Benjamin – 1748. 116p. (English Linguistics Series 1500-1800) – 9 – us UMI [400]
DES INSTITUTIONS OUVRIERES AU 19E SIECLE – 1866. (Condition of 19th century French working class series) – 9 – fr Hachette [305]
LES INSTITUTIONS OUVRIERES DE MULHOUSE ET DES ENVIRONS / Veron, Eugene – (Condition of 19th C. French working class series). 1866 – 9 – fr Hachette [305]
LES INSTITUTIONS POLITIQUES ET ADMINISTRATIVES DU PAYS DE LANGUEDOC DU 13E SIECLE AUX GUERRES DE RELIGION. / Dognon, Paul – Toulouse: E. Privat, 1895. xviii/652p – 1 – us U.W. Library [944]
INSTITUTIONUM DIALECTICARUM...LIBRO OCTO / Fonseca, P – (Missing: Title page) – [Coloniae, 1591] – 8mf – 9 – CA-15/1 – ne IDC [100]
INSTITUTIONUM THEOLOGICARUM... / Haunold, C – Ingolstadii, 1659 – 7mf – 9 – CA-53/1 – ne IDC [240]
Instituto Bacteriologico de Nova-Goa *see* ARQUIVOS INDO-PORTUGUESES DE MEDICINA E HISTORIA NATURAL
Instituto coloniale fascista. Roma *see*
– ANNUARIO DELLE COLONIE ITALIANE E DEI PAESI VICINI
– ANNUARIO DELL'IMPERO ITALIANO
Instituto Coloniale Italiano *see* RIVISTA COLONIALE
Instituto Cultural Argentino-Ruso *see* ARGENTINA Y LA U.R.S.S.
INSTITUTO DE 2ND...CURSO 1898 A 1899 / Suarez Quintero, Valentin – (Tambien curso 1899 a 1900) – Badajoz: Tip. Uceda Hermanos, 1900 – 1 – sp Bibl Santa Ana [370]
INSTITUTO DE DEFENSA LEGAL (IDL) – Lima. 97 docs. 1986-1991 – 52mf – 9 – ne IDC [320]
Instituto de Estudios Africanos *see* AFRICA EN EL PENSAMIENTO DE DONOSO CORTES
INSTITUTO DE ESTUDIOS LEGALES Y SOCIALES DEL URUGUAY (IELSUR) = INSTITUTE FOR LEGAL AND SOCIAL STUDIES IN URUGUAY – Montevideo. 10 docs. 1987-1990 – 9mf – 9 – ne IDC [320]
Instituto De Salubridad y Enfermedades Tropicales *see* REVISTA
INSTITUTO DE SEGUNDA ENSENANZA DE MERIDA. MEMORIA DEL CURSO 1934-35 / Dominguez, Manuel – Merida: A. Rodriguez, 1936 – 1 – sp Bibl Santa Ana [946]
Instituto fascista dell'Africa italiana. Roma *see* ANNUARIO DELL'AFRICA ITALIANA E DELLE ISOLE ITALIANE DELL'EGEO
INSTITUTO GENERAL TECNICO DE BADAJOZ. MEMORIA DEL CURSO DE 1904 A 1905... / Gonzalez Cuadrado, Antonio – (Tambien curso 1906-1907; 1907-1908; 1908-1909; 1909-1910; 1910-1911; 1911-1912; 1912-1913; 1913-1914; 1914-1915; 1916-1917) – Badajoz: Tip. La Minerva Extremena, 1906 – 1 – sp Bibl Santa Ana [370]
Instituto Geografico *see*
– ANUARIO ESTADISTICO DE ESPANA
– CENSO DE POBLACION DE ESPANA SEGUN EL EMPADRONAMIENTO DE...1887, TOMO 1-3
– CONSIDERACIONES DEMOGRAFICAS SOBRE EL CENSO DE BUENOS AIRES
– ESTADISTICA DE LA EMIGRACION E INMIGRACION DE ESPANA EN 1882-1895
– ESTADISTICA MORTUORIA DE LA CIUDAD DE BUENOS AIRES
– MEMORIA DE LOS TRABAJOS REALIZADOS
– MEMORIA ELEVADA AL CONSEJO DE MINISTROS
– MEMORIA SOBRE LA ESTADISTICA GENERAL DE ESPANA
– MEMORIAS. TOMO 1-12
– LA MORTALIDAD INFANTIL EN BUENOS AIRES. ESTUDIO COMPARATIVO...
– MOVIMIENTO DE LA POBLACION DE ESPANA. ANOS 1861-1870
– MOVIMIENTO DE POBLACION DE LA PLATA
– NOMENCLATOR DE ESPANA DE 1888, TOMO 1-5
– NUEVO NOMENCLATOR DE LAS CIUDADES
– PRESUPUESTOS GENERALES DE LA ISLA FILIPINAS
– RESENA GEOGRAFICA Y ESTADISTICA DE ESPANA
Instituto Geologico y Minero de Espana *see* MAPA GEOLOGICO DE ESPANA
Instituto GeologicoMinero de Espana Madrid *see* MAPA GEOLOGICO DE ESPANA. ESCALA 1:50000
INSTITUTO HISTORICO E GEOGRAPHICO BRASILEIRO... / ed by Bayle, Constantino – Madrid: Razon y Fe, 1927 – 1 – sp Bibl Santa Ana [972]
Instituto Historico e Geographico Brasileiro. Rio de Janeiro *see* REVISTA TRIMENSAL
Instituto Laboral Garcia de Paredes *see*
– MEMORIA. CURSO 1957-58
– MEMORIA DEL CURSO 1959-60
– MEMORIA DEL CURSO ACADEMICO 1960-61, 1961-62
Instituto Laboral "Garcia de Paredes". Trujillo *see* PROGRAMA DE ACTOS QUE SE CELEBRARAN CON MOTIVO DEL 10TH ANIVERSARIO DE LA IMPLANTACION DE LA ENSENANZA LABORAL EN TRUJILLO
Instituto Laboral General Moscardo *see* MEMORIA DEL CURSO ACADEMICO 1956-57
Instituto Latinoamericano de Doctrina y Estudios Sociales *see* DOCUMENTACION SOCIAL CATOLICA LATINOAMERICANA DOCLA
INSTITUTO LATINOAMERICANO DE SERVICIOS LEGALES ALTERNATIVOS (ILSA) = LATIN AMERICAN INSTITUTE FOR ALTERNATIVE LEGAL SERVICES – Bogota. 53 docs. 1983-1991 – 43mf – 9 – ne IDC [340]
INSTITUTO MILITAR PESTOLOZZIANO DE MADRID, OBRA DEL EXTREMENO MANUEL GODOY / Guerra Guerra, Arcadio – Badajoz: Imp. Dip. Provincial, 1963 – sp Bibl Santa Ana [350]
Instituto Nacional de 2nd Ensenanza. Caceres *see*
– MEMORIA DEL CURSO 1935 A 1936, 1936 A 1937
– MEMORIA DEL CURSO DE 1934 A 1935
INSTITUTO NACIONAL DE 2ND ENSENANZA DE BADAJOZ...1926 – Badajoz: Tip. La Economica, 1926 – sp Bibl Santa Ana [946]
INSTITUTO NACIONAL DE ENSENANZA MEDIA MASCULINO "ZURBARAN". BADAJOZ. MEMORIA INFORMATIVA – Badajoz: Imp. Comercial, 1968 – 1 – sp Bibl Santa Ana [380]
Instituto Nacional de Estadistica *see*
– NOMENCLATOR DE LAS CIUDADES, VILLAS, LUGARES, ALDEAS Y DEMAS ENTIDADES DE POBLACION DE ESPANA...
– RESE NA ESTADISTICA DE LA PROVINCIA DE BADAJOZ
– RESENA ESTADISTICA DE LA PROVINCIA DE BADAJOZ
INSTITUTO NACIONAL DE ESTADISTICA. NOMENCLATOR DE LAS CIUDADES DE ESPANA. PROVINCIA DE BADAJOZ – Madrid: Rivadeneira, 1950 – 1 – sp Bibl Santa Ana [946]
Instituto Nacional de Industria *see*
– EL PLAN DE BADAJOZ. RESUMEN INFORMATIVO DE SU SITUACION EN FIN DE 1962
– EL PLAN DE BADAJOZ. SU REALIDAD ACTUAL
Instituto Nacional de Industria. Secretaria Gestora del Plan *see* LEY Y REGLAMENTO SOBRE EL PLAN DE OBRAS Y COLONIZACION, INDUSTRIALIZACION Y ELECTRIFICACION DE LA PROVINCIA DE BADAJOZ
EL INSTITUTO NACIONAL DE PREVISION DE LABORATORIO INICIAL Y PREPARADOR DEL AMBIENTE ESPANOL PARA LA SEGURIDAD SOCIAL / Leal Ramos, Leon – Madrid: Ministerio de Trabajo Publicaciones del Instituto Nacional de Prevision, 1950 – sp Bibl Santa Ana [946]
Instituto Oswaldo Cruz *see* MEMORIAS
Instituto Panamericano de Geografia e Historia *see* CATALOGO DE LA EXPOSICION DE LIBROS DE GEOGRAFIA E HISTORIA DE VENEZUELA, CARACAS, AGOSTO DE 1946
INSTITUTO PENEDENSE : ORGAM DO INSTITUTO PENEDENSE – Penedo, Alagoas. 10 Maio 1903 – 1,5,6 – bl Biblioteca [072]
L'INSTITUTRICE DE PROVINCE / Frapie, Leon – Paris: Fasquelle, 1897. 352p. (Les Femmes Collection) – 4mf – 9 – $10.00 – fr Bibl Nationale [370]
INSTITUTS DE CHYMIE, OU PRINCIPES ELEMENTAIRES DE CETTE SCIENCE / Demachy, Jacques Francois – Paris, 1766 – 1 – us U.W. Library [540]
LES INSTITUTS DE TECHNOLOGIE: BILAN D'UNE ANNEE DE FONCTIONEMENT / Algeria. Centre de Coordination des Instituts de Technologie – 1970. BNE-8706 1 – 9 – ne IDC [324]
LES INSTITUTS FAMILIAUX DE NOTRE PROVINCE : ECOLES DE BONHEUR: BIBLIOGRAPHIE ANALYTIQUE D'UNE MAGNIFIQUE FORMULE D'EDUCATION FEMININE, 1937-1961 / Marie-Libermann, Soeur – 1961. SEM105P4 – 1mf – 9 – cn Bibl Nat [370]
INSTITUZIONI BOTANICHE / Targioni-Tozzetti, O – 3rd ed Firenze, 1813. v. 1, 642 pp., 17 pls; v. 2, 552 pp.; v. 3, 684 pp. B-906 2 – 8 – ne IDC [580]
INSTITUZIONI DI BOTANICA PRACTICA / Nocca, D – Pavia, 1808-1809. 3 Pts. B-920 2 – 8 – ne IDC [580]
A INSTRUCCAO : ORGAO DO CLUB LITTERARIO GONCALVES DIAS – Maceio, Alagoas. 29 Jun 1884 – 1,5,6 – bl Biblioteca [072]
A INSTRUCCAO : ORGAO DO COLLEGIO – JOSE DE ALENCAR – S. Luiz do Quitunde, Alagoas. 1-7 Out 1883 – 1,5,6 – bl Biblioteca [072]

Instruccion *see* INSTRUCCION DE ENFERMOS Y MODO DE APLICAR LOS REMEDIOS A TODO GENERO DE ENFERMEDADES...

INSTRUCCION CURATIVA DE LAS CALENTURAS CONOCIDAS...COMO TABARDILLO / Amar y Arguedas, J – Madrid, 1775 – 6mf – 9 – sp Cultura [616]

INSTRUCCION CURATIVA DE LAS VIRUELAS / Amar y Arguedas, J – Madrid, 1774 – 4mf – 9 – sp Cultura [615]

INSTRUCCION CURATIVA Y PRESERVATIVA DE LOS DOLORES DE COSTADO Y PULMONES / Amar y Arguedas, J – Madrid, 1777 – 4mf – 9 – sp Cultura [610]

INSTRUCCION DE ENFERMOS Y MODO DE APLICAR LOS REMEDIOS A TODO GENERO DE ENFERMEDADES... / Instruccion – Madrid, 1728 – 4mf – 9 – sp Cultura [615]

INSTRUCCION DE LOS BARBEROS FLEBOTONIANOS... / Munoz, A – Valencia, 1621 – 3mf – 9 – sp Cultura [615]

INSTRUCCION DE MUSICA SOBRE LA GUITARRA ESPANOLA.. / Sanz, Gasper – 3V. 1697 – 2 – us Sibley [780]

INSTRUCCION DE MUSICA SOBRE LA GUITARRA ESPANOLA, Y METODO DE SVS PRIMEROS RUDIMENTOS, HASTA TANERLA CON DESTREZA / Sanz, Gasper – Zaragoca. 1697. BP-754 1 – 9 – ne IDC [780]

INSTRUCCION DE UN PASSAJERO... GUADALUPE – 1697 – 9 – 1.50f – sp Bibl Santa Ana [910]

INSTRUCCION GENERAL SOBRE LA MANERA DE REDACTAR LOS DOCUMENTOS PUBLICOS SUJETOS A REGISTRO EN LAS PROVINCIAS DE CUBA Y PUERTO-RICO : EDICION OFICIAL – Madrid: Imprenta Nacional, 1879 – 1mf – 9 – $1.50 – LLMC 92-317 – us L.L.M.C. [340]

INSTRUCCION PARA DEFENSA DE LOS CONJUNTOS HISTORICO-ARTISTICOS / Ministerio de Education Nacional – Caceres, Madrid: Graficas Varela, 1965 – 1 – sp Bibl Santa Ana [700]

INSTRUCCION PARA LA VISITA / Spain. Laws, Statutes, etc – 1790 – 9 – 1.50f – sp Bibl Santa Ana [324]

INSTRUCCION PASTORAL ESTABLECIDAS.. / Delgado Moreno, Mateo – 1815 – 9 – 1.50f – sp Bibl Santa Ana [946]

INSTRUCCION PASTORAL QUE EL EXCMO. E ILTMO. SENOR...DIRIGE A LOS FIELES DE SU DIOCESIS SOBRE LA DEVOCION AL S. CORAZON DE JESUS / Perez Munoz, Adolfo – Badajoz: Tip. Uceda hermanos, 1918 – 1 – sp Bibl Santa Ana [240]

LA INSTRUCCION PRIMARIA EN FILIPINAS. DESDE 1596 HASTA 1868 / Barrantes Moreno, Vicente – Madrid: Imp. de la Iberia, s.a. – 1 – sp Bibl Santa Ana [946]

INSTRUCCION PROVISIONAL...CONTRIBUCION – 1821 – 9 – 1.50f – sp Bibl Santa Ana [946]

LA INSTRUCCION PUBLICA EN EL ECUADOR DE 1830 A 1930 / Tobar Donoso, Julio – Madrid: Razon y Fe, 1931 – 1 – sp Bibl Santa Ana [370]

INSTRUCCION SOBRE CUMPLIMIENTO PASCUAL Y VIDA RELIGIOSA EN LAS HERMANDADES SINDICALES DE LABRADORES / Rodriguez Amaya, Esteban – Badajoz: Imp. Provincial, 1946 – sp Bibl Santa Ana [240]

INSTRUCCION SOBRE LA PESTE / Mercado, M – Zaragoza, 1648 – 4mf – 9 – sp Cultura [616]

INSTRUCCION SOBRE MODO DE TRANSPORTAR PLANTAS VIVAS / Gomez Ortega, Casimiro – 1779 – 1mf – 9 – Pta1,000.00 – 84-7848-135-4 – sp Pentalfa [580]

INSTRUCCIONES IMPORTANTES QUE...SR.D....COMUNICA A TODOS... / Varela, Cipriano – Plasencia, s.i., 1828 – 1 – sp Bibl Santa Ana [946]

INSTRUCCIONES PARA COMBATIR ALGUNOS PARASITOS DEL OLIVO. 1897 – 9 – 1.50f – sp Bibl Santa Ana [630]

INSTRUCCIONES PARA LA DEFENSA DE LOS CONJUNTOS HISTORICO-ARTISTICOS / Ministerio de Educacion Nacional – Caceres – 1 – sp Bibl Santa Ana [700]

INSTRUCCIONES PARA...LA CONSERVACION Y AUMENTO DE LAS POBLACIONES / Fernandez, F – Madrid, 1769 – 3mf – 9 – sp Cultura [304]

INSTRUCCIONES SOBRE LAPIDAS / Sanguino y Michel, Juan – Caceres: Tip. Enc. y Lib. Jimenez, 1905 – 1 – sp Bibl Santa Ana [946]

INSTRUCCION...INTERNOS...COLEGIO DE HUMANIDADES DE CACERES – 1829 – 9 – 1.50f – sp Bibl Santa Ana [370]

INSTRUCCION...PLAN ADMINISTRATIVO... AYUNTAMIENTOS – 1822 – 9 – 1.50f – sp Bibl Santa Ana [340]

INSTRUCCION...TOMAR EL PURGANTE DE MR. LE ROY – 1829 – 9 – 1.50f – sp Bibl Santa Ana [610]

INSTRUCIONES.. / Varela, Cipriano – 1828 – 9 – 1.50f – sp Bibl Santa Ana [240]

INSTRUCTIO MEDICORUM APPOLLINEAM AGGREDIENTIBUS VALDE UTILIS / Lillo y Herrero, G – Madrid, 1679 – 9mf – 9 – sp Cultura [610]

INSTRUCTIO SACERDOTUM LOCUPLETISSIMA / Toledo, Francisco de – Lugduni, 1649 – 22mf – 8 – ne Slangenburg [240]

INSTRUCTION DONNEE PAR...IMPERATRICE ET LEGISLATRICE DE TOUTES LES RUSSIES.. / Catherine 2, Tsarina of Russia – Traduit en francais par Balthasar. Nouvelle ed, augmentee. Lausanne, 1769. 204p. Only Swiss printing of Catherine II's Nakaz. BR-9094/1 – 9 – ne IDC [947]

INSTRUCTION GENERALE POUR LA TEINTURE DES LAINES ET MANUFACTURES DE LAINES DE TOUTES COULEURS, & POUR LA CULTURE DES DROGUES OU INGREDIENS QU'ON Y EMPLOYE / Delormois – Paris: Impr. de F. Muguet, 1671 – 1 – us U.W. Library [670]

INSTRUCTION PASTORALE DE MONSEIGNEUR L'EVEQUE DE TROYES / Boulogne, E A de – Sur l'impression des mauvais livres et notamment sur les nouvelles oeuvres completes de Voltaire et Rousseau. Paris. A. Le Clere. 1821 – 9 – fr Hachette [440]

L'INSTRUCTION PUBLIQUE AU CANADA: PRECIS HISTORIQUE ET STATISTIQUE / Chauveau, Pierre J O – Quebec?: A. Cote, 1876. 00593. (Pre-1900 Canadiana) – 9 – cn C.I.H.M. [310]

L'INSTRUCTION PUBLIQUE DANS LA PROVINCE DE QUEBEC... / Magnan, C-J – 2e ed. Quebec: [s.n.], 1934. SEM105P1271 – 1mf – 9 – Can$2.25 – cn Bibl Nat [971]

L'INSTRUCTION PUBLIQUE DANS LA PROVINCE DU QUEBEC / Cazes, Paul de – Quebec: A. Cote, 1884. 04372. (Pre-1900 Canadiana) – 9 – cn C.I.H.M. [370]

INSTRUCTION SUR LE CHOLERA – Paris [1848?] – us Res Libr [616]

INSTRUCTIONAL INNOVATOR – v25-30, no.1. 1980-Jan 1985 – 1,5,6,9 – us UMI [073]

INSTRUCTIONAL SCIENCE – v1-13. 1972-84 – 1,5,6,13 – sz Elsevier [500]

INSTRUCTIONS ADDRESSEES...A LA COMMISSION ETABLIE POUR TRAVAILLER A L'EXECUTION DU PROJET D'UN NOUVEAU CODE DE LOIS / Catherine 2, Tsarina of Russia – St. Petersburg, 1769. 286p. Early French translation of Catherine's Nakaz published in Russia. BR-9095/1 – 9 – ne IDC [947]

INSTRUCTIONS CRETIENNES / Vaudelin, le P G – 1715 – 9 – fr I.C.S. [240]

INSTRUCTIONS FOR CHILDREN / Keach, Benjamin – 1685 – 1 – 6.26 – us Baptist [240]

INSTRUCTIONS FOR RIGHT SPELLING / Fox, George & Hookes, Ellis – 1673. 168p. (English Linguistics Series 1500-1800) – 9 – us UMI [420]

INSTRUCTIONS IN CRIMINAL CAUSES PASSED UPON BY THE COURTS OF MISSOURI / Pattison, Everett Wilson – St. Louis: Gilbert, 1902. 607p. LL-1320 – 1 – us L of C Photodup [340]

INSTRUCTIONS POPULAIRES SUR LA PRIERE / Lobry, J-B – (Includes bibliographical references) – 3e ed. Paris: Louis Vives, 1883 – 1mf – 9 – 0-8370-7478-9 – 1986-1478 – us A.T.L.A. [240]

INSTRUCTIONS POPULAIRES SUR LE SYMBOLE DES APAOTRES / Lobry, J-B – (Includes bibliographical references) – 5e ed. Paris: Louis Vives, 1885 – 2mf – 9 – 0-8370-7479-7 – 1986-1479 – us A.T.L.A. [240]

INSTRUCTIONS POPULAIRES SUR LES SACREMENTS / Lobry, J-B – (Includes bibliographical references) – 3e ed. Paris: Louis Vives, 1883 – 1mf – 9 – 0-8370-7480-0 – 1986-1480 – us A.T.L.A. [240]

INSTRUCTIONS POUR DEUX CAR EMES ET UN MOIS DE MARIE / Lobry, J-B – (Includes bibliographical references) – 5e ed. Paris: Louis Vives, 1885 – 1mf – 9 – 0-8370-7481-9 – 1986-1481 – us A.T.L.A. [240]

INSTRUCTIONS SUR LE FAICT DE LA GUERRE / Du Bellay, Guillaume – Paris. M. Vascosan. 1548. (Strategy of War Series) – 9 – fr Hachette [355]

INSTRUCTIONS TO CHRISTIAN CONVERTS / Clark, Dougan – Chicago: Publishing Association of Friends, 1889 – 1mf – us A.T.L.A. [240]

INSTRUCTIONS TO JURIES AND DECLARATIONS OF LAW / Helton, Peter – Springfield, MO: Tuthill, 1892. 599p. LL-890 – 1 – us L of C Photodup [340]

INSTRUCTIONS TO JURIES ESPECIALLY ADAPTED TO THE LAWS OF TEXAS / Goad, George Washington – Springfield, MO: Democrat, 1893. 561p. LL-669 – 1 – us L of C Photodup [340]

INSTRUCTOR – (v. 78- 1968- 5,6. v. 85- 1975- 9) – v. 5- 1895- – 1 – us UMI [370]

THE INSTRUCTOR – (Cont: Parish School Advocate and Family Instructor) – [Bay Verte, N.B.?: s.n.], 1860- – 9 – cn C.I.H.M. [370]

THE INSTRUCTOR / ed by Harpell, J J – Gardenvale, nov 1934-dec 1935 – 1r – 1 – Can$60.00 – cn Can Microfilming [072]

THE INSTRUCTOR – Montreal: J.E.L. Miller, no 1(Apr 28 1835)- – 9 – cn C.I.H.M. [370]

THE INSTRUCTOR *see* THE PARISH SCHOOL ADVOCATE AND FAMILY INSTRUCTOR

INSTRUCTOR'S MANUAL FOR WEED MANAGEMENT – 1986 – 148p – it F.A.O. [631]

EL INSTRUIDO EN LA CORTE...ESTREMENO (SIC) / Jara de Soto, Clara – 1789 – 9 – 1.50f – sp Bibl Santa Ana [946]

INSTRUKTAZH SEL'SKOKHOZIAISTVENNOI KOOPERATSII I EGO OSNOVNYE PROBLEMY / Makhov, V N – M., L., 1926 – 2mf – 9 – COR-489/1 – ne IDC [334]

INSTRUKTSIIA NO. 1 DLIA SOSTAVLENIIA PROIZVODSTVENNYKH PROGRAMM NA BLIZHAISHEE VREMIA – [Petrograd: Gosplan, 192-] – 1 – CSUX91-B3197 – us Hoover Inst Photo [330]

INSTRUKTSIIA O PORIADKE KRATKO-SROCHNOGO KREDITOVANIIA KUSTARNO-PROMYSLOVOI KOOPERATSII I OPERATIVNYI UCHET : SCHETOVODSTVO I OTCHETNOST'V PROMYSLOVOJ KOOPERATSII. VYP.2 / Belokurov, N G & Lapshov, Il – M., 1930 – 1mf – 9 – COR-411/1 – ne IDC [334]

INSTRUKTSIIA ORGANIZATSII AM R.K.P. BOLSHEVIKOV O EDINOM PARTI INOM BILETE / T S.K.R.K.P.(bolsh.) – Moskva: Gos. izdvo, 1920 – 1 – CSUX89-B7427 – us Hoover Inst Photo [320]

INSTRUMENT SOCIETY OF AMERICA *see* TRANSACTIONS

THE INSTRUMENTAL ASSISTANT / Holyoke, Samuel – Vol. I. Containing instructions for the violin, German flute, bass-viol, and hautboy...also a selection of favorite airs, marches &c. Exeter, N.H.: H. Ranlet n.d.? Bound and filmed with Vol. II. MUSIC 123, Item 13 and MUSIC 1995 – 1 – us L of C Photodup [780]

THE INSTRUMENTAL ASSISTANT / Holyoke, Samuel – Vol. II. Containing a selection of minuets, airs, duettos, rondos and marches; with instructions for the French-horn and bassoon. Exeter, N.H.: Ranlet and Norris, 1807. MUSIC 123, Item 13 and MUSIC 1995 – 1 – us L of C Photodup [780]

THE INSTRUMENTAL DIRECTOR CONTAINING RULES FOR ALL MUSICAL INSTRUMENTS. – Fifth edition. 1836 – 9 – us Sibley [780]

THE INSTRUMENTAL MUSICIAN, NO. 2 – Containing a large number of marches, quick-steps, waltzes, hornpipes, contra dances, cotillions &c. Arranged in three parts, for the flute, violin, clarionet, bass-viol, &c. May 1, 1843. To be issued once in two months. To be complete in six numbers. Boston: Elias Howe, Jr., 1843. "The People's Quadrille" is for five instruments and includes figures. MUSIC 1989, Item 5 – 1 – us L of C Photodup [780]

INSTRUMENTALMUSIK – v1-3. 1963-75 – 1 – us I.U. Libraries [390]

INSTRUMENTATION TECHNOLOGY – (v12-. 1965-. 5,6. v22-. 1975-. 9) – 1- 1954- – 1 – us UMI [621]

INSTRUMENTS AND CONTROL SYSTEMS – 1-1928- – 1,5,6,9 – us UMI [680]

INSTRUMENTS AND CONTROL SYSTEMS – v1-28 1928-55 – 1,5,6 – us Princeton Micro [620]

INSTRUMENTS AND EXPERIMENTAL TECHNIQUES – v1-37. 1958-94 – 1,5 – $150.00v – us UMI [619]

INSULA – Madrid. v. 1-11; 14-18; 24-26. 1946-1956; 1959-1963; 1969-1971 – 1 – us NY Public [073]

INSULA – v. 1-. 1946- – 1 – us UMI [410]

INSULA – v1-. 1 enero 1946-. Madrid. -m. Revista bibliografica de ciencias y letras – 1 – us U.W. Library [073]

THE INSULAR CASES / Randolph, Carman Fitz – New York? 1901 37 p. LL-1216 – 1 – us L of C Photodup [340]

THE INSULAR CASES, COMPRISING THE RECORDS, BRIEFS, AND ARGUMENTS OF COUNSEL IN THE INSULAR CASES OF THE OCTOBER TERM, 1900 / U.S. Supreme Court – Washington, Govt. Print. Off., 1901. 1075 p. LL-1419 – 1 – us L of C Photodup [340]

THE INSULAR DAILY PRESS – Manila: The Insular Daily Press, jul 17,19-20,22-24,27-31; aug 1-9,18,22-23,25-28,30 1899 – us Res Libr [072]

INSULATION – v2-16. 1956-70.Continued by: Insulation Circuits – 1 – us UMI [073]

INSULATION GUIDE – 1985- – 1 – us UMI [073]

INSULATION/CIRCUITS – (v.25-. 1979- 5,6,9) – v.16-. 1970- – 1 – us UMI [073]

INSURANCE ADVOCATE – (v85-. 1974-. 5,6. v86-. 1975-. 9) – v. 1-. 1890- – 1 – us UMI [336]

INSURANCE AND FINANCE CHRONICLE – (Cont: Insurance Society. Cont by: The Chronicle) – Montreal: R.W. Smith, [1886-1898] – 9 – cn C.I.H.M. [360]

INSURANCE AND FINANCE CHRONICLE *see* INSURANCE SOCIETY

INSURANCE BUYER'S GUIDE – (v.23 .1980 5,6,9) – v.1. 1957 – 1 – us UMI [073]

INSURANCE CONFERENCE PLANNER – v. 12-. 1976- – 1,5,6,9 – us UMI [336]

INSURANCE COUNSEL JOURNAL *see* DEFENSE COUNSEL JOURNAL

INSURANCE EXCHANGE MAGAZINE – (v51-53. 1975-77. 5,6,9) – v. 1-53. 1931-1977 – 1 – us UMI [336]

INSURANCE FORUM – v.1. 1974 – 1,5,6,9 – us UMI [073]

THE INSURANCE GUIDE – Sweetsburg, Canada. avr 1871 – 1r – 1 – Can$20.00 – cn Can Microfilming [073]

INSURANCE IN ISRAEL 1974 / Israel. Prime Minister's Office. Ministry of Finance. Superintendent of Insurance – Jerusalem, 1975. 23, 123, 20 p. (Special Series no. 508). Text also in Hebrew – 9 – 3.00 – is I.T.T.I. [336]

INSURANCE INDUSTRY – (v.5 .1980 5,6,9) – v.1. 1976 – 1 – us UMI [073]

INSURANCE INSTITUTE FOR HIGHWAY SAFETY: STATUS REPORT – (v.15 .1980 5,6,9) – v.1. 1966 – 1 – us UMI [073]

INSURANCE JOURNAL – v.1-2. 1923-24. Superseded by yInsurance Journal of Southern California. – 1 – us UMI [073]

INSURANCE JOURNAL – (v.58-. 1979- 5,6,9) – v.5-. 1927- – 1 – us UMI [073]

INSURANCE JOURNAL OF SOUTHERN CALIFORNIA – v.3-5. 1925-27. Superseded by Insurance Journal – 1 – us UMI [073]

THE INSURANCE LAW JOURNAL – (Additional vols to be filmed) – St Louis, New York: D T & L H Potter/C C Hine. v1-41. 1871-1912 – 491mf – 9 – $736.00 – LLMC 84-492 – us L.L.M.C. [073]

THE INSURANCE LAW OF CANADA : LIFE, FIRE, MARINE, ACCIDENT, GUARANTEE, HAIL, BURGLARY, EMPLOYERS' LIABILITY... / Laverty, F J – Montreal: John Lovell & Son, Limited, 1911. SEM105P1866 – 14mf – 9 – Can$31.50 – cn Bibl Nat [340]

THE INSURANCE LAWS OF THE STATE OF NEW YORK. / Cumming, Robert Cushing – New York, Baker, Voorhis, 1899. 653 p. LL-751 – 1 – us L of C Photodup [340]

INSURANCE MAPS / Sanborn Map Company – 1883-1950, The Sanborn fire insurance maps of Kansas – 1 – us KS Hist [910]

INSURANCE MARKET PLACE – (v.17 .1979 5,6,9) – v.12. 1974 – 1 – us UMI [336]

INSURANCE PLAN OF THE CITY OF MONTREAL – Montreal: The Author, 1909-1915. SEM35P153 – 1r – 1 – Can$31.00 – cn Bibl Nat [360]

INSURANCE PLAN OF THE CITY OF MONTREAL / Underwriters Survey Bureau – Montreal: The Bureau. 15v. 1918-1930. SEM35P154 – 1 – Can$48.00 – cn Bibl Nat [360]
INSURANCE PLAN OF THE CITY OF QUEBEC, CANADA – Rev. by the Underwriters Surveys Bureau Montreal, 1922. SEM35P134 – 1r – 1 – Can$15.00 – cn Bibl Nat [360]
INSURANCE POLICIES / Ottawa County. Ohio. Carroll Township. Board of Trustees – 1r – 1 – $32.50r – us Archival [324]
INSURANCE RECORD – 1863- – 1. ; 5,6,9 – apply; v.113- – us UMI [336]
INSURANCE SOCIETY – (Cont by: Insurance and Finance Chronicle) – Montreal: C.E. Goad, [1881-1885] – 9 – cn C.I.H.M. [360]
INSURANCE SOCIETY *see* INSURANCE AND FINANCE CHRONICLE
INSURANCE SUPERVISION IN ISRAEL / Israel. Laws, Statutes, etc – Jerusalem: Ministry of Finance, Superintendent of Insurance, 1965. 75p. LL-12040 – 1 – us L of C Photodup [340]
L'INSURGE – Politique et social. no. 1-42. Paris. janv-oct 1937 – 1 – fr A.C.R.P.P. [073]
INSURGENT SOCIALIST – Eugene, OR. 1972-1985 – 4r – 1 – $200.00 – R04990 – us Library Micro [320]
INSURGENT SOCIOLOGIST – v. 1-. 1969- – 1. ; 5,6,9 – apply; v.6- – us UMI [300]
THE INSURGENTS ADMIT THAT THEY LACK THE SYMPATHIES OF THE CIVIL POPULATION – Valencia, 193? Fiche W961. (Blodgett Collection of Spanish Civil War Pamphlets) – 9 – us H.U. College Libr [946]
LAS INSURRECCIONES EN CUBA : APUNTES PARA LA HISTORIA POLITICA DE ESTA ISLA EN EL PRESENTE SIGLO / Zaragoza, Justo – 2v. 1872-73 – 1r – 1 – us Ross [972]
INTEGER CURSUS PHILOSOPHICUS / Oviedo, F de – Lugduni. 2v. 1640 – 21mf – 9 – CA-25/1 – ne IDC [100]
INTEGRAL TRANSFORMS AND SPECIAL FUNCTIONS / ed by Prudnikov, A P – 9,5,1 – us Gordon [510]
INTEGRATED EDUCATION – v. 1-. 1963- – 1. ; 5,6,9 – apply; v.13- – us UMI [370]
INTEGRATED ENVIRONMENTAL CARTOGRAPHY : A TOOL FOR RESEARCH AND LAND-USE PLANNING – 1987 – 56p – 9 – 92-3-102347-0 – fr UNESCO [333]
INTEGRATED FERROELECTRICS : AN INTERNATIONAL JOURNAL / ed by Taylor, George W – 1,5,9 – us Gordon [621]
INTEGRATED MANAGEMENT OF COASTAL ZONES – 1992 – 175p – it F.A.O. [650]
INTEGRATED TECHNOLOGY TRANSFER / Richardson, Jacques – (A guide to the effective use of technology in developing countries from papers in UNESCO journal, Impact of Science on Society) – 1979. 162p. – 9 – $9.50 – 0-912338-20-2 – us Lomond [338]
INTEGRATING CROPS AND LIVESTOCK IN WEST AFRICA – 1983 2nd print 1985 – 120p – it F.A.O. [630]
INTEGRATING NUTRITION INTO AGRICULTURAL AND RURAL DEVELOPMENT PROJECTS : A MANUAL – 1982 2nd print 1984 – 63p – it F.A.O. [640]
INTEGRATING NUTRITION INTO AGRICULTURAL AND RURAL PROJECTS : SIX CASE STUDIES – 1984 – 141p – it F.A.O. [640]
INTEGRATION, COMPETITION AND THE AUSTRALIAN ACCOUNTING INDUSTRY / Anderson, Don – 1984. 26p – 9 – 1.00f – at Libertarian Micro [320]
L'INTEGRATION DES HARKIS DE VANVEY ET DE BAIGNEUX-LES-JUIFS (COTE D'OR) A LA SOCIETE FRANCAISE / Petonnet, C – 9 – F20.00 – fr Ethnologie [305]
L'INTEGRATION ECONOMIQUE DES JEUNES NON SCOLARISES ET DESCOLARISES (AVANT PROJET) / Rwanda. Ministere du Plan. Ministere de la Jeunesse – Kigali, 1978 – 2mf – 9 – DE-317/1 – ne IDC [370]
INTEGRATION OF FOOD AND AGRICULTURAL POLICY WITH MACROECONOMIC POLICY : METHODOLOGICAL CONSIDERATIONS IN A LATIN AMERICAN PERSPECTIVE – 1992 – 84p – it F.A.O. [339]
INTEGRATION OF GENERAL AND TECHNICAL AND VOCATIONAL EDUCATION – 1986 – 355p – 9 – 92-3-102088-9 – fr UNESCO [370]
INTEGRATION OF TECHNICAL AND VOCATIONAL EDUCATION INTO SPECIAL EDUCATION – 1977 – 224p – 9 – 92-3-101438-2 – fr UNESCO [370]
THE INTEGRATION OF THE PERSONALITY / Jung, Carl Gustav – Trans. by Stanley M. Dell. New York, Toronto: Farrar & Rinehart, (c1939). 313p, illus. PR-apply; UWM; 1 – us U.W. Library [616]
INTEGRATIVE FACHTEXTSORTENSTILISTIK : DARGESTELLT AN HISTORIOGRAPHISCHEN FACHTEXTEN DES ENGLISCHEN / Baumann, Klaus-Dieter – 1992 – 4mf – 9 – DM98.00 – 3-89349-480-4 – gw Hänsel [410]
INTEGRATIVE PHYSIOLOGICAL AND BEHAVIORAL SCIENCE *see* PAVLOVIAN JOURNAL OF BIOLOGICAL SCIENCE
INTEGRIERTE MODELLKONZEPTE : ENTWURF EINES KLASSIFIKATIONSSCHEMAS / Schoettle, Holger Hans – 1995 – 2mf – 9 – DM80.00 – 3-8267-2141-1 – gw Hänsel [330]
THE INTEGRITY OF SCRIPTURE: PLAIN REASONS FOR REJECTING THE CRITICAL HYPOTHESIS / Smith, John – New York: Fleming H. Revell, 1902. 1 fiche – 9 – us A.T.L.A. [240]
INTELLECT – (v. 97- 1969- 5,6. v. 98- 1970-9. See also: USA Today) – 1915- – 1 – us UMI [370]
INTELLECTUAL CULTURE OF THE COPPER ESKIMO / Rasmussen, Knud – 1932 – 8 – BN 366 2 – ne IDC [306]
INTELLECTUAL CULTURE OF THE IGLULIK ESKIMOS / Rasmussen, Knud – 1929 – 8 – BN-362 2 – ne IDC [306]
THE INTELLECTUAL DEVELOPMENT OF SCOTLAND / Macpherson, Hector Carswell – London; New York: Hodder and Stoughton, [1911?] – 1mf – us A.T.L.A. [941]
THE INTELLECTUAL DEVELOPMENT OF THE CANADIAN PEOPLE: AN HISTORICAL REVIEW / Bourinot, John George – Toronto: Hunter, Rose, 1881. 00197. (Pre-1900 Canadiana) – 9 – cn C.I.H.M. [971]
INTELLECTUAL LIFE IN HUNGARY PAMPHLET COLLECTION – 1936?-1961 – 1 reel – 1 – CSUXANL5746-B – us Hoover Inst Photo [100]
INTELLECTUAL LIFE IN POLAND PAMPHLET COLLECTION – 1924-1951 – 1 reel – 1 – CSUXANL6579-B – us Hoover Inst Photo [100]
INTELLECTUAL LIFE IN RUSSIA PAMPHLET COLLECTION – 1914?-1951? – 1 reel – 1 – CSUXANR3213-B – us Hoover Inst Photo [100]
INTELLECTUAL LIFE IN THE SOVIET UNION PAMPHLET COLLECTION – 1951-1959 – 1 reel – 1 – CSUXANR3219-B – us Hoover Inst Photo [100]
THE INTELLECTUAL OBSERVER: A REVIEW OF NATURAL HISTORY, MICROSCOPIC RESEARCH, AND RECREATIVE SCIENCE – London, 1862-68 – 3 – us Readex [500]
INTELLECTUAL PROPERTY LAW : AN INTERNATIONAL ANALYTICAL REVIEW JOURNAL / ed by Melser, Allen S – 9,5,1 – us Harwood [340]
INTELLECTUALS AND THE SPANISH MILITARY REBELLION – London, 1937. Fiche W962. (Blodgett Collection of Spanish Civil War Pamphlets) – 9 – us H.U. College Libr [946]
L'INTELLIGENCE – Journal du droit commun puis Journal de la reforme sociale. Paris. sept 1837-mars 1840 – 1 – fr A.C.R.P.P. [073]
INTELLIGENCE ACTIVITIES IN THE PHILIPPINES DURING THE JAPANESE OCCUPATION / U.S. Army. Far East Command – 1948. 2 v – 1 – 25.00 – us L of C Photodup [950]
INTELLIGENCE DIGEST – (1979- 5,6,9) – 1946-. Continues: Review of World Affairs – 1 – us UMI [320]
INTELLIGENCE DIVISION, OPNAV, COMBAT NARRATIVES / U.S. Navy – (With printed guide) – 1989 – 3r – 1 – $255.00 – S3175 – us Scholarly Res [355]
INTELLIGENCE REPORTS ON SOUTHERN NIGERIA / Great Britain. Colonial Office. Nigeria – A collection of unpublished reports prepared by British colonial officials, 1930?-1943? – 1 – us Res Libr [960]
INTELLIGENCE REPORTS ON THE WAR IN THE ATLANTIC, 1942-45 / U.S. Department of Navy. Naval Security Group. Command Headquarters – (With printed guide) – 1980 – 1r – 1 – $85.00 – D3257 – us Scholarly Res [355]
INTELLIGENCE SERIES / U.S. Army. Far East Command – 1948-51. 10v – 1 – 207.00 – us L of C Photodup [950]
INTELLIGENCER – (1901-1992.-524r) – Belleville, 1993 – 20r – 1 – cn Preston [971]
INTELLIGENCER – Ames. Iowa. 1877-1913 – 1 – us UMI [071]
INTELLIGENCER / Church Missionary Society – 1849-1927 – 1 – uk Microform Academic [073]
INTELLIGENCER – Doylestown. Pa. 1973- – 1 – us UMI [071]
INTELLIGENCER – Edwardsville. Ill. 1869- – 1 – us UMI [071]
INTELLIGENCER – Lancaster. Pa. 1864-1928 – 1 – us UMI [071]
INTELLIGENCER – Lexington. Va. 1823-1831 – 1 – us UMI [071]
INTELLIGENCER – Wheeling. West Virginia. 1852-1900; 1911-16; 1928- – 1 – us UMI [071]
INTELLIGENCER JOURNAL – Lancaster. Pa. 1841-1845; 1928- – 1 – us UMI [071]
INTELLIGENT MACHINES JOURNAL – v.1-2. 1979-80. Superseded by Infoworld – 1,5,6,9 – us UMI [000]
INTELLIGENTSIIA DLIA KOGO SKAZKA, DLIA KOGO BYL / Gordon, D M – Tashkent: Tip. Shtaba Turk. voen. okruga, 1916- – 1 – CSUX88-B8491 – us Hoover Inst Photo [947]
INTELLIGENTSIIA I REVOLIUTSIIA : SB. STATEI / Pokrovskii, MN et al – M., n.d. 181p – 2mf – 9 – ne IDC [320]
INTELLIGENTSIIA I REVOLIUTSIIA : SBORNIK STATE I / ed by Pokrovskogo et al – Moskva: Dom pechati, [192-?] – 1 – CSUX88-B7662 – us Hoover Inst Photo [947]
INTELLIGENZ-BLATT *see* INTELLIGENZ-BLATT DER FREIEN STADT FRANKFURT
INTELLIGENZBLATT *see* GEMEINNUETZIGES WOCHENBLATT
INTELLIGENZ-BLATT DER FREIEN STADT FRANKFURT – (Cont by: Intelligenz-Blatt, feb 16, 1819. Frankfurter Nachrichten und Intelligenz-Blatt, oct 11, 1910) – Frankfurt/Main. 1918-oct 31, 1933 – 52r – 1 – gw Mikrofilm [072]
INTELLIGENZ-BLATT DER STADT HOF *see* NEUES HOEFER INTELLIGENZ-BLATT
INTELLIGENZ-BLATT FUER DEN BEZIRK DER KOENIGLICHEN REGIERUNG ZU DANZIG – Danzig (Gdansk), Poland. 1844 (incomplete) – 1r – 1 – gw Mikrofilm [943]
INTELLIGENZBLATT FUER DIE OBERAEMTER BIBERACH UND WALDSEE *see* ANZEIGER VOM OBERLAND
INTELLIGENZBLATT FUER DIE PROVINZ OBERHESSEN – (Cont by: Friedberger Intelligenzblatt, 1854. Anzeiger fuer Oberhessen, sep 19, 1866. Oberhessischer Anzeiger, jan 5, 1869) – Friedberg. jan 4, 1834-mar 28, 1943. jul 30, 1949-apr 29, 1950 – 1 – gw Mikrofilm [072]
INTENDANTSKOE DELO – Zhurnal po voprosam voennago i podriadnago khoziastva. 4 v. Spb. 1909-10. BR-2352 2 – 8 – ne IDC [073]
INTENDED ACTIONS AND UNINTENDED CONSEQUENCES / Flew, Anthony – 1fiche (29x) – 9 – 1.00f – at Libertarian Micro [320]
INTENDENCIA DE EXTREMADURA: CIRCULAR / Eizalde, Bernardo – 1821 – 9 – 1.50f – sp Bibl Santa Ana [946]
INTENSIFIED PLANT BREEDING AND SEED PRODUCTION IN POLAND – 1985 – 340p – it F.A.O. [631]
INTENSIVE CARE MEDICINE – v.1-7, 1974-81. Continues European journal of intensive care medicine. ISSN:0342-4642 – 1,5,6,9,13 – 112.00v – us UMI [617]
INTENSIVE CARE NURSING – v1- . 1985- – 1,5,6,9 – us UMI [073]
INTENSIVE MULTIPLE-USE FOREST MANAGEMENT IN KERALA – 1982 – 146p – it F.A.O. [634]
INTENSIVE MULTIPLE-USE FOREST MANAGEMENT IN THE TROPICS : ANALYSIS OF CASE STUDIES FROM INDIA, AFRICA, LATIN AMERICAN AND THE CARIBBEAN – 1985 – 197p – it F.A.O. [634]
INTENSIVE SHEEP PRODUCTION IN THE NEAR EAST – 1983 – 77p – it F.A.O. [636]
INTENTIONS, THE DECAY OF LYING, PEN, PENCIL AND POISON, THE CRITIC AS ARTIST, THE TRUTH OF MASKS / Wilde, Oscar – London: James R. Osgood, McIlvaine and Co., 1891 – 1 roll – 1 – 1-55879-754-8 – uk Libr Preservation [840]
L'INTER *see* L'ACTION UNIVERSITAIRE
INTER ALIA : STATE BAR OF NEVADA – (Title varies: v1-38, No 1 as Nevada State Bar Journal. Superseded by Nevada Lawyer) – v1-57. 1937-1992 – 9 – $435.00 set – us Hein [340]
INTER ALIA *see* NEVADA LAWYER
INTER AVIA – 1946-62 – 1 – 344.00 – us L of C Photodup [629]
INTERACTIVE LEARNING INTERNATIONAL: ILI – v1-. 1984- – 1,5,6,9 – us UMI [370]
Interafrican Committee for Hydraulic Studies. Documentation Center. Ouagadougou, Upper Volta *see*
– CATALOG
– CATALOG OF THE DOCUMENTATION CENTER, INTERAFRICAN COMMITTEE FOR HYDRAULIC STUDIES
INTERAKTIONSHANDLUNGEN IM RUSSISCHUNTERRICHT / Matijaschtschuk, Evelyn – 1992 – 9 – DM98.00 – 3-89349-538-X – gw Hänsel [370]
INTER-ALLIED ARMISTICE COMMISSION, 1918-1920 / Great Britain. War Office – WO 144 – 13r – 1 – us Ross [941]
Interamerican Children's Institute. Montevideo *see*
– BOLETIN
– NOTICIARIO
INTER-AMERICAN DEVELOPMENT BANK ACT. RELEASE NUMBER 1, OCT. 25, 1960 / U.S. Securities and Exchange Commission – 9 – us UMI [336]
INTER-AMERICAN DEVELOPMENT BANK RELEASE – no1. 25 Oct 1960 (all publ) – 1mf – 9 – $1.50 – LLMC 89-005 – us L.L.M.C. [340]
INTERCEPTED JAPANESE MESSAGES : THE DOCUMENTS OF MAGIC, 1938-1945 – (Guide also sold separately: $10.00) – 1980 – 15 rolls – 9 – $1,125.00 – Dist. us Scholarly Res – us L of C Photodup [355]
INTERCEPTED JAPANESE MESSAGES : THE DOCUMENTS OF MAGIC, 1938-1945 / Japan. Ministry of Foreign Affairs – (Includes guide) – 15r – 1 – $1,275.00 – D3254 – us Scholarly Res [950]
INTERCHANGE – v15, no.2-. 1984- – 1,5,6,9 – us UMI [073]
INTERCHANGE ON EDUCATION – v14, no.2-v15, no.1. 1983-84 – 1,5,6,9 – us UMI [073]
INTERCHURCH WORLD MOVEMENT OF NORTH AMERICA – 2v. 1924? – 2 – us A.T.L.A. [073]
INTER-CITY EXPRESS – Oakland. Calif. 1969- – 1 – us UMI [071]
THE INTERCITY EXPRESS – Oakland, CA. 1969-70; 1973-89 – 53r – 1 BC02547 – $2,650.00 – us Library Micro [071]
INTERCOCTA MANUAL : TOWARDS AN INTERNATIONAL ENCYCLOPAEDIA OF SOCIAL SCIENCE TERMS / Riggs, Fred W – 1988 – vi/166p – 9 – 92-3-102556-2 – fr UNESCO [301]
INTERCOLLEGIATE LAW JOURNAL – New York. v1-2. 1891-93 – 1 – $35.00 – us Hein [073]
THE INTERCOLLEGIATE LAW JOURNAL – (Cont by: University Law Review) – New York. v1-2. 1891-93 (all publ) – 7mf – 9 – $10.50 – LLMC 84-493 – us L.L.M.C. [073]
THE INTERCOLLEGIATE LAW JOURNAL *see* THE UNIVERSITY LAW REVIEW
Intercollegiate Prohibition Association *see* PAPERS
INTERCOLLEGIATE SOCIALIST – New York. v. 1-6. Feb 1913-May 1918 – 1 – us NY Public [335]
INTERCOLONIAL COURIER – Tenterfield. Jan 10 1908-Dec 29 1911 – 9 – at Pascoe [072]
THE INTERCOLONIAL JOURNAL OF COMMERCE *see*
– THE TRADE REVIEW
– THE TRADE REVIEW AND INTERCOLONIAL JOURNAL OF COMMERCE
Intercolonial Railway Claims Commission *see* INTERCOLONIAL RAILWAY CLAIMS COMMISSION...: JOHN B. BERTRAND, ET AL., CLAIMANTS..
INTERCOLONIAL RAILWAY CLAIMS COMMISSION...: JOHN B. BERTRAND, ET AL., CLAIMANTS.. / Intercolonial Railway Claims Commission – 1883?. 03440. (Pre-1900 Canadiana) – 9 – cn C.I.H.M. [340]
INTERCOLONIAL TRADE: OUR ONLY SAFEGUARD AGAINST DISUNION / Haliburton, Robert Grant – Ottawa: G. Desbarais, 1868. 05646. (Pre-1900 Canadiana) – 9 – cn C.I.H.M. [971]

INTERCOM – 1- 1959- – 1. ; 5,6. ; 9 – apply; v.12-; v.84- – us UMI [010]

INTER-COUNTRY COMPARISON OF AGRICULTURAL PRODUCTION AGGREGATES – 1986 – 64p – it F.A.O. [338]

INTERDENOMINATIONAL FOREIGN MISSION ASSOCIATION : NEWS – 1950-83 (complete) – 2r – 1 – ATLA S0449 – us A.T.L.A. [073]

THE INTERDENOMINATIONAL HOLINESS BEREAN – Berlin [Kitchener, Ont]: J.M. Kerr, [1890?-19–] – 9 – cn C.I.H.M. [230]

Interdenominational Theological Center *see* JOURNAL

THE INTERDICT : ITS HISTORY AND ITS OPERATION: WITH SPECIAL ATTENTION TO THE TIME OF POPE INNOCENT 3, 1198-1216 / Krehbiehl, Edward B – Washington: American Historical Association, 1909. (Prize essays of the American Historical Association; 1907) – 1mf – us A.T.L.A. [240]

INTERDISCIPLINARY ANALYSIS AND RESEARCH / ed by Chubin, Daryl – Jan 1986. 482p.ISBN: 0-912338-54-7 – 9 – 19.75 – us Lomond [500]

INTERDISCIPLINARY PERSPECTIVES – v. 8-1976- Supersedes yPerspectives – 1,5,6,9 – us UMI [999]

L'INTERDIT *see* L'ACTION UNIVERSITAIRE

INTERECONOMICS – 1985- – 1 – us UMI [330]

INTERESSANTE BLAETTER – Berlin. oct 1, 1915. feb 11, 1916. jul 28-sep 22, 1916 (incomplete) – 1 – gw Mikrofilm [073]

THE INTERESTS OF THE FARMER INDEFINITELY POSTPONED / Bascom, John – 2p – 9 – 1.00f – at Libertarian Micro [335]

L'INTERET CIVIQUE – Quebec, Canada. 4 fev 1930-v1 n6. 15 fev 1930 – 1r – 1 – Can$25.00 – cn Can Microfilming [072]

L'INTERET DE QUEBEC : PUBLIE PAR L'ASSOCIATION CATH. VOYAGEURS DE COMMERCE – Quebec, Canada. 25 oct 1933 – 1r – 1 – Can$25.00 – cn Can Microfilming [380]

L'INTERET GENERAL – Levis, Canada. 24 jul 1930 – 1r – 1 – Can$25.00 – cn Can Microfilming [072]

L'INTERET GENERAL – Port-au-Prince: Imp Aug A Heraux, v1 n1-7. may-jul 1899 – 1 sheet – 9 – us Res Libr [072]

L'INTERET PUBLIC – Trois-Rivieres, Canada. 30 dec 1904-23 jun 1905 – 1r – 1 – Can$35.00 – cn Can Microfilming [072]

INTERFACE : JOURNAL OF NEW MUSIC RESEARCH – Lisse. v1-19. 1972-90 – 5,9 – Dfl2,090.00; Dfl110.00v – ne Swets [780]

INTERFACE : REVUE DE L'ACFAS – Montreal. v5 n1. jan/fev 1984-nov/dec 1992 – 3r – 1 – Can$60.00 – cn Can Microfilming [072]

INTERFACE – v.1 .1978 – 1,5,6,9 – us UMI [073]

INTERFACE AGE – v. 1-. 1975- – 1. – apply; v.3- 1978- 5,6,9 – us UMI [510]

INTERFACE AGE-COMPUTING FOR BUSINESS – 1985-. -m – 1 – us UMI [073]

INTERFACES – v. 1-. 1970- – 1. 1977-.; ; 5,6,9 – us UMI [330]

INTERFERENCIAS / Bayle, Constantino – Madrid: Razon y Fe, 1930 – 1 – sp Bibl Santa Ana [946]

INTERGOVERNMENTAL PERSPECTIVE – (1979-5,6,9) – 1975- – 1 – us UMI [320]

L'INTERIEUR DES COMITES REVOLUTIONNAIRES OU LES ARISTIDES MODERNES / Ducancel – (French Theatre Series). Paris. Barba, an III. 1794 – 9 – fr Hachette [820]

INTERIGHTS, THE INTERNATIONAL CENTRE FOR THE LEGAL PROTECTION OF HUMAN RIGHTS – London. 30 docs. 1984-1991 – 19mf – 9 – ne IDC [340]

INTERIM COLORADO COMPREHENSIVE OUTDOOR RECREATION PLAN, 1974 / Colorado Division of Parks and Outdoor recreation – Denver: The Division, [1974?] – us Res Libr [978]

DAS INTERIM IN WUERTTEMBERG / Bossert, Gustav – Halle: Verein fuer Reformationsgeschichte, 1895. ([Schriften des Vereins fuer Reformationsgeschichte; Bd. 46-47]) – 1mf – us A.T.L.A. [240]

INTERIM ORDERS OF GOVERNMENT ON THE RECOMMENDATIONS OF THE BOMBAY ECONOMIC AND INDUSTRIAL SURVEY COMMITTEE – (Filmed with: Pakistan Press Yearbook) – [s.l: s.n.], 1941 – 1 – us Res Libr [950]

AN INTERIM PROGRAMME OF INDUSTRIAL ESTATES OF INDONESIA / Gaztambide, Juan B – SE-5516 1. 1961 – 9 – ne IDC [338]

INTERIM REPORT 1966 / Hong Kong. Special Committee on Higher Education – Hong Kong, 1966 – 1mf – 9 – DE-180/1 – ne IDC [370]

INTERIM REPORT OF A. G. ETHERINGTON, SHIPPING ECONOMICS/ACCOUNTS AND STATISTICS EXPERT IN INDONESIA / United Nations. Bureau of Technical Assistance Operations – SE 5465 1. v. 2 only. 1960- – 9 – ne IDC [338]

INTERIM REPORT ON EDUCATION IN A RURAL AREA ... : BEING THE EDUCATION SECTION OF THE FACT FINDING REPORTS ON THE ILO PILOT PROJECT AREA / Calcott, D – Ibadan, 1967 – 3mf – 9 – DE-128/1 – ne IDC [370]

INTERIM REPORT ON THE EUROPEAN RECOVERY PROGRAMME / Iceland. Organization for European Economic Cooperation – v. II. Iceland. Long-Term Programme. Paris. Dec 1948. BD-1665 1 – 9 – ne IDC [330]

INTERIM REPORT ON THE EUROPEAN RECOVERY PROGRAMME. VOL. 2. LONG-TERM PROGRAMME OF DENMARK / Organization for European Economic Cooperation – Paris. Dec 1948 – 9 – ne IDC [948]

INTERIM REPORT ON THE EUROPEAN RECOVERY PROGRAMME. VOL. 2. PORTUGUESE LONG-TERM PROGRAMME / Organization for European Economic Cooperation – Paris. Dec 1948. BD-1733 1 – 9 – ne IDC [946]

INTERIM REPORT ON THE EUROPEAN RECOVERY PROGRAMME. VOL. 2. THE AUSTRIAN LONG-TERM PROGRAMME 1952-53 / Organization for European Economic Cooperation – Paris. 1948. BD-1609 1 – 9 – ne IDC [943]

INTERIM REPORT ON THE SIX-DAY WEEK / Singapore. Commission of Inquiry into Education – Singapore, 1962 – 1mf – 9 – DE-261/1 – ne IDC [370]

INTERIM REPORT TO THE CONGRESS OF MICRONESIA : 2ND CONG, 4TH REG SESS, JUL 8, 1968 / Future Political Status Commission [TTPI (U.S.)] – n.p, n.d. – 3mf – 9 – $4.50 – LLMC 82-100F, Title 35 – us L.L.M.C. [323]

INTERIM REVIEW OF DEVELOPMENT IN MALAYA UNDER THE SECOND FIVE-YEAR PLAN / Malaysia – Kuala Lumpur. 1963. BD-585 1 – 9 – ne IDC [338]

INTERIM-REPORT ON THE EUROPEAN RECOVERY PROGRAMME. VOL. 2. LONG-TERM PROGRAMME OF SWEDEN / Organization for European Economic Cooperation – Paris. Dec 1948. BD-1747 1 – 9 – ne IDC [948]

INTERIM-REPORT ON THE EUROPEAN RECOVERY PROGRAMME. VOL. 2. THE LONG-TERM PROGRAMME FOR THE UNITED KINGDOM / United Kingdom. Organization for European Economic Cooperation – Paris. 1948. BD-1775 1 – 9 – ne IDC [338]

THE INTERIOR *see* THE CONTINENT

THE INTERIOR CASTLE = MORADAS : OR, THE MANSIONS / Teresa of Avila, St – (In English. Includes appendix of Spanish correspondence from Saint Teresa) – London: Thomas Baker, 1893 – 1mf – 9 – 0-8370-7027-9 – 1986-1027 – us A.T.L.A. [080]

INTERIOR DECORATOR *see* INTERIORS

INTERIOR DEPARTMENT APPOINTMENT PAPERS : ALASKA, 1871-1907 – 6r – 1 – M1245 – us Nat'l Archives [324]

INTERIOR DEPARTMENT APPOINTMENT PAPERS: / U.S. Department of the Interior. Office of the Secretary – (State of California, 1849-1907. 29 rolls. M732. Printed guide. Idaho, 1862-1907, 17 rolls. M693. Printed guide. Territory of New Mexico, 1850-1907. 18 rolls. M750. Printed guide. Territory of Oregon, 1849-1907. 10 rolls. M814. Printed guide. Territory of Wisconsin, 1849-1907. 9 rolls. M831. Printed guide) – 1 – us Nat'l Archives [324]

INTERIOR DEPARTMENT APPOINTMENT PAPERS: MISSISSIPPI / U.S. Department of the Interior – 1849-1907. 4 rolls. M849 – 1 – us Nat'l Archives [324]

INTERIOR DEPARTMENT APPOINTMENT PAPERS: NEW YORK / U.S. Department of the Interior – 1849-1906. 5 rolls. M1022 – 1 – us Nat'l Archives [324]

INTERIOR DEPARTMENT APPOINTMENT PAPERS: NORTH CAROLINA / U.S. Department of the Interior – 1849-92. 1 roll. M950 – 1 – us Nat'l Archives [324]

INTERIOR DEPARTMENT TERRITORIAL PAPERS: / U.S. Department of the Interior. Office of the Secretary – (Alaska, 1869-1911. 17 rolls. M430. Printed guide. Arizona, 1868-1913. 8 rolls. M429. Printed guide. Colorado, 1861-88. 1 roll. M431. Printed guide. Dakota, 1863-89. 3 rolls. M310. Printed guide. Idaho, 1864-90. 3 rolls. M191. Printed guide. Montana, 1867-89. 2 rolls. M192. Printed guide. New Mexico, 1851-1914. 15 rolls. M364. Printed guide. Utah, 1850-1902. 6 rolls. M428. Printed guide. Washington, 1854-1902. 4 rolls. M189. Printed guide. Wyoming, 1870-90. 6 rolls, M204. Printed guide) – 1 – us Nat'l Archives [324]

INTERIOR LANDSCAPE INDUSTRY – v1-. 1984- – 1,5,6,9 – us UMI [073]

INTERIORS – (Cont by: Contract Interiors. Former titles: Upholsterer (1888-feb 15 1916); Upholsterer and Interior Decorator (mar 1916-dec 1934/jan 1935); Interior Decorator (feb 1935-oct 1940)) – New York, 1888-1916; v57-136 jan 1917-may 1977 1; v128-136 aug 1968-may 1977 5; v135-136 aug 1975-may 1977 9 – 1,5,9 – us UMI [740]

THE INTERLINEAR LITERAL TRANSLATION OF THE GREEK NEW TESTAMENT : WITH THE AUTHORIZED VERSION CONVENIENTLY PRESENTED IN THE MARGINS FOR READY REFERENCE – New York City: Arthur Hinds, [189-?] – 2mf – 9 – 0-8370-9416-X – 1986-3416 – us A.T.L.A. [220]

INTER-LOCAL PROGRESSIVE – (Library has: v.1, no.1 (October 1939)) – New York: Interlocal Progressive Culinary Workers of Greater New York, 1939- – 1 – CSUX89-S125 – us Hoover Inst Photo [331]

INTERLOCKING DIRECTORATES / U.S. Congress. House. Committee on Banking and Currency – Washington, 1913 – 4mf – 9 – $5.00f – us Ross [332]

INTERMARKET – 1956-61 – 2r – 1 – DM150.00 – gw Mikro Press [072]

INTERMARKET – Duesseldorf, West Germany. 1956-61 (incomplete) – 2r – 1 – gw Mikrofilm [073]

INTERMEDIA – v. 1-. 1974- – 1. – apply; v.2-1978- 5,6,9 – us UMI [700]

L'INTERMEDIAIRE DES CHERCHEURS ET CURIEUX – Paris. 1894 – 1 – fr A.C.R.P.P. [073]

INTERMEDIATE LEADER – Oct 1924-61. (Formerly: Intermediate Leader's B.Y.P.U. Quarterly. 1924-39) – 1 – 264.95 – us Baptist [240]

INTERMEDIATE PUPIL, 13-16 YEARS – (Intermediate Teacher, 13-16 Years. 1948. 48.65; 1) – 1948 – 1 – 47.88 – us Baptist [240]

INTERMEDIATE TEACHER, UNIFORM SERIES – Oct 1940-61 – 1 – 231.98 – us Baptist [240]

INTERMEDIATE TEACHER'S AND PUPIL BOOK, YEARS 1-4 – 1928-33 – 1 – 120.61 – us Baptist [240]

INTERMEDIATE WEEKLY – 1929-31 – 1 – 33.25 – us Baptist [240]

INTERMEDIO – Bogota. Columbia. 1956-1957 – 1 – us UMI [072]

INTERMENT RECORD NO. 1-4051 / Highland Cemetery, Geary County, KS – 1871-1930 – 1 – us KS Hist [920]

INTERMEZZO : EINE BUERGERLICHE KOMOEDIE MIT SINFONISCHEN ZWISCHENSPIELEN IN ZWEI AUFZUEGEN / Strauss, Richard – Berlin: Adolph Fuerstner, c1924 – 1r – 1 – us U.W. Library [780]

INTER-MOUNTAIN – Elkins. West Virginia. -w. 1896-1903, 1907-44, 1953- – 1 – us UMI [071]

INTER-MOUNTAIN ADVOCATE – Salt Lake City. Utah. 1895-1897 – 1 – us UMI [071]

INTERMOUNTAIN JEWISH NEWS – Denver. Col. 1935-48. 1963-67 – 1 – us A.J.P.C. [071]

INTERMOUNTAIN LIBERAL *see* NEVADA LIBERAL

INTER-MOUNTAIN NEWS – Burney, CA. 1963; 1966; 1970; 1977; 1979- – 15+ r – 1 – $750.00 ($50.00y) – B02086 – us Library Micro [071]

INTER-MOUNTAIN PRESS – Manhattan. Mont. 1956- – 1 – us UMI [071]

INTERMURAL LAW REVIEW – New York University School of Law. v1-23. 1945-68 (all publ) – 27mf – 9 – $40.50 – LLMC 84-494 – us L.L.M.C. [073]

INTERNAL AUDITOR – v. 6- 1949- – 1. ; 5,6,9 – apply; v.33- – us UMI [380]

INTERNAL EVIDENCES OF THE GENUINENESS OF THE GOSPELS / Norton, Andrews – 1856 – 9 – us A.T.L.A. [240]

INTERNAL REVENUE ACTS OF THE UNITED STATES : REVENUE ACT OF 1954 WITH LEGISLATIVE HISTORIES AND CONGRESSIONAL DOCUMENTS / ed by Reams, Bernard D Jr – v1-11 – 9 – $305.00 set – 0-89941-540-7 – us Hein [340]

INTERNAL REVENUE ACTS OF THE UNITED STATES : REVENUE ACTS OF 1953-1972 WITH LEGISLATIVE HISTORIES, LAWS AND CONGRESSIONAL DOCUMENTS / ed by Reams, Bernard D Jr – 48v. 1953-1972 – 9 – $1,735.00 set – 0-89941-624-1 – us Hein [340]

INTERNAL REVENUE ACTS OF THE UNITED STATES, 1909-1950 : LEGISLATIVE HISTORIES AND ADMINISTRATIVE DOCUMENTS – (With guide and analytical index ISBN: 0-930342-94-1) – 144v – 9 – $4,795.00set – 0-930342-69-0 – LC 78-71405 – us Hein [340]

INTERNAL REVENUE ACTS OF THE UNITED STATES 1950-1951 : LEGISLATIVE HISTORIES, LAWS AND ADMINISTRATIVE DOCUMENTS / U.S. Internal Revenue Service; ed by Reams, Bernard D Jr – v1-7. 1950-51 – 9 – $298.00 set – 0-89941-703-5 – us Hein [340]

INTERNAL REVENUE ASSESSMENT LISTS / U.S. Internal Revenue Service – (Alabama, 1865-66. 6 rolls. M754. Printed guide. Arkansas, 1865-66. 2 rolls. M755. Printed guide. California, 1862-66. 33 rolls. M756. Printed guide. Territory of Colorado, 1862-66. 3 rolls. M757. Printed guide. Connecticut, 1862-66. 23 rolls. M758. Printed guide.. Delaware, 1862-66. 8 rolls. M759. Printed guide. District of Columbia. 1862-66. 8 rolls. M760. Printed guide. Florida, 1865-66. 1 roll. M761. Printed guide. Georgia, 1865-66. 8 rolls. M762. Printed guide. Territory of Idaho, 1865-66. 1 roll. M763. Printed guide. Illinois, 1862-66. 63 rolls. M764. Printed guide. Indiana, 1862-66. 42 rolls. M765. Printed guide. Minnesota, 1862-66. 3 rolls. M774. Missouri 1862-65. 22 rolls. M776. New York and New Jersey, 1862-66. 218 rolls. M603.) – 1 – us Nat'l Archives [324]

INTERNAL REVENUE ASSESSMENT LISTS FOR ALABAMA, 1865-1866 – Districts 1-3. M754-0001 to M754-0006 – 1 – us A.G.L.L. [978]

INTERNAL REVENUE FORMS COLLECTION : BEGINNING THRU 1994 / U.S. Internal Revenue Service. Office of the Chief Counsel. Library – (7 annual suppl to main coll between 1987-1993/94 204mf $306.00. Standing order for future suppl $45.00y. Special form locator, annually updated, $15.00y. LLMC 84-368) – IRS, Office of Chief Counsel Library. Main coll – 1508mf – 9 – $650.00 – LLMC 84-368 – us L.L.M.C. [336]

THE INTERNAL REVENUE RECORD AND CUSTOMS BULLETIN – (Lacking: v41 1895) – New York: Church. v1-40. 1865-94 (all publ) – 60mf – 9 – $270.00 – LLMC 82-927 – us L.L.M.C. [073]

INTERNAL STATISTICS / Sudan. Dept. of Statistics – 6v. in 1. 1962-72. Lacking: 1969. BNE-7614 1 – 9 – ne IDC [310]

THE INTERNATINAL FORUM FOR LOGOTHERAPY – v1-5. 1978-82 – 1 – us UMI [073]

HET INTERNATIONAAL MARITIEM RECHT / Beer Poortugael, J C C den – Breda, 1888 – 9 – 8mf – ILM-1630/1 – ne IDC [327]

INTERNATIONAL – London, UK. 7 Mar 1863-15 Nov 1871 – 1 – uk British Libr Newspaper [072]

INTERNATIONAL – London, UK. Feb-Jul 1863 – 1 – uk British Libr Newspaper [072]

THE INTERNATIONAL – Johannesburg. Republic of South Africa. Sept. 1915-Sept. 1919, Jan. 1923-Sept. 1924 (gaps) – 1 – 35.00r – us Hoover Inst Photo [072]

INTERNATIONAL ABSTRACTS IN OPERATIONS RESEARCH – v1-29. 1961-84 – 1,5,6,13 – sz Elsevier [000]

INTERNATIONAL ABSTRACTS OF BIOLOGICAL SCIENCES – v.1- 1954- – 5,6,9 – us UMI [574]

INTERNATIONAL ABSTRACTS OF BIOLOGICAL SCIENCES *see* CURRENT AWARENESS IN BIOLOGICAL SCIENCES (CABS)

INTERNATIONAL AEROSPACE ABSTRACTS – v. 1-13. 1961-1973 – 1,5,6. 70.00; 1,5,6 – apply; y – us Princeton Micro [629]

INTERNATIONAL AEROSPACE ABSTRACTS: INDEXES – v. 1-13. 1961-1973 – 1,5,6. 70.00; 1,5,6 – apply; y – us Princeton Micro [629]

INTERNATIONAL AFFAIRS – 1955-1973 (1-11); Lacking: 1973 (7,12) – 582mf – 9 – ne IDC [327]

INTERNATIONAL AFFAIRS – (v. 1-8, 20-39. 249.00v; 9. v. 9-19, 40-45. 2413.50v; WDS; 9) – v. 1-45. London. 1922-69 – 9 – $24450.00 – uk Dawson [327]

INTERNATIONAL AFFAIRS – v1-43 1922-1967 – 1,5,6 – us Princeton Micro [327]

International African Institute. London *see*
- CUMULATIVE BIBLIOGRAPHY OF AFRICAN STUDIES

INTERNATIONAL AGRICULTURE SERIES / Minnesota. College of Agriculture. Institute of Agriculture – nos.1-13. 1966-71 – 1,5,6 – us Spaulding [630]

INTERNATIONAL ALERT – London. 17 docs. 1986-1990 – 11mf – 9 – ne IDC [320]

INTERNATIONAL ALLIANCE OF WOMEN *see* JUS SUFFRAGII

L'INTERNATIONAL ANARCHISTE – no. 2-4. Marseille. oct-nov 1886 – 1 – fr A.C.R.P.P. [073]

INTERNATIONAL AND COMPARATIVE LAW QUARTERLY – v1-19. 1952-70.8 reels – 1 – $350.00 – us Trans-Media [340]

INTERNATIONAL ANESTHESIOLOGY CLINICS – v. 1-. 1962- – 1. – apply; v.13- 1975- 5,6,9 – us UMI [617]

INTERNATIONAL ANTIFASCIST SOLIDARITY: AN APPEAL TO THE WOMEN OF AMERICA / Montseny, Frederica – N.Y., 1938? Fiche W 1061. (Blodgett Collection of Spanish Civil War Pamphlets) – 9 – us H.U. College Libr [946]

INTERNATIONAL APPLIED MECHANICS – v2-29. 1966-93 – 1,5 – $150.00v – us UMI [621]

INTERNATIONAL ARBITRATIONS : HISTORY AND DIGEST OF THE INTERNATIONAL ARBITRATIONS TO WHICH THE UNITED STATES HAS BEEN A PARTY / Moore, John Bassett – Washington: GPO. v1-6. 1898 – 64mf – 9 – $96.00 – LLMC 80-912 – us L.L.M.C. [340]

INTERNATIONAL ARBITRATIONS / Moore, John Bassett – 3r – 1 – $100.00 – us Trans-Media [340]

International Archives for the Women's Movement. Amsterdam *see*
- CATALOG OF THE LIBRARY
- CATALOG OF THE LIBRARY OF THE INTERNATIONAL ARCHIVES FOR THE WOMEN'S MOVEMENT

INTERNATIONAL ARCHIVES OF ALLERGY AND IMMUNOLOGY – v48-102. 1975-93 – 1,5,9 – us UMI [616]

INTERNATIONAL ARCHIVES OF OCCUPATIONAL AND ENVIRONMENTAL HEALTH – v. 13-47. 1954-80 – 1,5,9 – 5066.00 – us UMI [073]

INTERNATIONAL ART PRINTER – Owen Sound [Ont]: A.M. Rutherford, [1895?-189- or 19–] – 9 – cn C.I.H.M. [680]

INTERNATIONAL ARTHURIAN SOCIETY BIBLIOGRAPHICAL BULLETIN – Hull. v1-14. 1949-62 – 5,9 – Dfl630.00; Dfl45.00v – ne Swets [073]

International Association for Mathematical Geology *see* JOURNAL

International Association of Bridge, Structural and Ornamental Ironworkers. Local 55 (Toledo, Ohio) *see* RECORDS

International Association of Criminalists. Russian Group *see* ZHURNAL UGOLOVNAGO PRAVA I PROTESSA

International Association of Factory Inspectors *see* PROCEEDINGS

INTERNATIONAL ASSOCIATION OF INDUSTRIAL ACCIDENT BOARDS AND COMMISSION REPORTER – (Also known as: The ABC Reporter. Lacking: 1938 nos 1,4. 1939 no 3. 1954-55) – v1-18. 1937-55 (all publ) – 16mf – 9 – $24.00 – LLMC 84-495 – us L.L.M.C. [073]

International Association of Instructors and Investigators in Poultry Husbandry *see* PROCEEDINGS OF THE MEETINGS FOR THE YEARS 1908, 1909 AND 1910

International Association of Jewish Lawyers and Jurists *see* BULLETIN

International Association of Machinists *see* THE MACHINIST

International Association of Officials of Bureaus of Labor. Factory Inspection and Industrial Commissions *see* PROCEEDINGS

International Association of Pupil Personnel Workers *see* JOURNAL

International Atomic Energy Agency *see*
- RAPPORT DE LA MISSION D'ASSISTANCE PRELIMINAIRE DE L'AGENCE INTERNATIONALE DE L'ENERGIE ATOMIQUE AU MAROC
- REPORT OF THE PRELIMINARY ASSISTANCE MISSION TO SUDAN

International Bank for Reconstruction and Development (World Bank) *see*
- THE ECONOMIC DEVELOPMENT OF JORDAN; REPORT OF A MISSION ORGANIZED BY THE IBRD AT THE REQUEST OF THE GOVERNMENT OF JORDAN
- THE ECONOMIC DEVELOPMENT OF MOROCCO: REPORT OF A MISSION ORGANIZED BY IBRD

INTERNATIONAL BAR JOURNAL – (Superseded by: International Legal Practitioner) – v1-10 1970-79 – 9 – $90.00 set – us Hein [340]

INTERNATIONAL BEHAVIOURAL SCIENTIST – v. 1-. 1969- – 1. – apply; v.10- 1978- 5,6,9 – us UMI [300]

INTERNATIONAL BIBLIOGRAPHY OF TRANSLATIONS = REPERTOIRE INTERNATIONAL DES TRADUCTIONS – (Trilingual edition: English/French/Spanish) – 1992 – 1323p – 9 – 92-3-002773-1 – fr UNESCO [010]

INTERNATIONAL BIBLIOGRAPHY ON CRIME AND DELIQUENCY *see* CRIME AND DELINQUENCY ABSTRACTS

INTERNATIONAL BIMETALLISM: SPEECH...LEGISLATIVE ASSEMBLY OF BRITISH COLUMBIA: JANUARY 24TH, 1894 / Baker, James – 1894?. 03977. (Pre-1900 Canadiana) – 9 – cn C.I.H.M. [336]

INTERNATIONAL BLACKLIST – A left – anarchist directory. 1 fiche (29x) – 9 – 1.00f – at Libertarian Micro [320]

INTERNATIONAL BOOK TRADE IN THE EIGHTEENTH CENTURY : BOOKSELLERS' ACCOUNTS, 1697-1803, FROM THE LUCHTMANS ARCHIVE – 1992 – 346mf – 9 – Dfl3,895.00 set – ne MMF Publ [380]

INTERNATIONAL BOOKBINDER : 1900-1955 / International Brotherhood of Bookbinders – (Coll title: Labor Union Periodicals, Pt 2) – 13r – 1 – $1,755.00 – 1-55655-306-4 – us UPA [680]

THE INTERNATIONAL BRIGADE – Hassocks, 1939? Fiche W963. (Blodgett Collection of Spanish Civil War Pamphlets) – 9 – us H.U. College Libr [946]

International Brotherhood of Bookbinders *see* INTERNATIONAL BOOKBINDER

INTERNATIONAL BULLETIN OF MISSIONARY RESEARCH – v.5-. 1981- – 1,5,6,9 – us UMI [240]

International Bureau of Education *see* DIRECTORY OF EDUCATIONAL DOCUMENTATION AND INFORMATION SERVICES

INTERNATIONAL BUREAU OF EDUCATION IN THE SERVICE OF EDUCATIONAL DEVELOPMENT / Suchodolski, Bogdan et al – 1979 – 152p – 9 – 92-3-101733-0 – fr UNESCO [370]

International Bureau of Fiscal Documentation *see* PUBLIC FINANCE FOR STABILITY AND GROWTH IN THE UNDERDEVELOPED EXPORT ECONOMY: A CASE STUDY OF THE REPUBLIC OF THE SUDAN

INTERNATIONAL BUSINESS LAWYER – International Bar Association. v1-17. 1979-89 – 9 – $300.00 set – us Hein [340]

INTERNATIONAL CANADA – v. 1-. 1970- – 1. – apply; v.9- 1978- – us UMI [360]

International Center for Aquaculture *see*
- ANNUAL REPORT
- AQUACULTURE DEVELOPMENTS IN PERU
- AQUACULTURE SURVEY IN JAPAN
- ECONOMIC ANALYSIS OF THE INLAND FISHERIES PROJECT IN EL SALVADOR
- FISHERIES OF TURKEY
- HONDURAS AQUACULTURE DEVELOPMENT PROJECT
- LAKE IZABAL FISHERIES SURVEY
- LAKE NICARAGUA FISHERIES SURVEY
- A PRELIMINARY SURVEY OF THE FRESHWATER FOOD FISHES OF ECUADOR
- PROGRESS REPORT ON THE DEVELOPMENT OF FISHERIES IN NORTHEAST BRAZIL
- RESEARCH AND DEVELOPMENT SERIES

INTERNATIONAL CENTRE FOR TRADE UNION RIGHTS – Prague, New York. 33 docs. 1988-1990 – 12mf – 9 – ne IDC [320]

INTERNATIONAL CENTRE FOR TRADE UNION RIGHTS – Prague, New York. 35 docs. 1988-1991 – 13mf – 9 – ne IDC [320]

INTERNATIONAL CHRISTIAN PRESS AND INFORMATION SERVICE – 1933-46 (complete) – 3r – 1 – ATLA S0526 – us A.T.L.A. [073]

INTERNATIONAL CLASS STRUGGLE – 1-3 (all publ). 1936-1937 – 2mf – 9 – $35.00 – us UPA [335]

INTERNATIONAL COCOA COUNCIL U.N. COCOA CONFERENCES / United Nations – 1966, 1967, 1972, 1975, 1979-1986 – E/F.21 E.212 F.209 R.80 S.108 – 9 – us U.N. Pubs [320]

INTERNATIONAL CODEN DIRECTORY – 9 – us Chemical [540]

THE INTERNATIONAL COLLECTION / Career Guidance Foundation – Contains over 650 catalogs from 40 countries – 315mf – 9 – $268.00 – us Career [370]

INTERNATIONAL COMMERCE – 1-76. 1940-70 – 1,; 5,6 – apply; v. 75-76. 1969-70. apply – us UMI [380]

INTERNATIONAL COMMERCE – v. 1-75. 1940-1969 – 1 – us Princeton Micro [380]

INTERNATIONAL COMMISSION OF JURISTS – Geneva. 209 docs. 1980-1991 – 146mf – 9 – ne IDC [340]

International Commission on Snow and Ice of the International Assoc. of Hydrological Sciences *see* AVALANCHE ATLAS

INTERNATIONAL COMMISSION ON THE CHRISTIAN APPROACH TO THE JEWS : NEWS SHEET – v2-12: 1932-34 (complete) – 1r – 1 – ATLA S0664C – us A.T.L.A. [073]

INTERNATIONAL COMMITTEE FOR HUMAN RIGHTS IN TAIWAN – The Hague, Vancouver, Seattle. 95 docs. 1980-1991 – 21mf – 9 – ne IDC [320]

International Committee of Coordination and Information to Aid Republican Spain *see*
- INFORMATION SERVICE
- LES OPERATIONS MILITAIRES EN ESPAGNE

INTERNATIONAL COMMUNICATIONS IN HEAT AND MASS TRANSFER – (Formerly: Letters in Heat and Mass Transfer. Elmsford) – v1-1974- – 5,6,9 – us UMI [073]

INTERNATIONAL COMPUTER LAWYER – (Ceased with v3 n1. Merged with: Computer Lawyer) – v1-3. 1993-1995 – 9 – $50.00set – us Hein [340]

INTERNATIONAL CONCILIATION – (Includes c.1: no. 271) – New York [etc.], 1907 – 1 – CSUXADM8409-S – us Hoover Inst Photo [978]

INTERNATIONAL CONCILIATION – v1-568 1907-68 – 1,5,6 – us Princeton Micro [320]

THE INTERNATIONAL CONFERENCE OF THE HAGUE / Ferguson, J F – The Hague, 1899 – 2mf – 1 – ILM-1183/1 – ne IDC [327]

INTERNATIONAL CONFERENCE ON EDUCATION : RECOMMENDATIONS 1934-1977 – 1979 – 430p – 9 – 92-3-101614-8 – fr UNESCO [370]

International Conference on the Peaceful uses of Atomic Energy *see* PROCEEDINGS

International Conference on the Peaceful Uses of Atomic Energy. Geneva. 1955. (First). "Atoms for Peace" *see* PROCEEDINGS

International Conference on Unemployment. First. Paris. 1910 *see* COMPTE RENDU..

International Congress for Progressive Thought. 1904: St. Louis *see* REPORT.

International Congress of Africanists. Addis Ababa *see* PAPERS SUBMITTED TO THE INTERNATIONAL CONGRESS OF AFRICANISTS

International Congress of Celtic Studies. Cardiff, Wales. 2nd, 1963 *see* CELTIC STUDIES IN WALES

International Congress of Charities, Correction, and Philanthropy. Chicago. 1893. Second Section *see* THE CARE OF DEPENDENT, NEGLECTED AND WAYWARD CHILDREN

International Congress of European and Western Ethnology. Stockholm, Sweden. 1951 *see* WORKING PAPERS

International Congress of Folklore *see* PAPERS

INTERNATIONAL CONGRESS ON THE TEACHING OF HUMAN RIGHTS, VIENNA, 12-16 SEPTEMBER 1978 – 1980 – 9 – 92-3-101781-0 – fr UNESCO [370]

INTERNATIONAL CONSERVATIVE INSIGHT – (Ceased v4 no 2 1989) – Vancouver. v1-4. 1986-1989 – 9 – Can$20.00y – cn Micromedia [320]

INTERNATIONAL CONSTRUCTION – (5,6,9 v14-1975-) – v1- 1962- – 1 – us UMI [690]

International Cooperation Administration *see* THE CORN PROJECT IN INDONESIA

INTERNATIONAL CORN RECIPES / Maize Week Exhibition, 1964 – (Prepared by wives of staff members of the U.S. Agency for International Development Mission in Indonesia). SE-10,762 1. 1964? – 9 – ne IDC [640]

International Council on Archives *see* SOURCES DE L'HISTOIRE DE L'AFRIQUE AU SUD DU SAHARA DANS LES ARCHIVES ET BIBLIOTHEQUES FRANCAISES

INTERNATIONAL COURT OF JUSTICE / United Nations – 9 – 2380.00; 1.90f – uk UNIMICRO [340]

UN International Court of Justice *see*
- ACTS AND DOCUMENTS
- BIBLIOGRAPHY OF THE ICJ

INTERNATIONAL COURTS OF ARBITRATION / Balch, T W – Ed 5. Philadelphia, 1914 – 1mf – 9 – ILM-643/1 – ne IDC [340]

INTERNATIONAL COVENANT ON CIVIL AND POLITICAL RIGHTS : 1ST-34TH SESSIONS / United Nations. Commission on Human Rights – 1977-1988 – E.367 F.391 R.145 S.284 – 9 – us U.N. Pubs [320]

INTERNATIONAL CRITICAL COMMENTARY – T. and T. Clark. 39v – 9 – $425.00 – us I.R.C. [220]

THE INTERNATIONAL CRITICAL COMMENTARY ON THE OLD AND NEW TESTAMENTS / Driver, Samuel Rolles et al – 1895-1950. 39v – 9 – $425.00 – us I.R.C. [220]

INTERNATIONAL DAILY NEWS – Houston, TX. 1989 – 30+ r – 1 – $1,500.00 ($300.00y) – H04077 – us Library Micro [071]

INTERNATIONAL DAILY NEWS – Los Angeles, CA. 1983 – 132+ r – 1 – $6,600.00 ($600.00y) – H04047 – us Library Micro [071]

INTERNATIONAL DAILY NEWS – San Francisco, CA. 1989 – 30+ r – 1 – $1,500.00 ($300.00y) – H04070 – us Library Micro [071]

INTERNATIONAL DEFENCE AND AID FUND FOR SOUTHERN AFRICA – Retrospective. 65 docs. 1967-1979 – 52mf – 9 – ne IDC [320]

INTERNATIONAL DEFENCE AND AID FUND FOR SOUTHERN AFRICA (IDAF) – London. 218 docs. 1980-1991 – 142mf – 9 – ne IDC [320]

INTERNATIONAL DEFENSE AND AID FOR SOUTHERN AFRICA-CANADA – 164 docs, 1980-1990 – 18mf – 9 – ne IDC [320]

INTERNATIONAL DIMENSIONS OF HUMAN RIGHTS / ed by Vasak, Karel – (Co-published with Greenwood Press Inc., Westport, Conn.) – rev ed 1982 – 9 – 92-3-101477-3 – fr UNESCO [320]

INTERNATIONAL DIMENSIONS OF HUMANITARIAN LAW – 1989 – xxii/328p – 9 – 92-3-102371-3 – Co-published with the Henry Dunant Institute and Martinus Nijhoff Publishers – fr UNESCO [340]

INTERNATIONAL DIRECTORY OF AGRICULTURAL ENGINEERING INSTITUTIONS – 1983 – 494p – it F.A.O. [060]

INTERNATIONAL DIRECTORY OF FISH INSPECTION AND QUALITY CONTROL INSTITUTES – 1984 – 149p – it F.A.O. [360]

INTERNATIONAL DIRECTORY OF RESEARCH INSTITUTIONS ON HIGHER EDUCATION / European Centre for Higher Education – 2nd rev ed – xv/134p – 9 – 92-3-002516-X – fr UNESCO [370]

INTERNATIONAL DIRECTORY OF YOUTH BODIES – 1990 – 9 – 92-3-002673-5 – Trilingual: English/French/Spanish – fr UNESCO [360]

INTERNATIONAL DOCUMENTATION AND COMMUNICATIONS CENTRE – Rome. 70 docs. 1980-1991 – 37mf – 9 – ne IDC [320]

INTERNATIONAL DYER; TEXTILE PRINTER, BLEACHER AND FINISHER – (v155-. 1976-. 5,6,9) – v. 1-. 1879- – 1 – us UMI [660]

INTERNATIONAL ECONOMIC AND ENERGY STATISTICAL REVIEW / U.S. Central Intelligence Agency – 1980-86 – 129mf – 9 – $160.00 – us Updata [310]
INTERNATIONAL ECONOMIC INDICATORS – (v.5-. 1979- 5,6,9) – v.4-. 1977- – 1 – us UMI [330]
INTERNATIONAL ECONOMIC INDICATORS AND COMPETITIVE TRENDS – v1-2. 1975-76. Continued by: International Economic Indicators – 1 – us UMI [330]
INTERNATIONAL ECONOMIC REVIEW – (v18-. 1977-. 5,6,9) – v. 1-. 1960- – 1 – us UMI [380]
INTERNATIONAL EDUCATION AND THE UNIVERSITY / ed by Calleja, James – 1994 – 262p – 9 – 92-3-102950-9 – Co-publ with Jessica Kingsley/UNESCO Publishing – fr UNESCO [370]
INTERNATIONAL ENTREPRENEURS – v5-6. May 1977-Apr 1978 – 1 – us UMI [073]
International Federation of Infantile and Juvenile Gynecology *see* PEDIATRIC AND ADOLESCENT GYNECOLOGY
INTERNATIONAL FELLOWSHIP OF RECONCILIATION – Alkmaar. 59 docs. 1980-1991 – 31mf – 9 – ne IDC [320]
INTERNATIONAL FICTION REVIEW – Fredericton. v1-21. 1974-94 – 9 – Can$20.00y – cn Micromedia [400]
International Film and Television Council *see* CINEMATOGRAPHIC INSTITUTIONS
INTERNATIONAL FINANCIAL STATISTICS – v. 1-21. 1948-1968 – 1,5,6 – us Princeton Micro [310]
INTERNATIONAL FINANCIAL STATISTICS – (v31-. 1978-. 5,6,9) – 1- 1948- – 1 – us UMI [336]
INTERNATIONAL FISHERMAN AND ALLIED WORKER : 1941-1951 / International Fishermen and Allied Workers of America – (Coll title: Labor Union Periodicals, Pt 3) – 1996 – 1r – 1 – $135.00 – 1-55655-617-9 – us UPA [331]
International Fishermen and Allied Workers of America *see* INTERNATIONAL FISHERMAN AND ALLIED WORKER
INTERNATIONAL FLOW OF TELEVISION PROGRAMMES / Varis, Tapio – 1986 – 62p – 9 – 92-3-102365-9 – fr UNESCO [380]
INTERNATIONAL FLOWS OF SELECTED CULTURAL GOODS – 1986 – 9 – 92-3-102438-8 – fr UNESCO [380]
INTERNATIONAL FLOWS OF SELECTED CULTURAL GOODS 1970-1987 – 1992 – 163P – 9 – 92-3-102792-1 – fr UNESCO [380]
INTERNATIONAL FORUM FOR LOGOTHERAPY – v1-15. 1978-92 (complete) – Inquire – 1 – ATLA S0812 – us A.T.L.A. [073]
International Foundation for Development Alternatives (IFDA), Nyon, Switzerland *see* IFDA THIRD SYSTEM PROJECT PAPERS
INTERNATIONAL FREQUENCY LIST / International Frequency Registration Board (IFRB) – 13th series of editions includes information recorded in the Master International Frequency Register – 9 – Sfr2,022.00 complete series; Sfr337.00 each edition – sz I.T.U. [380]
International Frequency Registration Board (IFRB) *see* INTERNATIONAL FREQUENCY LIST
INTERNATIONAL FRIESIAN STRAIN COMPARISON TRIAL : A WORLD PERSPECTIVE – 1988 – 459p – it F.A.O. [636]
International Fur and Leather Workers' Union of the United States and Canada *see* FUR WORKER
INTERNATIONAL GLOSSARY OF HYDROLOGY – 2nd rev ed 1993 – 413p – 9 – 92-3-002745-6 – Co-published with the World Meteorological Organization (WMO) – fr UNESCO [627]
INTERNATIONAL GROUNDWATER RESOURCES LAW – 1986 – 74p – it F.A.O. [340]
INTERNATIONAL GYMNAST – (See also: Gymnast) – v19-. 1977- – 1,5,6,9 – us UMI [790]
INTERNATIONAL HELSINKI FEDERATION FOR HUMAN RIGHTS – Vienna. 118 docs. 1982-1991 – 60mf – 9 – ne IDC [320]
INTERNATIONAL HERALD / International Working Men's Association – no. 1-81 (all publ). 1872-1873 – 1 reel – 1 – $75.00 – us UPA [335]
INTERNATIONAL HERALD TRIBUNE – Paris. France. 1887-1940; 1944; 1946- – 1 – us UMI [072]
INTERNATIONAL HERALD TRIBUNE – (Yrly reel count varies) – Paris, 1985- – inquire – us Ross [072]
INTERNATIONAL HISTORY OF PAPER AND PAPER MAKING : THE LOEBER COLLECTION OF THE FOUNDATION FOR DUTCH PAPER HISTORY / Loeber, E G – (Available separately. Watermarks. 246mf. Dfl4,920.00 (index only 44mf Dfl350.00); Drawings. 82mf. Dfl1,640.00 (index only 16mf Dfl225.00); Photos. 262mf. Dfl5,240.00 (index only Dfl315.00); Dictionary. 78mf. Dfl1,560) – 668mf – 9 – Dfl12,400.00 – ne MMF Publ [680]
INTERNATIONAL HUMAN RIGHTS LAW GROUP – Washington D.C. 128 docs. 1980-1990 – 59mf – 9 – ne IDC [340]
INTERNATIONAL HUMANIST – 1981-86 (complete) – 1r – 1 – ATLA S0867 – us A.T.L.A. [073]
INTERNATIONAL INDEX TO ART EXHIBITION CATALOGUES, 1895-1991 – 867mf – 9 – Dfl9,995.00 – ne MMF Publ [700]
INTERNATIONAL INDEX TO FILM PERIODICALS – 1972-. Covers over 100 film magazines in more than 20 countries. 3 main categories: General Subjects, Film, and Biography. Includes abstracts. Cumulative updating four times per year plus annual cumulation back to 1987 – 9 – uk FIAF [790]
INTERNATIONAL INDEX TO TELEVISION PERIODICALS – 1979-. Covers over 100 international media journals. 3 main categories: General Subjects, Programmes and TV Films, and Biography. Includes abstracts. Cumulative updating four times a year plus annual cumulation back to 1987 – 9 – uk FIAF [380]
International Institute for the Unification of Private Law *see* UNIDROIT PROCEEDINGS AND PAPERS
International Institute of Social History. Amsterdam *see*
- 72 INVENTORIES TO THE ARCHIVES OF THE IISH
- CHINESE PEOPLE'S MOVEMENT, SPRING 1989
- OWENITE MINUTE BOOKS, 1838-1845
- RUSSIAN EMIGRE JOURNALS 1855-1917

International Institute of Social History (IISH), Amsterdam *see*
- LABOR ISSUES IN INDONESIA, 1979-1995
- THE SARVODAYA MOVEMENT IN INDIA IN THE 1950S

INTERNATIONAL INSTITUTE ON TAX AND BUSINESS PLANNING. NEW YORK UNIVERSITY : DOING BUSINESS IN... – v1-3. 1974-75 – 1,5,6 – $45.00 – us Hein [073]
International Instituut vor Sociale Geschiedenis. Amsterdam *see* ALFABETISCHE CATALOGUS VON DE BOEKEN EN BROCHURES VAN HET INTERNATIONAL INSTITUUT.
INTERNATIONAL INTERACTION – v1- 1973- – 1,5,6,9 – us UMI [320]
INTERNATIONAL INTERACTIONS / ed by Starr, H – 1974 – 1,5,9 – us Gordon [320]
INTERNATIONAL INTRODUCTIONS OF INLAND AQUATIC SPECIES – 1988 – 328p – it F.A.O. [639]
International Irrigation Congress *see* OFFICIAL PROCEEDINGS
INTERNATIONAL JOINT COMMISSION – 446mf – 9 – us UMI [978]
INTERNATIONAL JOINT COMMISSION – (Reports on water quality in the Great Lakes, 1972-1982) – 446mf – 9 – $1180.00 – us UMI [550]
INTERNATIONAL JOURNAL FOR NUMERICAL AND ANALYTICAL METHODS IN GEOMECHANICS – v1- 1977- – 1,5,6,9 – us UMI [550]
INTERNATIONAL JOURNAL FOR NUMERICAL METHODS IN ENGINEERING – v1- 1969- – 1,5,6,9 – us UMI [620]
INTERNATIONAL JOURNAL FOR NUMERICAL METHODS IN FLUIDS – v.1. 1981 – 1,5,6,9 – us UMI [073]
INTERNATIONAL JOURNAL FOR PARASITOLOGY – v1- 1971- – 5,6,9 – us UMI [073]
INTERNATIONAL JOURNAL FOR PHILOSOPHY OF RELIGION – (v11- 1980- 5,6,9) – v1- 1970- – 1 – us UMI [200]
INTERNATIONAL JOURNAL OF ADULT AND YOUTH EDUCATION – v. 1-16. 1949-64 – 1 – us UMI [073]
INTERNATIONAL JOURNAL OF AIR POLLUTION *see* AIR AND WATER POLLUTION
INTERNATIONAL JOURNAL OF AMERICAN LINGUISTICS – Chicago.v1-52.1917-86 – 1,5,6 – us Princeton Micro [400]
INTERNATIONAL JOURNAL OF AMERICAN LINGUISTICS – Native American Texts Series. v. 1-. 1976- – 1,5,6 – us UMI [400]
INTERNATIONAL JOURNAL OF AMERICAN LINGUISTICS. NATIVE AMERICAN TEXT SERIES – Chicago.v1-2. 1976-77 – 1,5,6 – us Princeton Micro [490]
INTERNATIONAL JOURNAL OF ANALYTICAL AND EXPERIMENTAL MODAL ANALYSIS – v1- . 1986- – 1,5,6,9 – us UMI [073]
INTERNATIONAL JOURNAL OF APOCRYPHA – nos 1-51. Mar 1905-Oct 1917 (complete) – 1r – 1 – ATLA B0036 – us A.T.L.A. [073]
INTERNATIONAL JOURNAL OF BEHAVIORAL DEVELOPMENT – v1-7. 1978-84 – 1,5,6,13 – sz Elsevier [073]
INTERNATIONAL JOURNAL OF BEHAVIORAL DEVELOPMENT (IJBD) – Amsterdam: North-Holland. v7 n1-v8 n4. 1984-85 – us Res Libr [150]
INTERNATIONAL JOURNAL OF BEHAVIORIAL GERIATRICS – v1-2. 1982-83 – 1,5,6,9 – us UMI [073]
INTERNATIONAL JOURNAL OF BIOCHEMISTRY – v1- 1970- – 5,6,9 – us UMI [073]
INTERNATIONAL JOURNAL OF BIO-CHROMATOGRAPHY / ed by Dandeu, Jean-Pierre & Kasai, Ken-Ichi – 9,5,1 – us Harwood [540]
INTERNATIONAL JOURNAL OF BIOMEDICAL COMPUTING – v1-15. 1970-84 – 1,5,6,13 – sz Elsevier [073]
INTERNATIONAL JOURNAL OF CANCER – v. 1-14. 1966-74 – 1,5,6 – us Princeton Micro [610]
INTERNATIONAL JOURNAL OF CARDIOLOGY – v1-6. 1981-84 – 1,5,6,13 – sz Elsevier [073]
INTERNATIONAL JOURNAL OF CEMENT COMPOSITES – v1-2 1979-80 – 1,5,6,9 – us UMI [690]
INTERNATIONAL JOURNAL OF CEMENT COMPOSITES AND LIGHTWEIGHT CONCRETE – v3-. 1981- – 1,5,6,9 – us UMI [073]
INTERNATIONAL JOURNAL OF CHEMICAL KINETICS – v. 1-. 1969- – 1,5,6,9 – us UMI [540]
INTERNATIONAL JOURNAL OF CHEMICAL KINETICS – v1-18. 1969-86 – 1,5,6 – us Princeton Micro [073]
INTERNATIONAL JOURNAL OF CHRONOBIOLOGY – 1975- – 1,5,9 – us Gordon [610]
INTERNATIONAL JOURNAL OF CIRCUIT THEORY AND APPLICATIONS – v. 1-. 1973- – 1,5,6,9 – us UMI [621]
INTERNATIONAL JOURNAL OF CLINICAL PHARMACOLOGY RESEARCH – v.1-. 1981- – 1,5,6,9 – us UMI [615]
INTERNATIONAL JOURNAL OF COAL GEOLOGY – v1-4. 1980-84 – 1,5,6,13 – sz Elsevier [550]
INTERNATIONAL JOURNAL OF COMPARATIVE AND APPLIED CRIMINAL JUSTICE – v. 1-. 1977- – 1,5,6,9 – us UMI [340]
INTERNATIONAL JOURNAL OF COMPARATIVE SOCIOLOGY – Leiden. v1-31. 1960-90 – 5,9 – Dfl3,100.00; Dfl100.00v – ne Swets [300]
INTERNATIONAL JOURNAL OF COMPUTATIONAL FLUID DYNAMICS / ed by Hamed, A et al – 9,5,1 – us Gordon [621]
INTERNATIONAL JOURNAL OF COMPUTER MATHEMATICS / ed by Evans, J E – 1965- – 1,5,9 – us Gordon [510]
INTERNATIONAL JOURNAL OF CONTROL – v.1-22. 1965-75 – 9 – 24330.00; 2415.00v – uk Dawson [000]
INTERNATIONAL JOURNAL OF CRUDE DRUG RESEARCH – (v1-12. Dfl60.00v; v13-26. Dfl100.00v; v27-28. Dfl170.00v) – Lisse. v1.28. 1961-90. Cont. as: International Journal of Pharmacognosy – 5,9 – Dfl2,460.00 – ne Swets [615]
INTERNATIONAL JOURNAL OF DERMATOLOGY – v. 1-. 1962- – 1. – apply; v.14- 1975- 5,6,9 – us UMI [616]
INTERNATIONAL JOURNAL OF DEVELOPMENTAL NEUROSCIENCE – v1- 1983- – 5,6,9 – us UMI [073]
INTERNATIONAL JOURNAL OF EARLY CHILDHOOD = REVUE INTERNATIONALE DE L'ENFANCE PRESCOLAIRE; REVISTA INTERNATIONAL DE LA INFANCIA PRE-ESCOLAR – (v12- 1980 5,6,9) – v1- 1969- – 1 – us UMI [305]
INTERNATIONAL JOURNAL OF EATING DISORDERS – v1-. 1981- – 1,5,6,9 – us UMI [073]
INTERNATIONAL JOURNAL OF EDUCATIONAL DEVELOPMENT – v1- 1981- – 5,6,9 – us UMI [073]
INTERNATIONAL JOURNAL OF EDUCATIONAL RESEARCH – (Formerly: Evaluation in Education. International Progress) – v1- 1977- – 5,6,9 – us UMI [073]
INTERNATIONAL JOURNAL OF ELECTRICAL ENGINEERING EDUCATION – (1985-. 5,6,9) – v1-. 1963- – 1 – us UMI [370]
INTERNATIONAL JOURNAL OF ELECTRONICS : THEORETICAL AND EXPERIMENTAL – v1-39 1965-75 – 9 – $24,540.00; $2414.00v – uk Dawson [621]
INTERNATIONAL JOURNAL OF ENERGY RESEARCH – v. 1-. 1977- – 1,5,6,9 – us UMI [621]
INTERNATIONAL JOURNAL OF ENGINEERING SCIENCE – v1- 1963- – 5,6,9 – us UMI [620]
INTERNATIONAL JOURNAL OF ENVIRONMENTAL ANALYTICAL CHEMISTRY / ed by Albaiges, J – 1971- – 1,5,9 – us Gordon [540]
INTERNATIONAL JOURNAL OF ENVIRONMENTAL STUDIES / ed by Rose, J & Pfafflin, J R – 1970- – 1,5,9 – us Gordon [360]
INTERNATIONAL JOURNAL OF ESTUARIAN AND COASTAL LAW *see* INTERNATIONAL JOURNAL OF MARINE AND COASTAL
INTERNATIONAL JOURNAL OF ETHICS – v1-54 1890-1944 – 1 – us Princeton Micro [170]
INTERNATIONAL JOURNAL OF FAMILY COUNSELING – v5- 1977- – 1,5,6,9 – us UMI [306]
INTERNATIONAL JOURNAL OF FAMILY COUNSELING *see* AMERICAN JOURNAL OF FAMILY THERAPY
INTERNATIONAL JOURNAL OF FUSION ENERGY – v1- 1977- – 1,5,6,9 – us UMI [621]
INTERNATIONAL JOURNAL OF GENERAL SYSTEMS / ed by Klir, G J et al – 1974- – 1,5,9 – us Gordon [600]
INTERNATIONAL JOURNAL OF GOVERNMENT AUDITING – v. 1-. 1971- – 1. ; 5,6,9 – apply; v.5- – us UMI [336]
INTERNATIONAL JOURNAL OF GROUP TENSIONS – (v.8 .1978 5,6,9) – v.1. 1971 – 1 – us UMI [073]
INTERNATIONAL JOURNAL OF HEALTH PLANNING & MANAGEMENT – v1-. 1985- – 1,5,6,9 – us UMI [610]
INTERNATIONAL JOURNAL OF HEAT AND FLUID FLOW – v.1-. 1979- – 1,5,6,9 – us UMI [073]
INTERNATIONAL JOURNAL OF HEAT AND MASS TRANSFER – v1- 1960- – 5,6,9 – us UMI [073]
INTERNATIONAL JOURNAL OF HEAT AND MASS TRANSFER – (With International Communications in Heat and Mass Transfer, 24 issues/y. £1,290.00. Back issues of journal available from UMI) – 18 issues/y. v36. 1993 – 9 – £908.00y – uk Elsevier Sci [621]
INTERNATIONAL JOURNAL OF HOSPITALITY MANAGEMENT – v1- 1982- – 5,6,9 – us UMI [640]
INTERNATIONAL JOURNAL OF HYDROGEN ENERGY – v1- 1976- – 5,6,9 – us UMI [621]
INTERNATIONAL JOURNAL OF IMMUNOPHARMACOLOGY – v1- 1979- – 5,6,9 – us UMI [615]
INTERNATIONAL JOURNAL OF IMMUNOTHERAPY – v1-. 1985- – 1,5,6,9 – us UMI [073]
INTERNATIONAL JOURNAL OF IMPACT ENGINEERING – v1- 1983- – 5,6,9 – us UMI [620]
INTERNATIONAL JOURNAL OF INFRARED AND MILLIMETER WAVES – (v5-15 1984-94 $125.00v) – v1-4. 1980-83 – 1,5 – $80.00v – us UMI [530]
INTERNATIONAL JOURNAL OF INSECT MORPHOLOGY AND EMBRYOLOGY – v1- 1972- – 5,6,9 – us UMI [590]
INTERNATIONAL JOURNAL OF INSTITUTIONAL MANAGEMENT IN HIGHER EDUCATION – (v.5-. 1981-. 5,6,9) – v.1-. 1977- – 1 – us UMI [370]

INTERNATIONAL JOURNAL OF INTERCULTURAL RELATIONS – v1- 1977- – 5,6,9 – us UMI [305]

INTERNATIONAL JOURNAL OF INVERTEBRATE REPRODUCTION – v1-7. 1979-84 – 1,5,6,13 – sz Elsevier [073]

INTERNATIONAL JOURNAL OF LAW AND PSYCHIATRY – v1- 1978- – 5,6,9 – us UMI [340]

INTERNATIONAL JOURNAL OF LAW LIBRARIES *see* INTERNATIONAL JOURNAL OF LEGAL INFORMATION

INTERNATIONAL JOURNAL OF LEGAL INFORMATION – (Title varies: v1-9 1973-81 as International Journal of Law Libraries) – v1-23. 1973-95 – 9 – $262.00 set – us Hein [340]

INTERNATIONAL JOURNAL OF LEGAL MEDICINE *see* ZEITSCHRIFT FUER RECHTSMEDIZIN

INTERNATIONAL JOURNAL OF LEPROSY – v.1-33. 1933-65. Superseded by International Journal of Leprosy and other Mycobacterial Diseases – 1 – us UMI [073]

INTERNATIONAL JOURNAL OF LEPROSY AND OTHER MYCOBACTERIAL DISEASES – (v.47-. 1979- 5,6,9) – v.34-. 1966- – 1 – us UMI [616]

INTERNATIONAL JOURNAL OF LIGHTWEIGHT CONCRETE – v1- 1979- – 1,5,6,9 – us UMI [690]

INTERNATIONAL JOURNAL OF MACHINE TOOL DESIGN AND RESEARCH *see* INTERNATIONAL JOURNAL OF MACHINE TOOLS AND MANUFACTURE

INTERNATIONAL JOURNAL OF MACHINE TOOLS AND MANUFACTURE – v1- 1961- – 5,6,9 – us UMI [680]

INTERNATIONAL JOURNAL OF MARINE AND COASTAL – (Title varies: v1-7 1986-92 as International Journal of Estuarian and Coastal Law) – v1-10. 1986-95 – 9 – $392.00 set – us Hein [340]

INTERNATIONAL JOURNAL OF MASS SPECTROMETRY AND ION PHYSICS – v1-60. 1968-84 – 1,5,6,13 – sz Elsevier [073]

INTERNATIONAL JOURNAL OF MECHANICAL ENGINEERING EDUCATION – v. 1-. 1973- – 1. ; 5,6,9 – apply; v.4- – us UMI [370]

INTERNATIONAL JOURNAL OF MECHANICAL SCIENCES – v1- 1960- – 5,6,9 – us UMI [073]

INTERNATIONAL JOURNAL OF MICROELECTRONICS PACKAGING MATERIALS AND TECHNOLOGIES / ed by Moresco, Larry L – 9,5,1 – us Gordon [621]

INTERNATIONAL JOURNAL OF MICROGRAPHICS AND OPTICAL TECHNOLOGY – v1- 1982- – 5,6,9 – us UMI [621]

INTERNATIONAL JOURNAL OF MIDDLE EAST STUDIES – v. 1- 1970- – 1. ; 5,6,9 – apply; v.7- – us UMI [320]

INTERNATIONAL JOURNAL OF MINERAL PROCESSING – v1-13. 1974-84 – 1,5,6,13 – sz Elsevier [622]

INTERNATIONAL JOURNAL OF MINING ENGINEERING – v1- 1983- – 1,5,6,9 – us UMI [622]

INTERNATIONAL JOURNAL OF MULTIPHASE FLOW – v1- 1974- – 5,6,9 – us UMI [073]

INTERNATIONAL JOURNAL OF MUSIC EDUCATION – v1-. 1983- – 1,5,6,9 – us UMI [073]

INTERNATIONAL JOURNAL OF NEURO-PHARMOCOLOGY *see* NEUROPHARMACOLOGY

INTERNATIONAL JOURNAL OF NEUROSCIENCE / ed by Weinstein, S – 1970- – 1,5,9 – us Gordon [610]

INTERNATIONAL JOURNAL OF NONDESTRUCTIVE TESTING – 1969- – 1,5,9 – us Gordon [620]

INTERNATIONAL JOURNAL OF NON-LINEAR MECHANICS – v1- 1966- – 5,6,9 – us UMI [530]

INTERNATIONAL JOURNAL OF NURSING STUDIES – v1- 1964- – 5,6,9 – us UMI [073]

INTERNATIONAL JOURNAL OF OFFENDER THERAPY AND COMPARATIVE CRIMINOLOGY – v. 1-. 1957- – 1. ; 9 – apply; v.18-6; v.19- – us UMI [360]

INTERNATIONAL JOURNAL OF OPINION AND ATTITUDE RESEARCH – v. 1-5. Mexico. 1947-51. – 49mf – 9 – ne IDC [073]

INTERNATIONAL JOURNAL OF ORAL AND MAXILLOFACIAL SURGERY – Copenhagen. v1-15. 1972-86 – 5,9 – Dfl1,800.00; Dfl120.00v – ne Swets [617]

INTERNATIONAL JOURNAL OF ORAL HISTORY – v.1. 1980 – 1,5,6,9 – us UMI [073]

INTERNATIONAL JOURNAL OF ORTHODONTIA *see* AMERICAN JOURNAL OF ORTHODONTICS

INTERNATIONAL JOURNAL OF ORTHODONTIA AND DENTISTRY FOR CHILDREN *see* AMERICAN JOURNAL OF ORTHODONTICS

INTERNATIONAL JOURNAL OF ORTHODONTIA AND ORAL SURGERY *see* – AMERICAN JOURNAL OF ORTHODONTICS

INTERNATIONAL JOURNAL OF ORTHODONTIA, ORAL SURGERY AND RADIOGRAPHY *see* AMERICAN JOURNAL OF ORTHODONTICS

INTERNATIONAL JOURNAL OF ORTHODONTICS – v. 1-15. 1962-77 – 1 – us UMI [073]

INTERNATIONAL JOURNAL OF PARALLEL PROGRAMMING – v1-22. 1972-94 – 1,5 – $80.00v – us UMI [000]

INTERNATIONAL JOURNAL OF PEDIATRIC HEMATOLOGY/ONCOLOGY / ed by Pochedly, Carl – 9,5,1 – us Harwood [618]

INTERNATIONAL JOURNAL OF PEDIATRIC OTORHINOLARYNGOLOGY – v1-8. 1979-84 – 1,5,6,13 – sz Elsevier [617]

INTERNATIONAL JOURNAL OF PHARMACEUTICS – v1-21. 1978-84 – 1,5,6,13 – sz Elsevier [073]

INTERNATIONAL JOURNAL OF PLASTICITY – v1- 1986- – 5,6,9 – us UMI [540]

INTERNATIONAL JOURNAL OF POLITICAL EDUCATION – v1-6. 1977-83 – 1,5,6,13 – sz Elsevier [073]

INTERNATIONAL JOURNAL OF POLYMERIC MATERIALS / ed by Prevorsek, D C – 1971- – 1,5,9 – us Gordon [540]

INTERNATIONAL JOURNAL OF PRESSURE VESSELS AND PIPING – v1-17. 1973-84 – 1,5,6,13 – sz Elsevier [073]

INTERNATIONAL JOURNAL OF PRIMATOLOGY – v1-15. 1980-94 – 1,5 – $65.00v – us UMI [590]

INTERNATIONAL JOURNAL OF PRODUCTION RESEARCH – (v.1-10. 249.00v; 9. v.11-13. 2413.00v; WDS; 9) – v.1-13. 1962-75 – 9 – 24130.00 – uk Dawson [338]

INTERNATIONAL JOURNAL OF PSYCHO-ANALYSIS – (1985-. 5,6,9) – v1-. 1920- – 1 – us UMI [616]

INTERNATIONAL JOURNAL OF PSYCHOANALYTIC PSYCHOTHERAPY – v.1-3.1972-74 – 1 – us UMI [616]

INTERNATIONAL JOURNAL OF PSYCHOLOGY – v14-19. 1979-84 – 1,5,6,13 – sz Elsevier [073]

INTERNATIONAL JOURNAL OF PUBLIC ADMINISTRATION – (1984-. 5,6,9) – v1-. 1979- – 1 – us UMI [073]

INTERNATIONAL JOURNAL OF QUANTUM CHEMISTRY – Quantum Biology Symposium. n. 1-. 1974- – 1. ; 5,6,9 – apply; n.3- – us UMI [540]

INTERNATIONAL JOURNAL OF QUANTUM CHEMISTRY – Quantum Chemistry Symposium. n. 1-. 1967- – 1,5,6,9 – us UMI [540]

INTERNATIONAL JOURNAL OF QUANTUM CHEMISTRY – v. 1-. 1967- – 1,5,6,9 – us UMI [540]

INTERNATIONAL JOURNAL OF RADIATION BIOLOGY – v.1-28. 1958-75 – 9 – 24350.00; 2413.00v – uk Dawson [574]

INTERNATIONAL JOURNAL OF RADIATION ONCOLOGY-BIOLOGY- PHYSICS – v1- 1976- – 5,6,9 – us UMI [616]

THE INTERNATIONAL JOURNAL OF RELIGIOUS EDUCATION – (Title varies) – v1-44. 1924-68 (complete) – 17r – 1 – ATLA S0136 – us A.T.L.A. [073]

INTERNATIONAL JOURNAL OF ROBOTICS RESEARCH – v. 1-. 1982- – 1,5,6,9 – us UMI [600]

INTERNATIONAL JOURNAL OF ROCK MECHANICS AND MINING SCIENCES AND GEOMECHANICS ABSTRACTS – v1- 1964- – 5,6,9 – us UMI [550]

INTERNATIONAL JOURNAL OF SATELLITE COMMUNICATIONS – v1-. 1983- – 1,5,6,9 – us UMI [621]

INTERNATIONAL JOURNAL OF SOCIOMETRY *see* HANDBOOK OF INTERNATIONAL SOCIOMETRY

INTERNATIONAL JOURNAL OF SOCIOMETRY AND SOCIATRY *see* HANDBOOK OF INTERNATIONAL SOCIOMETRY

INTERNATIONAL JOURNAL OF SOLIDS AND STRUCTURES – (Back issues of journal available from UMI) – 24 issues/y. v30. 1993 – 9 – £1,059.00y – uk Elsevier Sci [530]

INTERNATIONAL JOURNAL OF SOLIDS AND STRUCTURES – v1- 1965- – 5,6,9 – us UMI [073]

INTERNATIONAL JOURNAL OF SPECIAL EDUCATION – Vancouver. v1-9. 1986-94 – 9 – Can$20.00y – cn Micromedia [370]

INTERNATIONAL JOURNAL OF SPORT PSYCHOLOGY – Rome. v1-11. 1970-80 – 5,9 – Dfl880.00; Dfl80.00V – ne Swets [150]

INTERNATIONAL JOURNAL OF SULFER CHEMISTRY *see* PHOSPHORUS AND SULFER AND THE RELATED ELEMENTS

INTERNATIONAL JOURNAL OF SYSTEMATIC BACTERIOLOGY – v1-25. 1951-75.Continues: International Bulletin of Bacteriological Nomenclature and Taxonomy – 1,5,6 – us Princeton Micro [576]

INTERNATIONAL JOURNAL OF SYSTEMS SCIENCE – v.1-6. 1970-75 – 9 – 24110.00; 2418.00v – uk Dawson [000]

INTERNATIONAL JOURNAL OF THE ADDICTIONS – (v.16-. 1981-. 5,6,9) – v.1-. 1966- – 1 – us UMI [360]

INTERNATIONAL JOURNAL OF THE ECONOMICS OF BUSINESS – 1995, Vol 2 – £114.00 – uk Carfax [330]

INTERNATIONAL JOURNAL OF THE LEGAL PROFESSION – 1995, Vol 2 – £179.00 – uk Carfax [340]

INTERNATIONAL JOURNAL OF THEORETICAL PHYSICS – (v15-33 1976-94 $125.00v) – v1-14. 1968-75 – 1,5 – $60.00v – us UMI [530]

INTERNATIONAL JOURNAL OF THERMOPHYSICS – v1-15. 1980-94 – 1,5 – $80.00v – us UMI [530]

INTERNATIONAL JOURNAL OF TISSUE REACTIONS – v.1. 1979 – 1,5,6,9 – us UMI [616]

INTERNATIONAL JOURNAL OF WATER RESOURCES DEVELOPMENT – 1995, Vol 11 – £225.00 – uk Carfax [333]

INTERNATIONAL JOURNAL OF WIRELESS INFORMATION NETWORKS – v1. 1994 – $65.00v – us UMI [621]

INTERNATIONAL JOURNAL OF WOMEN'S STUDIES – v1- 1978- – 1,5,6,9 – us UMI [305]

INTERNATIONAL JURIDICAL ASSOCIATION BULLETIN – v1-10. 1932-42 (all publ) – 18mf – 9 – $27.00 – LLMC 84-496 – us L.L.M.C. [073]

International Labour Defense *see* IT'S HAPPENING IN SPAIN, TOLD BY THE VICTIMS THEMSELVES

INTERNATIONAL LABOUR DOCUMENTATION : CUMULATIVE CATALOGUE OF THE ILO LIBRARY / International Labour Organisation – (1978-90 Sfr780.00 ISBN: 92-2-108075-7) – 17 – sz I.L.O. [331]

INTERNATIONAL LABOUR DOCUMENTATION: CUMULATIVE EDITION, 1965-69 / International Labour Office. Geneva. Central Library – 1970.-112,000 entries 16 reels.-ISBN: 0-8161-1275-4 – 1 – $585.00 – uk Hall [331]

International Labour Office. Geneva. Central Library *see* INTERNATIONAL LABOUR DOCUMENTATION: CUMULATIVE EDITION, 1965-69

International Labour Office. International Social Security Association *see* SOCIAL INSURANCE IN THE KINGDOM OF LIBYA

International Labour Office. Library *see* CATALOGUE SYSTEMATIQUE DES PUBLICATIONS SUR LA RUSSIE (1917-25) SE TROUVANT DANS LA BIBLIOTHEQUE DU BUREAU INTERNATIONAL DU TRAVAIL

International Labour Organisation *see*
- BULLETIN D'INFORMATIONS SOCIALES 1974-1992
- CO-OPERATIVE INFORMATION
- EMPLOYMENT AND INCOME POLICIES FOR IRAN
- EQUIPMENT PLANNING GUIDES FOR VOCATIONAL AND TECHNICAL TRAINING AND EDUCATION PROGRAMMES
- ILO PUBLICATIONS AND DOCUMENTS
- INFORMATIONS COOPERATIVES 1928-1968
- INTERNATIONAL LABOUR DOCUMENTATION
- INTERNATIONAL LABOUR REVIEW
- LEGISLACION SOCIAL DE AMERICA LATINA.
- MINUTES OF THE GOVERNING BODY
- MULTINATIONAL ENTERPRISES PROGRAMME
- OFFICIAL BULLETIN
- PROJECT REPORT CONCERNING WORKERS EDUCATION IN LIBYA
- RAPPORT AU GOUVERNEMENT DE LA REPUBLIQUE ALGERIENNE SUR LA SITUATION ET LE DEVELOPPEMENT DU MOUVEMENT COOPERATIF
- RAPPORT AU GOUVERNEMENT DE LA REPUBLIQUE ALGERIENNE SUR LE DEVELOPPEMENT DU MOUVEMENT COOPERATIF RESEAU COOPERATIF D'APPROVISIONNEMENT DANS LE SECTEUR AGRICOLE
- RAPPORT AU GOUVERNEMENT DE LA REPUBLIQUE ALGERIENNE SUR LES STATISTIQUES DU TRAVAIL
- RAPPORT AU GOUVERNEMENT DE LA REPUBLIQUE LIBANAISE SUR LE DEVELOPPEMENT DE L'ARTISANAT
- RAPPORT AU GOUVERNEMENT DE LA REPUBLIQUE LIBANAISE SUR LE DEVELOPPEMENT DU MOUVEMENT COOPERATIF ET LE DEVELOPPEMENT RURAL
- RAPPORT AU GOUVERNEMENT DE LA REPUBLIQUE LIBANAISE SUR L'ORGANISATION ADMINISTRATIVE ET LA MECANISATION DE LA CAISSE NATIONALE DE SECURITE SOCIALE
- RAPPORT AU GOUVERNEMENT DE L'ALGERIE SUR LA READAPTION PROFESSIONNELLE ET L'EMPLOI DES INVALIDES
- RAPPORT AU GOUVERNEMENT DE L'ALGERIE SUR L'ADMINISTRATION DU TRAVAIL
- RAPPORT AU GOUVERNEMENT DE L'ALGERIE SUR L'ORGANISATION ET L'EQUIPEMENT DU CENTRE DU TRAVAIL DU CUIR DE DJIDJELLI
- RAPPORT AU GOUVERNEMENT DU LIBAN SUR UNE CONTRIBUTION DU B.I.T. A UN PROGRAMME DE FORMATION DES AGENTS DE L'ADMINISTRATION DU TRAVAIL FORMATION EN MATIERE D'INSPECTION DU TRAVAIL (JANVIER-JUILLET 1964)
- RAPPORT AU GOUVERNEMENT DU MAROC SUR LA SECURITE SOCIALE
- RAPPORT AU GOUVERNEMENT DU ROYAUME DU MAROC SUR LA FORMATION, L'EDUCATION ET LA VULGARISATION COOPERATIVES DANS LE SECTEUR ARTISANAL
- RAPPORT AU GOUVERNEMENT DU ROYAUME DU MAROC SUR LA FORMATION PROFESSIONNELLE RURALE
- RAPPORT AU GOUVERNEMENT DU ROYAUME DU MAROC SUR LA MECANISATION ET L'AUTOMATION AU SIEN DE LA CAISSE NATIONALE DE SECURITE SOCIALE
- RAPPORT AU GOUVERNEMENT DU ROYAUME DU MAROC SUR LA SITUATION ET LE DEVELOPPEMENT DU MOUVEMENT COOPERATIF
- RAPPORT AU GOUVERNEMENT DU ROYAUME DU MAROC SUR LES POSSIBILITES D'AMELIORATION DE L'ORGANISATION ADMINISTRATIVE DE LA CAISSE NATIONALE DE SECURITE SOCIALE
- RAPPORT AU GOUVERNEMENT DU ROYAUME DU MAROC SUR L'ORGANISATION ADMINISTRATIVE DE LA CAISSE NATIONALE DE SECURITE SOCIALE
- RAPPORT AU GOUVERNEMENT DU ROYAUME DU MAROC SUR L'ORIENTATION ET LA SELECTION PROFESSIONELLES
- RAPPORT SUR L'EDUCATION OUVRIERE EN REPUBLIQUE ALGERIENNE
- RAPPORT SUR L'EDUCATION OUVRIERE EN REPUBLIQUE ALGERIENNE DEMOCRATIQUE ET POPULAIRE
- REPORT ON AN ILO CONTRIBUTION TO TRAINING PROGRAMMES FOR LABOUR ADMINISTRATION OFFICIALS IN IRAQ, JORDAN, LIBYA AND SYRIA
- REPORT ON THE FAMILY BUDGET SAMPLE SURVEY, 1958-1959, AND ON NEW CONSUMER PRICE INDICES IN THE SOUTHERN REGION OF THE UNITED ARAB REPUBLIC (EGYPT)
- REPORT ON WORKERS' EDUCATION IN LIBYA
- REPORT TO THE GOVERNMENT OF JORDAN ON SURVEY OF SMALL-SCALE AND HANDICRAFT INDUSTRIES
- REPORT TO THE GOVERNMENT OF JORDAN ON THE FURTHER DEVELOPMENT OF THE MANPOWER ASSESSMENT PROGRAM
- REPORT TO THE GOVERNMENT OF JORDAN ON THE ORGANISATION OF A MANPOWER ASSESSMENT AND PLANNING PROGRAM
- REPORT TO THE GOVERNMENT OF LIBYA ON CO-OPERATIVE EDUCATION AND

TRAINING
- REPORT TO THE GOVERNMENT OF LIBYA ON SOCIAL INSURANCE
- REPORT TO THE GOVERNMENT OF LIBYA ON SOCIAL SECURITY
- REPORT TO THE GOVERNMENT OF LIBYA ON THE ADMINISTRATION OF THE NATIONAL SOCIAL INSURANCE INSTITUTION AND THE INVESTMENTS OF ITS FUNDS
- REPORT TO THE GOVERNMENT OF LIBYA ON THE BRINGING INTO OPERATION OF THE SOCIAL INSURANCE LAW NR. 53 OF 1957
- REPORT TO THE GOVERNMENT OF LIBYA ON THE ROLE OF HANDICRAFTS IN A RAPIDLY DEVELOPING ECONOMY
- REPORT TO THE GOVERNMENT OF LIBYA ON VOCATIONAL TRAINING
- REPORTS AND RECORDS OF PROCEEDINGS OF THE INTERNATIONAL LABOUR CONFERENCE
- REVUE INTERNATIONALE DU TRAVAIL 1921-1977
- SERIE LEGISLATIVE 1920-1965
- SOCIAL AND LABOUR BULLETIN
- WEP RESEARCH WORKING PAPERS
- WORKER'S MANAGEMENT IN ALGERIA
- YEAR BOOK OF LABOUR STATISTICS 1935-36 TO 1995
- YEARBOOK OF LABOUR STATISTICS

INTERNATIONAL LABOUR REVIEW – 1- 1921- – 1. ; 5,6. ; 9 – apply; v.97-; v.113- – us UMI [650]

INTERNATIONAL LABOUR REVIEW / International Labour Organisation – Geneva. 1965 (Apr.) Social Security and ILO Technical Cooperation in Libya. BNE-1406 1 – 9 – ne IDC [331]

INTERNATIONAL LABOUR REVIEW – v. 1-112. 1921-75 – 1,5,6 – us Princeton Micro [380]

International Ladies Garment Workers' Union *see*
- GERECHTIGKEIT
- GIUSTIZIA
- JUSTICE
- DER YUNION ARBEITER

INTERNATIONAL LADIES GARMENT WORKERS UNION, LOCAL 48, ITALIAN CLOAK, SUIT AND SKIRT MAKERS' UNION – New York, NY, 1920-1965 – 5r – 1 – us I.H.R.C. [331]

INTERNATIONAL LAW : ACHIEVEMENT AND PROSPECTS / Bedjaoui, Mohammed – 1992 – 1244p – 9 – 92-3-102716-6 – Co-published with Martinus Nijhoff, Netherlands – fr UNESCO [340]

INTERNATIONAL LAW / ed by Butler, W E – (Coll includes selected titles on public & private international law from the catalogue & bibliography of international law compiled & edited by the Marquis de Olivart & from other major reference aids. The project includes all consequential titles in whatever language: bibliographies, treaty colls, textbks, treatises & monographs wh are rare, significant or unobtainable. Titles are also listed individually and can be purchased separately) – 3,284 titles – 9 – ne IDC [327]

INTERNATIONAL LAW *see*
- L'ACTION DIRECTE EXERCEE PAR LA VICTIME D'UN ACCIDENT ...
- ANALYSIS OF FOOTE'S ...
- ARREDONDO'S HISTORICAL PROOF OF SPAIN'S TITLE TO GEORGIA
- ARS BELLI ET PACIS
- DIE AUFGABE DES RICHTERS ...
- DER AUSLAENDER VOR DEM STANDESAMT
- LA BELGIQUE ET L'ARBITRAGE OBLIGATOIRE A LA DEUXIEME CONFERENCE DE LA PAIX
- DER BESTAND DER FREIEN STADT DANZIG ...
- DAS BEUTERECHT ...
- DIE BEWAFFNETE NEUTRALITAET 1780-1783 ...
- THE BIBLIOGRAPHY OF INTERNATIONAL LAW AND ...
- EL BOLETIN DIPLOMATICO
- THE BOOK OF PEACE: ...
- LA BOUSSOLE MORALE ET POLITIQUE DES HOMMES, ...
- HET BUITENLANDSCH STRAFVONNIS
- THE BUREAU OF NATURALIZATION...
- IL CANALE DI SUEZ
- CATALOGUE DE LA BIBLIOTHEQUE DU MINISTERE DES AFFAIRES ETRANGERES
- CATALOGUE OF THE WORKS RELATIVE TO THE LAW OF NATIONS AND DIPLOMACY IN THE LIBRARY OF THE DEPARTMENT OF STATE
- CATALOGUE OF WORKS RELATING TO THE LAW OF NATIONS AND DIPLOMACY IN THE LIBRARY OF THE DEPARTMENT OF STATE OF THE UNITED STATES
- LA CESSAZIONE DEL MANDATO INTERNAZIONALE
- LE CODE DE L'AIR; ...
- COLUMBIA AND THE UNITED STATES
- LES COMMISSIONS ...
- COMPENDIO ... DEL DERECCHO DE GENTES NATURAL, ...
- LA CONFERENCIA INTERNACIONAL DE DERECHO MARITIMO DE BRUSELAS – 1922
- DES CONFLITS DE LOIS...DU TESTAMENT SOUS-SEING PRIVE
- CONNAISSEMENTS ET REGLES DE LA HAYE
- CORRESPONDANCE DIPLOMATIQUE...
- DE ARMIS ILLICITIS
- DE CAPTIVIS, ET POSTLIMINIO REVERSIS
- DE FOEDERUM JURE: ...
- DE JURE SOCIETATIS ARMORUM ...
- DE LA CONDITION JURIDIQUE DES SOCIETES ETRANGERES EN FRANCE ...
- DE LA JUSTICE ...
- DE LA PROCEDURE SUIVIE ...
- DE LA PROPRIETE PRIVEE ...
- DE L'APPLICATION DU ... ENTRE LA FRANCE ET LA SARDAIGNE ...
- DE L'ASILE ACCORDE AUX VAISSEAUX DE GUERRE ...
- DE L'EXTRADITION
- DE L'ORIGINE ET DES FONCTIONS DES CONSULS
- DE L'UNIFICATION...
- DE L'UNIFICATION DU DROIT RELATIF A LA LETTRE DE CHANGE ET AU BILLET A ORDRE
- DE REBUS INTER IOANNEM ET...
- DEL FORO COMPETENTE PER LE AZIONI SUCCESSORIE ...
- DELINEATIO IURIS DIVINI, ...
- DERECHO INTERNACIONAL MARITIMO
- DEVLETLER HUSUSI HUKUKU
- DIRITTO INTERNAZIONALE E ...
- LE DIVORCE ET LA SEPARATION DE CORPS ...
- LE DOMICILE DES ETRANGERS EN FRANCE
- LE DROIT DES ETRANGERS A LA PROPRIETE COMMERCIALE
- LE DROIT INTERNATIONAL ...
- LE DROIT INTERNATIONAL DE LA NAUFRAGE DU "TITANIC"
- LE DROIT INTERNATIONAL PUBLIC MARITIME ...
- DROIT ROMAIN: DE L'ACTION DE DOL ...
- DROIT ROMAIN: DETERMINATION DES ELEMENTS DU LITIGE ...
- DU BORNAGE EN DROIT ROMAIN
- DU DROIT DE LA GUERRE SUR TERRE ...
- DUTCH INTERNATIONAL LAW...
- DIE EHELICHEN GUETERVERHAELTNISSE DER AUSLAENDER, ...
- EINFUEHRUNG IN DAS ANGEWANDTE VOELKERRECHT
- EINSEITIGE ABHAENGIGKEITSVERHAELT-NISSE ...
- ENGLISH LAW AND PRACTICE RELATING TO ESTATES OF PERSONS DYING DOMICILED ABROAD...
- L'ESCAUT ET LA NEUTRALITE PERMANENTE DE LA BELGIQUE...
- L'ESCAUT FLEUVE INTERNATIONAL ...
- L'ETAT ET LES COMPAGNIES ...
- ETUDE SUR LA NATIONALITE DE LA FEMME ETRANGERE QUI EPOUSE UN SUJET OTTOMAN
- ETUDE SUR L'ACQUISITION DU DROIT DE CITE A ROME ...
- FOREIGN AND HOME LAW
- FORMULAIRE DES CONSULATS
- FRANCE ET ANGLETERRE...
- DIE FRANZOESISCHEN MANDATSGEBIETE KAMERUN UND TOGO
- THE FRENCH LAW OF MARRIAGE...
- THE FRENCH LAW OF MARRIAGE, MARRIAGE CONTRACTS AND DIVORCE ...
- DIE FRIEDENSFAHRT DEUTSCHER KIRCHENMAENNER NACH ENGLAND
- FUERZA EXTRATERRITORIAL DE LAS LEYES SUCESORIAS
- GESPRAECH UND DISCURSEN ...
- GREAT BRITAIN AND THE PANAMA-CANAL
- GRUNDRISS DES ... SEERECHTS
- GRUND-SAESSE DES VOELCKER-RECHTS...
- LES GUERRES D'IDIOME ET DE NATIONALITE
- DE HAGUE RULES IN DE BRUSSELSCHE CONVENTIE 1924
- HALBSOUVERAENITAET
- HANDBOOK OF TREATIES, ... COMMERCE AND NAVIGATION BETWEEN GREAT BRITAIN AND FOREIGN POWERS, ... 1907
- HANDBUCH DER INTERNATIONALEN NACHLASSBEHANDLUNG ...
- EL HISPANO-AMERICANISMO
- HISTOIRE DES GUERRES ... TRAITE DE WESTPHALIE, ...
- HISTORIAM NOVARUM LEGUM DE FLUMINUM COMMUNIUM NAVIGATIONE
- HISTORICO-IURIDICA DE MODERNO USU CONSTITUTIONIS PACIS PUBLICAE ...
- HUGO DE GROOT EN ZIJN RECHTSPHILOSOPHIE
- HUGO GROTIUS: VON DER FREIHEIT DES MEERES
- HUWELIJKEN VAN NEDERLANDERS IN HET BUITENLAND...
- ICONOGRAPHIE VAN HUGO GROTIUS
- INDIAN TREATIES AND SURRENDERS
- DE INHOUD DER OVEREENKOMSTEN IN HET INTERNATIONAAL PRIVAATRECHT
- HET INTERNATIONAAL MARITIEM RECHT
- INTERNATIONAL LAW AND AUTOCRACY
- INTERNATIONAL LAW AND DIPLOMACY OF ...
- INTERNATIONALE WECHSELPRAXIS
- DAS INTERNATIONALE WECHSELRECHT OESTERREICHS
- INTERNATIONALES EHE- UND KINDSCHAFTSRECHT
- L'INTERNATIONALISATION DES CAPITAUX...
- DIE INTERNATIONALISIERUNG DER ELBE
- LA JUSTICE PENALE INTERNATIONALE
- KATECHISMUS DES VOELKERRECHTS
- THE LAW OF DOMICILE IN ITS RELATION TO SUCCESSION ...
THE LAW OF NATIONS, INVESTIGATED...
- THE LAW OF WAR...
- THE LEAGUE ON TRIAL
- LIMITATION OF SHIPOWNER'S LIABILITY AND ...
- LIMITES ENTRE LAS REPUBLICAS DEL ECUADOR Y DEL PERU
- DIE LOESING VON OESTERREICHISCHEN, ... EHEN IN UNGARN
- LES LOIS DE LA GUERRE ET LES DEUX CONFERENCES DE LA HAYE (1899-1907)
- LE MANDAT SUR LA PALESTINE
- THE MANDATES SYSTEM
- LES MANDATS INTERNATIONAUX
- MANUEL DE DROIT ...
- MANUEL ELEMENTAIRE ...
- DES MARCHES A TERME SUR DEVISES ETRANGERES
- MODERN SPECIFIC SETTLEMENTS...
- DAS MODERNE KRIEGSRECHT ...
- DAS MODERNE VOELKERRECHT ...
- THE MONROE MISSION TO FRANCE 1794-96
- DIE NACHTEILE IM VOELKERRECHT
- LA NACIONALIDAD Y EL DOMICILIO
- DIE NATIONALITAET DER HANDELSGESELLSCHAFTEN WAEHREND DES KRIEGES.
- LA NATIONALITE DES SOCIETES EN TUNISIE
- LA NATIONALITE DU SLESVIG
- DENATIONALITEIT VAN DE VEREENIGING ...
- LA NATURALISATION
- NEDERLANDSCH OF BELGISCH?
- NEUTRAL RIGHTS...
- LA NEUTRALITE SUR L'ESCAUT
- THE NEUTRALITY OF...
- NOTES ON THE HAGUE RULES, 1921
- LA NOUVELLE VOIE MARITIME LE CANAL DE PANAMA
- NOZIONI ELEMENTARI DI DIRITTO PENALE INTERNAZIONALE E DELLE PROCEDURE AD ESSO ATTINENTI
- LE NUOVE LEGGI SUL MATRIMONIO ...
- OUTLINE OF INTERNATIONAL LAW
- L'OUVERTURE DU CANAL DE PANAMA ...
- PALESTINE MANDATE ...
- DER PANAMAKANAL...
- THE PEACE CONFERENCE...
- POLITISCHE BETRACHTUNGEN UEBER DIE GROSSEN VORTHEILE
- LA POLIZZA DI CARICO ...
- POUR LA SOCIETE DES NATIONS
- PRINCIPIOS ...
- DAS PROBLEM DER MEERESFREIHEIT...
- PROPRIETA TERRITORIALE
- LA QUESTION DES NEUTRES...
- QUESTIONI DI DIRITTO INTERNAZIONALE ...
- DAS RECHT DER STAATSANGEHOERIGKEIT ... SEIT DEM JAHRE 1870
- DIE RECHTFERTIGUNG DES VOELKERRECHTS AUS DEM STAATSWILLEN
- DIE RECHTLICHE NATUR DER NATURALISATION
- DER RECHTSERWERB VOM NICHTBERECHTIGTEN
- DIE RECHTSVERHAELTNISSE UND DER RECHTSSCHUTZ DES AUSLANDSDEUTSCHTUMS, ...
- ROBERT VON MOHL
- A SMALL COLLECTION OF VALUABLE TRACTS...HERRING FISHERY...
- LES SOCIETES ETRANGERES EN FRANCE ...
- THE SOVEREIGNTY OF THE BRITISH SEAS
- DAS STAATSINTERESSE ALS GRUNDLAGE DES VOELKERRECHTS
- STAATSVERTRAEGE ...
- LE STATUT INTERNATIONAL DU CHEQUE
- DIE STRAFBARKEIT EINER IN DEN KONSULARGEBIETEN BEGANGENEN BIGAMIE ...
- DER STREIT UM DIE FREIHEIT DER MEERE ...
- STUDIES IN STATECRAFT
- LE SUCCESSIONI SECONDO IL DIRITTO INTERNAZIONALE PRIVATO ITALIANO
- DER SUEZKANAL
- SUL PROGRETTO DI UNA LEGGE INTERNAZIONALE SUL DIRITTO CAMBIARIO
- A TENTATIVE LIST OF TREATY COLLECTIONS
- TENUITVOERLEGGING VAN BUITENLANDSCHE ARBITRALE VONNISSEN
- THEORIE DES VOELKERRECHTS
- THE THEORY OF THE STATE
- THREE TRACTS RELATIVE TO SPANISH AND PORTUGUEZE AFFAIRS ...
- TRAITE DE LA PERTE ET DE LA RESTITUTION DES TITRES AU PORTEUR ...
- TRAITE ... DE L'EXTRADITION ...
- LES TRAITES DE COMMERCE ...
- LES TRAITES PASSES LE 28 MAI 1902 ...
- TREATIES AND CORRESPONDENCE,...TO BOTH HOUSES OF PARLIAMENT,...
- TREATIES BETWEEN THE UNITED STATES OF AMERICA AND CHINA, JAPAN, LEWCHEW AND SIAM,...
- UEBER DIE COUPONSPROCESSE ...
- UNIFICATION DEL DERECHO COMERCIAL
- L'UNIFICATION DU DROIT DU CHANGE
- L'URTO DI NAVI ...
- VEREINBARUNGEN UEBER DEN GERICHTSSTAND IM INTERNATIONALEN RECHTSVERKEHR
- DIE VERJAEHRUNGSEINREDE...
- VERSO L'UNIFICAZIONE DEL DIRITTO DEL MARE
- DIE VOELKER UND DAS MEER ...
- DAS VOELKERRECHT DER ZUKUNFT
- VOELKERRECHT UND VOELKERPOLITIK
- DIE VOELKERRECHTLICHE ANERKENNUNG VON MANDSCHUKUO
- DER VOELKERRECHTLICHE SCHUTZ...AUF HOHER SEE
- DAS WASSERGEBIET FINNLANDS ...
- DIE WIRKUNG DER AUFHEBUNG DER GOLDKLAUSELN
- WIRKUNGSKREIS DES STRAFGESETZES, ...
- DIE WIRTSCHAFTLICHEN VERTRAEGE DEUTSCHLANDS

INTERNATIONAL LAW:... / Bowen, H W – New York, London, 1896 – 2mf – 1 – ILM-694/1 – ne IDC [327]

INTERNATIONAL LAW:... / Griffith, W – [London], n.d. – 2mf – 1 – ILM-181/1 – ne IDC [327]

INTERNATIONAL LAW;... / Halleck, H W – San Francisco, 1861 – 10mf – 1 – ILM-189/1 – ne IDC [327]

INTERNATIONAL LAW AND AUTOCRACY / Butler, G G – London, New York, Toronto, 1917 – 1mf – 9 – ILM-1704/1 – ne IDC [327]

INTERNATIONAL LAW AND DIPLOMACY OF ... / Benton, E J – Baltimore, 1908 – 4mf – 9 – ILM-1695/1 – ne IDC [327]

INTERNATIONAL LAW BULLETIN *see*
COLUMBIA JOURNAL OF TRANSNATIONAL LAW

INTERNATIONAL LAW CODIFIED... / Fiore, P – New York, 1918 – 9mf – 1 – ILM-175/1 – ne IDC [327]

INTERNATIONAL LAW COMMISSION : MAIN COMMISSION – GENERAL SERIES / United Nations – (1st – 11th Sessions: 1948-1959. A/CN.4/1-122. E.196; 12th – 14th Sessions: 1960-1962. A/CN.4/123-148; 15th – 37th Sessions: 1963-1985. A/CN.4/149-400. E.471) – 9 – us U.N. Pubs [340]

INTERNATIONAL LAW DIGESTS (AMERICAN) – Coverage includes Wharton, Moore and Hackworth – 7r – 1 – $250.00 – us Trans-Media [340]

INTERNATIONAL LAW IN CONNEXION WITH... / Hamel, F H – London, 1863 – 2mf – 1 – ILM-790/1 – ne IDC [327]

INTERNATIONAL LAW IN SOUTH AFRICA / Baty, T – London, 1900 – 2mf – 9 – ILM-1072/1 – ne IDC [340]

INTERNATIONAL LAW STUDIES – US Naval War College. v1-62 + 2 indexes. 1900-77 (all publ) – 206mf – 9 – $309.00 – LLMC 79-452 – us L.L.M.C. [073]

INTERNATIONAL LAW TIMES OF PEACE / Cheng, P – Shanghai, 1933 – 2mf – 1 – ILM-3782/1 – ne IDC [327]
INTERNATIONAL LAWYER – (Supersedes American Bar Association, Section of International and Comparative Law. Bulletin) – v1-28. 1966-1994 – 9 – $640.00 set – us Hein [340]
INTERNATIONAL LAWYER (ABA) – v1-28. 1966-94 – 1,5,6 – $720.00 – us Hein [073]
INTERNATIONAL LEAGUE FOR HUMAN RIGHTS – New York. 261 docs. 1980-1991 – 81mf – 9 – ne IDC [320]
INTERNATIONAL LEGAL MATERIALS – American Society of International Law. v1-34. 1962-95 – 9 – $1,776.00 set – us Hein [340]
INTERNATIONAL LEGAL PERSPECTIVES – Northwestern University. v1-6. 1987-1994 – 9 – $87.00 set – us Hein [340]
INTERNATIONAL LEGAL PRACTITIONER *see* INTERNATIONAL BAR JOURNAL
INTERNATIONAL LEGAL PRACTITIONERS – v5-14. 1980-92 – 9 – $50.00 run – us Hein [340]
INTERNATIONAL MAILER *see* PALETTE AND GRAVER, 1919-1923 : INTERNATIONAL MAILER, 1946-1955
INTERNATIONAL MANAGEMENT – v. 1- 1946- – 1. ; 5,6. ; 9 – apply; v.25-; v.31- – us UMI [650]
INTERNATIONAL MARINE INSURANCE RULES / Carver, T G – London, 1899 – 1mf – 1 – ILM-3749/1 – ne IDC [327]
INTERNATIONAL MEAT WORKER *see* MEAT OF IT, 1945-1966 : INTERNATIONAL MEAT WORKER, 1946-1948
INTERNATIONAL MENTAL HEALTH RESEARCH NEWSLETTER – (1974-75. 1,5,6. 1975. 9) – v1-17. 1959-75 – 1 – us UMI [616]
INTERNATIONAL METAL WORKER, 1902-1905 : UNITED WELDORS' NEWS, 1941-1945 / United Metal Workers' International Union of AmericaUnited Brotherhood of Weldors, Cutters and Helpers of America – (Coll title: Labor Union Periodicals, Pt 1) – 1r – 1 – $135.00 – 1-55655-237-8 – us UPA [331]
THE INTERNATIONAL MICROFORM JOURNAL OF AESTHETIC-PLASTIC SURGERY : TRANSACTIONS OF THE SECOND CONGRESS OF THE INTERNATIONAL SOCIETY OF AESTHETIC PLASTIC SURGERY JERUSALEM, JUNE 1973 – us Striker [617]
INTERNATIONAL MIGRATION REVIEW – v. 1-. 1964- – 1. ; 5,6. ; 9 – apply; v.5-; v.9- – us UMI [310]
INTERNATIONAL MIGRATION TODAY / ed by Appleyard, Reginald & Stahl, Charles – 1988 – 2v/668p – 9 – Co-published with the University of Western Australia – fr UNESCO [304]
International Military Tribunal *see*
- PROSECUTION EXHIBITS SUBMITTED TO THE INTERNATIONAL MILITARY TRIBUNAL
- TRIAL OF MAJOR WAR CRIMINALS
- TRIAL OF MAJOR WAR CRIMINALS BEFORE THE INTERNATIONAL MILITARY TRIBUNAL, NUREMBERG
- TRIALS OF WAR CRIMINALS BEFORE THE NUREMBERG MILITARY TRIBUNALS UNDER CONTROL COUNCIL LAW NO.10

International Military Tribunal for the Far East *see*
- COURT PAPERS, JOURNAL, EXHIBITS, AND JUDGMENTS..., 1900-48
- EXHIBITS
- GENERAL SUMMATION
- NARRATIVE SUMMARY OF RECORD
- PROCEEDING. JUDGEMENT
- PROCEEDINGS IN CHAMBER
- SUMMARY OF EVIDENCE
- TRANSCRIPT OF PROCEEDINGS
- TRIAL OF MAJOR WAR CRIMINALS

International Missionary Council and the Conference of British Missionary Societies *see* ARCHIVES
INTERNATIONAL MISSIONARY COUNCIL ARCHIVES 1910-1961 / World Council of Churches, Geneva – (Includes printed guide) – 7,029mf – 9 – ne IDC [240]
INTERNATIONAL MOLDERS AND FOUNDRY WORKERS JOURNAL : 1864-1955 / International Molders' and Foundry Workers' Union – (Coll title: Labor Union Periodicals, Pt 1) – 32r – 1 – $4,320.00 – 1-55655-238-6 – us UPA [331]
International Molders' and Foundry Workers' Union *see* INTERNATIONAL MOLDERS AND FOUNDRY WORKERS JOURNAL
International Monetary Fund *see*
- REPORTS AND SUMMARY PROCEEDINGS
- STAFF PAPERS

International Monetary Fund and World Bank. Library *see* ECONOMICS AND FINANCE: INDEX TO PERIODICAL ARTICLES, 1947-71
INTERNATIONAL MONTHLY MAGAZINE OF LITERATURE, SCIENCE, AND ART *see* HARPER'S
INTERNATIONAL MORALITY; OR,... / Atkinson, G – London, 1851 – 2mf – 9 – ILM-1591/1 – ne IDC [340]
INTERNATIONAL MOVEMENT AGAINST ALL FORMS OF DISCRIMINATION AND RACISM – Tokyo. 17 docs. 1988-1991 – 9mf – 9 – ne IDC [320]
International Museum of Photography at George Eastman House *see*
- BRITISH MASTERS OF THE ALBUMEN PRINT
- CATALOG..
- INDEX TO AMERICAN PHOTOGRAPHIC COLLECTIONS
- LIBRARY CATALOG OF THE INTERNATIONAL MUSEUM OF PHOTOGRAPHY AT GEORGE EASTMAN HOUSE

INTERNATIONAL MUSICIAN / American Federation of Musicians – New York. 1909-76. 20 reels – 1 – 372.00 – us L of C Photodup [780]
INTERNATIONAL NEWS: PROVISIONAL INTERNATIONAL CONTACT COMMISSION FOR THE NEW COMMUNIST – (4th Int'l). v1-12. no. 4 (all publ). 1939-50 – 1 reel – 1 – $115.00 – us UPA [335]
INTERNATIONAL NURSING REVIEW – (v. 12-1965- 5,6. v. 17- 1970- 9) – 1- 1954- – 1 – us UMI [610]
International Ophtalmological Congress 14, 1933 *see* STANDARDISATION OF TONOMETERS
INTERNATIONAL OPHTHALMOLOGY CLINICS – v. 1-. 1961- – 1. – apply; v.15- 1975- 5,6,9 – us UMI [617]
International Order of the King's Daughters and Sons. Ohio Branch *see* RECORDS
INTERNATIONAL ORGANIZATION – 1- 1947- – 1,5,6,9 – us UMI [320]
INTERNATIONAL ORTHOPAEDICS / Societe internationale de Chirurgie Orthopedique et de Traumatologie – v1-5, 1977-81. ISSN: 0341-2695 – 1,5,6,9,13 – 96.00v – us UMI [617]
International Penal and Prison Commission *see* BULLETIN DE LA COMMISSION INTERNATIONALE PENALE ET PENITENTIAIRE
INTERNATIONAL PENAL POLICY / Frank, H – N.p., [1935] – 1mf – 1 – ILM-2472/1 – ne IDC [327]
INTERNATIONAL PERSPECTIVES – (Cont: External Affairs 1972. Incorporated within: Peacekeeping and International Relations at v20 no 2 1991) – Toronto. v1-19. 1972-90 – 9 – Can$20.00y – cn Micromedia [320]
INTERNATIONAL PERSPECTIVES *see*
- EXTERNAL AFFAIRS
- PEACEKEEPING AND INTERNATIONAL RELATIONS

INTERNATIONAL PETROLEUM ABSTRACTS – v1- 1973- – 1,5,6,9 – us UMI [660]
THE INTERNATIONAL PHILATELIST – (Absorbed: The Canadian Journal of Philately. Absorbed: The Philatelic Fraud Reporter. Absorbed: One Dime) – Toronto: W.S. Weatherston, [1892-1893] – 9 – cn C.I.H.M. [760]
International Phonetic Association *see* JOURNAL
International Photoengravers Union of North America *see*
- PALETTE AND GRAVER, 1919-1923 : INTERNATIONAL MAILER, 1946-1955
- PLATE MAKERS' CRITERION, 1907-1909 : AMERICAN PHOTO-ENGRAVER, 1908-1955

INTERNATIONAL PLANT QUARANTINE TREATMENT MANUAL – 1984 – 230p – it F.A.O. [630]
International Plate Printers', Die Stampers' and Engravers' Union of North America *see* PLATE PRINTER, 1902-1932
INTERNATIONAL POLITICAL SCIENCE REVIEW – v1-5. 1980-1984 (all publ) – 5,6 – $60.00 – us Hein [320]
INTERNATIONAL POPULATION CENSUS : PACIFIC RIM – (Includes data for any country which borders the outer edge of the Pacific Ocean, excluding the U.S. and Canada) – 1 – us Primary [310]
INTERNATIONAL POPULATION CENSUS PUBLICATIONS, 1945-1967. SEGMENT 1 – Based on International Population Census Bibliography, prepared by the Population Research Center of the Univ. of Texas. – 1 – us Primary [310]
INTERNATIONAL POPULATION CENSUS PUBLICATIONS, POST-1967 : SEGMENT 3 – (Based on International Population Census Bibliography, prepared by the Population Research Center of the University of Texas) – 1 – us Primary [310]
INTERNATIONAL POPULATION CENSUS PUBLICATIONS, PRE-1945. SEGMENT 2 – Based on International Population Census Bibliography, prepared by the Population Research Center of the University of Texas. – 1 – us Primary [310]
INTERNATIONAL PRESS CORRESPONDENCE (IMPRECOR') – London. 1921-37 – 1 – uk World [380]
International Printing Pressman and Assistants' Union of North America *see* AMERICAN PRESSMAN, 1890-1955 : SERVICE BUREAU NEWS BULLETIN OF THE INTERNATIONAL PRINTING PRESSMEN AND ASSISTANTS' UNION OF NORTH AMERICA, 1937- 1952
INTERNATIONAL PRIVATE LAW IN SCOTLAND... / Gibb, A D – Edinburgh, 1928 – 1mf – 1 – ILM-536/1 – ne IDC [327]
INTERNATIONAL PROPERTY INVESTMENT JOURNAL – 1983- – 1,5,9 – us Harwood [650]
INTERNATIONAL PROPERTY INVESTMENT JOURNAL *see* HOFSTRA PROPERTY LAW JOURNAL
International Public Relations Association *see* IPRA REVIEW
INTERNATIONAL RAILWAY AND STEAM NAVIGATION GUIDE *see* THE INTERNATIONAL RAILWAY GUIDE
THE INTERNATIONAL RAILWAY GUIDE – (Cont by: International Railway and Steam Navigation Guide) – Montreal: Montreal Print and Pub. Co, [1866-1869] – 9 – cn C.I.H.M. [380]
International Reading Association *see* CONVENTION PAPERS
INTERNATIONAL REALITIES / Brown, P M – New York, 1917 – 3mf – 1 – ILM-3711/1 – ne IDC [327]
INTERNATIONAL RECOGNITION OF SOVEREIGNTY / Indonesia. Kementerian Penerangan – SE-10,475 1. 1949? – 9 – ne IDC [950]
International Red Aid. Spain. (Socorro Rojo de Espana) *see* SEIS MESES DE SOLIDARIDAD ANTIFASCISTA
International Refugee Organization *see* OCCUPATIONAL SKILLS OF REFUGEES
INTERNATIONAL REVIEW – London. no. 1-3 (all publ). 1889 – 1 reel – 1 – $65.00 – us UPA [335]
INTERNATIONAL REVIEW – New York. 1-4 2+1 (all publ). 1936-39 – 5mf – 9 – $50.00 – us UPA [073]
INTERNATIONAL REVIEW OF CRIMINAL POLICY / United Nations – 53 fiches – 9 – 100.00; 1.90f – uk UNIMICRO [360]
INTERNATIONAL REVIEW OF CRIMINAL POLICY / United Nations – (Nos. 1-4. ST/SOA/Ser.M/1-4. E.13 F.13; Nos. 5-22 and Addenda. ST/SOA/SerM/5-22 and Add. E/F/S.61; Nos. 21-31. ST/SOA/Ser.M/21-31. E.27 F.28 S.29; Nos. 32-37. ST/ESA/Ser.M/32-37. E.13 F.16 F.15) – 9 – us U.N. Pubs [360]
INTERNATIONAL REVIEW OF LAW AND ECONOMICS – (v3-. 1983-. 5,6,9) – v1-. Jun 1981- – 1 – us UMI [340]
INTERNATIONAL REVIEW OF MISSIONS – v1-44. 1912-55 (complete) – 14r – 1 – ATLA S0070 – us A.T.L.A. [073]
INTERNATIONAL REVIEW OF NATURAL FAMILY PLANNING – v1- 1977- – 1,5,6,9 – us UMI [360]
INTERNATIONAL REVIEW OF PSYCHIATRY – 1989- 5v – 9 – £205.00 – 0954-0261 – uk Carfax [616]
INTERNATIONAL REVIEW OF PSYCHO-ANALYSIS – (1985-. 5,6,9) – v1-. 1974- – 1 – us UMI [616]
INTERNATIONAL REVIEW OF SLAVIC LINGUISTICS – (v.4 .1979 5,6,9) – v.1. 1976 – 1 – us UMI [460]
INTERNATIONAL REVIEW OF SOCIAL HISTORY – (1983-. 1,5,6,9) – v1- .1956- – 1 – us UMI [073]
INTERNATIONAL REVIEWS OF IMMUNOLOGY / ed by Bona, Constantin – 9,5,1 – us Harwood [616]
THE INTERNATIONAL SCHOOL FOUNDATION – SE-11,543 1. 1961? – 9 – ne IDC [370]
INTERNATIONAL SEA-BORNE TRADE STATISTICS YEARBOOK (MARINE TRANSPORT) / United Nations – E.7 – 9 (ST/ESA/STAT/Ser.C/66-68) – us U.N. Pubs [380]
INTERNATIONAL SECURITY – (v4- 1979- 5,6,9) – v1- 1976 – 1 – us UMI [320]
INTERNATIONAL SHEEP BREEDS – 1939-1945 – 7 – uk Microform Academic [636]
INTERNATIONAL SOCIAL SCIENCE JOURNAL – (Eng. ed.). 1- 1949- – 1. ; 5,6. ; 9 – apply; v.23-; v.28- – us UMI [300]
INTERNATIONAL SOCIALIST – Highland Park, CA. 1969-1975 – 2r – 1 – $100.00 – R03242 – us Library Micro [071]
International Socialist Congress *see* BULLETIN OF THE LABOUR AND SOCIALIST INTERNATIONAL
International Socialist Congress. 1st. 1889 *see* PROTOKOLL DES INTERNATIONALEN ARBEITER-CONGRESSES ZU PARIS
International Socialist Congress. 7th. 1907 *see*
- COMPTE RENDU ANALYTIQUE PUBLIE PAR LE SECRETARIAT DU BUREAU SOCIALISTE INTERNATIONAL
- REPORT

International Socialist Congress. 8th. 1910 *see* INTERNATIONALER SOZIALISTEN-KONGRESS ZU KOPENHAGEN, AUG. 28 BIS SEPT. 3, 1910
International Socialist Congress. 9th. 1912 *see* AUSSERORDENTLICHER INTERNATIONALER SOZIALISTEN-KONGRESS ZU BASEL AM NOV. 24 UND 25, 1912
INTERNATIONAL SOCIALIST REVIEW – Chicago. 1-18 2+8 (all publ). 1900-18 – 6r – 1 – $695.00 – us UPA [330]
INTERNATIONAL SOCIALIST REVIEW – Chicago, IL. -m. July 1900-June 1907. 4 reels – 1 – uk British Libr Newspaper [073]
INTERNATIONAL SOCIALIST REVIEW – London. -m. Jul 1900-Jun 1906. (3 reels) – 1 – uk British Libr Newspaper [072]
INTERNATIONAL SOCIALIST REVIEW – New York. v1-17. 1940-56 – 2r – 1 – us Ross [073]
INTERNATIONAL SOCIALIST REVIEW / Socialist Workers Party – 1-24. 1940-63 – 65mf – 9 – $265.00 – us UPA [335]
INTERNATIONAL SOCIETY OF BARRISTERS QUARTERLY – v1-29. 1966-1994 – 9 – $330.00 set – us Hein [340]
INTERNATIONAL SPACE SAFETY AND RESCUE SYMPOSIA : FIRST, SECOND AND THIRD – 1975 – 11mf – 9 – $20.00 – 0-87703-239-4 – us Univelt [629]
INTERNATIONAL SPACE SAFETY AND RESCUE SYMPOSIA : FOURTH, FIFTH, AND SIXTH – 1975 – 11mf – 9 – $20.00 – 0-87703-240-8 – us Univelt [629]
INTERNATIONAL SPACE SAFETY AND RESCUE SYMPOSIA : NINTH, TENTH, AND ELEVENTH, 1976-78 – (Suppl to v54, Science and Technology) – 1982 – 6mf – 9 – $15.00 – 0-87703-223-8 – us Univelt [629]
INTERNATIONAL SPACE SAFETY AND RESCUE SYMPOSIA : THIRTEENTH AND FOURTEENTH, 1980-81 – (Suppl to v54, Science and Technology) – 1982 – 5mf – 9 – $15.00 – 0-87703-224-6 – us Univelt [629]
INTERNATIONAL SPACE SAFETY AND RESCUE SYMPOSIUM : TWELFTH, 1979 – (Suppl to v54, Space and Technology) – 1982 – 5mf – 9 – $12.00 – 0-87703-222-X – us Univelt [629]
INTERNATIONAL STANDARD BOOK NUMBERS LISTING – Pub. Jan and Jul – 17 – £195.00v – uk Whitaker [070]
INTERNATIONAL STATISTICS MICROFICHE LIBRARY – (Statistical publications on international intergovernmental organizations. Printed index available) – 1983- – 9 – Apply for prices – us CIS [310]
International Stereotyper and Electrotypers Union *see* INTERNATIONAL STEREOTYPER AND ELECTROTYPERS UNION JOURNAL
INTERNATIONAL STEREOTYPER AND ELECTROTYPERS UNION JOURNAL : 1906-1955 / International Stereotyper and Electrotypers Union – (Coll title: Labor Union Periodicals, Pt 2) – 18r – 1 – $2,430.00 – 1-55655-307-2 – us UPA [680]
THE INTERNATIONAL STUDENT – (Lacking: v1-23,26) – v24-46. Oct 1926-May 1949 – 2r – 1 – ATLA S0496 – us A.T.L.A. [073]

INTERNATIONAL STUDIES IN THE PHILOSOPHY OF SCIENCE – 1992- 7v – 9 – £131.00 – 0269-8595 – uk Carfax [500]

International Sunday-School Convention of the United States and British American Provinces *see* THE DEVELOPMENT OF THE SUNDAY-SCHOOL, 1780-1905

INTERNATIONAL SURGERY – v1- 1938- 1; v55- 5,6; v61- 9 – us UMI [617]

INTERNATIONAL SURVEY OF BOOK PRODUCTION DURING THE LAST DECADES : DIVISION OF STATISTICS ON CULTURE AND COMMUNICATION, OFFICE OF STATISTICS – 1985 – iv/87p – 9 – 92-3-102040-4 – fr UNESCO [070]

INTERNATIONAL SYMPOSIUM ON EARTH GRAVITY MODELS AND RELATED PROBLEMS / Rapp, R R – 1972 – 1,5,6,9 – $10.00 – us A.G.U. [550]

INTERNATIONAL TAX AND BUSINESS LAWYER – (1985- 5,6,9) – v1- 1983- – 1 – us UMI [340]

INTERNATIONAL TAX AND BUSINESS LAWYER – University of California at Berkeley. v1-13. 1983-95 – 9 – $226.00 set – us Hein [340]

INTERNATIONAL TAX JOURNAL – v1-21. 1974-1995 – 9 – $429.00set – us Hein [340]

International Telecommunication Union *see* SUMMARY OF MONITORING INFORMATION RECEIVED BY THE BR

INTERNATIONAL TELECOMMUNICATIONS UNION (ITU) . CCITT AND CCIR DOCUMENT3 – (Updated Every 120 Days) – Information Handling Services – 5 – us Info Handling [380]

INTERNATIONAL TELEVISION: THE JOURNAL OF THE INTERNATIONAL TELEVISION ASSOCIATION – v1-. 1983- – 1,5,6,9 – us UMI [073]

INTERNATIONAL TERRORISM : TWO LEAGUE OF NATIONS CONVENTIONS, 1934-1937 / ed by Dubin, Martin – 1990 – 9 – inquire – us Ross [340]

INTERNATIONAL THESAURUS OF CULTURAL DEVELOPMENT : SUB-SAHARAN AFRICA – (English/French) – 1985 – 9 – 92-3-002300-0 – fr UNESCO [306]

INTERNATIONAL TIMES – London, UK. 1966-1970 – 1r – $50.00 – R63603 – us Library Micro [072]

INTERNATIONAL TOURISM QUARTERLY – 1971-92. Continued annually – 1 – uk World [338]

INTERNATIONAL TRADE, 1971-88 : SPECIAL STUDIES SERIES / ed by Kesaris, Paul – (1971-81: ISBN 0-89093-506-8. $1,320.00; 1982-85: 9r ISBN 0-89093-551-3. $1,025.00; 1985-88: ISBN 1-55655-146-0. $1,210.00) – 1982 – 1 – us UPA [380]

INTERNATIONAL TRADE CENTER / United Nations – 1968-1986 – E/F.12 E.160 F.162 R.124 S.149 – 9 (UNCTAD/GATT) – us U.N. Pubs [320]

International Trade Centre UNCTAD GATT *see* MOROCCO: THE MARKET FOR SELECTED MANUFACTURED PRODUCTS FROM DEVELOPING COUNTRIES

INTERNATIONAL TRADE FORUM – 1964- 1; v11- 1975- 5,6,9 – us UMI [380]

INTERNATIONAL TRADE FROM THE 17TH CENTURY AMSTERDAM / Burlamacchi Archive – $5,550.00 – us UPA [380]

INTERNATIONAL TRADE LAW JOURNAL *see* MARYLAND JOURNAL OF INTERNATIONAL LAW AND TRADE

INTERNATIONAL TRADE REVIEW – 1969- 1; 1975- 5,6,9 – us UMI [380]

International Trade Union Committee of Negro Workers *see* NEGRO WORKER

International Typographical Union *see* BULLETIN OF THE INTERNATIONAL TYPOGRAPHICAL UNION

International Union of Brewery, Flour, Cereal, Soft Drink and Distillery Workers of America *see* BREWERY WORKER

International Union of Electrical Radio and Machine Workers *see* IUE

International Union of Electrical, Radio and Machine Workers *see* IUE-CIO NEWS

International Union of Flour and Cereal Mill Employees *see* EIGHT HOUR MILLER

International Union of Mine, Mill and Smelter Workers *see*
– CIO NEWS
– MINE-MILL UNION

International Union of Shipwrights, Joiners and Caulkers of America *see* JOURNAL OF LABOR

INTERNATIONAL VIEWPOINT – Montreuil, France: Presse-Edition-Communication, [1982- – 1 – CSUXALM3009-S – us Hoover Inst Photo [944]

INTERNATIONAL WILDLIFE – v1- 1971- 1; v4- 5,6,9 – us UMI [590]

International Woman Suffrage Alliance *see* JUS SUFFRAGII

INTERNATIONAL WOMEN'S NEWS *see* JUS SUFFRAGII

INTERNATIONAL WOMEN'S RIGHTS ACTION WATCH – South Minneapolis. 28 docs. 1987-1991 – 7mf – 9 – ne IDC [320]

INTERNATIONAL WOMEN'S YEAR WORLD CONFERENCE : MEXICO CITY – 1975 – (Includes printed index) – 65mf – 9 – $185.00 – us UNIFO [350]

INTERNATIONAL WOODWORKER – Portland, OR. 20 Mar 1946-27 Dec 1961. 4 rolls – 1 – us U.O. Library [071]

INTERNATIONAL WORK GROUP FOR INDIGENOUS AFFAIRS – Copenhagen. 83 docs. 1980-1991 – 135mf – 9 – ne IDC [320]

INTERNATIONAL WORKER – New York, N.Y.: International Workers Party, 197u – 1 – CSUX89-S111 – us Hoover Inst Photo [331]

International Working Association *see* L'EGALITE

International Working Men's Association *see*
– INTERNATIONAL HERALD
– PAPERS OF THE INTERNATIONAL WORKINGMEN'S ASSOCIATION, 1868-1877

INTERNATIONAL YEARBOOK OF EDUCATION – 9 – fr UNESCO [370]

L'INTERNATIONALE – communiste. Dir. Raymond Pericat. no. 3-5, 7-11, 13, 15-29, 35. Paris. mars-dec 1919 – 1 – fr A.C.R.P.P. [073]

L'INTERNATIONALE / L'Union Communiste – puis Revue mensuelle no. 1-40. Paris. nov 1933-38 – 1 – fr A.C.R.P.P. [335]

DIE INTERNATIONALE : ANARCHOSYNDIKALISTISCHES ORGAN / ed by Sekretariat der Internationalen Arbeiter-Assoziation – Amsterdam, aug 1934-apr 1935 – 1r – 1 – Dist. gw Mikrofilm – gw Misc Inst [072]

DIE INTERNATIONALE – Berlin, 1924-26 – 1 – Dist. gw Mikrofilm – gw Misc Inst [072]

DIE INTERNATIONALE – Zeitschrift fuer die revolutionare arbeiterbewegung....v1-4. 1927-31. -m. (Serial publications of German trade unions in the Memorial Library, University of Wisconsin-Madison.) – 1 – us U.W. Library [073]

DIE INTERNATIONALE : ZEITSCHRIFT FUER PRAXIS UND THEORIE DES MARXISMUS – Berlin, Leipzig. v1,no1-v15,no9-10. Apr 1915-Sept/Oct 1932. German periodical on Marxist theory and practice. 117 fiches – 9 – $445.00 – us UPA [335]

DIE INTERNATIONALE *see*
– NORDDEUTSCHE ALLGEMEINE ZEITUNG

INTERNATIONALE BIBLIOGRAPHIE ZUR DEUTSCHEN KLASSIK 1750-1850 / ed by Stiftung Weimarer Klassik – (3 index vols are available in printed form ca DM834.00 set ISBN: 3-598-32885-0) – (mf ed 1997) – 91mf (1:24) – 9 – diazo DM3,790.00 silver DM4,390.00 – 3-598-32883-4 – silver ISBN: 3-598-32884-2 – gw Saur [430]

L'INTERNATIONALE COMMUNISTE – Organe bimensuel du Comite executif de l'Internationale communiste. Petrograd puis Paris. mai 1919-aout 1939 – 1 – fr A.C.R.P.P. [073]

L'INTERNATIONALE COMMUNISTE / Organe du Comite Executif de l'Internationale Communiste – Moscow, Petrograd, Paris. v1,no.1-v21,no.8. May 1919-Aug 1939. French ed. of Kommunistische Internationale. 298 fiches – 9 – $1,060.00 – us UPA [335]

INTERNATIONALE FREIZUEGIGKEIT DES KAPITALS UND UNTERENTWICKELTE LAENDER / Gaebler, Joachim – Heidelberg, 1963 – 3mf – DM76.00 – 3-89349-982-2 – gw Hänsel [337]

INTERNATIONALE GELDSCHULDEN / Hartmann, G – Freiburg i. B., Tuebingen, 1882 – 1mf – 1 – ILM-2979/1 – ne IDC [327]

INTERNATIONALE GESELLSCHAFT FUER MENSCHENRECHTE = INTERNATIONAL SOCIETY FOR HUMAN RIGHTS – Frankfurt/Main. 270 docs. 1980-1991 – 174mf – 9 – ne IDC [320]

Internationale Jugendbibliothek. Muenchen *see*
– KATALOGE DER INTERNATIONALEN JUGENDBIBLIOTHEK

INTERNATIONALE JUGENDKORRESPONDENZ – Berlin, Germany.1920-21 – 1 – gw Mikrofilm [072]

INTERNATIONALE KIRCHLICHE ZEITSCHRIFT – (Cont: Revue Internationale de Theologie) – v1-60. 1893-1970 (complete) – 15r – 1 – ATLA S0176 – us A.T.L.A. [073]

DER INTERNATIONALE KLASSENKAMPF *see* GEGEN DEN STROM

INTERNATIONALE KLASSENKAMPF *see* GEGEN DEN STROM

INTERNATIONALE KORRESPONDENZ : IK UEBER ARBEITERBEWEGUNG, SOZIALISMUS UND AUSWAERTIGE POLITIK. AUSGABE W – Berlin, 1916-17 – 1 – Dist. gw Mikrofilm – gw Misc Inst [073]

INTERNATIONALE KORRESPONDENZ : IK UEBER ARBEITERBEWEGUNG, SOZIALISMUS UND AUSWAERTIGE POLITIK. AUSGABE W – Berlin, apr 1916-mar 1917 – 1r – 1 – DM75.00 – gw Mikro Press [073]

INTERNATIONALE LITERATUR : ZENTRALORGAN DER INTERNATIONALEN VEREINIGUNG REVOLUTIONAERER SCHRIFTSTELLER – (Title change: Internationale Literatur/Deutsche Blaetter) – Moskau (Moskva), U.S.S.R. 1933-1945 – 13r – 1 – gw Mikrofilm [072]

INTERNATIONALE LITERATUR/DEUTSCHE BLAETTER *see* INTERNATIONALE LITERATUR

INTERNATIONALE LITERATUR-UND MUSIKBERICHTE – v.1-13, 1894-1908 – 1 – 92.00 – us L of C Photodup [780]

INTERNATIONALE MUSIK-SACHLEXIKA, TEIL 1 : VOM 17. BIS ZUM FRUEHEN 19. JAHRHUNDERT – 1999 – ca 120mf (1:24) in 2 installments – 9 – diazo ca DM3,400.00 (silver ca DM4,200.00) – 3-598-33862-7 – silver ISBN: 3-598-33863-5 – gw Saur [780]

INTERNATIONALE PRESSE-KORRESPONDENZ : DEUTSCHE AUSGABE – Berlin, Wien. v1 no 1-v13 no 27 Sep 1921-Mar 1933. Documents and resolutions of the International Communist Party – 356mf – 9 – $910.00 – us UPA [335]

DAS INTERNATIONALE SEERECHT / Attlmayr, F von – Wien. 2v. 1903 – 10mf – 9 – ILM-318/1 – ne IDC [340]

INTERNATIONALE SITUATIONNISTE / L'Internationale Situationniste – Bulletin central edite par les sections. Dir. G.-E. Debord. no. 1-12. Paris. juin 1958-sept 1969 – 1 – fr A.C.R.P.P. [073]

L'INTERNATIONALE SYNDICALE ROUGE / Communist International. Comite Executif – Bulletin. Red. en chef A. Losovsky. Moscou, Paris. oct 1921-oct 1933, aout 1934. absorbe par: Correspondance syndicale internationale – 1 – fr A.C.R.P.P. [073]

INTERNATIONALE TENDENZEN IN DER TIERGESUNDHEITSUEBERWACHUNG UND DARAUS ABGELEITETE SCHLUSSFOLGERUNGEN FUER DIE ANPASSUNG DES NATIONALEN TIERSEUCHENBERICHTSSYSTEMS / Kroschewski, Klaus – 1993 – 2mf – 9 – DM98.00 – 3-89349-714-5 – gw Hänsel [636]

Internationale Vereinigung fuer Germanische Sprach- und Literaturwissenschaft *see* BERICHT UEBER DEN ERSTEN KONGRESS, ROM, 5.-10. SEPTEMBER 1955

Internationale Vereinigung fuer Germanische Sprach- und Literaturwissenschaft. Kongress *see* IVG, BERICHT UEBER DEN ERSTEN KONGRESS, ROM, 5.-10. SEPTEMBER 1955

INTERNATIONALE WECHSELPRAXIS / Boettger, F – Leipzig, n.d. – 2mf – 9 – ILM-3487/1 – ne IDC [327]

DAS INTERNATIONALE WECHSELRECHT OESTERREICHS / Bettelheim, E – Wien, 1904 – 3mf – 9 – ILM-3235/1 – ne IDC [327]

INTERNATIONALE ZEITSCHRIFT FUER ALLGEMEINE SPRACHWISSENSCHAFT – Leipzig, 1884-1890. 5v. Suppl – 61mf – 9 – H-1381/2 – ne IDC [400]

INTERNATIONALE ZEITSCHRIFT FUER METALLOGRAPHIE *see* ZEITSCHRIFT FUER METALLKUNDE

INTERNATIONALE ZEITSCHRIFT FUER PSYCHOANALYSE / Internationalen Psychoanalytischen Vereinigung – 1913-37 (I-XXIII). devenu: Internationale Zeitschrift und Imago. 1939-41 (XXIV-XXVI). Wien – 1 – fr A.C.R.P.P. [073]

INTERNATIONALEN – Stockholm, Sweden. 1979- – 1 – sw Kungliga [072]

INTERNATIONALEN: HUVUDORGAN FOR KOMMUNISTISKA ARBETARFORBUNDET (SVENSK SEKTION AV FJARDE INTERNATIONALEN) – Nr. 4 (1974)-. Stockholm: Kommunistiska arbetarforbundet, 1974- – 1 – us U.W. Library [073]

Internationalen Psychoanalytischen Vereinigung *see* INTERNATIONALE ZEITSCHRIFT FUER PSYCHOANALYSE

DIE INTERNATIONALEN RECHTSBEZIEHUNGEN... / Cohnitz, E – Berlin, Leipzig, 1920 – 2mf – 1 – ILM-3266/1 – ne IDC [327]

DIE INTERNATIONALEN VERTRAEGE UEBER DIE NORDSEEFISCHEREI / Gutmann, F – Borna, Leipzig, 1912 – 2mf – 1 – ILM-2314/1 – ne IDC [327]

Internationaler Germanisten-Kongress *see*
– DICHTUNG, SPRACHE, GESELLSCHAFT
– SPAETZEITEN UND SPAETZEITLICHKEIT
– TRADITION UND URSPRUENGLICHKEIT

INTERNATIONALER SCHUTZ VON ANLEIHEGLAEUBIGERN / Domke, M – Wien, 1934 – 1mf – 1 – ILM-3054/1 – ne IDC [327]

INTERNATIONALER SOZIALISTEN-KONGRESS ZU KOPENHAGEN, AUG. 28 BIS SEPT. 3, 1910 / International Socialist Congress. 8th. 1910 – Berlin, Buchhandlung Vorwaerts (H. Weber), 1910 – 1 – $35.00r – us Hoover Inst Photo [335]

INTERNATIONALES EHE- UND KINDSCHAFTSRECHT / Bergmann, A – Berlin. 3v. 1926-28 – 22mf – 9 – ILM-3329/1 – ne IDC [327]

INTERNATIONALES EHESCHLIESSUNGSRECHT... / ed by Garnier, A – Bern, 1884 – 3mf – 1 – ILM-3694/1 – ne IDC [327]

INTERNATIONALES JAHRBUCH FUER POLITIK UND ARBEITERBEWEGUNG – Berlin, 1912-15 – 2r – 1 – Dist. gw Mikrofilm – gw Misc Inst [320]

INTERNATIONALES JAHRBUCH FUER POLITIK UND ARBEITERBEWEGUNG – Berlin, 1912-15 – 2r – 1 – DM220.00 – gw Mikro Press [320]

L'INTERNATIONALISATION DES CAPITAUX... / Becque, E – Montpelier, 1912 – 9 – 5mf – ILM-3259/1 – ne IDC [327]

DIE INTERNATIONALISIERUNG DER ELBE / Duerkop, K – Magdeburg, 1931 – 1mf – 9 – ILM-1882/1 – ne IDC [327]

INTERNATSIONAL I VO INA : SBORNIK STATE I / Chernov, Viktor Mikhailovich – Izd. 2-e. Petrograd: Partii a sotsialistov-revoliut sionerov, 1917 – 1 – CSUX89-B7309 – us Hoover Inst Photo [320]

INTERNATSIONAL I VOINA : SBORNIK STATE I / Chernov, Viktor Mikhailovich & Gardenin, U – Geneve: "Zhizn", 1915 – 1 – CSUX89-B7311 – us Hoover Inst Photo [947]

INTERNATSIONAL MOLODEZHI – Moscow. 14v. 1929-41 – 1 – 115.00 – us L of C Photodup [335]

L'INTERNAZIONALE – Philadelphia, PA, 1909 – 13mf or 1r – 1,9 – us I.H.R.C. [978]

INTERNAZIONALE – London, UK. 12 Jan-5 May 1901 – 1 – uk British Libr Newspaper [072]

INTERNET REFERENCE SERVICES QUARTERLY : A JOURNAL OF INNOVATIVE INFORMATION PRACTICE, TECHNOLOGIES AND RESOURCES / ed by Martin, Lyn Elizabeth M – v1 n1. 1997- – 1,9 – $48.00 in US $67.20 outside hardcopy subsc – us Haworth [020]

DER INTERNIST – v. 1-21. 1960-80 – 1,5,9 – 1748.00 – us UMI [616]

INTERNIST – (1979 5,6,9) – 1959 – 1 – us UMI [073]

Internoscia, Jerome *see* A NEW CODE OF INTERNATIONAL LAW

INTER-OCEAN – Bartley. Neb. 1899-1901; 1909-1942; 1945-1947 – 1 – us UMI [071]

Inter-Ocean Publishing Co *see* HISTORY OF THE CITY OF CHICAGO

INTER-PARLIAMENTARY UNION – Geneva. 136 docs. 1980-1991 – 110mf – 9 – ne IDC [323]

INTERPLAY BETWEEN HUMAN SOCIETY AND THE BIOSPHERE – 250p – 9 – 92-3-102747-6 – fr UNESCO [550]

INTERPRETACION DE LA POLITICA AGRARIA JUSTICIALISTA / Emery, Carlos Alberto – [Buenos Aires, 1952?] – 1 – CSUXAHZ2870-B – us Hoover Inst Photo [320]

INTERPRETACIONES ACTUALES SOBRE LA AGRESION / Moros Planelles, Alfonso – 1mf – 9 – Pta1,000.00 – 84-85422-58-9 – sp Pentalfa [150]

INTERPRETACION...HORACIO FLACO / Saa Maldonado, Manuel – 1878 – 9 – 1.50f – sp Bibl Santa Ana [450]
INTERPRETATION – v1- 1947- 1; v25- 5,6; v29- 9 – us UMI [240]
INTERPRETATION : A JOURNAL OF BIBLE AND THEOLOGY – v1-10. 1947-56 (complete) – 2r – 1 – ATLA S0032 – us A.T.L.A. [073]
DIE INTERPRETATION DES NEUEN TESTAMENTS IN DER VALENTINIANISCHEN GNOSIS (T.U.U. 3-37/3) / Barth, C – Leipzig, 1911 – 2mf – 9 – ne Slangenburg [240]
AN INTERPRETATION OF CHRISTIANITY (CCC68) / Chao, Tzu-ch'en – (In Chinese) – Shanghai: Association Press of China, 1948 – 1r – 1 – 1984-B500 – us A.T.L.A. [240]
INTERPRETATION UND KRITIK EINIGER GRUNDBEGRIFFE DER SPAETPHILOSOPHIE FICHTES : DARGESTELLT AN DEN "EINLEITUNGSVORLESUNGEN IN DIE WISSENSCHAFTSLEHRE" VON 1813 / Lautemann, Willi – Frankfurt a.M, 1970 – 2mf – 9 – DM62.00 – 3-89349-773-0 – gw Hänsel [190]
INTERPRETATIONS ERRONEES ET FAUX MONUMENTS = AN INDEPENDENT EXAMINATION OF THE ASSUAN AND ELEPHANTINE ARAMAIC PAPYRI : REMARQUES SUR QUELQUES INSCRIPTIONS RECEMMENT EDITEES: SUIVIES D'UN SOMMAIRE ANALYTIQUE DE L'OUVRAGE / Belleli, Lazare – Casal Montferrat: Rossi et Lavagno, 1909 – 1mf – 9 – 0-8370-7284-0 – 1986-1284 – us A.T.L.A. [470]
L'INTERPRETE – Alfred, Ontario. 20 aut 1886-v5 n247. 10 jun 1891 – 1r – 1 – Can$55.00 – cn Can Microfilming [072]
L'INTERPRETE – St-Victor d'Alfred (Ont.) 1886- SEM35P24 – 1r – 1 – Can$15.00 – cn Bibl Nat [073]
O INTERPRETE : FOLHA THEATRAL – Aracaju, 26 Nov 1882 – 1,5,6 – bl Biblioteca [072]
THE INTERPRETER / Cowell, John – 1607. 580p. (English Linguistics Series 1500-1800) – 9 – us UMI [420]
THE INTERPRETER OF WORDS AND TERMS : USED EITHER IN THE COMMON OR STATUTE LAWS OF THIS REALM AND IN TENURES AND JOCULAR CUSTOMS / Cowell, D – (With an appendix containing the Ancient Names of Places in England) – London: J Place, 1701 – 4mf – 9 – $6.00 – LLMC 97-107 – us L.L.M.C. [340]
INTERPRETER RELEASES : AN INFORMATION SERVICE ON IMMIGRATION, NATURALIZATION AND RELATED PROBLEMS – (Includes selected decisions of the Board of Immigration Appeals. LLMC does not have permission to update after v63. Missing: v1-6) – New York: American Council for Nationalities Service. v1-63. 1924-86 – 549mf – 9 – $823.00 – LLMC 81-511 – us L.L.M.C. [340]
THE INTERPRETER WITH HIS BIBLE / Waffle, Albert Edward – New York: A.D.F. Randolph, 1891.1 fiche – 9 – us A.T.L.A. [240]
EIN INTERPRETIERENDES WOERTERBUCH DER NOMINALABSTRAKTA IM "NARRENSCHIFF" SEBASTIANS BRANTS VON ABENTEUER BIS ZWIETRACHT : "HIE FINDT MAN DER WELT GANTZEN LUFF" (EINE VORRED IN DAS NARREN SCHYFF / Benkartek, Dietmar – 1995 – 6mf – 9 – DM125.00 – 3-8267-2275-2 – gw Hänsel [430]
INTERPRETING INTERNATIONAL COMPARISONS OF STUDENT ACHIEVEMENT / Goldstein, Harvey – 1995 – 38p – 9 – 92-3-103082-5 – fr UNESCO [370]
INTERPRETING THE CONSTITUTION: INAUGURAL LECTURE OF THE PROFESSOR OF POLITICAL THEORY AND GOVERNMENT, DELIVERED AT THE COLLEGE ON 1 DECEMBER 1955 / Rees, John Collwyn – Swansea, Wales Univ. Coll. of Swansea 1956 33 p. LL-2309 – 1 – us L of C Photodup [340]
AN INTERPRETIVE INQUIRY OF PRESERVICE TEACHERS' REFLECTIONS AND DEVELOPMENT DURING A FIELD-BASED ELEMENTARY PHYSICAL EDUCATION METHODS COURSE / Sebren, Mary A & Barrett, Kate R – 192 – 3mf – 9 – $12.00 – us Microform Publ [790]
AN INTERPRETIVE INQUIRY OF THE PROFESSIONAL LIFE HISTORIES OF SELECTED WOMEN DANCE/PHYSICAL EDUCATORS / Clark, Dawn & Robinson, Sarah M – 1992 – 3mf – 9 – $12.00 – us Microform Publ [790]
L'INTERPROVINCIAL – Hull, Canada. 19 fev 1910 – 1r – 1 – Can$25.00 – cn Can Microfilming [072]
INTERRACIAL BOOKS FOR CHILDREN – v.1-6. 1966-75 – 1 – us UMI [800]
INTERRACIAL BOOKS FOR CHILDREN, BULLETIN – (v.10-. 1979- 5,6,9) – v.7-. 1976- – 1 – us UMI [800]
INTERRACIAL NEWS SERVICE – 1951-59 – 1 – $50.00 – us Presbyterian [240]
INTERRACIAL REVIEW : A JOURNAL FOR CHRISTIAN DEMOCRACY – New York. v1-39. 1928-66 – 8r – 1 – us Ross [240]
THE INTERREGNUM (A.D. 1648-1660); STUDIES OF THE COMMONWEALTH, LEGISLATIVE, SOCIAL, AND LEGAL / Inderwick, Frederick Andrew – London: S. Low, Marston, Searle & Rivington, 1891. 340p – 1 – us U.W. Library [941]
INTERREGNUM PACIFICATOR AND PROSPECTUS FOR "THE RIGHTS OF MAN" – (Temporary National Party Greenback newspaper) – Salem, OH. Dec 27 1880 – 1r – 1 – us Western Res [071]
INTERRELATIONSHIPS AMONG STRESS, SOCIAL SUPPORT, HEALTH BEHAVIORS AND SELF-ASSESSED HEALTH STATUS / Colwell, Gregory B & Seffrin, John R – 1992 – 2mf – 9 – $8.00 – us Microform Publ [613]
INTERRELIGIOUS NEWSLETTER – New York, NY. May 1976-Nov 1985 – 1 – us A.J.P.C. [071]
L'INTERROGATION – Rigaud, Canada. v28 n2. 4 jan 1957-v28 n103. 31 dec 1957 – 1r – 1 – Can$50.00 – cn Can Microfilming [072]
INTERROGATION RECORDS PREPARED FOR WAR CRIMES : PROCEEDINGS AT NUERNBERG, 1945-1947 – M1270 – 31r – $713.00 – us Nat'l Archives [340]
INTERROGATOIRE DE MAISTRE URBAIN GRANDIER – Paris. 1634 – 9 – fr Hachette [360]
THE INTER-STATE COMMERCE ACT; AN ANALYSIS OF ITS PROVISIONS / Dos Passos, John Randolph – New York, Putnam's, 1887. 125 p. LL-1707 – 1 – us L of C Photodup [340]
THE INTERSTATE COMMERCE ACT AND FEDERAL ANTI-TRUST LAWS, INCLUDING THE SHERMAN ACT; THE ACT CREATING THE BUREAU OF CORPORATIONS. / Snyder, William Lamartine – New York: Baker, Voorhis, 1906. LL-1154 – 1 – us L of C Photodup [340]
INTERSTATE COMMERCE ACTS ANNOTATED / U. S. Interstate Commerce Commission – Washington: GPO. v1-22. 1927-77 (all publ) – 215mf – 9 – $322.00 – LLMC 79-428 – us L.L.M.C. [340]
INTERSTATE COMMERCE COMMISSION REPORTS / U.S. Interstate Commerce Commission – (Updates planned) – 1st series: v1-367. 1887-1984 (all publ); 2nd series: v1-7. 1984-91 – 3731mf – 9 – $5,596.00 – LLMC 78-220 – us L.L.M.C. [324]
INTERSTATE COMMERCE COMMISSION REPORTS *see*
- GARTNER'S NOTES TO THE INTERSTATE COMMERCE COMMISSION REPORTS
- ICC ACTIVITIES

THE INTERSTATE COMMERCE LAW / Hamilton, Adelbert – Northport, Long Island, N.Y., Thompson, 1887. 219 p. LL-171 – 1 – us L of C Photodup [340]
INTERSTATE COMPACT FOR EDUCATION – v. 12-15. 1979-81 – 1,5,6,9 – us UMI [370]
INTER-STATE EXTRADITION / Hawley, John Gardner – Detroit, 1890. 172p. LL-1269 – 1 – us L of C Photodup [340]
Inter-State Historical Co *see* HISTORY OF MOWER COUNTY
Inter-State Publishing Co *see*
- BIOGRAPHICAL AND HISTORICAL RECORD OF WAYNE AND APPANOOSE COUNTIES
- HISTORICAL AND BIOGRAPHICAL RECORD OF BLACK HAWK COUNTY
- HISTORY OF CLAYTON COUNTY
- HISTORY OF CLINTON COUNTY
- HISTORY OF DEKALB COUNTY
- HISTORY OF FLOYD COUNTY
- HISTORY OF HENDRICKS COUNTY
- HISTORY OF HENRY COUNTY
- HISTORY OF HOCKING VALLEY
- HISTORY OF JACKSON COUNTY
- HISTORY OF LA SALLE COUNTY
- HISTORY OF LOGAN COUNTY
- HISTORY OF LOWER SCIOTO VALLEY
- HISTORY OF MCHENRY COUNTY
- HISTORY OF SANGAMON COUNTY
- HISTORY OF SCOTT COUNTY
- HISTORY OF WAYNE COUNTY
- HISTORY OF WHITE COUNTY
- AN ILLUSTRATED HISTORY OF SKAGIT AND SNOHOMISH COUNTIES

INTER-STATE TATTLER – New York. v1-8.1925-32 – 1r – 1 – us Ross [071]
Inter-synodical Foreign Missionary Convention for Men *see* MEN AND THE MODERN MISSIONARY ENTERPRISE
INTERVALLING-EFFEKT DER BETAFAKTOREN AM DEUTSCHEN AKTIENMARKT / Sauer, Egbert – 1993 – 2mf – 9 – DM98.00 – 3-89349-666-1 – gw Hänsel [332]
LA INTERVENCION DEL ABOGADO EN LA CONSTITUCION DE LAS SOCIEDADES MERCANTILES / Cuellar Grajera, Antonio – Badajoz: Dip. Provincial, 1966. Sep. REE – sp Bibl Santa Ana [946]
LA INTERVENCION FEDERAL EN LA PROVINCIA DE BUENOS AIRES, 5 DE ENERO A 5 DE MAYO DE 1944 / Ojea, Julio Oscar – Buenos Aires: Goyena, 1945. 158p. LL-8018 – 1 – us L of C Photodup [340]
LAS INTERVENCIONES MILITARES EN LA ARGENTINA, 1900-66 / Canton, Dario – [S.l.: s.n., n.d.] – 1 – CSUXAGP8629-B – us Hoover Inst Photo [355]
INTERVENTION IN SCHOOL AND CLINIC *see* ACADEMIC THERAPY
INTERVENTIONS AT THE KLEINSCHMIDT CENTENNIAL / Hammerich, L L et al – BN 461 2. v17. 1951 – 8 – ne IDC [999]
INTERVENTSIIA NA SEVERE V DOKUMENTAKH / Mintz, Il – Moskva: Parti inoe izdvo, 1933 – 1 – CSUX88-B9122 – us Hoover Inst Photo [947]
INTERVIEWING THE CABINET: THE COPYRIGHT ASSOCIATION LAY THEIR CASE BEFORE THE GOVERNMENT: ABLE SPEECH BY THE PRESIDENT OF THE ASSOCIATION / Copyright Association of Canada – s.l.: s.n., 1889?. 03773. (Pre-1900 Canadiana) – 9 – cn C.I.H.M. [971]
INTERVIEWS FOR TRANSITION IN WESTERN UGANDA, 1891-1901 : TRANSCRIPTS OF INTERVIEWS CONDUCTED BETWEEN MAR 1968 AND APR 1969 / Steinhart, Edward I – [Evanston, 1970?] – us Res Libr [960]
INTERVIEWS FROM VILLAGES IN THE NJOMBE DISTRICT, TANZANIA / Graham, James – [s.l.] Microsystems, Inc, 1967 – us Res Libr [960]
INTERVIEWS WITH US GOVERNMENT OFFICIALS CONCERNING THE NIGERIA-BIAFRA WAR, 1971-72 / Robison, David – [s.l: s.n.], 1972 – us Res Libr [960]
INTERVIROLOGY – v5-. 1975- – 1,5,9 – us UMI [616]
INTERVOX – (Ceased no 9 1990) – Halifax. nos 1-9. 1987/88-1990 – 9 – Can$20.00y – cn Micromedia [073]
DIE INTERZESSIONSBESCHRAENKUNGEN FUER FRAUEN... / Breer, H – Wuerzburg, 1936 – 1mf – 1 – ILM-3024/1 – ne IDC [327]
INTESTATE SUCCESSION IN THE STATE OF NEW YORK / Remsen, Daniel Smith – New York: Baker, Voorhis, 1886. 150p. LL-1437 – 1 – us L of C Photodup [340]
INTESTINAL ABSORPTION – (See also: Intestinal Absorption and Related Topics) – v15- 1973 1; v21- 5,6,9 – us UMI [616]
INTESTINAL ABSORPTION AND RELATED TOPICS – v. 1-14. 1965-1972 – 1 – us UMI [616]
INTHUSATHANAM – Jaffna, Sri Lanka. 11 Sept 1889-31 Jan 1981 – 15r – 1 – us L of C Photodup [072]
L'INTIERO RAGGVAGLIO DEL SVCCESSO DI FAMACOSTA / Martinengo, N – N.p., [1571] – 1mf – 9 – H-8316/1 – ne IDC [956]
INTIKAM – Geneva. Yayimliyan: Yeni Osmanlilar, 1900-1902 – 9 – $25.00 – us MEDOC [956]
INTIMAS (POESIAS DE LOS TIEMPOS IDOS) / Sanchez-Arjona, Vicente – Sevilla: Graficas Tirvia, Tomo 1. 1954 – 1 – sp Bibl Santa Ana [810]
INTIMAS (POESIAS DE LOS TIEMPOS IDOS) / Sanchez-Arjona, Vicente – Sevilla: Graficas Tirvia, Tomo 2. 1954 – 1 – sp Bibl Santa Ana [810]
INTIMAS.POESIAS / Real, Enrique – 1897 – 9 – 1.50f – sp Bibl Santa Ana [810]
INTIMATE LETTERS OF JAMES GIBBONS HUNEKER, COLLECTED AND EDITED BY JOSEPHINE HUNEKER / Huneker, James – New York: Issued for subscribers only by Boni and Liveright, 1924. 322p – 1 – us U.W. Library [920]
INTIQAD-I KITAB – (Dawrah-'i 1: shumarah-'i 1-12; dawrah-'i 2: shumarah-'i 1-8; dawrah-'i 3: shumarah-'i 1-12; dawrah-'i 4: shumarah-'i 1, 3 (2 Day 1334-Aban/Azar 1347[23 Dec 1955-Oct/Dec 1968])) – Tehran: Intisharat-i Nil, 1955- – 1 reel – 1 – $45.00 – us MEDOC [950]
INTISARI – SE-898 1. 1963-1971 – 9 – ne IDC [073]
INTISARI ROMAN INDONESIA, MASA BALAI PUSTAKA S/D MASA ANGK. 45 / Sabaruddin, Ahmad – SE-4686 1. 1963 – 9 – ne IDC [950]
INTO EUROPE – 1967-1970 – 9 – us Primary [073]
L'INTOLERANCE RELIGIEUSE ET LA POLITIQUE / Bouche-Leclercq, A – Paris: E. Flammarion, 1911 – 1mf – us A.T.L.A. [240]
INTOXICANTS AND OPIUM IN ALL LANDS AND TIMES : A TWENTIETH-CENTURY SURVEY OF INTEMPERANCE, BASED ON A SYMPOSIUM OF TESTIMONY FROM ONE HUNDRED MISSIONARIES AND TRAVELERS / Crafts, Wilbur F et al – Washington, D.C.: International Reform Bureau, 1904, c1900 – 1mf – us A.T.L.A. [306]
INTOXICATING LIQUORS; THE LAW RELATING TO THE TRAFFIC IN INTOXICATING LIQUORS AND DRUNKENNESS / Woollen, William Watson – Cincinnati, Anderson, 1910. 2 v. LL-1252 – 1 – us L of C Photodup [340]
INTRAMURAL LAW JOURNAL *see* QUEEN'S LAW JOURNAL
INTRAMURAL LAW REVIEW *see*
- AMERICAN UNIVERSITY LAW REVIEW
- SAINT LOUIS UNIVERSITY LAW JOURNAL

L'INTRANSIGEANT – Paris, France. 15 Jul 1880-11 Jun 1940 – 212r – 1 – uk British Libr Newspaper [072]
L'INTRANSIGEANT – Paris. Red. en chef, H. De Rochefort. 15 juil 1880-10 juin 1940, 13 mai 1947-sept 1948 – 1 – fr A.C.R.P.P. [073]
INTRAREGIONAL LABOUR MOBILITY AND AGRICULTURAL DEVELOPMENT IN THE NEAR EAST : PHENOMENON, IMPACT AND POLICY IMPLICATIONS – 1990 – 73p – it F.A.O. [331]
INTRATESTER AND INTERTESTER RELIABILITY WHEN USING THE CHATILLON HAND-HELD DYNAMOMETER TO MEASURE FORCE PRODUCTION IN THE UPPER AND LOWER EXTREMITIES / Jefferson, LouAnne M – 1994 – 2mf – $8.00 – us Microform Publ [574]
INTRAVENOUS THERAPY NEWS – v11-. 1984- – 1,5,6,9 – us UMI [617]
INTRAVENOUS THERAPY NEWS *see* AMERICAN JOURNAL OF INTRAVENOUS THERAPY AND CLINICAL NUTRITION
L'INTREPIDE – Shawinigan-Sud, Canada. v4 n22. 17 fev 1966 – 1r – 1 – Can$25.00 – cn Can Microfilming [072]
INTRIGA Y AMOR / Hurtado, Antonio – 1872 – 9 – 1.50f – sp Bibl Santa Ana [830]
L'INTRIGANTE OU L'ECOLE DES FAMILLES / Etienne – (French Theatre Series). Le Normant et Barba. 1813 – 9 – fr Hachette [820]
INTRIGAS DE LOS RUSOS EN ESPANA; COMO Y POR QUE SALI DEL MINISTERIO DE DEFENSA NACIONAL / Prieto, Indalecio – Montevideo, 1940. Fiche W1119. (Blodgett Collection of Spanish Civil War Pamphlets) – 9 – us H.U. College Libr [946]
L'INTRIGUE AU CHATEAU / Catrufo, G – (Parts) – Ms copy – 1 – us Sibley [780]
INTRODUCAO A GEOGRAFIA DAS COMUNICACOES BRASILEIROS / Travassos, Mario – Rio de Janeiro. 1942 – 1 – us Res Libr [972]
INTRODUCCION A LA FILOSOFIA 1. INTRODUCCION Y LOGICA / Frutos Cortes, Eugenio – Zaragoza: Tip. Libreria General, 1943 – sp Bibl Santa Ana [160]
INTRODUCCION A LA FILOSOFIA 2. PSICOLOGIA Y ETICA / Frutos Cortes, Eugenio – Zaragoza: Tip. Libreria General, 1943 – sp Bibl Santa Ana [170]
INTRODUCCION A LA HISTORIA ECLESIASTICA DEL TUCUMAN, 1535 A 1590. BUENOS AIRES, 1934 / Cabrera, Pablo – Madrid: Razon y Fe, 1935 – 1 – sp Bibl Santa Ana [240]
INTRODUCCION A LA HISTORIA NATURAL / Bowles, Guillermo – 1782 – 2mf – 9 – Pta1,500.00 – 84-7848-223-7 – sp Pentalfa [500]

INTRODUCCION A LA POESIA DE LA SENORITA ARMINO / Coronado, Carolina – 1850 – 9 – 1.50f – sp Bibl Santa Ana [410]

INTRODUCCION A UN TRATADO DE POLITICA / Costa y Martinez, Joaquin – 1881 – 1 – us I.U. Libraries [320]

INTRODUCCION A UNA OBRA HISTORICA / Barrado Font, Francisco – Madrid: Imp. Sucesores de M.Minuesa de los Rios, 1901 – sp Bibl Santa Ana [946]

INTRODUCCION AL DERECHO, VERSION TAQUIGRAFICA DE CARLOS ARGENTA ESTABLE / Jimenez de Arechaga, Eduardo – Montevideo, Organizacion Taquigrafica Medina 194-? 342 p. LL-4107 – 1 – us L of C Photodup [340]

INTRODUCCION AL ESTUDIO DEL PROBLEMA AGRARIO ARGENTINO / Frigerio, Reinaldo A – Buenos Aires: Ediciones "Clase Obrera", [1953] – 1 – CSUXAHZ6461-B – us Hoover Inst Photo [630]

INTRODUCCION...QUE SE RECITO...SEVILLA / Forner Segarra, Juan Pablo – 1796 – 9 – 1.50f – sp Bibl Santa Ana [840]

INTRODUCING POPULATION CONCEPTS IN RURAL WOMEN'S PROGRAMMES – 1981 – 50p – it F.A.O. [307]

INTRODUCING THE MINISTRY OF EDUCATION / Thailand. Ministry of Education – Bangkok, 1980 – 1mf – 9 – DE-299/1 – ne IDC [370]

INTRODUCTIO AD HISTORIAM NATURALEM / Scopoli, Giovanni Antonio – Prague. 1777. B-5737 2 – 9 – ne IDC [574]

INTRODUCTIO GENERALIS IN REM HERBARIAM / Rivinus, A Q – (Ordo Plantarum quae sunt flore irregulari monopetalo Ordo Plantarum quae sunt flore irregulari tetrapetalo. Ordo Plantarum quae sunt flore irregulari pentapetalo). 4 pts. Lipsiae. 1690-99. B-288 – 8 – ne IDC [580]

INTRODUCTIO MUSICAE THEORETICAE DIDACTICAE, IN QUA PRAICIPUA EJUS PRINCIPIA, CUM PRIMIS VERO MATHEMATICA / Gibelius, O – Bremae. 1660. BP-295 1 – 9 – ne IDC [780]

INTRODUCTION : L'ETUDE DU DROIT DE LA MER / Alessandri – Paris, n.d. – 1mf – 9 – ILM-1606/1 – ne IDC [340]

INTRODUCTION A LA CHYMIE, OU A LA VRAYE PHYSIQVE / Arnaud, Enrico – Lyon, 1655 – 1 – us U.W. Library [610]

INTRODUCTION A LA LITTERATURE ORALE LEBOUE : ANALYSE ETHNO-SOCIOLOGIQUE / Ndoye, Mbengue nee Mariama – 1981 – us Res Libr [390]

INTRODUCTION A LA SCIENCE POLITIQUE / Meynaud, J – F60.00 – fr Ethnologie [320]

INTRODUCTION A L'ETUDE DE DROIT PENAL INTERNATIONAL : ESSAI D'HISTOIRE ET DE CRITIQUE SUR LA COMPETENCE CRIMINELLE DANS LES RAPPORTS AVEC L'ETRANGER / Donnedieu de Vabres, H – Paris, 1922 – 6mf – 1 – ILM-2269/1 – ne IDC [327]

INTRODUCTION A L'ETUDE DE LA LITERATURE JAPONAISE / Rosny, Leon de – Cours pratique de japonais, 2eme annee. no. 6. Paris: Ernest Leroux. 1896 – 9 – $5.00 – fr Orientalistes [480]

INTRODUCTION A L'ETUDE DE LA LITTERATURE ORALE DES VOUTE, CAMEROUN CENTRAL / N'Goura, C – Approche ethnolinguistique – 9 – F90.00 – fr Ethnologie [306]

INTRODUCTION A L'ETUDE DES CULTES POPULAIRES DANS LE PERCHE / Bensa, A – (Departements de l'Eure-et-Loir et Loir-et-Cher) – 9 – F30.00 – fr Ethnologie [944]

INTRODUCTION A L'ETUDE DES SERRURES BAMBARA / Tesi, P – 9 – F30.00 – fr Ethnologie [306]

INTRODUCTION A L'ETUDE DU LAIT / O'Connor, C B & Tripathi, B R – 1991 – 9 – $6.00 – 92-9053-215-7 – et ILRI [630]

INTRODUCTION A L'ETUDE D'UN GENRE SATIRICO-LAUDATIF : LE TAASU-WOLOF / Thiam, Mamadou Cherif – 1979 – us Res Libr [470]

INTRODUCTION A L'HISTOIRE DE L'ASIE, DE L'AFRIQUE, ET DE L'AMERIQUE / Bruzen la Martiniere, Antoine A – Amsterdam, Zacharie Chatelain. 1735 – 9 – 27.00 – fr Orientalistes [900]

INTRODUCTION A UN NOUVEAU SYSTEME D'HARMONIE PAR ABRAMO BASEVI... / Basevi, A – Florence: G G Guidi, 1865 – 1 – us Sibley [780]

INTRODUCTION AU MALGACHE / Faublee, Jacques – Paris: G P Maisonneuve, 1946 – 1 – us Res Libr [490]

INTRODUCTION AU NOUVEAU TESTAMENT / Goguel, Maurice – 4v. in 5. 1922-26 – 1 – us A.T.L.A. [240]

INTRODUCTION AU NOUVEAU TESTAMENT / Goguel, Maurice – (Tome 1: Les Evangelis Synoptiques. Paris 1923 9mf; Tome 2: Le Quatrieme Evangile. Paris 1923 10mf; Tome 3: Le Livre des Actes. Paris 1922 7mf; Tome 4/1: Les Epitres Pauliniennes. Premiere Partie. Paris 1925 7mf) – 8 – ne Slangenburg [220]

INTRODUCTION AUX ETUDES LITURGIQUES / Cabrol, Fernand – Paris: Bloud, 1907 – 1mf – us A.T.L.A. [240]

INTRODUCTION AUX MELODIES GREGORIENNES / D'Agen, Boyer – Paris: H. Oudin, 1894 – 1mf – us A.T.L.A. [780]

INTRODUCTION AUX OUVRAGES DE VOLTAIRE / Flottes, J BM – Par homme du monde qui a lu avec fruit ces ouvrages immortels. Montpellier. Impr. de Tournel. 1816. XIII – 9 – fr Hachette [440]

INTRODUCTION AUX SOURCES DE L'HISTOIRE DU CULTE CHRETIEN AU MOYEN AGE / Vogel, C – Spoleto, 1966 – 7mf – 8 – Dfl28.00 – ne Slangenburg [240]

L'INTRODUCTION DE L'IMPRIMERIE AU CANADA UNE BREVE HISTOIRE / Fauteux, Aegidius – Montreal: Compagnie de Papier Rolland, 1957. SEM16P139 – 1r – 5 – Can$9.00 – cn Bibl Nat [070]

AN INTRODUCTION INTO THE GREEKE TONGUE / Reeve, Edmund – 1650. 96p. (English Linguistics Series 1500-1800) – 9 – us UMI [450]

INTRODUCTION O THE ART OF PLAYING THE PIANOFORTE / Clementi, M – London: Clementi et al, 1803? – 1 – us Sibley [780]

INTRODUCTION OF UNIVERSAL PRIMARY EDUCATION : 1. WITHIN FIFTEEN YEARS (1960-1975). 2. WITHIN TEN YEARS (1960-1970) / Pakistan. Planning Commission. Education and Training – 1959 – 1mf – 9 – DE-579/1 – ne IDC [370]

THE INTRODUCTION TO A NEW PHILOSOPHY / Bergson, Henri – Boston: J.W. Luce, 1912.108p. Trans. by Sidney Littman – 1 – us U.W. Library [120]

INTRODUCTION TO AFRICAN PASTURELAND PRODUCTION, WITH SPECIAL REFERENCE TO FARM AND RANGELAND ENVIRONMENTS OF EASTERN AFRICA – 1980 – 204p – it F.A.O. [338]

INTRODUCTION TO AGRICULTURAL PLANNING – 1975 – 123p – it F.A.O. [338]

INTRODUCTION TO AMERICAN LAW...11TH ED / Walker, Timothy – Boston, Little, Brown, 1905. 692 p. LL-154 – 1 – us L of C Photodup [340]

INTRODUCTION TO CHRISTIAN MISSIONS / Johnson, Thomas Cary – Richmond, Va.: For Sale by Presbyterian Commitee of Publication, c1910 – 1mf – us A.T.L.A. [240]

INTRODUCTION TO CHRISTIAN THEOLOGY...OR, THE PROLEGOMENA OF SYSTEMATIC THEOLOGY / Smith, Henry Boynton – New York: A.C. Armstrong, 1883. 1 fiche – 9 – us A.T.L.A. [240]

AN INTRODUCTION TO CHURCH HISTORY (CCC271) = CHIAO HUI SHIH CHI JU WEN : THE APOSTOLIC AND POST-APOSTOLIC AGES / Ridgely, L B – (In Chinese) – Hankow: Committee on Church Literature of the General Synod of the Chung Hwa Sheng Kung Hui, 1915 – 1r – 1 – 1984-6610 – us A.T.L.A. [240]

AN INTRODUCTION TO CONCHOLOGY, OR, ELEMENTS OF THE NATURAL HISTORY OF MOLLUSCUS ANIMALS / Johnston, G – 1850. Z-591/2 – 8 – ne IDC [590]

AN INTRODUCTION TO CUDWORTH'S TREATISE CONCERNING ETERNAL AND IMMUTABLE MORALITY : WITH LIFE OF CUDWORTH AND A FEW CRITICAL NOTES / Scott, William Robert – London, New York: Longmans, Green, 1891 – xii/67p – 1 – us U.W. Library [190]

AN INTRODUCTION TO DOGMATIC THEOLOGY: BASED ON LUTHARDT / Weidner, Revere Franklin – New York: Fleming H. Revell, 1895. 1 fiche – 9 – us A.T.L.A. [240]

AN INTRODUCTION TO ECCLESIASTES : WITH NOTES AND APPENDICES / McNeile, Alan Hugh – (Includes appendixes and index) – Cambridge: University Press; New York: Macmillan [distributor], 1904 – 1mf – 9 – 0-8370-6220-9 – 1986-0220 – us A.T.L.A. [220]

AN INTRODUCTION TO ENGLISH CHURCH ARCHITECTURE, 11TH TO 16TH CENTURY / Bond, Francis – 1913. 2v. H-1236-2 – 8 – ne IDC [941]

AN INTRODUCTION TO ENGLISH CHURCH ARCHITECTURE FROM THE ELEVENTH TO THE SIXTEENTH CENTURY / Bond, Francis – London, New York: Oxford University Press, 1913 – 3mf – us A.T.L.A. [720]

AN INTRODUCTION TO ENGLISH INDUSTRIAL HISTORY / Allsopp, Henry – London: G. Bell & Sons, 1912. xi,160p. maps – 1 – us U.W. Library [380]

AN INTRODUCTION TO ENTOMOLOGY, OR, ELEMENTS OF THE NATURAL HISTORY OF INSECTS / Kirby, W F & Spence, W – London, 1818-26.4v. Z-1390/2 – 8 – ne IDC [590]

INTRODUCTION TO ERGONOMICS IN FORESTRY IN DEVELOPING COUNTRIES – 1992 – 207p – it F.A.O. [620]

AN INTRODUCTION TO ETHICS / Murray, John Clark – (Includes bibliographical references & index) – Boston: De Wolfe, Fiske, c1891 – 1mf – 9 – 0-8370-6228-4 – 1986-0228 – us A.T.L.A. [170]

INTRODUCTION TO FISHERIES MANAGEMENT : ADVANTAGES, DIFFICULTIES AND MECHANISMS – 1992 – 63p – it F.A.O. [650]

INTRODUCTION TO GREEK AND LATIN PALEOGRAPHY / Thompson, E M – 1912 – 9 – ne IDC [410]

AN INTRODUCTION TO HERALDRY: WITH NEARLY ONE THOUSAND ILLUSTRATIONS, INCLUDING THE ARMS OF ABOUT FIVE HUNDRED DIFFERENT FAMILIES / Clark, Hugh; ed by Planche, J R – 18th ed. rev. and corrected. London: Bell & Daldy, 1866. viii,279p – 1 – us U.W. Library [920]

AN INTRODUCTION TO HISTORICAL THEOLOGY : BEING A SKETCH OF DOCTRINAL PROGRESS FROM THE APOSTOLIC ERA TO THE REFORMATION / Stoughton, John – London: Religious Tract Society, [1880?] – 2mf – us A.T.L.A. [240]

AN INTRODUCTION TO INDONESIAN LINGUISTICS / Brandstetter, R – 1916 – 1 – uk Microform Academic [490]

INTRODUCTION TO INTER-CULTURAL STUDIES : OUTLINE OF A PROJECT FOR ELUCIDATING AND PROMOTING COMMUNICATIONS BETWEEN CULTURES – 1983 – 221p – 9 – 92-3-101850-7 – fr UNESCO [370]

AN INTRODUCTION TO JUNG'S PSYCHOLOGY / Fordham, Frieda – London, Baltimore: Penguin Books, (1953). 127p – 1 – us U.W. Library [150]

AN INTRODUCTION TO LANGUAGES, LITERARY AND PHILOSOPHICAL / Bayly, Anselm – 1758. 313p. (English Linguistics Series 1500-1800) – 9 – us UMI [400]

AN INTRODUCTION TO LOGICK, SCHOLASTICK AND RATIONAL / Bentham, Edward – 1773. 147p. (English Linguistics Series 1500-1800) – 9 – us UMI [160]

AN INTRODUCTION TO MEDICAL LITERATURE INCLUDING A SYSTEM OF PRACTICAL NOSOLOGY / Young, T – London, 1813 – 11mf – ne IDC [610]

AN INTRODUCTION TO MEDICAL LITERATURE, INCLUDING A SYSTEM OF PRACTICAL NOSOLOGY / Young, T – M 230. 1813 – 9 – ne IDC [610]

AN INTRODUCTION TO MILK / O'Connor, C B & Tripathi, B R – 1991 – 9 – $6.00 – 92-9053-214-9 – et ILRI [630]

INTRODUCTION TO POLICY ANALYSIS IN SCIENCE AND TECHNOLOGY – 1982 – 93p – 9 – 92-3-101725-X – fr UNESCO [320]

AN INTRODUCTION TO PROTESTANT DOGMATICS / Lobstein, Paul – Chicago?: A.M. Smith, 1902. 1 fiche – 9 – us A.T.L.A. [240]

INTRODUCTION TO PSYCHOLOGICAL THEORY / Bowne, Borden Parker – New York: Harper, 1887, c1886 – 1mf – us A.T.L.A. [150]

INTRODUCTION TO ROMAN LAW, IN TWELVE ACADEMICAL LECTURES / Hadley, James – New York: D.Appleton and Company, 1873. 332p. With: Histoire Poetique du Quinzieme Siecle by P. Champion. 1 reel. 1261 – 1 – us U.W. Library [340]

AN INTRODUCTION TO THE ART OF READING WITH ENERGY AND PROPRIETY / Rice, John – 1765. 247p. (English Linguistics Series 1500-1800) – 9 – us UMI [420]

AN INTRODUCTION TO THE ARTICLES OF THE CHURCH OF ENGLAND / Maclear, George Frederick & William, Watkin Wynn – (Includes bibliographical references and index) – [rev ed]. London; New York: Macmillan, 1896 – 2mf – 9 – 0-8370-8694-9 – 1986-2694 – us A.T.L.A. [240]

AN INTRODUCTION TO THE BIRDS OF AUSTRALIA / Gould, J – London, 1848. viii,134p. Z/1775/2 – 8 – ne IDC [590]

INTRODUCTION TO THE BOOK OF ISAIAH : WITH AN APPENDIX CONTAINING THE UNDOUBTED PORTIONS OF THE TWO CHIEF PROPHETIC WRITERS IN A TRANSLATION / Cheyne, Thomas Kelly – (Includes indexes) – London: Adam & Charles Black, 1895 – 2mf – 9 – 0-8370-2648-2 – 1985-0648 – us A.T.L.A. [220]

AN INTRODUCTION TO THE BOOKS OF EZRA, NEHEMIAH, AND ESTHER / Sayce, Archibald Henry – London: Religious Tract Society, 1889. 1 fiche – 9 – us A.T.L.A. [240]

AN INTRODUCTION TO THE BOOKS OF THE APOCRYPHA / Oesterley, William Oscar Emil – New York: Macmillan, (1946), c1935. 345p – 1 – us U.W. Library [240]

AN INTRODUCTION TO THE BOOKS OF THE OLD TESTAMENT / Oesterly, William Oscar Emil & Robinson, T H – 1934 – 9 – $15.00 – us I.R.C. [220]

INTRODUCTION TO THE BOOKS OF THE OLD TESTAMENT : WITH ANALYSES AND ILLUSTRATIVE LITERATURE / Stearns, Oakman S – (Includes bibliographies) – Boston:Silver, Burdett, 1888 – 1mf – 9 – 0-8370-5378-1 – 1985-3378 – us A.T.L.A. [220]

INTRODUCTION TO THE CANONICAL BOOKS OF THE OLD TESTAMENT / Cornill, Carl Heinrich – London: Williams & Norgate, 1907. 2 fiches – 9 – us A.T.L.A. [240]

INTRODUCTION TO THE CATHOLIC EPISTLES / Gloag, Paton James – Edinburgh: T &T Clark, 1887 – 1mf – 9 – 0-8370-3310-1 – 1985-1310 – us A.T.L.A. [220]

AN INTRODUCTION TO THE CREEDS / Maclear, George Frederick – London, New York: Macmillan, 1901 – 1mf – us A.T.L.A. [240]

AN INTRODUCTION TO THE CREEDS AN TO THE TE DEUM / Burn, A E – London: Methuen, 1899 – 1mf – us A.T.L.A. [240]

AN INTRODUCTION TO THE CREEDS (CCC221) / Lin, Pu-chi – (In Chinese) – [Peiping, China]: Church Literature Committee of the Chung Hua Sheng Kung Hui, 1933 – 1r – 1 – 1984-B500 – us A.T.L.A. [220]

INTRODUCTION TO THE CRITICAL STUDY OF ECCLESIASTICAL HISTORY / Dowling, John Goulter – London: Printed for J.G.& F. Rivington, 1838 – 1mf – us A.T.L.A. [240]

AN INTRODUCTION TO THE DEPARTMENT OF EDUCATIONAL TECHNIQUE / Thailand. Ministry of Education. Department of Educational Techniques – Bangkok, 1978 – 1mf – 9 – DE-292/1 – ne IDC [370]

AN INTRODUCTION TO THE DEPARTMENT OF TEACHER TRAINING 1976-1979 / Thailand. Department of Teacher Training – (In Thai. Missing: 1976-1978) – Bangkok – 2mf – 9 – DE-283/1 – ne IDC [370]

AN INTRODUCTION TO THE EARLY HISTORY OF CHRISTIAN DOCTRINE : TO THE TIME OF THE COUNCIL OF CHALCEDON / Bethune-Baker, James Franklin – London: Methuen, 1903 – 2mf – us A.T.L.A. [240]

INTRODUCTION TO THE ECONOMICS OF FISHERIES MANAGEMENT – 1992 – 41p – it F.A.O. [338]

INTRODUCTION TO THE EDUCATIONAL SCIENCES / Mialaret, G – 1986 – 106p – 9 – 92-3-102302-0 – fr UNESCO [370]

AN INTRODUCTION TO THE FEDERAL PROBATION SYSTEM – Washington: FJC, 1976 – 3mf – 9 – $4.50 – LLMC 95-823 – us L.L.M.C. [340]

AN INTRODUCTION TO THE GEORGIST PHILOSOPHY AND MOVEMENT / Council of Georgist Organizations – 6p – 9 – 1.00f – at Libertarian Micro [335]

THE INTRODUCTION TO THE GOSPEL OF JOHN / Clarke, James Freeman – Boston: G H Ellis, 1890 – 1mf – 9 – 0-8370-2672-5 – 1985-0672 – us A.T.L.A. [220]
AN INTRODUCTION TO THE GRAMMAR OF THE KUI OR KANDH LANGUAGE / Letchmajee, Lingum – 2nd rev ed. Calcutta: Bengal Secretariat Press, 1902 – 1 – us Res Libr [490]
AN INTRODUCTION TO THE HISTORY OF EDUCATIONAL THEORIES / Browning, Oscar – Toronto: W. Gage, 1886. 00283. (Pre-1900 Canadiana) – 9 – cn C.I.H.M. [370]
AN INTRODUCTION TO THE HISTORY OF THE DEVELOPMENT OF LAW / Morris, M F – Washington: John Byrne & Co, 1916 – 4mf – 9 – $6.00 – LLMC 95-158 – us L.L.M.C. [340]
INTRODUCTION TO THE JOHANNINE WRITINGS / Gloag, Paton James – (Includes bibliographical references & index) – London: James Nisbet, 1891 – 2mf – 9 – 0-8370-3311-X – 1985-1311 – us A.T.L.A. [220]
AN INTRODUCTION TO THE LATIN TONGUE – Anon. 1758. 195p. (English Linguistics Series 1500-1800) – 9 – us UMI [450]
INTRODUCTION TO THE LAW OF REAL PROPERTY / Bigelow, Harry Augustus – 2nd ed. St. Paul, West, 1934. 95 p. LL-749 – 1 – us L of C Photodup [340]
AN INTRODUCTION TO THE LIFE OF JESUS : AN INVESTIGATION OF THE HISTORICAL SOURCES / Anthony, Alfred Williams – (Includes index) – Boston: Silver, Burdett, 1896 – 1mf – 9 – 0-8370-2106-5 – 1985-0106 – us A.T.L.A. [240]
INTRODUCTION TO THE LIFE OF JESUS: AN INVESTIGATION OF THE HISTORICAL SOURCES / Anthony, Alfred Williams – Boston: Silver, Burdett, 1896. 1 fiche – 9 – us A.T.L.A. [240]
INTRODUCTION TO THE LITERATURE OF EUROPE : IN THE FIFTEENTH, SIXTEENTH AND SEVENTEENTH CENTURIES / Hallam, Henry – London: John Murray, 1837-39 – 4 rolls – 1 – 1-55879-029-2 – uk Libr Preservation [410]
AN INTRODUCTION TO THE LITERATURE OF THE NEW TESTAMENT / Moffatt, James – (Includes bibliographies and indexes) – New York: Charles Scribner, 1911 – 2mf – 9 – 0-8370-9490-9 – 1986-3490 – us A.T.L.A. [220]
AN INTRODUCTION TO THE MAKING OF LATIN / Clarke, John – 1721. 293p. (English Linguistics Series 1500-1800) – 9 – us UMI [450]
AN INTRODUCTION TO THE NATURAL SYSTEM OF BOTANY / Lindley, J – London. 1830. B-6024 2 – 8 – ne IDC [580]
AN INTRODUCTION TO THE NEW TESTAMENT / Davidson, Samuel – 3v. 1848-1851 – 9 – us A.T.L.A. [240]
AN INTRODUCTION TO THE NEW TESTAMENT / Dods, Marcus – New York: Thomas Whittaker, 1888 – 1mf – 9 – 0-8370-2938-4 – 1985-0938 – us A.T.L.A. [220]
INTRODUCTION TO THE NEW TESTAMENT = INTRODUCTION AU NOUVEAU TESTAMENT : 1., THE EPISTLES OF ST. PAUL: PARTICULAR INTRODUCTION / Godet, Frederic Louis – (In English. Includes bibliographical references) – Edinburgh: T & T Clark, 1894 – 2mf – 9 – 0-8370-9387-2 – 1986-3387 – us A.T.L.A. [220]
INTRODUCTION TO THE NEW TESTAMENT = INTRODUCTION AU NOUVEAU TESTAMENT, TOME 2 : THE COLLECTION OF THE FOUR GOSPELS AND THE GOSPEL OF ST. MATTHEW / Godet, Frederic Louis – (In English) – Edinburgh: T & T Clark, 1899 – 1mf – 9 – 0-8370-3320-9 – 1985-1320 – us A.T.L.A. [220]
INTRODUCTION TO THE NEW TESTAMENT / Michaelis, Johann David – Trans. from the 4th German ed. by Herbert Marsh. 1823 – 9 – us A.T.L.A. [240]
AN INTRODUCTION TO THE OLD TESTAMENT / Wright, Charles Henry Hamilton – New York: Thomas Whittaker, 1891. 1 fiche – 9 – us A.T.L.A. [240]
INTRODUCTION TO THE OLD TESTAMENT / McFadyen, John Edgar – New York: A.C. Armstrong, 1906. 1 fiche – 9 – us A.T.L.A. [240]
AN INTRODUCTION TO THE OLD TESTAMENT IN GREEK / Swete, Henry Barclay – 1900 – 9 – $21.00 – us I.R.C. [220]
AN INTRODUCTION TO THE OLD TESTAMENT IN GREEK / Swete, Henry Barclay – Cambridge: University Press, 1914. 626p. 2 fiches – 9 – us A.T.L.A. [240]
AN INTRODUCTION TO THE PENTATEUCH / Chapman, Arthur Thomas – (Includes bibliographical references and index) – Cambridge: University Press; New York: G P Putnam [distributor], 1911 – 1mf – 9 – 0-8370-6727-8 – 1986-0727 – us A.T.L.A. [220]
INTRODUCTION TO THE PHILOSOPHY OF RELIGION / Caird, John – New York: Macmillan, 1894. 1 fiche – 9 – us A.T.L.A. [240]
INTRODUCTION TO THE SCIENCE OF LAW : SYSTEMATIC SURVEY OF THE LAW AND PRINCIPLES OF LEGAL STUDY / Gareis, Karl – 3rd rev German ed. N.Y.: The Macmillan Co, 1911 (reprint 1924) – 5mf – 9 – $7.50 – LLMC 95-187 – us L.L.M.C. [340]
AN INTRODUCTION TO THE SINGING OF PSALM-TUNES, IN A PLAIN AND EASY METHOD / Tufts, John – With a collection of tunes in three parts. 10th ed. Boston: Samuel Gerrish, 1738. MUSIC 1152 – 1 – us L of C Photodup [780]
AN INTRODUCTION TO THE SKILL OF MUSICK IN THREE BOOKS / Playford, J – 1683. 10th ed., corrected and enlarged – 9 – us Sibley [780]
AN INTRODUCTION TO THE SKILL OF MUSICK: IN THREE BOOKS / Playford, J – Ed. 19. London. 1730. BP-736 1 – 9 – ne IDC [780]
INTRODUCTION TO THE SOLUTION OF THE PROBLEMS OF THE PYRAMID / Davie, John G – Griffin, GA, printed in U.S.A., 1934. pt.1-8 in 1v. 922p – 1 – us U.W. Library [150]
AN INTRODUCTION TO THE STUDY OF CHRISTIAN APOLOGETICS / Gray, Arthur R – Sewanee, Tenn.: University Press at the University of the South, c1912 – 1mf – us A.T.L.A. [240]
AN INTRODUCTION TO THE STUDY OF EFFORTS AT CHRISTIAN REUNION / Bouquet, A C – Cambridge: W. Heffer, 1914 – 1mf – us A.T.L.A. [240]
AN INTRODUCTION TO THE STUDY OF FISHES / Guenther, A C LG – Z-2113 2. 1880 – 8 – ne IDC [590]
INTRODUCTION TO THE STUDY OF FORAMINIFERA / Carpenter, W B – Ray Society. 1862 – 1. 42.00; ; 7 – uk Microform Academic [580]
INTRODUCTION TO THE STUDY OF HISTORY / Langlois, CV & Seignobos, C – New York: H. Holt, [1898?] – 1mf – us A.T.L.A. [900]
INTRODUCTION TO THE STUDY OF INDIAN LANGUAGES WITH WORDS, PHRASES, AND SENTENCES TO BE COLLECTED / Powell, J W – Washington: GPO. 1877 – 1 – us KS Hist [490]
INTRODUCTION TO THE STUDY OF MORTUARY CUSTOMS AMONG NORTH AMERICAN INDIANS / Yarrow, Henry Crecy – Washington. 1880 – 1 – us Res Libr [390]
AN INTRODUCTION TO THE STUDY OF NEW TESTAMENT GREEK / Moulton, James Hope – (Includes indexes) – London: Charles H Kelly, 1895 – 1mf – 9 – 0-8370-9298-1 – 1986-3298 – us A.T.L.A. [450]
AN INTRODUCTION TO THE STUDY OF OBADIAH / Peckham, George A – (In English and Hebrew) – Chicago: University of Chicago Press, 1910 – 1mf – 9 – 0-8370-9811-4 – 1986-3811 – us A.T.L.A. [220]
AN INTRODUCTION TO THE STUDY OF ROMAN LAW / Cushing, Luther Stearns – Boston Little: Brown, 1854 – 3mf – 9 – $4.50 – LLMC 95-198 – us L.L.M.C. [340]
AN INTRODUCTION TO THE STUDY OF THE ACTS OF THE APOSTLES / Stifler, James M – New York:Fleming H. Revell, c1892 – 1mf – 9 – 0-8370-5420-6 – 1985-3420 – us A.T.L.A. [220]
INTRODUCTION TO THE STUDY OF THE BOOKS OF THE NEW TESTAMENT / Kerr, John Henry – Chicago: Fleming H. Revell, 1892. 1 fiche – 9 – us A.T.L.A. [240]
AN INTRODUCTION TO THE STUDY OF THE CHALDEE LANGUAGE : COMPRISING A GRAMMAR (BASED UPON WINER'S), AND AN ANALYSIS OF THE TEXT OF THE CHALDEE PORTION OF THE BOOK OF DANIEL / Longfield, George – (Includes bibliography and index) – London: Whittaker; Dublin: Hodges, Smith, 1859 – 1mf – 9 – 0-8370-9165-9 – 1986-3165 – us A.T.L.A. [470]
INTRODUCTION TO THE STUDY OF THE DECISIONS OF THE SUPREME COURT OF OHIO. / Rockel, William Mahlon – Norwalk, Ohio: Laning 1902. 75p. LL-618 – 1 – us L of C Photodup [340]
INTRODUCTION TO THE STUDY OF THE DEPENDENT, DEFECTIVE, AND DELINQUENT CLASSES : AND OF THEIR SOCIAL TREATMENT / Henderson, Charles Richmond – Boston, U.S.A.: D.C. Heath, 1901 – 1mf – us A.T.L.A. [305]
INTRODUCTION TO THE STUDY OF THE GOSPEL OF ST LUKE / MacLean, John Patterson – Cincinnati: Robert Clarke, 1895.1 fiche – 9 – us A.T.L.A. [240]
INTRODUCTION TO THE STUDY OF THE GOSPELS / Westcott, Brooke Foss – 1862 – 9 – us A.T.L.A. [240]
INTRODUCTION TO THE STUDY OF THE GREEK DIALECTS : GRAMMAR, SELECTED INSCRIPTIONS, GLOSSARY / Buck, Carl Darling – (Includes index) – Boston: Ginn, c1910 – 1mf – 9 – 0-8370-9209-4 – 1986-3209 – us A.T.L.A. [450]
AN INTRODUCTION TO THE STUDY OF THE MIDDLE AGES (375-814) / Emerton, Ephraim – Boston: Ginn, 1888 – 1mf – us A.T.L.A. [900]
AN INTRODUCTION TO THE STUDY OF THE NEW TESTAMENT / Davidson, Samuel – 2v. 1882 – 9 – us A.T.L.A. [240]
AN INTRODUCTION TO THE STUDY OF THE ROMAN LAW / Cushing, Luther Stearns – Boston, Little, Brown, 1854. 243 p. LL-4095 – 1 – us L of C Photodup [340]
INTRODUCTION TO THE STUDY OF THEOLOGY / Drummond, James – London: Macmillan, 1884.1 fiche – 9 – us A.T.L.A. [240]
INTRODUCTION TO THE SYNOPTIC GOSPELS / Gloag, Paton James – (Includes indexes) – Edinburgh: T & T Clark, 1895 – 1mf – 9 – 0-8370-3312-8 – 1985-1312 – us A.T.L.A. [220]
INTRODUCTION TO THE TEXTUAL CRITICISM OF THE GREEK NEW TESTAMENT / Nestle, Eberhard – New York: G.P. Putnam's, 1901. 1 fiche – 9 – us A.T.L.A. [240]
AN INTRODUCTION TO THE TEXTUAL CRITICISM OF THE NEW TESTAMENT / Warfield, Benjamin Breckinridge – New York: Thomas Whittaker, 1886?. 1 fiche – 9 – us A.T.L.A. [240]
AN INTRODUCTION TO THE TROCHILIDAE / Gould, J – London, 1861. Z/1778/2 – 8 – ne IDC [590]
INTRODUCTION TO THE...OLD TESTAMENT: WITH...ILLUSTRATIVE LITERATURE / Stearns, Oakman Sprague – Boston: Silver, Burdett, 1888. 1 fiche – 9 – us A.T.L.A. [240]
INTRODUCTION TO TROPICAL FISH STOCK ASSESSMENT : EXERCISES – 1992 – 102p – it F.A.O. [639]
INTRODUCTIONS IN FRENSSHE FOR HENRY THE YONGE ERLE OF LYNCOLN / Valence, Pierre – 1528. 127p. (English Linguistics Series 1500-1800) – 9 – us UMI [440]
AN INTRODUCTORIE FOR TO LERNE TO REDE TO PRONOUNCE, AND TO SPEKE FRENCHE TREWLY / Du Wes, Giles – 1532. 207p. (English Linguistics Series 1500-1800) – 9 – us UMI [440]
AN INTRODUCTORY ADDRESS, DELIVERED BEFORE THE LAW CLASS OF TRANSYLVANIA UNIVERSITY, ON THE 9TH OF NOV. 1839 / Marshall, Thomas Alexander – Lexington, Ky: Finnell & Virden, 1839. 16,3p. LL-462 – 1 – us L of C Photodup [340]
INTRODUCTORY CATECHISM, VOL 2 (CCC344) = CHI TU CHIAO TSIN PU WEN TI / Yang, Tzu-hung; ed by Price, P F – (In Chinese) – [s.l: s.n, 1938] – 1r – 1 – 1984-6683 – us A.T.L.A. [240]
INTRODUCTORY GRAMMATICAL REMARKS ON THE PERSIAN LANGUAGE / Hadley, George – 1776. 217p. (English Linguistics Series 1500-1800) – 9 – us UMI [490]
AN INTRODUCTORY HEBREW GRAMMAR : WITH PROGRESSIVE EXERCISES IN READING AND WRITING / Davidson, Andrew Bruce – (Includes English-Hebrew and Hebrew-English vocabularies) – 18th ed. Edinburgh: T & T Clark, 1909 – 1mf – 9 – 0-8370-9222-1 – 1986-3222 – us A.T.L.A. [470]
INTRODUCTORY HEBREW METHOD AND MANUAL / Harper, William Rainey – 4th ed. New York: Charles Scribner, 1888, c1886 – 1mf – 9 – 0-8370-9152-7 – 1986-3152 – us A.T.L.A. [470]
INTRODUCTORY HINTS TO ENGLISH READERS OF THE OLD TESTAMENT / Cross, John A – London: Longmans, Green, 1882 – 1mf – 9 – 0-8370-3410-8 – 1985-1410 – us A.T.L.A. [220]
AN INTRODUCTORY LECTURE ON THE STUDY OF ECCLESIASTICAL HISTORY / Hatch, Edwin – London: Rivingtons, 1885 – 1mf – us A.T.L.A. [240]
INTRODUCTORY LESSONS ON CHRISTIAN EVIDENCES / Whately, Richard – Cincinnati: Poe & Hitchcock, 1864. 1 fiche – 9 – us A.T.L.A. [240]
INTRODUCTORY SKETCH OF THE BANTU LANGUAGES / Werner, A – London. 1919. BA-377 2 – 8 – ne IDC [490]
INTRODUCTORY STUDIES IN GERMAN LITERATURE / Hochdoerfer, Richard – Chautauqua, NY: The Chautauqua Press, 1904 – 1r – 1 – us U.W. Library [430]
AN INTRODUCTORY STUDY OF ETHICS / Fite, Warner – (Includes bibliographical references and index) – New York: Longmans, Green, 1906, c1903 – 1mf – 9 – 0-8370-6043-5 – 1986-0043 – us A.T.L.A. [170]
INTRODUZIONE AD UN NOUVE SISTEMA D'ARMONIA / Basevi, A – Firenze: Tip. Tofani, 1862 – 1 – us Sibley [780]
INTRODUZIONE AL DIRITTO CIVILE INTERNAZIONALE ITALIANO / Gabba, C F – Roma, 1906 – 1mf – 1 – ILM-3641/1 – ne IDC [327]
INTRODVCTIO IN LINGVAM ARABICAM... / Radtmann, B – Francofvrti, 1588 – 1mf – 9 – H-8410/1 – ne IDC [470]
INTRONISATION DE SA GRANDEUR MGR. ELPHEGE GRAVEL, PREMIER EVEQUE DE NICOLET: SUIVIS SIC DE SON MANDEMENT D'ENTREE ET DE RENSEIGNEMENTS INTERESSANTS SUR LE NOUVEAU DIOCESE / Camirand, Wilfrid – 1895. 00394. (Pre-1900 Canadiana) – 9 – cn C.I.H.M. [240]
INTRUDER IN THE DUST – Concordance to the novel – 7mf – 9 – us UMI [420]
INTU CATANAM *see* HINDU ORGAN
INUIT MONTHLY – Canada, 1973-76 – 1 – cn Commonwealth Micro [072]
INUKTITUORUTIT : GRAMMAIRE PUREMENT ESQUIMAUDE / Schneider, Lucien – Quebec: Ministere des Richesses naturelles..., 1972. SEM105P938 – 8mf – 9 – Can$20.25 – cn Bibl Nat [490]
INUKTITUORUTIT: GRAMMAIRE PUREMENT ESQUIMAUDE / Schneider, Lucien – Quebec: Centre de Documentation..., 1978 i.e. 1979. SEM105P936 – 2mf – 9 – Can$4.50 – cn Bibl Nat [490]
INUKTITUT – Ottawa. nos 59-77. 1985-94 – 9 – Can$20.00y – cn Micromedia [306]
INVALID (HARBIN, CHINA) – (Includes c.1: 1936:Nov.15) – Kharbin: Izd-vo Kharbinskogo obshchestva pomoshchi invalidam, 19uu – 1 – CSUXADP4998-S – us Hoover Inst Photo [950]
DER INVALIDE : HISTORISCH-ROMANTISCHE BILDER NEUERER ZEIT / Spindler, Carl – Gera: C B Griesbach, 1897 – 1r – 1 – us U.W. Library [830]
INVANTAIRE DES DEUS LANGUES, FRANCOISE ET LATINE / Monet, P – 1636 – 9 – fr I.C.S. [450]
INVARIANTE KLASSIFIZIERUNG ELEKTRONENMIKROSKOPISCHER AUFNAHMEN VON EISEINGEBETTETEN BIOLOGISCHEN MAKROMOLEKUELEN / Schatz, Michael – 1992 – 179p – DM98.00 – 3-89349-454-5 – gw Hänsel [530]
INVASION AND METASTASIS – v1-. 1981- – 1,5,9 – us UMI [610]
L'INVASION DE LA MER / Verne, Jules – Paris: J. Hetzel, 1905. 331p. 4 fiches. (Literature Collection) – 9 – 10.00 – fr Bibl Nationale [830]
L'INVASION DE LA VENDEE : LA BATAILLE DE TORFOU... / Arnault, Charles – Lucon: Pacteau, 1930 – 1 – F55.98 – fr Armell [944]
INVENTAIRE CHRONOLOGIQUE / Dionne, Narcisse Eutrope – Quebec, 1905-09. SEM105P507 – 10mf – 9 – Can$22.50 – cn Bibl Nat [010]

INVENTAIRE CHRONOLOGIQUE DES LIVRES, BROCHURES, JOURNEAUX ET REVUES PUBLIES EN DIVERSES LANGUES DANS ET HORS LA PROVINCE DE QUEBEC / Dionne, Narcisse Eutrope – Quebec, 1912. SEM105P508 – 1mf – 9 – Can$2.25 – cn Bibl Nat [010]

INVENTAIRE DES ARCHIVES DES AFFAIRES ETRANGERES DE L'ETAT INDEPENDANT DU CONGO ET DU MINISTERE DES COLONIES, 1885-1914 – Bruxelles, 1955 – us Res Libr [327]

INVENTAIRE DES SCEAUX DE LA COLLECTION CLAIRAM BAULT A LA BIBLIOTHEQUE NATIONALE / Demay, G – Paris, 1885-1886. 2v – 5mf – 9 – F150.00 – fr F.F.G. [920]

INVENTAIRE DES SCEAUX DE LA FLANDRE / Demay – 2v. Paris, 1873 – 4mf – 9 – F120.00 – fr F.F.G. [920]

INVENTAIRE DES SCEAUX DE LA NORMANDIE / Demay – Paris, 1881 – 2mf – 9 – F60.00 – fr F.F.G. [920]

INVENTAIRE DES SCEAUX DE L'ARTOIS ET DE LA PICARDIE / Demay – Paris, 1877 – 3mf – 9 – F90.00 – fr F.F.G. [920]

INVENTAIRE GENERAL DES PEINTURES DU MUSEE DU CHATEAU DE VERSAILLES / Constant, Claire – 1979. (Plus de cinq mille oeuvres majeures identifiea1es et reproduites) – 9 – fr Réunion [760]

INVENTAIRE MANUSCRIT DE LA COLLECTION FRIEDRICHS (ESTAMPES) – 19th c. – fr Armell [760]

LES INVENTAIRES DES ARCHIVES NATIONALES DE PARIS / Paris. Archives Nationales – (Includes a suppl of 73 inventories on 2047mf £7,445. Separate sections available: Section Ancienne (Pre-1789) 3082mf £13,890; Section Moderne (1789-1940) et Contemporaine(since 1940) 1830mf £7,385; Archives Privees 1429mf £5,215; La Revolution Francaise 1104mf £4,360; Les Beaux-Arts 378mf £1,320) – 773 inventories on 8388mf – 9 – £25,360.00 – uk Chadwyck [020]

INVENTAIRES ET DOCUMENTS PUBLIES PAR ORDRE DE L'EMPEREUR : LAYETTES DU TRESOR DES CHARTES / ed by Teulet, A et al – (Missing: v4-5) – Paris. 5v. 1863-1901 – 78mf – ne IDC [944]

INVENTAIRES ET DOCUMENTS PUBLIES PAR ORDRE DE L'EMPEREUR. LAYETTES DU TRESOR DES CHARTES / ed by Teulet, A et al – (Missing: v4-5) – Paris, 1863-1901. 5v – 78mf – 9 – H-666/2 – ne IDC [324]

INVENTARIO DE...MUSEO...BADAJAZ / Romero de Castilla, Tomas – 1896 – 9 – $1.50f – sp Bibl Santa Ana [900]

INVENTARIO GENERAL DE RAGISTROS CEDULARIOS DEL ARCHIVO GENERAL DE INDIAS DE SEVILLA... / Rubio Moreno, Luis – Madrid: Razon y Fe, 1929 – 1 – sp Bibl Santa Ana [350]

INVENTARIOS E TESTAMENTOS / Brazil. Sao Paulo. Departamento do Archivo do Estado – v.1-42. 1920-73 – 1 – us Res Libr [972]

INVENTION AND TECHNOLOGY – 1985- – 1 – us UMI [073]

INVENTIONES MATHEMATICAE – v. 1-61. 1966-80 – 1,5,9 – 9379.00 – us UMI [073]

INVENTIONS, 2-PART, HARPSICHORD / Bach, Johann Sebastian – 1st ed. Leipsic: Bureau de musique/Vienne: Hoffmeister & Comp., 1802 – 1 – us Sibley [780]

INVENTIONS, 3-PART, HARPSICHORD / Bach, Johann Sebastian – 1st ed. Leipsic: Bureau de musique/Vienne: Hoffmeister & Comp, 1802 – 1 – us Sibley [780]

INVENTIONS AND TRADE / Reid, Struan – 1994 – 48p – 9 – 92-3-102926-6 – fr UNESCO [380]

INVENTO CERES O SEA METODO DE PROCEDER...PROPIO POR DIEZ ANOS / Alvarez Guerra, Andres – 1827 – 9 – $1.50f – sp Bibl Santa Ana [999]

INVENTORIES AND GUIDES TO DIPLOMATIC ARCHIVES / France. Ministry of Foreign Affairs, Paris – 172mf – 9 – AA-301/1 – ne IDC [025]

INVENTORIES AND GUIDES TO DIPLOMATIC ARCHIVES / The Netherlands. Ministry of Foreign Affairs. The Hague. – 19mf – 9 – AA-201-207/1 – ne IDC [025]

INVENTORIES OF CHRIST CHURCH CANTERBURY / ed by Wickham Legg, J & ST John Hope, W H – H 1227 2. 1902 – 8 – ne IDC [025]

INVENTORIES OF CHRISTCHURCH, CANTERBURY / ed by Legg, J Wickham & Hope, W H ST John – Westminster, 1902 – 8mf – 9 – ne IDC [240]

INVENTORIES OF THE HOUGHTON MANUCRIPT COLLECTION / Harvard University. Houghton Library – 331mf – 9 – £1,490.00 – uk Chadwyck [090]

INVENTORIES OF THE MANUSCRIPT COLLECTIONS / South African Library, Cape Town – Cape Town, South African Library, [19-?] – us Res Libr [090]

INVENTORIES TO OFFICIAL FILES / Central Zionist Archives. Jersualem – Berlin: The Central Zionist Office, 1911-1920 – 5mf – ne IDC [270]

INVENTORIES TO OFFICIAL FILES / Central Zionist Archives. Jersualem – Cologne: The Central Zionist Office, 1905-1911 – 2mf – ne IDC [270]

INVENTORIES TO OFFICIAL FILES / Central Zionist Archives. Jersualem – Jersualem: Department of Organization of the Zionist Organization, 1935-1948 – 5mf – ne IDC [270]

INVENTORIES TO OFFICIAL FILES / Central Zionist Archives. Jerusalem – Keren Hayesod (Palestine Foundation Fund), Central European Office. Berlin. 1920-26. In Hebrew. BJ-72-304 1 – 9 – ne IDC [956]

INVENTORIES TO OFFICIAL FILES / Central Zionist Archives. Jerusalem – The Central Zionist Office. Cologne. 1905-11. In German. BJ-72-302 1 – 9 – ne IDC [956]

INVENTORIES TO OFFICIAL FILES / Central Zionist Archives. Jersualem – Vienna: The Central Zionist Office, 1897-1905 – 2mf – ne IDC [270]

INVENTORIES TO OFFICIAL FILES: DEPARTMENT OF ORGANIZATION OF THE ZIONIST ORGANIZATION, JERUSALEM, 1935-1948 / Central Zionist Archives. Jerusalem – In Hebrew. BJ-72-305 1 – 9 – ne IDC [956]

INVENTORIES TO OFFICIAL FILES. KEREN HAYESOD (PALESTINE FOUNDATION FUND), CENTRAL EUROPEAN OFFICE / Central Zionist Archives. Jerusalem – Berlin, 1920-1926 – 1mf – ne IDC [270]

INVENTORIES TO OFFICIAL FILES: THE CENTRAL ZIONIST OFFICE, BERLIN, 1911-1920 / Central Zionist Archives. Jerusalem – In German. BJ-72-303 1 – 9 – ne IDC [956]

INVENTORIES TO OFFICIAL FILES: THE CENTRAL ZIONIST OFFICE, VIENNA, 1897-1905 / Central Zionist Archives. Jerusalem – In German. BJ-72-301 1 – 9 – ne IDC [956]

INVENTORIES TO PRIVATE ARCHIVES OF A. KLEE, 1875-1943 / Central Zionist Archives. Jerusalem – 2mf – ne IDC [320]

INVENTORIES TO PRIVATE ARCHIVES OF D. IDELOVITCH, 1863-1943 / Central Zionist Archives. Jersualem – 2mf – ne IDC [320]

INVENTORIES TO PRIVATE ARCHIVES OF D. YELLIN, 1864-1941 / Central Zionist Archives. Jerusalem – 2mf – ne IDC [470]

INVENTORIES TO PRIVATE ARCHIVES OF H. SZOLD, 1860-1945 / Central Zionist Archives. Jerusalem – 1mf – ne IDC [320]

INVENTORIES TO PRIVATE ARCHIVES OF L. MOTZKIN, 1867-1933 / Central Zionist Archives. Jerusalem – 1mf – ne IDC [320]

INVENTORIES TO PRIVATE ARCHIVES OF M. USSISCHKIN, 1863-1941 / Central Zionist Archives. Jersualem – 6mf – ne IDC [320]

INVENTORIES TO PRIVATE ARCHIVES OF S. LEVIN, 1867-1935 / Central Zionist Archives. Jerusalem – 1mf – ne IDC [320]

INVENTORIES TO PRIVATE ARCHIVES OF THE BENEI MOSHE SOCIETY / Central Zionist Archives. Jersualem – Odessa, Warsaw, Jaffa, 1890-1896 – 1mf – ne IDC [270]

INVENTORIES TO PRIVATE ARCHIVES OF Y. BARZILAI-EISENSTADT, 1856-1918 / Central Zionist Archives. Jersualem – 1mf – ne IDC [320]

INVENTORIES TO PRIVATE ARCHIVES OF Y. GRUENBAUM, 1879-1970 / Central Zionist Archives. Jerusalem – BJ-72-403/1 – 9 – ne IDC [956]

INVENTORY AND SALES BILLS / Hancock County. Ohio. Probate Court – 1855-1925 – 12r – 1 – $32.50r – us Archival [324]

INVENTORY AND VALUATION / Holkham Hall. Norfolk. England – 1842. etc – 1 – uk Microform Academic [025]

AN INVENTORY FOR ASSESSMENT OF ATTITUDES OF HIGH SCHOOL STUDENTS TOWARD HEALTH-REALTED PHYSICAL FITNESS / Blackwell, E B – 1990 – 1mf – 9 – $4.00 – us Microform Publ [150]

INVENTORY OF COUNTY ARCHIVES–NO. 2. ALLEN COUNTY (FORT WAYNE) / Indiana Historical Records Survey – Indianapolis, 1939. (Indiana Reel 4). (The Cox Library Collection) – 5 – us Americana [978]

INVENTORY OF DATA SOURCES IN SCIENCE AND TECHNOLOGY / Committee on Data for Science and Technology of the International Council of Scientific Unions – 1982 – 229p – 9 – 92-3-102048-X – fr UNESCO [500]

INVENTORY OF HOLDINGS OF CERTAIN CLASSES OF MATERIALS / Midwest Inter-Library Center. Chicago – 1952. Rev. 1957 – 1 – us Res Libr [020]

INVENTORY OF MONUMENTS AT PAGAN / Pichard, Pierre – 4v – 9 – Co-published with Kiskadale and EFEO – fr UNESCO [930]

INVENTORY OF SEMINARY-RELATED MSS IN THE A.R. WENTZ LIBRARY. (MIMEO) / Lutheran Theological Seminary – Gettysburg, PA. 1977 – 1mf – 9 – ne IDC [240]

INVENTORY OF THE CHURCH ARCHIVES OF TENNESSEE / Nashville. Tennessee. Church Archives – Also includes: Nashville Baptist Assoc., 1939; Oconee Baptist Assoc., 1942; Guide to Church Vital Statistics in Tenn., 1942; Guide to Vital Statistics in the Church Records of Conn., 1942. 1392p – 1 – us Baptist [240]

INVENTORY OF THE CONTENTS OF HOLKHAM HALL / Holkham Hall. Norfolk. England – 1774 – 1 – uk Microform Academic [650]

INVENTORY OF THE COUNTY ARCHIVES / Dougherty County. Georgia – No.47, 1941. Indexed. 5 fiches. F-0667 – 9 – us A.G.L.L. [978]

INVENTORY OF THE COUNTY ARCHIVES. / Jefferson County. Georgia – No.81, 1940. Indexed. 5 fiches. F-0728 – 9 – us A.G.L.L. [978]

INVENTORY OF THE COUNTY ARCHIVES. / Lee County. Georgia – No.88, 1942. v1: Historical Sketch. 2 fiches. F-0729 – 9 – us A.G.L.L. [978]

INVENTORY OF THE COUNTY ARCHIVES. / Richmond County. Georgia – No.121, 1939. Indexed. 4 fiches. F-0731 – 9 – us A.G.L.L. [978]

INVENTORY OF THE COUNTY ARCHIVES OF ARKANSAS: BAXTER / Baxter County. Arkansas – 1942. 2 fiches.F-0023 – 9 – us A.G.L.L. [978]

INVENTORY OF THE COUNTY ARCHIVES OF ARKANSAS: BENTON / Benton County. Arkansas – 1941. 3 fiches.F-0024 – 9 – us A.G.L.L. [978]

INVENTORY OF THE COUNTY ARCHIVES OF ARKANSAS: CARROLL / Carroll County. Arkansas – 1942. 3 fiches.F-0035 – 9 – us A.G.L.L. [978]

INVENTORY OF THE COUNTY ARCHIVES OF ARKANSAS: MADISON / Madison County. Arkansas – 1942. 2 fiches.F-0046 – 9 – us A.G.L.L. [978]

INVENTORY OF UGANDA DOCUMENTARY MATERIALS – Madison: Collection Maintenance Office, Memorial Library, University of Wisconsin, 1981 – us Res Libr [020]

INVENTORY OF UNPUBLISHED MATERIAL FOR AMERICAN RELIGIOUS HISTORY IN PROTESTANT CHURCH ARCHIVES AND OTHER REPOSITORIES / Allen, William Henry – Washington, D.C.: Carnegie Institution of Washington, 1910. (Carnegie Institution of Washington publication; no. 137. Papers of the Department of Historical Research) – 1mf – us A.T.L.A. [240]

INVENTORY OF UNPUBLISHED MATERIAL FOR AMERICAN RELIGIOUS HISTORY IN PROTESTANT CHURCH ARCHIVES AND OTHER REPOSITORIES / Allison, William Henry – 1910 – 1 – 9.59 – us Baptist [240]

INVENTORY RECORD / Wyandot County. Ohio. County Home – 1897-1903 – 1r – 1 – $32.50r – us Archival [324]

INVENTORY REPORTS / Libya. Ministry of Planning and Development. El Khums and Misratah – 2v. BNE-1303 1 – 9 – ne IDC [330]

INVENTORY TO THE FILES OF HERBERT LOUIS, FIRST VISCOUNT SAMUEL (FIRST HIGH COMMISSIONER FOR PALESTINE), 1914-1962 / Israel State Archives – Comp. by E. Mizrachi. Jerusalem. 1965. BJ-72-501 1 – 9 – ne IDC [956]

INVENTORY TO THE FILES OF THE GERMAN CONSULATE IN PALESTINE, 1842-1939 / Israel State Archives – BJ-72-500 1 – 9 – ne IDC [956]

INVENTORY TO THE RECORDS OF THE CHIEF SECRETARY'S OFFICE, 1918-1925 / Israel State Archives – Pt. 1. Government of Palestine. Comp. by B. Eshel. Jerusalem. 1966. BJ-72-502 1 – 9 – ne IDC [956]

INVENTO.TERCER CUADERNO. INVENTOS DE CERES – 1828 – 9 – 1.50f – sp Bibl Santa Ana [890]

INVENTUM NOVUM EX PERCUSSIONE THORACIS HUMANI / Auenbrugger, L – M-34. 1761 – 9 – ne IDC [611]

INVERNESS ADVERTISER ETC – Scotland, UK. 19 Jan 1849-1850; 1851-85. -w. 35 1/2 reels – 1 – uk British Libr Newspaper [072]

INVERNESS COURIER – 1 – £42.00r – uk Scot News [072]

INVERNESS COURIER – Scotland. -w. 1870-90. Lacking 1885. 25 1 2 reels – 1 – uk British Libr Newspaper [072]

INVERNESS JOURNAL AND NORTHERN ADVERTISER – Scotland, UK. 3 Apr 1840; 5 Jan 1844-26 Dec 1845; 2 Jan 1856-30 Jun 1848. -w. 2 reels – 1 – uk British Libr Nowspapor [072]

INVERNESS-SHIRE, 1837 : BRITISH ISLES CENSUS DIRECTORIES PROJECT, SCOTLAND. VOL 41 – 1mf – 9 – A$9.00 – at Vine [941]

INVERSE PROBLEMS – v1- . 1985- – 1,5,6,9 – £356.00 – uk I.O.P. [530]

INVERSE PROBLEMS IN ENGINEERING / ed by Dulikravich, G S & Gladwell, G M L – 9,5,1 – us Gordon [620]

INVERURIE ADVERTISER – 1 – £42.00r – uk Scot News [072]

INVERURIE AND DISTRICT ADVERTISER – Scotland, UK. 8 May-19 Jun, 14 Aug-Dec 1959; 1960-81. -w. 23 1/2 reels – 1 – uk British Libr Newspaper [072]

INVERURIE HERALD – 1 – £42.00r – uk Scot News [072]

INVEST CANADA – (Ceased v7 1990/91) – Toronto. v1-7. 1984-1990/91 – 9 – Can$20.00y – cn Micromedia [332]

INVESTIGACION DE LA NATURALEZA Y CAUSAS DE LA RIQUEZA DE LAS NACIONES / Smith, Adam – Valladolid, 1794 – 31mf – 9 – sp Cultura [946]

INVESTIGACION INDUSTRIAL / Honduras. Direccion General de Estadistica y Censos – 1953-58, 60, 62 – 1 – 23.00 – us L of C Photodup [338]

INVESTIGACIONES HISTORICAS. TOMO 2. CARACAS, 1927 / Davila, Vicente – Madrid: Razon y Fe, 1930 – 1 – sp Bibl Santa Ana [946]

INVESTIGACIONES...BANOS DE MONTEMAYOR Y BEJAR / Martinez Serrano, Francisco – (Quinta Memoria. 1843. 1.50f; 9) – 1843. Cuarta memoria – 9 – 1.50f – sp Bibl Santa Ana [946]

O INVESTIGADOR BRASILEIRO – Bahia, Brazil. Nov-Dec 1831; 8 Jan 1832 – 1 – bl Biblioteca [072]

O INVESTIGADOR CONSTITUCIONAL – '(s.l.')- Sao Luis, Brazil. 13 Oct 1836 – 1,5,6 – bl Biblioteca [072]

O INVESTIGADOR MARANHENSE – '(s.l.')-Sao Luis, Brazil. 16 Apr-16 Aug 1836 – 1,5,6 – bl Biblioteca [072]

INVESTIGATION AND TRIAL PAPERS RELATING TO THE ASSASINATION OF PRESIDENT LINCOLN / U.S. Army. Judge Advocate General – 16 rolls. M599. Printed guide – 1 – us Nat'l Archives [324]

INVESTIGATION AND TRIAL PAPERS RELATING TO THE ASSASSINATION OF PRESIDENT LINCOLN / U.S. Department of State – 16 rolls. M599 – 1 – us Nat'l Archives [976]

AN INVESTIGATION INTO PAIN THRESHOLD, PAIN TOLERANCE AND AUGMENTATION REDUCTION LEVELS AMONG RUGBY PLAYERS / Tahu, Hector – 1980 – 2mf – 9 – $8.00 – us Microform Publ [790]

AN INVESTIGATION INTO THE GRIEF PROCESS AND THE EMOTIONAL RESTABILIZATION OF THE DIVORCEE WITH SOME POSSIBLE IMPLICATIONS FOR THE MINISTER AS A THERAPEUTIC AGENT / Arnold, Robert E – 1982 – 1 – 10.24 – us Baptist [240]

AN INVESTIGATION INTO THE STATE OF CRISIS MANAGEMENT PLANS AT NATIONAL COLLEGIATE ATHLETIC ASSOCIATION DIVISION 1-A ATHLETIC DEPARTMENTS / Wingate, Allison M – University of North Carolina at Chapel Hill, 1995 – 2mf – 9 – $8.00 – PE3624 – us Microform Publ [790]

AN INVESTIGATION OF ANATOMICAL STRUCTURES ASSOCIATED WITH THE SITE OF MEDIAL TIBIAL STRESS SYNDROME, OFTEN REFERRED TO AS "SHIN SPLINTS" / Beck, Belinda R & Osternig, Louis R – 1991 – 2mf – 9 – $8.00 – us Microform Publ [617]

AN INVESTIGATION OF ATHLETE SATISFACTION WITH THE SPORT TEAM SELECTION PROCESS / Neu, Lois – 1993 – 2mf – $8.00 – us Microform Publ [150]

INVESTIGATION OF COMMUNIST AGGRESSION: TENTH INTERIM REPORT OF HEARINGS... WASHINGTON, DC, DECEMBER 1,2,AND 3, 1954 / U.S. Congress. House. Select Committee on Communist Aggression – Washington, Govt. Print. Off., 1954. 174p. LL-2312 – 1 – us L of C Photodup [340]

INVESTIGATION OF MINERAL DEPOSITS IN THE HASHEMITE KINGDOM OF JORDAN / Mackay & Schnellmann – London. 1953 – 9 – ne IDC [338]

AN INVESTIGATION OF MINISTERIAL COUNSELING SUPPORT: PROBLEMS, AND A PROPOSED MODEL / Kinchen, Thomas A – 1982 – 1 – 7.52 – us Baptist [240]

AN INVESTIGATION OF NORTH CAROLINA HIGH SCHOOL FOOTBALL COACHES : THEIR KNOWLEDGE OF CONDITIONING AND STRENGTHENING THE ATHLETE / Cook, Ben T – University of North Carolina at Chapel Hill, 1995 – 1mf – 9 – $4.00 – PE3586 – us Microform Publ [613]

AN INVESTIGATION OF OUTDOOR ADVENTURE LEADERSHIP AND PROGRAMMING PREPARATION IN PHYSICAL EDUCATION BACCALAUREATE DEGREE PROGRAMS / Uhlendorf, Karen J – 1988 – 404p 5mf – 9 – $20.00 – us Microform Publ [370]

INVESTIGATION OF PHYSICAL SELF-PERCEPTIONS, FITNESS BEHAVIOR, AND PROGRAM SELECTION AMONG FITNESS PARTICIPANTS IN THREE FITNESS CLUB ENVIRONMENTS / Kiefiuk, Deborah S – Temple University, 1995 – 2mf – 9 – $8.00 – PSY1847 – us Microform Publ [150]

AN INVESTIGATION OF SELF-EFFICACY AND CONTROL THEORY WITH ELITE DISTANCE RUNNERS / Martin, Jeffrey J & Gill, Diane L – 1992 – 2mf – 9 – $8.00 – us Microform Publ [150]

INVESTIGATION OF TELEPHONE COMPANIES : LETTER FROM THE SECRETARY OF COMMERCE AND LABOR IN RESPONSE TO A SENATE RESOLUTION OF MAY 28, 1908 / U.S. Bureau of Labor – Washington, 1910 – 4mf – 9 – $5.00f – us Ross [380]

AN INVESTIGATION OF THE CAREER MOBILITY PATTERNS OF NCAA DIVISION 1-A HEAD FOOTBALL COACHES / Giles, Scott L – Brigham Young University, 1995 – 1mf – 9 – PE 3646 – us Microform Publ [790]

AN INVESTIGATION OF THE ETHICAL DILEMMAS IN THE PRACTICE OF EUTHANASIA / Hipps, Richard Sherrill – 1982 – 1 – $5.00 – us Baptist [170]

AN INVESTIGATION OF THE ORGANIZATIONAL STRUCTURE AND POTENTIAL FOR INTERGROUP CONFLICT BETWEEN PHYSICAL EDUCATION AND ATHLETIC DEPARTMENTS IN THREE SECONDARY SCHOOLS / Wyatt, T J – 1991 – 2mf – 9 – $8.00 – us Microform Publ [370]

AN INVESTIGATION OF THE PROCESS OF CHANGE IN THE MAJOR CONTEMPORARY SCHOOLS OF PSYCHOTHERAPY / Gilburth, Kenneth Riley – 1981 – 1 – 5.36 – us Baptist [240]

AN INVESTIGATION OF THE QUALIFICATIONS OF CONTRACT ADVISORS FOR PROFESSIONAL ATHLETES / Smith, Gregory K P & Jackson, Michael W – 1991 – 2mf – 9 – $8.00 – us Microform Publ [790]

AN INVESTIGATION OF THE RELATIONSHIP BETWEEN MEASURES OF KINESTHESIS AND SLECTED ASPECTS OF PERFORMANCE IN BEGINNER SKIING / Solymosi, Frank – 1980 – 2mf – 9 – $8.00 – us Microform Publ [790]

INVESTIGATIVE AND CELL PATHOLOGY – v. 1-. 1978- – 1,5,6,9 – us UMI [616]

INVESTIGATOR – London. 1843 – 1 – uk Microform Academic [073]

INVESTIGATOR – Omaha, NE. -w. Feb 1906-Apr 1907; Mar-Jun 1908 – 1 – us NE Hist [071]

INVESTIGATOR *see* LONDON INVESTIGATOR

THE INVESTIGATOR – Toronto: J.T. White, [1872-189- or 19–] – 9 – cn C.I.H.M. [073]

INVESTISSEMENT ET FINANCEMENT : ORIGINE ET EMPLOI DES FONDS DE GRANDES SOCIETES / Malissen, M – F50.00 – fr Ethnologie [332]

INVESTISSEMENTS PUBLICS ET PARAETATIQUES BELGES. REALISATIONS 1948-1953 ET PROGRAMME 1954-1957 / Belgium. Commission Economique Interministerielle. Groupe d'Etude des Investissements Publics – (Belgian public and parastatal investments. 1948-1953 Outlays and 1954-1957 Program). (Bruxelles). 1954. BD-1619 1 – 9 – ne IDC [336]

INVESTISSEMENTS PUBLICS ET PARAETATIQUES BELGES. REALISATIONS 1948-1954 ET PROGRAMME 1955-1957 / Belgium. Commission Economique Interministerielle. Groupe d'Etude des Investissements Publics – (Belgian public and parastatal investments. 1948-1954 Outlays and 1955-1957 Program). BD-1620 1 – 9 – ne IDC [336]

INVESTISSEMENTS PUBLICS ET PARAETATIQUES BELGES. REALISATIONS 1948-1955 ET PROGRAMME 1956-1958 / Belgium. Commission Economique Interministerielle. Groupe d'Etude des Investissements Publics – (Belgian public and parastatal investment. 1948-1955 Outlays and 1956-1958 Program). BD-1621 1 – 9 – ne IDC [336]

INVESTMENT ADVISERS ACT OF 1940 RELEASES / U.S. Securities and Exchange Commission – nos 1-358. 7 Oct 1940-22 Jan 1973 (all publ) – 31mf – 9 – $46.50 – LLMC 84-362 – us L.L.M.C. [340]

INVESTMENT AND ADVISORS ACT OF 1940. RELEASE NUMBER 1-358, OCT. 7, 1940-JAN. 22, 1973 / U.S. Securities and Exchange Commission – The series will continue in the SEC Docket – 9 – us UMI [336]

INVESTMENT COMPANY ACT OF 1940. RELEASE NUMBER 1-7639, SEPT. 23, 1940-JAN. 26, 1973 / U.S. Securities and Exchange Commission – The series will continue in the SEC Docket – 9 – us UMI [336]

INVESTMENT COMPANY ACT OF 1940 RELEASES / U.S. Securities and Exchange Commission – (no 7143 was never released) – nos 1-7639. 23 Sept 1940-26 Jan 1973 (all publ) – 298mf – 9 – $447.00 – LLMC 84-363 – us L.L.M.C. [340]

INVESTMENT EFFECTIVENESS IN INDUSTRIAL SECTOR IN THE SYRIAN ARAB REPUBLIC / Syria. State Planning Organization – F. S. Katabi. 1970. BNE-9731 1 – 9 – ne IDC [338]

INVESTMENT: NEW POLICIES AND PROCEDURES ON INDONESIA'S FOREIGN CAPITAL INVESTMENT / Indonesia – Includes legislation. SE-8482 1. 1967? – 9 – ne IDC [336]

INVESTMENT OPPORTUNITIES UNDER THE SEVEN YEAR PLAN 1964-1970 / Jordan. Development Board – 9 – ne IDC [336]

INVESTOR-OWNED HOSPITAL REVIEW – v.6-9. 1973-76. Superseded by Review, Federation of American Hospitals – 1 – us UMI [073]

INVESTOR-OWNED HOSPITAL REVIEW *see* FAH REVIEW

INVESTORS AND TRADERS GUIDE – 3rd ed. Jones & Baker Securities, 1920 – 1mf – 9 – $1.50 – LLMC 92-204 – us L.L.M.C. [340]

INVESTORS CHRONICLE – 1945-1994 – 1 – F873.00 – sz Infoprint [072]

INVESTORS CHRONICLE – (Backfiles. 1) – Great Britain. 1945- – 1 – us Primary [072]

INVESTORS CHRONICLE – Subscription – 1 – F786.00 – sz Infoprint [072]

INVESTORS' GUARDIAN – 1863-1973 – 1 – £3,700.00 – uk World [073]

INVESTORS' MONTHLY MANUAL – London, UK. 15 Oct 1864-Jun 1930. -m. 57 1/2 reels – 1 – uk British Libr Newspaper [073]

O INVICTO : ORGAO OFICIAL DO VISCONDE FUTEBOL CLUBE – Manaus, Amazonas. 12 Ago-23 Dez 1967 – 1,5,6 – bl Biblioteca [072]

THE INVISIBLE INFLUENCE / Canon, Alexander – In Indonesian. SE-6711 1. 1966 – 9 – ne IDC [950]

THE INVISIBLE LODGE = UNSICHTBARE LOGE / Jean Paul – (In English) – New York: U S Book Co (successors to J W Lovell) c1883 – 1r – 1 – us U.W. Library [430]

THE INVITATION ANSWERED : A REPLY TO DR. J. KENT STONE'S "INVITATION HEEDED": AND TO HIS HOLINESS, POPE PIUS THE NINTH'S INVITATION TO THE VATICAN COUNCIL / Smythe, W Herbert – (Includes bibliographical references) – New York: Pliny F Smith, 1871 – 1mf – 9 – 0-8370-8789-9 – 1986-2789 – us A.T.L.A. [230]

AN INVITATION TO BANDUNG REGION; OPAL OF THE ORIENT / Admawiria, Sam Suhaedi – (Appendix in Indonesian). SE-3671 1. 1962? – 9 – ne IDC [950]

THE "INVITING-IN" FEAST OF THE ALASKAN ESKIMO / Hawkes, E W – BN 243 2. 1913 – 8 – ne IDC [306]

IN-VITRO-INFEKTION VON HUMANEN ENDOTHELZELLEN MIT ZYTOMEGALIEVIRUS / Oltrogge, Jens – 2nd ed 1992 – 101p – DM98.00 – 3-89349-452-9 – gw Hänsel [616]

INVOCATION DU PEUPLE A DIEU – (signe G.B., date: Prison d'Angers, 30 avril 1833), 8 p. Les Saint-Simoniens, 1825-1834. 7004 – 9 – fr Hachette [335]

INVOLUNTARY, UNMERITED, PERPETUAL, ABSOLUTE, HEREDITARY SLAVERY EXAMINED, 1753-1819 / Barrow, David – 1 – 5.00 – us Baptist [240]

INVOLVING THE LAITY OF THE NORTH DUNEDIN BAPTIST CHURCH IN A PROGRAM OF PARTICIPATION IN THE PREACHING EVENT / Shaddock, Daniel Kenneth – 1 – 5.36 – us Baptist [240]

THE INWARD GOSPEL : SOME FAMILIAR DISCOURSES ADDRESSED TO RELIGIOUS WHO FOLLOW THE RULES OF ST. IGNATIUS / Strappini, Walter Diver – London: Burns and Oates, 1909 – 1mf – 9 – 0-8370-7025-2 – 1986-1025 – us A.T.L.A. [240]

HET INWENDIG WOORD : EENIGE BLADZIJDEN UIT DE GESCHIEDENIS DER HERVORMING / Maronier, J H – Amsterdam: Tj. van Holkema, 1890 – 1mf – us A.T.L.A. [240]

DEN INWENDIGHEN CHRISTENEN / Bernieres de Louvigny, Jean de – Antwerpen, 1675 – 11mf – 8 – ne Slangenburg [240]

INYO INDEPENDENT – Independence, CA. 1870-84; 1901- – 52+ r – 1 – $2,600.00 ($80.00y) – C02303 – us Library Micro [071]

INYO INDEPENDENT – Independence. Calif. -w. 1950-66 – 1 – us UMI [071]

INYO REGISTER – Bishop, CA. 1909-58 – 52+ r – 1 BC02070 – $2,600.00 – us Library Micro [071]

INYO REGISTER – Bishop. Calif. -w. 1946-58 – 1 – us UMI [071]

Inzenga, G *see* FUNGHI SICILIANI STUDII

INZHENERNOE DELO – 1904-05 – 8 – BR-2351 2 – ne IDC [947]

IOAN : BVGENHAGII POMERANI IN HIOB ANNOTATIONES / Bugenhagen, J – [Zwickau, 1527] – 1mf – 9 – ne IDC [240]

IOANNIS BVGENHAGII POMERANI COMMENTARIUS, IN QUATUOR CAPITA PRIORIS EPISTOLAE AD CORINTHIOS,... / Bugenhagen, J – VVittembergae, 1530 – 5mf – 9 – ne IDC [240]

IOANNIS BVGENHAGII...PUBLICA, DE SACRAMENTO CORPORIS ET SANGUINIS CHRISTI... / Bugenhagen, J – [VVittembergae, 1528] – 3mf – 9 – ne IDC [240]

IOANNIS BVGENHAGUE POMERANI ANNOTATIONES AB IPSO IAM EMISSAE. IN DEUTERONOMIUM. IN SAMUELEM PROPHETA ID EST DUOS LIBROS REGU... / Bugenhagen, J – [Basel, 1524] – 8mf – 9 – ne IDC [240]

IOANNIS CANTACUZENI EXIMPERATORIS HISTORIARUM LIBRI 4 (CSHB 2-4) : GRAECE ET LATINE / Schopeni, Lud. – Bonnae. v1-3. 1828-1832 – Dfl112.00 – ne Slangenburg [240]

IOANNIS COLETI ENARRATIO IN PRIMAM EPISTOLAM S. PAULI AD CORINTHIOS / Colet, John – London: George Bell, 1874. 1 fiche – 9 – us A.T.L.A. [240]

IOANNIS SARESBERIENSIS EPISCOPI CARNOTENSIS POLICRATICI.. / John of Salisbury, Bishop of Chartres – Oxonnii: Typographeo Clarendoniano, 1909. 2v. C.C.J. Webb, ed – 1 – us U.W. Library [920]

IOANNIS SCYLITZAE OPE AB IMM. BEKKERO SUPPLETUS ET EMENDATUS (CSHB 34, 35) / Cedrenus, Georgius – Bonnae. v1-2. 1838-1839 – Dfl109.00 – ne Slangenburg [240]

I.O.C. ASSEMBLY *see* BRUUN MEMORIAL LECTURES

IOC World Congress on Sport Sciences *see* PROCEEDINGS

Iodkovskii, AN *see* KHRONOLOGICHESKII PERECHEN' ZAKONOV SOIUZA SSR PO SOSTOIANIIA NA 1 IIULIA 1935 G

IOFC *see*
- COMMITTEE FOR THE DEVELOPMENT AND MANAGEMENT OF FISHERY RESOURCES OF THE GULFS
- REPORT OF THE 4TH SESSION OF THE COMMITTEE FOR THE DEVELOPMENT AND MANAGEMENT OF FISHERIES IN THE SOUTHWEST INDIAN OCEAN. ZANZIBAR, TANZANIA, NOV 1986
- REPORT OF THE 5TH SESSION OF THE COMMITTEE FOR THE DEVELOPMENT AND MANAGEMENT OF FISHERIES IN THE BAY OF BENGAL. BANGKOK, MARCH 1987
- REPORT OF THE 5TH SESSION OF THE COMMITTEE FOR THE DEVELOPMENT AND MANAGEMENT OF FISHERIES IN THE SOUTHWEST INDIAN OCEAN
- REPORT OF THE 6TH SESSION OF THE COMMITTEE FOR THE DEVELOPMENT AND MANAGEMENT OF FISHERIES IN THE BAY OF BENGAL
- REPORT OF THE 6TH SESSION OF THE COMMITTEE FOR THE DEVELOPMENT AND MANAGEMENT OF FISHERIES IN THE SOUTHWEST INDIAN OCEAN
- REPORT OF THE 7TH SESSION OF THE COMMITTEE FOR THE DEVELOPMENT AND MANAGEMENT OF FISHERIES IN THE BAY OF BENGAL
- REPORT OF THE 8TH SESSION OF THE COMMITTEE FOR MANAGEMENT OF INDIAN OCEAN TUNA. COLOMBO, SRI LANKA, 1985
- REPORT OF THE 9TH SESSION OF THE COMMITTEE FOR THE MANAGEMENT OF INDIAN OCEAN TUNA. COLOMBO, SRI LANKA, DECEMBER 1986
- REPORT OF THE 9TH SESSION OF THE INDIAN OCEAN FISHERY COMMISSION
- REPORT OF THE 10TH SESSION OF THE COMMITTEE FOR THE MANAGEMENT OF INDIAN OCEAN TUNA
- REPORT OF THE 11TH SESSION OF THE COMMITTEE FOR THE MANAGEMENT OF INDIAN OCEAN TUNA

Ioffe, Adolf Abramovich *see* MIRNOE NASTUPLENIE

Iohannes Daventriae *see* CHRISTIANAE VERITATIS TELUM, SEU FIDEI CATAPULTA IN PLEROSQUE PSEUDOPROPHETAS, PRAESERTIM IN BERN

IOHANNIS ABBATIS VICTORIENSIS LIBER CERTARUM HISTORIARUM (MGH 7: 36.BD) – Tom. 1-2. 1909-1910 – Dfl39.00 – ne Slangenburg [240]

IOHANNIS PORTA DE ANNONIACO LIBER DE CORONATIONE KAROLI 4 IMPERATORIS (MGH 7: 35.BD) – 1913 – Dfl13.00 – ne Slangenburg [240]

IONAE VITAE SANCTORUM COLUMBANI, VEDASTIS, IOHANNIS (MGH 7: 37.BD) – 1905 – Dfl28.00 – ne Slangenburg [240]

IONAS PROPHETA... / Bugenhagen, J – VVittenberge, 1550 – 9mf – 9 – ne IDC [240]

IONE BULLETIN – Ione OR. June 12 19 Aug 7 Sep 11 1913 – 1 – us U.O. Library [071]

IONE INDEPENDENT – Ione, OR. -w. 13 Apr 1916-19 Jun 1931. 3 rolls – 1 – us U.O. Library [071]

IONE JOURNAL – Ione OR. Apr 28 May 19 26 Sep 22 1915, Oct 6-20 Nov 3 Dec 1 1915, Jan 19-Mar 23 Apr 12 1916 – 1 – us U.O. Library [071]

IONE PROCLAIMER – Ione OR. June 25-Dec 10 1909 – 1 – us U.O. Library [071]

IONE VALLEY ECHO – Ione, CA. 1895-1898 – 1r – 1 – $50.00 – C03605 – us Library Micro [071]

Ionev, R *see* LIUBOV BEZ LIUBVI

IONICA / Cory, William Johnson – London: George Allen, 1891 – 1 roll – 1 – 1-55879-169-8 – uk Libr Preservation [890]

IONN, EKSARKH BOLGARSKII / Kalaidovich, K F – Moscow, 1824. BR-10,330/1 – 9 – ne IDC [949]
IONNIS CALVIN COMMENTARII IN EPISTOLAM PAULI AD ROMANOS – 1540 – 1 – us A.T.L.A. [240]
IORDANIS ROMANA ET GETICA (MGH 1: 5.BD. 1.TEIL) / ed by Mommsen, Theodor – 1882 – Dfl28.00 – ne Slangenburg [240]
Iordanskh, N I *see* ZEMSKII LIBERALIZM
Iordanskii, N N *see* KOOPERATSIIA V SHKOLE
Iorish, Il *see* MATERIALY O MONGOLAKH, KALMYKAKH I BURIATAKH V ARKHIVAKH LENINGRADA
IOSIF IAKOVLEVICH LORKISH PAMPHLET COLLECTION – 1966 – 1 – CSUXANS1215-B – us Hoover Inst Photo [920]
Iota *see* THE ADVENTURES OF A PROTESTANT IN SEARCH OF A RELIGION
IOVIANUS : DIE FRAGMENTE SEINER SCHRIFTEN, DIE QUELLEN ZU SEINER GESCHICHTE, SEIN LEBEN UND SEINE LEHRE (T.U.U. 2-17/2) / Haller, W – Leipzig, 1897 – 3mf – 9 – ne Slangenburg [240]
IOVRNAL DE VAVIGATION DV VOYAGE DE LA COSTE DE GVINEE, ISLES DE L'AMERIQVE ET INDES D'ESPAGNE SVR LE VAISSEAV DV ROY LE FAVCON FRANCOIS ARME PAR L'ORDRE DE SAMAIESTE POVR LA ROYALLE COMPAGNIE DE LA SSIENTE – [S.l: s.n., 19–?] – us Res Libr [910]
IOWA : CODE ANNOTATED – St Paul: West Pub Co, 1949-Mar 1996 update – 9 – $1,693.00 set – us Hein [340]
IOWA : SESSION LAWS OF AMERICAN STATES AND TERRITORIES – 1838-1995 – 9 – $816.00 set – us Hein [340]
Iowa *see*
- OFFICIAL REGISTER
- REPORTS AND OPINIONS (A-G)
- REPORTS, POST-NRS
- REPORTS, PRE-NRS
- STATE LABOR REPORTS

IOWA AGE – Clinton. Iowa. 1869-1871 – 1 – us UMI [071]
IOWA ATTORNEY GENERAL REPORTS AND OPINIONS – (6 1896-1978 $245.00. 9 1979-1986, 1988-1994 $98.00. 1987 not available) – 1896-1994 – 6,9 – $343.00set – us Hein [340]
THE IOWA BAND / Adams, Ephraim – Boston: Congregational Publ Society, 1870 – 1mf – 9 – 0-8370-6240-3 – 1986-0240 – us A.T.L.A. [240]
IOWA BYSTANDER – Des Moines. Iowa. 1967- – 1 – us UMI [071]
Iowa. Census *see* THE 1840 IOWA CENSUS
IOWA FARM ECONOMIST / Iowa State University. Cooperative Extension Service in Agriculture and Home Economics – No.1-12.1935-46. 1 reel – 1,5 – us Spaulding [330]
IOWA FARM SCIENCE / Iowa State University. Cooperative Extension Service in Agriculture and Home Economics – No.1-14.1946-71 – 1,5 – us Spaulding [630]
Iowa Historical and Biographical Co *see*
- HISTORY OF FREMONT COUNTY
- HISTORY OF MONTGOMERY COUNTY

IOWA: ITS HISTORY AND ITS FOREMOST CITIZENS / Brigham, Johnson – (Chicago: S. J. Clarke Publ. Co., 1915). Vol. 1-3. Iowa Reel 1. (The Cox Library Collection) – 5 – us Americana [978]
THE IOWA JEWISH NEWS – Des Moines. Iowa. 1932-52 – 1 – us A.J.P.C. [071]
IOWA LAW BULLETIN *see* IOWA LAW REVIEW
IOWA LAW REVIEW – (First 10 volumes of this series are titled the "Iowa Law Bulletin". Add vols as copyright expires) – v1-5. 1915-1920 – 20mf – $30.00 – LLMC 95-103 – us L.L.M.C. [073]
IOWA LAW REVIEW – (v1-70 1915-85 on reel or mf $900.00. v71-80 1985-95 on mf $305.00) – v1-80. 1915-95 – 5,6,9 – $1,205.00 set – us Hein [340]
Iowa. Laws, Statutes, etc *see* HERRICK AND DOXSEE'S PROBATE LAW AND PRACTICE OF THE STATE OF IOWA.
IOWA LAWYER – (Title varies: v1-50 no 7 as News Bulletin Iowa State Bar Association) – v1-55. 1940-95 – 9 – $360.00 set – us Hein [340]
IOWA LEGAL INQUISITOR – (Lacking: 1853 no 2) – v1-2. 1851-53 (all publ) – 7mf – 9 – $10.50 – LLMC 84-497 – us L.L.M.C. [073]
IOWA PIONEER LAWMAKERS' ASSOCIATION REUNIONS – 11v. 1886, 1890-1909 (all publ) – 21mf – 9 – $31.50 – LLMC 84-498 – us L.L.M.C. [073]
IOWA POSTAL CARD – Fayette. Iowa. 1882-1910 – 1 – us UMI [071]
IOWA REFORM – Davenport. Iowa. 1887-1917; 1928-40 – 1 – us UMI [071]
Iowa. Secretary of State *see* THE OFFICIAL REGISTER OF IOWA 1911-12
IOWA SOUTHERN BAPTIST – Des Moines, IA. 1986-1991. 250p – 1 – $12.32 – us Baptist [071]
IOWA STAR – Des Moines. Iowa. 1849-1854 – 1 – us UMI [071]
Iowa. State Bar Association *see* PROCEEDINGS 1874-1968
IOWA STATE BAR ASSOCIATION NEWS BULLETIN – v1- 1940-up to copyright – 9 – LLMC 84-501 – us L.L.M.C. [073]
IOWA STATE BAR ASSOCIATION PROCEEDINGS – 1v. 1874-81 (all publ) – 3mf – 9 – $4.50 – LLMC 84-499 – us L.L.M.C. [073]
IOWA STATE BAR ASSOCIATION PROCEEDINGS – (Lacking: 81st pt 1. 84th pt 2) – v1-103. 1895-1976 – 85mf – 9 – $127.00 – LLMC 84-500 – us L.L.M.C. [073]
IOWA STATE BAR ASSOCIATION QUARTERLY – v1-3. 1929-32 (all publ) – 5mf – 9 – $7.50 – LLMC 84-502 – us L.L.M.C. [073]
IOWA STATE DEMOCRAT – Newton. Iowa. 1898-1901 – 1 – us UMI [071]
IOWA STATE JOURNAL – Des Moines. Iowa. 1857-1859 – 1 – us UMI [071]
IOWA STATE REPORTER – Waterloo. Iowa. 1871-72 – 1 – us UMI [071]
Iowa State University. Agricultural Experiment Station *see*
- BULLETIN
- CIRCULAR
- COMPLETE LIST OF PUBLICATIONS
- PRESS BULLETIN
- REPORT OF THE DIVISION OF AGRICULTURE
- REPORT ON AGRICULTURAL RESEARCH

Iowa State University. College of Agriculture. Center for Agricultural and Rural Development *see*
- CAED REPORT
- CARD REPORT

Iowa State University. Cooperative Extension Service in Agriculture and Home Economics *see*
- ANNUAL REPORT OF THE AGRICULTURAL EXTENSION DIVISION
- EMERGENCY LEAFLETS
- EXTENSION BULLETIN
- EXTENSION CIRCULAR
- FARM FACTS
- FARM OUTLOOK
- FARM SCIENCE REPORTER
- HOME ECONOMICS BULLETIN
- HOME ECONOMICS CIRCULAR
- IOWA FARM ECONOMIST
- IOWA FARM SCIENCE
- PAMPHLET

Iowa State University. Iowa Agriculture and Home Economics Experiment Station *see*
- ANNUAL REPORT
- BULLETIN P
- RESEARCH BULLETIN
- SPECIAL REPORT

IOWA STATE UNIVERSITY REGULATORY CONFERENCES ON PUBLIC UTILITY VALUATION AND THE RATE MAKING PROCESS – (Lacking: 2nd 1963 p123-4. 4th 1965) – 1st to 24th conferences. 1962-85 – 100mf – 9 – $150.00 – LLMC 84-503 – us L.L.M.C. [340]
Iowa. Supreme Court *see* IOWA SUPREME COURT REPORTS
IOWA SUPREME COURT REPORTS / Iowa. Supreme Court – (Pre-NRS run: v1-50 1855-79 369mf $553.00. Vols after v186 to be filmed once they fall out of copyright) – v1-186. 1855-1919 – 1711mf – 9 – $2,566.00 – LLMC 80-806 – us L.L.M.C. [340]
IOWA SUPREME COURT REPORTS *see*
- BRADFORD'S CASES
- GREENE'S REPORTS
- MORRIS' REPORTS

IOWA TERRITORIAL GAZETTE – Burlington. Iowa. and Burlington Advertiser. 1839-40 – 1 – us UMI [071]
IOYFULL NEWES OUT OF THE NEW FOUND WORLD / Monardes, N – M 381. 1580 – 9 – ne IDC [910]
Ipatieff, Vladimir N *see* THE LIFE OF A CHEMIST
(I.P.C. DE BELLEY). REPARTIES SUCCINCTES A L'ABREGE DES CONTROVERSES DE M. CHARLES DRELINCOURT...ENSEMBLES LES ANTITHESES PROTESTANTES... / Camus, J P – Caen. 2v. 1638 – 11mf – 9 – CA-99/1 – ne IDC [240]
IPC (INSTITUTE FOR INTERCONNECTING AND PACKAGING FITTINGS INDUSTRY) – Standards. Printed index. Updated every 60 days – 6,9 – us Info Handling [680]
IPEPA HLANGA ZULU PM'BURG – 24 Apr 1903-22 Apr 1904 – 1 roll – 1 – sa Microfile [960]
IPF UND JAGSTZEITUNG : BA DER SCHWAEBISCHE ZEITUNG – Ellwangen-Leutkirch, Germany. 2 Jan 1975- – 117r (1975-1990) – 1 – gw Mikrofilm [072]
IPFC *see*
- COUNTRY REPORTS PRESENTED AT THE 5TH SESSION OF THE INDO-PACIFIC FISHERY COMMISSION WORKING PARTY OF EXPERTS ON INLAND FISHERIES AND PAPERS
- PAPERS CONTRIBUTED TO THE WORKSHOP ON STRATEGIES FO THE MANAGEMENT OF FISHERIES AND AQUACULTURE IN MANGROVE ECOSYSTEMS, AND COUNTRY STATUS REPORTS ON INLAND FISHERIES
- PAPERS CONTRIBUTED TO THE WORKSHOP ON THE USE OF CYPRINIDS IN THE FISHERIES MANAGEMENT OF LARGER INLAND WATER BODIES OF THE INDO-PACIFIC
- PAPERS PRESENTED AT THE 6TH SESSION OF THE STANDING COMMITTEE ON RESOURCES RESEARCH AND DEVELOPMENT
- PAPERS PRESENTED AT THE 7TH SESSION OF THE INDO-PACIFIC FISHERY COMMISSION WORKING PARTY ON FISH TECHNOLOGY AND MARKETING
- PAPERS PRESENTED AT THE 8TH SESSION OF THE INDO-PACIFIC FISHERY COMMISSION WORKING PARTY ON FISH TECHNOLOGY AND MARKETING
- REPORT OF THE 3RD SESSION OF THE INDO-PACIFIC FISHERY COMMISSION WORKING PARTY OF EXPERTS ON INLAND FISHERIES AND REPORT OF THE WORKSHOP ON STRATEGIES FOR THE MANAGEMENT OF FISHERIES AND AQUACULTURE IN MANGROVE ECOSYSTEMS. BANGKOK, 1986
- REPORT OF THE 4TH SESSION OF THE COMMITTEE FOR THE DEVELOPMENT AND MANAGEMENT OF FISHERIES IN THE SOUTH CHINA SEA. KUALA LUMPUR, 1984
- REPORT OF THE 4TH SESSION OF THE INDO-PACIFIC FISHERY COMMISSION WORKING PARTY OF EXPERTS ON INLAND FISHERIES
- REPORT OF THE 5TH SESSION OF THE INDO-PACIFIC FISHERY COMMISSION WORKING PARTY OF EXPERTS ON INLAND FISHERIES AND REPORT OF THE WORKSHOP ON TILAPIA IN CAPTURE AND CULTURE-ENHANCED FISHERIES IN THE INDO-PACIFIC FISHERY COMMISSION COUNTRIES
- REPORT OF THE 7TH SESSION OF THE COMMITTEE FOR THE DEVELOPMENT AND MANAGEMENT OF FISHERIES IN THE SOUTH CHINA SEA
- REPORT OF THE 7TH SESSION OF THE WORKING PARTY OF EXPERTS ON AQUACULTURE
- REPORT OF THE 8TH SESSION OF THE INDO-PACIFIC FISHERY COMMISSION WORKING PARTY ON FISH TECHNOLOGY AND MARKETING
- REPORT OF THE INDO-PACIFIC FISHERY COMMISSION EXPERT CONSULTATION ON INLAND FISHERIES OF THE LARGER INDO-PACIFIC ISLANDS. BANGKOK, 1986
- REPORTS AND PAPERS PRESENTED AT THE INDO-PACIFIC FISHERY COMMISSION ON EXPERT CONSULTATION ON INLAND FISHERIES OF THE LARGER INDO-PACIFIC ISLANDS. BANGKOK, JUNE 1986

IPIRANGA ACREANO : PORTA VOZ DO ROTARY CLUB DE XAPURI – Xapuri, Acre. Dez 1961-Mar 1962 – 1,5,6 – bl Biblioteca [072]
Ipnocausto, Paulo *see*
- CARTA DE BARTOLO
- LA CORNEJA SIN PLUMAS

IPPOLITA ED ARICIA. [DRAMMA IN CINQUE ATTI] / Traetta, T – Ms, [176-?] – 1 – us Sibley [780]
IPQ: INTERNATIONAL PHILOSOPHICAL QUARTERLY – v1- 1961- – 1,5,6,9 – us UMI [100]
IPRA REVIEW / International Public Relations Association – v. 3-. 1979- – 5,6,9 – us UMI [380]
IPS PAPERS – Beirut: Institute for Palestine Studies, n1,3-4,7-9,14. 1979-80 – 1r – 1 – us Res Libr [956]
IPSA CHIEREGHINII CONCHYLIA / Brusina, S – Z-456 2. 1870 – 8 – ne IDC [590]
IPSA LINNAEI CONCHYLIA / Hanley, S – Z-564 2. 1855 – 8 – ne IDC [590]
IPSE, IPSA-IPSE, IPSA, IPSUM, WHICH? : THE LATIN VARIOUS READINGS, GENESIS III. 15 / Quigley, Richard F – (Includes appendix of correspondence) – New York: Fr Pustet, [1890?] – 2mf – 9 – 0-8370-6933-5 – 1986-0933 – us A.T.L.A. [220]
Ipsen, Lillas F *see* CARDIOVASCULAR AND BODY COMPOSITION RESPONSES TO AEROBIC DANCE TRAINING OF VARYING FREQUENCIES AND TOTAL PROGRAM LENGTHS
IPSG NEWSLETTER – London, UK. Journal of Indian Progressive Study Group (England). Oct 1971- – 1 – uk British Libr Newspaper [073]
IPSWICH 1634-1892 – (Mf 1-7: Vital Records 1664-1734. Mf 8-12: B,I,M,D 1663-1733. Mf 13-20: Vital Records 1734-83. Mf 21-26: B,I,M,D 1734-83. Mf 27-36: Vital Records 1705-1860. Mf 37-43: B,I,M,D 1748-1859. Mf 44-49: Vital Records 1935-1889. Mf 50: Out-of-Town Marriages 1648-1799. Mf 51-56: Town Records 1634-1662. Mf 57-63: Town Records 1634-1674. Mf 64-70: Town Records 1674-96. Mf 71-75: Town Records 1696-1720. Mf 76-84: Town & Land 1634-1757. Mf 85-88: Death Index 1850-1940. Mf 89-93: Marriage Index 1850-1953. Mf 94-97: Birth Index 1850-1943. Mf 98-102: B,D,M 1830-66. Mf 103-109: B,M,D 1867-92. Mf 110-114: Intentions 1860-89. Mf 115-119: Intentions 1890-1910. Mf 120-122: Deaths 1892-1921. Mf 123: Marriages 1892-1900) – (mf ed 1990) – 123mf – 9 – 0-87623-103-2 – us Holbrook [920]
IPSWICH 1648-1849 – (Mf 1T: Vital Records 1664-1732. Mf 1T-3T: Publishments 1708-34. Mf 2T-5T: Deaths & Births 1687-1739. Mf 4T,10T,12T-13T: Marriages & Intents 1693-1783. Mf 5T-10T,18T: Births & Baptisms 1672-1809. Mf 10T-12T: Deaths & Births 1734-83. Mf 14T-18T,25T: Intentions 1753-1849. Mf 19T-20T: Births 1749-1844. Mf 20T-22T: Marriages 1748-1849. Mf 22T-25T: Deaths 1775-1849. Mf 25T-26T: Births 1828-49. Mf 26T-27T: Marriages & Deaths 1844-49. Mf 28T: Out-of-Town Marriages 1648-1799) – (mf ed 1997) – 28mf – 9 – 0-87623-272-1 – us Holbrook [920]
Ipswich. Fine Arts Club *see* CONSTABLE AND OLD SUFFOLK ARTISTS
IPSWICH JOURNAL. (DAILY IPSWICH JOURNAL.-DAILY JOURNAL; WEEKLY IPSWICH JOURNAL.-WEEKLY JOURNAL) – England. Jan 1833-Jul 1902.-d,-w. 62mqn reels – 1 – uk British Libr Newspaper [072]
IPSWICH MERCURY – Ipswich, England. -w. 1981. 2 reels – 1 – uk British Libr Newspaper [072]
IPW-BERICHTE – 1972-1989 – 442mf – 1 – DM2,519.40 – gw Mikro Press [073]
IQBAL AS A THINKER – Essays by eminent scholars. (3rd ed.). Lahore: Sh. M. Ashraf, (1960). viii,304p. 1 reel. 1291 – 1 – us U.W. Library [290]
IQTICAD EL-DJAZAIRI *see* EL-IQTICAD EL-DJAZAIRI
IR TEHILLAH / Feinstein, A L – Warsaw. 1886. BJ-290-3 1 – 9 – ne IDC [947]
IR VILNAH / Maggid-Steinschneider, H N – Vilna, 1900 – 5mf – 9 – ne IDC [910]
IRA : "SAKURA" – Koetaradja, Atjeh Sinbun (2603 ?). 23p – 46mf – 9 – ne IDC [999]
IRAD KELLEY PAPERS *see* KELLEY, IRAD, PAPERS, MS 485
IRADE-I MILLIYE – Sivas, 1919-1922 – 9 – $35.00 – us MEDOC [956]
Irama Baru *see* MINANG MODERN INDONESIA DAN MALAJA
IRAMA MINANG MODERN AND INDONESIA POPULER / Sjaiful Nawas – SE 4199 1. 1962 – 9 – ne IDC [950]
IRAN : THE MAKING OF U.S. POLICY, 1977-1980 – (With 2-vol printed guide & index £630.00) – 565mf – 9 – £2,940.00 – uk Chadwyck [327]
IRAN – (Numrah-'i 1-32, 132-193 (15 Muharram 1288-11 Ramazan 1290[Mar 1871-Nov 1873]). Missing issues: 33-131) – Tehran, 1871-? – 1 reel – 1 – $60.00 – us MEDOC [950]

IRAN – Tehran. Shumarah-i 1-216 (11 Muharram 1288 – 7 Rabi' al-Avval [2 April 1871-24 April 1874]) – 1 reel – 1 – $195.00 – us MEDOC [950]
Iran *see*
- A GUIDE TO THE IRAN'S 5TH PLAN
- REPORT ON SEVEN YEAR DEVELOPMENT PLAN FOR THE PLAN ORGANIZATION OF THE IMPERIAL GOVERNMENT OF IRAN
- RUZNAMAH-'I RASMI-I KISHVAR-I SHAHANSHAHI-I IRAN
- THIRD FIVE-YEAR DEVELOPMENT PLAN LAW

Iran. Iran Plan and Budget organization *see* SUMMARY OF THE 5TH NATIONAL DEVELOPMENT PLAN 1973-1978
Iran. Iran Trade and Industry Publication. (suppl. nr. 200) *see* THE 5TH PLAN
Iran. Laws, Statutes, etc *see* MAJMU'AH SALYANAH
Iran. Plan Organization *see*
- FOURTH NATIONAL DEVELOPMENT PLAN, 1968-1972
- REVIEW OF THE SECOND SEVEN YEAR PLAN PROGRAM OF IRAN
- REVISED SECOND SEVEN-YEAR DEVELOPMENT PLAN, SEPT 1955-SEPT 1962

IRAN VA JAHAN – (Missing issues: 198-202, 204-217, 219-221, 227-229) – Paris: Iran Center for Documents, Shumarah-'i 1-280 (10 Shahrivar 1359-Aban 1365 [1 Sep 1980-Nov 1986]) – 2r – 1 – $50.00 – us MEDOC [950]
IRAN VA JAHAN – (Some issues missing) – Paris: Iran Center for Documents. Shumarah-i 1-280 (10 Shahrivar 1359-Aban 1365 [1 Sep 1980-Nov 1986]) – 9 – $75.00 – us MEDOC [956]
THE IRAN-CONTRA AFFAIR : THE MAKING OF A SCANDAL, 1983-1988 – (With 2-vol printed guide & index £630.00) – 664mf – 9 – £2,940.00 – uk Chadwyck [327]
IRAN-I ABAD – Tehran. Shumarah-'i 1-13 (Farvardin 1339-Farvardin 1340 [March 1960-March 1961]) – 1 reel – 1 – $90.00 – us MEDOC [950]
IRAN-I AZAD – (Sal-i 1: shumarah-'i 5-7, 9-15; sal-i 2: shumarah-'i 1-5, 18-19, 23-25; sal-i 3: shumarah-'i 27, 31-37; sal-i 4: shumarah-'i 38-41; sal-i 5: shumarah-'i 44-47; sal-i 6: shumarah-'i 51, 53-55 (Isfand 1341-Khurdad 1347[Feb/Mar 1963-Jun 1968])) – Secheron, Switzerland: Jibhah-'i Milli-i Iran, 1963- – 1 reel – 1 – $25.00 – us MEDOC [950]
IRAN-I BASTAN / ed by Azad, 'Abd al-Rahman Sayf – Tihran: Kanun-i Iran-i Bastan. Sal-i 1, shumarah-i 1-48; sal-i 2, shumarah-i 1-45; sal-i 3, shumarah-i 1-13 (Day 1311-Shahrivar 1314 [January 1933-September 1935]) – $50.00 – us MEDOC [470]
Irani, Behram S *see* CHALLENGES TO PRESS FREEDOM IN INDIA, 1947 TO 1963
IRAN-I IMRUZ / ed by Nazirzadah – Tihran: Sal-i 1, shumarah-i 1-sal-i 4, shumarah-i 2 (Isfand 1317-Tir 1321 [March 1939-July 1942]) – $150.00 – us MEDOC [470]
IRANIAN NATIONAL CENSUS – 1976-1977 – 455mf – 9 – $400.00 – us MEDOC [304]
IRANIAN NATIONAL CENSUS – 1986-1987 – ca 1065mf – 9 – $1,240.00 – us MEDOC [956]
IRANIAN OPPOSITION TO THE SHAH / ed by Behn, Wolfgang – (Includes a detailed printed catalogue with an index in arabic) – 790mf – ne IDC [260]
IRANIANS AND GREEKS IN SOUTH RUSSIA / Rostovtzeff, M – Oxford. 1922. BU-543 2 – 8 – ne IDC [360]
IRANSHAHR – (Dawrah-'i 1, shumarah-'i 1–dawrah-'i 6, shumarah-'i 2 (shumarah musalsal-i 1-233) (28 Mihr 1357-3 Urdibihisht 1363[20 Oct 1978-23 Apr 1984]). (Note: vol. 2-6 published in Arlington, Virginia by Intisharat-i Iranshahr.)) – London: Intisharat-i Tirazh, 1978- – 2r – 1 – $200.00 – us MEDOC [950]
IRAQ – (v2, 1935. Part 1. $3.00. v3, 1936. Part 1. $2.00. v4, 1937. $4.00. v8. 1946. $10.00. v9-10. 1947-48. $12.00v. v11-12. 1949-50. $10.00v. v13. 1951. $10.00. v14-15. 1952-53. $10.00v. v16-17. 1954-55. $12.00v. v18. 1956. $10.00) – v.1, 1934. Part 1 – 9 – $10.00 – us I.R.C. [930]
Iraq *see*
- ALWAQAI ALIRAQIYA: OFFICIAL GAZETTE OF THE REPUBLIC OF IRAQ
- AL-WAQA'I AL-IRAQIYAH
- THE FIVE YEARS ECONOMIC PLAN, 1965/1969, (LAW NO. 87 OF 1965)
- NATIONAL DEVELOPMENT PLAN FOR 1970-1974

Iraq. Agricultural Bank *see* ANNUAL REPORTS, 1936/1937 – 1972-1973
Iraq. Board of Development and Ministry of Development *see* SECOND DEVELOPMENT WEEK SHA'ABAN 1376
Iraq. Central Statistical Organization *see* STATISTICS OF FOREIGN TRADE, 1960-1975
Iraq. Development Board *see* FIRST DEVELOPMENT PLAN, 1951-1956
Iraq. Development Board and Ministry of Development *see* MAJOR IRRIGATION PROJECTS
Iraq. Ministry of Education *see* ANNUAL REPORT ON EDUCATIONAL STATISTICS 1961/62-1964/65
Iraq. Ministry of Guidance *see*
- THE FIVE YEARS DETAILED ECONOMIC PLAN FOR 1961/62-1965/66
- PROVISIONAL ECONOMIC PLAN

Iraq. Planning Board *see* THE GENERAL OUTLINE OF THE FIVE-YEAR ECONOMIC AND SOCIAL DEVELOPMENT PLAN OF IRAQ FOR THE YEARS 1970-74
Iraq. Planning Board and Ministry of Planning *see* NATIONAL DEVELOPMENT PLAN, 1970-1974
THE IRAQ TIMES – Baghdad: Times Press Ltd, 1948-50 6r; 1953-55 9r; 1956-may 1964 29r – 44r – 1 – us Res Libr [072]
IRAQGATE : SADDAM HUSSEIN, U.S. POLICY AND THE PRELUDE TO THE PERSIAN GULF WAR, 1980-1994 – (Printed guide & index only £630.00) – 1995 – ca 1,900 documents – 9 – £2,940.00 – uk Chadwyck [327]
Irazusta, Julio *see* PER ON Y LA CRISIS ARGENTINA
IRBITSKII I ARMAROCHNY I LISTOK – (Includes c.1: 1901:Jan.31, Feb.12-13) – Irbit: Irbitskii i armochny i komitet, 18uu – 1 – CSUXADP4206-S – us Hoover Inst Photo [947]
Irby, H L *see* THE ORNITHOLOGY OF THE STRAITS OF GIBRALTAR
IRCD BULLETIN – Information Retrieval Center on the Disadvantaged. v. 12-. 1977 – 1,5,6,9 – us UMI [305]
IRCD BULLETIN – v12-15, no.3-4. Summer 1977-Summer-Fall 1980 – 1,5,6,9 – us UMI [073]
IRDISCHE LIEBE : EINE ALLTAGSGESCHICHTE / Buelow, Frieda, Freiin von – Dresden: C Reiszner, 1905 – 1 – us U.W. Library [830]
Ireland *see*
- ANCIENT LAWS OF IRELAND
- DEVELOPMENT PLANS
- PROGRAMME FOR ECONOMIC EXPANSION
- PROGRAMME FOR ECONOMIC EXPANSION PROGRESS REPORT FOR SIX MONTHS ENDED 30 SEP 1960
- PROGRAMME FOR ECONOMIC EXPANSION PROGRESS REPORT FOR SIX MONTHS TO 31 MAR 1960
- PROGRAMME FOR ECONOMIC EXPANSION PROGRESS REPORT FOR THE PERIOD TO SEP 1959
- PROGRESS REPORT ON THE PROGRAMME FOR ECONOMIC EXPANSION FOR SIX MONTHS TO 30 SEP 1960
- PROGRESS REPORT ON THE PROGRAMME FOR ECONOMIC EXPANSION FOR SIX MONTHS TO 30 SEP 1961
- PROGRESS REPORT ON THE PROGRAMME FOR ECONOMIC EXPANSION FOR SIX MONTHS TO 30 SEP 1963
- PROGRESS REPORT ON THE PROGRAMME FOR ECONOMIC EXPANSION FOR SIX MONTHS TO 31 MAR 1961
- PROGRESS REPORT ON THE PROGRAMME FOR ECONOMIC EXPANSION FOR SIX MONTHS TO 31 MAR 1962
- PROGRESS REPORT ON THE PROGRAMME FOR ECONOMIC EXPANSION FOR SIX MONTHS TO 31 MAR 1963
- REPORTS, PRE-1894
- SECOND PROGRAMME FOR ECONOMIC EXPANSION
- SECOND PROGRAMME FOR ECONOMIC EXPANSION PROGRESS REPORT FOR 1964
- SECOND PROGRAMME FOR ECONOMIC EXPANSION PROGRESS REPORT FOR 1965
- TRACTS AND TREATISES, 1613-1769

IRELAND, 1811 : BRITISH ISLES CENSUS DIRECTORIES PROJECT, IRELAND. VOL 5 – 3mf – 9 – A$21.00 – at Vine [941]
IRELAND, 1815 : BRITISH ISLES CENSUS DIRECTORIES PROJECT, IRELAND. VOL 6 – 3mf – 9 – A$21.00 – at Vine [941]
IRELAND, 1820 : BRITISH ISLES CENSUS DIRECTORIES PROJECT, IRLAND – (In prep) – at Vine [941]
IRELAND, 1824 : BRITISH ISLES CENSUS DIRECTORIES PROJECT, IRELAND – (In prep) – at Vine [941]
IRELAND, 1829 : BRITISH ISLES CENSUS DIRECTORIES PROJECT, IRELAND. VOL 2 – 3mf – 9 – A$21.00 – at Vine [941]
IRELAND, 1832 : BRITISH ISLES CENSUS DIRECTORIES PROJECT, IRELAND. VOL 1 – 4mf – 9 – A$27.00 – at Vine [941]
IRELAND, 1833 : BRITISH ISLES CENSUS DIRECTORIES PROJECT, IRELAND. VOL 14 – 3mf – 9 – A$21.00 – at Vine [941]
IRELAND, 1845 : BRITISH ISLES CENSUS DIRECTORIES PROJECT, IRELAND. VOL 13 – 11mf – 9 – A$69.00 – at Vine [941]
IRELAND, 1868 : BRITISH ISLES CENSUS DIRECTORIES PROJECT, IRELAND. VOL 3 – 12mf – 9 – A$75.00 – at Vine [941]
IRELAND, 1877 : BRITISH ISLES CENSUS DIRECTORIES PROJECT, IRELAND. VOL 4 – 11mf – 9 – A$69.00 – at Vine [941]
IRELAND, 1928 : BRITISH ISLES CENSUS DIRECTORIES PROJECT, IRELAND – at Vine [941]
IRELAND, 1931 : BRITISH ISLES CENSUS DIRECTORIES PROJECT, IRELAND – (In prep) – at Vine [941]
IRELAND AND CANADA: STUDIES IN COMPARATIVE CONSTITUTIONAL LAW AND POLITICS / Bellot, Hugh Hale L – London: Reeves & Turner, 1893. 03567. (Pre-1900 Canadiana) – 9 – cn C.I.H.M. [971]
IRELAND AND HER CHURCHES / Godkin, James – London: Chapman and Hall, 1867. xxxv,623p – 1 – us U.W. Library [941]
IRELAND AND THE ANGLO-NORMAN CHURCH : A HISTORY OF IRELAND AND IRISH CHRISTIANITY FROM THE ANGLO-NORMAN CONQUEST TO THE DAWN OF THE REFORMATION / Stokes, George Thomas – London: Hodder & Stoughton, 1889 – 1mf – us A.T.L.A. [240]
IRELAND AND THE EMPIRE: A SPEECH DELIVERED BEFORE THE ST PATRICK'S SOCIETY, IN NORDHEIMER'S HALL, MONTREAL, ON ST PATRICK'S DAY, 1885 / Davin, Nicholas Flood – Ottawa: s.n., 1885 (Ottawa: Citizen). 02592. (Pre-1900 Canadiana) – 9 – cn C.I.H.M. [971]
IRELAND: AS SHE IS, AS SHE HAS BEEN, AND AS SHE OUGHT TO BE / Clancy, James J – New York: T. Kelly, 1877. 331p.3 pl – 1 – us U.W. Library [941]
Ireland. (Eire) *see* IRIS OIFIGIUIL
IRELAND IN THE NINETEENTH CENTURY – Key texts in Anglo-Irish literature. Over 500 works by some eighty authors of the 19th cent. 1000 fiches in set – 9 – PS4000.00 – ie European Micro [941]
Ireland, James *see* THE LIFE OF THE REV. JAMES IRELAND
Ireland, John *see*
- THE CHURCH AND MODERN SOCIETY
- PAPERS

Ireland, Joseph Norton *see* RECORDS OF THE NEW YORK STAGE, FROM 1750 TO 1860
Ireland. King's Council *see* ROLL OF THE PROCEEDINGS OF THE KING'S COUNCIL IN IRELAND (RS69)
Ireland. Laws, Statutes, etc *see*
- STATUTES AT LARGE
- THE STATUTES AT LARGE, PASSED IN THE PARLIAMENTS HELD IN IRELAND

Ireland. Ministry of External Affairs *see* IRELAND'S LONG TERM PROGRAMME (1949-1953)
Ireland. National Library *see*
- IRISH TOPOGRAPHICAL PRINTS AND DRAWINGS IN THE NATIONAL LIBRARY OF IRELAND
- MANUSCRIPT SOURCES OF THE HISTORY OF IRISH CIVILIZATION
- SOURCES FOR THE HISTORY OF IRISH CIVILIZATION, ARTICLES IN IRISH PERIODICALS

IRELAND OVER ALL – Ireland.7 Apr 1922 – 1 – ie Microforms [072]
Ireland. Parliament *see* THE PRINTED RECORDS OF THE PARLIAMENT OF IRELAND, 1613-1800
Ireland. Parliament. House of Commons *see* TRANSCRIPTS OF DEBATES
Ireland. Public Records Office *see* ANNUAL REPORTS OF THE DEPUTY KEEPER OF THE PUBLIC RECORDS IN IRELAND
IRELAND'S LONG TERM PROGRAMME (1949-1953) / Ireland. Ministry of External Affairs – Dublin. 1948. BD-438 1 – 9 – ne IDC [338]
IRELAND'S POSITION EXPLAINED AND JUSTIFIED: THE RED HAND OF ULSTER / Gahan, James Joseph – Quebec: s.n., 1873 (Quebec: L'Evenement). 04276. (Pre-1900 Canadiana) – 9 – cn C.I.H.M. [971]
IRENAEUS GEGEN DIE HAERETIKER : BUCH 4-5 (T.U.U. 3-35/2) / Ter-Minassiantz, E – Leipzig, 1910 – 4mf – 9 – ne Slangenburg [240]
THE IRENAEUS TESTIMONY TO THE FOURTH GOSPEL; ITS EXTENT, MEANING, AND VALUE / Lewis, Frank Grant – Chicago: Univ. of Chicago Press, 1908. 64p – 1 – us U.W. Library [240]
IRENICS AND POLEMICS : WITH SUNDRY ESSAYS IN CHURCH HISTORY / Bacon, Leonard – New York: Christian Literature, 1895 – 1mf – us A.T.L.A. [240]
IRENICUM WESLEYANUM, OR, PROPOSALS FOR UNION WITH WESLEYAN METHODISTS / Wordsworth, Christopher – Lincoln: J. Williamson; London: Rivingtons, 1876 – 1mf – us A.T.L.A. [240]
Iret, J L M *see* VOYAGE EN BARBARIE
IRFAN – Siverek, Urfa, 1923-19? – 9 – $20.00 – us MEDOC [956]
IRIAN BARAT DAERAH KITA / Indonesia – SE-4933 1. 1962? – 9 – ne IDC [950]
Iriarte, Juan de *see*
- GRAMATICA LATINA
- OBRAS SUELTAS. TOMO 1
- OBRAS SUELTAS. TOMO 2

Iriarte, Tomas *see*
- COLECCION DE OBRAS. TOMO 1
- COLECCION DE OBRAS. TOMO 2
- COLECCION DE OBRAS. TOMO 3
- COLECCION DE OBRAS. TOMO 4
- COLECCION DE OBRAS. TOMO 5
- COLECCION DE OBRAS. TOMO 6
- LA SENORITA MALCRIADA

Iriarte-A G, Joaquin *see* VERA, FRANCISCO. SENECA. MADRID, 1934
IRIDEARUM GENERA / Ker, J B – Bruxellis. 1827. B-5189 2 – 8 – ne IDC [580]
EL IRIS – Badajoz, 1889-1890 – 5 – sp Bibl Santa Ana [073]
IRIS – 1830-31 – 9mf – 9 – £75.00 – uk Chadwyck [800]
IRIS – Badajoz.1889-90 – 9 – 1.50f – sp Bibl Santa Ana [072]
IRIS : DEUTSCHE ENTOMOLOGISCHE ZEITSCHRIFT – Dresden, 1884/1888-1943. v1-57 – 312mf – 9 – Z-936/2 – ne IDC [590]
IRIS : A DRAMA IN FIVE ACTS / Pinero, Arthur Wing – London: W. Heinemann, 1902 – 1 roll – 1 – 1-55879-466-2 – uk Libr Preservation [820]
IRIS – Haverhill. Mass. 1832-1834 – 1 – us UMI [071]
IRIS : EIN TASCHENBUCH / ed by Jacobi, Johann Georg – Zuerich. 10v. 1803-12 – 36mf – 9 – subsc: DM270.00 diazo DM300.00 silver – gw Olms [430]
IRIS AN AIRM – Ireland.25 Sept-23 Dec 1922 – 1 – ie Microforms [072]
IRIS OIFIGIUIL / Ireland. (Eire) – Dublin, 1959-71 – 9r – 1 – us Ross [324]
IRIS PARANAENSE : FOLHA LITTERARIA, AGRICOLA, COMMERCIAL E NOTICIOSA – Curitiba, 19 Oct 1873 – 1,5,6 – bl Biblioteca [072]
Irisarri, Pantaleon *see* REFLEXIONES...ESPOSA DONA MARIA ROSARIO MENDOZA Y..
DIE IRISCHE KANONENSAMMLUNG / ed by Wasserschleben, H – Leipzig. Zweite Auflage. 1885 – 6mf – 8 – ne Slangenburg [240]
IRISH ADVOCATE – Drogheda. Ireland. -w. 14 Oct 1848-14 Apr 1849. (19 ft) – 1 – uk British Libr Newspaper [072]
IRISH ADVOCATE AND ACHILL MISSIONARY HERALD – Dublin, Ireland.1879-80. -w. 1 reel – 1 – uk British Libr Newspaper [072]
IRISH AGRICULTURISTS ETC – Ireland.1849. -w. 1/4 reel – 1 – uk British Libr Newspaper [072]
IRISH AMERICAN – New York. Weekly Aug 12 1849-Feb 1915. Incomplete – 1 – us NY Public [073]
IRISH ANTI-APARTHEID MOVEMENT (IAAM) – Dublin. 95 docs. 1980-1990 – 17mf – 9 – ne IDC [320]
AN IRISH BEAUTY OF THE REGENCY / Calvert, Frances Pery; ed by Blake, Warrenne – London: John Lane – New York: John Lane Company, 1911 – 1r – 1 – us U.W. Library [920]
IRISH BOOKLOVER – 63 mf – Ir£50.00 – ie Microforms [420]

THE IRISH BUILDER – 1859-?. 654 fiches. Indexed – 9 – PS1200.00 – ie European Micro [073]
IRISH BULLETIN – Dublin, Ireland.12 Jul 1919-13 Dec 1921 – 1 – ie Microforms [072]
IRISH CANADIAN – Toronto, Canada. 1863-92 – 18r – 1 – $1,170.00 – cn Library Assoc [971]
THE IRISH CANADIAN : ST PATRICK'S DAY SOUVENIR NUMBER – Montreal, Canada. mar 1905 – 1r – 1 – Can$25.00 – cn Can Microfilming [073]
THE IRISH CAUSE: A LECTURE DELIVERED IN THE ADELAIDE STREET RINK, ON SATURDAY EVENING, NOVEMBER 20TH, 1886 / Davitt, Michael – Toronto: s.n., 1886 (Toronto: Irish Canadian). 02601. (Pre-1900 Canadiana) – 9 – cn C.I.H.M. [971]
IRISH CHRISTIAN ADVOCATE – Belfast, Ireland. 1885-96. -d.12 reels – 1 – uk British Libr Newspaper [072]
IRISH CITIZEN – Dublin, Ireland.25 May 1912-Aug 1920 – 1 – ie Microforms [072]
IRISH CITIZEN – New York. v1. 1867-68 – 1r – 1 – us Ross [071]
IRISH CITIZEN – New York. Weekly. New York Oct 19 1867-Oct 19 1868 – 1 – us NY Public [073]
IRISH CITIZEN ARMY BULLETIN – Ireland.13 Dec 1934-15 May 1935 – 1 – ie Microforms [072]
IRISH DAILY INDEPENDENT – Dublin, Ireland. Irish Independent. -d. 18 Dec 1891-Dec 1913. 92 reels – 1 – uk British Libr Newspaper [072]
THE IRISH DAILY INDEPENDENT AND IRISH INDEPENDENT – 1 – Ir£9,000.00 – ie Microforms [941]
IRISH DEMOCRAT – Ireland.Mar-Dec 1937 – 1 – ie Microforms [072]
IRISH DEMOCRAT *see* IRISH FREEDOM
IRISH DIGEST – 1938-67 – 1 – uk Microform Academic [800]
IRISH EASTERN COUNTIES HERALD – Athy. Ireland. -w. 13 Feb-13 Mar 1849. (5 ft) – 1 – uk British Libr Newspaper [072]
IRISH ESSAYS : AND OTHERS / Arnold, Matthew – London: Smith, Elder, 1882 – 1 roll – 1 – 1-55879-195-7 – uk Libr Preservation [840]
IRISH ESSAYS: AND OTHERS / Arnold, Matthew – London: Smith, Elder & Co., 1882. xiv,1 leaf, 308p – 1 – us U.W. Library [840]
IRISH ETHNOLOGY PAMPHLET COLLECTION – 1978 – 9 – us Hoover Inst Photo [941]
IRISH EXAMINER – Dublin, Ireland.30 Sept 1848-17 Feb 1879. -w.1/2 reel – 1 – uk British Libr Newspaper [072]
IRISH EXILE – Ireland.Mar-Dec 1921 – 1 – ie Microforms [072]
THE IRISH EXPRESS – Montreal, Canada. v1 n6. 4 May 1866 – 1r – 1 – Can$20.00 – cn Can Microfilming [072]
IRISH FARMERS GAZETTE ETC – (Farmers Gazette, 1878-80) – Dublin, Ireland. 1861-77; 1881-84 – 23r – 1 – uk British Libr Newspaper [072]
THE IRISH FOLK SONG SOCIETY JOURNAL – London. 1904-32 – 1 – 23.00 – us L of C Photodup [780]
IRISH FOREIGN RELATIONS PAMPHLET COLLECTION – 1918 – 1r – 1 – us Hoover Inst Photo [941]
IRISH FREEDOM – Ireland.Nov 1910-1914 – 1 – ie Microforms [072]
IRISH FREEDOM – Ireland.Nov 1926-1937 – 1 – ie Microforms [072]
IRISH FREEDOM – (Irish Democrat 1945-) – London, UK. 1939-80 – 4r – 1 – uk British Libr Newspaper [072]
IRISH FRONT – Ireland.11 May 1935 – 1 – ie Microforms [072]
THE IRISH GLEANER – Quebec, Canada. v2 n3. 11 jun 1921 – 1r – 1 – Can$25.00 – cn Can Microfilming [072]
Irish, H C *see* A REVISION OF THE GENUS CAPSICUM WITH A SPECIAL REFERENCE TO GARDEN VARIETIES
IRISH HAMMER AND PLOUGH – Ireland.22 May-16 Oct 1926 – 1 – ie Microforms [072]
IRISH HISTORY, 1901 TO 1921, PAMPHLET COLLECTION – 1914-1975 – 4r – 1 – us Hoover Inst Photo [941]
IRISH HISTORY, 1922 TO THE PRESENT, PAMPHLET COLLECTION – 1922-1992 – 2r – 1 – us Hoover Inst Photo [941]
IRISH INDEPENDENT – Dublin: Printed & publ by the proprietors at the Offices, 1905- ; 1956-oct 1977; jul-aug 1978; nov-dec 1980; nov-dec 1981 – 1 – us Res Libr [072]
IRISH INDEPENDENT – Ireland.-d. 1905- – 1 – PS27.50r – ie European Micro [072]
IRISH INDEPENDENT – (Sunday Independent also available 8r per y $70.00r) – 1905- – 24r per y – 1 – inquire – us Ross [072]
THE IRISH INDEPENDENT – 1905- – 1 – ie Microforms [941]
IRISH JOURNAL OF MEDICAL SCIENCE – 1957 – 1 – uk Microform Academic [616]
IRISH JURIST – 1935-60 – 1 – uk Microform Academic [073]
IRISH JURIST AND LOCAL GOVERNMENT REVIEW : TOGETHER WITH REPORTS, STATUTES, ORDERS, RULES AND REGULATIONS – (Title varies: v1-4 as New Irish Jurist and Local Government Review) – Dublin. v1-5. 1900-05 – 1 – $80.00 – us Hein [072]
THE IRISH LAND AND LABOUR QUESTION, ILLUSTRATED IN THE HISTORY OF RALAHINE AND CO-OPERATIVE FARMING / Craig, Edward Thomas – London: Truebner & Co., 1893. xii,(3)-204p. Illus., incl. ports – 1 – us U.W. Library [331]
IRISH LAW REPORTS – 1839-1893 – 1 – £2,400.00 – uk World [340]
IRISH LAW TIMES – (Updates planned) – v1-46. 1867-1912 – 455mf – 9 – $682.00 – LLMC 84-504 – us L.L.M.C. [073]
THE IRISH LIBER HYMNORUM / Bernard, J & Atkinson, R – (Vol 1: Text and introduction; vol 2: Translations and notes) – 1898 – 12mf – 8 – Dfl42.00 – ne Slangenburg [941]
IRISH LITANIES / Plummer, Charles – 1925 – 3mf – 8 – ne Slangenburg [240]
IRISH LITERARY MAGAZINES *see* LITERARY MAGAZINES OF THE IRISH RENAISSANCE
IRISH LITERARY PERIODICALS 1700-1950 – 4 mf – Ir£5.00 – ie Microforms [420]
THE IRISH MANUSCRIPT COLLECTION / Royal Irish Academy – 1700-1900. 194 reels with printed guide – £7,995.00 – uk World [941]
IRISH MEDIEVAL MONASTERIES ON THE CONTINENT / Fuhrmann, J – Washington D.C., 1927 – 3mf – 8 – Dfl13.00 – ne Slangenburg [720]
IRISH MONASTICISM, ORIGINS AND EARLY DEVELOPMENT / Ryan, John – London, 1939 – 10mf – 8 – Dfl35.00 – ne Slangenburg [240]
IRISH MONASTICISM. ORIGINS AND EARLY DEVELOPMENT / Ryan, John – Dublin, 1931; Madrid: Razon y Fe, 1932 – 1 – sp Bibl Santa Ana [240]
THE IRISH NATION – Ireland.2 Jan 1909-24 Dec 1910 – 1 – ie Microforms [072]
THE IRISH NATION – Ireland.24 Jun 1916-26 May 1917 – 1 – ie Microforms [072]
THE IRISH NATION – New York. v1-2. 1881-83 – 1r – 1 – us Ross [071]
IRISH NATION AND THE PEASANT – Dublin, Ireland. -w. 2 Jan 1909-15 Oct, 3 Dec 1910. 1 1 2 reels – 1 – uk British Libr Newspaper [072]
IRISH NATIONAL GUARD – Dublin, Ireland.22 Apr-18 Jul 1848. -w. 17 feet – 1 – uk British Libr Newspaper [072]
IRISH NEWS ETC. (BELFAST) – Aug 15 1891-Aug 1915; Sep 22 1915-Jun 22 1917; Jul 3-Dec 29 1917; 1918-Aug 1925; Jan-Mar 1926; Apr 10-Jun 30 1926; Jul 19-Sep 1926; Oct 11 1926-Mar 20 1930; Apr 1930-Jan 19 1971; Mar 10 1971-84; 1986-87; Jan 2-Jan 30 1988; Feb-Apr 1988; May 3 1988-89; Jul 1990-Jun 1997 – 516r – 9 – uk British Libr Newspaper [072]
IRISH OPINION – Dublin, Ireland.17 Jun 1916-28 Apr 1917 – 1 – ie Microforms [072]
IRISH PAMPHLETS, C. 1700-1850 / Catholic University of America, Washington D.C. – (Includes a printed guide) – 1,070mf – 9 – ne IDC [420]
IRISH PAMPHLETS: THE LOUGH FEA AND THORPE COLLECTION – 650 titles mostly from the 1640s. 55 fiches – 9 – PS500.00 – ie European Micro [080]
IRISH PEASANT (THE PEASANT) – Dublin, Ireland.1903-26 Dec 1908 – 1 – ie Microforms [072]
IRISH PEDIGREES: OR, THE ORIGIN AND STEM OF THE IRISH NATION / O'Hart, John – Dublin, 1876. 2v – 1 – us U.W. Library [920]
IRISH PEOPLE – Dublin, Ireland. 16 Sep 1899-7 Nov 1903; 30 Sep 1905-27 Mar 1909.-w. 6 reels – 1 – uk British Libr Newspaper [072]
IRISH PEOPLE – Dublin, Ireland (1865-66) and New York, NY (1867-69) – 1 – Ir£20.00 – ie Microforms [072]
THE IRISH PEOPLE – Ireland.29 Feb-11 Apr 1936 – 1 – ie Microforms [072]
THE IRISH PEOPLE – Ireland.Sept 1899-Mar 1909 – 1 – ie Microforms [072]
THE IRISH PEOPLE – New York, 1867-1869 – 1 – Ir£45.00 – ie Microforms [941]
IRISH PEOPLE WAR SPECIAL – Ireland.16 Jul-20 Aug 1922 – 1 – ie Microforms [072]
IRISH POLITICAL AND RADICAL NEWSPAPERS OF THE TWENTIETH CENTURY – 145 titles. 118 reels – 1 – ie Microforms [072]
IRISH PRESS – 1930- – 12r per y – 1 – inquire – us Ross [072]
IRISH PRESS – Dublin, Ireland, 1930-1950.,-1978-date.-12 reels per year – 113r – 1 – ie Microforms [941]
IRISH PRESS – Ireland.-d. 1931- – 1 – PS27.50r – ie European Micro [072]
THE IRISH PRESS 1931-1950 – 1 – Ir£2,000.00 – ie Microforms [941]
THE IRISH PRESS (PHILADELPHIA, PA.: 1918) – (Library has: v.1,no.1-v.3,no.52; Mar. 23, 1918-Mar. 12, 1921; a few are mutilated) – Philadelphia, Pa.: [s.n.], 1918- – 1 – CSUX87-S410 – us Hoover Inst Photo [978]
THE IRISH QUESTION: WITH SPECIAL REFERENCE TO HOME RULE IN CANADA: SPEECHES / Blake, Edward – By Edward Blake, E. J. C. Morton and Robert W. Hamilton. Thursday, August 4th, 1892. 1892? 00175. (Pre-1900 Canadiana) – 9 – cn C.I.H.M. [971]
THE IRISH RACE IN CALIFORNIA, AND ON THE PACIFIC COAST / Quigley, Dr – San Francisco: A. Roman & Co., Publ., 1878. California Reel 2. (The Cox Library Collection) – 5 – us Americana [978]
IRISH RAILWAY GAZETTE ETC – Ireland.4 Nov 1844-13 May 1850. -w. 3 reels – 1 – uk British Libr Newspaper [072]
THE IRISH REFORMATION, OR, THE ALLEGED CONVERSION OF THE IRISH BISHOPS AT THE ACCESSION OF QUEEN ELIZABETH, AND THE ASSUMED DESCENT OF THE PRESENT ESTABLISHED HIERARCHY IN IRELAND, FROM THE ANCIENT IRISH CHURCH, DISPROVED / Brady, W Maziere – London: Longmans, Green, 1867 – 1mf – us A.T.L.A. [240]
IRISH REPUBLICAN ARMY PAMPHLET COLLECTION – 197?-1983 – 1r – 1 – us Hoover Inst Photo [941]
IRISH REVIEW – 1911-14.4v. 26 fiches – 9 – Ir£15.00 – ie Microforms [073]
IRISH SAINTS IN GREAT BRITAIN / Moran, Patrick Francis – (Includes bibliographical references) – Dublin: M H Gill: Browne & Nolan, 1879 – 1mf – 9 – 0-8370-6921-1 – 1986-0921 – us A.T.L.A. [240]
THE IRISH SENTINEL – Quebec, Canada. 7 fev 1872-v1 n24. 18 jul 1872 – 1r – 1 – Can$35.00 – cn Can Microfilming [072]
THE IRISH SITUATION: SPEECH OF MR. BLAKE, M. P., AT GLASGOW, DECEMBER, 1898 / Blake, Edward – Dublin, 1899. 02298. (Pre-1900 Canadiana) – 9 – cn C.I.H.M. [971]
THE IRISH SPELLING-BOOK – Anon. 1740. 369p. (English Linguistics Series 1500-1800) – 9 – us UMI [420]
IRISH TEMPERENCE AND LITERARY GAZETTE – Ireland. -w. Nov 1836-29 Sept 1838. 1 reel – 1 – uk British Libr Newspaper [072]
IRISH TIMES – 1 – sz Infoprint [072]
IRISH TIMES – Dublin. Ireland. -d. 1861-65. (20 reels) – 1 – uk British Libr Newspaper [072]
THE IRISH TIMES – 1859- – 1 – ie Irish Times [072]
THE IRISH TIMES – Dublin: Irish Times Ltd, jul 1938-jan 1975; apr 1975-jul 1976; sep-oct 1976; feb-aug, oct-nov 1, dec 1977; jan-mar 2 1978 – 1 – us Res Libr [072]
IRISH TOPOGRAPHICAL PRINTS AND DRAWINGS IN THE NATIONAL LIBRARY OF IRELAND / Ireland. National Library – Part 1. Hardcopy catalogue to entire collection. 17th to 19th Century – 1 – ie Microforms [941]
IRISH TRIBUNE – Dublin, Ireland.10 Jun-8 Jul 1848. -w. 12 feet – 1 – uk British Libr Newspaper [072]
THE IRISH VINDICATOR AND CANADA ADVERTISER *see* THE IRISH VINDICATOR AND CANADA GENERAL ADVERTISER
THE IRISH VINDICATOR AND CANADA GENERAL ADVERTISER – (Title varies: The Irish Vindicator and Canada Advertiser; The Vindicator; The Vindicator and Canadian Advertiser) – Montreal, Canada. 12 dec 1828-7 nov 1837 – 4r – 1 – Can$50.00r – cn Can Microfilming [072]
IRISH VOLUNTEER – Dublin, Ireland.7 Feb 1914-22 Apr 1916 – 1 – ie Microforms [072]
IRISH WAR NEWS – Ireland.Apr 1916 – 1 – ie Microforms [072]
IRISH WEEKLY AND ULSTER EXAMINER – Belfast: Irish News. -w. Running title: Irish Weekly, Belfast – 1 – us U.W. Library [073]
Irish, William Norman *see* HEBREW CHARTS
IRISH WORK – Ireland.19 Dec 1914 – 1 – ie Microforms [072]
IRISH WORKER – Dublin, Ireland. -m. March-June 1893. 10 ft – 1 – uk British Libr Newspaper [072]
IRISH WORKER – Dublin. Ireland. -w. 3 Jan-28 Nov 1914. (26 ft) – 1 – uk British Libr Newspaper [072]
THE IRISH WORKER – Dublin, Ireland.11 Oct 1930-12 Mar 1932 – 1 – ie Microforms [072]
THE IRISH WORKER – Dublin, Ireland.16 Jun 1923-9 May 1925 – 1 – ie Microforms [072]
THE IRISH WORKER – Dublin, Ireland.27 May 1911-5 Dec 1914 – 1 – ie Microforms [072]
IRISH WORKERS' VOICE – Dublin, Ireland.9 Apr 1932-13 Jun 1936 – 1 – ie Microforms [072]
IRISH WORKERS' WEEKLY – Dublin, Ireland.22 Apr 1939-1 Nov 1941 – 1 – ie Microforms [072]
IRISH WORLD AND AMERICAN INDUSTRIAL LIBERATOR – New York. v1-81. 1870-1950 – 39r – 1 – us Ross [071]
THE IRISH WORLD AND AMERICAN INDUSTRIAL LIBERATOR – New York. Nov 5 1870-Dec 1950. Incomplete – 1 – us NY Public [073]
IRISH-AMERICAN – New York. v1-68. 1849-1915 – 19r – 1 – us Ross [071]
IRISHMAN – Ireland. 1819-25 – 1 – Ir£40.00 – ie Microforms [072]
THE IRISHMAN – Belfast, Ireland. v. 1-2. Jan. 15, 1916-Feb. 10, 1917 – 1 – us NY Public [941]
THE IRISHMAN – Dublin, Ireland.1916-16 Aug 1919 – 1 – ie Microforms [072]
THE IRISHMAN – Galway. Ireland. -sw. 6 May-12 Dec 1835. (36 ft) – 1 – uk British Libr Newspaper [072]
THE IRISHMAN – Montreal, Canada. v1 n2. 12 jun-v1 n3. 19 jun 1858 – 1r – 1 – Can$25.00 – cn Can Microfilming [072]
THE IRISHMAN = AN T-EIREANNACH – Ireland.Jul 1910-Oct 1913 – 1 – ie Microforms [072]
THE IRISHMAN IN CANADA / Davin, Nicholas Flood – London: Sampson Low, Marston & Co.; Toronto: Maclean, c1877. 02593. (Pre-1900 Canadiana) – 9 – cn C.I.H.M. [305]
IRKA: ROMAN / Jungfer, Victor – Karlsbad: Adam Kraft, 1945. 383p – 1 – us U.W. Library [830]
Irkutsk. (Province). Gosudarstvennyi arkhiv *see* REVOLIUTSIONNOE DVIZHENIE V IRKUTSKOI GUBERNII V PERIOD PERVOI RUSSKOI REVOLIUTSII
IRKUTSKII KOOPERATOR – Irkutsk, 1916-17 n4 – 6mf – 9 – COR-598/1 – ne IDC [334]
IRKUTSKIIA GUBERNSKIIA VIEDOMOSR / Russia – 1859, 1871-98 – 1 – $269.00 – us L of C Photodup [947]
LES IRLANDAIS EN AMERIQUE AVANT COLOMB: D'APRES LA LEGENDE ET L'HISTORIE: COLONISATION DE L'IRLAND IT MIKLA / Gaffarel, Paul – Paris: Institut geographique de Paris, 1890. 04325. (Pre-1900 Canadiana) – 9 – cn C.I.H.M. [971]
L'IRLANDE LIBRE – Organe de la colonie irlandaise a Paris. Paris. juin 1897-oct 1898, avr 1900 – 1 – fr A.C.R.P.P. [073]
IRMELA : EINE GESCHICHTE AUS ALTER ZEIT / Steinhausen, Heinrich – 47. Aufl. Stuttgart: J F Steinkopf, [1950] – 1r – 1 – us U.W. Library [830]
Irmer, G *see* DIE VERHANDLUNGEN SCHWEDENS UND SEINER VERBUENDETEN MIT WALLENSTEIN UND DEM KAISER VON 1631 BIS 1634

IRODALMI UJSAG – Budapest. Hungary. -w. 2 Nov 1950-26 Mar, 10 Sep, 3 Dec 1955, 7 Jan-20 Oct 1956. (3 reels) – 1 – uk British Libr Newspaper [072]

IRODALMI UJSAG – Paris. France. -w. Feb 1962-Dec 1965. (3 reels) – 1 – uk British Libr Newspaper [072]

IROMANYOK / Hungary. Nemzetgyueles – v. 1-32. 1920-26 – 1 – 52.00 – us L of C Photodup [943]

IROMANYOK / Hungary. Orszaggyules. Felsohaz – v. 1-197. 1865 68-1944. (1865-72, 1915-18 and scattered issues wanting) – 1 – 1,297.00 – us L of C Photodup [943]

IRON AGE – Middletown. N.Y. v105-168 1920-51 – 1,5,6 – us Princeton Micro [670]

IRON AGE – New York – $175.00y – us Fairchild Micro [670]

IRON AGE – (v. 195- 1965- 5,6. v. 205-1970- 9) – 11- 1873- – 1 – us UMI [600]

IRON AND COAL TRADES REVIEW – Middlesbrough and London. 6 Oct 1869-Dec 1886. -w. 30 reels – 1 – uk British Libr Newspaper [073]

IRON AND STEEL ENGINEER – 1- 1924- 1; v42- 5,6; v54- 9 – us UMI [670]

Iron and Steel Institute *see* 67 SPECIAL REPORTS AND BIBLIOGRAPHIES

Iron and Steel Institute. London *see*
- CARNEGIE SCHOLARSHIP MEMOIRS
- JOURNAL

THE IRON CARDINAL : THE ROMANCE OF RICHELIEU / McCabe, Joseph – New York: J. McBride, 1909 – 1mf – us A.T.L.A. [240]

IRON CITY – Pittsburgh. Pa. and Pittsburgh Weekly Chronicle. 1841-42 – 1 – us UMI [071]

THE IRON HORSE / Ballantyne, Robert Michael – London: Nisbet, 1871?. 07472. (Pre-1900 Canadiana) – 9 – cn C.I.H.M. [830]

IRON VALLEY REPORTER – Dover. Ohio. 1872-1900 – 1 – us UMI [071]

IRONBRIDGE WEEKLY JOURNAL AND BOROUGH OF WENLOCK ADVERTISER – England. Boro' of Wenlock Express – Wenlock & Ludlow Express. -w. 17 July 1869-4 March 1882. Lacking July-Dec 1874. 11 reels – 1 – uk British Libr Newspaper [072]

IRONCLADS IN ACTION : A SKETCH OF NAVAL WARFARE FROM 1855 TO 1895, WITH SOME ACCOUNT OF THE DEVELOPMENT OF THE BATTLESHIP IN ENGLAND / Wilson, Herbert Wrigley – Introd. by Captain A.T. Mahan. 5th ed. 2v. 1897 – 9 – uk Libr Preservation [941]

IRONIAS / Sanchez-Arjona, Vicente – Sevilla: Artes Graficas, Tomo 1. 1948 – 1 – sp Bibl Santa Ana [810]

IRONIAS / Sanchez-Arjona, Vicente – Sevilla: Graf. Tirvia, Tomo 4. 1954 – 1 – sp Bibl Santa Ana [810]

IRONIAS / Sanchez-Arjona, Vicente – Sevilla: Graficas Tirvia, Tomo 5. 1955 – 1 – sp Bibl Santa Ana [810]

IRONIAS / Sanchez-Arjona, Vicente – Sevilla: Imp. Carlos Acuna, Tomo 2. 1953 – 1 – sp Bibl Santa Ana [810]

IRONIAS / Sanchez-Arjona, Vicente – Sevilla: Imp. Carlos Acuna, Tomo 3. 1953 – 1 – sp Bibl Santa Ana [810]

IRONIAS / Sanchez-Arjona, Vicente – Sevilla: Imprenta Cuadrado, Tomo 6. 1958 – 1 – sp Bibl Santa Ana [810]

IRONIAS Y SUTILEZAS CON HONORES / Sanchez-Arjona, Vicente – Sevilla: Imp. Alvarez, 1960 – 1 – sp Bibl Santa Ana [810]

IRONMAKING AND STEELMAKING – v1- 1974- – 1,5,6,9 – us UMI [670]

L'IROQUOIS : HUMORISTIQUE / ed by Berthelot, Hector – Montreal, Canada. 24 mai-21 jun 1890 – 1r – 1 – Can$25.00 – cn Can Microfilming [072]

THE IROQUOIS AND THE JESUITS: THE STORY OF THE LABORS OF CATHOLIC MISSIONARIES AMONG THESE INDIANS / Donohoe, Thomas – Buffalo, N.Y.: Buffalo Catholic Publication Co., 1895, c1894. 02076. (Pre-1900 Canadiana) – 9 – cn C.I.H.M. [971]

THE IROQUOIS BEACH / Coleman, Arthur Philemon – 1898? 03211. (Pre-1900 Canadiana) – 9 – cn C.I.H.M. [910]

IROQUOIS COUNTY TIMES – Watseka. Ill. 1959- – 1 – us UMI [071]

IROQUOIS FALLS ENTERPRISE – Ontario, CN. 1963- – 1r per yr – 1 – Can$57.00r – cn Commonwealth Micro [072]

IROQUOIS INDIANS: A DOCUMENTARY HISTORY – 8000 documents dated from the early 1600s to the 1920s – 1 – us Primary [975]

THE IROQUOIS TRAIL, OR, FOOTPRINTS OF THE SIX NATIONS: IN CUSTOMS, TRADITIONS AND HISTORY / Beauchamp, William M – Fayetteville, NY, 1892. 04555. (Pre-1900 Canadiana) – 9 – cn C.I.H.M. [970]

DER IRRE VON ST JAMES : AUS DEM REISETAGEBUCHE EINES ARZTES / Galen, Philipp – 7. Aufl. St Louis, Mo: Louis Lange, 1924 – 1 – us U.W. Library [920]

IRRGARTEN GOTTES : ODER, DIE KOMOEDIE DES CHAOS / Winckler, Josef – Jena: E Diederichs, 1922 – 1r – 1 – us U.W. Library [820]

IRRIGATION AGE – (1985-. 1,5,6) – v17-. 1982- – 9 – us UMI [631]

IRRIGATION BULLETIN – Manteca, CA. 1910-17 – 4r – 1 – $200.00 – B02417 – us Library Micro [073]

THE IRRIGATION BULLETIN – Ripon, CA. 1910-13 – 2r – 1 – $100.00 – B02709 – us Library Micro [071]

IRRIGATION BY GRAVITY FROM THE RIVER ATBARA / Sudan. Ministry of Irrigation and Hydroelectric Power – Bell, H. 1956? BNE-7671 1 – 9 – ne IDC [631]

IRRIGATION CANAL LINING / Kraatz, DB – 1977 – 199p – it F.A.O. [627]

IRRIGATION IN AFRICA SOUTH OF THE SAHARA – 1986 – 181p – it F.A.O. [631]

IRRIGATION JOURNAL – v1- 1951- 1; v26-1976- 5,6,9 – us UMI [627]

THE IRRIGATION OF THE JORDAN VALLEY / Masar, Ilhami – Jordan. Ministry of Economy. 1956 – 9 – ne IDC [956]

IRRIGATION PRACTICE AND WATER MANAGEMENT – 1978 – 86p – it F.A.O. [631]

IRRIGATION SCIENCE – v.1-2, 1978-80. ISSN: 0342-7188 – 1,5,6,9,13 – 79.00v – us UMI [627]

IRRIGATION USERS' ORGANIZATIONS IN THE LEGISLATION AND ADMINISTRATION OF CERTAIN LATIN AMERICAN COUNTRIES – 1983 – 94p – it F.A.O. [631]

IRRIGATOR – Selma, CA. 1886-1928 – 21r – 1 – $1,050.00 – B02993 – us Library Micro [071]

DIE IRRTUMSLOSIGKEIT JESU CHRISTI UND DER CHRISTLICHE GLAUBE : VIER BAENDEN DER "GOTTESOFFENBARUNG IN JESU CHRISTO" UND ZU DIESER SCHRIFT / Schwartzkopff, Paul – Giessen: J Ricker, 1897 – 1mf – 9 – 0-8370-4615-7 – 1985-2615 – us A.T.L.A. [240]

IRS CUMULATIVE BULLETIN : 1922-1990 / U.S. Treasury Department – (Updates planned) – 1206mf – 9 – $1,809.00 – LLMC 79-416 – us L.L.M.C. [324]

IRS CUMULATIVE BULLETIN *see*
- CUMULATIVE BULLETIN, INCOME TAX RULINGS
- TREASURY DECISIONS, 1899-1966

Irsay, Stephen d' *see* ALBRECHT VON HALLER

Irson, Cl *see* NOUVELE METHODE POUR APPRENDRE FACILEMENT LES PRINCIPES DE LA LANGUE

IRURAC BAT – Bilbao, Spain. July 1856-Sept 16 1856 – 1r – 1 – us L of C Photodup [072]

Irvin, Samuel M *see* DIARY AND JOURNAL KEPT AT IOWAY MISSION IN KANSAS

Irvine, Leigh *see*
- HISTORY OF CALIFORNIA
- HISTORY OF HUMBOLDT COUNTY

IRVINE TODAY – Irvine, CA. 1979-87 – 12r – 1 – $600.00 – R02313 – us Library Micro [071]

IRVINE WORLD NEWS – Irvine, CA. 1972-91 – 69r – 1 – $3,450.00 – R02315 – us Library Micro [071]

Irving, David *see*
- THE HISTORY OF SCOTISH POETRY
- HITLER'S WAR
- HUNGARIAN UPRISING, 1956

Irving, Edward *see*
- THE CHURCH AND STATE RESPONSIBLE TO CHRIST
- THE COLLECTED WRITINGS OF EDWARD IRVING
- THE COMING OF MESSIAH IN GLORY AND MAJESTY

IRVING GOLD SCRAPBOOK *see* GOLD, IRVING, SCRAPBOOK

Irving, Henry *see* THE DRAMA

Irving, M *see* A LIST OF INSCRIPTIONS ON CHRISTIAN TOMBS OR MONUMENTS IN THE PUNJAB, NORTH-WEST FRONTIER PROVINCE, KASHMIR AND AFGHANISTAN; POSSESSING HISTORICAL OR ARCH. INTEREST

Irving, Theodore *see* THE CONQUEST OF FLORIDA...HERNANDO DE SOTO

Irving, Washington *see*
- THE DISCOVERY AND CONQUEST OF THE NEW WORLD, CONTAINING THE LIFE AND VOYAGES OF CHRISTOPHER COLUMBUS
- NOTEBOOKS
- NOTEBOOKS CONTAINING QUERIES, EXTRACTS FROM PRINTED SOURCES, ETC. RELATING TO ASTORIA
- WORKS

IRVINGISM : IN ITS RISE, PROGRESS, AND PRESENT STATE / Baxter, Robert – London: J. Nisbet, 1836 – 1mf – us A.T.L.A. [240]

THE IRVINGTON STORIES / Dodge, Mary Mapes – Illus. by F.O.C. Darley.4th ed. New York: J. O'Kane, 1867. 263p – 1 – us U.W. Library [830]

Irwin, James W *see* HATCH ACT DECISIONS

Irwin, Melinda L *see* DEVELOPMENT OF AN ANTHROPOMETRIC REGRESSION EQUATION TO PREDICT BODY DENSITY IN AFRICAN AMERICAN WOMEN

Irwin, R L *see* DEVELOPMENT OF A COLLEGIATE LICENSING ADMINISTRATIVE PARADIGM

I.S. AKSAKOV V EGO PIS'MAKH / Aksakov, I S – Moscow, St. Petersburg, 1888-96. 4v. BR-9052 2 – 8 – ne IDC [460]

IS ATHLETE BURNOUT MORE THAN JUST STRESS? A SPORT COMMITMENT PERSPECTIVE / Raedeke, Thomas D – University of Oregon, 1995 – 3mf – 9 – $12.00 – PSY 1900 – us Microform Publ [150]

IS CHRISTIANITY TRUE? : ANSWERS FROM HISTORY, THE MONUMENTS, THE BIBLE, NATURE, EXPERIENCE, AND GROWTH OF CHRISTIANITY / Blaikie, William Garden et al – (Includes index) – Philadelphia: Rice & Hirst, c1897 – 1mf – 9 – 0-8370-3730-1 – 1985-1730 – us A.T.L.A. [230]

IS DUET 'NE WELT! : SCHWAENKE UND GESCHICHTEN / Henze, Wilhelm – Bad Pyrmont: F Gersbach, 1922 – 1r – 1 – us U.W. Library [830]

IS GOD KNOWABLE? / Iverach, James – London: Hodder & Stoughton, 1887 – 1mf – 9 – 0-8370-4608-4 – 1985-2608 – us A.T.L.A. [210]

IS IT MARY OR THE LADY OF THE JESUITS? / Fulton, Justin Dewey – Toronto: Willard Tract Depository, 1889?. 03272. (Pre-1900 Canadiana) – 9 – cn C.I.H.M. [971]

IS IT POSSIBLE TO SURVIVE? / Werkheiser, Don – 1fiche (29x) – 9 – 1.00f – at Libertarian Micro [320]

IS MUHAMMAD A TRUE PROPHET? / Hassan, Abdulkadir – SE-4116 1 – 9 – ne IDC [260]

IS MY BIBLE TRUE?: WHERE DID WE GET IT? / Leach, Charles – Chicago: Fleming H. Revell, 1897. 1 fiche – 9 – us A.T.L.A. [240]

IS PROTESTANTISM A FAILURE?: THE QUESTION CONSIDERED IN FIVE LECTURES: ALSO A DISCOURSE ON CHRISTIAN MONOTHEISM / Cordner, John – s.l.: s.n., 1869 (Montreal: J. Lovell). 00237. (Pre-1900 Canadiana) – 9 – cn C.I.H.M. [971]

IS ROMANISM REAL CHRISTIANITY? / Newman, Francis William & Abbot, Francis Ellingwood – Toledo, OH: Index Association, 1872 – 1mf – 9 – 0-8370-3915-0 – 1985-1915 – us A.T.L.A. [240]

IS THE BIBLE INSPIRED? / Brookes, James Hall – St. Louis: Gospel Book & Tract Depository, [ca 1883] – 1mf – 9 – 0-8370-2469-2 – 1985-0469 – us A.T.L.A. [220]

IS THE BIBLE TRUE? : SEVEN ADDRESSES / Brookes, James Hall – St Louis: Chas B Cox, [ca 1877] – 1mf – 9 – 0-8370-2470-6 – 1985-0470 – us A.T.L.A. [220]

IS THE FASCIST REBELLION IN SPAIN A POPULAR MOVEMENT? / Spain. Embajada. United States – Washington, DC, n.d. Fiche W1181. (Blodgett Collection of Spanish Civil War Pamphlets) – 9 – us H.U. College Libr [946]

IS THE LORD AMONG US? / Huntington, DeWitt C – 1904 – 9 – us A.T.L.A. [240]

IS THERE A GOD? / Wieman, Henry Nelson & Macintosh, Douglas Clyde & Otto, Max Carl – Introd. by Charles Clayton Morrison. Chicago: Willet, Clark, 1932. 328p – 1 – us U.W. Library [240]

IS THERE A RELATIONSHIP BETWEEN PRENATAL EXERCISE AND POSTPARTUM DEPRESSION / Stephenson, Sheryl L & Bleutler, Sharon A – 1993 – 2mf – 9 – $8.00 – us Microform Publ [150]

IS THERE AN UNDERGROUND OPPOSITION IN THE SOVIET UNION? / Association for a Free Russia – President Count Nicholas Tolstoy, 15p. With Annual Report, 1983, 16p – 9 – 1.00f – at Libertarian Micro [335]

IS THERE ANY CONNECTION BETWEEN THE ESKIMO LANGUAGE AND THE URALIAN / Thalbitzer, W – BN 419 2. 1928 – 8 – ne IDC [490]

IS THIS PAUL AT ATHENS IN THE MIDST OF THE AREOPAGUS? (ACTS XVIII, V22-15 (SIC): NO, IT IS FATHER GIRAUD IN THE PROVINCE OF QUEBEC BEFORE THE CRIMINAL COURT / Giraud, Philippe – Quebec?: s.n., 1900?. 04321. (Pre-1900 Canadiana) – 9 – cn C.I.H.M. [971]

I.S.A. (Instrument Society of America) *see* TRANSACTIONS

ISA (INSTRUMENT SOCIETY OF AMERICA) – Standards. Printed index. Updated every 60 days – 6,9 – us Info Handling [680]

ISA LOMUZI – v1-9. Sep 1931-Mar 1940 (incomplete) – 1r – 1 – ATLA S0704C – us A.T.L.A. [073]

ISAAC ASIMOV'S SCIENCE FICTION MAGAZINE – v. 1- 1977- – 1,5,6,9 – us UMI [830]

ISAAC CASAUBON, 1559-1614 / Pattison, Mark – Oxford: Clarendon Press, 1892 – 2mf – us A.T.L.A. [240]

ISAAC DE PINTO, SA VIE ET SES OEUVRES / Wijler, J S – Apeldoorn, 1923 – 2mf – ne IDC [100]

Isaac Hobhouse and Co *see* HOBHOUSE LETTERS, 1722-55

Isaac, Max *see* FACTS ABOUT BANKRUPTCY YOU OUGHT TO KNOW

ISAAC MCCOY: EARLY INDIAN MISSIONS / Wyeth, Walter N – 1895 – 1 – 8.54 – us Baptist [240]

ISAAC MCCOY PAPERS / McCoy, Isaac – 1808-74. In Kansas State Historical Society. Guide – 1 – us KS Hist [240]

ISAAC REID PAPERS *see* REID, ISAAC, PAPERS, MS 4704

ISAAC WATTS : HIS LIFE AND WRITINGS, HIS HOMES AND FRIENDS / Hood, Edwin Paxton – London: Religious Tract Society, [1875?] – 1mf – us A.T.L.A. [240]

Isaacs, Abram S *see* STORIES FROM THE RABBIS

ISABEL 1, REINA DE ESPANA Y MADRE DE AMERICA. MADRID, 1943 / Gomez de Mercado y Miguel, F – Madrid: Razon y Fe, 1947 – 1 – sp Bibl Santa Ana [946]

ISABEL PERON : INOCENTE O CULPABLE? / Deheza, Jose A – [Buenos Aires?]: Ediciones Cuenca del Plata, 1st ed 1983 – 1 – CSUXAJA7837-B – us Hoover Inst Photo [330]

ISABELLE AND HELEN MCFARLAND DIARIES *see* MCFARLAND, ISABELLE AND HELEN, DIARIES

Isacovich, Marcelo *see* ARGENTINA ECONOMICA Y SOCIAL

Isaev, A A *see*
- ARTELI V ROSSII
- NASTOIASHCHEE I BUDUSHCHEE RUSSKOGO OBSHCHESTVENNOGO KHOZIAISTVA

Isaevich, I D *see* GRODSKIE I ZEMSKIE AKTY-VAZNEISHII ISTOCHNIK PO AGRARNOI ISTORII RECHI POSPOLITOI V XVI-XVIII VV

ISAFOLD – Reykjavik, Iceland. -w. 6 Jan 1894-31 Dec 1914; 21 April 1917-12 Jan 1921. 1917, 1919 imperfect. 11 reels – 1 – uk British Libr Newspaper [072]

ISAGOGE ARTIS MUSICAE AD INCIPIENTIUM CAPTUM MAXIME ACCOMMODATA / Demantius, J C – Editio Quinta. 1611 – 9 – us Sibley [780]

ISAGOGE ARTIS MUSICAE, AD INCIPIENTIUM CAPTUM MAXIME ACCOMMODATA / Demantius, J C – P 233. 1632 – 9 – ne IDC [780]

ISAGOGE HISTORICA APOLOGETICA DE LAS INDIAS OCCIDENTALES Y ESPECIAL DE LA PROVINCIA DE SAN VICENTE DE CHIAPA Y GUATEMALA, DE LA ORDEN DE PREDICADORES. GUATEMALA, 1935 / Bayle, Constantino – Madrid: Razon y Fe, 1936 – 1 – sp Bibl Santa Ana [972]

ISAGOGE IN MUSICEN HENRICI GLAREANI / Glarean, Heinrich – 1516 – 9 – us Sibley [780]

ISAGOGE IN MUSICEN HENRICI GLAREANI HELVETII POE. LAV. E QUIBUSQUARBONIS AUTHORIBUS / Glareanus, H L – P 687. 1516 – 9 – ne IDC [780]

ISAGOGES MUSICAE LIBRI DUO.. / Schneegass, Cyriacus – 1591 – 5,15 – us Sibley [780]

ISAIAH 40-66 : WITH THE SHORTER PROPHECIES ALLIED TO IT / ed by Arnold, Matthew – London: Macmillan, 1875 – 1mf – 9 – 0-8370-2115-4 – 1985-0115 – us A.T.L.A. [220]

ISAIAH: A STUDY OF CHAPTERS I-XII / Mitchell, Hinckley Gilbert – New York: Thomas Y. Crowell, 1897. 1 fiche – 9 – us A.T.L.A. [240]

ISAIAH CHAPTERS XL-LV / Smith, Sydney – 1944 – 9 – $10.00 – us I.R.C. [220]

ISAIAH, HIS LIFE AND TIMES AND THE WRITINGS WHICH BEAR HIS NAME / Driver, Samuel Rolles – New York: A.D.F. Randolph, (1883). 1 fiche – 9 – us A.T.L.A. [220]

ISAIAH ONE AND HIS BOOK ONE / Douglas, George C M – An essay and an exposition. 1895? – 1 – us A.T.L.A. [240]

ISAIAH XL-LXVI – ed. Arnold. The great prophecy of Israel's restoration. London: Macmillan, 1896. 65p – 1 – us U.W. Library [220]

ISAIE 28-33 : ETUDE DE TRADITION TEXTUELLE / Laberge, Leo – (D'apres la Pesitto, le texte de Qumran, la Septante et le texte massoretique) – 1977 – 9 – Can$60.00 – 0-88769-002-5 – cn Nash Info [200]

ISAMAILI/ISMAILI – Bombay: Ismailia Association for India. illus. -w. In Gujarati and English – 1 – us U.W. Library [073]

ISANG BANSA, ISANG WIKA – Manila, Philippines: United Pub. Co., c1976. 307p. ill. map. Tagalog language-readers – 1 – us U.W. Library [490]

ISANG DIPANG LANGIT / Hernandez, Amado V – Quezon City: Tamaraw Pub Co, 1961 – us Res Libr [950]

Isar, Yudhishthir Raj *see* CHALLENGE TO OUR CULTURAL HERITAGE

Isbell, Irving J *see* CANADIAN MINING OPINION

Iscaro, Rubens *see*
- DIALOGOS SINDICALES ENTRE PERONISTAS Y COMUNISTAS
- HISTORIA DEL MOVIMIENTO SINDICAL
- PROBLEMAS DE ORIENTACI ON Y TACTICA DEL MOVIMIENTO SINDICAL

Iselin, Isaak *see* FILOSOFISCHE UND PATRIOTISCHE TRAEUME EINES MENSCHENFREUNDES

Iselin, Jacob Christoph *see* NEU-VERMEHRTES HISTORISCH UND GEOGRAPHISCHES ALLGEMEINES LEXICON (AEL, ABT.1;9)

Iselin, L E *see* EINE BISHER UNBEKANNTE VERSION DES ERSTEN TEILES DER "APOSTELLEHRE" (T.U.U. 1-13/1B)

Isely, Christian H *see* LETTERS

Isenberg, CW *see* DICTIONARY OF THE AMHARIC LANGUAGE

Isenberg, Karl *see* DER EINFLUSS DER PHILOSOPHIE CHARLES BONNETS AUF FRIEDRICH HEINRICH JACOBI

Iserloh, E *see* DER KAMPF UM DIE MESSE IN DEN ERSTEN JAHREN DER AUSEINANDERSETZUNG MIT LUTHER

ISERLOHNER KREISANZEIGER *see* OEFFENTLICHER ANZEIGER FUER DIE GRAFSCHAFT LIMBURG

ISERLOHNER KREISANZEIGER UND ZEITUNG *see* OEFFENTLICHER ANZEIGER FUER DIE GRAFSCHAFT LIMBURG

Isert, P E *see* HERBARIUM

Isert, Paul Erdmann *see*
- REISE NACH GUINEA UND DEN CARIBAISCHEN..
- VOYAGE EN GUINEE ET DANS LES ILES CARAIBES, EN AMERIQUE
- VOYAGES EN GUINEE ET DANS LES ILES CARAIBES EN AMERIQUE.

Isham, William S *see* JOURNALS

Ishaq al-Jundi, Khalil ibn *see* MALIKI LAW

Ishikawa, Matsutaro *see*
- OHRAI-MONO BUNRUI SHUSEI
- OHRAI-MONO BUNRUISHUSEI JOSHIYO OHRAI-HEN

Ishikawa, T *see*
- BERTANAM KAPAS DI DJAWA
- NANDOER KAPAS ING TANAH DJAWA

Ishirkov, A *see* LES BULGARES EN DOBROUDJA; APERCU HISTORIQUE ET ETHNOGRAPHIQUE

ISHM (INTERNATIONAL SOCIETY FOR HYBRID MICROELECTRONICS) – Printed index. Updated every 60 days – 6,9 – us Info Handling [600]

ISHMAEL / Braddon, Mary Elizabeth – British Fiction Archive: Unit 5 – 9 – uk Bell [830]

ISHMAEL AND THE CHURCH / Cheeseman, Lewis – Philadelphia: Parry and McMillan, 1856 – 1mf – us A.T.L.A. [240]

ISHQ-NAME / Firishta, Abdulmacid ibn – [14–?] – us Res Libr [956]

ISIBUTO SAMAVO – Newtondale, South Africa. 1 Jan 1843-31 Jul 1844. 1 reel – 1, 16 diazo available at reduced price – sa SA Libr [072]

Isidore de Seville, Saint *see*
- DE ECCLESIASTICIS OFFICIIS, FRAGMENTOS (SIECLE 9-10)
- OPERA OMNIA...FAUSTINO AREVALO...TOMUS OCTAVUS ET ULTIMUS
- OPERA OMNIA...FAUSTINO AREVALO...TOMUS QUARTUS...
- OPERA OMNIA...RECENSENTE FAUSTINO AREVALO...
- OPERA OMNIA...RECENSENTE FAUSTINO AREVALO, TOMO 6
- OPERA OMNIA...RECENSENTE FAUSTINO AREVALO, TOMUS PRIMUS ET SECUNDUS
- OPERA OMNIA...RECENSENTE FAUSTINO AREVALO...TOMI TERTIUS ET QUARTUS...
- QUAESTIONES IN PENTATEUCHUM (SIECLE 8)

Isidorus Hispalensis *see* DE ECCLESIASTICIS OFFICIIS (CCSL 113)

ISIGIDIMI SAMA-XOSA – Lovedale, South Africa. 1 Aug 1873-1 Dec 1884. 4 reels – 1, 16 diazo available at reduced price – sa SA Libr [072]

ISIK – Giresun: Giresun Matbaasi, 1918-1923 – 9 – $20.00 – us MEDOC [956]

ISIK – Izmir. Imtiyaz Sahibi: Ruscuklu Fahri. Umumi Nesriyat Mueduerue: Ibrahim. No. 30 (13 Mayis 1933) – 9 – $20.00 – us MEDOC [956]

ISIS – v1- 1913- 1; v59- 5,6; v66- 9 – us UMI [900]

ISIS – v1-33. 1913-41.An international review devoted to the history of science and its cultural influences – 1,5,6 – us Princeton Micro [500]

ISIS : WOMEN'S INTERNATIONAL CROSS-CULTURAL EXCHANGE – Geneva. 28 docs. 1984-1991 – 24mf – 9 – ne IDC [320]

ISIS CUMULATIVE BIBLIOGRAPHY 1913-65: A BIBLIOGRAPHY OF THE HISTORY OF SCIENCE FORMED FROM ISIS CRITICAL BIBLIOGRAPHIES 1-90, 1913-65 / Whitrow, Magda – v1-2. 1971. Microfiche ed., 1983 – 17mf – 9 – £105.00 – uk Mansell Publ [500]

ISIS INTERNATIONAL – Rome, Santiago. 83 docs. 1980-1991 – 73mf – 9 – ne IDC [320]

L'ISIS MODERNE – Revue des sciences nouvelles. Dir. G. Morand-Bussiere. no. 1-6. Paris. oct 1896-mars 1897 – 1 – fr A.C.R.P.P. [500]

ISIS Y SERAPIS EN LA ESPANA PAGANA : PREANUNCIOS DE DOCTRINAS Y DE VIRTUDES CRISTIANAS / Tormo, Elias – Madrid, 1944 – sp Bibl Santa Ana [240]

ISITUNYWA SENNYANGA – Mount Coke (King William's Town), South Africa. 1 Aug-31 Dec 1850. 1 reel – 1, 16 diazo available at reduced price – sa SA Libr [072]

ISK – MITTEILUNGSBLATT DES INTERNATIONALEN SOZIALISTISCHEN KAMPFBUNDES – (Cont as: Sozialistische Warte 1933-40) – Berlin, 1926-32 – 3r – 1 – DM225.00 – gw Mikro Press [072]

ISK – MITTEILUNGSBLATT DES INTERNATIONALEN SOZIALISTISCHEN KAMPFBUNDES – (Cont by: Sozialistische Warte, Paris) – Berlin, Stuttgart. 1926-32 – 1 – Dist. gw Mikrofilm – gw Misc Inst [073]

ISK – MITTEILUNGSBLATT DES INTERNATIONALEN SOZIALISTISCHEN KAMPFBUNDES – (Cont by: Sozialistische Warte, Paris, 1933-40) – Berlin, Stuttgart. 1933 – 1 – Dist. gw Mikrofilm – gw Misc Inst [073]

Iskandar, N S *see* TJINTA TANAH AIR

ISKRA : CENTRAL'NYJ ORGAN ROSSIJSKOJ SOCIAL'DEMOKRATICESKOJ RABOCEJ PARTII – Muenchen, London, Geneve, 1900-05 – 1 – us NY Public [335]

ISKRA – Kazanluk, Bulgaria. 1953-Apr 1968; 1976-79 (incomplete) – 5r – 1 – us L of C Photodup [949]

ISKRA – Munich, DE. 15 Jan 1949-Dec 1975 – 5r – 1 – uk British Libr Newspaper [072]

ISKRA – Munich, Germany. semimonthly, -irr. 1975- – 1 – us U.W. Library [949]

ISKRA : ROSSIISKAIA SOTSIAL-DEMOKRATICHESKAIA RABOCHAIA PARTIIA – v1-5. 1900-05 – 1r – 1 – us Ross [947]

ISKRA / Rossiiskoi Sotsialdemokraticheskoi rabochei partii – v. 1-112. 1900-05. B-1485 2 – 8 – ne IDC [320]

ISKUSSTVA – Zurnal illiustririvannyi muzyki, zivopisi, skulptury, arkhitektury i slovesnosti. v. 1-6. Spb. 1860. BR-3215 2 – 8 – ne IDC [700]

ISKUSSTVO – Moscow. 1-3. 1923-1927 – 1 – us NY Public [073]

ISKUSSTVO I KHUDOZHESTVENNAIA PROMYSHLENNOST' – Ezhemesiachnoe ill. izdanie Imp. Obshchestva pooshchreniia. v. 1-38. Peterburge, Spb. 1898-1902. BR-3217 2 – 8 – ne IDC [073]

ISKUSSTVO I PECHATNOE DELO – Zhurnal. v. 1-2. Kiev. 1909-10. BR-3218 2 – 8 – ne IDC [073]

ISKUSSTVO KINO – (1984-95 available 3r per y) – Russia, 1999- – 3r per y standing order – 1 – us Ross [072]

ISKUSSTVO KNIGI DREVNEI RUSI / Svirin, A N – Moscow, 1964. BR-10,492/1 – 9 – ne IDC [947]

ISKUSSTVO V IUZHNOI ROSSII – Zhivopis', grafika, khudozhestvennaia pechat. Kiev. 1913 14. Available: 1913, nr. 4-5-6; 1914, nr. 5-6. BR-3219 2 – 8 – ne IDC [760]

ISKUSSTVO, ZHIVOPIS', GRAFIKA, KHUDOZHESTVENNAIA PECHAT – Kiev. 1911-12. BR-3216 2 – 8 – ne IDC [760]

Isla, Jose Francisco *see*
- CARTAS DE JUAN DE LA ENCINA
- HISTORIA DE FRAY GERUNDIO DE CAMPAZAS. TOMO 1
- HISTORIA DE FRAY GERUNDIO DE CAMPAZAS. TOMO 2
- REFLEXIONES CRISTIANAS
- TRIUNFO DEL AMOR

ISLAH *see* AL-ISLAH

L'ISLAM – Organe hebdomadaire democratique des Musulmans algeriens. Dir. Sadek Denden. IV-VI, no. 100-206. Alger. 1912-14. devenu par fusion: L' Ikdam. Hebdomadaire de defense. v. .voir a ce titre – 1 – fr A.C.R.P.P. [073]

DER ISLAM : ZEITSCHRIFT FUER GESCHICHTE UND KULTUR DES ISLAMISCHEN ORIENTS – Strassburg, 1910-1942. v1-26 – 177mf – 9 – I-491c/2 – ne IDC [260]

ISLAM, A CHALLENGE TO FAITH / Zwemer, Samuel Marinus – New York, 1907 – 7mf – 8 – ne Slangenburg [260]

L'ISLAM ALGERIEN EN L'AN 1900 / Doutte, Edmond – (Filmed with: Traditions historiques et legendaires du Soudan occidental par Maurice Delafosse 1870-1926) – Alger-Mustapha: Giralt, 1900 – 1 – us Res Libr [260]

ISLAM AND CHRISTIAN MUSLIM RELATIONS – 1995, Vol 6 – £83.00 – uk Carfax [260]

ISLAM AND CHRISTIANITY IN INDIA AND THE FAR EAST / Wherry, E M – New York: F.H. Revell, c1907 – 1mf – us A.T.L.A. [240]

ISLAM AND THE ORIENTAL CHURCHES : THEIR HISTORICAL RELATIONS / Shedd, William Ambrose – Philadelphia: Presbyterian Board of Publication and Sabbath-School Work, 1904 – 1mf – us A.T.L.A. [230]

ISLAM AND THE RACE QUESTION / Kamil, Abd-al-Aziz Abd-al-Qadir – 1970 – 65p – 9 – 92-3-100833-1 – fr UNESCO [260]

L'ISLAM AU IVE-XE SIECLE / Mez, Adam – Traduit de l'allemand par Leon Bercher et Gerard Lecomte. 1976 – 9 – fr Orientalistes [260]

L'ISLAM AU SERVICE DU PEUPLE / Toure, Ahmed Sekou – 2nd ed. Conakry: Bureau de presse de la presidence de la republique, 1977 – us Res Libr [260]

ISLAM DALAM TINDJAUAN MA-DI-LOG. (MATERIALISME-DIALEKTIKA-LOGIKA) / Tan Malaka – SE 10,226 1. 1950 – 9 – ne IDC [335]

ISLAM DAN ANDA, PERTJIKAN PERMENUNGAN WAK HADJI / Anwar, Rosihan – SE-4511 1. 1962 – 9 – ne IDC [950]

ISLAM DAN DEMOKRASI / Amrullah, Abdul Malik Karim – SE-11,742 1. 1945? – 9 – ne IDC [956]

ISLAM DAN NEGARA / Jahja, Muchtar – SE-10,878 1. 1946 – 9 – ne IDC [260]

ISLAM DAN SOSIALISME / Tjokroaminoto, Umar Said – SE 4226 1. 1963 – 9 – ne IDC [335]

L'ISLAM DANS L'AFRIQUE OCCIDENTALE / Le Chatelier, Alfred – Paris: G Steinheil, 1899 – 1 – us Res Libr [260]

ISLAM DI SOEMATERA. OLEH HAMKA / Amrullah, Abdul Malik Karim – Medan, Badan Pembangoen Semangat Islam (2605 ?). 37p – 6mf – 9 – ne IDC [260]

L'ISLAM EN GUINEE : FOUTA-DAILLON / Marty, Paul – Paris: E Leroux, 1921 – 1 – us Res Libr [960]

L'ISLAM EN MAURITANIE ET AU SENEGAL – Paris: E Leroux, 1915-16 – 1 – us Res Libr [960]

L'ISLAM ET LA CIVILISATION FRANCAISE / Ouane, Ibrahima Mamadou – Avignon: Presses universelles 1957 – us Res Libr [260]

L'ISLAM ET LA POLITIQUE MUSULMANE FRANCAISE EN AFRIQUE OCCIDENTALE FRANCAISE / Arnaud, Robert – Paris: Comite de l'Afrique Francaise, 1912 – 1 – us Res Libr [960]

L'ISLAM ET LE TERROIR AFRICAINE / Cardaire, Michel – Koulouba, Mali, 1954 – 1 – us Res Libr [260]

L'ISLAM ET LES TRIBUS DANS LA COLONIE DU NIGER / Marty, Paul – [2. ser.] Paris: P Geuthner, 1931 – 1 – us Res Libr [960]

ISLAM, HER MORAL AND SPIRITUAL VALUE A RATIONAL AND PSYCHOLOGICAL STUDY. / Leonard, Arthur Glyn – Forward by Syed Ameer Ali. London: Luzac, 1909 160p – 1 – us U.W. Library [260]

ISLAM MECMUASI – (Mueduer-i Mes'ul: Halim Sabit. Nos. 2-5, 13, 15, 19, 24-36 (13 Subat 1329-10 Eyluel 1331[1913-1915])) – Istanbul: Tanin Matbaasi, Matbaa-i Osmaniye Matbaa-i Hayriye ve Suerekasi, Tecim Matbaasi, Necm-i Istikbal Matbaasi, 1913-1918 – 7mf – 9 – $105.00 – us MEDOC [949]

ISLAM, PHILOSOPHY AND SCIENCE / Hamidullah, Muhammad et al – 1981 – 168p – 9 – 92-3-101951-1 – fr UNESCO [260]

ISLAM THE STRAIGHT PATH / Morgan, Kenneth William – In Indonesian. SE-4547 1. v. 2 only. 1963 – 9 – ne IDC [260]

ISLAM UND CHRISTENTUM IM KAMPF UM DIE EROBERUNG DER ANIMISTISCHEN HEIDENWELT / Simon, G – Berlin, 1914 – 8mf – 8 – ne Slangenburg [240]

ISLAM UND CHRISTENTUM IM MITTELALTER / Fritsch, Erdmann – Breslau, 1930 – 3mf – 8 – ne Slangenburg [260]

ISLAM-FICHE / ed by Graham, William A & Waldman, Marilyn R – (Includes a printed guide and plastic binder) – 207mf – 9 – Gld2,395.00 – ne IDC [260]

ISLAMIC CITIES AND CONSERVATION / Antoniou, Jim – 1981 – 109p – 9 – 92-3-101919-8 – fr UNESCO [900]

ISLAMIC CULTURE – Hyderabad, Deccan, 1927-1965. v1-39 – 366mf – 9 – I-116/2 – ne IDC [260]

ISLAMIC HERITAGE OF BENGAL / ed by Michell, George – 1984 – 9 – 92-3-102174-5 – fr UNESCO [950]

ISLAMISME CONTRE "NATURISME" AU SOUDAN FRANCAIS : ESSAIS DE PSYCHOLOGIE POLITIQUE COLONIALE / Brevie, J – Paris: E Leroux, 1923 – 1 – us Res Libr [260]

L'ISLAMISME ET LE CHRISTIANISME EN AFRIQUE / Bonet-Maury, Gaston – Paris: Hachette, 1906 – 1mf – us A.T.L.A. [210]

ISLAND CREEK BAPTIST CHURCH. SPARTA, GEORGIA : CHURCH RECORDS – 1806-1947 – 1 reel – 1 – $57.61 – us Baptist [240]

ISLAND EXPRESS DE L'ILE – Ile des Soeurs, Verdun, Canada. 14 dec 1977 – 1r – 1 – Can$25.00 – cn Can Microfilming [900]

ISLAND GUARDIAN – Charlottetown, Canada. 1887-94 – 3r – 1 – $204.00 – cn Library Assoc [971]

ISLAND NIGHT'S ENTERTAINMENTS : CONSISTING OF THE BEACH OF FALESA, THE BOTTLE IMP, THE ISLE OF VOICES / Stevenson, Robert Louis – London: Cassell & Company, 1893 – 1 roll – 1 – 1-55879-956-7 – uk Libr Preservation [830]

THE ISLAND OF MADAGASCAR : A SKETCH, DESCRIPTIVE AND HISTORICAL / Phelps, John Wolcott – New York: J B Alden, 1885 – 1 – us Res Libr [960]

ISLAND PACKET – Beaufort. S.C. 1973- – 1 – us UMI [071]

ISLAND WAPPATO – Portland OR. Nov 1936 Jan Apr 1937, Feb Aug 1938, Oct 1941 – 1 – us U.O. Library [071]

ISLAND WAPPATO – Sauvie Island, OR. 1936-41 – 1 – 17.00 – us Oregon Hist [071]

ISLAND WAPPATO – Sauvies Island OR. Nov 1936, Jan Apr 1937, Feb Aug 1938, Oct 1941 – 1 – us U.O. Library [071]

ISLAND WAPPATO – Sayuies Island. Or. 1937-1941 – 1 – us UMI [071]

ISLANDER – Charlottetown, Canada. 1842-71 – 12r – 1 – $780.00 – cn Library Assoc [971]

THE ISLANDER – Anna Maria. Fl. -w. 1958- – 1 – us P.K. Yonge [071]

THE ISLANDER – Awali, Bahrain. Oct 1860-Jan 1969 – 2r – 1 – uk British Libr Newspaper [072]

THE ISLANDER – Toronto.v1-4, 1973-77 – 1 – 225.00 – cn McLaren [971]

ISLANDS' CULTURE AND DEVELOPMENT – (Texts in English and French) – 1992 – 245p – 9 – 92-3-002741-3 – fr UNESCO [307]

THE ISLANDS OF THE PACIFIC : FROM THE OLD TO THE NEW: A COMPENDIOUS SKETCH OF MISSIONS / Alexander, James McKinney – New York: American Tract Society, c1895 – 2mf – 9 – 0-8370-6000-1 – 1986-0000 – us A.T.L.A. [240]

ISLANDSKE FOLKESAGN OG AEVENTYR / Arnason, Jon – 1877 – 1 – us I.U. Libraries [390]

Islankin, FB *see*
- KONTRAKTATSIIA, SBYT I SNABZHENIE V SEL'SKO-KHOZIAISTVENNYKH KREDITNYKH TOVARISHCHESTVAKH
- KREDITNYE I KOMISSIONNO-BANKOVSKIE OPERATSII V SEL'SKOKHOZIAISTVENNYKH KREDITNYKH TOVARISHCHESTVAKH

LAS ISLAS MALVINAS Y EL SECTOR ANTARTICO ARGENTINO / Argentine Republic. Comision Nacional del Antartico – Buones Aires: Ministerio de Relaciones Exteriores y Culto, 1948 – 1 – CSUXADJ8088-B – us Hoover Inst Photo [910]

L'ISLE DE LA RAISON OU LES PETITS HOMMES. COMEDIE EN TROIS ACTES / Marivaux, Pierre C – (Utopias in the Enlightenment series). 1727 – 9 – fr Hachette [410]

L'ISLE DES ESCLAVES. COMEDIE EN UN ACTE, REPRESENTEE POUR LA PREMIERE FOIS PAR LES COMEDIENS ITALIENS DU ROI, LE LUNDI 5 MARS 1725 / Marivaux, Pierre C – (Utopias in the Enlightenment series). 1725 – 9 – fr Hachette [820]

L'Isle, Guillaume de *see* ATLAS GEOGRAPHIQUE

ISLE OF ISLAY 1851 CENSUS INDEX : ARGYLL AND WEST SCOTLAND CENSUS INDEX, PART 13 / Macinnes, John & Gibson, Peter – 1997 – 2mf – 9 – ca A$19.95 – at Seanachas [920]

ISLE OF MAN, 1824 : BRITISH ISLES CENSUS DIRECTORIES PROJECT, ENGLAND – (In prep) – at Vine [941]

ISLE OF MAN, 1837 : BRITISH ISLES CENSUS DIRECTORIES PROJECT, ENGLAND. VOL 197 – 1mf – 9 – A$9.00 – at Vine [941]

ISLE OF MAN, 1936 : BRITISH ISLES CENSUS DIRECTORIES PROJECT, ENGLAND – at Vine [941]

ISLE OF MAN COURIER *see* RAMSEY COURIER AND NORTHERN ADVERTISER

ISLE OF MAN EXAMINER ETC – May 25 1889-93; 1946-Dec 20 1974; 1975-81; 1986; Jan 7-28 1987; Jul 28 1987-90; Jul 1991-96 – 94 1/2r – 9 – uk British Libr Newspaper [072]

ISLE OF SKYE (NORTH) 1851 CENSUS INDEX : ARGYLL AND WEST SCOTLAND CENSUS INDEX, PART 3 / Gibson, Peter & Macinnes, John – 1994 – 2mf – 9 – A$19.95 – 0-646-17517-3 – at Seanachas [920]

ISLE OF SKYE (SOUTH) AND THE SMALL ISLES 1851 CENSUS INDEX : ARGYLL AND WEST SCOTLAND CENSUS INDEX, PART 4 / Gibson, Peter & Macinnes, John – 1994 – 2mf – 9 – A$19.95 – 0-646-17516-5 – at Seanachas [920]

ISLE OF WIGHT COUNT PRESS ETC – Nov 29 1884-Dec 24 1885; 1886-88; Jan 5-Dec 28 1889; 1890-96; Jan 2-Dec 24 1897; 1898-1900; Jan 5-Dec 28 1901; 1902; Jan 3-Dec 26 1903; 1904-96 – 214 1/2r – 9 – uk British Libr Newspaper [072]

ISLE OF WIGHT (HANTS), 1844 : BRITISH ISLES CENSUS DIRECTORIES PROJECT, ENGLAND – (In prep) – at Vine [941]

ISLE OF WIGHT (HANTS), 1852 : BRITISH ISLES CENSUS DIRECTORIES PROJECT, ENGLAND – at Vine [941]

ISLE OF WIGHT (HANTS), 1859 : BRITISH ISLES CENSUS DIRECTORIES PROJECT, ENGLAND. VOL 22 – 1mf – 9 – A$9.00 – at Vine [941]

ISLE OF WIGHT (HANTS), 1867 : BRITISH ISLES CENSUS DIRECTORIES PROJECT, ENGLAND. VOL 101 – 2mf – 9 – A$15.00 – at Vine [941]

ISLE OF WIGHT (HANTS), 1875 : BRITISH ISLES CENSUS DIRECTORIES PROJECT, ENGLAND. VOL 93 – 2mf – 9 – A$15.00 – at Vine [941]

LES ISLES SAMOA ET L'ARRANGEMENT ANGLO-ALLEMAND / Voission, Louis P – Paris: Plon-Nourrit, 1900 – 1mf – 9 – $1.50 – LLMC 82-100C Title 26 – us L.L.M.C. [327]

ISLETON JOURNAL – Rio Vista, CA. 1936-37; 1960-62 – 2r – 1 – $100.00 – B02704 – us Library Micro [071]

ISLINGTON AND HOLLOWAY PRESS *see* HOLLOWAY PRESS

ISLINGTON GAZETTE – London, 1856- – 265+ r – 1 – uk British Libr Newspaper [072]

ISLINGTON NEWS – London, UK. 1892 – 1r – 1 – uk British Libr Newspaper [072]

Ismail, A Hamid *see* FAR EASTERN ECONOMIC REVIEW INDEX ON MICROFICHE

Isma'il, Hakki *see* DIVAN

Ismail Ja'kub, T *see* TEUNGKU TJHI'DI TIRO

ISMAILIA; A NARRATIVE OF THE EXPEDITION TO CENTRAL AFRICA FOR THE SUPPRESSION OF THE SLAVE TRADE, ORGANIZED BY ISMAIL, KHEDIVE OF EGYPT / Baker, Samuel White – 2nd ed. London: Macmillan, 1879. 20+524p. Illus., ports. Includes appendix and index – 1 – us U.W. Library [960]

Ismet *see* DIVAN

Isnard, Achille N *see* OBSERVATIONS SUR LE PRINCIPE QUI A PRODUIT LES REVOLUTIONS DE FRANCE, DE GENEVE ET D'AMERIQUE, DANS LE DIX-HUITIEME SIECLE

ISO (INTERNATIONAL ORGANIZATION FOR STANDARDIZATION) – English language collection. Printed index. Updated every 60 days – 6,9 – us Info Handling [380]

ISO WORLD – v5-. 1982- – 1,5,6,9 – us UMI [330]

Isogawa, Hiroaki *see* THE ECONOMIC EFFECTS OF GOVERNMENT ASSISTANCE IN COMMERCIAL RESORT DEVELOPMENT

Isoiamo, A *see* CURRICULUM DEVELOPMENT IN PRIMARY EDUCATION, PAPUA NEW GUINEA SITUATION

ISOKAN – (Backfiles and standing orders available) – Nigeria, 1990- – 5 – inquire – us Ross [960]

ISOKINETIC EVALUATION OF PEAK TORQUE VALUES FOLLOWING CLOSED AND OPEN KINETIC CHAIN EXERCISE TRAINING PROGRAMS / Reed, Cathy A – Springfield College, 1995 – 2mf – 9 – $8.00 – PE3618 – us Microform Publ [611]

ISOKINETIC EVALUATION OF THE POSTERIOR ROTATOR CUFF MUSCULATURE FOLLOWING A STRENGTHENING PROGRAM UTILIZING RUBBER TUBING / O'Brian, Jeanne M & Redmond, Charles J – 1992 – 2mf – $8.00 – us Microform Publ [612]

ISOKO CLANS OF THE NIGER DELTA / Welsh, James William – 1937 – us Res Libr [307]

THE ISOKO MSS : A LUNGU VIEW OF THEIR OWN HISTORY / ed by Watson, William – [Sl: s.n., 195-?] – us Res Libr [960]

ISOKO Y'AMAJYAMBERE / Kagame, P Alegisi – [Kabgayi, Rwanda?]: Ibitabo By'injijura Muco (Editions morales), 1949-1951 – 1 – us Res Libr [960]

ISOLATION AND PURIFICATION / ed by Lochmiller, Charles – 1,5,9 – us Gordon [660]

ISOLDE UND TRISTAN : DIE GESCHICHTE EINER JUNGEN LIEBE / Jansen-Runge, Edith – Bodenhausen: Fackeltraeger-Verlag, 1943 – 1r – 1 – us U.W. Library [390]

ISOLDE WEISSHAND : EIN ROMAN AUS ALTER ZEIT / Lucka, Emil – Berlin: S Fischer, 1909 – 1r – 1 – us U.W. Library [830]

ISOLIERUNG UND SEQUENZIERUNG EINER MITOCHONDRIALEN FORM DER KATALYTISCHEN UNTEREINHEIT DER CYCLO-ADENOSIN-3',5'-MONOPHOSPHAT-ABHAENGIGEN PROTEINKINASE AUS RINDERLEBER / Schwertner, Heiko – 1993 – 2mf – 9 – DM98.00 – 3-89349-732-3 – gw Hänsel [540]

Isopescul, Octavian *see* DER PROPHET MALACHIAS

Isore, Andre *see* LA GUERRE ET LA CONDITION PRIVEE DE LA FEMME

ISOTOPENPRAXIS : ISOTOPES IN ENVIRONMENTAL AND HEALTH STUDIES / ed by Krumbiegel, Peter – 9,5,1 – us Gordon [333]

ISPANSKIIA NARODNYIA PESNI. LIUBOV I NENAVIST / Bal'mont, K D – Moscow, 1911. BR-518 2 – 8 – ne IDC [440]

ISPOLNENIE ZHELANII / Kaverin, V – Leningrad, 1937.430p – 1 – us U.W. Library [460]

ISPOLZOVANIE IZBYTOCHNOSTI V INFORMATSIONNYKH SISTEMAKH : TRUDY VTOROGO SIMPOZIUMA, LENINGRAD, 6-10 IIUNIA 1966 G / ed by Zheleznova, N A – Leningrad: Izd-vo "Nauka," Leningradskoe otd-nie, 1970 – us Res Libr [947]

ISPOVIED KOMISSARA : PODROBNOE OPISANIE KOMMUNISTICHESKAGO STROIA V ROSSII / Beliaev, V – New York: Izd. Amerikansko-russkago pechatnago i izdatelskago kooperativa, 1921 – 1 – CSUX88-B7702 – us Hoover Inst Photo [947]

ISPRITIZMA – (Mueduer: Bahaeddin. No. 1 (1 Kanunisani 1325[1909])) – Istanbul: Tanin Matbaasi, 1909 – 1mf – 9 – $12.00 – us MEDOC [949]

ISR : INTERDISCIPLINARY SCIENCE REVIEWS – (1982-. 1,5,6,9) – v1-. 1976- – 1 – us UMI [500]

ISR – No. 7-34, 37-48, 50, 53-85. Paris. juin 1923-oct 1926 – 1 – fr A.C.R.P.P. [073]

ISRAEEL EN DE VOLKEN / Costa, I da – Ed. 2. Haarlem. 1876. BJ-262-16 1 – 9 – ne IDC [956]

ISRAEL : NATIONAL SECURITY FILES, 1963-69 / Johnson, Lyndon B – (With printed guide) – 1982 – 1 – $320.00 – 0-89093-388-X – us UPA [956]

Israel *see*
- THE ISRAEL ECONOMY, 1950-1970, 1970-1980
- KITAB AL-QAWANIN
- MAJMU'AT AL-ANZIMAH
- MAJMU'AT AL-NASHARAT
- MASHRU'AT AL-QAWANIN
- QAWANIN DAWLAT ISRA'IL

ISRAEL AMONG THE NATIONS : A STUDY OF THE JEWS AND ANTISEMITISM / Leroy-Beaulieu, Anatole – London: W. Heinemann; New York: G.P. Putnam, 1895 – 1mf – us A.T.L.A. [270]

ISRAEL AND HUMAN RIGHTS / Pevsner, Isaiah – Tel-Aviv: Israel Association for Human Rights, 1969. 24p. LL-12042 – 1 – us L of C Photodup [340]

ISRAEL AND PALESTINE – 1971-81 1; 1975-81 5,6,9 – us UMI [320]

ISRAEL BALANCE OF PAYMENTS 1966-1976 / Israel. Prime Minister's Office – Jerusalem, 1977. 25, 35, 22 p. (Special Series no. 549). Text also in Hebrew – 9 – 2.00 – is I.T.T.I. [380]

Israel. Bank of Israel. Research Department *see*
- ANNUAL REPORT OF THE BANK OF ISRAEL
- ECONOMIC REVIEW

Israel. Central Bureau of Statistics *see* SHENATON STATISTI LE-ISRAEL

ISRAEL CHEMICAL INDUSTRY: BACKGROUND AND DEVELOPMENT / Israel. Ministry of Commerce, Industry and Tourism. Chemical Division – Jerusalem. Apr 1977. 67 p. Diagr – 9 – 2.00 – is I.T.T.I. [324]

ISRAEL COUNTRY PROGRAMME PROPOSAL FOR UNITED NATIONS DEVELOPMENT PROGRAMME ASSISTANCE 1972-1976 / Israel. Prime Minister's Office. Technical Assistance Department – Oct 1972. 62p – 9 – $2.00 – is I.T.T.I. [956]

ISRAEL ECONOMIC DEVELOPMENT, PAST PROGRESS AND PLAN FOR THE FUTURE FINAL DRAFT / Israel. Economic Planning Authority – Jerusalem. 1968. BD-594 1 – 9 – ne IDC [338]

Israel. Economic Planning Authority *see*
- DEVELOPMENT PLAN FOR THE NATIONAL ECONOMY 1971-1975
- ISRAEL ECONOMIC DEVELOPMENT, PAST PROGRESS AND PLAN FOR THE FUTURE FINAL DRAFT
- NATIONAL ECONOMIC DEVELOPMENT PLAN 1971-1975
- NATIONAL ECONOMIC PLAN 1974-1983
- PROPOSED DIRECTIVES FOR PREPARING A FIVE-YEAR DEVELOPMENT PLAN FOR THE NATIONAL ECONOMY, 1965-70
- TARGETS AND OUTLINE OF THE 4-YEAR DEVELOPMENT PLAN, 1963-67

ISRAEL ECONOMIST – Jerusalem, IS. 1972-1976 – 4r – $200.00 – R63572 – us Library Micro [330]

THE ISRAEL ECONOMY, 1950-1970, 1970-1980 / Israel – Ministry of Finance. The Economic Planning Authority – 9 – ne IDC [339]

ISRAEL EXPLORATION JOURNAL (IEJ) – (1952-1956. $4.00y) – 1950-51 – 9 – $12.00 – us I.R.C. [930]

ISRAEL FOREIGN TRADE: GENERAL SUMMARY / Israel. Prime Minister's Office – Jerusalem, 1975. 35, 45, 31 p. (Special Series no. 498). Text also in Hebrew – 9 – 3.00 – is I.T.T.I. [380]

ISRAEL GOVERNMENT PUBLICATIONS. RESHIMAT PIRSUME HA-MEMSHALA – (In English and Hebrew; Ceased after 1975) – Jerusalem, 1972 Index 1948-1975 – 73mf – 9 – J-81-44/1 – ne IDC [324]

ISRAEL IN THE MEDITERRANEAN ECOSYSTEM / Israel. Ministry of the Interior – Israel national report to the Conference of the Coastal States of the Mediterranean Region for the Protection of the Mediterranean Sea. Monaco. 9-14 Jan 1978. By David Greenberg and Richard A. Hellman. Jerusalem, 1978. 70 p – 9 – 2.00 – is I.T.T.I. [574]

Israel. Jerusalem Municipality *see* DAVID BEN-GURION: 1886-1973

Israel, John *see* THE CHINESE STUDENT MOVEMENT 1927-1937

ISRAEL JOURNAL OF CHEMISTRY – v. 1-10. 1963-1972 – 1,5,6 – us Princeton Micro [540]

ISRAEL JOURNAL OF MATHEMATICS – (v1-6. Dfl90.00v; v7-45. Dfl140.00v) – Jerusalem. v1-45. 1963-83 – 5,9 – Dfl6,000.00 – ne Swets [510]

ISRAEL JOURNAL OF PSYCHIATRY AND RELATED SCIENCES – v.18-. 1981- – 1,5,6,9 – us UMI [610]

ISRAEL LAW REVIEW – (v1-19 1966-84 on reel $192.50. v20-28 1985-94 on mf $233.00) – v1-28. 1966-94 – 5,6,9 – $426.00 set – us Hein [340]

Israel. Laws, Statutes, etc *see* INSURANCE SUPERVISION IN ISRAEL

ISRAEL MEDICAL BIBLIOGRAPHY : 1948-1971 – Court of Israel. Jerusalem, 1964-1977 – 55mf – ne IDC [610]

ISRAEL MEDICAL BIBLIOGRAPHY: 1948-1959 / Israel. Ministry of Health; ed by Nevenberger, Nadia – 1960-61, 1962-63, 1964-65, 1966-67, 1968-69, 1970-71. Jerusalem. Summary also in Hebrew – 9 – 52.00 – is I.T.T.I. [610]

ISRAEL MEDICAL BIBLIOGRAPHY. 1948-1971 – Jerusalem, 1964-1977 – 55mf – 9 – J-81-6/1 – ne IDC [610]

Israel. Ministry for Foreign Affairs. Cultural Relations Department *see* A REVIEW OF THE ARTS AND SCIENCES IN ISRAEL

Israel. Ministry of Agriculture *see*
- ECOLOGICAL RESEARCH ON DEVELOPMENT OF ARID ZONES (MEDITERRANEAN DESERTS) WITH WINTER PRECIPITATION
- THE FLORA OF WALLS IN ISRAEL
- FURTHER OBSERVATIONS ON THE EFFECT OF SEED ORIGIN ON COPPICE REGENERATION IN EUCALYPTUS CAMALDULENSIS DEHN
- GO, RENEW THE FACE OF THE LAND.'
- IDENTIFICATION OF PESTS AND DISEASES IN FIELD AND VEGETABLE CROPS
- NEWSLETTER
- AN OUTLINE OF THE FIVE YEAR PLAN FOR ISRAELS AGRICULTURE, 1966/7-1970/1
- PUBLICATIONS
- A QUANTITATIVE APPROACH TO PLANNING AGRICULTURAL RESEARCH: THE CASE OF CITRUS
- SCIENTIFIC ACTIVITIES
- SMALL LIFT-IRRIGATION PROJECTS FOR UPLAND CROPS IN MONSOON REGIONS

Israel. Ministry of Agriculture. Center for Cooperation with Developing Countries *see* COMPETITION PROGRAMMES DESIGNED TO PROMOTE GRAIN PRODUCTION

Israel. Ministry of Agriculture Fisheries Division *see* BAMIDGEH

Israel. Ministry of Agriculture. Institute for Technology and Storage of Agricultural Products *see* SCIENTIFIC ACTIVITIES

Israel. Ministry of Agriculture. Institute of Plant Protection *see* SCIENTIFIC ACTIVITIES

Israel. Ministry of Agriculture. Institute of Soils and Water *see* SCIENTIFIC ACTIVITIES

Israel. Ministry of Agriculture. Water Commissioner *see* ANNUAL OPERATION OF A COASTAL GROUNDWATER BASIN AT A PRESCRIBED RELIABILITY LEVEL

Israel. Ministry of Commerce, Industry and Tourism *see*
- PATTERNS OF SOME GEOLOGICAL CHARACTERISTICS FROM OIL FIELDS IN THE GULF OF SUEZ
- PROSPECTS OF COAL AND LIGNITE IN NORTHERN NEGEV

Israel. Ministry of Commerce, Industry and Tourism. Chemical Division *see* ISRAEL CHEMICAL INDUSTRY: BACKGROUND AND DEVELOPMENT

Israel. Ministry of Commerce, Industry and Tourism. Geological Survey *see* ABSTRACTS OF PAPERS PRESENTED AT THE 1974-76 SEMINAR OF THE GEOLOGICAL SURVEY OF ISRAEL

Israel. Ministry of Education and Culture *see*
- ATIQOT
- CURRICULUM THEORY AND CONSTRUCTION
- PHYSICAL EDUCATION AND SPORT IN THE JEWISH HISTORY AND CULTURE
- THE PHYSICAL EDUCATOR AND THE COACH: SIMILARITIES AND DISSIMILARITIES
- PHYSICAL EXERCISE AND ACTIVITY FOR THE AGING
- PLAY IN PHYSICAL EDUCATION AND SPORT

Israel. Ministry of Education and Culture. Antiquities Division *see* ATIKOTH

Israel. Ministry of Education and Culture. Sports Authority *see* 1974 PROCEEDINGS OF THE SOCIETY ON THE HISTORY OF PHYSICAL EDUCATION AND SPORT IN ASIA AND PACIFIC AREA

Israel. Ministry of Finance *see* NATIONAL ECONOMIC PLAN, 1974-1978

Israel. Ministry of Foreign Affairs. Cultural Relations Department *see* ARIEL

Israel. Ministry of Foreign Affairs. Information Department *see* KUNEITRA

Israel. Ministry of Foreign Affairs. International Cooperation Division *see* UPPER SHIRE VALLEY DEPARTMENT PROJECT (KASUPE MWANZA)

Israel. Ministry of Health *see* ISRAEL MEDICAL BIBLIOGRAPHY: 1948-1959

Israel. Ministry of Health. Chronic Diseases and Rehabilitation. Israel Cancer Registry *see* MANUAL

Israel. Ministry of Housing *see* POPULATION AND BUILDING IN ISRAEL 1948-1973

Israel. Ministry of Immigrant Absorption *see*
- GENERAL CONDITIONS OF EMPLOYMENT IN ISRAEL FOR PROFESSIONALS
- IMMIGRATION AND ABSORPTION 1970-1975

Israel. Ministry of Justice *see*
- LAWS OF THE STATE OF ISRAEL
- QOVEZ HA-TAGGNOT
- RESHUMOT
- RESHUMOT: HUGGE TAGZIV
- SEFER HA-HUGGIM SHEL MEMSHELET HA-MANDAT
- YOMAN HA-PATENTIM

Israel. Ministry of Justice. Supreme Court *see* TAQZIR PISQE DIN SHEL BET HA-MISHPAT HA-ELYON

Israel. Ministry of Labour. Productivity Institute *see* ANNUAL REPORT OF THE MINISTRY OF LABOUR, ISRAEL

Israel. Ministry of Police *see* ANNUAL REPORT

Israel. Ministry of Religious Affairs. Christian Affairs Department *see*
- CHRISTIAN NEWS FROM ISRAEL

Israel. Ministry of Social Welfare *see* SAAD

Israel. Ministry of the Interior *see*
- ENVIRONMENTAL EDUCATION IN ISRAEL: ISRAEL NATIONAL REPORT TO THE UNITED NATIONS CONFERENCE ON ENVIRONMENTAL EDUCATION
- ISRAEL IN THE MEDITERRANEAN ECOSYSTEM
- THE LEGAL FRAMEWORK FOR THE PREVENTATION AND CONTROL OF WATER POLLUTION IN ISRAEL
- SELECTED PAPERS ON THE ENVIRONMENT IN ISRAEL

Israel. Ministry of the Interior. Environmental Protection Service *see* SECOND ANNUAL ACTIVITY REPORT

Israel. Ministry of Transport Meteorological Service *see* AIR POLLUTION METEOROLOGY IN ISRAEL

Israel. National Insurance Institute *see*
- REDISTRIBUTION THROUGH NATIONAL INSURANCE IN ISRAEL BY INCOME AND DEMOGRAPHIC GROUPS
- STUDY OF COMPENSATION AND REHABILITATION PROCEDURES AND THEIR IMPACT ON REHABILITATION OF ROAD ACCIDENT VICTIMS IN ISRAEL
- TENTH INTERNATIONAL CONGRESS OF GERONTOLOGY

Israel. Prime Minister's Office *see*
- ADVANCES IN ISRAEL RESEARCH ON WATER DESALINATION
- ALTERNATIVE ENERGY SOURCES FOR THE ISRAEL ECONOMY 1973-2000
- COMPARISON AND FIT OF THE TWO AND SIX BAND K.P. MODELS FOR THE BAND EDGE STRUCTURE OF PB, SN, TE 1-X X
- CYANIDES: DECOMPOSITION AND DETERMINATION
- DEMOGRAPHIC CHARACTERISTICS OF THE POPULATION
- DRUGS, BRAIN AND BEHAVIOR
- FOUR YEAR DEVELOPMENT PLAN OF ISRAEL, 1950-53 SUMMARY
- IMMIGRATION TO ISRAEL 1948-1972
- INPUTS IN RESEARCH AND DEVELOPMENT IN ACADEMIC INSTITUTIONS 1970/71
- ISRAEL BALANCE OF PAYMENTS 1966-1976
- ISRAEL FOREIGN TRADE: GENERAL SUMMARY
- NATIONAL SUMMARY ISRAEL
- NUCLEAR DATA AND LOW ENERGY: NUCLEAR RESEARCH IN ISRAEL
- PROSPECTS FOR BIOCHEMICAL ENGINEERING AND TECHNOLOGY IN ISRAEL
- ROAD ACCIDENTS WITH CASUALTIES: 1974
- SCIENTIFIC RESEARCH IN ISRAEL
- SOCIETY IN ISRAEL: SELECTED STATISTICS

Israel. Prime Minister's Office. Atomic Energy Commission. Research Laboratories *see*
- ANNUAL REPORT

Israel. Prime Minister's Office. Bureau of the Advisor on Arab Affairs *see* MINORITY GROUPS IN ISRAEL, WITHIN THE GREEN LINE

Israel. Prime Minister's Office. Center for Demographical Problems *see* THE POPULATION OF ISRAEL

Israel. Prime Minister's Office. Central Bureau of Statistics *see*
- DIAGNOSTIC STATISTICS OF HOSPITALIZED PATIENTS 1971
- FOREIGN TRADE STATISTICS
- STATISTICAL ABSTRACT OF ISRAEL

Israel. Prime Minister's Office. Committee for Air Pollution Research in Israel *see* REPORT

Israel. Prime Minister's Office. Industry Science University in Israel *see* OPPORTUNITIES AND PROBLEMS OF A YOUNG COUNTRY: AN EXPLANATORY STUDY

Israel. Prime Minister's Office. Information Services Administration. Government Press Office *see*
- EDITORIALS IN THE HEBREW PRESS

Israel. Prime Minister's Office. International Council of the Aeronautical Sciences (ICAS) *see* PROCEEDINGS OF THE NINTH CONGRESS

Israel. Prime Minister's Office. Israel National Committee on Biosphere and Environment Water Quality in Israel. Committee on Water Quality *see* REPORT

Israel. Prime Minister's Office. Ministry of Agriculture *see* PROCEEDINGS OF THE ISRAEL-FRANCE SYMPOSIUM ON BEHAVIOR OF PESTICIDES IN SOIL

Israel. Prime Minister's Office. Ministry of Education and Culture *see* SCHOOLS AND KINDERGARTENS 1973/1974

Israel. Prime Minister's Office. Ministry of Finance. Superintendent of Insurance *see* INSURANCE IN ISRAEL 1974

Israel. Prime Minister's Office. Ministry of Immigrant Absorption and the Jewish Agency, Aliya and Absorption Dept *see* IMMIGRATION TO ISRAEL 1976

Israel. Prime Minister's Office. Ministry of the Interior. Local Authorities in Israel 1973 74 *see* PHYSICAL DATA

Israel. Prime Minister's Office. Ministry of the Interior. Local authorities in Israel 1973 74 *see* FINANCIAL DATA

Israel. Prime Minister's Office. National Council for Research and. Development. Desalination and Technical Forecasting *see* PROCEEDINGS OF THE TENTH NATIONAL SYMPOSIUM ON DESALINATION

Israel Prime Minister's Office. Negev Research Institute *see* REPORT FOR YEAR 1970/71

Israel. Prime Minister's Office. Technical Assistance Department *see* ISRAEL COUNTRY PROGRAMME PROPOSAL FOR UNITED NATIONS DEVELOPMENT PROGRAMME ASSISTANCE 1972-1976

ISRAEL SPEAKS – (Library has: Vol. 3, no.1-v.5, no. 14; v.7, no. 21-22, 24; v. 8, no. 1-6 (March 1949-Aug. 1951); Nov., Dec. 25, 1953; Jan.-March 1954) – New York, N.Y.: Israel Speaks, Inc., [1949]- – 1 – CSUX86-S317 – us Hoover Inst Photo [978]

ISRAEL SPEAKS – (V3, No1, (4 Feb. 1949)-v11, No5, (29 Mar. 1957); Continues: Haganah Speaks) – New York, N.Y. – us A.J.P.C. [270]

Israel State Archives *see*
- GOVERNMENT PUBLICATIONS LISTS
- INVENTORY TO THE FILES OF HERBERT LOUIS, FIRST VISCOUNT SAMUEL (FIRST HIGH COMMISSIONER FOR PALESTINE), 1914-1962
- INVENTORY TO THE FILES OF THE GERMAN CONSULATE IN PALESTINE, 1842-1939
- INVENTORY TO THE RECORDS OF THE CHIEF SECRETARY'S OFFICE, 1918-1925
- JERUSALEM. INVENTORY TO THE FILES OF HERBERT LOUIS, FIRST VISCOUNT SAMUEL (FIRST HIGH COMMISSIONER FOR PALESTINE), 1914-1962
- JERUSALEM. INVENTORY TO THE RECORDS OF THE CHIEF SECRETARY'S OFFICE, 1918-1925

Israel. State Corporations. ZIM Shipping Lines *see* REPORTS AND ACCOUNTS

Israel. State Records *see*
- CONVENTIONS AND AGREEMENTS: TREATY SERIES
- PATENTS AND DESIGNS JOURNAL
- TRADE MARKS JOURNAL

Israel. Szold Institute *see*
- AN ANNOTATED BIBLIOGRAPHY ON THE FAMILY AND RELATED TOPICS, PART 2
- AN ANNOTATED BIBLIOGRAPHY ON THE FAMILY AND RELATED TOPICS, PART 4
- ENHANCING THE EFFECTIVENESS OF KIBBUTZ ULPANIM

ISRAEL TODAY AND THE JEWISH TIMES *see* JEWISH TIMES

ISRAEL UND JUDA BEI AMOS UND HOSEA : NEBST EINEM EXKURS UEBER HOS. 1-3 / Seesemann, Otto – (Includes bibliographical references) – Leipzig:Dieterich, 1898 – 1mf – 9 – 0-8370-5216-5 – 1985-3216 – us A.T.L.A. [220]

ISRAEL UND JUDA BEI AMOS UND HOSEA NEBST EINEM EXKURS UEBER HOS. 1-3 / Seesemann, Otto – Leipzig, 1898 – 1mf – 9 – DM48.00 – 3-89349-347-6 – gw Hänsel [220]

ISRAEL VENGE. OU EXPOSITION NATURELLE DES PROPHETIES HEBRAIQUE QUE LES CHRETIENS APPLIQUENT A JESUS, LEUR PRETENDU MISSIE / Orobio, Isaac – (D'Holbach series). 1770 – 9 – fr Hachette [270]

ISRAEL WILLIAMS PAPERS, 1730-1785 / Williams, Israel – Massachusetts Historical Society – 1r – 1 – $85.00 – us UMI [920]

Israel. Yad Vashem. Remembrance Authority *see*
- GUIDE TO UNPUBLISHED MATERIALS OF THE HOLOCAUST PERIOD
- HOLOCAUST

Israel. Zahal. Israel Defence Forces *see*
- MAARAHOT
- SKEERA HODSHIT

DER ISRAELI – Ein Centralorgan fuer das orthodoxe Judenthum. 79 v. Mainz, Frankfurt a.M. 1860-1938; v. 30-32 published together with "vJeschurun". 1889-91. Lacking: 1860, v. 1 (3); 1861, v. 2 (4); 1861, v. 2 (13-17); 1861, v. 2 (20); 1861, v. 2 (26); 1861, v. 2 (39-50); 1862, v. 3 (2-9), 1862 v. 3 (12-21), 1862 v.3 (23); 1862, v. 3 (25-30); 1862, v. 3 (32); 1862, v. 3 (36-38); 1862, v. 3 (38-40); 1. BJ-23-22a 1 – 9 – ne IDC [270]

ISRAELI COUNCIL FOR ISRAELI-PALESTINIAN PEACE – Tel-Aviv. 45 docs. 1983-1991 – 9mf – 9 – ne IDC [320]

Israeli, Samuel Michael *see* THE NATURE OF THE LIABILITY OF SHAREHOLDERS OF A CORPORATION, UNDER STATUTE IMPOSING A LIABILITY ADDITIONAL TO THAT FOR STOCK SUBSCRIBED.

ISRAELIETISCH NIEUWS- EN ADVERTENTIEBLAD VOOR NEDERLAND – Amsterdam, 1901-1904 – 19mf – 9 – J-261-127/1 – ne IDC [073]

ISRAELIETISCH WEEKBLAD – (Cont. as: Weekblad voor Israelieten. Amsterdam, 1855(Aug. 17)-1884. v1-29) – Amsterdam, 1851-1855(July 27) – 218mf – 9 – J-261-120/1 – ne IDC [073]

ISRAELIETISCHE LETTERBODE – Amsterdam, 1875-1888. v1-12 – 33mf – 9 – J-261-46/1 – ne IDC [073]

ISRAELIETISCHE NIEUWSBODE – Amsterdam, 1875-1893. v1-18 – 109mf – 9 – J-261-128/1 – ne IDC [073]

ISRAELIT : EIN CENTRALORGAN FUER DAS ORTHODOXE JUDENTHUM – (1889-1891, v30-32 published together with Jeschurun; Some vols missing) – Mainz, Frankfurt a.M., 1860-1938. 79v – 2,211mf – 9 – J-23-22a/1 – ne IDC [270]

ISRAELIT – Mainz, Germany. v1-11, 14-57, 61-79. 1860-1938 – 31r – 1 – us Ross [072]

ISRAELIT – Mainz. v. 1-11, 14-57, 61-79. May 15 1860-Nov 3 1938. Incomplete – 1 – us NY Public [072]

ISRAELIT DES NEUNZEHNTEN JAHRHUNDERTS – v. 1-9. Meiningen. Hersfeld. Frankfurt a.M. 1839-1840-48. Lacking: 1839-41, v.1-2; 1842, v.3 (49); 1846, v.7 (31 p.133-36); 1847; 1848. – 44mf – 9 – ne IDC [073]

ISRAELITE – Cincinnati, Ohio. 1854-1927; 1958-68 – 1 – us A.J.P.C. [071]

ISRAELITE – Las Vegas. Nev. 1965- – 1 – us UMI [071]

L'ISRAELITE ALGERIEN – Organe des interets du judaisme en general et du judaisme d'Algerie en particulier. no. 1-22. Oran. 1900 – 1 – fr A.C.R.P.P. [270]

ISRAELITE OSTRACA FROM SAMARIA / Reisner, George A – 1924 – 9 – $10.00 – us I.R.C. [930]

THE ISRAELITE PRESS – (In Yiddish. v30 n16 23 feb 1940-23 jan 1983f 48r Can$65.00) – Winnipeg. v25 n9. 29 jan 1935-25 feb 1938 – 1r – 1 – Can$65.00 – cn Can Microfilming [072]

THE ISRAELITE PRESS – Winnipeg, CN. v25 no 9. 1935-1938 – 1r – 1 – Can$65.00 – cn Can Microfilming [072]

THE ISRAELITE PRESS – Winnipeg, CN. v30 no 16. 1940-1983f – 48r – 1 – Can$65.00r – cn Can Microfilming [072]

DIE ISRAELITEN IN DER WUESTE / Bach, C P E – Ein Oratorium in Musikgesetzt. 1775 – 5,9 – us Sibley [780]

ISRAELITISCHE ANNALEN – Ein Centralblatt fuer Geschichte, Literatur und Cultur der Israeliten aller Zeiten und Laender. Frankfurt a.M. v1-3. 1839-41. Complete. 1 reel. B109 (Leo Baeck Institute. German-Jewish Periodicals, Pt 2) – 1 – $75.00 – us UPA [305]

DER ISRAELITISCHE LEHRER – Wochenschrift fuer die allgemeinen Angelegenheiten des Judenthums und insbesondere des israelitischen Lehrerstandes. Darmstadt, Mainz. v1-12. 1861-1872. Lacking v12. 1 reel. B114 (Leo Baeck Institute. German-Jewish Periodicals, Pt 1) – 1 – $75.00 – us UPA [270]

ISRAELITISCHE LETTERBODE. 1-12, NO. 2. 1875/76-1888 – 1 – us NY Public [073]

ISRAELITISCHE MONATSCHRIFT = ISRAELITE MONTHLY – (In German) – Berlin, DE. v1 no1 28 Jan 1886-v24 no12 17 Dec 1909 – 1r – 1 – $35.00 – cn Can Microfilming [072]

DAS ISRAELITISCHE PFINGSTFEST UND DER PLEJADENKULT : EINE STUDIE / Grimme, Hubert – Paderborn:Ferdinand Schoeningh, 1907 – 1mf – 9 – 0-8370-3400-0 – 1985-1400 – us A.T.L.A. [230]

ISRAELITISCHE UND JUEDISCHE GESCHICHTE / Zahn, Adolph – Guetersloh: C. Bertelsmann, 1895. 1 fiche – 9 – us A.T.L.A. [270]

DER ISRAELITISCHE VOLKSFREUND – Cincinnati. Ohio. 1858-59 – 1 – us A.J.P.C. [071]

DER ISRAELITISCHE VOLKSLEHER – Eine Monatsschrift erbaulichen und belehrenden inhalts, zur Kenntnis des Judenthums. Frankfurt a.M. v1-10, 1851-60. Complete. 2 reels. B117 (Leo Baeck Institute. German-Jewish Periodicals, Pt 1) – 1 – $135.00 – us UPA [270]

ISRAELITISCHE WOCHEN-SCHRIFT / ed by Treuenfels, A & Rahmer, M – Breslau. Magdeburg. v.1-25. 1870-94. Lacking: 1885, (p. 207-end). – 451mf – 9 – ne IDC [270]

ISRAELITISCHE WOCHENSCHRIFT : EINE ALLGEMEINE ZEITUNG DES JUDENTHUMS – v1-25. 1870-94 – 5r – 1 – us Ross [270]

ISRAELITISCHE WOCHENSCHRIFT – Berlin, 1899 n12-1905 n52 – 1 – Dist. gw Mikrofilm – gw Misc Inst [072]
ISRAELITISCHE WOCHENSCHRIFT – Magdeburg. v. 1-12, 14, 16-25. 1870-1881, 1883, 1885-1894 – 1 – us NY Public [073]
ISRAELITISCHER JUGENDFREUND – Berlin, 1898 – 1 – Dist. gw Mikrofilm – gw Misc Inst [072]
ISRAELITISCHER LANDES-LEHRER-VEREIN IN BOEHMEN – Mitteilungen des israelitischen Landes-Lehrervereines in Boehmen. Prague. v1-23. 1895-1917. Incomplete. 1 reel. B113 (Leo Baeck Institute. German-Jewish Periodicals, Pt 2) – 1 – $75.00 – us UPA [270]
ISRAELITISCHER LEHRER UND CANTOR = ISRAELITE READER AND CANTOR – (In German) – Berlin, DE. no1 Jan 1886-no11 1909 – 1r – 1 – $35.00 – cn Can Microfilming [072]
ISRAELITISCHES FAMILIENBLATT : AUSGABE FUER GROSS-BERLIN – Berlin, 1929-38 – 7r – 1 – Dist. gw Mikrofilm – gw Misc Inst [073]
ISRAELITISCHES FAMILIENBLATT – Hamburg, DE. 1930-38 – 7r – 1 – gw Mikrofilm [072]
ISRAELITISCHES FAMILIENBLATT – Hamburg. v10-30. 1908-28 – 8r – 1 – us Ross [270]
ISRAELITISCHES FAMILIENBLATT – (v37(33-45) has not been published. Some vols missing) – Hamburg, Berlin, 1898-1938. v1-40 – 28r – 9 – J-23-32/3 – ne IDC [956]
ISRAELITISCHES GEMEINDEBLATT – Cologne. 1888-1921. Lacking: 1888-96 (1); 1897-99; 1901; 1905-10; 1912. – 209mf – 9 – ne IDC [073]
ISRAELITISCHES PREDIGT- UND SCHULMAGAZIN / ed by Philippson, L – Magdeburg. v1-3. 1834-36. – 15mf – 9 – ne IDC [270]
ISRAELITISCHES WOCHENBLATT FUER DIE SCHWEIZ – Zurich. Oct. 4, 1929-Dec. 30, 1960 – 1 – us NY Public [073]
ISRAELS HEROLD – (New York). 1849 – 1 – us A.J.P.C. [470]
ISRAEL'S IDEAL: STUDIES IN OLD TESTAMENT THEOLOGY / Adams, John – Edinburgh: T. & T. Clark, 1909. 1 fiche – 9 – us A.T.L.A. [240]
ISRAEL'S MESSIANIC HOPE TO THE TIME OF JESUS : A STUDY IN THE HISTORICAL DEVELOPMENT OF THE FORESHADOWINGS, OF THE CHRIST IN THE OLD TESTAMENT AND BEYOND / Goodspeed, George Stephen – (Includes indexes) – New York: Macmillan, 1900 – 1mf – 9 – 0-8370-3339-X – 1985-1339 – us A.T.L.A. [270]
ISRAEL'S MONTHLY MAGAZINE – (New York). 1900-02 – 1 – us A.J.P.C. [073]
ISRAEL'S POSITION ON THE JORDAN CANAL PROJECT : AN ADDRESS BY AMBASSADOR ABBA EBAN BEFORE THE UNITED NATIONS SECURITY COUNCIL ON OCT 30, 1953 / Eban, Abba – New York: Israel Office of Information, 1953 – us Res Libr [956]
ISRAEL'S WISDOM LITERATURE / Rankin, OS – 1936 – 9 – $10.00 – us I.R.C. [220]
ISRAELSMISSIONEN – (Lacking some issues) – 1935-40 – 1r – 1 – ATLA S0664D – us A.T.L.A. [073]
ISRAIL FI AL-ISTIRATIJIYAH AL-AMIRIKIYAH FI AL-THAMANINAT / Mansur, Kamil – Bayrut: Muassasat al-Dirasat al-Filastiniyah, 1980 – 1 – us Res Libr [956]
ISRAIL WA-"MASHRU KARTIR" / Shufani, Ilyas – Bayrut: Muassasah al-Dirasat al-Filastiniyah, 1980 – 1 – us Res Libr [956]
ISSAC BACKUS PAPERS *see* BACKUS, ISSAC, PAPERS, MS 71
Issel, Ernst *see*
- DER BEGRIFF DER HEILIGKEIT IM NEUEN TESTAMENT
- DIE LEHRE VOM REICHE GOTTES IM NEUEN TESTAMENT
- DIE REFORMATION IN KONSTANZ

ISSLEDOVANIIA PO OTECHESTVENNOMU ISTOCHNIKOVEDENIIU – Leningrad, 1964.BR-10,759/1 – 9 – ne IDC [947]
ISSLEDOVANIIA TERMODINAMICHESKIKH SVOISTV ZHIDKOGO VODORODA / Pashkov, V V & Marinin, V S – Moskva: In-t vysokikh temperatur AN SSSR, 1979 – us Res Libr [947]
ISSN International Centre *see* ISSN REGISTER
ISSN REGISTER : MICROFICHE EDITION / ISSN International Centre – (1977-95 cum ed F9,800.00) – Paris, 1996 – 4 issues + cum indexes – 9 – F2,400.00 – ISSN 1022-100X – fr I.S.S.N. [020]
THE ISSUE OF KIKUYO : A SERMON / Henson, Hensley – London, New York: Macmillan, 1914 – 1mf – us A.T.L.A. [240]
ISSUES AND ANSWERS – New York, 1960-71 – 212mf – 9 – $5.00f – us Ross [320]
ISSUES IN BANK REGULATION – (1981-. 1,5,6,9) – v1-. 1977- – 1 – us UMI [073]
ISSUES IN CHILD MENTAL HEALTH – (See also: Psychosocial Process) – v5-. 1977- – 1,5,6,9 – us UMI [150]
ISSUES IN CHILD MENTAL HEALTH *see*
- FAMILY AND CHILD MENTAL HEALTH JOURNAL
- PSYCHOSOCIAL PROCESS

ISSUES IN COMPREHENSIVE PEDIATRIC NURSING – (v7-. 1983-. 5,6,9) – v1-. May 1976- – 1 – us UMI [073]
ISSUES IN COOPERATION AND POWER – Riverside, 1980-1981 – 1r – 1 – $50.00 – R04092 – us Library Micro [071]
ISSUES IN COOPERATION AND POWER – v.1. 1980 – 1,5,6,9 – us UMI [073]
ISSUES IN CORRECTIONS SLIM / U.S. National Institute of Justice – 1987. 300 documents – 9 – $240.00 – us N.C.J.R.S. [360]
ISSUES IN HEALTH CARE OF WOMEN – (v4 1983 5,6,9) – v1-4 1978-83 – 1 – us UMI [618]
ISSUES IN HEALTH CARE OF WOMEN *see* HEALTH CARE FOR WOMEN INTERNATIONAL
ISSUES IN LAW AND MEDICINE – v1-10. 1985-1996 – 9 – $300.00set – us Hein [340]
ISSUES IN MENTAL HEALTH NURSING – (v6-. 1984-. 5,6,9) – v1-. Spring 1978- – 1 – us UMI [073]
ISSUES IN RADICAL THERAPY – v10-. 1982- – 1,5,6,9 – us UMI [073]
ISSUES IN REPRODUCTIVE AND GENETIC ENGINEERING – 1,5,69 – us UMI [660]
ISSUES MANAGEMENT: HOW YOU CAN PLAN, ORGANIZE AND MANAGE FOR THE FUTURE / Coates, Joseph F – 1986. 142p. ISBN:0-912338-56-3 – 9 – $12.50 – us Lomond [650]
IST DAS LIBERALE JESUSBILD MODERN? / Gruetzmacher, Richard Heinrich – (Includes bibliographical references) – Berlin: Edwin Runge, 1907 – 1mf – 9 – 0-8370-9475-5 – 1986-3475 – us A.T.L.A. [240]
IST DER PENTATEUCH VON MOSES VERFASST? / Stern, Jakob E Molchow – Berlin: M. Poppelauer, 1881. 1 fiche – 9 – us A.T.L.A. [220]
IST DER SONNTAG HEIDNISCHEN, PAEPSTLICHEN ODER CHRISTLICHEN URSPRUNGS? / Rauschenbusch, August – Cleveland, O[hio]: H. Schulte, 1886 – 1mf – us A.T.L.A. [240]
IST DIE FORDERUNG EINES MODERNEN CHRISTENTUMS UND EINER MODERNEN THEOLOGIE BERECHTIGT? / Hahn, Traugott – Riga: Jonck & Poliewsky, 1903. 1 fiche – 9 – us A.T.L.A. [240]
IST DIE REDE DES PAULUS IN ATHEN EIN URSPRUENGLICHER BESTANDTEIL DER APOSTELGESCHICHTE (T.U.U. 3-39/1A) / Harnack, Adolf von – Leipzig, 1913 – 1mf – 9 – ne Slangenburg [240]
IST DIE THEOLOGIE WISSENSCHAFT? : AKADEMISCHE REDE ZUM GEBURTSFESTE DES HOECHSTSELIGEN GROSSHERZOGS KARL FRIEDRICH AM 22. NOVEMBER, 1887.... / Holsten, Carl – (Includes addenda) – Heidelberg:J Hoerning, 1887 – 1mf – 9 – 0-8370-3628-3 – 1985-1628 – us A.T.L.A. [240]
IST DOELLINGER HAERETIKER? / Hoetzl, Petrus – (Includes bibliographical references) – 2. Aufl. Muenchen: Rudolph Oldenbourg, 1870 – 1mf – 9 – 0-8370-8462-8 – 1986-2462 – us A.T.L.A. [240]
IST DUNS SCOTUS INDETERMINIST? : BGPHMA 5/4 / Minges, P – Muenster, 1905 – 3mf – 9 – ne Slangenburg [240]
IST DUNS SCOTUS INDETERMINIST? / Minges, P – Muenster, 1905 – 3mf – 8 – ne Slangenburg [100]
IST GOTT PERSOENLICH? : ERNEUTE UNTERSUCHUNG DES PROBLEMS DER GOTTESFRAGE / Fricke, Gustav Adolf – (Includes bibliographical references) – Leipzig: Georg Wigand, 1896 – 1mf – 9 – 0-8370-4954-7 – 1985-2954 – us A.T.L.A. [210]
ISTANBUL EKSPRES – Istanbul: Tan Matbaasi, aug 30, 1951-aug 1955 – 9r – 1 – us Res Libr [072]
ISTANBUL TICARET – Istanbul, Turkey. Feb 27 1958-Dec 1962; July 9 1965-Oct 25 1991 – 18r – 1 – us L of C Photodup [072]
ISTANBUL'UN KARA VE DENIZDEN HUECM VE MUEDAFAASI HAKKINDA BIR KAC SOEZ / Pasa, Mahmud Mutar – Istanbul: Kitabhane-i Islam ve Askeri, 1326 [1910] – $18.00 – us MEDOC [956]
ISTAR UND SALTU; EIN ALTAKKADISCHES LIED / Zimmern, Heinrich – Leipzig. 1916. BNE-20,040 1 – 9 – ne IDC [470]
Istel, Edgar *see* DAS KUNSTWERK RICHARD WAGNERS
ISTINA – v1- 1954- 1; v21- 1976- 5,6,9 – us UMI [240]
ISTINA – Paris. 1954-72 – 5 – fr A.C.R.P.P. [073]
ISTINA – Zhurnal obshchedostupnyi literaturnyi, obshchestvenno-ekonomicheskii i politicheskii. nr. 1-5. Spb. 1906. Lacking: nr. 5. BR-4122 2 – 8 – ne IDC [330]
ISTINNOE POVESTVOVANIE ILI ZHIZN' GAVRIILA DOBRYNINA / Dobrynin, G – (1752-1823). Spb. 1872. BR-6141 2 – 8 – ne IDC [947]
ISTIRAK – Istanbul, 1. sene, nos. 1-20 (13 Subat 1325-2 Eyluel 1326 [27 Feb 1909-16 Sep 1910]) – 42mf – 9 – $275.00 – us MEDOC [949]
ISTIRAK ETMEDIGIMIZ HAREKAT / Nuri, Celal – [Istanbul]: Matbaa-yi Orhaniye, 1917 – $40.00 – us MEDOC [956]
ISTITUTIONI HARMONICHE / Zarlino, G – 1558 – 9 – us Sibley [780]
ISTITUTIONI HARMONICHE / Zarlino, G – 1562 – 9 – us Sibley [780]
ISTITUTIONI HARMONICHE / Zarlino, G – 1573 – 9 – us Sibley [780]
ISTITUZIONI DI DIRITTO COMMERCIALE NORD-AMERICANO / Lefebvre d'Ovidio, Antonio – Roma, Edizioni italiane 1945? 132 p. LL-387 – 1 – us L of C Photodup [340]
ISTKUSSTVO KINO. (CINEMA ART) – Moscow. U.S.S.R. 1966- – 1 – us UMI [790]
ISTLEVAIUSHCHIIA LICHINY / Sologub, F – Kniga razskazov. M. 1907. BR-861 2 – 8 – ne IDC [460]
ISTOCHNIKI DLIA UDEL'NAGO PERIODA RUSSKOI ISTORII / Pogodin, M P – Odessa. 1848. BR-8306 2 – 8 – ne IDC [947]
ISTOCHNIKI I POSOBIIA DLIA IZUCHENIIA PERMSKAGO KRAIA / Smysliaev, D – Perm', 1876 – 8 – BR-7271 2 – ne IDC [947]
ISTOCHNIKI PO ISTORII RUSSKO-SKANDINAVSKIKH OTNOSHENII V RUKOPISNYKH SOBRANIIAKH G. LENINGRADA / Rukhmanova, E D & Kurskov, Iu.V – BR-10,873/1 – 9 – ne IDC [947]
ISTOCHNIKI PO ISTORII SKANDINAVSKIKH STRAN V LENINGRADSKOM OTDELENII INSTITUTA ISTORII AN SSSR / Liublinskii, VS – BR-10,959/1 – 9 – ne IDC [948]
ISTOCHNIKI PRAVA I SUDA V DREVNEI ROSSII / Diuvernua, N L – M. 1869. BR-9512 1 – 9 – ne IDC [947]
ISTOCHNIKI SOVETSKOGO GRAZHDANSKOGO PRAVA – Moscow, 1938. 2v. BR-9354/1 – 9 – ne IDC [340]
ISTOCHNIKOVEDENIE ISTORII RUSSKOGO DOREVOLIUTSIONNOGO DRAMATICHESKOGO TEATRA / Petrovskaia, I F – Leningrad, 1971.199p. BR-10,746/1 – 9 – ne IDC [790]
ISTOCHNIKOVEDENIE ISTORII SSSR / Tikhomirov, M N – v1: S drevneishego vremeni do kontsa XVIII veka. Uchebnoe posobie. Moscow, 1962. 495p. BR-10,660/1 – 9 – ne IDC [947]
ISTORIA CRITICA... / Cromaziano, A – N.p., n.d. – 4mf – 1 – ILM-152/1 – ne IDC [327]
L'ISTORIA DELLA BASILI CA DIACONALE COLLEGIATA, E PARROCCHIALE DI S. MARIA IN COSMEDIN DI ROMA / Crescimbeni, Giovanni Mario – O 1048. 1715 – 9 – ne IDC [240]
ISTORIA DESCRIZIONE DE TRE REGNI CONGO, MATAMBA ET ANGOLA / Cavazzi, Giovanni Antonio – Bologna. BA-106 2 – 8 – ne IDC [960]
ISTORIA PROLETARIATA SSSR – Moscow. no. 1-8. 1930-1931 – 1 – us NY Public [335]
ISTORIA SSSR – (U.S.S.R. History). Moscow. U.S.S.R. 1961- – 1 – us UMI [947]
ISTORIA...DELLA SACRA LEGA CONTRA SELIM,... / Foglietta, U – Genova, 1598 – 8mf – 9 – H-8397/1 – ne IDC [956]
ISTORICA DESCRIZIONE DE TRE REGNI CONGO, MATAMBA ET ANGOLA SITUATI. CAPUCCINI. CACAZZI DA MONTECUCCOLO / Fortunatus, A – A-105. 1687 – 9 – ne IDC [960]
ISTORICHESKAIA IZVESTIIA – Izdavaemyia Istoricheskim obshchestvom pri Imp. Moskovskom universitete. M. 1916 (1-4); 1917 (1-2). BR-4124 2 – 8 – ne IDC [947]
ISTORICHESKAIA KOLLEKTSIA ERMITAZHNOGO SOBRANIIA RUKOPISEI / Al'shits, D N – Moscow, 1968. 158p. Description of the early part of the collection that came to Saltykov-Shchedrin Library from the Hermitage. BR-10,851/1 – 9 – ne IDC [020]
ISTORICHESKI PREGLED – Sofiia. 1945-56 (6). Lacking: 1945-46, v. 2 (1); 1946-1947-49, 1950, v. 3-6; 1950-51, v. 7 (2-6); 1951-52, v. 8 (2); 1955, v. 11; 1957, v. 13 (1). BR-7703 2 – 8 – ne IDC [940]
ISTORICHESKIE AFORIZMY / Pogodin, M P – M. 1836. BR-8334 2 – 8 – ne IDC [947]
ISTORICHESKIE OCHERKI I RASSKAZY / Shubinskii, S N – ed. 6. Spb. 1911. BR-7899 2 – 8 – ne IDC [947]
ISTORICHESKIE RAZSKAZY I BYTOVYE OCHERKI / Karnovich, E P – Spb. 1824. BR-6050 2 – 8 – ne IDC [947]
ISTORICHESKII ARKHIV – Moscow, 1955-62.Bimonthly, Institute of History of the Academy of Sciences. BR-11,050/1 – 9 – ne IDC [947]
ISTORICHESKII OBZOR DEIATEL' NOSTI KOMITETA MINISTROV – 4v. Spb. 1902-03. BR-4249 2 – 8 – ne IDC [947]
ISTORICHESKII OBZOR UCHEBNIKOV OBSHCHEI I RUSSKOI GEOGRAFII, IZDANNYKH SO VREMENI PETRA VELIKAGO PO 1876 GOD. (1710-1876 G.) / Vesin, L – Spb. 1876. BR-7034 2 – 8 – ne IDC [947]
ISTORICHESKII OCHERK KOOPERATSII V ROSSII / Kheisin, ML – Pg., 1918 – 2mf – 9 – COR-133/1 – ne IDC [334]
ISTORICHESKII SLOVAR' 86 OTSTEV I KATALOG ILI BIBLIOTEKA STAROVERCHESKOI TSERKVI / Liubopytnyi, P – Saratov. 1914. BR-7137 2 – 8 – ne IDC [010]
ISTORICHESKII VIESTNIK – v. 1-150. 1880-1917 – 1 – 1,478.00 – us L of C Photodup [947]
ISTORICHESKII ZHURNAL – Moscow. (Historical Journal). 15 V. 1931-45 – 3 – us Readex [900]
ISTORICHESKII ZHURNAL – Moscow. (v. 1-6, 1931-1936 entitled Bor'ba Klassov.) 1931-1945 – 1 – us UMI [947]
ISTORICHESKII ZHURNAL DLIA, VSEKH – v. 1-12. Spb. 1908; v. 1-5. 1909. BR-4123 2 – 8 – ne IDC [947]
ISTORICHESKOE OBOZRENIE – Sbornik Istoricheskogo obshchestva S.-Peterburgskogo universiteta. v. 1-21. Spb. 1890-1916. B-1221 2 – 8 – ne IDC [947]
ISTORICHESKOE OPISANIE STAVROPIGIAL'NOGO VOSKRESENSKOGO, NOVYI IERUSALEM IMENUEMOGO MONASTYRIA / Leonid, Arkhimandrit – M. 1876. BR-11,096 1 – 9 – ne IDC [240]
ISTORIIA ARKHEOGRAFII V DOREVOLIUTSIONNOI ROSSII / Korneva, II & Tal'man, E M & Epshtein, D M – Uchebnoe posobie. Moscow, 1969. 227p BR-10,766/1 – 9 – ne IDC [025]
ISTORIIA BIBLIOTEKI AKADEMII NAUK SSSR, 1714-1964 / Luppov, S P; ed by Filippov, M S – 1964. BR-11,306 1 – 9 – ne IDC [500]
ISTORIIA DREVNIKH PLEMEN VERKHENI OBI PO RASKOPKAM BLIZ S. BOL'SHAIA RECHKA / Griaznov, M P – In: MIA. v. 48. M., L. 1956. BU-570 2 – 8 – ne IDC [947]
ISTORIIA DVORIANSKOGO SOSLOVIIA V ROSSII / Lablochkov, M – Spb. 1876. BR-6041 2 – 8 – ne IDC [947]
ISTORIIA EVREISKOGO RABOCHEGO DVIZHENIIA V ROSSII PO NEIZDANNYM ARKHIVNYM MATERIALAM / Bukhbinder, Naum Abramovich – Leningrad: Akademicheskoe izd-vo, 1925 – 1 – CSUX89-B6462 – us Hoover Inst Photo [947]

ISTORIIA EVREISKOI PECHATI V ROSSII V SVIAZI S OBSHCHESTVENNYMI TECHENIIAMI / Tsinberg, S L – Petrograd. 1915. Discussion of Jewish periodical press (Yiddish, Russian and Hebrew) to 1881; among other questions, inevitably, relations with censorship. BR-9263 1 – 9 – ne IDC [947]

ISTORIIA FILOSOFII – 2 ed v1-6. Kazan'. 1939-40. B-1541 2 – 8 – ne IDC [100]

ISTORIIA GEOGRAFICHESKOI KARTY. OCHERK I UKAZATEL' LITERATURY / Bagrov, L S – Petrograd. 1917. BR-7059 2 – 8 – ne IDC [910]

ISTORIIA GIMNAZICHESKAGO OBRAZOVANIIA V ROSSII (XVIII I XIX VEK) / Aleshintsev, I – St. Petersburg, 1912. ix,346,vip. BR-11,036 2 – 8 – ne IDC [947]

ISTORIIA GORODA MOSKVY / Zabelin, I – Moscow: I Kushneryov's Printing House, 1905 – 7mf – 9 – $70.00 – us Ross [947]

ISTORIIA GOSUDARSTVENNOI ORDENA LENINA BIBLIOTEKI SSSR IMENI V.I. LENINA ZA 100 LET, 1862-1962 – Moscow, 1962. 279p BR-11,001/1 – 9 – ne IDC [025]

ISTORIIA GOSUDARSTVENNOI ORDENA TRUDOVOGO KRASNOGO ZNAMENI PUBLICHNOI BIBLIOTEKI IMENI M.E. SALTYKOVA-SHCHEDRINA – Leningrad, 1963.435p. BR-10,841/1 – 9 – ne IDC [025]

ISTORIIA GRAZHDANSKOI VOINY / Rabinovich, S E – Moscow, 1933 – 1 – 35.00r – us Hoover Inst Photo [947]

ISTORIIA I ORGANIZATSIIA ARKHIVNOGO DELA V SSSR (1917-1945 GG.) / Maksakov, V V – Moscow, 1969. 431p. BR-10,772/1 – 9 – ne IDC [025]

ISTORIIA I ORGANIZATSIIA SOVETA VSEROSSIISKIKH KOOPERATIVNYKH S"EZDOV / Khizhniakov, V V – M., 1919 – 1mf – 9 – COR-227/1 – ne IDC [334]

ISTORIIA I OSNOVNYE NAPRAVLENIIA DEIATEL'NOSTI LENINGRADSKOGO GOSUDARSTVENNOGO TEATRAL'NOGO MUZEIA / Kochetov, AN – BR-10,927/1 – 9 – ne IDC [790]

ISTORIIA IMP. AKADEMII NAUK V PETERBURGE / Pekarskii, P P – 2v. Spb. 1870-73. BR-7753 2 – 8 – ne IDC [370]

ISTORIIA IMP. MOSKOVSKOGO UNIVERSITETA, NAPISANNAIA K STOLETNEMU EGO IUBILEIU / Shevyrev, S – M. 1855. BR-7854 2 – 8 – ne IDC [947]

ISTORIIA IMPERATORSKAGO VOL'NAGO EKONOMICHESKAGO OBSHCHESTVA S 1765 DO 1865 GODA / Khodnev, A I – Spb. 1865. BR-6007 2 – 8 – ne IDC [330]

ISTORIIA ISTORICHESKOI NAUKI V SSSR – Dooktiabrskii period. Bibliografiia. Moscow, 1965. 703p. BR-10,764/1 – 9 – ne IDC [947]

ISTORIIA KHRAMA KHRISTA SPASITELIA V MOSKVE – Moscow: M Volchaninov's Printing-House, 1891 – 4mf – 9 – $40.00 – us Ross [947]

ISTORIIA KNIGI NA RUSI / Bakhtiarov, A A – Spb. 1890. BR-4557 2 – 8 – ne IDC [460]

ISTORIIA KNIGI OT EIA POIAVLENIIA DO NASHIKH VREMEN / Egger, Emile – Perevod s frantsuzskago. Spb, 1900 – 8 – BR-4597 2 – ne IDC [947]

ISTORIIA KNIGI V ROSSII / Librovich, S F – v. 1-2. Spb. 1913-14. BR-4579 2 – 8 – ne IDC [947]

ISTORIIA KRASNOGO OKTIABRIA : SATIRA V STIKHAKH V 3-KH GLAVAKH / Dol – Moskva: Gos. izd-vo, 1922 – 1 – CSUX88-B7279 – us Hoover Inst Photo [947]

ISTORIIA MAKHNOVSKOGO DVIZHENIIA (1918-1921 GG.) / Arshinov, Petr Andreevich – Berlin: Izd. "Gruppy russkikh anarkhistov v germanii", 1923 – 1 – CSUX88-B1690 – us Hoover Inst Photo [947]

ISTORIIA MEDITSINY V ROSSII / Rikhter, V – 3v. M. 1814-20. BR-7814 2 – 8 – ne IDC [610]

ISTORIIA MOLDAVII – Dokumenty i materialy. Kishenev, 1955-1969. v. 3:2; 4-5 – 1 – 35.00r – us Hoover Inst Photo [947]

ISTORIIA NA APRILSKOTO VUZSTANIE / Strashimirov, D T – v. 1-3. Plovdiv. 1907. BR-3917 2 – 8 – ne IDC [947]

ISTORIIA NA SOFIISKIIA UNIVERSITET SV. KLIMENT OKHRODSKI PREZ PURVOTO MU POLUSTOLETIE, 1888-1938 / Arnaudov, M P – Sofiia, 1939. 647p. BR-3813 2 – 8 – ne IDC [370]

ISTORIIA PROLETARIATA SSSR – 22 v. M. 1930-35. BR-5649 2 – 8 – ne IDC [947]

ISTORIIA PROLETARIATA SSSR – Moscow, 1930-31 – 1r – 1 – us Ross [335]

ISTORIIA PROLETARIATA SSSR – Moscow. nos. 1-22. 1930-35. Missing no. 16, 1933 – 1 – 90.00 – us Hoover Inst Photo [947]

ISTORIIA RABOCHEGO I PROFESSIONALNOGO DVIZHENIIA DEREVOOBDELOCHNIKOV DO REVOLIUTSII 1917 GODA / Ainzaft, Samuil Semenovich; ed by Milonova, U. – Moskva: T SK Derevoobdelochnikov SSSR, 1928 – 1 – CSUX89-B7262 – us Hoover Inst Photo [947]

ISTORIIA RABOCHEI KOOPERATSII V ROSSII : OCHERKI PO ISTORII RABOCHEGO KOOPERATIVNOGO DVIZHENIIA (1864-1917 GG.) / Balabanov, MS – Kiev, 1923 – 3mf – 9 – COR-7/1 – ne IDC [334]

ISTORIIA RAZVITIIA MEDITSINY I ZDRAVOOKHRANENIIA V ROSSII – Obzor dokumental'nykh materialov. Moscow, Leningrad, 1958. 99p. BR-10,718/1 – 9 – ne IDC [610]

ISTORIIA RIMSKOGO PRAVA / Pokrovskii, Iosif Alekseevich – Izd. 3., ispravlennoe i dopolnennoe. Petrograd, Izdanie iuridicheskogo knizhnogo sklada "Pravo", 1917. 430p. LL-4049 – 1 – us L of C Photodup [340]

ISTORIIA RUSSKAGO PRAVA OT IZDANIIA SOBORNAGO ULOZHENIIA TSARIA ALEKSEIA MIKHAILOVICHA DO IZDANIIA SVODA ZAKONOV / Chislov, PI – Moscow, 1894. 317p. History of Russian law from 1649-1832 based on the author's lectures at Moscow University. BR-9511/1 – 9 – ne IDC [947]

ISTORIIA RUSSKOGO TEATRA DO POLOVINY XVIII STOLETIIA / Morozov, P O – Spb. 1889. BR-7716 2 – 8 – ne IDC [790]

ISTORIIA RUSSKOI ARMII I FLOTA / ed by Grishinskii, A S – Moscow, 1911 – 1 – $35.00r – us Hoover Inst Photo [947]

ISTORIIA RUSSKOI ARMII I FLOTA = HISTORY OF THE RUSSIAN ARMY AND NAVY / ed by Grishinskii, A S et al – Moscow: Publ Society "Obrazovanie". 15v – 57mf – 9 – $400.00 – us Ross [355]

ISTORIIA RUSSKOI DETSKOI LITERATURY / Babushkina, A P – M. 1948. BR-6083 2 – 8 – ne IDC [460]

ISTORIIA RUSSKOI ETNOGRAFII / Pypin, AN – Spb. v1-4. 1890-1892 – 33mf – 9 – ne IDC [947]

ISTORIIA RUSSKOI I VSEOBSCHEI / Mezhov, VI – (A history of Russian and Universal literature). 1872 – 3 – us Readex [947]

ISTORIIA RUSSKOI I VSEOBSHCHEI SLOVESNOSTI / Mezhov, VI – Bibliograficheskie materialy. s 1855 do 1870. goda vkl. Spb. 1872. BR-7156 2 – 8 – ne IDC [947]

ISTORIIA RUSSKOI I VSEOBSHCHEI SLOVESNOSTI – St. Petersburg. Bibliograficheskie materialy. (History of Russian and Universal Literature. Bibliography Materials). 1872 – 3 – us Readex [460]

ISTORIIA RUSSKOI KRITIKI – II. M., L. 1958. BR-1297 2 – 8 – ne IDC [460]

ISTORIIA RUSSKOI LITERATURY 18 VEKA – Bibliograficheskii ukazatel'. Leningrad, 1968. 500p. BR-6185/2 – 8 – ne IDC [460]

ISTORIIA RUSSKOI LITERATURY 19 VEKA. ZAPISKI SLUSHATELEI, REDAKTIROVANNIIA PROFESSOROM / Speranskii, M N – M. 1914. BR-4100 2 – 8 – ne IDC [460]

ISTORIIA RUSSKOI LITERATURY KONTSA 19-NACHALA 20 VEKA – Bibliograficheskii ukazatel'. Moscow, Leningrad, 1963. 519p. BR-1301/2 – 8 – ne IDC [460]

ISTORIIA RUSSKOI LITERATURY SIBIRI V DVUKH TOMAKH : AKADEMIIA NAUK SSSR, SIBIRSKOE OTDELENIE, INSTITUT ISTORII, FILOLOGII I FILOSOFII / ed by Postnov, I U S – Novosibirsk: the Institute, [1974-]. v1 1975; v2 1974; v2 pt 2 1974 – us Res Libr [460]

ISTORIIA RUSSKOI LITERATURY V TREKH TOMAKH – v. 1-2. M. 1958-63. BR-6186 2 – 8 – ne IDC [460]

ISTORIIA RUSSKOI OBSHCHESTVENNOI MYSLI / Ivanov-Razumnik, R I – 2v. Spb. 1907. B-1316 2 – 8 – ne IDC [460]

ISTORIIA RUSSKOI OBSHCHESTVENNOI MYSLI / Ivanov-Razumnik, R I – Ed. 2. Petrograd. 1918. BR-1309 2 – 8 – ne IDC [460]

ISTORIIA RUSSKOI SLOVESTNOSTI, DREVNEI I NOVOI / Galakhov, A D – Ed 3. v1-2. 1894 – 8 – BR-6031 2 – ne IDC [390]

ISTORIIA RUSSKOI ZHURNALISTIKI 18 VEKA / Berkov, P N – 1952. BR-6098 2 – 8 – ne IDC [380]

ISTORIIA SLAVIANSKOI FILOLOGII / Iagich, V – St. Petersburg, 1910. B/2273/2 – 8 – ne IDC [460]

ISTORIIA SOSLOVII V ROSSII / Kliuchevskii, V O – Ed. 2. M. 1914. BR-6054 2 – 8 – ne IDC [947]

ISTORIIA SOVETSKOI ARKHEOGRAFII – Uchebnoe posobie. Moscow, 1966-67. 6v.BR-10,771/1 – 9 – ne IDC [025]

ISTORIIA SSSR – Ukazatel' sovetskoi literatury za 1917-1952 gg. v. 1-2. M. 1956-58. BR-3537 2 – 8 – ne IDC [460]

ISTORIIA, STATISTIKA, LITERATURA PISCHEBUMAZHNAGO PROIZVODSTVA / Mel'nikov, N P & Mel'nikov, P N – Vodianye znaki (filigran'.). Budushchee pischebumazhnago proizvodstva. Spb. 1906. BR-7700 2 – 8 – ne IDC [947]

ISTORIIA TEATRAL'NOGO OBRAZOVANIIA V ROSSII (17-18 VV.) / Vsevolodskii-Gerngross, V N – v1. Spb. 1913. BR-7965 2 – 8 – ne IDC [790]

ISTORIIA UDELOV ZA STOLETIE IKH SUSHCHESTVOVANIIA – v. 1-3. Spb. 1902. BR-4250 2 – 8 – ne IDC [947]

ISTORIIA UKRAJINS'KOHO ORNAMENTU / Pavluts'kii, G – Kiev. 1927. BR-10,044 1 – 9 – ne IDC [390]

ISTORIIA UKRAJINS'KOJI LITERATURY / Vozniak, M – v. 1-3. L'vov. 1920-24. BR-4101 2 – 8 – ne IDC [460]

ISTORIIA V LICHAKH O TSARE BORISE FEODOROVICHE GODUNOVE / Pogodin, M P – M. 1868. BR-8307 2 – 8 – ne IDC [920]

ISTORIIA VOENNAGO ISKUSSTVA, KAK NAUKA / Baiov, A K – St. Petersburg, 1912. B-2234 2 – 8 – ne IDC [621]

ISTORIJA MEDICINY V ROSSII / Richter, W M – R 7814. 3 v. 1814-1820 – 9 – ne IDC [947]

ISTORIK I SOVREMENNIK – Berlin. v. 1-5. 1922-24 – 1 – us NY Public [335]

ISTORIK I SOVREMENNIK : ISTORIKO-LITERATURNYI SBORNIK – Berlin. v1-5. 1922-24 – 1r – 1 – us Ross [460]

ISTORIK MARKSIST – Moscow. (Marxist Historian). 94 NOS. 1926-40 – 3 – us Readex [947]

ISTORIK MARKSIST – Moscow. U.S.S.R. 1926-41 – 1 – us UMI [947]

ISTORIKCHESKI PREGLED NA BULGARSKATA TS'RKVA / Drinov, M S – Vienna. 1869. BR-3817 – 8 – ne IDC [940]

ISTORIK-MARKSIST – Moscow. 1926-May 1941 – 1 – 35.00r – us Hoover Inst Photo [335]

ISTORIKO POLITICHESKIE PIS'MA I ZAPISKI V PRODOLZHENII KRYMSKOI VOINY, 1853-1856 / Pogodin, M P – M. 1874. BR-4831 2 – 8 – ne IDC [947]

ISTORIKO-ASTRONOMICHESKIE ISSLEDOVANIIA – Red. L. G. Kulikovskii. v. 1-8. M. 1955-62. BR-115 2 – 8 – ne IDC [520]

ISTORIKO-IURIDICHESKIE AKTY PEREKHODNOI EPOKHI XVII-XVIII VEKOV / ed by Pobedonostsev, K P – Moscow, 1887. 295p. BR-11,135/1 – 9 – ne IDC [340]

ISTORIKO-KRITICHESKIE OTRYVKI / Pogodin, M P – M. 1846-67. BR-8342 2 – 8 – ne IDC [947]

ISTORIKO-RODOSLOVNOE OBSHCHESTVO – Letopis. Moscow. no. 5-12. 1906-1907 – 1 – us NY Public [920]

ISTORIKO-STATICHESKOE OBOZRENIE UCHEBNOGO ZAVEDENII S. PETERBURGSKOGO UCHEBNOGO OKRUGA S 1715 PO 1828 VKLIUCHITEL'NO / Voronov, A S – v. 1. Spb. 1849. BR-7962 2 – 8 – ne IDC [947]

ISTORYCHKO-HEOHRAFICHNYI ZBIRNYK VSEUKRAJINS' KOI AKADEMII NAUK – Vydae Komisiia dlia skladannia Istorychno-Heohrafichnoho Slovnyka Ukrajiny. v. 1-4. Kiev. 1927-31. BR-3443 2 – 8 – ne IDC [947]

ISTORYCHNI DZHERELA TA JIKH VYKORYSTANNIA – 6v. available. Kiev. 1964-71. BR-11,295 1 – 9 – ne IDC [947]

ISTORYCHNY I KALENDAR AL'MANAKH CHERVONOYI KALYNY – L'viv, etc. 1928-1929, 1934-35 – 1 – us NY Public [520]

ISTRA – Zagreb, Yugoslavia. 20 Feb 1932; Sept 1938-1940 – 1r – 1 – us L of C Photodup [949]

ISTRUZIONE EMANATA DA CATERINA SECONDA, IMPERATRICE E LEGISLATRICE DI TUTTA LA RUSSIA...TRADOTTA NUOVAMENTE DAL FRANCESE IN LINGUA TOSCANA / Catherine 2, Empress of Russia – Firenze, 1769. 160p. Italian ed. of Catherine II's Nakaz. BR-9096/1 – 9 – ne IDC [947]

ISU INDEPENDENT NEWS – Weirton. West Virginia. 1951-1961 – 1 – us UMI [071]

ISUE-ISUE DI-DALAM RIWAYAT PELAJARAN MALAYSIA = CONTEMPORARY ISSUES IN MALAYSIAN EDUCATION : SEMINAR 1974 / Malaysia. Malaysian Association for Education – (In English) – Kuala Lumpur, 1974 – 3mf – 9 – DE-214/1 – ne IDC [370]

ISULE ET OROVESE / Lemercier – (French Theatre Series). Paris. Barba, an XI. 1803 – 9 – fr Hachette [820]

ISUS MLADENETS / Esenin, Sergei – Petrograd. BR-1051 2 – 8 – ne IDC [460]

ISVESTIJA – Moskau, 1966-1993ff – 57r – 1 – DM8,550.00 – In zusammenarbeit mit Norman Ross Publishing Inc, New York – gw Mikro Press [949]

ISWELA KITE ENGLISH AND DUNDEE NATAL (NEWSPAPER) – 25 Sept 1912-2 Jun 1915 – 1 roll – 1 – sa Microfile [072]

IT HEITELAN – Leeuwarden, Netherlands. 1,8 Mar 1919; 3 Apr 1920-25 Dec 1926 – 6r – 1 – uk British Libr Newspaper [949]

IT IS NEVER TOO LATE TO MEND / Reade, Charles L – British Fiction Archive: Unit 2 – 9 – uk Bell [830]

IT IS WRITTEN: A CAREFUL STUDY OF THE GOSPELS / Bacon, Thomas Scott – New York: W.B. Ketcham, 1891. 1 fiche – 9 – us A.T.L.A. [240]

I.T. MAGAZINE *see*
– CANADIAN DATASYSTEMS
– INFO CANADA

A ITABIRA – Itabira-de-Matto-Dentro, 13 Aug 1893-13 Nov 1894 – 1,5,6 – bl Biblioteca [072]

ITACOATIARA – Cidade de Itacoatiara, Amazonas. 21 Dez 1874 – 1,5,6 – bl Biblioteca [072]

ITACOATIARA : SEMANARIO INDEPENDENTE NOTICIOSO E DE PROPAGANDA – Itacoatiara, Amazonas. 27 Nov-Dez 1927; Fev-18 Nov 1928 – 1,5,6 – bl Biblioteca [072]

ITAK ITOG / Shershenevich, V – M. 1926. BR-158 2 – 8 – ne IDC [460]

ITALA UND VULGATA / Roensch, Hermann – Marburg, 1875 – 11mf – 8 – Dfl39.00 – ne Slangenburg [240]

ITALA UND VULGATA / Roensch, Hermann – Marburg: N.G. Elwert, 1875. 526p. 2 fiches – 9 – us A.T.L.A. [240]

L'ITALIA – Chicago, IL: Gentile & Durante, [1886- [1919-oct 3 1948]; jan 8 1950-jun 16 1957; 1958-59; 1961-62; 1965; Sunday issues only for 1919-jul 17 1938 – 1 – us Res Libr [071]

L'ITALIA – San Francisco, CA. 1897-1925 – 70r – 1 BO2838 – $3,500.00 – us Library Micro [071]

ITALIA – Bulletin bimensuel d'informations. Edite par la concentration antifasciste italienne. Dir. Filippo Turati. no. 1-67. Paris. avr 1929-juil 1932. mq no. 6, 17, 44 – 1 – fr A.C.R.P.P. [073]

L'ITALIA EVANGELICA – Florence, Italy. 1 Jan 1881-27 Dec 1907 – 10r – 1 – uk British Libr Newspaper [072]

ITALIA NOSTRA – London, UK. 8 Sept 1928-7 Jun 1940 – 1 – uk British Libr Newspaper [072]

ITALIA OGGI – 1986- – 4r per y – 5 – inquire – us Ross [072]

ITALIA OGGI – 1986-1995 – 4r per y – 5,6 – Sfr962.00 – sz Infoprint [072]

ITALIA SACRA SIVE DE EPISCOPIS ITALIAE / Ughelli, Ferd.; ed by Coleti, NiC – Ed 2a. Venetiis. Tom 1-10. 1717-1722 – 228mf – 9 – Dfl798.00 – ne Slangenburg [440]

L'ITALIA SOCIALISTA – Rome, 10 Jun 1947-30 Jan 1949 (imperfect) – 3r – 1 – uk British Libr Newspaper [072]

THE ITALIAN : OR, THE CONFESSIONAL OF THE BLACK PENITENTS. A ROMANCE / Radcliffe, Ann Ward – London: Printed for T. Cadell Jun. and W. Davies (successors to Mr. Cadell)..., 1797 – 2 rolls – 1 – 1-55879-265-1 – uk Libr Preservation [830]

ITALIAN ACTORS' UNION – 1939-1963 – 1r – 1 – us I.H.R.C. [331]

THE ITALIAN AIR FORCE IN SPAIN – London, 1938? Fiche W968. (Blodgett Collection of Spanish Civil War Pamphlets) – 9 – us H.U. College Libr [946]
ITALIAN BOOKS, 1601-1700 – 131r – 1 – $8,200.00 $1,200.00y – us OmniSys [440]
ITALIAN BOOKS BEFORE 1601 – 1965- – 605r – 1 – $37,000.00 $1,200.00y – us OmniSys [440]
ITALIAN DRAMA – 262r – 1 – $16.050,00 – us OmniSys [440]
ITALIAN DRAWINGS FOR JEWELRY 1700-1875 / Cooper Union Museum for the Arts of Decoration. New York – 1940 – 9 – $4.90 – uk Chadwyck [740]
ITALIAN DRAWINGS OF THE 18TH AND 19TH CENTURIES AND SPANISH DRAWINGS OF THE 17TH THROUGH 19TH CENTURIES / Olsen, Sandra Haller & McCullagh, Susanne Folds – (196p accompanying text) – 1979 – 3 color mf – 15 – $54.00f – 0-226-68803-8 – us Chicago [740]
ITALIAN DUETS AND C. 1500 LONDON: [CA. 1790-1810] – (Binder's title: A Collection of Arias Duets, Trios etc. in vocal or orchestral score, published separately) – 1 – us Sibley [780]
ITALIAN ECHO – Providence. R.I. -w. 1952- – 1 – us UMI [071]
AN ITALIAN GRAMMAR WRITTEN IN LATIN BY SCIPIO LENTULO A NEAPOLITANE: AND TURNED IN ENGLISHE / Granthan, Henry – 1575. 164p. (English Linguistics Series 1500-1800) – 9 – us UMI [440]
ITALIAN IN THE POLITICAL LIFE OF BOSTON / Serino, Gustave – 1r – 1 – us I.H.R.C. [320]
ITALIAN MANUSCRIPTS – 15th century. Caesar, Cicero, Horace, etc. Holkham MSS. 317, 327, 328, 331, 341, 369, 388, 409, 418. Holkham Hall, Norfolk, England – 1 – uk Microform Academic [450]
ITALIAN MUSIC MANUSCRIPTS IN THE BRITISH LIBRARY, LONDON – Four sections trace development from 1640 to 1820 – 1 – us Primary [780]
THE ITALIAN NEWS – Boston, MA. 1921- – us I.H.R.C. [071]
ITALIAN PRESS – Utica, NY, Aug. 1-Dec. 19, 1930; Jan. 6-Mar. 6, 1931 – 22mf or 1r – 1,9 – us I.H.R.C. [978]
THE ITALIAN PRESS = LA STAMPA ITALIANA – Kansas City: A J Tolsa. dec 25 1931-jan 3 1941 – 3r – 1 – us Res Libr [071]
ITALIAN PRISONERS IN SPAIN / Spain. Embajada. Great Britain – N.Y., 1937. Fiche W1175. (Blodgett Collection of Spanish Civil War Pamphlets) – 9 – us H.U. College Libr [946]
ITALIAN REVIEW – Providence. R.I. 1924-1925 – 1 – us UMI [071]
ITALIAN SCHOOL – (Over 1,200 artists, over 6,000 reproductions) – 101mf – 9 – $555.00 – 0-907006-07-8 – uk Mindata [750]
Italian Socialist Party *see* AVANTI!
THE ITALIAN-AMERICAN COMMUNITY OF SAN FRANCISCO / Paoli, Deanna M – June 1970 – 1r – 1 – us I.H.R.C. [306]
ITALIAN-AMERICAN HERALD – (In English) – Philadelphia, PA. 1960-63 – 2r – 1 – $170.00 – D3373 – us Scholarly Res [071]
THE ITALIAN-AMERICAN HOME AS INFLUENCED BY FACTORS OF FAMILY DISORGANIZATION / Fasano, Frank Paul – 1931 – 1r – 1 – us I.H.R.C. [302]
ITALIAN-FRENCH COLONY – Reno, NV. 1908-09 – 1r – 1 – $50.00 – U04674 – us Library Micro [071]
ITALIANO – London, UK. 1 May 1926-5 Dec 1928 – 1 – uk British Libr Newspaper [072]
ITALIANO – London, UK. 18 Sept-23 Oct 1909 – 1 – uk British Libr Newspaper [072]
ITALIANS IN SPAIN / Friends of Democracy and Independence in Spain – London. 1937. Fiche W 900. (Blodgett Collection of Spanish Civil War Pamphlets) – 9 – us H.U. College Libr [946]
ITAL'IANSKAIA RUKOPISNAIA KNIGA V SOBRANII GOSUDARSTVENNOI PUBLICHNOI BIBLIOTEKI.. / Bernadskaia, E V – Describes 250 Italian mss. in GPB (5th-18th cents.). BR-10,871/1 – 9 – ne IDC [010]
ITALIANSKIIA KOMEDII I INTERMEDII, PREDSTAVLENNYIA PRI DVORE IMP. ANNY IOANNOVNY V 1733-1735 GG. TEKSTY / ed by Peretts, V N – Petrograd. 1917. BR-7759 2 – 8 – ne IDC [820]
L'ITALIE MYSTIQUE : HISTOIRE DE LA RENAISSANCE RELIGIEUSE AU MOYEN AGE / Gebhart, Emile – Paris: Hachette, 1893 – 1mf – us A.T.L.A. [240]
ITALIEN : ERLEBNISSE DEUTSCHER IN ITALIEN / ed by Molo, Walter Ritter von – Berlin: Wegweiser, 1921 – 1r – 1 – us U.W. Library [945]
ITALIEN INDEX : BILDDOKUMENTATION ZUR KUNST IN ITALIEN – 1991-1992 – 620 fiches (1:24) – 9 – silver DM9,800.00 – 3-598-33130-4 – gw Saur [700]
ITALIENISCHE ANALEKTEN ZUR REICHSGESCHICHTE DES 14. JAHRHUNDERTS (1310-1378) (MGH SCHRIFTEN..: 11.BD) / Mommsen, Theodor – 1952 – Dfl22.00 – ne Slangenburg [240]
ITALIENISCHE REISE : MIT DEN ZEICHNUNGEN GOETHES, SEINER FREUNDE UND KUNSTGENOSSEN / Goethe, Johann Wolfgang von; ed by Graevenitz, George von – Leipzig: Insel-Verlag, 1912 – 1r – 1 – us U.W. Library [910]
ITALISCHE NORMANN IN DEUTSCHER HELDENSAGE / Panzer, Friedrich Wilhelm – (Includes bibliographical references) – Frankfurt am Main: M Diesterweg, 1925 – 1r – 1 – us U.W. Library [410]
L'ITALO AMERICANO – New Orleans, LA, 1899 (July 9) – 2mf or 1r – 1,9 – us I.H.R.C. [978]
ITALO AMERICANO – Sun Valley, CA. 1944 – 28+ r – 1 – $140.00 ($50.00y) – R04127 – us Library Micro [071]
L'ITALO AUSTRALIANO – (Italian language) – Sydney, Mar 11 1905-Jan 30 1909 – 9 – at Pascoe [072]
L'ITALO-AMERICANO – Nuova Orleans: S Calafiore, sep 22 1917-oct 19 1918 – 1r – 1 – us Res Libr [071]
L'ITALO-CANADESE – Montreal, Canada. 15 mar 1894-v2 n29. 13 jul 1895 – 1r – 1 – Can$30.00 – cn Can Microfilming [072]
ITALY : ANNUARIO STATISTICO ITALIANO 1878-1965 / Italy. Istituto Centrale di Statistica – (Coll title: European Official Statistical Serials, 1841-1984) – 384mf – 9 – £2,015.00 – uk Chadwyck [945]
ITALY / Balzani, Ugo – London: Society for Promoting Christian Knowledge; New York: E. & J.B. Young, 1883. 340p – 1 – us U.W. Library [900]
ITALY : A POEM / Rogers, Samuel – London: John Murray, 1823-1828 – 1 roll – 1 – 1-55879-259-7 – uk Libr Preservation [810]
Italy *see*
– GAZZETTA UFFICIALE DELLA REPUBBLICA ITALIANA
– LIBYA TREATY
– PROGRAMMA ECONOMICO NAZIONALE PER IL QUINQUENNIO 1966-70
ITALY, 1918-41 : REPORTS / U.S. Military Intelligence – 9 reels with printed guide – 1 – $965.00 – us UPA [355]
ITALY AND HER INVADERS 376-814 / Hodgkin, Thomas – H-270 2. v1-8. 1880-1899 – 8 – ne IDC [945]
Italy. Comitato interministeriale per la recostruzione. Segreteria per il programma di sviluppo economico *see* LINEMENTI DEL PROGRAMMA DI SVILUPPO DELL'OCCUPAZIONE E DEL REDDITO IN ITALIA (1955-1964)
Italy. Direzione Generale Della Statistica *see* ANNUARIO STATISTICO ITALIANO
Italy. Dogane e Imposte Indirette. Direzione Generale delle *see* BOLLETTINO UFFICIALE
ITALY FROM DANTE TO TASSO (1300-1600), ITS POLITICAL HISTORY.. / Cotterill, Henry Bernard – New York: Frederick A. Stokes company, 1919. xxviii,617p. illus – 1 – us U.W. Library [945]
ITALY IN THE THIRTEENTH CENTURY / Sedgwick, Dwight – Boston: Houghton Mifflin, 1912 – 2mf – us A.T.L.A. [945]
Italy. Istituto Centrale di Statistica *see*
– ANNALI DI STATISTICA
– ITALY
– MOVIMENTO DELLA POPOLAZIONE E CAUSE DI MORTE
– STATISTICA GIUDIZIARIA CIVILE E COMMERCIALE
Italy. Laws, Statutes, etc *see*
– BULLETTINO SETTIMANALE DELLE LEGGI E DEI DECRETI DEL REGNO D'ITALIA
– RACCOLTA UFFICIALE DELLE LEGGI E DEI DECRETI DEL REGNO D'ITALIA
Italy. Legislature. Seventh *see* PARLIAMENTARY PAPERS
Italy. Ministero del Bilancio *see*
– OUTLINE OF DEVELOPMENT OF INCOME AND EMPLOYMENT IN ITALY IN THE TEN-YEAR PERIOD 1955-1964
– PROGETTO DI PROGRAMMA DI SVILUPPO ECONOMICO PER IL QUINQUENNIO 1965-1969
– PROGRAMMA DI SVILUPPO ECONOMICO 1965-1969 PER IL QUINQUENNIO 1966-1970. PRESENTATA DEL MINISTERIO DEL BILANCIO ON. PIERACCINI, E APPROVATA DA CONSIGLIO DEI MINISTRI IL 29 OTT 1965
– PROGRAMMA DI SVILUPPO ECONOMICO PER IL QUINQUENNIO 1965-69
– PROGRAMMA DI SVILUPPO ECONOMICO PER IL QUINQUENNIO 1966-70
Italy. Ministero delle Finanze *see* BOLLETTINO DI STATISTICA E LEGISLAZIONE COMPARATA
Italy. Ministero di Giustizia e dei Culti *see* GRAZIA E GIUSTIZIA
Italy. Organization for European Economic Cooperation *see* GENERAL MEMORANDUM ON THE 1950/51 AND 1951/52 PROGRAMMES. ITALY
Italy. Parlamento. Legislatura *see* ATTI PARLAMENTARI
ITALY THROUGH DUTCH EYES. DUTCH 17TH CENTURY LANDSCAPE ARTISTS IN ITALY / Michigan. University. Museum of Art – 1964 – 9 – 4.90 – uk Chadwyck [700]
O ITAMBACURY : ORGAO DEDICADO AOS INTERESSES DO POVO – Itambacury, 31 May 1930; Dec 1932; Jan-Mar, May-Dec 1934; Jan-Feb 1935 – 1,5,6 – bl Biblioteca [072]
ITAPECERICA : ORGAM OFFICIAL MUNICIPAL E DO P.R.M. – Itapecerica, 5 Dec 1926; 13 Apr 1930 – 1,5,6 – bl Biblioteca [072]
O ITAPECERICA – Itapecerica, 8-22 Sep 1895 – 1,5,6 – bl Biblioteca [072]
O ITAPEMIRINENSE : JORNAL NOTICIOSO, LITTERARIO, COMMERCIAL E AGRICOLA – Villa do Itapemirim, 23 Jul 1876 – 1,5,6 – bl Biblioteca [072]
ITEM – Hammonton. N.J. 1872-77 – 1 – us UMI [071]
ITEM – Huntsville. Tex. -w. 1853-1901, 1928- – 1 – us UMI [071]
ITEM – Mobile. Ala. 1912-1916 – 1 – us UMI [071]
ITEM – New Orleans. La. 1911-58 – 1 – us UMI [071]
ITEM – New Oxford. Pa. 1889-1923; 1925-1943; 1945- – 1 – us UMI [071]
ITEM – O'Neill, NE. -w. Jan 1884-Jan 1892, scattered issues missing – 1 – us NE Hist [071]
ITEM – Picayune. Miss. 1936-1966 – 1 – us UMI [071]
ITEM – Port Chester. N.Y. 1966- – 1 – us UMI [071]
ITEM – Richmond. Ind. 1878-1879; 1881-1905 – 1 – us UMI [071]
THE ITEM – Mount Carmel. Pa. 1903-1908 – 1 – us UMI [071]
THE ITEM – Mount Carmel. Pa. -sw. 1896-1902 – 1 – us UMI [071]
THE ITEM – Williamsport, PA., 1888 – 13 – $25.00r – us I.M.R. [071]
ITEMS / Social Science Research Council – (v30- . 1976- . 5,6,9) – v. 1-. 1947- – 1 – us UMI [300]
DAS ITENERARIUM PEREGRINORUM (MGH SCHRIFTEN..: 18.BD) : EINE ZEITGENOESSISCHE ENGLISCHE CHRONIK ZUM 3. KREUZZUG IN URSPRUENGLICHER GESTALT / Mayer, H E – 1962 – Dfl32.00 – ne Slangenburg [240]
ITER AD FODINAS 1733 / Linnaeus, Carl – Iter Dalekarlicum. 1734; Iter ad Experos. 1735. B-168 2 – 8 – ne IDC [580]
ITER HISPANICUM / Loefling, P – Stockholm. 1758. B-886 2 – 8 – ne IDC [580]
ITER LAPPONICUM / Linnaeus, Carl – Holmiae. 1732. B-169 2 – 8 – ne IDC [580]
ITER PALAESTINUM, ELLER RESA TIL HELIGA LANDET FOERRAETTAD FRAN AR 1749 TIL 1752, MED BEKRIFTNINGAR, ROEN, ANMAERKNINGAR, OEFVER DE MAERKVAERDIGASTE NATURALIER / Hasselquist, F – Stockholmiae. 1757. B-2586 2 – 8 – ne IDC [580]
ITER PER POSEGANAM SCLAVONIAE PROVINCIAM / Piller, M & Mitterpacher, L – B-2457 2. 1783 – 8 – ne IDC [940]
ITER PERSICO-TURCICUM / Bornmuller, J – 1892-93 – 7 – uk Microform Academic [910]
ITET. 7-37 / Russia. (1917-R.S.F.S.R.). Tsentral'nyi Irmii vspolnitel'nyi Komitet – 1 – us L of C Photodup [947]
L'ITINERAIRE D' OU-K'ONG (751-790) / Levi, S & Chavannes, E – Note additionelle: le Kipin. S. 9. v. 6. JA. 1895. BU-594 2 – 8 – ne IDC [910]
ITINERAIRE DE QUEBEC A CHICAGO / Gerard, Arsene Gilbert – Montreal: Beauchemin & Valois, 1868. 03329. (Pre-1900 Canadiana) – 9 – cn C.I.H.M. [910]
ITINERAIRES RUSSES EN ORIENT / Khitrowo, B – Geneve, 1889 – Dfl32.00 – ne Slangenburg [240]
ITINERARIO – (Appears three times a year in the English language) – Leiden, 1975-1987 including index – 60mf – 9 – ne IDC [073]
ITINERARIO / Centre for the History of European Expansion, University of Leiden – (1975-1976 entitled: Newsletter/Nieuwsbrief (English/Dutch)) – Leiden, 1975-1987 – 60mf – ne IDC [940]
ITINERARIO DE RIO GUADIANA Y TODOS SUS AFLUENTES / Spain. Direccion general de Obras publicas – 1883 – 9 – 1.50f – sp Bibl Santa Ana [910]
ITINERARIO DE UN VIAGE (SIC) / Lujan, Francisco – (2a parte. 1837.1.50f; 9) – 1837 – 9 – 1.50f – sp Bibl Santa Ana [910]
ITINERARIOS DE EL REI D. SEBASTIAO... / Verissimo Serano, Joaquin – Madrid: Arch. Ibero Americano, 1964 – 1 – sp Bibl Santa Ana [946]
ITINERARIUM PARADISI... / Raulin J – Venetiis, 1585 – 4mf – 9 – CA-89/1 – ne IDC [240]
ITINERARY NOTES OF PLANTS / Griffith, W – Posthumous papers, v. 2. Calcutta. 1848. B-7412 2 – 8 – ne IDC [580]
THE ITINERARY OF JOHN LELAND IN OR ABOUT THE YEARS 1535-1543 / ed by Toulmin Smith, Lucy – H 1125 2. 5 v. 1907-1910 – 8 – ne IDC [910]
ITO – Amsterdam, 1911-1914. Special edition 1916-1918 – 8mf – 9 – J-261-129/1 – ne IDC [073]
Ito, Sayuri *see* THE CHOREOGRAPHY AND PERFORMANCE OF A JAPANESE FOLK TALE
Ito, Takeo *see* CHINA'S CHALLENGE IN MANCHURIA
ITOGI 7-MI DNE I – (Includes c.1: no.1 1940: June 17-no.2 (1940:June 25)) – New York: [s.n.], 1940- – 1 – CSUXADP7406-S – us Hoover Inst Photo [947]
ITOGI 10% VYBOROCHNOGO OBSLEDOVANII A OTDELNYKH KHOZI A ISTV V...GODU PO SIBIRSKOMU KRAI U : SIBIRSKI I KRAEVO I STATISTICHESKI I OTDEL. ITOGI DESI ATI PROT SENTNOGO OBSLEDOVANII A OTDELNYKH KHOZI A ISTV V...GODU PO SIBIRSKOMU KRAI U – (Includes c.1: 1927) – Novosibirsk: [Otdel], 19uu – 1 – CSUXAKZ1794-S – us Hoover Inst Photo [947]
ITOGI POLITIKI MITROPOLITOV SERGII A I EVLOGII A / Gorchakov, Mikhail Konstantinovich – Parizh: Izd-vo "Dolo i zlo", 1929- – 1 – CSUX89-B1657 – us Hoover Inst Photo [320]
ITOGI POSLEDGOL / Russia. (1917-R.S.F.S.R.). Tsentral'ania komissiia pomoshchi golodaiushchim – 15 X 1922G.-I VIII 1923G. Moscow. 1923. (The results of the last famine, Oct. 15, 1922-Aug. 1, 1923.) – 1 – 35.00r – us Hoover Inst Photo [324]
ITOGI RABOTY PO ZEMLEUSTROISTVU TRUDI ASHCHEGOSIA EVREISKOGO NASELENIIA V BELORUSSKOI SOTSIALISTICHESKOI SOVETSKOI RESPUBLIKE : STENOGRAFICHESKII OTCHET ZASEDANIIA PREZIDIUMATSIK BSSR OT 25 DEK. 1926 G / Byelorussian S.S.R. TS entralny vykana uchny kamit et – Minsk: Izdanie sekretariata T SIK BSSR, 1927 – 1 – CSUX91-B2447 – us Hoover Inst Photo [947]
ITOGI SEMI DNE I *see* ITOGI 7-MI DNE I
ITOGI VSESOIUZNOI PEREPISI NASELENIIA 1989 GODA : TOM 1. CHISLENNOST' RAZMESHCHENIE NASELENIIA SSSR. CHAST' 1 / Gosudarstvennyi komitet SSSR po statistike – (Part 1 of 24 parts) – Minneapolis: East View Publications, 1992 – 5mf – 9 – $39.95 – 1-879944-07-3 – us East View [304]

ITOGI VSESOIUZNOI PEREPISI NASELENIIA 1989 GODA : TOM 1. CHISLENNOST' RAZMESHCHENIE NASELENIIA SSSR. CHAST' 2 / Gosudarstvennyi komitet SSSR po statistike – (Part 2 of 24 parts) – Minneapolis: East View Publications, 1992 – 6mf – 9 – $39.95 – 1-879944-08-1 – us East View [304]

ITOGI VSESOIUZNOI PEREPISI NASELENIIA 1989 GODA : TOM 1. CHISLENNOST' RAZMESHCHENIE NASELENIIA SSSR. CHAST' 3 / Gosudarstvennyi komitet SSSR po statistike – (Part 3 of 24 parts) – Minneapolis: East View Publications, 1992 – 5mf – 9 – $39.95 – 1-879944-09-X – us East View [304]

ITOGI VSESOIUZNOI PEREPISI NASELENIIA 1989 GODA : TOM 10. RASPREDELENIE ZANIATOGO NASELENIIA SSSR PO OTRASLIAM NARODNOGO KHOZIAISTVA / Statisticheskii komitet Sodruzhestva Nezavisimykh Gosudarstv – (Part 21 of 24 parts) – Minneapolis: East View Publications, 1993 – 6mf – 9 – $39.95 – 1-879944-21-9 – us East View [304]

ITOGI VSESOIUZNOI PEREPISI NASELENIIA 1989 GODA : TOM 11. ZANIATIIA NASELENIIA SSSR. CHAST' 1 / Statisticheskii komitet Sodruzhestva Nezavisimykh Gosudarstv – (Part 22 of 24 parts) – Minneapolis: East View Publications, 1993 – 4mf – 9 – $39.95 – 1-879944-28-6 – us East View [304]

ITOGI VSESOIUZNOI PEREPISI NASELENIIA 1989 GODA : TOM 12. PRODOLZHITEL'NOST-PROZHIVANIIA NASELENIIA SSSR V MESTE POSTOIANNOGO ZHITEL'STVA / Statisticheskii komitet Sodruzhestva Nezavisimykh Gosudarstv – (Part 24 of 24 parts) – Minneapolis: East View Publications, 1993 – 8mf – 9 – $39.95 – 1-879944-32-4 – us East View [304]

ITOGI VSESOIUZNOI PEREPISI NASELENIIA 1989 GODA : TOM 2. VOZRAST I SOSTOIANIE V BRAKE NASELENIIA SSSR. CHAST' 1 / Gosudarstvennyi komitet SSSR po statistike – (Part 4 of 24 parts) – Minneapolis: East View Publications, 1992 – 7mf – 9 – $39.95 – 1-879944-10-3 – us East View [304]

ITOGI VSESOIUZNOI PEREPISI NASELENIIA 1989 GODA : TOM 2. VOZRAST I SOSTOIANIE V BRAKE NASELENIIA SSSR. CHAST' 2 / Gosudarstvennyi komitet SSSR po statistike – (Part 5 of 24 parts) – Minneapolis: East View Publications, 1992 – 7mf – 9 – $39.95 – 1-879944-11-1 – us East View [304]

ITOGI VSESOIUZNOI PEREPISI NASELENIIA 1989 GODA : TOM 3. CHISLO I SOSTAV SEMEI V SSSR / Statisticheskii komitet Sodruzhestva Nezavisimykh Gosudarstv – (Part 6 of 24 parts) – Minneapolis: East View Publications, 1993 – 6mf – 9 – $39.95 – 1-879944-14-6 – us East View [304]

ITOGI VSESOIUZNOI PEREPISI NASELENIIA 1989 GODA : TOM 4. CHISLO ROZHDENNYKH DETEI V SSSR / Statisticheskii komitet Sodruzhestva Nezavisimykh Gosudarstv – (Part 7 of 24 parts) – Minneapolis: East View Publications, 1993 – 4mf – 9 – $39.95 – 1-879944-15-4 – us East View [304]

ITOGI VSESOIUZNOI PEREPISI NASELENIIA 1989 GODA : TOM 5. ZHILISHCHENYE USLOVIIA NASELENIIA SSSR / Statisticheskii komitet Sodruzhestva Nezavisimykh Gosudarstv – (Part 8 of 24 parts) – Minneapolis: East View Publications, 1993 – 4mf – 9 – $39.95 – 1-879944-16-2 – us East View [304]

ITOGI VSESOIUZNOI PEREPISI NASELENIIA 1989 GODA : TOM 6. UROVEN' OBRAZOVANIIA NASELENIIA SSSR. CHAST' 1 / Statisticheskii komitet Sodruzhestva Nezavisimykh Gosudarstv – (Part 9 of 24 parts) – Minneapolis: East View Publications, 1993 – 7mf – 9 – $39.95 – 1-879944-18-9 – us East View [304]

ITOGI VSESOIUZNOI PEREPISI NASELENIIA 1989 GODA : TOM 6. UROVEN' OBRAZOVANIIA NASELENIIA SSSR. CHAST' 2 / Statisticheskii komitet Sodruzhestva Nezavisimykh Gosudarstv – (Part 10 of 24 parts) – Minneapolis: East View Publications, 1993 – 7mf – 9 – $39.95 – 1-879944-19-7 – us East View [304]

ITOGI VSESOIUZNOI PEREPISI NASELENIIA 1989 GODA : TOM 6. UROVEN' OBRAZOVANIIA NASELENIIA SSSR. CHAST' 3 / Statisticheskii komitet Sodruzhestva Nezavisimykh Gosudarstv – (Part 11 of 24 parts) – Minneapolis: East View Publications, 1993 – 7mf – 9 – $39.95 – 1-879944-22-7 – us East View [304]

ITOGI VSESOIUZNOI PEREPISI NASELENIIA 1989 GODA : TOM 6. UROVEN' OBRAZOVANIIA NASELENIIA SSSR. CHAST' 4 / Statisticheskii komitet Sodruzhestva Nezavisimykh Gosudarstv – (Part 12 of 24 parts) – Minneapolis: East View Publications, 1993 – 8mf – 9 – $39.95 – 1-879944-29-4 – us East View [304]

ITOGI VSESOIUZNOI PEREPISI NASELENIIA 1989 GODA : TOM 7. NATSIONAL'NYI SOSTAV NASELENIIA SSSR. CHAST' 1 / Statisticheskii komitet Sodruzhestva Nezavisimykh Gosudarstv – (Part 13 of 24 parts) – Minneapolis: East View Publications, 1993 – 7mf – 9 – $39.95 – 1-879944-23-5 – us East View [304]

ITOGI VSESOIUZNOI PEREPISI NASELENIIA 1989 GODA : TOM 7. NATSIONAL'NYI SOSTAV NASELENIIA SSSR. CHAST' 2 / Statisticheskii komitet Sodruzhestva Nezavisimykh Gosudarstv – (Part 14 of 24 parts) – Minneapolis: East View Publications, 1993 – 8mf – 9 – $39.95 – 1-879944-30-8 – us East View [304]

ITOGI VSESOIUZNOI PEREPISI NASELENIIA 1989 GODA : TOM 7. NATSIONAL'NYI SOSTAV NASELENIIA SSSR. CHAST' 4 / Statisticheskii komitet Sodruzhestva Nezavisimykh Gosudarstv – (Part 16 of 24 parts) – Minneapolis: East View Publications, 1993 – 5mf – 9 – $39.95 – 1-879944-24-3 – us East View [304]

ITOGI VSESOIUZNOI PEREPISI NASELENIIA 1989 GODA : TOM 7. NATSIONAL'NYI SOSTAV NASELENIIA SSSR. CHAST' 5 / Statisticheskii komitet Sodruzhestva Nezavisimykh Gosudarstv – (Part 17 of 24 Parts) – Minneapolis: East View Publications, 1993 – 6mf – 9 – $39.95 – 1-879944-25-1 – us East View [304]

ITOGI VSESOIUZNOI PEREPISI NASELENIIA 1989 GODA : TOM 7. NATSIONAL'NYI SOSTAV NASELENIIA SSSR. CHAST' 6 / Statisticheskii komitet Sodruzhestva Nezavisimykh Gosudarstv – (Part 18 of 24 parts) – Minneapolis: East View Publications, 1993 – 5mf – 9 – $39.95 – 1-879944-26-X – us East View [304]

ITOGI VSESOIUZNOI PEREPISI NASELENIIA 1989 GODA : TOM 8. ISTOCHNIKI SREDSTV SUSHCHESTVOVANIIA NASELENIIA SSSR / Statisticheskii komitet Sodruzhestva Nezavisimykh Gosudarstv – (Part 19 of 24 parts) – Minneapolis: East View Publications, 1993 – 5mf – 9 – $39.95 – 1-879944-17-0 – us East View [304]

ITOGI VYBOROV I SOSTAV DEPUTATOV MESTNYKH SOVETOV DEPUTATOV TRUDI ASHCHIKHSI A : OTDEL PO VOPROSAM RABOTY SOVETOV PREZIDIUMA VERKHOVNOGO SOVETA SSSR – (Includes c.1: 1969, 1971) – Moskva: Izd-vo Izvestii a Sovetov deputatov trudi ashchikhsi a SSSR, 1961 – 1 – CSUXAKY6091-S – us Hoover Inst Photo [947]

ITOGI VYBOROV V GORSOVETY... : VSEROSSI ISKAI A T SENTRALNAI A IZBIRATELNAI A KOMISSII A – (Includes c.1: 1927) – Moskva, Leningrad: Moskovski i rabochi i, 1928- – 1 – CSUXAKY5354-S – us Hoover Inst Photo [947]

ITOGI VYPOLNENIIA NARODNOKHOZI-AISTVENNOGO PLANA SSSR I SOIUZNYKH RESPUBLIK V 1964 G / U.S.S.R. Tsentralnoe Statisticheskoe Upravlenie – M. 1965. BD-789 1 – 9 – ne IDC [310]

ITOGI VYPOLNENIIA VTOROGO PIATILETNEGO PLANA RAZVITIIA NARODNA-KHOZIAISTVENNYI SOIUZA SSR / U.S.S.R. Gosudarstvennaia Planovaia Komissiia – M. 1939. BD-748 1 – 9 – ne IDC [338]

ITON HATSAIR – Amsterdam, 1929-1936. v1-7 – 9mf – 9 – J-261-47/1 – ne IDC [073]

ITON MACBI – Haarlem, 1936-1939. v1-3 – 1mf – 9 – J-261-48/1 – ne IDC [073]

...ITS AIMS AND OBJECTS / Catholic Truth Society of Ottawa – Ottawa?: The Society, 1891 Or 1892. 00517. (Pre-1900 Canadiana) – 9 – cn C.I.H.M. [240]

IT'S HAPPENING IN SPAIN, TOLD BY THE VICTIMS THEMSELVES / International Labour Defense – N.Y., 1937. Fiche W967. (Blodgett Collection of Spanish Civil War Pamphlets) – 9 – us H.U. College Libr [946]

ITS ORIGIN, RISE, DECLINE AND FALL / Peter, Robert et al – 1896. Indexed. F-0508 – 4mf – 9 – us A.G.L.L. [370]

IT'S UP TO THE WOMEN / Roosevelt, Eleanor – New York: Frederick A. Stokes Company, 1933. x,263p – 1 – us U.W. Library [305]

I-TSING – A Record of Buddhist Religion. Transl. by J. Takakusu. Oxford. 1896. BCH-939 2 – 8 – ne IDC [290]

I-TSING – A record of the Buddhist religion as practised in India and the Malay Archipelago (A.D. 671-695). 1896. Reel 4001 – 1 – ja CEACS [290]

ITTIHAD – Izmir, 1908-19? – 9 – $20.00 – us MEDOC [956]

ITTIHAD *see* AL-ITTIHAD

ITTIHAD-I BUZURG – (Cont: Jibhah-'i Milli-i Iran. Shumarah-'i 20-36 (7 Tir 1358-17 Mihr 1358[29 Jun 1979-16 Oct 1979]). Missing issues: 33-34) – Tehran: Jibhah-'i Milli dar rah-i Ittihad-i buzurg, 1979 – 1r – 1 – us MEDOC [950]

ITTIHAD-I ISLAM VE ALMANYA / Nuri, Celal – Istanbul: Yeni Osmanli Matbaa ve Kitabhanesi, 1333 [1917] – $10.00 – us MEDOC [956]

ITTIHAD-I JAVAN – (Shumarah-'i 7-12, 19, 24-27, 30-31, 33-35, 37-39, 41-49, 51-57 (23 Murdad 1358-7 Shahrivar 1360[14 Aug 1979-29 Aug 1981])) – Tehran, 1979 – 1 reel – 1 – $115.00 – us MEDOC [950]

ITTIHAD-I MARDUM – (Cont: Sawgand. Dawrah-'i 1: shumarah-'i 1-70 (23 Mihr 1358-44 Isfand 1359[15 Oct 1979-23 Feb 1981]). Missing issues: 11-21, 46-47, 58, 61, 63-64, 66-67. Also includes Sawgand, dawrah-i 2, shumarah-i 20-22 (22 Murdad 1358-16 Mihr 1358[14 August 1979-8 October 1979])) – [Tehran]: Ittihad-i Dimukratik-i Mardum-i Iran, 1979- – 1r – 1 – $25.00 – us MEDOC [950]

ITTIHAD-I OSMANI = LA FEDERATION OTTOMANE – Geneva: Heyet-i Muettefikiyye-i Osmaniyye, 1903-19? – 9 – $25.00 – us MEDOC [956]

ITTILA'AT : 28 HAZAR RUZ-I TARIKH-I IRAN VA JAHAN – Tehran: Ittila'at, 1972?- – 1 reel – 1 – $50.00 – us MEDOC [950]

ITTILLAAT – Tihran, Iran: Muassasah-i Ittilaat, jul 10 1926- – 1 – us Res Libr [072]

Iturbide, Agustin *see*
– CORRESPONDENCIA Y DIARIO MILITAR. 1810-1814. TOMO 3
– PAPERS

Iturrios, J *see* ELIAS DE TEJADA, F. LAS DOCTRINAS POLITICAS DE LA EDAD MEDIA. MADRID, 1946

ITZEHOER WOCHENBLATT – (Title change: Nord-deutsche Rundschau, 20 Aug 1949) – Itzehoe, Germany. 1976- – ca 7r per yr – 1 – gw Mikrofilm [072]

ITZEHOER WOCHENBLATT – (Title change: Norddeutsche Rundschau, 20 Aug 1949) – Itzehoe, West Germany. 1976- – ca 7r per yr – 1 – gw Mikrofilm [072]

IUBILEI PETRA VELIKAGO / Mezhov, VI – Bibliograficheskii ukazatel'. Spb. 1881. BR-7157 2 – 8 – ne IDC [010]

IUBILEI PREDATELEI I UBI IT S, 1917-1927 / Burtsev, Vladimir Lvovich – Paris: Rapid-Impr., 1927 – 1 – CSUX88-B3963 – us Hoover Inst Photo [947]

THE IUDYCYALL OF VRYNS – London, [1527] – 4mf – 9 – ne IDC [610]

IUE / International Union of Electrical Radio and Machine Workers – 1949- – 1 – us UMI [330]

IUE NEWS – Washington, DC. v1-22. 1949-71 – 8r – 1 – us Ross [330]

IUE-CIO NEWS : 1949-1955 / International Union of Electrical, Radio and Machine Workers – (Coll title: Labor Union Periodicals, Pt 1) – 2r – 1 – $270.00 – 1-55655-239-4 – us UPA [331]

IUGO-ZAPADNYI FRONT (OBZOR FONDA NO. 102) / U.S.S.R. Army – M. 1940. TsARKKA BR-11,080 1 – 9 – ne IDC [355]

IULII CAESARIS SCALIGERI EXOTICARUM EXERCITATIONUM, LIBER QUINTUS: DE SUBTILITATE, AD HIERONYMUM CARDANUM; IN EXTREMO DUO SUNT INDICES; PRIOR BREUIUSCULUS, CONTINENS SENTENTIAS NOBILIORES; ALTER OPULENTISSIMUS, PENE OMNIA COMPLECTENS / Scaliger, Julius Caesar, – Lutetia: Ex officina typographica Michaelis Vascosani, 1557 – 1 – us U.W. Library [574]

Iung, Theodore *see* LA GUERRE ET LA SOCIETE, STRATEGIE TACTIQUE ET POLITIQUE

Iunior, Arnobius *see* OPERA MINORA

I'UNITA – Rome, IT. 1966-1974 – 42r – $2,100.00 – R63617 – us Library Micro [072]

IUNOSHESKOE DVIZHENIE V MOSKVE 1917 GOD / Atsarkin, Aleksandr Nikolaevich – Moskva: Molodai a gvardii a, 1930 – 1 – CSUX89-B6456 – us Hoover Inst Photo [947]

IUNOST' VALERIIA BRIUSOVA / Mochul'skii, K – "Novyi Zhurnal". v. 54. 1958. BR-1444 2 – 8 – ne IDC [073]

IURIDICHESKAIA BIBLIOGRAFIIA IZDAVAEMAIA DEMIDOVSKIM IURIDICHESKIM LITSEEM – v. 1-33. Iaroslav'. 1886-93; v. 1-50. 1907-17. BR-7112 2 – 8 – ne IDC [340]

IURIDICHESKAIA GAZETA – 1993 – 1 – sz Infoprint [947]

IURIDICHESKAIA GAZETA – (Backfile through 1998 $85r) – 1999- – 2r per y – 1 – $160.00 standing order – us Ross [340]

IURIDICHESKAIA LITERATURA – Annotirovannyi ukazatel' otechestvennykh bibliograficheskikh posobii, izdannykh v 1831-1970 gg. M. 1972. BR-11,258 – 9 – ne IDC [340]

IURIDICHESKIE POSLOVITSY I POGOVORKI RUSSKOGO NARODA / Illiustrov, I – M., 1885 – 1mf – 9 – R-9020/1 – ne IDC [947]

IURIDICHESKIE PREDPOSYLKI RUSSKIKH OSNOVNYKH ZAKONOV / Kotliarevskii, S A – M. 1912. BR-9510 1 – 9 – ne IDC [321]

IURIDICHESKII SLOVAR' – M., 1953 – 14mf – 9 – R-8688/1 – ne IDC [340]

IURIDICHESKII VESTNIK – Ed. by N. Kalachov. Spb. 1860 61-1864. BR-957 1 – 9 – ne IDC [340]

IURIDICHESKII VESTNIK / Moscow. Law Society. St. Petersburg. Law Society – M. 1867-92. Journal with a liberal orientation founded by the Moscow Law Society and published with the cooperation of the St. Petersburg Law Society. Articles treat theory of civil and criminal law, legal history and philosophy, international law, and so forth. Not published in second half of 1868 nor from January 1870-March 1871. Lacking: 1867-68, (9) 1885, 1892. BR-9570 1 – 9 – ne IDC [340]

IURIS ALLEGATION...ENRIQUEZ DE GUZMAN CON...SUCESION DEL CONDADO DE ALBA DE ALISTE – 1612 – 9 – 1.50f – sp Bibl Santa Ana [340]

IURIS ECCLESIASTICI GRAECORUM HISTORIA ET MONUMENTA / Pitra, J B – Romae. v1-2. 1864-68 – Dfl378.00 – ne Slangenburg [240]

IURIS NATURAE ET GENTIUM... / Audisio, G – Romae, 1852 – 5mf – 9 – ILM-1773/1 – ne IDC [340]

IURISCONSULTI PRAECLARISSIMI / Gutierrez, Juan – (Libri III. 1618. 1.50f; 9. Libri IV. 1611.1.50f; BSA; 9) – Libri II. 1618 – 9 – 1.50f – sp Bibl Santa Ana [240]

Iusdorff, J *see* AIR AVEC 24 VARIATIONS POUR L'ETUDE DE LA FLUTE, OP. 1

Iuvenal *see* DECLARACION...SOBRE LAS SATIRAS DE..

IUVENCI CARMINA / Arevalo, Faustino – 1792 – 9 – 1.50f – sp Bibl Santa Ana [780]

Iuzhakova, S N *see* BOL'SHAIA ENTSIKLOPEDIIA

IUZHNO-RUSSKII POTREBITEL' *see* IUZNYI POTREBITEL'

IUZHNYI FRONT (PROTIV VRANGELIA) 27 SENTIABRIA-10 DEKABRIA 1920 G. ORGANIZATSIIA, SOSTAV I BOEVYE DEISTVIIA / U.S.S.R. Army – Obzor, sostavlennyi po dokumentam Tsentral'nogo Arkhiva RKKA fond no. 101. Comp. by D. Oznobishim. M. 1940. TsARKKA. BR11,079 1 – 9 – ne IDC [355]

IUZHNYI KOOPERATOR – (Missing: 1913 n20. 1916 n2, 4) – Odessa, 1913-17 n2 – 36mf – 9 – COR-709/1 – ne IDC [334]

IUZHNYI MUZYKAL'NYI VESTNIK – Odessa, 1915-16 (bimonthly) – 8mf – 9 – us Ross [780]

IUZHNYI SBORNIK – Ucheno-literaturnyi zhurnal. Odessa. 1859. B-1757 2 – 8 – ne IDC [073]

IUZIO SO LA ENFERMEDAD QUE...AFLIGE A TOLEDO... / Vazquez, J – Toledo, 1631 – 1mf – 9 – sp Cultura [610]

IUZNYI POTREBITEL' – (Cont by: Iuzhno-russkii potrebitel'. Khar'kov, 1914 n1-6 – 1918 n4. Missing: 1914 n6. 1917 n2-4, 10-12. 1918 n1) – Khar'kov, 1914 n1-5 – 22mf – 9 – COR-708/1 – ne IDC [334]

IVA FIRST BAPTIST CHURCH. IVA, SOUTH CAROLINA : CHURCH RECORDS – 1906-16, 1922-49, 1967-72. Formerly: Mizpah, 1890-1912.252p – 1 – 11.34 – us Baptist [240]

IVA. PIATAIA KNIGA STIKHOV / Gorodetskii, S – Spb. 1913. BR-1124 2 – 8 – ne IDC [460]

IVAN GREET'S MASTERPIECE, ETC / Allen, Grant – London: Chatto & Windus, 1893. 05046. (Pre-1900 Canadiana) – 9 – cn C.I.H.M. [830]

Ivanoff, J *see* LES BULGARES DEVANT LE CONGRES DE LA PAIX

Ivanov, A *see*
- OLONETSKI SBORNIK
- UKAZATEL' KNIG, BROSHIUR, ZHURNAL'NYKH I GAZETNYKH STATEI I ZAMETOK NA RUSSKOM IAZYKE O CHUVASHAKH, V SVIAZI S DRUGIMI INORODTSAMI, SREDNIAGO POVOLZH'IA, S 1756 PO 1906 G. KAZAN', 1907

Ivanov, G *see*
- GORNITSA
- OSIP MANDEL'SHTAM
- OTVET G.G. STRUVE I FILIPPOVU
- PETERBURGSKIE ZIMY
- PETERBURGSKIE ZIMY IZD. IMENI CHEKHOVA
- PORTRET BEZ SKHODSTVA
- RASPAD ATOMA
- SADY
- VERESK

Ivanov, G O *see* GUMILEVE

Ivanov, I *see* STAROBALGARSKI RAZKAZI

Ivanov, P A *see* OBOZRENIE SOSTAVA I USTROISTVA REGULIARNOI RUSSKOI KAVALERII OT PETRA VELIKOGO I DO NASHIKH DNEI

Ivanov, P P *see* KHOZIAISTVO DZHUIBARSKIKH SHEIKHOV. K.ISTORII FEODAL'NOGO ZEMLEVLADENIIA V SREDNEI AZII V XVI-XVII VV

Ivanov, Pl *see*
- OPISANIE GOSUDARSTVENNOGO ARKHIVA STARYKH DEL
- SBORNIK PALEOGRAFICHESKIKH SNIMKOV S POCHERKOV DREVNEGO I NOVAGO PIS'MA RAZNYKH PERIODOV VREMENI, IZDANNYI DLIA VOSPITANNIKOV MEZHEVAGO VEDOMSTVA

Ivanov, S V *see* ALEUT HUNTING HEADGEAR AND ITS ORNAMENTATION

Ivanov, V *see*
- BOROZDY I MEZHI
- CHELOVEK
- COR ARDENS
- DIONIS I PRADIONISIISTVO
- KORMCHIIA ZVEZDY
- MLADENCHESTVO
- NEZHNAIA TAINA
- O NOVEISHIKH TEORETICHESKIKH ISKANIIAKH V OBLASTI KHUDOZHESTVENNOGO SLOVA
- PEREPISKA IZ DVUKH UGLOV
- PO ZVEZDAM
- PROMETEI
- PROZRACHNOST'
- RODNOE I VSELENSKOE
- SVET VECHERNII

Ivanov, V V *see* VSEMIRNYI KONGRESS" BAPTISTOV" V" LONDONE V" 1905 GODU

Ivanov, Vl *see*
- KAPITALY KREDITNOGO KOOPERATIVA (IKH ZNACHENIE I ORGANIZATSIIA)
- VKLADNYE OPERATSII KREDITNYKH KOOPERATIVOV

Ivanov, Viacheslav *see* ELEMENTA

Ivanov-Razumnik, R I *see*
- DUSHA FUTURIZMA
- FUTURIZM I VESHCH
- ISTORIIA RUSSKOI OBSHCHESTVENNOI MYSLI
- LITERATURA I OBSHCHESTVENNOST'
- RUSSKAIA LITERATURA OT SEMIDESIATYKH GODOV DO NASHIKH DNEI
- RUSSKAJA LITERATURA 20 VEKA (1890-1915 GG.)
- O SMYSLE ZHIZNI
- VERSHINY

IVANOVSKAI A OBLAST : ORGAN OBLISPOLKOMA – (Library has: Sept., Nov.-Dec. 1936; Jan.-Apr. 1937) – Ivanovo: Gos. izd-vo Ivanovsko i oblasti, 1936-1937. 2v – 1 – CSUX90-S201 – us Hoover Inst Photo [947]

Ivanovskii, A O *see* MAN'CHZHURSKAIA KHRESTOMATIIA

Ivask, I *see* OSIP MANDEL'SHTAM, SOBRANIE SOCHINENII

Ivask, U G *see*
- GRIGORII NIKOLAEVICH GENNADI
- OPISANIE RUSSKIKH KNIZHNIKH ZNAKOV

IVDICIVM ERASMI ALBERI, DE SPONGIA ERASMI ROTEROD... / Alber, E – [Hagenau, 1524] – 1mf – 9 – ne IDC [240]

Ivens, W G *see* A DICTIONARY OF THE LANGUAGE OF BUGOTU, SANTA ISOBEL ISLAND, SOLOMON ISLANDS

Iverach, James *see*
- EVOLUTION AND CHRISTIANITY
- IS GOD KNOWABLE?
- ST. PAUL
- THEISM IN THE LIGHT OF PRESENT SCIENCE AND PHILOSOPHY

Ives, Charles L *see* BIBLE DOCTRINE OF THE SOUL, OR, MAN'S NATURE AND DESTINY AS REVEALED

Ives, Charles Linnaeus *see*
- THE BIBLE DOCTRINE OF THE SOUL

Ives, Rollin A *see* A TREATISE ON MILITARY LAW

IVG, BERICHT UEBER DEN ERSTEN KONGRESS, ROM, 5.-10. SEPTEMBER 1955 / ed by Internationale Vereinigung fuer Germanische Sprach- und Literaturwissenschaft. Kongress – [s.l.]: Die Vereinigung, 1958 (Verona: Stamperia Valdonega) – 1 – us U.W. Library [430]

IVHS JOURNAL : R AND D, OPERATIONAL TESTING, AND DEPLOYMENT OF INTELLIGENT VEHICLE-HIGHWAY SYSTEMS / ed by Chen, Kan – 9,5,1 – us Gordon [624]

Ivimey, Joseph *see* MEMOIR OF WILLIAM FOX, ESQ. FOUNDER OF THE SUNDAY SCHOOL SOCIETY

Ivkin, A *see* NOVAIA RUSSKAIA BIBLIOTEKA, ZAKLIUCHAIUSHCHAIA V SEBE DO 15000 NAZVANII KNIG, VYSHEDSHIKH S 1850 PO 1 OKT. 1877 G. ENTSIKLOPEDICHESKII (PREDMETNYI) UKAZATEL'

Ivkov, Iu. P *see* OBZOR BIBLIOGRAFICHESKIKH IZDANII GOS. PUBLICHNOI BIBLIOTEKI ZA 1917-1957 GG

Ivnev, R *see* GEROI ROMANA

IVOR WILKS : PHYLLIS FERGUSON COLLECTION OF MATERIAL ON GHANA – Chicago, University of Chicago, Photoduplication Dept, 1974 – us Res Libr [960]

IVORY COA LA COTE D'IVIORE EN CHIFFRES : ANNUAIRE STATISTIQUE DE LA COTE D'IVOIRE 1975 / Ivory Coast. Ministere du Plan – (Coll title: African Official Statistical Serials, 1867-1982) – 3mf – 9 – £25.00 – uk Chadwyck [960]

Ivory Coast *see*
- L'ECONOMIE IVOIRIENNE
- JOURNAL OFFICIEL
- JOURNAL OFFICIEL DE LA COTE D'IVOIRE
- JOURNAL OFFICIEL DE LA REPUBLIQUE DE LA COTE D'IVOIRE
- LOI-PLAN DE DEV. ECONOMIQUE SOCIAL ET CULTUREL POUR LES ANNEES 1967, 1968, 1969 ET 1970 (LOI NO. 67-302)
- LA LOI-PROGRAMME TRIENNALE. POUR 1975-1976-1977

Ivory Coast. Conseil Economique et Social *see* RAPPORT SUR L'EVOLUTION ECONOMIQUE ET SOCIALE DE LA COTE D'IVOIRE, 1960-1964

Ivory Coast. Ministere de l'Education Nationale et de la Recherche Scientifique *see* PROGRAMME D'EDUCATION CIVIQUE ET MORALE DANS L'ENSEIGNEMENT PRIMAIRE

Ivory Coast. Ministere des Finances *see* PERSPECTIVES DECENNALES DE DEVELOPPEMENT ECONOMIC, SOCIAL ET CULTUREL (1960-1970)

Ivory Coast. Ministere du Plan *see*
- DEUXIEME ESQUISSE DU PLAN QUINQUENNAL DE DEVELOPPEMENT 1971-1975
- IVORY COA LA COTE D'IVIORE EN CHIFFRES
- PLAN QUINQUENNAL DE DEVELOPPEMENT ECONOMIQUE, SOCIAL ET CULTUREL 1971-1975
- TROISIEME PLAN QUADRIENNAL DE DEVELOPPEMENT ECONOMIQUE ET SOCIAL, 1958-1962

Ivory Coast. Ministry of Information *see* DISCOURS PRONONCES PAR FELIX HOUPHOUET-BOIGNY

Ivory Coast. Office National de Formation Professionnelle *see*
- ENSEIGNEMENT TECHNIQUE ET FORMATION PROFESSIONNELLE
- LE SYSTEME DE FORMATION EN COTE D'IVOIRE

L'IVROGNERIE ET LA LOI DES LICENCES / Bedard, J -E – [Quebec: s.n., 1903 ?]. SEM105P1673 – 1mf – 9 – Can$2.25 – cn Bibl Nat [971]

IVRY ANOKHI – (Missing 1864/1865-1865/1866 v1-2. 1882/1883 v19) – Brody. v1-26. 1864-1890 – 157mf – 9 – J-91-44/1 – ne IDC [072]

IVSTIFICATIE DES MAGISTRAETS TOT LEYDEN IN HOLLANDT, TEGHENS DE CALUMNIEN, TER SAKEN VANDE DIFFERENTEN / Coornhert, D V – 1597. BME-242 1 – 9 – ne IDC [240]

IVW-AUFLAGENMELDUNGEN – (Publ started in Wiesbaden) – Bonn. 1950-55 – 5r – 1 – gw Mikrofilm [072]

Iwan-Mueller, Ernest Bruce *see* LORD MILNER AND SOUTH AFRICA

Iwanowa, Gora *see* DER NATIONALE GEDANKE BEI HEINRICH VON KLEIST

I-WEN TSA-CHIH – (Arts and Literary Magazine). v. 1 (1-6), v. 2 (1-12), v. 3 (1, 2). Peking. 1943-45. BCH-792 2 – 8 – ne IDC [700]

Iyer, LAK *see*
- KRISHNA DIWAN BAHADUR. THE TRAVANCORE TRIBES AND CASTES
- THE MYSORE TRIBES AND CASTES

IYO WILIWE NTA RUNGU / Kagame, Alexis – Kabgayi [Rwanda]: Les Editions Royales, 1949 – 1 – us Res Libr [960]

IZ CHEGO VYROSLI KOOPERATIVY / Kablukov, N A – M., 1916 – 1mf – 9 – COR-37/1 – ne IDC [334]

IZ CHUZHEZEMNYKH POETOV / Bal'mont, K D – Spb. 1909. BR-519 2 – 8 – ne IDC [460]

IZ DEREVNI / Engel'gardt, A N – 12 pisem 1872-87. Ed. 3. Spb. 1897. BR-10,570-2 – 8 – ne IDC [460]

IZ EVREISKIKH POETOV / Khodasevich, V – Spb. 1922. BR-695 2 – 8 – ne IDC [460]

IZ ISTORII FABRIK I ZAVODOV MOSKVY I MOSKOVSKOI GUBERNII (KONETS XVIII-NACHALO XX V.) – Obzor dokumentov. Moscow, 1968.335p. BR-10,941/1 – 9 – ne IDC [025]

IZ ISTORII GORODA MOSKVY / Nazarevskii, V – Moscow: Sytin Publishers, 1896 – 4mf – 9 – $40.00 – us Ross [947]

IZ ISTORII GRAZHDANSKOI VOINY V ROSSII / Bystrianskii, Vadim – Peterburg: Gos. idz-vo, 1921 – 1 – CSUX88-B1824 – us Hoover Inst Photo [355]

IZ ISTORII KNIGI, BIBLIOTECHNOGO DELA I BIBLIOGRAFII V SIBIRI / Akademiia nauk SSSR. Sibirskoe otdelenie, Gosudarstvennaia publichnaia nauchno- tekhnicheskaia biblioteka; ed by Kartashov, N S – Novosibirsk: Nauka, Sibirskoe otd-nie, 1969 – us Res Libr [947]

IZ ISTORII KRAKHA LEVYKH ESEROV V TURKESTANE / Nikishov, P P – Frunze: Kyrgyzstan, 1965. 178p – 2mf – 9 – ne IDC [320]

IZ ISTORII RABOCHIKH ARTELEI NA ZAPADE I V ROSSII : OT UTOPISTOV DO NASHIKH DNEI / Pazhitnov, K A – Pg., 1924 – 3mf – 9 – COR-87/1 – ne IDC [334]

IZ ISTORII RANNEGO RUSSKOGO SIMVOLIZMA / Gudzii, N – "Iskusstvo". nr. 4. 1927. BR-3268 2 – 8 – ne IDC [460]

IZ ISTORII RASKOLA PERVOI POLOVINY 18 VEKA. (PO NEIZDANNYM PAMIATNIKAM) / Smirnov, P S – Spb. 1908. BR-7877 2 – 8 – ne IDC [947]

IZ ISTORII RUSSKOI DO REVOLIUTSIONNOI ARKHEOGRAFII / Sofinov, PG – Moscow, 1957. 157p. Survey of documentary publication projects in Russia before the Revolution. BR-10,773/1 – 9 – ne IDC [070]

IZ ISTORII RUSSKOI DRAMY / Rezanov, V I – (Shkol'-nye deistva XVII-XVIII vv. i teatr iezuitov). M. 1910. BR-7812 2 – 8 – ne IDC [460]

IZ ISTORII RUSSKOI FILOSOFII 18 I 19 VEKOV / ed by Shchipanov, I I – Sbornik statei. M. 1952. BR-7841 2 – 8 – ne IDC [100]

IZ ISTORII TSENTRAL'NOGO GOSUDARSTVENNOGO ARKHIVA DREVNIKH AKTOV SSSR / Dremina, G A – Moscow, 1959. 69p. BR-10,709/1 – 9 – ne IDC [947]

IZ ISTORII VILENSKOI PUBLICHNOI BIBLIOTEKI / Milovidov, A I – Vil'na. 1911. BR-4624 2 – 8 – ne IDC [020]

IZ LEKTSII PO DIPLOMATIKE, CHITANNOI V SPB. ARKHEOLOGICHESKOM INSTITUTE / Likhachev, N P – St. Petersburg, 1905-06.BR/10,036/2 – 8 – ne IDC [460]

IZ MIROVOI POEZII / Bal'mont, K D – Berlin. 1921. BR-520 2 – 8 – ne IDC [460]

IZ MRAKA K SVETU / Minskii, N – Izbrannye stikhotvoreniia. Berlin. Petersburg. M. Izd. 1922. BR-804 2 – 8 – ne IDC [460]

IZ NEDAVNIAGO PROSHLAGO / Gershuni, Grigorii Andreevich – Moskva: "Zemli a i voli a", 1917 – 1 – CSUX89-B7329 – us Hoover Inst Photo [947]

IZ NEDR T SARSKOGO FLOTA K VELIKOMU OKTI ABRI U : IZ VOSPOMINANI I O REVOLIUTSII 1917-1927 / Dybenko, Pavel Efimovich – Moskva: "Voen. vestnik", 1928 – 1 – CSUX89-B6550 – us Hoover Inst Photo [320]

IZ NEOPUBLIKOVANNAGO ILI ZABYTOGO / Erenburg, I – Prostor (Alma Ata), 4. 1965. BR-3654 2 – 8 – ne IDC [460]

IZ PROSHLOGO RUSSKOI ZHURANLISTIKI / Evgen'ev-Maksimov, V & Maksimov, D – Stat'i materiali. L. 1930. BR-2070 2 – 8 – ne IDC [380]

IZ PROSHLOGO RUSSKOI ZHURNALISTIKI / Maksimov, D & Evgen'ev-Maksimov, V – L. 1930. BR-3325 2 – 8 – ne IDC [073]

IZ RAZYSKANII O SOCHINENIIAKH V.A. ZHUKOVSKAGO / Rezanov, V I – 2v. Spb. 1906-16 – 8 – BR-7813 2 – ne IDC [947]

IZ RUSSKIKH POETOV – Berlin. 1921. BR-1854 2 – 8 – ne IDC [460]

IZ TRAGEDII "PROLOG, ILI SON VO SNE" / Akhmatova, A – Novyi mir 6. M. 1964. BR-1098 2 – 8 – ne IDC [460]

IZ VOSPOMINANI I POLITICHESKOGO KATORZHANINA : 1908-1914 GG / Genkin, Iosif Isaevich – Petrograd: Izd. Petrogradskogo soveta rabochikh i krasnoarme iskikh deputatov, 1919 – 1 – CSUX89-B7323 – us Hoover Inst Photo [320]

IZ VOSPOMINANII / Chukovskii, K – Sovetskii pisatel'. M. 1959. BR-2028 2 – 8 – ne IDC [460]

IZ VOSPOMINANII I PEREPISKI FABRICHNAGO INSPEKTORA PERVAGO PRIZYVA / Ianzhul, I I – Spb, 1907 – 9 – BR-10 085 1 – ne IDC [338]

IZ ZAPISOK AGRARNIKA / Belokurov, Ivan Nikolaevich – Moskva: Izd-vo Vses. ob-va politkatorzhan i ss.-poselent sev, 1926 – 1 – CSUX88-B1898 – us Hoover Inst Photo [630]

IZ ZHIZNI RUSSKIKH DEIATELEI 18 VEKA / Korsakov, D A – Kazan'. 1891. BR-6060 2 – 8 – ne IDC [460]

Izaguirre, Fray Bernardino *see* HISTORIA DE LAS MISIONES FRANCISCANAS

Izard, John *see* ASSESSING LEARNING ACHIEVEMENT

Izates, Esther *see* BRIEFE AN EINE CHRISTLICHE FREUNDIN UEBER DIE GRUNDWAHRHEITEN DES JUDENTHUMS

IZBANDA – (La Victoire). no. 3-6. Paris. avr-nov 1934 – 1 – fr A.C.R.P.P. [073]

IZBORNIK / Gorodetskii, S – Stikhi 1905-1915 gg. M. 1916. BR-1125 2 – 8 – ne IDC [460]

IZBRANNAIA BIBLIOTEKA RUSSKAGO GENEALOGA. (BIBLIOGRAFICHESKII OPYT). 1 / Savelov, L M – M. 1895. BR-7248 2 – 8 – ne IDC [920]

IZBRANNOE / Aseev, N – M. 1948. BR-899 2 – 8 – ne IDC [460]

IZBRANNOE / Esenin, Sergei – M. 1946. BR-1052 – 8 – ne IDC [460]

IZBRANNOE / Esenin, Sergei – M. 1952. BR-1053 2 – 8 – ne IDC [460]

IZBRANNOE / Gumilev, Nikolai Sepanovich – S predisloviem N. Otsupa. Paris. 1959. BR-1140 2 – 8 – ne IDC [460]

IZBRANNOE / Kamenskii, V – L. 1948. BR-941 2 – 8 – ne IDC [460]

IZBRANNOE / Maiakovskii, Vladimir – M. 1943. BR-969 2 – 8 – ne IDC [460]

IZBRANNOE / Maiakovskii, Vladimir – M. 1948. BR-971 2 – 8 – ne IDC [460]

IZBRANNOE / Maiakovskii, Vladimir – M., L. 1945. BR-970 2 – 8 – ne IDC [460]

IZBRANNYE PEREVODY / Pasternak, B – M. 1940. BR-1013 2 – 8 – ne IDC [460]

IZBRANNYE PROIZVEDENIIA / Esenin, Sergei – 2v. Regensburg. 1946. BR-1054 2 – 8 – ne IDC [460]

IZBRANNYE PROIZVEDENIIA / Kheraskov, M M – L. 1961. BR-6127 2 – 8 – ne IDC [460]

IZBRANNYE PROIZVEDENIIA / Maiakovskii, Vladimir – M. 1949. BR-972 2 – 8 – ne IDC [460]

IZBRANNYE PROIZVEDENIIA / Reisner, L – M. 1958. BR-1230 2 – 8 – ne IDC [947]

IZBRANNYE PROIZVEDENIIA RUSSKIKH MYSLITELEI VTOROI POLOVINY 18 VEKA / ed by Shchipanov, I I – 2v. M. 1952. BR-7840 2 – 8 – ne IDC [000]

IZBRANNYE PROIZVEDENIIA V DVUKH TOMAKH / Aseev, N – v. 1: Stikhotvoreniia. v. 2: Poemy i perovody. 1953. BR-900 2 – 8 – ne IDC [460]

IZBRANNYE PROIZVEDENIIA V DVUKH TOMAKH / Maiakovskii, Vladimir – 2v. M. 1953. BR-973 2 – 8 – ne IDC [460]

IZBRANNYE RABOTY I STAT'I / Boiarenko, A G – M. 2v. 1925-26 – 6mf – 9 – COR-195/1 – ne IDC [334]

IZBRANNYE SOCHINENIIA / Novikov, N I – M., L. 1951. BR-7732 2 – 8 – ne IDC [950]

IZBRANNYE STATI. FILOSOFIIA, KRITIKA, POLEMIKA / Antonovich, M A – Leningrad, 1938. BR-10,545 1 – 9 – ne IDC [100]

IZBRANNYE STIKHI / Aseev, N – M. 1930. BR-901 2 – 8 – ne IDC [460]

IZBRANNYE STIKHI / Aseev, N – M. 1938. BR-902 2 – 8 – ne IDC [460]

IZBRANNYE STIKHI / Aseev, N – M. 1947. BR-903 2 – 8 – ne IDC [460]

IZBRANNYE STIKHI / Maiakovskii, Vladimir – M. 1932. BR-974 2 – 8 – ne IDC [460]

IZBRANNYE STIKHI / Maiakovskii, Vladimir – M. 1936. BR-975 2 – 8 – ne IDC [460]

IZBRANNYE STIKHOTVORENIIA I POEMY / Aseev, N – M. 1951. BR-904 2 – 8 – ne IDC [460]

IZBRANNYE STIKHOTVORENIIA. IZD. IMENI CHEKHOVA / Akhmatova, A – New York. 1952. BR-1095 2 – 8 – ne IDC [460]

IZBRANNYIA SOCHINENIIA / Karamzin, Nikolai M – (Pervyi period, 1783-1801). pt. 1. M. 1884. BR-6200 2 – 8 – ne IDC [460]

IZBRANNYIA STICHOTVORENIIA V ODNOM TOME / Esenin, Sergei – Paris. 1927. BR-1055 2 – 8 – ne IDC [460]

Izd Obshchestva dlia sodeistviia arte l'nomu delo v Rossii *see* ARTEL'NOE DELO

Izd Soiuza soiuzov promyslovoi i proizvoditel'no-trudovoi koop. Sev. r-na "Artel'trudsoiuza" *see* ARTEL'NOE DELO

IZDANIE VSEROSSIISKOGO TSENTRAL'NOGO SOIUZA POTREBITEL'SKIKH OBSHCHESTV *see* OB'EDINENIE

IZDANIIA PROIZVEDENIIA KLASSIKOV MARKSIZMA-LENINIZMA V SSSR / Levin, LA & Savitskaia, R M – M. 1955. BR-5716 2 – 8 – ne IDC [335]

IZDANIIA TSENTROSOIUZA ZA 25 LET (1898-1923) : SISTEMATICHESKII UKAZATEL' / Merkulov, A V – Moscow, 1924 – 2mf – 9 – COR-536/1 – ne IDC [334]

IZGADDA = PERSIAN AMERICAN COURIER – New York City: J E Werda, sep 12, 1917-jun 30, 1920 – us Res Libr [071]

Izgoev, A S *see*
- OBSHCHINNOE PRAVO
- RUSSKOE OBSHCHESTVO I REVOLIUTSIIA
- ZAMECHANIIA K PROEKTU OBSHCHEGO KOOPERATIVNOGO ZAKONA

IZGREV – (Cont by: Vecherni Novini) – Sofia, Bulgaria. Oct 29 1944-July 1951 – 8r – 1 – us L of C Photodup [072]

IZGREV – Sofia. Bulgaria. -d. 25 Nov 1944-25 Jan 1948. (8 reels) – 1 – uk British Libr Newspaper [949]

IZIASHCHNAIA LITERATURA – v. 7. Spb. 1883-85. Lacking: 1885 (1). B-1741 2 – 8 – ne IDC [460]

IZLER – Giresun, 1925-1927 – 9 – $20.00 – us MEDOC [956]

IZLOZHENIE POSTANOVLENII O TSENZURE I PECHATI – St. Petersburg, Imp. Akad. Nauk, 1865. iv, 221p. BR-9243 1 – 9 – ne IDC [380]

IZMENENIE POLOZHENIIA ZHENSHCHINY I DEMOGRAFICHESKOE RAZVITIE SEMI : PO MATERIALAM SOTSIALNO-DEMOGRAFICHESKIKH OBSLEDOVANII / Volkov, A – (Filmed with: Dinamika izmeneniia polozheniia dagestanskoi zhenshchiny i semiia/S Gadzhieva) – Moskva: In-t konkretnykh sotsialnykh issledovanii AN SSSR, 1972 – us Res Libr [947]

IZMENENIIA PROFESSIONALNO-KVALIFIKATSIONNOI STRUKTURY ZHENSKOGO TRUDA I SEMIA / Sonin, M – (Filmed with: Dinamika izmeneniia polozheniia dagestanskoi zhenshchiny i semiia/S Gadzhieva) – Moskva: In-t konkretnykh sotsialnykh issledovanii AN SSSR, 1981 – us Res Libr [947]

IZMENENIIA STRUKTURY SOTSIALNYKH ROLEI ZHENSHCHIN V RAZVITOM SOTSIALISTICHESKOM OBSHCHESTVE I MODEL SEMI / Iankova, Z – (Filmed with: Dinamika izmeneniia polozheniia dagestanskoi zhenshchiny i semiia/S Gadzhieva) – Moskva: In-t konkretnykh sotsialnykh issledovanii AN SSSR 1972 – us Res Libr [947]

IZMIR DOKUZ EYLUEL SERGISI – Izmir. Sahib-i Imtiyaz ve Mueduer-i Mes'ul: Mecdi Sadreddin. Nos. 4-7 (8), 9-16, 18 (17), 18 (22), (7-25 Eyluel 1927) – 9 – $35.00 – us MEDOC [956]

IZO : VESTNIK OTDELA IZOBRAZITELNYKH ISKUSSTV N.K.P. VESTNIK OTDELA IZOBRAZITELNYKH ISKUSSTV N.K.P. – (Includes c.1: no.1 1921:Mar.10) – Moskva: Otdel, 1921- – 1 – CSUXAKB0408-S – us Hoover Inst Photo [947]

IZOBLICHENIE SHTUNDISTSKOI BOGOPROTIVNOI ERESI NA OSNOVANII SVYASHCHENNAGO PISANIYA, SVYASHCHENNAGO PREDANIYA I ISTORICHESKIKH" PAMYATNIKOV" = AN EXPOSURE OF THE IMPIOUS STUNDIST HERESY ON THE BASIS OF THE SACRED SCRIPTURE, HOLY TRADITION AND HISTORIC RELICS / Opoichenko, Iakov – Nikolaev, 1891 – 1r – 1 – $9.24 – us Baptist [240]

IZOL'DA / Odoevsteva, I – Roman. Paris. 1929. BR-1224 2 – 8 – ne IDC [460]

IZOTOPY / Selinov, I P – Moskva: Nauka. v3. 1970 – us Res Libr [072]

IZQUIERDA – Montevideo. Nacional, popular, socialista. Ana9o 1, no. 1-ana9o 2, no. 70; Jan. 12, 1968-July 11, 1969. Missing: no. 68, 1969 – 1 – 35.00r – us Hoover Inst Photo [335]

LA IZQUIERDA LIBERAL – Badajoz, 1922. 1 numero – 5 – sp Bibl Santa Ana [073]

LA IZQUIERDA NACIONAL Y EL FIP / Galasso, Norberto – Buenos Aires: Centro Editor de America Latina, 1983 – 1 – CSUXAHZ6188-B – us Hoover Inst Photo [320]

IZQUIERDA, PERONISMO Y SOCIALISMO NACIONAL / Eggers Lan, Conrado – Buenos Aires: Ediciones Busqueda, 1972 – 1 – CSUXADJ8463-B – us Hoover Inst Photo [320]

IZQUIERDA REPUBLICANA – Plasencia y despues Caceres, 1832 – 5 – sp Bibl Santa Ana [073]

Izquierdo, Adolfo *see* EL PADRE LA CALLE (PRIMER CENTENARIO DE SU MUERTE)

Izquierdo Hernandez, Manuel *see* GODOY

IZRAELITA – Warsaw. 1-25, 27-43, 45-48. 1866-90, 1892-1908, 1910-13 – 1 – us NY Public [073]

IZSELJENEC – Sao Paolo, Brazil, 1930 – 1mf or 1 reel – 9,1 – us I.H.R.C. [972]

IZSLEDOVANIIA, ZAMECHANIIA I LEKTSII O RUSSKOI ISTORII / Pogodin, M P – v. 1-7. M. 1846-57. BR-8308 2 – 8 – ne IDC [947]

IZTOCHNIIAT VAPROS; POLITICHESKA I DIPLOMATICHESKA ISTORIIA / Genov, G P – v. 1-2. Sofiia. 1925-26. BR-3861 2 – 8 – ne IDC [940]

IZUCHENIE RAIONA I POSTROENIE GODOVOGO OPERATIVNO-KHOZIAISTVENNOGO PLANA SEL'SKOKHOZIAISTVENNOGO KREDITNOGO TOVARISHCHESTVA / Natsentov, D I & Vasys', IM – M., 1929 – 2mf – 9 – COR-397/1 – ne IDC [334]

IZVESTIA – Moscow. U.S.S.R. 1961- – 1 – us UMI [072]

IZVESTII A AZERBA IDZHANSKOGO T SENTRALNOGO STATISTICHESKOGO UPRAVLENII A – (Includes c.1: 1922:Jan./Feb.) – Baku: Upravlenie, 1921 – 1 – CSUXAKZ0159-S – us Hoover Inst Photo [947]

IZVESTII A BRI ANSKOGO GUBERNSK. ISPOLNITELNOGO KOMETETA SOVETOV RABOCHIKH, KRESTI ANSKIKH I KRASNOARME ISKIKH DEPUTATOV I GUBKOMA R.K.B. (B) [SIC] – (Includes c.1: 1921:Nov.7) – Briansk: Bri anskii gubispolkom, 19uu – 1 – CSUXAHZ3158-S – us Hoover Inst Photo [947]

IZVESTII A DANILOVSKOGO UEZDNOGO ISPOLNITELNOGO KOMITETA SOVETOV KRESTI ANSKIKH, RABOCHIKH I KRASNOARME ISKIKH DEPUTATOV – (Includes c.1: 1921:Nov.5) – Danilov: Uispolkom, 19uu – 1 – CSUXANR4597-S – us Hoover Inst Photo [947]

IZVESTII A ELATOMSKOGO UEZDNOGO KOMITETA ROSSI ISK. KOMMUNI PARTII (BOLSHEVIKOV) – (Includes c.1: 1921:Nov.7) – Sasovo: Ukompart, 1920 – 1 – CSUXANR4553-S – us Hoover Inst Photo [947]

IZVESTII A GLAVNOGO NEFTI ANOGO KOMITETA – (Includes c.1: 1918:Dec.-1919:Jan.; 1919:Apr.-May) – [Moskva: Komitet, 1918-1919] – 1 – CSUXAKY6116-S – us Hoover Inst Photo [947]

IZVESTII A GLAVPOLITPROSVETA – (Includes c.1: no.1 1921:Sept.//) – [Moskva]: Gos. izd-vo, 1921 – 1 – CSUXAKZ3057-S – us Hoover Inst Photo [947]

IZVESTII A KALI AZINSKOGO UISPOLKOMA, UEZDNOGO KOMITETA ROS. KOM PAR (BOLSHEVIKOV) I UEZDNOGO OTDELENII A ROSTA – (Includes c.1: 1921:Nov.6) – Kaliazin: Gos. tip., 1918 – 1 – CSUXALC3359-S – us Hoover Inst Photo [947]

IZVESTII A KERCHENSKOGO IKRUZHNOGO ISPOLKOMA I OKRKOMA RKP – (Includes c.1: 1922:Mar.12) – [Kerch: s.n., 1921 – 1 – CSUXANR5211-S – us Hoover Inst Photo [947]

IZVESTII A KHLOPCHATO-BUMAZHNO I PROMYSHLENNOSTI : ORGAN VSESOI UZNOGO OBEDINENII A KHLOPCH.-BUMAZHNO I PROMYSHLENNOSTI – (Includes c.1: v.2:no.6 1932:June-v.2:no.12 (1932:Dec.)) – Moskva: Gos. izd-vo legko i promyshlennosti, 1931 – 1 – CSUXAKZ1596-S – us Hoover Inst Photo [947]

IZVESTII A KOMISSARIATA GORODSKIKH KHOZI A ISTV SOI UZA KOMMUN SEVERNO I OBLASTI – (Includes c.1: no.1 1918:Sept.25, no.3/4-no.5/6, no.8, no.10; no.12-no.14, no.16, no.19, no.23-no.24/25 1918:Dec.21) – [Petrograd]: Komissariat, 1918- – 1 – CSUXAKY5420-S – us Hoover Inst Photo [947]

IZVESTII A (MOSCOW,R.S.F.S.R.: 1921) *see* IZVESTII A VYSSHEGO SOVETA NARODNOGO KHOZI A ISTVA

IZVESTII A NARODNOGO KOMISSARIATA PO PRODOVOLSTVII U – (Includes c.1: 1918:no.1-no.22/23; 1919:no.1/2-no.17/20; 1920:no.1/2-no.3/5) – Moskva: Komissariat, 1918-1920 – 1 – CSUXAKY5580-S – us Hoover Inst Photo [947]

IZVESTII A NARODNOGO KOMISSARIATA PO PRODOVOLSTVII U : KRESTI ANSKI I NOMER – (Includes c.1: no.6 1920:Nov.7) – Moskva: Komissariat, 19uu – 1 – CSUXAKY5586-S – us Hoover Inst Photo [947]

IZVESTII A NARODNOGO KOMISSARIATA PO PRODOVOLSTVII U NOV. 1918- *see* IZVESTII A NARODNOGO KOMISSARIATA PO PRODOVOLSTVII U

IZVESTII A NARODNOGO KOMISSARIATA ZDRAVOOKHRANENII A – (Library has: Aug. 25 1918; Feb. 1, May 25, July 15 1919; Mar. 15, Aug. 10, Nov. 1, no 7/11 1920) – Moskva: Komissariat, 1918-1925. 8v – 1 – CSUX89-S608 – us Hoover Inst Photo [947]

IZVESTII A PETROGRADSKAGO GORODSKOGO OBSHCHESTVENNAGO UPRAVLENII A – (Includes c.1: no.25 1918:Apr.17-no.26, no.32-no.47; no.49-no.66, no.68-no.69 1918:Sept.21) – [Petrograd]: Upravlenie, -1918 – 1 – CSUXAKY5391-S – us Hoover Inst Photo [947]

IZVESTII A PETROGRADSKAGO GORODSKOGO OBSHCHESTVENNAGO UPRAVLENII A NO. 55-NO. 63 *see* IZVESTII A PETROGRADSKAGO GORODSKOGO OBSHCHESTVENNAGO UPRAVLENII A

IZVESTII A PETROGRADSKOGO GORODSKOGO OBSHCHESTVENNOGO UPRAVLENII A NO. 64/65-NO. 69 *see* IZVESTII A PETROGRADSKAGO GORODSKOGO OBSHCHESTVENNAGO UPRAVLENII A

IZVESTII A SAMARSKOGO GUBERNSKOGO SOI UZA POTREBITELNYKH OBSHCHESTV – (Includes c.1: no.10 1921:Aug.1) – Samara: Soi uz, 1920 – 1 – CSUXAKY6082-S – us Hoover Inst Photo [947]

IZVESTII A SARATOVSKOGO SOVETA RABOCHIKH I KR.-ARM. DEPUTATOV, GUBISPOLKOMA, GUBKOMA VKP I GUBPROFSOVETA *see* IZVI ESTII A SARATOVSKAGO SOVIETA RABOCHIKH, SOLDATSKIKH I KRESTI ANSKIKH DEPUTATOV I RA IONNAGO ISPOLNITELNAGO KOMITETA

IZVESTII A SOVETA RABOCHIKH I KRESTI AN. DEPUTATOV GORODA ROSTOVA, I AROSLAVSKO I GUB – (Includes c.1: 1919:Nov.7) – [Rostov]: Tip. A.Kh. Oppel, 1918 – 1 – CSUXANR5178-S – us Hoover Inst Photo [947]

IZVESTII A SOVETOV DEPUTATOV TRUDI ASHCHIKHSI A SSSR *see* ALFAVITNO-PREDMETNYI UKAZATEL K DEKRETAM, POSTANOVLENIIAM I RASPORI AZHENIIAM

IZVESTII A T SENTRALNOGO KOMITETA VSESOI UZNOGO LENINSKOGO KOMMUNISTICHESKOGO SOI UZA MOLODEZHI – (Includes c.1: v.14:no.9 1933:May) – Moskva: Molodai a gvardii a, 192u – 1 – CSUXAKY6401-S – us Hoover Inst Photo [335]

IZVESTII A VITEBSKOGO GUBISPOLKOMA I GUBKOMA R.K.P. (BOLSHEVIKOV) – (Includes c.1: 1919:Nov.7; 1921:Nov.7; 1922:Mar.12) – Vitebsk: [s.n.], 191u – 1 – CSUXANR5114-S – us Hoover Inst Photo [947]

IZVESTII A VSEBASHKIRSKOGO T SENTRALNOGO ISPOLNITELNOGO KOMITETA SOVETOV RABOCHIKH, KRESTI ANSKIKH, KRASNOARME ISKIKH DEPUTATOV I BASHKIRSKOGO OBLASTNOGO KOMITETA RKP (BOLSHEVIKOV) – (Includes c.1: 1921:Nov.6) – Sterlitamak: Bashgosizdatelstvo, 1920 – 1 – CSUXANR5098-S – us Hoover Inst Photo [947]

IZVESTII A VSETATARSKOGO T SENTRALNOGO ISPOLNITELN. KOMITETA SOVETOV R., K. I K.D., OBLASTNOGO KOMITETA R.K.P. (B). I KAZANSKOGO SOVETA R. I K. DEPUTATOV – (Includes c.1: 1922:Mar.12) – Kaznan: TATROSTA, 19uu – 1 – CSUXAHZ3214-S – us Hoover Inst Photo [947]

IZVESTII A VYSHNEVOLOT SKOGO UEZDNOGO SOVDEPA – (Includes c.1: 1919:Nov.7) – [Vyshni i Volochek]: Ispolnitelny i komitet, 1918 – 1 – CSUXAKG2029-S – us Hoover Inst Photo [947]

IZVESTII A VYSSHEGO SOVETA NARODNOGO KHOZI A ISTVA – (Library has: 1921-1922; issues missing after March, 1922) – Moskva: [s.n.], 1921- – 1 – CSUX89-S583 – us Hoover Inst Photo [947]

IZVESTII A VYSSHEGO SOVETA NARODNOGO KHOZI A ISTVA NO. 5- *see* IZVI ESTII A VYSSHAGO SOVI ETA NARODNAGO KHOZI A ISTVA

IZVESTIIA – 1917 – 1 – sz Infoprint [947]

IZVESTIIA – (1995-98 4r $200. Backfile 1917-94 $85r. No of reels varies from yr to yr) – 1999- – 3r per y – 1 – $200.00 standing order – us Ross [072]

IZVESTIIA – 3. Garino-Amgunskaia ekspeditsiia, 1926 g. L. 1929. BR-3228 2 – 8 – ne IDC [370]

IZVESTIIA – In 1926 cont. as: Severo-kavkazskogo universiteta. Rostov na Donu. 1918-28. Lacking: 1918-24. BR-5834 2 – 8 – ne IDC [073]

IZVESTIIA – Moscow: Izvestiia, 1917- – 2mf – 9 – $199.95y – us East View [320]

IZVESTIIA – Nos. 7-129. 1867-1917. Incomplete – 1 – 92.00 – us L of C Photodup [306]

IZVESTIIA – NR. 1-3. Spb. 1911. BR-4129 2 – 8 – ne IDC [460]

IZVESTIIA – v. 1. Iakutsk. 1915. BR-3224 2 – 8 – ne IDC [947]

IZVESTIIA – v. 1. Vologda. 1922. BR-3242 2 – 8 – ne IDC [370]

IZVESTIIA – v. 1-10. Perm'. 1922-36. Lacking: 1932-33, v. 8. BR-1759 2 – 8 – ne IDC [370]

IZVESTIIA – v. 1-10. Spb. 1852-61. B-186 2 – 8 – ne IDC [072]

IZVESTIIA – v. 1-2. Irkutsk. 1934-35. Lacking: 1934 (1). BR-3223 2 – 8 – ne IDC [370]

IZVESTIIA – v. 1-2. L. 1928-30. BR-3229 2 – 8 – ne IDC [370]

IZVESTIIA – v. 1-3. Vologda. 1914-16. BR-3243 2 – 8 – ne IDC [370]

IZVESTIIA – v. 1-33 (4). Kazan'. 1878-1925. Lacking: 1922, v. 32 (3-4). B-1432 2 – 8 – ne IDC [930]

IZVESTIIA – v. 1-4. Odessa. 1912-14. Lacking: 1912, v. 1 (1-5, 9-12); 1913, v. 2 (2, 9-12); 1914, v. 3 (7-12); 1915, v. 4 (7-12). BR-4314 2 – 8 – ne IDC [370]
IZVESTIIA – v. 1-4. Petrograd, Tiflis. 1923-27. BR-3225 2 – 8 – ne IDC [930]
IZVESTIIA – v. 1-4. Tiflis. 1904-15. Lacking: 1915 (4). BR-3226 2 – 8 – ne IDC [930]
IZVESTIIA – v. 1-53. 1887-1916. Lacking: 1887-96, v. 1-25; 1904, v. 36; 1905-06, v. 38; 1909-13, v. 42-50. B-1490 2 – 8 – ne IDC [025]
IZVESTIIA – v. 1-66. Spb. 1901-18. (v. 63-65, 1917-18 as Izvestiia Arkheologicheskoi kommissii. v. 66, 1918 as Izvestiia Gosudarstvennoi Rossiiskoi arkheologicheskoi kommissii). B-1430 2 – 8 – ne IDC [073]
IZVESTIIA – v. 1-7. M. 1912-16. Lacking: 1914, v. 4. BR-4126 2 – 8 – ne IDC [370]
IZVESTIIA – v. 1-84. Tomsk. 1889-1929. Lacking: v. 83. B-1747 2 – 8 – ne IDC [073]
IZVESTIIA – v. 1-9. Spb. 1898-1903 – 8 – ne IDC [370]
IZVESTIIA – Vladivostok. 1899-1916. Lacking: 1911 12 (44). BR-3419 2 – 8 – ne IDC [073]
IZVESTIIA – Moskva: Izd-vo "Izvestiia", [1991-]. jan-dec 1992 – us Res Libr [072]
IZVESTIIA AKADEMII NAUK SSSR – Otdelenie Literatury i iazyka. Moscow, 1940-71.v1-30.BR/5832/2 – 8 – ne IDC [500]
IZVESTIIA AKADEMII NAUK SSSR = BULLETIN DE L'ACADEMIE DES SCIENCES DE L'URSS. CLASSE DES SCIENCES TECHNIQUES : OTDELENIE TEKHNICHESKIKH NAUK – Moskva: Izd-vo Akademii nauk SSSR, [-1958]. 1950-52 – us Res Libr [500]
IZVESTIIA AKADEMII NAUK SSSR = BULLETIN DE L'ACADEMIE DES SCIENCES DE L'USSR. SERIE BIOLOGIQUE : SERIIA BIOLOGICHESKAIA – Moskva: Izd-vo Akademii nauk SSSR, 1939-92. n2. 1950-52 – us Res Libr [574]
IZVESTIIA AKADEMII NAUK SSSR = BULLETIN OF THE ACADEMY OF SCIENCES OF THE USSR. PHYSICAL SERIES, 1954-91 : SERIIA FIZICHESKAIA – Moskva: Izd-vo Akademii nauk SSSR, [-1992]. v14-16 n2. 1950-52 – us Res Libr [500]
IZVESTIIA AKADEMII NAUK SSSR : SERIIA GEOFIZICHESKAIA – Moskva: Izd-vo Akademii nauk SSSR, 1951-64. n2-6. 1951; n1-3 1952 – 4r – 1 – us Res Libr [900]
IZVESTIIA AKADEMII NAUK SSSR : SERIIA GEOGRAFICHESKAIA – Moskva: Izd-vo Akademii nauk SSSR. n2-3. 1952 – us Res Libr [900]
IZVESTIIA AKADEMII NAUK SSSR : SERIIA GEOGRAFICHESKAIA I GEOFIZICHESKAIA – Moskva: Izd-vo Akademii nauk SSSR, [-1951]. v14 1950; v15 n1 jan/feb 1951 – 2r – 1 – us Res Libr [900]
IZVESTIIA AKADEMII NAUK SSSR. OTDELENIE LITERATURY I IAZYKA – Moskva, Izdatel Stvo: Akademii nauk SSSR, 1941-1961. 6 no. a year – 1 – us U.W. Library [460]
IZVESTIIA CHELIABINSKOGO OBSHCHESTVA POTREBITELEI RABOCHIKH I SLUZHASHCHIKH – (Missing: 1913 n32-34) – Cheliabinsk, 1909-15 n48 – 20mf – 9 – COR-596/1 – ne IDC [334]
IZVESTIIA IMPERATORSKAGO NIKOLAEVSKOI VOENNOI AKADEMII (I LETOPIS' VOENNOI PECHATI) – Nauchnobibliograficheskii zhurnal. Spb. 1910-14. BR-7632 2 – 8 – ne IDC [073]
IZVESTIIA MINSKAGO OBSHCHESTA LIUBITELEI ESTESTVOZNANIIA, ETNOGRAFII I ARKHEOLOGII – God 1912. pt. 1. Minsk. 1914. BR-3230 2 – 8 – ne IDC [930]
IZVESTIIA MOSKOVSKOGO LITERATURNO-KHUDOZHESTVENNOGO KRUZHKA – (v.1 & v.3: Kommerchesko-technicheskoe otdelenie; v.2 & v.4: Ekonomicheskoe otdelenie) – v. 1-4. M. 1913-16. B-1457 2 – 32mf – 8 – R-3231/2 – ne IDC [460]
IZVESTIIA MOSKOVSKOGO NARODNOGO BANKA – (Missing: 1917 n1-6, 10-12) – Moscow, 1916-18 n10 – 14mf – 9 – COR-594/1 – ne IDC [334]
IZVESTIIA O ZANIATIIAKH 4-OGO ARKHEOLOGICHESKOGO S'EZDA V KAZANI – v. 1-10. Kazan'. 1877. Lacking: 1877 (8). B-1751 2 – 8 – ne IDC [930]
IZVESTIIA OBSHCHESTVA ARKHEOLOGII, ISTORII I ETNOGRAFII PRI IMPERATORSKOM KAZANSKOM UNIVERSITETE – (Missing: V32(3-4) 1922) – Kazan', v1-33(4). 1878-1925 – 385mf – 9 – 1432/2 – ne IDC [947]
IZVESTIIA OBSHCHESTVA FINANSOVYKH REFORM – v. 1-12. Spb. 1910-15. BR-3232 2 – 19mf – 8 – R-3232/2 – ne IDC [332]
IZVESTIIA OBSHCHESTVA OBSLEDOVANII I IZUCHENIIA AZERBAJDZHANA – (Lacking: v1-3) – Baku. v1-7. 1926-1928/29 – 8 – BR-4050 2 – ne IDC [947]
IZVESTIIA OBSHCHESTVA RASPROSTRANENIIA PRAVILNYKH SVEDENII O EVERIAKH I EVEISTVE – Sbornik statei. v1. 1912 – 8 – BR-3233 2 – ne IDC [947]
IZVESTIIA OBSHCHESTVA REVNITELEI RUSSKAGO ISTORICHESKAGO PROSVESHCHENIIA V PAMIAT' IMPERATORA ALEKSANDRA 3 – v1-5. Spb. 1900-04. BR-3234 2 – 8 – ne IDC [947]
IZVESTIIA OBSHCHESTVA SLAVIANSKOI KUL'TURY – v. 1 (1-2); v. 2 (1). M. 1912-13. BR-3235 2 – 8 – ne IDC [947]
IZVESTIIA OBSHCHEZEMSKOI ORGANIZATSII – v. 1-10. M. 1905, 1906. BR-4125 2 – 8 – ne IDC [073]
IZVESTIIA OMGUBSOIUZA – (Cont by: Kooperativnaia niva. Omsk, 1923 n1-4 – 1924 n2. Missing: 1922. 1923 n8) – Omsk, 1923 n1-19 – 13mf – 9 – COR-615/1 – ne IDC [334]
IZVESTIIA PERMSKOGO GORODSKOGO OBSHCHESTVA POTREBITELEI : KOOPERATIVNYI ZHURNAL – (Missing: 1914 n19-... . 1916 n16-21) – Perm', 1913-17 n2 – 22mf – 9 – COR-595/1 – ne IDC [334]
IZVESTIIA PETERSBURGSKOGO KOMISSARIATA PO DELAM NATSIONAL'NOSTEI – Petrograd. 1919. Available: v. 1. BR-3236 2 – 8 – ne IDC [947]
IZVESTIIA PETROGRADSKOGO SOVETA RABOCHIKH I KRASNOARMEISKIKH DEPUTATOV – Petrograd. 1918-1921. Gaps – 1 – 35.00r – us Hoover Inst Photo [335]
IZVESTIIA PO NARODNOMU OBRAZOVANIIU – v. 1-14. Spb. 1904-17. Lacking: v. 1 (1-3), v. 12 (5). BR-3238 2 – 8 – ne IDC [073]
IZVESTIIA PSKOVSKOGO GUBSOIUZA – (Cont by: Vestnik Pskovskoi kooperatsii. Pskov, 1923 n19-24. Missing: 1922 n1-2) – Pskov, 1922-23 n18 – 18mf – 9 – COR-565/1 – ne IDC [334]
IZVESTIIA RUSSKAGO GENEALOGICHESKAGO OBSHCHESTVA – v. 1-4. Spb. 1900-11. BR-3240 2 – 8 – ne IDC [073]
IZVESTIIA RUSSKAGO SOBRANIIA – v1-3. Spb. 1903; v1-2. 1904 – 8 – BR-4127 2 – ne IDC [947]
IZVESTIIA SAMARSKOGO OBSHCHESTVA NARODNYKH UNIVERSITETOV – NR. 1-20. Samara. 1910. BR-4128 2 – 8 – ne IDC [370]
IZVESTIIA SOVETA PO DELAM STRAKHOVANIIA RABOCHIKH – (Lacking: 1914 n3) – Spb, 1913-16 – 8 – BR-9277 2 – ne IDC [331]
IZVESTIIA SOVETOV DEPUTATOV TRUDIASHCHIKHSIA SSSR – Moskva: Prezidium Verkhovnogo Soveta SSSR, jul 1938-oct 7 1977 – 1 – us Res Libr [947]
IZVESTIIA SOVETOV NARODNYKH DEPUTATOV SSSR – Moskva: Prezidium Verkhovnogo Soveta SSSR, 1977-91. oct 8, 1977-jun 1991 – us Res Libr [072]
IZVESTIIA S-PETERBURGSKOGO OBSHCHESTVA MUZYKAL'NYKH SOBRANII – (From 1903 with a suppl: Muzykal'naia bibliografiia) – St Petersburg, 1896-1908 (irregular) – 22mf – 9 – us Ross [780]
IZVESTIIA TAMBOVSKOI UCHENOI ARKHIVNOI KOMMISSII – (Missing: V1-2 1884; v4 1885) – Tambov. v1-57. 1884-1917 – 140mf – 9 – 1489/1 – ne IDC [947]
IZVESTIIA TVERSKOGO GUBSOIUZA – (Cont by: Ekho tverskoi kooperatsii. Tver', 1925-29 n20. Missing: 1920 n3-4, 7-8. 1921 n14-19, 21, 23-29, 31, 34. 1922 n6, 13, 17. 1923 n4) – Tver', 1920-24 n24 – 124mf – 9 – COR-706/1 – ne IDC [334]
IZVESTIIA VOLOGDSKOGO OBSHCHESTVA SEL'SKOGO KHOZIAISTVA – (Cont by: Severnyi khoziain. Vologda, 1911-19 n11. Missing: 1917 n21, 23-24. 1918 n1-10, 16, 19-21. 1919 n1) – Vologda, 1910 – 75mf – 9 – COR-680/1 – ne IDC [334]
IZVESTIIA VOSTOCHNO-SIBIRSKOGO OTDELA IMPERATORSKOGO RUSSKOGO GEORGRAFICHESKOGO OBSHCHESTVA – (Missing: V1-9 1878-1879; v10(3-4) 1879; v27(3-4) 1896) – Irkutsk. v1-46. 1878-1921 – 267mf – 9 – 1755/2 – ne IDC [947]
IZVESTIIA VYSOCHAISHE UCHREZHDENNAGO KOMITETA POPECHITEL'STVA O RUSSKOI IKONOPISI – v. 1-2. Spb. 1902-03. BR-3205 2 – 8 – ne IDC [947]
IZVESTIIA VYSSHIKH UCHEBNYKH ZAVEDENII – Pravovedenie. L. 1957-Available: 1957-69. BR-8280 2 – 8 – ne IDC [340]
IZVESTIIA VYSSHIKH UCHEBNYKH ZAVEDENII : STROITELSTVO I ARKHITEKTURA – Novosibirsk: Novosibirskii inzhenerno-stroitelnyi in-t, 1958-81. n4-6 1978; n7-8 1979 – us Res Libr [720]
IZVESTIIA ZAGRANICHNAGO SEKRETARIATA ORGANIZATSIONNAGO KOMITETA ROSSIISKOI / Sotsialdemokraticheskoi Rabochei Partii – Zurich. Feb. 22, 1915-Feb. 5, 1916, nos. 1-3; Jan. 18, 1917, no. 8 and "Prilozhenie k no. 8" – 1 – 35.00r – us Hoover Inst Photo [335]
IZVESTIJA SAMARSKOGO OBSHCHESTVA POTREBITELEI "SAMOPOMOSHCH" – (Cont by: Samopomoshch'. Samara, 1918-19 n7. Missing: 1916 n2, 7-8. 1917 n3-1918 n12. 1919 n1-5) – Samara, 1916-17 – 8mf – 9 – COR-676/1 – ne IDC [334]
IZVESTIYA – Leningrad, Moscow, U.S.S.R. -d. 1917-63. 1917-1932 imperfect. 113 reels – 1 – uk British Libr Newspaper [947]
IZVESTIYA NARODNAGO KOMISSARIATA PO VOENNYM DELAM – Moscow. May 1918-Sep 1921.-w. mqn reel – 1 – uk British Libr Newspaper [072]
IZVESTIYA SOVETSKOI MEDITSINY. (IZVESTIYA NARODNOGO KOMISSARIATA ZDRAVOOKRANENIYA) – Moscow. 15 May-25 Jul 1918; 25 Aug 1918-Dec 1921.-w. 28 ft – 1 – uk British Libr Newspaper [073]
IZVI ESTII A GELSINGFORSSKAGO SOVI ETA DEPUTATOV ARMII, FLOTA I RABOCHIKH – (Includes c.1: 1917:July 14, Aug.9; 1918:Feb.22, 26-28) – [Gelsingfors]: Tip. "Izvi esti i", 19uu – 1 – CSUXANR1569-S – us Hoover Inst Photo [947]
IZVI ESTII A GORNAGO OTDI ELA – (Library has: July-Sept. 1918) – [Moskva]: [s.n.], 1918 – 1 – CSUX89-S592 – us Hoover Inst Photo [947]
IZVI ESTII A KRESTI ANSKIKH DEPUTATOV – (Includes c.1: 1906:May 30) – S.-Peterburg: I.I. Subbotin, 1906 – 1 – CSUXALC2514-S – us Hoover Inst Photo [947]
IZVI ESTII A (MOSCOW, R.S.F.S.R.: 1918 *see* IZVI ESTII A VYSSHAGO SOVI ETA NARODNAGO KHOZI A ISTVA
IZVI ESTII A MOSKOVSKOGO OBLASTNOGO SOVI ETA NARODNAGO KHOZI A ISTVA – (Includes c.1: v.1 1918) – [Moskva: Sovi et, 1918] – 1 – CSUXAKZ1775-S – us Hoover Inst Photo [947]
IZVI ESTII A OTDI ELA PO TOPLIVU VYSSHAGO SOVIETA NARODNAGO KHOZI A ISTVA – (Library has: June-July, 1918) – Moskva: Otdi el, 1918 – 1 – CSUX89-S907 – us Hoover Inst Photo [947]
IZVI ESTII A OTDI ELA TOPLIVA VYSSHAGO SOVIETA NARODNAGO KHOZI A ISTVA *see* IZVI ESTII A OTDI ELA PO TOPLIVU VYSSHAGO SOVIETA NARODNAGO KHOZI A ISTVA
IZVI ESTII A SARATOV. SOVIETA RABOCHIKH, KRASNOARME ISKIKH I KRESTI ANSKIKH DEPUTATOV I RA IONNAGO ISPOLNITELNAGO KOMITETA *see* IZVI ESTII A SARATOVSKAGO SOVIETA RABOCHIKH, SOLDATSKIKH I KRESTI ANSKIKH DEPUTATOV I RA IONNAGO ISPOLNITELNAGO KOMITETA
IZVI ESTII A SARATOVSKAGO SOVIETA RABOCHIKH, SOLDATSKIKH I KRESTI ANSKIKH DEPUTATOV I RA IONNAGO ISPOLNITELNAGO KOMITETA – (Library has holdings (incomplete) from Jan. 3-June 22, 1918; Feb. 29-June 10, 1928) – Saratov: Izvi estii a, 1917-1960 – 1 – CSUX87-S263 – us Hoover Inst Photo [947]
IZVI ESTII A TVERSKOGO SOVI ETA RABOCHIKH, KRESTI ANSKIKH I KRASNO-ARME ISKIKH DEPUTATOV – (c.1: 1918:June 22) – [Tver]: Tip. Tverskogo gub. komissariata upravlenii a, 19uu – 1 – CSUXANR5134-S – us Hoover Inst Photo [947]
IZVI ESTII A VYSSHAGO SOVI ETA NARODNAGO KHOZI A ISTVA – (Library has Oct 19-24, Nov. 3, 1918) – Moskva: [s.n.], 1918 – 1 – CSUX89-S585 – us Hoover Inst Photo [947]
IZVIESTIIA PO LITERATURIE, NAUKAMI BIBLIOGRAFII / Tovarishchestvo MO Vol'f. Leningrad – 7v. 1897-1904 – 1 – 46.00 – us L of C Photodup [460]
IZVIESTIIA VOENNO-KHOZIAISTVENNAGO SOVIETA NARODNAGO KOMISSARIATA PO VOENNYM DIELAM / Russian S.F.S.R. Voenno-khoziaistvennyi sovet – (Includes c.1: no.1 1918:May 15) – Moskva: Sovet, 1918 – 1 – CSUXALJ6415-S – us Hoover Inst Photo [355]
IZWI LABANTU – East London, South Africa. 4 Jun 1901-16 Apr 1909. 1 reel. Lacking: 1903-07 – 1, 16 diazo available at reduced price – sa SA Libr [072]
IZWI LAMA AFRIKA – East London, South Africa. 8 May 1931-27 Feb 1932. 1 reel – 1, 16 diazo available at reduced price – sa SA Libr [072]
IZWI LAMA SWAZI – Mbabane, South Africa. 13 Feb-3 Jul 1934. 1 reel – 1, 16 diazo available at reduced price – sa SA Libr [072]
Izzet *see*
– DIVAN
– DIVANCE
Izzet Beg *see* DIVAN
Izzi, Sueleyman *see* TARIH-I IZZI
J, A *see* A COMPLEAT ACCOUNT OF THE PORTUGUEZE LANGUAGE
THE J. EDGAR HOOVER OFFICIAL AND CONFIDENTIAL FILE / ed by Theoharis, Athan – 17r – 1 – $1,940.00 – 1-55655-164-9 – us UPA [324]
J EHAN DE WA VRIN *see* RECUEIL DES CRONIQUES ET ANCHIENNES ISTORIES DE LA GRANT BRETAGNE (RS39)
J. ENOCH POWELL PAMPHLET COLLECTION – 1969 – 9 – us Hoover Inst Photo [941]
J. Frank Lewis and Co *see* THE MARYLAND DIRECTORY, 1880
J. FRANKLIN LITTLE, SENATE SERVICE 1910-1912 : SENATE PAGE – 1mf – 9 – $5.00 – us Scholarly Res [320]
J. GAUDENZ VON SALIS-SEEWIS / Frey, Adolf – (Includes bibliographical references and index) – Frauenfeld: J Huber, 1889 – 1r – 1 – us U.W. Library [920]
J. ROBERT OPPENHEIMER : FBI SECURITY FILE / U.S. Federal Bureau of Investigation – 1979 – 4r – 1 – $340.00 – S1761 – us Scholarly Res [360]
J. SLOVENSKY / Culen, Konstantin – Winnipeg, Canada: Kanadsky Slovak, 1954 – 1 reel – 1 – us I.H.R.C. [920]
J W Mansfield and Co *see* LEDGER
J. Whitaker and Sons *see* WHITAKER'S ISBN LISTING
J.A. LEISEWITZENS JULIUS VON TARENT : ERLAEUTERUNG UND LITERARHISTORISCHE WUERDIGUNG / Kuehlhorn, Walther – (Includes bibliographical references) – Halle a.d. Saale: M Niemeyer, 1912 – 1r – 1 – us U.W. Library [430]
Jaap Kunst Centre for Ethnomusicology *see* MUSIC AND DANCE IN SURINAM
JAAPA / American Academy of Physician Assistants – (Cont: Journal of the American Academy of Physician Assistants) – Montvale. v7-10. 1994-97+ 1,5*,9 – 1,5,9 – D16286.01 – us UMI [610]
JAARBOEK DER INDOLOGEN VEREENIGING, 1918-1919 – Leiden, 1918 – 3mf – 9 – ne IDC [950]
JAARBOEK VAN 5764 (1913-1914), UITGEGEVEN DOOR DE CENTRALE ORGANISATIE VOOR DE RELIGIEUZE EN MOREELE VERHEFFING DER JODEN IN NEDERLAND – Amsterdam. 1913. BJ-262-27 1 – 9 – ne IDC [949]
JAARBOEKEN VOOR DE ISRAELIETEN IN NEDERLAND – 's-Gravenhage, 1835-1838. v1-4 – 20mf – 9 – J-261-49/1 – ne IDC [270]
JAARBOEKEN VOOR DE ISRAELIETEN OF JODEN, BINNEN HET KONINKRIJK HOLLAND – Amsterdam, 1808(1) – 1mf – 9 – J-261-50/1 – ne IDC [270]
JAARBOEKEN VOOR WETENSCHAPPELIJKE THEOLOGIE – Utrecht, 1(1845)-13(1856) – 136mf – 9 – Dfl476.00 – ne Slangenburg [073]
JAARBOEKJE DER NEDERLANDSCHE ORNITHOLOGISCHE VEREENIGING – 9 – ne IDC [590]
JAARBOEKJE DER NEDERLANDSCHE ORNITHOLOGISCHE VEREENIGING *see* VERSLAGEN EN MEDEDEELINGEN VAN DE NEDERLANDSCHE ORNITHOLOGISCHE VEREENIGING

JAARVERSLAG DER ANTI-WOEKER VEREENIGING – Medan, 1931-1938. No 1-7 – 3mf – 9 – ne IDC [060]
JAARVERSLAG DER DELI PLANTERS VEREENIGING – 1914-1938 – 34mf – 9 – ne IDC [631]
JAARVERSLAG DER DELI SPOORWEG-MAATSCHAPPIJ – Amsterdam, 1883/1884-1949 – 58mf – 9 – ne IDC [060]
JABEZ BUNTING : A GREAT METHODIST LEADER / Rigg, James Harrison – London: Charles H. Kelly, [19-?] – 1mf – us A.T.L.A. [240]
Jablonowski, A *see* AKADEMIA KIJOWSKO-MOHILANSKA
Jablonski, Walter *see* VOM SINN DER GOETHESCHEN NATURFORSCHUNG
Jablonskis, K *see* LIETUVISKI ZODZIAI SENOSIOS LIETUVOS RASTINIU KALBOJE
Jabotinski Institute, Tel Aviv *see* EZEL MOVEMENT ARCHIVES, 1936-1948
Jabotinsky, V *see* STATE ZIONISM
JACA – JOURNAL OF THE ASSOCIATION FOR COMMUNICATION ADMINISTRATION *see* ACA BULLETIN
JACEP – (Journal of the American College of Emergency Physicians). v.1-8. 1972-79. Superseded by Annals of Emergency Medicine – 1 – us UMI [073]
JACEP *see* ANNALS OF EMERGENCY MEDICINE
JACK BRAG : BY THE AUTHOR OF "SAYINGS AND DOINGS,"–"MAXWELL," ETC / Hook, Theodore Edward – London: Richard Bentley, 1837 – 2r – 1 – 1-55879-162-0 – uk Libr Preservation [920]
JACK CANUCK – Toronto. v7 n8. 1 sep 1917 – 1r – 1 – Can$25.00 – cn Can Microfilming [072]
Jack, D T *see* ECONOMIC SURVEY OF SIERRA LEONE
Jack, J W *see*
– THE DATE OF THE EXODUS IN THE LIGHT OF EXTERNAL EVIDENCE
– SAMARIA IN AHAB'S TIME, HARVARD EXCAVATIONS AND THEIR RESULTS
Jack, James W *see* DAYBREAK IN LIVINGSTONIA
JACK JOHNSON IN THE RING AND OUT / Johnson, Jack – Chicago, 1927 – 1r – 1 – us Ross [790]
JACK SHEPPARD : A ROMANCE / Ainsworth, William Harrison – London: R. Bentley, 1839 – 2 rolls – 1 – 1-55879-257-0 – uk Libr Preservation [830]
Jack, W *see* DESCRIPTIONS OF MALAYAN PLANTS
JACKANAPES / Ewing, Juliana Horatia – British Fiction Archive: Unit 1 – 9 – uk Bell [830]
Jackel, A J *see* SYSTEMATISCHE UBERSICHT DER VOEGEL BAYERNS
Jackman, William James *see* LEGAL FEATURES OF COMMERCE REGULATION
JACKPOT – Issue Nos. 1-5 Spring 1941-Spring 42 – 5mf – 15 – $31.95 – us Comics [760]
JACKPOT – Issue Nos. 6-9 Summer 42-Spring 43 – 5mf – 15 – $31.95 – us Comics [760]
Jackson, Abner *see* DISCOURSES
Jackson, Andrew *see* PAPERS
Jackson, Andrew 2 *see* ACCOUNT BOOKS, MS 1880
JACKSON, ANDREW, 2, ACCOUNTS, MS 1880 – (Containing data on the purchase, sale, birth, marriage, and death of slaves at the Hermitage, 1845-1877, and a receipt book of Andrew 2 and Sarah Jackson, 1845-1877) – Nashville, TN. 1845-77 – 1r – 1 – us Western Res [978]
JACKSON BAPTIST CHURCH. BUTTS COUNTY. GEORGIA : CHURCH RECORDS – 1851-89 – 1 – 13.50 – us Baptist [240]
Jackson, BD *see*
– GUIDE TO THE LITERATURE OF BOTANY
– GUIDE TO THE LITERATURE OF BOTANY; A CLASSIFIED SELECTION OF BOTANICAL WORKS, INCLUDING NEARLY 6,000 TITLES NOT GIVEN IN PRITZEL "THESAURUS"
JACKSON COUNTY FLORIDIAN – Marianna. Fl. 1958- – 1 – us UMI [071]
JACKSON COUNTY FLORIDIAN – Marianna. Fl. -w. 1933-1936, 1937, 1938-1958, 1980- – 1 – us P.K. Yonge [071]
JACKSON COUNTY NEWS – Medford, OR. -w. 10 Oct 1924-15 Oct 1926. 2 rolls. Set incl. Clarion (Medford) – 1 – us U.O. Library [071]
JACKSON COUNTY NEWS – Ravenswood. West Virginia. 1878-79 – 1 – us UMI [071]
JACKSON COUNTY TIMES – Jacksonville, OR. 11 Mar 1977-31 Aug 1977. 1 roll – 1 – us U.O. Library [071]
JACKSON COUNTY TIMES – Ocean Springs. Miss. 1936-1949 – 1 – us UMI [071]
JACKSON CRITERION – Jackson, NE. -w. Jul 1896-Jan 1902, scattered issues missing – 1 – us NE Hist [071]
JACKSON FIRST BAPTIST CHURCH. JACKSON, LOUISIANA : CHURCH RECORDS – 1835-1958 – 1 – 59.76 – us Baptist [240]
JACKSON FIRST BAPTIST CHURCH. JACKSON, MISSOURI : CHURCH RECORDS – 1856-1905 – 1 – 10.26 – us Baptist [240]
Jackson, Francis Marris *see*
– INDEX TO THE LIBRARY EDITION OF THOMAS JACKSON'S LIFE OF CHARLES WESLEY
– WESLEYAN METHODIST MAGAZINE
Jackson, G K *see* NEW MISCELLANEOUS MUSICAL WORK
Jackson, George *see*
– SIXTY YEARS IN TEXAS
– TEACHING OF JESUS
– THE TEACHING OF JESUS
Jackson, George H *see* THE MEDICINAL VALUE OF FRENCH BRANDY
Jackson, Henry Latimer *see* THE FOURTH GOSPEL AND SOME RECENT GERMAN CRITICISM
JACKSON HERALD – Ripley. West Virginia. -w. 1935-66 – 1 – us UMI [071]
Jackson, Holbrook *see* BERNARD SHAW
Jackson, J G *see* AN ACCOUNT OF TIMBUCTOO AND HOUSA, TERRIT. IN THE INTERIOR OF AFRICA
Jackson, John *see*
– IN LEPER-LAND
– LEPERS: THIRTY-SIX YEARS' WORK AMONG THEM...IN INDIA AND THE EAST, 1874-1910
– MARY REED
Jackson, Michael *see*
– A STUDY OF THE PERCEIVED EFFECTS OF THE REPEAL OF THE PENNSYLVANIA INTERSCHOLASTIC ATHLETIC ASSOCIATION CONSTITUTIONAL BYLAW ARTICLE 11, SECTION 2
– A SURVEY OF THE DESIRED EDUCATIONAL PREPARATION AND EMPLOYMENT MARKET FOR HIGH SCHOOL ATHLETIC TRAINERS IN METROPOLITAN WASHINGTON, DC AS PERCEIVED BY HIGH SCHOOL ATHLETIC DIRECTORS
Jackson, Michael W *see*
– THE IDENTIFICATION OF THE MINIMUM QUALIFICATIONS FOR TENNIS TEACHING PROFESSIONALS TO BE HIRED AT MANAGED TENNES FACILITIES IN THE UNITED STATES
– AN INVESTIGATION OF THE QUALIFICATIONS OF CONTRACT ADVISORS FOR PROFESSIONAL ATHLETES
– A STUDY OF HIGH SCHOOL TRACK AND FIELD OUTDOOR CHAMPIONSHIPS BASED ON THE EVENTS ENDORSED BY THE NATIONAL FEDERATION OF STATE HIGH SCHOOL ASSOCIATIONS
– SURVEY OF AQUATIC PROGRAMS AND AQUATIC FACILITY ACCESSIBILITY FEATURES AVAILABLE TO AND UTILIZED BY PHYSICALLY HANDICAPPED STUDENTS AT FOUR-YEAR PENNSYLVANIA COLLEGES AND UNIVERSITIES
Jackson, Mississippi *see* MISCELLANEOUS EARLY NEWSPAPERS
Jackson, Nathaniel P *see* SELECT TEXAS STATUTES, ANNOTATIONS AND FORMS AND NOTARIES' MANUAL, EMBRACING CONSTITUTIONAL AND STATUTORY PROVISIONS AFFECTING INTEREST, PROPERTY RIGHTS UNDER MARITAL CONTRACTS, AND EXEMPTIONS.
JACKSON PRESS – Bellevue. Iowa. -w. 1852-54 – 1 – us UMI [071]
Jackson, Robert Houghwout *see* THE CASE AGAINST THE NAZI WAR CRIMINALS
JACKSON SENTINEL – Maquoketa. Iowa. -w. 1951- – 1 – us UMI [071]
Jackson, Sheldon *see*
– COLLECTION
– CORRESPONDENCE
– CRUISE OF THE U.S. REVENUE MARINE STEAMER BEAR
– PHOTOGRAPH COLLECTION
– SCRAPBOOKS
– TRAVEL DIARIES
Jackson, Susan A *see* ELITE ATHLETES IN FLOW
Jackson, T *see*
– THE CENTENARY OF WESLEYAN METHODISM
– THE LIVES OF EARLY METHODIST PREACHERS, CHIEFLY WRITTEN BY THEMSELVES,...
Jackson, Thomas *see*
– THE LIFE OF JOHN GOODWIN
– RECOLLECTIONS OF MY OWN LIFE AND TIMES
Jackson, Thomas Jefferson *see* RESEARCHES IN NON-EUCLIDIAN GEOMETRY AND THE THEORY OF RELATIVITY: A SYSTEMATIC STUDY OF TWENTY FALLACIES IN THE GEOMETRY OF RIEMANN
Jackson, W Rufus *see* MISSOURI DEMOCRACY
Jackson, William *see*
– THE PHILOSOPHY OF NATURAL THEOLOGY
– PHILOSOPHY OF NATURAL THEOLOGY: AN ESSAY IN CONFUTATION OF THE SCEPTICISM
Jackson, William V *see* CATALOG OF BRAZILIAN ACQUISITIONS OF THE LIBRARY OF CONGRESS, 1964-1974
THE JACKSONIAN – Wooster. Ohio. 1881-1899 – 1 – us UMI [071]
JACKSON'S OXFORD JOURNAL – Oxford. England. -w. 1756-66; 1826-37 (1756-66 imperfect). (6mqn reels) – 1 – uk British Libr Newspaper [072]
JACKSONS OXFORD JOURNAL – (Also known as: Oxford Journal) – May 5 1753-Dec 27 1755; 1756-71; Jan 4-May 2 1772; May 15 1773; Jan 4 1777-Nov 27 1779; 1780-82; Feb 1 1783-Dec 25 1786; Jan 20 1787-Dec 18 1790; 1791-1826; Jan 6 1827-Dec 19 1829; 1930-Dec 29 1832; 1833-1908; Jan 2-29 1909; 1910-27; Jan 4-Nov 28 1928; 1986-Jun 1991; 1992-Sep, Oct 7-Dec 23 1993; 1994-Jun 1997 – 127 1/2r – 1 – uk British Libr Newspaper [072]
JACKSONVILLE AMERICAN – Jacksonville. Fl. -w. 1949-1956 – 1 – us P.K. Yonge [071]
JACKSONVILLE BULLETIN – Jacksonville OR. Feb 15 1964-Feb 18 1974 – 1 – us U.O. Library [071]
JACKSONVILLE MINER – Jacksonville OR. Jan 1 1932-Jan 18 1935 – 1 – us U.O. Library [071]
JACKSONVILLE NUGGET – Jacksonville OR. Feb 5 1977-Jan 22 1981 – 1 – us U.O. Library [071]
JACKSONVILLE OREGON REPORTER GAZETTE TIMES – Jacksonville OR. July 17 1963 – 1 – us U.O. Library [071]
JACKSONVILLE POST – Jacksonville, OR. -w. 6 July 1907-25 June 1937. – 3r – 1 – us U.O. Library [071]
JACKSONVILLE REVEILLE – Jacksonville OR. Jan 11 June 6 13 27 1868, July 4 11 Sep 5 Nov 14 1868 – 1 – us U.O. Library [071]
JACKSONVILLE SEAFARER – v1-33 no 12 1952-84 – 1,5,6,9 – us UMI [623]
JACKSONVILLE SENTINEL – Jacksonville OR. Sep 1 1961-Dec 28 1962 – 1 – us U.O. Library [071]
JACKSONVILLE SENTINEL – Jacksonville, OR. -w. 22 May 1903-14 Apr 1905. 1 roll – 1 – us U.O. Library [071]
JACL REPORTER – (Library has: v.1, no. 1-v.5, no. 6; Jan. 1945-June 1949) – Salt Lake City, Utah: Japanese American Citizens' League, 1945- – 1 – CSUX86-S210 – us Hoover Inst Photo [978]
Jacob *see* AUX FEMMES
JACOB ALBRIGHT AND HIS CO-LABORERS / Yeakel, Reuben – Cleveland, O[hio]: Evangelical Association, c1883 – 1mf – us A.T.L.A. [240]
Jacob, B *see* DAS ERSTE BUCH DER TORA
JACOB BOEHMES DEUTSCHES CHRISTENTUM / Elert, W – Berlin: E. Ringe, 1914. (Biblische Zeit- und Streifragen, IX. Serie; 6. Heft) – 1mf – us A.T.L.A. [240]
Jacob, Edgar *see* THE DIVINE SOCIETY, OR, THE CHURCH'S CARE OF LARGE POPULATIONS
Jacob, G *see* A NEW LAW-DICTIONARY: CONTAINING, THE INTERPRETATION AND DEFINITION OF WORDS AND TERMS...
Jacob, Georg *see* DAS HOHELIED
Jacob, Karl *see* DIE GROSSEN KRIEGE IN DER GESCHICHTE DES DEUTSCHEN VOLKES
Jacob, Margaret C *see* FREEMASONRY
Jacob, Michael P *see* COLLEGE WOMEN ATHLETES' KNOWLEDGE AND PERCEPTIONS OF TITLE 9
Jacob of Edessa *see* A LETTER BY MAR JACOB, BISHOP OF EDESSA, ON SYRIAC ORTHOGRAPHY
Jacob, Son of Aaron *see* THE BOOK OF ENLIGHTENMENT FOR THE INSTRUCTION OF THE INQUIRER
JACOB THOMSON : EIN VERGESSENER DICHTER DES ACHTZEHNTEN JAHRHUNDERTS / Schmeding, G – Braunschweig, 1889 – v/94p – 9 – DM48.00 – 3-89349-065-5 – gw Hänsel [430]
JACOB UNREST (MGH 6: 11.BD) : OESTERREICHISCHE CHRONIK / ed by Grossmann, K – 1957 – Dfl28.00 – ne Slangenburg [240]
Jacob, W *see* DIE HANDSCHRIFTLICHE UEBERLIEFERUNG DER SOGENANNTEN HISTORIA TRIPARTITA DES EPIPHANIUS-CASSIDOR (T.U.U. 5-59)
JACOBI FABRI STAPULENSIS ELEMENTA MUSICALIA AD CLARISSIMU VIRU NICOLAUM DE HAQUEUILLE INQUISITORIUM PRESIDETEM / Faber Stapulensis, J – P 361. 1500 – 9 – ne IDC [780]
Jacobi, Franz *see* DAS THORNER BLUTGERICHT 1724
Jacobi, Johann Georg *see* IRIS
Jacobi, Wilhelm Heinrich *see* DIE PHILOSOPHIE DER PERSOENLICHKEIT NACH FRIEDRICH HEINRICH JACOBI
JACOBITE REBELLIONS: TRACTS FROM THE HOME OFFICE LIBRARY – 1715 and 1745 – 1 – uk Microform Academic [941]
Jacobowski, Ludwig *see* KLINGER UND SHAKESPEARE
Jacobs, Aletta Henriette *see* LA FEMME ET LE FEMINISME. COLLECTION DE LIVRES, PERIODIQUES, ETC..
JACOB'S BAND MONTHLY – (V11 only) – Boston: W Jacobs, 1916-1927 – 3mf – 9 – us Sibley [780]
Jacobs, E *see* HEINRICH WINCKEL UND DIE REFORMATION IM SUEDLICHEN NIEDERSACHSEN
Jacobs, H *see* COMPLETE AAS MICROFICHE SERIES COLLECTION
Jacobs, Henry Eyster *see*
– A CHRONICLE OF THE AUGSBURG CONFESSION – A QUESTION OF LATINITY
– THE ENGLISH AUGSBURG CONFESSION OF 1536
– A HISTORY OF THE EVANGELICAL LUTHERAN CHURCH IN THE UNITED STATES
– THE LUTHERAN CYCLOPEDIA
– THE LUTHERAN MOVEMENT IN ENGLAND DURING THE REIGNS OF HENRY 8TH AND EDWARD 6TH AND ITS LITERARY MONUMENTS
– MARTIN LUTHER
Jacobs, J *see* JEWISH DIFFUSION OF FOLK-TALES
Jacobs, Joseph *see* AS OTHERS SAW HIM
Jacobsen, Jerome V *see* EDUCATIONAL FORMATIONS OF THE JESUITS...
Jacobsohn, Jacob *see* MITTEILUNGEN DES GESAMTARCHIVS DER DEUTSCHEN JUDEN
Jacobson, B J *see* THE RELATIONSHIP BETWEEN SPORT-CONFIDENCE, COMPETITIVE ORIENTATION AND PERFORMANCE ON A MUSCULAR LEG-ENDURANCE TASK
Jacobson, J *see* MITTHEILUNGEN AUS DER KOENIGSBERGER UNIVERSITAETS-AUGENKLINIK 1877-1879
Jacobson, Johann Carl Gottfried *see* TECHNOLOGISCHES WOERTERBUCH ODER ALPHABETISCHE ERKLAERUNGEN ALLER NUETZLICHEN MECHANISCHEN KUENSTE, MANUFAKTUREN..
Jacobson, Lynn B *see* THE RELAPSE PREVENTION MODEL AND EXERCISE MAINTENANCE BEHAVIOR
Jacobson, Phyllis C *see* A HISTORICAL DOCUMENTATION, AN INSTRUCTIONAL MANUAL AND AN ANNOTATED BIBLIOGRAPHY OF SELECTED FOLK DANCES OF PUERTO RICO
Jacobstein, J Myron *see* SUPREME COURT OF THE U.S. HEARINGS AND REPORTS ON SUCCESSFUL AND UNSUCCESSFUL NOMINATIONS OF SUPREME COURT JUSTICES BY THE SENATE JUDICIARY COMMITTEE
JACOBSTOWN BAPTIST CHURCH. WRIGHTSTOWN, NEW JERSEY : CHURCH RECORDS – 1785-c1943, 1842-1910. list of members, Original Deed, etc – 1 – 25.92 – us Baptist [240]
Jacobstroer, Bernhard *see* DIE ROMANTECHNIK BEI FRIEDRICH GERSTAECKER
Jacobszoon, Mattheus *see* DIE PROPHETIEN DER PROPHETEN
JACOBUS ARMINIUS : EEN BIOGRAFIE / Maronier, J H – Amsterdam: Y. Rogge, 1905 – 1mf – us A.T.L.A. [240]

JAHRBUCH / Verband der Bergarbeiter Deutschlands – Bochum. 1921, 1923, 1926. (Serial publications of German trade unions in the Memorial Library, University of Wisconsin-Madison) – 1 – us U.W. Library [330]

JAHRBUCH / Verband der Bergbauindustriearbeiter Deutschlands – Bochum. 1930-31. (Serial publications of German trade unions in the Memorial Library, University of Wisconsin-Madison.) – 1 – us U.W. Library [330]

JAHRBUCH / Verband der Brauerei- und Muehlenarbeiter und verwandter Berufsgenossen – Berlin. 1912, 1914-15. (Serial publications of German trade unions in the Memorial Library, University of Wisconsin-Madison.) – 1 – us U.W. Library [330]

JAHRBUCH / Verband der Fabrikarbeiter Deutschlands – 1912, 1925, 1927-28, 1930-31. Hannover. Serial publications of German trade unions in the Memorial Library, University of Wisconsin-Madison.) – 1 – us U.W. Library [330]

JAHRBUCH / Verband der Maler, Lackierer, Anstreicher, Tuencher und Weissbinder Deutschlands – 1921, 1927-31. Hamburg. (Serial publications of German trade unions in the Memorial Library, University of Wisconsin-Madison) – 1 – us U.W. Library [330]

JAHRBUCH / Verband der Nahrungsmittel- und Getraenkearbeiter – 1928-31. Berlin. (Serial publications of German trade unions in the Memorial Library, University of Wisconsin-Madison.) – 1 – us U.W. Library [330]

JAHRBUCH / Verein fuer Geschichte der Deutschen in Boehmen. Prague – Prag, Im Selbstverlage des Vereines fuer Geschichte der Deutschen in Boehmen. 1.-3. Jahrg.; 1926-1930 33. Film Mas 8957 – 1 – us H.U. Library [943]

JAHRBUCH / Zentralverband der Maurer Deutschlands – 1907-10. Hamburg. Continued as: Deutscher Bauarbeiterverband. At head of title 1910 Zentralverbande der Maurer und Bauhilfsarbeiter. (Serial publications of German trade unions in the Memorial Library, University of Wisconsin-Madison.) – 1 – us U.W. Library [330]

JAHRBUCH / Zentralverband der Schuhmacher – 1918 19, 1921, 1923-31. Nurnberg. (Serial publications of German trade unions in the Memorial Library, University of Wisconsin-Madison.) – 1 – us U.W. Library [330]

JAHRBUCH / Zentralverband deutscher Konsumgenossenschaften – v1-31. 1903-33. (Serial publications of German trade unions in the Memorial Library, University of Wisconsin-Madison.) – 1 – us U.W. Library [330]

JAHRBUCH.. / Allgemeiner deutscher Gewerkschaftsbund. Ortsausschuss Muenchen – Muenchen. v23 24, 28-32. 1920-29. Title and subtitle varies. (Serial publications of German trade unions in the Memorial Library, University of Wisconsin-Madison) – 1 – us U.W. Library [073]

JAHRBUCH.. / Gesamtverband der Christlichen Gewerkschaften Deutschlands – Berlin. 1908, 1930, 1932. Some vols. issued as Schriften; some include Bericht. (Serial publications of German trade unions in the Memorial Library, University of Wisconsis-Madison) – 1 – us U.W. Library [330]

JAHRBUCH DER ANGESTELLTENBEWEGUNG – Berlin. 1913. (Serial publications of German trade unions in the Memorial Library, University of Wisconsin-Madison.) – 1 – us U.W. Library [331]

JAHRBUCH DER DEUTSCHEN SCHILLERGESELLSCHAFT – Stuttgart, 1957-59 – 1r – 1 – DM75.00 – gw Mikro Press [943]

JAHRBUCH DER ERFINDUNGEN UND FORTSCHRITTE AUF DEN GEBIETEN DER PHYSIK UND CHEMIE, DER TECHNOLOGIE UND MECHANIK, DER ASTRONOMIE UND METEOROLOGIE – Leipzig, 1865-1901. v. 1-37 – 3 – us Readex [500]

JAHRBUCH DER FRAUENARBEIT – v6-8. 1930-32. Verband der weiblichen Handels- und Buroangestellten. (Serial publications of German trade unions in the Memorial Library, University of Wisconsin-Madison.) – 1 – us U.W. Library [331]

JAHRBUCH DER FREIEN GENERATION / Freie Generation – v.2, n.3, 9-12. 1907-08; 1910. 1 fiche (29x) – 9 – 1.00f – at Libertarian Micro [320]

JAHRBUCH DER JUEDISCH-LITERARISCHEN GESELLSCHAFT – (Includes Index) – Frankfurt a.M. 1903-32. v1-22 – 171mf – 9 – ne IDC [470]

JAHRBUCH DER KOENIGLICH PREUSSISCHEN KUNSTSAMMLUNGEN – (Continued as: JAHRBUCH DER PREUSSICHEN KUNSTSAMMLUNGEN. Berlin. 1919-28. v1 -49. Index 1891. v1-10.) – Berlin, 1880-1918. v1-39. – 448mf – 9 – ne IDC [700]

JAHRBUCH DER KUNSTHISTORISCHEN SAMMLUNGEN IN WIEN : JAHRBUCH DER KUNSTHISTORISCHEN SAMMLUNGEN DES ALLERHOECHSTEN KAISERHAUSES. – Wien. 1883-1925. v1-36; 1926-28. n.s. v1-2. – 913mf – 9 – ne IDC [700]

JAHRBUCH DER MUSIKBIBLIOTHEK PETERS – Leipzig. v1-47. 1894-1940 – 94mf – ne IDC [780]

JAHRBUCH DER MUSIKBIBLIOTHEK PETERS / Musikbibliothek Peters – Leipzig. 1894-1939. 3 reels – 1 – 76.00 – us L of C Photodup [780]

JAHRBUCH DER SEELE / Thoma, Hans – Jena: E Diederichs, 1922 – 1r – 1 – us U.W. Library [750]

JAHRBUCH DER WELTPOLITIK / Deutsches Auslandswissenschaftliches Institut – Berlin. 1941-1944. 1941 is "2. unveraenderte Auflage", published 1942. Title varies; 1941, Jahrbuch fuer Politik und Auslandskunde. Film Mas C 686 – 1 – us H.U. Library [320]

JAHRBUCH DES BUNDES / German Baptict Convention – 1878-1959 60 – 1 – 173.04 – us Baptist [240]

JAHRBUCH DES DEUTSCHEN RECHTES – Berlin. On film: v1, pt.2-v39; 1903-41. LL-0245 – 1 – us L of C Photodup [340]

JAHRBUCH DES KOENIGLICHEN BOTANISCHEN GARTENS UND DES BOTANISCHEN MUSEUMS ZU BERLIN-DAHLEM – Berlin, 1881-1889. v1-5 – 24mf – 9 – 8567/1 – ne IDC [580]

JAHRBUCH DES KUNSTHISTORISCHEN INSTITUTES *see* KUNSTGESCHICHTLICHES JAHRBUCH DER K.K. ZENTRAL-KOMMISSION...

JAHRBUCH DES VOELKERRECHTS – Muenchen, Leipzig, 1911/1912-1919/1926. v1-9 – 80mf – 9 – IL-3/1 – ne IDC [340]

JAHRBUCH: ERGAENZUNGSHEFT / Deutsches Archaeologisches Institut – Berlin. Heft 1-6 1888-1905. Film Mas 8163 – 1 – us H.U. Library [930]

JAHRBUCH FUER BREMISCHE STATISTIK / Bremen. Statistisches Landesamt – v. 1-46. 1876-1915 16. 1875-80, 1881 wanting – 1 – 166.00 – us L of C Photodup [943]

JAHRBUCH FUER DEUTSCHNATIONALE HANDLUNGSGEHILFEN – v1-7, 9-10, 12-14, 17-21. 1900-20. -ann. (Serial publications of German trade unions in the Memorial Library, University of Wisconsin-Madison.) – 1 – us U.W. Library [331]

JAHRBUCH FUER DIE AMTLICHE STATISTIK DES BREMISCHEN STAATS / Bremen. Statistisches Amt – v. 1-8. 1868-75 – 1 – 52.00 – us L of C Photodup [943]

JAHRBUCH FUER GENEALOGIE, HERALDIK UND SPHRAGISTIK, 1893-1913 – Jelgava (Mitau). 7v. 1894-1914 – 83mf – 9 – ne IDC [920]

JAHRBUCH FUER GENEALOGIE, HERALDIK UND SPHRAGISTIK. 1893-1913 – Jelgava (Mitau). 7v. 1894-1914 – 83mf – 9 – ne IDC [920]

JAHRBUCH FUER JUDISCHE GESCHICHTE UND LITERATUR – Berlin. v1-31. 1898-1937 – 3r – 1 – us Ross [470]

JAHRBUCH FUER JUEDISCHE GESCHICHTE UND LITERATUR – Berlin. 1898-1938. 31v. – 110mf – 9 – ne IDC [270]

JAHRBUCH FUER JUEDISCHE GESCHICHTE UND LITERATUR – Berlin. bd 1-31. 1898-1937 – 1 – us NY Public [270]

JAHRBUCH FUER KUNSTGESCHICHTE *see* KUNSTGESCHICHTLICHES JAHRBUCH DER K.K. ZENTRAL-KOMMISSION...

JAHRBUCH FUER LITURGIEWISSENSCHAFT – v1-15. 1921-35 (complete) – Inquire – 1 – ATLA 1993-S500 – us A.T.L.A. [073]

JAHRBUCH FUER PSYCHOANALYTISCHE UND PSYCHOPATHOLOGISCHE FORSCHUNGEN – t. I-V. 1909-13. devenu: Jahrbuch der Psychanalyse. t. VI. 1914 – 1 – fr A.C.R.P.P. [073]

JAHRBUCH FUER SEXUELLE ZWISCHENSTUFEN 1.1899-23.1923 (HQ, 20) : UNTER BESONDERER BERUECKSICHTIGUNG DER HOMOSEXUALITAET – 1899-1923 (mf ed 1996) – 80mf – 9 – DM1,620.00 – 3-89131-132-X – gw Fischer [610]

JAHRBUCH FUER VOLKSLIEDFORSCHUNG – (Beihefte) – Berlin, Leipzig. v1-7. 1928-1941 – 18mf – ne IDC [780]

JAHRBUCH FUER VOLKSLIEDFORSCHUNG – Berlin, Leipzig. v1-7; Beihefte 1928-1941 – 18mf – 9 – ne IDC [780]

JAHRBUCH UEBER DIE FORTSCHRITTE DER MATHEMATIK – v. 1-68. 1868-1942 – 1,5,6 – us Princeton Micro [510]

JAHRBUECHER / Sozialdemokratische Partei Deutschlands – 1946-1968/69 – 1 – DM300.00 – gw Mikro Press [943]

JAHRBUECHER DER DEUTSCHEN MALAKOZOOLOGISCHEN GESELLSCHAFT – Frankfurt am Main. v1-14. 1874-1887 – 107mf – ne IDC [590]

JAHRBUECHER DER DEUTSCHEN MALAKOZOOLOGISCHEN GESELLSCHAFT – Frankfurt am Main. v1-14. 1874-1887 – 107mf – 9 – ne IDC [590]

JAHRBUECHER DER GEWAECHSKUNDE / Sprengel, K P J et al – 3v. Berlin. 1820. B-1013 2 – 8 – ne IDC [630]

JAHRBUECHER DER INSEKTENKUNDE... / ed by Klug, F – Berlin. v1. 1834 – 6mf – 9 – ne IDC [590]

JAHRBUECHER DER LITERATUR – Wien, 1818-49 (mf ed 1991) – 357mf – 9 – DM3,500.00 – 3-89131-038-2 – gw Fischer [430]

JAHRBUECHER DER MEDIZIN ALS WISSENSCHAFT / ed by Marcus, Adalbert Friedrich & Schelling, Friedrich Wilhelm Joseph – Tuebingen, 1806-08 – 11mf – 9 – subsc: DM84.00 diazo DM98.00 silver – gw Olms [610]

JAHRBUECHER DER WAHREN INSPIRATIONS-GEMEINDEN – v1-42; v1-58; v1-42. 1733-1883 (complete) – 13r – 1 – ATLA S0518 – us A.T.L.A. [240]

JAHRBUECHER DES FRAENKISCHEN REICHES UNTER KOENIG PIPPIN / Oelsner, L – Leipzig, 1871 – 10mf – ne IDC [944]

JAHRBUECHER DES VEREINS VON ALTERTHUMSFREUNDEN – Bonn. v1-146. 1842-1941 – 995mf – 9 – H-360c/2 – ne IDC [030]

JAHRBUECHER FUER JUEDISCHE GESCHICHTE UND LITERATUR / ed by Bruell, Nehemias – Frankfurt, 1874-90. Hildesheim, 1989 – 23mf – 9 – DM200.00 diazo DM230.00 silver – gw Olms [270]

JAHRBUECHER FUER JUEDISCHE GESCHICHTE UND LITERATUR – Frankfurt a/M. 1874, 1876, 1877, 1879, 1883-85, 1887, 1889, 1890. Complete. 1 reel. B133 (Leo Baeck Institute. German-Jewish Periodicals, Pt 1) – 1 – $75.00 – us UPA [270]

JAHRBUECHER FUER KULTUR UND GESCHICHTE DER SLAVEN – Breslau, 1924-35. N.S.v1-11(4). – 107mf – 8 – ne IDC [947]

JAHRBUECHER FUER MUSIKALISCHE WISSENSCHAFT – Leipzig. v1-2. 1863-1867 – 15mf – 9 – ne IDC [780]

JAHRBUECHER FUER PROTESTANTISCHE THEOLOGIE – 1(1875)-18(1892) – 222mf – 9 – Dfl777.00 – ne Slangenburg [073]

JAHRBUECHER FUER PROTESTANTISCHE THEOLOGIE – Leipzig. v1-18. 1875-1892 – 222mf – 9 – ne IDC [240]

JAHRBUECHER FUER STATISTIK UND LANDESKUNDE / Wuerttemberg – 1866-1951 52. 1876, 1938-50 wanting – 1 – 442.00 – us L of C Photodup [310]

JAHRBUECHER FUER WISSENSCHAFTLICHE BOTANIK / ed by Pringsheim, N – Berlin. v1-15. 1858-1884 – 108mf – 9 – ne IDC [580]

JAHRBUECHER FUER WISSENSCHAFTLICHE BOTANIK – Pringsheim. v72-91. 1930-43 – 1,5,6 – us Princeton Micro [580]

JAHRBUECHER FUER WISSENSCHAFTLICHE KRITIK – Stuttgart, Tuebingen (Jan 1827-Juni 1833); Berlin (Juli 1833-Dez 1846) (mf ed 1990) – 261mf – 9 – DM1,820.00 – 3-89131-035-8 – gw Fischer [100]

DIE JAHRE DER REAKTION: HISTORISCHE SKIZZE / Bernstein, Aaron David – Berlin: M. Bading, 1881.iv,260p – 1 – us U.W. Library [943]

JAHRE UND ZEITEN : ERINNERUNGEN / Wiechert, Ernst Emil – Erlenbach-Zuerich: E Rentsch, [1948, c1949] – 1r – 1 – us U.W. Library [080]

JAHRES- UND RECHENSCHAFTSBERICHT / Zentralverband der Glasarbeiter und -Arbeiterinnen Deutschlands – Berlin. 1921 23. Title varies slightly. (Serial publications of German trade unions in the Memorial Library, University of Wisconsin-Madison.) – 1 – us U.W. Library [330]

JAHRES-BERICHT.. / Arbeiter-Sekretariat. Muenchen – v1-4, 8-11, 17-21 22. 1898-1918 19. (Serial publications of German trade unions in the Memorial Library, University of Wisconsin-Madison) – 1 – us U.W. Library [330]

JAHRESBERICHT / Arbeiter-Sekretariat. Nuremberg – v20. 1914-20. (Serial publications of German trade unions in the Memorial Library, University of Wisconsin-Madison) – 1 – us U.W. Library [330]

JAHRESBERICHT / Deutsche Angestelltenschaft. Gau Brandenburg-Pommern – Berlin. 1929. (Serial publications of German trade unions in the Memorial Library, University of Wisconsin-Madison.) – 1 – us U.W. Library [330]

JAHRESBERICHT / Deutsche Mathematiker-Vereinigung. Bielefeld – v. 1-50. 1890-1941 – 1,5,6 – us Princeton Micro [510]

JAHRESBERICHT / Deutscher Tabakarbeiter-Verband – Bremen. 1908, 1910, 1922 24, 1928-29. (Serial publications of German trade unions in the Memorial Library, University of Wisconsin-Madison.) – 1 – us U.W. Library [330]

JAHRESBERICHT / Historischer Verein fuer die Graftschaft Ravensberg zu Bielefeld – Bielefeld. v. 1-56; 1877-1951. Film Mas C 302 – 1 – us H.U. Library [073]

JAHRESBERICHT / Verband der Bergarbeiter Deutschlands – Bochum. 1907 08. (Serial publications of German trade unions in the Memorial Library, University of Wisconsin-Madison.) – 1 – us U.W. Library [330]

JAHRESBERICHT / Verband der Bergbauindustriearbeiter Deutschlands. Bezirk Saarbruecken – 1930-32. Saarbrucken. (Serial publications of German trade unions in the Memorial Library, University of Wisconsin-Madison.) – 1 – us U.W. Library [330]

JAHRESBERICHT / Verband der deutschen Buchdrucker – Berlin. 1919-31. Title varies: Bericht. Includes some suppls. for regional unions. (Serial publications of German trade unions in the Memorial Library, University of Wisconsin-Madison.) – 1 – us U.W. Library [330]

JAHRESBERICHT / Verband der Gemeinde- und Staatsarbeiter – 1919-21. Berlin. (Serial publications of German trade unions in the Memorial Library, University of Wisconsin-Madison.) – 1 – us U.W. Library [330]

JAHRESBERICHT / Verband der Steinsetzer, Pflasterer und Berufsgenossen Deutschlands. Berlin – 1907-08, 1910 11, 1912, 1914 15. (Serial publications of German trade unions in the Memorial Library, University of Wisconsin-Madison.) – 1 – us U.W. Library [330]

JAHRESBERICHT / Verband deutscher Berufsfeuerwehrmaenner – 1925. Berlin. (Serial publications of German trade unions in the Memorial Library, University of Wisconsin-Madison.) – 1 – us U.W. Library [330]

JAHRESBERICHT / Verein fuer Geschichte der Stadt Nuernberg – Nuernberg. Vereinsjahr 3-61, 65-76; 1880-1938, 1942-53. Film Mas C 424 – 1 – us H.U. Library [943]

JAHRESBERICHT / Verein fuer Naturkunde in OEsterreich, Ob der Enns, Linz – v1-44 1870-1918 – 1 – us U.W. Library [500]

JAHRESBERICHT / Zentralverband der Lederarbeiter und Arbeiterinnen Deutschlands – 1912-13, 1915. Berlin. (Serial publications of German trade unions in the Memorial Library, University of Wisconsin-Madison.) – 1 – us U.W. Library [330]

JAHRESBERICHT.. / Arbeiter-Sekretariat. Bremen – v3, 1902. (Serial publications of German trade unions in the Memorial Library, University of Wisconsin-Madison) – 1 – us U.W. Library [330]

JAHRESBERICHT DER AKTIENGESELLSCHAFT REICHSKOHLENVERBAND – Berlin, 1920-38 – 2r – 1 – DM240.00 – gw Mikro Press [380]

JAHRESBERICHT DER DEUTSCHEN MATHEMATIKER-VEREINIGUNG / ed by Enestrom, G – 1910-13 – 7 – uk Microform Academic [510]

JAHRESBERICHT DER ORTSVERWALTUNG FUER.../ZENTRALVERBAND.. / Zentralverband der Schuhmacher. Zahlstelle Berlin – 1923 24, 1925 27. Berlin. Title from cover. Description based on: 1923-24. (Serial publications of German trade unions in the Memorial Library, University of Wisconsin-Madison.) – 1 – us U.W. Library [330]

JAHRESBERICHT DER POLLICHIA, EINES NATURWISSENSCHAFTLICHEN VEREINS DER BAYERISCHEN PFALZ – (Cont. as: Mitteilungen der Pollichia 1888-1936 v47-97) – Landau, Neustadt a.d. Haardt. v1-46. 1843-1888 – 100mf – ne IDC [500]

JAHRESBERICHT DER SCHLESISCHEN GESELLSCHAFT FUER VATERLAENDISCHE CULTUR, 1850-1933 *see* UEBERSICHT DER ARBEITEN UND VERAENDERUNGEN DER SCHLESISCHEN GESELLSCHAFT FUER VATERLAENDISCHE CULTUR, 1824-1849

JAHRESBERICHT DES ENTOMOLOGISCHEN VEREINS ZU STETTIN – (Continued as ENTOMOLOGISCHE ZEITUNG. Stettin, 1840-1914. v.1-75. Continued as STETTINER ENTOMOLOGISCHE ZEITUNG. Stettin, 1915-1942. v.76-103) – Stettin, 1839. v.1 – 778mf – 1,5,6 – ne IDC [590]

JAHRESBERICHT DES PHYSIKALISCHEN VEREINS ZU FRANKFURT AM MAIN / Physikalischer Verein. Frankfurt am Main – 15v 1858-1931 – 1 – $92.00 – us L of C Photodup [530]

JAHRESBERICHT DES VEREINS FUER DIE BERGBAULICHEN INTERESSEN – Essen, 1861-1913; 1925-30; 1934-36 – 5r – 1 – DM375.00 – gw Mikro Press [943]

JAHRESBERICHT FOR THE PACIFIC COLONIES ONLY, 1898-1908 = GERMAN COLONIAL ADMINISTRATION ANNUAL REPORTS – 1r – 1 – PMB Doc401 – at Pacific Mss [980]

JAHRESBERICHT FUER DAS GESCHAFTSJAHR / Deutscher Metallarbeiterverband. Verwaltungsstelle. Berlin – Berlin. 1918-19, 1921-22, 1924, 1926-27. (Serial publications of German trade unions in the Memorial Library, University of Wisconsin-Madison.) – 1 – us U.W. Library [330]

JAHRESBERICHT UEBER DAS GESCHAFTSJAHR / Deutscher Verkehrsbund – Berlin. 1929. (Serial publications of German trade unions in the Memorial Library, University of Wisconsin-Madison.) – 1 – us U.W. Library [330]

JAHRESBERICHT UEBER DIE ERSCHEINUNGEN AUF DEM GEBIETE DER GERMANISCHEN PHILOLOGIE – Berlin, etc. v. 1-22; 1879-1900. Film Mas C 681 – 1 – us H.U. Library [400]

JAHRESBERICHT UEBER DIE FORTSCHRITTE DER KLASSISCHEN ALTERTUMSWISSENSCHAFT – Leipzig. O. R. Reisland. Bd. 1-285; 1873-1955. No more published. Superseded by Lustrum; internationale Forschungsberichte aus dem Bereich des klassischen Altertums. Title varies slightly. Includes Index, v. 1-87. Film Mas C 675 – 1 – us H.U. Library [930]

JAHRESBERICHT UEBER DIE FORTSCHRITTE DER KLASSISCHEN ALTERTUMSWISSENSCHAFT, 1899-1909 – Leipzig. v100-144. 1900-1910 – 283mf – 9 – ne IDC [400]

JAHRESBERICHT UEBER DIE FORTSCHRITTE DER THIERCHEMIE – bd.1-bd.49. 1871-1922 – 3 – us Readex [540]

JAHRESBERICHT UEBER DIE TAETIGKEIT DES ZENTRALVORSTUNDES / Deutscher Lederarbeiter-Verband – Berlin. 1922, 1925-27. illus. (Serial publications of German trade unions in the Memorial Library, University of Wisconsin-Madison.) – 1 – us U.W. Library [330]

JAHRESBERICHT UEBER NEUERUNGEN UND LEISTUNGEN AUF DEM GEBIET DES PFLANZENSCHUTZES / Hollrung, M – v. 1-10. Berlin. 1898-1907. B-7454 2 – 8 – ne IDC [580]

JAHRESBERICHT UND ABRECHNUNG / Verband der deutschen Hutarbeiter – Altenberg. 1919. tables. (Serial publications of German trade unions in the Memorial Library, University of Wisconsin-Madison.) – 1 – us U.W. Library [330]

JAHRESBERICHTE DER FABRIKINSPEKTOREN : JAHRESBERICHTE DER GEWERBEAUFSICHTSBEAMTEN UND BERGBEHOERDEN BERLIN – Berlin, 1875-1937/38 – 41r – 1 – DM3,075.00 – gw Mikro Press [670]

JAHRESBERICHTE DER GESCHICHTSWISSENSCHAFT / Historische Gesellschaft zu Berlin – Berlin, E. S. Mittler. v.1.-36. 1878-1913. Superseded in 1918 by Jahresberichte der duetschen Geschichte. Film Mas C 390 – 1 – us H.U. Library [073]

JAHRESBERICHTE DER VERWAITUNGSBEHOSDEN / Hamburg – Hamburg.1877-1927. 16 reels – 1 – 23.00r – us L of C Photodup [943]

JAHRESBERICHTE UEBER DIE FORTSCHRITTE DER CHEMIE UND VERWANDTER TEILE ANDERER WISSENSCHAFTEN – 1847-1899 – 1 – us Princeton Micro [540]

JAHRESBRIEFE DES BERNEUCHENER KREISES – 1(1931)-5(1936) – 19mf – 9 – Dfl67.00 – ne Slangenburg [073]

JAHRESBUCH / Verband der Maler, Lackierer, Anstreicher, Tuencher und Weissbinder Deutschlands – 1911-12. Hamburg. (Serial publications of German trade unions in the Memorial Library, University of Wisconsin-Madison.) – 1 – us U.W. Library [330]

EIN JAHRHUNDERT RHEINISCHE MISSION / Bonn, A – 1928 – 1 – us A.T.L.A. [240]

EIN JAHRTAUSEND LATEINISCHER HYMNENDICHTUNG / Dreves, G M & -Blume, J – Leipzig. v1-2. 1909 – 18mf – 8 – Dfl63.00 – ne Slangenburg [450]

JAHWES WOHNSTAETTEN: NACH DEN ANSCHAUUNGEN DER ALTEN HEBRAEER / Westphal, Gustav – Giessen: Alfred Toepelmann, 1908. 1 fiche – 9 – us A.T.L.A. [270]

JAI HIND – Hubli, India. 1947-54 – 4r – 1 – us L of C Photodup [072]

JAI HIND – Rajkot, India. Apr-Sept 1966 – 2r – 1 – us L of C Photodup [072]

JAIL ADMINISTRATION DIGEST – v. 1-. 1978- – 1,5,6,9 – us UMI [340]

JAIL CALENDAR / Sedgwick County. Kansas. Sheriff – 1886-1907 – 1 – us KS Hist [360]

JAIL RECORDS OF SHAWNEE COUNTY, KANSAS / Shawnee County. Kansas. Sheriff – 1890-97, 1935-48 – 1 – us KS Hist [360]

JAIL REGISTER / Van Wert County. Ohio. Sheriff – 1874-1912 – 1r – 1 – $32.50r – us Archival [324]

JAIL REGISTER / Wyandot County. Ohio. Sheriff – 1849-1918 – 1r – 1 – $32.50r – us Archival [324]

JAIL REGISTERS / Defiance County. Ohio. Sheriff – 1871-1951 – 2r – 1 – $32.50r – us Archival [324]

JAIL REGISTERS / Erie County. Ohio. Sheriff – 1957-1963 – 2r – 1 – $32.50r – us Archival [324]

JAIL REGISTERS / Fulton County. Ohio. Sheriff – 1869-1927 – 2r – 1 – $32.50r – us Archival [324]

JAIL REGISTERS / Lucas County. Ohio. Toledo, City Police Department – 1872-1921 – 32r – 1 – $32.50r – us Archival [324]

JAIL REGISTERS (WOMEN) / Lucas County. Ohio. Toledo, City Police Department – 1910-1921 – 4r – 1 – $32.50r – us Archival [324]

JAIME 1 : DIEZMOS, TESTAMENTO; CONQUISTA DE VALENCIA (SIECLE 13) – Barcelona – 1r – 5,6 – sp Cultura [946]

JAIME 1 Y LUGARTENENCIA DEL INFANTE PEDRO (ANNO 1231-1276) – Barcelona – 1r – 5,6 – sp Cultura [946]

Jaime, G *see* DE KOULIKORO A TOMBOUCTOU A BORD DU "MAGE", 1889-1890

Jaimes Freyre, Ricardo *see* HISTORIA DEL DESCUBRIMIENTO DE TUCUMAN, SEGUIDA DE INVESTIGACIONES HISTORICAS

THE JAINA GAZETTE – Lucknow: Bharat Jaina Mahamandal. [v 9 n10-v14]. oct 1913-1918 – us Res Libr [950]

Jaipur. India (State). Development and Planning Department *see* FIVE YEAR PLAN OF JAIPUR STATE

JAIPUR PORTFOLIO OF ARCHITECTURAL DETAILS / Winton Jacob, S – 10 v. London. 1890. BI-587 2 – 8 – ne IDC [720]

JAIRE – Badajoz, 1954 y 1955 – 5 – sp Bibl Santa Ana [073]

Jajasan, Bakti *see* RUDJAK MANIS

Jajasan, Karya Pariwisata *see* MAKASSAR. SULSELRA, ITS CULTURE, ARTS AND BEAUTY

JAJASAN KEBUDAJAAN INDONESIA MALUKU – Kesenian Maluku; programma. Ambon, 1954?. 32p.illus.SEM-3397/1 – 9 – ne IDC [950]

Jajasan Kebudajaan Sulawese Selatan dan Tenggara *see* BINGKISAN

Jajasan Penerbit Pantjasila *see* BERITA FAKTA INDONESIA AND INTERNASIONAL

Jajasan Penerbitan "Djiwa Baru" *see* BHAKTI; MADJALAH BULANAN TENTANG PENDIDIKAN DALAM KELUARGA

JAJASAN PUSAT KEBUDAJAAN – Stichting Cultureel Centrum Oost-Indonesie. Ende/ Flores, Arnoldus, 1949. 107p. BSE-14265-66/1 – 9 – ne IDC [950]

JAK NIE NALEZY MOWIC I PISAC PO POLSKU / Krynski, A A – Warszawa. 1921. BR-8022 2 – 8 – ne IDC [943]

Jakarta *see*
- DJAKARTA PRESS SUMMARY
- EDITORIALS FROM DJAKARTA PRESS

THE JAKARTA TIMES – Jakarta: Zein Effendi, sep 23 1972-jan 21 1974 – us Res Libr [072]

Jakarta. Universitas Indonesia *see*
- THE GOVERNMENT'S PROGRAM ON INDUSTRIES; A PROGRESS REPORT
- SOME DATA ON THE POPULATION OF DJABRES: A VILLAGE IN CENTRAL JAVA
- SOME FACTS CONCERNING THE UNIVERSITY OF INDONESIA
- SPEECH DELIVERED ON SIXTH DIES NATALIS OF UNIVERSITAS INDONESIA, ON 2D FEB., 1956, AT BANDUNG, BY PROF. BAHDER DJOHAN
- SPEECH ON SEVENTH DIES NATALIS OF UNIVERSITAS INDONESIA ON FEB. 2ND, 1957, AT DJAKARTA, BY PROF. BAHDER DJOHAN
- SPEECH ON THE 4TH DIES NATALIS OF THE UNIVERSITY OF INDONESIA ON FEB. 4, 1954
- SPEECH ON THE FIFTH DIES NATALIS OF THE UNIVERSITY OF INDONESIA ON 10TH FEB., 1955 AT BANDUNG, BY PROF. BAHDER DJOHAN
- SUMMARY OF LECTURE AT CEREMONY OF THE 8TH DIES NATALIS OF THE UNIVERSITY OF INDONESIA
- SUMMARY OF THE ANNUAL REPORT FOR 1950 OF THE INSTITUTE FOR LINGUISTIC AND CULTURAL RESEARCH
- SUMMARY OF THE ANNUAL REPORT FOR 1951 OF THE INSTITUTE FOR LINGUISTIC AND CULTURAL RESEARCH

Jakarta. Universitas Indonesia. Fakultas Ekonomi *see* READINGS IN ECONOMICS

Jakarta. Universitas Indonesia. Fakultas Kedokteran *see* MORE DOCTORS FOR INDONESIA; A PICTURE STORY OF THE AFFILIATION BETWEEN THE SCHOOLS OF MEDICINE OF THE UNIVERSITY OF INDONESIA IN DJAKARTA AND THE UNIVERSITY OF CALIFORNIA IN SAN FRANCISCO

Jakarta. Universitas Indonesia. Fakultas Sastra *see* PEDOMAN SEMENTARA

JAKKO : DER ROMAN EINES JUNGEN / Weidenmann, Alfred – 4. Aufl. Stuttgart: Loewes (F Carl), 1941 – 1r – 1 – us U.W. Library [830]

JAKOB AYRERS "SIDEA", SHAKESPEARES "TEMPEST" UND DAS MAERCHEN / Fouquet, Karl – (Includes bibliographical references) – Marburg a.L.: N G Elwert, 1929 – 1r – 1 – us U.W. Library [410]

JAKOB FRIEDRICH FRIES : AUS SEINEM HANDSCHRIFTLICHEN NACHLASSE / Henke, Ernst Ludwig Theodor – Leipzig: F.A. Brockhaus, 1867 – 1mf – us A.T.L.A. [240]

JAKOB WASSERMANN UND SEIN WERK / Wassermann-Speyer, Julie – Wien: Deutsch-Oesterreichischer Verlag, 1923 – 1r – 1 – us U.W. Library [430]

JAKOBS, DES HANDWERKSGESELLEN WANDERUNGEN DURCH DIE SCHWEIZ / Gotthelf, Jeremias; ed by Hunziker, Rudolf – Muenchen: Verlegt von Eugen Rentsch im Delphin-Verlag, 1917 – 1 – us U.W. Library [830]

DER JAKOBUSBRIEF: NACH LEHRANSCHAUUNGEN UND ENTSTEHUNGSVERHAELTNISSEN / Feine, Paul – Eisenach: M. Wilckens, 1893. 1 fiche – 9 – us A.T.L.A. [220]

DER JAKOBUSBRIEF UND DIE NEUERE KRITIK / Weiss, Bernhard – Leipzig: A Deichert (Georg Boehme), 1904 – 1mf – 9 – 0-8370-7437-1 – 1986-1437 – us A.T.L.A. [220]

Jakovlev, IA A *see* K VOPROSU O SOTSIALISTICHESKOM PEREUSTROISTVE SELSKOGO KHOZIAISTVA

Jakubowicz, M *see* GRAMMATYKA JEZYKA POLSKIEGO

Jal *see* DICTIONNAIRE CRITIQUE DE BIOGRAPHIE ET D'HISTOIRE

Jal, A *see* GLOSSAIRE NAUTIQUE

Jalal-al-Din, al Suyuti *see* A HISTORY OF THE TEMPLE OF JERUSALEM

Jalisco. Mexico *see*
- EL ESTADO DE JALISCO
- EL ESTADO DEL JALISCO: PERIODICO OFICIAL DEL GOBIERNO

Jaloux, Edmond *see* DU REVE A LA REALITE

JAMA, THE JOURNAL OF THE AMERICAN MEDICAL ASSOCIATION / American medical association – (1964- 5,6. 1970- 9) – 1-1883- – 1 – us UMI [610]

JAMAICA : ANNUAL ABSTRACT OF STATISTICS 1947-1968 / Jamaica. Department of Statistics – (1964 not publ. 1947 not available. Coll title: Latin American and Caribbean Official Statistical Serials, 1821-1982) – 9 – £7.00f (set £385.00 46mf) – uk Chadwyck [972]

JAMAICA : STATISTICAL ABSTRACT 1972-1976 / Jamaica. Department of Statistics – (Coll title: Latin American and Caribbean Official Statistical Serials, 1821-1982) – 14mf – 9 – £7.00f (set £385.00 46mf) – uk Chadwyck [972]

Jamaica *see*
- ABSTRACTS OF WILLS PROVED IN 1625-1792
- FIVE YEAR INDEPENDENCE PLAN, 1963-1968
- FIVE-YEAR DEVELOPMENT PROGRAMME, 1955/56-1959/60
- A NATIONAL PLAN FOR JAMAICA, 1957-1967
- TEN-YEAR PLAN OF DEVELOPMENT (1946/47-1955/56)

JAMAICA: 1836-1937 AND 1945 – M.A.P. East Ardsley west yorks, Published October 1991 – 42r – 1 – uk Microform Academic [972]

JAMAICA ARISE! : THE POLITICAL AND LABOUR GUIDE [OFFICIAL ORGAN OF THE PNP] 1947-50. VOLS 1-4 FROM THE RICHARD HARK COLLECTION – 4mf – 9 – uk Microform Academic [320]

Jamaica. Assembly *see*
- JOURNALS
- JOURNALS OF THE ASSEMBLY OF JAMAICA, 1663-1826

Jamaica. Central Planning Unit *see*
- SECOND FIVE YEAR PLAN 1970-75
- TEN-YEAR PLAN, 1962-1971

JAMAICA CHRISTIAN CHRONICLE – (People's Paper). Kingston. Jamaica. -w. 3 May 1888, 6 Apr 1893-10 Nov 1894. (Very imperfect). (38 ft) – 1 – uk British Libr Newspaper [072]

JAMAICA CHURCHMAN – Kingston, Jamaica. -m. Sept 1899-Sept 1915. Lacking Jan 1903. 2 reels – 1 – uk British Libr Newspaper [073]

JAMAICA COUNCIL FOR HUMAN RIGHTS (JCHR) – Kingston. 177 docs. 1980-1990 – 29mf – 9 – ne IDC [320]

JAMAICA CREOLE – Kingston. Jamaica. -d. 24 Sep 1878, 9, 24 Jan, 8, 24 Feb, 11, 24 Mar, 9 Apr, 10 May, 9 Jul, 9 Aug 1879. (10 ft) – 1 – uk British Libr Newspaper [072]

JAMAICA DAILY TELEGRAPH – Kingston, Jamaica. 10, 27 Apr 1899-31 Dec 1909.-d. 58 reels – 1 – uk British Libr Newspaper [072]

Jamaica. Department of Statistics *see*
- JAMAICA

JAMAICA DESPATCH AND JAMAICA GAZETTE – Kingston. Jamaica. -d. 1 Jan-21 Apr 1840. (1 reel) – 1 – uk British Libr Newspaper [072]

JAMAICA GAZETTE – Kingston. v75-93. 1952-70 – 24r – 1 – us Ross [072]

Jamaica Labour Movement *see* MASSES

JAMAICA LABOUR WEEKLY : 1938-1939 FROM THE RICHARD HARK COLLECTION – 3mf – 9 – uk Microform Academic [073]

JAMAICA MAIL – Kingston, Jamaica. 2 Jan 1930-13 Jun 1931.-d 9 reels – 1 – uk British Libr Newspaper [072]

THE JAMAICA MAROONS: HOW THEY CAME TO NOVA SCOTIA: HOW THEY LEFT IT / Brymner, Douglas – 1894? 02111. (Pre-1900 Canadiana) – 9 – cn C.I.H.M. [971]

JAMAICA MERCURY – (Royal Gazette). Kingston. Jamaica. -w. May 1779-Dec 1781, 1815. (3 reels) – 1 – uk British Libr Newspaper [072]

Jamaica. Ministry of Education *see*
- ANNUAL REPORT 1975/76-1983/84
- DIRECTORY OF EDUCATIONAL INSTITUTIONS 1983-1984
- EARLY CHILDHOOD EDUCATION PROGRAMME
- EDUCATION STATISTICS 1974/75-1984/85
- THE EDUCATION THRUST OF THE 70'S

Jamaica. Ministry of Education. Planning Division *see* FIVE YEAR EDUCATION PLAN 1978-1983

JAMAICA PEOPLE'S NATIONAL PARTY : PAMPHLETS, LEAFLETS, ETC. 1938-1956 – 12mf – 9 – uk Microform Academic [320]
JAMAICA POST – Kingston, Jamaica. 11 Oct 1892-8 Apr 1899.-tw. 13 reels – 1 – uk British Libr Newspaper [072]
JAMAICA QUEEN'S VOICE – New York. N.Y. 1967- – 1 – us UMI [071]
JAMAICA STANDAARD – Kingston, 1938(Apr 4)-1939(Dec 23) – 10r – 1,5,6 – ne IDC [072]
JAMAICA STANDARD – Montego Bay. Jamaica. -sw. 9 Jan 1839-Apr 1840. (44 ft) – 1 – uk British Libr Newspaper [072]
JAMAICA TIMES – Kingston, Jamaica. 25 Aug 1900-24 Jun 1922; 4 Jan 1930-30 Jul 1938; 7 Jan-30 Sep, 23 Dec 1939-14 Sep 1940; 3 Mar 1951-27 Jun 1953; 22 Jun 1957-22 Jan 1963 (1939, 40 imperfect).-w. 50 reels – 1 – uk British Libr Newspaper [072]
JAMAICA TIMES – Kingston. Jamaica. -w. 3 Mar 1951-27 Jun 1953, 22 Jun 1957-26 Jan 1963. (7 reels) – 1 – uk British Libr Newspaper [072]
JAMAICA WITNESS – Falmouth. Jamaica. -w. 15 Jan 1877-4 Oct 1878, 6 Jan-1 May 1879, 1 Jan 1883-1 Oct 1887. (Imperfect). (1 reel) – 1 – uk British Libr Newspaper [072]
THE JAMAICAN – Kingston. Jamaica. -sw. 2 Nov-28 Dec 1907. (31 ft) – 1 – uk British Libr Newspaper [072]
JAMAICAN WEEKLY GLEANER – (1988-1992.-10r) – Toronto, 1993 – 2r – 1 – cn Preston [971]
JAMAICAN WEEKLY GLEANER – Kingston. Jamaica. 1958- – 1 – us UMI [072]
Jamandreu, Paco *see* EVITA FUERA DEL BALC ON
Jambert *see* LES SAINTS
JAM-E-JAMSHED – Bombay, India. 1947-Jul 1987 – 125r – 1 – us L of C Photodup [072]
JAMES A. GARFIELD FAMILY PAPERS *see* GARFIELD, JAMES A., FAMILY PAPERS MS 4575
JAMES A. GARFIELD PAPERS – (With guide) – 177r – 1 – $6,195.00 – Dist. us Scholarly Res – us L of C Photodup [975]
JAMES AND LUCRETIA MOTT: LIFE AND LETTERS / ed by Hallowell, Anna Davis – Ed. by their granddaughter, Anna Davis Hallowell. 1884 – 9 – us A.T.L.A. [240]
JAMES BACKUS PAPERS, MS 1548 / Backus, James – 1791-1833. 1 reel – 1 – us Western Res [920]
THE JAMES BAY AND NORTHERN QUEBEC AGREEMENT – Quebec: Editeur officiel du Quebec, c1976. SEM105P446 – 6mf – 9 – Can$13.50 – cn Bibl Nat [971]
James, Bob *see*
– A READER OF AUSTRALIAN ANARCHISM, 1886-96
– WHAT IS COMMUNISM? AND OTHER ANARCHIST ESSAYS
JAMES BUCHANAN AND HARRIET (LANE) JOHNSTON PAPERS – (With guide) – 4r – 1 – $140.00 – Dist. us Scholarly Res – us L of C Photodup [975]
THE JAMES BUCHANAN PAPERS, 1781-1893 – 60r – 1 – $3680.00 – us UMI [920]
James, C Roger et al *see* EFFECTS OF FATIGUE ON MECHANICAL AND MUSCULAR COMPONENTS OF PERFORMANCE DURING DROP LANDINGS
JAMES CALVERT : OR, FROM DARK TO DAWN IN FIJI / Vernon, R (Mrs) – 2nd ed. New York: Fleming H Revell, [189-] – 1mf – 9 – 0-8370-6710-3 – 1986-0710 – us A.T.L.A. [920]
James, Charles *see* A COLLECTION OF THE CHARGES, OPINIONS AND SENTENCES OF GENERAL COURTS-MARTIAL
James, Charles F *see* THE STRUGGLES FOR RELIGIOUS LIBERTY IN VIRGINIA
James, Charles R *see* EFFECTS OF OVERUSE INJURY PRONENESS AND TASK DIFFICULTY ON JOINT KINETIC VARIABILITY DURING LANDING
JAMES CONNOLLY PAMPHLET COLLECTION – 191?-1975 – 1r – 1 – us Hoover Inst Photo [941]
James, Croake *see*
– CURIOSITIES OF LAW AND LAWYERS
JAMES DUANE DOTY PAPERS, MS 1090 / Doty, James Duane – 1820-40. Collection includes letters, deeds, legal opinions relating in part to Indian matters and lands in Wisconsin. 1 reel – 1 – us Western Res [920]
James, Francis Bacon *see* THE OHIO LAW OF OPINION EVIDENCE, EXPERT AND NON-EXPERT
JAMES FRANCIS EDWARD, THE OLD CHEVALIER / Haile, Martin – With 11 photogravure illus. London: J.M. Dent & Co; New York: E.P. Dutton & Co., 1907. xii,479,(1)p. 11 ports. on 10 pl – 1 – us U.W. Library [920]
James, Frank A J L *see* CHEMISTRY AND THEOLOGY IN MID-VICTORIAN LONDON
JAMES FRASER, SECOND BISHOP OF MANCHESTER : A MEMOIR, 1818-1885 / Hughes, Thomas – London, New York: Macmillan and Co, 1987 – 1r – 1 – us U.W. Library [920]
JAMES FREEMAN CLARKE : AUTOBIOGRAPHY, DIARY AND CORRESPONDENCE / ed by Hale, Edward Everett – Boston: Houghton, Mifflin, 1891 – 1mf – us A.T.L.A. [240]
JAMES G. BIRNEY AND HIS TIMES : THE GENESIS OF THE REPUBLICAN PARTY WITH SOME ACCOUNT OF ABOLITION MOVEMENTS IN THE SOUTH BEFORE 1828 / Birney, William – New York: D. Appleton, 1890, c1889 – 2mf – us A.T.L.A. [320]
JAMES G. SWAN PAPERS (1852-1907) – Vancouver, BC: University of British Columbia Library, 1994 – 9r – 1 – Can$100.00r – cn U.B.C. Preserve [971]
James, George Francis *see* HANDBOOK OF UNIVERSITY EXTENSION; WITH AN INTRODUCTION BY E.J. JAMES
JAMES GILMOUR OF MONGOLIA : HIS DIARIES, LETTERS, AND REPORTS / Gilmour, James; ed by Lovett, Richard – (Includes index) – London: Religious Tract Society, 1892 – 1mf – 9 – 0-8370-6053-2 – 1986-0053 – us A.T.L.A. [240]
JAMES HARRIS FAIRCHILD, OR, SIXTY-EIGHT YEARS WITH A CHRISTIAN COLLEGE / Swing, Albert Temple – New York: F.H. Revell, c1907 – 1mf – us A.T.L.A. [240]
James, Henry *see*
– LECTURES AND MISCELLANIES
– THE SECRET OF SWEDENBORG
– WILLIAM WETMORE STORY AND HIS FRIENDS
James, Herbert A *see* SCHOOL IDEALS
JAMES HOGG / Douglas, George Brisbane – Edinburgh, London: Oliphant, Anderson & Ferrier, [1899] – 1r – 1 – 1-55879-273-2 – uk Libr Preservation [920]
James Island. Charleston County. South Carolina. St. James Episcopal Church *see* RECORDS
James, J D *see* THE GENUINENESS AND AUTHORSHIP OF THE PASTORAL EPISTLES
THE JAMES J. HILL PAPERS – (Pt 1, Personal and Private Series, 1874, 1877-1916: 17r $1,635.00; Pt 2, Pre-Railroad Business Series, 1866-78: 4r $380.00; Pt 3, Railroad Series, 1877-98: 27r $2,600.00. With printed guides) – 1 – $4,385.00 set – us UPA [920]
James, John Henry *see* MILITARY COMMISSIONS FOR THE TRIAL OF CITIZENS
James, Joseph H *see* THE LIFE OF MRS. MARY D. JAMES
JAMES JOYCE QUARTERLY – (v14- 1976-5,6,9) – v1- 1963- – 1 – us UMI [420]
JAMES K. POLK PAPERS – (With guide) – 67r – 1 – $2,345.00 – Dist. us Scholarly Res – us L of C Photodup [975]
James, King L *see* HISTORY OF SHAWNEE COUNTY AND REPRESENTATIVE CITIZENS
THE JAMES M. COMLY PAPERS / Comly, James M – (With printed guide) – 3r – 1 – $255.00 – D3170 – Dist. us Scholarly Res – us Ohio Hist [070]
JAMES M. PARKER DAYBOOK *see* PARKER, JAMES M., DAYBOOK, MS 2067
James, M R *see*
– APOCRYPHA ANECDOTA
– APOCRYPHA ANEDOCTA
– THE APOCRYPHAL NEW TESTAMENT
– THE TESTAMENT OF ABRAHAM
JAMES MACPHERSON : AN EPISODE IN LITERATURE / Smart, John Semple – London: D. Nutt, 1905 – 1 roll – 1 – 1-55879-861-7 – uk Libr Preservation [420]
JAMES MADISON / Gay, Sydney Howard – Boston & NY: Houghton, Mifflin & Co, 1899 – 4mf – 9 – $6.00 – LLMC 96-029 – us L.L.M.C. [975]
JAMES MADISON PAPERS – 28r – 1 – $980.00 – Dist. us Scholarly Res – us L of C Photodup [975]
JAMES MADISON'S NOTES OF DEBATES IN THE FEDERAL CONVENTION OF 1789 : AND THEIR RELATION TO A MORE PERFECT SOCIETY OF NATIONS / Scott, James Brown – New York: Oxford UP, American Branch, 1918 – 2mf – 9 – $3.00 – LLMC 95-078 – us L.L.M.C. [323]
JAMES MARTINEAUS ETHIK : DARSTELLUNG, KRITIK UND PAEDAGOGISCHE KONSEQUENZEN / Wilkinson, John J – Leipzig, 1898 – 2mf – 9 – DM62.00 – 3-89349-299-2 – gw Hänsel [170]
JAMES MERLE: AN AUTOBIOGRAPHY / Black, William – Edited i.e. written by W. Black. British Fiction Archive: Unit 4 – 9 – uk Bell [920]
JAMES MONROE PAPERS – 11r – 1 – $385.00 – Dist. us Scholarly Res – us L of C Photodup [975]
THE JAMES MONROE PAPERS – (With printed guide) – Rare Books and Manuscript Division: The New York Public Library, Astor, Lenox and Tilden Foundations 1995 – ca 8r – 1 – ca $680.00 – D3336 – us Scholarly Res [320]
JAMES MONROE PAPERS IN VIRGINIA REPOSITORIES – (With printed guide) – 13r – 1 – $1,105.00 – D3186 – us Nat'l Archives [975]
James, Montague Rhodes *see* PSALMS OF THE PHARISEES, COMMONLY CALLED THE PSALMS OF SOLOMON
JAMES PATTISON PAPERS, 1777-81 / Pattison, James – BRRAM – 1 – uk Microform Academic [920]
James, Philip Gilbert *see* BRITISH POLICY IN RELATION TO THE GOLD COAST 1815-1850
James, Robert *see*
– DICTIONNAIRE UNIVERSEL DE MEDECINE (AEL, ABT.3;3.2)
– A MEDICAL DICTIONARY, INCLUDING PHYSIC, SURGERY, ANATOMY, CHIMISTRY AND BOTANY (AEL, ABT 3;3.1)
James, S P *see* A MONOGRAPH OF THE ANOPHELES MOSQUITOES OF INDIA
JAMES SKINNER : A MEMOIR / Trench, Maria – London: K. Paul, Trench, 1883 – 1mf – us A.T.L.A. [240]
James, T S *see* THE HISTORY OF THE LITIGATION AND LEGISLATION RESPECTING PRESBYTERIAN CHAPELS AND CHARITIES IN ENGLAND AND IRELAND BETWEEN 1861 AND 1849
JAMES, THE LORD'S BROTHER / Patrick, William – (Includes an appendix and indexes) – Edinburgh: T & T Clark, 1906 – 1mf – 9 – 0-8370-4674-2 – 1985-2674 – us A.T.L.A. [220]
James, William *see*
– A FULL AND CORRECT ACCOUNT OF THE CHIEF NAVAL OCCURRENCES OF THE LATE WAR BETWEEN GREAT BRITAIN AND THE UNITED STATES OF AMERICA, PRECEDED BY... AMERICAN ACCOUNTS OF THEIR NAVAL ACTIONS FOUGHT PREVIOUS TO THAT PERIOD
– THE NAVAL HISTORY OF GREAT BRITAIN, FROM THE DECLARATION OF WAR BY FRANCE, 1793, TO THE ACCESSION OF GEORGE 4, 1820
– A PLURALISTIC UNIVERSE
Jameson, A B *see* LEGENDS OF THE MADONNA AS REPRESENTED IN THE FINE ARTS
Jameson, C *see* MAGNETIC RESONANCE REVIEW
Jameson, D *see* COMMENTS ON MOLECULAR AND CELLULAR BIOPHYSICS
Jameson, J Franklin *see* ESSAYS IN THE CONSTITUTIONAL HISTORY OF THE UNITED STATES IN THE FORMATIVE PERIOD, 1775-1789
Jameson, W *see* SYNOPSIS PLANTARUM AEQUATORIENSIUM
JAMESTOWN NEWS – Jamestown, NV. 1908 – 1r – 1 – $50.00 – U04848 – us Library Micro [071]
JAMIAT AL-RIYAD.KULLIYAT AL-ULUM – Bulletin of the Faculty of Science, Riyadh University. v1-10. 1969-79 – 1 – us UMI [370]
Jamieson, D G *see* INDEX TO OBITUARIES AND DEATH NOTICES IN THE NEW ZEALAND MEDICAL JOURNAL 1886-FEBRUARY 1981
Jamieson, Robert *see*
– EASTERN MANNERS ILLUSTRATIVE OF THE OLD TESTAMENT HISTORY
– THE HISTORICAL BOOKS OF THE HOLY SCRIPTURES
– INSPIRATION OF THE HOLY SCRIPTURES
– THE PENTATEUCH AND THE BOOK OF JOSHUA
Jamin, J *see*
– CONTACTS ET ANTAGONISMES CULTURELS EN PAYS KIKUYU (KENYA)
– LA TENDERIE AUX GRIVES CHEZ LES ARDENNAIS DU PLATEAU
Jammes, Francis *see* LES GEORGIQUES CHRETIENNES: POEME COURONNE PAR L'ACADEMIE FRANCAISE
JAMMU AND KASHMIR / Jammu and Kashmir. India. Census Commissioner – Jammu: Ranbir Govt Press. pts1-4. 1941 – us Res Libr [324]
THE JAMMU AND KASHMIR GOVERNMENT GAZETTE / Kashmir – Jammu. Apr. 4, 1963-Mar. 1967 – 1 – us NY Public [324]
Jammu and Kashmir. India. Census Commissioner *see* JAMMU AND KASHMIR
Jampel, Sigmund *see*
– DAS BUCH ESTHER
– VOM KRIEGSSCHAUPLATZE DER ISRAELITISCHEN RELIGIONSWISSENSCHAFT
– DIE WIEDERHERSTELLUNG ISRAELS UNTER DEN ACHAEMENIDEN
JAMTLANDS ALLEHANDA *see* JAMTLANDS TIDNING
JAMTLANDS TIDNING – (Jamtlands Allehanda, 1889-95) – Ostersund, Sweden. 1895-1957, 1960 – 185r – 1 – sw Kungliga [072]
JAN OF THE WINDMILL / Ewing, Juliana Horatia – British Fiction Archive: Unit 1 – 9 – uk Bell [830]
JAN YUG – Delhi, India. 10 Aug 1952-1953 – 1r – 1 – us L of C Photodup [072]
JANARAJAYE GASAT PATRAYA / Sri Lanka – 1967- – 1 – 130.00y – us L of C Photodup [950]
JANASAKTI – (Oriya language) – Cuttack, India. Jul-Sept 1966 – 1r – 1 – us L of C Photodup [072]
JANASAKTI – Patna, India. 1954 – 1r – 1 – us L of C Photodup [072]
JANASATTA – Ahmedabad, India. Jul-Sept 1966 – 1r – 1 – us L of C Photodup [072]
JANATA – Bombay, 1948, 1949-54 (all incompl) – 1 – us Hoover Inst Photo [072]
Janauschek, PL *see* ORIGINUM CISTERCIENSUM
JANAYUGA – New Delhi, India. Sept 1973-11 May 1985 – 27r – 1 – us L of C Photodup [072]
JANAYUGA (JANYUG) – Lucknow, India. 1954; 1957-60; 1962-63 – 7r – 1 – us L of C Photodup [072]
JANE / Corelli, Marie – British Fiction Archive: Unit 1 – 9 – uk Bell [830]
JANE ADDAMS PAPERS, 1860-1960 / Addams, Jane – 82r – 1 – $5,910.00 – us UMI [305]
JANE AUSTEN'S SAILOR BROTHERS: BEING THE ADVENTURES OF SIR FRANCIS AUSTEN, G.C.B., ADMIRAL OF THE FLEET, AND REAR-ADMIRAL CHARLES AUSTEN / Hubback, John Henry & Hubback (Brown), Edith Charlotte – 1906 – 9 – $20.00 – uk Libr Preservation [920]
JANE EYRE : AN AUTOBIOGRAPHY / Bronte, Charlotte – London: Smith, Elder and Co., 1847 – 2 rolls – 1 – 1-55879-264-3 – uk Libr Preservation [830]
Jane, Frederick T *see* HERESIES OF SEA POWER
Janelle, Christopher M *see* THE RELATIONSHIP OF PHYSICAL SELF-PERCEPTION TO INJURY POTENTIAL OF COLLEGE FOOTBALL ATHLETES
Janelle, Joseph-Emile *see* LA FAMILLE JANELLE
Janentzky, Christian *see* JOHANN CASPAR LAVATER
Janer, F *see*
– CATALOGO DEL MUSEO DE CIENCIAS NATURALES
– MADRID. MUSEO ARQUEOLOGICO NACIONAL INVENTARIO DE LA SECCION DE ETNOGRAFIA
Janet, Paul *see*
– THE MATERIALISM OF THE PRESENT TIME
– THE THEORY OF MORALS
Janeway, Thomas Leiper *see* MEMOIR OF THE REV. JACOB J. JANEWAY
JANG BERONTAK DAN JANG MENJERAH / Bachtiar Djamily – SE-4087 1. 1962 – 9 – ne IDC [950]
Janitschek, Ellinor *see* IM UMSTRITTENEN GEBIET
Janitschek, H *see* LEONE BATTISTA ALBERTI'S KLEINERE KUNSTTHEORETISCHE SCHRIFTEN

Jank, Martin *see* ECKERT AUF GROSSFAHRT
Jankowski, Joachim *see* EINFLUSS VON WASSERDAMPF AUF DEN ABLAUF DER HETEROGEN KATALYSIERTEN OXIDATIVEN KUPPLUNG VON METHAN
JANMABHOOMI – Bombay, India. 1958; 1964-Aug 1966 – 10r – 1 – us L of C Photodup [072]
JANMABHOOMI – Coorg, India. 1962 – 1r – 1 – us L of C Photodup [072]
JANMABHUMI – Masulipatam: M Krishnarao. v1 n1-25 dec 4 1919-may 27 1929; v2 n1-v5 n50 dec 2 1920-nov 27 1924-7. Dec 1919-Nov 1926 – 3r – 1 – us Res Libr [072]
Jann, Adelhelm *see* DIE KATHOLISCHEN MISSIONEN IN INDIEN, CHINA UND JAPAN
Janneau, Guillaume *see* L'APPRENTISSAGE DANS LES METIERS D'ART
Jannequin, C *see* LE PREMIER LIVRE...A QUATRE VOIX.
Jannequin, Claude *see* VOYAGE DE LYBIE AU SENEGAL, LE LONG DU NIGER AVEC LE DESCRIPTION DES HABITANTS QUI SONT LE LONG DE CE FLEUVE, LEURS COUTUMES ET FACONS DE VIVRE, LES PARTICULARITES LES PLUS REMARQUABLES DE'CES PAYS
Janney, Samuel M *see*
- HISTORY OF THE RELIGIOUS SOCIETY OF FRIENDS...
- MEMOIRS OF SAMUEL M. JANNEY
- PEACE PRINCIPLES EXEMPLIFIED IN THE EARLY HISTORY OF PENNSYLVANIA

Jannsen, Johannes *see* GESCHICHTE DES DEUTSCHEN VOLKES SEIT DEM AUSGANG DES MITTELALTERS
Jansen, Brigitte E S *see*
- EINIGE GEDANKEN ZUR AUSDIFFERENZIERUNG VON STAAT UND RECHT
- GEISTESGESCHICHTLICHE ASPEKTE DES GENOSSENSCHAFTLICHEN BILDUNGSGEDANKENS
- ZUM VERSTAENDNIS VON BILDUNG UND AUSBILDUNG IN DER SOZIALLEHRE V. A. HUBERS (1800-1869) UNTER BESONDERER BERUECKSICHTIGUNG DER DIFFERENZ SEINER FRUEH UND SPAETSCHRIFTEN

JANSEN ENIKELS WERKE (MGH 8: 3.BD) : 1. ABT: DIE WELTCHRONIK, 1891. 2. ABT: FUERSTENBUCH, 1900 – Dfl84.00 – ne Slangenburg [240]
Jansen, G H *see* AFRO-ASIA AND NON-ALIGNMENT
JANSEN NEWS – Jansen, NE. -w. Nov 1916-Apr 1925 – 1 – us NE Hist [071]
Jansen, Werner *see* ABSONDERLICHE CHARAKTERE BEI WILHELM RAABE
LE JANSENISME CONVULSIONNAIRE ET L'AFFAIRE DE LA PLANCHETTE : D'APRES LES ARCHIVES DE LA BASTILLE / Gagnol, abbe – Paris: Libraire generale catholique, 1911 – 1mf – 9 – 0-8370-8424-5 – 1986-2424 – us A.T.L.A. [240]
Jansenius, Corn. *see*
- AUGUSTINUS SEU DOCTRINA SANCTI AUGUSTINI DE HUMANAE NATURAE SANITATE
- NOTARUM SPONGIA QUIBUS ALEXIPHARMACUM CIVIBUS SYLVAE-DUCENSIBUS, ASPERSIT GISBERTUS VOETIUS MINISTER SYLVAE-DUCENSIS
- PENTATEUCHUS, SIVE COMMENTARIUS IN QUINQUE LIBROS MOYSIS
- TETRATEUCHUS SIVE COMMENTARIUS IN SANCTA JESU CHRISTI EVANGELIA

Jansenius, Corneil Jansen dit *see* LE MARS FRANCAIS OU LA GUERRE DE FRANCE
Jansen-Runge, Edith *see* ISOLDE UND TRISTAN
JANSON, COBB, PEARSON AND CO SOLICITORS. ARCHIVES / Guildhall Library, London – 1728-1928. 44 reels with printed guide – £1,700.00 – uk World [340]
Janson, John M *see* COLLECTION OF BOOKLETS AND PAMPHLETS OBTAINED IN 1965-66 IN THE LOWER CONGO
Janssen, H Q *see*
- ACTEN VAN DE CLASSICALE EN SYNODALE VERGADERINGEN DER VERSCHILLENDEN GEMEENTEN IN HET LAND VAN CLEEF, STICHT VAN KEULEN EN AKEN 1571-1589 (DE WERKEN..2,2)
- BESCHEIDEN AANGAANDE DE KERKHERVORMING IN VLAANDEREN (DE WERKEN..3,3)
- BRIEVEN UIT ONDERSCHEIDENE KERKELIJKE ARCHIEVEN (DE WERKEN..3,2)
- BRIEVEN UIT ONDERSCHEIDENE KERKELIJKE ARCHIEVEN (DE WERKEN..3,4)

Janssen, H Q. *see*
- ACTEN VAN DE CLASS. EN SYNOD. VERG. DER VERSCH. GEMEENTEN IN HET LAND VAN CLEEF
- DE SYNODE TE EMDEN IN 1571

Janssen, Johannes *see* SCHILLER ALS HISTORIKER
Janssen, N A *see* EEN WOORD OVER HET GREGORIAANSCH
Janssen, O *see* L'EXPRESSIVITE CHEZ SALVIEN DE MARSEILLE, 1
Janssen, R *see* DAS JOHANNES-EVANGELIUM NACH DER PARAPHRASE DES NONNUS PANOPOLITANUS (T.U.U. 2-23/4)
Jantzen Family *see* HISTORY
Jantzen Hillsboro Creamery *see* RECORDS
Jantzen, Peter *see* RECORDS OF THE HILLSBORO CREAMERY
JANUAE CLAVIS: OR, LILLY'S SYNTAX EXPLAINED / Banks, Jonathan – 1679. 83p. (English Linguistics Series 1500-1800) – 9 – us UMI [420]
JANUS : CENTRAL-MAGAZIN FUER GESCHICHTE UND LITERAERGESCHICHTE DER MEDIZIN, AERZTLICHER BIOGRAPHIK, EPIDEMIOGRAPHIK, MEDICINISCHE GEOGRAPHIE UND STATISTIK. NEUE FOLGE / ed by Bretschneider, H et al – Gotha. 2v. 1851-52 – 12mf – 9 – subsc: DM84.00 diazo DM98.00 silver – gw Olms [614]
JANUS : ZEITSCHRIFT FUER GESCHICHTE UND LITERATUR DER MEDICIN / ed by Henschel, A W E Th – Breslau. 3v. 1846-48 – 31mf – 9 – subsc: DM210.00 diazo DM240.00 silver – gw Olms [610]
Janus Cornarius *see* ANTHOLOGIA GRAECA: SELECTA EPIGRAMMATA GRAECA LATINE UERSA, EX SEPTEM EPIGRAMMATUM GRAECORUM LIBRIS; ACCESSERUNT...EPIGRAMMATA, RECENS UERSA, AB ANDREA ALICIATO, OTTOMARO LUSCINIO, AC IANO CORNARIO ZUICCAUIENSI
JANUS – THE EDINBURGH LITERARY ALMANAC – 1826 – 6mf – 9 – £50.00 – uk Chadwyck [800]
JANYUG *see* JANAYUGA (JANYUG)
Janze, Comte de *see* VERTICAL LAND
Janzen, D M *see* HISTORY OF FIRST BAPTIST CHURCH, WILLIAM LAKE, BRITISH COLUMBIA, CANADA
Janzen, Tami M *see* SPONTANEOUS KICKING IN INFANTS
JAOCS *see* JOURNAL OF THE AMERICAN OIL CHEMISTS' SOCIETY
Japan *see*
- CATALOGUE (ILLUSTRATED)
- CODE CIVIL DE L'EMPIRE DU JAPON
- JAPANESE ARCHIVAL MATERIAL ON KOREA
- MEMORIALS OF THE EMPIRE OF JAPAN
- NIPPON BOEKI NENPYO
- OUTLINE OF NEW AND ECONOMIC DEVELOPMENT PLAN
- TAISHO SHOWA-KI KEIZAI TOKEI SHIRYO

JAPAN, 1914-1918 / U.S. Department of State – (Series: U.S. Confidential Diplomatic Post Records: Japan.) 1983. Part 1 – 1 – $1,210.00 – 0-89093-503-3 – us UPA [950]
JAPAN, 1914-41 : CONFIDENTIAL U.S. DIPLOMATIC POST RECORDS – (Part 1, 1914-18: ISBN 0-89093-503-3. $1,210.00; Part 2, 1919-29: ISBN 0-89093-504-1. $5,500.00; Part 3, 1930-41. ISBN 0-89093-505-X. $8,805.00. All with printed guides) – 1983. Over 150,000 pages of reports, unpublished records of U.S. diplomats, minutes of meetings, translations of official Japanese documents – 1 – $14,735.00 set – us UPA [975]
JAPAN, 1918-41 : REPORTS / U.S. Military Intelligence – 31 reels with printed guide – 1 – $2,985.00 – us UPA [324]
JAPAN, 1919-1929 / U.S. Department of State – (Series: U.S. Confidential Diplomatic Post Records: Japan.) 1983. Part 2 – 1 – $5,500.00 – 0-89093-504-1 – us UPA [950]
JAPAN, 1930-1941 / U.S. Department of State – (Series: U.S. Confidential Diplomatic Post Records: Japan.) 1983. Part 3 – 1 – $8,805.00 – 0-89093-505-X – us UPA [950]
JAPAN ACADEMY: PROCEEDINGS – v26-53. 1950-77 – 1,5,6 – us Princeton Micro [073]
JAPAN AND ITS OCCUPIED TERRITORIES DURING WORLD WAR 2 : 1942-45 / U.S. Office of Strategic Services – 1977. Series: OSS State Department Intelligence and Research Reports, Pt 1 – 1 – $1,540.00 – 0-89093-117-8 – us UPA [950]
JAPAN AND ITS REGENERATION / Cary, Otis – (Includes index) – rev ed. New York: Student Volunteer Movt for Foreign Missions, 1908, c1904 – 1mf – 9 – 0-8370-6094-X – 1986-0094 – us A.T.L.A. [240]
JAPAN AND ITS RESCUE : A BRIEF SKETCH OF THE GEOGRAPHY, HISTORY, RELIGION AND EVANGELIZATION OF JAPAN / Hail, A D – Nashville,TN: Cumberland Presbyterian Publ House, 1898 – 1mf – 9 – 0-8370-6061-3 – 1986-0061 – us A.T.L.A. [240]
JAPAN CHRISTIAN ACTIVITY NEWS – 1974-88 (complete) – 3r – 1 – ATLA S0433 – us A.T.L.A. [240]
JAPAN CHRISTIAN QUARTERLY – (1986- . 5,6,9) – v1- . 1926- – 1 – us UMI [073]
JAPAN CHRISTIAN QUARTERLY – v1-40. 1926-78 (complete) – 13r – 1 – ATLA S0073 – us A.T.L.A. [073]
JAPAN CHRONICLE – Kobe. Japan. -d. 1 Mar 1929-11 Apr 1937, 24 Jul 1938-25 Dec 1940. (41 reels) – 1 – uk British Libr Newspaper [072]
JAPAN CIVIL LIBERTIES UNION – Tokyo. 24 docs. 1987-1988 – 9mf – 9 – ne IDC [320]
JAPAN CIVIL LIBERTIES UNION – Tokyo. 32 docs. 1987-1991 – 12mf – 9 – ne IDC [320]
JAPAN CORRESPONDENCE, 1856-1905 : REGISTERS, 1856-1905 / British Foreign Office – (With printed guide) – 6r – 1 – $510.00 – S0056-05 – us Scholarly Res [324]
JAPAN CORRESPONDENCE, 1856-1948 : CONFLICT OVER KOREA, 1883-1893 / British Foreign Office – (With printed guide) – 65r – 1 – $5,525.00 – S0183-93 – us Scholarly Res [324]
JAPAN CORRESPONDENCE, 1856-1948 : DOMINANCE OF THE GENRO, 1906-1913 / British Foreign Office – (With printed guide) – 47r – 1 – $3,995.00 – S0406-13 – us Scholarly Res [324]
JAPAN CORRESPONDENCE, 1856-1948 : THE EARLY MEIJI PERIOD, 1868-1875 / British Foreign Office – (With printed guide) – 61r – 1 – $5,185.00 – S0168-75 – us Scholarly Res [324]
JAPAN CORRESPONDENCE, 1856-1948 : EMERGENCE OF A MILITARY CLIQUE, 1930-1936 / British Foreign Office – (With printed guide) – 38r – 1 – $3,230.00 – S0430-36 – us Scholarly Res [324]
JAPAN CORRESPONDENCE, 1856-1948 : EMERGENCE OF JAPAN AS A PACIFIC POWER, 1914-1923 / British Foreign Office – (With printed guide) – 73r – 1 – $6,205.00 – S0414-23 – us Scholarly Res [324]
JAPAN CORRESPONDENCE, 1856-1948 : THE END OF FEUDAL RULE, 1856-1867 / British Foreign Office – (With printed guides) – 48r – 1 – $4,080.00 – S0156-67 – us Scholarly Res [324]
JAPAN CORRESPONDENCE, 1856-1948 : THE OCCUPATION, 1946-1948 / British Foreign Office – (With printed guide) – 85r – 1 – $7,225.00 – S0446-49 – us Scholarly Res [324]
JAPAN CORRESPONDENCE, 1856-1948 : PERIOD OF INTENSE WESTERNIZATION, 1876-1882 / British Foreign Office – (With printed guides) – 59r – 1 – $5,015.00 – S0176-82 – us Scholarly Res [324]
JAPAN CORRESPONDENCE, 1856-1948 : REGISTERS, 1906-1919 / British Foreign Office – (With printed guide) – 3r – 1 – $255.00 – S0106-19 – us Scholarly Res [324]
JAPAN CORRESPONDENCE, 1856-1948 : RISE OF THE KWANGTUNG ARMY, 1924-1929 / British Foreign Office – (With printed guide) – 15r – 1 – $1,275.00 – S0424-29 – us Scholarly Res [324]
JAPAN CORRESPONDENCE, 1856-1948 : THE RUSSO-JAPANESE WAR, 1905 / British Foreign Office – (With printed guide) – 57r – 1 – $4,845.00 – S0205 – us Scholarly Res [324]
JAPAN CORRESPONDENCE, 1856-1948 : THE SINO-JAPANESE WAR, 1937-1941 / British Foreign Office – (With printed guide) – 48r – 1 – $4,080.00 – S0437-41 – us Scholarly Res [324]
JAPAN CORRESPONDENCE, 1856-1948 : THE SINO-JAPANESE WAR AND EXPANSIONISM, 1894-1904 / British Foreign Office – (With printed guide) – 78r – 1 – $6,630.00 – S0194-04 – us Scholarly Res [324]
JAPAN CORRESPONDENCE, 1856-1948 : THE WAR IN THE PACIFIC, 1942-1945 / British Foreign Office – (With printed guide) – 28r – 1 – $2,380.00 – S0442-45 – us Scholarly Res [324]
JAPAN CORRESPONDENCE, 1856-1951 : THE RESTORATION OF SOVEREIGNTY, 1949-1951 / British Foreign Office – (Guide also sold separately $20.00 S0449-51.G) – 39r – 1 – $4,875.00 1500 1996 – S0449-51 – us Scholarly Res [950]
JAPAN ECONOMIC JOURNAL – Japan, 1963-70 – 8r – 1 – inquire – us Ross [330]
Japan. Economic Planning Agency *see*
- BASIC PLAN FOR ECONOMIC SOCIETY 1973-1977
- ECONOMIC AND SOCIAL DEVELOPMENT PLAN 1967-1971
- MEDIUM-TERM ECONOMIC PLAN 1964-1968
- NEW ECONOMIC AND SOCIAL DEVELOPMENT PLAN, 1970-1975

Japan. Economic Planning Board *see* ECONOMIC SELF-SUPPORT 5-YEAR PLAN, DECIDED BY THE CABINET MEETING ON 23 DECEMBER 1955
JAPAN EVANGELISTIC BAND – Jul 1917; Sep 1934-1949 (complete) – 1r – 1 – ATLA S0543 – us A.T.L.A. [073]
Japan. Imperial Academy *see* PROCEEDINGS
JAPAN IN WORLD POLITICS / Kawakami, Kiyoshi Karl – New York: The Macmillan Co., 1917. xxvii,300p – 1 – us U.W. Library [950]
Japan. Keizai Kikakucho *see*
- NEW LONG-RANGE ECONOMIC PLAN OF JAPAN, 1961-70
- NEW LONG-RANGE ECONOMIC PLAN OF JAPAN (FY1958-FY1962

JAPAN, KOREA AND THE SECURITY OF ASIA : SPECIAL STUDIES, 1970-80 / ed by Kesaris, Paul – 1981. 4 reels with printed guide – 1 – $440.00 – 0-89093-384-7 – us UPA [950]
JAPAN, KOREA AND THE SECURITY OF ASIA, 1946-76 / U.S. Central Intelligence Agency – 1982. Series: CIA Research Reports – 1 – $480.00 – 0-89093-450-9 – us UPA [950]
JAPAN, KOREA, SOUTHEAST ASIA AND THE FAR EAST GENERALLY / U.S. Office of Strategic Services – 1979. Series: OSS State Department Intelligence and Research Reports, Pt 8 – 1 – $690.00 – 0-89093-345-6 – us UPA [950]
Japan. Laws, Statutes, etc *see* KAMPO
JAPAN MAIL – (Japan Weekly Mail Summary Japan Mail Summary). Yokohama. Japan. -w. 21 Jun 1873-23 Dec 1893. (Wanting 1876, 1888, 1890, 1891). (10 reels) – 1 – uk British Libr Newspaper [072]
Japan. Ministry of Agriculture and Forestry *see*
- NIHON RINSEISHI CHOSA SHIRYO
- TOCHI KEIZAI SHIRYO

Japan. Ministry of Foreign Affairs *see* INTERCEPTED JAPANESE MESSAGES
Japan. Ministry of War *see*
- RIKUGUN. OSAMU BUTAI. EISEIHO DAN KYUKYUHO
- SENDJINKOEN. PENOENTOEN BAGI BALATENTARA DAI NIPPON. DITERDJEMAHKAN OLEH M. JOELI. DIPERIKSA SERTA DIPERBAIKI OLEH. T. ITJIKI

Japan. Office for Research on R and D Economic Planning Agency *see* THE NEW COMPREHENSIVE NATIONAL DEVELOPMENT PLAN (SUMMARY) AND ITS IMPLEMENTATION
JAPAN OFFICIAL GAZETTE – July 1883-Dec 1994 – 1041r – Y10,410,000 – ja Japan Micro [950]
Japan. Patent Office *see*
- PATENT PUBLICATIONS IN NUMERICAL ORDER, 1990
- PUBLISHED UNEXAMINED PATENT APPLICATIONS IN NUMERICAL ORDER, 1990
- PUBLISHED UNEXAMINED UTILITY MODEL APPLICATIONS IN NUMERICAL ORDER, 1990
- UTILITY MODEL PUBLICATIONS IN NUMERICAL ORDER, 1990

JAPAN PLASTICS AGE – (v15-. 1977-. 5,6,9) – v. 1- 1963- Title varies: Japan Plastic Age News – 1 – us UMI [660]
JAPAN PLASTICS INDUSTRY ANNUAL – (1977- . 5,6,9) – v. 1-. 1958 – 1 – us UMI [600]
Japan. Prefectures *see*
- MEIJI KYOIKU TOKEI SHIRYO
- TAISHO SHOWA KYOIKU TOKEI SHIRYO

JAPAN QUARTERLY – (v.27 .1980 5,6,9) – v.1. 1954 – 1 – us UMI [073]

Japan. Shisokyoku. Thought Control Bureau. Japanese Ministry of Education *see* SHISOKYOKU YOKO

Japan Society of Accounting *see* KAIKEI

JAPAN THROUGH WESTERN EYES : MANUSCRIPT RECORDS OF TRADERS, TRAVELLERS, MISSIONARIES AND DIPLOMATS, 1853-1941. PART 1: SOURCES FROM THE WILLIAM R. PERKINS LIBRARY, DUKE UNIVERSITY – (Guide included) – Marlborough: Adam Matthew Publications, 1996 – 20r – 1 – $2450.00 – uk Matthew [950]

JAPAN TIMES – 1897- – 1 – us UMI [072]

JAPAN TIMES – Tokyo. Japan. Dec 1941-Dec 1945 – 1 – 35.00r – us Hoover Inst Photo [072]

THE JAPAN TIMES – Tokyo. 1897-1994 – 779r – 1 – Y5,717,600 – ja Yushodo [950]

JAPAN TODAY AND TOMORROW – (annual). Osaka. Japan. 1927-39. (2 reels) – 1 – uk British Libr Newspaper [072]

Japan. (Tokugawa Feudal Government) *see* RYUEI HINAMI-KI

JAPAN TRADE MONTHLY – Tokyo. Japan. 1960-1962 – 1 – us UMI [072]

JAPAN WEEKLY MAIL – Yokohama. Japan. -w. 7 Jan 1871-25 Dec 1897. (Wanting 1872-77, 1889, 1893, 1895, 1896). (19 reels) – 1 – uk British Libr Newspaper [072]

JAPAN WEEKLY TIMES – (Japan Times. Weekly ed. Japan Times and Mail. Weekly ed.). Tokyo. Japan. -w. 27 Mar 1897-23 Dec 1922. (51 reels) – 1 – uk British Libr Newspaper [072]

JAPANESE AMERICAN NEWS – San Francisco, CA. Sept 1912-Jul 1932 – 60r – 1 – $3,000.00 – C02823 – us Library Micro [071]

THE JAPANESE AMERICAN REVIEW – (Library has: v.39, no.2047, 2049, 2051, 2053-2059, 2061-v.41, no.2125; Jan. 14, 28, Feb. 11, 25-May 20, June 3, 1939-Nov. 29, 1941) – New York: Nippon Publishing Co., 1939-1941. 3v – 1 – CSUX86-S117 – us Hoover Inst Photo [978]

JAPANESE AMERICAN WEEKLY NEWS -SEPT. 13, 1902 *see* THE JAPANESE-AMERICAN

JAPANESE ARCHIVAL MATERIAL ON KOREA / Japan – Includes documents and correspondence of the Japanese Legation in Seoul (1894-1905) and the Japanese Residency General in Korea (1906-1910), basic source material for the study of the history of modern Korea, international relations in the Far East, and Japanese policy and actions in Korea during the critical sixteen years preceding the annexation – 1 – $35.00r – us Hoover Inst Photo [950]

THE JAPANESE ARCHIVES *see* NIHONSI KANKEI SHIRYO

Japanese Biochemical Society *see* JOURNAL OF BIOCHEMISTRY

JAPANESE CAMP NEWSPAPERS – (15 Japanese- and English-language papers available. Apply for complete listing) – 1942-45 – 1 – $40.00r outside US – Dist. us Scholarly Res – us L of C Photodup [071]

JAPANESE CANADIAN RESEARCH COLLECTION – Vancouver, BC: University of British Columbia Library, Facilities and Preservation Office, 1996 – 11r – 1r – Can$100.00r – cn U.B.C. Preserve [971]

JAPANESE CITY DIRECTORY – West Coast. 1928 – 1r – 1 – $50.00 – D133 – us Library Micro [910]

JAPANESE GOVERNMENT DOCUMENTS AND CENSORED PUBLICATIONS – ((Pre-1946) Japanese thought control police materials 3r L9400015. Naimusho Keihokyoku, 1910 (Japanese police intelligence reports) 3r L9400016. Censored issues of Gakan (My Views) 3r L9400027. Kokuhon, organ of Kokuhonsha, established in 1924 3r L9400031. Koron (Public Opinions) 8r L9400033. Gekkan Nihon (Japanese Monthly) 3r L9400035. Kokumin hyoron (National Review) 4r L9400036. Kosaku mondai ni kansuru shiryo (Documents pertaining to farm tenancy question) 4r L9400042. Sayoku undo ni kansuru shiryo, 1922-1940 (Documents concerning Japanese left-wing movements) 4r L9400043. Musan seito ni kansuru shiryo (Materials concerning Japanese proletarian political parties) 4r L9400044. Rodo mondai ni kansuru shiryo (Materials on Japanese labor problems, 1917-1939) 9r L9400045. Documents on Japanese police activities, 1921-1945 4r L9400046. Documents on Japanese police activities, 1912-1946 15r L9400047. Man ju dai nikki (Great daily records of documents received concerning Manchurian Incident-classified) 4r L9400049. Taisho 3-4 nen Kaigun senshi (History of the Naval warfare during the war of 1914-15) 3r L9400052. Showa 6-7-nen jihen Kaigun senshi (History of the Naval warfare in the incident of 1931-32) 3r L9400059. Pre-war (i.e., pre-1946) Japanese government materials, 1913-1945 5r L9400060. Foreign affairs documents, 1917-1945 6r L9400061. Taisei Yokusankai Kyoryoku Kaigi kankei shorui (Documents concerning the meetings to cooperate with the Imperial Rule Assistance Association), 1941-1942 4r L9400062. Gaimusho genson kiroku mokuroku (Catalog of extant documents in Gaimusho) 3r L9400065. Japanese mongraphs compiled under auspices of SCAP, 1945-1954 12r L9400068. Banned Japanese Publications, 1919-1943 57r L9400077. Banned Japanese Publications, 1923-1944 12r L9400078. In Japanese) – 230r – 1 – $8,050.00 in US $40.00r outside – L9400014-9400078 – Dist. us Scholarly Res – us L of C Photodup [324]

JAPANESE JOURNAL OF ANTIBIOTICS – (v.32-. 1979- 5,6,9) – v.21-. 1968- – 1 – us UMI [610]

JAPANESE JOURNAL OF APPLIED PHYSICS – (v16- 1977- 16 (microjacket) Y126,000y) – v1- 1962- – 6 – Y63,000y – ja Journal of Physics [621]

JAPANESE JOURNAL OF BOTANY – v. 2-11. 1924-41 – 1,5,6 – us Princeton Micro [580]

JAPANESE JOURNAL OF MEDICAL SCIENCE AND BIOLOGY – v. 1-23. 1948-1970 – 1,5,6 – us Princeton Micro [610]

JAPANESE JOURNAL OF MICROBIOLOGY – v. 1-19. 1957-1975 – 1,5,6 – us Princeton Micro [576]

JAPANESE JOURNAL OF PHARMACOLOGY – v1- 1951- 1; v25- 1975- 5,6,9 – us UMI [615]

JAPANESE JOURNAL OF RELIGIOUS STUDIES – (1986- . 5,6,9) – v1- . 1974- – 1 – us UMI [200]

JAPANESE LANGUAGE PROGRAM AT THE UNIVERSITY OF MICHIGAN / U.S. War Department. General Staff. G-2 Division – 1943-46 – 1 – $35.00 – us L of C Photodup [480]

JAPANESE MACHINATIONS / Slamet, Mas – SE 12,090 1. 4 v. 1946 – 9 – ne IDC [950]

JAPANESE MANUSCRIPTS / School of Oriental and African Studies, London – (Includes a printed guide) – 294mf – 9 – ne IDC [480]

JAPANESE MINISTRY OF FOREIGN AFFAIRS, 1868-1945 – (Showa Documents, 1926-1945 722r. Unindexed Documents 52r. Special Studies 185r. Ppaers of the Parliamentary Vice Minister Matsumoto Tadao 76r. Biographical Materials 6r. Documents of the International Military Tribunal, GHQ, SCAP 94r. Treaties 13r. Telegraphs 164r. Meiji-Taisho Documents, 1867-1912 804r. Checklist available. In Japanese) – 2,116r – 1 – $40.00r outside US – Dist. us Scholarly Res – us L of C Photodup [324]

JAPANESE MONOGRAPHS ON THE WAR IN THE PACIFIC – (In English. Guide to Japanese Monographs on the War in the Pacific 1r L9400093. Japanese Monographs on the War in the Pacific 14r L9400094. Japanese Studies on Manchuria 3r L9400095) – 18r – 1 – $630.00 set in US $40.00r outside – L9400093-L9400095 – Dist. us Scholarly Res – us L of C Photodup [355]

JAPANESE NEWSPAPERS – (Some titles in Japanese; some in English; Akahata: Tokyo, July 1955-Feb 1958; 1959-1960. 8 reels. L9400100; Asahi Evening News: Tokyo, 1969-1974; 1977-1990. 62 reels. L9400101; Choson Sinbo: Tokyo, 1962-1965; 1968. 7 reels. L9400102; Hokkai Taimushu: Sapporo, 1940; Feb-Apr, 1941; July-Nov 1941; Feb-Oct 1942. 17 reels. L9400103; Hokkaidu Shimbun: Sapporo, Nov 1942-Dec 1945. 12 reels. L9400104; Japan Advertiser: Tokyo, Jan 1916-June 1938. 72 reels. L9400105; Japan Times (International Airmail edition): Tokyo, 1977-1987. 31 reels. L9400106; Japan Times Weekly (International edition): Tokyo, 1964-1969; 1977; 1988-1989. 11 reels, L9400107; Nippon Dokusho Shimbun: Tokyo, Mar 1937-1960; 1962-1964. 6 reels. L9400108; Nippon Times: Tokyo, Jan 1946-1954. 14 reels. L9400109; Osaka Mainichi and the Tokyo Nichi Nichi: Osaka, July 1922-1925; Apr 1926-May 1927; 1932-1940. 25 reels. L9400110; Osaka Mainichi: Osaka, Jan 1941-1945. 12 reels. L9400111; Otaru Shimbun: Otaru, 1938; Jan 1940-Apr 1941; Sept-Oct 1941. 8 reels. L9400112; People's Korea: Tokyo, Jan 1967-1989. 8 reels. L9400113; Teikoku Diagaku Shimbun: Tokyo, Apr 1929-May 1944; May-June 1946. 6 reels. L9400114) – 299r – 1 – $10,465.00 – Dist. us Scholarly Res – us L of C Photodup [072]

JAPANESE RELOCATION CAMP AND ASSEMBLY CENTER NEWSPAPERS – (Mostly in English) – 22r – 1 – $770.00 set in US $40.00r outside – L9400013 – Dist. us Scholarly Res – us L of C Photodup [978]

JAPANESE RESOURCES REFERENCE NOTEBOOKS, 1945-1947 – 6r – 1 – M1199 – us Nat'l Archives [355]

JAPANESE RULE IN FORMOSA / Takekoshi, Yosaburo – Transl. by G. Braithwaite. London. 1907. BCH-863 2 – 8 – ne IDC [950]

JAPANESE SPONSORED GOVERNMENTS IN CHINA / Mote, Frederick W – 1937-1945. 1954 – 1 – 35.00r – us Hoover Inst Photo [950]

JAPANESE TECHNOLOGY REVIEWS: SECTION A : ELECTRONICS / ed by Ikoma, Toshiaki – 9,5,1 – us Gordon [621]

JAPANESE TECHNOLOGY REVIEWS: SECTION B : COMPUTERS AND COMMUNICATIONS / ed by Ikoma, Toshiaki – 9,5,1 – us Gordon [621]

JAPANESE TECHNOLOGY REVIEWS: SECTION E : BIOTECHNOLOGY / ed by Ikoma, Toshiaki – 9,5,1 – us Gordon [660]

JAPANESE WOOD-BLOCK PRINTS IN THE BRITISH MUSEUM / British Museum – (Fully-detailed captions. Over 6,000 images) – 139mf – 9 – $580.00 – 0-907006-33-7 – uk Mindata [760]

THE JAPANESE-AMERICAN – (Library has: v.25, no.1200, 1202; v.32, no.1582-v.33, no.1743; v.40, no.2134-v.41, no.2195; English sect. only: v.38, no.2011, 2013, 2041, 2043, 2045; July 19) – New York: H. Hoshi [etc.], 1900-1941. 41v – 1 – CSUX86-S115 – us Hoover Inst Photo [978]

JAPANESE-AMERICAN CITIZENS' LEAGUE REPORTER *see* JACL REPORTER

JAPANESE-AMERICAN COMMERCIAL WEEKLY SEPT. 20, 1902-DEC. 22, 1923 *see* THE JAPANESE-AMERICAN

JAPANESE-AMERICAN EVACUATION CLAIMS ACT : ADJUDICATIONS OF THE ATTORNEY GENERAL; PRECEDENT DECISIONS UNDER JAPANESE-AMERICAN EVACUATION CLAIMS ACT, 1950-1956 / U.S. Department of Justice – Washington, GPO: 1956 (all publ) – 5mf – 9 – $7.50 – LLMC 84-114 – us L.L.M.C. [340]

JAPANESE-AMERICAN WAR RELOCATION CAMPS : U.S. DEPARTMENT OF INTERIOR WAR RELOCATION AUTHORITY REPORTS. 1942-1945 EVACUATION OF JAPANESE-AMERICANS FROM WEST COAST USA – 4r – 1 – $200.00 – B63003 – us Library Micro [324]

JAPAN'S PACIFIC MANDATE / Clyde, P H – New York, 1935 – 3mf – 1 – ILM-1933/1 – ne IDC [327]

THE JAPAN-U.S. SEMICONDUCTOR CASES : DOCUMENTARY CASE STUDIES IN INTERNATIONAL TRADE – Study 1. With printed guide – 9 – $1,240.00 – 0-89093-987-X – us UPA [380]

JAPCA *see* JOURNAL OF THE AIR POLLUTION CONTROL ASSOCIATION

Japheth ben Eli *see* A COMMENTARY ON THE BOOK OF DANIEL

LE JAPON / Breton de la Martiniere, J B J – ou Moeurs, Usages et Costumes des Habitants de cet Empire. Paris: Nepveu. 1818 – 9 – 30.00 – fr Orientalistes [390]

Japon, Cuentas del *see* BARCELONA, 1933

LE JAPON DE NOS JOURS ET LES ECHELLES DE L'EXTREME-ORIENT / Bousquet, Georges – Paris, Hachette. 1877 – 9 – 25.00 – fr Orientalistes [950]

LE JAPON EN 1867 / Layrle, J – La vie japonaise, les villes et les habitants. Le regime politique et l'etablissement des europeens. Paris, P. Dupont. 1868 – 9 – 5.00 – fr Orientalistes [950]

LE JAPON ET LA QUESTION JAPONAISE / Delprat, Charles – Paris, E. Dentu. 1868 – 9 – 5.00 – fr Orientalistes [950]

LE JAPON ET SES DERNIERS TRAITES AVEC LES PUISSANCES EUROPEENNES / Pages, Leon – Paris: Charles Douniol. 1859 – 9 – 5.00 – fr Orientalistes [950]

LE JAPON ILLUSTRE / Humbert, Aime – Paris: L'Hachette et Cie. 1870 – 9 – 25.00 – fr Orientalistes [950]

LE JAPON POLITIQUE ECONOMIQUE ET SOCIAL / Dumolard, Henry – 4eme ed. Paris, Armand Colin. 1905 – 9 – 10.00 – fr Orientalistes [950]

LE JAPON PRATIQUE / Regamey, Felix – Paris. 1891 – 9 – 10.00 – fr Orientalistes [950]

LE JAPON SES INSTITUTIONS, SES PRODUITS, SES RELATIONS AVEC L'EUROPE / Montblanc, C de – Paris: Bureaux de la Revue Contemporaine. 1867 – 9 – 5.00 – fr Orientalistes [950]

EL JAPON SU EVOLUCION, CULTURA, RELIGIONES / Domenzain, Moises – Madrid: Razon y Fe, 1943 – 1 – sp Bibl Santa Ana [306]

LE JAPON VRAI / Martin, Felix – Paris. 1898 – 9 – 10.00 – fr Orientalistes [950]

Japp, Alexander Hay *see*
- MASTER-MISSIONARIES
- THREE GREAT TEACHERS OF OUR OWN TIME

Jaquet, FG P *see* COLLECTION OF UNPUBLISHED INVENTORIES TO ARCHIVES ON ASIA AND OCEANIA

A JAR OF HONEY FROM MOUNT HYBLA / Hunt, Leigh – London: Smith, Elder, 1848 – 1 roll – 1 – 1-55879-661-4 – uk Libr Preservation [999]

Jara de Soto, Clara *see* EL INSTRUIDO EN LA CORTE...ESTREMENO (SIC)

Jaraiz de la Vera. Ayuntamiento *see*
- FERIA Y FIESTAS DE JARAIZ DE LA VERA 1974
- FIESTAS DEL TABACO Y DEL PIMIENTO 1980
- GUION DE FERIAS Y FIESTAS. AGOSTO 1959

Jaratt, Jennifer *see* WHAT FUTURISTS BELIEVE

Jarava, J *see*
- HISTORIA DE LAS YERVAS Y PLANTAS...
- PROBLEMAS O PREGUNTAS PROBLEMATICAS ANSI DE AMOR...Y ACERCA DEL VINO

JARDEN *see* HA-JARDEN

JARDIN DE LA MALMAISON / Ventenat, E P – Paris. 1803-04. B-484 2 – 8 – ne IDC [580]

LE JARDIN DE PLASIR / Mollet, Andre – Stocholme. H. Kayser, 1651. 41p., pl. (Architecture Series) – 9 – fr Hachette [720]

JARDIN DEL ALMA CRISTIANA / Diaz Tanco, Vasco – 1552 – 9 – 1.50f – sp Bibl Santa Ana [810]

LE JARDIN FLEURISTE,... / ed by Lemaire, C – Gand. 4v. 1851-1854 – 31mf – 9 – ne IDC [944]

LE JARDIN LITTERAIRE ILLUSTRE – Montreal: s.n. [1898] – 9 – cn C.I.H.M. [440]

Jardine, Douglas James *see* THE MAD MULLAH OF SOMALILAND

Jardine, Robert *see* WHAT TO BELIEVE

Jardine, W *see*
- THE BIRDS OF GREAT BRITAIN AND IRELAND
- BRITISH SALMONIDAE
- ILLUSTRATIONS OF ORNITHOLOGY
- ORNITHOLOGICAL SYNONYMS
- ORNITHOLOGIE. SUN-BIRDS

Jardrinet *see* STATISTIQUE DU DEPARTEMENT DE SAMBRE-ET-MEUSE

JARFALLA NYHETER – Stockholm, Sweden. 1982-87 – 1 – sw Kungliga [072]

JARFALLA NYHETER *see* VASTERORT

JARGON OU LANGAGE DE L'ARGOT REFORME / Chereau, O – 1741 – 9 – fr I.C.S. [440]

JARHESBUCH DER WISSENSCHAFTLICHEN ANSTALTEN ZU HAMBURG – Hamburg. v1-30. 1884-1913 – 50mf – ne IDC [500]

JARIDAH AL-RASMIYAH *see* AL-JARIDAH AL-RASMIYAH

JARIDAH AL-RASMIYAH LI-HUKUMAT DUBAYY WA-TAWABI'IHA *see* AL-JARIDAH AL-RASMIYAH LI-HUKUMAT DUBAYY WA-TAWABI'IHA

JARIDAT AL-SHAB / ed by Egyptian Socialist Party – (Missing: 1981(122)) – Cairo, 1979-1981 – 50mf – 9 – NE-20325/1 – ne IDC [260]

Jarman, Thomas *see* A TREATISE ON WILLS

Jarnagin *see* A HANDBOOK OF IOWA

Jarnowick, JG *see* SONATE POUR LE VIOLON AVEC ACCOMPAGNEMENT DE BASSE
JARRAPELLEJOS / Trigo, Felipe – Madrid: Renacimiento, 1914 – sp Bibl Santa Ana [946]
Jarrel, Willis Anselm *see*
– THE GOSPEL IN WATER, OR CAMPBELLISM
– OLD TESTAMENT ETHICS VINDICATED
Jarrett, Devereux *see* SERMONS ON VARIOUS AND IMPORTANT SUBJECTS..
Jarrett, Harold Reginald *see* THE GAMBIA
Jarric, P du *see* HISTOIRE DES CHOSES PLUS MEMORABLES ADVENUES TANT EZ INDES ORIENTALES, QUE AUTRES PAIS DE LA DESCOUVERTE DES PORTUGAIS, EN L'ESTABLISSEMENT ET PROGREZ DE LA FOY CHRESTIENNE, ET CATHOLIQUE...
Jarrin, Francisco *see* MORAL
EL JARRO RITUAL LUSITANO DE LA COLECCION CALZADILLA / Garcia y Bellido, Antonio – Madrid, 1957 – 1 – sp Bibl Santa Ana [946]
JARROW CHRONICLE AND TYNESIDE NEWS – England. -w. 1 Apr-16 Dec 1871. (33 ft) – 1 – uk British Libr Newspaper [072]
JARROW EXPRESS – England. -w. Dec 1873-Dec 1913. 36 1 2 reels – 1 – uk British Libr Newspaper [072]
JARROW GUARDIAN – England. -w. Jan 1872-Dec 1880. (9 reels) – 1 – uk British Libr Newspaper [072]
JARROW LABOUR HERALD – England. -w. 6 Apr 1906-15 Mar 1907. (1 reel) – 1 – uk British Libr Newspaper [072]
Jarry, Alfred *see* LE SURMALE, ROMAN MODERNE
Jartoux, P *see* LETTRE...
JARVA NYHETER *see* VASTERORT
Jarvis, Robert Edward Lee *see* THE MAKING OF A CHRISTIAN
JAS – v3-7, 1929-33 – 1 – us I.U. Libraries [073]
JASA: JOURNAL OF THE AMERICAN STATISTICAL ASSOCIATION – v1 1888-1; 1968- 5,6; 1975- 4 x 6 in. 9 – us UMI [310]
Jasani, Bhupendra *see* OUTER SPACE
JASEN'. VIDENIE DREVA. (STIKHI) / Bal'mont, K D – M. 1916. BR-521 2 – 8 – ne IDC [460]
JASH, JOURNAL OF THE ASSOCIATION FOR THE SEVERELY HANDICAPPED *see* AAESPH REVIEW
JASH: JOURNAL OF THE ASSOCIATION FOR THE SEVERELY HANDICAPPED – v.5-. 1980- – 1,5,6,9 – us UMI [370]
Jaspan, Helen *see* CASEWORK SOSIAL DI INDONESIA; PEDOMAN KANTONG
Jaspan, M A *see* SOCIAL STRATIFICATION AND SOCIAL MOBILITY IN INDONESIA; TREND REPORT AND ANNOTATED BIBLIOGRAPHY
Jaspan, Mervyn Aubrey *see* ETHNIC AND SOCIAL RELATIONS IN INDONESIA
JASPER COUNTY DEMOCRAT – Rensselaer. Ind. -w. 1898-1910, 1915-48 – 1 – us UMI [071]
JASPER REPUBLICAN – Rensselaer. Ind. 1875-1876 – 1 – us UMI [071]
Jaspers, E *see* FUNDAMENTAL AND APPLIED RESEARCH ON THE BRINE SHRIMP ARTEMIA SALINA (L.) IN BELGIUM
Jaspers, Karl *see* NIETZSCHE UND DAS CHRISTENTUM
Jaspersen, Ursula *see* GEORG TRAKL
Jass en, Raul *see* ORACIONES PARA LA REVOLUCION JUSTICIALISTA
Jassin, Hans Bague *see* GEMA TANAH AIR, PROSA DAN PUISI 1942-1948
Jastrow, Marcus *see* A DICTIONARY OF THE TARGUMIM, THE TALMUD BABLI AND YERUSHALMI, AND THE MIDRASHIC LITERATURE
Jastrow, Morris *see*
– A DICTIONARY OF THE TARGUMIM
– A FRAGMENT OF THE BABYLONIAN "DIBBARRA" EPIC
– THE RELIGION OF BABYLONIA AND ASSYRIA
Jaubert, Amedee *see* RELATION DU GHANAT ET DES COUTUMES DE SES HABITANTS
Jaubert de Passa, M *see* CANALES DE RIEGO DE CATALUNA Y REINO DE VALENCIA...
Jaubert, H F *see*
– GLOSSAIRE DU CENTRE DE LA FRANCE
– ILLUSTRATIONES PLANTARUM ORIENTALIUM
Jaubert, J *see* CONTRIBUTION A L'ETUDE DU PALEOLITHIQUE ANCIEN ET MOYEN DES CAUSSES
Jaubert, J B *see* RICHESSES ORNITHOLOGIQUES DU MIDI DE LA FRANCE
Jaubert, Pierre *see* DES CAUSES DE LA DEPOPULATION ET DES MOYENS D'Y REMEDIER
Jaume Saint-Hilaire, J H *see*
– EXPOSITION DES FAMILLES NATURELLES
– PLANTES DE LA FRANCE
Jaumenne, N-D J *see* L'IMPARTIAL
Jaunet, Jacques *see* ORAISON FUNEBRE DE (...)CHARLES-FERDINAND D'ARTOIS, PRONONCEE AU SERVICE SOLENNEL(...)LE 10 AVRIL, DANS L'EGLISE DES HERBIERS (VENDEE)
Jaunez-Sponville *see* LA PHILOSOPHIE DE RURAVEBOHNI, PAYS DONT LA DECOUVERTE SEMBLE D'UN GRAND INTERET POUR L'HOMME, OU RECIT DIALOGUE DES MOYENS PAR LESQUELS LES RURAVEHEUXIS HABITANTS DE CE PAYS ONT ETE CONDUITS AU VRAI ET SOLIDE BONHEUR
JAURETCHE : UNA VIDA AL SERVICIO DE LA REVOLUCION NACIONAL / Neyre, Juan Carlos et al – Buenos Aires: Grupo Editor de Buenos Aires, 1965 – 9 – us Hoover Inst Photo [972]
Jauretche, Arturo *see* EL RETORNO AL COLONIAJE
Java *see*
– BOEKOE PETOENDJOEK PRAKTEK TEKNIK BAGI PEMIMPIN SEINENDAN
– JAWA BOEI GIYUGUN. DJAWA BOEI GIYUGUN KYOREN-KYOTEI
– KOBIJITSU KENKUSHO. TJANDI PANATARAN
– LAWS, STATUTES, ETC...
– NAIMUBU. BUNKYO KYOKU. NICHI MA JITEN. KAMOES BAHASA NIPPON-INDONESIA
– SAIKO SHIKIKAN. KETERANGAN SAIKOO SIKIKAN. TENTANG HAL TOEROET MENGAMBIL BAHAGIAN DALAM PEMERINTAHAN NEGERI DAN PENDJELASAN PEMERINTAH
– SIHOBU. GUNSEI KEIZIREI KAISETU
JAVA ANNUAL DIRECTORY AND ALMANAC – 1816. Batavia, 1816. BSE-20,026 1 – 9 – ne IDC [950]
JAVA GAZETTE / British Chamber of Commerce for the NEI – London. 1947-50. – 13mf – 9 – ne IDC [073]
Java Instituut *see* DJAWA
JAVA. (Japanese Military Administration 1942-45) *see*
– BUNKYOKYOKU. DIDIKAN BOEDI PEKERTI
– JAWA HOKOKAI
– PELADJARAN BAHASA NIPPON
HET JAVAANSCHE TONEEL. I. WAJANG POERWA / Kats, J – Weltevreden, 1923. BSE-332/1 – 9 – ne IDC [950]
JAVAANSE VOLKSVERTONINGEN, BIJDRAGE TOT DE BESCHRIJVING VAN LAND EN VOLK / Pigeaud, T – Batavia, 1938 – 7mf – 9 – SE-20,212/1 – ne IDC [950]
JAVANAN-I TUDAH – Tehran: Hizb-i Tudah-'i Iran. Sal-i 1, shumarah-'i 1-4 (Shahrivar 1359-Day 1359 [Sep 1980-Dec 1980]) – 1 reel – 1 – $25.00 – us MEDOC [950]
O JAVARY : ORGAM INDEPENDENTE, LITTERARIO E NOTICIOSO – Benjamin Constant, Amazonas. 18 Jan-Dez 1916; Fev-Ago, Nov-Dez 1917; Jan-13 Fev 1918 – 1,5,6 – bl Biblioteca [072]
Javasche Bank *see* REPORT OF THE PRESIDENT OF THE JAVA BANK ON MARCH 10TH, 1948 AND JULY 9TH, 1949
Javasche Bank. Batavia *see*
– REPORT 1941-53
– VERSLAGEN DER JAVASCHE BANK
JAVASCHE COURANT, 1828-1939 / Netherlands. Royal Library. The Hague. Newspaper Department – (1828-37.-134mf.Dfl835.00 silver; 1838-47.-149mf. Dfl930.00 silver; 1848-57.-210mf.Dfl1,315.00 silver; 1858-67.-185mf.Dfl1,155.00 silver; 1868-77. 247mf. Dfl1,545.00 silver; 1878-87.-325mf.Dfl2,030.00 silver; 1888-92.-259mf.Dfl1,615.00 silver; 1893-97.-257mf. Dfl1,615.00 silver; 1898-1902.-256mf.Dfl1,615.00 silver; 1903-07.-285mf.Dfl1,780.00 silver; 1908-12.-336mf. Dfl2,100.00 silver; 1913-17.-564mf.Dfl2,275.00 silver; 1918-22.-580mf.Dfl3,625.00 silver; 1923-27.-500mf. Dfl3,125.00 silver; 1928-32.-606mf.Dfl3,785.00 silver; 1933-39.-760mf.Dfl4,735.00 silver) – Official gazette. KB002 – 5453mf – 9 – Dfl35,640.00 silver – ne MMF Publ [324]
Javens, J A *see* EFFECT OF ACUPUNCTURE TENS ON SECOND DEGREE ANKLE SPRAINS
Javierre, A *see* MADRID. ARCHIVO HISTORICO NATIONAL. SECCION DE ORDENES MILITARES. GUIA DE LA SECCION DE ORDENES MILITARES
Javierre, Jose Maria et al *see* CONTROL DE NATALIDAD. INFORME PARA EXPERTOS, LLOS DOCUMENTOS DE ROMA
JAWA BOEI GIYUGUN. DJAWA BOEI GIYUGUN KYOREN-KYOTEI / Java – Djakarta ? 2603. 3v – 59-66mf – 9 – ne IDC [950]
JAWA, DESZELFS GEDAANTE, BEKLEEDING EN INWENDIGE STRUCTUUR / Junghuhn, F W – Ed. 2. Amsterdam, 1853. 4v. Atlas – 34mf – 9 – ne IDC [950]
JAWA HOKOKAI : PERATOERAN-PERATOERAN HIMPOENAN KEBAKTIAN RAKJAT (BOELAN 2 TAHOEN 2604) / JAVA. (Japanese Military Administration 1942-45) – Djakarta, Panitia Persiapan Himpoenan Kebaktian Rakjat, 2604. 47p – 191mf – 9 – ne IDC [350]
JAWA NENKAN – Djakarta, Jawa Shinbunsha, 2604. 473p – 199-204mf – 9 – ne IDC [950]
Jawitz, Z *see* SEFER JAWITZ
THE JAWS OF DEATH: A NOVEL / Allen, Grant – London: Jarrold, 1896. 05047. (Pre-1900 Canadiana) – 9 – cn C.I.H.M. [830]
JAX AIR NEWS – Jacksonville. Fla. 1952- – 1 – us P.K. Yonge [071]
Jaxa-Roniker, Bogdan H *see* THE RED EXECUTIONER DZIERJINSI, THE GOOD HEART
Jay, Cyrus *see* THE LAW
Jay, John *see* PAPERS
Jay, Milton *see* HISTORY OF JAY COUNTY INCLUDING WORLD WAR RECORD
Jay, William *see*
– THE AUTOBIOGRAPHY OF THE REV. WILLIAM JAY
– LECTURES ON FEMALE SCRIPTURE CHARACTERS
– THE WORKS OF THE REV. WILLIAM JAY
Jayabharathi *see* INDIAN FILMS AND FILM WORLD, 1976
Jayakar, M R *see* PAPERS, 1916-1925
Jayewardene, Gustavus *see* CENTENARY SOUVENIR, 1851-1951
Jayne, Ebenezer *see* JAYNE'S HYMNAL
JAYNE'S HYMNAL / Jayne, Ebenezer – Misc. information. 1909 – 1 – 5.00 – us Baptist [240]
JAZZ : A QUARTERLY OF AMERICAN MUSIC – Nos. 1-5 (all publ). Oct 1958-Winter 1960. (Jazz Periodicals) – 1 reel – 1 – $70.00 – us UPA [780]
JAZZ – v1, nos. 1-10 (all publ). Jul 1938-Mar 1941. (Jazz Periodicals) – 1 reel – 1 – $55.00 – us UPA [780]
JAZZ, 1990-1993 – 17mf – 9 – uk Microform Academic [780]
JAZZ, BLUES, SOUL AND ROCK : CONTEMPORARY MUSIC JOURNALS – (Pt 1: New Musical Express and predecessors, 1946-71; Pt 2: Blues and Soul, 1967-1987) – 1 – us Primary [073]
JAZZ DIGEST – v1-3, no. 6 (all publ). Jan Feb 1972-Jun 1974. (Jazz Periodicals) – 1 reel – 1 – $95.00 – us UPA [780]
JAZZ HOT / Federation International des Hot Clubs Francais – nos. 1-32; n.s. nos. 1-288. Mar 1935-Jul 1939; Mar 1945-Nov 1972. (Jazz Periodicals) – 11r – 1 – $1,235.00 – us UPA [780]
JAZZ INFORMATION – v1-2, no. 16. Sep 1939-Nov 1941. (Jazz Periodicals) – 1 reel – 1 – $85.00 – us UPA [780]
JAZZ MAGAZINE – Dir. D. Filipachi et F. Tenot. no. 1-125. Paris. dec 1954-65 – 1 – fr A.C.R.P.P. [073]
JAZZ MAGAZINE – nos. 1-148. Dec 1954-Nov 1967. (Jazz Periodicals) – 7r – 1 – $895.00 – us UPA [780]
JAZZ PERIODICALS : 1914-77 – Collection of 22 titles. Individual titles available separately: Australian Jazz Quarterly; Clef; The Discophile; Hip; H.R.S. Society Rag; Jazz; Jazz: A Quarterly of American Music; Jazz Digest; Jazz Hot; Jazz Information; Jazz Magazine; Jazz Quarterly; The Jazz Record; Jazz Session; Les cahiers du Jazz; MATRIX; Music and Rhythm; NAJE Educator; The Needle; Playback; Ragtime Review; The Second Line – 41r – 1 – $3,670.00 – us UPA [780]
JAZZ QUARTERLY / Jazz Quarterly Society – v. -2, no. 4 (all publ). Spring 1942- . (Jazz Periodicals) – 1 reel – 1 – $55.00 – us UPA [780]
Jazz Quarterly Society *see* JAZZ QUARTERLY
THE JAZZ RECORD – nos. 1-60 (all publ). Feb 1943-Nov 1947. (Jazz Periodicals) – 1 reel – 1 – $95.00 – us UPA [780]
JAZZ SESSION / Hot Club of Chicago – nos. 1-13 (all publ). Sep 1944-Jul 1946. (Jazz Periodicals) – 1 reel – 1 – $60.00 – us UPA [780]
JAZZ TIMES – 1985-. -m – 1 – us UMI [073]
J.B. Beers and Co *see* HISTORY OF GREENE COUNTY
J.B. FISCHERS ZUSAETZE (SIC) ZU EINEM VERSUCH EINER NATURGESCHICHTE VON LIVLAND,... / Fischer, J B – Riga, 1784 – 4mf – 9 – ne IDC [574]
JCA NEWS – Los Angeles, CA.Jewish Centers Assoc. of Los Angeles. 1976-80 – 1 – us A.J.P.C. [071]
JCU : JOURNAL OF CLINICAL ULTRASOUND – v1- 1973- – 1,5,6,9 – us UMI [616]
JE SAIS TOUT – Paris. 1922-juil 1939 – 1 – fr A.C.R.P.P. [073]
JE SUIS LE VERITABLE PERE DUCHESNE, FOUTRE – 30 no. Paris. nov-dec 1790, no. 1-355. janv 1791-mars 1794 – 1 – fr A.C.R.P.P. [073]
JE SUIS PARTOUT – Le grand hebdomadaire de la vie mondiale. Paris. 29 nov 1930-16 aout 1944. N'a pas paru du 7 juin 1940 au 7 fevr 1941 – 1 – fr A.C.R.P.P. [073]
JE VOIS TOUT : ILLUSTRE HUMORISTIQUE – Montreal, Canada. 2 avr 1910-v1 n14. 22 oct 1910 – 1r – 1 – Can$30.00 – cn Can Microfilming [072]
Jeaffreson, John C *see*
– A BOOK ABOUT LAWYERS
– PLEASANTRIES OF ENGLISH COURTS AND LAWYERS
JEAN ASTRUC ET LA CRITIQUE BIBLIQUE AUX 18E SIECLE / Lods, Adolphe – Strasbourg. 1924. B-2334 2 – 8 – ne IDC [900]
Jean, B *see* VIE DE SAINTE MARIE MADELEINE. BARCELONA
LE JEAN BAPTISTE – Pawtucket. R.I. 1897-1932 – 1 – us UMI [071]
Jean Baptiste Theodore Baumes *see* TOPOGRAPHIE DE LA VILLE DE NISMES ET DE SA BANLIEUE
JEAN DE PARIS / Goddard D'Aucourt de Saint-Just – (French Theatre Series). Paris. Vente. 1812 – 9 – fr Hachette [820]
JEAN DOMINIQUE, SAINT DOMINIQUE... – Madrid: Razon y Fe, 1927 – 1 – sp Bibl Santa Ana [240]
JEAN ET SEBASTIEN CABOT: LEUR ORIGINE ET LEURS VOYAGES, ETUDE D'HISTOIRE CRITIQUE; SUIVIE D'UNE CARTOGRAPHIE, D'UNE BIBLIOGRAPHIE ET D'UNE CHRONOLOGIE DES VOYAGES...1497 A 1550.. / Harrisse, Henry – Paris: Leroux, 1882. 05392. (Pre-1900 Canadiana) – 9 – cn C.I.H.M. [910]
JEAN ETIENNE LIOTARD, 1702-1789, JOHANN HEINRICH FUESSLI, 1741-1825 / Reunion des musees nationaux. Paris – 1948. 16 illus. 1 fiche – 9 – fr Réunion [700]
JEAN GEILER DE KAYSERSBERG, PREDICATEUR A LA CATHEDRALE DES STRASBOURG, 1478-1510 : ETUDE SUR SA VIE ET SON TEMPS / Dacheux, L – Paris: C. Delagrave; Strasbourg: Derivaux, 1876 – 2mf – us A.T.L.A. [240]
JEAN GUITON ET LE SIEGE DE LA ROCHELLE / Blanchon, Pierre – 1911 – 1 – $50.00 – us Presbyterian [944]
JEAN JACQUES SERVAN-SCHREIBER PAMPHLET COLLECTION – 197? – 9 – us Hoover Inst Photo [944]
JEAN LE THEOLOGIEN : LES GRANDES TRADITIONS D'ISRAEL. L'ACCORD DES ECRITURES D'APRES LE QUATRIEME EVANGILE (ETB) / Braun, F M – Paris, 1964. – Dfl28.00 – ne Slangenburg [240]
JEAN LE THEOLOGIEN : SA THEOLOGIE. LE CHRIST, NOTRE SEIGNEUR (ETB) / Braun, F M – Paris, 1972 – Dfl25.00 – ne Slangenburg [240]
JEAN LE THEOLOGIEN : SA THEOLOGIE. LE MYSTERE DE JESUS CHRIST (ETB) / Braun, F M – Paris, 1966. – Dfl22.00 – ne Slangenburg [240]
JEAN MARIE GUYAUS RELIGIONSPHILOSOPHIE (L'IRRELIGON DE L'AVENIR) / Schumm, Felix – Tuebingen, 1913 – 2mf – DM62.00 – 3-8267-3075-5 – gw Hänsel [200]
JEAN PAUL : WELTGEDANKEN UND GEDANKENWELT / ed by Benz, Richard – (Includes bibliographical references & index) – Stuttgart: Alfred Kroener, c1938 – 1 – us U.W. Library [430]

Jean Paul *see*
- THE INVISIBLE LODGE
- LEBEN DES QUINTUS FIXLEIN
- WERKE

JEAN PAUL MARAT, THE PEOPLE'S FRIEND / Bax, Ernest Belfort – 2nd ed. London: G. Richards, 1901. xvi,353p – 1 – us U.W. Library [920]

JEAN PAULS VERHAELTNIS ZU ROUSSEAU : NACH DEN HAUPT-ROMANEN DARGESTELLT / Kommerell, Max – (Includes bibliographical references) – Marburg a.L.: N G Elwert, 1924 – 1 – us U.W. Library [410]

JEAN RAISIN – Revue joyeuse et vinicole. Dir. Gustave Mathieu. no. 1-10. Paris. 15 oct 1854-mars 1855 – 1 – fr A.C.R.P.P. [073]

JEAN RIVARD : SCENES DE LA VIE REELLE / Gerin-Lajoie, Antoine – Nouv. ed. Montreal: J B Rolland, 1877. SEM16P143 – 1r – 5 – Can$9.00 – cn Bibl Nat [830]

JEAN SAUVAGNARGUES PAMPHLET COLLECTION – 1974 – 9 – us Hoover Inst Photo [944]

JEAN TE THEOLOGIEN ET SON EVANGILE DANS L'EGLISE ANCIENNE (ETB) / Braun, F M – Paris, 1964 – Dfl30.00 – ne Slangenburg [240]

JEAN-ADAM MOEHLER ET L'ECOLE CATHOLIQUE DE TUBINGUE, 1815-1840 : ETUDE SUR LA THEOLOGIE ROMANTIQUE EN WURTTEMBERG ET LES ORIGINES GERMANIQUES DU MODERNISME / Vermeil, Edmond – Paris: A. Colin, 1913 – 2mf – us A.T.L.A. [240]

LE JEAN-BAPTISTE / ed by Gauvin, A – Montreal, Canada. 6 nov 1840-8 jan 1841 – 1r – 1 – Can$30.00 – cn Can Microfilming [072]

LE JEAN-BAPTISTE : JOURNAL COMMERCIAL – Quebec, Canada. 24 jun 1880 – 1r – 1 – Can$25.00 – cn Can Microfilming [380]

LE JEAN-BAPTISTE – Quebec, Canada. 24 jun 1890-1892 (Noces d'Or); 1902 (Noces de Diamant); 1904-1907; 24 jun 1922 – 1r – 1 – Can$40.00 – cn Can Microfilming [072]

JEAN-BAPTISTE BLANCHARD AU DAHOMEY. : JOURNAL DE LA CAMPAGNE PAR UN MARSOUIN / Badin, Adolphe – Paris: A Colin, 1895 – us Res Libr [960]

JEAN-DOMINIQUE MANSI ET LES GRANDES COLLECTIONS CONCILIAIRES : ETUDE D'HISTOIRE LITTERAIRE: SUIVIE.. / Quentin, Henri – Paris: E. Leroux, 1900 – 1mf – us A.T.L.A. [240]

JEAN-JACQUES ROUSSEAU, A SES DERNIERS MOMENTS: TRAIT HISTORIQUE: EN UN ACTE ET EN PROSE: REPRESENTE POUR LA PREMIERE FOIS, A PARIS, PAR LES COMEDIENS ITALIENS ORDINAIRES DU ROI, LE 31 DECEMBRE 1790 / Bouilly, Jean Nicolas – Paris: Brunet, 1791 – 1 – us U.W. Library [820]

Jean-Louis *see* LA REGIME FINANCIER DU GOUVERNEMENT MERCIER: EXPOSE PAR UN CULTIVATEUR

JEANNE D'ARC ET LE DROIT DES GENS / Defourny, P – Paris, 1888 – 1mf – 1 – ILM-4093/1 – ne IDC [327]

JEANNE D'ARC ET SES COMPAGNONS D'ARMES DU PAYS NANTAIS... / Durville, Georges – [1898] – 1 – F50.00 – fr Armell [920]

JEANNE LA FILEUSE: EPISODE DE L'EMIGRATION FRANCO-CANADIENNE AUX ETATS-UNIS / Beaugrand, Honore – Fall River, MA, 1878. 03033. (Pre-1900 Canadiana) – 9 – cn C.I.H.M. [971]

Jeanneney, J M *see* TABLEAUX STATISTIQUES RELATIFS A L'ECONOMIE FRANCAISE ET L'ECONOMIE MONDIALE

LE JEANNOIS – St-Felicien, Canada. 4 jul 1978-10 jan 1979 – 1r – 1 – Can$35.00 – cn Can Microfilming [072]

Jeanroy, A *see* GIOSUE CARDUCCI, L'HOMME ET LE POETE

Jean-Yvon *see* LA VOIX METROPOLITAINE

Jebb, Camilla *see* MARY WOLLSTONECRAFT

JEC : JOURNAL JECISTE MENSUEL – Ville Saint-Laurent, janv fev 1935-nov 1964. SEM35P181 – 6r – 1 – Can$283.00 – cn Bibl Nat [073]

JEC – Montreal. v1 n3. mar 1935-v11 n11. nov 1945 – 1r – 1 – Can$35.00 – cn Can Microfilming [072]

Jedaiah Ha-Penini (Jedaiah ben Abraham Bedersi) *see* OHEV NASHIM

JEDERMANN : GESCHICHTE EINES NAMENLOSEN / Wiechert, Ernst Emil – Muenchen: A Langen/G Mueller, 1935, c1931 – 1r – 1 – us U.W. Library [830]

JEDINSTVO – (In Yugoslavian) – Canada, 1948-70 – 23r – 1 – cn Commonwealth Micro [072]

JEDINSTVO = UNITY – Gary, IN: Carpathian-Russian Unity. v1 n1-v2 n5,6,7. mar 1942-jul/aug/sep 1943 – us Res Libr [073]

JEDINSTVO *see* EDINSTVO JEDINSTVO

JEDNOSC = UNITY – (In Polish) – Philadelphia, PA. 1929-63 – 12r – 1 – $1,020.00 – D3382 – us Scholarly Res [071]

JEDNOSC POLEK : SEMI-MONTHLY POLISH LANGUAGE FRATERNAL NEWSPAPER – Cleveland, Ohio. 11 Jan 1966-5 Apr 1988 – 4r – 1 – us Western Res [071]

JEDNOTA – Middletown, PA, 1893-1940 – 15r – 1 – us I.H.R.C. [978]

JEDNOTA : WEEKLY CATHOLIC SLOVAK NEWSPAPER – Cleveland, OH. 20 Nov 1895-13 June 1900 – 2r – 1 – us Western Res [071]

JEDNOTA BRATRSKA – (Lacking some pgs and issues) – v11-60. 1933-88 – Inquire – 1 – ATLA S0638 – us A.T.L.A. [073]

JEDNOTA, ST CYRIL AND METHODIUS LODGE NO 3 – Minneapolis, MN, 1896-1907 – 1 reel – 1 – us I.H.R.C. [240]

Jeens, C H *see* MEMORIALS OF JOHN MCLEOD CAMPELL, D.D.

Jeep, I *see* ZUR UEBERLIEFERUNG DES PHILOSTORGIOS (T.U.U. 2-17/3B2)

THE JEEP: ITS DEVELOPMENT AND PROCUREMENT UNDER THE QUARTERMASTER CORP, 1940-1942 / U.S. Army. Quartermaster Corp. General Administrative Services – 1943 – 1 – $26.00 – us L of C Photodup [629]

Jefatura de obras publicas de la provincia de Badajoz *see* ESCALOFON DE CAPATACES Y CAMINEROS DE LA MISMA EN 31 DE DICIEMBRE DE 1959

Jefatura provincial Servicio Pesca Continental, Caza y Parques Nacionales *see* CATALOGO EXPOSICION DE TROFEOS DE CAZA MAYOR 1970

Jefferies, Richard *see*
- FIELD AND HEDGEROW
- THE GAMEKEEPER AT HOME

Jefferis, Shelly J *see* AEROBIC CERTIFICATION

Jefferson *see* MUSIC PART BOOKS

JEFFERSON BAPTIST CHURCH. JEFFERSON COUNTY. SOUTH CAROLINA : CHURCH RECORDS – 1899-1977 – 1 – 30.06 – us Baptist [240]

Jefferson, Charles Edward *see* CHARACTER OF JESUS

JEFFERSON CITY FIRST BAPTIST CHURCH. JEFFERSON CITY, TENNESSEE : CHURCH RECORDS – Apr 1834-Feb 1987 – 1 – 152.64 – us Baptist [240]

Jefferson County. Georgia *see* INVENTORY OF THE COUNTY ARCHIVES.

Jefferson County, KS *see*
- CEMETERY TOMBSTONE AND OBITUARY CARDS
- OBITUARY CARD FILES BRO-CLY
- OBITUARY CARD FILES GOB-SCH
- OBITUARY CARD FILES SCH-ZWY

JEFFERSON COUNTY RECORD – (Set incl. Jefferson County Searchlight (Metolius)) – Metolius, OR. -w. 28 Oct 1915-29 Sept 1923. – 2r – 1 – us U.O. Library [071]

JEFFERSON COUNTY REPUBLICAN – Fairfield. Iowa. 1897-1916; 1917 – 1 – us UMI [071]

JEFFERSON COUNTY SEARCHLIGHT – Metolius OR. Apr 15-Oct 21 1915 – 1 – us U.O. Library [071]

JEFFERSON COUNTY SENTINEL – Boulder. Mont. 1886-1904 – 1 – us UMI [071]

JEFFERSON COUNTY UNION – Fort Atkinson. Wis. 1890-1938; 1963-1967 – 1 – us UMI [071]

JEFFERSON COUNTY-HER PIONEERS AND PEOPLE / McKnight, William J – Genealogical and biographical records. Chicago, J. H. Beers and Co., 1917. Vols. 1-2. Pennsylvania Reel 25. (The Cox Library Collection) – 5 – us Americana [978]

JEFFERSON DAVIS AS A REPRESENTATIVE OF CIVILIZATION / Du Bois, WE B – 1890. and A constructive critique of wage theory. 1891. Ms. no. 77-8. One reel – 1 – 15.00 – us Partington [976]

JEFFERSON FIRST BAPTIST CHURCH. JEFFERSON, GEORGIA : CHURCH RECORDS – Jun 1866-Sep 1973 – 1 – 63.63 – us Baptist [240]

Jefferson, LouAnne M *see* INTRATESTER AND INTERTESTER RELIABILITY WHEN USING THE CHATILLON HAND-HELD DYNAMOMETER TO MEASURE FORCE PRODUCTION IN THE UPPER AND LOWER EXTREMITIES

Jefferson, New Hampshire. Jefferson Baptist Church *see* RECORDS

Jefferson. Ohio. Bethel Union Baptist Church *see* CHURCH RECORDS, MS 1585

Jefferson. Ohio. First Baptist Church *see* CHURCH RECORDS, MS 642

THE JEFFERSON PAPERS OF THE UNIVERSITY OF VIRGINIA, 1732-1828 – (With printed guide) – 10r – 1 – $850.00 – D3188 – Dist. us Scholarly Res – us Nat'l Archives [975]

THE JEFFERSON REPUBLICAN – Ranson. West Virginia. 1944-1955 – 1 – us UMI [071]

JEFFERSON REVIEW – Jefferson, OR. -w. 19 Jan 1901-. – 1 – us U.O. Library [071]

JEFFERSON STAR – Jefferson, PA., 1851 – 13 – $25.00r – us I.M.R. [071]

Jefferson, Thomas *see*
- PAPERS
- A SUMMARY VIEW OF THE RIGHTS OF BRITISH AMERICA
- THOMAS JEFFERSON PAPERS, 1705-1827
- WRITINGS OF THOMAS JEFFERSON

JEFFERSON VALLEY NEWS – Whitehall. Mont. 1956-1959; 1966- – 1 – us UMI [071]

JEFFERSONIAN – Cambridge. Ohio. -w. 1886, 1899, 1905 – 1 – us UMI [071]

JEFFERSONIAN – Jefferson, PA., 1854-1859 – 13 – $25.00r – us I.M.R. [071]

JEFFERSONIAN – Jefferson, PA., 1859-1871 – 13 – $25.00r – us I.M.R. [071]

JEFFERSONIAN AMERICANA – 9 – $4,505.00 – us UPA [975]

JEFFERSONIAN BROOKVILLE – Brookville, PA., 1834-1835 – 13 – $25.00r – us I.M.R. [071]

JEFFERSONIAN DEMOCRAT – Brookville. Pa. -w. 1958-68 – 1 – us UMI [071]

JEFFERSONIAN DEMOCRAT – Jefferson, PA., 1886-1983 – 13 – $25.00r – us I.M.R. [071]

JEFFERSONIAN DEMOCRAT : WEEKLY REPUBLICAN NEWSPAPER – Chardon, Ohio. 1854-65 – 5r – 1 – us Western Res [071]

JEFFERSONIAN GAZETTE – Lawrence. Kan. 1899-1920 – 1 – us UMI [071]

JEFFERSONIAN REPUBLIC – Jefferson City. Mo. 1831-1840 – 1 – us UMI [071]

JEFFERSONIAN/BROOKVILLE DEMO – Jefferson, PA., 1871-1886 – 13 – $25.00r – us I.M.R. [071]

JEFFERSON'S REPORTS / Virginia. Supreme Court. General Court – (A Pre-NRS title) – 1v. 1730-1740 and 1768-1772 (all publ) – 2mf – 9 – $3.00 – LLMC 91-043 – us L.L.M.C. [340]

JEFFERSONVILLE BAPTIST CHURCH. JEFFERSONVILLE, GOERGIA : CHURCH RECORDS – (272p) – 1849-1894 – 1 reel – 1 – $12.24 – us Baptist [240]

Jeffery, A *see* THE QUR'AN AS SCRIPTURE

Jeffery, Arthur *see* THE FOREIGN VOCABULARY OF THE QUR'AN

Jeffrey, William H *see* SUCCESSFUL VERMONTERS-GAZETTER OF CALEDONIA, ESSEX, AND ORLEANS COUNTIES

Jeffreys, Arcelia T *see* EXPERIENCES AND RELATIONS IN THE WORK OF WOMEN TEACHER/COACHES

Jeffreys, Letitia D *see* ANCIENT HEBREW NAMES

Jeffreys, Mervyn David Waldegrave *see* OLD CALABAR AND NOTES ON THE IBIBIO LANGUAGE

Jeffs, Robin *see* FAST SERMONS TO PARLIAMENT: REPRODUCTIONS IN FACSIMILE WITH NOTES

JEFREN AND ABU GHALAY SILICA SAND / Libya. Ministry of Industry – Bulletin no 1. Ayler, M.F.P. BNE-1204 1 – 9 – ne IDC [550]

Jehan De Wavrin *see* A COLLECTION OF CHRONICLES AND ANCIENT HISTORIES OF GREAT BRITAIN (RS40)

JEHOVAH, THE REDEEMER GOD : THE SCRIPTURAL INTERPRETATION OF THE DIVINE NAME JEHOVAH / Tyler, Thomas – (Includes bibliographical references) – London: Ward, 1861 – 1mf – 9 – 0-8370-5593-8 – 1985-3593 – us A.T.L.A. [220]

JEHOVAH-JESUS : THE ONENESS OF GOD, THE TRUE TRINITY / Weeks, Robert Dodd – (Includes appendixes and index) – New York: Dodd, Mead, 1880, c1876 – 1mf – 9 – 0-8370-5666-7 – 1985-3666 – us A.T.L.A. [240]

JEHOVAH-JOVIS UND DIE DREI SOEHNE NOAH'S : EIN BEITRAG ZUR VERGLEICHENDEN GOETTERLEHRE / Glaser, Eduard – Muenchen: Hermann Lukaschik, 1901 – 1mf – 9 – 0-8370-3307-1 – 1985-1307 – us A.T.L.A. [220]

JEHRINGS JAHRBUECHER FUER DIE DOGMATIK DES BURGERLICHEN RECHTS – Jena. v. 1-90. 1857-1942; Index. 1857-1906 – 1 – 362.00 – us L of C Photodup [943]

JEHUDA HALEVI : ZWEIUNDNEUNZIG HYMNEN UND GEDICHTE / Rosenzweig, F – Berlin, 1927 – 7mf – 8 – ne Slangenburg [810]

JEHUDA HALEVI: EIN DIWAN / Bernhard, E – Berlin. BJ-421-51 1 – 9 – ne IDC [890]

JEHUDA HALEVI, SECHZIG HYMNEN UND GEDICHTE / Rosenzweig, F – 2v. Constance. 1924. BJ-421-56 1 – 9 – ne IDC [270]

JEHUDA HALEVI. ZWEIUNDNEUNZIG HYMNEN UND GEDICHTE / Rosenzweig, F – Berlin, 1927 – 7mf – 8 – ne Slangenburg [780]

JEHUDA HALEWI / Kaufmann, David – Versuch einer Charakteristik. Breslau. 1877. BJ-33-19 1 – 9 – ne IDC [180]

JEHUDA HALEWI / Kaufmann, David – Versuch einer Charakteristik. Breslau. 1877. BJ-421-55 1 – 9 – ne IDC [920]

Jekyll, G *see* A TREATISE ON THE RIGHT USE OF THE FATHERS IN THE DECISION OF CONTROVERSIES EXISTING AT THIS DAY IN RELIGION

Jelin, Elizabeth *see* FAMILY, HOUSEHOLD AND GENDER RELATIONS IN LATIN AMERICA

Jellicoe, S *see* THE SEPTUAGINT AND MODERN STUDY

JELLY BEAN JAMBOREE SUMMER WEEKLY READER – (v.6 .1980 5,6,9) – v.1. 1975 – 1 – us UMI [800]

Jelusich, Mirko *see* SICKINGEN UND KARL 5

JEMS: A JOURNAL OF EMERGENCY MEDICAL SERVICES – (1985-. 5,6,9) – 1980- – 1 – us UMI [617]

JEMTLANDS TIDNING – Ostersund, Sweden. 1845-89 – 16r – 1 – sw Kungliga [072]

JEN – (Journal of Emergency Nursing) – v1- 1975- 1; v4- 1978- 5,6,9 – apply; v.4-1978- 5,6,9 – us UMI [610]

JEN MIN JIH PAO – Peking, CC. 1970 – 2r – $100.00 – R63599 – us Library Micro [072]

JEN MIN JIH PAO SO YIN – Peking. Incomplete. CH-917 2. 1951-1968 – 9 – ne IDC [073]

JENA FIRST BAPTIST CHURCH (FORMERLY SALEM BAPTIST CHURCH). JENA, LOUISIANA : CHURCH RECORDS – Feb 1850-Sep 1872. 88p – 1 – 5.00 – us Baptist [240]

JENAISCHE ALLGEMEINE LITERATUR-ZEITUNG : MIT ERGAENZUNGSBLAETTERN, INTELLIGENZBLAETTERN UND REGISTERN – (1842-48 als Neue Jenaische allgemeine Literatur-Zeitung) – Jena, 1804-41 (mf ed 1992) – 680mf – 9 – DM4,700.00 – 3-89131-049-8 – gw Fischer [430]

JENAISCHE POLITISCHE EXTRA POST – Jena, Germany. 1783 – 1 – gw Mikrofilm [072]

JEN-CHIEN-SHIH – Human World. v. 1-42. Shanghai. 1934-35. BCH-277 2 – 8 – ne IDC [000]

Jendro, Frank *see* EINGRIFFSQUALITAET UND RECHTLICHE REGELUNG POLIZEILICHER VIDEOAUFNAHMEN

Jenish, Daniel *see* PHILOSOPHISCH-KRITISCHE-VERGLEICHUNG UND WURDIGUNG VON VIERZEHN ALTERN UND NEUERN SPRACHENS EUROPENS

Jenkins, Barry *see* THE VARIOUS EFFECTS OF CRYOGENIC MODALITIES WITH REGARDS TO RESTRICTION OF BLOOD VOLUME IN THE MALE FOREARM

Jenkins, Charles Francis *see* QUAKER POEMS

Jenkins, Deborah *see* BRITISH EMPLOYERS' CONFEDERATION ARCHIVE

Jenkins, F *see* TOUR IN ARRACAN

Jenkins, Floyd Thomas, jr *see* THE DESIGN AND IMPLEMENTATION OF A PROGRAM OF MINISTRY TO NON-PARTICIPATING RESIDENT MEMBERS OF BEREA BAPTIST CHURCH

Jenkins, George *see* A BIBLIOGRAPHY OF NIGERIAN HISTORY

Jenkins, Herbert *see* THE LIFE OF GEORGE BORROW
Jenkins, John Stilwell *see* THE NEW CLERK'S ASSISTANT, OR BOOK OF PRACTICAL FORMS; CONTAINING NUMEROUS PRECEDENTS AND FORMS FOR ORDINARY BUSINESS TRANSACTIONS.
Jenkins, Stanley John *see* THE ADMINISTRATION OF CECIL JOHN RHODES AS PRIME MINISTER OF THE CAPE COLONY, 1890-1896
JENKINSBURG BAPTIST CHURCH. BUTTS COUNTY. GEORGIA : CHURCH RECORDS – 1912-41 – 1 – 12.60 – us Baptist [240]
Jenkinson, H *see* THE LATER COURT HANDS IN ENGLAND FROM THE FIFTEENTH TO THE SEVENTEENTH CENTURY
Jenks, Jeremiah W *see*
– THE IMMIGRATION PROBLEM
– THE IMMIGRATION PROBLEM: A STUDY OF AMERICAN IMMIGRATION CONDITIONS AND NEEDS
– POLITICAL AND SOCIAL SIGNIFICANCE OF THE LIFE AND TEACHINGS OF JESUS
JENKS' PORTLAND GAZETTE – Portland, ME: Elezer A Jenks, oct 31 1803-mar 12 1805 – us Res Libr [071]
Jenkyn, William *see* EXPOSITION UPON THE EPISTLE OF JUDE
Jenman, G S *see* A HANDLIST OF THE JAMAICA FERNS AND THEIR ALLIES
JEN-MIN JIH-PAO – (Reel 1-3. 1950.4 months per reel. 21 issues lacking. Reel 4-13. 1951-55. 6 months per reel.27 issues lacking. Reel 14-22. 1956-58. 4 months per reel. 8 issues lacking. Reel 23-31. 1959-61. 4 months per reel. Complete. Reel 32.1962. Jan-Jun. Complete. Reel 33.1962. Jul-Dec. Lacking 14-31 Dec. Reel 34-41. 1963-66. 6 months per reel. Complete. Reel 42.1967. Jan-Jun. 3 issues lacking. Reel 44-45. 1968. Complete. Reel 46.1969. Jan-Jul. 1 issue lacking) – Peking. People's Daily – 1 – 35.00r – us Hoover Inst Photo [072]
JEN-MIN WEN-HSUEH – (People's Literature). v. 1-18. Peking. 1949-66. Lacking: v. 4 (2-6, 8, 9) 1952. BCH-918 2 – 8 – ne IDC [480]
Jenner, Edward *see* AN INQUIRY INTO THE CAUSES AND EFFECTS OF THE VARIOLAE VACCINAE
Jenner, Henry *see* EARLY DRAWINGS AND ILLUMINATIONS
Jenness, D *see*
– A COMPARATIVE VOCABULARY OF THE WESTERN ESKIMO DIALECTS
– ESKIMO STRING FIGURES
– THE LIFE OF THE COPPER ESKIMOS
– THE MYTHS AND TRADITIONS FROM NORTHERN ALASKA, THE MACKENZIE DELTA, AND CORONATION GULF
– A NEW ESKIMO CULTURE IN HUDSON BAY
– ORIGIN OF THE COPPER ESKIMOS AND THEIR COPPER CULTURE
– SONGS OF THE COPPER ESKIMOS
Jennings, A *see* THE EFFECT OF PERCEPTION OF PERFORMANCE OUTCOMES ON MOOD FOLLOWING EXERCISE
Jennings, Abraham G *see*
– THE LAST DAYS OF JESUS CHRIST ON THE EARTH, OR, THE DIVINE RECORD OF THE GREAT ATONEMENT
– LAST DAYS OF JESUS CHRIST ON THE EARTH, OR, THE DIVINE...GREAT ATONEMENT
– MOSAIC RECORD OF THE CREATION EXPLAINED
Jennings, Arthur C *see* THE MEDIAEVAL CHURCH AND THE PAPACY
Jennings, Henry J *see* CARDINAL NEWMAN
Jennings, Kathleen *see* LOUISVILLE'S FIRST FAMILIES
Jenny, Hans Heinrich *see* DIE AMERIKANISCHEN ANTITRUST-GESETZE, EINE UNTERSUCHUNG IHRES WESENS UND ZWECKES IN DER MODERNEN AMERIKANISCHEN MARKTWIRTSCHAFT
Jenny, Heinrich Ernst *see* HALLER ALS PHILOSOPH
JENS BAGGESEN : EN LITTERAER-PSYKOLOGISK STUDIE / Clausen, Julius – (Includes bibliographical references) – Kobenhavn: Brodrene Salmonsen, 1895 – 1 – us U.W. Library [430]
Jens, Walter *see* VON DEUTSCHER REDE
JENSEITS : DRAMA IN 5 AKTEN / Hasenclever, Walter – Berlin: E Rowohlt, 1920 – 1r – 1 – us U.W. Library [820]
JENSEITSMOTIVE IM DEUTSCHEN VOLKSMAERCHEN / Siuts, Hans – 1911 – 1 – us I.U. Libraries [390]
Jensen, Barbara E *see*
– CONQUERING ANXIETY IN GRADE SCHOOL AGED SWIMMERS THROUGH THE USE OF IMAGINATIVE PLAY
– THE IMPACT OF PROJECT ADVENTURE ACTIVITIES ON SELF-PERCEPTION
– THE INFLUENCE OF FITNESS-ORIENTED PHYSICAL ACTIVITY ON THE PHYSICAL SELF-PERCEPTION AND GLOBAL SELF-WORTH OF BOYS AND GIRLS
– MODIFICATION AND REVISION OF THE LEADERSHIP SCALE FOR SPORT
– TESTOSTERONE AND PHYSICAL ACTIVITY
Jensen, Herman *see* A PRACTICAL TAMIL READING BOOK FOR EUROPEAN BEGINNERS
Jensen, J Marinus *see* HISTORY OF PROVO
Jensen, Marian *see* COMPARISON OF RISK FACTORS FOR CORONARY HEART DISEASE IN SEDENTARY AND PHYSICALLY ACTIVE COLLEGE STUDENTS
Jensen, P *see*
– ASSYRISCH-BABYLONISCHE MYTHEN UND EPEN
– TEXTE ZUR ASSYRISCH-BABYLONISCHEN RELIGION
Jensen, Petrus *see* DE INCANTAMENTIS NONNULLIS SUMERICO-ASSYRIIS
Jensen, T *see* BRYOLOGIA DANICA
Jensen, Wilhelm *see*
– EDDYSTONE
– NIRWANA
– UM DEN KAISERSTUHL
Jenty, C *see* METHODO DE HACER LA AMPUTACION DEL MUSLO...
JEN-WEN – Humanities. v. 1-8 (10). Shanghai. 1930-37. (Including a list of new books and a monthly periodical index). BCH-278 2 – 8 – ne IDC [580]
JEPHET INB ALI THE KARAITE : A COMMENTARY ON THE BOOK OF DANIEL / ed by Margoliouth, David Samuel – Oxford v1-pt 3 1889 – 9mf – 8 – ne Slangenburg [220]
Jephson, A *see* FRIENDLY AND COMPASSIONATE ADDRESS TO ALL SERIOUS AND WELL DISPOSED METHODISTS,...
Jepson, W L *see*
– A FLORA OF CALIFORNIA
– THE TREES OF CALIFORNIA
O JEQUITINHONHA : FOLHA POLITICA, LITTERARIA E NOTICIOSA – Diamantina, 27 May 1863; Jan-Aug, Oct-Dec 1869; Apr 1870; 9 Jun 1872 – 1,5,6 – bl Biblioteca [072]
Jerahmeel *see* CHRONICLES
Jerdon, T C *see*
– THE BIRDS OF INDIA
– ILLUSTRATIONS OF INDIAN ORNITHOLOGY
– THE MAMMALS OF INDIA
JEREMIA / Coerper, F – Elberfeld: Evangelische Ges., 1900. 1 fiche – 9 – us A.T.L.A. [240]
JEREMIA IM FRUEHJUDENTUM UND URCHRISTENTUM (T.U.U. 5-118) / Wolff, C – 1976 – 5mf – 9 – ne Slangenburg [240]
JEREMIA UND SEINE ZEIT: DIE GESCHICHTE DER LETZEN FUENFZIG JAHRE DES VOREXILISCHEN JUDA / Erbt, Wilhelm – Goettingen: Vandenhoeck & Rup., 1902. 1 fiche – 9 – us A.T.L.A. [270]
THE JEREMIAD – (Lafayette). 1900 – 1 – us A.J.P.C. [073]
JEREMIAH : A DRAMA IN NINE SCENES / Zweig, Stefan – New York: The Viking Press, 1929 – 1 – us U.W. Library [820]
JEREMIAH : THE MAN AND HIS MESSAGE / Gillies, James Robertson – (Includes a chronological table) – London: Hodder & Stoughton, 1907 – 1mf – 9 – 0-8370-3289-X – 1985-1289 – us A.T.L.A. [220]
JEREMIAH : PRIEST AND PROPHET / Meyer, Frederick Brotherton – New York: Fleming H Revell, c1894 – 1mf – 9 – 0-8370-4408-1 – 1985-2408 – us A.T.L.A. [220]
JEREMIAH AND HIS LAMENTATIONS : WITH NOTES, CRITICAL, EXPLANATORY AND PRACTICAL: DESIGNED FOR BOTH PASTORS AND PEOPLE / Cowles, Henry – New York: D Appleton, 1880, c1869 – 1mf – 9 – 0-8370-6098-2 – 1986-0098 – us A.T.L.A. [220]
JEREMIAH, HIS LIFE AND TIMES / Cheyne, Thomas Kelly – New York: A.D.F. Randolf, (1888). 1 fiche – 9 – us A.T.L.A. [240]
JEREMIAH. HIS TIME AND HIS WORK / Welch, A C – Oxford, 1955 – Dfl22.00 – ne Slangenburg [220]
JEREMIAH THE PROPHET : A STUDY IN PERSONAL RELIGION / Calkins, R – New York, 1930 – 7mf – 8 – ne Slangenburg [240]
JEREMIAH THEUS / Middleton, Margaret Simons – ca.1952. Typescript draft with ms. emendations. 5 fiches – 9 – us South Carolina Historical [025]
JEREMIAH WALKER: GEORGIA GENERAL BAPTIST / Gardner, Robert G – 1976. 49p – 1 – 5.00 – us Baptist [920]
JEREMIAS : A DRAMA IN NINE SCENES / Zweig, Stefan – New York: The Viking Press, 1929 – 1r – 1 – us U.W. Library [820]
JEREMIAS : EINE DRAMATISCHE DICHTUNG IN NEUN BILDERN / Zweig, Stefan – Leipzig: Insel-Verlag, 1922 – 1r – 1 – us U.W. Library [820]
Jeremias, Alfred *see*
– DIE BABYLONISCH-ASSYRISCHEN VORSTELLUNGEN VOM LEBEN NACH DEM TODE
– BABYLONISCHES IM NEUEN TESTAMENT
JEREMIAS GOTTHELF / Bartels, Adolf – Leipzig: G H Meyer, 1902 – 1 – us U.W. Library [430]
JEREMIAS GOTTHELF : EINE EINFUEHRUNG IN SEINE WERKE / Muschg, Walter – Muenchen: Lehnen, c1954 – 1 – us U.W. Library [430]
JEREMIAS GOTTHELF : DAS KIRCHLICHE LEBEN IM SPIEGEL SEINER WERKE / Hutzli, Walther – (Includes bibliographical references) – Bern: B Haller, c1953 – 1 – us U.W. Library [430]
JEREMIAS METRIK / Giesebrecht, Friedrich – Goettingen: Vandenhoeck & Ruprecht, 1905 – 1mf – 9 – 0-8370-3274-1 – 1985-1274 – us A.T.L.A. [470]
JEREMIA'S PROFETIEEN TEGEN DIE VOLKEREN / Bleeker, Louis Hendrik Karel – Cap. XXV, XLVI-XLIX. Groningen: J.B. Wolters, 1894. 1 fiche – 9 – us A.T.L.A. [240]
JEREMY BENTHAM AND AMERICAN JURISPRUDENCE / Reeves, Jesse Siddall – Address delivered at the tenth annual meeting of the Indiana State Bar Association, July 11-12, 1906. n.p., 1906 26 p. LL-1079 – 1 – us L of C Photodup [340]
THE JEREMY ROBINSON PAPERS – 4r – 1 – $140.00 – Dist. us Scholarly Res – us L of C Photodup [355]
JEREMY TAYLOR / Gosse, Edmund – London: Macmillan, 1903 – 1mf – us A.T.L.A. [240]
Jerez de Los Caballeros *see* ORDENANZAS. ORDENANZAS. ORDENANZAS PARA EL GOBIERNO DE LA M.M. Y M.L. CIUDAD DE XEREZ DE LOS CABALLEROS PROBADAS POR LOS SENORES DEL REAL...
Jerez de los Caballeros. Badajoz *see* FERIA Y FIESTAS, 1945
Jerez, Francisco de *see* VERDADERA... CONQUISTA DE MEJICO
JERILDERIE HERALD – Jan 7 1898-Dec 24 1931 – 9 – at Pascoe [072]
Jerome, A *see* LA VIE INTELLECTUELLE DANS UNE ABBAYE LORAINE AU 17E ET 18E SIECLES
JEROME SAVONAROLA : A SKETCH / O'Neil, J L – Boston: Marlier, Callanan, 1898 – 1mf – us A.T.L.A. [240]
LE JEROMIEN : CAMPAGNE MUNICIPALE – St-Jerome, Canada. 30 mai 1961; v1 n2. 20 jun 1961 – 1r – 1 – Can$25.00 – cn Can Microfilming [971]
DIE JEROMIN-KINDER : ROMAN / Wiechert, Ernst Emil – Muenchen: K Desch, 1945 – 1r – 1 – us U.W. Library [830]
Jeronimo de Guadalupe *see* SANCTISSIMI MAXIMIGNE...
Jeronimo de Santa Cruz, M *see* LIBRO PRIMERO DE LA ARITMETICA EN EL CUAL SE CONTIENEN LAS SIETE ESPECIES PRINCIPALES
JERONIMO ZAPATA, NATURAL DE AZUAGA, EN NOTAS DE BIBLIOGRAFIA FRANCISCANA / Castro, Manuel – Madrid: Graf. Calleja, 1968 – 1 – sp Bibl Santa Ana [240]
Jeronimos *see*
– ORDINIS S. HIERONYMI...OBSERVATIONIS... MEMORIALE ADDITIONALE
– ORDINIS S. HIERONYMI...OBSERVATIONIS... SUMMARIUM
Jerphanion, Gabriel J *see* STATISTIQUE DU DEPARTEMENT DE LA LOZERE
Jerrold, Douglas *see* ESPANA; IMPRESIONES Y REFLEJOS
JERROLD, TENNYSON AND MACAULAY / Stirling, James Hutchison – Edinburgh: Edmonston & Douglas, 1868 – 1 roll – 1 – 1-55879-621-5 – uk Libr Preservation [840]
Jerrold, Walter *see* THOMAS HOOD
JERRY T. VERKLER, SENATE SERVICE 1963-1974 : STAFF DIRECTOR OF THE SENATE INTERIOR AND INSULAR AFFAIRS COMMITTEE – 2mf – 9 – $10.00 – us Scholarly Res [320]
JERSEY BAPTIST CHURCH. LIBERTY ASSOCIATION. DAVIDSON COUNTY. NORTH CAROLINA : CHURCH RECORDS – 1784-May 1964 – 1 – 63.45 – us Baptist [240]
THE JERSEY JEWISH VOICE – Bayonne. N.J. 1932 – 1 – us A.J.P.C. [071]
JERSEY JOURNAL – Jersey City. N.J. 1867- – 1 – us UMI [071]
JERSEY SHORE HERALD – Jersey Shore, PA. -w 1889-1912 – 13 – $25.00r – us I.M.R. [071]
JERSEY SHORE VIDETTE – Jersey Shore, PA. -w 1890-1912 – 13 – $25.00r – us I.M.R. [071]
JERSIAIS – Saint Helier. 6 Jan-29 Sept 1838; 11 Apr 1840 – 1 – uk British Libr Newspaper [072]
JERSUALEM PO CLIPPINGS ARCHIVE 1933-1977. PROMINENT PEOPLE – 1929mf – ne IDC [956]
Jerte, Ayuntamiento de *see*
– CENTENARIO DE UN EPISODIO DE LA GUERRA DE LA INDEPENDENCIA OCURRIDO EL 21 DE AGOSTO DE 1809
– FERIAS Y FIESTAS DE SAN GIL ABAD, SEPTIEMBRE, 1953
– FERIAS Y FIESTAS DE SAN GIL ABAD, SEPTIEMBRE DE 1952
JERUSALEM / Blake, William – Parts 1 to 4 (Copy E) – 14 – uk Microform Academic [810]
JERUSALEM : THE EMANATION OF THE GIANT ALBION / Blake, William – [S.l.]: Printed by W. Blake, 1804 – 1 roll – 1 – 1-55879-666-5 – uk Libr Preservation [810]
JERUSALEM : PHOTOGRAPHIC STUDY OF MONUMENTS OF THE HOLY CITY FROM THE JUDAIC ERA TO THE PRESENT DAY / Salzmann, Auguste – Collections of the Department of Prints and Photographs – 1r – 1 – $50.00 – fr Bibl Nationale [930]
JERUSALEM – '(s.l.')-Curitiba, Brazil. 1 Sep 1898-15 Jul 1902 – 1,5,6 – bl Biblioteca [072]
JERUSALEM AND EAST MISSION ARCHIVE 1842-1976 / Middle East Centre, St. Antony's College, Oxford – (Includes printed guide) – 2,574mf – 9 – ne IDC [240]
JERUSALEM DELIVREE: POEME HEROIQUE / Tasso, Torquato – Amsterdam: La Compagnie, 1756. 2v in 1.lxvi,405p. 5 fiches. (Literature Collection) – 9 – 12.00 – fr Bibl Nationale [810]
JERUSALEM. INVENTORY TO THE FILES OF HERBERT LOUIS, FIRST VISCOUNT SAMUEL (FIRST HIGH COMMISSIONER FOR PALESTINE), 1914-1962 / Mizrachi, E – Jerusalem, 1965 – 1mf – 9 – ne IDC [324]
JERUSALEM. INVENTORY TO THE RECORDS OF THE CHIEF SECRETARY'S OFFICE, 1918-1925 : PT 1: GOVERNMENT OF PALESTINE / Eshel, B – Jerusalem, 1966 – 1mf – 9 – ne IDC [324]
JERUSALEM POST – 1919-1995 – 12 times per yr – 1 – F2,003.00 – sz Infoprint [072]
JERUSALEM POST – Jerusalem, IS. 1977-1987 – 9r – $450.00 – R63573 – us Library Micro [072]
JERUSALEM POST – (Preceded by THE PALESTINE POST 1932-1950. by PALESTINE BULLETIN 1925-32. by PALESTINE WEEKLY 1919-31) – Dec 1919-June 1994 – 310r and 229mf – 1 – ne IDC [072]
THE JERUSALEM POST – Jerusalem, [Israell]: Palestine Post Publ Ltd, apr 23 1950-feb 1997 – us Res Libr [072]
JERUSALEM POST CLIPPINGS ARCHIVE – (A printed list is included) – 1933 onwards – 1,929mf – 9 – ne IDC [072]
Jerusalem Post. Jerusalem. Clippings Archive *see* PROMINENT PEOPLE
JERUSALEM STAR – London. 1895-96 – 1 – uk Microform Academic [073]
Jervis, John B *see*
– JOHN B. JERVIS PAPERS, 1795-1885
– SIR JOHN JERVIS ON THE OFFICE AND DUTIES OF CORONERS WITH FORMS AND PRECEDENTS

Jervis, W Henley *see*
- THE GALLICAN CHURCH
- THE GALLICAN CHURCH AND THE REVOLUTION

JESAIA / Guthe, Hermann – Tuebingen: J C B Mohr (Paul Siebeck), 1906, c1905 – 1mf – 9 – 0-8370-9477-1 – 1986-3477 – us A.T.L.A. [220]

JESAIA UND JEREMIA : IHR LEBEN UND WIRKEN AUS IHREN SCHRIFTEN / Koestlin, Friedrich – Berlin: G Reimer, 1879 – 1mf – 9 – 0-8370-3979-7 – 1985-1979 – us A.T.L.A. [220]

JESAJA 53 : DAS PROPHETENWORT VOM SUEHNLEIDEN DES GOTTESKNECHTES / Dalman, Gustaf – (Includes bibliographical references) – 2. umgearb. Aufl. Leipzig:J.C. Hinrichs, 1914 – 1mf – 9 – 0-8370-2809-4 – 1985-0809 – us A.T.L.A. [220]

JESAJA MIT DEN UEBRIGEN AELTEREN PROPHETEN / Ewald, Heinrich – Goettingen: Vandenhoeck, 1867. 2 fiches – 9 – us A.T.L.A. [240]

JESAJA UND ASSUR...UNTERSUCHUNG ZUR POLITIK DES PROPHETEN JESAJA / Wilke, Fritz – Leipzig: Dieterich, 1905. 1 fiche. 8370-5849-X – 9 – us A.T.L.A. [240]

JESAJA UND SEINE ZEIT / Meinhold, Johannes – (Includes bibliographical references) – Freiburg i.B: J C B Mohr, 1898 – 1mf – 9 – 0-8370-6281-0 – 1986-00281 – us A.T.L.A. [240]

DIE JESAJAERZAEHLUNGEN: JESAJA 36-39 / Meinhold, Johannes – Goettingen: Vandenhoeck & Ruprecht, 1898. 1 fiche. 8370-4380-8 – 9 – us A.T.L.A. [240]

Jeschke, Gunnar *see* FEHLER BEI DER MESSUNG UND AUSWERTUNG VON FESTKOERPER-MAS-NMR-SPEKTREN

JESCHURUN – Berlin. v. 1-17. 1914-1930 and Hebrew suppl. v. 1-7. 1920-1926 – 1 – us NY Public [270]

JESCHURUN – Breslau, 1868 n1-2, 1871 n1, 1871/72 n1-4, 1873/78 n1-2 – 1 – Inquire at Mikrofilmarchiv for details – gw Misc Inst [072]

JESCHURUN – (Continued as ALLGEMEINE ISRAELITISCHE WOCHENSHRIFT. Ed. by A. Levin, M.A. Klausner v. 4-15. Berlin. 1894-1906. Lacking: 1892-93, v. 1-2; 1895, v. 4 (47, 49, 51); 1898, v. 7 (36).) – Berlin. 1892-95. v1-4 – 302mf – 9 – ne IDC [073]

JESCHURUN : EIN MONATSBLATT ZUR FOERDERUNG JUEDISCHEN GEISTES UND JUEDISCHEN LEBENS, IN HAUS, GEMEINDE UND SCHULE. – (Merged with v"DER ISRAELIT" in 1889.) – Frankfurt a.M. Hannover. 1855-88. v1-21. – 248mf – 9 – ne IDC [073]

JESCHURUN : MONATSSCHRIFT FUER LEHRE UND LEBEN IM JUDENTUM – Berlin, 1(1914)-17(1930) – 197mf – 9 – Dfl690.00 – ne Slangenburg [073]

JESCHURUN : MONATSSCHRIFT FUER LEHRE UND LEBEN IM JUDENTUM – Berlin. v1-17. 1914-30 – 4r – 1 – us Ross [270]

JESCHURUN – Organ fuer die geistigen und sozialen Interessen des Judenthums. Posen. v1-4. 1901-1904. Complete. 3 reels. B140 (Leo Baeck Institute. German-Jewish Periodicals, Pt 1) – 1 – $205.00 – us UPA [270]

JESCHURUN : ZEITSCHRIFT FUER DIE WISSENSCHAFT DES JUDENTHUMS – Lemberg, Breslau, etc., 1856-1878 – 34mf – 9 – ne IDC [270]

JESCHURUN. MONATSSCHRIFT FUER LEHRE UND LEBEN IM JUDENTUM – Berlin. v1-17. 1914-1930 – 197mf – 9 – ne IDC [240]

JESHURUN – (New York). 1915 – 1 – us A.J.P.C. [073]

Jespersen, Otto *see* GROWTH AND STRUCTURE OF THE ENGLISH LANGUAGE

Jessaint, Claude LB *see* DESCRIPTION TOPOGRAPHIQUE DU DEPARTEMENT DE LA MARNE

"JESSE CHISHOLM" / Matthews, Warren L – 1 – us KS Hist [920]

Jesse, John Heneage *see* MEMOIRS OF THE PRETENDERS AND THEIR ADHERENTS

Jessen, C F G *see* PRASIOLAE GENERIS ALGARUM MONOGRAPHIA

Jessen, Karl Detlev *see*
- HEINSES STELLUNG ZUR BILDENDEN KUNST UND IHRER AESTHETIK
- HERZENSERGIESSUNGEN EINES KUNSTLIEBENDEN KLOSTERBRUDERS

Jessen, Paul *see*
- DIE HEILIGE PFLICHT
- DER KRAUTSTEIG

JESSENIA AND OENOCARPUS : NEOTROPICAL OIL PALMS WORTHY OF DOMESTICATION – 1988 – 196p – it F.A.O. [580]

Jessenius, F *see* AUFFGEDECKTE LARVE DAVIDIS GEORGII

JESSLETON-NORTH BORNEO NEWS – Sabath. Federation of Malaysia. and Sabah Times. 1958- – 1 – us UMI [072]

Jessopp, Augustus *see*
- BEFORE THE GREAT PILLAGE
- THE COMING OF THE FRIARS AND OTHER HISTORIC ESSAYS
- JOHN DONNE

Jessup, Henry Harris *see*
- THE MOHAMMEDAN MISSIONARY PROBLEM
- THE SETTING OF THE CRESCENT AND THE RISING OF THE CROSS
- SYRIAN HOME LIFE
- THE WOMEN OF THE ARABS

Jessup, Walter Edgar *see* LAW AND SPECIFICATIONS FOR ENGINEERS AND SCIENTISTS

JESTEDSKY OBZOR – Liberec, Czechoslovakia. Jun 1937-Sept 1938 – 1r – 1 – us L of C Photodup [072]

JESTEM POLAKIEM – London, UK. 4 Aug 1940-15 May/1 Jun 1941 – 1 – uk British Libr Newspaper [072]

THE JESTER – Montreal, Canada. v1 n5. 15 mar 1878-v3 n2. 27 jun 1879 – 1r – 1 – Can$30.00 – cn Can Microfilming [072]

Jestin, R *see* LE VERBE SUMERIEN

JESU BLUT, EIN GEHEIMNIS / Fiebig, Paul – Tuebingen: J.C.B. Mohr, 1906. 1 fiche – 9 – us A.T.L.A. [240]

JESU HISTORIQUE / Piepenbring, Charles – Paris: Emile Nourry, 1909. 1 fiche – 9 – us A.T.L.A. [240]

JESU MUTTERSPRACHE : DAS GALILAEISCHE ARAMAEISCH IN SEINER BEDEUTUNG FUER DIE ERKLAERUNG DER REDEN JESU UND DER EVANGELIEN UEBERHAUPT / Meyer, Arnold – (Includes bibliographical references and indexes) – Freiburg i.B.: J C B Mohr (Paul Siebeck), 1896 – 1mf – 9 – 0-8370-7171-2 – 1986-1171 – us A.T.L.A. [470]

JESU PREDIGT IN IHREM GEGENSATZ ZUM JUDENTUM : EIN RELIGIONGESCHICHTLICHER VERGLEICH / Bousset, Wilhelm – Goettingen:Vandenhoeck & Ruprecht, 1892 – 1mf – 9 – 0-8370-2420-X – 1985-0420 – us A.T.L.A. [240]

JESUCRISTO A TRAVES DE LAS EDADES. INSTRUCCION PASTORAL DIRIGIDA A SUS DIOCESANOS CON MOTIVO DEL 19TH CENTENARIO DE LA REDENCION DEL GENERO HUMANO... / Martinez Zarate, Jose de Jesus – Madrid: Razon y Fe, 1934 – 1 – sp Bibl Santa Ana [240]

JESUCRISTO REDENTOR / Goma, Isidoro – Barcelona, 1933; Madrid: Razon y Fe, 1933 – 1 – sp Bibl Santa Ana [240]

JESUCRISTO REDENTOR. PROGRAMA PARA LOS CIRCULOS DE ESTUDIO DE ACCION CATOLICA DE LA DIOCESIS DE CORIS. CURSO 1938-1939 / Junta Diocesana de Accion Catolica. (Coria) – Caceres: Editorial Extremadura, s.a. – 1 – sp Bibl Santa Ana [240]

DER JESUIT : CHARAKTERGEMAELDE AUS DEM ERSTEN VIERTEL DES ACHTZEHNTEN JAHRHUNDERTS / Spindler, Carl – 3. Aufl. Stuttgart: Hallberger, [1904?] – 1r – 1 – us U.W. Library [430]

JESUIT EDUCATION : ITS HISTORY AND PRINCIPLES VIEWED IN THE LIGHT OF MODERN EDUCATIONAL PROBLEMS / Schwickerath, Robert – (Includes index) – 2nd ed. St Louis, MO: B Herder, 1904, c1903 – 2mf – 9 – 0-8370-7587-4 – 1986-1587 – us A.T.L.A. [370]

JESUIT RELATIONS, AND ALLIED DOCUMENTS : TRAVELS AND EXPLORATIONS OF THE JESUIT MISSIONARIES IN NEW FRANCE, 1610-1791 / ed by Thwaites, R G – (Index v72-73) – Cleveland. v1-71. 1896-1901 – 423mf – 9 – ne IDC [240]

JESUIT RELATIONS AND ALLIED DOCUMENTS, 1610-1791 – 508mf – 9 – $965.00 – us UPA [240]

JESUIT RELATIONS OF NEW FRANCE – 9r – 1 – $650.00 – us OmniSys [240]

A JESUIT SCIENTIST AND THE REPUBLIC – n.p., n.d. Fiche W970. (Blodgett Collection of Spanish Civil War Pamphlets) – 9 – us H.U. College Libr [946]

UN JESUITA "A PALOS", JERONIMO DEL PORTILLO / Bayle, Constantino – Madrid: Missionalia Hispanica, 1945 – 1 – sp Bibl Santa Ana [240]

LOS JESUITAS DESDE SUS ORIGENES HASTA NUESTROS DIAS; APUNTES HISTORICOS / Rosa, Enrico – Madrid: Administracion de Razon y Fe, 1924. 477p. Trans. from the Italian – 1 – us U.W. Library [240]

JESUITAS EN EL MAR... / Plattner, Felix Alfredo – Madrid: Missionalia Hispanica, 1955 – 1 – sp Bibl Santa Ana [240]

LOS JESUITAS EN LA PROVINCIA DE QUITO DE 1570 A 1774 / Bayle, Constantino – Madrid: Razon y Fe, 1945 – 1 – sp Bibl Santa Ana [240]

LOS JESUITAS GERMANOS EN LA CONQUISTA ESPIRITUAL DE HISPANO AMERICA. SIGLOS 16-17 / Sierra, Vicente D – Buenos Aires, 1944; Madrid: Missionalia Hispanica, 1946 – 1 – sp Bibl Santa Ana [240]

JESUITEN-FABELN : EIN BEITRAG ZUR CULTURGESCHICHTE / Duhr, Bernhard – (Includes bibliographical references and index) – 2., unveraend Aufl. Freiburg i.B.; St Louis, MO: Herder, 1892 – 2mf – 9 – 0-8370-7457-6 – 1986-1457 – us A.T.L.A. [240]

DER JESUITEN-ORDEN : NACH SEINER VERFASSUNG UND DOCTRIN, WIRKSAMKEIT UND GESCHICHTE / Huber, Johannes – Berlin: C.G. Luederitz, 1873 – 2mf – us A.T.L.A. [240]

LES JESUITES CHASSES DE LA MACONNERIE / Bonneville, Nicolas de – (La Maconnerie ecossaise comparee avec les trois Professions et le Secret des Templiers. Memete des quatre Voeux de la Compagnie de S. Ignace et des quatre Grades de la Maconnerie de S. Jean) – Orient de Londres. 1788 – 9 – fr Hachette [321]

LES JESUITES-MARTYRS DU CANADA / Bressani, Francisco Giuseppe – Montreal: Compagnie d'Impr. Canadienne, 1877. 02837. (Pre-1900 Canadiana) – 9 – cn C.I.H.M. [971]

JESUITS : ALCVNE LETTERE DELLE COSE DEL GIAPPONE – Roma, 1584 – 2mf – 9 – H-8364/1 – ne IDC [956]

JESUITS : RERVM A SOCIETATE IESV IN ORIENTE... – Coloniae, 1574 – 6mf – 9 – H-8344/1 – ne IDC [956]

JESUITS! = JESUITES / Feval, Paul – (In English) – Baltimore: John Murphy, 1879, c1878 – 1mf – 9 – 0-8370-7459-2 – 1986-1459 – us A.T.L.A. [240]

THE JESUITS: A REPLY TO THE REV. J. J. ROY, OF WINNIPEG, DELIVERED AT ST PATRICK'S CHURCH, OTTAWA, MONDAY, MARCH 25TH, 1889 / Drummond, Lewis Henry – s.l.: s.n., 1889?. 02776. (Pre-1900 Canadiana) – 9 – cn C.I.H.M. [971]

THE JESUITS AND THE GREAT MOGUL / Melagan, Edward – London, Madrid: Razon y Fe, 1933 – 1 – sp Bibl Santa Ana [240]

THE JESUITS IN GREAT BRITAIN : AN HISTORICAL INQUIRY INTO THEIR POLITICAL INFLUENCE / Walsh, Walter – London: G. Routlegde; New York: E.P. Dutton, 1903 – 1mf – us A.T.L.A. [240]

THE JESUITS IN MALABAR / Ferroli, Domenico – 2v. 1939-51 – 1 – us A.T.L.A. [240]

THE JESUITS IN NORTH AMERICA IN THE SEVENTENTH CENTURY / Parkman, Francis – Boston: Little, Brown, 1867 – 2mf – us A.T.L.A. [240]

THE JESUITS: THEIR ORIGIN, HISTORY, AIMS, PRINCIPLES, IMMORAL TEACHINGS.. / Austin, Benjamin Fish – 1889. 07066. (Pre-1900 Canadiana) – 9 – cn C.I.H.M. [240]

THE JESUITS UNMASKED : BEING AN ILLUSTRATION OF THE EXISTING EVILS OF POPERY IN A PROTESTANT GOVERNMENT... / Parker, William – London: L B Seeley & Son, 1823 – us Res Libr [240]

JESUS / Bousset, Wilhelm – New York: Putnam's, 1906. 1 fiche – 9 – us A.T.L.A. [240]

JESUS / Bousset, Wilhelm – Tuebingen: J.C.B. Mohr, 1907. 1 fiche – 9 – us A.T.L.A. [240]

JESUS : HIS SELF-INTROSPECTION / Armitage, Thomas – New York: Putnam's, 1877 – 1mf – 9 – 0-8370-2112-X – 1985-0112 – us A.T.L.A. [920]

JESUS / Neumann, Arno – (Transl fr German. Includes bibliographical references and index) – London: Adam and Charles Black; New York: Macmillan [distributor], 1906 – 1mf – 9 – 0-8370-4572-X – 1985-2572 – us A.T.L.A. [240]

JESUS : AN UNFINISHED PORTRAIT / Norden, Charles van – NY: Funk & Wagnalls, 1906 – 1mf – 9 – 0-8370-56195 – 1985-3619 – us A.T.L.A. [240]

JESUS : WAS ER UNS HEUTE IST / Koenig, Alfred – Freiburg i. B:Paul Waetzel, 1903 – 1mf – 9 – 0-8370-4423-5 – 1985-2423 – us A.T.L.A. [240]

JESUS: AN UNFINISHED PORTRAIT / Van Norden, Charles – New York: Funk & Wagnalls, 1906.1 fiche. 8370-5619-5 – 9 – us A.T.L.A. [240]

JESUS AND MODERN RELIGION / Rumball, Edwin Alfred – Chicago: Open Court, 1908. 1 fiche – 9 – us A.T.L.A. [240]

JESUS AND MY CHARACTER (CCC71) = CHI TU YU WO TI JEN KO / Chao, Tzu-ch'en – (In Chinese) – Shanghai: Publication Dept., National Committee, YMCAs of China, 1925 – 1r – 1 – 1984-B500 – us A.T.L.A. [240]

JESUS AND THE GOSPEL: CHRISTIANITY JUSTIFIED IN THE MIND OF CHRIST / Denney, James – New York: A.C. Armstrong, 1909. 1 fiche – 9 – us A.T.L.A. [240]

JESUS AND THE GREEKS: OR, EARLY CHRISTIANITY IN THE TIDEWAY OF HELLENISM / Fairweather, William – Edinburgh: T. & T. Clark, 1924. xvi,407p. With: The Royal Woman by H. Mann. 1 reel.1297 – 1 – us U.W. Library [240]

JESUS AND THE MEN ABOUT HIM / Dole, Charles Fletcher – Boston: G H Ellis, 1888 – 1mf – 9 – 0-8370-2947-3 – 1985-0947 – us A.T.L.A. [240]

JESUS AS A PENOLOGIST : READ BEFORE THE NATIONAL PRISON CONGRESS, KANSAS CITY, MO., NOVEMBER, 1901 / Barrows, Samuel June – Louisville, KY.: Press of the Industrial School Gem, 1902 – 1mf – 9 – 0-8370-2191-X – 1985-0191 – us A.T.L.A. [240]

JESUS AT THE WELL, JOHN 4, 1-42 / Taylor, William MacKergo – New York: A.D.F. Randolph, 1884. 1 fiche – 9 – us A.T.L.A. [240]

JESUS (CCC291) = YEH SU / Surdam, T Janet – (In Chinese) – 1st ed. Hong Kong: Council on Christian Literature for Overseas Chinese, 1958 – 1r – 1 – 1984-6630 – us A.T.L.A. [240]

JESUS (CCC325) : A LIFE OF JESUS TAKEN FROM THE RECORDS OF MATTHEW, MARK AND LUKE / ed by Willmott, Lesslie Earl et al – (In Chinese) – Chengtu, Szechwan: Canadian Mission Press, 1936 – 1r – 1 – 1984-6664 – us A.T.L.A. [220]

JESUS CHRIST AND THE PEOPLE / Pearse, Mark Guy – 190- – 9 – us A.T.L.A. [240]

JESUS CHRIST AND THE PRESENT AGE : BEING THE TWENTY-FIFTH FERNLEY LECTURE / Chapman, James – London: C.H. Kelly, 1895 – 1mf – us A.T.L.A. [240]

JESUS CHRIST BEFORE HIS MINISTRY / Stapfer, Edmond – New York: Charles Scribner, 1896. 1 fiche – 9 – us A.T.L.A. [240]

JESUS CHRIST: CONFERENCES DELIVERED AT NOTRE DAME IN PARIS / Lacordaire, Henri Dominique – New York: Scribner, Welford, 1870. 1 fiche – 9 – us A.T.L.A. [240]

JESUS CHRIST D'APRES MAHOMET OU LES NOTIONS ET LES DOCTRINES MUSULMANES SUR LE CHRISTIANISME / Sayous, E – Paris, 1880 – Dfl13.00 – ne Slangenburg [230]

JESUS CHRIST DURING HIS MINISTRY / Stapfer, Edmond – New York: Charles Scribner, 1897. 1 fiche – 9 – us A.T.L.A. [240]

JESUS CHRIST ET LES CROYANCES MESSIANIQUES DE SON TEMPS / Colani, Timothee – 2e rev augm ed. Strasbourg: Treuttel & Wurtz, 1864 – 1mf – 9 – 0-8370-2706-3 – 1985-0706 – us A.T.L.A. [240]

JESUS CHRIST IN THE TALMUD, MIDRASH, ZOHAR, AND THE LITURGY OF THE SYNAGOGUE / Laible, Heinrich – Cambridge: Deighton, Bell, 1893.1 fiche – 9 – us A.T.L.A. [270]

JESUS CHRIST PENDANT SON MINISTERE / Stapfer, Edmond – Paris: Librairie Fischbacher, 1897. 1 fiche – 9 – us A.T.L.A. [240]

JESUS CHRIST THE DIVINE MAN : HIS LIFE AND TIMES / Vallings, James Frederick – (Includes bibliographical references) – NY: Anson D F Randolph, [c1887] – 1mf – 9 – 0-8370-5614-4 – 1985-3614 – us A.T.L.A. [240]

JESUS CHRISTUS UND PAULUS / Feine, Paul - Leipzig: J.C. Hinrichs, 1902. 1 fiche - 9 - us A.T.L.A. [240]
JESUS DE NAZARETH, ETUDES CRITIQUES / Reville, Albert - Paris, 1906. (Religion Series) - 9 - 15.00 - fr Bibl Nationale [240]
JESUS DEVANT CAIPHE ET PILATE: OU, PROCES DE JESUS-CHRIST / Dupin, Andre Marie Jean Jacques - Paris: F.H. Barba, 1864.1 fiche - 9 - us A.T.L.A. [240]
JESUS, DOCTOR / Caron, Max - Madrid: Razon y Fe, 1927 - 1 - sp Bibl Santa Ana [240]
JESUS EN DE ZIEL : EEN GEESTELIJCKE SPIEGEL VOOR 'T GEMOED. BESTAANDE UYT VEERTIG AANGENAME EN STICHTELIJCKE SINNE-BEELDEN. VERVAT IN DRIE DEELEN / Luyken, J - (161-168 bound at the end) - Amsterdam, 1685 - 3mf - 9 - O-3113/1 - ne IDC [760]
JESUS EN DE ZIEL : EEN GEESTELIJCKE SPIEGEL VOOR 'T GEMOED. BESTAANDE UYT VEERTIG AANGENAME EN STICHTELIJKE SINNE-BEELDEN. VERVAT IN DRIE DEELEN / Luyken, J - Amsterdam, 1680 - 2mf - 9 - O-3239/1 - ne IDC [760]
JESUS EN DE ZIEL. EEN GEESTELIJCKE SPIEGEL VOOR 'T GEMOED / Luiken, J - O 674. 1687.m - 9 - ne IDC [240]
JESUS EN DE ZIEL. EEN GEESTELIJKE SPIEGEL VOOR 'T GEMOED / Luiken, J - O 675. 1722 - 9 - ne IDC [240]
JESUS ET L'OUVRIER: DISCOURS PRONONCE A L'EGLISE ST SAUVEUR, QUEBEC, FETE DU TRAVAIL, 4 SEPTEMBRE 1893 / Defoy, Henri - Quebec: s.n., 1893 (Quebec: L. Brousseau). 04217. (Pre-1900 Canadiana) - 9 - cn C.I.H.M. [971]
Jesus, Gabriel de *see*
- DIOS ESTA AQUI
- VIDA GRAFICA DE SANTA TERESA DE JESUS
- VIDA GRAFICA DE SANTA TERESA DE JESUS. LA SANTA DE LA RAZA. VOLUMEN 1
- VIDA GRAFICA DE SANTA TERESA DE JESUS. TOMO 4. MADRID, 1935
- VIDA...DE SANTA TERESA DE JESUS...

THE JESUS I KNOW (CCC313) / Wang, K'uei-sheng & H S Feng - (In Chinese) - Shanghai: Christian Literature Society, 1935 - 1r - 1 - 1984-6652 - us A.T.L.A. [240]
THE JESUS I KNOW (CCC335) = NGO SUO JEN SHIH TI YEH SU / Wu, Yao-tsung - (In Chinese) - Shanghai: Association Press of China, 1929 - 1r - 1 - 1984-6674 - us A.T.L.A. [240]
JESUS IM NEUNZEHNTEN JAHRHUNDERT / Weinel, Heinrich - (Includes index of names) - Neue Bearbeitung. Tuebingen: J C B Mohr (Paul Siebeck), 1907, c1905 - 1mf - 9 - 0-8370-5743-4 - 1985-3743 - us A.T.L.A. [240]
JESUS IN BILDERN AUS SEINEM LEBEN / Zuendel, Friedrich - (Includes bibliographical references) - 2., neu durchgearbeitete und verm. AufL Zuerich: S Hoehr, 1885 - 1mf - 9 - 0-8370-5976-3 - 1985-3976 - us A.T.L.A. [240]
JESUS IN MODERN CRITICISM: A LECTURE / Schmiedel, Paul Wilhelm - London: Adam & Charles Black, 1907. 1 fiche - 9 - us A.T.L.A. [240]
JESUS IN MODERN LIFE / Logan, Algernon Sydney - Philadelphia:J B Lippincott, 1888 - 1mf - 9 - 0-8370-4169-4 - 1985-2169 - us A.T.L.A. [240]
JESUS IN THE QUR'AN / Parrinder, Geoffrey - London, 1965 - 4mf - 8 - Dfl19.00 - ne Slangenburg [260]
JESUS NAZARENUS UND DIE ERSTE CHRISTLICHE ZEIT : MIT DEN BEIDEN ERSTEN ERZAEHLERN / Volkmar, Gustav - Zuerich: Caesar Schmidt, 1882 - 1mf - 9 - 0-8370-9330-9 - 1986-3330 - us A.T.L.A. [240]
THE JESUS OF HISTORY AND THE JESUS OF TRADITION IDENTIFIED / Solomon, George - London: Reeves and Turner, 1880.1 fiche - 9 - us A.T.L.A. [240]
JESUS OF NAZARETH : 1: HIS PERSONAL CHARACTER 2: HIS ETHICAL TEACHINGS 3: HIS SUPERNATURAL WORKS: THREE LECTURES... / Broadus, John Albert - 3rd ed. New York: A C Armstrong, 1890 - 1mf - 9 - 0-8370-2462-5 - 1985-0462 - us A.T.L.A. [240]
JESUS OF NAZARETH / Clodd, Edward - London: Kegan Paul, Trench, 1889. 1 fiche - 9 - us A.T.L.A. [240]
JESUS OF NAZARETH: AN HISTORICAL AND CRITICAL SURVEY OF HIS LIFE AND TEACHING / Giran, Etienne - London: Sunday School Assoc., 1907. 1 fiche - 9 - us A.T.L.A. [240]
JESUS OF NAZARETH IN THE LIGHT OF TODAY / Russell, Elbert - Philadelphia: John C. Winston, 1909. 1 fiche - 9 - us A.T.L.A. [240]
THE JESUS OF THE EVANGELISTS, HIS HISTORICAL CHARACTER VINDICATED / Row, Charles Adolphus - New York: James Pott, 1884. 1 fiche - 9 - us A.T.L.A. [240]
JESUS ON THE HOLY MOUNT / Sanderson, Joseph - New York: American Tract Society, 1869. 1 fiche - 9 - us A.T.L.A. [240]
JESUS OR CHRIST? : ESSAYS: BEING THE HIBBERT JOURNAL SUPPLEMENT FOR 1909 - Boston: Sherman, French; London: Williams and Norgate, 1909 - 1mf - 9 - 0-8370-4721-8 - 1985-2721 - us A.T.L.A. [240]
JESUS OR PAUL? / Meyer, Arnold - New York: Harper & Brothers, 1909. 1 fiche - 9 - us A.T.L.A. [240]
JESUS: SEVEN QUESTIONS : CHAPTERS IN RECONSTRUCTION / Warschauer, Joseph - (Includes bibliographical references) - London: James Clarke, 1908 - 1mf - 9 - 0-8370-4647-5 - 1985-2647 - us A.T.L.A. [240]
JESUS THE JEW: AND OTHER ADDRESSES / Weinstock, Harris - New York: Funk & Wagnalls, 1902.1 fiche - 9 - us A.T.L.A. [240]
JESUS: THE LAST GREAT INITIATE / Schure, Edouard - Chicago: Yogi Pub. Soc., 1908.1 fiche - 9 - us A.T.L.A. [240]
JESUS THE MESSIAH IN PROPHECY AND FULFILMENT: A REVIEW AND REFUTATION OF THE NEGATIVE THEORY OF MESSIANIC PROPHECY / Dewart, Edward Hartley - Toronto: W. Briggs; Montreal: C. W. Coates; Halifiax: S. F. Huestis, 1891. 02649. (Pre-1900 Canadiana) - 9 - cn C.I.H.M. [971]
JESUS THE SON OF MARY, OR, THE DOCTRINE OF THE CATHOLIC CHURCH UPON THE INCARNATION OF GOD THE SON : CONSIDERED IN ITS BEARINGS UPON THE REVERENCE SHEWN BY CATHOLICS TO HIS BLESSED MOTHER / Morris, John Brande - (Includes bibliographical references and index) - London: James Toovey. 2v. 1851 - 4mf - 9 - 0-8370-8842-9 - 1986-2842 - us A.T.L.A. [240]
JESUS THROUGH THE EYES OF THE CHINESE NATION (CCC193) = CHUNG-HUA MIN TSU YEN LI TI YEH SU / Hsu, Sung-shih - (In Chinese) - Shanghai: Publication Dept., National Committee, YMCAs of China, 1934 - 1r - 1 - 1984-B500 - us A.T.L.A. [240]
JESUS UND DAS ALTE TESTAMENT: EIN... WORT AN DIE EVANGELISCHEN CHRISTEN / Meinhold, Johannes - Freiburg i.B.: J.C.B. Mohr, 1896. 1 fiche - 9 - us A.T.L.A. [240]
JESUS UND DIE HEIDENMISSION / Meinertz, M - Muenster i.W., 1925 - 16mf - 8 - ne Slangenburg [240]
JESUS UND DIE NEUTESTAMENTLICHE SCHRIFTSTELLER / Hausrath, Adolrf - Berlin. bd 1-2. 1908-1909 - Dfl74.00 - ne Slangenburg [220]
JESUS UND DIE NEUTESTAMENTLICHEN SCHRIFTSTELLER / Hausrath, Adolf - Berlin 2 Baende 1908-1909 - 21mf - 8 - ne Slangenburg [220]
JESUS UND DIE RELIGIONSGESCHICHTE : VORTRAG AUF DEM ERSTEN RELIGIONSWISSENSCHAFTLICHEN KONGRESS IN STOCKHOLM / Larsen, H Martensen - (Transl fr the Danish) - Freiburg i. B: J C B Mohr (Paul Siebeck), 1898 - 1mf - 9 - 0-8370-4385-9 - 1985-2385 - us A.T.L.A. [240]
JESUS UND PAULUS / Kaftan, Julius - Tuebingen: J.C.B. Mohr, 1906. 1 fiche - 9 - us A.T.L.A. [240]
JESUS UND SEINE PREDIGT: EIN VOLKSHOCHSCHULKURSUS / Thieme, Karl - Giessen: Alfred Toepelmann, 1908. 1 fiche - 9 - us A.T.L.A. [240]
JESUS' VIEW OF HIMSELF IN MARK'S GOSPEL: AN INDUCTIVE STUDY / Moxom, Phillip Stafford - Pittsfield, MA: Sun Printing, 1904. 1 fiche - 9 - us A.T.L.A. [240]
JESUS' WAY : AN APRRECIATION OF THE TEACHING IN THE SYNOPTIC GOSPELS / Hyde, William de Witt - Boston: Houghton, Mifflin, 1902 - 1mf - 9 - 0-8370-3714-X - 1985-1714 - us A.T.L.A. [240]
JESUS-CHRIST D'APRES MAHOMET OU LES NOTIONS ET LES DOCTRINES MUSULMANES SUR LE CHRSTIANISME / Sayous, E - Paris, 1880 - 3mf - 8 - ne Slangenburg [260]
JESUS-CHRIST PAR L. CL. FILLION / Vie, N -S de - Madrid: Razon y Fe, 1923 - 1 - sp Bibl Santa Ana [240]
JESUS-MESSIAS: DER HERR UND SEIN VOLK / Roentsch, Johannes - Leipzig: J.C. Hinrichs, 1882. 1 fiche - 9 - us A.T.L.A. [240]
JET - v1- 1951- 1; v35- 5,6; v51- 9 - us UMI [073]
JET LINE - Great Falls. Mont. 1956-1957 - 1 - us UMI [071]
Jeter, Helen Rankin *see* THE CHICAGO JUVENILE COURT
Jeter, J B *see* SEAL OF HEAVEN, OR, THE IMPRESSION OF DIVINE TRUTH ON A CANDID MIND
JETP LETTERS - v1- 1965- - 1,5,6 - us A.I.P. [530]
LE JEU DE L'IDENTITE ET DE LA DIFFERENCE. LE CAS D'ESSE ZOGBEDJI, MINI-DIASPORA ADANGME DANS LE SUD-EST DU TOGO / Corminboeuf, C - 9 - F130.00 - fr Ethnologie [306]
LE JEU DE ROBIN ET MARION / Halle, Adam de la - Manuscript, Paris, 1872 - 1 - us Sibley [780]
Jeulin, Paul *see* HISTOIRE LAPIDAIRE DU CHATEAU DE NANTES
JEUNE AFRIQUE - 1967-1974 - 2 times per yr - 6 - F1,500.00 - sz Infoprint [072]
JEUNE AFRIQUE - 1975-1988 - 2 times per yr - 6 - F2,100.00 - sz Infoprint [072]
JEUNE AFRIQUE - 1989-1995 - 2 times per yr - 6 - F2,350.00 - sz Infoprint [072]
JEUNE AFRIQUE - 1993-1995 - 5 times per yr - 1 - F2,800.00 - sz Infoprint [072]
JEUNE AFRIQUE - (Also available 1967-1992 on 16mm) - 1993- - 5r per y - 1 - inquire - us Ross [072]
JEUNE AFRIQUE (ACTION) - 1955-1960 - Cumul - 6 - F2,800.00 - sz Infoprint [072]
JEUNE AFRIQUE (ACTION) - 1961-1966 - Annual - 6 - F1,200.00 - sz Infoprint [072]
JEUNE AFRIQUE (ACTION) - (Also available on CD-ROM) - 1961-1966 - 1r per y - 5,6 - Sfr267.00 - sz Infoprint [960]
JEUNE AFRIQUE AND AFRIQUE MAGAZINE - 1993-1995 - 7 times per yr - 1 - F3,300.00 - sz Infoprint [072]
JEUNE AFRIQUE ECONOM. - 1989-1995 - 2 times per yr - 6 - F2,450.00 - sz Infoprint [072]
JEUNE AFRIQUE MAGAZINE - 1993-1995 - 2 times per yr - 1 - F1,800.00 - sz Infoprint [072]
JEUNE AFRIQUE MAGAZINE - (Also available on 35mm and CD-ROM) - 1984-1995 - 1r per y - 5,6 - Sfr401.00 - sz Infoprint [960]
JEUNE AFRIQUE MAGAZINE - v1-. Dec 1983- - 1,5,6,9 - us UMI [073]
JEUNE AFRIQUE PLUS - 1989-1991 - 1r per y - 5,6 - Sfr401.00 - sz Infoprint [960]
LE JEUNE AGE - Pointe-Gatineau, Canada. v1 n7. 15 jul 1878-v1 n19. 15 jan 1879 - 1r - 1 - Can$25.00 - cn Can Microfilming [072]
LE JEUNE ANNAM - Tribune de liberation nationale. Saigon. Mars 1926 - 1 - fr A.C.R.P.P. [073]
JEUNE FORCE DE FRANCE - Fond. Jean Balestre. no. 1-29. Paris. nov 1942-juil aout 1944. mq no. 28 - 1 - fr A.C.R.P.P. [073]
LA JEUNE GARDE - Organe des jeunesses socialistes S.F.I.O. de la Seine. Paris. juil 1936-mai 1938, fevr 1939 - 1 - fr A.C.R.P.P. [073]
LE JEUNE HOMME ET LA LITTERATURE: LECTURE FAITE AU CERCLE VILLE-MARIE DE MONTREAL / Bedard, MH - Montreal: E. Senecal, 1892. 03539. (Pre-1900 Canadiana) - 9 - cn C.I.H.M. [890]
LA JEUNE INDOCHINE - no. 1-12. Saigon. 10 nov 1927-2 fevr 1928 - 1 - fr A.C.R.P.P. [073]
UNE JEUNE MERE DANS LES PRISONS DE FRANCO / Fidalgo Carasa, Pilar - Paris, 1939? Fiche W 884. (Blodgett Collection of Spanish Civil War Pamphlets) - 9 - us H.U. College Libr [946]
LE JEUNE OUVRIER - Revue destinee au patronage des apprentis et des jeunes ouvriers. Angers. sept 1856-61 - 1 - fr A.C.R.P.P. [073]
JEUNE QUEBEC - Montreal, Canada. 17-23 jan 1967-28 fev- v1 n7. 6 mar 1967 - 1r - 1 - Can$30.00 - cn Can Microfilming [072]
JEUNE REPUBLIQUE - Pour une gauche unie et constructive au service de l'homme. Dir. Marc Sangnier. Paris. juin 1920-juin 1940, oct 1944-juin 1972 - 1 - fr A.C.R.P.P. [073]
JEUNESSE : ORGANE GENERAL DE L'A. C.J.C. J.A.C. - J.E.C. - J.I.C. - J.O.C. - J.U.C. - Montreal, 10 oct 1935-v8 n12. dec 1942 - 1r - 1 - Can$50.00 - cn Can Microfilming [072]
LA JEUNESSE BLANCHE: POESIES / Rodenbach, Georges - Paris: E. Fasquelles, 1913. 220p. 3 fiches. (Literature Collection) - 9 - 8.00 - fr Bibl Nationale [810]
LA JEUNESSE DE CALVIN / Lefranc, Abel - Paris: Fischbacher, 1888 - 1mf - us A.T.L.A. [240]
LA JEUNESSE DE MONTALEMBERT: CONFERENCE FAITE AU CERCLE VILLE-MARIE DE MONTREAL / Bourassa, Gustave - Montreal: E. Senecal, 1895. 03808. (Pre-1900 Canadiana) - 9 - cn C.I.H.M. [360]
LA JEUNESSE DE ROBESPIERRE ET LA CONVOCATION DES ETATS GENERAUX EN ARTOIS / Paris, Auguste Joseph - Arras: Vve. Rousseau-Leroy, 1870. 6 fiches. (Political Science Collection). (Historical Studies Series) - 9 - 15.00 - fr Bibl Nationale [323]
LA JEUNESSE DU DUC DE RICHELIEU OU LE LOVELACE FRANCAIS / Monvel, Duval de & Monvel, Boutet de - French Theatre Series. Paris. Barba, an V. 1796 - 9 - fr Hachette [820]
JEUNESSE ET REVOLUTION / Union de la Jeunesse Socialiste Congolaise - Brazzaville, Feb. 1977-Feb. 1978.-24 issues - 1r - 1 - $49.50 - us African Imprint [072]
LA JEUNESSE OUVRIERE : JOURNAL JOCISTE - Montreal. v1 no 1-v 10 no 16. 1944-1954. SEM35P180 - 10r - 1 - Can$417.00 - cn Bibl Nat [073]
JEUNESSE OUVRIERE (1956) - Montreal, 1956- SEM35P335 - 1r - 1 - Can$15.00 - cn Bibl Nat [072]
LA JEUNESSE SOCIALISTE / Groupe des Etudiants Socialistes - Revue mensuelle de socialisme scientifique. no. 1-11 12. Toulouse. 1895 - 1 - fr A.C.R.P.P. [073]
Jeunesses National-Populaires *see* ESSOR
Jeuthe, Lothar *see* FRIEDRICH DE LA MOTTE FOUQUE ALS ERZAEHLER
JEUX DE FICELLE LAPONS / Delaporte, Y - 9 - F30.00 - fr Ethnologie [306]
JEUX ET JOUETS DE L'OUEST AFRICAIN : T. 1 AND 2 / Beart, Charles - Dakar: IFAN, 1955 - 1 - F451.63 - fr Armell [306]
JEVERISCHE WOECHENTLICHE ANZEIGEN UND NACHRICHTEN - (Title changes: Affiches, Annonces et avis divers de Jever, from 1812; Woech entliche Anzeigen und Nachrichten von Jever, 5 Mar 1813; Jeverisches Wochenblatt , from 1817) - Jever, West Germany. 1978- - ca 6r per yr - 1 - gw Mikrofilm [072]
JEVERISCHES WOCHENBLATT *see* JEVERISCHE WOECHENTLICHE ANZEIGEN UND NACHRICHTEN
THE JEW - (New York). 1823-25 - 1 - us A.J.P.C. [073]
JEW AND GENTILE : BEING A REPORT OF A CONFERENCE OF ISRAELITES AND CHRISTIANS REGARDING THEIR MUTUAL RELATIONS AND WELFARE / Goodwin, E P et al - New York:Revell, c1890 - 1mf - 9 - 0-8370-2724-1 - 1985-0724 - us A.T.L.A. [230]
THE JEW AND HUMAN SACRIFICE = HUMAN BLOOD AND JEWISH RITUAL / Strack, Hermann Leberecht - London: Cope and Fenwick, 1909. 1 fiche - 9 - us A.T.L.A. [270]
THE JEW AS PATRIOT / Peters, Madison Clinton - New York: Baker & Taylor, 1902 - 1mf - us A.T.L.A. [305]
JEWELER AND OPTICIAN - v12-14. 1912-14 - 1 - us UMI [740]
Jewell County. Kansas. School District No. 106 *see* RECORDS
Jewell, Pliny *see* THE JEWELL REGISTER, CONTAINING A LIST OF THE DESCENDANTS OF THOMAS JEWELL

THE JEWELL REGISTER, CONTAINING A LIST OF THE DESCENDANTS OF THOMAS JEWELL / Jewell, Pliny – 1860 – 1 – $50.00 – us Presbyterian [920]
THE JEWELLERY GALLERY / Victoria and Albert Museum. London – (Includes printed index and catalogue) – 1984 – 24 colour mf – 15 – $756.00 – 0-907696-13-9 – uk Emmett [730]
Jewett, Ann E *see*
- CURRICULUM DEVELOPMENT FOR EXERCISE BEHAVIORAL CHANGE
- DEVELOPMENT OF AN INVENTORY TO ASSESS MULTICULTURAL EDUCATION ATTITUDES, COMPETENCIES AND KNOWLEDGE OF PHYSICAL EDUCATION PROFESSIONALS
- VALUE ORIENTATIONS OF PRESERVICE PHYSICAL EDUCATION TEACHERS

Jewett, Frances Gulick *see* LUTHER HALSEY GULICK
Jewett, Sarah Orne *see* THE MATE OF THE DAYLIGHT, AND FRIENDS ASHORE
JEWETT'S BOOK OF DUETS, TRIOS, AND QUARTETS – The duets composed and arranged for two violins and two flutes; the trios for three violins and three flutes; and a beautiful selection and arrangement of quartets for four instruments. Boston: John P. Jewett & Co., 1851. Includes: "Pot Pourri for two flutes, on popular airs, comprising Hail Columbia, Oh Susanna, The Last Rose of Summer, and Sweet Home, with variations." MUSIC 1086 – 1 – us L of C Photodup [780]
JEWISH ADVANCE – Chicago. Ill. 1878 – 1 – us A.J.P.C. [071]
THE JEWISH ADVANCE – Detroit. Mich. 1904 – 1 – us A.J.P.C. [071]
THE JEWISH ADVOCATE – Rochester, NY. 1898 – 1 – us A.J.P.C. [071]
JEWISH ADVOCATE AND CONNECTICUT HEBREW RECORD – Boston. Mass. 1923-36 – 1 – us A.J.P.C. [071]
JEWISH ADVOCATE SPRINGFIELD SPECIAL – Boston. Mass. 1923-24 – 1 – us A.J.P.C. [071]
Jewish Agency for Palestine *see*
- CONSTITUTION
- THE HISTORICAL CONNECTION OF THE JEWISH PEOPLE WITH PALESTINE
- MEMORANDA
- MEMORANDUM
- MEMORANDUM ON ACTS OF ARAB AGGRESSION TO ALTER BY FORCE THE SETTLEMENT ON THE FUTURE GOVERNMENT OF PALESTINE
- MEMORANDUM ON BRITISH POLICY IN PALESTINE SINCE THE ADOPTION OF THE GENERAL ASSEMBLY'S PALESTINE RESOLUTION
- MEMORANDUM ON THE JEWISH AGENCY WITH APPENDIX OF DOCUMENTS
- MEMORANDUM TO UNITED NATIONS

Jewish Agency for Palestine. Jerusalem *see*
- EVIAN CONFERENCE
- THE INFLUENCE OF JEWISH COLONISATION ON ARAB DEVELOPMENT IN PALESTINE
- JEWISH CASE BEFORE THE ANGLO-AMERICAN COMMITTEE OF INQUIRY ON PALESTINE
- THE JEWISH PLAN FOR PALESTINE
- MEMORANDUM ON THE POSITION OF THE JEWISH COMMUNITIES IN ORIENTAL COUNTRIES
- MEMORANDUM ON THE PROBLEM OF THE DISPLACED AND INSECURE JEWS IN EUROPE
- MEMORANDUM SUBMITTED TO THE ANGLO-AMERICAN COMMITTEE OF INQUIRY
- OBSERVATIONS ON THE SUPPLEMENTARY MEMORANDUM BY THE GOVERNMENT OF PALESTINE
- POLITICAL SURVEY, 1946-1947
- REPLY TO THE GOVERNMENT OF PALESTINE'S MEMORANDUM ON THE ADMINISTRATION OF PALESTINE UNDER THE MANDATE
- ZIONISM AND THE ARAB WORLD

Jewish Agency for Palestine. Lake Success, New York *see* SUPPLEMENTARY MEMORANDUM ON ACTS OF ARAB AGGRESSION TO ALTER BY FORCE THE SETTLEMENT ON THE FUTURE GOVERNMENT OF PALESTINE
Jewish Agency for Palestine. London *see*
- DOCUMENTS AND CORRESPONDENCE RELATING TO PALESTINE, AUG 1939-MAR 1940
- JEWISH CASE AGAINST THE PALESTINE
- JEWS AND ARABS IN PALESTINE
- MEMORANDUM ON THE "REPORT OF THE COMMISSION ON THE PALESTINE DISTURBANCES OF AUGUST 1929."MAY 1929. BJ-28-129/1
- MEMORANDUM SUBMITTED TO THE PALESTINE ROYAL COMMISSION ON BEHALF OF THE JEWISH AGENCY FOR PALESTINE
- PALESTINE AND THE BRITISH TAX-PAYER
- PALESTINE WHITE PAPER OF OCT 1930: MEMORANDUM
- PALESTINIAN ARABS UNDER THE BRITISH MANDATE
- PROMISES AND AFTERTHOUGHTS

Jewish Agency for Palestine. New York *see* MEMORANDUM ON TRUSTEESHIP FOR PALESTINE
THE JEWISH ALTAR : AN INQUIRY INTO THE SPIRIT AND INTENT OF THE EXPIATORY OFFERINGS OF THE MOSAIC RITUAL: WITH SPECIAL REFERENCE TO THEIR TYPICAL CHARACTER / Leighton, John – NY: Funk & Wagnalls, 1886 – 1mf – 9 – 0-8370-4086-8 – 1985-2086 – us A.T.L.A. [270]
JEWISH AMERICAN – Dallas, TX. 1938-41 – 1 – us A.J.P.C. [071]
JEWISH AMERICAN ARCHIVES – 1948-1995 – 6,1 – sz Infoprint [071]
JEWISH AMERICAN WOMEN'S MAGAZINE AND GAZETTE – New York, NY. In Yiddish. -w. Jan 1929-Dec 1931. 6 reels – 1 – uk British Libr Newspaper [073]
THE JEWISH AND THE CHRISTIAN MESSIAH / Stanton, Vincent Henry – Edinburgh: T.&T. Clark, 1886. 1 fiche – 9 – us A.T.L.A. [270]
THE JEWISH BANNER – (New York). 1905 – 1 – us A.J.P.C. [073]
JEWISH BIOGRAPHICAL ARCHIVE SUPPLEMENT = JUEDISCHES BIOGRAPHISCHES ARCHIV (JBA) SUPPLEMENT / Schmuck, Hilmar; ed by Lapide, Pinchas – 1998 – ca 120mf – 9 – diazo ca DM4,520.00 silver ca DM4,920.00 – 3-598-33513-X – silver ISBN: 3-598-33516-4 – gw Saur [920]
JEWISH BULLETIN – Omaha, NE. -w. Apr 1919-Apr 1921 – 1 – us NE Hist [071]
JEWISH BULLETIN – Omaha. Neb. 1919-21 – 1 – us A.J.P.C. [071]
JEWISH BULLETIN OF NORTHERN CALIFORNIA – San Francisco, CA. 1946- – 36+ r – 1 – $1,800.00 ($90.00y) – C02824 – us Library Micro [071]
THE JEWISH BUSINESS RECORD – New York. N.Y. 1916-18 – 1 – us A.J.P.C. [071]
JEWISH CALENDAR / Besse, Henry T – Syracuse: Wesleyan Methodist Publishing House, 1895. 1 fiche – 9 – us A.T.L.A. [270]
JEWISH CASE AGAINST THE PALESTINE / Jewish Agency for Palestine. London – White Paper. 1939. BJ-28-139 1 – 9 – ne IDC [956]
JEWISH CASE BEFORE THE ANGLO-AMERICAN COMMITTEE OF INQUIRY ON PALESTINE / Jewish Agency for Palestine. Jerusalem – 1947. BJ-28-144 1 – 9 – ne IDC [956]
JEWISH CHARITIES – Baltimore. Md. 1910-21 – 1 – us A.J.P.C. [071]
JEWISH CHAUTAUQUA SOCIETY. ASSEMBLY. JEWISH CHAUTAUQUA ASSEMBLY RECORD – 21 July 1899-1903 – 1 – us A.J.P.C. [060]
THE JEWISH CHESS JOURNAL – (New York). 1906 – 1 – us A.J.P.C. [790]
THE JEWISH CHILDREN'S WORLD – (New York). 1917-18 – 1 – us A.J.P.C. [830]
JEWISH CHRONICLE – 1841- 1; 1841-95 5,6 – us UMI [270]
JEWISH CHRONICLE – 1 – F1,572.00 – sz Infoprint [072]
JEWISH CHRONICLE – 1841-1888 – Cumul – 1 – sz Infoprint [072]
JEWISH CHRONICLE – 1889-1968 – 1 – sz Infoprint [072]
JEWISH CHRONICLE – 1969-1993 – 1 – sz Infoprint [072]
JEWISH CHRONICLE – Baltimore. Md. 1873-75 – 1 – us A.J.P.C. [071]
JEWISH CHRONICLE – Baltimore. v. 1 no. 1-5, 8-9, 15-16, 18-22, 35-44, 47; v. 2 no. 1. Jan-Dec 1875 – 1 – us NY Public [071]
JEWISH CHRONICLE – Boston. Mass. 1891-93 – 1 – us A.J.P.C. [071]
JEWISH CHRONICLE – Mobile. Ala. 1899-1901 – 1 – us A.J.P.C. [071]
JEWISH CHRONICLE – Pittsburgh. Pa. 1962-68 – 1 – us A.J.P.C. [071]
JEWISH CHRONICLE – (Syracuse, New York). v7 n37 (30 Mar 1951); v8 n12 (12 Oct 1951)-v8 n13 (19 Oct 1951); v8 n27 (4 Jan 1952) – us A.J.P.C. [270]
THE JEWISH CHRONICLE – (Index, 1841-1982) – London, England. 1841- – 1 – us Primary [072]
THE JEWISH CHRONICLE = SEFER ZICARON – (In English. Special Suppl: Tercentenary of the Resettlement of the Jews in the British Isles, 3 Nov 1961. Centenary issue: n3788 14 Nov 1941) – London, GB. v70 no1 12 Nov 1911-(no3969) 4 May 1961 – 1r – 1 – $35.00 – cn Can Microfilming [072]
JEWISH CHRONICLE INDEX – 1 – F655.00 – sz Infoprint [072]
JEWISH CHRONICLE INDEX – 1841-1880 – Cumul – 1 – F11,351.00 – sz Infoprint [072]
JEWISH CHRONICLE INDEX – 1881-1890 – Cumul – 1 – F2,270.00 – sz Infoprint [072]
JEWISH CHRONICLE INDEX – 1891-1895 – Cumul – 1 – F1,441.00 – sz Infoprint [072]
JEWISH CHRONICLE INDEX – 1896- 1900 – Cumul – 1 – F3,318.00 – sz Infoprint [072]
JEWISH CHRONICLE INDEX – 1901-1915 – Cumul – 1 – F524.00 – sz Infoprint [072]
JEWISH CHRONICLE INDEX – 1983-1984 – Cumul – 1 – F917.00 – sz Infoprint [072]
JEWISH CHRONICLE INDEX – 1985-1994 – Cumul – 1 – F524.00 – sz Infoprint [072]
JEWISH CHURCH IN ITS RELATIONS TO THE JEWISH NATION AND TO THE GENTILES / Korr, Samuel C – Cincinnati: William Scott, 1866.1 fiche – 9 – us A.T.L.A. [270]
THE JEWISH CHURCH IN ITS RELATIONS TO THE JEWISH NATION AND TO THE "GENTILES" : OR, THE PEOPLE OF THE CONGREGATION IN THEIR RELATIONS TO THE PEOPLE OF THE LAND, AND TO THE PEOPLES OF THE LANDS / Kerr, Samuel C – (Includes appendix) – Cincinnati: William Scott, 1866 – 1mf – 9 – 0-8370-3892-8 – 1985-1892 – us A.T.L.A. [270]
THE JEWISH CIVIC LEADER – Framingham. Mass. 1961-67 – 1 – us A.J.P.C. [071]
THE JEWISH CIVIC LEADER – Worcester. Mass. 1960-67 – 1 – us A.J.P.C. [071]
JEWISH COLLECTION – (Writings of Rabbi Isaac Mayer Wise. Includes guide with biography) – 15r – 1 – $1250.00 – us UMI [270]
JEWISH COMMENT – Baltimore. Md. 1900-18 – 1 – us A.J.P.C. [071]
JEWISH COMMUNITY BULLETIN – (Dec. 1948-Jan. 1949; Apr. 1949-May 1949; Nov. 1949-Apr. 1950; Sept. 1950-Oct. 1950; Feb. 1967; Nov. 1967; Mar. 1968-June 1968; Continued by: Jewish Community Journal) – Peoria, Illinois – 1 – us A.J.P.C. [270]
JEWISH COMMUNITY BULLETIN – Los Angeles, CA.1954-86 – 1 – us A.J.P.C. [071]
JEWISH COMMUNITY BULLETIN – San Francisco. Calif. 1946-1963 – 1 – us UMI [071]
THE JEWISH COMMUNITY BULLETIN CONSOLIDATED WITH EMANU-EL – San Francisco. Calif. 1895-49 – 1 – us A.J.P.C. [305]
JEWISH COMMUNITY JOURNAL – Peoria, IL. 1968-83 – 1 – us A.J.P.C. [071]
JEWISH COMMUNITY NEWS – Belleville, IL. 1972-84 – 1 – us A.J.P.C. [071]
JEWISH CONNECTION – (V1, No1, (Mar. 1981)-v8, No1, (fall 1987); Lacking: v1, No2; v5, No1) – New York, N.Y. – 1 – us A.J.P.C. [073]
JEWISH CONSERVATOR – Chicago. Ill. 1904-05 – 1 – us A.J.P.C. [071]
JEWISH CRITERION – Pittsburgh. Pa. 1958-62 – 1 – us A.J.P.C. [071]
JEWISH CURRENT EVENTS – Elmont, NY. 1974-86 – 1 – us A.J.P.C. [071]
JEWISH CURRENT EVENTS – Fall River. Mass. 1959-65 – 1 – us A.J.P.C. [071]
JEWISH DAILY EAGLE = DER KANADER ADLER – (Anniversary nos in Yiddish: 1927, 1932, 1938, 1958 1r Can$70.00. Souvenir nos in English: 1927, 1932, 1938, 1958 1r Can$50.00) – Montreal, Canada. 30 aut 1907-dec 1965; 2 jan 1966-jan 1988 – 123r – 1 – Can$140.00r – cn Can Microfilming [072]
JEWISH DAILY FORWARD – (Available in Yiddish or English. Backfiles 1897- $80r) – 1999- – 2r per y – 1 – $15.00y standing order – us Ross [072]
JEWISH DAILY FORWARD – (In Russian) – 1999- – 1r per y – 1 – $75.00r standing order – us Ross [072]
JEWISH DAILY FORWARD – (In Yiddish) – New York, 1897-1998 – 676r – 1 – $39,990.00 – us Ross [071]
JEWISH DAILY FORWARD – (Missing: 1900 (May-June)) – New York, 1897-1992 – 654r – 1,5,6 – ne IDC [071]
THE JEWISH DAILY FORWARD *see* THE JEWISH FORWARD
JEWISH DAILY FORWARD (NEW-YORK) – 1897-1995 – 1 – F1,484.00 – sz Infoprint [071]
THE JEWISH DAILY PRESS – Cleveland. Ohio. 1908-13 – 1 – us A.J.P.C. [071]
JEWISH DAILY PRESS AND "DER WEG" – Detroit. Mich. 1920 – 1 – us A.J.P.C. [071]
JEWISH DEAF – New York. N.Y. 1915-25 – 1 – us A.J.P.C. [073]
JEWISH DIALOG – Montreal, Quebec, Canada. 1972-83 – 1 – us A.J.P.C. [072]
JEWISH DIFFUSION OF FOLK-TALES / Jacobs, J – (Jewish Ideals). London. 1896. BJ-421-14 1 – 9 – ne IDC [390]
JEWISH DISPLACED PERSONS : PERIODICALS FROM THE COLLECTIONS OF THE YIVO INSTITUTE / Yivo Institute – $3,635.00 – 1-55655-210-6 – us UPA [270]
THE JEWISH DRAMATIC WORLD – (New York). 1909 – 1 – us A.J.P.C. [790]
JEWISH EDUCATION – (v.48 .1979 5,6,9) – v.1. 1929 – 1 – us UMI [270]
THE JEWISH ENCYCLOPEDIA – A descriptive record of the history, religion, literature and customs of the Jewish people from earliest times to the present day. Isidore Singer projector and managing ed. New York. 1901-06. B-6017-6028 2 – 226mf – 8 – ne IDC [270]
THE JEWISH ENCYCLOPEDIA – New York, London. v1-12. 1902-1906 – 226mf – 9 – Dfl791.00 – ne Slangenburg [270]
JEWISH EXAMINER – Brooklyn, NY. 10 Jan 1936-26 Dec 1941. Continues: Brookly Jewish Examiner. Continued by: The Examiner – 1 – us A.J.P.C. [071]
JEWISH EXPONENT – Philadelphia. Pa. 1887-1955 – 1 – us A.J.P.C. [071]
THE JEWISH FARMER – (New York). 1891-92 – 1 – us A.J.P.C. [630]
THE JEWISH FESTIVALS / Lehrman, Simon Maurice – London: Shapiro, Vallentine & Co., 1936.Illus. by Vivienne S. Lehrman. 191p. illus. plates (2 fold.) – 1 – us U.W. Library [270]
THE JEWISH FORWARD – New York, NY. 1897-1989 – 1 – inquire – us Ross [071]
JEWISH FREE PRESS – St. Louis. Mo. 1885-87 – 1 – us A.J.P.C. [071]
JEWISH GAZETTE – Manchester, England. 1950; 1955-81. -w. 22 reels – 1 – uk British Libr Newspaper [072]
JEWISH GAZETTE – Manchester, England. 9 Jan-31 Dec 1976; 1977-82. -w. 6 1/2 reels – 1 – uk British Libr Newspaper [072]
THE JEWISH GAZETTE – New York. N.Y. 1876-27 – 1 – us A.J.P.C. [071]
JEWISH GENEALOGICAL CONSOLIDATED SURNAME INDEX – 3mf – 9 – $7.50 – us A.G.L.L. [920]
JEWISH GENEALOGICAL SOCIETY PUBLICATIONS – Teaneck, NJ: Association of Jewish Genealogical Society – 24mf – 9 – $60.00 – us A.G.L.L. [920]
JEWISH GUARDIAN – London. v. 1-12. Oct 3 1919-Aug 14 1931 – 1 – us NY Public [072]
THE JEWISH GUARDIAN – (In English. National weekly) – London, GB. v11 no545 7 Mar 1930-v12 no619 7 Aug 1931 – 1r – 1 – $25.00 – cn Can Microfilming [072]
THE JEWISH GUARDIAN – New York, NY. 1898 – 1 – us A.J.P.C. [071]
THE JEWISH GUARDIAN – New York, NY. 1912 – 1 – us A.J.P.C. [071]
JEWISH HERALD – Boston. Mass. 1893-94 – 1 – us A.J.P.C. [071]
JEWISH HERALD – Houston. Texas. 1911-13 – 1 – us A.J.P.C. [071]
JEWISH HERALD – Providence. R.I. -w. 1952-58 – 1 – us UMI [071]
THE JEWISH HERALD = FOLKS-SHTIME – (In Yiddish) – Montreal, CN. v3 no 28. 1927 – 1r – 1 – Can$25.00 – cn Can Microfilming [072]
THE JEWISH HERALD – New York, NY. 1894 – 1 – us A.J.P.C. [071]
Jewish Historical Society of England *see* TRANSACTIONS OF THE JEWISH HISTORICAL SOCIETY OF ENGLAND

JEWISH HISTORICAL SOCIETY OF GREATER HARTFORD – Hartford, CT. 1974-82 – 1 – us A.J.P.C. [071]

THE JEWISH HISTORICO-CRITICAL SCHOOL OF THE NINETEENTH CENTURY / Stern, Nathan – New York, 1901. 1 fiche – 9 – us A.T.L.A. [240]

JEWISH HOLOCAUST DURING WORLD WAR 2 PAMPHLET COLLECTION – 1942-1985 – 1 reel – 1 – CSUXANN0299-B – us Hoover Inst Photo [943]

JEWISH HOME PRAYER-BOOK / Jewish Ministers Association of America – New York: Phillip Cowen, 1888. 1 fiche – 9 – us A.T.L.A. [270]

THE JEWISH HOME PRAYER-BOOK : A MANUAL OF HOUSEHOLD DEVOTION / ed by Jewish Ministers' Association of America – New York: Publ for the Jewish Ministers' Assoc [by] Philip Cowen, 1888, c1887 – 1mf – 9 – 0-8370-3783-2 – 1985-1783 – us A.T.L.A. [270]

JEWISH IMMIGRATION TO THE UNITED STATES : FROM 1881 TO 1910 / Joseph, Samuel – New York: Columbia University, 1914. (Studies in history, economics and public law; v59, whole no. 4: no. 145) – 1mf – us A.T.L.A. [304]

THE JEWISH INSTITUTE QUARTERLY – New York, NY. 1924-30 – 1 – us A.J.P.C. [073]

JEWISH JOURNAL – Brooklyn, NY. 1979-87 – 1 – us A.J.P.C. [071]

JEWISH JOURNAL – New Brunswick, NJ. 1968-81 – 1 – us A.J.P.C. [071]

THE JEWISH JOURNAL – New York. N.Y. 1889-1906 – 1 – us A.J.P.C. [071]

JEWISH JOURNAL OF GREATER L.A – Los Angeles, CA.1986-87 – 1 – us A.J.P.C. [071]

JEWISH JOURNAL OF RARITAN VALLEY – Highland Park, NJ. 1981-85 – 1 – us A.J.P.C. [071]

JEWISH JOURNAL/JEWISH VOICE – Highland Park, NJ. 1985 – 1 – us A.J.P.C. [071]

JEWISH LEDGER – Hartford. Conn. 1929-37; 1958-68 – 1 – us A.J.P.C. [071]

THE JEWISH LEDGER – New Orleans. La. 1951-60 – 1 – us A.J.P.C. [071]

JEWISH LIFE – 1933-74 – 1 – us UMI [270]

JEWISH LIFE – (v.4 .1980 5,6,9) – v.1. 1975 – 1 – us UMI [270]

JEWISH LIFE IN THE MIDDLE AGES / Abrahams, Israel – New York, London: MacMillan & Co., 1911.xxvi,452p – 1 – us U.W. Library [270]

JEWISH MESSENGER – (New York), 1857-1902 – 1 – us A.J.P.C. [073]

JEWISH MESSENGER – New York. v. 1-92. 1857-1902 – 1 – us NY Public [071]

JEWISH MESSENGER – New York. Nv. v1-92. 1857-1902 – 15r – 1 – us Ross [270]

THE JEWISH MESSIAH: A CRITICAL HISTORY OF THE MESSIANIC IDEA AMONG THE JEWS / Drummond, James – London: Longmans, Green, 1877. 1 fiche – 9 – us A.T.L.A. [270]

JEWISH METHOD OF SLAUGHTER COMPARED WITH OTHER METHODS / Dembo, Isaak Aleksandrovich – London: Kegan Paul, Trench, 1894. 1 fiche – 9 – us A.T.L.A. [240]

Jewish Ministers Association of America *see* JEWISH HOME PRAYER-BOOK

Jewish Ministers' Association of America *see* THE JEWISH HOME PRAYER-BOOK

JEWISH MISSIONARY MAGAZINE – v1-15. Jan 1921-Aug 1935 (complete) – 4r – 1 – ATLA S0483 – us A.T.L.A. [073]

JEWISH MONITOR – Birmingham. Ala. 1960-65 – 1 – us A.J.P.C. [071]

THE JEWISH MONTHLY – Rochester, NY. 1898 – 1 – us A.J.P.C. [071]

JEWISH MORNING TIMES – New York. N.Y. Morgen-zeitung. 1906 – 1 – us A.J.P.C. [071]

THE JEWISH MUSICAL WORLD AND THEATER MAGAZINE – (New York). 1923 – 1 – us A.J.P.C. [780]

THE JEWISH NATION – New York. N.Y. 1909-10 – 1 – us A.J.P.C. [071]

The Jewish National and University Library. Jerusalem *see* THE COLLECTIVE CATALOGUE OF HEBREW MANUSCRIPTS

Jewish National and University Library, Jerusalem *see* CLASSIFIED CATALOGUE (DEWEY DECIMAL SYSTEM)

Jewish National and University Library. Jerusalem *see*
- ALPHABETICAL CATALOGUES
- FINDING AIDS TO MANUSCRIPT AND ARCHIVE COLLECTIONS (ALL UNPUBLISHED)
- JUDAICA COLLECTION CARD CATALOGUE
- MARTIN BUBER ARCHIVE

Jewish National Fund (Keren Kayemeth Leisrael) *see*
- FACTS AND FIGURES, 5709 (OCT 1948-SEP 1949)
- TWENTY-FIVE YEARS OF THE JEWISH NATIONAL FUND

JEWISH NEWS – Detroit. Mich. -w. 1942- – 1 – us UMI [071]

JEWISH NEWS – Newark. N.J. 1946- – 1 – us UMI [071]

JEWISH NEWS – Richmond, VA. 1983-85 – 1 – us A.J.P.C. [071]

THE JEWISH NEWS – Detroit. Mich. 1942-62 – 1 – us A.J.P.C. [071]

THE JEWISH NEWS – Newark. N.J. 1959-67 – 1 – us A.J.P.C. [071]

JEWISH NEWS-MORRIS-SUSSEX – Ledgewood, NJ. 1979-83 – 1 – us A.J.P.C. [071]

THE JEWISH NEWSPAPER – Los Angeles, CA.28 Feb-6 Jun 1985. Missing issues – 1 – us A.J.P.C. [071]

JEWISH NEWSPAPERS FROM LATVIA – (Inquire for complete listing) – 7r – 1 – $490.00 set – us Ross [072]

JEWISH OBSERVER – 1963-1995 – 6,1 – sz Infoprint [071]

THE JEWISH OBSERVER OF THE EAST BAY – Oakland, CA. 1968-78 – 1 – us A.J.P.C. [071]

JEWISH OPINION – New York. N.Y. 1949-52 – 1 – us A.J.P.C. [071]

THE JEWISH PEOPLE AND PALESTINE / Weizmann, C – (Statements before the Palestine Royal Peel Commission). 25 Nov 1936. BJ-28-22 1 – 9 – ne IDC [956]

THE JEWISH PEOPLE FROM HOLOCAUST TO NATIONHOOD : ARCHIVES OF THE CENTRAL BRITISH FUND FOR WORLD JEWISH RELIEF, 1933-1960 – 1 – us Primary [270]

JEWISH PERIODICALS, MISCELLANEOUS – 1889-1921 – 1r – 1 – us Ross [270]

JEWISH PICTORIAL LEADER – Pittsburgh, PA. Jan 1952; Apr 1953 – 1 – us A.J.P.C. [071]

THE JEWISH PLAN FOR PALESTINE / Jewish Agency for Palestine. Jerusalem – Memorandum and Statements presented to U.N.S.C.O.P. 1947. BJ-28-149 1 – 9 – ne IDC [956]

THE JEWISH POST – Winnipeg, CN. v17 no 2. 1941-1980 – 27r – 1 – Can$65.00r – cn Can Microfilming [072]

THE JEWISH POST – Winnipeg. v17 n2. 9 jan 1941-31 dec 1980 – 27r – 1 – Can$65.00 – cn Can Microfilming [072]

JEWISH POST AND OPINION – (v46-. Sept 1979-. 5,6,9) – v3, no.27-. Oct 1935- – 1 – us UMI [073]

JEWISH PRESS – Brooklyn, NY. v20-23. 1970-73 – 7r – 1 – us Ross [071]

JEWISH PRESS – New York. N.Y. 1961-67 – 1 – us A.J.P.C. [071]

JEWISH PRESS – Omaha, NE. -w. Dec 1920-Dec 1959; Jan 1963 to date – 1 – us NE Hist [071]

JEWISH PRESS – Omaha. Neb. 1920-53 – 1 – us A.J.P.C. [071]

JEWISH PRESS – (The voice of the Torah Jewry). 1962-June 1970 – 1 – us NY Public [290]

THE JEWISH PROGRESS – San Francisco, CA. 1897-98 (broken series) – 1r – 1 – $50.00 – B02825 – us Library Micro [071]

THE JEWISH PROGRESS – San Francisco. Calif. 1878-96 – 1 – us A.J.P.C. [071]

JEWISH PUBLICATONS ON MICROFICHE, RARE RUSSIAN – (Inquire for complete listing) – 225mf – 9 – $990.00 – us Ross [090]

JEWISH QUARTELY – 1953-1995 – 6,1 – sz Infoprint [071]

JEWISH QUARTERLY REVIEW – (Missing: v15-17 1912-1926. v22-24 1932-1933. v36-41 1946-1950) – London. v1-20. 1888-1908; Philadelphia. NS v1-49. 1910-1959 – 582mf – 9 – ne IDC [270]

JEWISH QUARTERLY REVIEW – n.s. v. 1-41. 1910-51 – 1,5,6 – us Princeton Micro [270]

THE JEWISH QUARTERLY REVIEW – (Includes index. NS: 1(1910)-55(1964/65) Dfl 1,708.00) – 1(1889)-20(1908) – 262mf – 9 – Dfl917.00 – ne Slangenburg [073]

THE JEWISH QUESTION OR DEBATES ON ZIONISM – (Philadelphia). 1900 – 1 – us A.J.P.C. [270]

JEWISH RECORD – Philadelphia. Pa. 1875-86 – 1 – us A.J.P.C. [071]

THE JEWISH RECORD – Chicago. Ill. 1911-22 – 1 – us A.J.P.C. [071]

THE JEWISH RECORD – (In English and Yiddish) – St Louis, MO. 1926-50 – 15r – 1 – $1,275.00 – D3368 – us Scholarly Res [071]

THE JEWISH RECORD – Toronto, CN. v8 no 1, v9 no 12. 1937 – 1r – 1 – Can$35.00 – cn Can Microfilming [072]

THE JEWISH RECORDER – New York. N.Y. 1893-95 – 1 – us A.J.P.C. [071]

JEWISH RELIGION IN THE TIME OF JESUS / Hollmann, Georg – Boston: American Unitarian Assoc., 1909.1 fiche – 9 – us A.T.L.A. [240]

JEWISH RELIGIOUS LIFE AFTER THE EXILE / Cheyne, Thomas Kelly – New York: Putnam's, 1898. 1 fiche – 9 – us A.T.L.A. [270]

THE JEWISH REPORTER – Las Vegas, NV. 1994 – 1+ r – 1 – $50.00 ($90.00y) – U04859 – us Library Micro [071]

JEWISH REVIEW – Providence. R.I. 1920-1925 – 1 – us UMI [071]

JEWISH REVIEW : WEEKLY JEWISH NEWSPAPER – Cleveland, OH. 1895-1899 – 2r – 1 – us Western Res [071]

JEWISH REVIEW AND OBSERVER : WEEKLY JEWISH NEWSPAPER – Cleveland, Oh. 1889-1958 – 29r – 1 – us Western Res [071]

THE JEWISH REVIEW AND OBSERVER – Cleveland. Ohio. 1959-62 – 1 – us A.J.P.C. [071]

Jewish Scientific Institute (YIVO) *see* YEDIES

JEWISH SCRIPTURES...IN THE LIGHT OF THEIR ORIGIN AND HISTORY / Fisk, Amos Kidder – New York: Scribner's, 1896. 2 fiches – 9 – us A.T.L.A. [270]

JEWISH SHEET MUSIC FROM THE VERNADSKY LIBRARY IN KIEV, UKRAINE – (Includes printed guide. Hardcopy printout of complete series $495) – 4r – 1 – $360.00 – us Ross [780]

JEWISH SOCIAL SERVICE QUARTERLY – v.1-32. 1924-55. Superseded by Journal of Jewish Communal Service – 1 – us UMI [360]

JEWISH SOCIOLOGY AND SOCIAL RESEARCH – Superseded by Contemporary Jewry.x. v2 1975-76 – 1 – us UMI [270]

JEWISH SOUTH – Richmond, VA. 1893-99 – 1 – us A.J.P.C. [073]

THE JEWISH SOUTH – Atlanta. Ga. 1877-79 – 1 – us A.J.P.C. [073]

THE JEWISH SPECTATOR – Memphis, TN. 1885, 1902 – 1 – us A.J.P.C. [071]

THE JEWISH SPIRIT – Portland. Or. 1916 – 1 – us A.J.P.C. [071]

JEWISH STANDARD – London. -w. Jan 1890-Jun 1891. (1 reel) – 1 – uk British Libr Newspaper [072]

THE JEWISH STANDARD – (In English. National weekly) – London, GB. v7 no26. 4 Oct 1946 – 1r – 1 – $25.00 – cn Can Microfilming [072]

THE JEWISH STAR – Edison, NJ. 1985 – 1 – us A.J.P.C. [071]

JEWISH STRUGGLE – London. -m. Dec 1945-Oct Nov 1946. (4 ft) – 1 – uk British Libr Newspaper [072]

JEWISH STUDENTS' ORGANISATION – New York. N.Y. 1925 – 1 – us A.J.P.C. [071]

JEWISH STUDIES : RARE PRINTED SOURCES FROM THE PARKES COLLECTION – Marlborough: Adam Matthew Publications, 1993 – 322mf – 9 – $2,750.00 – uk Matthew [260]

JEWISH STUDIES GENERAL CATALOGUE – (Periodicals and newspapers 28,523mf + 4,120r Dfl711,720. Bibliography 3,107mf Dfl17,200. History 2,345mf Dfl16,530. Philosophy and religion 1,023mf Dfl7,110.00. Languages and literature 2,594mf Dfl18,560.00. Collected papers, jubilee and memorial vols 760mf Dfl4,810.00. All titles can be purchased separately) – 9 – ne IDC [470]

JEWISH STUDIES IN MEMORY OF ISRAEL ABRAHAMS – New York, 1927 – 9 – ne IDC [270]

THE JEWISH TABERNACLE AND ITS FURNITURE, IN THEIR TYPICAL TEACHINGS / Newton, Richard – New York: Robert Carter, 1878, c1863 – 1mf – 9 – 0-8370-4579-7 – 1985-2579 – us A.T.L.A. [270]

JEWISH TELEGRAPH – Manchester, England. 2 Mar 1956-24 Dec 1958; 1959-30 Dec 1960; 1961-83. -w. 24 reels – 1 – uk British Libr Newspaper [072]

Jewish Telegraphic Agency *see*
- BULLETIN
- COMMUNITY NEWS REPORTER

Jewish Telegraphic Agency, Inc *see* DAILY NEWS BULLETIN

THE JEWISH TEMPLE AND THE CHRISTIAN CHURCH : A SERIES OF DISCOURSES ON THE EPISTLE TO THE HEBREWS / Dale, Robert William – 2nd ed. London:Hodder and Stoughton, 1871 – 1mf – 9 – 0-8370-2803-5 – 1985-0803 – us A.T.L.A. [220]

JEWISH TEMPLE AND THE CHRISTIAN CHURCH: DISCOURSES ON THE EPISTLE TO THE HEBREWS / Dale, Robert William – London: Hodder & Stoughton, 1871. 1 fiche – 9 – us A.T.L.A. [220]

Jewish Theological Seminary *see* LUTZKI CATALOG OF BIBLICAL MANUSCRIPTS

Jewish Theological Seminary. Hebrew Manuscript Catalogs *see* RABBINIC MSS. CATALOG

JEWISH THEOLOGICAL SEMINARY OF AMERICA *see* COLLECTIONS FROM THE JEWISH THEOLOGICAL SEMINARY OF AMERICA

Jewish Theological Seminary of America *see* COLLECTIONS

JEWISH TIDINGS – Rochester. N.Y. 1887-94 – 1 – us A.J.P.C. [071]

JEWISH TIMES – Baltimore. Md. 1958-68 – 1 – us A.J.P.C. [071]

JEWISH TIMES – (Israel Today and the Jewish Times 1968-72) – Glasgow, Scotland, UK. 23 Oct 1964-Jul 1972 – 5r – 1 – uk British Libr Newspaper [072]

JEWISH TIMES – Los Angeles. Calif. 1930-31 – 1 – us A.J.P.C. [071]

JEWISH TIMES – Miami Beach, Fla., v2, no. 16 (20 Apr. 1983); v2, no. 18 (4 May 1983) – us A.J.P.C. [270]

JEWISH TIMES – Montreal. v1 n1. 10 dec 1897-v17 n15. 10 apr 1914f – 7r – 1 – Can$70.00 – cn Can Microfilming [072]

JEWISH TIMES – New York. N.Y. 1869-79 – 1 – us A.J.P.C. [071]

JEWISH TIMES – Toronto, Ontario. 9 Nov 1979-20 Dec 1985. English. Incomplete – 1 – us A.J.P.C. [072]

THE JEWISH TIMES – Brookline, MA. 1978-83 – 1 – us A.J.P.C. [071]

THE JEWISH TIMES – Downsview, Ont., Canada.1979-85 – 1 – us A.J.P.C. [072]

THE JEWISH TIMES – New Orleans, LA.14 Mar 1975-27 Mar 1981. English. Some issues missing – 1 – us A.J.P.C. [071]

THE JEWISH TIMES – New Orleans, LA.1894 – 1 – us A.J.P.C. [071]

THE JEWISH TIMES AND OBSERVER – San Francisco, CA. 1892-1911 (broken series) – 1r – 1 – $50.00 – B02826 – us Library Micro [071]

JEWISH TRIBUNE – San Francisco. Calif. 1936-47 – 1 – us A.J.P.C. [071]

JEWISH TRIBUNE – St. Louis. Mo. 1879-84 – 1 – us A.J.P.C. [071]

JEWISH TRIBUNE – Westchester, CT.sic 1978-81 – 1 – us A.J.P.C. [071]

THE JEWISH TRIBUNE – Bombay, 1936 n6-1940 n2 – 1 – Inquire at Mikrofilmarchiv for details – gw Misc Inst [072]

JEWISH VETERAN – Washington. D.C. 1963-64 – 1 – us A.J.P.C. [071]

JEWISH VOICE – (In Yiddish and English) – Reading, PA. 1923-24 – 1r – 1 – $85.00 – D3388 – us Scholarly Res [071]

JEWISH VOICE – St. Louis. Mo. 1888-1920 – 1 – us A.J.P.C. [071]

THE JEWISH VOICE – Cincinnati. Ohio. 1911-12 – 1 – us A.J.P.C. [071]

THE JEWISH VOICE – Edison, NJ. 1977-85 – 1 – us A.J.P.C. [071]

THE JEWISH VOICE – Houston, TX. 1937-38 – 1 – us A.J.P.C. [071]

THE JEWISH VOICE – Philadelphia. Pa. 1934 – 1 – us A.J.P.C. [071]

JEWISH VOICES – Cincinnati, Ohio. v1 n1 (Nov 1989)-v2 n2 (Mar 1991) – us A.J.P.C. [073]

JEWISH WEEKLY NEWS – Springfield. Mass. 1952-68 – 1 – us A.J.P.C. [071]

JEWISH WESTERN BULLETIN – Vancouver, BC. 9 Jun 1939; 20 May-30 Sept 1948; 23 Mar 1956; 12 Sept 1958; 14 Dec 1978 – 1 – us A.J.P.C. [072]

THE JEWISH WESTERN BULLETIN – Vancouver, CN. v20 no 1. 1952-1964 – 5r – 1 – Can$65.00r – cn Can Microfilming [072]

THE JEWISH WESTERN BULLETIN – Vancouver, CN. v40 no 1. 1972-1977 – 3r – 1 – Can$65.00r – cn Can Microfilming [072]

THE JEWISH WOMAN'S HOME JOURNAL – (New York). 1922-23 – 1 – us A.J.P.C. [073]

THE JEWISH WOMEN'S JOURNAL – New York, NY. v1 n4 (Summer 1993)-v2 n4 (Dec 1994) – us A.J.P.C. [073]

JEWISH WORLD – Albany, NY. 1979-86 – 1 – us A.J.P.C. [071]

JEWISH WORLD – London. Feb 14 1873-Feb 1 1934. Incomplete – 1 – us NY Public [270]

JEWISH WORLD – London. n1-185. 1873-76 – 1r – 1 – us Ross [072]

THE JEWISH WORLD – New York. N.Y. 1902-04 – 1 – us A.J.P.C. [071]

THE JEWISH WORLD – Philadelphia. Pa. 1914-42 – 1 – us A.J.P.C. [071]

THE JEWISH WORLD IN THE TIME OF JESUS / Guignebert, Charles – Trans. from the French by S.H. Hooke. New York: Dutton, 1939. xiv,288p – 1 – us U.W. Library [240]

JEWISH WORLD OF LONG ISLAND – Commack, NY. 1976-86 – 1 – us A.J.P.C. [071]

JEWISH YEARBOOKS AND CALENDARS : FROM THE NATIONAL LIBRARY OF RUSSIA, ST PETERSBURG – 51mf – 9 – $300.00 coll – us Ross [030]

THE JEWISH-AMERICAN PEOPLE'S CALENDAR – (New York). 1894-1900 – 1 – us A.J.P.C. [073]

JEWS AND ARABS IN PALESTINE / Jewish Agency for Palestine. London – Some Current Questions. 1936. BJ-28-135 1 – 9 – ne IDC [956]

THE JEWS AND THE ISRAELITES: THEIR RELIGION, PHILOSOPHY, TRADITIONS AND LITERATURE, IN CONNECTION WITH THEIR PAST AND PRESENT CONDITION, AND THEIR FUTURE PROSPECTS / Freshman, Charles – Toronto: A. Dredge, 1870. 03259. (Pre-1900 Canadiana) – 9 – cn C.I.H.M. [270]

THE JEWS AND THEIR EVANGELIZATION / Gidney, William Thomas – London: Student Volunteer Missionary Union, 1899 – 1mf – 9 – 0-8370-6119-9 – 1986-0119 – us A.T.L.A. [240]

JEWS AND WORLD WAR 2 PAMPHLET COLLECTION – 194?-1945 – 1 reel – 1 – CSUXANN2559-B – us Hoover Inst Photo [305]

JEWS BEHIND THE IRON CURTAIN / American Jewish Committee. Library of Jewish Information – New York. 1949-61. BJ-212-3 1 – 9 – ne IDC [947]

THE JEWS IN AMERICA : A SHORT STORY OF THEIR PART IN THE BUILDING OF THE REPUBLIC: COMMEMORATING THE TWO HUNDRED AND FIFTIETH ANNIVERSARY OF THEIR SETTLEMENT / Peters, Madison Clinton – Philadelphia: J.C. Winston, 1905 – 1mf – us A.T.L.A. [305]

THE JEWS OF PHILADELPHIA : THEIR HISTORY FROM THE EARLIEST SETTLEMENTS TO THE PRESENT TIME : A RECORD OF EVENTS AND INSTITUTIONS, AND OF LEADING MEMBERS OF THE JEWISH COMMUNITY IN EVERY SPHERE OF ACTIVITY / Morais, Henry Samuel – Philadelphia: Levytype, 1894 – 2mf – us A.T.L.A. [270]

THE JEWS: THEIR CUSTOMS AND CEREMONIES / Myers, Emmanuel Moses – New York: R. Worthington, 1879. 1 fiche – 9 – us A.T.L.A. [270]

JEWSBURY: THE COLLECTED WRITINGS OF GERALDINE JEWSBURY (1812-1880) – Marlborough: Adam Matthew Publications, 1994 – 6r – 1 – $725.00 – uk Matthew [305]

Jezequel, Jules *see* IMPRESSIONS D'ESPAGNE, 15 JOURS EN ESPAGNE REPUBLICAINE, 11-25 NOVEMBRE 1937

JEZUICI W POLSCE / Zaleski, S S J – 5v. Lwow. 1900-06. BR-5563 2 – 8 – ne IDC [240]

JEZUS EN DE ZIEL : EEN GEESTELYKE SPIEGEL VOOR 'T GEMOED, BESTAANDE IN VEERTIG AANGENAAME EN STICHTELYKE ZINNEBEELDEN. VERVAT IN DRIE DEELEN. NEVENS HET EEUWIGE VADERLAND EN DESZELFS VREUGDE / Luyken, J – Amsterdam, 1704 – 3mf – 9 – O-3240/1 – ne IDC [760]

JEZUS IN DE ISLAM / Bakker, FL – Den Haag, 1955 – 1mf – 8 – ne Slangenburg [260]

J.F. Glidden Publishing Co *see* DE KALB CHRONICLE SOUVENIR

J.G. HERDERS HUMANITAETSIDEE ALS AUSDRUCK SEINES WELTBILDES UND SEINER PERSOENLICHKEIT / Dobbek, Wilhelm – (Includes bibliographical references and index) – [Braunschweig]: G Westermann, 1949 – 1 – us U.W. Library [430]

J.G. SCHUMMEL : LEBEN UND SCHAFFEN EINES SCHRIFTSTELLERS UND REFORMPAEDOGOGEN: EIN BEITRAG ZUR GESCHICHTE DER PAEDAGOGISCHEN LITERATUR DER AUFKLAERUNGSZEIT / Weigand, Georg – (Includes bibliographical references) – Frankfurt am Main: M Diesterweg, 1925 – 1 – us U.W. Library [430]

J.H. Beers and Co *see*
- ARMSTRONG COUNTY: HER PEOPLE PAST AND PRESENT
- BIOGRAPHICAL ANNALS OF LANCASTER COUNTY
- BIOGRAPHICAL ANNALS OF LEBANON COUNTY
- BIOGRAPHICAL MEMOIRS OF GRATIOT COUNTY
- COMMEMORATIVE BIOGRAPHICAL RECORD OF CENTRE, CLINTON, UNION AND SNYDER COUNTIES
- COMMEMORATIVE BIOGRAPHICAL RECORD OF DUTCHESS COUNTY
- COMMEMORATIVE BIOGRAPHICAL RECORD OF HARTFORD COUNTY, CONNECTICUT
- COMMEMORATIVE BIOGRAPHICAL RECORD OF NORTHEASTERN PENNSYLVANIA
- COMMEMORATIVE BIOGRAPHICAL RECORD OF ROCK, GREEN, GRANT, IOWA AND LAFAYETTE COUNTIES
- COMMEMORATIVE BIOGRAPHICAL RECORD OF THE COUNTIES OF SANDUSKY AND OTTAWA
- COMMEMORATIVE BIOGRAPHICAL RECORD OF THE UPPER LAKE REGION
- COMMEMORATIVE BIOGRAPHICAL RECORD OF THE UPPER WISCONSIN
- COMMEMORATIVE BIOGRAPHICAL RECORD OF THE WEST SHORE OF GREEN BAY
- COMMEMORATIVE BIOGRAPHICAL RECORD OF WASHINGTON COUNTY
- COMMEMORATIVE BIOGRAPHICAL RECORD OF WAYNE AND HOLMES COUNTIES
- COMMEMORATIVE BIOGRAPHICAL RECORDS OF THE COUNTIES OF HURON AND LORAIN
- COMMEMORATIVE BIOGRAPHICAL RECORDS OF ULSTER COUNTY
- COMMEMORATIVE HISTORICAL AND BIOGRAPHICAL RECORD OF WOOD COUNTY
- GENEALOGICAL AND BIOGRAPHICAL RECORD OF NEW LONDON COUNTY, CONNECTICUT
- GENEALOGICAL FAMILY HISTORY OF AND BIOGRAPHY OF SCHUYLKILL COUNTY
- HISTORY OF BERKSHIRE COUNTY
- HISTORY OF HARRISON AND CARROLL COUNTIES
- HISTORY OF MCKEAN, ELK, CAMERON AND POTTER COUNTIES
- HISTORY OF THE GREAT LAKES
- UPPER LAKE REGION

J.-H. NEWMAN : ESSAI DE PSYCHOLOGIE RELIGIEUSE / Grappe, Georges – Paris: P.-J. Beduchaud, 1902. (Les Grands hommes de l'Eglise au XIXe siecle; 2) – 1mf – us A.T.L.A. [240]

Jha, Hari Bansh *see* BUDDHIST ECONOMICS AND THE MODERN WORLD

Jhering, Rudolf von *see* DER ZWECK IM RECHT, VON RUDOLPH VON JHERING.

JHERINGS JAHRBUCHER FUER DIE DOGMATIK DES BURGERLICHEN RECHTS – Jena. On film: v1-90; 1857-1942; index 1857-1906. LL-0226 – 1 – us L of C Photodup [340]

JI LU YI RI BAO – China. Sept 1948-Jun 1949. 27 ill. DL61f – 9 – 95.00 – cc Globe [072]

JIA – China, 1950-51. For women and children. ED25f – 9 – $50.00 – cc Globe [305]

JIAJING ANXI XIAN ZHI, 1552 – Records of Anxi County in the reign of Jiajing. 8 vols. Comp. by Lin Younian. F A43. (Rare Local Records in Chinese...1420-1507) – 9 – $22.50 – cc Microforms [950]

JIAJING BAOYING XIAN ZHILUE, 1538 / Jiangsu Province. China – Abstracts from the records of Baoying County in the reign of Jiajing. 4 vols. Comp. by Wen Renquan. F A13. (Rare Local Records in Chinese...1420-1507) – 9 – $9.00 – cc Microforms [950]

JIAJING BAZHOU ZHI, 1548 / Hebei Province. China – Records of Bazhou in the reign of Jiajing. 9 vols. Comp. by Zhou Fujun. F A6. (Rare Local Records in Chinese...1420-1507) – 9 – $18.00 – cc Microforms [950]

JIAJING CHANGDE FU ZHI, 1526 / Hunan Province. China – Records of Changde Prefecture in the reign of Jiajing. 20v. Comp. by Chen Hongmo. (Rare Local Records in Chinese...1420-1507). F A86 – 9 – $63.00 – cc Microforms [950]

JIAJING CHANGYUAN XIAN ZHI, 1541 / Henan Province. China – Records of Changyuan County in the reign of Jiajing. 9 vols. Comp. by Liu Fang. F A75. (Rare Local Records in Chinese...1420-1507) – 9 – $18.00 – cc Microforms [950]

JIAJING CHIZHOU FU ZHI, 1545 – Records of Chizhou Prefecture in the reign of Jiajing. 9 vols. Comp. by Wang Chong. F A31. (Rare Local Records in Chinese...1420-1507) – 9 – $36.00 – cc Microforms [950]

JIAJING CHUN'AN XIAN ZHI, 1524 / Zhejiang Province. China – Records of Chun'an County in the reign of Jiajing. 17 vols. Comp. by Yao Mingwan. F A20. (Rare Local Records in Chinese...1420-1507) – 9 – $40.50 – cc Microforms [950]

JIAJING DENGZHOU ZHI, 1564 / Henan Province. China – Records of Dengzhou in the reign of Jiajing. 16 vols. Comp. by Pan Tingnam. F A70. (Rare Local Records in Chinese...1420-1507) – 9 – $27.00 – cc Microforms [950]

JIAJING DONGXIANG XIAN ZHI, 1524 / Jiangxi Province. China – Records of Dongxiang County in the reign of Jiajing. 2v. Comp. by Rao Wenbi.F/A 53. (Rare Local Records in Chinese...1420-1507) – 9 – $13.50 – cc Microforms [950]

JIAJING GANZHOU FU ZHI, 1536 / Jiangxi Province. China – Records of Ganzhou Prefecture in the reign of Jiajing. 5 vols. Comp. by Tong Tianxi. F A50. (Rare Local Records in Chinese...1420-1507) – 9 – $40.50 – cc Microforms [950]

JIAJING GAOCHUN XIAN ZHI, 1562 / Jiangsu Province. China – Records of Gaochun County in the reign of Jiajing. 4 vols. Comp. by Liu Qidong. F A11. (Rare Local Records in Chinese...1420-1507) – 9 – $13.50 – cc Microforms [950]

JIAJING GUANGPING FU ZHI, 1550 / Hebei Province. China – (Records of Guangping Prefecture in the Reign of Jiajing, 16 vols.) Comp. by Chen Fei. F A2. (Rare Local Records in Chinese...1420-1507) – 9 – $31.50 – cc Microforms [950]

JIAJING GUANGSHAN XIAN ZHI, 1556 / Henan Province. China – Records of Guangshan County in the reign of Jiajing. 9 vols. Comp. by Shen Shaoqing. F A69. (Rare Local Records in Chinese...1420-1507) – 9 – $18.00 – cc Microforms [950]

JIAJING GUSHI XIAN ZHI, 1542 / Henan Province. China – Records of Gushi County in the reign of Jiajing. 10 vols. Comp. by Ge Chen. F A76. (Rare Local Records in Chinese...1420-1507) – 9 – $22.50 – cc Microforms [950]

JIAJING HAIMEN XIAN ZHI, 1597 / Jiangsu Province. China – Records of Haimen County in the reign of Jiajing. 6 vols. Comp. by Cui Tong. F A19. (Rare Local Records in Chinese...1420-1507) – 9 – $18.00 – cc Microforms [950]

JIAJING HANYANG FU ZHI, 1546 / Hubei Province. China – Records of Hanyang Prefecture in the reign of Jiajing. 3 vols. Comp. by Zhu Yi. (Rare Local Records in Chinese...1420-1507). F A82 – 9 – $27.00 – cc Microforms [950]

JIAJING HEJIAN FU ZHI, 1540 / Hebei Province. China – Records of Hejian Prefecture in the reign of Jiajing. 28 vols. Comp. by Fan Shen. F A1. (Rare Local Records in Chinese...1420-1507) – 9 – $81.00 – cc Microforms [950]

JIAJING HENGZHOU FU ZHI, 1536 / Hunan Province. China – Records of Hengzhou Prefecture in the reign of Jiajing. 9 vols. Comp. by Yang Pei. (Rare Local Records in Chinese...1420-1507). F A89 – 9 – $27.00 – cc Microforms [950]

JIAJING HONGYA XIAN ZHI, 1562 / Sichuan Province. China – Records of Hongya County in the Reign of Jiajing. 5 vols. Compiled by Zhang Keda. F A100. (Rare Local Records in Chinese...1420-1507) – 9 – $13.50 – cc Microforms [950]

JIAJING HUI ZHILUE, 1560 / Guangdong Province. China – Excerpts from the records of Hui in the reign of Jiajing. Comp. by Yang Zaiming. (Rare Local Records in Chinese...1420-1507). F A97 – 9 – $9.00 – cc Microforms [950]

JIAJING HUI'AN XIAN ZHI, 1525 – Records of Hui'an County in the reign of Jiajing. 13 vols. Comp. by Zhang Yue. F A38. (Rare Local Records in Chinese...1420-1507) – 9 – $22.50 – cc Microforms [950]

JIAJING HUIZHOU FU ZHI, 1556 / Guangdong Province. China – Records of Huizhou Prefecture in the reign of Jiajing. 16 vols. Comp. by Yang Zaiming. (Rare Local Records in Chinese...1420-1507). F A93 – 9 – $58.50 – cc Microforms [950]

JIAJING JIANGYIN XIAN ZHI, 1548 / Jiangsu Province. China – Records of Jiangyin County in the reign of Jiajing. 21 vols. Comp. by Zhang Gun. F A16. (Rare Local Records in Chinese...1420-1507) – 9 – $49.50 – cc Microforms [950]

JIAJING JIANNING FU ZHI, 1541 – Records of Jianning Prefecture in the reign of Jiajing. 20 vols. Comp. by Wang Dian. F A37. (Rare Local Records in Chinese...1420-1507) – 9 – $90.00 – cc Microforms [950]

JIAJING JIANPING XIAN ZHI, 1531 – Records of Jianping County in the reign of Jiajing. 2 vols. Comp. by Yao Wenye. F A36. (Rare Local Records in Chinese...1420-1507) – 9 – $18.00 – cc Microforms [950]

JIAJING JIANYANG XIAN ZHI, 1553 – Records of Jianyang County in the reign of Jiajing. 16 vols. Comp. by Feng Jike. F A41. (Rare Local Records in Chinese...1420-1507) – 9 – $54.00 – cc Microforms [950]

JIAJING JIUJIANG FU ZHI, 1527 / Jiangxi Province. China – Records of Jiujiang Prefecture in the reign of Jiajing. 16 vols. Comp. by He Fei. F A52. (Rare Local Records in Chinese...1420-1507) – 9 – $49.50 – cc Microforms [950]

JIAJING KAIZHOU ZHI, 1534 / Henan Province. China – Records of Kaizhou in the reign of Jiajing. 10 vols. Comp. by Wang Chongging. F A66. (Rare Local Records in Chinese... 1420-1507) – 9 – $22.50 – cc Microforms [950]

JIAJING KUNSHAN XIAN ZHI, 1538 / Jiangsu Province. China – Records of Kunshan County in the reign of Jiajing. 16 vols. Comp. by Fang Peng. F A10. (Rare Local Records in Chinese...1420-1507) – 9 – $45.00 – cc Microforms [950]

JIAJING LAIWU XIAN ZHI, 1548 / Shandong Province. China – Records of Laiwu County in the reign of Jiajing. 8 vols. Comp. by Chen Ganyu. F A57. (Rare Local Records in Chinese...1420-1507) – 9 – $13.50 – cc Microforms [950]

JIAJING LANYANG XIAN ZHI, 1546 / Henan Province. China – Records of Lanyang County in the reign of Jiajing. 10 vols. Comp. by Li Xicheng. F A78. (Rare Local Records in Chinese...1420-1507) – 9 – $27.00 – cc Microforms [950]

JIAJING LINQU XIAN ZHI, 1552 / Shandong Province. China – Records of Linqu County in the reign of Jiajing. 4 vols. Comp. by Feng Weimin. F A56. (Rare Local Records in Chinese...1420-1507) – 9 – $13.50 – cc Microforms [950]

JIAJING LONGQING ZHI, 1535 / Hebei Province. China – Records of Longqing in the reign of Jiajing. 10 vols. Comp. by Xie Tinggui. F A9. (Rare Local Records in Chinese...1420-1507) – 9 – $22.50 – cc Microforms [950]

JIAJING LONGXI XIAN ZHI, 1535 – Records of Longxi County in the reign of Jiajing. 8 vols. Comp. by Lin Kui and others. F A42. (Rare Local Records in Chinese...1420-1507) – 9 – $22.50 – cc Microforms [950]

JIAJING LUEYANG XIAN ZHI, 1552 / Shanxi, Shaanxi and Ganso Provinces. China – Records of Lueyang County in the Reign of Jiajing. 2 vols. Compiled by Li Yuchan. F A106. (Rare Local Records in Chinese... 1420-1507) – 9 – $9.00 – cc Microforms [950]

JIAJING LUSHAN XIAN ZHI, 1552 / Henan Province. China – Records of Lushan County in the reign of Jiajing. 3 vols. Comp. by Sun Duo. F A73. (Rare Local Records in Chinese...1420-1507) – 9 – $31.50 – cc Microforms [950]

JIAJING MAHU FU ZHI, 1555 / Sichuan Province. China – Records of Mahu Prefecture in the Reign of Jiajing. 7 vols. Compiled by Yu Chengxun. F A99. (Rare Local Records in Chinese...1420-1507) – 9 – $13.50 – cc Microforms [950]
JIAJING MIANYANG ZHI, 1531 / Hubei Province. China – Records of Mianyang in the reign of Jiajing. 4 vols. Comp. by Tong Chengxu. F A83. (Rare Local Records in Chinese.1420-1507) – 9 – $27.00 – cc Microforms [950]
JIAJING NEIHUANG XIAN ZHI,1537 / Henan Province. China – Records of Neihuang County in the reign of Jiajing. 2 vols. Comp. by Dong Xian. F A71. (Rare Local Records in Chinese...1420-1507) – 9 – $9.00 – cc Microforms [950]
JIAJING NINGGUO FU ZHI, 1536 – Records of Ningguo Prefecture in the reign of Jiajing. 10 vols. Comp. by Li Mo. F A29. (Rare Local Records in Chinese...1420-1507) – 9 – $27.00 – cc Microforms [950]
JIAJING NINGXIA XINZHI, 1540 / Shanxi, Shaanxi and Ganso Provinces. China – New Records of Ningxia in the Reign of Jiajing. 8 vols. Compiled by Hu Ruli. F A107. (Rare Local Records in Chinese...1420-1507) – 9 – $40.50 – cc Microforms [950]
JIAJING PU'AN ZHOU ZHI, APPROX. 1537 / Guizhou and Yunnan Province. China – Records of Pu'an District in the Reign of Jiajing. 10 vols. Compiled by Shen Xu. F A103. (Rare Local Records in China...1420-1507) – 9 – $13.50 – cc Microforms [950]
JIAJING PUJIANG XIAN ZHI, 1556 / Zhejiang Province. China – Records of Pujiang County in the reign of Jiajing. 8 vols. Comp. by Mao Fengshao. F A25. (Rare Local Records in Chinese...1420-1507) – 9 – $18.00 – cc Microforms [950]
JIAJING QINGZHOU FU ZHI, 1565 / Shandong Province. China – Records of Qingzhou Prefecture in the reign of Jiajing. 18 vols. Comp. by Feng Weine. F A55. (Rare Local Records in Chinese...1420-1507) – 9 – $90.00 – cc Microforms [950]
JIAJING QINZHOU ZHI, APPROX. 1529 / Guangdong Province. China – Records of Qinzhou in the reign of Jiajing. 9 vols. Comp. by Lin Xiyuan. (Rare Local Records in Chinese...1420-1507). F A92 – 9 – $27.00 – cc Microforms [950]
JIAJING QIZHOU ZHI, 1529 / Hubei Province. China – Records of Qizhou in the reign of Jiajing, 9 vols. Comp. by Gan Ze. (Rare Local Records in Chinese...1420-1507). F A84 – 9 – $22.50 – cc Microforms [950]
JIAJING RENHUA XIAN ZHI, APPROX. 1529 / Guangdong Province. China – Records of Renhua County in the Reign of Jiajing. 5 vols. Compiled by Hu Ju'an. F A96. (Rare Local Records in Chinese...1420-1507) – 9 – $9.00 – cc Microforms [950]
JIAJING RUIJIN XIAN ZHI, 1542 / Jiangxi Province. China – Records of Ruijin County in the reign of Jiajing. 8 vols. Comp. by Lin Younian. F A54. (Rare Local Records in Chinese...1420-1507) – 9 – $13.50 – cc Microforms [950]
JIAJING SHAOWU FU ZHI, 1543 – Records of Shaowu Prefecture in the reign of Jiajing. 15 vols. Comp. by Chen Rang. F A40. (Rare Local Records in Chinese...1420-1507) – 9 – $58.50 – cc Microforms [950]
JIAJING SHOUZHOU ZHI, 1550 – Records of Shouzhou in the reign of Jiajing. 3 vols. Comp. by Shu Yonglu. F A33. (Rare Local Records in Chinese...1420-1507) – 9 – $27.00 – cc Microforms [950]
JIAJING SINAN FU ZHI, 1537 / Guizhou and Yunnan Province. China – Records of Sinan Prefecture in the Reign of Jiajing. 8 vols. Compiled by Zhong Tian. F A102. (Rare Local Records in Chinese...1420-1507) – 9 – $18.00 – cc Microforms [950]
JIAJING SUZHOU ZHI, 1537 – Records of Suzhou in the reign of Jiajing. 8 vols. Comp. by Yu Hong. F A30. (Rare Local Records in Chinese...1420-1507) – 9 – $18.00 – cc Microforms [950]
JIAJING TAIPING XIAN ZHI, 1540 / Zhejiang Province. China – Records of Taiping County in the reign of Jiajing. 8 vols. Comp. by Ye Liangpei. F A22. (Rare Local Records in Chinese...1420-1507) – 9 – $22.50 – cc Microforms [950]
JIAJING TAIYUAN XIAN ZHI, 1551 / Shanxi, Shaanxi and Ganso Provinces. China – Records of Taiyuan County in the Reign of Jiajing. 6 vols. Compiled by Gao Ruxing. F A105. (Rare Local Records in Chinese... 1420-1507) – 9 – $18.00 – cc Microforms [950]
JIAJING TIANCHANG XIAN ZHI, 1550 – Records of Tianchang County in the reign of Jiajing. 7 vols. Comp. by Wang Xin. F A35. (Rare Local Records in Chinese...1420-1507) – 9 – $27.00 – cc Microforms [950]
JIAJING TONGLING XIAN ZHI, 1563 – Records of Tongling County in the reign of Jiajing. 8 vols. Comp. by Li Shiyuan and others. F A34. (Rare Local Records in Chinese...1420-1507) – 9 – $18.00 – cc Microforms [950]
JIAJING WEISHI XIAN ZHI, 1548 / Henan Province. China – Records of Weishi County in the reign of Jiajing. Comp. by Wang Xin. F A72. (Rare Local Records in Chinese... 1420-1507) – 9 – $36.00 – cc Microforms [950]
JIAJING WEIYANG ZHI, 1542 / Jiangsu Province. China – Records of Weiyang County in the reign of Jiajing. 38 vols. Comp. by Sheng Yi. F A15. (Rare Local Records in Chinese...1420-1507) – 9 – $54.00 – cc Microforms [950]
JIAJING WENGYUAN XIAN ZHI, APPROX. 1529 / Guangdong Province. China – Records of Wengyuan County in the reign of Jiajing. Comp. by Li Kongming. (Rare Local Records in Chinese...1420-1507). F A95 – 9 – $9.00 – cc Microforms [950]
JIAJING WENZHOU FU ZHI, 1537 / Zhejiang Province. China – Records of Wenzhou Prefecture in the reign of Jiajing. 8 vols. Comp. by Zhang Fujing. F A21. (Rare Local Records in Chinese...1420-1507) – 9 – $18.00 – cc Microforms [950]
JIAJING WUCHENG XIAN ZHI, 1525 / Shandong Province. China – Records of Wucheng County in the reign of Jiajing. 10 vols. Comp. by You Qi. F A58. (Rare Local Records in Chinese...1420-1507) – 9 – $18.00 – cc Microforms [950]
JIAJING WUDING ZHOU ZHI, 1548 / Shandong Province. China – Records of Wuding District in the reign of Jiajing. 2 vols. Comp. by Liu Dian. F A62. (Rare Local Records in Chinese...1420-1507) – 9 – $9.00 – cc Microforms [950]
JIAJING WUKANG XIAN ZHI, 1550 / Zhejiang Province. China – Records of Wukang County in the reign of Jiajing. 8 vols. Comp. by Luo Wensheng. F A27. (Rare Local Records in Chinese...1420-1507) – 9 – $18.00 – cc Microforms [950]
JIAJING XIAJIN XIAN ZHI, 1540 / Shandong Province. China – Records of Xiajin County in the reign of Jiajing. 5 vols. Comp. by Yi Shizhong. F A61. (Rare Local Records in Chinese...1420-1507) – 9 – $18.00 – cc Microforms [950]
JIAJING XIANGCHENG XIAN ZHI, 1551 / Henan Province. China – Records of Xiangcheng County in the reign of Jiajing. 8 vols. Comp. by Lin Luan. F A64. (Rare Local Records in Chinese...1420-1507) – 9 – $13.50 – cc Microforms [950]
JIAJING XIAYI XIAN ZHI, 1548 / Henan Province. China – Records of Xiayi County in the reign of Jiajing. 8 vols. Comp. by Huang Huchen. F A74. (Rare Local Records in Chinese...1420-1507) – 9 – $22.50 – cc Microforms [950]
JIAJING XINCHANG XIAN ZHI, 1579 / Zhejiang Province. China – Records of Xinchang County in the reign of Wanli. 13 vols. Comp. by Tian Guan. F A24. (Rare Local Records in Chinese...1420-1507) – 9 – $36.00 – cc Microforms [950]
JIAJING XIONGCHENG, 1533 / Hebei Province. China – Records of Xiongcheng in the reign of Jiajing. V. 1-2. Comp. By Wang Qi. F A7. (Rare Local Records in Chinese...1420-1507) – 9 – $9.00 – cc Microforms [950]
JIAJING XUNDIAN FU ZHI, 1550 / Guizhou and Yunnan Province. China – Records of Xundian Prefecture in the Reign of Jiajing. 2 vols. Compiled by Wang Shangyong. F A104. (Rare Local Records in Chinese... 1420-1507) – 9 – $18.00 – cc Microforms [950]
JIAJING XUZHOU ZHI, 1541 / Henan Province. China – Records of Xuzhou in the reign of Jiajing. 8 vols. Comp. by Zhang Liangzhi. F A67. (Rare Local Records in Chinese...1420-1507) – 9 – $27.00 – cc Microforms [950]
JIAJING YANLING ZHI, 1535 / Henan Province. China – Records of Yanling in the reign of Jiajing. 8 vols. Comp. by Liu Ren. (Rare Local Records in Chinese...1420-1507) – 9 – 20.00 – cc Microforms [950]
JIAJING YANPING FU ZHI, 1525 – Records of Yanping Prefecture in the reign of Jiajing. 23 vols. Comp. by Zheng Qingyun. F A39. (Rare Local Records in Chinese...1420-1507) – 9 – $63.00 – cc Microforms [950]
JIAJING YINGSHAN XIAN ZHI, 1540 / Hubei Province. China – Records of Yingshan County in the reign of Hongzhi, 10 vols. Comp. by Yan Mu. (Rare Local Records in Chinese...1420-1507). F A81 – 9 – $13.50 – cc Microforms [950]
JIAJING YONGFENG XIAN ZHI, 1544 / Jiangxi Province. China – Records of Yongfeng County in the reign of Jiajing. 4 vols. Comp. by Guan Jing. F A49. (Rare Local Records in Chinese...1420-1507) – 9 – $13.50 – cc Microforms [950]
JIAJING YOUXI XIAN ZHI, APPROX. 1552 – Records of Youxi County in the reign of Jiajing. 7 vols. Comp. by Tian Xu. F A44. (Rare Local Records in Chinese...1420-1507) – 9 – $18.00 – cc Microforms [950]
JIAJING YUNYANG XIAN ZHI, 1541 / Sichuan Province. China – Records of Yunyang County in the Reign of Jiajing. 2 vols. Compiled by Yang Luan. F A101. (Rare Local Records in Chinese...1420-1507) – 9 – $13.50 – cc Microforms [950]
JIAJING ZHANGDE FU ZHI, 1523 / Henan Province. China – Records of Zhangde Prefecture in the reign of Jiajing. 8 vols. Comp. by Cui Xian. F A63. (Rare Local Records in Chinese...1420-1507) – 9 – $36.00 – cc Microforms [950]
JIAJING ZICHUAN XIAN ZHI, 1546 / Shandong Province. China – Records of Zichuan County in the reign of Jiajing. 2 vols. Comp. by Wang Cong. F A60. (Rare Local Records in Chinese...1420-1507) – 9 – $9.00 – cc Microforms [950]
JIANG SHEN RI KAN – 1923-25 – 9 – 1100.00 – cc Globe [073]
JIANGHAN LUNTAN – Flubei Tribune. 1986. F/P 275 – 9 – $4.50f – cc Microforms [073]
Jiangsu Province. China *see*
– HONGZHI JURONG XIAN ZHI, 1496
– JIAJING BAOYING XIAN ZHILUE, 1538
– JIAJING GAOCHUN XIAN ZHI, 1562
– JIAJING HAIMEN XIAN ZHI, 1597
– JIAJING JIANGYIN XIAN ZHI, 1548
– JIAJING KUNSHAN XIAN ZHI, 1538
– JIAJING WEIYANG ZHI, 1542
– LONGQING HAIZHOU ZHI, 1572
– LONGQING YIZHEN XIAN ZHI, 1567
– WANLI TONGZHOU ZHI, APPROX. 1579
JIANGXI MINGUO RIBAO – The Republican Daily, Jiangxi Province ed. Apr, Jul, Sept, Nov 1929; Jun-Dec 1930; Jan-Sept 1931; Feb-Dec 1933; 1934-36; Jan-Jul, Oct 1937-Dec 1944; Jan, Mar-Sept, Nov-Dec 1945; Jan 1946-May 1949. 28 reels. M B23 – 1 – $1,260.00 – cc Microforms [072]
Jiangxi Province. China *see*
– JIAJING DONGXIANG XIAN ZHI, 1524
– JIAJING GANZHOU FU ZHI, 1536
– JIAJING JIUJIANG FU ZHI, 1527
– JIAJING RUIJIN XIAN ZHI, 1542
– JIAJING YONGFENG XIAN ZHI, 1544
– LONGQING LINJIANG FU ZHI, 1572
– LONGQING RUICHANG XIAN ZHI, 1567
– ZHENGDE JIANCHANG FU ZHI, 1516
– ZHENGDE NANKANG FU ZHI, 1515
– ZHENGDE YUANZHOU FU ZHI, 1514
JIANGXI RIBAO – China. Jiangxi Daily, 1985- . M-D64 – 1 reel/y – 1 – $55.00r – cc Microforms [072]
JIANGZHU XUEBAO – Architectural Journal. In Chinese but English abstracts to the main articles. F 3 – 9 – 4.00f – cc Microforms [073]
JIANKANG BAO – Health Gazette. China. In Chinese. Current subscription. Annual delivery. Jul-Dec 1979. 1 reel; 1980- . 1 reel per yr. M D6 – 1 – $40.00r – cc Microforms [072]
JIANSHE – Construct Monthly. Aug 1919-Dec 1920. M C11. In Chinese – 1 – $110.00 – cc Microforms [073]
JIANZHU JIEGOU XUEBAO – Journal of Building Structures. In Chinese, with English abstracts of the main articles. F p86 – 9 – $4.00f – cc Microforms [690]
JIAOYU YANJIU – (1979-84 $3.50f; 1987 $4.50f) – Educational Research. In Chinese but Table of Contents in English in each issue. F p24 – 9 – cc Microforms [073]
JIAS NEWS – Montreal, Quebec, Canada. 1966-83. Jewish Immigrant Aid Services of Canada – 1 – us A.J.P.C. [072]
JIAWU ZHONGRI ZHANZHENG (SHANGCE). SHEN XUANHUAI DANGAN ZILIAO XUANJI ZHISAN – Selection of Archival Materials in the Possession of Shen Xuanhuai, Part III: The Sino-Japanese War of 1894-95, v1. Comp. by Chen Xulu and others. 4 fiches. F H171 – 9 – 4.00f – cc Microforms [950]
JIAYIN ZAZHI – The Tiger. -m. May 1914-Oct 1915. 2 reels. M C35 – 1 – $80.00 – cc Microforms [073]
JIAYIN ZHOUBAO – The Tiger Weekly. Jul 1925-Feb 1927. 1 reel. M C36 – 1 – $40.00 – cc Microforms [073]
JIBHAH – (Nashriyah-'i milliyun-i Iran. Sal-i 1-2; shumarah-'i 2-97 (1 Mihr 1360-21 Farvardin 1366[23 Sep 1981-11 April 1987]). Missing Issues: 1, 6, 12-13, 15, 23-24, 38, 52, 70-71, 75-79, 84, 86, 90, 95) – Tehran (1981-1983); London (1983-1987) – 2r – 1 – $25.00 – us MEDOC [950]
JIBHAH-'I MILLI-I IRAN – (Continued by: Ittihad-i Buzurg. Dawrah-'i jadid: shumarah-'i 1-19 (12 Isfand 1357-31 Khurdad 1358[3 Mar 1979-21 Jun 1980])) – Tehran: Jibhah-'i Milli-i Iran – 1 reel – 1 – $25.00 – us MEDOC [950]
JIBHAH-'I MILLI-I IRAN – [Tehran]: Asnad-i Jibhah-'i Milli-i Duvvum. (30 Tir 1339-31 Shahrivar 1342 [21 Jul 1940-22 Sep 1943]) – 1 reel – 1 – $25.00 – us MEDOC [950]
JIBHAH-'I MILLI-I IRAN *see* ITTIHAD-I BUZURG
JICHUANG – Machine Tool. In Chinese but English abstracts to the main articles. F p113 – 9 – $4.50f – cc Microforms [073]
JICHUANG YU YEYA – Machine Tool and Hydraulics. 1982-. F P251 – 9 – $4.50f – cc Microforms [073]
JIDDISH PROTOCOLBOEK VAN DE NED. ISRS. GEMEENTE IN NIJMEGEN / Leer, W van – (Bijdragen en Mededeelingen). v. 4. Arnhem. 1901. BJ-262-32 1 – 9 – ne IDC [305]
JIDISHE CAJTUNG = JEWISH JOURNAL – (In Yiddish) – Bayern, DE. no30(98). 22 Apr 1947 – 1r – 1 – $25.00 – cn Can Microfilming [072]
JIE FANG – A political magazine begun in Apr 1937. 134 issues. 53 ill. DL52f – 9 – 250.00 – cc Globe [073]
JIE FANG – China. 1958-62.37 ill. Published by the Communist Party of China, Shanghai branch. PT26f – 9 – 130.00 – cc Globe [072]
JIE FANG RI BAO – China. News Daily of the Central Committee of the Communist Party. May 1941-Mar 1943.DL6 – 9 – 675.00 – cc Globe [072]
JIEFANG – (1958 $35.00r; 1960-62 $55.00r) – Liberation. Jul 1958-Feb 1962. F P260 – 1 – cc Microforms [073]
JIEFANG JUN BAO – People's Liberation Army Daily. 1987- . M/D 116 – 1 – $55.00r – cc Microforms [072]
JIEFANG JUNBAO = PEOPLE'S LIBERATION ARMY DAILY – (Yrly reel count varies) – 1992- – 1 – us Ross [072]
JIEFANG RIBAO – Liberation Daily. China. In Chinese. Current Subscription, Annual Delivery. Backfiles supplied on request. 1979-87, 1 reel/y; 1988- , 2 reels/y. M/D13 – 1 – $55.00r – cc Microforms [072]
JIEFANG YU GAIZAO – Liberation and Transformation. Sep 1919-Sep 1922. M C3. In Chinese – 1 – $90.00 – cc Microforms [073]
JIEFANGJUN YIXUE ZAZHI – Medical Journal of Chinese People Liberation Army. In Chinese but English abstracts to the main articles. F p167 – 9 – 4.00f – cc Microforms [073]
JIEPOU XUEBAO – Acta Anatomica Sinica. In Chinese but English abstracts to the main articles. F p50 – 9 – 4.00f – cc Microforms [073]
JIGUANG – Laser Journal. In Chinese but English abstracts to the main articles. F p112 – 9 – $4.50f – cc Microforms [073]
JIGUANG KEXUE YU JISHU – Laser Science and Technology. 1981-. F P242 – 9 – $4.50f – cc Microforms [073]
JIHOCESKA PRAVDA – Budweis, Czechoslovakia. 1956-65 – 9r – 1 – us L of C Photodup [072]
JIH-PEN P'ING-LUN – (Japan Review). 18 v. Shanghai, Chungking, Nanking. 1932-45. Monthly. Lacking: v. 6-12, 1935-40; v. 13 (1, 2, 10-?) 1941; v. 14 (1-?) 1941; v. 15 (1, 4-9) 1942; v. 16 (1-3, 5, 6, 12-14) 1943; v. 18 (4-12) 1945. BCH-281 1 – 9 – ne IDC [073]

JIJI SHIMPO – Japan, 1882-1936 – 559r – 1 – inquire – us Ross [950]
JIJI SHIMPO – March 1882-December 1936 (last no.) – 559r – 1 – Y5,590,000 – ja Japan Micro [950]
JILIANG JISHU – Measurement Technique. 1983-84.F/P 287 – 9 – $4.50f – cc Microforms [073]
JILIANG XUEBAO – Journal of Measurement. In Chinese but English abstracts to the main articles. F p119 – 9 – $4.50f – cc Microforms [073]
JILIN DAXUE XUEBAO – (Shehui Kexue Ban). Journal of Jilin University, Social Sciences. In Chinese but Table of Contents in English in each issue. F p215 – 9 – $4.50f – cc Microforms [073]
JILIN DAXUE ZIRAN KEXUE XUEBAO – Acta Scientiarum Naturalium Universitatis Jilinensis. In Chinese but English abstracts to the main articles. F p189 – 9 – $4.50f – cc Microforms [073]
JILIN RIBAO – Jilin Daily. 1983-. M D79 – 1 – $55.00r – cc Microforms [072]
Jillson, Willard R *see*
– THE BIG SANDY VALLEY
– THE KENTUCKY LAND GRANTS, 1782-1924
THE JILT, (ETC.) / Reade, Charles L – British Fiction Archive: Unit 2 – 9 – uk Bell [830]
JILUYU RIBAO = HEBEI-SHANDONG-HENAN DAILY – 1944, 1946-1948 – 5r – $325.00 – cc Microforms [950]
JIM THORPE TIMES-NEWS – Jim Thorpe, PA. -w 1954-1967 – 13 – $25.00r – us I.M.R. [071]
Jimack, Peter D *see* LA GENESE ET LA REDACTION DE L'EMILE
JIMBOLIAER ZEITUNG – Hatzfeld (Jimbolia), Rumaenien. 3 Apr-17 Jul 1938 – 1r – 1 – gw Mikrofilm [949]
Jimenez Andrades, Ildefonso *see* RECUERDOS DE MI CAMPANA EN RUSIA
Jimenez, Antonio *see* ERUDICION EVANGELICA...SANTA ORACION
Jimenez Arias, Diego *see*
– LEXICON ECCLESIASTICUM...CONCILIS
– LEXICON...ADICIONES DE JUAN DE LAMA ESCUDERO
– LEXICON...DIVORUM VITIS
– SACRIS BIBLIIS
– TABLAS REFORMADAS SEGUN EL CALENDARIO GREGORIANO
Jimenez de Arechaga, Eduardo *see* INTRODUCCION AL DERECHO, VERSION TAQUIGRAFICA DE CARLOS ARGENTA ESTABLE
Jimenez de la Espada, Marcos *see*
– CORRESPONDENCIA DEL DOCTOR BENITO ARIAS MONTANO CON EL LICENCIADO JUAN DE OVANDO
– NO FUE TEA, FUE BARRENO
Jimenez de la Llave, Luis *see* LAPIDA ROMANA INEDITA DEL VILLAR DEL PEDROSO
JIMENEZ DE SAMANIEGO, JOSE, GENERAL DE LA ORDEN Y OBISPO DE PLASENCIA, EN LA INMACULADA EN LA LITERATURA FRANCISCANO-ESPANOLA / Uribe, Angel – Archivo Ibero Americano, 1955 – 1 – sp Bibl Santa Ana [240]
Jimenez de Savariego, J *see* TRATADO DE PESTE, DONDE SE CONTIENEN LAS CAUSAS, PRESERVACION Y CURA
Jimenez de Zalamea, Fr. Juan *see* SERMON...LA LIMPIEZA DE LA VIRGEN EN SU INMACULADA
Jimenez Guillen, F *see*
– ANIMADVERSIONES...ACERCA DE LA RECETA DEL UNGUENTO DE MERCURIO
– RESPUESTA A LOS PARECERES...ACERCA DEL MAL...EN SEVILLA
Jimenez, Juan *see* VIDA Y...D. JUAN DE RIBERA...OBISPO DE BADAJOZ
Jimenez Navarro, E et al *see* ARQUEOLOGIA DE MAGACELA
Jimenez Navarro, Ernesto *see* LA COLECCION DE LAPIDAS DE D. CLAUDIO CONSTANZO
Jimenez Priego, Teresa *see* GUADALUPE EN LOS SIGLOS 17; 18
Jimenez Quilez, Manuel *see* WHEELS WITHIN WHEELS; HOW RUSSIA USES UNITED NATIONS AGAINST SPAIN
Jimenez Rodriguez, Fernando *see* MERIDA, ROMA DE OCCIDENTE. GUION LITERARIO PARA UN DOCUMENTAL CINEMATOGRAFICO
Jimenez Rueda, Julio *see* HEREJIAS Y SUPERTICIONES EN LA NUEVA ESPANA. LOS HETERODOXOS EN MEJICO
Jimenez Salas, Maria *see* VIDA Y OBRAS DE DON JUAN PABLO FORNER Y SEGARRA, MADRID, 1944
Jimenez Samaniego, Jose *see*
– CONSTITUTIONES ET ACTA GENERALIUM
– PROLOGO GALEATO.RELACION...DE AGREDA
– STATUTORUM...FAMILIA...OBSERVANTIAE... SANCTI FRANCISCI
– SYNODO DEL OBISPADO DE PLASENCIA
– VIDA DE JUAN DUNS SCOTO
– VIDA...JUAN DUNSIO ESCOTO
Jimenez, Sebastian *see*
– CONCORDANTIAE IURIS CANONICI CUM LEGIBUS PARTITARUM...
– CONCORDIANTAE...GLOSSEMATIBUSQUE GREGORII LOPEZ
Jimenz Vasco, Felipe *see* COMO NACE UN MONASTERIO Y MUERE UN CESAR
JIN RONG SHIBAO – Financial Times.1987- . M/D 117 – 1 – $34.00r – cc Microforms [072]
JIN WAN BAO – China. Tonight.1986-. M-D97 – 1 – $55.00r – cc Microforms [072]
JINAN XUEBAO – (1981-82 $4.50f; 1983 $3.50f) – (Zhexue Shehui Kexue Ban). Journal of Jinan University, Philosophy & Social Science. In Chinese but Table of Contents in English in each issue. F p211 – 9 – cc Microforms [073]
JINARATNAKOSA: AN ALPHABETICAL REGISTER OF JAIN WORKS AND AUTHORS / Velankar, Hari Damodar – Poona: Bhandarkar Oriental Research Institute, 1944. Text and commentary in English – 1 – us U.W. Library [280]
JINDAISHI YANJIU – Studies on Chinese Modern History. In Chinese. F p16 – 9 – $4.50f – cc Microforms [073]
JINDAISHI ZILIAO – v1-60. 1954-85.Materials on Modern Chinese History. Comp. by the Institute of Modern History, Chinese Academy of Social Sciences. 156 fiches. F-H12–F-H56-5 – 9 – $715.50 – cc Microforms [950]
JINDAISHI ZILIAO ZHUANKAN DIERHAO: XU SHUZHENG DIANGAO – Special series on modern history, No.2: Xu Shuzheng's telegrams. Comp. by the Institute of Modern History, Chinese Academy of Social Sciences. 4 fiches. F-H59 – 9 – $22.50 – cc Microforms [950]
JINDAISHI ZILIAO ZHUANKAN DIYIHAO: 1919 NIAN NANBEI YIHE ZILIAO HUIBIAN – Special series on modern history, No.1: Accumulated materials on the 1919 peace negotiations between the northern and southern governments in China.Comp. by the Institute of Modern History, Chinese Academy of Social Sciences. 6 fiches. F-H58 – 9 – 4.00f – cc Microforms [950]
JINDAISHI ZILIAO ZHUANKAN: HUAGIAO YU XINHAI GEMING – Special Series on Modern History: Overseas Chinese and the Revolution of 1911. Comp. by the Institute of Modern History, Chinese Academy of Social Sciences. 4 fiches. F H63 – 9 – $18.00 – cc Microforms [950]
JINDAISHI ZILIAO ZHUANKAN: SHANGDONG YIHETUAN ANJUAN. YIHETUAN ZILIAO CONGBIAN SHANGXIACE – Special series on modern history; materials on the Boxer Uprising, v1-2. The Boxer Uprising in Shandong province. 8 fiches. F-H60 – 9 – $49.50 – cc Microforms [950]
JINDAISHI ZILIAO ZHUANKAN: XINHAI GEMING ZILIAO LEIBIAN – Special series on modern history: Classified compilations of materials on the Revolution of 1911. Comp. by the Institute of Modern History, Chinese Academy of Social Sciences. 5 fiches.F-H62 – 9 – $22.50 – cc Microforms [950]
JINDAISHI ZILIAO ZHUNGKAN: TAIPING TIANGUO ZILIAO – Materials on modern history: supplement: The Taiping Uprising. Comp. by the Institute of Modern History, Chinese Academy of Social Sciences. 3 fiches. F-H61 – 9 – $13.50 – cc Microforms [950]
JINDAISHI ZILIAO, ZONG 1 HAO – (Serial no.2. 2 fiches. F/H13. Serial no.3-5. 3 fiches each. F/H14-F/H16. Serial no.6-10. 2 fiches each. F/H17-F/H21. Serial no.11. 3 fiches. F/H22. Serial no.12-23. 2 fiches each. F/H23-F/H34. Serial no.24. 10 fiches. F/H35. Serial no.25. 7 fiches. F/H36. Serial no.26. 3 fiches. F/H37. Serial no.27-29. 2 fiches each. F/H38-F/H40. Serial no.30. 3 fiches. F/H41. Serial no.31-38. 2 fiches each. F/H42-F/H49. Serial no.39-41. 3 fiches each. F/H50-F/H52. Serial no.42-43. 3 fiches each. F/H53-F/H54. Serial no.44-45. 3 fiches each. F/H55-F/H56) – Materials on modern Chinese history. Serial no.1. Comp. by the Institute of Modern History, Chinese Academy of Social Sciences. 2 fiches. F-H12 – 9 – 4.00f – cc Microforms [950]
JING DAI SHI ZI LIAO – Ed. by the Academy of Science and History. Subject matter includes politics, economics, and culture. 123 ill. HG17 – 9 – 110.00 – cc Globe [073]
JINGJI CANKAO – China. Economic Information. -d. 1986-. M-D90 – 1 – $55.00r – cc Microforms [072]
JINGJI YANJIU – (1978-83 $3.50f; 1984 $4.50f) – Economic Research. In Chinese but Table of Contents in English in each issue. F p4 – 9. – cc Microforms [330]
JINGJIXUE ZHOUBAO = ECONOMIC WEEKLY – China. 1983-88. M-D53 – 1 reel/y – 1 – $28.00r – cc Microforms [330]
JINGLISHE XIAOSHUO YUEBAO – Short stories of the Jingli Society. -m. Sept-Oct 1907. 3 fiches. F-C30 – 9 – $25.00 – cc Microforms [830]
JINGTI RIBAO = ECONOMIC DAILY – Continues Zhongguo Caimo Bao (China Finance and Trade Journal) after 1983. China. In Chinese. Current subscription. Annual delivery. 1981- , 1 reel/y. M D25 – $55.00r – cc Microforms [072]
JINMIN NIPPO – Japan, 1977- – 1 – inquire – us Ross [950]
JINQIAN HUI ZILIAO – Source materials relating to the Money Society. Comp. by Nie Chongqi. 3 fiches. F-H82 – 9 – $21.00 – cc Microforms [950]
JINRUIGAKU ZASHI, 1886-1964 : JOURNAL OF THE ANTHROPOLOGICAL SOCIETY OF JAPAN – (In English) – v1-72 – 24r – 1 – $840.00 set in US $40.00r outside – L9400097 – Dist. us Scholarly Res – us L of C Photodup [306]
JINSHU RECHULI = HEAT TREATMENT OF METALS – 1982- . F/P255 – 9 – $4.50f – cc Microforms [073]
JINSUI RIBAO = SHANXI-SUIYUAN DAILY – China. 1 Jul 1946-1 May 1949. 6 reels.M-B22 – 1 – $300.00 – cc Microforms [072]
Jirecek, C J *see*
– DAS FUERSTENTHUM BULGARIEN
– GESCHICHTE DER BULGAREN
JIS (JAPANESE INDUSTRIAL STANDARDS) – The English language collection. Printed index. Updated every 60 days – 6,9 – us Info Handling [380]
JISABU, JIHENG'ELE, IFIKA NI JINONGONONGO, JOSONEKE MU LIMOUNDU NI PUTU, KUA MON'ANGOLA JAKIM RIA MATTA / Cordeiro da Matta, J D – (Filmed with his Ensaio de diccionario kimbundu-portuguez) – Lisboa: Typo. e Stereotypia Moderna, 1891 – us Res Libr [470]
JISKRA – Jihlava, Czechoslovakia. 1956-Mar 1960 – 2r – 1 – us L of C Photodup [072]
JISUAN SHUXUE – (1981 $3.50f; 1979-80, 1983 $4.50f) – Mathematica Numerica Sinica. In Chinese but English abstracts to the main articles. F p118 – 9 – cc Microforms [073]
JISUANJI KEXUE = COMPUTER SCIENCE – 1981-. F-P231 – 9 – $4.50f – cc Microforms [073]
JISUANJI XUEBAO – Chinese Journal of Computers. In Chinese but English abstracts to the main articles. F p93 – 9 – $4.50f – cc Microforms [073]
JISUANJI YANJIU YU FAZHAN – Computer Research & Development.1986. F/P 269 – 9 – $4.50f – cc Microforms [073]
JIU GOU SHIBAO – Au Secours de la Patrie (National Salvation Times). Dec 1935-Feb 1938. 1 reel. M/B 13 – 1 – $50.00 – cc Microforms [072]
JIU ZHONGGUO GONGZHAISHI ZILIAO, 1894-1949 (ZHONGGUO JINDAI JINGJISHI CANKAO ZILIAO CONGSHU) – Series of reference materials on the economic history of modern China: Materials on the history of government bonds in the old China, 1894-1949. Comp. by Qian Jiaju. 5 fiches. F-H148 – 9 – $22.50 – cc Microforms [950]
JIXIE GONGCHENG XUEBAO – Chinese Journal of Mechanical Engineering. In Chinese but English abstracts to the main articles. F p47 – 9 – 4.00f – cc Microforms [073]
JIYUTO – TOMOSHIBI – MESAMASHI – (Antecedents of Tokyo Asahi) – 1884-88 – 12r – 1 – inquire – us Ross [950]
JIZHONG DAOBAO = CENTRAL HEBEI HERALD – China. 12 Aug 1946-1948. 5 reels. M-B21 – 1 – $250.00 – cc Microforms [072]
J.J. HERNANDEZ ARREGUI : DEL PERONISMO AL SOCIALISMO / Galasso, Norberto – [Buenos Aires, Argentina]: Ediciones del Pensamiento Nacional, c1986 – 1 – CSUXAHZ7487-B – us Hoover Inst Photo [320]
J.-J. OLIER, 1608-1657, CURE DE SAINT-SULPICE ET FONDATEUR DES SEMINAIRES / Fruges, G-M, de – Paris: Chez l'Auteur, [1904] – 5mf – 9 – Can$11.25 – cn Bibl Nat [240]
J.-J. ROUSSEAU : LE PROTESTANTISME ET LA REVOLUTION FRANCAISE / Dide, Auguste – Paris: Ernest Flammarion, [1911?] – 1mf – us A.T.L.A. [240]
J.J. ROUSSEAU A L'ASSEMBLEE NATIONALE / Aubert de Vitry, Francois J P – Paris. 1789 – 9 – fr Hachette [190]
J.J. ROUSSEAU, ARISTOCRATE / Lenormant, Charles F – Paris. 1790 – 9 – fr Hachette [190]
J.J. WILHELM HEINSE UND DIE AESTHETIK ZUR ZEIT DER DEUTSCHEN AUFKLAERUNG : EINE PROBLEMGESCHICHTLICHE STUDIE / Utitz, Emil – (Includes bibliograpical references) – Halle: M Niemeyer, 1906 – 1r – 1 – us U.W. Library [430]
J.K. LAVATER UND DIE RELIGIOESEN STROEMUNGEN DES ACHTZEHNTEN JAHRHUNDERTS : VERSUCH EINER SEELENKUNDLICHEN DEUTUNG IN GEISTESGESCHICHTLICHEM RAHMEN / Forssman, Julius – (Includes bibliographical references) – Riga: Verlag der Akt.-Ges. "Ernst Plates", 1935 – 1r – 1 – us U.W. Library [100]
J'L DE L'AGRICULTEUR ET DES TRAVAUX DE LA CHAMBRE D'AGRICULTURE DU BAS-CANADA – v5 n1. sep 1857-v5 n12. aut 1858 – 1 – cn Can Microfilming [072]
JL: JORNAL DE LETRAS, ARTES E IDEIAS – Lisbao. v2-. 1982-. biweekly. illus – 1 – us U.W. Library [073]
J.L. McDonough and Co *see* HISTORY OF RANDOLPH, MONROE AND PERRY COUNTIES
J.M. Armstrong and Company *see* BIOGRAPHICAL ENCYCLOPEDIA OF KENTUCKY
JM NUNEZ PONTE. QUIEN A SIDO ALGUIEN EN VENEZUELA?. NUESTRO GRAN APOSTOL / Bayle, Constantino – Madrid: Razon y Fe, 1939 – 1 – sp Bibl Santa Ana [240]
J.M. Runk and Co *see*
– BIOGRAPHICAL AND GENEALOGICAL HISTORY OF THE STATE OF DELAWARE
– COMMEMORATIVE BIOGRAPHICAL CYCLOPEDIA OF DAUPHIN COUNTY
– COMMEMORATIVE BIOGRAPHICAL ENCYCLOPEDIA OF THE COUNTIES OF HUNTINGTON, MUFFLIN, JUNIATA AND PERRY
JMJ REGLAMENTO PARA EL COLEGIO DE SENORITAS...SAGRADA FAMILIA... PLASENCIA / Colegio de la Inmaculada Concepcion – 1871 – 9 – sp Bibl Santa Ana [240]
JMPT : JOURNAL OF MANIPULATIVE AND PHYSIOLOGICAL THERAPEUTICS – v1-19. 1978-96 – 1,5,6,9 – $80.00r – us Williams [615]
J.M.R. LENZ UND SEINE SCHRIFTEN : NACHTRAEGE ZU DER AUSGABE VON L. TIECK UND IHREN ERGAENZUNGEN / Lenz, Jakob Michael Reinhold; ed by Dorer-Egloff, Edward – Baden: J Zehnder, 1857 – 1r – 1 – us U.W. Library [430]
J.O. Wright & Co *see* PRICE LIST OF THE BARLOW LIBRARY
JOACHIM BURSER'S HORTUS SICCUS / Juel, H O – (Symbolae Botanicae Upsalienses, v. 2, pt. 1). Uppsala. 1936. B-1073 2 – 8 – ne IDC [580]
Joachim, Harold Henry *see* A STUDY OF THE ETHICS OF SPINOZA
JOACHIM HEINRICH CAMPE. EIN LEBENSBILD AUS DEM ZEITALTER DER AUFKLAERUNG / Leyser, J – Braunschweig 1877 – 1 – DM50.00 – gw Mikro Press [920]
JOACHIM MURAT ROI DES DEUX SICILIES / Doin, Ernest – Montreal: C O Beauchemin & fils, 1879. SEM105P465 – 1mf – 9 – Can$2.25 – cn Bibl Nat [830]
JOACHIM VADIAN, DER REFORMATOR UND GESCHICHTSSCHREIBER VON ST GALLEN / Goetzinger, Ernst – Halle: Verein fuer Reformationsgeschichte, 1895. (Schriften des Vereins fuer Reformationsgeschichte; 13. Jahrg., Schrift 50) – 1mf – us A.T.L.A. [240]

JOACHIM VON RIBBENTROP PAMPHLET COLLECTION – 1937-1943 – 1 reel – 1 – CSUXANR9559-B – us Hoover Inst Photo [920]

Joalland, Jules *see* LE DRAME DE DANKORI

JOAN: A TALE / Broughton, Rhoda – British Fiction Archive: Unit 4 – 9 – uk Bell [830]

JOAN OF ARC : AN EPIC POEM / Southey, Robert – Bristol: Printed by Bulgin and Rosser, for Joseph Cottle, 1796 – 1 roll – 1 – 1-55879-291-0 – uk Libr Preservation [810]

JOAN OF ARC, THE MAID / Tuckey, Janet – New York: G.P. Putnam's sons, 1880. 224p – 1 – us U.W. Library [944]

JOANNES BISCHOF VON EPHESOS : DER ERSTE SYRISCHE KIRCHENHISTORIKER / Land, J P N – Leyden, 1856 – Dfl19.00 – ne Slangenburg [240]

Joannes, Bischof von Ephesos *see* THE THIRD PART OF THE ECCLESIASTICAL HISTORY OF JOHN, BISHOP OF EPHESUS

Joannes, de Garlandia *see* COMPENDIUM ALCHEMIAE; CUM DICTIONARIO EIUSDEN ARTIS ATQUE DE METALLORUM TINCTURA PRAEPARATIO NEQ

Joannes, de Janduno *see* QUAESTIONES IN LIBROS DE COELO ET MUNDO ARISTOTELIS STAGIRITAE

JOANNIS ALBERTI BANNI DISSERTATIO EPISTOLICA, DE MUSICAE NATURA, ORIGINE, PROGRESSU UND DENIQUE STUDIO BENE INSTITUENDO. LUGDUNI BATAVORUM, EX OFFICINA ISAACI / Ban, J A – Commelini. 1637. BP-147 1 – 9 – ne IDC [780]

JOANNIS SARESBERIENSIS EPISCOPI CARNOTENSIS POLICRATICI / ed by Webb, C C J – H 1237 2. 2 v. 1909 – 8 – ne IDC [240]

Joannou, Petros-Perikles *see* DIE ERFAHRUNG IN PLATONS IDEENLEHRE

Joaquim de Vasconcellos, Francesco de Hollanda *see* VIER GESPRAECHE UEBER DIE MALEREI, GEFUEHRT ZU ROM

JOB AND PRELUDE FOR TROMBONES / Moore, Jeff – 1982 – 1 – 5.00 – us Baptist [240]

JOB AND SOLOMON, OR, THE WISDOM OF THE OLD TESTAMENT / Cheyne, Thomas Kelly – (Includes bibliographies and index) – New York: Thomas Whittaker, 1887 – 1mf – 9 – 0-8370-9370-8 – 1986-3370 – us A.T.L.A. [220]

JOB SAFETY AND HEALTH *see* OCCUPATIONAL SAFETY AND HEALTH ADMINISTRATION REPORTS

JOB SATISFACTION AMONG SECONDARY LEVEL TEACHERS / Lambeth, Kelly K & Myers, Betty – 1991 – 1mf – 9 – $4.00 – us Microform Publ [150]

JOBBER RETAILER – (1980 5,6,9) – 1977 – 1 – us UMI [073]

Jobson, F J *see* THE ECCLESIASTICAL PRINCIPLES AND POLITY OF THE WESLEYAN METHODISTS...

Jobson, R *see* THE GOLDEN TRADE OR A DISCOVERY OF THE RIVER GAMBRA

Jocelyn Brook, E *see* UITERSTE WILLE VAN EEN MOEDER AAN HAAR TOEKOMENDE KIND

Jochelson, W *see*
- THE ALEUT LANGUAGE AND ITS RELATION TO THE ESKIMO DIALECTS
- PAST AND PRESENT SUBTERRANEAN DWELLINGS OF THE TRIBES OF NORTH EASTERN ASIA AND NORTH WESTERN AMERICA

Jockers, Ernst *see* SOZIALE POLARITAET IN GOETHES KLASSIK

LE JOCKEY – Sport. Sportsman, vie sportive, turf et jockey reunis. Dir. G. Baltazzi. Paris. 1893, janv-juin 1895, 1911, janv-aout 1914 – 1 – fr A.C.R.P.P. [073]

Jockey Club. South Carolina *see* RECORDS

JOCOSERIA / Browning, Robert – London: Smith, Elder, 1883 – 1 roll – 1 – 1-55879-884-6 – uk Libr Preservation [800]

Jodl, Alfred *see* WAR DIARIES AND CORRESPONDENCE

JOE LOUIS SCRAPBOOKS, 1935-1944 – (Includes guide) – 304mf – 9 – £1,140.00 – uk Chadwyck [790]

Joecher, Christian Gottlieb *see* ALLGEMEINES GELEHRTEN-LEXICON

Joel, M *see*
- LEWI BEN GERSON ALS RELIGIONSPHILOSOPH
- VERHAELTNISS ALBERT DES GROSSEN ZU MOSES MAIMONIDES

JOENKOEPINGS DAGBLAD – Joenkoeping, 1872-75 – 9 – sw Kungliga [072]

JOENKOEPINGSBLADET – Joenkoeping, 1843-72 – 9 – sw Kungliga [072]

JOERG WICKRAMS ROMANTECHNIK / Fauth, Gertrud – Straßburg, 1914 – 1mf – DM48.00 – 3-8267-3102-6 – gw Hänsel [430]

Joergen, Juan *see* DON BOSCO

Joerger, M J *see* WALDVEILCHEN

Joerlin, E *see* PARTES FRUCTIFICATIONIS, SEU PRINCIPIA BOTANICES ILLUSTRATA

Joganich, T G *see* INFLUENCE OF IN-SHOE ORTHOTICS ON LOWER EXTREMITY FUNCTION IN CYCLING

Jogjakarta. Indonesia *see*
- ANGGARAN KEUANGAN DAERAH ISTIMEWA JOGJAKARTA
- BALAI PENELITIAN BATIK
- DJAWATAN PENERANGAN
- PEKAN RAYA WINDU KEMERDEKAAN REPUBLIK INDONESIA
- STATISTIK PEMERINTAH DAERAH ISTIMEWA JOGJAKARTA

Jogjakarta. Indonesia. Institut Agama Islam Negeri *see* SUNAN KALIDJAGA

Jogjakarta. Indonesia. Museum Sono Budojo *see* A BRIEF GUIDE TO THE SONO BUDOJO MUSEUM

Jogjakarta. Indonesia. Universitas Gadjah Mada. Fakultas Ilmu Pasti dan Alam *see* BUKU PENERANGAN

JOH. CASPAR LAVATER 1741-1801 : EIN LEBENSBILD / Voemel, Alexander – (Includes bibliographical references) – Elberfeld: Buchhandlung des Erziehungs-Vereins, [1923?] – 1 – us U.W. Library [240]

JOH. CHR. GOTTSCHEDS STERBENDER CATO / Gottsched, Johann Christoph; ed by Lachmann, Otto F – Leipzig: P Reclam [1885] – 1r – 1 – us U.W. Library [430]

JOH. FRIEDRICH REICHARDT UEBER DIE DEUTSCHE CONISCHE OPER... / Reichardt, Johann F – Hamburg: Carl Ernst Bohn, 1774 – 2mf – 9 – us Sibley [780]

JOH. GOTTFR. HERDER ZWISCHEN RIGA UND BUECKEBURG : DIE AESTHETIK UND SPRACHPHILOSOPHIE DER FRUEHZEIT NACH IHREN EXISTENZIELLEN MOTIVEN / Kuentzel, Gerhard – (Includes bibliographical references) – Frankfurt a.M.: M Diesterweg, 1936 – 1 – us U.W. Library [100]

JOH. SEB. BACH / Halten, A van – Utrecht: Bazar, [1885] – 1 – us Sibley [780]

Johann, A E *see* IM STROM

JOHANN ADAM MOEHLER / Woerner, B – Regensburg, 1866 – 6mf – 8 – Dfl25.00 – ne Slangenburg [200]

JOHANN ADAM MOEHLER DER SYMBOLIKER / Friedrich, Johann – Muenchen, 1894 – 2mf – 8 – ne Slangenburg [290]

JOHANN ADAM MOEHLER, DER SYMBOLIKER : EIN BEITRAG ZU SEINEM LEBEN UND SEINER LEHRE: AUS SEINEN EIGENEN UND ANDEREN UNGEDRUCKTEN PAPIEREN / Friedrich, Johann – Muenchen: C.H. Beck, 1894 – 1mf – us A.T.L.A. [920]

JOHANN ADOLPH SCHEIBENS, CRITISCHER MUSIKUS. NEUE, VERMEHRTE UND VERBESSERTE AUFLAGE / Scheibe, Johann Adolph – P 757. 1745 – 9 – ne IDC [780]

JOHANN AGRICOLA VON EISLEBEN : EIN BEITRAG ZUR REFORMATIONSGESCHICHTE / Kawerau, Gustav – Berlin: W. Hertz, 1881 – 1mf – us A.T.L.A. [240]

JOHANN ALBRECHT 1, HERZOG VON MECKLENBURG / Schreiber, Heinrich – Halle: Verein fuer Reformationsgeschichte, 1899 (Schriften des Vereins fuer Reformationsgeschichte; 16. Jahrg., Schrift 64) – 1mf – us A.T.L.A. [240]

JOHANN AMOS COMENIUS ALS THEOLOG : EIN BEITRAG ZUR COMENIUSLITERATUR / Criegern, Hermann Ferdinand – Leipzig: C.F. Winter, 1881 – 1mf – us A.T.L.A. [240]

JOHANN ARNDT, DER VERFASSER DES "WAHREN CHRISTENTUMS" : EIN CHRISTLICHES LEBENSBILD / Winter, Friedrich Julius – Leipzig: Verein fuer Reformationsgeschichte, 1911. ([Schriften des Vereins fuer Reformationsgeschichte; Bd. 101-102] – 1mf – us A.T.L.A. [240]

JOHANN ARNDTS VIER BUECHER VOM WAHREN CHRISTENTHUM AUFS NEUE AUSGEFERTIGET VON JOACHIM LANGEN / Arndt, Johann; ed by Langen, Joachim – Halle, 1734. BO-867 1 – 9 – ne IDC [240]

JOHANN BALTHASAR SCHUPP : BEITRAEGE ZU SEINER WUERDIGUNG / Luehmann, Johann – (Includes bibliographical references) – Marburg a.L.: N G Elwert, 1907 – 1r – 1 – us U.W. Library [430]

JOHANN BRENZ / Hartmann, Julius & Jaeger, Karl – Hamburg: F. Perthes, 1840-1842 – 3mf – us A.T.L.A. [240]

JOHANN CALVIN : SEINE KIRCHE UND SEIN STAAT IN GENF / Kampschulte, FW – Leipzig: Duncker & Humblot, 1869-99 – 3mf – us A.T.L.A. [240]

JOHANN CASPAR LAVATER / Janentzky, Christian – Frauenfeld: Huber, 1928 – 1r – 1 – us U.W. Library [920]

JOHANN CHRISTIAN KRUEGER ALS LUSTSPIELDICHTER / Wittekindt, Wilhelm – 1995 – 1mf – 9 – DM48.00 – 3-8267-3138-7 – gw Hänsel [430]

JOHANN CHRISTIN: DER RICHTER VON ORB *see* DIE GESCHICHTE DES RICHTERS VON ORB

Johann, Ernst *see* GEORG BUECHNER IN SELBSTZEUGNISSEN UND BILDDOKUMENTEN

JOHANN FAUST : EIN ALLEGORISCHES DRAMA VON FUENF AUFZUEGEN: ZUM ERSTENMAHL AUFGEFUEHRT AUF DER KOENIGL. PRAGER SCHAUBUEHNE VON DER VON BRUNIANISCHEN GESELLSCHAFT, 1775 / Lessing, G C; ed by Thurn, R Payer von – Wien: Rosenbaum, 1911 – 1 – us U.W. Library [430]

JOHANN FRIEDRICH AUGUST TISCHBEIN : LEBEN UND WERK / Franke, Martin – (Mit umfassendem Werkverzeichnis) – 1993 – 11mf – 9 – DM175.00 – 3-89349-698-X – gw Hänsel [700]

JOHANN FRIEDRICH FREIHERR COTTA VON COTTENDORF (1764-1832) : EIN BEITRAG ZUR BERUFSGESCHICHTE DER VERLEGER / Muench, Roger – 1993 – 9mf – 9 – DM148.00 – 3-89349-700-5 – gw Hänsel [070]

JOHANN GABRIEL SEIDL / Fuchs, Karl – (Includes bibliographical references) – Wien: Carl Fromme, 1904 – 1r – 1 – us U.W. Library [920]

JOHANN GABRIEL SEIDL, SEINE SAGEN UND GESCHICHTEN.. / Seidl, Johann Gabriel – 1881 – 1 – us I.U. Libraries [390]

JOHANN GEORG ALBRECHTSBERGERS... GRUENDLICHE ANWEISUNG ZUR COMPOSITION / Albrechtsberger, Johann G – 1790 – 9 – us Sibley [780]

JOHANN GEORG HAMANN ALS KRITIKER DER DEUTSCHEN LITERATUR / Hilpert, Walter – (Includes bibliographical references) – Koenigsberg i.Pr.: P Escher, 1933 – 1r – 1 – us U.W. Library [430]

JOHANN GEORG HAMANN IN SEINER BEDEUTUNG FUER DIE STURM- UND DRANGPERIODE / Minor, Jacob – Frankfurt a/M.: Ruetten & Loening, 1881 – 1r – 1 – us U.W. Library [430]

JOHANN GEORG JACOBIS IRIS / Manthey-Zorn, Otto – (Includes bibliographical references) – [S.l.: s.n.], 1905 (Zwickau: Druck von J Herrmann) – 1 – us U.W. Library [430]

JOHANN GEORG ZIMMERMANN U. JOHANN GOTTFRIED HERDER : NACH BISHER UNGEDRUCKTEN BRIEFEN / Bonin, Daniel – Worms: [s.n.], 1910 – 1r – 1 – us U.W. Library [920]

JOHANN GERHARD ONCKEN, HIS LIFE AND WORK / Cooke, John H – London. 1800-79 – 1 – $6.54 – us Baptist [240]

JOHANN GOTTFRIED HERDER : SEIN LEBEN IN SELBSTZEUGNISSEN, BRIEFEN UND BERICHTEN / ed by Reisiger, Hans – Berlin: Im Propylaeen-Verlag, c1942 – 1 – us U.W. Library [430]

JOHANN GOTTFRIED HERDER : DER WEG, DAS WERK, DIE ZEIT / Baete, Ludwig – (Includes bibliographical references and index) – Stuttgart: S Hirzel, 1948 – 1 – us U.W. Library [430]

Johann Gottfried Herder Institute. Marburg-Lahn. Library *see* ALPHABETICAL CATALOG

JOHANN GOTTFRIED SCHADOW : DAS BLUECHER-DENKMAL IN ROSTOCK UNTER BESONDERER BERUECKSICHTIGUNG DES VERWENDETEN MATERIALS BRONZE / Schmidt, Martin H – 1992 – 9 – DM98.00 – 3-89349-496-0 – gw Hänsel [730]

JOHANN GOTTFRIED SCHADOWS AUSEINANDERSETZUNG MIT JOHANN WOLFGANG V. GOETHE – BEZOGEN AUF DIE JAHRE 1800 BIS 1823 / Schmidt, Martin H – 1994 – 2mf – DM80.00 – 3-8267-2055-5 – gw Hänsel [700]

JOHANN GOTTFRIED SEUME ALS MENSCH, DICHTER, PATRIOT UND DENKER / Kohut, Adolph – Berlin: Gotthold Auerbach, [1910?] – 1r – 1 – us U.W. Library [920]

JOHANN HEERMANN (1585-1647) : EIN BEITRAG ZUR GESCHICHTE DER GEISTLICHEN LYRIK IM SIEBZEHNTEN JAHRHUNDERT / Hitzeroth, Carl – (Includes bibliographical references) – Marburg a.L.: N G Elwert, 1907 – 1r – 1 – us U.W. Library [430]

JOHANN HEINRICH VOSS / Herbst, Wilhelm – (Includes bibliographical references and index) – Leipzig: B G Teubner, 1872-1876 – 1r – 1 – us U.W. Library [430]

JOHANN HUEBNERS CURIEUSES NATUR-KUNST-GEWERCK-UND HANDLUNGS-LEXICON (AEL, ABT 1;26) : GESAMTEDITIN ALLER DEUTSCHSPRACHIGEN AUSGABEN: 1. 1712; 2.1714; 3.1717; 4.1722; 5.1727; 6.1731; 7.1736; 8.1739; 9.1741; 10.1746; 11.1755; 12. 1762; 13.1776; 14.1792 – 1712-1792 (mf ed 1995) – 140mf – 9 – DM2,500.00 DM220.00f – 3-89131-199-0 – gw Fischer [030]

JOHANN JAENICKE : DER EVANGELISCH-LUTHERISCHE PREDIGER AN DER BOEHMISCHEN- ODER BETHLEHEMS-KIRCHE ZU BERLIN, NACH SEINEM LEBEN UND WIRKEN / Ledderhose, Karl Friedrich – Berlin: Im Selbstverlage des Herausgebers: In Commission bei F. Beck, 1863 – 1mf – us A.T.L.A. [240]

JOHANN JAKOB VON WILLEMER : DER MENSCH UND BUERGER / Mueller, Adolf – (Includes bibliographical references) – Frankfurt am Main: Englert und Schlosser, 1925 – 1r – 1 – us U.W. Library [943]

JOHANN JOACHIM WINCKELMANN : AUSGEWAEHLTE BRIEFE / ed by Uhde-Bernays, Hermann – Leipzig: Insel-Verlag, 1925 – 1 – us U.W. Library [860]

JOHANN KARL PASSAVANT. EIN CHRISTLICHES CHARAKTERBILD / Helfferich, Adolf – 1867 – 1 – us A.T.L.A. [920]

JOHANN KARL WEZEL : SEIN LEBEN UND SEINE SCHRIFTEN / Kreymborg, Gustav – (Includes bibliographical references) – [Vechta, Germany]: Vechtaer Druckerei und Verlag, 1913 – 1r – 1 – us U.W. Library [430]

JOHANN KASPAR FRIEDRICH MANSO : DER SCHLESISCHE SCHULMANN, DICHTER UND HISTORIKER / Lux, Konrad – (Includes bibliographical references) – Leipzig: Quelle & Meyer, 1908 – 1 – us U.W. Library [920]

JOHANN KASPAR LAVATER : EINE SKIZZE SEINES LEBENS UND WIRKENS / Muncker, Franz – (Includes index) – Stuttgart: J G Cotta, 1883 – 1r – 1 – us U.W. Library [920]

JOHANN KLAJ : EIN BEITRAG ZUR DEUTSCHEN LITERATURGESCHICHTE DES 17. JAHRHUNDERTS / Franz, Albin – (Includes bibliographical references) – Marburg a.L.: N G Elwert, 1908 – 1r – 1 – us U.W. Library [430]

JOHANN KNIPSTRO : DER ERSTE GENERALSUPERINTENDENT VON POMMERN-WOLGAST: SEIN LEBEN UND WIRKEN / Bahlow, F – Halle: Verein fuer Reformationsgeschichte, 1898 (Schriften des Vereins fuer Reformationsgeschichte; 16. Jahrg., Schrift 62 – 1mf – us A.T.L.A. [240]

JOHANN LORENZ MOSHEIM : EIN BEITRAG ZUR KIRCHENGESCHICHTE DES ACHTZEHNTEN JAHRHUNDERTS / Heussi, Karl – Tuebingen: J.C.B. Mohr, 1906 – 1mf – us A.T.L.A. [240]

JOHANN NEUDOERFER'S NACHRICHTEN VON KUENSTLERN UND WERKLEUTEN IN NUERNBERG / Lochner, G W R – (Quellenschriften fuer Kunstgeschichte. v. 10. Wien. 1875). BO-517j 1 – 9 – ne IDC [700]

JOHANN NEUDOERFER'S NACHRICHTEN VON KUENSTLERN UND WERKLEUTEN IN NUERNBERG / Lochner, G W R – Wien. v10. 1875 – 4mf – ne IDC [700]

JOHANN OEKOLAMPAD UND OSWALD MYCONIUS, DIE REFORMATOREN BASELS : LEBEN UND AUSGEWAEHLTE SCHRIFTEN / Hagenbach, K R – Elberfeld: R.L. Friderichs, 1859 – 2mf – us A.T.L.A. [240]

JOHANN PETER UZ : ZUM HUNDERTSTEN TODESTAGE DES DICHTERS / Petzet, Erich – Ansbach: E Bruegel, 1896 – 1r – 1 – us U.W. Library [430]

JOHANN REUCHLIN : SEIN LEBEN UND SEINE WERKE / Geiger, Ludwig – Leipzig: Duncker & Humblot, 1871 – 2mf – us A.T.L.A. [240]

JOHANN RIST ALS WELTLICHER LYRIKER / Kern, Oskar – (Includes bibliographical references) – Marburg a.L.: N G Elwert, 1919 – 1 – us U.W. Library [430]

JOHANN RIST UND DAS NIEDERDEUTSCHE DRAMA DES 17. JAHRHUNDERTS : EIN BEITRAG ZUR DEUTSCHEN LITERATURGESCHICHTE / Heins, Otto – (Includes bibliographical references (3rd-4th prelim. leaves)) – Marburg a.L.: Elwert, 1930 – 1r – 1 – us U.W. Library [430]

JOHANN SAMUEL TRAUGOTT GEHLERS PHYSIKALISCHES WOERTERBUCH : NEU BEARBEITET VON BRANDES, GMELIN, HORNER, MUNCKE, PFAFF / Gehler, ST & Brandes – Leipzig, 1825-1845 (mf ed 1993) – 215mf – 9 – DM1,540.00 – 3-89131-164-8 – gw Fischer [055]

JOHANN TETZEL DER ABLASSPREDIGER / Paulus, Nikolaus – 1995 – 1mf – 9 – DM48.00 – 3-8267-3154-9 – gw Hänsel [240]

JOHANN ULRICH VON KOENIG : EIN BEITRAG ZUR LITTERATURGESCHICHTE DES 18. JAHRHUNDERTS / Rosenmueller, Max Clemens – (Includes bibliographical references) – [S.l.: s.n.] 1896 (Leipzig-Reudnitz: Druck von A Hoffmann) – 1r – 1 – us U.W. Library [430]

JOHANN VON STAUPITZ UND DIE ANFAENGE DER REFORMATION / Keller, Ludwig – Leipzig: S. Hirzel, 1888 – 1mf – us A.T.L.A. [240]

JOHANN WESSEL : EIN BILD AUS DER KIRCHENGESCHICHTE DES XV. JAHRHUNDERTS / Friedrich, Johann – Regensburg: G.J. Manz, 1862 – 1mf – us A.T.L.A. [240]

JOHANN WICLIF UND SEINE ZEIT : ZUM FUENFHUNDERTJAEHRIGEN WICLIFJUBILAEUM, 31. DEZEMBER 1884 / Buddensieg, Rudolf – Halle: Verein fuer Reformationsgeschichte. 1885. ([Schriften des Vereins fuer Reformationsgeschichte; Bd. 8-9]) – 1mf – us A.T.L.A. [240]

JOHANN WILHELM SIMLER : DIE REZEPTION DES OPITZ-BAROCK IN DER DEUTSCHEN SCHWEIZ / Schumacher, Joachim – Heidelberg, 1933 – 1mf – 9 – DM48.00 – 3-89349-789-7 – gw Hänsel [430]

Johannas *see* DOLOMITE IN INDONESIA

JOHANNEAN PROBLEM: A RESUME FOR ENGLISH READERS / Gilmore, George W – Philadelphia: Presbyterian Board of Publications, 1895 – 9 – us A.T.L.A. [240]

DIE JOHANNEISCHE ANSCHAUUNG VOM LEBEN / Schrenck, Erich von – Leipzig: A. Deichert, 1898. 1 fiche – 9 – us A.T.L.A. [240]

DAS JOHANNEISCHE EVANGELIUM NACH SEINER EIGENTHUEMLICHKEIT GESCHILDERT UND ERKLAERT / Luthardt, Christoph Ernst – 2v. 1875-76 – 1 – us A.T.L.A. [240]

DIE JOHANNEISCHE URSPRUNG DES VIERTEN EVANGELIUMS / Luthardt, Christoph Ernst – Leipzig: Doerffling & Franke, 1874. 1 fiche – 9 – us A.T.L.A. [240]

DE JOHANNEISKA SMABREFVENS URSPRUNG / Hjelt, Arthur – Helsinki: Frenckellska Tryck., 1901. 1 fiche – 9 – us A.T.L.A. [240]

JOHANNES A LASCO / Bartels, Petrus – Elberfeld: R.L. Friderichs, 1860. (Leben und ausgewaehlte Schriften der Vaeter und Begruender der reformierten Kirche; 9. T., 1. Heft) – 1mf – us A.T.L.A. [240]

JOHANNES A LASCO UND DER SACRAMENTSSTREIT : EIN BEITRAG ZUR GESCHICHTE DER REFORMATIONSZEIT / Kruske, L – Leipzig: Dieterich, 1901 – 1mf – us A.T.L.A. [240]

Johannes a S Thoma *see*
- CURSUS PHILOSOPHICUS THOMISTICUS, SECUNDUM EXACTAM, VERAM ET GENUINAM ARISTOTELIS...
- CURSUS THEOLOGICI IN PRIMAM SECUNDAM PARTEM D. THOMAE

Johannes, Adolf *see* COMMENTAR ZU DER WEISSAGUNG DES PROPHETEN OBADJA

Johannes Agricola aus Eisleben *see*
- CONFESSION VND BEKENTNIS JOHANNS AGRICOLE EISSLEBENS VOM GESETZE GOTTES
- HUNDERT VND DREISSIG GEMEYNER FRAGESTUECKE FUER DIE IUNGEN KINDER YNN DER DEUDSCHEN MEYDLIN SCHULE ZU EYSSLEBEN

Johannes Amundesham *see* ANNALES MONASTERII S. ALBANI (CHRONIA..5)

JOHANNES BLANKENFELD : EIN LEBENSBILD AUS DEN ANFAENGEN DER REFORMATION / Schnoering, Wilhelm – Halle a.d.S.: Verein fuer Reformationsgeschichte, 1905. (Schriften des Vereins fuer Reformationsgeschichte; 23.Jahrg., Schrift 86) – 1mf – us A.T.L.A. [240]

JOHANNES BRENZ : LEBEN UND AUSGEWAEHLTE SCHRIFTEN / Hartmann, Julius – Elberfeld: R.L. Friderichs, 1862. (Leben und ausgewaehlte Schriften der Vaeter und Begruender der lutherischen Kirche; 6. T.) – 1mf – us A.T.L.A. [240]

JOHANNES BRENZ UND DIE REFORMATION IN HERZOGTUM WIRTEMBERG [SIC] / Hegler, Alfred – Freiburg i.B.: J.C.B. Mohr, 1899 – 1mf – us A.T.L.A. [240]

JOHANNES BRINCKERINCK EN ZIJN KLOOSTER TE DIEPENVEEN / Kuehler, W J – Rotterdam, 1908 – Dfl30.00 – ne Slangenburg [240]

JOHANNES BUENDERLIN VON LINZ UND DIE OBEROESTERREICHISCHEN TAEUFERGEMEINDEN IN DEN JAHREN 1525-31 / Nicoladoni, Alexander – (Includes index) – Berlin: R Gaertner, 1893 – 1mf – 9 – 0-8370-8927-1 – 1986-2927 – us A.T.L.A. [920]

JOHANNES CALVIN : EIN LEBENSBILD ZU SEINEM 400. GEBURTSTAG AM 10. JULI 1909 / Lang, August – Leipzig: Verein fuer Reformationsgeschichte, 1909. (Schriften des Vereins fuer Reformationsgeschichte; 26. Jahrg., Schrift 99) – 1mf – us A.T.L.A. [240]

JOHANNES CALVIN : REDE ZUR FEIER DER 400. WIEDERKEHR DES GEBURTSTAGES CALVINS / Holl, Karl – Tuebingen: J.C.B. Mohr, 1909 – 1mf – us A.T.L.A. [240]

Johannes de Oxenedes *see* CHRONICA (RS13)

JOHANNES DER TAEUFER UND DIE PARTEIEN SEINER ZEIT: EIN ZEITSPIEGEL / Weber, Th – Gotha: F.A. Perthes, 1870. 1 fiche – 9 – us A.T.L.A. [240]

JOHANNES GOSSNER : EIN LEBENSBILD AUS DER KIRCHE DES NEUNZEHNTEN JAHRHUNDERTS / Dalton, Hermann – Friedenau-Berlin: Buchhandlung des Gossnerschen Mission, 1898 – 2mf – us A.T.L.A. [240]

Johannes, H *see* ZARRAH-ZARRAH FISIKA MODERN..

JOHANNES HUS : EIN LEBENSBILD / Friedrich, Johann – Frankfurt am Main: Verlag fuer Kunst und Wissenschaft, 1864 – 1mf – us A.T.L.A. [240]

JOHANNES HUS : EIN LEBENSBILD AUS DER VORGESCHICHTE DER REFORMATION / Lechler, Gotthard Victor – Halle: Verein fuer Reformationsgeschichte, 1889. ([Schriften des Vereins fuer Reformationsgeschichte; Bd. 28]) – 1mf – us A.T.L.A. [240]

Johannes Isaaci, Hollandus *see* OPUS VEGETABILE, AUSS NIEDERLANDISCHEN MANUSCRIPTIS VERHOCHDEUTCHET, VON SOHN SENDIVOGII, GENANT J. F. H. S

JOHANNES KESSLERS SABBATA : ST. GALLER REFORMATIONSCHRONIK 1523-1539 / Kessler, Johannes – (Die Evangelischen Kantone und die Waldenser in den Jahren 1663 und 1664 / von Gerold Meyer von Knonau) – Leipzig: Verein fuer Reformationsgeschichte, 1911. ([Schriften des Vereins fuer Reformationsgeschichte; Bd. 103-104]) – 1mf – us A.T.L.A. [240]

JOHANNES KNADES SELBSTERKENNTNIS : HISTORISCHE ERZAEHLUNG AUS DER ZEIT DER REFORMATION / Quandt, Clara – 3. Aufl. Braunschweig: Grueneberg (Wollermann & Neumeyer) 1889 – 1r – 1 – us U.W. Library [830]

JOHANNES MATHESIUS : EIN LEBENS- UND SITTEN-BILD AUS DER REFORMATIONSZEIT / Loesche, Georg – Gotha: F.A. Perthes, 1895 – 3mf – us A.T.L.A. [240]

Johannes Parisiensis *see* DE UTRAQUE POTESTATE PAPALI ET REGALI

JOHANNES PASSION. SELECTIONS / Bach, Johann Sebastian – Ms, after 1863 – 1 – us Sibley [780]

JOHANNES RUYSBROEC : EEN BIJDRAGE TOT DE KENNIS VAN DE ONTWIKKELING DER MYSTIEK / Otterloo, A A V – Amsterdam, 1874 – 7mf – 8 – ne Slangenburg [290]

JOHANNES SCOTUS ERIGENA : EIN BEITRAG ZUR GESCHICHTE DER PHILOSOPHIE UND THEOLOGIE IM MITTELALTER / Huber, Johannes – London: J.J. Lentner, 1861 – 2mf – us A.T.L.A. [240]

JOHANNES SCOTUS ERIGENA UND DESSEN GEWAEHRSMAENNER IN SEINEM WERKE DE DIVISIONE NATURAE LIBRI V / Draeseke, Johannes – Leipzig: Dietrich, 1902 – 1mf – us A.T.L.A. [240]

JOHANNES TAULER UND DIE GOTTESFREUNDE / Baehring, Bernhard – Hamburg: Agentur des Rauhen Hauses, 1853 – 1mf – us A.T.L.A. [240]

JOHANNES VON DAMASKUS : EINE PATRISTISCHE MONOGRAPHIE / Langen, Joseph – Gotha: F.A. Perthes, 1879 – 1mf – us A.T.L.A. [240]

JOHANNES VON MIQUEL. SEIN ANTEIL AM AUSBAU DES DEUTSCHEN REICHES BIS ZUR JAHRHUNDERTWENDE / Herzfeld, Hans – Band 1-2. Detmold, 1937 – 1 – DM100.00 – gw Mikro Press [943]

JOHANNES VON MUELLER UND DIE FRANZOESISCHE LITERATUR / Herzog, Peter – (Includes bibliographical references) – Frauenfeld: Huber, 1937 – 1r – 1 – us U.W. Library [410]

JOHANNES WTENBOGAERT EN ZIJN TIJD / Rogge, Hendrik Cornelis – Amsterdam: Y. Rogge, 1874-76. 3v – 1 – us U.W. Library [920]

DIE JOHANNES-APOKALYPSE (T.U.U. 1.7/1) / Weiss, Bernhard – Leipzig, 1891 – 4mf – 9 – ne Slangenburg [240]

JOHANNESBURG GAZETTE – Johannesburg. South Africa. 1900-01 – 1 – sa State Libr [072]

Johannesburg, Public Library *see* CATALOGUE OF BANTU, KHOISAN AND MALAGASY IN THE STRANGE COLLECTION OF AFRICANA

Johannesburg Public LibraryPretoria State Library *see*
- STRANGE LIBRARY OF AFRICANA: AUTHOR-TITLE CATALOGUE
- STRANGE LIBRARY OF AFRICANA: SUBJECT CATALOGUE

JOHANNESBURG TIMES – Johannesburg. South Africa. 1895-98 – 1 – sa State Libr [072]

Johannesburg. University of Witwatersrand. Dept of Commerce *see* NATIVE URBAN EMPLOYMENT

DAS JOHANNESEVANGELIUM / Holtzmann, Oskar – Darmstadt: Johannes Waitz, 1887.1 fiche – 9 – us A.T.L.A. [240]

DAS JOHANNES-EVANGELIUM NACH DER PARAPHRASE DES NONNUS PANOPOLITANUS (T.U.U. 2-23/4) / Janssen, R – Leipzig, 1903 – 2mf – 9 – ne Slangenburg [240]

JOHANNES-KOMMENTARE AUS DER GRIECHISCHEN KIRCHE (T.U.U. 5-89) / Reuss, J – Berlin, 1964 – 9mf – 9 – ne Slangenburg [240]

Johann-Gottfried-Herder-Institut. Marburg/ Lahn, Germany *see* ALPHABETISCHER KATALOG DER BIBLIOTHEK DES JOHANN-GOTTFRIED-HERDER-INSTITUTS

THE JOHANNINE EPISTLES / Dodd, C H – Harper. 1946 – 9 – $10.00 – us I.R.C. [240]

JOHANNINE LITERATURE AND THE ACTS OF THE APOSTLES / Forbes, Henry Prentiss – New York: G.P. Putnam, 1907. 1 fiche – 9 – us A.T.L.A. [240]

THE JOHANNINE LITERATURE AND THE ACTS OF THE APOSTLES / Forbes, Henry Prentiss – (Includes index) – New York:G.P. Putnam, 1907 – 1mf – 9 – 0-8370-3161-3 – 1985-1161 – us A.T.L.A. [220]

JOHANNINE PROBLEMS AND MODERN NEEDS / Purchas, H T – London: Macmillan, 1901.1 fiche – 9 – us A.T.L.A. [240]

THE JOHANNINE THEOLOGY : A STUDY OF THE DOCTRINAL CONTENTS OF THE GOSPEL AND EPISTLES OF THE APOSTLE JOHN / Stevens, George Barker – (Includes indexes) – New York:Charles Scribner, 1894 – 1mf – 9 – 0-8370-5406-0 – 1985-3406 – us A.T.L.A. [220]

THE JOHANNINE THEOLOGY...DOCTRINAL CONTENTS OF THE GOSPEL AND EPISTLES / Stevens, George Barker – New York: Charles Scribner, 1894. 1 fiche – 9 – us A.T.L.A. [240]

JOHANNINE VOCABULARY : A COMPARISON OF THE WORDS OF THE FOURTH GOSPEL WITH THOSE OF THE THREE / Abbott, Edwin Abbott – (Includes appendix on the use of prepositions in the Gospels) – London: Adam and Charles Black, 1905 – 1mf – 9 – 0-8370-2013-1 – 1985-0013 – us A.T.L.A. [220]

JOHANNINE VOCABULARY:...THE WORDS OF THE FOURTH GOSPEL WITH THOSE OF THE THREE / Abbott, Edwin Abbott – London: Adam & Charles Black, 1905. 1 fiche – 9 – us A.T.L.A. [240]

JOHANNIS CODAGNELLI ANNALES PLACENTINI (MGH 7: 23.BD) – 1901 – Dfl13.00 – ne Slangenburg [240]

Johannis de Trokelowe *see* CHRONICA ET ANNALES 1259-1296, 1307-1324, 1392-1406 (CHRONIA..3)

JOHANNIS DE WICLIF TRACTATUS DE OFFICIO PASTORALI E CODICE VINDOBONENSI / Wycliffe, John; ed by Lechler, Gotthard Victor – Lipsiae: Typis A. Edelmanni, 1863 – 1mf – us A.T.L.A. [240]

Johanns, P *see* VERS LE CHRIST PAR LE VEDANTA

Johannsen, Christa *see* AN EINEN JUENGLING IM FELDE

Johannson, J-O *see* SOCIAL ASPECTS OF SPORT PARTICIPATION OF SWEDISH ATHLETES WITH DISABILITIES

Johanny, Erichio *see* DE ONTOLOGICAE DEI EXISTENTIS ARGUMENTATIONIS 6

Johansen, A C J *see* RANDERS FJORDS NATURHISTORIE

Johansen, Ernst *see* RUANDA

Johansen, Michelle K *see* GENDER DIFFERENCES IN WALKING WITH RESPECT TO MOVEMENT OF THE PELVIS

Johansson, J V *see* ETUDES SUR DENIS DIDEROT

JOHN O'GROAT JOURNAL – 1 – £42.00r – uk Scot News [072]

JOHN A LASCO : HIS EARLIER LIFE AND LABOURS : A CONTRIBUTION TO THE HISTORY OF THE REFORMATION IN POLAND, GERMANY, AND ENGLAND / Dalton, Hermann – London: Hodder and Stoughton, 1886 – 1mf – us A.T.L.A. [240]

THE JOHN A. LENT COLLECTION ON ASIAN MASS COMMUNICATIONS / ed by Lent, John A & Svobodny, Dolly – 1820-1984. 1500 titles. 350mf. Printed card indexes included – 9 – us A.T.B.I. [380]

JOHN AINSWORTH, PIONEER KENYA ADMINISTRATOR, 1864-1946 : BEING THE HITHERTO UNPUBLISHED MEMOIRS OF COLONEL JOHN D AINSWORTH / Ainsworth, John Dawson; ed by Goldsmith, F H – London: Macmillan; New York: St Martin's Press, 1955 – us Res Libr [920]

JOHN AND QUMRAN / ed by Charlesworth, J H – London, 1972 – 5mf – 8 – ne Slangenburg [220]

JOHN AND SEBASTIAN CABOT: THE DISCOVERY OF NORTH AMERICA / Beazley, Charles Raymond – London: Fisher Unwin, 1898. 03632. (Pre-1900 Canadiana) – 9 – cn C.I.H.M. [971]

JOHN ANGELL JAMES : A REVIEW OF HIS HISTORY, CHARACTER, ELOQUENCE, AND LITERARY LABOURS : WITH DISSERTATIONS ON THE PULPIT AND THE PRESS, ACADEMIC PREACHING, COLLEGE REFORM, ETC. / Campbell, John – London: John Snow, 1860 – 1mf – us A.T.L.A. [240]

JOHN B. ANDREWS MEMORIAL SYMPOSIUM ON LABOR LEGISLATION AND SOCIAL SECURITY, MEMORIAL UNION, THE UNIVERSITY OF WISCONSIN, NOV. 4 AND 5, 1949 – Proceedings. s.l.: s.n., 1949? – 1 – us U.W. Library [331]

JOHN B. GOUGH : THE APOSTLE OF COLD WATER / Martyn, Carlos – New York: Funk & Wagnalls, 1893 – 1mf – us A.T.L.A. [240]

JOHN B. JERVIS PAPERS, 1795-1885 / Jervis, John B – 13r – 1 – $965.00 – us UMI [920]

THE JOHN BEECHER PAPERS, 1899-1972 – (Guide available separately $20.00) – 14r – 1 – $1,207.50 – us UMI [920]

JOHN BIDWELL, PIONEER / Bidwell, John – Marcus Benjamin. 1907 – 1 – 15.00 – us Library Micro [978]

JOHN BRECK FAMILY PAPERS *see* BRECK, JOHN, FAMILY PAPERS, MS 4675

JOHN BROWN IN CANADA: A MONOGRAPH / Hamilton, James Cleland – 1894?. 05650. (Pre-1900 Canadiana) – 9 – cn C.I.H.M. [971]

JOHN BROWN LETTERS / Brown, John – 1 reel – 1 – $75.00 – us UMI [920]

JOHN BROWN'S RAID – 1 – us Ross [976]

JOHN BULL – London. -w. 17 Dec 1820-Dec 1833. (13 reels) – 1 – uk British Libr Newspaper [072]

JOHN BULL AND CO.: THE GREAT COLONIAL BRANCHES OF THE FIRM, CANADA, AUSTRALIA, NEW ZEALAND AND SOUTH AFRICA / O'Rell, Max – New York: C. Webster, 1894. 00236. (Pre-1900 Canadiana) – 9 – cn C.I.H.M. [321]

JOHN C. CALHOUN / Holst, Herman E von – Boston & NY: Houghton, Mifflin & Co, 1899 – 4mf – 9 – $6.00 – LLMC 96-028 – us L.L.M.C. [975]

JOHN CABOT, THE DISCOVERER OF NORTH AMERICA AND SEBASTIAN, HIS SON: A CHAPTER OF THE MARITIME HISTORY OF ENGLAND UNDER THE TUDORS, 1496-1557 / Harrisse, Henry – London: Stevens, 1896. 05393. (Pre-1900 Canadiana) – 9 – cn C.I.H.M. [910]

JOHN CALVIN : HIS LIFE, LETTERS, AND WORK / Reyburn, Hugh Y – London, New York: Hodder and Stoughton, 1914 – 1mf – us A.T.L.A. [240]

JOHN CALVIN : THE ORGANISER OF REFORMED PROTESTANTISM, 1509-1564 / Walker, Williston – New York: Putnam, 1906 – 2mf – us A.T.L.A. [240]

John Carter Brown Library. Providence *see* BIBLIOTHECA AMERICANA

JOHN CASSIAN / Chadwick, O – 1950 – 4mf – 8 – ne Slangenburg [240]

JOHN COLLIER PAPERS, 1922-1968 / Collier, John – 59r – 1 – $4325.00 – us UMI [305]

JOHN D. ROCKEFELLER INTERVIEW, 1917-20 – (William O. Inglis, interviewer. Rockefeller discusses his early life, his critics, the Standard Oil Company, the public perception of him, as well as his insights on the expansion of the multi-million dollar oil business. Text-fiche edition) – 19mf – 11 – $175.00 – us UPA [920]

JOHN D. SPAHR PAPERS *see* SPAHR, JOHN D., PAPERS

JOHN DAY VALLEY RANGER – (Set incl. Long Creek Ranger: East Oregon Ranger (John Day)) – John Day, OR. -w. 6 Mar 1931-20 Aug 1948. 6 rolls. – 1 – us U.O. Library [071]

JOHN DE WYCLIFFE, D.D. : A MONOGRAPH / Vaughan, Robert – London: Seeleys, 1853 – 1mf – us A.T.L.A. [240]

JOHN DONNE : SOMETIME DEAN OF ST. PAUL'S, A.D. 1621-1631 / Jessopp, Augustus – Boston: Houghton, Mifflin, 1897 – 1mf – us A.T.L.A. [240]

JOHN EDWARD BRUCE PAPERS : FROM THE HOLDINGS OF THE SCHOMBURG CENTER FOR RESEARCH IN BLACK CULTURE, MANUSCRIPTS, ARCHIVES AND RARE BOOKS DIVISION: THE NEW YORK PUBLIC LIBRARY, ASTOR, LENOX AND TILDEN FOUNDATIONS – (Guide sold separately for $20.00 which covers other Schomburg Center collections) – 1995 – ca 4r – 1 – ca $340.00 – 1167-6 – us L of C Photodup [070]

JOHN EDWARD BRUCE PAPERS – (Printed guide available for $20.00) – Schomburg Center for Research in Black Culture, 1995 – 4r – 1 – $340.00 – D3305P27 – us Scholarly Res [070]

John, Edward Mills *see* JOHN'S AMERICAN NOTARY AND COMMISSIONER OF DEEDS MANUAL.

THE JOHN ERICSSON COLLECTION OF THE AMERICAN SWEDISH HISTORICAL FOUNDATION / The American Swedish Foundation; ed by Meixner, Esther Chilstrom – (With printed guide) – 1839-1889 – 8r – 1 – $680.00 – S1848 – us Scholarly Res [355]

John, Eugenie *see* ROMANE UND NOVELLEN

JOHN F. KENNEDEY UNIVERSITY LAW REVIEW – v1-6. 1988-1995 – 9 – $49.00 set – us Hein [340]

THE JOHN F. KENNEDY 1960 CAMPAIGN, PART 1 : POLLS, ISSUES, AND STRATEGY – (With printed guide) – 10r – 1 – $1,160.00 – 0-89093-917-9 – us UPA [323]

THE JOHN F. KENNEDY 1960 CAMPAIGN, PART 2 : SPEECHES, PRESS CONFERENCE AND DEBATES – (With printed guide) – 12r – 1 – $1,385.00 – 0-89093-918-7 – us UPA [323]

JOHN F. KENNEDY ASSASSINATION / ed by Svobodny, Dolly – Books, journals, government reports, original material. Includes printed, eye-readable index; yearly update of materials. 300 microfiche. 1963-76 – 9 – 350.00 – us Creative [977]

JOHN F. KENNEDY ASSASSINATION IN DALLAS AND THE SUBSEQUENT COVERAGE IN THE WORLD'S MAJOR NEWSPAPERS – (Includes original Dallas Daily News as well as national and international papers from the New York Irish World to the Washington Post to the Zuerich Zeitung) – 8r – 1 – $400.00 – R05003 – us Library Micro [320]

John F. Kennedy Library. Boston *see*
- ERNEST HEMINGWAY
- ERNEST HEMINGWAY: CATALOG OF THE MANUSCRIPTS, CORRESPONDENCE AND OTHER MATERIAL..

THE JOHN F. KENNEDY NATIONAL SECURITY FILES, 1961-63 – (Series: National Security Files. Africa 9r $1,385.00 Index $265.00. Asia and the Pacific 10r $1,160.00 Index $245.00. Latin America 10r $1,160.00 Index $245.00. The Middle East 3r $345.00 Index $85.00. USSR and Eastern Europe 3r $370.00 Index $95.00. Vietnam 7r $810.00 Index $170.00. Western Europe 10r $1,160.00 Index $245.00) – us UPA [324]

THE JOHN F. KENNEDY PRESIDENTIAL ORAL HISTORY COLLECTION, PART 1 : THE WHITE HOUSE AND EXECUTIVE DEPARTMENTS – (Microfilm ed 1-55655-077-4 $1,150.00) – 9 – $1,150.00 – 1-55655-053-7 – us UPA [324]

THE JOHN F. KENNEDY PRESIDENTIAL ORAL HISTORY COLLECTION, PART 2 : THE CONGRESS, THE JUDICIARY, PUBLIC FIGURES AND PRIVATE INDIVIDUALS – (Microfilm ed 1-55655-078-2 $1,450.00) – 9 – $1,450.00 – 1-55655-054-5 – us UPA [324]

THE JOHN FITCH PAPERS – 3r – 1 – $105.00 – Dist. us Scholarly Res – us L of C Photodup [623]

JOHN FITZGERALD KENNEDY ASSASSINATION : A MICROFILM DOCUMENTARY – (Includes articles from US and foreign newspapers and magazines, plus Kennedy's biography) – 1917-63 – 1r – 1 – $50.00 – B40016 – us Library Micro [977]

John Fitzgerald Kennedy Library *see* RECORDS OF THE KENNEDY ADMINISTRATION, 1961-1963

JOHN FLETCHER HURST : A BIOGRAPHY / Osborn, Albert Sherman – New York: Eaton & Mains, 1905 – 2mf – us A.T.L.A. [240]

THE JOHN FOSTER DULLES ORAL HISTORY COLLECTION : FROM THE COLLECTIONS OF THE PRINCETON UNIVERSITY LIBRARIES – (With printed guide) – 1994 – 13r – 1 – $1,105.00 – D3301 – us L of C Photodup [327]

JOHN G. PATON : LATER YEARS AND FAREWELL: A SEQUEL TO JOHN G. PATON – AN AUTOBIOGRAPHY / Langridge, Albert Kent & Paton, Frank Hyme Lyall – (Includes index) – New York: Hodder and Stoughton, [1910?] – 1mf – 9 – 0-8370-6203-9 – 1986-0203 – us A.T.L.A. [920]

JOHN G. PATON : MISSIONARY TO THE NEW HEBRIDES: AN AUTOBIOGRAPHY / Paton, John Gibson – new ed. New York: Fleming H Revell, c1898 – 3mf – 9 – 0-8370-6406-6 – 1986-0406 – us A.T.L.A. [920]

JOHN GILL PRATT PAPERS / Pratt, John Gill – 1834-99. In Kansas State Historical Society. Guide – 1 – us KS Hist [920]

JOHN H. CLIFFORD, ESQ., ATTORNEY-GENERAL, &C / Clifford, John Henry – Boston: Elder, 1854. 141p. LL-219 – 1 – us L of C Photodup [340]

JOHN H. NEWMAN : THE CONCEPT OF INFALLIBLE DOCTRINAL AUTHORITY / Dibble, R A – Washington, D.C., 1955 – 9mf – 8 – ne Slangenburg [240]

JOHN HALL, PASTOR AND PREACHER : A BIOGRAPHY / Hall, Thomas Cuming – New York: F.H. Revell, c1901 – 1mf – us A.T.L.A. [240]

THE JOHN HAY PAPERS – 23r – 1 – $805.00 – Dist. us Scholarly Res – us L of C Photodup [320]

JOHN HAYSLIP PAPERS *see* HAYSLIP, JOHN, PAPERS, MS 2944

JOHN HENRY / Chappell, Louis Watson – 1933 – 1 – us I.U. Libraries [390]

JOHN HENRY INGRAM'S POE COLLECTION – (Guide sold separately $10.00) – 1967 – 9r – 1 – $765.00 – D3183 – us Scholarly Res [420]

JOHN HOWARD AND THE PRISON WORLD OF EUROPE / Dickson, Richard W – Webster, MA: Frederick Charlton, 1982 – 5mf – 9 – $7.50 – LLMC 92-112 – us L.L.M.C. [360]

JOHN HOWARD AND THE PRISON-WORLD OF EUROPE : FROM ORIGINAL AND AUTHENTIC DOCUMENTS / Dixon, Hepworth – New York: R. Carter, 1850 – 1mf – us A.T.L.A. [240]

JOHN HOWLAND: A MAYFLOWER PILGRIM / ed by Howland, William – 1926 – 1 – 5.00 – us Baptist [240]

JOHN HUSS : THE COMMENCEMENT OF RESISTANCE TO PAPAL AUTHORITY ON THE PART OF THE INFERIOR CLERGY / Wratislaw, A H – London: S.P.C.K.; New York: E. & J.B. Young, 1882 – 1mf – us A.T.L.A. [240]

JOHN HUSS : HIS LIFE, TEACHINGS AND DEATH, AFTER FIVE HUNDRED YEARS / Schaff, David Schley – New York: Scribner, 1915 – 1mf – us A.T.L.A. [240]

JOHN HUSS / Mussolini, Benito – Trans. by Clifford Parker. New York: A.& C. Boni, 1929.vi,225p – 1 – us U.W. Library [920]

JOHN HUSS AND THE PRESBYTERIANS AND REFORMED / Good, James I – [S.l.: s.n., 1915?] – 1mf – us A.T.L.A. [240]

JOHN INGLESANT : A ROMANCE / Shorthouse, Joseph Henry – London: Macmillan and Co., 1881 – 1 roll – 1 – 1-55879-976-1 – uk Libr Preservation [830]

JOHN INGLESANT / Shorthouse, Joseph Henry – British Fiction Archive: Unit 1 – 9 – uk Bell [830]

JOHN JAY / Pellew, George – Boston & NY: Houghton, Mifflin & Co, 1899 – 4mf – 9 – $6.00 – LLMC 96-031 – us L.L.M.C. [975]

THE JOHN KEATS MEMORIAL VOLUME – Issued by the Keats House Committee, Hampstead. Illus. London, New York: John Lane Company, 1921.xx,276p. 4 pl. 6 facs. including portraits. Ed. by Dr. G.C. Williamson. 1 reel. 1296 – 1 – us U.W. Library [420]

JOHN KEBLE : A BIOGRAPHY / Lock, Walter – Boston: Houghton, Mifflin, 1893 – 1mf – us A.T.L.A. [240]

JOHN KENNETH MACKENZIE : MEDICAL MISSIONARY TO CHINA / Bryson, Mary Isabella – New York: Fleming H Revell, 1891 – 1mf – 9 – 0-8370-6249-7 – 1986-0249 – us A.T.L.A. [920]

JOHN KERR PAPERS, MS 330 / Kerr, John – 1788-92; 1800-22; 1839 – 3r – 1 – us Western Res [920]

JOHN KNOX : A BIOGRAPHY / Brown, P Hume – London: A. and C. Black, 1895 – 2mf – us A.T.L.A. [240]

JOHN KNOX : A BIOGRAPHY / Macmillan, D – London: A. Melrose, 1905 – 1mf – us A.T.L.A. [240]

JOHN KNOX : THE HERO OF THE SCOTTISH REFORMATION / Cowan, Henry – New York: G.P. Putnam, 1905. (Heroes of the Reformation; 7) – 2mf – us A.T.L.A. [240]

JOHN KNOX : HIS IDEAS AND IDEALS / Stalker, James – New York: A.C. Armstrong, 1904 – 1mf – us A.T.L.A. [240]

JOHN KNOX / Innes, Alexander Taylor – Edinburgh: Oliphant, Anderson & Ferrier, 1905 – 1mf – us A.T.L.A. [240]

JOHN KNOX / Taylor, William MacKergo – 1885 – 1 – us A.T.L.A. [240]

JOHN KNOX, 1505-1572 : EIN ERINNERUNGSBLATT ZUR VIERTEN ZENTENARFEIER / Mulot, R – Halle a.d.S.: Verein fuer Reformationsgeschichte, 1904 (Schriften des Vereins fuer Reformationsgeschichte; 22. Jahrg., Schrift 84) – 1mf – us A.T.L.A. [240]

JOHN KNOX AND THE CHURCH OF ENGLAND : HIS WORK IN HER PULPIT AND HIS INFLUENCE UPON HER LITURGY, ARTICLES, AND PARTIES : A MONOGRAPH FOUNDED UPON SEVERAL IMPORTANT PAPERS OF KNOX NEVER BEFORE PUBLISHED / Lorimer, Peter – London: Henry S. King, 1875 – 1mf – us A.T.L.A. [240]

JOHN KNOX AND THE REFORMATION / Lang, Andrew – London; New York: Longmans, Green, 1905 – 1mf – us A.T.L.A. [240]

THE JOHN KNOX LITURGY, OR, SCOTTISH "BOOK OF COMMON ORDER": A LECTURE DELIVERED BEFORE THE ST STEPHEN'S CHURCH GUILD, ST JOHN, N.B., AND PUBLISHED AT THE REQUEST OF THE GUILD / Fotheringham, Thomas Francis – With an introduction by A. Pollok. St. John, N.B., s.n., 1898 (St. John, N.B.: E. Armstrong). 05598. (Pre-1900 Canadiana) – 9 – cn C.I.H.M. [971]

JOHN M. BERRIEN PAPERS / Berrien, John M – University of North Carolina Library. Guide – 1 – $54.00 – us U.N.C. Southern Hist [920]

John M. Gresham and Co *see*
- BIOGRAPHICAL AND HISTORICAL CYCLOPEDIA OF WESTMORELAND COUNTY
- BIOGRAPHICAL AND HISTORICAL SOUVENIR FOR COUNTIES OF CLARK, CRAWFORD, HARRISON, FLOYD, JEFFERSON, JENNINGS, SCOTT AND WASHINGTON
- BIOGRAPHICAL CYCLOPEDIA OF THE COMMONWEALTH OF KENTUCKY

DR. JOHN M. HENDERSON PAPERS *see* HENDERSON, DR. JOHN M., PAPERS, MS 533

JOHN MACKENZIE : SOUTH AFRICAN MISSIONARY AND STATESMAN / Mackenzie, William Douglas – (Includes index) – New York: A C Armstrong, 1902 – 2mf – 9 – 0-8370-6271-3 – 1986-0271 – us A.T.L.A. [920]

JOHN MARCHMONT'S LEGACY / Braddon, Mary Elizabeth – British Fiction Archive: Unit 5 – 9 – uk Bell [830]

John, Marquis of Butet *see* THE COPTIC MORNING SERVICE FOR THE LORD'S DAY

JOHN MARSHALL : COMPLETE CONSTITUTIONAL DECISIONS / Dillon, John M – (Edited with annotations historical, critical and legal) – Chicago: Callaghan, 1903 – 3mf – 9 – $13.50 – LLMC 84-249 – us L.L.M.C. [323]

JOHN MARSHALL AND THE CONSTITUTION : A CHRONICLE OF THE SUPREME COURT / Corwin, Edward A – New Haven: Yale UP, 1921 – 3mf – 9 – $4.50 – LLMC 92-234 – us L.L.M.C. [323]

JOHN MARSHALL DAY, CELEBRATION BY THE RHODE ISLAND BAR ASSOCIATION AND BROWN UNIVERSITY, FEBRUARY 4, 1901: ADDRESS BY HON. LE BARON BRADFORD COLT. / Rhode Island Bar Association – Providence: Rhode Island Printing Co., 1901. 53p. LL-199 – 1 – us L of C Photodup [340]

JOHN MARSHALL; LIFE, CHARACTER AND JUDICIAL SERVICES. / Dillon, John Forrest – Centenary ed. Chicago, Callaghan, 1903. 3 v. LL-1255 – 1 – us L of C Photodup [340]

JOHN MASON NEALE, D.D. : A MEMOIR / Towle, Eleanor A – London, New York: Longmans, Green, 1906 – 1mf – us A.T.L.A. [240]

THE JOHN MAYNARD KEYNES PAPERS IN KING'S COLLEGE, CAMBRIDGE – (With printed catalogue £58.00 ISBN: 0-85964-233-X) – 170r – 1 – £11,125.00 – uk Chadwyck [330]

JOHN MITCHELL PAPERS, 1885-1919 / Mitchell, John N – (Includes records of United Mine Workers) – 55r – 1 – $3640.00 – us UMI [920]

JOHN MUIR PAPERS, 1858-1957 / Muir, John; ed by Limbaugh, R H & Lewis, K E – (With printed guide and index £27.00) – 51r and 53mf – 1,9 – £3,090.00 – uk Chadwyck [920]

JOHN NICHOLSON PAPERS / Nicholson, John – 1772-1819. (In Pa. State Archives). 21 reels. Guide – 1 – us Penn Hist [920]

JOHN NICHOLSON PAPERS, 1772-1819 / Pennsylvania Historical and Museum Commission – (With printed guide) – 21r – 1 – $1,785.00 – D3292 – us Nat'l Archives [978]

John, of Damascus, Saint *see*
- FRAGMENTE VORNICAENISCHER KIRCHENVAETER AUS DEN SACRA PARALLELA
- ST. JOHN DAMASCENE ON HOLY IMAGES (PROS TOUS DIABALLONTAS TAS HAGIAS EIKONAS)

John of Salisbury, Bishop of Chartres *see* IOANNIS SARESBERIENSIS EPISCOPI CARNOTENSIS POLICRATICI..

JOHN OSBORNE SARGENT PAPERS, 1831-1912 / Sargent, John Osborne – Massachusetts Historical Society – 4r – 1 – $305.00 – us UMI [920]

JOHN P. GREEN PAPERS, MS 3379 / Green, John P – (Correspondence, speeches, financial and legal records) – 1968-1910 – 6r – 1 – us Western Res [920]

John Peckham *see* REGISTRUM EPISTOLARUM FRATRIS JOHANNIS PECKHAM (RS77)

THE JOHN PENDLETON KENNEDY PAPERS / Kennedy, John Pendleton; ed by Boles, John B – (Guide sold separately $10.00) – 1973 – 27r – 1 – $2,295.00 – S1616 – us Scholarly Res [920]

JOHN PENRY : THE SO-CALLED MARTYR OF CONGREGATIONALISM AS REVEALED IN THE ORIGINAL RECORD OF HIS TRIAL AND IN DOCUMENTS RELATED THERETO / Burrage, Champlin – Oxford: University Press; London: H. Frowde, 1913 – 1mf – us A.T.L.A. [240]

JOHN PRESTON DAVIS PAPERS : FROM THE HOLDINGS OF THE SCHOMBURG CENTER FOR RESEARCH IN BLACK CULTURE, MANUSCRIPTS, ARCHIVES AND RARE BOOKS DIVISION: THE NEW YORK PUBLIC LIBRARY, ASTOR, LENOX AND TILDEN FOUNDATIONS – (Guide sold separately for $20.00 covers all coll under "Literature and the Arts" D3305.G6) – 1995 – ca 5r – 1 – ca $425.00 – D3305P24 – Dist. us Scholarly Res – us L of C Photodup [070]

JOHN Q.A. CAMPBELL DIARIES *see* CAMPBELL, JOHN Q.A., DIARIES MS 3560

JOHN RICHARD BRINKLEY VS. KANSAS STATE BOARD OF MEDICAL REGISTRATION AND EXAMINATION, ET AL / Brinkley, John Richard – 1 – us KS Hist [610]

JOHN RICHARD BRINKLEY VS. THE KANSAS CITY STAR / Brinkley, John Richard – 1 – us KS Hist [978]

JOHN ROBINSON : THE PILGRIM PASTOR / Davis, Ozora S – Boston: Pilgrim Press, c1903 – 1mf – us A.T.L.A. [240]

JOHN ROGERS: THE COMPILER OF THE FIRST AUTHORISED ENGLISH BIBLE; THE PIONEER OF THE ENGLISH REFORMATION; AND ITS FIRST MARTYR...A GENEALOGICAL ACCOUNT OF HIS FAMILY. / Chester, Joseph Lemuel – London: Longman, Green, Longman, and Roberts, 1861. xii,452p – 1 – us U.W. Library [920]

JOHN RUSKIN : A SKETCH OF HIS LIFE, HIS WORK, AND HIS OPINIONS WITH PERSONAL REMINISCENCES... / Spielmann, Marion Harry – London, New York: Cassel and Co., 1900 – 1 roll – 1 – 1-55879-768-8 – uk Libr Preservation [110]

JOHN RUSKIN, SALE AND EXHIBITION CATALOGUES – 22mf – 1 – us UMI [700]

JOHN RUSKIN, THE PRE-RAPHAELITE BROTHERHOOD AND ARTS AND CRAFTS MOVEMENT – (The Ruskin, Holman Hunt, Fairfax Murray, Spielman and related collection from the John Rylands University Library, Manchester and the Manchester Art Gallery collection) – 1 – us Primary [700]

JOHN RUTLEDGE PAPERS / Rutledge, John – 1782-1872. University of North Carolina Library. Guide – 1 – $36.00 – us U.N.C. Southern Hist [920]

John Rylands Library *see* BULLETIN

JOHN RYLANDS UNIVERSITY LIBRARY, DEANSGATE CATALOGUE OF PRINTED BOOKS – 1,081mf – 9 – £5, 460.00 – uk Chadwyck [020]

John Rylands University Library, Manchester *see*
- ANTI-SLAVERY MATERIALS, REGIONAL RECORDS AND OTHER PAMPHLETS
- METHODIST ARCHIVES CATALOGUES

John Rylands University Library. Methodist Archives *see* A CATALOGUE OF MANUSCRIPTS AND RELICS, ENGRAVINGS AND PHOTOGRAPHS, MEDALS, BOOKS AND PAMPHLETS, POTTERY, MEDALLIONS, ETC...

JOHN S. BROWN PAPERS / Brown, John S – 1818-1907. In Kansas State Historical Society – 1 – us KS Hist [920]

John S Slater Fund *see* PROCEEDINGS AND REPORTS

JOHN SAINT JOHN AND ANNA GREY: A ROMANCE OF OLD NEW BRUNSWICK / Currie, Margaret Gill – Toronto: Printed by W. Briggs, 1897. 02246. (Pre-1900 Canadiana) – 9 – cn C.I.H.M. [830]

JOHN SHERMAN, AND DHOYA. BY GANCONAGH [I.E. W.B. YEATS] / Yeats, William Butler – London: T.F. Unwin, 1891 – 1 roll – 1 – 1-55879-542-1 – uk Libr Preservation [420]

JOHN SMITH, THE SE-BAPTIST AND THE PILGRIM FATHERS HELWYS AND BAPTIST ORIGINS / Burgess, Walter H – 1911 – 1 – 14.07 – us Baptist [240]

SIR JOHN SOANE'S MUSEUM : THE ILLUMINATED MANUSCRIPTS / London. Sir John Soane's Museum – 3r – 14 – £670.00 – uk Chadwyck [090]

SIR JOHN SOANE'S MUSEUM : THE ITALIAN DRAWINGS / London. Sir John Soane's Museum – (With catalogue) – 3r – 14 – £670.00 – uk Chadwyck [740]

SIR JOHN SOANE'S MUSEUM : ARCHITECTURAL AND ORNAMENTAL DRAWINGS / London. Sir John Soane's Museum – (With printed catalogue & index ISBN: 0-85964-187-2 £130) – 55r – 14 – £7,550.00 coll – uk Chadwyck [720]

JOHN STEINBECK COLLECTION / Steinbeck, John – (Index and annotated bibliography 1r $50.00 B40502) – Salinas, CA: John Steinbeck Library – 1 – $250.00 – B40501 – us Library Micro [420]

JOHN STUART MILL : A CRITICISM: WITH PERSONAL RECOLLECTIONS / Bain, Alexander – London: Longmans, Green, 1882 – 1mf – us A.T.L.A. [320]

JOHN STUART MILL : THE ECONOMIC, POLITICAL AND FEMINIST PAPERS – The J.S. Mill and Harriet and Helen Taylor Collection from the British Library of Political and Economic Science, London – 1 – us Primary [320]

JOHN THE BAPTIST : THE FORERUNNER OF OUR LORD: HIS LIFE AND WORK / Houghton, Ross C – (Includes index) – New York: Hunt & Eaton, 1889 – 1mf – 9 – 0-8370-3675-5 – 1985-1675 – us A.T.L.A. [920]

JOHN THE BAPTIST / Kraeling, C H – New York, 1951 – 4mf – 8 – ne Slangenburg [220]

JOHN THE BAPTIST / Meyer, Frederick Brotherton – New York:Fleming H. Revell, c1900 – 1mf – 9 – 0-8370-4409-X – 1985-2409 – us A.T.L.A. [920]

JOHN THOMAS PAPERS, 1693-1839 / Thomas, John – Massachusetts Historical Society – 3r – 1 – $225.00 – us UMI [920]

JOHN TYNDALL, NATURAL PHILOSOPHER, 1820-1893: CATALOGUE OF CORRESPONDENCE, JOURNALS AND COLLECTED PAPERS / Friday, James R & MacLeod, Roy M & Shepherd, Philippa – 1974. Microform original. 34 fiches – 9 – £125.00 – uk Mansell Publ [500]

John Walworth Family *see* WALWORTH FAMILY PAPERS, MS 1901

JOHN WESLEY / Overton, John H – London: Methuen, 1891 – 1mf – us A.T.L.A. [240]

JOHN WESLEY POWELL AND THE ANTHROPOLOGY OF THE CANYON COUNTRY / Fowler, D D et al – 1969 – 9 – $5.00f – us Ross [970]

JOHN WESLEY'S LIBRARY, HOUSED IN WESLEY'S HOUSE, 49 CITY ROAD, LONDON, E.C.1 / London. -Wesley's Chapel – n.d. – 1mf – 9 – ne IDC [240]

JOHN WICLIF : HIS LIFE, TIMES, AND TEACHING / Pennington, Arthur Robert – London: S.P.C.K.; New York: E. & J.B. Young, 1884 – 1mf – us A.T.L.A. [240]

JOHN WILLIAM BURGON : LATE DEAN OF CHICHESTER: A BIOGRAPHY, WITH EXTRACTS FROM HIS LETTERS AND EARLY JOURNALS / Goulburn, Edward Meyrick – London: J. Murray, 1892 – 2mf – us A.T.L.A. [240]

JOHN WILLIAM COOKE / Cooke, John William – [Buenos Aires]: Editorial del Noroeste: distribuidor en capital, Troisi y Vaccaro, [1974?] – 1 – CSUXADL6977-B – us Hoover Inst Photo [920]

JOHN WYCLIFFE AND HIS ENGLISH PRECURSORS / Lechler, Gotthard Victor – London: Religious Tract Society, [1884?] – 2mf – us A.T.L.A. [240]

JOHN WYCLIFFE AND THE FIRST ENGLISH BIBLE : AN ORATION / Storrs, Richard Salter – (Includes bibliographical references) – New York:Anson D.F. Randolph, 1880 – 1mf – 9 – 0-8370-5430-3 – 1985-3430 – us A.T.L.A. [220]

John Zube *see* COLLECTED WORKS OF LYSANDER SPOONER

JOHNNY LUDLOW / Wood, Ellen – (Series 1-6). British Fiction Archive: Unit 1 – 9 – uk Bell [830]

JOHN'S AMERICAN NOTARY AND COMMISSIONER OF DEEDS MANUAL. / John, Edward Mills – 4th ed. Chicago, Callaghan, 1931. 523 p. LL-566 – 1 – us L of C Photodup [340]

Johns, David *see* NY DIKISIONARY MALAGASY

JOHNS HOPKINS MAGAZINE – (v. 24- 1973- 5,6. v. 26- 1975- 9) – v. 1- 1950- – 1 – us UMI [610]

JOHNS HOPKINS MEDICAL JOURNAL – (v. 130-151. 1972-82. 5,6. v. 140-151. 1977-82. 9) – v. 1-151. 1889-1982 – 1 – us UMI [610]

JOHNS HOPKINS MEDICAL JOURNAL – v1-96. 1889-1955 – 1,5,6 – us Princeton Micro [616]

Johns Hopkins University *see* STUDIES IN HISTORICAL AND POLITICAL SCIENCE

JOHNS HOPKINS UNIVERSITY STUDIES IN HISTORICAL AND POLITICAL SCIENCE / ed by Adams, Herbert B – Seies 18. Nos. 10-12. Thom, William Taylor. The Struggle for religious freedom in Virginia: The Baptists. 1900. Thomas, David. The Virginia Baptist. 180p – 1 – 6.30 – us Baptist [323]

John's Island. South Carolina. St. John's (Episcopal) Church *see* RECORDS

Johns, J H *see* HISTORY OF THE ROCK PRESBYTERIAN CHURCH IN CECIL CO., MD

Johnsen, Julia Emily *see*
- LIMITATIONS OF POWER OF SUPREME COURT TO DECLARE ACTS OF CONGRESS UNCONSTITUTIONAL
- SPECIAL LEGISLATION FOR WOMEN

THE JOHNSON ADMINISTRATION AND PACIFICATION IN VIETNAM : THE ROBERT KOMER-WILLIAM LEONHART FILES, 1966-68 – 1993 – 15r – 1 – $1,785.00 – 1-55655-474-5 – us UPA [320]

Johnson, Allen *see* READINGS IN AMERICAN CONSTITUTIONAL HISTORY, 1776-1876

Johnson, Amandus *see* THE SWEDISH SETTLEMENTS ON THE DELAWARE

Johnson and Co *see* HISTORY OF PEORIA COUNTY

Johnson, Andrew *see* PAPERS

Johnson, Arthur Henry *see* THE NORMANS IN EUROPE

Johnson, Arthur N *see* BRITISH FOREIGN MISSIONS, 1837-97

Johnson, Brenda M *see* VALIDATION OF A MODIFIED CLOSED CIRCUIT, OXYGEN DILUTION RESIDUAL VOLUME METHOD

Johnson, C *see*
- THE FERN ALLIES; A SUPPLEMENT TO THE FERNS OF GREAT BRITAIN
- THE FERNS OF GREAT BRITAIN

Johnson C Smith University *see* QUARTERLY REVIEW OF HIGHER EDUCATION AMONG NEGROES

Johnson C. Smith University *see* QUARTERLY REVIEW OF HIGHER EDUCATION AMONG NEGROES

Johnson, Carrie P *see* HISTORY OF CLINTON AND CLADWELL COUNTIES

JOHNSON CITIZEN – Johnson, NE. -w. May-Jul 1898; Sep 1898-Feb 1899 – 1 – us NE Hist [071]

Johnson, Clifton *see* THE PARSON'S DEVIL

JOHNSON COUNTY COURIER – Sterling, NE. -w. Nov 1895-Feb 1896; Apr-Jun 1896; Aug 1896-Nov 1906; Mar 1907-Nov 1971 – 1 – us NE Hist [071]

JOHNSON COUNTY HERALD – Overland Park. Kan. -w. 1942-56 – 1 – us UMI [071]

JOHNSON COUNTY JOURNAL – Tecumseh, NE. -w. Nov 1879-Apr 1896, scattered issues missing; Jun-Oct 1896; Dec 1896-Mar 1899; Jun 1899; Nov 1899-Dec 1903; Mar 1908-Sept 1929 – 1 – us NE Hist [071]

JOHNSON COUNTY JOURNAL – Tecumseh. Neb. 1879-1929 – 1 – us UMI [071]

JOHNSON COUNTY, KENTUCKY, A HISTORY OF THE COUNTRY AND GENEALOGY OF ITS PEOPLE UP TO 1927 / Hall, Mitchel – Louisville: The Standard Press, 1928. v1, Kentucky Reel 7; v2, Kentucky Reel 8. (The Cox Library Collection) – 5 – us Americana [978]

JOHNSON COUNTY PRESS – Franklin. Ind. 1865-1869 – 1 – us UMI [071]

JOHNSON COUNTY TRIBUNAL – Tecumseh, NE. -w. Dec 1898-Jan 1901; Apr 1901-Nov 1909 – 1 – us NE Hist [071]

Johnson, Crisfield *see* CENTENNIAL HISTORY OF ERIE COUNTY

Johnson, D LaMont *see* COMPUTERS IN THE SCHOOLS

Johnson, D W *see* THE GEOLOGY OF THE ALBUQUERQUE SHEET

Johnson, Dave R *see* SELF-EFFICACY OF MALE AND FEMALE GOLFERS AT DIFFERING ABILITY LEVELS

Johnson, Donald McIntosh *see* INDIAN HEMP: A SOCIAL MENACE

Johnson, E Polk *see* A HISTORY OF KENTUCKY AND KENTUCKIANS

Johnson, Elias Finley *see*
- ELEMENTS OF THE LAW OF NEGOTIABLE CONTRACTS
- ILLUSTRATIVE CASES UPON THE LAW OF BILLS AND NOTES

Johnson, Elias Henry *see* THE RELIGIOUS USE OF IMAGINATION

Johnson, Elizabeth Frienech *see* WECKHERLIN'S ECLOGUES OF THE SEASONS...

Johnson, Francis *see* MISCELLANEOUS COLLECTION OF 20 VOCAL AND INSTRUMENTAL COMPOSITIONS

Johnson, Frank W *see* A HISTORY OF TEXAS AND TEXANS

Johnson, Franklin *see*
- THE CHRISTIAN'S RELATION TO EVOLUTION
- THE QUOTATIONS OF THE NEW TESTAMENT FROM THE OLD

Johnson, Harrison *see* HISTORY OF NEBRASKA

Johnson, J B *see* HISTORY OF VERNON COUNTY PAST AND PRESENT

Johnson, Jack *see* JACK JOHNSON IN THE RING AND OUT

Johnson, James *see* YORUBA HEATHENISM

Johnson, James B *see* MY LAND

Johnson, James D *see* DETROIT CITY DIRECTORY 1857-58

Johnson, Jana A *see* VALIDATION OF THE MAXIMAL MET PREDICTION EQUATIONS ON THE SCHWINN AIR-DYNE

Johnson, Jay R *see* A SURVEY OF DIVISION 2 ATHLETIC AND PHYSICAL EDUCATION FISCAL TRENDS FOR THE NEXT TWENTY YEARS

Johnson, John *see* PAPERS OF JOHN JOHNSON

Johnson, John J *see* POLITICAL CHANGE IN LATIN AMERICA

Johnson, L *see* SYSTEMS RESEARCH AND INFORMATION SCIENCE

Johnson, Lionel Pigot *see* POEMS

Johnson, Lyndon B *see*
- CRISIS IN PANAMA AND THE DOMINICAN REPUBLIC
- DAILY DIARY OF PRESIDENT JOHNSON (1963-69)
- ISRAEL
- MINUTES AND DOCUMENTS OF THE CABINET MEETINGS OF PRESIDENT LYNDON B. JOHNSON (1963-69)
- THE NATIONAL ECONOMY UNDER PRESIDENT JOHNSON: ADMINISTRATIVE HISTORIES

Johnson, Martin *see* PAPERS

THE JOHNSON NATIONAL DRILLERS JOURNAL – v22-27 1950-55 – 1 – us UMI [620]

JOHNSON NEWS – Johnson, NE. -w. Oct 1892; Oct-Dec 1895; Feb 1896-Mar 1899; Jun 1899; May 1901-Jun 1902; Aug 1902-Aug 1942 – 1 – us NE Hist [071]

Johnson, Osa *see* PAPERS

Johnson, Ovid Frazer, Jr *see* LAW OF MECHANICS' LIENS IN PENNSYLVANIA

JOHNSON RAG – Johnson, NE. 25 Nov 1970- . -w. Lacks scattered issues – 1 – us NE Hist [071]

Johnson, Ralph *see* THE SCHOLARS GUIDE FROM THE ACCIDENCE TO THE UNIVERSITY

Johnson, Richard *see* GRAMMATICAL COMMENTARIES

Johnson, Robert *see* ESSAIES OR RATHER IMPERFECT OFFERS

Johnson, Robert A *see* HISTORY OF THE REFORMATION IN GERMANY

Johnson, Robert F *see* GEOLOGY AND BAUXITE DEPOSITS OF THE CENTRAL RIAU ISLANDS, INDONESIA

Johnson, Robert Flynn *see* AMERICAN PRINTS, 1870-1950

Johnson, Rossal James *see* READINGS IN BUSINESS ADMINISTRATION AND ECONOMICS

Johnson, Roy M *see* OKLAHOMA HISTORY-SOUTH OF THE CANADIAN

Johnson, S Jangaba M *see* WRITINGS OF S. JANGABA M. JOHNSON

Johnson, Samuel *see* THE PLAN OF A DICTIONARY OF THE ENGLISH LANGUAGE

Johnson, Sid S *see* TEXANS WHO WORE GRAY

Johnson, Susan L *see* THE EFFECT OF THREE TRAINING METHODS ON THE TEACHING PREPARATION OF COUNSELOR-TEACHERS IN A RESIDENT ENVIRONMENTAL EDUCATION PROGRAM

Johnson, Susan M *see* THE EFFECT OF MUTUAL CHOICE PLACEMENT ON THE SATISFACTION OF STUDENT AND COOPERATING TEACHERS IN PHYSICAL EDUCATION
Johnson, Thomas Cary *see*
– INTRODUCTION TO CHRISTIAN MISSIONS
– THE LIFE AND LETTERS OF BENJAMIN MORGAN PALMER
– THE LIFE AND LETTERS OF ROBERT LEWIS DABNEY
– VIRGINIA PRESBYTERIANISM AND RELIGIOUS LIBERTY IN COLONIAL AND REVOLUTIONARY TIMES
Johnson, Tom L *see*
– PAPERS
– TOM L. JOHNSON PAPERS, SERIES 1, MS 3651
JOHNSON, TOM L., PAPERS, MS 4021 – (Series 2 of the Tom L. Johnson Papers) – 1901-1909 – 1r – 1 – us Western Res [350]
Johnson, W F *see* HISTORY OF COOPER COUNTY
Johnson, Walter Seely *see* THE CLAUSE COMPROMISSOIRE, ITS VALIDITY IN QUEBEC
Johnson, William *see* JOHNSON'S DIGEST OF NEW YORK CASES, 1799-1836
Johnson, William B *see* THE GOSPEL DEVELOPED THROUGH THE GOVERNMENT AND ORDER OF THE CHURCHES OF JESUS CHRIST
JOHNSON'S CHANCERY APPEALS REPORTS / New York. (State) – (A Pre-NRS title) – v1-7. 1814-23 (all publ) – 42mf – 9 – $63.00 – LLMC 80-001 – us L.L.M.C. [340]
JOHNSON'S DIGEST OF NEW YORK CASES, 1799-1836 / Johnson, William – Philadelphia: E F Backhus. 2nd corr ed. 2v. 1837-38 (all publ) – 15mf – 9 – $22.50 – LLMC 79-520 – us L.L.M.C. [340]
Johnson's Island Military Prison. Johnson's Island, Lake Erie *see* RECORDS
JOHNSON'S READY LEGAL ADVISER. / Chase, George – New York: Johnson, 1880. 308p. LL-1618 – 1 – us L of C Photodup [340]
JOHNSON'S TENNESSEE HARMONY – 1821 – 1 – 5.00 – us Baptist [240]
Johnston, Alexander J *see* JOHNSTON'S REPORTS OF CASES DETERMINED IN THE COURT OF APPEAL OF NEW ZEALAND
Johnston, Ann *see* NEW TECHNOLOGIES AND DEVELOPMENT
Johnston, B D *see* A STUDY OF THE RELATIONSHIP OF "WITHITHNESS" TO ALT-PE AND MONITORING IN MIDDLE SCHOOL PHYSICAL EDUCATION
JOHNSTON BAPTIST CHURCH. EDGEFIELD COUNTY. SOUTH CAROLINA : CHURCH RECORDS – 1875-1914 – 1 – 17.82 – us Baptist [240]
JOHNSTON CITY, ILLINOIS. WILLIAMS PRAIRIE BAPTIST CHURCH – Church Records, 1872-1903. 288p – 1 – $12.96 – us Baptist [240]
Johnston, David E *see* A HISTORY OF MIDDLE NEW RIVER SETTLEMENTS AND CONTIGUOUS TERRITORY
Johnston, David L *see* THE EFFECTS OF FUNCTIONAL ISOMETRIC WEIGHT TRAINING IN CONJUNCTION WITH DYNAMIC WEIGHT TRAINING ON TWO BENCH PRESS MEASUREMENT TESTS
Johnston, Denis Foster *see* ANALYSIS OF SOURCES OF INFORMATION ON THE POPULATION OF THE NAVAHO
Johnston, Edgar Lisle (Ted) *see* MISCELLANEOUS PAPERS, AUTOBIOGRAPHICAL MEMOS, FAMILY CERTIFICATES AND "SOGERINUMU" MAGAZINE OF THE SOGERI HIGH SCHOOL, MAPS AND PHOTOGRAPHS, 1934-1990
JOHNSTON FIRST -GRANITEVILLE GENERAL SIX PRINCIPLE BAPTIST CHURCH. ROHDE ISLAND : CHURCH RECORDS – Organized Jun 20, 1771-Sept 1908 (Foster First (Scituate)merged with Johnston First in 1837) 162p – 1 – us Baptist [240]
Johnston, Frances Benjamin *see*
– THE CARNEGIE SURVEY OF THE ARCHITECTURE OF THE SOUTH
– PAPERS
Johnston, G *see* AN INTRODUCTION TO CONCHOLOGY, OR, ELEMENTS OF THE NATURAL HISTORY OF MOLLUSCUS ANIMALS
Johnston, Graydon *see* THE MARRIAGE LAWS OF NEW YORK STATE
Johnston, H H *see*
– LIBERIA
– LIVINGSTONE AND THE EXPLORATION OF CENTRAL AFRICA
– THE UGANDA PROTECTORATE
Johnston, Harriet L *see*
– PAPERS
Johnston, Harry Hamilton *see* LIBERIA
Johnston, Henry P *see* THE CORRESPONDENCE AND PUBLIC PAPERS OF JOHN JAY
Johnston, Howard Agnew *see*
– THE BEATITUDES OF CHRIST
– BEATITUDES OF CHRIST
– BIBLE CRITICISM AND THE AVERAGE MAN
– MOSES AND THE PENTATEUCH
– STUDIES FOR PERSONAL WORKERS
Johnston, J Stoddard *see* MEMORIAL HISTORY OF LOUISVILLE
Johnston, J W *see* THE ILLUSTRATED SKETCH BOOK AND DIRECTORY OF JEFFERSON CITY AND COLE COUNTY
Johnston, J Wesley *see* THE BAPTISM OF FIRE
Johnston, James *see* MISSIONARY POINTS AND PICTURES
Johnston, James F *see* THE SUSPENDING POWER AND THE WRIT OF HABEAS CORPUS
Johnston, James Finlay Weir *see* THE CHEMISTRY OF COMMON LIFE
Johnston, John Octavius *see* LIFE AND LETTERS OF HENRY PARRY LIDDON, D.D., D.C.L., LL.D., CANON OF ST PAUL'S CATHEDRAL, AND SOMETIME IRELAND PROFESSOR OF EXEGESIS IN THE UNIVERSITY OF OXFORD
Johnston, Julia Harriette *see* THE LIFE OF ADONIRAM JUDSON
Johnston, Kelli D *see* THE RELATIONSHIP BETWEEN BLOOD TESTOSTERONE LEVELS AND BODY COMPOSITION IN PHYSICALLY ACTIVE, YOUNG ADULT MEN
Johnston, Mary *see* THE LONG ROLL
Johnston, R Keigh *see* HUNTING AND HUNTED IN THE BELGIAN CONGO
Johnston, Sir Harry Hamilton *see*
– A HISTORY OF THE COLONIZATION OF AFRICA BY ALIEN RACES
– A SURVEY OF THE ETHNOGRAPHY OF AFRICA AND THE FORMER RACIAL AND TRIBAL MIGRATIONS IN THAT CONTINENT
Johnston, William *see*
– LETTER TO E.T. SMYTH, BENTON COUNTY, AL, 1854
– A PRONOUNCING AND SPELLING DICTIONARY
Johnstone, James *see* MY EXPERIENCES IN MANIPUR AND THE NAGA HILLS
Johnstone, Robert *see* FIRST EPISTLE OF PETER: REVISED TEXT, WITH INTRODUCTION AND COMMENTARY
JOHNSTON'S REPORTS OF CASES DETERMINED IN THE COURT OF APPEAL OF NEW ZEALAND / Johnston, Alexander J – v1-3. 1867-77. Wellington: G Didsbury. 1872-77 (all publ) – 18mf – 9 – $27.00 – LLMC 96-014 – us L.L.M.C. [340]
JOHNSTOWN FREE PRESS – Johnstown, PA. 1901. 1 roll – 13 – $25.00r – us I.M.R. [071]
Johnstown, Pennsylvania *see* MISCELLANEOUS EARLY NEWSPAPERS
Johow, Frederico *see* ESTUDIOS SOBRE LA FLORA DE LAS ISLAS DE JUAN FERNANDEZ...CON UNA INTODUCCION...POR DON ROBERTO POEHLMANN
Johst, Hanns *see*
– AVE EVA
– ICH GLAUBE!
– KUNTERBUNT
– MUTTER
– MUTTER OHNE TOD – DIE BEGEGNUNG
– WECHSLER UND HAENDLER
JOINT ARMY-NAVY INTELLIGENCE STUDIES (JANIS), 1944-1945 / U. S. Strategic Bombing Survey – RG 243. M1169. 20 rolls – 1 – us Nat'l Archives [355]
Joint Committee on Future Status Subcommittees [TTPI (U.S.)] *see* FOURTEEN QUESTIONS
Joint Committee on Future Status [TTPI (U.S.)] *see*
– DRAFT COMPACT OF FREE ASSOCIATION
– REPORT ON 4TH ROUND OF STATUS NEGOTIATIONS
– REPORT ON 7TH ROUND OF STATUS NEGOTIATIONS
– REPORT ON 8TH ROUND OF STATUS NEGOTIATIONS
– REPORT ON THE 3RD ROUND OF STATUS NEGOTIATIONS
– SUMMARY OF FUTURE POLITICAL FUTURE STATUS TALKS
Joint Committee on Future Status [TTPI (U.S.)] Eastern Districts Subcommittee *see*
– HEARINGS IN TRUK, PONAPE AND THE MARSHALL ISLANDS, JUL 1973
– REPORT TO THE 5TH CONGRESS OF MICRONESIA
Joint Committee on Future Status [TTPI (U.S.)] Western Districts Subcommittee *see*
– HEARINGS IN YAP, PALAU AND THE MARIANAS, JUL 1973
– REPORT TO THE 5TH CONGRESS OF MICRONESIA
Joint East African Board *see* ANNUAL REPORT FOR THE YEAR ENDED...OF THE JOINT EAST AFRICAN BOARD FOR PROMOTING THE AGRICULTURAL, COMMERCIAL AND INDUSTRIAL DEVELOPMENT OF KENYA, NYASALAND, TANGANYIKA, UGANDA AND ZANZIBAR
JOINT ECONOMIC PLAN FOR RYUKYU ISLANDS, FY 1962-1966 / Ryukyu Islands. (United States). Office of Plans and Programs, and Department of Plans and Statistics – D 1465 1. 1960 – 9 – ne IDC [338]
JOINT EXPEDITION WITH THE IRAQ MUSEUM AT NUZI / Chiera, E – (American Schools of Oriental Research, v. 1-5). v. 1-5. Paris-Philadelphia. 1927-34 – 9 – ne IDC [930]
JOINT FAO/WHO EXPERT COMMITTEE ON BRUCELLOSIS, FIFTH REPORT : GENEVA, 1970 – 1971 – 76p – it F.A.O. [636]
THE JOINT IMC/CBMS MISSIONARY ARCHIVES / School of Oriental and African Studies, London – (Includes printed guide) – 2,517mf – 9 – ne IDC [240]
JOINT LABOR-MANAGEMENT TRUST FUNDS AND HISTORY OF THE COVERAGE OF NON-PROFIT HOSPITALS / U.S. Senate. Committee on Labor and Public Welfare – 2v in 1bk – 9 – $30.00 set – 0-89941-417-6 – us Hein [360]
JOINT LETTER OF THE ARCHBISHOP AND BISHOPS...ANNOUNCING THE SUPPRESSION BY THE HOLY SEE OF CERTAIN HOLIDAYS – Halifax: Halifax Print. Co., 1893. 03213. (Pre-1900 Canadiana) – 9 – cn C.I.H.M. [240]
JOINT LETTER OF THE SPANISH BISHOPS TO THE BISHOPS OF THE WHOLE WORLD CONCERNING THE WAR IN SPAIN – London, 1938. Fiche W974. (Blodgett Collection of Spanish Civil War Pamphlets) – 9 – us H.U. College Libr [946]
JOINT LETTER OF THE SPANISH BISHOPS TO THE BISHOPS OF THE WHOLE WORLD; THE WAR IN SPAIN – N.Y., 1937. Fiche W973. (Blodgett Collection of Spanish Civil War Pamphlets) – 9 – us H.U. College Libr [946]
Joint Panel on Oceanographic Tables and Standards Editorial Panel *see* PROCESSING OF OCEANOGRAPHIC STATION DATA
JOINT PASSENGER TARIFF TO THE CANADIAN NORTH-WEST, NORTHERN MINNESOTA, DAKOTA AND TRANSCONTINENTAL POINTS VIA CANADIAN ROUTES – Montreal: Canadian Pacific Railway, [1888] – 9 – cn C.I.H.M. [380]
JOINT PRESS READING SERVICE, MOSCOW – Moscow, Mar 1944-31 Dec 1956 – 75r – 1 – us L of C Photodup [073]
JOINT PROCEEDINGS / American Congress n Surveying and Mapping – (Ceased publ. Cont by: Proceedings of the American Society of Photogrammetry fall technical meeting; Proceedings of the American Congress on Surveying and Mapping fall convention. Cont in part in 1980 by: Technical papers of the American Society of Photogrammetry, Fall Technical Meeting and American Congress on Surveying and Mapping; Technical papers on the American Congress on Surveying and Mapping Fall Technical Meeting) – Falls Church. v1. Fall 1979* – 1 – D16404 – us UMI [520]
JOINT PUBLICATIONS RESEARCH SERVICE *see* TRANSDEX
JOINT RESOLUTION REGARDING THE STATUS OF THE TTPI : MESSAGE FROM THE PRESIDENT OF THE U.S., LYNDON B. JOHNSON, TRANSMITTING SAME / U.S. Congress – 90th Congr, 1st Sess, Hse Doc n159, aug 21, 1967. Washington: GPO, 1967 – 1mf – 9 – $1.50 – LLMC 82-100F, Title 33 – us L.L.M.C. [323]
JOINT RESOLUTION TO PROVIDE A CIVIL GOVERNMENT FOR THE TRUST TERRITORY OF THE PACIFIC ISLANDS (TTPI) / US Congress – Hse jnt rept no 391. Washington: GPO, 1948 – 1mf – 9 – $1.50 – LLMC 82-100F Title 96 – us L.L.M.C. [324]
THE JOINT STOCK ACT OF CONNECTICUT, FROM THE REVISED STATUTES. / Connecticut. Laws, Statutes, etc – 3d ed. New Haven: Peck, 1876. 93p. LL-603 – 1 – us L of C Photodup [340]
THE JOINT TRIAL CALENDARS IN THE WESTERN DISTRICT OF MISSOURI / Steinstra, Donna – Washington: FJC, 1985 – 1mf – 9 – $1.50 – LLMC 95-369 – us L.L.M.C. [340]
Jolibois *see* LA HAUTE MARNE ANCIENNE ET MODERNE
JOLIETTE ILLUSTRE: NUMERO SOUVENIR DE SES NOCES D'OR, 1843-93 / Gervais, Albert – Quebec: A. Gervais, 1893?. 03337. (Pre-1900 Canadiana) – 9 – cn C.I.H.M. [971]
JOLIETTE-JOURNAL – Joliette, Canada. 3 dec 1947-14 avr 1965 – 14r – 1 – Can$70.00r – cn Can Microfilming [072]
JOLIETTE-JOURNAL / L'ETOILE DU NORD – Joliette, Canada 21 avr 1965-28 oct 1992 – 60r – 1 – Can$75.00r – cn Can Microfilming [072]
Jolivet, A et al *see* ESQUISSES ALLEMANDES
LA JOLLA BREAKERS – La Jolla, CA. 1906 – 1r – 1 – $50.00 – C03607 – us Library Micro [071]
Jolliffe, Jill *see* THE EAST TIMOR QUESTION, (C1900) 1975-1996
Jollivet, Th. M Ad *see* HISTORIQUE DE LA TRAITE ET DU DROIT DE VISITE
Jolly, John *see* GOLD SPRING DIARY
JOLLY LEAVES – (New York). 1910 – 1 – us A.J.P.C. [830]
Jolowitz, Heimann *see* BIBLIOTHECA AEGYPTIACA
Joly de Maizeroy, P G *see* THEORIE DE LA GUERRE
Joly de Saint-Vallier *see* REFLEXIONS SUR L'ELOGE DE M. DE VOLTAIRE PAR M. D'ALEMBERT
Joly, Monique *see* BIBLIOGRAPHIE ANALYTIQUE DE L'OEUVRE DE MARCEL CLEMENT, LICENCIE ES LETTRES, DIPLOME D'ETUDES SUPERIEURES DE PHILOSOPHIE (SORBONNE)...
JOM (JOURNAL OF METALS) – v26- 1974- – 1,5,6,9 – us UMI [660]
JOM: JOURNAL OF OCCUPATIONAL MEDICINE – (v.21-. 1979- 5,6) – v.10-. 1968- – 1 – us UMI [073]
JOMA: DER MISCHNATRAKTAT VERSOEHNUNGSTAG / Strack, Hermann Leberecht – Berlin: H. Reuther, 1888. 1 fiche – 9 – us A.T.L.A. [270]
Jomelli, N *see* ASTIANATTE
Jomini, A H de *see* PRECIS DE L'ART DE LA GUERRE, OU NOUVEAU TABLEAU ANALYTIQUE DES PRINCIPALES COMBINAISONS DE LA STRATEGIE
JONAH IN FACT AND FANCY / Banks, Edgar J – C.1899. Chicago – 1 – us A.T.L.A. [240]
THE JONAH LEGEND : A SUGGESTION OF INTERPRETATION / Simpson, William – (Includes bibliographical references and index) – London: Grant Richards, 1899 – 1mf – 9 – 0-8370-5264-5 – 1985-3264 – us A.T.L.A. [220]
Jonas, F *see* ANSICHTEN UEBER AESTHETIK UND LITERATUR
Jonas, Fritz *see* SCHILLERS BRIEFE
Jonas, J *see*
– ANNOTATIONES IVSTI IONAE, IN ACTA APOSTOLORVM. CVM INDICE
– DAS SIBEND CAPITTEL DANIELIS VON DES TUERCKEN GOTTES LESTERUNG VND SCHRECKLICHER MOERDEREY MIT VNTERRICHT JUSTI JONE
Jonas, J B E *see* BURG NEIDECK
JONA'S NURSING SCAN IN ADMINISTRATION – v1- . 1986- – 1,5,6,9 – us UMI [073]
Jonathan Brierley *see* SIDELIGHTS ON RELIGION
JONATHAN EDWARDS / Allen, Alexander V G – Boston: Houghton, Mifflin, 1889 – 1mf – us A.T.L.A. [240]
JONATHAN EDWARDS : A RETROSPECT / ed by Gardiner, H Norman – Boston: Houghton, Miffling, 1901 – 1mf – us A.T.L.A. [240]

JONATHAN SWIFT UND G. CH. LICHTENBERG : ZWEI SATIRIKER DES ACHTZEHNTEN JAHRHUNDERTS / Meyer, Richard M – Berlin: W Hertz, 1886 – 1r – 1 – us U.W. Library [410]

DIE JONATHAN'SCHE PENTATEUCH-UEBERSETZUNG IN IHREM VERHAELTNISSE ZUR HALACHA : EIN BEITRAG ZUR GESCHICHTE DER AELTESTEN SCHRIFTEXEGESE / Gronemann, S – (Includes bibliographical references) – Leipzig: Robert Friese, 1879 – 1mf – 9 – 0-8370-3404-3 – 1985-1404 – us A.T.L.A. [220]

Jonckers, D *see* ORGANISATION SOCIO-ECONOMIQUE DES MINYANKA DU MALI

Jones *see*
- HISTORY OF LINCOLN, ONEIDA AND VILAS COUNTIES
- HISTORY OF WOOD COUNTY

Jones, A G *see* NATIVE RELIGIONS AND CHRISTIANITY (CCC204)

Jones, A H M *see* CITIES OF THE EASTERN ROMAN PROVINCES

Jones, Adam Leroy *see* EARLY AMERICAN PHILOSOPHERS

Jones, Arthur E *see* THE AULNEAU COLLECTION, 1734-45

Jones, Bassett *see* HERM'AELOGIUM: OR, AN ESSAY AT THE RATIONALITY OF THE ART OF SPEAKING

Jones, Burr W *see* THE LAW OF EVIDENCE IN CIVIL CASES

Jones, C *see* THE LIVING DIALECT OF CARDINGTON, SHROPSHIRE

Jones, Charles C *see* THE RELIGIOUS INSTRUCTION OF THE NEGROES IN THE UNITED STATES

Jones, Charles C, Jr *see*
- BIOGRAPHICAL SKETCHES OF THE DELEGATES FROM GEORGIA TO THE CONTINENTAL CONGRESS
- THE HISTORY OF GEORGIA

Jones, Charles Henry *see* LIVINGSTONE'S AND STANLEY'S TRAVELS IN AFRICA..

Jones, Charles P *see* AN APPEAL TO THE SONS OF AFRICA

Jones, Clement J *see* MASS MEDIA CODES OF ETHICS AND COUNCILS

Jones, D *see* A JOURNAL OF TWO VISITS MADE TO SOME NATIONS OF INDIANS ON THE WEST SIDE OF THE RIVER OHIO, IN THE YEARS 1772 AND 1773

Jones, D N *see* PARROTS AND SUNFLOWERS IN NORTHERN NEW SOUTH WALES

Jones, David Lewis *see* BRITISH AND IRISH BIOGRAPHIES 1840-1940

Jones, Dwight Arven *see*
- THE BUSINESS CORPORATIONS LAW.
- THE BUSINESS CORPORATIONS LAW...AND OTHER LAWS CONCERNING BUSINESS CORPORATIONS IN THE STATE OF NEW YORK
- THE LAW AND PRACTICE UNDER THE STATUTES IN THE STATE OF NEW YORK
- A TREATISE ON THE CONSTRUCTION OR INTERPRETATION OF COMMERCIAL AND TRADE CONTRACTS
- A TREATISE ON THE NEGLIGENCE OF MUNICIPAL CORPORATIONS

Jones, Ebenezer *see* STUDIES OF SENSATION AND EVENT

Jones, Ernest *see* PAPERS ON PSYCHO-ANALYSIS

Jones, F *see* ANALYSE STYLISTIQUE DE QUELQUES OEUVRES DU PAYS DOGON SUIVIE D'UN ESSAI D'ANALYSE SEMANTIQUE

Jones, Frederick Augustus *see*
- THE DATES OF GENESIS
- DATES OF GENESIS: A COMPARISON

Jones, Garth N *see*
- DEVELOPMENT OF ADMINISTRATIVE AND MANAGEMENT PERSONNEL FOR INDONESIA'S PUBLIC SERVICE: APPROACHES AND PROBLEMS
- EDUCATION FOR GOVERNMENT ADMINISTRATION IN RURAL INDONESIA: SOME CONSIDERATIONS
- SOME CRITICAL AREAS CONCERNING TECHNICAL ASSISTANCE IN PUBLIC ADMINISTRATION FOR INDONESIA

Jones, Gilmer Andrew *see* JONES' QUIZZER, CONSISTING OF NORTH CAROLINA SUPREME COURT QUESTIONS AND ANSWERS, FROM SEPTEMBER TERM, 1898, TO AUGUST TERM, 1920

Jones, H V *see* CATALOGUE OF PARLIAMENTARY PAPERS RELATING TO AFRICA

Jones, Harold W *see* ANTI-ACHITOPHEL

Jones, Harry W *see* WOMAN'S PIETY AND ITS BEAUTY

Jones, Henry Arthur *see*
- THE LIARS
- REPRESENTATIVE PLAYS, BY HENRY ARTHUR JONES

Jones, Hugh *see* AN ACCIDENCE TO THE ENGLISH TONGUE

Jones, Idwal *see* THE VINEYARD

Jones, J A *see* THE BUNHILL MEMORIALS

Jones, J E *see* HISTORY OF COLUMBIA COUNTY

Jones, James *see* GENERAL LEGAL FORMS AND PRECEDENTS, FOR ORDINARY USE AND WITH EXPLANATORY CHANGES ADAPTED TO SPECIAL CASES.

Jones, James Edward *see* THE IMPLEMENTATION OF A PERENNIAL PROGRAM OF EVANGELISM

Jones, Jeffrey R *see* COLONIZATION AND ENVIRONMENT

Jones, Jesse Henry *see* KNOW THE TRUTH

Jones, John *see* PRACTICAL PHONOGRAPHY

Jones, John Cynddylan *see* PRIMEVAL REVELATION

Jones, John Daniel *see* THE GLORIOUS COMPANY OF THE APOSTLES

Jones, John David Rheinallt *see* THE R.J. COLLECTION

Jones, John G *see* A CONCISE HISTORY OF THE INTRODUCTION OF PROTESTANTISM INTO MISSISSIPPI AND THE SOUTHWEST

Jones, John Paul *see*
- PAPERS
- PAPERS OF JOHN PAUL JONES

Jones, John Peter *see*
- INDIA'S PROBLEM, KRISHNA OR CHRIST
- THE MODERN MISSIONARY CHALLENGE

Jones, John T *see* JOURNEAUX DES SIEGES...ESPAGNE

Jones, Leonard Augustus *see*
- FORMS IN CONVEYANCING, COMPRISING PRECEDENTS FOR ORDINARY USE, AND CLAUSES ADAPTED TO SPECIAL AND UNUSUAL CASES
- FRAUDULENT MORTGAGES OF MERCHANDISE
- LEGAL FORMS; INCLUDING FORMS IN CONVEYANCING, TOGETHER WITH GENERAL LEGAL AND BUSINESS FORMS.
- THE LEGAL NATURE OF THE ROLLING-STOCK OF RAILROADS
- A TREATISE ON THE LAW OF LANDLORD AND TENANT.
- A TREATISE ON THE LAW OF LIENS, COMMON LAW, STATUTORY, EQUITABLE AND MARITIME
- A TREATISE ON THE LAW OF MORTGAGES OF REAL PROPERTY
- A TREATISE ON THE LAW OF MORTGAGES ON PERSONAL PROPERTY
- A TREATISE ON THE LAW OF PLEDGES, INCLUDING COLLATERAL SECURITIES

Jones, Lottie E *see* HISTORY OF VERMILION COUNTY

Jones, Mary *see* THE STORY OF MARY JONES AND HER BIBLE

Jones, Matt B *see* HISTORY OF THE TOWN OF WAITSFIELD

Jones, Philip Lovering *see* A RESTATEMENT OF BAPTIST PRINCIPLES

Jones, Pomroy *see* ANNALS OF AND RECOLLECTIONS OF ONEIDA COUNTY

JONES' QUIZZER, CONSISTING OF NORTH CAROLINA SUPREME COURT QUESTIONS AND ANSWERS, FROM SEPTEMBER TERM, 1898, TO AUGUST TERM, 1920 / Jones, Gilmer Andrew – Atlanta, Foote & Davies Co., 1921 280 p. LL-925 – 1 – us L of C Photodup [340]

Jones, Richard *see* THE GROWTH OF THE IDYLLS OF THE KING

Jones, Rowland *see*
- THE CIRCLES OF GOMER, OR AN ESSAY TOWARDS AN INVESTIGATION AND INTRODUCTION TO THE ENGLISH, AS AN UNIVERSAL LANGUAGE
- HEROGLYFIC
- THE ORIGIN OF LANGUAGE AND NATIONS

Jones, Rufus M *see*
- A BOY'S RELIGION FROM MEMORY
- ELI AND SYBIL JONES
- THE QUAKERS IN THE AMERICAN COLONIES
- SPIRITUAL REFORMERS IN THE 16TH AND 17TH CENTURIES
- STUDIES IN MYSTICAL RELIGION

Jones, Samuel Arthur *see* COLLECTANEA THOMAS CARLYLE, 1821-1855

Jones, Samuel M *see* "GOLDEN RULE" PAPERS 1896-1904

Jones, Samuel Porter *see*
- LIGHTNING FLASHES AND THUNDERBOLTS
- SERMONS AND SAYINGS, FIRST SERIES
- SERMONS BY SAM JONES AND SAM SMALL
- SERMONS, WITH A HISTORY OF HIS LIFE BY THEODORE M. SMITH

Jones, Scervant *see* ARGUMENTS FOR AND AGAINST A BAPTIST THEOLOGICAL SCHOOL AT WILLIAMSBURG, VA

Jones, Spencer *see* ENGLAND AND THE HOLY SEE

Jones, T F E *see* THE GOLD COAST AND THE FANTIS

Jones, T G *see* THE BAPTISTS

Jones, T Percy *see* FIRMILIAN: OR, THE STUDENT OF BADAJOZ

Jones, T R *see*
- A MONOGRAPH OF THE ENTOMOSTRACA OF THE CRETACEOUS FORMATION OF ENGLAND
- A MONOGRAPH OF THE TERTIARY ENTOMOSTRACA OF ENGLAND

Jones, T R et al *see* A MONOGRAPH OF THE FORAMINIFERA OF THE CRAG

Jones, Thomas *see* THE BRITISH LANGUAGE IN ITS LUSTRE, OR A COPIOUS DICTIONARY OF WELSH AND ENGLISH

Jones, W *see* A TREATISE ON THE ART OF MUSIC

Jones, W F R S *see* THE PRACTICE OF INTEREST

Jones, William *see*
- A GRAMMAR OF THE PERSIAN LANGUAGE
- THE JUBILEE MEMORIAL OF THE RELIGIOUS TRACT SOCIETY
- PHYSIOLOGICAL DISQUISITIONS

Jones, William Caswell *see* A PRACTICAL TREATISE UPON THE JURISDICTION OF, AND PRACTICE IN, THE COUNTY AND PROBATE COURTS OF ILLINOIS.

Jones, William K *see* NOTES ON THE HISTORY AND THE MATERIAL CULTURE OF THE TONKAWA INDIANS

Jones, WN *see* THE NORTH CAROLINA MANUAL OF LAW AND FORMS FOR JUSTICES OF THE PEACE, COUNTY OFFICERS, LAWYERS, AND BUSINESS MEN.

Jonesborough, Maine. Jonesborough and Addison Baptist Church *see* RECORDS

JONES-GOLDSMITH-JOHNSON FAMILY PAPERS, 1745-1929 – Ed. by Thomas J. Rieder. Related Guide Book included in purchase of set of 4 rolls; may be purchased separately from publisher – 1 – us Ohio Hist [975]

HET JONG LEVEN – Amsterdam. v1-9. 1910-1920 – 25mf – ne IDC [949]

HET JONG LEVEN – v. 1-9. Amsterdam. 1910-20. BJ-261-51 1 – 9 – ne IDC [073]

LA JONGLEUSE: LEGENDE CANADIENNE / Casgrain, Henri-Raymond – Montreal: Beauchemin & Valois, 1884. 02053. Pre-1900 Canadiana) – 9 – cn C.I.H.M. [830]

JONKOPINGSPOSTEN – Jonkoping, Sweden. 1865-1978 – 530r – 1 – sw Kungliga [072]

JONKOPINGSPOSTEN – (Varnamotidningen, 1979-81) – Jonkoping, Sweden. 1979- – 1 – sw Kungliga [072]

Jonson, Ben *see* THE ENGLISH GRAMMAR

Jonson, Linnea M *see* SELF-PERCEPTION AND MOTOR PROFICIENCY OF HEARING-IMPAIRED CHILDREN

Jonssen, F *see*
- EDDA SNORRA STURLUSONAR
- DEN NORSK-ISLANDSKE SKJALDEDIGTNING

JOODSCH HULPBETOON – Amsterdam. v1. 1933 – 4mf – ne IDC [949]

HET JOODSCH IN NEDERLAND / Voorzanger, J L & Polak, J E – Amsterdam. 1915 – 4mf – ne IDC [430]

JOODSCH ZAANDAM – Zaandam. Nos 1-3. 1939-1940 – 1mf – 9 – ne IDC [949]

DE JOODSCHE GEMEENTE VAN AMERSFOORT / Zwarts, J – Amersfoort. 1927. BJ-262-76 1 – 9 – ne IDC [949]

DE JOODSCHE GIDS – Amsterdam. v1-3. 1928-1930 – 27mf – ne IDC [949]

DE JOODSCHE JEUGDKRANT – Amsterdam. v1-7. 1928-1935 – 158mf – ne IDC [949]

HET JOODSCHE KOMPAS – Rotterdam. v1(1-7). 1932-1933 – 1mf – ne IDC [949]

DE JOODSCHE KRONIEK – Amsterdam. v1. 1912 – 22mf – 9 – ne IDC [949]

DE JOODSCHE MIDDENSTANDER – Amsterdam. v1-9. 1931-1940 – 155mf – ne IDC [949]

DE JOODSCHE PRINS – Amsterdam, 25 July 1912-7 Aug 1913 – 11mf – ne IDC [949]

DE JOODSCHE STAAT – Amsterdam. Nos 1-14. 1933-1934 – 2mf – 9 – ne IDC [949]

DE JOODSCHE STEM – Rotterdam. Nos 1-3. 1929 – 1mf – 9 – ne IDC [949]

DE JOODSCHE VOLKSSTEM – Amsterdam. Nos 1-3. 1918 – 1mf – 9 – ne IDC [949]

JOODSCHE VRIENDENKRING – (Missing: 1931 v1(1,2); 1936 v6(10-12); 1937 v7(1-7), 10-12)) – Venlo. v1-8. 1931-1939 – 13mf – 9 – ne IDC [949]

DE JOODSCHE WACHTER – Amsterdam. v1-57. 1905-1966(4) – 485mf – 9 – ne IDC [949]

DE JOODSCHE WACHTER – Rotterdam. v. 1-36. Jan. 5, 1905-May 3, 1940. Johore Bahrue. 1957-1966 – 1 – us NY Public [073]

HET JOODSCHE WEEKBLAD – Amsterdam. v1-3. 1941-1943 – 35mf – 9 – ne IDC [949]

HET JOODSCHE WEEKBLAD – (Missing: V1(9)) – Amsterdam. v1(1-10). 1940 – 2mf – 9 – ne IDC [072]

DE JOODSE GEMEENTE TE GRONINGEN / Mendels, I – Ed. 2. Groningen. 1910. BJ-262-38 1 – 9 – ne IDC [956]

Jordan *see*
- AL-JARIDAH AL-RASMIYAH.
- SUMMARY OF THE SEVEN YEAR PLAN FOR ECONOMIC DEVELOPMENT, 1964-1970

Jordan, A *see*
- BREVIARIUM PLANTARUM NOVARUM
- ICONES AD FLORAM EUROPAE NOVO FUNDAMENTO INSTAURANDAM SPECTANTES

Jordan, A. *see*
- OBSERVATIONS SUR PLUSIEURS PLANTES NOUVELLES, RARES, OU CRITIQUES DE LA FRANCE
- PUGILLUS PLANTARUM NOVARUM PRAESERTIUM GALLICARUM

Jordan. Arab Bank Limited *see* ANNUAL REPORT OF THE BOARD OF DIRECTORS. BALANCE SHEET AND PROFIT/LOSS ACCOUNT FOR THE YEARS 1947-1977

Jordan, C F *see* AMAZONIAN RAIN FOREST

Jordan. Central Bank *see*
- ANNUAL REPORT
- ANNUAL REPORTS
- BALANCE OF PAYMENTS, 1964-1976
- FINANCIAL POLICY IN JORDAN

Jordan. Chamber of Commerce and Industry *see*
- INDUSTRY OF JORDAN; INCLUDING A CLASSIFIED DIRECTORY, INDUSTRIAL FIRMS AND PRODUCTS AND BASIC INFORMATION ABOUT JORDAN
- JORDAN ECONOMY: SPECIAL ECONOMIC BULLETIN PREPARED ON THE OCCASION OF THE FIFTH ANNUAL MEETING OF THE ARAB CHAMBERS OF COMMERCE

Jordan. Chamber of Commerce and Industry. Amman *see* JORDANIAN ECONOMY IN 1954; A SPECIAL ECONOMIC BULLETIN ON THE OCCASION OF THE 4TH

Jordan. Chamber of Commerce and Industry. Economic progress in the Hashemite Kingdom of Jordan. Amman *see* REMARKS AND STATISTICS ON THE OCCASION OF THE THIRD CONFERENCE OF THE CHAMBER OF COMMERCE

Jordan, Claude *see* LA CLEF DU CABINET DES PRINCES DE L'EUROPE

Jordan. Currency Board *see* REPORT

Jordan. Currency Control *see* BALANCE OF PAYMENTS

Jordan, D S *see*
- THE FISHES OF NORTH AND MIDDLE AMERICA
- THE FISHES OF SAMOA
- THE GENERA OF FISHES FROM LINNAEUS TO CUVIER, 1758-1833
- GUIDE TO THE STUDY OF FISHES

Jordan, D S et al *see* A CATALOGUE OF THE FISHES OF JAPAN

Jordan, David Starr *see*
- PAPERS
- STANDETH GOD WITHIN THE SHADOW

Jordan de Asso, Ignacio *see*
- CARTAS ERUDITAS DE ALGUNOS LITERATOS ESPANOLES
- INSTITUCIONES DEL DERECHO CIVIL DE CASTILLA

Jordan. Department of Co-operative Societies *see* ANNUAL REPORT OF THE DEPARTMENT OF CO-OPERATIVE SOCIETIES, JORDAN

Jordan. Department of Customs *see* ANNUAL REPORT CUSTOMS, EXCISE, TRADE AND INDUSTRY

Jordan. Department of Land and Surveys *see* ANNUAL REPORT

Jordan. Department of Statistics *see*
- ANALYSIS OF THE POPULATION STATISTICS OF JORDAN
- CENSUS OF AGRICULTURE, 1953
- EXTERNAL TRADE STATISTICS
- FIRST CENSUS OF POPULATION AND HOUSING, 18 NOV 1961
- FLOW OF GOODS IN THE JORDAN ECONOMY
- THE JORDAN ECONOMY: SOME ECONOMIC INDICATORS
- MANUFACTURING INDUSTRIAL CENSUS, 1967
- MANUFACTURING INDUSTRY IN JORDAN: REPORT ON THE INDUSTRIAL CENSUS OF 1959
- THE NATIONAL ACCOUNTS
- POPULATION AND LABOUR FORCE IN THE AGRICULTURE SECTOR, 1967
- POPULATION CENSUS AND INTERNAL MIGRATION FOR AMMAN, JERUSALEM, ZARQA RUSEIFA, IRBID AND AQABA, 1967
- REPORT ON AGRICULTURE CENSUS, 1965
- REPORT ON LABOUR AND INDUSTRIAL SURVEY IN THE KINGDOM (JORDAN)
- STATISTICAL YEAR BOOK
- SURVEY OF AGRICULTURAL LAND IRRIGATED BY ARTESIAN WELLS

Jordan. Development Bank *see* ECONOMIC DEVELOPMENT IN JORDAN: FRAMEWORK AND TARGETS, 1960/1969

Jordan. Development Board *see*
- 5 YEAR PHASED PROGRAM OF ECONOMIC DEVELOPMENT AS REVISED
- 5 YEAR PROGRAM FOR ECONOMIC DEVELOPMENT 1962-1967
- ANNUAL REPORT OF THE DEVELOPMENT BOARD, JORDAN
- FIVE-YEAR PHASED PROGRAMME OF ECONOMIC DEVELOPMENT
- INVESTMENT OPPORTUNITIES UNDER THE SEVEN YEAR PLAN 1964-1970
- SEVEN YEAR PLAN FOR ECONOMIC DEVELOPMENT OF JORDAN, 1964-1970
- SEVEN YEAR PROGRAM FOR ECONOMIC DEVELOPMENT, 1964-70

THE JORDAN ECONOMY: SOME ECONOMIC INDICATORS / Jordan. Department of Statistics – 2v. 1960 65-1967. BNE-9772 1 – 9 – ne IDC [310]

JORDAN ECONOMY: SPECIAL ECONOMIC BULLETIN PREPARED ON THE OCCASION OF THE FIFTH ANNUAL MEETING OF THE ARAB CHAMBERS OF COMMERCE / Jordan. Chamber of Commerce and Industry – 1955. BNE-9747/1 – 9 – ne IDC [956]

Jordan, Frank C *see* ROSTER OF PUBLIC OFFICIALS OF CALIFORNIA

Jordan, H *see*
- ARMENISCHE IRENAEUSFRAGMENTE (T.U.U. 3-36/3)
- DIE BINNENMOLLUSKEN DER NOERDLICH GEMAESSIGTEN LAENDER VON EUROPA UND ASIEN UND DER ARKTISCHEN LAENDER

Jordan, Horst W *see* DER EINFLUSS DES SUPREME COURT AUF DIE POLITIK DER U.S.A. VON 1789 BIS ZUM ENDE DES ZWEITEN WELTKRIEGS.

Jordan. Industrial Development Bank *see* ANNUAL REPORT AND BALANCE SHEET

Jordan, J W *see*
- GENEALOGICAL AND PERSONAL HISTORY OF ALLEGHENY VALLEY
- GENEALOGICAL AND PERSONAL HISTORY OF FAYETTE COUNTY

Jordan, John W *see*
- HISTORY OF DELAWARE COUNTY AND ITS PEOPLE
- HISTORY OF FAYETTE COUNTY, PENNSYLVANIA

Jordan. Jordan Development Bank *see* DIRECTORS ANNUAL REPORT

Jordan, K *see* DIE BISTUMSGRUENDUNEN HEINRICHS DES LOEWEN (MGH SCHRIFTEN..: 3.BD)

Jordan. Kuwait fund for Arab Economic Development *see* LOAN AGREEMENT (JERUSALEM POWER PROJECT) BETWEEN JORDAN AND KUWAIT FUND

Jordan, Lewis G *see* NEGRO BAPTIST HISTORY

Jordan, Louis Henry *see* MODERNISM IN ITALY

Jordan, Mary C *see* A COMPARISON OF INTERMITTENT EXERCISE AND RELAXATION VERSUS STEADY STATE EXERCISE ON FITNESS LEVELS AND ATTITUDES IN SEVENTH GRADE GIRLS

Jordan. Ministry of Economy *see*
- CENSUS OF MINING AND MANUFACTURING INDUSTRIES IN JORDAN, 1954
- TABLES ON AGRICULTURAL STATISTICS

Jordan. Ministry of Finance *see*
- BUDGET LAW
- REPORT

Jordan. Ministry of National Economy *see* EAST JORDAN VALLEY: A SOCIAL AND ECONOMIC SURVEY, 1961

Jordan. National Planning Council *see* THREE YEAR DEVELOPMENT PLAN 1973-1975

THE JORDAN OLIVE OIL INDUSTRY / U.S. Department of State – A study made at the request of the Jordan Government by provision of TCA Point IV. 1953. BNE-9787 1 – 9 – ne IDC [634]

Jordan, Ronald *see* BODENNUTZUNG IN VENEZUELA

Jordan. U.N. Dept. of Economic and Social Affairs *see* ORGANIZATION AND ADMINISTRATION OF SOCIAL WELFARE PROGRAMMES, A SERIES OF COUNTRY STUDIES

Jordan. U.N. Development Programme *see* GENERAL REPORT ON THE GROUND-WATER INVESTIGATION OF THE AZRAQ BASIN PREPARED FOR THE GOVERNMENT OF JORDAN

Jordan. U.S. Operations Mission to Jordan *see*
- ANNUAL REPORT OF TECHNICAL SERVICE FOR ECONOMIC DEVELOPMENT AND TECHNICAL SERVICE FOR PUBLIC WORKS
- A REPORT TO THE KINGDOM OF JORDAN AND THE GOVERNMENT OF THE UNITED STATES OF AMERICA ON THE JOINT POINT 4 ACTIVITIES

Jordan. Unrwa *see* JORDAN-VALLEY AGRICULTURAL ECONOMIC SURVEY

JORDAN VALLEY EXPRESS – Jordan Valley, OR. -w. 17 May 1918-19 Feb 1925. 1 roll – 1 – us U.O. Library [071]

Jordan, W *see* W.J. AGAINST J.W.

Jordan, Wilhelm *see*
- LIEBE WAS DU LIEBEN DARFST
- SCHAUM
- SEIN ZWILLINGSBRUDER
- TAUSCH ENTTAEUSCHT

Jordan, William George *see*
- BIBLICAL CRITICISM AND MODERN THOUGHT
- PROPHETIC IDEAS AND IDEALS:...PROPHETIC LITERATURE OF THE HEBREW PEOPLE

JORDANIAN ECONOMY IN 1954; A SPECIAL ECONOMIC BULLETIN ON THE OCCASION OF THE 4TH / Jordan. Chamber of Commerce and Industry. Amman – annual meeting of the Arab Chambers of Commerce. 1954. BNE-9749 1 – 9 – ne IDC [380]

JORDAN-VALLEY AGRICULTURAL ECONOMIC SURVEY / Jordan. Unrwa – Oct 1954. BNE-9816 1 – 9 – ne IDC [630]

JORDBRUKARNAS FORENINGSBLAD – Stockholm, Sweden. 1930-70 – 115r – 1 – sw Kungliga [330]

Jorden, W *see* DAS CLUNIAZENSISCHE TOTENGEDAECHTNISWESEN (910-954)

JORDON HIGH SCHOOL YEARBOOK – Trail Blazer, Long Beach, CA. 1936-92 – 11r – 1 – $550.00 – R60011 – us Library Micro [370]

Jordon, William J *see* WILLIAM J. JORDAN PAPERS, MS P.P.

Jorge, Eduardo F *see* INDUSTRIA Y CONCENTRACION ECONOMICA

JORGE RICARDO BEJARANO NARINO, SU VIDA SUS INFORTUNIOS, SU TALLA HISTORICA / Bayle, Constantino – Madrid: Razon y Fe, 1939 – 1 – sp Bibl Santa Ana [946]

Jorgensen, A D *see* DEN NORDISKE KIRKES

Jorgensen, Arlo G *see* A NEW HYDROSTATIC METHOD

Jorgensen, Simon Emanuel *see* FOLK OG KIRKE PAA MADAGASKAR

Joriaen Ketel *see* HEILSAME LEERE ENDE NUTTE ONDERWYSINGE VAN ENEN GODVRUCHTIGEN MAN SIJN KYNDER

Joriaensz, Thijs *see*
- EEN CHRISTELIJCKE SENTBRIEF, GESCHREUEN WTER GEUANCKENISSE
- EEN CHRISTELIJCKE SENTBRIEF, GESCHREUEN WTER GEUANCKNISSE...WAARACHTER NOG EEN SENTBRIEF EN EEN LIEDEKEN
- EEN CHRISTELIJCKE SENTBRIEF, VAN DE SENDINGHE, INLEYDINGHE ENDE COEMSTE JESU CHRISTI IN DESER WERELT

Joris, David *see*
- D'ALDERCHRISTELICSTE RELIGION ODER CERIMONIEN DIE MEN SACRAMENTLIJCKEN TER BETERINGE DES LICHAEMS CHRISTI INDER GHEMEENTEN BRUYCKEN SAL. ANDER MAEL VERBETERT ENDE GHEMEERDERT VAN DEN AUTHEUR SELUE
- ANTWOORT VNDE ONDERRICHT D.J. OF DER WYSEN WIJSHEYT ODER MENSCHELIJCKE GHELEERTHEYDT NIET NUTLIJCK ODER NOOTWENDICH SY VOOR DEN GHELOOUIGHEN. DIE H. GODTLIJCKE SCHRIFT TE BETH TE VERSTAEN, ALS SOMMIGHE MEENEN?
- CATECHESIS DAT IS, ONDERWIJSLICK GESPRECK, TUSSCHEN VADER VNDE SOON
- CHRISTELIJCKE WAERSCHOUWINGHE. DATMENT NIEMANT OM SIJN GHELOOF EN BEHOORT TE BELEYDIGHEN NOCH TE VERVOLGEN, VEELE MIN TE DOODEN
- CHRISTLIJCKE SENDTBRIEUEN, INHOLDENDE SEER VEELE VNDE VERSCHEYDENE SCHOONE GODTLIJCKE VERMANINGHEN VNDE ONDERRICHTINGHEN
- A COLLECTION OF 16TH CENTURY MANUSCRIPTS, MANY OF WHICH HAVE NEVER APPEARED IN PRINT
- A COLLECTION OF TRACTATEN
- HET DERDE BOECK DER CHRISTLIJCKER SENDBRIEVEN
- ERNSTELIJCK KLAGE, LEER VNDE ONDERWYSINGHE, OUER DEN NYDIGHEN BLOETDORSTIGHEN AARDT BELIALS YEMANDEN OM T'GELOOF OF DIE WETH HAERDER CONSCIENTIEN TE MOGEN VERVOLGEN ODER TE DOODEN 1544
- EEN GODTLIJCKE ANTWOORDT VNDE CORT ONDERWIJS
- HANDT BOECXKEN: INHOLDENDE VELE GODLIJCKE TROUHERTIGHE VADERLIJCKE VERMANINGHEN VNDE LEERINGEN
- EEN NOOTWENDICH VERMANEN VNDE BEDACHTE REDEN, ALLEN GHOETWILLIGHEN IN EEN OPSIEN TER BETERINGE VOORGESCHREUEN
- ONSCHULDT DAUIDS JORIS. GEDAEN VNDE GEPRESENTEERT AN DIE WOLGEBORENE VROUW, VROUW ANNA, GHEBORENE GRAUINNE VAN OLDENBURCH
- ONSCHULDT DAUIDS JORISZ. GEDAEN VNDE GEPRESENTEERT AN DIE WOLGEBORENE VROUW, VROUW ANNA, GHEBORENE GRAUINNE VAN OLDENBURCH INT JAER 1540
- ONTDECKINGE VAN DAT PUNCT UNDE DIE REDEN ONS HEEREN CHRISTI JESU WOORDT: VAN DIE REIN VAN HERTEN SYN
- SEER SCHOONE AENWYSINGEN VNDE GRONDIGE ONTDECKINGEN VAN DIE VERBORGHEN WYSHEYDT GODES
- EN SUYUERLIJCKE BEWIJSREDEN VAN GODES WOORT
- HET TWEEDE BOECK DER CHRISTLIJCKER SENDBRIEUEN
- DAT TWEEDE HANDT-BOECXKEN. DEN INNERLIJCKEN WTTRECK OF GEESTELIJCKE PELGRIMAGIE, CORTELIJCK WTGHESPROKEN
- TWONDER-BOECK: WAER IN DAT VAN DER WERLDT AEN VERSLOTEN GHEOPENBAERT IS. OPT NIEUW GHECORRIGEERT VNDE VERMEERDERT BY DEN AUTHEUR SELUE
- TWONDERBOECK. WIE EEN DIE ICK, SEYT DIE HERE, SENDEN SAL ONTFANGT IN MINEN NAEM, DY ONTFANGT MY
- VAN DIE AART, BLINDTHEYT, DWALINGHE VNDE DUYSTERNISSE DESER ARGE BOOSE WERLT
- VAN DIE RECHTE WARE KENTENISSE CHRISTI VNDE KRAFT DES ALDERHEYLICHSTEN GHELOOFS
- VAN DIE VREEMDE TONGHEN OF TALEN DER MENSCHEN, AEN V MYNE KINDEREN VERSCHREUEN
- VERCLARINGHE VANT VADER ONSE. OP EEN NIEUW WEDER MET ALDER NEERSTICHEYT DEURSIEN
- VERKLARINGHE DER SCHEPPENISSEN AN V MIJN BEMINDE KINDEREN VNDE GHEBROEDERS
- WAERACHTIGE AENWYSINGHE VNDE CLAER VERHAEL VAN DIE WEDERBRENGHINGHE DES MENSCHEN
- WAERSCHOUWINGHE VOOR DEN DACH DES HEEREN

LA JORNADA – Mexico City, Mexico. 1991 – 12r – 1 – us L of C Photodup [072]

JORNADA HEROICA DEL PUEBLO Y PARA EL PUEBLO : DIEZ Y SIETE DE OCTUBRE – [Buenos Aires?, 1949?] – 1 – CSUXAHZ7417-B – us Hoover Inst Photo [972]

JORNADAS DE EDUCACION ESPECIAL. 1970 / Centro de Educacion Especial – Caceres: Tip. Extremadura, 1971 – 1 – sp Bibl Santa Ana [370]

O JORNAL – Lisbon. No.14-250, 1 Aug 1975-1 Feb 1980. Incomplete. (Portuguese Revolution of 1974. Newspapers from Portugal publ. from 21 Feb 1971 to 15 Feb 1980, collected and filmed by University of Wisconsin-Madison libraries.) – 1 – us U.W. Library [072]

O JORNAL – Paraiba do Norte, 20 Nov 1923-23 Dec 1924 – 1,5,6 – bl Biblioteca [072]

O JORNAL – Rio de Janeiro, 17 Jun 1919-Dec 1921; Jan-Jun, Oct-Dec 1922; Jan 1923-28 Apr 1974 – 1,5,6 – bl Biblioteca [072]

O JORNAL : SEMANARIO DA GENTE ACREANA – Rio Branco, Acre. 5 Out 1974; 5 Set 1977-Jun 1979; Out 1979-Jun 1980; Dez 1980; Abr 1981; Jul-Set 1981; Nov 1982 – 1,5,6 – bl Biblioteca [072]

JORNAL A MEMORIA – Rio Branco, Acre. 6 Ago-7 Set 1985 – 1,5,6 – bl Biblioteca [072]

O JORNAL BAPTISTA : ORGAO DA CONVENSAO BAPTISTA BRASILEIRA – Manaus, Amazonas. 24-31 Maio, Nov 1928; Out, Dez 1929; Jan, Abr, Jul 1930; Set 1931; Abr 1934; 4 Ago 1938 – 1,5,6 – bl Biblioteca [072]

O JORNAL BATISTA – Brazil. 1901-20, 1944, 1947 – 1 – 302.19 – us Baptist [240]

JORNAL CORRENTE *see*
- DIARIO DE PERNAMBUCO
- ESTADO DE MINAS
- JORNAL DO BRASIL
- JORNAL DO COMMERCIO
- SUPLEMENTO LITERARIO DO MINAS GERAIS

JORNAL CORRENTE. O MONITOR *see* O MONITOR CAMPISTA

JORNAL DA CIDADE – Belo Horizonte, Brazil. 1976-78 – 1 – bl Biblioteca [072]

JORNAL DA LABREA : ORGAO DO GOVERNO MUNICIPAL – S. Luiz da Labrea, Amazonas. 1 Mar 1897 – 1,5,6 – bl Biblioteca [072]

JORNAL DA LAVOURA : ORGANO ESPECIAL DA LAVOURA DO MARANHAO – '(s.l.')-Sao Luiz, Brazil. 15 Jun 1875-30 Dec 1876 – 1,5,6 – bl Biblioteca [072]

JORNAL DA PRO-FEDERACAO : DAS ASSOCIACOES DE MORADORES DO ACRE – Rio Branco, Acre. Out 1985 – 1,5,6 – bl Biblioteca [072]

JORNAL DA SAUDE – Rio Branco, Acre. Mar-Ago 1985 – 1,5,6 – bl Biblioteca [072]

JORNAL DA SOCIEDADE PHILOMATICA MARANHENSE – '(s.l.')-Sao Luiz, Brazil. Oct 1846; Jun 1847 – 1,5,6 – bl Biblioteca [072]

JORNAL DAS ALAGOAS – Maceio, Alagoas. 17 Abr 1874; Maio 1877; Mar, 9 Out 1878 – 1,5,6 – bl Biblioteca [072]

JORNAL DE ANNUNCIOS – Rio de Janeiro, Brazil. 5 May-16 Jun 1821 – 1 – bl Biblioteca [072]

JORNAL DE CURVELLO – Curvello, 10 Oct 1928; Nov-Dec 1929; Jan 1931-Dec 1932; 19 Jan 1938 – 1,5,6 – bl Biblioteca [072]

O JORNAL DE CURVELO – Curvelo, 28 Aug 1955; Jul-Oct 1956 – 1,5,6 – bl Biblioteca [072]

JORNAL DE DEBATES – Maceio, Alagoas. 29 Jul-Ago 1900; 9-14 Jun 1903 – 1,5,6 – bl Biblioteca [072]

JORNAL DE DOMINGO : ORGAM DA SOCIEDADE – GABINETE LITTERARIO TOBIAS BARRETO – Aracaju, 13 Apr, 4, 25 May 1890 – 1,5,6 – bl Biblioteca [072]

JORNAL DE INSTRUCCAO E RECREIO – '(s.l.')-Sao Luiz, Brazil. 15 Feb 1845-20 Jan 1846 – 1,5,6 – bl Biblioteca [072]

JORNAL DE LAFAYETTE – Conselheiro Lafayette, Sep-Dec 1937; Jan-May, 6 Aug 1938 – 1,5,6 – bl Biblioteca [072]

JORNAL DE LAVRAS : ORGAM INDEPENDENTE, DEDICADO AOS INTERESSES COLLECTIVOS – Lavras, 1 Jan-29 May 1938 – 1,5,6 – bl Biblioteca [072]

JORNAL DE LETRAS – Rio de Janeiro. 1955-58; 1973-78 – 1 – 60.00 – us L of C Photodup [073]

JORNAL DE LETRAS – Rio de Janeiro. Brazil. -m. Jul-Nov 1952, Feb 1953-Dec 1965. (5 reels) – 1 – uk British Libr Newspaper [072]

JORNAL DE LETRAS – Rio de Janeiro, July 1949-Dec 1987 – 1,5,6 – bl Biblioteca [072]

JORNAL DE MACEIO – Maceio, Alagoas. 9 Out 1861 – 1,5,6 – bl Biblioteca [072]

JORNAL DE MACEIO *see* PARTIDO LIBERAL

JORNAL DE MINAS – S. Joao Del-Rei, Sept, Nov 1970; Mar, May-28 Sept 1971 – 1,5,6 – bl Biblioteca [072]
O JORNAL DE MINAS – Ouro Preto, 2 Jan 1890-15 Jul 1891 – 1,5,6 – bl Biblioteca [072]
JORNAL DE NOTICIAS – Maceio, Alagoas. 5 Jul, Set 1892; 25 Fev 1893 – 1,5,6 – bl Biblioteca [072]
JORNAL DE QUELUZ – Conselheiro Lafaiete, Brazil. Mar 1926-Sept 1930. Very incomplete – 1 – bl Biblioteca [072]
JORNAL DE SERGIPE – Aracaju, 11 Feb 1879-Jul 1881; Feb, Aug-Oct 1882; 29 Nov 1884 – 1,5,6 – bl Biblioteca [072]
JORNAL DE UBERABA : ORGAO RELIGIOSO, LITTERARIO, SCIENTIFICO E NOTICIOSO – Uberaba, 25 Jul 1897 – 1,5,6 – bl Biblioteca [072]
JORNAL DE UBERLANDIA – Uberlandia, Brazil. 1941; Feb-Mar 1942 – 1 – bl Biblioteca [072]
JORNAL DO ACRE : ORGAM INDEPENDENTE – Rio Branco, Acre. 9 Jan-1 Maio 1916 – 1,5,6 – bl Biblioteca [072]
JORNAL DO AMAZONAS – Manaos, Amazonas. 16 Abr 1875-Ago 1878; Jun-Set 1880; Jan, Abr-Maio 1882; Set, Dez 1883; Jan-Abr 1884; Jan-Fev, Abr, Set-Dez 1885; Fev-Dez 1886; Jan, Mar, Maio-Jun, Nov 1887; Fev, Abr-Jul, Set-Out, Dez 1888; 23 Maio 1889 – 1,5,6 – bl Biblioteca [072]
JORNAL DO ARACAJU – Aracaju, 23 Feb 1870; Jan, Mar-Dec 1872; Jan-Dec 1873; Jan-Oct, Dec 1874; Jan-Jul, Sep-Dec 1875; Jun 1876-12 Oct 1878 – 1,5,6 – bl Biblioteca [072]
JORNAL DO BRASIL – (Cont of: Jornal Corrente) – Rio de Janeiro, 9 Apr 1891-. Incomplete – 1,5,6 – bl Biblioteca [072]
JORNAL DO BRASIL – Rio de Janeiro, Brazil. -d. March 1972-Dec 1975. 99 reels – 1 – uk British Libr Newspaper [072]
JORNAL DO BRASIL – Rio de Janeiro: [s.n.], 1938-43 – 64r – 1 – us Res Libr [072]
JORNAL DO BRAZIL – Rio de Janeiro. Brazil. 1965- – 1 – us UMI [072]
JORNAL DO COMERCIO – Lisbon. 21 22 Feb 1971-3 Sept 1976. Incomplete. (Portuguese Revolution of 1974. Newspapers from Portugal publ. from 21 Feb 1971 to 15 Feb 1980, collected and filmed by University of Wisconsin-Madison libraries.) – 1 – us U.W. Library [072]
JORNAL DO COMERCIO – Lisbon, Portugal. -d. 5 Oct 1942-31 Dec 1946; 5 Sept-31 Dec 1948; 10 Aug 1949-23 Dec 1950. Imperfect. 26 reels – 1 – uk British Libr Newspaper [072]
JORNAL DO COMERCIO – Nanuque, Brazil. Dec 1968; Jan-Mar 1969 – 1 – bl Biblioteca [072]
JORNAL DO COMERCIO – Rio de Janeiro: Typ. d'Emile-Seignot Plancheb, [oct 1899-1901]; 1930-apr 1941; may 15 1941-dec 15 1942; 1943-aug 1 1944; may-jul 1945; aug 16 1945-55; 1956-apr 1980; jun 1980-81 – us Res Libr [380]
JORNAL DO COMMERCIO : ADVOGA OS INTERESSES DO COMMERCIO, DA LAVOURA E DA INDUSTRIA – Aracaju, 26 Jul, Aug, Sep 1877; 30 Jan 1878 – 1,5,6 – bl Biblioteca [072]
JORNAL DO COMMERCIO – (Cont of: Jornal Corrente) – Rio de Janeiro, 1 Oct 1827- – 1,5,6 – bl Biblioteca [072]
JORNAL DO COMMERCIO : HEBDOMADARIO INDEPENDENTE – Itacoatiara, Amazonas. 4 Jul 1914-Dez 1916; Abr-Dez 1917; Jan-Maio, Set-29 Dez 1918 – 1,5,6 – bl Biblioteca [072]
JORNAL DO COMMERCIO – Jaragua-AL, Brazil. 22 Fev 1880 – 1 – bl Biblioteca [380]
JORNAL DO COMMERCIO – Juiz de Fora, 8 Apr, Sept 1897; Jun-Jul 1898;Dec 1901; Nov-Dec 1912; Apr 1913; 25 Aug 1920 – 1,5,6 – bl Biblioteca [072]
JORNAL DO COMMERCIO – Pilar, Alagoas. 11 Out 1880 – 1,5,6 – bl Biblioteca [072]
JORNAL DO COMMERCIO – '(s.l.')-BA, Brazil. 26 out 1833 – 1,5,6 – bl Biblioteca [072]
JORNAL DO COMMERCIO – '(s.l.')-Sao Luiz, Brazil. 8 Jun 1858-31 Dec 1860 – 1,5,6 – bl Biblioteca [072]
JORNAL DO COMMERCIO *see* O SPECTADOR BRASILEIRO
JORNAL DO DOMINGO : NOTICIOSO, LITTERARIO E JOCO-SERIO – Maceio, Alagoas. 9 Ago-14 Set 1879 – 1,5,6 – bl Biblioteca [072]
JORNAL DO FUNDAO – Fundao. No.1417-1727; 10 Mar 1974-15 Feb 1980. Incomplete. (Portuguese Revolution of 1974. Newspapers from Portugal publ. from 21 Feb 1971 to 15 Feb 1980, collected and filmed by University of Wisconsin-Madison libraries.) – 1 – us U.W. Library [072]
JORNAL DO INTERIOR – Manaus, Amazonas. 20 Fev-5 Mar 1982 – 1,5,6 – bl Biblioteca [072]
JORNAL DO NORTE : JORNAL INDEPENDENTE E COMMERCIAL – Manaos, Amazonas. 1 Out 1924 – 1,5,6 – bl Biblioteca [072]
JORNAL DO NORTE – [s.l.] 26 Abr 1872 – 1,5,6 – bl Biblioteca [072]
JORNAL DO OESTE – Divinopolis, 17 Feb-Aug, 27 Oct 1951 – 1,5,6 – bl Biblioteca [072]
JORNAL DO PAO D'ASSUCAR : PERIODICO IMPARCIAL E NOTICIOSO – Pao d'Assucar, Alagoas. 10 Dez 1876 – 1,5,6 – bl Biblioteca [072]
JORNAL DO PENEDO – (Cont: O Penedense) – Penedo, Alagoas. 9 Jan 1875-Dez 1877; Jan-Fev, Set-Dez 1878; Jan 1879-Dez 1881; Abr, Jul 1883; Jun, Out 1884; Jul 1886; Ago 1889-Dez 1891 – 1,5,6 – bl Biblioteca [072]
JORNAL DO PENEDO : ORGAM DO PARTIDO REPUBLICANO CONSERVADOR – Penedo, Alagoas. 27 Out 1912-Fev 1914; Set-Dez 1914; Jun 1949-15 Out 1950 – 1,5,6 – bl Biblioteca [072]
JORNAL DO PENEDO *see* O PENEDENSE
JORNAL DO PILAR – Pilar, Alagoas. 13 Jan-Abr, Jun-Dez 1874; Jan 1875; Dez 1878; Jan-Mar, Jul-12 Out 1879 – 1,5,6 – bl Biblioteca [072]
JORNAL DO POVO : O ACRE TAMBEM PARA OS ACREANOS – Rio Branco, Acre. 13 Dez 1952-Maio 1953; Jun 1954-Set 1956; Mar-5 Abr 1957 – 1,5,6 – bl Biblioteca [072]
JORNAL DO POVO – Manaus, Amazonas. 16 Nov 1945 – 1,5,6 – bl Biblioteca [072]
JORNAL DO PURUS : ORGAM DO PARTIDO REPUBLICANO FEDERAL – S. Luiz de Labrea, Amazonas. 12 Abr-Dez 1911; Jan-Mar, Jul-1 Dez 1912 – 1,5,6 – bl Biblioteca [072]
JORNAL DO RIO BRANCO : ORGAO DOS INTERESSES DOS MORADORES DO RIO BRANCO – Boa Vista do Rio Branco, Amazonas. Nov 1916-Nov 1917 – 1,5,6 – bl Biblioteca [072]
JORNAL DO RIO NEGRO – Manaos, Amazonas. 28 Ago 1867-13 Jun 1868 – 1,5,6 – bl Biblioteca [072]
JORNAL DO SERVIDOR : UM ORGAO DA SOCIBENE A SERVICO DE SEUS ASSOCIADOS – Rio Branco, Acre. 5 Fev-Jul, 28 Out 1967 – 1,5,6 – bl Biblioteca [072]
JORNAL DO SINDICATO – [s.l.] Set 1975 – 1,5,6 – bl Biblioteca [072]
JORNAL DO TRAIPU – Traipu, Alagoas. 11 Nov 1877; Jun, 26 Out 1884 – 1,5,6 – bl Biblioteca [072]
O JORNAL DOS ANNUNCIOS – '(s.l.')-Sao Luis, Brazil. 1-15 Mar 1831 – 1,5,6 – bl Biblioteca [072]
JORNAL DOS MUNICIPIOS – Patos de Minas, Brazil. Dec 1956; Jan, Dec 1977 – 1 – bl Biblioteca [072]
JORNAL EVANGELICO – 1972-92 (complete) – 10r – 1 – ATLA S0481 – us A.T.L.A. [073]
JORNAL MARANHENSE – Sao Luis, 9 Jul 1841-1 Jul 1842 – 1,5,6 – bl Biblioteca [072]
JORNAL NOVO – Lisbon. no. 1-1341; 17 Apr 1975-26 Sept 1979. Incomplete. (Portuguese Revolution of 1974. Newspapers from Portugal publ. from 21 Feb 1971 to 15 Feb 1980, collected and filmed by University of Wisconsin-Madison libraries.) – 1 – us U.W. Library [072]
JORNAL OFFICIAL – Manaos, Amazonas. 7 Jan-28 Fev 1882 – 1,5,6 – bl Biblioteca [072]
JORNAL OFFICIAL : ORGAM DA PREFEITURA DE TARAUACA – Villa Seabra, Acre. 16 Abr 1916-14 Abr 1918 – 1,5,6 – bl Biblioteca [072]
JORNAL OFFICIAL : ORGAO DE PUBLICIDADE DOS ACTOS DA ADMINISTRACAO – Rio Branco, Acre. 13 Jan 1925-31 Dez 1926 – 1 – bl Biblioteca [350]
JORNAL PEQUENO – Manaos, Amazonas. Jul 1954 – 1,5,6 – bl Biblioteca [072]
JORNAL PEQUENO : VESPERTINO INDEPENDENTE – Manaos, Amazonas. 4-22 Jul 1911 – 1,5,6 – bl Biblioteca [072]
JORNAL POPULAR : FOLHA CONSAGRADA AOS INTERESSES DA PROVINCIA – (Cont of: O Diario Popular) – Aracaju, 24 May, 19 Jun 1879 – 1,5,6 – bl Biblioteca [072]
JORNAL POPULAR *see* DIARIO POPULAR
JORNAL SCIENTIFICO, ECONOMICO E LITTERARIO, OU COLLECCAO DE PECAS, MELHORIAS, RELACOENS, VIAGENS, POESIAS E ANEDOCTAS : MIXTO DE INSTRUCCAO E RECREIO ACCOMMODADO A TODO O GENNERO DE LEITORES – Rio de Janeiro, May-Jul 1826 – 1,5,6 – bl Biblioteca [072]
JORNAL SPORTIVO : ORGAM EXCLUSVIAMENTE SPORTIVO – Manaos, Amazonas. 12 Abr-24 Maio 1914 – 1,5,6 – bl Biblioteca [072]
AO JORNALISTA DR. SILVEIRA JOSE NERY – Manaos, Amazonas. 1900 – 1,5,6 – bl Biblioteca [072]
O JORNALSINHO : PERIODICO CRITICO E HUMORISTICO – Manaus, Amazonas. 6 Out-15 Nov 1902 – 1,5,6 – bl Biblioteca [072]
Jos. Dussault & Cie *see* LE PETIT JOURNAL
JOSE ANTONIO EN LA CARCEL DE MADRID DEL 14 DE MARZO AL 6 DE JUNIO DE 1936 / Antiguedad, Alfredo R – Interesante reportaje con Raimundo Fernandez-Cuesta. Cegama, 1939? Fiche W 721. (Blodgett Collection of Spanish Civil War Pamphlets) – 9 – us H.U. College Libr [946]
JOSE ASUNCION SILVA; ENSAYO BIOGRAFICO CON DOCUMENTOS INEDITOS / Miramon, Alberto – Bogota, 1937. Bibliografia general, p191-194 – 1 – us U.W. Library [972]
JOSE BONIFACIO O MOCO / Faria, Julio Cezar de – Sao Paulo, 1944 – 8mf – 8 – ne Slangenburg [920]
JOSE DE ALENCAR : ORGAO DO CLUB LITTERARIO JOSE DE ALENCAR – Maceio, Alagoas. Maio-Out 1883; Maio, Jul-Ago 1884; Maio, 25 Jul 1885 – 1,5,6 – bl Biblioteca [072]
JOSE LOPEZ DE TORO Y RAMON PAZ REMOLAR / Barrado Manzano, Arcangel – Madrid: Archivo Ibero-Americano, 1959 – 1 – sp Bibl Santa Ana [946]
JOSE MARIA VARGAS / Dominguez, Rafael – Caracas, 1930; Madrid: Razon y Fe, 1931 – 1 – sp Bibl Santa Ana [920]
JOSE MAZZINI. ENSAYO ITALIA / Diaz Perez, Nicolas – 1876 – 9 – $1.50f – sp Bibl Santa Ana [920]
JOSE MORENO NIETO / Blanco Garcia, Francisco – Madrid: Saenz de Jubera, 1909 – sp Bibl Santa Ana [440]
JOSE SANCHEZ ARJONA / Blanco Garcia, Francisco – Madrid: Saenz de Jubera, 1909 – sp Bibl Santa Ana [440]
JOSEF FILSERS ENDE : LEDZDER BRIEFWEXEL UND BOLIDISCHES DESDAMEND / Kirschner, Max – Muenchen: F Eher, 1942 – 1r – 1 – us U.W. Library [920]
JOSEF VIKTOR WIDMANN : EIN LEBENSBILD / Widmann, Elisabeth & Widmann, Max – (Includes bibliographical references and index) – Frauenfeld; Leipzig: Huber & Co. 2v. 1922-24 – 1 – us U.W. Library [430]
JOSEF VON GOERRES : ZUM 150. GEBURTSTAG (25. JANUAR 1926) / Schellberg, Wilhelm – Koeln, 2nd rev ed 1926 – 1mf – 9 – DM48.00 – 3-89349-737-4 – gw Hänsel [920]
JOSEF VON GOERRES : ZUM 150. GEBURTSTAGE (25. JANUAR 1926) / Schellberg, Wilhelm – 2. verb. Aufl. Koeln: Gilde-Verlag, 1926 – 1r – 1 – us U.W. Library [943]
JOSEF WEINHEBER / Koch, Franz – Muenchen: A Langen, G Mueller, 1942 – 1 – us U.W. Library [430]
Josenhans, Joseph *see* ATLAS DER EVANGELISCHEN MISSIONS-GESELLSCHAFT ZU BASEL
Josenhans, Walther *see* LORD BYRON UND DIE POLITIK
JOSEPH / Bitaube, Paul Jeremie – Paris: Deschamps, 1826. 4 fiches. (Literature Collection) – 9 – $10.00 – fr Bibl Nationale [830]
JOSEPH – Breslau, 1879 – 1r – 1 – Inquire at Mikrofilmarchiv for details – gw Misc Inst [072]
JOSEPH : ISRAELITISCHE JUGENDZEITUNG – Breslau. v1. 1879 (complete) – 1r – 1 – $60.00 – us UPA [270]
JOSEPH 2 UND KATHARINA VON RUSSLAND : IHR BRIEFWECHSEL / ed by Arneth, A von – Wien, 1869 – 5mf – 9 – ne IDC [943]
JOSEPH 2 UND LEOPOLD VON TOSCANA : IHR BRIEFWECHSEL VON 1781 BIS 1790 / ed by Arneth, A von – Wien. 2v. 1872 – 10mf – 9 – ne IDC [943]
Joseph a Sancta Barbara *see*
– HET GEESTELYCK KAERT-SPEL MET HERTEN TROEF, OFT HET SPEL DER LIEFDE
JOSEPH ALLEINE : HIS COMPANIONS AND TIMES: A MEMORIAL OF "BLACK BARTHOLOMEW," 1662 / Stanford, Charles – London: Jackson, Walford, and Hodder, [1861?] – 1mf – us A.T.L.A. [240]
JOSEPH AMIOT ET LES DERNIERS SURVIVANTS DE LA MISSION FRANCAISE A PEKIN (1780-1795) / Rochemonteix, C de – Paris, 1915 – 7mf – 9 – HTM-232/1 – ne IDC [944]
JOSEPH AND MOSES, THE FOUNDERS OF ISRAEL : BEING THEIR LIVES AS READ IN THE LIGHT OF THE OLDEST PROPHETIC WRITINGS OF THE BIBLE / Blake, Buchanan – Edinburgh: T & T Clark, 1902 – 1mf – 9 – 0-8370-9444-5 – 1986-3444 – us A.T.L.A. [220]
Joseph Ben Joshua *see* CHRONICLE
Joseph, Corbett *see* THE REFORMERS
JOSEPH COSTISELLA : BIBLIOGRAPHIE DESCRIPTIVE / Martel, Louise – 1964. SEM105P4 – 1mf – 9 – cn Bibl Nat [920]
Joseph, Don *see* SHOP TALK ON SPAIN. THE TRADE UNIONS AND THE WAR IN SPAIN
Joseph, Edward L *see* HISTORY OF TRINIDAD WITH TRINIDAD ALMANAC
JOSEPH EN EGYPTE / Vergote, J – Univ. of Louvain, 1959. In French – 9 – $10.00 – us I.R.C. [240]
Joseph, Eugen *see* DAS HEIDENROESLEIN
JOSEPH GOEBBELS PAMPHLET COLLECTION – 1935-1943 – 1 reel – 1 – CSUXANR9530-B – us Hoover Inst Photo [355]
JOSEPH GOERRES UND DIE PRESSEPOLITIK DER DEUTSCHEN REAKTION : EIN BEITRAG ZUR GOERRESFORSCHUNG / Poelnitz, Goetz Freiherr von – Koeln, (1930) – lxiv – 9 – DM48.00 – 3-89349-064-7 – gw Hänsel [320]
JOSEPH GOERRES UND DIE PRESSEPOLITIK DER DEUTSCHEN REAKTION : EIN BEITRAG ZUR GOERRESFORSCHUNG / Poelnitz, Goetz, Freiherr von – Koeln: J P Bachem, [1936] – 1r – 1 – us U.W. Library [943]
JOSEPH H. CHOATE, NEW ENGLANDER, NEW YORKER, LAWYER, AMBASSADOR / Strong, Theron George – New York, Dodd, Mead, 1917. 390 p. LL-212 – 1 – us L of C Photodup [340]
JOSEPH HERALD – Joseph, OR. -w. 10 Jan 1902-14 Apr 1949. – 1 – us U.O. Library [071]
JOSEPH HILLEBRAND : SEIN LEBEN UND WERK / Schreiber, Hans Ulrich – (Includes bibliographical references) – Giessen: [s.n.], 1937 – 1r – 1 – us U.W. Library [920]
JOSEPH JORTZ : EL SANTO INCOMPARABLE / Barrado Manzano, Arcangel – Madrid: Arch. Ibero Americano, 1964 – 1 – sp Bibl Santa Ana [240]
JOSEPH L. BRISTOW PAPERS / Bristow, Joseph L – 1894-1925. In Kansas State Historical Society. Guide – 1 – us KS Hist [920]
JOSEPH LUDWIG COLMAR. BISCHOF VON MAINZ 1802-1818 : EIN ZEIT- UND LEBENSBILD / Selbst, Joseph – Mainz, 1902. 55p – DM50.00 – 3-89349-176-7 – gw Hänsel [240]
JOSEPH PILSUDSKI / Merezhkovskii, Dmitrii – Tr. from the Russian by Harriet E. Kennedy. London: S. Low, Marston & Co., 1921. 20p – 1 – us U.W. Library [920]
Joseph, S A *see* MISHBEZET HA-TARSHISH
JOSEPH S. ASSEMANI ET LA CELEBRATION DU CONCILE LIBANAIS MARONITE DE 1736 / Mafoud, P – Roma, 1965 – Dfl13.00 – ne Slangenburg [240]
Joseph, Samuel *see* JEWISH IMMIGRATION TO THE UNITED STATES
Joseph, Stanislaus *see* THE GROWTH OF AFRICAN LITERATURE
JOSEPH TUCKERMAN ON THE ELEVATION OF THE POOR : A SELECTION FROM HIS REPORTS AS MINISTER AT LARGE IN BOSTON / Hale, E E – Boston: Roberts Brothers, 1874 – 1mf – us A.T.L.A. [240]

JOSEPH VON GOERRES ALS LITTERARHISTORIKER / Wibbelt, Augustin – (Includes bibliographical references) – Koeln: J P Bachem, 1899 – 1r – 1 – us U.W. Library [430]

JOSEPH VON LASSBERG : MITTLER UND SAMMLER; AUFSAETZE ZU SEINEM 100. TODESTAG / ed by Bader, Karl Siegfried – (Includes bibliographical references) – Stuttgart: F Vorwerk: 1955 – 1 – us U.W. Library [920]

JOSEPHINE. PARURES, DECORS ET JARDINS / Reunion des musees nationaux. Paris – 1969. illus. 1 fiche – 9 – fr Réunion [700]

Joseph-Marie, Soeur *see* BIBLIOGRAPHIE ANALYTIQUE DE L'ABBE ANSELME LONGPRE, PH.L., TH.L., B.D.C. DU DIOCESE DE SAINT-HYACINTHE, PREMIERE PARTIE (1927-1947)

Josepho Catalano Presbytero *see* DE CODICE SANCTI EVANGELII, LIBRI 3

Josephs, Ray *see* ARGENTINE DIARY

Josephus, Flavius *see*
- BELLUM JUDAICUM
- THE COMPLETE WORKS OF FLAVIUS JOSEPHUS
- FLAVII IOSEPHI ANTIQUITATUM IUDAICARUM EPITOME
- JOZEF FLAWJUSZ DZIEJE WOJNY ZYDOWSKIEJ PRZECIWKO RZYMIANOM

JOSEPHUS UND LUCAS : DER SCHRIFTSTELLERISCHE EINFLUSS DES JUEDISCHEN GESCHICHTSCHREIBERS AUF DEN CHRISTLICHEN / Krenkel, Max – (Includes bibliographical references) – Leipzig: H Haessel, 1894 – 1mf – 9 – 0-8370-3999-1 – 1985-1999 – us A.T.L.A. [220]

JOSHUA AND THE LAND OF PROMISE / Meyer, Frederick Brotherton – London: Morgan & Scott, [1893?] – 1mf – 9 – 0-8370-4410-3 – 1985-2410 – us A.T.L.A. [220]

JOSHUA HAGGARD'S DAUGHTER / Braddon, Mary Elizabeth – British Fiction Archive: Unit 5 – 9 – uk Bell [830]

JOSIAH ALLEN'S WIFE AS A P.A. AND P. I. SAMENTHA AT THE CENTENNIAL. / Holley, Marietta – Hartford: American, 1891. 580p.illus – 1 – us U.W. Library [920]

JOSIAH WARREN: THE FIRST AMERICAN ANARCHIST / Bailie, William – 1906. Also: Libertarian Party,1978 Platform. 2 fiches (24x) – 9 – 1.00f – at Libertarian Micro [320]

JOSIP BROZ TITO PAMPHLET COLLECTION – 1944-1980 – 1 reel – 1 – CSUXANQ7257-B – us Hoover Inst Photo [320]

Joslin, James Elliott *see* THE FORMULATION AND USE OF A STAFF POLICY MANUAL WITHIN THE GREENE COUNTY BAPTIST ASSOCIATION

Joslyn, F W *see* HISTORY OF KANE COUNTY

Joslyn, R W *see* HISTORY OF KANE COUNTY

Josodharmodjo, S B *see* A BRIEF OUTLINE ON THE ASPECTS OF THE JAVANESE WAYANG KULIT

Joss, Gottlieb *see* DIE VEREINIGUNG CHRISTLICHER KIRCHEN

Josslyn, William *see* ECCE REGNUM, OR, AN INQUIRY INTO THE...REVELATION OF THE GLORY OF THE KINGDOM OF GOD

Jost, I M *see* OFFENES SENDSCHREIBEN AN HERRN. STRECKFUSS

Jost, I M BJ-91-88 1 *see* ZIVYON

Jost, Theodor *see* MECHANISIERUNG DES LEBENS UND MODERNE LYRIK

Jost, Walter *see* VON LUDWIG TIECK ZU E.T.A. HOFFMANN

Jostes, Franz *see*
- DIE TEPLER BIBELUBERSETZUNG
- DIE WALDENSER UND DIE VORLUTHERISCHE DEUTSCHE BIBELUEBERSETZUNG

JOSUAE IMPERATORIS HISTORIA ILLUSTRATA ATQUE EXPLICATA / Masius, A – Antwerpiae. 1574. Index. B-2187 2 – 8 – ne IDC [900]

LA JOTA ARAGONESA / Hurtado y Nunez de Arce, G – 1866 – 9 – 1.50f – sp Bibl Santa Ana [830]

JOTHAM MEEKER PAPERS / Meeker, Jotham – 1825-64. In Kansas State Historical Society. Guide – 1 – us KS Hist [240]

Joua, Ferdinand *see* ENTRETIEN SUR LES SAINT-SIMONIENS ET LE SAINT-SIMONISME

Jouan, P *see* NOTES DE LEXICOGRAPHIE HEBRAIQUE

Jouanny, Joseph *see* LE TISSAGE DE LA SOIE DANS LE BAS-DAUPHINE

Joubert, Henri *see* L'ESPAGNE DE FRANCO; SYNTHESE DE TROIS CONFERENCES DONNEES DU 17 JANVIER AU 10 FEVRIER 1938

Joubert, L *see* TRAITE DU RIS

Joucla, E *see* BIBLIOGRAPHIE DE L'AFRIQUE OCCIDENTALE FRANCAISE

Joukhadar, I *see* PROJECT REPORT ON LABOUR LEGISLATION AND LABOUR ADMINISTRATION IN LIBYA

Joulord *see* MANUEL FRANCAIS-DAHOMEEN

JOUNT COMMITTEE ON CONTINUING LEGAL EDUCATION (US) ALI-ABA CLE REVIEW *see* ALI-ABA CLE REVIEW

LE JOUR – Beirut: s.n. 1956-sep 14 1963 – 26r – 1 – us Res Libr [072]

LE JOUR – (Filmed with: Le Progres de Fraserville 23 mar-19 oct 1888. Le Journal de Fraserville v4 n44. 26 oct 1888-17 jan 1913) – Riviere-du-Loup, Canada. 4 dec 1884-16 mar 1888 – 4r – 1 – Can$55.00r – cn Can Microfilming [072]

LE JOUR / ed by Harvey, Jean-Charles – Montreal, Canada. 16 sep 1937-29 jun 1946 – 2r – 1 – Can$50.00r – cn Can Microfilming [072]

LE JOUR : HEBDO – Montreal. Hebdo. 4 fev 1977-13 jan 1978 – 2r – 1 – Can$65.00r – cn Can Microfilming [072]

LE JOUR – Paris. janv-juin 1896 – 1 – fr A.C.R.P.P. [073]

LE JOUR : QUOTIDIEN – Montreal, 28 fev 1974-24 aut 1976 – 14r – 1 – Can$65.00r – cn Can Microfilming [072]

LE JOUR DE LA FETE DES ARBRES: QUELQUES CONSEILS AUX CULTIVATEURS SUR LA PLANTATION DES ARBRES FORESTIERS ET D'ORNEMENT / Chapais, Jean Charles – Montreal: E. Senecal, 1884. 02869. (Pre-1900 Canadiana) – 9 – cn C.I.H.M. [630]

Jourdain, Silvester *see* A DISCOVERY OF THE BARMUDAS

Jourdain, Victor *see* LA LEGISLATION FRANCAISE SUR LES COALITIONS OUVRIERES, SON EVOLUTION AU XIXE SIECLE

Jourdan, A J L *see* DICTIONAIRE DES SCIENCES MEDICALES (AEL, ABT 3;16)

Jourdan et al *see* RECUEIL GENERAL DES ANCIENNES LOIS FRANCAISES ... L'AN 420 JUSQU'A LA REVOLUTION DE 1789

Jourdan, George V *see* THE MOVEMENT TOWARDS CATHOLIC REFORM IN THE EARLY XVI CENTURY

Jourdier, Auguste *see*
- DE L'EMANCIPATION DES SERFS EN RUSSIE. ETUDE SUR LA QUESTION AU 16 MARS 1861. EXPOSE ET CRITIQUES DU PROJET DU COMITE DE REDACTION. AVEC UNE CARTE ET TABLEAUX STATISTIQUES
- DES FORCES PRODUCTIVES, DESTRUCTIVES ET IMPRODUCTIVES DE LA RUSSIE

JOURNAL / AAUW (American Association of University Women) – (1968-70 5,6) – 1882-1978 – 1 – us UMI [360]

JOURNAL / Academy of Marketing Science – v1- 1973- 1,5,6; v3- 1975- 9 – us UMI [380]

JOURNAL – Aiken. S.C. and Review. 1885-1935 – 1 – us UMI [071]

JOURNAL / Air Pollution Control Association – (5, 6 1971- ; 9 1975-) – v1- 1951- – 1 – us UMI [360]

JOURNAL / Alabama Academy of Science – v1- 1924- 1; v46- 1975- 5,6,9 – us UMI [500]

JOURNAL – Albuquerque. N.M. 1881-86 – 1 – us UMI [071]

JOURNAL – Alexandria. Va. -w. 1950- – 1 – us UMI [071]

JOURNAL – (Also known as: Semi-Weekly Journal) – Yreka, CA. 1861-78; 1880-87; 1890-1944; 1946-59 – 46r – 1 BC03118 – $2,300.00 – us Library Micro [073]

JOURNAL – Altavista. Va. 1950- – 1 – us UMI [071]

JOURNAL / American Ceramic Society – v1-37. 1918-54 – 1,5,6 – us Princeton Micro [740]

JOURNAL / American Dietetic Association – Chicago, Boston.1960-66. v36-49. M-20/2 – 8 – ne IDC [610]

JOURNAL / American Dietetic Association – v7-31. 1931-49 – 1,5,6 – us Princeton Micro [610]

JOURNAL / American Health Care Association – (Cont by: Provider) – Washington. v1-12 jul 1975-feb 1986 1*; v9-12 jan 1983-feb 1986 5*,9 – 1,5,9 – D14122 – us UMI [360]

JOURNAL / American Irish Historical Society – v1-30 1898-1932 – 1 – us Princeton Micro [941]

JOURNAL / American Leather Chemists' Association – Easton. v46-92 jan 1951- 1; v66-92 jan 1971- 5; v72-92 jan-dec 1977 9* – 1,5,9 – D761 – us UMI [670]

JOURNAL / American Leather Chemists' Association – v34-50. 1939-55 – 1,5,6 – us Princeton Micro [540]

JOURNAL / American Oil Chemists' society – v1-32. 1924-55 – 1,5,6 – us Princeton Micro [660]

JOURNAL / American Oriental Society – v1-29 1849-1908 – 1 – us Princeton Micro [950]

JOURNAL / American Statistical Association – v. 1-63. 1888-1968 – 1,5,6 – us Princeton Micro [310]

JOURNAL / American Temperance Union – v. 1-29. Jan 1837-Dec 1865. v. 21, no. 1-5; v. 29, no. 10 wanting – 1 – 81.00 – us L of C Photodup [360]

JOURNAL / American Water Works Association – v13-47 1925-55 – 1,5,6 – us Princeton Micro [624]

JOURNAL – Anthony. Kan. 1881-82 – 1 – us UMI [071]

JOURNAL / AORN (Association of Operating Room Nurses) – (1974- . 5,6. 1976- . 9) – v1- . 1963- – 1 – us UMI [610]

JOURNAL / Architectural Association – 1936-59 – 1 – uk Microform Academic [720]

JOURNAL / ASCE (American Society of Civil Engineers). Technical Councils – v103-1977- – 1,5,6,9 – us UMI [624]

JOURNAL / ASCE (American Society of Civil Engineers.) Water Resources Planning and Management Division – v102- 1976- – 1,5,6,9 – us UMI [333]

JOURNAL – Ashland. Neb. 1897-1907 – 1 – us UMI [071]

JOURNAL / ASHRAE (American Society of Heating, Refrigerating and Air-Conditioning Engineers) – v1- 1959- – 1,5,6,9 – us UMI [621]

JOURNAL / Association international des Travailleurs. Section de la Suisse Romande – 1865-66 – 1 – us Res Libr [330]

JOURNAL / Association of Official Analytical Chemists – v1-66. 1915-83 – 1,5,6 – us Princeton Micro [630]

JOURNAL / Association of Teachers of Japanese – (1975- . 5,6,9) – 1963- – 1 – us UMI [370]

JOURNAL – Auburn, CA. 1914-1988 – 180r – 1 BC02027 – $9,000.00 – us Library Micro [073]

JOURNAL – Auburn. California. -w. 1914-67 – 1 – us UMI [071]

JOURNAL / Australian Institute of Agricultural Science – v. 45-. 1979- – 5,6,9 – us UMI [630]

JOURNAL / Australian Mathematical Society – v. 1-15. 1959-73 – 1,5,6 – us Princeton Micro [510]

JOURNAL – Azusa. Calif. 1924-1929 – 1 – us UMI [071]

JOURNAL – Bank Public Relations and Marketing Association. v51-54. 1965-69. Continued by: Bank Marketing Management – 1 – us UMI [336]

JOURNAL / Bath and West and Southern Counties Society – London. 1853-1906 – 3 – us Readex [941]

JOURNAL – Battle Creek. Mich. 1872-1911; 1912-1914 – 1 – us UMI [071]

JOURNAL – Battle Creek. Mich. -w. 1852-63, 1867-79 – 1 – us UMI [071]

JOURNAL – Beacon. N.Y. 1925-27 – 1 – us UMI [071]

JOURNAL – Belgrade. Mont. 1907-1908 – 1 – us UMI [071]

JOURNAL / Biological Sciences Curriculum Study – v. 1-2. 1978-79 – 1,5,6,9 – us UMI [580]

JOURNAL – Blaine. Wash. 1900-1950 – 1 – us UMI [071]

JOURNAL / Blantyre Mission – 1888-1911 and 1918-19 – 1 – uk Microform Academic [240]

JOURNAL / Board of Arts and Manufactures for Upper Canada – 1861-68 – 1 – 220.00 – cn McLaren [971]

JOURNAL / Bray, W – (Coll title: The People Called Methodists, Phase 3: Primary Sources, 1801-1850) – 5mf – 9 – MP-693/1 – ne IDC [240]

JOURNAL – Bucyrus, Ohio. 1853-1900 – 21r – 1 – $32.50r – us Archival [071]

JOURNAL – Caldwell. Kan. 1883-1894 – 1 – us UMI [071]

JOURNAL / Canada. Fisheries Research Board of Canada – (1972- . 5,6. 1975- . 9) – v. 1- 1934- – 1 – us UMI [639]

JOURNAL / Canada. Fisheries Research Board of Canada – v.15-36. 1958-79 – 1,5,6 – 221151.00 – us Princeton Micro [324]

JOURNAL / Canadian Ceramic Society – v1-42. 1932-73 – 1,5,6 – us Princeton Micro [073]

JOURNAL / Canadian Institute of Food Science and Technology – v1-12 1968-79. Continues: Canadian Institute of Food Technology: Journal – 1,5,6 – us Princeton Micro [660]

JOURNAL / Canadian Medical Association – Association medicale Canadienne – (v. 94-. 1966- 5,6. v. 102-. 1970- 9) – 1- 1911- – 1 – us UMI [610]

JOURNAL – Central Falls. R.I. 1899-1900 – 1 – us UMI [071]

JOURNAL / Chamber of Commerce. Constantinople – Istanbul, Turkey. -w. Jan. 1907-14 Nov. 1914, 5 Jan. 1918-28 Feb. 1921. 9 reels – 1 – uk British Libr Newspaper [380]

JOURNAL / Charleston Siege – 1780. Anon. diary of a member of the Corps of British Engineers. 1 fiche – 9 – us South Carolina Historical [978]

JOURNAL / Chartered Institution of Building Services – v1- 1978- – 1,5,6,9 – us UMI [690]

JOURNAL / Chemical Society – (1965- . 5,6. 1976- . 9) – 1849- – 1 – us UMI [540]

JOURNAL / Chemical Society. London – London. v1-78. 1847-1900 – 22r – 5 – inquire – us Ross [540]

JOURNAL / Chemical Society. London – v. 1-128. 1841-1965 – 1,5,6 – us Princeton Micro [540]

JOURNAL – Cheney. Kan. 1884-87 – 1 – us UMI [071]

JOURNAL – Chinook. Mont. 1942-1948 – 1 – us UMI [071]

JOURNAL – Coffeyville. Kan. 1972- – 1 – us UMI [071]

JOURNAL – Coffeyville. Kan. and Sun. 1880-1920 – 1 – us UMI [071]

JOURNAL – Coffeyville. Kan. -w. 1875-1920 – 1 – us UMI [071]

JOURNAL – Colonial Heights. Va. 1950-1955 – 1 – us UMI [071]

JOURNAL – Columbus. Neb. 1870-1917; 1934-1958 – 1 – us UMI [071]

JOURNAL – Commerce. Tex. -w. 1901-10, 1913- – 1 – us UMI [071]

JOURNAL – Corning. N.Y. -w. 1840-1902 – 1 – us UMI [071]

JOURNAL – Covington. Ky. 1848-1876 – 1 – us UMI [071]

JOURNAL – Crawfordsville. Ind. 1880; 1895-1904; 1955 – 1 – us UMI [071]

JOURNAL – Crawfordsville. Ind. and Review. 1955- – 1 – us UMI [071]

JOURNAL – Crawfordsville. Ind. w. 1863-1865; 1870-1871; 1875-1885; 1887-1889 – 1 – us UMI [071]

JOURNAL – Cripple Creek. Col. -w. 1894-98 – 1 – us UMI [071]

JOURNAL / Currie, James – 1776. BRRAM – 1 – uk Microform Academic [920]

JOURNAL / Cushing, William B – 1861-65. 1 roll. M1034 – 1 – us Nat'l Archives [324]

JOURNAL – Dayton. Ohio. 1940-48 – 1 – us UMI [071]

JOURNAL – Dighton. Kan. -w. 1886-92 – 1 – us UMI [071]

JOURNAL / Electrochemical Society – (v. 112-1965- 5,6. v. 117- 1970- 9) – 93- 1948- – 1 – us UMI [621]

JOURNAL – Ellenville. N.Y. 1973- – 1 – us UMI [071]

JOURNAL / Epsilon Pi Tau – v. 1-. 1974- – 1. 1977-.; ; 5,6,9 – us UMI [370]

JOURNAL – Eureka. Mont. 1910-1928 – 1 – us UMI [071]

JOURNAL / Evangelical Theological Society – v12- 1977- 1; v21- 1978- 5,6,9 – us UMI [240]

JOURNAL – Evansville. Ind. 1871-1936 – 1 – us UMI [071]

JOURNAL – Fairfield. Iowa. 1880-1881; 1904-1921 – 1 – us UMI [071]

JOURNAL – Falls City. Neb. 1869-1908; 1950- – 1 – us UMI [071]

JOURNAL – Fergus Falls. Minn. 1954- – 1 – us UMI [071]

JOURNAL / Forsyth, John R – 1849 – 1 – us KS Hist [920]

JOURNAL – Forsyth. Mont. 1908-1909 – 1 – us UMI [071]

JOURNAL / Franklin Institute. Philadelphia – v1-318. 1826-1984 – 1,5,6 – us Princeton Micro [600]
JOURNAL – Freeport. Ill. 1856-57; 1866-67; 1883-1913 – 1 – us UMI [071]
JOURNAL – Freeport. Ill. -w. 1848-82 – 1 – us UMI [071]
JOURNAL – Friday Harbor. Wash. -w. 1906-50 – 1 – us UMI [071]
JOURNAL – Galata. Mont. 1911-1920 – 1 – us UMI [071]
JOURNAL – Garnett. Kan. 1874-1912 – 1 – us UMI [071]
JOURNAL / Good, Adolphus Clemens – 1892 – 1 – $50.00 – us Presbyterian [240]
JOURNAL / Great Britain. Board of Trade – 1886-1960 – 1 – uk Microform Academic [324]
JOURNAL / Great Britain. Parliament. House of Commons – 155 v. 1547-1900 – 3 – us Readex [324]
JOURNAL / Great Britain. Parliament. House of Commons – Index. 1547-1900 – 3 – us Readex [324]
JOURNAL – Greenwood. S.C. 1895-1917 – 1 – us UMI [071]
JOURNAL / Hardin County. Ohio. Courthouse Building Commission – 1912-1917 – 1r – 1 – $32.50r – us Archival [324]
JOURNAL / Harvard University. Arnold Arboretum – v. 24. 1943; v. 27. 1950; v. 36-42. 1957-59. B-134 2 – 8 – ne IDC [580]
JOURNAL – Haverhill. Mass. 1958- 1965 – 1 – us UMI [071]
JOURNAL – Hemingford, NE. -w. Oct 1908-Oct 1909; Jan 1910; Aug 1911-Oct 1915 – 1 – us NE Hist [071]
JOURNAL – Herrin. Ill. 1913-1949 – 1 – us UMI [071]
JOURNAL – Hiawatha. Kan. 1889-1895 – 1 – us UMI [071]
JOURNAL / Huron County. Ohio. District Court – 1876-1897 – 1r – 1 – $32.50r – us Archival [324]
JOURNAL – (Index also available) – Santa Clara, CA. 1928-65 – 26r – 1 – $1,300.00 – B02946 – us Library Micro [073]
JOURNAL / Indian Chemical Society. Calcutta – v1-32. 1924-55 – 1,5,6 – us Princeton Micro [540]
JOURNAL / Indian Mathematical Society. Madras – v1-19. 1934-55 – 1,5,6 – us Princeton Micro [510]
JOURNAL – Indianapolis. Ind. 1857-65 – 1 – us UMI [071]
JOURNAL / Institute of Actuaries – 1850-to date – 1,9 – uk Microform Academic [310]
JOURNAL / Institute of Metals – v1-101. 1909-1973 – 1,5,6 – us Princeton Micro [660]
JOURNAL / Institute of Petroleum – 1-59. 1914-73 – 1,5,6 – us UMI [660]
JOURNAL / Institute of Petroleum – v1-26. 1914-1940 – 1,5,6 – us Princeton Micro [660]
JOURNAL / Institution of Mechanical Engineers. Railway Division – 1970-71 – us UMI [625]
JOURNAL / Interdenominational Theological Center – v1- . 1973- – 1,5,6,9 – us UMI [240]
JOURNAL / International Association for Mathematical Geology – v. 1- 1969- – 1,5,6 – us UMI [550]
JOURNAL / International Association of Pupil Personnel Workers – v. 1- 1957- – 1. 1976-; ; 56,9 – us UMI [370]
JOURNAL / International Phonetic Association – v. 1- 1971- – 1. ; 5,6,9 – apply; v.5- – us UMI [400]
JOURNAL / Iron and Steel Institute. London – v4-183 1872-1956 – 1,5,6 – us Princeton Micro [670]
JOURNAL – Isleton, CA. 1924-41; 1960-62 – 13r – 1 BC02316 – $650.00 – us Library Micro [071]
JOURNAL – Ithaca. N.Y. 1870; 1872- – 1 – us UMI [071]
JOURNAL – Jacksonville. Fla. 1901- – 1 – us UMI [071]
JOURNAL – Jamestown. N.Y. -w. 1826-70 – 1 – us UMI [071]
JOURNAL / Kansas. Bar Association – 1932-1; 1971- 5,6; 1977- 9 – us UMI [340]
JOURNAL / Kansas entomological society – 1928- 1; 1971- 5,6; 1977- 9 – us UMI [574]
JOURNAL – Knoxville. Tenn. 1885- – 1 – us UMI [071]
JOURNAL – La Cygne. Kansas. -w. 1870- – 1 – us UMI [071]
JOURNAL – Lafayette. Indiana. Also, Courier and pred. 1850-1919, 1920- – 1 – us UMI [071]
JOURNAL – Lancaster. Pa. -sw. 1816-18 – 1 – us UMI [071]
JOURNAL – Lancaster. Pa. -w. 1796-1816, 1819-36, 1841-45 – 1 – us UMI [071]
JOURNAL – Lane. Kan. 1913-1919 – 1 – us UMI [071]
JOURNAL – Lansing. Mich. -d. 1888-93, 1896-1910 – 1 – us UMI [071]
JOURNAL – Lansing. Mich. -w. 1892-96 – 1 – us UMI [071]
JOURNAL – Las Vegas, NV. 25 Apr 1929 – 1r – 1 – $50.00 – U04601 – us Library Micro [978]
JOURNAL / Leproserie du Village Segregation d'Akata-Palime, Togo – 9 – F40.00 – fr Ethnologie [610]
JOURNAL / Linnean Society – 1869 – 7 – uk Microform Academic [580]
JOURNAL / London Mathematical Society – v1-44 1926-69 – 1,5,6 – us Princeton Micro [510]
JOURNAL – Long Pine. Neb. 1883-1943 – 1 – us UMI [071]
JOURNAL – Lorain. Ohio. 1923- – 1 – us UMI [071]
JOURNAL / Lunsford, Isaac – (Methodist Preacher of Tenn.) Nov 1791-95 – 1 – 5.32 – us Baptist [978]
JOURNAL / McKay, Donald – 1870 1 – us KS Hist [978]
JOURNAL – Macomb. Ill. 1956- – 1 – us UMI [071]
JOURNAL – Mansfield. Ohio. 1930-1953 – 1 – us UMI [071]
JOURNAL / The Marine Biological Association – 1889-to date – 7,9 – uk Microform Academic [580]
JOURNAL – Marlington. West Virginia. 1951-1968 – 1 – us UMI [071]
JOURNAL – Martinsburg. West Virginia. 1912-1924; 1926-1929; 1933- – 1 – us UMI [071]
JOURNAL – Massac. Ill. 1872-1878 – 1 – us UMI [071]
JOURNAL / Mathematical Society of Japan – (Supersedes in part: Physico-Mathematical Society of Japan Journal). v. 1-23. 1949-71 – 1,5,6 – us Princeton Micro [510]
JOURNAL / Meeker, Jotham – 1832-55 – 1 – us KS Hist [978]
JOURNAL – Meriden. Conn. 1886-1940; 1946- – 1 – us UMI [071]
JOURNAL / Methodist Episcopal Church. Southwestern Conference – 1870-1905 – 1 – us KS Hist [978]
JOURNAL / Michigan School Board – v1-1956- 1; v21- 5,6; v24- 9 – us UMI [370]
JOURNAL – Middletown. Ohio. 1865-1866; 1948- – 1 – us UMI [071]
JOURNAL / Military Service Institution of the United States – v1-39. 1879-1906 – 1 – us UMI [355]
JOURNAL – Milwaukee. Wis. 1884-1909; 1921- – 1 – us UMI [071]
JOURNAL / Mine Ventilation Society of South Africa – (See also: Mine Ventilation Society of South Africa. Monthly Bulletin) – v10-1957- 1; v31- 5,6,9 – us UMI [622]
JOURNAL / Missouri Dental Association – 1917- 1; 1971- 5,6; 1975- 4 x 6 in. 9 – us UMI [617]
JOURNAL – Missouri State Medical Association. v.1-49. 1904-52. Superseded by Missouri Medicine – 1 – us UMI [610]
JOURNAL – Moundsville. West Virginia. -w. 1910-15 – 1 – us UMI [071]
JOURNAL – Muscatine. Iowa. 1856- – 1 – us UMI [071]
JOURNAL – Muscatine. Iowa. -w. 1851-54 – 1 – us UMI [071]
JOURNAL / National Association for Women Deans, Administrators, and Counselors – v37- 1973- 1,5,6; v40- 9 – us UMI [370]
JOURNAL / National Association for Women Deans and Counselors – v1-36 1938-73 1; v35-36 5,6 – us UMI [370]
JOURNAL / National Cancer Institute – v1-1940- 1; v37- 5,6; v58- 9 – us UMI [616]
JOURNAL / National Cancer Institute – v1-71. 1942-83 – 1,5,6 – us Princeton Micro [610]
JOURNAL – Nevada. Iowa. -w. 1895-1900 – 1 – us UMI [071]
JOURNAL / New England Water Works Association – v1- 1882- 1; v84- 5,6; v91- 9 – us UMI [628]
JOURNAL / New England Water Works Association – (Boston.) v. 41-84. 1927-1970 – 1,5,6 – us Princeton Micro [010]
JOURNAL / New York State Nurses Association – v4- 1973- 1,5,6; 1976- 9 – us UMI [073]
JOURNAL – Newburgh. N.Y. 1864-1874; 1876-1886; 1889-1917 – 1 – us UMI [071]
JOURNAL – Newburgh. N.Y. -w. 1841-1843 – 1 – us UMI [071]
JOURNAL – Newport. R.I. and Weekly News. 1874-1927 – 1 – us UMI [071]
JOURNAL – North Sacramento. Calif. -w. 1945-58 – 1 – us UMI [071]
JOURNAL – Northfork, CA. Jul 1977-80 – 3r – 1 – $150.00 – B02529 – us Library Micro [073]
JOURNAL – Norwich. N.Y. 1816-1830 – 1 – us UMI [071]
JOURNAL – Oklahoma City. Okl. 1964- – 1 – us UMI [071]
JOURNAL / Operations Research Society of America – v1-3. 1952-55 – 1 – us UMI [510]
JOURNAL / Orissa Historical Research Society – v. 1-16 (4). Bhubaneswar. 1952-68. BI-222 1 – 9 – ne IDC [950]
JOURNAL / OtoLaryngological Society of Australia – v1- 1961- 1; v3- 5,6; v4- 9 – us UMI [073]
JOURNAL – Ottawa. Kan. and pred. -w. 1865-68, 1870-1902 – 1 – us UMI [071]
JOURNAL – Paden City. West Virginia. 1965- – 1 – us UMI [071]
JOURNAL / Peck, John Mason – 1854-56. 114p – 1 – 5.00 – us Baptist [240]
JOURNAL – Pensacola. Fl. 1905-54 – 1 – us P.K. Yonge [071]
JOURNAL – Pensacola. Fl. 1955-59 – 1 – us UMI [071]
JOURNAL – Peoria. Ill. 1951-55 – 1 – us UMI [071]
JOURNAL / Pharmaceutical Society of Japan. Tokyo – v. 47-70. 1927-50 – 1,5,6 – us Princeton Micro [610]
JOURNAL / Physical Society of Japan – .v 1-43. 1946-77 – 1,5,6 – us Princeton Micro [530]
JOURNAL – Plattsmouth. Neb. 1890-1902; 1904-1962 – 1 – us UMI [071]
JOURNAL – Poughkeepsie. N.Y. 1960- – 1 – us UMI [071]
JOURNAL : A PROJECT OF THE AMERICAN CIVIL LIBERTIES UNION FOUNDATION, INC – v1-. 1984- – 1,5,6,9 – us UMI [323]
JOURNAL – Providence. R.I. 1830-1833 – 1 – us UMI [071]
JOURNAL – puis politique et litteraire D'Indre-et-Loire. Tours. 1809-15 – 1 – fr A.C.R.P.P. [073]
JOURNAL – Racine. Wis. -w. 1858-1912 – 1 – us UMI [071]
JOURNAL / Rathbun, Nathan – 1817-1849 – 1 reel – 1 – us Archival [920]
JOURNAL / Rathbun, Nathan – 1817-49 – 1r – 1 – $32.50r – us Archival [073]
JOURNAL – Rensselaer. Ind. 1898-1902 – 1 – us UMI [071]
JOURNAL / Rhodes-Livingstone Institute – 1944-65 – 7 – uk Microform Academic [960]
JOURNAL – Rochester, NV. Jan-May 1913 – 1r – 1 – $50.00 – U04732 – us Library Micro [071]
JOURNAL – Rock Hill. S.C. 1901-04 – 1 – us UMI [071]
JOURNAL – Rockport. Ind. 1933-1966 – 1 – us UMI [071]
JOURNAL / Royal Agricultural Society of England – 1933 to date – 1 – uk Microform Academic [630]
JOURNAL / Royal Agricultural Society of England – v. 1-133. 1840-1972 – 1,5,6 – us Princeton Micro [330]
JOURNAL / Royal Anthropological Institute of Great Britain and Ireland – v. 1-95. 1871-1965 – 1 – us UMI [306]
JOURNAL / Royal Army Veterinary Corps – v. 21-24. 1950-1953 – 1 – us UMI [636]
JOURNAL / Royal Asiatic Society – 1834- – 1 – uk Microform Academic [950]
JOURNAL / Royal Horticultural Society – xv 75-100 1950-75 1; v96-100 5,6 – us UMI [631]
JOURNAL / Royal Institute of Philosophy – 1926-1980 – 1 – uk Microform Academic [100]
JOURNAL / Royal Miscroscopical Society – v. 1-88. 1878-1968 – 1,5,6 – us Princeton Micro [576]
JOURNAL / Royal Society of Health – v1-1879- 1; v96- 5,6,9 – us UMI [610]
JOURNAL – Sacramento. Calif. 1970- – 1 – us UMI [071]
JOURNAL – Saint Paul. Kan. 1901-1953 – 1 – us UMI [071]
JOURNAL – Salina. Kan. and predecessors. -w., sw. 1885-1917 – 1 – us UMI [071]
JOURNAL – Salina. Kan. -d. 1887- – 1 – us UMI [071]
JOURNAL – San Lorenzo, CA. 1945-1946; 1948-1960; 1967-70 – 9r – 1 – $450.00 – B02900 – us Library Micro [073]
JOURNAL – Sandusky. Ohio. -w. 1879-1900 – 1 – us UMI [071]
JOURNAL – Sarasota. Fl. 1952- – 1 – us UMI [071]
JOURNAL / Shawnee County. Kansas. Board of Commissioners – 1855-62 – 1 – us KS Hist [978]
JOURNAL – Shreveport. La. 1895- – 1 – us UMI [071]
JOURNAL – Sidney. Ohio. 1863-1904 – 1 – us UMI [071]
JOURNAL – Sioux City. Iowa. 1864- – 1 – us UMI [071]
JOURNAL / Snowden, Gilbert T – 1783-85 – 1 – $50.00 – us Presbyterian [920]
JOURNAL / Societe d'archeologie lorraine et du musee historique lorrain – Nancy, 1852-94 – 7r – 1 – $585.00 – us UPA [944]
JOURNAL / Societe des americanistes de Paris – N.S.v.1-15. 1903-23 – 1 – 60.00 – us L of C Photodup [073]
JOURNAL / La Societe des Amis de la Constitution Monarchique – Par Fontanes. no. 1-27. Paris. dec 1790-juin 1791 – 1 – fr A.C.R.P.P. [944]
JOURNAL / Society for the Propagation of the Gospel in Foreign Parts – v. 1-50, and appendix. 1707-1870 – 1 – uk Microform Academic [240]
JOURNAL / Society of Chemical Industry – v. 1-69. 1881-1950 – 1,5,6 – us Princeton Micro [540]
JOURNAL – Society of Cinematologists. v1-5. 1961-65 – 1 – us UMI [410]
JOURNAL / Society of Cosmetic Chemists – v1-34. 1947-83 – 1,5,6 – us Princeton Micro [540]
JOURNAL / Society of Glass Technology – v. 1-5. 1917-1921. V. 25-39. 1941-1955 – 1,5,6 – us Princeton Micro [660]
JOURNAL / Society of Glass Technology. Sheffield – (v1-10 $248.00v; v11-43 $2410.00v) – v1-43 1917-59. All pub – 1 – $24,400.00 – uk Dawson [660]
JOURNAL / Society of Motion Picture and Television engineers – v. 11-37. 1927-1941 – 1,5,6 – us Princeton Micro [621]
JOURNAL / Society of Plastics Engineers – (See now: Plastics Engineering) – v1-29 1944-73 1; v22-29 5,6 – us UMI [624]
JOURNAL / Society of Research Administrators – v1- 1969- 1; v9- 5,6,9 – us UMI [370]
JOURNAL / Society of Telegraph Engineers and Electricians. London – v1-17. 1872-88 – 1,5,6 – us Princeton Micro [621]
JOURNAL / South African Institute of Mining and Metallurgy – v12-56. 1911-1956 – 1,5,6 – us Princeton Micro [622]
JOURNAL / South African Institution of Engineers – v16-49. 1917-51 – 1,5,6 – us Princeton Micro [620]
JOURNAL – South Bend. Wash. -w. 1890-98, 1900-05, 1907-56 – 1 – us UMI [071]
JOURNAL – South Pasadena. Calif. 1963- – 1 – us UMI [071]
JOURNAL – South San Francisco. Calif. -w. 1943-50 – 1 – us UMI [071]
JOURNAL – Southbridge. Mass. 1861-1900 – 1 – us UMI [071]
JOURNAL – Spartanburg. S.C. 1950- – 1 – us UMI [071]
JOURNAL – Springville. N.Y. and preds. 1867- – 1 – us UMI [071]
JOURNAL – Stevens Point. Wis. -w. 1873-1917, 1919-20 – 1 – us UMI [071]
JOURNAL – Tekamah. Neb. 1900-1918 – 1 – us UMI [071]
JOURNAL – (Title changes: Journal in Franckfurt am Main, 1724; Frankfurter Journal, 3 Mar 1873) – Frankfurt-Main, Germany. 1840-60 – 64r – 1 – gw Mikrofilm [072]
JOURNAL / Trades and Labour Congress – v3-35, no. 3. 1924-Mar 1956 – 1 – cn Precision [380]

JOURNAL – Tupelo. Miss. 1882-1897; 1900; 1902-1920; 1922-1924; 1926-1931; 1933- – 1 – us UMI [071]
JOURNAL – Tupelo. Miss. -sw. 1924-35 – 1 – us UMI [071]
JOURNAL / United Mine Workers – Washington. D.C. 1967-1970 – 1 – us UMI [331]
JOURNAL / United Reformed Church History Society – (1985-. 5,6,9) – 1973- – 1 – us UMI [240]
JOURNAL / U.S. Army. Quartermaster Corps. St. Louis Arsenal – 1844-50 – 1 – us KS Hist [324]
JOURNAL / U.S. Indian Claims Commission – 32 fiches – 9 – $110.00 – us UPA [305]
JOURNAL / University Film Association – v1-1949- 1; v29- 5,6,9 – us UMI [410]
JOURNAL – Utica. N.Y. 1902-1906 – 1 – us UMI [071]
JOURNAL – (v13- . 5,6. v18- . 9) – 1- 1958- – 1 – us UMI [330]
JOURNAL / Walker, William – 1866-69 – 1 – us KS Hist [978]
JOURNAL / Warburg Institute – London. v1-7. 1937-44.Continued by: Journal of the Warburg and Courtauld Institutes. v8-32. 1946-69. Lacking: v8, 1945; v23, 1960. O-525/1 – 9 – ne IDC [073]
JOURNAL / Warner, Sarah Gildersleeve – 6 Apr 1856-24 Mar 1892. With Thomas Paisley Warner, Journal, 1 Sept 1852-23 May 1868, 1870-25 Dec 1907 – 1 – us A.T.L.A. [240]
JOURNAL / Washington Academy of Sciences – v1-69. 1911-79 – 1,5,6 – us Princeton Micro [500]
JOURNAL / Washington Academy of Sciences – (v62- . 1972- . 5,6. v67- . 1977- . 9) – v1- . 1911- – 1. ; 5,6. ; 9 – apply; v.62-; v.67- – us UMI [500]
JOURNAL / Water Pollution Control Federation – Formerly: Sewage and Industrial Wastes. v1-18 1928-46 – 1,5,6 – us Princeton Micro [628]
JOURNAL / Water Pollution Control Federation – v1-27 1928-55 – 1,5,6 – us Princeton Micro [628]
JOURNAL / Water Pollution Control Federation – (v38- . 1966- . 5,6. v47- . 1975- . 9) – v. 1- 1928- – 1 – us UMI [628]
JOURNAL – Waukesha. Wis. 1889-91 – 1 – us UMI [071]
JOURNAL – (Weekly independent newspaper) – New Lisbon, OH. Apr 19 1867-Apr 4 1870 – 2r – 1 – us Western Res [071]
JOURNAL / West of Scotland Iron and Steel Institute – 1946-47, 1952-53 – 1 – uk Microform Academic [670]
JOURNAL – Westerly. R.I. 1888-1891 – 1 – us UMI [071]
JOURNAL – Whiting. Kan. 1898-1925 – 1 – us UMI [071]
JOURNAL / Whitsitt, William H – v1. 334p – 1 – 11.69 – us Baptist [240]
JOURNAL / Williamsburgh. South Carolina. Board of Commissioners – 1788-1811. 1 fiche – 9 – us South Carolina Historical [978]
JOURNAL – Willows. Calif. 1944- – 1 – us UMI [071]
JOURNAL – Wilmington. Ohio. 1868-1913 – 1 – us UMI [071]
JOURNAL – Wooster. Ohio. and Democratic Times. 1836-40 – 1 – us UMI [071]
JOURNAL / Wyandot County. Ohio. Supreme Court – 1846-1885 – 1r – 1 – $32.50r – us Archival [324]
JOURNAL – Yreka. California. -w.1946-59 – 1 – us UMI [071]
JOURNAL.. / Columbia University. Ancient Near Eastern Society – v1-13. 1968-81 – 1 – us UMI [073]
JOURNAL.. / Methodist Episcopal Church. Missouri Conference – 1849-64 – 1 – us KS Hist [978]
JOURNAL... / Coker, Daniel – Baltimore, 1820 – 1r – 1 – us Ross [073]
JOURNAL / American College of Nursing Home Administrators – (Cont by: Journal of long term care administration) – Silver Spring. v1 Fal 1972-Sum 1973* – 1 – D9138 – us UMI [610]
JOURNAL / Anthropological Institute of Great Britain and Ireland – (Ceased publ) – New York. v1. 1871-72 – 1 – D3359 – us UMI [301]
LE JOURNAL – Chambly, Canada. 3 mai 1966-v4 n43. 24 dec 1969 – 1r – 1 – Can$45.00 – cn Can Microfilming [072]
LE JOURNAL / ed by Francoeur, Louis et al – Quebec, Canada. 14 dec 1929-15 jun 1936 (hebdo); 20 jun 1936-28 oct 1938 (quotidien) – 11r – 1 – Can$40.00r – cn Can Microfilming [072]
LE JOURNAL = THE JOURNAL – Grand-Mere, Canada. 23 mar 1923-v3 n22. 22 aut 1925 – 1r – 1 – Can$40.00 – cn Can Microfilming [072]
LE JOURNAL = THE JOURNAL – Lachute, Canada. 20 sep 1978 – 1r – 1 – Can$20.00 – cn Can Microfilming [072]
LE JOURNAL / ed by Laventure, Felix – St-Bruno, Canada. v1 n14. 17 oct 1968-v6 n43. 24 dec 1974 – 2r – 1 – Can$60.00r – cn Can Microfilming [072]
LE JOURNAL – Lowell, MA. v1 n4. 23 avr 1916-v1 n13. 25 jun 1916 – 1r – 1 – Can$25.00 – cn Can Microfilming [071]
LE JOURNAL – puis Messager du matin. no. 1-96. Paris. 28 juil-31 oct 1848 – 1 – fr A.C.R.P.P. [073]
LE JOURNAL : QUOTIDIEN / ed by Forget, L-J – Montreal, Canada. 16 dec 1899-7 mar 1905 – 11r – 1 – Can$60.00r – cn Can Microfilming [072]
LE JOURNAL – Quotidien, litteraire, artistique et politique. Fond. Fernand Xau. Paris. 28 sept 1892-juin 1944 – 1 – fr A.C.R.P.P. [073]
O JOURNAL – Senna Madureira, Acre. 10 Fev-Set, Nov-8 Dez 1918 – 1,5,6 – bl Biblioteca [072]
THE JOURNAL – Albany, CA. 1988-1993 – 5r – 1 – $250.00 – B06007 – us Library Micro [073]
THE JOURNAL – (Cont: Stanstead Journal) – Rock-Island, 30 jun 1982-31 dec 1991 – 37r – 1 – Can$75.00 – cn Can Microfilming [072]
THE JOURNAL – Hemingford. Neb. 1908-1915 – 1 – us UMI [071]
THE JOURNAL = THE JOURNAL – Huntingdon, Canada. 4 nov 1952-v10 n25. 24 dec 1969 – 1r – 1 – Can$60.00 – cn Can Microfilming [072]
THE JOURNAL – South San Francisco, CA. 1943-50 – 5r – 1 – $250.00 – C03006 – us Library Micro [071]
THE JOURNAL – Technological Horizons in Education – v1- 1974- 1,5,6; v2- 9 – us UMI [370]
THE JOURNAL *see*
– THE GRAHAMSTOWN JOURNAL
– STANSTEAD JOURNAL
JOURNAL / American Association of Instructors and Investigators in Poultry Husbandry – (Ceased publ. Superseded by: Poultry Science) – New Brunswick. v1-7. nov 1914-jul 1921* – 1 – D12332 – us UMI [636]
JOURNAL. 75 V / Great Britain. Parliament. House of Commons – 1901-74. With Index – 3 – us Readex [324]
JOURNAL, 1765-1766, AND LETTER-BOOKS, 1772-1776 / Bardsley, S – (Coll title: The People Called Methodists, Phase 2: Primary Sources 1738-1800) – 21mf – 9 – MP-612/1 – ne IDC [240]
JOURNAL, 1773-1819 / Barrit, J – (Coll title: The People Called Methodists, Phase 2: Primary Sources 1738-1800) – 2mf – 9 – MP-613/1 – ne IDC [240]
JOURNAL, 1829-1835 / Hallam, J – (Coll title: The People Called Methodists, Phase 3: Primary Sources, 1801-1850) – 16mf – 9 – MP-686/1 – ne IDC [240]
JOURNAL, 1841-1851, 1853-1859 / Samuel, P – (Coll title: The People Called Methodists, Phase 3: Primary Sources, 1801-1850) – 3mf – 9 – MP-679/1 – ne IDC [240]
LE JOURNAL A UN SOU – Dir. Tony Revillon. no. 1-16. Paris. 7-22 dec 1879 – 1 – fr A.C.R.P.P. [073]
JOURNAL, ACTS AND PROCEEDINGS OF THE CONVENTION : WHICH FORMED THE CONSTITUTION OF THE UNITED STATES: PUBLISHED UNDER THE DIRECTION OF THE PRESIDENT – Boston: Thomas B Wait, 1819 – 6mf – 9 – $9.00 – LLMC 90-359 – us L.L.M.C. [340]
JOURNAL ADMINISTRATIF DE 1939 A 1943 / Documents Mangareviens – 9 – F40.00 – fr Ethnologie [306]
JOURNAL AMERICA – Huntingdon, PA. -w 1859-1870 – 13 – $25.00r – us I.M.R. [071]
JOURNAL. AMERICAN LIBRARY ASSOCIATION. HEALTH AND REHABILITATIVE LIBRARY SERVICES DIVISION *see* HRLSD JOURNAL
JOURNAL AMUSANT – Journal illustre, journal d'images, journal comique, critique, satirique et hebdomadaire. Paris. 1866-67, 1878-90 – 1 – fr A.C.R.P.P. [073]
JOURNAL AND ACCOUNT BOOK / Carter, John & Simerwell Elizabeth – 1861-1881 – 1 – us KS Hist [920]
JOURNAL AND ADVOCATE / Select Knights of Canada – Toronto: Select Knights of Canada, [1890?-189- or 19–] – 9 – cn C.I.H.M. [360]
JOURNAL AND ARGUS – Petaluma. Calif. 1864-1872 – 1 – us UMI [071]
JOURNAL AND CORRESPONDENCE, 1882-1886 / Gray, Elizabeth (nee McEwen) – 1r – at Pacific Mss [920]
JOURNAL AND GUIDE – Norfolk. Va. -w. 1916- – 1 – us UMI [071]
JOURNAL AND INVENTORIES / Belle Springs Creamery. Abilene, Kansas – 1892-98 – 1 – us KS Hist [025]
JOURNAL AND LETTERS OF THE ASIATIC SOCIETY OF BENGAL / Asiatic Society of Bengal – Calcutta. 1936-58. S. 4. v1.24. – 136mf – 8 – ne IDC [073]
JOURNAL AND MESSENGER – v1-63. 1831-94 (complete) – 28r – 1 – ATLA R0105 – us A.T.L.A. [073]
JOURNAL AND MESSENGER, CENTRAL NATIONAL BAPTIST PAPER – 1831-1920 – 1 – 1714.79 – us Baptist [240]
JOURNAL AND NEWS – Santa Clara. Calif. -w. 1966- – 1 – us UMI [071]
JOURNAL AND OFFICIAL GAZETTE / Workmen's Club – Working Men's Club and Institute Union. London. -w. 15 May 1875-9 Feb 1878. (1 reel) – 1 – uk British Libr Newspaper [330]
JOURNAL AND PROCEEDINGS / Institution of Mechanical Engineers – 1921-59 – 1,5,6 – us Princeton Micro [621]
JOURNAL AND PROCEEDINGS / Royal Society of New South Wales – v.2; 9-111. 1868; 1876-1978 – 1,5,6 – 483.00 – us Princeton Micro [500]
JOURNAL AND PROCEEDINGS OF THE ASIATIC SOCIETY OF BENGAL – N.S. Calcutta. v1-30. 1905-1935 – 416mf – 9 – ne IDC [950]
JOURNAL AND PROCEEDINGS OF THE INSTITUTION OF AGRICULTURAL ENGINEERS *see* AGRICULTURAL ENGINEER
JOURNAL AND PROCEEDINGS OF THE INSTITUTION OF BRITISH AGRICULTURAL ENGINEERS *see* AGRICULTURAL ENGINEER
JOURNAL AND REPORT OF JAMES L. CATHCART AND JAMES HUTTON, AGENTS APPOINTED BY THE SECTY. OF THE NAVY TO SURVEY TIMBER RESOURCES BETWEEN THE MERMENTAU AND MOBILE RIVERS, 1818-19 / U.S. Bureau of Land Management – 1roll. M8 – 1 – us Nat'l Archives [324]
JOURNAL AND TRANSACTIONS / Electrochemical Society – v1-102. 1902-55 – 1,5,6 – us Princeton Micro [540]
JOURNAL AND TRIBUNE – Logansport. Ind. 1876-1920 – 1 – us UMI [071]
JOURNAL ANGLICAN *see* CANADIAN CHURCHMAN
JOURNAL ANNUEL DE LA STE. HISTORIQUE DE LA VALLEE DE LA CHATEAUGUAY – Huntingdon. v1 n1 1968-n25. 1992 – 1r – 1 – cn Can Microfilming [073]
JOURNAL ASIATIQUE – Paris, 1822-1941 – 1929mf – 9 – ne IDC [950]
JOURNAL ASIATIQUE OU RECUEIL DE MEMOIRES, D'EXTRAITS ET DE NOTICES – Paris. 1823-24, 1826-27, 1930-38. devenu: Nouveau journal asiatique ou Recueil – 1 – fr A.C.R.P.P. [073]
JOURNAL BELGE DE NEUROLOGIE ET DE PSYCHIATRIE *see*
– ACTA NEUROLOGICA BELGICA
JOURNAL BOOKS OF SCIENTIFIC MEETINGS, 1660-1800 / Royal Society – $1,740.00 – 0-89093-875-X – us UPA [015]
JOURNAL BRITANNIQUE / ed by Maty, M – The Hague. 24v. 1750-1757 – 130mf – 9 – ne IDC [941]
LE JOURNAL CHALEUR – New Richmond, Canada. 19 mar 1975-29 dec 1991 – 18r – 1 – Can$70.00r – cn Can Microfilming [072]
LE JOURNAL (CHAMBLY, QUEBEC) – Chambly. v1-11. 1966-78. SEM35P255 – 11r – 1 – Can$616.00 – cn Bibl Nat [072]
LE JOURNAL CHOC *see* LE CHOC DES IDEES
JOURNAL COMMERCIAL DE POINTE A PITRE – French West Indies. 1841-1842; 1844; 1864 – apply; 32M; 1 – us UMI [072]
Journal Company Print. Lawrence, Kansas *see* SPECIMENS OF CUSTOM WORK
JOURNAL CONSTRUCTO – Quebec, [ca 1963]-. SEM35P329 – 36r – 1 – cn Bibl Nat [690]
JOURNAL CONTACT LAVAL – Ville de Laval, Canada. 13 fev; 3 jul 1974 – 1r – 1 – Can$25.00 – cn Can Microfilming [072]
JOURNAL D' EXTREME ORIENT – Saigon, Vietnam. 1956 – 1 – us Res Libr [072]
JOURNAL DA TARDE – Sao Paulo, 1 May-Jun 1867; Mar-30 Apr 1979 – 1,5,6 – bl Biblioteca [072]
JOURNAL DA TARDE – Sao Paulo, 10 Nov 1878-4 Aug 1881 – 1,5,6 – bl Biblioteca [072]
JOURNAL D'ABBEVILLE ET DE L'ARRONDISSEMENT – Feuille politique, agricole, commerciale, litteraire et d'annonces. devenu: Le Pilote de la Somme. Journal d'Abbeville et de l'arrondissement. Abbeville. 1842-47 – 1 – fr A.C.R.P.P. [073]
LE JOURNAL D'AGRICULTURE – Montreal: G.E. Desbarats, [1877-1879] – 9 – cn C.I.H.M. [630]
LE JOURNAL D'AGRICULTURE – St-Hyacinthe, Canada. 29 sep 1869-12 fev 1873 – 1r – 1 – Can$40.00 – cn Can Microfilming [630]
LE JOURNAL D'AGRICULTURE *see* LE JOURNAL D'AGRICULTURE ILLUSTRE
LE JOURNAL D'AGRICULTURE CANADIEN – Montreal: W Evans, [1844?-1845?] – 9 – cn C.I.H.M. [630]
JOURNAL D'AGRICULTURE ET D'HORTICULTURE – Montreal, Canada. 8 jan 1898-19 sep 1936 – 12r – 1 – Can$60.00r – cn Can Microfilming [630]
LE JOURNAL D'AGRICULTURE ET D'HORTICULTURE *see* LE JOURNAL D'AGRICULTURE ILLUSTRE
JOURNAL D'AGRICULTURE ET PROCEDES DE LA SOCIETE D'AGRICULTURE DU BAS-CANADA / La Societe d'Agriculture du Bas-Canada – (Becomes: Journal d'Agriculture et Transactions de la Societe d'Agriculture du Bas-Canada jan 1849-avr 1853) – Montreal, jan-dec 1848 – 2r – 1 – Can$75.00r – cn Can Microfilming [630]
JOURNAL D'AGRICULTURE ET TRANSACTIONS DE LA SOCIETE D'AGRICULTURE DU BAS-CANADA *see* JOURNAL D'AGRICULTURE ET PROCEDES DE LA SOCIETE D'AGRICULTURE DU BAS-CANADA
LE JOURNAL D'AGRICULTURE ILLUSTRE – Montreal: E Senecal, [1879-1897] – 9 – cn C.I.H.M. [630]
LE JOURNAL D'AGRICULTURE ILLUSTRE – Montreal, fev 1877-22 dec 1897 – 3r – 1 – Can$65.00 – cn Can Microfilming [072]
JOURNAL D'ALSACE – Elsaesser Journal. Strasbourg. juin-dec 1873 – 1 – fr A.C.R.P.P. [073]
JOURNAL, DALTON TRANSACTIONS / Chemical Society. London – 1972-75 – 1,5,6 – us Princeton Micro [540]
JOURNAL D'ANALYSE MATHEMATIQUE – v1-3. 1951-55 – 1,5,6 – us Princeton Micro [073]
JOURNAL D'ANTOINE GALLAND PENDANT SON SEJOUR A CONSTANTINOPLE: 1672-1673 / Galland, Antoine – Publie par C. Schefer. Paris, E. Leroux, 1881, 2 t. en 1 v., xvii-286 plus 220 p. French Voyagers in the Medditeranean 16th to 18th Centuries. 6006 – 9 – fr Hachette [944]
LE JOURNAL D'ARTHABASKA – Arthabaska, Canada. 5 oct 1877-5 oct 1878 – 1r – 1 – Can$25.00 – cn Can Microfilming [072]
JOURNAL D'ATHENES – Greece. -w. 22 Feb 1879-25 Feb 1883; 7 March-25 May 1886. Imperfect. 1 reel – 1 – uk British Libr Newspaper [949]
JOURNAL DE BARR *see* BARRER KANTONS-BLATT
JOURNAL DE BEAUNE – Beaune (Cote-d'Or), March 1855 – Dec. 1893 – 18r – 1 – fr Armell [073]
JOURNAL DE BOTANIQUE, APPLIQUEE A L'AGRICULTURE, A LA PHARMACIE, A LA MEDECINE... / ed by Desvaux, A N – Paris, 1813-1814. 4v – 20mf – 9 – ne IDC [580]
JOURNAL DE BOTANIQUE NEA1ERLANDAISE / Miquel, F A W – Amsterdam, etc., 1861. 384 pp., 3 pls. B-7148 1 – 9 – ne IDC [580]

JOURNAL DE BOTANIQUE, REDIGE PAR UNE SOCIETE DE BOTANISTES / ed by Desvaux, A N – Paris. 2v. 1808-1809 – 16mf – 9 – ne IDC [580]
JOURNAL DE CE QUI S'EST FAIT A ROME DANS L'AFFAIRE DES CINQ PROPOSITIONS / Saint-Amour, L G de – Amsterdam, 1662 – Dfl105.00 – ne Slangenburg [240]
JOURNAL DE CE QUI S'EST PASSE A LA TOUR DU TEMPLE, PENDANT LA CAPTIVITE DE LOUIS XVI, ROI DE FRANCE / Clery, Jean Baptiste Cant Hanet – Londres: Baylis, 1798. SEM105P952 – 3mf – 9 – Can$6.75 – cn Bibl Nat [944]
JOURNAL DE CHAMBLY – Chambly. v11-20. ca 1978-1987. SEM35P213 – 18r – 1 – Can$796.00 – cn Bibl Nat [072]
JOURNAL DE CHAMBLY (1989) – Chambly. v22 no 32 (11 Avril 1989)-. SEM35P336 – 9r – 1 – Can$522.00 – cn Bibl Nat [072]
LE JOURNAL DE CHATEAUBRIANT : POLITIQUE, LITTERAIRE (...) – (Numerous missing numbers) – Hebd., Chateaubriant (Loire-Atlantique), janv. 1889-dec. 1948 (nombreux no. manq.) – 7r – 1 – F4,042.84 – fr Armell [320]
JOURNAL DE CHIMIE PHYSIQUE ET DE PHYSIOCHIMIE BIOLOGIQUE – v. 1-56. 1903-1959 – 1,5,6 – us Princeton Micro [530]
JOURNAL DE COMINES – et des environs. Comines. mai 1908-juin 1914 – 1 – fr A.C.R.P.P. [073]
LE JOURNAL DE COMPTON NEWS *see* ECHO DE COMPTON NEWS
JOURNAL DE CONCHYLIOLOGIE – (Index 1850-1892, v1-40) – Paris. v1-84. 1850-1940/1941 – 668mf – 9 – ne IDC [590]
JOURNAL DE CONSTANTINOPLE ET DES INTERETS ORIENTAUX – devenu par fusion: Journal de Constantinople. Echo de l'Orient. Constantinople. oct 1843-46, fevr 1848-53 – 1 – fr A.C.R.P.P. [073]
LE JOURNAL DE CULTIVATEUR ET DE L'OUVRIER – Sorel, Canada. v1 n2. 26 fev 1876-v2 n52. 9 fev 1878 – 1r – 1 – Can$75.00 – cn Can Microfilming [631]
JOURNAL DE FRANCOISE / ed by Barry, Robertine – Montreal, Canada. 29 mar 1902-15 avr 1909 – 2r – 1 – Can$40.00r – cn Can Microfilming [072]
LE JOURNAL DE FRASERVILLE *see* LE JOUR
LE JOURNAL DE FRONTENAC – Cowansville, Canada. v5 n8. 21 jul 1965; 22 fev 1967-29 sep 1971 – 1r – 1 – Can$50.00 – cn Can Microfilming [072]
LE JOURNAL DE FRONTENAC – La Guadeloupe, Canada. v5 n8. 21 jul 1965; 22 fev 1967-v14 n6. 29 sep 1971 – 1r – 1 – Can$50.00 – cn Can Microfilming [072]
JOURNAL DE GENEVE – 12r per y – 1 – inquire – us Ross [073]
JOURNAL DE GENEVE – 1970-1995 – 6r per y – 5,6 – Sfr1,069.00 – sz Infoprint [944]
JOURNAL DE GENEVE – 1993-1995 – 12 times per yr – 1 – F5,000.00 – sz Infoprint [072]
JOURNAL DE GENEVE – Geneva: [s.n.] jul 1938-feb 1948; aug 16 1948-apr 1976 – us Res Libr [949]
JOURNAL DE GENEVE – Geneva. Switzerland. 1975- – 1 – us Primary [949]
JOURNAL DE GENEVE – National, politique et litteraire. no. 1-118. Geneve. janv-avr 1917. mq no. 19, 93 – 1 – fr A.C.R.P.P. [949]
JOURNAL DE GENEVE – Switzerland. -d. 8 Nov 1914-9 Aug 1919; 1 Jan-30 Jun 1938. 36 reels – 1 – uk British Libr Newspaper [949]
JOURNAL DE GYNECOLOGIE OBSTETRIQUE ET BIOLOGIE DE LA REPRODUCTION – v1-1972- 1; v6- 1977- 5,6,9 – us UMI [618]
JOURNAL DE JURISPRUDENCE – Dedie a Son Altesse serenissime electorale palatine. Bouillon. 1763-mai 1764 (I-VI) – 1 – fr A.C.R.P.P. [073]
JOURNAL DE JURISPRUDENCE COMMERCIALE ET MARITIME. – Marseille. On film: v1-91, 93-114; 1820-1913, 1915-37. LL-0227 – 1 – us L of C Photodup [340]
JOURNAL DE LA CONTRE-REVOLUTION – Redige par M. Suleau a Neuwied sur le Rhin. no. 1, 3. 1791-92 – 1 – fr A.C.R.P.P. [073]
JOURNAL DE LA LIBERTE DE LA PRESSE – devenu: Le Tribun du peuple ou le Defenseur des droits de l'homme. no. 1-43. Paris. sept 1794-avr 1796 – 1 – fr A.C.R.P.P. [073]
JOURNAL DE LA LIBRAIRIE OU CATALOGUE HEBDOMADAIRE CONTENANT PAR ORDRE ALPHABETIQUE LES LIVRES, TANT NATIONAUX QU'ETRANGERS – Paris. 1764-79 (II-XVII) – 1 – fr A.C.R.P.P. [010]
JOURNAL DE LA MONTAGNE – Paris. juin 1793-nov 1794 – 1 – fr A.C.R.P.P. [073]
JOURNAL DE LA PARFUMERIE FRANCAISE – Paris, France. -f. 15 Jan 1897-10 July 1914. 5 reels – 1 – uk British Libr Newspaper [073]
JOURNAL DE LA REPUBLIQUE – Le journal de la guerre. juil 1870-fevr 1871 – 1 – fr A.C.R.P.P. [073]
JOURNAL DE LA REPUBLIQUE FRANCAISE, PAR MARAT... – (Cont. as: Le Publiciste de la Republique francaise,...) – [Paris], 1792-1793 (6-242) – 19mf – 9 – ne IDC [944]
JOURNAL DE LA ROER *see* AACHENER ZEITUNG
JOURNAL DE LA SOCIETE DES AMERICANISTES DE PARIS – 1895-1976 – 9 – fr I.C.S. [970]
JOURNAL DE LA SOCIETE HONGROISE DE STATISTIQUE / Magyar Statisztikai Tarsasag. Budapest – v.1-23, 1923-45 – 1 – 92.00 – us L of C Photodup [310]
JOURNAL DE LA SOCIETE IMPERIALE ET CENTRALE D'HORTICULTURE – Paris. v1-12 1855-1866; S.2 v1-12 1867-1878; S.3 v1-21 1879-1899; S.4 v1-8 1900-1907 – 930mf – 9 – ne IDC [630]
LE JOURNAL DE LA SOLIDARITE FRANCAISE – no. 41, 46, 61. Paris. juin-dec 1935 – 1 – fr A.C.R.P.P. [073]
JOURNAL DE LA VIENNE, DES DEUX-SEVRES ET DE LA VENDEE – Gazette des provinces de l'Ouest. Poitiers. 1861 – 1 – fr A.C.R.P.P. [073]
JOURNAL DE L'AGRICULTURE, DU COMMERCE, DES ARTS ET DES FINANCES / ed by Pont, Pierre-Samuel du – Jul 1765-Nov 1766. Series: French Economists of the 18th Century – 21 fiches – 9 – $80.00 – us UPA [630]
JOURNAL DE L'AGRICULTURE, DU COMMERCE ET DES FINANCES – Paris. juil 1765-74, 1780-83 – 1 – fr A.C.R.P.P. [073]
JOURNAL DE L'AIN – Bourg. 1848 – 1 – fr A.C.R.P.P. [073]
JOURNAL DE L'ARRONDISSEMENT DE SAINT-ETIENNE – (7 missing numbers) – Hebd, Saint-Etienne (Loire), oct. 1808-dec 1810 (7 no. manq.) – 1r – 1 – F227,71 – fr Armell [073]
JOURNAL DE L'ASSOCIATION CANADIENNE DE LA FORMATION PROFESSIONELLE *see* CANADIAN VOCATIONAL JOURNAL
JOURNAL DE LAVAL ET DE LA MAYENNE – Laval, March 1895 – Jan. 1914 – 8r – 1 – fr Armell [944]
JOURNAL DE L'ECLAIRAGE AU GAZ – Paris, France. -w. Apr 1866-Dec 1906 – 11r – 1 – uk British Libr Newspaper [624]
JOURNAL DE LECTURE, OU RECUEIL POUR LES OISIFS – Paris, Amsterdam. 12v. 1775-1778 – 87mf – 9 – ne IDC [440]
JOURNAL DE L'EDUCATION – Montreal: J.B. Rolland, [1880] – 9 – cn C.I.H.M. [370]
JOURNAL DE L'EDUCATION *see* JOURNAL DE L'INSTRUCTION PUBLIQUE
LE JOURNAL DE L'EST – Ville St-Michel. v1 n10. 12 jun 1952-v1 n33. 20 nov 1952 – 1r – 1 – Can$30.00 – cn Can Microfilming [072]
LE JOURNAL DE LEVIS – Levis, Canada. v1 n2. 18 avr 1865-v2 n90. 16 nov 1866 – 1r – 1 – Can$35.00 – cn Can Microfilming [072]
JOURNAL DE L'EXPLOITATION DES CORPS GRAS INDUSTRIELS – Paris. (Les Corps gras industriels). -m Jul 1874-Aug 1914; Jan 1927-Feb 1928. 16 reels – 1 – uk British Libr Newspaper [338]
JOURNAL DE L'EXPOSITION / ed by Barthe, Ulrich – Quebec, 12,13 sep 1894 – 1r – 1 – Can$25.00 – cn Can Microfilming [900]
LE JOURNAL DE L'ILE JESUS / ed by Chevalier, J-Guy – Ville de Laval, Canada. 5 dec 1962-3 aut 1966 – 2r – 1 – Can$50.00r – cn Can Microfilming [072]
LE JOURNAL DE L'ILLINOIS – Kankakee, Chicago, IL. 20 fev 1857-7 jan 1859 – 1r – 1 – Can$50.00 – cn Can Microfilming [071]
JOURNAL DE L'INDUSTRIEL ET DU CAPITALISTE – Publ. par une societe d'ingenieurs civils. Paris. 1836-40 – 1 – fr A.C.R.P.P. [073]
JOURNAL DE L'INSTRUCTION PUBLIQUE – Montreal: J.B. Rolland, [1880?-1898] – 9 – cn C.I.H.M. [370]
JOURNAL DE L'INSTRUCTION PUBLIQUE – Quebec, Canada. jan 1857-juin 1879 – 3r – 1 – Can$50.00r – cn Can Microfilming [073]
JOURNAL DE L'INSTRUCTION PUBLIQUE *see*
– JOURNAL DE L'EDUCATION
– THE JOURNAL OF EDUCATION
– THE JOURNAL OF EDUCATION FOR LOWER CANADA
JOURNAL DE LONDRES – London, UK. 10 Sept-29 Oct 1909 – 1 – uk British Libr Newspaper [072]
LE JOURNAL DE LONGUEUIL – Longueuil, Canada. 22 jan 1892 – 1r – 1 – Can$20.00 – cn Can Microfilming [072]
JOURNAL DE L'OUEST – Poitiers. 1901 – 1 – fr A.C.R.P.P. [073]
JOURNAL DE LOUIS 16 ET DE SON PEUPLE OU LE DEFENSEUR DE L'AUTEL, DU TRONE ET DE LA PATRIE – Paris, nov 1790-aout 1792 (I-X) – 1 – fr A.C.R.P.P. [073]
JOURNAL DE LUNEVILLE – Republicain. Luneville. 1923-39 – 1 – fr A.C.R.P.P. [073]
JOURNAL DE MADAGASCAR – Franco-malgache. Tananarive. fevr 1923-mai 1925 – 1 – fr A.C.R.P.P. [073]
LE JOURNAL DE MAGOG – (Cont by: Le Nouveau Journal 29 jun 1966-20 dec 1967) – Magog, Canada. 4 nov 1964-28 jun 1966 – 2r – 1 – Can$55.00r – cn Can Microfilming [072]
JOURNAL DE MARSEILLE – Marseille. 1898 – 1 – fr A.C.R.P.P. [073]
JOURNAL DE MATHEMATIQUES PURES ET APPLIQUEES – Series 1-9. 1836-1982. Continues: Annales de Mathematiques pures et appliquees – 1,5,6 – us Princeton Micro [510]
JOURNAL DE MATHEMATIQUES PURES ET APPLIQUES – s1. v1- s9. v57 1836-1976 – 1,5,6 – us UMI [510]
JOURNAL DE MECANIQUE – v. 1-15. 1962-1976 – 1,5,6 – us UMI [621]
LE JOURNAL DE MEDECINE = QUEBEC MEDICAL JOURNAL – Quebec, Canada. 2 jan 1826-oct 1827 – 1r – 1 – Can$30.00 – cn Can Microfilming [610]
JOURNAL DE MES VOYAGES [SUIVI DE] LETTRES DE DESRIDELIERES-LEROUX FAITES A SON PERE ET A DIVERSES AUTRES PERSONNES / Desridelieres-Leroux – 18th cent – 1 – F209.68 – fr Armell [910]
JOURNAL DE MONACO : BULLETIN OFFICIEL DE LA PRINCIPAUTE – v101-110. 1958-67 – 7r – 1 – us Ross [324]
JOURNAL DE MONSIEUR SULEAU – Redige a Coblentz et dedie a toutes les puissances. Paris, Neuwied sur le Rhin. avr 1791-avr 1792 – 1 – fr A.C.R.P.P. [073]
JOURNAL DE MONTREAL / ed by Peladeau, Pierre – Montreal, Canada. 15 jun 1964-31 dec 1992 – 549r – 1 – cn Can Microfilming [072]
JOURNAL DE MOSCOU – Hebdomadaire politique, economique, social et litteraire. Moscou. avr 1934-avr 1939 – 1 – fr A.C.R.P.P. [073]
JOURNAL DE MUSIQUE / Lagard, N de – (12 issues in 1v. Each issue signed by the composer) – Paris: Prault et Duchesne, 1758 – 1 – us Sibley [780]
JOURNAL DE NAVIGATION DE L'INFERNET DANS LE PACIFIQUE, 1874-76 / Augarde, L – 9 – F40.00 – fr Ethnologie [910]
JOURNAL DE NAVIGATION DU VOYAGE DE LA COSTE DE GUINEE. / Des Marchais, Etienne Renaud – Holograph – 1 – us Res Libr [910]
JOURNAL DE NEUBOURG – Dir. E. Dumont. Rouen. 1932-36 – 1 – fr A.C.R.P.P. [073]
JOURNAL DE NEUROLOGIE *see*
– ACTA NEUROLOGICA BELGICA
JOURNAL DE NEUROLOGIE ET DE PSYCHIATRIE *see*
– ACTA NEUROLOGICA BELGICA
JOURNAL DE NOEL – Quebec, Canada. 25 dec 1906 – 1r – 1 – Can$25.00 – cn Can Microfilming [240]
JOURNAL DE NOEL DES FACTEURS DE QUEBEC – Quebec, Canada. 1920 – 1r – 1 – Can$25.00 – cn Can Microfilming [072]
JOURNAL DE PAQUES – Quebec, Canada. 7 avr 1906; 1907; 1911 – 1r – 1 – Can$25.00 – cn Can Microfilming [240]
JOURNAL DE PARIS – Paris. National, politique, et litteraire. janv-juin 1869, Janv-juin 1875, janv-avr 1876 – 1 – fr A.C.R.P.P. [073]
JOURNAL DE PARIS – puis de Paris et des departemens. 1777-juin 1827. devenu: Nouveau journal de Paris et des departemens. Feuille administrative, commerciale, industrielle et litteraire. no. 1-679. aout 1827-juin 1829. devenu: La France nouvelle. Nouveau journal de Paris. Politique, litteraire et industriel. no. 680-2109. juin 1829-juin 1833. devenu: Journal de Paris. Nouvelliste du matin et du soir. juin 1833-mai 1840. Paris. 1777-97, 21 mars 1798-22 sept 1800, 21 mai 1801-1839 – 1 – fr A.C.R.P.P. [073]
JOURNAL DE PARIS, OU POSTE DU SOIR – Paris, 1784-1793, 1805(May)-1811 – 571mf – 9 – ne IDC [944]
JOURNAL DE PHARMACIE ET DE CHIMIE – Series 1-9. 1809-1942 – 1,5,6 – us Princeton Micro [615]
JOURNAL DE PHYSIQUE – Series 1-8. 1872-1949. Continues: Journal de Physique et le Radium – 1,5,6 – us Princeton Micro [530]
JOURNAL DE PHYSIQUE *see* OBSERVATIONS ET MEMOIRES SUR LA PHYSIQUE, SUR L'HISTOIRE NATURELLE ET SUR LES ARTS...
JOURNAL DE PHYSIQUE, DE CHIMIE, D'HISTOIRE NATURELLE ET DES ARTS – Paris. v.1-39, 40-67, 68-96. 1773-1823 – 3 – us Readex [500]
JOURNAL DE QUEBEC / ed by Cauchon, Joseph & Cote, Augustin – Quebec, Canada. 1 dec 1842-1 oct 1889 – 36r – 1 – Can$50.00r – cn Can Microfilming [072]
JOURNAL DE QUEBEC – Quebec, 1853-1882 – 12r – 1 – cn Preston [971]
LE JOURNAL DE QUEBEC – Quebec, Canada. 1842-53; 1862-73 – 31r – 1 – $2,015.00 – cn Library Assoc [971]
LE JOURNAL DE QUEBEC – Quebec, Canada. 6 mar 1967-31 dec 1992 – 324+ r – 1 – cn Can Microfilming [072]
LE JOURNAL DE QUEBEC AU SAGUENAY – Chicoutimi, 8 nov 1973-3 oct 1981f – 61r – 1 – Can$70.00 – cn Can Microfilming [072]
LE JOURNAL DE QUEBEC ET LE TOMBEAU DE CHAMPLAIN / Drapeau, Stanislas – Quebec: s.n., 1867 (Quebec: Canadien). 02762. (Pre-1900 Canadiana) – 9 – cn C.I.H.M. [971]
LE JOURNAL DE RICHMOND = RICHMOND JOURNAL / ed by Poirier, Osias – Asbestos, Canada. 28 jan 1954-30 mar 1965 – 1r – 1 – Can$50.00 – cn Can Microfilming [073]
LE JOURNAL DE RIMOUSKI – Rimouski, Canada. 10 jun-10 aut 1899 – 1r – 1 – Can$30.00 – cn Can Microfilming [072]
LE JOURNAL DE ROME – Paris. v2 n248. 27 oct 1882; v2 n250. 29 oct 1882 – 1r – 1 – Can$25.00 – cn Can Microfilming [072]
JOURNAL DE ROUTE DE HENRI DUVEYRIER, PUBLIE ET ANNOTE PAR CH. MAUNOIR ET H. SCHIRMER; PRECEDE D'UNE BIOGRAPHIE DE H. DUVEYRIER... / Duveyrier, Henri – Paris: Challamel, 1905 – 1 – F125.24 – fr Armell [910]
JOURNAL DE ROUTE D'UN CAPORAL DE TIRAILLEURS DE LA MISSION SAHARIENNE, 1898-1900 / Guilleux, Charles – [Belfort: Impr J Spitzmuller] – us Res Libr [960]
LE JOURNAL DE ROYAN – Marennes. 22 mai 1859-8 mai 1860, 2 9 juil 1876-79 – 1 – fr A.C.R.P.P. [073]
LE JOURNAL DE SAINT-HYACINTHE – St-Hyacinthe, Canada. v1 n3. 7 oct 1861-v7 n77. 3 aut 1868 – 2r – 1 – Can$50.00r – cn Can Microfilming [072]
JOURNAL DE SAINT-LAURENT – Ville de St-Laurent, Canada. 19 fev 1963 – 1r – 1 – Can$20.00 – cn Can Microfilming [072]
LE JOURNAL DE SAINT-LEONARD – Ville St-Leonard, Canada. 9 aut 1978-6 dec 1987 – 6r – 1 – Can$65.00 – cn Can Microfilming [072]
JOURNAL DE SAINT-PETERSBOURG – no. 79-232. Saint-Petersbourg. 1840. mq no. 157 – 1 – fr A.C.R.P.P. [073]
LE JOURNAL DE SAINT-ROCH – Quebec, Canada. 14 dec 1874-12 fev 1876 – 1r – 1 – Can$35.00 – cn Can Microfilming [072]
JOURNAL DE SAONE-ET-LOIRE – Macon, July 1826 – Jan. 1921 – 5r – fr Armell [944]
JOURNAL DE SAVERNE – Saverne, France. 1817-1940 – 1 – fr A.C.R.P.P. [072]

LE JOURNAL DE SHERBROOKE – (Cont by: Le Sherbrookois 23 oct 1968) – Sherbrooke, Canada. v3 n46. 4 dec 1966-avr 1968 – 1r – 1 – Can$45.00 – cn Can Microfilming [072]
JOURNAL DE SMYRNE – Commercial, politique et litteraire. Smyrne. 1834-38 – 1 – fr A.C.R.P.P. [073]
LE JOURNAL DE SOREL – Sorel, Canada. 22 aut 1867-1 oct 1869 – 1r – 1 – Can$75.00 – cn Can Microfilming [072]
LE JOURNAL DE ST BRUNO (1977) – St. Bruno. v10-12. 1977-79. SEM35P278 – 3r – 1 – Can$143.00 – cn Bibl Nat [072]
LE JOURNAL DE ST BRUNO (1982) – St. Bruno. v16- 1982-. SEM35P214 – 20r – 1 – Can$973.00 – cn Bibl Nat [072]
JOURNAL DE ST-HUGUES – St-Hugues, 1 mai 1881 – 1r – 1 – Can$25.00 – cn Can Microfilming [072]
JOURNAL DE ST-LEONHARD – Ville St-Leonhard, 29 dec 1966-19 oct 1971f – 1r – 1 – Can$65.00 – cn Can Microfilming [072]
LE JOURNAL DE TOURAINE – Touraine, Canada. dec 1967-v9 n4. 27 oct 1976 – 1r – 1 – Can$25.00 – cn Can Microfilming [072]
JOURNAL DE TOURCOING – (18 missing numbers) – Tourcoing (Nord), Sept 1885-Sept 1888 – 5r – 1 – fr Armell [944]
JOURNAL DE TOURCOING – Tourcoing (Nord), June 1889-June 1890 – 2r – fr Armell [944]
LE JOURNAL DE WATERLOO / ed by Seguin, J-O & Dagenais, Gerard – Waterloo, Canada. v1 n26. 23 mai 1882-5 oct 1956 – 16r – 1 – Can$50.00r – cn Can Microfilming [072]
JOURNAL DE ZOOLOGIE – Paris. v1-6. 1872-1877 – 63mf – 9 – ne IDC [590]
JOURNAL DE ZOOLOGIE, COMPRENANT LES DIFFERENTES BRANCHES DE CETTE SCIENCE – Paris, 1872-77 – 3 – us Readex [590]
JOURNAL D'EDUCATION – Quebec: L Brousseau, 1881-[1882] – 9 – cn C.I.H.M. [370]
JOURNAL DER DISTRIKTE MINDEN, BIELEFELD UND RINTELN – (Cont by: Oeffentliche Anzeigen des Weserdepartements, apr 4 1810) – Bielefeld, 1809-10 – 1 – Inquire at Mikrofilmarchiv for details – gw Misc Inst [350]
JOURNAL DER PHYSIK / Annalen der Physik – Halle, 1790-94 – 3 – us Readex [530]
JOURNAL DER PHYSIK 1.1790-8.1794. NEUES JOURNAL DER PHYSIK 1.1795-4.1797 – Halle, Leipzig, 1790-1797 (mf ed 1993) – 41mf – 9 – DM560.00 – 3-89131-162-1 – gw Fischer [530]
JOURNAL DER PRACTISCHEN ARZNEYKUNDE UND WUNDARZNEYKUNST 1. 1795-98. 1844 / ed by Hufeland, C W – 1795-1844 (mf ed 1994) – 536mf – 9 – DM7,800.00 – 3-89131-190-7 – gw Fischer [610]
JOURNAL DER TONKUNST / ed by Koch, Heinrich C – 1795. 2v – 9 – us Sibley [780]
JOURNAL DES AMIS – I-II, no. 1-18. Paris. janv-juin 1793 – 1 – fr A.C.R.P.P. [073]
JOURNAL DES AMIS DE LA CONSTITUTION – no. 1-41. Paris. nov 1790-sept 1791. En janv 1792 elements repris par: Journal des debats de la Societe des amis de la Constitution. voir a ce titre – 1 – fr A.C.R.P.P. [073]
JOURNAL DES ARTISTES – Revue pittoresque consacree aux artistes et aux gens du monde. Le sous-titre varie. Paris. 1827-avr 1848 – 1 – fr A.C.R.P.P. [073]
LE JOURNAL DES ARTS – Chronique hebdomadaire de l'Hotel Drouot. Dir.-gerant Aug. Dalligny. Paris. 31 janv 1879-1900, 1910 – 1 – fr A.C.R.P.P. [073]
LE JOURNAL DES AUBAINES – Quebec, Canada. 4 avr-10 oct 1935 – 1r – 1 – Can$25.00 – cn Can Microfilming [072]
JOURNAL DES BEAUX-ARTS ET DES SCIENCES – Par M. l'Abbe Aubert. Paris. 1768 (I-IV) – 1 – fr A.C.R.P.P. [073]
JOURNAL DES CAMPAGNES – Quebec: Leger Brousseau, no 1 (9 fev 1882)- no 51 (28 dec 1901). SEM35P337 – 18r – 1 – Can$732.00 – cn Bibl Nat [072]
LE JOURNAL DES CAMPAGNES – Quebec, 9 fev 1882-24 avr 1897 – 4r – 1 – Can$40.00 – cn Can Microfilming [072]
JOURNAL DES CLUBS OU SOCIETES PATRIOTIQUES – Dedie aux amis de la Constitution, membres des differents clubs francais. no. 1-47. Paris. nov 1790-sept 1791 – 1 – fr A.C.R.P.P. [073]
LE JOURNAL DES DEBATS – Toronto. suppl 12 fev 1858; 3 mar 1858-v1 n34. 27 avr 1858 – 1r – 1 – Can$50.00 – cn Can Microfilming [072]
JOURNAL DES DEBATS DE LA SOCIETE DES AMIS DE LA CONSTITUTION SEANTE AUX JACOBINS A PARIS – Paris. juin 1791-93. En janv 1792 reprend les elements de: Journal des amis de la Constitution et se divise en 2 s. numerotees separement: Debats et Correspondance – 1 – fr A.C.R.P.P. [073]
JOURNAL DES DEBATS ET DES DECRETS – 29 aout 1789-15 juil 1805. devenu: Journal de l'Empire. 16 juil 1805-31 mars 1814. devenu: Journal des debats politiques et litteraires. 1er avr 1814-20 mars 1815. devenu: Journal de l'Empire. 21 mars-7 juil 1815. devenu: Journal des debats politiques et litteraires. 8 juil 1815. Paris. 5 mai-1er sept 1789, 29 aout 1789-aout 1944 – 1 – fr A.C.R.P.P. [073]
JOURNAL DES DEBATS ET LOIX... – (Cont. as: Journal de l'Empire) – Paris, 1805-1815 – 297mf – 9 – ne IDC [944]
LE JOURNAL DES DEBATS LEGISLATIFS ET LITTERAIRES DU CANADA – Toronto: [s.n., 1858] (Toronto: J. Blackburn) – 9 – cn C.I.H.M. [323]
JOURNAL DES DEBATS POLITIQUES ET LITTERAIRES – Paris: Impr de le Normant, 1919-28 – 32r – 1 – us Res Libr [073]
JOURNAL DES DEBATS, POLITIQUES ET LITTERAIRES – Paris. -d 1872-99. 68 reels – 1 – uk British Libr Newspaper [072]
JOURNAL DES DEPARTEMENTS MERIDIONAUX ET DES DEBATS DES AMIS DE LA LIBERTE ET DE L'EGALITE DE MARSEILLE – Marseille. mars 1792-mai 1793 – 1 – fr A.C.R.P.P. [073]
JOURNAL DES ECONOMISTES – Paris. Revue de la science economique et de la statistique. 1850, 1866-1904 – 1 – fr A.C.R.P.P. [073]
JOURNAL DES ETATS GENERAUX / ed by Hodey, Le – Paris. avr 1789-sept 1791 – 1,5 – Fr1.27 – fr A.C.R.P.P. [073]
JOURNAL DES ETUDIANS – Quebec, Canada. 12 dec 1840-27 fev 1841 – 1r – 1 – Can$25.00 – cn Can Microfilming [072]
JOURNAL DES ETUDIANTS *see* L'INSTITUT
LE JOURNAL DES ETUDIANTS / Universite de Montreal – (Cont by: L'Etudiant 21 dec 1911-29 jan 1915. Cont by: L'Escholier 14 oct 1915-4 mai 1917. Cont by: Le Quartier-Latin 9 jan 1919-20 nov 1970. Cont by: Vol 54 a Vol 57 sep 1971-15 avr 1975) – Montreal, Canada. 12 oct 1895-7 mai 1896 – 12r – 1 – Can$130.00r – cn Can Microfilming [360]
LE JOURNAL DES ETUDIANTS DE L'UNIVERSITE DE SHERBROOKE – (Includes: L'Estrien mar-avr 1956. Le Vert et Or mai 1956-oct 1957. Campus Estrien nov 1957-18 avr 1961. Le Nouveau Campus Estrien 28 sep 1961-5 oct 1961. Campus Estrien 12 oct 1961-6 avr 1965; 21 sep 1965-9 avr 1969. Vol 15 20 oct 1969-4 fev 1970. Vol 16 dec 1969-avr 1970. Campus Estrien 8 sep 1970-16 avr 1971. Presse Campus 9 sep 1971-20 jan 1976. L'Ouvre-Boite sep 1974-dec 1974. Caucus 1976-fev 1978. Le Collectif 5 oct 1977-11 avr 1983) – Sherbrooke, dec 1955 – 3r – 1 – Can$65.00 – cn Can Microfilming [072]
JOURNAL DES FABRICANTS DE SUCRE – Paris, France. -w. April 1869-Dec 1885 – 8r – 1 – uk British Libr Newspaper [660]
JOURNAL DES FAITS – Tous les journaux dans un. Paris. avr-juin 1850, janv-9 fevr 1854 – 1 – fr A.C.R.P.P. [073]
JOURNAL DES FAMILLES – Montreal: J.E. Belair, [1887-1888] – 9 – cn C.I.H.M. [073]
LE JOURNAL DES FAMILLES : RECUEIL DE LITTERATURE – Quebec: G.A.Lavoie, [1881] – 9 – cn C.I.H.M. [073]
JOURNAL DES IMPARTIAUX – Redige par M. Salles de la Salle. no. 1-19. Paris. fevr-avr 1790. mq no. 17 – 1 – fr A.C.R.P.P. [073]
JOURNAL DES JEUNESSES MUSICALES *see* LE JOURNAL DES JEUNESSES MUSICALES DU CANADA
LE JOURNAL DES JEUNESSES MUSICALES DU CANADA – (Cont by: Le Journal Musical Canadien jun 1954-6 mai 1961. Cont by: Journal des Jeunesses Musicales jan 1962-avr 1976) – Montreal, oct 1951-oct 1952 – 1r – 1 – Can$75.00 – cn Can Microfilming [073]
JOURNAL DES MERES ET DES JEUNES FILLES – Recueil religieux et litteraire. Paris. 1844-47 (I-III) – 1 – fr A.C.R.P.P. [073]
JOURNAL DES MINES – v1-38. 1794-1815 – 3 – us Readex [622]
JOURNAL DES MISSIONS EVANGELIQUES – (Lacking some pgs) – v1-162. 1826-89 – 73r – 1 – ATLA S0113 – us A.T.L.A. [073]
JOURNAL DES MISSIONS EVANGELIQUES – Paris. v1-115. 1826-1940 – 1326mf – 9 – ne IDC [240]
JOURNAL DES MISSIONS EVANGELIQUES / Societe des Missions Evangeliques – Paris. 1826-1969 – 1 – fr A.C.R.P.P. [240]
JOURNAL DES NATIONS – Geneva, Switzerland. -d. 3 June 1936-7 Oct 1938; 9 June 1939-9 May 1940. Imperfect. 5 reels – 1 – uk British Libr Newspaper [949]
JOURNAL DES OPERATIONS DE L'ARMEE LORS DE L'INVASION DU CANADA EN 1775-76 / Badeaux, Jean Baptiste – Montreal: E. Senecal, 1871. 00074. (Pre-1900 Canadiana) – 9 – cn C.I.H.M. [971]
JOURNAL DES OUVRIERS – Feuille populaire et economique. no. 1-24. Paris. sept-dec 1830. mq no. 3, 19 – 1 – fr A.C.R.P.P. [073]
JOURNAL DES PATES ET PAPIERS – (Suppl to: Canadian Papermaker 1994) – Toronto. v5- 1989- – 9 – Can$20.00y – cn Micromedia [680]
LE JOURNAL DES PAYS D'EN HAUT – Sainte-Adele, Canada. 25 fev 1967-dec 1991 – 30r – 1 – Can$70.00r – cn Can Microfilming [072]
JOURNAL DES PYRENEES ORIENTALES – Perpignan. 24 mars 1848-8 mai 1852 – 1 – fr A.C.R.P.P. [073]
LE JOURNAL DES RIVIERES – Bedford, Canada. 20 sep 1972; 29 avr/5 mai 1973-v1 no 40. 1/7 juil 1973 – 1r – 1 – Can$30.00 – cn Can Microfilming [072]
JOURNAL DES SAVANS D'ITALIE – Amsterdam. 1748-49 (I-III) – 1 – fr A.C.R.P.P. [073]
JOURNAL DES SAVANTS – 1911-1968 – 1,5,6 – us Princeton Micro [400]
JOURNAL DES SAVANTS – Paris. janv-mars 1665, 1666-nov 1792, janv-juin 1797, sept 1816-1981 – 1 – fr A.C.R.P.P. [073]
JOURNAL DES SCAVANS / ed by Belaval, Y – Paris. 210v. 1665-1910 – 1766mf – 9 – subsc: DM11,485.00 – gw Olms [440]
LE JOURNAL DES SPECIAUX DE LA SEMAINE – Montreal. 16 sep 1958-v2 n22. 23 fev 1960 – 1r – 1 – Can$45.00 – cn Can Microfilming [072]
JOURNAL DES SPECTACLES – Contenant l'analyse des differentes pieces qu'on a representees sur tous les theatres de Paris. Paris. juil 1793-janv 1794 (I-III) – 1 – fr A.C.R.P.P. [073]
JOURNAL DES TELECOMMUNICATIONS – v1-27. 1934-60.Continues: Journal Telegraphique – 1,5,6 – us Princeton Micro [621]
JOURNAL DES THEATRES, OU LE NOUVEAU SPECTATEUR SERVANT DE REPERTOIRE UNIVERSEL DES SPECTACLES – Redige par Le Fuel de Mericourt. Paris. avr 1776-juin 1778 – 1 – fr A.C.R.P.P. [073]
JOURNAL DES TRAVAILLEURS – Paris. France. -w. 4-22 25 Jun 1848. (10 ft) – 1 – uk British Libr Newspaper [331]
JOURNAL DES TRIBUNAUX – Lausanne. On film: v1-50; 1853-1902. Lacking: v23-24; 1875-76. LL-0240 – 1 – us L of C Photodup [340]
JOURNAL DES TROIS-RIVIERES : HEBDO – Trois-Rivieres, Canada. v1 n21. 27 mai 1881; v1 n22. 3 jun 1881 – 1r – 1 – Can$25.00 – cn Can Microfilming [072]
LE JOURNAL DES TROIS-RIVIERES – (NS: 7 dec 1892-17 jan 1893 1r Can$30.00) – Trois-Rivieres, Canada. 19 mai 1865-19 mar 1891 – 9r – 1 – Can$30.00r – cn Can Microfilming [072]
LE JOURNAL DES TROIS-RIVIERES – Trois Rivieres, Canada. 1865-73 – 6r – 1 – $390.00 – cn Library Assoc [971]
LE JOURNAL DES TROIS-RIVIERES – Trois-Rivieres, Canada. 28 aut 1847-31 dec 1853 – 1r – 1 – Can$50.00 – cn Can Microfilming [072]
JOURNAL DES USINES A GAZ – Paris. -f. May 1877-Dec 1891; Jan 1903-Dec 1909 – 10r – 1 – uk British Libr Newspaper [338]
LE JOURNAL DES VEDETTES – Montreal. v1-25. 1954-1978. SEM35P94 – 21r – 1 – Can$1,055.00 – cn Bibl Nat [073]
LE JOURNAL DES VEDETTES – Montreal. v2 n30. 13 mai 1956-23 dec 1967 – 1r – 1 – Can$50.00 – cn Can Microfilming [072]
JOURNAL DES VILLES ET DES CAMPAGNES, DES CURES, DES MAIRES, DES FAMILLES – Paris. 3,9,11,13 nov 1842, 1845-54, juil 1855-59, 2 oct 1863-65, 1868-28 fev 1892, 28 fev 1893, 1 mars 1894, 1 mars 1895 – 1 – fr A.C.R.P.P. [073]
JOURNAL D'ETAT ET DU CITOYEN – devenu: Mercure national ou Journal d'Etat et du citoyen. Paris. aout 1789-aout 1790 – 1 – fr A.C.R.P.P. [073]
JOURNAL DOLLARD – Ville St-Laurent. v1 n2. 28 mar 1958 – 1r – 1 – Can$20.00 – cn Can Microfilming [072]
LE JOURNAL D'OUTREMONT – Outremont, mai 1983-dec 1991 – 4r – 1 – Can$75.00 – cn Can Microfilming [072]
JOURNAL DRUMMOND *see* L'IDEE OUVRIERE
JOURNAL DU CAMP – (Nouvelles de France et du Monde: 16 Aug-2 Sept 1940) – London, UK. 24 Jul-15 Aug 1940 – 1 – uk British Libr Newspaper [072]
LE JOURNAL DU CAP – (Cont by: Hebdo du Cap v4 n47 11 aut 1971-30 oct 1974. Cont by: Hebdo du Cap-de-la-Madeleine 7 nov 1974-29 dec 1980) – Cap-de-la-Madeleine, Canada. 13 sep 1967-4 aut 1971 – 13r – 1 – Can$75.00r – cn Can Microfilming [072]
LE JOURNAL DU CAP *see* HEBDO DU CAP
JOURNAL DU CLUB DES CORDELIERS – Societe des amis des droits de l'homme et du citoyen. Par Sinties et Momoro. no. 1-10. Paris. juin-aout 1791 – 1 – fr A.C.R.P.P. [073]
JOURNAL DU COMMERCE – Paris. 1er germinal an VII-6e jour complementaire an VII. 21 mars-21 sept 1799 – 1 – fr A.C.R.P.P. [073]
JOURNAL DU COMMERCE DE LA VILLE DE LYON ET DU DEPARTEMENT DU RHONE – Lyon. dec 1826-aout 1828, dec 1835-juil 1844 – 1 – fr A.C.R.P.P. [073]
JOURNAL DU COMMERCE, POLITIQUE ET LITTERAIRE – Paris. 20 dec 1819-21 mars 1848 – 1 – fr A.C.R.P.P. [073]
JOURNAL DU CULTIVATEUR : CHAMBRE D'AGRICULTURE DU BAS-CANADA – Montreal, Canada. mai 1853-avr 1857 – 1r – 1 – Can$34.50 – cn Can Microfilming [631]
JOURNAL DU DEPARTEMENT DE LA MARNE – Par une Societe d'amis de la Republique. no. 1-512. Chalons-sur-Marne. 19 juin 1796-25 avr 1800. BM. Reims Per. CH. IX. 2 – 1 – fr A.C.R.P.P. [073]
JOURNAL DU DEPARTEMENT DES BOUCHES DU WESER – Bremen, feb 2 1812-oct 26 1813 – 2r – 1 – Inquire at Mikrofilmarchiv for details – gw Misc Inst [943]
JOURNAL DU DIMANCHE – Edite par France-soir. Paris. 1953-54 – 1 – fr A.C.R.P.P. [073]
JOURNAL DU DIMANCHE – Litterature, poesie, histoire, voyages, sciences. Red. en chef Leo Lespes. no. 1-48 avec 2 prosp. Paris. sept 1846-aout 1847. mq no – 1 – fr A.C.R.P.P. [073]
JOURNAL DU DIMANCHE – Montreal, Canada. 22 dec 1883-7 mar 1885 – 1r – 1 – Can$30.00 – cn Can Microfilming [072]
JOURNAL DU DROIT ADMINISTRATIF – v. 1-61. 1853-1913 – 1 – 302.00 – us L of C Photodup [944]
JOURNAL DU DROIT INTERNATIONAL – v1-63 1874-1936 – 1 – $600.00 – us L of C Photodup [340]
JOURNAL DU GENIE CIVIL, DES SCIENCES ET DES ARTS A L'USAGE DES INGENIEURS – Paris. 1829 – 1 – fr A.C.R.P.P. [073]
LE JOURNAL DU NORD-OUEST – Rouyn, Canada. v1 n8. 16 oct 1974-v1 n18. 28 oct 1974 – 1r – 1 – Can$25.00 – cn Can Microfilming [072]
LE JOURNAL DU NOUVEAU MAGOG – Magog, 1976 – 1r – 1 – Can$25.00 – cn Can Microfilming [072]
JOURNAL DU PETROLE – Paris. -m. May 1901-Dec 1905 – 3r – 1 – uk British Libr Newspaper [660]
JOURNAL DU PEUPLE – Dir. Sebastien Faure. no. 1-299. Paris. 6 fevr-3 dec 1899. mq no. 169, 185, 277 – 1 – fr A.C.R.P.P. [073]

JOURNAL DU PEUPLE – Feuille du dimanche. Red.-gerant Felix Avril. 4e-9e annee. Paris. 1837-30 avr 1842. mq 23 fevr-6 avr 1841 – 1 – fr A.C.R.P.P. [073]

JOURNAL DU PEUPLE – Montreal, Canada. v1 n4. 15 jun 1842; v1 n6. 29 jun 1842 – 1r – 1 – Can$25.00 – cn Can Microfilming [072]

JOURNAL DU PEUPLE – Par M. Boyer. no. 1-193; prosp. de janv 1792. fevr-aout 1792 – 1 – fr A.C.R.P.P. [073]

JOURNAL DU PEUPLE – Politique, litteraire, artistique et social. Dir. Henri Fabre. Paris. 9 fevr 1916-9 juin 1929 – 1 – fr A.C.R.P.P. [073]

LE JOURNAL DU PEUPLE – Quotidien. Red.-Fond. A. Arnould, L. Noir, U. Fonvielle, A. Humbert, G. Casse, G. Puissant, F. Enne, E. Mourot, G. Cavalier. Paris. 1er juil-6 sept 1870 – 1 – fr A.C.R.P.P. [073]

LE JOURNAL DU PEUPLE / ed by Vekeman, G & Denault, Amedee – Montreal, Canada. 2 fev-26 avr 1895 – 1r – 1 – Can$30.00 – cn Can Microfilming [072]

LE JOURNAL DU VIEUX-MONTREAL – (Cont by: La Cite mar 1986-jun 1986f) – Montreal, fev 1981-nov 1985 – 1r – 1 – Can$50.00 – cn Can Microfilming [072]

JOURNAL DU VOYAGE DU CHEVALIER CHARDIN EN PERSE ET AUX INDES ORIENTALES, PAR LA MER NOIRE ET PAR LA COLCHIDE. PREMIERE PARTIE QUI CONTIENT LE VOYAGE DE PARIS A ISPAHAN / Chardin, Jean – Londres, M. Pitt, 1686, viii-349-5 p., ill. French Voyagers in the Mediterranean 16th to 18th Centuries. 5980 – 9 – fr Hachette [949]

JOURNAL DU VOYAGE DU SIEUR DELBEE, AUX ISLES, DANS LA COSTE DE GUYNEE EN L'ANNEE 1669 POUR L'ETABLISSEMENT DU COMMERCE EN CES PAYS, ET LA PRESENTE : : AVEC LA DESCRIPTION PARTICULIERE DU ROYAUME D'ARDRES; ET DE CE QUI S'EST PHASSE ENTRE LES FRANCAIS ET LE ROI / Elbee, Sieur d' – (African library series). 1671 – 9 – fr Hachette [910]

JOURNAL D'UN SPAHI AU SOUDAN, 1897-1899 / Labour, Gaston – Paris. 1909 – 1 – us Res Libr [910]

JOURNAL D'UN VOYAGE SUR LES COTES D'AFRIQUE ET AUX INDES D'ESPAGNE – (African Library). 1723 – 9 – fr Hachette [910]

JOURNAL D'UNE EXPEDITION CONTRE LES IROQUOIS EN 1687: LETTRES ET PIECES RELATIVES AU FORT SAINT-LOUIS DES ILLINOIS / Baugy, Louis Henri – Paris: E. Leroux, 1883. 03503. (Pre-1900 Canadiana) – 9 – cn C.I.H.M. [971]

JOURNAL D'UNE EXPEDITION DE D'IBERVILLE / Beaudoin, Jean – Publie avec une introd. et des notes par A. Gosselin. Evreux: 1900. 03501. (Pre-1900 Canadiana) – 9 – cn C.I.H.M. [910]

JOURNAL D'UNE EXPEDITION ENTREPRISE DANS LE BUT D'EXPLORER LE COURS ET L'EMBOUCHURE DU NIGER / Lander, Richard & Lander, John – Traduction de l'anglais. Paris, Paulin. 1832 – 9 – $20.00 – fr Orientalistes [910]

LE JOURNAL D'UNE SAPHISTE / Montfort, Charles – Paris: Offenstadt, 1902. 216p. (Les Femmes Collection) – 3mf – 9 – $8.00 – fr Bibl Nationale [306]

JOURNAL ECCLESIASTIQUE – ou Bibliotheque raisonnee des sciences ecclesiastiques. Paris. 1789-juil 1792 – 1 – fr A.C.R.P.P. [073]

JOURNAL ENCYCLOPEDIQUE – puis ENCYCLOPEDIQUE OU UNIVERSEL. Liege puis Bouillon, Bruxelles. 1756-93 – 1 – fr A.C.R.P.P. [073]

JOURNAL ETRANGER – puis ou Notice exacte et detaillee des ouvrages de toutes les nations etrangeres en fait d'arts, de sciences, de litterature, etc.. Paris. avr 1754-58, 1760-sept 1762 – 1 – fr A.C.R.P.P. [073]

LE JOURNAL EXPRESS – Montreal, Canada. 20 oct 1960-v1 n7. 3 dec 1960 – 1r – 1 – Can$25.00 – cn Can Microfilming [072]

JOURNAL, FARADAY TRANSACTIONS 2 / Chemical Society. London – v. 68-71. 1972-75 – 1,5,6 – us Princeton Micro [540]

JOURNAL, FINANCIAL PUBLIC RELATIONS ASSOCIATION – v.50-51. 1965. Continued by: Journal. Bank Public Relations and Marketing Assoc – 1 – us UMI [073]

LE JOURNAL FLECHOIS, LITTERAIRE, AGRICOLE ET COMMERCIAL – (7 missing numbers) – Hebd., La Fleche (Sarthe), oct. 1878-juin 1942 (7 no. manq.) – 12r – 1 – F6,660.58 – fr Armell [400]

JOURNAL FOR INDUSTRIAL NURSES – (See also: Occupational Health) – v1-14. 1949-1963 – 1 – us UMI [610]

JOURNAL FOR PAPER CONVERTERS – 1933-34. Superseded by yPaper converters and envelope industry – 1 – us UMI [600]

JOURNAL FOR PAPER CONVERTERS *see* PAPER CONVERTERS AND ENVELOPE INDUSTRY

JOURNAL FOR RESEARCH IN MATHEMATICS – 1977- – 9 – us UMI [073]

JOURNAL FOR SCIENTIFIC RESEARCH *see* ONO-MEDEDELINGEN

JOURNAL FOR SPECIAL EDUCATORS – v.15-1978- – 1,5,6,9 – us UMI [073]

JOURNAL FOR SPECIAL EDUCATORS OF THE MENTALLY RETARDED – v6- 1969- 1; v7-5,6; v14- 9 – us UMI [370]

JOURNAL FOR THE EDUCATION OF THE GIFTED – (1983-. 1,5,6,9) – v1-. 1978- – 1 – us UMI [073]

JOURNAL FOR THE STUDY OF THE OLD TESTAMENT – (1985-. 5,6,9) – Issues 1-. 1976- – 1 – us UMI [220]

JOURNAL FOR THE THEORY OF SOCIAL BEHAVIOR – (1982-. 1,5,6,9) – v1-. 1971- – 1 – us UMI [073]

JOURNAL FOR VOCATIONAL SPECIAL NEEDS EDUCATION – (1983-. 1,5,6,9) – v1-. 1978- – 1 – us UMI [073]

JOURNAL FRANCAIS – London, UK. 1 Nov 1910-2 Apr 1912 – 1 – uk British Libr Newspaper [072]

JOURNAL FRANCAIS – London, UK. 24 Sept 1891-13 Jul 1893 – 1 – uk British Libr Newspaper [072]

JOURNAL FUER AUSERLESENE THEOLOGISCHE LITERATUR – v1-6 no 1. 1804-11 (complete) – 2r – 1 – ATLA S0076 – us A.T.L.A. [073]

JOURNAL FUER CHEMIE UND PHYSIK – Nurnberg. Bd.1-69. 1811-33 – 3 – us Readex [530]

JOURNAL FUER DEUTSCHE FRAUEN VON DEUTSCHEN FRAUEN GESCHRIEBEN, 1 (1805)-2 (1806) – (Selene 1 (1807)-2 (1808) zugleich als Fortsetzung des Journals fuer deutsche Frauen) – 1805-1808 (mf ed 1994) – 47mf – 9 – DM590.00 – 3-89131-128-1 – gw Fischer [305]

JOURNAL FUER DIE BOTANIK – Gottingen, 1799-1803 – 3 – us Readex [580]

JOURNAL FUER DIE BOTANIK / ed by Schrader, H A – (Cont. as.: Neues Journal fuer die Botanik. Goettingen, 1805-1810) – Goettingen, 1799-1803 [1804] – 69mf – 8 – ne IDC [580]

JOURNAL FUER DIE FREYMAURER – Wien. v1-12. 1784-1787 – 36mf – 9 – ne IDC [360]

JOURNAL FUER DIE LIEBHABER DER ENTOMOLOGIE / ed by Scriba, L G – Frankfurt. v1. [1790-]1791 – 6mf – 9 – ne IDC [590]

JOURNAL FUER DIE LIEBHABER DES STEINREICHS UND DER KONCHYLIOLOGIE – (Cont. as FUER DIE LITERATUR UND KENNTNISS DER NATURGESCHICHTE, SONDERLICH DER CONCHYLIEN UND DER STEINE. Weimar. 1782-85. v1-2; Cont. as NEUE LITERATUR UND BEITRAEGE ZUR KENNTNIS DER NATURGESCHICHTE, VORZUEGLICH DER CONCHYLIEN UND FOSSILIEN. Leipzig. 1784-87. v1-4) – Weimar, 1774-80.v1-6. 1782-85, v1-2. 1784-87, v1-4. – 101mf – 8 – ne IDC [590]

JOURNAL FUER DIE LIEBHABER DES STEINREICHS UND DER KONCHYLIOLOGIE – Weimar, 1774-80 – 3 – us Readex [560]

JOURNAL FUER DIE REINE UND ANGEWANDTE MATHEMATICK – v1- 1826-1; 1970- 5,6; v272- 1975- 9 – us UMI [510]

JOURNAL FUER DIE REINE UND ANGEWANDTE MATHEMATIK – v. 1-186. 1826-1944 – 1,5,6 – us Princeton Micro [510]

JOURNAL FUER ORNITHOLOGIE *see* NAUMANNIA

JOURNAL FUER PRAKITSCHE CHEMIE – New Series. v. 1-162. 1870-1943 – 1,5,6 – us Princeton Micro [540]

JOURNAL GAZETTE – Ft. Wayne. IN. 1884- – 1 – us UMI [071]

JOURNAL GAZETTE – Mattoon. Ill. 1943- – 1 – us UMI [071]

JOURNAL GAZETTE – Sidney. Ohio. 1905-1909 – 1 – us UMI [071]

JOURNAL GAZETTE (LAUNCESTON EDITION) – 1991-92; Jan 7-Jun 24 1993; Jul-Dec 1993; Jan 8-Jun 25 1994; Jul 9-Dec 23 1994; 1995-96 – 5 1/2r – 9 – uk British Libr Newspaper [072]

JOURNAL GENERAL – Par M. l'abbe Fontenai. Paris. 1er fevr 1791-10 aout 1792 – 1 – fr A.C.R.P.P. [073]

JOURNAL GENERAL DE FRANCE: SUPPLEMENT – puis Partie d'agriculture et d'economie rurale. Paris. 1787-6 janv 1790 – 1 – fr A.C.R.P.P. [073]

JOURNAL GENERAL DE LA COUR ET DE LA VILLE – Gautier. Paris. sept 1789-aout 1792 – 1 – fr A.C.R.P.P. [073]

JOURNAL GENERAL DE LA LITTERATURE DE FRANCE OU... – Paris, Strasbourg. v1-29. 1798-1826 – 328mf – 9 – ne IDC [440]

JOURNAL GENERAL DE L'EUROPE – ou Mercure national et etranger. Liege puis Herve puis Paris. juil 1791-aout 1792 – 1 – fr A.C.R.P.P. [073]

JOURNAL GENERAL DE L'IMPRIMERIE ET DE LA LIBRAIRIE – (Some missing vols) – Paris. v1-36 1857-1891; v56-61 1912-1917 – 2204mf – 9 – ne IDC [680]

JOURNAL HEALTH AND REHABILITATIVE LIBRARY SERVICES – v.2. 1976. Continued by: H R L S D Journal – 1,5,6,9 – us UMI [073]

JOURNAL HEBDOMADAIRE DE L'ARRONDISSEMENT DE SAINT-CALAIS (SARTHE) – (1 missing no. Becomes: L'Anille april 1830-march 1832) – Hebd., Saint-Calais – 1r – 1 – F212,53 – fr Armell [073]

JOURNAL HERALD – Dayton. Ohio. 1949- – 1 – us UMI [071]

JOURNAL HISTORIQUE DES EVENEMENS ARRIVES A SAINT-EUSTACHE – Montreal: Par J Jones, 1838. SEM16P150 – 1r – 5 – Can$9.00 – cn Bibl Nat [971]

JOURNAL HISTORIQUE DU VOYAGE FAIT AU CAP DE BONNE-ESPERANCE / La Caille, Nicolas-Louis de – Paris, Guillyn. 1763 – 9 – 12.50 – fr Orientalistes [910]

JOURNAL IN FRANCKFURT AM MAIN *see* JOURNAL

JOURNAL INEDIT DU SECOND SEJOUR AU SENEGAL (3 DECEMBRE 1786 – 25 DECEMBRE 1787) / Boufflers, Stanislas Jean de – Paris: Editions de la Revue politique et Litteraire (Revue Bleue) et de la Revue Scientifique, 1905 – 1 – us U.W. Library [960]

JOURNAL, INFO-ECONOMIQUE – Montreal. dec 1980-v1 n4. mars 1981 – 1r – 1 – Can$25.00 – cn Can Microfilming [072]

JOURNAL (JAMA) / American Medical Association – v1-159. 1883-1955 – 1,5,6 – us Princeton Micro [616]

JOURNAL, JAN 1888-MAR 1894 – Ms. from Furman University. 200p – 1 – 7.00 – us Baptist [240]

JOURNAL JUDICIAIRE DE L'INDO-CHINE FRANCAISE – Saigon. 1890-95. v1-5. – 59mf – 9 – ne IDC [073]

JOURNAL L'ACTION *see* L'ACTION DE MONTCALM

LE JOURNAL L'ARCHIPEL – Verdun, Canada. v2 n9. oct 1973 – 1r – 1 – Can$25.00 – cn Can Microfilming [072]

JOURNAL LAVAL – Laval, Canada. 9 mai 1973-v2 n7. 26 nov 1974 – 1r – 1 – Can$20.00 – cn Can Microfilming [072]

JOURNAL LE MAS-KA – St-Hyacinthe, Canada. 13 sep 1972 – 1r – 1 – Can$20.00 – cn Can Microfilming [072]

JOURNAL LE NORD – (Includes: Le Progres du Nord 2 dec 1954-27 mai 1960) – Montreal. v3 n42. 10 sep 1953-18 nov 1954 – 3r – 1 – Can$60.00 – cn Can Microfilming [072]

JOURNAL LE RIVERAIN – Ste-Anne des Monts, 10 jun 1986-29 dec 1991 – 5r – 1 – Can$70.00 – cn Can Microfilming [072]

JOURNAL L'HISTOIRE *see* L'HISTOIRE

JOURNAL LITTERAIRE – Sallengre, Saint-Hyacinthe. La Haye. mai juin 1713-22, 1728-37 (I-XXIV) – 1 – fr A.C.R.P.P. [073]

JOURNAL L'OUTLET DE MAGOG – Magog, 1976 – 1r – 1 – Can$25.00 – cn Can Microfilming [072]

JOURNAL MANUSCRIT / Kapea – Houailou, Nouvelle-Caledonie. 1884-1906 – 9 – F30.00 – fr Ethnologie [306]

JOURNAL MESSENGER – Manassas. Va. 1931-43; 1952- – 1 – us UMI [071]

JOURNAL METROPOLE / ed by Gagnon, Marcel-A – Montreal, Canada. 2 sep 1959-2 dec 1960 – 1r – 1 – Can$45.00 – cn Can Microfilming [072]

LE JOURNAL METROPOLITAIN – Trois-Rivieres, Canada. 8 sep 1971 – 1r – 1 – Can$20.00 – cn Can Microfilming [072]

JOURNAL, MS 1236 / Benyon, B G – 1813-14 – 1r – 1 – us Western Res [355]

JOURNAL, MS 3506 / Indiana. Morgan Raid Commission – Proceedings, Apr 4-Oct 22, 1867 – 1 – us Western Res [976]

LE JOURNAL MUNICIPAL CANADIEN – Montreal, Canada. v12 n5. mai 1916 – 1r – 1 – Can$25.00 – cn Can Microfilming [072]

JOURNAL MUSICAL – Bull. Int. Critique de la Bibliogr. Musicale. Geneva. v1-3, n1-53. 1896-1898 – 1 – us Schnase [780]

LE JOURNAL MUSICAL CANADIEN *see* LE JOURNAL DES JEUNESSES MUSICALES DU CANADA

JOURNAL NEWS – Hamilton. Ohio. 1938- – 1 – us UMI [071]

JOURNAL; NEWS – Pensacola. Fl. 1960- – 1 – us UMI [071]

THE JOURNAL NEWS – Nyack. N.Y. 1945- – 1 – us UMI [071]

JOURNAL NUN'S ISLAND – Ile des Soeurs, Verdun. 18 oct 1979; 6 mar 1980; v-n-. 16 oct 1980 – 1r – 1 – Can$25.00 – cn Can Microfilming [072]

JOURNAL OF, 1773-1832 / Littlejohn, John – 1 – 31.43 – us Baptist [240]

JOURNAL OF A FOURTEEN DAYS' RIDE THROUGH THE BUSH FROM QUEBEC TO LAKE ST JOHN / Davenport, Mrs. – Quebec?: s.n., 1872 (Quebec: Printed at the Daily Mercury Office). 02509. (Pre-1900 Canadiana) – 9 – cn C.I.H.M. [910]

JOURNAL OF A HARPOONER ON BOARD THE WHALING SHIP MASSACHUSETTS, 1836-1840 / Brett, James Warden – 1r – 1 – at Pacific Mss [920]

THE JOURNAL OF A MISSION TO THE INTERIOR OF AFRICA : IN THE YEAR 1805... / Park, Mungo – London: Printed for John Murray, by W. Bulmer, 1815 – 1 roll – 1 – 1-55879-752-1 – uk Libr Preservation [960]

JOURNAL OF A RESIDENCE IN ASHANTEE / Dupuis, J – London. 1824. BA-147 2 – 8 – ne IDC [960]

JOURNAL OF A RESIDENCE IN ASHANTI / Dupuis, J – 1824 – 7 – uk Microform Academic [920]

JOURNAL OF A RESIDENCE IN THE BURMHAN EMPIRE, AND MORE PARTICULARLY AT THE COURT OF AMARAPOORAH / Cox, H – London, 1821 – 5mf – 9 – ne IDC [950]

JOURNAL OF A SECOND EXPEDITION INTO THE INTERIOR OF AFRICA, FROM THE BIGHT OF BENIN TO SOCCATOO / Clapperton, Hugh – London. 1829. BA-292 2 – 8 – ne IDC [910]

JOURNAL OF A SECOND EXPEDITION TO AFRICA / Clapperton, Hugh – 1829 – 7 – uk Microform Academic [910]

JOURNAL OF A SECOND VOYAGE FOR THE DISCOVERY OF A NORTH-WEST PASSAGE FROM THE ATLANTIC TO THE PACIFIC / Parry, W E – BN 334 2. 1824 – 8 – ne IDC [910]

JOURNAL OF A THIRD VOYAGE FOR THE DISCOVERY OF A NORTH-WEST PASSAGE FROM THE ATLANTIC TO THE PACIFIC / Parry, W E – BN 335 2. 1826 – 8 – ne IDC [910]

JOURNAL OF A THREE YEARS' RESIDENCE IN ABYSSINIA : IN FURTHERANCE OF THE OBJECTS OF THE CHURCH MISSIONARY SOCIETY / Gobat, Samuel – London: Hatchard, 1834 – 1mf – us A.T.L.A. [240]

JOURNAL OF A TOUR TO NIAGARA FALLS IN THE YEAR 1805 / Bigelow, Timothy – Boston: J. Wilson, 1876. 00131. (Pre-1900 Canadiana) – 9 – cn C.I.H.M. [910]

JOURNAL OF A VOYAGE FOR THE DISCOVERY OF A NORTH-WEST PASSAGE FROM THE ATLANTIC TO THE PACIFIC / Parry, W E – ed. 2. London. 1821. BN-333 2 – 8 – ne IDC [910]

JOURNAL OF A VOYAGE IN BAFFIN'S BAY AND BARROW STRAITS / Sutherland, P C – BN 408 2. 2v. 1852 – 8 – ne IDC [910]

JOURNAL OF A VOYAGE TO GREENLAND, IN YEAR 1821 / Manby, G W – BH-486 2. 1823 – 8 – ne IDC [910]

JOURNAL OF A VOYAGE TO THE NORTHERN WHALE-FISHERY / Scoresby, W – BH 500 2. 1823 – 8 – ne IDC [910]
A JOURNAL OF A VOYAGE TO THE SOUTH SEAS IN HIS MAJESTY'S SHIP THE ENDEAVOUR / Parkinson, S – London. 1784. B-5632 2 – 8 – ne IDC [580]
JOURNAL OF ABNORMAL AND SOCIAL PSYCHOLOGY – American Psychological Association. Albany, NY.v40-41, 1945-46; v49, 1954; v53, 1956; v55, 1957. M-19/2 – 8 – ne IDC [150]
JOURNAL OF ABNORMAL CHILD PSYCHOLOGY – v1-22. 1973-94 – 1,5 – $90.00v – us UMI [150]
JOURNAL OF ABNORMAL PSYCHOLOGY – (v. 70- 1965- 5,6. v. 75- 1970- 9) – v. 1- 1906- – 1 – us UMI [150]
JOURNAL OF ABNORMAL PSYCHOLOGY – v1-92. 1906-83 – 1,5,6 – us Princeton Micro [150]
JOURNAL OF ACADEMIC LIBRARIANSHIP – v. 1-. 1975- – 1,5,6,9 – us UMI [020]
JOURNAL OF ACCOUNTANCY – (v. 127- 1969- 5,6. v. 139- 1975- 9) – v. 1- 1905- – 1 – us UMI [650]
JOURNAL OF ACCOUNTING AND ECONOMICS – v1-6. 1979-84 – 1,5,6,13 – sz Elsevier [650]
JOURNAL OF ACCOUNTING, AUDITING AND FINANCE – v. 1-. 1977- – 1,5,6,9 – us UMI [650]
JOURNAL OF ACCOUNTING EDUCATION – 1,5,69 – us UMI [650]
JOURNAL OF ADDICTIVE DISEASES / ed by Stimmel, Barry – v1- 1981- – 1, 9 ($325.00 in US $455.00 outside hardcopy subsc) – us Haworth [360]
JOURNAL OF ADHESION – 1969- – 1,5,9 – us Gordon [600]
JOURNAL OF ADOLESCENT CHEMICAL DEPENDENCY *see* JOURNAL OF CHILD AND ADOLESCENT SUBSTANCE ABUSE
JOURNAL OF ADULT DEVELOPMENT – v1. 1994 – $65.00v – us UMI [370]
JOURNAL OF ADULT EDUCATION *see* ADULT EDUCATION
JOURNAL OF ADVERTISING *see* ADVERTISING MAGAZAINE
JOURNAL OF ADVERTISING RESEARCH – v1- 1960- 1; v9- 5,6; v15- 9 – us UMI [380]
JOURNAL OF AERONAUTICAL SCIENCES *see* AEROSPACE ENGINEERING
JOURNAL OF AEROSOL SCIENCE – v1- 1970- – 5,6,9 – us UMI [540]
JOURNAL OF AEROSPACE EDUCATION – (See also: Aviation/Space) – v1-5. 1974-1978 – 1,5,6. ; 9 – apply; v.3-5 – us UMI [629]
JOURNAL OF AESTHETICS AND ART CRITICISM – v14- 1955- 1; v29- 5,6; v35- 9 – us UMI [780]
JOURNAL OF AFFECTIVE DISORDERS – v1-7. 1979-84 – 1,5,6,13 – sz Elsevier [616]
JOURNAL OF AFRICAN CIVILIZATIONS – 1985- – 1 – us UMI [960]
JOURNAL OF AFRICAN EARTH SCIENCES – v1- 1984- – 5,6,9 – us UMI [550]
JOURNAL OF AFRICAN HISTORY – v1- 1960- 1; v10- 5,6; v16- 9 – us UMI [960]
JOURNAL OF AFRICAN LANGUAGE AND LINGUISTICS – 1984- – 1 – us UMI [470]
JOURNAL OF AFRICAN LAW – (v1-28 1957-84 on reel $290.00. v29-38 1985-94 on mf $202.00) – v1-38. 1957-94 – 5,6,9 – $492.00 set – us Hein [340]
JOURNAL OF AFRICAN STUDIES – (v.7 9. 1980 83. 5,6,9) – v.1 9.1974 83 – 1 – us UMI [073]
JOURNAL OF AGING AND JUDAISM – v1- . 1986- – 1,5,6,9 – us UMI [618]
JOURNAL OF AGING AND SOCIAL POLICY / ed by Bass, Scott A & Morris, Robert – v1- 1989- – 1, 9 ($175.00 in US $245.00 outside hardcopy subsc) – us Haworth [360]
JOURNAL OF AGRICULTURAL AND FOOD CHEMISTRY – v1- 1953- – 1,5,6,9 – us A.C.S. [660]
JOURNAL OF AGRICULTURAL AND FOOD INFORMATION / ed by Frank, Robyn – v4 n1. 1997- – 1,9 – $85.00 in US $119.00 outside hardcopy subsc – us Haworth [630]
JOURNAL OF AGRICULTURAL ECONOMICS RESEARCH *see* AGRICULTURAL ECONOMICS RESEARCH
JOURNAL OF AGRICULTURAL EDUCATION *see* JOURNAL OF THE AMERICAN ASSOCIATION OF TEACHER EDUCATORS IN AGRICULTURE
JOURNAL OF AGRICULTURAL RESEARCH / U.S. Department of Agriculture – v1-78. 1913-49.460 fiches – 9 – 640.00 – us Updata [630]
JOURNAL OF AGRICULTURAL RESEARCH – v. 1-78. 1913-1949 – 1,5,6 – us Princeton Micro [630]
JOURNAL OF AGRICULTURAL RESEARCH – Washington. v1-63. 1913-1941 – 1093mf – 9 – ne IDC [630]
JOURNAL OF AGRICULTURAL SCIENCE – v. 66-77. 1966-71 – 1,5,6 – us Princeton Micro [630]
JOURNAL OF AGRICULTURAL SCIENCE – (v.92 .1979 5,6,9) – v.1 .1905 – 1 – us UMI [630]
JOURNAL OF AGRICULTURAL TAXATION AND LAW – v5-. 1983- – 1,5,6,9 – us UMI [073]
JOURNAL OF AGRICULTURAL TAXATION AND LAW *see* AGRICULTURAL LAW JOURNAL
JOURNAL OF AGRICULTURE – (Cont by: The Nova Scotia Journal of Agriculture) – Halifax, N.S.: A and W MacKinlay, [1865-1866?] – 9 – cn C.I.H.M. [630]
THE JOURNAL OF AGRICULTURE AND HORTICULTURE – Montreal, Canada. 1 jan 1898-13 jun 1936 – 12r – 1 – Can$60.00r – cn Can Microfilming [630]
JOURNAL OF AGROMEDICINE : INTERFACE OF HUMAN HEALTH AND AGRICULTURE / ed by Schumann, Stanley H – v3 n1. 1996- – 1,9 – $135.00 in US $189.00 outside hardcopy subsc – us Haworth [073]
JOURNAL OF AIR LAW *see* JOURNAL OF AIR LAW AND COMMERCE
JOURNAL OF AIR LAW AND COMMERCE – (v1-50 1930-85 on reel $560.00. v51-60 1985-95 on mf $282.00. Title varies: v1-9, 1930-38 as Journal of Air Law. Cumulative index v1-35 1930-69. Suspended Oct 1942-Jan 1947) – Southern Methodist University. v1-60. 1930-95 – 9 – $842.00 set – us Hein [340]
JOURNAL OF ALCOHOL AND DRUG EDUCATION – v1-20 1955-75 1; v21- 1975- 5,6,9 – us UMI [610]
JOURNAL OF ALLERGY – v1-26. 1929-55 – 1,5,6 – us Princeton Micro [610]
JOURNAL OF ALLERGY AND CLINICAL IMMUNOLOGY – (v. 36- 1965- 5,6. v. 45- 1970- 9) – 1- 1929- – 1 – us UMI [610]
JOURNAL OF ALLIED HEALTH – 1972- 1; 1975- 5,6; v5- 9 – us UMI [616]
JOURNAL OF AMBULATORY CARE MANAGEMENT – (v.3 .1980 5,6,9) – v.1. 1978 – 1 – us UMI [617]
JOURNAL OF AMBULATORY CARE MARKETING / ed by Meadow, H Lee – v1- 1987- – 1, 9 ($75.00 in US $105.00 outside hardcopy subsc) – us Haworth [610]
JOURNAL OF AMERICAN COLLEGE HEALTH – v30-. 1982- – 1,5,6,9 – us UMI [073]
JOURNAL OF AMERICAN ETHNIC HISTORY – 1981- – 1,5,6,9 – us UMI [306]
JOURNAL OF AMERICAN ETHNIC HISTORY – 1985-. -q – 1 – us UMI [073]
JOURNAL OF AMERICAN FOLKLORE – v. 1-74. 1888-1961 – 1 – us Princeton Micro [390]
JOURNAL OF AMERICAN FOLKLORE – (v. 81- 1968- 5,6. v. 88- 1975- 9) – v. 1- 1888- – 1 – us UMI [970]
JOURNAL OF AMERICAN HISTORY – (New Haven, Conn.). v. 1-29. 1907-1935 – 1 – us Princeton Micro [970]
JOURNAL OF AMERICAN HISTORY – (v55- 1968- 5,6. v62- 1975- 9) – 1- 1914- – 1 – us UMI [975]
JOURNAL OF AMERICAN STUDIES – v1- 1967- 1; v10- 5,6,9 – us UMI [320]
JOURNAL OF AN EXPEDITION TO EXPLORE THE COURSE AND TERMINATION OF THE NIGER / Lander, Richard & Lander, John – 3v. London. 1832. BA-154 2 – 8 – ne IDC [910]
JOURNAL OF AN EXPEDITION TO EXPLORE THE COURSE AND TERMINATION OF THE NIGER / Lander, Richard & Lander, John – 3v. London. 1832. BA-332 2 – 8 – ne IDC [900]
JOURNAL OF AN EXPEDITION TO EXPLORE THE COURSE AND TERMINATION OF THE NIGER : WITH A NARRATIVE OF A VOYAGE DOWN THAT RIVER TO ITS TERMINATION / Lander, Richard – New York. 2v. 1832 – 1r – 1 – us Ross [910]
JOURNAL OF ANALYTIC SOCIAL WORK / ed by Brandell, Jerrold R – (Cont: Journal of Independent Social Work) – v1- 1993- – 1,9 ($95.00 in US $133.00 outside hardcopy subsc) – us Haworth [360]
JOURNAL OF ANALYTICAL AND APPLIED PYROLYSIS – v1-6. 1979-84 – 1,5,6,13 – sz Elsevier [073]
JOURNAL OF ANALYTICAL CHEMISTRY – v7-48. 1952-93 – 1,5 – $240.00v – us UMI [540]
JOURNAL OF ANALYTICAL TOXICOLOGY / ed by Baselt, Randall – 1977-96 – 1,5 – $100.00v subsc $270.00 nonsubsc 1 ($75.00v subsc $270.00 nonsubsc 5) – ISSN 0146-4760 – us Preston Publ [615]
JOURNAL OF ANATOMY AND PHYSIOLOGY – London, 1867-1939. V.1-73 – 813mf – 9 – ne IDC [611]
JOURNAL OF ANDROLOGY – 1980 – 1,5,6,9 – us UMI [073]
JOURNAL OF ANIMAL SCIENCE – v1- 1942- 1; v34- 5,6; v40- 9 – us UMI [636]
JOURNAL OF ANIMAL SCIENCE – v1-14. 1942-55 – 1,5,6 – us Princeton Micro [590]
JOURNAL OF ANTHROPOLOGICAL RESEARCH – v29- 1973- 1,5,6; v32- 9 – us UMI [301]
JOURNAL OF ANTIBIOTICS – Tokyo. v1-36. 1947-83.Eng. ed – 1,5,6 – us Princeton Micro [610]
JOURNAL OF ANTIBIOTICS. SERIES B – v.6-20. 1953-67. Superseded by Japanese Journal of Antibiotics – 1 – us UMI [615]
JOURNAL OF ANXIETY DISORDERS – 1,5,69 – us UMI [150]
JOURNAL OF APPLIED AQUACULTURE / ed by Webster, Carl David – v6 n1. 1996- – 1,9 – $150.00 in US $210.00 outside hardcopy subsc – us Haworth [630]
JOURNAL OF APPLIED BEHAVIORAL SCIENCE – (v.7- 1971- 5,6. v.11- 1975- 9) – v.1- 1965- – 1 – us UMI [150]
JOURNAL OF APPLIED CHEMISTRY AND BIOTECHNOLOGY – v. 1-25. 1951-1977 – 1,5,6 – us Princeton Micro [540]
JOURNAL OF APPLIED CHEMISTRY OF THE USSR *see* RUSSIAN JOURNAL OF APPLIED CHEMISTRY
JOURNAL OF APPLIED COMMUNICATIONS RESEARCH – v1- 1973- 1; v4- 5,6,9; – us UMI [621]
JOURNAL OF APPLIED ELECTROCHEMISTRY – (1983-. 5,6,9) – v1-. 1971- – 1 – us UMI [073]
JOURNAL OF APPLIED MANAGEMENT – (v.4-. 1979- 5,6,9) – v.2-. 1977- – 1 – us UMI [650]
JOURNAL OF APPLIED MATHEMATICS AND MECHANICS – v22- 1958- – 5,6,9 – us UMI [510]
JOURNAL OF APPLIED MECHANICS : (SERIES E OF THE ASME TRANSACTIONS) – v17- 1950-. v32-. v43- – 1,5,6,9 – us UMI [621]
JOURNAL OF APPLIED MECHANICS AND TECHNICAL PAPERS – v. 6- 1965- – 1,5,6 – us UMI [621]
JOURNAL OF APPLIED MECHANICS AND TECHNICAL PHYSICS – v6-35. 1965-94 – 1,5 – $80.00v – us UMI [621]
JOURNAL OF APPLIED METALWORKING – 1979- – 1,5,6,9 – us UMI [670]
JOURNAL OF APPLIED NUTRITION – v1- 1947- 1; v28- 5,6,9 – us UMI [612]
JOURNAL OF APPLIED PHOTOGRAPHIC ENGINEERING – (v.5 .1975 5,6,9) – v.1. 1975- – 1 – us UMI [073]
JOURNAL OF APPLIED PHYSICS – v1- 1931- – 1,5,6,9 – us A.I.P. [621]
JOURNAL OF APPLIED PHYSIOLOGY – v1-41 1948-76 1; v20-41 1965-76 5,6; v28-41 1970-76 9 – us UMI [612]
JOURNAL OF APPLIED PHYSIOLOGY – v58-. 1985- – 1,5,6,9 – us UMI [073]
JOURNAL OF APPLIED PHYSIOLOGY: RESPIRATORY, ENVIRONMENTAL AND EXERCISE PHYSIOLOGY – v42-57, no.6. 1977-84 – 1,5,6,9 – us UMI [073]
JOURNAL OF APPLIED POLYMER SCIENCE – v. 1-. 1959- – 1,5,6,9 – us UMI [660]
JOURNAL OF APPLIED POLYMER SCIENCE – v1-31. 1959-86 – 1,5,6 – us Princeton Micro [073]
JOURNAL OF APPLIED POLYMER SCIENCE: SYMPOSIA – Nos.1-40. 1965-86 – 1,5,6 – us Princeton Micro [073]
JOURNAL OF APPLIED PSYCHOLOGY – v1-64. 1917-79 – 1,5,6 – us Princeton Micro [150]
JOURNAL OF APPLIED PSYCHOLOGY – (v.49- 1965- 5,6. v.54- 1970- 9) – v.1- 1917- – 1 – us UMI [150]
JOURNAL OF APPLIED SPECTROSCOPY – v2-59. 1965-93 – 1,5 – $80.00v – us UMI [621]
JOURNAL OF APPLIED STATISTICS – 1974- 20v – 9 – £251.00 – 0266-4763 – uk Carfax [310]
JOURNAL OF APPLIED TOXICOLOGY – v1-. 1981- – 1,5,6,9 – us UMI [073]
JOURNAL OF AQUATIC FOOD PRODUCT TECHNOLOGY : ...AN INTERNATIONAL JOURNAL DEVOTED TO FOODS FROM MARINE AND INLAND WATERS OF THE WORLD / ed by Pigott, George M – v5 n1. 1996- – 1,9 – $150.00 in US $210.00 outside hardcopy subsc – us Haworth [660]
JOURNAL OF ARAB AFFAIRS – v.1-. 1981- – 1,5,6,9 – us UMI [956]
JOURNAL OF ARCHAEOLOGICAL METHOD AND THEORY – v1. 1994 – $65.00v – us UMI [930]
JOURNAL OF ARCHAEOLOGICAL RESEARCH – v1-2. 1993-94 – $65.00v – us UMI [930]
JOURNAL OF ARCHITECTURAL RESEARCH – (See also: Architectural Research and Teaching) – v3-. 1974- – 1,5,6,9 – us UMI [720]
JOURNAL OF ART AND DESIGN EDUCATION – 1982- 12v – 9 – £216.00 – 0260-9991 – uk Carfax [370]
JOURNAL OF ARTHROPLASTY – v1-. 1986- – 1,5,6,9 – us UMI [610]
JOURNAL OF ARTS MANAGEMENT AND LAW *see* JOURNAL OF ARTS MANAGEMENT, LAW AND SOCIETY
JOURNAL OF ARTS MANAGEMENT, LAW AND SOCIETY – (v1-13 1971-on reel $165.00. v14-25 1984-96 on mf $243.00. Title varies: v1-11 1971-81 as Performing Arts Review; v12-21 1982-1992 as Journal of Arts Management and Law) – Helen Dwight Reid Educational Foundation. v1-25. 1971-96 – 9 – $408.00 set – us Hein [340]
JOURNAL OF ASIAN AND AFRICAN STUDIES – Leiden. v1-25. 1966-90 – 5,9 – Dfl2,000.00; Dfl80.00v – ne Swets [950]
JOURNAL OF ASIAN HISTORY – v1- 1967- 1; v10- 5,6,9 – us UMI [950]
JOURNAL OF ASIAN STUDIES – (v. 29- 1969- 5,6. v. 35- 1975- 9) – v. 1- 1941- – 1 – us UMI [950]
JOURNAL OF ASIA-PACIFIC BUSINESS / ed by Quraeshi, Zahir A – v1 n1. 1995- – 1,9 – $95.00 in US $133.00 outside hardcopy subsc – us Haworth [650]
JOURNAL OF ASSISTED REPRODUCTION AND GENETICS – (v3-9 1986-92 $90.00v. v10-11 1993-94 $160.00v) – v1-2. 1984-85 – 1,5 – $60.00v – us UMI [612]
JOURNAL OF ATMOSPHERIC AND TERRESTRIAL PHYSICS – v1- 1950- – 5,6,9 – us UMI [550]
JOURNAL OF ATMOSPHERIC CHEMISTRY – v1-. 1983- – 1,5,6,9 – us UMI [073]
JOURNAL OF AUDIOVISUAL MEDIA IN MEDICINE – v. 1- 1978 – 1,5,6,9 – us UMI [610]
JOURNAL OF AUTISM AND DEVELOPMENTAL DISORDERS – v1-24. 1971-94 – 1,5 – $90.00v – us UMI [610]
JOURNAL OF AUTOMATED REASONING – v1-. 1985- – 1,5,6,9 – us UMI [073]
JOURNAL OF AVIATION MEDICINE *see* AEROSPACE MEDICINE
JOURNAL OF BACTERIOLOGY – v. 1-124. 1916-75 – 1,5,6 – us Princeton Micro [576]
JOURNAL OF BACTERIOLOGY – (v. 89- 1965- 5,6. v. 101- 1970- 9) – 1- 1916- – 1 – us UMI [576]
JOURNAL OF BANKING AND FINANCE – v1-8. 1977-84 – 1,5,6,13 – sz Elsevier [073]
JOURNAL OF BANKING LAW – New York, NY. v1-7. 1882-88 – 9 – LLMC 84-505 – us L.L.M.C. [073]
JOURNAL OF BASIC WRITING – v.1. 1975- – 1,5,6,9 – us UMI [073]
JOURNAL OF BEHAVIOR THERAPY AND EXPERIMENTAL PSYCHIATRY – v1- 1970- – 5,6,9 – us UMI [150]
JOURNAL OF BEHAVIORAL MEDICINE – v1-17. 1978-94 – 1,5 – $80.00v – us UMI [610]
JOURNAL OF BIBLE AND RELIGION – (Cont by: American Academy of Religion Journal) – v1-16. 1933-48 (complete) – 3r – 1 – ATLA S0033 – us A.T.L.A. [073]
JOURNAL OF BIBLE AND RELIGION *see* JOURNAL OF THE AMERICAN ACADEMY OF RELIGION
JOURNAL OF BIBLICAL LITERATURE – Middletown. v1-82. 1881-1963 – 425mf – 9 – Dfl1,488.00 – ne IDC [220]

JOURNAL OF BIBLICAL LITERATURE – v. 1-1881- – 1. ; 5,6. ; 9 – apply; v.89-; v.95- – us UMI [240]
JOURNAL OF BIBLICAL LITERATURE – v. 1-59. 1882-1940 – 1 – us Princeton Micro [240]
JOURNAL OF BIOCHEMICAL AND BIOPHYSICAL METHODS – v1-10. 1979-84 – 1,5,6,13 – sz Elsevier [574]
JOURNAL OF BIOCHEMISTRY / Japanese Biochemical Society – v. 1-76. 1922-74 – 1,5,6 – us Princeton Micro [540]
JOURNAL OF BIOCOMMUNICATION – (v.7 .1980 5,6,9) – v.1. 1974 – 1 – us UMI [574]
JOURNAL OF BIOELECTRICITY – (1984-. 5,6,9) – v1-. 1982- – 1 – us UMI [073]
JOURNAL OF BIOENERGETICS AND BIOMEMBRANES – v1-26. 1970-94 – 1,5 – $80.00v – us UMI [574]
JOURNAL OF BIOETHICS – v4-5. Spring-Summer 1982-1984 – 1,5,6,9 – us UMI [073]
JOURNAL OF BIOLOGICAL CHEMISTRY – v. 1-252. 1905-1977 – 1,5,6 – us Princeton Micro [540]
JOURNAL OF BIOLOGICAL CHEMISTRY – (v. 241- 1966- 5,6. v. 245- 1970- 9) – v. 1-1905- – 1 – us UMI [540]
THE JOURNAL OF BIOLOGICAL EXPERIENCE – v1-3. Summer 1978-Spring 1981 – 1 – us UMI [574]
JOURNAL OF BIOLOGICAL SCIENCES – v1-1958- 1; v18- 1975- 5,6,9 – us UMI [574]
JOURNAL OF BIOMECHANICS – v1- 1968- – 5,6,9 – us UMI [574]
JOURNAL OF BIOMEDICAL ENGINEERING – (1982-. 1,5,6,9) – v1-. 1979- – 1 – us UMI [073]
JOURNAL OF BIOMEDICAL MATERIALS RESEARCH – v. 1-. 1967- – 1,5,6,9 – us UMI [615]
JOURNAL OF BIOPHYSICAL AND BIOCHEMICAL CYTOLOGY – v.1-11. 1955-61. Superseded by Journal of Cell Biology – 1 – us UMI [574]
JOURNAL OF BLACK PSYCHOLOGY – (v.6 .1979 5,6,9) – v.1. 1974 – 1 – us UMI [073]
JOURNAL OF BONE AND JOINT SURGERY – (v. 47- 1965- 5,6; v. 52- 1970- 9) – Series A. 1- 1919- – 1 – us UMI [617]
JOURNAL OF BOTANY / ed by Hooker, W J – London. 4v. 1834-1842 – 34mf – 9 – ne IDC [580]
JOURNAL OF BOTANY AND KEW GARDEN MISCELLANY / ed by Hooker, W J – London. 9v. 1849-1857 – 71mf – 9 – ne IDC [580]
THE JOURNAL OF BOTANY, BEING A SECOND SERIES OF THE BOTANICAL MISCELLANY – London, 1834-1842 – 3 – us Readex [580]
JOURNAL OF BOTANY, BRITISH AND FOREIGN / ed by Seemann, Berthold Carl et al – (1929-1942. v67-80. Sfr271.00) – London, 1863-1941. v1-79 – 685mf – 8 – ne IDC [580]
JOURNAL OF BRITISH STUDIES – v.1. 1961 – 1,5,6,9 – us UMI [073]
JOURNAL OF BROADCASTING – 1- 1956- 1; v13- 5,6; v19- 9 – us UMI [380]
JOURNAL OF BROADCASTING *see* JOURNAL OF BROADCASTING AND ELECTRONIC MEDIA
JOURNAL OF BROADCASTING AND ELECTRONIC MEDIA – (v1-28 1956-84 on reel $293.00. v29-39 1985-95 on mf $365.00. Title varies: v1-28 1956-84 as Journal of Broadcasting) – v1-39. 1956-95 – 5,6,9 – $606.00 set – us Hein [380]
JOURNAL OF BURN CARE AND REHABILITATION – (1983-. 1,5,6,9) – v1-. 1980- – 1 – us UMI [617]
JOURNAL OF BUSINESS – v. 1-13. 1928-1940 – 1 – us Princeton Micro [073]
JOURNAL OF BUSINESS – (v. 50- 1977- 9) – v. 1- 1928- – 1. ; 5,6 – apply; v.42- – us UMI [650]
JOURNAL OF BUSINESS AND FINANCE LIBRARIANSHIP / ed by Popovich, Charles J – v1- 1989- – 1, 9 ($75.00 in US $105.00 outside hardcopy subsc) – us Haworth [020]
JOURNAL OF BUSINESS AND PSYCHOLOGY – v1- . 1986- – 1,5,6,9 – us UMI [073]
JOURNAL OF BUSINESS EDUCATION – 1976- – 9 – us UMI [073]
JOURNAL OF BUSINESS EDUCATION – (v.44-58. 1968-83. 5,6. v.46-58. 1970-83. 9) – v.1-58. 1928-83 – 1 – us UMI [370]
JOURNAL OF BUSINESS ETHICS: JBE – (v3-. 1984-. 5,6,9) – v1-. 1982- – 1 – us UMI [073]
JOURNAL OF BUSINESS FINANCE AND ACCOUNTING – (1982-. 1,5,6,9) – v1-. 1974- – 1 – us UMI [073]
JOURNAL OF BUSINESS RESEARCH – v1-12. 1973-84 – 1,5,6,13 – sz Elsevier [073]
JOURNAL OF BUSINESS STRATEGY – v.1 .1980 – 1,5,6,9 – us UMI [073]
JOURNAL OF BUSINESS-TO-BUSINESS MARKETING : ...INNOVATIONS IN APPLIED BUSINESS AND INDUSTRIAL MARKETING RESEARCH / ed by Lichtenthal, J David – v3 n1. 1996- – 1,9 – $150.00 in US $210.00 outside hardcopy subsc – us Haworth [650]
JOURNAL OF CANADIAN ART HISTORY = ANNALES D'HISTOIRE DE L'ART CANADIEN – (Publ delay at v15 1992) – Montreal. v1-16. 1974-93 – 9 – Can$20.00y – cn Micromedia [700]
JOURNAL OF CANADIAN FICTION – (v1-4 1976-75 Can$28.00y. nos15-36 Can$20.00y. Ceased no 35/36 1986) – Montreal. v1-4. 1972-75; nos 15-35/36. 1976-86 – 9 – Price varies – cn Micromedia [420]
JOURNAL OF CANADIAN PETROLEUM TECHNOLOGY – 1984- – 1,5,6,9 – us UMI [660]
JOURNAL OF CANADIAN PHYSIOTHERAPY ASSOCIATION – v.1-24. 1939-72 – 1 – us UMI [615]
JOURNAL OF CANADIAN STUDIES = REVUE D'ETUDES CANADIENNES – (v1-6 1966-71 Can$100.00. v1-11 1966-76 Can$20.00y. Index 1966-86 Can$20.00 v7-10 1972-75 Can$100.00. v11-19 1976-84 Can$50.00y. v 12-30 1977-96 Can$28.00y) – Peterborough. v1-30. 1966-1995/96 – 5,9 – Price varies – cn Micromedia [971]
JOURNAL OF CANCER EDUCATION – 1,5,69 – us UMI [616]
JOURNAL OF CANCER RESEARCH AND CLINICAL ONCOLOGY – v.56-101, 1948-81. ISSN: 0171-5216 – 1,5,6,9,13 – 132.00v – us UMI [616]
JOURNAL OF CANCER RESEARCH AND CLINICAL ONCOLOGY *see* ZEITSCHRIFT FUER KREBSFORSCHUNG UND KLINISCHE ONKOLOGIE
JOURNAL OF CARBOHYDRATE CHEMISTRY – (1984-. 5,6,9) – v1-. 1982- – 1 – us UMI [073]
JOURNAL OF CARDIOVASCULAR MEDICINE – (1984-. 5,6,9) – v5-9. 1980-84 – 1 – us UMI [610]
JOURNAL OF CARDIOVASCULAR NURSING – v1- . 1986- – 1,5,6,9 – us UMI [073]
JOURNAL OF CARDIOVASCULAR SURGERY – Torino. v1-17. 1960-76 – 5,9 – Dfl1,700.00; Dfl100.00v – ne Swets [617]
JOURNAL OF CAREER EDUCATION – 1972- 1; 1976- 5,6,9 – us UMI [370]
JOURNAL OF CELL BIOLOGY – (v.80-. 1979-5,6,9) – v.12-. 1962- – 1 – us UMI [574]
JOURNAL OF CELL SCIENCE – (1983-. 1,5,6,9) – v1-. 1966- – 1 – us UMI [073]
JOURNAL OF CELLULAR BIOCHEMISTRY – v.18-. 1982- – 1,5,6,9 – us UMI [540]
JOURNAL OF CELLULAR PHYSIOLOGY – v. 1-70. 1932-1967 – 1,5,6 – us Princeton Micro [612]
JOURNAL OF CEMENT AND CONCRETE RESEARCH *see* CEMENT AND CONCRETE RESEARCH
JOURNAL OF CHARLES J. DEBLOIS, CAPTAIN'S CLERK, ABOARD THE U.S.S. MACEDONIAN / Deblois, Charles J – 1818-19. M876 – 1r – 1 – us Nat'l Archives [920]
JOURNAL OF CHARLES MASON KEPT DURING THE SURVEY OF THE MASON AND DIXON LINE, 1763-68 / U.S. Department of State – 1 roll. M86 – 1 – us Nat'l Archives [975]
JOURNAL OF CHEMICAL AND ENGINEERING DATA – v1- 1956- – 1,5,6,9 – us A.C.S. [660]
JOURNAL OF CHEMICAL CRYSTALLOGRAPHY – (v23-24 1993-94 $120.00v. Cont: Journal of Crystallographic and Spectroscopic Research) – v1-22. 1971-92 – 1,5 – $80.00v – us UMI [540]
JOURNAL OF CHEMICAL DEPENDENCY TREATMENT / ed by Finnegan, Dana – v1- 1987- – 1, 9 ($175.00 in US $245.00 outside hardcopy subsc) – us Haworth [615]
JOURNAL OF CHEMICAL ECOLOGY – (v8-14 1982-88 $150.00v. v15-20 1989-94 $225.00v) – v1-7. 1975-81 – 1,5 – $80.00v – us UMI [574]
JOURNAL OF CHEMICAL EDUCATION – (v. 43- 1966- 5,6. v. 47- 1970- 9) – 1- 1924- – 1 – us UMI [370]
JOURNAL OF CHEMICAL EDUCATION – v1-32. 1924-55 – 1,5,6 – us Princeton Micro [540]
JOURNAL OF CHEMICAL INFORMATION AND COMPUTER SCIENCES – v1- 1961- – 1,5,6,9 – us A.C.S. [540]
JOURNAL OF CHEMICAL PHYSICS / American Institute of Physics – Lancaster, PA, New York. 1933-39. v1-7. – 222mf – 8 – ne IDC [073]
THE JOURNAL OF CHEMICAL PHYSICS – v1-. 1933- – 1,5,6,9 – us A.I.P. [530]
JOURNAL OF CHEMICAL TECHNOLOGY AND BIOTECHNOLOGY – v1-25. 1951-75 – 1,5,6 – us Princeton Micro [660]
JOURNAL OF CHILD AND ADOLESCENT SUBSTANCE ABUSE / ed by DePiano, Frank & Hasselt, Vincent B Van – v1-1989- – 1, 9 ($145.00 in US $203.00 outside hardcopy subsc) – us Haworth [360]
JOURNAL OF CHILD LANGUAGE – (v.6 .1979 5,6,9) – v.1 .1974 – 1 – us UMI [400]
JOURNAL OF CHILD PSYCHOLOGY AND PSYCHIATRY – (Back issues of journal available from UMI) – 8 issues/y. v34. 1993 – 9 – £180.00y – uk Elsevier Sci [150]
JOURNAL OF CHILD PSYCHOLOGY AND PSYCHIATRY – v1- 1960- – 5,6,9 – us UMI [150]
JOURNAL OF CHILD SEXUAL ABUSE : RESEARCH, TREATMENT AND PROGRAM INNOVATIONS FOR VICTIMS, SURVIVORS AND OFFENDERS / ed by Geffner, Robert A – v5 n1. 1996- – 1,9 – $85.00 in US $119.00 outside hardcopy subsc – us Haworth [360]
JOURNAL OF CHIROPRACTIC – v19-. 1982- – 1,5,6,9 – us UMI [073]
JOURNAL OF CHIROPRACTIC *see* ACA JOURNAL OF CHIROPRACTIC
JOURNAL OF CHRISTIAN EDUCATION – v1-3. 1980-82 – 1 – us UMI [370]
JOURNAL OF CHRISTIAN JURISPRUDENCE – (Superseded by Liberty, Life and Family) – Regent University. v1-8. 1980-90 – 9 – $90.00 set – us Hein [340]
JOURNAL OF CHRISTIAN JURISPRUDENCE *see* LIBERTY, LIFE AND FAMILY
JOURNAL OF CHRISTIAN NURSING: A QUARTERLY PUBLICATION OF NURSES CHRISTIAN FELLOWSHIP – v1-. Spring 1984- – 1,5,6,9 – us UMI [073]
JOURNAL OF CHRISTIAN RECONSTRUCTION – (1985- . 5,6,9) – v1- . 1974- – 1 – us UMI [073]
JOURNAL OF CHROMATOGRAPHIC SCIENCE / ed by Gordon, Bert & Walker, John Q. – 1962-96 – 1,5 – $100.00v subsc $240.00v nonsubsc 1 ($75.00v subsc $240 nonsubsc 5) – ISSN 0021-9665 – us Preston Publ [540]
JOURNAL OF CHROMATOGRAPHY – v1-311. 1958-84 – 1,5,6,13 – sz Elsevier [073]
JOURNAL OF CHRONIC DISEASES – St. Louis, New York. 1960, 1962, 1963, 1965, 1966. M-22/2 – 8 – ne IDC [616]
JOURNAL OF CHRONIC DISEASES – v.1-. 1955- – 5,6,9 – us UMI [616]
JOURNAL OF CHRONIC FATIGUE SYNDROME : MULTIDISCIPLINARY INNOVATIONS IN RESEARCH, THEORY AND CLINICAL PRACTICE / ed by Klimas, Nancy – v2 n1. 1996- – 1,9 – $125.00 in US $175.00 outside hardcopy subsc – us Haworth [616]
JOURNAL OF CHURCH AND STATE – (v1-26 1959-84 on reel $299.00. v27-37 1985-95 on mf $225.00) – Baylor University. v1-37. 1959-95 – 5,6,9 – $529.00 set – us Hein [240]
JOURNAL OF CLASSROOM INTERACTION – v12- 1976- 1,5,6; v13- 1977- 9 – us UMI [370]
JOURNAL OF CLIMATOLOGY – v1- 1981- – 1,5,6,9 – us UMI [550]
JOURNAL OF CLINICAL AND EXPERIMENTAL GERONTOLOGY – (1984-. 5,6,9) – v1-. 1979- – 1 – us UMI [618]
JOURNAL OF CLINICAL AND EXPERIMENTAL PSYCHOPATHOLOGY – v10-21 1949-1960 – 1 – us UMI [616]
JOURNAL OF CLINICAL ENDOCRINOLOGY AND METABOLISM – (v. 26-45. 1966-77 5,6. v. 30-45 1970-77 9) – 1-45. 1941-77 – 1 – us UMI [610]
JOURNAL OF CLINICAL ENDOCRINOLOGY AND METABOLISM – v1-15. 1941-55 – 1,5,6 – us Princeton Micro [616]
JOURNAL OF CLINICAL EPIDEMIOLOGY – 1,5,69 – us UMI [614]
JOURNAL OF CLINICAL IMMUNOASSAY / Clinical Ligand Assay Society – v6-. 1983- – 1,5,6,9 – us UMI [073]
JOURNAL OF CLINICAL IMMUNOLOGY – (v4-14 1984-94 $80.00v) – v1-3. 1981-83 – 1,5 – $60.00v – us UMI [612]
JOURNAL OF CLINICAL INVESTIGATION – (v. 30- 1951- 1. v. 49 1970- 9) – 1- 1904- – 5,6 – us UMI [610]
JOURNAL OF CLINICAL INVESTIGATION – v1-32. 1924-52 – 1,5,6 – us Princeton Micro [073]
JOURNAL OF CLINICAL LABORATORY AUTOMATION – v1-. 1981- – 1,5,6,9 – us UMI [073]
JOURNAL OF CLINICAL MICROBIOLOGY – v1-1975- 1,5,6; v3- 1976- 9 – us UMI [616]
JOURNAL OF CLINICAL MONITORING – v1-. 1985- – 1,5,6,9 – us UMI [616]
JOURNAL OF CLINICAL NUTRITION *see* AMERICAN JOURNAL OF CLINICAL NUTRITION
JOURNAL OF CLINICAL PATHOLOGY – v1 1947- 1; v18- 5,6; v28- 9 – us UMI [616]
JOURNAL OF CLINICAL PERIODONTOLOGY – (v1-9. Dfl100.00v; v10-13. Dfl130.00v) – Copenhagen. v1-13. 1974-86 – 5,9 – Dfl1,420.00 – ne Swets [617]
JOURNAL OF CLINICAL PSYCHIATRY – v. 39-. 1978- – 1,5,6,9 – us UMI [150]
JOURNAL OF CLINICAL PSYCHOLOGY – 1-1945- 1; v21- 5,6; v30- 9 – us UMI [150]
JOURNAL OF CLINICAL PSYCHOLOGY IN MEDICAL SETTINGS – v1. 1994 – $65.00v – us UMI [610]
JOURNAL OF CLINICAL PSYCHOPHARMACOLOGY – v1-16. 1981-96 – 16r – 1,5,6,9 – $80.00r – us Williams [615]
JOURNAL OF CLUSTER SCIENCE – v1-5. 1990-94 – 1,5 – $65.00 – us UMI [540]
JOURNAL OF COLLEGE AND UNIVERSITY FOODSERVICE / ed by Khan, Mahmood A – v3 n1. 1997- – 1,9 – $60.00 in US $84.00 outside hardcopy subsc – us Haworth [640]
JOURNAL OF COLLEGE AND UNIVERSITY LAW – (v.6.1979 5,6,9) – v.1. 1973 – 1 – us UMI [340]
JOURNAL OF COLLEGE AND UNIVERSITY STUDENT HOUSING – (v.9 .1979 9) – v.1. 1971 – 1 – us UMI [073]
JOURNAL OF COLLEGE PLACEMENT – v1-1940- 1; v31- 5,6; v37- 9 – us UMI [370]
JOURNAL OF COLLEGE STUDENT PSYCHOTHERAPY / ed by Whitaker, Leighton C – v1- 1986- – 1, 9 ($225.00 in US $315.00 outside hardcopy subsc) – us Haworth [615]
JOURNAL OF COMBUSTION TOXICOLOGY – v. 3-. 1976- – 1,5,6,9 – us UMI [610]
JOURNAL OF COMMERCE : BRITISH COLUMBIA EDITION – British Columbia, CN. 1962-73 – 26r – 1 – cn Commonwealth Micro [073]
JOURNAL OF COMMERCE – Chicago. Ill. 1920- – 1 – us UMI [071]
JOURNAL OF COMMERCE : COMBINED EDITION – (1974-82 36r. 1983-July 1989 14r) – Vancouver, British Columbia, CN. 1974-July 1989 – 50r – 1 – cn Commonwealth Micro [073]
JOURNAL OF COMMERCE – (Cont by: San Francisco Journal) – San Francisco, CA. 1874-1885; 1906-1908; 1912-1920 – 35r – 1 – $1,750.00 – C03496 – us Library Micro [071]
JOURNAL OF COMMERCE : A MONTHLY REVIEW OF INDUSTRY, COMMERCE AND FINANCE / ed by Foley, M S et al – (With index) – Montreal, Canada. 20 aug 1875-oct 1932 – 70r – 1 – Can$60.00r – cn Can Microfilming [380]
JOURNAL OF COMMERCE – Montreal, Canada. -w. 5 Oct 1877; March 1919-June 1922. 3 1 2 reels – 1 – uk British Libr Newspaper [072]
JOURNAL OF COMMERCE – New York City, NY. 1958- – 366+ r – 1 – $18,300.00 ($510.00) – R04912 – us Library Micro [073]
JOURNAL OF COMMERCE – Portland OR. Mar 30 June 7 1853 + – 1 – us U.O. Library [071]
JOURNAL OF COMMERCE : PRAIRIE EDITION – British Columbia, CN. 1962-73 – 26r – 1 – cn Commonwealth Micro [073]

JOURNAL OF COMMERCE : WEEKLY EDITION – British Columbia, CN. 1951-61 – 19r – 1 – cn Commonwealth Micro [073]
JOURNAL OF COMMERCE *see* LIVERPOOL JOURNAL OF COMMERCE
JOURNAL OF COMMERCE AND COMMERCIAL BULLETIN – New York, N.Y. Oct 26, 1903-1910 – 1 – us Res Libr [380]
JOURNAL OF COMMERCE AND COMMERCIAL NEW YORK – New York, 1829-47 – us Ross [380]
JOURNAL OF COMMERCE AND COMMERCIAL NEW YORK – New York. Jan. 1828-June 30, 1948 – 1 – us NY Public [071]
THE JOURNAL OF COMMERCE AND COMMERCIAL, NEW YORK – Commercial precedents, selected from the column of replies and decisions of the New York Journal of Commerce. Hartford, Conn: American Publishing Co., 1881. 588p. LL-403 – 1 – us L of C Photodup [340]
JOURNAL OF COMMERCE AND INDEPENDENT REVIEW – Los Angeles, CA. 1975 – 4r – 1 – $200.00 – R03300 – us Library Micro [073]
JOURNAL OF COMMERCE AND SHIPPING TELEGRAPH *see* LIVERPOOL JOURNAL OF COMMERCE
JOURNAL OF COMMERCE REVIEW – Los Angeles, CA. 1976-1980 – 29r – 1 – $1,450.00 – R03301 – us Library Micro [073]
JOURNAL OF COMMERCE REVIEW *see* LOS ANGELES DAILY JOURNAL OF COMMERCE
JOURNAL OF COMMERCIAL BANK LENDING – (v.62-. 1979- 5,6,9) – v.50-. 1967- – 1 – us UMI [073]
JOURNAL OF COMMON MARKET STUDIES – v1-33. 1962-1995 – 9 – $360.00set – us Hein [380]
JOURNAL OF COMMUNICATION – v1- 1951- 1; v24- 5,6; v25- 1975- 9 – us UMI [380]
JOURNAL OF COMMUNICATION – 1985-. -q – 1 – us UMI [073]
JOURNAL OF COMMUNICATION DISORDERS – v1-17. 1968-84 – 1,5,6,13 – sz Elsevier [616]
JOURNAL OF COMMUNITY DEVELOPMENT – (Cont by: Main Street at v2 1988) – Belfast, PEI. v1. 1987 – 9 – Can$20.00y – cn Micromedia [307]
JOURNAL OF COMMUNITY DEVELOPMENT *see* MAIN STREET
JOURNAL OF COMMUNITY PRACTICE : MULTIDISCLIPLINARY INNOVATIONS IN RESEARCH, THEORY AND CLINICAL PRACTICE SPONSORED BY THE ASSOCIATION FOR CUMMUNITY ORGANIZATION AND SOCIAL ADMINISTRATION (ACOSA) / ed by Weil, D S W Marie – v3 n1. 1996- – 1,9 – $105.00 in US $147.00 outside hardcopy subsc – us Haworth [360]
JOURNAL OF COMMUNITY PSYCHOLOGY – v. 1- 1973- – 1,5,6 – us UMI [150]
JOURNAL OF COMPARATIVE ADMINISTRATION – v1-5. 1969-74. Continued by: Administration and Society – 1 – us UMI [073]
JOURNAL OF COMPARATIVE ADMINISTRATION *see* ADMINISTRATION AND SOCIETY
JOURNAL OF COMPARATIVE AND PHYSIOLOGICAL PSYCHOLOGY – (v. 59-1965- 5,6. v. 70- 1970- 9) – v. 41- 1948- – 1 – us UMI [150]
JOURNAL OF COMPARATIVE AND PHYSIOLOGICAL PSYCHOLOGY – v1-96. 1921-82 – 1,5,6 – us Princeton Micro [150]
JOURNAL OF COMPARATIVE BUSINESS AND CAPITAL MARKET LAW – v1-6. 1978-84. Continues: Journal of comparative corporate law and security regulation – 1,5,6,13 – sz Elsevier [073]
JOURNAL OF COMPARATIVE BUSINESS AND CAPITAL MARKET REVIEW *see* UNIVERSITY OF PENNSYLVANIA JOURNAL OF INTERNATIONAL BUSINESS LAW
JOURNAL OF COMPARATIVE CORPORATE LAW AND SECURITIES REGULATION *see* UNIVERSITY OF PENNSYLVANIA JOURNAL OF INTERNATIONAL BUSINESS LAW
JOURNAL OF COMPARATIVE FAMILY STUDIES – (v1-9 1970-78 Can$20.00y) – Calgary. v1- 1970- – 9 – Can$28.00y – cn Micromedia [306]
JOURNAL OF COMPARATIVE LEGISLATION AND INTERNATIONAL LAW – 1896-1951 – 13r – 1 – $500.00 – us Trans-Media [340]
JOURNAL OF COMPARATIVE NEUROLOGY – Philadelphia. v120-128.1963-66. M-23/2 – 8 – ne IDC [073]
JOURNAL OF COMPARATIVE NEUROLOGY – Philadelphia. v133-188. 1968-79 – 5,9 – Dfl3,920.00; Dfl70.00v – ne Swets [610]
JOURNAL OF COMPARATIVE NEUROLOGY – v. 1-131. 1891-1967 – 1,5,6 – us Princeton Micro [590]
JOURNAL OF COMPARATIVE PHYSIOLOGY – v20-153.1924-83 – 1,5,9 – 25,773.00 – us UMI [073]
JOURNAL OF COMPARATIVE PHYSIOLOGY *see* ZEITSCHRIFT FUER VERGLEICHENDE PHYSIOLOGIE
JOURNAL OF COMPARATIVE PHYSIOLOGY: A. SENSORY, NEURAL AND BEHAVIORAL PHYSIOLOGY – v154-. 1984- – 1,5,6,9 – us UMI [073]
JOURNAL OF COMPARATIVE PHYSIOLOGY: B. BIOCHEMICAL, SYSTEMIC AND ENVIRONMENTAL PHYSIOLOGY – v154-. 1984- – 1,5,6,9 – us UMI [073]
JOURNAL OF COMPARATIVE PSYCHOLOGY – v97-. 1983- – 1,5,6,9 – us UMI [073]
JOURNAL OF COMPUTATIONAL CHEMISTRY – v1-7. 1980-86 – 1,5,6 – us Princeton Micro [073]
JOURNAL OF COMPUTER-ASSISTED MICROSCOPY – v1-6. 1989-94 – 1,5 – $65.00v – us UMI [578]
JOURNAL OF COMPUTER-BASED INSTRUCTION – (v3-. 1976-. 5,6,9) – v. 1-. 1974- – 1 – us UMI [510]
JOURNAL OF COMPUTERS AND STRUCTURES *see* COMPUTERS AND STRUCTURES
JOURNAL OF COMPUTERS IN MATHEMATICS AND SCIENCE TEACHING – (1983-. 1,5,6,9) – v1-. 1981- – 1 – us UMI [073]
JOURNAL OF CONCHOLOGY *see* QUARTERLY JOURNAL OF CONCHOLOGY
JOURNAL OF CONFLICT RESOLUTION – (v15-. 1971-. 5,6. v19-. 1975-. 9) – v. 1- 1957- – 1 – us UMI [073]
JOURNAL OF CONSTITUTIONAL AND PARLIAMENTARY STUDIES – (v6-. 1972-. 5,6. v9-. 1975-. 9) – v. 1- 1967- – 1 – us UMI [073]
JOURNAL OF CONSTRUCTION ENGINEERING AND MANAGEMENT – v109- 1983- – 1,5,6,9 – us UMI [690]
JOURNAL OF CONSTRUCTIONAL STEEL RESEARCH – v1-4. 1981-84 – 1,5,6,13 – sz Elsevier [670]
JOURNAL OF CONSULTING AND CLINICAL PSYCHOLOGY – (v. 29- 1965- 5,6. v. 34- 1970- 9) – v. 1- 1937- – 1 – us UMI [150]
JOURNAL OF CONSULTING AND CLINICAL PSYCHOLOGY – v1-51. 1936-83 – 1,5,6 – us Princeton Micro [150]
JOURNAL OF CONSUMER CREDIT MANAGEMENT – v1-12 1969-80 1; v5-12 5,6; v8-12 9 – us UMI [073]
JOURNAL OF CONSUMER POLICY – v6-. 1983- – 1,5,6,9 – us UMI [073]
JOURNAL OF CONSUMER POLICY *see* ZEITSCHRIFT FUER VERBRAUCHERPOLITIK
JOURNAL OF CONSUMER PRODUCT FLAMMABILITY – (See also: Consumer Product Flammability) – v3- 1976- – 1,5,6,9 – us UMI [360]
JOURNAL OF CONSUMER RESEARCH – (v.8-. 1981-. 5,6,9) – v.1-. Jun 1974- – 1 – us UMI [380]
JOURNAL OF CONTEMPORARY ASIA – v1- 1970- 1; v4- 5,6; v6- 9 – us UMI [950]
JOURNAL OF CONTEMPORARY BUSINESS – v1-11 1972-82 1; v4-11 5,6,9 – us UMI [073]
JOURNAL OF CONTEMPORARY HEALTH LAW AND POLICY – Catholic University of America, D.C. v1-11. 1985-95 – 9 – $133.00 set – us Hein [340]
JOURNAL OF CONTEMPORARY HISTORY – 1-3. 1966-1968 – 1 – us UMI [900]
JOURNAL OF CONTEMPORARY LAW – v1- 1974- 1,5,6; v2- 9 – us UMI [073]
JOURNAL OF CONTEMPORARY LEGAL ISSUES – University of San Diego. v1-5. 1987-94 – 9 – $47.00 set – us Hein [340]
JOURNAL OF CONTEMPORARY STUDIES – v.4-. 1981- – 1,5,6,9 – us UMI [073]
JOURNAL OF CONTINUING EDUCATION IN FAMILY MEDICINE – v. 23-24. 1977-78 – 1,5,6,9 – us UMI [610]
JOURNAL OF CONTINUING EDUCATION IN O.R.L. AND ALLERGY – v. 39-40. 1977-78 – 1,5,6,9 – us UMI [610]
JOURNAL OF CONTINUING EDUCATION IN ORTHOPEDICS – v. 6-. 1978- – 1,5,6,9 – us UMI [617]
JOURNAL OF CONTINUING EDUCATION IN PEDIATRICS – Superseded by PEDIATRICS DIGEST v20 1978 – 1,5,6,9 – us UMI [610]
JOURNAL OF CONTINUING EDUCATION IN UROLOGY – Superseded by UROLOGY DIGEST v16 and v18 1977 and 79 – 1,5,6,9 – us UMI [610]
JOURNAL OF CONVENTION AND EXHIBITION MANAGEMENT / ed by Abbott, Je'Anna Lanza – v1 n1. 1997- – 1,9 – $95.00 in US $133.00 outside hardcopy subsc – us Haworth [650]
JOURNAL OF COOPERATIVE EDUCATION – (v.16 .1979 5,6,9) – v.1. 1964 – 1 – us UMI [073]
JOURNAL OF COORDINATION CHEMISTRY – 1971- – 1,5,9 – us Gordon [540]
JOURNAL OF COORDINATION CHEMISTRY / ed by Williams, Peter A – 9,5,1 – us Gordon [540]
JOURNAL OF CORPORATE ACCOUNTING AND FINANCE – v1-4. 1989-93 – 9 – $105.00 set – us Hein [650]
JOURNAL OF CORPORATE TAXATION – v1- 1974- 1,5,6; v3- 9 – us UMI [336]
JOURNAL OF CORPORATION LAW – University of Iowa. v1-20. 1976-95 – 9 – $403.00 set – us Hein [340]
JOURNAL OF CORPORATION LAW – v1-19. 1975-94 – 1,5,6 – $405.00 – us Hein [073]
JOURNAL OF CORRECTIONAL EDUCATION – v1- 1949- 1; v23- 5,6; v29- 9 – us UMI [360]
JOURNAL OF COUNSELING AND DEVELOPMENT: JCD – v63, no.1-. Sept 1984- – 1,5,6,9 – us UMI [073]
JOURNAL OF COUNSELING PSYCHOLOGY – v. 1-26. 1954-79 – 1,5,6 – us Princeton Micro [150]
JOURNAL OF COUNSELING PSYCHOLOGY – (v. 15- 1968- 5,6. v. 17- 1970- 9) – v. 1- 1954- – 1 – us UMI [150]
JOURNAL OF COUNSELING SERVICES – v. 1-. 1976- – 1,5,6,9 – us UMI [370]
JOURNAL OF COUPLES THERAPY / ed by Brothers, Barbara Jo – v1- 1989- – 1,9 ($125.00 in US $175.00 outside hardcopy subsc) – us Haworth [306]
JOURNAL OF CREATIVE BEHAVIOR – v1- 1967- 1; v5- 5,6; v9- 9 – us UMI [300]
JOURNAL OF CRIME AND JUSTICE – (1985-. 5,6,9) – v1-. 1978- – 1 – us UMI [340]
JOURNAL OF CRIMINAL JUSTICE – v1- 1973- – 5,6,9 – us UMI [360]
JOURNAL OF CRIMINAL LAW AND CRIMINOLOGY – v1-86. 1910-96 – 1,5,6 – $2,160.00 – us Hein [073]
JOURNAL OF CRIMINAL LAW, CRIMINOLOGY AND POLICE SCIENCE – (Add vols as copyright expires) – American Institute of Criminal Law and Criminology. v1-10. 1910-20 – 75mf – $112.00 – LLMC 95-107 – us L.L.M.C. [073]
JOURNAL OF CRIMINAL LAW (LONDON) – v1-59. 1937-95 – 9 – $1,203.00 set – us Hein [340]
JOURNAL OF CRITICAL ANALYSIS – v1- 1969- 1; v2- 5,6; v6- 9 – us UMI [370]
JOURNAL OF CROP PRODUCTION : INNOVATIONS IN PRACTICE, THEORY AND RESEARCH / ed by Basra, Amarjit S – v1 n1. 1997- – 1,9 – $95.00 in US $133.00 outside hardcopy subsc – us Haworth [630]
JOURNAL OF CROSS-CULTURAL GERONTOLOGY – v1-. 1986- – 1,5,6,9 – us UMI [618]
JOURNAL OF CRYSTAL GROWTH – v1-70. 1967-84 – 1,5,6,13 – sz Elsevier [073]
JOURNAL OF CRYSTALLOGRAPHIC AND SPECTROSCOPIC RESEARCH *see* JOURNAL OF CHEMICAL CRYSTALLOGRAPHY
JOURNAL OF CUNEIFORM STUDIES – v1- 1947- 1; v24- 5,6; v27- 9 – us UMI [410]
JOURNAL OF CUSTOMER SERVICE IN MARKETING AND MANAGEMENT : INNOVATIONS OF SERVICE, QUALITY AND VALUE / ed by Winston, William J – v2 n1. 1996- – 1,9 – $125.00 in US $175.00 outside hardcopy subsc – us Haworth [650]
JOURNAL OF CYBERNETICS – v1- 1971- 1; v6- 5,6,9 – us UMI [000]
JOURNAL OF DAIRY RESEARCH – v1- 1929- 1; v38- 5,6; v43- 9 – us UMI [636]
JOURNAL OF DAIRY SCIENCE – v. 1-38. 1917-1955 – 1,5,6 – us Princeton Micro [636]
JOURNAL OF DATA COLLECTION *see* VIEWPOINTS, THE JOURNAL FOR DATA COLLECTION
JOURNAL OF DENTAL EDUCATION – v14-18 1949-1954 – 1 – us UMI [617]
JOURNAL OF DENTAL PRACTICE ADMINISTRATION: JDPA – v1-. 1984- – 1,5,6,9 – us UMI [073]
JOURNAL OF DENTAL RESEARCH – v1- 1919- 1; v54- 1975- 5,6,9 – us UMI [617]
JOURNAL OF DENTAL RESEARCH – v. 1-20. 1919-1941 – 1,5,6 – us Princeton Micro [617]
JOURNAL OF DENTISTRY FOR CHILDREN – v1- 1933- 1; v36- 5,6; v42- 9 – us UMI [617]
THE JOURNAL OF DESIGN AND MANUFACTURES / ed by Cole, Henry – (Essential resource for study of early industrial design) – London. 6v. 1849-52 – 19mf – 9 – $100.00 – 0-907006-63-9 – uk Mindata [760]
JOURNAL OF DEVELOPMENT ECONOMICS – v1-16. 1974-84 – 1,5,6,13 – sz Elsevier [338]
JOURNAL OF DEVELOPMENTAL AND BEHAVIORAL PEDIATRICS – v2-17. 1981-96 – 1,5,6,9 – $80.00r – us Williams [618]
JOURNAL OF DEVELOPMENTAL AND PHYSICAL DISABILITIES – v1-6. 1988-94 – 1,5 – $65.00 – us UMI [616]
JOURNAL OF DEVELOPMENTAL PHYSIOLOGY – v5-. 1983- – 1,5,6,9 – us UMI [073]
JOURNAL OF DHARMA – (1986- . 5,6,9) – v1- . 1975- – 1 – us UMI [280]
JOURNAL OF DIAGNOSTIC MEDICAL SONOGRAPHY – v1-. 1985- – 1,5,6,9 – us UMI [616]
JOURNAL OF DIALYSIS – v1-4. 1977-80 – 1 – us UMI [616]
JOURNAL OF DIFFERENTIAL GEOMETRY – v. 2-6. 1968-1972 – 1,5,6 – us Princeton Micro [510]
JOURNAL OF DISEASES OF CHILDREN *see* AMERICAN JOURNAL OF DISEASES OF CHILDREN
JOURNAL OF DISPERSION SCIENCE AND TECHNOLOGY – (1984-. 5,6,9) – v1-. 1980- – 1 – us UMI [073]
JOURNAL OF DISPUTE RESOLUTION – (Title varies: 1984-87 as Missouri Journal of Dispute Resolution) – University of Missouri-Columbia, 1984-95 – 9 – $175.00 set – us Hein [340]
JOURNAL OF DISTANCE EDUCATION – Ottawa. v1-9. 1986-94 – 9 – Can$20.00y – cn Micromedia [370]
JOURNAL OF DISTRICT OF COLUMBIA BAR ASSOCIATION OF THE DISTRICT OF COLUMBIA *see* JOURNAL OF THE BAR ASSOCIATION OF THE DISTRICT OF COLUMBIA
JOURNAL OF DIVORCE AND REMARRIAGE / ed by Everett, Craig A – v1- 1977- – 1,9 ($325.00 in US $455.00 outside hardcopy subsc) – us Haworth [306]
JOURNAL OF DOCUMENTARY REPRODUCTION – v. 1-5. 1938-42 – 1 – 19.00 – us L of C Photodup [770]
JOURNAL OF DRUG TARGETING / ed by Florence, A T & Lee, V H L – 9,5,1 – us Harwood [615]
JOURNAL OF DYNAMIC SYSTEMS, MEASUREMENT AND CONTROL – v93- 1971- 1,5,6; v98- 9 – us UMI [073]
JOURNAL OF DYNAMICS AND DIFFERENTIAL EQUATIONS – v1-6. 1989-94 – 1,5 – $65.00v – us UMI [510]
JOURNAL OF EARLY ADOLESCENCE – v1-. 1981- – 1,5,6,9 – us UMI [073]
JOURNAL OF EAST-WEST BUSINESS / ed by Kaynak, Erdener – v2 n1. 1996 – 1,9 – $95.00 in US $133.00 outside hardcopy subsc – us Haworth [650]
JOURNAL OF ECCLESIASTICAL HISTORY – v17- 1966- 1; v22- 5,6; v27- 9 – us UMI [240]
JOURNAL OF ECOLOGY / British Ecological Society – Cambridge. v1-8. 1913-1921 – 46mf – 9 – ne IDC [574]
JOURNAL OF ECOLOGY – v. 63-64. 1975-76 – 1,5,6 – us Princeton Micro [574]
JOURNAL OF ECONOMETRICS – v1-26. 1973-84 – 1,5,6,13 – sz Elsevier [330]
JOURNAL OF ECONOMIC AND SOCIAL MEASUREMENT – v1-12. 1972-84.Continues: Review of public data use – 1,5,6,13 – sz Elsevier [330]
JOURNAL OF ECONOMIC BEHAVIOR AND ORGANIZATION – v1-5. 1980-84 – . 1.5,6,13 – sz Elsevier [650]

JOURNAL OF ECONOMIC DYNAMICS AND CONTROL – v1-8. 1979-84 – 1,5,6,13 – sz Elsevier [650]
JOURNAL OF ECONOMIC EDUCATION – v1- 1969- 1; v8- 5,6,9 – us UMI [370]
JOURNAL OF ECONOMIC ENTOMOLOGY – v2- 1909- 1; v62- 5,6; v69- 9 – us UMI [630]
JOURNAL OF ECONOMIC ENTOMOLOGY – v.1-49. 1908-56 – 1,5,6 – 22460.00 – us Princeton Micro [590]
JOURNAL OF ECONOMIC HISTORY – v1- 1941- 1; v29- 5,6; v35- 9 – us UMI [330]
JOURNAL OF ECONOMIC ISSUES – v1- 1967- 1; v7- 5,6; v9- 9 – us UMI [330]
JOURNAL OF ECONOMIC LITERATURE – v1- 1963- 1; v8- 5,6; v13- 9 – us UMI [330]
JOURNAL OF ECONOMIC PSYCHOLOGY – v1-5. 1981-84 – 1,5,6,13 – sz Elsevier [073]
JOURNAL OF ECONOMICS *see* ZEITSCHRIFT FUER NATIONALOEKONOMIE
JOURNAL OF ECONOMICS EDUCATION – v1- 1969- 1; v8- 1976- 5,6,9 – us UMI [370]
JOURNAL OF ECUMENICAL STUDIES – (v1-21 1961-84 on reel $236.00. v22-32 1985-95 on mf $242.00) – v1-32. 1964-95 – 5,6,9 – $478.00 set – us Hein [340]
JOURNAL OF EDUCATION – v1- 1875- 1; v151- 5,6; v157- 9 – us UMI [370]
JOURNAL OF EDUCATION – (Ceased v21 1975) – Vancouver. v1-21. 1957-75 – 5 – Can$130.00 – cn Micromedia [370]
JOURNAL OF EDUCATION *see* THE JOURNAL OF EDUCATION FOR LOWER CANADA
THE JOURNAL OF EDUCATION – (Cont: The Journal of Education for Lower Canada) – Montreal: Dept of Public Instruction, [1867-1879?] – 9 – cn C.I.H.M. [370]
THE JOURNAL OF EDUCATION AND AGRICULTURE FOR THE PROVINCE OF NOVA SCOTIA – Halifax [N.S.]: A and W Mackinlay, [1858-1860] – 9 – cn C.I.H.M. [370]
JOURNAL OF EDUCATION FINANCE – (v1-10 1975-85 on reel $110.00. v11-21 1986-96 on mf $236.00) – Western Kentucky University. v1-21. 1975-96 – 5,6,9 – $346.00 set – us Hein [370]
JOURNAL OF EDUCATION FOR LIBRARIANSHIP – (v11-24. Summer 1970-Spring 1984. 5,6. v16-24. Summer 1975-Spring 1984. 9) – v1-24. Summer 1960-Spring 1984 – 1 – us UMI [073]
JOURNAL OF EDUCATION FOR LIBRARY AND INFORMATION SCIENCE – v25-. Summer 1984- – 1,5,6,9 – us UMI [073]
THE JOURNAL OF EDUCATION FOR LOWER CANADA – (Cont by: Journal of Education) – Montreal: Dept of Education, [1857-1867] – 9 – cn C.I.H.M. [370]
THE JOURNAL OF EDUCATION FOR LOWER CANADA *see* THE JOURNAL OF EDUCATION
JOURNAL OF EDUCATION FOR NOVA SCOTIA – [S.l.: s.n. 1851-1853] – 9 – cn C.I.H.M. [370]
JOURNAL OF EDUCATION FOR ONTARIO, TORONTO – 1848-77 – 5r – 1 – $325.00 – cn Library Assoc [971]
JOURNAL OF EDUCATION FOR SOCIAL WORK – v1- 1965- 1; v9- 5,6; v12- 9 – us UMI [073]
JOURNAL OF EDUCATION FOR TEACHING – 1974- 19v – 9 – £188.50 – 0260-7476 – uk Carfax [370]
JOURNAL OF EDUCATION FOR TEACHING: JET – v9-. 1983- – 1,5,6,9 – us UMI [073]
THE JOURNAL OF EDUCATION FOR THE PROVINCE OF NOVA SCOTIA – (Cont by: Journal of Education, Nova Scotia) – [Halifax, N.S.?: s.n. 1866-between 1881 and 1887] – 9 – cn C.I.H.M. [370]
THE JOURNAL OF EDUCATION FOR THE PROVINCE OF NOVA SCOTIA *see* JOURNAL OF EDUCATION, NOVA SCOTIA
JOURNAL OF EDUCATION, NOVA SCOTIA – (Cont: The Journal of Education for the Province of Nova Scotia) – [Halifax, N.S.?: s.n. between 1881 and 1887-19–] – 9 – cn C.I.H.M. [370]
JOURNAL OF EDUCATION, NOVA SCOTIA *see* THE JOURNAL OF EDUCATION FOR THE PROVINCE OF NOVA SCOTIA
JOURNAL OF EDUCATIONAL ADMINISTRATION AND FOUNDATIONS – (Vols 1-3 filmed as "EAF: Journal of Educational Administration and Foundations") – Ottawa. v1-9. 1986-94 – 9 – Can$20.00y – cn Micromedia [370]
JOURNAL OF EDUCATIONAL ADMINISTRATION AND HISTORY – v1- 1968- 1; v8- 5,6,9 – us UMI [370]
JOURNAL OF EDUCATIONAL COMMUNICATION – v. 1- 1975- – 1,5,6,9 – us UMI [073]
JOURNAL OF EDUCATIONAL EQUITY AND LEADERSHIP – v.1-. 1980- – 1,5,6,9 – us UMI [370]
JOURNAL OF EDUCATIONAL MEASUREMENT – v1- 1964- 1; v15- 5,6,9 – us UMI [370]
JOURNAL OF EDUCATIONAL PSYCHOLOGY – (v. 58- 1967- 5,6. v. 61- 1970- 9) – v. 1- 1910- – 1 – us UMI [150]
JOURNAL OF EDUCATIONAL PSYCHOLOGY – v1-71. 1910-79 – 1,5,6 – us Princeton Micro [370]
JOURNAL OF EDUCATIONAL RESEARCH – v1- 1920- 1; v60-76 5,6; v69-76 9 – us UMI [370]
JOURNAL OF EDUCATIONAL RESEARCH – v. 1-38. 1920-1945 – 1 – us Princeton Micro [370]
JOURNAL OF EDUCATIONAL SOCIOLOGY – v. 1-19. 1927-1945 – 1 – us Princeton Micro [300]
THE JOURNAL OF EDUCATIONAL SOCIOLOGY – Albany. v1-18. 1927-1945 – 141mf – 9 – ne IDC [370]
JOURNAL OF EDUCATIONAL STATISTICS – v1- 1976- – 1,5,6,9 – us UMI [370]
JOURNAL OF EDUCATIONAL TELEVISION – 1975- 19v – 9 – £216.00 – 0260-7417 – uk Carfax [370]
JOURNAL OF EDUCATIONAL THOUGHT – v1- 1967- 1; v5- 5,6; v10- 9 – us UMI [370]
JOURNAL OF EDUCATIONAL THOUGHT – (v1-8 1967-74, 9-11 1975-77 Can$100.00. v 12-19 1978-85 Can$50.00y. v20-29 1986-95 Can$20.00y) – Calgary. v1-28. 1967-94 – 5,9 – Price varies – cn Micromedia [370]
JOURNAL OF EGYPTIAN ARCHAEOLOGY – London. v1-9. 1914-1923 – 54mf – 9 – ne IDC [930]
THE JOURNAL OF EGYPTIAN ARCHAEOLOGY – v1-. 1914-. London: Egypt Exploration Society. ill. plates, facsims. semiannual, 1920-; quarterly, 1914-19; annual, 1976-. Bibliographies included – 1 – us U.W. Library [073]
JOURNAL OF ELDER ABUSE AND NEGLECT / ed by Wolf, Rosalie S & Aderson, Susan McMurray – v1- 1989- – 1, 9 ($225.00 in US $315.00 outside hardcopy subsc) – us Haworth [360]
JOURNAL OF ELECTROANALYTICAL CHEMISTRY – (v.67-116. 1976-80. 1,5,6,9) – v1-174. 1959-84 – 1,5,6,13 – sz Elsevier [073]
JOURNAL OF ELECTRON SPECTROSCOPY AND RELATED PHENOMENA – v1-35. 1972-84 – 1,5,6,13 – sz Elsevier [073]
JOURNAL OF ELECTROSTATICS – v1-16. 1974-84 – 1,5,6,13 – sz Elsevier [073]
JOURNAL OF ELIZA WILSON BAGEHOT, 1850-1921 / Bagehot, Eliza Wilson – 5r – 1 – $325.00 – us UMI [305]
JOURNAL OF EMBRYOLOGY AND EXPERIMENTAL MORPHOLOGY – (1983-. 1,5,6,9) – v1-. 1953- – 1 – us UMI [574]
JOURNAL OF EMBRYOLOGY AND EXPERIMENTAL MORPHOLOGY – (v. 1-5. 247.50v; 9. v. 6-10. 2412.00v; WDS; 9) – v. 1-10. London. 1953-62 – 2495.00 – uk Dawson [590]
JOURNAL OF EMERGENCY MEDICINE – v1- 1983- – 5,6,9 – us UMI [610]
JOURNAL OF EMOTIONAL ABUSE : INTERVENTIONS, RESEARCH, AND THEORIES OF PSYCHOLOGICAL MALTREATMENT, TRAUMA, AND NONPHYSICAL AGGRESSION / ed by Geffner, Robert A & Rossman, B B Robbie – v1 n1. 1997- – 1,9 – $85.00 in US $119.00 outside hardcopy subsc – us Haworth [150]
JOURNAL OF EMPLOYMENT COUNSELING – v3- 1966- 1; v8- 5,6; v12- 9 – us UMI [380]
JOURNAL OF ENDOCRINOLOGY / Society of Endocrinology – v. 1-67. 1939-75 – 1,5,6 – us Princeton Micro [612]
JOURNAL OF ENDODONTICS – (v.6 .1980 5,6,9) – v.1. 1975 – 1 – us UMI [073]
JOURNAL OF ENDODONTICS – v9-22. 1983-96 – 1,5,6,9 – $80.00r – us Williams [617]
JOURNAL OF ENERGY – v1- 1977- – 1,5,6,9 – us UMI [621]
JOURNAL OF ENERGY AND DEVELOPMENT – University of Colorado. v1-19. 1975-94 – 9 – $242.00 set – us Hein [333]
JOURNAL OF ENERGY AND NATURAL RESOURCES LAW – v1-13. 1983-95 – 9 – $594.00 set – us Hein [340]
JOURNAL OF ENERGY ENGINEERING – v109- 1983- – 1,5,6,9 – us UMI [621]
JOURNAL OF ENGINEERING AND APPLIED SCIENCE – v1- 1980- – 5,6,9 – us UMI [620]
JOURNAL OF ENGINEERING DESIGN – 1992- 4v – 9 – £192.50 – 0954-4828 – uk Carfax [620]
JOURNAL OF ENGINEERING FOR INDUSTRY : (SERIES B OF THE ASME TRANSACTIONS) – (v86- 1964- . v92- 1970-) – v81- 1959- – 1,5,6,9 – us UMI [620]
JOURNAL OF ENGINEERING FOR POWER : (SERIES A OF THE ASME TRANSACTIONS) – (v87- 1965-. v92- 1970-) – v81- 1959- – 1,5,6,9 – us UMI [621]
JOURNAL OF ENGINEERING MATERIALS AND TECHNOLOGY – v95- 1973- 1,5,6; v98- 1976- 9 – us UMI [620]
JOURNAL OF ENGINEERING MECHANICS – v109- 1983- – 1,5,6,9 – us UMI [620]
JOURNAL OF ENGINEERING PHYSICS – v8-65. 1965-93 – 1,5 – $80.00v – us UMI [621]
JOURNAL OF ENGINEERING PRODUCTION – (5,6,9 1984-) – v1- 1977- – 1 – us UMI [620]
JOURNAL OF ENGLISH AND GERMANIC PHILOLOGY – v1- 1897- 1; v68- 5,6; v74- 9 – us UMI [420]
JOURNAL OF ENGLISH AND GERMANIC PHILOLOGY – Bloomington. v1-39. 1897-1940 – 443mf – 9 – ne IDC [420]
JOURNAL OF ENGLISH AND GERMANIC PHILOLOGY – v. 1-62. 1897-1963 – 1 – us Princeton Micro [400]
JOURNAL OF ENHANCED HEAT TRANSFER / ed by Webb, Ralph L – 1,5,9 – us Gordon [660]
JOURNAL OF ENTEROSTOMAL THERAPY – v9-. 1982- – 1,5,6,9 – us UMI [615]
JOURNAL OF ENTOMOLOGY – London. v1-2. 1862-1866 – 20mf – 9 – ne IDC [400]
THE JOURNAL OF ENTOMOLOGY: DESCRIPTIVE AND GEOGRAPHICAL – London. 1862-66 – 3 – us Readex [590]
JOURNAL OF ENVIRONMENTAL ENGINEERING – v109-. 1983- – 1,5,6,9 – us UMI [628]
JOURNAL OF ENVIRONMENTAL LAW AND LITIGATION – University of Oregon. v1-10. 1986-95 – 9 – $81.00 set – us Hein [340]
JOURNAL OF ENVIRONMENTAL PLANNING AND MANAGEMENT – 36v – 9 – £153.00 – 0964-0568 – uk Carfax [333]
JOURNAL OF ENVIRONMENTAL POLYMER DEGRADATION – v1-2. 1993-94 – $65.00v – us UMI [660]
JOURNAL OF ENVIRONMENTAL SCIENCE – v2- 1959- 1; v14- 5,6; v18- 9 – us UMI [333]
JOURNAL OF ENVIRONMENTAL SCIENCE AND HEALTH: PART A. ENVIRONMENTAL SCIENCE AND ENGINEERING – (1984-. 5,6,9) – v11-. 1976- – 1 – us UMI [628]
JOURNAL OF ENVIRONMENTAL SCIENCE AND HEALTH: PART B. PESTICIDES, FOOD CONTAMINANTS AND AGRICULTURAL WASTES – (1984-. 5,6,9) – v11-. 1976- – 1 – us UMI [628]
JOURNAL OF ENVIRONMENTAL SCIENCE AND HEALTH: PART C. ENVIRONMENTAL CARCINOGENESIS REVIEWS – v1-. 1983- – 1,5,6,9 – us UMI [628]
JOURNAL OF ENVIRONMENTAL SCIENCE AND HEALTH: PART D. ENVIRONMENTAL HEALTH SCIENCES – v13. 1978-79 – 1 – us UMI [628]
JOURNAL OF ENZYME INHIBITION / ed by Smith, H J – 9,5,1 – us Harwood [574]
JOURNAL OF ETHNIC STUDIES – (v.9-. 1981-. 5,6,9) – v.1-. 1973- – 1 – us UMI [305]
JOURNAL OF ETHNOPHARMACOLOGY – v1-12. 1979-84 – 1,5,6,13 – sz Elsevier [073]
JOURNAL OF EUGENIE DE GUERIN / Guerin, Eugenie de; ed by Trebutien, G S – London: Simpkin, Marshall, 1865 – 2mf – us A.T.L.A. [240]
JOURNAL OF EUROMARKETING / ed by Kaynak, Erdener – v6 n1. 1996- – 1,9 – $175.00 in US $245.00 outside hardcopy subsc – us Haworth [650]
JOURNAL OF EUROPEAN STUDIES – v1- 1971- 1; v6- 5,6,9 – us UMI [940]
JOURNAL OF EVIDENCE PHOTOGRAPHY – v. 1-. 1969- – 1,5,6,9 – us UMI [360]
JOURNAL OF EVOLUTIONARY BIOCHEMISTRY AND PHYSIOLOGY – v5-30. 1969-94 – 1,5 – $80.00v – us UMI [612]
JOURNAL OF EXPERIENTIAL EDUCATION – (v.3 .1980 5,6,9) – v.1. 1978 – 1 – us UMI [073]
JOURNAL OF EXPERIMENTAL BIOLOGY – (1983-. 1,5,6,9) – v7-. 1930- – 1 – us UMI [574]
JOURNAL OF EXPERIMENTAL BOTANY – v1- 1950- 1; v22- 5,6; v27- 9 – us UMI [580]
JOURNAL OF EXPERIMENTAL EDUCATION – 1- 1932- 1; v35-51 5,6; v44-51 9 – us UMI [370]
JOURNAL OF EXPERIMENTAL EDUCATION – v. 1-26. 1932-1958 – 1,5,6 – us Princeton Micro [370]
JOURNAL OF EXPERIMENTAL MARINE BIOLOGY AND ECOLOGY – v1-84. 1967-84 – 1,5,6,13 – sz Elsevier [574]
JOURNAL OF EXPERIMENTAL MEDICINE – (v.149 .1979 5,6,9) – v.1. 1896 – 1 – us UMI [073]
JOURNAL OF EXPERIMENTAL PSYCHOLOGY – v. 1-108. 1916-79 – 1,5,6 – us Princeton Micro [150]
JOURNAL OF EXPERIMENTAL PSYCHOLOGY – (v69-103. 1965-74. 5,6. v83-103. 1970-74. 9. See also: Journal of Experimental Psychology: General) – v1-103. 1916-74 – 1 – us UMI [150]
JOURNAL OF EXPERIMENTAL PSYCHOLOGY: ANIMAL BEHAVIOR PROCESSES – v.1-1975- – 1,5,6,9 – us UMI [150]
JOURNAL OF EXPERIMENTAL PSYCHOLOGY: ANIMAL BEHAVIOR PROCESSES – v1-9. 1975-83 – 1,5,6 – us Princeton Micro [150]
JOURNAL OF EXPERIMENTAL PSYCHOLOGY: GENERAL – v. 104- 1975- – 1,5,6,9 – us UMI [150]
JOURNAL OF EXPERIMENTAL PSYCHOLOGY. HUMAN LEARNING AND MEMORY – v. 1-. 1975- – 1,5,6,9 – us UMI [150]
JOURNAL OF EXPERIMENTAL PSYCHOLOGY: HUMAN LEARNING AND MEMORY – v1-9. 1975-83 – 1,5,6 – us Princeton Micro [150]
JOURNAL OF EXPERIMENTAL PSYCHOLOGY. HUMAN PERCEPTION AND PERFORMANCE – v. 1-. 1975- – 1,5,6,9 – us UMI [150]
JOURNAL OF EXPERIMENTAL PSYCHOLOGY: HUMAN PERCEPTION AND PERFORMANCE – v1-9. 1975-83 – 1,5,6 – us Princeton Micro [150]
JOURNAL OF EXPERIMENTAL ZOOLOGY – Philadelphia. v1-65. 1904-1933 – 663mf – 9 – ne IDC [590]
JOURNAL OF EXPERIMENTAL ZOOLOGY – Philadelphia. v165-210. 1968-79 – 5,9 – Dfl3,680.00; Dfl80.00v – ne Swets [590]
JOURNAL OF EXPERIMENTAL ZOOLOGY – v. 1-164. 1904-1967 – 1,5,6 – us Princeton Micro [590]
JOURNAL OF FAMILY COUNSELING – v1- 1973- 1,5,6; v3- 9 – us UMI [306]
JOURNAL OF FAMILY HISTORY – v. 1- 1976- – 1,5,6,9 – us UMI [300]
JOURNAL OF FAMILY ISSUES – (1983-1,5,6,9) – v1- 1980- – 1 – us UMI [306]
JOURNAL OF FAMILY ISSUES – (v1-5 1980-84 on reel $70.00. v6-16 1985-95 on mf $308.00) – v1-16. 1980-95 – 5,6,9 – $378.00 set – us Hein [073]
JOURNAL OF FAMILY LAW – v1- 1961- 1; v10- 5,6; v15-16 9 – us UMI [340]
JOURNAL OF FAMILY PRACTICE – (1982-. 1,5,6,9) – v1-. 1974- – 1 – us UMI [616]
JOURNAL OF FAMILY PSYCHOTHERAPY : THE QUARTERLY JOURNAL OF CASE STUDIES, TREATMENT REPORTS, AND STRATEGIES IN CLINICAL PRACTICE / ed by Trepper, Terry S – (Continues: Journal of Psychotherapy and the Family) – v1- 1990- – 1,9 ($175.00 in US $245.00 outside hardcopy subsc) – us Haworth [616]
JOURNAL OF FAMILY SOCIAL WORK / ed by Bardill, Donald R – (Continues: Journal of Social Work and Human Sexuality) – v1-1994- – 1,9 ($60.00 in US $84.00 outside hardcopy subsc) – us Haworth [306]
JOURNAL OF FAMILY VIOLENCE – v1-9. 1986-94 – 1,5 – $65.00v – us UMI [360]
JOURNAL OF FARM ECONOMICS – v. 7-51. 1925-1969 – 1,5,6 – us Princeton Micro [630]
JOURNAL OF FARM ECONOMICS *see* AMERICAN JOURNAL OF AGRICULTURAL ECONOMICS
JOURNAL OF FEMINIST FAMILY THERAPY / ed by MacKune-Karrer, Betty – v1- 1989- – 1,9 ($175.00 in US $245.00 outside hardcopy subsc) – us Haworth [305]
JOURNAL OF FINANCE – v1- 1946- 1; v29- 5,6; v30- 9 – us UMI [336]
JOURNAL OF FINANCIAL ECONOMICS – v1-13. 1974-84 – 1,5,6,13 – sz Elsevier [332]

JOURNAL OF FIRE RETARDANT CHEMISTRY – (See also: Fire Retardant Chemistry) – v3-. 1976- – 1,5,6,9 – us UMI [670]

JOURNAL OF FIRE SCIENCES – v1-. 1983- – 1,5,6,9 – us UMI [073]

JOURNAL OF FLUENCY DISORDERS – v1-9. 1976-84 – 1,5,6,13 – sz Elsevier [616]

JOURNAL OF FLUID MECHANICS – v1- 1956- 1; v45- 5,6; v73- 9 – us UMI [530]

JOURNAL OF FLUID MECHANICS – v1-47 1956-71 – 1,5,6 – us Princeton Micro [620]

JOURNAL OF FLUIDS ENGINEERING – v95- 1973- 1,5,6; v98- 9 – us UMI [073]

JOURNAL OF FLUORESCENCE – v1-4. 1991-94 – 1,5 – $65.00v – us UMI [530]

JOURNAL OF FLUORINE CHEMISTRY – v1-26. 1971-84 – 1,5,6,13 – sz Elsevier [073]

JOURNAL OF FOOD PRODUCTS MARKETING : INNOVATIONS IN FOOD ADVERTISING, FOOD PROMOTION, FOOD PUBLICITY, FOOD SALES PROMOTION / ed by Stanton, John L Jr – v3 n1. 1996- – 1,9 – $90.00 in US $126.00 outside hardcopy subsc – us Haworth [650]

JOURNAL OF FOOD SCIENCE – v1- 1936- 1; v30- 5,6; v41- 9 – us UMI [660]

JOURNAL OF FORECASTING – v.1-. 1982- – 1,5,6,9 – us UMI [073]

JOURNAL OF FOREIGN MEDICAL SCIENCE AND LITERATURE – 1-N.S. 4. 1810-1824 – 1 – us UMI [610]

JOURNAL OF FORENSIC SCIENCES – (v. 17- 1972- 5,6. v. 20- 1975- 9) – v. 1- 1956- – 1 – us UMI [360]

JOURNAL OF FORESTRY – v47- 1949- 1; v68- 5,6; v74- 9 – us UMI [634]

JOURNAL OF FORESTRY – v1-53. 1902-55 – 1,5,6 – us Princeton Micro [634]

JOURNAL OF FREE RADICALS IN BIOLOGY AND MEDICINE *see* ADVANCES IN FREE RADICAL BIOLOGY AND MEDICINE

JOURNAL OF FUNDS / Ottawa County. Ohio. Carroll Township. Township Clerk – 1888-1905 – 1r – 1 – $32.50r – us Archival [324]

JOURNAL OF FUSION ENERGY – v1-13. 1981-94 – 1,5 – $65.00v – us UMI [621]

JOURNAL OF FUTURES MARKETS – v1-. 1981- – 1,5,6,9 – us UMI [073]

JOURNAL OF FUTURES MARKETS – v1-6. 1981-86 – 1,5,6 – us Princeton Micro [332]

JOURNAL OF GAMBLING BEHAVIOR – v1-. 1985- – 1,5,6,9 – us UMI [073]

JOURNAL OF GAY AND LESBIAN PSYCHOTHERAPY / ed by Scasta, David L – v1- 1989- – 1, 9 ($75.00 in US $105.00 outside hardcopy subsc) – us Haworth [150]

JOURNAL OF GAY AND LESBIAN SOCIAL SERVICES : ISSUES IN PRACTICE, POLICY AND RESEARCH / ed by Kelly, James J – v4 n1. 1996- – 1,9 – $60.00 in US $84.00 outside hardcopy subsc – us Haworth [305]

JOURNAL OF GENDER STUDIES – 1995, Vol 4 – £101.00 – uk Carfax [305]

JOURNAL OF GENERAL AND APPLIED MICROBIOLOGY – (v. 14- 1968- 5,6. v. 16- 1970- 9) – v. 11- 1965- – 1 – us UMI [576]

JOURNAL OF GENERAL CHEMISTRY OF THE USSR *see* RUSSIAN JOURNAL OF GENERAL CHEMISTRY

JOURNAL OF GENERAL EDUCATION – v9- 1955- 1; v20- 5,6; v27- 9 – us UMI [370]

JOURNAL OF GENERAL MICROBIOLOGY – v1-103. 1947-77 – 1,5,6 – us Princeton Micro [073]

JOURNAL OF GENERAL PHYSIOLOGY – 1-41. 1918-1958 – 1 – us UMI [612]

JOURNAL OF GENERAL PHYSIOLOGY – New York, 1919-1941. V.1-24 – 377mf – 9 – ne IDC [612]

JOURNAL OF GENERAL PHYSIOLOGY – v1-8. 1918-25 – 1,5,6 – us Princeton Micro [073]

JOURNAL OF GENETIC PSYCHOLOGY – v. 1-53. 1891-1938 – 1 – us Princeton Micro [370]

JOURNAL OF GENETICS / ed by Bateson, W & Punnett, R C – Cambridge, 1910-1941. v1-41. Lacking: v.39-40 – 352mf – 9 – ne IDC [575]

JOURNAL OF GEOCHEMICAL EXPLORATION – v1-22. 1972-84 – 1,5,6,13 – sz Elsevier [073]

JOURNAL OF GEODYNAMICS – 1,5,69 – us UMI [550]

JOURNAL OF GEOGRAPHY – v1- 1902- 1; v68- 5,6; v74- 9 – us UMI [910]

JOURNAL OF GEOGRAPHY IN HIGHER EDUCATION – 1977- 17v – 9 – £188.50 – 0309-8265 – uk Carfax [370]

JOURNAL OF GEOLOGY – v1- 1893- 1; v73- 5,6,9 – us UMI [550]

JOURNAL OF GEOLOGY – v. 1-57. 1893-1949 – 1 – us Princeton Micro [550]

JOURNAL OF GEOMORPHOLOGY – (Ceased publication with v. 5, no. 4. 1942.) v. 1-5. 1938-1942 – 1,5,6 – us Princeton Micro [550]

JOURNAL OF GEOPHYSICAL RESEARCH – (1896-1900 $25.00 1,5,6,13. 1901-05 $25.00 1,5,6,13. 1906-10 $25.00 1,5,6,13. 1911-15 $25.00 1,5,6,13. 1916-20 $25.00 1,5,6,13. 1921-25 $25.00 1,5,6,13. 1926-30 $25.00 1,5,6,13. 1931-58 $30.00 per 2 yrs 1,5,6,13. 1959-61 v64-66 $50.00y 1,5,6,13. 1962 v67 $75.00 1,5,6,13. 1963 v68 $75.00 1,5,6,13. 1964-67 v69-72 $75.00 1,5,6,13. 1968-69 v73-74 $100.00y 1,5,6,13. 1970-75 v75-80 $100.00y 1,5,6,13. 1971-75 v76-80 $100.00y 9. 1976 v81 $100.00 1,5,6,13 $150.00 9. 1977 v82 $100.00 1,5,6,13 $220.00 9. 1978 v83 $125.00 1,5,6,13 $280.00 9. 1979 v84 $135.00 1,5,6,13 $350.00 9. 1980 v85 $160.00 1,5,6,13 $435.00 9. 1981 v86 $220.00 1,5,6,13 $570.00 9. 1982 v87 $320.00 1,5,6,13 $680.00 9. 1992 v97 $2,555.00. 1993 v98 $2,800.00. 1994v99 $3065.00; 1995 v100 $3510.00) – Printed indexes available – us A.G.U. [550]

JOURNAL OF GEOPHYSICS – v. 40-48. 1974-80 – 1,5,9 – 662.00 – us UMI [073]

JOURNAL OF GEOPHYSICS – ZEITSCHRIFT FUER GEOPHYSIK *see* ZEITSCHRIFT FUER GEOPHYSIK

THE JOURNAL OF GEORGE FOX / Fox, George – Cambridge: University Press, 1911 – 3mf – us A.T.L.A. [240]

JOURNAL OF GEOTECHNICAL ENGINEERING – v109- 1983- – 1,5,6,9 – us UMI [620]

JOURNAL OF GERIATRIC DRUG THERAPY / ed by Cooper, James – v1- 1986- – 1, 9 ($225.00 in US $315.00 outside hardcopy subsc) – us Haworth [615]

JOURNAL OF GERMAN-AMERICAN STUDIES – v11-15. 1976-80 – 1 – us UMI [073]

JOURNAL OF GERONTOLOGICAL SOCIAL WORK / ed by Dobrof, Rose – v1- 1978- – 1, 9 ($275.00 in US $385.00 outside hardcopy subsc) – us Haworth [360]

JOURNAL OF GERONTOLOGY – v1- 1946- 1; v20- 5,6; v31- 9 – us UMI [618]

JOURNAL OF GLASS STUDIES-INDEX – v1-15, 1959-73. 85p. 1976. 2 fiches. Fiche no. 6666 – 9 – $5.00 – us Corning Mus [740]

JOURNAL OF GLOBAL MARKETING / ed by Kaynak, Erdener – v1- 1987- – 1, 9 ($200.00 in US $280.00 outside hardcopy subsc) – us Haworth [337]

JOURNAL OF GOVERNMENT INFORMATION – (Cont: Government Publications Review. Back issues available from UMI) – 6 issues/ y. v21. 1994 – 9 – £168.00y – uk Elsevier Sci [320]

JOURNAL OF GRAPH THEORY – v. 1-. 1977- – 1,5,6,9 – us UMI [510]

JOURNAL OF GRAPH THEORY – v1-10. 1977-86 – 1,5,6 – us Princeton Micro [330]

JOURNAL OF GREAT LAKES RESEARCH – v1- 1975- 1; v3- 1977- 5,6,9 – us UMI [550]

JOURNAL OF GUIDANCE AND CONTROL – (1981-. 1,5,6,9) – v1-. 1978- – 1 – us UMI [073]

JOURNAL OF GUIDANCE, CONTROL, AND DYNAMICS – v5-. 1982- – 1,5,6,9 – us UMI [073]

JOURNAL OF H. M. S. ENTERPRISE: ON THE EXPEDITION IN SEARCH OF SIR JOHN FRANKLIN'S SHIPS BY BEHRING STRAIT 1850-55 / Collinson, Richard – With a memoir of his other services – 9 – cn C.I.H.M. [910]

JOURNAL OF HAND SURGERY – v. 1-. 1976- – 1,5,6,9 – us UMI [617]

JOURNAL OF HAND SURGERY – JOURNAL OF THE BRITISH SOCIETY FOR SURGERY OF THE HAND *see* HAND

JOURNAL OF HARD MATERIALS / ed by Brookes, C A – (Ceased pub 1994) – UK: 10P Publishing Ltd, 1993.-v4 – 1,5,6,9 – £105.00 – uk I.O.P. [621]

JOURNAL OF HAZARDOUS MATERIALS – v1-10 1976-84 – 1,5,6,13 – sz Elsevier [620]

JOURNAL OF HEAD TRAUMA REHABILITATION – v1- . 1986- – 1,5,6,9 – us UMI [073]

JOURNAL OF HEALTH AND SOCIAL BEHAVIOR – (v.12- 1971- 5,6. v.16- 1975- 9) – v.1- 1960- – 1 – us UMI [300]

JOURNAL OF HEALTH AND SOCIAL POLICY / ed by Feit, Marvin D – v1- 1989- – 1, 9 ($200.00 in US $280.00 outside hardcopy subsc) – us Haworth [610]

JOURNAL OF HEALTH CARE CHAPLAINCY / ed by Rutz, Kathy – v1- 1987- – 1, 9 ($85.00 in US $119.00 outside hardcopy subsc) – us Haworth [240]

JOURNAL OF HEALTH CARE MARKETING – (1985- 5,6,9) – v1- 1986- – 1 – us UMI [380]

JOURNAL OF HEALTH CONDUCTED BY AN ASSOCIATION OF PHYSICIANS – 1-4. 1829-33 – 1 – us UMI [610]

JOURNAL OF HEALTH, PHYSICAL EDUCATION, AND RECREATION – v1-26. 1930-55 – 1 – us Princeton Micro [790]

JOURNAL OF HEALTH, PHYSICAL EDUCATION, RECREATION – 1-45 1930-74 1; 1969-74 5,6 – us UMI [790]

JOURNAL OF HEALTH POLITICS, POLICY AND LAW – v. 1. 1976- – 1,5,6,9 – us UMI [340]

JOURNAL OF HEALTH POLITICS, POLICY AND LAW – (v1-9 1976-85 on reel $176.00. v10-20 1985-95 on mf $348.00) – Duke University. v1-20. 1976-95 – 5,6,9 – $524.00 set – us Hein [340]

JOURNAL OF HEART TRANSPLANTATION – (1986- . 5,6,9) – v4- . 1984- – 1 – us UMI [617]

JOURNAL OF HEAT TRANSFER : SERIES C OF THE ASME TRANSACTIONS – (v87-1965-. v92- 1970-) – v81- 1959- – 1,5,6,9 – us UMI [621]

JOURNAL OF HEAT TREATING – v.1-. 1979- – 1,5,6,9 – us UMI [600]

JOURNAL OF HELLENIC STUDIES – 1880-1900 – 1 – us UMI [900]

JOURNAL OF HERBS, SPICES AND MEDICINAL PLANTS / ed by Craker, Lyle E – v4 n1. 1996- – 1,9 – $125.00 in US $175.00 outside hardcopy subsc – us Haworth [580]

JOURNAL OF HEREDITY – v. 1-67. 1910-1976 – 1,5,6 – us Princeton Micro [630]

JOURNAL OF HEREDITY – (v. 56- 1965- 5,6. v. 61- 1970- 9) – 1- 1910- – 1 – us UMI [575]

JOURNAL OF HIGHER EDUCATION – v1-26. 1930-55 – 1,5,6 – us Princeton Micro [370]

JOURNAL OF HIGHER EDUCATION – (v40-1969- 5,6. v46- 1975- 9) – v1- 1930- – 1 – us UMI [370]

THE JOURNAL OF HIS AMERICAN MISSION / Bourne, Hugh – 1844-46. BRRAM – 1 – uk Microform Academic [240]

JOURNAL OF HIS VOYAGE ROUND THE WORLD IN H.M.S. "RESOLUTION" / Cook, James – 1772-75. National Maritime Museum. Ms JOD 20.37; Ms 1702 – 1 – uk Microform Academic [910]

JOURNAL OF HISTOCHEMISTRY AND CYTOCHEMISTRY – Baltimore. 1953-57. v1-5. 2220/2 – 8 – ne IDC [073]

JOURNAL OF HISTOCHEMISTRY AND CYTOCHEMISTRY – v1-32. 1953-84 – 1,5,6,13 – sz Elsevier [073]

JOURNAL OF HISTORICAL STUDIES – v1-5, no.2. 1975-82 – 1,5,6,9 – us UMI [900]

JOURNAL OF HIV/AIDS PREVENTION AND EDUCATION FOR ADOLESCENTS AND CHILDREN / ed by Morales, Julio & Bok, Marcia – v1 n1. 1997- – 1,9 – $60.00 in US $84.00 outside hardcopy subsc – us Haworth [360]

JOURNAL OF H.M.S. ENTERPRISE, 1850-55 / Collinson, Richard – BN 168 2. 1889 – 8 – ne IDC [910]

JOURNAL OF H.M.S. ENTERPRISE, ON THE EXPEDITION IN SEARCH OF SIR JOHN FRANKLIN'S SHIPS BY BEHRING STRAIT, 1850-55 / Collinson, Richard – Ed. by T.B. Collinson. 1889 – 9 – $20.00 – uk Libr Preservation [910]

JOURNAL OF HOLISTIC MEDICINE – v.2-. 1980 – 1,5,6,9 – us UMI [073]

JOURNAL OF HOME ECONOMICS – v1- 1909- 1; v61- 5; v64- 1969- 9 – us UMI [640]

JOURNAL OF HOME ECONOMICS EDUCATION – (Publ delay at v30 1991) – Edmonton. v29-33. 1990-94 – 9 – Can$20.00y – cn Micromedia [640]

JOURNAL OF HOMOSEXUALITY / ed by Cecco, John P De – v1- 1974- – 1, 9 ($275.00 in US $385.00 outside hardcopy subsc) – us Haworth [305]

JOURNAL OF HOSPITAL MARKETING / ed by Winston, William J – v1- 1986- – 1, 9 ($200.00 in US $280.00 outside hardcopy subsc) – us Haworth [650]

JOURNAL OF HOSPITALITY AND LEISURE MARKETING : THE INTERNATIONAL FORUM FOR RESEARCH, THEORY AND PRACTICE / ed by Knutson, Bonnie – v4 n1. 1996- – 1,9 – $75.00 in US $105.00 outside hardcopy subsc – us Haworth [650]

JOURNAL OF HOUSING – v1- 1944- 1; v29- 5,6; v32- 9 – us UMI [360]

JOURNAL OF HOUSING FOR THE ELDERLY / ed by Pastalan, Leon A – v1- 1983- – 1, 9 ($200.00 in US $280.00 outside hardcopy subsc) – us Haworth [360]

JOURNAL OF HUMAN BEHAVIOR IN THE SOCIAL ENVIRONMENT : A PROFESSIONAL JOURNAL / ed by Feit, Marvin D & Wodarski, John S – v1 n1. 1997- – 1,9 – $45.00 in US $63.00 outside hardcopy subsc – us Haworth [150]

JOURNAL OF HUMAN RELATIONS – v1-21 1952-73 1; v19-21 5,6 – us UMI [300]

JOURNAL OF HUMAN RESOURCES – v1- 1966- 1; v6- 5,6; v10- 9 – us UMI [650]

JOURNAL OF HUMAN STRESS – (v.5 7. 1979 81. 5,6,9) – v.1 7. 1975-81 – 1 – us UMI [073]

JOURNAL OF HUMANISTIC PSYCHOLOGY – v1- 1961- 1; v8- 5,6; v15- 9 – us UMI [300]

JOURNAL OF HYDRAULIC ENGINEERING – v109- 1983- – 1,5,6,9 – us UMI [627]

JOURNAL OF HYDROLOGY – v1-74. 1963-84 – 1,5,6,13 – sz Elsevier [550]

JOURNAL OF HYGIENE – v1-53. 1901-55 – 1,5,6 – us Princeton Micro [613]

JOURNAL OF HYGIENE – (v.82 .1979 5,6,9) – v.1. 1901 – 1 – us UMI [073]

JOURNAL OF HYGIENE AND HERALD OF HEALTH *see* HEALTH

JOURNAL OF ICHTHYOLOGY – (v24-. 1984-. 5,6,9) – v10-. 1970- – 1 – us UMI [073]

JOURNAL OF IMMUNOASSAY – (1984-. 5,6,9) – v1-. 1980- – 1 – us UMI [073]

JOURNAL OF IMMUNOLOGICAL METHODS – v1-75. 1971-84 – 1,5,6,13 – sz Elsevier [073]

JOURNAL OF IMMUNOPHARMACOLOGY – (1984-. 5,6,9) – v1-. 1978- – 1 – us UMI [073]

THE JOURNAL OF... IN PENNSYLVANIA, 1774 / Prevost, Augustine – BRRAM – 1 – uk Microform Academic [920]

JOURNAL OF INCLUSION PHENOMENA – v1-. 1983- – 1,5,6,9 – us UMI [073]

JOURNAL OF INDEPENDENT SOCIAL WORK *see* JOURNAL OF ANALYTIC SOCIAL WORK

JOURNAL OF INDIAN ART AND INDUSTRIES – 1-17. 1886-1916 – 1 – us UMI [740]

THE JOURNAL OF INDIAN ART AND INDUSTRY – London, 1884-1916 – 5r – 1 – £290.00 – uk Chadwyck [700]

JOURNAL OF INDIAN HISTORY – Allahabad, Trivandrum. 1921-60. v1-38 – 285mf – 8 – ne IDC [073]

JOURNAL OF INDIAN PHILOSOPHY – (v12-1984- 5,6,9) – v1- Oct 1970- – 1 – us UMI [100]

JOURNAL OF INDIVIDUAL PSYCHOLOGY – (Merged with: Individual Psychologist to form: Individual Psychology. Former titles: Individual Psychology News (oct 1 1940-jul 1 9141); Individual Psychology Bulletin (oct 1941-51); American Journal of Individual Psychology (1952-56)) – Austin. v1-37 oct 1940-nov 1981. cum index v2-28 1941-72 1; v29-37 may 1957-nov 1981 5,9 – 1,5,9 – D7717 – us UMI [150]

JOURNAL OF INDIVIDUAL PSYCHOLOGY *see*
- INDIVIDUAL PSYCHOLOGIST
- INDIVIDUAL PSYCHOLOGY

JOURNAL OF INDUSTRIAL AFFAIRS – 1995, Vol 4 – £94.00 – uk Carfax [338]

JOURNAL OF INDUSTRIAL ENGINEERING *see* AIIE TRANSACTIONS

JOURNAL OF INDUSTRIAL HYGIENE – v1-14. 1919-32 – 1 – us UMI [073]

JOURNAL OF INDUSTRIAL IRRADIATION TECHNOLOGY – v1-. 1983- – 1,5,6,9 – us UMI [073]

JOURNAL OF INDUSTRIAL TEACHER EDUCATION – v1- 1963- 1; v11- 5,6,9 – us UMI [370]

JOURNAL OF INFECTIOUS DISEASE – v. 1-103. 1904-1958 – 1,5,6 – us Princeton Micro [610]

JOURNAL OF INFECTIOUS DISEASE PHARMACOTHERAPY : ANTIMICROBIAL EVALUATION, DEVELOPMENT AND CLINICAL APPLICATION / ed by Bosso, John A – v2 n1. 1996- – 1,9 – $75.00 in US $105.00 outside hardcopy subsc – us Haworth [615]

JOURNAL OF INFORMATION AND IMAGE MANAGEMENT: JIIM – v16-. 1983- – 1,5,6,9 – us UMI [000]
JOURNAL OF INFORMATION RECORDING MATERIALS / ed by Stopperka, Klaus – 9,5,1 – us Gordon [540]
JOURNAL OF INFORMATION SCIENCE – v1-9. 1979-84 – 1,5,6,13 – sz Elsevier [000]
JOURNAL OF INFORMATION SCIENCE, LIBRARIANSHIP AND ARCHIVES ADMINISTRATION / UNESCO – v.1- 1979- – 1,5,6,9 – us UMI [073]
JOURNAL OF INORGANIC AND NUCLEAR CHEMISTRY – v.1-43. 1955-81. Continued as Polyhedron – 5,6,9 – us UMI [073]
JOURNAL OF INORGANIC AND ORGANOMETALLIC POLYMERS – v1-4. 1991-94 – 1,5 – $65.00v – us UMI [540]
JOURNAL OF INORGANIC BIOCHEMISTRY – v1-22. 1971-84 – 1,5,6,13 – sz Elsevier [073]
JOURNAL OF INORGANIC NUCLEAR CHEMISTRY – London. v1-13. 1955-60. 779/2 – 8 – ne IDC [073]
JOURNAL OF INSECT BEHAVIOR – v1-7. 1988-94 – 1,5 – $80.00v – us UMI [590]
JOURNAL OF INSECT PHYSIOLOGY – v1- 1957- – 5,6,9 – us UMI [590]
JOURNAL OF INSECT PHYSIOLOGY – (With Insect Biochemistry and Molecular Biology, 20 issues/y. £891.00y. Back issues of journal available from UMI) – 12 issues/y. v39. 1993 – 9 – £522.00y – uk Elsevier Sci [590]
JOURNAL OF INSECT PHYSIOLOGY – Z-184 2. v1-11. 1957-1965 – 8 – ne IDC [073]
JOURNAL OF INSTRUCTIONAL DEVELOPMENT – (v.3 .1979 5,6,9) – v.1. 1977 – 1 – us UMI [073]
JOURNAL OF INSTRUCTIONAL PSYCHOLOGY – (v.6 .1979 5,6,9) – v.1. 1974- – 1 – us UMI [073]
JOURNAL OF INSURANCE – v1- 1940- 1; v32- 5,6; v38- 9 – us UMI [336]
JOURNAL OF INTEGRAL EQUATIONS – v1-7. 1978-84 – 1,5,6,13 – sz Elsevier [073]
JOURNAL OF INTERAMERICAN STUDIES AND WORLD AFFAIRS – v1- 1959- 1; v17- 5,6,9 – us UMI [970]
JOURNAL OF INTERDISCIPLINARY CYCLE RESEARCH – (v1-9. Dfl70.00v; v10-21. Dfl140.00v) – Lisse. v1-21. 1970-90 – 5,9 – Dfl2,310.00 – ne Swets [500]
JOURNAL OF INTERLIBRARY LOAN, DOCUMENT DELIVERY AND INFORMATION SUPPLY / ed by Morris, Leslie R – v1- 1990- – 1, 9 ($90.00 in US $126.00 outside hardcopy subsc) – us Haworth [020]
JOURNAL OF INTERNATIONAL AFFAIRS – v1- 1947- 1; v23- 5,6; v29- 9 – us UMI [327]
JOURNAL OF INTERNATIONAL CONSUMER MARKETING / ed by Kaynak, Erdener – v1- 1988- – 1, 9 ($200.00 in US $280.00 outside hardcopy subsc) – us Haworth [380]
JOURNAL OF INTERNATIONAL ECONOMICS – v1-17. 1971-84 – 1,5,6,13 – sz Elsevier [337]
JOURNAL OF INTERNATIONAL FOOD AND AGRIBUSINESS MARKETING / ed by Kaynak, Erdener – v1- 1989- – 1, 9 ($150.00 in US $210.00 outside hardcopy subsc) – us Haworth [380]
JOURNAL OF INTERNATIONAL HOSPITALITY, LEISURE AND TOURISM MANAGEMENT 1090 A MULTINATIONAL AND CROSS-CULTURAL JOURNAL OF APPLIED RESEARCH / ed by Khan, Mahmood A – v1 n1. 1997- – 1,9 – $85.00 in US $119.00 outside hardcopy subsc – us Haworth [650]
JOURNAL OF INTERNATIONAL LAW AND ECONOMICS *see* GEORGE WASHINGTON JOURNAL OF INTERNATIONAL LAW AND ECONOMICS
JOURNAL OF INTERNATIONAL LAW AND PRACTICE – Detroit College of Law. v1-5. 1992-1995 – 9 – $48.00set – us Hein [340]
JOURNAL OF INTERNET CATALOGING : THE INTERNATIONAL QUARTERLY OF DIGITAL ORGANIZATION, CLASSIFICATION, AND ACCESS / ed by Carter, Ruth C & Brisson, Roger – v1 n1. 1997- – 1,9 – $65.00 in US $91.00 outside hardcopy subsc – us Haworth [020]
JOURNAL OF INTERPROFESSIONAL CARE – 1992- 7v – 9 – £137.50 – 0884-3988 – uk Carfax [613]
JOURNAL OF INTERVENTION RADIOLOGY – v1- . 1986- – 1,5,6,9 – us UMI [073]
JOURNAL OF IRRIGATION AND DRAINAGE ENGINEERING – v109- 1983- – 1,5,6,9 – us UMI [627]
JOURNAL OF ITALIAN LINGUISTICS – 1984- – 1,5,6,9 – us UMI [440]
THE JOURNAL OF JASTRO – 1,5,6,9 – us UMI [073]
JOURNAL OF JAZZ STUDIES – v1- 1973- 1; v4- 5,6,9 – us UMI [780]
JOURNAL OF JEWISH ART – (v.7 .1980 5,6,9) – v.1. 1974- – 1 – us UMI [073]
JOURNAL OF JEWISH COMMUNAL SERVICE – (v.57-. 1980- 5,6,9) – v.32-. 1956- – 1 – us UMI [360]
THE JOURNAL OF JEWISH THOUGHT AND PHILOSOPHY / ed by Wolfson, Elliot R – 9,5,1 – us Harwood [470]
JOURNAL OF JOHN LANDRETH ON AN EXPEDITION TO THE GULF COAST, NOV. 15, 1818-MAY 19, 1819 / U.S. Navy. Office of Naval Records and Library – 1roll. T12 – 1 – us Nat'l Archives [910]
JOURNAL OF JURISPRUDENCE – 1821 – 1 – us UMI [340]
THE JOURNAL OF JURISPRUDENCE – Edinburgh. v1-35. 1857-91 (all publ) – 104mf – 9 – $468.00 – LLMC 82-904 – us L.L.M.C. [073]
JOURNAL OF JUVENILE LAW – (None publ 1987-88) – University of La Verne. v1-16. 1977-95 – 9 – $165.00 set – us Hein [340]
JOURNAL OF LABELLED COMPOUNDS AND RADIOPHARMACEUTICALS – v. 12-. 1976- – 1,5,6,9 – us UMI [540]
JOURNAL OF LABOR / International Union of Shipwrights, Joiners and Caulkers of America – (Lacks numerous issues) – Paducah, KY. 1904-07 – 1r – 1 – us Ross [331]
JOURNAL OF LABOR – Paducah, Kentucky. v. 2-4. Nov 4 1904-July 20 1907. Incomplete – 1 – us NY Public [331]
JOURNAL OF LABOR ECONOMICS – v1-. 1983- – 1,5,6,9 – us UMI [331]
JOURNAL OF LABOR RESEARCH – v.1. 1980 – 1,5,6,9 – us UMI [331]
JOURNAL OF LABORATORY AND CLINICAL MEDICINE – (v. 65- 1965- 5,6. v. 75- 1970- 9) – 1- 1915- – 1 – us UMI [610]
JOURNAL OF LABORATORY AND CLINICAL MEDICINE – v1-46. 1915-55 – 1,5,6 – us Princeton Micro [610]
JOURNAL OF LANGUAGE, SPEECH AND HEARING SERVICES IN THE SCHOOLS – v.3. 1972. Continued by Language, speech and hearing services in schools – 1 – us UMI [370]
JOURNAL OF LARYNGOLOGY AND OTOLOGY – v75- 1961- 1; 1965- 5,6; v79- 9 – us UMI [617]
JOURNAL OF LARYNGOLOGY AND OTOLOGY – London. v74-80(2). 1960-66. M-24/2 – 8 – ne IDC [073]
JOURNAL OF LATIN AMERICAN STUDIES – v1- 1969- 1; v8- 5,6,9 – us UMI [320]
JOURNAL OF LAW – Philadelphia. v1. 1830-31 – 1 – $40.00 – us Hein [073]
THE JOURNAL OF LAW – Philadelphia. v1 nos 1-24. 1830-31 (all publ) – 9 – LLMC 84-506 – us L.L.M.C. [073]
JOURNAL OF LAW AND COMMERCE – University of Pittsburgh. v1-14. 1981-95 – 9 – $248.00 set – us Hein [340]
JOURNAL OF LAW AND ECONOMIC DEVELOPMENT *see* GEORGE WASHINGTON JOURNAL OF INTERNATIONAL LAW AND ECONOMICS
JOURNAL OF LAW AND ECONOMICS – v1- 1958- 1; v21- 1978- 5,6,9 – us UMI [340]
JOURNAL OF LAW AND ECONOMICS – University of Chicago. v1-38. 1958-95 – 9 – $408.00 set – us Hein [340]
JOURNAL OF LAW AND POLICY – Brooklyn Law School. v1-4. 1993-96 – 9 – $36.00 set – us Hein [340]
JOURNAL OF LAW AND RELIGION – (v1-2 1983-84 on reel $49.00. v3-10 1985-94 on mf $143.00) – Hamline University. v1-10. 1983-94 – 5,6,9 – $192.00 set – us Hein [340]
JOURNAL OF LAW AND SOCIETY – (Title varies: v1-8 as British Journal of Law and Society) – v1-21. 1974-94 – 9 – $256.00 set – us Hein [340]
JOURNAL OF LAW AND TECHNOLOGY – Georgetown University. v1-5. 1986-1990 – 9 – $65.00 set – us Hein [340]
JOURNAL OF LAW AND TECHNOLOGY *see* IDEA
JOURNAL OF LAW AND THE ENVIRONMENT – University of Southern California. v1-5. 1985-87 (all publ) – 9 – $25.00 set – us Hein [340]
JOURNAL OF LAW MEDICINE AND ETHICS – (Title varies: v1-9. No.3, 1973-1981, as Medicolegal News; v1-20, 1982-1992, as Law, Medicine and Health Care) – v1-23. 1973-95 – 9 – $240.00 set – us Hein [340]
JOURNAL OF LEGAL EDUCATION – (v.32-. 1981-. 5,6,9) – v.1-. 1948- – 1 – us UMI [340]
JOURNAL OF LEGAL MEDICINE – American College of Legal Medicine. v1-16. 1979-95 – 9 – $318.00 set – us Hein [340]
JOURNAL OF LEGAL MEDICINE – v.1. 1979 – 1,5,6,9 – us UMI [340]
JOURNAL OF LEGAL MEDICINE *see* LEGAL ASPECTS OF MEDICAL PRACTICE
JOURNAL OF LEGAL STUDIES – University of Chicago. v1-25. 1972-96 – 9 – $457.00 set – us Hein [340]
JOURNAL OF LEGAL STUDIES – v. 1- 1972- – 1. ; 5,6,9 – apply; v.5- – us UMI [340]
JOURNAL OF LEGAL STUDIES EDUCATION – v1-13. 1983-95 – 9 – $126.00 set – us Hein [340]
JOURNAL OF LEGISLATION – (See also: Notre Dame Journal of Legislation) – v3-. 1976- – 1,5,6,9 – us UMI [340]
JOURNAL OF LEGISLATIVE ASSEMBLY / Newfoundland – 1866-1900: 18r. Index for Assembly Journal, 1r. Legislative Council: Journals, 3r. Statutes, 3r – 25r – 1 – $1,625.00 set – cn Library Assoc [971]
JOURNAL OF LEISURABILITY – v.7-. 1980-. Continues yLeisurability – 1,5,6,9 – us UMI [073]
JOURNAL OF LESBIAN STUDIES / ed by Rothblum, Esther D – v1 n1. 1997- – 1,9 – $75.00 in US $105.00 outside hardcopy subsc – us Haworth [305]
JOURNAL OF LETRAS – Rio de Janeiro, BL. 1969-1983 – 8r – $400.00 – R04176 – us Library Micro [073]
THE JOURNAL OF LIBERAL RELIGION – v1-9. 1939-49 (complete) – Inquire – 1 – ATLA 1994-S521 – us A.T.L.A. [073]
JOURNAL OF LIBERTARIAN STUDIES – v.1- 1977- – 5,6,9 – us UMI [073]
JOURNAL OF LIBRARY ADMINISTRATION / ed by Lee, Sul H – v1- 1980- – 1, 9 ($115.00 in US $161.00 outside hardcopy subsc) – us Haworth [020]
JOURNAL OF LIBRARY AUTOMATION – (v.3- 1970- 5,6. v.8- 1975- 9) – v.1- 1968- – 1 – us UMI [510]
JOURNAL OF LIBRARY HISTORY, PHILOSOPHY AND COMPARATIVE LIBRARIANSHIP – v1- 1966- 1; v6- 5,6; v10- 9 – us UMI [020]
JOURNAL OF LIGHTWAVE TECHNOLOGY – Monthly – 9,6 – $600.00 in US $672.00 outside – us Optical Soc [621]
JOURNAL OF LIGHTWAVE TECHNOLOGY / Optical Society of AmericaInstitute of Electrical and Electronic Engineers – (v11. 1993. $386.00, $401.00 outside of North America) – v1- 1983-. -m – 9 – us Optical Soc [621]
JOURNAL OF LINGUISTICS – v1- 1965- 1; v12- 1976- 5,6,9 – us UMI [400]
JOURNAL OF LIQUID CHROMATOGRAPHY – (1984-. 5,6,9) – v1-. 1978- – 1 – us UMI [073]
JOURNAL OF LOGGING – v11-12,no.3. 1980-Mar 1981 – 1 – us UMI [073]
JOURNAL OF LOGGING AND SAWMILLING – v12,no.4-12. Apr-Dec 1981 – 1 – us UMI [073]
JOURNAL OF LOGGING MANAGEMENT – v8,no.6-v10,no.10. Jul 1977-Nov 1979 – 1 – us UMI [073]
JOURNAL OF LORD MACARTNEY'S EMBASSY TO CHINA / Alexander, W – 1791-94 – 1 – uk Microform Academic [950]
JOURNAL OF LOW TEMPERATURE PHYSICS – v1-97. 1969-94 – 1,5 – $60.00v – us UMI [530]
JOURNAL OF LT. CHARLES GAUNTT (U.S.S. MACEDONIAN), JULY 29, 1818-JUNE 18, 1821 / U.S. Navy. Office of Naval Records and Library – 1roll. M875 – 1 – us Nat'l Archives [355]
JOURNAL OF LT. COMMANDER WILLIAM B. CUSHING, MAY 1961-FEB 1965 / U.S. Navy. Office of Naval Records and Library – 1roll. M1034 – 1 – us Nat'l Archives [355]
JOURNAL OF LT. THOMAS A. DORIN (U.S.S. BRANDYWINE AND U.S.S. FALMOUTH), 1826-34 / U.S. Navy. Office of Naval Records and Library – 1roll. M981 – 1 – us Nat'l Archives [355]
JOURNAL OF LUMINESCENCE – v1-32. 1970-84 – 1,5,6,13 – sz Elsevier [530]
JOURNAL OF MACROECONOMICS – v.1. 1979 – 1,5,6,9 – us UMI [339]
JOURNAL OF MACROMOLECULAR CHEMISTRY – v1. 1966 – 1 – us UMI [073]
JOURNAL OF MACROMOLECULAR SCIENCE: PART A. CHEMISTRY – (1984-. 5,6,9) – v1-. 1967- – 1 – us UMI [073]
JOURNAL OF MACROMOLECULAR SCIENCE: PART B. PHYSICS – (1984-. 5,6,9) – v1-. 1967- – 1 – us UMI [073]
JOURNAL OF MACROMOLECULAR SCIENCE: PART C. REVIEWS IN MACROMOLECULAR CHEMISTRY – v1-21. 1967-82 – 1 – us UMI [073]
JOURNAL OF MACROMOLECULAR SCIENCE: PART D. REVIEWS IN POLYMER TECHNOLOGY – v1-2. 1971 – 1 – us UMI [073]
JOURNAL OF MACROMOLECULAR SCIENCE. REVIEWS IN MACROMOLECULAR CHEMISTRY AND PHYSICS – (1984-. 5,6,9) – v22-. 1982- – 1 – us UMI [073]
JOURNAL OF MAGNETISM AND MAGNETIC MATERIALS – v1-44. 1976-84 – 1,5,6,13 – sz Elsevier [073]
JOURNAL OF MAINTENANCE IN THE ADDICTIONS : INNOVATIONS IN RESEARCH, THEORY AND PRACTICE / ed by Payte, J Thomas – v1 n1. 1997- – 1,9 – $60.00 in US $84.00 outside hardcopy subsc – us Haworth [616]
THE JOURNAL OF MAJOR GEO. WASHINGTON / Washington, George – 1754 – 9 – 5.00 – us Scholars' Facs [975]
JOURNAL OF MAJOR ROBERT ROGERS : CONTAINING AN ACCOUNT OF THE SEVERAL EXCURSIONS HE MADE UNDER THE GENERALS WHO COMMANDED THE CONTINENT OF NORTH AMERICA DURING THE LATE WAR / Rogers, Robert – London: J Millan, 1765. SEM105P886 – 3mf – 9 – Can$6.75 – cn Bibl Nat [971]
JOURNAL OF MAMMALIAN EVOLUTION – v1-2. 1993-94 – $60.00v – us UMI [570]
JOURNAL OF MAMMALOGY – v. 1-32. 1919-1951 – 1 – us Princeton Micro [590]
JOURNAL OF MAMMALOGY – v. 33- 1952- – 1. ; 5,6,9 – apply; v.58- – us UMI [590]
JOURNAL OF MANAGEMENT – v1- 1975- 1; v4- 1978- 5,6,9 – us UMI [650]
JOURNAL OF MANAGEMENT AND BUSINESS CONSULTING – v.1. 1976. Superseded by Journal of Applied Management – 1 – us UMI [650]
JOURNAL OF MANAGEMENT IN ENGINEERING – v1- 1985- – 1,5,6,9 – us UMI [620]
JOURNAL OF MANAGEMENT STUDIES – (1982-. 1,5,6,9) – v1-. 1964- – 1 – us UMI [650]
JOURNAL OF MARINE ENVIRONMENTAL ENGINEERING / ed by Bruno, Michael S – 9,5,1 – us Gordon [628]
JOURNAL OF MARINE RESEARCH – v. 1-31. 1937-1973 – 1,5,6 – us Princeton Micro [550]
JOURNAL OF MARINE RESOURCE ECONOMICS – v1-. 1982- – 1,5,6,9 – us UMI [333]
JOURNAL OF MARITAL AND FAMILY THERAPY – v. 5- 1979-. Supersedes Journal of Marriage and Family Counseling – 1,5,6,9 – us UMI [300]
JOURNAL OF MARITIME LAW AND COMMERCE – v1- 1969- 1; v9- 1977- 5,6,9 – us UMI [340]
JOURNAL OF MARKETING – (v. 33- 1969- 5,6. v. 39- 1975- 9) – v. 1- 1936- – 1 – us UMI [380]
JOURNAL OF MARKETING CHANNELS : DISTRIBUTION SYSTEMS, STRATEGY, AND MANAGEMENT / ed by Rosenbloom, Bert – v5 n1. 1995- – 1,9 – $160.00 in US $224.00 outside hardcopy subsc – us Haworth [650]
JOURNAL OF MARKETING FOR HIGHER EDUCATION / ed by Hayes, Thomas J – v1- 1988- – 1, 9 ($160.00 in US $224.00 outside hardcopy subsc) – us Haworth [380]
JOURNAL OF MARKETING FOR MENTAL HEALTH *see* JOURNAL OF NONPROFIT AND PUBLIC SECTOR MARKETING

JOURNAL OF MARKETING RESEARCH – v1- 1964- 1; v6- 5,6; v12- 9 – us UMI [380]
JOURNAL OF MARRIAGE AND FAMILY COUNSELING – v. 1-4 1975-78 – 1,5,6,9 – us UMI [300]
JOURNAL OF MARRIAGE AND THE FAMILY – (v31- 1969- 5,6 v37- 1975- 9) – v1- 1939- – 1 – us UMI [306]
JOURNAL OF MATERIALS FOR ENERGY SYSTEMS – v1- . 1979- – 1,5,6,9 – us UMI [621]
JOURNAL OF MATERIALS SCIENCE – (1983- 5,6,9) – v1- 1966- – 1 – us UMI [620]
JOURNAL OF MATERIALS SCIENCE LETTERS – v1- 1982- – 1,5,6,9 – us UMI [620]
JOURNAL OF MATERIALS SYNTHESIS AND PROCESSING – v1-2. 1993-94 – $65.00v – us UMI [660]
JOURNAL OF MATHEMATICAL BIOLOGY – v.1-12, 1974-81. ISSN: 0303-6812 – 1,5,6,9,13 – 123.00v – us UMI [574]
JOURNAL OF MATHEMATICAL ECONOMICS – v1-13. 1974-84 – 1,5,6,13 – sz Elsevier [330]
JOURNAL OF MATHEMATICAL PHYSICS – v1-. 1960- – 1,5,6,9 – us A.I.P. [510]
JOURNAL OF MATHEMATICAL SCIENCES – (Cont: Journal of Soviet Mathematics) – v1-72. 1973-94 – 1,5 – $85.00v – us UMI [510]
JOURNAL OF MATHEMATICAL SOCIOLOGY – 1970- – 1,5,9 – us Gordon [300]
JOURNAL OF MATHEMATICAL SOCIOLOGY / ed by Doreian, Patrick – 9,5,1 – us Gordon [301]
JOURNAL OF MECHANICAL ENGINEERING SCIENCE – v1- 1959- 1; 1976- 5,6,9 – us UMI [621]
JOURNAL OF MECHANICAL WORKING TECHNOLOGY – v1-11. 1977-84 – 1,5,6,13 – sz Elsevier [073]
JOURNAL OF MECHANISMS, TRANSMISSIONS, AND AUTOMATION IN DESIGN – v105- 1983- – 1,5,6,9 – us UMI [620]
JOURNAL OF MEDICAL EDUCATION – v1- 1926- 1; v39- 5,6; v51- 9 – us UMI [610]
JOURNAL OF MEDICAL EDUCATION *see* ACADEMIC MEDICINE
JOURNAL OF MEDICAL EDUCATION (FORMERLY: ASSOCIATION OF AMERICAN MEDICAL COLLEGES: BULLETIN AND MEDICAL EDUCATION) – v1-56. 1926-81 – 1,5,6 – us Princeton Micro [610]
JOURNAL OF MEDICAL ENTOMOLOGY – v12- 1975- 1,5,6; v13- 1976- 9 – us UMI [616]
JOURNAL OF MEDICAL HUMANITIES AND BIOETHICS – v6-. 1985- – 1,5,6,9 – us UMI [073]
JOURNAL OF MEDICAL MICROBIOLOGY – (1982-. 1,5,6,9) – v1-. 1968- – 1 – us UMI [073]
JOURNAL OF MEDICAL PRACTICE MANAGEMENT – v1-11. 1985-96 – 11r – 1,5,6,9 – $65.00r – us Williams [610]
JOURNAL OF MEDICAL RESEARCH – v. 1-44. 1896-1924 – 1,5,6 – us Princeton Micro [610]
JOURNAL OF MEDICAL SYSTEMS – v1-18. 1977-94 – 1,5 – $65.00v – us UMI [610]
JOURNAL OF MEDICAL TECHNOLOGY *see*
– AMERICAN JOURNAL OF MEDICAL TECHNOLOGY
– JOURNAL OF THE AMERICAN MEDICAL TECHNOLOGISTS
JOURNAL OF MEDICINAL CHEMISTRY – v1- 1959- – 1,5,6,9 – us A.C.S. [612]
JOURNAL OF MEDICINE AND PHILOSPHY – (1985- 5,6,9) – v1- 1976- – 1 – us UMI [610]
JOURNAL OF MEDICINE: EXPERIMENTAL AND CLINICAL – v. 1-4. 1970-73 – 1,5,6 – us Princeton Micro [616]
JOURNAL OF MEDIEVAL AND RENAISSANCE STUDIES – v1- 1971- 1; v3- 5,6; v6- 9 – us UMI [073]
JOURNAL OF MEDIEVAL HISTORY – v1-10. 1975-84 – 1,5,6,13 – sz Elsevier [073]
JOURNAL OF MEMBRANE BIOLOGY – v. 1-57. 1969-80 – 1,5,9 – 4788.00 – us UMI [073]
JOURNAL OF MEMBRANE SCIENCE – v1-21. 1977-84 – 1,5,6,13 – sz Elsevier [540]
JOURNAL OF MENTAL DEFICIENCY RESEARCH – v16- 1972- 1,5,6; v19- 9 – us UMI [073]
JOURNAL OF MENTAL HEALTH – 1992- 2v – 9 – £153.00 – 0963-8237 – uk Carfax [616]
JOURNAL OF MENTAL HEALTH COUNSELING *see* AMHCA JOURNAL
JOURNAL OF METABOLIC RESEARCH – (All published.) v. 1-8. 1922-1926 – 1 – us Princeton Micro [616]
JOURNAL OF METALS – Superseded by JOM (Journal of Metals) – 1. 1971-74.; ; 5,6 – us UMI [600]
JOURNAL OF MICROELECTRONIC SYSTEMS INTEGRATION – v1-2. 1993-94 – $60.00v – us UMI [621]
JOURNAL OF MICROMECHANICS AND MICROENGINEERING – v1. 1991 – 1,5,6,9 – £149.00 – uk I.O.P. [621]
JOURNAL OF MICROSURGERY – v.1. 1979 – 1,5,6,9 – us UMI [617]
THE JOURNAL OF MIND AND BEHAVIOR – (1984-. 5,6,9) – v1-. Spring 1980- – 1 – us UMI [073]
JOURNAL OF MINERAL LAW AND POLICY *see* JOURNAL OF NATURAL RESOURCES AND ENVIRONMENTAL LAW
JOURNAL OF MINING SCIENCE – v1-30. 1965-94 – 1,5 – $80.00v – us UMI [622]
JOURNAL OF MINISTRY IN ADDICTION AND RECOVERY / ed by Albers, Robert H – v3 n1. 1996- – 1,9 – $120.00 in US $168.00 outside hardcopy subsc – us Haworth [616]
JOURNAL OF MINISTRY MARKETING AND MANAGEMENT / ed by Stevens, Robert E & Loudon, David L – v2 n1. 1996- – 1,9 – $75.00 in US $105.00 outside hardcopy subsc – us Haworth [650]
JOURNAL OF MINNESOTA PUBLIC LAW *see* HAMLINE JOURNAL OF PUBLIC LAW AND POLICY
JOURNAL OF MISSISSIPPI HISTORY – (1979 5,6,9) – 1978 – 1 – us UMI [073]
JOURNAL OF MODERN AFRICAN STUDIES – v1- 1963 1; v14- 1976- 5,6,9 – us UMI [960]
JOURNAL OF MODERN HISTORY – v. 1-14. 1929-1942 – 1 – us Princeton Micro [900]
JOURNAL OF MODERN HISTORY – (v. 41- 1969- 5,6) – v. 1- 1929- – 1 – us UMI [900]
JOURNAL OF MOLECULAR CATALYSIS – v1-26. 1975-84 – 1,5,6,13 – sz Elsevier [073]
JOURNAL OF MOLECULAR ELECTRONICS – (1984-. 5,6,9) – v1-. 1975- – 1 – us UMI [621]
JOURNAL OF MOLECULAR ELECTRONICS *see* ADVANCED MATERIALS FOR OPTICS AND ELECTRONICS
JOURNAL OF MOLECULAR EVOLUTION – v. 1-16. 1971-80 – 1,5,9 – 2880.00 – us UMI [073]
JOURNAL OF MOLECULAR LIQUIDS – v1-30. 1967-84 – 1,5,6,13 – sz Elsevier [073]
JOURNAL OF MOLECULAR STRUCTURE – v1-118. 1967-84 – 1,5,6,13 – sz Elsevier [073]
JOURNAL OF MONETARY ECONOMICS – v1-14. 1975-84 – 1,5,6,13 – sz Elsevier [332]
JOURNAL OF MONEY, CREDIT, AND BANKING – v1- 1969- 1; v3- 5,6; v7- 9 – us UMI [336]
JOURNAL OF MORAL EDUCATION – v1- 1970- 1; v6- 1976- 5,6,9 – us UMI [370]
JOURNAL OF MORAL EDUCATION – 1972- 22v – 9 – £76.00 – 0305-7240 – uk Carfax [370]
JOURNAL OF MORPHOLOGY – Philadelphia. v125-162. 1968-79 – 5,9 – Dfl3,040.00; Dfl80.00v – ne Swets [590]
JOURNAL OF MORPHOLOGY – v. 1-123. 1887-1967 – 1,5,6 – us Princeton Micro [590]
JOURNAL OF MULTICULTURAL SOCIAL WORK / ed by Anda, Diane de – v4 n1. 1996- – 1,9 – $125.00 in US $175.00 outside hardcopy subsc – us Haworth [360]
JOURNAL OF MUSCLE RESEARCH AND CELL MOTILITY – (1983-. 5,6,9) – v1-. 1980- – 1 – us UMI [073]
JOURNAL OF MUSCULOSKELETAL PAIN : INNOVATIONS IN RESEARCH, THEORY AND CLINICAL PRACTICE / ed by Russell, I Jon – v4 n1. 1996- – 1,9 – $125.00 in US $175.00 outside hardcopy subsc – us Haworth [616]
JOURNAL OF MUSIC THEORY – (v.24$. 1980 5,6,9) – v.1. 1957 – 1 – us UMI [073]
JOURNAL OF MUSIC THERAPY – (v.17-. 1980-. 5,6,9) – v.1-. 1964- – 1 – us UMI [780]
JOURNAL OF MUSICK – 1810 – 1 – us UMI [780]
JOURNAL OF MUSICOLOGICAL RESEARCH / ed by Locke, R – (Formerly: Music and man) – 1,5,9 – us Gordon [780]
JOURNAL OF MUSICOLOGY: JM – (1985- . 5,6,9) – v1- . 1982- – 1 – us UMI [073]
JOURNAL OF MYCOLOGY – (Cont as: Mycologia. New York v1-33 1909-1941) – Columbus, Ohio. v1-13. 1885-1908 – 365mf – 9 – ne IDC [580]
JOURNAL OF NATURAL HISTORY – v.1-9. 1967-75 – 9 – 2490.00; 2413.00v – uk Dawson [574]
JOURNAL OF NATURAL PHILOSOPHY, CHEMISTRY, AND THE ARTS – v1-36 1802-13 – 1,5,6 – us Princeton Micro [500]
A JOURNAL OF NATURAL PHILOSOPHY, CHEMISTRY, AND THE ARTS. LONDON – (1797-1813. 3) – 1797-1801 – 3 – us Readex [500]
JOURNAL OF NATURAL PRODUCTS – Washington, DC, v59. 1996- – 1,5,6,9 – Co-publ with American Society of Pharmacognosy – us A.C.S. [660]
JOURNAL OF NATURAL RESOURCES AND ENVIRONMENTAL LAW – (Title varies: v1-7 1985-92 as Journal of Mineral Law and Policy) – University of Kentucky. v1-9. 1985-94 – 9 – $121.00 set – us Hein [340]
JOURNAL OF NEAR EASTERN STUDIES – v1-45. 1942-86 – 1 – us Princeton Micro [956]
JOURNAL OF NEAR EASTERN STUDIES, 1942 *see* AMERICAN JOURNAL OF SEMITIC LANGUAGES AND LITERATURES
JOURNAL OF NEGRO EDUCATION – v1- 1932- 1; v41- 5,6; v44- 9 – us UMI [305]
JOURNAL OF NEGRO EDUCATION – Lancaster, PA. v1-34. 1932-65 – 10r – 1 – us Ross [370]
JOURNAL OF NEGRO EDUCATION – v1-24. 1932-55 – 1,5,6 – us Princeton Micro [370]
JOURNAL OF NEGRO HISTORY – v. 1-25. 1916-1940 – 1 – us Princeton Micro [975]
JOURNAL OF NEGRO HISTORY – (v. 50- 1965- 5,6. v. 55- 1970- 9) – 1- 1916- – 1 – us UMI [975]
JOURNAL OF NEGRO HISTORY – v67, no.4-. Winter 1982- – 1,5,6,9 – us UMI [073]
JOURNAL OF NERVOUS AND MENTAL DISEASE – v120-184. 1954-96 – 1,5,6,9 – $110.00r – us Williams [616]
JOURNAL OF NETWORK AND SYSTEMS MANAGEMENT – v1-2. 1993-94 – $65.00v – us UMI [621]
JOURNAL OF NEURAL TRANSMISSION – v.1-52, 1950-81. Title varies. ISSN: 0300-9564 – 1,5,6,9,13 – 135.00v – us UMI [073]
JOURNAL OF NEURO-AIDS : A FORUM DEVOTED TO ADVANCES IN THE NEUROLOGY AND NEUROBIOLOGY OF HUMAN IMMUNODEFICIENCY VIRUS (HIV), AIDS AND RELATED VIRAL INFECTIONS OF THE NERVOUS SYSTEM / ed by Price, Richard W – v1 n1. 1996- – 1,9 – $125.00 in US $175.00 outside hardcopy subsc – us Haworth [616]
JOURNAL OF NEUROBIOLOGY – v. 1-. 1969- – 1,5,6,9 – us UMI [610]
JOURNAL OF NEUROBIOLOGY – v1-17. 1969-86 – 1,5,6 – us Princeton Micro [073]
JOURNAL OF NEUROCHEMISTRY – v.1-33. 1956-79 – 5,6,9 – us UMI [540]
JOURNAL OF NEUROCYTOLOGY – (1983-. 5,6,9) – v1-. 1972- – 1 – us UMI [073]
JOURNAL OF NEUROGENETICS / ed by Hall, Jeffery C – 9,5,1 – us Harwood [575]
JOURNAL OF NEUROIMMUNOLOGY – v1-6. 1981-84 – 1,5,6,13 – sz Elsevier [073]
JOURNAL OF NEUROLINGUISTICS – 1,5,69 – us UMI [400]
JOURNAL OF NEUROLOGY – v. 158-226. 1947-80 – 1,5,9 – 7245.00 – us UMI [073]
JOURNAL OF NEUROLOGY *see* ZEITSCHRIFT FUER NEUROLOGIE
JOURNAL OF NEUROLOGY, NEUROSURGERY AND PSYCHIATRY – v1- 1926- 1; v34- 5,6; v39- 9 – us UMI [616]
JOURNAL OF NEUROPATHOLOGY AND EXPERIMENTAL NEUROLOGY – (v. 24- 1965- 5,6. v. 29- 1970- 9) – v. 1- 1942- – 1 – us UMI [616]
JOURNAL OF NEUROPHYSIOLOGY – v. 1-31. 1938-1968 – 1,5,6 – us Princeton Micro [616]
JOURNAL OF NEUROPHYSIOLOGY – (v. 28- 1965- 5,6. v. 33- 1970- 9) – 1- 1938- – 1 – us UMI [612]
JOURNAL OF NEUROSCIENCE METHODS – v1-12. 1979-84 – 1,5,6,13 – sz Elsevier [073]
JOURNAL OF NEUROSURGERY – 1944-74 1; 1971-74 5,6 – us UMI [610]
JOURNAL OF NEUROSURGICAL NURSING – (v.11 .1979 5,6,9) – v.1 .1969 – 1 – us UMI [073]
JOURNAL OF NEUROSURGICAL SCIENCES – 1973- 1; 1975- 5,6,9 – us UMI [617]
JOURNAL OF NEURO-VISCERAL RELATIONS *see* ACTA NEUROVEGETATIVA
JOURNAL OF NON-CRYSTALLINE SOLIDS – v1-67. 1969-84 – 1,5,6,13 – sz Elsevier [073]
JOURNAL OF NONDESTRUCTIVE EVALUATION – v1-13. 1980-94 – 1,5 – $65.00v – us UMI [620]
JOURNAL OF NON-NEWTONIAN FLUID MECHANICS – v1-16. 1976-84 – 1,5,6,13 – sz Elsevier [073]
JOURNAL OF NONPARAMETRIC STATISTICS / ed by Ahmad, Ibrahim A – 9,5,1 – us Gordon [510]
JOURNAL OF NONPROFIT AND PUBLIC SECTOR MARKETING / ed by Self, Donald R – (Continues: Journal of Marketing for Mental Health) – v1- 1992- – 1,9 ($160.00 in US $224.00 outside hardcopy subsc) – us Haworth [650]
JOURNAL OF NON-WHITE CONCERNS IN PERSONNEL AND GUIDANCE – v1- 1972- 1,5,6; v4- 9 – us UMI [073]
JOURNAL OF NUCLEAR BIOLOGY AND MEDICINE – Superseded by Journal of Nuclear Medicine and allied sciences – 1; 1975-1975 5,6,9 – us UMI [616]
JOURNAL OF NUCLEAR ENERGY – v1- 1974- – 5,6,9 – us UMI [621]
JOURNAL OF NUCLEAR ENERGY *see* ANNALS OF NUCLEAR SCIENCE AND ENGINEERING
JOURNAL OF NUCLEAR MATERIALS – v1-129. 1959-84 – 1,5,6,13 – sz Elsevier [073]
JOURNAL OF NUCLEAR MEDICINE – v1- 1960- 1; v12- 5,6; v17- 9 – us UMI [616]
JOURNAL OF NUCLEAR MEDICINE AND ALLIED SCIENCES – v. 21-. 1977- – 1,5,6,9 – us UMI [616]
JOURNAL OF NUCLEAR MEDICINE TECHNOLOGY – v1- 1973- 1; v4- 5,6,9 – us UMI [616]
JOURNAL OF NURSE-MIDWIFERY – v20-29. 1975-84 – 1,5,6,13 – sz Elsevier [073]
JOURNAL OF NURSING CARE – v11-. 1978- – 1,5,6,9 – us UMI [073]
JOURNAL OF NURSING EDUCATION – v1- 1962- 1; v11- 5,6; v14- 9 – us UMI [610]
JOURNAL OF NURSING QUALITY ASSURANCE – v1- . 1986- – 1,5,6,9 – us UMI [073]
JOURNAL OF NURSING STAFF DEVELOPMENT – v1-. Apr 1985- – 1,5,6,9 – us UMI [073]
JOURNAL OF NUTRACEUTICALS, FUNCTIONAL AND MEDICAL FOODS : PRODUCT DEVELOPMENT, COMMERCIALIZATION, AND POLICY ISSUES / ed by Childs, Nancy M – v1 n1. 1997- – 1,9 – $120.00 in US $168.00 outside hardcopy subsc – us Haworth [660]
JOURNAL OF NUTRITION – v1- 1928- 1,5,6; v105- 9 – us UMI [612]
JOURNAL OF NUTRITION – v1-57. 1928-55 – 1,5,6 – us Princeton Micro [615]
JOURNAL OF NUTRITION EDUCATION – v1- 1969- 1; v4- 5,6; v8- 9 – us UMI [073]
JOURNAL OF NUTRITION FOR THE ELDERLY / ed by Natow, Annette B – v1- 1980- – 1, 9 ($300.00 in US $420.00 outside hardcopy subsc) – us Haworth [618]
JOURNAL OF NUTRITION IN RECIPE AND MENU DEVELOPMENT : INNOVATIONS IN NUTRITIONAL PRODUCTS, DIETARY SUBSTITUTES, AND MEDICAL ISSUES IN FOOD PRODUCT DEVELOPMENT / ed by Khan, Mahmood A – v2 n1. 1996- – 1,9 – $125.00 in US $175.00 outside hardcopy subsc – us Haworth [613]
JOURNAL OF NUTRITIONAL IMMUNOLOGY / ed by Spallholz, Julian E – v4 n1. 1996- – 1,9 – $120.00 in US $168.00 outside hardcopy subsc – us Haworth [073]
JOURNAL OF NUTRITIONAL MEDICINE – 1992- 4v – 9 – £202.50 – 0955-6664 – uk Carfax [610]
JOURNAL OF OBSTETRIC, GYNECOLGIC, AND NEONATAL NURSING *see* AWHONN'S CLINICAL ISSUES IN PERINATAL AND WOMEN'S HEALTH NURSING
JOURNAL OF OBSTETRICS AND GYNAECOLOGY – 1980- 13v – 9 – £119.00 – 0144-3615 – uk Carfax [618]
JOURNAL OF OBSTETRICS AND GYNAECOLOGY OF THE BRITISH COMMONWEALTH – (See also: British Journal of Ostetrics and Gynaecology) – v1-81. 1902-74 – 1 – us UMI [618]

JOURNAL OF OBSTETRICS AND GYNECOLOGY OF THE BRITISH EMPIRE – v. 43-80. 1936-73 – 1,5,6 – us Princeton Micro [618]
JOURNAL OF OCCUPATIONAL ACCIDENTS – v1-6. 1976-84 – 1,5,6,13 – sz Elsevier [360]
JOURNAL OF OCCUPATIONAL AND ENVIRONMENTAL MEDICINE – v28-38. 1986-96 – 11r – 1,5,6,9 – $85.00r – us Williams [610]
JOURNAL OF OCCUPATIONAL AND ORGANIZATIONAL PSYCHOLOGY – (v48-61. Dfl90.00v; v62-63. Dfl140.00v) – London. v48-63. 1975-90 – 5,9 – Dfl1,540.00 – ne Swets [150]
JOURNAL OF OCCUPATIONAL MEDICINE – v.1-9. 1959-67. Superseded by JOM: Journal of Occupational Medicine – 1 – us UMI [073]
JOURNAL OF OCCUPATIONAL REHABILITATION – v1-4. 1991-94 – $60.00v – us UMI [360]
JOURNAL OF OFFENDER COUNSELING – v.1. 1980 – 1,5,6,9 – us UMI [073]
JOURNAL OF OFFENDER REHABILITATION / ed by Pallone, Nathaniel J – v1- 1976- – 1, 9 ($225.00 in US $315.00 outside hardcopy subsc) – us Haworth [360]
JOURNAL OF OIL AND FAT INDUSTRIES *see* JOURNAL OF THE AMERICAN OIL CHEMISTS' SOCIETY
JOURNAL OF OPTICAL TECHNOLOGY – Monthly – 9,6 – $1,635.00 in US $1,662.00 outside – us Optical Soc [621]
JOURNAL OF OPTIMIZATION THEORY AND ITS APPLICATIONS – v1-83. 1967-94 – 1,5 – $80.00v – us UMI [510]
JOURNAL OF OPTOMETRIC EDUCATION – (v.6 .1980 5,6,9) – v.1. 1975 – 1 – us UMI [370]
JOURNAL OF ORAL MEDICINE – v1- 1946- 1; v26- 5,6; v31- 9 – us UMI [617]
JOURNAL OF ORAL PATHOLOGY – Copenhagen. v1-15. 1972-86 – 5,9 – Dfl1,800.00; Dfl120.00v – ne Swets [610]
JOURNAL OF ORGANIC CHEMISTRY – Baltimore, 1936-40. v1-5 Lacking: v5, 1940, p449-560. – 41mf – 9 – ne IDC [073]
THE JOURNAL OF ORGANIC CHEMISTRY – v1- 1936- – 1,5,6,9 – us A.C.S. [073]
JOURNAL OF ORGANIC CHEMISTRY OF THE USSR *see* RUSSIAN JOURNAL OF ORGANIC CHEMISTRY
JOURNAL OF ORGANIZATIONAL BEHAVIOR MANAGEMENT / ed by Mawhinney, Thomas C – v1- 1977- – 1, 9 ($250.00 in US $350.00 outside hardcopy subsc) – us Haworth [650]
JOURNAL OF ORGANOMETALLIC CHEMISTRY – Incorporating Subject Reviews and Annual Surveys. v1-278. 1963-84 – 1,5,6,13 – sz Elsevier [073]
JOURNAL OF ORIENTAL RESEARCH – Madras. v1-27. 1927-1957/1958 – 130mf – 9 – ne IDC [950]
JOURNAL OF ORIENTAL RESEARCH OF THE UNIVERSITY OF MADRAS – (1945-1950 have not been published) – Madras. v-19. 1937-1964 – 163mf – 9 – ne IDC [950]
JOURNAL OF ORIENTAL STUDIES / Hong Kong University Press – Hong Kong. v1-7. 1954-1969 – 61mf – 9 – ne IDC [950]
JOURNAL OF ORTHOMOLECULAR PSYCHIATRY – v. 3-. 1974- – 1,5,6,9 – us UMI [616]
THE JOURNAL OF ORTHOPAEDIC AND SPORTS PHYSICAL THERAPY – v1-24. 1979-96 – 1,5,6,9 – $80.00r – us Williams [617]
JOURNAL OF OUTDOOR EDUCATION – (1980 5,6,9) – 1966 – 1 – us UMI [073]
JOURNAL OF PAINT TECHNOLOGY – v38-47 1966-75 1; v43-47 1871-75 5,6 – us UMI [600]
JOURNAL OF PAINT TECHNOLOGY – v38-47. 1966-75 – 1,5,6 – us Princeton Micro [073]
JOURNAL OF PALEONTOLOGY – (v. 39- 1965- 5,6. v. 44- 1970- 9) – 1- 1927- – 1 – us UMI [560]
JOURNAL OF PALESTINE STUDIES – v1- 1971- 1,5,6; v6- 9 – us UMI [073]
JOURNAL OF PALLIATIVE CARE – Montreal. v1-10. 1985/86-1994 – 9 – Can$20.00y – cn Micromedia [615]
JOURNAL OF PARASITOLOGY – Urbana. v1-27. 1914-1941 – 204mf – 9 – ne IDC [616]
JOURNAL OF PARASITOLOGY – v. 41-50. 1955-1964 – 1 – us UMI [576]
JOURNAL OF PARASITOLOGY – v1-41. 1914-55 – 1,5,6 – us Princeton Micro [590]
JOURNAL OF PARTNERSHIP TAXATION – v1-. 1984- – 1,5,6,9 – us UMI [073]
JOURNAL OF PASTORAL COUNSELING – (1985-. 5,6,9) – v1-. 1966- – 1 – us UMI [073]
JOURNAL OF PASTORAL PSYCHOTHERAPY *see* AMERICAN JOURNAL OF PASTORAL COUNSELING
JOURNAL OF PATHOLOGY – (1984-. 5,6,9) – v97-. 1969- – 1 – us UMI [610]
JOURNAL OF PATHOLOGY AND BACTERIOLOGY – v. 1-92. 1892-1966 – 1,5,6 – us Princeton Micro [616]
JOURNAL OF PATHOLOGY AND BACTERIOLOGY – v1-96. 1892-1968 – 1 – us UMI [610]
JOURNAL OF PEACE RESEARCH – (1981-. 1,5,6,9) – v1-. 1964- – 1 – us UMI [073]
JOURNAL OF PEDIATRIC PSYCHOLOGY – (v15-19 1990-94 $90.00v) – v1-14, 1976-89 – 1,5 – $60.00v – us UMI [150]
JOURNAL OF PEDIATRICS – (v. 66- 1965- 5,6; v. 76- 1970- 9) – v. 1- 1932- – 1 – us UMI [618]
JOURNAL OF PEDIATRICS – v1-47. 1932-55 – 1,5,6 – us Princeton Micro [618]
JOURNAL OF PENSION BENEFITS – v1-2. 1993-1995 – 9 – $45.00set – us Hein [340]
JOURNAL OF PENSION PLANNING AND COMPLIANCE – (Title varies: v1-3 n2 as Pension and Profit Sharing Tax Journal) – v1-19. 1974-1994 – 9 – $425.00set – us Hein [340]
JOURNAL OF PERINATAL AND NEONATAL NURSING – v1- . 1987- – 1,5,6,9 – us UMI [073]
JOURNAL OF PERIODONTAL RESEARCH – Copenhagen. v1-21. 1966-86 – 5,9 – Dfl2,520.00; Dfl120.00v – ne Swets [617]
JOURNAL OF PERIODONTOLOGY – v1- 1930- 1; v41- 5,6,9 – us UMI [617]
JOURNAL OF PERSONALITY – (v. 33- 1965- 5,6. v. 38- 1970- 9) – v. 1- 1932- – 1 – us UMI [150]
JOURNAL OF PERSONALITY AND SOCIAL PSYCHOLOGY – v. 1-37. 1965-79 – 1,5,6 – us Princeton Micro [150]
JOURNAL OF PERSONALITY AND SOCIAL PSYCHOLOGY – (v. 17- 1971- 5,6. v. 31- 1975- 9) – v. 1- 1965- – 1 – us UMI [150]
JOURNAL OF PERSONALITY ASSESSMENT – 1936- 1; v35- 5,6; v39- 9 – us UMI [150]
JOURNAL OF PETROLEUM TECHNOLOGY – v1- 1949- 1; v17- 5,6; v28- 9 – us UMI [660]
JOURNAL OF PETROLOGY – v1- 1960- 1; v15- 5,6; v17- 9 – us UMI [550]
JOURNAL OF PETROLOGY – v. 1-9 and CUM. IND. 1-5. Oxford. 1960-68 – 9 – 2480.00; 9.00v – uk Dawson [550]
JOURNAL OF PHARMACEUTICAL AND BIOMEDICAL ANALYSIS – v1- 1983- – 5,6,9 – us UMI [615]
JOURNAL OF PHARMACEUTICAL CARE IN PAIN AND SYMPTOM CONTROL : INNOVATIONS IN DRUG DEVELOPMENT, EVALUATION AND USE / ed by Lipman, Arthur G – v4 n1. 1996- – 1,9 – $125.00 in US $175.00 outside hardcopy subsc – us Haworth [615]
JOURNAL OF PHARMACEUTICAL MARKETING AND MANAGEMENT / ed by Smith, Mickey C – v1- 1986- – 1, 9 ($200.00 in US $280.00 outside hardcopy subsc) – us Haworth [650]
JOURNAL OF PHARMACEUTICAL SCIENCES – v1- 1912- 1,5,6; 1970- 9 – us UMI [615]
JOURNAL OF PHARMACEUTICAL SCIENCES – v1-44. 1912-55 – 1,5,6 – us Princeton Micro [615]
JOURNAL OF PHARMACEUTICAL SCIENCES – v85. 1996- – 1,5,6,9 – Co-publ with American Pharmaceutical Association – us A.C.S. [540]
JOURNAL OF PHARMACEUTICAL SCIENCES: PRACTICAL PHARMACY EDITION – v1-16. 1940-55 – 1,5,6 – us Princeton Micro [615]
JOURNAL OF PHARMACOEPIDEMIOLOGY / ed by Fincham, Jack E – v1- 1990- – 1, 9 ($125.00 in US $175.00 outside hardcopy subsc) – us Haworth [614]
JOURNAL OF PHARMACOKINETICS AND BIOPHARMACEUTICS – v1-22. 1973-94 – 1,5 – $80.00v – us UMI [615]
JOURNAL OF PHARMACOLOGICAL METHODS – v1-12. 1978-84 – 1,5,6,13 – sz Elsevier [073]
JOURNAL OF PHARMACOLOGY AND EXPERIMENTAL THERAPEUTICS – Baltimore. 1934-41. v50-73. – 212mf – 8 – ne IDC [073]
JOURNAL OF PHARMACOLOGY AND EXPERIMENTAL THERAPEUTICS – v1-279. 1909-96 – 1,5,6,9 – $125.00r – us Williams [615]
JOURNAL OF PHARMACY AND LAW – Ohio Northern University. v1-4. 1992-1995 – 9 – $39.00 set – us Hein [615]
JOURNAL OF PHARMACY AND PHARMACOLOGY – v. 1-27. 1949-1975 – 1,5,6 – us Princeton Micro [615]
JOURNAL OF PHARMACY TEACHING / ed by Buerki, Robert A – v5 n1. 1996- – 1,9 – $105.00 in US $147.00 outside hardcopy subsc – us Haworth [615]
JOURNAL OF PHENOMENOLOGICAL PSYCHOLOGY – (v.11 .1980 5,6,9) – v.1. 1970 – 1 – us UMI [073]
JOURNAL OF PHILADELPHIA COLLEGE OF PHARMACY *see* AMERICAN JOURNAL OF PHARMACY AND THE SCIENCES SUPPORTING PUBLIC HEALTH
JOURNAL OF PHILOLOGY – v. 1-35. 1868-1920 – 1 – us Princeton Micro [400]
JOURNAL OF PHILOSOPHICAL LOGIC – (v13-1984- 5,6,9) – v1- Feb 1972- – 1 – us UMI [160]
JOURNAL OF PHILOSOPHICAL STUDIES – v1-6 1926-31 – 1 – us UMI [100]
JOURNAL OF PHILOSOPHY – v1-57 1904-60 – 1 – us Princeton Micro [100]
JOURNAL OF PHILOSOPHY OF EDUCATION – 1967- 27v – 9 – £197.00 – 0309-8249 – uk Carfax [370]
JOURNAL OF PHOTOCHEMISTRY – v1-26. 1972-84 – 1,5,6,13 – sz Elsevier [073]
THE JOURNAL OF PHOTOGRAPHIC SCIENCE : BEFORE 1953: SECTION B OF THE PHOTOGRAPHIC JOURNAL – (In 1954 The Photographic Journal was divided into 2pts, A and B, and from then on pt B contained the purely scientific articles on photography. In 1953, pt B began to be publ separately. Individual yrs available separately) – v1-31. 1953-83 – 4r + 30mf – 1,9 – £370.00 – uk Chadwyck [770]
JOURNAL OF PHYSICAL AND CHEMICAL REFERENCE DATA – v1-. 1972- – 1,5,6 – us A.I.P. [530]
JOURNAL OF PHYSICAL CHEMISTRY / ed by Bancroft, W D et al – (1929-52, v33-56. 8) – New York, 1896-1940. v1-44 – 919mf – 8 – ne IDC [073]
JOURNAL OF PHYSICAL CHEMISTRY – v. 1-10. 1896-1906 – 1 – us UMI [540]
JOURNAL OF PHYSICAL CHEMISTRY – v1- 1896- – 1,5,6,9 – us A.C.S. [073]
JOURNAL OF PHYSICAL EDUCATION AND RECREATION – v. 46- 1975- – 1,5,6,9 – us UMI [370]
JOURNAL OF PHYSICS A : MATHEMATICAL AND GENERAL – v1-. 1968- – 1,5,6,9 – £1174.00 – uk I.O.P. [510]
JOURNAL OF PHYSICS AND CHEMISTRY OF SOLIDS – (Back issues of journal available from UMI) – 12 issues/y. v54. 1993 – 9 – £869.00y – uk Elsevier Sci [530]
JOURNAL OF PHYSICS AND CHEMISTRY OF SOLIDS – v1- 1956- – 5,6,9 – us UMI [540]
JOURNAL OF PHYSICS B : ATOMIC, MOLECULAR AND OPTICAL PHYSICS – v1-. 1968- – 1,5,6,9 – £956.00 – uk I.O.P. [530]
JOURNAL OF PHYSICS C : CONDENSED MATTER – v1-. 1989- – 1,5,6,9 – £1,940.00 – uk I.O.P. [530]
JOURNAL OF PHYSICS D : APPLIED PHYSICS – v1- 1968- – 1,5,6,9 – £521.00 – uk I.O.P. [621]
JOURNAL OF PHYSICS (USSR) – v. 1-11. 1939-1947 – 1,5,6 – us Princeton Micro [530]
JOURNAL OF PHYSIOLOGY – v. 1-253. 1878-1975 – 1,5,6 – us Princeton Micro [612]
JOURNAL OF PHYSIOLOGY – (v. 212- 1971- 5,6. v. 244- 1975- 9) – v. 150- 1960- – 1 – us UMI [612]
JOURNAL OF PIPELINES – v1-5. 1981-84 – 1,5,6,13 – sz Elsevier [073]
JOURNAL OF PLANT NUTRITION – (1984-. 5,6,9) – v1-. 1979- – 1 – us UMI [073]
JOURNAL OF PLANT NUTRITION AND SOIL SCIENCE *see* ZEITSCHRIFT FUER PFLANZENERNAEHRUNG UND BODENKUNDE
JOURNAL OF PLASMA PHYSICS – (v21- 1979- 5,6,9) – v1- 1967- – 1 – us UMI [530]
JOURNAL OF PODIATRIC EDUCATION – (See also: Journal of Podiatric Medical Education) – v1-4. 1970-73 – 1 – us UMI [617]
JOURNAL OF PODIATRIC MEDICAL EDUCATION – (See also: Journal of Podiatric Education) – v5- 1974- 1; v8- 5,6,9 – us UMI [617]
JOURNAL OF POLICE SCIENCE AND ADMINISTRATION – v.1. 1973 – 1,5,6,9 – us UMI [073]
JOURNAL OF POLICY ANALYSIS AND MANAGEMENT – v.1-. 1981- – 1,5,6,9 – us UMI [320]
JOURNAL OF POLICY ANALYSIS AND MANAGEMENT – v1-6. 1981-87 – 1,5,6 – us Princeton Micro [650]
JOURNAL OF POLICY MODELLING – v1-6. 1979-84 – 1,5,6,13 – sz Elsevier [000]
JOURNAL OF POLITICAL AND MILITARY SOCIOLOGY – v1- 1973- 1,5,6; v4- 9 – us UMI [073]
JOURNAL OF POLITICAL AND MILITARY SOCIOLOGY – 1985-. -q – 1 – us UMI [073]
JOURNAL OF POLITICAL ECONOMY – v. 1-77. 1892-1969 – 1 – us Princeton Micro [330]
JOURNAL OF POLITICAL ECONOMY – (v. 77-1969- 5,6. v. 85- 1977- 9) – v. 1- 1892- – 1 – us UMI [330]
JOURNAL OF POLITICS – v15- 1953- 1; v31- 5,6; v37- 9 – us UMI [320]
JOURNAL OF POLYMER SCIENCE – A, General Papers; B, Polymer Letters; C, Polymer Symposia; and D. v1-62.1946-62 – 1,5,6 – us Princeton Micro [073]
JOURNAL OF POLYMER SCIENCE – New York. v1-33. 1946-58. 146/2 – 8 – ne IDC [073]
JOURNAL OF POLYMER SCIENCE – Part A: General Papers. v. 1-3. 1963-65 – 1,5,6,9 – us UMI [530]
JOURNAL OF POLYMER SCIENCE – Part C: Polymer Symposia. v. 1-39. 1963-71 – 1,5,6,9 – us UMI [540]
JOURNAL OF POLYMER SCIENCE – Part D: Macromolecular Reviews. v. 1-6. 1967-72 – 1,5,6,9 – us UMI [540]
JOURNAL OF POLYMER SCIENCE – Polymer physics ed. V. 4-. 1966- – 1,5,6,9 – us UMI [540]
JOURNAL OF POLYMER SCIENCE: GENERAL PAPERS – v1-3. 1963-65 – 1,5,6 – us Princeton Micro [540]
JOURNAL OF POLYMER SCIENCE: MACROMOLECULAR REVIEWS – v. 7-. 1973- – 1,5,6,9 – us UMI [540]
JOURNAL OF POLYMER SCIENCE: MACROMOLECULAR REVIEWS – v4-16. 1970-81 – 1,5,6 – us Princeton Micro [073]
JOURNAL OF POLYMER SCIENCE: POLYMER CHEMISTRY – v4-24. 1966-86 – 1,5,6 – us Princeton Micro [073]
JOURNAL OF POLYMER SCIENCE: POLYMER CHEMISTRY EDITION – v. 4-. 1966- – 1,5,6,9 – us UMI [540]
JOURNAL OF POLYMER SCIENCE: POLYMER LETTERS – v1-24. 1963-86 – 1,5,6 – us Princeton Micro [073]
JOURNAL OF POLYMER SCIENCE: POLYMER LETTERS EDITION – v. 1-. 1963- – 1,5,6,9 – us UMI [540]
JOURNAL OF POLYMER SCIENCE: POLYMER PHYSICS – v4-24. 1966-86 – 1,5,6 – us Princeton Micro [073]
JOURNAL OF POLYMER SCIENCE: POLYMER SYMPOSIA – Nos.1-73. 1963-85 – 1,5,6 – us Princeton Micro [073]
JOURNAL OF POLYMER SCIENCE: POLYMER SYMPOSIA – v. 40-. 1973- – 1,5,6,9 – us UMI [540]
JOURNAL OF POPULAR CULTURE – v1- 1967- 1; v5- 5,6; v9- 9 – us UMI [073]
JOURNAL OF POPULAR CULTURE – Bowling Green, OH. v1-11. 1967-78 – 154mf – 9 – $5.00f – us Ross [073]
JOURNAL OF POPULATION. BEHAVIORAL, SOCIAL AND ENVIRONMENTAL ISSUES – v. 1-2. 1978-79 – 1,5,6,9 – us UMI [300]
JOURNAL OF PORTFOLIO MANAGEMENT – v1- 1974- 1; v5- 5,6,9 – us UMI [332]
JOURNAL OF POST SUTLER / Fort Harker. Kansas – Nov 1867-Nov 1868 – 1 – us KS Hist [025]
JOURNAL OF POTATO PRODUCTION AND POSTHARVEST HANDLING – v1 n1. 1997- – 1,9 – $75.00 in US $105.00 outside hardcopy subsc – us Haworth [630]

JOURNAL OF POVERTY : INNOVATIONS ON SOCIAL, POLITICAL AND ECONOMIC INEQUALITIES / ed by Kilty, Keith M et al – v1 n1. 1997- – 1,9 – $45.00 in US $63.00 outside hardcopy subsc – us Haworth [339]
JOURNAL OF POWER SOURCES – v1-13. 1976-84 – 1,5,6,13 – sz Elsevier [621]
JOURNAL OF PRACTICAL APPROACHES TO DEVELOPMENT HANDICAP – Calgary. v13-17. 1989-94 – 9 – Can$20.00y – cn Micromedia [360]
JOURNAL OF PRACTICAL NURSING – (See also: Practical Nursing) – v13- 1963- 1; v28- 5,6,9 – us UMI [610]
JOURNAL OF PRAGMATICS – v1-8 1977-84 – 1,5,6,13 – sz Elsevier [400]
JOURNAL OF PRESBYTERIAN HISTORY – v1-61. 1901-87 – 1 – 420.00 – us Presbyterian [240]
JOURNAL OF PRESBYTERIAN HISTORY – (v.58-. 1980- 5,6,9) – v.40-. 1962- – 1 – us UMI [240]
JOURNAL OF PREVENTION – v.1. 1980 81 – 1,5,6,9 – us UMI [073]
JOURNAL OF PREVENTION AND INTERVENTION IN THE COMMUNITY / ed by Ferrari, Joseph R – (Formerly: Prevention in Human Services) – v1- 1981- – 1, 9 ($250.00 in US $350.00 outside hardcopy subsc) – us Haworth [614]
JOURNAL OF PRIMARY PREVENTION – v2-. 1981- – 1,5,6,9 – us UMI [614]
JOURNAL OF PRISON AND JAIL HEALTH – v2-. 1982- – 1,5,6,9 – us UMI [360]
JOURNAL OF PRISON DISCIPLINE AND PHILANTHROPY – 1-N.S.58. 1845-1919 – 1 – us UMI [360]
JOURNAL OF PRISON DISCIPLINE AND PHILANTHROPY (1845-1920) AND THE PRISON JOURNAL (1921-1986) – 1972-86 – 6r – 1 – $510.00 – S1867 – us Scholarly Res [073]
JOURNAL OF PRISON HEALTH – 1980 81 – 1,5,6,9 – us UMI [073]
JOURNAL OF PROCEEDINGS / Kansapolis Association – June 7, 1856 to December 27, 1857 – 1 – us KS Hist [978]
JOURNAL OF PROCEEDINGS / New York. (City) Board of Estimate and Apportionment – 1879-1941. (Wanting some) – 1 – 3,109.00 – us L of C Photodup [336]
JOURNAL OF PROCEEDINGS OF COUNCIL / Chippewa and Munsee Indians – 1870-1881 – 1 – us KS Hist [305]
JOURNAL OF PROCEEDINGS OF THE GRAND DIVISION, S. OF T. OF NOVA SCOTIA *see* JOURNAL OF THE PROCEEDINGS OF THE GRAND DIVISION OF THE SONS OF TEMPERANCE OF THE PROVINCE OF NOVA SCOTIA AT THE QUARTERLY SESSION...
JOURNAL OF PROCEEDINGS.V.1-. 1880- / Essex Field Club – 1 – us UMI [580]
JOURNAL OF PRODUCTS LIABILITY – v1- 1977- – 5,6,9 – us UMI [360]
JOURNAL OF PROFESSIONAL ISSUES IN ENGINEERING – v109- 1983- – 1,5,6,9 – us UMI [620]
JOURNAL OF PROFESSIONAL NURSING – v1-. 1985- – 1,5,6,9 – us UMI [073]
JOURNAL OF PROFESSIONAL SERVICES MARKETING / ed by Winston, William J – v1- 1985- – 1, 9 ($225.00 in US $315.00 outside hardcopy subsc) – us Haworth [650]
JOURNAL OF PROGRAMMED INSTRUCTION – v. 1-3. 1962-1964 – 1 – us UMI [370]
JOURNAL OF PROGRESSIVE HUMAN SERVICES – v1- 1990- – 1, 9 ($95.00 in US $133.00 outside hardcopy subsc) – us Haworth [360]
JOURNAL OF PROMOTION MANAGEMENT / ed by Crane, F G – v4 n1. 1996- – 1,9 – $95.00 in US $133.00 outside hardcopy subsc – us Haworth [650]
JOURNAL OF PROPERTY MANAGEMENT – v1- 1934- 1; v40- 5,6; v41- 9 – us UMI [336]
JOURNAL OF PROPRIETARY RIGHTS – v1-7. 1988-1995 – 9 – $185.00set – us Hein [340]
JOURNAL OF PROSTHETIC DENTISTRY – v1- 1951- 1; v25- 5,6; v35- 9 – us UMI [617]
JOURNAL OF PROTEIN CHEMISTRY – v1-13. 1982-94 – 1,5 – $90.00v – us UMI [540]
JOURNAL OF PSYCHEDELIC DRUGS – v1- 1967- 1; v3- 5,6; v8- 9 – us UMI [610]
JOURNAL OF PSYCHIATRIC EDUCATION *see* ACADEMIC PSYCHIATRY
JOURNAL OF PSYCHIATRIC NURSING AND MENTAL HEALTH SERVICES – v1- 1963- 1; v9- 5,6,9 – us UMI [610]
JOURNAL OF PSYCHIATRIC RESEARCH – v1- 1956- – 5,6,9 – us UMI [616]
JOURNAL OF PSYCHIATRY AND LAW – v1- 1973- 1; v4- 5,6,9 – us UMI [340]
JOURNAL OF PSYCHOACTIVE DRUGS – 1985- – 1 – us UMI [073]
JOURNAL OF PSYCHOLINGUISTIC RESEARCH – v1-23. 1971-94 – 1,5 – $85.00v – us UMI [400]
JOURNAL OF PSYCHOLOGY AND CHRISTIANITY – v1-. 1982- – 1,5,6,9 – us UMI [073]
JOURNAL OF PSYCHOLOGY AND HUMAN SEXUALITY / ed by Coleman, Eli – v1- 1988- – 1, 9 ($225.00 in US $315.00 outside hardcopy subsc) – us Haworth [150]
JOURNAL OF PSYCHOLOGY AND THEOLOGY – (1980 5,6,9) – 1973 – 1 – us UMI [150]
JOURNAL OF PSYCHOPATHOLOGY AND BEHAVIORAL ASSESSMENT – v1-16. 1979-94 – 1,5 – $65.00v – us UMI [150]
JOURNAL OF PSYCHOSOCIAL ONCOLOGY / ed by Christ, Grace H & Zabora, James R – v1- 1983- – 1, 9 ($275.00 in US $385.00 outside hardcopy subsc) – us Haworth [616]
JOURNAL OF PSYCHOSOMATIC RESEARCH – v1- 1956- – 5,6,9 – us UMI [616]
THE JOURNAL OF PSYCHOSOPHY – Toronto: First School of Practical Psychosophy, [1899] – 9 – cn C.I.H.M. [130]
JOURNAL OF PSYCHOTHERAPY AND THE FAMILY *see* JOURNAL OF FAMILY PSYCHOTHERAPY
JOURNAL OF PSYCHOTHERAPY INTEGRATION – v1-4. 1991-94 – 1,5 – $65.00v – us UMI [150]
JOURNAL OF PUBLIC ECONOMICS – v1-25. 1972-84 – 1,5,6,13 – sz Elsevier [336]
JOURNAL OF PUBLIC HEALTH DENTISTRY – v1- 1941- 1; v26- 5,6; v36- 9 – us UMI [617]
JOURNAL OF PUBLIC LAW – v. 17-22. 1968-73 – 1. ; 5,6 – apply; v.20-22 – us UMI [340]
JOURNAL OF PUBLIC LAW *see* EMORY LAW JOURNAL
JOURNAL OF PULP AND PAPER SCIENCE – (Contained in: Pulp and Paper Canada from 1989) – Don Mills – cn Micromedia [670]
JOURNAL OF PULP AND PAPER SCIENCE *see* PULP AND PAPER CANADA
JOURNAL OF PURE AND APPLIED ALGEBRA – v1-34. 1971-84 – 1,5,6,13 – sz Elsevier [073]
JOURNAL OF QUANTITATIVE CRIMINOLOGY – v1-10. 1985-94 – 1,5 – $65.00v – us UMI [360]
JOURNAL OF QUANTITATIVE SPECTROSCOPY AND RADIATIVE TRANSFER – v1- 1961- – 5,6,9 – us UMI [540]
THE JOURNAL OF RACE DEVELOPMENT / ed by Blakeslee, G H et al – Worcester. 12v. 1910-1922 – 67mf – 9 – ILM-3744/1 – ne IDC [575]
JOURNAL OF RADIO LAW – v1-2. 1931-32 – 1,5,6 – us Princeton Micro [073]
JOURNAL OF RADIOANALYTICAL CHEMISTRY – v1-87. 1968-84 – 1,5,6,13 – sz Elsevier [073]
JOURNAL OF RADIOLOGICAL PROTECTION – v1-. 1981- – 1,5,6,9 – £113.00 – uk I.O.P. [530]
JOURNAL OF RAMAN SPECTROSCOPY – (1982-. 1,5,6,9) – v1-. 1973- – 1 – us UMI [073]
JOURNAL OF RATIONAL EMOTIVE THERAPY – The journal of the Institute for Rational-emotive Therapy. v1-. 1983- – 1,5,6,9 – us UMI [073]
JOURNAL OF READING – v1- 1957- 1; v12- 5,6; v19- 9 – us UMI [370]
JOURNAL OF READING BEHAVIOR – v1- 1969- 1; v5- 5,6; v8- 9 – us UMI [073]
JOURNAL OF REAL ESTATE TAXATION – v1- 1973- 1,5,6; v5- 9 – us UMI [073]
JOURNAL OF RECEPTOR RESEARCH – (1984-. 5,6,9) – v1-. 1980- – 1 – us UMI [574]
JOURNAL OF RECONSTRUCTIVE MICROSURGERY – v1-. 1984- – 1,5,6,9 – us UMI [617]
JOURNAL OF REFORM *see* SPIRITUAL UNIVERSE AND JOURNAL OF REFORM
JOURNAL OF REFUGEE RESETTLEMENT – v1- 1980/81- – 1,5,6,9 – us UMI [360]
JOURNAL OF REHABILITATION – v1-46. 1935-80 – 10r – 1 – us Ross [617]
JOURNAL OF RELIGION – v1- 1921- 1; v49- 5,6; v57- 1977- 9 – us UMI [240]
JOURNAL OF RELIGION – v. 1-26. 1921-1946 – 1 – us Princeton Micro [240]
JOURNAL OF RELIGION – v1-29. 1921-49 (complete) – 8r – 1 – ATLA S0010 – us A.T.L.A. [073]
JOURNAL OF RELIGION *see* AMERICAN JOURNAL OF THEOLOGY
THE JOURNAL OF RELIGION – 1(1921)-30(1950) – 326mf – 9 – Dfl1,141.00 – ne Slangenburg [073]
THE JOURNAL OF RELIGION – Chicago. v1-30. 1921-1950 – 326mf – 9 – ne IDC [240]
JOURNAL OF RELIGION AND AGING *see* JOURNAL OF RELIGIOUS GERONTOLOGY
JOURNAL OF RELIGION AND GERONTOLOGY *see* JOURNAL OF RELIGIOUS GERONTOLOGY
JOURNAL OF RELIGION IN DISABILITY AND REHABILITATION : INNOVATIONS IN MINISTRY FOR INDEPENDENT LIVING / ed by Blair, William A & Davidson, Dana – v3 n1. 1996- – 1,9 – $105.00 in US $147.00 outside hardcopy subsc – us Haworth [360]
JOURNAL OF RELIGION IN PSYCHOTHERAPY *see* AMERICAN JOURNAL OF PASTORAL COUNSELING
JOURNAL OF RELIGIOUS AND THEOLOGICAL INFORMATION / ed by Miller, William C – v2 n1. 1996- – 1,9 – $48.00 in US $67.20 outside hardcopy subsc – us Haworth [240]
JOURNAL OF RELIGIOUS ETHICS – (v.8-. 1980-. 5,6,9) – v.1-. 1973- – 1 – us UMI [170]
JOURNAL OF RELIGIOUS GERONTOLOGY / ed by Sapp, Stephen – (Continues: Journal of Religion and Aging and Journal of Religion and Gerontology) – v1- 1990- – 1,9 ($140.00 in US $196.00 outside hardcopy subsc) – us Haworth [200]
JOURNAL OF RELIGIOUS PSYCHOLOGY – v5-7. 1912-1915 (complete) – 1r – 1 – ATLA 1994-S519 – us A.T.L.A. [073]
JOURNAL OF RELIGIOUS THOUGHT – v1- 1943- 1; v28- 5,6; v33- 9 – us UMI [200]
JOURNAL OF REPRODUCTION AND FERTILITY – v15-31. 1968-72 – 1,5,6 – us Princeton Micro [618]
JOURNAL OF REPRODUCTIVE IMMUNOLOGY – v1-6. 1979-84 – 1,5,6,13 – sz Elsevier [073]
JOURNAL OF REPRODUCTIVE MEDICINE – v6-31. 1971-86 – 1,5,6 – us Princeton Micro [618]
JOURNAL OF RESEARCH / U.S. National Bureau of Standards – (all sections). v1-82. 1928-77 – 1,5,6 – us Princeton Micro [073]
JOURNAL OF RESEARCH AND DEVELOPMENT IN EDUCATION – v1- 1967- 1; v9- 5,6,9 – us UMI [073]
JOURNAL OF RESEARCH IN CRIME AND DELINQUENCY – (v1-21 1964-84 on reel $160.00. v22-32 1985-95 on mf $334.00) – v1-32. 1964-95 – 5,6,9 – $494.00 set – us Hein [360]
JOURNAL OF RESEARCH IN MUSIC EDUCATION – v1- 1953- 1; v18- 5,6; v23- 9 – us UMI [780]
JOURNAL OF RESEARCH IN PHARMACEUTICAL ECONOMICS / ed by Smith, Mickey C – v1- 1989- – 1, 9 ($160.00 in US $224.00 outside hardcopy subsc) – us Haworth [330]
JOURNAL OF RESEARCH IN READING – (v.4-. 1981-. 5,6,9) – v.1-. 1978- – 1 – us UMI [370]
JOURNAL OF RESEARCH IN SCIENCE TEACHING – v. 1-. 1963- – 1,5,6,9 – us UMI [370]
JOURNAL OF RESEARCH IN SCIENCE TEACHING – v1-23. 1963-86 – 1,5,6 – us Princeton Micro [073]
JOURNAL OF RESEARCH OF THE NBS: SECTION A: PHYSICS AND CHEMISTRY – v63A-81A. 1959-77 – 1,5,6 – us Princeton Micro [073]
JOURNAL OF RESEARCH OF THE NBS: SECTION B: MATHEMATICS AND MATHEMATICAL PHYSICS – v63B-81B. 1959-77 – 1,5,6 – us Princeton Micro [073]
JOURNAL OF RESEARCH OF THE NBS: SECTION C: ENGINEERING AND INSTRUMENTATION – v63C-76C 1959-72 – 1,5,6 – us Princeton Micro [620]
JOURNAL OF RESEARCH OF THE NBS: SECTION D: RADIO PROPAGATION – v63D-69D. 1959-65 – 1,5,6 – us Princeton Micro [073]
JOURNAL OF RESEARCH ON COMPUTING IN EDUCATION *see* AEDS JOURNAL
JOURNAL OF RESTAURANT AND FOODSERVICE MARKETING / ed by Bowen, John – v2 n1. 1997- – 1,9 – $60.00 in US $84.00 outside hardcopy subsc – us Haworth [650]
JOURNAL OF RETAIL BANKING – (v.3-. 1981-. 5,6,9) – v.1-. 1979- – 1 – us UMI [336]
JOURNAL OF RETAILING – (v. 44- 1968- 5,6. v. 51- 1975- 9) – v. 1- 1925- – 1 – us UMI [380]
JOURNAL OF RHEOLOGY – v. 22-. 1978- – 1,5,6,9 – us UMI [530]
JOURNAL OF RHEOLOGY – v1-27. 1957-83 – 1 – us Princeton Micro [530]
JOURNAL OF RHEUMATOLOGY – (v.6 .1979 5,6,9) – v.1. 1974 – 1 – us UMI [073]
THE JOURNAL OF RICHARD NORWOOD 1639-1640, SURVEYOR OF BERMUDA / Norwood, Richard – 9 – 15.00 – us Scholars' Facs [910]
JOURNAL OF RISK AND INSURANCE – v1- 1932- 1; v41- 5,6; v43- 9 – us UMI [073]
JOURNAL OF ROBOTIC SYSTEMS – v1-. Spring 1984- – 1,5,6,9 – us UMI [629]
JOURNAL OF RURAL STUDIES – v1- 1985- – 5,6,9 – us UMI [305]
JOURNAL OF RUSSIAN LASER RESEARCH – (Cont: Journal of Soviet Laser Research) – v1-15. 1980-94 – 1,5 – $90.00v – us UMI [621]
JOURNAL OF RUSSIAN STUDIES – v. 1-1959- – 1,5,6,9 – us UMI [460]
JOURNAL OF SACRED LITERATURE – v. 1-NS2. 1848-1868 – 1 – us UMI [240]
JOURNAL OF SAFETY RESEARCH – v13-1982- – 5,6,9 – us UMI [360]
JOURNAL OF SCHOOL HEALTH – v1- 1928-1; v41- 5,6; v45- 9 – us UMI [370]
JOURNAL OF SCHOOL PSYCHOLOGY – v1-1963- 1; v12- 5,6; v13- 9 – us UMI [150]
JOURNAL OF SCIENCE, AND ANNALS OF ASTRONOMY, BIOLOGY, GEOLOGY, INDUSTRIAL ARTS, MANUFACTURES, AND TECHNOLOGY – v. 1-22. 1864-1885 – 1 – us UMI [500]
JOURNAL OF SCIENCE AND MATHEMATICS EDUCATION IN SOUTHEAST ASIA – (1983-. 1,5,6,9) – v1-. 1978- – 1 – us UMI [073]
JOURNAL OF SCIENCE AND THE ARTS – v. 1-5. 1817-1818 – 1 – us UMI [500]
JOURNAL OF SCIENCE EDUCATION AND TECHNOLOGY – v1-3. 1992-94 – 1,5 – $80.00 – us UMI [500]
JOURNAL OF SCIENTIFIC COMPUTING – v1-9. 1986-94 – 1,5 – $65.00v – us UMI [000]
JOURNAL OF SCIENTIFIC INSTRUMENTS – v15-18. 1938-1941 – 38mf – 9 – ne IDC [680]
JOURNAL OF SECONDARY EDUCATION – v1-46 1925-71 1; 1961- 5,6 – us UMI [370]
JOURNAL OF SECTIONAL PROCEEDINGS / British Association for the Advancement of Science – Montreal: The Association, [1883?-19-?] – 9 – cn C.I.H.M. [500]
JOURNAL OF SECURITY ADMINISTRATION AND PRIVATE POLICE – v.1. 1978 – 1,5,6,9 – us UMI [073]
JOURNAL OF SEDIMENTARY PETROLOGY – v. 1-36. 1931-1966 – 1 – us Princeton Micro [550]
JOURNAL OF SEGMENTATION IN MARKETING : INNOVATIONS IN MARKET IDENTIFICATION AND TARGETING / ed by Weinstein, Art T – v1 n1. 1997- – 1,9 – $65.00 in US $91.00 outside hardcopy subsc – us Haworth [650]
JOURNAL OF SEMITIC STUDIES – v1- 1956-1; v16- 5,6; v20- 9 – us UMI [305]
JOURNAL OF SEMITIC STUDIES – 1(1956)-13(1968) – 89mf – 9 – Dfl312.00 – ne Slangenburg [073]
JOURNAL OF SEX AND MARITAL THERAPY – v1- 1974- 1,5,6; v2- 9 – us UMI [613]
JOURNAL OF SIKH STUDIES – (Lacking: v1 p79-88) – v1-15. 1974-88 – Inquire – 1 – ATLA S0778 – us A.T.L.A. [073]
JOURNAL OF SMALL BUSINESS AND ENTREPRENEURSHIP – (Mf available to 1994 only) – Toronto. v6-11. 1989-1993/94 – 9 – Can$20.00y – cn Micromedia [650]
JOURNAL OF SMALL FRUIT AND VITICULTURE / ed by Gough, Robert E – v3 n1. 1995- – 1,9 – $75.00 in US $105.00 outside hardcopy subsc – us Haworth [630]
JOURNAL OF SOCIAL AND CLINICAL PSYCHOLOGY – v1-. 1983- – 1,5,6,9 – us UMI [073]

JOURNAL OF SOCIAL ISSUES / Society for the Psychological Study of Social Issues – v. 1-26. 1945-70 – 1 – us Princeton Micro [150]
JOURNAL OF SOCIAL ISSUES – (v. 25- 1969- 5,6. v. 31- 1975- 9) – v. 1- 1945- – 1 – us UMI [360]
JOURNAL OF SOCIAL POLICY – (v.8 .1979 5,6,9) – v.1. 1972 – 1 – us UMI [073]
JOURNAL OF SOCIAL PSYCHOLOGY – v. 1-11. 1930-1940 – 1 – us Princeton Micro [300]
JOURNAL OF SOCIAL SCIENCE – v. 1-12. 1865-1866 – 1 – us UMI [300]
JOURNAL OF SOCIAL SCIENCE, CONTAINING THE PROCEEDINGS OF THE AMERICAN ASSOCIATION – 1-46. 1869-1909 – 1 – us UMI [300]
JOURNAL OF SOCIAL SERVICE RESEARCH / ed by Gillespie, David F – v1- 1977- – 1, 9 ($250.00 in US $350.00 outside hardcopy subsc) – us Haworth [360]
JOURNAL OF SOCIAL STUDIES RESEARCH – v. 1- 1977- – 1,5,6,9 – us UMI [300]
JOURNAL OF SOCIAL THERAPY – v.1-7. 1954-61 – 1 – us UMI [300]
JOURNAL OF SOCIAL WORK AND HUMAN SEXUALITY *see* JOURNAL OF FAMILY SOCIAL WORK
JOURNAL OF SOCIAL WORK PRACTICE – 1992- 7v – 9 – £86.00 – 0265-0533 – uk Carfax [360]
JOURNAL OF SOCIETY OF PUBLIC TEACHERS OF LAW *see* LEGAL STUDIES
JOURNAL OF SOCIOLOGY AND SOCIAL WELFARE – (v.6 .1979 5,6,9) – v.1. 1973 – 1 – us UMI [360]
JOURNAL OF SOIL AND WATER CONSERVATION – v1- 1941- 1; v30- 5,6; v31- 9 – us UMI [333]
JOURNAL OF SOIL SCIENCE – v. 1-19. 1949 50-1968. London – 9 – 24110.00; 6.00v – uk Dawson [550]
JOURNAL OF SOLAR SCIENCES – v1-. 1982- – 1,5,6,9 – us UMI [073]
JOURNAL OF SOLUTION CHEMISTRY – v1-23. 1972-94 – 1,5 – $120.00v – us UMI [540]
THE JOURNAL OF SOMATIC EXPERIENCE – v4-. 1981- – 1 – us UMI [574]
JOURNAL OF SOURCES IN EDUCATIONAL HISTORY – 1978- 16v – 9 – £188.00y – 0140-671X – uk Carfax [370]
JOURNAL OF SOUTH AMERICAN EARTH SCIENCES – 1,5,69 – us UMI [550]
JOURNAL OF SOUTHEAST ASIAN EARTH SCIENCES – v1- 1986- – 5,6,9 – us UMI [550]
JOURNAL OF SOUTHERN AFRICAN AFFAIRS – Publ. of Southern African Research Assoc. and Afro-American Studies, Univ. of Maryland. -q – 1 – us U.W. Library [073]
JOURNAL OF SOUTHERN AFRICAN STUDIES – 1995, Vol 21 – £104.00 – uk Carfax [960]
JOURNAL OF SOUTHERN HISTORY – v1- 1935- 1; v35- 5,6; v41- 9 – us UMI [978]
JOURNAL OF SOVIET LASER RESEARCH *see* JOURNAL OF RUSSIAN LASER RESEARCH
JOURNAL OF SOVIET MATHEMATICS *see* JOURNAL OF MATHEMATICAL SCIENCES
JOURNAL OF SPACE LAW – (v1-12 1973-84 on reel $144.00. v13-15 1985-87 on mf $60.00) – University of Mississippi. v1-15. 1973-87 – 5,9 – $204.00 set – us Hein [340]
JOURNAL OF SPANISH STUDIES; TWENTIETH CENTURY – v1- 1973- 1,5,6; v4- 9 – us UMI [073]
JOURNAL OF SPECIAL EDUCATION TECHNOLOGY – (v.3-. 1980-. 5,6,9) – v.1-. 1978- – 1 – us UMI [370]
JOURNAL OF SPECULATIVE PHILOSOPHY – v1-22 1867-93 – 1 – us UMI [100]
JOURNAL OF SPEECH AND HEARING DISORDERS – (v.45-. 1980- 5,6,9) – v.13-. 1948- – 1 – us UMI [073]
JOURNAL OF SPEECH AND HEARING RESEARCH – (v.23 .1980 5,6,9) – v.1. 1958 – 1 – us UMI [073]
JOURNAL OF SPEECH DISORDERS – v.1-12. 1936-47. Superseded by Journal of Speech and Hearing Disorders – 1 – us UMI [073]
JOURNAL OF SPELEAN HISTORY – v1-3. 1968-70 – 9mf – 9 – $5.00f – us Ross [500]
JOURNAL OF SPORTS MEDICINE *see* AMERICAN JOURNAL OF SPORTS MEDICINE
JOURNAL OF SPORTS MEDICINE AND PHYSICAL FITNESS – Torino. v1-28. 1961-88 – 5,9 – Dfl3,080.00; Dfl110.00v – ne Swets [610]
JOURNAL OF SPORTS SCIENCES – v1-. 1983- – 1,5,6,9 – us UMI [073]
JOURNAL OF STAFF DEVELOPMENT – v1-. 1980- – 1,5,6,9 – us UMI [650]
JOURNAL OF STATE GOVERNMENT *see* SPECTRUM
JOURNAL OF STATE TAXATION – v1-14. 1982-96 – 9 – $290.00set – us Hein [340]
JOURNAL OF STATISTICAL COMPUTATION AND SIMULATION / ed by Krutchkoff, R G – 1972- – 1,5,9 – us Gordon [510]
JOURNAL OF STATISTICAL PHYSICS – v1-77. 1969-94 – 1,5 – $100.00v – us UMI [530]
JOURNAL OF STATISTICAL PLANNING AND INFERENCE – v1-10. 1977-84 – 1,5,6,13 – sz Elsevier [073]
JOURNAL OF STEROID BIOCHEMISTRY AND MOLECULAR BIOLOGY – v1- 1970- – 5,6,9 – us UMI [540]
JOURNAL OF STORED PRODUCTS RESEARCH – v1- 1965- – 5,6,9 – us UMI [073]
JOURNAL OF STRAIN ANALYSIS – v. 1-10. 1965-75 – 1 – us UMI [621]
JOURNAL OF STRAIN ANALYSIS FOR ENGINEERING DESIGN – v. 11-. 1976- – 1,5,6,9 – us UMI [621]
JOURNAL OF STRUCTURAL CHEMISTRY – (Continues: Journal of Structural Chemistry of the USSR) – v1-35. 1960-94 – 1,5 – $100.00v – us UMI [540]
JOURNAL OF STRUCTURAL ENGINEERING – v109- 1983- – 1,5,6,9 – us UMI [620]
JOURNAL OF STRUCTURAL GEOLOGY – v1- 1979- – 5,6,9 – us UMI [550]
JOURNAL OF STRUCTURAL LEARNING / ed by Scandura, J M – 1968- – 1,5,9 – us Gordon [150]
JOURNAL OF STRUCTURAL MECHANICS – v1- 1972- – 1,5,6,9 – us UMI [620]
JOURNAL OF STUDENT FINANCIAL AID – v1- 1971- 1; v7- 5,6,9 – us UMI [370]
JOURNAL OF STUDIES IN TECHNICAL CAREERS – (v.4-. 1982-. 5,6,9) – v.1-. 1978- – 1 – us UMI [370]
JOURNAL OF STUDIES ON ALCOHOL – (See also: Quarterly Journal of Studies on Alcohol) – v36- 1975- 1,5,6; v37- 9 – us UMI [360]
JOURNAL OF SUBSTANCE ABUSE TREATMENT – v1- 1984- – 5,6,9 – us UMI [360]
JOURNAL OF SUPERCONDUCTIVITY – (v4-6 1991-93 $90.00v. 1994 $180.00v) – v1-3, 1988-90 – 1,5 – $60.00v – us UMI [530]
JOURNAL OF SUPRAMOLECULAR STRUCTURE – v.1-. 1972- – 1 – us UMI [540]
JOURNAL OF SUPRAMOLECULAR STRUCTURE AND CELLULAR BIOCHEMISTRY – v.15-17. 1981 – 1,5,6,9 – us UMI [540]
JOURNAL OF SURGICAL ONCOLOGY – (v.16-. 1981-. 5,6,9) – v.1-. 1969- – 1 – us UMI [617]
JOURNAL OF SURVEYING ENGINEERING – v109- 1983- – 1,5,6,9 – us UMI [620]
JOURNAL OF SUSTAINABLE AGRICULTURE : INNOVATIONS FOR LONG-TERM AND LASTING MAINTENANCE AND ENHANCEMENT OF AGRICULTURAL RESOURCES, PRODUCTION, AND ENVIRONMENTAL QUALITY / ed by Poincelot, Raymond P – v7 n1. 1996- – 1,9 – $120.00 in US $168.00 outside hardcopy subsc – us Haworth [630]
JOURNAL OF SUSTAINABLE FORESTRY / ed by Berlyn, Graeme P – v4 n1. 1997- – 1,9 – $95.00 in US $133.00 outside hardcopy subsc – us Haworth [630]
JOURNAL OF SYMBOLIC LOGIC – (1985- . 5,6,9) – v1- . 1936- – 1 – us UMI [073]
JOURNAL OF SYMBOLIC LOGIC – v1-34 1936-69 – 1,5,6 – us Princeton Micro [160]
JOURNAL OF SYSTEMS AND SOFTWARE – v1-4. 1979-84 – 1,5,6,13 – sz Elsevier [073]
JOURNAL OF SYSTEMS MANAGEMENT – v1- 1948- 1; v19- 5,6; v26- 9 – us UMI [650]
JOURNAL OF TAXATION – v1- 1954- 1; v48- 5,6,9 – us UMI [336]
JOURNAL OF TAXATION OF INVESTMENTS – v1-. 1983- – 1,5,6,9 – us UMI [073]
JOURNAL OF TEACHER EDUCATION – (v. 20- 1969- 5,6. v. 26- 1975- 9) – v. 1- 1950- – 1 – us UMI [370]
JOURNAL OF TEACHING IN INTERNATIONAL BUSINESS / ed by Kaynak, Erdener – v1- 1989- – 1, 9 ($120.00 in US $168.00 outside hardcopy subsc) – us Haworth [370]
JOURNAL OF TEACHING IN SOCIAL WORK / ed by Vigilante, Florence & Lewis, Harold – v1- 1987- – 1, 9 ($150.00 in US $210.00 outside hardcopy subsc) – us Haworth [370]
JOURNAL OF TECHNICAL TOPICS IN CIVIL ENGINEERING – v109- 1983- – 1,5,6,9 – us UMI [624]
JOURNAL OF TECHNOLOGY – 1956- 1; 1974- 5,6; 1975- 4 x 6 in. 9 – us UMI [600]
JOURNAL OF TEMPERANCE – Prescott [Ont] : 'oEvangelizer" Office, [1864-1865] – 9 – cn C.I.H.M. [170]
JOURNAL OF TERRAMECHANICS – v1- 1964- – 5,6,9 – us UMI [073]
JOURNAL OF TERTIARY EDUCATIONAL ADMINISTRATION – (v6-. May 1984-. 5,6,9) – v1-. 1979- – 1 – us UMI [073]
JOURNAL OF THE ABRAHAM LINCOLN ASSOCIATION *see* PAPERS OF THE ABRAHAM LINCOLN ASSOCIATION
JOURNAL OF THE ACADEMY OF MANAGEMENT *see* ACADEMY OF MANAGEMENT JOURNAL
THE JOURNAL OF THE ACOUSTICAL SOCIETY OF AMERICA – v1-. 1929- – 1,5,6,9 – us A.I.P. [530]
JOURNAL OF THE AEROSPACE SCIENCES – v. 1-29. 1934-62 – 1 – us UMI [629]
JOURNAL OF THE AEROSPACE SCIENCES – v9-29. 1941-62 – 1 – us Princeton Micro [629]
JOURNAL OF THE AEROSPACE SCIENCES *see* AIAA JOURNAL
JOURNAL OF THE AFRICAN SOCIETY – v1-34. Oct 1901-Apr 1935 – us UMI [073]
JOURNAL OF THE AFRICAN SOCIETY / African Society – (Cont by: Journal of the Royal African Society) – London. v1-34. oct 1901-apr 1935* – 1 – D14338 – us UMI [960]
JOURNAL OF THE AIR POLLUTION CONTROL ASSOCIATION / Air Pollution Control Association – (Cont by: JAPCA. Former title: Air Repair (jul 1951-feb 1955)) – Pittsburgh. cum index 1-15 1951-1965; v1-36 jul 1951-dec 1986 1; v21-36 jan 1971-dec 1986 5; v25-36 jan 1975-dec 1986 9 – 1,5,9 – D6210 – us UMI [360]
JOURNAL OF THE AMERICAN ACADEMY OF CHILD AND ADOLESCENT PSYCHIATRY – v10-35. 1971-96 – 1,5,6,9 – $110.00r – us Williams [616]
JOURNAL OF THE AMERICAN ACADEMY OF DERMATOLOGY / American Academy of Dermatology – St Louis. v1-38. jul 1979-jun 1998+ – 1,5,9 – D11875 – us UMI [616]
JOURNAL OF THE AMERICAN ACADEMY OF MATRIMONIAL LAWYERS – University of Wisconsin. v1-12. 1985-1994 – 9 – $120.00 set – us Hein [340]
JOURNAL OF THE AMERICAN ACADEMY OF PHYSICIAN ASSISTANTS *see* JAAPA
JOURNAL OF THE AMERICAN ACADEMY OF PSYCHOANALYSIS / American Academy of Psychoanalysis – New York. v1-25. 1973-Win 1997+ 1,5*,9 – 1,5,9 – D11046 – us UMI [616]
JOURNAL OF THE AMERICAN ACADEMY OF RELIGION / American Academy of Religion – (Mf ed includes American Academy of Religion Bulletin, and the Council on the Study of Religion Bulletin (v1-6). Former titles: Journal of the National Association of Biblical Instructors (1933-36); Journal of Bible and Religion (jan/mar 1937-oct 1966)) – Chico. cum index 1-25 1933-57; v1-65 1933-Win 1997+ 1; v38-65 mar 1970-Win 1997+ 5; v44-65 mar 1976-Win 1997+ 9 – 1,5,9 – D1480 – us UMI [240]
JOURNAL OF THE AMERICAN ANIMAL HOSPITAL ASSOCIATION / American Animal Hospital Association – (Former title: Animal Hospital (feb 1965-nov 1967)) – South Bend. v1- feb 1965- 1*; v15- jan 1979- 5*,9 – 1,5,9 – D2765 – us UMI [636]
JOURNAL OF THE AMERICAN ASSOCIATION OF CEREAL CHEMISTS / American Association of Cereal Chemists – (Cont by: Cereal Chemistry) – Hutchinson. cum index 1-6 oct 1915-nov 1921; v1-8 oct 1915-dec 1923 – 1 – D5132 – us UMI [660]
JOURNAL OF THE AMERICAN ASSOCIATION OF INSTRUCTORS AND INVESTIGATORS IN POULTRY HUSBANDRY – v.1-7. 1914-21. Superseded by Poultry Science – 1 – us UMI [073]
JOURNAL OF THE AMERICAN ASSOCIATION OF NEPHROLOGY NURSES AND TECHNICIANS *see* AANNT JOURNAL
JOURNAL OF THE AMERICAN ASSOCIATION OF NURSE ANESTHETISTS *see* AANA JOURNAL
JOURNAL OF THE AMERICAN ASSOCIATION OF TEACHER EDUCATORS IN AGRICULTURE / American Association of Teacher Educators in Agriculture – (Cont by: Journal of Agricultural Education) – College Station. v1-29 apr 1961-Win 1988 1*; v19-29 mar 1978-Win 1988 5*,9 – 1,5,9 – D11422 – us UMI [630]
JOURNAL OF THE AMERICAN ASSOCIATION OF UNIVERSITY WOMEN *see* AAUW JOURNAL
JOURNAL OF THE AMERICAN AUDITORY SOCIETY *see* EAR AND HEARING
JOURNAL OF THE AMERICAN CERAMIC SOCIETY / American Ceramic Society – (Vols 5-16 (jan 1922-dec 1933) & v25 (1942) include v1-12 n6 (1922-jun 1933) & v21 n1-4 (jan-apr 1942) of: American Ceramic Society Bulletin. Vols 5-57 (1922-74) include v1-53 of: Ceramic Abstracts) – Columbus. cum index 1-38 1918-55; v1-80 jan 1918-dec 1997+ 1; v51-80 jan 1968-dec 1997+ 5; v60-80 jan 1977-dec 1997+ 9 – 1,5,9 – D1542 – us UMI [730]
JOURNAL OF THE AMERICAN CERAMIC SOCIETY *see* AMERICAN CERAMIC SOCIETY BULLETIN
JOURNAL OF THE AMERICAN CHEMICAL SOCIETY / American Chemical Society – Washington. v1-28 1879-dec 1906 – 1 – D5801 – us UMI [540]
JOURNAL OF THE AMERICAN CHEMICAL SOCIETY – New York. v1-45. 1879-1923 – 1162mf – 9 – ne IDC [540]
JOURNAL OF THE AMERICAN CHEMICAL SOCIETY – v1- 1879- – 1,5,6,9 – us A.C.S. [073]
JOURNAL OF THE AMERICAN COLLEGE HEALTH ASSOCIATION – (1966-82. 1,5,6,9) – v1-30. 1952-82 – 1 – us UMI [073]
JOURNAL OF THE AMERICAN CONCRETE INSTITUTE *see* ACI MATERIALS JOURNAL
JOURNAL OF THE AMERICAN DENTAL ASSOCIATION / American Dental Association – (Former titles: Official Bulletin of the National Dental Association (nov 1913-oct 1914); Journal of the National Dental Association (mar 15 1915-jul 1922); Journal of the American Dental Association (aug 1922-dec 1936); Journal of the American Dental Association and the Dental Cosmos (jan 1937-dec 1938)) – Chicago. v1-128 nov 1913-dec 1997+ 1; v60-128 jan 1960-dec 1997+ 5; v80-128 jan 1970-dec 1997+ 9 – 1,5,9 – D602 – us UMI [617]
JOURNAL OF THE AMERICAN DENTAL ASSOCIATION *see* JOURNAL OF THE AMERICAN DENTAL ASSOCIATION
JOURNAL OF THE AMERICAN DENTAL ASSOCIATION AND THE DENTAL COSMOS *see* JOURNAL OF THE AMERICAN DENTAL ASSOCIATION
JOURNAL OF THE AMERICAN DIETETIC ASSOCIATION / American Dietetic Association – Chicago. v1-65 jun 1925-dec 1974 1; v66-97 jan 1975-dec 1997+ 1,5,9 – 1,5,9 – D11400 – us UMI [613]
JOURNAL OF THE AMERICAN FORENSIC ASSOCIATION / American Forensic Association – (Cont by: Argumentation and advocacy) – Columbia. v1-24 jan 1964-Spr 1988 1; v13-24 Sum 1976-Spr 1988 5*; v13-24 Sum 1976-Spr 1988 9 – 1,5,9 – D6485 – us UMI [634]
JOURNAL OF THE AMERICAN FOUNDRYMEN'S ASSOCIATION *see* TRANSACTIONS
JOURNAL OF THE AMERICAN GEOGRAPHICAL AND STATISTICAL SOCIETY *see* BULLETIN
JOURNAL OF THE AMERICAN GEOGRAPHICAL SOCIETY OF NEW YORK *see* BULLETIN
JOURNAL OF THE AMERICAN GERIATRICS SOCIETY – v39-44. 1991-96 – 6r – 1,5,6,9 – $95.00r – us Williams [618]
JOURNAL OF THE AMERICAN INSTITUTE OF ARCHITECTS *see* AIA JOURNAL
JOURNAL OF THE AMERICAN INSTITUTE OF PLANNERS / American Institute of Planners – (Cont: Planners journal. Cont by: Journal of the American Planning Association) – Washington. cum index v31-36 1965-1967, cum index v37-40 1971-1974; v9-44 1944-oct 1978 1*; v43-44 jan 1977-oct 1978 5,9 – 1,5,9 – D2001.01 – us UMI [710]

JOURNAL OF THE AMERICAN LISZT SOCIETY – (v.5 1979 1,5,9) – v.1 1977 – 1 – us UMI [073]

JOURNAL OF THE AMERICAN MEDICAL TECHNOLOGISTS / American Medical Technologists – (Merged with: American Journal of Technology, to form: Journal of Medical Technology. Cont in pt by: AMT Events. Former title: Journal of the American Medical Technologists (apr 1940-apr/may 1959); Official Journal of the American Medical Technologists (aug 1959-nov/dec 1965)) – Park Ridge. v1-45 1939-dec 1983 1; v36-45 jan 1974-dec 1983 5; v39-45 jan 1977-dec 1983 9 – 1,5,9 – D8705 – us UMI [610]

JOURNAL OF THE AMERICAN MEDICAL TECHNOLOGISTS *see*
- AMERICAN JOURNAL OF MEDICAL TECHNOLOGY
- AMT EVENTS

JOURNAL OF THE AMERICAN OIL CHEMISTS' SOCIETY / American Oil Chemists' Society – (Cont by: JAOCS – Journal of the American Oil Chemists' Society. Former titles: Journal of Oil and Fat Industries(jul 1924-dec 1926); Oil and Fat Industries (jan 1927-oct 1931); Oil and Soap (jan 1932-dec 1946)) – Champaign. v1-56 jul 1924-dec 1979 1; v42-56 jan 1965-dec 1979 5; v47-56 jan 1970-dec 1979 9 – 1,5,9 – D131 – us UMI [660]

JOURNAL OF THE AMERICAN ORIENTAL SOCIETY / American Oriental Society – New Haven. cum index 1-20; v1-117 oct 1843-dec 1997+ 1; v91-117 jan 1971-dec 1997+ 5; v96-117 jan 1976-dec 1997+ 9 – 1,5,9 – D2181 – us UMI [950]

JOURNAL OF THE AMERICAN ORIENTAL SOCIETY – Boston. v1-61. 1849-1941 – 527mf – 9 – ne IDC [978]

JOURNAL OF THE AMERICAN PHARMACEUTICAL ASSOCIATION / American Pharmaceutical Association – (Cont in pt: Journal of the American Pharmaceutical Association wh in Jan 1940 was divided into a practical pharmacy ed and a scientific ed. Cont by: American Pharmacy. Former title: Journal of the American Pharmaceutical Association – Practical Pharmacy edition) – Washington. v1-20 jan 1940-dec 1959 ns 21-2,3-17 jan 1960-dec 1977 1; ns 11-17 jan 1971-dec 1977 5; ns 16-17 jan 1976-dec 1977 9 – 1,5,9 – D18 – us UMI [615]

JOURNAL OF THE AMERICAN PLANNING ASSOCIATION *see* JOURNAL OF THE AMERICAN INSTITUTE OF PLANNERS

JOURNAL OF THE AMERICAN PODIATRIC MEDICAL ASSOCIATION – v75-. 1985- – 1,5,6,9 – us UMI [073]

JOURNAL OF THE AMERICAN PODIATRY ASSOCIATION – (v65-74. 1975-1984. 9) – v1-74. 1907-84 – 1,5,6 – us UMI [073]

JOURNAL OF THE AMERICAN PUBLIC HEALTH ASSOCIATION *see*
- AMERICAN JOURNAL OF PUBLIC HEALTH
- AMERICAN JOURNAL OF PUBLIC HYGIENE

JOURNAL OF THE AMERICAN SOCIETY FOR INFORMATION SCIENCE / American Society for Information Science – (Former title: American Documentation (Win 1950-oct 1969)) – New York. v1-48 jan 1950-dec 1997+ 1; v20-48 jan 1969-dec 1997+ 5; v26-48 jan 1975-dec 1997+ 9 – 1,5,9 – D1423 – us UMI [020]

JOURNAL OF THE AMERICAN SOCIETY FOR PSYCHICAL RESEARCH / American Society for Psychical Research – (Former titles: Journal of the American Society of Psychical Research (jan 1907-dec 1927); Psychic Research (1928-dec 1931)) – New York. v1-91 jan 1907-oct 1997+ 1; v59-91 jan 1965-oct 1997+ 5; v70-91 jan 1976-oct 1997+ 9 – 1,5,9 – D10 – us UMI [150]

JOURNAL OF THE AMERICAN SOCIETY OF ASSOCIATION EXECUTIVES – v.1-14. 1949-62. Superseded by yAssociation Management – 1 – us UMI [650]

JOURNAL OF THE AMERICAN SOCIETY OF CLU – v38-. 1984- – 1,5,6,9 – us UMI [073]

JOURNAL OF THE AMERICAN SOCIETY OF NEPHROLOGY – v1-7. 1990-96 – 1,5,6,9 – $100.00r – us Williams [616]

JOURNAL OF THE AMERICAN STATISTICAL ASSOCIATION – (Index) – Boston, Washington. v1-35. 1888-1940 – 438mf – 9 – ne IDC [310]

JOURNAL OF THE AMERICAN TRIAL LAWYERS ASSOCIATION – v.31-34. 1965-72. Continued as Journal of the Association of Trial Lawyers of America – 1 – us UMI [073]

JOURNAL OF THE AMERICAN VENEREAL DISEASE ASSOCIATION / American Venereal Disease Association – (Cont by: Sexually Transmitted Diseases) – Birmingham. v1-3. sep 1974-dec 1976* – 1 – D11301 – us UMI [616]

JOURNAL OF THE AMERICAN VETERINARY MEDICAL ASSOCIATION / American Veterinary Medical Association – (Absorbed: Scientific Proceedings of the American Veterinary Medical Association (1965). Former title: American Veterinary Review (jan 1877-sep 1915)) – Schaumburg. v1'-211 1877-dec 1997+ 1; v146-211 jan 1965-dec 1997+ 5; v156-211 jan 1970-dec 1997+ 9 – 1,5,9 – D159 – us UMI [636]

JOURNAL OF THE ANCIENT NEAR EASTERN SOCIETY – (1985- . 5,6,9) – v14- . 1982- – 1 – us UMI [073]

JOURNAL OF THE ANDHRA HISTORICAL RESEARCH SOCIETY *see* THE QUARTERLY JOURNAL OF THE ANDHRA HISTORICAL RESEARCH SOCIETY

JOURNAL OF THE ANNUAL ENCAMPMENT / Grand Army of the Republic. Department of the Potomac – 17TH-27TH. 1885-95 – 1 – 19.00 – us L of C Photodup [976]

JOURNAL OF THE ANTHROPOLOGICAL SOCIETY OF BOMBAY / Anthropological Society of Bombay – Bombay. 1886-1936; v1-15. n.s. v1-10. 1946-58. – 229mf – 8 – ne IDC [306]

JOURNAL OF THE ARMED FORCES – Washington. 1863-1963 – 1 – 3266.00 – us L of C Photodup [073]

JOURNAL OF THE ASIATIC SOCIETY OF BENGAL – (1856, Index v1-23) – Calcutta. v1-74. 1832-1910 – 1389mf – 9 – ne IDC [950]

JOURNAL OF THE ASIATIC SOCIETY OF PAKISTAN / Asiatic Society of Pakistan – Dacca. 1956-63. v1-8. – 45mf – 8 – ne IDC [950]

JOURNAL OF THE ASSOCIATION FOR COMPUTING MACHINERY – (v.25 .1978 5,6,9) – v1.. 1954 – 1 – us UMI [073]

JOURNAL OF THE ASSOCIATION FOR PHYSICAL AND MENTAL REHABILITATION *see* AMERICAN CORRECTIVE THERAPY JOURNAL

JOURNAL OF THE ASSOCIATION FOR THE CARE OF CHILDREN IN HOSPITALS – (v.8-. 1979- 1,5,6,9) – v.1-. 1972- – 1 – us UMI [073]

JOURNAL OF THE ASSOCIATION OF MILITARY SURGEONS OF THE UNITED STATES – v.10-19. 1901-1906. Continued by:military surgeon – 1 – us UMI [610]

JOURNAL OF THE ASSOCIATION OF PHYSICAL AND MENTAL REHABILITATION *see* AMERICAN CORRECTIVE THERAPY JOURNAL

JOURNAL OF THE ASSOCIATION OF TRIAL LAWYERS OF AMERICA – (v.37. 1978. 5,6,9) – v.35-37. 1974-78 – 1 – us UMI [073]

JOURNAL OF THE ASTRONAUTICAL SCIENCES – (In 3 pts: Vols 1-19 1954-June 1972 $100.00. Vols 20-26 July 1972-78 $100.00. Vols 27-33 1979-86 $200.00.) – v1-33. 1954-86 – 6 – $300.00 set – us Univelt [629]

JOURNAL OF THE AUDIO ENGINEERING SOCIETY *see* AES

JOURNAL OF THE AUSTRALIAN CHIROPRACTORS' ASSOCIATION – v14- . 1984- – 1,5,6,9 – us UMI [073]

JOURNAL OF THE AUTOMATIC NERVOUS SYSTEM – v1-11. 1979-84 – 1,5,6,13 – sz Elsevier [073]

JOURNAL OF THE BAR ASSOCIATION OF THE DISTRICT OF COLUMBIA – (Title varies: v1 no 1-v2 no 3 as Bulletin of the Bar Association of the District of Columbia. v2 no 4-v7 no 6 as Journal of District of Columbia Bar Association of the District of Columbia. v33 no 11-v40 no 9 as D.C. Bar Journal) – v1-41. 1934-74 (all publ) – 9 – $550.00 set – us Hein [340]

JOURNAL OF THE BEVERLY HILLS BAR ASSOCIATION *see* BEVERLY HILLS BAR ASSOCIATION JOURNAL

JOURNAL OF THE BIHAR AND ORISSA RESEARCH SOCIETY – (Cont as: Journal of the Bihar Research Society. 1943-1960 v29(3)-46) – [Patna]. v1-29(2). 1915-1943 – 442mf – 9 – ne IDC [950]

JOURNAL OF THE BOARD OF AGRICULTURE *see* AGRICULTURE

JOURNAL OF THE BOARD OF TRUSTEES AND MINUTES OF COMMITTEES AND INSPECTORS OF THE FREEDMAN'S SAVINGS AND TRUST COMPANY – 1865-74. 2 rolls. M874 – 1 – us Nat'l Archives [324]

JOURNAL OF THE BOMBAY HISTORICAL SOCIETY / Bombay Historical Society – Bombay. 1928-39. v1-5. – 35mf – 8 – ne IDC [950]

JOURNAL OF THE BOMBAY NATURAL HISTORY SOCIETY – Bombay etc. v1-64. 1886-1967 – 1162mf – 9 – ne IDC [500]

JOURNAL OF THE BRITISH ARCHAEOLOGICAL ASSOCIATION – London. v1-50 1845-1894; N.S. v1-26 1895-1920 – 708mf – 9 – ne IDC [930]

JOURNAL OF THE BURMA RESEARCH SOCIETY / Burma Research Society – Rangoon. 1911-65. v1-48. Lacking: v32(2); v34(2) – 391mf – 8 – ne IDC [950]

JOURNAL OF THE CANADIAN CHURCH HISTORICAL SOCIETY – (v1-27 1950-85 $100.00v. v28-37 1986-95 Can$20.00y 9) – Toronto v1-37. 1950-95 – 5,9 – Price varies – cn Micromedia [240]

JOURNAL OF THE CANADIAN SOCIETY FOR THE PREVENTION OF CRUELTY TO CHILDREN – (Cont by: Empathic Parenting v7 1984) – Midland. v1-6. 1978-83 – 9 – Can$20.00y – cn Micromedia [360]

JOURNAL OF THE CANADIAN SOCIETY FOR THE PREVENTION OF CRUELTY TO CHILDREN *see* EMPATHIC PARENTING

JOURNAL OF THE CEYLON BRANCH OF THE ROYAL ASIATIC SOCIETY / Royal Asiatic Society of Great Britain. Ceylon Branch – (Index. 1845-90) – Colombo. 1859-1949. v1-38. n.s. 1. 1950-59. v1-6 – 350mf – 8 – ne IDC [950]

THE JOURNAL OF THE CHARTERED SOCIETY OF MASSAGE & MEDICAL GYMNASTICS – v1-29. 1915-43 – 1 – us UMI [073]

THE JOURNAL OF THE CHARTERED SOCIETY OF PHYSIOTHERAPY – v29-33. 1944-47 – 1 – us UMI [073]

JOURNAL OF THE CHEMICAL SOCIETY – (Chemical Communications. 1972-84. Dalton Transactions. 1972-84. Faraday Transactions I. 1972-84. Faraday Transactions II. 1972-84. Perkin Transactions I. 1972-84. Perkin Transactions II. 1972-84) – Royal Society of Chemistry, Great Britain. Available to current subscribers to the equivalent printed editions – 1 – us UMI [073]

JOURNAL OF THE CHEMICAL SOCIETY – Royal Society of Chemistry, Great Britain. 1948-71. All sections including Proceedings and Memoirs (1948-64). Available to current subscribers of equivalent printed editions – 1 – us UMI [073]

JOURNAL OF THE CHEMICAL SOCIETY *see* FARADAY DISCUSSIONS OF THE CHEMICAL SOCIETY

JOURNAL OF THE CHEMICO-AGRICULTURAL SOCIETY OF ULSTER – Belfast, Ireland. Oct 1849-Sept 1867. -w. 1 reel – 1 – uk British Libr Newspaper [630]

JOURNAL OF THE CLEVELAND BAR ASSOCIATION *see* CLEVELAND BAR JOURNAL

JOURNAL OF THE COLLEGE OF SCIENCE, KING SAUD UNIVERSITY – (1984-. 5,6,9) – v13-. 1982- – 1 – us UMI [500]

JOURNAL OF THE COMMUNITY DEVELOPMENT SOCIETY – (v15-. 1984-. 5,6,9) – v1-. 1970- – 1 – us UMI [073]

JOURNAL OF THE CONGRESS OF THE CONFEDERATE STATES OF AMERICA – 76mf – 9 – $225.00 – us UPA [320]

JOURNAL OF THE COPYRIGHT SOCIETY OF THE U.S.A. / Copyright Society of the U.S.A. – (Includes index v1-10) – v1-41. 1953-94 – 1,5,6 – $405.00 – us Hein [070]

JOURNAL OF THE DERBYSHIRE ARCHAEOLOGICAL AND NATURAL HISTORY SOCIETY / Derbyshire Archaeological and Natural History Society – London. 1879-1920. v1-42. Lacking: 1886, v. 8. – 217mf – 8 – ne IDC [930]

JOURNAL OF THE EARLY REPUBLIC – v.1-. 1981- – 1,5,6,9 – us UMI [900]

JOURNAL OF THE ECONOMIC AND SOCIAL HISTORY OF THE ORIENT – Leiden. v1-33. 1958-90 – 5,9 – Dfl3,300.00; Dfl100.00v – ne Swets [300]

JOURNAL OF THE EXECUTIVE PROCEEDINGS / U.S. Congress. Senate – v. 1-107. 1789-1965 – 1 – 2,554.00 – us L of C Photodup [324]

JOURNAL OF THE EXECUTIVE PROCEEDINGS OF THE U.S. SENATE / U.S. Congress. Senate – (Updates planned) – Washington: GPO. v1-134. 1828-1992 – 1970mf – 9 – $2,955.00 – LLMC 78-084 – us L.L.M.C. [073]

JOURNAL OF THE EXECUTIVE PROCEEDINGS OF THE U.S. SENATE, 1789-1823 / U.S. Senate – 3r – 1 – M1252 – us Nat'l Archives [324]

THE JOURNAL OF THE FELLOWSHIP OF ST ALBAN AND ST SERGIUS – 1933-34 – 4mf – 9 – Dfl19.00 – ne Slangenburg [073]

JOURNAL OF THE FORUM COMMITTEE ON FRANCHISING *see* FRANCHISE LAW JOURNAL (ABA)

JOURNAL OF THE FRANKLIN INSTITUTE – (Back issues of journal available from UMI) – 6 issues/y. v330. 1993 – 9 – £385.00 – uk Elsevier Sci [500]

JOURNAL OF THE FRANKLIN INSTITUTE – v287- 1969- – 5,6,9 – us UMI [500]

THE JOURNAL OF THE FRENCH CANADIAN MISSIONARY SOCIETY – Montreal: [s.n., 1872-18– or 19–] – 9 – cn C.I.H.M. [240]

JOURNAL OF THE GENERAL ASSEMBLY : 1ST GENERAL AND 1ST SPECIAL SESS, 1965 / Congress of Micronesia – Saipan: Congress of Micronesia. 2v. 1965 – 34mf – 9 – $51.00 – LLMC 82-100F Title 85 – us L.L.M.C. [323]

JOURNAL OF THE GENERAL CONFERENCE *see* METHODIST CHURCH (U.S.) UNITING CONFERENCE

JOURNAL OF THE GIFTED CHILD – v.1 .1979 – 1,5,6,9 – us UMI [073]

JOURNAL OF THE GUJERAT RESEARCH SOCIETY / Gujarat Research Society – Bombay. 1939-65. v1-27(2). Lacking: v. 27 (1). – 8 – ne IDC [950]

JOURNAL OF THE GYPSY LORE SOCIETY, 1888-1973 / The Gypsy Lore Society – 1974 – 6r – 1 – $510.00 – S1854 – us Scholarly Res [306]

THE JOURNAL OF THE HISTORICAL SOCIETY OF NIGERIA, 1956-1980 – March 1990, M.A.P. West Yorkshire – 5r – 1 – uk Microform Academic [960]

JOURNAL OF THE HISTORY OF BIOLOGY – (v17-. 1984-. 5,6,9) – v1-. 1968- – 1 – us UMI [574]

JOURNAL OF THE HISTORY OF IDEAS – v1-1940- – 1,5,6; v36- 9 – us UMI [000]

JOURNAL OF THE HISTORY OF IDEAS – v1-21 1940-60 – 1 – us Princeton Micro [100]

JOURNAL OF THE HISTORY OF MEDICINE AND ALLIED SCIENCES – v1-12. 1946-57 – 1,5,6 – us Princeton Micro [073]

JOURNAL OF THE HISTORY OF MEDICINE AND THE ALLIED SCIENCES – v1- 1946- 1; v26- 5,6; v32- 9 – us UMI [610]

JOURNAL OF THE HISTORY OF PHILOSOPHY – v1- 1963- 1; v9- 5,6; v19- 9 – us UMI [100]

JOURNAL OF THE HORTICULTURAL SOCIETY OF LONDON – London. v1-9 1846-1854; N.S. 1866-1920 – 639mf – 9 – ne IDC [580]

JOURNAL OF THE HOUSE OF COMMONS – (Available for every session from 1982/1983) – Published annually – 9 – £58.00 per session – uk Chadwyck [324]

JOURNAL OF THE HOUSE OF COMMONS / Great Britain. House of Commons – (Available for every session from 1982/83) – 1982/83-1997/98 – 9 – £58.00 per session – uk Chadwyck [941]

JOURNAL OF THE ILLINOIS STATE HISTORICAL SOCIETY – (v64-77, no.2. Spring 1971-Summer 1984. 5,6. v70-77, no.2. Feb 1977-Summer 1984. 9) – v1-77, no.2. Apr 1908-Summer 1984 – 1 – us UMI [073]

JOURNAL OF THE IMPEACHMENT PROCEEDINGS BEFORE THE U.S. SENATE, 1798-1805 / U.S. Senate – 1r – 1 – M1253 – us Nat'l Archives [324]

JOURNAL OF THE INDIAN LAW INSTITUTE – (v1-26 1958-84 on reel $527.00. v27-35 1985-93 on mf $195.00) – v1-35. 1958-93 – 5,6,9 – $722.00 set – us Hein [340]

JOURNAL OF THE INDIAN MUSICOLOGICAL SOCIETY / Indian Musicological Society – (Former title: Sangeet Kala Vihar: English suppl jan/mar-dec 1970) – Baroda. v1-11 jan 1970-dec 1980 1; v4-11 jan 1973-dec 1980 5; v5 1974. v11 mar-dec 1980 9 – 1,5,9 – D8805 – us UMI [780]

JOURNAL OF THE INDIAN SOCIETY OF ORIENTAL ART / Indian Society of Oriental Art – Calcutta. 1933-1952 53. v1-19. Special no 1961 (Tagore) and special no 1965-66. Lacking: 1943-44. v11-12. – 136mf – 8 – ne IDC [700]

JOURNAL OF THE INSTITUTE FOR SOCIOECONOMIC STUDIEES *see* SOCIOECONOMIC STUDIES

JOURNAL OF THE INSTITUTE FOR SOCIOECONOMIC STUDIES – (With index v1-6- 1976-80) – v1-11. 1976-86 – 9 – $132.00 set – us Hein [300]

JOURNAL OF THE INSTITUTE OF METALS / Institute of Metals – London. 1920-40. v23-66. – 537mf – 8 – ne IDC [660]

JOURNAL OF THE INSTITUTE OF PERSONNEL MANAGEMENT – 1946-51 – 1 – us UMI [650]

JOURNAL OF THE INSTITUTION OF BRITISH AGRICULTURAL ENGINEERS *see* AGRICULTURAL ENGINEER

JOURNAL OF THE INSTITUTION OF CIVIL ENGINEERS – London. v7-16. 1937-1941 – 118mf – 9 – ne IDC [624]

JOURNAL OF THE INTER-AMERICAN FOUNDATION – v1-5 1978-81 – 1 – us UMI [977]

JOURNAL OF THE INTERNATIONAL ACADEMY OF PREVENTIVE MEDICINE – (v.6 .1979 5,6,9) – v1. 1974 – 1 – us UMI [073]

JOURNAL OF THE INTERNATIONAL ASSOCIATION OF BUDDHIST STUDIES – v.1. Apr. 1978 – 1,5,6,9 – us UMI [280]

JOURNAL OF THE KANSAS BAR ASSOCIATION – v1-64. 1932-95 – 9 – $720.00 set – us Hein [340]

JOURNAL OF THE LEGAL PROFESSION – University of Alabama. v1-19. 1976-95 – 9 – $178.00 set – us Hein [340]

JOURNAL OF THE LEGISLATIVE PROCEEDINGS OF THE U.S. SENATE, 1789-1817 / U.S. Senate – 28r – 1 – M1251 – us Nat'l Archives [324]

JOURNAL OF THE LESS-COMMON METALS – v1-103. 1959-84 – 1,5,6,13 – sz Elsevier [540]

JOURNAL OF THE LOCKWOOD EXPEDITION ON THE NORTH COAST OF GREENLAND / Lockwood Expedition – 31 Apr-1 Jun 1882. 1 roll. T298 – 1 – us Nat'l Archives [550]

JOURNAL OF THE MALAYAN BRANCH OF THE ROYAL ASIATIC SOCIETY / Royal Asiatic Society. Malayan Branch – Singapore. 1923-65. v1-38. Lacking: v. 1-16 (1, 2, 4); – 441mf – 8 – ne IDC [950]

JOURNAL OF THE MAMMALOGICAL SOCIETY OF JAPAN – (Missing: v1(1)) – Tokyo. v1-2. 1952-1961 – 6mf – 9 – ne IDC [590]

JOURNAL OF THE MARINE BIOLOGICAL ASSOCIATION OF THE UNITED KINGDOM – London. v1-24. 1889-1940 – 322mf – 9 – ne IDC [574]

JOURNAL OF THE MASSACHUSETTS ASSOCIATION OF BOARDS OF HEALTH *see* AMERICAN JOURNAL OF PUBLIC HYGIENE

JOURNAL OF THE MECHANICS AND PHYSICS OF SOLIDS – v1- 1952- – 5,6,9 – us UMI [073]

JOURNAL OF THE MINISTRY OF AGRICULTURE *see* AGRICULTURE

JOURNAL OF THE MISSOURI BAR – (Supersedes: Missouri Bar Journal) – v1-51. 1945-95 – 9 – $631.00 set – us Hein [340]

JOURNAL OF THE MISSOURI BAR *see* – MISSOURI BAR JOURNAL

JOURNAL OF THE MISSOURI DENTAL ASSOCIATION – v60, no.3-v64, no.6. May-Jun 1980-Nov-Dec 1984 – 1,5,6,9 – us UMI [073]

JOURNAL OF THE MOSCOW PHYSICAL SOCIETY – v1-3. 1991-93. Publ. ceased – 1,5,6,9 – uk I.O.P. [530]

JOURNAL OF THE MOUNT SINAI HOSPITAL – v.1-36. 1934-69. Superseded by Mount Sinai Journal of Medicine – 1 – us UMI [073]

JOURNAL OF THE NATIONAL ASSOCIATION OF ADMINISTRATIVE LAW JUDGES – v1-15. 1981-95 – 9 – $133.00 set – us Hein [340]

JOURNAL OF THE NATIONAL ASSOCIATION OF BIBLICAL INSTRUCTORS *see* JOURNAL OF THE AMERICAN ACADEMY OF RELIGION

JOURNAL OF THE NATIONAL ASSOCIATION OF REFEREES IN BANKRUPTCY *see* – AMERICAN BANKRUPTCY LAW JOURNAL

JOURNAL OF THE NATIONAL CONFERENCE OF REFEREES IN BANKRUPTCY *see* – AMERICAN BANKRUPTCY LAW JOURNAL

JOURNAL OF THE NATIONAL DENTAL ASSOCIATION *see* JOURNAL OF THE AMERICAN DENTAL ASSOCIATION

JOURNAL OF THE NATIONAL INDIAN ASSOCIATION – (Cont as: Indian Magazine. 1886-1924 v181-630. Some missing vols) – Bristol. v1-180. 1871-1885 – 447mf – 9 – ne IDC [950]

JOURNAL OF THE NEUROLOGICAL SCIENCES – v1-66. 1964-84 – 1,5,6,13 – sz Elsevier [073]

JOURNAL OF THE NEW HARBINGER – v1. 1971-73 – 1 – us UMI [330]

JOURNAL OF THE NEW YORK BOTANICAL GARDEN – New York. v1-22. 1900-1921 – 119mf – 9 – ne IDC [580]

JOURNAL OF THE NIGER / Lander, Richard – 1832 – 7 – uk Microform Academic [910]

JOURNAL OF THE OHIO FOLKLORE SOCIETY – 1965-78 – 1 – us UMI [073]

JOURNAL OF THE OKLAHOMA BAR ASSOCIATION *see* OKLAHOMA BAR JOURNAL

JOURNAL OF THE OKLAHOMA STATE MEDICAL ASSOCIATION – v1- 1909- 1; v64- 5,6; v69- 9 – us UMI [616]

JOURNAL OF THE OPERATIONAL RESEARCH SOCIETY – v.1-. 1950- – 5,6,9 – us UMI [073]

JOURNAL OF THE OPTICAL SOCIETY OF AMERICA A – Monthly – 9,6 – $837.00 in US $855.00 outside – us Optical Soc [073]

JOURNAL OF THE OPTICAL SOCIETY OF AMERICA A: OPTICS AND IMAGE SCIENCE – (v1-9. 1984-92. $490.00v, $44.00 per issue. v10. 1993. $530.00, $545.00 outside North America) – v1-. 1984-. -m – 9 – us Optical Soc [073]

JOURNAL OF THE OPTICAL SOCIETY OF AMERICA B – Monthly – 9,6 – $837.00 in US $855.00 outside – us Optical Soc [073]

JOURNAL OF THE OPTICAL SOCIETY OF AMERICA B: OPTICAL PHYSICS – (v1-9. 1984-92. $490.00v, $44.00 per issue. v10. 1993. $530.00, $545.00 outside North America) – v1-. 1984-. -m – 9 – us Optical Soc [073]

JOURNAL OF THE PAKISTAN HISTORICAL SOCIETY / Pakistan Historical Society – Karachi. 1953-55. v1-3 – 20mf – 8 – ne IDC [950]

JOURNAL OF THE PALESTINE ORIENTAL SOCIETY – Jerusalem. v1-21. 1920-1948 – 84mf – 9 – ne IDC [956]

JOURNAL OF THE PARLIAMENTS OF THE COMMONWEALTH *see* PARLIAMENTARIAN

JOURNAL OF THE PARLIAMENTS OF THE EMPIRE *see* PARLIAMENTARIAN

JOURNAL OF THE PATENT AND TRADEMARK OFFICE SOCIETY – (Title varies: v1-66 1918-84 as Journal of the Patent Office Society) – v1-77. 1918-95 – 9 – $1,243.00 set – us Hein [340]

JOURNAL OF THE PATENT OFFICE SOCIETY *see* JOURNAL OF THE PATENT AND TRADEMARK OFFICE SOCIETY

THE JOURNAL OF THE PHOTOGRAPHIC SOCIETY : THE OFFICIAL ORGAN OF THE ROYAL PHOTOGRAPHIC SOCIETY OF GREAT BRITAIN / Great Britain. Royal Photographic Society – (Individual yrs available separately. Renamed: The Photographic Journal in 1876/77) – v1-123. 1853-1983 – 48r + 51mf – 1,9 – £2,935.00 – uk Chadwyck [770]

JOURNAL OF THE PHYSICAL SOCIETY OF JAPAN / Physical Society of Japan – (v1-6 1946-51 Y16,000r. v7-9 1952-54 Y16,000r. v10-11 1955-56 Y16,000r. v12-20 1957-65 Y16,000y. v21-63 1966-94 Y16,00half-y. v64 1995 Y16,000y. v66 1997 Y32,000y) – v21-66, 1966-97. Monthly (Nos 1-12 + index) – 5 – Y75,000y Y6,800ea – ja Physical Soc [530]

JOURNAL OF THE PROCEEDINGS OF THE GRAND DIVISION OF THE SONS OF TEMPERANCE OF THE PROVINCE OF NOVA SCOTIA AT THE QUARTERLY SESSION... / Sons of Temperance of North America. Grand Division of Nova Scotia – (Cont by: Sons of Temperance of North America, Grand Division of Nova Scotia. Journal of Proceedings of the Grand Division, S. of T. of Nova Scotia) – [Yarmouth, NS?]: The Division, [1848 or 1849]-1876 (Yarmouth [NS]: H C Flint) – 9 – cn C.I.H.M. [240]

JOURNAL OF THE PROCEEDINGS OF THE LINNEAN SOCIETY. BOTANY – London. v1-51. 1857-1937 – 542mf – 9 – ne IDC [580]

JOURNAL OF THE PROCEEDINGS OF THE PARTY FROM THE RIVER MACKENZIE TOWARDS CAPE BATHURST / Pullen, W J S – BN 354. 2. Lacking: p. 67-E. 1852 – 9 – ne IDC [910]

JOURNAL OF THE PUNJAB HISTORICAL SOCIETY / Punjab Historical Society – Lahore. 1911-29. v1-10. – 64mf – 8 – ne IDC [950]

JOURNAL OF THE PUNJAB UNIVERSITY HISTORICAL SOCIETY / Punjab University. Historical Society – Lahore. 1932-60. v1-11 – 41mf – 8 – ne IDC [950]

JOURNAL OF THE ROYAL AERONAUTICAL SOCIETY *see* AERONAUTICAL JOURNAL

JOURNAL OF THE ROYAL AFRICAN SOCIETY – v35-43 (136-171). Jul 1935-Apr 1944 – 1 – us UMI [073]

JOURNAL OF THE ROYAL AFRICAN SOCIETY *see* – AFRICAN AFFAIRS – JOURNAL OF THE AFRICAN SOCIETY

JOURNAL OF THE ROYAL ASIATIC SOCIETY, BOMBAY BRANCH / Royal Asiatic Society. Bombay Branch – (Annual Reports 1933-35, 1964-65.) – n.s. 1925-62. v. 1-35. – 132mf – 8 – ne IDC [950]

JOURNAL OF THE ROYAL ASIATIC SOCIETY, BOMBAY BRANCH / Royal Asiatic Society. Bombay Branch – Bombay. 1841-1923. v1-26 – 338mf – 8 – ne IDC [950]

JOURNAL OF THE ROYAL ASIATIC SOCIETY OF BENGAL / Royal Asiatic Society of Bengal – Calcutta. 1935-58. Science Ser. 3 v1-24. – 77mf – 8 – ne IDC [950]

JOURNAL OF THE ROYAL ASIATIC SOCIETY OF GREAT BRITAIN AND IRELAND : NORTH CHINA BRANCH – Shanghai. v1-3 1858-1860; N.S. v1-73 1864-1948 – 398mf – 9 – ne IDC [950]

THE JOURNAL OF THE ROYAL ASIATIC SOCIETY OF GREAT BRITAIN AND IRELAND – London. v1-20 1834-1863; N.S. v1-92 1865-1960 – 1454mf – 9 – ne IDC [941]

JOURNAL OF THE ROYAL SOCIETY OF HEALTH – v103, no.1-. Feb 1983- – 1,5,6,9 – us UMI [073]

JOURNAL OF THE ROYAL SOCIETY OF MEDICINE – v.71- 1978- – 1,5,6,9 – us UMI [073]

JOURNAL OF THE SCHOOL OF LANGUAGES – (1984-. 5,6,9) – v1-. 1977- – 1 – us UMI [400]

JOURNAL OF THE SECRETARY OF THE SENATE, 1789-1845 / U.S. Senate – 1r – 1 – M1254 – us Nat'l Archives [324]

JOURNAL OF THE SIEGE OF QUEBEC, 1759 / Coates, E – 1 – uk Microform Academic [920]

THE JOURNAL OF THE SIND HISTORICAL SOCIETY / Sind Historical Society – Karachi. 8v. 1934-48 – 1 – $23.00r – us L of C Photodup [073]

JOURNAL OF THE SOCIETY OF ARCHIVISTS – 14v- – 9 – £46.50 – 0037-9816 – uk Carfax [025]

JOURNAL OF THE SOUTH AFRICAN ORNITHOLOGIST'S UNION – Pretoria. v1-4. 1905/1906-1908 – 16mf – 9 – ne IDC [590]

JOURNAL OF THE SOUTH CAROLINA COURT OF GENERAL SESSIONS, 1769-1776 – South Carolina: Department of Archives and History, 1995 – 1r – 1 – $85.00 – us Scholarly Res [340]

JOURNAL OF THE STATE BAR OF CALIFORNIA *see* CALIFORNIA STATE BAR JOURNAL

JOURNAL OF THE STRAITS BRANCH OF THE ROYAL ASIATIC SOCIETY / Royal Asiatic Society of Great Britain. Straits Branch – Singapore. 1878-1922. v1-86. – 305mf – 8 – ne IDC [950]

JOURNAL OF THE STUDENT AMERICAN MEDICAL ASSOCIATION – v.1-5. 1952-56. Superseded by New Physician – 1 – us UMI [073]

JOURNAL OF THE SUFFOLK ACADEMY OF LAW – v1-10. 1980-95 – 9 – $66.00 set – us Hein [340]

JOURNAL OF THE TELEGRAPH – v. 1-46. 1867-1914 – 1,5,6 – us Princeton Micro [621]

THE JOURNAL OF THE TIMES – Halifax, NS: Macallaster & Paine, [1858-186-?] – 9 – cn C.I.H.M. [971]

JOURNAL OF THE TOWN PLANNING INSTITUTE – London, England. 1923/24-1951/52. With printed Finding List – 1 – £35.00r – uk Altair [710]

JOURNAL OF THE UNITED PROVINCES HISTORICAL SOCIETY / United Provinces Historical Society – Calcutta, Bombay, etc. 1917-52. v1-25. n.s. v1-5. 1953-57. – 196mf – 8 – ne IDC [950]

JOURNAL OF THE UNIVERSITY OF BOMBAY – (Some missing vols) – Bombay etc. v1-29. 1932-1961 – 406mf – 9 – ne IDC [370]

JOURNAL OF THE VIGILANCE ASSOCIATION FOR THE DEFENCE OF PERSONAL RIGHTS – London, 1881-1886 – 13mf – 9 – ne IDC [360]

JOURNAL OF THE VOYAGE OF THE USS NONSUCH UP THE ORINOCO, 1819 / U.S. Department of State – 1roll. M83 – 1 – us Nat'l Archives [910]

JOURNAL OF THE WEST CHINA BORDER RESEARCH SOCIETY – v1-15. 1922-1946 – 74mf – 9 – ne IDC [950]

JOURNAL OF THEOLOGICAL STUDIES – v1-1899- 1; v22- 5,6; v26- 9 – us UMI [240]

JOURNAL OF THEOLOGICAL STUDIES – 1(1900)-50(1949) – 422mf – 9 – Dfl1,477.00 – ne Slangenburg [073]

JOURNAL OF THEOLOGY FOR SOUTHERN AFRICA – 1972-88.Continued annually – 1 – uk World [240]

JOURNAL OF THEOLOGY FOR SOUTHERN AFRICA – (1985-. 5,6,9) – 1972- – 1 – us UMI [240]

JOURNAL OF THEORETICAL PROBABILITY – v1-7. 1988-94 – 1,5 – $65.00v – us UMI [510]

JOURNAL OF THERAPEUTIC HUMOR – v1. 1980 – 1,5,6,9 – us UMI [073]

JOURNAL OF THERMAL ANALYSIS – (1982-. 1,5,6,9) – v1-. 1969- – 1 – us UMI [073]

JOURNAL OF THERMAL BIOLOGY – v1-1975- – 5,6,9 – us UMI [574]

JOURNAL OF THORACIC AND CARDIOVASCULAR SURGERY – (v. 44-1965- 5,6; v. 59- 1970- 9) – v. 1- 1931- – 1 – us UMI [617]

JOURNAL OF THORACIC IMAGING – 1985- – 1,5,6,9 – us UMI [610]

JOURNAL OF THOUGHT – v1- 1966- 1; v11-5,6; v12- 9 – us UMI [073]

JOURNAL OF TISSUE CULTURE METHODS: TISSUE CULTURE ASSOCIATION MANUAL OF CELL, TISSUE, AND ORGAN CULTURE PROCEDURES – (1985-. 5,6,9) – v6-. 1980- – 1 – us UMI [612]

JOURNAL OF TOXICOLOGY AND ENVIRONMENTAL HEALTH – v. 1-. 1975- – 1,5,6,9 – us UMI [615]

JOURNAL OF TOXICOLOGY. CLINICAL TOXICOLOGY – v19-. 1982- – 1,5,6,9 – us UMI [073]

JOURNAL OF TOXICOLOGY. CUTANEOUS AND OCULAR TOXICOLOGY – (1984-. 5,6,9) – v1-. 1982- – 1 – us UMI [073]

JOURNAL OF TOXICOLOGY. TOXIN REVIEWS – (1984-. 5,6,9) – v1-. 1982- – 1 – us UMI [073]

JOURNAL OF TRACE AND MICROPROBE TECHNIQUES – v1-. 1982- – 1,5,6,9 – us UMI [073]

JOURNAL OF TRANSACTIONS : SOCIETY FOR PROMOTING THE STUDY OF RELIGIONS – nos1-8. 1931-34 (complete) – Inquire – 1 – ATLA 1994-S512 – us A.T.L.A. [073]

JOURNAL OF TRANSNATIONAL MANAGEMENT DEVELOPMENT : THE OFFICIAL PUBLICATION OF THE INTERNATIONAL MANAGEMENT DEVELOPMENT ASSOCIATION / ed by Cordell, Victor V – v2 n1. 1995- – 1,9 – $175.00 in US $245.00 outside hardcopy subsc – us Haworth [650]

JOURNAL OF TRANSPORT HISTORY – (1985-. 5,6,9) – v1-. 1953- – 1 – us UMI [380]

JOURNAL OF TRANSPORTATION ENGINEERING – v109-. 1983- – 1,5,6,9 – us UMI [073]

JOURNAL OF TRANSPORTATION LAW, LOGISTICS AND POLICY – (v1-52 1933-85 on reel $830.00. v53-62 1985-95 on mf $312.00. Title varies: v1-51 1933-84 as ICC Practitioners' Journal. v52-61 1985-94 as Transportation Practitioners' Journal) – v1-62. 1933-95 – 5,6,9 – $1,142.00 set – us Hein [340]

JOURNAL OF TRAUMA : INJURY, INFECTION AND CRITICAL CARE – (Also available on CD-ROM: 1985-89 $395.00) – v1-41. 1961-96 – 1,5,6,9 – $110.00r – us Williams [616]

JOURNAL OF TRAUMATIC STRESS – v1-7. 1988-94 – 1,5 – $65.00v – us UMI [616]
JOURNAL OF TRAVEL AND TOURISM MARKETING / ed by Chon, K S (Kaye) – v5 n1. 1996- – 1,9 – $80.00 in US $112.00 outside hardcopy subsc – us Haworth [650]
A JOURNAL OF TRAVELS INTO THE ARKANSA TERRITORY, DURING THE YEAR 1819... / Nuttall, Thomas – Philadelphia: Palmer, 1821 – 1 – F155.60 – fr Armell [910]
JOURNAL OF TREE FRUIT PRODUCTION / ed by Autio, Wesley R – v1 n1. 1996- – 1,9 – $95.00 in US $133.00 outside hardcopy subsc – us Haworth [630]
JOURNAL OF TROPICAL GEOGRAPHY – Singapore, Kuala Lumpur. 1959-64. v.13-19 – 23mf – 8 – ne IDC [910]
JOURNAL OF TROPICAL PEDIATRICS – (v30-. 1984-. apply: 5,6,9) – v26-. Feb 1980- – 1 – us UMI [073]
THE JOURNAL OF TROPICAL PEDIATRICS – v13-16. 1967-70 – 1 – us UMI [073]
THE JOURNAL OF TROPICAL PEDIATRICS – v1-5. 1955-59 – 1 – us UMI [073]
THE JOURNAL OF TROPICAL PEDIATRICS AND AFRICAN CHILD HEALTH – v5-13. 1959-67 – 1 – us UMI [073]
JOURNAL OF TROPICAL PEDIATRICS AND ENVIRONMENTAL CHILD HEALTH – v17-25. 1971-79 – 1 – us UMI [073]
JOURNAL OF TURFGRASS MANAGEMENT : DEVELOPMENTS IN BASIC AND APPLIED TURFGRASS RESEARCH / ed by Torello, William A – v1 n1. 1995- – 1,9 – $90.00 in US $126.00 outside hardcopy subsc – us Haworth [630]
A JOURNAL OF TWO VISITS MADE TO SOME NATIONS OF INDIANS ON THE WEST SIDE OF THE RIVER OHIO, IN THE YEARS 1772 AND 1773 / Jones, D – 1875 – 1 – us A.T.L.A. [240]
JOURNAL OF UKRAINIAN GRADUATE STUDIES – Zhurnal vyshchykh ukrainoznaychykh studii. v1-4. 1976-79 – 1 – us UMI [460]
JOURNAL OF UKRAINIAN STUDIES – (1983-. 1,5,6,9) – Zhurnal ukrainoznavchykh studii. v5-. 1980- – 1 – us UMI [460]
JOURNAL OF ULTRASOUND IN MEDICINE – v.1-. 1982- – 1,5,6,9 – us UMI [616]
THE JOURNAL OF UNIFIED SCIENCE (ERKENNTNIS) – v8 Jun 1939-Apr 1940 – 1 – us UMI [100]
JOURNAL OF URBAN ANALYSIS AND PUBLIC MANAGEMENT / ed by Altman, S – 1,5,9 – us Gordon [600]
JOURNAL OF URBAN HISTORY – (1983-. 1,5,6,9) – v1-. 1974- – 1 – us UMI [073]
JOURNAL OF URBAN LAW *see* UNIVERSITY OF DETROIT MERCY LAW REVIEW
JOURNAL OF URBAN PLANNING AND DEVELOPMENT – v109-. 1983- – 1,5,6,9 – us UMI [073]
JOURNAL OF UROLOGY – v1-156. 1917-96 – 1,5,6,9 – $105.00r – us Williams [616]
JOURNAL OF VACUUM SCIENCE AND TECHNOLOGY: A AND B – v1A+B-. 1983- – 1,5,6 – us A.I.P. [530]
JOURNAL OF VACUUM SCIENCE AND TECHNOLOGY: A: VACUUM, SURFACES, AND FILMS – v1A-. 1983- – 1,5,6 – us A.I.P. [530]
JOURNAL OF VACUUM SCIENCE AND TECHNOLOGY: B: MICROELECTRONICS PROCESSING AND PHENOMENA – v1B-. 1983- – 1,5,6 – us A.I.P. [073]
JOURNAL OF VASCULAR RESEARCH – v30-1993- – us UMI [616]
JOURNAL OF VASCULAR SURGERY – v1-. 1984- – 1,5,6,9 – us UMI [617]
JOURNAL OF VEGETABLE CROP PRODUCTION / ed by Robbins, M LeRon – v2 n1. 1997- – 1,9 – $90.00 in US $126.00 outside hardcopy subsc – us Haworth [631]
JOURNAL OF VESTIBULAR RESEARCH – 1,5,69 – us UMI [612]
JOURNAL OF VETERINARY MEDICAL EDUCATION – v1- 1974- 1; v3- 5,6,9 – us UMI [636]
JOURNAL OF VETERINARY ORTHOPEDICS – 1979 – 1,5,6,9 – us UMI [073]
JOURNAL OF VIBRATION, ACOUSTICS, STRESS, AND RELIABILITY IN DESIGN – v105-. 1983- – 1,5,6,9 – us UMI [073]
JOURNAL OF VIRGINIA EDUCATION *see* – VIRGINIA JOURNAL OF EDUCATION
JOURNAL OF VIROLOGICAL METHODS – v1-10. 1980-84 – 1,5,6,13 – sz Elsevier [073]
JOURNAL OF VIROLOGY – v1- 1967- 1; v7- 5,6; v15- 9 – us UMI [610]
JOURNAL OF VIROLOGY – v1-60. 1967-86 – 1,5,6 – us Princeton Micro [073]
JOURNAL OF VISUAL IMPAIRMENT AND BLINDNESS – v. 71- 1977- – 1,5,6,9 – us UMI [370]
THE JOURNAL OF VOCATIONAL RESEARCH – (v9-. 1984-. 5,6,9) – v1-. Winter 1976- – 1 – us UMI [073]
JOURNAL OF VOLCANOLOGY AND GEOTHERMAL RESEARCH – v1-22. 1976-84 – 1,5,6,13 – sz Elsevier [550]
JOURNAL OF VOLUNTARY ACTION RESEARCH – 1985- – 1 – us UMI [073]
JOURNAL OF VOYAGE FROM SALEM TOWARDS ST KITTS OF BRIG ADVENTURE – 1807 – 1 reel – 1 – $68.00 – cn Library Assoc [910]
JOURNAL OF WARRANTS ISSUED / Fulton County. Ohio. Auditor – 1850-1870 – 1r – 1 – $32.50r – us Archival [324]
JOURNAL OF WARRANTS REDEEMED / Wyandot County, Ohio, Treasurer – 1845-1847 – 1r – 1 – $32.50r – us Archival [324]
JOURNAL OF WATER RESOURCES PLANNING AND MANAGEMENT – v109-. 1983- – 1,5,6,9 – us UMI [333]
JOURNAL OF WATERWAY, PORT, COASTAL AND OCEAN ENGINEERING – v109- 1983- – 1,5,6,9 – us UMI [627]
JOURNAL OF WILDLIFE MANAGEMENT – (v. 43- 1979- 5,6,9) – v. 1- 1937- – 1 – us UMI [639]
JOURNAL OF WIND ENGINEERING AND INDUSTRIAL AERODYNAMICS – v1-19. 1975-84 – 1,5,6,13 – sz Elsevier [073]
JOURNAL OF WINE RESEARCH – 1992- 4v – 9 – £188.50 – 0957-1264 – uk Carfax [640]
JOURNAL OF WOMEN AND AGING / ed by Garner, J Dianne – v1- 1989- – 1, 9 ($175.00 in US $36.00 outside hardcopy subsc) – us Haworth [618]
JOURNAL OF WOOD CHEMISTRY AND TECHNOLOGY – (1984-. 5,6,9) – v1-. 1981- – 1 – us UMI [073]
JOURNAL OF WORLD PREHISTORY – v1-8. 1987-94 – 1,5 – $65.00v – us UMI [500]
JOURNAL OF YOUTH AND ADOLESCENCE – v1- 1972- – 1,5,6 – us UMI [305]
JOURNAL OF YOUTH AND ADOLESCENCE – v1-23. 1972-94 – 1,5 – $95.00v – us UMI [305]
JOURNAL OFFICIAL / United Arab Republic – 1949-1966. Cairo – 1 – us NY Public [956]
JOURNAL OFFICIAL DE LA REPUBLIQUE ALGERIENNE / Algeria – (1980-. approx.23.00y; 1) – 1970-79. 10 reels – 1 – 230.00 – us L of C Photodup [324]
JOURNAL OFFICIEL – 1900-1995 – 3 times per yr – 6 – F2,400.00 – sz Infoprint [072]
JOURNAL OFFICIEL / Algeria – (Premier partie. Lois et decrets. 1927-juin 1936, 1937-39, avr 1943-44, oct 1957-58. 1. Deuxieme partie. Decrets, arretes, textes divers. 1927-37, juin 1943-44. 1. Troisieme partie. Texte arabe. 1927-29. 1) – fr A.C.R.P.P. [960]
JOURNAL OFFICIEL / Algeria – puis de la Republique algerienne; de la Republique algerienne democratique et populaire. juil 1962-70 – 1 – fr A.C.R.P.P. [960]
JOURNAL OFFICIEL / Congo. (Brazzaville) – 1960, 1962-70 – 1 – fr A.C.R.P.P. [960]
JOURNAL OFFICIEL / Dahomey – aout 1894-1928, 1949, 1953-55. Annexes 1953-56 – 1 – fr A.C.R.P.P. [960]
JOURNAL OFFICIEL / Dahomey – Porto Nova. v69-81. 1958-70. 6 reels – 1 – $60.00r – us Ross [324]
JOURNAL OFFICIEL / Dahomey. Porto Novo – 1957-1967- – 1 – us NY Public [960]
JOURNAL OFFICIEL / French Equatorial Africa – A.E.F. mars 1910-27, 1929-38, 1940-45, 1947-aout 1959 – 1 – fr A.C.R.P.P. [960]
JOURNAL OFFICIEL / French Guinea – 1901-26, 1930-44, 1947-sept 1958 – 1 – fr A.C.R.P.P. [073]
JOURNAL OFFICIEL / French Polynesia – Papeete. v106-117. 1957-68 – 5r – 1 – us Ross [324]
JOURNAL OFFICIEL / French Sudan – fevr 1921, 1922-nov 1958 – 1 – fr A.C.R.P.P. [960]
JOURNAL OFFICIEL / French Sudan – Koulouba. 1951-Oct. 1958 – 1 – us NY Public [960]
JOURNAL OFFICIEL / French West Africa – A.O.F. oct 1895-1900, 1905-aout 1959 – 1 – fr A.C.R.P.P. [960]
JOURNAL OFFICIEL / French West Africa – Goree. 1952-1959 – 1 – us NY Public [960]
JOURNAL OFFICIEL / Gabon – juil 1904-oct 1908 – 1 – fr A.C.R.P.P. [960]
JOURNAL OFFICIEL / Gabon-Congo – juin 1887-88 – 1 – fr A.C.R.P.P. [960]
JOURNAL OFFICIEL : GAZETI YA LETA YA REPUBLIKA Y'URWANDA / Rwanda – v1-10. 1962-71 – 3r – 1 – us Ross [324]
JOURNAL OFFICIEL / Guinea. French – Conakry. 1948-Sept. 1958 – 1 – us NY Public [960]
JOURNAL OFFICIEL / Indochina. French – 1889-1950 – 1 – fr A.C.R.P.P. [073]
JOURNAL OFFICIEL / Ivory Coast – 1895-1927, 1930-38, 1940-42, 1946-58 – 1 – fr A.C.R.P.P. [960]
JOURNAL OFFICIEL / Malagasy Republic – v74-86. 1958-70 – 16r – 1 – us Ross [324]
JOURNAL OFFICIEL / Martinique. French West Indies – Port de France. Jan. 6, 1940-Oct. 12, 1940; 1941-1946 – 1 – us NY Public [324]
JOURNAL OFFICIEL / Oubangui-Chari-Tchad – 1907 – 1 – fr A.C.R.P.P. [960]
JOURNAL OFFICIEL – Paris, FR. 1975-1981 – 23r – $1,150.00 – R63611 – us Library Micro [073]
JOURNAL OFFICIEL / Senegal – 1888-95, 1901-27, 1930-39, 1947-58, 1960-66, Juil 1967-71 – 1 – fr A.C.R.P.P. [073]
JOURNAL OFFICIEL / Senegal – Dakar. Feuille officielle du Senegal et dependances. 1856-1961. Gaps – 1 – 35.00r – us Hoover Inst Photo [324]
JOURNAL OFFICIEL / Senegal. Parliament – Debats Parliamentaires de l'Assemblee. St. Louis. 1963-1967, nos. 61-152; 1968, nos. 1-11. Missing: nos. 67-78, 91-124, 128-130 – 1 – 35.00r – us Hoover Inst Photo [324]
JOURNAL OFFICIEL / Silesia. Upper – Commission interalliee de gouvernement et de plebiscite de Haute-Silesie. Oppeln. fevr 1920-juin 1922 – 1 – fr A.C.R.P.P. [073]
JOURNAL OFFICIEL / Togo – 1956-60 – 1 – fr A.C.R.P.P. [073]
JOURNAL OFFICIEL / Tunisia – (1980-. ca $50.00y) – 1970-79 – 17r – 1 – $360.00; outside North America add $1.25r – us L of C Photodup [324]
JOURNAL OFFICIEL / United Arab Republic – v76-94. 1949-67. Cairo. 7 reels – 1 – $60.00r – us Ross [324]
LE JOURNAL OFFICIEL / France – (Yrly mf count varies. Various eds available: Lois et decrets 1869- . Documents de l'Assemblee Nationale. Documents du Senat. Debats de l'Assemblee Nationale. Debats du Senat) – 9 – inquire for prices – us Ross [072]
JOURNAL OFFICIEL DE LA COTE D'IVOIRE / Ivory Coast – 1904-1965. Gaps – 1 – 35.00r – us Hoover Inst Photo [324]
JOURNAL OFFICIEL DE LA GUADELOUPE / Guadeloupe. French West Indies – 1852-1947 – 1 – us UMI [324]
JOURNAL OFFICIEL DE LA HAUTE-VOLTA / Upper Volta – oct 1919-27 – 1 – fr A.C.R.P.P. [960]
JOURNAL OFFICIEL DE LA MARTINIQUE / Martinique. French West Indies – 1834-1947 – 1 – us UMI [324]
JOURNAL OFFICIEL DE LA NOUVELLE-CALEDONIE / New Caledonia – Noumea. v94-112. 1949-67 – 9r – 1 – us Ross [324]
JOURNAL OFFICIEL DE LA POLYNESIE FRANCAISE / Polynesia. French – 1965-70 – 1 – fr A.C.R.P.P. [950]
JOURNAL OFFICIEL DE LA REPUBLIC DU MALI / Mali – puis de la Federation. avril 1959-68 – 1 – fr A.C.R.P.P. [073]
JOURNAL OFFICIEL DE LA REPUBLIQUE ALGERIENNE DEMOCRATIQUE ET POPULAIRE – Algiers, 1953-70 – 20r – 1 – us Ross [324]
JOURNAL OFFICIEL DE LA REPUBLIQUE AUTONOME DU TOGO – v28-32; ns: v3-15. 1947-70 – 12r – 1 – us Ross [324]
JOURNAL OFFICIEL DE LA REPUBLIQUE CENTRAFRICAINE – Bangui. v1-12. 1959-70 – 3r – 1 – us Ross [324]
JOURNAL OFFICIEL DE LA REPUBLIQUE CENTRAFRICAINE / Central African Republic – aout 1959-70 – 1 – fr A.C.R.P.P. [960]
JOURNAL OFFICIEL DE LA REPUBLIQUE DE COTE D'IVOIRE – Abidjan. v1-12. 1958-70 – 10r – 1 – us Ross [324]
JOURNAL OFFICIEL DE LA REPUBLIQUE DE HAUTE-VOLTA / Upper Volta – 1960-70 – 1 – fr A.C.R.P.P. [960]
JOURNAL OFFICIEL DE LA REPUBLIQUE DE HAUTE-VOLTA – v6-12. 1964-70 – 2r – 1 – us Ross [324]
JOURNAL OFFICIEL DE LA REPUBLIQUE DE LA COTE D'IVOIRE / Ivory Coast – 1960-70 – 1 – fr A.C.R.P.P. [960]
JOURNAL OFFICIEL DE LA REPUBLIQUE DU CONGO – Brazzaville, 1958-69 – 6r – 1 – us Ross [324]
JOURNAL OFFICIEL DE LA REPUBLIQUE DU CONGO / Congo. Republic – Brazzaville. 1958-1967 – 1 – us NY Public [960]
JOURNAL OFFICIEL DE LA REPUBLIQUE DU DAHOMEY / Dahomey – dec 1963-nov 1969 – 1 – fr A.C.R.P.P. [960]
JOURNAL OFFICIEL DE LA REPUBLIQUE DU MALI – v2-11. 1960-69 – 7r – 1 – us Ross [324]
JOURNAL OFFICIEL DE LA REPUBLIQUE DU NIGER / Niger – 1933-1959 complete – 1 – 35.00r – us Hoover Inst Photo [324]
JOURNAL OFFICIEL DE LA REPUBLIQUE DU NIGER / Niger – 1959-1967. Niamey – 1 – us NY Public [324]
JOURNAL OFFICIEL DE LA REPUBLIQUE DU NIGER / Niger – 1960-70 – 1 – fr A.C.R.P.P. [960]
JOURNAL OFFICIEL DE LA REPUBLIQUE DU NIGER – v26-35. 1959-68 – 5r – 1 – us Ross [324]
JOURNAL OFFICIEL DE LA REPUBLIQUE DU SENEGAL – v95-114. 1950-69 – 12'r – 1 – us Ross [324]
JOURNAL OFFICIEL DE LA REPUBLIQUE DU TCHAD – Fort-Lamy, 1959-66 – 3r – 1 – us Ross [324]
JOURNAL OFFICIEL DE LA REPUBLIQUE FEDERALE DU CAMEROUN – Yaounde, 1956-70 – 15r – 1 – us Ross [324]
JOURNAL OFFICIEL DE LA REPUBLIQUE FRANCAISE / France – 1789- – 1 – us UMI [324]
JOURNAL OFFICIEL DE LA REPUBLIQUE FRANCAISE / France – (5 sept 1870-80. 1. Ed. du soir. 6 sept 1870-19 mars 1871. 1) – fr A.C.R.P.P. [323]
JOURNAL OFFICIEL DE LA REPUBLIQUE FRANCAISE / France – (8 sept 1944-86. 1,5) – 1881-1924, 25 aout 1944 – 1 – fr A.C.R.P.P. [323]
JOURNAL OFFICIEL DE LA REPUBLIQUE FRANCAISE / France – La Commune. Ed. du matin. 20 mars-24 mai 1871 et ed. du soir 21 mars-19 mai 1871 – 1 – fr A.C.R.P.P. [323]
JOURNAL OFFICIEL DE LA REPUBLIQUE FRANCAISE / France – Lois et decrets depuis 1869. Approx. 300 fiches per year – 9 – fr Journal Officiel [340]
JOURNAL OFFICIEL DE LA REPUBLIQUE FRANCAISE : LOIS ET DECRETS – 1921- – 9 – inquire – us Ross [340]
JOURNAL OFFICIEL DE LA REPUBLIQUE GABONAISE / Gabon – juil 1959-70 – 1 – fr A.C.R.P.P. [960]
JOURNAL OFFICIEL DE LA REPUBLIQUE GABONAISE – Libreville, [Gabon]. v1-11. 1959-69 – 5r – 1 – us Ross [324]
JOURNAL OFFICIEL DE LA REPUBLIQUE GUINEE – Guinea-Conakry. v1-12. 1958-70 – 3r – 1 – us Ross [324]
JOURNAL OFFICIEL DE LA REPUBLIQUE ISLAMIQUE DE MAURITANIE / Mauritania – 1959-sept 1969 – 1 – fr A.C.R.P.P. [960]
JOURNAL OFFICIEL DE LA REPUBLIQUE ISLAMIQUE DE MAURITANIE – Mauritania. v9. 1967 – 1r – 1 – us Ross [324]
JOURNAL OFFICIEL DE LA REPUBLIQUE KHMERE / Cambodia – Phnom Penh. Bi-weekly. Oct. 10, 1970-Jun 30, 1973. Formerly: Journal Officiel du Cambodge. Incomplete – 1 – us UMI [950]
JOURNAL OFFICIEL DE LA REPUBLIQUE SOUDANAISE / Sudan – janv-sept 1960 – 1 – fr A.C.R.P.P. [073]
JOURNAL OFFICIEL DE LA REPUBLIQUE TUNISIENNE – Tunisia. v67-75, 101-111. 1949-68 – 20r – 1 – us Ross [324]
JOURNAL OFFICIEL DE L'AFRIQUE OCCIDENTALE FRANCAISE / France – Paris. Jan. 1905-Aug. 1959. Missing v. 54, nos. 2972-2974 – 1 – 35.00r – us Hoover Inst Photo [960]

JOURNAL OFFICIEL DE L'EMPIRE FRANCAIS / France – (Ed. du matin. 1869-4 sept 1870. 1. Ed. du soir. 1869-5 sept 1870. 1) – fr A.C.R.P.P. [323]
JOURNAL OFFICIEL DE MADAGASCAR / Malagasy Republic – nov 1957-69 – 1 – fr A.C.R.P.P. [960]
LE JOURNAL OFFICIEL DES COMMUNAUTES EUROPEENES – (Publ also available in English and other languages of Europe) – 1971- – 9 – inquire – us Ross [340]
JOURNAL OFFICIEL DES ILES SAINT-PIERRE ET MIQUELON – Saint-Pierre and Miquelon. v79-105. 1944-70 – 11r – 1 – us Ross [324]
JOURNAL OFFICIEL DES POSSESSIONS DU CONGO FRANCAIS / Congo. (French) – juil 1904-10 – 1 – fr A.C.R.P.P. [960]
JOURNAL OFFICIEL DU CAMBODGE / Cambodia – Phnom Penh. 1958?-Oct 7, 1970. Bi-weekly. Incomplete – 1 – us UMI [950]
JOURNAL OFFICIEL DU CAMBODGE – Cambodia. v14-17. 1958-61 – 6r – 1 – us Ross [324]
JOURNAL OFFICIEL DU GOUVERNEMENT EGYPTIEN / Egypt – Cairo. Jan 1922-Dec 1938 gaps – 1 – 35.00r – us Hoover Inst Photo [956]
JOURNAL OFFICIEL DU HAUT-SENEGAL-NIGER – aout 1906-21 – 1 – fr A.C.R.P.P. [960]
JOURNAL OFFICIEL DU ROYAUME DU LAOS – Vientiane, [Laos]. v3-18. 1955-70 – 7r – 1 – us Ross [324]
JOURNAL OFFICIEL DU TCHAD / Chad – oct 1959-67 – 1 – fr A.C.R.P.P. [960]
JOURNAL OFFICIEL DU TERRITOIRE DU NIGER / Niger – 1938-39 – 1 – fr A.C.R.P.P. [073]
JOURNAL OFICIEL... / Somaliland. French – (Lacks 6 issues) – 1955-63 – 3r – 1 – us Ross [960]
JOURNAL, PERKIN TRANSACTIONS 1 / Chemical Society. London – 1972-75 – 1,5,6 – us Princeton Micro [540]
JOURNAL, PERKIN TRANSACTIONS 2 / Chemical Society. London – 1972-75 – 1,5,6 – us Princeton Micro [540]
JOURNAL PIE – no. 1-15. Paris. janv-mars 1792. suivi de: Journal royaliste voir a ce titre – 1 – fr A.C.R.P.P. [073]
JOURNAL POLITIQUE ET COMMERCIAL DE LA POINTE-A-PITRE – devenu: Journal commercial, economique et maritime de la Pointe-a-Pitre. devenu: Journal commercial de Pointe-a-Pitre. Pointe-a-Pitre. 1819-31 – 1 – fr A.C.R.P.P. [073]
LE JOURNAL POPULAIRE : CATHOLIQUE – Montreal, Canada. 29 mar 1894-31 mai 1895 – 1r – 1 – Can$30.00 – cn Can Microfilming [072]
JOURNAL POUR TOUS – Ottawa, Ontario. 27 jul 1878-v1 n50. 14 aut 1879 – 1r – 1 – Can$35.00 – cn Can Microfilming [072]
JOURNAL POUR TOUS – Ottawa: P N Bureau, [1878-1880] – 9 – cn C.I.H.M. [073]
JOURNAL, PRESBYTERIAN HISTORICAL SOCIETY – v1-39. 1901-61. Superseded by Journal of Presbyterian History – 1 – us UMI [240]
JOURNAL PRESS DISPATCH – Redwood City. Calif. -w. 1949-54 – 1 – us UMI [071]
JOURNAL REFLEXE – Ville d'Anjou. v1 n13. 26 mar 1970-v1 n17. 28 avr 1970 – 1r – 1 – Can$25.00 – cn Can Microfilming [072]
JOURNAL, REPORT AND LETTERBOOK, 1882-1906 / Gray, William – 1r – at Pacific Mss [980]
JOURNAL REVOLUTIONNAIRE DE TOULOUSE – ou Le Surveillant du Midi. no. 1-104. Toulouse. sept 1793-sept 1794 – 1 – fr A.C.R.P.P. [073]
JOURNAL ROYALISTE – Par M. le Comte de Barruel-Beauvert. Paris. mars-aout 1792 (I-II). suite de: Journal pie voir a ce titre – 1 – fr A.C.R.P.P. [073]
LE JOURNAL (SAINT-BRUNO-DE-MONTARVILLE, QUEBEC, 1968) – St. Bruno. v1-10. 1968-77. SEM35P275 – 6r – 1 – Can$260.00 – cn Bibl Nat [072]
LE JOURNAL SAINT-BRUNO-DE-MONTARVILLE, QUEBEC, 1979) – St. Bruno. v12-16. 1979-82. SEM35P277 – 4r – 1 – Can$158.00 – cn Bibl Nat [072]
JOURNAL, SECTION A: INORGANIC, PHYSICAL, AND THEORETICAL CHEMISTRY / Chemical Society. London – 1966-1971 – 1,5,6 – us Princeton Micro [540]
JOURNAL, SECTION B: PHYSICAL ORGANIC CHEMISTRY / Chemical Society. London – 1966-1971 – 1,5,6 – us Princeton Micro [540]
JOURNAL, SECTION C: ORGANIC CHEMISTRY / Chemical Society. London – 1966-1971 – 1,5,6 – us Princeton Micro [540]
JOURNAL, SECTION D: CHEMICAL COMMUNICATIONS / Chemical Society. London – 1965-75 – 1,5,6 – us Princeton Micro [540]
JOURNAL STANDARD – Falls Church. Va. -w. 1946- – 1 – us UMI [071]
JOURNAL STANDARD – Freeport. Ill. 1914- – 1 – us UMI [071]
JOURNAL STAR – Peoria. Ill. (Morning and Evening). 1955- – 1 – us UMI [071]
JOURNAL TELEGRAPHIQUE – v2-57. 1872-1933. See also: Journal des Telecommunications – 1,5,6 – us Princeton Micro [380]
LE JOURNAL TEMISCAMIEN – Ville-Marie, Canada. 27 jun 1974; v1 n1. 22 aut 1974 – 1r – 1 – Can$25.00 – cn Can Microfilming [072]
JOURNAL TOWN AND COUNTRY ADVERTISER – Providence. R.I. 1799-1801 – 1 – us UMI [071]
JOURNAL TRIBUNE – Marysville. Ohio. 1971- – 1 – us UMI [071]
JOURNAL UNIVERSEL – no. 1-20. Gand. 14 avr-21 juin 1815. Connu sous le nom de: Moniteur de Gand – 1 – fr A.C.R.P.P. [073]
JOURNAL UNIVERSEL – ou Revolution des royaumes. Par Audouin. Paris. nov 1789-oct 1791 – 1 – fr A.C.R.P.P. [073]
JOURNAL VERDUN = VERDUN JOURNAL – Verdun, Canada. 26 oct 1953 – 1r – 1 – Can$25.00 – cn Can Microfilming [072]
LA JOURNAL VRAI – 1932-34 – 1 – fr A.C.R.P.P. [073]
THE JOURNAL, WITH OTHER WRITINGS.. / Woolman, John – London & Toronto: J.M. Dent & sons Ltd.; New York: E.P. Dutton, 1922. xix,250p. (Everyman's Library, ed. by Ernest Rhys. Biography. No.402) – 1 – us U.W. Library [920]
JOURNAL-AMERICAN – New York. N.Y. 1937-1966 – 1 – us UMI [071]
JOURNAL-COMPASS – Coronado. Calif. -w. 1948-52 – 1 – us UMI [071]
JOURNAL-DEMOCRAT – Dodge City. Kan. 1905-1908 – 1 – us UMI [071]
JOURNALISM AND POLITICS – (Series One: The Papers of C.P. Scott, 1846-1932 from the John Rylands University Library of Manchester; Part 1: C.P. Scott's General Correspondence ca 1870-1934, and Political Diaries, 1911-1928) – Marlborough: Adam Matthew Publications, 1992 – 22r – 1 – $2,600.00 – uk Matthew [070]
JOURNALISM HISTORY – v1- 1974- 1; v4-1977- 5,6,9 – us UMI [380]
LE JOURNALISTE CANADIEN-FRANCAIS – Montreal, Canada. jul 1926-v2 n4. oct 1927; ns: v1 n5. sep 1955; v4 n29. aut/sep 1960 – 1r – 1 – Can$35.00 – cn Can Microfilming [072]
LE JOURNALISTE OU L'AMI DES MOEURS / Lombard De Langres – (French Theatre Series). Paris. Barba. 1797 – 9 – fr Hachette [820]
JOURNALISTIEK OP JAVA / Wormser, C W – Deventer, 1941 – 1mf – 9 – SE-1447/1 – ne IDC [070]
JOURNAL-REGISTER – Hebron. Neb. and preds. 1892-1969 – 1 – us UMI [071]
JOURNAL-REPUBLICAN – Massac. Ill. 1916-1920 – 1 – us UMI [071]
JOURNALS / Allen County. Ohio. Circuit Court – 1885-1912 – 2r – 1 – $32.50r – us Archival [324]
JOURNALS / Allen County. Ohio. Common Pleas. Criminal Div – 1861-1933 – 8r – 1 – $32.50r – us Archival [324]
JOURNALS / Allen County. Ohio. Common Pleas. Juvenile Div – 1906-1948 – 4r – 1 – $32.50r – us Archival [324]
JOURNALS / Allen County. Ohio. District Court – 1861-1884 – 1r – 1 – $32.50r – us Archival [324]
JOURNALS / Canada. Parliament. House of Commons – 28th-34th Parliaments. 1970-93 – 5 – cn Micromedia [324]
JOURNALS / Canada. Parliament. Senate – 1970-93. 28th-34th Parliaments – 5 – cn Micromedia [324]
JOURNALS / Dickinson County. Kansas. Board of Commissioners – 1861-83 – 1 – us KS Hist [978]
JOURNALS / Ford County. Kansas. Board of Commissioners – 1873-1904 – 1 – us KS Hist [978]
JOURNALS / Fulton County. Ohio. Common Pleas. Civil Division – 1850-1861 – 1r – 1 – $32.50r – us Archival [324]
JOURNALS / Fulton County. Ohio. Probate Court – 1864-1959 – 25r – 1 – $32.50r – us Archival [324]
JOURNALS / Hardin County, Ohio. Probate Court – 1886-1909 – 5r – 1 – $32.50r – us Archival [324]
JOURNALS / Heintzelman, Samuel – 1854-55 – 1 – 255.00 – us L of C Photodup [920]
JOURNALS / Henry County. Ohio. Common Pleas. Civil Division – 1847-1870 – 2r – 1 – $32.50r – us Archival [324]
JOURNALS / Henry County. Ohio. District Court – 1852-1884 – 1r – 1 – $32.50r – us Archival [324]
JOURNALS / Henry County. Ohio. Supreme Court – 1847-1877 – 1r – 1 – $32.50r – us Archival [324]
JOURNALS / Huron County. Ohio. Common Pleas. Civil Division – 1817-1879 – 9r – 1 – $32.50r – us Archival [324]
JOURNALS / Huron County. Ohio. Supreme Court – 1874 – 1r – 1 – $32.50r – us Archival [340]
JOURNALS / Isham, William S – 1886-1895, Diary entries, copies of letters, and other documents relating to Isham's duties as a constable and businessman in Ohio; Winona, Minnesota; and Superior, Nebraska – 1 – us KS Hist [920]
JOURNALS / Jamaica. Assembly – v1-14. 1663-1826 – 5r – 1 – us Ross [324]
JOURNALS / Leathers, Harrison – 1862-1865 – 1r – 1 – $32.50r – us Archival [976]
JOURNALS / Lucas County. Ohio. Board of County Commissioners – 1835-1973 – 78r – 1 – $32.50r – us Archival [324]
JOURNALS / Lucas County. Ohio. Common Pleas. Civil Division – 1835-1940 – 124r – 1 – $32.50r – us Archival [324]
JOURNALS / Menkel, Peter – 1875-1897 – 1 – $50.00 – us Presbyterian [920]
JOURNALS / Prince Edward Island. House of Assembly – 1867-1920; Legislative Council. Debates, Journals and Proceedings. To 1893; Statutes; Index to Journals and Debates – 28r – 1 – $1,820.00 set – cn Library Assoc [971]
JOURNALS / Putnam County. Ohio. Probate Court – 1853-1889 – 4r – 1 – $32.50r – us Archival [324]
JOURNALS / Saskatchewan. Legislative Assembly – 1906-20 – 9r – 1 – $585.00 – cn Library Assoc [971]
JOURNALS / Sheldon, Henry Olcott – 1817-82 – 3r – 1 – $32.50r – us Archival [073]
JOURNALS / Sheldon, Henry Olcott – 1817-82.3 reels – 1 – us Archival [920]
JOURNALS / Van Wert County. Ohio. Common Pleas. Civil Division – 1837-1907 – 12r – 1 – $32.50r – us Archival [324]
JOURNALS / Van Wert County. Ohio. District Court – 1842-1884 – 1r – 1 – $32.50r – us Archival [324]
JOURNALS / Van Wert County. Ohio. Probate Court – 1852-1910 – 8r – 1 – $32.50r – us Archival [324]
JOURNALS / Walker, William – undated, Journals of William Walker, the provisional governor of Nebraska Territory, edited by William E. Connelley – 1 – us KS Hist [920]
JOURNALS / Wood County. Ohio. Common Pleas. Civil Division – 1820-1935 – 35r – 1 – $32.50r – us Archival [324]
JOURNALS / Wyandot County. Ohio. Probate Court – 1883-1914 – 6r – 1 – $32.50r – us Archival [324]
JOURNALS, 1764, 1783, 1785, 1788, 1792-1799 / Bosanquet, M – (Coll title: The People Called Methodists, Phase 2: Primary Sources 1738-1800) – 4mf – 9 – MP-620/1 – ne IDC [240]
JOURNALS, 1790, 1792, 1794-1795, 1797-1798, 1800-1806 / Bosanquet, M – (Coll title: The People Called Methodists, Phase 2: Primary Sources 1738-1800) – 4mf – 9 – MP-621/1 – ne IDC [240]
JOURNALS, 1765-1794 / Valton, J – (Coll title: The People Called Methodists, Phase 2: Primary Sources 1738-1800) – 31mf – 9 – MP-636/1 – ne IDC [240]
JOURNALS, 1796-1807, 1813-1814, 1832-1833, 1837-1842 / Tooth, M – (Coll title: The People Called Methodists, Phase 3: Primary Sources, 1801-1850) – 12mf – 9 – MP-680/1 – ne IDC [240]
JOURNALS, 1803-1804, 1808-1813, 1816-1820, 1842-1852 / Bourne, H – (Coll title: The People Called Methodists, Phase 3: Primary Sources, 1801-1850) – 38mf – 9 – MP-684/1 – ne IDC [240]
JOURNALS, 1807-1815 / Bosanquet, M – (Coll title: The People Called Methodists, Phase 2: Primary Sources 1738-1800) – 2mf – 9 – MP-622/1 – ne IDC [240]
JOURNALS, 1875-97; ESTATE, 1897-99 / Sewell, J F – 34 fiche – 9 – sa SA Libr [960]
JOURNALS AND APPENDICES / Canada. Upper Canada. House of Assembly – 13 Jan 1825-10 Feb 1840.Printed index available – 1 – cn Commonwealth Micro [072]
JOURNALS AND ESSAYS / Todd, John P – 1809-1830 – 1 – $50.00 – us Presbyterian [240]
JOURNALS AND LETTERS / Rice, Luther – 1815-23.381p – 1 – 13.33 – us Baptist [240]
JOURNALS AND MINUTES OF THE PENNSYLVANIA ASSEMBLY, 1776-1790 / Pennsylvania. Assembly – 1975 – 3r – 1 – $255.00 – S1864 – us Scholarly Res [978]
JOURNALS AND SERMONS / Simpson, Archibald – 1748-84. 64 fiches – 9 – us South Carolina Historical [240]
JOURNALS, BRIDGES, ROADS, DITCHES / Van Wert County. Ohio. Board of County Commissioners – 1838-1930 – 1r – 1 – $32.50r – us Archival [324]
JOURNALS, BRIGANTINE HOPE / Ingraham, Joseph – 1790-92 – 1 – $18.00 – us L of C Photodup [920]
JOURNALS, COUNTY HOME / Fulton County. Ohio. Board of County Commissioners – 1913-1928 – 1r – 1 – $32.50r – us Archival [324]
JOURNALS, COUNTY HOME / Henry County. Ohio. Board of County Commissioners – 1913-1987 – 2r – 1 – $32.50r – us Archival [324]
JOURNALS, COUNTY HOME / Ottawa County. Ohio. Board of County Commissioners – 1927-1951 – 1r – 1 – $32.50r – us Archival [324]
JOURNALS, COUNTY HOME / Wood County. Ohio. Board of County Commissioners – 1938-1953 – 2r – 1 – $32.50r – us Archival [324]
JOURNALS IN MICROFORM – (Catalog avail. on request) – 1,9 – us Alper [073]
JOURNALS, LEDGERS, MEMO BOOK / Rice, Luther – 1810-26. 758p – 1 – 26.53 – us Baptist [240]
JOURNALS OF ALL THE PARLIAMENTS DURING REIGN OF ELISABETH, BOTH LORDS AND COMMONS / Simonds D'Ewes – London. 1682 – 33mf – 8 – ne IDC [941]
JOURNALS OF THE ASSEMBLY OF JAMAICA, 1663-1826 / Jamaica. Assembly – (With printed guide) – 1972 – 7r – 1 – $595.00 – S1843 – us Scholarly Res [972]
JOURNALS OF THE CONTINENTAL CONGRESS / U.S. Continental Congress – v1-34. 1774-89 (all publ) – 167mf – 9 – $250.00 – LLMC 78-080 – us L.L.M.C. [323]
JOURNALS OF THE CONTINENTAL CONGRESS *see*
- INDEX TO THE JOURNALS OF THE CONTINENTAL CONGRESS, 1774-1789
- INDEX TO THE PAPERS OF THE CONTINENTAL CONGRESS, 1774-1789
- SECRET JOURNAL OF THE CONTINENTAL CONGRESS, 1775-1788

JOURNALS OF THE CONTINENTAL CONGRESS, 1774-1789 / U.S. Continental Congress – 1904-37. 1774-80 ONLY – 4r – 1 – $140.00 – Dist. us Scholarly Res – us L of C Photodup [324]
JOURNALS OF THE HOUSE OF BURGESSES OF VIRGINIA, 1619-1776 / Virginia. House of Burgesses; ed by Kennedy, John Pendleton & McIlwaine, Henry Read – (Includes printed guide) – 1985 – 4r – 1 – $340.00 – S1856 – Co-publ with the Virginia State Library – us Scholarly Res [978]
JOURNALS OF THE SHIP LLOYD, 1767-72 / Lloyd. (Ship) – From National Maritime Museum, Greenwich. BRRAM – 1 – uk Microform Academic [910]

THE JOURNALS OF THOMAS A. DORNIN, U.S. NAVY / Dornin, Thomas A – 1826-55. 1 roll. M981 – 1 – us Nat'l Archives [324]
JOURNALS OF TRIP TO LIBERIA, 1868 / Pinney, John B – Also: letters pertaining to the liberian college. 1879. 352p – 1 – 12.32 – us Baptist [240]
JOURNAL...SUR L'ENFANCE ET LA JEUNESSE DE LOUIS XIII (1601-1628) / Heroard, Jean – (v2. 1610-1628. Paris: F. Didot, 1868. 03764) – v1. 1601-10. Paris, F. Didot, 1868. 03763. (Pre-1900 Canadiana) – 9 – cn C.I.H.M. [920]
JOURNAL-TIMES – Racine. Wis. 1856-1866; 1881- – 1 – us UMI [071]
JOURNAUX, CHAMBRE D'ASSEMBLEE, BAS-CANADA = JOURNALS, HOUSE ASSEMBLY, LOWER-CANADA – Quebec, 17 dec 1792-26 aut 1837 – 18r – 1 – Can$30.00r – cn Can Microfilming [324]
JOURNAUX, CONSEIL LEGISLATIF, BAS-CANADA = JOURNALS, LEGISLATIVE COUNCIL, LOWER CANADA – Quebec, 1792-1837 – 4r – 1 – Can$50.00r – cn Can Microfilming [324]
JOURNAUX DIVERS – (Includes: Il Secolo, Milano v36 n12518 24-26 fev 1901. Avanti, Roma v5 n1515 28 fev 1901. Dibattimenti, Roma v4 n8 24 fev 1901. Il Messagero, Roma v23 n59 28 fev 1901. Il Nuovo Fan Fulla, Roma v2 n57 28 fev 1901. L'Osservatore Romano, Roma v41 n46 24 fev 1901. La Patria, Roma v2 n54 23 fev 1901 + v2 n56 25 fev 1901. Il Travaso, Roma v2 n8 24 fev 1901) – 1r – 1 – Can$40.00 – cn Can Microfilming [072]
JOURNAUX DU CONSEIL SPECIAL DU BAS-CANADA – Quebec, Canada. 18 avr 1838-9 fev 1841 – 1r – 1 – Can$35.00 – cn Can Microfilming [324]
JOURNAUX PUBLIES PAR LES PRISONNIERS DE GUERRE ALLEMANDS EN FRANCE 1946-1948 / Germany – (AUFKLAERER (DER). Depot 135.- Clermont-Ferrand. AUSBLICK. Depot 94. – Angouleme. AUSLESE (DIE). Depot 164.- Nimes. BAUSTEIN (DER). Der Rundblick des Depot 141.- Saint-Fons. BERGEWART devient DER LAGERSPIEGEL. Depot 155.- Chambery. BRUECKE (DIE). Depot 131.- Clermont-Ferrand. CHAMP DE MARS RUNDSCHAU.- La Rochelle. DEPOT ECHO. Depot 153. DEPOT ZEITUNG.- Valenciennes. DROME-ARDECHE. Depot 147.- Montelimar. ECHO. Depot 121.- Saint-Paul-d'Eyjeaux (Haute-Vienne). ECHO (DAS) DES LAGERS 301.- Cherbourg. GEMEINSCHAFT (DIE). Depot 223. – Villeneuve-Saint-Georges. HAUTVILLER ZEITUNG.- Dijon) – 11 reels – 1 – fr A.C.R.P.P. [943]
JOURNAUX PUBLIES PAR LES PRISONNIERS DE GUERRE ALLEMANDS EN FRNACE 1946-1948, 2 – (HEUTE UND MORGEN DEPOT 172.- Vernet d'Ariege. IN DER FREMDE. Depot 133.- Brioude. KAMERAD (DER) AUS AMBROISE DES DEPOT PGA 41. KLEINE WELT. Depot 124. – Gueret. KUBUCK (DER). Depot 103.- Haguenau. L.I.D. LAGER INFORMATIONS DIENST. Depot 15.- Bizerte. LAGER BOTE. Depot 85.- Besancon. LAGER (DAS) ECHO. Depot 101.- Mutzig. LAGERBOTE (DER). Depot 125.- Brantome. LAGERBOTE (DER). Depot 132.- Allier-Troncais. LAGER POST (DIE). Depot 171.- Camp des Sables (Haute-Savoie). LAGER POST (DIE). Depot 201. – Epinal. LAGER ZEITUNG DES LAGERS 91.- Poitiers. LAGER ZEITUNG DES LAGERS 127.- Chateauroux. LAGER ZEITUNG DES P.G. DES DEPOT 88. – Lons-le-Saunier. LAGER ZEITUNG P.G. DEPOT 158.- Gap (Hautes-Alpes). LAGER ZEITUNG.- Neuland. LAGER ZEITUNG. Depot 82. Zaunkoenig. – Chalon-sur-Saone. LAGER ZEITUNG. Depot 142.- Bourg-en-Bresse. LAGER ZEITUNG. P.G. Depot 102.- Colmar. LAGER ZEITUNG. Depot 151. – Marseille. LAGER ZEITUNG. Depot 163.- Larzac (Aveyron). LAGER ZEITUNG. Depot 105.- Strasbourg. LAGER ZEITUNG (DIE). Depot 189.- Bayonne. LAGER ZEITUNG. Depot 104.- Mulhouse. LAGER ZEITUNG 128. Depot 402.- Thoree. MISTRAL. Depot 154.- Sorgues (Vancluse). N.T.N. Neueste Tremoulier Nachrichter.- Tulle. NACHRICHT (DIE).- Grenoble. NACHRICHTER (DER). – Rouen. NACHSCHLAG. Lager Post.- Nevers. NEUE LAGER ZEITUNG. Depot 15. – Bizerte. PAROLE (DIE). Depot 134.- Cantal. PAROLE (DIE). Lagerzeitung des Depot 221.- Cormeilles. RING (DER).- Laon. RIVIERA BOTE. Depot 159. – Nice. RUNDSCHAU (DIE). Depot. 224.- Evreux. STACHELDRAHT (DER). Depot 152.- Aubagne. STACHELDRAHT FUNK devient DER WEGWEISER.- Lens. UMSCHAU. Depot 22.- Beauvais. UNSER NACHRICHTENBLATT.- Belfort. UNTER UNS.- Metz. WELT (DIE) UND WIR. Depot 92.- Vendee. ZAUNGAST. Depot 114.- Lorient. ZEITSPIEGEL (DER). Depot 183.- St-Medard-en-Jalles (Gironde). ZITADELLE (DIE). Depot 23.- Amiens) – 11 bobines cont'd – 1 – fr A.C.R.P.P. [943]
JOURNEAUX DES SIEGES...ESPAGNE / Jones, John T – 1821 – 9 – 1.50f – sp Bibl Santa Ana [946]
LA JOURNEE DE LA PETITE MENAGERE / Valette – Paris: D. Delarue, n.d. 239p. (Les Femmes Collection) – 3mf – 9 – $8.00 – fr Bibl Nationale [640]
LA JOURNEE INDUSTRIELLE – Quotidien de l'industrie, du commerce et de l'agriculture. Fond. Et. Bernard-Precy. Paris. 14 mars 1918-38, janv-juin 1940 – 1 – fr A.C.R.P.P. [073]
LA JOURNEE RELIGIEUSE OU INSTRUCTIONS PRATIQUES / Saint-Pierre, Antoine de – Paris. v1-2. 1869 – v1 5mf; v2 4mf – 8 – Dfl32.00 – ne Slangenburg [240]
JOURNEES D'INFORMATION ET DE DISCUSSION SUR LE DEVELOPPEMENT INDUSTRIEL DE L'ALGERIE / Algeria. Centre European pour le Developpement Industriel – 1970. BNE-8619 1 – 9 – ne IDC [330]
A JOURNEY FROM PRINCE OF WALES'S FORT IN HUDSON'S BAY, TO THE NORTHERN OCEAN / Hearne, S – BN 247 2. 1795 – 8 – ne IDC [910]
A JOURNEY TO CANADA / Gurney, Jane Tritton – 1887?. 05133. (Pre-1900 Canadiana) – 9 – cn C.I.H.M. [910]
THE JOURNEYMAN, AND ARTIZANS' LONDON AND PROVINCIAL CHRONICLE – London. -w. 12 Jun-4 Sep 1825. (14 ft) – 1 – uk British Libr Newspaper [330]
JOURNEYS AMONG THE GENTLE JAPS IN THE SUMMER OF 1895, WITH A SPECIAL CHAPTER ON THE RELIGIONS OF JAPAN / Thomas, Joseph Llewelyn – London: S. Low, Marston, 1897. x,266p. fold. map – 1 – us U.W. Library [950]
JOURNEY'S BEHIND THE NEWS: SCRIPTS – 1941-57 – 1 – 2284.00 – us Princeton Micro [380]
JOURS DE GUINEE / Espagnat, Pierre d' – Paris, Librairie academique Didier, Perrin et Cie. 1899 – 9 – 10.00 – fr Orientalistes [960]
JOURS TROUBLES, PAGES D'EPOPEE AFRICAINE / Dufays, Felix – Ixelles, Belgium: R Weverbergh, 1928 – us Res Libr [960]
Jousse, Mathurin *see*
– L'ART DE CHARPENTERIE.
– L'ART DE CHARPENTERIE DE MATHURIN JOUSSE
– LE SECRET D'ARCHITECTURE.
Jousset, Edouard *see* INFLUENCE DES MACHINES SUR LA CLASSE OUVRIERE
Jouvancy, Joseph de *see* DE LA MANIERE D'APPRENDRE ET D'ENSEIGNER
Jouve, J *see* THE FOREST OF HERMANSTADT. A MELODRAMA, IN TWO ACTS
Jouy *see* LA VESTALE
Jouy, Esmerard *see* FERNAND CORTEZ OU LA CONQUETE DU MEXIQUE
Jouy (ouvrier menusier) *see* ADDRESSE AUX PROLETAIRES ET OUVRIERS FRANCAIS SUR LA SITUATION PRESENTE.
Jovellanos, Melchor Gaspar de *see*
– CARTA SOBRE LA LONJA DE MALLORCA
– ELOGIO DE CARLOS 3
– ELOGIO DE VENTURA RODRIGUEZ
– INFORME SOBRE JUEGOS, ESPECTACULOS Y DIVERSIONES PUBLICAS
– INFORME SOBRE LEY AGRARIA
– MEMORIA EN QUE SE REBATEN CALUMNIAS CONTRA LA JUNTA CENTRAL
– MEMORIAS SOBRE EL CASTILLO DE BELLVER
EL JOVEN Y EL ZAPATERO / Mendoza, Antonio – 1846 – 9 – 1.50f – sp Bibl Santa Ana [830]
LA JOVEN Y EL ZAPATERO / Muscat, Eduardo y – 1846 – 9 – 1.50f – sp Bibl Santa Ana [830]
Jovin, Tom *see* BIOIMAGING
Jowett, Benjamin *see* EPISTLES OF ST PAUL TO THE THESSALONIANS, GALATIANS AND ROMANS: WITH CRITICAL NOTES AND DISSERTATIONS
Jowett, John Henry *see*
– EPISTLES OF ST PETER
– HIGH CALLING: MEDITATIONS ON ST PAUL'S LETTER TO THE PHILIPPIANS
Jowitt, P W *see*
– CIVIL ENGINEERING SYSTEMS
– TEACHING AIDS IN HYDROLOGY
JOY DAVIS INDEX *see*
– INDEX TO THE NORTHERN TERRITORY TIMES AND GAZETTE
THE JOY OF SERVICE / Miller, James Russell – New York: Thomas Y Crowell, c1898 – 1mf – 9 – 0-8370-7243-3 – 1986-1243 – us A.T.L.A. [240]
Joyce, James Wayland *see*
– ACTS OF THE CHURCH, 1531-1885
– HANDBOOK OF THE CONVOCATIONS, OR, PROVINCIAL SYNODS OF THE CHURCH OF ENGLAND
– THE SWORD AND THE KEYS
Joyce, Joseph Asbury *see*
– ADOPTION AND LEGITIMATION OF CHILDREN
– A TREATISE ON ELECTRIC LAW, COVERING THE LAW GOVERNING ALL ELECTRIC CORPORATIONS, USES AND APPLIANCES.
– TREATISE ON THE LAW GOVERNING NUISANCES.
Joyce, Patrick Weston *see* THE STORY OF ANCIENT IRISH CIVILISATION
JOYEULSE ADVENUE ET NOUVELLE ENTREE DES ROY ET ROYNE...EN CESTE VILLE DE NANTES (1518) / Praud de la Nicolliere-Teijeiro, Stephane – 19th cent – 1 – F120.50 – fr Armell [910]
JOYEUSE ENTREE DE L'EMPEREUR MAXIMILIEN I A GAND, EN 1508 / Volkaersbeke, P K de – (Description d'un livre perdu). O 1091 1. 1850 – 9 – ne IDC [920]
Joyner, A Barry *see* DESCRIPTIVE AND PREDICTIVE DISCRIMINANT ANALYSIS OF THE GOLF ABILITY OF COLLEGE MALES
JOYRIDE : MANIFESTATIONS OF THE 1890S BICYCLE CRAZE IN TORONTO / Cossarin, Mark A & Morrow, Don – 1993 – 2mf – 9 – $8.00 – us Microform Publ [790]
JOZEF FLAWJUSZ DZIEJE WOJNY ZYDOWSKIEJ PRZECIWKO RZYMIANOM / Josephus, Flavius – 1906. 573p. ill – 1 – us U.W. Library [930]
JOZEF PILSUDSKI, JAKIM GO ZNALEM / Wasilewski, Leon – Warszawa: "Roj", 1935. 233p. 1 reel. 1247 – 1 – us U.W. Library [920]
JOZEF PILSUDSKI PAMPHLET COLLECTION – 1919-1959 – 1 reel – 1 – CSUXANL6743-B – us Hoover Inst Photo [947]
JPL NEWS – Montreal, Quebec. Jan/Feb 1982-Mar 1983 – 1 – us A.J.P.C. [072]
JPRS *see* TRANSDEX
JQ. JOURNALISM QUARTERLY – v1- 1924- 1; v46- 5,6; v52- 9 – us UMI [070]
JR – v1-. 1984- – 1,5,6,9 – us UMI [073]
J.R. GRAVES : LIFE, TIMES AND TEACHINGS / Hailey, O L – 1909 – 1 – $5.00 – us Baptist [240]
DE J.S.E'ER – Eindhoven. v-3. 1936-1939 – 8mf – 9 – ne IDC [949]
JSK-MITTEILUNGSBLATT *see* SOZIALISTISCHE WARTE
JUAN D. PERON : EL PENSAMIENTO Y AMOR A LOS HUMILDES DEL PRIMER TRABAJADOR ARGENTINO – [N.P. 1946?] – 1 – CSUXADP9928-B – us Hoover Inst Photo [320]
JUAN DE BORBONY BATTEMBERG / Estrella Estralla, Jose Emilio – Madrid: Graf. Menor, 1966 – sp Bibl Santa Ana [920]
JUAN DE LA TORRE (DE J.A. LAVALLE. INFORME) / Fernandez Duro, Cesareo – Madrid: Fortanet, 1885. B.R.A.H. vii/pp. 223-228 – 1 – sp Bibl Santa Ana [920]
Juan de los Angeles *see*
– DIALOGOS DE LA CONQUISTA...DIOS
– OBRAS MISTICAS DEL ANOTADAS Y PRECEDIDAS DE UNA INTRODUCCION...POR EL P. FR. JAIME SALA. PARTE 1...
– OBRAS MISTICAS...OBRA PREPARADA POR EL P. FR. JAIME SALA Y REVISADA POR EL P. FR. GREGORIO FUENTES...
– EL REINO DE DIOS
– TRIUMPHOS DEL AMOR DE DIOS
JUAN DE LOS ANGELES...EN LA INMACULADA EN LA LITERATURA FRANCISCANO-ESPANOLA / Uribe, Angel – Archivo Ibero Americano, 1955 – 1 – sp Bibl Santa Ana [240]
JUAN DE PADILLA / Barrantes Moreno, Vicente – 1855-56. 2 tomas – 9 – $1.50f – sp Bibl Santa Ana [920]
JUAN DE SAN ESTEBAN O DE SAUCEDILLA. JUAN TORIBIO ARROYA EN LOS CUSTODIOS Y PROVINCIALES DE LA PROVINCIA DE SAN JOSE / Perez, Lorenzo – Archivo Ibero Americano, 1924 – 1 – sp Bibl Santa Ana [946]
Juan del Santisimo Sacramento, Fray *see* VIAJE Y PEREGRINACION DE JERUSALEN
JUAN DOMINGO PERON : A HISTORY / Alexander, Robert Jackson – Boulder, Colo.: Westview Press, 1979 – 1 – CSUXADH2498-B – us Hoover Inst Photo [320]
JUAN DONOSO CORTES E LA NOBILTA / Maresca, Giovanni – (Ano 13. Nov.-Dic. 1965, no 73, pp. 729-734) – Madrid: Hidalguia, 1965 – 1 – sp Bibl Santa Ana [920]
JUAN JOSE DE VERTIZ Y SALADO, GOBERNADOR Y VIRREY DE BUENOS AIRES. ENSAYO BASADO EN DOCUMENTOS INEDITOS DEL ARCHIVO GENERAL DE INDIAS / Torre Revello, Jose – Buenos Aires, 1932; Madrid: Razon y Fe, 1933 – 1 – sp Bibl Santa Ana [320]
JUAN JUSTINIANO Y ARRIBAS / Blanco Garcia, Francisco – Madrid: Saenz de Jubera, 1909 – sp Bibl Santa Ana [440]
JUAN MACIAS, INCLITA GLORIA DE EXTREMADURA Y DE LA IGLESIA / Fernandez Sanchez, Teodoro – Badajoz: Dip. Provincial, 1976. Sep. REE – 1 – sp Bibl Santa Ana [240]
JUAN MARTIN ROCO. SENOR DE CAMPOFRIO / Solar y Taboada, Antonio & Rujula, Jose de – Badajoz: A. Arqueros, 1928 – 1 – sp Bibl Santa Ana [920]
JUAN PERON AND THE RESHAPING OF ARGENTINA / ed by Turner, Frederick C & Miguens, Jose Enrique – Pittsburgh, PA: University of Pittsburgh Press, c1983 – 1 – CSUXADP1507-B – us Hoover Inst Photo [320]
JUAN PERON VS. SPRUILLE BRADEN : THE STORY BEHIND THE BLUE BOOK / Frank, Gary – Lanham, MD: University Press of America, c1980 – 1 – CSUXADQ2514-B – us Hoover Inst Photo [320]
JUAN PERON Y EL TERCER MUNDO : TERCERA POSICION Y EL TERCER MUNDO: IMPORTANCIA DEL PENSAMIENTO Y ACCION DE PERON EN LA CONSTITUCION Y DESARROLLO DEL TERCER MUNDO / Universidad Nacional de Litoral. Instituto de Estudio de la Realidad Nacional y del Tercer Mundo – Santa Fe, [Argentina]: La Universidad, 1974 – 1 – CSUXADJ7533-B – us Hoover Inst Photo [320]
JUAN RAMON JIMENEZ EN SU OBRA / Diez Canedo, Enrique – Mexico: El Colegio de Mexico, 1944 – 1 – sp Bibl Santa Ana [920]
JUAN VAZQUEZ DE LA PARRA, EL EXTREMENO AL QUE AMO COMO A UN HIJO SAN MARTIN DE PORRES / Munoz de San Pedro, Miguel – Badajoz: Imp. Diput. Prov. Sep. de la Revista de Estudios Extremenos – 1 – sp Bibl Santa Ana [920]
JUAN VAZQUEZ EN LA CATEDRAL DE PLASENCIA / Gomez Guillen, Roman – Badajoz: Dip. Provincial, 1973. Sep. REE – 1 – sp Bibl Santa Ana [240]
Juana Sardon, Amalio de la *see* EL CERDO DE TIPO IBERICO EN LA PROVINCIA DE BADAJOZ
Juanini, J *see*
– CARTAS ESCRITAS A LOS MUY NOBLES DOCTORES...SE DIZE QUE EL SAL AZIDOY ALCALI...
– NUEVA IDEA PHYSICA NATURAL DEMOSTRATIVA, ORIGEN DE LAS MATERIAS QUE MUEVEN LAS COSAS
Juarez, Carlos Arturo *see* HORA CRUCIAL EN LA ARGENTINA
Juarez, Ernesto *see* HIGIENE Y PROFILAXIS EN EL MEDIO RURAL
Juarez, Juan C *see* LOS TRABAJADORES EN FUNCI ON SOCIAL
Juarez, Roberto *see* ATENTADOS POLITICOS EN LA ARGENTINA
Juarez Sanchez-Rubio, Cipriano *see* EVOLUCION DE LA ENERGIA ELECTRICA EN LA PROVINCIA DE BADAJOZ
JUBELSCHRIFT ZUM NEUNZIGSTEN GEBURTSTAG DES DR. L. ZUNZ / Curatorium der Zunz-Stiftung – Berlin: Louis Gerschel, 1884. 1 fiche – 9 – us A.T.L.A. [920]
Jubera, A *see* DECHADO Y REFORMACION DE TODAS LAS MEDICINAS COMPUESTAS, RENALES...

JUBILACIONES FERROVIARIAS : LA INFLUENCIA DE LA ACCION SINDICAL DE LOS TRABAJADORES EN LA FORMACION DE LAS LEYES / Bramuglia, Juan Atilio – Buenos Aires: La Union ferroviaria, 1941 – 1 – CSUXADJ0168-B – us Hoover Inst Photo [331]

JUBILAEUMSSCHRIFT (HEFT 100) / Friedensburg, Walter et al – Leipzig: Verein fuer Reformationsgeschichte, 1910. (Schriften des Vereins fuer Reformationsgeschichte; 27. Jahrg., Schrift 100) – 1mf – us A.T.L.A. [240]

JUBILEE DAYS – Boston, 1872 – 1r – 1 – £60.00 – uk Chadwyck [780]

THE JUBILEE MEMORIAL OF HORTON COLLEGE, BRADFORD, CONTAINING THE SERMON PREACHED AT THE JUBILEE SERVICE, 2 AUG 1854; ALSO / Godwin, Benjamin – Historical and biographical sketchBY B. Evans – 1 – 5.00 – us Baptist [240]

JUBILEE MEMORIAL OF THE AMERICAN BIBLE SOCIETY : BEING A REVIEW OF ITS FIRST FIFTY YEARS' WORK / Ferris, Isaac – (Includes appendixes) – New York: American Bible Society, 1867 – 1mf – 9 – 0-8370-6042-7 – 1986-0042 – us A.T.L.A. [220]

THE JUBILEE MEMORIAL OF THE RELIGIOUS TRACT SOCIETY : CONTAINING A RECORD OF ITS ORIGIN, PROCEEDINGS AND RESULTS, A.D. 1799 TO A.D. 1849 / Jones, William – (Includes appendixes and index) – London: Religious Tract Society, 1850 – 2mf – 9 – 0-8370-6268-3 – 1986-0268 – us A.T.L.A. [240]

JUBILEE MEMORIALS, 1860-1910 / Fernando, J S A – Colombo: Industrial Home Press, 1910 – 9 – us Res Libr [240]

THE JUBILEE OF THE METHODIST NEW CONNEXION : BEING A GRATEFUL MEMORIAL OF THE ORIGIN, GOVERNMENT AND HISTORY OF THE DENOMINATION / Allin, Thomas et al – London, 1848 – 5mf – 9 – ne IDC [240]

THE JUBILEE OF THE METHODIST NEW CONNEXION; BEING A GRATEFUL MEMORIAL OF THE ORIGIN, GOVERNMENT AND HISTORY OF THE DENOMINATION / Allin, Thomas et al – London, 1848. 450p – 5mf – 9 – ne IDC [240]

JUBILEE, PATRIOTIC AND OTHER POEMS / Awde, Robert – Toronto: W. Briggs: Montreal: C. Coates; Halifax: S. Huestis, 1887. 00070. (Pre-1900 Canadiana) – 9 – cn C.I.H.M. [810]

THE JUBILEE PHILATELIST – (Merged with: The Mount Royal Stamp News. Merged to become: The Jubilee Philatelist and Mount Royal Stamp News) – Smith's Falls, Ont: Jubilee Stamp and Pub. Co, [1899-1900] – 9 – cn C.I.H.M. [760]

THE JUBILEE PHILATELIST *see*
- THE JUBILEE PHILATELIST AND MOUNT ROYAL STAMP NEWS
- THE MOUNT ROYAL STAMP NEWS

THE JUBILEE PHILATELIST AND MOUNT ROYAL STAMP NEWS – (Cont: The Jubilee Philatelist) – Smith's Falls, Ont: Jubilee Stamp and Pub. Co, [1900] – 9 – cn C.I.H.M. [760]

THE JUBILEE PHILATELIST AND MOUNT ROYAL STAMP NEWS *see*
- THE JUBILEE PHILATELIST
- THE PHILATELIC AND ADVOCATE

JUBILEE PROGRAMME: INCLUDING A BRIEF RETROSPECT OF HER MAJESTY'S REIGN AND OTHER INTERESTING INFORMATION: DEMONSTRATION...OTTAWA, JUNE 30TH & JULY 1ST, 1887 – Ottawa, 1887. 03045. (Pre-1900 Canadiana) – 9 – cn C.I.H.M. [971]

THE JUBILEE REMEMBRANCER – Halifax, NS: Jubilee Committee of the Nova Scotia Auxiliary of the British and Foreign Bible Society, [1853-1854] – 9 – cn C.I.H.M. [240]

THE JUBILEE SINGERS AND THEIR CAMPAIGN FOR TWENTY THOUSAND DOLLARS / Pike, G D – Boston: Lee and Shepard; New York: Lee, Shepard and Dillingham, 1873, c1872 – 1mf – us A.T.L.A. [240]

A JUBILEE SOUVENIR, 1876-1926 / Lakshapatiya. Ceylon. St Matthias' Church – Deshiwala: Pearl Press, 1926 – us Res Libr [950]

JUBILEE STANDARD – v. 1. 1845 – 1 – us UMI [240]

THE JUBILEE STORY OF THE CHINA INLAND MISSION : WITH PORTRAITS, ILLUSTRATIONS AND MAPS / Broomhall, Marshall – London: Morgan & Scott, 1915 – 1mf – us A.T.L.A. [240]

JUBILEE VOLUME...JUNE 22-24, 1885 / Royal Statistical Society. Great Britain – London: E. Stanford, 1885. xv,372p. illus., map, charts, diagrs. Some of the papers in French – 1 – us U.W. Library [510]

THE JUBILEE YEAR: AN ORATION / Alward, Silas – 1887. 06077. (Pre-1900 Canadiana) – 9 – cn C.I.H.M. [971]

JUBILEE...AND MEMORIAL EXERCISES / Acadia College. Halifax – 1889. Halifax. 02385. (Pre-1900 Canadiana) – 9 – cn C.I.H.M. [370]

JUBILEUM-NUMMER, 1910-1935 / Sin, Po – Batavia, 1935 – 6mf – 9 – SE-1614/1 – ne IDC [950]

Juchereau-Duchesnay, Marguerite *see* BIO-BIBLIOGRAPHIE DE MONSIEUR JEAN VALLERAND, B.A., LICENCIE ES LETTRES, DIPLOME DE L'UNIVERSITE DE MONTREAL EN JOURNALISME, CRITIQUE MUSICAL

JUCO REVIEW / National Junior College Athletic Association – (1985-. 1,5,6) – 1976- – 9 – us UMI [073]

THE JUDAEN – Montreal, CN, 1917-1970 – 1r – 1 – Can$30.00 – cn Can Microfilming [072]

JUDAIC STUDIES: MIQRA'OT GEDOLOT – (v1. Torah: Genesis. $12.00. v2. Torah: Exodus. $12.00. v3. Torah: Leviticus. $10.00. v4. Torah: Numbers. $10.00. v5. Torah: Deuteronomy. $10.00. v6. Megilloth: Song of Songs, Ruth, Lamentations, Ecclesiastes, Esther. $10.00. v7 Former Prophets: Joshua, Judges, 1st & 2nd Samuel, 1st & 2nd Kings and writings, 1st and 2nd Chronicles. $24.00. v8. Latter Prophets: Isaiah, Jeremiah. $12.00. v9. Latter Prophets: Ezekiel, Book of the Twelve. $12.00. v10. Writings: Psalms, Proverbs, Job, Daniel, Ezra, Nehemiah. $18.00) – 9 – us I.R.C. [270]

JUDAICA : FORSCHUNGEN ZUR HELLENISTISCH-JUEDISCHEN GESCHICHTE UND LITTERATUR / Willrich, Hugo – (Includes index of names) – Goettingen: Vandenhoeck & Ruprecht, 1900 – 1mf – 9 – 0-8370-5860-0 – 1985-3860 – us A.T.L.A. [270]

JUDAICA COLLECTION CARD CATALOGUE / Jewish National and University Library. Jerusalem – (Includes printed index) – 549mf – 9 – J-10-1/1 – ne IDC [020]

JUDAICA, FESTSCHRIFT / Cohen, H – Berlin. 1912. BJ-100-18 1 – 9 – ne IDC [270]

JUDAICA LIBRARIANSHIP – New York, NY. Fall 1983-Spring 1985 – 1 – us A.J.P.C. [071]

JUDAISM / Abrahams, Israel – (Includes bibliography) – London: Archibald Constable, 1907 – 1mf – 9 – 0-8370-2033-6 – 1985-0033 – us A.T.L.A. [270]

JUDAISM AND CHRISTIANITY: A SKETCH OF THE PROGRESS OF THOUGHT / Toy, Crawford Howell – Boston: Little, Brown, 1890. 1 fiche – 9 – us A.T.L.A. [270]

JUDAISM AND ITS HISTORY / Geiger, Abraham – New York: Bloch, 1911. 1 fiche – 9 – us A.T.L.A. [270]

JUDAISM AT ROME / Huidekoper, Frederic – 1877 – 9 – us A.T.L.A. [270]

JUDAISM AT THE WORLD'S PARLIAMENT OF RELIGIONS : COMPRISING PAPERS ON JUDAISM READ AT THE PARLIAMENT, AT THE JEWISH DENOMINATIONAL CONGRESS, AND AT THE JEWISH PRESENTATION – (Includes index) – Cincinnati:Publ by the Union of American Hebrew Congregations – 1mf – 9 – 0-8370-5599-7 – 1985-3599 – us A.T.L.A. [270]

Judaism.Liturgy. Fes *see* AHAVAT HA-KADMONIM

JUDAISTIC CHRISTIANITY : A COURSE OF LECTURES / Hort, Fenton John Antony – (Includes index of biblical citations) – Cambridge; New York: Macmillan, 1894 – 1mf – 9 – 0-8370-9791-6 – 1986-3791 – us A.T.L.A. [240]

JUDAS : ORGAO HUMORISTICO – Maceio, Alagoas. 12 Mar-9 Abr 1898 – 1,5,6 – bl Biblioteca [072]

JUDAS : ROMAN / Strauss und Torney, Lulu von – Stuttgart: Deutsche Verlags-Anstalt, 1922 – 1r – 1 – us U.W. Library [830]

Judd, Charles Hubbard *see* LABORATORY EQUIPMENT FOR PSYCHOLOGICAL EXPERIMENTS

JUDD FAMILY DIARIES – 1861-64 – 1 – us KS Hist [978]

DER JUDE – Berlin. v. 1-10 no. 1. Apr 1916-Mar 1928 – 1 – us NY Public [270]

DER JUDE – Breslau, 1777 n1-27 – 1 – Inquire at Mikrofilmarchiv for details – gw Misc Inst [943]

DER JUDE – Ein Journal fuer Gewissens-Freiheit. Altona. v1, 1835. Complete. 1 reel. B165 (Leo Baeck Institute. German-Jewish Periodicals, Pt 2) – 1 – $75.00 – us UPA [270]

DER JUDE – New York, NY. 1895 – 1 – us A.J.P.C. [071]

DER JUDE : PERIODISCHE BLAETTER FUER RELIGION UND GEWISSENS-FREIHEIT – Altona. v1-2. 1832-33. Complete. 1 reel. B164 (Leo Baeck Institute. German-Jewish Periodicals, Pt 2) – 1 – $75.00 – us UPA [270]

DER JUDE : EINE WOCHENSCHRIFT – Leipzig. v1-9. 1768-1772. Complete. 1 reel. B482 (Leo Baeck Institute. German-Jewish Periodicals, Pt 1) – 1 – $75.00 – us UPA [270]

DER JUDE : EINE WOCHENSCHRIFT / ed by Seelig, Gottfried – Leipzig, 1768-72. Hildesheim, 1992 – 50mf – 9 – DM380.00 diazo DM450.00 silver – gw Olms [270]

JUDE : EINE MONATSSCHRIFT – Berlin. v1-10. 1916-28 – 3r – 1 – us Ross [270]

JUDE : SONDERHEFT 1-5 – Berlin, Wien. v1-8. 1916-1924 – 111mf – 9 – ne IDC [270]

DE JUDEER – Laren. v1-10. 1928-1939 – 6mf – 9 – ne IDC [270]

DIE JUDEN IN HOLLAND / Seeligmann, S – (Festskrift David Simonsen). Kobenhavn. 1923. BJ-262-55 1 – 9 – ne IDC [949]

DIE JUDEN VON BARNOW / Franzos, Karl Emil – 6e. Auf. Berlin. 1899 – 1 – us Res Libr [800]

DAS JUDENCHRISTENTUM IN DEN PSEUDOKLEMENTINEN (T.U.U. 5-70) / Strecker, G – Berlin, 1958 – 6mf – 9 – ne Slangenburg [240]

DIE JUDENFRAGE : ALS RACEN- , SITTEN- , UND CULTURFRAGE: MIT EINER WELTGESCHICHTLICHEN ANTWORT / Duehring, Eugen Karl – 2. verb. Aufl. Karlsruhe: H Reuther, 1881 – 1mf – 9 – 0-8370-2073-5 – 1985-0073 – us A.T.L.A. [270]

DIE JUDENFRAGE AUF DEM WIENER KONGRESS / ed by Baron, S – Wien. Berlin. 1920. BJ-23-105 1 – 9 – ne IDC [321]

DIE JUDENFRAGE UND DER SOZIALISTISCHE JUDENSTAAT / Syrkin, N – Bern. 1898. BJ-28-53 1 – 9 – ne IDC [956]

DAS JUDENGRAB – AUS BIMBOS SEELENWANDERUNGEN : ZWEI ERZAEHLUNGEN / Huch, Ricarda – Leipzig: Insel-Verlag, [1916?] – 1r – 1 – us U.W. Library [830]

DAS JUDENTHUM / Guedemann, Moritz – Wien: R. Loewit, 1902 – 9 – us A.T.L.A. [270]

DAS JUDENTHUM IN GEGENWART UND ZUKUNFT / Hartmann, Eduard von – Leipzig: Wilhelm Friedrich, 1885 – 1mf – 9 – 0-8370-5997-6 – 1985-3997 – us A.T.L.A. [270]

DAS JUDENTHUM UND DAS WESEN DES CHRISTENTUMS / Eschelbacher, Joseph – Berlin: Poppelauer, 1905. 1 fiche – 9 – us A.T.L.A. [240]

JUDENTUM UND JUDENCHRISTENTUM IM JUSTINS DIALOG MIT TRYPHO (T.U.U. 3-39/1B) / Harnack, Adolf von – Leipzig, 1913 – 1mf – 9 – ne Slangenburg [240]

OS JUDEUS PORTUGUESES EM AMSTERDAM / Mendes dos Remedios, J – Coimbra. 1911. BJ-262-39 1 – 9 – ne IDC [949]

JUDEX MATERARUM...INSINGULIS / Lopez de Tovar, Gregorio – 1611 – 9 – 1.50f – sp Bibl Santa Ana [946]

JUDGE – v. 1-116. 1881-1939 – 1 – us UMI [340]

JUDGE ADVOCATE GENERAL OF THE ARMY OPINIONS / U.S. Army. Judge Advocate General – Washington: GPO. v1-3. 1917-19 (all publ) – 30mf – 9 – $45.00 – LLMC 84-227 – us L.L.M.C. [340]

THE JUDGE ADVOCATE JOURNAL – (No issues between 1945-bulletin no 1 1948) – v1-v2 no 3. Jun 1944-Fall/Winter 1945; bulletins 1-48 1948-76 (all publ) – 9 – $81.00 – LLMC 84-239 – us L.L.M.C. [073]

JUDGE AND JURY : A POPULAR EXPLANATION FOR THE LEADING TOPICS IN THE LAW OF THE LAND / Abbott, Benjamin Vaughan – New York: Harper & Bros, 1880 – 5mf – 9 – $7.50 – LLMC 92-102 – us L.L.M.C. [360]

JUDGE BURNHAM'S DAUGHTERS – Boston: D. Lothrop Co., 1888. 339p – 1 – us U.W. Library [830]

JUDGEMENT / Gray, Robert – London: Bell & Daldy, 1864 – 1mf – us A.T.L.A. [240]

THE JUDGEMENT OF THE FLOOD / Heraud, John Abraham – London: James Fraser, 1834 – 1r – 1 – 1-55879-736-X – uk Libr Preservation [240]

JUDGEMENT RECORDS OF THE U.S. CIRCUIT COURT FOR THE SOUTHERN DISTRICT OF NEW YORK / U.S. Circuit and District Courts. New York – 1794-1840. 8 rolls. M882 – 1 – us Nat'l Archives [324]

JUDGES AND RUTH / Watson, Robert Alexander – New York: A.C. Armstrong, 1890. 1 fiche – 9 – us A.T.L.A. [240]

JUDGES AND RUTH: INTRODUCTION, REVISED VERSION WITH NOTES / Thatcher, Griffithes Wheeler – New York: Henry Frowde, 1904?.1 fiche – 9 – us A.T.L.A. [240]

JUDGES JOURNAL (ABA) – v1-30. 1962-1991 – 9 – $168.00 set – us Hein [340]

JUDGES OF THE UNITED STATES : PUBLISHED UNDER THE AUSPICES OF THE BICENTENNIAL COMMITTEE OF THE JUDICIAL CONFERENCE OF THE UNITED STATES – 1st ed 1978. Washington: GPO, 1980 – 6mf – 9 – $9.00 – LLMC 95-013A – us L.L.M.C. [340]

JUDGES OF THE UNITED STATES : PUBLISHED UNDER THE AUSPICES OF THE BICENTENNIAL COMMITTEE OF THE JUDICIAL CONFERENCE OF THE UNITED STATES – 2nd ed 1983. Washington: GPO, 1983 – 8mf – 9 – $12.00 – LLMC 95-013B – us L.L.M.C. [340]

THE JUDGE'S ROLE IN THE SETTLEMENT OF CIVIL SUITS / Lacey, Frederick B – Washington, 1977 – 1mf – 9 – $1.50 – LLMC 95-804 – us L.L.M.C. [340]

JUDGESHIP CREATION IN THE FEDERAL COURTS : OPTIONS FOR REFORM / Baar, Carl – Washington: FJC, Feb 1981 – 1mf – 9 – $1.50 – LLMC 95-310 – us L.L.M.C. [340]

JUDGING EDUCATIONAL RESEARCH BASED ON EXPERIMENTS AND SURVEYS / Wolf, Richard M – 1993 – 96p – 9 – 92-803-1149-2 – fr UNESCO [370]

JUDGMENT DE CONSEIL SOUVERAIN / Canada. Quebec – (Cont by: Judgment de Conseil superieur) – v1-4. 1663-1707 (all publ) – 49mf – 9 – $73.00 – LLMC 81-069 – us L.L.M.C. [340]

JUDGMENT DE CONSEIL SOUVERAIN *see* JUDGMENT DE CONSEIL SUPERIEUR

JUDGMENT DE CONSEIL SUPERIEUR / Quebec. Canada – (Cont: Judgment de Conseil Souverain) – v5-6. 1705-16 – 26mf – 9 – $39.00 – LLMC 81-070 – us L.L.M.C. [340]

JUDGMENT DE CONSEIL SUPERIEUR *see* JUDGMENT DE CONSEIL SOUVERAIN

JUDGMENT INDEXES, DIRECT / Van Wert County. Ohio. Common Pleas. Civil Division – 1838-1921 – 5r – 1 – $32.50r – us Archival [324]

JUDGMENT INDEXES, DIRECT / Wyandot County. Ohio. Common Pleas. Civil Division – 1845-1919 – 4r – 1 – $32.50r – us Archival [324]

JUDGMENT INDEXES, REVERSE / Van Wert County. Ohio. Common Pleas. Civil Division – 1838-1900 – 3r – 1 – $32.50r – us Archival [324]

JUDGMENT INDEXES, REVERSE / Wyandot County. Ohio. Common Pleas. Civil Division – 1845-1919 – 4r – 1 – $32.50r – us Archival [324]

THE JUDGMENT OF A CATHOLICKE ENGLISHMAN LIVING IN BANISHMENT FOR HIS RELIGION / Parsons, Robert – 1608 – 9 – 10.00 – us Scholars' Facs [240]

THE JUDGMENT OF URINES / Record, R – 1679. M 394 – 9 – ne IDC [610]

JUDGMENT RECORDS OF THE U.S. CIRCUIT COURT FOR THE SOUTHERN DISTRICT OF NEW YORK, 1794-1840 – 8 – 1 – M882 – us Nat'l Archives [340]

JUDGMENT RECORDS OF THE U.S. DISTRICT COURT FOR THE SOUTHERN DISTRICT OF NEW YORK / U.S. Circuit and District Courts. New York – 1795-1840. 16 rolls – 1 – M934 – us Nat'l Archives [324]

JUDGMENTS / Sierra Leone. Supreme Court – 1922-55, 1960-72. 8 reels – 1 – $316.00 – us African Imprint [340]

JUDGMENTS OF THE U.N. ADMINISTRATIVE TRIBUNAL / United Nations – 1950-1982 – E.54 F.58 – 9 (AT/DEC/1-300) – us U.N. Pubs [350]

JUDGMENTS OF THE UNITED NATIONS ADMINISTRATIVE TRIBUNAL / United Nations – Issued irreg. since 1950. 40 fiches – 9 – $70.00; $1.90f – uk UNIMICRO [340]

JUDICATURE – v1- 1917- 1; v55- 5,6; v61- 9 – us UMI [340]

JUDICIAL CENTENNIAL BANQUET GIVEN AT THE LENOX LYCEUM, NEW YORK, FEBRUARY 4TH, 1890 / New York State Bar Association – New York: American Bank Note Co., 1890 29p. LL-373 – 1 – us L of C Photodup [340]

THE JUDICIAL CHRONICLE, BEING A LIST OF THE JUDGES OF THE COURTS OF COMMON LAW AND CHANCERY IN ENGLAND AND AMERICA AND OF THE CONTEMPORARY REPORTS / Gibbs, George – Cambridge Mass.: Munroe, 1834. 55p. LL-2258 – 1 – us L of C Photodup [340]

THE JUDICIAL CODE; BEING THE JUDICIARY ACT OF THE CONGRESS OF THE UNITED STATES, APPROVED MARCH 3, A.D. 1911 / U. S. Laws, Statutes, etc – Chicago, Callaghan, 1911. 254 p. LL-1462 – 1 – us L of C Photodup [340]

THE JUDICIAL CONFERENCE AND ITS COMMITTEE ON COURT ADMINISTRATION / Hunter, Elmo B – Washington: FJC, 1986 – 1mf – 9 – $1.50 – LLMC 95-397 – us L.L.M.C. [340]

THE JUDICIAL CONFERENCE OF THE U.S., REPORTS AND PROCEEDINGS – THE ADMINISTRATIVE OFFICE OF THE U.S. COURTS, ANNUAL REPORTS – (Lacking: 1943-44 for the Judicial Conference. 1942 report of the ASdministrative Office. 1984-88 for both) – 1940-43; 1989 – 209mf – 9 – $313.00 – LLMC 80-411 – us L.L.M.C. [340]

JUDICIAL DIARY / Drayton, William – 1784. 2 fiches – 9 – us South Carolina Historical [978]

THE JUDICIAL DICTIONARY OF WORDS AND PHRASES JUDICIALLY INTERPRETED / Stroud, Frederick – 1v. 1835-1912. London: Sweet & Maxwell, 1890 – 11mf – 9 – $16.50 – LLMC 95-448 – us L.L.M.C. [340]

JUDICIAL DISCIPLINE AND REMOVAL IN THE U.S. / Wheeler, Russell R & Levin, Leo – Washington: GPO, 1987 – 1mf – 9 – $1.50 – LLMC 95-304 – us L.L.M.C. [340]

JUDICIAL DRAMAS : OR THE ROMANCE OF FRENCH CRIMINAL LAW / Spicer, Henry – London: Tinsley Bros, 1872 – 5mf – 9 – $7.50 – LLMC 92-133 – us L.L.M.C. [340]

JUDICIAL LAYMENS ASSOCIATION BULLETIN – v1-2. 1937, 1941 (all publ) – 1mf – 9 – $1.50 – LLMC 84-508 – us L.L.M.C. [073]

THE JUDICIAL POWER OF THE UNITED STATES / Harris, Robert Jennings – University, LA: Louisiana State University Press, 1940. 238p. LL-217 – 1 – us L of C Photodup [340]

THE JUDICIAL POWER OF THE UNITED STATES IN SOME OF ITS ASPECTS. / Matthews, Stanley – New Haven, Conn.: Hoggson & Robinson, 1888. 39p. LL-190 – 1 – us L of C Photodup [340]

JUDICIAL REFORMS PROPOSED BY THE COMMISSION FOR THE CODIFICATION OF THE STATUTES. FIRST REPORT. / Quebec. (Province). Commission to Consolidate the General Statutes – Quebec, 1882. 262p. LL-1663 – 1 – us L of C Photodup [340]

JUDICIAL REGULATION OF ATTORNEYS' FEES : BEGINNING THE PROCESS AT PRETRIAL / Willging, Thomas E – Washington: GPO, 1985 – 1mf – 9 – $1.50 – LLMC 95-318 – us L.L.M.C. [340]

JUDICIAL REVIEW UNDER THE CLEAN AIR ACT AND FEDERAL WATER POLLUTION CONTROL ACT / Currie, David P – Washington, 19 Oct 1976 (all publ) – 2mf – 9 – $3.00 – LLMC 94-344 – us L.L.M.C. [340]

JUDICIAL SABBATICALS / Robbins, Ira P – Washington: FJC, 1987 – 1mf – 9 – $1.50 – LLMC 95-335 – us L.L.M.C. [340]

JUDICIAL SETTLEMENT OF CONTROVERSIES BETWEEN STATES OF AMERICAN UNION : CASES DECIDED IN THE SUPREME COURT OF THE UNITED STATES: COLLECTED AND EDITED BY JAMES B. SCOTT – New York: Oxford UP, American Branch. 2v. 1918 – 20mf – 9 – $30.00 – LLMC 95-065 – us L.L.M.C. [323]

JUDICIAL STATISTICS. / Bannatyne, Andrew – Glasgow, Graham, 1863. 30 p. LL-2255 – 1 – us L of C Photodup [340]

JUDICIAL WRITING MANUAL – Washington: FJC, 1991 – 1mf – 9 – $1.50 – LLMC 95-371 – us L.L.M.C. [340]

JUDICION – Vacaville, CA. 1885-87 – 1r – 1 – $50.00 – B03057 – us Library Micro [071]

JUDICIUM DEI ET SPONSI NOSTRI, QUID CUM IMAGINIBUS, SEU SIMULACHRIS AGENDUM SIT, ETC / Haetzer, L – Augsburg. 1524. BME-49 – 9 – ne IDC [240]

JUDICIUM PACIFICI SALOMONIS CHRISTI DOMINI NOSTRI / Bottens, Fulg. OF M – Gandavi, 1713 – 5mf – 8 – ne Slangenburg [240]

EL JUDIO EN LA EPOCA COLONIAL; UN ASPECTO DE LA HISTORIA RIOPLATENSE / Lewin, Boleslao – Buenos Aires: Colegio Libre de Estudias Superiores, 1939. 158p. facsims. bibliog – 1 – us U.W. Library [972]

LOS JUDIOS EN EXTREMADURA / Munoz de la Pena, Arsenio – Badajoz: (Imprenta Diputacion Provincial), 1970. Sepr. Revista Estudios Extremenos – 1 – sp Bibl Santa Ana [305]

DAS JUDISCHE LITERATURBLATT = JEWISH LITERARY JOURNAL – (In German) – Magdeburg, DE. v6 no1 1 Jan 1877-v15 no52 23 Dec 1886 – 1r – 1 – $55.00 – cn Can Microfilming [072]

JUDISCHE MORGENPOST = JEWISH MORNING POST – (In Yiddish) – Vienna, AU. v8 no29. Jul 1924 – 1r – 1 – $25.00 – cn Can Microfilming [072]

DIE JUDISCHE PRESSE = THE JEWISH PRESS – (In German) – Berlin, DE. v17 no1 7 Jan 1886-v49 no52 27 Dec 1918 – 3r – 1 – $50.00 – cn Can Microfilming [072]

DER JUDISCHE WILLE = THE JEWISH WILL – (In German. Monthly) – Berlin, DE. v1 no1 Apr 1918-no6 Feb 1919 – 1r – 1 – $25.00 – cn Can Microfilming [072]

DAS JUDISHE WOKHENBLAT = JEWISH WEEKLY – (In Yiddish) – Bedzin, PL. v3 no32 29 Apr 1927-v5 no36 31 May 1929 – 1r – 1 – $35.00 – cn Can Microfilming [072]

DOS JUDISZE TOGBLAT – (Missing: Several vols) – Warsaw, Odessa. v1-11. 1929-1939 – 17r – 1 – J-92-27/3 – ne IDC [072]

JUDITH, AN OLD ENGLISH EPIC FRAGMENT – Ed. by Albert S. Cook. Boston, London: D.C. Heath and Co., 1904. xxiv,72p. Bibliography – 1 – us U.W. Library [810]

JUDITH BASIN PRESS – Stanford. Mont. 1951-1954; 1958-1959; 1966- – 1 – us UMI [071]

JUDITH BASIN STAR – Hobson. Mont. 1947-1955 – 1 – us UMI [071]

JUDITH IN DER DEUTSCHEN LITERATUR / Baltzer, Otto – (Includes bibliographical references) – Berlin: W de Gruyter & Co, 1930 – 2r – 1 – us U.W. Library [430]

JUDITH, LYRIC DRAMA / Chadwick, George Whitefield – Text by William Chauncy Langdon. 1900. Holograph score, in ink. At end: score finished Dec. 12, 1900. music 3075 – 1 – us L of C Photodup [780]

JUDITH SHAKESPEARE: A ROMANCE / Black, William – British Fiction Archive: Unit 4 – 9 – uk Bell [830]

Judson, A H *see* AN ACCOUNT OF THE AMERICAN BAPTIST MISSION TO THE BURMAN EMIPRE

Judson, Adoniram *see* LETTERS TO GARDNER COLBY, 1846-49

Judson, Ann H *see* ANN H. JUDSON: A MEMORIAL

THE JUDSON CENTENNIAL, 1814-1914 : CELEBRATED IN BOSTON, MASS., JUNE 24-25, IN CONNECTION WITH THE CENTENARY OF THE AMERICAN BAPTIST FOREIGN MISSION SOCIETY / ed by Grose, Howard B & Haggard, Fred P – Philadelphia: Published for the American Baptist Foreign Mission Society [by] American Baptist Publication Society, c1914 – 1mf – us A.T.L.A. [240]

Judson, Edward *see*
– ADONIRAM JUDSON
– THE INSTITUTIONAL CHURCH
– THE LIFE OF ADONIRAM JUDSON

Judson, Emily C *see*
– EMILY C. JUDSON: A MEMORIAL
– MEMOIR OF SARAH B. JUDSON: MEMBER OF THE AMERICAN MISSION TO BURMAH

THE JUDSON OFFERING : INTENDED AS A TOKEN OF CHRISTIAN SYMPATHY WITH THE LIVING, AND A MEMENTO OF CHRISTIAN AFFECTION FOR THE DEAD / ed by Dowling, John – New York: L. Colby, 1847, c1846 – 1mf – us A.T.L.A. [240]

Judson, S *see* BIOGRAPHICAL AND DESCRIPTIVE WORKS ON THE REV. JOHN WESLEY

Judson, Sarah B *see* SARAH B. JUDSON: A MEMORIAL

JUE WU – Published during the May movement. One issue, Jan 1920.3 ill. DL68f – 9 – 30.00 – cc Globe [073]

JUEDISCH-ARABISCHE POESIEN AUS VORMUHAMMEDISCHER ZEIT : EIN SPECIMEN AUS FLEISCHERS SCHULE ALS BEITRAG ZUR FEIER SEINES JUBILEUMS / Delitzsch, Franz – Leipzig: Doerffling & Franke, 1874 – 1mf – 9 – 0-8370-2870-1 – 1985-0870 – us A.T.L.A. [470]

JUEDISCH-BABYLONISCHE ZAUBERTEXTE / ed by Stuebe, Rudolph – (Commentary in German. Text in Aramaic and German. Includes bibliographical references) – Halle (Saale): J Krause, 1895 – 1mf – 9 – 0-8370-8388-5 – 1986-2388 – us A.T.L.A. [470]

EIN JUEDISCH-CHRISTLICHES PSALMBUCH AUS DEM ERSTEN JAHRHUNDERT (T.U.U. 3-35/4) / Harnack, Adolf von – Leipzig, 1910 – 3mf – 9 – ne Slangenburg [240]

JUEDISCHE ALLGEMEINE ZEITUNG *see* JUEDISCH-LIBERALE ZEITUNG

DIE JUEDISCHE APOKALYPTIK / Bousset, Wilhelm – Berlin: Reuther & Reichard, 1903. 1 fiche – 9 – us A.T.L.A. [270]

JUEDISCHE ARBEITS- UND WANDERFUERSORGE – Berlin, 1927/28-1929/30 (incomplete) – 1 – Dist. gw Mikrofilm – gw Misc Inst [360]

DIE JUEDISCHE BIBELEXEGESE / Bacher, Wilhelm – Trier: Sigmund Mayer, 1892. 1 fiche – 9 – us A.T.L.A. [220]

DIE JUEDISCHE DICHTER DER PROVENCE / Zunz, L – (Zur Geschichte und Literatur). Berlin. 1845. BJ-421-28 1 – 9 – ne IDC [470]

JUEDISCHE ESCHATOLOGIE VON DANIEL BIS AKIBA / Volz, Paul – (Includes index) – Tuebingen: J C B Mohr (Paul Siebeck), 1903 – 1mf – 9 – 0-8370-7274-3 – 1986-1274 – us A.T.L.A. [270]

JUEDISCHE FAMILIEN-FORSCHUNG – Berlin, 1924-38 (incomplete) – 1 – Dist. gw Mikrofilm – gw Misc Inst [900]

JUEDISCHE FAMILIEN-FORSCHUNG – Berlin, 1925-38 – 1r – 1 – Dist. gw Mikrofilm – gw Misc Inst [900]

JUEDISCHE FAMILIEN-FORSCHUNG – Mitteilungen der Gesellschaft fuer Juedische Familien-Forschung. Berlin. v1-14. 1925-38. Complete. 1 reel. B184 (Leo Baeck Institute. German-Jewish Periodicals, Pt 2) – 1 – $75.00 – us UPA [270]

DIE JUEDISCHE FRAU – Berlin, 1925-27 – 1r – 1 – Dist. gw Mikrofilm – gw Misc Inst [073]

DIE JUEDISCHE FRAU – UEberparteiliche Halbmonatsschrift fuer alle Lebensinteressen der juedischen Frau. Berlin, v1-3, 1925-27. Complete. B186 (Leo Baeck Institute. German-Jewish Periodicals, Pt 2) – 1r – 1 – $75.00 – us UPA [305]

DIE JUEDISCHE FRAU ALS MUTTER : EIN BILD IM UMBRUCH? ZUR HISTORISCHEN STELLUNG UND FUNKTION DER MUTTER IN DER JUEDISCHEN FAMILIE / Herwig, Rachel Monika – 1993 – 3mf – 9 – DM98.00 – 3-89349-756-0 – gw Hänsel [270]

JUEDISCHE GEMEINDEZEITUNG FUER DIE ISRAELITSICHEN GEMEINDEN WUERTTEMBERGS – Stuttgart. v1-15. 1924-1938. Lacking v2 and v13. B475 (Leo Baeck Institute. German-Jewish Periodicals, Pt 1) – 2r – 1 – $135.00 – us UPA [270]

DER JUEDISCHE HANDWERKER – (Cont: Handwerk und Gewerbe, since oct 1925) – Berlin 1935-38 (incomplete) – 1 – Dist. gw Mikrofilm – gw Misc Inst [072]

DER JUEDISCHE HANDWERKER – Organ des gesamten Juedischen Mittelstandes. Berlin. v1-30. 1909-1938. Lacking v1-6, 1909-1914. 1 reel. B192 (Leo Baeck Institute. German-Jewish Periodicals, Pt 1) – 1 – $75.00 – us UPA [270]

JUEDISCHE MODERNE : ZEITSCHRIFT FUER JUEDISCHE BELLETRISTIK UND KRITIK. / ed by Birnbaum, N – Berlin. 1897. v1(1-5) – 2mf – 9 – ne IDC [290]

JUEDISCHE MONATSHEFTE – Frankfurt a.M. v1-8. 1914-21. Incomplete. 1 reel. B215 (Leo Baeck Institute. German-Jewish Periodicals, Pt 2) – 1 – $75.00 – us UPA [270]

DIE JUEDISCHE PRESSE – Berlin. 1870-1923. v1-54. Lacking: parts of 1902, 1903, 1906, 1909, 1910, 1914, 1919 – 1,042mf – 9 – ne IDC [900]

DIE JUEDISCHE PRESSE – Berlin, 1870-73 (incomplete), 1876, 1879-1902, 1904-07, 1909, 1912-16, 1918, 1919 n28, 1920 n49 – 1 – Dist. gw Mikrofilm – gw Misc Inst [070]

DIE JUEDISCHE PRESSE – Berlin, 1872-79, 1881-1914, jul 2 1915-jun 30 1916, 1918, 1920-aug 30 1923 (incomplete) – 20r – 1 – Dist. gw Mikrofilm – gw Misc Inst [070]

DIE JUEDISCHE PRESSE – Berlin. v1-54. 1869-1923. Lacking misc. issues. 18 reels. B219 (Leo Baeck Institute. German-Jewish Periodicals, Pt 1) – 1 – $1,225.00 – us UPA [270]

JUEDISCHE PRESSZENTRALE – Zuerich. und Juedisches Familienblatt fuer die Schweiz. Zurich. jahrg. 1 (1)-23 (1061). 15 Dec 1918-10 May 1940 – 1 – us NY Public [073]

JUEDISCHE REVUE – Mukatschewo (Mukacevo), Ukraine Jun 1936-Nov 1938 – 1r – 1 – gw Mikrofilm [072]

JUEDISCHE RUNDSCHAU – Berlin. 1905-10, 1919-20, 1922-Nov. 8, 1938 – 1 – us NY Public [073]

JUEDISCHE RUNDSCHAU – Berlin, 1905-38 (incomplete) – 1 – Dist. gw Mikrofilm – gw Misc Inst [072]

JUEDISCHE RUNDSCHAU – Berlin. Germany. sept. 1924-Nov. 1938 (gaps) – 1 – 35.00r – us Hoover Inst Photo [072]

JUEDISCHE RUNDSCHAU – (Title varies. Some missing nos) – Berlin, 1895-1938 – 26r – 1,5,6 – ne IDC [270]

JUEDISCHE RUNDSCHAU / Zionistische Vereinigung fuer Deutschland – Berlin, 1905-38 – 11r – 1 – us Ross [072]

JUEDISCHE RUNDSCHAU – MACCABI – Basel, 1947-49 (incomplete) – 1 – Dist. gw Mikrofilm – gw Misc Inst [270]

JUEDISCHE SCHULZEITUNG – Hamburg. v. 1-14. 1925-1938 – 1 – us NY Public [073]

JUEDISCHE SKIZZEN / Perles, Felix – Leipzig. 1912. BJ-100-10 1 – 9 – ne IDC [270]

DER JUEDISCHE STUDENT – Berlin, 1907-08, 1914 n10, 1922 n3-5, 1929 n1-10, 1931-33 (incomplete) – 1 – Dist. gw Mikrofilm – gw Misc Inst [073]

JUEDISCHE STUDENT – (Missing: v3 1906/1907) – Berlin. v1-30. 1902-1933 – 120mf – 9 – ne IDC [270]

JUEDISCHE STUDIEN / Wohlgemuth, J – Frankfurt a.Main. 1928. BJ-100-23 1 – 9 – ne IDC [260]

JUEDISCHE THEOLOGIE: AUF GRUND DES TALMUD UND VERWANDTER SCHRIFTEN / Weber, Ferdinand – Leipzig: Doerffling & Franke, 1897. 1 fiche – 9 – us A.T.L.A. [270]

JUEDISCHE TURNZEITUNG – Berlin, 1910, 1912-13 n8 – 1 – Dist. gw Mikrofilm – gw Misc Inst [790]

DAS JUEDISCHE VOLK – Berlin, 1937-38 – 1 – Dist. gw Mikrofilm – gw Misc Inst [072]

DER JUEDISCHE VOLKSSOZIALIMUS / Arlosoroff, C – Berlin, 1919. BJ-28-2 1 – 9 – ne IDC [270]

JUEDISCHE VOLKSSTIMME – Bruenn, feb 1900-sep 1934 (incomplete) – 2r – 1 – Inquire at Mikrofilmarchiv for details – gw Misc Inst [943]

JUEDISCHE VOLKSSTIMME – Unabhaengiges, unparteiisches Wochenblatt. Bruenn. v1-34? 1900-1934? Lacking misc. issues. 2 reels. B240 (Leo Baeck Institute. German-Jewish Periodicals, Pt 1) – 1 – $135.00 – us UPA [270]

JUEDISCHE VOLKS-ZEITUNG – Cracow. v1-2. 1902-1903 – 1r – 1 – J-92-7/3 – ne IDC [072]

JUEDISCHE VOLKSZEITUNG *see* JUEDISCHES VOLKSBLATT

JUEDISCHE VOLKSZEITUNG FUER OSTDEUTSCHLAND *see* JUEDISCHES VOLKSBLATT

JUEDISCHE WELT-RUNDSCHAU – Jerusalem. 10 Mar 1939-20 May 1940 – 1 – gw Mikrofilm [270]

DER JUEDISCHE WILLE – Berlin, 1918-1919/20, 1933-37 (incomplete) – 1 – Dist. gw Mikrofilm – gw Misc Inst [072]

DIE JUEDISCHE WITWE : BUEHNENSPIEL IN FUENF AKTEN / Kaiser, Georg – Potsdam: G Kiepenheuer, 1920 – 1r – 1 – us U.W. Library [820]

JUEDISCHE WOCHENSCHAU – Buenos Aires, apr 26-dec 27 1940, apr 25-nov 24 1941, 1942-50 (incomplete) – 1 – Inquire at Mikrofilmarchiv for details – gw Misc Inst [972]

JUEDISCHE WOHLFAHRTSPFLEGE UND SOZIALPOLITIK – Berlin, 1929-38 (incomplete) – 1 – Dist. gw Mikrofilm – gw Misc Inst [360]

JUEDISCHE ZEITSCHRIFT FUER WISSENSCHAFT UND LEBEN / ed by Geiger, Abraham – Breslau. 1862-75. 11v. – 44mf – 9 – ne IDC [270]

JUEDISCHE ZEITSCHRIFT FUER WISSENSCHAFT UND LEBEN / ed by Geiger, Abraham – Breslau, 1862-75. Hildesheim, 1989 – 44mf – 9 – DM350.00 diazo DM400.00 silver – gw Olms [270]

Der Juedischen Gemeinde zu Berlin *see* GEMEINDEBLATT

JUEDISCHER FRAUENBUND VON DEUTSCHLAND – Blaetter des Juedischen Frauenbundes fuer Frauenarbeit und Frauenbewegung. Berlin. v1-14. 1924-1938. Lacking misc. issues. 1 reel. B187 (Leo Baeck Institute. German-Jewish Periodicals, Pt 1) – 1 – $75.00 – us UPA [270]

JUEDISCHER KULTURBUND HAMBURG – Monatsblaetter des...Hamburg. v1-3. 1836-38. Complete. 1 reel. B211 (Leo Baeck Institute. German-Jewish Periodicals, Pt 2) – 1 – $75.00 – us UPA [270]

JUEDISCHER VOLKSBOTE – Blaetter zur Foerderung der geistigen und wirtschaftlichen Interessen der juedischen Landbevoelkerung. Frankfurt a/M. v1-37?, 1908-15?. Complete. 1 reel. B237 (Leo Baeck Institute. German-Jewish Periodicals, Pt 1) – 1 – $75.00 – us UPA [270]

JUEDISCHES ARCHIV : MITTEILUNGEN DES KOMITEES "JUEDISCHES KRIEGSARCHIV" – Berlin, Wien. 1915-18, 1920 – 1r – 1 – Dist. gw Mikrofilm – gw Misc Inst [025]

JUEDISCHES ARCHIV – Mitteilungen des Komitees "Juedisches Kriegsarchiv." 1915-18. Vienna, Berlin. v1-9. 1920. Complete. B173 (Leo Baeck Institute. German-Jewish Periodicals, Pt 2) – 1r – 1 – $75.00 – us UPA [270]

JUEDISCHES ARCHIV – Zeitschrift fuer Juedisches Museal- und Buchwesen, Geschichte, Volkskunde und Familienforschung. Vienna, v1-2, 1927-29. Complete. B174 (Leo Baeck Institute. German-Jewish Periodicals, Pt 2) – 1r – 1 – $75.00 – us UPA [270]

JUEDISCHES GEMEINDEBLATT – Bremen, 1932-36 (incomplete) – 1 – Inquire at Mikrofilmarchiv for details – gw Misc Inst [943]

JUEDISCHES GEMEINDEBLATT – Mitteilungen der Juedischen Reformgemeinde zu Berlin. Berlin. v1-21. 1918-1938. Lacking: v21, 1938, nos. 6-8. B429 (Leo Baeck Institute. German-Jewish Periodicals, Pt 1) – 1r – 1 – $75.00 – us UPA [270]

JUEDISCHES GEMEINDEBLATT *see* MITTEILUNGEN DER JUEDISCHEN REFORMGEMEINDE ZU BERLIN

JUEDISCHES GEMEINDEBLATT FUER DIE ISRAELITISCHE GEMEINDE ZU FRANKFURT A.M – Frankfurt a/M. v1-16, 1922-38. Complete. B442 (Leo Baeck Institute. German-Jewish Periodicals, Pt 1) – 2r – 1 – $135.00 – us UPA [270]

JUEDISCHES GEMEINDEBLATT FUER DIE SYNAGOGENGEMEINDE BRESLAU *see* BRESLAUER JUEDISCHES GEMEINDEBLATT

JUEDISCHES GEMEINDEBLATT FUER DIE SYNAGOGEN-GEMEINDEN IN PREUSSEN UND NORDDEUTSCHLAND *see* VERWALTUNGSBLATT DES PREUSSISCHEN LANDESVERBANDES JUEDISCHER GEMEINDEN

JUEDISCHES GEMEINDEBLATT UND NACHRICHTENBLATT DER GEMEINDEVERWALTUNG DER ISRAELITSCHEN RELIGIONSGEMEINDE ZU LEIPZIG – Leipzig. v1-14. 1925-38. Lacking: v13, 1937; v14, 1938, all except no. 34. B453 (Leo Baeck Institute. German-Jewish Periodicals, Pt 1) – 2r – 1 – $135.00 – us UPA [270]

JUEDISCHES LEBEN IN KOENIGSBERG/PR. IM 20. JAHRHUNDERT / Jacoby, Yoram K – (Includes bibliographical references and index) – Wuerzburg: Holzner Verlag, 1983 – 10r – 1 – us U.W. Library [943]

JUEDISCHES LEXICON : EIN ENZYKLOPAEDISCHES HANDBUCH DES JUEDISCHEN WISSENS; MIT UEBER 2000 ILLUSTRATIONEN, BEILAGEN UND TABELLEN / ed by Herlitz, G & Kirschner, B – Berlin, 1927-1930 – 51mf – ne IDC [270]

JUEDISCHES LITERATURBLATT – Magdeburg, Berlin. v1-37? 1872-1916? Complete. B212 (Leo Baeck Institute. German-Jewish Periodicals, Pt 1) – 2r – 1 – $135.00 – us UPA [270]

JUEDISCHES NACHRICHTENBLATT : AUSGABE BERLIN – Berlin, nov 23 1938-jan 22 1943 – 1 – Dist. gw Mikrofilm – gw Misc Inst [943]

JUEDISCHES VOLKSBLATT – (Cont by: Juedische Volkszeitung, jul 31 1914; Juedische Zeitung fuer Ostdeutschland, feb 13 1925) – Breslau, aug 31 1900-apr 30 1937 (incomplete) – 4r – 1 – Inquire at Mikrofilmarchiv for details – gw Misc Inst [943]

JUEDISCHES VOLKSBLATT – Spb. v8. 1888 – 1r – 1 – J-92-4/3 – ne IDC [072]

JUEDISCHES VOLKSBLATT – (Title varies. Missing: several pgs. v5-11 1900-05; v15 1909) – Breslau. v4-19. 1899-1913 – 106mf – 9 – J-23-47/1 – ne IDC [072]

JUEDISCHES VOLKSBLATT – Unabhaengiges Organ fuer die Interessen von Gemeinde, Schule und Haus. Breslau. v1-44. 1896-1937. Lacking 1896-99 and misc. issues. B234 (Leo Baeck Institute. German-Jewish Periodicals, Pt 1) – 4r – 1 – $270.00 – us UPA [270]

JUEDISCHES VOLKSBLATT – Zur Belehrung und Unterhaltung auf Juedischem Gebiet. Leipzig. v1-13. 1854-1866. Lacking misc. issues. B233 (Leo Baeck Institute. German-Jewish Periodicals, Pt 1) – 1r – 1 – $75.00 – us UPA [270]

JUEDISCHES VOLKSBLATT *see* JUEDISCHES WOCHENBLATT

JUEDISCHES WOCHENBLATT – (Cont by: Juedisches Volksblatt, 1919 n4) – Bonn, 1919-23 – 1 – Inquire at Mikrofilmarchiv for details – gw Misc Inst [943]

JUEDISCH-LIBERALE ZEITUNG – Berlin. 1921-1936. Lacking misc. issues. 2 reels. B252 (Leo Baeck Institute. German-Jewish Periodicals, Pt 1) – 1 – $135.00 – us UPA [270]

JUEDISCH-LIBERALE ZEITUNG – (Cont by: Juedische Allgemeine Zeitung, nov 7 1934) – Berlin, 1922-36 n37 (incomplete) – 1 – Dist. gw Mikrofilm – gw Misc Inst [072]

JUEDISCH-THEOLOGISCHES SEMINAR – Festschrift zum 75 jaehrigen Bestehen des juedischtheologischen Seminars. 2 v. Breslau. 1929. BJ-100-33 1 – 9 – ne IDC [270]

JUEGOS ANTIGUOS EN AMERICA / ed by Bayle, Constantino – Madrid: Razon y Fe, 1943 y 1944 – 1 – sp Bibl Santa Ana [740]

JUEGOS INFANTILES DE EXTREMADURA / Hernandez de Soto, Sergio – 1884 – 1 – sp Bibl Santa Ana [946]

Juel, H O *see* JOACHIM BURSER'S HORTUS SICCUS

Juelg, B *see* MONGOLISCHE MAERCHEN-SAMMLUNG. DIE NEUN MAERCHEN DES SIDDHI-KUER

Juelicher, Adolf *see* EINLEITUNG IN DAS NEUE TESTAMENT

Juenger, Friedrich Georg *see*
- NIETZSCHE
- DIE SILBERDISTELKLAUSE
- DER TAURUS

DER JUENGLING / Hasenclever, Walter – Leipzig: K Wolff, 1913 – 1r – 1 – us U.W. Library [830]

Juengst, Hugo C *see* FLAMMENZEICHEN

Juengst, Johannes *see*
- KULTUS- UND GESCHICHTSRELIGION (PELAGIANISMUS UND AUGUSTINISMUS)
- PIETISTEN
- DIE QUELLEN DER APOSTELGESCHICHTE

DIE JUENGSTE KRITIK DES GALATERBRIEFES : AUF IHRE BERECHTIGUNG / Gloel, Johannes – (Includes bibliographical references) – Erlangen: Andr Deichert, 1890 – 1mf – 9 – 0-8370-9698-7 – 1986-3698 – us A.T.L.A. [220]

DER JUENGSTE TAG – Giessen. mar 6-dec 30, 1848 – 1 – gw Mikrofilm [072]

Juergens, Cheryl A *see* A KINETIC AND KINEMATIC COMPARISON OF THE GRAB AND TRACK STARTS IN COMPETITIVE SWIMMING

Juergensen, Hans *see* HENRIK IBSENS EINFLUSS AUF HERMANN SUDERMANN

Juerrns, J F *see* GRONDIG ONDERWYS IN DE GREGORIAANSCHE CHOORZANG OF CHORAL

JUEWU – Consciousness. 1920. F C9. In Chinese – 9 – $9.00 – cc Microforms [073]

Juez, Antonio *see*
- DEFENSA CIUDADANA
- EXPOSICION JUEZ
- GUERRAS DE RETAGUARDIA
- RAZA ESPANOLA

Juez Nieto, Antonio *see*
- ALDABADAS
- HACIA LAS RUTAS NUEVAS
- LUIS DE MORALES. EL DIVINO
- POR NUESTROS CAMINOS
- SOY UN POBRE PEREGRINO...

JUF NEWS – Chicago, Ill., v6, no. 10 (Dec. 1978)-v7, no. 9 (Nov. 1979); some lacking – us A.J.P.C. [270]

JUGANTAR – Calcutta, India. 12 Jul 1952-1954; 1965-Aug 1966 – 12r – 1 – us L of C Photodup [072]

LE JUGE A PAIX, ET OFFICIER DE PAROISSE, POUR LA PROVINCE DE QUEBEC / Burn, Richard – Montreal: Fleury Mesplet, 1789. SEM35P59 – 1r – 1 – Can$16.00 – cn Bibl Nat [971]

JUGEMENS SUR QUELQUES OUVRAGES NOUVEAUX – Avignon. 1744-45 (I-XI) – 1 – fr A.C.R.P.P. [073]

JUGEMENT DE NOS SEIGNEURS LES COMMISSAIRES NOMMEZ PAR LE ROY AU FAIT DES PERSONNES RELIGIEUSES ET AUTRES POSSEDEES DU MALIN ESPRIT, A AUSSONNE – Paris. 1662 – 9 – fr Hachette [360]

LE JUGEMENT DE SALOMON / Chaigniez – (French Theatre Series). Paris. An Theatre, an X. 1802 – 9 – fr Hachette [820]

LE JUGEMENT DERNIER DES ROIS / Marechal, Sylvain – (French Theatre Series). Paris. Impr. D.F. Patris, an II. 1793 – 9 – fr Hachette [820]

JUGEMENT DES LORDS DU COMITE JUDICIAIRE DU CONSEIL PRIVE SUR L'APPEL DE DAME HENRIETTE BROWN... / Grande-Bretagne, Privy Council Judicial Committee – [Montreal?]: [s.n.], [1875]. SEM105P1448 – 1mf – 9 – Can$2.25 – cn Bibl Nat [324]

[LE JUGEMENT DU BERGER PARIS] A SELECTION OF FAVORITE AURS IN THE GRAND BALLET CALLED LE JUGEMENT DU BERGER PARIS AS PERFORMED... AT THE KING'S THEATRE / Steibelt, Daniel – London: J Dale, [1805?] – 1 – us Sibley [780]

JUGEND : EIN LIEBESDRAMA IN DREI AUFZUEGEN / Halbe, Max – Berlin: G Bondi, 1911 – 1r – 1 – us U.W. Library [820]

JUGEND IM KAMPF *see* FORUM UND TRIBUNE

JUGEND OHNE GOETHE / Kommerell, Max – Frankfurt a.M.: V Klostermann, [1931] – 1r – 1 – us U.W. Library [430]

JUGEND UND TECHNIK – 1966-1974, 1976-1983 – 425mf – 1 – DM2,422.50 – gw Mikro Press [370]

JUGEND UND WELT / Arnheim, Rudolf – I Herausgegeben von Rudolf Arnheim, E.L. Schiffer Cl. With. Berlin-Gruenwald, Williams & Co. c 1928 326 p. Film Mas 8917 – 1 – us H.U. Library [360]

DER JUGENDBUND – Duesseldorf. v1-18. 1925-1932? Lacking misc. issues. B254 (Leo Baeck Institute. German-Jewish Periodicals, Pt 1) – 1r – 1 – $75.00 – us UPA [270]

DIE JUGENDDICHTUNG FRIEDRICH HOELDERLINS / Grosch, Rudolf – 1995 – 1mf – 9 – DM48.00 – 3-8267-3134-4 – gw Hänsel [430]

JUGENDFREUDE – Stuttgart, Germany. 1886, 1895-1901 – 1 – gw Mikrofilm [072]

Jugie, Martin *see*
- HISTOIRE DU CANON DE L'ANCIEN TESTAMENT DANS L'EGLISE GRECQUE ET L'EGLISE RUSSE
- NESTORIUS ET LA CONTROVERSE NESTORIENNE
- THEOLOGIA DOGMATICA CHRISTANORUM ORIENTALIUM

JUGOSLOVENKI SVIJET – New York, July 23 1908-June 30 1913; Jan 2 1914-June 20 1920 – 16r or 1mf – 9,1 – us I.H.R.C. [975]

JUGOSLOVENSKA ZASTAVA – Chicago, New York, St. Louis, Pittsburgh. v16(1919):14 – us I.H.R.C. [071]

JUGOSLOVENSKI GOSPODAR – Chicago, IL. 1907 – 1mf or 1r – 9,1 – us I.H.R.C. [975]

JUGOSLOVENSKI KOMERCIJALNI BILTEN – Yugoslavia. Jugoslovenski komercijalne novine. -sw. 1960-70. 9 reels – 1 – uk British Libr Newspaper [072]

JUGOSLOVENSKI OBZOR – Milwaukee, WI. 1929, 1938 – 2mf or 1r – 9,1 – us I.H.R.C. [975]

EL JUGUETE CAIDO / Vega Mateos, Celestino – Villanueva de la Serena: Tip. Lucas Alonso Garcia, 1940 – sp Bibl Santa Ana [946]

EL JUGUETE CAIDO. NOTAS BIBLIOGRAFICAS DE PEREZ COMENDADOR / Vega Mateos, Celestino – Plasencia: Editorial Sanchez Rodrigo, 1970 – sp Bibl Santa Ana [920]

Juhle, Werner *see* ILIAMNA VOLCANO AND ITS BASEMENT

Juhlin-Dannfelt, H J B *see* ON THE DIATOMS OF THE BALTIC SEA

Juhn, Kurt *see* DER HEXENHAMMER

Juhnke, Richard *see* WOHLAU

JUICIO CRITICO DE DONOSO CORTES / Perez Cortes y Garcia Camacho, Angel – 1894 – 9 – $1.50f – sp Bibl Santa Ana [440]

EL JUICIO DE PARIS VERDADERO DESENGANO DEL AGUA / Fernandez, F – Madrid, 1755 – 2mf – 9 – sp Cultura [615]

JUICIO DEL TRATADO DE EDUCACION DE POZZI / Munoz, Juan Bautista – 1778 – 1mf – 9 – Pta1,000.00 – 84-7848-285-7 – sp Pentalfa [370]

EL JUICIO POLITICO COMO INSTRUMENTO DE OPRESION : MEMORIAL PRESENTADO AL H. SENADO DE LA NACION, CONSTITUIDO EN TRIBUNAL, POR EL DEFENSOR DEL DR. D. BENITO A. NAZAR ANCHORENA,...DE LA CORTE SUPREMA DE JUSTICIA Y EL PROCURADOR GENERAL DE LA NACION / Drago, Mariano Jose – Buenos Aires, 1946 – 1 – CSUXADJ1806-B – us Hoover Inst Photo [320]

JUICIO PRACTICO SOBRE LAS VIRTUDES MEDICINALES... / Fernandez Barea, M – Granada, 1761 – 2mf – 9 – sp Cultura [610]

LE JUIF ERRANT / Piccini, Caigniez & Piccini, Alexandre – French Theatre Series. Paris. Barba. 1812 – 9 – fr Hachette [820]

LES JUIFS D'AFRIQUE DU NORD ENTRE L'ORIENT ET L'OCCIDENT / Chouraqui, A – F40.00 – fr Ethnologie [305]

Juillerat, B *see* OBJETS DU HAUT-SEPIK, NOUVELLE-GUINEE

JUIN – Politique, economique, litteraire. no. 1-47. Paris. fevr 1946-7 janv 1947 – 1 – fr A.C.R.P.P. [073]

JUIN 36 – Trente-six. Organe de la Federation socialiste de la Seine, S.F.I.O. puis Organe du Parti socialiste ouvrier et paysan. Dir. Marceau Pivert. Paris. fevr 1938-39 – 1 – fr A.C.R.P.P. [073]

Jukes, Andrew John *see*
- CHARACTERISTIC DIFFERENCES OF THE FOUR GOSPELS
- THE CHARACTERISTIC DIFFERENCES OF THE FOUR GOSPELS
- THE LAW OF THE OFFERINGS IN LEVITICUS 1-7
- LAW OF THE OFFERINGS IN LEVITICUS I-VII
- NAMES OF GOD IN HOLY SCRIPTURES: A REVELATION OF HIS NATURE AND RELATIONSHIPS
- THE NEW MAN AND THE ETERNAL LIFE
- THE SECOND DEATH AND THE RESTITUTION OF ALL THINGS

- THE TYPES OF GENESIS BRIEFLY CONSIDERED AS REVEALING THE DEVELOPMENT OF HUMAN NATURE

Jukes, Joseph Beete see NARRATIVE OF THE SURVEYING VOYAGE OF H.M.S. FLY; COMMANDED BY CAPT. F. P. BLACKWOOD IN TORRES STRAIT, NEW GUINEA, AND OTHER ISLANDS IN THE EASTERN ARCHIPELAGO 1842-1846..

JULES FERRY, 1832-1893 / Reclus, Maurice – Paris: Flammarion, [1947] – us Res Libr [920]

JULIA : EIN TRAUERSPIEL IN DREI AKTEN – NEBST EINER VORREDE UND EINER ABHANDLUNG / Hebbel, Friedrich – Leipzig: J J Weber, 1851 – 1r – 1 – us U.W. Library [820]

JULIA GONZAGA : EIN LEBENSBILD AUS DER GESCHICHTE DER REFORMATION IN ITALIEN / Benrath, Karl – Halle: Verein fuer Reformationsgeschichte, 1900 (Schriften des Vereins fuer Reformationsgeschichte; 16. Jahrg., Schrift 65 – 1mf – us A.T.L.A. [240]

JULIA OU LES SOUTERRAINS DU CHATEAU DE MAZZINI / Sewrin – (French Theatre Series). Paris. Chez le libraire "Au Theatre du Vaudeville." an VII. 1798 – 9 – fr Hachette [820]

JULIAN DER ABTRUENNIGE : GESCHICHTLICHER ROMAN / Dahn, Felix – Leipzig: Breitkopf und Haertel. 3v in 2. 1898 – 1 – us U.W. Library [830]

JULIAN GAZETTE – Julian, NE. -w. May-Nov 1899 – 1 – us NE Hist [071]

JULIAN HUXLEY : SCIENTIST AND WORLD CITIZEN 1887-1975 / Baker, J R – 1978 – 184p – 9 – 92-3-101461-7 – fr UNESCO [500]

JULIAN, OR, SCENES IN JUDEA / Ware, William – 2v. 1885, c1841 – 1 – us A.T.L.A. [240]

JULIAN, PHILOSOPHER AND EMPEROR : AND THE LAST STRUGGLE OF PAGANISM AGAINST CHRISTIANITY / Gardner, Alice – New York: G.P. Putnam, 1906, c1895. (Heroes of the nations) – 1mf – us A.T.L.A. [240]

JULIAN THE EMPEROR : CONTAINING GREGORY NAZIANZEN'S TWO INVECTIVES AND LIBANIUS' MONODY : WITH JULIAN'S EXTANT THEOSOPHICAL WORKS / King, CW – London: G. Bell, 1888. (Bohn's classical library) – 1mf – us A.T.L.A. [240]

JULIAN VON ECLANUM (T.U.U. 1-15/3A) / Bruckner, A – Leipzig, 1897 – 3mf – 9 – ne Slangenburg [240]

JULIANA HORATIA EWING AND HER BOOKS / Ewing, Juliana Horatia – British Fiction Archive: Unit 1 – 9 – uk Bell [830]

JULIANUS APOSTATA IN DER DEUTSCHEN LITERATUR / Philip, Kaete – (Includes bibliographical references and index) – Berlin: W de Gruyter & Co, 1929 – 2r – 1 – us U.W. Library [430]

Julien, E see BOSSUET ET LES PROTESTANTS

Julien, S see
- MEMOIRES SUR LES CONTREES OCCIDENTALES TRADUITS DU SANSCRIT EN CHINOIS EN L'AN 648 PAR HIOUEN-THSANG ET DU CHINOIS EN FRANCAIS
- METHODE POUR DECHIFFRER LES NOMS SANSCRITS DANS LES LIVRES CHINOIS

JULIET GRENVILLE; OR, THE HISTORY OF THE HUMAN HEART / Brooke, H – London, 1774. 3v – 10mf – 9 – ne IDC [830]

JULIO CESAR : COMMENTARIORUM BELLI GALLIA – Madrid, SP. S.15 – 1,5 – sp Cultura [945]

JULIUS CAHN'S OFFICIAL THEATRICAL GUIDE – New York. v. 1-2, 4-6, 8-9. 1896 97-1897, 1899 1900-1901 02, 1903 04-1904 05 – 1 – us NY Public [790]

JULIUS CAHN'S OFFICIAL THEATRICAL GUIDE – New York. v1-9. 1896-1905 – 2r – 1 – us Ross [790]

JULIUS FUCIK PAMPHLET COLLECTION – 1973 – 9 – us Hoover Inst Photo [970]

JULIUS GROSSES ERZAEHLENDE DICHTUNGEN / Naegel, Andreas – (Includes bibliographical references) – Zeulenroda: B Sporn, 1938 – 1r – 1 – us U.W. Library [430]

JULIUS LEOPOLD KLEIN ALS DRAMATIKER / Glatzel, Max – Stuttgart: Metzler, 1914 – 1r – 1 – us U.W. Library [430]

JULIUS MOSEN : EIN DEUTSCHER DICHTER UND VOLKSMANN / Zimmer, Fritz Alfred – (Includes bibliographical references) – Dresden: Verlag Heimatwerk Sachsen, v. Baensch Stiftung, 1938 – 1r – 1 – us U.W. Library [430]

JULIUS PINCAS DIT PASCIN / Voss, Hans – Frankfurt a.M., 1956 – 1mf – DM48.00 – 3-89349-849-4 – gw Hänsel [700]

Jullien, Jean-Auguste see
- HISTOIRE ANECDOTIQUE ET RAISONNEE DU THEATRE ITALIEN
- HISTOIRE DU THEATRE DE L'OPERA COMIQUE

Jully, Antony see MANUEL DES DIALECTES MALGACHES, COMPRENANT SEPT DIALECTES

Jumariam see RESEARCH IN INDONESIAN AND REGIONAL LANGUAGES

JUMHURI-I ISLAMI – (Sal-i 1, shumarah-'i 1-sal-i 10, shumarah-'i 3902 (9 Khurdad 1358-28 Aban 1371[30 May 1979-19 Nov 1992]). Missing issues: 649, 659-676, 768, 771, 773, 779, 789, 813, 878, 894, 1492, 1521-1522, 1524-1529, 1668, 1743, 1892, 1954, 2196, 2389, 2402, 2555, 2560, 2603-2605, 2695, 2701, 2744, 2840-2845, 2878, 3040-3041, 3043-3141, 3145, 3176, 3184, 3448-3450, 3687, 3716, 3750) – Tehran: Hizb-i Jumhuri-i Islami – 54r – 1 – $2,000.00 – us MEDOC [950]

Jumilhac, P B de see LA SCIENCE ET LA PRATIQUE DU PLAIN-CHANT

JUNBISH – (Shumarah-'i 1-27,51-69,75-88 (20 Isfand 1356-21 Urdibihisht 1359[11 Mar 1978-11 May 1980])) – Tehran, 1979-1980 – 1 reel – 1 – $35.00 – us MEDOC [950]

JUNCTION CITY BULLETIN – Junction City, OR. -w. 4 Aug 1899-18 Jul 1901. 1 roll – 1 – us U.O. Library [071]

Junction City. Kansas. Church of the Covenant see PARISH RECORDS

Junction City. Kansas. First Presbyterian Church see RECORDS

JUNCTION CITY TIMES – Junction City, OR. -w. 10 Oct 1891-6 Dec 1984 – 1 – us U.O. Library [071]

Jundt, Andre see LE DEVELOPPEMENT DE LA PENSEE RELIGIEUSE DE LUTHER JUSQU'EN 1517

Jundt, Auguste see
- LES AMIS DE DIEU AU QUATORZIEME SIECLE
- LES CENTURIES DE MAGDEBOURG, OU, LA RENAISSANCE DE L'HISTORIOGRAPHIE ECCLESIASTIQUE AU SEIZIEME SIECLE
- HISTOIRE DU PANTHEISME POPULAIRE AU MOYEN AGE ET AU SEIZIEME SIECLE

JUNE 21, 1914-SEPT. 27, 1914 see SUNDAY TRANSCRIPT

Jung, Andreas see PHOTOADDITION VON APLPHA-MORPHOLINOACRYLONITRIL AN 8-CHINOLINCARBONSAEUREMETHYLESTER

Jung, Carl Gustav see THE INTEGRATION OF THE PERSONALITY

Jung, Hermann see DIE BETEILIGUNG DER RELIGIONSGESELLSCHAFTEN AN STAATLICHEN AUFGABEN

Jung, J see OPUSCULA BOTANICO-PHYSICA

Jung, Rudolf see
- GOETHES BRIEFWECHSEL MIT ANTONIE BRENTANO 1814-1821
- STUDIEN ZUR SPRACHAUFFASSUNG GEORG CHRISTOPH LICHTENBERGS

Jung, Werner see VOM NULLPUNKT ZUR WENDE

Jungbauer, Gustav see DA MENSCH MUASS A FREUD HABN

Jungbluth, Guenther see UNTERSUCHUNGEN ZU HEINRICH VON VELDEKE

JUNGBORN : JUGEND-ORGAN DES VERBANDES DER BERGARBEITER DEUTSCHLANDS – Bochum, 1920-22 – 1r – 1 – Inquire at Mikrofilmarchiv for details – gw Misc Inst [622]

JUNGBORN : JUGEND-ORGAN DES VERBANDES DER BERGARBEITER DEUTSCHLANDS – Bochum, Germany. 1920-1922 – 1r – 1 – gw Mikrofilm [073]

DER JUNGDEUTSCHE – Berlin. Jan 1929-June 1933 – 1 – us NY Public [073]

DER JUNGDEUTSCHE see DER JUNG-DEUTSCHE ORDEN

DER JUNG-DEUTSCHE ORDEN – (Founded in Muenchen. Cont as: Der Jungdeutsche, Kassel. Since feb 1 1925 publ in Berlin. Cont by: Nordische Zeitung, jul 11 1933. Deutsche Staatsbuerger Zeitung, sep 1 1933) – Berlin, 1921-33 – 1 – Dist. gw Mikrofilm – gw Misc Inst [943]

JUNGDEUTSCHLAND-POST – Berlin, 1921 n1-24, 1925 n1-15 – 1 – Dist. gw Mikrofilm – gw Misc Inst [072]

DAS JUNGE DEUTSCHLAND – Berlin, 1926 n10, 12, 1927 n2, 1929, 1930 (incomplete), 1931, 1933-43 (incomplete) – 1 – Dist. gw Mikrofilm – gw Misc Inst [072]

DER JUNGE DONOSCO CORTES (1809-1836) / Schramm, Edmund – Pp. 248-310 – sp Bibl Santa Ana [920]

DER JUNGE EICHENDORFF / Krueger, Hermann Anders – 1995 – 1mf – 9 – DM48.00 – 3-8267-3137-9 – gw Hänsel [430]

DIE JUNGE GARDE : ZENTRALORGAN DER SOZIALISTISCHEN JUGEND DEUTSCHLANDS – Berlin, 1918-23 – 1 – Dist. gw Mikrofilm – gw Misc Inst [943]

DIE JUNGE GARDE : ZENTRALORGAN DER SOZIALISTISCHEN JUGEND DEUTSCHLANDS – Berlin, nov 2 1918-aug 15 1923 – 1r – 1 – DM90.00 – gw Mikro Press [943]

JUNGE GENERATION – 1966-1989 – 592mf – 1 – DM3,374.40 – gw Mikro Press [370]

DER JUNGE GENOSSE – Berlin-Schoeneberg, 1921-24 – 1r – 1 – Dist. gw Mikrofilm – gw Misc Inst [072]

DER JUNGE GOETHE / Vietor, Karl – Leipzig: Quelle & Meyer, 1930 – 1r – 1 – us U.W. Library [920]

DER JUNGE GOETHE ALS SOZIALERZIEHER / List, Friedrich – (Includes bibliographical references) – Giessen: W Huch, 1922 – 1r – 1 – us U.W. Library [430]

DER JUNGE HALLER : NACH SEINEM BRIEFWECHSEL MIT JOHANNES GESSNER AUS DEN JAHREN 1728-1738 / Vetter, Ferdinand – (Includes bibliographical references) – Bern: A Francke, 1909 – 1r – 1 – us U.W. Library [920]

DER JUNGE HEINSE / Schurig, Arthur – (Includes bibliographical references) – Muenchen: G Mueller, 1912 – 1r – 1 – us U.W. Library [430]

DER JUNGE HERDER UND WINCKELMANN / Berger, Arnold Erich – Halle a.d.S.: M Niemeyer, 1903 – 1r – 1 – us U.W. Library [430]

DER JUNGE JOSEF GOERRES UND FRIEDRICH HOELDERLINS HYPERION / Bianchi, Lorenzo – (Includes bibliographical references) – Heidelberg: Weiss, 1926 – 1r – 1 – us U.W. Library [430]

JUNGE KIRCHE – (Lacking: v19 p645-64) – v1-35. Jun 1933-1974 – 22r – 1 – ATLA S0105 – us A.T.L.A. [073]

DER JUNGE MYSTIKER, ODER, DIE DREI LETZTEN FESTZEITEN AUS SEINEM LEBEN : EINE BIOGRAPHISCHE SKIZZE / Fritz, Dr. – Leipzig: K.F. Koehler, [1839?] – 1mf – us A.T.L.A. [240]

DER JUNGE PIONIER see DIE TROMMEL

JUNGE PIONIER see TROMMEL

DER JUNGE STURMTRUPP – Berlin, jul 22-nov 1 1931, jan 1-oct 15 1932 – 1 – Dist. gw Mikrofilm – gw Misc Inst [943]

DER JUNGE TIECK UND SEINE MAERCHENKOMOEDIEN / Brodnitz, Kaethe – (Includes bibliographical references) – Muenchen: Walhalla-Verlag, 1912 – 1 – us U.W. Library [430]

JUNGE WELT : AUSGABE B – Berlin, mai-aug 1952 – 1r – 1 – Dist. gw Mikrofilm – gw Misc Inst [072]

JUNGE WELT – Berlin. 1939 n3-1944 n4 – 1r – 1 – gw Mikrofilm [073]

JUNGE WELT – Berlin, 1950- – 1 – Dist. gw Mikrofilm – gw Misc Inst [072]

JUNGE WELT – v. 1-6. Apr 1939-Mar Apr 1944 – 5 – 28.00 – us L of C Photodup [943]

DER JUNGE WIELAND : WESENSBESTIMMUNG SEINES GEISTES / Hoppe, Karl – (Includes bibliographical references) – Leipzig: J J Weber, 1930 – 1r – 1 – us U.W. Library [430]

DAS JUNGE ZENTRUM – Berlin. aug 1924-jul 1933 – 2r – 1 – gw Mikrofilm [073]

Jungel, Eberhard see UNTERWEGS ZUR SACHE

JUNGENS, MAENNER UND MOTORE / Stoll, Friedrich Albert Robert – Berlin: Volksverband der Buecherfreunde, 1940.86p. illus – 1 – us U.W. Library [355]

Junger, Ewig see ZHIZNBORBA

JUNGERMANNIARUM AMERICANARUM PUGILLUS / Notaris, G de – Mem. Acad. Sc. S. 2(16). Torino. 1855. B-6520 2 – 8 – ne IDC [999]

Jungfer, Victor see IRKA: ROMAN

DIE JUNGFRAU VON ORLEANS IN DER DICHTUNG / Grenzmann, Wilhelm – (Includes bibliographical references) – Berlin: W de Gruyter & Co, 1929 – 2r – 1 – us U.W. Library [430]

DIE JUNGFRAU VON ORLEANS IN DER DICHTUNG : SHAKESPEARE, VOLTAIRE, SCHILLER / Kummer, Carl Ferdinand – (Includes bibliographical references) – Wien: A Hoelder, 1874 – 1r – 1 – us U.W. Library [410]

JUNGFRAUENGEBURT = THE VIRGIN BIRTH / Gruetzmacher, Richard H – (In English. Includes bibliographical references) – New York: Eaton & Mains; Cincinnati: Jennings & Graham, c1907 – 1mf – 9 – 0-8370-3416-7 – 1985-1416 – us A.T.L.A. [240]

JUNG-HSIEN CHIH – 1929, 15. BCH-761 2 – 8 – ne IDC [950]

Junghuhn, F W see
- JAWA, DESZELFS GEDAANTE, BEKLEEDING EN INWENDIGE STRUCTUUR
- PRAEMISSA IN FLORA CRYPTOGAMICAM JAVAE INSULAE
- TOPOGRAFISCHE UND NATURWISSENSCHAFTLICHE REISEN DURCH JAVA

JUNGLE GODS / Hoffman, Carl von; ed by Lohrke, Eugene – New York: H Holt, [c1929] – us Res Libr [290]

JUNGMAEDEL AUF DEM KOELLINGSHOF / Perzl, Irmgard – Reutlingen: Ensslin & Laiblin, 1941 – 1r – 1 – us U.W. Library [943]

Jungmann, Bernardus see
- TRACTATUS DE GRATIA
- TRACTATUS DE NOVISSIMIS
- TRACTATUS DE VERA RELIGIONE
- TRACTATUS DE VERBO INCARNATO

Jungmann, J A see
- GEWORDENE LITURGIE
- DIE STELLUNG CHRISTI IM LITURGISCHEN GEBET. L.T.Q 19/20

Jungniss, J see DIE BRESLAUER RITUALIEN

JUNGSOZIALISTEN IN DER SPD – Misc. publications. University of Wisconsin Libraries, Madison, 1986 – 1 – us U.W. Library [335]

JUNGSOZIALISTISCHE BLAETTER – Nuernberg, Germany. Jan 1922-Jul 1931 – 2r – 1 – gw Mikrofilm [072]

JUNGSOZIALISTISCHE BLAETTER – Nuernberg, Jan 1922-Jul 1931 – 2r – 1 – DM240.00 – gw Mikro Press [335]

JUNG-SPARTAKUS / Jung-Spartakusbundes – Berlin. Zeitschrift fuer Arbeiterkinder. Jan. 1, 1921-Dec. 1924. Aug. 5, 1925 – 1 – $35.00r – us Hoover Inst Photo [320]

Jung-Spartakusbundes see JUNG-SPARTAKUS

JUNGVOLK – Berlin, 1915 – 1r – 1 – Dist. gw Mikrofilm – gw Misc Inst [072]

JUNGVOLK – Zentralstelle fuer die arbeitende jugend Deutschlands. 1913-21. illus. - ann. (Serial publications of German trade unions in the Memorial Library, University of Wisconsin-Madison.) – 1 – us U.W. Library [331]

JUNIATA HERALD – Juniata, NE. -w. Nov 1877-Oct 1879; Jan 1880-Nov 1917 – 1 – us NE Hist [071]

JUNIATA HERALD – Mifflintown, PA. -w 1889-1912 – 13 – $25.00r – us I.M.R. [071]

JUNIATA SENTINEL – Ebensburg, PA., 1971-1975 – 13 – $25.00r – us I.M.R. [071]

JUNIATA SENTINEL – Mifflintown, PA. -w 1860 – 13 – $25.00r – us I.M.R. [071]

JUNIATA STAR – Mifflintown, PA. -w 1897-1899 – 13 – $25.00r – us I.M.R. [071]

JUNIATA TRIBUNE – Mifflintown, PA. -w 1891-1896; 1918-1932; 1962-1970 – 13 – $25.00r – us I.M.R. [071]

JUNIATA TRUE DEMOCRAT – Mifflintown, PA. Circa 1866 – 13 – $25.00r – us I.M.R. [071]

Juniolus see FALLACY DETECTED IN A LETTER TO THE REV. MR. JOHN WESLEY, MASTER OF ARTS, WHEREIN HIS 'FREE THOUGHTS ON THE STATE OF PUBLIC AFFAIRS' AND HIS 'CALM ADDRESS TO THE AMERICANS' ARE CONSIDERED AND COMPARED

JUNIOR BOOKSHELF – 1936- 1; 1970- 5,6; 1976- 4 x 6 in. 9 – us UMI [010]

JUNIOR BOY – 1930-31 – 1 – 9.45 – us Baptist [240]

JUNIOR COLLEGE JOURNALIST – v. 1-2. 1972-74 – 1 – us UMI [070]

JUNIOR EDUCATION – (1983-. 1,5,6,9) – v1-. 1977- – 1 – us UMI [073]

JUNIOR EDUCATION SPECIAL – v1-. 1982- – 1,5,6,9 – us UMI [073]

JUNIOR EXTENSION CIRCULAR / South Dakota. Agricultural Extension Service. State College of Agriculture and Mechanic Arts – nos.1-42. 1919-21 – 1,5,6 – us Spaulding [630]

JUNIOR GAZETTE – Salem OR. July 20 1934, Apr 6 1935 – 1 – us U.O. Library [071]

JUNIOR GIRL – 1930-31 – 1 – 9.38 – us Baptist [240]

THE JUNIOR HERALD – Lincoln, NE. 1919-20 – 1 – us A.J.P.C. [071]

JUNIOR HIGH-MIDDLE SCHOOL BULLETIN – 1962- 1; 1978- 5,6,9 – us UMI [370]

JUNIOR LEADER – 1924-55. (Formerly: The Junior Leader's B.Y.P.U. Quarterly. 1925-39) – 1 – 209.23 – us Baptist [240]

THE JUNIOR LEAGUE HAND-BOOK : DEVOTED TO JUNIOR LEAGUE METHODS OF WORK / Bartlett, S T – Toronto: W. Briggs; Montreal: C. Coates; Halifax: S. Huestis, 1897. 03384. (Pre-1900 Canadiana) – 9 – cn C.I.H.M. [360]

JUNIOR QUARTERLY – Jan 1930-61 – 1 – 223.30 – us Baptist [240]

JUNIOR SCHOLASTIC – 1937- 1; 1970- 5,6; 1975- 4 – us UMI [370]

JUNIOR TEACHER'S AND PUPIL BOOK, YEARS 1-4 – 1923-28 – 1 – 119.00 – us Baptist [240]

JUNIOR TRAINING UNION QUARTERLY – 1922-61 – 1 – 186.34 – us Baptist [240]

JUNIOR WEEKLY – 1931 – 1 – 5.74 – us Baptist [240]

Juniu, Susana *see* MUSIC

Junius, Franciscus *see* DE PICTURA VETERUM LIBRI TRES

Junius, H *see*
- EMBLEMATA
- EMBLEMATA, AD D. ARNOLDUM COBELIUM. EIUSDEM AENIGMATUM LIBELLUS, AD D. ARNOLDUM ROSENBERGUM
- DE EMBLEMATA VAN HADRIANUS JUNIUS

Junk *see* CATALOGUS COLEOPTERORUM

Junk, Victor *see* ALEXANDER

Junk, W *see* BIBLIOGRAPHIA BOTANICA

Junker, C L *see*
- ZWANZIG COMPONISTEN, EINE SKIZZE
- ZWANZIG COMPONISTEN, EINE SKIZZE VON C. L. JUNKER

Junker, H *see*
- DAS GOETTERDEKRET UEBER DAS ABATON
- DIE ONURIS-LEGENDE

Junker, K *see* PORTFEULLE FUR MUSIKLIEBHABER

DIE JUNKER, ROMAN / Zobeltitz, Fedor Karl Maria Hermann August von – Berlin: Ullstein, 1918. 443p – 1 – us U.W. Library [830]

Junker, W *see* REISEN IN AFRIKA; 1875, 1876

Junod, Henri A *see* GRAMMAIRE RONGA SUIVIE D'UN MANUEL DE CONVERSATION ET D'UN VOCABULAIRE RONGA-PORTUGAIS-FRANCAIS-ANGLAIS

JUNTA DE AGRICULTURA...ENSENANZA AGRICOLA / Paredes Guillen, Vicente – 1871 – 9 – 1.50f – sp Bibl Santa Ana [630]

JUNTA DE ARANCELES. PROYECTO DE DICTAMEN RESPECTO...AL ARANCEL DE 23 DE MARZO DE 1906 – Madrid, 1906 – 7mf – 9 – sp Cultura [946]

Junta de Cofradias de Penitencia *see* HORARIO E ITINERARIO DE LAS PROCESIONES DE SEMANA SANTA...1962

Junta de Cofradias de Penitencia y C.I.T.E. *see*
- SEMANA SANTA. BADAJOZ, 1968
- SEMANA SANTA. BADAJOZ, 1969, 70

Junta Diocesana de Accion Catolica. (Coria) *see* JESUCRISTO REDENTOR. PROGRAMA PARA LOS CIRCULOS DE ETUDIO DE ACCION CATOLICA DE LA DIOCESIS DE CORIS. CURSO 1938-1939

Junta Diocesano de Accion Catolica. (Coria) *see* REGLAMENTO DE LOS SECRETARIOS DE CARIDAD DE ACCION CATOLICA

LA JUNTA PARA AMPLIACION DE ESTUDIOS. RECTIFICACION Y COMENTARIOS / Bayle, Constantino – Madrid: Razon y Fe, 1924 – 1 – sp Bibl Santa Ana [946]

Junta Provincial de Educacion Fisica y Deportes *see*
- ANUARIO DEPORTIVO 1969
- ELECCION AL MEJOR DEPORTISTA PROVINICAL DE BADAJOZ-1970

Junta Provincial de Fomento Pecuario *see*
- LABOR DESARROLLADA DESDE SU CREACION HASTA FIN DE DICIEMBRE DE 1951
- MEMORIA-INDICE DE LOS TRABAJOS EFECTUADOS DURANTE LOS ANOS 1938-1944. INCLUSIVES

Junta Provincial de Fomento Pecuario. Badajoz *see*
- CURSILLO SOBRE EXPLOTACIONES OVINAS EN SU ASPECTO DE PRODUCCION DE LANA
- GANADO LANAR
- PRIMER CONCURSO PROVINCIAL DE GANADO LANAR

Junta Provincial de Informacion, Turismo y Educacion Popular *see*
- CACERES. MAPA GUIA TURISTICO PROVINCIAL
- RUTA DE LA ALTA EXTREMADURA, CUNA DE LOS CONQUISTADORES

Junta Provincial de Turismo *see*
- ALCANTARA (CACERES)
- CACERES
- CATALOGO DEL CONCURSO-EXPOSICION DE FOTOGRAFIAS SOBRE TEMAS CACERENOS
- CORIA (CACERES)
- GUADALUPE (CACERES)
- HERVAS (CACERES)
- TRUJILLO, CUNA DE CONQUISTADORES. MONTANCHEZ, EL BALCON DE EXTREMADURA

JUNTURA TIMES – Juntura OR. Jan 16 1914, Apr 30 May 7 21 1915 – 1 – us U.O. Library [071]

Juranville, Clarisse *see* LA CIVILITE DES PETITES FILLES

Juras Reales, Baron de *see* EL ESPIRITU DEL SIGLO

THE JURASSIC FLORA / Seward, A C – 1900-04 – 7 – uk Microform Academic [550]

LAS JURDES ETUDE DE GEOGRAPHIA HUMAINE / Legendre, Maurice – Bordeaux: Feret fils, edoteurs, 1927 – 1 – sp Bibl Santa Ana [550]

LAS JURDES Y SU LEYENDAS / Barrantes Moreno, Vicente – 1891 – 9 – $1.50f – sp Bibl Santa Ana [390]

JURIDIC STATUS OF THE CATHOLIC CHURCH AND RELIGIOUS ORDERS UNDER THE CONSTITUTIONAL MONARCHY – n.p., 193? Fiche W977. (Blodgett Collection of Spanish Civil War Pamphlets) – 9 – us H.U. College Libr [946]

JURIDICAL ARGUMENTS AND COLLECTIONS / Hargrave, Francis – London: Robinson, 1797-99. 2v. LL-993 – 1 – us L of C Photodup [340]

JURIDICAL REVIEW – (Add vols as copyright expires) – Edinburgh. v1-23. 1889-1912 – 133mf – 9 – $199.00 – LLMC 84-509 – us L.L.M.C. [073]

JURIDICAL SOCIETY PAPERS – Papers read before the Juridical Society. v1-4. 1855-74 (all publ) – 25mf – 9 – $37.50 – LLMC 84-510 – us L.L.M.C. [340]

JURIDICAL TECHNIQUES AND THE JUDICIAL PROCESS / Epstein, A L – 7 – uk Microform Academic [340]

LA JURIDICTION DES EGLISES ET LES CONFLICTS DE LOIS EN MATIERE DE MARIAGE EN BULGARIE / Ghenadieff, M – Paris, 1939 – 2mf – 1 – ILM-3013/1 – ne IDC [327]

JURIDICTION EXERCEE PAR L'ARCHEVEQUE DE ROUEN / Gosselin, Auguste – Evreux: Impr. de l'Eure, 1895. 03475. (Pre-1900 Canadiana) – 9 – cn C.I.H.M. [240]

JURIESPRUDENSI INDONESIA, AGIAN PERDATA / Pudjosubroto, R Santoso – SE-5419 1. 1964 – 9 – ne IDC [340]

Jurieu, P *see*
- APOLOGIE POUR LA REFORMATION, POUR LES REFORMATEURS, ET POUR LES REFORMEZ
- LA POLITIQUE DU CLERGE DE FRANCE
- PREJUGEZ LEGITIMES CONTRE LE PAPISME

JURIMETRICS – 1959- 1; 1970- 5,6; 1977- 4 x 6 in. 9 – us UMI [600]

JURIMETRICS JOURNAL (ABA) – (Title varies; v1-7. 1959-1965, as M.U.L.L. Modern Uses of Logic in Law) – v1-32. 1959-1992 – 9 – $265.00 set – us Hein [340]

THE JURISDICTION AND PRACTICE AT LARGE IN CITY JUDGES', MAYORS', AND JUSTICES' COURTS OF THE STATE OF INDIANA...2ND ED / Spalding, Hugh Mortimer – Cincinnati, Wilstach, Baldwin, 1876. 789 p. LL-1293 – 1 – us L of C Photodup [340]

JURISDICTION OF SUBMERGED LANDS IN AMERICAN SAMOA, GUAM, AND THE VIRGIN ISLANDS : HEARING BEFORE THE SUBCOMMITTEE ON TERRITORIAL AND INSULAR AFFAIRS OF THE HOUSE COMMITTEE ON INTERIOR AND INSULAR AFFAIRS / American Samoa. US Congress – 93rd Congress 1st sess 25 Sept 1973. Washington: GPO, 1974 – 1mf – 9 – $1.50 – LLMC 95-041 – us L.L.M.C. [327]

JURISDICTION OF THE FEDERAL COURTS. REV. ED / Thayer, Amos Madden – St. Louis, Brewer 1900. 52 p. LL-1222 – 1 – us L of C Photodup [340]

JURISDICTION, PRACTICE, AND PECULIAR JURISPRUDENCE OF THE COURTS OF THE UNITED STATES / Curtis, Benjamin Robbins – (2nd ed., Boston, Little, Brown, 1896. 341 p. LL-1276) – Boston, Little, Brown, 1880. 298 p. LL-1301 – 1 – us L of C Photodup [340]

Jurispridencia del Tribunal Supremo *see* CODIGO PENAL PARA LAS ISLAS DE CUBA Y PUERTO RICO

JURISPRUDENCE, LAW AND ETHICS : PROFESSIONAL ETHICS / Kinkead, Edgar Benton – New York: the Banks Publ Co, 1905 – 4mf – 9 – $6.00 – LLMC 95-178 – us L.L.M.C. [170]

JURISPRUDENCIA – Maceio, Alagoas. 5 Ago, Dez 1894; Fev-7 Mar 1895 – 1,5,6 – bl Biblioteca [072]

JURISPRUDENCIA ARGENTINA – Buenos Aires. On film: v1-211; 1918-71; indexes: 1918-66. LL-0285 – 1 – 3151.00 – us L of C Photodup [340]

JURISPRUDENCIA CIVIL / Spain. Tribunal Supremo – Madrid. On film: v1-224; 1855-1936. LL-0152 – 1 – us L of C Photodup [340]

JURISPRUDENCIA CRIMINAL / Spain. Tribunal Supremo – Madrid. On film: v1-136; 1871-1937. LL-0151 – 1 – us L of C Photodup [340]

JURIST – v19- 1959- 1; v31- 5,6; v37- 9 – us UMI [340]

JURIST – London. v1-30. 1837-67 (v19-30 as n.s. v1-12) – 1 – $1,040.00 – us Hein [073]

THE JURIST : A JOURNAL FOR LAW STUDENTS AND THE PROFESSION – (Lacking: v5 p93-136) – London. v1-5. 1887-91 (all publ) – 18mf – 9 – $27.00 – LLMC 84-512 – us L.L.M.C. [073]

THE JURIST : OR QUARTERLY JOURNAL OF JURISPRUDENCE AND LEGISLATION – London. v1-4. 1827-33 (all publ) – 9 – LLMC 84-513 – us L.L.M.C. [073]

THE JURIST – Suffolk University Law School, 1926-28 (all publ) – 9 – LLMC 84-511 – us L.L.M.C. [073]

THE JURIST, NEW SERIES : CONTAINING REPORTS OF CASES DTERMINED IN THE COURTS OF LAW AND EQUITY, AND...IN THE ADMIRALTY AND ECCLESIASTICAL COURTS, WITH A GENERAL DIGEST OF ALL THE REPORTS PUBLISHED / Great Britain – (All vols have a pt2, serving same purpose as with v6-18 of Old Series. v4 New Series, 1858 sees expansion of coverage to include a section on Divorce and Probate courts) – v1-12. 1855-67. London: Sweet/ Stevens, 1856-57 – 276mf – 9 – $414.00 – LLMC 95-268 – us L.L.M.C. [340]

THE JURIST, OLD SERIES : CONTAINING REPORTS OF CASES DETERMINED IN THE COURTS OF LAW AND EQUITY, AND...IN THE ADMIRALTY AND ECCLESIASTICAL COURTS, WITH A GENERAL DIGEST OF ALL REPORTS PUBLISHED / Great Britain – (v6-18 have a pt2 containing articles on legal subjects, all important statutes, miscellaneous legal information etc. v11 1847 has a suppl book) – v1-18. 1837-54: London: Sweet/ Stevens, 1838-55 (all publ) – 340mf – 9 – $510.00 – LLMC 95-267 – us L.L.M.C. [340]

JURISTISCHE ABHANDLUNG UEBER DIE FLOEHE / Goethe, Johann Wolfgang von – 1995 – 1mf – 9 – DM48.00 – 3-8267-3119-0 – gw Hänsel [340]

JURISTISCHE BLAETTER – v.92-103, 1970-81. v.1-91 incomplete. Prices upon request. ISSN: 0022-6912 – 1,5,6,9,13 – 95.00v – us UMI [073]

JURISTISCHE WOCHENSCHRIFT.. – Organ des deutschen anwalt-vereins. Berlin. 1881-1939.Suppl., 1900-02. General register, 1879-1900 – 1 – 1334.00 – us L of C Photodup [943]

JURNALUL DE DIMINEATA – Bucharest. Rumania. -d. 14 Nov 1944-10 Jul 1947. (Imperfect). (5 reels) – 1 – uk British Libr Newspaper [949]

THE JUROR: BEING A GUIDE TO CITIZENS SUMMONED TO SERVE AS JURORS / Reilly, Andrew Jackson – Philadelphia, Campbell, 1873. 108 p. LL-1280 – 1 – us L of C Photodup [340]

O JURUA : ORGAO INDEPENDENTE, NOTICIOSO E DEFENSOR DOS INTERESSES DA COLETIVIDADE – Cruzeiro do Sul, Acre. 15 Fev-Set, Nov-Dez 1953; Jan-Set, Dez 1954; Jan-Mar, Jun, Set, Nov-Dez 1955; Jan, Abr-Ago, Out-Dez 1956; Jan, Mar-Maio, Set-Dez 1957; Abr-Dez 1958; Jan-Jun 1959; Jan-Set 1960; Maio 1961; Fev-Set 1962; Jan-Mar 1963; Jan-Set 1964; Jan-Nov 1965; Jan-Dez 1966; Jan-Ago 1967; Jan, Maio-Dez 1968; Ago 1969; Abr-Nov 1970; Jan-20 Abr 1971 – 1,5,6 – bl Biblioteca [072]

O JURUAENSE : ORGAO INDEPENDENTE DEFENSOR DOS INTERESSES GERAES DO DEPARTAMENTO – Cruzeiro do Sul, Acre. 24 Fev 1916-Jan 1920; Jan 1921; Jan-11 Fev 1923 – 1,5,6 – bl Biblioteca [072]

JURUPA THIS WEEK – Riverside, CA. 1993 – 1+ r – 1 – $50.00 ($50.00y) – R04093 – us Library Micro [071]

THE JURY – Saint John, NB: "Jury" Pub. Co, [1886-1888] – 9 – cn C.I.H.M. [340]

JURY CHARGES / Trott, Nicholas – 1703-07, 1972. 8 fiches – 9 – us South Carolina Historical [025]

JURY SELECTION PROCEDURES IN U.S. DISTRICT COURTS / Bermant, Gordon – Washington: FJC, June 1982 – 1mf – 9 – $1.50 – LLMC 95-372 – us L.L.M.C. [340]

JURY SERVICE IN LENGTHLY CIVIL TRIALS / Cecil, Joe S et al – Washington: GPO, 1988 – 1mf – 9 – $1.50 – LLMC 95-336 – us L.L.M.C. [340]

THE JURY SYSTEM–DEFECTS AND PROPOSED REMEDIES / Train, Arthur Cheney – Philadelphia, American Academy of Political and Social Science 1910 p. 175-184. LL-1467 – 1 – us L of C Photodup [340]

THE JURYMAN'S HANDBOOK / Brown, Alec – London: The Harvill Press, 1951 – 2mf – 9 – $3.00 – LLMC 94-280 – us L.L.M.C. [340]

JUS POTANDI : ODER, DEUTSCHES ZECHRECHT: COMMENTBUCH DES MITTELALTERS NACH DEM ORIGINAL VON 1616 MIT EINLEITUNG / ed by Oberbreyer, Max – (Includes bilbiographical references) – 6. Aufl. Heilbronn: Henninger, [1890?] – 1r – 1 – us U.W. Library [943]

JUS SUFFRAGII / International Woman Suffrage Alliance – (Cont. as: The International Women's News. International Alliance of Women. London 1929(5)-1982. Some missing vols) – London, 1906-1929(4) – 190mf – 9 – ne IDC [320]

JUS SUFFRAGII – International Woman Suffrage Alliance. Rotterdam. -m. Sept 1906-16. Continued by: International Woman Suffrage News – 1 – us U.W. Library [073]

Jusserand, Jean Adrien Antoine Jules *see* SHAKESPEARE IN FRANCE UNDER THE ANCIEN REGIME

Jussieu, A H L de *see*
- DE EUPHORBIACEARUM GENERIBUS MEDICIQUE EARUNDEM VIRIBUS TENTAMEN
- GENERA PLANTARUM
- HERBARIUM
- MEMOIRE SUR LE GROUPE DES RUTACEES
- MEMOIRES SUR LES RUTACEES

Just *see* BOTANISCHER JAHRESBERICHT

JUST AS I AM / Braddon, Mary Elizabeth – British Fiction Archive: Unit 5 – 9 – uk Bell [830]

JUST BETWEEN OURSELVES – v.1-8. 1962-69. Superseded by PLA Newsletter – 1 – us UMI [073]

JUST FRIEDRICH WILHELM ZACHARIAE UND SEIN RENOMMIST : EIN BEITRAG ZUR LITTERATUR- UND KULTURGESCHICHTE DES 18. JAHRHUNDERTS / Zimmer, Hans – (Includes bibliographical references) – Leipzig: Rossberg, 1892 – 1 – us U.W. Library [430]

Just, Klaus Guenther *see*
- AFRIKANISCHE TRAUERSPIELE
- ROEMISCHE TRAUERSPIELE
- TUERKISCHE TRAUERSPIELE

JUSTA REPULSA / Feijoo Montenegro, Benito J – 1749 – 1mf – 9 – Pta1,000.00 – 84-7848-010-2 – sp Pentalfa [946]

JUSTA REPULSA...TEATRO CRITICO...FRANCISCO SOTO Y MARNE / Feyjoo, B Geronimo – 1749 – 9 – 1.50f – sp Bibl Santa Ana [440]
JUSTAS LITERARIAS DE SAN JUAN ORGANIZADAS POR EL EXCELENTISIMO AYUNTAMIENTO DE BADAJOZ / Badajoz – Badajoz: Dip. Prov., 1944 – sp Bibl Santa Ana [946]
JUSTAS POETICAS SEVILLANAS DEL SIGLO 16 (1531-1542) – Valencia: Edit Catalia, 1955 – sp Bibl Santa Ana [810]
LA JUSTESSE DE LA LANGUE FRANCOISE / Girard – 1718 – 9 – fr I.C.S. [440]
Justi, F *see* DER BUNDEHESH, ZUM ERSTEN MALE HERAUSGEGEBEN, TRANSCRIBIRT, UEBERSETZT UND MIT GLOSSAR VERSEHEN
A JUSTICA – Cidade do Pomba, 4 Feb 1909; Apr 1919; 6 Jun 1920 – 1,5,6 – bl Biblioteca [072]
A JUSTICA : JUSTICIARIO – RELIGIOSO – LITERARIO – NOTICIOSO – Oliveira, 15 Jan, 30 Mar 1939 – 1,5,6 – bl Biblioteca [072]
A JUSTICA SOCIAL E FEITA PELO POVO / Argentina. Direccion General de Relaciones Culturales y Difusion – [Buenos Aires?: Direc cao Geral das Rela coes de Cultura e Difusao, 1950?] – 1 – CSUXADN3886-B – us Hoover Inst Photo [360]
JUSTICE – 1884-1914. Radical journal – 1 – uk World [340]
JUSTICE – Grass Valley OR. Apr 1893 – 1 – us U.O. Library [071]
JUSTICE : ILLUSTRE – Quebec, Canada. 8 avr 1916 – 1r – 1 – Can$25.00 – cn Can Microfilming [072]
JUSTICE / International Ladies Garment Workers' Union – Official Organ. New York. v. 1-48. Jan 18 1919-1968 – 1 – us NY Public [330]
JUSTICE – Jersey City. N.J. Gerechtigkeit. 1919-55 – 1 – us A.J.P.C. [071]
JUSTICE – London. 64 docs. 1980-1991 – 43mf – 9 – ne IDC [340]
JUSTICE – London, Great Britain. 1884-1914 – 1 – uk Microform Academic [072]
JUSTICE – New York. v1-64. 1919-82 – 24r – 1 – us Ross [071]
JUSTICE : OFFICIAL ORGAN OF THE INTERNATIONAL LADIES GARMENT WORKERS UNION – New York: The Union. v1 n1-3,5-50. 1919 – us Res Libr [331]
JUSTICE : ORGAN OF THE SOCIAL DEMOCRACY – London, 1884-1925 – 32r – 1 – uk British Libr Newspaper [335]
LA JUSTICE – Biddeford, ME. v16 n17. 24 aut 1911-v47. 14 jan 1944 – 1r – 1 – Can$25.00 – cn Can Microfilming [071]
LA JUSTICE : CAMPAGNE POLITIQUE MUNICIPALE – OPPOSE A MEDERIC MARTIN – Montreal, Canada. v1 n5. 9 mar 1928 – 1r – 1 – Can$25.00 – cn Can Microfilming [971]
LA JUSTICE – Central Falls. R.I. 1906-1910 – 1 – us UMI [071]
LA JUSTICE : CONSERVATEUR-NATIONALISTE – (Edition hebdo: 4 jan-28 dec 1895 1r Can$50.00) – Quebec, Canada. 9 jan 1886-24 mar 1892 – 1 – Can$50.00 – cn Can Microfilming [072]
LA JUSTICE / ed by Garceau, Napoleon – Drummondville, Canada. v2 n11. 5 sep 1902-v3 n44. 2 mar 1906 – 1r – 1 – Can$35.00 – cn Can Microfilming [072]
LA JUSTICE – Holyoke, MA. v43 n1. 13 nov 1941-23 aut 1956 – 3r – 1 – Can$50.00r – cn Can Microfilming [071]
LA JUSTICE : INDEPENDANT – Montreal, Canada. v1 n2. 14 jun 1923; v1 n7. 19 jul 1923 – 1r – 1 – Can$25.00 – cn Can Microfilming [072]
LA JUSTICE – Moderation, fermete, independance, indulgence. Dir. A. Rouge. no. 1-5, 7-9, 11, 13, 15-16, 18. Tamatave. dec 1893-avr 1894 – 1 – fr A.C.R.P.P. [073]
LA JUSTICE – Newcastle, New Brunswick. 12 avr 1906; v1 n22. 18 oct 1906 – 1r – 1 – Can$25.00 – cn Can Microfilming [072]
LA JUSTICE – Organe des revendications du peuple musulman algerien. Red. en chef Adoulhak. Alger. oct 1934-avr 1938 – 1 – fr A.C.R.P.P. [073]
LA JUSTICE – Ottawa, Ontario. 1 jun 1912-25 sep 1914 – 1r – 1 – Can$40.00 – cn Can Microfilming [072]
LA JUSTICE – Paris. Journal quot. republicain. Fond., G. Clemenceau. 16 janv 1880-8 nov 1910, 18 fevr-31 dec 1911, 6 mars 1912-29 sept 1913, 20 mars-2 juil 1914, 6 avr-23 dec 1916, 1918-16 janv 1931, 17 janv-18 juil 1939, 1 fevr-8 juin 1940 – 1 – fr A.C.R.P.P. [073]
LA JUSTICE – Quebec, 1891-1892 – 1r – 1 – cn Preston [971]
LA JUSTICE – Sanford, ME. 27 mai 1943 – 1r – 1 – Can$20.00 – cn Can Microfilming [071]
THE JUSTICE – (Waltham, Mass.) v40, no. 5 (Oct. 6,1987)-v40, no. 8 (Oct. 17,1987) Lacking: v40, no. 6 (Oct. 13, 1987) – us A.J.P.C. [340]
JUSTICE A QUI DE DROIT – Levis: Imp. du journal "Le Quotidien", 1895? SEM105P393 – 1mf – 9 – Can$2.25 – cn Bibl Nat [320]
JUSTICE AND AUTHORITY IN ENGLAND, C1540-C1800: COUNTY QUARTER SESSIONS AND RELATED RECORDS – Series 1: Cheshire – 1 – us Primary [941]
JUSTICE AND SHERIFF AND ATTORNEY'S ASSISTANT. / Morrison, Charles Robert – (Rev. ed. Concord, N.H.: Sanborn, 1888. 557p. LL-828) – Manchester, N.H., 1872. 464p. LL-838 – 1 – us L of C Photodup [340]
JUSTICE ASSISTANCE NEWS – (1982-. applyl; 1,5,6,9) – v1-. 1980- – 1 – us UMI [073]
JUSTICE AUX CANADIENS-FRANCAIS / Bouthillier Chavigny, Charles de – Saint John, N. B.: Daily News, 1874. 00225. (Pre-1900 Canadiana) – 9 – cn C.I.H.M. [971]
JUSTICE AUX MINORITES: PROTECTION DE L'INDUSTRIE NATIONALE: PROTECTION ET DEVELOPPEMENT DE L'AGRICULTURE / Bisaillon, Francois Joseph – Lettre de F. J. Bisaillon, candidat conservateur aux electeurs du comte de Laval. 1896? 00830. (Pre-1900 Canadiana) – 9 – cn C.I.H.M. [971]
JUSTICE IN MICRONESIA – v1 n1-2. sep 1977-jan 1978 (all publ?) – 3mf – 9 – $4.50 – LLMC 82-100F, Title 66 – us L.L.M.C. [340]
THE JUSTICE OF THE PEACE – (Issues for Apr 1906-May 1907 were never publ) – Lancaster Co, PA. v1-8. 1899-Oct 1907 (all publ) – 14mf – 9 – $21.00 – LLMC 84-514 – us L.L.M.C. [073]
JUSTICE OF THE PEACE AND COUNTY BOROUGH : POOR LAW UNION AND PARISH LAW RECORDER – London. v1-1837- – 9 – LLMC 84-515 – us L.L.M.C. [073]
JUSTICE OF THE PEACE DOCKETS / Sedgwick County. Kansas. Wichita Township – 1870-73 – 1 – us KS Hist [340]
LA JUSTICE PENALE INTERNATIONALE / Caloyanni, M A – Varsovie, 1929 – 1mf – 9 – ILM-2075/1 – ne IDC [327]
JUSTICE QUARTERLY – v1-. Mar 1984- – 1,5,6,9 – us UMI [073]
LA JUSTICE REVOLUTIONNAIRE A NANTES... / Lallie, Alfred – Nantes: Cier, 1896 – 1 – F230.56 – fr Armell [340]
LA JUSTICE SOCIALE – Journal des interets democratiques. Dir. Abbe Naudet. Bordeaux puis Paris. juil 1893-juil 1906 – 1 – fr A.C.R.P.P. [073]
LA JUSTICE SOCIALE EST LA PIERRE ANGULAIRE DU JUSTICIALISME / Argentina. Direccion General de Relaciones Culturales y Difusion – [Buenos Aires?: Direction generale des relations culturelles et de diffusion, 1950?] – 1 – CSUXADN3874-B – us Hoover Inst Photo [360]
JUSTICE, SOCIALISM AND DEMOCRACY / Hayek, F A – 2fiches (29x) – 9 – 1.00f – at Libertarian Micro [320]
JUSTICE STUDIES / Dominican Province of Saint Joseph – 1977-80.1 reel – 1 – us A.T.L.A. [073]
JUSTICE SUSPENDED / Marsh, Richard – London: Chatto & Eindus, 1913 – 5mf – 9 – $7.50 – LLMC 92-225 – us L.L.M.C. [830]
JUSTICE SYSTEMS JOURNAL – v1-17. 1974-1995 – 9 – $212.00 set – us Hein [340]
JUSTICE TO THE JEW : THE STORY OF WHAT HE HAS DONE FOR THE WORLD / Peters, Madison Clinton – London, New York: F.T. Neely, c1899 – 1mf – us A.T.L.A. [305]
JUSTICE WITHOUT LAW : A RECONSIDERATION OF THE "BYOARD EQUITABLE POWERS" OF THE FEDERAL COURTS, 31 AUG 1988 – n.p., n.d. – 2mf – 9 – $3.00 – LLMC 94-366 – us L.L.M.C. [340]
THE JUSTICES' MANUAL OF STATUTE, JUDICIAL AND ELEMENTARY LAW, WITH APPROPRIATE FORMS. / Bundy, Charles Smith – (2nd Ed. Washington, Byrne, 1896. 435 p. LL-563. 1) – Washington, Law Reporter Print, 1880. 496 p. LL-60 – 1 – us L of C Photodup [340]
JUSTICES' OATHS/MAYORS' CERTIFS / Huron County. Ohio. Clerk of Courts – 1860-1883 – 1r – 1 – $32.50r – us Archival [324]
THE JUSTICES' PRACTICE UNDER THE LAWS OF MARYLAND. / Latrobe, John Hazelhurst Boneval – (5th ed. Baltimore, Lucas 1856. 622 p. LL-774. 8th ed. Baltimore, Lucas 1889. 652 p. LL-559) – 2nd ed. Baltimore, Lucas 1835 456 p. LL-948 – 1 – us L of C Photodup [340]
JUSTICIA – 1914-26. Scattered issues wanting – 1 – 87.00 – us L of C Photodup [972]
LA JUSTICIA BAJO LA DICTADURA / Salazar Alonso, Rafael – Madrid: Editorial Reus, 1930 – 1 – sp Bibl Santa Ana [360]
LA JUSTICIA REVOLUCIONARIA EN ESPANA / Castilla, Juan de – Buenos Aires, 193? Fiche W 781. (Blodgett Collection of Spanish Civil War Pamphlets) – 9 – us H.U. College Libr [946]
LA JUSTICIA SOCIAL ES REALIZADA POR EL PUEBLO / Argentina. Direccion General de Relaciones Culturales y Difusion – [Buenos Aires?, 1950?] – 1 – CSUXADN3898-B – us Hoover Inst Photo [360]
JUSTICIA SOCIAL Y REFORMA CONSTITUCIONAL : CONTRIBUCION AL ESTUDIO DE LA DOCTRINA DE LA JUSTICIA SOCIAL Y DEL PROBLEMA DE LA REVISION CONSTITUCIONAL EN LA REPUBLICA ARGENTINA / Dana Montano, Salvador M – Santa Fe [Republica Argentina]: Impr. de la Universidad, 1949 – 1 – CSUXADQ6504-B – us Hoover Inst Photo [340]
JUSTICIA Y CARACTER DE LA GUERRA NACIONAL ESPANOLA / Getino, Luis G – Salamanca, 1937. Fiche W911. (Blodgett Collection of Spanish Civil War Pamphlets) – 9 – us H.U. College Libr [946]
EL JUSTICIALISMO : SU HISTORIA, SU PENSAMIENTO Y SUS PROYECCIONES / Frenkel, Leopoldo – Buenos Aires: Editorial Legasa, [1984] – 1 – CSUXAHZ7479-B – us Hoover Inst Photo [360]
EL JUSTICIALISMO FRENTE AL COMUNISMO / Baldassarre, Pedro B – Buenos Aires: El Ateneo, [1951] – 1 – CSUXAJA7258-B – us Hoover Inst Photo [360]
JUSTIFICACIONES HISTORICAS / Bayle, Constantino – Madrid: Razon y Fe, 1924 – 1 – sp Bibl Santa Ana [946]
JUSTIFICATION DE LA DOMINATION PORTUGAISE EN ASIE / Freitas, S de – Paris, Lille, 1882 – 4mf – 1 – ILM-1054/1 – ne IDC [327]
JUSTIFICATION DE LA DOMINATION PORTUGAISE EN ASIE / Freitas, S de – Paris, Lille, n.d. – 4mf – 1 – ILM-3926/1 – ne IDC [327]
JUSTIN, AUGUSTIN, BERNHARD UND LUTHER : DER ENTWICKLUNGSGANG CHRISTLICHER WAHRHEITSERFASSUNG IN DER KIRCHE ALS BEWEIS FUER DIE LEHRE DER REFORMATION / Dieckhoff, August Wilhelm – Leipzig: Justus Naumann, 1882 – 1mf – us A.T.L.A. [240]
Justin the Martyr, Saint *see* THE APOLOGIES OF JUSTIN MARTYR. TO WHICH IS APPENDED THE EPISTLE TO DIOGNETUS
Justinard, Leopold Victor *see* UN GRAND CHEF BERBERE
Justiniano Arribas, Juan *see*
– ALONSO PEREZ DE GUZMAN
– CRISTOBAL COLON
– HERNAN CORTES
– HERNANDO CORTES
– POESIAS SELECTAS
– ROGER DE FLOR
Justinianus *see* INSTITUTIONES; DIGESTUM (BOOKS 40-50); NOVELLAE CONSTITUTIONES
JUSTINS DES MAERTYRERS LEHRE VON JESUS CHRISTUS : DEM MESSIAS UND DEM MENSCHGEWORDENEN SOHNE GOTTES: EINE DOGMENGESCHICHTLICHE MONOGRAPHIE / Feder, Alfred Leonhard – Freiburg im Breisgau, St. Louis, Mo.: Herder, 1906 – 1mf – us A.T.L.A. [240]
JUSTINUS KERNERS SAEMTLICHE POETISCHE WERKE / Kerner, Justinus; ed by Gaismaier, Josef – (Includes bibliographical references and index) – Leipzig: M Hesse. 4v. [1905?] – 1 – us U.W. Library [800]
JUSTITIA – Dept. Penerangan Senat Mahasiswa Fak. 1966-69. v1-4 (3). BSE-1726/1. Some missing issues. Title varies: Pro Justitia, 1966, v1. TEN 1162 – 9 – ne IDC [950]
Justo, Juan Bautista *see*
– SEPARACI ON DE LA IGLESIA DEL ESTADO
– SOCIALISMO
JUSTRO POLSKI – London, UK. Jul, Nov, Dec 1943 – 1 – uk British Libr Newspaper [072]
JUSTUS FALCKNER : MYSTIC AND SCHOLAR, DEVOUT PIETIST IN GERMANY, HERMIT ON THE WISSAHICKON, MISSIONARY ON THE HUDSON / Sachse, Julius Friedrich – Philadelphia: Printed for the author, 1903 (Lancaster: New Era) – 1mf – us A.T.L.A. [240]
JUSTUS LIEBIGS ANNALEN DER CHEMIE *see* LIEBIGS ANNALEN DER CHEMIE
JUSTUS MOESER / Kreyssig, Friedrich Alexander Theodor – Berlin: Nicolai, 1857 – 1r – 1 – us U.W. Library [920]
JUSTUS MOESER'S APPROACH TO HISTORY / Bossenbrook, William John – (Includes bibliographical references) – Chicago, IL: Private edition, Distributed by the University of Chicago Libraries, 1938 – 1 – us U.W. Library [900]
Juta, E H P *see* PEMUNGUTAN HASIL HUTAN
JUTRO POLSKI – London, UK. 24 Dec 1944- – 1 – uk British Libr Newspaper [072]
Jutzi, S C et al *see* MANAGEMENT OF VERTISOLS IN SUB-SAHARAN AFRICA
Juvenal *see* SATURARUM LIBRI 5; MIT ERKLARENDEN ANMERKUNGEN VON L. FRIEDLAENDER
O JUVENIL – Bom-Successo, 26 May 1892; May, Nov 1893; May-Aug 1894; Mar 1900; Dec 1912; Apr 1940; Jan-Jun, Aug-24 Dec 1979 – 1,5,6 – bl Biblioteca [072]
O JUVENIL : LEITURAS INFANTS – Pao d'Assucar, Alagoas. 1 Fev 1892 – 1,5,6 – bl Biblioteca [072]
JUVENILE COURT LAWS IN THE UNITED STATES : SUMMARY BY STATES / Hart, Hastings Hornell – New York: Charities, 1910. 150p. LL-1558 – 1 – us L of C Photodup [340]
THE JUVENILE COURT LAWS OF THE STATE OF COLORADO / Colorado. Laws, Statutes, etc – Denver: Juvenile Improvement Association of Denver 1905. 80p. LL-353 – 1 – us L of C Photodup [340]
JUVENILE COURT LAWS OF THE UNITED STATES : TOPICAL SUMMARY OF THEIR MAIN PROVISIONS / Hiller, Francis Hemperley – New York: National Probation Association, 1933. 82p. LL-1233 – 1 – us L of C Photodup [340]
THE JUVENILE COURT OF DENVER, CONCERNING ITS JUDGE, CONCERNING ITS WORK, WHAT IT HAS DONE, WHAT IT IS DOING, WHAT IT HOPES TO DO – Denver, 1913 23 p. LL-421 – 1 – us L of C Photodup [340]
JUVENILE ENTERTAINER – Pictou, NS: W Milne, [1831-18–] – 9 – cn C.I.H.M. [790]
JUVENILE FORGET-ME-NOT – 1829-37 – 27mf – 9 – £230.00 – uk Chadwyck [830]
JUVENILE GAZETTE – v. 1. 1819-1820 – 1 – us UMI [830]
JUVENILE JUSTICE – 1949- 1; 1972- 5,6; 1975- 4 x 6 in. 9 – us UMI [360]
JUVENILE JUSTICE PUBLICATIONS OF THE U.S. DEPT. OF JUSTICE (SLIM) / U.S. Juvenile Justice Clearinghouse (NCJRS) – (1981-85. 180 documents. $130.00; 1985-88. 62 documents. $130.00) – 1975-81. Full-text copies of 164 documents from 6 agencies, indexed – 9 – $125.00 – us N.C.J.R.S. [360]
JUVENILE KEEPSAKE – 1829-30 – 3mf – 9 – £25.00 – uk Chadwyck [830]
JUVENILE MAGAZINE – v. 1-4. 1811-1813 – 1 – us UMI [830]
JUVENILE MAGAZINE *see* THE SNOW DROP OR JUVENILE MAGAZINE
JUVENILE MIRROR – v. 4. 1812 – 1 – us UMI [830]
JUVENILE MISCELLANY – NS1- 1826-1834 – 1 – us UMI [830]

JUVENILE MISSIONARY HERALD – 1845-1908 – 1 – 763.00 – us Baptist [240]
JUVENILE PORT-FOLIO AND LITERARY MISCELLANY *see* PARLOUR COMPANION
JUVENILE PORT-FOLIO, AND LITERARY MISCELLANY – v. 1-4. 1812-1816 – 1 – us UMI [800]
THE JUVENILE PRESBYTERIAN – Montreal: Printed and issued for the Lay Association by J Lovell, [1856-186-?] – 9 – cn C.I.H.M. [240]
JUVENILE REPOSITORY – v. 1. 1811 – 1 – us UMI [073]
JUVENILE RESTITUTION SLIM / U.S. Juvenile Justice Clearinghouse (NCJRS) – 1986. 64 documents – 9 – $35.00 – us N.C.J.R.S. [360]
LA JUVENTUD ANARQUISTA: FACTOR DETERMINATIVO DE LA GUERRA Y DE LA REVOLUCION / Briones, Mariano – Barcelona, 1937? Fiche W 763. (Blodgett Collection of Spanish Civil War Pamphlets) – 9 – us H.U. College Libr [946]
LA JUVENTUD ESPANOLA CONTINUA SU LUCHA / Claudin, Fernando – Mexico, 1940. Fiche W 802. (Blodgett Collection of Spanish Civil War Pamphlets) – 9 – us H.U. College Libr [946]
LA JUVENTUD: FACTOR DE LA VICTORIA / Carrillo, Santiago – Barcelona, 1937. Fiche W 776. (Blodgett Collection of Spanish Civil War Pamphlets) – 9 – us H.U. College Libr [946]
LA JUVENTUD QUE DEFIENDE MADRID; CONFERENCIA NACIONAL DE JUVENTUDES / Munoz Arconada, Felipe – Valencia, 1937. Fiche W 1065. (Blodgett Collection of Spanish Civil War Pamphlets) – 9 – us H.U. College Libr [946]
JUVENTUD REBELDE – Havana. 22 Oct 1965-Dec 1976 – 1 – 35.00r – us Hoover Inst Photo [073]
LA JUVENTUD Y LA HORA / Escardo, Florencio – Buenos Aires: [s.n.], 1948 – 1 – CSUXADH5651-B – us Hoover Inst Photo [305]
LA JUVENTUD Y LOS CAMPESINOS / Alvarez, Segis – Valencia, 1937. Fiche W 711. (Blodgett Collection of Spanish Civil War Pamphlets) – 9 – us H.U. College Libr [946]
JUVENTUD Y...DESENCANTO / Sanchez-Arjona, Vicente – Sevilla: Imp. Carlos Acuna, 1953 – 1 – sp Bibl Santa Ana [810]
Juynboll, T G J *see* CHRONICON SAMARITANUM
J.V. VON SCHEFFELS GESAMMELTE WERKE... MIT EINER BIOGRAPHISCHEN EINLEITUNG VON JOHANNES PROELSS / Scheffel, Joseph Viktor von – Stuttgart, A. Bonz & comp., 1907. 6v. Film Mas 8546 – 1 – us H.U. Library [800]
J.W. Burke and Co *see* HISTORY OF CLINCH COUNTY
J.W. Lewis Publishing Co *see*
– HISTORY OF CLINTON AND FRANKLIN COUNTIES
– HISTORY OF NORFOLK COUNTY
JWB CIRCLE – (New York). 1946-67 – 1 – us A.J.P.C. [073]
J.W.V. BEACON – New York, NY. 1978-81 – 1 – us A.J.P.C. [071]
K – Revue de la poesie. Dir. Alain Gheerbrant et Henri Parisot. no. 1-3. Paris. juin 1948-mai 1949 – 1 – fr A.C.R.P.P. [073]
K 40-LETIIU UCHENO-LITERATURNOI DEIATEL'NOSTI PROFESSORA I AKADEMIKA A.N. VESELOVSKAGO. 1859-1902 / Simoni, P K – Spb. 1906. BR-7256 2 – 8 – ne IDC [460]
K AGRARNOMU VOPROSU V ROSSII : MYSLI I TSIFRY / Voblyi, KG – Kiev, 1917 – 1mf – 9 – COR-15/1 – ne IDC [334]
K BIBLIOGRAFII TSERKOVNO-SLAVIANSKIKH PECHATNYKH IZDANII V ROSSII / Kaluzhniatskii, E – Saint Petersburg, 1886. 46p. BR-4676/2 – 8 – ne IDC [947]
K DESIATILETIIU OKTIABRSKOI REVOLIUTSII : DOKLAD NA 8TH MOSKOVSKOM GUBERNSKOM SEZDE PROFSOIUZOV 12 OKTIABRIA 1927 GODA / Bukharin, Nikolai Ivanovich – Moskva: Gos. izd-vo, 1927 – 1 – CSUX88-B1284 – us Hoover Inst Photo [947]
K EVREISKOMU VOPROSU / Marks, K – Perevod pod red. A. Lunacharskii. Petrograd, 1919 – 8 – B-1557 2 – ne IDC [947]
K ISTORII "BALAGANCHIKA" / Chulkov, G I – (In "Kul'tura teatra"). nr. 7-8. 1921. BR-3258 2 – 8 – ne IDC [460]
K ISTORII IZDANIIA IZVESTII I UCHENYKH ZAPISOK VTOROGO OTDELENIIA IMP. AKADEMII NAUK. (1852-1863) / Sreznevskii, 6 – Spb. 1905. BR-4826 2 – 8 – ne IDC [947]
K NASHEI POLEMIKIE S STAROOBRIADISAMI : DOPOLNENTIA I POPRAVKI K POLEMIKIE OTNOSITEL'NO OBSHCHEI ETA POSTANOVKI I OTNOSITEL'NO... / Golubinskii, E E – Moskva: Tip. Ob-va rasprostraneniia poleznykh knig, 1905 – 1mf – us A.T.L.A. [240]
K NOVYM BEREGAM – Moscow. no. 1-3. Apr-Aug 1923 – 1 – us NY Public [780]
K. PH. MORITZ' GOETTERLEHRE : EIN DOKUMENT DES GOETHESCHEN KLASSIZISMUS / Fahrner, Rudolf – (Includes bibliographical references (p.[31])) – Marburg-Lahn: N G Elwert, 1932 – 1r – 1 – us U.W. Library [200]
K POEME, STIKHOTVORENIE. DEN' POEZII 1962 / Akhmatova, A – M. 1962. BR-1099 2 – 8 – ne IDC [460]
K POZNANII U ARMII / Gerua, Aleksandr Vladimirovich – S-Peterburg: Tip. A S Suvorina, 1907 – 1 – CSUX89-B681 – us Hoover Inst Photo [947]
K SINEI ZVEZDE / Gumilev, Nikolai Sepanovich – Neizdannye stikhi 1918 g. Berlin. 1923. BR-1141 2 – 8 – ne IDC [460]
K SIRO-TURETSKOI EPIGRAFIKE SEMIRECH'IA / Kokovtsov, P K – IAN. 1909. BU-713 2 – 8 – ne IDC [410]
K STOLETIIU GEROICHESKOI BOR'BY ZA NASHU I VASHU SVOBODU / Akademia Nauk SSSR Institut slaviano Vediniia – Surveys of materials relating to the 1863 Polish uprising in a number of repositories in Moscow and Leningrad. BR-10,672/1 – 9 – ne IDC [947]
K TEORII KOOPERATIZMA : OCHERKI / Evdokimov, Andrei Aandreevich – M., 1909 – 1mf – 9 – COR-22/1 – ne IDC [334]
K VOPROSU O MUNITSIPAL'NO-KOOPERATIVNOI ORGANIZATSII NARODNOGO PRODOVOL'STVIIA V SEVERNOI OBLASTI / Pekarskii, V F – Pg., 1918 – 1mf – 9 – COR-344/1 – ne IDC [334]
K VOPROSU O PRAVE GOSUDARSTVA NA ZEMLIU / Karadzhe-Iskrov, N P – Irkutsk, 1928. 22p. Essay on system of state ownership of land in Soviet Union. BR-9626/1 – 9 – ne IDC [335]
K VOPROSU O SOTSIALISTICHESKOM PEREUSTROISTVE SELSKOGO KHOZIAISTVA : MATERIALY ISSLED. NKRKI SSSR / ed by Jakovlev, IA A – L., M., 1928 – 6mf – 9 – COR-476/1 – ne IDC [334]
K VOPROSU O STROITEL'STVE KOOPERATISII : TEZ. K 19 GUBPARTKONFERENTSII – M., 1925 – 1mf – 9 – COR-152/1 – ne IDC [334]
KA ES ATKLAHJU MODERNISUMU (WILTIGU MAHZIBU) STARP AMERIKANU BAPTISTEEM UN KAPEHZ ES NODIBINAJU ANGLU-AMERIKANU MISSIONES BEEDRIBU = HOW I DISCOVERED MODERISM AMONG AMERICAN BAPTISTS, AND WHY I FOUNDED THE RUSSIAN MISSIONARY SOCIETY / Fetler, William – (Part of an 8-item unit) – Riga: Derigu Rakstu Apgahdneeziba, 1924 – 1r – 1 – us Baptist [240]
KA MEI RI LUM (MOTHER HIGHLAND) – Shillong, India. 1961-68 – 1 – us Res Libr [072]
KA PYRTA U RI LUM (VOICE OF THE HILLMAN) – Shillong, India. 1957-66 – 1 – us Res Libr [072]
HET KAAPSCHE HANDELSBLAD EN ZEE KRONIJK – Cape Town, South Africa. 13 Jan-24 Mar 1843. 1 reel – 1, 16 diazo available at reduced price – sa SA Libr [072]
KA'ARAT HA-KESEL / Ezobi, J; ed by Steinschneider, M – Berlin. 1860. BJ-421-72 1 – 9 – ne IDC [470]
Kab, M S *see* KACHESTVO I STANDART V PROMKOOPERATSII
KABA SI GADIH RANTI DENGAN SI BUDHANG SAMAN / Sjamsuddin, Sutan – SE 4725 1. 1961 – 9 – ne IDC [950]
KABA TJURITO SITI SJAMSIAH / Sjamsuddin, Sutan – SE 5444 1. 1961 – 9 – ne IDC [950]
Kabalevsky, D B *see* MUSIC AND EDUCATION
Kabanov, AK *see* OPISANIE AKTOV SOBRANIIA GRAFA A.S. UVAROVA: AKTY ISTORICHESKIE
KABBALA DENUDATA: THE KABBALA UNVEILED. – The Book of Concealed Mystery; The Greater Holy Assembly; The Lesser Holy Assembly.Trans. into Eng. from the Latin & collated with the original Chaldee and Hebrew text, by S.L. MacGregor Mathers. London: G. Redway, 1887. viii,359p. plates, tables – 1 – us U.W. Library [270]
Kabel, Michael *see* DE BETEKENIS VAN HET WOORD SOLITUDO IN DE COLL. VAN CASSIANUS
KABINET VAN NEDERLANDSCHE EN KLEEFSCHE OUDHEDEN... / Rademaker, A – (J.H. Reisig, Ed.). Amsterdam, 1792-1803 – 8 vols – 9 – ne IDC [700]
Kabisch, Richard *see* DAS VIERTE BUCH ESRA
Kablukov, N A *see*
– IZ CHEGO VYROSLI KOOPERATIVY
– KUSTARNAIA PROMYSHLENNOST'I EE SVIAZ'S KOOPERATIVAMI
– MELKOE KHOZIAISTVO I KOOPERATSIIA
– OB USLOVIIAKH RAZVITIIA KREST'IANSKOGO KHOZIAISTVA V ROSSII
Kabore, O *see* NIULI ZAMZAM... LES OISEAUX S'EBATTENT
KABUL TO KANDAHAR / Diver, Maud – London: P. Davies, 1935. 191p. 2 maps – 1 – us U.W. Library [950]
Kabuzan, V M *see* ZASELENIE NOVOROSSI
LA KABYLIE ET LES COUTUMES KABYLES / Hanoteau, Gal Adolphe – 2e ed. – Paris: Challamel, 1893 – fr Armell [390]
Kachenovskii, D I *see*
– O KATERAKH I PRIZOVOM SUDOPROIZVODSTVE V OTNOSHENII K NEITRAL'NOI TORGOVLE
– THE PRIZE LAW, PARTICULARLY WITH REFERENCE TO THE DUTIES AND OBLIGATIONS OF BELLIGERENTS AND NEUTRALS
KACHESTVO I STANDART V PROMKOOPERATSII : MATERIALY SEKTORA PROIZVODSTVENNO-TEKHNICHESKOI RATSIONALIZATSII VSEKOPROMSOIUZA / Golubkova, SN & Karnaukhov, DE; ed by Kab, M S – M., 1931 – 1mf – 9 – COR-420/1 – ne IDC [334]
THE KACHINS / Gilhodes, C – Religion and customs. 1922 – 1 – us A.T.L.A. [949]
Kachorovskii, K R *see* NARODNOE PRAVO
KADESH-BARNEA : ITS IMPORTANCE AND PROBABLE SITE: WITH THE STORY OF A HUNT FOR IT: INCLUDING STUDIES OF THE ROUTE OF THE EXODUS AND THE SOUTHERN BOUNDARY OF THE HOLY LAND / Trumbull, Henry Clay – (Includes indexes) – 3rd rev ed. Philadelphia: John D Wattles, 1895 – 2mf – 9 – 0-8370-9833-5 – 1986-3833 – us A.T.L.A. [956]
KADESH-BARNEA / Trumbull, Henry Clay – Scribners, 1884 – 9 – $18.00 – us I.R.C. [930]
KADIMA – Tilburg, 1946-1953 – 4mf – 9 – ne IDC [999]
KADIMAH – Delft. v1. 1910-1911 – 3mf – 9 – ne IDC [999]
KADIMAH – (Missing: 1926-1928(1-2)) – Amsterdam. v1-6. 1926-1933 – 4mf – 9 – ne IDC [999]
KADIN – (Sahib-i Imtiyaz: Mustafa Ibrahim, Mueduer: Enis Avni. Nos. 1 (13 Tesrinievvel 1324[1908]), 4 (3 Tesrinisani 1324[1908])) – Selanik: Asir Matbaasi, 1908-1909 – 1mf – 9 – $12.00 – us MEDOC [949]
Kadmin [Abramovich, N I] *see* PADENIE DINASTII
KADRY GOSUDARSTVENNOGO I KOOPERATIVNOGO APPARATA SSSR / Bineman, IM & Kheinman, S A – M., 1930 – 4mf – 9 – COR-144/1 – ne IDC [334]
Kaefer, Karl *see* DIE BETRIEBSRECHNUNG
DIE KAEFER VON MITTELEUROPA / Ganglbauer, L – 2780 2. 4 v. 1892-1904 – 8 – ne IDC [590]
Kaehler, Martin *see*
– DER SOGENANNTE HISTORISCHE JESUS UND DER GESCHICHTLICHE, BIBLISCHE CHRISTUS
– DIE UNIVERSITAETEN UND DAS OEFFENTLICHE LEBEN
KAELAN. A SHORT GUIDE TO THE LARA DJONGGRANG TEMPLE GROUP – Trans. by Mardijo. Rev. by M. Juska. 1963. SE-6577- – 9 – ne IDC [280]
KAELAN. A SHORT GUIDE TO THE LARA DJONGGRANG TEMPLES – Trans. by Mardijo. SE-2788 1. 1958 – 9 – ne IDC [280]
Kaelan. Indonesia *see*
– PETUNDJUK TJANDI..
– A SHORT GUIDE TO THE LARA DJONGGRANG TEMPLE GROUP
Kaemmel, Otto *see*
– CHRISTIAN WEISE
– DIE ERHEBUNG PREUSSENS IM JAHRE 1813 UND DIE REKONSTRUKTION DES STAATES
Kaempchen, Paul Ludwig *see* DIE NUMINOSE BALLADE
Kaempf, Saul Isaac *see*
– DIE ERSTEN MAKAMEN AUS DEM TACHKEMONI ODER DIVAN DES CHARISI
– DAS HOHELIED
– DIE INSCHRIFT AUF DEM DENKMAL MESA'S KOENIGS VON MOAB
– MAMTIK SOD
– NICHTANDALUSISCHE POESIE ANDALUSISCHER DICHTER AUS DEM XI, XII UND XIII JAHRHUNDERT
DIE KAEMPFE UND LEIDEN DER EVANGELISCHEN AUF DEM EICHSFELDE WAEHREND DREIER JAHRHUNDERTE / Wintzingeroda-Knorr, Levin Freiherr von – Halle: Verein fuer Reformationsgeschichte, 1892-1893. ([Schriften des Vereins fuer Reformationsgeschichte; Bd. 36, 42]) – 1mf – us A.T.L.A. [240]
KAEMPFEN UND LACHEN : ERLEBNISSE: MIT EINER SELBSTDARSTELLUNG DES VERFASSERS "HEIMAT UND HERKUNFT" / Pleyer, Wilhelm – Leipzig: P Reclam, 1944, c1941 – 1r – 1 – us U.W. Library [920]
DER KAEMPFER – Berlin, 1959-61, apr 1 1968-81 – 2r – 1 – Dist. gw Mikrofilm – gw Misc Inst [072]
DER KAEMPFER – Chemnitz, DE. 1921-33 – 31r – 1 – gw Mikrofilm [072]
DER KAEMPFER *see* WESTFAELISCHER KAEMPFER
Kaempfer, Engelbert *see*
– HISTOIRE NATURELLE, CIVILE, ET ECCLESIASTIQUE DE L'EMPIRE DU JAPON
– ICONES SELECTAE PLANTARUM
DIE KAEMPFERIN – Berlin, 1927-32 – 1r – 1 – Dist. gw Mikrofilm – gw Misc Inst [072]
DIE KAEMPFERIN – Leipzig, Germany. 1919-20; 1921 (incomplete) – 1r – 1 – gw Mikrofilm [072]
Kaempffer, Adolf *see*
– RITT GEN MITTERNACHT
– DER TOD AN DER GRENZE
Kaerle, Joseph *see* CHRESTOMATHIA TARGUMICO-CHALDAICA
DIE KAESEREI IN DER VEHFREUDE : EINE GESCHICHTE AUS DER SCHWEIZ / Gotthelf, Jeremias; ed by Bloesch, Hans – (Includes bibliographical references) – Erlenbach, Zuerich: E Rentsch, 1922 – 1 – us U.W. Library [830]
Kaeslin, Hans *see* ALBRECHT V. HALLERS SPRACHE IN IHRER ENTWICKLUNG DARGESTELLT
Kaestner, Erhart *see* WAHN UND WIRKLICHKEIT IM DRAMA DER GOETHEZEIT
KAETCHEN SCHOENKOPF : EINE FRAUENGESTALT AUS GOETHES JUGENDZEIT / Vogel, Julius – Leipzig: Klinkhardt & Biermann, 1920 – 1r – 1 – us U.W. Library [430]
DAS KAETHCHEN VON HEILBRONN : GROSSES HISTORISCHES SCHAUSPIEL MIT GESANG IN 5 AKTEN / Kleist, Heinrich von – Aarau: H R Sauerlaender, 1899 – 1r – 1 – us U.W. Library [820]
KAETHI DIE GROSSMUTTER / Gotthelf, Jeremias; ed by Bohnenblust, Gottfried – (Includes bibliographical references) – Erlenbach, Zuerich: E Rentsch, 1916 – 1 – us U.W. Library [830]
KAETHI, DIE GROSSMUTTER, ODER, DER WAHRE WEG DURCH JEDE NOT : EINE ERZAEHLUNG FUER DAS VOLK / Gotthelf, Jeremias; ed by Vetter, Ferdinand – Bern: Schmid & Francke, 1900 – 1 – us U.W. Library [830]
Kafengauz, B B I T *see* POSOSHKOV
KAFFIR EXPRESS – Lovedale. South Africa. -m. Oct 1870-Feb, May, Jun, Sep. 1871, May 1872. (11 ft) – 1 – uk British Libr Newspaper [072]
KAFFIR EXPRESS *see* SOUTH AFRICAN OUTLOOK
KAFFRARIAN – King William's Town, South Africa. 14 May 1864-13 May 1865. 1 reel – 1, 16 diazo available at reduced price – sa SA Libr [072]

KAFFRARIAN RECORDER – King William's Town, South Africa. 15 Aug 1863-6 Feb 1864. 1 reel – 1, 16 diazo available at reduced price – sa SA Libr [072]
KAFIR-ENGLISH DICTIONARY / Appleyard, J W – 1845 – 14 fiche – 9 – sa SA Libr [490]
KAFIYA LI IBN AL-HAJIB / Uthman ibn Umar, called Ibn al-Hajib – Rome, 1592 – 1mf – 9 – H-8441/1 – ne IDC [956]
Kafka, Franz *see* DER HEIZER
Kaftan, Julius *see*
- DAS CHRISTENTUM UND DIE PHILOSOPHIE
- JESUS UND PAULUS
- DAS VERHAELTNIS DES EVANGELISCHEN GLAUBENS ZUR LOGOSLEHRE
- ZUR DOGMATIK

KAGAKU SHIRYO SHUSEI = COLLECTION OF WAKA (31 SYLLABLE JAPANESE POEM), RENGA (LINKED VERSE), HAIKAI (17 SYLLABLE VERSE), KYOKA (COMIC POEM) AND SENRYU (SATIRICAL POEM) IN THE CUSTODY OF THE SEIKADO LIBRARY / Seikado Library. Tokyo – (First Series: General considerations and indexes. 50 reels. Printed guide. Y475,000. Second Series: Anthologies of poems collected by Imperial Command. 38 reels. Printed guide. Y356,000. Third Series: Anthologies of poems collected by private persons. 62 reels. Printed guide. Y594,000. Fourth Series: Collected poetical works of the Emperors and other persons. 46 reels. Printed guide. Y436,000. Last Series: Poetry contests and poetry parties; linked verses and syllabled verses; comic poems and satirical poems. 56 reels. Printed guides. Y515,000) – 1,133 manuscripts and printed books in 3,192v – 252r – 1 – ja Yushodo [800]
Kagame, Alexis *see* IYO WILIWE NTA RUNGU
Kagame, P Alegisi *see*
- INDYOHESHA-BIRAYI
- ISOKO Y'AMAJYAMBERE

Kaganovich, A *see* FEODOSII FEDOROVICH SHCHEDRIN 1751-1825
Kagwa, Apolo *see*
- BASAKABAKA BE BUGANDA
- THE BOOK OF THE GANDA CLANS
- THE CLANS OF THE BAGANDA
- EKITABO KY'EKIKA KYA NSENENE

KAHARINGAN, RELIGI DAN PENGHIDUPAN DI PEHULUAN KALIMANTAN / Sarwoto Kertopiduro – SE 4688 1. 1963 – 9 – ne IDC [950]
KAHEL : CARNET DE VOYAGE / Sanderval, Aime Olivier – Paris: F Alcan, 1893 – us Res Libr [910]
Kahle, Paul *see* DIE ARABISCHEN BIBELUEBERSETZUNGEN: TEXTE MIT GLOSSAR UND LITERATURUEBERSICHT
Kahle, Wilhelm *see* GOETHE UND DAS CHRISTENTUM
Kahn, Leon *see* LE COMITE DE BIENFAISANCE
Kahnis, Karl Friedrich August *see*
- DIE DEUTSCHE REFORMATION
- DER GANG DER KIRCHE IN LEBENSBILDERN
- UEBER DAS VERHAELTNISS DER ALTEN PHILOSOPHIE ZUM CHRISTENTHUM

Kahn-Wallerstein, Carmen *see* AUS GOETHES LEBENSKREIS
KAHOKU-SHO SHIN-KEN SHISATSU HOKOKU – Peking. Rural conditions in Hopeh Province (Ho-pei sheng Chin hsien). 1939. (J 612.221 P35k) – 1 – 35.00r – us Hoover Inst Photo [305]
KAHTOU MAGAZINE – (v1-4 1983-86 Can$115.00. Ceased v10 no 4 1992) – Vancouver. v1-10. 1983-92 – 1 – Can$60.00y – cn Micromedia [073]
KAHTOU NEWS – v1- 1992- – 1 – Can$60.00y – cn Micromedia [971]
Kahu, M *see* DAS F.R. KREUTZWALD-LITERATURMUSEUM
Kai, Burhaneddin *see* DIVAN
Kaibel, Georg *see* INSCRIPTIONES GRAECAE, SICILIAE ET ITALIAE
Kaibel, George *see* DE PHRYNICHO SOPHISTA
KAIDAH BAHASA INDONESIA / Slametmuljana, R B – v2 only. 1960- – 9 – SE-5013 1 – ne IDC [490]
Kaidalov, A B et al *see* SURVEYS IN HIGH ENERGY PHYSICS
Kaidanov, I K *see* KRATKOE IZLOZHENIE DIPLOMATII ROSSIISKAGO DVORA
Kaidanov, N I *see*
- SISTEMATICHESKII KATALOG DELAM DEPARTAMENTA TAMOZHENNYKH SBOROV
- SISTEMATICHESKII KATALOG DELAM DEPARTAMENTA VNESHNEI TORGOVLI..
- SISTEMATICHESKII KATALOG DELAM GOSUDARSTVENNOI KOMMERTS-KOLLEGII
- SISTEMATICHESKII KATALOG DELAM KOMMISSII O KOMMERTSII I O POSHLINAKH, KHRANIASHCHIMSIA V ARKHIVE DEPARTAMENTA TAMOZHENNYKH SBOROV
- SISTEMATICHESKII KATALOG DELAM SIBIRSKOGO PRIKAZA, MOSKOVSKOGO KOMMISSARSTVA I DRUGIKH BYVSHIKH UCHREZHDENII PO CHASTI PROMYSHLENNOSTI I TORGOVLI, KHRANIASHCHIMSIA V ARKHIVE

DAS KAIDOKI : EIN REISETAGEBUCH AUS DER KAMAKURA-ZEIT / Mittenzwei, Peter – Frankfurt a.M., 1978 – 3mf – 9 – DM76.00 – 3-89349-777-3 – gw Hänsel [950]
KAIFA BAO – China. Development Weekly. 1986-. M-D112 – 1 – $28.00r – cc Microforms [072]
KAIGUN SEIDO ENKAKU = HISTORY OF THE NAVY SYSTEM – 14r – 1 – inquire – us Ross [355]
Kaihatu, J E *see* ASURANSI PENGANGKUTAN
KAIKEI = THE ACCOUNTING / Japan Society of Accounting – v1-55/2, 1917-1944. 324 books – 54r – 1 – Y400,000.00 – ja Yushodo [650]
KAIN UND ABEL IN DER AGADA DEN APOKRYPHEN, DER HELLENISTISCHEN, CHRISTLICHEN UND MUHAMMEDANISCHE LITERATUR / Aptowitzer, V – Vienna. Leipzig. 1922. BJ-32-33 1 – 9 – ne IDC [230]
KAIN UND ABEL IN DER DEUTSCHEN DICHTUNG / Brieger, Auguste – (Includes bibliographical references) – Berlin: W de Gruyter & Co, 1934 – 2r – 1 – us U.W. Library [430]
KAINAI NEWS – (Ceased v24 no 22 1991) – Standoff. v1-24. 1968/69-1991 – 1 – Price varies – cn Micromedia [073]
KAIROS – Braamfontein, South Africa. v1-8. 1969-76; 1983-85 (complete) – Inquire – 1 – ATLA S0406 – us A.T.L.A. [073]
KAIROS : AN INDEPENDENT QUARTERLY OF LIBERAL RELIGION – nos 1-29. 1975-83 (complete) – 1r – 1 – ATLA S0409 – us A.T.L.A. [073]
KAIROS *see* CHRISTIAN COUNCIL QUARTERLY
Kaisenberg, Moritz von *see* KOENIG JEROME NAPOLEON
DER KAISER ALS ARZT : GENREBILD IN EINEM AUFZUGE / Langer, Anton – Wien: [s.n., 18–?] – 1 – us U.W. Library [820]
Kaiser, Bernd *see* EIGNUNG VON UNTERSCHIEDLICH KONSERVIERTEN GEWEBEPROBEN VON MAJA CRISPATA UND CARCINUS MAENAS, ZUR UNTERSUCHUNG DES GENETISCHEN POLYMORPHISMUS IN POPULATIONEN MITTELS RAPD-FINGERPRINTING
Kaiser, Bruno *see*
- AUSGEWAEHLTE WERKE
- DER FREIHEIT EINE GASSE

KAISER CONSTANTIN UND DIE CHRISTLICHE KIRCHE : FUENF VORTRAEGE / Schwartz, Eduard – Leipzig: B.G. Teubner, 1913 – 1mf – us A.T.L.A. [240]
Kaiser, E *see* PALAEONTOLOGISCHE ABHANDLUNGEN
Kaiser, Georg *see*
- DIE JUEDISCHE WITWE
- KANZLIST KREHLER

KAISER HEINRICH 4 : DRAMATISCHES GEDICHT IN ZWEI ABTHEILUNGEN / Saar, Ferdinand von – 2., verb. Aufl. in einem Band. Heidelberg: G Weiss, 1872 – 1r – 1 – us U.W. Library [810]
Kaiser, Ilse *see* DIE FREUNDE MACHEN DEN PHILOSOPHEN, DER ENGLAENDER, DER WALDBRUDER
THE KAISER IN EXILE : THE ARCHIVE OF FORMER KAISER WILHELM 2 OF GERMANY DURING HIS STAY IN THE NETHERLANDS, 1918-1941 / Koen, DT – (With printed inventory. Pt 1: 1040mf. Installments may be purchased separately) – 1996 – ca 3000mf in 3 installments – 9 – Dfl50,400 set Dfl16,800 per installment – ne MMF Publ [943]
KAISER JULIANUS / Geffcken, Johannes – Leipzig: Dietrich, 1914 – 1mf – us A.T.L.A. [943]
Kaiser, Oscar *see* DER DUALISMUS LUDWIG TIECKS ALS DRAMATIKER UND DRAMATURG
Kaiser, Paul *see* DER KIRCHLICHE BESITZ IM ARRONDISSEMENT AACHEN GEGEN ENDE DES 18. JAHRHUNDERTS UND SEINE SCHICKSALE IN DER SAEKULARISATION DURCH DIE FRANZOESISCHE HERRSCHAFT
KAISER ROTBART : ROMAN / Strobl, Karl Hans – Budweis: Verlagsanstalt Moldavia, c1935 – 1r – 1 – us U.W. Library [830]
DER KAISER UND DIE PROTESTANTEN IN DEN JAHREN 1537-1539 / Rosenberg, Walter – Halle a.S.: Verein fuer Reformationsgeschichte, 1903. (Schriften des Vereins fuer Reformationsgeschichte; 20. Jahrg., Schrift 77) – 1mf – us A.T.L.A. [940]
Kaiser, W *see* DIE GOETTERWELT DER ALTEN DEUTSCHEN
KAISERCHRONIK EINES REGENSBURGER GEISTLICHEN (MGH 8: 1.BD. 1.ABT) – (1. Bd. 2. Abt.: Der Trierer Silvester. Das Annolied. 1895) – 1895 – Dfl53.00 – ne Slangenburg [240]
KAISERIN MARIA THERESIA UND KURFUERSTIN MARIA ANTONIA VON SACHSEN : BRIEFWECHSEL 1747-1772 / ed by Lippert, W – Leipzig, 1908 – 9mf – 9 – ne IDC [943]
Kaiserliches Gouvernement Van Deutsch Neu-Guinea (Imperial Government of German New Guinea) *see* CORRESPONDENCE FILES, ALPHABETICAL SINGLE NUMBER SERIES, 1911-1914
DAS KAISERREICH AM SCHEIDEWEG / Eschenburg, Theodor – Berlin, 1929 – 1 – DM30.00 – gw Mikro Press [943]
KAISERTUM UND HERZOGSGEWALT IM ZEITALTER FRIEDRICHS 1 (MGH SCHRIFTEN..: 9.BD) : STUDIEN ZUR POLITISCHEN UND VERFASSUNGSGESCHICHTE DES HOHEN MITTELALTERS / Mayer, Th. et al – 1944 – Dfl35.00 – ne Slangenburg [240]
KAJIAN KECICIRAN = DROPOUT STUDY / Malaysia. Ministry of Education – (In English) – Kuala Lumpur, 1973 – 2mf – 9 – DE-209/1 – ne IDC [370]
KAK BOLSHEVIKI ZAKHVATILI VLAST NA RUSI / Grimm, Ervin Davidovich – Rostovna Donu: "Nar. polza", 1919 – 1 – CSUX88-B8420 – us Hoover Inst Photo [947]
KAK DELAT' STIKHI / Maiakovskii, Vladimir – M. 1931. BR-976 2 – 8 – ne IDC [460]
KAK DELAT' STIKHI / Maiakovskii, Vladimir – M. 1940. BR-977 2 – 8 – ne IDC [460]
KAK KOOPERATSIIA SOZDAET KREST'IANSKOE BOGATSTVO / Serebriakov, F S – M., 1926 – 1mf – 9 – COR-511/1 – ne IDC [334]
KAK KREST'IANINU OBZAVESTIS' MASHINOI / Vasilevskii, N M – Moscow, 1926 – 1mf – 9 – COR-476/1 – ne IDC [334]
KAK MOZHNO KONCHIT VOINU I KAKOVY SPRAVEDLIVYIA USLOVIIA MIRA / Bulanov, Leonid Petrovich – Petrograd: Po zakazu Izd-vo "Voli a naroda": Izd-vo "Edinenie", 1917 – 1 – CSUX88-B9231 – us Hoover Inst Photo [947]
KAK NADO USTROIT UPRAVLENIE SVOBODNOI ROSSIEI / Finkel, IM – Moskva: Tip. A Pett sman, 1917 – 1 – CSUX89-B695 – us Hoover Inst Photo [350]
KAK NAROD DOBILSIA SVOIKH PRAV; KAK ZAKRIEPIT SVOBODU / Azvitskii, Valeriiloilovich – Moskva: Izd. D. A. Makovskago, 1917 – 1 – CSUX88-B1694 – us Hoover Inst Photo [947]
KAK ORGANIZOVAT' KREDITNUIU RABOTU V PROMYSLOVOI KOOPERATSII / Iakhontov, P V – M., 1929 – 2mf – 9 – COR-458/1 – ne IDC [334]
KAK ORGANIZOVAT' KREST'IANSKOE KHOZIAISTVO V NECHERNOZEMNOI POLOSE / Chaianov, A V – Ed 2. M., L., 1926 – 1mf – 9 – COR-229/1 – ne IDC [334]
KAK ORGANIZOVAT' SEL'SKOKHOZIAISTVEN-NOE KREDITNOE TOVARISHCHESTVO / Beliaev, V N – M., L., 1928 – 1mf – 9 – COR-372/1 – ne IDC [334]
KAK ORGANIZOVAT'I VESTI POTREBITEL'SKOE OBSHCHESTVO : TEKST, ZAKONY, USTAVY, INSTRUKTSII I PR / Merkulov, A V & Kheisin, ML – Spb., 1914 – 4mf – 9 – COR-74/1 – ne IDC [334]
KAK OTKRYT' SEL'SKOKHOZIAISTVENNOE TOVARISHCHESTVO PO PERERABOTKE PRODUKTOV / Kancher, E S – Spb., 1913 – 1mf – 9 – COR-42/1 – ne IDC [334]
KAK PROIZOSHLA RUSSKAIA REVOLIUTSIIA / Dainskii, Ivan – Moskva: Izd. D. I A. Makovskago, 1917 – 1 – CSUX88-B5087 – us Hoover Inst Photo [947]
KAK PROSHLI VYBORY VO 2-IU GOSUDARSTVENNUIU DUMU / Smirnov, A – Spb., 1907. 294p – 4mf – 9 – ne IDC [320]
KAK RABOCHIE I KRESTIANE SBROSII TSARIA, POMESHCHIKOV I KAPITALISTOV / Aroslavskii, Emelian – Moskva: Gos. izdvo, 1927 – 1 – CSUX88-B5795 – us Hoover Inst Photo [947]
KAK RABOTAT' REVIZIONNOI KOMISSII SEL'SKO-KHOZIAISTVENNOGO KREDITNOGO TOVARISHCHESTVA / Barantsov, MS – L., 1926 – 2mf – 9 – COR-371/1 – ne IDC [334]
KAK SOSTAVIT' OTCHET SEL'SKOKHOZIAISTVENNOGO KREDITNOGO TOVARISHCHESTVA / Kil'chevskii, V A – M., 1927 – 1mf – 9 – COR-384/1 – ne IDC [334]
KAK SOSTAVIT' PLAN DEIATEL'NOSTI SEL'SKOGO OBSHCHESTVA POTREBITELEI / Dneprovskii, S P – M., 1927 – 2mf – 9 – COR-324/1 – ne IDC [334]
KAK UCHREDIT' I OTKRYT' KRDITNOE TOVARISHCHESTVO / Shmidt, G R – L., 1924 – 1mf – 9 – COR-409/1 – ne IDC [334]
KAK USTROIT' I VESTI KREDITNOE TOVARISHCHESTVO : PIS'MA KREST'IANINA IVANA BODROGO K DIADE AKIMU MAKSIMOVICHU / Serebriakov, F S; ed by Shefler, M E – M., 1927 – 2mf – 9 – COR-402/1 – ne IDC [334]
Kakabadze, S S *see* GRUZINSKIE DOKUMENTY INSTITUTA NARODOV AZII AN SSSR
KAKAIA RAZNITSA MEZHDU CHASTMYM BANKOM I KREDITNYM TOVARISHCHESTVOM : IZ BESED NA KOOP. KURSAKH / Kil'chevskii, V A – Smolensk, 1913 – 1mf – 9 – COR-47/1 – ne IDC [334]
THE KAKAMORA REPORTER – Honiara. n4, 7, 10-46. jun 1970-jul 1975 – 1r – 1 – PMB Doc414 – at Pacific Mss [072]
Kalachov, N V *see*
- AKTY, OTNOSIASHCHIESIA DO IURIDICHESKAGO BYTA DREVNEI ROSSII
- ARKHIVY, IKH GOSUDARSTVENNYE ZNACHENIE, SOSTAV I USTROISTVO
- ARTELI V DREVNEI I NYNESHNEI ROSSII
- PREDVARITEL'NYIA IURIDICHESKIIA SVEDENIIA DLIA POLNAGO OB IASNENIIA RUSSKOI PRAVDY
- RAZBOR SOCHINENIIAG ANDREEVSKAGO "O NAMESTNIKAKH, VOEVODAKH I GUBERNATORAKH"

KALADIT OKALLUKTUALLAIT. KALADISUT KABLUNATUDLO – v. 1-4. 1859-63. BH-459 2 – 8 – ne IDC [999]
Kalaidovich, K F *see*
- IONN, EKSARKH BOLGARSKII
- OBSTOIATEL'NOE OPISANIE SLAVIANO-ROSSIISKIKH RUKOPISEI, KHRANIASHCHIKHSIA...V BIBLIOTEKE...F.A. TOLSTOGO

Kalaidovich, P *see* OPYT SLOVARIA RUSSKIKH SINONIMOV
AL KALAM – Bangalore, India. 1946-Jun 1953; 1957-60; 1962; Jun-Dec 1963 – 12r – 1 – us L of C Photodup [072]
AL KALAM – Mangalore, India. 1961 – 1r – 1 – us L of C Photodup [072]
DER KALAM IN DER JUEDISCHEN LITERATUR / Schreiner, M – Berlin. 1895. (Dreizehnter Bericht ueber die Lehranstalt fuer die Wissenschaft des Judenthums in Berlin). BJ-33-12 1 – 9 – ne IDC [270]
Kalb, J S *see* WEIGHT TRAINING ECONOMY AS A FUNCTION OF INTENSITY OF THE SQUAT AND OVERHEAD PRESS EXERCISE
Kalchbrenner, C *see* ICONES SELECTAE HYMENOMYCETUM HUNGARIAE PER S. SCHULZER ET C. KALCHBRENNER OBSERVATORIUM ET DELINEATORUM
Kalckstein, Carl von et al *see* NATIONALE UND HUMANISTISCHE ERZIEHUNG
KALE LID – Venice. 1593. BJ-43-34 1 – 9 – ne IDC [956]
THE KALEIDOSCOPE – San Bernardino. Calif. 1891-1894 – 1 – us UMI [071]
THE KALELA DANCE: ASPECTS OF SOCIAL RELATIONSHIPS AMONG URBAN AFRICANS IN NORTHERN RHODESIA / Clyde Mitchell, J – 7 – uk Microform Academic [960]
KALEM – Nos. 1-130 (1324-1327 [1908-1911]) – 32mf – 9 – $63.00 – us MEDOC [949]
KALENDAR / American Carpatho-Russian Youth – Pittsburgh. 1949-54, 1958-62, 1964-73 – 1 – 46.00 – us L of C Photodup [360]

KALENDAR I ZAPISNAI A KNIZHKA VOLOSTNOGO STATISTIKA I KORRESPONDENTA T SENTRALN. STATISTICHESK. UPRAVLENII A UKRAINY NA... : T SENTRALNOE STATISTICHESKOE UPRAVLENIE UKRAINY – (c.1: 1922) – Kharkov: [Upravlenie], 19uu – 1 – CSUXAKY6534-S – us Hoover Inst Photo [947]

KALENDARIUM HUMANAE VITAE / Farley, Robert – (The Kalender of Mans Life). O-249. 1638 – 9 – ne IDC [520]

KALENDERGESCHICHTEN / Gotthelf, Jeremias; ed by Hunziker, Rudolf & Bloesch, Hans – (Includes bibliographical references) – Erlenbach, Zuerich: Eugen Rentsch. 2v. 1931-32 – 1 – us U.W. Library [830]

Kales, Albert Martin *see*
- CASES ON PERSONS AND DOMESTIC RELATIONS, SELECTED FROM DECISIONS OF ENGLISH AND AMERICAN COURTS
- CONDITIONAL AND FUTURE INTERESTS AND ILLEGAL CONDITIONS AND RESTRAINTS IN ILLINOIS
- CONTRACTS AND COMBINATIONS IN RESTRAINT OF TRADE

Kalette, Linda E *see*
- PAPERS
- PAPERS, 1776-1865

KALEVALA – The Kalevala. 1888 – 1 – us I.U. Libraries [390]

Kalfelis, Petros *see* DIE AUSWIRKUNGEN DER FABRIKARBEIT AUF DAS TRADITIONALE ROLLENVERHALTEN DER FRAU IN MEGARA, GRIECHENLAND

KALGOORLIE MINER – Australia. 1901-32.-d. 80mqn reels – 1 – uk British Libr Newspaper [072]

KALGOORLIE WESTERN ARGUS. (WESTERN ARGUS) – Australia. 30 Jul 1896-20 Jun 1922.-d. 57mqn reels – 1 – uk British Libr Newspaper [072]

KALI KONTO PROJECT: SELOREDJO DAM AND POWER STATION / Indonesia. Kementerian Pekerdjaan Umum dan Tenaga – Contents: (1) Specification for purchase. (2) Specification for construction. SE-5537 1. 2v. 1962 – 9 – ne IDC [624]

KALIDA RECORD – Kalida, Ohio. 1919-21 – 1r – 1 – $32.50r – us Archival [071]

Kalidasa *see*
- BIRTH OF THE WAR GOD (KUMARASAMBHAVA)
- RAGHUVANSA/KUMARA SAMBHAVA

KALIFORNIER IDISHER SHTERN = CALIFORNIA JEWISH STAR – Los Angeles, San Francisco. 1924 – 1 – us A.J.P.C. [071]

KALINGA – (Oriya language) – Cuttack, India. Jul-Sept 1966 – 1r – 1 – us L of C Photodup [072]

Kalinin, M I *see* ZNACHENIE SEL'SKOKHOZIAIST VENNYKH KOMMUN V SOVETSKOM STROITEL'STVE

Kalinin, V A *see* SISTEMATICHESKII KATALOG BIBLIOTEKI NIKOLAEVSKOI INZHENERNOI AKADEMII I UCHILISHCHA

Kalinka, V *see* DER VIERJAEHRIGE POLNISCHE REICHSTAG, 1788 BIS 1791

Kalinychev, F I *see* GOSUDARSTVENNAIA DUMA V ROSSII

Kalisch, Isador *see*
- SEFER YETSIRAH...A BOOK ON CREATION, OR, THE JEWISH METAPHYSICS OF REMOTE ANTIQUITY
- SKETCH OF THE TALMUD

Kalisch, Isidor *see* A SKETCH OF THE TALMUD

Kalisch, Marcus Moritz *see*
- THE BOOK OF JONAH
- THE PROPHECIES OF BALAAM (NUMBERS 22 TO 24)

Kalischer, Alfred Christlieb *see* HEINRICH HEINE'S VERHAELTNIS ZUR RELIGION

Kalischer, H *see* DRISCHATH ZION ODER ZIONS HERSTELLUNG

Kalischer, Salomon *see* GOETHE ALS NATURFORSCHER UND HERR DU BOIS-REYMOND ALS SEIN KRITIKER

KALISH, MAX, SCRAPBOOK, MS P.P. – 1909-1992 – 1 reel – 1 – us Western Res [730]

KALISHER LEBEN = KALISHER LIFE – (In Yiddish) – Kalisz, PL. v3 no3. 12 Apr 1929 – 1r – 1 – $25.00 – cn Can Microfilming [072]

Kalitin, N *see* SLOVO I MYSL'

Kaliuzhnaia, G P *see* PRAVOVYE FORMY MONOPOLII VNESHNEI TORGOVLI SSSR V IKH ISTORICHESKOM RAZVITII

Kalkbrenner, C *see* KURZER ABRISZ DER GESCHICHTE DER TONKUNST ZUM VERGNUEGEN DER LIEBHABER DER MUSIK

KALKINMA PLANI UCUNCU BES YIL (1973-1977), 1973 YILI PROGRAMI / Turkey. Devlet Planlama Teskilati – (Third Five Year Development Plan (1973-1977), 1973 Draft Annual Program). Ankara. 1972. BD-1772 1 – 9 – ne IDC [338]

Kalkoff, Paul *see*
- DIE ANFAENGE DER GEGENREFORMATION IN DEN NIEDERLANDEN
- BRIEFE, DEPESCHEN, UND BERICHTE UEBER LUTHER VOM WORMSER REICHSTAGE 1521
- DIE DEPESCHEN DES NUNTIUS ALEANDER VOM WORMSER REICHSTAGE 1521

Kalkschmidt, Till *see* DER DEUTSCHE FRONTSOLDAT

Kallen, G *see* DE AUCTORITATE PRESIDENDI IN CONCILIO GENERALI

Kalm, Peter *see* EN RESA TILL NORRA AMERICA

KALMAR LANS TIDNING – Kalmar, Sweden. 1979- – 1 – sw Kungliga [072]

KALMYTSKIIA ZAGADKI I POSLOVITSY / Kotvich, V L – Spb, 1905 – 8 – BU-402 2 – ne IDC [947]

Kal'nev, Mikhail A *see* SBORNIK" 17-TI GLAVNEISHIKH" PROTOVOSEKTANTSKIKH"

THE KALPA-SUTRA AND NAVA TATVA / Bhadrabahu – 1848 – 1 – uk Microform Academic [280]

DAS KALTE HAUS, OBERSCHLESIEN : NOVELLEN / Koehler, Willibald – Prag: Noebe, 1944 – 1 – us U.W. Library [830]

Kaltenbach, J H *see* MONOGRAPHIE DER FAMILIEN DER PFLANZENLAEUSE

Kalthoff, Albert *see*
- DAS CHRISTUS-PROBLEM
- DIE ENTSTEHUNG DES CHRISTENTUMS
- WAS WISSEN WIR VON JESUS?

Kalund, Kr. *see* KATALOG OVER DE OLDNORSK-ISLANDSKE HANDSKRIFTER I KOEBENHAVNS OFFENTLICHER BIBLIOTHEKER

Kaluzhniatskii, E *see*
- K BIBLIOGRAFII TSERKOVNO-SLAVIANSKIKH PECHATNYKH IZDANII V ROSSII
- KIRILLOVSKOE PIS'MO Y RUMYN

KALUZHSKII KOOPERATOR – Kaluga, 1926-27 n15 – 8mf – 9 – COR-599/1 – ne IDC [334]

KALUZHSKII VESTNIK KOOPERATSII I SEL'SKOGO KHOZIAISTVA *see* VESTNIK KALUZHSKOI KOOPERATSII

Kalweit, Paul *see*
- DIE STELLUNG DER RELIGION IM GEISTESLEBEN

Kamal, Youssouf *see* MONUMENTA CARTOGRAPHICA AFRICAE ET AEGYPTI

Kamali, Iris *see* DIE RELATIVE HAEUFIGKEIT DES HARNBLASENKARZINOMS AN UNAUSGEWAEHLTEM BIOPSIEGUT DER JAHRE 1977-79...

Kamanin, I M *see* VODIANI ZNAKY NA PAPERI UKRAJINS'KIKH DOKUMENTIV XVI I XVII VV. (1566-1651)

Kamanin, IM *see* PALEOGRAFICHESKII IZBORNIK

Kamarovskii, L A *see*
- MEZHDUNARODNOE PRAVO PO LEKTSIIAM
- MEZHDUNARODNOE PRAVO V 19 VEKE
- O MEZHDUNARODNOM SUDE
- NACHALO NEVMESHATEL'STVA; RASSUZHDENIE
- O NOVEISHEI LITERATURE MORSKAGO I VOENNAGO PRAVA
- OBZOR SOVREMENNOI LITERATURY PO MEZDUNARODNOMU PRAVU
- OSNOVNYE VOPROSY NAUKI MEZHDUNARODNAGO PRAVA
- PERVOE TREKHLETIE INSTITUTA MEZHDUNARODNOGO PRAVA, 1873-76
- PRAVO I MIR V MEZHDUNARODNYKH OTNOSHENIIAKH
- VOPROS O MEZHDUNARODNOI ORGANIZATSII SOEDINENNYE SHTATY EVROPY

KAMBA CUSTOMARY LAW; NOTES TAKEN IN THE MACHAKOS DISTRICT OF KENYA COLONY / Penwill, D J – Kampala: East African Literature Bureau 1972. 122p. LL-12044 – 1 – us L of C Photodup [340]

Kambra, K *see*
- DUO. POUR LE VIOLON ET VIOLA
- THREE SONATINAS, OP. 14

KAMBUJA – Phnom-Penh. 6 janv 1943-27 fevr 1945 – 1 – fr A.C.R.P.P. [073]

KAMBUJA SURIYA – Phnom-Penh. 1927-46, 1948. mq: 1929 – 1 – fr A.C.R.P.P. [073]

KAMCHATSKAI A PRAVDA : ORGAN KAMCHATSKOGO OBKOMA, PETROPAVLOVSKOGO GK VKP (B) I OBLASTNOGO SOVETA DEPUTATOV TRUDI ASHCHIKHSI A – (Includes c.1: 1945:Mar.27) – Petropavlovsk-na-Kamchatke: "Kamchatskai a pravda", 193u – 1 – CSUXANQ9893-S – us Hoover Inst Photo [947]

KAMEL UND NADELOEHR: EINE KRITISCH-EXEGETISCHE STUDIE UEBER MT. 19, 24 UND PARAL / Aicher, Georg – Muenster i.W.: Aschendorff, 1908. 1 fiche – 9 – us A.T.L.A. [240]

KAMEN' / Mandelstam, Osip E – Stikhi. Ed. 2. Petrograd. 1916. BR-1172 2 – 8 – ne IDC [460]

"KAMEN VERY" STEFANA IAVORSKAGO / Morev, I – Spb, 1804 – 8 – BR-7711 2 – ne IDC [920]

Kamenev, L B *see*
- KUDA I KAK VEDET SOVETSKAIA VLAST' KREST'IANSTVO?
- MEZHDU DVUMIA REVOLIUTSIIAMI

Kameneva, S S *see* FRONTY KRASNOI ARMII I FLOTA

KAMENNOUGOLNAI A PROMYSHLENNOST DONET SKOGO BASSE INA V... / DONET SKI I GOSUDARSTVENNY I KAMENNOUGOLNY I TREST "DONUGOL", NAUCHNO-IZDATELSKOE BI URO – (Includes c.1: 1923/1925) – [Kharkov]: Donugol, 19uu – 1 – CSUXAKZ0497-S – us Hoover Inst Photo [947]

Kamenskii, V *see*
- DEVUSHKI BOSIKOM
- IZBRANNOE
- KNIGA O EVREINOVE
- POEMY
- PUSHKIN I DANTES
- STEN'KA RAZIN
- STIKHI I POEMY
- ZEMLIANKA
- ZHIZN'S MAIAKOVSKIM

DER KAMERAD – Liberec, Czechoslovakia. Dec 1936-Aug 1938 – 1r – 1 – us L of C Photodup [072]

KAMERAD MIT DEM HAARIGEN GESICHT / Schwab, Guenther – Wien: W Frick, 1941 – 1r – 1 – us U.W. Library [430]

KAMERAD UND KAMERADIN : BUNTE BILDER, GEDANKEN UND WORTE AUS DEN MORGENFEIERN IM DEUTSCHEN RUNDFUNK / Kinau, Rudolf – Hamburg: Quickborn-Verlag, 1941 – 1r – 1 – us U.W. Library [840]

KAMERADEN : CHRONIK EINER JUGEND / Sturm, Stefan – Karlsbad: A Kraft, 1943 – 1r – 1 – us U.W. Library [830]

KAMERADEN UNTERM SPATEN / Strauss, Eberhard – Oldenburg i.O.: G Stalling, [1935] – 1r – 1 – us U.W. Library [830]

KAMERADSCHAFT : SCHRIFTEN JUNGER DEUTSCHER – Bruessel, Amsterdam, London. nov 1937-feb 1940 – 1 – Inquire at Mikrofilmarchiv for details – gw Misc Inst [072]

KAMERADSCHAFT : SCHRIFTEN JUNGER DEUTSCHER – Bruessel-Amsterdam-London. Nov 1937-Feb 1940 – 1 – gw Mikrofilm [949]

Kamerlingh Onnes Laboratorium. Leiden *see* COMMUNICATIONS

KAMERSTUKKEN / Netherlands. Cabinet and Parliament – Published correspondence between the Cabinet and Members of Parliament. 1960/61- – 9 – ne Sdu MICRO [324]

KAMERVRAGEN / Netherlands. Parliament – Collection of written questions by the Members of Parliament to the executive branch of government, and resulting responses. Available from 1945- – 9 – ne Sdu MICRO [323]

KAMI YO NO MAKI / Rosny, Leon de – Histoire des dynasties divines. Paris. 1884 – 9 – 15.00 – fr Orientalistes [950]

KAMIKAZE. KERA PUTIH – SE-6384 1 – 9 – ne IDC [950]

Kamil, A *see* AFAK

Kamil, Abd-al-Aziz Abd-al-Qadir *see* ISLAM AND THE RACE QUESTION

Kaminer, I *see* SHIREI

Kaminka, A I *see*
- MEHKARIM BE-MIKRA VA-TALMUD UVE-SIFRUT RABBANIT
- SEFER HA-YOVEL LE-AHARON KAMINKA
- VTORAIA GOSUDARSTVENNAIA DUMA

Kaminskaia, PD *see*
- OCHERKI TRUDOVOGO PRAVA
- SOVETSKOE TRUDOVOE PRAVO

Kaminskii, GN *see* SEL'SKOKHOZIAISTVENNAIA KOOPERATSIIA

KAMINSTEIN LEGISLATIVE HISTORY PROJECT *see* THE DOCUMENTS REFERRED TO IN THE KAMINSTEIN LEGISLATIVE HISTORY PROJECT

KAMLOOPS AND DISTRICT MINING GAZETTE – Kamloops [BC]: W W Clarke and F E Young, [1899?-1900?] – 9 – cn C.I.H.M. [622]

KAMLOOPS INLAND SENTINEL – Kamloops, British Columbia, CN. May 1880-1916 – 17r – 1 – cn Commonwealth Micro [072]

THE KAMLOOPS PHONOGRAPHER – Kamloops, BC: St. Louis Mission, [1892-1893?] – 9 – cn C.I.H.M. [621]

KAMLOOPS SENTINEL – (1924-1971.-85r) – Kamloops, No1976-1987Ju – 131r – 1 – cn Preston [971]

KAMLOOPS STANDARD AND SENTINEL – Kamloops, British Columbia, CN. Jul 1897-Jul 1924 – 13r – 1 – cn Commonwealth Micro [072]

KAMLOOPS WAWA – [Kamloops, BC: J.-M R LeJeune, 1891-1923] – 9 – cn C.I.H.M. [240]

Kammerer, A *see* ESSAI SUR L'HISTOIRE ANTIQUE D'ABYSSIENIE

DER KAMMERSAENGER : DREI SZENEN / Wedekind, Frank – 4. Aufl. Berlin: B Cassirer, 1909 – 1r – 1 – us U.W. Library [820]

KAMOES BAHASA INDONESIA-NIPPON DAN NIPPON INDONESIA / Adinegoro, Djamaludin – Medan, 2602. 1942. 1011. 197p – 1-3mf – 9 – ne IDC [950]

KAMOES HARIAN. NIPPON-INDONESIA; INDONESIA-NIPPON / Poerwadarminta, W J S – (Microfiche Nos 136-137) – Djakarta: Toko Boekoe Pendidikan, 2602 – 2mf – 9 – SE-2002/1 – ne IDC [950]

KAMOES HARIAN. NIPPON-INDONESIA; INDONESIA-NIPPON. TJETAKAN KETIGA, DITAMBAH DAN DIPERBAIKI / Poerwadarminta, W J S – (Microfiche Nos 138-140) – Djakarta: Pendidikan, (2603) – 3mf – 9 – SE-2002/1 – ne IDC [950]

KAMOES INDONESIA / Harahap, Elisa Sutan – SE-10,909 1. 1942 – 9 – ne IDC [950]

KAMOES LEUTIK SOENDA-INDONESIA / Satjadibrata, R – (Microfiche Nos 152-153) – Djakarta: Gunseikanbu Kokumin Tosyokyoku (Bale Poestaka), 2605 – 2mf – 9 – SE-2002/1 – ne IDC [950]

KAMOES SOENDA-MELAJOE / Satjadibrata, R – (Microfiche Nos 154-158) – Djakarta: Gunseikanbu Kokumin Tosyokyoku (Balai Poestaka), 2604 – 5mf – 9 – SE-2002/1 – ne IDC [950]

LE KAMOURASKA – La Pocatiere, 8 fev 1978-22 dec 1991 – 14r – 1 – Can$70.00 – cn Can Microfilming [072]

Kamp, Otto *see* ARMELEUTSLIEDER

Kampen. Netherlands. Ordinances, Local Laws, etc *see* BOECK VAN RECHTEN DER STAD KAMPEN: DAT GULDEN BOECK

DER KAMPF – Berlin. v. 1-2. July 1927-July 1928 – 1 – us NY Public [073]

DER KAMPF – (Cont by: Der Sozialistische Kampf, Paris) – Prag (Praha), Czechoslovakia. May 1934-Sept 1938. Ausg. f. Oesterreich: Jul 1934-Apr 1938 – 1 – gw Mikrofilm [072]

DER KAMPF = STRUGGLE – Toronto, CN. v6 no 308, v14 no 701. 1932-1939 – 1r – 1 – Can$40.00 – cn Can Microfilming [072]

DER KAMPF : SUEDBAYERISCHE TAGESZEITUNG DER UNABHAENGIGEN SOZIALDEMOKRATIE – Muenchen, DE. 1919-1920 – 1r – 1 – DM75.00 – gw Mikro Press [943]

DER KAMPF : SUEDBAYERISCHE TAGESZEITUNG DER UNABHAENGIGEN SOZIALDEMOKRATIE – Muenchen, Germany. 1919-20 – 1r – 1 – gw Mikrofilm [072]

DER KAMPF – Vienna. v. 1-26. Oct. 1907-1933 – 1 – us NY Public [073]

DER KAMPF – Wien, 1907-34 – 7r – 1 – DM1,330.00 – gw Mikro Press [072]

DER KAMPF – Wien, Austria. 1907-Jan 1934 – 7r – 1 – gw Mikrofilm [072]

DER KAMPF *see* DER SOZIALISTISCHE KAMPF

KAMPF : SOZIALDEMOKRATISCHE MONATSSCHRIFT – Vienna. v1-26. 1907-33 – 6r – 1 – us Ross [320]

Kampf, C A von *see* LITTERATUR DES GESAMMTEN SOWOHL NATUERLICHEN ALS POSITIVEN VOELKERRECHTS

KAMPF DEM TODE : ROMAN / Adler, Hans – Muenchen: Knorr & Hirth, c1929 – 1r – 1 – us U.W. Library [830]

DER KAMPF DER GEGENWART; EIN DRAMATISCHER VERSUCH IN 5 AKTEN / Katzer, Friedrich Xavier – Milwaukee: Milwaukeer Seebote, 1873. 194p – 1 – us U.W. Library [820]
DER KAMPF DER LUTHERISCHEN KIRCHE UM LUTHERS LEHRE VOM ABENDMAHL IM REFORMATIONSZEITALTER : IM ZUSAMMENHANG MIT DER GESAMMTEN LEHRENTWICKLUNG DIESER ZEIT / Schmid, Heinrich – Leipzig; J.C. Hinrichs, 1868 – 1mf – us A.T.L.A. [240]
DER KAMPF IM SPESSART : ERZAEHLUNG / Schuecking, Levin – Berlin, Leipzig: Enck-Verlag, [1924?] – 1r – 1 – us U.W. Library [830]
Kampf, Leopold *see* ON THE EVE
DER KAMPF MIT DEM DRACHEN : ZEHN KAPITEL VON DER GEGENWART DES DEUTSCHEN SCHRIFTTUMS UND VON DER KRISE DES DEUTSCHEN GEISTESLEBENS / Forst de Battaglia – Berlin: Verlag fuer Zeitkritik, 1931 – 1 – us U.W. Library [430]
DER KAMPF MIT DEM FREUND ODER VERWANDTEN IN DER DEUTSCHEN LITERATUR BIS UM 1300 / Harms, Wolfgang – (Includes bibliographical references and index) – Muenchen: Eidos, 1963 – 1 – us U.W. Library [430]
DER KAMPF; SOZIALDEMOKRATISCHE MONATSSCHRIFT – v. 1-27. 1907-1934. (13 scattered issues wanting) – 1 – 119.00 – us L of C Photodup [943]
DER KAMPF UM DIE MESSE IN DEN ERSTEN JAHREN DER AUSEINANDERSETZUNG MIT LUTHER / Iserloh, E – Muenster, 1952 – 1mf – 8 – ne Slangenburg [240]
DER KAMPF UM DIE SCHRIFT IN DER DEUTSCH-EVANGELISCHEN KIRCHE DES NEUNZEHNTEN JAHRHUNDERTS / Gennrich, Paul – Berlin: Reuther & Reichard, 1898 – 1mf – 9 – 0-8370-8575-6 – 1986-2575 – us A.T.L.A. [220]
DER KAMPF UM GLATZ : AUS DER GESCHICHTE DER GEGENREFORMATION IN DER GRAFSCHAFT GLATZ / Wiese, Hugo von – Halle: Verein fuer Reformationsgeschichte, 1896 (Schriften des Vereins fuer Reformationsgeschichte; 14. Jahrg., Schrift 54) – 1mf – us A.T.L.A. [240]
KAMPF UM IRLAND : ERZAEHLUNG / Auerswald, Annmarie von; ed by Plenzat, Karl – Leipzig: H Eichblatt, c1943 – 1r – 1 – us U.W. Library [830]
KAMPF UM PREUSSEN : SCHAUSPIEL / Heynicke, Kurt – Leipzig: Schauspiel-Verlag, 1926 – 1r – 1 – us U.W. Library [820]
EIN KAMPF UM ROM / Dahn, Felix – Leipzig: Breitkopf und Haertel. 3v. 1898 – 1 – us U.W. Library [830]
EIN KAMPF UM ROM : HISTORISCHER ROMAN / Dahn, Felix – Leipzig: Breitkopf und Haertel. 3v. 1904 – 1 – us U.W. Library [830]
KAMPF UM SPANIEN: DIE GESCHICHTE DER LEGION CONDOR. BEARB. IM AUFTRAG DES REICHSLUFTFAHRTMINISTERIUMS; MIT 16 BILDTAFELN UND 5 KARTEN. 41.-60. TAUSEND. OLDENBURG I.O / Beumelburg, Werner – Berlin: G. Stalling. 1942 – 1 – us U.W. Library [946]
KAMPF UM THURANT : EIN ROMAN AUS DEM 13. JAHRHUNDERT / Allmers, Robert – [Stuttgart: Deutsche Verlags-Anstalt, 1931] – 1r – 1 – us U.W. Library [830]
KAMPFBEREIT – Paris-Oslo. Feb-Sept 1937 – 1 – gw Mikrofilm [072]
KAMPFER – Liberec, Czechoslovakia. Aug 1933-Jun 1934 (5 scattered issues) – 1r – 1 – us L of C Photodup [072]
KAMPFJUGEND : GEDICHTE / Schenk, Walter – 3., erw. Aufl. Berlin: Arbeiterjugend-Verlag, 1927 – 1r – 1 – us U.W. Library [810]
KAMPFRUF – Essen, Germany. 1922-26 (incomplete) – 1 – gw Mikrofilm [072]
DAS KAMPFSIGNAL *see* DIE FACKEL
Kamphausen, Adolf *see*
- DIE BERICHTIGTE LUTHERBIBEL: REKTORATSREDE MIT ANMERKUNGEN
- DIE CHRONOLOGIE DER HEBRAEISCHEN KOENIGE: EINE GESCHICHTLICHE UNTERSUCHUNG
- DAS LIED MOSES: DEUT. 32:1-43

KAMPO / Japan. Laws, Statutes, etc – Official gazette. Tokyo. On film: 1887-1930. LL-02048 – 1 – us L of C Photodup [340]
DER KAMPRUF – Wien: Buchdruckerei "Albrecht Durer", sep 16 1930-1932 – 1r – 1 – us Res Libr [073]
DER KAMPS UM BADAJOZ UN FRUHJAHR / Brodruch, Karl – 1861 – 9 – 1.50f – sp Bibl Santa Ana [946]
Kampschulte, FW *see*
- JOHANN CALVIN
- DIE UNIVERSITAET ERFURT IN IHREM VERHAELTNISSE ZU DEM HUMANISMUS UND DER REFORMATION

KAMUS BAHASA DJERMAN; DJERMAN-INDONESIA DAN INDONESIA-DJERMAN / Situmorang, F – SE 3943 1. 1951? – 9 – ne IDC [950]
KAMUS DJEPANG-INDONESIA / Sastranegara, Rd. M – SE 4471 1. 1962 – 9 – ne IDC [950]
KAMUS DJERMAN-INDONESIA / Aetius, Br – SE-4327 1. 1962 – 9 – ne IDC [950]
KAMUS INDONESIA-TIONGHOA / Pao, Ssu-ching – SE-4042 1. 1952 – 9 – ne IDC [950]
KAMUS INTERNASIONAL / Raliby, Osman – SE-2239 1. 1956 – 9 – ne IDC [950]
KAMUS PELADJARAN INDONESIA-RUSIA; 7000 KATA / Teselkin, Avenir Stepanovich – SE 4654 1. 1964 – 9 – ne IDC [950]
KAMUS POLITIK / Nasution, Amir Taat – SE-11,090 1. 1962 – 9 – ne IDC [320]
KAMUS POLITIK / Nasution, Amir Taat – SE-2073 1. 1956 – 9 – ne IDC [320]
KAMUS POPULER – By Habeyb. 1966?. SE-6294/1 – 9 – ne IDC [950]
KAN PO : BERITA PEMERINTAH – Djakarta, Gunseikanbu, Bahagian Kikakuka, 2602-2605. n1-74 – 277-319mf – 9 – ne IDC [950]
KANA JAWA SHIMBUN – Nos. 1-86. Jan. 1, 2604-Aug. 18, 2605 – 320-329mf – 9 – ne IDC [073]
Kana, Nicodemus Lulu *see* A PRELIMINARY STUDY OF THE EAST SUMBANESE SOCIAL ORGANIZATION AND RELIGION
KANAD – (Mueessisi: Ismail Hami, Sahib-i Imtiyaz: Hueseyin Huesnue, Sermuharriri: Tahsin Nahid. No. 4 (28 Tesriniewel 1326[1910])) – Istanbul: Muesterek uel-Menfaa-i Osmani Sirketi Matbaasi, 1910 – 1mf – 9 – $12.00 – us MEDOC [949]
KANADA SHINBUN = THE CANADA DAILY NEWS – Vancouver, BC. Sept-Dec 1941 – 1r – 1 – Can$125.00 – cn U.B.C. Preserve [072]
KANADAI MAGYARSAG – (In Hungarian) – Canada, 1951-77 – 1 – cn Commonwealth Micro [072]
KANADA-KURIER *see*
- HAMILTON JOURNAL
- KITCHENER JOURNAL
- MONTREALER ZEITUNG

KANADE = CANADA – Montreal, CN. v1 no 3. 1925 – 1r – 1 – Can$25.00 – cn Can Microfilming [072]
KANADER NAYES = CANADIAN NEWS – (In Yiddish and English) – Toronto, CN. v1. 1935-1954 – 1r – 1 – Can$60.00 – cn Can Microfilming [072]
KANADER ZHURNAL = CANADIAN JOURNAL – Montreal, CN, 1940 – 1r – 1 – Can$25.00 – cn Can Microfilming [072]
KANADI ISKAI A ZHIZN = CANADIAN LIFE – (Includes c.1: v.1:no.1 1921:Dec. 2-v.13:no.62 (1933:June); LACKS many issues) – Vinnipeg: Russkoe pravoslavnoe obshchestvo "Prosvi eshchenie", 1921- – 1 – CSUXAKG0864-S – us Hoover Inst Photo [947]
KANADIISKY FARMER – Winnipeg, Canada. 11 Apr 1928-8 Oct 1973.-w. 46 reels – 1 – uk British Libr Newspaper [630]
DER KANAEDER IDISHER SHRAYBER = THE CANADIAN YIDDISH WRITER – Montreal, CN, 1916 – 1r – 1 – Can$25.00 – cn Can Microfilming [072]
KANAGAWA SHIMBUN – Japan, 1940-61 – 84r – 1 – inquire – us Ross [072]
KANAGAWA SHIMBUN – November 1940-December 1994 – 516r – 1 – Y5,508,000 – ja Japan Micro [950]
KANAKEE VALLEY POST – De Motte. Ind. 1937-1962 – 1 – us UMI [071]
Kanarskii, S M *see* UGOLOVNYI KODEKS SOVETSKIKH RESPUBLIK
KANATA KOURIER – Kanata, Ja1990-1991Ju – 3r – 1 – cn Preston [971]
KANATA KOURIER-STANDARD – (Ju1991-1992De.-5r) – Kanata, 1993 – 3r – 1 – cn Preston [971]
KANATA STANDARD – Kanata, Ja1990-1991Ju – 3r – 1 – cn Preston [971]
KANAURI VOCABULARY / Bailey, T G – 1911 – 1 – uk Microform Academic [490]
THE KANAWHA GAZETTE – Charleston. West Virginia. 1877-1886 – 1 – us UMI [071]
KANAWHA VALLEY LEADER – Nitro. West Virginia. -w. 1912-40, 1958-66 – 1 – us UMI [071]
Kancher, E S *see*
- KAK OTKRYT' SEL'SKOKHOZIAISTVENNOE TOVARISHCHESTVO PO PERERABOTKE PRODUKTOV
- RUKOVODSTVO PO SEL'SKOI KOOPERATSII

KAND VA KAV – London: Dawrah-'i 1, shumarah-'i 1-8 (Azar 1353-Pa'iz 1357 [Nov/Dec 1974- Aut 1978])-dawrah-'i 2, shumarah-'i 1-3 (Bahar 1359-Zimistan 1359 [Spring 1980- Winter 1980/81]) and supplements 1-6 – 1 reel – 1 – $85.00 – us MEDOC [072]
Kanda, Kiichiro *see* HUANG-MING-WEN-HAI
Kandidov, Boris Pavlovich *see* SEKTANTSTVO I MIROVAYA VOINA
Kandler, Gunther *see* ZWEITSINN. VORSTUDIEN ZU EINER THEORIE DER SPRACHLICHEN
Kandra, K *see* MAGYAR MYTHOLOGIA
KANE DAILY REPUBLICAN – Kane, PA., 1894-1899 – 13 – $25.00r – us I.M.R. [071]
Kane, E K *see* ARCTIC EXPLORATIONS
KANE LEADER – Kane, PA., 1885-1888 – 13 – $25.00r – us I.M.R. [071]
KANE REPUBLICAN – Kane, PA., 1894-1979 – 13 – $25.00r – us I.M.R. [071]
KANE WEEKLY BLADE – Kane, PA., 1879-1882 – 13 – $25.00r – us I.M.R. [071]
Kanehira, R *see*
- FLORA MICRONESICA
- FORMOSAN TREES INDIGENOUS TO THE ISLAND

K'ANG CHAN SHIH KO CHI, VOL 5 (CCC126) / Feng, Yu-hsiang – (In Chinese) – [s.l: s.n, 1945] – 1r – 1 – 1984-B500 – us A.T.L.A. [240]
Kang, H -Y *see* THE EFFECT OF VARIOUS LIFTING INTENSITIES IN RELEASE OF HUMAN GROWTH HORMONE
K'ANG YU-WEI I-KAO – A collection of manuscripts left by the late K'ang Yu'wei to his daughter. (2268 0343. 19) – 1 – 35.00r – us Hoover Inst Photo [090]
KANG ZHAN RI BAO – China. Jan-Feb 1946. 3 ill. DL37f – 9 – 30.00 – cc Globe [072]
KANGAROO OUT OF HIS ELEMENT – Australia. 19 Oct-30 Nov 1914. 6 ft – 1 – uk British Libr Newspaper [072]
K'ANG-JIH CHAN-CHENG SHIH-CH'I SHEN-KAN-NING PIEN-CH'U TS'AI-CHENG.. – Collection of historical abstracts on the finance and economy of the Shen-Kan-Ning Border Regions during the war of resistance against Japan – 1 – 83.00 – us Chinese Res [950]
KANGRI ZHANZHENG SHIQI DE BALUJUN HE XINSIJUN (ZHONGGUO XIANDAISHI ZILIAO CONGKAN) – Series of materials on contemporary Chinese history: The Eighth Route Army and New Fourth Army during the War of Resistance against Japan. Comp. by Renmin Chubanshe, 1953. 7 fiches. F/H129 – 9 – $24.50 – cc Microforms [950]
KANGRI ZHANZHENG SHIQI JIEFANGQU DE GAIQUANG (ZHONGGUO XIANDAISHI ZILIAO CONGKAN) – Series of materials on contemporary Chinese history: A General account of the situation in liberated areas during the War of Resistance against Japan.Comp. by Renmin Chubanshe, 1953. 2 fiches. F-H130 – 9 – 4.00f – cc Microforms [950]
KANG-YONG-QIAN SHIQI CHENGXIANG RENMIN FANKANG DOUZHENG ZILIAO – Materials on people's resistance during the reigns of Kangxi, Yongzheng, Qiantong, v1-2. Comp. by the Institute of Qing Dynasty History, People's University. 1 reel. M-H76 – 5 – $40.00 – cc Microforms [950]
KANGZHAN – Resistance. 1937-38. 1 reel. M/C 80 – 1 – $55.00 – cc Microforms [073]
KANGZHAN RIBAO – (Journal of the War of Resistance). China. Sept 1940-Jun 1946. M B16 – 4r – 1 – $200.00 – cc Microforms [072]
Kanitz, FP *see* DONAU-BULGARIEN UND DER BALKAN
KANIVA TIMES – 1939-1974. KT1-16 – 16r – 1 – at Corangamite [072]
O KANIVETE : HUMORISTICO – "APOLITICO" – ESPORTIVO – NOTICIOSO – UM ORGAO PARA O BEM DAS CAUSAS PUBLICAS – Uba, 28 Feb 1960; Sep 1965; Feb, Sep, Dec 1971; Jun 1972; Oct 1973; Jan, Mar-Apr, Sep, Nov-Dec 1974; Feb-Mar, Jun-Aug, Nov 1975; Jan, Mar-Apr, Jul-Sep, Dec 1976; Apr 1977; Jan, Mar, May, Jul-Oct, Dec 1979; Jan-Dec 1980 – 1,5,6 – bl Biblioteca [072]
Kanne, Friedrich August *see* (WIENER) ALLGEMEINE MUSIKALISCHE ZEITUNG
Kano, Marshall *see* THE RELATIONSHIP BETWEEN AEROBIC FITNESS AND DIET COMPOSITION IN ADULT FEMALES
DER KANON DES ALTEN TESTAMENTS : NACH DEN UEBERLIEFERUNGEN IN TALMUD UND MIDRASCH / Fuerst, Julius – Leipzig: Doerffling und Franke, 1868 – 1mf – 9 – 0-8370-3220-2 – 1985-1220 – us A.T.L.A. [220]
DER KANON DES ALTEN TESTAMENTS: EIN ABRISS / Budde, Karl – Giessen: J. Ricker (Toepelmann), 1900. 1 fiche – 9 – us A.T.L.A. [240]
DER KANON UND DIE KRITIK DES NEUEN TESTAMENTS IN IHRER GESCICHTLICHEN AUSBILDUNG UND GESTALTUNG / Hilgenfeld, Adolf – (Includes index) – Halle: C E M Pfeffer, 1863 – 1mf – 9 – 0-8370-3584-8 – 1985-1584 – us A.T.L.A. [220]
KANONISCH UND APOKRYPH / Hoelscher, Gustav – Naumburg a.S.: Lippert, 1905. 1 fiche – 9 – us A.T.L.A. [240]
KANPO : JAPANESE GOVERNMENT OFFICIAL GAZETTE – 1883-1990 – 1 – us Ross [950]
KAN-PU HSUEH-HSI TZU-LIAO – Study materials for Cadres. pts. 1-4, 6-22, 27, 30, 34-36, 41-44, 51. 1950-52. BCH-845 1 – 9 – ne IDC [335]
KANRIDOO : DJALAN JANG HAROES DILALOEI OLEH PEGAWAI NEGERI... / Kataoka, S – Djakarta ? Gunseikanbu Soomubu Zinzika (2604 ?). 92p – 88-89mf – 9 – ne IDC [950]
KANSAN – Kansas City. Kan. 1916- – 1 – us UMI [071]
KANSAN – Newton. Kan. 1872-78 – 1 – us UMI [071]
KANSAN TOVERI – New York Mills, MN. 1897-1898 – 1r – 1 – us I.H.R.C. [975]
Kansapolis Association *see* JOURNAL OF PROCEEDINGS
KANSAS : SESSION LAWS OF AMERICAN STATES AND TERRITORIES – 1855-1995 – 9 – $1,386.00 set – us Hein [340]
KANSAS : STATUTES ANNOTATED – Topeka: Office of Revisor of Statutes, 1964-Mar 1996 update – 9 – $1,382.00 set – us Hein [340]
Kansas *see*
- REPORTS AND OPINIONS (A-G)
- REPORTS, POST-NRS
- REPORTS, PRE-NRS
- STATE LABOR REPORTS

KANSAS; A GUIDE TO THE SUNFLOWER STATE – Comp. & written by the Federal Writers' Project (WPA). 1949. American Guide Series. Indexed. 9 fiches. F-1309 – 9 – us A.G.L.L. [978]
KANSAS APPELLATE REPORTS / Kansas. Court of Appeals – (No Pre-NRS vols. No updates planned) – v1-10. 1895-1900 (all publ) – 33mf – 9 – $148.00 – LLMC 84-136 – us L.L.M.C. [340]
KANSAS ATTORNEY GENERAL REPORTS AND OPINIONS – (6 1864-1959, 1961-1979 $105.00. 9 1979-1994 $85.00) – 1864-1994 – 6,9 – $195.00 set – us Hein [340]
Kansas. Bar Association *see* JOURNAL
KANSAS BAR ASSOCIATION REPORTS PROCEEDINGS – (Lacking: 1st-2nd meetings) – 1st to 49th annual meetings. 1884-1931 (all publ) – 38mf – 9 – $171.00 – LLMC 84-516 – us L.L.M.C. [073]
Kansas. Board of Statehouse Commissioners *see* RECORDS
KANSAS BREEZE – Topeka. Kan. 1894-95 – 1 – us UMI [071]
KANSAS CATHOLIC – Kansas City. Kan. 1890-1898 – 1 – us UMI [071]
KANSAS CHIEF – White Cloud (Troy). Kan. 1857-1899 – 1 – us UMI [071]
KANSAS CITY DAILY RECORD – Kansas City, Missouri. On film: v89-149; 1932-62. LL-013 – 1 – us L of C Photodup [340]
KANSAS CITY JEWELER AND OPTICIAN – v1-12. 1901-12 – 1 – us UMI [740]
KANSAS CITY JEWISH CHRONICLE – Kansas City. Mo. 1920-50 – 1 – us A.J.P.C. [071]
KANSAS CITY JEWISH CHRONICLE – Kansas City. Mo. 1954-67 – 1 – us A.J.P.C. [071]
KANSAS CITY LAW REPORTER – v1 nos 1-7. 1888 (all publ) – 9 – LLMC 84-517 – us L.L.M.C. [073]
KANSAS CITY LAW REVIEW *see* UMKC LAW REVIEW

KANSAS COMMONER – Wichita. Kan. -w. 1887-1913 – 1 – us UMI [071]
KANSAS COSMOS – Council Grove. Kan. 1881-1886 – 1 – us UMI [071]
Kansas. Court of Appeals *see* KANSAS APPELLATE REPORTS
KANSAS DAILY COMMONWEALTH – Topeka. Kan. 1869-88 – 1 – us UMI [071]
KANSAS DEMOCRAT – Hiawatha. Kansas. 1883-1924 – 1 – us UMI [071]
Kansas entomological society *see* JOURNAL
KANSAS FARMER – Topeka. Kan. 1863-92 – 1 – us UMI [071]
Kansas. Fort Dodge *see* HEADQUARTERS RECORDS
Kansas. Fort Scott *see* HEADQUARTERS RECORDS
KANSAS GAZETTE – Enterprise. Kan. 1876-78 – 1 – us UMI [071]
Kansas. Governor, 1883-85 (Governor Glick) *see* GOVERNOR'S CORRESPONDENCE RELATING TO LUKE SHORT
KANSAS HERALD – Hiawatha. Kan. 1876-1883 – 1 – us UMI [071]
KANSAS HERALD – Kansas, Ohio. 1928 – 1r – 1 – $32.504 – us Archival [071]
KANSAS HERALD OF FREEDOM – Lawrence. Kan. 1854-59 – 1 – us UMI [071]
KANSAS HISTORY – v.1. 1978 – 1,5,6,9 – us UMI [073]
Kansas Infantry. 1st Regiment (Colored) *see* RECORDS
KANSAS JOURNAL OF LAW AND PUBLIC POLICY – v1-4. 1991-1995 – 9 – $65.00set – us Hein [340]
KANSAS KIN – v1-3. Item B. SW16-0038 – 5 – us A.G.L.L. [073]
KANSAS LAW JOURNAL – v1-5. 1885-87 (all publ) – 21mf – 9 – $31.50 – LLMC 84-518 – us L.L.M.C. [073]
KANSAS NEW ERA – Valley Falls. Kan. 1875-77 – 1 – us UMI [071]
KANSAS STAATS-ANZEIGER – Atchison. Kan. 1881-1913 – 1 – us UMI [071]
Kansas. State Bar Association *see* PROCEEDINGS
Kansas. State Board of Dental Examiners *see* MINUTES OF MEETINGS
Kansas State Historical Society *see* FAMILY RECORDS: EARLY LYON COUNTY SETTLERS
Kansas State Historical Society, Manuscripts Department *see* HOLDINGS
Kansas. State Penitentiary *see*
- CONVICTS..
- RECORDS

Kansas State Temperance Union *see* RECORDS
Kansas. State University. Agricultural Experiment Station *see*
- AGRICULTURAL ECONOMICS REPORT
- ANNUAL WHEAT NEWSLETTER
- BIENNIAL REPORT
- BULLETIN
- CIRCULAR
- MINUTES, STATION CONFERENCE
- REPORT
- RESEARCH PAPERS
- RESEARCH PUBLICATIONS

Kansas. State University of Agriculture and Applied Science. Division of College Extension *see* EXTENSION BULLETIN
Kansas. State University of Agriculture and Applied Science. Extension Service *see* EXTENSION CIRCULAR
Kansas. Supreme Court *see*
- KANSAS SUPREME COURT REPORTS
- MCCAHON'S TERRITORY REPORTS
- ROLL OF ATTORNEYS OF THE STATE OF KANSAS

KANSAS SUPREME COURT REPORTS / Kansas. Supreme Court – (Pre-NRS: v1-29 1862-83 236mf $354.00. Vols after v144 still in copyright) – v1-144. 1862-1936 – 1424mf – 9 – $2,136.00 – LLMC 84-135 – us L.L.M.C. [340]
KANSAS SUPREME COURT REPORTS *see* MCCAHON'S TERRITORY REPORTS
Kansas Town and Land Company *see* LETTER PRESS VOLUMES FROM THE COLLECTION OF THE KANSAS TOWN AND LAND CO., INC. (JULY 27, 1887)
KANSAS TRIAL BRIEF. / Marshall, John – Kansas City, Mo.: Pipes-Reed Book Co., 1905. 1056p. LL-910 – 1 – us L of C Photodup [340]
KANSAS TRIBUNE – Lawrence. Kan. -w. 1863-83 – 1 – us UMI [071]
KANSAS UNIVERSITY LAWYER – v1-2. 1895-96 (all publ) – 9 – LLMC 84-519 – us L.L.M.C. [073]
KANSAS VIM – McPherson. Kansas. 1888-1891 – 1 – us UMI [071]
KANSAS WEEKLY COMMONWEALTH – Topeka. Kan. -w. 1869-88 – 1 – us UMI [071]
KANSAS-A CYCLOPEDIA OF STATE HISTORY AND PROMINENT PERSONS – Supplementary vol. of personal history and reminiscence.Chicago, 1912. v3. Kansas Reel 1. (The Cox Library Collection) – 5 – us Americana [978]
KANSAS-A CYCLOPEDIA OF THE STATE HISTORY AND PROMINENT PERSONS / ed by Blackmar, Frank W – Chicago: Standard Publ. Co., 1912. v1-2. Kansas Reel 1. (The Cox Library Collection) – 5 – us Americana [978]
Kansas.Census *see*
- CENSUS OF THE TERRITORY OF KANSAS, FEBRUARY 1855
- MORTALITY SCHEDULES, 1860
- MORTALITY SCHEDULES, 1880
- SOCIAL STATISTICS, 1870
- SOCIAL STATISTICS, AGRICULTURAL & INDUSTRIAL SCHEDULES, 1860
- STATE CENSUS, 1855
- STATE CENSUS, 1875

KANSASKE ROZHELEDY – Wilson, KS. -w. 1 Feb 1905-27 May 1914 – 1 – us NE Hist [071]
KANSTYTUTSYI A (1937) *see* KANSTYTUTSYI A (ASNO UNY ZAKON) BELARUSKAI SAVETSKAI SATSYI ALISTYCHNAI RESPUBLIKI
KANSTYTUTSYI A (ASNO UNY ZAKON) BELARUSKAE SATSYI ALISTYCHNAE SAVETSKAE RESPUBLIKI / Byelorussian S.S.R. – Mensk: T SVK B.S.S.R., 1927 – 1 – CSUX91-B2684 – us Hoover Inst Photo [947]
KANSTYTUTSYI A (ASNO UNY ZAKON) BELARUSKAI SAVETSKAI SATSYI ALISTYCHNAI RESPUBLIKI / Byelorussian S.S.R. – Minsk: Dzi arzha unae vydavetstva BSSR, 1960 – 1 – CSUX91-B2358 – us Hoover Inst Photo [947]
KAN-SU HSIANG-SHIH LU – List of successful candidates in the imperial examination in Kansu province: 1873, 1875, 1876, 1888, 1889, 1894, 1900, 1903. 1 reel – 1 – 14.00 – us Chinese Res [950]
KAN-SU JIH-PAO – Lauchow, Kansu. Sep 1, 1949-. Scattered issues missing. 2 reels – 1 – 27.50 – us Chinese Res [072]
KANT AND SPENCER : A CRITICAL EXPOSITION / Bowne, Borden Parker – Boston: Houghton Mifflin, 1912 – 2mf – us A.T.L.A. [140]
KANT ET FICHTE ET LE PROBLEME DE L'EDUCATION / Duproix, Paul – (Includes bibliographical references) – Paris: Fischbacher, 1895 – 1mf – 9 – 0-8370-8569-1 – 1986-2569 – us A.T.L.A. [190]
Kant, Immanuel *see*
- FUNDAMENTAL PRINCIPLES OF THE METAPHYSIC OF ETHICS
- IMMANUEL KANT'S CRITIQUE OF PURE REASON
- KRITIK DER REINEN VERNUNFT
- THE PHILOSOPHY OF LAW; AN EXPOSITION OF THE FUNDAMENTAL PRINCIPLES OF JURISPRUDENCE AS THE SCIENCE OF RIGHT

KANTEERAVA – Mangalore, India. Apr 1944-1953; 1957-62 – 9r – 1 – us L of C Photodup [072]
Kantemir, A D *see*
- RELIATSII KN. A. D. KANTEMIR IZ LONDONA
- SOCHINENIIA, PIS'MA I IZBRANNYE PEREVODY

Kanter, Hermann *see* STUDIEN ZU DEN ACTA APOSTOLORUM DER CHESTER BEATTY-PAPYRI
KANTOBERITA – Djakarta. Indonesia. 1967-68 – 1 – us UMI [072]
Kanton *see* MITTEILUNGEN AUS DEM GEOGRAPHISCHEN INSTITUT DER SUN-YATSEN UNIVERSITAT, 1930-1931
Kantor, M *see*
- O KOOPERATSII
- OCHERKI TEORII I ISTORII KOOPERATSII
- OSNOVY KOOPERATIVNOI POLITIKI RKP(B)
- V POMOSHCH' UCHITELIU – STROITELIU DEREVENSKOI KOOPERATSII

KANTOR PUSAT MISI. MINIMUM PROGRAM HAL AGAMA, PENGADJARAN, SOSIAL, SERTA KESEHATAN RA'JAT DARI PIHAK GEREDJA ROEM KATOLIK – Indonesian and Dutch on opposite pages. SE-6850 1. 1949 – 9 – ne IDC [240]
Kantorovich, Ia. A *see*
- KOLLEKTIVNYI DOGOVOR
- PRAVOVYE OSNOVY KHOZIAISTVENNOGO STROIA SSSR

KANTS DING AN SICH – EIN UNLOESBARES PROBLEM? : EINE REKONSTRUKTION DES KANTISCHEN DINGES AN SICH AUF GRUND SEINER HISTORISCH-SYSTEMATISCHEN ABLEITUNG VON PLATON, ARISTOTELES, LOCKE UND LEIBNIZ / Wilmers, Anne – 1993 – 3mf – 9 – DM98.00 – 3-89349-752-8 – gw Hänsel [190]
KANT'S ETHICS : A CRITICAL EXPOSITION / Porter, Noah – Chicago: S.C. Griggs & Co., 1886 – 1 – us U.W. Library [190]
KANTS FORMBEGRIFF UND SYSTEMENTWUERFE / Maier, Dieter – Frankfurt a.M., 1979 – 2mf – 9 – DM62.00 – 3-89349-637-8 – gw Hänsel [110]
KANUN-I ESASI – Cairo: Osmanli Ittihad ve Terakki Cemiyeti Misir Suebesi. Muharriri: Seyh Alizade Hoca Muhiddin, 1896-1899 – 9 – $25.00 – us MEDOC [956]
KANUNNAME-YI HUEMAYUN TICARET-I BAHRIYE – Istanbul: Tasvir-i Efkar Gazetehanesi, 1280 [1864] – 9 – $35.00 – us MEDOC [380]
KANURI SONGS : WITH A TRANSLATION AND INTRODUCTORY NOTE / Patterson, John Robert – Lagos: Govt Painter, 1926 – us Res Libr [780]
Kanzler, Melanie *see* DIE EINFLUSSNAHME DER AMERIKANISCHEN BESATZUNGSMACHT AUF DIE BERLINER KULTURPOLITIK IN DEN NACHKRIEGSJAHREN, 1945-1947
KANZLIST KREHLER : TRAGIKOMOEDIE IN DREI AKTEN / Kaiser, Georg – Potsdam: G Kiepenheuer, 1922 – 1r – 1 – us U.W. Library [820]
KAO KOSANA GAN – Vientiane. Laos. 1952-1968 – 1 – us UMI [072]
KAO-CHOU FU-CHIH – 1827, 16, 1. BCH-626 2 – 8 – ne IDC [950]
KAOGU XUEBAO – Acta Archaeologia Sinica. In Chinese but English abstracts to the main articles. F p19 – 9 – $4.50f – cc Microforms [073]
K'AO-KU – Archeology. Peiping, 1934-37. 6v. Semi-annual. BCH-283/1 – 9 – ne IDC [930]
KAOKU – Archaeology. In Chinese but Table of Contents in English in each issue. F p18 – 9 – $4.50f – cc Microforms [073]
K'AO-KU HSUEH-PAO – Journal of Archeology. v. 1-3, 5-25, 29-36. Peking. 1936-65. quarterly, semi-annual. BCH-284 2 – 8 – ne IDC [073]
K'AO-KU. (T'UNG-HSUN) – (Archeology). (5). 1955-66. Lacking: 1959; (11-12) 1960-(6) 1961; (7-12) 1962; (7-12) 1963; (2, 9) 1964. BCH-813 2 – 8 – ne IDC [930]
KAO-YAO HSIEN-CHIH – 1826, 22, 1. BCH-623 2 – 8 – ne IDC [950]
KAPAL TUDJUH – 1953?-1956. Lacking: 1953?-55, v1-3; 1956, v4 (2-3). BSE-1727/1 – 9 – ne IDC [950]
KAPATID/ASSOCIATION FOR THE RELEASE AND AMNESTY OF DETAINEES IN THE PHILIPPINES – Manila. 74 docs. 1980-1990 – 13mf – 9 – ne IDC [320]
Kapea *see* JOURNAL MANUSCRIT
Kapelrud, Arvid S *see* BAAL IN THE RAS SHAMRA TEXTS
KAPITAL PROTIV TRUDA : CHTO TAKOE LOKAUTY / Garvi, Petr Abramovich – Petrograd: "Rabochai a biblioteka", 1917 – 1 – CSUX89-B7321 – us Hoover Inst Photo [330]
KAPITALISME DAN IMPERIALISME ADALAH DJAHAT / Sukarno, Pres. Indonesia – SE 5453 1. 1964 – 9 – ne IDC [025]
KAPITAL-JOURNAL – London, UK. 17 Jun 1912 – 1 – uk British Libr Newspaper [072]
KAPITALY GOSUDARSTVENNO I TORGOVLI SSSR / Fridman, Saadii Lazarevich; ed by Trakhtenberga, I A – Moskva: Izd. Gosplana RSFSR, 1927 – 1 – CSUX89-B2339 – us Hoover Inst Photo [330]
KAPITALY KREDITNOGO KOOPERATIVA (IKH ZNACHENIE I ORGANIZATSIIA) / Ivanov, VI – M., 1927 – 1mf – 9 – COR-380/1 – ne IDC [334]
KAPITALY KREST'IANSKOGO KHOZIAISTVA I EGO KREDITOVANIE PRI AGRARNOI REFORME / Chaianov, A V – M., 1918 – 1mf – 9 – COR-230/1 – ne IDC [334]
Kapitan, J C *see* MASALAH TUBERCULOSA DI PERUSAHAAN
KAPITUELASYONLAR – K.D. Sancakiyan Matbaasi, 1329 [1913] – 9 – $20.00 – us MEDOC [380]
Kaplan, Leah E *see*
- A DESCRIPTIVE ANALYSIS OF CORPORATE HEALTH PROMOTION ACTIVITY EVALUATIONS
- HEALTH BELIEFS, HEALTH VALUES, AND PREVENTIVE HEALTH PROMOTION ACTIVITIES OF AFRICAN- AND EURO-AMERICAN WOMEN
- VARIABLES RELATED TO KNOWLEDGE LEVELS OF AGING AND PLANNING FOR FUTURE AGING OF TEXAS HIGH SCHOOL GRADUATES

Kaplan, Linda *see* THE EFFECT OF WRIST WEIGHT ON THE HEMODYNAMIC RESPONSE TO EXERCISE IN CORONARY ARTERY DISEASE
Kaplan, Susan *see* OCCUPATIONAL THERAPY IN HEALTH CARE
Kapnist, PI *see* KKRATKOE OBOZRENIE NAPRAVLENIIA..
Kapnist, V V *see* SOBRANIE SOCHINENII
Kapp, Julius *see* WAGNER
Kappel, A W *see* BRITISH AND EUROPEAN BUTTERFLIES AND MOTHS (MACROLEPIDOPTERA)
Kappenberg, Hans *see* DER BILDLICHE AUSDRUCK IN DER PROSA EDUARD MOERIKES
Kappler, Charles J *see* KAPPLER'S INDIAN AFFAIRS
Kappler, Helmut *see* DER BAROCKE GESCHICHTSBERGRIFF BEI ANDREAS GRYPHIUS
KAPPLER'S INDIAN AFFAIRS : LAWS AND TREATIES / Kappler, Charles J – (With suppl vol 1975. Also part of LLMC's Native American Collection Titles 4130 + 4133) – Washington: GPO. v1-5. 1903-41 – 60mf – 9 – $90.00 – LLMC 88-003 – us L.L.M.C. [324]
Kaprelian, Edward K *see* PHOTOGRAPHICA
Kaptein, A *see* PSYCHOLOGY AND HEALTH
KAPTIN. DEFICIT PEMERINTAH PADJAK-PADJAK DAN PEMBANGUNAN / Adisumarta, R J – SE-5778 1. 1962? – 9 – ne IDC [950]
DE KAPUCIJNEN IN DE NEDERLANDEN EN HET PRINSBISDOM LUIK / Hildebrand, P OF M Cap. – Antwerpen. v1-10. 1945-1956 – Dfl364.00 – ne Slangenburg [240]
KAPUNDA HERALD – Australia. Jan 1885-Jul 1893.-w. 6 reels – 1 – uk British Libr Newspaper [072]
Kapustin, MN *see*
- DIPLOMATICHESKIE SNOSHENIIA ROSSII S ZAPADNOIU EVROPOIU VO VTOROI POLOVINE XVII-GO VEKA
- OBOZRENIE PREDMETOV MEZHDUNARODNOGO PRAVA

Kapustin, S Ia *see* DREVNEE RUSSKOE PORUCHITEL'STVO
KAR – (SEE ALSO Kar (Aksariyat). Shumarah-'i 1-152 (19 Isfand 1357-18 Murdad 1361[10 Mar 1979-9 Aug 1982]). Missing issues 146-152) – [Tehran]: Sazman-i Chirik'ha-yi Fada'i-i Khalq, 1979-1982 – 2r – 1 – $100.00 – us MEDOC [950]
KAR (AKSARIYAT) – (SEE ALSO Kar. Shumarah-'i 62-149 (21 Khurdad 1359-28 Bahman 1359[14 Jun 1980-17 Feb 1981]). Missing issues: 63-64, 66, 90-91, 104-112, 125, 139, 143-144) – [Tehran]: Sazman-i Fada'iyan-i Khalq – 2r – 1 – $75.00 – us MEDOC [950]
KAR INTERNATIONAL – Arlington, VA: Kar Committee, International, Nos. 1-3 (Feb, Mar, Apr 1981) – 9 – $25.00 – us MEDOC [956]
KARA BELA – Istanbul: Mahmud Bey Matbaasi, 1326 [1910] – $25.00 – us MEDOC [470]
KARA DENIZ VAKI SAMSUN LIMANI IMTIYAZINE DAIR HUEKUMET-I OSMANIYE CANIBINDAN IMTIYAZIN MUENAKASAI MUAMELAT... – Konstantiniye [Istanbul]: Matbaa-yi Ebuezziya – 9 – $20.00 – us MEDOC [380]
Karabchevskii, N P *see* OKOLO PRAVOSUDIIA
Karabegov, A I *see* REFORMA SUDEBNYKH USTAVOV V SVIAZI S SOVREMENNYM SOSTOIANIEM PRAVOSUDIIA
Karacelebizade, Abduelaziz *see*
- RAVAT UEL-EBRAR
- SUELEYMANNAME

KARACHI COMMERCE – Karachi, Pakistan. -w. Jan 1951-Dec 1956; Jan-Dec 1959. 7 reels – 1 – uk British Libr Newspaper [072]
Karadzhe-Iskrov, N P *see*
- K VOPROSU O PRAVE GOSUDARSTVA NA ZEMLIU
- NOVEISHAIA EVOLIUTSIIA ADMINISTRATIVNOGO PRAVA

Karadzic, Vuk Stefanovic *see* VUKOVA PREPISKA

KARAFUTO NICHINICHI SHIMBUN – Japan, 1910-42 – 152r – 1 – inquire – us Ross [072]

KARAFUTO NICHINICHI SHIMBUN – May 1910-Jan 1942 – 152r – 1 – Y3,400,000 – ja Japan Micro [950]

Karageorgis, Fevronia *see* PERCEPTIONS OF THE IMPORTANCE AND ACHIEVEMENT OF STUDENT TEACHING OBJECTIVES

KARAGOEZ SALNAMESI – (1326[1910]. – 2mf. $100.00; 1327[1911]. – 2mf. $100.00; 1328[1912]. – 3mf. $100.00; 1329[1913]. – 2mf. $100.00) – 9 – us MEDOC [949]

KARAIMISCHE TEXTE IM DIALEKT VON TROKI / Kowalski, T – PAU. MCO. no. 11. Krakow. 1929. BU-306 2 – 8 – ne IDC [460]

KARAKTER EN HERKOMST VAN DEN JACOBUSBRIEF / Toxopeus, Hendrik Jan – Amsterdam: J. Clausen, 1906. 1 fiche – 9 – us A.T.L.A. [240]

Karamyshev, IP *see* SBORNIK TSIRKULIAROV I RAPORIAZHENII PO DELAM PECHATI..

KARAMZIN, AVTOR / Sipovskii, V V – "Pisem russkogo puteshestvennika". Spb. 1899. BR-7859 2 – 8 – ne IDC [460]

Karamzin, N M *see*
- SOCHINENIIA

Karamzin, Nikolai M *see*
- IZBRANNYIA SOCHINENIIA
- NEIZDANNYE SOCHINENIIA I PEREPISKA
- PEREPISKA S LAFATEROM
- SOCHINENIIA

DIE KARAS : ROMAN / Vuorio, Anelma Kaarina Kojonen – Wien: W Frick, 1944 – 1r – 1 – us U.W. Library [830]

Karass, A V *see* SOVETSKOE PROMYSHLENNOE PRAVO

Karataev, I *see*
- BIBLIOGRAFICHESKIIA ZAMETKI O STARO-SLAVIANSKIKH PECHATNYKH IZDANIIAKH 1491-1730
- OPISANIE SLAVIANO-RUSSKIKH KNIG NAPECHATATANNYKH KIRILLOVSKIMI BUKVAMI. 1491 PO 1652

Karataev, N K *see* OCHERKI PO ISTORII EKONOMICHESKIKH NAUK V ROSSII 18 VEKA

Karataev, S *see* BIBLIOGRAFIIA FINANSOV PROMYSHLENNOSTI I TORGOVLI:SO VREMEN PETRA VELIKOGO PO NASTOIASHCHEE VREMIA (S 1714 PO 1879 G, VKL.)

KARATELNYE EKSPEDITSII V PRIBALTIISKOM KRAEV 1905-1907 GG : PO MATERIALAM II GOSUDARSTVENNOI DUMY / Anson, P – Leningrad: Rabochee izdvo "Pribo i", 1926 – 1 – CSUX88-B1647 – us Hoover Inst Photo [947]

Karatygina, E S *see* SEL'SKOKHOZIAIST-VENNAIA KOOPERATSIIA I GOSPROMYSHLENNOST'

Karawan, Ariel *see* THE EFFECTS OF TWELVE WEEKS OF WALKING OR EXERSTRIDING ON UPPER BODY MUSCULAR STRENGTH AND ENDURANCE

KARAWANKEN-BOTE – Krainburg (Kranj), Jugoslavien. 15 Nov 1941- 31 Dec 1943 – 2r – 1 – gw Mikrofilm [949]

Karbowiak, Antoni *see* DZIEJE EDUCACYJNE POLAKOW NA OBZYZNIE

DIE KARDINAELE UND IHRE POLITIK UM DIE MITTE DES 13. JAHRHUNDERTS : UNTER DEN PAEPSTEN INNOCENZE 4., ALEXANDER 4., URBAN 4., CLEMENS 4., (1243-68) / Maubach, Jos – (Includes index) – Bonn: Carl Georgi, 1902 – 1mf – 9 – 0-8370-7650-1 – 1986-1650 – us A.T.L.A. [240]

KARDINAL JOHN HENRY NEWMAN : EIN BEITRAG ZUR RELIGIOESEN ENTWICKLUNGSGESCHICHTE DER GEGENWART / Blennerhassett, Charlotte, Lady – Berlin: Gebrueder Paetel, 1904 – 2mf – us A.T.L.A. [240]

Kardos, A *see* HISTOIRE DE LA LITTERATURE HONGROISE

Kardouche, GK *see* UNITED ARAB REPUBLIC: CASE STUDY OF AID THROUGH TRADE AND REPAYMENT OF DEBT IN GOODS OR LOCAL CURRENCIES

Kareev, N *see* UKAZATEL' SOTSIOLOGICHESKOI LITERATURY

Kareh, Rashid *see* ONE HUNDRED YEARS OF FABIAN PUBLISHING

Karelin, A A *see* OBSHCHINNOE VLADENIE V ROSSII

Karelin, GS *see* ENUMERATIO PLANTARUM IN DESERTIS SONGORIAE ORIENTALIS

KARELO-MURMANSKI I KRA I – (Includes c.1: 1926:no.21-22; 1927:no.2-1929:no.1; 1929:no.4/5-1931:no.1/2; 1931:no.7/8; 1932:no.1/2-7/8; 1933:no.1/2-no.9/10; 1934:no.1/2-7/8, 12-1935:no.4) – Leningrad: Sovnarkom A.K.S.S.R. i Pravlenie Murmansko i zhel. dor., 1926-. 10v – 1 – CSUXAKZ2897-S – us Hoover Inst Photo [947]

KARET – Institute for Rubber Research and Development. Bogor, Indonesia. 1950-64, v1-15 (1). Lacking issues. BSE-828/1 – 9 – ne IDC [660]

Karev, D S *see*
- UGOLOVNOE ZAKONODATEL'STVO SSSR O SOIUZNYKH RESPUBLIK: SBORNIK
- UGOLOVNONPROTSESSUAL'NOE ZAKONODATEL'STVO SSSR I SOIUZNYKH RESPUBLIKI SBORNIK

KARGAR – (Sal-i 1 shumarah-'i 1-10 (1 Farvardin 1358-17 Murdad 1358[21 Mar 1979-8 Aug 1979])) – [Tehran]: Tribun-i azad-i mardum-i zahmatkash, 1979- – 1 reel – 1 – $25.00 – us MEDOC [950]

KARGAR, BIH PISH – (Shumarah-'i 1-7[Mar 1979]-(30 Mihr 1358[Oct 22 1979]). Missing issue: 2) – Tehran: Sazman-i Paykar dar rah-i azadi-i tabaqah-'i kargar – 1 reel – 1 – $25.00 – us MEDOC [950]

KARIKATUER – (Mueduer-i Mes'ul: M. Hilmi, Mueduer: Turhan. Nos. 4, 5, 8 (20 Mart-17 Nisan 1330[1914])) – Istanbul Matbaa-i Hayriye ve Suerekasi, 1913-1914 – 1mf – 9 – $12.00 – us MEDOC [949]

Karinskii, N M *see*
- OBRAZTSY PIS'MA DREVNEISHEGO PERIODA ISTORII RUSSKOI KNIGI
- SLAVIANSKAIA PALEOGRAFIIA. LEKTSII... ARKHEOLOGICHESKOM INSTITUTE

KAR-INTERNATIONAL – Los Angeles: Kar International, Kar Committee, (fall 1980, Feb 1981-Jun 1982, Jun 1983) – 9 – $25.00 – us MEDOC [956]

Karjadi, mas *see* PERATURAN MENGHANTAR ORANG HUKUMAN (PESAKITAN)

KARJALAN TALOUS JA TILASTO *see* EKONOMIKA I STATISTIKA KARELII

KARJALAN-MUURMANNIN ALUEEN VIESTI JAN. 5-10, 1925- *see* VESTNIK KARELO-MURMANSKOGO KRAIA

KARJALAN-MUURMANNIN SEUTU NOV. 1926- *see* KARELO-MURMANSKI I KRA I

KARJALAN-MUURMANNIN SEUTU OCT. 1926 *see* KARELO-MURMANSKI I KRA I

KARL 5. UND DIE DEUTSCHE REFORMATION / Baumgarten, Hermann – Halle: Verein fuer Reformationsgeschichte, 1889. (Schriften des Vereins fuer Reformationsgeschichte; 7. Jahrg., 2. Stueck, Nr. 27) – 1mf – us A.T.L.A. [240]

KARL CHRISTIAN PLANCK UND DIE DEUTSCHE ERNEUERUNGSBEWEGUNG NACH 1870 / Ruelius, Hermann – Frankfurt a.M., 1938 – 1mf – 9 – DM48.00 – 3-89349-318-2 – gw Hänsel [430]

KARL CHRISTIAN THALHEIM PAMPHLET COLLECTION – 1961-1965 – 1r – 1 – us Hoover Inst Photo [943]

KARL DIETRICH BRACHER PAMPHLET COLLECTION – 1952-1966 – 1r – 1 – us Hoover Inst Photo [943]

Karl, Freiherr de *see* BRIEFE AN FRIEDRICH BARON DE LA MOTTE FOUQUE VON CHAMISSO, CHEZY, COLLIN...

KARL GUTZKOW ALS DRAMATIKER : MIT BENUETZUNG UNVEROEFFENTLICHTER STUECKE / Metis, Eduard – Stuttgart: Metzler, 1915 – 1r – 1 – us U.W. Library [430]

KARL GUTZKOW AS LITERARY CRITIC WITH SPECIAL EMPHASIS ON THE PERIOD 1852-1862 / McConkey, Elizabeth – (Includes bibliographical references) – Private ed. Chicago, IL: Distributed by University of Chicago Libraries, 1941 – 1r – 1 – us U.W. Library [430]

KARL HEINRICH : ERZAEHLUNG / Meyer-Foerster, Wilhelm – Stuttgart: Deutsche Verlags-Anstalt, 1903 – 1r – 1 – us U.W. Library [430]

KARL HENCKELL, EIN MODERNER DICHTER : STUDIE / Blei, Franz – Zuerich: Verlags-Magazin (J Schabelitz), 1895 – 1r – 1 – us U.W. Library [430]

KARL LLEWELLYN PAPERS, SECTION F : NATIONAL CONFERENCE OF COMMISSIONERS ON UNIFORM STATE LAWS / Llewellyn, Karl N – (Price includes Twining's "Karl Llewellyn Papers," 1986 (hard copy)) – 2r – 5 – $295.00 – us Hein [340]

KARL LLEWELLYN PAPERS, SECTION G : THE SACCO-VANZETTI CASE / Llewellyn, Karl N – (Price includes Twining's "Karl Llewellyn Papers", 1986 (hard copy)) – 2r – 5 – $295.00 – us Hein [340]

KARL LLEWELLYN PAPERS, SECTION I : AMERICAN INDIANS AND PRIMITIVE LAW / Llewellyn, Karl N – (Price includes Twining's "Karl Llewellyn Papers", 1986 (hard copy)) – 9r – 5 – $990.00 – us Hein [340]

KARL LLEWELLYN PAPERS, SECTION J : THE UNIFORM COMMERICAL CODE / Llewellyn, Karl N – (Price includes Twining's "Karl Llewellyn Papers", 1986 (hard copy)) – 25r – 13 – $1,250.00 – 0-89941-567-9 – us Hein [340]

KARL LLEWELLYN PAPERS, SECTION R : CORRESPONDENCE / Llewellyn, Karl N – (Price includes Twining's "Karl Llewellyn Papers", 1986 (hard copy)) – 3r – 5 – $395.00 – us Hein [340]

KARL MARKS I EGO VREMI A / Berlin, Pavel Abramovich – Moskva: "Krasnai a nov", 1923 – 1 – CSUX89-B6534 – us Hoover Inst Photo [335]

KARL MARX : LEBEN UND WERK (1818-1883). NEUREZEPTION DER POLIS-IDEE UND ESCHATOLOGIE AUS JUEDISCH-CHRISTLICHER GEISTESTRADITION. BEITRAEGE ZUR POLITISCHEN THEORIE / Wittig, Horst E – 1993 – 2mf – 9 – DM80.00 – 3-89349-794-3 – gw Hänsel [320]

KARL MARX RIWAJATHIDUP SINGKAT DENGAN URAIAN TENTANG MARXISME / Lenin, Vladimir Ilyich – SE-10,588 1. 1962 – 9 – ne IDC [335]

KARL MARX UEBE DIE POLYTECHNISCHE BILDUNGSIDEE UND DER EINFLUSS SEINER ERZIEHUNGSIDEOLOGIE AUF DIE SOZIALISTISCHE PAEDAGOGIK UND VORSCHULERZIEHUNG IN DER EHEM. UDSSR / Wittig, Horst E – 1993 – 2mf – 9 – DM80.00 – 3-89349-796-X – gw Hänsel [370]

Karl, Mauricio *see* EL COMUNISMO EN ESPANA. CINCO ANOS EN EL PARTIDO

KARL MAX LICHNOWSKY PAMPHLET COLLECTION – 191? – 9 – us Hoover Inst Photo [943]

KARL ODEBREKT, UHE BAPTISTI ELU-JA UMBERPOORAMISE LUGU = KARL ODEBREKT, THE LIFE OF A BAPTIST AND THE STORY OF HIS TURNABOUT / Ruhl, Gustav – (One part of sa six-part item) – Revel: Tallinna Sinodi kirjastus, 1885 – 1r – 1 – $20.88 – us Baptist [240]

KARL PHILIPP MORITZ ALS AESTHETIKER / Dessoir, Max – (Includes bibliographical references) – Berlin: C Duncker, 1889 – 1r – 1 – us U.W. Library [110]

KARL RUDOLF HAGENBACH : EINE FRIEDENSGESTALT AUS DER STREITENDEN KIRCHE DER GEGENWART / Eppler, Christoph Friedrich – Gueterlsoh: C. Bertelsmann, 1875 – 1mf – us A.T.L.A. [240]

KARL SIMROCKS AUSGEWAEHLTE WERKE IN ZWOELF BAENDEN / Simrock, Karl Joseph; ed by Klee, Gotthold – Leipzig: Max Hesse, [1907?] – 1 – us U.W. Library [800]

KARL SPINDLER, EIN BEITRAG ZUR GESCHICHTE DES HISTORISCHEN ROMANS UND DER UNTERHALTUNGSLEKTUERE IN DEUTSCHLAND : NEBST EINER ANZAHL BISHER UNGEDRUCKTER BRIEFE SPINDLERS / Koenig, Joseph – (Includes bibliographical references) – Leipzig: Quelle & Meyer, 1908 – 1 – us U.W. Library [430]

KARL VON HOLTEIS ROMANE : EIN BEITRAG ZUR GESCHICHTE DER DEUTSCHEN UNTERHALTUNGS-LITERATUR / Landau, Paul – Leipzig: M Hesse, 1904 – 1 – us U.W. Library [430]

KARL VON RAUMER UND SEIN BEITRAG ZUR VOLKSBILDUNG IM 19. JAHRHUNDERT / Dorweiler, Joachim – 1994 – 2mf – DM80.00 – 3-8267-2046-6 – gw Hänsel [370]

Karlowicz, J *see* SLOWNIK GWAR POLSKICH

KARLSHAMNS ALLEHANDA – (Olofstroms Nyheter, 1963-64) – Karlshamn, Sweden. 1848-1976 – 1 – sw Kungliga [072]

KARLSHAMNS ALLEHANDA *see* BLEKINGE LANS TIDNING

KARLSHORSTER ANZEIGER – (Incl suppl) – Berlin-Karlshorst, nov 1925-26, apr-dec 1927, jul 1929-32, apr 1933-aug 2 1934 – 19r – 1 – Dist. gw Mikrofilm – gw Misc Inst [943]

KARLSHORSTER ANZEIGER *see* KARLSHORSTER LOKALANZEIGER

KARLSHORSTER LOKALANZEIGER – (Filmed with Karlshorster Anzeiger) – Berlin, apr-dec 1937 – 1 – Dist. gw Mikrofilm – gw Misc Inst [943]

KARLSKOGA BERGSLAGSKURIREN *see* OREBROKURIREN

KARLSKOGA TIDNING – Nora, Karlskoga, Sweden. 1883- – 1 – sw Kungliga [072]

KARLSKOGA-DEGERFORS ALLEHANDA *see* NERIKES ALLEHANDA

KARLSKOGAKURIREN – OErebro, 1945-54 – 9 – sw Kungliga [072]

KARLSKOGAKURIREN – OErebro, 1994- – 9 – sw Kungliga [072]

KARLSKOGAKURIREN – Orebro, Sweden. 1955 – 5r – 1 – sw Kungliga [072]

KARLSKOGAKURIREN *see*
- OREBRO-BERGSLAGSKURIREN
- OREBROKURIREN

KARLSKRONA WECKOBLAD – Karlskrona, Sweden. 1753-1908 – 68r – 1 – sw Kungliga [072]

KARLSRUHER BEOBACHTER – Karlsruhe, Germany. 1848 – 1r – 1 – gw Mikrofilm [072]

KARLSRUHER INTELLIGENZ- UND TAGBLATT *see* KARLSRUHER INTELLIGENZ-UND WOCHENBLATT

KARLSRUHER INTELLIGENZ- UND WOCHENBLATT – (Title changes: Karlsruher Unterhaltungs- und Intelligenzblatt, 3 Jan 1819; Karlsruher Intelligenz- und Tageblatt, 1 Jan 1833; Karlsruher Tagblatt, 1 Jan 1843) – Karlsruhe, Germany. 1848-49 – 1r – 1 – gw Mikrofilm [072]

KARLSRUHER TAGBLATT *see* KARLSRUHER INTELLIGENZ- UND WOCHENBLATT

KARLSRUHER UNTERHALTUNGS- UND INTELLIGENZBLATT *see* KARLSRUHER INTELLIGENZ- UND WOCHENBLATT

KARLSRUHER ZEITUNG : ORGAN DER PROVISORISCHEN REGIERUNG (15 MAY-24 JUN 1849) – Karlsruhe, Germany. 1848-30 Dec 1849 – 3r – 1 – gw Mikrofilm [072]

KARLSTADSTIDNINGEN – Karlstad, 1917- – 1 – sw Kungliga [072]

KARLSTADSTIDNINGEN – Karlstad, Sweden. 1879-1917 – 34r – 1 – sw Kungliga [072]

Karlweis, C *see* DAS GROBE HEMD

Karmann, Anton *see* METHODISCHE UND SYSTEMATISCHE UNTERSUCHUNGEN ERKENNTNISTHEORETISCH WICHTIGER SACHLICHER GRUNDPROBLEME IN DER PLATONISCHEN IDEENLEHRE

KARNAK. ETUDE TOPOGRAPHIQUE ET ARCHEOLOGIQUE AVEC UN APPENDICE COMPRENANT LES PRINCIPAUX TEXTES HIEROGLYPHIQUES / Mariette, A – Leipzig, 1875. BNE-364 1 – 9 – ne IDC [930]

KARNAMAK I ARTAKHSHIR PAPAKAN / ed by Antia, E E K – (The original Pahlavi text, with transliteration in Avesta characters, translations into English and Gujarati and selections from the Shahnameh) – Bombay, 1900 – 4mf – NE-20158/1 – ne IDC [490]

Karnaukhov, DE *see* KACHESTVO I STANDART V PROMKOOPERATSII

Karner, Friedrich Karl *see* DIE BEDEUTUNG DES VERGELTUNGSGEDANKENS FUER DIE ETHIK JESU, DARGESTELLT IM ANSCHLUSS AN DIE SYNOPTISCHEN EVANGELIEN

Karni, R S *see*
- FROM PRINTED CATALOGUE TO DATA BASE
- INDONESIAN MONOGRAPHS

Karnovich, E P *see*
- ISTORICHESKIE RAZSKAZY I BYTOVYE OCHERKI
- ZAMECHATEL'NYE BOGATSTVA CHASTNYKH LITS V ROSSII

KAROO FARMER *see* DIE AFRIKANER

KARPATEN-RUNDSCHAU : WOCHENSCHRIFT FUER GESELLSCHAFT, POLITIK, KULTUR – Kronstadt (Brasov), Romania. 1976- – 1 – gw Mikrofilm [949]

KARPATENRUNDSCHAU – 1976- – 1r per y – 1 – us Ross [072]

KARPATENRUNDSCHAU – Rumaenien, 1976-1992ff – 17r – 1 – DM1,275.00 – gw Mikro Press [949]

KARPATHEN-POST – Kaesmark (Kesmarok), Czechoslovakia. 1920-41 – 4r – 1 – gw Mikrofilm [072]

KARPATORUSSKI KALENDAR' LEMKO-SOIUZA NA... – Yonkers, NY: Lemko-Soiuz, 1930-71 – us Res Libr [520]

KARPATORUSSKIJ NARODNYJ KALENDAR' – Perth Amboy, NJ. 1944-1946 – 1r – 1 – us I.H.R.C. [978]

KARPATORUSSKIJE NOVOSTI – 1-3, Oct 1943-1945 – 1 – us Res Libr [073]

KARPATO-RUSSKOE SLOVO = CARPATHO-RUSSIAN WORD – New York: Carpatho Russian National Committee, jun 1935-38 – us Res Libr [073]
KARPATS'KA ZORIA = CARPATHIAN STAR – New York: Carpathian Star Pub Co, oct 1951-52 – us Res Libr [073]
Karpeles, Gustav *see*
– DIWAN DES JEHUDA HALEVI
– HEINRICH HEINE
– HEINRICH HEINE'S BIOGRAPHIE
– HEINRICH HEINE'S LIFE TOLD IN HIS OWN WORDS
Karpov, G F *see* KRITICHESKII OBZOR RAZRABOTKI GLAVNYKH RUSSKIKH ISTOCHNIKOV PO ISTORII MALOROSSII...1654-30 MAIA 1672
Karpovich, M *see* MOE ZNAKOMSTVO S MANDEL'SHTAMOM; NOVYI ZHURNAL
Karrer, O *see* MEISTER ECKEHART
Karsch, F *see* ENTOMOLOGISCHE NACHRICHTEN
DIE KARSCHIN – Muenchen: Muenchener Buchverlag, [1943] – 1r – 1 – us U.W. Library [800]
Karsen, Fritz *see* HENRIK STEFFENS ROMANE
Karskii, E F *see*
– BELORUSY. IAZYKH BELORUSSKOGO NARODA
– LISTI UNDOL'SKOGO, OTRYVOK KIRILLOVSKOGO EVANGELIJA XI V. FOTOTIPICHESKOE VOSPROIZVEDINIE TEKSTA I ISSLEDOVANIE PIS'MA I IAZYKA
– OBRAZTSY SLAVIANSKOGO, KIRILLOVSKOGO PIS'MA S X DO XVIII VEK
– RUSSKAIA PRAVDA PO STAREISHEMU SPISKU. VVEDENIE, TEKST, SNIMKI, PEREVOD, UKAZATELI AVTOROV I SLOVARNOGO SOSTAVA
Karsten, B A *see* MYCOLOGICA FENNICA
Karsten, GKW H *see* FLORAE COLUMBIAE TERRARUMQUE ADJACENTIUM SPECIMINA SELECTA
Karsten, P A *see* ICONES SELECTAE HYMENOMYCETUM FENNIAE
Kartashov, N S *see* IZ ISTORII KNIGI, BIBLIOTECHNOGO DELA I BIBLIOGRAFII V SIBIRI
Kartavov,D A *see* BIBLIOGRAFICHESKIIA IZVESTIIA O REDNIKH KNIGAKH. NO. 2
KARTENSPIEL : AUFGABENBUCH KLEINER PROSA / Heyse, Ulrich – Muenchen: K Alber, 1942 – 1r – 1 – us U.W. Library [830]
KARTERIA – Athens, Greece. -w. 1 June 1877-9 Nov 1878. 2 reels – 1 – uk British Libr Newspaper [949]
KARTOCHNYE DOMIKI SOVIETSKAGO STROITELSTVA / Damanskaia, Avgusta Filippovna – Berlin: Tip. "Ne ie t se it", 1921 – 1 – CSUX88-B3555 – us Hoover Inst Photo [330]
KARTOGRAFIIA ROSSII XVIII VEKA / Fel', S E – Moscow, 1960. 226p. BR-6159/2 – 8 – ne IDC [910]
Kartosoewirjo, SM *see* HALOEAN POLITIK ISLAM
Kartschoke, Christopher *see* THE DIFFERENCE BETWEEN PARTICIPATION IN INTERCOLLEGIATE ATHLETICS AND ACADEMIC PERFORMANCE BASED ON TIME USE
Kartsov, S V *see* OPYT SLOVARIA PSEVDONIMOV RUSSKIKH PISATELEI
Karwas, Marcia R *see* FEMININITY AND MASCULINITY
KAS TE TAHDI IRR, BAPTISTI? = WHO ARE THEY, THOSE BAPTISTS? – Jelgawa: J.W. Steffenhagen, 1866. Publ. No. 6298 b. One of five items on a reel – 1 – us Baptist [240]
KASAI – 1959(Dec 30)-1960 Oct 31) – 1r – 1,5,6 – ne IDC [960]
Kasai, Ken-Ichi *see* INTERNATIONAL JOURNAL OF BIO-CHROMATOGRAPHY
KASA'ID TEVFIK – Istanbul, 1304 – 1mf – 9 – $6.00 – us MEDOC [949]
Kasatkin, V N *see* OSNOVNYE UZAKONENII I RASPORIAZHENIIA PO NARODNOMU PROSVESHCHENIIU
Kasch, Fritz *see* LEOPOLD F.G. VON GOECKINGK
KASCH-UL-NICAB – Journal arabe politique hebdomadaire. Dir. L. Emin Arslan. no. 1-12. Paris. aout-nov 1894 – 1 – fr A.C.R.P.P. [073]
Kashifi, Husayn Vaiz *see* THE ANVAR-I SUHAILI, OR THE LIGHTS OF CANOPUS
Kashin, N P *see*
– A. N. OSTROVSKII, N. S. LESKOV RUKOPISI, PEREPISKA, DOKUMENTY
KASHKUL – Tehran: Shumarah-'i 1-40 (15 Safar 1325-11 Rabi sani 1326 [30 Mar 1907-12 May 1908]) – 1 reel – 1 – $50.00 – us MEDOC [950]
Kashmir *see* THE JAMMU AND KASHMIR GOVERNMENT GAZETTE
KASHMIR POST – Jammu, India. 1962-64 – 3r – 1 – us L of C Photodup [072]
KASHMIR TIMES – Jammu, India. 1972-93 – 51r – 1 – us L of C Photodup [072]
Kasim Sulaiman *see* MENUDJU PRIBADI JANG MULIA DAN TINGGI
Kasim Sutan Mohammad Sjah *see* MERDU; NJANJIAN2 UNTUK KL. 5 DAN 6 S.R
Kasim Sutan Mohammed Sjah *see* DJIKA MALAM DIPADANG PASIR
KASPAR KLEE VON GEROLZHOFEN : DAS LEBENSBILD EINES ELSAESSISCHEN EVANGELISCHEN PFARRERS UM DIE WENDE DES 16. ZUM 18. JAHRHUNDERT / Beck, Hermann – Halle: Verein fuer Reformationsgeschichte, 1901. (Schriften des Vereins fuer Reformationsgeschichte; 19. Jahrg., Schrift 71) – 1mf – us A.T.L.A. [240]
KASSEL UND AHNABERG : STUDIEN ZUR GESCHICHTE VON STADT UND KLOSTER IM MITTELALTER / Buck, Herbert – Frankfurt a.M., 1968 – 3mf – 9 – DM76.00 – 3-89349-365-4 – gw Hänsel [943]
KASSELER VOLKSBLATT – Kassel, 1892-93; 1894-1919; 1921-27; 1928-1933 – 72r – 1 – DM5,400.00 – gw Mikro Press [072]
KASSELER VOLKSBLATT – Kassel, Germany. 1892-1893; Jun 1894-1919; 1921-27; Jun 1928-27 Feb 1933 – 1 – gw Mikrofilm [072]
KASSELSCHE ALLGEMEINE ZEITUNG – Kassel, Germany. 1848; Jul-Dec 1849 – 3r – 1 – gw Mikrofilm [072]
Kassewitz, Joseph *see* DARLEGUNG DER DICHTERISCHEN TECHNIK UND LITTERARHISTORISCHEN STELLUNG VON GOETHES ELEGIE "ALEXIS UND DORA"
Kassil, L *see* MAIAKOVSKII-SAM
Kassin, Saul M *see* AN EMPIRICAL STUDY OF RULE 11 SANCTIONS
KASTALIA – Wien, jul 1912-jul 1915 – 2r – 1 – gw Mikrofilm [072]
KASTAMONU – (Nos. 2174, 2190, 2194, 2197, 2214, 2219, 2222, 2245, 2255, 2267, 2272, 2284, 2778 (31 Tesrinievvel 1332[1919]-16 Subat 1929)) – Kastamonu: Vilayet Matbaasi. Cikaran: Kastamonu Vilayeti, 1873-? – 1mf – 9 – $40.00 – us MEDOC [949]
Kasznica, Stanislaw *see* NAJWAZNIEJSZE WYNIKI SPISU LUDNOSCI I SPISU ZWIERZAD DOMOWYCH WEDLUG STANU Z DN. 31 GRUDNIA 1910 R
Kat, A I M *see* DE GESCHIEDENIS DER KERKMUZIEK IN DE NEDERLANDEN SEDERT DE HERVORMING
Kataev, I *see* OBZOR RUKOPISNYKH PAMIATNIKOV PO ISTORII SLOBODSKOI UKRAINY, KHRANIASHCHIKHSIA V VOENNO-UCHENOM ARKHIVE V S-PETERBURGE
Kataev, IM *see* OPISANIE AKTOV SOBRANIIA GRAFA A.S. UVAROVA: AKTY ISTORICHESKIE
DIE KATAKOMBENGEMAELDE UND IHRE ALTEN COPIEN / Wilpert, J – Freiburg im Breisgau, 1891 – 7mf – 8 – Dfl28.00 – ne Slangenburg [240]
KATALLAGETE – 1965- 1; 1970- 5,6; 1976- 4 x 6 in.9 – us UMI [073]
KATALOG / Leningrad. Rukopisnyi Fond Biblioteki. LIIZhTa – Comp. by I.V. Shkliar. L. 1969. BR-10,931 1 – 9 – ne IDC [620]
KATALOG / Rukopisi M I Glinki – Leningrad, 1950.100p. BR-10,901/1 – 9 – ne IDC [780]
KATALOG / Rukopisi N A Nekrasova – R.P. Matorina, comp. Moscow, 1939. 79p. Describes Nekrasov mss. in the MS division of the Lenin Library (GBL). BR-11,015/1 – 9 – ne IDC [460]
KATALOG / Rukopisi S A Esenina – Comp. by R. B. Zaborova. L. 1970. BR-11,115 – 9 – ne IDC [920]
KATALOG AKTOV 14, 15, 16 I 17 VV., PRINESENNYKH V DAR MOSKOVSKOMU PUBLICHNOMU MUZEIU PAVLOM ALEKSANDROVICHEM MUKHANOVYM / Lenin Library. P.A. Mukhanov Collection – Spb. 1865. BR-11,187 1 – 9 – ne IDC [947]
KATALOG, ALPHABETISCHER, DER DISSERTATIONEN DER UNIVERSITAETSBIBLIOTHEK DER HUMBOLDT-UNIVERSITAET BERLIN, BIS 1974 – Hildesheim, 1989 – 458mf – 9 – DM3,400.00 diazo DM3,900.00 silver – gw Olms [020]
KATALOG, ALPHABETISCHER, DER KINDER- UND JUGENDBUCHABTEILUNG DER STAATSBIBLIOTHEK ZU BERLIN PREUSSISCHER KULTURBESITZ – Hildesheim, 1994 – 64mf – 9 – DM620.00 daizo DM690.00 silver – gw Olms [020]
KATALOG, ALPHABETISCHER, DER MUSIKSAMMLUNG DER STAATSBIBLIOTHEK BERLIN PREUSSISCHER KULTURBESITZ – Hildesheim, 1990 – 537mf – 9 – DM5,300.00 diazo DM5,700.00 silver – gw Olms [780]
KATALOG, ALPHABETISCHER, DER STAATSBIBLIOTHEK ZU BERLIN PREUSSISCHER KULTURBESITZ – Hildesheim, 1987 – 3199mf – 9 – DM24,800.00 diazo DM28,800.00 silver – gw Olms [020]
KATALOG, ALPHABETISCHER, DER STADT- UND UNIVERSITAETSBIBLIOTHEK BERN – Hildesheim, 1991 – 1502mf – 9 – DM8,400.00 diazo DM9,800.00 silver – gw Olms [020]
KATALOG, ALPHABETISCHER, DER UNIVERSITAETSBIBLIOTHEK GRAZ – Hildesheim, 1984 – 711mf – 9 – DM7,200.00 diazo DM8,600.00 silver – gw Olms [020]
KATALOG, ALPHABETISCHER ZENTRAL-, DER ZUERCHERISCHEN BIBLIOTHEKEN – Hildesheim, 1990 – 1357mf – 9 – DM8,800.00 diazo DM9,900.00 silver – gw Olms [020]
KATALOG, ALTER, DER MUSIKDRUCKE DER OESTERREICHISCHEN NATIONALBIBLIOTHEK – Hildesheim, 1985 – 249mf – 9 – DM3,900.00 diazo DM4,500.00 silver – gw Olms [780]
KATALOG ARABSKIKH RUKOPISEI INSTITUTA NARODOV AZII AN SSSR – Moscow, 1960-65. 3v. 136p; 77p; 199p. BR-10,974/1 – 9 – ne IDC [010]
KATALOG ARKHIVNYKH DOKUMENTOV PO SEVERNOI VOINE 1700-1721 GG – Leningrad, 1959. 433p. BR-10,933/1 – 9 – ne IDC [947]
KATALOG ARKHIVOVEDCHESKOI LITERATURY, 1917-59 GG – Moscow, 1961. 191p. BR-10,649/1 – 9 – ne IDC [025]
KATALOG ARKHIVOVEDCHESKOI LITERATURY I SBORNIKOV DOKUMENTOV (1960-1963 GG.) – Moscow, 1964. 138p. BR-10,650/1 – 9 – ne IDC [025]
KATALOG ARKHIVOVEDCHESKOI LITERATURY I SBORNIKOV DOKUMENTOV (1964-1967 GG.) – Moscow, 1970. 183p. BR-10,651/1 – 9 – ne IDC [025]
KATALOG BIBLIOTEKI ALEKSANDROVSKAGO VOENNAGO UCHILISHCHA – Ed. by V. Kedrin. M. 1901. BR-4737 2 – 8 – ne IDC [370]
KATALOG BIBLIOTEKI IMP. ALEKSANDROVSKAGO LITSEIA – Osnovnoi otdel. Spb. 1900. BR-4507 2 – 8 – ne IDC [370]
KATALOG BIBLIOTEKI IMP. ARCHEOLOGICHESKOI KOMMISSII – Spb. 1904. Suppl. 1-2. Spb. 1907-10. BR-5937 2 – 8 – ne IDC [930]
KATALOG BIBLIOTEKI IMP. KHAR'KOVSKAGO UNIVERSITETA – Pervoe-vtoroe prodolzhenie. Khar'kov. 1884-1900. BR-5912 2 – 8 – ne IDC [370]
KATALOG BIBLIOTEKI IMP. MOSKOVSKAGO TEKHNICHESKAGO UCHILISHCHA – Ed. 2. M. 1900. BR-5941 2 – 8 – ne IDC [370]
KATALOG BIBLIOTEKI IMP. MOSKOVSKAGO UNIVERSITETA / Reis, F F – M. 1831-32. BR-7234 2 – 8 – ne IDC [370]
KATALOG BIBLIOTEKI IMP. NOVOROSSIISKAGO UNIVERSITETA – Odessa. 1878-93. BR-5913 – 8 – ne IDC [370]
KATALOG BIBLIOTEKI IMP. S-PETERBURGSKAGO ISTORIKO-FILOLOGICHESKAGO INSTITUTA – D-E, M-N, G-ZH-O. Spb. 1897, 1901. BR-4544 2 – 8 – ne IDC [370]
KATALOG BIBLIOTEKI MUZEIA D.G. BURYLINA V. G. IVANOVO-VOZNESENSKE – Ivanovo-Voznesensk. 1915. BR-5942 2 – 8 – ne IDC [010]
KATALOG BIBLIOTEKI MUZEIA DREVNOSTEI – Spb. 1896. Suppl. 1. Spb. 1901. BR-5918 2 – 8 – ne IDC [010]
KATALOG BIBLIOTEKI NIKOLAEVSKOI AKADEMII GENERAL'NAGO SHABA / Kvitnitskii Vil'k – Spb. 1866-73. BR-5959 2 – 8 – ne IDC [020]
KATALOG BIBLIOTEKI OBSHCHESTVA ISPYTATELEI PRIRODY PRI IMP. KHAR'KOVSKOM UNIVERSITETE – Khar'kov. 1911. BR-4814 2 – 8 – ne IDC [370]
KATALOG BIBLIOTEKI PERVAGO MOSKOVSKAGO OBSHCHESTVA TREZVOSTI – M. 1908. BR-5915 2 – 8 – ne IDC [010]
KATALOG BIBLIOTEKI SEMINARII PRI ISTORIKOFILOLOGICHESKOM FAKUL'TETE IMP. MOSKOVSKAGO UNIVERSITETA – Sost. V. A. Sheffer. M. 1895. BR-5916 2 – 8 – ne IDC [370]
KATALOG BIBLIOTEKI SLUZHASHCHIKH V MINISTERSTVE FINANSOV – Ed. 5. Spb. 1900. BR-5940 2 – 8 – ne IDC [336]
KATALOG BIBLIOTEKI UCHENAGO KOMITETA MINISTERSTVA GOSUDARSTVENNYKH IMUSHCHESTV – Spb. 1865. BR-5938 2 – 8 – ne IDC [010]
KATALOG BIBLIOTEKI VILENSKAGO VOENNAGO SOBRANIIA / Melekii – Ed. 2. Vil'na. 1908. BR-6997 2 – 8 – ne IDC [460]
KATALOG BIBLIOTEKI VTOROGO OTDELENIIA SOBSTVENNOI EGO IMP. VELICHESTVA KANTSELIARII – Spb. 1880. BR-5920 2 – 8 – ne IDC [010]
KATALOG DER ALTEN SAMMLUNG DER UNIVERSITAET KOPENHAGEN (BIBLIOTHECA UNIVERSITATIS HAFNIENSIS) 1486-1970 – Hildesheim, 1992 – 572mf – 9 – DM4,800.00 diazo DM5,800.00 silver – gw Olms [020]
KATALOG DER ARMENISCHEN HANDSCHRIFTEN DES HERRN ABGAR JOANNISSIANY ZU TIFLIS / Finck, FN – Leipzig, Marburg, 1903 – 3mf – 9 – ne IDC [460]
KATALOG DER AUSSTELLUNG ZUM 10. ARCHAEOLOGISCHEN KONGRESS IN RIGA 1896 – Riga. 1896. BR-9835 1 – 9 – ne IDC [930]
KATALOG DER BIS 1957 IM ZENTRALKATALOG BADEN-WUERTTEMBERG NACHGEWIESENEN WERKE VON MARTIN LUTHER – 5mf – 9 – DM120.00 – gw Olms [240]
KATALOG DER DEUTSCHEN BUECHEREI LEIPZIG IN DER DEUTSCHEN BIBLIOTHEK = CATALOG OF THE DEUTSCHEN BUECHEREI LEIPZIG IN DER DEUTSCHEN BIBLIOTHEK : GESAMTARCHIV DES DEUTSCHSPRACHIGEN SCHRIFTTUMS SEIT 1913 – Hildesheim, 1988 – 2532mf – 9 – DM19,800.00 diazo DM22,800.00 silver – gw Olms [010]
KATALOG DER ECHTEN SPINNEN (ARANEAE) DES PALAEARKTISCHEN GEBIETES / Reimoser, E – Z 2193 2. 1919 – 8 – ne IDC [590]
KATALOG DER EIERSAMMLUNG / Nehrkorn, A – 1899. Z 1987 – 9 – ne IDC [590]
KATALOG DER FILMSAMMLUNG / Kindermann, Jurgen – v1-24, 1500-1750. Verfilmung von Musikdrucken und Musikhandschriften zur deutschen Musikgeschichte von 1500-1750 – 1 – DM10.00v – gw D.M.A. [000]
KATALOG DER HAUPTBIBLIOTHEK IN DEN FRANCKESCHEN STIFTUNGEN HALLE – Hildesheim, 1993 – 99mf – 9 – DM920.00 diazo DM1,100.00 silver – gw Olms [020]
KATALOG DER IN DER PALAEARCTISCHEN REGION LEBENDEN BINNECONCHYLIEN / Westerlund, C A – Berlin, Karlshamn. 1890. BZ-862 2 – 8 – ne IDC [590]
KATALOG DER JUDAICA UND HEBRAICA – (Ceased publication) – Frankfurt am Main. v1. 1932 – 7mf – ne IDC [470]
KATALOG DER KOENIGLICHEN BIBLIOTHEK KOPENHAGEN. AUSLAENDISCHE AELTERE SAMMLUNG : DRUCKSCHRIFTEN MIT DEN ERSCHEINUNGSJAHREN 1454-1949 – Hildesheim, 1987 – 822mf – 9 – DM4,800.00 diazo DM5,800.00 silver – gw Olms [020]
KATALOG DER LIBRETTI : OESTERREICHISCHE NATIONALBIBLIOTHEK, WIEN. MUSIKSAMMLUNG – Hildesheim, 1985 – 52mf – 9 – DM750.00 diazo DM900.00 silver – gw Olms [780]
KATALOG DER MASONICA-SAMMLUNG DER UNIVERSITAETSBIBLIOTHEK POZNAN/ POSEN – Hildesheim, 1989 – 46mf – 9 – DM330.00 diazo DM420.00 silver – gw Olms [020]
KATALOG DER MUSIKDRUCKE DER NATIONALBIBLIOTHEK ZU PRAG-NARODNI KNIHORNA – Hildesheim, 1991 – 158mf – 9 – DM1,300.00 diazo DM1,500.00 silver – gw Olms [780]
KATALOG DER MUSIKHANDSCHRIFTEN : OESTERREICHISCHE NATIONALBIBLIOTHEK,WIEN. MUSIKSAMMLUNG – Hildesheim, 1984 – 106mf – 9 – DM1,600.00 diazo DM1,800.00 silver – gw Olms [780]

KATALOG DER OESTERREICHISCHEN NATIONALBIBLIOTHEK WIEN : DRUCKSCHRIFTEN 1501-1929 – Hildesheim, 1982 – 808mf – 9 – DM7,200.00 diazo DM8,600.00 silver – gw Olms [020]

KATALOG DER ORNAMENTSTICH-SAMMLUNG DES K.K. OESTERREICHISCHEN MUSEUMS FUER KUNST UND INDUSTRIE – Wien, 1865 – 1mf – ne IDC [700]

KATALOG DER ORNAMENTSTICH-SAMMLUNG DES KUNSTGEWERBE-MUSEUMS, BERLIN – Leipzig, 1894 – 6mf – ne IDC [700]

KATALOG DER SALO COHN'SCHEN SCHENKUNGEN / Wachstein, B – Wien. 2v. 1911-1914 – 5mf – ne IDC [943]

KATALOG DER UNIVERSITAETSBIBLIOTEK WROCLAW/BRESLAU – Hildesheim, 1990 – 847mf – 9 – DM11,800.00 diazo DM13,800.00 silver – gw Olms [020]

KATALOG DER UNIVERSITAETSBIBLIOTHEK WIEN : DRUCKSCHRIFTEN BIS ZUM ERSCHEINUNGSJAHR 1931 – Hildesheim, 1983 – 693mf – 9 – DM5,100.00 diazo DM5,900.00 silver – gw Olms [020]

KATALOG DER ZENTRALBIBLIOTHEK DER LANDBAUWISSENSCHAFT, BONN – (Alphabetischer Gesamtkatalog 1847-Apr 1986. Schlagwortkatalog 1960-Apr 1986) – 1986 – 275 fiches (1:42) – 9 – silver DM6,400.00 – 3-598-30288-6 – gw Saur [630]

KATALOG DER ZENTRALBIBLIOTHEK DER MEDIZIN, KOELN : HOCHSCHULSCHRIFTEN BIS ES 1976 – (Autoren-Sachtitel Katalog/ Schlagwort Index. 176 silver fiches. DM3,400.00 ISBN 3-598-30353-X. Dissertations Katalog. 170 silver fiches. (1:42) DM4,980.00 ISBN 3-598-30354-8.) – 1984 – 176mf (1:42) – 9 – Published by Norbert Gaertner, FRG – gw Saur [020]

KATALOG DES KUNSTHISTORISCHEN INSTITUTS IN FLORENZ = CATALOG OF THE INSTITUTE FOR THE HISTORY OF ART IN FLORENCE : SECOND SUPPLEMENT / Kunsthistorisches Institut in Florenz. Biblioteca dell'Instituto di Storia dell'Arte – 1972. 14,100 cards on 4 reels – 1 – $220.00 export $265.00 – 0-8161-1337-8 – uk Hall [700]

KATALOG DES KUNSTHISTORISCHEN INSTITUTS IN FLORENZ = CATALOG OF THE INSTITUTE FOR THE HISTORY OF ART IN FLORENCE : THIRD SUPPLEMENT / Kunsthistorisches Institut. Florenz. – 1976. 17,200 cards on 4 reels – 1 – $230.00 export $280.00 – 0-8161-1412-9 – uk Hall [700]

KATALOG DZIEL TRESCI PRZYSLOWIOWEJ SKLADAJACYCH BIBLJOTEKE IGNACEGO BERNSTEINA / Bernstein, Ignatz – 2v, complete. 1900. Bibliography of proverbs – 1 – us I.U. Libraries [390]

KATALOG GRECHESKIKH RUKOPISEI LENINGRADSKIKH KHRANILISHCH / Granstrem, E E – 8 pts. Includes index. BR-10,782/1 – 9 – ne IDC [020]

KATALOG INDIISKIKH RUKOPISEI / Mironov, N D – Catalogus codicum manuscriptorum Indicorum qui in Academiae Imperialis Scientiarum Petropolitanae Museo Asiatico asservantur. (Katalogi Aziatiskogo muzeia Imp. Akademii nauk, v. 1). Petrograd. 1914. BR-9889 1 – 9 – ne IDC [010]

KATALOG INDIISKIKH RUKOPISEI ROSSIISSKOI PUBLICHNOI BIBLIOTEKI / Mironov, N D – Sobranie I.P. Minaeva i nekotorye drugie. Petrograd. 1918. BR-10,885 1 – 9 – ne IDC [010]

KATALOG IZDANII IMP. AKADEMII NAUK – 1. Izdaniia na russkom iazyke. Spb. 1888. BR-4820 2 – 8 – ne IDC [370]

KATALOG IZDANII IMP. AKADEMII NAUK – 1. Izdaniia na russkom iazyke. Spb. 1902. BR-4821 2 – 8 – ne IDC [370]

KATALOG IZDANII IMP. AKADEMII NAUK – 2. Izdaniia na inostrannykh iazykakh. Spb. 1877. BR-4822 2 – 8 – ne IDC [370]

KATALOG IZDANII IMP. AKADEMII NAUK – 2. Izdaniia na inostrannykh iazykakh. Spb. 1891. BR-4823 2 – 8 – ne IDC [370]

KATALOG IZDANII IMP. AKADEMII NAUK – 2. Izdaniia na inostrannykh iazykakh. Spb. 1905. BR-4824 2 – 8 – ne IDC [370]

KATALOG IZDANII OTDELENIIA RUSSKAGO IAZYKA I SLOVESTNOSTI IMP. AKADEMII NAUK – Spb. 1911, Apr, Sep; 1912, Apr. BR-4827 2 – 8 – ne IDC [370]

KATALOG IZDANII PO KUSTARNOI PROMYSHLENNOSTI I PROMYSLOVOI KOOPERATSII – Moscow, 1930 – 1mf – 9 – COR-533/1 – ne IDC [334]

KATALOG KARTINNOI GALLEREI – (Moskovskii Publichnyi i Rumiantsovskii Muzei). M. 1912. BR-4752 2 – 8 – ne IDC [700]

KATALOG KNIG BIBLIOTEKI ALEKSEIA PETROVICHA BAKHRUSHINA – M. 1911-12. B-5943 2 – 8 – ne IDC [020]

KATALOG KNIG DLIA DETEI I VZROSLYKH IZDANNYKH KNIZHNYMI MAGAZINAMI I-VA M. O. VOL'F – Spb., M. 1903. BR-5668 2 – 8 – ne IDC [020]

KATALOG KNIG I RUKOPISEI BIBLIOTEK LAZAREVSKAGO INSTITUTA VOSTOCHNYKH IAZYKOV – M. 1888. BR-7118 2 – 8 – ne IDC [370]

KATALOG KNIG PO OBSHCHESTVENNO-IURIDICHESKIM NAUKAM (SISTEMATICHESKII KATALOG KNIZHNYKH MAGAZINOV T-VA M.O. VOL'F) – Saint Petersburg, Moscow, n.d., 55p. Catalog of books, including law, offered for sale by M.O. Wolf, bookdealers. BR-5666/2 – 8 – ne IDC [070]

KATALOG KNIG PO SEL'SKOMU KHOZIAISTVU, SADOVODSTVU, LESOVODSTVU, DOMASHNEMU KHOZIAISTVU, ZHIVOTNOVODSTVU, PCHELOVODSTVU I.T.P. IZD. M. O. VOL'F – Spb. 1913. BR-5671 2 – 8 – ne IDC [010]

KATALOG KNIG POSTUPIVSHIKH V BIBLIOTEKU GOSUDARSTVENNOI DUMY S 1 IIULIA 1913 G. PO 1 IIULIA 1914 G – Petrograd. 1914. BR-4517 2 – 8 – ne IDC [020]

KATALOG KNIG POSTUPIVSHIKH V BIBLIOTEKU GOSUDARSTVENNOI DUMY S 1 IIULIA 1914 G. PO 1 IIULIA 1915 G – Petrograd. 1915. BR-4518 2 – 8 – ne IDC [020]

KATALOG KNIG RUSSKAGO OTDELENIIA TURKESTANSKOI PUBLICHNOI BIBLIOTEKI / Dmitrovskii, N V – Spb. Br-5869 2 – 8 – ne IDC [010]

KATALOG KNIG V OTDELA REVEL'SKOI MORSKOI – Ofitserskoi Biblioteki. Revel'. 1912. BR-4786 2 – 8 – ne IDC [020]

KATALOG KNIG ZA 1891 G – Izd. Russkago Obshchestva knigoprodavtsev i izdatelei. Spb. 1892. BR-5684 2 – 8 – ne IDC [010]

KATALOG KNIG ZA 1892 G – Izd. Russkago Obshchestva knigoprodavtsev i izdatelei. Spb. 1893. BR-5685 2 – 8 – ne IDC [010]

KATALOG KNIGAM, RUKOPISIAM I KARTAM, NA KITAISKOM, MAN'DZHURSKOM, MONGOL' SKOM, TIBETSKOM I SANSKRITSKOM IAZYKAKH, NAKHODIASHCHIMSIA V BIBLIOTEKE AZIIATSKAGO DEPARTAMENTA – Spb. 1843. BR-7121 2 – 8 – ne IDC [950]

KATALOG KNIG/BIBLIOTHEQUE DE VOLTAIRE / Biblioteka Vol'tera – Catalogue des livres. Leningrad, 1961. 1166p. BR-10,867/1 – 9 – ne IDC [010]

KATALOG KNIZHNAGO MAGAZINA I IURIDICHESKAGO IZDATEL' STVA PRAVOVEDENIE I.K. GOLUBEVA, NO.75, 79 – Moscow, 1911-12.2v. Catalogues of the book dealer and publisher, I. K. Golubev, who dealt in law books. BR-5676/2 – 8 – ne IDC [340]

KATALOG KNIZHNAGO MAGAZINA I IURIDICHESKAGO IZDATEL'STVA ZAKONOVEDENIE I.I. ZUBKOVA – Catalog of bookdealer and law publisher, I.I. Zubkov; Petrograd. 1916. 96p BR-5678/2 – 8 – ne IDC [340]

KATALOG KNIZHNAGO MAGAZINA I IURIDICHESKAGO IZDATEL'STVA ZAKONOVEDENIE I.I. ZUBKOVA – Catalog of bookdealer and law publisher, I.I. Zubkov; Saint Petersburg. 1912. 96p BR-5677/2 – 8 – ne IDC [340]

KATALOG KNIZHNAGO MAGAZINA "NOVAGO VREMENI" A. S. SUVORINA – Petrograd. 1915. BR-5691 2 – 8 – ne IDC [010]

KATALOG KNIZHNAGO MAGAZINA NOVAGO VREMENI A.S. SUVORINA: KATALOG IURIDICHESKAGO OTDELA – Saint Petersburg, 1911. 2v. Catalog of law books offered for sale by the bookdealer, Savorin. BR-5690/2 – 8 – ne IDC [340]

KATALOG KNYHARNI LITERATURNO-NAUKOVOHO VISTNYKA – Kyiv. 1912. BR-5681 2 – 8 – ne IDC [460]

KATALOG KOPENHAGEN, ALPHABETISCHER DER KOENIGLICHEN BIBLIOTHEK KOPENHAGEN : ALPHABETISCHER KATALOG DER DAENISCHEN UND NORWEGISCHEN ABTEILUNG 1474-1959 – Hildesheim, 1995 – 685mf – 9 – DM7,800.00 diazo DM9,400.00 silver – gw Olms [010]

KATALOG LETUCHIKH IZDANII I IKH PEREPECHATOK – Manifesty, ukazy i drugiia pravitel'stvennyia rasporiazheniia v otdel'nykh izdaniiakh i perepechatkakh. Spb. 1895. BR-7119 2 – 8 – ne IDC [010]

KATALOG MASONSKIKH RUKOPISEI MOSKOVSKOGO PUBLICHNOGO I RUMIANTSEVSKOGO MUZEEV / Russia – M. 1900. BR-9816 1 – 9 – ne IDC [360]

KATALOG NO. 31 PO ISTORII I GENEALOGII (NOVYKH PRIOBRETENII) – Antikvarnaia knizhnaia torgovlia S. P. Trusova. Spb. 1907. BR-5692 2 – 8 – ne IDC [920]

KATALOG ODESSKOI GORODSKOI PUBLICHNOI BIBLIOTEKI – v. 1-3, 5. Odessa. 1901-10. BR-5945 2 – 8 – ne IDC [020]

KATALOG ODOBRENNYKH KNIG – Izdaniia M. O. Vol'f. Spb., M. 1914. BR-5672 2 – 8 – ne IDC [460]

KATALOG OVER DE OLDNORSK-ISLANDSKE HANDSKRIFTER I KOEBENHAVNS OFFENTLICHER BIBLIOTHEKER / Kalund, Kr. – N.p., n.d. – 11mf – 9 – ne IDC [090]

KATALOG PEDAGOGICHESKOI BIBLIOTEKI PO NACHAL'NOMU NARODNOMU OBRAZOVANIIU – Spb. 1910. BR-5946 2 – 8 – ne IDC [370]

KATALOG P'ESAM CHLENOV OBSHCHESTVA RUSSKIKH DRAMATICHESKIKH PISATELEI I OPERNYKH KOMPOZITOROV – Moscow, 1895. BR-7122 1 – 9 – ne IDC [790]

KATALOG PISEM I DRUGIKH MATERIALOV ZAPADNOEVROPEISKIKH UCHENYKH I PISATELEI XVI-XVIII VV. IZ SOBRANIIA P.P. DUBROVSKOGO – Leningrad, 1963.105p. BR-10,856/1 – 9 – ne IDC [010]

KATALOG (POLNYI) 1831 GODA ROSSIISKIM KNIGAM ATLASAM – knizhnago magazina I. Zankina. Spb. 1831. BR-7217 2 – 8 – ne IDC [460]

KATALOG (POLNYI) MUZYKAL'NYKH SOCHINENII IZDANNYKH V ROSSII – St. Petersburg, 1908. BR-7218/2 – 8 – ne IDC [780]

KATALOG PROIZVEDINII CHLENOV SOIUZA DRAMATICHESKIKH MUZYKAL'NYKH PISATELEI – St. Petersburg, 1910. BR-7123 1 – 9 – ne IDC [790]

KATALOG RAZSMOTRENNYKH INOSTRANNOIU TSENZUROIU SOCHINENII ZAPRESHCHENNYKH DOZVOLENNYKH S ISKLIUCHENIIAMI S 1-GO IIULIA 1871 G. PO 1-E IANVARIA 1897 G – Spb. 1898. BR-5947 2 – 8 – ne IDC [460]

KATALOG REKOPISOW / Paris. Biblioteka Polska – Krakow, 1939- – 1 – us U.W. Library [025]

KATALOG RUKOPISEI / U.S.S.R. Istoriia Leningrada; ed by Pishvanova, V I & Glushkov, T P – L. 1954 – 9 – ne IDC [947]

KATALOG RUSSKIKH ILLIUSTRIROVANNYKH IZDANII 1725-1860 GG / Obol'ianinov, N – v. 1-2. M. 1914-15. BR-4364 2 – 8 – ne IDC [760]

KATALOG RUSSKIKH KNIG / Martynov, N G – Izd. knizhnago magazina Ia.A. Isakova. Spb. 1868-69. BR-7145 2 – 8 – ne IDC [010]

KATALOG RUSSKIKH KNIG BIBLIOTEKI A. I. BORTNEVSKAGO S 1868 PO 1898 G – Odessa. 1897. BR-5949 2 – 8 – ne IDC [460]

KATALOG RUSSKIKH KNIG BIBLIOTEKI IMP. S -PETERBURGSKAGO UNIVERSITETA – v. 1-2. Spb. 1897-1902. BR-5948 2 – 8 – ne IDC [370]

KATALOG RUSSKIKH KNIG IZDANNYKH IMP. AKADEMIEIU NAUK I NAKHODIASHCHIKHSIA V PRODAZHE U EIA KOMMISSIONEROV 1857 – Spb. 1857. BR-4817 2 – 8 – ne IDC [370]

KATALOG RUSSKIKH KNIG PRINESENNYKH V DAR UNIVERSITETU V PENNSIL'VANII SHARLEMAIN' TAUER – Spb. 1902. BR-4783 2 – 8 – ne IDC [370]

KATALOG SANSKRITSKIM, MONGOL'SKIM, TIBETSKIM, MAN'DZHURSKIM I KITAISKIM KNIGAM I RUKOPISIAM V BIBLIOTEKE IMP. KAZANSKAGO UNIVERSITETA KHRANIASHCHIKHSIA – Kazan'. 1834. BR-4485 2 – 8 – ne IDC [950]

KATALOG SBORNIKOV DOKUMENTOV, IZDANNYKH ARKHIVNYMI UCHREZHDENIIAMI SSSR 1917-1960 GG – Moscow, 1961. 110p. BR-10,750/1 – 9 – ne IDC [010]

KATALOG SIRIISKIKH RUKOPISEI LENINGRADA / Pigulevskaia, N V – Moscow, Leningrad, 1960. 230p. BR-10,670/1 – 9 – ne IDC [010]

KATALOG SOBRANIIA RUKOPISEI PROF. I. V. POMIALOVSKOGO NYNE PRINADLEZHASHCHIKH IMP. PUBLICHNOI BIBLIOTEKE / Abramovich, D I – St. Petersburg, 1914. 180p. BR-11,208 1 – 9 – ne IDC [010]

KATALOG, SYSTEMATISCHER... *see* SYSTEMATISCHER KATALOG...

KATALOG, SYSTEMATISCHER, DER KARTENABTEILUNG IN DER STAATSBIBLIOTHEK ZU BERLIN PREUSSISCHER KULTURBESITZ, BIS 1945 – (Subject index and guide is available separately DM20.00) – Hildesheim, 1991 – 597mf – 9 – DM3,300.00 diazo DM3,800.00 silver – gw Olms [020]

KATALOG, SYSTEMATISCHER, DER STAATSBIBLIOTHEK ZU BERLIN PREUSSISCHER KULTURBESITZ, BIS 1955 – (Subject index and guide is also sold separately DM20.00) – Hildesheim, 1988-1991 – 6,226mf – 9 – DM29,800.00 diazo DM35,800.00 silver – gw Olms [020]

KATALOG UCHEBNIKOV, RAZRESHENNYKH DLIA UPOTREBLENIIA V TSERKOVNO-PRIKHODSKIKH SHKOLAKH – (V. A. Krandievskii, Red.). M. 1899. Index. BR-5951 2 – 8 – ne IDC [460]

KATALOG UCHEBNYKH KNIG I POSOBII (SISTEMATICHESKII KATALOG KNIZHNAGO MAGAZINA T-VA M. O. VOL'F) – Spb., M. n.d. BR-5669 2 – 8 – ne IDC [460]

KATALOG VOENNO-UCHENAGO ARKHIVA GLAVNAGO SHTABA – Materialy o voinakh, v kotorykh uchastvovali russkiia voiska. Ed. 2. Spb. 1898. BR-7120 2 – 8 – ne IDC [010]

KATALOG VOENNO-UCHENOGO ARKHIVA GLAVNOGO SHTABA / Russia; ed by Bender, M O – Ed. 2. 4v. Spb. 1905-14. BR-10,824 1 – 9 – ne IDC [010]

KATALOG ZHURNALA "VESTNIK EVROPY" ZA 25 LET, 1866-1890, S ALFAVITNYM UKAZATELEM IMEN AVTOROV – (M. M. Stasiukvi, Red.). 1891. BR-237 2 – 8 – ne IDC [073]

KATALOGE DER ALPENVEREINS BUECHEREI = CATALOGS OF THE ALPINE ASSOCIATION LIBRARY. 1970 : AUTORENKATALOG / Alpenvereins Buecherei. Munich – (Available on microfilm by request) – 28,700 cards – 9 – $400.00 – 0-8161-0849-8 – uk Hall [790]

KATALOGE DER BIBLIOTHEK DES DEUTSCHEN ARCHAEOLOGISCHEN INSTITUTES = CATALOGS FROM THE LIBRARY OF THE GERMAN INSTITUTE OF ARCHAEOLOGY. 1969 : AUTOREN UND PERIODICA KATALOGE / Deutsches Archaeologisches Institut. Rome. – (Available on microfilm by request) – 92,000 cards – 9 – $840.00 – uk Hall [930]

KATALOGE DER BIBLIOTHEK DES DEUTSCHEN ARCHAEOLOGISCHEN INSTITUTES = CATALOGS FROM THE LIBRARY OF THE GERMAN INSTITUTE OF ARCHAEOLOGY. 1969 : SYSTEMATISCHER KATALOG / Deutsches Archaeologisches Institut. Rome. – (Available on microfilm by request) – 84,000 cards – 9 – $445.00 – uk Hall [930]

KATALOGE DER BIBLIOTHEK DES DEUTSCHEN ARCHAEOLOGISCHEN INSTITUTES = CATALOGS FROM THE LIBRARY OF THE GERMAN INSTITUTE OF ARCHAEOLOGY. 1969 : ZEITSCHRIFTEN-AUTHORENKATALOG / Deutsches Archaeologisches Institut. Rome. – (Available on microfilm by request) – 37,000 cards – 9 – $365.00 – uk Hall [930]

KATALOGE DER BIBLIOTHEK DES INSTITUTS FUER WELTWIRTSCHAFT = CATALOGS FROM THE LIBRARY OF THE INSTITUTE FOR WORLD ECONOMICS : BEHOERDENKATALOG / Institut fuer Weltwirtschaft. Bibliothek. Kiel – (Available on microfilm by request) – 1967 – 170,000 cards – 1 – $1,198.00 – uk Hall [330]

KATALOGE DER BIBLIOTHEK DES INSTITUTS FUER WELTWIRTSCHAFT = CATALOGS FROM THE LIBRARY OF THE INSTITUTE FOR WORLD ECONOMICS : KOERPERSCHAFTENKATALOG / Institut fuer Weltwirtschaft. Bibliothek. Kiel – (Available on microfilm by request) – 1967 – 238,000 cards – 1 – $1,555.00 – uk Hall [330]

KATALOGE DER BIBLIOTHEK DES INSTITUTS FUER WELTWIRTSCHAFT = CATALOGS FROM THE LIBRARY OF THE INSTITUTE FOR WORLD ECONOMICS : PERSONENKATALOG / Institut fuer Weltwirtschaft. Bibliothek. Kiel – 1966 – 30r – 1 – $3,585.00 – 0-8161-1466-8 – uk Hall [330]

KATALOGE DER BIBLIOTHEK DES INSTITUTS FUER WELTWIRTSCHAFT = CATALOGS FROM THE LIBRARY OF THE INSTITUTE FOR WORLD ECONOMICS : REGIONENKATALOG / Institut fuer Weltwirtschaft. Bibliothek. Kiel – (1968. 85,000 cards. $595.00 export $720.00; Available on microfilm by request) – 1967 – 849,000 cards – 1 – $6,220.00 – uk Hall [330]

KATALOGE DER BIBLIOTHEK DES INSTITUTS FUER WELTWIRTSCHAFT = CATALOGS FROM THE LIBRARY OF THE INSTITUTE FOR WORLD ECONOMICS : SACHKATALOG / Institut fuer Weltwirtschaft. Bibliothek. Kiel – 1968 – 167r – 1 – $8,560.00 – 0-8161-1344-0 – uk Hall [330]

KATALOGE DER BIBLIOTHEK DES INSTITUTS FUER WELTWIRTSCHAFT = CATALOGS FROM THE LIBRARY OF THE INSTITUTE FOR WORLD ECONOMICS : TITELKATALOG / Institut fuer Weltwirtschaft. Bibliothek. Kiel – (Available on microfilm by request) – 1968 – 240,000 cards – 1 – $1,555.00 – uk Hall [330]

KATALOGE DER BIBLIOTHEK DES INSTITUTS FUER ZEITGESCHICHTE = CATALOGS FROM THE LIBRARY OF THE INSTITUTE FOR CONTEMPORARY HISTORY : ALPHABETISCHER KATALOG / Institut fuer Zeitgeschichte – (Available on microfilm by request) – 62,200 cards – 1 – $510.00 – uk Hall [900]

KATALOGE DER BIBLIOTHEK DES INSTITUTS FUER ZEITGESCHICHTE = CATALOGS FROM THE LIBRARY OF THE INSTITUTE FOR CONTEMPORARY HISTORY : BIOGRAPHISCHER KATALOG / Institut fuer Zeitgeschichte – (Available on microfilm by request) – 16,000 cards – 1 – $120.00 – uk Hall [900]

KATALOGE DER BIBLIOTHEK DES INSTITUTS FUER ZEITGESCHICHTE = CATALOGS FROM THE LIBRARY OF THE INSTITUTE FOR CONTEMPORARY HISTORY : ERSTER NACHTRAGSBAND 1973. ALPHABETISCHER KATALOG / Institut fuer Zeitgeschichte – 2r – 1 – $170.00 – 0-8161-1404-8 – uk Hall [900]

KATALOGE DER BIBLIOTHEK DES INSTITUTS FUER ZEITGESCHICHTE = CATALOGS FROM THE LIBRARY OF THE INSTITUTE FOR CONTEMPORARY HISTORY / Institut fuer Zeitgeschichte – 1967 – 1 – uk Hall [900]

KATALOGE DER BIBLIOTHEK DES INSTITUTS FUER ZEITGESCHICHTE = CATALOGS FROM THE LIBRARY OF THE INSTITUTE FOR CONTEMPORARY HISTORY : LAENDERKATALOG / Institut fuer Zeitgeschichte – (Available on microfilm by request) – 24,000 cards – 1 – $175.00 – uk Hall [900]

KATALOGE DER BIBLIOTHEK DES INSTITUTS FUER ZEITGESCHICHTE = CATALOGS FROM THE LIBRARY OF THE INSTITUTE FOR CONTEMPORARY HISTORY : SACHKATALOG / Institut fuer Zeitgeschichte – (Available on microfilm by request) – 94,500 cards – 1 – $655.00 – uk Hall [900]

KATALOGE DER BIBLIOTHEK DES ZENTRALINSTITUTS FUER KUNSTGESCHICHTE IN MUENCHEN = CATALOGUES OF THE LIBRARY OF THE CENTRAL INSTITUTE FOR THE HISTORY OF ART IN MUNICH – (Alphabetischer Katalog 1982-1985. 220 fiches silver 3-598-30349-1. DM3,280.00. Aufsatzkatalog 1983/1985. 231 fiches. Silver 3-598-30391-2. DM2,600.00 1984. 480 fiches. Silver 3-598-30351-3. DM 5,800.00. Supplement. 94 fiches. Silver 3-598-30350-0. DM3,800.00) – 1982-1991 – 1,025 fiches (1:42) – 9 – silver DM13,6000.00 – 3-598-30348-3 – gw Saur [020]

KATALOGE DER BIBLIOTHEK...: SACHKATALOG / Institut fuer Weltwirtschaft. Kiel. Bibliothek – 1968.-1,129,000 cards 167 reels.-ISBN: 0-8161-1344-0 – 1 – $7780.00 – uk Hall [330]

KATALOGE DER FRANKFURTER UND LEIPZIGER BUCHMESSEN 1594-1860 = CATALOGUES OF THE FRANKFURT AND LEIPZIG BOOK FAIRS / ed by Fabian, Bernhard – (Also available separately: Michaelismesse 1594- Michaelismesse 1699 211mf DM3,100.00 diazo DM3,800.00 silver. Ostermesse 1700- Ostermesse 1759 126mf DM1,300.00 diazo DM1,600.00 silver. Michaelismesse 1759-Michaelismesse 1800 141mf DM1,800.00 diazo DM2,200.00 silver. Ostermesse 1801- Michaelismesse 1860 453mf DM2,400.00 diazo DM2,900 silver) – Hildesheim, 1977-85 – 931mf – 9 – DM8,200.00 diazo DM9,800.00 silver – gw Olms [070]

KATALOGE DER INTERNATIONALEN JUGENDBIBLIOTHEK = CATALOGS OF THE INTERNATIONAL YOUTH LIBRARY. 1968 : ALPHABETISCHER KATALOG / Internationale Jugendbibliothek. Muenchen – (Available on microfilm by request) – 55,300 cards – 9 – $598.00 – uk Hall [010]

KATALOGE DER INTERNATIONALEN JUGENDBIBLIOTHEK = CATALOGS OF THE INTERNATIONAL YOUTH LIBRARY. 1968 : ILLUSTRATORENKATALOG / Internationale Jugendbibliothek. Muenchen – (Available on microfilm by request) – 31,200 cards – 9 – $360.00 – uk Hall [010]

KATALOGE DER INTERNATIONALEN JUGENDBIBLIOTHEK = CATALOGS OF THE INTERNATIONAL YOUTH LIBRARY. 1968 : LAENDERKATALOG / Internationale Jugendbibliothek. Muenchen – (Available on microfilm by request.) – 52,300 cards – 9 – $475.00 – uk Hall [010]

KATALOGE DER INTERNATIONALEN JUGENDBIBLIOTHEK = CATALOGS OF THE INTERNATIONAL YOUTH LIBRARY. 1968 : SYSTEMATISCHER KATALOG / Internationale Jugendbibliothek. Muenchen – (Available on microfilm by request) – 23,900 cards – 9 – $240.00 – uk Hall [010]

KATALOGE DER INTERNATIONALEN JUGENDBIBLIOTHEK = CATALOGS OF THE INTERNATIONAL YOUTH LIBRARY. 1968 : TITELKATALOG / Internationale Jugendbibliothek. Muenchen – (Available on microfilm by request) – 47,700 cards – 9 – $475.00 – uk Hall [010]

KATALOGE DER TECHNISCHEN INFORMATIONSBIBLIOTHEK (TIB) HANNOVER = CATALOGUE OF THE TECHNICAL INFORMATION LIBRARY HANNOVER : ALPHABETISCHER KATALOG BIS 1982 : KONFERENZKATALOG BIS 1983 – 1983 – 664 fiches (1:42) – 9 – silver DM4,800.00 – 3-598-30445-5 – gw Saur [020]

KATALOG-PERECHEN', KNIG IZD. M. O. VOL'F. 1853-1913 – Spb., M. 1913. BR-5659 2 – 8 – ne IDC [460]

Katanian, V A *see*
– MAIAKOVSKII

Katanov, N F *see* OPYT IZSLEDOVANIIA URIANKHAISKAGO IAZYKA

Kataoka, S *see* KANRIDOO

Kate, L ten *see* GEMEENSCHAP TUSSEN DE GOTTISCHE SPRAEKE EN DE NEDERDUYTSCHE VERTOONT

Kate, Lambert ten *see* AENLEIDING TOT DE KENNISE VAN HET VERHEVENE DEEL DER NEDERDUITSCHE SPRAKE

DIE KATECHESE IN DER ERZDIOEZESE KOELN UNTER DEN KURFUERSTEN MAX HEINRICH BIS MAX FRANZ. 1650-1801 / Miebach, Peter – Koeln, 1926 – 9 – DM48.00 – 3-89349-248-8 – gw Hänsel [240]

KATECHISMUS DER CHRISTKATHOLISCHEN LEHRE ZUM GEBRAUCHE DER GROESSEREN SCHUELER, (WELCHE DEN KLEINEN KATECHISMUS GELERNT HABEN) NACH ANLEITUNG DES RELIGIONS-HANDBUCHS / Overberg, Bernhard – Muenster, 29th ed 1835 – 2mf – 9 – DM62.00 – 3-89349-358-1 – gw Hänsel [240]

KATECHISMUS DER KOMPOSITIONSLEHRE / Riemann, H – Leipzig: Hesse, 1889 – 1 – us Sibley [780]

KATECHISMUS DES GENERALBASS-SPIELS / Riemann, H – Leipzig: Hesse, 1889 – 1 – us Sibley [780]

KATECHISMUS DES VOELKERRECHTS / Bischof, H – Leipzig, 1877 – 2mf – 9 – ILM-2423/1 – ne IDC [327]

KATECHISMUS FUER DIE KATHOLISCHEN PFARRSCHULEN DER VEREINIGTEN STAATEN / Faerber, Wilhelm – St Louis, MO: B Herder, c1895 – 1mf – 9 – 0-8370-7062-7 – 1986-1062 – us A.T.L.A. [240]

Kategile, J A *see* FUTURE OF LIVESTOCK INDUSTRIES IN EAST AND SOUTHERN AFRICA

DIE KATEGORIEN- U. BEDEUTUNGSLEHRE DES DUNS SCOTUS / Heidegger, M – Tuebingen, 1916 – 5mf – 8 – ne Slangenburg [100]

KATEI BUNKO = KATEI COLLECTION OF EDO LITERATURE AND DRAMATIC WORKS – Printed books. 1,159 items in 2,032v – 72r – 1 – Y650,000.00 – ja Yushodo [480]

KATENLUED / Lau, Fritz – 6. Aufl. Hamburg: M Glogau, 1921 – 1r – 1 – us U.W. Library [830]

DER KATER : ANTIFASCHISTISCH-SATYRISCHE ZEITUNG – Paris. 3 Jun 1933 (nur 1 nr. ersch.) – 1r – 1 – gw Mikrofilm [073]

O KATERAKH I PRIZOVOM SUDOPROIZVODSTVE V OTNOSHENII K NEITRAL'NOI TORGOVLE / Kachenovskii, D I – Moscow, 1855. 191p. Early Monograph on the Law of Prize with respect to neutral trade. BR-9148/1 – 9 – ne IDC [340]

KATERI, LYS DES AGNIERS / ed by Bechard, Henri – Kahnawake. v1 n1. Printemps 1960-n112. Printemps 1988 – 1r – 1 – Can$60.00 – cn Can Microfilming [072]

Katerkamp, Theodor *see* DENKWUERDIGKEITEN AUS DEM LEBEN DER FUERSTIN AMALIA VON GALLITZIN

Kath, Lydia *see*
– DER BAUERNKANZLER
– DIE SCHULTZEN-KATHRIN

THE KATHAKOSA (OR TREASURY OF STORIES) / Tawney, T H – 1895 – 1 – uk Microform Academic [830]

DIE KATHAREN (MGH SCHRIFTEN..: 12.BD) / Borst, A – 1953 – Dfl30.00 – ne Slangenburg [240]

KATHARINA KNIE : EIN SEILTAENZERSTUECK IN VIER AKTEN / Zuckmayer, Carl – Berlin: Im Propylaeen-Verlag, c1929 – 1r – 1 – us U.W. Library [790]

KATHARSIS ZWISCHEN DIESSEITS UND JENSEITS : EINE EMPIRISCH-REZIPROKE, PSYCHO-SOZIALE STUDIE DYNAMISCHER PROZESSE ZWISCHEN THERAPIE, POLITIK, KULTUR UND RELIGION / Weidkuhn, Wilmar – 1993 – 2mf – 9 – DM80.00 – 3-89349-782-X – gw Hänsel [150]

HEKATHEMERINE – Athena: s.n., 1956-apr 20 1967; sep 15 1974-jun 1987; mar-jun 1989 – us Res Libr [949]

KATHEMERINE – Athens. Greece. -d. 1946-55. (28 reels) – 1 – uk British Libr Newspaper [949]

KATHMANDU VALLEY : NEPALESE HISTORIC MONUMENTS IN NEED OF PRESERVATION / Sanday, John – 1982 – 9 – 92-3-101992-9 – fr UNESCO [910]

KATHOLICISMUS, PROTESTANTISMUS UND UNGLAUBE = CATHOLICITY, PROTESTANTISM AND INFIDELITY : EIN AUFRUF AN ALLE ZUR RUECKKEHR ZU CHRISTENTHUM UND KIRCHE / Weninger, Francis Xavier – (Includes bibliographical references) – 4. Aufl. Mainz: Franz Kirchheim, 1864 – 1mf – 9 – 0-8370-8632-9 – 1986-2632 – us A.T.L.A. [240]

KATHOLICISMUS UND PROTESTANTISMUS GEGENUEBER DER SOCIALEN FRAGE / Uhlhorn, Gerhard – Goettingen: Vendenhoeck und Ruprecht, 1887 – 1mf – us A.T.L.A. [240]

DER KATHOLIK = THE CATHOLIC – (In German. Weekly) – Mainz, DE. Special Edition: 25 Jan 1934 – 1r – 1 – $25.00 – cn Can Microfilming [072]

KATHOLIKON : TIJDSCHRIFT VOOR BESCHAAFDE ROOMSCH-KATHOLIJKEN – Breda, 1827-1830 – 38mf – 9 – Dfl133.00 – ne Slangenburg [073]

KATHOLISCH ODER JESUITISCH? : DREI ZEITGESCHICHTLICHE UNTERSUCHUNGEN / Nippold, Friedrich – Leipzig: G. Reichardt, 1888 – 1mf – us A.T.L.A. [240]

EINE KATHOLISCHE BELEUCHTUNG DER AUGSBURGISCHEN KONFESSION : POLEMISCHE STUDIE / Thieme, Karl – (Includes bibliographical references) – Leipzig: Duerr, 1898 – 1mf – 9 – 0-8370-8794-5 – 1986-2794 – us A.T.L.A. [240]

KATHOLISCHE DOGMATIK / Kuhn, Johannes von – 1846-57 – 1 – us A.T.L.A. [240]

DIE KATHOLISCHE KIRCHE IN ARMENIEN / Weber, S – Freiburg Brsg., 1903 – Dfl35.00 – ne Slangenburg [240]

DIE KATHOLISCHE KIRCHE UND IHR RECHT IN DEN PREUSSISCHEN RHEINLANDEN / Stutz, Ulrich – Bonn, 1915 – 35p – 9 – DM48.00 – 3-89349-074-4 – gw Hänsel [240]

KATHOLISCHE KIRCHENZEITUNG *see* PETRUSBLATT

DER KATHOLISCHE MODERNISMUS / Schnitzer, Joseph – Berlin: Protestantischer Schriftenvertrieb, 1912 – 1mf – us A.T.L.A. [240]

KATHOLISCHE RELIGIONSLEHRE FUER DIE VIER OBERSTEN KLASSEN DER GELEHRTENSCHULEN UND FUER GEBILDETE MAENNER – 2. verb. Aufl. Regensburg; New York: Friedrich Pustet, 1890-91 – 4mf – 9 – 0-8370-8376-1 – 1986-2376 – us A.T.L.A. [370]

KATHOLISCHE SOZIALPOLITISCHE KORRESPONDENZ – (Missing: Jul-Dec 1887) – Moenchengladbach, Krefeld. Jul 1891-Aug 1928 – 3r – 1 – DM225.00 – gw Mikro Press [072]

KATHOLISCHE SOZIALPOLITISCHE KORRESPONDENZ – Moenchengladbach-Krefeld, Germany. Jul 1891-Aug 1928 – 3r – 1 – gw Mikrofilm [240]

DER KATHOLISCHE VOLKSBOTE – (Title change: Trier'scher Volksbote, 1 Jun 1849) – Trier, Germany. 25 Aug 1848-Jun 1850 – 1r – 1 – gw Mikrofilm [072]

KATHOLISCHE VOLKSZEITUNG – (Bereichsausgabe der Germania, Berlin) – Berlin, jan-mar 1892, jul-sep 1897 – 2r – 1 – Dist. gw Mikrofilm – gw Misc Inst [943]

KATHOLISCHE VOLKSZEITUNG – (In German) – Baltimore, MD. 1870-76 – 3r – 1 – $255.00 – D3367 – us Scholarly Res [071]

KATHOLISCHE WELTANSCHAUUNG UND FREIE WISSENSCHAFT : EIN POPULAERWISSENSCHAFTLICHER VORTRAG UNTER BERUECKSICHTIGUNG DES SYLLABUS PIUS 10 UND DER ENZYKLIKA "PASCENDI DOMINICI GREGIS" / Wahrmund, Ludwig – (Includes bibliographical references) – Muenchen: J F Lehmann, 1908 – 1mf – 9 – 0-8370-8719-8 – 1986-2719 – us A.T.L.A. [240]

DIE KATHOLISCHEN BRIEFE (T.U.U. 1-8/3) / Weiss, Bernhard – Leipzig, 1892 – 4mf – 9 – ne Slangenburg [240]

DIE KATHOLISCHEN MISSIONEN – Aachen, etc. Bd. 1-69; 1873-1950. "Zeitschrift des paepstlichen Werkes der Glaubensverbreitung." Subtitle varies. Film Mas C 441 – 1 – us H.U. Library [073]

DIE KATHOLISCHEN MISSIONEN IN INDIEN, CHINA UND JAPAN : IHRE ORGANISATION UND DAS PORTUGIESISCHE PATRONAT VOM 15. BIS INS 18. JAHRHUNDERT / Jann, Adelhelm – Paderborn: F. Schoeningh, 1915 – 2mf – us A.T.L.A. [240]

KATHOLISCHER LITERATURKALENDER – Freiburg im Breisgau, Herder & Co, etc. 1-5; 1891-97. No issues for 1895, 1896. 1893 published as "Erganzungsheft zum 2. Jahrg." Film Mas C 292 – 1 – us H.U. Library [430]

KATHOLISCHER LITERATURKALENDER – (v6-14 1902-14 as katholischer Literaturkalender) – v1-15. 1891-1926 – 45mf – 9 – DM560.00 – 3-89131-050-1 – gw Fischer [430]

DIE KATHOLISCH-THEOLOGISCHE FAKULTAET ZU MARBURG : EIN BEITRAG ZUR GESCHICHTE DER KATHOLISCHEN KIRCHE IN KURHESSEN UND NASSAU / Mirbt, Carl – Marburg: N G Elwert, 1905 – 1mf – us A.T.L.A. [240]

KATHOLIZISMUS UND REFORMATION : KRITISCHES REFERAT UEBER DIE WISSENSCHAFTLICHEN LEISTUNGEN DER NEUEREN KATHOLISCHEN THEOLOGIE AUF DEM GEBIETE DER REFORMATIONSGESCHICHTE / Koehler, Walther E – Giessen: A. Toepelmann, 1905 – 1mf – us A.T.L.A. [240]

AL-KATIB – Jerusalem, 1979-1991. – mujallad 1, adad 1-mujallad 12, adad 138 (Nov 1979-Dec 1991 – 5r – 1 – $175.00 – us MEDOC [949]

KATIE NEWSLETTER / Auburn University. Extension Service – No.1-446. 1970-82. 1 reel – 1, 5 – us Spaulding [630]

Katili, John A *see* GEOLOGI

KATILINA / Kuernberger, Ferdinand – Hamburg: Hoffmann und Campe, 1855 – 1 – us U.W. Library [820]

KATILINA IM DRAMA DER WELTLITERATUR : EIN BEITRAG ZUR VERGLEICHENDEN STOFFGESCHICHTE DES ROEMERDRAMAS / Speck, Hermann Berthold Georg – Leipzig: Hesse, 1906 – 1r – 1 – us U.W. Library [410]

KATIP CELEBI / Tahir, Mehmed – Dersaadet [Istanbul]: Kanaat Matbaasi, 1331 [1916] – $12.00 – us MEDOC [470]

Katip Celebi *see* TUHFET EL-KIBARF I ESFAR EL-BIHAR

KATJANG TANAH / Sukadis Sosroprawiro, R – SE 5269 1. 1958 – 9 – ne IDC [950]

Katjavivi, Peter H see HISTORY OF RESISTANCE IN NAMIBIA
Katkov, MN see SOBRANIE PEREDOVYKH STATEI "MOSKOVSKIKH VEDOMOSTEI" 1863-1887
Kato, Harubumi see DIAGNOSTIC AND THERAPEUTIC ENDOSCOPY
KATOLICKE NOVINY – Nadas, Slovakia. 1896-1900, 1902-1906 – 4r – 1 – us I.H.R.C. [947]
KATOLICKE NOVINY – Prague, Czechoslovakia. -w. Jan 1954-Dec 1970. 4 reels – 1 – uk British Libr Newspaper [072]
DE KATOLIJKE : LETTERKUNDIG TIJDSCHRIFT VOOR GODSDIENST EN WETENSCHAPPEN – Deventer, 1822-1824 – 37mf – 9 – Dfl130.00 – ne Slangenburg [073]
KATOLIK – Chicago, IL: Bohemian Benedictine Press, [sep 14 1917-1945]; 1946-dec 19 1975 – us Res Libr [240]
KATOOMBA CITY NEWS – May 23 1924 – 9 – at Pascoe [072]
KATOOMBA DAILY – Dec 18 1920-May 9 1939 – 9 – at Pascoe [072]
KATORGA I SSYLKA – Moscow, 1921-35. Incomplete. BR-9555 1 – 9 – ne IDC [947]
KATORGA I SSYLKA – Moscow. no. 1-116. 1921-1935. Index for 1921-1930 – 1 – us NY Public [320]
KATORGA I SSYLKA – Moscow. nos. 1-116 and index. 1921-35 – 1 – 35.00r – us Hoover Inst Photo [947]
KATORGA I SSYLKA : VSESOIUZNOE OBSHCHESTVO POLITKATORZHAN I SSYL'NOPOSELENTISEV – Moscow. v1-15. 1921-35 – 12r – 1 – us Ross [947]
Katre, S M see NEW INDIAN ANTIQUARY
KATRINEHOLMSKURIREN – Katrineholm, Sweden. 1916-78 – 297r – 1 – sw Kungliga [072]
KATRINEHOLMSKURIREN – Katrineholm, Sweden. 1979- – 1 – sw Kungliga [072]
Kats, J see HET JAVAANSCHE TONEEL. I. WAJANG POERWA
Kats, R R see SOTSIAL'NOE STRAKHOVANIE; SBORNIK ZAKONODATEL'NYKH I DIREKTIVNYKH MATERIALOV
Katsaros, Kristina see THE ATMOSPHERE-OCEAN SYSTEM
Katsh, A I see
- THE ANTONIN GENIZAH IN THE SALTYKOV-SHCHEDRIN PUBLIC LIBRARY IN LENINGRAD
- CATALOGUE OF HEBREW MANUSCRIPTS PRESERVED IN THE USSR
- HEBREW AND JUDEO-ARABIC MSS. IN THE COLLECTIONS OF THE USSR
- HEBREW AND JUDEO-ARABIC MSS IN THE COLLECTIONS OF THE USSR. M., 1962

Kattenbusch, Ferdinand see
- DAS APOSTOLISCHE SYMBOL
- DIE KIRCHEN UND SEKTEN DES CHRISTENTUMS IN DER GEGENWART
- LUTHERS STELLUNG ZU DEN OECUMENISCHEN SYMBOLEN

Katter, F see ENTOMOLOGISCHE NACHRICHTEN
Katterfeld, Anna see LEUCHTENDES LEBEN
KATTOWITZER ZEITUNG – Katowice, Poland. Oct 1927-Feb 1938 – 1r – 1 – us L of C Photodup [943]
KATTOWITZER ZEITUNG – (Title change: Oberschlesische Zeitung, 1 Sep 1942) – Kattowitz (Katowice), Poland. 5 May-30 Sept 1923; Sept 1925-32; 1933-43 – 53r – 1 – gw Mikrofilm [943]
Katushkina, LG see OT DANTE DO TASSO. KATALOG PISEM I SOCHINENII ITAL'IANSKIKH GUMANISTOV V SOBRANII LOII SSSR
Katwijk, AF van see LEXICON COMMODIANEUM. DISS
Katz, Bill see
- THE ACQUISITIONS LIBRARIAN
- THE REFERENCE LIBRARIAN

Katzenelson, I see HA-MA'AGAL
Katzer, Friedrich Xavier see DER KAMPF DER GEGENWART; EIN DRAMATISCHER VERSUCH IN 5 AKTEN
Katzew, Henry see SOLUTION FOR SOUTH AFRICA
KATZ/PRINCE COLLECTION : FROM THE HOLDINGS OF THE SCHOMBURG CENTER FOR RESEARCH IN BLACK CULTURE, MANUSCRIPTS, ARCHIVES AND RARE BOOKS DIVISION: THE NEW YORK PUBLIC LIBRARY, ASTOR, LENOX AND TILDEN FOUNDATIONS – (Guide which covers all coll under "Antebellum America and Slavery" sold separately for $20.00 D3305.G2) – 1995 – 3r – 1 – $255.00 – Dist. us Scholarly Res – us L of C Photodup [470]
Kau Besin, AF see
- NJANJIAN KANAK-KANAK, DENGAN ARANSEMEN PIANO
- SEDJARAH MUSIK DI EROPAH

KAUCHUK I REZINA (MOSCOW, R.S.F.S.R.: 1937) see KAUCHUK I REZINA: ORGAN NARODNOGO KOMISSARIATA TI AZHELO I PROMYSHLENNOSTI
KAUCHUK I REZINA: ORGAN NARODNOGO KOMISSARIATA TI AZHELO I PROMYSHLENNOSTI – (Includes c.1: 1939) – Moskva: GONTI NKTP SSSR, 1937 – 1 – CSUXAKZ6829-S – us Hoover Inst Photo [947]
KAUENER ZEITUNG – Kaunas, Lietuva (Kowno, U.S.S.R.). 3 Jan-5 Jul 1994 – 2r – 1 – gw Mikrofilm [943]
KAUENER ZEITUNG – Kaunas. USSR. -d. 3 Jan-5 Jul 1944. (2 reels) – 1 – uk British Libr Newspaper [072]
Kauffman, Angelica see RECORDS OF PICTURES PAINTED IN ITALY, 1781-1798
Kauffman, C H see THE AGARICACEAE OF MICHIGAN
Kauffman, Daniel see MENNONITE CHURCH HISTORY
Kauffmann, Georg F see HARMONISCHE SEELEN LUST MUSICALISCHER GOENNER UND FREUNDE
Kaufhold, Karl Heinrich see PREUSSISCHE STATISTIK
Kaufman, IM see
- RUSSKIE BIOGRAFICHESKIE I BIBLIOGRAFICHESKIE SLOVARI
- RUSSKIE ENTSIKLOPEDII

Kaufman, Wayne S see VALIDATION OF THE MAXIMAL MET PREDICTION EQUATIONS ON THE SCHWINN AIR-DYNE
DER KAUFMANN – Biberach, jul 1 1902-nov 5 1904 – 1r – 1 – Inquire at Mikrofilmarchiv for details – gw Misc Inst [380]
Kaufmann, Barbara E see THE IMPACT OF "WINNING WEIGHS" WEIGHT CONTROL PROGRAM ON PERCEIVED BODY IMAGE
Kaufmann, David see
- GESAMMELTE SCHRIFTEN VON DAVID KAUFMANN
- GESCHICHTE DER ATTRIBUTENLEHRE
- GESCHICHTE DER ATTRIBUTENLEHRE IN DER JUEDISCHEN RELIOGIONSPHILOSOPHIE VON SAADIA BIS MAIMUNI
- JEHUDA HALEWI
- PAUL DE LAGARDE'S JUEDISCHE GELEHRSAMKEIT: EINE ERWIEDERUNG
- DIE SINNE
- STUDIEN UEBER SALOMON IBN GABIROL

Kaufmann, Frank see ARBEITSLOSIGKEIT ZWISCHEN LOHN UND EFFIZIENZ
Kaufmann, Guenter see DAS KOMMENDE DEUTSCHLAND; DIE ERZIEHUNG DER JUGEND IM REICH ADOLF HITLERS
Kaufmann, Herman Ezechiel see DIE ANWENDUNG DES BUCHES HIOB IN DER RABBINISCHEN AGADAH
Kaufmann, Max see
- HEINES CHARAKTER UND DIE MODERNE SEELE
- HEINES LIEBESLEBEN

Kaufmann, R von et al see LIVESTOCK SYSTEMS RESEARCH IN NIGERIA'S SUBHUMID ZONE
KAUKASIEN, NORDKAUKASIEN, ASERBEIDSCHAN, ARMENIEN, GEORGIEN, GESCHICHTLICHER UMRISS / Nikuradse, Alexander – Muenchen: Hoheneichen verlag, c1942. 349p. illus. maps – 1 – us U.W. Library [947]
KAUKASISCHE POST – Tiflis (Tbilissi), U.S.S.R. 1908-12 (incomplete); 1918-22 (incomplete) – 4r – 1 – gw Mikrofilm [947]
Kaul, A see OSNOVY I PRAKTIKA SOVETSKOGO PRAVA; SBORNIK STATEI
Kaulen, Franz see SPRACHLICHES HANDBUCH ZUR BIBLISCHEN VULGATA
Kaulfuss, G F see
- ENUMERATIO FILICUM, QUAS IN ITENERE CIRCA TERRAM LEGIT
- ENUMERATO FILICUM AND OTHER ARTICLES
- DAS WESEN DER FARRENKRAEUTER

Kaups, Richard see
- HEA SONUM JA EESTI BAPTISTI KOGUDUSED
- ILMUTUSTRAAMATU SELETUS
- VIISKUMMEND AASTAT APOSTLITE RADADEL, 1884-1934

Kausch, J J see PSYCHOLOGISCHE ABHANDLUNG UEBER DEN EINFLUSS DER TOENE UND INS BESONDERE DER MUSIK AUF DIE SEELE
KAUTENBERGER, PETER G., DIARY, MS MICR – (Diary of this private soldier in the American Civil War, commenting on his experiences whith the 46th Illinois Vounteer Infantry regiment, Company C, which participated in the seige of Mobile, AL, and later, garrison duty) – 1865 – 1r – 1 – us Western Res [920]
KAUTIONSFREIES KREIS-WOCHENBLATT FUER DEN KREIS ADENAU UND UMGEGEND – Adenau, jan 7 1853-66 – 1 – Dist. gw Mikrofilm – gw Misc Inst [943]
KAUTSCHUK UND GUMMI KUNSTSTOFFE – v14-28. 1961-75 – 1,5,6 – us Princeton Micro [073]
Kautsky, Karl see ETHIK UND MATERIALISTISCHE GESCHICHTSAUFFASSUNG
Kautz, Robert E see COMPARING TORT LIABILITY KNOWLEDGE OF FUTURE TEACHER COACHES AND CURRENT PRACTICING TEACHER COACHES
Kautzsch, E see DIE GENESIS: MIT AUSSERER UNTERSCHEIDUNG DER QUELLENSCHRIFTEN
Kautzsch, Emil see
- DIE BLEIBENDE BEDEUTUNG DES ALTEN TESTAMENTS
- DIE POESIE UND DIE POETISCHEN BUECHER DES ALTEN TESTAMENTS

Kautzsch, Emil F see
- DIE APOKRYPHEN UND PSEUDEPIGRAPHEN DES ALTEN TESTAMENTS
- DIE ARAMAISMEN IM ALTEN TESTAMENT UNTERSUCHT

Kavanagh, Julia see WOMEN OF CHRISTIANITY
Kavass, Igor I see
- HUMAN RIGHTS, EUROPEAN POLITICS, AND THE HELSINKI ACCORD
- HUMAN RIGHTS, THE HELSINKI ACCORDS AND THE UNITED STATES

Kaverin, V see ISPOLNENIE ZHELANII
KAVI – Valka, 1910-13 – 1r – 1 – $75.00 – us Ross [072]
KAVI – Valka, De 1910 a 1913 – 1 reel – 1 – Sfr120.00 – sz Infoprint [947]
KAVKAZ – Munich. 1951-1954 – 1 – 35.00r – us Hoover Inst Photo [072]
KAVKAZSKII SBORNIK – v. 1-22. Tiflis. 1876-1901. B-1503 2 – 8 – ne IDC [073]
KAVKAZSKJI KNIZHNYI VESTNIK – Ezhemesiachnyi bibliograficheskii zhurnal. Tiflis. 1900-01. BR-4315 2 – 8 – ne IDC [010]
KAVKAZTSY ILI PODVIGI I USPEKHI ZAMECHATEL'NYKH LITS DEISTVOVAVSHIKH – V 1-3. Spb. 1857-59. BR-3201 2 – 8 – ne IDC [460]
Kavussanu, Maria et al see THE EFFECTS OF SINGLE VERSUS MULTIPLE MEASURES OF BIOFEEDBACK ON BASKETBALL FREE THROW SHOOTING PERFORMANCE
Kawakami, Kiyoshi Karl see JAPAN IN WORLD POLITICS
KAWAN TENTARA – Djakarta. 1949-51. v1-2 (1-17). TEN 1181. Lacking some issues. BSE-1732/1 – 9 – ne IDC [950]
Kawase, Kazuma see
- EDO BUNGAKU SOKWAN
- EDOJIDAI RYUZU JIBIKI DAIHUSEI
- MONOGATARI BUNGAKU SOKWAN

Kawase, Kazuma et al see EDO BAKUFU KANKOBUTSU SHUSHEI
KAWEAH COMMONWEALTH – Kaweah, CA. – 1r – 1 – $50.00 – B02321 – us Library Micro [071]
Kawerau, Gustav see
- DE DIGAMIA EPISCOPORUM
- HIERONYMUS EMSER
- JOHANN AGRICOLA VON EISLEBEN
- LUTHER IN KATHOLISCHER BELEUCHTUNG
- PAUL GERHARDT
- DIE VERSUCHE, MELANCHTHON ZUR KATHOLISCHEN KIRCHE ZURUECKZUFUEHREN

Kawerau, Waldemar see
- HANS SACHS UND DIE REFORMATION
- HERMANN SUDERMANN
- DIE REFORMATION UND DIE EHE
- THOMAS MURNER UND DIE DEUTSCHE REFORMATION
- THOMAS MURNER UND DIE KIRCHE DES MITTELALTERS

KAWHIA SETTLER AND RAGLAN ADVERTISER – New Zealand, 19 Jul 1902-15 Jun 1904 (imperfect) – 1r – 1 – uk British Libr Newspaper [072]
KAWI-BALINEESCH-NEDERLANDSCH WOORDENBOEK... / Tuuk, H N van der; ed by Brandes, J – Batavia, 1897-1912.- v1-4 – 65mf – 9 – SE-93/1 – ne IDC [430]
KAWI-DJARWA. DAMELANIPOEN W.J.S. POERWADARMINTA / Poerwadarminta, W J S – (Microfiche No 141) – Djakarta: Bale Poestaka, 2603 – 1mf – 9 – SE-2002/1 – ne IDC [950]
KAWKAB IFRIQIYA – Kaoukeb Ifrika puis Al-Kawkab al-Gaza-iri. Alger. 1908-juil 1914 – 1 – fr A.C.R.P.P. [073]
KAWKAB-OUL-MASCHRIK – Titre francais: L'Astre d'Orient. no. 1-36. Paris. juin 1882-mai 1883. mq no. 33 – 1 – fr A.C.R.P.P. [073]
Kay, Joseph see FREE TRADE IN LAND
Kay, William see CRISIS HUPFELDIANA
KAYASARE HINDA – (English and Gujarati languages) – Bombay, India. 1944-65; 1967-Apr 1981 – 47r – 1 – us L of C Photodup [072]
KAYGU – Trabzon, 1918-1919 – 9 – $57.00 – us MEDOC [956]
Kayguli, Sultan see DIVAN
Kaygulu, Efendi see DIVAN
KAYHAN – (Shumarah-'i 10799-11248 (13 Shahrivar 1358-11 Farvardin 1360[4 Sep 1979-31 Mar 1981]); shumarah-'i 11537-12117 (7 Farvardin 1362-28 Isfand 1362[27 Mar 1983-18 Mar 1984]). Missing issues: 10844, 10846, 10849, 10968, 11027, 11039-11045, 11074, 11107, 11110, 11113-11115, 11137, 11147, 11159, 11167, 11186, 11191, 11542, 11585, 11610, 11671, 11702, 11730, 11861, 11865, 11874, 11885, 12009, 12103) – Tehran – 27r – 1 – $500.00 – us MEDOC [950]
Kaynak, Erdener see
- JOURNAL OF EAST-WEST BUSINESS
- JOURNAL OF EUROMARKETING
- JOURNAL OF GLOBAL MARKETING
- JOURNAL OF INTERNATIONAL CONSUMER MARKETING
- JOURNAL OF INTERNATIONAL FOOD AND AGRIBUSINESS MARKETING
- JOURNAL OF TEACHING IN INTERNATIONAL BUSINESS

Kayser, August see DIE THEOLOGIE DES ALTEN TESTAMENTS
Kayser, Brigitte see MOEGLICHKEITEN UND GRENZEN INDIVIDUELLER FREIHEIT
Kayser, Christian Gottlob see VOLLSTAENDIGES BUECHER-LEXIKON, ENTHALTEND ALLE VON 1750 IN DEUTSCHLAND UND DEN ANGRENZENDEN LAENDERN GEDRUCKTEN BUECHER
Kayser, Gabriel see
- BIBLIOGRAPHIE D'OUVRAGES AYANT TRAIT A L'AFRIQUE EN GENERAL DANS SES RAPPORTS AVEC L'EXPLORATION AND LA CIVILISATION DE SES CONTREES...
- BIBLIOGRAPHIE D'OUVRAGES AYANT TRAIT A L'AFRIQUE EN GENERAL DANS SES RAPPORTS AVEC L'EXPLORATION, ET LA CIVILISATION DE CES CONTREES

Kayser, J C see DEUTSCHLANDS SCHMETTERLINGE, MIT BERUECKSICHTIGUNG SAEMMTLICHER EUROPAEISCHER ARTEN
KAYSERI – Kayseri. Mesul Mueduerue: Hamdi. No. 41 (8 Mart 1926) – 9 – $20.00 – us MEDOC [949]
KAYSERLICH-PRIVILEGIRTE HAMBURGISCHE NEUE ZEITUNG – (Several title changes: 1806 Hamburgische Neue Zeitung. 1824 Hamburgische Address-Comtoir-Nachrichten. 1826 Hamburgische Neue Zeitung. 1831 Neue Zeitung. 1838 Hamburger Neue Zeitung) – Hamburg, DE. 1767-1826 – 55r – 1 – gw Mikrofilm [072]
Kayserling, M see
- BIBLIOTECA ESPANOLA-PORTUGUEZA-JUDAICA
- MENASSE BEN ISRAEL, SEIN LEBEN UND WIRKEN
- NOTES SUR LA LITTERATURE DES JUIFS HISPANO-PORTUGAIS
- SEPHARDIM

KAZACHESTVO DONA, KUBANI I TEREKA V REVOLIUTSII 1905-1907 GG / Muzhev, I F – Ordzhonikidze, 1963 – 1 – $35.00r – us Hoover Inst Photo [947]
KAZACH'I DUMY – Sofia, Bulgaria. Feb-Jun 1922 – 1r – 1 – us L of C Photodup [949]
KAZACHI I NABAT = KOZACK Y POPLACH – (Includes c.1: no.11 1933:Nov.1-no.16 (1934:Sept.1); no.18 1934:Oct.18-no.24 (1937:June 30); no.30 1940:Jan.5) – Praha: G. Cap cikov, 193u – 1 – CSUXAHZ3430-S – us Hoover Inst Photo [947]
KAZACHI I PUT (PARIS, FRANCE) – (Library has no. 1, 3-6 (Oct. 1934-Oct. 1936)) – Paris: "Kazachi i put", 1934- – 1 – CSUX88-S490 – us Hoover Inst Photo [947]

KAZACHI I VESTNIK = DER KOSAKENBOTE : ORGAN KAZACHEGO NAT SIONALNOGO DVIZHENII A – (Includes c.1: v.6:no.1=no.92 1951:June 15-; v.7:no.1=no.94 1952: Jan.15) – Praga: Kasakenb uro, 193u – 1 – CSUXAKF0210-S – us Hoover Inst Photo [947]
Kazachiago Komiteta pri T S.I.K.S.R.K.S. i K.D. *see* TRUDOVOE KAZACHESTVO
KAZAKHSTAN, EKONOMIKA I ZHIZN' – (Comes in Russian) – 1 – sz Infoprint [330]
KAZAKHSTANSKAI A PRAVDA – (Library has holdings (incomplete) from between Mar. 16, 1945 and Dec. 21, 1945) – Alma-Ata: Kommunisticheskai a partii a Kazakhstana, 19uu – 1 – CSUX88-S475 – us Hoover Inst Photo [947]
KAZAKHSTANSKAIA PRAVDA = THE TRUTH OF KAZAKHTAN – (Comes in Russian) – 1920- – 1 – sz Infoprint [947]
KAZAKHSTANSKAYA PRAVDA – Kazakhstan, USSR. 1962-1980 – 20r – $1,000.00 – B63588 – us Library Micro [072]
KAZAKHSTANSKAYA PRAVDA – Kazakhstan. U.S.S.R. (Alma-Ata). 1955-1970 – 1 – us UMI [072]
Kazakova, Iskhaka *see* BICH NARODA
Kazan. Academy *see* SISTEMATICHESKII KATALOG KNIG FUNDAMENTAL'NOI BIBLIOTEKI KAZANSKOI DUKHOVNOI AKADEMII
Kazan Universitet. Russia *see*
- PROTOKOLY ZASIEDANII OBSHCHESTVA ESTESTVOISPYTATELEI PRI IMPERATORSKOM KAZANSKOM UNIVERSITETIE
- TRUDY IURIDICHESKAGO OBSHCHESTVA, SOSTOIASCHCHAGO PRI IMP. KAZANSKOM UNIVERSITETE
- UCHENYE ZAPISKI I. KAZANSKOGO UNIVERSITETA PO OTDELENIIU ISTORIKO-FILOLOGICHESKIKH I POLITIKO-IURIDICHESKIKH NAUK
- UCHENYE ZAPISKI KAZANSKOGO GOSUDARSTVENNOGO UNIVERSITETA

Kazancigil, Ali *see* STATE IN GLOBAL PERSPECTIVE
Kazanir, A S *see* KOMMENTARII K UGOLOVNO-PROTSESSUAL'NOMU KODEKSU MOLDAVSKOI SSR
KAZANSKIE GUBERNSKIE VEDOMOSTI – 1838-1917 – 94r – 1 – $8,400.00 coll – us Ross [072]
KAZANSKIE IZVESTIIA – 1811-20 – 6r – 1 – $480.00 – us Ross [072]
Kazanskii, P E *see*
- NARODNOST'I GOSUDARSTVO
- VLAST' VSEROSSIISKAGO IMPERATORA
- VSEOBSHCHIE ADMINISTRATIVNYE SOIUZY GOSUDARSTV
- VVEDENIE K KURSE MEZHDUNARODNOGO PRAVA

Kazim *see* DIVANCE
Kazimi, Avnullah [Mehmet Selim] *see* DIVAN-I OERFI VE AVNULLAH KAZIMI
KAZIRNA *see* AL-KAZIRNA
Kaznacheev, Aleksandr IUr'evich *see* INSIDE A SOVIET EMBASSY
Kaznelson, B *see*
- KITVEI NAHMAN SYRKIN
- THE NEXT STAGE IN PALESTINE
- REACTION AND PROGRESS IN PALESTINE
- REVOLUTIONARY CONSTRUCTIVISM

KC BLAETTER – Monatsschrift der im Kartell-Convent der Verbindungen deutscher Studenten Juedischen Glaubens vereinigten Korporationen. Cologne, Berlin. v1-23. 1910-1933. Complete. B261 (Leo Baeck Institute. German-Jewish Periodicals, Pt 1) – 2r – 1 – $135.00 – us UPA [270]
KCT – Itacoatiara, Amazonas. 8 Jun-Dez 1917; Ago-31 Out 1918 – 1,5,6 – bl Biblioteca [072]
KCT : ORGAM INDEPENDENTE, DEFENSOR DO DIREITO E DA VERDADE – Manaos, Amazonas, 3-13 Mar 1927 – 1,5,6 – bl Biblioteca [072]
Keach, Benjamin *see*
- BREACH REPAIRED IN GOD'S WORSHIP
- EXAMINATION OF MR. ISAAC MARLOW'S TWO PAPERS, ONE CALLED A DISCOURSE AGAINST SINGING, ETC., THE OTHER, AN APPENDIX
- INSTRUCTIONS FOR CHILDREN
- SPIRITUAL MELODY, CONTAINING THREE HUNDRED SACRED HYMNS
- TROPOLOGIA: A KEY TO OPEN SCRIPTURE-METAPHORS

KEADILAN; MADJALAH PEMOEDA SOSIALIS INDONESIA – (Lacking: 1946, V.1(2-3, 5-6)) – Modjokerto, 1946 – 4mf – 9 – ne IDC [300]
Keane, A H *see* AFRICA
Keane, John *see* REPORT ON IRRIGATION IN CEYLON
Keane, John J *see* CHRISTIAN EDUCATION IN AMERICA
KEARAH KEMAKMOERAN DAN KEADILAN SOSIAL DI LAPANGAN EKONOMI / Dipokusumo, S – SE-5346 1. 1945 – 9 – ne IDC [338]
KEARNEY COUNTY DEMOCRAT – Minden, NE. -w. Jan 1886-Jun 1893 – 1 – us NE Hist [071]
KEARNEY COUNTY NEWS – Minden, NE. -w. (-sw 1962-67). Mar 1960 to date – 1 – us NE Hist [071]
KEARNEY DAILY HUB – Kearney, NE. Jun 1889 to date – 1 – us NE Hist [071]
KEARNEY DAILY NEWS – Kearney, NE. (-sw 1919-20). Sep 1893; Aug 1896; Sep 1896-Aug 1899; Oct 1899-Aug 1900; Oct 1900-Sep 1901; Nov 1901-Jun 1902, scattered issues missing; Aug 1902-Apr 1938; Apr 1939-Dec 1941 – 1 – us NE Hist [071]
KEARNEY MORNING TIMES – Kearney, NE. -d. Jun 1909-Oct 1917 – 1 – us NE Hist [071]
KEARNEY WEEKLY TIMES – Kearney, NE. Aug 1880-Aug 1882, scattered issues missing; Sep 1882-Aug 1889; Dec 1892; Aug 1895-Jan 1901; Apr 1901-Dec 1909; Jun 1910-Jan 1913 – 1 – us NE Hist [071]
KEARNY COUNTY ADVOCATE – Lakin. Kan. 1885-1920 – 1 – us UMI [071]
Keary, Charles Francis *see*
- OUTLINES OF PRIMITIVE BELIEF AMONG THE INDO-EUROPEAN RACES
- THE VIKINGS IN WESTERN CHRISTENDOM, A.D. 789 TO A.D. 888

Keary, W H *see* REPORT ON ALL THE HOLKHAM ESTATES
Keasbey, Edward Quinton *see* THE LAW OF ELECTRIC WIRES IN STREETS AND HIGHWAYS
Keate, Henry *see* GUIDE TO MARINE INSURANCE
Keating *see* LIVINGSTON COUNTY DIRECTORY 1873-1874
Keatinge, Maurice Walter *see* THE GREAT DIDACTIC OF JOHN AMOS COMENIUS
Keatley, Hettie A *see* A COMPENDIUM OF EDENBURG AND EDENBURG PEOPLE
KEATS / Murry, John Middleton – (Studies in Keats). 4th ed. rev. and enl. London: Cape, (1955). 322p. illus. First ed. publ. in 1930 with title: Studies in Keats – 1 – us U.W. Library [420]
KEAT'S GREAT ODES; A RECONSIDERATION OF THE FIVE ODES WHICH REDEEM ROMANTICISM / Megally, Shafik – Zug, 1974. BNE-386/1 – 9 – ne IDC [420]
Keats, John *see*
- ENDYMION
- LETTERS OF JOHN KEATS TO FANNY BRAWNE
- MANUSCRIPT MATERIAL
- THE POETICAL WORKS OF JOHN KEATS

KEBANGOENAN : MADJALAH RASMI KABOEPATEN KARO – (Lacking: 1946 v1 (1-4,7)) – Kabandjahe, 1946-1947 – 4mf – 9 – ne IDC [950]
Kebbaj, Abd el Khalek *see* LES LEGUMINEUSES, LES GRAINES OLEAGINEUSES CONDIMENTAIRES ET DIVERSES AU MAROC; ETUDE STATISTIQUE, 1965
KEBEBASAN JANG KELIMA ADALAH SENDJATA KITA; SALAH SATU PEDOMAN PELAKSANAAN MANIPOL / Sukarno, Pres. Indonesia – SE 5325 1. 1965 – 9 – ne IDC [025]
KEBEC / Dufresne, Guy – 1958. SEM35P109 – 1r – 1 – Can$15.00 – cn Bibl Nat [890]
KEBEC *see* ETOILES DE KEBEC
Keble, John *see*
- THE CHRISTIAN YEAR
- OCCASIONAL PAPERS AND REVIEWS
- SERMONS, ACADEMICAL AND OCCASIONAL
- STUDIA SACRA

KEBOEDAJAAN TIMOER – Djakarta, Keimin Bunka Shidosho, 2603-2605. 3v – 330-336mf – 9 – ne IDC [073]
KEBUDAJAAN DALAM PEMBANGUNAN SEMESTA / Rachman, Asj'ari, Abd – SE-4047 1. 1961 – 9 – ne IDC [950]
Keck, Karl Heinrich *see* DIE GUDRUNSAGE
KEDAH GOVERNMENT GAZETTE – Kedah, [Malaysia], 1958-70 – 6r – 1 – us Ross [324]
KEDAULATAN RAKJAT – Jogjakarta. Indonesia. 1957-1959; 1961- – 1 – us UMI [072]
KEDEM, KOVEZ LE-HEKER KADMONIYYOT YISRA'EL – Ed. by E. L. Sukenik. v. 1-2. Jerusalem. 1942, 1945. BJ-100-182 1 – 9 – ne IDC [900]
Keding, Karl *see* FELDGEISTLICHER BEI LEGION CONDOR: SPANISCHES KRIEGSTAGEBUCH EINES EVANGELISCHEN LEGIONSPFARRERS
KEDLESTON HALL, DERBYSHIRE: ACCOUNTS AND PAPERS RELATING TO THE BUILDING – c.1758-70 – 1 – uk Microform Academic [941]
KEDOEDOEKAN BANGSA TIONGHOA DI INDONESIA; DE POSITIE DER CHINEEZEN IN INDONESIE / Liem, Khiam Soen – In Indonesian and Dutch. SE-4679 1. 1947 – 9 – ne IDC [305]
Keedy, John Lincoln *see* TEACHERS' BOOK OF OLD TESTAMENT HEROES
Keele, Alan F *see* KONKORDANZ ZU WALTER KEMPOWSKIS "DEUTSCHER CHRONIK"
Keele. Staffordshire *see* PARISH REGISTERS
Keeler, Bronson C *see* A SHORT HISTORY OF THE BIBLE
Keeler, Charles *see* SAN FRANCISCO AND THEREABOUTS
Keeler, L W *see*
- EX SUMMA PHILIPPI CANCELLARII QUESTIONES DE ANIMA
- EX SUMMA PHILIPPI CANCELLARII QUESTIONES DE ANIMA. OPUSC. ET TEXTUS SER. SCHOL. FASC. 20

Keeling, A E *see* EMINENT METHODIST WOMEN
Keen, James T *see* A MANUAL FOR NOTARIES PUBLIC, JUSTICES OF THE PEACE, AND THEIR EMPLOYERS IN MASSACHUSETTS
Keenan, Karen A *see* THE EFFECT OF HEAT AND COLD ON ANKLE STABILITY
Keenan, S *see* EDUCATION AND TRAINING OF USERS OF SCIENTIFIC AND TECHNICAL INFORMATION
Keene, Derek *see* HISTORICAL GAZETTEER OF LONDON BEFORE THE GREAT FIRE
Keene, New Hampshire. Keene Baptist Church *see* MANUSCRIPT HISTORIES
Keener, John *see*
- PUBLIC LAND LAWS OF THE UNITED STATES

Keener, William Albert *see* A SELECTION OF CASES ON THE LAW OF PRIVATE CORPORATIONS
Keep, J *see* WEST AMERICAN SHELLS
KEEPING POSTED WITH NCSY – New York, NY. 1962-83. National Conference of Synagogue Youth – 1 – us A.J.P.C. [071]
KEEPING THE LAND ALIVE. SOIL EROSION: ITS CAUSES AND CURES – 1983 – 95p – it F.A.O. [631]
KEEPSAKE – 1828-57 – 115mf – 9 – £725.00 – uk Chadwyck [800]
Keerl, Philipp Friedrich *see* DIE EINHEIT DER BIBLISCHEN URGESCHICHTE (1 MOS 1-3)
Keersmaecker, Jacob de *see*
- IN DIT TEGENWOORDIGHE BOECXKEN ZIJN VEEL SCHOONE ENDE LIEFLIJCKE BRIEUEN, VAN EENEN GHENAEMT JACOB DE KEERSMAECKER
- IN DIT TEGENWOORDIGHE BOECXKEN ZIJN VEEL SCHOONE ENDE LIEFLIJCKE BRIEUEN, VAN EENEN GHENAEMT JACOB DE KEERSMAECKER

KEESING'S ARCHIV DER GEGENWART – Essen/Wien, 1931-Juli 1945 – 11r – 1 – DM1,100.00 – gw Mikro Press [072]
KEESING'S CONTEMPORARY ARCHIVES – Part 1: 1931-75; Part 2: 1976-80 – 9 – us Primary [025]
Keetch, Anita *see* EFFECTS OF ADHESIVE SPRAY AND PREWRAP ON TAPED ANKLE INVERSION BEFORE AND AFTER EXERCISE
KEETMANSHOOPER NACHRICHTEN – Keetmanshoop, South West Africa. 1911 – 1 – sa State Libr [072]
KEETMANSHOOPER ZEITUNG – Keetmanshoop, South West Africa. 1912-14 – 1 – sa State Libr [072]
Keeves, John P *see* NATIONAL EXAMINATIONS
Keezer, Frank H *see* THE LAW OF MARRIAGE AND DIVORCE
Keffer, Frank M *see* HISTORY OF THE SAN FERNANDO VALLEY
KEGAGALAN ILMU BAHASA MODERN DALAM MENGHADAPI SOAL2 BAHASA ABAD KEDUA PULUH / Alisjahbana, Sutan Takdir – SE-5331 1965 – 9 – ne IDC [950]
KEHIDUPAN SUKU-SUKU IRIAN BARAT / Slamet, Ina E – SE 5634 1. 1964 – 9 – ne IDC [950]
KEHLER ZEITUNG : BA DES OFFENBURGER TAGEBLATTS – Kehl, West Germany. 6 Oct 1978- – ca 9r per yr – 1 – gw Mikrofilm [072]
Kehr, C *see* DER CHRISTLICHE RELIGIONS-UNTERRICHT
Kehr, PF *see* REGESTA PONTIFICUM ROMANORUM
Kehrein, Josef *see* BIOGRAPHISCH-LITERARISCHES LEXIKON DER KATHOLISCHEN DEUTSCHEN DICHTER, VOLKS-UND JUNGENDSCHRIFTSTELLER IM 19. JAHRHUNDERT
Kehukee Baptist Association. North Carolina *see* MATERIALS
Keidel, Heinrich *see* DIE DRAMATISCHEN VERSUCHE DES JUNGEN GRILLPARZER
Keifer, Joseph Warren *see* SLAVERY AND FOUR YEARS OF WAR
KEIGHLEY LABOUR JOURNAL – Yorkshire. 1894-1902 – 1 – uk Microform Academic [072]
Keigwin, Charles Albert *see* CASES IN COMMON LAW ACTIONS.
Keil, Carl Friedrich *see*
- COMMENTAR UEBER DEN BRIEF AN DIE HEBRAEER
- COMMENTAR UEBER DIE BRIEFE DES PETRUS UND JUDAS

Keil, E et al *see* PARTICLE ACCELERATORS
Keil, Heinrich *see* GRAMMATICI LATINI
Keil, Karl Friedrich *see* COMMENTARY ON THE BOOKS OF KINGS
Keil, Richard *see* GOETHE, WEIMAR UND JENA IM JAHRE 1806
Keil, Robert *see*
- AUS KLASSISCHER ZEIT
- GOETHE, WEIMAR UND JENA IM JAHRE 1806

Keilin, A D *see* MORSKOE PRAVO
DIE KEILINSCHRIFTEN AM EINGANGE DER QUELLGROTTE DES SEBENEH-SU / Schrader, Eberhard – (Discussion in German; texts in Akkadian and German) – Berlin: Koenigl Akademie der Wissenschaften, 1885 – 1mf – 9 – 0-8370-8617-5 – 1986-2617 – us A.T.L.A. [470]
KEILINSCHRIFTLICH BIBLIOTHEK : SAMMLUNG VON ASSYRISCHEN UND BABYLONISCHEN TEXTEN / ed by Schrader, Eberhard – Berlin. 6v. 1889-1900 – 29mf – 9 – ne IDC [956]
KEILINSCHRIFTLICHES TEXTBUCH ZUM ALTEN TESTAMENT / Winckler, Hugo – (Akkadian texts and German Translations. Includes bibliographical references) – 2. neu bearb Aufl. Leipzig: J C Hinrichs, 1903 – 1mf – 9 – 0-8370-7276-X – 1986-1276 – us A.T.L.A. [220]
Keill, J *see* THE ANATOMY OF THE HUMANE BODY
Keilmann, Wilhelm *see* PALLA TOA
KEILSCHRIFT URKUNDEN AUS BOGHARSKOEI – Staatliche Museum zu Berlin. Vorderasiatische Abt. v. 29-34. Berlin. 1938. BNE-416 – 9 – ne IDC [930]
KEILSCHRIFTLICHE ACTEN-STUECKE AUS BABYLONISCHEN STAEDTEN : VON STEINEN UND TAFELN DES BERLINER MUSEUMS IN AUTOGRAPHIE, TRANSSCRIPTION UND UEBERSETZUNG / Peiser, Felix Ernst – (Discussion in German. Texts in German and Akkadian) – Berlin: Wolf Peiser, 1889 – 1mf – 9 – 0-8370-7320-0 – 1986-1320 – us A.T.L.A. [470]
KEILSCHRIFTTEXTE : ZUM GEBRAUCH BEI VORLESUNGEN / ed by Abel, Ludwig – (In Akkadian and German) – Berlin: W Spemann, 1890 – 1mf – 9 – 0-8370-8560-8 – 1986-2560 – us A.T.L.A. [470]
Keim, Theodor *see* DER GESCHICHTLICHE CHRISTUS
Keiper, Wilhelm *see* FRIEDRICH LEOPOLD STOLBERGS JUGENDPOESIE
Keiser, C E *see* SELECTED TEMPLE DOCUMENTS
Keiter, Heinrich *see*
- HEINRICH HEINE
- KONFESSIONELLE BRUNNENVERGIFTUNG

KEITERS KATHOLISCHER LITERATURKALENDER *see* KATHOLISCHER LITERATURKALENDER
Keith, Arthur Berriedale *see*
- IMPERIAL UNITY AND THE DOMINIONS
- THE SAMKHYA SYSTEM
- SPEECHES AND DOCUMENTS ON INDIAN POLICY, 1750-1921

KEITH CO. NEWS – Ogallala. Neb. 1885-1964 – 1 – us UMI [071]

KEITH COUNTY NEWS – Ogallala, NE. -w. (-sw 1946 to date). Sept 1885-Jul 1892; Aug 1895-Feb 1904, scattered issues missing; May 1904-Jul 1913; Oct 1913 to date – 1 – us NE Hist [071]

Keith, G *see* TRAVELS AND VOYAGES

Keith, J B *see* FORTRESS GWALIOR

KEITH'S COLLECTION OF INSTRUMENTAL MUSIC – containing marches, quicksteps, waltzes, airs, cotillons sic, contra-dances, hornpipes, quadrilles (arranged with figures) Scotch and Irish jigs, reels, strathspeys, arranged for brass, wooden, and strings instruments. No. 1. To be completed in six numbers. Boston: Keith's Music Publishing House, 1844. Music is arranged in four parts. MUSIC 1992 – 1 – us L of C Photodup [780]

KEIZER NEWS – Salem, OR. -w. 11 Feb 1965-29 May 1968. 2 rolls – 1 – us U.O. Library [071]

KEIZERTIMES – Keizer OR. Mar 7 1980 + – 1 – us U.O. Library [071]

KEJSARDOEMETS QVINNOR = FRAUEN DES KAISERREICHS : SKISSER FRAN DET NAPOLEONSKA PARIS / Wachenhusen, Hans – (Swedish translation from German) – Stockholm: Associations-Boktryckeriet, 1870 – 1r – 1 – us U.W. Library [430]

KEKOEATAN PROLETAR / Sandra – SE 4189 1. 1946 – 9 – ne IDC [950]

Kekuatov, K V *see*
- KOOPERATSIIA I PRAVO
- ZAKON OB USTROISTVE SEL'SKOGO KREDITA I ZEMSTVO

Kelaart, E F *see*
- FLORA CALPENSIS
- PRODROMUS FAUNAE ZEYLANICAE

KELAPA – Bandung: G. Kolff, 195?. BSEM-3058/1 – 9 – ne IDC [950]

KELCHIS ADVANCE – Tillamook, OR. 18 Dec 1880-28 Mar 1882. 1 roll – 1 – us U.O. Library [071]

KELEBEK – Sene 1-2, nos 1-77 (1339-1340) – 23mf – 9 – $175.00 – us MEDOC [949]

KELEDOR, HISTOIRE AFRICAINE / Roger, Jacques F – Paris, A. Nepveu. 1828 – 9 – 7.50 – fr Orientalistes [960]

Kelemina, Jakob *see* UNTERSUCHUNGEN ZUR TRISTANSAGE

KELENGKAPAN TARICH NABI MUHAMMAD / Chalil, H Munawar – Indonesian or Arabic. SE-4747 1. v. 1 only. 1964- – 9 – ne IDC [950]

KELET – Nyiregyhaza, Hungary. 1962-72 – 16r – 1 – us L of C Photodup [072]

KELETI SZEMLE (REVUE ORIENTALE POUR LES ETUDES OURALO-ALTAIQUES) – Budapest. 1900-32. v1-21. – 125mf – 8 – ne IDC [490]

Kelham, R *see* A DICTIONARY OF THE NORMAN OR OLD FRENCH LANGUAGE

Kelker, Luther R *see* HISTORY OF DAUPHIN COUNTY

Kelland, Clarence Budington *see* QUIZZER NO. 20; BEING QUESTIONS AND ANSWERS ON INSURANCE.

Kelland, Jill *see* THE LEVEL OF PROFESSIONALISM AMONG THERAPEUTIC RECREATION PRACTITIONERS IN ALBERTA, CANADA

Kelleher-Walsh, Barbara J *see* DEVELOPMENT OF A CHILD INJURY DATA BASE FOR USE IN BIOMECHANICS RESEARCH

Keller, Gabriele *see* MONITORING UND GEOTECHNISCHE ANALYSE VON MASSENBEWEGUNGEN IN FLYSCH UND FALTEN-MOLASSE DES GUNZESRIEDER TALS (OBERALLGAEU)

Keller, Gottfried *see*
- ABRAHAM A SANCTA CLARA (1644-1709)
- AUSGEWAEHLTE ERZAEHLUNGEN
- DIE DREI GERECHTEN KAMMACHER
- DAS FAEHNLEIN DER SIEBEN AUFRECHTEN
- GESAMMELTE GEDICHTE
- DER GRUENE HEINRICH
- NOVELLEN
- ROMEO UND JULIA AUF DEM DORFE
- ZUERICHER NOVELLEN

Keller, Ludwig *see*
- EIN APOSTEL DER WIEDERTAEUFER
- GESCHICHTE DER WIEDERTAEUFER UND IHRES REICHS ZU MUENSTER
- JOHANN VON STAUPITZ UND DIE ANFAENGE DER REFORMATION
- DIE REFORMATION UND DIE AELTEREN REFORMPARTEIEN
- DIE WALDENSER UND DIE DEUTSCHEN BIBELUEBERSETZUNGEN
- ZUR GESCHICHTE DER ALTEVANGELISCHEN GEMEINDEN

Keller, Rudi *see* UEBER DEN BEGRIFF DER PRAESUPPOSITION

Kellermann, Benzion *see*
- DER MIDRACH ZUM I. BUCHE SAMUELIS UND SEINE SPUREN BEI KIRCHENVAETERN UND IN DER ORIENTALISCHEN SAGE.
- DER MIDRASCH ZUM I. BUCHE SAMUELIS UND SEINE SPUREN BEI KIRCHENVAETERN

Kelley, B C *see* AN EXAMINATION OF A MODEL OF BURNOUT IN DUAL-ROLE TEACHER-COACHES

Kelley, Fanny *see* FANNY KELLEY V. SARAH L. LARIMER, ET AL

Kelley, Francis Clement *see* MEXICO, EL PAIS DE LOS ALTARES ENSANGRENTADOS. DOCUMENTOS Y NOTAS DE EBER COLE BYAM

Kelley, Henry Smith *see*
- A TREATISE ON CRIMINAL LAW AND PRACTICE: COMPRISING GENERALLY THE STATUTES OF MISSOURI.
- A TREATISE ON THE LAW RELATING TO THE POWERS AND DUTIES OF JUSTICES OF THE PEACE, CONSTABLES, ETC., ETC., IN THE STATE OF MISSOURI.

KELLEY, IRAD, PAPERS, MS 485 – 1791-1875 – 2r – 1 – us Western Res [650]

Kelley, Kristi S *see* AN ASSESSMENT OF THE HEALTH HABITS AND COUNSELING PRACTICES OF PHYSICIANS

Kelley, Robert *see*
- 100 YEARS OF THE COMMERCIAL APPEAL 1840-1940

KELLEYTOWN BAPTIST CHURCH. DARLINGTON COUNTY. HARTSVILLE, SOUTH CAROLINA : CHURCH RECORDS – 1923-72. (Fragments of 1923-65) – 1 – 5.00 – us Baptist [240]

Kellie, E I *see* A HISTORY OF BETHLEHEM BAPTIST ASSOCIATION

Kellison, Barbara *see* THE RIGHTS OF WOMEN IN THE CHURCH

Kellner, David *see*
- TREULICHER UNTERRICHT IM GENERAL-BASS

Kellner, Heinrich *see* HELLENISMUS UND CHRISTENTHUM, ODER, DIE GEISTIGE REAKTION DES ANTIKEN HEIDENTHUMS GEGEN DAS CHRISTENTHUM

Kellner, Johann C *see* SIX FUGUES FOR THE ORGAN OR HARPSICHORD

Kellner, Karl Adam Heinrich *see*
- HEORTOLOGY
- HEORTOLOGY SIC; A HISTORY OF THE CHRISTIAN FESTIVALS FROM THEIR ORIGIN TO THE PRESENT DAY

Kellner, Maximilian *see*
- THE ASSYRIAN MONUMENTS ILLUSTRATING THE SERMONS OF ISAIAH
- DELUGE IN THE IZDUBAR EPIC AND IN THE OLD TESTAMENT
- THE PROPHECIES OF ISAIAH

KELLOCK'S LIST OF STEAMSHIPS AND SAILING VESSELS FOR SALE – Liverpool, England. Oct 1895-1906 – 1r – 1 – uk British Libr Newspaper [380]

Kellogg, Frank B *see* PAPERS

Kellogg, Moses Eastman *see* THE VISION OF THE EVENING AND THE MORNING

Kellogg, Samuel Henry *see* THE BOOK OF LEVITICUS

Kellogg, SH *see* A GRAMMAR OF THE HINDI LANGUAGE...HIGH HINDI, BRAJ, EASTERN HINDI...ALSO COLLOQUIAL DIALECTS OF RAJPUTANA, KUMAON, AVADH, RIWA, BHOJPUR, MAGADHA, MAITHILA, ETC

Kelly, Bernard William *see* HISTORICAL NOTES ON ENGLISH CATHOLIC MISSIONS

Kelly, E *see* THE FRENCH LAW OF MARRIAGE...

Kelly, Edward *see* DIARY

Kelly, Fred T *see* THE STROPHIC STRUCTURE OF HABAKKUK

Kelly, H *see* A WORD TO THE WISE

Kelly, Helen G *see* A STUDY OF INDIVIDUAL DIFFERENCES IN BREATHING CAPACITY

Kelly, Herbert *see* THE CHURCH AND RELIGIOUS UNITY

Kelly, James *see* THE ETERNAL PURPOSE OF GOD IN CHRIST JESUS OUR LORD

Kelly, James J *see* JOURNAL OF GAY AND LESBIAN SOCIAL SERVICES

Kelly, John Eogan *see* PEDRO DE ALVARADO, CONQUISTADOR. PRINCETON, 1932

Kelly, K Patrick *see* EFFECT OF CHRONIC COCAINE ON SELECTED PHYSIOLOGICAL RESPONSES DURING REST AND EXERCISE IN RATS

Kelly, Kathryn D *see* THE RELATIONSHIP OF PELVIC GIRDLE ASYMMETRIES AND LOW BACK PAIN

Kelly, Luke E *see* MICROCOMPUTER ASISTANCE FOR EDUCATORS IN PRESCRIBING ADAPTED PHYSICAL EDUCATION

Kelly, M *see* [BLUEBEARD] THE GRAND MARCH...FOR THE PIANOFORTE...

Kelly, Mary E H *see* SAND IN THEIR CRAWS

Kelly, Thomas E *see* WHO'S WHO IN MISSISSIPPI

Kelly, William *see*
- AN EXPOSITION OF THE GOSPEL OF MARK
- REVELATION

THE KELLYS AND THE O'KELLYS; OR, LANDLORDS AND TENANTS : A TALE OF IRISH LIFE / Trollope, Anthony – London: Henry Colburn, 1848 – 1 roll – 1 – 1-55879-979-6 – uk Libr Preservation [830]

KELLY'S DIRECTORIES – From Guildhall Library, London. 1841, 1851, 1861 – 1 – uk Microform Academic [941]

KELLY'S LONDON DIRECTORIES, 1900-1902 – 16r – 1 – uk Microform Academic [910]

Kel'man, E I *see*
- SOVETSKOE PRAVO PERED INOSTRANNYMI SUDAMI
- SOVETSKOE PRAVO ZA RUBEZHEM

KELOEARGA DAN ROEMAH TANGGA NIPPON. DISALIN DENGAN MERDEKA...OLEH TUN SRI LANANG / Akimoto, S – Medan ? Departemen Keboedajaan Soematera Timoer, 2604. 62p – 4mf – 9 – ne IDC [950]

Kelsall, J *see* MANUAL OF THE BELLARY DISTRICT

Kelsey, Dandridge E *see* DIARIES

KELSEYVILLE SUN – Kelseyville, CA. 1903-40 (broken series) – 5r – 1 – $250.00 – B02322 – us Library Micro [071]

THE KELSONIAN – Kelso. Wash. -w. 1906-12, 1914-20 – 1 – us UMI [071]

THE KELSONIAN TRIBUNE – Kelso, Wash. -w, d. 1923-26 – 1 – us UMI [071]

KELSUS TEXTE / Gloeckner, O – (Lietzmann, Kleine Texte, nr.151). Bonn. 1924. B-95 1 – 9 – ne IDC [400]

KELTIC RESEARCHES; STUDIES IN THE HISTORY AND DISTRIBUTION OF THE ANCIENT GOIDELIC LANGUAGE AND PEOPLES / Nicholson, Edward Williams Byron – London, New York: H. Frowde, Oxford University Press, 1904. xviii,211p. Plates,maps – 1 – us U.W. Library [490]

Keltie, Sir John Scott *see* HISTORY OF GEOGRAPHY

KELUARGA – Incomplete. SE-854 1. 1952-1971 – 9 – ne IDC [073]

KELUARGA BERENTJANA – Djakarta, 1967-72 (1-22). TEN 1199. Lacking: 1967(1-2). BSE-1740/1 – 9 – ne IDC [950]

KELUARGA SEDJAHTERA – Djakarta, Lembaga Keluarga Berentjana Nasional Indonesia. 1969-70 (1-10). TEN 1200. Lacking: 1969 (4).BSE-1741/1 – 9 – ne IDC [950]

Kelvin, William Thomson *see* REPRINT OF PAPERS ON ELECTROSTATICS AND MAGNETISM

Kemal, Ahmed *see* KITAB-I SUBHAT UEL-AHBAR

Kemal, Namik *see* AKIF BEY

Kemalpasazade *see* DIVAN

KEMANA BEKAS PEJUANG BERSENDJATA? / Sutomo – SE 10,630 1. 1952 – 9 – ne IDC [950]

KEMBALI KEPADA TJINTA KASIHMU / Tolstoi, Lev N – SE 6432 1. 1950.n – 9 – ne IDC [460]

KEMBANG PANTJAWARNA (BATJAAN ANAK2 UMUR 10-12 TAHUN) DITJERITAKAN KEMBALI / Sastrawinata, Saleh – SE 5195 1. 1964 – 9 – ne IDC [950]

Kemble, Fanny *see* RECORDS OF LATER LIFE

Kemble, J M *see* CODEX DIPLOMATICUS AEVI SAXONICI

KEMBLE PROMPT BOOKS IN THE GARRICK CLUB, LONDON / Garrick Club. London – (Complete collection covering period 1710-1821. With library index cards and printed guide. Individual fiches available) – 1986 – 104mf – 9 – $660.00 – 1-900853-70-1 – uk Mindata [790]

KEMENANGAN 2 SOSIALISME DI BULGARIA: TJATATAN 2 PENINDJAUAN DI BULGARIA / Amir – 1963. SE-5029 1 – 9 – ne IDC [949]

Kemenova, E V *see* OPISANIE RUKOPISEI A.I. GERTSENA

KEMENTERIAN PENERANGAN / East Indonesia – 1 year East Indonesia. SE-4925/1. Dec. 24, 1946-47 – 9 – ne IDC [950]

KEMENTERIAN PENERANGAN : SIARAN KILAT – Jogjakarta, 1946. Nos. 2,4,5 – 1mf – 9 – ne IDC [950]

KEMENTERIAN PENERANGAN : SIARAN KILAT – (Lacking: Pamphlet Nos. 2,7,11,13,15-17,19,20,22,24,26-28,35,39,41) – Djakarta, 1946. 45 pamphlets – 13mf – 9 – ne IDC [950]

KEMERDEKAAN INDONESIA; KUMPULAN PERTAMA / Subronto, K Atmodjo – SE 3946 1. 1962 – 9 – ne IDC [950]

Kemmer, A *see* CHARISMA MAXIMUM

Kemmerer, Frances *see* UTILIZING EDUCATION AND HUMAN RESOURCE SECTOR ANALYSES

Kemmerich, D H *see* GRUND-SAESSE DES VOELCKER-RECHTS...

Kemp *see* HEROES OF SAN JACINTO

Kemp, Dennis *see* NINE YEARS AT THE GOLD COAST

Kemp, John *see* "WHAT I REMEMBER OF THE BATTLE OF THE BLUE, AND INCIDENTS CONNECTED WITH IT"

Kemper, Dirk *see* MISSBRAUCHTE AUFKLAERUNG?

Kempis, Thomas a *see* L'IMITATION DE JESUS-CHRIST

Kempner, Alfred *see* BRENTANOS JUGENDDICHTUNGEN

Kempowski, Walter *see* KONKORDANZ ZU WALTER KEMPOWSKIS "DEUTSCHER CHRONIK"

KEMPTNER ZEITUNG – Kempten, Germany. 1848-Mar 1849 – 1r – 1 – gw Mikrofilm [072]

KEMPTON RURAL PRESS – Kempton, PA., 1888-1889 – 13 – $25.00r – us I.M.R. [071]

KEMPTVILLE TELEGRAM – (Some issues missing) – Ontario, CN. 1901-08 – 3r – 1 – cn Commonwealth Micro [072]

KEMPTVILLE WEEKLY ADVANCE – Kemptville, Ontario, CN. 1881- – 2r per yr – 1 – Can$55.00r – cn Commonwealth Micro [072]

Kenaani, J *see* HA-HAYYIM HA-KALKALIYYIM BI-ZEFAT U-VI-SEVIVOTEHA

KENANGAN BAHAGIA / Sutomo – SE 10,426 1. 1950? – 9 – ne IDC [950]

Kendall, H B *see*
- HISTORY OF THE PRIMITIVE METHODIST CHURCH
- THE ORIGIN AND HISTORY OF THE PRIMITVE METHODIST CHURCH
- 'WHAT HATH GOD WROUGHT!'

Kendig, Abby E G *see* HEINRICH HEINE'S AN ESSAY, READ BEFORE THE MONDAY CLUB, MAY 21ST, 1883

Kendrick, J R *see* DUELING (A SERMON)

Kendrick, Nathaniel *see* A SERMON DELIVERED IN THE CHAPEL OF THE BAPTIST LITERARY AND THEOLOGICAL SEMINARY, HAMILTON, NEW YORK, 19 MAR 1824

Kendrick, R J *see* A COMPARISON OF ISOMETRIC STRENGTH TEST RESULTS BETWEEN LOW BACK INJURED PATIENTS AND NORMALS

Kendrick, T D *see* SAINT JAMES IN SPAIN

Kendrick, Zebulon V *see*
- EFFECTS OF CALORIC RESTRICTION AND RESISTIVE EXERCISE ON THE RESTING ENERGY EXPENDITURE OF WEIGHT-REDUCED OBESE WOMEN
- EFFECTS OF THYMOPENTIN ON THE RESPONSES OF HYPOTHALAMIC-PITUITARY-ADRENAL AXIS TO A HIGH INTENSITY DYNAMIC EXERCISE PROTOCOL

KENEDER ADLER = THE JEWISH DAILY EAGLE – (Special Issues: 20th Anniversary – 1927; Centennial – First Jew Elected M.P. in Canada – 1932; 30th Anniversary – 1938; 50th Golden Jubilee – 1957 1r Can$50.00. In Yiddish 1r Can$70.00) – Montreal, CN. v2 no 263. 1908-1956 – 114r – 1 – Can$70.00r – cn Can Microfilming [072]

KENEDER ADLER – Montreal. (Jewish Daily Eagle). Oct 1908-Dec 1965. Incomplete – 1 – us NY Public [072]

DER KENEDER ALDER – Montreal, 1908-65 – 114r – 1 – us Ross [072]

KENEDER ID = THE CANADIAN JEW – Montreal, Quebec. 1935; 1938; 1941 – 1 – us A.J.P.C. [072]

KENESAW KALEIDOSCOPE – Kenesaw, NE. -w. Nov 1892-Jan 1896, scattered issues missing; Apr 1896-May 1898; Jan 1899-Jan 1901; May 1901-Jan 1913, scattered issues missing – 1 – us NE Hist [071]

KENESAW TIMES – Kenesaw, NE. -w. Mar 1974-Jul 1975 – 1 – us NE Hist [071]

KENESET – Odessa. 1917. BJ-91-45 1 – 9 – ne IDC [800]
KENESET – Tel Aviv. 1928. One issue only. Lacking: Nr. 2. BJ-91-90 1 – 9 – ne IDC [956]
KENESET HA-GEDOLAH / ed by Suwalski, I – v. 1-4. Warsaw. 1890-91. BJ-422-36 1 – 9 – ne IDC [470]
KENESET YISRA'EL – Warsaw. 1886-89. BJ-91-46 1 – 9 – ne IDC [470]
Kenfield, Scott D *see* AKRON AND SUMMIT COUNTY
KENG PO – Djakarta. Indonesia. 1953-54; 1956-57 – 1 – us UMI [072]
Kengne Pokam, E *see* LA RELIGION FACE AU POUVOIR POLITIQUE AU CAMEROUN
KENILWORTH OBSERVER – Jan 12-Dec 14 1995 – 8r – 9 – uk British Libr Newspaper [072]
KENILWORTH WEEKLY NEWS – England. 24 May 1949- – 56+ r – 1 – uk British Libr Newspaper [072]
Kennan, George *see* SIBERIA AND THE EXILE SYSTEM
Kennard, Richard *see* GILFIELD BAPTIST CHURCH, PETERSBURG, VIRGINIA, 1803-1903
KENNEBEC JOURNAL – Augusta, Maine. -w. 1825-1913 – 1 – us UMI [071]
KENNEBEC VALLEY, MAINE / Whitney – 1887. Maine Reel 2. (The Cox Library Collection) – 5 – us Americana [978]
KENNEDY ASSASSINATION – Dallas, TX. v1-10 L.A. Metro, A-Z; International A-Z – 8r – 1 – $400.00 – R05003 – us Library Micro [071]
Kennedy, Benjamin Hall *see* ELY LECTURES ON THE REVISED VERSION OF THE NEW TESTAMENT
Kennedy, C M *see* THE INFLUENCE OF CHRISTIANITY UPON INTERNATIONAL LAW
THE KENNEDY CLAN AND TIERRA REDONDA / Lynch, Alice Clare – San Francisco: Marnell & Co, Jan 1935 – 1r – 1 – $50.00 – B40254 – us Library Micro [978]
Kennedy, Gladys *see* EARLY HISTORY OF MOBILE BAPTISTS
Kennedy, H A A *see* ST. PAUL'S CONCEPTIONS OF THE LAST THINGS
Kennedy, Harold W *see* LEGAL SUPPORT FOR LOS ANGELES COUNTY'S STRICT AIR POLLUTION CONTROL PROGRAM
Kennedy, Harry Angus Alexander *see* SOURCES OF NEW TESTAMENT GREEK
Kennedy, Inez A *see* RECOLLECTIONS OF THE PIONEERS OF LEE COUNTY
Kennedy, James *see*
- NOTE-LINE IN THE HEBREW SCRIPTURES
- OBSERVATIONS ON PROFESSOR W. R. SMITH'S ARTICLE "BIBLE."

Kennedy, James Henry *see* THE BENCH AND BAR OF CLEVELAND
Kennedy, James Houghton *see*
- NATURAL THEOLOGY AND MODERN THOUGHT
- SECOND AND THIRD EPISTLES OF ST PAUL TO THE CORINTHIANS

Kennedy, John *see*
- BOOK OF DANIEL FROM THE CHRISTIAN STANDPOINT
- OLD TESTAMENT CRITICISM AND THE RIGHTS OF THE UNLEARNED
- ON THE BOOK OF JONAH
- THE PENTATEUCH
- A POPULAR ARGUMENT FOR THE UNITY OF ISAIAH

Kennedy, John F *see*
- APPOINTMENT BOOK OF PRESIDENT KENNEDY (1961-1963)
- MEMORIAL COLLECTION OF NEWSPAPERS ON MICROFILM CHRONICLING EVENTS OF THE ASSASSINATION
- PRESIDENT KENNEDY AND THE PRESS (1961-1963)
- PROFILES IN COURAGE

Kennedy, John Pendleton *see*
- THE JOHN PENDLETON KENNEDY PAPERS
- JOURNALS OF THE HOUSE OF BURGESSES OF VIRGINIA, 1619-1776

Kennedy, Margrit I *see* BUILDING COMMUNITY SCHOOLS
Kennedy, R J Sinclair *see* NON-EXTINCTION OF CHRISTIANITY
Kennedy, Robert Francis *see* WE MUST MEET OUR DUTY AND CONVINCE THE WORLD THAT WE ARE JUST FRIENDS AND BRAVE ENEMIES
Kennedy, Robert P *see* HISTORICAL REVIEW OF LOGAN COUNTY
Kennedy, S O *see* A BIOMECHANICAL ANALYSIS OF CHILDREN'S BALANCE BEHAVIOR
Kennedy, Sir Alexander B W *see* PETRA: ITS HISTORY AND MONUMENTS
Kennedy, Vans *see*
- PRACTICAL REMARKS ON THE PROCEEDINGS OF GENERAL COURTS MARTIAL
- A TREATISE ON THE PRINCIPLES AND PRACTICE OF MILITARY LAW

Kennedy, William *see* TEXAS: THE RISE, PROGRESS, AND PROSPECTS OF THE REPUBLIC OF TEXAS
Kennedy, William S *see*
- MESSIANIC PROPHECY, AND THE LIFE OF CHRIST
- THE PLAN OF UNION, OR, A HISTORY OF THE PRESBYTERIAN AND CONGREGATIONAL CHURCHES OF THE WESTERN RESERVE

Kennel, A (Albert) *see* BURLEIGH, SHREWSBURY U. LEICESTER IN SCHILLERS MARIA STUART
KENNEL GAZETTE – Toronto: H B Donovan, 1889-[189–19–] – 9 – cn C.I.H.M. [630]
KENNEN UND SAMMELN : EIN VERZEICHNIS DER SCHRIFTEN VON URSULA SCHLEGEL / Schlegel, Ursula; ed by Laschke, Birgit & Welzel, Barbara – 1995 – 1mf – 9 – DM60.00 – 3-8267-2088-1 – gw Hänsel [700]
Kenner, James B *see* THE PRACTICE IN INDIANA UNDER THE LAWS FOR CONSTRUCTING DITCHES AND DRAINS
Kenner, S A *see* UTAH AS IT IS
Kenneth, H *see* LAND TENURE: PROCEEDINGS OF THE INTERNATIONAL CONFERENCE ON LAND TENURE AND RELATED PROBLEMS IN WORLD AGRICULTURE, HELD AT MADISON, WISCONSIN, 1951
Kennicott, Benjaminus *see* VETUS TESTAMENTUM HEBRAICUM
Kennington, Anna *see* THE RELATIONSHIP OF ATHLETIC PARTICIPATION AND INACTIVITY TO FATTY FOOD SELECTION IN SENIOR CITIZENS
Kenny, Michael *see* THE ROMANCE OF THE FLORIDAS. THE FINDING OF THE FOUNDING. NEW YORK, 1934
Kenrick, Francis Patrick *see* THE PRIMACY OF THE APOSTOLIC SEE VINDICATED
Kenrick, Peter Richard *see* THE VALIDITY OF ANGLICAN ORDINATIONS AND ANGLICAN CLAIMS TO APOSTOLICAL SUCCESSION EXAMINED
Kenrick, William *see* A RHETORICAL GRAMMAR OF THE ENGLISH LANGUAGE
Kensdale, W E N *see* CATALOGUE OF THE ARABIC MANUSCRIPTS PRESERVED IN THE UNIVERSITY LIBRARY, IBADAN, NIGERIA
Kensei-Bunko *see* OHRAI-MONO BUNRUISHUSEI JOSHIYO OHRAI-HEN
KENSINGTON AND HAMMERSMITH REPORTER – (Missing: Apr-Dec 1904) – London, 5 Jul 1879-28 Dec 1906 – 26r – 1 – uk British Libr Newspaper [072]
KENSINGTON NEWS AND WEST LONDON TIMES – London, Jan-Nov 1869; Jan 1876-Dec 1888; Jan 1931-Jul 1972 – 48r – 1 – uk British Libr Newspaper [072]
KENSINGTON PO (KENSINGTON NEWS AND POST) – London. 1918-72.-w. 62mqn reels – 1 – uk British Libr Newspaper [072]
KENT, 1823 : BRITISH ISLES CENSUS DIRECTORIES PROJECT, ENGLAND. VOL 210 – 2mf – 9 – A$15.00 – at Vine [941]
KENT, 1846 : BRITISH ISLES CENSUS DIRECTORIES PROJECT, ENGLAND – at Vine [941]
KENT, 1855 : BRITISH ISLES CENSUS DIRECTORIES PROJECT, ENGLAND. VOL 251 – 10mf – 9 – A$63.00 – at Vine [941]
KENT, 1862 : BRITISH ISLES CENSUS DIRECTORIES PROJECT, ENGLAND – at Vine [941]
KENT, 1895 : BRITISH ISLES CENSUS DIRECTORIES PROJECT, ENGLAND. VOL 247 – 13mf – A$81.00 – at Vine [941]
KENT AND SUSSEX COURIER – Turnbridge Wells, England. Jun 1873-Dec 1981 (missing 1897, 1911). -w. 180 reels – 1 – uk British Libr Newspaper [072]
KENT ARCHAEOLOGICAL SOCIETY : RECORDS BRANCH – (Coll title: Publications of the English Record Societies, 1835-1972...) – v1-19 + 3 add. vols. 1912-66 – 91mf – 9 – £670.00 – uk Chadwyck [930]
KENT (CANTERBURY, CHATHAM, MAIDSTONE, ROCHESTER AND STROOD), 1805 : BRITISH ISLES CENSUS DIRECTORIES PROJECT, ENGLAND. VOL 170 – 1mf – 9 – A$9.00 – at Vine [941]
Kent, Charles Foster *see* THE MESSAGES OF ISRAEL'S LAWGIVERS
KENT COAST REGISTER OF HOTELS, BOARDING HOUSES AND APARTMENTS – London. 6 Jul-30 Sep 1893. -w. 10 ft – 1 – uk British Libr Newspaper [072]
KENT COAST TIMES ETC – (East Kent Times, etc. 1897-) – Ramsgate, England. 17 May 1866-1980 – 158r – 1 – uk British Libr Newspaper [072]
Kent County Archives. Maidstone *see* WYKEHAM-MARTIN PAPERS
KENT COUNTY ATLAS – East Greenwich. R.I. 1850-1853 – 1 – us UMI [071]
KENT COUNTY ATLAS – Phenix. R.I. 1850-1852 – 1 – us UMI [071]
KENT COUNTY NEWS – East Greenwich. R.I. 1913-1914 – 1 – us UMI [071]
Kent, Dorman B E *see* VERMONTERS
KENT (EAST), 1847 : BRITISH ISLES CENSUS DIRECTORIES PROJECT, ENGLAND – at Vine [941]
Kent, George O *see* A CATALOG OF FILES AND MICROFILMS OF THE GERMAN FOREIGN MINISTRY ARCHIVES
KENT HERALD – Canterbury, England. 1824-70. -w. 18 1/2 reels – 1 – uk British Libr Newspaper [072]
Kent, J *see* TWELVE ANTHEMS AND A MORNING AND EVENING SERVICE WITH EIGHT ANTHEMS
Kent, James *see* COMMENTARIES ON AMERICAN LAW
Kent, Josiah C *see* NORTHBOROUGH HISTORY, NORTHBOROUGH, MASS
Kent, M Chris *see* A SATRICAL INTERPRETATION OF THE HISTORY OF SELECTED PERSONS, EVENTS AND ORGANIZATIONS IN AMERICAN PHYSICAL EDUCATION
KENT MESSENGER AND GRAVESEND TELEGRAPH & DARTFORD NEWS – England. Kent Messenger – North Kent edition. -w. 1906-69. 103 reels – 1 – uk British Libr Newspaper [072]
KENT MESSENGER AND MAIDSTONE TELEGRAPH – England. -w. 12 Aug 1871-Dec 1891. 20 reels – 1 – uk British Libr Newspaper [072]
Kent, Otis *see* KENT'S DIGEST OF DECISIONS UNDER THE FEDERAL SAFETY APPLIANCES ACTS
Kent, Roland Grubb *see* THIRTY YEARS OF ORIENTAL STUDIES
KENT STREET MAPS / British Ordnance Survey – 1994 – 5mf – 15 – $28.50 – us Comics [941]
Kent, W H *see* A MANUAL OF CHURCH HISTORY
KENT (WEST), 1847 : BRITISH ISLES CENSUS DIRECTORIES PROJECT, ENGLAND. VOL 58 – 4mf – 9 – A$27.00 – at Vine [941]
Kent, William *see*
- DRAWINGS AND PLANS FOR HOLKHAM HALL, NORFOLK
- MEMOIRS AND LETTERS OF JAMES KENT, LL.D., LATE CHANCELLOR OF THE STATE OF NEW YORK

KENTISH EXPRESS *see* ASHFORD AND ALFRED NEWS
KENTISH GAZETTE – Canterbury. England. -w. Jan 1772-Dec 1776; Jan 1804-Jul 1806. (4 reels) – 1 – uk British Libr Newspaper [072]
KENTISH GUARDIAN – Ashford, England. 29 Sept 1868-12 Jan 1869. -w. 1/4 reel – 1 – uk British Libr Newspaper [072]
KENTISH INDEPENDENT – London. -w. 1843-1981. (177 reels) – 1 – uk British Libr Newspaper [072]
KENTISH MERCURY – (South East London Mercury). London. -w. Jan 1834-April 1981. (185 reels) – 1 – uk British Libr Newspaper [072]
KENTISH POST, OR CANTERBURY NEWS LETTER – England. -sw. 1 5 Jan 1726-16 20 July 1768. Lacking 1727, 1734, 1735, 1742, 1744. 12 1 2 reels – 1 – uk British Libr Newspaper [072]
KENT'S COMMENTARIES. / Snyder, Emil William – Detroit, Collector 1895 4 v. On film: v. 4. LL-307 – 1 – us L of C Photodup [340]
KENT'S DIGEST OF DECISIONS UNDER THE FEDERAL SAFETY APPLIANCES ACTS / Kent, Otis – Washington: GPO, 1910 (all publ) – 1mf – 9 – $4.50 – LLMC 84-391 – us L.L.M.C. [340]
KENT'S DIRECTORIES – From Bodleian Library, Oxford. 1745, 1777, 1787 – 1 – uk Microform Academic [941]
KENTUCKY – 9r – 1 – $720.00 – us Scholarly Res [370]
KENTUCKY : ATTORNEY GENERAL OPINIONS – (1908-59 on reel $35.00. 1968-94 and 10yr index (1980-1989) on mf $730.00. 1960-67 not available) – 1908-94 – 9 – $765.00 set – 0-89941-535-0 – us Hein [340]
KENTUCKY : SESSION LAWS OF AMERICAN STATES AND TERRITORIES – 1792-1995 – 9 – $1,691.00 set – us Hein [340]
Kentucky *see*
- CEMETERY RECORDS OF MARION, CLARK, & TAYLOR COUNTIES.
- THE CHURCH OF THE MOTHER OF GOD, A CENTENNIAL CHRONICLE.
- DUTIES AND FUNCTIONS OF KENTUCKY COUNTY GOVERNMENT
- FIRST CENSUS OF KENTUCKY, 1790
- GUIDE AND CHECK LIST OF COUNTY GOVERNMENTAL ORGANIZATION & COUNTY RECORD SYSTEM, PAST & PRESENT OF KENTUCKY COUNTIES
- REPORTS AND OPINIONS (A-G)
- REPORTS, POST-NRS
- REPORTS, PRE-NRS
- SALEM ON RENNIX CREEK

THE KENTUCKY – By Thomas D. Clark, 1942. Hist. and biog. sketches. Indexed. Rivers of America Series. 7 fiches. F-0463 – 9 – us A.G.L.L. [978]
KENTUCKY, A HISTORY OF THE STATE – By W.H. Perrin et al, 1887. Indexed. 16 fiches. F-0166 – 9 – us A.G.L.L. [978]
KENTUCKY AGRI-BUSINESS QUARTERLY / University of Kentucky. Department of Agricultural Economics – No.1-39/40. 1970-79. 3 fiches – 9 – us Spaulding [650]
KENTUCKY AGRI-BUSINESS SPOTLIGHT / University of Kentucky. Department of Agricultural Economics – No.1-112. 1969-79. 5 fiches – 9 – us Spaulding [650]
Kentucky. Agricultural Experiment Station *see*
- ANNUAL REPORT
- BULLETIN
- CIRCULAR
- FARM EC.-MISC
- KENTUCKY ANIMAL SCIENCE RESEARCH REPORTS
- KENTUCKY FARM AND HOME SCIENCE
- KENTUCKY FRUIT NOTES
- MISCELLANEOUS PUBLICATIONS
- NEWSPAPER BULLETIN
- PROGRESS REPORTS
- REGULATORY BULLETIN

Kentucky. Agricultural Extension Service *see*
- ANNUAL REPORT
- CIRCULAR
- GREENHOUSE VEGETABLE GROWER'S NEWSLETTER
- KENTUCKY FARM ANALYSIS GROUP SUMMARY
- KENTUCKY FARM ECONOMICS
- LEAFLETS
- LIVESTOCK AND MEAT MKTNG. INFO
- MISCELLANEOUS
- NOTES ON THE KENTUCKY AGRICULTURAL SITUATION
- RS
- SPECIAL FOLDERS
- SPOTS AND ROTS
- TIMELY NOTE ON SOIL AND CROPS

KENTUCKY ANIMAL SCIENCE RESEARCH REPORTS / Kentucky. Agricultural Experiment Station – 1954-71 – 1,5,6 – us Spaulding [636]
KENTUCKY ANTE-BELLUM PORTRAITURE – By Edna Talbott Whitley, 1957. Biog. sketches of portrait subjects. Indexed. 15 fiches. F-1303 – 9 – us A.G.L.L. [920]
KENTUCKY AT BOGOR; A REVIEW AFTER SIX YEARS / Seay, William A – (Review of work of Univ. of Kentucky-AID Project with Univ. of Indonesia, Bogor, Java). SE 11,572 1. 1963 – 9 – ne IDC [370]
THE KENTUCKY BAPTIST – Franklin, Kentucky. May 17, 1866-June 22, 1867. 192p – 1 – 6.72 – us Baptist [240]
Kentucky Baptist Convention *see* MOUNTAIN NEWS AND VIEWS
Kentucky Baptist Historical Society *see* PUBLICATIONS, NO. 3
KENTUCKY BAR ASSOCIATION PROCEEDINGS – (Cont as: Kentucky State Bar Association Proceedings 1st-33rd 1902-34) – 1st to 33rd annual meetings. 1882-84; 1902-34 (all publ) – 38mf – 9 – $171.00 – LLMC 84-520 – us L.L.M.C. [073]
KENTUCKY BAR JOURNAL *see* KENTUCKY BENCH AND BAR

KENTUCKY BENCH AND BAR – (Title varies: v1-35 no 3 1936-71 as Kentucky State Bar Journal. v35 no 4-38 1971-74 as Kentucky Bar Journal) – v1-59. 1936-95 – 9 – $522.00 set – us Hein [340]
KENTUCKY CEMETERY RECORDS, V1 / Kentucky Records Research Committee – 1960. Item F. 471p. Includes index. SW16-0028 – 5 – us A.G.L.L. [920]
Kentucky. Census *see*
– MORTALITY SCHEDULES, 1850
– MORTALITY SCHEDULES, 1860
– MORTALITY SCHEDULES, 1870
– MORTALITY SCHEDULES, 1880
– SECOND CENSUS OF KENTUCKY, 1800
KENTUCKY COURT AND OTHER RECORDS, V2 / ed by Ardery, MrS W B – Item G. From wills, deeds, orders, suits, church minutes, marriages, old bibles and tombstone inscriptions. 257p Includes index. SW16-0028 – 5 – us A.G.L.L. [920]
Kentucky. Court of Appeals *see*
– KENTUCKY LAW REPORTER
– KENTUCKY OPINIONS
THE KENTUCKY CULTURE SERIES: A BASIC LIBRARY OF KENTUCKIANA – Selected from A Bibliography of Kentucky History by J. Winston Coleman – 9 – us Primary [978]
Kentucky. Dept. of Mines and Minerals *see* STATE LABOR REPORTS
KENTUCKY FARM ANALYSIS GROUP SUMMARY / Kentucky. Agricultural Extension Service – 1962-69 – 1,5,6 – us Spaulding [630]
KENTUCKY FARM AND HOME SCIENCE / Kentucky. Agricultural Experiment Station – v. 1-8, no. 3. 1955-62 – 1,5,6 – us Spaulding [630]
KENTUCKY FARM BUSINESS ANALYSIS PROGRAM; ANNUAL SUMMARY / University of Kentucky. Cooperative Extension Service – 1970-83.1 reel – 1,5 – us Spaulding [650]
KENTUCKY FARM ECONOMICS / Kentucky. Agricultural Extension Service – v. 1-245. 1957-69 – 1,5,6 – us Spaulding [630]
KENTUCKY FOREIGN LANGUAGE QUARTERLY – v.1-13. 1954-66. Continued as Kentucky Romance Quarterly – 1 – us UMI [400]
KENTUCKY FRUIT NOTES / Kentucky. Agricultural Experiment Station – v. 1-4. 1938-51 – 1,5,6 – us Spaulding [634]
KENTUCKY GAZETTE – 18 Aug 1787-12 Jan 1910 – 27r – 1 – $1,620.00 – us OmniSys [071]
KENTUCKY GAZETTE – Lexington. Ky. 1793-1819; 1822-30; 1833-; 1844 – 1 – us UMI [071]
KENTUCKY GENEALOGIST – v1-2 by Martha P. Miller. Item K. SW16-0028 – 5 – us A.G.L.L. [920]
KENTUCKY HISTORICAL SOCIETY COMMUNIQUE – v1-3. Very incomplete. 1 fiche. F-0397 – 9 – us A.G.L.L. [978]
KENTUCKY IN RETROSPECT; NOTEWORTHY PERSONAGES & EVENTS IN KENTUCKY HISTORY, 1792-1967 – 1967. Sesquicentennial ed. publ. in 1942. Includes new material for 175th Anniv. ed. 4 fiches. F-1318 – 9 – us A.G.L.L. [978]
KENTUCKY IN THE NATION'S HISTORY / McElroy, Robert M – New York: Moffat, Yard and Co., 1909. Kentucky Reel 1. (The Cox Library Collection) – 5 – us Americana [978]
THE KENTUCKY JEWISH POST AND OPINION – Louisville, KY. 1978-86 – 1 – us A.J.P.C. [071]
KENTUCKY JOURNAL – (Republican Auxiliary. Washington, KY. 1806-10. Political Theatre. Lancaster, KY. 1808-10. Globe. Richmond, KY. 1809-10. Telegraph. Georgetown, KY. 1811-13. Instructer. Paris, KY. 1818. People's Friend. Danville, KY. 1818-19. Eagle. Maysville, KY. 1814-20. Weekly Messenger. Russelville, KY. 1814-20. Union. Washington, KY. 1814-20) – Frankfort, KY. 1795. Sold with following titles as one unit – 3 – us Readex [071]
KENTUCKY KENTUCKY REVISED STATUTES ANNOTATED – Charlottesville, Michie Company: 1973 edition thru Mar 1996 update – 9 – 1,216.00set – us Hein [340]
THE KENTUCKY LAND GRANTS, 1782-1924 / Jillson, Willard R – Louisville: The Standard Printing Co., 1925. Kentucky Reel 8. (The Cox Library Collection) – 5 – us Americana [978]
KENTUCKY LAW JOURNAL – (Add vols as copyright expires) – v1-8. 1913-1920 – 21mf – $31.50 – LLMC 90-323 – us L.L.M.C. [073]
KENTUCKY LAW JOURNAL – Louisville. v1-2. 1881-82 – 1 – $40.00 – us Hein [073]
KENTUCKY LAW JOURNAL – (v1-73 1913-85 on reel or mf $885.00. v74-82 1985-94 on mf $243.00) – v1-82. 1913-94 – 5,6,9 – $1,128.00 set – us Hein [340]
KENTUCKY LAW REPORTER : UNREPORTED / Kentucky. Court of Appeals – (Pre-NRS: v1-8 1880-86 67mf $100.00) – v1-33. 1880-1908 (all publ) – 324mf – 9 – $485.00 – LLMC 84-138 – us L.L.M.C. [340]
KENTUCKY LAWS MADE PLAIN. / Morris, Charles Harwood – Sedalia? Mo. Bankers Law, 1906. 100p. LL-251 – 1 – us L of C Photodup [340]
Kentucky. Laws, Statutes, etc *see*
– ACTS OF THE GENERAL ASSEMBLY OF THE COMMONWEALTH OF KENTUCKY
– CIVIL AND CRIMINAL CODES OF PRACTICE OF KENTUCKY; REV. AND COR. TO JULY 1, 1908
KENTUCKY MICROFORMS : LIBRARY SCIENCE – 189mf – 9 – $460.40 – us OmniSys [020]
KENTUCKY MISSION MONTHLY – Louisville, Ky. 1902-15. Merged with western recorder, 1919. 2350p – 1 – 82.25 – us Baptist [240]
KENTUCKY NEW ERA – Hopkinsville. Ky. 1946- – 1 – us UMI [071]
Kentucky. Office of the Governor *see* CATALOGUE OF RECORDS, DOCUMENTS, PAPERS, ETC. OF KENTUCKY GOVERNORS, 1792-1926
KENTUCKY OPINIONS : UNREPORTED / Kentucky. Court of Appeals – (With 2 digest vols. A Pre-NRS title) – v1-13. 1864-86 (all publ) – 33mf – 9 – $225.00 – LLMC 84-139 – us L.L.M.C. [340]
KENTUCKY PIONEER AND COURT RECORDS : ABSTRACTS OF EARLY WILLS, DEEDS AND MARRIAGES FROM COURT HOUSES AND RECORDS OF OLD BIBLES, CHURCHES AND GRAVEYARDS, AND CEMETERIES / ed by McAdams, MrS Harry K – Genealogical material from authentic sources. 1929. Item B. Indexed. 342p SW16-0027 – 5 – us A.G.L.L. [920]
KENTUCKY POST – Cincinnati. Ohio. and Kentucky Times Star. 1958- – 1 – us UMI [071]
KENTUCKY POST – Covington. Ky. and Times Star. 1903-09, 1910- – 1 – us UMI [071]
KENTUCKY. PRESBYTERY (ASSOCIATION PRES. CH. OF N.A.) *see* MINUTES
KENTUCKY RECORDS : EARLY WILLS AND MARRIAGES, OLD BIBLE RECORDS, AND TOMBSTONE INSCRIPTIONS / ed by Ardery, MrS W B – 1969. Orig. publ. 1926. Indexed. 4 fiches. F-0851 – 9 – us A.G.L.L. [920]
Kentucky Records Research Committee *see* KENTUCKY CEMETERY RECORDS, V1
THE KENTUCKY RESOLUTIONS OF 1798 : AN HISTORICAL STUDY / Warfield, Ethelbert, D – 2nd ed. New York/London: G P Putnam's Sons, 1894 – 3mf – 9 – $4.50 – LLMC 95-089 – us L.L.M.C. [323]
KENTUCKY REVISED STATUTES ANNOTATED – Charlottesville: Michie Company, 1973-Mar 1996 update – 9 – $1,132.00 set – us Hein [340]
THE KENTUCKY REVIVAL / McNemar, Richard – 1 – 5.53 – us Baptist [240]
KENTUCKY ROMANCE QUARTERLY – v.14-. 1967-. Continues yKentucky Foreign Language Quarterly – 1 – us UMI [440]
KENTUCKY SCHOOL JOURNAL – v. 1-50. 1923-72 – 1 – us UMI [370]
KENTUCKY SKETCHES – Historical and biographical sketches, Kentucky, 1882-88.With particular coverage of Bourbon, Christian, Fayette, Harrison, Scott, Todd and Trigg Counties. With an index of many more by Bailey F. Davis. Perin ed. 5578p – 1 – 195.23 – us Baptist [920]
Kentucky. State Bar Association *see* PROCEEDINGS
KENTUCKY STATE BAR ASSOCIATION PROCEEDINGS *see* KENTUCKY BAR ASSOCIATION PROCEEDINGS
KENTUCKY STATE BAR JOURNAL – v1-27. 1936-63 – 39mf – 9 – $130.00 – LLMC 84-521 – us L.L.M.C. [073]
KENTUCKY STATE BAR JOURNAL *see* KENTUCKY BENCH AND BAR
Kentucky State Historical Society *see*
– GENERAL INDEX TO THE 43 VOLUMES OF THE REGISTER.
– REGISTERS
Kentucky. Supreme Court *see* KENTUCKY SUPREME COURT REPORTS
KENTUCKY SUPREME COURT REPORTS / Kentucky. Supreme Court – (Pre-NRS: v1-84 1785-1886 623mf $934.00. Vols after v247 still in copyright) – v1-247. 1785-1933 – 2333mf – 9 – $3,499.00 – LLMC 80-807 – us L.L.M.C. [340]
KENTUCKY SUPREME COURT REPORTS *see*
– KENTUCKY LAW REPORTER
– KENTUCKY OPINIONS
Kentucky. Synod (Pres. Ch. in the U.S.A.) *see* MINUTES, 1802-1810
KENTUCKY VITAL RECORDS AND STATISTICS: BIRTH, MARRIAGE AND DEATH STATISTICS – 1911-1938. V158-0033 to V158-0084 – 1 – us A.G.L.L. [310]
KENTUCKY VITAL RECORDS & STATISTICS: BIRTH, MARRIAGE AND DEATH RECORDS – 1852-1910. V158-0001 to v158-0032. Alpha by county – 5 – us A.G.L.L. [310]
KENYA / Leys, N – London. 1925. BA-410 2 – 8 – ne IDC [960]
KENYA : STATISTICAL ABSTRACT 1955-1976 / Kenya (formerly British East Africa). Ministry of Economic Planning and Development. Statistics Division – (Coll title: African Official Statistical Serials, 1867-1982) – 52mf – 9 – £380.00 – uk Chadwyck [960]
Kenya *see*
– DEVELOPMENT PLAN, 1964-1970
– DEVELOPMENT PLAN FOR THE PERIOD 1965/66 TO 1969/70
– DEVELOPMENT PLANS
– THE DEVELOPMENT PROGRAMME, 1954-57
– GOVERNMENT PUBLICATIONS
– PROGRESS REPORT ON THE THREE-AND-A-HALF-YEAR DEVELOPMENT PLAN
Kenya and E.A.H.C *see* ANNUAL DEPARTMENTAL REPORTS
Kenya. Central Bureau of Statistics *see* EDUCATIONALE TRENDS 1973-1977
Kenya (formerly British East Africa). Ministry of Economic Planning and Development. Statistics Division *see* KENYA
Kenya. International Institute for Educational Planning *see* THE KENYA LITERACY PROGRAMME
Kenya. Kenya Education Commission *see* REPORT
Kenya. Land Commission.Carter Commission *see* MINUTES OF EVIDENCE
THE KENYA LITERACY PROGRAMME : A VIEW FROM BELOW: REPORT OF AN IIEP RESEARCH REVIEW WORKSHOP HELD AT NAIROBI, KENYA, NOVEMBER 1989 / Kenya. International Institute for Educational Planning – Paris, 1991 – 2mf – 9 – DE-675/1 – ne IDC [370]
Kenya. Ministry for Finance and Planning *see* DEVELOPMENT PLAN FOR THE PERIOD 1974 TO 1978
Kenya. Ministry of Education *see* TRIENNIAL SURVEY AND ANNUAL REPORT 1961/63-1984
Kenya. National Assembly. House of Representatives *see* OFFICIAL REPORT
Kenya. National Committee on Educational Objectives and Policies *see* REPORT...
KENYA NOTES AND NEWS – nos 1-13. 1929-36 (complete) – 1r – 1 – ATLA S0710A – us A.T.L.A. [073]
Kenyon, F G *see* THE PALEOGRAPHY OF GREEK PAPYRI
Kenyon, Frederic G *see* ROBERT BROWNING AND ALFRED DOMETT
KENYON REVIEW – v1-32 1939-70 1; 1969-70 5,6,9 – us UMI [073]
KENYON REVIEW – N S 1-. 1979- – 1,5,6,9 – us UMI [420]
Keokuk, Iowa *see* MISCELLANEOUS EARLY NEWSPAPERS
KEPADA PARTAI : KUMPULAN SANDJAK – 1965 – 9 – SE-5309 1 – ne IDC [950]
KEPES KALVIN KALENDARIUM – 1956-92 (complete) – Inquire – 1 – ATLA S0576 – us A.T.L.A. [073]
Kephart, Cyrus Jeffries *see* THE PUBLIC LIFE OF CHRIST
Keplinger, Lewis Walter *see* PAPERS AND SCRAPBOOK OF LEWIS WALTER KEPLINGER
Keppel, Henry *see* A SAILOR'S LIFE UNDER FOUR SOVEREIGNS
Keppen, P *see*
– MATERIALY DLIA ISTORII PROSVESHCHENIIA V ROSSII
– SOBRANIE SLAVIANSKIKH PAMIATNIKOV
– SPISOK RUSSKIM PAMIATNIKAM, SLUZHASHCHIM K SOSTAVLENIIU ISTORII KHUDOZHESTV I OTECHESTVENNOI PALEOGRAFII
Keppler, J A *see* COLLECTION OF CARTOONS
Keppler, Paul Wilhelm von *see* AUS KUNST UND LEBEN
KEPUTUSAN-KEPUTUSAN TENTANG PERKARA PIDANA / Saleh, Ruslan – 1961 – 9 – SE-3831 1 – ne IDC [350]
Ker, J B *see* IRIDEARUM GENERA
Ker, James Campbell *see* POLITICAL TROUBLE IN INDIA, 1907-1917
KERALA CHRONICLE – Trichur, India. 1962-Apr 1964 – 5r – 1 – us L of C Photodup [072]
KERALA GAZETTE / Kerala. India – Trivadrum. 1963-1966 – 1 – us NY Public [324]
Kerala. India *see* KERALA GAZETTE
THE KERALA KAUMUDI – Trivandrum, India. Jul-Sept 1966 – 1r – 1 – us L of C Photodup [072]
KERANG NEW TIMES – 1921-1971 – 59mf – 9 – at Corangamite [980]
KERANG SHIRE RATES – 1899-1962 – 562mf – 9 – at Corangamite [980]
KERANG SHIRE VARIOUS MINUTES – 1881-1946 – 69mf – 9 – at Corangamite [350]
Kerber, Georg *see* DIE RELIGIONSGESCHICHTLICHE BEDEUTUNG DER HEBRAEISCHEN EIGENNAMEN DES A.T
Kerckhoffs, August *see* DANIEL CASPER VON LOHENSTEIN'S TRAUERSPIELE
KERDJANTARA: SUARA LEMBAGA PENELITIAN DAJA TENAGA DAN PERALATAN PERHUTANAN – Bogor, 1962-63(1-6). TEN 1206. BSE-1743/1 – 9 – ne IDC [950]
KEREM HEMED – v. 1-9. Vienna, Berlin. 1833-56. BJ-91-47 1 – 9 – ne IDC [470]
Kereszty, L *see* A MAGYAR ES MAGYARORSZAGI IDOESZAKI SAJTO IDOERENDI ATTEKINTESE, 1705-1867
Kergoat, J *see* PAYSAN AU DAHRA ORIENTAL (ALGERIE) DJEBEL BISSA
Kerharo, J *see* SORCIERS, FETICHEURS ET GUERISSEURS DE LA COTE D'IVOIRE – HAUTE-VOLTA
KERK EN EREDIENST – 1(1945)-13(1958) – 113mf – 9 – Dfl396.00 – ne Slangenburg [073]
KERK EN VREDE – (Cont and filmed with: Militia Christi) – v38-46. 1983-91 (complete) – Inquire – 1 – ATLA S0376A – us A.T.L.A. [073]
KERK EN VREDE *see* MILITIA CHRISTI
KERK EN WERELD – (Lacking: nos 1-7 and 1939-43) – 1937; 1938; 1944-58; 1973-88 – 9r – 1 – ATLA S0595 – us A.T.L.A. [073]
DIE KERKBODE – Vereinigde blad van die Ned. Geref. kerke van Suid-Afrika. 1849-1962 – 1 – us A.T.L.A. [240]
KERKELIJK LEESBLAD : TEN DIENSTE DER CLEEFS- EN GELDERLANDSCHE CATHOLIJKEN – 1(1800)-2(1801) – 21mf – 9 – Dfl47.00 – ne Slangenburg [073]
KERKELIJKE BIBLIOTHEEK : VOORNAMELIJK VOOR DE ROOMSCH-CATHOLYKEN IN NEDERLAND – (Tweede deel. Mengelwerk, 1795. 8mf; Uittreksels en Beoordelingen 1795. 6mf; Kerk-Nieuws. 1795. 5mf) – 8 – Dfl3.50ea – ne Slangenburg [240]
KERKELIJKE BIBLIOTHEEK : VOORNAMELIJK VOOR DE ROOMSCH-CATHOLYKEN IN NEDERLAND. MENGELWERK- UITTREKSELS EN BEOORDEELINGEN-KERKNIEUWS – Amsterdam/Grave, 1(1794)-2(1795) – 9 – Dfl147.00 – ne Slangenburg [073]
HET KERKELYK EN WERELTLYK DEVENTER / Dumbar, Gerhard – Arnhem. Deel 1. 1752 – Dfl105.00 – ne Slangenburg [240]
KERKERAADS-PROTOCOLLEN DER HOLLANDSCHE GEMEENTE TE LONDEN 1569-1571 (DE WERKEN..1,1) / ed by Kuyper, A – Utrecht, 1870 – Dfl25.00 – ne Slangenburg [240]
KERKHISTORISCH ARCHIEF – (1870...Studien en Bijdragen op 't Gebied der Historische Theologie. 1885...Archief voor Nederlandsche Kerkgeschiedenis) – 1(1857)-4(1866) – 24mf – 9 – Dfl84.00 – ne Slangenburg [073]
KERKHISTORISCHE STUDIEN / Sepp, Christiaan – Leiden: E.J. Brill, 1885 – 1mf – us A.T.L.A. [240]
Kerl, Georg *see* ROBESPIERRES KIRCHENPOLITIK

KERMAN NEWS – Kerman, CA. 1971-72; 1981- – 10+ r – 1 – $500.00 ($50.00y) – B02324 – us Library Micro [071]
LA KERMESSE – Montreal, Canada. 14-19 oct 1895 – 1r – 1 – Can$25.00 – cn Can Microfilming [072]
LA KERMESSE – Quebec: L Brousseau, [1892-1893] – 9 – cn C.I.H.M. [072]
La Kermesse. Canada *see* LE MONUMENT
KERMESSE-JOURNAL – Montreal, Canada. 2-10 jun 1884 – 1r – 1 – Can$25.00 – cn Can Microfilming [072]
KERN COUNTY – 1909-35 – 26r – 1 – $1,300.00 – P00041 – us Library Micro [910]
KERN COUNTY INCLUDING BAKERSFIELD – Kern Co, CA. 1899; 1936-1949 – 14r – 1 – $700.00 – D043 – us Library Micro [978]
KERN COUNTY SURVEY / U.S. Library of Congress. Prints and Photographs Division – 415 views from Kern County, CA in the late 1880's. 4 maps. 1 reel. P&P43 – 1 – 23.00r – us L of C Photodup [080]
KERN COUNTY WHO'S WHO / Wilson, Grove – Bakersfield: Wiley K. Peterson, 1941. California reel 39. (Cox Library Collection) – 5 – us Americana [920]
KERN DRESSDINISCHER MERCKWUERDIGKEITEN – Dresden, Germany. 1700-1772 (incomplete); 1781 – 1 – gw Mikrofilm [072]
Kern Institute, University of Leiden *see* INDONESIAN ARCHAEOLOGICAL PHOTOGRAPHS
Kern, Jack C *see* TENNIS RACKET COEFFICIENT OF RESTITUTION UNDER STATIC AND DYNAMIC CONDITIONS
Kern, Josephus *see* DE SACRAMENTO EXTREMAE UNCTIONIS
KERN, LOS ANGELES, SAN BERNARDINO, SAN DIEGO, SAN LUIS OBISPO, SANTA BARBARA AND VENTURA COUNTIES – Kern Co, CA. 1875 – 1r – 1 – $50.00 – D044 – us Library Micro [978]
KERN, LOS ANGELES, SAN BERNARDINO, SAN DIEGO, SAN LUIS OBISPO, SANTA BARBARA AND VENTURA COUNTIES – Los Angeles Co, CA. 1875 – 1r – 1 – $50.00 – D044 – us Library Micro [978]
KERN, LOS ANGELES, SAN BERNARDINO, SAN DIEGO, SAN LUIS OBISPO, SANTA BARBARA AND VENTURA COUNTIES – San Bernardino Co, CA. 1875 – 1r – 1 – $50.00 – D044 – us Library Micro [978]
KERN, LOS ANGELES, SAN BERNARDINO, SAN DIEGO, SAN LUIS OBISPO, SANTA BARBARA AND VENTURA COUNTIES – San Luis Obispo Co, CA. 1875 – 1r – 1 – $50.00 – D044 – us Library Micro [380]
KERN, LOS ANGELES, SAN BERNARDINO, SAN DIEGO, SAN LUIS OBISPO, SANTA BARBARA AND VENTURA COUNTIES – Santa Barbara Co, CA. 1875 – 1r – 1 – $50.00 – D044 – us Library Micro [978]
KERN, LOS ANGELES, SAN BERNARDINO, SAN DIEGO, SAN LUIS OBISPO, SANTA BARBARA AND VENTURA COUNTIES – Ventura Co, CA. 1875 – 1r – 1 – $50.00 – D044 – us Library Micro [978]
KERN MELODISCHER WISSENSCHAFFT / Mattheson, J – 1737 – 9 – us Sibley [780]
Kern, Oskar *see* JOHANN RIST ALS WELTLICHER LYRIKER
Kern, Otto *see* INSCRIPTIONES GRAECAE
KERN VALLEY SUN – Kernville. Calif. 1959-1967 – 1 – us UMI [071]
KERNEL AND THE HUSK : LETTERS ON SPIRITUAL CHRISTIANITY / Abbott, Edwin Abbott – (Includes glossary) – Boston: Roberts Bros, 1887 – 1mf – 9 – 0-8370-2014-X – 1985-0014 – us A.T.L.A. [240]
Kerner, Justinus *see* JUSTINUS KERNERS SAEMTLICHE POETISCHE WERKE
Kerner, Justinus Andreas Christian *see* THE SEERESS OF PREVOST; BEING REVELATIONS CONCERNING THE INNER-LIFE OF MAN, AND THE INTER-DIFFUSION OF A WORLD OF SPIRITS IN THE ONE WE INHABIT
Kerner, Miroslav *see* DOCUMENTS ON SOVIET MILITARY LAW AND ADMINISTRATION
Kerner, R J *see*
- THE BALKAN CONFERENCES AND THE BALKAN ENTENTE, 1930-1935
- SLAVIC EUROPE
- SLAVIC EUROPE: A SELECTED BIBLIOGRAPHY IN THE WESTERN EUROPEAN LANGUAGES, COMPRISING HISTORY, LANGUAGES AND LITERATURES

Kerner von Marilaun, A *see*
- DIE ABHAENGIGKEIT DER PFLANZENGESTALT VON KLIMA UND BODEN
- NOVAE PLANTARUM SPECIES

Kernholt, Otto *see* VOM GHETTO ZUR MACHT: DIE GESCHICHTE DES AUFSTIEGS DER JUDEN AUF DEUTSCHEN BODEN
Keroack, Christopher R *see* THE EFFECTS OF ALPHA-TOCOPHEROL ON METABOLIC DETERMINATIONS IN GRADED EXERCISE
KEROVEZ – Cracow. 1642. Cowley. BJ-43-36 1 – 9 – ne IDC [470]
KEROVEZ – Prague. 1629. Cowley. BJ-43-35 1 – 9 – ne IDC [470]
Kerr *see* THE STORY OF OKLAHOMA CITY
Kerr, Dianne L *see* AN HIV EDUCATION NEEDS ASSESSMENT OF SELECTED TEACHER MEMBERS OF THE AMERICAN SCHOOL HEALTH ASSOCIATION AND THE AMERICAN HOME ECONOMICS ASSOCIATION
Kerr, James Manford *see*
- KERR'S MINES AND WATER CASES ANNOTATED
- PRACTICE ON ATTACHMENT AND GARNISHMENT OF PROPERTY IN THE STATE OF OHIO
- A SELECTION OF ADJUDICATED CRIMINAL FORMS AND PRECEDENTS OF INDICTMENTS AND INFORMATIONS.

Kerr, John *see* JOHN KERR PAPERS, MS 330
Kerr, John Henry *see* INTRODUCTION TO THE STUDY OF THE BOOKS OF THE NEW TESTAMENT
Kerr, Kathleen A *see* DIFFERENTIATION OF ETHNIC CULTURE REGIONS USING LABAN MOVEMENT ANALYSIS
Kerr, Malcolm H *see* AMERICA'S MIDDLE EAST POLICY
Kerr, Robert *see*
- A GENERAL HISTORY AND COLLECTION OF VOYAGES AND TRAVELS, ARRANGED IN SYSTEMATIC ORDER
- THE KING OF MEN
- KING OF MEN: THE BLANK IN HIS HISTORY, ITS FILLING UP AND LESSONS
- PIONEERING IN MOROCCO

Kerr, S R *see* A COMPARATIVE STUDY OF LEISURE LIFESTYLES
Kerr, Samuel C *see*
- JEWISH CHURCH IN ITS RELATIONS TO THE JEWISH NATION AND TO THE GENTILES
- THE JEWISH CHURCH IN ITS RELATIONS TO THE JEWISH NATION AND TO THE "GENTILES"

Kerrich, G J *see*
- FIVE ARTICLES ON INSECTS
- INSECT PARASITES OF OTHER INSECTS

KERR'S MINES AND WATER CASES ANNOTATED : AMERICAN, ENGLISH AND CANADIAN / Kerr, James Manford – Chicago: Callaghan. 1v. 1912 (all publ) – 9 – LLMC 95-135 – us L.L.M.C. [340]
KERRY ADVOCATE – Tralee, Ireland. -w. 25 July 1914-6 May 1916. 1 1 2 reels – 1 – uk British Libr Newspaper [072]
KERRY EVENING POST – Tralee. Ireland. -d. 2 Jan 1828-29 Sep 1917. (89 reels) – 1 – uk British Libr Newspaper [072]
KERRY EVENING STAR – Tralee, Ireland. -w. 29 Sept 1902-12 March 1914. 11 1 2 reels – 1 – uk British Libr Newspaper [072]
KERRY EXAMINER AND MUNSTER GENERAL OBSERVER – Tralee. Ireland. -w. 11 Aug 1840-19 Oct 1849, 1 Mar 1850-8 Aug 1854, 5 Jan 1855-11 Mar 1856. (11 reels) – 1 – uk British Libr Newspaper [072]
KERRY INDEPENDENT – Tralee, Ireland. 28 Oct 1880-10 Jan, 5, 12 Jul 1884. (imperfect).-w. 3 reels – 1 – uk British Libr Newspaper [072]
KERRY NEWS – Kerry, Ireland. 1924-41. 29 reels – 1 – ie Microforms [072]
KERRY PEOPLE – Tralee, Ireland.27 Sept 1902-1903; 1905-14 Mar 1914; 24 Nov-15 Dec 1917; 12 Jan-9 Feb, 22, 29 Jun, 28 Sept 1918-3 Sept 1921; Jan-Aug 1922. -d. 12 3/4 reels – 1 – uk British Libr Newspaper [072]
KERRY PRESS – Tralee, Ireland. 28 Jul 1914-11 May 1916.-w. 2 reels – 1 – uk British Libr Newspaper [072]
KERRY REPORTER – Kerry, Ireland. 1924-35. 17 reels – 1 – ie Microforms [072]
KERRY STAR – Tralee, Ireland. 15 May 1861-27 Mar 1863.-w. 1mqn reels – 1 – uk British Libr Newspaper [072]
KERRY WEEKLY REPORTER AND COMMERCIAL ADVERTISER – Tralee, Ireland. 3 Feb 1883-14 Aug 1920.-w. 33 reels – 1 – uk British Libr Newspaper [072]

KERRYMAN – Kerry, Ireland. 1904-80. 460 reels – 1 – ie Microforms [072]
Kersaint, Armand G S *see*
- DE LA CONSTITUTION ET DU GOUVERNEMENT QUI POURRAIENT CONVENIR A LA REPUBLIQUE FRANCAISE
- MOYENS PROPOSES A L'ASSEMBLEE NATIONALE POUR RETABLIR LA PAIX ET L'ORDRE DANS LES COLONIES

Kersey, John *see*
- DICTIONARIUM ANGLO-BRITANNICUM: OR, A GENERAL ENGLISH DICTIONARY
- A NEW ENGLISH DICTIONARY

Kershaw, J C *see* BUTTERFLIES OF HONGKONG AND SOUTH-EAST CHINA
KERSHAW SECOND BAPTIST CHURCH. KERSHAW, SOUTH CAROLINA : CHURCH RECORDS – 1916-72 – 1 – 42.03 – us Baptist [240]
Kershaw, W L *see* HISTORY OF PAGE COUNTY
Kersopoulos, J G *see*
- BULGARIE
- BULGARIE: OUVRAGES ET ARTICLES DE REVUES PARUS DE 1613 A 1937

Kerssebomn, W *see* ESSAYS IN POLITICAL ARITHMETIC
Kerssenbrock, H *see* BELLI MONASTERIENSIS CONTRA ANABAPTISTICA MONSTRA
Kersten *see* WIELANDS VERHAELTNIS ZU LUCIAN
KERTONEGORO. DIKTAT KULIAH UNTUK TINGKAY DOCTORAL. POLITIK PEREKONOMIAN – SE-5842 1. 1963? – 9 – ne IDC [320]
Kerviler, Rene *see* RENE KERVILER
Kerwick, Andrew *see* A REPORT OF THE TRIALS OF THE CARAVATS AND SHANAVESTS, AT THE SPECIAL COMMISSION, FOR THE SEVERAL COUNTIES OF TIPPERARY, WATERFORD, AND KILKENNY.
DAS KERYGMA PETRI (T.U.U. 1-11/1) / Dobschuetz, E V – Leipzig, 1893 – 3mf – 9 – ne Slangenburg [240]
KERYGMA UND DOGMA – 1(1955)-12(1966) – 73mf – 9 – Dfl256.00 – ne Slangenburg [073]
Kerzhentsev, V *see* BIBLIOTEKA KOMMUNISTA
KESARI – Poona, India. 2 Jul 1943-27 Sept 1949; 17 Jan 1954-Sept 1991 – 128r – 1 – us L of C Photodup [072]
Kesaris, Paul *see*
- ASIA, 1980-94
- CHINA, 1911-41
- CHINA, 1970-80
- EUROPE AND NATO, 1970-94
- GERMANY, 1919-41
- INTERNATIONAL TRADE, 1971-88
- JAPAN, KOREA AND THE SECURITY OF ASIA
- LATIN AMERICA, 1962-94
- THE MAGIC DOCUMENTS
- MANHATTAN PROJECT
- THE MIDDLE EAST, 1970-94
- MULTINATIONAL CORPORATIONS, OPEC, CARTELS, FOREIGN INVESTMENTS, AND TECHNOLOGY TRANSFER, 1971-88
- NUCLEAR WEAPONS, ARMS CONTROL, AND THE THREAT OF THERMONUCLEAR WAR
- THE SOVIET UNION, 1970-80
- VIETNAM AND SOUTHEAST ASIA

Keseberg, Kerstin *see* ZUM ZUSAMMENHANG VON IDENTIFIKATION MIT DEM GRUPPENREPRAESENTANTEN UND REGIONALER IDENTITAET
KESESATAN HAKIM (RECHTERLIJKE DWALING) / Suparto, R – SE 4311 1. 26 Mei 1961 – 9 – ne IDC [950]
KESIMPOELAN2 DAN KEPOETOESAN2 MOETAMAR DI MALINO / Indonesia. Malino Conference, 1946 – 1946? – 9 – SE-6880 1 – ne IDC [950]
Keskula, DR *see* THE RELIABILITY OF AN ISOKINETIC MEASUREMENT PROTOCOL FOR THE POSTERIOR ROTATOR CUFF MUSCULATURE
Kessel, Johann C *see* UNTERRICHT IM GENERALBASSE ZUM GEBRAUCHE FUER LEHRER UND LERNENDE..
Kessinger, L *see* HISTORY OF BUFFALO COUNTY, WISCONSIN
Keßler, Aloys Wilhelm *see* DIE BEDEUTUNG DER IM ART. 119 I 2 DER REICHSVERFASSUNG AUSGESPROCHENEN GLEICHBERECHTIGUNG DER GESCHLECHTER DE LEGE FERENDA FUER DIE PERSONENRECHTLICHE STELLUNG DER EHEFRAU

Kessler, Franz Josef *see* SINN UND UMSETZUNG EINES VERTRIEBSWIRTSCHAFTLICHEN MARKETING-KONZEPTES IM PRODUKTIONSBETRIEB IM ALLGEMEINEN UND SPEZIELL AM BEISPIEL DER KFZ-ZULIEFERINDUSTRIE
Kessler, Hans *see* DIE PSALMEN
Kessler, Hugo *see* DER FUENFFUESSIGE JAMBUS BEI CHRISTIAN DIETRICH GRABBE
Kessler, Johannes *see* JOHANNES KESSLERS SABBATA
Kessler, Lina *see* VERGLEICHENDE RELIGIONSWISSENSCHAFT UND INSPIRATION DER HEILIGEN SCHRIFT
Kestemont, P *see* ETUDE DES POTENTIALITES D'ELEVAGE INTENSIF DU GOUJON, GOBIO GOBIO, L. REPRODUCTION ET CROISSANCE LARVAIRE
Kester, Howard A *see* HOWARD A. KESTER PAPERS, 1923-1972
DAS KESTNERBUCH / Kuppers, Paul Erich – Hannover, H. Bohme 1919 – 1 – us U.W. Library [760]
KESTON COLLEGE – Kent. 405 docs. 1980-1991 – 183mf – 9 – ne IDC [370]
KETAVIM LE-TOLEDOT HIBBAT ZIYYON / ed by Druyanov, A – 3v. Odessa. Tel Aviv. 1919-32. BJ-290-1 1 – 9 – ne IDC [956]
KETAVIM NIVHARIM / Levin, I L (Pseudonym Yahalal) – 2v. Warsaw. 1911. BJ-422-45 1 – 9 – ne IDC [470]
Kethan, J *see* COMPENDIO DE LA SALUD HUMANA, ZARAGOZA, 1494
Kethudazade 'Arif *see* DIVAN
KETIGA KALINJA 17 AGOESTOES / Sukarno, Pres. Indonesia – SE 4208 1. 1947 – 9 – ne IDC [025]
Ketner, Kenneth Laine *see* CHARLES S. PEIRCE MICROFICHE COLLECTION
Kett, H.F. and Co *see* PAST AND PRESENT OF WARREN COUNTY, ILLINOIS 1877
KETTELER WACHT – Koeln, West Germany. Jan 1953-Dec 1975 – 1 – gw Mikrofilm [072]
Ketteler, Wilhelm Emmanuel, Freiherr von *see*
- DIE ARBEITERFRAGE UND DAS CHRISTENTHUM
- DAS UNFEHLBARE LEHRAMT DES PAPSTES NACH DER ENTSCHEIDUNG DES VATICANISCHEN CONCILS

Kettelhoit, T *see* DE SQUAMIS LEPIDOPTERORUM
KETTERING EVENING TELEGRAPH *see* EVENING TELEGRAPH
Kettlewell, Samuel *see*
- THE AUTHORSHIP OF THE DE IMITATIONE CHRISTI
- THOMAS A. KEMPIS AND THE BROTHERS OF COMMON LIFE
- THOMAS A. KEMPIS AND THE BROTHERS OF THE COMMON LIFE

Kettner, Gustav *see*
- UEBER DEN RELIGIOESEN GEHALT VON LESSINGS NATHAN DEM WEISEN
- UEBER LESSINGS EMILIA GALOTTI
- UEBER LESSINGS MINNA VON BARNHELM

DER KETZER-KATALOG DES BISCHOFS MARUTA VON MAIPHERKAT (T.U.U. 2-19/1B) / Harnack, Adolf von – Leipzig, 1899 – 1mf – 9 – ne Slangenburg [240]
DIE KETZERTAUFANGELEGENHEIT IN DER ALTCHRISTLICHEN KIRCHE NACH CYPRIAN : MIT BESONDERER BERUECKSICHTIGUNG DER KONZILIEN VON ARLES UND NICAEA / Ernst, Johann – Mainz: F. Kirchheim, 1901 – 1mf – us A.T.L.A. [240]
KEUANGAN DAN BANK – Djakarta: Perbankan Nasional Swasta. Aug 1967/68. v1-2(1-10). TEN 1212. Lacking: 1968, v1(7-8). BSE-1744/1 – 9 – ne IDC [950]
Keune, O *see* MAENNER, DIE NAHRUNG SCHUFEN
KEUR VAN GRAFSTEENEN OP DE NEDERL.-PORTUG.-ISRAEL. BEGRAAFPLAATS TE OUDERKERK AAN DEN AMSTEL / Castro, H D de – Leiden, 1883. BJ-262-14 1 – 9 – ne IDC [410]
Keussen, H *see* DIE MATRIKEL DER UNIVERSITAET KOELN 1389 BIS 1559 (PGRG 4)
Kevisi, John (?) *see* DIARY
KEVUZAT HAKHAMIM – Vienna. 1861. BJ-100-180 1 – 9 – ne IDC [520]
KEW CITY COUNCIL MINUTE BOOKS – 1861-1946 – 276mf – 9 – at Corangamite [910]
KEXUE TONGBAO – Science Bulletin. In Chinese. F p76 – 9 – $4.50f – cc Microforms [073]

KEY EDUCATION STATISTICS 1981-1986 / Singapore. Ministry of Education – Singapore, 1982-1986 – 6mf – 9 – DE-254/1 – ne IDC [370]

Key, Francis Scott *see*
- DEFENCE OF FORT M'HENRY-STAR-SPANGLED BANNER
- THE STAR SPANGLED BANNER

A KEY INTO THE LANGUAGE OF AMERICA / Williams, Roger – 1643. 221p. (English Linguistics Series 1500-1800) – 9 – us UMI [400]

Key, J *see* EIGHTEEN MARCHES FOR 2 VIOLINS, [FLUTES OR HAUTBOYS], 2 FRENCH HORNS AD LIB AND A BASS

THE KEY OF THE FRENCH TONGUE / Pujolas, J – 1690. 301p. (English Linguistics Series 1500-1800) – 9 – us UMI [440]

THE KEY OF THE HOLY TONGUE / Martinius, Petrus – 1593. 491p. (English Linguistics Series 1500-1800) – 9 – us UMI [400]

"KEY PERSONS" FILES OF THE PRESIDENT'S COMMISSION ON THE ASSASSINATION OF PRESIDENT KENNEDY, 1963-1964 – 34r – 1 – M1289 – us Nat'l Archives [324]

KEY STATISTICS ON VOCATIONAL TRAINING 1983-1989 / Singapore. Vocational and Industrial Training Board – Singapore – 2mf – 9 – DE-582/1 – ne IDC [370]

KEY TO BAILLAIRGE'S STEREOMETRICAL TABLEAU: NEW SYSTEM OF MEASURING ALL BODIES...BY ONE AND THE SAME RULE / Baillairge, Charles – Quebec: C. Darveau, 1876. 02494. (Pre-1900 Canadiana) – 9 – cn C.I.H.M. [510]

THE KEY TO LIFE (CCC154) / Ho, Shih-ming – (In Chinese) – 1st ed. Hong Kong: Council on Christian Literature for Overseas Chinese, 1959 – 1r – 1 – 1984-B500 – us A.T.L.A. [240]

KEY TO NORTH AMERICAN BIRDS / Coues, E – Z-2064 2. 1872 – 8 – ne IDC [590]

A KEY TO STORY'S EQUITY JURISPRUDENCE, CONTAINING OVER EIGHT HUNDRED QUESTIONS / Guernsey, Rocellus Sheridan – New York, Diossy, 1876. 133 p. LL-270 – 1 – us L of C Photodup [340]

KEY TO THE APOCALYPSE, OR, REVELATION OF JESUS CHRIST TO ST JOHN / Brunson, Alfred – Cincinnati: Walden & Stowe, 1881. 1 fiche – 9 – us A.T.L.A. [240]

A KEY TO THE ART OF LETTERS; OR, ENGLISH A LEARNED LANGUAGE, FULL OF ART, ELEGANCY AND VARIETY / Lane, A – 1700. 143p. (English Linguistics Series 1500-1800) – 9 – us UMI [400]

A KEY TO THE BIRDS OF AUSTRALIA / Hall, R – Melbourne, 2nd ed. London,Melbourne, 1906. Z/1790/2 – 8 – ne IDC [590]

A KEY TO THE EXERCISES OF THE NEW METHOD OF LEARNING THE HEBREW LANGUAGE / Herxheimer, S – London: Franz Thimm, 1866 – 1mf – 9 – 0-8370-9247-7 – 1986-3247 – us A.T.L.A. [470]

A KEY TO THE NARRATIVE OF THE ACTS OF THE APOSTLES / Norris, John Pilkington – London: Rivingtons, 1877. 1 fiche – 9 – us A.T.L.A. [240]

KEY TO THE SYSTEM OF VICTORIAN PLANTS / Mueller, Ferdinand Jakob Heinrich von – 2v. Melbourne. 1887-88. B-8063 1 – 9 – ne IDC [580]

KEY TRENDS AND ISSUES IMPACTING LOCAL GOVERNMENT RECREATION AND PARK ADMINISTRATION IN THE 1990S / Whyte, Digby N B & Martin, W Donald – 1992 – 4mf – 9 – $16.00 – us Microform Publ [790]

KEY WEST ENQUIRER – Key West. Fl. 1834-36 – 1 – us P.K. Yonge [071]

KEY WEST GAZETTE – Key West. Fl. 1831-32 – 1 – us P.K. Yonge [071]

A KEY WORD INDEX TO THE NOTES IN AMERICAN NEGLIGENCE CASES – Chicago. 1v. 1914 (all publ) – 2mf – 9 – $3.00 – LLMC 84-699E – us L.L.M.C. [340]

KEYA PAHA PRESS – Springview, NE. -w. Feb-Sep 1887 – 1 – us NE Hist [071]

KEYBOARD MUSIC / ed by Hul, Dick van den – (Individual titles available and the set icludes a printed guide) – From Dutch music libraries – 1425mf – 9 – MS-1-1287/1 – ne IDC [780]

KEYBOARD MUSIC, 1600-1820 – 1997 – 500mf – 9 – ne MMF Publ [780]

Keydel, Oscar F *see* DEEDS OF VALOR

KEYES' APPEALS REPORTS / New York. (State) – (A Pre-NRS title) – v1-4. 1863-68 (all publ) – 30mf – 9 – $45.00 – LLMC 80-011 – us L.L.M.C. [340]

Keyes, C R *see* MISSOURI GEOLOGICAL SURVEY

Keyes, Wade *see* AN ESSAY ON THE LEARNING OF PARTIAL, AND OF FUTURE INTERESTS IN CHATTELS PERSONAL

Keyfitz, Nathan *see* POPULATION IN INDONESIA, THE SHORT AND LONG RUN

KEYHOLE FOR ROGER WILLIAMS' KEY / Ely, William D – 1892 – 1 – $5.00 – us Baptist [240]

THE KEYNOTE – New York City – 1 – £115.00 – uk Chadwyck [780]

THE KEYNOTE – v1-29. Nov 1883-Jan 1897 – 1 – 1050.00 – us Opus [073]

KEYS OF SAINT PETER...CONNECTED WITH THE HISTORY OF SYMBOLISM AND IDOLATRY / Bunsen, Ernest de – London: Longmans, Green, 1867. 1 fiche – 9 – us A.T.L.A. [240]

THE KEYS OF THE KINGDOM : OR, THE UNFAILING PROMISE / Moriarty, James Joseph – New York: Catholic Publ Society; London: Burns & Oates, c1885 – 1mf – 9 – 0-8370-7005-8 – 1986-1005 – us A.T.L.A. [230]

KEYS TO HIDDEN TREASURE AND THE ARGUS – Las Vegas, NV. 26 Sep 1926 – 1r – 1 – $50.00 – U04602 – us Library Micro [071]

KEYS TO THE WORD, OR, HELP TO BIBLE STUDY / Pierson, Arthur Tappan – New York: A.D.F. Randolph, 1887.1 fiche – 9 – us A.T.L.A. [240]

Keyser, Leander Sylvester *see* THE RATIONAL TEST

Keyserlin, Hermann Alexander *see* DAS REISETAGEBUCH EINES PHILOSOPHEN

Keyserling, A *see* THE GEOLOGY OF RUSSIA IN EUROPE AND THE URAL MOUNTAINS

Keyserling, Alfred *see* GRAF ALFRED KEYSERLING ERZAEHLT

Keyserling, Eduard von *see* DIE SPINNEN AMERIKAS

Keyserling, Hermann Alexander *see* AMERIKA, DER AUFGANG EINER NEUEN WELT

Keyssner, Gustav *see*
- AUSGEWAEHLTE WERKE

THE KEYSTONE AND WOMAN'S COLUMN – v1-14 no 9 (all publ) 1899-1913 – 2r – 1 – $225.00 – us UPA [360]

KEYSTONE BAPTIST – Philadelphia, PA. Pennsylvania Baptist General Convention. 1922-Nov 1930 – 1 – 24.15 – us A.B.H.S. [073]

KEYSTONES OF FAITH : OR, WHAT AND WHY WE BELIEVE / Calkins, Wolcott – (Includes bibliographical references and index) – New York:Baker and Taylor, c1888 – 1mf – 9 – 0-8370-3100-1 – 1985-1100 – us A.T.L.A. [240]

KEYSTONES OF FAITH, OR, WHAT AND WHY WE BELIEVE / Calkins, Wolcott – New York: Baker and Taylor, 1888. 1 fiche – 9 – us A.T.L.A. [240]

KEYWORD INDEX TO SERIAL TITLES – (Also available quarterly for £330.00 UK + VAT E.U. £336.00 oversees) – 9 – £125.00y UK + VAT E.U. £131.00y overseas – uk British Libr Docs [020]

KEYWORD INDEX TO SERIAL TITLES (KIST) / British Library. Document Supply Centre – (Subscription 1994, quarterly updates. £330.00 in UK £336.00 overseas. Single set £125.00 in UK £131.00 overseas) – Alphabetical list by keyword of the Centre's collection of 450,000 serials – 9 – uk British Libr Humanities [010]

KFKB Radio, Milford, KS *see* RECEPTION REPORTS AND LETTERS RECEIVED

K.G. Saur Verlag *see* TARNSCHRIFTEN 1933 BIS 1945

KGALAGADI DISTRICT DEVELOPMENT PLAN 1989-1995 / Botswana. Kgalagadi District – Gaborone, 1990 – 4mf – 9 – ne IDC [338]

KGATLENG DISTRICT DEVELOPMENT PLAN 1989-1995 / Botswana. Kgatleng District – Gaborone, 1990 – 3mf – 9 – ne IDC [338]

K.H. PEDOMAN TABLIGH / Machfudz, Shiddig – SE-5850 1. v. 1 only. 1955 – 9 – ne IDC [073]

Khabachev, A E *see* ENTSIKLOPEDIIA PCHELOVODSTVA L

KHABAR'NAMAH – (Shumarah-'i 12-62 (11 Bahman 1358-Tir 1360[31 Jan 1980-Jun 1981]). Missing issues: 1-11, 14, 17-22) – [Tehran]: Chirik'ha-yi Fada'i-i Khalq-i Iran – 1 reel – 1 – $55.00 – us MEDOC [950]

KHABAR'NAMAH-'I JANG – (Shumarah-'i 4, 7-9 (29 Mihr 1359-10 Azar 1359[21 Oct 1980-1 Dec 1980])) – [Tehran]: Jabhah-'i Milli-i Iran – 1 reel – 1 – $25.00 – us MEDOC [950]

KHABAR'NAMAH-'I JIBHAH-'I MILLI-'I IRAN – (Shumarah-'i 1-36 (Urdibihisht 1347-Farvardin 1353[Apr/May 1968-Mar/Apr 1974]). Missing issues: 31-35) – Tehran: Jabhah-'i Milli-'i Iran – 1 reel – 1 – $30.00 – us MEDOC [950]

Khafi Khan *see* MUNTAKHAB AL-LUBAB

Khakbar, Dalpatram Pranjivan *see* REPORT ON THE ARCHITECTURAL AND ARCHAEOLOGICAL REMAINS IN THE PROVINCE OF KACHH

KHAKI – Ottawa, Ontario. v4 n25. 24 sep 1945 – 1r – 1 – Can$25.00 – cn Can Microfilming [072]

KHAKI: THE ARMY BULLETIN / Ottawa. Minister of National Defence – v.1-4, no. 25; May 5, 1943-Sept 23, 1945 – 1 – 165.00 – cn McLaren [971]

KHALA *see* AFLAK

Khalafov, MS *see* MEROPRIIATIIA SOVETSKOI VLASTI V AZERBAIDZHANE V OBLASTI TRUDOVOGO PRAVA (1917-18)

Khalanskii, MG *see* VELIKORUSSKIIA BYLINY KIEVSKOGO TSIKLA

Khalatnikov, I M *see* PHYSICS REVIEWS

KHALIJ-I FARS – (Sal-i 1: shumarah-'i 1-16 (19 Tir 1358-3 Azar 1358[10 Jul 1979-24 Nov 1979])) – Ahwaz, 1979- – 1 reel – 1 – $25.00 – us MEDOC [950]

KHALIL ED-DAHIRY – Texte arabe, publie par Ravaisse – 9 – fr Orientalistes [470]

KHALQ – (Continues Aflak. Sal-i 1, shumarah-'i 15-sal 5, shumarah-'i 66 (10 Shahrivar 1304-31 Urdibihisht 1305[1 Sep 1925-21 May 1926])) – 1 – us MEDOC [950]

KHALQ-I MUSALMAN – (Shumarah-'i 1-18 (25 Murdad 1358-18 Azar 1358[11 Aug 1979-9 Dec 1979]). Irregular periodicity) – Tehran: Hizb-i Jumhuri-i Khalq-i Musalman, 1979- – 1 reel – 1 – $25.00 – us MEDOC [950]

KHALSA SEWAK – Chandigarh, India. May 1967-Mar 1968; Jul 1968-Feb 1970 – 7r – 1 – us L of C Photodup [072]

KHALYK KENESI = THE SOVIET OF KAZAKHSTAN – (Comes in Kazakh) – 1990- – 1 – sz Infoprint [947]

Khan, Abid Ali *see* MEMOIRS OF GAUR AND PANDUA

Khan, Mahmood A *see*
- JOURNAL OF COLLEGE AND UNIVERSITY FOODSERVICE
- JOURNAL OF INTERNATIONAL HOSPITALITY, LEISURE AND TOURISM MANAGEMENT 1090 A MULTINATIONAL AND CROSS-CULTURAL JOURNAL OF APPLIED RESEARCH
- JOURNAL OF NUTRITION IN RECIPE AND MENU DEVELOPMENT

Khan, Riza Q. *see* RELATION DE L'AMBASSADE AU KHAREZM

THE KHAN'S WEEKLY – [Toronto?: s.n., 1895-189- or 19–] – 9 – cn C.I.H.M. [072]

KHAO CHATURAT : THAI-LANGUAGE WEEKLY NEWS MAGAZINE – (Sept 1981-Dec 1981 $50.00v; Jan 1982-Dec 1983 $100.00y; Jan 1984-Jun 1984 $50.00v) – Bangkok, Thailand – 1 – us Asia Libr [072]

KHAO CO HOC / Hanoi. Institute d'Archeologie. Comite des Sciences Sociales du Viet-Nam – Red. en chef Pham huy Thong. no. 1-9 10. Hanoi. juin 1969-juin 1971 – 1 – fr A.C.R.P.P. [073]

KHAO PHANIT – Bangkok, Thailand. 1971; 1973-74; 1983-91 – 40r – 1 – us L of C Photodup [072]

KHAO PHANIT : THAI-LANGUAGE DAILY NEWSPAPER – (Jan 1975-Dec 1978 $150.00y; Jan 1979-Dec 1980 $200.00y) – Bangkok, Thailand – 1 – us Asia Libr [072]

KHAO PHISET : THAI-LANGUAGE WEEKLY NEWS MAGAZINE – (Jul 1986-Dec 1986 $50.00v; Jan 1987-Dec 1991 $100.00v) – Bangkok, Thailand. Formerly: Wiwat – 1 – us Asia Libr [073]

KHAOSAN PATHET LAO : LAO-LANGUAGE DIALY NEWS SUMMARY – (Jan 1975-Dec 1975 $150.00v; Jan 1984-Dec 1986 $200.00y) – Vientiane, Laos. Mimeograph format – 1 – us Asia Libr [072]

Khaparde, G S *see* PAPERS, 1914-1919

KHARBIN *see* KHARBIN TORGOVY I

KHARBIN TORGOVY I – (Includes c.1: v.3:no.89 1933:Jan.1) – [Kharbin: s.n.], 19uu – 1 – CSUXAKG4168-S – us Hoover Inst Photo [947]

KHARBINSKOE VREMI A – (Library has holdings (incomplete) from between Jan 3, 1932 and Apr. 13, 1937) – Kharbin: "Kharbinskoe vremi a", 1931- – 1 – CSUX87-S34 – us Hoover Inst Photo [947]

Khar'kov. University *see* ZAPISKI IMPERATORSKAGO KHAR'KOVSKOGO UNIVERSITETA

KHAR'KOVSKAIA GUB – Materialy po zemlevladeniiu i zemledelliiu krest'ianskiia obshchestva Khar'kovskoi gub. 1886. BRZ-199/2 – 8 – ne IDC [947]

KHAR'KOVSKAIA GUB – Ocherk ekonomicheskoi zhizni Krest'ianskogo naseleniia Starobel'skago uezda i prichin ego zadolzhennosti, 1843-1893. Khar'kov. 1893. BRZ-206 2 – 8 – ne IDC [330]

KHAR'KOVSKAIA GUB – Pereseleniia Krest'ian Khar'kovskoi gub.1908. BRZ-207/2 – 8 – ne IDC [947]

KHAR'KOVSKAIA GUB – Statisticheskii ezhegodnik 1907-08. BRZ-202/2 – 8 – ne IDC [947]

KHAR'KOVSKAIA GUB – Statisticheskii ezhegodnik 1913 g. Khar'kov. 1914. BRZ-203 2 – 8 – ne IDC [310]

KHAR'KOVSKAIA GUB – Statisticheskii spravochnik po Khar'kovskoi gubernii. Ed. 2. Khar'kov. 1914. BRZ-205 2 – 8 – ne IDC [310]

Kharkovskoe gubernskoe statisticheskoe bi uro *see* BI UDZHETY KRESTI AN KHARKOVSKO I GUBERNII V 1922-23 GODU

Khartoum. Press Centre, People's Court *see* TRANSCRIPTS AND SUMMARIES OF THE TRIAL OF ROLF STEINER

KHARTOUM WORKSHOP ON ARID LANDS MANAGEMENT : PROCEEDINGS / ed by Mabbutt, J A – 1979 – 97p – pb – $5.00 – 92-808-0044-2 – ja U.N. Univ [333]

Kharuzin, N *see* OBZOR DOKUMENTOV OTNOSIASHCHIKHSIA K ISTORII BALTIISKOGO KRAIA I KHRANIASHCHIKHSIA V MOSKOVSKIKH ARKHIVAKH MINISTERSTV..

Khasbulatov, A I *see* BOR'BA TRUDIASHCHIKHSIA CHECHENOINGUSHETII V PERVOI REVOLIUTSII 1905-1907 GG

KHASKOVSKA TRIBUNA – Khaskovo, Bulgaria. Sept 1959-1982 – 23r – 1 – us L of C Photodup [949]

Khatti, Humayum Sharif *see*
- THE TURKISH CONSTITUTION PROCLAIMED UNDER MIDHAT PASHA

Khauer, Frank *see* NATIONALSOZIALISTISCHE POLITIK IN SUEDOSTEUROPA

Khauke, F A *see* KREST'IANSKOE ZEMEL'NOE PRAVO

Khauke, OA *see* RUSSKOE ZEMLE USTROITEL'NOE ZAKONODATEL'STVO

KHAVERSHAFT = FRIENDSHIP – (In Yiddish) – Lodz, PL. no3(15) Mar 1948-(12/13)(40/41) Aug 1948 – 1r – 1 – $25.00 – cn Can Microfilming [072]

DI KHAZONIM-VELT = THE CANTOR'S WORLD – (In Yiddish) – Warsaw, PL. v3 no16. Feb 1935 – 1r – 1 – $25.00 – cn Can Microfilming [072]

Kheifets, Ila *see*
- OSNOVY PATENTNOGO PRAVA
- PROMYSHELENNYE PRAVA I IKH KHOZIAISTVENNOE ZNACHENIE V SOIUZE SSR I NA ZAPADE

Kheinman, S A *see* KADRY GOSUDARSTVENNOGO I KOOPERATIVNOGO APPARATA SSSR

Kheisin, M L *see*
- 50 LET POTREBITEL'SKOI KOOPERATSII V ROSSII
- ORGANIZATSIIA UPRAVLENIIA POTREBITEL'SKIKH OBSHCHESTV I IKH SOIUZOV
- RABOCHII KLASS I KOOPERATSIIA
- RABOCHII VOPROS V KOOPERATSII
- V POMOSHCH' RABOTNIKAM V POTREBITEL'NYKH OBSHCHESTVAKH

Kheisin, ML *see*
- CHTO MOZHET DAT' KOOPERATSIIA RABOCHIM
- ISTORICHESKII OCHERK KOOPERATSII V ROSSII
- KAK ORGANIZOVAT'I VESTI POTREBITEL'SKOE OBSHCHESTVO
- KOOPERATSIIA V SEL'SKOM KHOZIAISTVE
- KREDITNAIA KOOPERATSIIA V ROSSII

Khemnitser, II *see* SOCHINENIIA I PIS'MA

Kheraskov, M M *see*
- IZBRANNYE PROIZVEDENIIA
- TVORENIIA

KHETI – v1- 1948- 1; v29- 1976- 5,6,9 – us UMI [630]

Khevenhiller, FChr. *see* ANNALES FERDINANDEI

KHILANDARSKIE LISTKI OTRYVOK KIRILLOVSKOI PIS'MENNOSTI XI-GO VEKA / Kulbakin, SM – St. Petersburg, 1900. BR-8050/2 – 8 – ne IDC [947]

KHIMICHESKII SOSTAVI FIZICHESKIIA SVOISTVA I ADOVITYKH VESHCHESTV, PRIMI ENI AEMYKH DLIA BOEVYKH TSIELEI / Andreev, I I – Petrograd: Tip. Shtaba Petrogradskago voen. okruga, 1916 – 1 – CSUX89-B3210 – us Hoover Inst Photo [947]

KHIMII A I OBORONA – (Library has: July 1935, Jan.-Oct. 1936) – Moskva: Zhurnalno-gazetnoe obedinenie, 1932-1938. 7v – 1 – CSUX89-S967 – us Hoover Inst Photo [947]

KHIMIK : VESTNIK KHIMICHESKOI TEKHNOLOGII I LABORATORNOI PRAKTIKI – (Missing: 1901/1902 v35-36) – Vil'na, 1900-1902 – 66mf – 9 – ne IDC [600]

KHIMIK – Vestnik khimicheskoi tekhnologii i laboratornoi praktiki. Vil' na. 1900-02. Lacking: 1901 02, v. 35-36. BR-8128 2 – 8 – ne IDC [460]

Khing, H D *see* L'OEUVRE LITTERAIRE DE NAN, AUTEUR CAMBODGIEN DE LA FIN DU XVIIIE SIECLE ET DU DEBUT DU XIXE

KHIRURGIIA – Ezhemesiachnoe izdanie. v. 1-36. M. 1897-1914. BR-8129 2 – 8 – ne IDC [617]

Khitrovo, N P *see* ZAKONODATEL'NYE PAMIATNIKI 16 I 17 STOLETTII

Khitrowo, B *see* ITINERAIRES RUSSES EN ORIENT

Khizhniakov, V V *see*
- ISTORIIA I ORGANIZATSIIA SOVETA VSEROSSIISKIKH KOOPERATIVNYKH S"EZDOV
- KOOPERATSIIA V SHKOLE
- REVIZIIA KOOPERATIVNYKH TOVARISHCHESTV
- SOSTAVLENIE KHOZIAISTVENNOGO PLANA V PROMYSLOVYKH TOVARISHCHESTVAKH I ARTELIAKH
- SPRAVOCHNAIA KNIZHKA DLIA SEL'SKOKHOZIAISTVENNYKH I SEL'SKOKHOZIAISTVENNYKH KREDITNYKH TOVARISHCHESTV
- UCHITES' REVIZII!
- ZEMSTVO I KOOPERATSIIA

KHLEBNAIA SEL'SKOKHOZIAISTVENNAIA KOOPERATSIIA I SOTSIALISTICHESKOE PEREUSTROISTVO KREST'IANSKOGO KHOZIAISTVA / Bauman, K Ia. – M., 1929 – 1mf – 9 – COR-461/1 – ne IDC [334]

Khlebnikov, N I *see*
- OBSHCHESTVO I GOSUDARSTVO V DO-MONGOL'SKII PERIOD RUSSKOI ISTORII
- PRAVO I GOSUDARSTVO V IKH OBOIUDNYKH OTNOSHENIIAKH

Khlebnikov, V *see*
- SLOVO KAK TAKOVOE
- SOBRANIE PROIZVEDENII
- STIKHOTVORENIIA I POEMY
- TE LI LE

KHLEBNOE DELO – Spb. 1907-14. Available: 1909, nrs. 94, 96, 98, 111, 121, 124; 1911, nrs. 306, 307, 353, 359-361; 1912, nrs. 428, 431, 432, 438. BR-8130 2 – 8 – ne IDC [073]

Khleboprodukt *see* OTCHET AKT SIONERNOGO OBSHCHESTVA "KHLEBOPRODUKT" ZA...G.

KHLESL'S, DES CARDINALS, DIRECTORS DES GEHEIMEN CABINETES KAISERS MATHIAS, LEBEN / Hammer-Purgstall, Josef von – Wien. 4v. 1847-1851 – 35mf – ne IDC [943]

KHLESL'S, DES CARDINALS, DIRECTORS DES GEHEIMEN CABINETES KAISERS MATHIAS, LEBEN / Hammer-Purgstall, Josef von – Wien. 4v. 1847-1851 – 35mf – 9 – ne IDC [943]

KHLET LAP – Bangkok, Thailand. Jul 1983-Jun 1984. Formerly: Sayam Mai – 1 – $50.00v – us Asia Libr [073]

KHLI EB I VOLI A : EZHENDI ELNY I [SIC] ORGAN FEDERAT SII SOI UZOV RUSSIKH RABOCHICKH – (Includes c.1: v.1:no.1 1919:Feb.26, v.1:no.23 (1919:July 31); v.2:no.37 1919:Nov.6) – New York, N.Y.: [Federat sii a], 1919- – 1 – CSUXAHZ2634-S – us Hoover Inst Photo [947]

KHLI EB I VOLI A (NEW YORK, N.Y.) *see* KHLI EB I VOLI A

KHLOPCHATO-BUMAZHNYE TOVARY – M., 1925 – 4mf – 9 – COR-757/1 – ne IDC [334]

KHLOPKOVOE DELO : ZHURNAL GLAVNOGO KHLOPKOVOGO KOMITETA – (Library has: Jan.-Aug. 1930) – Tashkent: Komitet, 1922-1930. 9v – 1 – CSUX90-S31 – us Hoover Inst Photo [947]

LE KHMER – Hebdomadaire independant pour la defense des interets du Cambodge. Phnom-Penh. 28 dec 1935-36 – 1 – fr A.C.R.P.P. [073]

Khmyrov, M D *see* GRAFINIA EKATERINA IVANOVNA GOLOVKINA I EE VREMIA

Kho, K G *see* BUSINESS TOPICS: A COLLECTION OF TEXTS WITH NOTES

KHOA HOC – Revue de vulgarisation agricole artisanale et scientifique en langue annamite. no. 1-232. Hanoi. 1er juil 1931-juil aout 1940. mq no. 35-36, no. 53., 228-229 – 1 – fr A.C.R.P.P. [073]

Khobragade, B D *see* ELECTION MANIFESTO OF THE REPUBLICAN PARTY OF INDIA, 1967

Khodasevich, V *see*
- DERZHAVIN
- IGOR' SEVERIANIN I FUTURIZM
- IZ EVREISKIKH POETOV
- MOLODOST'
- NEKROPOL'
- O PUSHKINE
- SCHASTLIVYI DOMIK
- SOBRANIE STIKHOV
- STAT'I O RUSSKOI POEZII
- TIAZHELAIA LIRA

KHODATAISTVO RUSSKIKH LITERATOROV OB OBLEGCHENII TSENZURY – London. 1895. BR-10.099 1 – 9 – ne IDC [460]

Khodnev, A I *see* ISTORIIA IMPERATORSKAGO VOL'NAGO EKONOMICHESKAGO OBSHCHESTVA S 1765 DO 1865 GODA

Khodorkovskii, VR *see* KINODOKUMENTY PO ISTORII SOVETSKOGO KINO, KHRANIASHCHIESIA V TSENTRAL'NOM GOSUDARSTVENNOM ARKHIVE KINOFOTOFONODOKUMENTOV (1917-1945)

Khodunov, M E *see* PRAKTICHESKII KOMMENTARII K USTAVU VNUTRENNEGO VODNOGO TRANSPORTA

Kholmogorskii, FD *see* OBSHCHIMI SILAMI K OBSHCHEMU BLAGU

Khomiakov, Aleksei Stepanovich *see* L'EGLISE LATINE ET LE PROTESTANTISME AU POINT DE VUE DE L'EGLISE D'ORIENT

KHONT-HON-NOFER : THE LANDS OF ETHIOPIA / Kumm, Hermann Karl Wilhelm – (Includes index and appendix) – London: Marshall, 1910 – 1mf – 9 – 0-8370-6133-4 – 1986-0133 – us A.T.L.A. [960]

KHOROSHO / Maiakovskii, Vladimir – Oktiabrskaia poema. M. 1927. BR-966 2 – 8 – ne IDC [460]

KHOROVOE I REGENTSKOE DELO – St Petersburg, 1909-17 (bimonthly) – 45mf – 9 – us Ross [780]

KHORSABAD, PT 1 : WITH CHAPTERS BY HENRI FRANKFORT AND THORKILD JACOBSEN / Loud, Gordon – 1937 – 9 – $8.50f – 0-226-49388-1 – us U.C. Orient [930]

Khosrau, Nassiri *see* SEFER NAMEH, RELATION DU VOYAGE EN SYRIE

Khouri-Saint-Pierre, Anastassia *see* ETUDE SUR LES STATISTIQUES

KHOZHDENIE SV. APOSTOLA I EVANGELISTA IOANNA BOGOSLOVA / Likhachev, N P – Po litsevym rukopisiam XV i XVI vekov. Spb. 1911. BR-10,309 1 – 9 – ne IDC [240]

KHOZI A ISTVENNY I OBZOR SEVERO-ZAPADNO I OBLASTI : SEVERO-ZAPADNOE OBLASTNOE EKONOMICHESKOE SOVESHCHANIE – (Library has: 1924/25-1925/26) – Leningrad: Izd-vo Sevzap ekoso, 1921 – 1 – CSUX90-S675 – us Hoover Inst Photo [947]

KHOZI A ISTVO I AKUTII / I AKUTSKAI A AVTONOMNAI A SOVESTKAI A SOT SIALISTICHESKAI A RESPUBLIKA, GOSUDARSTVENNAI A PLANOVAI A KOMISSII A – (Library has: Mar./Apr. 1927) – I Akutsk: Izd. I Akutizdata, 1925-1928. 4v – 1 – CSUX90-S119 – us Hoover Inst Photo [947]

KHOZI A ISTVO I EGO ORGANIZAT SII A. SERII A I – (Library has: vol. 1-10, 1920) – Moskva: Redakt sionno Izdatelski i otdel V.S.N.Kh., 1920- – 1 – CSUX89-S646 – us Hoover Inst Photo [947]

KHOZI A ISTVO IVANOVSKO I OBLASTI / ORGAN OBLISPOLKOMA – Ivanovo: Gos. izd.-vo Ivanovsko i obl., 1936. 1v – 1 – CSUX90-S569 – us Hoover Inst Photo [947]

KHOZI A ISTVO IVANOVSKO I PROMYSHLENNO I OBLASTI : ORGAN OBLISPOLKOMA, ETC – (Library has: Jan.-Apr. 1932; Mar.-May, July 1934; 1935; Jan.-Feb. 1936) – Moskva, Ivanovo: Ogiz RSFSR, izd-vo Ivansko i promyshl. obl, 1929-1936. 8v – 1 – CSUX90-S566 – us Hoover Inst Photo [947]

KHOZI A ISTVO NA NOVYKH PUTI AKH : ORGAN STALINGRADSKO I GUBERNSKO I PLANOVO I KOMISSII (GUBPLAN) – Stalingrad: Komissii a, 1924-1928. 5v – 1 – CSUX90-S113 – us Hoover Inst Photo [947]

KHOZI A ISTVO SEVERA : EZHEMESI ACHNY I POLITIKO-EKONOMICHESKI I ZHURNAL SEVERNO I KRAEVO I PLANOVO I KOMISSII – (Library has: Dec. 1929; Jan., Mar.-Dec. 1930; Jan.-Aug. 1931; Jan.-Apr. 1933; Jan.-Aug. 1934; 1935-1936) – Arkhangelsk: Izd. Severnogo kra iplana, 1929-1936. 8v – 1 – CSUX90-S147 – us Hoover Inst Photo [320]

KHOZI A ISTVO URALA : POLITIKO-EKONOMICHESKI I ZHURNAL URALSKOGO OBLASTNOGO ISPOLNITELNOGO KOMITETA SOVETOV RABOCHIKH, KRESTI ANSKIKH, KRASNOARME ISKIKH I KAZACHIKH DEPUTATOV – (Library has: Apr.-July, Dec. 1928; Jan., Mar.-Sept. 1929; Oct. 1930; Jan.-June 1931; July/Aug. 1932; Jan.-Feb., Apr. 1933; May/June 1935) – Sverdlovsk: Izd. Sverdlovskogo oblplana, 1925-1935. 10v – 1 – CSUX90-S141 – us Hoover Inst Photo [320]

KHOZIAIN : ZHURNAL SEL'SKAGO KHOZIAISTVA I EKONOMII – (Lacking: 1894 v1. 1896 v3 n37. 1897 v4 n3,41,43,45,51-52. 1898-99 v5-6. 1900 v7 n17,30,34-36. 1901 v8 n40. 1902 v9 n4-6,8,13,22,24,26-30,40-47. 1903 v10 n7, 12,19,31-37,46. 1904 v11 n29,36,40-42,51. 1905 v12 n15,34-35) – Spb. 1894-1905 n42 – 359mf – 8 – R-8131/2 – ne IDC [330]

KHOZIAISTVENNYE DOGOVORY I KHOZRASCHET; SBORNIK POSTANOVLENII, PRIKAZOV I INSTRUKTSII, OTNOSIASHCHIKHSIA K RECHNOMU TRANSPORTU – 2nd ed. Moscow, 1950. 259p. BR-9266/1 – 9 – ne IDC [330]

KHOZIAISTVO – Ezhenedel'nyi sel'skokhoziaistvennyi i ekonomicheskii zhurnal. Kiev. 1906-16. Lacking: 1906-08 (22, 43), 1911 (36), 1913 (4-10). 1914 (28-50), 1915 (1-50), 1916 (7-8, 11-14, 21-28, 31-50). BR-2300 2 – 231mf – 8 – R-2300/2 – ne IDC [073]

KHOZIAISTVO DZHUIBARSKIKH SHEIKHOV. K.ISTORII FEODAL'NOGO ZEMLEVLADENIIA V SREDNEI AZII V XVI-XVII VV / Ivanov, P P – M., L. 1954. BU-747 2 – 8 – ne IDC [947]

KHOZRASCHET V PROMKOOPERATSII / Genkin, D M – M., L., 1932 – 2mf – 9 – COR-418/1 – ne IDC [334]

KHRAM PRAVOSLAVNO-KHRISTIANSKII = THE ORTHODOX CHRISTIAN TEMPLE / Krasnovskii, N – Moscow, 1888. One of 13 titles on reel – 1 – 86.44 – us Baptist [240]

KHRESHCHATIK – (Backfile through 1998 $85r) – 1999- – 2r per y – 1 – $160.00 standing order – us Ross [072]

KHRESTOMATIIA KRITICHESKIKH MATERIALOV PO RUSSKOI LITERATURE 18 VEKA / Orishin, A D – L'vov. 1959. BR-7740 2 – 8 – ne IDC [460]

KHRESTOMATIIA PO ISTORII PERVOI RUSSKOI REVOLIUTSII 1905 G : POSOBIE DLIA KABINETOV OBSHCHESTVOVEDENIIA BIBLIOTEK, SHKOL I STUPENI, SOVPARTSHKOL, SHKOL FABZAVUCHAI KRESTIANSKOI MOLODEZHII DLIA UCHITELEI SHKOL L STUPENI / Belousov, Semen Nikitich – Moskva: Gos. izd-vo, [192-] – 1 – CSUX88-B822 – us Hoover Inst Photo [947]

KHRISTIANIN – Ezhemesiachnoe izdanie dlia vsekh ishchushchikh istinu i liubiashchikh Gospoda. Spb. 1906-12, 1914. Lacking: 1906 (1); 1907 (4); 1914. BR-1565 2 – 8 – ne IDC [073]

KHRISTIANIN – Zhurnal tserkovno-obshchestvennoi zhizni nauki i literatury. Sergiev Posed. 1907-16. Lacking: 1908 (10-12), 1914 (5-7); 1916 (5-12). BR-1566 1 – 9 – ne IDC [073]

KHRISTIANSKI POBORNIK = CHRISTIAN ADVOCATE – St. Petersburg, 1909-1912. Methodist. 1,391p – 1 – $55.64 – us Baptist [073]

KHRISTIANSTVO I AKTIVNOST' CHELOVEKA / Berdiaev, N A – Paris: YMCA Press, [193-] – us Res Libr [240]

KHRISTO BOTEV / Topencharov, Vladimir – 1982 – 87p – 9 – 92-3-101489-7 – fr UNESCO [460]

KHRISTOS I ANTIKHRIST / Merezhkovskii, Dimitrii – Trilogiia. 3 v. (v. I, II Ed. 3; v. III Ed. 2). Spb. 1906. BR-794 2 – 8 – ne IDC [240]

KHRISTOS I ANTIKHRIST / Merezhkovskii, Dimitrii – Trilogiia. 5 v. Berlin. 1922. BR-758 2 – 8 – ne IDC [240]

KHRIZANTEMY – Ezhenedel'nyi khudozhestvenno-illiustrirovannyi zhurnal. v. 1-3. Spb. 1909. BR-1567 2 – 8 – ne IDC [073]

KHRIZOPRAS – Khudozhestvenno-literaturnyi sbornik izdatel'stva "Samotsvet". v. 1. M. 1906-07. BR-1836 2 – 8 – ne IDC [073]

KHRONIKA – (Library has: 1918, no.2) – Moskva: Kinematograficheski i komitet Narodnogo komissariata prosveshchenii a, 191u – 1 – CSUX90-S5 – us Hoover Inst Photo [947]

KHRONIKA / Naukove Tovaristvo Imeni Shevchenka – Lemberg. no. 1-59. 1900-1914 – 1 – us NY Public [400]

KHRONIKA / Naukove Tovaristvo Imeni Shevchenka – Lvov. n1-59. 1900-14 – 1r – 1 – us Ross [460]

KHRONIKA ARKHEOLOGIJI TA MYSTETSTVA – v. 1-3. Kiev. 1930-31. BR-1568 2 – 8 – ne IDC [073]

KHRONIKA LENINGRADSKOGO OBSHCHESTVA BIBLIOFILOV, 5 IANVARIA-20 IIUNIA 1930 G / Leningradskoe obshchestvo bibliofilov – Leningrad: Izd. L.O.B., 1931 – 1 – us U.W. Library [947]

KHRONIKA NEDAVNEI STARINY – Iz arkhiva kniazia Obolenskago-Neledinskago-Meletskago. Spb. 1876. BR-6009 2 – 8 – ne IDC [010]

KHRONIKA UCHREZHDENII MELKAGO KREDITA – Ezhemesiachnoe prilozhenie k zhurnalu "Sel'skii vestnik". Kiev. 1907-12. Lacking: 1907 (2, 4, 7-8, 10-12); 1910 (3, 5); 1912 (1-7, 10). BR-1572 2 – 8 – ne IDC [073]

KHRONIKA UCHREZHDENII MELKOGO KREDITA : EZHEMESIACHNOE PRILOZHENIE K ZHURNALU "SEL'SKII VESTNIK" – (Missing: 1907 n2, 4, 7-8, 10-12; 1910 n3, 5; 1912 n1-7, 10) – Kiev, 1907-12 – 54mf – 9 – R-1572/2 – ne IDC [334]

KHRONOLOGICHESKII PERECHEN' IMMUNITETNYKH GRAMOT 16 V – Catalogue of 16th cent. charters of immunity. S.M. Kashtanov, V.D. Nazarov and B.N. Floria, comps. BR-11,045/1 – 9 – ne IDC [947]

KHRONOLOGICHESKII PERECHEN' ZAKONOV SOIUZA SSR PO SOSTOIANIIA NA 1 IIULIA 1935 G / Iodkovskii, AN & Mashukovs, V A – Ed. 2. 1935. BR-9345 1 – 9 – ne IDC [947]

KHRONOLOGICHESKII SPISOK UCHENYKH I LITERATURNYKH TRUDOV I IZDANII L.N. MEIKOVA / Simoni, P K – Spb. 1905. BR-7255 2 – 8 – ne IDC [460]

KHRONOLOGICHESKII UKAZATEL' KNIG I BROSHIUR, VYSHEDSHIKH NA GRUZINSKOM IAZYKE S 1629 PO 1883. G – Tiflis. 1883. BR-4386 2 – 8 – ne IDC [460]

KHRONOLOGICHESKOE SOBRANIE ZAKONOV ESTONSKOI SSR, UKAZOV PREZIDIUMMA VERKHOVNOGO SOVETA I POSTANOVLENII PRAVITEL'STVA ESTONSKOI SSR – Tallin, 1953. 2v. v1: 1940-1941, v2: 1944-1947 – 13mf – 9 – ne IDC [340]

KHRONOLOGICHESKOE SOBRANIE ZAKONOV LATVIISKOI SSR, UKAZOV PREZIDIUMA VERKHOVNOGO SOVETA LATVIISKOI SSR I POSTANOVLENII PRAVITEL'STVA LATVIISKOI SSR; 1940-1959 – Riga, 1960 – 6mf – 9 – ne IDC [340]

KHRONOLOGICHESKOE SOBRANIE ZAKONOV LITOVSKOI SSR, UKAZOV PREZIDIUMA VERKHOVNOGO SOVETA I POSTANOVLENII PRAVITEL'STVA LITOVSKOI SSR – Vilnius. 6v. 1957-1959 – 64mf – 9 – ne IDC [340]

KHRONOLOGICHESKOE SOBRANIE ZAKONOV PREZIDIUMA VERKHOVNOGO SOVETA I POSTANOVLENII PRAVITEL'STVA RSFSR – Moscow, 1958-60.8v. BR-8478/1 – 9 – ne IDC [520]

KHRONOLOGICHESKOE SOBRANIE ZAKONOV TURKMENSKOI SSR, UKAZOV PREZIDIUMA VERKHOVNOGO SOVETA, POSTANOVLENII I RASPORIAZHENII PRAVITEL'STVA TURKMENSKOI SSR – Ashkhabad, 1960-63. 4v.BR-8479/1 – 9 – ne IDC [520]

Khrushchev, Nikita Sergeevich *see*
- EMPATPULUH TAHUN REVOLUSI SOSIALIS OKTOBER BESAR
- PIDATO DALAM SIDANG SOVJET TERTINGGI URSS, 21 DESEMBER 1957

Khudiakov, P *see* DELOPROIZVODSTVO I KORRESPONDENTSIIA SEL'SKOKHOZIAISTVENNYKH KOOPERATIVNYKH ORGANIZATSII

KHUDOZHESTVENNAIA GAZETA – Spb. 1836-1841. Lacking: 1838-39, 1841. B-1694 2 – 8 – ne IDC [073]

KHUDOZHESTVENNAIA LITERATURA RUSSKAIA I PEREVODNAIA 1917-1925 GG. UKAZATEL' STATEI I RETSENZII / Matsuev, N I – M. 1926. B-1060 2 – 8 – ne IDC [460]

KHUDOZHESTVENNII TRUD – Moscow, 1923-24 – 19mf – 9 – $130.00 – us Ross [790]

KHUDOZHESTVENNO-BIBLIOGRAFICHESKII SBORNIK – (Izd. A. E. Burtsev). pt. 6-71, 73-80. Spb. 1908. BR-4337 2 – 8 – ne IDC [460]

O KHUDOZHESTVENNOI PROZE. GORN / Belyi, A – Izdanie Moskovskogo Proletkul'ta. v. 2-3. 1919. BR-578 2 – 8 – ne IDC [460]

KHUDOZHESTVENNY I TRUD – Peterburg: Izd. Otdela izobrazitelnykh iskusstv pri narodnom komissariate po prosveshchenii u, 191. 1v – 1 – CSUX89-S934 – us Hoover Inst Photo [947]

KHUDOZHESTVENNYE SOKROVISHCHA ROSSII = ART TREASURES OF RUSSIA / ed by Benois, A & Prakhov, A – St Petersburg: Society for the Encouragement of Artists, 1901-07 – 55mf – 9 – $380.00 – us Ross [740]

KHUDOZHESTVENNYI FOL'KLOR – Organ fol'klornoi podsektsii literaturnoi sektsii GAKhN. v. 1-5. M. 1926-29. BR-2021 2 – 8 – ne IDC [390]

KHUDOZHESTVENNYIA NOVOSTI – Prilozhenie k zhurnalu "Vestnik iziashchnykh iskusstv". v. 1-8. Spb. 1884-90. B-1696 2 – 8 – ne IDC [073]

KHUDOZHNIK – Illiustrirovannyi zhurnal iziashchnoi literatury i iskusstva. Spb. 1891-92. Lacking: 1892 (5). B-1697 2 – 8 – ne IDC [073]

KHUDOZHNIK I ZRITEL' – Moscow, 1924 – 11mf – 9 – $75.00 – us Ross [790]

KHUDOZHNIKI I MYSLITELI. II KNIGA LITERATURNO-KRITICHESKIKH OCHERKOV / Abramovich, N Ia – M. 1911. BR-1956 2 – 8 – ne IDC [460]

Khuen, Joseph Cajetan *see* MAGNUS IN ORTU: MAXIMUS IN MERIDIE: MAJOR IN OCCASU SEMPERQUE SERENISSIMUS PRINCIPUM SOL MAXIMILIANUS EMANUEL

Khunrath, Heinrich *see* AMPHITHEATRUM SAPIENTIAE AETERNAE, SOLIUS, VERAE

KHUTOR : NOVYI PRAKTICHESKII SEL'SKO-KHOZIAISTVENNYI ZHURNAL – (Missing: 1908 n8; 1912 n5; 1914 n12) – Spb., 1906-15 – 202mf – 9 – R-1574/2 – ne IDC [334]

KHUTORIANIN : EZHENEDEL'NOE IZDANIE, POSVIASHCHENNOE INTERESAM MESTNOGO SEL'KOGO KHOZIAISTVA, PROMYSHLENNOSTI I TORGOVLI – (Missing: 1896-1906; 1907 n29; 1908 n18, 31, 46; 1909 n22, 39; 1910 n32; 1911 n2, 49-50; 1912 n3, 12-13, 40, 52; 1913-17) – Poltava, 1896-1917 – 290mf – 9 – R-1575/1 – ne IDC [334]

KHUTORSKOE KHOZIAISTVO – Prilozhenie k zhurnalu "Selskii khoziain." Spb. 1906-17. Incomplete. BR-2246 2 – 100mf – 8 – R-2246/2 – ne IDC [073]

KHUTTAT EL TANMEYA EL IQTISADEYA WA EL IJTIMAEYA LIL-SANAWAT EL KHAMS, 1963-1968 / Libya. Ministry of Planning and Development – (Five-Year Economic and Social Plan for the Period 1963-1968). Tripoli. 1964. BD-1369 1 – 9 – ne IDC [330]

Khuwarazmu *see* THE ALGEBRA OF MOHAMMED BEN MUSA

KHWAM TOK LONG TRAIPHAKHI...KHAO THAI...TRIPARTITE AGREEMENT BETWEEN THE GOVERNMENTS OF SIAM, THE UNITED STATES OF AMERICA AND THE UNITED KINGDOM OF GREAT BRITAIN AND NORTHERN IRELAND. / Thailand. Treaties, etc – Bangkok, 1946 1 v. (various pagings). LL-10019 – 1 – us L of C Photodup [324]

KIAMA INDEPENDENT – Jul 21 1863-Dec 30 1897; Jan 3 1942- Dec 22 1956 – 9 – at Pascoe [072]

Kiamichi Baptist Assembly. Oklahoma *see* CORRESPONDENCE AND RECORDS, 1944-55

Kiang Su. Provincial Sinological Library *see* CHIANG-SU SHENG-LI KUO-HSUEH T'U-SHU-KUAN NIEN-K'AN

Kiang, Wen-han *see*
- CHRISTIANITY AND MARX-LENINISM (CCC205)
- WHAT IS THE CHRISTIAN FAITH? (CCC206)

Kiangsi. China. (Province) *see*
- CHIANG-HSI MIN-CHENG KUNG-PAO
- CHIANG-HSI SHENG-CHENG FU KUNG-PAO

UN KIBBOUTZ DE GALILEE / Le Diraison, C – 9 – fr Hachette [360]

KIBBUTZ JOURNAL – New York, New York, No. 1 (Jan. 1984)-no. 10 (Mar. 1990) – us A.J.P.C. [270]

Kick, Friedrich *see* DIE ENTWICKLUNG DER WERKZEUGE

THE KICKLEBURYS ON THE RHINE BY MR. M.A. TITMARSH / Thackeray, William Makepeace – London: Smith, Elder, & Co., 1850 – 1 roll – 1 – 1-55879-341-0 – uk Libr Preservation [830]

Kickx, J *see* FLORA BRUXELLENSIS

KID : KRIMINALROMAN / Albert, Albrecht – Berlin: Aufwaerts-Verlag M Klieber, c1943 – 1r – 1 – us U.W. Library [830]

Kidd, B J *see*
- DOCUMENTS ILLUSTRATIVE OF THE CONTINENTAL REFORMATION
- THE THIRTY-NINE ARTICLES

Kidd, J B *see* SELECTED LETTERS OF WILLIAM BRIGHT

Kidd, S *see*
- CATALOGUE OF THE CHINESE LIBRARY OF THE ROYAL ASIATIC SOCIETY
- CHINA, OR, ILLUSTRATION OF THE SYMBOLS, PHILOSOPHY,... EDUCATION, AND LITERATURE OF THE CHINESE

Kidd, Thomas *see* TRACTS AND MISCELLANEOUS CRITICISMS OF THE LATE RICHARD PORSON, ESQ. REGIUS GREEK PROFESSOR IN THE UNIVERSITY OF CAMBRIDGE

Kidder, Frank E *see* THE ARCHITECTS AND BUILDERS HANDBOOKS

Kiddle, Henry *see* THE DICTIONARY OF EDUCATION AND INSTRUCTION: A REFERENCE BOOK AND MANUAL ON THE THEORY AND PRACTICE OF TEACHING.

KIDD'S OWN JOURNAL: FOR INTER-COMMUNICATIONS ON NATURAL HISTORY, POPULAR SCIENCE. – London, 1852-54. v.1-5 – 3 – us Readex [500]

Kidgell, J *see* ORIGINAL FABLES

KIDNAPPED : BEING MEMOIRS OF THE ADVENTURES OF DAVID BALFOUR IN THE YEAR 1751 / Stevenson, Robert Louis – London: Cassell, 1886 – 1 roll – 1 – 1-55879-677-0 – uk Libr Preservation [830]

Kidner, FD *see* SACRIFICE IN THE OLD TESTAMENT

KIDNEY AND BLOOD PRESSURE RESEARCH – v1-. 1978- – 1,5,9 – us UMI [612]

KIDNEY INTERNATIONAL – v. 1-18. 1972-80 – 1,5,9 – 1418.00 – us UMI [073]

KIDUNG SISWA: LAGU2 KRISTEN DALAM BAHASA INGGERIS, DJERMAN DAN PERANTJIS. HYMNS, WITHOUT MUSIC; ENGLISH, GERMAN AND FRENCH WORDS / ed by Pakun, R M – SE-10,702 1. 1962 – 9 – ne IDC [240]

Kieffer, Patricia E *see* THE RELATIONSHIP OF SPORT INVOLVEMENT AND SEX ROLE CLASSIFICATION OF COLLEGE FEMALES

Kiefiuk, Deborah S *see* INVESTIGATION OF PHYSICAL SELF-PERCEPTIONS, FITNESS BEHAVIOR, AND PROGRAM SELECTION AMONG FITNESS PARTICIPANTS IN THREE FITNESS CLUB ENVIRONMENTS

Kiel, Friedrich *see* EIGHT SHORT MELODIOUS PIECES FOR PIANOFORTE DUET

Kiel, Herman Gottlieb *see* THE CENTENNIAL BIOGRAPHICAL DIRECTORY OF FRANKLIN COUNTY

KIEL-ALTONAER DEMOKRATISCHES WOCHENBLATT – Kiel, Germany. 7 Jan-1 Feb 1849 – 1r – 1 – gw Mikrofilm [072]

KIELER DEMOKRATISCHES WOCHENBLATT – Kiel, Germany. 19 Nov-14 Dec 1848 – 1 – gw Mikrofilm [072]

KIELER NACHRICHTEN – Kiel, West Germany. 1968- – ca 9r per yr – 1 – gw Mikrofilm [072]

DIE KIELER SPROTTEN : DIE GESCHICHTE EINES FISCHEREIPRODUKTES AM BEISPIEL DER STANDORTE KIEL-ELLERBEK UND ECKERNFOERDE MIT EINEM SCHWERPUNKT 1871-1914/18 UND EINEM AUSBLICK IN DIE GEGENWART / Szadkowski, Karin – 1995 – 2mf – 9 – DM80.00 – 3-8267-2273-6 – gw Hänsel [630]

KIELER ZEITUNG – Germany. -d. 13 Jan 1916-19 Oct 1918. Imperfect. 8 reels – 1 – uk British Libr Newspaper [072]

Kieninger, Carmen *see* AMBULANTE SOZIALE DIENSTE IN DER ALTENHILFE

Kienow, Nancy L *see* DEATH EDUCATION AND DEATH ANXIETY IN STUDENT NURSE AIDES

DER KIENTOPP *see* KINOBRIEFE

Kier, Martin *see* SOLDATEN DES KOENIGS

Kier, P O *see* BEDARF ES EINER BESONDEREN INSPIRATIONSLEHRE?

Kierkegaard, Soren *see*
- AF EN ENDNU LEVENDES PAPIRER
- EN BLADARTIKEL
- DOMMER SELV!
- ENTEN–ELLER
- HVAD CHRISTUS DOMMER OM OFFICIEL CHRISTENDOM
- INDOVELSE I CHRISTENDOM
- EN LITERAIR ANMELDELSE
- OIEBLIKKET
- OM BEGREBET IRONI
- EN OPBYGGELIG TALE
- S. KIERKEGAARD'S BLADARTIKLER
- STADIER PAA LIVETS VEI
- TO TALER VED ALTERGANGEN OM FREDAGEN
- TRE TALER VED TAENKTE LEILIGHEDER

KIERUNKI – Warsaw. v. 1 no. 1-v. 6 no. 281. May 20 1956-Nov 5 1961. Incomplete – 1 – us NY Public [073]

Kierzkowski, Leon *see* TROIS LETTRES ADRESSEES A R. LAFLAMME DE LA VILLE DE MONTREAL:...APPEL AU TRIBUNAL DE L'OPINION PUBLIQUE

DIE KIESELSCHALIGEN BACILLARIEN ODER DIATOMEEN / Kuetzing, F T – Nordhausen. 1844. B-7112 1 – 9 – ne IDC [580]

Kiesgen, Laurenz *see* HEINRICH VON KLEIST

Kiessmann, Rudolf *see* UNTERSUCHUNGEN UEBER DIE MOTIVE DER ROBIN-HOOD-BALLADEN

Kiester, J A *see* THE HISTORY OF FARIBAULT COUNTY

Kiev. Central Archive *see* OPISI AKTOVYKH KNIG KIEVSKAGO TSENTRAL'NAGO ARKHIVA

Kiev. Dukhovnoi Akademii. Library *see* SISTEMATICHESKII KATALOG KNIG BIBLIOTEKI KIEVSKOI DUKHOVNOI AKADEMII

Kiev. Pecherskoi Library *see* SISTEMATICHESKII KATALOG KNIG BIBLIOTEKI KIEVO-PECHERSKOI LAVRY

Kiev. Universytet *see* ZAPYSKY

KIEVLIANIN – v. 1-3. Kiev. 1840-50. BR-3199 2 – 8 – ne IDC [947]

KIEVSKAIA AKADEMIIA S POLOVINY 18 V. DO PREOBRAZOVANIIA V 1819 G / Serebrennikov, V – Kiev. 1897. BR-7852 2 – 8 – ne IDC [370]

KIEVSKAIA AKADEMIIA V PERVOI POLOVINE 18 STOLETIIA / Vishnevskii, D – Novyе dannye otnoshchiesia k istorii etoi Akademii za ukazannoe vremia. Kiev. 1903. BR-7954 2 – 8 – ne IDC [947]

KIEVSKAIA MYSL' – Kiev, Russia, 1914-16 – 4r – 1 – us Ross [072]

KIEVSKAIA STARINA : ESHEMESIACHNYI ISTORICHESKII ZHURNAL – (Cont. as: Ukraina. Kiev, 1907. 1v. Index for 1882-1906: Poltava, 1911. 219p) – Kiev. v1-94. 1882-1906 – 1303 mf – 9 – 1239/2 – ne IDC [947]

KIEVSKAIA STARINA. EZHEMESIACHNYI ISTORICHESKII ZHURNAL – (Cont as: Ukraina, Kiev 1907 1v. Index for 1882-1906: Poltava 1911 219p) – Kiev. v1-94. 1882-1906 – 1303mf – 9 – ne IDC [947]

KIEVSKIE GUBERNSKIE VEDOMOSTI, 1838-1917 – 136r – 1 – $12,000.00 coll $100.00r – us Ross [072]

KIEVSKII KOMMUNIST – Kiev. Mar. 13-18, 1919 – 1 – 35.00r – us Hoover Inst Photo [335]

Kiewiet, C W de *see* THE ANATOMY OF SOUTH AFRICAN MISERY

KIKIS HABIS TIAP-TIAP PERBUATAN KONTRA-REVOLUSIONER / Sukarno, Pres. Indonesia – SE 4733 1 Djuli 1963 di Djakarta – 9 – ne IDC [324]

Kikuchi, Yoshio *see* GOBANKATA DAIDAIKI

KIKUYU : THE ARCHBISHOP OF CANTERBURY, EASTER, 1915 / Davidson, Randall Thomas – London: Macmillan, 1915 – 1mf – us A.T.L.A. [240]

KIKUYU NEWS – v129-216. Sep 1934-1958 (complete) – 1r – 1 – ATLA S0523 – us A.T.L.A. [073]

Kilbourn, John Kenyon *see* FAITHS OF FAMOUS MEN IN THEIR OWN WORDS

Kilbourne, John D *see* THE THOMAS PENN PAPERS

Kilbourne, John R *see* BUILDING A BRIDGE BETWEEN ATHLETICS AND ACADEMICS

Kil'chevskii, V A *see*
- KAK SOSTAVIT' OTCHET SEL'SKOKHOZIAISTVENNOGO KREDITNOGO TOVARISHCHESTVA
- KAKAIA RAZNITSA MEZHDU CHASTMYM BANKOM I KREDITNYM TOVARISHCHESTVOM
- KOOPERATSIIA I PARTIIA
- KOOPERATSIIA I REVOLIUTSIIA
- OBSHCHESTVENNO-KOOPERATIVNAIA SHKOLA
- ORGANIZATSIIA MESTNYKH KOOPERATIVNYKH KURSOV
- PRAVA I OBIAZANNOSTI CHLENA KREDITNOGO KOOPERATIVA
- ROBERT QUEN I OSNOVY POTREBITEL'SKOI KOOPERATSII
- SEL'SKOKHOZIAISTVENNOE KREDITNOE TOVARISHCHESTVO – ORGANIZATOR RAIONA
- UKAZANIIA PRAVLENIIAM KREDITNYKH KOOPERATIVOV DLIA SAMOPROVERKI

KILDARE AND WICKLOW CHRONICLE – Athy. Ireland. -w. 17 Feb-3 Mar 1849. (4 ft) – 1 – uk British Libr Newspaper [072]

KILDERNE TIL SAKSES OLDHISTORIE / Olrik, Axel – v1-2. 1892-94 – 1 – us I.U. Libraries [390]

Kilgore, Bruce M *see* WILDERNESS IN A CHANGING WORLD ANTHOLOGY

Kilgore, Damon Y *see* THE BIBLE IN PUBLIC SCHOOLS

Kilham, A *see* IN- AND OUT-LETTERS, 1795-1799, RELATING TO THE FORMATION OF THE METHODIST NEW CONNEXION

Kilian, Werner *see* HERWEGH ALS UEBERSETZER

Kilianus, C *see* ETYMOLOGICUM TEUTONICAE LINGUAE SIVE DICTIONARIUM TEUTONICO-LATINUM

Kilinskii, A *see* ZAKONY O TRUDE V UCHREZHDENIIAKH SSSR ZA GRANITSEI

KILKENNEY PEOPLE – Ireland. 1896-1920 (missing Aug-Sep 1917).-w. 22 reels – 1 – uk British Libr Newspaper [072]

KILKENNY JOURNAL – Ireland. -w. 1832-1900. Lacking 23 Dec 1893-19 June 1895. 67 reels – 1 – uk British Libr Newspaper [072]

KILKENNY MODERATOR – Ireland. -w. 1828-40, 1881, 1885, 1900-2. 18 reels – 1 – uk British Libr Newspaper [072]

KILLARNEY ECHO – Ireland. 26 Aug 1899-Dec 1917.-w. 14mqn reels – 1 – uk British Libr Newspaper [072]

Killen, James Miller *see* OUR FRIENDS IN HEAVEN

Killen, W D *see*
- THE ANCIENT CHURCH
- THE ECCLESIASTICAL HISTORY OF IRELAND
- THE FRAMEWORK OF THE CHURCH
- HISTORY OF CONGREGATIONS OF THE PRESBYTERIAN CHURCH IN IRELAND AND BIOGRAPHICAL NOTICES OF EMINENT PRESBYTERIAN MINISTERS AND LAYMEN
- THE IGNATIAN EPISTLES ENTIRELY SPURIOUS

Killgore, Garry L *see* THE EFFECTS OF SURFACE TYPE ON PLANTAR PRESSURE DISTRIBUTION AND RUNNING KINEMATICS

Killinger, Manfred, Freiherr von *see* DAS WAREN KERLE

Killits, John M *see* TOLEDO AND LUCAS COUNTY 1623-1923

Killmer, Karen J *see* THE DIFFERENCE IN COACH ROLE MODEL BEHAVIORS FOR MALE AND FEMALE ATHLETES

Killy, Walther *see* GROSSE DEUTSCHE LEXIKA

KILMARNOCK ADVERTISER AND AYRSHIRE REVIEW – Scotland. 22 Aug-12 Dec 1868.-w. 13 ft – 1 – uk British Libr Newspaper [072]

KILMARNOCK CHRONICLE, AND COUNTY ADVERTISER – Scotland. Jan 1854-Aug 1855.-w. 1 reel – 1 – uk British Libr Newspaper [072]

KILMARNOCK HERALD – Scotland. Nov 1882-Apr 1955. 42 reels – 1 – uk British Libr Newspaper [072]

KILMARNOCK HERALD AND WEST COUNTY ADVERTISER – Scotland. Jan 1845-May 1848.-w. 1 reel – 1 – uk British Libr Newspaper [072]

KILMARNOCK JOURNAL AND AYRSHIRE ADVERTISER – Scotland. 1844-May 1857. 5 reels – 1 – uk British Libr Newspaper [072]

KILMARNOCK PIONEER – Scotland. Oct 1870-May 1871.-w. 7 ft – 1 – uk British Libr Newspaper [072]

Kilmarnock. Scotland. St. Andrew's Parish Churchyard *see* REGISTER OF BURIALS

KILMARNOCK STANDARD – 1 – £42.00r – uk Scot News [072]
KILMARNOCK STANDARD – Scotland. -w. 1876-91. 6 reels – 1 – uk British Libr Newspaper [072]
KILMARNOCK WEEKLY POST – Scotland. Nov 1856-Oct 1865.-w. 8 reels – 1 – uk British Libr Newspaper [072]
KILMENY / Black, William – British Fiction Archive: Unit 4 – 9 – uk Bell [830]
KILOBAUD – (See also: Kilobaud Microcomputing) – v1-24. 1977-1978 – 1,5,6,9 – us UMI [510]
KILOBAUD MICROCOMPUTING – v. 25-. 1979- – 1,5,6,9 – us UMI [510]
KILSYTH CHRONICLE – 1 – £42.00r – uk Scot News [072]
KILSYTH CHRONICLE – (Available As a Standing Order) – 1923 – 1. 235 – £42.00r – uk Scot News [072]
Kilty, Keith M et al *see* JOURNAL OF POVERTY
Kim, Dae Tschong *see* BERTOLT BRECHT UND DIE GEISTESWELT DES FERNEN OSTENS
Kim, H D *see* DIFFERENTIAL EFFECTS OF STRENGTH TRAINING AND ENDURANCE TRAINING ON PARAMETERS REALTED TO RESISTANCE TO GRAVITATIONAL FORCES
Kim, Jong-Il. *see* THE EFFECTS OF GLASNOST AND PERESTROIKA ON THE SOVIET SPORT SYSTEM
Kim, Kyoung N *see* THE EFFECTS OF HIGH SPATIAL CONSTRAINTS IN DETERMINING THE NATURE OF THE SPEED-ACCURACY TRADE-OFF IN AIMED HAND MOVEMENTS
Kim, Kyunghee *see* THE STATUS OF DANCE IN KOREAN HIGHER EDUCATION
Kim, M P *see* V.I. LENIN I ISTORIIA KLASSOV I POLITICHESKIKH PARTII V. ROSSII / AON PRI TSK KPSS
KIM VAN KIEU TAN TRUYEN – Poeme annamite, traduit et annote par Abel Des Michels. 1884 – 9 – fr Orientalistes [810]
KIMBERLEY CITIZEN – Kimberley, South Africa. 11 Aug 1897-24 Dec 1898. 1 reel. Title varies: S.A. Citizen, Aug-Dec 1897; The Citizen, Dec 1897-Jul 1898; The Kimberley Elector, Jul-Aug 1898; Burgers Vriend – 1, 16 diazo available at reduced price – sa SA Libr [072]
THE KIMBERLEY COLONIST – Kimberley, South Africa.27 Mar-20 Apr 1897. 1 reel – 1, 16 diazo available at reduced price – sa SA Libr [072]
KIMBERLEY ELECTOR *see* KIMBERLEY CITIZEN
KIMBERLY AND KURUMAN DIOCESAN MAGAZINE – (Cont by: Highway) – v2-7. 1937-46 (complete) – 1r – 1 – ATLA S0727 – us A.T.L.A. [073]
KIMBERLY AND KURUMAN DIOCESAN MAGAZINE *see* HIGHWAY
KIMBERLY FREE PRESS *see* THE WEEKLY FREE PRESS
Kime, J *see* PLASMA AND ERYTHROCYTE LACTATE CONCENTRATIONS IN HUMANS AFTER SUBMAXIMAL EXERCISE
Kimedoncius, J *see* VANDER DOOPE ONSES HEEREN JESU CHRISTI, BEKENTNISSE DOOR DIERICK PHILIPS
Kimmell, J A *see* 20TH CENTURY HISTORY OF FINDLAY AND HANCOCK COUNTY AND REPRESENTATIVE CITIZENS
Kimura, Iris F *see*
- BIOMECHANICAL COMPARISON OF SUPPORT PROVIDED BY THE AIRSTIRRUP ANKLE TRAINING BRACE™ PRE- AND POST-EXERCISE
- THE HIGH JUMP AS PERFORMED BY THE 1979 UNITED STATES OUTDOOR FEMALE RECORD HOLDER: A BIOMECHANICAL ANALYSIS
- INFLUENCE OF THE STRENGTH SHOE AND THREE PLYOMETRIC DRILLS ON THE STRENGTH, VELOCITY, AND JUMPING ABILITY OF HIGH SCHOOL FOOTBALL PLAYERS
- PEAK TORQUE RELIABILITY OF BIODEX B-2000 ISOKINETIC DYNAMOMETER DURING CONCENTRIC LOADING OF BACK FLEXORS AND EXTENSORS

KINABALY TIMES AND SUNDAY TIMES – Jesselton. North Borneo. 1965-1967 – 1 – us UMI [072]
KINAH AL GEZEIROT HA-KEHILLOT DI-K"K OKRAYNE – Amsterdam. 1649. BJ-43-38 1 – 9 – ne IDC [470]
KINAH AL GEZEIROT HA-KEHILLOT DI-K"K OKRAYNE – Prague. 1648. BJ-43-37 1 – 9 – ne IDC [470]
Kinane, Thomas H *see* MARY IMMACULATE, MOTHER OF GOD
Kinau, Rudolf *see*
- EIN FROEHLICH HERZ
- KAMERAD UND KAMERADIN

Kincaide, H R *see* BIENNIAL REPORT OF THE SECRETARY OF STATE OF THE STATE OF OREGON 1897-1898
KINCARDINE NEWS – Ontario, CN. 1978-80 – 6r – 1 – cn Commonwealth Micro [072]
KINCARDINESHIRE, 1837 : BRITISH ISLES CENSUS DIRECTORIES PROJECT, SCOTLAND. VOL 42 – 1mf – 9 – A$9.00 – at Vine [941]
KINCARDINESHIRE OBSERVER *see* LAURENCE KIRK OBSERVER
KINCARDINSHIRE OBSERVER – 1 – £42.00r – uk Scot News [072]
Kinchen, Thomas A *see* AN INVESTIGATION OF MINISTERIAL COUNSELING SUPPORT: PROBLEMS, AND A PROPOSED MODEL
KINCH'S HENLEY ADVERTISER – England. Henley Advertiser. -w. 7 May 1870-11 Jan 1908. 28 reels – 1 – uk British Libr Newspaper [072]
DOS KIND = THE CHILD – (In Yiddish) – Warsaw, PL. v13 no3. Oct 1936 – 1r – 1 – $25.00 – cn Can Microfilming [072]
DAS KIND : NOVELLE / Grimm, Hermann Friedrich – New York: E Steiger, [1886?] – 1r – 1 – us U.W. Library [830]
DAS KIND DER MADELEINE MONTCORNET / Kraenzlein, Kurt – Hamburg: Hanseatische Verlagsanstalt, 1943 – 1r – 1 – us U.W. Library [830]
DAS KIND DES TORFMACHERS : EINE ERZAEHLUNG / Griese, Friedrich – Muenchen: A Langen/G Mueller, 1937 – 1r – 1 – us U.W. Library [830]
KIND WORD SERIES – 1866-1929 – 1 – 575.89 – us Baptist [240]
KINDAPOSTEN – Vimmerby, Sweden. 1894-1903 – 3r – 1 – sw Kungliga [072]
KINDAPOSTEN *see* VIMMERBY TIDNING
Kindberg, N C *see* EUROPEAN AND NORTH AMERICAN BRYINEAE
KINDER BOTE – v1-50. 1886-1936 – Inquire – 1 – ATLA 1994-S006 – us A.T.L.A. [073]
DIE KINDER DER EXCELLENZ : ROMAN / Wolzogen, Ernst von – Stuttgart: J Engelhorn [1888?] – 1r – 1 – us U.W. Library [830]
KINDER FREIHEIT = CHILDREN'S FREEDOM – New York City, NY, 1932 – 1r – Can$25.00 – cn Can Microfilming [071]
Kinder, George D *see* HISTORY OF PUTMAN COUNTY
Kinder, Robin *see* HUMANITIES COLLECTIONS
DI KINDER SHUL = THE CHILDREN SCHOOL – (Monthly) – New York City, NY. v1 no 1. 1932-1933 – 1r – Can$25.00 – cn Can Microfilming [071]
DER KINDERBOTE – (Lacking: v67 no22) – v53-58. 1940-1955 – Inquire – 1 – ATLA 1994-S008 – us A.T.L.A. [073]
KINDER-BOTE AND JUNIOR-MESSENGER – v51-52. 1937-38 (complete) – Inquire – 1 – ATLA 1994-S007 – us A.T.L.A. [073]
DER KINDERFREUND – Bremen, feb-oct 1856, aug 1857-mar 1858 – 1r – 1 – Inquire at Mikrofilmarchiv for details – gw Misc Inst [370]
DER KINDERFREUND – Bremen, Germany. Feb-Okt 1856; Aug 1857-Marz 1958 – 1r – 1 – gw Mikrofilm [072]
KINDERGARTEN AND FIRST GRADE *see* AMERICAN CHILDHOOD
KINDERLAND = CHILDREN'S WORLD – (In Yiddish) – Warsaw, PL. v3 no2. Jul/Aug 1933 – 1r – 1 – $25.00 – cn Can Microfilming [072]
KINDERLAND = CHILDREN'S WORLD – (Monthly) – New York City, NY. v1 no 1. 1930 – 1r – Can$25.00 – cn Can Microfilming [071]
KINDERLEGENDE / Leitgeb, Josef – Berlin: Wiking Verlag, [1945?] – 1r – 1 – us U.W. Library [830]
KINDERLIEDER UND GESCHICHTEN / Seidel, Heinrich – 5. Aufl. Stuttgart: Union Deutsche Verlagsgesellschaft, [190-?] – 1r – 1 – us U.W. Library [800]
Kindermann, Heinz *see*
- FERDINAND RAIMUND
- HEBBEL UND DAS WIENER THEATER SEINER ZEIT
- HOELDERLIN UND DAS DEUTSCHE THEATER
- KLOPSTOCKS ENTDECKUNG DER NATION

Kindermann, Jurgen *see* KATALOG DER FILMSAMMLUNG
KINDERMUND : AUSSPRUECHE UND SCENEN AUS DEM KINDERLEBEN / Schoenthan, Paul von – Leipzig: P. Reclam jun., [1886?] – 1r – 1 – us U.W. Library [080]
KINDERPOST – Essen, Germany. Apr 1930-Mar 1931 – 1 – gw Mikrofilm [072]
KINDERSPEL UND KINDERLUST IN ZUID-NEDERLAND / Cock, Alfons de – 1902-08 – 1 – us I.U. Libraries [390]
KINDERTHRAENEN : ZWEI ERZAEHLUNGEN / Wildenbruch, Ernst von – 3. Aufl. Berlin: Freund & Jeckel, 1884 – 1r – 1 – us U.W. Library [430]
DIE KINDERWELT – Leipzig, Germany. 1926-30 – 1 – gw Mikrofilm [072]
KINDERZEICHNUNGEN : UNTERSUCHUNG VON KINDERZEICHNUNGEN DER SCHULEINGANGSUNTERSUCHUNG DES HAUPTGESUNDHEITSAMTES BREMEN UNTER BESONDERER BERUECKSICHTIGUNG WISSENSCHAFTLICHER ERKENNTNISSE UEBER DEREN AUSSAGEFAEHIGKEIT / Leiers, Bastian – 1995 – 2mf – 9 – DM80.00 – 3-8267-2265-5 – gw Hänsel [150]
KINDEX – v1-3. 1965-94 – 9 – $147.00set – us Hein [340]
KINDGERECHTE BESTIMMUNG DER TRANSEPITHELIALEN POTENTIALDIFFERENZ AM RESPIRATORISCHEN EPITHEL DER NASE / Hofmann, Thomas – 1995 – 2mf – 9 – DM80.00 – 3-8267-2087-3 – gw Hänsel [611]
KINDNYTT – Boras, 1992 – 9 – sw Kungliga [072]
KINE WEEKLY – 1907-71. With printed list – 1 – £8,500.00 – uk World [790]
KINEMA – Zuerich, jul 5 1913-14, jan 9-aug 14 1915, sep 29-oct 7 1916, jan 5-dec 21 1918, jan 4-oct 25 1919 – 4r – 1 – gw Mikrofilm [790]
A KINEMATIC AND KINETIC ANALYSIS OF THE OVERGRIP GIANT SWING ON THE UNEVEN PARALLEL BARS / Witten, W – 1990 – 2mf – 9 – $8.00 – us Microform Publ [790]
THE KINEMATIC VARIABLES RELATED TO THE EFFICIENCY OF THROWING : FOOTBALL / Heppe, Robert A & Evans, Gail G – 1992 – 2mf – 9 – $8.00 – us Microform Publ [612]
"Der Kinematograph" *see* DER PRAKTIKUS
DER KINEMATOGRAPH – (Publ since 1923 in Berlin) – Duesseldorf. 1907-mar 30, 1935 – 23r – 1 – gw Mikrofilm [790]
DER KINEMATOGRAPH *see* DER PRAKTIKUS
KINEMATOGRAPHISCHE MONATSHEFTE – Berlin. apr 1921-jul 1933 – 2r – 1 – gw Mikrofilm [790]
KINEMATOGRAPHISCHE RUNDSCHAU – Berlin, Wien. feb 1, 1907-dec 15, 1908. 1909-jul 28, 1910. jul 7-dec 29, 1912 – 4r – 1 – gw Mikrofilm [790]
KINEMATOGRAPHISCHE WOCHENSCHAU / ed by Gaumont – Berlin. 1910 n38-66. 1912 n8-47 (incomplete) – 1 – gw Mikrofilm [790]
A KINETIC AND KINEMATIC COMPARISON OF THE GRAB AND TRACK STARTS IN COMPETITIVE SWIMMING / Juergens, Cheryl A – Oregon State University, 1995 – 2mf – 9 – $8.00 – PE 3657 – us Microform Publ [612]
KINETICS AND CATALYSIS – v1-34. 1960-93 – 1,5 – $120.00v – us UMI [540]
King, Albert Barnes *see* THE PURPLE AND SCARLET WOMAN AND HER RELATIVES
KING ALFRED'S VERSION OF THE CONSOLATIONS OF BOETHIUS / Sedgefield, Walter John – Oxford: Clarendon Press, 1900 – 1mf – us A.T.L.A. [190]
KING ARTHUR AND THE TABLE ROUND: TALES CHIEFLY AFTER THE OLD FRENCH OF CRESTIEN OF TROYES, WITH AN ACCOUNT OF ARTHURIAN ROMANCE. / Newell, William Wells – Boston, New York: Houghton, Mifflin, 1897. 2v – 1 – us U.W. Library [830]
King, C W *see* THE GNOSTICS AND THEIR REMAINS, ANCIENT AND MEDIEVAL
KING CHARLES 5, A PERSONAL MEMOIR / Gore, John – New York: Charles Scribner's Sons, 1941. xx,464p, front., illus, pl., ports – 1 – us U.W. Library [941]
King, Charles Daly *see* THE ORAGEAN VERSION
KING CITY HERALD – King City, CA. 1914-1932 – 6r – 1 – $300.00 – C03257 – us Library Micro [071]
King, CW *see*
- EARLY CHRISTIAN NUMISMATICS AND OTHER ANTIQUARIAN TRACTS
- JULIAN THE EMPEROR

King, David *see* THE PRINCIPLES OF GEOLOGY EXPLAINED, AND VIEWED IN THEIR RELATIONS TO REVEALED AND NATURAL RELIGION
King, E J *see* THE SACRED HARP
King, Edward George *see* THE YALKUT ON ZECHARIAH
King, Edward T *see* GENEALOGY OF SOME EARLY AMERICAN FAMILIES IN PRESTON COUNTY
KING EDWARD THE SIXTH, SUPREME HEAD : AN HISTORICAL SKETCH, WITH AN INTRODUCTION AND NOTES / Lee, Frederick George – London: Burns and Oates; New York: Catholic Publication Society Co., 1886 – 1mf – us A.T.L.A. [941]
King, Ernest J *see* OFFICIAL PAPERS OF FLEET ADMIRAL ERNEST J. KING
King, H C *see* RECORDS AND DOCUMENTS CONCERNING SERGEANT'S INN, FLEET STREET
King, Henry Churchill *see*
- RECONSTRUCTION IN THEOLOGY
- THEOLOGY AND THE SOCIAL CONSCIOUSNESS

King, Henry Melville *see*
- THE BAPTISM OF ROGER WILLIAMS
- RELIGIOUS LIBERTY
- WHY WE BELIEVE THE BIBLE

King, Henry T *see* SKETCHES OF PITT COUNTY 1704-1910
King, J *see* A VOYAGE TO THE PACIFIC OCEAN
King, J M *see* LIVESTOCK WATER NEEDS IN PASTORAL AFRICA IN RELATION TO CLIMATE AND FORAGE
KING JAMES 1 OF ENGLAND TO KING CHRISTIAN 4 OF DENMARK: ROYAL CORRESPONDENCE, 1603-1625 / Great Britain – 1 – us Primary [941]
King, James M *see* A STATEMENT CONCERNING THE FIRST YEAR'S ACTIVE WORK OF THE LEAGUE, AND ITS PURPOSES FOR THE IMMEDIATE FUTURE
King, John *see*
- LECTURES UPON JONAH
- SERMONS

King, Josiah *see* THE EXAMINATION AND TRYAL OF OLD FATHER CHRISTMAS
King, L W *see*
- BABYLONIAN MAGIC AND SORCERY
- THE LETTERS AND INSCRIPTIONS OF HAMMURABI, KING OF BABYLON
- THE SCULPTURES AND INSCRIPTIONS OF DARIUS 1, KING OF PERSIA, 548-485 BC
- STUDIES IN EASTERN HISTORY. CHRONICLES CONCERNING EARLY BABYLONIAN KINGS

King, Leonard William *see* FIRST STEPS IN ASSYRIAN
King, Man *see* THE PIONEER (CCC245)
THE KING OF COURT POETS; A STUDY OF THE WORK, LIFE AND TIME OF LODOVICO ARIOSTO / Gardner, Edmund Garratt – New York: E.P. Dutton, 1906. xix,395p. 9 pl. incl. front., ports., facsim. 3 fold. geneal. tab – 1 – us U.W. Library [440]
THE KING OF MEN : THE BLANK IN HIS HISTORY, ITS FILLING UP AND LESSONS / Kerr, Robert – Mitchell, IA: R Kerr, 1879 – 1mf – 9 – 0-8370-3891-X – 1985-1891 – us A.T.L.A. [240]
KING OF MEN: THE BLANK IN HIS HISTORY, ITS FILLING UP AND LESSONS / Kerr, Robert – Mitchell, IA: R. Kerr, 1879. 1 fiche – 9 – us A.T.L.A. [240]
THE KING OF THE SCHNORRERS : GROTESQUES AND FANTASIES / Zangwill, Israel – London: W. Heinemann, 1894 – 1 roll – 1 – 1-55879-711-4 – uk Libr Preservation [830]
KING PHILIP'S WAR / Ellis, George W. et al – 1906. Item E. Based on the archives and records of MA, Plymouth, RI & CT & contemporary letters & accounts with biog. and topograph. notes. Indexed, 326p.SW16-0084 – 5 – us A.G.L.L. [978]
King, Spencer B *see* AUTOBIOGRAPHY, 1880-1945
King, Susan E *see* THE ENROLLMENT AND PERSISTENCE OF AFRICAN-AMERICAN DOCTORAL STUDENTS IN PHYSICAL EDUCATION AND RELATED DISCIPLINES
King, T *see* A CHECK TO UNCHARITABLENESS
'KING TAUFA' / Collocott, E E V – 1r – 1 – at Pacific Mss [980]

King, Thomas Starr *see* SUBSTANCE AND SHOW
King, W *see* A MONOGRAPH OF THE PERMIAN FOSSILS OF ENGLAND
King, William Harvey *see* HISTORY OF HOMEOPATHY AND ITS INSTITUTIONS IN AMERICA; THEIR FOUNDERS, BENEFACTORS, FACULTIES, OFFICERS, HOSPITALS..
KING WILLIAMS TOWN GAZETTE – King Williams Town, South Africa. 14 Aug 1856-30 Dec 1874. 18 reels – 1, 16 diazo available at reduced price – sa SA Libr [072]
KINGCREST BAPTIST CHURCH (FORMERLY: EMMANEUL). VANCOUVER, BRITISH COLUMBIA. CANADA : CHURCH RECORDS – 1911-Sep 1969 – 1 – 67.12 – us Baptist [240]
THE KINGDOM AND PEOPLE OF SIAM : WITH A NARRATIVE OF THE MISSION TO THAT COUNTRY IN 1855 / Bowring, J – (Missing: v1) – London. 2v. 1857 – 9mf – 9 – ne IDC [950]
THE KINGDOM AND THE FARM / Feeman, Harlan L – New York: Fleming H. Revell, c1914 – 1mf – us A.T.L.A. [240]
KINGDOM (BASILEIA): AN EXEGETICAL STUDY / Boardman, George Dana – New York: Scribner's, 1899. 1 fiche – 9 – us A.T.L.A. [240]
THE KINGDOM IN HISTORY AND PROPHECY / Chafer, Lewis Sperry – New York: Fleming H. Revell, c1915 – 1mf – us A.T.L.A. [240]
THE KINGDOM IN INDIA : ITS PROGRESS AND ITS PROMISE / Chamberlain, Jacob – (Includes index) – New York: Fleming H Revell, c1908 – 1mf – 9 – 0-8370-6032-X – 1986-0032 – us A.T.L.A. [240]
THE KINGDOM IN THE CRADLE / Atkins, James – Nashville, Tenn.: Publishing House of the M.E. Church, South, 1905 – 1mf – us A.T.L.A. [240]
THE KINGDOM OF GOD : AN ESSAY IN THEOLOGY / Schwab, Laurence Henry – New York: E P Dutton, 1897 – 1mf – 9 – 0-8370-5172-X – 1985-3172 – us A.T.L.A. [240]
THE KINGDOM OF GOD AND AMERICAN LIFE / Brewster, Chauncey B – New York: Thomas Whittaker, 1912 – 1mf – us A.T.L.A. [240]
KINGDOM OF GOD BIBLICALLY AND HISTORICALLY / Candlish, James S – Edinburgh: T. & T. Clark, 1884. 1 fiche – 9 – us A.T.L.A. [240]
KINGDOM OF GOD: CHRIST'S TEACHING ACCORDING TO THE SYNOPTICAL GOSPELS / Bruce, Alexander Balmain – New York: Scribner's, 1896. 1 fiche – 9 – us A.T.L.A. [240]
KINGDOM OF GOD IN THE WRITINGS OF THE FATHERS / Herrick, Henry Martyn – Chicago: University of Chicago, 1903. 1 fiche – 9 – us A.T.L.A. [240]
THE KINGDOM OF GOD IN THE WRITINGS OF THE FATHERS / Herrick, Henry Martyn – (Includes index) – Chicago: University of Chicago Press, 1903 – 1mf – 9 – 0-8370-3570-8 – 1985-1570 – us A.T.L.A. [240]
THE KINGDOM OF GOD ON EARTH / Belaney, Robert – London: Thomas Baker, 1896 – 1mf – 9 – 0-8370-6962-9 – 1986-0962 – us A.T.L.A. [230]
THE KINGDOM OF GOD, OR, WHAT IS THE GOSPEL? / Dunn, Henry – (Includes indexes) – London: Simpkin, Marshall, 1868 – 1mf – 9 – 0-8370-8664-7 – 1986-2664 – us A.T.L.A. [240]
THE KINGDOM OF HEAVEN: WHAT IT IS AND HOW WE ENTER IT / Walpole, George Henry Somerset – London: Elliot Stock, 1909. 1 fiche – 9 – us A.T.L.A. [240]
KINGDOM OF LESOTHO ELECTORS' LIST FOR THE NATIONAL ASSEMBLY ELECTION IN JANUARY 1970 – (Includes the 1969 Report of the Constituency Delimination Commission) – 15r – 1 – $742.50 – us African Imprint [324]
THE KINGDOM OVERSEAS *see* WORK AND WORKERS IN THE MISSION FIELD
THE KINGDOMS OF AFRICA / Garlake, Peter S – Oxford: Elsevier-Phaidon, 1978. 152p. ill., facsim., maps, plans, ports.Bibliography. Includes index.(The Making of the Past) – 1 – us U.W. Library [960]
Kinglake, Alexander William *see* EOTHEN, OR, TRACES OF TRAVEL BROUGHT HOME FROM THE EAST
Kingman Park Civic Association *see* PUBLICATIONS
KING'S BAPTIST CHURCH. TAYLORSVILLE, KENTUCKY : CHURCH RECORDS – 1805-1989 – 1 – $123.15 – us Baptist [240]
THE KING'S BUSINESS – Los Angeles, CA. 1910-1970 – 12r – 1 – $600.00 – R04059 – us Library Micro [071]
King's College, Cambridge *see* MANORIAL COURT ROLLS AND VILLAGE SURVEYS
KING'S COLLEGE UNIVERSITY MAGAZINE – [Halifax, NS?: s.n, 1871-18– or 19–] (Halifax, NS: J Bowes) – 9 – cn C.I.H.M. [370]
KING'S CONFLICTING CIVIL CASES IN THE TEXAS REPORTS / Texas. Supreme Court – v1-3. 1840-1911 – 17mf – 9 – $25.50 – LLMC 91-030 – us L.L.M.C. [340]
THE KING'S COUNCIL IN ENGLAND DURING THE MIDDLE AGES / Baldwin, J F – H-1204 2. 1913 – 8 – ne IDC [941]
KING'S COUNSEL : JOURNAL OF THE FACULTY OF LAWS SOCIETY – (Lacking: 1940-47; 1949-50; 1966; 1968; 1981-82) – King's College, University of London, 1936-85 – 9 – LLMC 84-5221 – us L.L.M.C. [073]
KINGS COUNTY, 1901 – 1r – 1 – $50.00 – D046 – us Library Micro [978]
KING'S COUNTY CHRONICLE – Birr, Ireland. 24 Sep 1845-Dec 1921. -w. 27 reels – 1 – uk British Libr Newspaper [072]
KING'S COUNTY NEWS – Hampton, Canada. 1894-98 – 2r – 1 – $136.00 – cn Library Assoc [971]
THE KING'S GREATEST BUSINESS / Gilbert, Paul James – New York: Fleming H Revell, 1909 – 1mf – 9 – 0-8370-6120-2 – 1986-0120 – us A.T.L.A. [240]
KINGS GROVE BAPTIST CHURCH. PICKENS COUNTY. SOUTH CAROLINA : CHURCH RECORDS – 1910-59.Minutes, 1910-31. Membership rolls, 1910-1959 – 1 – 8.15 – us Baptist [240]
KING'S HIGHWAY – (Lacking some issues) – 1890-1967 – 9r – 1 – ATLA S0330 – us A.T.L.A. [073]
KINGS MOUNTAIN FIRST BAPTIST CHURCH. KINGS MOUNTAIN, NORTH CAROLINA : CHURCH RECORDS – 1944-63. WMU Records. 1917-62 – 1 – 63.95 – us Baptist [240]
THE KING'S MOUNTAIN MEN – By Katherine Keogh White, 1924. Item K.The story of the battle with sketches of thef American soldiers who took part. Includes militia roster and sundry pension declarations. Indexed, 271p. SW16-0054 – 5 – us A.G.L.L. [975]
KINGS MOUNTAIN SECOND BAPTIST CHURCH. KINGS MOUNTAIN, NORTH CAROLINA : CHURCH RECORDS – 1940-63 – 1 – 18.45 – us Baptist [240]
Kingsbury, G W *see*
- HISTORY OF DAKOTA TERRITORY, SOUTH DAKOTA, ITS HISTORY AND ITS PEOPLE
- ILLUSTRATED HISTORY OF KENNEBEC COUNTY

THE KINGSBURG RECORDER – Kingsburg, CA. 1904-20; 1925-33; 1937; 1941-43; 1945-46; 1950; 1973- – 39+ r – 1 – $1,950.00 ($90.00y) – B02327 – us Library Micro [071]
Kingsbury, Harmon *see* LAW AND GOVERNMENT
Kingsford, Anna Bonus *see* THE VIRGIN OF THE WORLD OF HERMES MERCURIUS TRISMEGISTUS
Kingsford, C L *see* THE FIRST ENGLISH LIFE OF KING HENRY THE FIFTH, WRITTEN IN 1513 BY AN ANONYMOUS AUTHOR KNOWN COMMONLY AS THE TRANSLATOR OF LIVIUS
Kingsford, W *see*
- THREE LETTERS TO THE REV. MR. WESLEY, CONTAINING REMARKS ON A PIECE LATELY PUBLISHED...
- A VINDICATION OF THE BAPTISTS FROM THE CRIMINALITY OF A CHARGE EXHIBITED AGAINST THEM BY THE REV. MR. WESLEY

Kingsley, Calvin *see*
- THE RESURRECTION OF THE DEAD
- ROUND THE WORLD

Kingsley, Charles *see*
- ALTON LOCKE, TAILOR AND POET
- CHARLES KINGSLEY
- THE HERMITS
- HISTORICAL LECTURES AND ESSAYS
- THE NOVELS, POEMS, AND MEMORIES OF CHARLES KINGSLEY
- TOWN AND COUNTRY SERMONS
- THE WATER-BABIES
- WESTMINSTER SERMONS

Kingsley, Florence Morse *see* STEPHEN
Kingsley, Henry *see*
- AUSTIN ELLIOT
- THE BOY IN GREY
- FIRESIDE STUDIES
- THE GRANGE GARDEN
- THE HARVEYS
- THE HILLYARS AND THE BURTONS
- LEIGHTON COURT
- MADEMOISELLE MATHILDE
- THE MYSTERY OF THE ISLAND
- NUMBER SEVENTEEN
- OAKSHOTT CASTLE, BY GRANBY DIXON
- OLD MARGARET
- RAVENSHOE
- THE RECOLLECTIONS OF GEOFFRY HAMLYN
- REGINALD HETHEREGE
- SILCOTES OF SILCOTE
- STRETTON
- TALES OF OLD TRAVEL RE-NARRATED
- VALENTIN

Kingsley, M H *see* TRAVELS IN WEST AFRICA, CONGO FRANCAIS, CORISCO AND CAMEROON
KINGSTON 1683-1849 – (Mf 1T-3T: Births & Deaths 1683-1859. Mf 3T-4T: Marriages 1726-68. Mf 4T: Publishments 1726-69. Mf 5T-13T: Births & Deaths 1744-1856. Mf 8T: Marriages 1768-1809. Mf 8T-9T: Publishments 1769-1809. Mf 13T-14T: Marriages 1809-44. Mf 14T-15T: Marriage Intentions 1809-49. Mf 15T-16T: Births 1843-49. Mf 16T: Marriages 1843-49. Mf 17T: Deaths 1843-49; Out-of-Town Marriages 1727-98) – (mf ed 1997) – 17mf – 9 – 0-87623-273-X – us Holbrook [920]
KINGSTON 1683-1900 – (Mf 1-7: Vital Records 1683-1882. Mf 8-10: Vital Records 1744-1896. Mf 11-13: Births & Deaths 1758-1894. Mf 14-16: Marrs & Intents 1809-83. Mf 17: Out-of-Town Marriages 1727-97. Mf 18-22: Church Records 1720-1880. Mf 18-19: Vital Records 1720-1858. Mf 23-31: Town Records 1717-68. Mf 26,31: Publishments 1762-69. Mf 32-36: Town Records 1769-95. Mf 37-42: Town Records 1796-1818. Mf 43-51: Town Records 1769-1810. Mf 52-58: Town Records 1818-50. Mf 59-66: Town Records 1838-71. Mf 67-68: School Records 1838-58. Mf 69-70: Taxes, Voters 1864-84. Mf 71: Rebellion Records 1861-65. Mf 72-73: Birth Index 1843-1921. Mf 74-75: Marr Index 1843-1921. Mf 75-76: Death Index 1843-1921. Mf 77-78: Vital Records 1843-53. Mf 79-82: Births 1854-1902. Mf 83-85: Marriages 1854-1902. Mf 86-88: Deaths 1854-99) – (mf ed 1992) – 88mf – 9 – 0-87623-154-7 – us Holbrook [920]
KINGSTON AND BRAY GAZETTE ETC *see* BRAY GAZETTE
KINGSTON AND THE LOYALISTS OF THE SPRING FLEET OF A.D. 1783: WITH REMINISCENCES OF EARLY DAYS IN CONNECTICUT.. / Bates, Walter – Ed. with notes by W.O. Raymond. Saint John, N.B.: Barnes, 1889. 03001.(Pre-1900 Canadiana) – 9 – cn C.I.H.M. [971]
KINGSTON CHRONICLE – Kingston, Canada. 1819-32 – 3r – 1 – $204.00 – cn Library Assoc [971]
KINGSTON CHRONICLE AND GAZETTE – Kingston, Canada. 1833-45 – 7r – 1 – $455.00 – cn Library Assoc [971]
THE KINGSTON DAILY NEWS – Kingston, Ontario, CN. Oct 1851-Dec 1886 – 34r – 1 – Can$65.00r – cn Commonwealth Micro [072]
KINGSTON DEANERY MAGAZINE – (Cont by: The Deanery Magazine) – Sussex, NB: [Deanery of Kingston, 1884?-1889?] – 9 – cn C.I.H.M. [240]
KINGSTON DEANERY MAGAZINE *see* THE DEANERY MAGAZINE
KINGSTON GAZETTE – Kingston, Canada. 1810-18 – 2r – 1 – $136.00 – cn Library Assoc [971]
KINGSTON HERALD – Kingston, Ontario. v23 n32. 22 nov 1842 – 1r – 1 – Can$25.00 – cn Can Microfilming [072]
KINGSTON WHIG-STANDARD – Kingston, Ontario. 1 Dec 1926-27 Mar 1939.-d. 148 reels – 1 – uk British Libr Newspaper [072]
KINGSTOWN AND BRAY OBSERVER – (Dublin Pictorial Advertiser 6 May 1871-) – Ireland, 7 May 1870-20 May 1871 – 1r – 1 – uk British Libr Newspaper [072]
KINGSTOWN EVENING JOURNAL, ETC – Wicklow, UK. 5 Jun-8 Sept 1863.-d. 1 reel – 1 – uk British Libr Newspaper [072]
KINGSTOWN GAZETTE ETC – County Dublin, Ireland. 19 Dec 1857-9 Jan 1858; 2 May 1868-17 Jul 1869. -w. 1/2 reel – 1 – uk British Libr Newspaper [072]
KINGS/TULARE COUNTIES – 1989- – 6+ r – 1 – $300.00 – P00042 – us Library Micro [910]
KINH-TE TAP-CHI – no. 1-19, suppl. Nam-Dinh, Hanoi. 1933-34, mq no. 18 – 1 – fr A.C.R.P.P. [073]
Kin-Hubbard *see* A BOOK OF INDIANA
KINI TERSERAH PADA BUNG KARNO / Sutomo – SE 10,987 1. 1965 – 9 – ne IDC [950]
Kinkead, Edgar Benton *see*
- THE COMPLETE LAW QUIZZER...THE OHIO SUPREME COURT EXAMINATION QUESTIONS FOR ADMISSION TO THE BAR
- JURISPRUDENCE, LAW AND ETHICS
- THE LAW OF PLEADING IN CIVIL ACTIONS AND DEFENSES UNDER THE CODE.
- A TREATISE ON THE LAW OF COURT PRACTICE AND PROCEDURE, CIVIL AND CRIMINAL.

Kinkel, Gottfried *see*
- OTTO DER SCHUETZ
- TANAGRA

Kinkel, Hans *see* LESSINGS DRAMEN IN FRANKREICH
Kinley, Joseph Macy *see* KINLEY'S AMERICAN AND ENGLISH PRECEDENTS.
KINLEY'S AMERICAN AND ENGLISH PRECEDENTS. / Kinley, Joseph Macy – Pt. I, Personal right. vol. I San Francisco, Crocker, 1899. 1030 p. LL-1511 – 1 – us L of C Photodup [340]
Kinloch, MG J *see* STUDIES IN SCOTTISH ECCLESIASTICAL HISTORY IN THE SEVENTEENTH AND EIGHTHEENTH CENTURIES
Kinloch, William Penney *see* THE CIRCLE OF CHRISTIAN DOCTRINE
Kinne, Asa *see*
- KINNE'S LAW COMPENDIUM
- QUESTIONS AND ANSWERS ON LAW

Kinne, La Vega George *see* PROCEDURE AND METHODS OF THE COURTS OF FINAL RESORT OF THE REPUBLIC OF MEXICO, THE UNITED STATES OF AMERICA, AND OF THE SEVERAL STAGES AND TERRITORIES OF THE UNION
Kinnebrew, J H *see* THE THEOLOGY OF FATHERHOOD
Kinner, J L *see* HISTORY OF HENRY COUNTY
KINNE'S LAW COMPENDIUM / ed by Kinne, Asa – (v1-5 under title "Questions and Answers on Law Alphabetically Arranged". v6-11 cover selected cases from the US and British Commonwealth starting 1844. Lacking: v7,10,11) – v1-11. 1844-55 (all publ) – 43mf – 9 – $64.50 – LLMC 95-020 – us L.L.M.C. [340]
Kinney, Abbot *see* THE CONQUEST OF DEATH
Kinnon, Colette M *see* NEW HORIZONS OF HUMAN KNOWLEDGE
KINNOR NA'IM / Luzzatto, S D – Vienna. 1825. BJ-422-55 1 – 9 – ne IDC [470]
KINO *see* KINOBRIEFE
KINO I FOTODOKUMENTY PO ISTORII VELIKOGO OKTIABRIA, 1917-1920 – Moscow, 1958. 354p. BR-10,742/1 – 9 – ne IDC [947]
KINO-ADRESSBUCH – Berlin, 1917 – 1 – gw Mikrofilm [790]
KINOBRIEFE – (Cont by: Der Kientopp, jan 1920. Kino, mar 1920) – Berlin. jan 5, 1919-jul 15, 1920 – 1 – gw Mikrofilm [790]
KINODOKUMENTY PO ISTORII SOVETSKOGO KINO, KHRANIASHCHIESIA V TSENTRAL'NOM GOSUDARSTVENNOM ARKHIVE KINOFOTOFONODOKUMENTOV (1917-1945) / Khodorkovskii, VR – Moscow, 1960. No.3,p165-206. BR-10,827/1 – 9 – ne IDC [790]
KINOFOTO PROMYSHLENNOST: SISTEMATIZ. SBORNIK.. – Moscow, 1936. 232p. First attempt to systematize normative materials on cinematography in the USSR; status juris: 1 Nov 1935. BR-9360/1 – 9 – ne IDC [340]
KINO-KALENDER – Wien, 1918 – 1 – gw Mikrofilm [790]
DER KINO-PRAKTIKUS *see* DER PRAKTIKUS
Kinross, John *see* DOGMA IN RELIGION AND CREEDS IN THE CHURCH
KINROSS-SHIRE, 1837 : BRITISH ISLES CENSUS DIRECTORIES PROJECT, SCOTLAND. VOL 43 – 1mf – 9 – A$9.00 – at Vine [941]

KINROSS-SHIRE ADVERTISER – Scotland, UK. 26 Jan 1850-26 Jul 1851. -w. 11 feet – 1 – uk British Libr Newspaper [072]
Kinsey, Clark *see* CLARK KINSEY LOGGING PHOTOGRAPHS
Kinsey, Robert Baldwin *see* A SERIOUS QUESTION
Kinsley, William Wirt *see* OLD FAITHS AND NEW FACTS
Kinsman, Frederick Joseph *see* PRINCIPLES OF ANGLICANISM
KINSMAN NEWS : WEEKLY GENERAL NEWSPAPER – Kinsman, OH. 14 May 1897 – 1r – 1 – us Western Res [071]
Kinzel, K *see* GESCHICHTE DER DEUTSCHEN LITERATUR
Kinzie, Juliette Augusta *see* WALTER OGILBY: A NOVEL
KINZIGTAL-NACHRICHTEN : BA DER FRANKFURTER NEUEN PRESSE – Schluechtern, Germany. 1 Jun 1983- – ca 6r per yr – 1 – gw Mikrofilm [072]
THE KINZUA PLANNING NEWSLETTER – 1961-65. (American Indian Periodicals In the Princeton University Library). 1 fiche – 9 – $45.00 – us UPA [305]
KIOKEE BAPTIST CHURCH. APPLING, GEORGIA : CHURCH RECORDS – 1790-1955 – 1 – 40.50 – us Baptist [240]
THE KIOKIO NIUS *see* MELANESIAN NIUS / THE KIOKIO NIUS
Kip, William Ingraham *see*
- THE CATACOMBS OF ROME AS ILLUSTRATING THE CHURCH OF THE FIRST THREE CENTURIES
- THE CHURCH OF THE APOSTLES
- THE EARLY CONFLICTS OF CHRISTIANITY
- THE EARLY DAYS OF MY EPISCOPATE
- HISTORICAL SCENES FROM THE OLD JESUIT MISSIONS
- THE UNNOTICED THINGS OF SCRIPTURE

Kiphuth, R *see* THE DIAGNOSIS AND TREATMENT OF POSTURAL DEFECTS
Kipka, Karl *see* MARIA STUART IM DRAMA DER WELTLITERATUR
Kipling, Rudyard *see*
- BARRACK-ROOM BALLADS AND OTHER VERSES
- LETTERS OF MARQUE
- LIFE'S HANDICAP
- THE PHANTOM 'RICKSHAW
- PLAIN TALES FROM THE HILLS
- THE SECOND JUNGLE BOOK

Kipp, Catherine G *see* WOMEN ON THE LAND; THE WOMEN'S LAND ARMY
Kipper, Karl *see* DIE ENTWICKLUNG DES ARBEITSHAUSES UNTER BESONDERER BERUECKSICHTIGUNG DER REFORMATORISCHEN BESTREBUNGEN UND DER VEHAELTNISSE IN WESTFALEN
A KIRALYI ITELOTABLAK FELULVIZSGALATI TANACSAINAK ELVI JELENTOSEGU HATAROZATAI. / Hungary. Itelotablak – Budapest. On film: v1-19; 1895-1917. LL-0244 – 1 – us L of C Photodup [340]
KIRBISCH, ODER, DER GENDARM, DIE SCHANDE UND DAS GLUECK : EIN EPISCHES GEDICHT / Wildgans, Anton – Leipzig: L Staackmann, 1927 – 1r – 1 – us U.W. Library [810]
Kirby, Elizabeth *see* CHAPTERS ON TREES. A POPULAR ACCOUNT OF THEIR NATURE AND USES
KIRBY MEMORIAL BAPTIST CHURCH. CHEROKEE COUNTY. GAFFNEY, SOUTH CAROLINA : CHURCH RECORDS – 1954-1973 – 1 – 25.02 – us Baptist [240]
Kirby, W F *see*
- BRITISH AND EUROPEAN BUTTERFLIES AND MOTHS (MACROLEPIDOPTERA)
- CATALOGUE OF THE COLLECTION OF DIURNAL LEPITOPTERA
- CENTURIE D'INSECTS, CONTENANT PLUSEIURS GENRES NOUVEAUX DECRITS DANS SA COLLECTION
- ELEMENTARY TEXT BOOK OF ENTOMOLOGY
- EUROPEAN BUTTERFLIES AND MOTHS
- A HAND-BOOK TO THE ORDER LEPIDOPTERA
- AN INTRODUCTION TO ENTOMOLOGY, OR, ELEMENTS OF THE NATURAL HISTORY OF INSECTS
- A MANUAL OF EUROPEAN BUTTERFLIES
- A SYNONYMIC CATALOGUE OF DIURNAL LEPIDOPTERA
- A SYNONYMIC CATALOGUE OF LEPIDOPTERA HETEOCERA
- A SYNONYMIC CATALOGUE OF NEUROPTERA ODONATA, OR DRAGONFLIES

Kirby, William Forsell *see* THE HERO OF ESTHONIA AND OTHER STUDIES IN THE ROMANTIC LITERATURE OF THAT COUNTRY
KIRBY'S REPORTS / Connecticut. Supreme Court – (A Pre-NRS title) – 1v. 1785-1788 (all publ) – 6mf – 9 – $9.00 – LLMC 94-002 – us L.L.M.C. [340]
Kirchbach, Wolfgang *see*
- DEUTSCHE SCHAUSPIELER UND SCHAUSPIELKUNST
- WAIBLINGER

DIE KIRCHE – 1978-85 – 1 – us A.T.L.A. [073]
DIE KIRCHE – Berlin, 1956-86 – 5r – 1 – Dist. gw Mikrofilm – gw Misc Inst [240]
DIE KIRCHE : EVANGELISCHE WOCHENZEITUNG – Berlin, dec 9 1945-dec 5 1948 (incomplete) – 1r – 1 – uk British Libr Newspaper [072]
DIE KIRCHE – v25-32, 1970-77.1 reel – 1 – us A.T.L.A. [073]
DIE KIRCHE DER GEGENWART : EINE MONATSCHRIFT FUER DIE REFORMIERTE SCHWEIZ – 1845-50 (complete) – 2r – 1 – ATLA B0253 – us A.T.L.A. [073]
DIE KIRCHE DER THOMASCHRISTEN : EIN BEITRAG ZUR GESCHICHTE DER ORIENTALISCHEN KIRCHEN / Germann, W – Guetersloh: C. Bertelsmann, 1877 – 2mf – us A.T.L.A. [240]
DIE KIRCHE DER WUESTE 1715 BIS 1787 : DAS WIEDERAUFLEBEN DES FRANZOESISCHEN PROTESTANTISMUS IM ACHTZEHNTEN JAHRHUNDERT / Schott, Theodor – Halle: Verein fuer Reformationsgeschichte, 1893. ([Schriften des Vereins fuer Reformationsgeschichte; Bd. 43-44]) – 1mf – us A.T.L.A. [240]
DIE KIRCHE GOTTES UND DIE BISCHOEFE : DENKSCHRIFT MIT RUECKSICHT AUF DAS ANGEKUENDIGTE ALLGEMEINE CONCILIUM ZUR KLAERUNG DER RELIGIOESEN LEBENSFRAGE / Liano, Heinrich St A von – (Includes bibliographical references) – Muenchen: J J Lentner, 1869 – 1mf – 9 – 0-8370-8920-4 – 1986-2920 – us A.T.L.A. [240]
DIE KIRCHE, IHR AMT, IHR REGIMENT : GRUNDLEGENDE SAETZE MIT DURCHGEHENDER BEZUGNAHME AUF DIE SYMBOLISCHEN BUECHER DER LUTHERISCHEN KIRCHE / Harnack, T – Nuernberg: U.E. Sebald, 1862 – 1mf – us A.T.L.A. [240]
KIRCHE IM SOZIALISMUS – 1973-90 (complete) – 4r – 1 – ATLA S0819 – us A.T.L.A. [073]
KIRCHE OG FOLK *see* CHURCH AND LIFE
KIRCHE. SCHWEIZERISCHE KIRCHE – v147-151, 1979-83 – 1 – us A.T.L.A. [073]
KIRCHE UND FERNSEHEN – Frankfurt/Main. 1955-73 – 10r – 1 – gw Mikrofilm [240]
KIRCHE UND KIRCHEN, PAPSTTHUM UND KIRCHENSTAAT / Doellinger, Ignaz von – 1992 – 5mf – DM98.00 – 3-89349-045-0 – gw Hänsel [240]
KIRCHE UND KUNST – v40-63. 1962-85 (complete) – 1r – 1 – ATLA S0785 – us A.T.L.A. [073]
KIRCHE UND MANN : MONATSZEITUNG FUER MAENNERARBEIT DER EVENGELISCHEN KIRCHE IN DEUTSCHLAND – (Ceased: 1976. Cont by: Evangelisches Monatsblatt) – v18-29. 1965-76 – 2r – 1 – ATLA S0202 – us A.T.L.A. [073]
KIRCHE UND MANN *see* EVANGELISCHES MONATSBLATT
KIRCHE UND RUNDFUNK – Frankfurt/Main. jan 21, 1949-96 – 43r – 1 – gw Mikrofilm [240]
KIRCHE UND RUNDFUNK – (Lacking: 1982 and some pgs) – 1961-93 – 51r – 1 – ATLA S0399 – us A.T.L.A. [073]
KIRCHE UND VOLK – v16-39. 1964-86 (complete) – 1r – 1 – ATLA S0856 – us A.T.L.A. [073]
DIE KIRCHE UNTERM KREUZ : ODER, BOTSCHAFTER DES HEILS IN CHRISTO – 1885 (complete) – 1r – 1 – ATLA 1993-S025 – us A.T.L.A. [073]
KIRCHE VON KURHESSEN WALDECK : KIRCHLICHES AMTSBLATT – (Lacking some pgs) – v86-105. 1971-90 – 3r – 1 – ATLA S0793 – us A.T.L.A. [073]
Kircheisen, F M *see* FELDZUGSERINNERUNGEN AUS DEM KRIEGSJAHRE 1908
DIE KIRCHEN- UND SCHULVISITATION IM SAECHSISCHEN KURKREISE VOM JAHRE 1555 / Schmidt, Wilhelm – Halle a.d.S.: Verein fuer Reformationsgeschichte, 1906. (Schriften des Vereins fuer Reformationsgeschichte; 24. Jahrg., Schrift 90, 92) – 1mf – us A.T.L.A. [240]
DIE KIRCHEN UND SEKTEN DES CHRISTENTUMS IN DER GEGENWART / Kattenbusch, Ferdinand – Tuebingen: J.C.B. Mohr, 1909. (Religionsgeschichtliche Volksbuecher fuer die deutsche christliche Gegenwart; 4. Reihe, 11./12. Heft) – 1mf – us A.T.L.A. [240]
KIRCHENBLATT DER EVANGELISCH LUTHERISCHEN SYNODE VON IOWA UND ANDEREN STAATEN – (Lacking some pgs) – v1-103. 1858-1960 – 40r – 1 – ATLA S0148 – us A.T.L.A. [073]
KIRCHENBLATT FUER DIE REFORMIERTE SCHWEIZ – (Filmed with: Die Zukunft die Kirche) – 1845-54; 1939-86 (incomplete) – 12r – 1 – ATLA S0124 – us A.T.L.A. [073]
KIRCHENBLATT FUER DIE REFORMIERTE SCHWEIZ *see* DIE ZUKUNFT DIE KIRCHE
KIRCHENBUCHS AND MINUTE BOOK / Trinity Lutheran Church, Otis, KS – 1877-1952 – 1 – us KS Hist [240]
DIE KIRCHENGESCHICHTE DER NICEPHORUS CALLISTUS XANTHOPUPOS UND IHRE QUELLEN (T.U.U. 5-98) / Gentz, G – Berlin, 1966 – 5mf – 9 – ne Slangenburg [240]
DIE KIRCHENGESCHICHTE DES EUSEBIUS (T.U.U. 2-21/2) / Nestle, E – Leipzig, 1901 – 5mf – 9 – ne Slangenburg [240]
KIRCHENGESCHICHTE HEUTE : GESCHICHTSWISSENSCHAFT ODER THEOLOGIE / ed by Kottje, R – Trier, 1970 – Dfl13.00 – ne Slangenburg [240]
DIE KIRCHENGESCHICHTE VON SPANIEN / Gams, Pius Bonifacius – Regensburg: G.J. Manz, 1862-1879 – 5mf – us A.T.L.A. [240]
KIRCHENGESCHICHTLICHE ABHANDLUNGEN UND UNTERSUCHUNGEN / Funk, Franz Xaver – Paderborn: F. Schoeningh, 1897-1907 – 4mf – us A.T.L.A. [240]
DER KIRCHENGESCHICHTLICHE ERTRAG DER EXEGETISCHEN ARBEITEN DES ORIGENES : 1. TEIL: HEXATEUCH UND RICHTERBUCH (T.U.U. 3-42/3A) / Harnack, Adolf von – Leipzig, 1918 – 3mf – 9 – ne Slangenburg [240]
DER KIRCHENGESCHICHTLICHE ERTRAG DER EXEGETISCHEN ARBEITEN DES ORIGENES : 2. TEIL: DIE BEIDEN TESTAMENTE MIT AUSSCHLUSS DES HEXATEUCHS UND DES RICHTERBUCHS (T.U.U. 3-42/4) / Harnack, Adolf von – Leipzig, 1919 – 3mf – 9 – ne Slangenburg [240]
DIE KIRCHENGESCHICHTSSCHREIBUNG : GRUNDZUEGE IHRER HISTORISCHEN ENTWICKLUNG / Nigg, W – Muenchen, 1934 – Dfl22.00 – ne Slangenburg [240]
KIRCHENGUETERFRAGE UND SCHMALKALDISCHER BUND : EIN BEITRAG ZUR DEUTSCHEN REFORMATIONSGESCHICHTE / Koerber, Kurt – Leipzig: Verein fuer Reformationsgeschichte, 1913. (Schriften des Vereins fuer Reformationsgeschichte; Jahrg. 30, 3 u. 4. Stueck, Nr. 111/12) – 1mf – us A.T.L.A. [240]
DER KIRCHENKAMPF : THE GUTTERIDGE-MICKLEM COLLECTION HELD IN THE BODLEIAN LIBRARY – 1988 – 678 fiches (1:24) + Intro and Index – 9 – silver DM9,400.00 – 3-598-32599-1 – gw Saur [019]
KIRCHENMUSIK – Duesseldorf. v. 1-7 no. II. 1938-1944 – 1 – us Schnase [780]
KIRCHENMUSIKALISCHES JAHRBUCH – Regensburg. v1-27. 1886-1932 – 89mf – 9 – ne IDC [780]
KIRCHENMUSIKALISCHES JAHRBUCH. – Regensburg, New York. 1876-1932, 1950. 3 reels – 1 – 54.00 – us L of C Photodup [780]
DIE KIRCHENPOLITIK DES KANZLERS MICHEL DE L'HOSPITAL / Geuer, F – Duisburg, 1877 – 1mf – 9 – DM48.00 – 3-89349-334-4 – gw Hänsel [320]
DIE KIRCHENPOLITIK KOENIG SIGMUNDS WAEHREND SEINES ROMZUGES (1431-1433) / Koch, Max – Leipzig, 1906 – 9 – DM48.00 – 3-89349-269-0 – gw Hänsel [943]
DIE KIRCHENRECHTSQUELLEN DES PARTRIARCHATS ALEXANDRIEN / Riedel, Wilhelm – Leipzig: A. Deichert, 1900 – 1mf – us A.T.L.A. [240]
DIE KIRCHENVAETER UND DAS NEUE TESTAMENT : BEITRAEGE ZUR GESCHICHTE DER ERKLAERUNG DER WICHTIGSTEN NEUTESTAMENTLICHEN STELLEN / Langen, Joseph – (Includes bibliographical references and indexes) – Bonn: Eduard Weber (R Weber & M Hochguertel), 1874 – 1mf – 9 – 0-8370-4050-7 – 1985-2050 – us A.T.L.A. [220]
DER KIRCHENVORSTAND NACH DEM RECHTE DER EVANGELISCH-LUTHERISCHEN LANDESKIRCHE DES KOENIGREICHS SACHSEN / Troll, Alfred – Leipzig, 1913 – 2mf – 9 – DM62.00 – 3-89349-352-2 – gw Hänsel [240]
KIRCHE-NYT – v17-38, 1966-86.2 reels – 1 – us A.T.L.A. [073]
Kircher, A *see* LINGUA AEGYPTIACA RESTITUTA OPUS TRIPARTITUM
Kircher, Athanasius *see*
- MAGNES SIVE DE ARTE MAGNETICA OPUS TRIPARTITUM
- MUSURGIA UNIVERSALIS SIVE ARS MAGNA CONSONI ET DISSONI IN 10 LIBROS DIGESTA
- MVSVRGIA VNIVERSALIS SIVE ARS MAGNA CONSONI ET DISSONI IN X LIBROS DIGESTA. ROMAE
- NEUE HALL- UND THONKUNST, ODER MECHANISCHE GEHEIM-VERBINDUNG DER KUNST UND NATUR

Kircher, Konrad *see* CONCORDANTIAE VETERIS TESTAMENTI GRAECAE, EBRAEIS, VOCIBUS RESPONDENTES
Kirchgeorg, Otto Hermann *see* DIE DICHTERISCHE ENTWICKLUNG J.F.W. ZACHARIAS
KIRCHLICHE AUTORITAET UND MACHT DER WISSENSCHAFT / Buchmann, Jacob – Breslau [Wroclaw]: Fiedler & Hentschel, 1874 – 1mf – 9 – 0-8370-9127-6 – 1986-3127 – us A.T.L.A. [210]
DIE KIRCHLICHE BAUKUNST DES ABENDLANDES, HISTORISCH UND SYSTEMATISCH DARGESTELLT / Dehio, G G & Bezold, G von – 2v. text and 5v. illus. Stuttgart. 1887-1901. BO-222 1 – 9 – ne IDC [720]
DER KIRCHLICHE BESITZ IM ARRONDISSEMENT AACHEN GEGEN ENDE DES 18. JAHRHUNDERTS UND SEINE SCHICKSALE IN DER SAEKULARISATION DURCH DIE FRANZOESISCHE HERRSCHAFT : EIN BEITRAG ZUR KIRCHEN- UND WIRTSCHAFTSGESCHICHTE DER RHEINLANDE / Kaiser, Paul – Aachen, 1906 – 9 – DM48.00 – 3-89349-119-8 – gw Hänsel [240]
KIRCHLICHE DISCIPLIN : IN DEN DREI ERSTEN CHRISTLICHEN JAHRHUNDERTEN / Probst, Ferdinand – Tuebingen: H. Laupp, 1873 – 1mf – us A.T.L.A. [240]
DIE KIRCHLICHE FRAGE UND IHRE PROTESTANTISCHE LOESUNG : IM ZUSAMMENHANGE MIT DEN NATIONALEN BESTREBUNGEN UND MIT BESONDERER BEZIEHUNG AUF DIE NEUESTEN SCHRIFTEN J.J.J. VON DOELLINGER'S UND BISCHOF VON KETTELER'S / Schenkel, Daniel – Elberfeld: R.L. Friderichs, 1862 – 1mf – us A.T.L.A. [240]
DAS KIRCHLICHE LEBEN DER EVANGELISCH-LUTHERISCHEN LANDESKIRCHE DES KOENIGREICHS SACHSEN / Drews, Paul – Tuebingen: J.C.B. Mohr, 1902. (Evangelische Kirchenkunde; 1. T.) – 1mf – us A.T.L.A. [240]
KIRCHLICHE MITTEILUNGEN AUS UND UEBER NORDAMERIKA, AUSTRALIEN UND NEU-GUINEA – 1843-66: 1869-1914 (complete) – 4r – 1 – ATLA S0158 – us A.T.L.A. [073]
DIE KIRCHLICHE ORDNUNG DER TAUFE / Beckman, J – Stuttgart, 1950 – 1mf – 8 – Dfl6.00 – ne Slangenburg [240]
KIRCHLICHE ZEITSCHRIFT – (Lacking some pgs and issues) – v1-68. 1876-1943 – 23r – 1 – ATLA S0138 – us A.T.L.A. [073]
KIRCHLICHE ZEITSCHRIFT – Schwerin, Rostock. v1-6. 1854-1859 – 76mf – 9 – ne IDC [240]
KIRCHLICHE ZEITSCHRIFT – Schwerin-Rostock, 1(1854)-6(1859) – 76mf – 9 – Dfl266.00 – ne Slangenburg [073]
DIE KIRCHLICHEN BENEDIKTIONEN IM MITTELALTER / Franz, Albert – Freiburg i.Br. v1-2. 1909 – 22mf – 8 – Dfl77.00 – ne Slangenburg [240]
DIE KIRCHLICHEN QUATERTEMBER : IHRE ENTSTEHUNG, ENTWICKLUNG UND BEDEUTUNG / Fischer, L – Muenchen, 1914 – 4mf – 8 – Dfl19.00 – ne Slangenburg [240]
DIE KIRCHLICHEN REUNIONSBESTREBUNGEN WAEHREND DER REGIERUNG KARLS 5. / Pastor, Ludwig, Freiherr von – Freiburg i.B., St. Louis, Mo.: Herder, 1879 – 2mf – us A.T.L.A. [240]

DIE KIRCHLICHEN SIMULTANVERHAELTNISSE DER RHEINPROVINZ UNTER BESONDERER BERUECKSICHTIGUNG DES RYSWICKER FRIEDENS / Beck, Dietrich – Weimar, 1934 – viii/129p – 9 – DM48.00 – 3-89349-211-9 – gw Hänsel [240]

DIE KIRCHLICHEN ZUSTAENDE IN OESTERREICH UND DAS ALLGEMEINE KONZIL IN ROM / Schoepf, Ignaz – (Includes bibliographical references) – Innsbruck: Wagner, 1869 – 1mf – 9 0-8370-8380-X – 1986-2380 – us A.T.L.A. [240]

KIRCHLICHER ZENTRALKATALOG BEIM EVANGELISCHEN ZENTRALARCHIV IN BERLIN / ed by Czubatynski, Uwe – 1997 – 216mf (1:42) – 9 – diazo DM4,800.00 silver DM5,800.00 – 3-598-32013-2 – silver ISBN: 3-598-32014-0 – gw Saur [240]

DIE KIRCHLICHKEIT DER S.G. KIRCHLICHEN THEOLOGIE / Gottschick, Johannes – (Includes bibliographical references) – Freiburg i.B.: J C B Mohr, 1890 – 1mf – 9 – 0-8370-8741-4 – 1986-2741 – us A.T.L.A. [240]

Kirchner, Erich *see* "INDUZIERTE HYPERVOLAEMIE" UND "KONTROLLIERTE VOLUMENANPASSUNG", ZWEI NEUE METHODEN ZUR PROPHYLAXE UND THERAPIE DER AKUTEN TONISCHEN KREISLAUFINSUFFIZIENS

Kirchner, O *see* ATLAS DER KRANKHEITEN UND BESCHAEDIGUNGEN

Kirchner, Rita *see* UNTERSUCHUNG ZUM SPRACHLICHEN MODEVERHALTEN

Kirchner, T *see*
- APOLOGIA, ODER VERANTWORTUNG DESS CHRISTLICHEN CONCORDIEN BUCHS JN WELCHER DIE WAHRE CHRISTLICHE LEHRE...VERTHEYDIGET:...
- ENCHIRIDION D. TIMOTHEI KIRCHNERI. JN WELCHEM DIE FUERNEMBSTEN HAUPTSTUCK DER CHRISTLICHEN LEHRE DURCH FRAG VND ANTWORT AUSS GOTTES WORT GRUENDTLICH ERKLAERET...
- HISTORI DESS SACRAMENTSTREITS DARINNEN KLAERLICH AUSSGEFUEHRET WIRDT WIE DIESE ZWYTRACHT ENTSTANDEN BISS AUFF VNSERE ZEIT CONTINUIRET...
- METHODICA EXPLICATIO PRAECIPVORVM CAPITVM DOCTRINAE COELESTIS...
- DAS DIE ZWEY VND VIERZIG ANHALTISCHE ARGUMENT WIDER DER VBISQUISTEN TREWME NOCH FEST STEHEN...

Kirchner, Werner *see* DER HOCHVERRATSPROZESS GEGEN SINCLAI

Kireev, A A *see*
- SLAVIANOFIL'STVO I NATSIONALIZM
- SOCHINENIIA

Kireevskii, Petr Vasil'evich *see* PESNI

Kirevskii, IV *see* POLNOE SOBRANIE SOCHINENII V DVUKH TOMAKH

KIRIAT SEFER, AUSFUEHRLICHER BIBIOGRAPHISCHER CATALOG... HEBRAEISCHER UND JUEDISCHER BUECHER UND HANDSCHRIFTEN, NACHGELASSEN VOM J. EMDEN, M.J. LEWENSTEIN U.A. ERSTE LIEFERUNG / Roest, M – Amsterdam, 1867 – 3mf – ne IDC [470]

KIRILLO-MEFODIEVSKII SBORNIK / Pogodin, M P – Moscow, 1865. 555p. BR-4204/2 – 8 – ne IDC [460]

Kirillov, A *see* GEOGRAFICHESKO-STATISTICHESKII SLOVAR' AMURSKOI PRIMORSKOI OBLASTEI

KIRILLOVSKOE PIS'MO Y RUMYN / Kaluzhniatskii, E – Entsiklopediia Slavianskoi Filologii. Petrograd, 1915. v4 (2). BR-10,485/1 – 9 – ne IDC [400]

Kirilov, J *see* ENUMERATIO PLANTARUM IN DESERTIS SONGORIAE ORIENTALIS

KIRJATH SEPHER – 1(1924)-50(1975) – 709mf – 9 – Dfl2,482.00 – ne Slangenburg [073]

KIRK ANBAR – Nos. 1-34 (1290-1293) – 21mf – 9 – $52.50 – us MEDOC [949]

Kirk, Edward Norris *see* LECTURES ON REVIVALS

KIRK FOLK / Anderson, Robert – Toronto: Westminster, 18--. 02402. (Pre-1900 Canadiana) – 9 – cn C.I.H.M. [240]

Kirk, Hiram van *see* A HISTORY OF THE THEOLOGY OF THE DISCIPLES OF CHRIST

Kirkaldy, G W *see* CATALOGUE OF THE HEMIPTERA (HETEROPTERA), WITH BIOLOGICAL AND ANATOMICAL REFERENCES

Kirkburton. Yorkshire. All Hallows *see* PARISH REGISTERS

Kirkby, J *see* THE IMPOSTOR DETECTED

Kirkby, John *see* A NEW ENGLISH GRAMMAR

KIRKCUDBRIGHTSHIRE, 1837 : BRITISH ISLES CENSUS DIRECTORIES PROJECT, SCOTLAND. VOL 44 – 1mf – 9 – A$9.00 – at Vine [941]

KIRKCUDBRIGHTSHIRE, 1852 : BRITISH ISLES CENSUS DIRECTORIES PROJECT, SCOTLAND. VOL 6 – 1mf – 9 – A$9.00 – at Vine [941]

KIRKEBYGNINGER OG DERES UDSTYR – 1934 – 1 – us I.U. Libraries [390]

KIRKELIG MAANEDSTIDENDE – v1-18. Mar 1855-1873 (complete) – 3r – 1 – ATLA S0247 – us A.T.L.A. [073]

KIRKELIG SAMLER – (Lacking: no 52 1917. p619-20 of original damaged) – v1-61. Oct 1872-May 1933 – 16r – 1 – ATLA S0229 – us A.T.L.A. [073]

KIRKE-NYT – v17-38. 1966-86 (complete) – 2r – 1 – ATLA S0853 – us A.T.L.A. [073]

Kirk-Greene, Anthony Hamilton Millard *see* THIS IS NORTHERN NIGERIA

Kirkham, E Bruce *see*
- A CONCORDANCE TO THE OLNEY HYMNS OF JOHN NEWTON AND WILLIAM COWPER
- A CONCORDANCE TO THE PLYMOUTH COLLECTION OF HYMNS AND TUNES

Kirkheaton. Yorkshire *see* PARISH REGISTERS

Kirkhengeim, A von *see* OBZOR IURIDICHESKOI LITERATURY ZA 1884-94 GG

KIRKINTILLOCH GAZETTE – Scotland. 15 Oct 1898-12 Aug 1938.-w. 16 reels – 1 – uk British Libr Newspaper [072]

KIRKINTILLOCH HERALD – Scotland. 18 Jul 1883; 23 Jun 1886-Dec 1974.-w. 74 reels – 1 – uk British Libr Newspaper [072]

KIRKINTILLOCH HERALD AND BISHOPBRIGGS HERALD – 1 – £42.00r – uk Scot News [072]

KIRKLAND BAPTIST CHURCH. TAFT, TENNESSEE : CHURCH RECORDS – 1908-63 – 1 – 8.64 – us Baptist [240]

Kirkland, Caroline Matilda Stansbury *see* THE EVENING BOOK: OR, FIRESIDE TALK ON MORALS AND MANNERS, WITH SKETCHES OF WESTERN LIFE

Kirkland, J V *see* APOSTOLIC HYMNS

Kirkland, R S *see* APOSTOLIC HYMNS

Kirkman, F B *see* THE BRITISH BIRD BOOK

Kirkpatrick, Alexander F *see*
- THE BOOK OF PSALMS
- DIVINE LIBRARY OF THE OLD TESTAMENT: ITS ORIGIN...AND PERMANENT VALUE
- FIRST BOOK OF SAMUEL
- SECOND BOOK OF SAMUEL

Kirkpatrick, Alexander Francis *see*
- THE DIVINE LIBRARY OF THE OLD TESTAMENT
- THE DOCTRINE OF THE PROPHETS
- THE FIRST BOOK OF SAMUEL
- THE SECOND BOOK OF SAMUEL

KIRKSTALL ABBEY / Owen, David E – Leeds, s.a. – 2mf – 8 – Dfl9.00 – ne Slangenburg [240]

THE KIRKSTALL ABBEY CHRONICALS, VOL 62 / Taylor, J – Leeds, 1932 – 3mf – 8 – Dfl13.00 – ne Slangenburg [240]

KIRKUS REVIEWS – (1983-. 5,6,9) – 1933- – 1 – us UMI [073]

Kirkus, William *see* RELIGION

KIRKWOOD FIRST BAPTIST CHURCH (NAME LATER CHANGED TO WETZEL MEMORIAL, STILL LATER TO KIRKWOOD). KIRKWOOD, MISSOURI : CHURCH RECORDS – 31 Jul 1870-31 Dec 1900 – 1 – 14.49 – us Baptist [240]

Kirkwood, Robert *see* A PLEA FOR THE BIBLE

Kirn, Otto *see* AUSGANGSPUNKT UND ZIEL DER EVANGELISCHEN DOGMATIK

Kirnberger, Johann P *see*
- ANLEITUNG ZUR SINGEKOMPOSITION
- CLAVIERUEBUNGEN
- GEDANKEN UEBER DIE VERSCHIEDENEN LEHRARTEN IN DER KOMPOSITION
- GEDANKEN UEBER DIE VERSCHIEDENEN LEHRARTEN IN DER KOMPOSITION ALS VORBEREITUNG ZUR FUGENKENNTNISZ
- GRUNDSAETZE DES GENERALBASSES ALS ERSTE LINIEN ZUR COMPOSITION
- GRUNDSAETZE DES GENERAL-BASSES ALS ERSTE LINIEN ZUR COMPOSITION
- DIE KUNST DES REINEN SATZES IN DER MUSIK
- LIEDER MIT MELODIEN. ZWEITE AUFLAGE
- DIE WAHREN GRUNDSAETZE ZUM GEBRAUCH DER HARMONIE
- DIE WAHREN GRUNDZAETZE ZUM GEBRAUCH DER HARMONIE ALS EIN ZUSATZ ZU DER KUNST DES REINEN SATZES IN DER MUSIK

KIRRIEMUIR HERALD – 1 – £42.00r – uk Scot News [072]

Kirrinnis, Herbert *see* GESCHICHTE DER FRIEDRICHSSCHULE ZU GUMBINNEN

Kirsanoff, Mary T *see* LIFE STRESS AND SOCIAL SUPPORT AS PREDICTORS OF ATHLETIC INJURY

Kirsch, Johann Peter *see* DIE LEHRE VON DER GEMEINSCHAFT DER HEILIGEN IM CHRISTL. ALTERTHUM

Kirschner, B *see* JUEDISCHES LEXICON

Kirschner, Max *see* JOSEF FILSERS ENDE

Kirschweng, Johannes *see* DAS TOR DER FREUDE

Kirshenbaum, G S *see* POLYMER NEWS

Kirsop, J *see* HISTORIC SKETCHES OF FREE METHODISM

Kirtikar, KR *see* INDIAN MEDICINAL PLANTS

Kirtland, Turhand *see* TURHAND KIRTLAND PAPERS, MS 3237

Kirwan, A V *see* CARRINGTON AND KIRWAN'S REPORTS

Kirwan, Richard *see* AN ESSAY ON THE ANALYSIS OF MINERAL WATERS

KIRYAH NE'EMANAH / Fuenn, S J – Vilna, 1860 – 4mf – 9 – ne IDC [910]

Kirzhnitz, A *see*
- DER IDISHER ARBAYTER
- DI YIDISHE PRESE IN DER GEVEZENER RUSLANDISHER IMPERIE
- DI YIDISHE PRESE IN RATNFARBAND
- DI YUDISHE PRESE IN DER GEVEZENER RUSLANDISHER IMPERIE

KIS UJSAG – Budapest. Hungary. -d. 31 Mar 1945-13 Jan 1948, 9 Aug 1949, 10 Aug 1952. (Imperfect). (17 reels) – 1 – uk British Libr Newspaper [072]

KISAH – Djakarta. Incomplete. SE-796 1. 1953-1957 – 9 – ne IDC [073]

KISAH KARTOSUWIRJO DAN MENJERAHNJA / Amak Sjariffudin – SE-4507 1. 1963 – 9 – ne IDC [950]

KISAH NABI ADAM / ed by Diradja, D M – SE-5053 1. 1963 – 9 – ne IDC [950]

KISALFOLD – (Some issues missing) – Gyor, Hungary. 1962-Jun 1991 – 57r – 1 – us L of C Photodup [072]

Kisch, C *see* ALEXANDER BLOK, PROPHET OF REVOLUTION

Kisch, I *see* HUWELIJKEN VAN NEDERLANDERS IN HET BUITENLAND...

Kisch, M S *see* LETTERS AND SKETCHES FROM NORTHERN NIGERIA

Kiselev, I F *see* DEISTVUIUSHCHIE RASPORIAZHENIIA PO MILITSII..

Kiselev, Ia. L *see*
- SBORNIK VAZHNEISHIKH POSTANOVLENII PO TRUDU

Kiselev, S V *see* DREVNIAIA ISTORIIA IUZHNOI SIBIRI

Kisliakov, E N *see* DLIA CHEGO NUZHNA SEL'SKOKHOZIAISTVENNAIA I PROMYSLOVAIA KOOPERATSIIA I KAK EE ORGANIZOVAT' V DEREVNE

Kislov, A A *see* IDEOLOGY AND POLITICS OF THE AMERICAN BAPTIST CHURCHES IN 1900-1917

Kissin, A A *see* OPYT RATSIONALIZATSII TORGOVOGO APPARATA

KIST *see* KEYWORD INDEX TO SERIAL TITLES (KIST)

Kistler, R *see* BASILICA

KISTORII ROSSI ISKO I REVOLIUTSII / Chaikin, Vadim Afanasevich – Moskva: Izd-vo Z.I. Grzhebina, 1922- – 1 – CSUX88-B7498 – us Hoover Inst Photo [320]

KIT AND KITTY / Blackmore, Richard Doddridge – British Fiction Archive: Unit 3 – 9 – uk Bell [830]

KIT: LAND RIGHTS NOW, EXTRACTS / Land Rights Lobby – With comments by John Zube. 1 fiche (29x) – 9 – 1.00f – at Libertarian Micro [320]

KITAB ADAB AL-DUNYA WA-AL-DIN / Mawardi, Ali ibn Muhammad – Cairo: s.n., 1800? 164p – 1 – us U.W. Library [260]

KITAB AL-AJURRUMIYA FI L-NAHW TA'LIF AL-SHAIK AL-IMAM AL-ALLAMAH MUHAMMAD IBN DAUDAL-SINHAJI AL-SHAHIR BI AJURRUM / Muhammad ibn Muhammad, al-Sinhaji, called Ibn Ajurrum – Romae, 1592 – 2mf – 9 – H-8440/1 – ne IDC [956]

LE KITAB AL-MOUHADARA WA-L-MOUDHAKARA DE MOISE IBN EZRA ET SES SOURCES / Schreiner, M – (Revue des etudes juives). v. 21, v. 22. 1890-91. BJ-421-48 1 – 9 – ne IDC [470]

KITAB AL-QAWANIN / Israel – (1977-. approx.20.00y; 1) – 1970-76 – 1 – 46.00 – us L of C Photodup [324]

KITAB PERUKUNAN / Alaydrus, Ali – SE-5026 1. 1963 – 9 – ne IDC [950]

KITAB SOERAT-MENJOERAT DALAM BAHASA INDONESIA / Zain, Sutan M – (Microfiche No 188) – Djakarta, Doenia Baroe (2602) – 1mf – 9 – SE-2002/1 – ne IDC [950]

KITAB UNDANG2 HUKUM DISIPLIN TENTARA (K.U.H.D.T.) SERTA KOMENTAR-KOMENTARNJA LENGKAP PASAL DEMI PASAL / Marjoto – SE-4633 1. 1958? – 9 – ne IDC [950]

KITAB-AL-FIHRIST MIT ANMERKUNGEN / ed by Fluegel, G – (Erster Band: den Text enthaltend von J. Roediger Leipzig, 1871 Dfl39.00. Zweiter Band: Anmerkungen und Indices von A. Mueller Leipzig, 1872 Dfl30.00) – ne Slangenburg [260]

KITAB-I AGAH – Tehran: Intisharat-i Agah. Jildi 1-4 (1360-1362 [1981-1983]) – 1 reel – 1 – $65.00 – us MEDOC [950]

KITAB-I CIHAN-NUEMA [NESRI TARIHI] / Nesri; ed by Unat, Faik Resit & Koeymen, Mehmed A – Ankara: Tuerk Tarih Kurumu Basimevi, 1949-1957 – 9 – $200.00 – us MEDOC [956]

KITAB-I JUM'AH – (Sal-i 1: shumarah-'i 1-36 (3 Murdad 1358-1 Khurdad 1359[26 Jul 1979-22 May 1980])) – Tehran: Intisharat-i Mazyar, 1979- – 5r – 1 – $75.00 – us MEDOC [950]

KITAB-I SUBHAT UEL-AHBAR / Kemal, Ahmed – 1289 [1873] – $13.00 – us MEDOC [956]

KITAB-I-YAMANI / Utbi – 1858 – 1 – uk Microform Academic [950]

KITAISKAIA BIBLIOTEKA I UCHENYE TRUDY CHLENOV IMP. ROSSIISKOI DUKHOVNOI I DIPLOMATICHESKOI MISSII V G. PEKINE / Aleksh, (Vinogradov) Ieromonakh – St. Petersburg, 1889. 87p. 4 tables. Prilozhenie. Katalog Kitaiskikh Knig Imp. Rossiiskoi dukhovnoi Missii v Pekine. St. Petersburg, 1889. 111p. BR-7051 2 – 8 – ne IDC [947]

Kitamura, S *see* FLORA OF AFGHANISTAN

KITASATO ARCHIVES OF EXPERIMENTAL MEDICINE – v. 1-17. 1917-1940 – 1,5,6 – us Princeton Micro [610]

KITASATO ARCHIVES OF EXPERIMENTAL MEDICINE – v1-17. 1917-40 – 1,5,6 – us Princeton Micro [073]

KITCHEN PLANNING – v1-18 1964-81 – 1 – us UMI [640]

KITCHENER JOURNAL / ed by German Publications Ltd – (Cont by: KANADA-KURIER) – Pickering, Ontario, Canada. 1972-1976; 1978-12 Sep 1980 – 1 – gw Mikrofilm [073]

KITCHENER-WATERLOO RECORD – Kitchener, Ontario, CN. 1907- – 24r per yr – 1 – Can$53.00r – cn Commonwealth Micro [072]

KITCHENER-WATERLOO RECORD *see* THE BERLIN RECORD

Kitchin, Claude *see* PAPERS

Kitchiner, William *see* THE ART OF INVIGORATING AND PROLONGING LIFE, BY FOOD, CLOTHES, AIR, EXERCISE, WINE, SLEEP, ETC.: OR, THE INVALID'S ORACLE

KITIMAT NORTHERN SENTINEL – Kitimat, British Columbia, CN. 1954-73 – 20r – 1 – cn Commonwealth Micro [072]

KITOVRAS, LEF AMERIKANSKII – v. 1-3. 1924. Available: v. 3. BR-3598 2 – 8 – ne IDC [978]

KITSAP AMERICA – Bremerton. Wash. 1924-25 – 1 – us UMI [071]

KITSAP COUNTY REVIEW – Bremerton, WA. 1903-25 – 10r – 1 – $500.00 – R05402 – us Library Micro [071]

Kitson, Arthur *see* THE MONEY QUESTION

KITTANNING GAZETTE – Kittanning, PA., 1832-1882 – 13 – $25.00r – us I.M.R. [071]

Kittanning, Pennsylvania *see* MISCELLANEOUS EARLY NEWSPAPERS

Kittel, J C *see* 25 CHORALE, MIT ACHTERLY GENERAL BAESSEN

Kittel, Rudolf *see*
- UEBER DIE NOTWENDIGKEIT UND MOEGLICHKEIT: EINER NEUEN AUSGABE DER HEBRAEISCHEN BIBEL
- ZUR THEOLOGIE DES ALTEN TESTAMENTS

Kittle, Warren Brance *see* NOTES ON THE LAW OF RULE DAYS IN VIRGINIA AND WEST VIRGINIA.

Kittlitz, F H von *see* DENKWUERDIGKEITEN EINER REISE NACH DEM RUSSISCHEN AMERIKA

Kitton, F G *see* THE POEMS AND VERSES OF CHARLES DICKENS

Kitton, Frederic George *see*
- CHARLES DICKENS
- CHARLES DICKENS BY PEN AND PENCIL
- THE DICKENS COUNTRY
- THE NOVELS OF CHARLES DICKENS

Kittredge, Tracy B *see* THE EVOLUTION OF GLOBAL STRATEGEY

Kitts, Eustace J *see*
- IN THE DAYS OF THE COUNCILS
- POPE JOHN THE TWENTY-THIRD AND MASTER JOHN HUSS OF BOHEMIA

KITVEI NAHMAN SYRKIN / Syrkin, N; ed by Kaznelson, B – Tel-Aviv. 1939. BJ-28-26 1 – 9 – ne IDC [956]

DIE KITZINGER *see* KITZINGER ZEITUNG

KITZINGER ZEITUNG – (Title change: Die Kitzinger) – Kitzingen, Germany. 1 Jun 1983- – ca 7r per yr – 1 – gw Mikrofilm [072]

KIUCHUK-KAINARDZHIISKII MIR 1774 GODA / Druzhinina, E I – Akademiia nauk SSSR, institut istorii. M. 1955. BR-10,520 1 – 9 – ne IDC [947]

KIVANDORLASI ELLENDOER – Budapest, Feb-March 1908 – 1r – 1 – us I.H.R.C. [947]

KIVANDORLASI ERTESITOE – Budapest, Nov 1903-1907 – 1r – 1 – us I.H.R.C. [947]

KIVANDORLO – Budapest, 1904-1905 – 1r – 1 – us I.H.R.C. [947]

KIWANIS MAGAZINE – 1917- 1; 1971- 5,6; 1977- 4 x 6 in. 9 – us UMI [073]

Kiwuwa, G H et al *see* CROSSBRED DAIRY CATTLE PRODUCTIVITY IN ARSI REGION, ETHIOPIA

KIYEVSKAYA MYSL' – Kiev. 1914-1916. Incomplete – 1 – us NY Public [073]

Ki-Zerbo, J et al *see* GENERAL HISTORY OF AFRICA

Kizevetter, A A *see* POSADSKAIA OBSHCHINA V ROSSII 18 ST

KIZIHRMAK – Sivas, 1912-1925 – 9 – $20.00 – us MEDOC [956]

Kjellman, F R *see*
- BIDRAG TIL KAENNEDOMEN OM SKANDINAVIENS ECTOCARPEER OCH TILOPTERIDER
- HANDBOK I SKANDINAVIENS HAFSALGFLORA

Kjer, J *see*
- DANSK-GROENLANDSK ORDBOG
- DANSK-GROENLANDSK ORDBOG, PLUS SUPPL

KKRATKOE OBOZRENIE NAPRAVLENIIA.. / Kapnist, Pl – Saint Petersburg, 1862. 84p. Summary of surveys prepared by Kapnist for the Tsar on orders of A.V. Golovnin. BR-9232/1 – 9 – ne IDC [380]

Klaar, Alfred *see*
- KOENIG OTTOKARS GLUECK UND ENDE
- DIE MARQUISE VON O–

Klabund *see*
- DEUTSCHE LITERATURGESCHICHTE IN EINER STUNDE
- DUMPFE TROMMEL UND BERAUSCHTES GONG
- DIE GEISHA O-SEN
- KLEINES KLABUND-BUCH
- LAOTSE
- LI-TAI-PE

KLADDERADATSCH – Berlin. may 7, 1848-86. jul 3, 1887-1940. may 18, 1941-sep 3, 1944 – 1 – gw Mikrofilm [073]

KLADDERADATSCH – Humoristisch-Satirisches Wochenblatt. May 1848-1906 – 1 – 337.00 – us L of C Photodup [073]

Klaehn, Friedrich Joachim *see*
- DAS GASTMAHL
- NACHT UEBER MALMAISON
- DER SERGEANT WEBER
- TIMM DER TOLPATSCH

Klaehn, Simone *see* DIE GEGENWAERTIGE SITUATION IN DER ALTENHILFE

KLAENGE AUS VERGANGENEN ZEITEN / Wagner, Philipp – New York: L W Schmidt, 1881 – 1r – 1 – us U.W. Library [943]

DIE KLAGELIEDER DES JEREMIAS / Loehr, Max – Goettingen: Vandenhoeck & Rup., 1891. 1 fiche – 9 – us A.T.L.A. [240]

DIE KLAGELIEDER DES JEREMIAS NACH RABBINISCHER AUSLEGUNG / Schoenfelder, Josef M – Muenchen: Ernst Stahl, 1887. 1 fiche – 9 – us A.T.L.A. [240]

DIE KLAGELIEDER DES JEREMIAS UND DER PREDIGER DES SALOMON / Raabe, Andreas – Leipzig: L. Fernau, 1880. 1 fiche – 9 – us A.T.L.A. [240]

Klages, Ludwig *see* GOETHE ALS SEELENFORSCHER

Klaic, Vjekoslav *see* SLIKE IZ SLAVENSKE POVJESTI

DER KLAINE CATECHISMUS / Huberinus, Caspar – [Augsburg: Philipp Ulhart, Vorrede 6. Jan. 1544]. [G.F.: 17.1] – 2mf – 9 – HUB-42/1 – ne IDC [240]

KLAMATH BASIN PROGRESS – Klamath Falls, OR. -d. 23 Feb 1928-23 Jul 1943. 5 rolls. Set incl. Malin Progress – 1 – us U.O. Library [071]

KLAMATH CHRONICLE – Klamath Falls OR. Aug 6 15 23 Sep 28 Dec 24 1911, Aug 15-23 Sep 28 Dec 24 1911 – 1 – us U.O. Library [071]

KLAMATH COUNTY COURIER – Klamath Falls, OR. -w. 5 Jul 1928-4 Aug 1932. 1 roll – 1 – us U.O. Library [071]

KLAMATH COUNTY STAR – Linkville OR. July 11 1890 – 1 – us U.O. Library [071]

KLAMATH FALLS EXPRESS – Klamath Falls, OR. -w. 26 May 1892-31 Aug 1911. 2 rolls – 1 – us U.O. Library [071]

KLAMATH NEWS – Klamath Falls, OR. -d. 13 Nov 1923-31 May 1942. 46 rolls – 1 – us U.O. Library [071]

KLAMATH REPUBLICAN – Klamath Falls, OR. -w. 6 Jul 1899-30 Nov 1914. 4 rolls – 1 – us U.O. Library [071]

KLAMATH STAR – Klamath Falls, OR. -w. 21 Mar 1895-7 Nov 1895. – 1 – us U.O. Library [071]

KLAMATH TRIBUNE – Chiloquin, OR. -m. Nov 1956-Aug 1961. 1 roll – 1 – us U.O. Library [071]

Klamp, Gerhard *see* UEBER DIE IDEE EINER METAPHYSIK IM SINNE DES KRITISCHEN REALISMUS

KLAPPER OP DE INHOUD VAN DE TIJDSCHRIFTEN IM INHEEMSE TALEN VAN HET JAVA-INSTITUUT – Poesaka Djawi, 1-15, 1922-30; Poesaka Soenda, 1-7, 1922-29; Poesaka Madhoera, 1, 1924. Djogjakarta: Java-Instituut, 1937. Th. Pagaud. 1937 – 1 – us U.W. Library [950]

Klaproth, J H *see*
- SUPPLEMENT AU DICTIONNAIRE CHINOIS-LATIN DU P. BASILE DE GLEMONA...
- VERZEICHNIS DER CHINESISCHEN UND MANDSCHUISCHEN BUECHER UND HANDSCHRIFTEN DER KOENIGLICHEN BIBLIOTHEK ZU BERLIN,...

Klaproth, Julius von *see*
- CHRESTOMATHIE MANDCHOU, OU RECUEIL DE TEXTES MANDCHOU
- ESSAI SUR LA LANGUE DU BORNOU, SUIVI DES VOCABULAIRES DU BEGHARMI, DU MANDARA ET DE TIMPOUCTOU

KLARALVSBYGDEN – Hagfors, Sweden. 1979-85 – 1 – sw Kungliga [072]

EYNE KLARE VNWEDERSPREKELIKE BEKENTENISSE UNDE ANWIJSINGE VTH DEN GRONT VNDE KRAFT DER HEYLIGER SCRIFT VORUATED, DAT DIE GHEHEELE CHRISTUS JESUS GODT VNDE MENSCE, MENSCHE VNDE GODT, GODES EINGEBORENE VNDE EERSTGEBORENE EYGEN SONE IS / Simons, Menno – BME-287 1 – 9 – ne IDC [240]

DIE KLARINETTE : ERZAEHLUNG / Schaffner, Jakob – Stuttgart: Deutsche Volksbuecher, 1942 – 1r – 1 – us U.W. Library [390]

DIE KLARINETTE BEI CARL MARIA VON WEBER / Sandner, Wolfgang – Frankfurt a.M., 1971 – 3mf – 9 – DM76.00 – 3-89349-721-8 – gw Hänsel [780]

Klasen, Franz *see* DIE INNERE ENTWICKLUNG DES PELAGIANISMUS

KLASIFIKASI PERSEPULUNAN DEWEY AND INDEKS RELATIF / Dewey, Melvil – SE-3324 1. Ed. 15. 1959 – 9 – ne IDC [020]

Klass, Gert von *see* DIE GROSSE ENTSCHEIDUNG

Klassen, N *see* TOVAROVEDENIE

KLASSEN UND ORDNUNGEN DES THIERREICHS / Bronn, H G – Z-209 2. v. 1, pt. 2. 1859 – 8 – ne IDC [590]

DER KLASSENKAMPF – (Missing: apr 16-may 14 1931) – Berlin, oct 1927-jul 1 1932 (incomplete) – 2r – 1 – Dist. gw Mikrofilm – gw Misc Inst [943]

DER KLASSENKAMPF: SOZIALISTISCHE POLITIK UND WIRTSCHAFT – Berlin. v. 1-6, no. 7; Oct. 1927-Juli 1932. Subtitle varies. No more published? Film Mas C 711 – 1 – us H.U. Library [073]

KLASSICHESKIIA RECHI. STIKHI 1922-1930 GG / Severianin, I – Belgrad. 1931. BR-1028 2 – 8 – ne IDC [460]

KLASSISCHE GESTALTUNG UND ROMANTISCHER EINFLUSS IN DEN DRAMEN HEINRICHS VON KLEIST / Willige, Wilhelm – (Includes bibliographical references) – Heidelberg: C Winter, 1915 – 1r – 1 – us U.W. Library [430]

KLASSISCHE SCHOENHEIT : JOHANN WINCKELMANN, G EPHRAIM LESSING / ed by Gleichen-Russwurm, Alexander von – Jena: E Diederichs, 1906 – 1 – us U.W. Library [840]

DER KLASSISCHE WIENER FRANZ GRILLPARZER / Ludwig, Alfred Josef – Wien: Amandus-Edition, 1946 – 1r – 1 – us U.W. Library [430]

KLASSITSIZM V SOVREMENNOI RUSSKOI POEZII / Mochul'skii, K – Sovremennye Zapiski. pt. 11. 1922. BR-3682 2 – 8 – ne IDC [460]

KLASSOVAI A BORBA I REVOLIUTSII A V ROSSII / Bukharin, Nikolai Ivanovich – Krasnoiarsk: Izd. Enise iskogo gub. agentstva V. T S.I.K. "T Sentropechat", [1919?] – 1 – CSUX89-B3866 – us Hoover Inst Photo [947]

KLASSOVAIA BORBA I REVOLIUTSIIA V ROSSII / Bukharin, Nikolai Ivanovich – Petrograd: Izd. Petrogradskogo soveta rabochikh i krasnoarme iskikh deputatov, 1919 – 1 – CSUX88-B2059 – us Hoover Inst Photo [947]

KLASSOVAIA BORBA V SOVETSKOI DEREVNE / Angarov, Aleksei Ivanovich – Moskva: Izd-vo Kommunistichesko i akademii, 1929 – 1 – CSUX89-B5475 – us Hoover Inst Photo [947]

KLASSOVOE GOSUDARSTVO I GRAZHDANSKOE PRAVO / Stuchka, Petr Ivanovich – M., 1924 – 1mf – 9 – ne IDC [340]

KLASSY I KOOPERATSIIA V DEREVNE SSSR : (K VOPR. O RAZMEZHEVANII POTREBITEL'SKOI I SEL'SKOKHOZIAISTVENNOI KOOPERATSII V SOVETSKOI DEREVNE) / Vlasov, M E – Moscow, 1925 – 2mf – 9 – COR-469/1 – ne IDC [334]

KLASSY I PARTII V SIBIRI NAKANUNE I V PERIOD VELIKOI OKTIABR'SKOI SOTSIALISTICHESKOI REVOLIUTSII – Tomsk, 1977. 193p – 3mf – 9 – ne IDC [320]

KLASYCYZM OSIPA MANDEL'SZTAMA / Przybylski, R – Wzpolczesnosc. no. 24. Dec 1964. BR-3696 2 – 8 – ne IDC [460]

KLASYCZNE PRZYSLOWIA W POLSZCZYZNIE / Sinko, T – Lwow Warszawa. 1939. B-1482 2 – 8 – ne IDC [999]

KLATSASSAN: AND OTHER REMINISCENCES OF MISSIONARY LIFE IN BRITISH COLUMBIA / Brown, Robert Christopher Lundin – London: Society for Promoting Christian Knowledge, 1873. 00316. (Pre-1900 Canadiana) – 9 – cn C.I.H.M. [240]

Klatt, Fritz *see*
- DIE GATTUNG LYSIMACHIA L., MONOGRAPHISCH BEARB
- GRIECHISCHES ERBE; DAS URBILD DER ANTIKE IM WIDERSCHEIN DES HEUTIGEN LEBENS

Klatzkin, J *see* KRISIS UND ENTSCHEIDUNG IM JUDENTUM

Klauber, E G *see*
- ASSYRISCHES BEAMTENTUM NACH BRIEFEN AUS DER SARGONIDENZEIT
- POLITISCH-RELIGIOESE TEXTE AUS DER SARGONIDENZEIT

Klauber, Ernst Georg *see*
- POLITISCH-RELIGIOESE TEXTE AUS DER SARGONIDENZEIT

Klaus, A *see* URSPRUNG UND VERBREITUNG DER DREIFALTIGKEITSMESSE

KLAUS GROTH : ZU SEINEM ACHTZIGSTEN GEBURTSTAGE / Bartels, Adolf – Leipzig: E Avenarius, 1899 – 1r – 1 – us U.W. Library [430]

Klauser, T *see* DER URSPRUNG DER BISCHOEFLICHEN INSIGNIEN UND EHRENRECHTE

Klausner, J G *see*
- HA-SHILO'AH
- SEFER KLAUSNER

Klausner, Joseph *see* DIE MESSIANISCHEN VORSTELLUNGEN DES JUEDISCHEN VOLKES IM ZEITALTER DER TANNAITEN

KLAVIERSCHULE, ODER ANWEISUNG ZUM KLAVIERSPIELEN FUER LEHRER UND LERNEDE... / Tuerk, Daniel G – Leipzig und Halle: Selbstverlag, 1789 – 8mf – 9 – us Sibley [780]

KLAVIERSCHULE, ODER ANWEISUNG ZUM KLAVIERSPIELEN FUER LEHRER UND LERNENDE / Tuerk, Daniel G – Leipzig. Halle. 1789. BP-493 1 – 9 – ne IDC [780]

Klawon, Dieter *see* GESCHICHTSPHILOSOPHISCHE ANSAETZE IN DER FRUEHROMANTIK

Kleban, Patricia L *see* THE RELATIONSHIP BETWEEN SHARED FAMILY RECREATION TIME AND EXPRESSED PARENT-ADOLESCENT CONFLICT

Kleber, John Christopher *see* VOID JUDICIAL AND EXECUTION SALES, AND THE RIGHTS, REMEDIES AND LIABILITIES OF PURCHASERS THEREAT.

Kleber, Peter et al *see* EARTH SPACE REVIEW

Klebs, A C *see* INCUNABULA SCIENTIFICA ET MEDICA

Klebs, J *see* DIE LANDESKULTURGESETZGEBUNG, DEREN AUSFUHRUNG UND ERFOLGE IM GROSSHERZOGTHUM POSEN

KLEE / Reunion des musees nationaux. Paris – 1972. 18 illus. 1 fiche – 9 – fr Réunion [700]

Klee, Gotthold *see*
- DER ABENTEUERLICHE SIMPLICISSIMUS
- KARL SIMROCKS AUSGEWAEHLTE WERKE IN ZWOELF BAENDEN
- WIELANDS WERKE

Kleeberg, J A G *see* MOLLUSCORUM BORUSSICORUM SYNOPSIS

Kleef, Rald *see* BESTIMMUNG VON HLA KLASSE 1 AN ZUR AUTOVACCINATION BESTIMMTEN, EPITHELMARKER-CHARAKTERISIERTEN TUMORZELLEN

Kleeman, Karen M *see* A FAMILY SYSTEMS ANALYSIS OF ANXIETY, DEPRESSION, AND SOMATIZATION IN GRADUATE NURSING STUDENTS

Kleiber, Ludwig *see* ZUR WIRTSCHAFTSPOLITIK OBERSCHWAEBISCHER REICHSSTAEDTE IM AUSGEHENDEN MITTELALTER

Klein, Felix *see*
- AMERICA OF TO-MORROW
- IN THE LAND OF THE STRENUOUS LIFE
- LES PARABOLES DE L'EVANGILE

Klein, Horst G *see* DAS VERHALTEN DER TELISCHEN VERBEN IN DEN ROMANISCHEN SPRACHEN EROERTERT AN DER INTERFERENZ VON ASPEKT UND AKTIONSART

Klein, J J *see* VERSUCH EINES LEHRBUCHS DER PRAKTISCHEN MUSIK IN SYSTEMATISCHER ORDNUNG ENTWORFEN

Klein, J T *see* HISTORIAE AVIUM PRODROMUS

Klein, Johannes *see* WALTER FLEX, EIN DEUTER DES WELTKRIEGES

Klein, John Frederick *see* BEITRAEGE ZU PAUL HEYSES NOVELLENTECHNIK

Klein, Judy L *see* RATINGS OF PERCEIVED EXERTION IN COLLEGE AGE MALES AND FEMALES OF HIGH AND LOW FITNESS LEVELS

Klein, Mary Frances Goldmann *see* PAPERS

Klein, Peter *see* ENTWICKLUNG EINES IMMUNTESTS FUER DEN EINSATZ IN DER RUECKSTANDSANALYTIK

Klein, S *see*
- BIBLIOGRAPHIE DER SCHRIFTEN WILHELM BACHERS NEBST EINEM HEBRAEISCHEN SACH- UND ORTSNAMENREGISTER
- SEFER ZIKKARON LE-ASHER GULAK VELI-SHEMU'EL KLEIN
- YAVNEH

Klein, S W *see*
- HA-EMET VE-HA-SHALOM EHAVU
- MI-PENEI KOSHET

Kleinberg, Alfred *see*
- DIE DEUTSCHE DICHTUNG IN IHREN SOZIALEN, ZEIT- UND GEISTESGESCHICHTLICHEN BEDINGUNGEN
- LUDWIG ANZENGRUBER

KLEINE BEITRAEGE ZU AKTUELLEN FRAGESTELLUNGEN IN DER MODERNEN KRIMINOLOGIE / Funk, Alfred – 1992 – 67p – 9 – DM75.00 – 3-89349-594-0 – gw Hänsel [360]

DAS KLEINE BLATT – Wien: Druck & Verlagsanstalt "Vorwarts" Swoboda & Co, 1928-33 – 24r – 1 – us Res Libr [072]

KLEINE CHRONIK : VIER ERZAEHLUNGEN / Zweig, Stefan – Leipzig: Insel-Verlag, [1929] – 1r – 1 – us U.W. Library [890]

DER KLEINE COCO – Goch, Germany. 1910-12 – 1 – gw Mikrofilm [072]

KLEINE DEUTSCHE LITERATURGESCHICHTE / Roos, Carl – Kobenhavn: Gyldendal, 1955 – 1r – 1 – us U.W. Library [430]

KLEINE ERZAEHLUNGEN / Peters, Friedrich Ernst – Goettingen: Deuerlich, 1941 – 1r – 1 – us U.W. Library [830]

KLEINE GENERAL-BASS-SCHULE / Mattheson, J – 1735 – 9 – us Sibley [780]

DER KLEINE GERD : HUMORISTISCH-MILITAERISCHE ERZAEHLUNG / Baudissin, Wolf Ernst Hugo Emil, Graf von – Berlin: Schreiter, [19–?] – 1r – 1 – us U.W. Library [830]

KLEINE HAUSAPOTHEKE / Vegesack, Siegfried von – Hamburg: Hammerich & Lesser, 1944 – 1r – 1 – us U.W. Library [800]

KLEINE HIEROGLYPHEN-GRAMMATIK (AUSZUG) NACH DEM WERK H. PROF. HEINRICH BRUGSCH, BERLING, HANDSCHRIFT / Meyer-Berlin, Richard – Berlin, 1913 – 1mf – DM48.00 – 3-8267-3073-9 – gw Hänsel [470]

DAS KLEINE JOURNAL – Berlin, may 1883-jun 1884, 1892-mar 1897, jul 1897-1902, apr 1903-sep 1905, 1906-14, jul 1915-nov 1918, 1925-mar 1935 – 65r – 1 – Dist. gw Mikrofilm – gw Misc Inst [072]

KLEINE KOPTISCHE STUDIEN 1-58 : SUBSIDIA BYZANTINA, VOL 1 / Lemm, O von – Leipzig, 1972 – 22mf – 8 – ne Slangenburg [240]

KLEINE LEUTE : DREI NOVELLEN / Hopfen, Hans – Berlin: F Schneider, 1880 – 1r – 1 – us U.W. Library [830]

KLEINE LITERARTURFIBEL : EINE ANLEITUNG ZUM VERSTAENDNIS SCHOENER LITERATUR / Hoefer, Karl-Heinz – (Includes bibliographical references and index) – Leipzig: Fachbuchverlag, 1967 – 1r – 1 – us U.W. Library [430]

DER KLEINE MARTIN / Franzos, Karl Emil – 3e. Auf. Stuttgart and Berlin. n.d – 1 – us Res Libr [890]

DER KLEINE MISSIONS-FREUND – Berlin, 1899-1922 – 1 – Dist. gw Mikrofilm – gw Misc Inst [240]

KLEINE MORGENZEITUNG *see*
- BRESLAUER ANZEIGER
- BRESLAUER MORGENZEITUNG

DER KLEINE NACHT-EXPRESS *see* NACHT-EXPRESS

KLEINE NORDISCHE ERZAEHLUNGEN / Dahn, Felix – Leipzig: Breitkopf & Haertel, 1898 – 1 – us U.W. Library [830]

DIE KLEINE PASSION : ROMAN / Wiechert, Ernst Emil – Berlin: G Grote, 1929 – 1r – 1 – us U.W. Library [830]

KLEINE PROSAISCHE SCHRIFTEN / Schwab, Gustav Benjamin; ed by Kluepfel, K – (Includes bibliographical references) – Freiburg i.Br: J C B Mohr, 1882 – 1r – 1 – us U.W. Library [430]

KLEINE ROMANE AUS DER VOELKERWANDERUNG / Dahn, Felix – (1. Felicitas. 9 Aufl. 1884. 2. Bissula. 6 Aufl. 1884. 3. Gelimer. 6 Aufl. 1885. 4. Die schlimmen Nonnen von Poitiers. 6 Aufl. 1886. 5. Fredigundis. 2 Aufl. 1886. 6. Attila. 4 Aufl. 1888. 7. Die Bataver. 5 Aufl. 1890. 8. Chlodovech. 6 Aufl. 1895. 9. Vom Chiemgau. 5 Aufl. 1896. 10. Ebroin. 4 Aufl. 1897. 11. Am Hof Herrn Karls. 4 Aufl. 1901. 12. Stilicho. 2 Aufl. 1900. 13. Der Vater und die Soehne. 3 Aufl. 1901) – Leipzig, Breitkopf und Haertel, 1884-1901. Film Mas C 494 – 1 – us H.U. Library [830]

DER KLEINE ROSENGARTEN : VOLKSLIEDER / Loens, Hermann – Jena: Eugen Diederichs, 1919 – 1r – 1 – us U.W. Library [780]

DER KLEINE SAEMANN – v2. 1899 (complete) – 1r – 1 – ATLA 1994-S027 – us A.T.L.A. [073]

KLEINE SCHRIFTEN / Scherer, Wilhelm – hrsg. von K. Burdach und E. Schmidt. Berlin, Weidmannsche Buchhandlung, 1893. 2 v. in l. Film Mas 7982 – 1 – us H.U. Library [800]

KLEINE SCHRIFTEN / Strauss, David Friedrich – Bonn: Emil Strauss, 1895 – 1 – us U.W. Library [430]

KLEINE SCHRIFTEN 1 : STUDIEN ZUR SPAETANTIKEN RELIGIONS-GESCHICHTE (T.U.U. 5-67) / Lietzmann, Hans; ed by Aland, Kurt – Berlin, 1958 – 9mf – 9 – ne Slangenburg [240]

KLEINE SCHRIFTEN 2 : STUDIEN ZUM NEUEN TESTAMENT (T.U.U. 5-68) / Lietzmann, Hans; ed by Aland, Kurt – Berlin, 1958 – 6mf – 9 – ne Slangenburg [240]

KLEINE SCHRIFTEN 3 : STUDIEN ZUR LITURGIE- UND SYMBOLSGESCHICHTE ZUR WISSENSCHAFTSGESCHICHTE (T.U.U. 5-74) / Lietzmann, Hans; ed by Kommission fuer spaetantike Religionsgeschichte – Berlin, 1962 – 7mf – 9 – ne Slangenburg [240]

KLEINE SCHRIFTEN RELIGIONS-GESCHICHTLICHEN INHALTS / Hausrath, Adolf – Leipzig: S. Hirzel, 1883 – 2mf – us A.T.L.A. [240]

KLEINE SCHRIFTEN (T.U.U. 5-83) / Altaner, Bruno – Berlin, 1967 – 11mf – 9 – ne Slangenburg [240]

KLEINE SCHRIFTEN ZUR LITTERATUR UND KUNST / Stahr, Adolf Wilhelm Theodor – Berlin: J Guttentag, 1871-1875 – 1r – 1 – us U.W. Library [430]

KLEINE SCHRIFTEN ZUR LITTERATUR UND KUNST / Stahr, Adolf Wilhelm Theodor – (v. 1. Biographisches. 1871. v. 2. Biographisches and kritisches. 1872. v. 3. Aus dem alten Weimar. 1875. v. 4. Aus meinen Lebenserinnerungen. Biographisches und kritisches. 1875) – Berlin, Gutlentag, 1871-75. 4 v. in 3. Film Mas 8517 – 1 – us H.U. Library [430]

KLEINE SING- UND SPIELSTUECKE FUER CLAVIER VON VERSCHIEDENEN MEISTERN – 3v. ca.1762-66. (Contains work of: C. P. E. Bach, Dandrieu, Graun, Marpurg, Nichelmann, Sack, Anon.) – 9 – us Sibley [780]

DAS KLEINE VOLKSBLATT – Vienna. Austria. -d. 5 Aug 1945-22 Apr 1948, 16 Nov 1948-31 Dec 1953. (Imperfect). (27 reels) – 1 – uk British Libr Newspaper [072]

KLEINER KATECHISMUS DER CHRISTLICHEN LEHRE : ZUM GEBRAUCH FUER KATHOLISCHE SCHULEN / Weninger, Francis Xavier – New York: Benziger, 1866, c1865 – 1mf – 9 – 0-8370-6859-2 – 1986-0859 – us A.T.L.A. [240]

KLEINERE ERZAEHLUNGEN / Gotthelf, Jeremias – (Includes bibliographical references) – Erlenbach, Zuerich: E Rentsch. 7v. 1912-29 – 1 – us U.W. Library [830]

KLEINERE ERZAEHLUNGEN = SHORT STORIES / Raabe, Wilhelm Karl – 4. Aufl. Berlin-Grunewald: Hermann Klemm, [189-?] – 1 – us U.W. Library [830]

KLEINERE SCHRIFTEN / Rosenzweig, F – Berlin, 1937 – 10mf – 8 – ne Slangenburg [100]

KLEINERE SCHRIFTEN / Rosenzweig, F – Berlin, 1937 – 10mf – 8 – ne Slangenburg [100]

Kleinert, Paul *see*
- ABRISS DER EINLEITUNG ZUM ALTEN TESTAMENT IN TABELLENFORM
- THE BOOK OF HABAKKUK
- THE BOOK OF JONAH
- THE BOOK OF MICAH
- THE BOOK OF NAHUM
- THE BOOK OF OBADIAH
- THE BOOK OF ZEPHANIAH
- DAS DEUTERONOMIUM UND DER DEUTERONOMIKER
- LUTHER IM VERHAELTNIS ZUR WISSENSCHAFT UND IHRER LEHRE
- O.R. HERTWIG'S TABELLEN ZUR EINLEITUNG IN DIE...BUECHER DES ALTEN TESTAMENTS
- DIE PROFETEN ISRAELS IN SOZIALER BEZIEHUNG
- ZUR CHRISTLICHEN KULTUS- UND KULTURGESCHICHTE

KLEINES ALPHABETISCHES WOERTERBUCH DER VORNEHMSTEN UND INTERESSANTESTEN ARTIKEL AUS DER MUSIKALISCHEN THEORIE. / Knecht, J H – 1795 – 9 – us Sibley [780]

EIN KLEINES BILD : ERZAEHLUNG AUS DER ZEIT DES DEUTSCH-FRANZOESISCHEN KRIEGES / Wichert, Ernst – Leipzig: Philipp Reclam jun., [189-?] – 1r – 1 – us U.W. Library [830]

KLEINES GOTTSCHED-DENKMAL : DEM DEUTSCHEN VOLKE ZUR MAHNUNG ERRICHTET / Reichel, Eugen – (Includes selections from Gottsched's works) – Berlin: Gottsched-Verlag, 1900 – 1r – 1 – us U.W. Library [430]

KLEINES KLABUND-BUCH : NOVELLEN UND LIEDER / Klabund – Leipzig: P Reclam, c1921 – 1r – 1 – us U.W. Library [800]

KLEINES PARADIES : TIERGESCHICHTEN / Steguweit, Heinz – 1. Aufl. der Feldpostausg. Guetersloh: C Bertelsmann, 1943 – 1r – 1 – us U.W. Library [830]

Kleinman, S *see* THE PERCEIVED INFLUENCE OF PARTICIPATION IN INTRAMURAL SPORTS ON PURPOSE, INTERPERSONAL RELATIONSHIP, AND AUTONOMY

Klein-Nicolai, G *see* EXERCITATIO HISTORICA DE ORIGINE LINGVAE ITALICAE EX BARBARORUM INCVRSIONIBUS NATAE

DIE KLEINSCHMETTERLINGE DER MARK BRANDENBURG UND EINIGER ANGRENZENDEN LANDSCHAFTEN / ed by Sorhagen, L – Berlin, 1886 – X, 367p – 8 – ne IDC [590]

Kleinschmidt, Juergen *see* UNTERSUCHUNGEN ZUR PROBLEMATIK BEI DER FESTSETZUNG VON MAXIMALEN IMMISSIONSKONZENTRATIONEN FUER OZON

Kleinschmidt, Karl *see* FRIEDRICH SCHILLER

Kleinschmidt, Samuel P *see*
- GRAMMATIK DER GROENLAENDISCHEN SPRACHE
- DEN GRØLANDSKE ORDBOG
- DEN GRONLANDSKE ORDBOG

Kleinsorge, John Arnold *see* BEITRAEGE ZUR GESCHICHTE DER LEHRE VOM PARALLELISMUS DER INDIVIDUAL- UND DER GESAMTENTWICKLUNG

EIN KLEINSTAATLICHER MINISTER DES ACHTZEHNTEN JAHRHUNDERTS / Hardenberg, Friedrich von – Leben and Wirken Friedrich August's, Freiherrn von Hardenberg. Hrsg. von einem Mitgleide der Familie. Leipzig, Duncker & Humboldt, 1877. xv, 276 p. Film Mas 8161 – 1 – us H.U. Library [920]

KLEINSTER KATECHISMUS ZUM NOTHWENDIGSTEN UNTERRICHT FUER DIE ERSTE KOMMUNION / Weninger, Francis Xavier – New York: Benziger, 1866, c1865 – 1mf – 9 – 0-8370-6860-6 – 1986-0860 – us A.T.L.A. [240]

KLEIST / Hegeler, Wilhelm – Berlin: Schuster & Loeffler – 1r – 1 – us U.W. Library [920]

KLEIST AND HEBBEL : A COMPARATIVE STUDY; THE NOVELS / Becker, Henrietta K – (Includes bibliographical references) – Chicago: Scott, Foresman, 1904 – 1r – 1 – us U.W. Library [430]

Kleist, Heinrich von *see*
- AMPHITRYON
- ERZAEHLUNGEN
- DIE HERMANNSSCHLACHT
- H.V. KLEISTS WERKE
- DAS KAETHCHEN VON HEILBRONN
- KLEIST'S HERMANNSSCHLACHT
- KLEISTS NOVELLEN
- DIE MARQUISE VON O–
- PENTHESILEA
- PRINZ FRIEDRICH VON HOMBURG
- WERKE
- DER ZERBROCHNE KRUG

KLEIST'S AMPHITRYON / Ruland, Wilhelm – 1995 – 1mf – 9 – DM48.00 – 3-8267-3130-1 – gw Hänsel [430]

KLEIST'S HERMANNSSCHLACHT : EIN GEDICHT AUF OESTERREICH / Kleist, Heinrich von; ed by Mueller-Guttenbrunn, Adam – Wien: Verlag des Kaiserjubilaeums-Stadttheaters, 1898 – 1 – us U.W. Library [820]

KLEISTS LUSTSPIEL "DER ZERBROCHENE KRUG" AUF DER BUEHNE / Buchtenkirch, Gustav – (Includes bibliographical references) – 1r – 1 – us U.W. Library [430]

KLEISTS NOVELLEN : "MICHAEL KOHLHAAS" UND "DIE HEILIGE CAECILIE" IM WORTLAUT DER ERSTEN FASSUNG / Kleist, Heinrich von – (Includes bibliographical references) – Heidelberg: C Winter, 1926 – 1r – 1 – us U.W. Library [830]

KLEISTS "PENTHESILEA" : ODER VON DER LEBENDIGEN FORM DER DICHTUNG / Schulze, Berthold – (Includes bibliographical references) – Leipzig: B G Teubner, 1912 – 1 – us U.W. Library [430]

KLEISTS UND ADAM MUELLERS FREUNSCHAFTSKRISE : ZWEI UNGEDRUCKTE BRIEFE ADAM MUELLERS ZUR GESCHICHTE DER ZEITSCHRIFT "PHOEBUS" / Muehlher, Robert – (Includes bibliographical references) – Wien: Europa-Verlag, c1948 – 1r – 1 – us U.W. Library [920]

KLEMENS VON ALEXANDREIA UND SEIN HELLENISCHES CHRISTENTUM / Pohlenz, M – Goettingen, 1943 – 2mf – 9 – ne Slangenburg [240]

KLEMENS VON ALEXANDRIEN UND SEINE ERKENNTNISPRINZIPIEN / Scherer, Wilhelm – Muenchen: J.J. Lentner, 1907 – 1mf – us A.T.L.A. [240]

DER KLEMENSROMAN UND SEINE GRIECHISCHEN QUELLEN (T.U.U. 3-40/2) / Heintze, W – Leipzig, 1914 – 3mf – 9 – ne Slangenburg [240]

DIE KLEMENSROMANE : IHRE ENTSTEHUNG UND IHRE TENDENZEN / Langen, Joseph – Gotha: Friedrich Andres Perthes, 1890 – 1mf – us A.T.L.A. [430]

Klemm, Christian Gottlob *see* DER AUF DEN PARNASS VERSETZTE GRUENE HUT

Klemm, Frederick Alvin *see* THE DEATH PROBLEM IN THE LIFE AND WORKS OF GERHART HAUPTMANN

Klemm, Guenther *see* CHRISTIAN MORGENSTERNS DICHTUNGEN VON "ICH UND DU"

Klemm, Wilhelm Bernhard *see* DER BERTIN-ALTAR AUS -OMER IM KAISER-FRIEDRICH-MUSEUM ZU BERLIN

Klemmt, Rolf *see* EINE MITTELHOCHDEUTSCHE EVANGELIENSYNOPSE DER PASSION CHRISTI

Klemperer, Victor *see* PAUL HEYSE

Kleppinger, Alison *see* GENDER DIFFERENCES IN SPORT ORIENTATION AND GOAL ORIENTATION

Klette, E T *see* DER PROCES UND DIE ACTA APOLLONII (T.U.U. 1-15/2)

Klette, E Theodore *see* DIE CHRISTENKATASTROPHE UNTER NERO

Kletzka, Renate *see* AESTHETIK DES JAHRMARKTS

Kleutgen, J *see* DIE PHILOSOPHIE DER VORZEIT

KLICH TRUDOVYKH KAZAKOV : ORGAN KAZACHI AGO KOMITETA PRI T S.I.K.S.R.K.S. I K.D. – Moskva: Kom-t, 1918- – 1 – CSUX89-S965 – us Hoover Inst Photo [947]

Kliemann, Julian-Matthias *see* POLITISCHE UND HUMANISTISCHE IDEEN DER MEDICI IN DER VILLA POGGIO A CAIANO

Klieneberger, H R *see* THE CHRISTIAN WRITERS OF THE INNER EMIGRATION

KLIENTENZENTRIERTE PSYCHOTHERAPIE/ BERATUNG UND WEIBLICHES SELBSTKONZEPT / Schumacher, Eva-Maria – 1994 – 2mf – DM80.00 – 3-8267-2061-X – gw Hänsel [150]

Klimas, Nancy *see* JOURNAL OF CHRONIC FATIGUE SYNDROME

KLIMATGEBIETE DER SACHSENGAENGER IN BRANDENBURG, POSEN UND SCHLESIEN / Lezius, Martin – Neudamm 1913 – 1 – DM30.00 – gw Mikro Press [550]

Klinckowsstroem, A von *see* UEBER DIE INSEKTEN UND SPINNENFAUNA ISLANDS UND DER FAEROEER

Kling, Christian Friedrich *see*
- THE FIRST EPISTLE OF PAUL TO THE CORINTHIANS
- DIE KORINTHER-BRIEFE
- THE SECOND EPISTLE OF PAUL TO THE CORINTHIANS

Klingberg, Fran J *see* "THE EDUCATION OF A KANSAN"

Klinger, Friedrich Maximilian *see*
- FAUSTS LEBEN, TATEN UND HOELLENFAHRT
- FAUSTUS, HIS LIFE, DEATH, AND DOOM

KLINGER UND SHAKESPEARE : EIN BEITRAG ZUR SHAKESPEAROMANIE DER STURM- UND DRANGPERIODE / Jacobowski, Ludwig – (Includes bibliographical references) – Dresden, Leipzig: E Pierson, 1891 – 1 – us U.W. Library [410]

Klinggraeff, H von *see* DIE HOEHEREN CRYPTOGAMEN PREUSSENS. EIN BEITRAG ZUR FLORA DER PROVINZ KOENIGSBERG 1858

KLINISCH KONTROLLIERTE UNTERSUCHUNGEN ZUR EFFEKTIVITAET DER LOKALANAESTHETIKA ULTRACAIN 2% SUPRARENIN UND ULTRACAIN D-S IN DER KINDERZAHNHEILKUNDE / Leiers, Christoph – 1995 – 1mf – 9 – DM60.00 – 3-8267-2216-7 – gw Hänsel [617]

KLINISCHE WOCHENSCHRIFT – v. 24 25-58. 1946 47-1980 – 1,5,9 – 5775.00 – us UMI [616]

KLINISCHE WOCHENSCHRIFT – v1-33. 1922-55 – 1,5,6 – us Princeton Micro [610]

Klinke, Otto *see* E.T.A. HOFFMANNS LEBEN UND WERKE

Klinkhamer, G *see* STICHTELYKE ZINNEBEELDEN EN BYBEL-STOFFEN

Klinkowstroem, C von *see* BRIEFE POLITISCHEN INHALTS VON UND AN FRIEDRICH VON GENTZ AUS DEN JAHREN 1799-1827

KLIO : BEITRAEGE ZUR ALTEN GESCHICHTE – Leipzig. v1-16. 1901-1920 – 220mf – 9 – ne IDC [930]

KLIPPANS DAGBLAD *see* HELSINGBORGS DAGBLAD

KLIPPANS TIDNING *see* NORDVASTRA SKANES TIDNINGAR ENGELHOLMS TIDNING

Klir, G J et al *see* INTERNATIONAL JOURNAL OF GENERAL SYSTEMS

Klise *see* THE COUNTY OF HIGHLAND

Klitzman, SH *see* GOVERNMENT IN THE SUNSHINE ACT

Kliuchevskii, V O *see*
- ISTORIIA SOSLOVII V ROSSII
- OCHERKI I RECHI
- OPYT I ISSLEDOVANIIA

Kloecker, Andreas *see*
- STRUKTUREN UND BEDINGUNGEN POLITISCHER PARTIZIPATION UND MITBESTIMMUNG IN DER KOMMUNALPOLITIK
- THEORIE UND PRAXIS REGIONALER KOMMUNIKATION

Kloepper, Albert *see*
- DER BRIEF AN DIE EPHESER
- DER BRIEF DES APOSTELS PAULUS AN DIE PHILIPPER
- DER ZWEITE BRIEF AN DIE THESSALONICHER

Klokman, Iu. R *see* FEL'DMARSHAL RUMIANTSEV V PERIOD RUSSKO-TURETSKOI VOINY 1768-1774. G.G

KLONDIKE : A MANUAL FOR GOLDSEEKERS / Bramble, Charles A – New York: R. Fenno, 1897. 02279. (Pre-1900 Canadiana) – 9 – cn C.I.H.M. [622]

THE KLONDIKE NUGGET – (Newspaper mf on 6r index on 62mf) – Dawson City, Yukon Territory, 1893-1903. Newspaper microfilm on 6 reels, index on 62 fiches – 1,9 – $120.00 set (Index $65.00 set 9) – us U.W. Libraries [072]

A KLONDIKE PICNIC: THE STORY OF A DAY / Donnelly, Eleanor Cecilia – New York; Cincinnati; Chicago: Benziger Bros., 1898. 02738. (Pre-1900 Canadiana) – 9 – cn C.I.H.M. [971]

KLONDYKE: THE YUKON (KLONDYKE) MINES, AND HOW TO REACH THEM – Issued by the British Columbia Development Association, Ltd. London: Crowther & Goodman, 1897?. 00862. (Pre-1900 Canadiana) – 9 – cn C.I.H.M. [971]

HET KLOOSTER TE WINDESHEIM EN ZIJN INVLOED / Acquoy, J G R – Utrecht. v1-3. 1875-1880 – Dfl74.00 – ne Slangenburg [240]

Kloosterhuis, H *see* AMBON NU!

Klopstock, Friedrich Gottlieb *see*
- AUSGEWAEHLTE DICHTUNGEN
- LA MESSIADE
- DER MESSIAS
- ODEN
- WINGOLF

KLOPSTOCK UND SCHUBART : BEZIEHUNGEN IM LEBEN UND DICHTEN / Bruestle, Wilhelm – (Includes bibliographical references) – Augsburg: Reichel, 1917 – 1r – 1 – us U.W. Library [430]

KLOPSTOCKS ENTDECKUNG DER NATION / Kindermann, Heinz – (Includes bibliographical references) – Danzig: A W Kafemann – Berlin: Junger & Duennhaupt, 1935 – 1r – 1 – us U.W. Library [430]

KLOPSTOCK'S JUGENDGESCHICHTE UND KLOPSTOCK UND DER MARKGRAF KARL FRIEDRICH VON BADEN : BRUCHSTUECKE EINER KLOPSTOCKBIOGRAPHIE / Strauss, David Friedrich – (Includes bibliographical references) – Bonn: E Strauss, 1878 – 1r – 1 – us U.W. Library [920]

KLOPSTOCKS LEBEN UND WERKE / WIELANDS LEBEN UND WERKE / Heinemann, Karl & Boxberger, R – (Includes bibliographical references) – Bielefeld: Velhagen & Klasing, 1899 – 1 – us U.W. Library [920]

KLOPSTOCKS ODEN : (LEIPZIGER PERIODE): EIN TEXTKRITISCHER BEITRAG ZUR LITERATURGESCHICHTE SEINER ZEIT / Pawel, Jaro – (Includes bibliographical references) – Wien: C Gerold, 1880 – 1r – 1 – us U.W. Library [430]

KLOPSTOCKS SENDUNG / Berger, Arnold Erich – Darmstadt: E Hofmann, 1924 – 1r – 1 – us U.W. Library [430]

KLORAN / Ku Klux Klan of Canada – 1925 – 9 – $15.00 – cn McLaren [360]

KLORKANT = CLARTE – (In Yiddish) – Paris, FR. no4 Jul 1930-no7 Nov 1930 – 1r – 1 – $25.00 – cn Can Microfilming [072]

Klose, Juergen *see* STABILITAETS- UND SENSITIVITAETSANALYSE IN DER VEKTOROPTIMIERUNG

Klose, W H *see* A STUDY OF GRILLPARZER'S AHNFRAU

Kloss, Erich *see* MAX KRETZER

Kloss, G *see* BIBLIOGRAPHIE DER FREIMAUREREI...

KLOSTER, PRIESTERMOENCH UND PRIVATMESSE / Nuszbaum, O – Bonn, 1961 – 6mf – 8 – Dfl25.00 – ne Slangenburg [240]

KLOSTER WENDHUSEN; URSULA / Heimburg, W – Stuttgart: Union Deutsche Verlagsgesellschaft, [1890?] – 1 – us U.W. Library [830]

DIE KLOSTERKIRCHE SAN CARLO ALLE QUATTRO FONTANE VON FRANCESCO BORROMINI IN ROM : EINE "INNOVATIVE REZEPTION" / Moehlenkamp, Annegret – 1992 – 144p – 9 – DM98.00 – 3-89349-610-6 – gw Hänsel [720]

DAS KLOSTERLAND DES ATHOS / Schmidtke, Alfred – Leipzig: J.C. Hinrichs, 1903 – 1mf – us A.T.L.A. [240]

Klostermann, August *see*
- DEUTEROJESAIA
- KORREKTUREN ZUR BISHERIGEN ERKLAERUNG DES ROEMERBRIEFES
- DAS MARKUSEVANGELIUM: NACH SEINEM QUELLENWERTHE FUER DIE EVANGELISCHE GESCHICHTE
- DER PENTATEUCH
- ZUR THEORIE DER BIBLISCHEN WEISSAGUNG UND ZUR CHARAKTERISTIK DES HEBRAEERBRIEFS

Klostermann, D et al *see* DIE BIBELFRAGE IN DER GEGENWART: FUENF VORTRAEGE

Klostermann, Erich *see*
- ANALECTA ZUR SEPTUAGINTA, HEXAPLA UND PATRISTIK
- EUSEBIUS SCHRIFT PERI TOON TOPIKOON ONOMATOON (T.U.U. 2-23/2B)
- GRIECHISCHE EXCERPTE AUS HOMILIEN DES ORIGENES (T.U.U. 1-12/3B)
- NACHLESE ZUR UEBERLIEFERUNG DER MATTHAEUSERKLAERUNG DES ORIGENES (T.U.U. 4-47/4)
- STUDIEN ZUM NEUEN TESTAMENT UND ZUR PATRISTIK (T.U.U. 5-77)
- UEBER DES DIDYMUS VON ALEXANDRIEN IN EPISTOLAS CANONICAS ENARRATIO (T.U.U. 2-28/2C)
- DIE UEBERLIEFERUNG DER JEREMIA-HOMILIEN DES ORIGENES (T.U.U. 2-16/3)
- ZUR UEBERLIEFERUNG DER MATTHAEUSERKLAERUNG DES ORIGENES (T.U.U. 4-47/2)

Klostermann-Berthold *see* NEUE HOMILIEN DES MAKARIUS/SYMEON

KLOSTERMANN'S GRUNDSTUECK : NEBST EINIGEN ANDREN BEGEBENHEITEN, DIE SICH IN DESSEN NACHBARSCHAFT ZUGETRAGEN HABEN / Rodenberg, Julius – Berlin: Gebrueder Paetel, 1891 – 1 – us U.W. Library [430]

Klotsch, J F *see* ICONES PLANTARUM RARIORUM HORTI REGII BOTANICI BEROLINENSIS

Klotzsch, J F *see*
- BEGONIACEEN-GATTUNGEN UND ARTEN
- LINNE'S NATUERLICHE PFLANZENKLASSE TRICOCCAE DES BERLINER HERBARIUM'S

Klucke, Walther Gottfried *see*
- BEFEHL IST BEFEHL
- LIEBE MUTTER

Kluegel, Georg Simon et al *see* MATHEMATISCHES WOERTERBUCH

Klueger, Hermann *see* UEBER GENESIS UND COMPOSITION DER HALACHA-SAMMLUNG EDUJOT

Klueh, John M *see* STORY OF THE CHILDHOOD AND PASSION OF THE LORD JESUS...IN THE WORDS OF THE EVANGELISTS

Kluepfel, K *see* KLEINE PROSAISCHE SCHRIFTEN

Klug, F *see* JAHRBUECHER DER INSEKTENKUNDE...

Klug, Gary A *see*
- 31P METABOLIC RESPONSES TO ACTIVITY OF NONSPECIFICALLY TRAINED MUSCLE TISSUE IN ELITE ENDURANCE ATHLETES AND IN HEALTHY, SEDENTARY SUBJECTS AS OBSERVED BY 31P MAGNETIC SPECTROSCOPY
- THE ABILITY OF SARCOPLASMIC RETICULUM TO REGULATE INTRACELLULAR CALCIUM FOLLOWING A FATIGUING BOUT OF EXERCISE
- A BIOCHEMICAL ANALYSIS OF THE EXERCISE-INDUCED DYSFUNCTION OF THE RAT GASTROCNEMIUS SARCO-PLASMIC RETICULUM CA2+-ATPASE PROTEIN
- A COMPARISON OF HYDROSTATIC WEIGHING AND DISPLACEMENT PLETHYSMOGRAPHY FOR DETERMINING BODY DENSITY OF YOUNG ELITE FEMALE GYMNASTS
- CORRELATION BETWEEN MUSCLE RELAXATION AND SARCOPLASMIC RETICULUM CA2+-ATPASE DURING FATIGUE

DIE KLUGE BAUERNTOCHTER : NACH DEM GLEICHNAMIGEN MAERCHEN DER BRUEDER GRIMM IN FUENF LUSTIGEN VORGAENGEN DER BUEHNE UEBERMITTELT / Guembel-Seiling, Max – Leipzig: Breitkopf & Haertel, 1918 – 1r – 1 – us U.W. Library [820]

Kluge, Hermann *see* GESCHICHTE DER DEUTSCHEN NATIONAL-LITERATUR

Kluh, John M *see* THE MANIFESTATION OF AGES

KLUIZENAARS IN LIMBURG / Welters, A – Heerlen, 1950 – Dfl19.00 – ne Slangenburg [240]

Klunzinger, C B *see* DIE KORALLTHIERE DES ROTHEN MEERES

Klutschak, H W *see* ALS ESKIMO UNTER DEN ESKIMOS

Knaepper, Matthias *see* EG-BINNENMARKT UND ENTWICKLUNG VON POLITIKFELDERN

Knapp *see* ILLUSTRATED HISTORY AND BIOGRAPHICAL RECORD OF LENAWEE COUNTY

Knapp, Clark D *see* A TREATISE ON THE LAWS OF THE STATE OF NEW YORK RELATING TO THE POOR, INSANE, IDIOTS AND HABITUAL DRUNKARDS.

Knapp, Ferdinand M *see* IDEOLOGY, TECHNOLOGY AND THE HISTORICAL AVANT GARDE

Knapp, H S *see* HISTORY OF THE MAUMEE VALLEY

Knapp, Jacob *see* AUTOBIOGRAPHY OF ELDER JACOB KNAPP

Knapp, Martin Wells *see*
- PENTECOSTAL AGGRESSIVENESS, OR, WHY I CONDUCTED THE MEETINGS OF THE CHESAPEAKE HOLINESS UNION AT BOWENS, MARYLAND
- REVIVAL KINDLINGS
- REVIVAL TORNADOES, OR, LIFE AND LABORS OF REV. JOSEPH H. WEBER

Knapp, Samuel Lorenzo *see* AMERICAN CULTURAL HISTORY, 1607-1829

Knappert, Jan *see* THE RELIGION OF ISRAEL

Knappert, L *see* DE OPKOMST VAN HET PROTESTANTISME IN EENE NOORD-NEDERLANDSCHE STAD

DAS KNAPPSCHAFTSWESEN IM RUHRKOHLENBEZIRK BIS ZUM ALLGEMEINEN PREUSSISCHEN BERGGESETZ VOM 24.6.1865 / Buelow, Wilhelm – 1 – DM30.00 – gw Mikro Press [330]

Knauff, Christopher W *see* DOCTOR TUCKER, PRIEST-MUSICIAN

Knaup, Werner *see* ALGEBRAISCHE STRUKTUREN IN EINFACHEN WARTESCHLANGEN-NETZEN

Knauss, Heinz *see* STUDIEN ZUM STIL VON GRIMMELSHAUSENS SIMPLICISSIMUS

Knauth, Paul *see*
- GOETHES SPRACHE UND STIL IM ALTER
- VON GOETHES SPRACHE UND STIL IM ALTER

DER KNECHT GOTTES ANDREAS NYLAND : ROMAN / Wiechert, Ernst Emil – Berlin: G Grote, 1926 – 1r – us U.W. Library [830]

Knecht, J H *see*
- GEMEINNUETZLICHES ELEMENTARWERK DER HARMONIE UND DES GENERALBASSES.
- KLEINES ALPHABETISCHES WOERTERBUCH DER VORNEHMSTEN UND INTERESSANTESTEN ARTIKEL AUS DER MUSIKALISCHEN THEORIE.

DER KNECHT JAHVES DES DEUTEROJESAIA / Giesebrecht, Friedrich – (Includes bibliographical references) – Koenigsburg i. Pr: Thomas & Oppermann, 1902 – 1mf – 9 – 0-8370-3275-X – 1985-1275 – us A.T.L.A. [220]

Knecht, John *see* THE EFFECTS OF EXERCISE ON THE STRENGTH OF THE LOW BACK

Kneeland, Stillman Foster *see*
- LAW, LAWYERS AND LAMBS
- A TREATISE ON THE LAW OF ATTACHMENTS IN CIVIL CASES.

Kneile, Karl *see* DIE FORMENLEHRE BEI JOHN LYLY

KNEKTERYM OTAZKAM PRIPRANEHO RIZENI / Stepan, J – Praha. 1966. BR-8766 1 – 9 – ne IDC [999]

Kneller, George Frederick *see* THE EDUCATIONAL PHILOSOPHY OF NATIONAL SOCIALISM

Knesebeck, Rosemarie von dem *see* RUDOLF PECHEL UND DIE "DEUTSCHE RUNDSCHAU" 1946-1961

Kneucker, J J *see* VORLESUNGEN UEBER BIBLISCHE THEOLOGIE UND MESSIANISCHE WEISSAGUNGEN DES ALTEN TESTAMENTS

Kneucker, Johann Jacob *see* DAS BUCH BARUCH: GESCHICHTE UND KRITIK, UEBERSETZUNG UND ERKLAERUNG

Knew, E *see* FLAYING AND CURING OF HIDES AND SKINS AS A RURAL INDUSTRY

KNIAZ' S.N. TRUBETSKOI I EGO OBSHCHEE FILOSOFSKOE MIROSOZERTSANIE / Lopatin, L M – 1906. BR-5767 2 – 8 – ne IDC [190]

KNIAZHNA TARAKANOVA I PRINTSESSA VLADIMIRSKAIA / Mel'nikov, P – Spb. 1868. BR-10,525 2 – 8 – ne IDC [947]

Kniazhnii, V *see* A. A. BLOK

Kniazhnin, Ia. B *see* SOCHINENIIA

THE KNICKERBOCKER MAGAZINE – 1833-65 – 1 – us UMI [073]

KNICKERBOCKER NEWS-UNION STAR – Albany. N.Y. 1937- – 1 – us UMI [071]

KNIGA – Ezhenedel'nyi kritiko-bibliograficheskii zhurnal. v. 1-25. Spb. 1906-07. Lacking: v. 22-23. B-1759 2 – 8 – ne IDC [073]

KNIGA ESFIR'. V TEKSTAKH: EVREISKOM-MASORETSKOM, GRECHESKOM, DREVNEM LATINSKOM I SLAVIANSKOM / Rozhdestvenskii, I – Spb. 1885. BR-4095 2 – 8 – ne IDC [400]

KNIGA I REVOLIUTSIIA – v1-3. 1920-23 – 1r – 1 – us Ross [335]

KNIGA I REVOLYUTZIYA – St. Petersburg. v. 1-3 no. 1, 3, 4. 1920-23 – 1 – us NY Public [335]

KNIGA O EVREINOVE / Kamenskii, V – Petrograd. 1917. BR-942 2 – 8 – ne IDC [460]

KNIGA O KNIGAKH – (Includes c.1: no.3 1924:May-no.4 (1924:May)) – [Moskva]: Gos. izd-vo, 1924 – 1 – CSUXAKZ2855-S – us Hoover Inst Photo [947]

KNIGA O KNIGAKH – Tolkovui ukazatel' dlia vybora knig vazhneishim otrasliam znanii. v. 1-2. M. 1892. BR-5952 2 – 8 – ne IDC [070]

KNIGA O LEONIDE ANDREEVE – Vospominaniia (Blok, Belyi i dr.). Ed. 2. (Izd. "Grzhebin"). Spb., Berlin. 1922. BR-3319 2 – 8 – ne IDC [920]

KNIGA O RUSSKIKH POETAKH POSLEDNIAGO DESIATILETIIA / Gofman, M & Piast, V – Spb., M. 1910. BR-1265 2 – 8 – ne IDC [460]

KNIGA OB ALEKSANDRE BLOKE / Chukovskii, K – Ed. 2. Berlin. 1922. BR-2030 2 – 8 – ne IDC [460]

KNIGA OB ALEKSANDRE BLOKE / Chukovskii, K – "Epokha". Spb. 1922. BR-2029 2 – 8 – ne IDC [460]

KNIGA OTRAZHENII I VTORAIA KNIGA OTRAZHENII / Annenskii, I F – St. Petersburg, 1909. BR-509 2 – 8 – ne IDC [460]

KNIGA OTRAZHENII. PROBLEMA GOGOLEVSKAGO IUMORA. DOSTOEVSKII DO KATASTROFY / Annenskii, I F – St. Petersburg, 1906. 213p. BR-1968 2 – 8 – ne IDC [460]

KNIGA PROROKA DANIILA, V DREVNESLAVIANSKOM PEREVODE / Evseev, I – Vvedenie i teksty. M. 1905. BR-172 2 – 8 – ne IDC [460]

KNIGA RAZLUK / Sologub, F – Razskazy. Spb. 1908. BR-864 2 – 8 – ne IDC [460]

KNIGA SKAZOK / Sologub, F – M. 1905. BR-865 2 – 8 – ne IDC [460]

KNIGA V ROSSII – Pod red. V.Ia. Adariukova i A. A. Sidorova. v. 1-2. M. 1924-26. BR-6209 2 – 8 – ne IDC [460]

KNIGA VELIKAGO GNEVA / Volynskii, A L – Kriticheskaia stat'i, zametki, polemika. Izd. Trud. Spb. 1904. BR-2214 2 – 8 – ne IDC [460]

KNIGA ZHIZNI / Gnedich, P P – Vospominaniia. 1855-1918. M. 1929. BR-9062 1 – 9 – ne IDC [700]

O KNIGAKH – Kritiko-bibliograficheskii zhurnal. v. 1-4. M. 1907. BR-7635 2 – 8 – ne IDC [073]

THE KNIGHT ERRANT – Buckhannon. West Virginia. 1896-1900 – 1 – us UMI [071]

Knight, George H *see* PATENT-OFFICE MANUAL, INCLUDING THE LAW AND PRACTICE OF CASES IN THE UNITED STATES PATENT OFFICE AND THE COURTS HOLDING A REVISORY RELATION THERETO

Knight, Helen C *see* LADY HUNTINGTON AND HER FRIENDS, OR, THE REVIVAL OF THE WORK OF GOD IN THE DAYS OF WESLEY, WHITEFIELD, ROMAINE, VENN, AND OTHERS IN THE LAST CENTURY

Knight, Henry JC *see* TEMPTATION OF OUR LORD...AS RELATED TO...MINISTRY AND AS A REVELATION OF HIS PERSON

Knight, J *see* ON THE CULTIVATION OF THE PLANTS BELONGING TO THE NATURAL ORDER OF PROTEAE
Knight, JC *see* THE PENTATEUCHAL NARRATIVE VINDICATED FROM THE ABSURDITIES CHARGED AGAINST IT BY THE BISHOP OF NATAL
Knight, Joseph *see* LIFE OF DANTE GABRIEL ROSSETTI
Knight, William *see*
- ASPECTS OF THEISM
- LECTURES ON SOME OF THE PROPHECIES CONCERNING THE RISE AND CHARACTER OF THE POWER COMMONLY CALLED ANTICHRIST

Knight, William Allen *see* SONG OF OUR SYRIAN GUEST
Knight, William H *see* HANDBOOK ALMANAC FOR THE PACIFIC STATES: AN OFFICIAL REGISTER AND BUSINESS DIRECTORY...CALIFORNIA AND OREGON; THE TERRITORIES...WASHINGTON, NEVADA AND UTAH;...COLONIES OF BRITISH COLUMBIA AND VANCOUVER
Knights, David B *see* IN SUPPORT OF THE RAISON D'ETRE
KNIGHTS LANDING NEWS – Knights Landing, CA. 1861-1862 – 1r – 1 – $50.00 – C03258 – us Library Micro [071]
THE KNIGHTS OF THE CROSS / Sienkiewicz, Henryk – Authorized and unabr. trans. from the Polish by Jeremiah Curtin. Boston: Little, Brown, 1900. 2v – 1 – us U.W. Library [830]
Knights or Honor. Imperial Lodge No671 (Upper Sandusky, Ohio) *see* RECORDS
KNIGHT'S PENNY MAGAZINE – v. 1-NS2. 1832-1846 – 1 – us UMI [073]
KNIGHT'S QUARTERLY MAGAZINE – v. 1-3. 1823-1824 – 1 – us UMI [073]
KNIGI GRAZHDANSKOI PECHATI 18 V / Petrov, SO – Katalog knig, khraniashchikhsia v gosudarstvennoi publichnoi biblioteke ukrainskoi SSR. Kiev. 1956. BR-7765 2 – 8 – ne IDC [020]
KNIGOVEDENIE – Ezhemesiachnyi bibliograficheskii zhurnal. M. 1894-97. Lacking: 1897 (1-2). B-1760 2 – 8 – ne IDC [073]
Knill, Richard *see* THE MISSIONARY'S WIFE, OR, A BRIEF ACCOUNT OF MRS. LOVELESS, OF MADRAS, THE FIRST MISSIONARY TO FOREIGN LANDS
Knippel, Richard *see* SCHILLERS VERHAELTNIS ZUR IDYLLE
DER KNITTELVERS DES JUNGEN GOETHE : EINE METRISCHE UND MELODISCHE UNTERSUCHUNG / Feise, Ernst – (Includes bibliographical references) – Leipzig: Roeder & Schunke, 1909 – 1r – 1 – us U.W. Library [430]
THE KNITTER / America's Textiles – (Supersedes: The Knitter.) Years: 1937-1971 – 1,5,6 – us Princeton Micro [331]
KNIZHNAI A TORGOVLI A – (Includes c.1: 1964-1971) – Moskva: "Kniga", 1964- – 1 – CSUXAKZ0062-S – us Hoover Inst Photo [947]
KNIZHNAIA LETOPIS – Leningrad. (Bibliographical Chronicle). 1907-59 – 3 – us Readex [010]
KNIZHNAIA LETOPIS' – Moscow: Knizhnaia palata, 1907- – 100mf – 9 – $495.00y – us East View [460]
KNIZHNIK – Zhurnal bibliograficheskii. Spb. 1898-1907. Lacking: 1898-99, 1902 (1), 1904 (2, 8), 1905-06, 1907 (2-8). B-1764 2 – 8 – ne IDC [073]
KNIZHNOE OBOZRENIE – Moscow: Ministerstvo pechati i informatsii Rossii, 1966- – 52mf – 9 – $89.95y – us East View [460]
KNIZHNYI MIR – Bibliograficheskii vestnik. Spb. 1902-05; 1908-11. Lacking: 1904 (4, 50, 52); 1909 (23); 1910 (1, p. 1-4). BR-4318 2 – 8 – ne IDC [073]
KNIZHNYI UGOL : KRITIKA-BIBLIOGRAFIIA-KHRONIKA – Petrograd. n1-8. 1918-22 – 1r – 1 – us Ross [010]
KNIZHNYI VESTNIK – Zhurnal knizhno-torgovoi izdatel'skoi i literaturnoi deiatelnosti v Rossii. Spb. 1884-1901. B-1766 2 – 8 – ne IDC [073]
KNIZHNYI VESTNIK – Zhurnal russkoi literaturnoi deiatel' nosti, knizhnoi torgovli, knigopechataniia i.t.p. v. 1-24. Spb. 1860-63. B-1765 2 – 8 – ne IDC [073]
KNIZHNYI VIESTNIK – St Petersburg, 1899 – 1r – 1 – us Ross [072]
KNIZNA REVUE – (Backfile through 1998 $85r) – Slovakia, 1999- – 1r per y – 1 – $80.00 standing order – us Ross [072]
KNIZNOYE OBOZRENIE – Moscow. U.S.S.R. -w. 1968- – 1 – us UMI [072]
KNJIGE MATICE SRPSKE – Collected works, Serbian history – 1 – us U.W. Library [949]
KNJIZEVNE NOVINE – Beograd.Jan 1969-Dec 1978 – 1 – 69.00 – us L of C Photodup [073]
KNJIZEVNI JADRAN – Split. Yugoslavia. -m. Jan 1952-Aug 1953. (1 reel) – 1 – uk British Libr Newspaper [949]
KNJIZEVNIK – Zagreb, Croatia. v1-9, 11. 1928-36, 1938 – 1 – us I.U. Libraries [073]
KNOB CREEK BAPTIST CHURCH. COLUMBIA, TENNESSEE : CHURCH RECORDS – Dec 1881-Oct 1986. Lacking Jan-Aug 1958. 1004p – 1 – 45.18 – us Baptist [978]
Knock, N A *see* DISPOSITIEN DER MERKWAARDIGSTE KERK-ORGELEN, WELKEN IN DE PROVINCIE FRIESLAND, GRONINGEN EN ELDERS AANGETROFFEN WORDEN
THE KNOCKER – Manhattan, NV. 1911 – 1r – 1 – $50.00 – U04628 – us Library Micro [071]
Knoebelspies, Karin *see* CHANCEN UND PERSPEKTIVEN EINER DEMOKRATISIERUNG DES RUNDFUNKSYSTEMS IN BRASILIEN
THE KNOEDLER LIBRARY ON MICROFICHE : THE COMPLETE TITLE INDEX OF 26,000 VOLUMES OF SALES, EXHIBITIONS AND SALONS IN THE KNOEDLER LIBRARY ON MICROFICHE – 55mf – 9 – $100.00 – us Knoedler [700]
THE KNOEDLER LIBRARY ON MICROFICHE : THE COMPLETE TITLE INDEX OF 26,000 VOLUMES OF SALES, EXHIBITIONS AND SALONS IN THE KNOEDLER LIBRARY ON MICROFICHE – 55mf – 9 – $100.00 – us Knoedler [380]
THE KNOEDLER LIBRARY ON MICROFICHE : EXHIBITION CATALOGUES – (Knoedler Gallery, New York, 1876-1971.-930mf. $3,096.90; New York (except Knoedler), 1876-1971.-1,010mf. $3,363.30; American, 1889-1970.-1,950mf. $6,498.37; British, 1813-1970.-1,715mf. $5,715.23; French, 1855-1971.-942mf. $3,139.22; German, 1888-1970.-712mf. $2,372.75; International, 1873-1970.-1,887mf. $6,288.43) – 9 – us Knoedler [700]
THE KNOEDLER LIBRARY ON MICROFICHE, 1 : AMERICAN AUCTIONS – (American Art Association, 1884-1939. – 296mf. $986.42; American Art Galleries, 1886-1929. – 474mf. $1,579.60; Anderson Art Galleries, 1911-1939. – 339mf. $1,129.72; Selected American Auctions (excluding American Art Association, American Art Galleries, Anderson Art Galleries and Philadelphia), 1835-1970. – 730mf. $2,432.72; Philadelphia Auctions, 1873-1970. – 177mf. $589.85) – 9 – us Knoedler [700]
THE KNOEDLER LIBRARY ON MICROFICHE, 2 : BRITISH AUCTIONS – (Christie's, 1792-1970. – 2,077mf. $7,198.20; Selected British Auctions (excluding Christie's & Sotheby's), 1748-1966. – 809mf. $2,696.00) – 9 – us Knoedler [700]
THE KNOEDLER LIBRARY ON MICROFICHE, 3 : FRENCH AUCTIONS – (Hotel Drouot, 1863-1970. – 1,442mf. $4,805.46; George Petit, 1883-1932. – 644mf. $2,146.13; Selected French Auctions (excluding Hotel Drouot, G. Petit, Charpentier & Palais Galleria), 1774-1970. – 391mf. $1,303.00; Charpentier, 1933-1960. – 301mf. $1,003.00; Palais Galleria, 1960-1970. – 287mf. $956.43) – 9 – us Knoedler [700]
THE KNOEDLER LIBRARY ON MICROFICHE, 4 : INTERNATIONAL AUCTIONS – (Selected International Auctions (excluding American, British, French, Belgian, Dutch & German), 1845-1970. – 473mf. $1,576.27; Belgian Auctions, 1819-1968. – 264mf. $879.78; Dutch Auctions, 1816-1970. – 400mf. $1,333.00; German Auctions, 1876-1970. – 639mf $2,132.80) – 9 – us Knoedler [700]
Knoop, Kaete *see* DIE ERZAEHLUNGEN EDUARD VON KEYSERLINGS
Knopf, R *see* DER ERSTE CLEMENSBRIEF (T.U.U. 2-20/1)
Knopf, Rudolf *see*
- DER ERSTE CLEMENSBRIEF
- DAS NACHAPOSTOLISCHE ZEITALTER
- DIE ZUKUNFTSHOFFNUNGEN DES URCHRISTENTUMS

Knortz, Karl *see*
- CHRISTENTUM UND KIRCHENTUM
- DEUTSCHES UND AMERIKANISCHES
- EPIGRAMME
- GOETHE UND DIE WERTHERZEIT
- HUMORISTISCHE GEDICHTE
- NEUE GEDICHTE

KNOSSOS NOTEBOOKS FROM THE ASHMOLEAN MUSEUM / Ashmolean Museum – 1900-29 – 1 – uk Microform Academic [930]
Knote, Walter *see* HERMANN LINGG UND SEINE LYRISCHE DICHTUNG
KNOTS UNTIED 1090 OR WAYS AND BY-WAYS IN THE HIDDEN LIFE OF AMERICAN DETECTIVES / McWatters, George S – Hartford/Chicago: J B Burr & Co, 1874 – 7mf – 9 – $10.50 – LLMC 92-178 – us L.L.M.C. [340]
Knott, R R *see* THE NEW AID TO MEMORY: PT. 4, ADAPTED TO THE NEW TESTAMENT
KNOVO I ARMII : ORGAN GLAVNOGO UPRAVLENII A VSEOBSHCHAGO VOENNOGO OBUCHENII A I GLAVNOGO UPRAVLENII A VOENNOUCHEBNYKH ZAVEDENI I – (Library has: 1920, no. 1-6; 9-18) – Moskva: Upr., 1920- – 1 – CSUX89-S975 – us Hoover Inst Photo [947]
KNOW THE TRUTH : A CRITIQUE ON THE HAMILTONIAN THEORY OF LIMITATION: INCLUDING SOME STRICTURES UPON THE THEORIES OF REV. HENRY L. MANSEL AND MR. HERBERT SPENCER / Jones, Jesse Henry – New York: Hurd and Houghton, 1865 – 1mf – 9 – 0-8370-3797-2 – 1985-1797 – us A.T.L.A. [210]
KNOWING AND DOING : LITERACY FOR WOMEN / Chlebowska, Krystyna – 1992 – 9 – 92-3-102803-0 – fr UNESCO [305]
Knowland, J B *see* EARLY NARRATIVES OF BERKS COUNTY
KNOWLE JOURNAL. (KNOWLE JOURNAL AND SOLIHULL ADVERTISER) – England. 8 Apr 1893-9 Feb 1901.-w. 7 reels – 1 – uk British Libr Newspaper [072]
KNOWLEDGE – (1983-. 1,5,6,9) – v1-. 1979- – 1 – us UMI [073]
KNOWLEDGE – v. 1-40. no. 583. 1881-1917 – 1 – us UMI [000]
THE KNOWLEDGE OF GOD : OBJECTIVELY CONSIDERED: BEING THE FIRST PART OF THEOLOGY CONSIDERED AS A SCIENCE OF POSITIVE TRUTH, BOTH INDUCTIVE AND DEDUCTIVE / Breckinridge, Robert J – New York: R. Carter; Louisville: A. Davidson, 1859, c1857 – 2mf – us A.T.L.A. [210]
THE KNOWLEDGE OF JESUS, THE MOST EXCELLENT OF THE SCIENCES / Carson, Alexander – Second ed., 1851 – 1 – us A.T.L.A. [240]
THE KNOWLEDGE OF MARY / Concilio, Januarius de – New York: Catholic Publ Society, 1878, c1877 – 1mf – 9 – 0-8370-8333-8 – 1986-2333 – us A.T.L.A. [240]
Knowles, Edward Randall *see* SUPREMACY OF THE SPIRITUAL
Knowles, James Davis *see* MEMOIR OF ANN H. JUDSON: MISSIONARY TO BURMA
Knowles, Morris, Inc *see* REPORT
Knowling, Richard John *see* THE EPISTLE OF ST JAMES: WITH AN INTRODUCTION AND NOTES
THE KNOWLTON ADVERTISER AND EASTERN TOWNSHIPS CHRONICLE – (Also: The Eastern Townships Advertiser 1 jun 1961-10 nov 1967) – Knowlton, Canada. 27 jun 1957-16 mai 1958 – 1r – 1 – Can$25.00 – cn Can Microfilming [072]
THE KNOWLTON ADVERTISER AND EASTERN TOWNSHIPS CHRONICLE *see* THE EASTERN TOWNSHIPS ADVERTISER
KNOWLTON NEWS AND BROME COUNTY ADVOCATE – Knowlton, Canada. v4 n7. 1 nov 1889-v88 n33. 12 dec 1935 – 1r – 1 – Can$35.00 – cn Can Microfilming [072]
Knox, Alexander *see* CONSIDERATIONS ON A SEPARATION OF THE METHODISTS FROM THE ESTABLISHED CHURCH, ADDRESSED TO SUCH OF THEM AS ARE FRIENDLY TO THAT MEASURE, AND PARTICULARLY TO THOSE IN THE CITY OF BRISTOL
KNOX COLLEGE MONTHLY – (Cont by: The Knox College Monthly and Presbyterian Magazine) – [Toronto?]: Metaphysical and Literary Society, [1883-1887] – 9 – cn C.I.H.M. [370]
KNOX COLLEGE MONTHLY *see* THE KNOX COLLEGE MONTHLY AND PRESBYTERIAN MAGAZINE
THE KNOX COLLEGE MONTHLY AND PRESBYTERIAN MAGAZINE – (Cont: Knox College Monthly) – Toronto: Alumni Association and the Metaphysical and Literary Society of Knox College, [1887-1896] – 9 – cn C.I.H.M. [370]
THE KNOX COLLEGE MONTHLY AND PRESBYTERIAN MAGAZINE *see* KNOX COLLEGE MONTHLY
KNOX COUNTY GAZETTEER AND FARMERS' AND LAND OWNERS' DIRECTORY – Springfield: 1888. Illinois Reel 33. (The Cox Library Collection) – 5 – us Americana [978]
KNOX COUNTY HONOR ROLL 1917-18-19 / Wagner Printing Co – Galesburg, 1920. (Illinois Reel 35). (The Cox Library Collection) – 5 – us Americana [978]
KNOX COUNTY RECORDER – Verdigre, NE. -w. Dec 1892; Apr-Dec 1896 – 1 – us NE Hist [071]
KNOX COUNTY REPUBLICAN – Mount Vernon. Ohio. -sw, w. 1881-1900 – 1 – us UMI [071]
KNOX COUNTY REPUBLICAN NEWS – Mount Vernon. Ohio. 1901-1921 – 1 – us UMI [071]
Knox, George William *see*
- DIRECT AND FUNDAMENTAL PROOFS OF THE CHRISTIAN RELIGION
- THE GOSPEL OF JESUS THE SON OF GOD
- THE MYSTERY OF LIFE

Knox, George William et al *see* THE CHRISTIAN POINT OF VIEW
Knox, Henry *see* HENRY KNOX PAPERS, 1719-1825
Knox, John *see*
- AN HISTORICAL JOURNAL OF THE CAMPAIGNS IN NORTH-AMERICA FOR THE YEARS 1757, 1758, 1759 AND 1760
- THE HISTORY OF THE REFORMATION OF RELIGION WITHIN THE REALM OF SCOTLAND

Knox, Kelly M *see* ENERGY COST OF WALKING WITH AND WITHOUT ARM ACTIVITY ON THE CROSS WALK DUAL MOTION CROSS TRAINER
Knox, Peter *see* PROGRAMME OF LAW STUDIES.
Knox, T F *see* THE TRUE STORY OF THE CATHOLIC HIERARCHY DEPOSED BY QUEEN ELIZABETH
KNOXVILLE FIRST BAPTIST CHURCH. KNOXVILLE, TENNESSEE : CHURCH RECORDS – 1843-1952 – 1 – 337.77 – us Baptist [240]
Knudtzon, J A *see*
- ASSYRISCHE GEBETE AN DEN SONNENGOTT. AUS DER ZEIT ASARHADDONS
- ASSYRISCHE GEBETE AN DEN SONNENGOTT FUER STAAT UND KOENIGLICHES HAUS

DER KNUEPPEL : SATIRISCHE ARBEITERZEITUNG – Berlin, 1925, 1927 n1-5 – 1 – Dist. gw Mikrofilm – gw Misc Inst [870]
Knueppelholz, Paul *see* DER MONOLOG IN DEN DRAMEN DES ANDREAS GRYPHIUS
Knuth, P E O W *see* HANDBOOK OF FLOWER POLLINATION
KNUTSFORD DIVISION GUARDIAN – (Also known as: Knutsford Guardian) – Aug 22-Dec 30 1891; 1911; 1939-Jun 18 1959; Aug 1959-75; 1977-80; 1985-91; Jan 8-Feb 26 1992; Mar 1992-96 – 113 1/2r – 9 – uk British Libr Newspaper [072]
KNUTSFORD GUARDIAN *see* KNUTSFORD DIVISION GUARDIAN
Knutson, Bonnie *see* JOURNAL OF HOSPITALITY AND LEISURE MARKETING
Knutson-Kaske, Jill A *see* A DESCRIPTION OF TRENDS EMERGING DURING YEARS THREE AND FOUR OF THE WISCONSIN COMPREHENSIVE ELEMENTARY HEALTH EDUCATION PILOT PROJECT
Knuttel Collection, Royal Library. The Hague *see* DUTCH PAMPHLETS, 1486-1750
Knuttel, Willem Pieter Cornelis *see* DE TOESTAND DER NEDERLANDSCHE KATHOLIEKEN TEN TIJDE DER REPUBLIEK
Knuttel, Willem Pieter Cornelius *see* NEDERLANDSCHE BIBLIOGRAPHIE VAN KERKGESCHIEDENIS
Koabel-Bagley, Patricia *see* ASSESSMENT OF THE NEED FOR CERTIFIED ATHLETIC TRAINERS IN NEW YORK STATE HIGH SCHOOLS
KOAIN CHOSA GEPPO = MONTHLY REPORTS OF THE BOARD OF DEVELOPMENT OF ASIA: JAPANESE EMPIRE – In Japanese. v1-3, 1940-1942 – 10r – 1 – Y90,000 – ja Yushodo [338]
Kobaudaisi *see* ZITU-GO KYAU. DO-ZI KYAU
Kobayashi, Takayoshi *see* NONLINEAR OPTICS

KOBE CHRONICLE – Kobe, Japan. Japan Chronicle. -w. 21 March 1900-22 May 1930; 7 Jan 1937-29 Dec 1938. 60 reels – 1 – uk British Libr Newspaper [072]
KOBEDINENII U: INFORMAT SIONNY I BI ULLETEN OBEDINENII A NAT SIONALNO-PROGRESSIVN. I DEMOKRATICH. RUSKO I EMIGRAT SII V KOROL. S.KH.S. – (Includes c.1: no.1) – Bielgrad: Russkai a tip., [1926- – 1 – CSUXANR5722-S – us Hoover Inst Photo [947]
Kobeko, D M *see* TSESAREVICH PAVEL PETROVICH (1754-1796)
Kobelt, W *see* ILLUSTRIRTES CONCHYLIENBUCH
Kober, Margarete *see* DAS DEUTSCHE MAERCHENDRAMA
Koberstein, Astrid Beate *see* DIE FUNDLANDSCHAFT GUSPINI, PROVINZ CAGLIARI, SARDINIEN
Koberstein, August *see* GRUNDRISS ZUR GESCHICHTE DER DEUTSCHEN NATIONALLITERATUR
Kobes, Alois *see*
- DICTIONNAIRE VOLOF-FRANCAIS
- GRAMMAIRE DE LA LANGUE VOLOFE

Kobes, Mgr *see* DICTIONNAIRE VOLOF-FRANCAIS
KOBIJITSU KENKUSHO. TJANDI PANATARAN / Java – Djakarta, Gunseikanbu Kokumin Tosyokyoku, 2605. 35p – 69mf – 9 – ne IDC [950]
Koblents, I N *see* A. I. BOGDANOV, 1692-1766
KOBLENZER VOLKSZEITUNG *see* COBLENZER VOLKSZEITUNG
KOBMAND B. J. LUND'S BESKRIVELSE AF GRONLAENDERNES ISFANGST / Birket-Smith, K – (Det gronlandske Selskabs Aarsskrift). Kobenhavn. 1931-32. BN-136 2 – 8 – ne IDC [306]
Kobner, Johann *see* SERMONS AND CONTROVERSIAL WRITINGS
KOCAELI – Izmit, 1920-19? – 9 – $20.00 – us MEDOC [956]
Koch, Adolf *see* DER SEMITISCHE INFINITIV
Koch, C L *see* DIE ARACHNIDEN. GETREU NACH DER NATUR
Koch, Ernst *see* GRIECHISCHE SCHULGRAMMATIK
Koch, Franz *see*
- DREI GOETHE-REDEN
- GEIST UND LEBEN
- JOSEF WEINHEBER
- VERGANGENHEIT UND GEGENWART IN EINS

Koch, Grace *see* COMPUTERISED INDEX OF AUSTRALIAN ABORIGINAL SONGS, CAPE YORK AREA
Koch, H *see*
- CYPRIAN UND DER ROEMISCHE PRIMAT (T.U.U. 3-35/1)
- CYPRIANISCHE UNTERSUCHUNGEN
- VINCENZ VON LERIN UND GENNADIUS (T.U.U. 3-31/2B)
- VIRGINES CHRISTI (T.U.U. 3-31/2C)

Koch, Hans *see*
- AUFSAETZE ZUR DEUTSCHEN LITERATURGESCHICHTE
- UNSERE LITERATURGESELLSCHAFT

Koch, Heinrich C *see*
- JOURNAL DER TONKUNST
- VERSUCH EINER ANLEITUNG ZUR COMPOSITION

Koch, Herbert *see* UEBER DAS VERHAELTNIS VON DRAMA UND GESCHICHTE BEI FRIEDRICH HEBBEL
Koch, Hugo *see* PSEUDO-DIONYSIUS AREOPAGITA IN SEINEN BEZIEHUNGEN ZUM NEUPLATONISMUS UND MYSTERIENWESEN
Koch, Johannes Guenther *see* GUTZKOWS THEORIE DES ROMANS IN SEINEM ROMAN "HOHENSCHWANGAU"
Koch, K H E *see*
- BEITRAEGE ZUR EINER FLORA DES ORIENTS
- MONOGRAPHIA GENERIS VERONICAE

Koch, K R *see* DIE KUESTE LABRADORS UND IHRE BEWOHNER
Koch, L *see*
- FORTAELLINGER AF DANMARKS KIRKEHISTORIE FRA 1517 TIL 1848
- FRA GRUNDTVIGIANISMENS OG DEN INDRE MISSIONS TID 1848-1898

Koch, M *see* WIE HABEN WIR ZAEHLEN UND RECHNEN GELERNT?
Koch, Max *see*
- AUGUST GRAF VON PLATENS SAEMTLICHE WERKE IN ZWOELF BAENDEN
- DEUTSCHE VERGANGENHEIT IN DEUTSCHER DICHTUNG
- FRANZ GRILLPARZER
- GESAMMELTE WERKE
- GESCHICHTE DER DEUTSCHEN LITTERATUR VON DEN AELTESTEN ZEITEN BIS ZUR GEGENWART
- GOTTSCHED UND DIE REFORM DER DEUTSCHEN LITERATUR IM ACHTZEHNTEN JAHRHUNDERT
- HELFERICH PETER STURZ
- DIE KIRCHENPOLITIK KOENIG SIGMUNDS WAEHREND SEINES ROMZUGES (1431-1433)
- QUELLENVERHAELTNISS VON WIELANDS OBERON

Koch, R *see* UNTERSUCHUNGEN UEBER DIE AETIOLOGIE DER WUNDINFECTIONSKRANKHEITEN
Koch, Stefan *see* UNTERSUCHUNG UND OPTIMIERUNG ALTERNATIVER ZAHNFUELLUNGS-COMPOSITE-MATERIALIEN AUF DER BASIS VON POLYBUTADIENEPOXID
Koch, W D J *see*
- SYNOPSIS FLORAE GERMANICAE ET HELVETICAE

Kochanowski, Bodo *see* DIE LICHTEN STUNDEN
Kocher, Pamela L *see* THE EFFECTS OF CHROMIUM SUPPLEMENTATION AND A LOW CARBOHYDRATE DIET ON HIGH-INTENSITY ENDURANCE PERFORMANCE
Kochetov, AN *see* ISTORIIA I OSNOVNYE NAPRAVLENIIA DEIATEL'NOSTI LENINGRADSKOGO GOSUDARSTVENNOGO TEATRAL'NOGO MUZEIA
Kochin, GE *see* MATERIALY DLIA TERMINOLOGICHESKOGO SLOVARIA DREVNEI RUSI
Kocourek, Albert *see* FORMATIVE INFLUENCES OF LEGAL DEVELOPMENT
O KODAK – Manacapuru, Amazonas. 16 Jun 1918 – 1,5,6 – bl Biblioteca [072]
Kodama, Yoshio *see* I WAS DEFEATED
KODEKS O BRAKE I SEME ARMI ANSKO I SOVETSKO I SOTSIALISTICHESKO I RESPUBLIKI / Armenian SSR – Erevan: "Aiastan", 1969 – 1 – CSUX91-B2262 – us Hoover Inst Photo [335]
KODEKS ZAKONA U ABPRAT SY BELARUSKAI SSR. RUSSIAN KODEKS ZAKONOV O TRUDE BELORUSSKOI SSR : OFITSIALNYI TEKST S IZMENENIIAMI NA 1 SENT. 1956 G. I S PRILOZHENIEM SISTEMATIZIROVANNYKH MATERIALOV / Byelorussian S.S.R. – Minsk: Gos. izd-vo BSSR, 1957 – 1 – CSUX91-B1738 – us Hoover Inst Photo [947]
KODEKS ZAKONOV O BRAKE, SEME I OPEKE : S POSTATEINYM KOMMENTARIEM / Gidulianov, Pavel Vasilevich – Leningrad: "Rabochi i sud", 1927 – 1 – CSUX90-B9292 – us Hoover Inst Photo [640]
KODEKS ZAKONOV O TRUDE ESTONSKO I SSR : OFITSIALNY I TEKST – Tallin: E esti Raamat, 1973 – 1 – CSUX91-B2403 – us Hoover Inst Photo [340]
KODUMAA – Tallinn, U.S.S.R. -w. Jan 1961-Dec 1970. 8 reels – 1 – uk British Libr Newspaper [947]
DET KOEBENHAVINSKE KIRKEFONDS ARBOG – 1966-80 (complete) – 1r – 1 – ATLA S0508 – us A.T.L.A. [073]
Koeberle, Justus *see*
- NATUR UND GEIST: NACH DER AUFFASSUNG DES ALTEN TESTAMENTS
- DIE TEMPELSAENGER IM ALTEN TESTAMENT: EIN VERSUCH

KOECI BEY RISALESI / Bey, Mustafa Koci – Istanbul: Matba'a-i Ebuezziya, 1303 [1887] – 2mf – 9 – $50.00 – us MEDOC [949]
KOEDUKTION ODER MAEDCHENBILDUNG? : EINE VERGLEICHENDE BETRACHTUNG ZWEIER LAENGSSCHNITTUNTERSUCHUNGEN UNTER DEM ASPEKT GESCHLECHTSSPEZIFISCHER UNTERSCHIEDE VOR UND IN DER KOEDUKAKTIVEN SCHULE / Amse, Corina – 1995 – 3mf – 9 – DM98.00 – 3-8267-2155-1 – gw Hänsel [370]
Koehl, Eduard *see* DIE GESCHICHTE DER FESTUNG GLATZ
Koehler, August *see* UEBER BERECHTIGUNG DER KRITIK DES ALTEN TESTAMENTS
Koehler Family *see* FAMILY REUNION MINUTE BOOKS
Koehler, Franz *see* FREI UND GEWISS IM GLAUBEN: BEITRAEGE ZUR VERTIEFUNG IN...DER CHRISTLICHE RELIGION
Koehler, Georg *see* ENTWICKLUNG UND ERPROBUNG EINES COMPUTERUNTERSTUETZTEN CURRICULUMS DES GRUNDLEGENDEN CHEMIEUNTERRICHTES FUER DIE SCHWERPUNKTTHEMEN "EINFUEHRUNG IN DIE CHEMIE" SOWIE "ATOMBAU UND CHEMISCHE BINDUNG"
Koehler, H *see* VON DER WELT ZUM HIMMELREICH, ODER, DIE JOHANNEISCHE DARSTELLUNG DES WERKES JESU CHRISTI
Koehler, Hans-Joachim *see* SIXTEENTH CENTURY PAMPHLETS IN GERMAN AND LATIN
Koehler, J *see* ZEITSCHRIFT FUER VOELKERRECHT UND BUNDESSTAATSRECHT
Koehler, Karen M *see* DEVELOPMENT AND VALIDATION OF A QUESTIONNAIRE FOR ASSESSING HABITUAL PHYSICAL ACTIVITY OF SIXTH-GRADE STUDENTS
Koehler, Karl *see* DER PROPHETISMUS DER HEBRAEER UND DIE MANTIK DER GRIECHEN
Koehler, Klaus *see* ZUR THEORETISCHEN BESTIMMUNG UND PRAKTISCHEN NUTZUNG MUSIKERZIEHERISCHER POTENZEN DES MUSIKKRITISCHEN SCHRIFTTUMS
Koehler, Reinhold *see* ZU HEINRICH VON KLEIST'S WERKEN
Koehler, Robert *see* CORRESPONDENCE
Koehler, Ruth *see* DIE SENDING DER FRAU IN DER DEUTSCHEN GESCHICHTE
Koehler, V *see* LUTHER UND DIE KIRCHENGESCHICHTE
Koehler, Walther E *see*
- BEITRAEGE ZUR GESCHICHTE DER MYSTIK IN DER REFORMATIONSZEIT
- DOKUMENTE ZUM ABLASSSTREIT VON 1517
- KATHOLIZISMUS UND REFORMATION
- LUTHER UND DIE LUEGE
- LUTHERS SCHRIFT AN DEN CHRISTLICHEN ADEL DEUTSCHER NATION

Koehler, Willibald *see*
- HERMANN STEHR
- DAS KALTE HAUS, OBERSCHLESIEN

Koek, Edwin Rowland *see* A TABLE OF WRITTEN LAW JUDICIALLY CONSIDERED BY THE SUPREME COURT OF THE STRAIGHTS SETTLEMENTS AND ON APPEAL THEREFROM, 1808-1898
Koelbing, Paul *see* DIE GEISTIGE EINWIRKUNG DER PERSON JESU AUF PAULUS
Koelle, Conrad *see* ERNST MORITZ ARNDTS FRAGMENTE UEBER MENSCHENBILDUNG IN IHRER PAEDAGOGISCHEN BEDEUTUNG
Koelle, Sigismund W *see* POLYGLOTTA AFRICANA, OR A COMPARATIVE VOCABULARY...
Koelling, Heinrich *see* VERSUCH EINER SCHRIFTGEMAESSEN...DEM HERRN JESU UND SEINER MUTTER
Koelmel, Rainer *see* DIE GESCHICHTE DEUTSCH-JUEDISCHER REFUGEES IN SCHOTTLAND
KOELNER SCHREINSURKUNDEN DES 12. JAHRHUNDERT (PGRG 1) / ed by Hoeniger, R – Bonn. 2bd. 1884-1894 – Dfl84.00 – ne Slangenburg [240]
KOELNER STADT-ANZEIGER – Koeln, West Germany. 1992- – 14r per yr – 1 – gw Mikrofilm [072]
KOELNER STADTANZEIGER – Cologne. 1979-80 – 22370.00y; CPC; 9 – gw Alpha Com [072]
DIE KOELNER WIRREN (1837) : STUDIEN ZU IHRER GESCHICHTE / Schroers, Heinrich – Berlin, Bonn, 1927 – xx/634p – 9 – DM98.00 – 3-89349-106-6 – gw Hänsel [943]
KOELNER-STADTANZEIGER – Koeln, 1949-1962 – 86r – 1 – DM6,450.00 – gw Mikro Press [943]
KOELNISCHE BLAETTER – (Title change: Koelnische Volkszeitung) – Koeln, Germany. 1 Apr 1866; 1869-31 May 1941 – 221r – 1 – gw Mikrofilm [072]
KOELNISCHE BLATTER – Koeln, 1860-1868 – 16r – 1 – DM1,200.00 – gw Mikro Press [072]
KOELNISCHE RUNDSCHAU – (Also Bereichsausgaben available: BERGHEIM, 1988- ; BERGISCH-GLADBACH, 1988- ; BERGISCH-GLADBACH, nur Lokalteil, nov 5 1957-60; BONN, Bonner Rundschau, Ausgabe Bonn-Land, mar 19 1946-sep 1949; BONN, Bonner Rundschau, oct 1 1949-69; EUSKIRCHEN, 1988- ; SIEGBURG, jan 4 1949-60, 1970- (cont by: Siegkreis Rundschau, oct 27 1949; Rhein-Sieg-Rundschau, jan 2 1970)) – Koeln, mar 19 1946- – 1 – Inquire at Mikrofilmarchiv for details – gw Misc Inst [072]
KOELNISCHE RUNDSCHAU : AUSGABE RHEINISCH BERGISCHER KREIS – (Cont by: Bergische Rundschau, oct 5 1949. Bergische Landeszeitung, aug 21 1952 (Bereichsausgaben der Koelnischen Rundschau)) – Bergisch Gladbach, mar 19 1946-may 25 1948. jun 1 1948-mar 31 1969 – 114r – 1 – gw Mikrofilm [072]
KOELNISCHE RUNDSCHAU – (Includes suppl: Rundschau am Sonntag) – Koeln, 1955-80 – us Res Libr [072]
KOELNISCHE RUNDSCHAU – Koeln. 1992- – 7r per yr – 1 – gw Mikrofilm [072]
KOELNISCHE RUNDSCHAU – Koeln, mar 19 1946-74 – 1 – gw Mikrofilm [072]
KOELNISCHE RUNDSCHAU: BERGISCHE LANDESZEITUNG *see* KOELNISCHE RUNDSCHAU
KOELNISCHE RUNDSCHAU: BERGISCHE RUNDSCHAU *see* KOELNISCHE RUNDSCHAU
KOELNISCHE VOLKS ZEITUNG – Cologne. Germany. Jul 1914-Aug 1919 – 1 – 35.00r – us Hoover Inst Photo [072]
KOELNISCHE VOLKSZEITUNG – Koeln, 1869-1941 – 203r – 1 – DM15,225.00 – gw Mikro Press [072]
KOELNISCHE VOLKSZEITUNG *see* KOELNISCHE BLAETTER
KOELNISCHE ZEITUNG – Cologne. Germany. June 1914-March 1920 (gaps) – 1 – 35.00r – us Hoover Inst Photo [072]
KOELNISCHE ZEITUNG – Koeln, Germany. 6 Oct 1803-1805; 1814-15; 1817-1943; Jan-Sept 1944; Nov 1944-Jan 1945 – 352r – 1 – gw Mikrofilm [072]
KOELNISCHER ANZEIGER : MIT KOELNER FREMDENBLATT – Koeln, Germany. 1848-49 – 2r – 1 – gw Mikrofilm [072]
KOELNISCHER KURIER / ed by Die Amerikanische Armee – 1945-1946 – 1r – 1 – DM75.00 – gw Mikro Press [072]
KOELNISCHER KURIER / ed by Die Amerikanische Armee – Koeln, West Germany. 2 Apr 1945-26 Feb 1946 – 1r – 1 – gw Mikrofilm [072]
KOEMIE ORIE – Amsterdam. v1-7(4). 1933-1940 – 33mf – 9 – ne IDC [949]
Koen, DT *see* THE KAISER IN EXILE
Koenekamp, Alfred Heinrich *see* DIE PREUSSISCHEN LANDWIRTSCHAFTLICHEN VERSUCHS- UND FORSCHUNGSANSTALTEN, LANDSBERG/W.
Koeneke, Irene Aniata *see* LETTERS RECEIVED
Koenen, H J *see* GESCHIEDENIS DER JODEN IN NEDERLAND
Koenig, A B *see* ANNALEN DER JUDEN IN DEN PREUSSISCHEN STAATEN, BESONDERS IN DER MARK BRANDENBURG
Koenig, Alfred *see* JESUS
Koenig, Arthur *see* DIE ECHTHEIT DER APOSTELGESCHICHTE DES HEILIGEN LUCAS: EIN WORT AN DEREN GEGNER
Koenig, B(runo) Emil *see* AUSGEBURTEN DES MENSCHENWAHNS IM SPIEGEL DER HEXENPROZESSE UND DER AUTO DA FES
Koenig, Eduard *see*
- ALTTESTAMENTLICHE KRITIK UND CHRISTENGLAUBE
- DE CRITICAE SACRAE ARGUMENTO E LINGUAE LEGIBUS REPETITO...GENESEOS CAPP, 1
- EINLEITUNG IN DAS ALTE TESTAMENT
- THE EXILES' BOOK OF CONSOLATION CONTAINED IN ISAIAH 40-66
- GESCHICHTE DES REICHES GOTTES BIS AUF JESUS CHRISTUS
- DER GLAUBENSACT DES CHRISTEN
- HEBRAEISCHE GRAMMATIK FUER DEN UNTERRICHT MIT UEBUNGSSTUECKEN UND WOERTERVERZEICHNISSEN
- NEUESTE PRINZIPIEN DER ALTTESTAMENTLICHEN KRITIK
- DER OFFENBARUNGSBEGRIFF DES ALTEN TESTAMENTES
- DIE ORIGINALITAET DES NEULICH ENTDECKTEN HEBRAEISCHEN SIRACHTEXTES
- DIE POESIE DES ALTEN TESTAMENTS
- PROPHETENIDEAL JUDENTUM UND CHRISTENTUM
- STILISTIK, RHETORIK, POETIK IN BEZUG AUF DIE BIBLISCHE LITTERATUR
- THEOLOGIE DES ALTEN TESTAMENTS

KOENIG EDUARD UND DER EINSIEDLER, EINE MITTELENGLISCHE BALLADE / Kurz, Albert – Erlangen, 1904 – 1mf – DM48.00 – 3-8267-3037-2 – gw Hänsel [420]
Koenig, F E *see*
- HISTORISCH-COMPARATIVE SYNTAX DER HEBRAEISCHEN SPRACHE

- STILISTIK, RHETORIK, POETIK IN BEZUG AUF DIE BIBLISCHE LITTERATUR KOMPARATIVISCH DARGESTELLT
Koenig, Heinrich *see* WAS IST DIE WAHRHEIT VON JESU?: ZEITFRAGE UND BEKENNTNISS
KOENIG HEINRICH 1 UND DIE HEILIGE LANZE / Holtzmann, W – Bonn, 1947 – Dfl9.00 – ne Slangenburg [240]
Koenig, Irina *see* VOM URSPRUNG DES GEISTES AUS DER GESCHLECHTLICHKEIT
KOENIG JEROME NAPOLEON : EIN ZEIT- UND LEBENSBILD NACH BRIEFEN DER FRAU VON SOTHEN UND DES REICHSERZKANZLERS VON DALBERG ETC / Kaisenberg, Moritz von – Leipzig, 1899 – 9 – DM48.00 – 3-89349-118-X – gw Hänsel [943]
Koenig, Joerg Udo *see* DER ERYTHROIDE ANIONENAUSTAUSCHER AE1
Koenig, Joseph *see*
- BEITRAEGE ZUR GESCHICHTE DER THEOLOGISCHEN FACULTAET IN FREIBURG
- KARL SPINDLER, EIN BEITRAG ZUR GESCHICHTE DES HISTORISCHEN ROMANS UND DER UNTERHALTUNGSLEKTUERE IN DEUTSCHLAND
Koenig, Joseph M *see* A COMPARISON OF BODY DENSITY AND PERCENT BODY FAT USING FUNCTIONAL RESIDUAL CAPACITY AND RESIDUAL VOLUME AND DEVELOPMENT OF IMMERSED FUNCTIONAL RESIDUAL CAPACITY AND RESIDUAL VOLUME PREDICTION FORMULAS
Koenig, K D E *see* ANNALS OF BOTANY
KOENIG KARL : EIN TRAUERSPIEL IN DREI AUFZUEGEN MIT EINEM VORSPIEL "DAS VOELKLEIN AUF DER HEIDE" / Wolzogen, Ernst von – Darmstadt: A Bergstraesser, 1914 – 1r – 1 – us U.W. Library [820]
Koenig, Karl *see* IM KAMPF UM GOTT UND UM DAS EIGENE ICH
KOENIG LIPIT-ISTAR'S VERGOETTLICHUNG; EIN ALTSUMERISCHES LIED / Zimmern, Heinrich – (Koenigl. Saechsischen Gesellschaft Wissensch., v. 68, pt. 5). Leipzig. 1916. BNE-20,041 1 – 9 – ne IDC [930]
DER KOENIG MIT DEM HANDGEPAECK / Steguweit, Heinz – Hamburg: Hanseatische Verlagsanstalt, [1941] – 1r – 1 – us U.W. Library [430]
KOENIG NICOLO, ODER, SO IST DAS LEBEN : SCHAUSPIEL IN DREI AUFZUEGEN UND NEUN BILDERN, MIT EINEM PROLOG / Wedekind, Frank – 3. Aufl. Muenchen: G Mueller, 1911 – 1r – 1 – us U.W. Library [820]
KOENIG OTTOKARS GLUECK UND ENDE : TRAUERSPIEL IN FUENF AUFZUEGEN / Grillparzer, Franz; ed by Waniek, Gustav – Wien: F Tempsky, 1903 – 1r – 1 – us U.W. Library [820]
KOENIG OTTOKARS GLUECK UND ENDE : EINE UNTERSUCHUNG UEBER DIE QUELLEN DER GRILLPARZER'SCHEN TRAGOEDIE / Klaar, Alfred – (Includes bibliographical references) – Leipzig: G Freytag, 1885 – 1r – 1 – us U.W. Library [430]
KOENIG SALOMO : EIN DRAMA IN DREI AKTEN / Hardt, Ernst – Leipzig: Insel-Verlag, 1915 – 1r – 1 – us U.W. Library [820]
"DER KOENIG VERDIENT KEIN DENKMAL" : MAJESTAETSBELEIDIGUNGEN IM KOENIGREICH HANNOVER ZUR ZEIT KOENIG GEORGS V. (1851-1866) / Reuter, Hans Ulrich – 1995 – 2mf – 9 – DM80.00 – 3-8267-2191-8 – gw Hänsel [943]
DER KOENIG VON SIDON / Lindau, Paul – Bremen: Verlag der Winking-Buecher, [191-?] – 1r – 1 – us U.W. Library [830]
Koeniger, Albert Michael *see*
- DIE BEICHT NACH CAESARIUS VON HEISTERBACH
- BURCHARD 1. VON WORMS UND DIE DEUTSCHE KIRCHE SEINER ZEIT (1000-1025)
DIE KOENIGHAEUSER : EINE ERZAEHLUNG AUS DEM ISERGEBIRGE / Leutelt, Gustav – 5. Aufl. Reichenberg: F Kraus, 1943 – 1r – 1 – us U.W. Library [830]
KOENIGLICH BERLINISCHE PRIVILEGIRTE STAATS- UND GELEHRTE ZEITUNG – (Cont: Berlinische privilegirte Zeitung, -1779. Cont by: Vossische Zeitung, 1912) – Berlin, 1784-88, 1791-93, 1795-96, aug 1 1798-apr 29 1800, oct 2 1800-dec 25 1806, apr 2-jul 30 1807, 1809-jun 30 1810, jan 24-may 11 1811, jul 2 1811-1911 – 1 – Inquire at Mikrofilmarchiv for details – gw Misc Inst [943]
KOENIGLICH BERLINISCHE PRIVILEGIRTE STAATS- UND GELEHRTE ZEITUNG *see*
- BERLINISCHE PRIVILEGIRTE ZEITUNG
- VOSSISCHE ZEITUNG
KOENIGLICH PRIVILEGIRTE BERLINISCHE ZEITUNG VON STAATS- UND GELEHRTEN SACHEN – Berlin, 1812-15 – 3r – 1 – DM225.00 – gw Mikro Press [072]
KOENIGLICH PRIVILEGIRTE BERLINISCHE ZEITUNG – (Vossiche Zeitung). Berlin, Germany. 1850-1919. (1161 reels) – 1 – uk British Libr Newspaper [072]
KOENIGLICH PRIVILEGIRTE MAGDEBURGISCHE ZEITUNG *see* MAGDEBURGISCHE ZEITUNG
KOENIGLICH PRIVILEGIRTER PREUSSISCHER VOLKSFREUND – Berlin, 1798-1800 (incomplete) – 2r – 1 – Dist. gw Mikrofilm – gw Misc Inst [943]
KOENIGLICH-BAIERISCHES SALZACH-KREIS-BLATT *see* OETTINGER UND BURGHAUSER ANZEIGER
KOENIGLICH-PREUSSISCHER STAATSANZEIGER *see*
- ALLGEMEINE PREUSSISCHE STAATS-ZEITUNG
KOENIGREICHS (DES MUENSTERISCHEN) VND WIDERTAUFFS AN VND ABGANG, BLUTHANDEL VND END, AUFF SAMBSTAG NACH SEBASTIANI 1536 – BME-155 1 – 9 – ne IDC [240]
DES KOENIGS LEIBWACHE : EINE JUGEND-ERZAEHLUNG / Nieritz, Gustav – 4. Aufl. Gütersloh: C Bertelsmann, [1909?] – 1r – 1 – us U.W. Library [830]
Koenigsberg. Regierungsbezirk *see* AMTSBLATT DER PREUSSISCHEN REGIERUNG ZU KOENIGSBERG
Koenigsberger, Bernhard *see* AUS MASORAH UND TALMUDKRITIK: EXEGETISCHEN STUDIEN
DER KOENIGSBERGER RUNDFUNK – (Cont by: Koenigsberger und Danziger Rundfunk, 1932. Ostfunk, apr 1 1933) – Koenigsberg, nov 2 1924-35. jun 28-dec 31 1936. jan 1-jul 1 1939 – 18r – 1 – gw Mikrofilm [790]
KOENIGSBERGER SKULPTUREN UND IHRE MEISTER 1255-1945 / Muehlpfordt, Herbert Meinhard – (Includes bibliographical references and indexes) – Wuerzburg: Holzner Verlag, 1970 – 10r – 1 – us U.W. Library [730]
KOENIGSBERGER TAGEBLATT – Kaliningrad, U.S.S.R. -d. 8 Jan 1918-31 July 1919. 3 reels – 1 – uk British Libr Newspaper [947]
KOENIGSBERGER UND DANZIGER RUNDFUNK *see* DER KOENIGSBERGER RUNDFUNK
KOENIGSBERG(I)SCHE GELEHRTE UND POLITISCHE ZEITUNG – Koenigsberg (Kaliningrad), Germany. 1764-68; 1771-72 – 1 – gw Mikrofilm [943]
Koenigsgarten, Hugo F *see* GRUNDVORSTELLUNGEN DER AMERIKANISCHEN WIRTSCHAFTS-ETHIK
DIE KOENIGSGLEICHNISSE DES MIDRASCH / Ziegler, I – Breslau. 1903. BJ-32-34 1 – 9 – ne IDC [270]
Koenigsloew, Eva von *see* DAS RELIGIOESE MOTIV ALS GESTALTENDE KRAFT DER DEUTSCHEN VOLKSSAGEN DER GEGENWART
KOENIGSMARK, THE LEGEND OF THE HOUNDS AND OTHER POEMS / Boker, George Henry – Philadelphia: J.B. Lippincott & Co., 1869. 244p – 1 – us U.W. Library [810]
DER KOENIGSTRAUM : ROMAN / Vogt, Helmut – Stuttgart: Deutsche Verlags-Anstalt, c1943 – 1r – 1 – us U.W. Library [830]
DIE KOENINGEN VON SABA...OP. 27 / Goldmark, C – (Vocal score) – Bremen: Schwers & Haake, [188-?] – 1 – us Sibley [780]
Koennecke, Gustav *see* SCHILLER, EINE BIOGRAPHIE IN BILDERN
KOENNEN DEUTSCHE GERICHTE BEI AUSLAENDERN... / Friedrich, C – Stolp, i. Pom., 1906 – 1mf – 1 – ILM-3463/1 – ne IDC [327]
Koenning, Josef *see* KOERPERTHERAPIE MIT KINDERN UND JUGENDLICHEN
Koeppen, C F *see* DIE RELIGION DES BUDDHA
Koepruelue, Mehmet Fuat *see* TUERKIYE TARIHI
Koerber, G W *see*
- LICHENOGRAPHIAE GERMANICAE SPECIMEN PARMELIACEARUM FAMILIAM CONTINENS
- SYSTEMA LICHENUM GERMANIAE
Koerber, Kurt *see* KIRCHENGUETERFRAGE UND SCHMALKALDISCHER BUND
Koerner, Gabriele-Elisabeth *see* NUCLEAR PHYSICS NEWS
Koerner, M *see* SKANDINAVISKA FOGLAR
Koerner, Theodor *see* THEODOR KOERNERS BRIEFWECHSEL MIT DEN SEINEN
KOEROGLU – (Mueduer-i Mes'ul: Ismail Sedat, Mueduer: A. Nureddin. No. 14 (19 Mart 1909)) – Kastamonu, 1907-? – 1mf – 9 – $12.00 – us MEDOC [949]
KOERPERTHERAPIE MIT KINDERN UND JUGENDLICHEN / Koenning, Josef – 1994 – 1mf – DM60.00 – 3-8267-2032-6 – gw Hänsel [615]
KOERS – 1964-90 – 10r – 1 – ATLA S0787 – us A.T.L.A. [073]
KOERSOES GOEROE NORMALIS JANG 2 TAHOEN LAMANJA / Dutch East Indies. Departement van Opvoeding, Kunsten en Wetenschappen – SE-4521 1. 7 v. lacking v. 2. 1948 – 9 – ne IDC [324]
Koerting, Heinrich *see* UEBER ZWEI RELIGIOESE PARAPHRASEN PIERRE CORNEILLE'S: L'IMITATION DE JESUS-CHRIST UND DIE LOUANGES DE LA SAINTE VIERGE
Koesfelt, Coenraad Z van *see* INSTITUTIONES MUSICAE..
Koester, Albert *see* DER BRIEFWECHSEL ZWISCHEN THEODOR STORM UND GOTTFRIED KELLER
Koester, H *see* SYNOPTISCHE UEBERLIEFERUNG BEI DEN APOSTOLISCHEN VAETERN (T.U.U. 5-65)
Koester, H M G *see* DEUTSCHE ENCYCLOPAEDIE ODER ALLGEMEINES REALWOERTERBUCH ALLER KUENSTE UND WISSENSCHAFTEN, (AEL, ABT 1;2)
DIE KOESTLICHE PERLE UND DIE INNERE MISSION : EINE PRAKTISCH-THEORETISCHE MEDITATION / Wacker, Emil – Guetersloh: C Bertelsmann, 1895 – 1mf – 9 – 0-8370-6785-5 – 1986-0785 – us A.T.L.A. [240]
Koestlin, Friedrich *see*
- JESAIA UND JEREMIA
- LEITFADEN ZUM UNTERRICHT IM ALTEN TESTAMENT FUER HOEHERE SCHULEN
- LEITFADEN ZUM UNTERRICHT IM NEUEN TESTAMENT FUER HOEHERE SCHULEN
Koestlin, Heinrich Adolf *see* GESCHICHTE DES CHRISTLICHEN GOTTESDIENSTES
Koestlin, Julius *see*
- DIE BEGRUENDUNG UNSERER SITTLICH-RELIGIOESEN UEBERZEUGUNG
- FRIEDRICH DER WEISE UND DIE SCHLOSSKIRCHE ZU WITTENBERG
- DER GLAUBE UND SEINE BEDEUTUNG FUER ERKENNTNIS, LEBEN UND KIRCHE
- LIFE OF LUTHER
- LUTHER UND J. JANSSEN
- THE THEOLOGY OF LUTHER IN ITS HISTORIAL DEVELOPMENT AND INNER HARMONY
Koestlin, Karl Reinhold von *see* RICHARD WAGNER'S TONDRAMA
Koetschau, Paul *see*
- BEITRAEGE ZUR TEXTKRITIK VON ORIGENES' JOHANNESCOMMENTAR (T.U.U. 2-28/2A)
- KRITISCHE BEMERKUNGEN ZU MEINER AUSGABE VON ORIGENES' EXHORTATIO, CONTRA CELSUM, DE ORATIONE
- DIE TEXTUEBERLIEFERUNG DER BUECHER DES ORIGENES GEGEN CELSUS (T.U.U. 1-6/1)
Koetzschke, R *see*
- RHEINISCHE URBARE, BD 2
- RHEINISCHE URBARE. BD 3
KOETZTINGER UMSCHAU – Koetzting, Germany. Mai 1956-Jul 1973 – 1 – gw Mikrofilm [072]
KOEYLUE – Izmir, 1908-1921 – 9 – $10.00 – us MEDOC [956]
Koeymen, Mehmed A *see* KITAB-I CIHAN-NUEMA [NESRI TARIHI]
Kogan *see* MODERNISTY I IKH PREDSHESTVENNIKI I KRITICHESKAIA LITERATURA O NIKH
Kogan, E R *see* OPIS' DOKUMENTAL'NYKH MATERIALOV LICHNOGO FONDA NO. 1996
Kogan, Iu. Ia *see* PROSVETITEL 18 VEKA
Kogan, P *see*
- LITERATURA VELIKOGO DESIATILETIIA
- OCHERKI PO ISTORII NOVEISHEI RUSSKOI LITERATURY
KOGO ISHCHESH', (MISTERIIA) / Minskii, N – Berlin. 1922. BR-806 2 – 8 – ne IDC [460]
KOGUTAD JUTLUSI = SELECTED SERMONS / Lige, B – Toronto: Oma Press, 1975. Includes sermons by Estonian Baptist pastors; 166p – 1 – 6.64 – us Baptist [240]
Koh, Roland *see* DOES GOD CARE FOR ME? (CCC191)
Kohaut J *see* AIRS ET DUO DU MARIAGE SECRET [COMEDIE LYRIQUE]
KOHELET : ODER, DER SALMONISCHEN PREDIGER / Graetz, Heinrich – (Text in German & Hebrew. Commentary in German) – Leipzig: C F Winter, 1871 – 1mf – 9 – 0-8370-3357-8 – 1985-1357 – us A.T.L.A. [220]
KOHELET / ed by Zederbaum, A – St. Petersburg. 1881. BJ-422-37 1 – 9 – ne IDC [470]
KOHIEREN VAN DE TIENDE PENNING 1543 = TAX ROLLS FOR THE TENTH PENNY 1543 / Netherlands. General State Archives – 313mf – 9 – Dfl3600.00 silver – ne MMF Publ [949]
Kohl, Horst *see* BISMARCK-JAHRBUCH
Kohler, F J et al *see* HAMMURABI'S GESETZ
Kohler, J *see*
- HAMMURABI'S GESETZ
Kohler, Josef *see* PHILOSOPHY OF LAW
Kohler, K *see* STUDIES IN JEWISH LITERATURE
Kohler, Minnie I *see* A 20TH CENTURY HISTORY OF HARDIN COUNTY
Kohlschmidt, Werner *see* HERDER-STUDIEN
Kohn-Zwilling, Isolde *see* UNTERSUCHUNGEN ZUM DIALOG BEI CHRISTOPHER FRY
K'O-HSUEH = SCIENCE – Shanghai, Jul 1915-Sep 1950 (incomplete) – 25r – 1 – $692.00 – us Chinese Res [500]
K'O-HSUEH – "Science". 32 v. Shanghai. 1915-50. monthly. Lacking: v. 25 (9-12) 1941; v. 26 (1-12) 1943; v. 27 (4) 1944; v. 28 (1) 1946; v. 31 (4-12) 1948; v. 32 (12) 1950. BCH-285 1 – 9 – ne IDC [500]
Kohut, Adolf *see*
- BERUEHMTE ISREALITISCHE MAENNER UND FRAUEN IN DER KULTURGESCHICHTE DER MENSCHHEIT
- HEINRICH VON KLEIST UND DIE FRAUEN
Kohut, Adolph *see*
- JOHANN GOTTFRIED SEUME ALS MENSCH, DICHTER, PATRIOT UND DENKER
- THEODOR KOERNER
Kohut, G A *see* SEMITIC STUDIES IN MEMORY OF REV. DR. ALEXANDER KOHUT
Koikylides, K M *see* AI PARA TON IORDANEN LAURAI KALAMOONOS KAI AGIOU GERASIMOU
KOINOTIKA NEA : LANGUE GRECQUE ET ANGLAISE – Montreal, Canada. 17 fev 1965-n4. 8 jun 1965 – 1r – 1 – Can$25.00 – cn Can Microfilming [072]
KO-JISHO SHUSEI = COLLECTION OF JAPANESE CLASSICAL LANGUAGE DICTIONARIES IN THE CUSTODY OF THE SEIKADO LIBRARY, TOKYO – 361 manuscripts and printed books in 2,137v – 178r – 1 – Y1,840,000.00 – ja Yushodo [480]
Kok, K J de *see* EMPIRES OF THE VELD
KOKALTIDNINGEN KIKAREN – Stockholm, 1994- – 9 – sw Kungliga [072]
KOKHEVEI YIZHAK – Vienna. 1845-73. BJ-91-49 1 – 9 – ne IDC [270]
Kokhomskii, S V *see* PRIMECHANIYA K EVANGELIYU V OBLICHENIE SHTUNDISTOV I PODOBNYKH IM SEKTANTOV
KOKKA = AN ILLUSTRATED MONTHLY JOURNAL OF THE FINE AND APPLIED ARTS OF JAPAN AND OTHER EASTERN COUNTRIES – Nos. 1-1149, 1889-1991 – 48r; 1 color r; 47 color mf – 1,14,15 – Y528,000; Y419,000 – ja Yushodo [700]
KOKKA – Tokyo, 1889-1977 – 42r b/w 47col mf – 1,15 – £2,200.00 1 £1,325.00 15 – uk Chadwyck [760]
KOKKAI KAIGIROKU = PROCEEDINGS OF THE NATIONAL DIET OF JAPAN, 1947-1972: THE HOUSE OF REPRESENTATIVES AND COUNCILORS, 1ST-69TH SESSION – 66r – 1 – Y554,000.00 – ja Yushodo [336]
KOKOGAKU ZASSHI = JOURNAL OF ARCHAEOLOGICAL SOCIETY OF NIPPON – (Lacking: v1-8. 1896-1910) – 1896-1920 – 8 – CH-430 2 – ne IDC [930]
Kokovtsov, P K *see*
- K SIRO-TURETSKOI EPIGRAFIKE SEMIRECH'IA
- YEVREYSKO-KHAZARSKAYA PEREPISKA V 10-OM VEKE
KOKSOAK – Schefferville, Canada. 20 dec 1967; v1 n2. 3 jan 1968 – 1r – 1 – Can$25.00 – cn Can Microfilming [072]
KOKSTAD ADVERTISER – Kokstad, South Africa. 20 May 1882-30 Dec 1911.27 reels – 1, 16 diazo available at reduced price – sa SA Libr [072]

KOKUGAKUIN ZASSHI – Kokugakuin University Journal. v. 1-45. Tokyo. 1894-1939. BCH-434 2 – 8 – ne IDC [073]
KOKUGOGAKU SHIRYO SHUSEI = DR. K. MATSUI COLLECTION OF JAPANESE CLASSICAL LANGUAGE IN THE CUSTODY OF THE SEIKADO LIBRARY, TOKYO – 472 manuscripts and printed books in 769v – 54r – 1 – Y565,000.00 – ja Yushodo [480]
KOKUMIN SHIMBUN – February 1890-October 1942 (last no.) – 397r – 1 – Y3,970,000 – ja Japan Micro [950]
KOKUMIN SHIMBUN – Japan, 1890-1942 – 397r – 1 – inquiure – us Ross [072]
KOL HA T'NUAH – New York, NY. Nov 1974-Mar 1985 – 1 – us A.J.P.C. [071]
KOL HAADAMA = CALL OF THE LAND – (In Yiddish and Spanish) – Mexico, MX. v2 no 2,3. 1945 – 1r – 1 – Can$25.00 – cn Can Microfilming [072]
KOL HA-AM – Tel Aviv. 1947-75. BJ-91-50 3 – 1 – ne IDC [956]
KOL HAAM = VOICE OF THE PEOPLE – (In Hebrew. Daily) – Tel Aviv, IS. v2 no12(no383). 16 May 1948 (Birth of Israel Issue) – 1r – 1 – $25.00 – cn Can Microfilming [072]
KOL HILLEL – Saskatoon, Saskatchewan.Dec 1949; May 1950; Mar 1951; Jan 1958 – 1 – us A.J.P.C. [072]
KOL KITVEI / Brandstaedter, M D – 3v. Warsaw. 1910-13. BJ-422-8 1 – 9 – ne IDC [470]
KOL KITVEI / Kovner, A H – Tel-Aviv. 1947. BJ-422-38 1 – 9 – ne IDC [470]
KOL KITVEI / Lilienblum, M L – 4v. Odessa. 1910-13. BJ-422-52 1 – 9 – ne IDC [470]
KOL KITVEI / Rabinovitz, A S – Cracow. 1904. v. 1. Jaffa. 1914; v. 2. Tel-Aviv. 1922; v. 3. BJ-422-68 1 – 9 – ne IDC [470]
KOL KORE = DIE BIBEL, DER TALMUD, UND DAS EVANGELIUM / Soloweyczyk, Elias – (In German) – Leipzig: F A Brockhaus, 1877 – 1mf – 9 – 0-8370-5325-0 – 1985-3325 – us A.T.L.A. [220]
KOL MEVASSER. SEFER HALAKHOT GEDOLOT. AL DEREKH HADASH / Reifmann, J – Prague. 1859. BJ-32-44 1 – 9 – ne IDC [270]
KOL NEHI MI-ZIYYON / Schlesinger, A J – Jerusalem. 1872. BJ-27-50 1 – 9 – ne IDC [270]
KOL SHIREI / Dolitzki, M M – v. 1. Newark. 1895. BJ-422-13 1 – 9 – ne IDC [470]
KOL SHIREI MAHALALEL / Gottlober, A B – 3v. 1890. BJ-422-22 1 – 9 – ne IDC [470]
KOL SIFREI / Smolenskin, P – Warsaw-Vilna. 6 v. 1905-10. BJ-422-89 1 – 9 – ne IDC [470]
KOL ZIMRAH / Eichenbaum, J – Leipzig. 1836. BJ-422-14 1 – 9 – ne IDC [490]
KOLAROVGRADSKA BORBA – Kolarovgrad, Bulgaria. 1951-63 – 6r – 1 – us L of C Photodup [949]
Kolb, Georg *see* WEGWEISER IN DIE MARIANISCHE LITERATUR
Kolb, Peter *see*
– DESCRIPTION DU CAP DE BONNE ESPERANCE
– DESCRIPTION DU CAP DE BONNE-ESPERANCE.
Kolbasov, Oleg Stepanovich *see* ZAKONODATEL' STVO O VODOPOL'ZOVANII V SSSR; PROBLEMY SOVERSHENSTVOVANIIA SOVETSKOGO ZAKONODATEL' STVA OB ISPOL'ZOVANII VODNYKH RESURSOV
Kolbe, E *see* TEXT ZU DEN ILLUSTRATIONEN AUS REUTER'S WERKEN
Kolbe, Pierre *see* DESCRIPTION DU CAP DE BONNE-ESPERANCE: OU L'ON TROUVE TOUT CE QUI CONCERNE L'HISTOIRE NATURELLE DU PAYS; ET L'ETABLISSEMENT DES HOLLANDAIS
Kolbenheyer, Erwin Guido *see*
– DIE BEGEGNUNG AUF DEM RIESENGEBIRGE
– DIE BRUECKE
– WEIHNACHTSGESCHICHTEN
Kolberg, A *see* AGENDA COMMUNIS
KOLCHAK ILI LENIN? : K VAM SOLDATY, KRESTI ANE I RABOCHIE! / Agelov, E – Rostov na Donu: "Narodnai a polza", 1919 – 1 – CSUX88-B5535 – us Hoover Inst Photo [320]
KOLCHAKOVSHCHINA / Burevii, Kost – Moskva: Gos. izd-vo, 1919 – 1 – CSUX88-B2661 – us Hoover Inst Photo [999]
KOLCHAN / Gumilev, Nikolai Sepanovich – Stikhi. Ed. 2. Berlin. 1923. Index. BR-3802 2 – 8 – ne IDC [460]
KOLCHAN / Gumilev, Nikolai Sepanovich – Stikhi. M., Petrograd. 1916. BR-1142 2 – 8 – ne IDC [460]
Kolde, T *see*
– LUTHER UND DER REICHSTAG ZU WORMS, 1521
– DAS RELIGIOESE LEBEN IN ERFURT BEIM AUSGANGE DES MITTELALTERS
Koldewey, Friedrich *see* HEINZ VON WOLFENBUETTEL
Koldewey, Paul *see* WACKENRODER UND SEIN EINFLUSS AUF TIECK
Koldewey, Robert *see* THE EXCAVATIONS AT BABYLON
KOLENU – (V. 1, no. 1 (April 1973); Vol. 3, no. 2 (May 1975)-v. 15, no. (Fall 1987)) – Ithaca, N.Y. – 1 – us A.J.P.C. [978]
Kolessa, Filaret, 1871-1947 *see* STUDII NAD POETICHNOIU TVORCHISTIU T. SHEVCHENKA
KOLGESPNIK UKRAINI – Kiev, USSR. May 1-Dec 30 1939; Feb 29-Dec 24 1940; Jan 16-Feb 27 1941 – 1r – 1 – us L of C Photodup [072]
Kolhoff, Ludger *see*
– BERUFLICHE BILDUNG IN DER REGION POITOU-CHARENTE (FRANKREICH)
– BERUFLICHE QUALIFIZIERUNG IM INFORMELLEN SEKTOR IN BERLIN-KREUZBERG
– WOHNRAUMVERSORGUNG FUER JUNGE ERWACHSENE IM BEREICH DER JUGEND-/ SOZIALHILFE DURCH SELBSTHILFEINITIATIVEN
– ZUSEHEN IST NICHT EXISTIEREN
Kolkhorst, FW *see* THE EFFECTS OF EXERCISE MODE ON POSTEXERCISE OXYGEN CONSUMPTION, URINARY NITROGEN, AND FAT UTILIZATION
KOLKHOZNIK TATARII – (Includes c.1: 1930:July 19) – Kazan': Tatobkom VKP (b), 192u – 1 – CSUXAHZ6942-S – us Hoover Inst Photo [947]
KOLKHOZNIK ZA KNIGOI – Leningrad. n1-10. 1930-31 – 1r – 1 – us Ross [460]
KOLKHOZNIK ZA KNIGOI – Leningrad. no. 1-10. Oct 28 1930-Oct 20 1931 – 1 – us NY Public [073]
KOLKHOZNOE PROIZVODSTVO : ORGAN NARODNOGO KOMISSARIATA ZEMLEDELII A SSSR – (Library has July 1945-Dec. 1953; May 1956; Jan. 1959-Dec. 1962; some issues missing) – Moskva: Komissariat, 1941-1962. 22v – 1 – CSUX89-S604 – us Hoover Inst Photo [947]
Kollarius, AF *see* ANALECTA MONUMENTORUM OMNIS AEVI VINDOBONENSIA
KOLLECTIVNOE ISPOL'ZOVANIE SEL'SKOKHOZIAISTVENNYKH MASHIN I ORUDII / Debu, K I – M., 1924 – 1mf – 9 – COR-471/1 – ne IDC [334]
KOLLEKTIVNYI DOGOVOR / Kantorovich, Ia. A – Leningrad, 1924.191p. Collective labor contracts in the Soviet Union and Tsarist Russia. Treats socio-economic and legal aspects with statistical data. BR-9419/1 – 9 – ne IDC [340]
Kollewijn, Roeland A *see* UEBER DEN EINFLUSS DES HOLLAENDISCHEN DRAMAS AUF ANDREAS GRYPHIUS
DIE KOLLISIONSNORMEN DES INTERNATIONALEN WECHSELRECHTES / Fiedler, H – Coburg, 1936 – 1mf – 1 – ILM-3251/1 – ne IDC [327]
Kollman, A *see*
– A PRACTICAL GUIDE TO THOROUGHBASS
– A SECOND PRACTICAL GUIDE TO THOROUGHBASS
Kollmann, Fritz *see* NOVALIS "HEINRICH VON OFTERDINGEN" UND DER "GUIDO" DES GRAFEN VON LOEBEN
Kollock, Florence E *see* WOMAN IN THE PULPIT
KOLLOID BEIHEFTE – v1-144. 1906-55 – 1,5,6 – us Princeton Micro [540]
KOLLOID ZEITSCHRIFT – See: Colloid and Polymer Science – us Princeton Micro [540]
Kollontai, A *see* PIS' MA K TRUDIASHCHEISIA MOLODEZHI
Kollontai, Alexandra *see* LA FEMME NOUVELLE ET LA CLASSE OUVRIERE
Kolmodin, Adolf *see* FRAN DE SVARTAS VAERLDSDEL
KOLNISCHE ZEITUNG – Cologne, Germany. Aug 1906-Apr 1936; Jan-May 1941 – 126r – 1 – us L of C Photodup [072]
KOLNS LEGENDEN, SAGEN, UND GESCHICHTEN – 1919-21 – 1 – us I.U. Libraries [390]
KOLO – Belgrade, Serbia, 1889. Nos.1-40, 1889-90 – 1 – us I.U. Libraries [073]
KOLO – Belgrade, Serbia, 1901. v1-5, 1901-03 – 1 – us I.U. Libraries [073]
KOLO – v1-9, 1963-71 – 1 – us I.U. Libraries [073]
KOLO – Zagreb, Croatia, 1842. v1-9, 1842-53 – 1 – us I.U. Libraries [073]
KOLOKOL : ORGAN RUSSKAGO OSVOBOZHDENIIA – Geneva, 1870 – 1r – 1 – us Ross [947]
KOLOKOL'CHIK – Literaturnaia gazeta na 1831 g. v. 1. Spb. 1831. Lacking: v. 1 (20). BR-3198 2 – 8 – ne IDC [073]
KOLONIAAL TIJDSCHRIFT : UITGAVE VAN DE VEREENIGING VAN AMBTENAREN BIJ HET BINNENLANDSCH BESTUUR VAN NEDERLANDSCH INDIE – (Index. 1912-31) – Batavia, 1912-1941. v1-30. – 357mf – 9 – ne IDC [073]
KOLONIAAL VERSLAG – 1849-1931. Bijlagen 1868-1870. Lacking 1855 – 1722mf – 9 – ne IDC [073]
KOLONIALE RUNDSCHAU – Leipzig. 1909-27 – 1 – 35.00r – us Hoover Inst Photo [073]
KOLONIALE STUDIEN – (Includes a printed bibliography) – Batavia, 1916/1917-1941. v1-25 – 258mf – 9 – ne IDC [950]
KOLONIAL'NYE MANDATY / Aleksandrov, B A – M., 1934 – 2mf – 9 – ILM-2527/1 – ne IDC [340]
KOLONIAL'NYE PROBLEMY – Moscow. 1933-1934, nos. 1-4 – 1 – 35.00r – us Hoover Inst Photo [323]
KOLONIE UND HEIMAT – Berlin, sep 1937-mar 1943 – 5r – 1 – Dist. gw Mikrofilm – gw Mikrofilm [943]
DE KOLONISATIE VAN DE PORTUGEESCH JOODSCHE NATIE IN SURINAME EN DE GESCHIEDENIS VAN DE JODEN SAVANNE / Oudschans Dentz, F – Amsterdam. 1927. BJ-262-42 1 – 9 – ne IDC [972]
DE KOLONIST *see* HET DAGBLAD
Koloskov, A *see*
– MAIAKOVSKII V BOR'BE ZA KOMMUNIZM
– ZHIZN' MAIAKOVSKOGO
KOLOZSVARI ESTILAP – Cluj, Romania. 1941-42 – 2r – 1 – us L of C Photodup [949]
Kolpakova, E *see* MATERIALY K BIBLIOGRAFII A. BLOKA ZA 1928-1957 GODY
Kolubovskii, Ia *see* FILOSOFSKII EZHEGODNIK
Kolvoord, John *see*
– THE VISION OF THE EVENING AND THE MORNING
– VISION OF THE EVENING AND THE MORNING: A STUDY OF THE PROPHECY OF DANIEL VIII
Komarov Botanical Institute, St. Petersburg *see*
– BARON FRIEDRICH AUGUST MARSCHALL VON BIEBERSTEIN, 1768-1826
– CARL BERNHARD TRINIUS, 1778-1844
– THE CAUCASIAN HERBARIUM
Komarov, M *see* SHEVCHENKO V LITERATURE I ISKUSSTVE
Komarov, V L *see* FLORA URSS
DER KOMET : ORGAN ZUR WAHRUNG DER INTERESSEN DER BESITZER VON SEHENSWUERDIGKEITEN UND SCHAUSTELLUNGEN JEDER ART – (Further title: Gemeinschaftsblatt) – Pirmasens, jan 6 1894-sep 23 1944 – 74r – 1 – gw Mikrofilm [790]
KOMETENTANZ : ASTRALE PANTOMIME IN ZWEI AUFZUEGEN / Scheerbart, Paul – Leipzig: Insel-Verlag, 1903 – 1r – 1 – us U.W. Library [820]
KOMI MU – ZYRI ANSKI I KRA I : IZDAVAEMY I OBKOMOM VKP(B), OBLASTNYM ISPOLNITELNYM KOMITETOM I OBLASTNYM BI URO KRAEVEDENII A AVTONOMNO I KOMI OBLASTI – (Library has: July 1928) – Ustsysolsk: Komitet, 1924- – 1 – CSUX90-S115 – us Hoover Inst Photo [947]
Komin, V V *see*
– BANKROTSTVO BURZHUAZNYKH I MELKOBURZHUAZNYKH PARTII ROSSII V PERIOD PODGOTOVKI I POBEDY VELIKOI OKTIABR'SKOI SOTSIALISTICHESKOI REVOLIUTSII
– BURZHUAZNYE I MELKOBURZHUAZNYE PARTII ROSII V OKTIABR'SKOI REVOLIUTSII I GRAZDANSKOI VOINE
THE KOMIN-KYOIKU – 22r – 1 – Y330,000 – ja Yushodo [370]
Komisarjevsky, Theodore *see* THE COSTUME OF THE THEATRE
DIE KOMISCHEN ELEMENTE DER ALTFRANZOESISCHEN CHANSONS DE GESTE / Theodor, Hugo – Halle, 1913 – 2mf – DM62.00 – 3-8267-3018-6 – gw Hänsel [440]
KOMISSIYA ISTORYCHNOI PISENNOSTY UKRAYINS'KI NARODNI DUMY / Akademiia Nauk. URSR. Kiev. Istorychna Sektziya – v. 1. 1927 – 1 – us NY Public [073]
Komite Nasional Pusat *see* BADAN PEKERDJA
Komitee der Antifaschistischen Widerstandskaempfer in der DDR *see* IMMER BEREIT FUER DIE VERTEIDIGUNG DER FREIHEIT DES VOLKES
KOMITEE FUER GRUNDRECHTE UND DEMOKRATIE = COMMITTEE FOR BASIC RIGHTS AND DEMOCRACY – Sensbachtal (bei Frankfurt/Main). 49 docs. 1980-1991 – 91mf – 9 – ne IDC [320]
Komitet po izobretatelstvu pri STO *see* VESTNIK KOMITETA PO IZOBRETATELSTVU
Komitet sodeistviia narodnostiam severnykh okrain pri Prezidiume VT SIK *see* SOVETSKII SEVER
KOMKYA = CHAGGA DAWN – (Library has: no. 99-174 (Nov. 15, 1957-Jan. 1, 1961);[missing 7 issues]) – Moshi, Tanzania: Chagga Council, 19uu – 1 – CSUX86-S80 – us Hoover Inst Photo [960]
KOMM MIT NACH MADEIRA : ERZAEHLUNG / Zerkaulen, Heinrich – Guetersloh: C Bertelsmann, 1943 – 1r – 1 – us U.W. Library [430]
DAS KOMMENDE DEUTSCHLAND; DIE ERZIEHUNG DER JUGEND IM REICH ADOLF HITLERS / Kaufmann, Guenter – Berlin: Junker und Duennhaupt, 1943. 376p. Illus. Ports. Map. 1 reel. 1293 – 1 – us U.W. Library [305]
KOMMENDE KIRCHE – Bremen, DE. 24 Sept 1936-25 Dez 1938 – 1r – 1 – gw Mikrofilm [072]
KOMMENDE KIRCHE – Bremen, sep 24 1936-dec 25 1938 – 1r – 1 – Inquire at Mikrofilmarchiv for details – gw Misc Inst [240]
DIE KOMMENDEN : UNABHAENGIGE ZEITSCHRIFT FUER FREIES GEISTESLEBEN – Freiburg, Germany. Okt 1946-25 Dec 1957 – 1 – gw Mikrofilm [072]
KOMMENTAR ZU DEN PROVERBIEN. THEIL I / Scheschet ben Isaac, Gerundi – Erlangen: Aug. Vollrath, 1893. 1 fiche.8370-5087-1 – 9 – us A.T.L.A. [220]
KOMMENTARII K POLOZHENIIU O TOVARISHCHESKIKH SUDAKH LATVIISKOI SSR – Ed.2, rev. Riga, 1968. 251p. BR-8482/1 – 9 – ne IDC [947]
KOMMENTARII K POLOZHENIIU O TOVARISHCHESKIKH SUDAKH LATVIISKOI SSR – Ed.2. Riga. 251p. 1968 – 3mf – 9 – ne IDC [340]
KOMMENTARII K UGOLOVNO-PROTSESSUAL'NOMU KODEKSU MOLDAVSKOI SSR / ed by Kazanir, A S & Santalov, A I – Kishinev, 1966. 375p. Commentary to the Moldavian Code of Criminal Procedure, as amended 1 Nov 1964. BR-8798/1 – 9 – ne IDC [340]
KOMMENTARII Z. G. MINTS / Vospominaniia o Bloke – Uchenye zapiski Tartuskogo universiteta. nr. 4. 1961. BR-3345 2 – 8 – ne IDC [460]
KOMMERANT *see* KOMMERSANT (DAILY)
KOMMERCHESKAIA GAZETA – [St Petersburg]: Tip Departmenta vnieshnei torgovli, 1827; 1829-34; 1840-60 – 8r – 1 – us Res Libr [072]
Kommerell, Max *see*
– JEAN PAULS VERHAELTNIS ZU ROUSSEAU
– JUGEND OHNE GOETHE
KOMMERSANT (DAILY) – Moscow: AO "Kommersant", 1992- – 4mf per year – 9 – $299.95y – us East View [330]
DEN KOMMERSANTA I ORIENTALISTA : ODNODNEVNAI A GAZETA STUDENTOV INSTITUTA ORIENTALNYKH I KOMMERCHESKIKH NAUK V KHARBINE – (Includes c.1: 1931:Jan) – [Karbin]: Komissii a po izyskanii u sredstv dli a nedostatochnykh studentov pri in-te, 19uu – 1 – CSUXANR2019-S – us Hoover Inst Photo [947]
Kommission fuer spaetantike Religionsgeschichte *see* KLEINE SCHRIFTEN 3
KOMMUN AKTUELLT – 1978-. Veckotidning utgiven av Kommunforbundet. Stockholm: Kommunforbundet, 1978. Forty issues yearly – 1 – us U.W. Library [948]

KOMMUNA : EZHEDNEVNAI A GAZETA VORONEZHSKOGO OBKOMA VKP(B), OBLISPOLKOMA, OBLPROFSOVETA I GORKOMA VKP(B) – (Includes c.1: 1936:Feb.23, 26-27, Mar.10-12, 15-16, 20-22, 24-27; 1936:Apr. 3, 5-8, 12, 16, 20-21, 23, 29; 1936:May5, 8, 10, 12-14, 16-18, 21, 24-28; 1936:June) – Voronezh: Izd-vo "Kommuna", 19uu – 1 – CSUXAHZ2701-S – us Hoover Inst Photo [947]

KOMMUNA – Petrograd. Nov. 7, 1918-Feb. 17, 1919 – 1 – 35.00r – us Hoover Inst Photo [335]

KOMMUNA PROLETARSKIKH MISSIONEROV : OTRYVKI IZ NEIZDANNAGO ROMANA "MIKHAIL" / Belotsvetov, N N – Berlin: "Pressa", 1921 – 1 – CSUX88-B6134 – us Hoover Inst Photo [947]

KOMMUNA (VORONEZH, R.S.F.S.R.) *see* KOMMUNA

KOMMUNAR – Moscow. Nov. 12, 19-21, 26-29, 1918; Mar. 9, 11-12, 29; Apr. 2-4, 23, 1919 – 1 – 35.00r – us Hoover Inst Photo [335]

KOMMUNAR – Moscow, USSR. Nov 12 1918-Apr 23 1919 – 1r – 1 – us L of C Photodup [072]

KOMMUNAR : ORGAN TUL. GUBISPOLKOMA SOVETOV RAB., KR. I KR.-ARM. DEPUTATOV I TULSKOGO GUBKOMA R.K.P. (BOLSH.) – (Includes c.1: 1922:Mar.12) – Tula: Gazetnai a tip. Gubsovnarkhoza, 191u – 1 – CSUXAHZ6919-S – us Hoover Inst Photo [947]

KOMMUNAR (TULA, R.S.F.S.R.) *see* KOMMUNAR

KOMMUNARKA UKRAINY – (In Ukranian) – Khar'kov, 1921-1933 – 152mf – 9 – $890.00 – us Ross [073]

DIE KOMMUNE – Berlin, 1927-33 – 1r – 1 – Dist. gw Mikrofilm – gw Misc Inst [943]

KOMMUNIKATIONSSTOERUNGEN BEI KINDERN MIT SYNDROMEN / Scheler, Elke Verena Ulrike – 1995 – 1mf – 9 – DM60.00 – 3-8267-2173-X – gw Hänsel [618]

KOMMUNISMUS – Vienna. v. 1-2. no. 32. Feb 1920-Sept 1921. Incomplete – 1 – us NY Public [335]

KOMMUNISMUS : ZEITSCHRIFT DER KOMMUNISTISCHEN INTERNATIONALE FUER DIE LAENDER SUEDOSTEUROPAS; ZEITSCHRIFT DER KOMMUNISTISCHEN INTERNATIONALE – Wien, v1,no1/2-v2,no31/32. Feb 1920-Sept 1921 – 32 fiches – 9 – $90.00 – us UPA [335]

DER KOMMUNIST – (Cont by: Kommunistische Arbeiterzeitung, Hamburg, feb 7 1920; Kommunist, Bremen, feb 21 1920; Rote Fahne, Berlin-Neukoelln, may 1 1920; Rote Fahne, Bremen, dec 1 1920; Nordwestdeutsches Echo, nov 1 1921; Rote Fahne, Berlin, mar 14 1924; Nordwestdeutsches Echo, Bremen, apr 1 1924; Arbeiter-Zeitung, jan 2 1925) – Bremen, Hamburg, Berlin. nov 27 1918-feb 1933 (incomplete) – 1 – Inquire at Mikrofilmarchiv for details – gw Misc Inst [335]

DER KOMMUNIST – Dresden, Germany. Nov 1918-Jan 1921 – 1r – 1 – gw Mikrofilm [072]

DER KOMMUNIST / ed by KP der Schweiz – Zuerich, Switzerland. Feb 1919-Jul 1922 – 1r – 1 – gw Mikrofilm [949]

DER KOMMUNIST – (Title changes: Kommunistische Arbeiterzeitung (Hamburg), 7 Feb 1920; Kommunist (Bremen), 21 Feb 1920; Kommunist (Neukoelln), 1 May 1920; Rote Fahne (Bremen) 1 Dec 1920; Nordwestdeutsches Echo (Bremen), 1 Nov 1921; Rote Fahne (Berlin), 14 Mar 1924; Arbeiter-Zeitung (Bremen) 2 Jan 1925) – Bremen-Hamburg-Berlin-Neukoelln, Germany. 1927-Feb 1933 – 1 – gw Mikrofilm [072]

KOMMUNIST – Armenia. U.S.S.R. (Yerevan). 1955- – 1 – us UMI [072]

KOMMUNIST – Baku. Aug. 27-31, Sept. 5, 7-17, 20-21, 1920 – 1 – 35.00r – us Hoover Inst Photo [335]

KOMMUNIST – Erivan, U.S.S.R. -d. Jan 1946-May 1948; Jan 1950-Dec 1957; April-Dec 1958; July 1960-Dec 1968. 37 reels – 1 – uk British Libr Newspaper [947]

KOMMUNIST : EZHEDNEVNAI A GAZETA DONSKOGO KOMITETA R.K.P. I DONISPOLKOMA – (Includes c.1: 1922:Mar.12) – Rostov-na-Donu: Komitet i Donispolkom, 1921 – 1 – CSUXAHZ6284-S – us Hoover Inst Photo [335]

KOMMUNIST – Moscow, 1924-52 – 19r – 1 – us Ross [335]

KOMMUNIST – Moscow. 1924-62 – 1 – 989.00 – us L of C Photodup [335]

KOMMUNIST – Moscow. U.S.S.R. 1935- – 1 – us UMI [073]

KOMMUNIST / Moskovskago Oblastnago Byuro R K P (bol'shevikov) – Moscow. no. 1-2, 4. 1918 – 1 – us NY Public [335]

KOMMUNIST : ORGAN T SENTRALN. I BAKINSK. KOMIT. AZERBA IDZH. KOMMUN. P. (BOLSHEVIKOV), AZT SIK'A I BAKSOVETA – (Includes c.1: 1921:Nov.7) – [Baku: s.n., 1920 – 1 – CSUXANR5733-S – us Hoover Inst Photo [335]

KOMMUNIST : ZHURNAL T SENTRALNOGO KOMITETA KOMMUNISTICHESKO I KIRGIZII – (Library has: Jan.-Apr., June, Aug.-Dec. 1958; Feb.-Mar., May-Aug. 1959) – Frunze: Zd-vo "Sovettik Kyrgyzstan", 1957- – 1 – CSUX89-S862 – us Hoover Inst Photo [335]

KOMMUNIST *see* DER KOMMUNIST

KOMMUNIST ARMENIA – Armenia, USSR. 1963; 1964-1966; 1968-1974 – 11r – $550.00 – B63585 – us Library Micro [320]

KOMMUNIST (BAKU, AZERBAIJAN) *see* KOMMUNIST

KOMMUNIST ESTONII – (Includes Jan. 1957-July 1958, Sept. 1958-. Library has: Jan. 1957-July 1958, Sept. 1958-1989, 11) – [Tallin: Izd-vo T SK Kompartii Estonii, 1953-1989 – 1 – CSUX90-S45 – us Hoover Inst Photo [335]

KOMMUNIST ESTONII *see* EESTI BOLSHEVIK

KOMMUNIST (FRUNZE, KIRGHIZ S.S.R.) *see* KOMMUNIST

KOMMUNIST KAZAKHSTANA : TEORETICHESKI I I POLITICHESKI I ZHURNAL T SK KP KAZAKHSTANA – (Library has: Jan. 1956-Dec. 1957) – Alma-Ata: Respublikanskoe gazetno-zhurnalnoe izd-vo pri T SK KP Kazakhstana, 1952-1957. 6v – 1 – CSUX90-S42 – us Hoover Inst Photo [335]

KOMMUNIST MOLDAVII – (Library has: Jan.1958-Dec.1960, Jan.1972-Dec.1979; missing Jan.1978) – Kishinev: Parti inoe izd-vo T SK KP Moldavii, 1956 – 1 – CSUX90-S559 – us Hoover Inst Photo [335]

KOMMUNIST (ROSTOV-NA-DONU, R.S.F.S.R.) *see* KOMMUNIST

KOMMUNIST TADZHIKISTANA : ORGAN T SENTRALNOGO KOMITETA STALINABADSKOGO GORKOMA KP TADZHIKISTANA I VERKHOVNOGO SOVETA TADZHIKSKO I SSR – (Includes c.1: 1945:Aug.1-5, 9-Sept.8, 11, 14-Oct.21, 24-Dec.5, 18-26, 29-30) – Dushanbe: Komitet, -1991 – 1 – CSUXANR6321-S – us Hoover Inst Photo [335]

KOMMUNIST TADZHIKISTANA – Tadzhikistan. U.S.S.R. (Dushanbe). 1955- – 1 – us UMI [072]

KOMMUNIST TADZHIKISTANA (DUSHANBE, TAJIKISTAN: 1925) *see* KOMMUNIST TADZHIKISTANA

KOMMUNIST TURKMENISTANA – (Library has: 1956, no.7-8; 1957, nos.1-8; 1958, 1959, nos.1-8) – Ashkabad: Kom-t, 1953-1959. 7v – 1 – CSUX90-S36 – us Hoover Inst Photo [335]

Kommunisticheskaia Akademiia *see* PECHAT' I REVOLIUTSIIA

Kommunisticheskaia Partiia Sovetskogo Soiuza *see* STENOGRAFICHESKII OTCHET

KOMMUNISTICHESKAIA PARTIIA SOVETSKOGO SOIUZA V REZOLIUTSIIAKH I RESHENIAKH S"EZDOV, KONFERENTSII I PLENUMOV TSK. 1898-1981 – 8th ed. M., 1970-1984. 14v. 2 guides – 94mf – 9 – ne IDC [320]

KOMMUNISTICHESKAIA REVOLIUTSIIA – Moscow. Dvukhnedel'nyi Zhurnal Politiki, Ekonomiki, Agitatsii i Propagandy. Sep 1920-Jun 1922, Aug 1922-Mar 1935. Scattered issues missing – 1 – 35.00r – us Hoover Inst Photo [073]

Kommunisticheskaya Akademiya. Moscow *see*
- PLAN ROBAT
- VESTNIK

KOMMUNISTICHESKI I TRUD : ORGAN MOSKOVSKOGO KOMITETA R.K.P. I MOSKOVSKOGO SOVETA R. I K.D. – (Library has holdings (incomplete) from between Nov. 13, 1920 and Feb. 5, 1922) – Moskva: [s.n.], 1920-1922. 1v – 1 – CSUX87-S280 – us Hoover Inst Photo [335]

KOMMUNISTICHESKI I TRUD *see* ALFAVITNO-PREDMETNYI UKAZATEL K POSTANOVLENIIAM I RASPORI AZHENIIAM MOSKOVSKOGO SOVETA R., K. I K.D. I EGO OTDELOV, OPUBLIKOVANNYKH V GAZETE "KOMMUNISTICHESKI I TRUD"

KOMMUNISTICHESKII INTERNATZIONAL – Moscow. May 1919-June 1943. Incomplete – 1 – us NY Public [073]

KOMMUNISTICHESKII INTERNATSIONAL Moscow. v1-25. 1919-43 – 17r – 1 – us Ross [335]

KOMMUNISTICHESKII TRUD *see* RABOCHAIA MOSKVA

KOMMUNISTICHESKOE PROSVESHCHENIE – Moscow. 1920-1925. Gaps – 1 – 35.00r – us Hoover Inst Photo [335]

KOMMUNISTISCHE ARBEITER-ZEITUNG – Berlin. v. 1; v. 3; v. 4, no. 3-v. 14, no. 2. Apr 29 1919-Feb 1933 – 1 – us NY Public [073]

KOMMUNISTISCHE ARBEITERZEITUNG – Berlin, 1921 n158-258 – 1r – 1 – Dist. gw Mikrofilm – gw Misc Inst [943]

KOMMUNISTISCHE ARBEITERZEITUNG – Essen, Germany. 1922-24 (incomplete) – 1r – 1 – gw Mikrofilm [072]

KOMMUNISTISCHE ARBEITERZEITUNG *see* – DER KOMMUNIST

DER KOMMUNISTISCHE GEWERKSCHAFTER – Berlin, 1921-26 – 1 – Dist. gw Mikrofilm – gw Misc Inst [072]

KOMMUNISTISCHE GEWERKSCHAFTER – 1922-1923. Madison: University of Wisconsin, 1977. Includes Supplements – 1 – us U.W. Library [073]

DIE KOMMUNISTISCHE INTERNATIONALE – Berlin. v. 1-20, no. 8. Aug 1919-Aug 10 1939. Incomplete – 1 – us NY Public [073]

DIE KOMMUNISTISCHE INTERNATIONALE – Moskau (Moskva), U.S.S.R. 1919. (Nos.1-718) – 1r – 1 – gw Mikrofilm [072]

DIE KOMMUNISTISCHE INTERNATIONALE – Moskau. n1-718. 1919 – 1r – 1 – DM75.00 – gw Mikro Press [072]

DIE KOMMUNISTISCHE INTERNATIONALE : ZEITSCHRIFT DES EXEKUTIVKOMITEES DER KOMMUNISTISCHEN INTERNATIONALE – (Publ in Berlin, jan 10-apr 19 1933) – Basel-Strassburg-Paris-Stockholm. jan 10 1933-may 1941 – 10r – 1 – Dist. gw Mikrofilm – gw Misc Inst [072]

KOMMUNISTISCHE INTERNATIONALE. BIBLIOTHEK *see* COMMUNIST INTERNATIONAL

KOMMUNISTISCHE PARTEI DEUTSCHLANDS – (Lacks: n13-14) – Berlin. n1-15. 1918-46 – 2r – 1 – us Ross [335]

Kommunistische Partei Deutschlands, Spartakusbund *see* SPARTAKUS

KOMMUNISTISCHE RAETE-KORRESPONDENZ – Berlin, 1919-20 (incomplete) – 1r – 1 – Dist. gw Mikrofilm – gw Misc Inst [943]

KOMMUNISTISCHEN INTERNATIONALE *see* PAMPHLETS

KOMMUNISTKA – Moscow. Organ Ts. K.V.K.P. (b) po rabote Sredi rabotnits i krest'ianok. 1920-1927. Missing: no. 2, 1922; no. 9, 1923; nos. 5-6, 1924 – 1 – 35.00r – us Hoover Inst Photo [335]

KOMMUNISTU-OTPUSKNIKU NAKAZ / Baratov, Boris – Moskva: Gos. izd-vo, 1921 – 1 – CSUX89-B5479 – us Hoover Inst Photo [320]

KOMOEDIE DER IRRUNGEN : EIN BEITRAG ZUR KULTURGESCHICHTE DES NEUNZEHNTEN JAHRHUNDERTS / Segesser, H – Zuerich: D Herzog, 1886 – 1r – 1 – us U.W. Library [430]

Komovskii, V D *see* BIBLIOGRAFIIA

Kompaneiskii, B N *see* OBSHCHII KURS SCHETOVODSTVA POTREBITEL'SKIKH OBSHCHESTV

KOMPANIE IN POLEN / Pecher, Erich – Wien: Deutscher Verlag fuer Jugend und Volk, 1942 – 1r – 1 – us U.W. Library [830]

KOMPAS – Djakarta, Indonesia. June 28 1965-Dec 1993 – 109r – 1 – us L of C Photodup [072]

KOMPAS BAHASA; BUKU LATIRAN BAHASA INDONESIA BAGI SEKOLAH LANDJUTAN ATAS / Samidi, A – SE 4467 1. v. 1, 2, 3 only. 1961 – 9 – ne IDC [950]

KOMPENDIUM DER BIBLISCHEN THEOLOGIE DES ALTEN UND NEUEN TESTAMENTS VON KONSTANTIN SCHLOTTMANN / Schlottmann, Konstantin; ed by Kuehn, Ernst – (Includes index) – Leipzig:Doerffling & Franke, 1889 – 1mf – 9 – 0-8370-5101-0 – 1985-3101 – us A.T.L.A. [220]

Kompert, Leopold *see* LEOPOLD KOMPERTS SAEMTLICHE WERKE IN ZEHN BAENDEN

DIE KOMPETENZEN DES VOELKERBUNDSRATES UND DER VOELKERBUNDSVERSAMMLUNG... / Grob, F – Berlin, 1933 – 4mf – 1 – ILM-4023/1 – ne IDC [327]

DIE KOMPOSITION DES BUCHES JES. C. 28-33: EIN REKONSTRUKTIONSVERSUCH / Brueckner, Martin – Halle a.S.: J. Krause, 1897. 1 fiche – 9 – us A.T.L.A. [240]

KOMPOSITON UND ENTSTEHUNGSZEIT DER ORACULA SIBYLLINA (T.U.U. 2-23/1) / Geffcken, J – Leipzig, 1902 – 2mf – 9 – ne Slangenburg [240]

O KOMPOZITSII "DVENADTSATI" / Oksenov, I – Kniga i revoliutsiia. nr. 1. 1923. BR-3285 2 – 8 – ne IDC [335]

KOMSOMOL I KOOPERATSIIA / Ershov, A – M., 1925 – 1mf – 9 – COR-151/1 – ne IDC [334]

KOMSOMOL I KOOPERATSIIA : REZOLIUTSII I POSTANOVLENIIA VKP(B), VLKSM, PRAVITEL'STV. I KOOP. ORGANOV / Levitas, I et al – M., 1928 – 3mf – 9 – COR-157/1 – ne IDC [334]

KOMSOMOL V STROITEL'STVE RABOCHEI KOOPERATSII : FORMY I METODY KOOP. RABOTY MOLODEZHI / Milov, V V – M., 1926 – 1mf – 9 – COR-172/1 – ne IDC [334]

KOMSOMOLET S TADZHIKISTANA – (Includes c.1: v.4237 1970:July 10-v.5420 ie. 6420 (1983:Dec.26); c.1: missing 76 issues; some issues slightly mutilated; c.2) – Dushanbe: [s.n.], 1938- – 1 – CSUX86-S282 – us Hoover Inst Photo [947]

KOMSOMOLET S UZBEKISTANA – (Includes c.71: no.6315 1970:July 1-no.9448 (1982:Dec.30); c.71: Some issues missing; c.72) – Tashkent: T SK KP Uzbekistana, -1990 – 1 – CSUX86-S285 – us Hoover Inst Photo [947]

KOMSOMOLETS NA KOOPERATIVNUIU UCHEBU / Matveev-Bodryi, N N – M., 1926 – 1mf – 9 – COR-168/1 – ne IDC [334]

KOMSOMOLII A : STRANITSY EPOPEI / Bezymenskii, Aleksandr – Moskva: Gos. izd-vo, 1927 – 1 – CSUX88-B8947 – us Hoover Inst Photo [947]

KOMSOMOL'SKAIA PRAVDA – (Backfile through 1998 $85r. 1925-28 (reels not available anywhere in US, either in paper or on film) 11r $935) – 1999- – 4r per y – 1 – $320.00 standing order – us Ross [072]

KOMSOMOLSKAIA PRAVDA – Moscow. U.S.S.R. 1942, 1945- – 1 – us UMI [335]

KOMSOMOLSKAIA ZHIZN' – Moscow, 1958-72.Lacking: 1958; 1965(15). BR-10,407/1 – 9 – ne IDC [947]

KOMSOMOLSKAYA PRAVDA – Moscow, U.S.S.R. -d. 1 July 1926; 13 Nov-23 Dec 1927; 18 Sept 1928-30 Dec 1931. 1927, 1928 very imperfect. 7 reels – 1 – uk British Libr Newspaper [947]

KOMSOMOLSKI I RABOTNIK: ZHURNAL T SK VLKSM – (Includes c.1: v.23:no.21 1945:Nov.-v.23:no.22; v.25:no.1-v.25:no.4, v.25:no.6-; v.25:no.19, v.26:no.12-v.26:no.16; 1948:Aug) – Moskva: Molodai a gvardii a, -1948 – 1 – CSUXAKY6372-S – us Hoover Inst Photo [947]

KOMSOMOL'SKIA PRAVDA – De 1925 a 1928 – 7r – 1 – Sfr840.00 – sz Infoprint [947]

KOMSOMOL'SKIA PRAVDA – (Standing order available from De 1994 +. 2r per year. Sfr240.00y) – 1929-1993 – 2 times per yr – 1 – Sfr225.00 – sz Infoprint [947]

KOMSOMOL'SKIE STIKHI / Maiakovskii, Vladimir – M. 1933. BR-978 2 – 8 – ne IDC [460]

KOMUNIST – Belgrade, Yugoslavia. May 1957-1960 – 3r – 1 – us L of C Photodup [949]

KOMUNIST – Beograd, 1976-79 – 4r – 1 – DM300.00 – gw Mikro Press [949]

KOMUNIST – (Later absorbed by: Radians'ka Ukraina) – Kiev, USSR. Oct 17 1940-Oct 3 1941; Mar 5-Dec 24 1942 – 2r – 1 – us L of C Photodup [072]

KOMUNIST UKRAINY – Kiev. v10-16. 1935-41 – 3r – 1 – us Ross [335]

KOMUNISTISHER VEG = COMMUNIST WAY – (In Yiddish) – Homel, UA. v2 no221. 23 Oct 1921-May 1926 (Supp't of "Poleskaya Pravda" – 2r – 1 – $30.00r – cn Can Microfilming [072]

LE KOMYEN CHEZ LES BAOULE / Lafarque, Fernand – (Africa series). 1970 – 9 – fr Hachette [306]

KOMYO NIPPO – Japan, 1977- – 1 – inquire – us Ross [950]

LES KON CAU DE LA DA'NYING / Ferreiros Espinosa, A – 9 – fr Hachette [999]
Kon, SK *see* MILK AND MILK PRODUCTS IN HUMAN NUTRITION
Konandreas, P A *see* CATTLE HERD DYNAMICS
Konandreas, P A et al *see* ECONOMIC TRADE-OFFS BETWEEN MILK AND MEAT PRODUCTION UNDER VARIOUS SUPPLEMENTATION LEVELS IN BOTSWANA
Kondrateu, K YA *see* SOVIET JOURNAL OF REMOTE SENSING
Kondrat'ev, N D *see*
- AGRARNYI VOPROS O ZEMLE I ZEMEL'NYKH PORIADKAKH
- MIROVOI KHLEBNYI RYNOK I PERSPEKTIVY NASHE GO KHLEBNOGO EKSPORTA
- PERSPEKTIVY RAZVITIIA SEL'SKOGO KHOZIAISTVA SSSR
- RAZVITIE KHOZIAISTVA KINESHEMSKOGO ZEMSTVA KOSTROMSKOI GUBERNII
- RYNOK KHLEBOV I EGO REGULIROVANIE VO VREMIA VOINY I REVOLIUTSII

Kondrateyv, I *see* SEDAIA STARINA MOSKVY
Koneffke, Gernot *see* MENSCHENBILDUNG UND KINDERARBEIT BEI PESTALOZZI UND OWEN
Konferenz der Gewerkschaftsvorstaende *see* PROTOKOLL DER KONFERENZ...19-23 FEBRUAR 1906
Der Konferenz der Mennoniten-Bruedergemeinde in Kanada *see* MENNONITISCHE RUNDSCHAU
Konferenz der Strassenwarter *see* PROTOKOLL DER VERHANDLUNGEN..
Konferenz von Vertretern der gewerkschaftlichen Organisationen und Angestelltenverbande *see* GESETZ UEBER DEN VATERLANDISCHEN HILFSDIENST
KONFESSIONELLE BRUNNENVERGIFTUNG / Keiter, Heinrich – 2. verb u verm Aufl. Essen (Ruhr): Fredebeul & Koenen, 1908 – 1mf – 9 – 0-8370-6989-0 – 1986-0989 – us A.T.L.A. [430]
DIE KONFESSIONELLE SCHULE : EIN VORTRAG / Graeber, H J – Ruhrort: Andreae, 1876 – 1mf – 9 – 0-8370-7633-1 – 1986-1633 – us A.T.L.A. [370]
DIE KONFUTATION DES AUGSBURGISCHEN BEKENNTNISSES : IHRE ERSTE GESTALT UND IHRE GESCHICHTE / Ficker, Johannes – (Prolegomonena and notes in German; texts in Latin. Includes bibliographical references) – Leipzig: Johann Ambrosius Barth, 1891 – 1mf – 9 – 0-8370-8814-3 – 1986-2814 – us A.T.L.A. [240]
DIE KONFUTATION DES VIERSTAEDTEBEKENNTNISSES : IHRE ENTSTEHUNG UND IHR ORIGINAL – (Includes bibliographical references) – Leipzig: Johann Ambrosius Barth, 1900 – 1mf – 9 – 0-8370-8849-6 – 1986-2849 – us A.T.L.A. [240]
Kongelige Bibliotek. Copenhagen *see* EARLY NINETEENTH CENTURY MANUSCRIPTS FROM KUMASI, GHANA
KONGELIGE DANSKE VIDENSKABERNES SELSKABS NATURVIDENSKABELIGE OG MATHEMATISKE AFHANDLINGER – Kjobenhavn. v3. 1828 – 8mf – 9 – ne IDC [500]
DET KONGELIGE DANSKE VIDENSKABERS SELSKABS SKRIVETER / Danske Videnskabernes selskab. Copenhagen – 1801-18 – 3 – us Readex [500]
KONGJIAN KEXUE XUEBAO – Chinese Journal of Space Science. In Chinese but English abstracts to the main articles. F p138 – 9 – $4.50f – cc Microforms [073]
KONGOLEESCHE VERTELLINGEN / Struyf, Ivon – Brugge: Excelsior, 1924-26 – us Res Libr [960]
KONGQI DONGLIXUE XUEBAO – Acta Aerodynamica Sinica. 1983-84. F/P 289 – 9 – $4.50f – cc Microforms [073]
KONGRES PENDIRIKAN INDONESIA MOEDA 28 DES. 1930 – 2 JAN. 1931 : DI SOERAKARTA – Weltevreden, 1931 – 3mf – 9 – ne IDC [320]
KONGRES RA'JAT INDONESIA 1 – Batavia-C., 1940 – 3mf – 9 – ne IDC [320]
KONGRESA GRAHMATA = CONGRESS BOOK / Kronlins, Janis – Speeches and Reports at the annual meeting of the Latvian Baptist Union in Liepja, Sept. 13-16, 1923, etc. Publ. No. 6348b. One of two items on reel. Total Pages 1,228 – 1 – us Baptist [240]
Kongress der Christlichen Gewerkschaften Deutschlands *see* NIEDERSCHRIFT DER VERHANDLUNGEN
Kongress der Gewerkschaften Deutschlands *see*
- PROTOKOLL DER VERHANDLUNGEN..
- PROTOKOLL DER VERHANDLUNGEN DES AUSSERORDENTLICHEN KONGRESSES DER GEWERKSCHAFTEN DEUTSCHLANDS

KONGRESSZEITUNG = CONGRESS BULLETIN – (In German) – Vienna, AU. v1 no2 9 Sep 1935-v1 no7 17 Sep 1935 – 1r – 1 – $30.00 – cn Can Microfilming [072]
KONGRESSZENTRALBLATT FUER DIE GESAMTE INNERE MEDIZIN – v.114-318, 1943-72 – 1,5,6,9,13 – us UMI [073]
KONGRESZEITUNG – Basel, 1927, 1931 (both incomplete) – 1 – Dist. gw Mikrofilm – gw Misc Inst [072]
KONI UNKTURNAI A TOVARNO-TRANSPORTNAI A STATISTIKA = STATISTIQUE CONJONCTURALE DU TRANSPORT DES MARCHANDISES/FREIGHT TRAFFIC STATISTICS : T SENTRALNOE STATISTICHESKOE UPRAVLENIE – (Includes c.1: no.1 1924:Aug.-; no.10, no.12-no.18/19, no.27 1926:Oct) – Moskva: Upravlenie, 1924- – 1 – CSUXAKZ6110-S – us Hoover Inst Photo [380]
KONICHI MINZOKU TOITSU SENSEN UNDO SHI / South Manchurian Railway. Shanghai – Dairen. A study of the Nationalist-Communist United Front against Japan. 414 p. 1939. (J 222.07 Mi37k) – 1 – 35.00r – us Hoover Inst Photo [335]
Konig, David Thomas *see* PLYMOUTH COURT RECORDS, 1686-1859
DER KONIGL / Svenska Vetenskapsakademien, Stockholm – Schwedischen Akademie der Wissenschaften Abhandlungen, aus der Naturlehre, Haushaltungskunst und Mechanik. Hamburg und Leipzig, 1739-79 – 3 – us Readex [574]
Koning, M *see* LEXICON HIEROGLYPHICUM SACRO-PROFANUM, OF WOORDBOEK VAN GEWYDE EN ONGEWYDE VOOR-EN ZINNEBEELDEN
HET KONINGLYK NEDER-HOOG-DUITSCH-HOOG-NEDER-DUITSCH DICTIONARIUM (AEL, ABT.2;3) / Kramer, Matthias – Nuernberg, 1719 (mf ed 1992) – 10mf – 9 – DM110.00 – 3-89131-063-3 – gw Fischer [430]
KONITZER NACHRICHTEN : NACHRICHTENBLATT FUER POMMERELLEN – Konitz (Chojnice), Poland. 21 Mar-6 Dec 1922 – 1r – 1 – gw Mikrofilm [943]
KONITZER TAGBLATT – Konitz (Chojnice), Poland. 23 Oct 1924-36; 10 Feb 1937-27 Aug 1939 – 14r – 1 – gw Mikrofilm [943]
Koniunkturnogo Instituta *see* EKONOMICHESKII BIULLETEN' KONIUNKTURNOGO INSTITUTA
Kon'iunkturnyi Institut. Moscow *see* EKONOMICHESKII BIULLETEN
Konjaev, K V *see* SPECTRAL ANALYSIS OF RANDOM PROCESSES AND FIELDS
KONJUNKTUR – London, UK. 3 Apr 1909-15 Aug 1914 – 1 – uk British Libr Newspaper [072]
DAS KONKLAVE PIUS' 4 : HISTORISCHE ABHANDLUNG / Mueller, Theodor – (Includes bibliographical references) – Gotha: Friedrich Andreas Perthes, 1889 – 1mf – 9 – 0-8370-8846-1 – 1986-2846 – us A.T.L.A. [920]
KONKORDANZ ZU WALTER KEMPOWSKIS "DEUTSCHER CHRONIK" / Kempowski, Walter; ed by Keele, Alan F – Hildesheim, 1994 – 9180p on 34mf – 9 – DM298.00 diazo DM330.00 silver – gw Olms [430]
KONKORDANZ ZUM TARGUM ONKELOS / Brederek, E – (Beihefte zur Zeitschrift fuer die Alttestamentliche Wissenschaft, v. 9). Gieszen. 1906. BNE-484 1 – 9 – ne IDC [470]
Kononov, A N *see* RODOSLOVNAIA TURKMEN
Konrad, Martin *see* ZEITBILDER ODER ERINNERUNGEN AN MEINE VEREWIGTEN WOHLTHAETER
Konrad, P *see* DR. AMBROSIUS MOIBANUS
KONSENS UND DISSENS IM BILDUNGSSYSTEM VON BADEN-WUERTTEMBERG : EIN BEITRAG ZUM VERHAELTNIS VON PARTIZIPATION UND SCHULREFORM NACH 1970 / Felgner, Harald – Heidelberg, 1977 – 3mf – 9 – DM76.00 – 3-89349-367-0 – gw Hänsel [370]
KONSERVATIVE POLITIK IM LETZTEN JAHRZEHNT DES KAISERREICHES BAND I / Westarp, Graf von – 1908-1914 – 1 – DM60.00 – gw Mikro Press [943]
KONSERVEN-ZEITUNG – Brunswick, Germany. 1907-15. -w – 6r – 1 – uk British Libr Newspaper [660]
KONSPEKT LEKTSII PO SEL'SKOKHOZIAISTVENNOI KOOPERATSII / Ostroumov, VI – Omsk, 1929 – 3mf – 9 – COR-269/1 – ne IDC [334]
DE KONST DER WIJSHEID / Gracian – Den Haag, 1696 – 5mf – 8 – ne Slangenburg [100]
KONSTANTIN KARLOVICH GROT KAK GOSUDARSTVENNYI OBSHCHESTVENNYI DEIATEL' / Grot, K I – v. 1-3. Petrograd, Aleksandrov. 1915. BR-8059 2 – 8 – ne IDC [947]
Konstantinov, G *see* REVOLIUTSIONNA ROMANTIKA V BALGARSKOTO VAZRAZHDANE
Konstantinov, M M *see* POSLEDNIE DNI KOLCHAKOVSHCHINY
KONSTANTINS DES GROSSEN KREUZERSCHEINUNG : EINE KRITISCHE UNTERSUCHUNG / Schroers, Heinrich – Bonn: Hanstein, 1913 – 1mf – us A.T.L.A. [240]
KONSTANZER POLITISCHE ZEITUNG *see* DER VOLKSFREUND
KONSTANZER ZEITUNG *see* DER VOLKSFREUND
KONSTANZISCHES INTELLIGENZBLATT *see* DER VOLKSFREUND
KONSTITUSI PARTAI KOMUNIS INDONESIA (P.K.I.) / Communist Party. Indonesia – 1956. SE-2077-1 – 9 – ne IDC [950]
KONSTITUSI SOBSI / Sentral Organisasi Buruh Seluruh Indonesia – SE 2242 1. 1955 – 9 – ne IDC [025]
KONSTITUTSII A (OSNOVNO I ZAKON) ESTONSKO I SOVETSKO I SOTSIALISTICHESKO I RESPUBLIKI : SIZMENENII AMI I DOPOLNENII AMI, PRINI ATYMI NA 4, 5, 6, 8 I 9 SESSII AKH VERKHOVNOGO SOVETA ESTONSKO I SSR PI ATOGO SOZYVA I NA 1, 2, 4, 5, 6, I 7 SESSII AKH VERKHOVNOGO SOVETA ESTONSKO I SSR SHESTOGO SOZYVA – Tallin: "E esti Raamat", 1965 – 1 – CSUX91-B2625 – us Hoover Inst Photo [340]
KONSTITUTSII A (OSNOVNO I ZAKON) ESTONSKO I SOVETSKO I SOTSIALISTICHESKO I RESPUBLIKI : SIZMENENII AMI I DOPOLNENII AMI, PRINI ATYMI NA 8 I 9 SESSII AKH VERKHOVNOGO SOVETA ESTONSKO I SSR SHESTOGO SOZYVA, 1, 3, 4, 5, 6, 7 I 8 SESSII AKH SEDMOGO SOZYVA I NA I SESSII VOSMOGO SOZYVA VERKHOVNOGO SOVETA ESTONSKO I SSR – Tallin: "E esti raamat", 1972 – 1 – CSUX91-B2649 – us Hoover Inst Photo [340]
KONSTITUTSII A (OSNOVNO I ZAKON) ESTONSKO I SOVETSKO I SOTSIALISTICHESKO I RESPUBLIKI : SIZMENENII AMI I DOPOLNENII AMI, PRINI ATYMI NA 8 SESSII VERKHOVNOGO SOVETA ESTONSKO I SSR CHETVERTOGO SOZYVA I 1, 2 I 3 SESSII AKH VERKHOVNOGO SOVETA ESTONSKO I SSR PI ATOGO SOZYVA – Tallin: Estonskoe gos. izd-vo, 1960 – 1 – CSUX91-B2627 – us Hoover Inst Photo [340]
KONSTITUTSII A ROSSI ISKO I SOTSIALISTICHESKO I FEDERATIVNO I SOVETSKO I RESPUBLIKI V OTVETAKH NA VOPROSY / Dranitsyn, Sergei Nikanorovich – 2-e izd. Moskva: Gos. izd-vo, 1922 – 1 – CSUX89-B4211 – us Hoover Inst Photo [320]
KONSTITUTSII A ROSSI ISKO I SOTSIALISTICHESKO I FEDERATIVNO I SOVETSKO I RESPUBLIKI V OTVETAKH NA VOPROSY / Dranitsyn, Sergei Nikanorovich – Peterburg: Gos. izd-vo, 1922 – 1 – CSUX89-B3862 – us Hoover Inst Photo [320]
KONSTITUTSIIA *see*
- KONSTITUTSIIA (OSNOVNO I ZAKON) ARMIANSKO I SOVETSKO I SOTSIALISTICHESKO I RESPUBLIKI
- KONSTITUTSIIA (OSNOVNO I ZAKON) ARMIANSKO I SOVETSKO I SOTSIALISTICHSKO I RESPUBLIKI
- KONSTITUTSIIA (OSNOVNO I ZAKON) AZERBA IDZHANSKO I SOVETSKO I SOTSIALISTICHESKO I RESPUBLIKI
- KONSTITUTSIIA (OSNOVNO I ZAKON) AZERBAIDHANSKO I SOVETSKO I SOTSIALISTICHESKO I RESPUBLIKI

KONSTITUTSIIA (1922) *see* OSNOVNO I ZAKON (KONSTITUTSIIA) SOVETSKO I SOTSIALISTICHESKO I RESPUBLIKI GRUZII
KONSTITUTSIIA (1937) *see* KONSTITUTSIIA (OSNOVNO I ZAKON) GRUZINSKO I SOVETSKO I SOTSIALISTICHESKO I RESPUBLIKI
KONSTITUTSIIA (OSNOVNO I ZAKON) ARMIANSKO I SOVETSKO I SOTSIALISTICHESKO I RESPUBLIKI : S IZMENENII AMI I DOPOLNENII AMI, PRINI ATYMI NA 6-9 SESSII AKH VERKHOVNOGO SOVETA ARMIANSKO I SSR PI ATOGO SOZYVA I NA I SESSII VERKHOVNOGO SOVETA ARMIANSKO I SSR SHESTOGO SOZYVA / Armenian SSR – Erevan: Armianskoe gos. izd-vo, 1963 – 1 – CSUX91-B2622 – us Hoover Inst Photo [340]
KONSTITUTSIIA (OSNOVNO I ZAKON) ARMIANSKO I SOVETSKO I SOTSIALISTICHESKO I RESPUBLIKI : S IZMENENII AMI I DOPOLNENII AMI PRINI ATYMI NA VOSMO I I DEVI ATO I SESSII AKH VERKHOVNOGO SOVETA ARMI ANSKO I SSR SHESTOGO SOZYVA / Armenian SSR – Erevan: Aiastan, 1967 – 1 – CSUX91-B2468 – us Hoover Inst Photo [340]
KONSTITUTSIIA (OSNOVNO I ZAKON) ARMIANSKO I SOVETSKO I SOTSIALISTICHESKO I RESPUBLIKI : S IZMENENII AMI I DOPOLNENII AMI, PRINI ATYMI NA VTORO I SESSII VERKHOVNOGO SOVETA ARMI ANSKO I SSR PI ATOGO SOZYVA / Armenian SSR – Erevan: Armianskoe gos. izd-vo, 1960 – 1 – CSUX91-B2360 – us Hoover Inst Photo [340]
KONSTITUTSIIA (OSNOVNO I ZAKON) ARMIANSKO I SOVETSKO I SOTSIALISTICHSKO I RESPUBLIKI : S IZM. I DOP., PRINI ATYMI NA 4. I 5. SESSII AKH VERKHOVNOGO SOVETA ARMIANSKO I SSR 5. SOZYVA / Armenian SSR – Erevan: Armianskoe gos. izd-vo, 1961 – 1 – CSUX91-B2618 – us Hoover Inst Photo [340]
KONSTITUTSIIA (OSNOVNO I ZAKON) AZERBA IDZHANSKO I SOVETSKO I SOTSIALISTICHESKO I RESPUBLIKI : S IZM. I DOP., PRINTI ATYMI NA 1, 2, 3 I 5 SESSII AKH VERKHOVNOGO SOVETA AZERBA IDZHANSKO I SSR 5. SOZYVA / Azerbaijan S.S.R. – Baku: Azerba idzshanskoe gos. izd-vo, 1961 – 1 – CSUX91-B3143 – us Hoover Inst Photo [340]
KONSTITUTSIIA (OSNOVNO I ZAKON) AZERBAIDHANSKO I SOVETSKO I SOTSIALISTICHESKO I RESPUBLIKI : S IZM. I DOP., PRINI ATYMI NA 1, 2, 4 I 5 SESSII AKH VERKHOVNOGO SOVETA AZERBAIDZHANSKO I SSR SHESTOGO SOZYVA / Azerbaijan S.S.R. – Baku: Azerbaidzhanskoe gos. izd-vo, 1965 – 1 – CSUX91-B2354 – us Hoover Inst Photo [340]
KONSTITUTSIIA (OSNOVNO I ZAKON) GRUZINSKO I SOVETSKO I SOTSIALISTICHESKO I RESPUBLIKI : SIZMENENII AMI I DOPOLNENII AMI, PRINI ATYMI NA DEVI ATO I SESSII VERKHOVNOGO SOVETA GRUZINSKO I SSR SHESTOGO SOZYVA – Tbilisi: T SK KP Gruzii, 1966 – 1 – CSUX91-B2443 – us Hoover Inst Photo [340]
KONSTITUTSIIA SOIUZA SSR I KONSTITUTSII SOIUZNYKH RESPUBLIK – Moscow, 1938. 273p. BR-9581/1 – 9 – ne IDC [947]
KONSTITUTSIIA SSSR I KONSTITUTSII SOVETSKIKH SOTSIALISTICHESKIKH RESPUBLIK – Moscow, 1937. 282p. BR-9580/1 – 9 – ne IDC [947]
KONSTITUTSIONNOE GOSUDARSTVO / Gessen, I V – 2d ed. Spb. 1905. BR-9747 1 – 9 – ne IDC [321]
KONSTITUTSIONNYI VESTNIK – Moscow: Konstitutsionnaia kommissiia Verkh. Soveta Rossii, 1990- – 50mf – 9 – $119.95y – us East View [320]
KONSTITUTSIOON (1940). RUSSIAN *see*
- KONSTITUTSII A (OSNOVNO I ZAKON) ESTONSKO I SOVETSKO I SOTSIALISTICHESKO I RESPUBLIKI

KONSTRUKTION IM MASCHINENAPPARATE-UND GERAETEBAU – v. 1-32. 1949-80 – 1,5,9 – 2664.00 – us UMI [073]
KONSULAT / Indonesia – New York. Incomplete. SE-768 1. 1965-1971 – 9 – ne IDC [950]
KONSUMENT – Maribor, Yugoslavia, 1929 – 1mf or 1 reel – 9,1 – us I.H.R.C. [947]
KONSUMENTBLADET *see* VI
Kont, J *see* LA HONGRIE LITTERAIRE ET SCIENTIFIQUE

KONTRAKTATSIIA, SBYT I SNABZHENIE V SEL'SKO-KHOZIAISTVENNYKH KREDITNYKH TOVARISHCHESTVAKH : ORGANIZATSIIA I FINANSIROVANIE / Islankin, FB – Ed.2. M., 1929 – 3mf – 9 – COR-382/1 – ne IDC [334]

KONTRAPUNKT / Odoevsteva, I – Stikhi. Paris. 1951. BR-1225 2 – 8 – ne IDC [460]

KONTROLNYE T SIFRY NARODNOGO KHOZI A ISTVA I KULTURY LENINGRADSKO I OBLASTI NA...G. : LENINGRADSKAI A OBLASTNAI A PLANOVAI A KOMISSII A – (Includes c.1: 1928-1930) – [S.l.]: Pribo i, 19uu – 1 – CSUXAKY6431-S – us Hoover Inst Photo [947]

KONTROLNYE TSIFRY NARODNOGO KHOZIAISTVA I SOTSIALNO-KURTURNOGO STROITELSTVA RSFSR – Moskva: Gos. izd-vo, [192-?] – 1 – CSUX88-B6445 – us Hoover Inst Photo [339]

KONTROL'NYE TSIFRY POTREBITEL'SKOI KOOPERATSII SSSR NA 1927-28 GOD – M., 1927 – 2mf – 9 – COR-328/1 – ne IDC [334]

KONTROLNYE TSIFRY RAZVITIIA NARODNOGO KHOZIAISTVA SSSR NA 1959-1965 GG / U.S.S.R. – M. 1959. BD-245 1 – 9 – ne IDC [947]

DIE KONTROVERSE UM DIE TRANSFERPROBLEMATIK 1924-1929 / Holthaus, Arno – 1992 – 9 – DM98.00 – 3-89349-512-6 – gw Hänsel [350]

KONTR-REVOLIUTSIIA I EE METODY : BELYI TERROR PREZHDEI TEPER / Bystrianskii, Vadim – Peterburg: Gos. izd-vo, 1920 – 1 – CSUX88-B1851 – us Hoover Inst Photo [947]

KONTSESSIONNYI DOGOVOR PRAVITEL'STVA SSSR S ANGLIISKIM OBSHCHESTVOM LENA GOLDFIELDS LIMITED – Moscow, 1925. 70p. BR-9030/1 – 9 – ne IDC [380]

DAS KONVERSENINSTITUT DES CISTERZIENSERORDENS / Hoffman, E – Freiburg Schw., 1905 – 2mf – 8 – Dfl9.00 – ne Slangenburg [240]

KONYA – (No. 183 (2932) (14 Tesrinisani 1928)) – Konya: Vilayet Matbaasi. Cikaran: Konya Vilayeti, 1871-1928 – 1mf – 9 – $10.00 – us MEDOC [949]

KONZENTRA-BLAETTER – Berlin, jun 6 1925-33 (incomplete) – 1 – Dist. gw Mikrofilm – gw Misc Inst [072]

KONZEPTE EINER ZENTRALEN EUROPAEISCHEN VERKEHRSWEGEPLANUNG : ANSATZPUNKTE, MOEGLICHKEITEN UND GRENZEN / Breuer, Joerg – 1994 – 1mf – DM60.00 – 3-89349-889-3 – gw Hänsel [337]

KONZERT RONDO K. 386, A MAJOR / Mozart, Wolfgang Amadeus – (Contains mm 136-54. Holograph) – From MS – 1 – us Sibley [780]

DAS KONZIL VON NICAEA : HABILITATIONSVORLESUNG / Bernoulli, Carl Albrecht – Freiburg i. B.: J.C.B. Mohr, 1896 – 1mf – us A.T.L.A. [240]

KONZILIENSTUDIEN ZUR GESCHICHTE DES 13. JAHRHUNDERTS : ERGAENZUNGEN UND BERICHTIGUNGEN ZU HEFELE-KNOEPFLER "CONCILIENGESCHICHTE" BAND V UND VI / Finke, Heinrich – Muenster: Regensberg, 1891 – 1mf – us A.T.L.A. [240]

DIE KONZILSPOLITIK KARLS 5 IN DEN JAHREN 1538-1543 / Korte, August – Halle a.d.S.: Verein fuer Reformationsgeschichte, 1905 (Schriften des Vereins fuer Reformationsgeschichte; 22. Jahrg., Schrift 85) – 1mf – us A.T.L.A. [240]

KONZILSTUDIEN / Schwartz, E – Strassburg, 1914 – Dfl9.00 – ne Slangenburg [240]

Kook, A J *see* AZKARAH, LE-MISHMAT AVRAHAM YIZHAK HA-KONEN KOOK

Kookogey, William P *see* PATENT LAW IN BRIEF

KOONDROOK AND BARHAM BRIDGE – Sep 30 1909-Dec 21 1968 – 9 – at Pascoe [072]

Koones, John Alexander *see* EVERYBODY'S LAW BOOK; LEGAL RIGHTS AND LEGAL REMEDIES.

Koontz, William H *see* HISTORY OF BEDFORD AND SOMERSET COUNTIES

HET KOOPCONTRACT IN DEN OVERZEESCHEN HANDEL / Craandijk, H – Amsterdam, 1921 – 3mf – 9 – Dfl 27 – ILM-3053/1 – ne IDC [380]

KOOPERAT SII A – (Library has: No. 54 (July 31, 1919)) – V Moskve: "Kooperat sii a", 1919 – 1 – CSUX89-S680 – us Hoover Inst Photo [947]

KOOPERATIV V RABOTE : PRAVDIVAIA GLAVA IZ ISTORII VYMYSHL. POTREBITEL'NOGO OBSHCHESTVA / Orlov, N A – Pg., 1918 – 1mf – 9 – COR-85/1 – ne IDC [334]

DI KOOPERATIVE BAVEGUNG (RUCH SPOLDZIELCZY) = CO-OP – (Polish monthly) – Warsaw, PL. v10 no11-12. Nov/Dec 1932 – 1r – 1 – $25.00 – cn Can Microfilming [072]

KOOPERATIVNAIA ARENDA ZEMLI : O TOM, KAK SOOBSHCHA ARENDUIUT ZEMLIU I ULUCHAIUT KHOZIAISTVO / Maslov, S L – M., 1914 – 1mf – 9 – COR-69/1 – ne IDC [334]

KOOPERATIVNAIA CHAINAIA : PT. 1: ORGANIZATSIIA CHAINYKH / Armand, L M – Ed 2. M., 1920 – 1mf – 9 – COR-321/1 – ne IDC [334]

KOOPERATIVNAIA MYSL' – Kiev, 1916-17 n6 – 7mf – 9 – COR-613/1 – ne IDC [334]

KOOPERATIVNAIA MYSL' – (Missing: 1918 n1-7, 9-11) – Vladikavkaz, 1918 – 2mf – 9 – COR-611/1 – ne IDC [334]

KOOPERATIVNAIA MYSL' – (Missing: 1921 n1-1922 n3, n14. 1923 n7-10) – Voronezh, 1921-23 n18 – 17mf – 9 – COR-612/1 – ne IDC [334]

KOOPERATIVNAIA MYSL' – (Missing: n1) – Stavropol', 1923 – 4mf – 9 – COR-614/1 – ne IDC [334]

KOOPERATIVNAIA NIVA *see* IZVESTIIA OMGUBSOIUZA

KOOPERATIVNAIA ORGANIZATSIIA MELKOGO KREDITA / Prokopovich, SN – M., 1919 – 1mf – 9 – COR-399/1 – ne IDC [334]

KOOPERATIVNAIA SIBIR *see* SEL'SKAIA KOOPERATSIIA

KOOPERATIVNAIA SIBIR' – (Missing: 1928 n20-21) – Novonikolaevsk (Novosibirsk), 1924-29 n3 – 142mf – 9 – COR-616/1 – ne IDC [334]

KOOPERATIVNAIA VIATKA – (Cont by: Kooperativnaia zhizn'. Viatka, 1922 n1-3[=9-11] – 1923 n31) – Viatka, 1922 n1-8 – 15mf – 9 – COR-602/1 – ne IDC [334]

KOOPERATIVNAIA ZHIZN' – (1917 n5-1918 n3 have not been publ. Missing: 1918 n8-end) – Moscow, 1912-20 – 69mf – 9 – COR-604/1 – ne IDC [334]

KOOPERATIVNAIA ZHIZN' – Ekaterinoslav, 1917 n1 – 2mf – 9 – COR-603/1 – ne IDC [334]

KOOPERATIVNAIA ZHIZN' : EZHEMESIACHNYI KOOPERATIVNYI I OBSHCHESTVENNO-EKONOMICHESKII ZHURNAL – Nikolaev, 1923 – 1mf – 9 – COR-605/1 – ne IDC [334]

KOOPERATIVNAIA ZHIZN' – (Missing: 1921 n1-1922 n8, 10-18) – Novonikolaevsk, 1921-23 n24 – 11mf – 9 – COR-606/1 – ne IDC [334]

KOOPERATIVNAIA ZHIZN' – (Missing: 1921-22 n5) – Iaroslavl', 1921-24 n10 – 18mf – 9 – COR-609/1 – ne IDC [334]

KOOPERATIVNAIA ZHIZN' – (Missing: n1-7) – Briansk, 1923 n1-12 – 3mf – 9 – COR-600/1 – ne IDC [334]

KOOPERATIVNAIA ZHIZN' – Samara, 1913-14 n10 – 6mf – 9 – COR-607/1 – ne IDC [334]

KOOPERATIVNAIA ZHIZN' – Tula, 1922 – 4mf – 9 – COR-608/1 – ne IDC [334]

KOOPERATIVNAIA ZHIZN' – Vladimir, 1923 – 4mf – 9 – COR-601/1 – ne IDC [334]

KOOPERATIVNAIA ZHIZN' *see* KOOPERATIVNAIA VIATKA

KOOPERATIVNAIA ZHIZN' KARELII – (Missing: 1922-23 n1) – Petrozavodsk, 1922-23 n16 – 4mf – 9 – COR-610/1 – ne IDC [334]

KOOPERATIVNO SELO – Sofia, Bulgaria. May 1958-87 – 35r – 1 – us L of C Photodup [949]

KOOPERATIVNOE DELO – (Missing: 1925 n8-1926 n2) – Orel, 1925-26 n4 – 4mf – 9 – COR-617/1 – ne IDC [334]

KOOPERATIVNOE DELO – Tomsk, 1922-24 – 18mf – 9 – COR-618/1 – ne IDC [334]

KOOPERATIVNOE DVIZHENIE V ROSSII : EGO TEORIIA I PRAKTIKA / Prokopovich, SN – Ed 2. M., 1918 – 5mf – 9 – COR-219/1 – ne IDC [334]

KOOPERATIVNOE DVIZHENIE V ROSSII / Prokopovich, SN – Spb., 1903 – 3mf – 9 – COR-100/1 – ne IDC [334]

KOOPERATIVNOE PTITSEVODSTVO *see* PTITSEVODSTVO

KOOPERATIVNOE SLOVO – (Missing: 1917 n10-12, 19-22) – Khar'kov, 1916-17 n39 – 13mf – 9 – COR-622/1 – ne IDC [334]

KOOPERATIVNOE SLOVO – (Missing: 1917 n14-22, 27-28) – Chita, 1916-17 – 10mf – 9 – COR-623/1 – ne IDC [334]

KOOPERATIVNOE SLOVO – (Missing: 1917 n4-1919 n1, 17-20. 1920 n11-12) – Smolensk, 1917-20 n21/22 – 14mf – 9 – COR-621/1 – ne IDC [334]

KOOPERATIVNOE SLOVO – (Missing: 1918 n4-5, 8-10, 13-14, 18-22) – Nizhnyi Novgorod, 1918 n1-23 – 5mf – 9 – COR-620/1 – ne IDC [334]

KOOPERATIVNOE STROITEL'STVO – Leningrad, 1926-29 – 95mf – 9 – COR-624/1 – ne IDC [334]

KOOPERATIVNOE VOSPITANIE DETEI I VOZROZHDENIE CHELOVECHESTVA / Frommett, B R – Pg., 1918 – 1mf – 9 – COR-278/1 – ne IDC [334]

KOOPERATIVNOE ZAKONODATEL'STVO / Voitsekhovskii, S F – Ed 2. M., 1914 – 1mf – 9 – COR-16/1 – ne IDC [334]

KOOPERATIVNOE ZAKONODATEL'STVO S PRILOZHENIEM DEKRETOV O VSEKH VIDAKH KOOPERATSII / Povolotskii, LI – Ed 3. M., 1926 – 4mf – 9 – COR-300/1 – ne IDC [334]

KOOPERATIVNOE ZHILISHCHE – Kiev, 1925-26 – 4mf – 9 – COR-619/1 – ne IDC [334]

O KOOPERATIVNOM IDEALE / Tugan-Baranovskii, M I – M., 1918 – 1mf – 9 – COR-223/1 – ne IDC [334]

KOOPERATIVNYE BI ULLETENI PRIKAMSKIKH SOI UZOV : IZDANIE PRIKAMSKOGO SOI UZA POTREBITELNYKH OBSHCHESTV I PRIKAMSKOGO KREDITNO-KOOPERATIVNOGO SOI UZA – (Includes c.1: no.1(1919:Aug.15)) – Sarapul: [s.n.], 1919- – 1 – CSUXANR6812-S – us Hoover Inst Photo [947]

KOOPERATIVNYE KRUZHKI : MATERIALY DLIA ZANIATII – M., 1925 – 2mf – 9 – COR-255/1 – ne IDC [334]

KOOPERATIVNYE KRUZHKI V DEREVNE / Ozerov, N I – M., L., 1926 – 2mf – 9 – COR-268/1 – ne IDC [334]

KOOPERATIVNYE OB'EDINENIIA MOSKOVSKOI OBLASTI – M., 1919 – 4mf – 9 – COR-717/1 – ne IDC [310]

KOOPERATIVNYE SOIUZY V SIBIRI (1908-1918 GG.) / Ilimskii, D I – M., 1919 – 2mf – 9 – COR-248/1 – ne IDC [334]

KOOPERATIVNYE TOVARISHCHESTVA I IKH KLASSIFIKATSIIA / Prokopovich, SN – M., 1919 – 1mf – 9 – COR-220/1 – ne IDC [334]

KOOPERATIVNYI APPARAT V SOVETSKOI ROSSII V 1920/21 GODU – M., 1921 – 2mf – 9 – COR-718/1 – ne IDC [310]

KOOPERATIVNYI BIULLETEN' – (Missing: 1922 n1-6, 11-end) – Kaluga, 1921-23 n6 – 11mf – 9 – COR-627/1 – ne IDC [334]

KOOPERATIVNYI BIULLETEN' – Ves'egonsk, 1924 – 1mf – 9 – COR-626/1 – ne IDC [334]

KOOPERATIVNYI BIULLETEN' SUMRAISOIUZA – Sumy, 1923-24 – 7mf – 9 – COR-628/1 – ne IDC [334]

KOOPERATIVNYI BYT – Riazan', 1923-24 – 5mf – 9 – COR-625/1 – ne IDC [334]

KOOPERATIVNYI INSTITUT I MUZEI / Antsyferov, A N – Khar'kov, 1914 – 1mf – 9 – COR-2/1 – ne IDC [334]

KOOPERATIVNYI INSTRUKTAZH I EGO METODY / Makhov, V N – Ed 2. Novonikolaevsk, 1924 – 3mf – 9 – COR-266/1 – ne IDC [334]

KOOPERATIVNYI KREDIT / Antsyferov, A N – Ed.2. Pg., 1918 – 1mf – 9 – COR-369/1 – ne IDC [334]

KOOPERATIVNYI KREDIT – Moscow, 1919-20 – 7mf – 9 – COR-630/1 – ne IDC [334]

KOOPERATIVNYI KREDIT : POLOZHENIE O KOOPERATIVNOM KREDITE 18-GO IANVARIA 1927 GODA, EGO OSNOVY I POSTATEINYI RAZBOR... / Shmidt, G R – L., 1927 – 2mf – 9 – COR-410/1 – ne IDC [334]

KOOPERATIVNYI KREDIT V SEVERO-ZAPADNOM KRAE – Minsk, 1913-14 – 4mf – 9 – COR-631/1 – ne IDC [334]

KOOPERATIVNYI LISTOK – (Missing: 1924, 1925 n1-23) – Vitebsk, 1924-26 n11 – 5mf – 9 – COR-632/1 – ne IDC [334]

KOOPERATIVNYI MIR – Moscow, 1917-18 – 14mf – 9 – COR-633/1 – ne IDC [334]

KOOPERATIVNYI MOLOT – Tula, 1919 – 1mf – 9 – COR-634/1 – ne IDC [334]

KOOPERATIVNYI PUT' – Odessa, 1927-28 – 5mf – 9 – COR-635/1 – ne IDC [334]

KOOPERATIVNYI PUT' – Samara, 1928-29 – 28mf – 9 – COR-636/1 – ne IDC [334]

KOOPERATIVNYI SBYT PRODUKTOV MELKOGO KHOZIAISTVA / Kulyzhnyi, A E – Ed 2. M. – 1mf – 9 – COR-56/1 – ne IDC [334]

KOOPERATIVNYI SBYT PRODUKTOV SEL'SKOGO KHOZIAISTVA / Kulyzhnyi, A E – Ed.3. M., 1918 – 2mf – 9 – COR-480/1 – ne IDC [334]

KOOPERATIVNYI SBYT PRODUKTOV SEL'SKOGO KHOZIAISTVA V ROSSII / Evdokimov, Andrei Aandreevich – Khar'kov, 1911 – 2mf – 9 – COR-23/1 – ne IDC [334]

KOOPERATIVNYI URAL – (Missing: n1, 3-5) – Ekaterinburg, 1921 n1-8 – 2mf – 9 – COR-637/1 – ne IDC [334]

[/KOOPERATIVNYI/] VESTNIK NIZHEGORODSKOI SOIUZA UCHREZHDENII MELKOGO KREDITA – Nizhnyi Novgorod, 1914-18 – 15mf – 9 – COR-629/1 – ne IDC [334]

KOOPERATIVNYI ZAKON I PRIMERNYE USTAVY OBSHCHESTVA POTREBITELEI I SOIUZA POTREBITEL'SKIKH OBSHCHESTV – M., 1917 – 1mf – 9 – COR-50/1 – ne IDC [334]

KOOPERATIVY / Bragin, M & Minin, M – Spb., 1907 – 1mf – 9 – COR-11/1 – ne IDC [334]

KOOPERATIVY I SOTSIALIZM / Semkovskii, S M – Pg., [1917] – 1mf – 9 – COR-106/1 – ne IDC [334]

KOOPERATOR – Iaroslavl', 1926-29 n18 – 40mf – 9 – COR-641/1 – ne IDC [334]

KOOPERATOR – (Missing: 1921 n1-13. 1922 n2-3, 6-12(p1-64), 13-14. 1924 n19-22) – Kursk, 1921-25 n4 – 61mf – 9 – COR-638/1 – ne IDC [334]

KOOPERATOR – (Missing: 1921 n1-2, 5-6) – Nikolaev, 1921-22 n2 – 2mf – 9 – COR-639/1 – ne IDC [334]

KOOPERATOR – Tambov, 1922-23 – 6mf – 9 – COR-640/1 – ne IDC [334]

O KOOPERATSII / Kantor, M – M., L., 1927 – 2mf – 9 – COR-198/1 – ne IDC [334]

O KOOPERATSII / Tolstoi, Lev N et al – Spb., 1911 – 1mf – 9 – COR-79/1 – ne IDC [334]

KOOPERATSII. SVOD TRUDOV MESTNYKH KOMITETOV PO 49 GUBERNIIAM EVROPEISKOI ROSSII / Borodaevskii, S V – Spb., 1904 – 2mf – 9 – COR-51/1 – ne IDC [334]

KOOPERATSIIA / Korotkov, M A – L., 1925 – 2mf – 9 – COR-204/1 – ne IDC [334]

KOOPERATSIIA : KRAT. OCHERKI TEORII I ISTORII KOOP. DVIZHENIIA I ZADACH SOV. KOOP. / Medvedev, V V – M., 1930 – 2mf – 9 – COR-211/1 – ne IDC [334]

KOOPERATSIIA – (Missing: 1914 n2-end) – Moscow, 1914-15 n1 – 2mf – 9 – COR-642/1 – ne IDC [334]

KOOPERATSIIA / Nikolaev, A A – Ed 3. M., 1918 – 1mf – 9 – COR-215/1 – ne IDC [334]

KOOPERATSIIA : SBORNIK STAT'EI O POTREBITEL'SKOI, SEL'SKOKHOZIAISTVENNOI I KREDITNOI KOOPERATSII – Tula, 1923 – 2mf – 9 – COR-203/1 – ne IDC [334]

KOOPERATSIIA : O TOM, KAK SOOBSHCHA MOZHNO VYGODNEE USTRAIVAT' SVOI KHOZ. DELA / Nikolaev, A A – Ed 2, Spb., 1908 – 2mf – 9 – COR-77/1 – ne IDC [334]

KOOPERATSIIA : UKAZATEL' LITERATURY – Khar'kov, 1918 – 2mf – 9 – COR-534/1 – ne IDC [334]

KOOPERATSIIA BSSR – Minsk, 1927 – 4mf – 9 – COR-719/1 – ne IDC [310]

KOOPERATSIIA I AGRONOMIIA (SBORNIK STATEI) – M., 1919 – 1mf – 9 – COR-479/1 – ne IDC [334]

KOOPERATSIIA I BOR'BA S DOROGOVIZNOI / Totomiants, V F – M., 1916 – 1mf – 9 – COR-118/1 – ne IDC [334]

KOOPERATSIIA I GORODSKOE SAMOUPRAVLENIE : OPYT OBOSNOVANIIA MUNITSIPAL'NOI PROGRAMMY KOOPERATOROV / Ostrovskii, V V – Pg., 1919 – 5mf – 9 – COR-217/1 – ne IDC [334]

KOOPERATSIIA I GOSTORGOVLIA SEVERO-ZAPADNOI OBLASTI I SEVERA SSSR NA 1925 GOD – L., M – 5mf – 9 – COR-721/1 – ne IDC [310]

KOOPERATSIIA I OBORONA SSSR – M., 1928 – 1mf – 9 – COR-722/1 – ne IDC [334]

KOOPERATSIIA I PARTIIA / Kil'chevskii, V A – Pg., 1919 – 1mf – 9 – COR-155/1 – ne IDC [334]

KOOPERATSIIA I PRAVO : SBORNIK ZAKLIUCHENNII IURISKONSUL'TA MOSKOVSKOGO NARODNOGO BANKA / Kekuatov, K V – M., 1914 – 3mf – 9 – COR-46/1 – ne IDC [334]

KOOPERATSIIA I PROSVESHCHENIE / Suzdal'tsev, K K – M., 1915 – 1mf – 9 – COR-113/1 – ne IDC [334]

KOOPERATSIIA I REVOLIUTSIIA / Kil'chevskii, V A – M., 1917 – 1mf – 9 – COR-156/1 – ne IDC [334]

KOOPERATSIIA I REVOLIUTSIIA : OT STAROI K NOVOI KOOPERATSII / Shliapnikov, D D – Kazan', 1920 – 1mf – 9 – COR-192/1 – ne IDC [334]

KOOPERATSIIA I SHKOLA : SBORNIK STATEI – M., 1925 – 2mf – 9 – COR-258/1 – ne IDC [334]

KOOPERATSIIA I SOTSIALIZM / Nikolaev, A A – Pg., 1918 – 1mf – 9 – COR-175/1 – ne IDC [334]

KOOPERATSIIA I SOTSIALIZM : SBORNIK STATEI / Meshcheriakova, N L – M., 1920 – 2mf – 9 – COR-171/1 – ne IDC [334]

KOOPERATSIIA I VOLOGODSKOE ARTEL'NOE MASLODELIE / Stepanovskii, I K – Vologda, 1922 – 1mf – 9 – COR-449/1 – ne IDC [334]

KOOPERATSIIA I ZHIZN' – (Missing: 1918 n11) – Samara, 1918-19 n3 – 10mf – 9 – COR-643/1 – ne IDC [334]

KOOPERATSIIA K 15 S"EZDU VKP(B) – M., 1927 – 2mf – 9 – COR-724/1 – ne IDC [334]

KOOPERATSIIA K 15-MUS S"EZDU VKP(B) – M., [1927] – 2mf – 9 – COR-160/1 – ne IDC [334]

KOOPERATSIIA NA 14 KONFERENTSII ROSSIISKOI KOMMUNISTICHESKOI PARTII (BOL'SHEVIKOV) : DOKLAD A.I. RYKOVA, PRENIIA PO DOKLADU I RESHENIE KONFERENTSII – M., 1925 – 2mf – 9 – COR-161/1 – ne IDC [334]

KOOPERATSIIA SEVERA – (Missing: 1921 n1-2, 4. 1922 n2. 1923 n2-3) – Vologda, 1921-23 – 51mf – 9 – COR-644/1 – ne IDC [334]

KOOPERATSIIA SREDI SLAVIAN / Boradaevskii, S V – Spb., 1912 – 1mf – 9 – COR-10/1 – ne IDC [334]

KOOPERATSIIA S.S.S.R. NA VNESHNEM RYNKE V 1925 G. (V T SIFRAKH) / Barou, Noah – V Londone: Izd. Moskovskogo nar. banka limited, 1926 – 1 – CSUX89-B3483 – us Hoover Inst Photo [947]

KOOPERATSIIA V 1923-24 GODU I V 1924-25 GODU – M., 1928 – 3mf – 9 – COR-720/1 – ne IDC [310]

KOOPERATSIIA V DEREVNE / Miliutin, V – Ed.2. M., 1925 – 1mf – 9 – COR-492/1 – ne IDC [334]

KOOPERATSIIA V RUSSKOI DEREVNE / Totomiants, V F – M., 1912 – 5mf – 9 – COR-117/1 – ne IDC [334]

KOOPERATSIIA V SEL'SKOM KHOZIAISTVE / Kheisin, ML – L., 1924 – 1mf – 9 – COR-521/1 – ne IDC [334]

KOOPERATSIIA V SHKOLE : KHRESTOMATIINYI SBORNIK / ed by Iordanskii, N N – M., L., 1926 – 2mf – 9 – COR-257/1 – ne IDC [334]

KOOPERATSIIA V SHKOLE : PRAKT. UKAZANIIA PO USTROISTVU I VEDENIIU SHKOL'NOGO KOOPERATIVA V GORODSKIKH SHKOLAKH / Khizhniakov, V V – M., 1924 – 1mf – 9 – COR-280/1 – ne IDC [334]

KOOPERATSIIA V SISTEME SOVETSKOGO KHOZIAISTVA / Sarab'ianov, V N – M., L., 1926 – 1mf – 9 – COR-187/1 – ne IDC [334]

KOOPERATSIIA V SOIUZE SSR / Sevruk, P N – Ed 2. M., L., 1926 – 2mf – 9 – COR-274/1 – ne IDC [334]

KOOPERATSIIA V SOVETSKOI DEEREVNE / Tsingevatov, I A – Moscow, Leningrad, 1927 – 2mf – 9 – COR-524/1 – ne IDC [334]

KOOPERATSIIA V SOVETSKOI ROSSII / Meshcheriakova, N L – M., 1922 – 1mf – 9 – COR-170/1 – ne IDC [334]

KOOPERATSIIA V ZAPADNOI EVROPE I ROSSII : SKHEMA STROITEL'STVA (SERIIA "KOOPERATIVNAIA SHKOLA, VYP. III) / Fishgendler, Abram Markovich – M., 1923 – 1mf – 9 – COR-224/1 – ne IDC [334]

O KOOPERIROVANII I KREDITOVANII BEDNOTY V KUSTARNO-PROMYSLOVOI KOOPERATSII – Ed.2. M., [1928] – 1mf – 9 – COR-436/1 – ne IDC [334]

KOOPVAARDIJ EN VISSCHERIJ – London, UK. Jul/Aug 1942-Jan/Feb 1945 – 1 – uk British Libr Newspaper [072]

Koorders, SH *see*
- ATLAS DER BAUMARTEN VON JAVA...
- BIJDRAGEN TOT DE KENNIS DER BOOMSOORTEN VAN JAVA
- EXKURSIONSFLORA VON JAVA...
- FLORA VON TJIBODAS...
- SUPPLEMENT...FLORA VON N.O. CELEBES,...
- VERSLAG EENER BOTANISCHE DIENSTREIS DOOR DE MINAHASA

Koorders-Schumacher, A *see* SYSTEMATISCHES VERZEICHNIS...

KO-ORDINASI DALAM REPUBLIK INDONESIA / Sutomo – SE 10,242 1. 1953 – 9 – ne IDC [950]

KOOTENAY MINING STANDARD – Rossland, BC: Standard Pub. Co, [1898?-189- or 19–] – 9 – cn C.I.H.M. [622]

Kopease, State College, PA *see* BASIC DESIGN PROCESS AND VISUAL COMMUNICATION PRODUCTS

KOPENHAGISCHER POST-REUTER – Kopenhagen, Daenemark. 1703-04 (incomplete); 1713 (incomplete); 1715-16 (incomplete); 1719-1723 (incomplete); 1729-30 (incomplete) – 1 – gw Mikrofilm [072]

KOPERASI RAKJAT DESA (K.R.D.) PRIMER / Sunardhi Shs – SE 5459 1. 1961 – 9 – ne IDC [490]

Kopfstein, Marcus *see* DIE ASAPH-PSALMEN

KOPINGS TIDNING – Koping, Sweden. 1855-97 – 18r – 1 – sw Kungliga [072]

Kopp, Georg Ludwig Karl *see* IDEEN ZU DER ORGANISATION DER TEUTSCHEN KIRCHE

Koppius, F *see* VITAE AC GESTA ABBATUM ADWERDENSIUM

KOPTISCHE AKTEN ZUM EPHESINISCHEN KONZIL VON JAHRE 431 (T.U.U. 2-26/2) / Kraatz, W – Leipzig, 1904 – 4mf – 9 – ne Slangenburg [240]

KOPTISCHE MISCELLEN, 1-148 : SUBSIDIA BYZANTIA / Lemm, O von – Leipzig, 1972 – 18mf – 8 – ne Slangenburg [290]

DER KOPTISCHE TEXT DER KIRCHENORDNUNG HIPPOLYTS (T.U.U. 5-58) / Till, W & Leipoldt, J – Berlin, 1954 – 2mf – 9 – ne Slangenburg [240]

DIE KOPTISCHE UEBERSETZUNG DER VIER GROSSEN PROPHETEN / Schulte, Adalbert – Muenster i.W.: Aschendorff, 1892. 1 fiche – 9 – us A.T.L.A. [240]

DIE KOPTISCHEN QUELLEN ZUM KONZIL VON NICAEA / Haase, Felix – Paderborn, 1920 – 3mf – 8 – ne Slangenburg [290]

KOPTISCHES HANDWOERTERBUCH / Siegelberg, W – Heidelberg, 1921 – 5mf – ne IDC [470]

KOPTSKIE RUKOPISI GOSUDARSTVENNOI PUBLICHNOI BIBLIOTEKI IMENI M.E. SALTYKOVA-SHCHEDRINA / Elanskaia, A I – Leningrad, 1969.151p. BR-10,876/1 – 9 – ne IDC [010]

KOPTSKIE TEKSTY GOSUDARSTVENNOGO ERMITAZHA / Ernshtedt, P V – Moscow, Leningrad, 1959. 191p. BR-10,928/1 – 9 – ne IDC [240]

KOPTSKIE TEKSTY GOSUDARSTVENNOGO MUZEIA IZOBRAZITEL'NYKH ISKUSSTV IMENI A.S. PUSHKINA / Ernshtedt, P V – Leningrad, 1959. 215p. BR-11,029/1 – 9 – ne IDC [240]

DIE KORALLE – Berlin, 1933-36 – 1 – Dist. gw Mikrofilm – gw Misc Inst [640]

DIE KORALLTHIERE DES ROTHEN MEERES / Klunzinger, C B – 3v. Berlin. 1877-79. BZ-2246 1 – 9 – ne IDC [590]

KORAN. AL QURAAN DAN TERDJEMAHNJA – In Indonesian and Arabic. SE-6122 v.m1-3. c.1965 – 9 – ne IDC [260]

KORAN. AL;QURAN-UL-HAKIM, BESERTA TERDJEMAH DAN TAFSIRNJA – Indonesian and Arabic. SE-6947 1. v. 1-2 only. 1961 – 9 – ne IDC [260]

THE KORAN; COMMONLY CALLED THE ALCORAN OF MOHAMMED / Sale, G – 1 – uk Microform Academic [260]

KORAN. QURAAN SUTJI DJARWA DJAWI DALAH TAFSIRIPUN – SE-4149 1. 1958 – 9 – ne IDC [260]

KORAN. TAFSIR QURAEN – SE-10,320 1. 1963 – 9 – ne IDC [260]

KORANTA EA BECOANA – Mafikeng, South Africa. 1 Jan 1901-31 Dec 1904 – 2r – 1,16 diazo available – sa SA Libr [072]

KORDOFAN AND THE REGION TO THE WEST OF THE WHITE NILE / Sudan. Intelligence Department – London: H M Stationery Off, 1912 – us Res Libr [960]

KOREA BOOKMAN – 1920-25 – 1 – us UMI [073]

KOREA FIELD – 1901-1905 – 1 – us UMI [240]

KOREA FOR CHRIST / Davis, George Thompson Brown – New York: Fleming H Revell, c1910 – 1mf – 9 – 0-8370-6104-0 – 1986-0104 – us A.T.L.A. [240]

KOREA FROM ITS CAPITAL : WITH A CHAPTER ON MISSIONS / Gilmore, George W – Philadelphia: Presbyterian Board of Publication and Sabbath-school Work, c1892 – 1mf – us A.T.L.A. [950]

Korea. (Government-General of Chosen, 1910-45) *see* CHOSEN SOTOKUFU

KOREA HERALD – 1965- – 1 – us UMI [072]

KOREA IN TRANSITION / Gale, James Scarth – (Includes index and appendixes) – New York: Eaton & Mains; Cincinnati: Jennings & Graham, c1909 – 1mf – 9 – 0-8370-6186-5 – 1986-0186 – us A.T.L.A. [950]

Korea. Korean Educational Development Institute *see*
- DEVELOPMENT STRATEGIES IN EDUCATION TOWARD THE FUTURE INDUSTRIAL SOCIETY
- EDUCATIONAL INDICATORS IN KOREA 1988
- A RECOMMENDATION FOR THE REINFORCEMENT OF COMPUTER EDUCATION IN PRIMARY AND SECONDARY SCHOOLS
- A STUDY ON THE AUTONOMY OF EDUCATIONAL ADMINISTRATION
- A STUDY ON THE FIFTH REVISION OF THE GENERAL GUIDELINES OF THE KOREAN SCHOOL CURRICULUM
- A SURVEY OF THE ATTITUDES ON EDUCATION IN KOREA
- THINKING AND EDUCATION

KOREA MAGAZINE – 1917-1919 – 1 – us UMI [950]

KOREA METHODIST – Seoul. Korea. 1904-05 – 1 – us UMI [240]

KOREA MISSION FIELD – 1904-1940 – 1 – us UMI [240]

Korea. North *see* SEVEN-YEAR PLAN, 1961-1967

Korea (Republic). Presidential Commission on Economic Restructuring *see* REALIGNING KOREA'S NATIONAL PRIORITIES FOR ECONOMIC ADVANCE

KOREA REVIEW – 1901-1906 – 1 – us UMI [950]

Korea. South *see*
- THE SECOND FIVE-YEAR ECONOMIC DEVELOPMENT PLAN, 1967-1971
- THE SECOND FIVE-YEAR PLAN FOR DEVELOPMENT OF SCIENCE AND TECHNOLOGY, 1967-1971
- THIRD FIVE-YEAR ECONOMIC DEVELOPMENT PLAN 1972-1976

Korea. South. Economic Development Council *see* THREE-YEAR ECONOMIC DEVELOPMENT PLAN (1960-1962)

Korea. South. Economic Planning Board *see*
- DRAFT FIRST FIVE-YEAR ECONOMIC PLAN, 1962-1966
- FIRST FIVE-YEAR ECONOMIC DEVELOPMENT PLAN (1962-1966), ADJUSTED VERSION
- FIRST FIVE-YEAR PLAN FOR TECHNICAL DEVELOPMENT SUPPLEMENT TO FIRST FIVE-YEAR ECONOMIC PLAN
- OVERALL RESOURCES BUDGET: 1969. SECOND FIVE-YEAR ECONOMIC DEVELOPMENT PLAN
- OVERALL RESOURCES BUDGET FOR 1971. THE TERMINAL YEAR OF THE SECOND FIVE YEAR DEVELOPMENT PLAN
- SUMMARY OF THE FIRST FIVE-YEAR ECONOMIC PLAN, 1962-1966

Korea. (Territory under U.S. Occupation, 1945-). Military Governor *see* HISTORY OF THE U.S. ARMY MILITARY GOVERNMENT IN KOREA, SEP 1945-30 JUN 1946

Korea. (Territory under U.S. Occupation, 1945-1948). Military Governor *see* MISCELLANEOUS ORDERS, APPOINTMENTS, ETC

KOREA TIMES – Los Angeles, CA. 1970 – 284+ r – 1 – $14,200.00 ($590.00y) – H03302 – us Library Micro [071]

THE KOREA TIMES – Seoul, jan 3 1956- – us Res Libr [072]

KOREA TIMES (EN ENGLAIS) – 1956-1995 – 12 times per yr – 1 – F1,978.00 – sz Infoprint [072]

KOREAN ARMISTICE NEGOTIATIONS, 1951-53 / United Nations Command – 11 rolls. T1152 – 1 – us Nat'l Archives [977]

KOREAN GOVERNOR-GENERAL'S OFFICIAL GAZETTE – (Suppl to Meiji & Taisho Era) – 1910-45 – 1 – us Ross [950]

THE KOREAN METHODIST – 1937-38 (incomplete) – 1r – 1 – ATLA S0717B – us A.T.L.A. [073]

KOREAN MILITARY ARMISTICE CONFERENCE DOCUMENTS / United Nations Command – Panmunjon, 1951-53 – 1 – $35.00r – us Hoover Inst Photo [950]

THE KOREAN NATIONAL HERALD – (Library has: no.1-2,4,6-48,50,101-153; Jan.21, 1942-Jan. 31, 1945) – Honolulu: Korean National Association of Hawaii, 1942- – 1 – CSUX86-S199 – us Hoover Inst Photo [950]

THE KOREAN PACIFIC WEEKLY-NATIONAL HERALD *see* THE KOREAN NATIONAL HERALD

KOREAN REPOSITORY – 1892; 1895-1898 – 1 – us UMI [950]

KOREAN REPOSITORY – (Missing: 1892 v1(1-2, 10-12); 1896 v3(7)) – Seoul, 1892, 1895-1898 – 42mf – 9 – ne IDC [950]

KOREAN REPOSITORY – v1-5. 1892-98 (complete) – 1r – 1 – ATLA S0058 – us A.T.L.A. [240]

KOREAN REPUBLIC – 1953-1965 – 1 – us UMI [072]

THE KOREAN SITUATION; THE KOREAN SITUATION NO. 2 / Federal Council of the Churches of Christ in America – 1919, 1920 – 1 – $50.00 – us Presbyterian [240]

KOREAN SKETCHES / Gale, James Scarth – Chicago: Fleming H Revell, c1898 – 1mf – 9 – 0-8370-6048-6 – 1986-0048 – us A.T.L.A. [950]

KOREAN TREATIES / Chung, H – New York, 1919 – 3mf – 1 – ILM-1700/1 – ne IDC [327]

KOREAN WAR STUDIES AND AFTER-ACTION REPORTS – $2,110.00 – 1-55655-125-8 – us UPA [950]

DER KOREN PLAN. DAS WIRTSCHAFTSPOLITISCHE KONZEPT DER BUNDESREGIERUNG / Austria. Bundesministerium fuer Finanzen – (The Koren Plan. The Economic Conceptions of the Federal Government). Wien. 1968. BD-1612 1 – 9 – ne IDC [338]

Koresec, V *see* HETHITISCHE STAATSVERTRAEGE

Koretskii, V M *see* "OBSHCHIE PRINTSIPY PRAVA" V MEZHDUNARODNOM PRAVE

Korevo, N N *see* OB IZDANIIAKH ZAKONOV ROSSIISKOI IMPERII 1830-1917

Korff, Hermann August *see*
- GEIST DER GOETHEZEIT
- GOETHES DEUTSCHE SENDUNG

Korff, Sergei Aleksandrovich *see* DVORIANSTVO I EGO SOSLOVNOE UPRAVLENIE ZA STOLIETIE 1762-1855 GODOV

KORIFEI ILI KLIUCH' LITERATURY – v. 1-11. Spb. 1802-07. B-1450 2 – 8 – ne IDC [460]

DIE KORINTHER-BRIEFE / Kling, Christian Friedrich – Bielefeld: Velhagen & Klasing, 1865. 1 fiche – 9 – us A.T.L.A. [240]

Korkunov, N M *see* GENERAL THEORY OF LAW

KORMCHIIA ZVEZDY / Ivanov, V – Kniga liriki. Spb. 1903. BR-735 2 – 8 – ne IDC [460]

THE KORN COLLECTION – (Includes a printed guide) – 1,594mf – 9 – ne IDC [350]

Korn, Heinz *see* GEHETZT UEBERS MEER

Korn, Karl *see* IN DER STILLE

Korn, Victor Emanuel *see* MANUSCRIPT COLLECTION

Kornatovskii, N *see* KRONSHTADSKII MIATEZH

Korneva, II *see* ISTORIIA ARKHEOGRAFII V DOREVOLIUTSIONNOI ROSSII

DER KORNGARTEN CODE : DIE ERFOLGSFORMEL FUER DIE ZUKUNFT / Schuermeyer, Manfred – 1993 – 2mf – 9 – DM80.00 – 3-89349-812-5 – gw Hänsel [330]

Kornilov, A A *see* OCHERKI PO ISTORII OBSHCHESTVENNAGO DVIZHENIIA I KREST'IANSKAGO DELA V ROSSII

KORNILOVSHCHINA / Chaadaeva, O N – Moskva: Molodai a gvardii a, 1930 – 1 – CSUX88-B4667 – us Hoover Inst Photo [947]

KORNWESTHEIMER ZEITUNG – Kornwestheim, Germany. 2 Jan 1909-31 Mar 1943 – 18r – 1 – gw Mikrofilm [072]

KOROIT BOROUGH COUNCIL MINUTE BOOKS – 1870-1985. KB1-8 – 8r – 1 – at Corangamite [910]

KOROIT BOROUGH COUNCIL RATE BOOKS – 1871-1983. 1901-6;8;11-13. KBR1-5 – 5r – 1 – at Corangamite [910]

KOROIT BOROUGH WATERWORKS – 1889-1983. KBWT1-3 – 3r – 1 – at Corangamite [910]

KOROIT HERALD – 1878-1886. KH1-6 – 6r – 1 – at Corangamite [072]

KOROIT SENTINEL – 1921-1941. KS1-7 – 7r – 1 – at Corangamite [072]

Korolenko, Vladimir G *see* OPIS DOKUMENTAL'NYKH MATERIALOV LICHNOGO FONDA NO.234

KOROLEVNA I RYTSARI / Belyi, A – Skazki. 1919. BR-565 2 – 8 – ne IDC [460]

KORONG VALE LANCE – Korong Vale, Australia. 10 Jan 1903-9 Jun 1906.-w. 2 1-2 reels – 1 – uk British Libr Newspaper [072]

KOROT HA-ITTIM / Mendel, Menahem (b. Aaron of Kamenets) – Vilna. 1840. BJ-27-53 1 – 9 – ne IDC [956]

Korotkov, M A *see*
- KOOPERATSIIA
- OCHERKI PO ISTORII RUSSKOI KOOPERATSII

KORREKTUREN ZUR BISHERIGEN ERKLAERUNG DES ROEMERBRIEFES / Klostermann, August – Gotha: Friedrich Andreas Perthes, 1881 – 1mf – 9 – 0-8370-9707-X – 1986-3707 – us A.T.L.A. [220]

DER KORRESPONDENT FUER DEUTSCHLANDS BUCHDRUCKER UND SCHRIFTGIESSER – Leipzig, Germany. 1875-1907 – 4r – 1 – gw Mikrofilm [072]

DER KORRESPONDENT VON UND FUER DEUTSCHLAND – Nuernberg. 1848-49 – 5r – 1 – gw Mikrofilm [072]

KORRESPONDENZ DER DEUTSCHNATIONALEN VOLKSPARTEI – Berlin, 1924 – 1 – Dist. gw Mikrofilm – gw Misc Inst [943]

KORRESPONDENZ DES REICHSVERBANDES GEGEN DIE SOZIALDEMOKRATIE – Berlin, 1907 n24-1909 – 1 – Dist. gw Mikrofilm – gw Misc Inst [943]

KORRESPONDENZBLATT – Berlin, 1905-25, 1927-30, 1933-39 (all incomplete) – 1 – Dist. gw Mikrofilm – gw Misc Inst [072]

KORRESPONDENZBLATT : FUER DIE MITGLIEDER DES GEWERKSCHAFTSBUNDES IN BONN-STADT UND BONN-LAND – Bonn, 16 Mar-15 Jun 1946 – 1r – 1 – DM75.00 – gw Mikro Press [072]

KORRESPONDENZBLATT / Verein zur Gruendung und Erhaltung einer Akademie fuer die Wissenschaft des Judenthums – Frankfurt a.M., Berlin. v1-11. 1920-30. Complete. B381 (Leo Baeck Institute. German-Jewish Periodicals, Pt 2) – 1r – 1 – $75.00 – us UPA [270]

KORRESPONDENZBLATT.. / Allgemeiner deutscher Gewerkschaftsbund – Berlin. v7-21, 23-25, 28, 33-36, 38-40. 1897-1930. Many incomplete. (Serial publications of German trade unions in the Memorial Library, University of Wisconsin-Madison) – 1 – us U.W. Library [073]

KORRESPONDENZ-BLATT DES VERBANDES DER DEUTSCHEN JUDEN – Berlin. nos. 1-14. 1908-1914. Complete. B375. (Leo Baeck Institute. German-Jewish Periodicals, Pt 1) – 1r – 1 – $75.00 – us UPA [270]

KORRESPONDENZ-BLATT DES VERBANDES DER DEUTSCHEN JUDEN – Berlin, oct 1907, may 1908-jun 1914 – 1r – 1 – Dist. gw Mikrofilm – gw Misc Inst [943]

KORRESPONDENZBLATT DES VEREINS FUER NIEDERDEUTSCHE SPRACHFORSCHUNG / Verein fuer Niederdeutsche Sprachforschung – Hamburg. v1-68 1876-1961. Film Mas C 617 – 1 – us H.U. Library [430]

KORRESPONDENZBLATT FUER DIE MITGLIEDER DES GEWERKSCHAFTSBUNDES IN BONN-STADT UND BONN-LAND – Bonn, mar 16-jun 15 1946 – 1r – 1 – Inquire at Mikrofilmarchiv for details – gw Misc Inst [331]

KORRESPONDENZBLATT FUER DIE MITGLIEDER DES GEWERKSCHAFTSBUNDES IN BONN-STADT UND BONN-LAND – Bonn, West Germany. 16 Mar-15 Jun 1946 – 1r – 1 – gw Mikrofilm [072]

Korsakov, D A *see*
- IZ ZHIZNI RUSSKIKH DEIATELEI 18 VEKA
- VOTSARENIE IMPERATRITSY ANNY IOANNANOVNY

Korsakov, P *see*
- MAIAK SOVREMENNOGO PROSVESHCHENIIA I OBRAZOVANNOSTI

Korsakov, V V *see* V PROSNUVSHEMSIIA KITAE

Korsh, V F *see* ETIUDY

Korsikov, O A *see* VOLVOCINEAE

KORT BEGRYP DER ZANG KUN IN DE LATIJNSCHE TAAL BESCHREVEN EN VAN J.H. GLAZEMAKER VERTAALT / Descartes, Rene – P 235. 1661 – 9 – ne IDC [950]

KORT EN GRONDIG ONDERWYS VAN DE TRANSPOSITIE BENEFFENS EENIGE KORTE AENMERKINGEN OVER DE MUSIEK DER OUDEN / Fischer, J P A – Utrecht. Willem Stouw. 1728. BP-269 1 – 9 – ne IDC [780]

KORT SANGH-BERICHT OP ZYNE ZIELROERENDE ZANGEN / Ban, J A – P 148. 1643 – 9 – ne IDC [780]

KORT UNDERRAETTELSE OM SKANDINAVISKA INSEKTERS ALLMAENNARE SKADA OCH NYTTA I HUSHALLNINGEN / Dahlbom, A G – Lund, 1837. vi, xxxvi, 340, xiip. 2pls. Z-1168 2 – 8 – ne IDC [590]

KORT VERSLAG VAN DE HANDELSVEREENIGING TE SOERABAIA – (In English and Dutch) – 1948-1956 – 28mf – 9 – ne IDC [380]

Korte, August *see* DIE KONZILSPOLITIK KARLS 5 IN DEN JAHREN 1538-1543

KORTE BERICHTEN – (Title varies) – nos 1-4,6. 1935-38 (complete) – 1r – 1 – ATLA S0712 – us A.T.L.A. [073]

EEN KORTE EN KLARE INSTRUCTIE OFTE ONDERWYSINGHE DER MUSYCKE / Domeslius, P – Amsterdam. 1648. BP-242 1 – 9 – ne IDC [780]

KORTE EN NOODIGSTE GRONDREGELEN VAN DE BASSUS-CONTINUUS / Fischer, J P A – Utrecht. Willem Stouw. 1731. BP-268 1 – 9 – ne IDC [780]

KORTE VERHANDELING OVER HET ZINGEN EN SPEELEN IN DE HERVORMDE KERK VAN NEDERLAND.. / Beyen, Petrus – 1790 – 9 – us Sibley [780]

KORTFATTAD REDOGORELSE OVER ARBETET, DESS ORGANISATION OCH UTVECKLING SAMT RAPPORT FRAN KOMMITTENS REVISORER / Svenska Hjaelpkommitten for Spanien – Stockholm, 1937 – 9 – us H.U. College Libr [946]

Korthals, PW *see* VERHANDELINGEN OVER DE NATUURLIJKE GESCHIEDENIS DER NEDERLANDSCHE OVERZEESCHE BEZITTINGEN,...

Kortum, Karl Arnold *see* LEBEN, MEYNUNGEN UND THATEN VON HIERONIMUS JOBS DEM KANDIDATEN, UND WIE ER SICH WEILAND VIEL RUHM ERWARB AUCH ENDLICH ALS NACHTSWAECHTER ZU SULZBURG STARB

Kortunov, OP *see* BIBLIOGRAFIIA OBSHCHESTVENNOI-POLITICHESKOI LITERATURY

Korzon, R *see* DZIEJE WOJEN I WOJSKOWOSCI W POLSCE

Korzon, T *see* WEWNETRZNE DZIEJE POLSKI ZA STANISLAWA AUGUSTA, 1764-1794

Kosch, Wilhelm *see* OESTERREICH IM DICHTEN UND DENKEN GRILLPARZERS

Koschaker, P *see* HAMMURABI'S GESETZ

Koschmieder, Arthur *see* HERDERS THEORETISCHE STELLUNG ZUM DRAMA

Kosciusko, Mississippi *see* MISCELLANEOUS EARLY NEWSPAPERS

KOSCIUSKO UNION – Warsaw. Ind. 1915-1919 – 1 – us UMI [071]

KOSHELEK – Satiricheskii zhurnal 1774. Novoe izd. v. 1. M. 1852. BR-3197 2 – 8 – ne IDC [073]

Koskolou, Maria D *see* ARTERIAL HYPOXEMIA AND PERFORMANCE DURING INTENSE EXERCISE

Koskull, Harald, Baron von *see* WIELANDS AUFSAETZE UEBER DIE FRANZOESISCHE REVOLUTION

DIE KOSMOGRAPHIE IN ARIOSTS ORLANDO FURIOSO / Strauch, Alfons – Bonn, 1918 – 1mf – DM48.00 – 3-8267-3058-5 – gw Hänsel [520]

KOSMOPOLIS – Ezhemesiachnyi mezhdunarodnyi zhurnal. Russkii otdel. Spb. 1897-98. BR-3196 2 – 8 – ne IDC [073]

KOSMORAMA – Copenhagen, 1954-93. Continued annually – 1 – £650.00 – uk World [790]

KOSMOS – (Cont: V.P. Journal) – Cobourg, Ont: Science Association of Victoria University, [1885-1886] – 9 – cn C.I.H.M. [500]

KOSMOS *see* VP JOURNAL

KOSMOS. ENTWURF EINER PHYSISCHEN WELTBESCHREIBUNG / Humboldt, Alexander von – Stuttgart, Tuebingen, 1845-1862. 5 vols. atlas. B-2533 2 – 8 – ne IDC [520]

KOSOVA – (No. 1577 (15 Temmuz 1325[1909])) – Skopje, Yugoslavia, 1877-? – 1mf – 9 – $10.00 – us MEDOC [949]

KOSRAE DISTRICT CHARTER, 1978 : AS APPROVED BY THE SEVENTH CONGRESS OF MICRONESIA / Federated States of Micronesia – 2nd reg sess. Saipan: the Congress, 14 Feb 1978 – 2mf – 9 – $3.00 – LLMC 82-100H Title 3 – us L.L.M.C. [324]

KOSSUTH COUNTY ADVANCE – Algona. Iowa. -w. 1951- – 1 – us UMI [071]

Kossuth, Lajos *see* MEMORIES OF MY EXILE

Kosteletzky, V F *see* ALLGEMEINE MEDIZINISCH-PHARMAZEUTISCHE FLORA,...

KOSTER / Gumilev, Nikolai Sepanovich – Stikhi. Ed. 2. Spb. 1922. BR-1143 2 – 8 – ne IDC [460]

KOSTER / Gumilev, Nikolai Sepanovich – Stikhi. Spb. 1918. BR-3729 2 – 8 – ne IDC [460]

Koster, Henry *see*
- TRAVELS IN BRAZIL IN THE YEARS 1809 TO 1815
- VIAGENS AO NORDESTE DO BRASIL

Kostermans, Andre Joseph Guillaume Henri *see* A MONOGRAPH OF THE GENUS HERITIERA DRY (STERCULIACEAE). INC. ARGYRODENDRON F.V.M. AND TARRIETIA BL

KOSTNICKE JISKRY – Prague, Czechoslovakia. -w. May 1949-Dec 1970. Imperfect. 6 reels – 1 – uk British Libr Newspaper [072]

Kostov, T *see* THE TRIAL OF TRAIECHO KOSTOV AND HIS GROUP

Kostrikin, V I et al *see* KRATKII SLOVAR' ARKHIVNOI TERMINOLOGII

KOSTROMSKAI A GUBERNII A V T SIFRAKH : KOSTROMSKO I GUBISPOLKOM, GUBERNSKOE STATISTICHESKOE BI URO – (Includes c.1: 1923/1924) – Kostroma: [Bi uro], 1925- – 1 – CSUXAKY6526-S – us Hoover Inst Photo [947]

KOSTROMSKIIA GUBERNSKIIA VIEDOMOSTI / Russia – 1838-51, 1894-1906 – 1 – $388.00 – us L of C Photodup [947]

KOSTROMSKOI KOOPERATOR – (Missing: 1913 n10. 1914-15) – Kostroma, 1913-17 n3 – 8mf – 9 – COR-645/1 – ne IDC [334]

Kostrzewa, Frank *see*
- DIE AKTUELLE WEITERENTWICKLUNG IN DER ANLAGE-UMWELTDEBATTE DER INTELLIGENZ
- ELEMENTE DESKRIPTIVER UND INFERENTIELLER STATISTIK UND IHRE VORLAEUFER
- ERNEST HEMINGWAY'S "NOW I LAY ME" UND "SOLDIER'S HOME"
- MERKMALE VERSTEHENS- UND BEHALTENSFOERDERNDER KONTEXTUELLER BEDEUTUNGSERKLAERUNGEN
- UNTERRICHT FUER SPAETAUSGESIEDELTE KINDER UND JUGENDLICHE

Kosygin, A *see*
- DIRECTIVES FOR THE FIVE YEAR PLAN FOR ECONOMIC DEVELOPMENT OF THE USSR FOR 1966-1970
- DIRECTIVES OF THE FIVE YEAR ECONOMIC DEVELOPMENT PLAN OF THE USSR FOR 1971-1975

Kot, Elizabeth G *see*
- CALIFORNIA CEMETRY INSCRIPTION SOURCES
- MISSOURI CEMETRY INSCRIPTION SOURCES

KOTA BESAR MALANG. THE INNERSIDE OF MALANG AND ITS ENVIRONS – SE-10,032 1. 1955 – 9 – ne IDC [950]

Kotarski, Mark *see* AN EVALUATION OF A HOME-BASED EXERCISE PROGRAM INVOLVING NON-EXERTIONAL HYPOXEMIC AND EXERTIONAL HYPOXEMIC CHRONIC OBSTRUCTIVE PULMONARY DISEASED PATIENTS

Kotei, S I A *see* BOOK TODAY IN AFRICA

Kotel'nikov, K G *see* KREST'IANSKOE DVIZHENIE V 1917 GODU

Kotenev, A L *see*
- SHANGHAI. ITS MIXED COURT AND COUNCIL
- SHANGHAI. ITS MUNICIPALITY AND THE CHINESE

KOTIA KOHTI – 1934-41 (complete) – 1r – 1 – ATLA S0694 – us A.T.L.A. [073]

Kotik, J *see* MAYNE ZIKHROYNES

KOTIK LETAEV. ROMAN / Belyi, A – Izd. Epokha. Spb. 1922. BR-566 2 – 8 – ne IDC [460]

KOTIMAA – (Lacking: 1973-74. 1977-79) – 1971-92 – Inquire – 1 – ATLA S0275 – us A.T.L.A. [073]

Kotkov, K *see* REVOLIUTSIIA 1905-1907 GODOV NA TERRITORII MORDOVII

Kotkylides, K M *see* AI PARA TON IORDANENS LAURAI KALAMOONOS KAI AGIOU GERASIMOU...

Kotliarevskii, S A *see* IURIDICHESKIE PREDPOSYLKI RUSSKIKH OSNOVNYKH ZAKONOV

KOTOBA NO TEBIKI : NIPPON-MELAJOE-DJAWA-SOENDA-MADOERA – Djakarta, 2603. 200p – 90-92mf – 9 – ne IDC [950]

Kotschy, T *see*
- ANALECTA BOTANICA
- DER LIBANON UND SEINE ALPENFLORA
- PLANTAE ARABIAE IN DITIONIBUS HEDSCHAS

Kottinger, Hermann Marcus *see* THE YOUTH'S LIBERAL GUIDE FOR THEIR MORAL CULTURE AND RELIGIOUS ENLIGHTENMENT

Kottje, R *see* KIRCHENGESCHICHTE HEUTE

Kotvich, V L *see*
- KALMYTSKIIA ZAGADKI I POSLOVITSY
- RUSSKIE ARKHIVNYE DOKUMENTY PO SNOSHENIIAM S OIRATAMI V 17 I 18 VV. IAN

Kotyska, Vaclav *see* UPLNY MISTOPISNY SLOVNIK KRALOVSTFI CESKEHO.

Kotzebue *see* MISANTHROPIE ET REPENTIR

Kotzebue, August von *see*
- DIE BIENE, 1808-1810
- ERHEITERUNGEN, 1811-1827
- DER FREIMUETHIGE, 1804-1811
- FUER GEIST UND HERZ, 1786
- DIE GRILLE, 1811-1812
- HEKATE, 1823
- LITERARISCHES WOCHENBLATT, 1818-1820
- LITTERARISCHES WOCHENBLATT
- POLITISCHE FLUGBLAETTER, 1814-1816
- ZWISCHEN POLEMIK UND KRITIK

KOTZEBUE IN ENGLAND : EIN BEITRAG ZUR GESCHICHTE DER ENGLISCHEN BUEHNE UND DER BEZIEHUNGEN DER DEUTSCHEN LITTERATUR ZUR ENGLISCHEN / Sellier, Walter – (Includes bibliographical references) – [S.l.: s.n.] 1901 (Leipzig: Druck von O. Schmidt) – 1r – 1 – us U.W. Library [430]

Kouban Hafezi, S *see* YAZD, FACE A LA "MODERNISATION" (IRAN)

KOUBE SHIMBUN – July 1900-Dec 1994 – 961r – 1 – Y11,658,000 – ja Japan Micro [072]

KOUMINTANG PARTY ORGANS AND NATIONALIST CHINESE GOVERNMENT GAZETTES, PRE-1949 – Nov 1919-45. 16 titles – 1 – 160.00 – us L of C Photodup [950]

THE KOURIER – Willow Creek, CA. 1967- – 17+ r – 1 – $850.00 ($50.00y) – B03104 – us Library Micro [071]

Kovalenskii *see* MOSKVA

Kovalenskii, Mikhail N *see* RUSSKAIA REVOLIUTSIIA V SUDEBNYKH PROTSESSAKH I MEMUARAKH

Kovalyov, L *see* MOSKVA

Kovatch-McMillan-Botkin Family *see* PAPERS

KOVEZ AL YAD – (Sefer ha-Asif). Berlin. Jerusalem. 1885-1903. BJ-100-181 1 – 9 – ne IDC [290]

KOVEZ HA-HEVRAH LA-HARIKAT – Erez-Yisra'el ve-Attikoteha. 4 v. Jerusalem. 1921-45. BJ-91-52 1 – 9 – ne IDC [956]

KOVEZ LE-ZIKHRO SHEL GEDALYAH UNNA / Unna, G – Kibbutz Rodges. 1940. BJ-100-85 1 – 9 – ne IDC [956]

KOVEZ MADDA'I LE-ZEKHER MOSHEH SCHORR / Schorr, M – New York. 1945. BJ-100-86 1 – 9 – ne IDC [900]

Kovner, A H *see* KOL KITVEI

KOVODELNIK – Prague, Czechoslovakia. Mar 1936-May 1938 (incomplete) – 1r – 1 – us L of C Photodup [072]

KOVSH – Leningrad. v. 1-4. 1925-1926 – 1 – us NY Public [073]

KOVYL'NYE VOINY – Joinville le Pont. (Organ of the Kalmuck national organization "Khalmsk tangachin tuk".) Nov. 1930-Feb. 1936, nos. 1-9, 11-15 – 1 – 35.00r – us Hoover Inst Photo [335]

Kowalski, Ellen M *see* MODELING AND MOTOR SEQUENCING STRATEGIES OF LEARNING DISABLED BOYS

Kowalski, T *see* KARAIMISCHE TEXTE IM DIALEKT VON TROKI

Kowan, Theodor Ira *see* THE LEGAL STENOGRAPHER

KOZA, KORMLENIE I UKHOD ZA NEI U / Barabanshchikova, V – Penza: [Izdatelskoe otdelenie Penzenskogo gub. zemelnogo otdela], 1920 – 1 – CSUX91-B3013 – us Hoover Inst Photo [999]

KOZAT SKY I VISTNYK 92 *see* KAZACHI I VESTNIK

Kozeluch, L *see*
- QUARTETS, STRING, OP. 32
- TROIS QUATUORS CONCERTANS POUR DEUX VIOLONS, ALTO ET BASSE

Kozhanyi, P M *see*
- RABOCHAIA KOOPERATSIIA I PROFSOIUZY
- RABOCHAIA KOOPERATSIIA ZA 10 LET SOVETSKOI VLASTI

KOZHEVENNO OBUVNAIA PROMYSHLENNOST' SSSR – (Leather and Shoe Industry of the USSR, 1922-40 and Leather and Shoe Industry; a Scientific-Technical and Production Journal, 1959-62) – 1 – 168.00 – us L of C Photodup [947]

KOZIGAZGATASI DONTVENYTAR. – Budapest. On film: v1-19; 1908-28. LL-0265 – 1 – us L of C Photodup [340]

Kozlov, K *see* RUSSKIE PISATELI POSLE GOGOLIA V OTZYVAKH KRITIKI

Kozlovskii, I *see* SIL'VESTR MEDVEDEV

Kozman, Fr. *see* TEXTES LEGITATIFS TOUCHANT LE CENOBITISME EGYPTIEN

Kozmenko, A S *see* UKAZATEL' LITERATURY PO ESTESTVENNO-ISTORICHESKOMU IZUCHENIIU TUL'SKOI GUBERNII

Koz'min, B *see* PISATELI SOVREMENNOI EPOKHI

Kozubskii, E *see* UKAZATEL' K 1-20 VYPUSKAM "SBORNIKA MATERIALOV DLIA OPISANIIA MESTNOSTEI I IMEN KAVKAZA". 1881-1894 G

KP der Schweiz *see* DER KOMMUNIST

K.P. POBEDONOSZEWS SAMMLUNG MOSKOWITISCHER STUDIEN UEBER DAS...LEBEN DER GEGENWART / Pobedonoszew, K P – Dresden: E. Pierson, 1902. 1 fiche – 9 – us A.T.L.A. [290]

THE KPELLE LANGUAGE IN LIBERIA: GRAMATICAL OUTLINE, COLLOQUIAL SENTENCES AND VOCABULARY / Westermann, Diedrich & Melzian, H J – Berlin. 1930. BA-596 2 – 8 – ne IDC [490]

KPL BULLETIN QUOTIDIEN : FRENCH-LANGUAGE DAILY NEWS SUMMARY – (Jul 1975-Dec 1975 $75.00v; Jan 1976-Dec 1986 $150.00y) – Vientiane, Laos. Mimeograph format – 1 – us Asia Libr [950]

KPL NEWS BULLETIN : ENGLISH-LANGUAGE DIALY NEWS SUMMARY – Vientiane, Laos. Jul 1984-Dec 1984. Mimeograph format – 1 – $75.00v – us Asia Libr [950]

KPOZNANII U KHARAKTERA GRAZHDANSKOI VOINY : BUNT V 5-M SI EVERNOM STRIELKOVOM POLKU 20 -II ULI A 1919 GODA / Aleksandrovich, V – Bielgrad: Russkai a tip., 1926 – 1 – CSUX89-B2711 – us Hoover Inst Photo [947]

KPR 1967- *see* KULTURNO-PROSVETITELNAI A RABOTA

KQCY TIMES – Quincy, CA. 1963 – 1r – 1 – $50.00 – B03638 – us Library Micro [071]

Kra, P *see* RELIGION IN MONTESQUIEU'S 'LETTRES PERSANES'

Kraatz, DB *see* IRRIGATION CANAL LINING

Kraatz, G *see* ENTOMOLOGISCHE MONATSBLAETTER

Kraatz, W *see* KOPTISCHE AKTEN ZUM EPHESINISCHEN KONZIL VON JAHRE 431 (T.U.U. 2-26/2)

Krabbe, G *see* ENTWICKLUNGSGESCHICHTE UND MORPHOLOGIE DER POLYMORPHEN FLECHTENGATTUNG CLADONIA

DE KRACHT VAN BUITENLANDSCHE VONNISSEN / Fresemann, Vietor, J – Groningen, 1865 – 4mf – 1 – ILM-2081/1 – ne IDC [327]

DEKRACHT VAN BUITENLANDSCHE VONNISSEN... / Ham, M G T van den – Utrecht, 1890 – 3mf – 1 – ILM-2036/1 – ne IDC [327]

Krack, Otto *see* GRABBE

DIE KRAEHEN : NOVELLEN / Stehr, Hermann – Berlin: S Fischer, 1921 – 1 – us U.W. Library [830]

Kraeling, C H *see* JOHN THE BAPTIST

Kraemer, Christoph *see* DAS STATIONAERE KRANKENGUT DES JAHRES 1988 DER UNIVERSITAETSKLINIKEN FUER KINDER- UND JUGENDPSYCHIATRIE LUEBECK UND KINDERNEUROPSYCHIATRIE ROSTOCK – EINE VERGLEICHENDE ANALYSIERENDE STUDIE

Kraemer, Gerhard *see* DIE ROEMISCH-BAROCKE STILKOMPONENTE IM WERK PETER ANTON VON VERSCHAFFELTS

Kraemer, Henry *see* SCIENTIFIC AND APPLIED PHARMACOGNOSY, INTENDED FOR THE USE OF STUDENTS IN PHARMACY,...PHARMACISTS,...FOOD AND DRUG ANALYSTS...PHARMACOLOGISTS

Kraemer, Michael *see* DIE UEBERLIEFERUNGSGESCHICHTE DER BERGPREDIGT

Kraemer, Wilhelm *see* SAEMTLICHE WERKE

Kraenzlein, Kurt *see* DAS KIND DER MADELEINE MONTCORNET

Kraetzschmar, Richard *see* DIE BUNDESVORSTELLUNG IM ALTEN TESTAMENT IN IHRER GESCHICHTLICHEN ENTWICKELUNG

Kraeutlein, Jonathan *see* DIE SPRACHLICHEN VERSCHIEDENHEITEN IN DEN HEXATEUCHQUELLEN

Kraevskij, V V *see* THEORY OF CURRICULUM CONTENT IN THE USSR

Krafft, H *see* DIE SOZIALE UND PRAKTISCHE WEISHEIT DER SPRUECHE SALOMOS: VORTRAG

Krafft, Jean Charles *see* RECUEIL D'ARCHITECTURE CIVILE.

Krafft, Johann Karl *see* PLANS, COUPES, ELEVATIONS DES PLUS BELLES MAISONS ET DES HOTELS CONSTRUITS A PARIS ET DANS LES ENVIRONS

Krafft, Wilhelm *see* DIE DEUTSCHE BIBEL VOR LUTHER

DER KRAFT-MAYR : EIN HUMORISTISCHER MUSIKANTEN-ROMAN / Wolzogen, Ernst von – Berlin: J Singer, [1933] – 1r – 1 – us U.W. Library [870]

DER KRAFT-MAYR : EIN HUMORISTISCHER MUSIKANTEN-ROMAN / Wolzogen, Ernst von – Stuttgart: J Engelhorn. 2v in 1. [1897?] – 1 – us U.W. Library [830]

Kragh, Karsten *see* CONTRIBUTORY NEGLIGENCE. A COMPARATIVE STUDY OF THE LAW OF TORTS (U.S.A., ENGLAND AND DENMARK)

Krahe, Hans *see* INDOGERMANISCHE SPRACHWISSENSCHAFT

KRAI OZIRISA. EGIPETSKIE OCHERKI / Bal'mont, K D – M. 1914. BR-522 2 – 8 – ne IDC [470]

Krainskii, V V *see*
- AGRARNYI VOPROS I KOOPERATSIIA
- OBSHCHINA I KOOPERATSIIA

KRAKAUER UND WARSCHAUER ZEITUNG *see* KRAKAUER ZEITUNG

KRAKAUER ZEITUNG – Cracow. Poland. -d. Mar 1941, Apr 1942-Jan 1945. (Imperfect). (13 reels) – 1 – uk British Libr Newspaper [943]

KRAKAUER ZEITUNG – Krakau, nov 12 1939-dec 10 1940. sep 2-oct 31 1941. 1944-jan 16 1945 – 9r – 1 – gw Mikrofilm [943]

KRAKAUER ZEITUNG – Krakow, Poland. Nov 1939-Jan 14 1945 – 22r – 1 – us L of C Photodup [072]

KRAKAUER ZEITUNG – (Many issues missing) – Krakau: Zeitungsverlag Krakau-Warschau, 1939-1945. 7v – 1 – CSUX85-S402 – us Hoover Inst Photo [943]

KRAKIVS'KI VISTI – Krakow, Poland. 1940-43 – 4r – 1 – us L of C Photodup [943]

Krall, William *see* ACCOUNT BOOKS

Kramer, Friedrich Oswald *see* DIE AETHIOPISCHE UEBERSETZUNG DES ZACHARIAS, ERSTES HEFT

Kramer, G W *see* THE WHAT, HOW, AND WHY OF CHURCH BUILDING

Kramer, Gustav *see* AUGUST HERMANN FRANCKE

Kramer, Matthias *see*
- DICTIONARIUM FRANTZOESICSH-TEUTSCH UND TEUTSCH-FRANTZOESISCHES WOERTERREGISTER UEBER KRAMERS DICTIONNAIRE (AEL, ABT.2;1)
- HET KONINGLYK NEDER-HOOG-DUITSCH-HOOG-NEDER-DUITSCH DICTIONARIUM (AEL, ABT.2;3)

Kramer, SN *see*
- FROM THE TABLETS OF SUMER
- SUMERIAN MYTHOLOGY

KRAMER UND FRIEMANN : EINE LEHRZEIT / Mueller, Fritz – 3. Aufl. der Feldausg. Guetersloh: C Bertelsmann, 1942 – 1r – 1 – us U.W. Library [920]

Kramme, Ulrike *see*
- ARAB-ISLAMIC BIOGRAPHICAL ARCHIVE (AIBA)
- CESKY BIOGRAFICKY ARCHIV A SLOVENSKY BIOGRAFICKY ARCHIV

Krammer, F *see* QUINTETTI, NOUVEAUS, POUR DEUX VIOLONS, DEUX ALTOS ET VIOLONCELLO

Krammer, Mario *see* THEODOR FONTANES ENGERE WELT

Kramp, Willy *see* GEIST UND GESELLSCHAFT

Krancke, Adolf *see* DIE BEIDEN FASSUNGEN VON SCHILLERS ABHANDLUNG "UEBER NAIVE UND SENTIMENTALISCHE DICHTUNG"

Krane, Vl *see* THE RELATIONSHIP BETWEEN ANXIETY AND ATHLETIC PERFORMANCE

Krane, Vikki *see* RELATIONSHIPS AMONG PERCEIVED LEADERSHIP STYLES, MEMBER SATISFACTION AND TEAM COHESION IN HIGH SCHOOL BASKETBALL TEAMS

Kraner, Christian Friedrich *see* UEBER SCHILLERS UNTERSCHEIDUNG VON NAIVER UND SENTIMENTALISCHER DICHTUNG

Kranichfeld, Rudolph *see*
- DAS BUCH DANIEL
- DE IIS, QUAE IN TESTAMENTO VETERE COMMEMORANTUR, PROPHETARUM SOCIETATIBUS

Kranikhfel'd, V *see* LITERATURNYE OTKLIKI

KRANKENPFLEGE IM KRANKENHAUS : BERUFLICHE SITUATION UND MOEGLICHKEITEN IHRER VERBESSERUNG / Waizenegger, Joachim – 1994 – 3mf – 9 – DM98.00 – 3-8267-2063-6 – gw Hänsel [360]

KRANKEN-PHYSIOGNOMIK / Baumgaertner, Karl Heinrich – (Atlas and text in Latin/German) – Stuttgart, Leipzig. 1839 (mf ed 1991) – 3 b/w + 4 color mf – 9,15 – DM240.00 – 3-89131-048-X – gw Fischer [610]

KRANSNYI ARKHIV – v. 1-103. 1922-1940 – 1 – us UMI [025]

Krantz, A *see* WANDALIA

KRANY I PUT (USMAN, RUSSIA) *see* KRASNY I PUT

Kranz, Jacob ben Wolf *see* OHEL YA'AKOV: AL HAMISHAH HUMSHE TORAH.

Kranz, Michael *see* DIE VERPACKUNGSVERORDNUNG

Krapf, J L *see* REISEN IN OSTAFRIKA: AUSGEFUEHRT IN DEN JAHREN 1837-1855

Krapf, Ludwig *see* A NIKA-ENGLISH DICTIONARY.

Krapp, George Philip *see* MODERN ENGLISH

Krappe, Alexander Haggerty *see*
- ETUDES DE MYTHOLOGIE ET DE FOLKLORE GERMANIQUE
- LA GENESE DES MYTHES

KRASHENYIA RYLA. TEATR I KNIGA / Remizov, A – Berlin. 1922. BR-822 2 – 8 – ne IDC [460]

Krasinski, Valerian *see* HISTORICAL SKETCH OF THE RISE, PROGRESS, AND DECLINE OF THE REFORMATION IN POLAND

KRASNAI A ARMII A (KHARKOV, UKRAINE) – (Library has no. 290 (May 24, 1928)) – Kharkov: Polit. upr. Ukr. voen. okruga, 1925-1934. 1v – 1 – CSUX89-S197 – us Hoover Inst Photo [947]

KRASNAI A BASHKIRII A – (Library has: v.9, no.28, 122 (Apr. 22, May 27 1928)) – Ufa: [s.n.], 19uu – 1 – CSUX89-S713 – us Hoover Inst Photo [947]

KRASNAI A KONNIT SA – (Library has: Jan.-Feb., July 1937) – Moskva: Voenizdat, 1932-1940. 9v – 1 – CSUX89-S876 – us Hoover Inst Photo [947]

KRASNAI A PRAVDA – (Includes c.1: 1921:Nov.7) – Orel: [Tip. "Trud"], 1920 – 1 – CSUXANR6160-S – us Hoover Inst Photo [947]

KRASNAI A STEP : ORGAN KALM. OBKOMA VKP(B), OBLISPOLKOMA I OBLPROFSOVETA – (Includes c.1: 1928:Jan.31, Feb.13, Mar.8-15, Apr.2-May 17, 21-24, June 4-7) – Astrakhan: Tip. Kalmizdata, 192u – 1 – CSUXANR6230-S – us Hoover Inst Photo [947]

KRASNAIA ARMIIA NA VNUTRENNEM FRONTE : BORBA S BELOGVARDEISKIMI VOSSTANIIAMI, POVSTANCHESTVOM I BANDITIZMOM / Buiskii, A – 2-e izd. Moskva: Gos. izd-vo, Otdel voen. litr-ry, 1927 – 1 – CSUX88-B7492 – us Hoover Inst Photo [355]

KRASNAIA LETOPIS – Moscow. Leningrad. 1922-34 – 1 – 35.00r – us Hoover Inst Photo [947]

KRASNAIA NOV' – 1921-31 – 1 – 209.00 – us L of C Photodup [073]

KRASNAIA NOV' – Moscow. U.S.S.R. 1921-1940 – 1 – us UMI [072]

KRASNAIA ZVEZDA – 1924 – 1 – sz Infoprint [947]

KRASNAIA ZVEZDA – Moscow. 1955- – 1 – us UMI [355]

KRASNAIA ZVEZDA – Moscow. Jan 1941-May 1952 gaps – 1 – 35.00r – us Hoover Inst Photo [947]

KRASNAIA ZVEZDA = RED STAR – (Backfile through 1998 $85r) – 1999- – 2r per y – 1 – $160.00 standing order – us Ross [072]

KRASNAIA ZVEZDA – (Some missing issues) – Moscow, USSR. Oct 1918-Apr 1919; 1925; 1929 no 160; 1930; 1932-77 – 90r – 1 – us L of C Photodup [947]

KRASNAIA ZVEZDA : TSENTRALYI ORGAN NARODNOGO KOMMISSARIATA OBORONY SOIUZA SSR – Moscow, [1939-45] – 12r – 1 – us Res Libr [947]

KRASNAYA NOV' – Moscow. 1921-38, oct-nov 1939, janv 1940 – 1 – fr A.C.R.P.P. [073]

KRASNAYA NOV' – Moscow. Nov 1921-Nov 1939; Mar 1940-May 1941; Jan-Aug 1942 – 1 – us NY Public [073]

KRASNOARME ISKAI A PRAVDA : ORGAN POLITUPRAVLENII A REVVOENSOVETA ZAPFRONTA – (Includes c.1: 1921:Nov.7; 1922:Mar.12) – Smolensk: [s.n.], 19uu – 1 – CSUXANR6087-S – us Hoover Inst Photo [947]

KRASNOARME ISKI I SPRAVOCHNIK – (Includes c.1: 1925:Oct.14) – Moskva: GVIZ, 192u – 1 – CSUXANR5983-S – us Hoover Inst Photo [947]

KRASNOARMEET S (MOSCOW, R.S.F.S.R.) – (Library has: no. 1-117, 1919-1927; some issues missing) – Moskva: Izd. Polit otdela Revoli ut sionnogo voennogo soveta respubliki, 1919-1928. 10v – 1 – CSUX90-S554 – us Hoover Inst Photo [947]

KRASNOE POMORE – (Library has: May, 1920) – Arkhangelsk: Izd. Gub. otdela Narodnogo obrazovanii a i Proletkulta, 1920 – 1 – CSUX89-S911 – us Hoover Inst Photo [947]

KRASNOE PRIAZOVE : EZHENEDELNAI A KRESTI ANSKAI A GAZETA – ORGAN AZOVSKOGO RA IKOMA VKP(B) I ISPOLKOMA SOVETOV – (Includes c.1: 1928:Apr.8-15) – Azov-Don: Tip. "Krasnoe Priazove", 19uu – 1 – CSUXANR6836-S – us Hoover Inst Photo [947]

KRASNOE PRIKAME – (Includes c.1: 1928:Apr.6, 28 May 1) – Sarapul: Gazetnoe izd-vo Okrispolkoma, 19uu – 1 – CSUXADQ2985-S – us Hoover Inst Photo [947]

KRASNOE ZNAMI A : ORGAN KUBCHERISPOLKOMA, KUBCHEROBLAST KOMA R.K.P. I KUBCHERSOVPROFA – (Includes c.1: 1921:Dec.4; 1922:Mar.12; 1928:Mar.21, Apr.10, 14, 20-22, May 8, 11-12) – Krasnodar: Gos. izd-vo Kubano-Chernom. otd-nie, 1920 – 1 – CSUXADQ3278-S – us Hoover Inst Photo [947]

KRASNOE ZNAMI A : ORGAN TIKHVINSKOGO UKOMA RKP(B) – (Includes c.1: 1921:Nov.7) – Tikhvin: ROSTA, 191u – 1 – CSUXADQ3007-S – us Hoover Inst Photo [947]

KRASNOE ZNAMI A (KRASNODAR, R.S.F.S.R.) *see* KRASNOE ZNAMI A

KRASNOE ZNAMI A (TIKHVIN, R.S.F.S.R.) *see* KRASNOE ZNAMI A

Krasnoff, Joanne B *see* THE INFLUENCE OF PHYSICAL CONDITIONING ON THE POST-MENOPAUSAL HOT FLASH

KRASNOI ARET S – (Includes c.1: 1906:Oct.21-29) – Krasnoi arsk: [s.n.], 1906- – 1 – CSUXADQ1036-S – us Hoover Inst Photo [947]

Krasnovskii, N *see* KHRAM PRAVOSLAVNO-KHRISTIANSKII

Krasnozhen, M *see* UKAZATEL' LITERATURY TSERKOVNAGO PRAVA PO 1910 G

KRASNY I BALTI ISKI I FLOT : ORGAN POLITICHESKOGO OTDELA REVOLI UT SIONNOGO VOENNOGO SOVETA BALTI ISKOGO FLOTA – (Includes c.1: 1919:July 10, Aug.20, 27, Sept.3, 10-13, 24, Oct.1, 7, Dec.11; 1920:Jan.6-10, Feb.28, Sept.14, 23-Oct.21, 26-28, Nov.2-4) – Petrograd: [s.n.], 1919 – 1 – CSUXANR6941-S – us Hoover Inst Photo [947]

KRASNY I FLOT – Moskva: Nar. komissariat voen.-morskogo flota SSSR, 19uu – 1 – CSUX89-S678 – us Hoover Inst Photo [947]

KRASNY I GORNI AK : ORGAN KRIVOROGSKOGO OKRPARKOMA, OKRISPOLKOMA I OKRPROFSOVETA – (Includes c.1: 1928:May 8-10, June 2-6, 8-9) – Krivo i Rog Okrparkom, 192u – 1 – CSUXANR7314-S – us Hoover Inst Photo [947]

KRASNY I KHOROVOD : POVI EST / Galich, Iurii – Riga: "Literatura", 1929. 2v – 1 – CSUX88-B7173 – us Hoover Inst Photo [460]

KRASNY I MIR : ORGAN KOSTROMSKOGO GUBERN.. ISPOLN. K-T SOVETOV I GUBK-TA R.K.P. (BOLSHEVIKOV) – (Includes c.1: 1919:Nov.7; 1921:Nov.6) – [Kostroma]: s.n., 191u – 1 – CSUXANR7199-S – us Hoover Inst Photo [947]

KRASNY I NABAT – (Includes c.1: 1919:Nov.7) – [S.l.]: Politotdel Voensoveta N-o i armii, 19uu – 1 – CSUXANR7181-S – us Hoover Inst Photo [947]

KRASNY I OFIT SER – (Library has: 1918, no. 1, 3; 1919, no. 1, 3/4, 6/7) – Moskva: Izd. Voenno-uchebnogo upravlenii a Vserossi iskogo glavnogo shtaba, 1918-1919. 2v – 1 – CSUX89-S973 – us Hoover Inst Photo [947]

KRASNY I OKTI ABR : IZDANIE SHENKURSKOGO OTDELENII A VSEROSSI ISKOGO KOMMUNISTICHESKOGO SOI UZA ZHURNALISTOV – (Includes: c.1: 1919:Nov.7) – Shenkursk: Sovetskai a tip., 191u – 1 – CSUXANR7107-S – us Hoover Inst Photo [947]

KRASNY I OKTI ABR – (Libray has: Nov. 7, 1919) – [Kineshma, R.S.F.S.R.]: Ispolnitelny i kom-t Kineshem. soveta rabochikh, kresti an. i krasnoarme iskikh deputatov, 19uu – 1 – CSUX89-S675 – us Hoover Inst Photo [947]

KRASNY I OKTI ABR (SHENKURSK, RUSSIA) *see* KRASNY I OKTI ABR

KRASNY I PAKHAR – Moskva: Izd. Narodnogo komissariata zemledelii a, 1919-1920. 2v – 1 – CSUX89-S806 – us Hoover Inst Photo [947]

KRASNY I PAKHAR : ORGAN ARDATOVSKOGO UEZDN. KOMITETA R.K.P. I UEZDNOGO ISPOLNITELN. KOMITETA – (Includes c.1: 1921:Nov.7) – Ardatov: Ispolnit. kom-t., 1921 – 1 – CSUXADQ5591-S – us Hoover Inst Photo [947]

KRASNY I PAKHAR : ORGAN STARORUSSKOGO SOVETA RABOCHIKH, KRESTI ANSKIKH I KRASNOARME ISKIKH DEPUTATOV I UEZDNOGO KOMITETA R.K.P. – (Includes c.1: 1919:Nov.7) – [Starai a Russa: s.n.], 19uu – 1 – CSUXADQ5606-S – us Hoover Inst Photo [947]

KRASNY I PAKHAR (ARDATOV, R.S.F.S.R.) *see* KRASNY I PAKHAR

KRASNY I PAKHAR (STARAI A RUSSA, R.S.F.S.R.) *see* KRASNY I PAKHAR

KRASNY I PUT : EZHEDNEVNAI A GAZETA USMANSKOGO UKOMPARTA I ISPOLKOMA – (Includes c.1: 1921:Nov.7) – Usman: [s.n.], 19uu – 1 – CSUXANR7083-S – us Hoover Inst Photo [947]

KRASNY I PUT : ORGAN KINESHEMSKAGO UEZDNOGO KOMITETA R.K.P. – (Library has: Nov. 7, 1918) – [Kineshma]: Komitet, 1918-1919. 2v – 1 – CSUX89-S779 – us Hoover Inst Photo [947]

KRASNY I PUT ZHELEZNODOROZHNIKA – (Library has: 1919: nos. 16-31, 34-38, 40-42, 49-50; 1920: nos. 7-12/13) – Moskva: Izd. Narod. komissariata pute i soobshchenii a, 1919-1920. 2v – 1 – CSUX89-S804 – us Hoover Inst Photo [947]

KRASNY I SEVER : ORGAN VOLOGODSKIKH: GUBERN KOMITETA VKP(B), GUB. ISPOLNITELN. KOMITETA S.R.KR. I KR. DEP. I GUB. SOVETA PROFESSIONALNYKH SOI UZOV – (Includes c.1: no.244=no.2231 1926:Oct.24) – Vologda: Tip. akt sionernogo o-va "Severny i pechatnik", 19uu – 1 – CSUXAHZ3381-S – us Hoover Inst Photo [947]

KRASNY I SPORT : ORGAN VSESOI UZNOGO KOMITETA PO DELAM FIZKULTURY I SPORTA PRI SOVNARKOME SSSR I VT SSPS – (Includes c.1: 1945:no.24=no.1171 June 19; 1945:no.32=no.1178 Aug.7; 1945:no.35=no.1181 Aug.21-; 1945:no.36=no.1182 Aug.28; 1945:no.38=no.1184 Sept.11-; 1945:n) – Moskva: [s.n.], 19uu – 1 – CSUXAHZ3232-S – us Hoover Inst Photo [947]

KRASNY I TRUBACH : ORGAN POLITOTDELA N GRUPPY ZAPFRONTA – (Includes c.1: no.30 1920:July 10-no.31 (1920:July 11)) – Gomel: Otdel, 19uu – 1 – CSUXAHZ2575-S – us Hoover Inst Photo [947]

KRASNY I UGLEKOP : ORGAN CHEREMKHOVSKOGO RA IONNOGO KOMITETA R.K.P., SOI UZA GORNORABOCHIKH I IRUGLI A – (Includes c.1: 1922:Mar.11) – Cheremkhovo: Ra ikom, 1921 – 1 – CSUXANR8828-S – us Hoover Inst Photo [947]

KRASNY I VES'EGONSK : ORGAN UEZDNO-GORODSKOGO KOMITETA VESEGONSKO I ORGANIZAT SII ROSSI ISKO I KOMMUNITICHESKO I PARTII – (Includes c.1: 1921:Nov.5, Dec.3) – Ves'egonsk: Komitet, 19uu – 1 – CSUXAHZ3476-S – us Hoover Inst Photo [947]

KRASNYI ARKHIV – Istoricheskii zhurnal. v. 1-106. M. 1922-41. BR-1596 2 – 8 – ne IDC [947]

KRASNYI BALTIISKII FLOT – Leningrad, USSR. Aug 20 1919-Sept 20 1921 – 1r – 1 – us L of C Photodup [072]

KRASNYI CHASOVOI KRONSHTADT / DOr, OL – Moskva: Literaturno-izdatelski i otdel polit. upr. revoliutsionnogo voen. soveta respubliki, 1920 – 1 – CSUX88-B6996 – us Hoover Inst Photo [947]

KRASNYI FLOT : ORGAN NARODNOGO KOMMISSARIATA VOENNO-MORSKOGO FLOTA SSSR – Moskva: Tip "Pravda" imeni Stalina, [jan-aug 29 1941] – us Res Libr [947]

KRASNYI KHOROVOD : ESKIZY / Galich, Iurii – Vladivostok: [s.n.], 1921 (Vladivostok: Tip. "Kommercheskai a") – 1 – CSUX88-B5484 – us Hoover Inst Photo [947]

KRASNYI PAIATS : POVIESTI STRASHNYKH LIET / Chirikov, Evgeni i Nikolaevich – Berlin: Mi edny i vsadnik, 1928 – 1 – CSUX88-B5761 – us Hoover Inst Photo [947]

KRASNYI ZVON – Ezhemesiachnyi belletristicheskii i publicheskii. v. 1. Spb. 1908-10. BR-3195 2 – 8 – ne IDC [460]

KRATKAIA ISTORIIA PERVOGO KADETSKOGO KORPUSA / Viskovatov, A – Spb. 1832. BR-7953 2 – 8 – ne IDC [947]

KRATKAIA ISTORIIA ROSSIISKOI DIPLOMATII / Dobroklonskii, S – Moscow, 1830. 154p. BR-9503 1 – 9 – ne IDC [947]

KRATKI I STATISTICHESKI I SPRAVOCHNIK : T SENTRALNOE UPRAVLENIE NARODNOKHOZI A ISTVENNOGO UCHETA GOSPLANA SSSR – (Includes c.1: 1935-1936) – Moskva: Upravlenie, 19uu – 1 – CSUXAKZ2602-S – us Hoover Inst Photo [947]

KRATKIE ZAMETKI O LETOPISNYKH PROIZVEDENIIAKH V RUKOPISNYKH SOBRANIIAKH MOSKVY / Tikhomirov, M N – Moscow, 1962. 181p. BR-10,663/1 – 9 – ne IDC [947]

KRATKII KURS KOOPERATSII / Chaianov, A V – Ed 3. M., 1925 – 1mf – 9 – COR-231/1 – ne IDC [334]

KRATKII KURS KOOPERATSII : KONSPEKT / Lobov, GZ – Rostov n/D, 1925 – 1mf – 9 – COR-262/1 – ne IDC [334]

KRATKII KURS PO POTREBITEL'SKOI KOOPERATSII / Leonov, V – Pg., 1918 – 2mf – 9 – COR-259/1 – ne IDC [334]

KRATKII KURS TSERKOVNAGO PRAVA PRAVOSLAVNOI TSERKVI / Bernikov, Ilya Stepanovich (1839-1915) – A short course of church law of the Orthodox Church. Kazan, 1913 – 1 – 59.28 – us Baptist [240]

KRATKII OBZOR SOBRANIIA RUKOPISEI, PRINADLEZHASHCHEGO PREOSVIASHCHENNOMU EPISKOPU PORFIRIIU, A NYNE KHRANIASHCHEGOSIA V IMP. PUBLICHNOI BIBLIOTEKE / Bychkov, I A – Spb. 1885. BR-11,157 1 – 9 – ne IDC [010]

KRATKII OBZOR SUVOROVSKOI LITERATURY / Petrushevskii, A – Russkoi, frantsuzskoi i nemetskoi po 1903 god. Spb. 1903. BR-7212 2 – 8 – ne IDC [460]

KRATKII OCHERK STOLETNEI DEIATEL NOSTI TIPOGRAFII GLAZUNOVYKH V SVIAZI S RAZVITIEMIKH KNIGOIZDATELSTVA 1803-1903 / Lisovskii, N M – Spb, 1903 – 8 – BR-4580 2 – ne IDC [947]

KRATKII OTCHET O NOVYKH POSTUPLENIIAKH (GBP) ZA 1947-1949 GG – Leningrad, 1952. 131p. BR-10,844/1 – 9 – ne IDC [025]

KRATKII OTCHET O NOVYKH POSTUPLENIIAKH (GPB) ZA 1939-1946 GG – Leningrad, 1951. 162p. BR-10,843/1 – 9 – ne IDC [025]

KRATKII OTCHET RUKOPISNOGO OTDELA (GPB) ZA 1914-1938 GG. SO VSTUPITEL'NYM ISTORICHESKIM OCHERKOM – Leningrad, 1940. 302p. BR-10,842/1 – 9 – ne IDC [025]

KRATKII SLOVAR' ARKHIVNOI TERMINOLOGII / ed by Kostrikin, V I et al – M., L., 1968 – 1mf – 9 – R-9885/1 – ne IDC [460]

KRATKII UKAZATEL'ARKHIVNYKH FONDOV OTDELA RUKOPISEI – Moscow, 1948. 253p. BR-11,007/1 – 9 – ne IDC [025]

KRATKOE IZLOZHENIE DIPLOMATII ROSSIISKAGO DVORA / Kaidanov, I K – Saint Petersburg, 1833. 2v. Early diplomatic history of Russia placing emphasis on treaty relations. Covers period from accession of Romanovs to Alexander I (1613-1825). BR-9476- – 9 – ne IDC [947]

KRATKOE NACHERTANIE RIMSKIKH. / Artemev, A I – Moscow, 1777. BR-9315 1 – 9 – ne IDC [947]

KRATKOE NACHERTANIE RUSSKOI ISTORII / Pogodin, M P – M. 1838. BR-8310 2 – 8 – ne IDC [947]

KRATKOE OPISANIE RUKOPISEI TSERKOVNOISTORICHESKOGO DREVNEKHRANILISHCHA PRI BRATSTVE SV. BL. VEL. KN. ALEKSANDRA NEVSKOGO – Vladimir, 1906. 157p. BR/7292/2 – 8 – ne IDC [947]

KRATKOE UCHENIE O PROPOVEDI = A SHORT STUDY ON PREACHING / Prokhanov, IS – Anapa, Kuban Province, Russia. 1911. 122p – 1 – $5.00 – us Baptist [240]

KRATKOSROCHNYE KOOPERATIVNYE KURSY : SBORNIK UCHEBNYKH PLANOV, PROGRAMM, METODICHESKIKH UKAZANII, SMET I INSTRUKTSII – M., 1925 – 3mf – 9 – COR-260/1 – ne IDC [334]

Kratzenberg, Andree *see* WECHSELKURSRISIKO UND EXPORTENTSCHEIDUNG

Kratzmann, Ernst *see* REGINA SEBALDI

Kratzmoeller, Wilhelm *see* DARSTELLUNG UND KRITIK DER LEHRE DES DESCARTES VON DER BILDUNG DES UNIVERSUMS

Kraus, Hans P *see* COLLECTION(SPANISH-AMERICAN DOCUMENTS)

Kraus, Joseph Martin *see* ETWAS VON IND XUBER MUSIK FUERS JAHR 1777

Kraus, Konrad *see* WINCKELMANN UND HOMER

Krause, A *see* DIE TLINKIT-INDIANER

Krause, B *see* DIE SCHOPFUNG. ORATORIUM, TEXT VON HOFBAUM. PARTITUR

Krause, J G *see* NEUER BUECHER-SAAL DER GELEHRTEN WELT ODER AUSFUEHRLICHE NACHRICHTEN VON ALLERHAND NEUEN BUECHERN UND ANDERN ZUR HEUTIGEN HISTORIE DER GELEHRSAMKEIT GEHOERIGEN SACHEN

Krausen, Edgar *see* URKUNDEN DES KLOSTERS RAITENHASLACH 1034-1350

Krauskopf, J *see* THE SERVICE-HYMNAL: WITH AN INTRODUCTORY SERVICE

Krauss, Alfred Ed *see* DIE LEHRE VON DER OFFENBARUNG

Krauss, Friedrich S *see* BOEHMISCHE KORALLEN AUS DER GOETTERWELT

Krauss, S *see*
- GRIECHISCHE UND LATEINISCHE LEHNWOERTER IM TALMUD, MIDRASCH UND TARGUM
- SEFER HA-YOVEL LI-SHEMU'EL KRAUSS

Kraussold, Lorenz *see* DIE SAGE VOM HEILIGEN GRAL UND PARCEVAL

Krauth, Charles Porterfield *see*
- A CHRONICLE OF THE AUGSBURG CONFESSION – A QUESTION OF LATINITY
- THE CONSERVATIVE REFORMATION AND ITS THEOLOGY

DER KRAUTSTEIG : DIE GESCHICHTE EINER KAMERADSCHAFT / Jessen, Paul – Darmstadt: L Kichler, c1942 – 1 – us U.W. Library [830]

KREATIVE PROZESSE IM UNTERRICHT / Falk, Brigitte – 1995 – 1mf – 9 – DM60.00 – 3-8267-2196-9 – gw Hänsel [370]

KREATIVITAETSFORSCHUNG UND JOY PAUL GUILFORD (1897-1987) – MATERIALIEN ZU EINER ERSTBEGEGNUNG / Pimmer, Hans – 1994 – 6mf – DM125.00 – 3-8267-2022-9 – gw Hänsel [150]

DIE KREATUR – Berlin, 1926-1929/30 – 1r – 1 – Dist. gw Mikrofilm – gw Misc Inst [073]

DIE KREATUR – Eine Zeitschrift. Berlin. v1-3. 1926-30. Complete. B594 (Leo Baeck Institute. German-Jewish Periodicals, Pt 2) – 1r – 1 – $75.00 – us UPA [270]

KREBS DURCH NIEDERFREQUENTE MAGNETFELDER? : EINE STUDIE UEBER DIE ROLLE DES MELATONINS BEI BLINDEN UND FELDEXPONIERTEN PERSONEN / Haubrich, Stefan – 1995 – 1mf – 9 – DM60.00 – 3-8267-2235-3 – gw Hänsel [616]

Krebs, E *see* MEISTER DIETRICH, SEIN LEBEN, SEINE WERKE, SEINE WISSENSCHAFT

Krebs, Kurt *see* SAECHSISCHE KRIEGSNOT IN DEN JAHREN 1806 BIS 1815

Krebs, Susanne M *see* BERUFLICHE REHABILITATION BEHINDERTER IN DER BUNDESREPUBLIK DEUTSCHLAND UND DER SCHWEIZ

Krebs, Werner *see* AUF DER WALZ VOR FUENFZIG JAHREN

KREDIT I KREDITNYE OPERATSII V SEL'SKOKHOZIAISTVENNYKH KOOPERATIVAKH / Trapeznikov, I F – M., 1927 – 3mf – 9 – COR-406/1 – ne IDC [334]

KREDIT I POTREBITEL'SKAIA KOOPERATSIIA / Zel'geim, V N – M., [1910] – 1mf – 9 – COR-31/1 – ne IDC [334]

KREDITNAIA KOOPERATSIIA V ROSSII : ISTORICHESKII OCHERK I SOVREMENNOE PLOZHENIE / Kheisin, ML – Ed.2. Pg., 1919 – 3mf – 9 – COR-408/1 – ne IDC [334]

KREDITNAIA KOOPERATSIIA V ROSSII / Prokopovich, SN – M., 1923 – 2mf – 9 – COR-400/1 – ne IDC [334]

KREDITNAIA KOOPERATSIIA ZAURAL'IA : PERMSKOGO / Panin, I – Ekaterinburg, 1917 – 2mf – 9 – COR-93/1 – ne IDC [334]

KREDITNYE I KOMISSIONNO-BANKOVSKIE OPERATSII V SEL'SKOKHOZIAISTVENNYKH KREDITNYKH TOVARISHCHESTVAKH / Islankin, FB – M., 1928 – 3mf – 9 – COR-383/1 – ne IDC [334]

KREDITNYE I SSUDO-SBEREGATEL'NYE TOVARISHCHESTVA / Kulyzhnyi, A E – Ed.4. Pg., 1918 – 1mf – 9 – COR-388/1 – ne IDC [334]

KREDITNYE OPERATSII SEL'SKOKHOZIAISTVENNYKH TOVARISHCHESTV / Merkulov, A V – M., 1923 – 1mf – 9 – COR-491/1 – ne IDC [334]

KREFELDER ANZEIGER – Krefeld, Germany. 1858 (6 Nos.) – 1 – gw Mikrofilm [072]

Krehbiehl, Edward B *see* THE INTERDICT

Krehbiel, H P *see*
- THE HISTORY OF THE GENERAL CONFERENCE OF THE MENNONITES OF NORTH AMERICA
- MENNONITE CHURCHES OF NORTH AMERICA

Krehbiel, Henry Edward *see* AFRO-AMERICAN FOLKSONGS

Kreibig, Gustav *see* DIE VERSOEHNUNGSLEHRE

Kreider, Eugene G *see* KREIDER'S INDEX OF NOTES IN THE ANNOTATED CASES

KREIDER'S INDEX OF NOTES IN THE ANNOTATED CASES / Kreider, Eugene G – (Covers all vols of all 3 titles in the Annotated Cases Series) – New York, San Francisco: Thompson Co, Bancroft-Whitney. 1v. 1922 (all publ) – 10mf – 9 – $15.00 – LLMC 84-695F – us L.L.M.C. [340]

Kreidler, Charles Ray *see* ANALYZED NEW YORK DECISIONS AND CITATIONS, 1914-1917, COVERING DUPLICATE REPORTS

Kreihing, I *see* EMBLEMATA ETHICO-POLITICA CARMINE EXPLICATA

DER KREIS ANGERBURG : EIN OSTPREUSSISCHES HEIMATBUCH / ed by Pfeiffer, Erich – (Includes bibliographical references and indexes) – Angerburg: Selbstverlag der Kreisgemeinschaft, 1973 – 1 – us U.W. Library [910]

DER KREIS CAMMIN : EIN POMMERSCHES HEIMATBUCH / ed by Flemming-Benz, Hasso Graf von – (Includes bibliographical references) – Wuerzburg: Holzner Verlag, 1970 – 1 – us U.W. Library [910]

DER KREIS GERDAUEN : EIN OSTPREUSSISCHES HEIMATBUCH / ed by Bachor, Oskar-Wilhelm – (Includes bibliographical references and index) – Wuerzburg: Holzner Verlag, 1968 – 1 – us U.W. Library [943]

DER KREIS GOLDAP : EIN OSTPREUSSISCHES HEIMATBUCH / ed by Mignat, Johannes – (Includes bibliographical references and index) – Wuerzburg: Holzner Verlag, 1965 – 1 – us U.W. Library [910]

KREIS HAMMSCHES WOCHENBLATT – (Cont by: Wochenblatt fuer die Stadt und den Kreis Hamm, jan 2, 1825. Westfaelischer Anzeiger, dec 11, 1850. Westfaelischer Anzeiger und Kurier, nov 1, 1949. Westfaelischer Anzeiger, apr 12, 1972) – Hamm. 1824-29. 1831-43. 1845-47. 1850-62. 1864-72. 1874. 1876-78. 1880-98. 1900-21. jul 1, 1922-mar 31, 1935. jul 2, 1935-apr 2, 1945. oct 28, 1949-57 – 1 – gw Mikrofilm [943]

DER KREIS JOHANNISBURG : EIN OSTPREUSSISCHES HEIMATBUCH / ed by Guttzeit, Johannes – (Includes bibliographical references and index) – Wuerzburg: Holzner, 1964 – 10r – 1 – us U.W. Library [910]
DER KREIS LOETZEN : EIN OSTPREUSSISCHES HEIMATBUCH / Meyhoefer, Max – (Includes bibliographical references and index) – Wuerzburg: Holzner, 1961 – 1 – us U.W. Library [430]
DER KREIS MOHRUNGEN : EIN OSTPREUSSISCHES HEIMATBUCH / Wrangel, Wolf, Freiherr von – (Includes bibliographical references and indexes) – Wuerzburg: Holzner Verlag, 1967 – 1 – us U.W. Library [910]
DER KREIS NEUSTETTIN : EIN POMMERSCHES HEIMATBUCH / ed by Stelter, Franz – (Includes bibliographical references and indexes) – Wuerzburg: Holzner Verlag, 1972 – 1 – us U.W. Library [910]
DER KREIS OSTERODE (OSTPR.) : DATEN ZUR GESCHICHTE SEINER ORTSCHAFTEN / Hartmann, Ernst of Osterode – (Includes index) – Wuerzburg: Holzner-Verlag, 1958 – 10r – 1 – us U.W. Library [910]
DER KREIS SCHLOSSBERG : EIN OSTPREUSSISCHES HEIMATBUCH / ed by Mietzner, Franz – (Includes bibliographical references and indexes) – Wuerzburg: Holzner Verlag, 1962 – 1 – us U.W. Library [910]
DER KREIS SENSBURG / Glass, Paul; ed by Bredenberg, Fritz von – (Includes bibliographical references and index) – Wuerzburg: Holzner Verlag, 1960 – 1 – us U.W. Library [910]
KREISANZEIGER FUER WETTERAU UND VOGELSBERG – Buedingen, 1988- – 7r per yr – 1 – Inquire at Mikrofilmarchiv for details – gw Misc Inst [072]
KREISBLATT *see* HINTERLAENDER ANZEIGER
KREIS-BLATT FUER DAS MUENSTERLAND – Muenster, may 6-9 1852, 1854-56 (incomplete), 1858-62 (incomplete) – 1 – gw Mikrofilm [943]
KREISBLATT FUER DEN KREIS ACHIM *see* ACHIMER KREISBLATT
KREISBLATT FUER DEN KREIS OSTERHOLZ *see* NORDDEUTSCHE VOLKSZEITUNG
Kreiskomitee Temesch der RKP *see* NEUE BANATER ZEITUNG
Kreisler, Emil *see*
– HEBBELS FRAUENGESTALTEN
– DER STOFF UND DIE QUELLE VON BAUERNFELDS LUSTSPIEL "DAS TAGEBUCH"
Kreisler, F *see*
– AUSTRIAN IMPERIAL HYMN: "GOTT ERHALTE UNSEREN KAISER"
– CAPRICE NO. 20, ARRANGED FOR VIOLIN AND PIANO BY KREISLER
– PRAELUDIUM AND ALLEGRO
– SARABANDE AND ALLEGRO
– LE TRILLE DU DIABLE
KREISNACHRICHTEN – Calw, Germany. 1 Sept 1983- – ca 7r per yr – 1 – gw Mikrofilm [072]
KREIS-ZEITUNG – Neutomischl (Nowy Tomysl), Poland. 1929-1939 – 9r – 1 – gw Mikrofilm [943]
KREISZEITUNG : ALLGEMEINER ANZEIGER FUER DIE GRAFSCHAFT HOYA – (Title change: Kreiszeitung fuer die Landkreise Diepholz und Verden, 24 Aug 1977; Kreiszeitung/Syker Zeitung, 22 May 1993) – Syke, West Germany. 1976- – ca 11r per yr – 1 – gw Mikrofilm [072]
KREISZEITUNG: BOEBLINGER BOTE – Boeblingen, 1987- – 8r per yr – 1 – Inquire at Mikrofilmarchiv for details – gw Misc Inst [072]
KREISZEITUNG FUER DEN KREIS ROTENBURG IN HANNOVER *see* ROTENBURGER ANZEIGER
KREISZEITUNG FUER DIE LANDKREISE DIEPHOLZ UND VERDEN *see* KREISZEITUNG
KREISZEITUNG WESERMARSCH – Nordenham, West Germany. 1 Sept 1978- – ca 6r per yr – 1 – gw Mikrofilm [072]
KREISZEITUNG/SYKER ZEITUNG *see* KREISZEITUNG
Krell, Leo *see* DEUTSCHE LITERATURGESCHICHTE
Krementz, Ph *see* DIE OFFENBARUNG DES HL. JOHANNES
Kremer, Hannes *see*
– "DU, MEIN VOLK"
– DER ERZBETER
– DER GEAECHTETE
– MORITATEN
Kremianskii, Ia. *see* BOR'BA ZA KACHESTVO V PROMKOOPERATSII
KREML' V MOSKVE, OCHERKI I KARTINY PROSHLOGO I NASTOIASHCHEGO / Fabritsius, M – Moscow: T Gagen, 1883 – 7mf – 9 – $70.00 – us Ross [947]
Kremnev, G M *see* RAZVITIE KOOPERATSII
Krempelhuber, A von *see*
– GESCHICHTE UND LITTERATUR DER LICHENOLOGIE VON DEN AELTESTEN ZEITEN BIS ZUM SCHLUSSE DES JAHRES 1865
– DIE LICHENEN-FLORA BAYERNS
Krenck *see* VERPONDINGSQUOHIER ZUTPHEN 1640-1650
Krenkel, Max *see*
– JOSEPHUS UND LUCAS
– VORLESUNGEN UEBER DIE GESCHICHTE DER MESSIANISCHEN IDEE
KREPOSTNOI PETERBURG PUSHKINSKOGO VREMENI / Iatsevich, Andrei Grigor'evich – Leningrad: Pushkinskoe obshchestvo, 1937 – 1 – us U.W. Library [947]
Kreppel, Friedrich *see* ZUR NATIONALFEIER
KRESHCHENYI KITAETS / Belyi, A – Roman. (Rasshirennaia redaktsiia "Prestupleniia Nikolaia Letaeva"). 1927. BR-567 2 – 8 – ne IDC [460]
Kress *see* MEDICAL PROFESSION OF SOUTHERN CALIFORNIA
Kressel, G *see* GUIDE TO THE HEBREW PRESS
KRESTANSKA REVUE – (1940-45 not publ) – 1927-88 – 14r – 1 – ATLA S0627 – us A.T.L.A. [073]
KRESTI ANIN I RABOCHI I : OBEDINENNY I ORGAN ISPOLNITELNAGO BI URO PRIMORSKAGO OBLASTNOGO SOVETA KRESTI ANSKIKH DEPUTATOV I VLADIVOSTOKSKAGO SOVETA RABOCHIKH I SOLDATSKIKH DEPUTATOV – (Includes c.1: 1918:Apr.9-10, 18, 20, 23, June 9, 21, 27) – [Vladivostok: s.n.], 1918 – 1 – CSUXANR8781-S – us Hoover Inst Photo [947]
KRESTI ANSKAI A GAZETA DLI A NACHINAI USHCHIKH CHITAT – (Library has no. 55-65 (Oct. 19-Dec. 31, 1931), 1-4,6,8,10 (Jan. 6-29, Feb. 12,28, Mar. 17, 1932)) – Moskva: T Sentr. kom-t VKP(b), 1930-1939. 1v – 1 – CSUX88-S493 – us Hoover Inst Photo [947]
KRESTI ANSKAI A PRAVDA (LUGA, R.S.F.S.R.) – (Library has: no. 127, 133, 146 (Nov. 10, 24, Dec. 29, 1928)) – Luga: Izd. Luzhskogo okruzhnogo kom-ta Vses. kommunistichesko i partii (bolshevikov) i Okruzhnogo ispolnitelnogo kom-ta Sovetov rabochikh, kresti anskikh i krasnoarme iskikh deputatov, 1918- – 1 – CSUX88-S518 – us Hoover Inst Photo [947]
KRESTI ANSKAI A PRAVDA (STALINGRAD, R.S.F.S.R.) – (Library has: no 35 (May 4, 1927), 48 (June 20, 1928)) – Stalingrad: Izd. Stalingradskogo gubkoma VKP(b) i gubispolkoma sovetov, 1921-1928 – 1 – CSUX88-S520 – us Hoover Inst Photo [947]
KRESTI ANSKAI A RUS – (Includes c.1: no.1 1921:May 25-no.20 (1921:Nov.6); no.33 1922:Mar.3) – Varshava: [s.n.], 1921- – 1 – CSUXADQ2972-S – us Hoover Inst Photo [947]
KRESTI ANSKAI A UKRAINA : ORGAN VSEUKRAINSKAGO OBEDINENNAGO KRESTI ANSKAGO SOVI ETA – (Includes c.1: 1925:Jan.20) – Wien: Serge Cernu senko-Sagajda cny, 192u – 1 – CSUXANR8803-S – us Hoover Inst Photo [947]
KRESTI ANSKAI A ZHIZN (VOLOGDA, R.S.F.S.R.) – (Library has no. 12-16, 18-20, 43-44 (Mar. 28-Apr. 25, May 16-30, Nov. 14-23, 1928)) – Vologda: "Kresti anskai a zhizn", 1923- – 1 – CSUX88-S522 – us Hoover Inst Photo [947]
KRESTI ANSKI I DEPUTAT – (Includes c.1: 1906:June 27, July 6) – S.-Petersburg: [s.n.], 1906 – 1 – CSUXADQ1763-S – us Hoover Inst Photo [947]
KRESTI ANSKIE BI UDZHETY KIEVSKO I GUBERNII V...G : KIEVSKOE GUBERNSKOE STATISTICHESKOE BI URO – (Includes c.1: 1922/1923-1923/1924) – Kiev: [Bi uro], 1924- – 1 – CSUXAKZ1567-S – us Hoover Inst Photo [947]
KRESTI ANSKIE BI UDZHETY PO ULI ANOVSKO I GUBERNII ZA... : ULI ANOVSKOE GUBERNSKOE STATISTICHESKOE BI URO – (Includes c.1: 1923/1924) – Sengilei: Bi uro, 1926- – 1 – CSUXAKZ2452-S – us Hoover Inst Photo [947]
KRESTI ANSKOE SLOVO : ORGAN LODE INOPOLSKOGO OKRUZHKOMA VKP(B), OKRISPOLKOMA, OKRPROFBI URO I OKRPOTREBSOI UZA – (Includes c.1: 1928:Apr.28) – Lode inoe pole: [s.n.], 19uu – 1 – CSUXADQ1531-S – us Hoover Inst Photo [947]
KRESTIANSKAIA GAZETA – Moskva: TSK VKP (b). [n1-132/133] jan 4-dec 1930 – us Res Libr [947]
KREST'IANSKAIA KOOPERATSIIA V SVOBODNOI ROSSII / Evdokimov, Andrei Aandreevich – Ed 2. M., 1917 – 1mf – 9 – COR-24/1 – ne IDC [334]
KREST'IANSKAIA ROSSIIA – (Backfile through 1998 $85r) – 1999- – 2r per y – 1 – $160.00 standing order – us Ross [630]
KREST'IANSKAIA ROSSIIA – (Founded in 1906, renewed in 1991) – 1 – sz Infoprint [947]
KREST'IANSKII BIUDZHET V 1922-23 GODU. IZD : TSENTRRAL'NOGO STATISTICHESKOGO UPRAVLENIIA / Litoshenko, LN – M., 1923 – 1mf – 9 – COR-207/1 – ne IDC [334]
KREST'IANSKII INTERNATSIONAL – Moscow. Apr.-Oct. 1924; Jan. 1925-May 1926 – 1 – 35.00r – us Hoover Inst Photo [073]
KREST'IANSKOE DELO – Bezpartiinyi zhurnal dlia krest'ian i sel'skoi intelligentsii. M. 1909-12. Lacking: 1909 (2-20), 1910 (3, 6, 9-12, 16, 19), 1911 (3, 6), 1912. BR-2350 2 – 8 – ne IDC [073]
KREST'IANSKOE DVIZHENIE V 1917 GODU / ed by Kotel'nikov, K G & Meller, V L – M., L. 1927. BR-8647 1 – 9 – ne IDC [460]
KREST'IANSKOE DVIZHENIE V ROSSII V 19-NACHALE 20 VV / Paina, E S – Obzor publikatsii gosudarstvennykh arkhivov SSSR. Moscow, 1963.81p. BR-10,752/1 – 9 – ne IDC [947]
KREST'IANSKOE KHOZIAISTVO : OCHERKI EKONOMIKI MELKOGO ZEMLEDELIIA / Maslov, S L – Ed.3. M., 1918 – 3mf – 9 – COR-484/1 – ne IDC [334]
KREST'IANSKOE KHOZIAISTVO I EGO INTERESY : LIGA AGRARNYKH REFORM SERIIA 5, NO. 2 / Makarov, N P – M., 1917 – 2mf – 9 – COR-209/1 – ne IDC [334]
KREST'IANSKOE KHOZIAISTVO I SEL'SKOKHOZIAISTVENNAIA KOOPERATSIIA / Maslov, S L – Pg., 1919 – 1mf – 9 – COR-485/1 – ne IDC [334]
KREST'IANSKOE KOOPERATIVNOE DVIZHENIE V ZAPADNOI SIBIRI / Makarov, N P – M., 1910 – 3mf – 9 – COR-65/1 – ne IDC [334]
KREST'IANSKOE ZEMEL'NOE PRAVO / Khauke, F A – Moscow, 1913. 382p. Guide to prevailing Russian legislation on peasant land holdings.B-2382/2 – 4mf – 8 – COR-131/1 – ne IDC [340]
KRESTNYI PUT VOIMIA RODINY : DVUKHLIETNIAIA VOINA KRASNAGO SIEVERA S BIELYMI UGOM, 1918-1920 GODA / Dreier, Vladimir Nikolaevich fon – [Berlin: s.n.], 1921 – 1 – CSUX89-B4239 – us Hoover Inst Photo [355]
KRESTOVYIA SESTRY / Remizov, A – Berlin, 1923. 175p. BR-823 2 – 8 – ne IDC [460]
Kretz, M *see* VON DER MESS, VND WER DER RECHT PRIESTER SEY
Kretzer, Max *see*
– DER BASSGEIGER
– BERLINER SKIZZEN
– DIE VERKOMMENEN
Kreutzer *see* LE BRIGAND
Kreutzer, R *see*
– POT-POURRI POPUR VIOLON AVEC ACCOMPAGNEMENT DE VIOLON ET BASSE
– QUATUORS, DEUX
– QUATUORS, TROIS
– TROIS SONATES POUR LE VIOLON AVEC ACCOMPAGNEMENT DE BASSE
DAS KREUZ UND DIE KREUZIGUNG : EINE ANTIQUARISCHE UNTERSUCHUNG NEBST NACHWEIS DER VIELEN SEIT LIPSIUS VERBREITETEN IRRTHUEMER: ZUGLEICH VIER EXCURSE UEBER VERWANDTE GEGENSTAENDE / Fulda, Hermann – (Includes appendixes on aspects of crucifixion. Includes indexes) – Breslau: Wilhelm Koebner, 1878 – 1mf – 9 – 0-8370-3216-4 – 1985-1216 – us A.T.L.A. [240]
Kreuzer, Wolfgang *see*
– BAU EINES RUNDLAUFTHERMOSTATEN FUER DAS FESTKOERPERDILATOMETER UND MESSUNG DES AUSDEHNUNGSVERHALTENS UND DER VOLUMENRELAXATION VON POLYMEREN
– VORHERSAGE DER SCHWINGFESTIGKEIT VON SCHWEISSVERBINDUNGEN AUF DER BASIS DES STATISTISCHEN GROESSENEINFLUSSES
KREUZ-ZEITUNG *see*
– NEUE PREUSSISCHE ZEITUNG
Krey, August C *see* PARALLEL SOURCE PROBLEMS IN MEDIEVAL HISTORY
Kreyenberg, Gotthold *see* GESCHICHTE DER POETISCHEN LITTERATUR DER DEUTSCHEN
Kreyenbuehl, Johannes *see* DIE NOTHWENDIGKEIT UND GESTALT EINER KIRCHLICHEN REFORM
Kreymborg, Gustav *see* JOHANN KARL WEZEL
Kreyssig, Friedrich Alexander Theodor *see* JUSTUS MOESER
Kriby, John B *see* NEW DEAL AGENCIES AND BLACK AMERICA
Kriebel, Howard Wiegner *see* THE SCHWENKFELDERS IN PENNSYLVANIA
Krieck, Ernst *see* LESSING UND DIE ERZIEHUNG DES MENSCHENGESCHLECHTS
KRIEG : EIN TEDEUM / Hauptmann, Carl – Leipzig: K Wolff, 1914 – 1r – 1 – us U.W. Library [810]
Krieg, Cornelius *see* ENCYKLOPAEDIE DER THEOLOGISCHEN WISSENSCHAFTEN NEBST METHODENLEHRE
KRIEG IN SPANIEN. BARBAREI UND ZIVILISATION; EIN ZEITDOKUMENT – Barcelona, 1938. Fiche W 979. (Blodgett Collection of Spanish Civil War Pamphlets) – 9 – us H.U. College Libr [946]
DER KRIEG UND DIE INFEKTION-SKRANKHEITEN / Mueller, Otfried – Tuebingen: Kloeres, 1915. 23p – 1 – us U.W. Library [943]
DER KRIEG UND DIE RELIGION : REDE AM 12. NOVEMBER 1914 / Deissmann, Gustav Adolf – Berlin: C. Heymann, 1914 – 1mf – us A.T.L.A. [240]
KRIEG UND FRIEDEN : MILITAERPOLITISCHE REVUE – Paris, Oct 1938-Sep 1939 (Nos. 1-4) – 1r – 1 – gw Mikrofilm [073]
KRIEG UND KULTUR / Smend, Rudolf – Tuebingen: Kloeres, 1915. 20p – 1 – us U.W. Library [000]
KRIEG UND KUNST / Lange, Konrad – Tuebingen: Kloeres, 1915. 32p – 1 – us U.W. Library [700]
Krieger, Erhard *see* ERNST THEODOR AMADEUS HOFFMANN
Krieger, Y *see* AL DEVAR HEVRAT MEYASSEDEI HA-YISHUV
DER KRIEGSBOTE – Windhoek, S.W.A.1916-19 – 1 – sa State Libr [072]
KRIEGSDICHTER ERZAEHLEN / ed by Velmede, August Friedrich – (Includes bibliographical references) – Muenchen: A Langen/G Mueller, [1942?] – 1r – 1 – us U.W. Library [430]
EINES KRIEGSKNECHTS ABENTEUER / Schuecking, Levin – Berlin: Carl Flemming und C T Wiskott, c1922 – 1r – 1 – us U.W. Library [830]
KRIEGSLIEDER AUS OESTERREICH / Schaukal, Richard von – Muenchen: G Mueller, 1914- – 1r – 1 – us U.W. Library [780]
DIE KRIEGSMARINE – Berlin, 1939-mar 2 1944 (incomplete) – 1 – Dist. gw Mikrofilm – gw Misc Inst [355]
KRIEGSMESSE 1914 : [EINE DICHTUNG] / Zerzer, Julius – Jena: E Diederichs, 1914 – 1r – 1 – us U.W. Library [810]
KRIEGSTAGE IN SUEDWEST / Willich, C – Pretoria, State Library, 1979. Orig. pub., Oldenburg: Gerhard Stalling, 1916. (Microfiche Reprint Series no.6). 2 fiche. Printed booklet – 9 – sa State Libr [960]
DAS KRIEGSVERHUETUNGSRECHT DES VOELKERBUNDES / Barandon, P – Berlin, 1933 – 5mf – 9 – ILM-4014/1 – ne IDC [340]
Krige, J *see* HISTORY AND TECHNOLOGY
Kriksunov, L *see* INFRARED SYSTEMS: FOR DETECTION, DIRECTION-FINDING AND AUTOMATIC TRACKING OF MOVING OBJECTS
KRILOF AND HIS FABLES / Krylov, Ivan Andreevich – By W.R.S. Ralston. 3rd ed., enl. London: Strahan, 1871. 268p., ill – 1 – us U.W. Library [390]
KRIMINALISTIKA / Shaver, B M & Vinburg, A I – Moscow, 1940. 200p. BR-9441/1 – 9 – ne IDC [360]
Krimphove, Frank *see* GLOBALE KONVERGENZ VON ZUFALLSSTRATEGIEN IN DER OPTIMIERUNG

DER KRIPPENWEG / Schaumann, Ruth – Muenchen: J Koesel & F Pustet, c1932 – 1r – 1 – us U.W. Library [430]
Krischer, Volker *see* UNTERSUCHUNG DER VERKERNUNG DER JAHRRINGSTRUKTUR SOWIE DER ROHDICHTE AN DOUGLASIEN [PSEUDOTSUGA MENZIESII (MIRB.) FRANCO] UNTERSCHIEDLICHER KRONENKLASSEN
DIE KRISE DER ALTEN WELT IM 3. JAHRHUNDERT N. ZW. UND IHRE URSACHEN / Altheim, Franz – (v.1. Die ausserroemische Welt. v.2. never publ. in this ed.. v.3. Goetter und Kaiser) – Mit beitraegen von E. Trautmann$Nehring. Berlin-Dahlem. 1943. Complete work published in rev. ed. under title: Niedergang der alten welt. Film Mas 8190 – 1 – us H.U. Library [900]
DIE "KRISE DES CHRISTENTUMS" : PROTESTANTISMUS UND KATHOLISCHE KIRCHE / Hettinger, Franz – Freiburg im Breisgau, St. Louis, Mo.: Herder, 1881 – 1mf – us A.T.L.A. [240]
KRISHNA DIWAN BAHADUR. THE TRAVANCORE TRIBES AND CASTES / Iyer, LAK – 3v. Trivandrum. 1937-41. BI-476 2 – 8 – ne IDC [306]
Krishna Rao, MV *see* THE GANGAS OF TALKAD: A MONOGRAPH ON THE HISTORY OF MYSORE FROM THE FOURTH TO THE CLOSE OF THE ELEVENTH CENTURY
Krishnamacharlu, C R *see* SUBJECT-INDEX TO THE ANNUAL REPORTS ON SOUTH-INDIAN EPIGRAPHY FROM 1887-1936
DIE KRISIS DES CHRISTENTHUMS IN DER MODERNEN THEOLOGIE / Hartmann, Eduard von – (Includes bibliographical references) – Berlin: Carl Duncker, 1880 – 1mf – 9 – 0-8370-8745-7 – 1986-2745 – us A.T.L.A. [240]
KRISIS UND ENTSCHEIDUNG IM JUDENTUM / Klatzkin, J – Berlin. 1921. BJ-28-59 1 – 9 – ne IDC [956]
KRISTDEMOKRATEN – Stockholm, Sweden. 1988- – 1 – sw Kungliga [072]
Kristensen, Evald Tang *see* VINDT MOLLE OG DENS EJERE
KRISTIANSTADS LANSDEMOKRATEN – Kristianstad, Sweden. 1932-57 – 99r – 1 – sw Kungliga [072]
KRISTIANSTADSBLADET – Kristianstad, Sweden. 1979-. Mellersta Skane, 1979-85 – 1 – sw Kungliga [072]
KRISTIANSTADSBLADET – (Mellersta Skane: 1971-77) – Kristianstad, Sweden. 1856-1978 – 540r – 1 – sw Kungliga [072]
KRISTIGA BALSS-THE CHRISTIAN VOICE – Riga, Latvia. Jul 1920-Aug 1940. Organ of the Latvian Baptist Union. Saweja Balss (The Voice of Isaiah), Jul 1920-Jun 1921 – 1 – 383.12 – us Baptist [240]
KRISTIGS WEHSTNESIS – Riga, Latvia. 1915, no.10; 1923-29. Ed. by William Fetler – 1 – 83.88 – us Baptist [240]
KRISTIN : EIN DEUTSCHES GRENZLANDMAEDEL / Lange, Mariluise – Reutlingen: Ensslin & Laiblin, 1943 – 1r – 1 – us U.W. Library [830]
DEN KRISTNA TANKENS TOLKNING AF JESU PERSON : EN BLICK PA DEN KRISTOLOGISKA UTVECKLINGEN INTILL NUTIDEN: TRE UTVIDGADE FOEREDRAG / Aulen, Gustaf – Uppsala: Norblad, [1910] – 1mf – us A.T.L.A. [240]
DEN KRISTNE BUDDHIST MISSION – (Lacking: v17-22 1942-47) – v9-38. 1934-63 – 3r – 1 – ATLA S0533 – us A.T.L.A. [073]
KRITERION – v1-7. 1900-07 – 1r – 1 – us Ross [290]
KRITICHESKIE ETIUDY / Lunacharskii, A V – L., knizhnyi sektor Gubono. 1925. BR-1379 2 – 8 – ne IDC [460]
KRITICHESKII OBZOR RAZRABOTKI GLAVNYKH RUSSKIKH ISTOCHNIKOV PO ISTORII MALOROSSII...1654-30 MAIA 1672 / Karpov, G F – Moscow, 1870. 179p. Materials relating to 17th century Ukraine. PR-11,179/1 – 9 – ne IDC [947]
KRITICHESKOE OBOZRENIE – Kritiko-bibliograficheskii zhurnal. M. 1907-09. B-1222 2 – 8 – ne IDC [460]
KRITICHESKOE OBOZRENIE – Zhurnal nauchnoi kritiki i bibliografii. M. 1879-80. B-1768 2 – 8 – ne IDC [460]
KRITIEK EN OPBOUW – Bandung. 1938-1950. v1-7 – 44mf – 9 – ne IDC [999]
KRITIK DER EPHESER- UND KOLOSSERBRIEFE / Holtzmann, Heinrich Julius – Leipzig: Wilhelm Engelmann, 1872. 1 fiche – 9 – us A.T.L.A. [240]
KRITIK DER EVANGELIEN UND GESCHICHTE IHRES UHRSPRUNGS / Bauer, Bruno – Berlin. 2 Baende 1850-1851 – 11mf – 8 – ne Slangenburg [240]
KRITIK DER EVANGELISCHEN GESCHICHTE / Bauer, Bruno – Leipzig 3 Baende 1841-1842 – 21mf – 8 – ne Slangenburg [240]
KRITIK DER FREIHEITSTHEORIEN : EINE ABHANDLUNG UEBER DAS PROBLEM DER WILLENSFREIHEIT / Mack, Joseph – (Includes bibliographical references and index) – Leipzig: Johann Ambrosius Barth, 1906 – 1mf – 9 – 0-8370-4260-7 – 1985-2260 – us A.T.L.A. [210]
KRITIK DER PAULINISCHEN BRIEFE / Bauer, Bruno – (Erste Abteilung: Der Ursprung der Galaterbriefe, Berlin 1850 2mf; Zweite Abteilung: Der Ursprung des ersten Korintherbriefes, Berlin 1851 2mf; Dritte und letzte Abteilung: Berlin 1852 3mf) – 8 – ne Slangenburg [240]
KRITIK DER REINEN VERNUNFT / Kant, Immanuel – Berlin: 1919 – xi/609p – 1 – us U.W. Library [190]
KRITIK DER REVIDIERTEN LUTHERBIBEL / Schwalb, Moritz – Berlin: Walther & Apolant, 1884.1 fiche – 9 – us A.T.L.A. [240]
KRITIK DES MIDRASCH SCHIR-HASCHIRIM, NACH DER MUENCHENER HANDSCHRIFT NO. 50 ORIENTAL / Chodowski, S – Berlin. 1877. BJ-32-35 1 – 9 – ne IDC [470]
KRITIK DES NEUEN TESTAMENTS VON EINEM GRIECHISCHEN PHILOSOPHEN DES 3. JAHRHUNDERTS (T.U.U. 3-37/4) / Harnack, Adolf von – Leipzig, 1911 – 3mf – 9 – ne Slangenburg [240]
KRITIK UND ERLAEUTERUNG DES GOETHE'SCHEN FAUST : NEBST EINEM ANHANGE ZUR SITTLICHEN BEURTHEILUNG GOETHE'S / Weisse, Christian Hermann – (Includes bibliographical references) – Leipzig: Reichenbach, 1837 – 1r – 1 – us U.W. Library [430]
KRITIK UND UEBERLIEFERUNG AUF DEM GEBIETE DER ERFORSCHUNG DES URCHRISTENTUMS / Krueger, Gustav – Gieszen: J. Ricker, 1903 – 1mf – us A.T.L.A. [240]
KRITIKA – Cracow. v. 8, no. 2-v. 16, no. 6. 1906-1914 – 1 – us NY Public [460]
KRITISCH EXEGETISCHES HANDBUCH UEBER DIE APOSTELGESCHICHTE / Meyer, H A W – Goettingen 3. Auflage 1861 – 9mf – 8 – ne Slangenburg [220]
KRITISCH EXEGETISCHES HANDBUCH UEBER DIE APOSTELGESCHICHTE / Meyer, H A W; ed by Wendt, Hans Hinrich – (Sechste, resp. siebente Auflage neu bearbeitet) – Goettingen, 1888 – 10mf – 8 – ne Slangenburg [220]
KRITISCH EXEGETISCHES HANDBUCH UEBER DIE BRIEFE AN DIE THESSALONICHER / Leunemann, Gottlieb – Goettingen: Vandenhoeck & Rup., 1878. 1 fiche – 9 – us A.T.L.A. [240]
KRITISCH EXEGETISCHES HANDBUCH UEBER DIE BRIEFE PAULI AN TIMOTHEUS UND TITUS / Weiss, Bernhard – Goettingen: Vandenhoeck & Rup., 1886. 1 fiche – 9 – us A.T.L.A. [240]
KRITISCH EXEGETISCHES HANDBUCH UEBER DIE EVANGELIEN DES MARKUS UND LUKAS / Meyer, Heinrich August Wilhelm – (Includes bibliographical references) – 7. Aufl. Goettingen: Vandenhoeck und Ruprecht, 1885 – 2mf – 9 – 0-8370-9721-5 – 1986-3721 – us A.T.L.A. [220]
KRITISCHE BEITRAEGE ZU DEN CONSTANTIN-SCHRIFTEN DES EUSEBIUS (T.U.U. 3-36/4) / Heikel, I A – Leipzig, 1911 – 2mf – 9 – ne Slangenburg [240]
KRITISCHE BEITRAEGE ZUR GESCHICHTE DER DICHTERSPRACHE KLOPSTOCK'S / Petri, Friedrich Karl Wilhelm – (Includes bibliographical references) – Greifswald: J Abel, 1894 – 1r – 1 – us U.W. Library [430]
KRITISCHE BELEUCHTUNG DES C.F. WEITZMANN'SCHEN HARMONIESYSTEMS, UND DES SCHRIFTENS: "DIE NEUE HARMONIELEHRE IM STREIT MIT DER ALTEN", VON F. J. KINKEL / Kunkel, F – Frankfurt am Main: F B Auffarth, 1863 – 1 – us Sibley [780]
KRITISCHE BEMERKUNGEN UA5BER GEGENSTAA5NDE AUS DEM PFLANZENREICHE / Medikus, F K – Mannheim, 1793. 303 pp. B-1324 2 – 8 – ne IDC [580]
KRITISCHE BEMERKUNGEN UEBER DIE EUROPAEISCHEN LEBERMOOSE MIT BEZUG AUF DIE EXEMPLARE DES EXSICCATENWERKES HEPATICAE EUROPAE EXSICCATAE / Schiffner, V – S. 1-29. Prag. 1901-43. B-5350 2 – 8 – ne IDC [580]
KRITISCHE BEMERKUNGEN UND ZUSAETZE ZU KURT SPRENGEL'S WERK: UEBER DEN BAU UND DIE NATUR DER GEWAECHSE / Link, J H F – Halle. 1812. B-5479 2 – 8 – ne IDC [580]
KRITISCHE BEMERKUNGEN ZU MEINER AUSGABE VON ORIGENES' EXHORTATIO, CONTRA CELSUM, DE ORATIONE : ENTGEGNUNG AUF DIE VON PAUL WENDLAND IN DEN GOETTINGISCHEN GELEHRTEN ANZEIGEN 1899 NR. 4. VEROEFFENTLICHTE KRITIK / Koetschau, Paul – Leipzig, J.C. Hinrichs, 1899 – 1mf – us A.T.L.A. [240]
KRITISCHE BRIEFE UEBER DIE TONKUN. / Marpurg, Friedrich Wilhelm – Bd. I-III, I-IV theil. 1759-64 – 2,9 – us Sibley [780]
KRITISCHE BRIEFE UEBER DIE TONKUNST MIT KLEINEN CLAVIERSTUECKEN UND SINGODEN / Marpurg, Friedrich Wilhelm – P 713. 3 v. 1760-1764 – 9 – ne IDC [780]
KRITISCHE EINLEITUNG IN DIE GESCHICHTE UND LEHRSAETZE DER ALTEN UND NEUEN MUSIK / Marpurg, Friedrich Wilhelm – 1759 – 9 – us Sibley [780]
KRITISCHE EINLEITUNG IN DIE GESCHICHTE UND LEHRSAETZE DER ALTEN UND NEUEN MUSIK / Marpurg, Friedrich Wilhelm – P 714. 1759 – 9 – ne IDC [780]
KRITISCHE GAENGE / Vischer, Friedrich Theodor – Stuttgart: J G Cotta, 1861-73 – 1 – us U.W. Library [430]
KRITISCHE GESCHICHTE DER THALMUD-UEBERSETZUNGEN ALLER ZEITEN UND ZUNGEN / Bischoff, Erich – Frankfurt: J. Kauffmann, 1899. 1 fiche – 9 – us A.T.L.A. [270]
KRITISCHE REVISION DER INSEKTENFAUNE DEUTSCHLANDS NACH DEM SYSTEM BEARBEITET / Panzer, G W F – Nuernberg, 1805-06. 2v.Z-1529/2 – 8 – ne IDC [590]
KRITISCHE RUNDSCHAU – Bremen, Germany. 1 Mar 1928-17 Feb 1935 – 1r – 1 – gw Mikrofilm [072]
KRITISCHE RUNDSCHAU – Bremen, mar 1 1928-feb 17 1935 – 1r – 1 – Inquire at Mikrofilmarchiv for details – gw Misc Inst [072]
KRITISCHE SENDSCHREIBEN UEBER DIE PROBEBIBEL / Cassel, Paulus – Berlin: Friedrich Schulze, 1885.1 fiche – 9 – us A.T.L.A. [240]
KRITISCHE THEORIE UND METAPHYSIK / Geyer, Carl-Friedrich – Darmstadt, 1980 – 250p – 9 – DM48.00 – 3-89349-025-6 – gw Hänsel [110]
KRITISCHE UEBERSICHT DER EUROPAEISCHEN VOEGEL / Schlegel, H – Leiden, etc. 1844. (Text in German and French). Z-1908 2 – 8 – ne IDC [590]
KRITISCHES JAHRBUCH – Hamburg: Actien-Gesellschaft, 1889-1890 – 1 – us U.W. Library [943]
KRITISCHES JOURNAL DER PHILOSOPHIE – v1-2 no 3. 1802-03 (complete) – 1r – 1 – ATLA S0054 – us A.T.L.A. [073]
KRITISCH-LITERAERISCHE UEBERSICHT DER REISENDEN IN RUSSLAND BIS ZUM 1700, DEREN BERICHTE BEKANNT SIND / Adelung, F von – Spb., Leipzig. 2v. 1846 – 17mf – 9 – ne IDC [910]
Kritz, Wilhelm *see* DIE EVANGELISCHE LEHRE
Krivenko, S N *see*
- NA RASPUT'I
- SOBRANIE SOCHINENII VNUTRENNIIA OBOZRENIIA, KHRONIKA I DR. STAT'I IZ "OTECHESTVENNYKH ZAPISOK" (1873-1884)

Krivitsky, Walter G *see* RUSIA EN ESPANA
Krivopolena, Maria Dmitrievna *see* BABUSHKINY STARINY
Krivosheeva, A *see* SOVETSKII FOL'KLOR
Krivosheina, P I *see* AGRO-KOOPERATIVNYI KRUZHOK
KRIZIS ISKUSSTVA / Berdiaev, N A – Izd. Lemana. M. 1918. BR-1995 2 – 8 – ne IDC [700]
Krocker, A J *see* FLORA SILESIACA RENOVATA
Kroeber, A L *see*
- AMERICAN CULTURE AND THE NORTHWEST COAST
- THE ESKIMO OF SMITH SOUND
- THE TRIBES OF THE PACIFIC COAST OF NORTH AMERICA

Kroeger, Arved *see* ORDENSDEUTSCHE
Kroeger, Timm *see*
- DER EINZIGE UND SEINE LIEBE
- HEIN WIECK
- NEUN NOVELLEN
- NOVELLEN
- DES REICHES KOMMEN
- DER SCHULMEISTER VON HANDEWITT
- UM DEN WEGZOLL

Kroenig, Gottlieb *see* DAS DASEIN GOTTES WISSENSCHAFTLICH BEWIESEN
DIE KROENUNGSOPFER : EIN MOZART-ROMAN / Watzlik, Hans – Karlsbad: A Kraft, 1944 – 1r – 1 – us U.W. Library [830]
Krohn, Barthold N *see* GESCHICHTE DER FANATISCHEN UND ENTHUSUASTISCHEN WIEDERTAEUFER VORNEHMLICH IN NIEDERDEUTSCHLAND. MELCHIOR HOFMANN UND DIE SECTE DER HOFMANNIANER
Krohn, Julius *see* SUOMALAISEN KIRJALLISUUDEN HISTORIA
Krok, T O B N *see* SVENSK BOTANISK LITERATUR
Krok, T OBN *see* ANTECKNINGAR TILL EN MONOGRAFI OEFVER VAEXTFAMILJEN VALERIANEAE. 1. VALERIANELLA HALL
KROKODIL – 1928-60 – 1 – 283.00 – us L of C Photodup [460]
KROKODIL – (1986-91 1r per y $85y; 1992-94 1r $85y. 1995-96 1r $85) – 1999- – 1r per y – 1 – $80.00 standing order – us Ross [072]
KROKODIL – Moscow, USSR. 1969-1988 – 19r – $950.00 – R63622 – us Library Micro [072]
KROKODIL (CROCODILE) – Moscow. U.S.S.R. 1961- – 1 – us UMI [460]
Kroll, Adam *see* SIX QUARTETTOS FOR A GERMAN FLUTE, VIOLIN, VIOLA AND VIOLONCELLO, WITH AN OCCASIONAL ACCOMPANYMENT FOR TWO FRENCH HORNS..
Kroll, Erwin *see* ERNST THEODOR AMADEUS HOFFMANN
Krombholz, J V von *see*
- CONSPECTUS FUNGORUM
- NATURGETREUE ABBILDUNGEN UND BESCHREIBUNGEN DES ESSBAREN SCHWAEMME

Kromrei, Ernst *see* GLAUBENSLEHRE UND GEBRAEUCHE DER AELTEREN ABESSINISCHEN KIRCHE
Kronauer, Fr *see* DIE WASSERNOT IM EMMENTHAL; FUENF MAEDCHEN; DURSLI DER BRANNTWEINLAEUTER
Kronenberg, Moritz *see* DIE ALL-EINHEIT
Kroner, T *see* FESTSCHRIFT
Krones, F von *see* AUS DEM TAGEBUCHE ERZHERZOG JOHANNS VON OESTERREICH 1810-1815
KRONICLE – Kincaid. Kan. 1886-1892 – 1 – us UMI [071]
KRONIK / Indonesia. Kementerian Penerangan – (Missing: 1963 v3-6; 1952-1953 v10-12; 1953-1954 v14-15; 1954 v17-20(1-2); 195? v22; 195? v24; 195? v8) – Djakarta, 1951-1963 – 113mf – 9 – SE-576/1 – ne IDC [950]
KRONIK DOKUMENTASI – Djakarta: Kementerian Penerangan, Bag. Dokumentasi, 19(52)-(69).39v. Some vols. also have Dutch or English.Some vols. issued by other subdivisions of the Departemen Penerangan – 1 – us U.W. Library [950]
KRONIKA – London, UK. 17 Nov 1962-28 Aug 1971 – 1 – uk British Libr Newspaper [072]
KRONIKA (NEW YORK: 1944) – (Library has: v.1,no.1-4,7-8,10-12; v.2,no.1,3-7,9-11; v.3,no.1-v.4,no.8; v.5, no.1-v.7,no.12; v.8,no.2-v9,no.3; Jan. 1944-Mar.1952) – New York: "Kronika" Hungarian Press, 1944- – 1 – CSUX86-S144 – us Hoover Inst Photo [947]
Kronlins, Janis *see*
- KONGRESA GRAHMATA
- MUHSU KORI UN DSEESMAS: LATWIJAS BAPTISTU DRAUDSCHU KORU WEHSTURES MATERIALU KRAHJUMS
- US AUGSCHU!: LATWI JA BAPTISTU DRAUDSCHU 75 GADU DARBIBAS APSKATS

KRONOBERGAREN – Vaxjo, 1979-93 – 1 – sw Kungliga [072]
DES KRONPRINZEN REGIMENT : ROMAN / Samarow, Gregor – 2. Aufl. Stuttgart: Deutsche Verlags-Anstalt, [18–] – 1r – 1 – us U.W. Library [830]
KRONSHTADSKII MIATEZH / Kornatovskii, N – Leningrad, 1931 – 1 – 35.00r – us Hoover Inst Photo [947]

KRONSTAEDTER ZEITUNG – Kronstadt (Brasov), Rumaenien. 10 Okt 1916-11 Jan (1917, incomplete) – 29r – 1 – gw Mikrofilm [949]
KROONE DER VIER HOOFT-DEUGHDEN, TOE-GHE-EYGENT AEN DE H. MAGHET ENDE MOEDER GODS MARIA : DOOR ERNEST VAN VEEN, ADVOCAET ENDE WERDEYN VAN SIJNE KONINGHL. MAJESTEYTS MUNTE DESER STEDE / Veen, E van – Sole ed. Brussel, 1644 – 1mf – 9 – O-3190/1 – ne IDC [760]
Kropat, A *see* DIE SYNTAX DES AUTORS DER CHRONIK VERGLICHEN MIT DER SEINER QUELLEN BEIHEFTE ZUR ZEITSCH. F. D. ALTTESTAMENTLICHE WISSENSCHAFT XVI
Kropatscheck, Friedrich *see* DAS SCHRIFTPRINZIP DER LUTHERISCHEN KIRCHE
KROPOTKIN AND LAW / Cahm, C – 1980, 13p – 9 – 1.00f – at Libertarian Micro [335]
KROPOTKIN ON LAW / Bax, C – 1980. 12p – 9 – 1.00f – at Libertarian Micro [335]
Kropotkin, Peter *see* MUTUAL AID
Kropotkin, Petr Alekseevich *see* MODERN SCIENCE AND ANARCHISM
Kroschewski, Klaus *see*
INTERNATIONALE TENDENZEN IN DER TIERGESUNDHEITSUEBERWACHUNG UND DARAUS ABGELEITETE SCHLUSSFOLGERUNGEN FUER DIE ANPASSUNG DES NATIONALEN TIERSEUCHENBERICHTSSYSTEMS
KROTKI SZKIS DO HISTORJI 1-GO POLSKIEGO KORPUSU / Dowbor-Musnicki, Josef – Wyd. 2-e. Warzszawa: Nak. P.S.W. "Plac owka", 1919. 3v in 1 – 1 – CSUX88-B5403 – us Hoover Inst Photo [999]
Krotoschiner, Hermann Alfred *see* DER SCHUTZ DES KREDITVERKEHRS VOR DEN GEFAHREN AUS ZU UMFANGREICHEN SICHERUNGSUEBEREIGNUNGEN
KROTOSCHINER ZEITUNG – Krotoschin (Krotoszyn), Poland. 18 Feb-31 Aug 1922; 19 Jun 1926-28 Sept 1932 – 4r – 1 – gw Mikrofilm [943]
KROVAVYI OPYT : OTKRYTOE PISMO BYVSHEGO MENSHEVIKA / Genkin, Aleksandr Borisovich – Moskva: Izd-vo Vseros. tsentr. ispolnitelnogo kom-ta sovetov r., s., k. i k. deputatov, 1919 – 1 – CSUX88-B7008 – us Hoover Inst Photo [947]
KROVAVYI TSAR : FANTAZIIA / Amfiteatrov, Aleksandr – Niulork: Izd. "Russkago golosa", 1919 – 1 – CSUX89-B6814 – us Hoover Inst Photo [460]
Kroy, Moshe *see* A CRITIQUE OF OBJECTIVISM
Kruchen, Gottfried *see* DIE BIBEL BERNHARD OVERBERGS
Kruchenykh, A *see*
– 15 LET RUSSKOGO FUTURIZMA. 1912-1927
– APOKALIPSIS V RUSSKOI LITERATURE
– FONETIKA TEATRA
– PRIEMY LENINSKOI RECHI. K IZUCHENIIU IAZYKA LENINA
– SDVIGOLOGIIA RUSSKOGO STIKHA
– SLOVO KAK TAKOVOE
– TE LI LE
– TSVETNAIA KLEI
Kruecken, O von *see* DAS GEISTIGE UNGARN; BIOGRAFICHES LEXIKON
Kruegel, Rudolf *see* DER BEGRIFF DES VOLKSGEISTES IN ERNST MORITZ ARNDTS GESCHICHTSANSCHAUUNG
Krueger, Ferdinand *see* WITTE LILJEN
Krueger, Gustav *see*
– DOGMA AND HISTORY
– DAS DOGMA VOM NEUEN TESTAMENT
– DAS DOGMA VON DER DREIEINIGKEIT UND GOTTMENSCHHEIT IN SEINER GESCHICHTLICHEN ENTWICKLUNG
– HISTORY OF EARLY CHRISTIAN LITERATURE IN THE FIRST THREE CENTURIES
– KRITIK UND UEBERLIEFERUNG AUF DEM GEBIETE DER ERFORSCHUNG DES URCHRISTENTUMS
– LUCIFER, BISCHOF VON CALARIS UND DAS SCHISMA DER LUCIFERIANER
– MONOPHYSITISCHE STREITIGKEITEN IM ZUSAMMENHANGE MIT DER REICHSPOLITIK
– DAS PAPSTTUM. SEINE IDEE UND IHRE TRAEGER
– DIE RELIGION DER GOETHEZEIT
– WAS HEISST UND ZU WELCHEN ENDE STUDIERT MAN DOGMENGESCHICHTE?
Krueger, Hermann Anders *see* DER JUNGE EICHENDORFF
Krueger, MS *see* BIBLIOGRAPHIA BOTANICA
Krueger, Paul *see*
– HELLENISMUS UND JUDENTUM IM NEUTESTAMENTLICHEN ZEITALTER
– PHILO UND JOSEPHUS: ALS APOLOGETEN DES JUDENTUMS
– DAS SYRISCH-MONOPHYSITISCHE MOENCHTUM IM TUR-AB(H)DIN VON SEINEN ANFAENGEN BIS ZUR MITTE DES 12. JAHRHUNDERTS
Krueger, Wilhelm *see* DIE AUFERSTEHUNG JESU IN IHRER BEDEUTUNG FUER DEN CHRISTLICHEN GLAUBEN
Krueger-Westend, Herman *see*
– GOETHE UND DER ORIENT
– GOETHE UND SEINE ELTERN
Kruemmer, G *see* DIE BERGARBEITER-VERHAELTNISSE IN GROSSBRITANNIEN
Kruenitz, Johann Georg *see* OEKONOMISCH-TECHNISCHE ENZYKLOPAEDIE..
Krug, Camille *see* LE CERTIFICAT D'HERITIER DANS LES DEPARTEMENTS DU BAS-RHIN, DU HAUT-RHIN ET DE LA MOSELLE D'APRES LA LOI D'INTRODUCTION DU DROIT FRANCAIS DU 1ER JUIN 1924
KRUG UND TINTENFASS : GEDICHTE / Baumbach, Rudolf – Leipzig: A G Liebeskind, 1887 – 1r – 1 – us U.W. Library [810]
Krug, Wilhelm Traugott *see* SCHELLING UND HEGEL. ODER DIE NEUESTE PHILOSOPHIE IM VERNICHTUNGSKRIEGE MIT SICH SELBST BEGRIFFEN
Kruger, J D L *see* BANTUSTAN
HET KRUIS GEPLANT IN EEN ONBEKEND NEGERLAND VAN MIDDEN-AFRIKA.. : VERHAAL VAN DE STICHTING DER SINT-ANTONIUS-MISSIE IN HET KRONINKRIJK OEROENDI / Burgt, Joannes Michael M van der – Boxtel-Burgakker: Procure der Witte Paters, 1921 – us Res Libr [960]
Kruitwagen, E *see* EEN MISSALE LEODIENSE GEDRUKT DOOR JOH. DE WESTFALIA TE LEUVEN (OVERDRUCK)
Krul, J H *see*
– EERLYCKE TYTKORTING BESTAENDE IN VERSCHEYDE RYMEN
– EERLYCKE TYTKORTING BESTAENDE IN VERSCHEYDE RYMEN GEMAECT
– MINNE-SPIEGEL ENDE WEG.WYSER.TER DEUGDEN
– MINNE-SPIEGEL TER DEUGHDEN
– PAMPIERE WERELD OFTE WERELDSCHE OEFFENINGE, BEGRIJPENDE IN VIER DEELEN MEEST ALLE DE RIJMEN
– PAMPIERE WERELD OFTE WERELDSCHE OEFFENINGE, WAER IN BEGREPEN ZIJN MEEST ALLE DE RIJMEN EN WERKEN VAN I.H. KRUL
Krumbacher, K *see* DER HEILIGE GEORG IN DER GRIECHISCHEN UEBERLIEFERUNG (ABAW.PPH 25/3)
Krumbiegel, Peter *see* ISOTOPENPRAXIS
Krummacher, Friedrich Wilhelm *see* THE RISEN REDEEMER
KRUMME WEGE ZUR UNFEHLBARKEIT / Buchmann, Jacob – (Includes bibliographical references) – Breslau [Wroclaw]: Fiedler & Hentschel, 1874 – 1mf – 9 – 0-8370-9128-4 – 1986-3128 – us A.T.L.A. [240]
Krummel, L *see* GESCHICHTE DER BOEHMISCHEN REFORMATION IM FUENFZEHNTEN JAHRHUNDERT
Krummel, Leopold *see* UTRAQUISTEN UND TABORITEN
Krusch, B *see*
– FREDEGARII ET ALIORUM CHRONICA (MGH 2: 2.BD)
– GREGORII TURONENSIS OPERA (MGH 2: 1.BD)
– PASSIONES VITAEQUE SANCTORUM AEVI MEROVINGICI ET ANTIQUORUM ALIQUOT (MGH 2: 3.BD)
– PASSIONES VITAEQUE SANCTORUM AEVI MEROVINGICI (MGH 2: 4.BD)
– PASSIONES VITAEQUE SANCTORUM AEVI MEROVINGICI (MGH 2: 5.BD)
– PASSIONES VITAEQUE SANCTORUM AEVI MEROVINGICI (MGH 2: 6.BD)
– PASSIONES VITAEQUE SANCTORUM AEVI MEROVINGICI (MGH 2: 7.BD)
– STUDIEN ZUR CHRISTLICH-MITTELALTERLICHEN CHRONOLOGIE
– VENANTI HONORI CLEMENTIANI FORTUNATI PRESBYTERI ITALICI OPERA PEDESTRIA (MGH 1: 4. 2.TEIL)
Kruschwitz, William Albin *see* A MISSIONS INFORMATION CONFERENCE MANUAL FOR THE SOUTHERN BAPTIST FOREIGN MISSION BOARD, RICHMOND, VIRGINIA
Kruse, Georg Richard *see* RICHARD WAGNERS TONDRAMEN
Kruse, Heinrich *see*
– BRUTUS
– DAS MAEDCHEN VON BYZANZ
– MARINO FALIERO
Kruse, Paul *see* DIE PAEDAGOGISCHEN ELEMENTE IN DER PHILOSOPHIE DES JAKOB BALMES
KRUSHENIE (ARMIIA) / Lappo-Danilevskaia, Nadezhda Aleksandrovna (Liutkevich) – (Berlin): Glagol, 1922. 368p. In Cyrillic characters. 1 reel.1246 – 1 – us U.W. Library [460]
Kruske, L *see* JOHANNES A LASCO UND DER SACRAMENTSSTREIT
Kruszka, Waclaw *see* SIEDM SIEDMIOLICI, CZYLI POT WIEKU ZYCIA:...HISTORJI POLSKIEJ W AMERYCE
Krutchkoff, R G *see* JOURNAL OF STATISTICAL COMPUTATION AND SIMULATION
KRUYDTBOECK OFT BESCHRIJVINGHE VAN ALLERLEYE GHEWASSEN, KRUYDEREN, HESTEREN, ENDE GHEBOOMTEN / Lobelius, M – Antwerpen. 1581. B-7669 2 – 8 – ne IDC [580]
KRUZHESKIYA BESEDY = FRIENDLY CONVERSATIONS / Pashkov, Vasilii A – St. Petersburg, 1880. 18p. Filmed with: Pamyati A.V. Pashkov, Recollections of A.V. Pashkov, St. Petersburg, 1904. 60p – 1 – $5.00 – us Baptist [240]
Krylov, Ivan Andreevich *see* KRILOF AND HIS FABLES
KRYMINALNA-PRATSESUALNY KODEKS BELARUSKAI SSR : NA BELARUSKAI I RUSKAI MOVAKH / Byelorussian S.S.R. – Minsk: Dzi arzha unae Vydavetstva BSSR, 1961 – 1 – CSUX91-B2237 – us Hoover Inst Photo [360]
KRYMINALNA-PRATSESUALNY KODEKS BELARUSKAI SSR (1923). RUSSIAN UGOLOVNO-PROTSESSUALNYI KODEKS BELORUSSKOI SSR : OFITSIALNYI TEKST S IZMENENIIAMI NA 15 APRELIA 1957 G. I S PRILOZHENIEM SISTEMATIZIROVANNYKH MATERIALOV / MINISTERSTVO IUSTITSII BELORUSKOI SSR / Byelorussian S.S.R. – Minsk: Gos. izd-vo BSSR, Rd. nauchno-tekh. lit-ry, 1957 – 1 – CSUX91-B1998 – us Hoover Inst Photo [360]
KRYMINALNA-PRATSESUALNY KODEKS BELARUSKAI SSR (1961). RUSSIAN UGOLOVNO-PROTSESSUALNYI KODEKS BELORUSSKOI SSR : OFITSIALNYI TEKST S IZMENENIIAMI NA 1 APRELIA 1971 G. I S PRILOZHENIEM POSTATEINOGO MATERIALA / MINISTERSTVO IUSTITSII BELORUSSKOI SSR / Byelorussian S.S.R. – Minsk: Belarus, 1971 – 1 – CSUX91-B2222 – us Hoover Inst Photo [360]
KRYMOV, IURII (BEKLEMISHEV, IURII SOLOMONOVICH) (1908-1941) – Opis' dokumental'nykh materialov lichnogo fonda No.593. Moscow, 1949. 14p. BR-10,692/1 – 9 – ne IDC [010]
KRYMSKI I KOLKHOZNIK : ORGAN OK VKP(B), KRYMT SIKA I SOI UZA KOLKHOZSOI UZOV – (Includes c.1: 1930:June 7) – Simferopol: [s.n.], 1930 – 1 – CSUXANR8766-S – us Hoover Inst Photo [947]
KRYMSKOE T SENTRALNOE STATISTICHESKOE UPRAVLENIE *see* BIULLETEN KRYMSKOGO T SENTRALNOGO STATISTICHESKOGO UPRAVLENII A
Krynski, A A *see* JAK NIE NALEZY MOWIC I PISAC PO POLSKU
KRYPTOGAMEN FLORA VON DEUTSCHLAND, OESTERREICH UND DER SCHWEIZ / Rabenhorst, G L – 1884-1910 – 7 – uk Microform Academic [580]
KRYPTOGAMEN-FLORA VON DEUTSCHLAND / Rabenhorst, G L – Leipzig. 1845-53. B-5282 2 – 8 – ne IDC [580]
KRYPTOGAMEN-FLORA VON DEUTSCHLAND / ed by Rabenhorst, G L – Leipzig. 1881-1941. ed. 2. v1-14 – 556mf – 8 – ne IDC [580]
KRYTYKA, MIESIECZNIK POSWIECONY SPRAWOM SPOLECZNYM, NAUCE I SZTUCE – Cracow, 1906-14 – 4r – 1 – us Ross [460]
Krzyzanowski, K *see* POLSKA BAJKA LUDOWA W UKADZIE SYSTEMATYCZNYM
KSATRYA DICTIONARY : KAMUS INGGERIS-INDONESIA / Nuh, Muhammad – SE-5869 1. 1964 – 9 – ne IDC [490]
KSATRYA VOCABULARY. KAMUS INGGERIS-INDONESIA, INDONESIA-INGGERIS / Nuh, Muhammad – SE-2074 1. 1950 – 9 – ne IDC [490]
Ksenofontov, F *see* GOSUDARSTVO I PRAVO (OPYT IZLOZHENIIA MARKSISTSKOGO UCHENIIA O SUSHCHESTVE GOSUDARSTVA I PRAVA). S PREDISLOVIEM N. V. KRYLENKO
Ksmendra *see* AVADANA KALPALATA, A COLLECTION OF LEGENDARY STORIES ABOUT THE BODHISATTVAS; WITH ITS TIBETAN VERSION
K'tut Tantri [pseud] *see* REVOLT IN PARADISE
Ku, Hung-Min *see* THE STORY OF A CHINESE OXFORD MOVEMENT
Ku Klux Klan of Canada *see*
– KLORAN
– MANUAL OF THE ORDER OF CITIZENSHIP
KU KLUX KLAN, OHIO KNIGHTS – 1923-24. 1 reel – 1 – us Ohio Hist [025]
KU KLUX KLAN. SELECT TITLES – 1871-1906 – 2r – 1 – us Ross [360]
Ku Ping-Yuan *see* CHUNG-KUO LAO-TUNG FA LING HUI-PIEN
K'UAI PAO = CHINESE EXPRESS – Toronto. v1-19, 1971-89 – 1 – $6,300.00 – cn McLaren [072]
KUAN-CH'A – (Observer). v. 1-5. Shanghai. 1946-48. Lacking: (12-13) 1946; (12) 1948. BCH-919 2 – 8 – ne IDC [073]
KUANG-CHOU HSUEH-PAO – (Canton Journal). v. 1 (1-2). Canton. 1937. BCH-793 2 – 8 – ne IDC [073]
KUANG-CHOU-SHIH SHIH-CHENG KAI-YAO / Canton. Municipal Administration – 1922. BCH-856 2 – 8 – ne IDC [305]
KUANG-CHOU-SHIH SHIH-CHENG LI-KUEI CHANG-CH'ENG HUI-PIEN – 1922 – 8 – BCH-846 2 – ne IDC [950]
KUANG-CHOU-SHIH-CHENG PAO-KAO HUI-PIEN – Collection By Wang Yun-sheng. 7 v. 1932-34. BCH-855 2 – 8 – ne IDC [080]
KUANG-HSI HSIANG-SHIH LU – List of successful candidates in the imperial examination in Kwangsi province: 1867, 1893, 1901, 1903. 1 reel – 1 – 12.00 – us Chinese Res [950]
KUANG-HSI JIH-PAO – Nanning, Kwangsi. Mar 1, 1961-Sep 25, 1965. Scattered issues missing. 1 reel – 1 – 15.00 – us Chinese Res [072]
KUANGSHAN JIXIE = MINING MACHINERY – 1981- . F/P229 – 9 – $4.50f – cc Microforms [622]
KUANG-TA-HSUEH-PAO / Canton. University – (Journal of Canton University). Canton. Jul-Sep 1958. BCH-796 2 – 8 – ne IDC [073]
KUANG-TA-HSUEH-PAO / Canton. University – (Journal of Canton University). v. 1 (1). Canton. 1949. BCH-795 2 – 8 – ne IDC [073]
KUANG-TA-HSUEH-PAO / Canton. University – (Journal of Canton University). v. 1. Hongkong. 1959. BCH-794 2 – 8 – ne IDC [073]
KUANG-TS'ANG HSUEH-HUI YEN-SHUO PAO / Shanghai. Kuang-ts'ang Society – (Kuang-ts'ang Society Lecture Bulletin). v. 1-4. Shanghai. 1916. BCH-797 2 – 8 – ne IDC [073]
KUANG-TUNG – Kuang-chou fu-chih, 1759 – 8 – BCH-586 2 – ne IDC [950]
KUANG-TUNG FU-I CH'UAN-SHU – Taxation of Kwangtung. 105 v. circa. 1780. BCH-839 2 – 8 – ne IDC [336]
KUANG-TUNG HSIANG-SHIH LU – List of sucessful candidates in the imperial examination in Kwangtung province: 1852, 1900. 1 reel – 1 – 12.00 – us Chinese Res [950]
KUANG-TUNG TAN-HSING FA-LING HUI-TSUAN / ed by Wu Nuan-sen – Collected Local Regulations of Kwangtung. 6 v. 1921. appendix. BCH-844 2 – 8 – ne IDC [340]
KUANG-TUNG T'UNG-CHIH – 1731, 64. BCH-584 2 – 8 – ne IDC [950]
KUASAILAH LAUTAN INDONESIA / Pardi, N – SE-4455 1. 1951 – 9 – ne IDC [950]
KUBA FIELD NOTES / Vansina, Jan – 1979 – 1 – us Res Libr [960]
KUBANSKII KOOPERATOR – (Missing: 1917-22. 1923 n8) – Krasnodar, 1917-24 – 30mf – 9 – COR-646/1 – ne IDC [334]
KUBANSKII SBORNIK; TRUDY KUBANSKOGO OBLASTNOGO STATISTICHESKOGO KOMITETA – (Missing: 1883, v1 (p1-vi, 1-79); 1910-1911, v15-16; 1916, v21) – Ekaterinodar. v1-21. 1883-1916 – 113mf – 9 – RET-5/1 – ne IDC [947]
Kube, Constanze *see* DIE PHILOSOPHISCHEN GRUNDLAGEN UND DIE POLITISCHE ZIELSTELLUNG DER PERSONALISTISCHEN GRUNDKONZEPTION VON KAROL WOJTYLA

Kube, Helga *see* DIE INDUSTRIEANSIEDLUNG IN LUDWIGSHAFEN AM RHEIN BIS 1892 (CHEMIE UND METALLVERARBEITUNG)
KUBOK METELEI / Belyi, A – (Chetvertaia simfoniia). 1908. BR-597 2 – 8 – ne IDC [460]
Kuchler, J *see* TROIS CONCERTANT, SIX, POUR DEUX VIOLONS ET BASSE. OP. 3
Kuchowicz, B *see* NUCLEAR AND RELATIVISTIC ASTROPHYSICS AND NUCLIDIC COSMOCHEMISTRY
Kucich, Greg *see* NINETEENTH-CENTURY CONTEXTS
Kuckuck, P *see* BEITRAEGE ZUR KENNTNIS DER ECTOCARPUS-ARTEN DES KIELER FOEHRDE
Kuczynski Godard, Maximo H *see* LA VIDA EN LA AMAZONIA PERUANA. OBSERVACION DE UN MEDICO. LIMA, 1944
Kuczynski, Juergen *see* DIE MENSCHENRECHTE
KUDA I KAK VEDET SOVETSKAIA VLAST' KREST'IANSTVO? / Kamenev, L B – L, 1925 – 3mf – 9 – COR-477/1 – ne IDC [334]
Kudaszewicz, Joseph *see* GESCHICHTE DER REFORMIRTEN KIRCHEN IN LITHAUEN
Kuder, F C *see* RAMAROW
Kudriavtsev, V A *see* BIBLIOGRAFICHESKII UKAZATEL' KNIG I STATEI PO NARODNOMU OBRAZOVANIIU ZA 1894 GOD
Kudryts'kyi, A V *see* ENTSYKLOPEDYCHNYI DOVIDNYK
Kuebeck, M von *see* METTERNICH UND KUEBECK
Kuebel, Franz Eberhard *see* DIE SOZIALE UND VOLKSWIRTHSCHAFTLICHE GESEZGEBUNG DES ALTEN TESTAMENTS
Kuebel, Johannes *see* GESCHICHTE DES KATHOLISCHEN MODERNISMUS
Kuebel, Robert *see*
- DER APOSTEL PAULUS: EINE MANN FUER UNSERE ZEIT: VORTRAG
- UEBER DEN UNTERSCHIED ZWISCHEN DER POSITIVEN UND DER LIBERALEN RICHTUNG IN DER MODERNEN THEOLOGIE

Kuechler, Friedrich *see* DIE STELLUNG DES PROPHETEN JESAJA ZUR POLITIK SEINER ZEIT
Kuechling, Eduard Hermann *see* STUDIEN ZUR SPRACHE DES JUNGEN GRILLPARZER
Kueck, Eduard *see* SICKINGEN UND LANDSCHAD
KUECUEK MECMUA – Diyarbakir: Vilayet Matbaasi, 1922-1923 – 9 – $10.00 – us MEDOC [956]
Kuegelgen, Constantin von *see*
- DIE ETHIK HULDREICH ZWINGLIS
- LUTHERS AUFFASSUNG DER GOTTHEIT CHRISTI
- DIE RECHTFERTIGUNGSLEHRE DES JOHANNES BRENZ

Kuegelgen, Wilhelm von *see* LEBENSERINNERUNGEN DES ALTEN MANNES IN BRIEFEN AN SEINEN BRUDER GERHARD
Kuehl, Ernst *see* DAS VERHAELTNISS DER MASSORA ZUR SEPTUAGINTA IM JEREMIA
Kuehl, W F *see* THE LIBRARY OF WORLD PEACE STUDIES
Kuehler, W J *see* JOHANNES BRINCKERINCK EN ZIJN KLOOSTER TE DIEPENVEEN
Kuehlhorn, Walther *see* J.A. LEISEWITZENS JULIUS VON TARENT
Kuehn, Ernst *see* KOMPENDIUM DER BIBLISCHEN THEOLOGIE DES ALTEN UND NEUEN TESTAMENTS VON KONSTANTIN SCHLOTTMANN
Kuehn, Julius *see* DIE KUNST ADALBERT STIFTERS
Kuehn, Walter *see* HEINRICH VON KLEIST UND DAS DEUTSCHE THEATER
Kuehne, Benno *see* UNSER HEILIGER VATER PAPST LEO 13
Kuehne, F Gustav *see* WITTENBERG UND ROM
Kuehnemann, Eugen *see*
- AUSWAHL
- GERHART HAUPTMANN – AUS DEM LEBEN DES DEUTSCHEN GEISTES IN DER GEGENWART

Kuehnhold, Marianne *see* HARMONIEN
K'UEI-CHOU FU-CHIH – 1827, 36. Lacking: ch. 20-36. BCH-734 2 – 8 – ne IDC [950]
K'UEI-CHOU FU-CHIH – 1891, 36, 1. BCH-735 2 – 8 – ne IDC [950]
KUEI-CHOU HSIANG-SHIH LU – List of successful candidates in the imperial examination in Kweichow province. 1870. 1 reel – 1 – 12.00 – us Chinese Res [950]
KUEI-CHOU JIH-PAO – Kweiyang, Kweichow. Nov. 28 1949-. Scattered issues missing. 7 reels – 1 – 148.75 – us Chinese Res [072]
KUEI-CHOU T'UNG-CHIH – 1697, 37. BCH-687 2 – 8 – ne IDC [950]
KUEI-HSIEN CHIH – 1934, 18. BCH-655 2 – 8 – ne IDC [950]
Kuekelhaus, Heinz *see* THOMAS DER PERLENFISCHER
KUELFOELDI MAGYARSAG – Budapest, Nov. 1, 1920-1925 – 4r – 1 – us I.H.R.C. [947]
KUELLIYAT-I (DIVAN-I) FUZULI – Istanbul, 1291 – 6mf – 9 – $36.00 – us MEDOC [949]
KUELLIYAT-I ES'AR RUHI' BAGDADI – Istanbul, 1287 – 5mf – 9 – $30.00 – us MEDOC [949]
KUELLIYAT-I FUZULI – Istanbul, 1296 – 5mf – 9 – $30.00 – us MEDOC [949]
KUELLIYAT-I HUDAYI – Istanbul, 1338/40 – 3mf – 9 – $18.00 – us MEDOC [949]
KUELLIYAT-I SA'IR ESREF – Istanbul, 1928 – 3mf – 9 – $18.00 – us MEDOC [949]
KUELLIYAT-I ZIYA PASA – Istanbul, 1343 – 4mf – 9 – $24.00 – us MEDOC [949]
Kuelpe, Ernst *see* DER CHRISTLICHE GLAUBE FUER DIE MENSCHEN DER GEGENWART: ZWOELF VORTRAEGE
Kuen, M *see* COLLECTIO SCRIPTORUM RERUM HISTORICO-MONASTICO-ECCLESIASTICARUM VARIORUM RELIGIOSORUM ORDINUM
KUENDER DEUTSCHER EINHEIT : DAS LEBEN ERNST MORITZ ARNDTS / Breitenkamp, Paul – Berlin: Haude & Spenersche Buchhandlung Max Paschke, 1938 – 1r – 1 – us U.W. Library [943]
Kuenen, Abraham *see*
- DE PROFETISCHE BOEKEN DES OUDEN VERBONDS
- HISTOIRE CRITIQUE DES LIVRES DE L'ANCIEN TESTAMENT
- AN HISTORICO-CRITICAL INQUIRY INTO THE ORIGIN AND COMPOSITION OF THE HEXATEUCH

KUENH UEL-AHBAR / Geliboeluelue, Mustafa Ali b. Ahmed – Istanbul: Takvimhane-i 'Amire, 1277 [1860] – 5v 30mf – 9 – $400.00 – us MEDOC [949]
Kuenkel, Hans *see*
- AUF DEN KARGEN HUEGELN DER NEUMARK
- SCHICKSAL UND LIEBE DES NIKLAS VON CUES

Kuenstle, Karl *see* IKONOGRAPHIE DER CHRISTLICHEN KUNST
KUENSTLERBRIEFE UEBERSETZT UND ERLAEUTERT VON DR. ERNST GUHL. ZWEITE UMGEARBEITETE UND SEHR VERMEHRTE AUFLAGE VON DR. ADOLF ROSENBERG / Guhl, Ernst – Berlin. 1880. BO-280 1 – 9 – ne IDC [700]
KUENSTLER-INVENTARE. URKUNDEN ZUR GESCHICHTE DER HOLLAENDISCHE KUNST DER 16TEN, 17TEN, 18TEN JAHRHUNDERTS / Bredius, A – Haag, 1915-1922 – 39mf – ne IDC [700]
DIE KUENSTLERISCHEN VORAUSSETZUNGEN DES GENTER ALTARS DER BRUEDER VAN EYCK / Fuerbringer, Hermann – Weida, 1914 – 9 – DM48.00 – 3-89349-259-3 – gw Hänsel [730]
KUENSTLICHE UND WOLGERISSENE FIGUREN, DER FUERNEMSTEN EVANGELIEN / Amman, J – O-1015 1. 1579 – 9 – ne IDC [240]
Kuentzel, G *see* PREUSSISCHE UND OESTERREICHISCHE ACTEN ZUR VORGESCHICHTE DES SIEBENJAEHRIGEN KRIEGES
Kuentzel, Gerhard *see* JOH. GOTTFR. HERDER ZWISCHEN RIGA UND BUECKEBURG
Kuenzel, Carl *see* ICH HABE MICH RASIEREN LASSEN
Kueper, Lic *see* DAS PRIESTERTHUM DES ALTEN BUNDES
Kuerbs, Harry *see* STUDIEN ZUR PFAHLDORFGESCHICHTE AUS FRIEDRICH THEODOR VISCHERS ROMAN "AUCH EINER"
KUERDLER / Tarihi ve Ictimai Tedkikat – Istanbul: Kitabhane-i Sudi, 1334 [1915] – $45.00 – us MEDOC [956]
Kuernberger, Ferdinand *see*
- DER AMERIKA-MUEDE
- FUENFZIG FEUILLETONS
- KATILINA
- NOVELLEN

Kuerschner, Joseph *see* PIERER'S KONVERSATIONS-LEXIKON (AEL, ABT.1;6.7)
KUERSCHNERS DEUTSCHER ITERATURKALENDER 1903-1917 *see* ALLGEMEINER DEUTSCHER LITERATURKALENDER, 1879-1882
KUERSCHNERS DEUTSCHER LITERATUR-KALENDER – Berlin, etc. Jahrg. 1-42; 1879-1925. Incomplete: lacks v. 39, 1917. Film Mas C 437 – 1 – us H.U. Library [430]
Kuersten, Hans *see* PANZER GREIFEN AN
Kuery, Hans *see* SIMON GRYNAEUS VON BASEL, 1725-1799
DIE KUESTE LABRADORS UND IHRE BEWOHNER / Koch, K R – BN 284 2. 1884 – 8 – ne IDC [971]
DAS KUESTENMEER IM FRIEDEN / Coenen, H W – Leipzig, 1933 – 2mf – 1 – ILM-2325/1 – ne IDC [327]
Kuester, H C *see*
- ORNITHOLOGISCHER ATLAS... DER AUSSEREUROPAEISCHEN VOEGEL
- SYSTEMATISCHES CONCHYLIEN-CABINET

Kuetzing, F T *see*
- DIE KIESELSCHALIGEN BACILLARIEN ODER DIATOMEEN
- PHYCOLOGIA GENERALIS
- PHYCOLOGIA GERMANICA
- PHYCOLOGICA GENERALIS ODER ANATOMIE DER TANGE
- PHYCOLOGICA GERMANICA
- SPECIES ALGARUM
- SYNOPSIS DIATOMEARUM
- TABULAE PHYCOLOGICAE
- TABULAE PHYCOLOGICAE ODER ABBILDUNGEN DER TANGE

Kufferath, Maurice *see* THE PARSIFAL OF RICHARD WAGNER
KUFI / Ali Ibn Hamid – Chach namah. Tr. by K. Fredunbeg. 2 v. Karachi. 1900-02. BI-772 2 – 8 – ne IDC [890]
Kugler, Bernhard *see* WALLENSTEIN
Kuh, Anton *see* BOERNE DER ZEITGENOSSE
Kuhlenbeck, L *see* GIORDANO BRUNOS EINFLUSS AUF GOETHE UND SCHILLER
Kuhn, Felix *see* LE CHRISTIANISME DE LUTHER
Kuhn, G J *see* DIE REFORMATOREN BERNS IM 16. JAHRHUNDERT
Kuhn, Johannes von *see*
- KATHOLISCHE DOGMATIK
- PHILOSOPHIE UND THEOLOGIE: EINE STREITSCHRIFT

Kuhn, M *see*
- FILICES AFRICANAE
- FILICES AFRICANEA
- FILICES DECKENIANAE

Kuhnau, J *see*
- FRISCHE CLAVIER FRUECHTE..
- NEUER CLAVIER UBUNG, ANDRER THEIL..
- NEUER CLAVIER UBUNG, ERSTER THEIL..

Kuhne *see* FOUR YEARS IN ASHANTEE BY THE MISSIONARIES RAMSEYER AND KUEHNE.
Kuhne, Berthold *see* NEUTESTAMENTLICHES WOERTERBUCH
Kuhn-Foelix, August *see* HEINRICH VON KLEIST
Kuhnlein, H et al *see* ECOLOGY OF FOOD AND NUTRITION
Kuhns, Oscar *see* THE GERMAN AND SWISS SETTLEMENTS OF COLONIAL PENNSYLVANIA
Kuhring, Otto *see* DAS SCHICKSAL DER WESTFAELISCHEN DOMAENENKAEUFER IN KURHESSEN
KUHRPFAELZISCHE TONSCHULE / Vogler, Georg Joseph – Mannheim. 1778. BP-769 1 – 9 – ne IDC [780]
Kuibyshev, V V *see*
- LENIN I KOOPERATSIIA
- ZADACHI VNUTRENNEI TORGOVLI I KOOPERATSIIA

Kuilman, L W *see* RICE DURING AND AFTER THE WAR. BIBLIOGRAPHY OF THE LITERATURE, 1940-47. 1949. WARTIME DEVELOPMENTS IN RICE
KUJAVISCHER BOTE – Hohensalza (Inowroclaw), Poland. 10 Jun 1924-27 Aug 1939 – 1 – gw Mikrofilm [943]
Kukolevskii, A G *see* GONKONG V SISTEME MIROVYKH EKONOMICHESKIKH SVIAZEI
Kukulka, Carl G *see* EFFECT OF MUSCLE LENGTH ON MOTOR UNIT FIRING BEHAVIOR IN HUMAN TIBIALIS ANTERIOR MUSCLE
KU-KUNG CHOU-K'AN / Peiping. Palace Museum – Palace Museum Weekly. v1-21. Peiping. 1929-36. BCH-286 2 – 8 – ne IDC [060]
KU-KUNG SHU-HUA CHI / Peiping. Palace Museum – (Collection of painting and calligraphy from Palace Museum). No 1-45 1930-34. BCH-814 2 – 8 – ne IDC [750]
KU-KUNG YUEH-K'AN / Peiping. Palace Museum – (Palace Museum Monthly). 44 nos. Peiping. 1929-33. BCH-288 1 – 9 – ne IDC [060]
Kulakova, L I *see* PETR ALEKSEEVICH PLAVIL'SHCHIKOV. 1760-1812
Kulbakin, SM *see* KHILANDARSKIE LISTKI OTRYVOK KIRILLOVSKOI PIS'MENNOSTI XI-GO VEKA
KULIAH KERDJA HUKUM INTERNASIONAL; PEMBAHASAN BUKU: STARKE 'AN INTRODUCTION TO INTERNATIONAL LAW,' TAHUN / Tirtaamidjaja, Nusjirwan – SE 6253 1. 1961-1962 – 9 – ne IDC [340]
Kulinich, A V *see* SERGEI ESENIN
Kulischer, M *see* DAS LEBEN JESU: EINE SAGE VON DEM SCHICKSALE UND ERLEBNISSEN DER BODENFRUCHT
Kulisher, IM *see* OBZOR RUSSKOGO I INOSTRANNOGO ZAKONODATEL'STVA O KOOPERATIVNYKH TOVARISHCHESTVAKH
Kulke, Eduard *see* ERINNERUNGEN AN FRIEDRICH HEBBEL
Kulp, George B *see* FAMILIES OF THE WYOMING VALLEY
DER KULT DER SHANG-DYNASTIE IM SPIEGEL DER ORAKELINSCHRIFTEN : EINE PALAEOGRAPHISCHE STUDIE ZUR RELIGION IM ARCHAISCHEN CHINA / Tsung-tung, Chang – Frankfurt a.M., 1970 – 4mf – 9 – DM90.00 – 3-89349-731-5 – gw Hänsel [290]
DER KULTISCHE KALENDER DER BABYLONIER UND ASSYRER / Landsberger, B – (Leipziger semitistische studien. v. 6, pt. 1-2. Leipzig. 1915). Leipzig. 1915. BNE-20,118 1 – 9 – ne IDC [290]
DIE KULTISCHEN GOTTHEITEN DER ESKIMOS / Thalbitzer, W – BN 415 2. 1928 – 8 – ne IDC [290]
KULTUR = CULTURE – Chicago, IL. v1 no 1,21. 1925-1926 – 1r – Can$25.00 – cn Can Microfilming [071]
DIE KULTUR DES MANAGEMENTS IM KULTURMANAGEMENT : ZU EINER THEORIE DES KULTURMANAGEMENTS / Lenders, Britta – 1995 – 3mf – 9 – DM98.00 – 3-8267-2101-2 – gw Hänsel [650]
KULTUR UN BILDUNG = CULTURE AND ILLUSTRATIONS – (Yiddish weekly) – Moscow, RU. no2 Aug 1918; no3-4 6 Sep 1918 – 1r – 1 – $25.00 – cn Can Microfilming [072]
KUL'TURA – (1991-93 1r per y $85y. 1994 2r $170y. 1995-98 1r per y $85) – 1999- – 1r per y – 1 – $80.00 standing order – us Ross [900]
KULTURA – 1 – sz Infoprint [947]
KULTURA – (Cont: Narodna Kultura) – 1975- – 1r per y – 1 – us Ross [072]
KULTURA – Prague, Czechoslovakia. 1957 (-1962) Kulturni tvorba. -w. 17 Feb 1957-27 Nov 1958; 5 Jan 1961-15 Aug 1968. 14 reels – 1 – uk British Libr Newspaper [072]
KULTURA *see* NARODNA KULTURA
KUL'TURA I SVOBODA – Sbornik pervyi. v. 1. Petrograd. 1918. BR-3206 2 – 8 – ne IDC [460]
KULTURA I ZHITTYA – Kiev, U.S.S.R. -w. 1967-70. 4 reels – 1 – uk British Libr Newspaper [947]
KULTURA I ZHIZN – Moscow, U.S.S.R. -f. Nov 1948-Feb 1951. 1 reel – 1 – uk British Libr Newspaper [947]
KULTURA I ZHYTTIA – (Backfile through 1998 $85r) – 1999- – 1r per y – 1 – $80.00 standing order – us Ross [072]
KULTURA LUDOWA SLOWIAN / Moszynski, K – Krakow. 3v. 1929-1939 – 43mf – 9 – ne IDC [947]
KUL'TURA RUSI EPOKHI OBRAZOVANIIA RUSSKOGO NATSIONAL' NOGO GOSUDARSTVA (KONETS 14-NACHALO 16 V.) / Likhachev, D S – L. 1946. BR-8093 2 – 8 – ne IDC [947]
KUL'TURA TEATRA – Zhurnal Moskovskikh akademicheskikh teatrov. no. 7 8. M. 1921. BR-8366 2 – 8 – ne IDC [790]
KULTURARBEIT ALS BESTANDTEIL SOZIALISTISCHER ERWACHSENENBILDUNG IN DER DDR / Pralle, Elka – Frankfurt a.M., 1976 – 3mf – 9 – DM76.00 – 3-89349-677-7 – gw Hänsel [306]
KULTURGESCHICHTE DER ROEMISCHEN KAISERZEIT / Grupp, Georg – Muenchen, Allgemeine Verlags-Gesellschaft m. b. h., 1903-04. 2 v. Film Mas 9095 – 1 – us H.U. Library [000]
DER KULTURKAEMPFER – Berlin, 1880-83, 1886-88 – 1 – Dist. gw Mikrofilm – gw Misc Inst [943]

KULTURNI ZIVOT – Bratislava, Czechoslovakia. -w. Jan-Dec 1955; Jan 1957-Dec 1965. 13 reels – 1 – uk British Libr Newspaper [072]

KULTURNO-PROSVETITELNAI A RABOTA : ORGAN KOMITETA PO DELAM KULTURNO-PROSVETITELNYKH UCHREZHDENI I PRI SOVETE MINISTROV RSFSR – (Library has: Jan., Mar.-July, Nov.-Dec. 1947; Apr.1948; May-Dec. 1951; Jan.-Apr., July-Dec. 1952; June-Dec. 1966; 1967-1969; Jan.-June 1970) – Moskva: Gos. izd-vo kulturno-prosvetitelno i literatury, 1945- – 1 – CSUX90-S563 – us Hoover Inst Photo [947]

KULTURNO-PROSVETITELNAI A RABOTA (MOSCOW, R.S.F.S.R.: 1945) *see* KULTURNO-PROSVETITELNAI A RABOTA

KULTURPOLITIK IM STAENDESTAAT : DIE ORGANISATION, FUNKTION UND INTENTION DES "BUNDES DER DEUTSCHEN SCHRIFTSTELLER OESTERREICHS" (BDSOE) VOR UND NACH DEM ANSCHLUß / Boehner, Claus-Peter – 1992 – 367p – 9 – DM98.00 – 3-89349-486-3 – gw Hänsel [320]

DIE KULTURWERTE DER DEUTSCHEN LITERATUR DES MITTELALTERS / Francke, Kuno – (Includes bibliographical references) – Berlin: Weidmannsche Buchhandlung, 1910 – 1r – 1 – us U.W. Library [430]

DIE KULTURWERTE DER DEUTSCHEN LITERATUR IN IHRER GESCHICHTLICHEN ENTWICKLUNG / Francke, Kuno – (Includes bibliographical references and index) – Berlin: Weidmannsche Buchhandlung, 1910-1928 – 1 – us U.W. Library [430]

DIE KULTURWERTE DER DEUTSCHEN LITERATUR VON DER REFORMATION BIS ZUR AUFKLAERUNG / Francke, Kuno – (Includes bibliographical references and index) – Berlin: Weidmannsche Buchhandlung, 1923 – 1 – us U.W. Library [430]

KULTURWILLE – Leipzig, 1924-32 – 2r – 1 – gw Mikrofilm [073]

KULTUS- UND GESCHICHTSRELIGION (PELAGIANISMUS UND AUGUSTINISMUS) : EIN BEITRAG ZUR RELIGIOESEN PSYCHOLOGIE UND VOLKSKUNDE / Juengst, Johannes – Giessen: J. Ricker, 1901 – 1mf – us A.T.L.A. [200]

Kulyzhnyi, A E *see*
- DEREVENSKAIA KOOPERATSIIA
- KOOPERATIVNYI SBYT PRODUKTOV MELKOGO KHOZIAISTVA
- KOOPERATIVNYI SBYT PRODUKTOV SEL'SKOGO KHOZIAISTVA
- KREDITNYE I SSUDO-SBEREGATEL'NYE TOVARISHCHESTVA
- KURS KREDIT NOI KOOPERATSII
- OCHERKI PO SEL'SKO-KHOZIASTVENNOI I KREDITNOI KOOPERATSIIA
- ORGANIZATSIIA KHLEBOTORGOVLI I KOOPERATIVNYI SBYT KHLEBA V ROSSII

Kulzhinskii, SK *see* OPISANIE KOLLEKTSII NARODNYKH PISANOK

Kumar, Pradeep *see* SUPERCONDUCTIVITY REVIEW

Kumm, Hermann Karl Wilhelm *see*
- KHONT-HON-NOFER
- THE SUDAN

Kummer, Carl Ferdinand *see* DIE JUNGFRAU VON ORLEANS IN DER DICHTUNG

Kummer, Friedrich *see*
- DEUTSCHE LITERATURGESCHICHTE DES NEUNZEHNTEN JAHRHUNDERTS

Kummer, Rolf *see* DIE FRANKFURTER BERICHTE GUSTAVS V. MEYERN-HOHENBERG

Kummerle, Salomon *see* ENCYCLOPEDIE DER EVANGELISCHEN KIRCHENMUSIK

KUMPULAN PERATURAN-PERATURAN 17 APRIL 1964 / Indonesia. Laws, Statutes, etc – SE-4804 1 – 9 – ne IDC [340]

KUMPULAN SEMINAR EKONOMI INDUSTRI / Rustam, Didong – SE 5436 1. 1964? – 9 – ne IDC [338]

KUNCHONG XUEBAO – Acta Entomologica Sinica. In Chinese but English abstracts to the main articles. F p42 – 9 – 4.00f – cc Microforms [073]

Kundler, Peter *see* ARCHIVES OF AGRONOMY AND SOIL SCIENCE

KUNEITRA / Israel. Ministry of Foreign Affairs. Information Department – Jerusalem. Feb 1975. 9 p. illus – 9 – 3.00 – is I.T.T.I. [324]

KUNENE-SAMBESI EXPEDITION / Baum, H – 8035 1. 1903 – 9 – ne IDC [910]

KUNG PAANO NAMUMUHAY AT GUMAGAWA ANG MGA TAO. / Agno, Lydia Navarro – Quezon City: JMC Press, c1975. xvi,264p. illus – 1 – us U.W. Library [480]

KUNG SHANG KUNG PAO – (Official Gazette of the Ministry of Industry and Commerce). 2 v. Nanking. 1928-30. Lacking: v. 1 (1-4) 1928; v. 2 (14-41) 1930. BCH-1074 1 – 9 – ne IDC [380]

KUNG SHANG PAN-YUEH K'AN – Shanghai, China. 1929-Jan 1936. Semi-monthly economic journal – 1 – 572.00 – us Chinese Res [330]

Kung, Tien-min *see*
- CHRISTIANITY IN THE T'ANG DYNASTY (CCC208)
- FROM BUDDHISM TO CHRISTIANITY (CCC207)

KUNGALVSPOSTEN – Kungalv, Sweden. 1979- – 1 – sw Kungliga [072]

Kungliga Biblioteket-Royal Library. Stockholm *see* UNION CATALOGUE OF FOREIGN LITERATURE IN SWEDISH RESEARCH LIBRARIES

KUNGSBACKA TIDNING – Kungsbacka, Sweden. 1978- – 1 – sw Kungliga [072]

KUNG-SHANG PAN-YUEH-K'AN – Semi-monthly Economic Journal. Shanghai, 1929-36. 8v. Lacking: 1929-30; v1-2; 1933, index v5; 1936. index v8.BCH-290/1 – 9 – ne IDC [330]

Kunik, A A *see* SBORNIK MATERIALOV DLIA ISTORII IMP. AKADEMII NAUK V 18 VEKE

KUNINGAS VLADISLAVAS DEMBSKIS : JO GYVENIMAS, RASTAI IRDARBAI / Sliupas, Jonas – Scranton, PA, 1916 – 1r – 1 – us I.H.R.C. [978]

Kunitzer, M *see* BET RABBI

Kunkel, F *see* KRITISCHE BELEUCHTUNG DES C.F. WEITZMANN'SCHEN HARMONIESYSTEMS, UND DES SCHRIFTENS: "DIE NEUE HARMONIELEHRE IM STREIT MIT DER ALTEN", VON F. J. KINKEL

KUNKEL'S MUSICAL REVIEW – St Louis, 1879-1905 – 1 – £765.00 – uk Chadwyck [780]

K'UN-MING HSIEN-CHIH – 1841; 1901, 10. Available: 1-6. BCH-661 2 – 8 – ne IDC [950]

Kunos, Ignatz *see* TUERKCE NINNILER

Kunow, Hanns von *see* MICHEL UND DIE SCHWESTERN

KUNST – 1931 – 1 – us I.U. Libraries [390]

DIE KUNST ADALBERT STIFTERS / Kuehn, Julius – (Includes bibliographical references) – 2. Aufl. Berlin: Junker und Duennhaupt, 1943 – 1 – us U.W. Library [430]

DIE KUNST DAS CLAVIER ZU SPIELEN. DRITTE, VERBESSERTE UND VERMEHRTE AUFLAGE / Marpurg, Friedrich Wilhelm – 1760 – 9 – us Sibley [780]

DIE KUNST DER ERZAEHLUNG / Wassermann, Jakob – Berlin: Bard Marquardt, [1904] – 1 – us U.W. Library [430]

DIE KUNST DER FUGUE DURCH HERRN JOHANN SEBASTIAN BACH...HERAUSGEBEN VON MARPURG / Bach, Johann Sebastian – c.1752 – 9 – us Sibley [780]

DIE KUNST DER INTERPRETATION : STUDIEN ZUR DEUTSCHEN LITERATURGESCHICHTE / Staiger, Emil – (Includes bibliographical references) – Zuerich: Atlantis Verlag, c1955 – 1 – us U.W. Library [430]

KUNST DER NATION – Berlin, 1933-45 – 1 – Dist. gw Mikrofilm – gw Mikrofilm [700]

DIE KUNST DES ORGELBAUES, THEORETISCH UND PRAKTISCH BESCHRIEBEN / Halle, J S – P 692. 1779 – 9 – ne IDC [780]

DIE KUNST DES REINEN SATZES IN DER MUSIK / Kirnberger, Johann P – 2v. Berlin. Koenigsberg. 1774-79. P-345 1 – 9 – ne IDC [780]

DIE KUNST DES REINEN SATZES IN DER MUSIK / Kirnberger, Johann P – Erster -zweyter theil. 1771-79 – 9 – us Sibley [780]

DIE KUNST, IHR WESEN UND IHRE GESETZE / Holz, Arno – Berlin: Issleib, 1891 – 1r – 1 – us U.W. Library [100]

DIE KUNST, IHR WESEN UND IHRE GESETZE : NEUE FOLGE / Holz, Arno – 2. Aufl. Berlin: W Issleib, 1893 – 1r – 1 – us U.W. Library [100]

DIE KUNST IM DRITTEN REICH – Muenchen, DE. 1937-39; 1940 (incomplete); 1941-42; 1943-44 (incomplete) – 1 – gw Mikrofilm [072]

KUNST IM KINO – Berlin. 1912 n1. 1913 n2, 4, 6, 8, 9, 13, 31. 1914 n21 – 1 – gw Mikrofilm [790]

KUNST ODER TRACTAT DER MALEREI DES CENNINO CENNINI DA COLLE DI VALDELSA / Ilg, Albert – (Quellenschriften fuer kunstgeschichte. v. 1. Wien. 1871). BO-517a 1 – 9 – ne IDC [700]

KUNST, RELIGION UND KULTUR : ANSPRACHE AN DIE HEIDELBERGER STUDENTENSCHAFT GEHALTEN BEI DER ANLAESSLICH SEINER ABLEHNUNG DES RUFS AN DIE BERLINER UNIVERSITAET VERANSTALTETEN FEIER / Thode, Henry – Heidelberg, 1901 – 9 – DM38.00 – 3-89349-295-X – gw Hänsel [100]

KUNST UND KUENSTLER – Berlin, 1921-1924/25 – 1 – Dist. gw Mikrofilm – gw Mikrofilm [700]

"KUNST UND KUENSTLER" 1902-1933 : EINE ZEITSCHRIFT IN DER AUSEINANDERSETZUNG UM DEN IMPRESSIONISMUS IN DEUTSCHLAND / Paas, Sigrun – Heidelberg, 1976 – 3mf – 9 – DM76.00 – 3-89349-390-5 – gw Hänsel [700]

KUNST UND KUENSTLER AM VORABEND DER REFORMATION : EIN BILD AUS DEM ERZGEBIRGE / Gurlitt, Cornelius – Halle: Verein fuer Reformationsgeschichte, 1890. ([Schriften des Vereins fuer Reformationsgeschichte; Bd. 29]) – 1mf – us A.T.L.A. [700]

KUNST UND LEBEN : VORTRAGE UND ABHANDLUNGEN ZUR DEUTSCHEN LITERATUR / Strich, Fritz – Bern: Francke, 1960 – 1r – 1 – us U.W. Library [430]

KUNST UND LITERATUR – 1966-1983 – 537mf – 1 – DM3,060.90 – gw Mikro Press [400]

DIE KUNST ZU MODULIREN UND ZU PRALUDIEN, EIN PRAKTISCHE BEITRAG ZUR HARMONIELEHRE... / Jadassohn, S – Leipzig: Breitkopf & Haertel, 1890 – 1 – us Sibley [780]

DIE KUNSTBESTREBUNGEN AM BAYERISCHEN HOFE UNTER DEN HERZOGEN ALBERT V UND WILHELM V / Stockbauer, J – (Quellenschriften fuer Kunstgeschichte...Wien, 1874, v8) – 9 – ne IDC [700]

KUNSTBUECHLEIN / Amman, J – Franckfurt am Mayn. 1599. BO-1017 1 – 9 – ne IDC [700]

KUNSTERNOVELLEN / Mann, Heinrich – Illustrationen Bert Heller, Auswahl und Nachwort Helga Bemmann, Berlin: Henschelverlag, 1961 – 1 – us U.W. Library [830]

DER KUNSTFREUND – Bozen, 1885-91. 1 reel – 1 – $85.00 – us UPA [720]

KUNSTGESCHICHTLICHE FORSCHUNGEN DES KOENIGLICH-PREUSSISCHEN HISTORISCHEN INSTITUT IN ROM – Leipzig. v1-3. 1910-1912 – 20mf – 9 – ne IDC [700]

KUNSTGESCHICHTLICHE GRUNDBEGRIFFE / Woelfflin, H – O 466. 1915 – 9 – ne IDC [700]

KUNSTGESCHICHTLICHES JAHRBUCH DER K.K. ZENTRAL-KOMMISSION... – (Cont as: Jahrbuch des Kunsthistorischen Institutes...Wien v5-14 1911-1920; Cont as: Jahrbuch fuer Kunstgeschichte...Wien v1(15) 1921/22; Cont as: Wiener Jahrbuch fuer Kunstgeschichte. Wien v2(16)-11 1923-1937;) – Wien. v1-4. 1907-1910. Suppls – 175mf – 9 – ne IDC [700]

Kunsthistorisches Institut. Florenz *see* MITTEILUNGEN

Kunsthistorisches Institut. Florenz. *see* KATALOG DES KUNSTHISTORISCHEN INSTITUTS IN FLORENZ

Kunsthistorisches Institut in Florenz. Biblioteca dell'Instituto di Storia dell'Arte *see* KATALOG DES KUNSTHISTORISCHEN INSTITUTS IN FLORENZ

Kunstmann, Walter G *see*
- DIE BABYLONISCHE GEBETSBESCHWOERUNG

KUNSTSTOFFE – v1-65 1911-75 – 1,5,6 – us Princeton Micro [620]

DAS KUNSTWERK RICHARD WAGNERS / Istel, Edgar – (Includes bibliographical references) – Leipzig: B G Teubner, 1910 – 1r – 1 – us U.W. Library [780]

KUNTERBUNT / Johst, Hanns – Bielefeld: Velhagen & Klasing, [1940] – 1r – 1 – us U.W. Library [830]

KUNTERES – Tel Aviv. 1919-29, 1943-44. BJ-91-53 1 – 9 – ne IDC [956]

Kunth, C S *see*
- EICHHORNIA, GENUS NOVUM E FAMILIA PONTEDERIACEARUM
- ENUMERATIO PLANTARUM OMNIUM HUCUSQUE COGNITARUM
- FLORA BEROLINENSIS SIVE ENUMERATIO VEGETABILIUM CIRCA BEROLINUM SPONTE CRESCENTIUM
- MALVACEAE, BUETTNERIACEAE. TILIACEAE
- MIMOSES ET AUTRES PLANTES LEGUMINEUSES DU NOUVEAU CONTINENT
- REVISION DE LA FAMILLE DES BIGNONIACEES
- REVISION DES GRAMINEES
- SYNOPSIS PLANTARUM AEQUINOCTIALIUM ORBIS NOVI

Kunth, CS *see*
- HERBARIUM
- SYNOPSIS PLANTARUM, QUAS IN ITINERE AD PLAGAM AEQUINOCTIALEM ORBIS NOVI

Kuntjaraningrat *see*
- DANCE AND LITERATURE IN JAVA
- PENDUDUK IRIAN BARAT
- VILLAGES IN INDONESIA

Kuntz, Marthe *see* OMBRES ET LUMIERES

Kuntze, C E O *see*
- REVISIO GENERUM PLANTARUM
- REVISIO GENERUM PLANTARUM VASCULARIUM

K'UN-YANG CHOU-CHIH – 1839; 1840, 16. BCH-666 2 – 8 – ne IDC [950]

Kunz, Dorothea E *see* THE EFFECTS OF A PROJECT LEARNING TREE WORKSHOP ON PRE-SERVICE TEACHERS' ATTITUDES TOWARD TEACHING ENVIRONMENTAL EDUCATION

Kunz, Grete *see* WAECHTER DER HEIMAT

Kunze, G *see*
- ANALECTA PTERIDOGRAPHICA
- DIE FARRNKRAEUTER IN KOLORIRTEN ABBILDUNGEN NATURGETREU ERLAEUTERT UND BESCHRIEBEN
- DIE GOTTESDIENSTLICHE SCHRIFTLESUNG 1

Kunze, Johannes *see*
- THE APOSTLES' CREED AND THE NEW TESTAMENT
- DIE GOTTESLEHRE DES IRENAEUS
- MARCUS EREMITA
- DAS NICAENISCH-KONSTANTINOPOLITA-NISCHE SYMBOL

Kunzemann, Gertrud *see*
- LAUTER KLEINIGKEITEN
- WIEDERGEBOREN

Kunzen, F L A *see* STUDIEN FUER TONKUENSTLER UND MUSIKFREUNDE...IN ZWEI THEILEN

KUO FENG – (National Wind). 8 v. Nanking. 1932-36. monthly. Lacking: v. 6 (11-12) 1935; v. 8 (5, 8, 11) 1936. BCH-292 1 – 9 – ne IDC [073]

KUO-CHI MAO-I CH'ING-PAO – Shanghai, China. Mar 1936-Aug 1937. Foreign trade bulletin – 1 – 72.00 – us Chinese Res [073]

KUO-CHI MAO-I TAO-PAO – "Foreign Trades Journal". 9 v. Shanghai. 1930-37. monthly. BCH-291 1 – 9 – ne IDC [073]

KUO-CHI MAO-I TAO-PAO – Shanghai, China. Apr 1930-Ju 1937. Foreign trade monthly – 1 – 234.00 – us Chinese Res [073]

KUO-CHI WEN-T'I YEN-CHIU – (Studies of International Problems). Peking. 1959. Lacking: v. 7-12. BCH-922 2 – 8 – ne IDC [950]

KUO-CHUN CHENG-KUNG SHIH-KAO – Taipei. Draft History of the Political Work in the Chinese Nationalist Armed Forces. 1960. (8922 6311) – 1 – 35.00r – us Hoover Inst Photo [950]

KUO-FENG PAO – (National Wind Magazine). nos. 1-35. Shanghai. 1910; nos. 1-17. 1911. BCH-293 1 – 9 – ne IDC [073]

KUO-HSUEH HUI-PIEN – (Sinology Magazine). v. 1-2. Tsinan. 1932-34. BCH-798 2 – 8 – ne IDC [073]

KUO-HSUEH LUN-TS'UNG – Sinological review. v. 1-2 (2). Peiping, Shanghai. 1927-29. BCH-294 2 – 8 – ne IDC [480]

KUO-KU YUEH-K'AN – Sinological monthly. v. 1-4. Peiping. 1919. BCH-298 2 – 8 – ne IDC [480]

KUO-LI HUA-PEI PIEN-I-KUAN KUAN-K'AN / National Institute of Compilation and Translation of North China – Bulletin. v. 1-2 (10). Peking. 1942-43. BCH-302 2 – 8 – ne IDC [480]

KUO-TS' UI HSUEH-PAO – Sinological journal. v. 1-7 (13). Shanghai. 1905-11. monthly. BCH-308 2 – 8 – ne IDC [480]

KU-PEN HSI-CH'U TS'UNG-K'AN – Collection of old texts of Chinese drama. 1st and 2nd series. BCH-882 2 – 8 – ne IDC [820]

KU-PEN HSI-CH'U TS'UNG-K'AN, CH'U-CHI – Shanghai. 112 plays – 1 – $35.00r – us Hoover Inst Photo [820]

Kuper, Hilda *see* THE SWAZI

Kuppers, Paul Erich *see* DAS KESTNERBUCH

Kuprhanovskii, P see MATERIALY K BIBLIOGRAFII A. BLOKA ZA 1928-1957 GODY
Kuprian, Herman see REALIDAD Y ESPIRITUALIDAD
Kuramoto, Anna K see MUSCULAR ENDURANCE IN WOMEN THROUGH ADULTHOOD
KU'RAN : MACHVMETIS SARACENORUM PRINCIPIS, EIUS' QUE SVCCESSORVM VITAE, ... – Zuerich, 1550 – 5mf – 9 – H-8282/1 – ne IDC [956]
KURANTY = CHIMES – Kiev. n1-10. may-oct 1918 – 4mf – 9 – $50.00 – us Ross [790]
Kurbatova, IN see MATERIALY ARKHIVA G.V. PLEKHANOVA
KURDISTAN / ed by Zadah, Muhammad Sadiq Mufti – Hamadan ['Ikbatan], Badi al-Zamani, Iran. Publisher: Abd al-Maiid, Nos. 32, 34, 35, 38, 37 (sic), 39, 40, 41, 44, 46, 48, 49, 50 (12, 25 Dec 1962; 5, 13, 16, 30 Jan 1963; 6, 13 Feb 1963; 5, 20 Mar 1963; 10, 17, 24 Apr 1963). New series?, nos. 20, 23 (Apr, Nov 1969) – 9 – $90.00 – us MEDOC [956]
KURDISTAN AND THE KURDS / Ghassemlou, Abdul Rahman – Prague: Pub. House of the Czechoslovak Academy of Sciences, 1965. 304p. Bibliog – 1 – us U.W. Library [950]
KUREJAS – Chicago, IL, 1900 – 1r – 1 – us I.H.R.C. [978]
DER KURIER – Berlin, Germany. 1962-66 – 14r – 1 – us L of C Photodup [072]
DER KURIER – Berlin. Germany. Nov. 1945-Dec. 1949. Missing Mar. 5, 1948 – 1 – 35.00r – us Hoover Inst Photo [072]
DER KURIER – Berlin, nov 12 1945-66 – 1 – Dist. gw Mikrofilm – gw Misc Inst [072]
KURIER – 1945- – 9 – inquire – us Ross [072]
KURIER CODZIENNY – Warsaw, Poland. Jul 1945-May 1953 – 12r – 1 – us L of C Photodup [943]
KURIER POLSKI – 1965 – 1 – sz Infoprint [947]
KURIER POLSKI – (Backfile 1965- $85r) – 1999- – 3r per y – 1 – $240.00 standing order – us Ross [072]
KURIER POLSKI – London, UK. 14 Dec 1959-16 Jan 1960 – 1 – uk British Libr Newspaper [072]
KURIER POLSKI – Warsaw, Poland. 1958-93 – 74r – 1 – us L of C Photodup [943]
KURIER POLSKI – Warsaw, Poland. -d. Sept 1957-Dec 1967. 31 reels – 1 – uk British Libr Newspaper [943]
KURIER SPORTOWY – Bydgoszcz, Poland. Jul-Aug 1945 – 1r – 1 – us L of C Photodup [943]
KURIER SZCZECINSKI – Szczecin, Poland. May-Nov 1948; Mar 1950-Apr 1980 – 61r – 1 – us L of C Photodup [943]
KURING-GAI HORNSBY RECORDER – Feb 2 1950-Dec 14 1960 – 9 – at Pascoe [072]
KURIREN – Norrkoping, Sweden. 1983-84 – 1 – sw Kungliga [072]
KURIREN – Uddevalla, Sweden. 1921-63 – 153r – 1 – sw Kungliga [072]
KURJER CLEVELANDSKI – Cleveland, Ohio. 1891 – 1r – 1 – $32.50r – us Archival [071]
KURJER POLSKI – Warsaw, Poland. Jan-Feb 1919; 1926-Aug 1939 – 28r – 1 – us L of C Photodup [943]
KURJER PORANNY – Warsaw, Poland. Jan-Feb 1919 – 1r – 1 – us L of C Photodup [943]
KURJER WARSZAWSKI – Warsaw. Jan 1 1909-July 1914; Jan 17 1923-July 29 1939. Not collated – 1 – us NY Public [072]
KURJER WARSZAWSKI – Warsaw, Poland. Jan-Feb 1919 – 1r – 1 – us L of C Photodup [943]
Kurland, Roselle see SOCIAL WORK WITH GROUPS
Kuroghlu see SPECIMENS OF POPULAR POETRY OF PERSIA
Kurono Maisaichi see NIPPONGO
KURPFALZBAIERISCHE BAMBERGER ZEITUNG see FRAENKISCHER MERKUR
KURS ISTORII RUSSKOGO VOENNOGO ISKUSSTVA / Baiov, A K – Spb. 1909. B-2235 2 – 8 – ne IDC [700]
KURS KREDIT NOI KOOPERATSII / Kulyzhnyi, A E – M., 1918 – 1mf – 9 – COR-261/1 – ne IDC [334]
KURS PSIKHOLOGII / Lopatin, L M – 1903. BR-5768 2 – 8 – ne IDC [150]
KURS SOVETSKOGO GRAZHDANSKOGO PRAVA / Stuchka, Petr Ivanovich – M. 3v. 1927-1931 – 12mf – 9 – 81.00 – ne IDC [340]
KURSACHSEN UND DIE DURCHFUEHRUNG DES PRAGER FRIEDENS 1635 / Duerbeck, Ernst – Leipzig, 1908 – 2mf – DM62.00 – 3-8267-3041-0 – gw Hänsel [943]
Kurskii, D I see SBORNIK STATEI I MATERIALOV PO VRACHNOMU I SEMEINOMU PRAVU
KURSKII KOOPERATOR – Kursk, 1928 – 4mf – 9 – COR-647/1 – ne IDC [334]
KURSKII SBORNIK : MATERIALY PO ETNOGRAFII KURSKOI GUBERNII – Kursk, 1901-1912 – 20mf – 9 – RET-6/1 – ne IDC [947]
Kurskov, Iu.V see ISTOCHNIKI PO ISTORII RUSSKO-SKANDINAVSKIKH OTNOSHENII V RUKOPISNYKH SOBRANIIAKH G. LENINGRADA
KURSUN – Manastir: Beynelmilel Ticaret Matbaasi. Mueduer-i Mes'ul: Es'ad, 1911 – 9 – $25.00 – us MEDOC [956]
KURSY PO KOOPERATSII / Manuilov, A A – M. 2v. 1912-1913 – 10mf – 9 – COR-59/1 – ne IDC [334]
KURSY PO KOOPERATSII PETROGRADSKOGO OBSHCHESTVA NARODNYKH UNIVERSITETOV – Pg., [1916] – 1mf – 9 – COR-60/1 – ne IDC [334]
Kurth, G see
- CHARTES DE L'ABBAYE DE SAINT-HUBERT EN ARDENNE
- CLOVIS. TOME 2

Kurtz, Johann Heinrich see
- BIBLISCHE GESCHICHTE: DER HEILIGEN SCHRIFT
- DER BRIEF AN DER HEBRAEER
- HISTORY OF THE OLD COVENANT
- LEHRBUCH DER KIRCHENGESCHICHTE
- TEXT-BOOK OF CHURCH HISTORY
- ZUR THEOLOGIE DER PSALMEN

Kurtz, Robert see ZUR PSYCHOLOGIE DER VOREXILISCHEN PROPHETIE IN ISRAEL
KURTZE ANLEYTUNGE VNND NACHRICHTUNGE WIE MAN D. EGIDIUM HUNNEN VND D. LUCAM OSIANDERN SAMPT JREM ANHANG EXAMINIEREN... / Huber, S – N.p., 1597 – 1mf – ne IDC [240]
KURTZE AUSSLEGUNG DER SONTAGS EUANGELIEN VNND CATECHISMI / Mathesius, Johannes – Nuernberg, 1563 – 7mf – ne IDC [240]
KURTZE EINLEITUNG IN EINIGE THEILE DER BERGWERCKS-WISSENSCHAFT / Lehmann, Johann Gottlob – Berlin, 1751. 8, 192, 5 p. Film Mas 8912 – 1 – us H.U. Library [622]
EIN KURTZE ERINNERUNG ETLICHER GSCHRIFFT DAR AUSZ MAN DEN KINDERTAUFF / Landtsperger, J – 1528. BME-65 1 – 9 – ne IDC [240]
KURTZE ERJNNERUNG VON GEGENWERTIGEM ZWEYTRACHT VBER DIE LEHRE VON DER GNADEN WAHL... / Huber, S – Muehlhausen, 1595 – 1mf – ne IDC [240]
KURTZE SCHLOSZREDE WIDER DEN IRSALL DER NEUEGEROTTENN TAUFFER; DARIN DER KINDERTAUFF BESTETTIGT. WIRD / Fuchsperger, O – Landshuet. 1528. BME-113 1 – 9 – ne IDC [240]
EIN KURTZE VNTTERRICHT DEN PFARHERRN VND PREDIGERN. VERORDENT, WES SIE DAS VOLCK WIDER ETLICHE VERFUERISCHE LERE, DER WIDERTAUFFER. AUSZ GOETTLICHER SCHRIFFT VERMANEN, VND VNTERRICHTEN SOLLEN / Althamer, A – 1528. BME-112 1 – 9 – ne IDC [240]
KURTZE VORSTELLUNG DER GANTZEN CIVIL-BAU-KUNST, WORINNEN ERSTLICH DIE VORNEHMSTEN KUNSTWOERTER, ... / Sturm, L C – Augsburg, 1718 – 1mf – ne IDC [720]
AIN KURTZE, WOLGEGRUENDTE AUSZLEGUNG UEBER DIE ZEHEN NACHGEENDEN EPISTELN S. PAULI / Bugenhagen, J – 1524. Verteuetscht durch L. Haetzer. BME-51 1 – 9 – ne IDC [240]
EIN KURTZER AUSZUG AUSS DER HEYLIGEN SCHRIFFT DARINNEN ANGEZEYGT WIRD WIE EIN BETRUEBT MENSCH BEGRIFFEN IN GROSSER ANGST VNND NOTH SCHREYT ZU GOTT VMB HILFF... / Huberinus, Caspar – Nuernberg: Johann Daubmann, [1550]. [G.F.: 7.14b] – 3mf – 9 – HUB-75/1 – ne IDC [240]
AIN KURTZER AUSZUG AUSS DER HAYLIGEN SCHRIFFT... / Huberinus, Caspar – [Augsburg: Philipp Ulhart], 1525. [G.F.: 7.1] – 2mf – 9 – HUB-66/1 – ne IDC [240]
EIN KURTZER BEGRIFF VON GUTEN WERCKEN / Greyffenberger, H – 1524. BME-24 1 – 9 – ne IDC [240]
AIN KURTZER EINFELTIGER BERICHT, VOM HAILIGEN SACRAMENT DESZ LEIBS VND BLUTS JESU CHRISTI. ITEM ZEHEN HAUPTARTICUL CHRISTLICHER LEERE / Rhegius, Urbanus – Augspurg, Ph. Vlhart. 1535. BME-110 1 – 9 – ne IDC [240]
KURTZER VND NUETZLICHER BERICHT VON DEM HEILSAMEN VND CHRISTLICHEM BUCH FORMULAE CONCORDIAE... / Hunnius, A – Magdeburgk, 1593 – 3mf – ne IDC [240]
EIN KURTZER VNTERRICHT AUFF D. GEORGEN MAIORS ANTWORT... / Amsdorff, N von – Basel, 1552 – 1mf – 9 – ne IDC [240]
KURTZER/DOCH AUSFUEHRLICHER BERICHT/ VON DEN MODIS MUSICIS, WELCHEN AUS DEN BESTEN/AELTESTEN/BERUEHMTESTEN UND / Matthaeus, C – Universitaet zu Koeningsberg. Koeningsberg. 1658. BP-397 1 – 9 – ne IDC [780]
KURTZGEFASSTES MUSICALISCHES LEXICON – Often attributed to Barnickel, C. Stoessel, and J. D. Stoessel. 1737 – 9 – us Sibley [780]
KURTZGEFASZTES MUSIKALISCHES LEXICON, WORINNEN EINE NUETZLICHE ANLEITUNG UND GRUENDLICHER BEGRIFF VON DER MUSIC ENTHALTEN – P 704. 1737 – 9 – ne IDC [780]
KURULTAY – Eskisehir. Sahib-i Imtiyaz: Idris Vehbi. No. 21 (22 Tesriniewel 1335 [1919]) – 9 – $10.00 – us MEDOC [956]
Kurultay, Dorduncu see TUERK OCAKLARI 1927 SENESI KURULTAY ZABITLERI
KURUN-I CEDIDE VE NAVOLYON'UN SUKUNTUNA KADAR ASR-I HAZIR MEBADISI / Hamid, V Ahmet – Istanbul: Matbaa-i Amire, 1924 – $30.00 – us MEDOC [956]
KURYER KATOLICKI – Toledo, Ohio. 1924 – 1r – 1 – $32.50r – us Archival [071]
KURYER TOLEDOSKI – Toledo, Ohio. 1925 – 1r – 1 – $32.50r – us Archival [071]
KURYER ZJEDNOCZENIA : MONTHLY AND SEMI-MONTHLY POLISH FRATERNAL ASSOCIATION NEWSPAPER – Cleveland, Oh. 31 May 1971-17 Dec 1987. – 3r – 1 – us Western Res [071]
Kurz, Albert see KOENIG EDUARD UND DER EINSIEDLER, EINE MITTELENGLISCHE BALLADE
Kurz, Heinrich see GESCHICHTE DER DEUTSCHEN LITERATUR
Kurz, Hermann see
- DIE BEIDEN TUBUS
- HERMANN KURZ' SAEMTLICHE WERKE
- INNERHALB ETTERS
- NOVELLENSCHATZ DES AUSLANDES
- REICHSTAEDTISCHE ERZAEHLUNGEN
- SCHILLER'S HEIMATHJAHRE
- SCHILLERS HEIMATJAHRE
- DER SONNENWIRTH

Kurz, Isolde see
- INNERHALB ETTERS
- DAS LEBEN MEINES VATERS
- DIE NACHT IM TEPPICHSAAL

Kurz, Joseph Felix, Freiherr von see PRINZESSIN PUMPHIA
Kurz, L see GREGORS DES GROSSEN LEHRE VON DEN ENGELN
Kurzbach, Herbert see FINNISCHE NOVELLE
KURZE ANWEISUNG ZUM GENERALBASSPIELEN... / Tuerk, Daniel G – Halle und Leipzig: Schwickert und Schwetschke, 1791 – 5mf – 9 – us Sibley [780]
KURZE ANWEISUNG ZUM KLAVIERSPIELEN / Tuerk, Daniel G – 1792 – 9 – us Sibley [780]
KURZE BESCHREIBUNG DER MATHEMATISCHEN, ASTRONOMISCHEN UND ASTROLOGISCHEN HEBRAEISCHEN HANDSCHRIFTEN DER FIRKOWITSCH'SCHEN SAMMLUNG IN DER KAISERLICHEN OEFFENTLICHEN BIBLIOTHEK ZU ST PETERSBURG / Gurland, J H – Spb., 1866 – 1mf – 9 – ne IDC [510]
KURZE DARSTELLUNG / Abicht, J H – Bayreuth, 1795 – 2mf – 9 – ILM-309/1 – ne IDC [340]
KURZE, DOCH HINLAENGLICHE ANWEISUNG ZUM GENERAL-BASSE / Hesse, Johann H – 1776 – 9 – us Sibley [780]
KURZE UN LEICHTE KLAVIERSTUCKE, W. 113, NO. 1, 2, 3, 10, 11 / Bach, C P E – Ms, 1766 – 1 – us Sibley [780]
KURZE UND SYSTEMATISCHE ANLEITUNG ZUM GENERAL-BASS, UND DER TONKUNST UEBERHAUPT, MIT EXEMPELN ERLAEUTERT / Bach, Johann M – Cassel. 1780. BP-634 1 – 9 – ne IDC [780]
Kurze, Volker see PHYSIKALISCHE CHARAKTERISIERUNG ULTRAFLEXIBLER LIPID-VESIKEL
KURZER ABRISZ DER GESCHICHTE DER TONKUNST ZUM VERGNUEGEN DER LIEBHABER DER MUSIK / Kalkbrenner, C – Berlin. 1792. BP-337 1 – 9 – ne IDC [780]
KURZER, DOCH HINLAENGLICHER... – Heydelberg: J J Haener, 1745 – 1 – us Sibley [780]
KURZER HAND-COMMENTAR ZUM ALTEN TESTAMENT see EXODUS ERKLAERT
KURZER HAND-COMMENTAR ZUM ALTEN TESTAMENT, ABT. 9 see DIE BUECHER DER KOENIGE
KURZER UMRISS EINER SYSTEMATISCHEN BESCHREIBUNG DER MANNIGFALTIGEN UMHUELLUNGEN DER SAAMEN / Medikus, F K – 1788. B-8137 1 – 9 – ne IDC [580]
KURZER UND DEUTLICHER UNTERRICHT VON DEM GENERAL-BASS.. / Reinhard, Leonhard – 1750 – 2 – us Sibley [780]
KURZER UND DEUTLICHER UNTERRICHT VON DEM GENERAL-BASS.. / Reinhard, Leonhard – 1767 – 2 – us Sibley [780]
KURZGEFASSTE ASSYRISCHE GRAMMATIK / Meissner, Bruno – Leipzig: J C Hinrichs, 1907 – 1mf – 9 – 0-8370-8457-1 – 1986-2457 – us A.T.L.A. [470]
KURZGEFASSTE GESCHICHTE DER LUTHERISCHEN BIBELUEBERSETZUNG BIS ZUR GEGENWART : MIT BERUECKSICHTIGUNG DER VORLUTHERISCHEN DEUTSCHEN BIBEL UND DER IN DER REFORMIERTEN SCHWEIZ GEBRAUCHTEN DEUTSCHEN BIBELN: EINE DENK- UND DANKSCHRIFT ZUR VIERHUNDERTJAEHRIGEN JUBELFEIER DER GEBURT LUTHERS / Grimm, Wilibald – (Includes bibliographical references) – Jena: Hermann Costenoble, 1884 – 1mf – 9 – 0-8370-3398-5 – 1985-1398 – us A.T.L.A. [220]
KURZGEFASSTE GESCHICHTE DER ORGEL AUS DEM FRANZOESISCHEN DES DOM BEDOS DE CELLES / Vollbeding, J C – Berlin. 1793. BP-771 1 – 9 – ne IDC [780]
KURZGEFASSTE GRAMMATIK DER BIBLISCHARAMAEISCHE SPRACHE / Marti, Karl – (Porta linguarum orientalium. Sammlung von Lehrbuechern fuer das Studium der orientalischen Sprachen. XVIII). Berlin. 1925. BNE-478 1 – 9 – ne IDC [470]
KURZGEFASSTE METHODE DEN GENERALBASS ZU ERLERNEN.. / Albrechtsberger, Johann G – ca. 1791 – 9 – us Sibley [780]
KURZGEFASSTE SYRISCHE GRAMMATIK / Noeldeke, Theodor – (In German and Syriac) – 2. verb Aufl. Leipzig: Chr Herm Tauchnitz, 1898 – 1mf – 9 – 0-8370-8603-5 – 1986-2603 – us A.T.L.A. [470]
KURZGEFASSTER UEBERBLICK UEBER DIE BABYLONISCHASSYRISCHE LITERATUR : NEBST EINEM CHRONOLOGISCHEN EXCURS, ZWEI REGISTERN UND EINEM INDEX ZU 1700 THONTAFELN DES BRITISH MUSEUM'S / ed by Bezold, Carl – (In German and Akkadian. Includes indexes) – Leipzig: Otto Schulze, 1886 – 1mf – 9 – 0-8370-8404-0 – 1986-2404 – us A.T.L.A. [470]
KURZGEFASSTES LEXICON DEUTSCHER PSEUDONYMER SCHRIFTSTELLER VON DER AELTERN BIS AUF DIE JUENGSTE ZEIT AUS ALLEN FAECHERN DER WISSENSCHAFTEN / Rassmann, F – Leipzig, 1830 – viii/248p – 9 – DM48.00 – 3-89349-235-6 – gw Hänsel [920]
KURZGEFASSTES MUSICALISCHES LEXICON... / Stoessel, C & Stoessel, J D; ed by Franz Schubert's copy – Chemnitz: Stoessel, 1737 – 5mf – ne IDC [780]
KURZGEFASSTES MUSIKALISCHES LEXIKON, ZUSAMMENGETRAGEN VON GEORG FRIEDRICH WOLF / Wolf, G F – Halle. 1792. BP-776 1 – 9 – ne IDC [780]
Kurzreiter, Heinrich see UEBER DIE HAMBURGER DRAMATURGIE UND CORNEILLES DISCOURS
KURZTGEFASSTES MUSICALISCHES LEXICON / Stössel, C & Stössel, J D – P 480. 1737 – 9 – ne IDC [780]

...ski, Auguste *see*
LES DEPUTES A L'ASSEMBLEE LEGISLATIVE DE 1791
- LES DEPUTES AUX CORPS LEGISLATIFS, CONSEIL DES CINQ CENTS, CONSEIL DES ANCIENS DE L'AN 4 A L'AN 7
- DICTIONNAIRE DES CONVENTIONNELS, STE D'HISTOIRE DE LA REVOLUTION FRANCAISE

Kuslansky, Gerald *see* PROSPECTS OF COAL AND LIGNITE IN NORTHERN NEGEV

Kusmen, Karhiwikarta *see* THE HISTORY OF PASUNDAN

Kusnetsov, N *see* MATERIALY DLIA FLORY KAVKAZA. FLORA CAUCASICA CRITICA

Kuss, E *see* MITBESTIMMUNG UND GERECHTER LOHN ALS ELEMENTE EINER NEUORDNUNG DER WIRTSCHAFT

KUSTAR'-KOOPERATOR – Moscow, 1925-27 – 26mf – 9 – COR-648/1 – ne IDC [334]

KUSTARNAIA PROMYSHLENNOST' SSSR : SBORNIK STATEI I MATERIALOV / ed by Lereda, S P – M., 1925 – 2mf – 9 – COR-428/1 – ne IDC [334]

KUSTARNAIA PROMYSHLENNOST'I EE SVIAZ'S KOOPERATIVAMI / Kablukov, N A – M., 1915 – 1mf – 9 – COR-38/1 – ne IDC [334]

KUSTARNAIA PROMYSHLENNOST'I PROMYSLOVAIA KOOPERATSIIA : MATERIALY III PLENUMA VSNKH RSFSR, 27 FEVR.-1 MARTA 1928 G – M., 1928 – 2mf – 9 – COR-425/1 – ne IDC [334]

KUSTARNAIA PROMYSHLENNOST'I PROMYSLOVAIA KOOPERATSIIA RSFSR : SBORNIK MATERIALOV – M., 1929 – 2mf – 9 – COR-427/1 – ne IDC [334]

KUSTARNAIA PROMYSHLENNOST'I PROMYSLOVAIA KOOPERATSIIA V NATSIONAL'NYKH RESPUBLIKAKH I OBLASTIAKH SSSR / ed by Enbaev, A M – M., 1928 – 3mf – 9 – COR-426/1 – ne IDC [334]

KUSTARNAIA ROSSIIA : OCHERKI / Denisiuk, N F – Petrograd: Tip. zhurn. "Sport i favority", 1918 – 1 – CSUX88-B8951 – us Hoover Inst Photo [333]

KUSTARNO-PROMYSLOVAIA KOOPERATSIIA NA NIZHEGORODSKOI IARMARKE 1927 G : SPRAVOCHNIK VSEKOPROMSOIUZA – M., 1927 – 1mf – 9 – COR-430/1 – ne IDC [334]

KUSTARNO-PROMYSLOVAIA KOOPERATSIIA RSFSR V 1927-28 GODU : STATISTICHESKII EZHEGODNIK – M., 1929 – 3mf – 9 – COR-431/1 – ne IDC [334]

KUSTARNO-REMESLENNAIA PROMYSHLENNOST' SSSR / Feigin, V – M., L., 1927 – 2mf – 9 – COR-452/1 – ne IDC [334]

KUSTARNY I KRA I : LENINSKOGO UKOMA VKP(B), UISPOLKOMA I UPROFBI URO – (Includes c.1: 1928:Feb.19) – Leninsk: Leninskai a gos. tip., 192u – 1 – CSUXAHZ6259-S – us Hoover Inst Photo [947]

Kutrzeba, S *see* GRUNDRISS DER POLNISCHEN VERFASSUNGSGESCHICHTE

Kutscher, Artur *see*
- GERHART HAUPTMANN
- LOENS-BREVIER
- DAS NATURGEFUEHL IN GOETHES LYRIK
- DAS NATURGEFUEHL IN GOETHES LYRIK BIS ZUR AUSGABE DER SCHRIFTEN 1789

Kutscher, Austin H *see* LOSS, GRIEF AND CARE

Kutter, Hermann *see*
- THEY MUST, OR, GOD AND THE SOCIAL DEMOCRACY
- WILHELM VON ST. THIERRY

Kutuzov, A I *see* SLOVAR' RUSSKO-SUAKHILI GAZETNOI LEKSIKI

Kuwait *see*
- AL-KUWAYT AL-YAWM
- THE FIRST FIVE YEAR DEVELOPMENT PLAN, 1967/68-1971/72

Kuwait. Central Statistical Office *see*
- MASHROU' AL ITAR AL'AM LIL KHITTA AL INMAIYYA AL KHAMSIYYA LIL SANAWAT 1990/91-1994/95
- STATISTICAL ABSTRACT
- YEARLY SUMMARY OF FOREIGN TRADE

Kuwait. Chamber of Commerce and Industry *see* ANNUAL REPORT ON ECONOMIC CONDITIONS IN KUWAIT

Kuwait. Commercial Bank *see* REPORT AND ACCOUNTS

Kuwait. Currency Board *see* ANNUAL REPORT OF THE CURRENCY BOARD, KUWAIT

Kuwait. Customs and Port Dept *see* STATISTICS ON TRADE

THE KUWAIT FUND SCHEME FOR THE QUARANTEE OF INTER-ARAB INVESTMENTS / Kuwait. Kuwait Fund for Arab Economic Development – Z. A. Nasr. 1972. BNE-9022 1 – 9 – ne IDC [338]

Kuwait. Gulf Bank *see* ANNUAL REPORT AND BALANCE SHEET, 1970-1975

Kuwait. Industrial and process engineering consultants. (Great Britain, London) *see* INDUSTRIAL SURVEY OF KUWAIT

Kuwait. Kuwait Foreign Trading, Contracting and Investment Company *see* ANNUAL REPORT

Kuwait. Kuwait Fund for Arab Economic Development *see*
- ANNUAL REPORTS, 1962/63-1975/76
- THE KUWAIT FUND SCHEME FOR THE QUARANTEE OF INTER-ARAB INVESTMENTS
- LOAN AGREEMENT BETWEEN JORDAN AND THE KUWAIT FUND
- LOAN AGREEMENT BETWEEN THE REPUBLIC OF SUDAN AND THE KUWAIT FUND FOR ARAB ECONOMIC DEVELOPMENT. DATED 25 MAR 1962. BNE-7658/1
- LOAN AGREEMENT (HAOUD EL HAMRA-ARZEW OIL PIPELINE PROJECT) BETWEEN THE DEMOCRATIC AND POPULAR REPUBLIC OF ALGERIA AND KUWAIT FUND FOR ARAB ECONOMIC DEVELOPMENT

Kuwait. Kuwait Investment Company *see* REPORT AND ACCOUNTS, 1966-1977

Kuwait. Kuwait University *see*
- GENERAL UNDERGRADUATE CATALOG 1985-1987
- UNIVERSITY OF KUWAIT IN YEARS 18

Kuwait. Ministry of Finance and Industry *see* FINANCIAL AND ECONOMIC STATEMENT

Kuwait. National Bank *see* ANNUAL REPORT OF THE BOARD OF DIRECTORS AND ACCOUNTS, 1953-1977

Kuyper, A *see* KERKERAADS-PROTOCOLLEN DER HOLLANDSCHE GEMEENTE TE LONDEN 1569-1571 (DE WERKEN..1,1)

Kuyper, Abraham *see*
- CALVINISM
- HET CALVINISME
- HET CALVINISME EN DE KUNST
- DIE MODERNE THEOLOGIE (DER MODERNISMUS)
- PANTHEISM'S DESTRUCTION OF BOUNDARIES
- UIT HET WOORD

KUZBASS – (Library has no. 274 (Nov. 25, 1928)) – Shcheglovsk: "Kuzbass", 1922- – 1 – CSUX88-S526 – us Hoover Inst Photo [947]

KUZBASS : ORGAN KOLCHUGINSKOGO RA IKOMA R.K.P., RA IKOMA GORNORABOCHIKH, RUDOISPOLKOMA I RUDOUPRAVLENII A – (Includes c.1: 1922:Mar.12) – Kolchugino: Ra ikom, 19uu – 1 – CSUXANR8738-S – us Hoover Inst Photo [947]

KUZBASS (KOLCHUGINO, RUSSIA) *see* KUZBASS

Kuzmin, M *see*
- ALEKSANDRIISKIIA PESNI
- DVUM
- GLINIANYE GOLUBKI
- GLINIANYIA GOLUBKI
- NEZDESHNIE VECHERA
- OSENNIIA OZERA
- PARABOLY
- PLAVAIUSHCHIE PUTESHESTVUIUSHCHIE
- SETI
- USLOVNOSTI

Kuz'mina, V D *see* RUSSKII DEMOKRATICHESKII TEATR 18 VEKA

Kuznetsova, T V *see* TSENTRAL'NYI GOSUDARSTVENNYI ISTORICHESKII ARKHIV SSSR V G. LENINGRADE. UCHEBNOE POSOBIE

KUZNITZA – Moscow. no. 1-3, 7. May-Jul, Dec 1920-Mar 1921 – 1 – us NY Public [460]

Kvacala, Jan *see* THOMAS CAMPANELLA

KVAELLSPOSTEN – Malmoe, 1995- – 9 – sw Kungliga [072]

KVAKARTIDSKRIFT – v1-12. 1974-85 (complete) – 1r – 1 – ATLA S0797 – us A.T.L.A. [073]

DER KVAL = THE SOURCE – Montreal, CN, 1922 – 1r – 1 – Can$25.00 – cn Can Microfilming [072]

KVALLSPOSTEN – Malmo, Sweden. 1948-78 – 462r – 1 – sw Kungliga [072]

KVALLSPOSTEN – Malmo, Sweden. 1979-89 – 1 – sw Kungliga [072]

KVALLSSTUNDEN *see* VASTMANLANDS NYHETER

Kvaskov, Ia. G *see* REFORMA BIBLIOTECHNAGO DELA. BIBLIOTECHNYIA KARTOCHKI PRI VNOV' VYKHODIASHCHIKH KNIGAKH

KVELOSA LOKA: ROMANS / Brigader, Anna – n.p.: Apgads Sejejs, 1949. 252p. With: Le Probleme de la Population en France by L. Rabinowicz. 1 reel. 1296 – 1 – us U.W. Library [460]

KVETY – Prague, Czechoslovakia, 1865. v2-7, 1867-72 – 1 – us I.U. Libraries [073]

KVETY – Prague, Czechoslovakia, 1879. v1-5, 8-60, 62-69, 72-73.1879-80, 1882-1912, 1914-15 – 1 – us I.U. Libraries [073]

KVETY AMERICKE – Omaha, NE. -m,w,sm. 15 Oct 1884-4 Jun 1919. Title varies – 1 – us NE Hist [071]

KVINNAN OCH HEMMET – Cedar Rapids, Iowa. 1893-1917. Incomplete – 1 – sw Kungliga [073]

KVINNORNAS TIDNING – Goteborg, Sweden. 1921-25 – 2r – 1 – sw Kungliga [073]

KVINNOSYN – Karlstad, 1988-94 – 1 – sw Kungliga [072]

Kvitnitskii Vil'k *see* KATALOG BIBLIOTEKI NIKOLAEVSKOI AKADEMII GENERAL'NAGO SHABA

KWANG-TUNG CHING-WU CHUANG-K'UANG / China. Kwangtung Provincial Government – Survey of the Police Administration in Kwangtung. Canton, 1928.2v., tables, charts. 1 reel – 1 – 32.00 – us Chinese Res [950]

KWARTALNIK HISTORYCZNY – Krakaw. v.1-47. 1887-1931 – 1 – 140.00 – us L of C Photodup [943]

KWARTALNIK HISTORYCZNY – Warsaw. 1887. Available: 1914-15, 1934-35. BR-5865 2 – 8 – ne IDC [306]

KWAYEDZA/UMTHUNYWA – Bulawayo, Rhodesia. 15 June 1985 – 3 rolls – 1 – sa Microfile [960]

Kwee, H *see* MEMBUAT ICE CREAM, COCKTAIL, PUDDING

Kwee, Kek Beng *see* WHO'S WHO IN NEW CHINA

Kwee, Oen Keng *see* PEDANG PEMBUNUH ASMARA

Kweetin, John *see* A HIDDEN JEWEL

KWENENG DISTRICT DEVELOPMENT PLAN 1989-1995 / Botswana. Kweneng District – Gaborone, 1990 – 3mf – 9 – ne IDC [338]

KWESTJA ROLNA W GALICJI / Ludkiewicx, Zdzislaw – Lwow, 1910 – 1r – 1 – us I.H.R.C. [947]

KWESTYA LITEWSKA W PRASIE POLSKIEJ – Warsaw. 1905 – 1 – 35.00r – us Hoover Inst Photo [073]

Kwik, Hok Tiang *see* OBAT-OBATAN DAN PEMBUATANNJA

KY LAN – no. 2-69. Saigon. 18 aout 1928-19 mai 1929. mq no. 50, 64-66, 68 – 1 – fr A.C.R.P.P. [073]

KYEMON – Rangoon, Burma. May 1970-73; Mar 1978-Sept 1988 – 53r – 1 – us L of C Photodup [072]

KYIOKOS – 1976-82 – 1 – us A.T.L.A. [240]

KYKLOS – v1- 1947- 1; v28- 1975- 5,6,9 – us UMI [073]

Kymeus, J *see* EIN ALT CHRISTLICH CONCILIUM FUR 1200 JAREN ZU GANGRA JNN PAPHLAGONIA GEHALTEN

KYNETON GUARDIAN – 1901-1920. KG1-20 – 20r – 1 – at Corangamite [072]

Kynett, Alpha Jefferson *see* OUR LAITY: AND THEIR EQUAL RIGHTS WITHOUT DISTINCTION OF SEX IN THE METHODIST EPISCOPAL CHURCH

KYODON NEWS LETTER – 1966-87 (complete) – 2r – 1 – ATLA S0588 – us A.T.L.A. [073]

(KYOKUTO KOKUSAI GUNJI SAIBAN KIROKU MOKUROKU OYOBI SAKUIN) / Mori, Kyozo – Tokyo, 1953. 21,293p. LL-10030 – 1 – us L of C Photodup [340]

DIE KYPRIEN : EIN HELLENISCHES EPOS IN ZWOELF GESAENGEN NEU GESCHAFFEN / Scheffer, Thassilo von – 2. Aufl. Wiesbaden: Dieterich, 1947 – 1r – 1 – us U.W. Library [450]

Kyriakos, A Diomedes *see* GESCHICHTE DER ORIENTALISCHEN KIRCHEN VON 1453-1898

Kyrieleis, Richard *see* MORITZ AUGUST VON THUEMMELS ROMAN "REISE IN DIE MITTAEGLICHEN PROVINZEN VON FRANKREICH"

KYRILLOS VON SKYTHOPOLIS (T.U.U. 4-49/2) / Schwartz, Eduard – Leipzig, 1939 – 7mf – 9 – ne Slangenburg [240]

KYRIOKOS. UUWF JOURNAL – v1-3. 1976-82 (complete) – 1r – 1 – ATLA S0342 – us A.T.L.A. [073]

KYRIOS – 1(1936)-6(1943) – 37mf – 9 – Dfl30.00 – ne Slangenburg [073]

KYRKA OCH FOLK – v45-66. 1968-89 (complete) – 9r – 1 – ATLA S0642 – us A.T.L.A. [073]

KYRKANS INFORMATIONCENTRAL : NEWS FROM THE CHURCH OF SWEDEN – v1-10. 1974-83 (complete) – 1r – 1 – ATLA S0644 – us A.T.L.A. [073]

KYST-OG INDLANDSKULTUR I DET ARKTISKE / Hatt, G – (Geografisk Tidskrift, v. 23, 1915 16). Kjobenhavn. 1916. BN-242 2 – 8 – ne IDC [306]

KYUSHU NIPPO (FUKURYU SHIMPO) – Aug 1887-1942 – 272r – 1 – Y2,176,000 – ja Japan Micro [950]

KYUSHU NIPPO FUKURYU SHIMPO – Japan, 1887-1942 – 272r – 1 – inquire – us Ross [950]

KYUSTENDILSKO DELO – Kyustendil, Bulgaria. Jul 1952-Feb 1959 – 2r – 1 – us L of C Photodup [949]

GUIDE TO MICROFORMS IN PRINT

AUTHOR
TITLE

Incorporating International Microforms in Print

VOL. 2

1999

L – Z

K·G·SAUR

Edited by:
Irene Izod

CIP-Kurztitelaufnahme der Deutschen Bibliothek
[Guide to microforms in print / Author, title]
Guide to microforms in print :
incorporating international microforms in print.
Author, title. – Munich : Saur
ISSN 0164-0747
Erscheint jährlich. – Früher im Verl. Meckler,
Westport, CT. – Aufnahme nach 1990

1990 –
Verl.-Wechsel

Library of Congress Catalog Card Number: 61-7082

Computer-controlled data preparation
and automatic data processing
by Microcomposition, München

Cover art by William Pownall

Printed and bound by Legoprint S.r.l., Trento, Italy

ISSN 0164-0747
ISBN 3-598-11392-7

Author-Title List
L–Z

Title main entries with references from authors, editors

L (Amuse), Coronel *see* RELACION DE LOS SITIOS Y DEFENSAS DE OLIVENZA, DE BADAJOZ Y DE CAMPO-MAYOR EN 1811 Y 1812 POR LAS TROPAS FRANCESAS DEL - EJERCITO DEL MEDIODIA EN ESPANA. TRADUCIDO POR E. SEGURA
L EBENSOHN, A D *see* SHIREI SEFAT KODESH
L Ehmann, FV Paul *see* GEOGRAFIA DEL JAPON. BARCELONA, 1929
L. SPOONER : FASCINATION WITH THE LAW / Creagh, M R – 1980. 11p – 9 – 1.00f – at Libertarian Micro [340]
L. TIECK ET LE THEATRE ESPAGNOL / Bertrand, Jean Jacques Achille – (Includes bibliographical references) – Paris: F Rieder, 1914 – 1r – 1 – us U.W. Library [790]
L. TOLSTOI I DOSTOEVSKII / Merezhkovskii, Dimitrii – 2v. Spb. 1901-02. BR-767 2 – 8 – ne IDC [460]
La Badie, Jean de *see* SERMONS
La Barre DuParq, Edouard *see* COMMENTAIRES SUR LE TRAITE "DE LA GUERRE" DE CLAUZEWITZ
La Barre, Francois Poullain de *see* DE L'EGALITE DES DEUX SEXES, DISCOURS PHYSIQUE ET MORALE OU L'ON VOIT L'IMPORTANCE DE SE DEFAIRE DES PREJUGEZ
La Bastide, M-A de *see* REPONSE AU LIVRE DE M. EVEQUE DE CONDOM
La Baume-Desdossat, Jacques Francois de *see* LA CHRISTIADE OU LE PARADIS RECONQUIS: POUR SERVIR DE SUITE AU "PARADIS PERDU" DE MILTON
La Bouillerie, Francois Alexandre Roullet de *see* ETUDES SUR LE SYMBOLISME DE LA NATURE
La Boutresse *see* LES FIEFS DU BOURBONNAIS, LA PALISSE
La Briere, Leon de *see* MADAME LOUISE DE FRANCE
La Brouee, C *see* LA VIE DU R.P. JEAN-FRANCOIS REGIS
La Bruyere, Jean de *see* CARACTERES: PAGES CHOISIES
La Cadena, Ramon Lacadena y Brualla *see* EL GRAN CARDINAL DE ESPANA, DON PEDRO GONZALEZ DE MENDOZA
La Caille, Nicolas-Louis de *see* JOURNAL HISTORIQUE DU VOYAGE FAIT AU CAP DE BONNE-ESPERANCE
La Chambre, Marin Cureau de *see* LES CARACTERES DES PASSIONS...
La Chatre, M *see* NOUVEAU DICTIONNAIRE UNIVERSEL
La Condamine, Charles-Marie de *see* LETTRE CRITIQUE SUR L'EDUCATION
La Croix *see* RELATION UNIVERSELLE DE L'AFRIQUE ANCIENNE ET MODERNE, OU L'ON VOIT CE QU'IL Y A DE REMARQUABLE TANT DANS LA TERRE FERME QUE DANS LES ILES, AVEC CE QUE LE ROI A FAIT DE MEMORABLE CONTRE LES CORSAIRES DE BARBARIE
La Croix, A P de *see* L'ART DE LA POESIE FRANCOISE ET LATINE
LA CUCARACHA RECORDS – Fresno Co, 1946-50 – 1 – 1 – $50.00 – B06089 – us Library Micro [978]
La Cuisse, Sr. de *see* LA REPERTOIRE DES BALS, OU THEORIE-PRACTIQUE DES CONTRADANSES...
La Curne de Sainte Palaye *see* DICTIONNAIRE HISTORIQUE DE L'ANCIEN FRANCOIS
La Dixmerie, Nicolas Bricaire de *see* LE SAUVAGE DE TAITI AUX FRANCAIS AVEC UN ENVOI AU PHILOSOPHE AMI DES SAUVAGES
La Faige *see* LES FIEFS DU BOURBONNAIS, LA PALISSE
La Farelle, FF de *see* DU PROGRES SOCIAL AU PROFIT DES CLASSES POPULAIRES OU INDIGENTES, SUIVI DE: PLAN D'UNE REORGANISATION DISCIPLINAIRE DES CLASSES INDUSTRIELLES EN FRANCE
...LA FEMME COMPOSITEUR.. / Soleniere, Eugene de – 1895 – 9 – us Sibley [780]
La Feuille, D de *see* LA SCIENCE DES HIEROGLYPHES, OU L'ART D'EXPRIMER PAR DES FIGURES SYMBOLIQUES, LES VERTUS, LES VICES...
La Follette, Robert M *see* PAPERS OF ROBERT M. LA FOLLETTE, 1876-1924
La Font de Saint-Yenne *see* EXAMEN D'UN ESSAI SUR L'ARCHITECTURE, AVEC QUELQUES REMARQUES SUR CETTE SCIENCE TRAITEE DANS L'ESPIRIT DES BEAUX-ARTS
La Garaye, Claude Toussaint Marot *see* CHYMIE HUDRAULIQUE, POUR EXTRAIRE LES SELS ESSENTIELS DES VEGETAUX ET DES MINERAUX, PAR LE MOYEN DE L'EAU PURE
La Glebe, Jean de *see* LE DIABLE EST AUX VACHES
La Grue, Th. *see* LA VRAYE INTRODUCTION A LA LANGUE FRANCOISE
La Harpe, Jean Francois de *see*
- COMMENTAIRE SUR LE THEATRE DE VOLTAIRE
- ELOGE DE VOLTAIRE

La Martelliere *see* ROBERT, CHEF DE BRIGANDS
La Masseliere, B de *see* LES DYNAMISMES SOCIO-POLITIQUES ET ECONOMIQUES DANS LA TRANSFORMATION DES PAYSAGES AGRAIRES DU KAYOR CENTRAL ET SEPTENTRIONAL, SENEGAL
La Mere, Vern J *see* VALIDATION OF EQUATIONS TO PREDICT LACTATE THRESHOLD, FIXED BLOOD LACTATE CONCENTRATIONS, AND PEAK VALUES FROM A 3200 METER PERFORMANCE TIME
La Mesnardiere, H J P de *see* LA POETIQUE
La Moiriniere, M M de *see* LES VERTUS DU VRAI PRELAT REPRESENTEES EN LA VIE DE MGR. L'EMINENTISSIME CARDINAL DE LA ROCHEFOUCAULT
La Monte, R R *see* MEN VERSUS THE MAN
La Mothe Le Vayer, F de *see* OEUVRES
La Motte, Ellen Newbold *see* THE BACKWASH OF WAR
La Motte-Fouque, Albertine Baronin de *see* BRIEFE AN FRIEDRICH BARON DE LA MOTTE FOUQUE VON CHAMISSO, CHEZY, COLLIN...
La Motte-Fouque, Friedrich Heinrich Karl *see*
- UNDINE
- UNDINE: EINE ERZAHLUNG VON FRIEDRICH BARON DE LA MOTTE FOUQUE

La Noue, O de *see*
- LE DICTIONNAIRE DES RIMES FRANCOISES
- LE GRAND DICTIONNAIRE DES RIMES FRANCOISES

La Perouse, Jean-Francois de G de *see* COPIES DE PIECES SUR LA PEROUSE, APPARTENANT A M. DE LAJARIETTE
La Perriere, Guillaume de *see* LE THEATRE DES BONS ENGINS, AUQUEL SONT CONTENUZ CENT EMBLEMES MORAULX
La Pichonnaye, Guillaume de *see* A PLAYNE TREATISE TO LEARNE IN A SHORT SPACE THE FRENCHE TONGUE
La Ramee, Pierre de *see*
- THE LATINE GRAMMAR OF P. RAMUS: TRANSLATED INTO ENGLISH
- THE RUDIMENTES OF P. RAMUS HIS LATINE GRAMMAR: ENGLISHED AND NEWLY CORRECTED

La Riviere, L de *see* HISTOIRE DE LA VIE ET MOEURS DE MARIE TESSONNIERE...
La Roque, Louis de *see* CATALOGUE DES GENTILSHOMMES DE NORMANDIE.
LA SCALA, 1778-1906; NOTE STORICHE E STATISTICHE / Cambiasi, P – (5th edition) – Milano etc.: G Ricordi & Co; New York: Boosey & Co, 1906 – 1 – us Sibley [780]
La Souchere, Elena de *see* GUERRE ET RELIGION
La Taille, J de *see* LA MANIERE DE FAIRE DES VERS EN FRANCOIS
La Vergne, Armand *see* TRENTE ANS DE VIE NATIONALE
La Vicomterie de Saint-Sanson *see* LES DROITS DU PEUPLE SUR L'ASSEMBLEE NATIONALE
La Voye, M de *see* TRAITE DE MUSIQUE, POUR BIEN ET FACILEMENT APPRENDRE A CHANTER ET COMPOSER, TANT POUR LES VOIX QUE POUR LES INSTRUMENTS
L.A. Williams and Co *see* HISTORY OF THE OHIO FALLS CITIES AND THEIR COUNTIES
La-Anyane, Seth *see* THE ECONOMIC ORGANISATION OF AGRICULTURAL PRODUCTION IN WEST AFRICA
Laar, Clemens *see* EINE MANNSCHAFT
LAB ANIMAL – v. 6-. 1977- – 1,5,6,9 – us UMI [590]
LAB WORLD – 1950- 1; 1971- 5,6; 1976- 4 x 6 in. 9 – us UMI [500]
Labadie, Laurance *see* WHAT IS MAN'S DESTINY?
Labanca, Baldassare *see* GESU CRISTO NELLA LETTERATURA CONTEMPORANEA STRANIERA E ITALIANA
IL LABARO – Rome, Italy. Il Labaro della reforma cattolica. -w, -m. 4 Oct, 10 Nov 1883; 16 Jan-1 March, 15 May, 15 Aug 1884; 9 March 1890-March 1898. 3 reels – 1 – uk British Libr Newspaper [072]
O LABARO : JORNAL INDEPENDENTE, LITTERARIO E NOTICIOSO – Pecanha, 22 Sep 1919; 7-22 Jan 1920 – 1,5,6 – bl Biblioteca [072]
Labarthe, Pierre *see*
- VOYAGE A LA COTE DE GUINEE
- VOYAGE AU SENEGAL PENDANT LES ANNEES 1784 ET 1785, D'APRES LES MEMOIRES DE LAJAILLE

LABARUM : ORGAO DA MACONARIA – Maceio, Alagoas. 18 Set 1874-30 Mar 1876 – 1,5,6 – bl Biblioteca [072]
Labasse, J *see* LES CAPITAUX ET LA REGION
Labat, Jean-Baptiste *see*
- NOUVELLE RELATION DE L'AFRIQUE OCCIDENTALE
- RELATION HISTORIQUE DE L'ETHIOPIE OCCIDENTALE: CONTENANT LA DESCRIPTION DES ROYAUMES DU CONGO, ANGOLLE ET MATAMBA
- VOYAGE DU CHEVALIER DES MARCHAIS EN GUINEE

LABATT'S DISTRICT REPORTS / California – v1-2. 1857-1858 – 8mf – 9 – $12.00 – LLMC 91-023 – us L.L.M.C. [340]
Labatut, Roger *see* CHANTS DE BEAUTE ET DE VIE RECUEILLIS CHEZ LES PEULS NOMADES DU NORD CAMEROUN
Labbe *see*
- NOVAE BIBLIOTHECAE MANUSCRIPT LIBRORUM THOMUS PRIMUS
- NOVAE BIBLIOTHECAE MANUSCRIPT LIBRORUM TOMUS SECUNDUS

L'Abbe, A *see* THE PRINCE OF WALES SARABAND
Labbe, Edith *see* BIBLIOGRAPHIE DE MONSIEUR L'ABBE HONORIUS PROVOST, L.TH., L.PH., DU SEMINAIRE DE QUEBEC, ARCHIVISTE A L'UNIVERSITE LAVAL
Labbe, Ph *see*
- ANNALES A MUNDI EXORDIO USQUE AD OBITUM ALEXII COMMENI IMPER. (CBH 9)
- ECLOGAE HISTORICORUM DE REBUS BYZANTINIS (CBH 1,3)
- NOTITIA DIGNITATUM IMPERII ROMANI (CBH 27)

Labbe, Ph. *see* DE HISTORIAE BYZANTINAE SCRIPTORIBUS EMITTENDIS PROTREPTICON
Labbe, Wilfrid *see* BIO-BIBLIOGRAPHIE ANALYTIQUE DE MGR LEONCE BOIVIN, P.D., B.S., L.D.C., D. TH.
Labelle, J H A *see* LE TRAIT D'UNION
Labelle, Jean Baptiste *see*
- O CANADA, MON PAYS, MES AMOURS
- LE RETOUR DU ZOUAVE: ROMANCE

Laberge, Gaetan *see* BIBLIOGRAPHIE ANALYTIQUE DU BASSON
Laberge, Leo *see* ISAIE 28-33
Laberge, Raymond-Marie *see* BIBLIOGRAPHIE ANALYTIQUE DE C.-J. MAGNAN
Laberthonniere, Lucien *see*
- ESSAIS DE PHILOSOPHIE RELIGIEUSE
- POSITIVISME ET CATHOLICISME
- LE REALISME CHRETIEN ET L'IDEALISME GREC

LABETTE COUNTY DEMOCRAT – Oswego. KS. 1879-81 – 1 – us UMI [071]
Labette County, KS *see* FUNERAL REGISTERS
LABIATARUM GENERA ET SPECIES / Bentham, G – London. 1832-36. B-33 2 – 8 – ne IDC [580]
Labillardiere, J J H de *see*
- ICONES PLANTARUM SYRIAE RARIORUM
- NOVAE HOLLANDIAE PLANTARUM SPECIMEN
- RELATION DU VOYAGE A LA RECHERCHE DE LA PEROUSE
- SERTUM AUSTROCALEDONICUM

Lablochkov, M *see* ISTORIIA DVORIANSKOGO SOSLOVIIA V ROSSII
O LABOR : HEBDOMADARIO LITTERARIO, INSTRUCTIVO E RECREATIVO – Maceio, Alagoas. 30 Maio-27 Jun 1892 – 1,5,6 – bl Biblioteca [072]
O LABOR – Januaria, Brazil. Mar 1923 – 1 – bl Biblioteca [072]
O LABOR : PELOS INTERESSES DO MUNICIPIO – Eugenopolis, 29 Mar, Jul, Oct, Dec 1953; Feb, Apr, Jun-Jul 1954 – 1,5,6 – bl Biblioteca [072]
LABOR ACTION – New York, NY. -w. 5 Jan 1942-22 Sept 1958. Lacking 1944. 7 reels – 1 – uk British Libr Newspaper [071]
LABOR ACTION / Workers Party. U.S.A – 4 2+6-22 2+19 (all publ). 1940-58 – 5r – 1 – $580.00 – us UPA [331]
LABOR ACTION NEWS – NY City, NY. 1940-1958 – 8r – 1 – $400.00 – R04925 – us Library Micro [331]
LABOR ADVOCATE – Nashville, Tenn. v. 13-49. Sept 12 1913-Feb 27 1941. Incomplete – 1 – us NY Public [331]
THE LABOR ADVOCATE – Toronto: Grip Print & Pub. Co, [1890-1891] – 9 – cn C.I.H.M. [331]
LABOR AGE / American Workers Party – 1-22 2+1 (all publ). 1913-33 – 4r – 1 – $460.00 – us UPA [331]
LABOR AND INDUSTRY IN BRITAIN – British Information Services. v1-14. 1943-56 (all publ) – 14mf – $63.00 – LLMC 84-347 – us L.L.M.C. [073]
LABOR ARBITRATION AWARDS / American Arbitration Association – (With bound index) – New York, 1959-73 – 350mf – 9 – $5.00f – us Ross [331]
LABOR ARBITRATION IN GOVERNMENT / American Arbitration Association – (With bound index) – New York, 1971-73 – 88mf – 9 – us Ross [331]
LABOR ARGUS – Charleston. West Virginia. 1906-11 – 1 – us UMI [071]
LABOR BULLETIN – Decatur. Ill. 1886-1896 – 1 – us UMI [331]
LABOR BULLETIN – Kansas City. Kan. 1940-57 – 1 – us UMI [331]
LABOR BULLETIN / Labor Research Front – 1-2 2+1 (all publ). 1936-1938 – 2mf – 9 – $35.00 – us UPA [330]
LABOR CALL – 1921-1953. LC1-20 – 20r – 1 – at Corangamite [072]
LABOR CHALLENGE (TORONTO, ONT.: 1945) – (Includes c.1: v.1:no.1 (1945:June 1) – v.5:no.2=no.67 (1949:Feb.); v.6:no.1=no.78 (1950:Jan.) – v.6:no.5=no.82 (1950:May); v.6:no.7=no.84 (1950:Mid-July)-; v) – Toronto: Labor Challenge, 1945 – 1 – CSUXALP7232-S – us Hoover Inst Photo [331]
LABOR DAILY : DAILY NEWS – Sydney, 1930-35 – 20r – 1 – A$620.00 silver A$540.00 vesicular – at Pascoe [072]
LABOR DESARROLLADA DESDE SU CREACION HASTA FIN DE DICIEMBRE DE 1951 / Junta Provincial de Fomento Pecuario – Badajoz: Junta Provincial de Fomento Pecuario, 1952 – 1 – sp Bibl Santa Ana [331]
THE LABOR DOLLAR / Andrews, Stephen Pearl – 3fiches (29x) – 9 – 1.00f – at Libertarian Micro [320]
LABOR EN EL EXILIO / Repetto, Nicolas – Buenos Aires: Editorial de La Vanguardia, 1949 – 1 – CSUXADH7698-B – us Hoover Inst Photo [331]
LABOR GAZETTE – Portland OR. May 10 1878 – 1 – us U.O. Library [071]
LABOR HERALD / American Federation of Labor. Missouri State Federation of Labor – Kansas City, Missouri. v. 10, no. 42-v. 37, no. 35. Nov 14 1913-Sept 27 1940. Incomplete – 1 – us NY Public [331]
LABOR HERALD – Rochester, New York. v. 1-22. Oct 9 1914-Sept 28 1935. Incomplete – 1 – us NY Public [071]
THE LABOR HERALD – San Francisco, CA. 1943-51 – 4r – 1 – $200.00 – C02829 – us Library Micro [071]
LABOR HISTORY – v1- 1960- 1; v11- 5,6; v16- 9 – us UMI [331]
LABOR IN THE SUDAN / U.S. Bureau of Labor Statistics – O'Grady-Jones, L. 1961. BNE-7696 1 – 9 – ne IDC [324]
LABOR INFORMATION BULLETIN – Bureau of Labor Statistics. v1-20. 1934-53 (all publ) – 53mf – 9 – $80.00 – LLMC 95-012 – us L.L.M.C. [340]
LABOR ISSUES IN INDONESIA, 1979-1995 : PRESS CLIPPINGS AND OTHER DOCUMENTATION FROM THE INDOC ARCHIVES / International Institute of Social History (IISH), Amsterdam – (With guide) – 1996 – 494mf – 9 – Dfl4,370.00 – ne MMF Publ [331]
LABOR LAW / Rotwein, Abraham – Brooklyn: Harmon, 1939. 259p. LL-1041 – 1 – us L of C Photodup [340]
LABOR LAW AND PRACTICE IN LEBANON / U.S. Department of Labor. Bureau of Labor Statistics – 1966. Clarke, J. BNE-19.716 1 – 9 – ne IDC [324]
LABOR LAW AND PRACTICE IN MOROCCO / U.S. Department of Labor. Bureau of Labor Statistics – 1964. Suter, A. C. BNE-3229 1 – 9 – ne IDC [324]
LABOR LAW JOURNAL – v1- 1949- 1; v20- 5,6; v27- 9 – us UMI [331]
LABOR LAWYER (ABA) – v1-11. 1985-95 – 9 – $205.00 set – us Hein [340]

LABOR LEADER – (Labour Leader). London. -w. 10 Oct-19 Dec 1891, 31 Mar 1894-28 Sep 1922. (35 reels) – 1 – uk British Libr Newspaper [331]
LABOR LEADER – v1-22. 1938-59. New York. 2 reels – 1 – $60.00r – us Ross [331]
THE LABOR LEADER – National Issue. A Catholic Viewpoint on Labor. New York. v. 1-22. 1938-Nov 1959. Incomplete – 1 – us NY Public [240]
LABOR, MANAGEMENT RELATIONS ACT (LMRA) – Taft-Hartley Act. 2v. 1947 – 9 – $60.00 set – 0-89941-195-9 – us Hein [331]
LABOR MARKET AND EMPLOYMENT SECURITY – 1956-1963 – 1 – us UMI [331]
LABOR MOBILIZATION; THE MOROCCAN EXPERIENCE / Andriamananjara, R – (University of Michigan Center for Research on Economic Development). 1971. BNE-3003 1 – 9 – ne IDC [960]
LABOR, NATIONALISM, AND POLITICS IN ARGENTINA / Baily, Samuel L – New Brunswick, N.J.: Rutgers University Press, [1967] – 1 – CSUXAHZ2903-B – us Hoover Inst Photo [331]
LABOR NEW DEALER – Portland OR. Feb 18 Sep 9 1938-Feb 7 1941 – 1 – us U.O. Library [071]
LABOR NEWS – Flint. Mich. 1945-1957 – 1 – us UMI [331]
LABOR NEWS – Long Beach. Calif. -w. 1943-48 – 1 – us UMI [331]
LABOR PARLAMENTARIA 1912-1916, 1920-1924, 1924-1928. BUENOS AIRES, 1928 / Cafferata, Juan F – Madrid: Razon y Fe, 1929 – 1 – sp Bibl Santa Ana [350]
LABOR POWER / Socialist Union Party – 1-2 (all publ). 1939-41 – 5mf – 9 – $40.00 – us UPA [335]
LABOR PRESS – Portland. Or. 1901-1913 – 1 – us UMI [331]
LABOR PROBLEMS IN A NEWLY INDEPENDENT COUNTRY: THE CASE OF INDONESIA / Hawkins, Everett D – SE-3337 1. 1959 – 9 – ne IDC [331]
THE LABOR QUESTION / Gladden, Washington – Boston: Pilgrim Press, c1911 – 1mf – us A.T.L.A. [240]
LABOR REALIZADA Y EN EJECUCION, BREVE RESENA : DIC. 1943-4 DE JUN. DE 1947. TRES ANOS DE LABOR / Argentina. Ministerio de Obras Publicas – [Buenos Aires, 1947]. 1v – 1 – CSUXAHZ6544-B – us Hoover Inst Photo [331]
THE LABOR RECORD – Williamsport, PA., 1886 – 13 – $25.00r – us I.M.R. [071]
LABOR RELATIONS IN ARGENTINA, BRAZIL, AND CHILE / Alexander, Robert Jackson – McGraw-Hill, 1962 – 1 – CSUXADH7732-B – us Hoover Inst Photo [331]
Labor Research Front *see* LABOR BULLETIN
LABOR REVIEW *see* ONTARIO LABOUR
LABOR STANDARD – v1-8. 1876-81 – 3r – 1 – us Ross [331]
LABOR STUDIES – 1985- – 1 – us UMI [331]
LABOR STUDIES JOURNAL – (v.4 .1979 5,6,9) – v.1. 1976 – 1 – us UMI [331]
LABOR UNION PERIODICALS, PART 1 : THE METAL TRADES – (Coll: Research Collections in Labor Studies. Individual titles listed separately. With printed guide) – 161r – 1 – $16,300.00 coll – us UPA [331]
LABOR UNION PERIODICALS, PART 1 *see*
- AF OFL AUTO WORKER
- AMALGAMATED JOURNAL
- AUTO WORKERS NEWS
- AUTO WORKER/THE SPARK PLUG
- BLACKSMITHS, DROP FORGERS AND HELPERS JOURNAL
- BOILERMAKERS-BLACKSMITHS JOURNAL
- CARRIAGE AND WAGON WORKERS JOURNAL, 1899-1908 : OFFICIAL JOURNAL, 1912-1915 : MESA EDUCATOR, 1944-1951
- CIO NEWS
- FE NEWS
- INTERNATIONAL METAL WORKER, 1902-1905 : UNITED WELDORS' NEWS, 1941-1945
- INTERNATIONAL MOLDERS AND FOUNDRY WORKERS JOURNAL
- IUE-CIO NEWS
- MACHINERY MOLDERS JOURNAL, 1888-1892 : VULCAN RECORD, 1868-1875
- THE MACHINIST
- MACHINISTS AND BLACKSMITHS' MONTHLY JOURNAL, 1870-1875 : THE BRASS WORKER, 1895-1896 : OFFICIAL JOURNAL, 1902-1904
- METAL POLISHER, BUFFER AND PLATER
- METAL WORKERS BULLETIN, 1910-1914 : WELDORS' JOURNAL, 1938-1941
- MINE-MILL UNION
- PATTERN MAKERS JOURNAL
- SHEET METAL WORKERS' JOURNAL
- THE SHIPBUILDER
- STEEL LABOR
- STOVE MOUNTERS' AND RANGE WORKERS' JOURNAL
- UE NEWS
- UNITED AUTOMOBILE WORKER

LABOR UNION PERIODICALS, PART 2 : THE PRINTING TRADES – (Coll title: Research Coll in Labor Studies. Pt 2 brings together 18 titles from 10 unions between 1866-1995. Individual titles listed separately. With printed guide) – 174r – 1 – $17,620.00 coll – us UPA [331]
LABOR UNION PERIODICALS, PART 2 *see*
- AMERICAN PRESSMAN, 1890-1955 : SERVICE BUREAU NEWS BULLETIN OF THE INTERNATIONAL PRINTING PRESSMEN AND ASSISTANTS' UNION OF NORTH AMERICA, 1937- 1952
- BUCHDRUCKER-ZEITUNG
- BULLETIN OF THE INTERNATIONAL TYPOGRAPHICAL UNION
- INTERNATIONAL BOOKBINDER
- INTERNATIONAL STEREOTYPER AND ELECTROTYPERS UNION JOURNAL
- LITHOGRAPHER'S BULLETIN, 1901-1904 : OFFICIAL PUBLICATION OF THE LITHOGRAPHER'S INTERNATIONAL PROTECTIVE AND BENEFICIAL ASSOCIATION, 1910-1913 : THE LITHOGRAPHER'S JOURNAL, 1918-1955
- PALETTE AND GRAVER, 1919-1923 : INTERNATIONAL MAILER, 1946-1955
- PLATE MAKERS' CRITERION, 1907-1909 : AMERICAN PHOTO-ENGRAVER, 1908-1955
- PLATE PRINTER, 1902-1932
- PRINTER'S CIRCULAR AND STATIONERS' AND PUBLISHERS' GAZETTE, 1866-1888 : AMERICAN MODEL PRINTER, 1879-1882 : CRAFTSMAN, 1884-1888
- TYPOGRAPHICAL JOURNAL

LABOR UNION PERIODICALS, PART 3 : FOOD AND AGRICULTURAL INDUSTRIES / ed by Danky, James P & Dubofsky, Melvyn – (Coll: Research Collections in Labor Studies. Individual titles listed separately. With printed guide) – 91r – 1 – $9,215.00 coll – us UPA [331]
LABOR UNION PERIODICALS, PART 3 *see*
- AFL CANNERY REPORTER, 1949-1954 : UNITED DAIRY FARMER, 1941, 1944-1945
- BAKERS' AND CONFECTIONERS' JOURNAL
- BREWERY WORKER
- BUTCHER WORKER
- BUTCHER WORKMAN
- CANNERY AND FIELD UNION NEWS, 1937 : CIO NEWS CANNERY WORKERS EDITION, 1938-1939 : UCAPAWA NEWS, 1939-1944 : FTA NEWS, 1945-1950
- CIGAR WORKERS OFFICIAL JOURNAL
- CIO NEWS
- DISTILLERY, RECTIFYING AND WINE WORKERS INTERNATIONAL JOURNAL
- EIGHT HOUR MILLER
- FISHERY WORKER
- FREE VOICE OF THE AMALGAMATED FOOD WORKERS
- FTA NEWS
- INTERNATIONAL FISHERMAN AND ALLIED WORKER
- MEAT OF IT, 1945-1966 : INTERNATIONAL MEAT WORKER, 1946-1948
- MEAT WORKER
- OFFICIAL JOURNAL OF THE AMALGAMATED MEATCUTTERS AND BUTCHER WORKMEN
- PACKINGHOUSE WORKER
- PROGRESS
- RURAL WORKER
- SHARECROPPER'S VOICE, 1935-1937 : SOUTHERN FARM LEADER, 1936 : STFU NEWS, 1938-1939 : TENANT FARMER, 1941-1942 : FARM WORKER, 1943-1944 : FARM LABOR NEWS, 1946-1951 : THE UNION FARMER, 1952-1953 : AGRICULTURAL UNIONIST, 1952-1954
- THE TOBACCO WORKER, 1897-1924, 1940-1943

LABOR UNION PERIODICALS, PARTS 1-3 – (Coll: Research Collections in Labor Studies) – 426r – 1 – $37,380.00 set – us UPA [331]
LABOR, WITH PRELUDES ON CURRENT EVENTS / Cook, Joseph – Boston: Houghton, Mifflin, c1880 – 1mf – us A.T.L.A. [331]
Laboratoire d'Ethnobotanique et d'Ethnozoologie *see* COURS D'ETHNOBOTANIQUE ET D'ETHNOZOOLOGIE (1969-1970)
LABORATORY ANIMAL SCIENCE – v. 13-19, 21-27. 1963-69, 1971-77 – 1,5,6 – us Princeton Micro [590]
LABORATORY EQUIPMENT FOR PSYCHOLOGICAL EXPERIMENTS / Judd, Charles Hubbard – v3 of a series of textbooks...to introduce the student to the methods and principles of scientific psychology. New York: C. Scribner's sons, 1907. xi,257p. illus – 1 – us U.W. Library [150]
LABORATORY INVESTIGATION – v1-75. 1952-96 – 1,5,6,9 – $105.00r – us Williams [610]
LABORATORY MANAGEMENT – 1963- 1; 1970- 5,6; 1976- 4 x 6 in. 9 – us UMI [650]
LABORATORY MEDICINE – v1- 1970- 1; v6-6; v8- 1977- 9 – us UMI [610]
LABORATORY PRACTICE – 1952- 1; 1971- 5,6; 1975- 4 x 6 in. 9 – us UMI [500]
LABOR-DAY SOUVENIR: UNDER THE AUSPICES OF THE ALLIED TRADES AND LABOR ASSOCIATION – Ottawa: Ottawa Print. Co., 1898.00785.(Pre-1900 Canadiana) – 9 – cn C.I.H.M. [971]
Laborde, A de *see* LES PRINCIPAUX MANUSCRITS A PEINTURES CONSERVES DANS L'ANCIENNE BIBLIOTHEQUE IMPERIALE PUBLIQUE DE SAINT-PETERSBOURG
Laborde, J-B de *see*
- ESSAI SUR LA MUSIQUE ANCIENNE ET MODERNE

Laborde, Jean B V *see* LES HOMMES ET LES ACTES DE L'INSURRECTION DE PARIS DEVANT LA PSYCHOLOGIE MORBIDE. LETTRES A M. LE DOCTEUR MOREAU DE TOURS
Laborde, Julio et al *see* EL LLAMADO "SOCIALISMO NACIONAL" ?ES SOCIALISMO?
Laborde, Maximilian *see* HISTORY OF THE SOUTH CAROLINA COLLEGE, FROM ITS INCORPORATION, DEC. 19, 1801 TO DEC. 19, 1865, INCLUDING SKETCHES OF ITS PRESIDENTS AND PROFESSORS
LABOR-HERALD – San Francisco. Calif. -w. 1943-51 – 1 – us UMI [331]
LABOR-MANAGEMENT RELATIONS ACT (TAFT-HARTLEY), 1947 : LEGISLATIVE HISTORY / U. S. National Labor Relations Board – Washington: GPO. 2bks. 1948 – 19mf – 9 – $28.50 – LLMC 80-038 – us L.L.M.C. [340]
LABOR-MANAGEMENT REPORTING AND DISCLOSURE ACT, 1959 (LANDUM-GRIFFIN) : LEGISLATIVE HISTORY / U. S. National Labor Relations Board – Washington: GPO. 2bks. 1959 – 22mf – 9 – $33.00 – LLMC 80-039 – us L.L.M.C. [340]
Laboulaye, Charles *see* LES DROITS DES OUVRIERS. ETUDE SUR L'ORDRE DANS L'INDUSTRIE
Labouliniere, Pierre *see*
- ANNUAIRE STATISTIQUE DU DEPARTEMENT DES HAUTES-PYRENEES, CONTENANT L'INTRODUCTION DU GRAND MEMOIRE STATISTIQUE POUR L'AN IX. 1801
- IDEE D'UN TABLEAU OU ETAT GENERAL DE LA FRANCE
- PLAN D'UNE STATISTIQUE GENERALE POUR LES SIX DEPARTEMENTS DE LA 27E DIVISION MILITAIRE (CI-DEVANT PIEMONT)

LABOUR ADVOCATE / Blackpool and District Labour Representation Committee – Blackpool, England. -m. Jan. 1910-Dec. 1914. (23 ft.) – 1 – uk British Libr Newspaper [331]
LABOUR ADVOCATE – Georgetown, Guyana. -w. 5 Jan 1958-27 March 1966. Imperfect. 1 reel – 1 – uk British Libr Newspaper [072]
LABOUR AND POLITICS IN LIBYA AND ARAB AFRICA / Norman, J – New York. 1964. BNE-906 1 – 9 – ne IDC [331]
LABOUR AND TRADES UNIONISM / Great Britain. Royal Commission and Select Committee – 1824-1906 – 1 – uk Microform Academic [331]
LABOUR CHALLENGE – (Cont by: Socialist Voice, 1977 v1-5 1970-74 Can$115.00. v6-7 1975-76 Can$115.00) – Montreal. v1-7. 1970-76 – 1 – cn Micromedia [331]
LABOUR CHALLENGER *see* SOCIALIST VOICE
THE LABOUR CHARTER FOR FRANCO'S SPAIN – London, 1938. Fiche W981. (Blodgett Collection of Spanish Civil War Pamphlets) – 9 – us H.U. College Libr [946]
LABOUR CHRONICLE – Liverpool. v1-2. 1894-1902 – 1r – 1 – us Ross [331]
LABOUR ECHO – Bradford. 1895-99 – 1 – uk Microform Academic [072]
LABOUR EDUCATION – 1964- 1; 1976- 5,6,9 – us UMI [370]
LABOUR ELECTOR – London, England. -sw. Jan 1893-Jan 1894. 27 ft – 1 – uk British Libr Newspaper [072]
LABOUR ELECTOR – London, England. -w. June 1888-April 1890. 1 reel – 1 – uk British Libr Newspaper [072]
LABOUR ELECTOR : THE ORGAN OF PRACTICAL SOCIALISM – Series 1: no. 1-9 (all publ). 1888. Series 2: v1-5 (all publ). 1889-94 – 1 reel – 1 – $90.00 – us UPA [335]
THE LABOUR FORCE, AUSTRALIA : STANDARD TABLES ON MICROFICHE – 9 – at Statistics [331]
THE LABOUR FORCE OF LIBYA / Libya. Ministry of Economy and Trade. Census and Statistical Department – Population Census Paper nr. (3). Tripoli. BNE-901 1 – 9 – ne IDC [331]
Labour, Gaston *see* JOURNAL D'UN SPAHI AU SOUDAN, 1897-1899
LABOUR GAZETTE / Canada. Department of Labour – (Ceased v78 1978) – Ottawa. v1-78. 1900-78 – 5 – Price varies – cn Micromedia [331]
LABOUR GAZETTE – Jul 1909-Jun 1911 – 1 – cn Precision [331]
LABOUR HISTORY : SERIES ONE: BRITISH LABOUR PARTY RESEARCH DEPARTMENT MEMORANDA AND INFORMATION PAPERS, 1941-1979 – (Part 1: July 1941-December 1961. $1,650.00. Part 2: 1962-1970, 151mf. $1,300.00. Part 3: 1970-1974, ca 185mf. $1,600.00; Part 4: November 1974-May 1979, 136mf. $1250.00) – Marlborough: Adam Matthew Publications, 1992 – 189mf – 9 – $1,650.00 – uk Matthew [331]
LABOUR HISTORY : SERIES TWO: MINUTE BOOKS AND PAPERS OF THE ROYAL ARSENAL CO-OPERATIVE SOCIETY, 1868-1986 – (Pt 1: Political Purposes Committee Minutes, 1922-1986 49mf $450.00 9. Pt 2: General Committee Minutes, July 1876-May 1930 35r $4.200.00 1. Pt 3: General Committee Minutes, May 1930-December 1970 25r $3000.00 1. Guides included) – Marlborough: Adam Matthew Publications, 1995 – 9,1 – uk Matthew [331]
LABOUR LAW AND PRACTICE IN THE KINGDOM OF LIBYA / U.S. Department of Labor – BLS Report nr. 297. Jan 1966. BNE-904 1 – 9 – ne IDC [324]
LABOUR LEADER – A Socialist Review of Politics, Economics and Industrialism. London etc. v. 5, no. 1-40, v. 9, no. 144-v. 33. Mar 31-Dec 29 1894; Jan 1897-Sept 28 1922 – 1 – us NY Public [335]
LABOUR LEADER – London. v5-33. 1894-1922 – 12r – 1 – us Ross [331]
LABOUR LEADER – -m. v.67, no.14-, July 1975-. Leeds, Independent Labour Publications – 1 – us U.W. Library [335]
LABOUR LEAGUE EXAMINER – (Labourer: 1875-Feb 1881) – London, UK. May 1874-Feb 1881 – 3r – 1 – uk British Libr Newspaper [072]
LABOUR MANAGEMENT – 1931-46 – 1 – us UMI [331]
LABOUR MONTHLY – London. 1921-80 – 1 – uk World [073]
LABOUR MONTHLY – London. A magazine of international labor. July 1921-Dec. 1964 – 1 – 35.00r – us Hoover Inst Photo [331]
LABOUR NEWS – Ireland.28 Nov 1936-2 Apr 1938 – 1 – ie Microforms [072]
LABOUR OPPOSITION OF NORTHERN IRELAND – Ireland.Mar 1925-Jun 1926 – 1 – ie Microforms [072]
Labour Party. Great Britain *see*
- MADRID, THE "MILITARY" ATROCITIES OF THE REBELS: A RECORD OF MASSACRE, MURDER, MUTILATION
- ORIGINS AND DEVELOPMENT AT LOCAL LEVEL

Labour Party. Great Britain. Archives *see* ARCHIVES OF THE BRITISH LABOUR PARTY
Labour Party. Great Britain. Birmingham *see* RECORDS
Labour Party. Great Britain. Cambridge City and County *see* RECORDS
Labour Party. Great Britain. Colne Valley *see* RECORDS
Labour Party. Great Britain. Conference *see* RECORDS

Labour Party. Great Britain. Doncaster *see* RECORDS
Labour Party. Great Britain. Gloucester *see* RECORDS
Labour Party. Great Britain. Hamilton *see* RECORDS
Labour Party. Great Britain. Huddersfield *see* RECORDS
Labour Party. Great Britain. Penistone *see* RECORDS
Labour Party. Great Britain. Peterborough *see* RECORDS
Labour Party. Great Britain. Pontypridd, Wales *see* RECORDS
Labour Party. Great Britain. Sheffield *see* RECORDS
Labour Party. Great Britain. South Shields *see* RECORDS
Labour Party. Great Britain. Stockport *see* RECORDS
Labour Party. Great Britain. Wansbeck *see* RECORDS
Labour Party. Great Britain. Wolverhampton *see* RECORDS
Labour Party. Great Britain. Woolwich *see* RECORDS
Labour Party. Great Britain. Wrexham *see* RECORDS
Labour Party, London *see* LABOUR WEEKLY
Labour Party. South Africa *see* MISCELLANEOUS DOCUMENTS
LABOUR PIONEER – Cardiff, Wales. -m. Feb-Dec 1900. 15 ft – 1 – uk British Libr Newspaper [072]
LABOUR POLITICS IN GLASGOW – 1 – uk Microform Academic [360]
LABOUR PRESS AND MINERS' AND WORKMEN'S EXAMINER – (The Miner). Stoke-on-Trent and Wolverhampton. England. -w. 4 Apr 1874-24 Aug 1878. (3 reels) – 1 – uk British Libr Newspaper [331]
LABOUR PROPHET AND LABOUR CHURCH RECORD – London, England. -w. Manchester & London. Jan 1892-Sept 1898. 1 reel – 1 – uk British Libr Newspaper [072]
THE LABOUR PROPHET AND LABOUR CHURCH RECORD – London. 1892-1897. v. 1-6 – 1 – 35.00r – us Hoover Inst Photo [331]
THE LABOUR QUESTION / George, Henry – 1fiche (29x) – 9 – 1.00f – at Libertarian Micro [320]
LABOUR, RECONSTRUCTION AND SOCIAL REFORM – The papers of Sir William Beveridge, 1879-1965 – 1 – us Primary [920]
LABOUR RESEARCH – 1917-92. Continued annually. Continues: The Monthly Circular of the Labour Research Department. Incorporates Social Service News – 1 – £1,225.00 – uk World [331]
Labour Research Department. London *see*
- THE MONTHLY CIRCULAR
- PAMPHLETS AND BOOKS

LABOUR REVIEW – (Cont by: Ontario Labour, 1978) – Don Mills, 1957-77 – 5 – Can$100.00 – cn Micromedia [331]
LABOUR SPOKESMAN – Basseterre, St. Kitts. -d. Jan 1958-Dec 1967. 19 reels – 1 – uk British Libr Newspaper [072]
LABOUR STANDARD – London, England. -w. 7 May 1881-4 July 1885. 2 reels – 1 – uk British Libr Newspaper [072]
LABOUR STANDARD – London. v. 1-4. May 7 1881-Nov 8 1884. Incomplete – 1 – us NY Public [331]
LABOUR STANDARD : AN ORGAN OF INDUSTRY – v1-5. 1-218 (all publ). 1881-1885 – 5r – 1 – $380.00 – us UPA [335]
LABOUR TRIBUNE – West Bromwich. England. -w. 6 Mar 1886-30 Jun 1894. (8 reels) – 1 – uk British Libr Newspaper [331]
LABOUR UNION JOURNAL – London, UK. 1892. -irr. 2 feet – 1 – uk British Libr Newspaper [072]
LABOUR WEEKLY : THE NEWSPAPER OF THE LABOUR PARTY / Labour Party, London – London, 1972-87 – 1 – us Hoover Inst Photo [335]
LABOUR WORLD : A JOURNAL DEVOTED TO THE INTERESTS OF ALL WHO TOIL – Series 1: v1-6, no. 9 (all publ). 1884-1890. Series 2: v1-2, 1-37 (all and last publ). 1890-91 – 3r – 1 – $95.00 – us UPA [335]
THE LABOUR WORLD – Johannesburg, South Africa. 24 May 1918-4 Dec 1920. 3 reels – 1, 16 diazo available at reduced price – sa SA Libr [072]
LABOURER – A Monthly Magazine of Politics, Literature, Poetry, etc. 1-4 (all publ). 1847-1848 – 15mf – 9 – $65.00 – us UPA [320]
LABOURER *see* LABOUR LEAGUE EXAMINER
LABOURER'S HERALD – London, UK. 1874-75. -irr. 5 feet – 1 – uk British Libr Newspaper [072]
LABOURERS' UNION CHRONICLE – (National Agricultural Labourers' Chronicle). Leamington. England. -w. Jun-Dec 1873, Jan 1875-Apr 1877. (2 reels) – 1 – uk British Libr Newspaper [331]
Labouret, Henri *see*
- LA CHASSE ET LA PECHE DANS LEURS RAPPORTS AVEC LES CROYANCES RELIGIEUSES PARMI LES POPULATIONS DU LOBI
- LES MANDING ET LEUR LANGUE

LABOUR'S ADVOCATE AND NORTHERN WEEKLY ADVERTISER – London, UK. 1847. -irr. 5 feet – 1 – uk British Libr Newspaper [072]
LABOUR'S VOICE – London, England. -m. May 1920. 1 ft – 1 – uk British Libr Newspaper [072]
Labourt, J *see*
- LE CHRISTIANISME DANS L'EMPIRE PERSE
- LE CHRISTIANISME DANS L'EMPIRE PERSE SOUS LA DYNASTIE SASSANIDE (224-632)

Labra y Cadrana, Rafael Maria de *see* LA ABOLICION DE LA ESOLAVITUD EN EL ORDERN ECONOMICO
THE LABRADOR COA NEW YORK, 1891. 513P., ILLUS., MAPS / Packard, A S – BN 332 2. 1891 – 8 – ne IDC [971]
LABRADOR ESKIMO *see* AMONG THE ESKIMOS OF LABRADOR
THE LABRADOR ESKIMO / Hawkes, E W – BN 245 2. 1916 – 8 – ne IDC [305]
LABRADOR: ITS DISCOVERY, EXPLORATION AND DEVELOPMENT / Gosling, W G – BN 228 2. 1910 – 8 – ne IDC [910]
LABRADOR: THE COUNTRY AND THE PEOPLE / Grenfell, W T – BN 230 2. 1910 – 8 – ne IDC [971]
LaBranche, Matthew *see* EFFECT OF BATTING STANCE ON GROUND REACTION FORCES, BAT VELOCITY, AND RESPONSE TIME
LABRENSE : PERIODICO IMPARCIAL DEDICADO AOS INTERESSES DO MUNICIPIO – Labrea, Amazonas. 11 Jun, Set, Dez 1889; Mar, 8 Ago 1890 – 1,5,6 – bl Biblioteca [072]
Labretonniere, PL C *see* STATISTIQUE DU DEPARTEMENT DE LA VENDEE
LaBrie, Hilda *see* BIO-BIBLIOGRAPHIE DE MONSEIGNEUR ELIAS ROY, P.A., DIRECTEUR NATIONAL DE L'UNION MISSIONNAIRE DU CLERGE ET ANCIEN SUPERIEUR DU COLLEGE DE LEVIS
Labrie, Jean-Marc *see* BIBLIOGRAPHIE ANALYTIQUE DES ECRITS DE JEAN HUBERT, EDITORIALISTE A L'ACTION
Labriolle, Marie-Rose de *see* LE 'POUR ET CONTRE' ET SON TEMPS
Labriolle, Pierre de *see*
- LA CRISE MONTANISTE
- SAINT AMBROISE
- LES SOURCES DE L'HISTOIRE DU MONTANISME

LABRIT *see* LATVIJAS JAUNATNE
LaBrosse, Jean Baptiste de *see* NEHIRO-IRINIUI AIAMIHE MASSINAHIGAN, SHATSHEGUTSH, MITINEKAPITSH, ISKUAMISKUTSH, NETSHEKATSH, MISHT', ASSINITSH, SHEKUTIMITSH, EKUANATSH, ASHUABMUSHUANITSH, PIAKUAGAMITSH...
Labrousse, Alain *see* ARGENTINE, REVOLUTION ET CONTRE-REVOLUTIONS
THE LABYRINTH / Hooke, SH – 1935 – 9 – $12.00 – us I.R.C. [240]
THE LABYRINTH / Seidel, Ina – New York: Farrar and Rinehart, 1932 – 1r – 1 – us U.W. Library [830]
LABYRINTHVS SIVE DE COMPOSITIONE CONTINVI LIBER VNVS / Froidmont, Libert – Antverpiae, 1631 – 1 – us U.W. Library [440]
Labzina, A E *see* VOSPOMINANIIA, (1763-1819)
LE LAC SAINT-JEAN – Roberval, Canada. v1 n1. 11 nov 1902-v13 n43. 26 oct 1916 – 2r – 1 – Can$50.00r – cn Can Microfilming [072]
LE LAC SAINT-JEAN / ed by Tielmans, Henri – Roberval, Canada. 14 jan 1898 – 1r – 1 – Can$25.00 – cn Can Microfilming [072]
LE LAC SAINT-JEAN / ed by Tremblay, F et al – Alma, Canada. 29 mai 1941-29 dec 1991 – 59r – 1 – Can$70.00r – cn Can Microfilming [072]
L'Academie Imperiale des Sciences. St. Petersbourg *see* MELANGES ASIATIQUES, TIRES DE L'ACADEMIE IMPERIALE DES SCIENCES DE ST. PETERSBOURG
LACARIDAD. CARTA PASTORAL. EXCMO. ADOLFO PEREZ MUNOZ DIRIGE AL CLERO Y FIELES DE SU DIOCESIS / Perez Munoz, Adolfo – Badajoz: Uceda Hnos, 1918 – 1 – sp Bibl Santa Ana [240]
Lacasse, Zacharie *see*
- DIFFICULTE SCOLAIRE DE MANITOBA PAR QUESTIONS ET REPONSES A LA PORTEE DE TOUS
- TROIS CONTES SAUVAGES
- UNE VISITE DANS LES ECOLES DU MANITOBA

LAC-AU-SAUMON – (Becomes: L'Echo du Lac dec 1919-avr 1926) – Quebec, Canada. oct-nov 1919 – 1r – 1 – Can$35.00 – cn Can Microfilming [072]
LACEDEMONE ANCIENNE ET NOUVELLE: OU L'ON VOIT LES MOEURS ET LES COUTUMES DES GRECS MODERNES, DES MAHOMETANS, ET DES JUIFS DU PAYS / Guillet de Saint-George, Georges – Paris, J. Ribou, 1676, 2 tomes en 1 v. xiv-666-19 p. French Voyagers in the Mediterranean 16th to 18th Centuries. 5968 – 9 – fr Hachette [949]
LACERBA – Dir. Giovanni Papini. Firenze. 1913-mars 1915 (I-III) – 1 – fr A.C.R.P.P. [073]
Lacerte, A B *see*
- BOIS-SINISTRE
- LA REINE DE NAINVILLE

Lacerte, E A Bourgeois *see*
- BOIS SINISTRE
- LE BRACELET DE FER.
- LE MYSTERIEUX MONSIEUR DE L'AIGLE
- L'OMBRE DU BEFFROI.
- ROXANE
- LE SPECTRE DU RAVIN.

Lacey, Frederick B *see* THE JUDGE'S ROLE IN THE SETTLEMENT OF CIVIL SUITS
Lacey, T A *see*
- MARRIAGE IN CHURCH AND STATE
- A ROMAN DIARY AND OTHER DOCUMENTS RELATING TO THE PAPAL INQUIRY INTO ENGLISH ORDINATIONS, MDCCCXCVI

Lacey, Thomas James *see* BEGINNING AT JERUSALEM
Lach, Friedrich *see* STEFAN GEORGES GEDICHTZYKLUS "PILGERFAHRTEN" IN EINZELANALYSEN
DAS LACHEN DES SERGEANTEN WASSENAAR / Horst, Cornelius van der & Petersen, Wilhelm – Hamburg: Hanseatische Verlagsanstalt, c1941/43 – 1r – 1 – us U.W. Library [830]
Lachenal, W de *see* OBSERVATIONES BOTANICO-MEDICAE
LACHENDES ALLGAEU : ALLERLEI SACHEN GESAMMELT UND AUFGESCHRIEBEN / Weitnauer, Alfred – (T.p. of v1 missing) – Lindau: J T Stettner, 1943 – 1r – 1 – us U.W. Library [870]
LACHESIS LAPPONICA, OR A TOUR IN LAPLAND / Smith, J E – 6143 2. 1811 – 8 – ne IDC [910]
LACHISH / Tufnell, Olga – 1940. 4v – 9 – $60.00 – us I.R.C. [930]
LACHISH I, THE LACHISH LETTERS / Torczyner, Harry – Oxford, 1938 – 9 – $10.00 – us I.R.C. [930]
Lachmann, Hans *see* GOTTSCHEDS BEDEUTUNG FUER DIE GESCHICHTE DER DEUTSCHEN PHILOLOGIE
Lachmann, Karl *see* GOTTHOLD EPHRAIM LESSINGS SAEMTLICHE SCHRIFTEN
Lachmann, Otto F *see*
- HEINRICH HEINE'S BUCH DER LIEDER
- JOH. CHR. GOTTSCHEDS STERBENDER CATO

THE LACHUTE NEWS : HEBDO – Lachute, Canada. v1 n11. 26 jul 1895-v70 n26. 30 mai 1918 – 1r – 1 – Can$28.00 – cn Can Microfilming [072]
THE LACHUTE WATCHMAN *see* THE WATCHMAN / THE LACHUTE WATCHMAN
Lack, T *see* DISPERSION AND SELF-PURIFICATION OF POLLUTANTS IN SURFACE WATER SYSTEMS
Lackington, J *see* MEMOIRS OF THE FIRST FORTY-FIVE YEARS OF THE LIFE OF JAMES LACKINGTON, THE PRESENT BOOKSELLER IN CHISWELL STREET, MOORFIELDS, LONDON, WRITTEN BY HIMSELF;...
Lackowitz, Ida *see* OTTILIE WILDERMUTHS GESAMMELTE WERKE
LaClair, Kirsten W *see* THE INFLUENCE OF GOAL SETTING ON INDIVIDUAL ENDURANCE SWIMMING PERFORMANCE
LACLOS 1741-1803. / Gaussy, Fernand – Paris. 1905 – 1 – us Res Libr [440]
LACNA SRDCE: ROMAN / Simacek, Matej Anastasia – Praze: Unie, 1918. 519p. With: Stesti zlateho hroznu by Vaclav Stech, Prague: J. Otto, 1915 and Mistr kampanus by Zikmund Winter, Chicago: Slavie, 1915 – 1 – us U.W. Library [460]
Lacombe de Prezel, H *see* DICTIONNAIRE ICONOLOGIQUE, OU INTRODUCTION A LA CONNOISSANCE DES PEINTURES, SCULPTURES, ESTAMPES, MEDAILLES, PIERRES GRAVEES, EMBLEMES, DEVISES ET C.
Lacombe, Patrice *see* LA TERRE PATERNELLE
LA LACONDA DE VAGOBONDI : OPERA BUFFA IN DUE ATTI / Paer, F – Partition. 2v. Ms 179- – 1 – us Sibley [780]
Laconia, New Hampshire. Laconia Baptist Church *see* RECORDS
Lacordaire, Henri Dominique *see*
- GOD AND MAN: CONFERENCES DELIVERED AT NOTRE DAME IN PARIS
- JESUS CHRIST: CONFERENCES DELIVERED AT NOTRE DAME IN PARIS
- THE LIFE OF SAINT DOMINICK

Lacordaire, J T *see* FAUNE ENTOMOLOGIQUE DES ENVIRONS DE PARIS
Lacoste, D *see* OBSERVATIONS SUR LA STATISTIQUE DU DEPARTEMENT DES BASSES-PYRENEES QUI PARUT EN L'ANNEE 1802, ET PROJETS D'AMELIORATION
Lacour, Auguste *see* HISTOIRE DE LA GUADELOUPE
Lacour, Paul *see* LES FEMMES DANS L'HISTOIRE: LES AMAZONES
Lacretelle, Pierre-Louis *see* DE L'ETABLISSEMENT DES CONNOISSANCES HUMAINES, ET DE L'INSTRUCTION PUBLIQUE DANS LA CONSTITUTION FRANCAISE
Lacroix, Celine *see* BIBLIGRAPHIE ANALYTIQUE DES TRAVAUX DE JOSEPH RISI, B.A., B.SC., D.SC., M.S.R.C.
Lacroix, Denise *see* LES ACTIVITES ET LES PUBLICATIONS DU CENTRE CANADIEN DES CERCLES LACORDAIRE ET SAINTE-JEANNE D'ARC DEPUIS SA FONDATION EN DECEMBRE 1939
Lacroix, Pablo *see* LA BIBLIOTECA DE JULES JANIN
Lacroix, PF *see*
- LES PARLERS DU SOUS-ENSEMBLE SONGHAY-ZARMA SEPTENTRIONAL. DOCUMENTS DE TERRAIN. DICTIONNAIRE FRANCAIS-TASAWAQ
- LES PARLERS DU SOUS-ENSEMBLE SONGHAY-ZARMA SEPTENTRIONAL. DOCUMENTS DE TERRAIN. DICTIONNAIRE TASAWAQ-FRANCAIS
- LES PARLERS DU SOUS-ENSEMBLE SONGHAY-ZARMA SEPTENTRIONAL. DOCUMENTS DE TERRAIN. LEXICOLOGIE TADAKSAHAK
- LES PARLERS DU SOUS-ENSEMBLE SONGHAY-ZARMA SEPTENTRIONAL. DOCUMENTS DE TERRAIN. LEXICOLOGIE TIHITIT ET TAGDALT

Lacroix, Ph. de *see* L'ART DE LA POESIE FRANCOISE ET LATINE
LACROSSE: THE NATIONAL GAME OF CANADA / Beers, William George – Montreal: Dawson Bros., 1869. 05682. (Pre-1900 Canadiana) – 9 – cn C.I.H.M. [790]
LACTANTII PLACIDI QUI DICITUR COMMENTARIOS IN STATII THEBAIDA IT COMMENTARIUM IN ACHILLEIDA RECENSUIT RICARDUS JAHNKE / Lactantius Placidus – Lipsiae, 1898. x,522p – 1 – us U.W. Library [450]
Lactantius Placidus *see*
- DIVINAE INSTITUTIONES, ETC
- LACTANTII PLACIDI QUI DICITUR COMMENTARIOS IN STATII THEBAIDA IT COMMENTARIUM IN ACHILLEIDA RECENSUIT RICARDUS JAHNKE

LACTATE THRESHOLD IN MASTERS ATHLETES AS COMPARED TO YOUNG ATHLETES / Allen, William K – 1983 – 1mf – 9 – $4.00 – us Microform Publ [790]
LAD – (Only backfile available) – 1994-95 – 1r per y – $85.00r – us Ross [072]
LAD NEWSLETTER – (v.2-4. 1976-78. 5,6,9) – Library Administration and Management Association. Library Administration Division. v.1-4. 1975-78 – 1 – us UMI [020]

LAD NEWSLETTER / American Library Association. Library Administration Division – (Cont by: Library Administration and Management Association. Newsletter) – Chicago. v1-4 jan 1975-sep 1978 1; v2-4 jan 1976-sep 1978 5*,9 – 1,5,9 – D10533 – us UMI [020]
LaDage, John H *see* DICTIONARY OF NAUTICAL TERMS
LADANG MENANTI; SADJAK-SADJAK RAKJAT VIETNAM – Translation of Come to the fields buffalo. In Indonesian. SE-4153 1 – 9 – ne IDC [950]
Ladas, S P *see* THE EXCHANGE OF MINORITIES: BULGARIA, GREECE AND TURKEY
Ladd, George Trumbull *see* THE DOCTRINE OF SACRED SCRIPTURE
Ladd, John *see* ARCHAEOLOGICAL INVESTIGATIONS IN THE PARITA AND SANTA MARIA ZONES OF PANAMA
Ladd, W C *see* MEMORANDUM ON A PROPOSED SUDAN INDUSTRIAL DEVELOPMENT BANK AND RELATED MATTERS
THE LADDER OF DIVINE ASCENT / Climacus, John – London, 1959 – 4mf – 8 – ne Slangenburg [240]
Laddey, Emma *see* VIER MAEDCHENLEBEN, ODER, DEUTSCH UND AMERIKANISCH
DIE LADE JAHVES / Meinhold, Johannes – Tuebingen: J.C.B. Mohr, 1900. 1 fiche – 9 – us A.T.L.A. [240]
Ladendorf, J M *see* THE REVOLT IN INDIA 1857-1858: ANNOTATED BIBLIOGRAPHY OF ENGLISH LANGUAGE MATERIALS
LADIES' AFTERNOON VISITOR – v. 1. 1806-1807 – 1 – us UMI [640]
LADIES AT HOME – Toronto: Ladies' Companion Pub. Co, [1893-18– or 19–] – 9 – cn C.I.H.M. [640]
LADIES' AUXILIARY FOR FEMALE EDUCATION *see* LADIES' COMMITTEE FOR AMELIORATING THE CONDITION OF WOMEN IN HEATHEN COUNTRIES, FEMALE EDUCATION...
THE LADIES' BAZAR – Toronto: The Ladies' Bazar Pub., Co, [1887?-18– or 19–] – 9 – cn C.I.H.M. [640]
LADIES' COMMITTEE FOR AMELIORATING THE CONDITION OF WOMEN IN HEATHEN COUNTRIES, FEMALE EDUCATION... – (Cont as: Ladies' Auxiliary for Female Education. London Nos 57-102 1873/1874-1884; Cont as: Woman's Work. London Nos 103-161 1885-1889.) – London. Nos 1-56. 1859-1873 – 85mf – 9 – ne IDC [370]
LADIES' COMPANION – Toronto: Ladies' Companion Pub. Co, [1893-189- or 19–] – 9 – cn C.I.H.M. [640]
LADIES' COMPANION AND LITERARY EXPOSITOR – v. 1-NS1. 1834-1844 – 1 – us UMI [640]
Ladies' Enterprise Association. Mound City, Kansas *see* BY-LAWS AND CONSTITUTION; MINUTES
LADIES' GARLAND – v. 1-4. 1824-1828 – 1 – us UMI [640]
LADIES' GARLAND AND FAMILY WREATH EMBRACING TALES, SKETCHES, INCIDENTS, HISTORY, POETRY, MUSIC – v.1-3sv.4. April 1837-December 1850 – 1 – us UMI [640]
THE LADIES GARMENT WORKER – v1-10 no 12 (all publ). 1910-18 – 2r – 1 – $195.00 – us UPA [331]
LADIES' HOME JOURNAL – v1- 1884- 1; v87-5,6,9 – us UMI [640]
LADIES' JOURNAL – 1884-96 – 1 – $75.00 – cn McLaren [640]
LADIES LITERARY CABINET – BEING A REPOSITORY OF MISCELLANEOUS LITERARY PRODUCTIONS, BOTH ORIGINAL and SELECTED, IN PROSE and VERSE. v. NS 1-7. May 15, 1819-December 21, 1822 – 1 – us UMI [410]
LADIES MAGAZINE – v. 1. March 1823-June 1824 – 1 – us UMI [073]
LADIES' MAGAZINE *see*
– AMERICAN LADIES' MAGAZINE
LADIES' MAGAZINE AND LITERARY GAZETTE *see* AMERICAN LADIES' MAGAZINE
LADIES MAGAZINE: OR, THE UNIVERSAL ENTERTAINER – v. 1-4. 1749-1753 – 1 – us UMI [073]
LADIES MUSEUM – v. 1. 1828-29 – 1 – us UMI [073]
LADIES' MUSEUM – v. 1-5sv.3. New and Improved Series. Jul 1798-Jun 1832 – 1 – us UMI [073]
THE LADIES MUSICAL JOURNAL – New York: I. and M. Paff, ca.1800. MUSIC 1047 – 1 – us L of C Photodup [780]
Ladies of the Maccabees of the World *see* WBA REVIEW
LADIES REPOSITORY – v. 1-36. 1841-1876 – 1 – us UMI [640]
LADIES' VISITOR – 1819-1820 – 1 – us UMI [640]
LADIES' WEEKLY MUSEUM – 1-3RD S. 6. June 28, 1788-October 25, 1817 – 1 – us UMI [073]
LADIES' WORLD – New York. v10-25. 1889-1904 – 3r – 1 – us Ross [640]
LADIES' WREATH – v. 1-17. 1846-1859 – 1 – us UMI [640]
Ladimir, Jules *see* LES GUERRES D'AFRIQUE DEPUIS LA CONQUETE D'ALGER PAR LES FRANCAIS JUSQU'A ET COMPRIS L'EXPEDITION DE KABYLIE EN 1858
Ladriere, Jean *see* CHALLENGE PRESENTED TO CULTURES BY SCIENCE AND TECHNOLOGY
LADY ABERDEEN'S ADDRESS: AT A PUBLIC MEETING HELD IN THE TOWN HALL, PORT ARTHUR, ON TUESDAY, SEPT. 25 / Aberdeen and Temair, Ishbel Gordon, Marchioness of – 189?. 06571. (Pre-1900 Canadiana) – 9 – cn C.I.H.M. [971]
LADY ADELAIDE('S OATH) / Wood, Ellen – British Fiction Archive: Unit 1 – 9 – uk Bell [830]
LADY ANNA / Trollope, Anthony – London: Chapman and Hall, 1874 – 1 roll – 1 – 1-55879-966-4 – uk Libr Preservation [830]
LADY AUDLEY'S SECRET / Braddon, Mary Elizabeth – British Fiction Archive: Unit 5 – 9 – uk Bell [830]
LADY AUDLEY'S SECRET / Braddon, Mary Elizabeth – London: Tinsley, 7th rev ed 1862 – 1 roll – 1 – 1-55879-978-8 – uk Libr Preservation [830]
LADY BYRON VINDICATED : A HISTORY OF THE BYRON CONTROVERSY, FROM ITS BEGINNING IN 1816 TO THE PRESENT TIME / Stowe, Harriet Beecher – Boston: Fields, Osgood, & Co., 1870 – 1 roll – 1 – 1-55879-450-6 – uk Libr Preservation [420]
LADY CONNIE / Ward, Mary Augusta – British Fiction Archive: Unit 2 – 9 – uk Bell [830]
LADY GRACE / Wood, Ellen – British Fiction Archive: Unit 1 – 9 – uk Bell [830]
LADY HUNTINGTON AND HER FRIENDS, OR, THE REVIVAL OF THE WORK OF GOD IN THE DAYS OF WESLEY, WHITEFIELD, ROMAINE, VENN, AND OTHERS IN THE LAST CENTURY / Knight, Helen C – New York: American Tract Society, c1853 – 1mf – us A.T.L.A. [240]
THE LADY LISLE / Braddon, Mary Elizabeth – British Fiction Archive: Unit 5 – 9 – uk Bell [830]
LADY NAIRNE AND HER SONGS / Henderson, George – Paisley, London: Alexander Gardner, 1900 – 1 roll – 1 – 1-55879-840-4 – uk Libr Preservation [780]
THE LADY OF THE ICE: A NOVEL / De Mille, James – With illustrations by C. G. Bush. New York: D. Appleton, 1870. 02631. (Pre-1900 Canadiana) – 9 – cn C.I.H.M. [830]
THE LADY OF THE LAKE : A POEM / Scott, Walter – Edinburgh: John Ballantyne and Co.; London: Longman, Hurst, Rees, and Brown, 2nd ed 1810 – 1 roll – 1 – 1-55879-651-7 – uk Libr Preservation [810]
LADY ROSE'S DAUGHTER / Ward, Mary Augusta – British Fiction Archive: Unit 2 – 9 – uk Bell [830]
LADY SILVERDALE'S SWEETHEART; AND OTHER TALES / Black, William – British Fiction Archive: Unit 4 – 9 – uk Bell [830]
A LADY TRAVELER IN THE TRANSVAAL / Heckford, Sarah – London. 1882 – 1 – us Res Libr [960]
LADY WINDERMERE'S FAN : A PLAY ABOUT A GOOD WOMAN / Wilde, Oscar – London: E. Mathews and J. Lane, 1893 – 1 roll – 1 – 1-55879-906-0 – uk Libr Preservation [820]
LADY'S BOOK *see* AMERICAN LADIES' MAGAZINE
LADY'S FRIEND – v1-10 (all publ). 1864-1873 – 4r – 1 – $395.00 – us UPA [640]
LADY'S MAGAZINE AND REPOSITORY OF ENTERTAINING KNOWLEDGE – 1-2. June 1792-May 1793 – 1 – us UMI [073]
THE LADY'S MILE / Braddon, Mary Elizabeth – British Fiction Archive: Unit 5 – 9 – uk Bell [830]
LADY'S MISCELLANY; OR THE WEEKLY VISITOR – v. 1-15. October 9, 1802-October 17, 1812 – 1 – us UMI [073]
LADY'S MONITOR – August 8, 1801-May 29, 1802 – 1 – us UMI [073]
THE LADY'S MONTHLY MUSEUM, 1798-1828 – Marlborough: Adam Matthew Publications, 1993 – 89mf – 9 – $800.00 – uk Matthew [305]
LADY'S PEARL – v. 1-4. June 1840-July, 1843 – 1 – us UMI [073]
LADY'S PICTORIAL : A NEWSPAPER FOR THE HOME – London, 1892-99 – 1r – 1 – us Ross [640]
LADYSMITH CHRONICLE – Ladysmith, British Columbia, CN. Aug 1957-90 – 30r – 1 – cn Commonwealth Micro [072]
LAE JOURNAL OF THE AMERICAN CRIMINAL JUSTICE ASSOCIATION – (v.42-. 1979- 5,6,9) – v.1-. 1942- – 1 – us UMI [073]
LAEKARTIDNINGEN – v.62-76. 1965-79 – 1,5,6 – app – us Princeton Micro [610]
Laemmer, Hugo *see* COELESTIS URBS IERUSALEM
LAENDERKATALOG AFRIKA DER UEBERSEE-DOKUMENTATION HAMBURG, 1971-1984 / ed by Deutsches UEbersee-Institut Hamburg – (Companion brochure in German, English, French and Spanish) – 1986 – 231 fiches (1:42) – 9 – diazo DM4,800.00 silver DM5,400.00 (silver DM5,400.00 ISBN: 3-598-30982-1) – 3-598-30981-3 – gw Saur [960]
Laengin, Theodor *see* DIE SPRACHE DES JUNGEN HERDER IN IHREM VERHAELTNIS ZUR SCHRIFTSPRACHE
Laennec, R T H *see* DE L'AUSCULTATION MEDIATE
LAERDA TIDNINGAR – Stockholm, 1745-1773 – 219mf – 9 – ne IDC [500]
DER LAEROVERKS-LEHRER : UNTERSUCHUNGEN UEBER DEN WISSENSCHAFTLICHEN LEHRER AN DEN HOEHEREN LEHRANSTALTEN SCHWEDENS / Deffke, Paul – 1994 – 2mf – 9 – DM62.00 – 3-8267-3092-5 – gw Hänsel [370]
Laet, Jean de *see* L'HISTOIRE DU NOUVEAU-MONDE OU DESCRIPTION DES INDES OCCIDENTALES
Laet, S J De *see* HISTORY OF HUMANITY, VOL. 1
DER LAEUFER VON MARATHON : HISTORISCHE GESCHICHTEN / Watzinger, Carl Hans – Karlsbad: A Kraft, 1942 – 1r – 1 – us U.W. Library [830]
Lafargue, Fernand *see*
– LE GOLI. CONTRIBUTION A L'ETUDE DES MASQUES BAOULE
– LA PALOMBIERE
– LA RELIGION TRADITIONNELLE DES ABIDJI
Lafarque, Fernand *see* LE KOMYEN CHEZ LES BAOULE
Lafauci, Jorge Santos *see* LA MUJER ARGENTINA ANTES Y DESPUES DE EVA PERON
LAFAYETTE BAPTIST CHURCH. LAFAYETTE, TENNESSEE : CHURCH RECORDS – 1849-1958 – 1 – 46.08 – us Baptist [240]
LAFAYETTE FIRST BAPTIST CHURCH. BLEDSOE ASSOCIATION. LAFAYETTE, TENNESSEE : CHURCH RECORDS – 1950-86 – 1 – 46.94 – us Baptist [240]
LAFAYETTE SUN AND MIDWEEK SUN *see* CONTRA COSTA SUN
LaFeillee, Francois de *see* METHODE NOUVELLE POUR APPRENDRE PARFAITEMENT LES REGLES DU PLAIN-CHANT..
LaFerriere, Ph *see* LA BATAILLE
LaFerriere, Philippe *see* LE PROGRES DE QUEBEC
L'Affillard, M *see* PRINCIPES TRES FACILES POUR BIEN APPRENDRE LA MUSIQUE
Laffitte, J *see*
– LE DAHOME
– LE PAYS DES NEGRES ET LA COTE DES ESCLAVES.
Laflamme, Claire *see*
– BIBLIOGRAPHIE ANALYTIQUE DE LA LITTERATURE MUSICALE CANADIENNE FRANCAISE
– L'EGLISE ORTHODOXE RUSSE; ORGANIZATION, DOGMES, HERESIES (DOUKHOBORSTES ET MOLOKANES)
Laflamme, J L K *see* LE GAULOIS
Laflamme, Joseph Clovis Kemner *see* L'ABBE H.-R. CASGRAIN
LE LAFONTAINE : CONSEIL LAFONTAINE CH. DE COLOMB – Montreal, Canada. avr 1917-v1 n7. dec 1917 – 1r – 1 – Can$25.00 – cn Can Microfilming [073]
LAFONTAINE ET SON TEMPS / DeCelles, Alfred Duclos – 1907. SEM105P512 – 3mf – 9 – Can$6.75 – cn Bibl Nat [920]
LAFONTAINE ET SON TEMPS / DeCelles, Alfred Duclos – 1912. SEM105P515 – 3mf – 9 – Can$6.75 – cn Bibl Nat [920]
LAFONTAINE ET SON TEMPS / DeCelles, Alfred Duclos – 1925. SEM105P545 – 3mf – 9 – Can$6.75 – cn Bibl Nat [920]
Lafontaine, H *see* PASICRISIE INTERNATIONALE
Lafontaine, L-B *see* L'AVENIR DE L'EST
Lafontaine, V *see* LES NOUVELLES
Laforest, Marthe *see* BIBLIOGRAPHIE ANALYTIQUE DE L'OEUVRE DE MARCEL DUBE
Laforgue, E *see* LES ERMITES DE LA BIGORRE
Laforgue, Henri *see* STATISTIQUE DES MALADIES OBSERVEES PENDANT L'ANNEE 1850.
Laforgue, Jules *see*
– OEUVRES COMPLETES
– OEUVRES COMPLETES DE JULES LAFORGUE
Lafuente, Carlos F *see* MAYO EN LA BIBLIOGRAFIA. BUENOS AIRES, 1961
LAG BULLETIN / Legal Action Group. London – (1980-. 5,6,9) – 1972- – 1 – us UMI [340]
Lagard, N de *see* JOURNAL DE MUSIQUE
Lagarde, Andre *see* THE LATIN CHURCH IN THE MIDDLE AGES
Lagarde, P A *see* RELIQUIAE IURIS ECCLESIASTICI ANTIQUISSIMAE
Lagarde, Paul de *see*
– REGISTER UND NACHTRAEGE ZU DER 1889 ERSCHIENENEN UEBERSICHT UEBER DIE IM ARAMAEISCHEN, ARABISCHEN UND HEBRAEISCHEN UEBLICHE BILDUNG DER NOMINA
– DIE REVIDIERTE LUTHERBIBEL DES HALLESCHEN WAISENHAUSES
– UEBERSICHT UEBER DIE IM ARAMAEISCHEN, ARABISCHEN UND HEBRAEISCHEN UEBLICHE BILDUNG DER NOMINA
Lagasca y Segura, M *see*
– AMENIDADES NATURALES DE LAS ESPANAS
– GENERA ET SPECIES PLANTARUM, QUAE AUT NOVAE SUNT, AUT NONDUM RECTE COGNOSCUNTUR
– MEMORIA SOBRE LAS PLANTAS BARRILLERAS DE ESPANA
Lagden, Godfrey *see* SOUTH AFRICAN NATIVE AFFAIRS COMMISSION, 1903-5
LAGEBERICHTE (1920-1929) UND MELDUNGEN (1930-1933) / Reichskommissar fuer die Ueberwachung der oeffentlichen Ordnung und Nachrichtensammelstelle im Reichsministerium des Innern; ed by Ritter, Ernst – 1979. Companion volume. Bestand R134 des Bundesarchivs Koblenz – 399 fiches (1:24) – 9 – silver DM3,200.00 – 3-598-10004-3 – gw Saur [943]
Lagergren, D *see*
– MISSION AND STATE IN THE CONGO
Lagerlof, Selma *see*
– CHRIST LEGENDS
– GOSTA BERLINGS SAGA...2. UPPLAGAN
Laggan Presbytery. Ireland *see* MINUTES, 1672-1700
LAGGARDS IN OUR SCHOOLS; A STUDY OF RETARDATION AND ELIMINATION IN CITY SCHOOL SYSTEMS / Ayres, Leonard Porter – New York: Charities Publication Committee, 1909.xv,236p. incl. tables, diagrs – 1 – us U.W. Library [370]
Lagneau, Gustave *see*
– ETUDE DEMOGRAPHIQUE DE LA DIMINUTION OU DE L'ACCROISSEMENT DES FAMILLES
– POPULATION DE PARIS: REMARQUES DEMOGRAPHIQUES SUR L'HABITAT URBAIN
Lagneau, Jules *see* DE L'EXISTANCE DE DIEU
LAGOA DOURADA : ORGAM DE DEFESA DOS INTERESSES DO MUNICIPIO – Lagoa Dourada, 1 Jan, Mar-15 Apr 1936 – 1,5,6 – bl Biblioteca [072]
LAGOS OBSERVER – Nigeria. -d. Mar 1882-Dec 1888. (1 reel) – 1 – uk British Libr Newspaper [072]
LAGOS STANDARD – Nigeria. -w. Feb 1895-Jan 1920. (18 reels) – 1 – uk British Libr Newspaper [072]
THE LAGOS STANDARD – Lagos. Nigeria. may 14, 21, 1913 – 1 – us NY Public [072]
LAGOS TIMES – Nigeria. -f. Nov 1880-Oct 1883. (32 ft) – 1 – uk British Libr Newspaper [072]

LAGOS WEEKLY RECORD – Nigeria. -w. Aug 1891-Dec 1913, May 1914-Dec 1921. (Imperfect). (8 reels) – 1 – uk British Libr Newspaper [072]
LAGRANDE CHRONICLE – LaGrande OR. Jan 12 May 3 1895, Jan 4 18 Nov 9 16 23 1906, Dec 21 28 1906, Jan 27 1907-Feb 26 1909 – 1 – us U.O. Library [071]
LAGRANDE DAILY CHRONICLE – LaGrande OR. June 15 Dec 14 1894, 1898 – Special Edition – 1 – us U.O. Library [071]
LAGRANDE GAZETTE – LaGrande, OR. 20,27 May 1892 – 1 – us U.O. Library [071]
LAGRANDE JOURNAL – LaGrande OR. May 27 1887, July 19 1889, Christmas 1900 – Industrial ed, Jan 19-Mar 16 1901 – 1 – us U.O. Library [071]
LAGRANDE MORNING STAR – LaGrande, OR. -d. 13 Jul 1907-8 Apr 1911. 2 rolls – 1 – us U.O. Library [071]
LAGRANDE OBSERVER – LaGrande, OR. -d. 1 Dec 1897-. – 1 – us U.O. Library [071]
LAGRANDE OBSERVER – LaGrande OR. May 27 1959 + – 1 – us U.O. Library [071]
LAGRANDE TIMES – LaGrande OR. July 1890 – 1 – us U.O. Library [071]
LAGRANDE WEEKLY OBSERVER – LaGrande, OR. 3 Jan 1908-6 Oct 1911 – 1 – us U.O. Library [071]
LAGRANDE WEEKLY STAR – LaGrande, OR. 23 Jul 1909-12 May 1911 – 1 – us U.O. Library [071]
Lagrange, Joseph Louis de *see*
- LECONS SUR LE CALCUL DES FONCTIONS
- MECANIQUE ANALYTIQUE
- THEORIE DES FONCTIONS ANALYTIQUES CONTENANT LES PRINCIPES DU CALCUL DIFFERENTIEL

Lagrange, Marie Joseph *see*
- CRITIQUE HISTORIQUE DU N.T
- CRITIQUE TEXTUELLE DU N.T
- ETUDES SUR LES RELIGIONS SEMITIQUES
- L'EVANGILE DE JESUS-CHRIST
- HISTOIRE ANCIENNE DU CANON DU N. TEST
- LE LIVRE DES JUGES
- LE MESSIANISME CHEZ LES JUIFS (150 AV.J.C. A 200 AP.J.C.)
- ST. ETIENNE ET SON SANCTUAIRE A JERUSALEM
- SAINT LUC
- SAINT MARC
- SAINT MATTHIEU
- ST. PAUL
- SAINT PAUL

Lagrange, P *see* ZACHARIE 9-14
Lagrave, H *see* NOTICES SUR LES OEUVRES DE THEATRE
Lagreze, Gustave Bascle de *see* LES NORMANDS DANS LES DEUX MONDES
LAGRIMAS DE SAN PEDRO / Fernandez de Ribera, Rodrigo – 1889 – 9 – $1.50f – sp Bibl Santa Ana [830]
Lagros de Langeron, Gabriel *see* MARIAGE PARISIEN
Lagrue *see* SUR LA RELIGION SAINT-SIMONIENNE
Laguna, A de *see*
- ANNOTACIONES IN GALENI INTERPRETES QUIBUS VARII LOCIS, IN QUOS HACTENUS IMPEGERUNT...
- DE ARTICULARI MORBO COMMENTARIUS
- METHODUS COGNOSCENDI EXTIRPANDIQUE ECRESCENTES IN VESICAE COLLO CARUNCULAS...
- QUATRO ELEGANTISIMAS Y GRAVISSIMAS ORATIONES DE M.T. CICERON CONTRA CATILINA...
- RERVM PRODIGIOSARVM QVAE IN VRBE CONSTANTINOPOLITANA, ...
- VITA GALENI PERGAMENI EX GALENOPSO

LAGUNA BEACH CITY DIRECTORIES – Orange Co, CA. 1935; 1941; 1947 – 3r – 1 – $150.00 – D071 – us Library Micro [910]
LAGUNA BEACH DAILY PILOT – Laguna Beach, CA. 1967 – 11r – 1 – $550.00 – H04017 – us Library Micro [071]
LAGUNA BEACH NEWS – South Co, CA. 1993 – 4+ r – 1 – $200.00 ($100.00y) – R04119 – us Library Micro [071]
LAGUNA NIGUEL NEWS – South Co, CA. 1993 – 4+ r – 1 – $200.00 ($100.00y) – R04120 – us Library Micro [071]
Laguna Sanz, Eduardo *see* 4 CONSEJO ECONOMICO SINDICAL
LA-HARAMAT KEREN YERUSHALAYIM VE-TOSHAVEHA – (Havazzelet, Jerusalem, 5635). 1875. BJ-27-204 1 – 9 – ne IDC [941]
Lahaye, R *see* LES ENTREPRISES PUBLIQUES AU MAROC; ESSAI D'ANALYSE DES FORMES D'ACTION MEDIATE DE LA PUISSANCE PUBLIQUE
Lahille, Abel *see* MES IMPRESSIONS SUR L'AFRIQUE OCCIDENTALE FRANCAISE
LAHIRNJA PANTJA-SILA / Sukarno, Pres. Indonesia – SE 5650 1. 1963 – 9 – ne IDC [324]
LAHIRNJA PANTJASILA; THE BIRTH OF PANTJASILA. OUTLINE OF FIVE PRINCIPLES OF THE INDONESIAN STATE / Sukarno, Pres. Indonesia – SE 6909 1. 2nd English ed. 1952 – 9 – ne IDC [324]
LAHKUSUD EESTIS = ESTONIAN SECTARIANISM / Ederberg, B – Rakvere, Estonia: Autor, Kirjastus, 1935. 140p – 1 – us Baptist [240]
Lahnstein, Ernst *see* ETHIK UND MYSTIK IN HEBBELS WELTANSCHAUUNG
LAHOLMS NYA TIDNING – Laholm, Sweden. 1880-93 – 14r – 1 – sw Kungliga [072]
LAHOLMS TIDNING – Laholm, Sweden. 1877 – 1 reel – 1 – sw Kungliga [072]
LAHOLMS TIDNING – Laholm, Sweden. 1979- – 1 – sw Kungliga [072]
Lahontan, Louis A de L d'A *see* NOUVEAUX VOYAGES DE MR LE BARON DE LAHONTAN DANS L'AMERIQUE SEPTENTRIONALE
LAHONTAN VALLEY NEWS *see* LOHONTAN DAILY NEWS
LAHONTAN VALLEY NEWS AND FALLON EAGLE STANDARD – Fallon, NV. 1972; 1980-1982 – 37+ r – 1 – $1,850.00 ($240.00y) – N04529 – us Library Micro [071]
LAHORE CHRONICLE – Pakistan. -d. June 1850-Nov 1868. 38 reels – 1 – uk British Libr Newspaper [072]
LAHRER ZEITUNG – Lahr-Schwarzwald, West Germany. 1 Sept 1978- – ca 9r per – 1 – gw Mikrofilm [072]
LAHUN 2 / Petrie, William Matthew Flinders & Brunton, Guy & Murray, M A – BSA, 1923 – 9 – $10.00 – us I.R.C. [930]
LAHUN I: THE TREASURE / Brunton, Guy – 1920 – 9 – $10.00 – us I.R.C. [930]
Laible, Heinrich *see* JESUS CHRIST IN THE TALMUD, MIDRASH, ZOHAR, AND THE LITURGY OF THE SYNAGOGUE
LAICISATION DE L'ASSISTANCE PUBLIQUE. / Bourneville, Desire Magloire – Paris: Bureau du Progres medical, 1881-91. 12 fasc. en 1 vol. 4 fiches. (Economics Collection) – 9 – 10.00 – fr Bibl Nationale [330]
LAICISME ET LAICITE... / Ligot, Maurice – Madrid: Razon y Fe, 1927 – 1 – sp Bibl Santa Ana [210]
LAICUS, OR, THE EXPERIENCES OF A LAYMAN IN A COUNTRY PARISH / Abbott, Lyman – New York: Dodd & Mead, 1872 – 1mf – us A.T.L.A. [240]
Laidlaw, Alexander Fraser *see* TRAINING AND EXTENSION IN THE COOPERATIVE MOVEMENT
LAIDLAW CHRONICLE – Laidlaw, OR. -w. 17 Nov 1905-25 Sept 1908. – 1r – 1 – us U.O. Library [071]
Laidlaw, Robert J *see* OUR RELIGION: AS IT WAS AND AS IT IS
Laidley, W S *see* HISTORY OF CHARLESTON AND KANAWHA COUNTY
Laidlow, John *see* THE BIBLE DOCTRINE OF MAN, OR, THE ANTHROPOLOGY AND PSYCHOLOGY OF SCRIPTURE
LAIENBREVIER / Schefer, Leopold – 17. Aufl. Berlin: Veit, 1878 – 1r – 1 – us U.W. Library [810]
LAIKO VEMA – Argyro-Castro, Albania. 1963-85 – 14r – 1 – us L of C Photodup [949]
LAILI AND MAJNUM: WOMEN OF PERSIA / Nizami – 1 – uk Microform Academic [900]
LA LAINE. NOUVELLE SERIE DES ETUDES SUR LE REGIME DES MANUFACTURES / Reybaud, Louis – (Condition of 19th C. French working class series). 1867 – 9 – fr Hachette [670]
Laine, PL *see* DICTIONNAIRE VERIDIQUE DES ORIGINES DES MAISONS NOBLES OU ANOBLIES DU ROYAUME DE FRANCE
Laing, Alexander G *see*
- TRAVELS IN THE TIMANEE, KOORANKO, AND SOOLIMA COUNTRIES IN WESTERN AFRICA
- VOYAGE DANS LE TIMANNI, LE KOURANKO ET LE SOULIMANA, CONTREES DE L'AFRIQUE OCCIDENTALE

LAIN'S DIRECTORY OF LONG ISLAND – Including a Business Directory of BROOKLYN, LONG ISLAND CITY AND THE TOWNS OF KING COUNTY BROOKLYN. 1878-1879 – 1 – us NY Public [978]
Laird, M *see* NARRATIVE OF AN EXPEDITION INTO THE INTERIOR OF AFRICA BY THE RIVER NIGER IN 1832-1834
Lairesse, Gerard de *see* GROOT SCHILDERBOEK
LAISSEZ FAIRE LIBERTARIANISM VERSUS ANARCHISM / Dolgoff, Sam – 1981, 4p. Also: The New Anarchism, 1973, 2p – 9 – 1.00f – at Libertarian Micro [335]
LE LAISSEZ-PASSER – (Cont by: La Prosperite Montreal jan 1967-mai 1978f) – Montreal, fev 1962-dec 1965 – 1r – 1 – Can$65.00 – cn Can Microfilming [072]
LE LAIT – v30-56 1950-76 – 1,5,6 – us Princeton Micro [660]
LAITY'S DIRECTORY FOR THE UNITED STATES *see* THE METROPOLITAN CATHOLIC ALMANAC AND LAITY'S DIRECTORY FOR THE UNITED STATES
LAITY'S DIRECTORY FOR THE YEAR OF OUR LORD *see*
- THE METROPOLITAN CATHOLIC ALMANAC
- THE U.S. CATHOLIC ALMANAC

Lajaille, Andre C *see* VOYAGE AU SENEGAL PENDANT LES ANNEES 1784 ET 1785 PUBLIE D'APRES LES MEMOIRES DE LAJAILLE
Lajoie, Jennifer M *see* THE CONTROL OF MOVEMENTS WHICH VARY IN ACCURACY AND COMPLEXITY
LAK LAK – Istanbul: Mahmud Bey Matbaasi, 1909 – 9 – $20.00 – us MEDOC [949]
THE LAKE / Moore, George – London: W. Heinemann, 1905 – 1 roll – 1 – 1-55879-771-8 – uk Libr Preservation [830]
LAKE CHARLES FIRST BAPTIST CHURCH. LAKE CHARLES, LOUISIANA : CHURCH RECORDS – Mar 1880-Sept 1888. Statistics, 1888-1910 – 1 – 15.21 – us Baptist [240]
LAKE CITY FIRST BAPTIST CHURCH. LAKE CITY, SOUTH CAROLINA : CHURCH RECORDS – 1842-1952. Deacons' Minutes. 1952-67 – 1 – 39.33 – us Baptist [240]
Lake City Publishing Co *see*
- PORTRAIT AND BIOGRAPHICAL ALBUM OF FAYETTE COUNTY
- PORTRAIT AND BIOGRAPHICAL ALBUM OF JEFFERSON AND VAN BUREN COUNTIES
- PORTRAIT AND BIOGRAPHICAL ALBUM OF POLK COUNTY
- PORTRAIT AND BIOGRAPHICAL ALBUM OF RACINE AND KENOSHA COUNTIES
- PORTRAIT AND BIOGRAPHICAL RECORD OF COOK AND DU PAGE COUNTIES
- PORTRAIT AND BIOGRAPHICAL RECORD OF EFFINGHAM, JASPER AND RICHLAND COUNTIES
- PORTRAIT AND BIOGRAPHICAL RECORD OF FORD COUNTY
- PORTRAIT AND BIOGRAPHICAL RECORD OF IROQUOIS COUNTY
- PORTRAIT AND BIOGRAPHICAL RECORD OF KANKAKEE COUNTY
- PORTRAIT AND BIOGRAPHICAL RECORD OF MACON COUNTY

LAKE COUNTY BEE – (Cont by: Lake County Record Bee) – Lakeport, CA. Sept 1895-1940 – 18r – 1 BC02334 – $900.00 – us Library Micro [071]
LAKE COUNTY BEE – Lakeport. Calif. -w. 1941- – 1 – us UMI [071]
LAKE COUNTY BEE *see* LAKE COUNTY RECORD BEE
LAKE COUNTY EXAMINER – Lakeview, OR. -w. 27 July 1883-. – 1 – us U.O. Library [071]
LAKE COUNTY FROM 1834-1872 / Ball, T H – Chicago: J.W. Goodspeed Publ., 1873. Indiana Reel 18. (The Cox Library Collection) – 5 – us Americana [978]
LAKE COUNTY GLOBE LEDGER – Hammond, Ind. -w. 1932- – 1 – us UMI [071]
LAKE COUNTY HERALD – Painesville. Ohio. -w. 1900-07, 1911-16, 1920-21 – 1 – us UMI [071]
LAKE COUNTY HISTORICAL SOCIETY RECORDS – (Minutes, annual reports, brochures, fliers, announcements, and clippings of this local historical society, which preserves the artifacts and archival records of Lake County, Ohio) – Mentor/ Kirtland Hills, Lake, OH. 1938-87 – 6r – 1 – us Western Res [978]
LAKE COUNTY INDEPENDENT – Libertyville. Ill. -w. 1894-1916 – 1 – us UMI [071]
LAKE COUNTY NEWS – Hammond. Ind. -w. 1893-1918 – 1 – us UMI [071]
Lake County. Ohio. Perry Township *see* RECORDS, MS 2026
Lake County. Ohio. Willoughby Township *see* RECORDS, MS 91
LAKE COUNTY RECORD – Upper Lake, CA. 1925-1926 – 1r – 1 – $50.00 – B03559 – us Library Micro [071]
LAKE COUNTY RECORD BEE – (Also known as: Lake County Bee) – Lakeport, CA. 1941- – 65+ r – 1 BC02335 – $3,450.00 ($360.00) – us Library Micro [071]
LAKE COUNTY RECORD BEE *see* LAKE COUNTY BEE
LAKE COUNTY REGISTER – Libertyville. Ill. -w. 1922-30 – 1 – us UMI [071]
LAKE COUNTY REPUBLICAN HERALD – Willoughby. Ohio. -sw. 1923-32 – 1 – us UMI [071]
LAKE COUNTY RUSTLER – Lakeview OR. June 11 1896-Oct 17 1901 – 1 – us U.O. Library [071]
LAKE COUNTY STAR – Crown Point. Ind. -w. 1882-97, 1901-50, 1952- – 1 – us UMI [071]
LAKE COUNTY TRIBUNE – Lakeview, OR. -w. 12 Apr 1929-25 Apr 1940 – 1 – us U.O. Library [071]
LAKE COUNTY TRIBUNE AND SILVER LAKE LEADER – Lakeview OR. Apr 12 1928-Apr 9 1929 – 1 – us U.O. Library [071]
LAKE ELSINORE TRIBUNE – Lake Elsinore, CA. 1949-1993 – 45r – 1 – $2,250.00 – R03262 – us Library Micro [071]
LAKE ELSINORE WILDOMAR NEWS – Lake Elsinore, CA. 1989 – 3+ r – 1 – $150.00 ($50.00y) – R04045 – us Library Micro [071]
LAKE FRONT NEWS – Port Clinton, Ohio. 1938-84 – 3r – 1 – $32.50r – us Archival [071]
LAKE HILL BAPTIST CHURCH. ORLANDO, FLORIDA : CHURCH RECORDS – Apr-May 1940 – 1 – 5.00 – us Baptist [240]
LAKE IZABAL FISHERIES SURVEY / International Center for Aquaculture – 1973. 1 reel – 1, 5 – us Spaulding [639]
Lake, Kirsopp *see*
- CODEX 1 OF THE GOSPELS AND ITS ALLIES
- THE HISTORICAL EVIDENCE FOR THE RESURRECTION OF JESUS CHRIST

LAKE LYRICS AND OTHER POEMS / Campbell, Wilfred – Saint John, N.B.: J. & A. McMillan, 1889. 00409. (Pre-1900 Canadiana) – 9 – cn C.I.H.M. [810]
LAKE MAGAZINE – 1892-93 – 1 – 60.00 – cn McLaren [800]
LAKE, MARIN, NAPA, SOLANO, SONOMA AND YOLO COUNTIES – Lake Co, CA. 1878-1879 – 1r – 1 – $50.00 – D049 – us Library Micro [978]
LAKE, MARIN, NAPA, SOLANO, SONOMA AND YOLO COUNTIES – Marin Co, CA. 1878-1879 – 1r – 1 – $50.00 – D049 – us Library Micro [978]
LAKE, MARIN, NAPA, SOLANO, SONOMA AND YOLO COUNTIES – Napa Co, CA. 1878-1879 – 1r – 1 – $50.00 – D049 – us Library Micro [978]
LAKE, MENDOCINO, NAPA AND SONOMA COUNTIES – Lake Co, CA. 1874 – 1r – 1 – $50.00 – D048 – us Library Micro [978]
LAKE, MENDOCINO, NAPA AND SONOMA COUNTIES – Mendocino Co, CA. 1874 – 1r – 1 – $50.00 – D048 – us Library Micro [978]
LAKE, MENDOCINO, NAPA AND SONOMA COUNTIES – Napa Co, CA. 1874 – 1r – 1 – $50.00 – D048 – us Library Micro [978]
LAKE, MENDOCINO, NAPA AND SONOMA COUNTIES – Sonoma Co, CA. 1874 – 1r – 1 – $50.00 – D048 – us Library Micro [978]
Lake Mohonk Conference of Friends of the Indians *see* ANNUAL REPORTS, 1883-1916, 1929
Lake Mohonk Conference on International Arbitration *see* ANNUAL REPORTS
Lake Mohonk Conference on the Indians *see* REPORT
LAKE, NAPA, MARIN, SOLANO, SONOMA AND YOLO COUNTIES – Solano Co, CA. 1878-1879 – 1r – 1 – $50.00 – D049 – us Library Micro [978]
LAKE, NAPA, MARIN, SOLANO, SONOMA AND YOLO COUNTIES – Sonoma Co, CA. 1878-1879 – 1r – 1 – $50.00 – D049 – us Library Micro [978]
LAKE, NAPA, MARIN, SOLANO, SONOMA AND YOLO COUNTIES – Yolo Co, CA. 1878-1879 – 1r – 1 – $50.00 – D049 – us Library Micro [978]

LAKE NICARAGUA FISHERIES SURVEY / International Center for Aquaculture – 1972. 1 reel – 1, 5 – us Spaulding [639]
LAKE OF TWO MOUNTAINS GAZETTE – Hudson, Canada. v19 n41. 9 jan 1969-v26 n43. Christmas 1975 – 3r – 1 – Can$60.00r – cn Can Microfilming [072]
LAKE OSWEGO DAILY REPORT – Lake Oswego OR. July 29 1968-Apr 21 1969 – 1 – us U.O. Library [071]
LAKE OSWEGO REVIEW – Lake Oswego, OR. -w. 19 sep 1929 – 1 – us U.O. Library [071]
Lake, P *see* A MONOGRAPH OF THE BRITISH CAMBRIAN TRILOBITES
THE LAKE ST JOHN REGION: THE GRANARY OF THE PROVINCE OF QUEBEC: A GUIDE FOR SETTLERS / ed by Buies, Arthur – Edited for the Quebec and Lake St. John Railway Co. by A. Buies. Quebec: Morning Chronicle Steam Print, 1891. 00346. (Pre-1900 Canadiana) – 9 – cn C.I.H.M. [971]
LAKE ST LOUIS OLD AND NEW: ILLUSTRATED: AND CAVELIER DE LA SALLE / Girouard, Desire – Columbian ed. (Montreal: Poirier, Bessette, 1893). 03441. (Pre-1900 Canadiana) – 9 – cn C.I.H.M. [971]
LAKE SUN – Kelseyville, CA. 1976-81; 1987-88 – 8r – 1 – $400.00 – B02323 – us Library Micro [071]
LAKE TAHOE AREA : ALPINE MEADOWS, DONNER LAKE, INCLINE, NORTHSTAR, SOUTH TAHOE, TAHOE CITY, ETC. – 1992- – 3+ r – 1 – $150.00 – P00043 – us Library Micro [910]
LAKE TAHOE NEWS – South Lake Tahoe, CA. 1961-72; 1976-84 – 18r – 1 – $900.00 – C03002 – us Library Micro [071]
LAKE TAHOE NEWS – Tahoe City, CA. 1973-84 – 7r – 1 CN03032 – $350.00 – us Library Micro [071]
LAKE TAHOE NEWS – Tahoe City, CA, NV. 1960; 1973-1984 – 7r – 1 – $350.00 – CU04759 – us Library Micro [071]
Lakebrink, B *see* HEGELS DIALEKTISCHE ONTOLOGIE UND DIE THOMISTISCHE ANALEKTIK
LAKELAND BOATING – v37-. 1982- – 1,5,6,9 – us UMI [073]
LAKELAND FIRST BAPTIST CHURCH. LAKELAND, FLORIDA : CHURCH RECORDS – 1897-Sep 1963 – 1 – 62.73 – us Baptist [240]
LAKE/MENDOCINO COUNTIES – 1992- – 3+ r – 1 – $150.00 – P00044 – us Library Micro [910]
LAKE/MENDOCINO/SONOMA – 1907-33 – 21r – 1 – $1,050.00 – P00128 – us Library Micro [910]
LAKEPORT DEMOCRAT – Lakeport, CA. 1887-1888; 1893 – 1r – 1 – $50.00 – B03265 – us Library Micro [071]
LAKE'S FALMOUTH PACKET *see* FALMOUTH PACKET
The Lakes. Presbytery (Assoc. Ref. Ch.) *see* MINUTES, 1829-1861
Lakeshore and Michigan Southern Railway System *see* RECORDS, MS 3912
THE LAKESHORE NEWS – (Cont by: Lakeshore News and West Island Chronicle 29 nov 1962-10 sep 1964. Cont by: News and Chronicle 17 sep 1964-20 jun 1984. Cont by: The Chronicle 27 jun 1984-24 dec 1991) – Pointe-Claire, Canada. v18 n9. 10 mai 1940-22 nov 1962 – 53r – 1 – Can$70.00r – cn Can Microfilming [072]
THE LAKESHORE NEWS *see* POINTE-CLAIRE RECORD
LAKESHORE NEWS AND WEST ISLAND CHRONICLE *see* THE LAKESHORE NEWS
LAKESHORE PRESS *see* POINTE-CLAIRE RECORD
LAKESHORE PRESS RECORD *see* POINTE-CLAIRE RECORD
LAKESIDE MONTHLY – v. 1-11. 1869-1874 – 1 – us UMI [073]
LAKESIDE NEWS – Lowell, OR. -w. 7 Oct 1971-19 Dec 1974; 24 Dec 1974. – 1r – 1 – us U.O. Library [071]
Lakeside. Ohio.Lakeside United Methodist Church *see* RECORDS
LAKESIDE SUN – Lakeside, NE. -w. Oct 1918-Jan 1920 – 1 – us NE Hist [071]
LAKEVIEW HERALD – Lakeview, OR. -w. 24 Oct 1907-23 Sep 1913. – 1 – us U.O. Library [071]
LAKEVIEW REGISTER – Lakeview OR. Nov 17 1898, July 20 1899 – 1 – us U.O. Library [071]

LAKEVILLE 1853-1902 – (Mf 1: Births 1853-69. Mf 2: Births 1869-92. Mf 3: Births 1893-1902. Mf 3: Marriages 1853-71. Mf 4: Marriages 1872-97. Mf 5: Marriages 1898-1903; Deaths 1853-69. Mf 6: Deaths 1870-90. Mf 7: Deaths 1891-1902) – (mf ed 1992) – 7mf – 9 – 0-87623-136-9 – us Holbrook [920]
LAKEWIEW BAPTIST CHURCH. HARTSVILLE, SOUTH CAROLINA : CHURCH RECORDS – 1944-76, 1979-81 – 1 – 38.57 – us Baptist [240]
LAKEWOOD BAPTIST CHURCH. GEORGETOWN COUNTY. SOUTH CAROLINA : CHURCH RECORDS – 1967-1972 – 1 – 5.54 – us Baptist [240]
LAKEWOOD HIGH SCHOOL YEARBOOK – Citadel, Long Beach, CA. 1958-93 – 10r – 1 – $500.00 – R60012 – us Library Micro [370]
Laki, Georgette *see* BIBLIOGRAPHIE ANALYTIQUE DE L'OEUVRE DE BRUNO LAFLEUR
LAKOLOSY VOLAMENA *see* NY LAKOLOSY VOLAMENA
Lakroum, M *see* L'ESSOR DU SALARIAT AU SENEGAL DANS L'ENTRE-DEUX-GUERRES, 1917-37
Laks, Johannes *see*
- ARKAMISTUULED KODUMAAL
- EVANGEELIUMI KRISTLASTE VABAKOGUDUSE AJALOOLINE ULEVAADE, 1905-1930
- MAELESTUSI ELUTEELT JA TOEOEMAALT

Lakshapatiya. Ceylon. St Matthias' Church *see* A JUBILEE SOUVENIR, 1876-1926
Laktaw, Pedro Serrano *see* DICCIONARIO HISPANO-TAGALOG
LAL BANGLA : EINE UNTERSUCHUNG DER URSACHEN UND FOLGEN KOMMUNISTISCHER HERRSCHAFT IN WESTBENGALEN / Olnhausen, Gerd von – 1992 – 4mf – 9 – DM98.00 – 3-89349-546-0 – gw Hänsel [320]
Lal, H *see* THE TRIBES AND CASTES OF THE CENTRAL PROVINCES OF INDIA
LALA PASA – (First in the Markopasa set) – No. 1 (1947) – 1mf – 9 – $10.50 – us MEDOC [949]
LALAKI DI TEGAL PATI; SADJAK-SADJAK SUNDA / Sajudi – SE 4465 1. 1963 – 9 – ne IDC [950]
Lalande, Jerome *see*
- MEMOIRE SUR L'INTERIEUR DE L'AFRIQUE

Lalande, M R *see* CONFITEMINI DOMINO [1705] AND CONFITEMINI [1699]. MOTETS A GRAND CHOEUR
LaLar *see* ABSTRACTS OF WILLS OF CHATHAM COUNTY, 1773-1817
LALAZAR. KAVKAZSKII SKAZ / Remizov, A – Berlin, 1922. 35p. BR-825 2 – 8 – ne IDC [460]
Lalevic, D et al *see* LIST OF PRINCIPAL RECOMMENDATIONS FOR AGRICULTURAL DEVELOPMENT IN LIBYA
Laliberte, Alfred *see* OEUVRE
Laliberte, Gerard *see* QUEBEC 9
Lalle, Henri *see* LA QUESTION DES REGLEMENTS D'ATELIER
Lallemand, Leon *see* HISTOIRE DES ENFANTS ABANDONNES ET DELAISSES
Lallie, Alfred *see*
- ALFRED LALLIE
- LE DIOCESE DE NANTES PENDANT LA REVOLUTION
- LE DISTRICT DE MACHECOUL, 1788-1793...
- ETUDES SUR LA TERREUR
- LA JUSTICE REVOLUTIONNAIRE A NANTES...
- LES PRISONS DE NANTES PENDANT LA REVOLUTION
- LES SOCIETES POPULAIRES A NANTES PENDANT LA REVOLUTION

Lalo, E *see* TROISIEME TRIO EN LA MIMEUR...OP. 26
Lalonde, Pierre *see* LE TELE-JOURNAL
LALOR'S SUPPLEMENT TO HILL AND DENIO'S REPORTS / New York. (State) – (A Pre-NRS title.) – 1v. 1842-44 (all publ) – 6mf – 9 – $9.00 – LLMC 80-051 – us L.L.M.C. [340]
Lalouette, Le P A *see* HISTOIRE ET ABREGE DES OUVRAGES LATINS, ITALIENS ET FRANCOIS, POUR ET CONTRE LA COMEDIE ET L'OPERA
Lalource *see*
- FORME GENERALE ET PARTICULIERE DE LA CONVOCATION ET DE LA TENUE DES ASSEMBLEES NATIONALES OU ETATS GENERAUX DE FRANCE, JUSTIFIEE PAR PIECES AUTHENTIQUES
- RECUEIL DE PIECES ORIGINALES ET AUTHENTIQUES CONCERNANT LA TENUE DES ETATS GENERAUX: D'ORLEANS EN 1560 SOUS CHARLES 9; DE BLOIS EN 1576 SOUS HENRI 3; DE BLOIS EN 1588 SOUS HENRI 3; DE PARIS EN 1614 SOUS LOUIS 13

Lam, Tak C *see* A COMPARISON OF THE LEADERSHIP BEHAVIOR OF WINNING AND LOSING HIGH SCHOOL BASKETBALL COACHES
Lama, Iris L *see* PULMONARY DIFFUSING CAPACITY AND EXERCISE-INDUCED HYPOXEMIA IN HIGHLY TRAINED ATHLETES
LAMA NEWSLETTER – Library Administration and Management Association. v. 5-. 1979- – 1,5,6,9 – us UMI [020]
Lama y Lena, Rafael *see* GRAMATICA ELEMENTAL DE LA LENGUA LATINA Y CASTELLANA
Lamack, Daniel D *see* ELECTROMYOGRAPHIC CHANGES DURING INTENSE ISOKINETIC STRENGTH TRAINING
Laman, Karl Eduard *see* DICTIONNAIRE KIKINGO-FRANCAIS, AVEC UNE ETUDE PHONETIQUE DECRIVANT LES DIALECTES LES PLUS IMPORTANTS DE LA LANGUE DITE KIKONGO
Lamande, Andre *see* LE VIE DE RENE VAILLIE, VAINQUEUR DE TOMBOUCTOU.
Lamar, James Sanford *see* THE ORGANON OF SCRIPTURE
Lamarck, J B A P M de *see*
- CATALOGUE ILLUSTRE DE LA COLLECTION LAMARCK
- ENCYCLOPEDIE METHODIQUE BOTANIQUE
- FLORA FRANCAIS
- FLORE FRANCAISE
- FLORE FRANCIASE
- HERBARIUM
- HISTOIRE NATURELLE DES ANIMAUX SANS VERTEBRES
- SYNOPSIS PLANTARUM IN FLORA GALLICA DESCRIPTIORUM
- TABLEAU ENCYCLOPEDIQUE ET METHODIQUE DES TROIS REGNES DE LA NATURE BOTANIQUE

Lamare, General *see* RELATION DES SIEGES ET DEFENSES DE BADAJOZ, D'OLIVENCA
Lamarque, Francois *see* STATISTIQUE DU DEPARTEMENT DU TARN
Lamartine, Alphonse M *see* DU DROIT AU TRAVAIL ET DE L'ORGANISATION DU TRAVAIL
THE LAMAS EVANGEL – (Lacking: nos 1-6 1942) – 1939-48 – 1r – 1 – ATLA S0666B – us A.T.L.A. [073]
LaMaster, Kathryn J *see* PRESERVICE TEACHERS AS MENTORS DURING AN EARLY FIELD EXPERIENCE THROUGH ELECTRONIC COMMUNICATION (E-MAIL)
LAMASTU, PAZUZU UND ANDERE DAEMONEN. EIN BEITRAG ZUR BABYL-ASSYR. DAEMONOLOGIE / Frank, C – (Mitteilungen der altorientalischen gesellschaft. v. 14, pt. 2). Leipzig. 1941. BNE-20,103 1 – 9 – ne IDC [290]
LAMB AND HAZLITT : FURTHER LETTERS AND RECORDS HITHERTO UNPUBLISHED / ed by Hazlitt, William Carew – New York: Dodd, Mead and Company, 1899 – 1 roll – 1 – 1-55879-850-1 – uk Libr Preservation [420]
Lamb, Charles *see*
- THE LETTERS OF CHARLES LAMB
- THE OLD BENCHERS OF THE INNER TEMPLE
- SPECIMENS OF ENGLISH DRAMATIC POETS, WHO LIVED ABOUT THE TIME OF SHAKESPEARE

Lamb, D *see* EXPLOITING THE TROPICAL RAIN FOREST
Lamb, Geoff *see* CAN EQUITY BE ORGANIZED?
Lamb, Jennifer A *see* HEALTH-RELATED FITNESS IN AND AMONG YOUTH
THE LAMB OF GOD : EXPOSITIONS IN THE WRITINGS OF ST. JOHN / Nicoll, William Robertson – New York: Macmillan, 1883 – 1mf – 9 – 0-8370-4589-4 – 1985-2589 – us A.T.L.A. [220]
LAMB OF GOD: EXPOSITIONS IN THE WRITINGS OF ST JOHN / Nicoll, William Robertson – New York: Macmillan, 1883. 1 fiche – 9 – us A.T.L.A. [240]
Lamb, S Ernest *see* THE STATUTES OF NEW SOUTH WALES OF RACTICAL UTILITY PASSED PRIOR TO 1894 AND STILL IN FORCE
Lamb, William *see* THE MELBOURNE PAPERS

Lamballe, Marie Therese Louise *see* SECRET MEMOIRS...BEING HER JOURNALS, LETTERS AND CONVERSATIONS DURING HER CONFIDENTIAL RELATIONS WITH MARIE ANTOINETTE
THE LAMBAS OF NORTHERN RHODESIA: A STUDY OF THEIR CUSTOMS AND BELIEFS / Doke, Clement Martin – London. 1931. BA-361 2 – 8 – ne IDC [306]
LAMBDA – 1980 – 1,5,6,9 – us UMI [073]
Lambda *see* THE TRUTH ABOUT THE BARCELONA EVENTS
Lambecht, D *see* DE SYNODE IN HET OUDE BISDOM DOORNIK GESITUEERD IN DE EUROPESE ONTWIKKELING
Lambecii, Petri *see* ORIGINES HAMBURGENSES SIVE RERUM HAMBURGENSIUS. LIBRI 2
Lambert, A B *see* A DESCRIPTION OF THE GENUS PINUS
Lambert, Christopher M *see* A COMPARISON OF SELECTED CORONARY HEART DISEASE RISK FACTORS IN WEIGHT TRAINED MALES
Lambert, Edouard *see* L'ANCETRE AMERICAIN DU DROIT COMPARE; LA DOCTRINE DU JUGE STORY
Lambert, Gerald P *see* THE RELATIONSHIP BETWEEN PHYSIOLOGICAL MEASUREMENTS AND CROSS-COUNTRY RUNNING PERFORMANCE
Lambert, J *see* LE BRESIL
Lambert, Jean-Henri *see* ESSAI D'HYGROMETRIE OU SUR LA MESURE DE L'HUMIDITE
Lambert, Joseph A *see* ENQUETE SUR LA LOI DE LA CONVENTION COLLECTIVE ET SON APPLICATION: ANALYSE DES DECISIONS DES TRIBUNAUX
Lambert le Tort *see* THE ROMANCE OF ALEXANDER: A COLLOTYPE FACSIMILE OF MS. BODLEY 264..
Lambert, Louis Aloisius *see*
- CATHOLIC BELIEF
- CHRISTIAN SCIENCE BEFORE THE BAR OF REASON
- NOTES ON INGERSOLL

Lambert, M *see* GRAMMAIRE OUOLOVE
Lambert, Maurice *see* ETUDE SUR LA PROTECTION DU SALAIRE A L'EGARD DU PATRON
LAMBERT TEN KATE : DE "GEMEENSCHAP TUSSEN DE GOTISCHE SPRAEKE EN DE NEDERDUYTSCHE",... / Hoeven, A van der – Diss. 's-Gravenhage, 1896 – 2mf – 9 – ne IDC [430]
Lamberts, J H *see* PYROMETRIE ODER VOM MAASSE DE FEUERS UND DER WARME BERLIN
Lambertson, William Purnell *see* THE CLOAK ROOM AND WEEKLY LETTER
Lambertz, Paul *see* DER FUENFFUESSIGE JAMBUS IN DEN DRAMEN FRIEDRICHS HALMS
LAMBETH AND SOUTHWARK ADVERTISER – (South London News etc, 1857-61) – London, UK. 23 Jun 1855-27 Jul 1861 – 4r – 1 – uk British Libr Newspaper [072]
Lambeth Conference *see* REPORTS
THE LAMBETH CONFERENCE (1930) – London, 1930 – 3mf – 8 – ne Slangenburg [240]
THE LAMBETH CONFERENCE (1948) – London, 1948 – 3mf – 8 – ne Slangenburg [240]
THE LAMBETH CONFERENCES OF 1867, 1878, AND 1888 : WITH THE OFFICIAL REPORTS AND RESOLUTIONS, TOGETHER WITH THE SERMONS PREACHED AT THE CONFERENCES / ed by Davidson, Randall Thomas – London: S.P.C.K.; New York: E.& J.B. Young, 1896 – 1mf – us A.T.L.A. [240]
Lambeth, Kelly K *see* JOB SATISFACTION AMONG SECONDARY LEVEL TEACHERS
LAMBETH PALACE LIBRARY : CATALOGUE OF PRINTED BOOKS – 544mf – 9 – £2,185.00 – uk Chadwyck [240]
Lambeth Palace Library *see*
- HERALDIC AND GENEALOGICAL MANUSCRIPTS, 16TH-17TH CENTURIES
- THE MEDIAEVAL MANUSCRIPT COLLECTION
- MISCELLANEOUS AMERICAN MANUSCRIPTS
- PAPERS OF THOMAS MURRAY 1593-1623
- "THE QUEEN ANNE CHURCHES"
- RECORDS OF THE COURT OF ARCHES, 1554-1911
- THE SHREWSBURY PAPERS

Lambeth Palace. Library *see*
- ACT BOOKS OF THE ARCHBISHOPS OF CANTERBURY: 1663-1914
- THE CAREW PAPERS
- CATALOGUE CARTE ANTIQUAE ET MISCELLANEAE

- CATALOGUE PRESENTATION DEEDS, AUGMENTATION BOOKS AND PARLIAMENTARY SURVEYS
- THE FULHAM PAPERS
- VISITATION RETURNS 1766-1815

Lambin, P P *see* RUSSKII BIBLIOGRAFICHESKII UKAZATEL' ZA 1855 GOD

Lambot, C *see* NORTH ITALIAN SERVICES OF THE 11TH CENTURY

Lamb-Roberts Funeral Home, Ottawa, KS *see* UNDERTAKERS REGISTER

Lambron de Lignim, H de *see* DOCUMENTS GENEALOGIQUES SUR LES FAMILLES DE TOURAINE

Lambros, Spyr P *see* CATALOGUE OF THE GREEK MANUSCRIPTS ON MOUNT ATHOS

Lambruschini, Luigi *see* SULL'IMMACOLATO CONCEPIMENTO DI MARIA

THE LAMBS : THEIR LIVES, THEIR FRIENDS, AND THEIR CORRESPONDENCE; NEW PARTICULARS AND NEW MATERIAL / Hazlitt, William Carew – London: Elkin Mathews; New York: C. Scribner's Sons, 1897 – 1 roll – 1 – 1-55879-277-5 – uk Libr Preservation [420]

LAMB'S BIOGRAPHICAL DICTIONARY OF THE UNITED STATES – v. 1-7. 1900-03 – 1 – 129.00 – us L of C Photodup [920]

Lambton, A K S *see* THREE PERSIAN DIALECTS

Lambton, Earl of Durham, John George *see* REPORT ON THE AFFAIRS OF BRITISH NORTH AMERICA

Lamech *see* CHRONICON EPHRATENSE

LAMENNAIS : SA VIE ET SES DOCTRINES / Boutard, Charles – Paris: Perrin, 1905-1913 – 3mf – us A.T.L.A. [920]

Lamennais, Felicite Robert de *see* ESSAY ON INDIFFERENCE IN MATTERS OF RELIGION

LAMENTACIONES DE JEREMIAS / Mogollon, Antonio – 1878 – 9 – 1.50f – sp Bibl Santa Ana [240]

LAS LAMENTACIONES, HIMNOS / Salas, Francisco Gregorio de – 1826 – 9 – $1.50f – sp Bibl Santa Ana [810]

LAMENTATIONES JEREMIAE PROPHETAE(...) / Nivers, Guillaume-G – Nannetis: N. Verger, 1730 – fr Armell [240]

LAMENTO ET DISPERATIONE DI SELIM GRAN TVRCO – N.p., [1571] – 1mf – 9 – H-8183/1 – ne IDC [956]

LA-MERHAV – Tel Aviv. 1954-71. Available; 1960-71. BJ-91-54 3 – 1 – ne IDC [956]

Lamiral, D H *see*
- L'AFRIQUE ET LE PEUPLE AFFRIQUAIN
- L'AFRIQUE ET LE PEUPLE AFRICAIN CONSIDERES DANS LEURS RAPPORTS AVEC NOTRE COMMERCE ET NOS COLONIES
- L'AFRIQUE ET LE PEUPLE AFRICAIN CONSIDERES SOUS TOUS LEURS RAPPORTS AVEC NOTRE COMMERCE ET NOS COLONIES. DEDIE AU COMMERCE ET AUX COLONS FRANCAIS
- MEMOIRE SUR LE SENEGAL PAR M. LAMIRAL, DEPUTE DE LA COLONIE DU SENEGAL, PRES L'ASSEMBLEE NATIONALE

Lamkin, Thomas Elwood *see* A HISTORY OF THE INTERPRETATION OF ROMANS 14:1-15:13, 1845-1980

Lamkin, Uel W *see* HISTORY OF HENRY COUNTY

Lamm, Henry *see* EPIGRAMS AND EXCERPTS SELECTED AND ARRANGED BY FRED C. MULLINIX.

Lamm, Martin *see* SWEDENBORG

Lammens, Henri *see* L'ARABIE OCCIDENTALE AVANT L'HEGIRE

Lammer Moor *see* BOWRING, GOBDEN AND CHINA: A MEMOIR

Lammers, Hans Heinrich *see* DIE VERWALTUNGS-AKADEMIE. EIN HANDBUCH FUER DEN BEAMTEN IM NATIONALSOZIALISTISCHEN STAAT..

Lamo, A *see* DISCORSO INTERNE ALLA SCOLTURA ET PITTURA

Lamoise *see* GRAMMAIRE DE LA LANGUE SERERE AVEC DES EXEMPLES ET DES EXERCICES

Lamond, Elizabeth *see* A DISCOURSE OF THE COMMON WEAL OF THIS REALM OF ENGLAND

Lamoneda, Ramon *see* EL CAMINO DE LA UNIDAD: UN DISCURSO SOCIALISTA

LaMontagna, R *see* VALIDITY AND RELIABILITY OF THE 20-METER SHUTTLE TEST IN AMERICAN FEMALES 19-34

Lamott, A *see* DAS SPEYERER DIOEZESANRITUALE VON 1512 BIS 1932

LaMotte, Antoine Houdar de *see* INES DE CASTRO

Lamouche, L *see* LA BULGARIE DANS LE PASSE ET LE PRESENT; ETUDE HISTORIQUE, ETHNOGRAPHIQUE, STATISTIQUE ET MILITAIRE

Lamouroux, J V F *see* DISSERTATIONS SUR PLUSIEURS ESPECES DE FUCUS

THE LAMP = DER LAMP – (In Yiddish and English) – New York City, NY. v2 no3 Feb 1954-Jan/Feb 1955 – 1r – 1 – $25.00 – cn Can Microfilming [071]

THE LAMP – Toronto: Toronto Branch of the Theosophical Society, [1894-1900?] – 9 – cn C.I.H.M. [290]

Lamp Light Press Staff *see*
- BUSINESS IDEA PUBLICATIONS
- IMMUNE SYSTEM HERBALS, APPROACHES, FOLKLORE

LAMPADA : HEBDOMADARIO SCIENTIFICO, LITTERARIO E PHILOTECHNICO – Maceio, Alagoas. 6, 19 Maio 1888 – 1,5,6 – bl Biblioteca [072]

O LAMPADARIO – Juiz de Fora, 24 Dec 1953 – 1,5,6 – bl Biblioteca [072]

LAMPADORAMA – Maceio, Alagoas. 1-20 Out 1884; 5 Abr 1885 – 1,5,6 – bl Biblioteca [072]

Lampe, Friedrich A *see*
- DE CYMBALIS VETERUM; LIBRI TRES
- DE CYMBALIS VETERUM LIBRI TRES

Lampe, J F *see*
- THE ART OF MUSICK
- A PLAIN AND COMPENDIOUS METHOD OF TEACHING THOROUGH BASS

Lamperez Romea, Vicente *see* INFORME SOBRE EL CONVENTO DE SAN BENITO DE ALCANTARA Y FALLECIMIENTO

LAMPERTI MONACHI HERSFELDENSIS OPERA (MGH 7: 38.BD) : ACCEDUNT ANNALES WEISSENBURGENSES – Ed 3a.1894 – Dfl35.00 – ne Slangenburg [240]

LAMPIRAN / Indonesia. Direktorat Film – SE-8566 1. 5v in 4. 1968 – 9 – ne IDC [790]

Lamprecht, Karl *see* DEUTSCHE GESCHICHTE

Lamprecht, Kurt *see* REGIMENT REICHSTAG

Lamy, A *see*
- COURS ET EXERCICES POUR LES STAGES DE RECYCLAGE DES MONITEURS
- ENQUETE SUR LE FRANCAIS DES ELEVES DE SIXIEME
- EXERCICES STRUCTURAUX
- L'EXPRESSION DU TEMPS

Lamy, B *see*
- DE L'ART DE PARLER
- NOUVELLES REFLEXIONS SUR L'ART POETIQUE
- LA RHETORIQUE

Lamy, Thomas Josephus *see*
- DISSERTATION DE SYRORUM FIDE ET DISCIPLINA IN RE EUCHARISTICA
- HYMNI ET SERMONES

LANARK CLIPPINGS – 1887-1954 – 1. 301-304; 1. 367-368 – £42.00r – uk Scot News [072]

THE LANARK ERA – (Some issues missing) – Lanark, Ontario, CN. 1895-1919 – 11r – 1 – cn Commonwealth Micro [072]

LANARK GAZETTE – 1 – £42.00r – uk Scot News [072]

LANARKSHIRE – 1916-1925 – 1. 315-324 – £42.00r – uk Scot News [072]

LANARKSHIRE – Hamilton, Scotland, UK. Jul 1905-1915. -w. 20 reels – 1 – uk British Libr Newspaper [072]

LANARKSHIRE, 1837 : BRITISH ISLES CENSUS DIRECTORIES PROJECT, SCOTLAND. VOL 26 – 2mf – 9 – A$15.00 – at Vine [941]

LANARKSHIRE (GLASGOW), 1805 : BRITISH ISLES CENSUS DIRECTORIES PROJECT, SCOTLAND. VOL 23 – 1mf – 9 – A$9.00 – at Vine [941]

LANARKSHIRE (GLASGOW), 1826 : BRITISH ISLES CENSUS DIRECTORIES PROJECT, SCOTLAND – at Vine [941]

LANARKSHIRE (GLASGOW), 1840 : BRITISH ISLES CENSUS DIRECTORIES PROJECT, SCOTLAND. VOL 3 – 3mf – 9 – A$21.00 – at Vine [941]

LANARKSHIRE (GLASGOW), 1845 : BRITISH ISLES CENSUS DIRECTORIES PROJECT, SCOTLAND. VOL 5 – 4mf – 9 – A$27.00 – at Vine [941]

LANCASHIRE, 1822 : BRITISH ISLES CENSUS DIRECTORIES PROJECT, ENGLAND – (In prep) – at Vine [941]

LANCASHIRE, 1834 : BRITISH ISLES CENSUS DIRECTORIES PROJECT, ENGLAND – (In prep) – at Vine [941]

LANCASHIRE, 1848 : BRITISH ISLES CENSUS DIRECTORIES PROJECT, ENGLAND. VOL 244 – 7mf – 9 – A$45.00 – at Vine [941]

LANCASHIRE, 1855 : BRITISH ISLES CENSUS DIRECTORIES PROJECT, ENGLAND – at Vine [941]

LANCASHIRE, 1903 : BRITISH ISLES CENSUS DIRECTORIES PROJECT, ENGLAND. VOL 111 – 8mf – 9 – A$51.00 – at Vine [941]

LANCASHIRE, 1913 : BRITISH ISLES CENSUS DIRECTORIES PROJECT, ENGLAND – at Vine [941]

LANCASHIRE AND CHESHIRE RECORD SOCIETY – (Coll title: Publications of the English Record Societies, 1835-1972...) – v1-109. 1879-1965 – 367mf – 9 – £1,930.00 – uk Chadwyck [941]

LANCASHIRE AND YORKSHIRE CO-OPERATOR AND USEFUL CLASSES' ADVOCATE – Series 1. nos. 1-6 (all publ). 1831. Series 2. nos. 1-12 (all publ). 1831-32. Series 3: nos. 1-10. (all and last publ). 1832 – 4mf – 9 – $55.00 – us UPA [335]

LANCASHIRE BEACON – Manchester. 1849-50 – 1 – uk Microform Academic [073]

LANCASHIRE (BLACKBURN), 1900 : BRITISH ISLES CENSUS DIRECTORIES PROJECT, ENGLAND – at Vine [941]

LANCASHIRE (BLACKBURN, BOLTON, LANCASTER, LIVERPOOL, MANCHESTER, PRESTON, ROCHEDALE, WARRINGTON, WIGAN), 1805 : BRITISH ISLES CENSUS DIRECTORIES PROJECT, ENGLAND. VOL 165 – 1mf – 9 – A$9.00 – at Vine [941]

LANCASHIRE EVENING POST – Lancashire – 1 – uk Microform Academic [072]

LANCASHIRE (EXC LIVERPOOL), 1864 : BRITISH ISLES CENSUS DIRECTORIES PROJECT, ENGLAND. VOL 3 – 6mf – 9 – A$39.00 – at Vine [941]

LANCASHIRE (FAR NORTH), 1829 : BRITISH ISLES CENSUS DIRECTORIES PROJECT, ENGLAND. VOL 126 – 2mf – 9 – A$15.00 – at Vine [941]

LANCASHIRE (FURNESS AND CARTMEL), 1849 : BRITISH ISLES CENSUS DIRECTORIES PROJECT, ENGLAND – at Vine [941]

LANCASHIRE (FURNESS AND CARTMEL), 1910 : BRITISH ISLES CENSUS DIRECTORIES PROJECT, ENGLAND – at Vine [941]

LANCASHIRE (LIVERPOOL), 1769 : BRITISH ISLES CENSUS DIRECTORIES PROJECT, ENGLAND – at Vine [941]

LANCASHIRE (LIVERPOOL), 1796 : BRITISH ISLES CENSUS DIRECTORIES PROJECT, ENGLAND – (In prep) – at Vine [941]

LANCASHIRE (LIVERPOOL), 1851 : BRITISH ISLES CENSUS DIRECTORIES PROJECT, ENGLAND – at Vine [941]

LANCASHIRE (LIVERPOOL), 1858 : BRITISH ISLES CENSUS DIRECTORIES PROJECT, ENGLAND. VOL 33 – 1mf – 9 – A$9.00 – at Vine [941]

LANCASHIRE (LIVERPOOL AND MANCHESTER), 1824 : BRITISH ISLES CENSUS DIRECTORIES PROJECT, ENGLAND – (In prep) – at Vine [941]

LANCASHIRE (LIVERPOOL AND MANCHESTER), 1837 : BRITISH ISLES CENSUS DIRECTORIES PROJECT, ENGLAND. VOL 198 – 1mf – 9 – A$9.00 – at Vine [941]

LANCASHIRE (MANCHESTER), 1773 : BRITISH ISLES CENSUS DIRECTORIES PROJECT, ENGLAND – (In prep) – at Vine [941]

LANCASHIRE (MANCHESTER AND SALFORD), 1813 : BRITISH ISLES CENSUS DIRECTORIES PROJECT, ENGLAND – at Vine [941]

LANCASHIRE (MANCHESTER AND SALFORD), 1832 : BRITISH ISLES CENSUS DIRECTORIES PROJECT, ENGLAND. VOL 201 – 4mf – 9 – A$27.00 – at Vine [941]

LANCASHIRE (MANCHESTER AND SALFORD), 1841 : BRITISH ISLES CENSUS DIRECTORIES PROJECT, ENGLAND. VOL 231 – 3mf – 9 – A$21.00 – at Vine [941]

LANCASHIRE (NORTH), 1851 : BRITISH ISLES CENSUS DIRECTORIES PROJECT, ENGLAND. VOL 133 – 2mf – 9 – A$15.00 – at Vine [941]

Lancashire Parish Register Society *see* PUBLICATIONS

LANCASHIRE (PART 1), 1824 : BRITISH ISLES CENSUS DIRECTORIES PROJECT, ENGLAND. VOL 145 – 4mf – 9 – A$27.00 – at Vine [941]

LANCASHIRE (PART 2), 1825 : BRITISH ISLES CENSUS DIRECTORIES PROJECT, ENGLAND. VOL 146 – 5mf – 9 – A$33.00 – at Vine [941]

LANCASHIRE (PART), 1816 : BRITISH ISLES CENSUS DIRECTORIES PROJECT, ENGLAND – (In prep) – at Vine [941]

LANCASHIRE (PRESTON), 1889 : BRITISH ISLES CENSUS DIRECTORIES PROJECT, ENGLAND. VOL 60 – 4mf – 9 – A$27.00 – at Vine [941]

LANCASHIRE (PRESTWICK), 1900 : BRITISH ISLES CENSUS DIRECTORIES PROJECT, ENGLAND – at Vine [941]

LANCASTER 1647-1905 – (Mf 1-8: Vital Records 1647-1816. Mf 9-10: Births 1776-1843. Mf 11-13: Deaths 1792-1844. Mf 14-17: Marriages 1815-56. Mf 18-19: Roads 1729-1862. Mf 20: Town Records 1652-70. Mf 20-22: Proprietors 1716-1837. Mf 23-31: Proprietors 1718-1744. Mf 32-37: Land Records 1659-1818. Mf 38-42: Town Records 1725-67. Mf 43-50: Town Records 1766-1800. Mf 51-59: Town Records 1800-23. Mf 60-63: Births 1843-1901. Mf 64: Marriages 1843-54. Mf 65: Deaths 1843-57. Mf 66-68: Marriages 1853-1905. Mf 69-71: Deaths 1858-1905) – (mf ed 1991) – 71mf – 9 – 0-87623-140-7 – us Holbrook [920]

THE LANCASTER ARGUS – (Cont by: The Lankastr Orgus) – St. John, NB: New Brunswick Insane Asylum, [1891?-1892 or 1893] – 9 – cn C.I.H.M. [360]

THE LANCASTER ARGUS *see* THE LANKASTR ORGUS

LANCASTER COUNTY CITIZEN – Lincoln, NE. -w. Dec 1915-Dec 1925 – 1 – us NE Hist [071]

LANCASTER FIRST BAPTIST CHURCH. LANCASTER, SOUTH CAROLINA : CHURCH RECORDS – 1894-1972 – 1 – 21.06 – us Baptist [240]

LANCASTER GAZETTEER – (Lancaster Gazette). Lancaster. England. -w. 20 Jun 1801-Dec 1830. (10 reels) – 1 – uk British Libr Newspaper [072]

LANCASTER GUARDIAN – England. -w. Jan 1860-Dec 1861. (2 reels) – 1 – uk British Libr Newspaper [072]

LANCASTER, HARRISBURG, LEBANON AND YORK GOPSILL'S DIRECTORY 1863/64 / Lyon, John – 1863. Pennsylvania Reel 26. (The Cox Library Collection) – 5 – us Americana [978]

Lancaster, Joseph Campbell, 1861-1916 *see* THE EXTENT TO WHICH THE TITLE OF A PURCHASER TO LAND, BOUGHT AT A SHERIFF'S SALE, IS AFFECTED BY ERROR IN THE PROCEEDINGS, IN PENNSYLVANIA

LANCASTER JOURNAL – Lancaster, PA., 1803-1812 – 13 – $25.00r – us I.M.R. [071]

Lancaster, N *see* METHODISM TRIUMPHANT

Lancaster. Presbytery (Pres. Ch. in the U.S.A.) *see* MINUTES, 1765-66

LANCASTER PRESS – Bethany, NE. -w. Mar. 1898-Aug. 1898 – 1 – us NE Hist [071]

Lancaster, W T *see* THE COUCHER BOOK OF THE CISTERCIAN ABBEY OF KIRKSTALL

Lancastre-Laboreiro e Souza de Villalobos, Anna *see* INFANTAS LUNTANAS REINAS DE ESPANA E INFANTAS ESPANOLAS REINAS DE PORTUGAL

LANCE – Portland OR. Nov 7 28 1931 – 1 – us U.O. Library [071]

LANCE – Topeka. Kansas. 1883-1896 – 1 – us UMI [071]

THE LANCE – Quebec, Canada. v1 n10. 16 oct 1875 – 1r – 1 – Can$25.00 – cn Can Microfilming [072]

Lance, Chevalier de la *see* TROIS SONATAS POUR LE CLAVECIN OU PIANOFORTE AVEC VIOLON OBLIGE...

LANCE CURIOSO EN VISITA PASTORAL, MISSIONALIA HISPANICA, 1948 / Bayle, Constantino – Missionalia Hispanica V, 1948 – 1 – sp Bibl Santa Ana [240]

LANCEFIELD EXAMINER – 1872-1882. 1876-1881 lost. LE1-2 – 2r – 1 – at Corangamite [072]

Lancelot, Claude *see*
- A GENERAL AND RATIONAL GRAMMAR
- GRAMMAIRE GENERALE ET RAISONNEE
- LA LOGIQUE OU L'ART DE PENSER
- A NEW METHOD OF LEARNING WITH GREATER FACILITY THE GREEK TONGUE
- NOUVELLE METHODE POUR APPRENDRE FACILEMENT ET EN PEU DE TEMPS LA LANGUE LATINE.

Lancelot, M *see* MEMOIRES TOUCHANT LA VIE DE MONSIEUR DE S. CYRAN

LANCET – 5,641mf – 9 – ne IDC [610]

LANCET – 1823-1964 – 1,5,6 – us Princeton Micro [610]

LANCET – (1966- 5,6. 1963- 9) – England. 1823- – 1 – us UMI [616]

A LANCETA : PERIODICO HUMORISTICO, NOTICIOSO DE GRANDE CIRCULACAO – Manaus, Amazonas. 24 Ago 1912-Mar 1913; Maio-Out 1914; Maio-9 Set 1915 – 1,5,6 – bl Biblioteca [072]

LA LANCETTE CANADIENNE – Montreal, Canada. 4 jan 1847-15 jun 1847 – 1r – 1 – Can$25.00 – cn Can Microfilming [072]

Lanchantin, Margaret M *see* THE HISTORY OF INTERCOLLEGIATE SWIMMING AT THE COLLEGE OF WILLIAM AND MARY (1928-1987)

Lancho Moreno, Juan Jose *see*
- ESTUDIO SOCIO-ECONOMICO DE UN MUNICIPIO RURAL
- LAS MUTUALIDADES LABORALES DE TRABAJADORES AUTONOMOS DE SERVICIOS, DE LA INDUSTRIA Y DE LAS ACTIVIDADES DIRECTAS PARA EL CONSUMO. COMPENDIO...

Lanciani, Rodolfo *see* ANCIENT ROME

Lancis y Sanchez, Antonio *see* ELEMENTOS DE DERECHO ELECTORAL; DESARROLLADOS CONFORME AL PROGRAMA Y EXPLICACIONES DEL PROFESOR TITULAR DE LA ASIGNATURA, EN LA UNIVERISDAD DE LA HABANA

Lancour, Harold *see* A BIBLIOGRAPHY OF SHIP PASSENGER LISTS, 1538-1825

Lanctot, Charles *see* MANUEL DU JUGE DE PAIX: COMPRENANT LA NATURE DES FONCTIONS DU JUGE DE PAIX, LA PROCEDURE REGULIERE AT LA PROCEDURE SOMMAIRE, LA RESPONSABILITE DES JUGES DE PAIX...ETC.

Lanctot, Mederic *see*
- L'INDEPENDANCE CANADIENNE
- LA PRESSE
- L'UNION NATIONALE

LAND – (Details on request) – Sydney – 1 – at Pascoe [072]

LAND – Stockholm, Sweden. 1970-78 – 29r – 1 – sw Kungliga [333]

LAND – Sydney, Jan 1 1954-Dec 31 1959; Jan 7 1965-Dec 26 1968 – at Pascoe [072]

THE LAND – Sydney, Australia. 24 Jul 1914-30 Jun 1922.-w. 12mqn reels – 1 – uk British Libr Newspaper [072]

LAND AND BUILDING NEWS *see* FREEHOLD LAND TIMES BUILDING NEWS

LAND AND FRESH-WATER MOLLUSCA (FROM CLARE ISLAND) / Stelfox, A W – Z 817 2. 1912 – 8 – ne IDC [590]

LAND AND FRESHWATER MOLLUSCA OF INDIA / Godwin-Austen, H H – Z-540 2. 3 v. 1882-1920 – 8 – ne IDC [590]

THE LAND AND FRESHWATER MOLLUSKS INDIGENOUS TO / Reeve, LA – or Naturalized in, the British Isles. Z 745 2. 1863 – 8 – ne IDC [590]

THE LAND AND ITS PEOPLE – King City, CA. Oct 1956-1982; 1986 – 6r – 1 – $300.00 – B02325 – us Library Micro [071]

LAND AND LABOR / Land Nationalisation Society – (Land Nationaliser). The organ of the Land Nationalisation Society. London. - m. Nov 1889-Nov 1914, Oct 1916-Mar 1921. (4 reels) – 1 – uk British Libr Newspaper [073]

LAND AND NATIONAL DEMOCRAT – Ireland.28 Apr-9 Aug 1923 – 1 – ie Microforms [072]

LAND AND NATURAL RESOURCES DIVISION JOURNAL – (v1-3 are titled (The Lands Division Journal. This title is also available as part of LLMC's Native American Collection as Title No. 3992)) – 1963-74 (all publ?) – 58mf – 9 – $87.00 – LLMC 88-015 – us L.L.M.C. [340]

LAND AND TREE TENURE IN HUMID WEST AFRIA : A BIBLIOGRAPHY / Francis, P & Bulfeta, Getachew – 1987 – 9 – $6.00 – 92-9053-153-3 – et ILRI [333]

LAND AND WATER – London. v. 1-79. 27 Jun 1866-27 May 1905. (Scattered issues wanting) – 1 – 974.00 – us L of C Photodup [941]

LAND AND WATER LAW REVIEW – (v1-30 1966-84 on reel $350.00. v20-31 1985-96 on mf $211.00. Supersedes: Wyoming Law Journal) – University of Wyoming. v1-31. 1966-96 – 5,6,9 – $561.00 set – us Hein [340]

LAND AND WATER RESOURCES SURVEY IN THE JEBEL MARRA AREA. FINAL REPORT / Sudan. FAO – 1968 – 9 – ne IDC [333]

LAND AND WATER SURVEYS FROM THE WADI JIZAN, KINGDOM OF SAUDI ARABIA: FINAL REPORT 1966 / Saudi Arabia – BNE-6606 1 – 9 – ne IDC [333]

LAND CLAIM CASE FILES OF THE U.S. DISTRICT COURT FOR THE EASTERN DISTRICT OF LOUISIANA, 1844-1880 – 16r – 1 – M1115 – us Nat'l Archives [340]

LAND CLAIMS CASE FILE / U.S. District Courts. Eastern District of Louisiana – RG21. M1115. 13 rolls – 1 – us Nat'l Archives [340]

LAND CLASSIFICATION PROGRAM PROPOSAL FOR THE TTPI / Sahara, Tamotsu – Honolulu: Land Study Bureau of the Uni of Hawaii, dec 1967 – 1mf – 9 – $1.50 – LLMC 82-100F, Title 75 – us L.L.M.C. [980]

DAS LAND DER DEIDE UND TIBET IM LICHTE DER ANTIKE / Herrmann, A – U-525 2. 1938 – 8 – ne IDC [960]

LAND DEVELOPMENT STUDIES – v1-. 1984- – 1,5,6,9 – us UMI [333]

LAND ECONOMICS – (1971-. 5,6. 1975-. 9) – 1- 1925- – 1 – us UMI [630]

LAND EN VOLK – Pretoria. South Africa. 1891-1907 – 1 – sa State Libr [072]

LAND EVALUATION CRITERIA FOR IRRIGATION : REPORT OF AN EXPERT CONSULTATION, ROME, 1979 – 1981 – 223p – it F.A.O. [631]

LAND EVALUATION FOR FORESTRY – 1984 2nd print 1987 – 132p – it F.A.O. [333]

LAND EVALUATION GUIDELINES FOR RAINFED AGRICULTURE : REPORT OF AN EXPERT CONSULTATION, ROME, 1979 – 1980 – 122p – it F.A.O. [630]

LAND, FOOD AND PEOPLE – 1984 2nd print 1985 – 96p – it F.A.O. [370]

LAND GRANT RECORDS / Ohio – Chillicothe Land Office, 1801-1811; Cincinnati Land Office, 1801-1806; Steubenville Land Office, 1788-1812; Zanesville Land Office, 1812-1820 – 1 – us Ohio Hist [978]

LAND GRANT RECORDS / Ohio – Marietta Land Office, 1800-29 – 1 – us Ohio Hist [333]

LAND GRANTS / South Carolina – 1735-52. 77 fiches – 9 – us South Carolina Historical [978]

LAND HOLDING AND LAND USAGE AMONG THE PLATEAU TONGA OF MAZABUKA DISTRICT : A RECONNAISSANCE SURVEY, 1945 / Allan, William et al – Cape Town: OUP, 1948 – us Res Libr [333]

Land, J P N *see*
- ANECDOTA SYRIACA
- JOANNES BISCHOF VON EPHESOS

LAND, LABOR AND LIQUOR: A CHAPTER IN THE POLITICAL ECONOMY OF THE PRESENT DAY / Burgess, William – Introd. by W. H. Howland. Toronto: S. Briggs; Toronto: Willard Tract Depository, 1887. 00337. (Pre-1900 Canadiana) – 9 – cn C.I.H.M. [971]

LAND LAWS OF THE UNITED STATES, 1776-1938 – (Titles also listed individually) – 141mf – 9 – $211.00 coll – LLMC 82-101 – us L.L.M.C. [340]

LAND LAWS OF THE UNITED STATES, 1776-1938 *see*
- DECISIONS OF THE INTERIOR DEPARTMENT IN PUBLIC LAND CASES AND LAND LAWS PASSED, 1838-1870
- DIGEST OF PUBLIC LAND LAWS OF THE UNITED STATES
- GENERAL PUBLIC ACTS OF CONGRESS RESPECTING THE SALE AND DISPOSITION OF PUBLIC LANDS
- HARRIS' PUBLIC LAND GUIDE
- THE PUBLIC DOMAIN, ITS HISTORY...AND DISPOSITION TO 1880
- PUBLIC LAND LAWS OF THE UNITED STATES
- PUBLIC LAND LAWS OF THE UNITED STATES, 1869-1882
- PUBLIC LAND LAWS OF THE UNITED STATES, 1882-1890
- PUBLIC LAND STATUTES AND REGULATIONS IN FORCE JUNE 1, 1938
- PUBLIC LAND STATUTES OF THE UNITED STATES
- U.S. MINERAL LANDS

LAND MANAGEMENT CONFERENCE PROCEEDINGS / Trust Territory of the Pacific Islands (U.S.) Div of Land Management – 1st-5th conference 1966, 1967, 1969, 1970, 1971. n.p, n.d. – 29mf – 9 – $43.50 – LLMC 82-100F, Title 69 – us L.L.M.C. [980]

LAND MANAGEMENT IN TIMOR; ORIENTING NOTES / Grader, Ch. J – SE-3890 1. 1950 – 9 – ne IDC [630]

LAND MARKS OF MONROE COUNTY / Boston Historic Co – Boston, 1895. New York Reel 22. (The Cox Library Collection) – 5 – us Americana [978]

LAND MARKS OF ORLEAN COUNTY – Syracuse, D. Mason and Co., 1894. New York Reel 29. (The Cox Library Collection) – 5 – us Americana [978]

LAND MARKS OF OSWEGO COUNTY – Syracuse, D. Mason and Co., 1895. New York Reel 30. (The Cox Library Collection) – 5 – us Americana [978]

LAND MARKS OF RENSSELAER COUNTY / Anderson, George B – Syracuse, D. Mason and Co., 1897. New York Reel 31. (The Cox Library Collection) – 5 – us Americana [978]

LAND MARKS OF STUEBEN COUNTY / Hakes & Aldrich – Philadelphia, D. Mason and Co., 1896. New York Reel 34. (The Cox Library Collection) – 5 – us Americana [978]

LAND MARKS OF TOMPKINS COUNTY – Including a history of Cornell University. Syracuse, D. Mason and Co., 1894. New York Reel 35. (The Cox Library Collection) – 5 – us Americana [978]

LAND MARKS OF WAYNE COUNTY / Cowles & Smith – Syracuse, D. Mason and Co., 1895. New York Reel 37. (The Cox Library Collection) – 5 – us Americana [978]

Land Nationalisation Society *see* LAND AND LABOR

LAND NATIONALIZATION AND LAND TAXATION / Cox, Harold – 2nd ed., 1906. Indexed, 229p. Orig. publ. 1892 – 9 – 1.00f – at Libertarian Micro [336]

THE LAND NATIONALIZATION BILL, 1948 / Burma. Laws, Statutes, etc – Rangoon, 1948. 41 p. LL-10034 – 1 – us L of C Photodup [324]

LAND OF EXILE : CONTEMPORARY KOREAN FICTION – 1993 – 9 – 92-3-102933-9 – Co-published with M.E. Sharpe Inc., which has exclusive sales rights in the USA and Canada – fr UNESCO [480]

THE LAND OF FAIR PLAY : A TEXT-BOOK OF AMERICAN CIVICS / Parsons, Geoffrey – New York/Chicago/Boston: Charles Scribner's Sons, 1920 – 3mf – 9 – $4.50 – LLMC 92-233 – us L.L.M.C. [340]

THE LAND OF ISRAEL : A TEXT BOOK ON PHYSICAL AND HISTORICAL GEOGRAPHY OF THE HOLY LAND EMBODYING THE RESULTS OF RECENT RESEARCH / Stewart, Robert Laird – (Includes bibliographical references and index) – [2nd ed]. New York: Fleming H Revell, c1899 – 1mf – 9 – 0-8370-6396-5 – 1986-0396 – us A.T.L.A. [956]

THE LAND OF THE MIDNIGHT SUN: SUMMER AND WINTER JOURNEYS THROUGH SWEDEN, NORWAY, LAPLAND AND NORTHERN FINLAND. ..BI.NEW YORK: HARPER AND BROTHERS, 1881. 2V. ILLUS. MAP. WITH: THE GERMANS BY I.A.R. WYLIE. 1 REEL. 1260 / Du Chaillu, Paul Belloni – 1 – us U.W. Library [910]

THE LAND OF THE PEAKS AND THE PAMPAS : SOUTH AMERICA OF YESTERDAY AND TO-DAY / Page, Jesse – London: Religious Tract Society, 1913 – 1mf – us A.T.L.A. [972]

LAND OF THE PHARAOHS – 34p – 9 – 92-3-102587-2 – Co-published with Childrens Press, Chicago, who have exclusive sales rights in the USA and Canada – fr UNESCO [930]

THE LAND OF THE VEDA : BEING PERSONAL REMINISCENCES OF INDIA, ITS PEOPLE, CASTES, THUGS, AND FAKIRS, ITS RELIGIONS, MYTHOLOGY, PRINCIPAL MONUMENTS, PALACES, AND MAUSOLEUMS / Butler, William – New York: Phillips & Hunt; Cincinnati: Cranston & Stowe, c1871 – 2mf – us A.T.L.A. [950]

LAND OWNERSHIP IN MICRONESIA / Wilson, William H & Toribiong, Johnson – n.p, sep 1970 – 6mf – 9 – $9.00 – LLMC 82-100F, Title 105 – us L.L.M.C. [980]

LAND OWNERSHIP MAPS / U.S. Library of Congress. Geography and Map Division – Pre-20th century. 1449 county maps relating to 1041 counties, mostly northeast and north central states, Virginia, California and Texas. Individual maps available – 1 – 5000.00 – us L of C Photodup [910]

LAND PROBLEMS AND THEIR SOLUTION IN THE FEDERAL REPUBLIC OF GERMANY / Bohnsack, G – Georgist, 1982. 9p – 9 – 1.00f – at Libertarian Micro [335]

LAND RECORDS OF NEW MEXICO / New Mexico. State Records Center and Archives – (Includes guide and calendar) – 1685-1849 – 63r – 1 – $15.00r – us NM Archives [978]

LAND REFORM AND STRUCTURAL ADJUSTMENT IN SUB-SAHARAN AFRICA : CONTROVERSIES AND GUIDELINES – 1992 – 332p – it F.A.O. [338]

LAND REFORM IN ALGERIA / U.S. Agency for international Development – Foster, P. W. Washington, D.C. 1970. BNE-8640 1 – 9 – ne IDC [333]

LAND REFORM IN ALGERIA, TUNISIA, THE UNITED ARAB REPUBLIC / U.S. Agency for International Development – Ed. 2. 1970. Foster, P. a.o. BNE-8743 1 – 9 – ne IDC [333]

Land Rights Lobby *see* KIT: LAND RIGHTS NOW, EXTRACTS

THE LAND RIGHTS OF INDIVIDUALS AMONG THE NYAKYUSA / Wilson, G – 7 – uk Microform Academic [960]

LAND SALES, DELINQUENT TAXES / Erie County. Ohio. Auditor – 1847-1879 – 1r – 1 – $32.50r – us Archival [324]

LAND SALES RECORDS / Fulton County. Ohio. Probate Court – 1932-1969 – 7r – 1 – $32.50r – us Archival [324]

LAND SALES RECORDS / Van Wert County. Ohio. Probate Court – 1856-1910 – 9r – 1 – $32.50r – us Archival [324]

LAND SALES: SWAMP LAND / Ottawa County. Ohio. Auditor – 1854-1858 – 1r – 1 – $32.50r – us Archival [324]

LAND SERVICE BULLETIN – (Lacking: v1-9) – US Dept of the Interior. v1-17. ?-1933 (all publ?) – 39mf – 9 – $58.00 – LLMC 84-523 – us L.L.M.C. [073]

LAND SURVEYS / Huron County. Ohio. Recorder – 1828 – 1r – 1 – $32.50r – us Archival [324]

Land, T *see*
- A LETTER TO THE REV. MR. WHITEFIELD, DESIGNED TO CORRECT HIS MISTAKEN ACCOUNT OF REGENERATION, OR THE NEW BIRTH;...
- A SECOND LETTER TO THE REV. MR. WHITEFIELD UPON THE FORMER SUBJECT OF REGENERATION OR THE NEW BIRTH,...

LAND TAX COMISSIONERS FOR THE CITY OF LONDON : LAND TAX ASSESSMENTS / Guildhall Library, London – 1692-1831. 135 reels with printed guide – £5,250.00 – uk World [336]

LAND TENURE COURSEBOOK / Crocombe, Ron – Uni of the Southern Pacific Ext Services. 2v. n.d. – 4mf – 9 – $6.00 – LLMC 82-100F, Title 73 – us L.L.M.C. [980]

LAND TENURE IN THE PACIFIC : A SYMPOSIUM / Pacific Science Congress. 10th. Div of Geography – n.p, n.d. – 1mf – 9 – $1.50 – LLMC 82-100F, Title 74 – us L.L.M.C. [980]

LAND TENURE IN THE YORUBA PROVINCES / Ward-Price, Henry Lewis – Lagos, 1939 – us Res Libr [333]

LAND TENURE PATTERNS IN THE TRUST TERRITORY OF THE PACIFIC : A HANDBOOK SERIES ISSUED FROM THE OFFICE OF THE STAFF ANTHROPOLOGISTS / Trust Territory of the Pacific Islands. (U.S.) – Guam, TTPI, 1958 – 4mf – 9 – $6.00 – LLMC 82-100F Title 12 – us L.L.M.C. [324]

LAND TENURE: PROCEEDINGS OF THE INTERNATIONAL CONFERENCE ON LAND TENURE AND RELATED PROBLEMS IN WORLD AGRICULTURE, HELD AT MADISON, WISCONSIN, 1951 / University of Wisconsin. Conference on World Land Tenure Problem; ed by Kenneth, H – Parsons – 1 – us U.W. Library [340]

LAND TENURE SYSTEMS AND FOREST POLICY – 1987 – 82p – it F.A.O. [333]

LAND TRANSFER REFORM: PROCEEDINGS OF A PUBLIC MEETING HELD IN...TORONTO, ON 12TH FEBRUARY, 1890 / Canada Land Law Amendment Association – Toronto: The Association, 1890. 00420. (Pre-1900 Canadiana) – 9 – cn C.I.H.M. [971]

DAS LAND UND DIE WELT – Muenchen. 136 docs. 1984-1991 – 34mf – 9 – ne IDC [320]

LAND UND FRAU – Berlin, apr 7 1917-jul 19 1919 – 1r – 1 – uk British Libr Newspaper [305]

LAND UND MEER – London, UK. Zeitung der Hamburg-Amerika Linie. 2 Jan 1906-10 Aug 1909 – 1 – uk British Libr Newspaper [072]

LAND- UND STADT-ZEITUNG – Coburg, Germany. Apr 1848-49; 22 Nov 1850 – 1r – 1 – gw Mikrofilm [072]
DIE LAND- UND SUESSWASSER-MOLLUSKEN VON JAVA / Mousson, J R A – Zuerich, 1849. iv/126p, 22 pls. – 4mf – 9 – ne IDC [590]
LAND USE – it F.A.O. [333]
LAND USE LAW AND ZONING DIGEST *see* ZONING DIGEST
LAND USE PLANNING APPLICATIONS : PROCEEDINGS OF THE FAO EXPERT CONSULTATION; ROME, 1990 – 1992 – 212p – it F.A.O. [333]
LAND UTILIZATION AND CROP PRODUCTION ESTIMATES FOR CYRENAICA 1956/1957 / Libya. Provincial Government of Cyrenaica. Statistics Division – Nazarat of Agriculture and Forests. BNE-1024 1 – 9 – ne IDC [310]
THE LAND WE LIVE IN – Sherbrooke, Canada. v1 n5. mai 1888-v4 n12. jul 1892 – 1r – 1 – Can$30.00 – cn Can Microfilming [073]
Landais, N *see* GRAND DICTIONNAIRE GENERAL ET GRAMMATICAL DES DICTIONNAIRES FRANCAIS
DER LANDARZT – Augsburg, 1794 – 1 – Dist. gw Mikrofilm – gw Misc Inst [610]
Landau, J L *see*
- DON ISAAC ABARBANEL
- NEGINOT

Landau, Katia *see* LE STALINISME EN ESPAGNE; TEMOIGNAGES DE MILITANTS REVOLUTIONNAIRES SAUVES DES PRISONS STALINIENNES
Landau, L *see* UNE COMMUNAUTE D'ORIGINE YEMENITE EN ISRAEL
Landau, Paul *see* KARL VON HOLTEIS ROMANE
Landau, Wilh, Freiherr von *see* BEITRAEGE ZUR ALTERTUMSKUNDE DES ORIENTS
Landauer, Kathleen *see* TROPICAL HOME GARDENS
LAND-BASED NAVY AND MARINE CORPS AIRCRAFT ACTION REPORTS, 1944-45 – 1993 – 36r – 1 – $828.00 set in US $30.00r outside – M1720 – us Nat'l Archives [355]
DER LANDBOTE – Krumau (Ceskij Krumlov), Czechoslovakia. 16 Okt 1928-3 Aug 1933 – 4r – 1 – gw Mikrofilm [072]
LANDBRUG OG BEBYGGELSE – 1956 – 1 – us I.U. Libraries [390]
Lander, Gerry *see* NEUTRON NEWS
Lander, John *see*
- JOURNAL D'UNE EXPEDITION ENTREPRISE DANS LE BUT D'EXPLORER LE COURS ET L'EMBOUCHURE DU NIGER
- JOURNAL OF AN EXPEDITION TO EXPLORE THE COURSE AND TERMINATION OF THE NIGER

Lander, Richard *see*
- CAPTAIN CLAPPERTON'S LAST EXPEDITION TO AFRICA
- JOURNAL D'UNE EXPEDITION ENTREPRISE DANS LE BUT D'EXPLORER LE COURS ET L'EMBOUCHURE DU NIGER
- JOURNAL OF AN EXPEDITION TO EXPLORE THE COURSE AND TERMINATION OF THE NIGER
- JOURNAL OF THE NIGER
- RECORDS OF CAPTAIN CLAPPERTON'S LAST EXPEDITION TO AFRICA. WITH SUBSEQUENT ADVENTURES OF THE AUTHOR

Landerer, Maximilian Albert *see* NEUESTE DOGMENGESCHICHTE
Landers, Susan K A *see* UNDERGRADUATE STUDENTS' PERCEIVED REASONS FOR SELECTION OF HEALTH PROMOTION AS A MAJOR
Landes. France (Department) *see* DESCRIPTION ABREGEE DU DEPARTEMENT DES LANDES
Landes, R *see* THE OJIBWA WOMAN
Landesen, Wera von *see*
- DIE ROTE KERZE
- DIE SONATE VON GRIEG

DIE LANDESKIRCHE – Bordesholm, oct 3 1920-dec 28 1924 – 1 – Inquire at Mikrofilmarchiv for details – gw Misc Inst [240]
LANDESKIRCHLICHEN VEREINIGUNG DER FREUNDE DER POSITIVE UNION : KIRCHLICHE MONATSSCHRIFT – (Lacks: v16-20 no 3) – v1-31. 1904-35 – 9r – 1 – ATLA S0061 – us A.T.L.A. [073]
DIE LANDESKULTURGESETZGEBUNG, DEREN AUSFUHRUNG UND ERFOLGE IM GROSSHERZOGTHUM POSEN / Klebs, J – Berlin, 1860 – 1 – DM30.00 – gw Mikro Press [943]
LANDESKUNDE VON TUWA / Leimbach, W – (Petermans Mitteilungen, Ergaenzungsheft nr. 222). Gotha. 1936. BU-330 2 – 8 – ne IDC [306]
LANDESPOST – Fuenfkirchen (Pecs), Hungary. 27 Feb 1927-25 Dec 1935 – 3r – 1 – gw Mikrofilm [072]
LANDESS FREE PRESS – Battle Mountain, NV. 1881-82 – 1r – 1 – $50.00 – U04409 – us Library Micro [071]
LANDESZEITUNG – (Cont by: Schweriner Volkszeitung, aug 14 1952) – Schwerin, apr 10 1946-aug 14 1952 – 9r – 1 – gw Mikrofilm [072]
LANDESZEITUNG – Schwerin, 1946-47 – 2r – 1 – DM150.00 – gw Mikro Press [072]
LANDESZEITUNG *see* SCHWERINER VOLKSZEITUNG
LANDESZEITUNG FUER DIE LUENEBURGER HEIDE – Lueneburg, West Germany. 1969- – ca 7r per yr – 1 – gw Mikrofilm [072]
DIE LANDGEMEINDEN DES KREISES LOETZEN : EIN BEITRAG ZUR BESIEDLUNG, BEVOELKERUNGSENTWICKLUNG UND WIRTSCHAFTSGESCHICHTE VOM 14. JAHRHUNDERT BIS 1945 / Meyhoefer, Max – (Includes bibliographical references) – Wuerzburg: Holzner, 1966 – 10r – 1 – us U.W. Library [910]
DIE LANDGEMEINDEN DES KREISES ORTELSBURG : EIN BEITRAG ZUR BESIEDLUNG, BEVOELKERUNGSENTWICKLUNG UND WIRTSCHAFTSGESCHICHTE VOM 14. JAHRHUNDERT BIS 1945 / Meyhoefer, Max – (Includes bibliographical references) – Wuerzburg: Holzner Verlag, 1967 – 1 – us U.W. Library [910]
LANDGEWINNUNGSARBEITEN IM BEREICH DER HALLIGEN AN DER SCHLESWIGSCHEN WEST KUESTE UND IHRE WIRTSCHAFTLICHE BEDEUTUNG / Bolten, Carl – Kiel, 1921 – 1 – DM30.00 – gw Mikro Press [333]
Landgraf, Arthur M *see*
- COMMENTARIUS PORRETANUS IN PRIMAM EPISTOLAM AD CORINTHIOS 1945 STUDI E TESTI 117
- EINFUEHRUNG IN DIE GESCHICHTE DER THEOLOGISCHEN LITERATUR DER FRUEHSCHOLASTIK

LANDGRAF PHILIPP VON HESSEN : M. BUTZERS BEDEUTUNG FUER DAS KIRCHLICHE LEBEN IN HESSEN: VORTRAEGE / Egelhaaf, Gottlob & Diehl Wilhelm – Halle a.S.: Verein fuer Reformationsgeschichte, 1904 (Schriften fuer Reformationsgeschichte; 22. Jahrg., Schrift 83) – 1mf – us A.T.L.A. [240]
Landis, Abb *see* DIGEST OF STATE LAWS REGULATING FRATERNAL BENEFICIARY SOCIETIES
Landis, James McCauley *see* CASES ON LABOR LAW.
DER LANDKREIS SAMLAND : EIN HEIMATBUCH DER EHEMALIGEN LANDKREISE KOENIGSBERG UND FISCHHAUSEN / ed by Gusovius, Paul – (Includes bibliographical references and index) – Wuerzburg: Holzner Verlag, 1966 – 1 – us U.W. Library [910]
Landle, K M *see* A SUBMAXIMAL TREADMILL WALKING PROTOCOL FOR PREDICTING MAXIMAL OXYGEN CONSUMPTION
LANDLESSNESS : A GROWING PROBLEM / Sinha, Radha – 1984 – 112p – it F.A.O. [333]
LANDLORD AND TENANT LAWS OF TEXAS / Hunt, Horace Washington – Bonham, Tex.: Bonham News, 1919. 56p. LL-361 – 1 – us L of C Photodup [340]
Landmann, Bernhard *see* PHYSIKALISCHE CHARAKTERISIERUNG DES GENOMS THERMOPHILER CLOSTRIDIEN MIT HILFE DER PULSED-FIELD AGAROSE GEL ELECTROPHORESIS
LANDMARK – Statesville. N.C. 1874-1876; 1880-1954 – 1 – us UMI [071]
THE LANDMARK – Montreal: J T Henderson, [1875-18–] – 9 – cn C.I.H.M. [971]
LANDMARK BANNER AND CHEROKEE BAPTIST – Atlanta and Augusta. Georgia. Oct 1859-65 – 1 – 24.57 – us Baptist [240]
LANDMARKS IN AMERICAN STAGE DESIGN – (Lists 78 productions) – 94mf – 9 – £445.00 – uk Chadwyck [790]
LANDMARKS IN CHRISTIAN HISTORY / Rowe, Henry Kalloch – New York: Scribner, c1911 – 1mf – us A.T.L.A. [240]
LANDMARKS IN HISTORY – 15-25 Jul 1969 – 1 – us UMI [380]
LANDMARKS IN THE HISTORY OF THE WELSH CHURCH / Edwards, Alfred George – London: John Murray, 1912 – 1mf – us A.T.L.A. [240]
LANDMARKS OF A LAWYER'S LIFETIME / Strong, Theron George – New York, Dodd, Mead, 1914. 552 p. LL-368 – 1 – us L of C Photodup [340]
LANDMARKS OF ALBANY COUNTY / Parker, Amasa J – Syracuse, D. Mason and Co., 1897. New York Reel 8. (The Cox Library Collection) – 5 – us Americana [978]
LANDMARKS OF NEW TESTAMENT MORALITY / Matheson, George – London: James Nisbet, 1888 – 1mf – 9 – 0-8370-4309-3 – 1985-2309 – us A.T.L.A. [230]
LANDMARKS OF SCIENCE – A comprehensive collection of the source materials in the history of science, comprising the significant contributions to the advancement of science and technology of the 15th$19th centuries – 3 – us Readex [500]
LANDMARKS OF SCIENCE – Catalog information cards. First set – 3 – us Readex [500]
LANDMARKS OF SCIENCE 2 – A continuation and extension of LANDMARKS OF SCIENCE. Journals and Monographs. Free catalog information cards. 12 segments – 3,9 – us Readex [500]
LANDMARKS OF THE DECCAN. A COMPREHENSIVE GUIDE TO THE ARCHAEOLOGICAL REMAINS / Syed Ali Asgar Bilgrami, A – Hyderabad, Deccan, 1927, 8, 226 pp., ills. BI-1045 2 – 8 – ne IDC [930]
DIE LAND-MOLUSKEN VON CELEBES / Sarasin, P B & Sarasin, C F – Wiesbaden, 1899 – 11mf – 9 – Z-764/2 – ne IDC [590]
LANDNUTZUNG UND WALDMERKMALE IN OSTTHUERINGEN : METHODEN UND GRENZEN DER DIGITALEN AUSWERTUNG VON SATELLITENDATEN / Weissflog, Gotthard – 1994 – 2mf – DM80.00 – 3-89349-896-6 – gw Hänsel [630]
Landolphe *see* MEMOIRES DU CAPITAINE LANDOLPHE, CONTENANT L'HISTOIRE DE SES VOYAGES PENDANT TRENTE-SIX ANS, AUX COTES D'AFRIQUE ET AUX DEUX AMERIQUES
Landon, Edward H *see* A MANUAL OF COUNCILS OF THE HOLY CATHOLIC CHURCH
Landon, Harry F *see* THE NORTH COUNTRY, A HISTORY OF JEFFERSON, ST LAWRENCE, OSWEGO, LEWIS AND FRANKLIN COUNTIES
Landon, Melville D *see* WIT AND HUMOR OF THE AGE
Landon, R B *see* DIARY AND LETTERS
Landor, Walter Savage *see*
- ANTONY AND OCTAVIUS
- CITATION AND EXAMINATION OF WILLIAM SHAKESPEARE, EUSEBY TREEN, JOSEPH CARNABY, AND SILAS GOUGH, CLERK.
- HEROIC IDYLS
- THE LAST FRUIT OFF AN OLD TREE
- POEMATA ET INSCRIPTIONES
- THE POEMS OF WALTER SAVAGE LANDOR

THE LANDOWNERS OF IRELAND / Hussey de Burgh, U H – 1878. 6 fiches – 9 – ie Microforms [941]
LANDOWNERS OF IRELAND 1878 / Hussey de Burgh, U H – 6 microfiche – Ir£5.00 – ie Microforms [333]
LAND-REFORM IN INDONESIA AND BASIC REGULATIONS GOVERNING THIS / Indonesia. Laws, Statutes, etc – SE-3255 1. 1961 – 9 – ne IDC [340]
Landreth, Lucius Scott *see* A BRIEF ANALYSIS OF SALE
Landrin *see* POTPOURRI FRANCOIS DE CONTRE-DANSE ANCIENNE
Landriot, Monseigneur, Archbishop of Rheims *see* THE VALIANT WOMAN
LANDRUM FIRST BAPTIST CHURCH. LANDRUM, SOUTH CAROLINA : CHURCH RECORDS – 1835-71, 1896-1950, 1954-72 – 1 – 41.09 – us Baptist [240]
Landrum, J BO *see* SPARTANBURG COUNTY
Landrum, John W *see* SERMON OUTLINES
Landry, Adolphe *see* PRINCIPES DE MORALE RATIONNELLE
THE LANDS DIVISION JOURNAL *see* LAND AND NATURAL RESOURCES DIVISION JOURNAL
LANDS FOR SALE, IN THE EASTERN TOWNSHIPS OF LOWER CANADA / British American Land Company – [London, England]: [the Company], [1835 ?]. SEM105P1401 – 1mf – 9 – Can$2.25 – cn Bibl Nat [333]
LANDS OF PLENTY: BRITISH NORTH AMERICA FOR HEALTH, SPORT AND PROFIT: A BOOK FOR ALL TRAVELLERS AND SETTLERS / Hall, Edward Hepple – Toronto: J. Campbell, 1879. 05336. (Pre-1900 Canadiana) – 9 – cn C.I.H.M. [971]
LANDS OF THE SLAVE AND THE FREE : OR, CUBA, THE UNITED STATES, AND CANADA / Murray, Henry Anthony – London. 2v. 1855 – 1r – 1 – us Ross [970]
Landsberg, Hans *see* OTTO ERICH HARTLEBEN
Landsberger, B *see* DER KULTISCHE KALENDER DER BABYLONIER UND ASSYRER
Landsberger, J *see* IGGERETH BAALE CHAJJIM
LANDSBERGER LAGER-CAJTUNG = LANDSBERG CAMP JOURNAL – (Yiddish in Latin characters) – Landsberg, DE. v1 no10. 14 Dec 1945 – 1r – 1 – $25.00 – cn Can Microfilming [072]
LANDSBERGER TAGBLATT : BA DER AUGSBURGER ALLGEMEINEN – Landsberg-Lech, West Germany. 1977- – ca 8r per yr – 1 – gw Mikrofilm [072]
LANDSBOROUGH TIMES – 1867. On Reel SAM AA (St. Arnaud Mercury 1864). LT1 – 1r – 1 – at Corangamite [072]
LANDSCAPE IN POETRY FROM HOMER TO TENNYSON : WITH MANY ILLUSTRATIVE EXAMPLES / Palgrave, Francis Turner – London, New York: Macmillan and Co., 1897 – 1 roll – 1 – 1-55879-593-6 – uk Libr Preservation [420]
LANDSCAPE INDUSTRY – (v20-. 1975-. 5,6. v21-. 1976-. 9) – 1955- – 1 – us UMI [631]
LANDSCAPE JOURNAL – v1-. 1982- – 1,5,6,9 – us UMI [073]
LANDSCAPE PAINTING : SUBJECT COLLECTIONS – (Individual titles not listed separately) – 41 catalogues on 53mf – 9 – £390.00 – uk Chadwyck [750]
LANDSCAPE PLANNING – v1-11. 1974-84 – 1,5,6,13 – sz Elsevier [073]
DIE LANDSCHAFT BEI TIECK UND IHRE HISTORISCHEN VORAUSSETZUNGEN / Donat, Walter FW K – (Includes bibliographical references) – Frankfurt am Main: M Diesterweg, 1925 – 1r – 1 – us U.W. Library [430]
Landsheere, G de *see* EMPIRICAL RESEARCH IN EDUCATION
LANDSHUTER ZEITUNG – Landshut, West Germany. 1977- – ca 12r per yr – 1 – gw Mikrofilm [072]
Landshuth, L E *see* AMMUDEI HA-AVODAH
LANDSKAB – v.62-. 1981- – 1,5,6,9 – us UMI [740]
LANDSKAP – (v.60-. 1979- 5,6,9) – v.5-. 1969-. Superseded by Landskab – 1 – us UMI [740]
LANDSKRONAPOSTEN – Landskrona, 1896-1952 – 41r – 1 – sw Kungliga [072]
LANDSKRONAPOSTEN *see*
- NORDVASTRA SKANES TIDNINGAR ENGELHOLMS OCH KLIPPANS TIDNING HOGANAS TIDNING ORESUNDSPOSTEN
- NORDVASTRA SKANES TIDNINGAR ENGELHOLMS TIDNING
- NORDVASTRA SKANES TIDNINGAR ENGELHOLMS TIDNING OCH KLIPPANS TIDNING

LANDSKRONER ZEITUNG – Landskron (Lanskroun), Germany. 4 Okt 1924-16 Okt 1938 – 5r – 1 – gw Mikrofilm [072]
LANDSLAYT = COMPATRIOTS – (In Yiddish) – New York City, NY. v1 no1 Jan 1947-v2 no4 May 1948 – 1r – 1 – $30.00 – cn Can Microfilming [071]
LANDSLIDE HAZARD ZONATION : A REVIEW OF PRINCIPLES AND PRACTICE / Varnes, David J – 1984 – 64p – 9 – 92-3-101895-7 – fr UNESCO [360]
Landsorganisationen i Sverige *see* NEWS OF THE SWEDISH TRADE UNION CONFEDERATION
DER LANDSTRASSE VERSCHWOREN : JOHANN GOTTFRIED SEUME / Mueller-Burbach, Heinrich – Berlin: Ruetten & Loening, 1957 – 1r – 1 – us U.W. Library [920]
LANDSTREICHER – (Figaro's Chronik. 3 Jan 1891-27 May 1893; Londoner Figaro-Chronik. 3 Jun 1893-28 Apr 1894. Londoner General-Anzeiger. 5 May 1894-16 Sept 1914) – London, UK. 7 Sept 1889-27 Dec 1890 – 1 – uk British Libr Newspaper [072]
Landtsperger, J *see*
- AIN CHRISTLICHE VNDERRICHTUNG
- AIN GRUENDTLICHER BERICHT VOM CHRISTLICHEN TAUFF

- EIN KURTZE ERINNERUNG ETLICHER GSCHRIFFT DAR AUSZ MAN DEN KINDERTAUFF
LANDWARDS *see* AGRICULTURAL ENGINEER
LANDWIRTSCHAFTLICE WOCHENSCHRIFT FUER DIE PROVINZ SACHSEN *see* ZEITSCHRIFT DES LANDWIRTSCHAFTLICHEN CENTRALVEREINS DER PROVINZ SACHSEN
LANDWIRTSCHAFTLICHE GESETZGEBUNG DES BUNDES / Switzerland. Laws, Statutes, etc – Zurich, Orell, Fussli, 1895. 168 p. LL-4006 – 1 – us L of C Photodup [340]
LANDWIRTSCHAFTLICHES WOCHENBLATT – Munich. DE. 28 Aug 1948-11 Jan 1964 – 32r – 1 – uk British Libr Newspaper [630]
LANDWORKER – 1978-. Incomplete. -m. Continues: Land Worker. London: The Landworker Publishing Co. Ltd – 1 – us U.W. Library [630]
Lane, A *see*
- A KEY TO THE ART OF LETTERS; OR, ENGLISH A LEARNED LANGUAGE, FULL OF ART, ELEGANCY AND VARIETY
- A RATIONAL AND SPEEDY METHOD OF ATTAINING TO THE LATIN TONGUE
Lane, Arthur *see* GREEK POTTERY
LANE COUNTY BEE – Mapleton OR. Dec 28 1934-Feb 15 1935 – 1 – us U.O. Library [071]
LANE COUNTY CITIZEN – Eugene OR. May 9 1900-Mar 23 1901 – 1 – us U.O. Library [071]
LANE COUNTY FUN GUIDE – Springfield OR. Apr 1964 – 1 – us U.O. Library [071]
LANE COUNTY GAZETTE – California. Kan. 1880-82 – 1 – us UMI [071]
LANE COUNTY HERALD – Dighton. Kan. 1885-92 – 1 – us UMI [071]
LANE COUNTY JOURNAL – Dighton. Kan. 1897-1911 – 1 – us UMI [071]
LANE COUNTY STAR – Springfield OR. May-June 1943 – 1 – us U.O. Library [071]
Lane, Henry Higgins *see* EVOLUTION AND CHRISTIAN FAITH
Lane, Samuel A *see* FIFTY YEARS AND OVER, AKRON AND SUMMIT COUNTY
Lane, Thomas *see*
- THE STUDENT'S GUIDE
- THE STUDENT'S GUIDE THROUGH LINCOLN'S INN
Lane, Tidence *see* COLLECTION OF DATA, 1784-1840
Lane, W C *see* A(MERICAN) L(IBRARY) A(SSOCIATION) PORTRAIT INDEX
Laneham, Robert *see* A LETTER: WHEARIN, PART OF THE ENTERTAINMENT UNTOO THE QUEENZ MAIESTY AT KILLINGWOORTH CASTLE IZ SIGNIFIED
Lane-Poole, Stanley *see*
- CATALOGUE OF ORIENTAL COINS IN THE BRITISH MUSEUM
- THE STORY OF TURKEY
LANESBORO 1765-1895 – (Mf 1-2: Town Records 1765-1816. Mf 3-5: B,M,D 1752-1858. Mf 6-8: B,M,D 1843-58. Mf 9: Births 1859-69. Mf 10: Births 1870-79. Mf 11: Births 1879-90. Mf 12: Births 1891-97; Marriages 1859-70; Mf 13: Marriages 1872-95. Mf 14: Marriages 1896-97; Deaths 1859-75. Mf 15: Deaths 1876-92. Mf 16: Deaths 1893-97. Mf 17-20: Marriage Intentions 1860-1948) – (mf ed 1983) – 20mf – 9 – us Holbrook [920]
THE LANEY TOWER – Oakland, CA: Lane College, 1965-76 – 1r – 1 – $50.00 – B02548 – us Library Micro [370]
Lanford, Lanny *see* THE LAST COMMANDMENT: A MUSICAL INTERPRETATION OF THE GREAT COMMISSION OF JESUS CHRIST
Lanfranc *see* A MOST EXCELLENT AND LEARNED WOORKE OF CHIRURGERIE
Lanfranco, G M *see* SCINTILLE DI MUSICA
Lang, Andrew *see*
- ADVENTURES AMONG BOOKS
- BALLADES AND VERSES VAIN
- ESSAYS IN LITTLE
- JOHN KNOX AND THE REFORMATION
- LETTERS ON LITERATURE
- THE LIFE AND LETTERS OF JOHN GIBSON LOCKHART FROM ABBOTSFORD AND MILTON LOCKHART AND OTHER ORIGINAL SOURCES
- LIFE, LETTERS, AND DIARIES OF SIR STAFFORD NORTHCOTE, FIRST EARL OF IDDESLEIGH
Lang, August *see*
- DIE BEDEUTUNG DER REFORMIERTEN THEOLOGIE FUER DIE RELIGIOESE LAGE DER GEGENWART
- DIE BEKEHRUNG JOHANNES CALVINS
- DER HEIDELBERGER KATECHISMUS
- JOHANNES CALVIN
- DIE REFORMATION UND DAS NATURRECHT
- ZWEI CALVIN-VORTRAEGE
- ZWINGLI UND CALVIN
Lang, Charles J *see*
- WHO'S WHO IN LOS ANGELES, 1924
- WHO'S WHO IN LOS ANGELES, 1925-1926
- WHO'S WHO IN LOS ANGELES, 1926-1927
- WHO'S WHO IN LOS ANGELES, 1927-1928
- WHO'S WHO IN LOS ANGELES, 1928-1929
- WHO'S WHO IN LOS ANGELES, 1930-1931
Lang, Cosmo Gordon *see* THE MIRACLES OF JESUS AS MARKS ON THE WAY OF LIFE
Lang, H *see* DAS LEBEN JESU UND DIE KIRCHE DER ZUKUNFT
Lang, Hartmut *see* DIE BEREDSAMKEIT J. ENOCH POWELLS
Lang, John Dunmore *see* RELIGION AND EDUCATION IN AMERICA
Lang, John Marshall *see* THE EXPANSION OF THE CHRISTIAN LIFE
Lang, Ludwig *see* UHLANDS DRAMATISCHE ARBEITSWEISE IN SEINEN HISTORISCHEN DRAMEN UND DRAMENENTWUERFEN
Lang, W *see* HISTORY OF SENECA COUNTY FROM THE CLOSE OF THE REVOLUTIONARY WAR TO JULY, 1880
Lang, Wilhelm *see* GOTTLOB DAVID HARTMANN
LANGAGES – Dir. Henri Didier. no. 1-28. Paris. mars 1966-72 – 5 – fr A.C.R.P.P. [073]
Langans, F *see* SLOVAR' IURIDICHESKII, ILI SVOD ROSSIISKIKH UZAKONENII, PO AZBUCHNOMU PORIADKU DLIA PRAKTICHESKOGO UPOTREBLENIIA IMP. MOSKOVSKOGO UNIVERSITETA V IURIDICHESKOM FAKUL'TETE
THE LANGASTR ORGUS *see* THE LANCASTER ARGUS
Langbein, August Friedrich Ernst *see* AFE LANGBEIN'S SAEMMTLICHE GEDICHTE
Langbein, Bernhard Adolf *see* DER CHRISTLICHE GLAUBE
Langbein, George Frederick *see* THE LAW AND PRACTICE OF THE MUNICIPAL COURT OF THE CITY OF NEW YORK UNDER THE GREATER NEW YORK CHARTER.
LANG-CH'IUNG HSIEN-CHIH – 1842, 10, 1. BCH-673 2 – 8 – ne IDC [950]
Langdell, Christopher Columbus *see*
- A BRIEF SURVEY OF EQUITY JURISDICTION.
- A SELECTION OF CASES ON THE LAW OF CONTRACTS, WITH A SUMMARY OF THE TOPICS COVERED BY THE CASES
- A SUMMARY OF EQUITY PLEADING
LANGDON CHEVES PAPERS / Cheves, Langdon, 1st – 202 fiches. Includes index and calendar – 9 – $1.50f – us South Carolina Historical [920]
Langdon, S *see*
- BABYLONIAN LITURGIES
- DIE NEUBABYLONISCHEN KOENIGSINSCHRIFTEN
- SUMERIAN AND BABYLONIAN PSALMS
- SUMERIAN LITURGICAL TEXTS
Langdon, Stephen *see* LA SYNTAXE DU VERBE SUMERIEN
Langdon, W B *see*
- A DESCRIPTIVE CATALOGUE OF THE CHINESE COLLECTION, NOW EXHIBITING AT ST GEORGE'S PLACE, HYDE PARK CORNER, LONDON,...
- TEN THOUSAND THINGS RELATING TO CHINA AND THE CHINESE
Langdon-Davies, John *see*
- THE CASE FOR THE GOVERNMENT
- THE SPANISH CHURCH AND POLITICS
Lange *see* HISTOIRE DE LA FILLE MALEFICIEE DE COURSON
Lange, Adolf *see* UEBER DIE SPRACHE DER GOTTSCHEDIN IN IHREN BRIEFEN
Lange, Carl Friedrich August *see* MALER MUELLERS JUGENDSPRACHE
Lange, E *see* FRANZ GRILLPARZER
Lange, Friedrich Albert *see* HISTOIRE DU MATERIALISME ET CRITIQUE DE SON IMPORTANCE A NOTRE EPOQUE
Lange, H *see* AUSLEGUNG VON SCHRIFTABSCHNITTEN ZUM ZWECK DES HOEHEREN SCHULUNTERRICHTS
Lange, Helene *see*
- DIE FRAU (HQ 1)
- HANDBUCH DER FRAUENBEWEGUNG (HQ 26)
- HIGHER EDUCATION OF WOMEN IN EUROPE
Lange, Horst *see* ULANENPATROUILLE
Lange, J M C *see*
- DESCRIPTIO ICONIBUS ILLUSTRATA PLANTARUM NOVARUM E FLORA HISPANICA
- PRODROMUS FLORAE HISPANICAE
Lange, Johann Peter *see*
- DER BRIEF DES JAKOBUS
- BUECHER EXODUS, LEVITICUS, NUMERII
- EVANGELIUM NACH JOHANNES
- DAS EVANGELIUM NACH JOHANNES
- THE GOSPEL ACCORDING TO MATTHEW
- GRUNDRISS DER BIBLISCHEN HERMENEUTIK
- GRUNDRISS DER CHRISTLICHEN ETHIK
- GRUNDRISS DER THEOLOGISCHEN ENCYKLOPAEDIE: MIT EINSCHLUSS DER METHODOLOGIE
- VIERTE BUCH MOSIS
Lange, Karl Julius *see* DER NORDISCHE MERKUR
Lange, Konrad *see* KRIEG UND KUNST
Lange, Mariluise *see* KRISTIN
Lange, Oscar Richard *see* THE PROBLEM OF FRANCO SPAIN; STATEMENT MADE ON APRIL 17 AT THE MEETING OF THE SECURITY COUNCIL
Langedijk, Karia *see* INDEX ICONOLOGICUS, 1250-1940
Langelier, J-Francois *see* L'AVENIR
Langelier, L N *see* LA PAIX
Langen, Albrecht *see* DIE HAFTUNG DES HERRSCHENDEN UNTERNEHMENS FUR VERBINDLICHKEITEN DER ABHANGIGEN GESELLSCHAFT BEI EINEM MULTINATIONALEN UNTERNEHMEN
Langen, Joachim *see*
- JOHANN ARNDTS VIER BUECHER VOM WAHREN CHRISTENTHUM AUFS NEUE AUSGEFERTIGET VON JOACHIM LANGEN
- EYN SERMON VONN MENSCHLICHER SACHWACHEIT
Langen, Joseph *see*
- JOHANNES VON DAMASKUS
- DIE KIRCHENVAETER UND DAS NEUE TESTAMENT
- DIE KLEMENSROMANE
- DIE TRINITARISCHE LEHRDIFFERENZ ZWISCHEN DER ABENDLAENDISCHEN UND DER MORGENLAENDISCHEN KIRCHE
Langen, Martin *see* GEBEN UND NEHMEN
Langenbahn, Hans-Juergen *see* DIE MATERIELLE KULTUR DER INGESSANA (REP. SUDAN)
LANGENBECKS ARCHIV FUER CHIRURGIE – v260-353. 1948-80 – 1,5,9 – 9800.00 – us UMI [617]
Langenbucher, Erich *see* EHE DIE SPUR SICH VERLIERT
Langenbucher, Hellmuth *see*
- ES KLINGT WIE EINE SAGE
- REITER IM KRIEG
- VON JUNGER LIEBE, LUST UND LEID
Langendorfer, Stephen *see* DEVELOPMENTAL RELATIONSHIPS BETWEEN THROWING AND STRIKING: A PRE-LONGITUDINAL TEST OF MOTOR STAGE THEORY
Langenhan, F *see* OPHTALMOTONOMETRIE
Langenmantel, E H *see* DISZ IST AIN ANZAYG:. DES SACRAMENT VND ANNDERS BETREFFEND
Langenscheidt, Paul *see* THIRTEEN NOVELS
Langer, Anton *see*
- DER HERR GEVATTER VON DER STRASSE
- DER KAISER ALS ARZT
Langer, Georg *see* DIE STRASSE DES UNRECHTS
Langeron, M *see* LE GENRE ALEURITES FOR (EUPHORBIACEES). SYSTEMATIQUE, ANATOMIE-PHARMACOLOGIE
Langerstein, Julius *see* DIE ENTVOLKERUNG DES PLATTEN LANDES IN POMMERN VON 1890-1905 UND IHRE URSACHEN
Langevin, Jean *see* COURS DE PEDAGOGIE, OU PRINCIPE D'EDUCATION
Langewiesche, Karl Robert *see* GOETHE
Langewiesche, Marianne *see* DIE DAME IN SCHWARZ
Langewiesche, Wilhelm *see* GOETHE
Langford, Ella Molloy *see* HISTORY OF JOHNSON COUNTY, ARKANSAS
Langford, John Alfred *see* RELIGIOUS SCEPTICISM AND INFIDELITY
LANGFRISTIGES INVESTITIONSPROGRAMM DES BUNDES / Austria – Wien. 1954 – 9 – ne IDC [330]
Langgaesser, Elisabeth *see* DAS UNAUSLOESCHLICHE SIEGEL
Langham, E James *see* A PROGRAM OF VISITATION FOR A CHURCH IN A SUBURBAN METROPOLIS
Langhorne, J *see* LETTERS ON RELIGIOUS RETIREMENT, MELANCHOLY AND ENTHUSIASM
Langill, Robert H *see* PREDICTION OF TRIATHLON PERFORMANCE FROM VENTILATORY THRESHOLD MEASUREMENTS
LANGKAH KE ATOERAN. BOEKOE SOERAT MENJOERAT DAN PIDATO-PIDATO DALAM BAHASA INDONESIA. TJETAKAN JANG KEDOEA / Rasad, BZ – (Microfiche Nos 145-146) – Djakarta: Poespa-Sari (2602) – 2mf – 9 – SE-2002/1 – ne IDC [950]
LANGLADE COUNTY SPECIAL – Antigo. Wis. 1891-1896 – 1 – us UMI [071]
Langle, H F M *see*
- TRAITE DE LA BASSE SOUS LE CHANT
- TRAITE D'HARMONIE ET DE MODULATION
Langles, L *see* ALPHABET MANTCHOU, REDIGE D'APRES LE SYLLABAIRE ET LE DICTIONNAIRE UNIVERSEL DE CETTE LANGUE
LANGLEY ADVANCE – British Columbia, CN. Jul 1931- – 2r per yr – 1 – Can$55.00r – cn Commonwealth Micro [072]
Langley, David Jet al *see* STUDENT COGNITION DURING MOTOR SKILL LEARNING
LANGLEY FIRST BAPTIST CHURCH. LANGLEY, SOUTH CAROLINA : CHURCH RECORDS – 1927-67 – 1 – 10.80 – us Baptist [240]
Langley, Thelma *see* BAPTIST FAMILY IN GLOBAL VILLAGE
Langlois, A *see* L'OUVRIER
Langlois, CV *see* INTRODUCTION TO THE STUDY OF HISTORY
Langlois, G E et al *see* LE CLAIRON
Langlois, Marguerite *see* LA BIBLIOTHEQUE MEDICALE DE L'HOTEL-DIEU DE QUEBEC, 17-18-19E SIECLES
Langmann, Philipp *see* DIE HERZMARKE
Langmesser, August *see* CONRAD FERDINAND MEYER UND JULIUS RODENBERG
LANGMUIR – v1- 1985- – 1,5,6,9 – us A.C.S. [073]
Langner, Erwin *see* DIE RELIGION GERHART HAUPTMANNS
LA LANGOSTA Y LAS ROTUACIONES / Moreno Marquez, Victor – Madrid: Estacion de Fitopatologia Agricola, 1940. Publicacion no 5 del Servicio de Lucha contra la langosta – 1 – sp Bibl Santa Ana [946]
LA LANGOUSTE DES ILES ST PAUL ET AMSTERDAM (JASUS PAULENSIS, HELLER 1862). BIOLOGIE ET PECHE / Duhamel, Georges – 9 – F50.00 – fr Ethnologie [590]
Langridge, Albert Kent *see* JOHN G. PATON
Langrod, G *see* LA SCIENCE ET L'ENSEIGNEMENT DE L'ADMINISTRATION PUBLIQUE AUX ETATS-UNIS
Langsdorff *see* PLANTES RECUILLIES PENDANT LE VOYAGE DES RUSSES AUTOUR DU MONDE
Langstaff, Annie Macdonald *see* FRENCH-ENGLISH, ENGLISH-FRENCH LAW DICTIONARY
LANGSTON BAPTIST CHURCH. LAURENS COUNTY. SOUTH CAROLINA : CHURCH RECORDS – 1832-99 – 1 – 28.44 – us Baptist [240]
Langston, George *see* HISTORY OF EASTLAND COUNTY
LANGSTON HUGHES COLLECTION : FROM THE HOLDINGS OF THE SCHOMBURG CENTER FOR RESEARCH IN BLACK CULTURE, MANUSCRIPTS, ARCHIVES AND RARE BOOKS DIVISION: THE NEW YORK PUBLIC LIBRARY, ASTOR, LENOX AND TILDEN FOUNDATIONS – (Guide which covers all coll under "Literature and the Arts" sold separately for $20.00 D3305.G6) – 1995 – 4r – 1 – $340.00 – D3305P18 – Dist. us Scholarly Res – us L of C Photodup [470]
LANGTIDSPROGRAMMET, 1962-1965 / Norway. Finans- og Toll departementet – (St. Meld. Nr. 60, 1960 61). Oslo. 1961. BD-202 1 – 9 – ne IDC [336]
LANGTIDSPROGRAMMET 1966-1969 / Norway. Finans- og Toll departementet – (St. Meld. Nr. 63, 1964 65). Oslo. 1965. BD-532 1 – 9 – ne IDC [336]
Langtry, John *see*
- COME HOME
- HISTORY OF THE CHURCH IN EASTERN CANADA AND NEWFOUNDLAND
LANGUAGE – Baltimore. v1-55. 1925-79 – 380mf – 9 – $5.00f – us Ross [400]
LANGUAGE AND COMMUNICATION – v1- 1981- – 5,6,9 – us UMI [400]
LANGUAGE AND SOCIETY = LANGUE ET SOCIETE – (Nos 38-41 1992 Can$60.00y 1. Ceased no 47 1994) – Ottawa. nos 1-47. 1979-94 – 9,1 – Can$20.00y – cn Micromedia [306]

LANGUAGE ARTS – (See also: Elementary English) – v52- 1975- – 1,5,6,9 – us UMI [400]

LANGUAGE COLLECTION / Bibliotheque Nationale – 7titles dealing with languages (English-Malabar, Flemish, Latin); Grammars (German); linguistic study on grammar; 3 eds. of a Latin grammar. 28 fiches. Titles available separately – 9 – 69.00 – fr Bibl Nationale [400]

LANGUAGE DISSERTATIONS – Philadelphia. v1-57. 1927-63 – 76mf – 9 – $5.00f – us Ross [400]

LANGUAGE IN SOCIETY – v1-. 1972- – 1 – us UMI [400]

LANGUAGE LEARNING – 1- 1948- 1; v21- 5,6; v25- 9 – us UMI [400]

LANGUAGE LEARNING AND COMMUNICATION – v1-3. 1982-84 – 1,5,6 – us Princeton Micro [400]

LANGUAGE MONOGRAPHS – Philadelphia. v1-27. 1925-67 – 38mf – 9 – $5.00f – us Ross [400]

THE LANGUAGE OF THE MISSISSAGA INDIANS OF SKUGOG: A CONTRIBUTION TO THE LINGUISTICS OF THE ALGONKIAN TRIBES OF CANADA / Chamberlain, Alexander Francis – Philadelphia: MacCalla & Co., 1892. 84p. Bibliog – 1 – us U.W. Library [490]

LANGUAGE PROBLEMS AND LANGUAGE PLANNING – 1980- – 1,5,6,9 – us UMI [400]

LANGUAGE, READING AND DEAFNESS / Athey, Irene & Geoffrion, Leo D & Wilson, Kirk – 1965-84. 3000 titles. 750mf. Printed card indexes included. Annual supplements – 9 – us A.T.B.I. [370]

LANGUAGE SCIENCES – (1975-77. 5,6. 1977. 9) – 1968-77 – 1 – us UMI [400]

LANGUAGE SCIENCES : AN EDUCATIONAL CHALLENGE / Bronckart, J -P – 1986 – 105p – 9 – 92-3-102332-2 – fr UNESCO [370]

LANGUAGE SCIENCES – v1- 1979- – 1,5,6,9 – us UMI [400]

LANGUAGE, SPEECH AND HEARING SERVICES IN SCHOOLS – (v.11-. 1980- 5,6,9) – v.4-. 1973- – 1 – us UMI [370]

LANGUAGE TEACHING ABSTRACTS – v.1-7. 1968-74. Continued as Language Teaching and Linguistics: Abstracts – 1 – us UMI [370]

LANGUAGE TEACHING AND LINGUISTICS: ABSTRACTS – (v.12-. 1979- 5,6,9) – v.8-. 1975- – 1 – us UMI [370]

LANGUAGE USE AMONG PUPILS IN BANDUNG, INDONESIA / Thomas, Murray – SE 5209 1. 1960? – 9 – ne IDC [490]

THE LANGUAGES OF THE NORTHERN HIMALAYAS / Bailey, T G – 1908 – 1 – uk Microform Academic [490]

LA LANGUE BISA; GRAMMAIRE ET DICTIONNAIRE / Prost, Andre – Ouagoudougou, Upper Volta. 1950 – 1 – us Res Libr [490]

LA LANGUE DES KEMANT EN ABYSSINIE / Conti Rossini, Carlo – Vienna: Commisssioned by A Holder, 1912 – us Res Libr [470]

LA LANGUE ET LA LITTERATURE HEBRAIQUES DEPUIS LA BIBLE JUSQU'A NOS JOURS / Slouschz, Nahum – Paris: E. Sansot, 1904. 1 fiche – 9 – us A.T.L.A. [470]

LA LANGUE FRANCAISE / Godard, J – 1620 – 9 – fr I.C.S. [440]

LANGUE FRANCAISE – no. 1-16. Paris. fevr 1969-72; 1985-1993 – 5 – fr A.C.R.P.P. [073]

LA LANGUE MALGACHE EN 30 FAMILLES DE MOTS : ESSAI DE REGROUPEMENT SYSTEMATIQUE DES THEMES DE LA LANGUE MALGACHE / Auber, Jacques – Tananarive, [Madagascar]: Impr officielle, 1957 – us Res Libr [470]

LA LANGUE MALGACHE ET LES ORIGINES MALGACHES-RAZAFINTSAMALA / Damantsoha – Tanararive: G. Pitot, 1928-29. 2v in 1.With: Midrash Hasirot Ve-Yiterot. 1 reel. 1251 – 1 – us U.W. Library [490]

LA LANGUE MANDE / Rambaud, J B – Paris, Imprimerie Nationale Emile Bouillon. 1896 – 9 – $5.00 – fr Orientalistes [490]

LA LANGUE MANDINGUE ET SES DIALECTES (MALINKE, BAMBARA, DIOULA) / Delafosse, Maurice – Paris: P Geuthner, 1929-55 – us Res Libr [470]

LA LANGUE SONGHAY, DIALECTE DYERMA / Ardant du Picq, Charles Pierre – Paris: Larose, 1933 – us Res Libr [470]

LANGUES MODERNES / Societe des Professeurs de Langues Vivantes – Paris, 1903-1940 – 352mf – 9 – ne IDC [400]

LES LANGUES MODERNES – Revue et bulletin de l'Association des professeurs de langues vivantes de l'enseignement public. Paris. juin 1903-mars 1940, 1945-73 – 1 – fr A.C.R.P.P. [073]

LANGUES NEO-LATINES / Societe d'etudes des Professeurs de Langues Meridionales – Bulletin. puis Bulletin de la Societe des langues neo-latines. Paris. 1936-1993 – 5 – fr A.C.R.P.P. [440]

LES LANGUES PERDUES DE LA PERSE ET DE L'ASSYRIE / Menant, Joachim – (Includes bibliographical references) – Paris: Ernest Leroux. 2v. 1885-86 – 2mf – 9 – 0-8370-8458-X – 1986-2458 – us A.T.L.A. [470]

Languet, Jean Joseph *see* CATECHISME DU DIOCESE DE SENS

Lanham, John C *see*
- MANUAL ON HOW TO DO A DIVORCE CASE IN THE MARSHALL ISLANDS TOGETHER WITH FORMS
- RULES OF APPELLATE PROCEDURE, 1983

Laniel-Le Francois, M *see* LES DANSEURS KACHINE HOPI

Laning, Jay Ford *see*
- OHIO CRIMINAL LAW AND PRACTICE; A PRACTICAL TREATISE, WITH DIRECTIONS AND FORMS
- THE OHIO LAW OF APPELLATE PROCEDURE AND THE PRACTICE INCIDENT TO APPEALS IN ALL OHIO COURTS.

Lanjuinais, J D *see* NOTICE DE L'OUVRAGE DE GREGOIRE INTITULE: DE LA LITTERATURE DES NEGRES

THE LANKASTR ORGUS – (Cont: The Lancaster Argus) – St. John, NB: New Brunswick Insane Asylum, [1892 or 1893-189- or 19–] – 9 – cn C.I.H.M. [360]

Lankester, E R *see* A MONOGRAPH OF THE FISHES OF THE OLD RED SANDSTONE OF BRITAIN

Lankey, Lori L *see* THE RELATIONSHIP BETWEEN PERSONALITY TYPE PREFERNCES AND LEVELS OF COPING RESOURCES AMONG CARDIAC REHABILITATION PARTICIPANTS AT THE UNIVERSITY OF WISCONSIN-A CROSSE

LANKWITZER NACHRICHTEN – Berlin, 1910-14, 1917-19, 1921-oct 1923 – 1 – Dist. gw Mikrofilm – gw Misc Inst [943]

Lanman, Charles *see* PAPERS

Lanmon, Dwight P *see* PAPERWEIGHTS: FLOWERS WHICH CLOTHE THE MEADOWS

LANNEN SUOMETAR – Astoria, OR. 10 Jan 1939-26 Jul 1946. 3 rolls – 1 – us U.O. Library [071]

LANNEN UUTISET – Astoria, OR. 26 July 1946-30 Mar 1951. – 2r – 1 – us U.O. Library [071]

Lanner, Josef *see* WALZER FUR PIANO. LES ADIEUX, OP. 185

Lanning, Aaron L *see* REMINISCENCES

Lanning, John Tate *see* REALES CEDULAS DE LA REAL Y PONTIFICIA DE LA UNIVERSIDAD DE MEXICO DE 1551 A 1816

Lansbergivs, F *see* VANDE VREMDE ENDE ONSCHRIFTMATIGHE MANIERE DER WEDER-DOOPSCHER LEERAREN HEYMELIJCKE GHEBEDEN

Lansdell, Henry *see*
- THE SACRED TENTH
- THE TITHE IN SCRIPTURE

Lansden, John M *see* HISTORY OF THE CITY OF CAIRO

LANSDOWNE BAPTIST CHURCH. EAST ST LOUIS, ILLINOIS : CHURCH RECORDS – 1903-56 – 1 – 205.65 – us Baptist [240]

LANSFORD LEADER – Lansford, PA. -w 1897-1912 – 13 – $25.00r – us I.M.R. [071]

Lansing, John Gulian *see* OUTLINES OF SPECIAL INTRODUCTION TO THE BOOKS OF THE OLD TESTAMENT

Lansing, Robert *see* DESK DIARIES

Lansing, William *see*
- FORMS OF CIVIL PROCEDURE ADAPTED TO PRACTICE AND PLEADING UNDER THE CODE OF CIVIL PROCEDURE OF THE STATE OF NEW YORK
- THE LAWYERS' AND CLERKS' ASSISTANT

LANSING'S SELECT CHANCERY CASES – New York. 1v. 1824-26 (all publ) – 1mf – 9 – $1.50 – LLMC 80-025 – us L.L.M.C. [340]

LANSING'S SUPREME COURT REPORTS / New York. (State). Supreme Court – v1-7. 1869-73 (all publ) – 47mf – 9 – $70.00 – LLMC 80-012 – us L.L.M.C. [340]

LANSPOSTEN – Orebro, Sweden. 1979- – 1 – sw Kungliga [072]

LANSTIDNINGEN – Ostersund, Sweden. 1924-78 – 276r – 1 – sw Kungliga [072]

LANSTIDNINGEN – Ostersund, Sweden. 1979- – 1 – sw Kungliga [072]

LANSTIDNINGEN – Sodertalje, Sweden. 1963-78 – 117r – 1 – sw Kungliga [072]

LANSTIDNINGEN – Sodertalje, Sweden. 1979- – 1 – sw Kungliga [072]

LANSTIDNINGEN OSTERGOTLAND – Linkoping, Sweden. 1979- – 1 – sw Kungliga [072]

LANSTIDNINGEN TIDNING FOR SKARABORGS LAN *see* MARIESTADS WECKOBLAD

Lantenay, Jeanne de *see* SI LES FEMMES SAVAIENT

LANTERN – Portland, OR. -w. 23 Dec 1897; 20 June 1902; 5 June, 30 July 1903. – 1 – us U.O. Library [071]

A LANTERNA : HEBDOMADARIO LITTERARIO, CRITICO E NOTICIOSO – Manaos, Amazonas. 26 Jun 1910 – 1,5,6 – bl Biblioteca [072]

LA LANTERNE / ed by Buies, Arthur – Montreal, Canada. 17 sep 1868-18 mar 1869 – 1r – 1 – Can$35.00 – cn Can Microfilming [072]

LA LANTERNE – devenu: Le Supplement. Paris. 6 juil 1884-1er aout 1914, 3 avr-25 dec 1920 – 1 – fr A.C.R.P.P. [073]

LA LANTERNE – Montreal, Canada. 5 nov 1903-v1 n4. fev 1904 – 1r – 1 – Can$25.00 – cn Can Microfilming [072]

LA LANTERNE – Paris. 22 avr 1877-17 mars 1928, 10 nov-22 dec 1928, dec 1938 – 1 – fr A.C.R.P.P. [073]

Lanthenas, Francois X. *see*
- BASES FONDAMENTALES DE L'INSTRUCTION PUBLIQUE
- BASES FONDAMENTALES DE L'INSTRUCTION PUBLIQUE ET DE TOUTE CONSTITUTION LIBRE
- DES SOCIETES POPULAIRES CONSIDEREES COMME UNE BRANCHE ESSENTIELLE DE L'INSTRUCTION PUBLIQUE
- RELIGION CIVILE PROPOSEE AUX REPUBLIQUES POUR BIEN DES GOUVERNEMENTS REPRESENTATIFS

Lantier, R *see* RESERVOIRS ET AQUEDUCS ANTIQUES DE MERIDA

Lantis, Margaret *see*
- THE ALASKAN WHALE CULT AND ITS AFFINITIES
- THE MYTHOLOGY OF KODIAK ISLAND, ALASKA

LANTMANNEN – Stockholm, Sweden. 1917-74 – 31r – 1 – sw Kungliga [330]

Lantz, C D *see* THE EFFECTS OF SOCIAL PHYSIQUE ANXIETY, GENDER, AGE, AND DEPRESSION ON PERCEIVED EXERCISE BEHAVIOR

Lantz, Christopher D *see* VALIDATION OF A CONCEPTUAL MODEL CHARACTERIZING COLLEGE STUDENT-ATHLETES' READINESS TO RETIRE FROM COMPETITIVE SPORT PARTICIPATION

Lanusse, M *see* DE L'INFLUENCE DU DIALECTE GASCON

Lanuza, Francisco de *see* HISTORIA DEL TRASLADO DEL COLEGIO DE ARTILLERIA DE BADAJOZ

LANVAEL : EIN DRAMA / Stucken, Eduard – 3. Aufl. Berlin: E Reiss, 1910 – 1r – 1 – us U.W. Library [820]

Lanz, K *see*
- ACTENSTUECKE UND BRIEFE ZUR GESCHICHTE KAISER KARL 5.
- CORRESPONDENZ DES KAISERS KARL 5.

EINE LANZE FUER RUMAENIEN / Dahn, F – Leipzig, 1883 – 2mf – 1 – ILM-1848/1 – ne IDC [327]

DER LANZELET DES ULRICH VON ZAZIKHOVEN / Richter, Werner – (Includes bibliographical references) – Frankfurt am Main: M Diesterweg, 1934 – 1r – 1 – us U.W. Library [943]

LANZHOU DAXUE XUEBAO – (1979-81 $4.50f; 1982, 1984 $3.50f) – (Shehui Kexue Ban). Journal of Langzhou University, Social Science. In Chinese but Table of Contents in English in each issue. F p214 – 9 – cc Microforms [073]

LANZHOU DAXUE XUEBAO – Ziran Kexueban. Journal of Lanzhou University, Natural Science. In Chinese but English abstracts to the main articles. F p188 – 9 – $4.50f – cc Microforms [073]

LANZHOU WANBAO = LANZHOU EVENING POST – (Jul-Dec 1980, 1r; 1981, 1r; 1983-85, 1r/y; 1986-87, 2r/y; 1988, 1r; 1989- , 2r/y) – China. As Lanzhou Bao (Lanhou Gazette) until 1985. M-D51 – 1 – $55.00r – cc Microforms [072]

Lanzi, L *see* THE HISTORY OF PAINTING IN ITALY FROM PERIOD OF THE REVIVAL OF THE FINE ARTS TO THE END OF THE EIGHTEENTH CENTURY

Lanzkowsky, Philip *see* PEDIATRIC REVIEWS AND COMMUNICATIONS

LAO DONG – Ten issues from 1929 and 1930. 2 ill. DL13f – 9 – 30.00 – cc Globe [073]

Lao Tzu *see* LIVRE DES RECOMPENSES ET DES PEINES

LAO-DONG – no. 2-20. Saigon. 6 dec 1938-14 juil 1939 – 1 – fr A.C.R.P.P. [073]

LAODONG BAO = LABOUR JOURNAL – As Shanghai Gongyun Bao (Journal of the Chinese workers movement) until 1984. 1983- . Shanghai, China. M-D40 – 1 reel/ y – 1 – $23.00r – cc Microforms [072]

LAODONGJIE – Labour Circles. 15 Aug 1920-19 Dec 1920. F C15. In Chinese – 9 – $18.00 – cc Microforms [073]

Laos *see*
- BULLETIN ADMINISTRATIF
- DEVELOPMENT PLANS:
- PLAN DE DEVELOPPEMENT ET SOCIAL, 1959/64

Laos (North). Presbytery (Presbyterian Church in the USA) *see* MINUTES, 1885-1898

LAOTSE : SPRUECHE / Klabund – Berlin-Zehlendorf: F Heyder, 1921 – 1r – 1 – us U.W. Library [180]

Lao-tse *see* DIE BAHN UND DER RECHTE WEG DES LAO-TSE (: TAO-TE-KING)

LAO-TUNG – (Labor). Peking. 1957-64. Lacking: 1957-61. BCH-923 2 – 8 – ne IDC [330]

Lao-tzu *see* TAO TE CHING (CCC211)

Laoust, Henri *see*
- ESSAI SUR LES DOCTRINES SOCIALES ET POLITIQUES DE TAKI-D-DIN-AHMAD B. TAIMIYA
- LE TRAITE DE DROIT PUBLIC D'IBN TAIMIYA

LAP CENTER FOR CUBAN STUDIES NEWSLETTER – London, UK. 1974-1976 – 1r – $50.00 – R63604 – us Library Micro [072]

LAP JOURNAL – Mexico, MX. (Dates unknown) – 3r – $150.00 – R04218 – us Library Micro [073]

LAPA = TORCH – Nuremburg: Gunnars Varpa. "Authorized by: Headquarters European Command. Civil Affairs Division." "Latvian Youth Magazine." 1946-48 – 1 – us U.W. Library [800]

LA LAPA DO CABOCLO, JANUARIA, BRESIL / Prous, A et al – 9 – F330.00 – fr Ethnologie [306]

THE LAPEER COUNTY REVIEW – Galion. Ohio. -w. 1865-70 – 1 – us UMI [071]

Lapene, Edouard *see* CONQUETE DE L'ANDALOUSIE

Laperriere, Augustin *see* DECISIONS OF THE SPEAKERS OF THE LEGISLATIVE ASSEMBLY AND HOUSE OF COMMONS OF CANADA, FROM 1841 TO JUNE 1872 WITH AN APPENDIX CONTAINING THE SPEAKERS' DECISIONS ON ELECTION PETITION RECOGNIZANCES

LAPERRIERE'S SPEAKER'S DECISIONS / Canada. General – 1v. 1841-70 (all publ) – 4mf – 9 – $6.00 – LLMC 81-013 – us L.L.M.C. [324]

LAPERRINE LE SAHARIEN / Lehuraux, Leon Joseph – Paris: Ed de l'encyclopedie de l'empire francais, [1947] – us Res Libr [960]

Lapeyre, Paul *see* REVOLUTION ET CONTRE-REVOLUTION EN ESPAGNE. LUEURS SUR L'ESPAGNE REPUBLICAINE

Lapeyrouse, P P de *see*
- FIGURES DE LA FLORE DES PYRENEES
- HISTOIRE ABREGEE DES PLANTES DES PYRENEES

LAPIDA FUNERARIA DE MONROY (CACERES) CON S. SOLAR / Pujol Puiguehi, Ana – Badajoz: Imp. Diputacion Povincial, 1974 – sp Bibl Santa Ana [946]

LAPIDA ROMANA INEDITA DE ALMENDRALEJO / Fita, Fidel & Rodriguez Villa, Antonio – Madrid: Tip. Fortanet, 1896 – sp Bibl Santa Ana [946]

LAPIDA ROMANA INEDITA DEL VILLAR DEL PEDROSO / Jimenez de la Llave, Luis – Madrid: Fortanet, 1891. B.R.A.H. 19, pp. 519-521 – sp Bibl Santa Ana [946]

LAPIDA ROMANA INEDITA, MERIDA / Fita, Fidel – Madrid: Fortanet, 1887. B.R.A.H. XI, pp. 454-455 – sp Bibl Santa Ana [946]
LAPIDA VISIGOTICA DE HERGUIJUELA / Roso de Luna, Mario – Madrid: Fortanet, 1903. B.R.A.H. 43, 1903, p. 554 – sp Bibl Santa Ana [920]
LAPIDAS EXTREMENAS DE LA EDAD ROMANA Y VISIGOTICA (SALVALEON, MERIDA, ALANGE Y VILLAFRANCA DE LOS BARROS) / Monsalud, Marques de – Madrid: Fortanet, 1905. B.R.A.H. 46, 1905, pp. 495-498 – 1 – sp Bibl Santa Ana [946]
LAPIDAS INEDITAS : MERIDA, LOARRE / Mosalud, Marques de – Madrid: Est. Tip. Fortanet, 1898. B.R.A.H. 32, 1898, pp. 5-9 – 1 – sp Bibl Santa Ana [946]
LAPIDAS INEDITAS DE MARCHAMALO, CACERES, PALENCIA Y LUGO / Fita, Fidel – Madrid: Tip. de Fortanet, 1900 – sp Bibl Santa Ana [946]
LAPIDAS ROMANAS. ALCOLLARIN / Pazos, Matias – Madrid: Fortanet, 1887. B.R.A.H. XI, pp. 447-449 – sp Bibl Santa Ana [946]
LAPIDAS ROMANAS DE BURGUILLOS / Fernandez Guerra, Aureliano – Madrid: Tip. Fortanet, 1889 – 1 – sp Bibl Santa Ana [946]
LAPIDAS ROMANAS DE GARLITOS, ARROYO DEL PUERCO Y ARAYA, EN EXTREMADURA / Fita, Fidel – Madrid: Fortanet, 1912. B.R.A.H. 60,pp. 431-442 – sp Bibl Santa Ana [946]
LAPIDAS ROMANAS DE JEREZ DE LOS CABALLEROS Y MORON DE LA FRONTERA / Fita, Fidel – Madrid: Fortanet, 1909. B.R.A.H. 54, pp. 527-531 – sp Bibl Santa Ana [946]
LAPIDAS ROMANAS INEDITAS / Fita, Fidel – Madrid: Tip. Fortanet, 1897 – sp Bibl Santa Ana [946]
LAPIDAS SEPULCRALES DE LA EDAD DEL BRONCE EN EXTREMADURA / Ramon y Fernandez, Jose – Madrid, 1951 – 1 – sp Bibl Santa Ana [946]
Lapide, Cornelius a *see* COMMENTARIA IN SCRIPTURAM SACRAM
Lapide, Pinchas *see* JEWISH BIOGRAPHICAL ARCHIVE SUPPLEMENT
Lapierre, Augustin *see* DECISIONS OF THE SPEAKERS OF THE LEGISLATIVE ASSEMBLY AND HOUSE OF COMMONS OF CANADA, FROM 1841 TO JUNE 1872..
Lapierre, Eugene *see* L'ACTION MUSICALE
LAPINE INTER MOUNTAIN – Lapine OR. Aug 30 Sep 20 1917, May 16 1918 – 1 – us U.O. Library [071]
Laplace, O *see* LE BOUQUINEUR
Laplace, Pierre Simon de *see*
- ESSAI PHILOSOPHIQUE SUR LES PROBABILITES.
- THE SYSTEM OF THE WORLD

Laplanche, M C de *see* DICTIONNAIRE, ICONOGRAPHIQUE DES CHAMPIGNONS SUPERIEURS...
LA-PLATA-POST : WOCHENBLATT DER DEUTSCHEN LA-PLATA-ZEITUNG – Buenos Aires, 1903, 1912 (single issue only), aug 4 1914-nov 8 1919, oct 2 1920-jun 28 1930, jan 2-jun 26 1931, 1933-jun 25 1936, 1937-aug 30 1939 – 59r – 1 – Inquire at Mikrofilmarchiv for details – gw Misc Inst [972]
Lapointe, Madeleine *see* BIBLIOGRAPHIE ANALYTIQUE DE L'OEUVRE DE MONSIEUR CHARLES-MARIE BOISSONNAULT, HISTORIEN, POETE, CRITIQUE ET PUBLICISTE
LaPointe-Crump, Janice D *see* DANCING IN DIXIE'S LAND
LA LAPONIE ET LA CORSE / Bonaparte, Roland – Geneve: R. Burkhardt, 1889 – fr Armell [944]
LAPORAN / Indonesia. Bank Negara – SE-264 1. 1946-1963 – 9 – ne IDC [336]
LAPORAN BUPATI TENTANG KEADAAN DAERAH KABUPATEN BOJOLALI / Bojolali, Indonesia (Kabupaten) – (Annual) – Bojolali. v1-3. 1967 – 3mf – 9 – SE-1362/1 – ne IDC [950]
LAPORAN ETHNOGRAFI DARI DAERAHKABUPATEN WANASABA / Sulardjo Pontjosutirto – SE 4306 1. 1961 – 9 – ne IDC [950]
LAPORAN KEPADA DEWAN PERWAKILAN RAKJAT DAERAH / Surabaya, Java – SE 4575 1 – 9 – ne IDC [950]
Laporan Perkembangan *see* BANK NEGARA INDONESIA UNIT 3
Laporan. Sekretariat D.P.R.D.G.R. *see* BANK PEMBANGUNAN-DAERAH DJAWA-TIMUR
LAPORAN TAHUNAN JABATAN PELAJARAN SABAH = ANNUAL REPORT 1978 / Sabah. Department of Education – (In Malay) – 2mf – 9 – DE-197/1 – ne IDC [370]
Laporte, M *see* LES EPITHETES
Laporte, Rebecca J *see* THE EFFECTS OF AMINO ACID SUPPLEMENTATION ON ENDURANCE PERFORMANCE
Lapp, John A *see* IMPORTANT FEDERAL LAWS
Lapparent, Albert A *see* TRAITE DE GEOLOGIE
LAPPERNE / Wiklund, Karl Bernhard – 1947 – 1 – us I.U. Libraries [390]
Lappi, Pietro *see* SACRAE MELODIAE UNICA
LAPPLAENDISCHE MAERCHEN, VOLKSSAGEN, RAETHSEL UND SPRICHWOERTER / Poestion, Josef Calasanz – 1886 – 1 – us I.U. Libraries [390]
Lappo-Danilevskaia, Nadezhda Aleksandrovna (Liutkevich) *see* KRUSHENIE (ARMIIA)
Lappo-Danilevskii, A S *see* ZAPISNAIA KNIGA KREPOSTNYM AKTAM 15-16 VV., IAVLENNYM V NOVGORODE D'IAKU D. ALIABEVU
Lapponi, Giuseppe *see* HYPNOTISM AND SPIRITISM
Lapshin, I I *see*
- FILOSOFSKOE ZNACHENIE PSIKHOLOGICHESKIKH VOZZRENII DZHEMSA
- VSELENSKOE CHUVSTVO

Lapshov, Il *see*
- INSTRUKTSIIA O PORIADKE KRATKO-SROCHNOGO KREDITOVANIIA KUSTARNO-PROMYSLOVOI KOOPERATSII I OPERATIVNYI UCHET
- SBORNIK POLOZHENII I INSTRUKTSII PO BUKHGALTERSKOMU UCHETU I OTCHETNOSTI SOIUZOV KUSTARNO-PROMYSLOVOI I LESNOI KOOPERATSII

Lapsley, Samuel Norvell *see* LIFE AND LETTERS OF SAMUEL NORVELL LAPSLEY
Lapsov, I *see* SISTEMATICHESKII UKAZATEL' KNIG I STATEI PO VNESHKOL'NOMU OBRAZOVANIIU
Lapworth, C *see* A MONOGRAPH OF BRITISH GRAPTOLITES
DER LAR : EINE OSTER-, PFINGST-, WEIHNACHTS- UND NEUJAHRSGESCHICHTE / Raabe, Wilhelm Karl – 2. Aufl. Braunschweig: G Westermann, 1890 – 1r – 1 – us U.W. Library [390]
LAR CATHOLICO – Juiz de Fora, 10 Feb 1957-Dec 1958; Jan-May, Jul-Dec 1959; Jan 1960; 15 Sep 1963 – 1,5,6 – bl Biblioteca [072]
O LAR CATHOLICO : REVISTA SOCIAL, RELIGIOSA, DEDICADA AS FAMILIAS – Cidade de Paracatu, 15 Jul 1897 – 1,5,6 – bl Biblioteca [072]
O LAR CATHOLICO : REVISTA SOCIAL, RELIGIOSA, DEDICADA AS FAMILIAS – Juiz de Fora, 3 May, Oct-Nov 1891; Mar-Jul, Sep 1892; Mai-Jun, Sep, Nov-Dec 1921; Jan 1922; May, Dec 1923; Jan, May-Jun 1924; Jan, Mar, Nov 1925; Feb 1926-25 Sep 1927 – 1,5,6 – bl Biblioteca [072]
LARA : A TALE; JACQUELINE, A TALE / Byron, George Gordon Byron – London: Printed for J. Murray, by T. Davison, 1814 – 1 roll – 1 – 1-55879-306-2 – uk Libr Preservation [830]
O LARANGEIRENSE – Laranjeiras, Brazil. Jan, Feb, Sept-Oct 1888 – 1 – bl Biblioteca [072]
Larber, G *see* SUI FUNGHI SAGGIO GENERALE. CON TAVOLE IN RAME ED UNA DESCRIZIONE E TAVOLA SINOTTICA DE FUNGHI MANGERECCI PIU COMMUNI D'ITALIA
DAS LARCENY ACT, 1916 / Hagel, K – 99 2. v. 1-3, incl. Registerband. 1960 – 8 – ne IDC [323]
Larcher, Louis Julien *see* LE DERNIER MOT SUR LES FEMMES...CONNAIS-TOI TOI-MEME
Larchey, L *see*
- DICTIONNAIRE HISTORIQUE D'ARGOT
- DICTIONNAIRE HISTORIQUE DE L'ARGOT PARISIEN
- LES EXCENTRICITES DE LA LANGUE FRANCAISE EN 1860
- LES EXCENTRICITES DU LANGAGE
- NOUVEAU SUPPLEMENT DU DICTIONNAIRE D'ARGOT

Lardizabal Uribe, Manuel *see* DISCURSO SOBRE LAS PENAS CRIMINALES EN ESPANA
Lardner, W B *see* HISTORY OF PLACER AND NEVADA COUNTIES
Laredo, B *see*
- METAPHORA MEDICINE ET CHIRURGIE...
- MODUS FACIENDI CUM ORDINE MEDICANDI...

THE LARGE AND SMALL GAME OF BENGAL AND THE NORTH-WESTERN PROVINCES OF INDIA / Baldwin, J H – Z-259 2. 1876 – 8 – ne IDC [590]
Large, Moina W *see* HISTORY OF ASHTABULA COUNTY
Largen, T L *see* HISTORY OF SHOAL CREEK ASSOCIATION, MISSOURI WITH HISTORY OF HER CHURCHES AND BIOGRAPHIES OF MINISTERS
THE LARGENESS OF THE IMAGERY IN THE DEUTERO-ISAIAH / Robinson, Benjamin Willard – Chicago: Geo W Danforth, 1906 – 1mf – 9 – 0-8370-4927-X – 1985-2927 – us A.T.L.A. [220]
Largent, Augustin *see* SAINT JEROME
LARGE-SCALE SYSTEMS – v1-11. 1974-84 – 1,5,6,13 – sz Elsevier [073]
LARGO CABALLERO DENUNCIA / Largo Caballero, Francisco – Buenos Aires, 1937. Fiche W770. (Blodgett Collection of Spanish Civil War Pamphlets) – 9 – us H.U. College Libr [946]
Largo Caballero, Francisco *see*
- DISCIPLINA UNIDAD TRIUMFO
- LARGO CABALLERO DENUNCIA
- QUE SE PUEDE HACER?

THE LARIAT – Virginia City, NV. Aug 1877 – 1r – 1 – $50.00 – U04792 – us Library Micro [071]
Larichev, Oleg I *see* PRACTICAL ASPECTS OF SCIENTIFIC AND TECHNOLOGICAL RESEARCH PROGRAMMING
Larionov, M, Zdanevich, I *see* MANIFEST FUTURISTOV
Larivee, Louis *see* TRUTH "SANS PEUR"
LARK – San Francisco, 1895-96 – 1r – 1 – us Ross [073]
LARKIN, ABEL, FAMILY PAPERS, MS 924 – 1790-1898 – 6r – 1 – us Western Res [978]
Larkin, James M *see* AEROBIC RESPONSES TO 12 WEEKS OF EXERSTRIDING OR WALKING TRAINING IN SEDENTARY ADULT WOMEN
Larkin, Thomas *see* THE PROTECTOR
Larkins, Clifford *see* A BIOMECHANICAL ANALYSIS OF THE SINGLE ARM VERSUS THE PARALLEL DOUBLE ARM TAKEOFFS IN THE TRIPLE JUMP
Larnac, Jean *see* HISTOIRE DE LA LITTERATURE FEMININE EN FRANCE
LARNE OBSERVER – Ireland, 23 Mar-2 Nov 1906 – 38ft – 1 – uk British Libr Newspaper [072]
LARNE REPORTER *see* LARNE WEEKLY REPORTER
LARNE TIMES – Ireland, 1893- – 137+ r – 1 – uk British Libr Newspaper [072]
LARNE WEEKLY REPORTER – (Larne Reporter, 1884-) – Ireland, 18 Mar 1865-5 Nov 1881; Apr-Dec 1884; 1886-Mar 1904 – 13r – 1 – uk British Libr Newspaper [072]
Larned, Ellen D *see* HISTORY OF WINDHAM COUNTY
Larner, John W Jr *see*
- THE PAPERS OF CARLOS MONTEZUMA, M.D
- PAPERS OF THE SOCIETY OF AMERICAN INDIANS, 1906-1946

Larose, ArT *see* LE DROIT DE VIVRE
Larose, P *see* LE CITOYEN
Larouche, J et al *see* LE QUOTIDIEN
LAROUSSE GRAND DICTIONNAIRE UNIVERSEL FRANCAIS DE XIX SIECLE / Larousse, Pierre – 17 v. 1866-90 – 1 – 377.00 – us L of C Photodup [440]
Larousse, Pierre *see*
- GRAND DICTIONNAIRE UNIVERSEL FRANCAIS
- LAROUSSE GRAND DICTIONNAIRE UNIVERSEL FRANCAIS DE XIX SIECLE

LARRA EN LA ESCUELA : ANTOLOGIA: ARTICULOS, POESIAS, ESCENAS, ETC. SELECCION, PROLOGO Y EPILOGO DE... / Larra, Fernando Jose de – Madrid: Razon y Fe, 1931 – 1 – sp Bibl Santa Ana [440]
Larra, Fernando Jose de *see* LARRA EN LA ESCUELA
Larrabee, William Clark *see*
- ASBURY AND HIS COADJUTORS
- LECTURES ON THE SCIENTIFIC EVIDENCES OF NATURAL AND REVEALED RELIGION
- WESLEY AND HIS COLABORERS

Larrivee, Pierrette *see* BIBLIOGRAPHIE DE MONSIEUR RICHARD JOLY, 1955 A 1963
Larroumet, Gustave *see* DERNIERS PORTRAITS
Larruga y Boneta, E *see* HISTORIA DE LA REAL Y GENERAL JUNTA DE COMERCIO, MONEDA Y MINAS...
Larsen, Asbjorn Lunge *see* PAUL HARRO-HARRING
Larsen, H Martensen *see* JESUS UND DIE RELIGIONSGESCHICHTE
Larsen, Michelle H *see* THE DEVELOPMENT OF SPIRITUAL HEALTH INSTRUCTIONAL STRATEGIES USING A SYSTEMS APPROACH MODEL
Larson, Bill *see* PREDICTORS OF SUCCESS ON THE NATIONAL ATHLETIC TRAINERS ASSOCIATION CERTIFICATION EXAMINATION
Larson, Everette E *see* CHRISTOPHER COLUMBUS COLLECTION OF THE LIBRARY OF CONGRESS
Larson, Lois A *see* THE EFFECT OF THE MENSTRUAL CYCLE ON BIOIMPEDANCE RELIABILITY
Lartigaut, A *see*
- LES PRINCIPES INFAILLIBLES DE LA PRONONCIATION
- LES PROGRES DE LA VERITABLE ORTOGRAFE

Lartigue, Jean J *see* MEMOIRE ACCOMPAGNANT LA REQUETE PRESENTEE A LA CHAMBRE D'ASSEMBLEE PAR LE CLERGE CATHOLIQUE DU BAS-CANADA, CONTRE L'ADMISSION DES NOTABLES DANS LES ASSEMBLEES DE FABRIQUE
Larue, Gilbert *see* L'AUTORITE
Larue, Michel *see* QUALITE DE L'EAU DE CONSOMMATION AU QUEBEC
THE LARVAE OF THE BRITISH BUTTERFLIES AND MOTHS / Buckler, W M – Ray Society – 1 – uk Microform Academic [590]
Larymore, Constance *see*
- A RESIDENT'S LIFE IN NIGERIA
- A RESIDENT'S WIFE IN NIGERIA

LARYNGOLOGIE, RHINOLOGIE OTOLOGIE UND IHRE GRENZGEBIETE *see* ZEITSCHRIFT FUER LARYNGOLOGIE, RHINOLOGIE, OTOLOGIE UND IHRE GRENZGEBIETE
LARYNGOSCOPE – v.1. 1896 – 1,5,6,9 – us UMI [073]
LAS VEGAS BUGLE – Las Vegas, NV. 1994 – 1+ r – 1 – $50.00 ($50.00y) – U04860 – us Library Micro [071]
LAS VEGAS ISRAELITE – Las Vegas, NV. 1965 – 15+ r – 1 – $750.00 ($60.00y) – N04600 – us Library Micro [071]
LAS VEGAS MAGAZINE – Las Vegas, NV. 1964 – 1r – 1 – $50.00 – U04907 – us Library Micro [071]
LAS VEGAS SENTINEL-VOICE – Las Vegas, NV. 1993 – 1+ r – 1 – $50.00 ($50.00y) – U04862 – us Library Micro [071]
THE LASCARIDS OF NICAEA : THE STORY OF AN EMPIRE IN EXILE / Gardner, Alice – London: Methuen, 1912 – 1mf – us A.T.L.A. [900]
Laschke, Birgit *see* KENNEN UND SAMMELN
LASCIANA NEBST DEN AELTESTEN EVANGELISCHEN SYNODALPROTOKOLLEN POLENS 1555-1561 / Dalton, Hermann – Berlin, 1898 – Dfl35.00 – ne Slangenburg [240]
Lasco, Johannes a *see* DEFENSIO VERAE SEMPERQVE IN ECCLESIA RECEPTAE DOCTRINAE DE CHRISTI DOMINI INCARNATIONE, ADUERSUS MENNONEM SIMONIS
Lascoux, J B *see*
- GASCONISMES CORRIGES
- LES PERIGORDINISMES

Lasegue, A *see* MUSEE BOTANIQUE DE B. DELESSERT
LASER CHEMISTRY / ed by Donovan, R J et al – 1983- – 1,5,9 – us Harwood [540]
LASER IN DER MATERIALBEARBEITUNG / Rasche, Christian – 1995 – 2mf – 9 – DM80.00 – 3-8267-2117-9 – gw Hänsel [621]
LASERS AND APPLICATIONS – v1-. Sept 1982- – 1,5,6,9 – us UMI [073]
LASERS IN ENGINEERING / ed by Mordike, B L – 9,5,1 – us Gordon [621]
LASERS IN THE LIFE SCIENCES / ed by Ben-hur, Ehud et al – 9,5,1 – us Harwood [621]
Laserstein, Kaete *see* DIE GESTALT DES BILDENDEN KUENSTLERS IN DER DICHTUNG
A LASH AT ENTHUSIASM, IN A DIALOGUE FOUNDED UPON REAL FACTS BETWEEN MRS. CLINKER AND MISS MARTHA STEADY / Hill, Richard – Shrewsbury, [1774] – 1mf – 9 – MP-494/1 – ne IDC [240]
Lasher, George *see* THE MINISTERIAL DIRECTORY OF THE BAPTIST CHURCHES
Lasius, E J *see* YAHWEH-ELOHIM: THE MEMORIAL NAME

LASKARIS : EINE DICHTUNG / Pfungst, Arthur – 5. Aufl. Frankfurt am Main: Neuer Frankfurter Verlag, 1926 – 1r – 1 – us U.W. Library [810]
Lasker, Eduard *see* WEGE UND ZIELE DER CULTURENTWICKLUNG
Lasker-Schueler, Else *see* DIE GESAMMELTEN GEDICHTE
Laskowski, J S *see* COAL PREPARATION
Laso de la Vega, Garcia *see*
– LA FLORIDA DEL INCA
– LA FLORIDA DEL INCA. HISTORIA DEL ADELANTADO HERNANDO DE SOTO. TOMO 1
Lassay, Armand-Leon de Madaillon de Lesparre, M de *see* RELATION DU ROYAUME DES FELICIENS
Lassels, R *see* THE VOYAGE OF ITALY
LASSEN ADVOCATE – Susanville, CA. Jan-Oct 1892; 1896- – 90+ r – 1 BC03027 – $4,500.00 ($110.00y) – us Library Micro [071]
LASSEN ADVOCATE MAIL – Susanville, CA. 1939 – 1r – 1 – $50.00 – B03029 – us Library Micro [071]
LASSEN COUNTY ADVOCATE – Susanville. Calif. -w. 1892, 1896-1915, 1943- – 1 – us UMI [071]
LASSEN COUNTY TIMES – Susanville, CA. Oct 1978- – 13+ r – 1 – $650.00 ($110.00y) – B03030 – us Library Micro [071]
LASSEN MAIL *see* LASSEN WEEKLY MAIL
LASSEN WEEKLY MAIL – (Also known as: Lassen Mail) – Susanville, CA. Sept 1918-Dec 1938 – 9r – 1 – $450.00 – B03028 – us Library Micro [071]
LASSEN/PLUMAS COUNTIES – 1941-50 – 9r – 1 – $450.00 – P00045 – us Library Micro [910]
Lasserre, Adrien *see* LA PARTICIPATION COLLECTIVE DES FEMMES A LA REVOLUTION FRANCAISE
Lasserre, Andre *see* LA SITUATION DES OUVRIERS DE L'INDUSTRIE TEXTILE DANS LA REGION LILLOISE
Lasserre, Enrique *see* NUESTRA SENORA DE LOURDES
Lasserre, G *see* LIBREVILLE
Lasso de la Vega Cotino, Garbriel *see* ELOGIOS EN LOOR...DON JAIME...DON FERNANDO CORTES
Lasso de la Vega, Garcia *see*
– HISTORIA DE LA FLORIDA
– HISTORIA...PERU...INCAS
– OBRAS
Lasso, Orlando di *see*
– PATROCINIUM MUSICES..
– PATROCINIUM MUSICES...CANTIONUM, QUAS MUTETAS VOCANT, OPUS NOVUM
– PATROCINIUM MUSICES...MAGNIFICAT ALIQUOT, QUATUOR, QUINQUE, SEX ET OCTO VOCUM
– PATROCINIUM MUSICES...MISSAE ALIQUOT QUINQUE VOCUM
– PATROCINIUM MUSICES...PASSIO QUINQUE VOCUM
L'Association des Anciens Eleves de l'enseignement Colonial. Chambre de Commerce. Lyon *see* LYON COLONIAL
L'Association Emile-Zola *see* BULLETIN
Lasson, Adolf *see* UEBER DEN ZUFALL
Lassus, J B A *see* REACTION DE L'ACADEMIE DES BEAUX ARTS CONTRE L'ART GOTHIQUE
Lasswell, DH *see* LES "SCIENCES DE LA POLITIQUE" AUX ETATS-UNIS
LAST 12 VERSES OF THE BIBLE ACCORDING TO ST MARK VINDICATED / Burgon, John William – Oxford: James Parker, 1871. 1 fiche – 9 – us A.T.L.A. [240]
THE LAST ABBOT OF GLASTONBURY AND OTHER ESSAYS / Gasquet, Francis Aidan – London: G. Bell, 1908 – 1mf – us A.T.L.A. [240]
THE LAST COMMANDMENT: A MUSICAL INTERPRETATION OF THE GREAT COMMISSION OF JESUS CHRIST / Lanford, Lanny – 1981 – 1 – 5.28 – us Baptist [240]
LAST DAY OF OUR LORD'S PASSION / Hanna, William – New York: Robert Carter, 1864. 1 fiche – 9 – us A.T.L.A. [240]
THE LAST DAYS OF JESUS CHRIST ON THE EARTH, OR, THE DIVINE RECORD OF THE GREAT ATONEMENT : INCLUDING THE BETRAYAL, SUFFERINGS, AND DEATH OF OUR LORD, AND HIS RESURRECTION AND ASCENSION, AS RECORDED BY THE EVANGELISTS / ed by Jennings, Abraham G – New York: N Tibbals, 1874, c1873 – 1mf – 9 – 0-8370-3779-4 – 1985-1779 – us A.T.L.A. [240]
LAST DAYS OF JESUS CHRIST ON THE EARTH, OR, THE DIVINE...GREAT ATONEMENT / Jennings, Abraham G – New York: N. Tibbals, 1874. 1 fiche – 9 – us A.T.L.A. [240]
THE LAST DAYS OF LORD BYRON : WITH HIS LORDSHIP'S OPINIONS ON VARIOUS SUBJECTS, PARTICULARLY ON THE STATE AND PROSPECTS OF GREECE / Parry, William – London: Knight and Lacey [etc., etc.], 1825 – 1 roll – 1 – 1-55879-741-6 – uk Libr Preservation [420]
THE LAST DAYS OF PAPAL ROME, 1850-1870 / Cesare, R de – London: A. Constable, 1909 – 2mf – us A.T.L.A. [945]
THE LAST DAYS OF UNOMUNO / Brouwer, Johannes – n.p. 1936? Fiche W 767. (Blodgett Collection of Spanish Civil War Pamphlets) – 9 – us H.U. College Libr [946]
THE LAST DEFENDER OF JERUSALEM / Dawson, Aeneas McDonell – Ottawa?: s.n., 1882 (Ottawa: "Free Press"). 02347. (Pre-1900 Canadiana) – 9 – cn C.I.H.M. [971]
THE LAST FRUIT OFF AN OLD TREE / Landor, Walter Savage – London: Edward Moxon, 1853 – 1 roll – 1 – 1-55879-841-2 – uk Libr Preservation [810]
THE LAST OF THE MILL CREEKS : EARLY LIFE IN NORTHERN CALIFORNIA / Moak, S – Chico, CA. 1923 – 1r – 1 – $50.00 – B40027 – us Library Micro [978]
LAST OF THE PROPHETS:...A STUDY OF...JOHN THE BAPTIST / Feather, J – Edinburgh: T. & T. Clark, 1894. 1 fiche – 9 – us A.T.L.A. [240]
LAST POST – (Ceased v7 1978/79) – Toronto. v1-7. 1969-78/79 – 9 – Can$20.00y – cn Micromedia [073]
THE LAST WILL AND TESTAMENT OF NICHOLAS JENSEN (SEP 1480) – Chicago: Ludlow Typograph Co, 1928 – 1mf – 9 – $1.50 – LLMC 91-072 – us L.L.M.C. [340]
THE LAST WILL AND TESTAMENT; TO WHICH IS ADDED TWO TREATISES NEVER BEFORE PUBLISHED IN ENGLISH / Basilius, Valentinus – London, 1671 – 1 – us U.W. Library [890]
LAST WILLS AND TESTAMENTS – (Last Wills and Testaments of Thirteen Patriarchs and Gospel of Nicodemus, the Believing Jew. Apocryphal biblical accounts) – Urbana, OH: Evan Banes, Jr, 1827 – 1r – 1 – us Western Res [220]
LAST YEARS OF ST PAUL / Fouard, Constant – New York: Longmans, Green, 1900.1 fiche – 9 – us A.T.L.A. [240]
THE LAST YEARS OF THE PROTECTORATE, 1656-1658 / Firth, Charles Harding – London; New York: Longmans, Green, 1909 – 2mf – us A.T.L.A. [240]
Lasteyrie, Jules de *see* RAPPORT RELATIF AU REGIME DES ESCLAVES DANS LES COLONIES FRANCAISES
LASTOCHKA – Zhurnal dlia dam i devits. 2 v. Spb. 1859-60. BR-3374 2 – 8 – ne IDC [073]
Laszlo, E *see* WORLD FUTURES
Latch, Edward Biddle *see* INDICATIONS OF THE SECOND BOOK OF MOSES CALLED EXODUS
THE LATCH-KEY – Toronto: [s.n, 1863-18–?] – 9 – cn C.I.H.M. [072]
LATE LYRICS AND EARLIER : WITH MANY OTHER VERSES / Hardy, Thomas – London: Macmillan, 1922 – 1 roll – 1 – 1-55879-684-3 – uk Libr Preservation [810]
LATE POLITICAL DECISIONS. / California. Supreme Court – Sacramento, State Journal, 1855. 14p. LL-2284 – 1 – us L of C Photodup [340]
LATEINAMERIKA : ABHAENGIGKEIT UND SELBSTBESTIMMUNG / Hirsch-Weber, Wolfgang – Opladen: Leske, 1972 – 1 – CSUXADQ2863-B – us Hoover Inst Photo [320]
DAS LATEINISCHE NEUE TESTAMENT IN AFRIKA ZUR ZEIT CYPRIANS (T.U.U. 3-33) / Soden, Hans, Freiherr von – Leipzig, 1909 – 10mf – 9 – ne Slangenburg [240]
LATEINISCHE UND DEUTSCHE JUGENDDICHTUNGEN : ERGAENZUNGSBAND MIT EINER BIBLIOGRAPHIE DER GRYPHIUS-DRUCKE / Gryphius, Andreas; ed by Wentzlaff-Eggebert, Friedrich-Wilhelm – Leipzig: K W Hiersemann, 1938 – 1 – us U.W. Library [810]
DIE LATEINISCHEN MITTELALTERLICHEN HANDSCHRIFTEN DER UNIVERSITAETSBIBLIOTHEK MUENCHEN – (Gesamtedition: Die Handschriften der Universitaetsbibliothek Muenchen) – 1995 – 2,207mf – 9 – DM39,500.00 – 3-89131-202-4 – gw Fischer [090]
Latendorf, Friedrich *see* AGRICOLA'S SPRICHWORTER
LATER ANNALS OF NATAL. / Hattersley, Allan Frederick – London, New York [etc]: Longmans, Green, [1938] – us Res Libr [960]
THE LATER COURT HANDS IN ENGLAND FROM THE FIFTEENTH TO THE SEVENTEENTH CENTURY / Jenkinson, H – (Cambridge Univ. Press). London. 1927. B-131 2 – 8 – ne IDC [410]
LATER LETTERS OF MARCUS DODS, D.D. : (LATE PRINCIPAL OF NEW COLLEGE, EDINBURGH) (1895-1909) / Dods, Marcus – London: Hodder and Stoughton, 1911 – 1mf – us A.T.L.A. [240]
LATERCULI PROVINCIARUM *see* NOTITIA DIGNITATUM, ACCEDUNT NOTITIA CONSTANTINOPOLITANAE ET LATERCULI PROVINCIARUM
THE LATEST – Benoni, South Africa, 1930-1932 – 1 reel – 1 – sa State Libr [960]
LATEST COLLECTION OF ORIGINAL AND SELECT HYMNS – New York. 1810 – 1 – 5.32 – us Baptist [240]
LATEST STATISTICS ON RADIO AND TELEVISION BROADCASTING / Division of Statistics on Culture and Communication. Office of Statistics – 1987 – 132p – 9 – 92-3-102468-X – fr UNESCO [380]
THE LATGALIAN CHRONICLE – Tilza, Latvia. Bi-monthly Organ of the Latgalian Gospel Mission and Orphan Home. v2, No. 15. October 1936. Publ. No. 6350a. Total Pages, 398. One of two items on reel – 1 – $15.92 – us Baptist [240]
LATGOLAS BOLSS – Sao Paulo: Arquivo cultural Letao. -w – 1 – us U.W. Library [073]
Latham, J *see* SYSTEMA ORNITHOLOGIAE, SIVE INDEX ORNITHOLOGICUS
Latham, M C *see*
– HUMAN NUTRITION IN TROPICAL AFRICA
– PLANNING AND EVALUATION OF APPLIED NUTRITION PROGRAMMES
Latham, Robert Gordon *see* OPUSCULA
Lathan, Robert *see*
– HISTORY OF HOPEWALL CHURCH
– HISTORY OF THE ASSOCIATE REFORMED SYNOD OF THE SOUTH
LATHATAR = HORIZON – Budapest, 1936-1941 – 3r – 1 – us I.H.R.C. [947]
Lathburg, Thomas *see* A HISTORY OF THE ENGLISH EPISCOPACY FROM THE PERIOD OF THE LONG PARLIAMENT TO THE ACT OF UNIFORMITY
Lathbury, D C *see*
– CORRESPONDENCE ON CHURCH AND RELIGION OF WILLIAM EWART GLADSTONE
– DEAN CHURCH
– MR. GLADSTONE
Lathbury, Thomas *see* A HISTORY OF THE CONVOCATION OF THE CHURCH OF ENGLAND
Lathief, Abdul Karim *see* THE INDONESIAN-ENGLISH DICTIONARY OF TERMINOLOGY
Latif, Chalid *see* DJAKARTA-KEBAJORAN. LIST OF STREET NAMES
Latif, Isom *see* MAP AND TOURIST GUIDE DJAWA-BALI
LATIFE – (Sahib-i Imtiyaz ve Mueduer-i Mes'ul: Hueseyin Huesnue, Sermuharriri: Fuad Talat. No. 2 (6) (25 Haziran 1327[1911])) – Istanbul: Tuerk Matbaasi, 1911 – 1mf – 9 – $12.00 – us MEDOC [949]
EL LATIFUNDIO, ENEMIGO DE LA NACION, UNA OPINION DE LOS COMUNISTAS ARGENTINOS – Buenos Aires: Editorial Problemas, 1941 – 1 – CSUXAHZ2786-B – us Hoover Inst Photo [320]
LATIHAN KADER PERUSAHAAN (MANAGEMENT TRAINING) / Aritonang, M – SE-5036 1. 1961 – 9 – ne IDC [650]
LATIHAN PERTJAKAPAN NIPPON / Poerwadarminta, W J S – (Microfiche No 142) – Djakarta: Pendidikan, 2602 – 1mf – 9 – SE-2002/1 – ne IDC [950]
Latilla, G *see* SIX QUARTETTOS
Latimer, Joseph W *see* BUREAUCRACY A LA MODE
Latimer, Robert Sloan *see* UNDER THREE TSARS
Latimer, William Thomas *see* A HISTORY OF THE IRISH PRESBYTERIANS
LATIN AMERICA – London. v1-5. 1967-71 – 29mf – 9 – $5.00f – us Ross [972]
LATIN AMERICA : THE PAGANS, THE PAPISTS, THE PATRIOTS, THE PROTESTANTS AND THE PRESENT PROBLEM / Brown, Hubert William – (Includes index) – New York: Fleming H Revell, 1901 – 1mf – 9 – 0-8370-6652-2 – 1986-0652 – us A.T.L.A. [240]
LATIN AMERICA, 1946-76 / U.S. Central Intelligence Agency – 1982. Series: CIA Research Reports – 1 – $480.00 – 0-89093-422-3 – us UPA [972]
LATIN AMERICA, 1962-94 : SPECIAL STUDIES SERIES / ed by Kesaris, Paul – (1962-80: 10r $1,105.00 ISBN 0-89093-454-1; Supplements, 1980-82: 3r $330.00 ISBN 0-89093-435-5; 1982-85: 7r $770.00 ISBN 0-89093-655-2; 1985-88: 12r $1,320.00 ISBN 0-55655-115-0; 1989-91: 14r $1,540.00 ISBN 1-55655-426-5; 1992-94: 14r $1,670.00 ISBN 1-55655-537-7) – 1 – us UPA [320]
LATIN AMERICA BRITISH DIPLOMATIC BLUE BOOKS – ie Microforms [941]
LATIN AMERICA BRITISH DIPLOMATIC BLUE BOOKS *see* BRITISH DIPLOMATIC BLUE BOOKS CONCERNING CENTRAL AND SOUTH AMERICA
LATIN AMERICAN: 1941-61 / U.S. Office of Strategic Services – 1981. Series: US State Department Intelligence and Research Reports, Pt 14 – 1 – $965.00 – us UPA [972]
LATIN AMERICAN AND CARIBBEAM OFFICIAL STATISTICAL SERIALS, 1821-1982 *see* JAMAICA
LATIN AMERICAN AND CARIBBEAN OFFICIAL STATISTICAL SERIALS *see*
– ANUARIO GENERAL DE ESTADISTICA
– HONDURAS
LATIN AMERICAN AND CARIBBEAN OFFICIAL STATISTICAL SERIALS, 1821-1982 – (Individual titles also listed and may be purchased separately) – 3,981mf – 9 – £17,080.00 coll – uk Chadwyck [972]
LATIN AMERICAN AND CARIBBEAN OFFICIAL STATISTICAL SERIALS, 1821-1982 *see*
– ARGENTINE REPUBLIC
– BAHAMAS
– BARBADOS
– BELIZE
– BERMUDA
– BOLIVIA
– BRAZIL
– BRITISH VIRGIN ISLANDS
– CARIBBEAN – GENERAL
– CHILE
– COSTA RICA
– CUBA
– DOMINICAN REPUBLIC
– ECUADOR
– EL SALVADOR
– GUADELOUPE
– GUATEMALA
– GUYANA
– GUYANE
– JAMAICA
– MARTINIQUE
– MEXICO
– MONTSERRAT
– NETHERLANDS ANTILLES
– NICARAGUA
– PANAMA
– PARAGUAY
– PERU
– PUERTO RICO
– ST LUCIA
– ST. VINCENT
– SURINAM
– TRINIDAD AND TOBAGO
– URUGUAY
– VENEZUELA
LATIN AMERICAN AND CARIBBEAN STATISTICAL SERIALS, 1821-1982 *see* ANTIGUA
LATIN AMERICAN BUSINESS REVIEW : INNOVATIONS IN THEORY, RESEARCH AND PRACTICE / ed by Dimon, Denise – v1 n1. 1997- – 1,9 – $80.00 in US $112.00 outside hardcopy subsc – us Haworth [650]
LATIN AMERICAN DOCUMENTS – (1960-67; 9) – 1968- – 20,201mf, 1,207r – 1 – $49,600.00 $70,950.00 – us OmniSys [972]
LATIN AMERICAN LITERARY REVIEWS – (1985- . 5,6,9) – v1- . 1972- – 1 – us UMI [800]
LATIN AMERICAN PAMPHLETS FROM YALE UNIVERSITY LIBRARY: SELECTIONS FROM 1600-1900 – (Argentina. 50 titles. $280.00; Bolivia. 226 titles. $1,150.00; Brazil. 123 titles. $580.00; Chile. 425 titles. $2,485.00;

Colombia. 169 titles. $870.00; Cuba. 32 titles. $190.00; Ecuador. 23 titles. $120.00; Guatemala. 21 titles. $120.00; Mexico. 6060 titles. $27,205.00; Paraguay. 13 titles. $90.00; Peru. 1936 titles. $8,550.00; Uruguay. 4 titles. $55.00; Venezuela. 188 titles. $1,050.00; Miscellaneous. 1325 titles. $145.00; Guide only. $815.00) – 10,685 fiches. Printed guide – 9 – $37,305.00 – us UPA [080]
LATIN AMERICAN PERSPECTIVES – (1983-. 1,5,6,9) – v1-. 1974- – 1 – us UMI [073]
LATIN AMERICAN PERSPECTIVES – (Series: Argentine 4r $200 R60100. Brazilian 91r $4,550 R60200. Central American 10r $500 R60300. Chilean 17r $850 R60400. Colombian 169r $8,450 R60500. Cuban 95r $4,750 R60600. Mexican 872r $43,600 R60700. Nicaraguan 8r $400 R60800. Uruguayan 9r $450 R60900. Fiche $1,000) – 1 – $58,275.00 coll – R6000 – us Library Micro [972]
LATIN AMERICAN POLITICAL REPORT – London, UK. 1977-1979 – 3r – $50.00 – R63605 – us Library Micro [072]
LATIN AMERICAN PULSE – 1970-83 – 1 – us UMI [972]
LATIN AMERICAN REPORT – 1956-68 – 1 – us UMI [073]
LATIN AMERICAN RESEARCH REVIEW – v1-1966- 1; v6- 5,6; v10- 9 – us UMI [972]
LATIN AMERICAN TRAVELS – 257r – 1 – $16,700.00 – us OmniSys [910]
LATIN AMERICAN WEEKLY REPORT – London, UK. 1979-1983 – 4r – $200.00 – R63565 – us Library Micro [072]
THE LATIN CHURCH IN THE MIDDLE AGES / Lagarde, Andre – Edinburgh: T. & T. Clark; New York: Putnam, 1915 – 2mf – us A.T.L.A. [240]
LE LATIN DE GREGOIRE DE TOURS / Bonnet, Max – Paris: Hachette, 1890 – 2mf – us A.T.L.A. [240]
THE LATIN HYMN-WRITERS AND THEIR HYMNS / Duffield, Samuel Willoughby; ed by Thompson, R E – New York: Funk & Wagnalls, 1889 – 2mf – us A.T.L.A. [780]
THE LATIN KINGDOM OF JERUSALEM, 1099 TO 1291 A.D. / Conder, C R – London: Committee of the Palestine Exploration Fund, 1897 – 2mf – us A.T.L.A. [240]
LATIN LANGUAGE AND GRAMMAR ADAPTED TO THE CAPACITIES OF CHILDREN AND FOR THE USE OF PARENTS IN THE WORK OF HOME EDUCATION / Dallas, Angus – Toronto: Hunter, Rose, 1878. 02256. (Pre-1900 Canadiana) – 9 – cn C.I.H.M. [971]
LATIN QUARTER – Los Angeles, CA. 1974-1975 – 1r – 1 – $50.00 – R04060 – us Library Micro [071]
Latin, Richard W *see* BODY COMPOSITION DETERMINATION OF OLDER MEN
LATINAE GRAMMATICAE / Duncan, Andrew – 1595. 129p. (English Linguistics Series 1500-1800) – 9 – us UMI [450]
THE LATINE GRAMMAR / Hoole, Charles – 1651. 330p. (English Linguistics Series 1500-1800) – 9 – us UMI [450]
THE LATINE GRAMMAR OF P. RAMUS: TRANSLATED INTO ENGLISH / La Ramee, Pierre de – 1585. 155p. (English Linguistics Series 1500-1800) – 9 – us UMI [450]
THE LATINS IN THE LEVANT : A HISTORY OF FRANKISH GREECE (1204-1566) / Miller, William – London: J. Murray, 1908 – 2mf – us A.T.L.A. [240]
LATITUDE OF SPORTSMANSHIP BEHAVIOR DEEMED ACCEPTABLE BY SPECTATORS OF BASKETBALL GAMES / Morrow, Ellen R – 1981 – 2mf – 9 – $8.00 – us Microform Publ [790]
THE LATON ARGUS – Laton, CA. 1914-1917 – 2r – 1 – $100.00 – B03609 – us Library Micro [071]
Latouche, De *see* L'ART DE BIEN PARLER FRANCOIS
Latour de Franqueville *see* ERRATA DE L'ESSAI SUR LA MUSIQUE ANCIENNE ET MODERNE (DE J.B. DE LABORDE), OU LETTRE A L'AUTEUR DE CET ESSAI, PAR MADAME
Latour, Frederick St. George de *see* THE LIFE OF CATHERINE BOOTH
Latour, Rene *see* ETUDE SUR LA RESERVE DES ENFANTS LEGITIMES
Latour, T *see* AIR FAVORI POUR LE PIANO-FORTE...
Latreille *see* RECHERCHES GEOGRAPHIQUES SUR L'AFRIQUE CENTRALE D'APRES LES ECRITS D'EDRISI ET DE LEON L'AFRICAIN
Latreille, A *see* LES FORCES RELIGIEUSES ET LA VIE POLITIQUE
Latrobe, John Hazelhurst Boneval *see* THE JUSTICES' PRACTICE UNDER THE LAWS OF MARYLAND.
LATTA BAPTIST CHURCH. DILLON COUNTY. SOUTH CAROLINA : CHURCH RECORDS – 1891-1972. Deacons' Minutes. 1962-72 – 1 – 50.27 – us Baptist [240]
LATTER DAY LUMINARY – 1818-25 – 1 – 104.16 – us Baptist [240]
LATTER DAY LUMINARY – Philadelphia, PA. 1818-25 – 1 – 55.75 – us A.B.H.S. [073]
LATTHI THAMNIAM TANG PHAK THI 15: TAMRA BAEP THAMNIAN NAI-RATCHASAMNAK – Phranakhon: 1923. 99p. In Thai – 1 – us U.W. Library [950]
Lattila, G *see*
- LA COMEDIA IN COMEDIA
- DON CALASCIONE

LATTIMORE BAPTIST CHURCH. KINGS MOUNTAIN ASSOCIATION. NORTH CAROLINA : CHURCH RECORDS – 1891-1962 – 1 – 19.35 – us Baptist [240]
Lattin, Ward Elgin *see* FEDERAL ADMINISTRATIVE REGULATORY AGENCIES AND THE DOCTRINE OF THE SEPARATION OF POWERS
Latvia *see* TABLE CHRONOLOGIQUE DES TRAITES CONCLUS PAR LA LETTONIE
Latvia. Ministere des Affaires Etrangeres *see* RECUEIL DES PRINCIPAUX TRAITES... 1918-1930
LATVIAN BAPTIST ASSOCIATION/UNION. STATISTIKA (STATISTICS) / GADA PARSKATS (ANNUAL REPORTS) – 1896-1909, 1911, 1913, 1920-1937, 1939. Publ. No. 6344a. One of three items on reel. Total pages 1,412 – 1 – us Baptist [240]
Latvian Baptist Churches. Baltic Association *see* PROTOKOLS/PROTOKOLI (MINUTES)
THE LATVIAN ECONOMIST = LATVIAN EKONOMIST (1928) – (Library has: 1928, 1930-1931, 1938) – Riga: The Ministry of finance, 1928- – 1 – CSUX90-S416 – us Hoover Inst Photo [947]
LATVIESU AVIZES – Latvia, 1827-66 – 10r – 1 – $750.00 – us Ross [072]
LATVIESU ZINAS – Ludwigsburg. Nov 22 1947-June 9 1949. Incomplete – 1 – us NY Public [072]
LATVIJA – Eutin, Germany. 1960-Sept 1986 – 8r – 1 – us L of C Photodup [072]
LATVIJAS JAUNATNE – (Ceased publication december 1993) – 1990-93 – 7r – 1 – Sfr840.00 – sz Infoprint [947]
LATVIJAS JAUNATNE = LATVIAN YOUTH – (Cont as: Labrit 1994-98 4r per y $340. 1990-93 7r $595) – Latvia, 1999- – 4r per y – 1 – $320.00y standing order – us Ross [072]
LATVIJAS KAREIVIS – Riga, Latvia, jul 1938-mar 1940 – 5r – 1 – us Res Libr [947]
LATVIJAS SAULE – Riga. v. 1-9. Jan 1923-Mar 1931 – 1 – us NY Public [073]
LATVIS – Riga. Aug 1923-Oct 1934. Incomplete – 1 – us NY Public [073]
LATVJU DAINAS. LATWJU DAINAS – 1922 – 1 – us I.U. Libraries [390]
LATWEESCHU BAPTISTU JAUNEESCHU PULZINU. GADA PAHRSKAT = LATVIA BAPTIST YOUTH SOCIETIES. ANNUAL REPORTS – 1905-1908. Publ. No. 6344c. One of three items on reel. Total pages, 1,412 – 1 – us Baptist [240]
LATWEESCHU BAPTISTU SABEEDRIBA PEHDEJOS DESMIT GADOS, NO 1904, LIHDS 1914 G. = LATVIAN BAPTIST ASSOCIATION, THE LAST TEN YEARS FROM 1904 TO 1914 / Lauberts, Peter – Publ. No. 6349b. One of three items on reel. Total Pages 146 – 1 – us Baptist [240]
LATWEESCHU RAKSTNEEZIBAS RAHDITAJS 1585-1925 / Missinsch, J – Riga. v1-2. 1924-1937 – 35mf – 9 – ne IDC [947]
Latysev, V V *see* INSCRIPTIONES ANTIQUAE ORAE SEPTENTRIONALIS PONTI EUXINI GRAECAE ET LATINAE
Latzel, R *see* DIE MYRIOPODEN DER OESTERREICHISCH-UNGARISCHEN MONARCHIE
Latzke, Rudolf *see* PETER ROSEGGER
Lau, Fritz *see*
- BRANDUNG
- EBB UN FLOT
- HELDEN TO HUS
- IN LUV UN LEE
- KATENLUED

Laube, Heinrich *see*
- CATO VON EISEN
- FRANZ GRILLPARZERS LEBENSGESCHICHTE
- GESAMMELTE SCHRIFTEN IN 15 (16) BAENDEN
- GESCHICHTE DER DEUTSCHEN LITERATUR
- GRAF ESSEX
- MEISTERDRAMEN
- MODERNE CHARAKTERISTIKEN

Lauber, Russell L *see* ATTITUDES ASSOCIATED WITH COMPETITIVE AGE-GROUP SWIMMING
Laubert, M *see* HISTORIA DE POLONIA
Lauberts, Peter *see*
- DEEWA ROKA MANA DSIHWE, 1904-1928
- LATWEESCHU BAPTISTU SABEEDRIBA PEHDEJOS DESMIT GADOS, NO 1904, LIHDS 1914 G.
- WAJ W. FETLERS IR BAPTISTS?

Laubman, Katherine M *see* A HISTORICAL-ETHNOGRAPHIC ACCOUNT OF A CANADIAN WOMAN IN SPORT, 1920-1938
Laud, William *see* A RELATION OF THE CONFERENCE BETWEEN WILLIAM LAUD, LATE LORD ARCHBISHOP OF CANTERBURY AND MR. FISHER THE JESUIT BY THE COMMAND OF KING JAMES OF EVER BLESSED MEMORY
Laudam, Jet al *see* PASTKAIDROJUMI BAPTISTU DRAUDSCHU LOZEKLEEM SAWEENIBAS PADOMES SUHDSIBAS LEETA
LAUDATE PUERI. ORACIONES Y CANTOS / Colegio de San Jose. Villafranca de los Barros (Badajoz) – Sevilla: Imp. La Gavidia, 1942 – sp Bibl Santa Ana [780]
LAUDATIO HUGONIS GROTII / Cras, H C – Amstelaedami, 1796 – 2mf – 1 – ILM-986/1 – ne IDC [327]
Lauder, Jean *see* PERSPECTIVES ON DEVELOPMENTAL NEUROBIOLOGY
LAUDERDALE COUNTY ENTERPRISE – Ripley. Tenn. 1957- – 1 – us UMI [071]
Laudermilk, Julie I *see* CATASTROPHIC INJURIES IN JUNIOR HIGH AND HIGH SCHOOL WRESTLING
Laudet, Fernand *see* L'INSTITUTEUR DES INSTITUTEURS. ST JEAN DE LA SALLE. PARIS, 1929
Laudonniere, R *see* HISTOIRE DE LA FLORIDE
Laudun D'Aigaliers, P de *see* L'ART POETIQUE FRANCOIS
Laue, Hellmuth *see* DIE OPERNDICHTUNG LORTZINGS
Laue, Ludwig *see* DIE COMPOSITION DES BUCHES HIOB: EIN LITTERAR-KRITIKISCHER VERSUCH
Lauenburgische Nachrichten *see* LUEBECKER NACHRICHTEN
Lauer, Edgar Jacob *see* THE NEW PRACTICE AND PROCEDURE IN THE MUNICIPAL COURT OF THE CITY OF NEW YORK UNDER THE MUNICIPAL COURT CODE (LAWS OF 1915, CHAP. 279).
Lauer, Joseph *see* SAHEL
Lauer, Paul E *see* CHURCH AND STATE IN NEW ENGLAND
DER LAUFEN : ERZAEHLUNG / Strauss, Emil – Muenchen: A Langen, G Mueller, 1934 – 1r – 1 – us U.W. Library [830]
Laufer, B *see*
- ARABIC AND CHINESE TRADE IN WALRUS AND NARWHAL IVORY
- EPIGRAPHISCHE DENKMAELER AUS CHINA
- THE REINDEER AND ITS DOMESTICATION
- SUPPLEMENTARY NOTES ON WALRUS AND NARWHAL IVORY

Lauff, Joseph von *see* MARIE VERWAHNEN
Laufs, Carl *see* EIN TOLLER EINFALL
THE LAUGHING ATOM – Bombay: R K Karanjia, oct 1-dec 24 1950 – 1r – 1 – us Res Libr [950]
LAUGHING HORSE – Berkeley etc. no. 5-21. 1923-1939 – 1 – us NY Public [073]
THE LAUGHLIN GAMBLER – Laughlin, NV. 1984-1991 – 23r – 1 – $1,150.00 – U04866 – us Library Micro [790]
LAUGHTER : AN ESSAY ON THE MEANING OF THE COMIC / Bergson, Henri – New York: Macmillan, 1911 – 1mf – us A.T.L.A. [100]
Laugier, M *see* NOUVEAU RECUEIL DE PLANCHES COLORIEES D'OISEAUX
Laugier, M A *see*
- ESSAI SUR L'ARCHITECTURE
- OBSERVATIONS SUR L'ARCHITECTURE

LAUKU AVIZE – (1988-92, 1r per y $85y. 1993 2r $170. 1994 3r $255. 1995-98 4r per y $320y) – Latvia, 1999- – 4r per y – 1 – $320.00 standing order – us Ross [072]
Laumann, E M *see* A LA COTE OCCIDENTALE D'AFRIQUE
Laumond, Jean C J *see* STATISTIQUE DU DEPARTEMENT DU BAS-RHIN
Laun, Uwe *see*
- PLASTIZITAET UND ANELASTIZITAET NANOKRISTALLINER MATERIALIEN
- UNTERSUCHUNGEN ZUR STEIGERUNG DER INTERPRETATIONSSICHERHEIT AKUSTO-MIKROSKOPISCHER BILDER

Launay, Adrien *see* LES MISSIONNAIRES FRANCAIS AU TONKIN
Launay, Couanier de *see* PIECES DIVERSES MANUS. OU IMPR. REUNIES PAR M. COUANIER DE LAUNAY ET CONCERNANT L'HISTOIRE DE LAVAL
Launay, G de *see* LA DIALECTIQUE
LAUNCERTON EXAMINER – 1 – F3,413.00 – sz Infoprint [072]
LAUNCESTON ADVERTISER – Launceston, 1830-42 – 1 – at Pascoe [072]
LAUNCESTON EXAMINER – 1981-1996 – 184r – 9 – at Pascoe [072]
LAUNCESTON EXAMINER – Australia, Jan 1850-30 Dec 1858; 19 Jan 1864-23 Feb 1871; 23 Jan 1875-30 Jun 1922; 1 Jan 1930-31 Mar 1931; 1 Aug 1933-30 Jul 1938; 2 Jan-31 Aug 1939; Jan 1952-Dec 1975 (imperfect) – 513r – 1 – uk British Libr Newspaper [072]
LAUNCESTON WEEKLY NEWS – England.19 Apr 1856-23 Dec 1858; 1859-66. -w.5 reels – 1 – uk British Libr Newspaper [072]
LAUNDRY JOURNAL – v. 57-70. 1950-May 1963 – 1 – us UMI [360]
LAUNDRY NEWS – (1979 5,6,9) – 1975 – 1 – us UMI [073]
Laune, Alfred *see* LA TRADUCTION DE L'ANCIEN TESTAMENT DE LEFEVRE D'ETAPLES
Laupacis, Benedict *see* LA BIBLIOGRAPHIE DU DROIT NATUREL DANS LA PHILOSOPHIE CHRETIENNE DU COMMENCEMENT DE L'EPOQUE JUSQU'AU DIXSEPTIEME SIECLE
Laur, Ernst *see* STAND DER FORSCHUNGSLEHRE AUF DEM GEBIETE DER WIRTSCHAFTSLEHRE DES LANDBAUES
LAURA SECORD, THE HEROINE OF 1812: A DRAMA: AND OTHER POEMS / Curzon, Sarah Anne – Toronto: C. Blackett Robinson, 1887. 02248. (Pre-1900 Canadiana) – 9 – cn C.I.H.M. [971]
THE LAURA SPELMAN ROCKEFELLER MEMORIAL COLLECTION : SERIES 3: APPROPRIATIONS, 1917-1945 – (Guide available Dec 1996 and may be purchased separately S3349.G $25.00) – 89r – 1 – $7.565.00 – S3349 – Co-publ with the Rockefeller Archive Center, North Tarrytown, NY, a Division of the Rockefeller univ – us Scholarly Res [975]
LAUREA EVANGELICA DE.. / Manrique, Angel – 1609 – 9 – 1.50f – sp Bibl Santa Ana [240]
LAUREL ADVOCATE – Laurel, NE. -w. Jun 1893 to date – 1 – us NE Hist [071]
THE LAUREL BUSH: AN OLD FASHIONED LOVE STORY / Craik, Dinah Maria – by the author of John Halifax, gentleman, &c. Montreal: Dawson, 1876. 05267. (Pre-1900 Canadiana) – 9 – cn C.I.H.M. [971]
EL LAUREL DE LA ZUBIA / Hurtado y Nunez de Arce, G – 1865 – 9 – 1.50f – sp Bibl Santa Ana [830]
LAUREL FIRST BAPTIST CHURCH. LAUREL, MISSISSIPPI : CHURCH RECORDS – 1905-66. (lacking 1921-27) – 1 – 40.91 – us Baptist [240]
LAUREL FORK BAPTIST CHURCH. MORRISTOWN, TENNESSEE : CHURCH RECORDS – 1855-1909 – 1 – 5.94 – us Baptist [240]
LAUREL HILL BAPTIST CHURCH. LEESVILLE, LOUISIANA : CHURCH RECORDS – 1869-1925. 576p – 1 – $25.92 – us Baptist [240]
LAUREL REVIEW – Brookville. Ind. 1887-1888 – 1 – us UMI [071]
Lauremberg, P *see* MUSOMACHIA: ID EST BELLUM MUSICALE
LAURENCE KIRK OBSERVER – (Kincardineshire Observer 1907-) – Laurence Kirk, Scotland, UK. 4 Jan-Dec 1907; 1908-81 – 40r – 1 – uk British Libr Newspaper [072]
Laurence, Margaret *see* A TREE FOR POVERTY
Laurence, Reginald Vere *see*
- LECTURES ON MODERN HISTORY
- LECTURES ON THE FRENCH REVOLUTION

LAURENCE STERNE AND GOETHE / Pinger, Wilhelm Robert Richard – (Includes bibliographical references) – Berkeley: University of California Press, 1920 – 1 – us U.W. Library [410]
LAURENCE STERNE UND JOHANN GEORG JACOBI / Longo, Joseph – (Includes bibliographical references) – Wien, Leipzig: J Eisenstein, 1898 – 1r – 1 – us U.W. Library [410]
LAURENCE WHISTLER – 1974. 5p., 2 illus. 1 fiche. Fiche no. 1031 – 9 – $2.50 – us Corning Mus [700]
LAURENS FIRST BAPTIST CHURCH. LAURENS, SOUTH CAROLINA : CHURCH RECORDS – 1834-1934, 1834-1959, 1961-1986; 295p; DEDICATION SERVICE BROCHURE, 18 May 1958; Membership Rolls, 1898-January 1987 – 1 – $17.33 – us Baptist [240]
Laurens, Henri *see* HENRY LAURENS PAPERS
Laurent, D *see* LA VILLEMARQUE, COLLECTEUR DE CHANTS POPULAIRES
Laurent, J *see* ABBAYES ET PRIEURES DE L'ANCIENNE FRANCE
Laurent, M *see* CONSIDERATIONS SUR LA POLITIQUE EXTERIEURE ET INTERIEURE DE LA FRANCE DEPUIS LA REVOLUTION DE 1830
Laurent, M A *see* LA RESILIATION DES BAUX RURAUX PAR SUITE DE LA GUERRE, COMMENTAIRE DE LA LOI DU 17 AOUT 1917
Laurent, Paul-Mathieu *see*
- DE LA MODERATION POLITIQUE
- LETTRE A UN LIBERAL
- SUR LES PRINCIPES FONDAMENTAUX DE LA THEORIE DES NOMBRES ET DE LA GEOMETRIE

THE LAURENTIAN AND HURONIAN SYSTEMS IN THE REGION NORTH OF LAKE HURON / Bell, Robert – Toronto: Warwick, 1892. 02328. (Pre-1900 Canadiana) – 9 – cn C.I.H.M. [910]
LAURENTIAN UNIVERSITY REVIEW – (Ceased v19 no 2 1987) – Sudbury. v1-19. 1968/69-1986/87 – 9 – Can$20.00y – cn Micromedia [370]
LES LAURENTIDES – St-Lin, Canada. v1 n33. 29 sep 1874-v3 n7. 10 sep 1878 – 1r – 1 – Can$30.00 – cn Can Microfilming [072]
LAURENTIE : REVUE / ed by Barbeau, Raymond – Montreal, oct 1957-oct 1962 – 1r – 1 – Can$40.00 – cn Can Microfilming [073]
LE LAURENTIEN – Shawinigan, Canada. v22 n2. 14 jan 1959-v24 n52. 27 dec 1961 – 1r – 1 – Can$45.00 – cn Can Microfilming [072]
Laurentium, F *see* DE PROBATIS SANCTORUM. HISTORIIS, PARTIM EX TOMIS ALOYSII LIPOMANI
Laurie, Thomas *see*
- DR. GRANT AND THE MOUNTAIN NESTORIANS
- THE ELY VOLUME
- WOMAN AND HER SAVIOUR IN PERSIA
- WOMAN AND THE GOSPEL IN PERSIA

LAURIER ET SON TEMPS / DeCelles, Alfred Duclos – Montreal, 1920. SEM105P520 – 3mf – 9 – Can$6.75 – cn Bibl Nat [920]
Laurier, Wilfred *see* DISCOURS DE SIR WILFRED LAURIER-ALFRED D. DECELLES
Laurier, Wilfrid *see* LE DEFRICHEUR
Laurin, Fernand *see* INSPECTION ET REGLEMENTATION CONCERNANT LA PREVENTION DES INCENDIES
Laurin, MT *see* LES INSTITUTEURS ET LE SYNDICALISME
Laury, Preston A *see* A HISTORY OF LUTHERAN MISSIONS
Laus de Boissy, L de *see* REFLEXIONS IMPARTIALES SUR LES ELOGES DE VOLTAIRE QUI ONT CONCOURU POUR LE PRIX DE L'ACADEMIE FRANCAISE EN 1779, A FERNEY, ET SE TROUVE A PARIS, CHEZ VALLEYRE, 1780
Lauser, Wilhelm *see* NOVELLEN
THE LAUSIAC HISTORY OF PALLADIUS / Butler, C – 2v. 1904 – 11mf – 8 – ne Slangenburg [240]
THE LAUSIAC HISTORY OF PALLADIUS / Butler, C – Pts 1-2. 1898. 2pts in 1v – 13mf – 9 – ne Slangenburg [240]
LAUSITZER RUNDSCHAU – Cottbus, 1946-47 – 1r – 1 – DM75.00 – gw Mikro Press [072]
LAUSITZER RUNDSCHAU – Goerlitz, East Germany. 20 Jul 1946-47 – 1r – 1 – gw Mikrofilm [072]
LAUSITZER RUNDSCHAU – (Publ in Bautzen until aug 14, 1952. Ausgabe Land und Stadt) – Cottbus. 1991 – 5r – 1 – gw Mikrofilm [072]
DIE LAUTE DER TOGGENBURGER MUNDARTEN / Wiget, Wilhelm – Zuerich, 1910 – 2mf – DM62.00 – 3-8267-3057-7 – gw Hänsel [390]
LAUTE UND FORMEN DER MAGNETISCHEN INSCHRIFTEN / Nachmanson, Ernst – (Includes bibliographical references and index) – Uppsala: Almqvist & Wiksells, 1903 – 1mf – 9 – 0-8370-9300-7 – 1986-3300 – us A.T.L.A. [450]
Lautemann, Willi *see* INTERPRETATION UND KRITIK EINIGER GRUNDBEGRIFFE DER SPAETPHILOSOPHIE FICHTES
LAUTER KLEINIGKEITEN : SZENEN AUS DEM BERUFS-ALLTAG / Kunzemann, Gertrud – Berlin-Schoeneberg: T Weicher, 1943, c1940 – 1r – 1 – us U.W. Library [830]
Lauterbach, K *see* DIE FLORA DER DEUTSCHEN SCHUTZGEBIETE IN DER SUEDSEE
LAUTERBACHER ANZEIGER : BA DES GIESSENER ANZEIGER – Lauterbach, Germany. 1 Jun 1983- – ca 5r per yr – 1 – gw Mikrofilm [072]
Lauth, Charles *see* RAPPORT GENERAL SUR L'HISTORIQUE ET LE FONCTIONNEMENT DE L'ECOLE MUNICIPALE DE PHYSIQUE ET DE CHIMIE INDUSTRIELLE
Lauth, Franz Joseph *see* AEGYPTISCH-ARAMAEISCHE INSCHRIFTEN
Lavaissiere de Lavergne, Alexandre de *see* LA RICHESSE DE LA FRANCE: FORTUNE ET REVENUES PRIVES
LAVAL MEDICAL – 1936-71 1; 1970-71 5,6 – us UMI [610]
LAVAL MEDICAL *see* VIE MEDICALE AU CANADA FRANCAIS
LAVAL THEOLOGIQUE ET PHILOSOPHIQUE – v1- 1945- 1; v32- 5,6,9 – us UMI [240]
LAVAL THEOLOGIQUE ET PHILOSOPHIQUE – 1(1945)-14(1958) – 115mf – 9 – Dfl403.00 – ne Slangenburg [073]
LAVAL THEOLOGIQUE ET PHILOSOPHIQUE – Quebec City. v1-14. 1945-1958 – 115mf – 9 – ne IDC [240]
LAVAL THEOLOGIQUE ET PHILOSOPHIQUE – Quebec: Presses de l'Universite. v1-1944/45-. SEM35P43 – 7r – 1 – Can$372.00 – cn Bibl Nat [240]
Lavallee, G *see* LA GAZETTE LITTERAIRE
Lavallee, Irene *see* LA VENTE DE L'ASSURANCE-VIE SELON LES BESOINS
Lavallee, Joseph *see* LETTRES D'UN MAMELUCK, OU TABLEAU MORAL ET CRITIQUE...DES MOEURS DE PARIS
Lavallee, P A M *see*
- ARBORETUM SEGREZIANUM
- LES CLEMATITES A GRANDES FLEURS

LAVAL-REPUBLICAIN – Laval, July 1909 – Nov. 1937 – 8r – fr Armell [944]
Lavardin, J de *see* HISTOIRE DE GEORGES CASTRIOT, SVRNOMME SCANDERBEG, ROY D'ALBANIE. CONTENANT SES ILLUSTRES FAICTS, D'ARMES, ET MEMORABLES VICTOIRES A L'ENCONTRE DES TURCS
Lavater, Johann Caspar *see*
- AUS LAVATERS BRIEFTASCHE
- DENKSCHRIFT ZUR HUNDERTSTEN WIEDERKEHR SEINES TODESTAGES

Lavater, Ludwig *see* DE RITIBUS ET INSTITUTIS ECCLESIAE TIGURINAE OPUSCULUM
IL LAVATORE ITALIANO – no. 1-43. Puteaux (Seine). 30 oct 1926-20 aout 1927. mq no. 14 – 1 – fr A.C.R.P.P. [073]
Lavau, G *see* PARTIS POLITIQUES ET REALITES SOCIALES
Laveaux, J -Ch. Thibault de *see*
- NOUVEAU DICTIONNAIRE DE LA LANGUE FRANCAISE

Lavedan, A *see* TRATADO DE LAS ENFERMEDADES EPIDEMICAS, PUTRIDAS, MALIGNAS, CONTAGIOSAS...
Laveille, E *see* THE LIFE OF FATHER DE SMET, S.J., 1801-1873
LAVEILLE LE CARDENAL MERCIER... – Madrid: Razon y Fe, 1927 – 1 – sp Bibl Santa Ana [240]
Laventure, Felix *see* LE JOURNAL
Laverdant, Gabriel-Desire *see* SOCIALISME CATHOLIQUE. LA DEROUTE DES CESARS. LA GAULE TRES CHRETIENNE ET LE CZAR ORTHODOXE
Laverde Ruiz, Gumersindo *see* ENSAYOS CRITICOS SOBRE FILOSOFIA, LITERATURA E INSTRUCCION PUBLICA
Laverdiere, C-H *see* HISTOIRE DU CANADA A L'USAGE DES MAISONS D'EDUCATION
Lavergne, Armand et al *see* LE COMBAT
LAVERNE COURIER – Laverne, CA. 1975-88 – 14r – 1 – $700.00 – R02340 – us Library Micro [071]
Laverty, F J *see* THE INSURANCE LAW OF CANADA
Lavery, Salluste *see* LE BON SENS
Lavigerie *see* L'ESCLAVAGE AFRICAIN, DISCOURS PRONONCE
Lavigne, A *see* EVANGILE SELON SAINT JEAN
Lavington, G *see*
- THE BISHOP OF EXETER'S ANSWER TO MR. J. WESELY'S LATE LETTER TO HIS LORDSHIP
- THE ENTHUSIASM OF METHODISTS AND PAPISTS COMPAR'D [PART 1]
- THE ENTHUSIASM OF METHODISTS AND PAPISTS COMPARED, PART 2

LAVINIA / Broughton, Rhoda – British Fiction Archive: Unit 4 – 9 – uk Bell [830]
Laviron, Gabriel *see* L'ARCHITECTURE CONTEMPORAINE ET LE STYLE GOTHIQUE
LAVISION Y LA VIDA / Sanz de Moreta, Emilio – Badajoz: Tip. Vda. de A. Arqueros, 1945 – 1 – sp Bibl Santa Ana [946]
Lavoie, Amedee *see* BIBLIOGRAPHIE RELATIVE A L'HISTOIRE DE LA NOUVELLE-FRANCE, 1516-1700
Lavoie, J-N *see* OPINIONS DE L'ILE JESUS
Lavoisier, Antoine-Laurent *see* OEUVRES
Lavondes, A *see* LES COLLECTIONS POLYNESIENNES DU MUSEE DU PALAIS DES BEAUX-ARTS, LILLE
IL LAVORATORE – Chicago and New York. Daily. July 1 1924-Sept 26 1931. Not collated. Incomplete – 1 – us NY Public [071]
IL LAVORATORE – Toronto. 1936-38 – 1 – 65.00 – cn McLaren [073]
IL LAVORATORE INDUSTRIALE – San Francisco, CA, 1912 – 1mf or 1r – 1,9 – us I.H.R.C. [978]
IL LAVORATORE ITALIANO – Pittsburg, KS, Aug. 31, 1906-Sep. 22, 1911 – 1r – 1 – us I.H.R.C. [978]
IL LAVORATORE ITALIANO – Pittsburg, KS, Jan. 5, 1912-Jan. 5, 1928 – 4r – 1 – us I.H.R.C. [978]
IL LAVORATORE ITALIANO – Pittsburgh, KS, Dec. 15, 1905-Aug. 24, 1906 – 1r – 1 – us I.H.R.C. [978]
LAVORO – 1992-1995 – 6r per y – 5,6 – Sfr1,123.00 – sz Infoprint [073]
LAVOURA E COMERCIO – Uberaba, 27 Oct 1978-30 Apr 1979 – 1,5,6 – bl Biblioteca [072]
O LAVRENCE – Lavras, 24 Jul, 11 Sep 1887 – 1,5,6 – bl Biblioteca [072]
Lavrin, J *see* FROM PUSHKIN TO MAYAKOVSKY
Lavrov, P A *see* PALEOGRAFICHESKOI OBOZRENIE KIRILLOVSKOGO PIS'MA
LAW – Chicago. v1-2. 1889-90 – 1 – $40.00 – us Hein [073]
LAW : ITS ORIGIN, GROWTH AND FUNCTION / Carter, James Coolidge – New York/London: G P Putnam's Sons, 1907 – 4mf – 9 – $6.00 – LLMC 95-145 – us L.L.M.C. [340]
LAW / Wilkinson, Richard James – Kuala Lumpur, Wallace. 1922-29. 2 pts. L.C. copy imperfect: pt. 2 wanting. LL-10023 – 1 – us L of C Photodup [340]
THE LAW – (Cont by: Law and Commerce after 1907) – New York. v1-7. 1905-09 (all publ) – 57mf – 9 – $85.00 – LLMC 84-524 – us L.L.M.C. [073]
THE LAW : A MONTHLY MAGAZINE OF LEGAL MATTERS – London. v1-2. 1874-75 (all publ) – 7mf – 9 – $10.50 – LLMC 84-543 – us L.L.M.C. [073]
THE LAW – Oklahoma City School of Law. nos 1-2. 1901 (all publ) – 1mf – 9 – $1.50 – LLMC 82-928 – us L.L.M.C. [073]
THE LAW : WHAT I HAVE SEEN, WHAT I HAVE HEARD AND WHAT I HAVE KNOWN / Jay, Cyrus – London: Tinsley Bros, 1868 – 4mf – 9 – $6.00 – LLMC 95-168 – us L.L.M.C. [340]
THE LAW ADVERTISER – London. v1-9. 1823-31 (all publ) – 61mf – 9 – $91.00 – LLMC 84-525 – us L.L.M.C. [073]
LAW AND APPELLATE RECORDS OF THE U.S. CIRCUIT COURT FOR THE EASTERN DISTRICT OF PENNSYLVANIA / U.S. Circuit and District Courts. Pennsylvania – 1790-1847. 26 rolls – 1 – M969 – us Nat'l Archives [324]
LAW AND COMMERCE *see* THE LAW
LAW AND CONTEMPORARY PROBLEMS – v1-1933- 1; v35- 5,6; v39- 9 – us UMI [360]
LAW AND CONTEMPORARY PROBLEMS – v1-57. 1933-94 – 1,5,6 – $990.00 – us Hein [073]
LAW AND COURT NEWS – Chicago. v1 no 1. 1940 (all publ) – 1mf – 9 – $1.50 – LLMC 84-535 – us L.L.M.C. [073]
THE LAW AND COVENANT: BEING THE RESTORATION OF TWO OF THE BOOKS OF MOSES : EACH IN TWO VERSIONS, AND DESIGNATED HEREIN AS THE SINAITIC TORA AND THE BOOK OF THE COVENANT: ACCORDING TO RECONTRUCTIVE CRITICISM / Martin, William Wallace – New York: Eaton & Mains; Cincinnati: Jennings & Pye, c1902 – 1mf – 9 – 0-8370-4302-6 – 1985-2302 – us A.T.L.A. [220]
THE LAW AND CUSTOMS OF THE STOCK EXCHANGE / Melsheimer, Rudolph Eyre – London: Sweet and Maxwell, 1891. 199p. LL-121 – 1 – us L of C Photodup [340]
LAW AND CYBERNETICS / Tenorio, Igor – Brasilia Editora de Brasilia 1972? 131 p. LL-8028 – 1 – us L of C Photodup [340]
LAW AND EDUCATIONAL PLANNING / Birch, Ian – 1994 – 86p – 9 – 92-803-1150-6 – fr UNESCO [340]
LAW AND EQUITY REPORTER – (Covers Am, Eng, Irish and Indian cases. Cont by: The Reporter) – New York: Cricton/Hurd & Houghton. v1-4. 1876-77 (all publ) – 35mf – 9 – $52.00 – LLMC 81-414 – us L.L.M.C. [073]
LAW AND EQUITY REPORTER *see* THE AMERICAN LAW TIMES REPORTS
THE LAW AND EQUITY REPORTER *see* THE REPORTER
LAW AND FORMS OF PRAYERS AND INSTRUCTIONS / Ashman, Louis S – Baltimore, Hepbron & Haydon, 1923. 421 p. LL-698 – 1 – us L of C Photodup [340]
LAW AND GOVERNMENT / Kingsbury, Harmon – 1849 – 9 – us A.T.L.A. [240]
LAW AND HISTORY REVIEW – v1-13. 1983-95 – 9 – $198.00set – us Hein [340]
LAW AND HUMAN BEHAVIOR – (v14-18 1990-94 $100.00v) – v1-13, 1977-89 – 1,5 – $65.00v – us UMI [340]
LAW AND INEQUALITY : A JOURNAL OF THEORY AND PRACTICE – University of Minnesota. v1-14. 1983-96 – 9 – $217.00 set – us Hein [340]
LAW AND JUSTICE : THE CHRISTIAN LAW REVIEW – (Title varies: no 1-41 as Quis Custodiet) – nos 1-127. 1962-95 – 9 – $272.00 set – us Hein [340]
LAW AND LABOR : A PERIODICAL ON THE LAW OF THE LABOR PROBLEM – New York: League for Industrial Rights. v1-14. 1919-32 (all publ) – 9 – LLMC 84-349 – us L.L.M.C. [073]
LAW AND LAUGHTER : ILLUSTRATED WITH PORTRAITS OF EMINENT MEMBERS OF THE BENCH AND BAR / Morton, George A & Malloch, D Macleod – London, Edinburgh: T N Foulis, 1913 – 4mf – 9 – $6.00 – LLMC 95-162 – us L.L.M.C. [870]
LAW AND LAUGHTER / Morton George A & Malloch, D Macleod – (Includes index) – Boston/London/Edinburgh: L Roy Phillips/T N Foulis, n.d. – 5mf – 9 – $7.50 – LLMC 91-075 – us L.L.M.C. [870]
LAW AND MILITARY OPERATIONS IN HAITI, 1994-1995 : LESSONS LEARNED FOR JUDGE ADVOCATES – Charlottesville, VA: Center for Law & Military Operations, 11 Dec 1995 – 5mf – 9 – $7.50 – LLMC 96-070 – us L.L.M.C. [340]
LAW AND ORDER – v1- 1953- 1; v20- 5,6; v23- 9 – us UMI [360]
LAW AND PHILOSOPHY – v1-13. 1981-94 – 9 – us Hein [340]
LAW AND PHILOSOPHY – (v3- 1984- 5,6,9) – v1- Apr 1982- – 1 – us UMI [340]
LAW AND POLICY IN INTERNATIONAL BUSINESS – v1- 1969- 1; v9- 5,6,9 – us UMI [340]
LAW AND POLICY IN INTERNATIONAL BUSINESS – Georgetown University. v1-26. 1969-95 – 9 – $618.00 set – us Hein [340]
THE LAW AND PRACTICE CONCERNING CONTROBERTED [I.E. CONTROVERTED] PARLIAMENTARY ELECTIONS IN THE PROVINCE OF CANADA / Notman, John – Quebec: Hunter, Rose and Co., 1863. SEM105P172 – 2mf – 9 – Can$4.50 – cn Bibl Nat [323]
THE LAW AND PRACTICE IN BANKRUPTCY. / Blumenstiel, Alexander – New York, Ward & Peloubet, 1878. 765 p. LL-1458 – 1 – us L of C Photodup [340]

THE LAW AND PRACTICE IN BANKRUPTCY UNDER THE NATIONAL BANKRUPTCY ACT OF 1898 / Collier, William Miller – (4th ed. by William Hotchkiss. 5th and rev. ed., with amendments and decisions to date, by Frank B. Gilbert. Albany, N.Y., Bender, 1905. 1038 p. LL-1655. 1. 4th ed. by William Hotchkiss. 10th ed. with amendments of statutes and rules, and all decisions to April 1, 1914. By Frank B. Gilbert. Albany, N.Y., Bender, 1914. 1513 p. LL-679. 1) – 3d ed. Albany, N.Y., Bender, 1900. 866 p. LL-678 – 1 – us L of C Photodup [340]

THE LAW AND PRACTICE IN PROCEEDINGS SUPPLEMENTARY TO EXECUTION. UNDER THE NEW YORK CODE / Riddle, Daniel S – (2nd ed. New York: Strouse, 1882. 380, 220p. LL-1275) – New York: Diossy & Cockcroft, 1866. 380p. Supplement. New York: Diossy, 1877. 128p. LL-1669 – 1 – us L of C Photodup [340]

THE LAW AND PRACTICE OF ATTACHMENT, UNDER THE CODE OF VIRGINIA. / Daniel, John Warwick – Lynchburg, Schaffter & Bryant, 1869. 304 p. LL-692 – 1 – us L of C Photodup [340]

THE LAW AND PRACTICE OF REFEREES AND REFERENCES UNDER THE CODE OF CIVIL PROCEDURE AND STATUTES OF THE STATE OF NEW YORK / Cooper, Morris – New York: Diossy, 1888. 434p. LL-625 – 1 – us L of C Photodup [340]

THE LAW AND PRACTICE OF THE MUNICIPAL COURT OF THE CITY OF NEW YORK UNDER THE GREATER NEW YORK CHARTER. / Langbein, George Frederick – (5th ed. New York, Baker, Voorhis, 1902. 628 p. LL-292. Suppl. New York, 1905. 147 p. LL-292) – 4th ed. New York, Banks, 1898. 609 p. LL-443 – 1 – us L of C Photodup [340]

THE LAW AND PRACTICE UNDER THE ACT FOR QUIETING TITLES TO REAL ESTATE IN UPPER CANADA / Turner, Robert J – Toronto, Adam, Stevenson, 1867. 84 p. LL-2217 – 1 – us L of C Photodup [340]

THE LAW AND PRACTICE UNDER THE STATUTES IN THE STATE OF NEW YORK / Jones, Dwight Arven – 6th ed. New York, Baker, Voorhis, 1900. 129 p. LL-1329 – 1 – us L of C Photodup [340]

LAW AND PSYCHOLOGY REVIEW – (v1-8 1975-84 on reel $65.00. v9-19 1985-95 on mf $134.00) – University of Alabama. v1-19. 1975-95 – 5,6,9 – $199.00 set – us Hein [340]

LAW AND SEXUALITY : A REVIEW OF LESBIAN AND GAY LEGAL ISSUES – Tulane University. v1-5. 1991-95 – 9 – $57.00 set – us Hein [340]

LAW AND SOCIAL INQUIRY *see* AMERICAN BAR FOUNDATION RESEARCH JOURNAL

LAW AND SOCIETY REVIEW – (1979-. 1,5,6,9) – v1-. 1966- – 1 – us UMI [073]

LAW AND SOCIETY REVIEW – (v1-18 1966-84 on reel $236.00. v19-26 1985-92 on mf $224.00) – v1-26. 1966-92 – 5,6,9 – $460.00 set – us Hein [340]

LAW AND SOCIETY REVIEW – v1-24. 1966-90 – 1,5,6 – $405.00 – us Hein [073]

LAW AND SPECIFICATIONS FOR ENGINEERS AND SCIENTISTS / Jessup, Walter Edgar – Englewood Cliffs, N.J., Prentice-Hall 1963 585 p. LL-2264 – 1 – us L of C Photodup [340]

THE LAW AND THE GOSPEL OF LABOR / Waring, Luther Hess – New York: Neale, 1907 – 1mf – us A.T.L.A. [240]

THE LAW AND THE PROPHETS / Watson, Frederick – London: T. Fisher Unwin, 1884. 1 fiche – 9 – us A.T.L.A. [240]

LAW AND THE SOCIAL ORDER *see* ARIZONA STATE LAW JOURNAL

LAW AS A MEANS TO AN END / Ihering, Rudolf von – New York: The Macmillan Co, 1914 (reprint 1924) – 6mf – 9 – $9.00 – LLMC 95-185 – us L.L.M.C. [340]

LAW ASSOCIATION FOR ASIA AND THE PACIFIC – Kensington. 57 docs. 1980-1992 – 82mf – 9 – ne IDC [340]

LAW AT A GLANCE / Carey, Thomas Joseph – (Rev. ed., New York: Excelsior 1911. 319p. LL-1001) – New York: Excelsior 1893. 317p. LL-998 – 1 – us L of C Photodup [340]

LAW BONDS: INDENTURE OF MORTGAGE; THE COMPANY TO THE HON. GEORGE EULAS FOSTER, THE HON. JOHN JOSEPH CALDWELL ABBOTT AND RICHARD BLADWORTH ANGUS, TRUSTEES: 2ND JUNE, 1888 / Canadian Pacific Railway Company – 1888? 02075. (Pre-1900 Canadiana) – 9 – cn C.I.H.M. [380]

THE LAW BOOK ADVISER : A JOURNAL OF LEGAL BIBLIOGRAPHY – (Lacking: nos 2-8) – Washington, DC: John Byrne & Co. v1 no 1. Sept 1984 – 1mf – 9 – $1.50 – LLMC 84-526 – us L.L.M.C. [073]

THE LAW BOOK BROKER – (Also known as: The Lawyer's Review) – v1 nos 1-10. 1915-16 (all publ) – 3mf – 9 – $4.50 – LLMC 84-527 – us L.L.M.C. [073]

LAW BOOK NEWS – (Lacking: v1 no 1 1888) – Philadelphia. v1-2. 1889-96 (all publ) – 3mf – 9 – $4.50 – LLMC 84-528 – us L.L.M.C. [073]

LAW BOOK NEWS : A MONTHLY REVIEW OF CURRENT LEGAL LITERATURE AND JOURNAL OF LEGAL BIBLIOGRAPHY – St Paul: West Publ Co. v1-2. 1894-95 (all publ) – 10mf – 9 – $15.00 – LLMC 84-529 – us L.L.M.C. [073]

LAW BOOK REVIEW DIGEST AND CURRENT LEGAL BIBLIOGRAPHY – Philadelphia. v1 nos 1-4. 1931-32 (all publ) – 2mf – 9 – $3.00 – LLMC 84-530 – us L.L.M.C. [073]

THE LAW BULLETIN OF THE STATE UNIVERSITY OF IOWA – v1-5. Oct 1891-Feb 1901 (all publ) – 22mf – 9 – $33.00 – LLMC 82-930 – us L.L.M.C. [073]

LAW CASE FILES OF THE U.S. CIRCUIT COURT FOR THE SOUTHERN DISTRICT OF NEW YORK / U.S. Circuit and District Courts. New York – 1790-1846. 43 rolls – 1 – M883 – us Nat'l Archives [324]

LAW CASE FILES OF THE U.S. DISTRICT COURT FOR THE SOUTHERN DISTRICT OF NEW YORK / U.S. Circuit and District Courts. New York – 1795-1844. 15 rolls – 1 – M937 – us Nat'l Archives [324]

THE LAW CENTRAL – Washington, DC. nos 1-3. 1881 (all publ) – 2mf – 9 – $3.00 – LLMC 82-931 – us L.L.M.C. [073]

THE LAW CHRONICLE : A MONTHLY JOURNAL – (Cont as: The Law Chronicle and Law Student's Magazine ns: v1-2. 1859-60 (all publ)) – v1-5. 1854-58. ns: v1-2. 1859-60 (all publ) – 14mf – 9 – $63.00 – LLMC 84-352 – us L.L.M.C. [073]

THE LAW CHRONICLE : OR JOURNAL OF JURISPRUDENCE AND LEGISLATION – Edinburgh. v1-4. 1829-31 (all publ) – 16mf – 9 – $24.00 – LLMC 84-531 – us L.L.M.C. [073]

LAW CHRONICLE AND ESTATE ADVERTISER *see* AUCTION REGISTER AND LAW CHRONICLE

THE LAW CHRONICLE AND LAW STUDENT'S MAGAZINE *see* THE LAW CHRONICLE

LAW CHRONICLE, COMMERCIAL AND BANKRUPTCY REGISTER *see* AUCTION REGISTER AND LAW CHRONICLE

LAW (CIVIL ACTION) RECORDS FOR THE U.S. DISTRICT COURT FOR THE EASTERN DISTRICT OF PENNSYLVANIA / U.S. Circuit and District Courts. Pennsylvania – 1789-1844. 40 rolls – 1 – M1057 – us Nat'l Archives [324]

THE LAW CLERK – (With v2 cont by: The Law Clerk and Municipal Assistant 1907-13) – London. v1-7. 1906-1913 – 7mf – 9 – $31.50 – LLMC 84-533 – us L.L.M.C. [073]

THE LAW CLERK AND MUNICIPAL ASSISTANT *see* THE LAW CLERK

LAW CLERK HANDBOOK : A HANDBOOK FOR LAW CLERKS TO FEDERAL JUDGES / Rubin, Alvin B & Bartell, Laura B – Washington: FJC, 1989 – 2mf – 9 – $3.00 – LLMC 95-346 – us L.L.M.C. [340]

LAW COLLECTION / Bibliotheque Nationale – 5titles on 27 fiches by Beaurepaire, Favre, Gin, Michel and Quetelet. Available separately – 9 – 67.00 – fr Bibl Nationale [080]

THE LAW COUNSELLOR – Cincinnati, OH. 1 issue Oct 1887 (all publ) – 1mf – 9 – $1.50 – LLMC 84-534 – us L.L.M.C. [073]

LAW, CRIME AND SOCIETY IN HANOVERIAN ENGLAND – 1714-1834. The Old Bailey Proceedings – 1 – us Primary [941]

LAW DAYS; OR, DIES JURIDICI, COMMONLY CALLED "TERMS OF COURT," THEIR APPLICATION TO COURTS IN GENERAL, AND PARTICULARLY TO THE MARINE COURT OF THE CITY OF NEW YORK / McAdam, David – New York, Diossy, 1874. 45 p. LL-620 – 1 – us L of C Photodup [340]

THE LAW DICTIONARY : DEFINING AND INTERPRETING THE TERMS OF WORDS OF ART AND EXPLAINING THE RISE, PROGRESS AND PRESENT STATE OF THE ENGLISH LAW, ABSTRACTED FROM THE LAST QUARTO EDITION / ed by Tomlins, Thomas Edlyne – 1v. 1762-1841. London: R Baldwin, 1810 – 11mf – 9 – $16.50 – LLMC 95-427 – us L.L.M.C. [340]

LAW ENFORCEMENT AND CRIMINAL JUSTICE: INFORMATION DATABASE – (Annual Update. 22125.00y; 9) – 1952-80. Ed. by R. Voight – 9 – 22400.00; 225.00t – us I.R.E. [340]

LAW ENFORCEMENT BULLETIN / U.S. Federal Bureau of Investigation – (v47- . 1978- . 5,6,9) – v. 1-. 1932- – 1 – us UMI [360]

LAW ENFORCEMENT COMMUNICATIONS – v1-1974- 1; v4- 5,6,9 – us UMI [360]

LAW ENFORCEMENT JOURNAL – v. 1-. 1970- – 1 – us UMI [360]

LAW ENFORCEMENT NEWS – v.1-. 1975- – 1 – us UMI [073]

THE LAW EXAMINATION JOURNAL AND LAW STUDENTS' MAGAZINE – v1-4. 1869-85 (all publ) – 27mf – 9 – $40.50 – LLMC 84-536 – us L.L.M.C. [073]

LAW EXAMINATIONS, EMBRACING EXAMINATION PAPERS FROM THE YEAR 1869 TO 1894 / Anderson Bros. Charlottesville, Va – 4th ed. Charlottesville 1894. 193 p. LL-413 – 1 – us L of C Photodup [340]

LAW FOR THE CLERGY: A COMPILATION OF THE STATUTES OF THE STATES OF ILLINOIS, INDIANA, IOWA, MICHIGAN, MINNESOTA, OHIO, AND WISCONSIN. / Hudson, Sanford Amos – Chicago: Griggs, 1877. 192p. LL-1658 – 1 – us L of C Photodup [340]

LAW FOR THE MASSES: FOR EVERY-DAY USE / Hastings, Truman – Cleveland: Schneider 1877. 281p. LL-342 – 1 – us L of C Photodup [340]

Law, Frederick Houk *see* SCIENCE IN LITERATURE; A COLLECTION OF LITERARY SCIENTIFIC ESSAYS..

THE LAW GAZETTE – (Lacking: v1-2,7-8) – London. v1-8. 1890-1894 (all publ) – LLMC 84-5381 – us L.L.M.C. [073]

THE LAW GAZETTE – London. 1v. 1822 (all publ) – 9 – LLMC 84-537 – us L.L.M.C. [073]

A LAW GLOSSARY OF THE LATIN, GREEK, NORMAN, FRENCH, AND OTHER LANGUAGES : INTERSPERSED IN THE COMMENTARIES BY SIR W. BLACKSTONE, AND VARIOUS LAW TREATISES UPON EACH BRANCH OF THE PROFESSION, TRANSLATED INTO ENGLISH AND ALPHABETICALLY ARRANGED – 2nd ed. London: J & W T Clarke. 1v. 1823 – 3mf – 9 – $4.50 – LLMC 95-425 – us L.L.M.C. [340]

LAW IN A FREE STATE / Donisthorpe. Wordsworth – 1895, 323p – 9 – 1.00f – at Libertarian Micro [335]

THE LAW IN THE PROPHETS / Leathes, Stanley – London: Eyre & Spottiswoode, 1891. 1 fiche – 9 – us A.T.L.A. [240]

LAW IN TRANSITION QUARTERLY – 1964-67 – 1 – us UMI [340]

LAW INSTITUTE JOURNAL – (v1-58 1927-84 on reel or mf $460.00. v59-69 1985-95 on mf $419.00) – Law Institute of Victoria. v1-69. 1927-95 – 5,6,9 – $879.00 set – us Hein [340]

LAW INSTITUTE JOURNAL – (v.54-. 1980-. 5,6,9) – v.1-. 1927- – 1 – us UMI [073]

LAW JOURNAL – New York. N.Y. 1888- – 1 – us UMI [340]

LAW JOURNAL – New York. N.Y. and pred. 1872- – 1 – us UMI [340]

THE LAW JOURNAL : ANNOTATED CASE REPORTS – London. v1-2. 1803-04 (all publ) – 9 – LLMC 84-539 – us L.L.M.C. [073]

THE LAW JOURNAL : NOTES OF CASES IN...LAW AND EQUITY – London. v1- 1866- – 9 – LLMC 84-541 – us L.L.M.C. [073]

THE LAW JOURNAL REPORTS *see* THE LAW JOURNAL / THE LAW JOURNAL REPORTS

THE LAW JOURNAL / THE LAW JOURNAL REPORTS / Great Britain. Courts of Chancery, King's Bench and Common Pleas – (Title change with v4 of New Series, 1835 to: The Law Journal Reports) – os: v1-9. 1822/23-1831. London: J W Paget/E B Ince, n.d-1831. ns: v1-94. 1832-1925. London: E B Ince/Proprietors of the Law Journal Reports, 1832-1925 (all publ) – 9 – LLMC 95-278 – us L.L.M.C. [340]

LAW, LAWYERS AND LAMBS / Kneeland, Stillman Foster – New York: Banks Law Publ Co, 1910 – 2mf – 9 – $3.00 – LLMC 95-154 – us L.L.M.C. [340]

THE LAW LECTURES TREATING OF THE RIGHTS WHICH RELATE TO THINGS REAL AND PERSONAL. / Pearson, Richmond Mumford – Raleigh: Edwards, Broughton, 1879. 523p. LL-1149 – 1 – us L of C Photodup [340]

THE LAW LEXICON : OR, DICTIONARY OF JURISPRUDENCE; EXPLAINING THE TECHNICAL WORDS AND PHRASES EMPLOYED IN SEVERAL DEPARTMENTS OF ENGLISH LAW; INCLUDING THE VARIOUS LEGAL TERMS USED IN COMMERCIAL BUSINESS... / ed by Wharton, John Jane Smith – 4th ed. London: Stevens. 1v. 1867 – 11mf – 9 – $16.50 – LLMC 95-455 – us L.L.M.C. [340]

THE LAW LIBRARIAN : A QUARTERLY JOURNAL – v1-2. 1887-90 (all publ) – 9 – LLMC 82-932 – us L.L.M.C. [073]

THE LAW LIBRARY – 23 reels – 1 – $750.00 – us Trans-Media [340]

THE LAW LIBRARY : A MONTHLY REVIEW OF LEGAL LITERATURE – Milwaukee. 1v (all publ) – 9 – LLMC 84-542 – us L.L.M.C. [073]

THE LAW LIBRARY – v1-16. 1833-37. ns: v1-88. 1837-61 (all publ) – 9 – apply for prices – LLMC 82-933 – us L.L.M.C. [020]

LAW LIBRARY BUILDINGS REPORTER – (A reprint of building plans, project programs and specifications, and assorted other planning documents related to Law Library construction or renovation from various university law libraries. Includes a cumulative index) – 63mf – 9 – $94.00 backfile – LLMC 81-800 – us L.L.M.C. [340]

LAW LIBRARY COLLECTION / United Nations – Documents and publications tailored to the needs of the Law Library – 9 – us Readex [340]

LAW LIBRARY JOURNAL – 1- 1908- 1; v64-5,6; v70- 9 – us UMI [340]

LAW LIBRARY JOURNAL – American Association of Law Libraries. v1-29-1908-1936 (all offered) – 44mf – $66.00 – LLMC 95-108 – us L.L.M.C. [073]

LAW LIBRARY JOURNAL – v. 1-35. 1908-42 – 1,5,6 – us Princeton Micro [340]

LAW LIBRARY PACKAGE PLAN / American Association of Law Libraries – (Annual retrospective mf ed) – American Association of Law Libraries, 1982/83-1993-94 – 305mf – 9 – $457.00 backfile ($50.00 standing order) – LLMC 83-200 – us L.L.M.C. [340]

THE LAW LIBRARY TO THE YEAR 2000 : STORING AND PRESERVING THE COLLECTIONS / Dupont, Jerry – Ann Arbor: University of Michigan Law Library, 1972 – 2mf – 9 – $3.00 – LLMC 82-999 – us L.L.M.C. [340]

LAW MAGAZINE AND REVIEW – Five series. 1828-1915.31 reels – 1 – $1,750.00 – us Trans-Media [340]

LAW, MEDICINE AND HEALTH CARE *see* JOURNAL OF LAW MEDICINE AND ETHICS

Law, N N *see* GAUTAMA BUDDHA

LAW NOTES – (Add vols as copyright expires) – New York: Thompson. v1-15. 1897-1912 – 45mf – 9 – $67.00 – LLMC 82-934 – us L.L.M.C. [073]

LAW NOTES : A MONTHLY MAGAZINE FOR LAW STUDENTS AND OTHERS – (Also known as: Gibson's Law Notes. Add vols as copyright expires) – London: Gibson. v1-31 + 4 indexes. 1882-1912 – 66mf – 9 – $297.00 – LLMC 84-545 – us L.L.M.C. [073]

LAW NR. 5 FOR THE ORGANIZATION OF PLANNING AND DEVELOPMENT AFFAIRS, AND THE REGULATIONS AND DECISIONS ISSUED THEREUNDER / Libya. Ministry of Planning and Development. Legislation. Economic Administration – Tripoli. 1965. BNE-707 1 – 9 – ne IDC [338]

LAW OF ADMINISTRATIVE PROCEDURE / Bulgaria. Laws, Statutes, etc – Sofia, Ministry of Justice, 1970. 38 p. LL-4202 – 1 – us L of C Photodup [340]

LAW OF ADMINISTRATIVE VIOLATIONS AND PUNISHMENTS / Bulgaria. Laws, Statutes, etc – Sofia, Ministry of Justice, 1970. 37 p. LL-4203 – 1 – us L of C Photodup [340]

LAW OF ASSOCIATIONS AND RELIGIOUS CONGREGATIONS OF JUNE 1, 1933 – n.p., 193? Fiche W993. (Blodgett Collection of Spanish Civil War Pamphlets) – 9 – us H.U. College Libr [946]

THE LAW OF ASYLUM IN ISRAEL HISTORICALLY AND CRITICALLY EXAMINED / Bissell, Allen Page – Leipzig: Theodor Stauffer, 1884 – 1mf – 9 – 0-8370-2350-5 – 1985-0350 – us A.T.L.A. [340]

THE LAW OF ATTACHMENT IN MARYLAND / Hodge, William L – Baltimore: Scrimger, 1895. 292p. LL-715 – 1 – us L of C Photodup [340]

THE LAW OF ATTACHMENTS IN MARYLAND / Hinkley, Edward Otis – Baltimore: Cushings & Bailey, 1869. 238p. LL-713 – 1 – us L of C Photodup [340]

THE LAW OF BANKRUPTCY, INCLUDING THE NATIONAL BANKRUPTCY LAW OF 1898. / Brandenburg, Edwin Charles – (2nd ed. Chicago, Callaghan, 1901. 988 p. LL-1459. 1) – Chicago, Callaghan, 1898. 692 p. LL-59 – 1 – us L of C Photodup [340]

THE LAW OF BARON AND FEMME; OF PARENT AND CHILD. / Reeve, Tapping – (2nd ed. New York, Banks, Gould, 1846. 493 (i.e. 466) 6 p. LL-1085. 3rd ed. Albany, Gould, 1874. 677p. LL-1086) – New Haven, Steele, 1816. 494 7 p., 1l.LL-863 – 1 – us L of C Photodup [340]

THE LAW OF BLOCKADE,... / Deane, J P – London, 1855 – 3mf – 1 – ILM-481/1 – ne IDC [327]

THE LAW OF BLOCKADE:... / Deane, H B – London, 1870 – 1mf – 1 – ILM-479/1 – ne IDC [327]

THE LAW OF CARRIERS OF GOODS AND PASSENGERS. / Redfield, Isaac Fletcher – Cambridge, Mass., Houghton, 1869. 599 p. LL-1123 – 1 – us L of C Photodup [340]

THE LAW OF CIVILIZATION AND DECAY : AN ESSAY ON HISTORY / Adams, Brooks – London, New York: Macmillan, 1896 – 1mf – us A.T.L.A. [900]

THE LAW OF COLLATERAL AND DIRECT INHERITANCE, LEGACY AND SUCCESSION TAXES, EMBRACING ALL AMERICAN AND MANY ENGLISH DECISIONS. / Dos Passos, Benjamin Franklin – 2d ed. St. Paul, West, 1895. 654 p. LL-1629 – 1 – us L of C Photodup [340]

THE LAW OF CONSTRUCTIVE CONTEMPT. THE SHEPHERD CASE REVIEWED / Thomas, John Lilburn – St. Louis, Thomas, 1904. 270 p. LL-1347 – 1 – us L of C Photodup [340]

THE LAW OF CONTRACTS / Parsons, Theophilus – (4th ed. Boston: Little, Brown, 1860. 2v. LL-944. 9th ed. Boston: Little, Brown, 1904. 3v. LL-1431) – Boston: Little, Brown, 1853-55. 2v. LL-821 – 1 – us L of C Photodup [340]

THE LAW OF CORPORATIONS, CONTAINING THE GENERAL STATUTES OF THE STATE OF ILLINOIS ON THE SUBJECT. / Root, James P – 6th ed. Chicago: Myers, 1895. 283p. LL-1349 – 1 – us L of C Photodup [340]

THE LAW OF CREEDS IN SCOTLAND : A TREATISE ON THE LEGAL RELATION OF CHURCHES IN SCOTLAND ESTABLISHED AND NOT ESTABLISHED, TO THEIR DOCTRINAL CONFESSIONS / Innes, Alexander Taylor – Edinburgh: W. Blackwood, 1867 – 2mf – us A.T.L.A. [240]

THE LAW OF CRIMINAL CONSPIRACIES AND AGREEMENTS / Wright, Robert Samuel – Philadelphia, Blackstone, 1887. 320 p. LL-1566 – 1 – us L of C Photodup [340]

THE LAW OF CROWN PRIVILEGE IN CANADA AND ELSEWHERE / Linstead, Stephen G – 1968 124 l. LL-202 – 1 – us L of C Photodup [340]

THE LAW OF DEFAMATION, LIBEL AND SLANDER IN CIVIL AND CRIMINAL CASES AS ADMINISTERED IN THE COURTS OF THE UNITED STATES OF AMERICA / Newell, Martin L – Chicago: Callaghan, 1890. 1025p. LL-266 – 1 – us L of C Photodup [340]

THE LAW OF DOMICIL... / Dicey, A V – London, 1879 – 5mf – 1 – ILM-3124/1 – ne IDC [327]

THE LAW OF DOMICILE IN ITS RELATION TO SUCCESSION ... / Bentwich, N – London, 1911 – 3mf – 9 – ILM-3113/1 – ne IDC [327]

THE LAW OF ELECTRIC WIRES IN STREETS AND HIGHWAYS / Keasbey, Edward Quinton – 2nd ed. Chicago, Callaghan, 1900. 358 p. LL-92 – 1 – us L of C Photodup [340]

THE LAW OF ELECTRICITY / Thompson, Seymour Dwight – St. Louis, Central Law Journal Co. 1891. 525 p. LL-1049 – 1 – us L of C Photodup [340]

THE LAW OF EMINENT DOMAIN. / Nichols, Philip – 2d ed. Albany, N.Y.: Bender, 1917. 2v. LL-451 – 1 – us L of C Photodup [340]

THE LAW OF EMPLOYED INVENTORS IN EUROPE / Neumeyer, Fredrik – Washington: Govt. Print. Off., 1963. 156p. LL-4208 – 1 – us L of C Photodup [340]

LAW OF EVIDENCE / Gorter, James Polk – Baltimore: Hepbron and Haydon, 1916. 295p. LL-479 – 1 – us L of C Photodup [340]

THE LAW OF EVIDENCE IN CIVIL CASES / Jones, Burr W – (2d ed. San Francisco, Bancroft-Whitney, 1911. 1368 p. LL-911) – San Francisco, Bancroft-Whitney, 1896. 3 v. LL-769 – 1 – us L of C Photodup [340]

THE LAW OF EXPERT AND OPINION EVIDENCE REDUCED TO RULES. / Lawson, John Davison – 2nd ed. Chicago, Flood, 1900. 655 p. LL-770 – 1 – us L of C Photodup [340]

THE LAW OF EXPERT TESTIMONY / Rogers, Henry Wade – St. Louis: Stevenson, 1883. 297p. LL-1241 – 1 – us L of C Photodup [340]

THE LAW OF FIELD-SPORTS / Smith, George Putnam – New York: Judd, 1886. 128p. LL-1556 – 1 – us L of C Photodup [340]

THE LAW OF FIRE INSURANCE / Ostrander, Dempster – Chicago: Rollins, 1892. 670p. LL-330 – 1 – us L of C Photodup [340]

LAW OF FORCIBLE ENTRY AND DETAINER, IN THE STATE OF ILLINOIS / Cunningham, William Bennett – Chicago, Regan 1885 155 p. LL-607 – 1 – us L of C Photodup [340]

LAW OF FOREIGN CORPORATIONS / Murfree, William Law – St. Louis, Mo.: Central Law Journal Co., 1893. 376p. LL-23 – 1 – us L of C Photodup [340]

THE LAW OF FORGIVENESS AS PRESENTED IN THE NEW TESTAMENT / Schulhof, John Maurice – Cambridge: Heffer, 1901.1 fiche – 9 – us A.T.L.A. [240]

THE LAW OF FRATERNITIES AND SOCIETIES... WITH SPECIAL REFERENCE TO THEIR INSURANCE FEATURE / Hirschl, Andrew Jackson – St. Louis: Stevenson, 1883. 74p. LL-277 – 1 – us L of C Photodup [340]

THE LAW OF FREEDOM AND BONDAGE IN THE UNITED STATES / Hurd, John C – Boston, N.Y.: Little, Brown & Co/D Van Nostrand. 2v. 1858 – 16mf – 9 – $24.00 – LLMC 92-108 – us L.L.M.C. [340]

THE LAW OF GROWTH AND OTHER SERMONS / Brooks, Phillips – New York: E.P. Dutton, 1902 – 1mf – us A.T.L.A. [240]

LAW OF HOTELS, BOARDING HOUSES AND LODGING HOUSES, PARTICULARLY ADAPTED TO THE STATE OF WISCONSIN / Scanlan, Charles Martin – Milwaukee: Riverside, 1890. 150p. LL-1352 – 1 – us L of C Photodup [340]

THE LAW OF HUSBAND AND WIFE / Stewart, David – San Francisco, Whitney, 1885. 749 p. LL-1084 – 1 – us L of C Photodup [340]

THE LAW OF HUSBAND AND WIFE, OF PARENT AND CHILD, GUARDIAN AND WARD, MASTER AND SERVANT / Reeve, Tapping – 4th ed., Albany, N.Y., Gould, 1888. 541 p. LL-1081 – 1 – us L of C Photodup [340]

THE LAW OF INJUNCTIONS / Hilliard, Francis – 3d ed. Philadelphia: Kay, 1874. 787p. LL-759 – 1 – us L of C Photodup [340]

THE LAW OF INNS, HOTELS AND BOARDING HOUSES. / Wandell, Samuel Henry – Rochester, N.Y., Williamson & Higbie, 1888. 271 p. LL-1319 – 1 – us L of C Photodup [340]

THE LAW OF INSOLVENCY / Cowdery, Jabez Franklin – San Francisco, Bancroft, 1880. 174 p. LL-785 – 1 – us L of C Photodup [340]

THE LAW OF INSURANCE, AS APPLIED TO FIRE, LIFE, ACCIDENT, GUARANTEE, AND OTHER NON-MARITIME RISKS / May, John Wilder – 3d ed. Boston: Little, Brown, 1891. 2v. LL-615 – 1 – us L of C Photodup [340]

THE LAW OF INSURANCE IN TEXAS. / Morse, Frederic Clarke – Austin, Tex.: Southern Law Book, 1917. 821p. LL-677 – 1 – us L of C Photodup [340]

LAW OF INTERNATIONAL WATER RESOURCES – 1980 – 335p – it F.A.O. [340]

LAW OF LAND WARFARE – Ann Arbor, MI: The Judge Advocate General's School, 1 Sep 1943 – 3mf – 9 – $4.50 – LLMC 96-072 – us L.L.M.C. [340]

(LAW OF LANDLORD AND TENANT) / Bengal. India (State) – A digest of the law of landlord and tenant in the provinces subject to the Lieutenant-Governor of Bengal. C.D. Field, Calcutta: Bengal Secretariat Press, 1879. 253p. Bibliog. references and index. 1 reel. 1232 – 1 – us U.W. Library [340]

THE LAW OF LANDLORD AND TENANT IN ONTARIO / Millstone, Maurice Shelly – Toronto: Blackstone, 1940. 80p. LL-2225 – 1 – us L of C Photodup [340]

THE LAW OF LIBEL: IN WHICH IS CONTAINED A GENERAL HISTORY OF THIS LAW IN THE ANCIENT CODES. / Holt, Francis Ludlow – 1st Amer. from the 2nd London ed. New York: Gould, Murden, 1818. 328p. LL-1638 – 1 – us L of C Photodup [340]

THE LAW OF LIS PENDENS AND IN PART OF MECHANICS' LIENS. / Clarke, Samuel Robinson – Toronto: Murray, 1889. 50p. LL-2224 – 1 – us L of C Photodup [340]

THE LAW OF MANDAMUS AND THE PRACTICE CONNECTED WITH IT, WITH AN APPENDIX OF FORMS / Moses, Halsey H – Albany: Gould, 1866. 268p. LL-250 – 1 – us L of C Photodup [340]

THE LAW OF MARRIAGE AND DIVORCE / Keezer, Frank H – Boston, Nagel, 1906. 609 p. LL-452 – 1 – us L of C Photodup [340]

LAW OF MECHANICS' LIENS IN PENNSYLVANIA / Johnson, Ovid Frazer, Jr – 2d ed. Philadelphia, Welsh, 1886. 512 p. L.O.C. copy imperfect: p. 25-32 wanting. LL-88 – 1 – us L of C Photodup [340]

THE LAW OF MINES AND MINING INJURIES / White, Edward Joseph – St. Louis, Thomas, 1903. 966 p. LL-1506 – 1 – us L of C Photodup [340]

THE LAW OF MINES, QUARRIES, AND MINERALS / MacSwinney, Robert Forster – 2nd ed. London: Sweet and Maxwell, 1897. 899p. LL-119 – 1 – us L of C Photodup [622]

THE LAW OF MORTGAGES, OF REAL AND PERSONAL PROPERTY / Hilliard, Francis – (3d ed. Boston: Little, Brown, 1864. 2v. LL-858) – 2d ed. Boston: Little, Brown, 1856. 2v. LL-788 – 1 – us L of C Photodup [340]

THE LAW OF MOTION PICTURES, INCLUDING THE LAW OF THE THEATRE TREATING OF THE VARIOUS RIGHTS OF THE AUTHOR, ACTOR. / Frohlich, Louis D – New York: Baker, Voorhis, 1918. 943p. LL-262 – 1 – us L of C Photodup [340]

THE LAW OF MUNICIPAL CORPORATIONS IN THE STATE OF OHIO. / Peck, Hiram David – 2d ed. Cincinnati: Clarke, 1883. 708p. LL-983 – 1 – us L of C Photodup [340]

THE LAW OF NATIONS, INVESTIGATED... / Duane, W J – Philadelphia, 1809 – 2mf – 9 – ILM-1016/1 – ne IDC [327]

THE LAW OF NATURALIZATION,... / Cutler, J – London, 1871 – 1mf – 1 – ILM-3387/1 – ne IDC [327]

THE LAW OF PATENTS FOR USEFUL INVENTIONS / Robinson, William C – Boston: Little-Brown. 3v. 1890 – 25mf – 9 – $37.50 – LLMC 82-504 – us L.L.M.C. [340]

THE LAW OF PERSONAL INJURIES IN MINES. / White, Edward Joseph – At. Louis, Thomas, 1905. 701 p. LL-254 – 1 – us L of C Photodup [340]

THE LAW OF PERSONAL INJURIES IN THE STATE OF ILLINOIS, AND THE REMEDIES AND DEFENSES OF LITIGANTS / Corbin, David Timothy – Chicago: Chicago Legal News Co., 1899 561p. LL-67 – 1 – us L of C Photodup [340]

THE LAW OF PLEADING IN CIVIL ACTIONS AND DEFENSES UNDER THE CODE. / Kinkead, Edgar Benton – 2nd ed. Cincinnati, Anderson, 1898. 2 v. LL-781 – 1 – us L of C Photodup [340]

THE LAW OF PRE-TRIAL INTERROGATION, 12 FEB 1986 – Washington: GPO, 1988 – 2mf – 9 – $3.00 – LLMC 94-360 – us L.L.M.C. [340]

THE LAW OF RADIO COMMUNICATION / Davis, Stephen Brooks – 1st ed. New York, McGraw-Hill, 1927. 206 p. LL-849 – 1 – us L of C Photodup [340]

THE LAW OF RAILROAD FENCES AND PRIVATE CROSSINGS. / Thornton, William Wheeler – Indianapolis, Bowen-Merrill, 1892. 590 p. LL-1050 – 1 – us L of C Photodup [340]

THE LAW OF RAILWAY ACCIDENTS IN MASSACHUSETTS / Hay, Gustavus – Boston: Little, Brown, 1897. 353p. LL-708 – 1 – us L of C Photodup [340]

THE LAW OF RAILWAYS...3RD ED / Redfield, Isaac Fletcher – Boston, Little, Brown, 1867. 2v. L.C. set incomplete: v. 2 wanting. LL-200 – 1 – us L of C Photodup [340]

THE LAW OF REAL ESTATE BROKERS, WITH 1917 SUPPLEMENT. / Gross, Fred Louis – New York, Ronald, 1917. 473, x, 123 p. LL-235 – 1 – us L of C Photodup [340]

THE LAW OF REAL ESTATE MORTGAGES IN ONTARIO / Millstone, Maurice Shelly – Toronto, Ont.: Blackstone, 1941. 149p. LL-2315 – 1 – us L of C Photodup [340]

LAW OF REAL PROPERTY. / Boone, Charles Theodore – San Francisco, Bancroft-Whitney, 1901. 3 v. LL-823 – 1 – us L of C Photodup [340]

THE LAW OF REAL PROPERTY AND LEASEHOLD ESTATES IN MARYLAND, ABRIDGED FROM LECTURES DELIVERED TO THE LAW SCHOOL OF THE UNIVERSITY OF MARYLAND / Venable, Richard Morton – Baltimore, Friedenwald 1892. 312, 64, 5, 2 p. LL-1611 – 1 – us L of C Photodup [340]

THE LAW OF REAL PROPERTY (BASED ON MINOR'S INSTITUTES) / Minor, Raleigh Colston – (2nd ed. Charlottesville, VA: Michie, 1928. 2v. LL-894) – Charlottesville, VA.: Anderson, 1908. 2v. LL-764 – 1 – us L of C Photodup [340]

LAW OF REAL PROPERTY, PART 4, INSTRUCTION PAPER / American School. Chicago – Prepared by Albert Martin Kales. Chicago, 1912, 161-226 p. LL-1203 – 1 – us L of C Photodup [340]

THE LAW OF RECEIVERS OF CORPORATIONS INCLUDING NATIONAL BANKS. / Gluck, James Fraser – New York: Banks, 1891. 580p. LL-826 – 1 – us L of C Photodup [340]

THE LAW OF RECEIVERSHIPS AS ESTABLISHED AND APPLIED IN THE UNITED STATES, GREAT BRITAIN AND HER COLONIES, WITH PROCEDURE AND FORMS / Smith, John Wilson – (Supplement to 1st ed. Rochester, N.Y.: Lawyers' Co-Operative, 1900. 154p. LL-1162) – Chicago: Lawyers' Co-Operative, 1897. 805p. LL-1162 – 1 – us L of C Photodup [340]

THE LAW OF REMEDIES FOR TORTS, OR PRIVATE WRONGS / Hilliard, Francis – Boston: Little, Brown, 1867. 595p. LL-1659 – 1 – us L of C Photodup [340]

THE LAW OF RIPARIAN RIGHTS, ALLUVION AND FISHERY / Doss, Lal Mohun – Calcutta: Thacker, Spink and Co., 1891. xxix,439p. (Tagore Law Lectures, 1889) – 1 – us U.W. Library [340]

THE LAW OF RITUALISM : EXAMINED IN ITS RELATION TO THE WORD OF GOD, TO THE PRIMITIVE CHURCH, TO THE CHURCH OF ENGLAND, AND TO THE PROTESTANT EPISCOPAL CHURCH IN THE UNITED STATES / Hopkins, John Henry – New York: Hurd and Houghton, 1866 – 1mf – us A.T.L.A. [240]

THE LAW OF SALES / Read, James Burton – New York, Appleton, 1923. 229 p. LL-1009 – 1 – us L of C Photodup [340]

THE LAW OF SALES OF PERSONAL PROPERTY / Hilliard, Francis – 3d ed. Philadelphia: Johnson, 1869. 672p. LL-878 – 1 – us L of C Photodup [340]

THE LAW OF SEARCH AND SEIZURE. / Cornelius, Asher Lynn – Indianapolis: Bobbs-Merrill 1926. 925p. LL-1421 – 1 – us L of C Photodup [340]

LAW OF SEPARATE SCHOOLS IN UPPER CANADA BY THE ROMAN CATHOLIC BISHOPS AND THE CHIEF SUPERINTENDENT OF SCHOOLS / Canada. Departement de l'Instruction Publique pour le Haut-Canada – Toronto: Printed by Lovell and Gibson, 1855. SEM105P333 – 1mf – 9 – Can$2.25 – cn Bibl Nat [370]

THE LAW OF SLANDER AND LIBEL IN CIVIL AND CRIMINAL CASES / Newell, Martin L – 4th ed. Chicago: Callaghan, 1924. 1109p. LL-253 – 1 – us L of C Photodup [340]

THE LAW OF TAXATION / Cooley, Thomas McIntyre – 4th ed. Chicago, Callaghan, 1924. 4 v. LL-1427 – 1 – us L of C Photodup [340]

THE LAW OF THE AIR / Hazeltine, H D – London, 1911 – 2mf – 1 – ILM-826/1 – ne IDC [327]

THE LAW OF THE APOTHECARY: A COMPENDIUM OF BOTH THE COMMON AND STATUTORY LAW GOVERNING DRUGGISTS AND CHEMISTS IN MASSACHUSETTS, MAINE, NEW HAMPSHIRE, VERMONT, RHODE ISLAND AND CONNECTICUT / Fall, George Howard – Boston: Irving P. Fox, c1894. 153p. Includes index – 1 – us U.W. Library [340]

THE LAW OF THE CANADIAN CONSTITUTION / Clement, William Henry Pope – Toronto: Carswell, 1892. 00684. (Pre-1900 Canadiana) – 9 – cn C.I.H.M. [971]

THE LAW OF THE CHURCH / Taunton, Ethelred L – A cyclopaedia of canon law for English-speaking countries. 1906 – 1 – us A.T.L.A. [240]

THE LAW OF THE FARM. / Thompson, Abram Warren – San Francisco,Whitney, 1876. 520 p. LL-1072 – 1 – us L of C Photodup [340]

THE LAW OF THE FEDERAL JUDICIARY. / Spear, Samuel Thayer – New York, Baker, Voorhis, 1883. 872 p. LL-99 – 1 – us L of C Photodup [340]

THE LAW OF THE OFFERINGS IN LEVITICUS 1-7 : CONSIDERED AS THE APPOINTED FIGURE OF THE VARIOUS ASPECTS OF THE OFFERING OF THE BODY OF JESUS CHRIST / Jukes, Andrew John – 7th ed. London: James Nisbet, 1869 – 1mf – 9 – 0-8370-3817-0 – 1985-1817 – us A.T.L.A. [220]

LAW OF THE OFFERINGS IN LEVITICUS I-VII / Jukes, Andrew John – London: James Nisbet, 1869. 1 fiche – 9 – us A.T.L.A. [220]

THE LAW OF THE SEA : A MANUAL OF THE PRINCIPLES OF ADMIRALTY LAW FOR STUDENTS, MARINERS, AND SHIP OPERATORS / Canfield, George L & Dalzell, Georg W – (With a summary of the navigation laws of the U.S. by Jasper Y. Brinton) – N.Y./London: D Appleton-Century Co., 1940 – 4mf – 9 – $6.00 – LLMC 92-237 – us L.L.M.C. [340]

LAW OF THE SEA INSTITUTE PUBLICATIONS SERIES – (Proceedings: v1-2 1990. Workshops: nos 1-9 1988. Papers: nos 1-37 1991. Special publ: nos 1-6 1977) – 224mf – 9 – $336.00 – LLMC 77/78-120 – us L.L.M.C. [073]

THE LAW OF THE SUSPENSION OF THE POWER OF ALIENATION IN THE STATE OF NEW YORK / Bolles, Albert Sidney – New York, Homans, 1891. 216 p. LL-817 – 1 – us L of C Photodup [340]

THE LAW OF TORTS. / Burdick, Francis Marion – 3d ed. Albany, N.Y., Banks, 1913. 612 p. LL-399 – 1 – us L of C Photodup [340]

THE LAW OF TORTS OR PRIVATE WRONGS / Hilliard, Francis – 3d. ed. Boston: Little, Brown, 1866. 2v. LL-1687 – 1 – us L of C Photodup [340]

THE LAW OF TRADE COMBINATION / Lyttleton, Alfred – 1894. 1 fiche (29x) – 9 – 1.00f – at Libertarian Micro [320]

THE LAW OF TRUSTS AND TRUSTEES AS DETERMINED BY THE DECISIONS OF THE PRINCIPAL ENGLISH AND AMERICAN COURTS / Flint, James Henry – San Francisco: Bancroft-Whitney, 1890. 572p. LL-325 – 1 – us L of C Photodup [340]

THE LAW OF USAGES AND CUSTOMS, WITH ILLUSTRATIVE CASES / Lawson, John Davison – St. Louis, Thomas, 1881. 552 p. LL-350 – 1 – us L of C Photodup [340]

THE LAW OF VOLUNTARY SOCIETIES, MUTUAL BENEFIT INSURANCE AND ACCIDENT INSURANCE / Niblack, William Caldwell – Chicago: Callaghan, 1894. 845p. LL-806 – 1 – us L of C Photodup [340]

THE LAW OF WAR... / Campbell, H – London, 1918 – 3mf – 9 – ILM-357/1 – ne IDC [327]

THE LAW OF WARRANTS OF ATTORNEY, COGNOVITS, AND CONSENTS OF JUDGES' ORDERS FOR JUDGMENT, WITH FORMS / Robinson, Benjamin Coulson – London: Richards, 1844. 246p. LL-1676 – 1 – us L of C Photodup [340]

THE LAW OF ZONING AND PLANNING / Rathkopf, Charles Allan – New York, Grosby, 1937. 415 p. LL-296 – 1 – us L of C Photodup [340]

LAW OFFICE ECONOMICS AND MANAGEMENT – v1-36. 1960-96 – 9 – $494.00 set – us Hein [330]

LAW OFFICER'S OPINIONS TO THE FOREIGN OFFICE : 1861-1939 / Parry, Clive – London: Public Record Office. Confidential Print – 6r – 1 – $300.00 – us Trans-Media [340]

LAW ON NAVIGATION IN SIAMESE WATERS. IN FORCE SEPTEMBER 1ST, 1905 / Thailand. Laws, Statutes, etc – Bangkok, The American Presbyterian Mission, 1905. 62 p. LL-10017 – 1 – us L of C Photodup [340]

LAW ON THE FIVE YEAR PLAN FOR THE DEVELOPMENT OF THE NATIONAL ECONOMY OF THE FEDERATIVE PEOPLE'S REPUBLIC OF YUGOSLAVIA IN THE PERIOD FROM 1947 TO 1951 / Yugoslavia – Beograd. 1947. BD-1783 1 – 9 – ne IDC [338]

LAW ON THE SEVEN YEAR PLAN FOR THE DEVELOPMENT OF THE GERMAN NATIONAL ECONOMY FROM 1959 TO 1965 / Germany. Democratic Republic – Berlin. 1959. BD-444 1 – 9 – ne IDC [338]

LAW PRACTICE MANAGEMENT (ABA) – (Title varies: v1-15 1975-1989 as Legal Economics) – v1-21. 1975-95 – 9 – $329.00 set – us Hein [650]

LAW PRIMER – n.p.,n.d. 15 p. LL-213 – 1 – us L of C Photodup [340]

LAW PRINTING LAWS. / Carroll, Edward, Jr – New York: Carroll 1909. 63p. LL-1219 – 1 – us L of C Photodup [340]

LAW QUARTERLY REVIEW – (Add vols as copyright expires) – v1-28. 1885-1912 – 146mf – 9 – $219.00 – LLMC 84-546 – us L.L.M.C. [073]

Law, R Craig *see* CARDIORESPIRATORY RESPONSES OF WORLD CLASS WHITEWATER SLALOM PADDLERS

LAW REFORM COMMISSION OF AUSTRALIA : PUBLICATIONS – (Annual update ca $100.00) – 1975-1996 no 1 – 9 – $1,775.00 set – us Hein [340]

LAW REFORM COMMISSION OF CANADA : PUBLICATIONS – 1971 thru update 1992. no 2. Annual update – 9 – $2,300.00 set – 0-89941-416-8 – us Hein [340]

LAW REFORM NOW: A PROGRAMME FOR THE NEXT THREE YEARS. / Haldane Society – London, Gollancz, 1947. 31 p. LL-2301 – 1 – us L of C Photodup [340]

THE LAW RELATING TO BANKS AND THEIR DEPOSITORS AND TO BANK COLLECTIONS / Bolles, Albert Sidney – New York, Homans, 1887. 522 p. LL-437 – 1 – us L of C Photodup [340]

THE LAW RELATING TO GAS AND WATER. / Michael, William Henry – London: Butterworths, 1884. 811p. LL-122 – 1 – us L of C Photodup [340]

THE LAW RELATING TO GENERAL VOLUNTARY ASSIGNMENTS FOR THE BENEFIT OF CREDITORS, AS PROVIDED FOR THE STATUTE OF 1860, AS AMENDED / Hawes, Granville Parker – New York: Baker, Voorhis, 1876. 126p. LL-1702 – 1 – us L of C Photodup [340]

THE LAW RELATING TO MASTER AND SERVANT. / Hertslet, Charles John Belcher – London: Crockford, 1850. 290p. LL-114 – 1 – us L of C Photodup [340]

THE LAW RELATING TO REAL ESTATE BROKERS, AS DECIDED BY THE AMERICAN COURTS / Rapalje, Stewart – New York, Strouse, 1893. 283 p. LL-1240 – 1 – us L of C Photodup [340]

THE LAW RELATING TO RIOTS AND UNLAWFUL ASSEMBLIES, TOGETHER WITH A VIEW OF THE DUTIES, POWERS AND LIABILITIES OF MAGISTRATES, CONSTABLES. / ed by Wise, Edward – 3d ed. London, Shaw, 1889. 188 p. LL-1701 – 1 – us L of C Photodup [340]

THE LAW RELATING TO WORKS OF LITERATURE AND ART: EMBRACING THE LAW OF COPYRIGHT. / Shortt, John – 2d ed. London: Reeves & Turner, 1884. 840p. LL-126 – 1 – us L of C Photodup [340]

THE LAW REPORTER – Boston: Weeks, Jordan/Bradbury, Soden. v1-4. 1839-1842 (all publ) – LLMC 95-212 – us L.L.M.C. [073]

THE LAW REPORTER / Great Britain. England – (Also known as: The Law Times Reports. Updates planned) – London: The Law Times. v1-133. 1859-1925 – 1392mf – 9 – $2,088.00 – LLMC 95-230 – us L.L.M.C. [324]

THE LAW REPORTER : JOURNAL DE JURISPRUDENCE – Montreal: H Ramsay, [1854] – 9 – cn C.I.H.M. [340]

LAW REPORTER (ATLA) – (Title varies: v1-31 1957-88 as ATLA Law Reporter) – v1-38. 1957-95 – 9 – $534.00 set – us Hein [340]

LAW REPORTS / Bengal. India (State) – 15 v. Calcutta. 1868-75. BI-667 – 8 – ne IDC [324]

LAW REPORTS : INDIAN APPEALS / India – London. 1872-1941. v1-69. – 414mf – 8 – ne IDC [950]

LAW REPORTS / Scotland. Courts – 81 reels – 1 – $3,000.00 – us Trans-Media [340]

LAW REPORTS: INDIAN APPEALS / Great Britain. Privy Council – v1-77. 1873-Jun 1950. 7 reels – 1 – $350.00 – us Trans-Media [340]

LAW REPORTS: PRE-1865 / Great Britain. Laws, Statutes, etc – Authentic editions. 206 reels – 1 – $9,500.00 – us Trans-Media [324]

LAW REPORTS: PRE-1865: ENGLISH NOMINATIVES / Great Britain. Laws, Statutes, etc – 330v. 64 reels. Index included – 1 – $2,800.00 – us Trans-Media [324]

LAW REVIEW / New York Law School – (See also: New York Law Forum) – v22-. 1976- – 1,5,6,9 – us UMI [340]

THE LAW REVIEW – v1-23. 1844-56 (all publ) – 9 – LLMC 84-547 – us L.L.M.C. [073]

LAW REVIEW DIGEST – v1-33. 1950-84 – 5,6 – $330.00 set – us Hein [340]

Law, Robert *see* THE TESTS OF LIFE: A STUDY OF THE FIRST EPISTLE OF ST JOHN

LAW, RULES AND REGULATIONS FOR THE GOVERNMENT OF DOCKS AND HARBORS OF PORTO RICO – San Juan: Bureau of...Transportation, 1912 – 1mf – 9 – $1.50 – LLMC 92-322 – us L.L.M.C. [323]

THE LAW SCHOOL CATALOGS – (150 American Law Schools) – 1979-93 – 276mf – 9 – $500.00 per releaxe – us Trans-Media [340]

THE LAW SCRUTINY : OR ATTORNIES' GUIDE – London: John Barlow, 1807 – 2mf – 9 – $3.00 – LLMC 91-001 – us L.L.M.C. [340]

LAW SOCIETY GAZETTE – 1903-62 – 7 – uk Microform Academic [073]

LAW SOCIETY JOURNAL – Law Society of New South Wales. v1-33. 1963-95 – 9 – $414.00 set – us Hein [340]

LAW SOCIETY OF GREAT BRITAIN PROCEEDINGS – (No meeting was held in 1907) – 1st to 37th meetings. 1874-1912 (all publ) – 93mf – 9 – $139.00 – LLMC 84-548 – us L.L.M.C. [073]

LAW SOCIETY OF MASSACHUSETTS JOURNAL – v1-13. 1929-49 (all publ) – 27mf – 9 – $121.00 – LLMC 84-549 – us L.L.M.C. [073]

LAW SOCIETY'S GAZETTE / Saskatchewan. Canada – v1-3. 1929-35 (all publ) – 5mf – 9 – $7.50 – LLMC 81-091 – us L.L.M.C. [340]

THE LAW SOCIETY'S GAZETTE AND REGISTER – (Add vols as copyright expires) – v1-9. 1903-12 – 10mf – 9 – $45.00 – LLMC 84-550 – us L.L.M.C. [073]

Law, Stephen D *see* LAW'S DIGEST OF AMERICAN CASES RELATED TO PATENTS AND COPYRIGHTS, 1789-1862

THE LAW STUDENT – Brooklyn. v1-20. 1923-43 (all publ) – 33mf – 9 – $49.50 – LLMC 84-552 – us L.L.M.C. [073]

THE LAW STUDENT – Chicago. v1 no 1. 1898 (all publ) – 1mf – 9 – $1.50 – LLMC 84-551 – us L.L.M.C. [073]

THE LAW STUDENT – (Lacking: v1 Jan/Feb 1947) – London. v1-3. 1947-49 (all publ) – 2mf – 9 – $9.00 – LLMC 84-553 – us L.L.M.C. [073]

THE LAW STUDENT – v1-20. 1923-43 – 1,5,6 – us Princeton Micro [073]

LAW STUDENT LIFE IN MOSKAU : THE LETTERS AND COURSE NOTES OF JOHN N. HAZARD, 1934-1939 – 46mf – 9 – ne IDC [340]

THE LAW STUDENT'S EXAMINATION CHRONICLE – London. v1-8. 1861-68 (all publ) – 14mf – 9 – $63.00 – LLMC 84-554 – us L.L.M.C. [073]

THE LAW STUDENT'S HELPER : A MONTHLY MAGAZINE – Detroit. v1-23. 1893-1915 (all publ) – 46mf – 9 – $207.00 – LLMC 84-555 – us L.L.M.C. [073]

THE LAW STUDENT'S JOURNAL – London. v1-39. 1879-1917 (all publ) – 114mf – 9 – $171.00 – LLMC 84-556 – us L.L.M.C. [073]

THE LAW STUDENT'S MAGAZINE – (Includes a suppl: Compendium of the Practice of Law issued in 1847, London) – London. v1-6. 1844-48. ns: v1-6. 1849-54 (all publ) – 9 – LLMC 84-557 – us L.L.M.C. [073]

THE LAW STUDENT'S MONTHLY – Philadelphia. v1 nos 1-12. 1889-90 – 7mf – 9 – $10.50 – LLMC 84-558 – us L.L.M.C. [073]

LAW STUDENTS' REVIEW AND QUIZ BOOK. / Whitman, Russell – Indianapolis, Bobbs-Merrill 1916 651 p. LL-411 – 1 – us L of C Photodup [340]

THE LAW TIMES – (Updates planned) – London. v1-210. 1843-1950 – 1304mf – 9 – $1,956.00 – LLMC 84-559 – us L.L.M.C. [073]

THE LAW TIMES REPORTS *see* THE LAW REPORTER

LAW TIMES (U.S.) COURTS REPORTS *see* THE AMERICAN LAW TIMES REPORTS

LAW TRACTS PUBLISHED IN THE LAW JOURNAL – London. v1-2. 1825-29 (all publ) – 9 – LLMC 84-540 – us L.L.M.C. [073]

Law, W *see* OF JUSTIFICATION BY FAITH AND WORKS

Lawaetz, Heinrich Wilhelm *see* HANDBUCH FUER BUECHERFREUNDE UND BIBLIOTHEKARE

THE LAW-FRENCH DICTIONARY. ALPHABETICALLY DIGESTED... TO WHICH IS ADDED THE LAW-LATIN DICTIONARY / ed by F O – London, 1701 – 6mf – ne IDC [340]

THE LAWFULNESS AND DUTY OR SEPARATION FROM CORRUPT MINISTERS AND CHURCHES EXPLAINED AND VINDICATED;... / Fraser, J – Edinburgh, 1744 – 3mf – 9 – MP-314/1 – ne IDC [240]

LAWH – May 1968-Winter 1975; Jun 1980 – 43mf – 9 – $200.00 – us MEDOC [950]

THE LAWIERS LOGIKE / Fraunce, Abraham – 1588. 329p. (English Linguistics Series 1500-1800) – 9 – us UMI [160]

Lawkland. Yorkshire *see* PARISH REGISTERS

Lawler, H J *see* THE ROSSLYN MISSAL

Lawless, Emily *see*
- THE BOOK OF GILLY
- A CHELSEA HOUSEHOLDER
- GRANIA
- HURRISH
- MAELCHO
- MAJOR LAWRENCE, FLS
- A MILLIONAIRE'S COUSIN
- PLAIN FRANCES MOWBRAY; AND OTHER TALES
- THE RACE OF CASTLEBAR
- TRAITS AND CONFIDENCES
- WITH ESSEX IN IRELAND

Lawley, M *see* BREVIARIUM AD USUM INISIGNIS ECCLESIAE EBORACENSIS, 1-2

LAWLOIT TIMES – 1929-1939. LLT1-3 – 3r – 1 – at Corangamite [072]

Lawlor, Denys Shyne *see* PILGRIMAGES IN THE PYRENEES AND LANDES

Lawlor, H *see* THE MARYROLOGY OF TALLAGHT

Lawlor, Hugh Jackson *see*
- EVSEBIANA
- THE PSALTER AND MARTYROLOGY OF RICEMARCH
- SOME WORTHIES OF THE IRISH CHURCH

LAWN AND GARDEN MARKETING – (v23-. 1984-. 5,6,9) – v11-. Sept 1972- – 1 – us UMI [073]

LAWN CARE INDUSTRY – (v.5-. 1981-. 5,6,9) – v.1-. 1977- – 1 – us UMI [631]

LAWN, GARDEN, OUTDOOR LIVING – v1-11. Mar 1962-Aug 1972 – 1 – us UMI [630]

LAWNDALE BAPTIST CHURCH. NORTH CAROLINA : CHURCH RECORDS – 1899-1963 – 1 – 33.30 – us Baptist [240]

Lawrance, M *see* A COLLECTION OF ROSES FROM NATURE

Lawrence *see* GRUNDY COUNTY DIRECTORY

LAWRENCE 1847-1849 – (Mf 1T-3T: Births 1847-49. Mf 3T-4T: Marriages 1847-49. Mf 4T-5T: Deaths 1847-49. Mf 5T-6T: Intentions 1847-49) – (mf ed 1997) – 6mf – 9 – 0-87623-274-8 – us Holbrook [920]

LAWRENCE 1847-1905 – (Mf 1-12: Births & Index 1847-62. Mf 13-20: Births & Index 1862-70. Mf 21-30: Births & Index 1871-76. Mf 31-39: Births & Index 1877-82. Mf 40-57: Births & Index 1882-91. Mf 58-74: Births & Index 1892-98. Mf 75-95: Births & Index 1899-1905. Mf 96-99: Birth Index 1906-09. Mf 100-108: Marriages/ Index 1847-59. Mf 109-116: Marriages/Index 1859-66. Mf 117-124: Marriages/Index 1867-72. Mf 125-132: Marriages/Index 1872-77. Mf 133-140: Marriages/Index 1878-82. Mf 141-155: Marriages/Index 1882-90. Mf 156-164: Marriages/Index 1891-95. Mf 165-179: Marriages/Index 1895-1902. Mf 180-194: Marriages/Index 1902-07. Mf 195-202: Deaths & Index 1847-63. Mf 203-211: Deaths & Index 1864-74. Mf 212-220: Deaths & Index 1874-81. Mf 221-227: Deaths & Index 1881-87. Mf 228-235: Deaths & Index 1888-92. Mf 236-250: Mf Deaths & Index 1893-99. Mf 251-277: Deaths & Index 1900-07) – (mf ed 1998) – 277mf – 9 – 0-87623-396-5 – us Holbrook [920]

Lawrence, Amos *see* EXTRACTS FROM THE DIARY AND CORRESPONDENCE...WITH A BRIEF ACCOUNT OF SOME INCIDENTS IN HIS LIFE

LAWRENCE AND HOUSEWORTH STEREO VIEWS / U.S. Library of Congress. Prints and Photographs Division – 860 stereoscopic halves. Points of interest in northern Calif. and western Nevada in the 1860's. 1 reel. P&P19 – 1 – 23.00r – us L of C Photodup [080]

LAWRENCE COLLECTION OF PHOTOGRAPHS IN IRELAND – Selected portions of the collection – 1 – ie Microforms [941]

LAWRENCE COUNTY PRESS – Monticello. Miss. 1938-1953 – 1 – us UMI [071]

Lawrence, David *see* NINE HONEST MEN

Lawrence, Edward Alexander *see* THE LIFE OF REV. JOEL HAWES, D.D., TENTH PASTOR OF THE FIRST CHURCH, HARTFORD, CONN

LAWRENCE ENTERPRISE – Lawrence, NE. -w. Jun-Nov 1928 – 1 – us NE Hist [071]

Lawrence, George Alfred *see* GUY LIVINGSTONE, OR, "THOROUGH"

LAWRENCE GUARDIAN – New Castle, PA. -w 1870-1889 – 13 – $25.00r – us I.M.R. [071]

THE LAWRENCE JOURNAL – New Castle, PA. -w 1849-1874 – 13 – $25.00r – us I.M.R. [071]

Lawrence, Kansas *see* MISCELLANEOUS EARLY NEWSPAPERS

Lawrence. Kansas. First Christian Church *see* CHRONOLOGICAL LIST OF MEMBERS

Lawrence Lande Collection *see* HISTORICAL RECORDS OF EARLY CANADA

LAWRENCE LOCOMOTIVE – Lawrence. NE. -w. Aug 1892; Apr 1896 to date – 1 – us NE Hist [071]

Lawrence, Margarette Woods *see* LIGHT ON THE DARK RIVER

Lawrence, Sarah *see* DESCENDANTS OF PHILIP HENRY

Lawrence, Thomas *see* HISTORICAL GENEALOGY OF THE LAWRENCE FAMILY, 1635-1858

Lawrence, William *see* PHILLIPS BROOKS

Lawrence, William Beach *see*
- A BRIEF OF THE AUTHORITIES UPON THE LAW OF IMPEACHABLE CRIMES AND MISDEMEANORS
- WILLIAM BEACH LAWRENCE VS. R.H. DANA, JR., ET AL

Lawrence Women's Club. Lawrence, Kansas *see* RECORDS

Lawrence-Archer, J H *see* MONUMENTAL INSCRIPTIONS OF THE BRITISH WEST INDIES FROM THE EARLIEST DATE, WITH GENEALOGICAL AND HISTORICAL ANNOTATIONS

LAWRENCEVILLE FIRST BAPTIST CHURCH. LAWRENCEVILLE, ILLINOIS : CHURCH RECORDS – Oct 1903 – Nov 1982 – 1 – 70.11 – us Baptist [240]

Lawrie, A Campbell *see* A GAZETTEER OF THE CENTRAL PROVINCE OF CEYLON, EXCLUDING WALAPANE

THE LAWS AND COURTS OF NORTHWEST AND INDIANA TERRITORIES / Howe, Daniel Wait – Indianapolis: Bowen-Merrill Co., 1886. 25p. LL-441 – 1 – us L of C Photodup [340]

THE LAWS AND CUSTOMS OF EGBA-LAND / Folarin, Abedesin – [n.p.]: ENA Printing Press. v1. 1939 – us Res Libr [306]

THE LAWS AND CUSTOMS OF THE YORUBA PEOPLE / Ajisafe, Ajayi Kolawole – Lagos: Kash & Klare Bookshop, 1946 – us Res Libr [960]

THE LAWS AND JURISPRUDENCE OF ENGLAND AND AMERICA / Dillon, John Forrest – (Series of lectures at Yale University,) – Boston: Little-Brown, 1895 – 5mf – 9 – $7.50 – LLMC 84-279 – us L.L.M.C. [340]

THE LAWS AND POLITY OF THE JEWS / Edersheim, Elisa Williamina – (Includes index) – London: Religious Tract Society, [1883] – 1mf – 9 – 0-8370-3709-3 – 1985-1709 – us A.T.L.A. [270]

LAWS AND REGULATIONS, ETC...SPECIALLY RELATING TO THE NATIVE POPULATION OF THE TRANSVAAL / Transvaal. Native Affairs Department – Pretoria: Govt Printer & Stationery Off, 1907 – us Res Libr [323]

LAWS AND RESOLUTIONS : IST TO 7TH CONGRESSES, JUL 1965-OCT 1978 / Congress of Micronesia – n.p, n.d. – 72mf – 9 – $108.00 – LLMC 82-100F, Title 30 – us L.L.M.C. [324]

LAWS AND RESOLUTIONS OF THE FEDERATED STATES OF MICRONESIA, 1979-1986 / Federated States of Micronesia – 1st Congress 2nd reg sess-4th Congress 3rd spec sess – 34mf – 9 – $51.00 – LLMC 82-100H Title 1 – us L.L.M.C. [324]

LAWS AND RESOLUTIONS OF THE STATE OF YAP, 1983-1984 / Federated States of Micronesia – 1st-2nd reg sess – 4mf – 9 – $6.00 – LLMC 82-100H Title 12 – us L.L.M.C. [324]

THE LAWS AND USAGES OF MARITIME WARFARE / Davis, G B & Sperry, C S – Washington D C, 1907 – 1mf – 1 – ILM-4092/1 – ne IDC [327]

LAWS APPLICABLE TO IMMIGRATION AND NATURALIZATION, 1953 / Avery, E – (Includes suppls 1-3) – Washington: GPO, 1952-59 (all publ) – 22mf – 9 – $33.00 – LLMC 81-502 – us L.L.M.C. [340]

LAWS APPLICABLE TO THE U.S. DEPARTMENT OF AGRICULTURE : REVISED EDITION, 1945 / US Dept of Agriculture. Office of the Solicitor – (Includes 1945-50 suppl) – Washington: GPO. v1-2. 1945; 1952 (all publ) – 29mf – 9 – $43.50 – LLMC 95-028 – us L.L.M.C. [340]

LAWS AUTHORIZING THE INCORPORATON OF CLUBS, SOCIETIES AND ASSOCIATIONS, FOR LITERARY, LIBRARY, SOCIAL RECREATIVE AND SPORTING PURPOSES / Snyder, William Lamartine – New York, Baker, Voorhis, 1881. 35 p. LL-695 – 1 – us L of C Photodup [340]

LAWS, BYE-LAWS, AND REGULATIONS. / Botanical Society of Edinburgh – Corrected to 1 October, 1841. Edinburgh, 1841 – 3 – us Readex [060]

LAW'S DIGEST OF AMERICAN CASES RELATED TO PATENTS AND COPYRIGHTS, 1789-1862 / Law, Stephen D – (Includes suppl) – 5th rev ed. New York: Arthur & Fred D Linn. 1v. 1877 (all publ) – 9 – LLMC 95-136 – us L.L.M.C. [340]

LAWS, ETC : ORDENAMIENTO DE LAS LEYES OBRERAS ARGENTINAS / Unsain, Alejandro M – 3rd ed actualizada al 1. de jun. de 1947. Buenos Aires: Editorial Losada, 1947 – 1 – CSUXADQ0985-B – us Hoover Inst Photo [340]

LAWS, ETC : SBORNIK ZAKONOV SSSR I UKAZOV PREZIDIUMA VERKHOVNOGO SOVETA SSSR / Soviet Union – (Includes c.1: 1938/1944-1949, 1938/1956, 1938/1958, 1938/1961; 1938/1967, 1938/1970:no.3, 1938/1975:no. 2) – Moskva: Izd. Vedomoste i Verkhovnogo Soveta SSSR, 19uu – 1 – CSUXAKY5657-S – us Hoover Inst Photo [340]

LAWS, ETC : SOBRANIE ZAKONOV I RASPORI AZHENI I RABOCHE-KRESTI ANSKOGO PRAVITELSTVA SOTSIALISTICHESKO I SOVETSKO I RESPUBLIKI GRUZII: IZDANIE UPRAVLENII A DELMAMI SOVETA NARODNYKH KOMISSAROV I EKONOMICHESKOGO SOVESHCHANII A SSRG / Georgian S.S.R. – (Includes c.1: 1934:no.21-22, 27-28) – Tiflis: Upravlenie, 19uu – 1 – CSUXAKZ1952-S – us Hoover Inst Photo [340]

LAWS, ETC. : EZHENEDELNIK KOMISSARIATA FINANSOV I SOVETA NARODNOGO KHOZI A ISTVA SEVERNO I OBLASTI / Russian S.F.S.R. – (Includes c.1: no.7 1918:Nov.24) – [Petrograd: Komissariat i Sovet], 1918 – 1 – CSUXAKZ2067-S – us Hoover Inst Photo [340]

THE LAW'S LUMBER ROOM / Watt, Francis – 2nd Series. London/New York: John Lane, 1848 – 3mf – 9 – $4.50 – LLMC 92-232 – us L.L.M.C. [340]

LAWS OF ALASKA PERTAINING TO CIVIL GOVERNMENT, MINES, AND LAND / Hall, Frederic – Los Angeles, Prack & Blech 1897 32 p. LL-546 – 1 – us L of C Photodup [340]

LAWS OF BUSINESS FOR ALL THE STATES OF THE UNION AND THE DOMINION OF CANADA / Parsons, Theophilus – Harford: Scranton, 1880. 848p. LL-1005 – 1 – us L of C Photodup [340]

THE LAWS OF CONTRAST OF COLOUR / Chevreul, M E – (Translated from the French) – England, 1861 – 1r – 1 – Can$50.00 – cn Can Microfilming [700]

THE LAWS OF FAESOLE : A FAMILIAR TREATISE ON THE ELEMENTARY PRINCIPLES AND PRACTICE OF DRAWING AND PAINTING..., VOLUME 1 / Ruskin, John – Sunnyside, Orpington, Kent: G. Allen, 1879 – 1 roll – 1 – 1-55879-383-6 – uk Libr Preservation [750]

LAWS OF INTESTACY IN THE DOMINION OF CANADA / Armstrong, J – Montreal: J. Lovell, 1885. 02199. (Pre-1900 Canadiana) – 9 – cn C.I.H.M. [971]

THE LAWS OF LAND WARFARE... / Baker, J R & Crocker, H G – Washington, DC. 1919 – 5mf – 9 – ILM-338/1 – ne IDC [340]

THE LAWS OF MANU : TRANSLATED WITH EXTRACTS FROM SEVEN COMMENTARIES / Buehler, G – (Hindu religious law) – Oxford: The Clarendon Press, 1886 – 8mf – 9 – $12.00 – LLMC 92-121 – us L.L.M.C. [340]

THE LAWS OF NATAL / Natal. Laws, Statutes, etc – Church St., 1890. 4v. On film: v. 3, 1879-89 (1890); Missing v. 1 and 2 (1845-78) and 4. Indexes. LL-12014 – 1 – us L of C Photodup [340]

THE LAWS OF NEW YORK FAVOR AND PROTECT WOMAN / Seymour, Raymond B – New York: The Man-Suffrage Association Opposed to Extension of Political Suffrage to Women. 1916?. 30p. LL-1212 – 1 – us L of C Photodup [340]

THE LAWS OF NEW YORK STATE RELATING TO GENERAL, RELIGIOUS AND NON-BUSINESS CORPORATIONS, TAXATION AND EXEMPTION, SUNDAY OBSERVANCE, MARRIAGE AND DIVORCE / Cumming, Robert Cushing – 7th ed. Albany, Banks, 1901. 321, 140p. LL-71 – 1 – us L of C Photodup [340]

LAWS OF THE CANAL ZONE, ISTHMUS OF PANAMA : ENACTED BY THE ISTHMIAN CANAL COMMISSION / Panama Canal Zone – Washington: GPO, 1906 – 4mf – 9 – $6.00 – LLMC 82-100D Title 2 – us L.L.M.C. [340]

LAWS OF THE CANAL ZONE, ISTHMUS OF PANAMA, 1904-1914 : ENACTED BY THE ISTHMIAN CANAL COMMISSION / McGuigan, J J – (The Commission was replaced in 1914 by a governor of the Panama Canal and the Panama Canal Company) – Mount Hope, CZ: Panama Canal Press, 1922 – 4mf – 9 – $6.00 – LLMC 82-100D Title 3 – us L.L.M.C. [340]

LAWS OF THE INNER KINGDOM / Clark, Henry W – London: R. Scott, 1909 – 1mf – us A.T.L.A. [240]

LAWS OF THE KINGDOM / Dykes, James Oswald – New York: Robert Carter, 1873. 1 fiche – 9 – us A.T.L.A. [240]

LAWS OF THE SEVERAL STATES IN REGARD TO INSURANCE COMPANIES FROM OTHER STATES AND COUNTRIES / Hine, Charles Cole – New York: The Insurance Monitor, 1874. 142p. LL-802 – 1 – us L of C Photodup [340]

LAWS OF THE STATE OF ISRAEL / Israel. Ministry of Justice – Jerusalem. 1948-. (added 2 v. of laws of the prestate period, published in new version) – 9 – 150.00; 6.00y – is I.T.T.I. [324]

THE LAWS OF THE UNITED STATES OF AMERICA, 1789-1796 – Philadelphia: Richard Folwell. 3v. 1796 (all publ) – 19mf – 9 – $28.50 – LLMC 95-006 – us L.L.M.C. [340]

LAWS OF THE UNITED STATES OF AMERICA, 1789-1815 – Philadelphia/Washington City: John Bioren & W John Duance/R C Weightman. 5v. 1815 (all publ) – 39mf – 9 – $59.00 – LLMC 95-007 – us L.L.M.C. [340]

THE LAWS OF THE UNITED STATES RELATING TO PATENTS AND TRADEMARKS. / Hill, Merritt B – Peoria, Ill.: Thurlow, 1889. 232p. LL-1632 – 1 – us L of C Photodup [340]

LAWS OF THE UNITED STATES RELATING TO THE IMPROVEMENT OF RIVERS AND HARBORS FROM AUGUST 11, 1790, TO MARCH 3, 1887. / U. S. Laws, Statutes, etc – Washington, Govt. Print. Off., 1887. 579 p. LL-1484 – 1 – us L of C Photodup [340]

LAWS OF WISCONSIN CONCERNING THE ORGANIZATION AND GOVERNMENT OF TOWNS, AND THE POWERS AND DUTIES OF TOWN OFFICERS AND BOARDS OF SUPERVISORS. / Haines, Elijah Middlebrook – Chicago, Keen; 1858. 189 p. LL-642 – 1 – us L of C Photodup [340]

LAWS RELATING TO FOREIGNERS AND FOREIGN CORPORATIONS / Emery, G F – London, 1908 – 3mf – 1 – ILM-3303/1 – ne IDC [327]

LAWS RELATING TO MECHANICS' LIENS, APPLICABLE TO NEW YORK CITY AND THE COUNTIES OF KINGS AND QUEENS, AND THE CITIES OF THE STATE OF NEW YORK. / Snyder, William Lamartine – New York, Baker, Voorhis, 1882. 52 p. LL-1383 – 1 – us L of C Photodup [340]

THE LAWS RELATING TO ROADS AND DITCHES, BRIDGES AND WATERCOURSES IN THE STATE OF OHIO. / Giauque, Florien – Cincinnati: Clarke, 1886. 780p. LL-836 – 1 – us L of C Photodup [340]

LAWS, STATUTES, ETC... / Java – Djakarta, Kokumin Tosyokyoku, 2604. 422p – 70-74mf – 9 – ne IDC [340]

LAWS, STATUTES, ETC CONSISTING OF THE ACTS OF THE LEEWARD ISLANDS IN FORCE IN ANTIGUA, 1690-1798, AND THE ACTS OF ANTIGUA, FROM 1668 TO 1804 – 1r – 1 – us Ross [323]

LAWS THE DETECTIVE SHOULD KNOW / Brooks, Joseph S – Kansas City, MO: C T Ludwig Detective Correspondence School Corp, 1915 – 3mf – 9 – $4.50 – LLMC 91-090 – us L.L.M.C. [340]

Lawson, George *see* PRACTICAL EXPOSITIONS OF THE WHOLE BOOK OF RUTH AND ESTHER

Lawson, John *see* LECTURES CONCERNING ORATORY

Lawson, John Davison *see*
- THE ADJUDGED CASES ON INSANITY AS A DEFENSE TO CRIME.
- THE LAW OF EXPERT AND OPINION EVIDENCE REDUCED TO RULES.
- THE LAW OF USAGES AND CUSTOMS, WITH ILLUSTRATIVE CASES
- LEADING CASES SIMPLIFIED
- THE MAKING OF A CONTRACT
- THE PRINCIPLES OF THE AMERICAN LAW OF CONTRACTS AT LAW AND IN EQUITY

Lawson, John Parker *see*
- THE EPISCOPAL CHURCH OF SCOTLAND
- HISTORY OF THE SCOTTISH EPISCOPAL CHURCH

Lawson, Marjorie Frances *see* SPANNUNG IN DER ERZAEHLUNG

Lawson, W D *see* WESLEYAN LOCAL PREACHERS

Lawson, W J *see* THE CANADIAN CONSTITUTION; A STUDY OF THE WRITTEN AND UNWRITTEN FEATURES OF OUR SYSTEM OF GOVERNMENT

LAWTON STANDARD – Lawton OR. Apr 13 1900 – 1 – us U.O. Library [071]

LAWTONVILLE BAPTIST CHURCH. HAMPTON COUNTY. ESTILL, SOUTH CAROLINA : CHURCH RECORDS – 1874-1968 – 1 – 52.34 – us Baptist [240]

LAWYER AND CLIENT : OR THE TRIALS AND TRIUMPHS OF THE BAR / Proctor, Lucien Brock – New York: S S Peloubet & Co, 1882 – 4mf – 9 – $6.00 – LLMC 91-015 – us L.L.M.C. [340]

LAWYER AND CLIENT; OR, THE TRIALS AND TRIUMPHS OF THE BAR / Proctor, Lucien Brock – (2nd ed. New York: Peloubet, 1883. 345p. LL-2352) – New York: Peloubet, 1882. 324p. LL-1076 – 1 – us L of C Photodup [340]

THE LAWYER AND MAGISTRATE – London. v1 nos 1-6. 1898-99 (all publ) – 3mf – 9 – $4.50 – LLMC 84-560 – us L.L.M.C. [073]

LAWYER AND UNITED STATES FORM-BOOK / Wells, John C – Montpellier, VT: John Wells, 1849 – 3mf – 9 – $4.50 – LLMC 91-086 – us L.L.M.C. [340]

LAWYER AND UNITED STATES FORM-BOOK / Wells, John C & Wells, H T – Montpellier?: John C Wells, 1852 – 4mf – 9 – $6.00 – LLMC 91-087 – us L.L.M.C. [340]

A LAWYER OF KENT: BARZILLAI SLOSSON AND HIS ACCOUNT BOOKS, 1794-1812 / Seymour, Mabel – New Haven: Yale, 1935. 35, 1p. LL-798 – 1 – us L of C Photodup [340]

LAWYER OF THE AMERICAS *see* UNIVERSITY OF MIAMI INTERAMERICAN LAW REVIEW

THE LAWYERS' AND CLERKS' ASSISTANT / Lansing, William – New York, Baker, Voorhis, 1898. 1252 p. LL-447 – 1 – us L of C Photodup [340]

LAWYERS AND LAWLESSNESS; AN ADDRESS DELIVERED BEFORE THE JOINT MEETING OF THE BAR ASSOCIATIONS OF ARKANSAS AND TEXAS, JULY 11, 1906, AT TEXARKANA / Spencer, Selden Palmer – n.p., 1906 16 p. LL-1192 – 1 – us L of C Photodup [340]

LAWYERS AND LAWMAKERS OF KENTUCKY / Levin, H – Chicago: Lewis Publishing Co., n.d. Kentucky Reel 4. (The Cox Library Collection) – 5 – us Americana [920]

THE LAWYERS AND LAWMAKERS OF KENTUCKY / Levin, H – Chicago, Lewis 1897 777 p. LL-947 – 1 – us L of C Photodup [340]

THE LAWYER'S AND MAGISTRATE'S MAGAZINE – v1-6. 1790-94 (all publ) – 9 – LLMC 84-564 – us L.L.M.C. [073]

Lawyers' Association of the 8th Judicial Circuit of Missouri *see* THE BENCH AND BAR

Lawyers Club of Detroit *see* BENCH AND BAR

LAWYERS COLLECTIVE – Bombay. 60 docs. 1986-1991 – 38mf – 9 – ne IDC [340]

LAWYERS' COMMITTEE FOR CIVIL RIGHTS UNDER LAW, SOUTHERN AFRICA PROJECT – Washington D.C. 103 docs. 1979-1991 – 31mf – 9 – ne IDC [320]

LAWYERS COMMITTEE FOR HUMAN RIGHTS – New York. 278 docs. 1980-1991 – 140mf – 9 – ne IDC [320]

LAWYERS' DIRECTORIES, 1868-1980 – 8941mf – 9 – $8,900.00 – LLMC 92-001A – us L.L.M.C. [340]

A LAWYER'S EXAMINATION OF THE BIBLE / Russell, Howard Hyde – (Includes index) – Chicago: Fleming H Revell, c1893 – 1mf – 9 – 0-8370-5003-0 – 1985-3003 – us A.T.L.A. [220]

THE LAWYER'S MAGAZINE : OR ATTORNEY'S AND SOLICITOR'S UNIVERSAL LIBRARY – (Lacking: v2) – London. v1-2. 1761-62 (all publ) – 6mf – 9 – $9.00 – LLMC 84-563 – us L.L.M.C. [073]

THE LAWYER'S MONTHLY – New York. v1 no 1. 1913 (all publ) – 1mf – 9 – $1.50 – LLMC 84-565 – us L.L.M.C. [073]

LAWYERS' REPORTS ANNOTATED, 1ST SERIES – New York: Lawyers' Co-op. vl-70 + 2 index vols. 1888-1905 (all publ) – 811mf – 9 – $1,216.00 – LLMC 78-046 – us L.L.M.C. [340]

LAWYERS' REPORTS ANNOTATED, 2ND SERIES – New York: Lawyers' Co-op. v1-52 + v1915A-1918F. 1906-19 (all publ) – 1023mf – 9 – $1,534.00 – LLMC 78-046A – us L.L.M.C. [340]

LAWYERS' REPORTS ANNOTATED, 2ND SERIES *see*
- THE COMPLETE L.R.A. DIGEST
- LRA DESKBOOK

LAWYERS REPORTS ANNOTATED, OLD SERIES, NEW SERIES, 3RD SERIES, LRA CASES CITED, COMPLETE DIGEST – 66 reels – 1 – $2,500.00 – us Trans-Media [340]

THE LAWYER'S REVIEW *see* THE LAW BOOK BROKER

THE LAWYER'S SCRAPBOOK – v1-2. 1909-12 (all publ) – 9 – LLMC 82-936 – us L.L.M.C. [073]

THE LAWYERS'S CLUB OF LOS ANGELES DOCKET – v1-3. 1937-39 (all publ) – 3mf – 9 – $4.50 – LLMC 84-561 – us L.L.M.C. [073]

THE LAWYERS'S CLUB OF NEW YORK PROCEEDINGS – v1-3. 1916-21 (all publ) – 7mf – 9 – $10.50 – LLMC 84-562 – us L.L.M.C. [073]

Lax, Gaspar *see*
- QUESTIONES PHISICALES
- SUMMA EXPONIBILIUM MAGISTRI GASPARIS LAX ARAGONENSIS
- SUMMA PARVORUM LOGICALIUM

Lay, GT *see* THE CHINESE AS THEY ARE

THE LAY OF THE LAST MINSTREL : A POEM / Scott, Walter – London: Printed for Longman, Hurst, Rees, and Orme; Edinburgh: A. Constable and Co. by James Ballantyne, 1805 – 1 roll – 1 – 1-55879-727-0 – uk Libr Preservation [810]

THE LAY PREACHER / Dennie, Joseph – 1796 – 9 – 15.00 – us Scholars' Facs [830]

LAY SERMONS / Blackie, John Stuart – New York: Scribner, 1881 – 1mf – us A.T.L.A. [240]

LAY SERMONS AND ADDRESSES : DELIVERED IN THE HALL OF BALLIOL COLLEGE, OXFORD / Caird, Edward – Glasgow: J. MacLehose; New York: Macmillan, 1907 – 1mf – us A.T.L.A. [240]

Laya *see* L'AMI DES LOIS

Laya, D *see* LA TRADITION PEULE DES ANIMAUX D'ATTACHE

Laya, Jean H *see* VOLTAIRE AUX FRANCAIS, SUR LEUR CONSTITUTION

LAYALI *see* AL-LAYALI

LAYAR TERKEMBANG / Alisjahbana, Sutan Takdir – SE-4909 1. 1963 – 9 – ne IDC [950]

Laycock, Thomas *see* MIND AND BRAIN

Laymann, P *see*
- COMPENDIUM MORALIS THEOLOGIAE
- THEOLOGIA MORALIS, LIBER QUINTUS DE SACRAMENTIS, ET SACRIFICIO, NOVAE LEGIS

A LAYMAN'S MIND ON CREED AND CHURCH / Templeton, John Stewart – London, New York: Macmillan, 1906 – 1mf – 9 – 0-8370-5577-6 – 1985-3577 – us A.T.L.A. [240]

LAYOUT FOR LIVING – Canada. v1-35. Feb. 1947-June Jul. 1950 – 1 – cn Precision [073]

Layrle, J *see*
- LE JAPON EN 1867
- LA RESTAURATION IMPERIALE AU JAPON

LAYS OF CANADA AND OTHER POEMS / Anderson, Duncan – Montreal: J. Lovell, 1890. 00011. (Pre-1900 Canadiana) – 9 – cn C.I.H.M. [810]

Layton, David *see* INNOVATIONS IN SCIENCE AND TECHNOLOGY EDUCATION

Lazarevskii, I *see* SOBRANIE VAZHNEISHIKH PAMIATNIKOV PO ISTORII DREVNIAGO RUSSKAGO PRAVA

Lazarevskij, I V *see* SREDI KOLLEKCIONEROV

Lazarus, John *see* TAMIL GRAMMAR

Lazarus, Josephine *see* THE SPIRIT OF JUDAISM

Lazarus, Moritz *see*
- AUS MEINER JUGEND
- DER PROPHET JEREMIAS

Lazarus, Paul *see* DAS BASLER KONZIL

Lazcano, Carlos Alberto *see* EL TRASPORTE TERRESTRE Y MIXTO EN EL DERECHO INTERNACIONAL PRIVADO, EL TRATADO DE DERECHO COMERCIAL TERRESTRE INTERNACIONAL DE MONTEVIDEO DEL 9 I.E. 19 DE MARZO DE 1940

Lazelle, Henry Martyn *see* MATTER, FORCE, AND SPIRIT, OR, SCIENTIFIC EVIDENCE OF A SUPREME INTELLIGENCE

Lazowski, D *see* GRAMATYKA JEZYKA POLSKIEGO

Lazure, N *see* LES VALEURS MORALES ET LA THEOLOGIE JOHANNIQUE (EVANGILE ET EPITRES)

Lazurtegui, Julio de *see* ESPANA ANTE EL HEMISFERIO DE OCCIDENTE

Lazzarini, G *see* ARNO ED AMAR MI DUOLE, FROM THE OPERA LA DISCORDIA CONJUGALE

LDP-KURIER – Frankfurt-Main, West Germany. 25 Sept 1946-1958 – 1 – gw Mikrofilm [072]

Le Baron, William Jr *see* PAST AND PRESENT OF KANE COUNTY

Le Batteux *see*
- LES BEAUX-ARTS REDUITS A UN MEME PRINCIPE
- TRAITE DE LA CONSTRUCTION ORATOIRE
- TRAITE DE L'ARRANGEMENT DES MOTS

Le Berre *see* GRAMMAIRE DE LA LANGUE PONGOUEE

Le Bon, G *see* LES CIVILISATIONS DE L'INDE

Le Breton, Anna Letitia Aikin *see* MEMOIR OF MRS. BARBAULD

Le Brun, A-L *see* THEATRE LYRIQUE

Le Buffe, Francis Peter *see* THE AMERICAN PHILOSOPHY OF LAW.

Le Camus de Mezieres, Nicolas *see*
- LA GENIE DE L'ARCHITECTURE OU L'ANALOGIE DE CET ART AVEC NOS SENSATIONS
- LE GUIDE DE CEUX QUI VEULENT BATIR

Le Caron, Louis *see* DE LA TRANQUILLITE D'ESPRIT, LIVRE SINGULIER

Le Chatelier, Alfred *see* L'ISLAM DANS L'AFRIQUE OCCIDENTALE

Le Clerc, Sebastien *see* TRAITE D'ARCHITECTURE.

Le Comte, LD *see* NOUVEAUX MEMOIRES SUR L'ETAT PRESENT DE LA CHINE

Le Coq, A von *see*
- DIE BUDDHISTISCHE SPAETANTIKE IN MITTELASIEN
- CHOTSCHO

Le Cour Grand Maison *see* RAPPORT PRELIMINAIRE D'ENQUETE DES ZONES D'EXTENSION DES SECTEURS PILOTES DIABO-BROBO

Le Diraison, C *see* UN KIBBOUTZ DE GALILEE

Le Fanu, J H *see* A MANUAL OF THE SALEM DISTRICT

Le Fanu, Joseph Sheridan *see* UNCLE SILAS

Le Faucheur, Michel *see* TRATADO DE LA ACCION DE EL ORADOR, U DE LA PRONUNCIACION Y DEL GESTO, OBRA MUY NECESARIA PARA TODOS LOS QUE SE DEDICAN A HABLAR EN PUBLICO

Le Fevre, J *see* DICTIONNAIRE DES RIMES FRANCOISES

Le Fort, Gertrud *see*
- DIE LETZTE AM SCHAFOTT
- DAS SCHWEISSTUCH DER VERONIKA

Le Gallienne, Richard *see*
- GEORGE MEREDITH
- SLEEPING BEAUTY AND OTHER PROSE FANCIES

Le Gallois, J-L *see* TRAITE DU RECITATIF DANS LA LECTURE

Le Gauffre, Le P Thomas *see* RECIT VERITABLE DE CE QUI S'EST FAIT ET PASSE AUX EXORCISMES DE PLUSIEURS RELIGIEUSES DE LA VILLE DE LOUVIERS

Le Gauffre, T *see* LA VIE DE CLAUDE BERNARD, DIT LE PAUVRE PRESTRE

Le Gaygnard, P *see* PROMPTUAIRE D'UNISONS

Le Govec, Vincent *see* QUAND LA VENDEE RESISTA

Le Grand d'Aussy, Pierre Jean Baptiste *see* FABLIAUX OR TALES

Le Gras *see* LA RHETORIQUE (SIC) FRANCOISE

Le Gray, Gustave *see* LE CAMP DE CHALONS, 1857

Le Guennec-Coppens, F *see* LES FEMMES ET LE MARIAGE DANS L'ILE DE LAMU (KENYA)

Le Herisse, A *see* L'ANCIEN ROYAUME DE DAHOMEY

Le Hir, Jean Louis *see* HISTOIRE DE L'ANNEE 1865

Le Huen, N *see* LE GRANT VOYAGE DE HIERUSALEM DIUISE EN DEUX PARTIES

Le Huong *see* TRUYEN TICH VIET-NAM

Le Jolis, A F *see* LISTE DES ALGUES MARINES DE CHERBOURG

Le Juge, Vasil von *see* DIE NOMINALSUFFIXE IM RUSSISCHEN

Le Maire, Jacques *see*
- LES VOYAGES DU SIEUR LE MAIRE AUX ILES CANARIES, CAP-VERD, SENEGAL ET GAMBIE
- LES VOYAGES DU SIEUR LE MAIRE AUX ILES CANARIES, CAP-VERT, SENEGAL ET GAMBIE SOUS M. DANCOURT, DIRECTEUR GENERAL DE LA COMPAGNIE ROYALE D'AFRIQUE

Le Mao, P *see* PEUPLEMENTS PISCICOLES ET TEUTHOLOGIQUES DU BASSIN MARITIME DE LA RANCE: IMPACT DE L'AMENAGEMENT MAREMOTEUR

Le Masson, Dom Inn. O Cart. *see*
- DISCIPLINA ORDINIS CARTUSIENSIS TRIBUS LIBRIS DISTRIBUTA
- LA VIE DE MESSIRE JEAN D'ARANTHON D'ALEX, EVEQUE ET PRINCE DE GENEVE

Le Mercier de la Riviere *see* L'HEUREUSE NATION, OU RELATIONS DU GOUVERNEMENT DES FELICIENS, PEOPLE SOUVERAINEMENT LIBRE SOUS L'EMPIRE ABSOLU DE SES LOIS

Le Monnier, Leon *see* HISTOIRE DE SAINT FRANCOIS D'ASSISE

Le More, Rene *see* D'ALGER A TOMBOUCTOU, DES RIVES DE LA LOIRE AUX RIVES DU NIGER

Le Morin, Jean *see* VERITES D'HIER?

Le Muet, Pierre *see*
- MANIERE DE BIEN BASTIR POUR TOUTES SORTES DE PERSONNES.
- TRAITE DES CINQ ORDRES D'ARCHITECTURE.

Le Noble, Jean Pierre F *see*
- AUX CHARPENTIERS DE PARIS, MAITRES ET OUVRIERS
- AUX OUVRIERS EN BATIMENT. UN MOT SUR LA CRISE ACTUELLE

Le Nordez, Albert Leon M *see* LE LIVRE DES FEMMES DE BIEN: 1. LA MERE

Le Paige *see* DICTIONNAIRE TOPOGRAPHIQUE, HISTORIQUE, GENEALOGIQUE ET BIBLIOGRAPHIQUE DU MAINE

Le Parquier, E *see* UNE ENQUETE SUR LE PAUPERISME ET LA CRISE INDUSTRIELLE DANS LA REGION ROUENNAISE EN 1788

Le Pautre, Antoine *see* LES OEUVRES D'ARCHITECTURE

Le Pelletier, Emile *see* MANUEL PRATIQUE DE LA LOI DU 12 JANVIER 1895 SUR LA SAISIE-ARRET AVEC UN FORMULAIRE COMPLET A L'USAGE DES JUGES DE PAIX, GREFFIERS, HUISSIERS, ET AUSSI DES PATRONS, EMPLOYES ET OUVRIERS

Le Pileu d'Apligny *see* TRAITE SUR LA MUSIQUE ET SUR LES MOYENS D'EN PERFECTIONNER L'EXPRESSION

Le Play, Frederic *see* LES OUVRIERS EUROPEENS. ETUDES SUR LES TRAVAUX, LA VIE DOMESTIQUE ET LA CONDITION MORALE DES POPULATIONS OUVRIERES DE L'EUROPE, D'APRES LES FAITS OBSERVES DE 1829 A 1879

Le Poitfevin, Gustave *see* LA REHABILITATION DE DROIT, COMMENTAIRE DE L'ARTICLE 10 DE LA LOI DU 5 AOUT 1899, MODIFIE PAR LA LOI DU 11 JUILLET 1900

Le Radonvilliers, P *see* DISCOURS PRONONCES DANS L'ACADEMIE FRANCAISE, LE 4 MARS 1979

Le Roux, Patrick *see* UNE INSCRIPTION FRAGMENTAIRE D'AUGUSTA EMERITA. EMERITA DE LUSITANIE A LA LUMIERE DES "HISTOIRES" DE TACITE

Le Roux, Ph.J *see* DICTIONNAIRE COMIQUE, SATYRIQUE, CRITIQUE, BURLESQUE, ETC

Le Roy, C *see* TRAITE DE L'ORTHOGRAPHE FRANCOISE

Le Roy, Chretien *see* LETTRE SUR L'EDUCATION PUBLIQUE AU SUJET DES EXERCICES DE L'ABBAYE ROYALE DE SOREZE

Le Roy, Edouard *see* DOGME ET CRITIQUE

Le Secq, Henri *see* OEUVRE

Le Strange, G *see* MESOPOTAMIA AND PERSIA UNDER THE MONGOLS IN THE 14TH CENTURY

Le Tac, Sixte *see* HISTOIRE CHRONOLOGIQUE DE LA NOUVELLE FRANCE, 1504-1632

Le Tellier, M *see* DEFENSE DES NOUVEAUX CHRESTIENS ET DES MISSIONARES DE LA CHINE...

Le Vaillant, Francois *see*
- NEW TRAVELS INTO THE INTERIOR PARTS OF AFRICA, BY THE WAY OF THE CAPE OF GOOD HOPE, IN THE YEARS 1783, 1784 AND 1785
- VOYAGE DANS L'INTERIEUR DE L'AFRIQUE PAR LE CAP DE BONNE ESPERANCE

Le Vasseur, Dom L O Cart. *see* EPHIMERIDES ORDINIS CARTUSIENSIS

Lea, Henry Charles *see*
- CHAPTERS FROM THE RELIGIOUS HISTORY OF SPAIN CONNECTED WITH THE INQUISITION
- A FORMULARY OF THE PAPAL PENITENTIARY IN THE THIRTEENTH CENTURY
- A HISTORY OF AURICULAR CONFESSION AND INDULGENCES IN THE LATIN CHURCH
- HISTORY OF SACERDOTAL CELIBACY IN THE CHRISTIAN CHURCH
- A HISTORY OF THE INQUISITION OF THE MIDDLE AGES
- THE INQUISITION IN THE SPANISH DEPENDENCIES
- THE MORISCOS OF SPAIN
- STUDIES IN CHURCH HISTORY

LEA VALLEY MERCURY – (Also known as: Cheshunt and Waltham Cross Mercury) – Oct 1974-Sep 24 1982; Oct 1982-96 – 104r – 1 – uk British Libr Newspaper [072]
Lea, W *see*
– AUTOBIOGRAPHY, 1870
– DIARIES, 1845-1846, 1848, 1850, 1852-1858, 1861, 1863, 1867
Leab, Daniel *see* COMMUNIST ACTIVITY IN THE ENTERTAINMENT INDUSTRY
Leach, A F *see*
– EDUCATIONAL CHARTERS AND DOCUMENTS A.D. 589-1909
– THE SCHOOLS OF MEDIEVAL ENGLAND
Leach, A J *see* A HISTORY OF ANTELOPE COUNTY, NEBRASKA 1868-1883
Leach, Charles *see* IS MY BIBLE TRUE?: WHERE DID WE GET IT?
LEACH'S ART OF DRESSMAKING – London, UK. Nos 30 & 31. -irr. 9 feet – 1 – uk British Libr Newspaper [640]
Leacock, Arthur Gordner *see* STUDIES IN THE LIFE OF ST. PAUL
Leadbeater, Charles Webster *see* SOME GLIMPSES OF OCCULTISM, ANCIENT AND MODERN
LEADER – Allahabad, India. Oct 1942-Sept 1967 – 77r – 1 – us L of C Photodup [072]
LEADER – Barberton. Ohio. -w. 1913-22 – 1 – us UMI [071]
LEADER – Boston, 1892-99 – 1 – £165.00 – uk Chadwyck [780]
LEADER – Chelan. Wash. -w. 1891-1925 – 1 – us UMI [071]
LEADER – Cottage Grove, OR. -w. 7 Dec 1895-8 Aug 1896; Jan 1901-27 Aug 1915; Commemorative Issue. – 1 – us U.O. Library [071]
LEADER – Dayton. Mont. 1911-1917 – 1 – us UMI [071]
LEADER – Eau Claire. Wis. 1896-1940; 1952-1970 – 1 – us UMI [071]
LEADER – Genoa. Neb. 1895-1911 – 1 – us UMI [071]
LEADER – Great Falls. Mont. 1954-1970 – 1 – us UMI [071]
LEADER – Linden. Mich. 1933-1969 – 1 – us UMI [071]
LEADER – Lostine OR. May-June 4 1902 – 1 – us U.O. Library [071]
LEADER – Lyndon. Kan. 1881-1883 – 1 – us UMI [071]
LEADER – Milwaukee. Wis. -d. 1911-39 – 1 – us UMI [071]
LEADER – Minerva. Ohio. -w. 1942- – 1 – us UMI [071]
LEADER – Montreal, Canada. v1 n1. oct-nov 1953; dec 1953-v1 n3. jan 1954 – 1r – 1 – Can$25.00 – cn Can Microfilming [072]
LEADER – Neligh. Neb. 1885-1962 – 1 – us UMI [071]
LEADER – New Concord. Ohio. 1968-1969 – 1 – us UMI [071]
LEADER – Oakdale. Calif. -w. 1954-58, 1961- – 1 – us UMI [071]
LEADER – Pittsburgh. Pa. 1870-1876; 1895-1923 – 1 – us UMI [071]
LEADER – Pontiac. Ill. -w. 1890-97, 1900-04 – 1 – us UMI [071]
LEADER – Port Townsend. Wash. 1888-1921 – 1 – us UMI [071]
LEADER – Port Townsend. Wash. -w. 1921-60 – 1 – us UMI [071]
LEADER – Pueblo. Colo. 1911-1913 – 1 – us UMI [071]
LEADER – Richfield. Kan. 1886-87 – 1 – us UMI [071]
LEADER – San Francisco. Calif. -w. 1941-55 – 1 – us UMI [071]
LEADER – San Mateo, CA. 1897-1915 – 103r – 1 – $5,150.00 – B02918 – us Library Micro [071]
LEADER – Staunton. Va. and predecessors. 1902- – 1 – us UMI [071]
LEADER – Topeka. Kan. -w. 1865-76 – 1 – us UMI [071]
LEADER – Union City. Pa. 1959-1969 – 1 – us UMI [071]
LEADER – v1-30. Oct 1875-1904 – 1 – 295.00 – us Opus [073]
LEADER – Waterford. Pa. -w. 1947-48, 1951- – 1 – us UMI [071]
LEADER – West Point. Miss. -w. 1902-27 – 1 – us UMI [071]
LEADER – Wilkes-Barre. Pa. 1889-1907 – 1 – us UMI [071]
LEADER *see* MEARNS LEADER
THE LEADER – Allahabad, India. -d. Jan 1939-Dec 1951. Lacking Jan-June 1933. 89 reels – 1 – uk British Libr Newspaper [072]
THE LEADER : FAMILY ILLUSTRATED WEEKLY – Maisonneuve, Canada. 1 nov 1919-v1 n2. 8 nov 1919 – 1r – 1 – Can$25.00 – cn Can Microfilming [640]
THE LEADER = LE GUIDE – Dorval et Lachine, Canada. 22 avr 1971 – 1r – 1 – Can$25.00 – cn Can Microfilming [072]
THE LEADER – Hinton. West Virginia. 1892-1902 – 1 – us UMI [071]
THE LEADER – Kampala. Uganda. jan 15, Feb, 15, 28, Mar. 15, Sept. 15, Dec. 15, 31, 1937; Mar. 31, July 31, 1938 – 1 – us NY Public [072]
THE LEADER – London. Mar 1850-Dec 1852. -w. 4 reels – 1 – uk British Libr Newspaper [072]
THE LEADER – Melbourne. Australia. -w. 4 Jan 1941-31 Dec 1952. (22 reels) – 1 – uk British Libr Newspaper [072]
THE LEADER – Pemberville, Ohio. 1887-1980 – 40r – 1 – $32.50r – us Archival [071]
THE LEADER – San Francisco, CA. 1902-04; 1906-55 – 27r – 1 BC02831 – $1,350.00 – us Library Micro [071]
THE LEADER – Toronto, Canada. -d. 21 Feb 1876-Oct 1878. 8 reels – 1 – uk British Libr Newspaper [072]
THE LEADER – Toronto, Canada. Semi-weekly edition. -sw. 13, 16 Jan, 3 July 1863-30 Sept 1864. 1 reel – 1 – uk British Libr Newspaper [072]
LEADER- INC. MEARNS LEADER – 1 – £42.00r – uk Scot News [072]
THE LEADER OF THE OPPOSITON, TO THE ELECTORS OF THE PROVINCE OF QUEBEC / Flynn, Edmund James – s.l.: s.n., 189?. 05576. (Pre-1900 Canadiana) – 9 – cn C.I.H.M. [971]
THE LEADER POST – Regina, Saskatchewan, CN. 1883- – 24r per yr – 1 – Can$53.00r – cn Commonwealth Micro [072]
LEADER REPUBLICAN – Gloversville. N.Y. 1937-55 – 1 – us UMI [071]
LEADER-CALL – Laurel. Miss. 1915-1920; 1937- – 1 – us UMI [071]
LEADER-COURIER – Osceola Mills, PA. -w 1889-1912 – 13 – $25.00r – us I.M.R. [071]
LEADER-DEMOCRAT – Richfield. Kan. 1888-89 – 1 – us UMI [071]
LEADER-DISPATCH – Piqua. Ohio. 1901-1917 – 1 – us UMI [630]
LEADER-ENTERPRISE – Montpelier, Ohio, 1924- – 14r – 1 – us Archival [978]
LEADER-ENTERPRISE – Montpelier, Ohio. 1975- – 14r – 1 – $32.50r – us Archival [071]
LEADER-HERALD – Gloversville. N.Y. 1955- – 1 – us UMI [071]
LEADER-INDEPENDENT – Greeley, NE. -w. Apr 1888-Apr 1891; Oct 1895-May 1906; Jan 1908-Dec 1924 – 1 – us NE Hist [071]
LEADERS – Brookhaven. Miss. -w. 1883-91, 1902-07, 1908-33 – 1 – us UMI [071]
LEADERS AND LEADING MEN OF THE INDIAN TERRITORY / O'Beirne, H F – Chicago: American Publishers' Assoc., 1891. Oklahoma Reel 2. (The Cox Library Collection) – 5 – us Americana [978]
LEADER'S DIGEST: WORTHWHILE LIFE INSURANCE SALES IDEAS – (See also: Leader's Magazine) – 1938-1939 – 1 – us UMI [336]
LEADERS IN THE NORTHERN CHURCH : SERMONS PREACHED IN THE DIOCESE OF DURHAM / Lightfoot, Joseph B – London; New York: Macmillan, 1890 – 1mf – us A.T.L.A. [240]
LEADER'S MAGAZINE – (See also: Leader's Digest: Worthwhile Life Insurance Sales Ideas) – 1939- 1; 1978- 5,6,9 – us UMI [336]
LEADERS OF 20TH CENTURY CHINA / Wu, Eugene – Monograph – 1 – 35.00r – us Hoover Inst Photo [950]
THE LEADERS OF PUBLIC OPINION IN IRELAND / Lecky, William Edward Hartpole – London: Saunders, Otley, 1861 – 1mf – us A.T.L.A. [240]
THE LEADERS OF PUBLIC OPINION IN IRELAND : SWITH-FLOOD-GRATTAN-O'CONNELL / Lecky, William Edward Hartpole – London: Longmans, Green, [18–?] – 1 roll – 1 – 1-55879-551-0 – uk Libr Preservation [941]
LEADERS OF THE REFORMATION / Dubbs, Joseph Henry – Philadelphia, Pa.: Heidelberg Press, c1898. (The World's benefactors series) – 1mf – us A.T.L.A. [240]
LEADERS QUARTERLIES FOR INTERMEDIATES AND JUNIORS – Jan 1922-Sep 1924 – 1 – 14.28 – us Baptist [240]
LEADERSHIP – v.1-. 1980- – 1,5,6,9 – us UMI [073]
LEADERSHIP : THE WILLIAM BELDEN NOBLE LECTURES / Brent, Charles H – New York: Longmans, Green, 1908 – 1mf – us A.T.L.A. [240]
LEADER-TRIBUNE – Marion. Ind. 1912-1968 – 1 – us UMI [071]
A LEADING CASE AS TO HOTEL-KEEPERS AND GUESTS; A SUMMARIZED OPINION WITH DECISION OF THE COURT OF APPEALS OF THE STATE OF NEW YORK / Hennessy, Joseph Patrick – New York: Ideal 1908. 12p. LL-924 – 1 – us L of C Photodup [340]
LEADING CASES, AMERICAN AND ENGLISH, ON THE LAW OF LEGAL TENDER AND MONEY. / Crandall, John J – Camden, N.J., Chew, 1899. 358 p. LL-303 – 1 – us L of C Photodup [340]
LEADING CASES IN MODERN EQUITY / Brett, Thomas – Philadelphia, Blackstone, 1888. 498 p. LL-1073 – 1 – us L of C Photodup [340]
LEADING CASES IN THE AMERICAN LAW OF REAL PROPERTY / Sharswood, George & Budd, Henry – Philadelphia: M Murphy. v1-4. 1883-1889 (all publ) – 31mf – 9 – $46.50 – LLMC 95-051 – us L.L.M.C. [340]
LEADING CASES SIMPLIFIED / Lawson, John Davison – San Francisco: Bancroft-Whitney. 3v in 1. 1892 (all publ) – 12mf – 9 – $18.00 – LLMC 95-044 – us L.L.M.C. [340]
LEADING CASES SIMPLIFIED / Lawson, John Davison – St. Louis, Thomas, 1884. 327 p. LL-486 – 1 – us L of C Photodup [340]
LEADING CASES UPON THE LAW OF TORTS / Chase, George – St. Paul: West, 1892. 299p. LL-419 – 1 – us L of C Photodup [340]
LEADING COMICS – Issue Nos. 1-5 Winter 41-42-Winter 42-43 – 5mf – 15 – $31.95 – us Comics [760]
LEADING COMICS – Issue Nos. 6-10 Spring 43-Spring 44 – 5mf – 15 – $31.95 – us Comics [760]
THE LEADING FACTS OF NEW MEXICAN HISTORY / Twitchell, Ralph E – (v2-3. New Mexico reel 2) – Cedar Rapids: The Torch Press, 1911, 1912, 1917.v1. New Mexico reel 1. (Cox Library Collection) – 5 – us Americana [978]
LEADING IDEAS OF THE GOSPELS: FIVE SERMONS / Alexander, William – London: Macmillan, 1872.1 fiche – 9 – us A.T.L.A. [240]
LEADING POINTS IN SOUTH AFRICAN HISTORY, 1486 TO MARCH 30, 1900, ARRANGED CHRONOLOGICALLY, WITH DATE-INDEX / Pratt, Edwin A – London: J. Murray, 1900.viii,384p – 1 – us U.W. Library [960]
LEADING TEACHERS OF ADULTS AND YOUTH TO STUDY THE HISTORICAL CONTEXTS OF SCRIPTURE / Frazier, Edwin Ray – 1982 – 1 – 5.00 – us Baptist [240]
LEADVALE BAPTIST CHURCH. WHITE PINE, TENNESSEE : CHURCH RECORDS – White Pine, Tennessee. Leadvale Baptist Church, 1851-August 1989 – 1 – $84.60 – us Baptist [240]
LEAFLET / Alabama. Agricultural Experiment Station – v. 1-78. 1934-69 – 1,5,6 – us Spaulding [630]
LEAFLET / Auburn University. Agricultural Experiment Station – No.79-101. 1970-82. 1 reel – 1, 5 – us Spaulding [630]
LEAFLET / Georgia. Agricultural Experiment Station. Athens – v. 1-47. 1954-65 – 1,5,6 – us Spaulding [630]
LEAFLET / Georgia. University. Agricultural Extension Service – v. 1-88. 1964-69 – 1,5,6 – us Spaulding [630]
LEAFLET / Georgia. University. George Foster Peabody School of Forestry – n.1-14. 1943-55 – 1,5 – us Spaulding [634]
LEAFLET / Montana. Agricultural Extension Service – nos.1-175. 1949-69 – 1,5,6 – us Spaulding [630]
LEAFLET / Tennessee. University. Agricultural Extension Service – n.1-143. Apr 1941-Mar 1957 – 1,5 – us Spaulding [630]
LEAFLET / Texas A & M University. Agricultural Experiment Station and Agricultural Extension Service – No.145-874A (revisions of pre-1970 publications); No.895-2056 – 1,5 – us Spaulding [630]
LEAFLET / University of Georgia. Agricultural Extension Service – No.89-360. 1970-82. 18 fiches – 9 – us Spaulding [630]
LEAFLET / Virginia. Agricultural Experiment Station. Blacksburg – 1953-62.n.1-4 – 1,5 – us Spaulding [630]
LEAFLET / Virginia. Polytechnic Institute. Extension Division – May 1954-Jan 1968. n.1-328 – 1,5 – us Spaulding [630]
LEAFLET 4H / Auburn University. Extension Service – v. 1-210. 1963-64 – 1,5,6 – us Spaulding [630]
LEAFLET (L-YPH) / Auburn University. Extension Service – 1,5,6 – us Spaulding [630]
LEAFLET YANR / Auburn University. Extension Service – No.1-130. 1978-82. 1 reel – 1, 5 – us Spaulding [630]
LEAFLET YE / Auburn University. Extension Service – No.2-10 (revisions only). 1972-78. 1 reel – 1, 5 – us Spaulding [630]
LEAFLET YEX / Auburn University. Extension Service – No.2-17.1970-82. 1 reel – 1, 5 – us Spaulding [630]
LEAFLET YF / Auburn University. Extension Service – No.1-18.1978-82. 1 reel – 1, 5 – us Spaulding [630]
LEAFLET YHE / Auburn University. Extension Service – No.23-205. 1970-82. 1 reel – 1, 5 – us Spaulding [630]
LEAFLET YM / Auburn University. Extension Service – No.4-47.1970-82. 1 reel – 1, 5 – us Spaulding [630]
LEAFLET YR / Auburn University. Extension Service – No. 1-44. 1971-78. 1 reel – 1, 5 – us Spaulding [630]
LEAFLETS / Blount, P Clavell – Four pages of leaflets on his National Ideas Scheme – 9 – 1.00f – at Libertarian Micro [335]
LEAFLETS / Clemson University. Agricultural Experiment Station – 1 fiche – 9 – us Spaulding [630]
LEAFLETS / Kentucky. Agricultural Extension Service – A-1 – 346. 1938-72 – 1,5,6 – us Spaulding [630]
LEAFLETS AND 3 SAMPLES OF ITS NEWSLETTER: "LIBERTAS REVIEW." / Society for Libertarian Life – 1fiche (24x) – 9 – 1.00f – at Libertarian Micro [320]
LEAFLETS OF BOTANICAL OBSERVATION AND CRITICISM / Greene, E L – 2v. Washington. 1903-12. B-912 2 – 8 – ne IDC [580]
THE LEAGUE – The organ of the National Anti-Corn Law League. London. -w. Sep 1843-Jul 1846. (2 reels) – 1 – uk British Libr Newspaper [073]
League for Industrial Democracy *see*
– INDUSTRIAL DEMOCRACY
– LID MONTHLY
THE LEAGUE IN OUR TIME / Gibberd, K – Oxford, 1933 – 3mf – 1 – ILM-4021/1 – ne IDC [327]
LEAGUE LEAFLET – London. Labour Woman. 1911-31.-m. 3mqn reels – 1 – uk British Libr Newspaper [072]
League of American Writers *see* BLACK AND WHITE
League of Arab States *see* REPORT ON THE SURVEY OF INDUSTRY AND THE POSSIBILITIES OF INDUSTRIAL DEVELOPMENT IN THE REPUBLIC OF SUDAN
LEAGUE OF NATIONS : OFFICIAL JOURNAL – London. v1-21 1920-1940 Index; London. 1920-1939 Special Supplement – 840mf – 9 – ne IDC [340]
LEAGUE OF NATIONS : RECORDS OF THE ASSEMBLIES. TEXT OF THE DEBATES. SPECIAL SUPPLEMENT – (Index) – Geneva, 1920-1946 – 445mf – 9 – ne IDC [340]
LEAGUE OF NATIONS : TREATY SERIES – (Index 9 vols) – Geneva. 205v. 1920-1946 – 1277mf – 9 – ne IDC [340]
League of Nations *see*
– LEAGUE OF NATIONS DOCUMENTS AND SERIAL PUBLICATIONS, 1919-1946
– LEAGUE OF NATIONS TREATY SERIES
– OFFICIAL JOURNAL
THE LEAGUE OF NATIONS AND THE RECOGNITION OF STATES / Graham, M W – Berkeley, 1933 – 1mf – 1 – ILM-1676/1 – ne IDC [327]

LEAGUE OF NATIONS CHRONICLE – (Library wants: v. 1 (Mr 1928)-v. 5, no. 1 (Ja 1932)) – Chicago: League of Nations Association of Illinois and Mid-West Office, 1928-1935 – 1 – CSUX86-S101 – us Hoover Inst Photo [340]
LEAGUE OF NATIONS DOCUMENTS AND SERIAL PUBLICATIONS, 1919-1946 / League of Nations – 1 – us Primary [340]
League of Nations. Health Mission to Spain *see* RAPPORT DE LA MISSION SANITAIRE DE LA SOCIETE DES NATIONS EN ESPAGNE, 28 DECEMBRE 1936-15 JANVIER 1937
LEAGUE OF NATIONS NEWS – v1-9. Sept 1923 – Apr 1932 – 22mf – 9 – $90.00 – us UPA [340]
LEAGUE OF NATIONS TREATY SERIES / League of Nations – (Cont by: United Nations Treaty Series) – v1-205 + 9 index vols. 1920-45 (all publ) – 9 – $1,639.00 – LLMC 79-454 – us L.L.M.C. [340]
LEAGUE OF NATIONS TREATY SERIES – (With 9 index volumes) – Law Library Microform Consortium. v1-205. 1920-1945 (all publ) – 9 – $1,639.00 set – us Hein [340]
LEAGUE OF NATIONS TREATY SERIES *see* UNITED NATIONS TREATY SERIES
LEAGUE OF NATIONS TREATY SERIES, 1920-1946 – 41r – 1 – $3000.00 – us Trans-Media [340]
League of Women Voters *see*
- PAPERS, PART 1
- PAPERS, PART 2
- PAPERS, PART 3

THE LEAGUE ON TRIAL / Beer, M – Boston, New York, 1933 – 9 – 5mf – ILM-4012/1 – ne IDC [327]
Leahy, Daniel F *see* THE AMERICAN LAW PRIMER, FOR PUBLIC AND PRIVATE SCHOOLS, FAMILIES, AND THE UNPROFESSIONAL GENERALLY
Leahy, Ethel C *see* WHO'S WHO ON THE OHIO RIVER AND ITS TRIBUTARIES
Leahy, Teresa *see* SENSE OF RHYTHM AND MOTOR RHYTHM ABILITY IN EDUCABLE MENTALLY RETARDED AND INTELLECTUALLY NORMAL CHILDREN
Leak, David *see* BIOCATALYSIS
Leake, Stephen Martin *see* PRINCIPLES OF THE LAW OF CONTRACTS
LEAKEY FIRST BAPTIST CHURCH. LEAKEY, TEXAS : CHURCH RECORDS – 1897, 1946-62 – 1 – 19.08 – us Baptist [240]
Leal Ramos, Leon *see*
- LA COLABORACION DE LA CAJA EXTREMENA DE PREVISION SOCIAL EN EL FOMENTO DE LAS CONSTRUCCIONES ESCOLARES
- CONFERENCIA SOBRE EL SEGURO DE MATERNIDAD DEDICADA ESPECIALMENTE A PATRONOS AGRICOLAS
- LA FAMILIA PREOCUPACION FUNDAMENTAL DEL ESTADO ESPANOL
- EL INSTITUTO NACIONAL DE PREVISION DE LABORATORIO INICIAL Y PREPARADOR DEL AMBIENTE ESPANOL PARA LA SEGURIDAD SOCIAL
- LA MORAL PROFESIONAL DEL EMPLEADO DE LA CAJA DE AHORROS
- EL REGIMEN OBLIGATORIO ESPANOL DE SUBSIDIOS FAMILIARES

Leale, Thomas Henry *see* A HOMILETIC COMMENTARY ON THE BOOK OF ECCLESIASTES
LA LEALTAD – Llerena, 1893 – 5 – sp Bibl Santa Ana [073]
Leaming, Thomas *see* A PHILADELPHIA LAWYER IN THE LONDON COURTS
LEAMINGTON ADVERTISER – England. -w. 27 Oct 1849-Dec 1862. Lacking 1851, 1852. 4 1 2 reels – 1 – uk British Libr Newspaper [072]
LEAMINGTON POST – (1993.-4r; 1907-1976.-70r) – Leamington, 1977-1992 – 42r – 1 – cn Preston [971]
LEAMINGTON PRESS – (Leamington Chronicle Leamington Royal Spa Chronicle Royal Leamington Spa Chronicle). England. -w. 13 Aug 1834-22 Sept 1842; 5 Feb-7 May 1859. (5 reels) – 1 – uk British Libr Newspaper [072]
LEAMINGTON SPA COURIER – England, 9 Aug 1828- – 221+ r – 1 – uk British Libr Newspaper [072]
LEAMINGTON SPA OBSERVER *see* ROYAL LEAMINGTON SPA OBSERVER
Leamy, Margaret Hanly *see* PARNELL'S FAITHFUL FEW
Leander, Richard *see* AUS DER BURSCHENZEIT
LEANDRO HERRERO / Blanco Garcia, Francisco – Madrid: Saenz de Jubera, 1909 – sp Bibl Santa Ana [440]
Leao, Antonio Carneiro *see* O BRAZIL E A EDUCACAO POPULAR
Leaper, D J *see* SURGICAL RESEARCH COMMUNICATIONS
Lear, Edward *see* LETTERS OF EDWARD LEAR
Lear, H L Sidney *see*
- FENELON, ARCHBISHOP OF CAMBRAI
- HENRI DOMINIQUE LACORDAIRE
- THE REVIVAL OF PRIESTLY LIFE IN THE SEVENTEENTH CENTURY IN FRANCE
- S. FRANCIS DE SALES

Lear, Henrietta Louisa Farrer *see* LIFE OF ROBERT GRAY, BISHOP OF CAPE TOWN AND METROPOLITAN OF AFRICA
LEARNING AND DEVELOPMENT – (Ceased v8 1976/77) – Montreal. v1-8. 1969/70-1976/77 – 9 – Can$20.00y – cn Micromedia [370]
LEARNING AND WORKING – 1986 – 348p – 9 – 92-3-101684-9 – fr UNESCO [370]
LEARNING DISABILITY QUARTERLY – (v.3-. 1980- 5,6,9) – v.1-. 1978- – 1 – us UMI [073]
LEARNING FROM CHINA : A REPORT ON AGRICULTURE AND THE CHINESE PEOPLE'S COMMUNES, BY AN F.A.O. STUDY MISSION, 1975 – 1978 – 120p – it F.A.O. [630]
LEARNING TO BE : THE WORLD OF EDUCATION TODAY AND TOMORROW / Faure, Edgar et al – 1982 – 313p – 9 – 92-3-101017-4 – fr UNESCO [370]
Leary, William *see*
- CIRCUITS AND MINISTERS, 1924-1980
- HANDLIST OF BAPTISMAL REGISTERS HELD AT THE RECORD OFFICE OF THE REGISTRAR GENERAL BY WILLIAM LEARY
- HANDLIST OF MARRIAGE REGISTERS OF THE METHODIST CHURCH HELD AT LOCAL RECORD OFFICES
- AN INDEX TO THE PRIMITIVE METHODIST WORLD, 1883 [AND] THE PRIMITIVE METHODIST, 1870, 1 AND 2 WILLIAM LEARY
- P[RIMITIVE] M[ETHODIST] CIRCUITS ABROAD
- PRIMITIVE METHODIST CIRCUITS [AND THEIR MINISTERS, TO 1932]
- PRIMITIVE METHODIST MINISTERS, FROM THE COMMENCEMENT TO THE YEAR 1932
- THE WATCHMAN
- WESLEYAN METHODIST MAGAZINE

Lease, Barbara J *see* THE DEVELOPMENT AND IMPLEMENTATION OF A COMPUTER-ASSISTED INSTRUCTION SERIES TO BE UTILIZED AS AN AID TO CURRICULUM METHODOLOGY IN PHYSICAL EDUCATION
Leask, G A *see* HYMN-WRITERS OF THE NINETEENTH CENTURY
LEATHER – 1867-1980 1; 1975-80 5,6,9 – us UMI [680]
LEATHER CRAFTSMAN – v1- 1985- – 1,5,6,9 – us UMI [740]
THE LEATHER INDUSTRY IN LIBYA / Libya. Ministry of Industry. Industrial Training and Service Department – 1Feb 1967. BNE-1208 1 – 9 – ne IDC [338]
LEATHERNECK – v5- 1921- 1; v54- 5,6; v60- 9 – us UMI [900]
Leathers, Harrison *see* JOURNALS
THE LEATHERWOOD GOD / Taneyhill, Richard H – 1869-70 – 9 – 10.00 – us Scholars' Facs [978]
Leathes, Stanley *see*
- CHARACTERISTICS OF CHRISTIANITY
- CHRIST AND THE BIBLE: FOUR LECTURES
- THE CHRISTIAN CREED
- THE CLAIMS OF THE OLD TESTAMENT: LECTURES
- FUTURE PROBATION
- THE GOSPEL ITS OWN WITNESS
- THE LAW IN THE PROPHETS
- OLD TESTAMENT PROPHECY: ITS WITNESS AS A RECORD OF DIVINE FOREKNOWLEDGE
- THE RELIGION OF THE CHRIST
- THE STRUCTURE OF THE OLD TESTAMENT: A SERIES OF POPULAR ESSAYS
- THE WITNESS OF ST. JOHN TO CHRIST
- THE WITNESS OF ST. PAUL TO CHRIST
- THE WITNESS OF THE OLD TESTAMENT TO CHRIST

Leavell, Frank H *see* DATA FROM HIS PAPERS ON BAPTIST INTERNATIONAL YOUTH CONFERENCE, 1931-1947
LEAVENING THE NATION ; THE STORY OF AMERICAN (PROTESTANT) HOME MISSIONS / Clark, Joseph B – New York: Baker & Taylor, 1903 – 1mf – us A.T.L.A. [240]
Leavens, Robert French *see* COLLECTED ADDRESSES AND WRITINGS
Leavenworth County. Kansas. Board of Commissioners *see* COMMISSIONER'S SIC JOURNAL
Leavenworth County. Kansas. District Court *see* ATTORNEY'S RECORD
Leavenworth County. Kansas. Little Stranger Church *see* RECORDS
LEAVENWORTH COUNTY PLAT BOOK / Missouri Publishing Company – 1878 – 1 – us KS Hist [978]
Leavenworth. Kansas. First Baptist Church *see*
- RECORDS

Leavenworth. Kansas. St. Paul Lutheran Church *see* RECORDS
Leavenworth. Kansas. Turnverein *see* RECORDS
LEAVES FROM A SPORTSMAN'S DIARY / Gillmore, Parker – London: W. Allen, 1893. 03199. (Pre-1900 Canadiana) – 9 – cn C.I.H.M. [790]
LEAVES FROM MY PORTFOLIO / Burr, W K – Belleville, Ont.: "Daily Ontario," 1880. 00351. (Pre-1900 Canadiana) – 9 – cn C.I.H.M. [920]
LEAVES OF GRASS / Whitman, Walt – Boston: Small, Maynard & Co., 1907, c1897. 455p – 1 – us U.W. Library [810]
Leavitt *see* HISTORY AND DIRECTORY OF KENT COUNTY, MICHIGAN
Leavitt, John McDowell *see*
- BIBLE LEAGUE ESSAYS IN BIBLE DEFENCE AND EXPOSITION
- REASONS FOR FAITH IN THIS NINETEENTH CENTURY

Leavitt, Joshua *see* THE CHRISTIAN LYRE
Lebaigue, Charles *see* MORCEAUX CHOISIS DE LITTERATURE FRANCAISE ET POESIE
Lebanon *see*
- AL-JARIDAH AL-RASMIYAH.
- STATE BUDGET OF LEBANON

LEBANON ADVERTISER – Lebanon, NE. -w. Mar 1912-Jun 1913; Jan 1914-Jun 1918 – 1 – us NE Hist [071]
Lebanon. Banque Al-Ahli *see* RAPPORT ANNUEL
Lebanon. Banque de Credit Agricole, Industriel et Foncier *see* REPORT OF THE BOARD OF DIRECTORS
Lebanon. Banque de la Mediterranee *see* RAPPORT ANNUEL
Lebanon. Banque de Liban *see* RAPPORT
LEBANON BAPTIST CHURCH. LEBANON, KENTUCKY : CHURCH RECORDS – 1864-1973 – 1 – 113.85 – us Baptist [240]
Lebanon. Beirut Riyad Bank *see* ANNUAL REPORTS, 1962-1976
Lebanon. Centre Beryte de Recherches Orientalis *see* LE REGIME DE L'ASSURANCE-MALADIE AU LIBAN
LEBANON COURIER – Lebanon, PA. -w 1851-1913 – 13 – $25.00r – us I.M.R. [071]
LEBANON CRITERION – Lebanon, OR. -w. 23 Jun 1910-31 Jul 1924. 4 rolls – 1 – us U.O. Library [071]
LEBANON DAILY NEWS – Lebanon, PA. -d 1961-1962 – 13 – $25.00r – us I.M.R. [071]
LEBANON DEMOCRAT – Lebanon, PA. (German) Circa 1851-1854 – 13 – $25.00r – us I.M.R. [071]
Lebanon. Development Studies Association *see* AL-INMA WA-AL-TASNIFI LUBNAN THIRD NATIONAL DEVELOPMENT CONFERENCE 18-20 APR 1968
Lebanon. Direction Centrale de la Statistique *see* RECENSEMENT DE L'INDUSTRIE AU LIBAN RESULTATS POUR 1964
Lebanon. Direction Generale des Douanes *see* STATISTIQUES DU COMMERCE EXTERIEUR
LEBANON EXPRESS – Lebanon, OR. 5 Mar 1887-6 Apr 1898; 24 July 1908-. – 1 – us U.O. Library [071]
LEBANON EXPRESS ADVANCE – Lebanon OR. Apr 15 1898-July 21 1908 – 1 – us U.O. Library [071]
Lebanon. Federation Nationale des Syndicats des Ouvriers et des Employes au Liban *see* DOCUMENTATION DU 1ER CONGRES: FEDERATION NATIONALE DES SYNDICATS DES OUVRIERS ET DES EMPLOYES AU LIBAN
Lebanon. Haut-Commissariat en Syrie et au Liban *see* STATISTIQUE DU COMMERCE EXTERIEUR DES ETATS DU LEVANT SOUS MANDAT FRANCAIS
Lebanon. International Bank for Reconstruction and Development *see* LOAN AGREEMENT (ELECTRIC POWER AND IRRIGATION PROJECTS) BETWEEN IBRD AND LITANI RIVER AUTHORITY
Lebanon. Laws, Statutes, etc *see* RECUEIL DES ARRETES ET DECISIONS DU GRAND LIBAN
LEBANON LEADER – Lebanon, NE. -w. Apr-Nov 1907, scattered issues missing; Jan 1908-Aug 1910; May-Oct 1911, scattered issues missing; Dec 1911-Oct 1912 – 1 – us NE Hist [071]
Lebanon. Ministere des Finances *see* FINAL ACCOUNTS, 1963-1974
Lebanon. Ministere du Plan *see*
- AL-IDARAT AL-MAHA-LIYYAH AL-BALADIYYAH FI LUBNAN
- AL-KHIDMAH AL-IJTIMAIYYAH AL-AHLIYYAH FI LUBNAN
- PLAN DE DEVELOPPEMENT, 1964-1968
- PLAN DE DEVELOPPEMENT, 1965-1969
- PLAN DE DEVELOPPEMENT 1972-1977
- PROGRAMME GLOBAL INTEGRE
- PROJET DU PLAN QUINQUENNAL 1964-1968
- PROPOSITIONS POUR LE PROJECT DE PLAN DE DEVELOPPEMENT 1964-1968
- RECUEIL DE STATISTIQUES LIBANAISES
- STATISTIQUES DU COMMERCE EXTERIEUR DU LIBAN

Lebanon. Office du Developpement Social *see* LES ACTES. DU 2 IEME SEMINAIRE D'ETUDES SUR LE DEVELOPPEMENT RURAL DANS LES PAYS DU BASSIN MEDITERRANEEN
Lebanon. Societe Nouvelle de la Banque de Syrie et du Liban. Assemblee generale ordinaire, 1964-1977 *see* PUBLICATIONS
Lebanon. University. Faculte de Droit et des Sciences Economiques. Etudes Economiques *see* BILAN DEMOGRAPHIQUE ET EVALUATION PERSPECTIVE DE L'EMPLOI AU LIBAN
Lebas, F et al *see* RABBIT
Lebassu d'Helf, Josephine *see*
- LA SAINT-SIMONIENNE

Lebed, D Z *see* DVA GODA RABOTY
Lebedev, A A *see*
- RUKOPISI TSERKOVNO-ARKHEOLOGICHESKAGO MUZEIA IMP. KIEVSKOI DUKHOVNOI AKADEMII
- RUSSKAIA BOGOSLOVSKAIA LITERATURA 1888-1892 GG

Lebedev, P S *see* GRAFY NIKITA I PETR PANINY
Lebedev, V *see* UKAZATEL' K RUSSKIM IZDANIIAM GRECHESKIKH I LATINSKIKH KLASSIKOV, AZBUK, RAZGOVOROV, GRAMMATIK I SLOVAREI OT NACHALA PO 1871
Lebedianskaia, A P, et al *see* PUTEVODITEL' PO ISTORICHESKOMU ARKHIVU MUZEIA
Lebegue, Nicolas *see* MOTETS POUR LES PRINCIPALES FESTES DE L'ANNEE
Lebel, Gilles *see* HORIZON 1980
Lebel, Roland *see*
- L'AFRIQUE OCCIDENTALE FRANCAISE DANS LA LITTERATURE FRANCAISE (DEPUIS 1870)
- LE LIVRE DU PAYS NOIR; ANTHOLOGIE DE LITTERATURE AFRICAINE

DOS LEBEN = THE LIFE – (Yiddish weekly and daily) – St-Petersburg, RU. no1. 28 Dec 1905 – 1r – 1 – $25.00 – cn Can Microfilming [072]
DAS LEBEN CYPRIANS VON PONTIUS : DIE ERSTE CHRISTLICHE BIOGRAPHIE (T.U.U. 3-39/3) / Harnack, Adolf von – Leipzig, 1913 – 2mf – 9 – ne Slangenburg [240]
DAS LEBEN DER LIUTBIRG (MGH DEUTSCHES..: 3.BD) – 1937 – Dfl6.00 – ne Slangenburg [240]
DAS LEBEN DES DEUTSCHEN VOLKS BEI BEGINN DER NEUZEIT / Ulmann, Heinrich – Halle: Verein fuer Reformationsgeschichte, 1893. ([Schriften des Vereins fuer Reformationsgeschichte; Bd. 41]) – 1mf – us A.T.L.A. [943]
DAS LEBEN DES HEILANDS DARGESTELLT / Frenssen, Gustav – Berlin:G Grote, 1907 – 1mf – 9 – 0-8370-3192-3 – 1985-1192 – us A.T.L.A. [240]
LEBEN DES HEILIGEN PAPSTES LEO 9 / Guibert, Archdeacon of Toulouse – Strassburg: F X le Roux, [1902?] – 1mf – 9 – 0-8370-8516-0 – 1986-2516 – us A.T.L.A. [920]
DAS LEBEN DES HEILIGEN SYMEON STYLITES (T.U.U. 3-32/4) / Lietzmann, Hans – Leipzig, 1908 – 4mf – 9 – ne Slangenburg [240]

DAS LEBEN DES HL. ROBERT VON MOLESME / Spahr, K – Freiburg Schw., 1944 – 2mf – 8 – Dfl9.00 – ne Slangenburg [240]
DAS LEBEN DES MICHELANGELO BUONARROTI / Condivi, Ascanio – O 517f. 1874 – 9 – ne IDC [730]
LEBEN DES QUINTUS FIXLEIN : AUS FUENFZEHN ZETTELKAESTEN GEZOGEN NEBST EINEM MUSSTEIL UND EINIGEN JUS DE TABLETTE / Jean Paul – Leipzig: P Reclam jun, [1887?] – 1r – 1 – us U.W. Library [430]
DAS LEBEN FRIEDRICH VON MATTHISSONS / Heers, Alois – (Includes bibliographical references) – Leipzig: Im Xenienverlag, 1913 – 1r – 1 – us U.W. Library [920]
DAS LEBEN GOETHES : NEU BEARBEITET UND EINGELEITET VON REINHARD BUCHWALD / Grimm, Hermann Friedrich – (Includes bibliographical references) – 3., durchgesehene Aufl. Stuttgart: A Kroener, 1940 – 1r – 1 – us U.W. Library [920]
DAS LEBEN IM BILD – Berlin, 1927-31 – 1r – 1 – Dist. gw Mikrofilm – gw Misc Inst [072]
DAS LEBEN JESU / Strausz, D F – Bonn, 1891 – 15mf – 8 – ne Slangenburg [240]
LEBEN JESU / Holtzmann, Oskar – Tuebingen: J.C.B. Mohr, 1901. 1 fiche – 9 – us A.T.L.A. [240]
LEBEN JESU / ed by Stork, Hans-Walter – 1990 – 30p + 5 color mf – ca DM620.00 – 3-89219-022-4 – gw Lengenfelder [240]
DAS LEBEN JESU: EINE SAGE VON DEM SCHICKSALE UND ERLEBNISSEN DER BODENFRUCHT / Kulischer, M – Leipzig: Otto Wigand, 1876. 1 fiche – 9 – us A.T.L.A. [240]
DAS LEBEN JESU IN URKUNDLICHER DARSTELLUNG...MARCUS, MATTHAEUS UND LUCAS / Wittichen, Carl – Jena: Hermann Dufft, 1876. 1 fiche. 8370-5887-2 – 9 – us A.T.L.A. [240]
DAS LEBEN JESU UND DIE KIRCHE DER ZUKUNFT / Lang, H – 1872 – 1 – us A.T.L.A. [240]
DAS LEBEN MEINES VATERS / Kurz, Isolde – 3. Aufl. Tuebingen: R Wunderlich, [19–?] – 1r – 1 – us U.W. Library [920]
LEBEN, MEYNUNGEN UND THATEN VON HIERONIMUS JOBS DEM KANDIDATEN, UND WIE ER SICH WEILAND VIEL RUHM ERWARB AUCH ENDLICH ALS NACHTSWAECHTER ZU SULZBURG STARB / Kortum, Karl Arnold; ed by Hoelscher, Eberhard – Hamburg: E Hauswedell, 1948 – 1 – us U.W. Library [830]
LEBEN MOSES : NACH AUFFASSUNG DER JUEDISCHEN SAGE / Beer, Bernhard – Leipzig: Oskar Leiner, 1863 – 1mf – 9 – 0-8370-2124-3 – 1985-0124 – us A.T.L.A. [920]
DAS LEBEN NACH DEM TODE : NACH DEN VORSTELLUNGEN DES ALTEN ISRAEL UND DES JUDENTUMS... / Schwally, Friedrich – (Includes bibliographical references & indexes) – Giessen: J Ricker, 1892 – 1mf – 9 – 0-8370-5174-6 – 1985-3174 – us A.T.L.A. [270]
LEBEN SCHLEIERMACHERS / Dilthey, Wilhelm – 1870 – 1 – us A.T.L.A. [240]
LEBEN UND SEELE UNSERES SOLDATENLIEDS IM WELTKRIEG / Schuhmacher, Wilhelm – (Includes bibliographical references) – Frankfurt am Main: M Diesterweg, 1928 – 1 – us U.W. Library [780]
LEBEN UND THATEN DES BERUEHMTEN RITTERS SCHNAPPHAHNSKI / Weerth, Georg – Hamburg: Hoffmann und Campe, 1849 – 1r – 1 – us U.W. Library [430]
LEBEN UND WIRKEN DES HOCHSELIGEN JOHANNES NEP. NEUMANN : AUS DER CONGREGATION DES ALLERH. ERLOESERS, BISCHOFS VON PHILADELPHIA / Berger, Johann – New York: Benziger, 1883 – 1mf – 9 – 0-8370-6565-8 – 1986-0565 – us A.T.L.A. [920]
DAS LEBENDE BILD – Berlin. feb 8, feb 15, mar 1, mar 22-apr 26, sep 6-20 1919. jun 26, oct 31 1920 – 1 – gw Mikrofilm [790]
DIE LEBENSANSCHAUUNGEN DER GROSSEN DENKER / Eucken, Rudolf – Berlin, 1922 – 8mf – 8 – ne Slangenburg [100]
LEBENS-ANSICHTEN DES KATERS MURR : NEBST FRAGMENTARISCHER BIOGRAPHIE DES KAPELLMEISTERS JOHANNES KREISLER IN ZUFAELLIGEN MAKULATURBLAETTERN / Hoffmann, Ernst Theordor Amadeus – Muenchen: Musarion Verlag, [19–?] – 1 – us U.W. Library [830]
LEBENSBESCHREIBUNG DES KK. KAPELLMEISTERS W.A. MOZART, AUS ORIGINALQUELLEN / Niemtschek, FX. – 2. vermehrte Aufl. Prag: Herrlische Buchhandlung, 1808 – 1 – us Sibley [780]
LEBENSBESCHREIBUNGEN BERUEHMTER MUSIKGELEHRTEN UND TONKUENSTLER... / Hiller, J – Leipzig, 1784 – 3mf – ne IDC [780]
LEBENSBESCHREIBUNGEN BERUEHMTER MUSIKGELEHRTEN UND TONKUENSTLER, NEUERER ZEIT. 1. THEIL / Hiller, Johann Adam – Leipzig: Dykischen Buchhandlung, 1784 – 1 – us Sibley [780]
LEBENSBESCHREIBUNGEN BERUEHMTER MUSIKGELEHRTEN UND TONKUENSTLZR / Hiller, Johann Adam – P 697. 1784 – 9 – ne IDC [920]
LEBENSBILDER UND LANDSCHAFT : LANDWIRTSCHAFT UND KUNST. VOM ERBE ZUM KULTURLAND / Bennigsen, Ingrid – 1993 – 2mf – 9 – DM98.00 – 3-89349-672-6 – gw Hänsel [750]
LEBENSDIENST : GESAMMELTE STUDIEN, ERFAHRUNGEN UND REDEN AUS DREI JAHRZEHNTEN / Wassermann, Jakob – Leipzig: Zurich: Grethlein und Co, c1928 – 1r – 1 – us U.W. Library [430]
LEBENSDRANG UND TODESVERLANGEN IN DER DEUTSCHEN LITERATUR VON 1850-1880 IM ZUSAMMENHANG MIT DER PHILOSOPHIE SCHOPENHAUERS / Arnold, Hans – Heidelberg, 1933 – 2mf – 9 – DM62.00 – 3-89349-747-1 – gw Hänsel [430]
LEBENSERINNERUNGEN / Groth, Klaus; ed by Wolff, Eugen – Kiel: Lipsius und Tischer, 1891 – 1r – 1 – us U.W. Library [920]
LEBENSERINNERUNGEN, BAND 3 : BRIEFE UND LEBENSABRISS / Schurz, Carl – Berlin, 1912 – 1 – DM30.00 – gw Mikro Press [943]
LEBENSERINNERUNGEN DES ALTEN MANNES IN BRIEFEN AN SEINEN BRUDER GERHARD / Kuegelgen, Wilhelm von; ed by Taube, Otto Freiherr von – Stuttgart: K F Koehler, c1951 – 1 – us U.W. Library [860]
LEBENSERINNERUNGEN UND LEBENSHOFFNUNGEN: 1832 BIS 1910 / Foerster, Wilhelm Julius – Berlin: G. Reimer, 1911.351p – 1 – us U.W. Library [943]
DIE LEBENSFRAGE DER SYSTEMATISCHEN THEOLOGIE DIE LEBENSFRAGE DES CHRISTLICHEN GLAUBENS : REDE ZUM ANTRITT DES AKADEMISCHEN LEHRAMTS AN DER UNIVERSITAET TUEBINGEN / Haering, Theodor – Tuebingen: J J Heckenhauer, 1895 – 1mf – 9 – 0-8370-5069-3 – 1985-3069 – us A.T.L.A. [240]
DER LEBENSGEHALT DER WISSENSCHAFTEN : WISSENSCHAFTSTHEORETISCHE GRUNDFRAGEN / Elsbach, A C – Berlin, Leipzig, 1926 – 1mf – 9 – DM38.00 – 3-89349-307-7 – gw Hänsel [100]
Lebensohn, A D *see* SHIREI SEFAT KODESH
Lebenson, A A *see* T-VO SKOROPECHATNI A.A. LEBENSON
LEBENSQUALITAET, HERZFREQUENZ UND HERZFREQUENZVARIABILITAET NACH AKUTEM MYOKARDINFARKT / Rentrop, Klaus W – 1995 – 1mf – 9 – DM60.00 – 3-8267-2221-3 – gw Hänsel [616]
LEBENSRAETHSEL : FUENF NOVELLEN / Riehl, Wilhelm Heinrich – Stuttgart: J G Cotta, 1888 – 1r – 1 – us U.W. Library [830]
DIE LEBENSSCHAU DES YUSTIMUS / Sanchez Morales, Narciso – 1 – sp Bibl Santa Ana [360]
LEBENSSCHWAENKE : HEITERE GESCHICHTEN / Blumenthal, Oscar – Berlin: Verlag der Lustigen Blatter, [191-?] – 1 – us U.W. Library [870]
DER LEBENSSTROM : GEDICHTE / Vegesack, Siegfried von – Berlin: E Schmidt, c1943 – 1r – 1 – us U.W. Library [810]
DIE LEBENSUHR DES GOTTLIEB GRAMBAUER : BEICHTE EINES EINFAELTIGEN HERZENS: ROMAN / Welk, Ehm – Berlin: Deutscher Verlag, c1938 – 1r – 1 – us U.W. Library [830]
LEBENSVERSICHERUNGEN BEI FEINDLAENDISCHEN GESELLSCHAFTEN / Herold, H W – Berlin, 1922 – 1mf – 1 – ILM-3801/1 – ne IDC [327]
Leber, [J M]C *see* COLLECTION DES MEILLEURS DISSERTATIONS, NOTICES ET TRAITES RELATIFS A L'HISTOIRE DE FRANCE
LEBERECHT HUEHNCHEN : JUBILIAEUMSAUSG. / Seidel, Heinrich – Stuttgart: J G Cotta, 1942 – 1r – 1 – us U.W. Library [830]
LEBERECHT HUEHNCHEN / Seidel, Heinrich – 2. Aufl. Stuttgart: J G Cotta, 1903 – 1r – 1 – us U.W. Library [830]
Lebert, H *see*
- BAU UND LEBEN DER SPINNEN
- VERZEICHNISS SCHLESINGER SPINNEN

Leberthon *see* CITY AND COUNTY OF SAN DIEGO
Lebeuf, Jean *see* HISTOIRE DE LA VILLE ET DE TOUT LE DIOCESE DE PARIS
Lebeuf, Jean Paul *see* LA CIVILISATION DU TCHAD...: SUIVI D'UNE ETUDE SUR LES BRONZES SAO, PAR RAYMOND LANTIER
Leblanc, C *see* L'INFRASTRUCTURE SCOLAIRE EN COTE D'IVOIRE
Leblanc, D *see* LA GAZETTE D'ARTHABASKA
Leblanc de Marconnay, Hyacinthe *see* VALENTINE OU LA NINA CANADIENNE COMEDIE EN UN ACTE
Leblond de Brumath, A *see* HISTOIRE POPULAIRE DE MONTREAL DEPUIS SON ORIGINE JUSQU'A NOS JOURS
Leblond, Gaspard-Michel *see* MEMOIRES POUR SERVIR A L'HISTOIRE DE LA REVOLUTION OPEREE DANS LA MUSIQUE PAR M. LE CHEVALIER GLUCK
Leblond, Marius-Ary *see* MADAGASCAR, CREATION FRANCAISE
LEBN UN SHOLEM = VIE ET PAIX – (In Yiddish) – Brussels, BE. 15 Apr 1955 – 1r – 1 – $20.00 – cn Can Microfilming [072]
Lebon, J *see* LE MONOPHYSISME SEVERIEN
Lebour, M V *see* THE PLANKTONIC DIATOMS OF NORTHERN SEAS
Lebrun, Constance MT *see* EFFECTS OF THE MENSTRUAL CYCLE AND ORAL CONTRACEPTIVES ON ATHLETIC PERFORMANCE
Lebrun, Isidore *see* TABLEAU STATISTIQUE ET POLITIQUE DES DEUX CANADAS
Lebrun-Tossa *see* VOLTAIRE, JUGE PAR LES FAITS
Lebrun-Tossa et Lesueur *see* ARABELLE ET VASCOS OU LES JACOBINS DE GOA
Lebzelter, Joseph *see* CARDIOPULMONARY RESPONSES TO UNSUPPORTED AND SUPPORTED ARM EXERCISE IN NORMAL SUBJECTS AND PATIENTS WITH OBSTRUCTIVE PULMONARY DISEASE
LECCION CRITICA A LOS LECTORES DE LA MEMORIA DE COSME DAMIAN SOBRE EL TEATRO / Garcia de la Huerta, Vicente – Madrid: Pantaleon Aznar, 1786 – 1 – sp Bibl Santa Ana [240]
LECCION CRITICA A LOS LECTORES DEL PAPEL INTITULADO : CONTINUACION DE LAS MEMORIAS CRITICAS DE COSME DAMIAN / Garcia de la Huerta, Vicente – Madrid: Imprenta Real, 1785 – 1 – sp Bibl Santa Ana [240]
LA LECCION DEL PASADO. ESPANA SALVA A EUROPA DEL COMUNISMO, BIOGRAFIAS / Spain. Servicio Nacional de Prensa y Propaganda – n.p., 1936? Fiche W1497. (Blodgett Collection of Spanish Civil War Pamphlets) – 9 – us H.U. College Libr [946]
LECCION HISTORICA AL PROFESOR PAREDES / Garcia de la Huerta, Vicente – Lorenzo de San Martin, 1786 – 1 – sp Bibl Santa Ana [946]
LAS LECCIONES DE ALMERIA / Dimitrov, Georgi – Barcelona, 1937? Fiche W 838. (Blodgett Collection of Spanish Civil War Pamphlets) – 9 – us H.U. College Libr [946]
LECCIONES DE CLAVE Y PRINCIPIOS DE HARMONIA / Bails, B – P-144 1. 1775 – 9 – ne IDC [780]
LECCIONES DE DERECHO MARITIMO... / Arias, A – Lima, 1876 – 5mf – 9 – ILM-1501/1 – ne IDC [340]
LECCIONES DE DERECHO POLITICO / Donoso Cortes, Juan Francisco – 1837 – 9 – 1.50f – sp Bibl Santa Ana [946]
LECCIONES DE DOCTRINA CRISTIANA... CUARTA EDICION / Soto y Mancera, Felix – Badajoz: Imp. de Vicente Rodriguez, 1921 – 1 – sp Bibl Santa Ana [240]
LECCIONES DE HISTORIA SAGRADA / Pedrajas y Nunez-Moreno, Eloy – 1899 – 9 – 1.50f – sp Bibl Santa Ana [946]
LECCIONES DE LENGUA FRANCESA / Soler Arques, Carlos – 1895 – 9 – 1.50f – sp Bibl Santa Ana [440]
LECCIONES DE MORAL / Rodriguez y Hernandez, Juan Antonio – 1852 – 9 – 1.50f – sp Bibl Santa Ana [240]
LECCIONES DE RITOS ROMANOS / Fuertes, Jose V – 1856 – 9 – 1.50f – sp Bibl Santa Ana [290]
Lecestre, Leon *see* ABBAYES, PRIEUR ES ET COUVENTS D'HOMMES EN FRANCE
Lechevalier, A *see* NOTE SUR LE MOUVEMENT DE LA POPULATION ET LA QUESTION DE LA NATALITE DANS LE CANTON DE CRIQUETCH-L'ESNEVAL
Lechevalier, J *see*
- AUX SAINT-SIMONIENS
- MISSION SAINT-SIMONIENNE. PROFESSION DE FOI DES SAINTS-SIMONIENS
- OUVERTURE D'UNE BIBLIOTHEQUE DE LA DOCTRINE SAINT-SIMONIENNE A PERPIGNAN

Lechevalier, Jules *see* RAPPORT SUR LES QUESTIONS COLONIALES
Lechler, G V *see* GESCHICHTE DER PRESBYTERIAL- UND SYNODALVERFASSUNG
Lechler, Gotthard Victor *see*
- DE THOMA BRADWARDINO COMMENTATIO
- GESCHICHTE DES ENGLISCHEN DEISMUS
- JOHANNES HUS
- JOHANNIS DE WICLIF TRACTATUS DE OFFICIO PASTORALI E CODICE VINDOBONENSI
- JOHN WYCLIFFE AND HIS ENGLISH PRECURSORS
- ROBERT GROSSETESTE, BISCHOF VON LINCOLN
- URKUNDENFUNDE ZUR GESCHICHTE DES CHRISTLICHEN ALTERTUMS

Lechner, Hermann *see*
- GRUNDZUEGE DER LITERATURGESCHICHTE
- LITERATURGESCHICHTE DES DEUTSCHEN SPRACHRAUMES

Leckie, Joseph H *see* AUTHORITY IN RELIGION
Lecky, Alexander G *see* IN THE DAYS OF LAGGAN PRESBYTERY, 1908
Lecky, William Edward Hartpole *see*
- THE LEADERS OF PUBLIC OPINION IN IRELAND
- THE MAP OF LIFE, CONDUCT, AND CHARACTER

Leclair, Jean-Marie *see* PREMIER (-SECOND) LIVRE DE SONATES
Lecler, A *see* DICTIONNAIRE TOPOGRAPHIQUE, ARCHEOLOGIQUE ET HISTORIQUE DE LA CREUSE
Leclerc, D *see* THE HISTORY OF PHYSICK
Leclerc, Marcel *see* BIBLIOGRAPHIE DE L'ILE D'ORLEANS
Leclerc, Max *see* CARTAS DO BRASIL
LeClercq, Ch *see* PREMIER ETABLISSEMENT DE LA FOY DANS LA NOUVELLE FRANCE
Leclercq, H *see*
- HISTOIRE DES CONCILES
- HISTOIRE DES CONCILES D'APRAES LES DOCUMENTS ORIGINAUX

Leclercq, Henri *see* L'AFRIQUE CHRETIENNE
Leclere, Adhemard *see*
- LE BUDDHISME AU CAMBODGE
- LES CODES CAMBODGIENS
- RECHERCHES SUR LA LEGISLATION CRIMINELLE ET LA PROCEDURE DES CAMBODGIENS

Leclere, Albert *see* PRAGMATISME, MODERNISME, PROTESTANTISME
Leclere, P-E *see* L'AMI DU PEUPLE
Leclerq, H *see*
- DICTIONNAIRE D'ARCHEA1OLOGIE CHRETIENNE ET DE LITURGIE
- L'ESPAGNE CHRETIENNE

L'Ecole francaise d'Extreme-Orient *see* BULLETIN
Lecompton, Kansas *see* MISCELLANEOUS NEWSPAPERS
Lecomte, L H *see*
- LES PARODIES THEATRALES EN FRANCE: HISTOIRE DU GENRE A TRAVERS DEUX SIECLES
- LES THEATRES DE PARIS ET LEUR REPERTOIRE: THEATRE DE L'ODEON 1797-1900

LeComte, LD *see* THE MEMOIRS AND OBSERVATIONS,... (HARRIS, J. NAVIGANTIUM ATQUE ITINERANTIUM BIBLIOTHECA...)
Lecomte, Maurice *see* CHARTES ET DOCUMENTS DE L'ABBAYE CISTERCIENNE DE PREUILLY
Lecomte, [P] H *see* ATLAS DES BOIS DE L'INDOCHINE
UNE LECON D'AGRICULTURE: CAUSERIES AGRICOLES / Barnard, Edouard Andre – Montreal: Burland-Desbarats, 1875. 03370. (Pre-1900 Canadiana) – 9 – cn C.I.H.M. [630]
Leconfield. Yorkshire *see* PARISH REGISTERS

LECONS D'ANGLAIS D'APRES LA METHODE NATURELLE: PREMIER LIVRE DU MAITRE / Ahern, John – Quebec: Dussault & Proulx, 1895. 00020. (Pre-1900 Canadiana) – 9 – cn C.I.H.M. [420]

LECONS DE CLAVECIN, ET PRINCIPES D'HARMONIE / Bemetzrieder, A – 1771 – 9 – us Sibley [780]

LECONS DE CLAVECIN, ET PRINCIPES D'HARMONIE / Bemetzrieder, A – P-160. 1771 – 9 – ne IDC [780]

LECONS DE FRANCAIS A L'USAGE DE L'ACADEMIE FRANCAISE / Daniel, J F – 1837 – 9 – fr I.C.S. [440]

LECONS DE PERSPECTIVE POSITIVE / Androuet du Cerceau, Jacques – O-1038 1. 1576 – 9 – ne IDC [760]

LECONS DE PHOTOGRAPHIE / Grenier, Henry Napoleon – Montreal: s.n, 1864. SEM105P342 – 1mf – 9 – Can$2.25 – cn Bibl Nat [760]

LECONS DE PHYSIQUE-CHIMIQUE: OU, APPLICATION DE LA CHIMIE MODERN A LA PHYSIQUE / Libes, Antoine – Paris: Libes, between 1792 and 1822 – 1 – us U.W. Library [540]

LECONS D'EPIGRAPHIE ASSYRIENNE : PROFESSEES AUX COURS LIBRES DE LA SORBONNE PENDANT L'ANNEE 1869 / Menant, Joachim – Paris: Maisonneuve, 1873 – 1mf – 9 – 0-8370-8532-2 – 1986-2532 – us A.T.L.A. [470]

LECONS, DOUZE, AVEC LEUR GOIGTE POUR LE PIANO-FORTE... / Steibelt, Daniel – Offenbach: Jean Andre, [1809] – 1 – us Sibley [780]

LECONS DU MARDI A LA SALPETRIERE. V. V.1887-1889 / Charcot, Jean Martin – (French Precursors of Psychiatry Series). Paris. Aux Bureaux Du Progres Medical et E. Lecrosnier et Babe. 1888-89 – 9 – fr Hachette [150]

LECONS SUR LA PHYSIOLOGIE ET LA PATHOLOGIE DU SYSTEME NERVEUX / Bernard, C – 2V. M 283. 1858 – 9 – ne IDC [610]

LECONS SUR LE CALCUL DES FONCTIONS / Lagrange, Joseph Louis de – Nouv. edition revue, corrigee et augmentee, Paris, chez Courcier, 1806, vi, 502 p. Histoire des Sciences XVIIe-XIXe Siecles. 7986 – 9 – fr Hachette [510]

LECONS SUR LES MALADIES DU SYSTEME NERVEUX / Charcot, Jean Martin – M 88. 3 v. 1872-1887 – 9 – ne IDC [616]

Leconte, J L *see* HISTOIRE GENERALE ET ICONOGRAPHIE DES LEPIDOPTERES ET DES CHENILLES DE L'AMERIQUE SEPTENTRIONALE

LeConte, Joseph *see*
- EVOLUTION: ITS NATURE, ITS EVIDENCES, AND ITS RELATION TO RELIGIOUS THOUGHT
- RELIGION AND SCIENCE...,OR, THE TRUTHS REVEALED IN NATURE AND SCRIPTURE
- SIGHT: AN EXPOSITION OF THE PRINCIPLES OF MONOCULAR AND BINOCULAR VISION

Lecoyer, J C *see* MONOGRAPHIE DU GENRE THALICTRUM

Lecreulx, Francois M *see* DESCRIPTION ABREGEE DU DEPARTEMENT DE LA MEURTHE

LECTIONARIUM – 15th cent. German manuscript. Lamentations with music in Gothic notation on three- or four-line staves – 9 – us Sibley [780]

LECTIONARIUM EVANGELIORUM / Holkham Hall. Norfolk. England – (Italian). 15th Century. Holkham Ms 18 – 1 – uk Microform Academic [240]

LECTIONARIUS – ca 30p + 6 color mf – ca DM620.00 – 3-89219-018-6 – gw Lengenfelder [090]

THE LECTIONARY = LECTIONNAIRES : ITS SOURCES AND HISTORY / Baudot, Jules – (Includes bibliographical references) – London: Catholic Truth Society; St Louis, MO: B Herder, 1910 – 1mf – 9 – 0-8370-7441-X – 1986-1441 – us A.T.L.A. [240]

LA LECTURA – Revista de Ciencias y de Artes. Madrid. v. 1-20. 1901-1920 – 1 – us NY Public [073]

LA LECTURA POPULAR – Manila, Philippine Islands. 3 Jan-25 Dec 1890; 12 Mar-1 Oct 1891 (imperfect) – 1r – 1 – uk British Libr Newspaper [072]

LECTURA Y VIDA – (1982-. 1,5,6,9) – 1980- – 1 – us UMI [370]

LECTURAS DE HISTORIA NACIONAL RELACIONADAS CON EL SANTISIMO SACRAMENTO. SANTIAGO DE CHILE, 1928 / Munoz Olave, Reinaldo; ed by Bayle, Constantino – Madrid: Razon y Fe, 1929 – 9 – sp Bibl Santa Ana [972]

LECTURAS PARA LA JUVENTUD. COLECCION DE BIOGRAFIAS HIJOS ILUSTRES DE ESPANA / Editorial Sanchez Rodrigo – Plasencia: Imp. Sanchez Rodrigo, 1962 – 1 – sp Bibl Santa Ana [920]

LECTURAS VENEZOLANAS / Briano-Iragorry, Mario – Caracas, 1930; Madrid: Razon y Fe, 1931 – 1 – sp Bibl Santa Ana [972]

LA LECTURE – Magazine litteraire. Paris. aout 1887-mars 1896 – 1 – fr A.C.R.P.P. [073]

LA LECTURE AU FOYER : JOURNAL LITTERAIRE – Montreal, Canada. 22 nov 1884 – 1r – 1 – Can$25.00 – cn Can Microfilming [073]

LA LECTURE AU FOYER – Montreal: [s.n, 1898-189-?] – 9 – cn C.I.H.M. [971]

LECTURE BEFORE STUDENTS OF PADJADJARAN UNIV. IN BANDUNG / Sukarno, Pres. Indonesia – SE 4486 1. May 2, 1958 – 9 – ne IDC [025]

A LECTURE; BEING THE THIRD OF A SERIES OF LECTURES, INTRODUCTORY TO A COURSE OF LECTURES NOW DELIVERING IN THE UNIVERSITY OF MARYLAND / Hoffman, David – Baltimore: Toy, 1826. 62p. LL-384 – 1 – us L of C Photodup [340]

A LECTURE ON HEADS... / Stevens, G A – London, 1799 – 2mf – 9 – ne IDC [840]

LECTURE ON IMPERIAL FEDERATION, DECEMBER 1888 / Dobell, Richard Reid – Quebec: s.n., 1888 (Quebec: Dawson). 02726. (Pre-1900 Canadiana) – 9 – cn C.I.H.M. [971]

LECTURE ON THE DREADFUL ABUSE OF HUMAN MAGNETISM... : IN THE MYSTERIES OF THE ROMAN CHURCH, AND HER DAUGHTERS / Smolnikar, Andrew B – Salem, [Ohio]: 1851 – 1r – 1 – us Western Res [240]

LECTURE ON THE EPISTLE OF JAMES / Wardlow, Ralph – Edinburgh: A. Fullarton, 1869. 1 fiche – 9 – us A.T.L.A. [240]

LECTURE ON THE FLORA OF AUSTRALIA / Mueller, Ferdinand Jakob Heinrich von – Ballarat. 1882. B-8064 1 – 9 – ne IDC [580]

A LECTURE ON THE LAW OF REPRESENTATIONS IN MARINE INSURANCE. / Duer, John – New York, Voorhies, 1844. 239 p. LL-111 – 1 – us L of C Photodup [340]

LECTURE OUTLINES ON THE THIRTY-NINE ARTICLES / Tait, Arthur James – London: Elliot Stock, 1910 – 1mf – 9 – 0-8370-8715-5 – 1986-2715 – us A.T.L.A. [240]

LECTURE PRONONCEE PAR E. PARENT DEVANT L'INSTITUT CANADIEN, JEUDI LE 19 NOVEMBRE 1846 / Parent, Etienne – Montreal: Impr. de la Revue Canadienne, 1846. SEM16P192 – 1r – 5 – Can$9.00 – cn Bibl Nat [330]

LECTURES / Boutroux, Emile [et al] – Princeton: Princeton University Press, 1914 – 1mf – us A.T.L.A. [240]

LECTURES : REVUE MENSUELLE DE BIBLIOGRAPHIE CRITIQUE / Fides. Service de bibliographie et de documentation – Montreal. v1 no 1-v10 no 10; n.s. v1 no 1- n.s. v12 no 9 10. 1946-1966. SEM16P305 – 4r – 5 – Can$134.00 – cn Bibl Nat [073]

LECTURES AND ESSAYS BY WILLIAM KINGDON CLIFFORD / Clifford, William Kingdon; ed by Stephen, Leslie & Pollock, Frederick – London: Macmillan, 1879 – 1 roll – 1 – 1-55879-224-4 – uk Libr Preservation [800]

LECTURES AND MISCELLANIES / James, Henry – New York: Redfield, 1852. 442p – 1 – us U.W. Library [850]

LECTURES AND NOTES ON SHAKESPEARE AND OTHER ENGLISH POETS / Coleridge, Samuel Taylor – London: George Bell and Sons, 1883 – 1 roll – 1 – 1-55879-749-1 – uk Libr Preservation [420]

LECTURES AND OTHER THEOLOGICAL PAPERS / Mozley, James Bowling – New York: E P Dutton, 1883 – 1mf – 9 – 0-8370-4030-2 – 1985-2030 – us A.T.L.A. [240]

LECTURES BY...JOHN M'CLINTOCK ON THEOLOGICAL ENCYCLOPAEDIA AND METHODOLOGY / M'Clintock, John – Cincinnati: Hitchcock & Walden, 1873 – 1mf – 9 – us A.T.L.A. [240]

LECTURES CHIEFLY EXPOSITORY ON ST PAUL'S EPISTLE TO THE PHILIPPIANS : WITH NOTES AND ILLUSTRATIONS / Hutchison, John – (Includes bibliographical references) – Edinburgh: T & T Clark, 1887 – 1mf – 9 – 0-8370-3703-4 – 1985-1703 – us A.T.L.A. [240]

LECTURES CHIEFLY EXPOSITORY ON ST PAUL'S FIRST AND SECOND EPISTLES TO THE THESSALONIANS : WITH NOTES AND ILLUSTRATIONS / Hutchison, John – Edinburgh: T & T Clark, 1884 – 1mf – 9 – 0-8370-3704-2 – 1985-1704 – us A.T.L.A. [220]

THE LECTURES COMPLETE OF FATHER GAVAZZI / Gavazzi, Alessandro – New York: M W Dodd, 1854, c1853 – 1mf – 9 – 0-8370-8574-8 – 1986-2574 – us A.T.L.A. [240]

LECTURES CONCERNING ORATORY / Lawson, John – 1758. 494p. (English Linguistics Series 1500-1800) – 9 – us UMI [400]

LECTURES DOCTRINAL AND PRACTICAL ON THE EPISTLE OF THE APOSTLE PAUL TO THE ROMANS – Edinburgh: William Blackwood, 1838 – 1mf – 9 – 0-8370-4076-0 – 1985-2076 – us A.T.L.A. [220]

LECTURES IN ANAESTHESIOLOGY *see* WFSA LECTURES

LECTURES IN DEFENCE OF THE CHRISTIAN FAITH / Godet, Frederic Louis – 2nd ed. 1883 – 9 – us A.T.L.A. [240]

LECTURES IN DEFENCE OF THE CHRISTIAN FAITH / Godet, Frederic Louis – Edinburgh: T. & T. Clark, 1895. 1 fiche – 9 – us A.T.L.A. [240]

LECTURES IN THE TRAINING SCHOOLS FOR KINDERGARTNERS / Peabody, Elizabeth Palmer – Boston: D.C. Heath & Company, 1886. 226p. 1 reel. 1249 – 1 – us U.W. Library [370]

LECTURES ON AGRICULTURAL PLANNING DELIVERED AT THE F.A.O. NEAR EAST REGIONAL TRAINING CENTRE ON AGRICULTURAL DEVELOPMENT PLANNING, CAIRO, 1963 – 1976 – 294p – it F.A.O. [338]

LECTURES ON ANGINA PECTORIS AND ALLIED STATES / Osler, W – New York, 1897 – 3mf – 9 – ne IDC [616]

LECTURES ON ARCHBISHOP LAUD : TOGETHER WITH A BIBLIOGRAPHY OF LAUDIAN LITERATURE AND THE LAUDIAN EXHIBITION CATALOGUE, ETC. / ed by Collins, William Edward – London: Allhallows Barking, E.C., A. Southey [distributor], 1895 – 1mf – us A.T.L.A. [240]

LECTURES ON BIBLE REVISION : WITH AN APPENDIX CONTAINING THE PREFACES TO THE CHIEF HISTORICAL EDITIONS OF THE ENGLISH BIBLE / Newth, Samuel – (Includes bibliographical references and index) – London: Hodder & Stoughton, 1881 – 1mf – 9 – 0-8370-4576-2 – 1985-2576 – us A.T.L.A. [220]

LECTURES ON BUTLER'S ANALOGY / Norris, John Pilkington – London: S.P.C.K., 1887. 1 fiche – 9 – us A.T.L.A. [240]

LECTURES ON CAUSES, PATHOLOGY AND TREATMENT OF JOINT DISEASES:.. / Bauer, Louis – New York: W. Wood, 1868.02287.(Pre-1900 Canadiana) – 9 – cn C.I.H.M. [616]

LECTURES ON CERTAIN DIFFICULTIES FELT BY ANGLICANS IN SUBMITTING TO THE CATHOLIC CHURCH / Newman, John Henry – London: Burns & Lambert, 1850 – 1 roll – 1 – 1-55879-384-4 – uk Libr Preservation [240]

LECTURES ON CHRISTIAN DOCTRINE / Peabody, Andrew Preston – 1857 – 9 – us A.T.L.A. [240]

LECTURES ON CHURCH DIFFICULTIES / Neale, John Mason – London: J.T. Hayes; New York: Pott & Amery, [1871?] – 1mf – us A.T.L.A. [240]

LECTURES ON COLET, FISHER, AND MORE, AT ST PAUL'S CATHEDRAL, 1894 / Mason, Arthur James – London: S.P.C.K.; New York: E.& J.B. Young, 1895 – 1mf – us A.T.L.A. [240]

LECTURES ON ECCLESIASTES DELIVERED IN WESTMINSTER ABBEY / Bradley, George Granville – Oxford: Clarendon Press, 1885 – 1mf – 9 – 0-8370-2434-X – 1985-0434 – us A.T.L.A. [220]

LECTURES ON EDUCATION / Mann, Horace – Boston: William B Fowle, 1848, c1845 – 1mf – 9 – 0-8370-7647-1 – 1986-1647 – us A.T.L.A. [370]

LECTURES ON ELOQUENCE AND MORAL PHILOSOPHY / Witherspoon, John – 1 – $50.00 – us Presbyterian [170]

LECTURES ON ENTOMOLOGY / Burton, J B – London, 1837 – 48p, 4pls – 8 – ne IDC [590]

LECTURES ON FEMALE SCRIPTURE CHARACTERS / Jay, William – 1854 – 9 – us A.T.L.A. [240]

LECTURES ON FOREIGN CHURCHES. FIRST SERIES / Candlish, Robert Smith – Edinburgh: W.P. Kennedy, 1845 – 2mf – us A.T.L.A. [240]

LECTURES ON FOREIGN CHURCHES, SECOND SERIES / Wilson, John – Edinburgh: W.P. Kennedy, 1846 – 1mf – us A.T.L.A. [240]

LECTURES ON GRAMMAR, RHETORIC / Davidson, Robert – 1 – $50.00 – us Presbyterian [400]

LECTURES ON LOGIC, MORAL PHILOSOPHY AND METAPHYSICS / Smith, Robert – 1 – $50.00 – us Presbyterian [160]

LECTURES ON MISSIONS AND EVANGELISM / Somerville, Andrew – Edinburgh: William Oliphant, 1874 – 1mf – 9 – 0-8370-6616-6 – 1986-0616 – us A.T.L.A. [240]

LECTURES ON MODERN HISTORY / Acton, John Emerich Edward Dalberg Acton, Baron; ed by Figgis, John Neville & Laurence, Reginald Vere – London, New York: Macmillan, 1906 – 1mf – us A.T.L.A. [900]

LECTURES ON NATURAL THEOLOGY, OR, NATURE AND THE BIBLE FROM THE SAME AUTHOR / Chadbourne, Paul Ansel – New York: G.P. Putnam, 1867. 1 fiche – 9 – us A.T.L.A. [240]

LECTURES ON POLITICAL ATHEISM AND KINDRED SUBJECTS : TOGETHER WITH SIX LEXTURES ON INTEMPERANCE : DEDICATED TO THE WORKING MEN OF THE UNITED STATES / Beecher, Lyman – Boston: J.P. Jewett; Cleveland, Ohio: Jewett, Proctor & Worthington, 1842, c1851. (Beecher's works; v1) – 1mf – us A.T.L.A. [210]

LECTURES ON PREACHING : DELIVERED BEFORE THE DIVINITY SCHOOL OF YALE COLLEGE IN JANUARY AND FEBRUARY, 1877 / Brooks, Phillips – New York: E.P. Dutton, 1877 – 1mf – us A.T.L.A. [240]

LECTURES ON PRIVATE CORPORATIONS / Ellis, Wade Hampton – Columbus, O., Heer, 190- 121 p. LL-517 – 1 – us L of C Photodup [340]

LECTURES ON PUBLIC INTERNATIONAL LAW / Angell, J B – Ann Arbor, n.d. – 2mf – 9 – ILM-2488/1 – ne IDC [340]

LECTURES ON REASON AND REVELATION / Preston, Thomas Scott – New York: Catholic Publ House, 1869, c1867 – 1mf – 9 – 0-8370-7093-7 – 1986-1093 – us A.T.L.A. [240]

LECTURES ON REVIVALS / Kirk, Edward Norris – Boston: Congregational Pub., 1875. viii,338p. 1 fiche – 9 – us A.T.L.A. [240]

LECTURES ON REVIVALS OF RELIGION / Finney, Charles G – c1868 – 9 – us A.T.L.A. [240]

LECTURES ON SCIENCE, PHILOSOPHY AND ART, 1907-8 / Columbia University – New York: The Columbia University Press, 1908. At head of title: Columbia University Lectures. Various pagings. (671p). Lectures were first publ. separately and each has separate title page – 1 – us U.W. Library [500]

LECTURES ON SOME OF THE GREAT MASTERS OF ART: AND ON THE RISE, PROGRESS AND DECAY OF MODERN ART IN EUROPE / Cassels, Robert – Edinburgh: A. Elliot, 1875. 05404. (Pre-1900 Canadiana) – 9 – cn C.I.H.M. [700]

LECTURES ON SOME OF THE PROPHECIES CONCERNING THE RISE AND CHARACTER OF THE POWER COMMONLY CALLED ANTICHRIST : AND THEIR REFERENCE TO THE CHURCH OF PAPAL ROME / Knight, William – London: Seeley, Jackson, and Halliday; Bristol: Chilcott, 1855 – 1mf – 9 – 0-8370-8438-5 – 1986-2438 – us A.T.L.A. [230]

LECTURES ON ST PAUL'S EPISTLE TO THE PHILIPPIANS / Vaughan, Charles John – 4th ed. London: Macmillan, 1882 – 1mf – 9 – 0-8370-5623-3 – 1985-3623 – us A.T.L.A. [220]

LECTURES ON SYSTEMATIC THEOLOGY / Finney, Charles G; ed by Fairchild, J H – Oberlin, Ohio: E.J. Goodrich, 1878 – 2mf – us A.T.L.A. [240]

LECTURES ON THE APOCALYPSE, OR, BOOK OF THE REVELATION OF ST. JOHN THE DIVINE / Maurice, Frederick Denison – 2nd ed. London: Macmillan, 1885 – 1mf – 9 – 0-8370-9718-5 – 1986-3718 – us A.T.L.A. [220]

LECTURES ON THE ATHEISTIC CONTROVERSY, 1836, DELIVERED AT SION CHAPEL, BRADFORD, YORKSHIRE / Godwin, Benjamin – 1 – 13.23 – us Baptist [240]

LECTURES ON THE ATOMIC THEORY; AND ESSAYS SCIENTIFIC AND LITERARY / Brown, Samuel – 2v. Edinburgh: Thomas Constable, 1858 – 1 – us U.W. Library [530]

LECTURES ON THE CALLING OF A CHRISTIAN WOMAN, AND HER TRAINING TO FULFIL IT / Dix, Morgan – 1883 – 9 – us A.T.L.A. [240]

LECTURES ON THE COMPARATIVE GRAMMAR OF THE SEMITIC LANGUAGES. / Wright, William – Cambridge: University Press, 1890 – 1 – us U.W. Library [470]

LECTURES ON THE COUNCIL OF TRENT : DELIVERED AT OXFORD 1892-93 / Froude, James Anthony – New York: Charles Scribner, 1896 – 1mf – 9 – 0-8370-8816-X – 1986-2816 – us A.T.L.A. [240]

LECTURES ON THE DOCTRINE OF ATONEMENT / Porter, John Scott – 1860 – 9 – us A.T.L.A. [240]

LECTURES ON THE EARLY HISTORY OF CHRISTIANITY IN ENGLAND : WITH SERMONS DELIVERED ON SEVERAL OCCASIONS / Coit, Thomas Winthrop – New York: D. Dana, Jr.; Troy, N.Y.: W.H. Young, 1859 – 1mf – us A.T.L.A. [240]

LECTURES ON THE EARLY HISTORY OF INSTITUTIONS / Maine, Henry S – (A sequel to Maine's "Ancient Law") – New York: Henry Holt & Co, 1888 – 5mf – 9 – $7.50 – LLMC 95-148 – us L.L.M.C. [340]

LECTURES ON THE ENGLISH POETS : DELIVERED AT THE SURREY INSTITUTION / Hazlitt, William – London: Printed for Taylor and Hessey, 1818 – 1 roll – 1 – 1-55879-354-2 – uk Libr Preservation [420]

LECTURES ON THE EPISTLE OF PAUL THE APOSTLE TO THE EPHESIANS: CHAPTER 1: EXPOSITORY AND PRACTICAL / Alves, William – St. John: J. & A. McMillan, 1867. 06078. (Pre-1900 Canadiana) – 9 – cn C.I.H.M. [240]

LECTURES ON THE EPISTLE TO THE HEBREWS / Lincoln, William – London: John F Shaw, 1873 – 1mf – 9 – 0-8370-7235-2 – 1986-1235 – us A.T.L.A. [220]

LECTURES ON THE EPISTLES OF ST JOHN / Lincoln, William – Boston: Believers' Book-Rooms, 1871?. 1 fiche – 9 – us A.T.L.A. [240]

LECTURES ON THE EPISTLES TO THE SEVEN CHURCHES OF ASIA / Windle, Henry E – London: James Nisbet, 1870. 1 fiche – 9 – us A.T.L.A. [240]

LECTURES ON THE FIRST PRAYER BOOK OF KING EDWARD 6TH / Dix, Morgan – New York: E.& J.B. Young, 1881 – 1mf – us A.T.L.A. [240]

LECTURES ON THE FRENCH REVOLUTION / Acton, John Emerich Edward Dalberg; ed by Figgis, John Neville & Laurence, Reginald Vere – London: Macmillan, 1910 – 1 roll – 1 – 1-55879-379-8 – uk Libr Preservation [944]

LECTURES ON THE HISTORY OF MORAL PHILOSOPHY IN ENGLAND / Whewell, William – London: J.W. Parker & Son, 1852 – xxxii/265p – 1 – us U.W. Library [170]

LECTURES ON THE HISTORY OF PREACHING / Broadus, John A – 1876 – 1 – us A.T.L.A. [240]

LECTURES ON THE HISTORY OF THE EASTERN CHURCH : WITH AN INTRODUCTION ON THE STUDY OF ECCLESIASTICAL HISTORY / Stanley, Arthur Penrhyn – (Includes index) – 2nd ed. London: John Murray; Oxford: J H & James Parker, 1862 – 2mf – 9 – 0-8370-9829-7 – 1986-3829 – us A.T.L.A. [240]

LECTURES ON THE HISTORY OF THE PAPAL CHANCERY : DOWN TO THE TIME OF INNOCENT 3RD / Poole, Reginald Lane – Cambridge: University Press; New York: Putnam [distributor], 1915 – 1mf – us A.T.L.A. [240]

LECTURES ON THE ORIGIN AND GROWTH OF RELIGION AS ILLUSTRATED BY THE RELIGION OF THE ANCIENT HEBREWS / Montefiore, Claude Goldsmid – (Includes bibliographical references and index) – 2nd ed. London: Williams and Norgate, 1893 – 2mf – 9 – 0-8370-9491-7 – 1986-3491 – us A.T.L.A. [270]

LECTURES ON THE ORIGIN AND GROWTH OF THE PSALMS / Murray, Thomas Chalmers – New York: Charles Scribner, 1880 – 1mf – 9 – 0-8370-4546-0 – 1985-2546 – us A.T.L.A. [220]

LECTURES ON THE PANTHEISTIC IDEA OF AN IMPERSONAL-SUBSTANCE-DEITY : AS CONTRASTED WITH THE CHRISTIAN FAITH CONCERNING ALMIGHTY GOD / Dix, Morgan – New York: Hurd & Houghton, 1864 – 1mf – 9 – 0-8370-2928-7 – 1985-0928 – us A.T.L.A. [210]

LECTURES ON THE PHILOSOPHY OF KANT AND OTHER PHILOSOPHICAL LECTURES & ESSAYS / Sidgwick, Henry – London, New York: Macmillan, 1905 – x/475p – 1 – us U.W. Library [190]

LECTURES ON THE PRESENT POSITION OF CATHOLICS IN ENGLAND : ADDRESSED TO THE BROTHERS OF THE ORATORY / Newman, John Henry – London: Burns & Lambert, 1851 – 1 roll – 1 – 1-55879-687-8 – uk Libr Preservation [240]

LECTURES ON THE PRESENT POSITION OF CATHOLICS IN ENGLAND / Newman, John Henry – London: Burns & Lambert, 1851 – 1mf – us A.T.L.A. [240]

LECTURES ON THE PROPHECIES OF ZECHARIAH / Wardlaw, Ralph; ed by Wardlaw J S – 2nd ed. Edinburgh: A Fullarton, 1869 – 1mf – 9 – 0-8370-9341-4 – 1986-3341 – us A.T.L.A. [220]

LECTURES ON THE REASONABLENESS OF CHRISTIANITY AND THE SHALLOWNESS OF UNBELIEF : MAN, GOD, DENIAL, FAITH / Vaughan, Roger William Bede – Baltimore: John B Piet, 1879 – 1mf – 9 – 0-8370-6953-X – 1986-0953 – us A.T.L.A. [230]

LECTURES ON THE RELIGION OF THE SEMITES / Smith, William Robertson – 1894 – 9 – us A.T.L.A. [290]

LECTURES ON THE REUNION OF THE CHURCHES / Doellinger, Ignaz von – 1872 – 1 – us A.T.L.A. [240]

LECTURES ON THE SCIENTIFIC EVIDENCES OF NATURAL AND REVEALED RELIGION / Larrabee, William Clark – 1855 – 9 – us A.T.L.A. [240]

LECTURES ON THE SPHERE AND DUTIES OF WOMAN / Burnap, George Washington – 1841 – 9 – us A.T.L.A. [240]

LECTURES ON THE TRUTH OF THE CHRISTIAN RELIGION / Cocker, BF – Detroit: J.M. Arnold, 1873 – 1mf – us A.T.L.A. [240]

LECTURES ON THE TWO ESTATES : THAT OF THE WEDDED IN THE LORD, AND THAT OF THE SINGLE FOR THE KINGDOM OF HEAVEN'S SAKE / Dix, Morgan – New York: Pott, Young, 1872 – 1mf – us A.T.L.A. [240]

LECTURES ON THE VEGETABLE KINGDOM, WITH SPECIAL REFERENCE TO THE FLORA OF AUSTRALIA / Woolls, W – 5177. 1879 – 9 – ne IDC [580]

LECTURES ON THE...EVIDENCES OF DIVINE REVELATION: ADDRESSED TO...WOMEN / Phillips, LF March – Cambridge: Deighton Bell, 1883. 1 fiche – 9 – us A.T.L.A. [240]

LECTURES ON THEOLOGY / Strong, Augustus Hopkins – Rochester: E R Andrews, 1876 – 1mf – 9 – 0-8370-2899-X – 1985-0899 – us A.T.L.A. [240]

LECTURES PRESENTED AT THE 5TH FAO/ SIDA WORKSHOP ON AQUATIC POLLUTION IN RELATION TO PROTECTION OF LIVING RESOURCES : SCIENTIFIC AND ADMINISTRATIVE BASES FOR MANAGMENT MEASURES; MANILA, 1977 – 1978 – 465p – it F.A.O. [360]

LECTURES PROLETARIENNES – Revue de documentation et de bibliographie. no. 1-3. Paris. 1936-37 – 1 – fr A.C.R.P.P. [073]

LECTURES TCHEQUES – 1944 – 1 – us I.U. Libraries [390]

LECTURES TO YOUNG WOMEN / Eliot, William G – 1890 – 9 – us A.T.L.A. [240]

LECTURES UPON JONAH : DELIVERED AT YORK, IN THE YEAR OF OUR LORD 1594 / King, John – (Includes bibliographical references & sermons) – Edinburgh: James Nichol, 1864 – 1mf – 9 – 0-8370-3898-7 – 1985-1898 – us A.T.L.A. [220]

LECTURES UPON THE PHILOSOPHY OF HISTORY / Shedd, William Greenough Thayer – Andover: W.F. Draper, 1856 – 1mf – us A.T.L.A. [900]

LECTURES UPON THE WHOLE EPISTLE OF ST PAUL TO THE PHILIPPIANS / Airay, Henry – Edinburgh: James Nichol, 1864. 1 fiche – 9 – us A.T.L.A. [240]

Lecuna, Vicente *see*
- CARTAS DEL LIBERTADOR. TOMOS 1 A 10
- DOCUMENTOS REFERENTES A LA CREACION DE BOLIVIA...

LECUTRES ON INTERNATIONAL LAW / Davis, C K – N.p., [1897] – 1mf – 1 – ILM-3743/1 – ne IDC [327]

L'Ecuyer, Paul *see* LE RICHELIEU

Leczinski, Stanislas, roi de Pologne *see* ENTRETIEN D'UN EUROPEEN AVEC UN INSULAIRE DU ROYAUME DE DUMOCALS. REPONSE A LA LETTRE D'UN AMI

LE-DAVID ZEVI. FESTSCHRIFT. DAVID HOFFMANN / Hoffmann, David – Berlin. 1914. BJ-100-39 1 – 9 – ne IDC [920]

Ledderhose, Karl Friedrich *see*
- JOHANN JAENICKE
- THE LIFE OF PHILIP MELANCHTHON

Ledebour, C F von *see*
- FLORA ALTAICA
- FLORE ROSSICA; SIVE, ENUMERATIO PLANTARUM

Ledebour, CF von *see* ICONES PLANTARUM NOVARUM VEL IMPERFECTE COGNITARUM FLORAM ROSSICAM

LEDERARBEITER-ZEITUNG – (Cont by: Die Lederwarte, 1934) – Berlin, 1913-34 – 1 – Dist. gw Mikrofilm – gw Misc Inst [670]

Lederer, Carl *see* DIE BIBLISCHE ZEITRECHNUNG

DIE LEDERWARTE *see* LEDERARBEITER-ZEITUNG

LEDGER / Aimar, C P – 1873-78.Charleston apothecary and plantation owner. 4 fiches – 9 – us South Carolina Historical [978]

LEDGER – Antioch. Calif. 1945-1958 – 1 – us UMI [071]

LEDGER – Attica. Ind. 1871-1872; 1882-1894; 1901-1911 – 1 – us UMI [071]

LEDGER – Brookhaven. Miss. 1875-1883 – 1 – us UMI [071]

LEDGER – Ellwood City. Pa. 1920- – 1 – us UMI [071]

LEDGER – Emporia. Kan. 1874-1881 – 1 – us UMI [071]

LEDGER – Fairfield. Iowa. 1853-1953; 1957- – 1 – us UMI [071]

LEDGER – Hemingford, NE. -w. Oct 1915-Aug 1935; Jan 1936 to date – 1 – us NE Hist [071]

LEDGER / J W Mansfield and Co – Port Vila, New Hebrides, 1903-13 – 1r – 1 – PMB 1127 – at Pacific Mss [650]

LEDGER – Lakeland. Fl. 1942-1971 – 1 – us P.K. Yonge [071]

LEDGER – Mexico. Mo. 1909- – 1 – us UMI [071]

LEDGER – Mexico. Mo. -w. 1876-1909 – 1 – us UMI [071]

LEDGER – Noblesville. Ind. 1874-1881 – 1 – us UMI [071]

LEDGER / Northwest Colony and Russell Townsite Company – 1871-74 – 1 – us KS Hist [978]

LEDGER – Reno, NV. 1899-1903 (broken series) – 1r – 1 – $50.00 – U04676 – us Library Micro [071]

LEDGER – Tacoma. Wash. 1883-1937 – 1 – us UMI [071]

LEDGER – Tacoma. Wash. -w. 1893-96 – 1 – us UMI [071]

LEDGER / Tefft House. Topeka, Kansas – 1868-70 – 1 – us KS Hist [978]

LEDGER / Wines, Francis – 1868-1872 – 1r – 1 – $32.50r – us Archival [920]

LEDGER *see* LEDGER DISPATCH

THE LEDGER – Millerstown, PA., 1876-1878 – 13 – $25.00r – us I.M.R. [071]

THE LEDGER – New York. v. 1-15. 1935-1948 – 1 – us NY Public [071]

THE LEDGER – Reedley, CA. Feb 1920-Apr 1921 – 1r – 1 – $50.00 – B02687 – us Library Micro [071]

LEDGER AND PROGRESS-NEWS *see* AMADOR DISPATCH

LEDGER DISPATCH – (Cont: Ledger; Weekly Ledger) – Antioch, CA. 1870-72; 1877-1902; 1901-36; 1945- – 321+ r – 1 BC02019 – $16,050.00 ($400.00y) – us Library Micro [071]

LEDGER GAZETTE – (Also known as: Antelope Valley Press) – Antelope Valley, CA. 1896-1909 (Scats); 1914-1915; 1917-1928; 1929-1983 – 134r – 1 – $6,700.00 – H04001 – us Library Micro [071]

LEDGER, MINUTES, AND BURIAL RECORDS / Mt. Auburn Cemetery, Topeka, KS – undated – 1 – us KS Hist [920]

LEDGER-DISPATCH : IONE PROGRESS-NEWS – Jackson, CA. 1981 – 32+ r – 1 – $1,600.00 – B02319 – us Library Micro [071]

LEDGER-DISPATCH – Norfolk. Va. 1952-1969 – 1 – us UMI [071]

LEDGERS / General Store (Tymochtee, Ohio) – 1824-1832 – 1r – 1 – $32.50r – us Archival [978]

LEDGERS / Miller Brothers Hardware Company, Onaga, KS – 1884-1906 – 1 – us KS Hist [380]

LEDGERS, DAY BOOKS / Hodges Brothers. Olathe, Kansas – 1888-1900 – 1 – us KS Hist [025]

LEDGERS OF PAYMENTS, 1818-72, TO U.S. PENSIONERS UNDER ACTS OF 1818 THROUGH 1858 / U.S. Treasury Department. Third Auditor's Office – 23 rolls – 1 – T718 – us Nat'l Archives [336]

LEDGER-STAR – Norfolk. Va. and pred. 1876- – 1 – us UMI [071]

Ledieu, Alcius *see* LES VILAINS DANS LES OEUVRES DES TROUVERES

LEDIGE FRAUEN – Berlin, 1928-29 n12 – 1r – 1 – Dist. gw Mikrofilm – gw Misc Inst [072]

Lednicki, W *see* RUSSIA, POLAND AND THE WEST

Ledoux, Claude Nicolas *see* L'ARCHITECTURE CONSIDEREE SOUS LE RAPPORT DE L'ART, DES MOEURS ET DE LA LEGISLATION

Leduc, G *see* L'ECONOMIE DE GUERRE DANS LES ETATS DE SYRIE ET DU LIBAN

Leduc, R *see* LA LIBRE PAROLE

LEDUC REPRESENTATIVE – Leduc, Alberta, CN. Jan 1907-1989 – 78r – 1 – cn Commonwealth Micro [072]

Ledyard, John *see* VOYAGES EN AFRIQUE

LEE 1738-1849 – (Mf 1T-2T: Publishments & Marriages 1776-1846. Mf 2T-3T: Births & Deaths 1738-1847. Mf 4T: Births 1825-45. Mf 4T-5T: Deaths 1775-1844. Mf 5T: Marriages 1844-50. Mf 5T-7T: Births 1844-50. Mf 7T-8T: Deaths 1844-50) – (mf ed 1997) – 8mf – 9 – 0-87623-275-6 – us Holbrook [920]

LEE 1844-1892 – (Mf 1-3: Birth Index 1844-92. Mf 4-5: Birth Index 1893-1926. Mf 6-7: Birth Index 1937-54. Mf 8-9: Marriage Index 1853-92. Mf 10-11: Marriage Index 1893-1945. Mf 12-13: Death Index 1844-96. Mf 14-15: Death Index 1897-1921. Mf 16-17: Death Index 1921-51. Mf 18-21: B,M,D 1844-55. Mf 22-26: Births 1855-92. Mf 27-31: Marriages 1853-93. Mf 32-36: Deaths 1854-92. Mf 37-42: Deaths 1893-1921. Mf 43-47: Deaths 1921-52) – (mf ed 1988) – 47mf – 9 – 0-87623-081-8 – us Holbrook [920]

Lee, Ada *see*
- DIARIES, 1934-1966
- AN INDIAN PRIESTESS

Lee, B W *see* A COMPARISON OF STANDING POSTURE BETWEEN FEMALE JUNIOR HIGH SCHOOL STUDENTS IN HONG KONG WITH AND WITHOUT BALLET TRAINING

Lee, Charles *see*
- THE IMPORTANCE OF CANADA CONSIDERED IN TWO LETTERS TO A NOBLE LORD

LEE COUNTY DEMOCRAT – Dixon. Ill. -w. 1871-72 – 1 – us UMI [071]

LEE COUNTY DEMOCRAT – Fort Madison. Iowa. -w. 1842-44 – 1 – us UMI [071]

Lee County. Georgia *see* INVENTORY OF THE COUNTY ARCHIVES.

LEE COUNTY MESSENGER – Bishopville. S.C. 1937-1939 – 1 – us UMI [071]

Lee, E E *see* PAPERS, 1876-1962

Lee, E Trumbull *see* A SHEAF OF WHEAT GATHERED FROM THE FIELD OF DIVINE REVELATION

Lee, Eliza Buckminster *see* LIFE OF JEAN PAUL FREDERIC RICHTER

LEE FAMILY PAPERS, 1535-1957 – Massachusetts Historical Society – 41r – 1 – $3055.00 – us UMI [920]

THE LEE FAMILY PAPERS, 1742-1795 – (With printed guide) – 8r – 1 – $680.00 – D3180 – us Scholarly Res [920]

Lee, Francis B *see* GENEALOGICAL AND PERSONAL MEMORIAL OF MERCER COUNTY

Lee, Frank Theodosius *see* POPULAR MISCONCEPTIONS AS TO CHRISTIAN FAITH AND LIFE
Lee, Frederick George *see*
- THE CHURCH UNDER QUEEN ELIZABETH
- GLIMPSES OF THE SUPERNATURAL
- A GLOSSARY OF LITURGICAL AND ECCLESIASTICAL TERMS
- KING EDWARD THE SIXTH, SUPREME HEAD
- MORE GLIMPSES OF THE WORLD UNSEEN
- REGINALD POLE, CARDINAL ARCHBISHOP OF CANTERBURY

Lee, Gerald Stanley *see* THE SHADOW CHRIST
Lee, Guy C *see* HISTORICAL JURISPRUDENCE
Lee, J Ross *see* A TREATISE ON THE ELEMENTS OF LAW
Lee, Jae Y et al *see* THE SOCIALIZATION OF BEGINNING PHYSICAL EDUCATION TEACHERS
Lee, Jarena *see* RELIGIOUS EXPERIENCE AND JOURNAL OF MRS. JARENA LEE: GIVING AN ACCOUNT OF HER CALL TO PREACH THE GOSPEL
Lee, Jesse *see* A SHORT HISTORY OF THE METHODISTS IN THE U.S. OF AMERICA, BEGINNING IN 1766 AND CONTINUED TILL 1809
Lee, John A R *see* TOWARDS REALISTIC COMMUNICATION POLICIES
Lee, J-Y *see* SPORT NATIONALISM IN THE MODERN OLYMPIC GAMES
Lee, L T *see* READINGS ON POPULATION FOR LAW STUDENTS
Lee, Luther *see*
- AUTOBIOGRAPHY OF THE REV. LUTHER LEE
- ECCLESIASTICAL MANUAL
- NATURAL THEOLOGY
- THE REVIVAL MANUAL
- UNIVERSALISM EXAMINED AND REFUTED
- WESLEYAN MANUAL
- WOMAN'S RIGHT TO PREACH THE GOSPEL

Lee, Mui Sin *see* SINGAPOREAN EDUCATION IN PERSPECTIVE
Lee, Peter H *see* SOURCEBOOK OF KOREAN CIVILIZATION
Lee, Siu Y *see* ALLOMETRIC SCALING OF GRIP STRENGTH BY BODY MASS AND LEAN BODY MASS IN COLLEGE-AGE MEN AND WOMEN
Lee, Su-Hsin *see* RECREATIONAL CHOICE BEHAVIOR
Lee, Sul H *see*
- COLLECTION MANAGEMENT
- JOURNAL OF LIBRARY ADMINISTRATION

Lee, T W *see* DYNAMIQUE DES POPULATIONS D'ANGUILLES, ANGUILLA ANGUILLA (L.), DES LAGUNES DU BASSIN D'ARCACHON
LEE TRAVELLER – Petersburg. Va. 1942- – 1 – us UMI [071]
Lee, V H L *see* JOURNAL OF DRUG TARGETING
Lee, W H K *see* TERRESTRIAL HEAT FLOW
Lee, Wau *see* PAPERS, MS 522
Lee, Y *see* THE ACUTE EFFECTS OF MODERATE ITENSITY CIRCUIT WEIGHT TRAINING ON LIPID-LIPOPROTEIN PROFILES
Leech, Samuel *see* THIRTY YEARS FROM HOME; OR, A VOICE FROM THE MAIN DECK
LEECHDOMS, WORTCUNNING AND STARCRAFT OF EARLY ENGLAND (RS35) : BEING A COLLECTION OF DOCUMENTS ILL. THE HISTORY OF SCIENCE IN THIS COUNTRY BEFORE THE NORMAN CONQUEST / ed by Cockayne, T O – 3v (v1 1864 v2 1865 v3 1866) – Dfl32.00v – ne Slangenburg [500]
Leedham-Green, Elisabeth *see* RENAISSANCE MAN: THE RECONSTRUCTED LIBRARIES OF EUROPEAN SCHOLARS, 1450-1700
LEEDS AND WEST RIDING EXPRESS – England. Leeds Express – Leeds Evening Express. -w, -d. 1859-70. 14 reels – 1 – uk British Libr Newspaper [072]
Leeds. City Archives *see* VYNER MANUSCRIPTS
LEEDS INTELLIGENCER – England, 1784-86; 1828-48; 1861-70; 1873; Jan-June 1881 – 40 1/2r – 1 – uk British Libr Newspaper [072]
THE LEEDS INTELLIGENCER, JULY 1754-JUNE 1866 – 63r – 1 – uk Microform Academic [072]
Leeds, Josiah Woodward *see* THE PRIMITIVE CHRISTIAN'S ESTIMATE OF WAR AND SELF-DEFENSE
LEEDS MERCURY – England, 1838-46 – 9r – 1 – uk British Libr Newspaper [072]
LEEDS MERCURY – Leeds. 1738-1939 – 1 – uk Microform Academic [072]
LEEDS PATRIOT – England. -w. 1829-32. 2 reels – 1 – uk British Libr Newspaper [072]
LEEDS TIMES – England. -w. 1838-46. (9 reels) – 1 – uk British Libr Newspaper [072]
LEEGE LUED : EEN LUSTIG SPILLWARK IN EEN TOERN / Wriede, Hinrich – Hamburg: Quickborn-Verlag, [1919] – 1 – us U.W. Library [820]
LEEGE LUED : EEN LUSTIG SPILLWARK IN EEN TOERN / Wriede, Hinrich – Hamburg: Quickborn-Verlag, [1919] – 1r – 1 – us U.W. Library [820]
LEEK COMET – England.6 Jan-10 Feb 1894. -w. 18 feet – 1 – uk British Libr Newspaper [072]
Leek. Staffordshire *see* PARISH REGISTERS
LEEK TIMES – England.1871-72; Mar 1912-1922. -w. 8 1/4 reels – 1 – uk British Libr Newspaper [072]
Leeke, William *see* THE HISTORY OF LORD SEATON'S REGIMENT, THE 52ND LIGHT INFANTRY AT THE BATTLE OF WATERLOO; TOGETHER WITH VARIOUS INCIDENTS CONNECTED WITH THAT REGIMENT..
LEEN-, KEURMEDIGE EN TYNSGOEDEREN : DE VAN DE SINT-SALVATOR-ABDIJ TE PRUEM IN GELDERLAND (LEENKAMER VAN KLARENBEEK) / ed by Maris, A J – Arnhem, 1934 – Dfl19.00 – ne Slangenburg [240]
Leenhardt, M *see* CORRESPONDANCE
Leenhardt, Maurice *see*
- CAHIERS MANUSCRITS DE COMPTES RENDUS DES CONFERENCES PASTORALES, NOUVELLE-CALEDONIE
- CARNETS, NOUVELLE-CALEDONIE, 1905-1919
- CENTENAIRE DE MAURICE LEENHARDT, ETHNOLOGUE
- LETTRES ECRITES DE NOUVELLE-CALEDONIE A SON PERE
- NOTES D'ETHNOLOGIE NEO-CALEDONIENNE
- RECENSEMENT ETHNOLOGIQUE DE LA VALLEE DE HOUAILOU

Leenheer, J de *see*
- THEATRUM STULTORUM JOCOSERIUM
- VIRGO MARIA MYSTICA SOLIS IMAGINE EMBLEMATICE EXPRESSA

LEER DER HERVORMDE KERK...UIT DE BRONNEN VOORGESTELD / Scholten, Johannes Henricus – Leiden, 1855 – 21mf – 8 – ne Slangenburg [290]
LEER EN LEVEN DER STATENVERVORMINGEN / Eysinga, W J M van – Groningen, 1908 – 1mf – 1 – ILM-1687/1 – ne IDC [327]
DE LEER VAN GOD / Doedes, Jacobus Izaak – Utrecht: Kemink en Zoon, 1871. 1 fiche – 9 – us A.T.L.A. [240]
DE LEER VAN HET MESSIASRIJK BIJ DE EERSTE CHRISTENEN / Blom, Abraham Herman – Dordrecht: P.K. Braat, 1863. 1 fiche – 9 – us A.T.L.A. [240]
Leer, W van *see* JIDDISH PROTOCOLBOEK VAN DE NED. ISRS. GEMEENTE IN NIJMEGEN
LEERBOEK DER SCHEIKUNDE / Berzelius, Jons Jakob – Rotterdam, P.H. van den Heuvell, 1834-42. 6v. ill – 1 – us U.W. Library [540]
DE LEERMEESTER DER ZEDEN : VERTOONT IN HORATIUS ZINNEBEELDEN, LIERZANGEN, ENZ. HET LOF VAN 'T LANDLEVEN, EN BESPIEGELING OP 'T LEVEN DER MENSCHEN, VERBEELT IN DE 4 GETYDEN DES JAARS. MET KOPERE PLATEN VERCIERT – Amsterdam, [c1695] – 3mf – 9 – O-3216/1 – ne IDC [760]
DE LEERMEESTER DER ZEDEN : VERTOONT IN HORATIUS ZINNEBEELDEN, LIERZANGEN, ENZ. LOF VAN 'T LANDLEVEN, EN BESPIEGELING OP 'T LEVEN DER MENSCHEN, VERBEELD IN DE VIER GETYDEN DES JAARS. MET VEELE UITMUNTENDE VERSEN VERMEERDERT. DE VYFDE DRUK. MET KOPERE PLATEN VERCIERT – Amsterdam, 1750 – 5mf – 9 – O-3186/1 – ne IDC [760]
DE LEERMEESTER DER ZEDEN, VERTOOND IN HORATIUS ZINNEBEELDEN, LIERZANGEN, ENZ. LOF VAN'T LANDLEVEN, EN BESPIEGELING OP 'T LEVEN DER MENSCHEN, VERBEELD IN DE VIER GETYDEN DES JAARS / Veen, O van – Amsterdam, 1781 – 5mf – 9 – O-3236/1 – ne IDC [740]
Leers, J D *see* FLORA HERBORNENSIS
HET LEERZAAM HUISRAAD / Luiken, J – O 353. 1711 – 9 – ne IDC [760]
HET LEERZAAM HUISRAED / Luiken, J – O 813. 1731 – 9 – ne IDC [760]
LEERZAME ZINNEBEELDEN / Spinniker, A – O 434. 1714 – 9 – ne IDC [760]
LEERZAME ZINNEBEELDEN, BESTAANDE IN CHRISTELYKE BEDENKINGEN DOOR VERGELYKINGE EENIGER SCHEPSELEN, ALS DIEREN, VOGELS, GEWASSEN, ETC. : STREKKENDE TOT ZEEDELESSEN TER DEUGD, EN AANMOEDIGING TOT GODZALIGHEID / Graauwhart, Hendrik – Amsterdam, 1758 – 3mf – 9 – O-3094/1 – ne IDC [760]
LEERZAME ZINNEBEELDEN; BESTAANDE IN CHRISTELYKE BEDENKINGEN DOOR VERGELYKINGE EENIGER SCHEPSELEN, ALS DIEREN, VOGELS, GEWASSEN ETC. : STREKKENDE TOT ZEEDELESSEN TER DEUGD, EN AANMOEDIGING TOT GODZALIGHEID / Graauwhart, Hendrik – 1st ed. Amsterdam, 1704 – 3mf – 9 – O-3073/1 – ne IDC [760]
Lees, George Robinson *see* VILLAGE LIFE IN PALESTINE
Lees, W N *see* BADSHAH NAMAH
Leeson, M A *see* DOCUMENTS AND BIOGRAPHY PERTAINING TO THE SETTLEMENT OF AND PROGRESS OF STARK COUNTY
LEESVILLE FIRST BAPTIST CHURCH. LEESVILLE, SOUTH CAROLINA : CHURCH RECORDS – 1946-53, 1958-72 – 1 – 18.45 – us Baptist [240]
Leete, Frederick Deland *see*
- CHRISTIAN BROTHERHOODS
- THE CHURCH IN THE CITY
- EVERY-DAY EVANGELISM

LEF : ZHURNAL LEVOGO FRONTA ISKUSSTVA – Moscow. n1-7. 1923-25 – 1r – 1 – us Ross [460]
LEF – Zhurnal levogo fronta iskusstva. 5 v. M. Petrograd. L. 1923-25. BR-1866 2 – 8 – ne IDC [073]
Lefaivre, Louise *see* BIBLIOGRAPHIE ANALYTIQUE DE L'OEUVRE DE L'ABBE JEAN HOLMES, UN DES FONDATEURS DE L'UNIVERSITE LAVAL
Lefebure, LF H *see* ATLAS BOTANIQUE,...
Lefebure, Victor *see* THE RIDDLE OF THE RHINE, CHEMICAL STRATEGY IN PEACE AND WAR..
Lefebvre, Alexis *see* MOIS DU SACRE-COEUR
Lefebvre d'Ovidio, Antonio *see* ISTITUZIONI DI DIRITTO COMMERCIALE NORD-AMERICANO
Lefebvre, Elois *see* LA VALLEE DE LA DIABLE
Lefebvre, Gerard *see* BIBLIOGRAPHIE DU REVEREND FRERE M.-CYRILLE COTE DES ECOLES CHRETIENNES
Lefebvre, J *see* L'OEUVRE DU QUATRIEME JOUR DE LA CREATION
Lefebvre, Marguerite *see* BIO-BIBLIOGRAPHIE DU CHANOINE LIONEL GROULX, D.TH., D.PH. ET PROFESSEUR A L'UNIVERSITE DE MONTREAL
LE-FERASHAT HITNAHALUT YEHUDEI TEIMAN BI-YERUSHALAYIM / Ratzaby, J – v. 1. Yerushalayim. 1948. BJ-27-80 1 – 9 – ne IDC [270]
Lefevre, F *see*
- COUTUMIERS LITURGIQUES DE PREMONTRE DU 13TH ET 14TH SIECLE
- LA LITURGIE DE PREMONTRE
- L'ORDINAIRE DE PREMONTRE D'APRES DES MANUSCRITS DU 12TH ET DU 13TH SIECLE
- LES ORDINAIRES DES COLLEGIALES S. PIERRE A LOUVAIN ET S. PIERRE ET S. PAUL A ANDERLECHT D'APRES DES MANUSCRITS DU 14TH SIECLES

Lefevre, Robert *see*
- CONSTITUTIONAL GOVERNMENT TODAY IN SOVIET RUSSIA
- LEFEVRE'S JOURNAL
- LIFT HER UP, TENDERLY
- MUST WE DEPEND UPON POLITICAL PROTECTION?
- THE NATURE OF MAN AND HIS GOVERNMENT
- PINE TREE AND RAP
- THE POWER OF CONGRESS
- RAISING CHILDREN FOR FUND AND PROFIT
- THIS BREAD IS MINE

LeFevre, Tannegui *see* A COMPENDIOUS WAY OF TEACHING ANCIENT AND MODERN LANGUAGES
LEFEVRE'S JOURNAL / Lefevre, Robert – Winter '73 – Fall '78. Complete. 3 fiches (24x) – 9 – 1.00f – at Libertarian Micro [320]
Lefevre-Witier, P *see* ETUDE ANTHROPO-BIOLOGIQUE DES GROUPES HMONG DE GUYANE, ENQUETE PRELIMINAIRE. RAPPORT DE MISSION CNRS
Leffson, August *see* IMMERMANNS ALEXIS
Lefizelier, Jules *see* COLLECTION DE DOCUMENTS MANUS. OU IMPR. CONCERNANT L'HISTOIRE DE LAVAL ET DU BAS-MAINE
Lefort, Joseph *see* ETUDES SUR LA MORALISATION ET LE BIEN-ETRE DES CLASSES OUVRIERES
Lefort-Lavauzelle *see* L'ORGANISATION SCIENTIFIQUE DES USINES
Lefranc, Abel *see*
- A LA DECOUVERTE DE SHAKESPEARE
- LA JEUNESSE DE CALVIN

Lefroy, H M *see* INDIAN INSECT LIFE: A MANUAL OF THE INSECTS OF THE PLAINS
Lefroy, William *see* THE CHRISTIAN MINISTRY
THE LEFT IN BRITAIN *see* PEACE NEWS
THE LEFT IN BRITAIN, PART 1 – (Updates: 1973-88, 1989-93. Publications and documents of groups, organisations and papers. Primary Social Sources. Includes case-bound bibliographical guides) – 1958-72 – 1,9 – us Primary [941]
THE LEFT IN BRITAIN, PART 2 – (1973-85. Available by year. Updates 1973-1988, 1989-93) – 1950-72 – 1,9 – 1200.00 – us Primary [941]
THE LEFT IN BRITAIN, PART 3 – (1973-87 update. Comprising "Socialist Commentary," 1973-78; "Socialist Standard" (official organ of the Socialist Party of Great Britain), 1973-78) – 1904-1972. Comprising "Socialist Commentary," 1934-72 and the "Socialist Standard" (official organ of the Socialist Party of Great Britain) – 1 – us Primary [941]
THE LEFT IN BRITAIN, PART 4 – (1975-87 update. Comprising "Peace News," 1936-74; 1975-78) – 1936-74 – 1 – us Primary [941]
THE LEFT IN BRITAIN, PART 5 : PEACE, PROTEST AND THE NUCLEAR THREAT – (Section 2: Annual Reports, Minutes and Other Records, 1973-80; Pamphlets and Serial Items, 1958-80; Section 3: Annual Reports, Minutes and other Records, Pamphlets, and Serial Items, 1981-85; Section 4: Annual Reports, Minutes and other Records 1986-1990) – Archives of the Campaign for Nuclear Disarmament, Section 1: 1958-72 – 1 – us Primary [941]
THE LEFT NEWS – 1936-47.Continues: The Left Book News – 1 – £190.00 – uk World [335]
LEFT RITES / Black, Bob – 1p – 9 – 1.00f – at Libertarian Micro [335]
LEFT VENTRICULAR FUNCTION DURING ISOMETRIC EXERCISE / Sagiv, Michael – 1982 – 2mf – 9 – $8.00 – us Microform Publ [790]
"LEFT WING" COMMUNISM: AN INFANTILE DISORDER / Lenin, Vladimir Ilyich – London: Communist Pary of Great Britian. Translation of Detskaia bolezn' "levizny" v kommunisme.. 95 p – 1 – us U.W. Library [335]
LEFTIST LEADERS OF INDIA / Chaudhuri, Bhawani Prasad – Foreward by R.S. Ruikar.Calcutta: Calcutta Book House, 1947.72p – 1 – us U.W. Library [920]
LEG LENGTH AND DISTANCE OF APPROACH STEPS FOR THE OPTIMAL SOCCER STYLE PLACEKICK / Olson, KR – 1992 – 2mf – 9 – $8.00 – us Microform Publ [790]
LEGA INTERNAZIONALE PER I DIRITTI E LA LIBERAZIONE DEI POPOLI = INTERNATIONAL LEAGUE FOR THE RIGHTS AND LIBERATION OF PEOPLES (INTERNATIONAL LELIO BASSO FOUNDATION) – Rome. 80 docs. 1980-1991 – 87mf – 9 – ne IDC [320]
LEGACY FOR ALL : THE WORLD'S MAJOR NATURAL, CULTURAL AND HISTORIC SITES – 1982 – 9 – 92-3-102025-0 – fr UNESCO [900]
LEGACY OF INFLATION AND LAND MONOPOLY / Blundell, VH – 1982. 13p – 9 – 1.00f – at Libertarian Micro [335]
Legal Action Group. London *see* LAG BULLETIN
LEGAL ADMINISTRATOR *see* LEGAL MANAGEMENT
THE LEGAL ADVERTISER – London. nos 1-26 + suppl nos 1-11. 1881-83 (all publ) – 9mf – 9 – $13.50 – LLMC 84-566 – us L.L.M.C. [073]
THE LEGAL ADVISER – (Lacking: v3. v4 nos 4,11.29,35,44. y5 no 45,47, v6 no 1) – Denver. v1-6. 1898-1902 (all publ) – 9 – LLMC 82-937 – us L.L.M.C. [073]

THE LEGAL ADVISOR / Carey, Thomas Joseph – New York: Excelsior, 1889. 317p. LL-1008 – 1 – us L of C Photodup [340]
LEGAL AID BRIEF CASE *see* NLADA BRIEFCASE
LEGAL AND INSTITUTIONAL FRAMEWORK FOR NATURAL RESOURCES MANAGEMENT – 1975 – 44p – it F.A.O. [340]
LEGAL AND INSTITUTIONAL RESPONSES TO GROWING WATER DEMAND – 1979 – 100p – it F.A.O. [640]
LEGAL AND OTHER LYRICS / Outram, George – London/Edingburgh/Boston: T N Foulis, 1916 – 3mf – 9 – $4.50 – LLMC 91-005 – us L.L.M.C. [810]
LEGAL AND STATE MEMORANDA / Coke, Edward – 16th and 17th cents. Holkham mss. 723, 725, 732A, 748A,B,C, 751. Holkham Hall, Norfolk, England – 1 – uk Microform Academic [941]
LEGAL ANTIQUITIES : A COLLECTION OF ESSAYS UPON ANCIENT LAWS AND CUSTOMS / White, Edward Joseph – St Louis, MO: F H Thomas Law Book Co, 1913 – 4mf – 9 – $6.00 – LLMC 95-157 – us L.L.M.C. [340]
LEGAL ASPECTS OF INTERNATIONAL JOINT VENTURES IN AGRICULTURE – 1990 – 80p – it F.A.O. [340]
LEGAL ASPECTS OF MEDICAL PRACTICE – (Title varies: v1-5 1973-1977 as Journal of Legal Medicine) – v1-17. 1973-1989 – 9 – $250.00 set – us Hein [340]
LEGAL ASPECTS OF MEDICAL PRACTICE – (v.8-. 1980- 5,6,9) – v.5-. 1977- – 1 – us UMI [340]
THE LEGAL, BANK, AND REPORTING DIRECTORY. / Bond & Weigley – Chicago 1882 253 p. LL-1094 – 1 – us L of C Photodup [340]
LEGAL BIBLIOGRAPHY OF THE BRITISH COMMONWEALTH – 31mf – 9 – us UMI [340]
Legal Bureau of the City of Hai Phong *see* CAC VAN KIEN PHAP LUAT PHUC VU CUOC VAN DONG NGHI QUYET 228 NQ/TW NGAY 12/1/1974 CUA BO CHINH TRI TRUNG UONG DANG
Legal Bureau, the Prime Minister's Office *see* TONG MUC LUC LUAT LE CUA NUOC VIET NAM DAN CHU CONG HOA
LEGAL CHATTER : A MONTHLY LEGAL MAGAZINE – Baltimore. v1-2. 1937-39 (all publ) – 4mf – 9 – $18.00 – LLMC 84-568 – us L.L.M.C. [073]
THE LEGAL CHRONICLE : A DIGEST OF PROCEEDINGS IN THE SUPERIOR COURTS OF LAW – London. v1 nos 1-2. 1844 (all publ) – 3mf – 9 – $4.50 – LLMC 84-569 – us L.L.M.C. [073]
THE LEGAL CIRCULAR – London. v1-3 nos 1-144. 1855-57 (all publ) – 16mf – 9 – $24.00 – LLMC 84-570 – us L.L.M.C. [073]
LEGAL COMPILATION : STATUTES, LEGISLATIVE HISTORY, EXECUTIVE ORDERS, REGULATIONS, GUIDELINES AND REPORTS / U.S. Environmental Protection Agency – (Includes index. Compilation organized as follows: General 9bks. Air 6bks. Water 12bks. Solid Waste 2bks. Pesticides 4bks. Radiation 3bks. Noise 3bks and Index 1bk) – Washington: GPO. 40v. 1974 – 237mf – 9 – $355.00 – LLMC 81-220 – us L.L.M.C. [324]
LEGAL DECISIONS AFFECTING COAL AND COKE; ABSTRACT OF DECISIONS OF AMERICAN COURTS / Street, Arthur Leonard Howell – New York, Coal Age, 1915. 128 p. LL-1110 – 1 – us L of C Photodup [340]
LEGAL DIARY – Dublin, Ireland.20 Oct 1847-1848; 1850-Oct 1853; 1891-96. -w. 4 1/2 reels – 1 – uk British Libr Newspaper [072]
LEGAL ECONOMICS *see* LAW PRACTICE MANAGEMENT (ABA)
LEGAL ETHICS / Drinker, Henry Sandwith – New York, Columbia, 1953. 448 p. L.O.C. copy imperfect: p. i-ii wanting. LL-637 – 1 – us L of C Photodup [340]
LEGAL ETHICS, THE DUTY OF THE HOUR; LECTURE DELIVERED BEFORE THE STUDENTS OF LAW DEPARTMENT OF UNION UNIVERSITY / Goodrich, William Winton – Albany?. 1905. 16p. LL-363 – 1 – us L of C Photodup [340]
THE LEGAL EXAMINER – (Lacking: v2-3) – London. v1-3. 1831-33 (all publ) – 8mf – 9 – $12.00 – LLMC 84-571 – us L.L.M.C. [073]
LEGAL EXAMINER: A JOURNAL OF GENERAL JURISPRUDENCE AND PUBLIC ECONOMY *see* THE LEGAL EXAMINER, WEEKLY REPORTER, AND JOURNAL OF MEDICAL JURISPRUDENCE
THE LEGAL EXAMINER AND LAW CHRONICLE – London. v1-5. 1833-35 (all publ) – 9 – LLMC 84-572 – us L.L.M.C. [073]
THE LEGAL EXAMINER, WEEKLY REPORTER, AND JOURNAL OF MEDICAL JURISPRUDENCE – (Title changes to: Legal Examiner: A Journal of General Jurisprudence and Public Economy (1854). Lacking: 1854-57) – London, 1852-57 (all publ) – 9 – LLMC 84-573 – us L.L.M.C. [073]
LEGAL FEATURES OF COMMERCE REGULATION / Jackman, William James – Minneapolis, University Extension Society 1912 394 2 p. LL-178 – 1 – us L of C Photodup [340]
LEGAL FORMS AND LAW OFFICE PRACTICE / Page, Bessie Nadine – Boston, 1938. 1v. LL-941 – 1 – us L of C Photodup [340]
LEGAL FORMS; INCLUDING FORMS IN CONVEYANCING, TOGETHER WITH GENERAL LEGAL AND BUSINESS FORMS. / Jones, Leonard Augustus – 6th ed. Indianapolis, Bobbs-Merrill Co., 1909. 1131 p. LL-1411 – 1 – us L of C Photodup [340]
THE LEGAL FRAMEWORK FOR THE PREVENTATION AND CONTROL OF WATER POLLUTION IN ISRAEL / Israel. Ministry of the Interior – Richard Laster. Jerusalem. 1976. 387 p – 9 – 6.00 – is I.T.T.I. [628]
THE LEGAL GAZETTE – v1-8. 1869-76 (all publ) – 35mf – 9 – $52.00 – LLMC 82-938 – us L.L.M.C. [073]
THE LEGAL GUIDE – London. v1-7. 1838-42 (all publ) – 9 – LLMC 84-574 – us L.L.M.C. [073]
LEGAL LAUGHS : A JOKE FOR EVERY JURY / Edwards, Gus C – Clarkesville, GA: Legal Publ Co, 1915 – 5mf – 9 – $7.50 – LLMC 95-147 – us L.L.M.C. [870]
LEGAL LITERATURE – (no1-4 have subtitle "A Quarterly Record") – London: Sweet & Maxwell. nos1-11. July 1899-Dec 1904. ns: nos1-11. July 1905-May 1911 (all publ) – LLMC 91-500 – us L.L.M.C. [073]
LEGAL LORE : CURIOSITIES OF LAW AND LAWYERS / ed by Andrews, William – London: William Andrews & Co, 1897 – 3mf – 9 – $4.50 – LLMC 95-192 – us L.L.M.C. [340]
LEGAL MANAGEMENT – (Title varies: v1-7 1982-88 as Legal Administrator) – Association of Legal Administrators: v1-14. 1982-95 – 9 – $153.00 set – us Hein [340]
LEGAL MASTERPIECES, SPECIMENS OF ARGUMENTATION AND EXPOSITION : BY EMINENT LAWYERS / ed by Veeder, Van Vechten – St Paul, MN: Keefe-Davidson Co. 2v. 1903 – 15mf – 9 – $22.50 – LLMC 95-144 – us L.L.M.C. [340]
LEGAL MASTERPIECES, SPECIMENS OF ARGUMENTATION AND EXPOSITION / ed by Veeder, Van Vechten – Chicago: Callaghan. 2v. 1912 – 15mf – 9 – $22.50 – LLMC 95-149 – us L.L.M.C. [340]
A LEGAL MONOGRAPH UPON PROVISIONAL REMEDIES UNDER THE CODE / Derby, John Sayward – New York, Peloubet, 1886. 322 p. LL-626 – 1 – us L of C Photodup [340]
THE LEGAL NATURE OF THE ROLLING-STOCK OF RAILROADS / Jones, Leonard Augustus – St. Louis, Jones, 1878. 42 p. LL-179 – 1 – us L of C Photodup [340]
LEGAL NEWS – Flint. Mich. 1949-69 – 1 – us UMI [340]
THE LEGAL NEWS – Montreal: R White, [1878-1897] – 9 – cn C.I.H.M. [340]
THE LEGAL NEWS – Montreal: v1-20, 1878-1897 (all publ) – 102mf – $153.00 – LLMC 93-100 – us L.L.M.C. [073]
LEGAL NOTES ON LOCAL GOVERNMENT – (ABA Section on Local Govt. Cont as: The American Municipal Law Review. Not available from LLMC) – v1-6. 1936-41 (all publ) – 11mf – 9 – $49.50 – LLMC 84-575 – us L.L.M.C. [073]
LEGAL OBSERVER AND SOLICITOR'S JOURNAL – (v1-46 entitled: Legal Observer, or Journal of Jurisprudence) – London. v1-52. 1830-56 (all publ) – 9 – LLMC 84-576 – us L.L.M.C. [073]
LEGAL OBSERVER, OR JOURNAL OF JURISPRUDENCE *see* LEGAL OBSERVER AND SOLICITOR'S JOURNAL
LEGAL OPINION : REAL ESTATE AND INSURANCE BULLETIN – Pennsylvania. v1-5. 1870-73 (all publ) – 9 – LLMC 82-939 – us L.L.M.C. [073]
LEGAL PHILADELPHIA, COMMENTS AND MEMORIES / Coxe, Robertson D – Philadelphia: Willim J Campbell, 1908 – 3mf – 9 – $4.50 – LLMC 92-171 – us L.L.M.C. [340]
LEGAL POLITICAL AND PERSONAL PAPERS / Coke, Edward – 16th cent. Holkham mss. 227, 249-252, 677, 681, 723, 724, 726-728, 764. Holkham Hall, Norfolk, England – 1 – uk Microform Academic [941]
LEGAL PRACTICE – v1 no 1 Jan-Feb 1934 (all publ) – 1mf – 9 – $1.50 – LLMC 82-940 – us L.L.M.C. [073]
THE LEGAL PRACTITIONER AND SOLICITOR'S JOURNAL – London, 1846-47 (all publ) – 9 – LLMC 84-577 – us L.L.M.C. [073]
LEGAL PRESS – Sacramento. Calif. -w. 1945- – 1 – us UMI [071]
THE LEGAL PROFESSION: ITS MORAL NATURE, AND PRACTICAL CONNECTION WITH CIVIL SOCIETY / Brooke, John T – Cincinnati, Derby, 1849. 24 p. LL-372 – 1 – us L of C Photodup [340]
LEGAL REFERENCE SERVICES QUARTERLY / ed by Berring, Robert C – v1- 1981- – 1, 9 ($140.00 in US $196.00 outside hardcopy subsc) – us Haworth [020]
THE LEGAL RELATIONS BETWEEN BENCH AND BAR; AN ADDRESS BEFORE THE SOUTHERN NEW HAMPSHIRE BAR ASSOCIATION, AT CONCORD. FEB 26, 1898 / Pillsbury, Albert Enoch – n.p., 1898. 29p. LL-1227 – 1 – us L of C Photodup [340]
LEGAL RELATIONSHIP OF STUDENT TEACHERS TO PUBLIC INSTITUTIONS OF HIGHER EDUCATION AND PUBLIC SCHOOLS / Hall, Gayle C – 1989 – 190p 2mf – 9 – $8.00 – us Microform Publ [370]
THE LEGAL REPORTER – Dublin. v1-3. 1840-43 (all publ) – 9 – LLMC 84-578 – us L.L.M.C. [073]
LEGAL RESEARCH IN THE SOUTH PACIFIC : A PRELIMINARY BIBLIOGRAPHY OF SELECTED AREAS AND ISSUES / Hall, Frederick Lee – (Covers American Samoa, Guam, Northern Marianas, Federated States of Micronesia and the Philippines) – Dec 31 1992 – 2mf – 9 – $3.00 – LLMC 92-400 – us L.L.M.C. [340]
LEGAL RESOURCE INDEX – Monthly cumulative index of over 720 law journals and other sources. Developed in cooperation and sponsorship of the American Association of Law Libraries – 5,17 – us I.A.C. [340]
THE LEGAL REVIEW – London, 1812-13 (all publ) – 9 – LLMC 84-579 – us L.L.M.C. [073]
LEGAL SERVICES BULLETIN *see* ALTERNATIVE LAW JOURNAL
LEGAL SERVICES IN RURAL AFRICA – 1985 – sz I.C.J. [340]
LEGAL SERVICES, MILITARY JUDGES' BENCHBOOK, 1966 : DEPARTMENT OF THE ARMY PAM. 27-9, 30 SEPTEMBER 1966 – Washington: GPO, 1996 – 10mf – 9 – $15.00 – LLMC 97-001 – us L.L.M.C. [340]
LEGAL SERVICES, MILITARY JUSTICE, ARMY REGULATION 27-10 : EFFECTIVE 24 JUNE 1996 – Washington: GPO, 1996 – 2mf – 9 – $3.00 – LLMC 97-003 – us L.L.M.C. [340]
LEGAL SERVICES, MILITARY JUSTICE, ARMY REGULATION 27-10 : EFFECTIVE 8 SEPTEMBER 1994 – Washington: GPO, 1994 – 2mf – 9 – $3.00 – LLMC 97-002 – us L.L.M.C. [340]
THE LEGAL STATUS OF FOREIGNERS IN INDONESIA / Gouw, Giok Siong – SE-4525 1. 1963 – 9 – ne IDC [323]
THE LEGAL STATUS OF FOREIGNERS IN THE U.S.S.R / Boguslavskii, Mark Moiseevich – Moscow, Foreign Languages Pub. House 196- 122 p. LL-4218 – 1 – us L of C Photodup [340]
LEGAL STATUS OF RURAL WOMEN : LIMITATIONS ON THE ECONOMIC PARTICIPATION OF WOMEN IN RURAL DEVELOPMENT – 1979 – 73p – it F.A.O. [340]
THE LEGAL STENOGRAPHER / Kowan, Theodor Ira – Cleveland, Cadillac Press, 1941 160 p. LL-354 – 1 – us L of C Photodup [340]
LEGAL STUDIES – (Supersedes: the Journal of Society of Public Teachers of Law N.S.) – v1-14. 1981-1994 – 9 – $300.00 set – us Hein [340]
LEGAL STUDIES FORUM – (v1-8 1976-84 on reel $81.00. v9-18 1985-94 on mf $230.00. Title varies: v1-8 1976-84 as ALSA Forum) – American Legal Studies Association. v1-18. 1976-94 – 5,6,9 – $311.00 set – us Hein [340]
LEGAL SUPPORT FOR LOS ANGELES COUNTY'S STRICT AIR POLLUTION CONTROL PROGRAM / Kennedy, Harold W – Los Angeles, 1957 24 p. LL-2263 – 1 – us L of C Photodup [340]
THE LEGAL TENDER CASES OF 1871 / U.S. Supreme Court – New York, Bankers' Magazine and Statistical Register, 1872. 137 p. LL-200 – 1 – us L of C Photodup [340]
LEGAL TENDER DURING THE ENGLISH AND IRISH BANK RESTRICTIONS / Fetter, Frank Whitson – 1950. 13p – 9 – $1.00f – at Libertarian Micro [332]
A LEGAL VIEW OF THE TRIAL OF CHRIST / Mabry, J C – Cincinnati: Standard Pub. Co., 1895. 1 fiche – 9 – us A.T.L.A. [240]
EL LEGALISMO DE HERNAN CORTES COMO INSTRUMENTO DE SU CONQUISTA / Valero Silva, Jose – Mexico: Universidad Autonoma de Mexico, 1965. Cuadernos. Ser. H. no 13 – sp Bibl Santa Ana [350]
O LEGALISTA – '(s.l.')-Sao Luis, Brazil. 15 Apr, Jun-8 Oct 1840 – 1,5,6 – bl Biblioteca [072]
Legare, Claire *see* BIBLIOGRAPHIE ANALYTIQUE DE M. JEAN-CHARLES FALARDEAU, SOCIOLOGUE, DIRECTEUR DU DEPARTEMENT DE SOCIOLOGIE A LA FACULTE DES SCIENCES SOCIALES DE L'UNIVERSITE LAVAL
Legare, Denise *see* BIBLIOGRAPHIE DE STANISLAS VACHON
Legare, Helene *see* BIBLIOGRAPHIE DE L'OEUVRE DE M. JEAN-BAPTISTE CAOUETTE, POETE CANADIEN
Legare, James *see* FINANCIAL ACCOUNTS
Legare, Jean-Paul *see* ENSEMBLE
Legault, Emile *see* LE CRIEUR
LEGEA NR. 1 PENTRU PLANUL GENERAL ECONOMIC AL REPUBLICII POPULARE ROMANE PE ANUL 1949 / Romania. Monitorul Oficial – pt. 1 A. Bucuresti. 1 Jan 1949. BD-790 1 – 9 – ne IDC [338]
THE LEGEND OF BADAJOZ, BEING AN EXTRACT FROM "THE SIEGE OF ALCAZAR." / McNeill-Moss, Geoffrey – London, 1937. Fiche W1014. (Blodgett Collection of Spanish Civil War Pamphlets) – 9 – us H.U. College Libr [946]
LEGEND. SPECULUM PERFECTIONIS. S. FRANCIS OF ASSISI: THE MIRROR OF PERFECTION / Francis of Assisi, Saint; ed by Paul Sabatier – Written by Brother Leo of Assisi; Trans. by Sebastian Evans. London: D. Nutt – 1 – us U.W. Library [920]
LEGENDA O LESSINGE = LESSING LEGENDE : LITERATURNO-KRITICHESKIE STATØEI / Mehring, Franz – (Includes bibliographical references) – Moskva: Academia. 2v. 1934 – 1 – us U.W. Library [430]
LEGENDE : AUS DEM ALLTAG DES KRIEGES / Wildgans, Anton – Wien: H Hellør, 1914 – 1r – 1 – us U.W. Library [430]
LEGENDE : AUS DEM ALLTAG DES KRIEGES / Wildgans, Anton – Wien: H Heller, 1914 – 1 – us U.W. Library [810]
LA LEGENDE DE DON JUAN / Gendarme de Bevotte, Georges – Paris: Hachette, 1911. 2v. (Les Femmes Collection) – 8mf – 9 – $20.00 – fr Bibl Nationale [390]
LA LEGENDE DE KERET / Virolleaud, Ch. – Paris, 1936 – 4mf – 8 – Dfl19.00 – ne Slangenburg [270]
LA LEGENDE DE M'PHOUMOU MA MAZONO / Malonga, Jean – Paris. 1954 – 1 – us Res Libr [960]
DIE LEGENDE DER H. JUNGFRAU UND MAERTYRIN SANKT KATHARINA / Bornstedt, Louise von – Muenster, 1838 – xvi/134p – 9 – DM48.00 – 3-89349-073-6 – gw Hänsel [240]
LEGENDE DER HEILIGEN / Luxemburg, Dionysius von – v1-2. 1844-45 – 1 – us I.U. Libraries [390]
LA LEGENDE DOREE DE MONTREAL / Morin, Victor – Montreal, 1949. SEM105P768 – 3mf – 9 – Can$6.75 – cn Bibl Nat [910]

LA LEGENDE D'UN PEUPLE / Frochette, Louis-Honore – Paris: La Librairie illustree, 1887. SEM16P50 – 1r – 5 – Can$9.00 – cn Bibl Nat [971]
LEGENDE EINIGER MUSIKHEILGEN / Marpurg, Friedrich Wilhelm – 1786 – 9 – us Sibley [780]
LA LEGENDE PHENICIENNE DE DANEL / Virolleaud, Ch. – Paris, 1936 – 10mf – 8 – Dfl35.00 – ne Slangenburg [270]
DIE LEGENDE VON DEM ERZWUNGENEN BRUDER / Luserke, Martin – Breslau: F Hirt, 1930 – 1r – 1 – us U.W. Library [390]
LEGENDES AFRICAINES / Dadie, Bernard Binlin – Paris: Seghers, [1954] – us Res Libr [390]
LEGENDES BRETONNES DU PAYS D'AVESSAC / L'Estourbeillon de la Garnache, Regis – 1882 – 1 – us I.U. Libraries [390]
LEGENDES CANADIENNES / Casgrain, Henri-Raymond – Quebec: J T Brousseau, 1861. SEM16P120 – 1r – 5 – Can$9.00 – cn Bibl Nat [971]
Legendre, Maurice see LAS JURDES ETUDE DE GEOGRAPHIA HUMAINE
LEGENDS AND LYRICS : A BOOK OF VERSES / Procter, Adelaide Anne – London: George Bell and Sons, 1877-1879 – 1 roll – 1 – 1-55879-242-2 – uk Libr Preservation [810]
LEGENDS AND POPULAR TALES OF THE BASQUE PEOPLE / Monteiro, Mariana – New York: A.C. Armstrong & Son, 1887. vi,274p – 1 – us U.W. Library [390]
LEGENDS, LOVES AND LOYALTIES OF OLD NEW ENGLAND – By Caroline Leonard Goodenough. Item H.Memories of the Leonard, Thompson & Hakell families. Indexed, 341p. SW16-0155 – 5 – us A.G.L.L. [978]
LEGENDS OF ANGRIA / Bronte, Charlotte – New Haven: Yale University Press; London: Humphrey Milford, Oxford University Press, 1933 – 1 roll – 1 – 1-55879-836-6 – uk Libr Preservation [830]
LEGENDS OF GENESIS / Gunkel, Hermann – Chicago: Open Court, 1901. 1 fiche – 9 – us A.T.L.A. [220]
LEGENDS OF NEW ENGLAND / Whittier, John Greenleaf – 1831 – 9 – 10.00 – us Scholars' Facs [830]
THE LEGENDS OF THE JEWS / Ginzberg, L – 7v. Index. Philadelphia. 1909-1910-38. BJ-32-32 1 – 9 – ne IDC [305]
LEGENDS OF THE MADONNA AS REPRESENTED IN THE FINE ARTS / Jameson, A B – O-1249 1. 1891 – 9 – ne IDC [240]
LEGENDS OF THE PATRIARCHS AND PROPHETS : AND OTHER OLD TESTAMENT CHARACTERS FROM VARIOUS SOURCES / Baring-Gould, Sabine – New York: Holt & Williams, 1872 – 1mf – 9 – 0-8370-2176-6 – 1985-0176 – us A.T.L.A. [220]
THE LEGENDS OF THE SAINTS : AN INTRODUCTION TO HAGIOGRAPHY / Delehaye, Hippolyte – London, New York: Longmans, Green, 1907 – 1mf – us A.T.L.A. [240]
Leger, Chazet et Buhan see IL FAUT UN ETAT OU LA REVUE DE L'AN 6
Leger, D see
– L'ETHNOMINERALOGIE ET LA VIE RELIGIEUSE DES BAHNAR JOLONG, PROVINCE DE KONTUM, VIETNAM
– PRESENTATION DES BAHNAR-JOLONG, PROTO-INDOCHINOIS DE LANGUE AUSTROASIATIQUE, PROVINCE DE KONTUM, VIETNAM DU SUD
Leger, J O see L'UNION AGRICOLE
Leger, L see
– NICOLAS GOGOL
– RECUEIL D'ITINERAIRES ET DE VOYAGES DANS L'ASIE CENTRALE ET L'EXTREME-ORIENT
Leger, Louis see
– CYRILLE ET METHODE
– LA MYTHOLOGIE SLAVE
Legerlotz, Gustav see PARZIVAL
LEGES ALAMANNORUM (MGH LEGES 2A: 5.BD. PARS 1A) – 1888 – Dfl22.00 – ne Slangenburg [240]
LEGES BURGUNDIORUM (MGH LEGES 2A: 2.BD. PARS 1A) – 1892 – Dfl22.00 – ne Slangenburg [240]
LEGES LANGOBARDORUM (MGH LEGES. 1: 4.BD) – 1868 – Dfl74.00 – ne Slangenburg [240]
LEGES NATIONUM GERMANICARUM (MGH LEGES. 1: 3.BD) : LEGES ALAMANNORUM.-LEGES BAIUWARIORUM.-LEGES BURGUNDIONUM.-LEX FRISIONUM – 1863 – Dfl67.00 – ne Slangenburg [240]
LEGES SAXONUM ET LEX THURINGORUM (MGH LEGES 4: 4.BD) – 1918 – Dfl9.00 – ne Slangenburg [240]
LEGES SAXONUM.- LEX THURINGORUM.- EDICTUM THEODERICI REGIS.- REMEDII CURIENSIS EPISCOPI CAPITULA.- LEX RIBUARIA.- LEX FRANCORUM CHAMAVORUM.- LEX ROMANA RAETICA CURIENSIS (MGH LEGES. 1: 5.BD) – 1875-1889 – Dfl42.00 – ne Slangenburg [240]
LEGES VISIGOTHORUM ANTIQUIORES (MGH LEGES 4: 5.BD) – 1894 – Dfl22.00 – ne Slangenburg [240]
LEGES VISIGOTHORUM (MGH LEGES 2: 1.BD) – 1902 – Dfl56.00 – ne Slangenburg [240]
Legeso, S see SOVETSKAIA KOOPERATSIIA
Legg, J Wickham see
– BREVIARIUM ROMANUM A FRANCISCO CARDINALE QUIGNONIO. ED. 1535
– ENGLISH CHURCH LIFE FROM THE RESTORATION TO THE TRACTARIAN MOVEMENT
– INVENTORIES OF CHRISTCHURCH, CANTERBURY
– THE REFORMED BREVIARY OF CARDINAL TOMMASI
– THE SARUM MISSAL
Legge, F see FORERUNNERS AND RIVALS OF CHRISTIANITY
LA LEGGE; MONITORE GUIDIZIARIO ED AMMINISTRATIVO DEL REGNO L'ITALIA. – Torino. On film: v1-52; 1861-1912. LL-0219 – 1 – us L of C Photodup [340]
LA LEGGE SULLA NATURALIZZAZIONE IN ITALIA / Esperson, P – Roma, 1886 – 1mf – 1 – ILM-3150/1 – ne IDC [327]
LA LEGGE UNIFORME SULLA CAMBIALE / Bracco, B – Padova, 1627 – 5mf – 1 – ILM-3762/1 – ne IDC [327]
Legge, W V see A HISTORY OF THE BIRDS OF CEYLON
Leggett, Conaway and Co see
– HISTORY OF MARION COUNTY
– HISTORY OF WYANDOT COUNTY
LA LEGION DU RHONE – Circulaire de liaison de la legion francaise des combattants et des volontaires de la revolution nationale du Rhone. no. 1. Lyon. 1er nov 1941; no. 11-60, 1er avr 1942-15 juil 1944. mq no. 15-17, 27 – 1 – fr A.C.R.P.P. [073]
LEGION LIAR – Las Vegas, NV. 1925-1955 – 1r – 1 – $50.00 – U04860 – us Library Micro [071]
THE LEGION OF MARCHING MADMEN / Blackledge, William James – London: S. Low, Marston & Co., 1936. ix,244p. illus – 1 – us U.W. Library [940]
Legipontius, O see HISTORIA REI LITERARIAE O.S.B.
LEGISLACION AGRARIA DE LA REPUBLICA ARGENTINA / Borea, Domingo – Buenos Aires: "Carlos Gide" Cooperativa Editorial, 1948 – 1 – CSUXAHZ6469-B – us Hoover Inst Photo [340]
LEGISLACION HIPOTECARIA PARA CUBA, PUERTO RICO Y FILIPINAS : EXTENSAMENTE ANOTADA Y CONCORDADA CON LA LEGISLACION ESPANOLA Y ULTRAMARINA, JURISPRUDENCIA, ETC... – (With appendices & index) – Madrid: Centro Editorial de Gongoro, 1912 – 9mf – 9 – $13.50 – LLMC 92-321 – us L.L.M.C. [323]
LEGISLACION LATINO-AMERICANA SOBRE PROPIEDAD INDUSTRIAL / Martinez Morales, Maria – Santiago de Chile, 1944. 90,4p. LL-8015 – 1 – us L of C Photodup [340]
LEGISLACION MEXICANA / Mexico. Laws, Statutes, etc. – Mexico: Imprenta del gobierno, en Palacio, 1872-73. 3v. LL-8016 – 1 – us L of C Photodup [340]
LEGISLACION SOBRE INDIOS DEL RIO DE LA PLATA EN EL SIGLO 16TH. MADRID. 1928 / Garcia Santillan, Juan Carlos; ed by Bayle, Constantino – Madrid: Razon y Fe, 1929 – 9 – sp Bibl Santa Ana [340]
LEGISLACION SOCIAL DE AMERICA LATINA. / International Labour Organisation – Ginebra, 1928-29. 2v. LL-8012 – 1 – us L of C Photodup [340]
LEGISLACION UNIFORME DE CHEQUES / Crespo, E – Buenos Aires, 1924 – 1mf – 1 – ILM-3380/1 – ne IDC [327]
LEGISLACION Y JURISPRUDENCIA PENAL EN AMERICA DEL SUR / MacLean y Estenos, Percy – Lima, Peru, Imprenta azul 1944. 102, 2 p. LL-8014 – 1 – us L of C Photodup [340]
LEGISLATIO (OFM) DE MUSICA SACRA. STUDIUM HISTORICO-IURIDICUM / Belluco, Bartolome – Madrid: Archivo Ibero Americano, 1960 – 1 – sp Bibl Santa Ana [240]
LEGISLATION AGAINST WEEDS / Dewey, Lyster Hoxie – Washington, Govt. Print. Off., 1896. 60 p. LL-652 – 1 – us L of C Photodup [340]
LEGISLATION CONTROLLING THE INTERNATIONAL BEEF AND VEAL TRADE – 1985 – 142p – it F.A.O. [340]
LA LEGISLATION EN MATIERE IMMOBILIERE EN EGYPTE; RECUEIL DES LOIS, REGLEMENTS ET INSTRUCTIONS ADMINISTRATIVES RELATIFS A LA PROPRIETE IMMOBILIERE / Egypt. Laws, Statutes, etc – Le Caire, Imprimerie nationale, 1893. 560 p. LL-12024 – 1 – us L of C Photodup [340]
LEGISLATION EN VIGUEUR EN MATIERE DE CONTRACT DE TRAVAIL ET DE L'EMPLOI / Algeria. Direction du Travail et de l'Emploi – 1969. BNE-8719 1 – 9 – ne IDC [332]
LEGISLATION EN VIGUEUR EN MATIERE DE FORMATION PROFESSIONNELLE ET D'APPRENTISSAGE / Algeria. Direction du Travail et de l'Emploi – 1969. BNE-8718 1 – 9 – ne IDC [332]
LA LEGISLATION FRANCAISE SUR LES COALITIONS OUVRIERES, SON EVOLUTION AU XIXE SIECLE / Jourdain, Victor – (Thesis). (Condition of 19th C. French working class series). 1898 – 9 – fr Hachette [944]
LEGISLATION, MAJOR SPEECHES AND ESSAYS, AND SPECIAL REPORTS, 1913-1960 / U. S. Federal Reserve System – Part One of Papers of the Federal Reserve System Series. 1983 – 1 – $1,830.00 – 0-89093-509-2 – us UPA [336]
LEGISLATION ON PRODUCTIVITY IN AGRICULTURE : A COMPARATIVE OUTLINE – 1985 – 80p – it F.A.O. [340]
LEGISLATION ON WILDLIFE AND PROTECTED AREAS IN AFRICA – 1984 – 165p – it F.A.O. [340]
LEGISLATION ON WILDLIFE, HUNTING AND PROTECTED AREAS IN SOME EUROPEAN COUNTRIES – 1980 – 54p – it F.A.O. [340]
LEGISLATION SUR LE TRAVAIL DES ENFANTS DANS LES MANUFACTURES. RECUEIL DES DOCUMENTS PARLEMENTAIRES, LEGISLATIFS ET STATISTIQUES / Tallon, Eugene & Maurice, Gustave – Condition of 19th C. French working class series. 1875 – 9 – fr Hachette [360]
LEGISLATIVE ASSEMBLY : VOTES AND PROCEEDINGS / New South Wales. Australia. Parliament – New South Wales, 1856-1900 – 116r – 1 – A$3,364.00 silver A$2,842.00 vesicular – at Pascoe [324]
LEGISLATIVE ASSEMBLY : VOTES AND PROCEEDINGS / Queensland. Australia. Parliament – Queensland, 1860-1901 – 47r – 1 – A$1,368.00 silver A$1,179.00 vesicular – at Pascoe [324]
LEGISLATIVE ASSEMBLY : VOTES AND PROCEEDINGS / Victoria. Australia. Parliament – Victoria, 1856-1901 – 73r – 1 – A$2,117.00 silver A$1,789.00 visicular – at Pascoe [324]
LEGISLATIVE ASSEMBLY DEBATES – (Includes a printed guide) – Delhi. 1921-47. v1-53. Lacking: 1928. v5 – 2,486mf – 8 – ne IDC [324]
LEGISLATIVE ASSEMBLY JOURNALS / Alberta – 1906-20 – 1r – 1 – $68.00 – cn Library Assoc [971]
LEGISLATIVE ASSEMBLY JOURNALS / British Columbia – 1872-1903; Sessional Papers; Statutes; Revised Statutes – 25r – 1 – $1,625.00 set – cn Library Assoc [971]
LEGISLATIVE ASSEMBLY JOURNALS / Manitoba – 1871-1900; Legislative Council. Journals. To 1876; Gazette; Statutes; Revised Statutes; Index to Journals – 24r – 1 – $1,560.00 – cn Library Assoc [971]
LEGISLATIVE ASSEMBLY JOURNALS / Ontario – 1867-1923; Sessional papers; Statutes; Revised Statutes; Index. – 209r – 1 – $13,585.00 set – cn Library Assoc [971]
LEGISLATIVE CHRONICLES OF THE CITY OF ALEXANDRIA / Caton, James R – Alexandria, VA: Newell-Cole Co., 1933. 244p. LL-761 – 1 – us L of C Photodup [340]
LEGISLATIVE COUNCIL : JOURNALS / New South Wales. Australia. Parliament – New South Wales, 1856-1900 – 56r – 1 – A$1,624.00 silver A$1,372.00 vesicular – at Pascoe [073]
LEGISLATIVE COUNCIL : JOURNALS / Queensland. Australia. Parliament – 1860-1901 – 39r – 1 – A$1,131.00 silver A$937.00 vesicular – at Pascoe [324]
LEGISLATIVE COUNCIL : JOURNALS / Tasmania. Australia. Parliament – Tasmania, 1856-1902 – 30r – 1 – A$912.00 silver A$786.00 vesicular – at Pascoe [324]
LEGISLATIVE COUNCIL : VOTES AND PROCEEDINGS / New South Wales. Australia. Parliament – New South Wales, 1824-55 – 11r – 1 – A$319.00 silver A$269.00 vesicular – at Pascoe [324]
LEGISLATIVE COUNCIL : VOTES AND PROCEEDINGS / Victoria. Australia. Parliament – Vicotria, 1852-1902 – 12r – 1 – A$348.00 silver A$294.00 vesicular – at Pascoe [324]
LEGISLATIVE COUNCIL : VOTES AND PROCEEDINGS / Western Australia. Australia. Parliament – 1870-1900 – 12r – 1 – A$374.00 silver A$322.00 vesicular – at Pascoe [324]
LEGISLATIVE COUNCIL DEBATES – 1925/26 through 1955/56 – 7r – $346.50 – us African Imprint [320]
LEGISLATIVE COUNCIL DEBATES / Basutoland. National Council. Maseru – mar 11-jun 6 1960; jan 9-apr 1961; mar 14-may 15 1962; nov 21 1962-feeb 15 1963; aug 20-oct 4 1963; nov 25 1963-apr 20 1964; nov 20-dec 9 1964 – us Res Libr [323]
LEGISLATIVE COUNCIL DEBATES / Eastern Bengal and Assam – 1v. Shillong. 1906-17. BI-60 2 – 8 – ne IDC [324]
LEGISLATIVE COUNCIL DEBATES / Madras – v. 1-16. 1937-48. BI-34 2 – 8 – ne IDC [323]
LEGISLATIVE COUNCIL DEBATES / North West Frontier Province. India – v. 1-11. Peshavar. 1932-36. BI-68 2 – 8 – ne IDC [324]
LEGISLATIVE COUNCIL DEBATES, 1918-1921 / Assam – Shillong. 1919-21. BI-62 2 – 8 – ne IDC [324]
LEGISLATIVE COUNCIL DEBATES, 1937-1939 / Bihar – v. 1-5. Bihar – Patna. 1937-40. BI-46 2 – 8 – ne IDC [324]
A LEGISLATIVE HANDBOOK RELATING TO THE PREPARATION OF STATUTES. / Willard, Ashton Rollins – Boston, Houghton, Mifflin, 1890. 281 p. LL-1622 – 1 – us L of C Photodup [340]
LEGISLATIVE HISTORY OF THE EMPLOYEE RETIREMENT INCOME SECURITY ACT OF 1974 – Washington: GPO. v1-3. 1989 – 9 – $75.00 set – 0-89941-705-1 – us Hein [340]
LEGISLATIVE HISTORY OF THE MILITARY JUSTICE ACT OF 1968, PL 90-632 / U.S. Law Branch Army LibraryArmy Court of Military Review – (Also serves as a suppl to: Index and Legislative History, UCMJ, 1950) – 1969; 1985 – 4mf – 9 – $6.00 – LLMC 87-320B – us L.L.M.C. [324]
LEGISLATIVE HISTORY OF THE MILITARY JUSTICE ACT OF 1983 / U.S. Army Legal Service Agency – (Also serves as suppl to: Index and Legislative History, UCMJ, 1950) – Washington, 1984; 1985 – 9mf – 9 – $13.50 – LLMC 87-320C – us L.L.M.C. [324]
A LEGISLATIVE HISTORY OF THE MOTOR CARRIER ACT, 1935. / Wagner, Warren Herbert – Denton, Md., Rue, 1935 155 p. LL-1475 – 1 – us L of C Photodup [340]
LEGISLATIVE HISTORY OF THE OMNIBUS INSUALR AREAS ACT OF 1979-1980 / U.S. Congress. Subcomm on National Parks and Insular Affairs – 96th Cong. 2nd sess. Washington: GPO, 1980 (mf ed) – 4mf – 9 – $6.00 – LLMC 95-038 – us L.L.M.C. [323]
LEGISLATIVE HISTORY OF THE OMNIBUS INSULAR AREAS ACT OF 1979-1980 : H.R. 3756 PUBLIC LAW 96-205 / American Samoa. US Congress. Subcomm National Parks and Insular Affairs – (Deals with American Samoa, Guam, the Northern Mariana Islands, the Trust Territory of the Pacific, and the Virgin Islands) – 96th Congress 2nd sess. Washington: GPO,

1980 – 4mf – 9 – $6.00 – LLMC 95-038 – us L.L.M.C. [327]

LEGISLATIVE HISTORY OF THE SECURITIES ACT OF 1933 AND SECURITIES EXCHANGE ACT OF 1934 / Ellenberger, J S & Mahar, E P – (Set contains 69 individual items including the law, documents, reports, hearings, bills, amendments and debates. Histories are not indexed by subject but they contain two section-by-section indices by Act section) – 1,5,6 – $125.00 – us Hein [340]

THE LEGISLATIVE MANUAL FOR THE STATE OF WISCONSIN / Turner, A J – Madison: Atwood and Culver, Printers, 1873. Wisconsin Reel 22. (The Cox Library Collection) – 5 – us Americana [978]

LEGISLATIVE PRINCIPLES OF SOIL CONSERVATION – 1977 – 73p – it F.A.O. [340]

LEGISLATIVE SCENE *see* ACA NEWS

LEGISLATIVE SERIES / Central Government of India – All series, 1854-1947 – 4081mf – 9 – ne IDC [323]

LEGISLATIVE SERIES / Provincial Government of India – All series, 1826-1941 – 9870mf – 9 – ne IDC [323]

LEGISLATIVE SOUVENIR MANUAL 1895-1896 / Steel, William A & Searl, Albert – Seattle, Tacoma, 1895. Washington reel 8. (Cox Library Collection) – 5 – us Americana [978]

LEGISLATIVE STUDIES QUARTERLY – (v.4-. 1979- 5,6,9) – v.1-. 1976- – 1 – us UMI [073]

LEGISLATIVE VETO OF AGENCY RULES AFTER U.S. V. CHADHA / Administrative Conference of the U.S. (ACUS) – Acus: 27th Pleanary Sess, 15 Dec 1983; Washington: GPO, 1984 – 2mf – 9 – $3.00 – LLMC 94-348 – us L.L.M.C. [340]

LA LEGITIMITE – Journal contre-revolutionnaire et anti-maconnique. Bordeaux. 1891-94 – 1 – fr A.C.R.P.P. [073]

LA LEGITIMITE – Toulouse and Bordeaux. -w, -m 4 Feb 1883-Dec 1898. 8 reels – 1 – uk British Libr Newspaper [072]

LEGKAIA PROMYSHLENMOST' – v. 1-19. 1922-40. NS. 1-16. 1941-58 – 1 – 370.00 – us L of C Photodup [943]

Legoazre de Kervelegan, Augustin *see* LETTRE DE M. AUGUSTIN LE GOAZRE DE KERVELEGAN, SENECHAL DE QUIMPER-CORENTIN, A M. BALAIS SUBDELEGUE...(17 NOV. 1788)

Legos, Patricia M *see*
- THE EFFECT OF REGULARLY SCHEDULED DAILY SUPERVISOR VERBAL FEEDBACK ON USE OF PERSONAL PROTECTIVE EQUIPMENT
- USE OF THE HEALTH BELIEF MODEL IN DETERMINING MAMMOGRAPHY SCREENING PRACTICE IN OLDER WOMEN

Legouve *see*
- EPICHARIS ET NERON OU CONSPIRATION POUR LA LIBERTE
- ETEOCLE
- LA MORT D'ABEL
- LA MORT D'HENRI 4, ROI DE FRANCE

Legouve, Ernest *see* EDITH DE FALSEN

Legoyt, Alfred *see*
- DES CHERTES EN FRANCE ET DE LEUR INFLUENCE SUR LE MOUVEMENT DE LA POPULATION
- DES CONDITIONS D'ACCROISSEMENT DE LA POPULATION FRANCAISE COMPAREE AUX AUTRES POPULATIONS EUROPEENES
- DES NAISSANCES ILLEGITIMES EN EUROPE
- DU PROGRES DES AGGLOMERATIONS URBAINES ET DE L'EMIGRATION RURALE: EN EUROPE ET PARTICULIEREMENT EN FRANCE
- LA FRANCE ET L'ETRANGER: ETUDES DE STATISTIQUE COMPAREE

Legrain, L *see* UR EXCAVATIONS, 3: ARCHAIC SEAL-IMPRESSIONS

Legrain, Paul Maurice *see* HEREDITE ET ALCOOLISME, ETUDE PSYCHOLOGIQUE ET CLINIQUE SUR LES DEGENERES BUVEURS ET LES FAMILLES D'IVROGNES

Legrand, Emile L *see* EPHEMERIDES DACES

Legrand, J J *see* LES COAPTATIONS SEXUELLES DES ONISCOIDEA

Legrand, Marc-Antoine *see* LE ROI DE COCAGNE, COMEDIE

Legras, Henri *see* LA TABLE LATINE D'HERACLEE (LA PRETENDUE LEX JULIA MUNICIPALIS)

Leguat, Francois *see* VOYAGE ET AVENTURES DE FR. LEGUAT EN DEUX ISLES DESERTES DES INDES ORIENTALES

Leguevel de Lacombe, B F *see* VOYAGE A MADAGASCAR ET AUX ILES COMORES

THE LEGULEIAN – ns: London. v1-4. 1850-64 (all publ) – 14mf – 9 – $21.00 – LLMC 84-581 – us L.L.M.C. [073]

Legum, Colin *see*
- COLIN LEGUM'S PRESS CUTTINGS VOLUMES, 1936-1987
- COLIN LEGUM'S THIRD WORLD REPORTS, 1982-1989
- COLIN LEGUM'S WRITINGS FROM 1940'S TO 1980'S

LEGUME INOCULANTS AND THEIR USE : A POCKET MANUAL JOINTLY PREPARED BY NIFTAL PROJECT AND FAO – 1984 – 63p – it F.A.O. [630]

LEGUME TREES AND OTHER FODDER TREES AS PROTEIN SOURCES FOR LIVESTOCK – 1992 – 358p – it F.A.O. [636]

LEGUMES IN HUMAN NUTRITION – 1982 – 160p – it F.A.O. [640]

LES LEGUMINEUSES, LES GRAINES OLEAGINEUSES CONDIMENTAIRES ET DIVERSES AU MAROC; ETUDE STATISTIQUE, 1965 / Kebbaj, Abd el Khalek – BNE-3061 1 – 9 – ne IDC [960]

THE LEGUMINOSAE OF TROPICAL AFRICA / Baker, E G – Ghent, 1926 – 950p – 8 – ne IDC [580]

LEHIGH PIONEER AND MAUCH CHUNK COURIER – Mauch Chunk, PA. 1830-31. Also incl. The Mauch Chunk Courier, 1831-33. 1 roll – 13 – $25.00r – us I.M.R. [071]

LEHIGH REGISTER WEEKLY – Allentown, PA. -w 1889-1912 – 13 – $25.00r – us I.M.R. [071]

LEHIGHTON TIMES – Lehighton, PA., 1971 – 13 – $25.00r – us I.M.R. [071]

Lehman, Steven L *see* THE EFFECT OF EXERCISE INTENSITY ON THE EXTENT OF AND RECOVERY FROM FATIGUE OF LONG DURATION

Lehmann, Alfred *see* DREIHEIT UND DREIFACHE WIEDERHOLUNG IM DEUTSCHEN VOLKSMAERCHEN

Lehmann, Arthur Heinz *see* HENGST MAESTOSO AUSTRIA

Lehmann, Christian *see* AUSFUEHRLICHE BESCHREIBUNG DES MEISSNISCHEN OBER-ERTZGEBUERGES

Lehmann, Ernst Gottlob *see* BILDER AUS DEM LEBEN JESU

Lehmann, G W *see* PAPERS

Lehmann, Heinrich *see* VOLKSGESETZBUCH. GRUNDREGEL UND BUCH I

Lehmann, Ignaz *see* AMERIKA'S GESETZE

Lehmann, J G C *see*
- ICONES ET DESCRIPTIONES NOVARUM ET MINUS COGNITARUM STIRPIUM
- MONOGRAPHIA GENERIS POTENTILLARUM
- NOVARUM ET MINUS COGNITARUM STIRPIUM PUGILLUS 1-10
- PLANTAE E FAMILIA ASPERIFOLIARUM NUCIFERAE
- PLANTAE PREISSIANAE SIVE ENUMERATIO PLANTARUM QUAS IN AUSTRALASIA OCC. ET ANNIS 1838-1841 COLLEGIT

Lehmann, Johann Gottlob *see* KURTZE EINLEITUNG IN EINIGE THEILE DER BERGWERCKS-WISSENSCHAFT

Lehmann, Karl *see* VERLOBUNG UND HOCHZEIT

Lehmann, Otto *see* DEUTSCHES VOLKSTUM IN VOLKSKUNST UND VOLKSSTRACHT

Lehmann, Peter Ambros *see* NOVA LITERARIA GERMANIAE COLLECTA HAMBURGI, 1703-1706; NOVA LITERARIA GERMANIAE ALLIORUMQUE EUROPAE REGNORUM COLLECTA HAMBURGI, 1707-1709

Lehmann, Ulf *see* DER GOTTSCHEDKREIS UND RUSSLAND

Lehmann-Hohenberg, Johannes *see* NATURWISSENSCHAFT UND BIBEL

Lehmayer, Martin *see* SHOULD JURIES IN CRIMINAL CASES BE JUDGES OF THE LAW AND FACT?

Lehmensick, Fritz *see* TEXT ZU MEINHOLD'S DEUTSCHEN MAERCHENBILDERN

Lehr *see* L'ALSACE NOBLE

LEHR- UND LESEBUCH ZUR SPRACHE DER MISCHNAH / Geiger, Abraham – 2pts. Breslau. 1845. BJ-412-7 1 – 9 – ne IDC [470]

LEHRBUCH DER ALTTESTAMENT. RELIGIONSGESCHICHTE / Smend, Rudolf – Freiburg i.B.: J.C.B. Mohr, 1899. 519p.2 fiches – 9 – us A.T.L.A. [240]

LEHRBUCH DER BIBLISCHEN THEOLOGIE DES NEUEN TESTAMENTS / Weiss, Bernhard – 6. verb. aufl. Berlin, 1895 – Dfl42.00 – ne Slangenburg [220]

LEHRBUCH DER CHRISTLICHEN DOGMENGESCHICHTE / Baur, Ferdinand Christian – Leipzig: Fues, 1867 – 1mf – us A.T.L.A. [240]

LEHRBUCH DER EINLEITUNG IN DAS ALTE TESTAMENT / Reusch, Franz Heinrich – (Includes bibliographies) – 2., verb Aufl. Freiburg i.B.: Herder, 1864 – 1mf – 9 – 0-8370-6936-X – 1986-0936 – us A.T.L.A. [220]

LEHRBUCH DER EINLEITUNG IN DAS NEUE TESTAMENT / Weiss, Bernhard – 3. verb. aufl. Berlin, 1897 – Dfl39.00 – ne Slangenburg [220]

LEHRBUCH DER GESCHICHTE DER PHILOSOPHIE / Windelband-Heimsoeth – Tuebingen, 1948 – 20mf – 8 – ne Slangenburg [100]

LEHRBUCH DER GRIECHISCHEN ANTIQUITAETEN / Hermann, Karl Freidrich – Neu hrsg. von H. Bluemmer und W. Dittenberger. Freiburg i.B.,J.C.B. Mohr, 1882-1913. 4 v. in 7. Film Mas 9160 – 1 – us H.U. Library [930]

LEHRBUCH DER HISTORISCHEN METHODE UND DER GESCHICHTSPHILOSOPHIE : MIT NACHWEIS DER WICHTIGSTEN QUELLEN UND HILFSMITTEL ZUM STUDIUM DER GESCHICHTE / Bernheim, Ernst – Leipzig: Duncker & Humblot, 1908 – 2mf – us A.T.L.A. [900]

LEHRBUCH DER KATHOLISCHEN GLAUBENS- UND SITTENLEHRE FUER DIE OBEREN KLASSEN DER HOEHEREN LEHRANSTALTEN OESTERREICHS / Martin, Konrad – Mainz: Franz Kirchheim. 3v. 1859 – 3mf – 9 – 0-8370-8453-9 – 1986-2453 – us A.T.L.A. [240]

LEHRBUCH DER KIRCHENGESCHICHTE / Deutsch, S M – Bonn: A. Marcus & E. Weber, 1909. (Sammlung theologischer Handbuecher. Fuenfter Teil, Kirchengeschichte) – 2mf – us A.T.L.A. [240]

LEHRBUCH DER KIRCHENGESCHICHTE : FUER ACADEMISCHE VORLESUNGEN UND ZUM SELBSTSTUDIUM / Brueck, Heinrich – (Includes bibliographical references and index) – 5., verb Aufl. Mainz: Franz Kirchheim, 1890 – 3mf – 9 – 0-8370-7370-7 – 1986-1370 – us A.T.L.A. [240]

LEHRBUCH DER KIRCHENGESCHICHTE : FUER STUDIERENDE / Kurtz, Johann Heinrich – Leipzig: A. Neumann, 1906 – 4mf – us A.T.L.A. [240]

LEHRBUCH DER KIRCHENGESCHICHTE / Marx, Jakob – (Includes bibliographies, chronological summary, and index) – 4., verb Aufl. Trier: Paulinus, 1908 – 3mf – 9 – 0-8370-6918-1 – 1986-0918 – us A.T.L.A. [240]

LEHRBUCH DER MECHANISCHEN NATURLEHRE / Fischer, Ernst Gottfried – 2nd ed. Berlin, 1819. 2v in 1 – 1 – us U.W. Library [530]

LEHRBUCH DER METAPHYSIK / Aschenbrenner, Michael – Landshut. 1830 – 1 – us Res Libr [110]

LEHRBUCH DER OEKOLOGISCHEN PFLANZENGEOGRAPHIE. / Warming, Eugenius – Berlin: Gebrueder Borntraeger, 1896. xii,412p – 1 – us U.W. Library [580]

LEHRBUCH DER PHILOSOPHISCHEN RECHTSWISSENSCHAFT... / Gros, K H – Ed 3. Tuebingen, 1815 – 4mf – 1 – ILM-1061/1 – ne IDC [327]

LEHRBUCH DER SAMARITANISCHEN SPRACHE UND LITERATUR : MIT FACSIMILE EINES SAMARITANISCHEN BRIEFES VOM GEGENWAERTIGEN HOHENPRIESTER DER SAMARITANER ZU NABLUS / Rosenberg, Isaak – Wien: A Hartleben, [1901] – 1mf – 9 – 0-8370-7420-7 – 1986-1420 – us A.T.L.A. [470]

LEHRBUCH DES DEUTSCHEN KIRCHENRECHTES / Mejer, Otto – Goettingen: Vandenhoeck und Ruprecht, 1869 – 2mf – us A.T.L.A. [240]

LEHRBUCH DES KATHOLISCHEN UND EVANGELISCHEN KIRCHENRECHTS / Friedberg, Emil – Leipzig, 1879 – Dfl39.00 – ne Slangenburg [240]

DIE LEHRE DER KIRCHE VON DER H. SCHRIFT NACH DER SCHRIFT SELBST GEPRUEFT : EINE VON DER HAAGER GESELLSCHAFT ZUR VERTHEIDIGUNG DER CHRISTLICHEN RELIGION GEKROENTE PREISSCHRIFT / Walz, K – Leiden: E J Brill, 1884 – 1mf – 9 – 0-8370-5695-0 – 1985-3695 – us A.T.L.A. [220]

DIE LEHRE DER ZWOELF APOSTEL (T.U.U. 1-2/1.2.) / Harnack, Adolf von – Leipzig, 1884 – 7mf – 9 – ne Slangenburg [240]

DIE LEHRE DES HEIL. CYPRIAN VON DER EINHEIT DER KIRCHE / Reinkens, Joseph Hubert – Wuerzburg: Stahel, 1873 – 1mf – us A.T.L.A. [240]

DIE LEHRE DES RABBI JESUA VON NAZARETH : NACH DEN EVANGELIEN UND MIT AUSSPRUECHEN AUS DEM ALTEN TESTAMENTE UND DEM TALMUD / Reichenbach, A – Muenchen: Carl Merhoff, 1882 – 1mf – 9 – 0-8370-7326-X – 1986-1326 – us A.T.L.A. [220]

DIE LEHRE SCHLEIERMACHERS VON DER ERLOESUNG / Stephan, Horst – Tuebingen: J.C.B. Mohr, 1901 – 1mf – us A.T.L.A. [240]

LEHRE UND GEBET IN DEN DREI ERSTEN CHRISTLICHEN JAHRHUNDERTEN / Probst, Ferdinand – Tuebingen: H. Laupp, 1871 – 1mf – us A.T.L.A. [240]

LEHRE UND WEHRE – v1-75. 1855-1929 (complete) – 18r – 1 – ATLA 1993-S504 – us A.T.L.A. [073]

DIE LEHRE VOM DREIEINIGEN GOTT IN DER SCHULE DES PETRUS LOMBARDUS / Schneider, J – Muenchen, 1961 – 7mf – 8 – ne Slangenburg [240]

DIE LEHRE VOM DREIEINIGEN GOTT IN DER SCHULE DES PETRUS LOMBARDUS / Schneider, J – Muenchen, 1961 – 7mf – 8 – ne Slangenburg [240]

DIE LEHRE VOM GEBET NACH DEM NEUEN TESTAMENT : EIN BEITRAG ZUR KENNTNIS UND WUERDIGUNG DES URSPRUENGLICHEN CHRISTENTHUMS / Christ, Paul – Leiden: E J Brill, 1886 – 1mf – 9 – 0-8370-2655-5 – 1985-0655 – us A.T.L.A. [220]

DIE LEHRE VOM REICHE GOTTES IM NEUEN TESTAMENT : EINE VON DER HAAGER GESELLSCHAFT ZUR VERTEIDIGUNG DER CHRISTLICHEN RELIGION GEKROENTE PREISSCHRIFT / Issel, Ernst – (Includes bibliographical references and list of biblical citations) – Leiden: E J Brill, 1891 – 1mf – 9 – 0-8370-3734-4 – 1985-1734 – us A.T.L.A. [220]

DIE LEHRE VOM REICHE GOTTES IN DEN SCHRIFTEN DES NEUEN TESTAMENTS : BEARBEITUNG EINER VON DER HAAGER GESELLSCHAFT ZUR VERTEIDIGUNG DER CHRISTLICHEN RELIGION GESTELLTEN AUFGABE / Schmoller, Otto – Leiden:E J Brill, 1891 – 1mf – 9 – 0-8370-5122-3 – 1985-3122 – us A.T.L.A. [220]

DIE LEHRE VON DEN SAKRAMENTEN IN IHRER GESCHICHTLICHEN ENTWICKELUNG INNERHALB DER ABENDLAENDISCHEN KIRCHE BIS ZUM CONCIL VOM TRIENT / Hahn, G L – Breslau: E. Morgenstern, 1864 – us A.T.L.A. [240]

DIE LEHRE VON DER ANFANGSLOSIGKEIT D. WELT BEI DEN MITTELALT. ARAB. PHILOSOPHEN : BGPHMA 3/4 / Worms, M – Muenster, 1900 – 2mf – 9 – ne Slangenburg [240]

DIE LEHRE VON DER EUCHARISTIE IN DEN DREI ERSTEN JAHRHUNDERTEN : HISTORISCH-THEOLOGISCHE ABHANDLUNG / Doellinger, Ignaz von – Mainz: in Commission bei Stenz, 1826. (Die Eucharistie in den drei ersten Jahrhunderten / dargestellt von Joh. Jos. Ign. Doellinger; 1. Abt.) – 1mf – us A.T.L.A. [240]

DIE LEHRE VON DER GEMEINSCHAFT DER HEILIGEN IM CHRISTL. ALTERTHUM : EINE DOGMENGESCHICHTLICHE STUDIE / Kirsch, Johann Peter – (Includes bibliographical references) – Mainz: Franz Kirchheim, 1900 – 1mf – 9 – 0-8370-6990-4 – 1986-0990 – us A.T.L.A. [240]

DIE LEHRE VON DER HARMONIK, MIT BEIGEFUSTAN NOTEBEISPIELEN / Hauptman, M – Leipzig: Breitkopf & Hartel, 1868 – 1 – us Sibley [780]

DIE LEHRE VON DER INNEREN MISSION / Wurster, Paul – (Includes bibliographical references and index) – Berlin: Reuther & Reichard, 1895 – 1mf – 9 – 0-8370-6552-6 – 1986-0552 – us A.T.L.A. [240]

DIE LEHRE VON DER KENOSE / Bensow, Oscar – Leipzig: A. Deichert, 1903. 1 fiche – 9 – us A.T.L.A. [240]

DIE LEHRE VON DER KIRCHE NACH DEM H. AUGUSTIN / Specht, Thomas – (Includes bibliographical references and indexes) – Paderborn: Ferdinand Schoeningh, 1892 – 1mf – 9 – 0-8370-6840-1 – 1986-0840 – us A.T.L.A. [240]

DIE LEHRE VON DER OFFENBARUNG : EIN BEITRAG ZUR PHILOSOPHIE DES CHRISTENTHUMS / Krauss, Alfred Ed – (Includes bibliographical references) – Gotha: Friedrich Andreas Perthes, 1868 – 1mf – 9 – 0-8370-3996-7 – 1985-1996 – us A.T.L.A. [240]
DIE LEHRE VON DER RECHTFERTIGUNG AUS DEM GLAUBEN IM KAMPFE DER GEGENWART : VORTRAG / Riggenbach, Eduard – (Includes bibliographical references) – Neukirchen: Erzeihungsverein, [1907] – 1mf – 9 – 0-8370-5278-5 – 1985-3278 – us A.T.L.A. [220]
DIE LEHRE VON DER STELLVERTRETENDEN GENUGTUUNG CHRISTI HISTORISCH-KRITISCH DARGESTELLT / Staab, Karl – Paderborn:Ferdinand Schoeningh, 1908 – 1mf – 9 – 0-8370-5432-X – 1985-3432 – us A.T.L.A. [240]
DIE LEHRE VON DER UEBERNATUERLICHEN GEBURT CHRISTI: CHRISTOLOGISCHE STUDIE / Lobstein, Paul – Freiburg i.B.: J.C.B. Mohr, 1896. 1 fiche – 9 – us A.T.L.A. [240]
DIE LEHRE VON DER UNFEHLBARKEIT DES PAPSTES AUS DER GESCHICHTE / Daniel, J – (Includes bibliographical references) – Hamburg: Wilhelm Jowien, [187-?] – 1mf – 9 – 0-8370-8733-3 – 1986-2733 – us A.T.L.A. [240]
DIE LEHRE VON DER VERSOEHNUNG / Bensow, Oscar – Guetersloh: C. Bertelsmann, 1904. 1 fiche – 9 – us A.T.L.A. [240]
DIE LEHRE VON DER WIEDERGEBURT AUF THEISTISCHER GRUNDLAGE : EIN BEITRAG ZUR ERNEUERUNG DER CHRISTLICHEN RELIGION / Andresen, Carl – 2. umgearb. Aufl. Hamburg: Lucas Graefe & Sillem, 1899 – 1mf – 9 – 0-8370-2508-7 – 1985-0508 – us A.T.L.A. [210]
DIE LEHRE VON DER ZWECKBESTIMMUNG DES MENSCHEN IM GRIECHISCH-ROEMISCHEN ALTERTUM UND IM JUEDISCHEN MITTELALTER / Heinemann, I – Breslau. 1926. BJ-33-9 1 – 9 – ne IDC [120]
DIE LEHREN DES BERGWERKSSTREIKES VOM MAI 1889 / Eschenbach, A – Berlin, 1889 – 1 – DM30.00 – gw Mikro Press [943]
DIE LEHREN DES JUDENTUMS NACH DEN QUELLEN : 1. TEIL: DIE GRUNDLAGEN DER JUEDISCHEN ETHIK / ed by Bernfield, Simon & Bamberger, F – 1996 – 2mf – 9 – DM62.00 – 3-8267-3199-9 – gw Hänsel [270]
DIE LEHREN DES JUDENTUMS NACH DEN QUELLEN : 2. TEIL: DIE SITTLICHEN PFLICHTEN DES EINZELNEN / ed by Bernfield, Simon & Bamberger, F – 1996 – 4mf – 9 – DM 90.00 – 3-8267-3200-6 – gw Hänsel [270]
DIE LEHREN DES JUDENTUMS NACH DEN QUELLEN : 3./4. TEIL IN EINEM BAND: 3. TEIL: DIE SITTLICHEN PFLICHTEN DER GEMEINSCHAFT. 4. TEIL. DIE LEHRE VON GOTT / ed by Bernfield, Simon & Bamberger, F – 1996 – 4mf – 9 – DM90.00 – 3-8267-3201-4 – gw Hänsel [270]
DIE LEHREN DES JUDENTUMS NACH DEN QUELLEN : 5. TEIL: JUDENTUM UND UMWELT / ed by Bernfield, Simon & Bamberger, F – 1996 – 6mf – 9 – DM118.00 – 3-8267-3202-2 – gw Hänsel [270]
DIE LEHRER DER MISCHNAH: IHR LEBEN UND WIRKEN / Braunschweiger, Moses – Frankfurt a.M.: J. Kauffmann, 1903. 1 fiche – 9 – us A.T.L.A. [240]
Lehrer, Harry Frederick *see* A MINISTRY OF MARRIAGE ENRICHMENT DESIGNED FOR CHURCH COUPLES
LEHRER ZWISCHEN KAISER UND FUEHRER : DER DEUTSCHE PHILOLOGENVERBAND IN DER WEIMARER REPUBLIK. EINE UNTERSUCHUNG ZUR SOZIALGESCHICHTE DER LEHRERORGANISATION / Hamburger, Franz – Heidelberg, 1974 – 4mf – 9 – DM90.00 – 3-89349-699-8 – gw Hänsel [060]
DIE LEHRERIN – (Cont by: Deutsche Lehrerinnenzeitung) – Berlin, 1917-19, 1924-26, 1928-34 – 4r – 1 – Dist. gw Mikrofilm – gw Misc Inst [370]
DIE LEHRERIN – Leipzig. v. 1-32. Oct 1884-11 Mar 1916. (Wanting v. 8; v. 10; v. 14; v. 20, no. 27-52; v. 26, no. 27-52; v. 32, no. 44-46) – 1 – 289.00 – us L of C Photodup [943]
LEHRERZEITUNG FUER WESTFALEN UND DIE RHEINPROVINZEN – Bielefeld, 1884, 1893-96 – 2r – 1 – Inquire at Mikrofilmarchiv for details – gw Misc Inst [370]
LEHREVALUATION ALS EINE MASSNAHME DER QUALITAETSSICHERUNG UND -VERBESSERUNG IN DER MEDIZINISCHEN AUSBILDUNG / Wilmer, Ruediger – 1994 – 3mf – DM98.00 – 3-89349-907-5 – gw Hänsel [370]
DAS LEHRGEDICHT DES KAREL VAN MANDER / Hoecker, R – (Quellenstudien zur hollaendischen kunstgeschichte. v. 8. Haag. 1916). BO-518f 1 – 9 – ne IDC [700]
Lehrman, Simon Maurice *see* THE JEWISH FESTIVALS
LEHRPLAN FUER DEN RELIGIONSUNTERRICHT UND DIE KINDERLEHRE DER EVANGELISCHEN KIRCHE DES KANTONS THURGAU – Frauenfeld: Lehrmittelverlag des evang Kirchenrates, 1907 – 1mf – 9 – 0-8370-7581-5 – 1986-1581 – us A.T.L.A. [370]
LEHRPLANGEBUNDENES UND LEHRPLANUNGSGEBUNDENES ERZAEHLEN IN KLASSE 1, UNTERSUCHT IM ZUSAMMENHANG MIT DER SOZIALEN SCHICHTUNG / Pausewang, Ute – 1994 – 3mf – DM98.00 – 3-89349-910-5 – gw Hänsel [370]
Lehr-Sptawinski, Tadeusz *see* GRAMATYKA HISTORYCZNA JEZYKA CZESKIEGO
DER LEHRSTUHL FUER RELIGIONSGESCHICHTE / Deissmann, Gustav Adolf – Berlin: Weidmann, 1914 – 1mf – us A.T.L.A. [240]
Lehuraux, Leon *see* BOU-SAADA, CITE DE BONHEUR
Lehuraux, Leon Joseph *see*
– LES FONDATEURS D'EMPIRE
– LAPERRINE LE SAHARIEN
– LE SAHARA; SES OASIS
– SUR LES PISTES DU DESERT
DER LEIB CHRISTI....EINE UNTERSUCHUNG ZUM URCHRISTLICHEN GEMEINDEGEDANKEN / Schmidt, Traugott – 1919 – 1 – us A.T.L.A. [240]
Leib, Fritz *see* ERZAEHLUNGSEINGAENGE IN DER DEUTSCHEN LITERATUR
Leibbrandt, H C V *see* [RESOLUSIES, 1655-1745, SERIES LM 2, 2A, 3, 4, 5, 7]
LEIBNIZ / Carr, Herbert Wildon – Boston: Little, Brown, and Co., 1929. vi,222p. With bibliog – 1 – us U.W. Library [190]
Leibniz *see* BREVIS DESIGNATIO MEDITATIONUM DE ORIGINIBUS GENTIUM
LEIBNIZ ET BOSSUET : ESSAI SUR LE PROTESTANTISME / Hugues, Edmond – Montauban: Victor Bertuot, 1871 – 1mf – us A.T.L.A. [240]
Leibniz, Gottfried Wilhelm von *see*
– ANNALES IMPERII OCCIDENTIS BRUNSVICENSES (768-1005)
– GESCHICHTLICHE AUFSAETZE UND GEDICHTE
– LEIBNIZ'S DEUTSCHE SCHRIFTEN
– LA MONADOLOGIE
– OPUSCULES ET FRAGMENTS INEDITES
LEIBNIZ-LEXICON, A DUAL CONCORDANCE TO LEIBNIZ'S PHILOSOPHISCHE SCHRIFTEN : TEIL 2: KONKORDANZ DES VOLLSTAENDIGEN VOKABULARS VOM TYP KEY-WORD-IN-CONTEXT / ed by Finster, Reinhard et al – (Part 1: Verzeichnis der Philosophischen Begriffe mit ausgewaehlten Stellen und ausfuehrlichem Kontext VII./4199 DM118.00) – Hildesheim, 1988 – 65mf – 3 – DM398.00 – gw Olms [100]
LEIBNIZ'S DEUTSCHE SCHRIFTEN / Leibniz, Gottfried Wilhelm von – Berlin: Veit und Comp., 1838-40. 2v. Includes bibliog. footnotes – 1 – us U.W. Library [190]
LEIBNIZ'S NEW ESSAYS CONCERNING THE HUMAN UNDERSTANDING : A CRITICAL EXPOSITION / Dewey, John – Chicago: S.C. Griggs, 1888 – 1mf – us A.T.L.A. [190]
Leibowitz, Arnold H *see* MEMORANDUM TO THE GUAM COMMISSION ON SELF-DETERMINATION
LEICESTER 1706-1891 – (Mf 1-3: Births 1706-1895. Mf 4-6: Birth Index 1725-1897. Mf 7-8: Intentions of Marriages 1722-1905. Mf 9-11: Intentions Index 1722-1905. Mf 12-13: Marriages 1726-1897. Mf 14-15: Marriage Index 1726-1897. Mf 16-17: Deaths 1729-1897. Mf 18-19: Death Index 1729-1897. Mf 20-34: General Records 1720-1787. Mf 35-37: Births & Deaths 1762-1843. Mf 38: Record of Births 1833-44. Mf 39-40: B,M,D 1843-51. Mf 41-44: Births 1851-91. Mf 45-47: Marriages 1851-91. Mf 48-51: Deaths 1851-91. Mf 52: B,M,D 1891-97) – (mf ed 1986) – 52mf – 9 – us Holbrook [920]
LEICESTER 1738-1849 – (Mf 1T: Marriages & Intentions 1722-46; Deaths 1741-87, 1808-30. Mf 1T-4T: Births 1716-87. Mf 1T-2T: Marriages & Intents 1744-87. Mf 4T-5T: Marriages & Intents 1787-1829. Mf 5T-7T: Births 1759-1849. Mf 7T: Deaths 1798-1839; Intentions 1828-49; Marriages 1823-44. Mf 8T: Births 1816-49; Deaths 1840-44. Mf 9T: Marriages & Deaths 1843-49) – (mf ed 1997) – 9mf – 9 – 0-87623-276-4 – us Holbrook [920]
LEICESTER CHRONICLE – England. -w. 6 Jan 1827-5 Jun 1915. (Wanting 1873). (65 reels) – 1 – uk British Libr Newspaper [072]
LEICESTER DAILY POST – England. -d. 1892-1915. (Wanting Jan-Apr 1897, Jan-Dec 1898, Jan-Dec 1911). (89 reels) – 1 – uk British Libr Newspaper [072]
Leicester. (Earls) *see* ESTATE RECORDS OF THE EARLS OF LEICESTER
LEICESTER JOURNAL – England. -w. 1829-52, 1890-1920. (30mqn reels) – 1 – uk British Libr Newspaper [072]
LEICESTER MERCURY – England.Jan-Oct 1950; Nov-Dec 1954; Jan-Feb 1955. -d.5 reels – 1 – uk British Libr Newspaper [072]
Leicester Secular Society *see* PAPERS
LEICESTERSHIRE, 1822 : BRITISH ISLES CENSUS DIRECTORIES PROJECT, ENGLAND – (In prep) – at Vine [941]
LEICESTERSHIRE, 1841 : BRITISH ISLES CENSUS DIRECTORIES PROJECT, ENGLAND. VOL 233 – 1mf – 9 – A$9.00 – at Vine [941]
LEICESTERSHIRE, 1848 : BRITISH ISLES CENSUS DIRECTORIES PROJECT, ENGLAND – at Vine [941]
LEICESTERSHIRE, 1850 : BRITISH ISLES CENSUS DIRECTORIES PROJECT, ENGLAND – at Vine [941]
LEICESTERSHIRE, 1854 : BRITISH ISLES CENSUS DIRECTORIES PROJECT, ENGLAND – at Vine [941]
LEICESTERSHIRE, 1877 : BRITISH ISLES CENSUS DIRECTORIES PROJECT, ENGLAND. VOL 36 – 10mf – 9 – A$63.00 – at Vine [941]
LEICESTERSHIRE, 1888 : BRITISH ISLES CENSUS DIRECTORIES PROJECT, ENGLAND – at Vine [941]
LEICESTERSHIRE, 1896 : BRITISH ISLES CENSUS DIRECTORIES PROJECT, ENGLAND – at Vine [941]
LEICESTERSHIRE, 1916 : BRITISH ISLES CENSUS DIRECTORIES PROJECT, ENGLAND – at Vine [941]
LEICESTERSHIRE, 1928 : BRITISH ISLES CENSUS DIRECTORIES PROJECT, ENGLAND – at Vine [941]
LEICESTERSHIRE (HINCKLEY AND LEICESTER), 1805 : BRITISH ISLES CENSUS DIRECTORIES PROJECT, ENGLAND. VOL 180 – 1mf – 9 – A$9.00 – at Vine [941]
LEICESTERSHIRE (LEICESTER), 1808 : BRITISH ISLES CENSUS DIRECTORIES PROJECT, ENGLAND – at Vine [941]
LEICESTERSHIRE MERCURY – Leicester. England. -w. 9 Jul 1836-24 Sep 1864. (11 reels) – 1 – uk British Libr Newspaper [072]
LEICESTERSHIRE (PIGOT'S), 1862 : BRITISH ISLES CENSUS DIRECTORIES PROJECT, ENGLAND. VOL 8 – 2mf – 9 – A$15.00 – at Vine [941]
LEICESTERSHIRE (WHITE'S), 1862 : BRITISH ISLES CENSUS DIRECTORIES PROJECT, ENGLAND. VOL 65 – 5mf – 9 – A$33.00 – at Vine [941]
Leich, J *see* LIBRI DUO DE CEREMONIIS AULAE BYZANTINAE (CBH 33)
LEI-CHOU FU-CHIH – 1811, 20, 1. BCH-634 2 – 8 – ne IDC [950]
DER LEICHTATHLET – Berlin, 1965-89 – 17r – 1 – Dist. gw Mikrofilm – gw Misc Inst [790]
LEICHTES LEHRBUCH DER HARMONIE, COMPOSITION UND DES GENERALBASSES, ZUM GEBRAUCHT FUR LIEBHABER DER MUSIK, ANGEHANDE UND FORTSCHREITENDE MUSICI UND COMPONISTEN... / Portmann, J G – Darmstadt: J J Wild, 1789 – 5 – us Sibley [780]
LEIDEN UND FREUDEN EINES SCHULMEISTERS / Gotthelf, Jeremias; ed by Baehler, Eduard – (Includes bibliographical references) – Erlenbach, Zuerich: E Rentsch. 2v. 1921 – 1 – us U.W. Library [830]
LEIDEN UND FREUDEN EINES SCHULMEISTERS / Gotthelf, Jeremias; ed by Vetter, Ferdinand – Bern: Schmid & Francke, 1898 – 1 – us U.W. Library [830]
DER LEIDENDE UND DER STERBENDE MESSIAS DER SYNAGOGE / Dalman, Gustaf – Berlin: H. Reuther, 1888. 1 fiche – 9 – us A.T.L.A. [240]
DER LEIDENDE UND DER STERBENDE MESSIAS DER SYNAGOGE IM ERSTEN NACHCHRISTLICHEN JAHRTAUSEND / Dalman, G H – Berlin, 1888 – 2mf – 8 – ne Slangenburg [270]
LEIERMANN UND FIEDELBOGEN : NEUE ERZAEHLUNGEN / Steguweit, Heinz – Wiesbaden: Deutsche Volksbuecher, 1941 – 1r – 1 – us U.W. Library [830]
Leiers, Bastian *see* KINDERZEICHNUNGEN
Leiers, Christoph *see* KLINISCH KONTROLLIERTE UNTERSUCHUNGEN ZUR EFFEKTIVITAET DER LOKALANAESTHETIKA ULTRACAIN 2% SUPRARENIN UND ULTRACAIN D-S IN DER KINDERZAHNHEILKUNDE
Leifchild, John *see*
– REMARKABLE FACTS
– REMARKABLE FACTS: ILLUSTRATIVE AND CONFIRMATORY OF...HOLY SCRIPTURE
Leifer, M *see*
– NATIONALISM, REVOLUTION AND EVOLUTION IN SOUTH-EAST ASIA
– THE PHILIPPINE CLAIM TO SABAH
LEIFUR – (In Icelandic) – Canada, 1883-86 – 1r – 1 – cn Commonwealth Micro [072]
Leigh, John G *see* THE SAMOAN CRISES AND ITS CAUSES
LEIGH WORLD – Leigh, NE. -w. Dec 1892; Nov 1895-Oct 1896, scattered issues missing; Aug 1897-Sept 1903; May 1908 to date – 1 – us NE Hist [071]
LEIGHTON BUZZARD OBSERVER & LINSLADE GAZETTE – England. -w. 1 Jan 1861; 10 March 1863-Dec 1889. 15 reels – 1 – uk British Libr Newspaper [072]
LEIGHTON COURT / Kingsley, Henry – British Fiction Archive: Unit 2 – 9 – uk Bell [830]
Leighton, John *see* THE JEWISH ALTAR
Leighton, Joseph Alexander *see* TYPICAL MODERN CONCEPTIONS OF GOD
Leighton, Robert Fowler *see* A HISTORY OF ROME. AMPLY ILLUSTRATED WITH MAPS, PLANS, AND ENGRAVINGS
Leighton, W A *see*
– THE BRITISH SPECIES OF ANGIOCARPUS LICHENS ELUCIDATED BY THEIR SPORIDIA
– THE LICHEN-FLORA OF GREAT-BRITAIN, IRELAND AND THE CHANNEL ISLANDS
– THE LICHENS OF CEYLON
LEILA ADA, THE JEWISH CONVERT : AN AUTHENTIC MEMOIR / Heighway, Osborn W Trenery – Philadelphia: Presbyterian Board of Publ, c1853 – 1mf – 9 – 0-8370-6262-4 – 1986-0262 – us A.T.L.A. [920]
Leimbach, Carl L *see*
– BEITRAEGE ZUR ABENDMAHLSLEHRE TERTULLIANS
– DAS PAPIASFRAGMENT
Leimbach, W *see* LANDESKUNDE VON TUWA
Leimdoerfer, David *see*
– DAS HEILIGE SCHRIFTWERK KOHELET IM LICHTE DER GESCHICHTE
– DER "PREDIGER SALMONIS" IN HISTORISCHER BELEUCHTUNG
Leimena, Johannes *see* THE DUTCH-INDONESIAN CONFLICT
Leineweber, Clemens Heinrich *see* LIEBE UND TOD
LEINSTER EXPRESS – Port Laoighise, Ireland. -w. Sept 1831-Dec 1871. 25 1 2 reels – 1 – uk British Libr Newspaper [072]
LEINSTER INDEPENDENT – Maryborough. Ireland. -w. 20 Dec 1834-26 Dec 1835, 9 Jul 1836-4 May 1839, 7 Oct 1839-18 Apr 1840. (2 reels) – 1 – uk British Libr Newspaper [072]
LEINSTER REFORMER – Carlow. Ireland. -sw. 12 Oct 1839-17 Jul 1841. (2 reels) – 1 – uk British Libr Newspaper [072]
Leinz, Anton *see* ANSPRACHEN FUER CHRISTLICHE MUETTERVEREINE
Leip, Hans *see*
– DIE BERGUNG
– DIE BLONDJAEGER
– LILIENCRON
– DAS MUSCHELHORN
– DER WIDERSCHEIN
Leipart, Theodor *see* DIE ARBEIT
Leipelt, Detlef *see* VERWENDUNG VON EINSTELLUNGSKONZEPTEN IN DER MARKTFORSCHUNG
Leipoldt, J *see* DER KOPTISCHE TEXT DER KIRCHENORDNUNG HIPPOLYTS (T.U.U. 5-58)

Leipoldt, Johannes *see*
- DIDYMUS DER BLINDE VON ALEXANDRIA
- DIDYMUS, DER BLINDE VON ALEXANDRIA (T.U.U. 2-29/3)
- DAS EVANGELIUM NACH THOMAS (T.U.U. 5-101)
- SAIDISCHE AUSZUEGE AUS DEM 8. BUCHE DER APOSTOLISCHEN KONSTITUTIONEN (T.U.U. 2-26/1B)
- SCHENUTE VON ATRIPE UND DIE ENTSTEHUNG DES NATIONAL AEGYPTISCHEN CHRISTENTUMS
- SCHENUTE VON ATRIPE UND DIE ENTSTEHUNG DES NATIONAL AEGYPTISCHEN CHRISTENTUMS (T.U.U. 2-25/1)

LEIPZIG 1813 : AUS DEN AKTEN DES KRIEGSARCHIVS DES GROSSEN GENERALSTABES, DES GEHEIMEN STAATSARCHIVS IN BERLIN,... / Pflugk-Harttung, J von – Gotha, 1913 – 6mf – 9 – ne IDC [943]

Leipzig. Hansetage. Hanserecesse *see* DIE RECESSE UND ANDERE AKTEN DER HANSETAGE, 1256-1430

LEIPZIGER FAERBER ZEITUNG – Leipzig, Germany. 1 Dec 1899-Nov 1909 – 5r – 1 – gw Mikrofilm [072]

LEIPZIGER LEHRERZEITUNG – Leipzig, 1916; 1920-21; 1923 – 4r – 1 – gw Mikrofilm [072]

LEIPZIGER LOCOMOTIVE – Leipzig, DE. 1843; Jul-Sep 1848 – 1 – gw Mikrofilm [072]

LEIPZIGER MONATSSCHRIFT FUER TEXTIL-INDUSTRIE – Leipzig, Germany. 1900-09 – 7,5r – 1 – gw Mikrofilm [072]

LEIPZIGER NEUESTE NACHRICHTEN UND HANDELSZEITUNG – Leipzig, Germany. 1918 – 2r – 1 – gw Mikrofilm [072]

DER LEIPZIGER PAPYRUSFRAGMENTE DER PSALMEN / ed by Heinrici, Carl Friedrich Georg – (Text in Greek. Discussion in German and Greek. Includes bibliographical references) – Leipzig: Duerr, 1903 – 1mf – 9 – 1986-3244 – us A.T.L.A. [220]

LEIPZIGER TAGEBLATT – Leipzig, Germany. -d. 1 Sept 1916-6 Aug 1919. Imperfect. 13 reels – 1 – uk British Libr Newspaper [072]

LEIPZIGER VOLKSHALLE – Leipzig, aug 27-dec 21 1850 – 1r – 1 – gw Mikrofilm [072]

LEIPZIGER VOLKSZEITUNG – (1947 1r DM75.00) – Leipzig, 1902-Mar 1927; Jan-Dec 1932 – 84r – 1 – DM6,300.00 – gw Mikro Press [072]

LEIPZIGER VOLKSZEITUNG – (Also Bereichsausgaben available: ALTENBURG, apr 1 1958-oct 31 1961, 1967-dec 25 1969, nur Kreisseiten; ALTENBURG, Osterlaender Volkszeitung: fuer die Kreise Altenburg und Schmoelln, 1993- ; BORNA/GEITHAIN, apr 1 1958-oct 27 1961, 1967-oct 15 1969 (incomplete), nur Kreisseiten; BORNA/ GEITHAIN, 1993-may 1996; BORNA, may 11 1996- ; DELITZSCH, apr 1 1958-oct 31 1961, apr 6 1965-feb 1 1970, nur Kreisseiten; DELITZSCH, 1993- ; DOEBELN, apr 1 1958-oct 31 1961, may 13 1962-63, feb 14 1967-jan 21 1970 (incomplete), nur Kreisseiten; EILENBURG, apr 1 1958-oct 31 1961, jan 9-oct 6 1963, feb 8 1967-aug 21 1969 (incomplete), nur Kreisseiten; EILENBURG, 1993- ; GEITHAIN, apr 1 1958-oct 31 1961, may 7 1967-dec 18 1969 (incomplete), nur Kreisseiten; GEITHAIN, may 11 1996- ; GRIMMA, apr 1 1958-oct 31 1961, feb 12 1967-nov 15 1969 (incomplete), nur Kreisseiten; GRIMMA, 1993- ; LEIPZIG-LAND, mar 11 1958-oct 31 1961, jun 3 1966-dec 18 1969 (incomplete), nur Kreisseiten; OSCHATZ, apr 4 1958-oct 31 1961, mar 24-nov 28 1963, feb 2-dec 8 1964, feb 7-sep 12 1965, mar 29-nov 18 1966, mar 15-dec 19 1967, feb 2-nov 15 1968, feb 5-oct 24 1969, nur Kreisseiten; SCHMOELLN, apr 1 1958-oct 28 1961, mar 17 1966-feb 28 1970, nur Kreisseiten; TORGAU, apr 1 1958-mar 31 1970 (incomplete), nur Kreisseiten; WURZEN, apr 2 1958-oct 31 1961, apr 1 1962-dec 18 1969 (incomplete), nur Kreisseiten; WURZEN, 1993-) – Leipzig, 1947, 1951- – 1 – Inquire at Mikrofilmarchiv for details – gw Misc Inst [072]

LEIPZIGER VOLKSZEITUNG – Leipzig, Germany. 1992- – 7r per yr – 1 – gw Mikrofilm [072]

LEIPZIGER VOLKSZEITUNG – Leipzig, Germany. Aug 1899-Dec 1900; 1962-Jun 1976 – 58r – 1 – us L of C Photodup [072]

LEIPZIGER VOLKSZEITUNG – Leipzig, Germany. May 1919-1923 – 1 – us Res Libr [072]

LEIPZIGER VOLKSZEITUNG – Leipzig. July 1914-June 1919. Missing: scattered issues – 1 – 35.00r – us Hoover Inst Photo [073]

LEIPZIGER ZEITUNG *see* LEIPZIGER ZEITUNGEN

LEIPZIGER ZEITUNGEN – (Title change: Leipziger Zeitung, 1810) – Leipzig, Germany. 1735; 1749-50, (incomplete); 1760 (incomplete); 1789 (incomplete), 1860 (incomplete) – 1r – 1 – gw Mikrofilm [072]

Leiris, Michel *see* L'AFRIQUE FANTOME

Leis, Hans J *see* THE EFFECTS OF TWO INSTRUCTIONAL CONDITIONS ON SPORT SKILL SPECIFIC ANALYTIC PROFICIENCY OF PHYSICAL EDUCATION MAJORS

LEISE BESCHWOERUNG : GEDICHTE / Granau, Johannes – Stuttgart: J Engelhorns Nachf. A Spemann, 1943 – 1r – 1 – us U.W. Library [810]

Leisenring, Jacob Shindel *see* LEISENRING'S BOOK OF FORMS

LEISENRING'S BOOK OF FORMS / Leisenring, Jacob Shindel – Philadelphia, Murphy, 1885. 1039 p. LL-288 – 1 – us L of C Photodup [340]

Leisler, J P A *see* NACHTRAEGE ZU BECHSTEINS NATURGESCHICHTE DEUTSCHLANDS

Leisring, V *see* BREVIARIUM ARTIS MUSICES

LEISTON OBSERVER – England. 1978-81. -w. 8 reels – 1 – uk British Libr Newspaper [072]

LEISURABILITY – v.1-. 1974-. Continued by Journal of Leisurability – 1 – us UMI [073]

THE LEISURE ACTIVITY SELECTION PROCESS : THE ROLE OF ACTIVITY AS AN ATTRACTOR / Gordon, William N & Lundegren, Herberta M – 1991 – 3mf – 9 – $12.00 – us Microform Publ [790]

LEISURE BEHAVIOR OF LESBIANS IN RELATION TO ALCOHOL CONSUMPTION / Lute, Linda K & Lundegren, Herberta M – 1992 – 1mf – 9 – $4.00 – us Microform Publ [790]

LEISURE PARTICIPATION AMONG INDIVIDUALS WITH TRAUMATIC BRAIN INJURY FOLLOWING DISCHARGE FROM A TRANSITIONAL FACILITY / Potter, Jacqueline S & Smith, Ralph W – 1992 – 2mf – 9 – $8.00 – us Microform Publ [790]

LEISURE PREFERENCE PATTERNS OF SECOND-GENERATION JAPANESE-AMERICANS OF SELECTED CITIES IN THE UNITED STATES / Ego, Michael M – 1980 – 3mf – 9 – $12.00 – us Microform Publ [790]

LEISURE SCIENCES – v. 1-. 1977- – 1,5,6,9 – us UMI [150]

LEISURE SOCIALIZATION AND ADULT AND CHILD RELATED DECISION-MAKING INTERACTIONS IN FAMILY RECREATIONAL ACTIVITIES / Yoshioka, Carlton F – 1981 – 2mf – 9 – $8.00 – us Microform Publ [306]

LEISURE STUDIES: THE JOURNAL OF THE LEISURE STUDIES ASSOCIATION – v1-. 1982- – 1,5,6,9 – us UMI [073]

LEISURE WORLD NEWS – Orange Co, CA. 1993 – 8+ r – 1 – $400.00 ($200.00y) – R04080 – us Library Micro [071]

Leitch, John *see* MAN TO MAN, THE STORY OF INDUSTRIAL DEMOCRACY

LEITCHFIELD FIRST BAPTIST CHURCH. LEITCHFIELD, KENTUCKY : CHURCH RECORDS – 1804-1959. 1227p – 1 – 55.22 – us Baptist [240]

Leite, N *see* L'ART RUPESTRE DE LA LAPA DO VEADO, JANUARIA, MONTALVANIA, BRESIL

Leite, Serafin *see* HISTORIA DELA COMPANIA DE JESUS NO BRASIL...

Leiteizen, G D *see* BOL'SHEVIKI, MEN'SHEVIKI I REVOLIUTSIONNAIA SOTSIAL-DEMOKRATIIA

LEITFADEN DER DEUTSCHEN LITERATURGESCHICHTE / Podlech, Alfred – (Includes bibliographical references and index) – Koeln-Braunsfeld: R Mueller, 1952 – 1r – 1 – us U.W. Library [430]

LEITFADEN DER DOGMATIK : ZUM GEBRAUCH BEI AKADEMISCHEN VORLESUNGEN / Heim, Karl – Halle a.S.: M. Niemeyer, 1912 – 1mf – us A.T.L.A. [240]

LEITFADEN DER INNEREN MISSION : ZUNAECHST FUER DEN BERUFSUNTERRICHT IN BRUEDER-, DIAKONEN- UND DIAKONISSEN-ANSTALTEN / Schaefer, Theodor – 2. verm u verb Aufl. Hamburg: Agentur des Rauhen Hauses, 1889 – 1mf – 9 – 0-8370-6513-5 – 1986-0513 – us A.T.L.A. [240]

LEITFADEN DER METRIK DER HEBRAEISCHEN POESIE: NEBST DEM ERSTEN BUCHE DER PSALMEN / Ley, Julius – Halle a.S.: Waisenhauses, 1887. 1 fiche – 9 – us A.T.L.A. [470]

LEITFADEN ZUM STUDIUM DER DOGMENGESCHICHTE / Loofs, Friedrich – Halle a.S.: M. Niemeyer, 1906 – 3mf – us A.T.L.A. [240]

LEITFADEN ZUM UNTERRICHT IM ALTEN TESTAMENT FUER HOEHERE SCHULEN / Koestlin, Friedrich – Frieburg i.B.: J.C.B. Mohr, 1894. 1 fiche – 9 – us A.T.L.A. [240]

LEITFADEN ZUM UNTERRICHT IM NEUEN TESTAMENT FUER HOEHERE SCHULEN / Koestlin, Friedrich – Freiburg i.B.: J.C.B. Mohr, 1893. 1 fiche – 9 – us A.T.L.A. [240]

Leitgeb, Josef *see* KINDERLEGENDE

Leith *see* CENSUS OF THE ISLAND OF BOMBAY

LEITH BURTH'S PILOT – England.1900-02. -w. 3 reels – 1 – uk British Libr Newspaper [072]

Leith, Scotland *see* MONUMENTAL INSCRIPTIONS

Leith-Ross, Sylvia *see*
- AFRICAN CONVERSATION-PIECE
- A FULANI GRAMMAR

LEITMERITZER TAGBLATT *see* DEUTSCHE ZEITUNG FUER DEN LEITMERITZER KREIS

LEITMERITZER ZEITUNG – Leitmeritz (Litomerice), Germany. 17 Nov 1922-30 Okt 1933 – 6r – 1 – gw Mikrofilm [072]

LEITMERITZER ZEITUNG – Litomerice, Czechoslovakia. Dec 1937-Oct 1938 (incomplete) – 1r – 1 – us L of C Photodup [072]

Leitnekker, E E *see* ANNOTIROVANNOE OPISANIE PISEM A.P. CHEKHOVU

Leitner, Franz *see* DER GOTTESDIENSTLICHE VOLKSGESANG IM JUEDISCHEN UND CHRISTLICHEN ALTERTUM

Leitner, Franz Xaver *see* DER HL. THOMAS VON AQUIN UEBER DAS UNFEHLBARE LEHRAMT DES PAPSTES

LEITRIM GAZETTE – Mohill, Ireland.1858-65; 4 Jan 1866-26 Sept 1867. -w.5 reels – 1 – uk British Libr Newspaper [072]

Leitrim, Ireland *see* LEITRIM OBSERVER

LEITRIM JOURNAL / Carrick-on-Shannon, Ireland – -w. Oct 1850-1868; 1870-72 – 712r – 1 – uk British Libr Newspaper [072]

LEITRIM OBSERVER / Carrick-on-Shannon, Ireland – 2 Jan 1904-6 Nov 1920. -w. 9mqn reels – 1 – uk British Libr Newspaper [072]

LEITRIM OBSERVER / Leitrim, Ireland – 1923-35 – 1 – ie Microforms [072]

LEITRUM AND LONGFORD ADVERTISER. (LEITRUM ADVERTISER) – Mohill, Ireland. Oct 1867-1916.-w. 17 reels – 1 – uk British Libr Newspaper [072]

Leitzmann, Albert *see*
- BRIEFE VON WILHELM VON HUMBOLDT AN FRIEDRICH HEINRICH JACOBI
- GOETHES ROEMISCHE ELEGIEN
- LICHTENBERGS BRIEFE AN JOHANN FRIEDRICH BLUMENBACH
- WILHELM VON HUMBOLDT
- WILHELM VON HUMBOLDTS BRIEFE AN KARL GUSTAV BRINKMANN
- WILHELM VON HUMBOLDTS SONNETTDICHTUNG

Leixner-Gruenberg, Otto von *see* ILLUSTRIERTE GESCHICHTE DES DEUTSCHEN SCHRIFTTHUMS IN VOLKSTHUEMLICHER DARSTELLUNG

Leizaola, Jesus Maria de *see* INCONTROVERTIBLE FACTS REGARDING THE DESTRUCTION OF GUERNICA: SPEECH

Lejamble, Georges *see* LE FOKONOLONA ET LE POUVOIR

Lejarza, Fidel de *see*
- BARRADO MANZANO, P. ARCANGEL O.F.M. LAS MISIONES FRANCISCANAS EN BOLIVIA CONFERENCIAS...
- FRANCISCANISMO DE CORTES Y CORTESANISMO DE LOS FRANCISCANOS

Lejean, Guillaume M *see*
- THEODORE 2, LE NOUVEL EMPIRE D'ABYSSINIE ET LES INTERETS FRANCAIS DANS LE SUD DE LA MER ROUGE
- VOYAGE AUX DEUX NILS EXECUTE DE 1860 A 1864 PAR ORDRE DE L'EMPEREUR
- VOYAGE EN ABYSSINIE EXECUTE DE 1862 A 1864

Lejeune *see* CLOVIS, POEME HEROI-COMIQUE AVEC DES REMARQUES HISTORIQUES ET CRITIQUES

LEKAH TOV – Prague. 1604. Cowley. BJ-43-39 1 – 9 – ne IDC [270]

LEKAR OCH SPEL – 1962 – 1 – us I.U. Libraries [390]

Lekhela, E P *see* A SURVEY OF THE DEVELOPMENT OF EDUCATION AMONG THE BATSWANA OF BOPHUTHATSWANA

Lekhela, Ernest Plaelo *see* THE DEVELOPMENT OF BANTU EDUCATION IN THE NORTH-WESTERN CAPE, 1840-1947

LE-KOROT HA-GEZEIROT BE-YISRA'-EL / Gurland, J – v. 1-8. Odessa. Krakau. 1886-92. BJ-290-17 1 – 9 – ne IDC [956]

LEKSIKON ROSSIISKOI, ISTORICHESKOI, GEOGRAFICHESKOI POLITICHESKOI I GRAZHDANSKOI / Tatishchev, V N – N.p., 1793. 3 vols – 13mf – 9 – R-8004/2 – ne IDC [460]

LEKSIKON SLAVENO-ROSSIISKII / Berynda, P – 2nd ed. Kutenskii monastyr. 1653. R-8383/2 – 5mf – 8 – ne IDC [460]

LEKSIKON TREIAZYCHNYI / Polikarpov, F – M., 1704 – 12mf – 9 – 453/2 – ne IDC [460]

LEKTSII PO GERENU O POLITIKE, SVIAZI I TORGOVLE GLAVNYKH NARODOV DREVNIAGO MIRA / Pogodin, M P – v. 1-2. M. 1835-36. BR-8311 2 – 8 – ne IDC [947]

LEKTSII PO ISOTRII FILOSOFII PRAVA / Turbetskoi, E N – M. 1907. BR-5793 2 – 8 – ne IDC [100]

LEKTSII PO SLAVIANO-RUSSKOI PALEOGRAFII, CHITANNYE V MOSKOVSKOM ARKHEOLOGICHESKOM INSTITUTE V 1908, 1909 I 1910 GG / Brandt, R F – Moscow, 1910. BR-10,316/1 – 9 – ne IDC [930]

Leland, Charles G *see* SUNSHINE IN THOUGHT

Leland, John *see* BOOKS AND PAMPHLETS BY OR ABOUT JOHN LELAND

Lelevich, G *see*
- GIPPOKRATOVO LITSO
- PO ZHURNALNYM OKOPAM
- VIA BRIUSOV

Lelievre, Julien *see* L'ENFANCE DIFFICILE, VICIEUSE OU DELINQUANTE ET L'ASSISTANCE PUBLIQUE DEPARTEMENTALE

Lelong, M H *see* LA LIBERIA INTIME

Lemaire, C *see* LE JARDIN FLEURISTE,...

Lemaire, C A *see*
- CACTEARUM GENERA NOVA SPECIESQUE NOVAE ET OMNIUM IN HORTO MONVILLIANO CULTARUM
- HERBIER GENERALE DE L'AMATEUR

Lemaire, Charles Francois Alexandre *see*
- AU CONGO
- VOYAGE AU CONGO

Lemaire, Ghyslaine *see* BIO-BIBLIOGRAPHIE ANALYTIQUE DE MONSIEUR HERVE BIRON, REDACTEUR EN CHEF AU JOURNAL LE NOUVELLISTE DES TROIS-RIVIERES, PRESIDENT DE LA SOCIETE D'HISTOIRE REGIONALE DES TROIS-RIVIERES

Lemaitre, Francois *see*
- GAZETTE PATRIOTIQUE
- LA SENTINELLE

Lemaitre, Jules *see* IMPRESSIONS DE THEATRE

Lemaitre, N *see* USSEL ET SON PAYS

LeMare, E *see*
- ROMEO ET JULIETTE, OVERTURE-FANTASIE
- [TRISTAN UND ISOLDE]. EINLEITUNG, ARRANGED FOR ORGAN BY E. LEMARE

LeMare, E H *see*
- AN DEN FRUHLING, OP. 43, NO. 6
- PEER GYNT NO. 1, OP. 46

Lemare, E H *see* MINUET IN A, TRANSCRIBED FOR THE ORGAN BY E.H. LEMARE

LeMare, Edwin *see* DANSE MACABRE

Lemare, P A *see* COURS DE LANGUE FRANCAISE

Lemarignier, J -F *see* ETUDE SUR LES PRIVILEGES D'EXEMPTION ET DE JURISDICTION ECCLESIASTIQUES DES ABBAYES NORMANDES

Lemau de la Jaisse, Pierre *see* CARTE GENERALE DE LA MONARCHIE FRANCOISE, CONTENANT L'HISTOIRE MILITAIRE, DEPUIS CLOVIS...JUSQU'A...LOUIS 15

Lemay, Clotilde *see* BIBLIOGRAPHIE ANALYTIQUE DE MAXINE, MEMBRE DE LA SOCIETE DES ECRIVAINS CANADIENS ET DE LA SOCIETE DES ECRIVAINS POUR LA JEUNESSE
Lemay, Leona *see* BIBLIOGRAPHIE ANALYTIQUE DE LA GENEALOGIE DANS LES COMTES DE SAINT-MAURICE, MASKINONGE, CHAMPLAIN
LeMay, Pamphile *see* LEON-PAMPHILE LE MAY ET SON OEUVRE
LeMayre, Marten *see* THE DUTCH SCHOOLE MASTER
LEMBAGA BAHASA INDONESIA. ISTILAH BAHASA INDONESIA. DIOESAHAKAN OLEH LEMBAGA BAHASA INDONESIA – Medan, Tokaigansyu Seityo, 2604. 5, 84p – 98mf – 9 – ne IDC [490]
Lembaga Da' wah Mahasiswa Islam (HMI) Djaja *see* API
LEMBAGA HIDUP / Amrullah, Abdul Malik Karim – SE-5292 1. 1955 – 9 – ne IDC [950]
LEMBAGA PENJELIDIKAN MASALAH BANGUNAN : ABSTRACTS SERVICE; MADJALAH BULANAN: BAGIAN DOKUMENTASI / Bandung, Indonesia – (Irregular. Missing: 1966(1-5,8,10,13-15); 1967(17-19); 1968(33,36); 1970(52-53)) – Bandung, 1966-1972(2) – 26mf – 9 – SE-1327/1 – ne IDC [950]
Lembeye, J *see* AVES DE LA ISLA DE CUBA
LEMBRANCA DA COMMEMORACAO CIVICA, PROMOVIDA NO 8 ANNIVERSARIO DO FALLECIMENTO DO MARECHAL FLORIANO PEIXOTO, PELA REDACCAO DO COMMERCIO DO AMAZONAS – [s.l.] 29 Jun 1903 – 1,5,6 – bl Biblioteca [072]
Lemen, Frank B *see* HISTORY OF THE LEMEN FAMILY OF ILLINOIS, VIRGINIA, AND ELSEWHERE, 1656-1898
Lemercier *see*
- AGAMEMNON
- CHRISTOPHE COLOMB
- ISULE ET OROVESE
- OPHIS
- PINTO OU LA JOURNEE D'UNE CONSPIRATION

LeMercier de La Riviere *see* DE L'INSTRUCTION PUBLIQUE OU CONSIDERATIONS MORALES ET POLITIQUES SUR LA NECESSITE, LA NATURE ET LA SOURCE DE CETTE INSTRUCTION
Lemercier, G *see* MONACHISME LAIQUE
Lemercier, Nepomucene *see*
- L'ATLANTIADE OU LA THEOGONIE NEWTONIENNE: POEME EN SIX CHANTS
- HEROLOGUES OU CHANTS DES POETES ROIS ET L'HOMME RENOUVELE, RECIT MORAL EN VERS
- LA MEROVEIDE OU LES CHAMPS CATALAUNIQUES: POEME
- LA PANHYPOCRISIADE OU LE SPECTACLE INFERNAL DE SEIZIEME SIECLE. SUITE DE LA PANHYPOCRISIADE OU LE SPECTACLE INFERNAL DU DIX-NEUVIEME SIECLE
- SUITE DE LA PANHYPOCRISIADE OU LE SPECTACLE INFERNAL DU DIX-NEUVIEME SIECLE

Lemery, Nicolas *see*
- COURS DE CHYMIE CONTENANT LA MANIERE DE FAIRE LES OPERATIONS
- TRAITE DE L'ANTIMOINE CONTENANT L'ANALYSE CHYMIQUE

Lemierre, D'Argy *see* CALAS OU LE FANATISME
Lemieux, Francois Xavier *see* DEBAT SUR L'ADRESSE, NOVEMBRE 1896-DISCOURS DE M.F.X. LEMIEUX
Lemire, J *see* LE CARDINAL MANNING ET SON ACTION SOCIALE
Lemke, M K *see*
- EPOKHA TSENZURNYKH REFORM 1859-1865 GODOV
- OCHERKI OSVOBODITELNAGO DVIZHENIIA "SHETSTIDESIATYKH GODOV"
- POCHEMU OSNOVANO VSEROSSIISKOE OBSHCHESTVO KNIZHNAGO DELA

LEMKO (PHILADELPHIA, PA.) – (Includes c.1: 1932:July 21-Aug.25, Sept.15-Oct.6, 27-1933:Oct.19; 1933:Nov.2, 16) – Philadelphia, Pa.: Lemko's Committee/Lemko Association of the United States and Canada, 1928-1940 – 1 – CSUXAHZ5919-S – us Hoover Inst Photo [947]
Lemley, John *see* WOMEN IN WHITE RAIMENT
Lemley, T R *see* A COMPARISON OF TWO INTERMITTENT EXTERNAL COMPRESSION DEVICES ON PITTING ANKLE EDEMA
Lemly, Samuel Conrad *see* NAVAL SUMMARY COURTS-MARTIAL
Lemm, O von *see*
- KLEINE KOPTISCHE STUDIEN 1-58
- KOPTISCHE MISCELLEN, 1-148

Lemme, Ludwig *see*
- HEILSTHATSACHEN UND GLAUBENSERFAHRUNG
- DIE RELIGIONSGESCHICHTLICHE BEDEUTUNG DES DEKALOGS

Lemoine, Albert J F *see* L'ALIENE DEVANT LA PHILOSOPHIE, LA MORALE ET LA SOCIETE
Lemoine, Charles Amedee *see* DES VOIES D'EXECUTION DES JUGEMENTS A ROME
Lemoine Moniere, Jean A *see* LIVRE DE COMPTE OU JOURNAL D'UN MARCHAND DE VILLE-MARIE, JEAN-ALEXIS LEMOINE MONIERE, DU 27 JUIN 1739 AU 8 JANVIER 1751
LEMOND PRESS – Alberta, CN. 1916-28 – 2r – 1 – cn Commonwealth Micro [072]
Lemonnier, Charles *see* QUEL BUT SE PROPOSENT LES SAINT-SIMONIENS?
Lemonnier, Leon *see* LA FEMME SANS PECHE
LEMOORE ADVANCE – Lemoore, CA. 1971- – 20+ r – 1 – $1,000.00 ($50.00y) – B02341 – us Library Micro [071]
Lempriere, John *see* UNIVERSAL BIOGRAPHY: CONTAINING A COPIOUS ACCOUNT, CRITICAL AND HISTORICAL, OF THE LIFE AND CHARACTER, LABORS AND ACTIONS OF EMINENT PERSONS, IN ALL AGES AND COUNTRIES, CONDITIONS AND PROFESSIONS.
LEMUEL SHAW PAPERS, 1648-1923 / Shaw, Lemuel – (Influential state jurist (1781-1861). Includes background material on Herman Melville, Shaw's son-in-law) – Massachusetts Historical Society – 65r – 1 – $4950.00 – us UMI [920]
LEMUR: MARS-AVRIL-MAI 1871 / Montegut, Maurice – Paris: E. Dentu, 1892. 421p. 5 fiches. (Literature Collection) – 9 – $12.00 – fr Bibl Nationale [944]
Lemus y Rubio, Pedro *see* ELEMENTOS... GRAMATICA CASTELLANA
LENA ELLERBROK : EN PLATTDUETSCH STUECKSCHEN UT OLE TIEDEN / Trede, Paul – 2. Opl. Garding: H Luehr & Dircks, 1916 – 1r – 1 – us U.W. Library [430]
Lena, P *see* TRANSFORMATION DE L'ESPACE RURAL DANS LE FRONT PIONNIER DU SUD-OUEST IVOIRIEN
Lenain De Tillemont, LS *see*
- HISTOIRE DES EMPEREURS ET DES AUTRES PRINCES QUI ONT REGNE DURANT LES SIX PREMIERS SIECLES DE L'EGLISE
- MEMOIRES POUR SERVIR A L'HISTOIRE ECCLESIASTIQUE DES SIX PREMIERS SIECLES

Lenard, Philipp Eduard Anton *see* IDEELLE KONTINENTALSPERRE
LENAU / Greiner, Leo – Berlin: Schuster & Loeffler, [1904] – 1r – 1 – us U.W. Library [920]
LENAU IN SCHWABEN : AUS DEM LETZTEN JAHRZEHNT SEINES LEBENS / Niendorf, Emma – 2. billige Ausg. Leipzig: F L Herbig, 1855 – 1r – 1 – us U.W. Library [920]
Lenau, Nikolaus *see*
- GEDICHTE
- NIKOLAUS LENAUS SAEMTLICHE WERKE IN ZWEI BAENDEN

LENAU UND DIE FAMILIE LOEWENTHAL : BRIEFE UND GESPRAECHE, GEDICHTE UND ENTWUERFE / ed by Castle, Eduard – (Includes bibliographical references) – Leipzig: M Hesse, 1906 – 1 – us U.W. Library [430]
LENAUS LEBEN : GROSSENTHEILS AUS DES DICHTERS EIGENEN BRIEFEN / Schurz, Anton Xaver – Stuttgart: J G Cotta, 1855 – 1r – 1 – us U.W. Library [920]
Lenclud, G *see* AGRICULTEURS (INTEGRAUX) SUR BRULIS EN ASIE DU SUD-EST
LEND A HAND – 1-18 2+2 (all publ). 1886-1897 – 107mf – 9 – $370.00 – us UPA [360]
LE LENDEMAIN – ou Esprit des feuilles de la veille. Paris. oct 1790-juin 1791 – 1 – fr A.C.R.P.P. [073]
Lenders, Britta *see* DIE KULTUR DES MANAGEMENTS IM KULTURMANAGEMENT
LENDLEASE ACTIVITIES IN THE CARIBBEAN DEFENSE COMMAND / U.S. Army. Caribbean Defense Command. Historical Section – Cap't. Cecil L. Munden. New Orleans. 1947. 222 p. 1 reel – 1 – 18.00 – us L of C Photodup [977]
Lenepveu, Veronique *see* ELEMENTS POUR UNE ETUDE DU SYSTEME ADVERBIAL DU FRANCAIS CONTEMPORAIN
Leneveu, Georges *see* LA SAPE: DRAME SOCIAL EN TROIS ACTES
Lenfant, Davidis *see* CONCORDANTIAE AUGUSTINIANAE
Lenglart, J *see* LES ZONES D'ACTIONS PRIORITAIRES INTEGREES (ZAPIS) DE L'EST CAMEROUN
Lenglet Du Fresnoy, Nicolas *see* HISTOIRE DE LA PHILOSOPHIE HERMETIQUE
Lenglet du Fresnoy, Nicolas *see* RECUEIL DE DISSERTATIONS, ANCIENNES ET NOUVELLES SUR LES APPARITIONS, LES VISIONS ET LES SONGES.
LA LENGUA DE PUERTO RICO. ENSAYOS / Rosario, Ruben del – San Juan. 1956 – 1 – us Res Libr [440]
LENGUA ESPANOLA. TOMO 1. ORTOGRAFIA, PROSODIA, MORFOLOGIA, ANALISIS / Malaga Garcia, Eduardo – Caceres: J. Garcia Floriano Cumbreno, 1932 – 1 – sp Bibl Santa Ana [440]
LENGUA ESPANOLA. TOMO 2 : SINTAXIS ORACIONAL GENERALIDADES DE GRAMATICA. METODOLOGIA DE LA GRAMATICA ESPANOLA / Malaga Garcia, Eduardo – Caceres: Imp. y Enc. de Garcia Floriano, 1932 – 1 – sp Bibl Santa Ana [440]
EL LENGUAJE CASTELLANO EN PUERTO RICO / Marxuach, Teofilo – San Juan. 19– – 1 – us Res Libr [440]
LENGUAJE. CURSO SEGUNDO / Hinojosa del Valle, Gregorio – Plasencia, Caceres: Editorial Sanchez Rodrigo, S.A., 1969 – 1 – sp Bibl Santa Ana [946]
Lengyel, Peter *see* APPROACHES TO THE SCIENCE OF SOCIO-ECONOMIC DEVELOPMENT
Lenhartz, Rolf *see* DIE LYRISCHE EINLAGE BEI THEODOR STORM
LENIN I KOOPERATSIIA / Kuibyshev, V V – M., 1925 – 1mf – 9 – COR-163/1 – ne IDC [334]
LENIN I KOOPERATSIIA / Lozovoi, A – Ed 2. M., 1925 – 3mf – 9 – COR-167/1 – ne IDC [334]
LENIN I PROBLEMY RUSSKOI LITERATURY KONTSA 19 NACHALA 20 V. ISSLEDOVANIIA I OCHERKI / Meilakh, B – Ed. 2. M. 1951. BR-1424 2 – 8 – ne IDC [335]
LENIN I PROBLEMY RUSSKOI LITERATURY KONTSA 19 NACHALA 20 V. ISSLEDOVANIIA I OCHERKI / Meilakh, B – Ed. 3. L. 1956. BR-1425 2 – 8 – ne IDC [335]
LENIN I PROBLEMY RUSSKOI LITERATURY KONTSA 19 NACHALA 20 VV. ISSLEDOVANIIA I OCHERKI / Meilakh, B – M. 1947. BR-1423 2 – 8 – ne IDC [335]
Lenin Library *see* ZAPISKI OTDELA RUKOPISEI GOSUDARSTVENNOI BIBLIOTEKI SSSR IMENI V.I. LENINA
Lenin Library. P.A. Mukhanov Collection *see* KATALOG AKTOV 14, 15, 16 I 17 VV., PRINESENNYKH V DAR MOSKOVSKOMU PUBLICHNOMU MUZEIU PAVLOM ALEKSANDROVICHEM MUKHANOVYM
Lenin, N *see* COLLECTED PAMPHLETS
LENIN O KUL'TURE I ISKUSSTVE – M. 1956. BR-1363 2 – 8 – ne IDC [335]
LENIN: THE MAN, THE THEORIST, THE LEADER / ed by Schapiro, L B – N.Y. 1967 – 1 – $35.00r – us Hoover Inst Photo [335]
LENIN TO KHRUSHCHEV: THE USSR IN RETROSPECT – (Checklist. 3) – External affairs. Catalog information cards gratis – 3 – us Readex [947]
LENIN TO KHRUSHCHEV: THE USSR IN RETROSPECT, 1917-56 – Internal Affairs – 3 – us Readex [947]
LENIN, V.I. O KOOPERATSII : STAT'I I RECHI / Meshcheriakova, N L – M., 1924 – 2mf – 9 – COR-165/1 – ne IDC [334]
Lenin, Vladimir Ilyich *see*
- ADJARANADJARAN KARL MARX: 1964
- ARTIKEL DAN PIDATO PADA ULANGTAHUN2 REVOLUSI OKTOBER
- CHTO DIELAT?: NABOLIEVSHIE VOPROSY NASHEGO DVIZHENIIA
- FRIEDRICH ENGELS
- GERAKAN PEMBEBASAN NASIONAL DI TIMUR
- KARL MARX RIWAJATHIDUP SINGKAT DENGAN URAIAN TENTANG MARXISME
- "LEFT WING" COMMUNISM: AN INFANTILE DISORDER
- O LITERATURE I ISKUSSTVE
- PELADJARAN DARI REVOLUSI
- PERANG PARTISAN
- THE SOVIETS AT WORK; THE INTERNATIONAL POSITION OF THE RUSSIAN SOVIET REPUBLIC AND THE FUNDAMENTAL PROBLEMS OF THE SOCIALIST REVOLUTION
- TENTANG DIALEKTIKA
- TENTANG KOPERASI

Leningrad *see* COMMENTARII ACADEMIAE SCIENTIARUM IMPERIALIS PETROPOLITANAE
Leningrad. Artilleriskii istoricheskii muzei *see* PUTEVODITEL' PO ISTORICHESKOMU ARKHIVU MUZEIA
Leningrad. Rukopisnyi Fond Biblioteki. LIIZhTa *see* KATALOG
Leningrad. Sovet rabochikh i soldatskikh deputatov *see* PROTOKOLY ZASEDANII ISPOLNITEL'NOGO KOMITETA I BIURO I. K
Leningrad. Universitet *see*
- VESTNIK LENINGRADSKOGO UNIVERSITETA

LENINGRADSKAI A GUBERNSKAI A KONFERENTSII A VKP(B) (23RD: 1926: LENINGRAD, R.S.F.S.R.) *see* DOKLADNA 23RD CHREZVYCHAINOI LENINGRADSKOI GUBERNSKOI KONFERENTSII VKP(B)
LENINGRADSKAI A OBLAST – (Library has: Jan.-Feb., May 1928) – Leningrad: Izd. Oblastnogo ispolkoma, 1928-1929. 2v – 1 – CSUX89-S878 – us Hoover Inst Photo [947]
LENINGRADSKAIA KOOPERATSIIA ZA 10 LET – L., 1928 – 10mf – 9 – COR-166/1 – ne IDC [334]
LENINGRADSKAIA POTREBITEL'SKAIA KOOPERATSIIA S OKTIABRIA 1924 G. PO APREL' 1927 G. – L., 1927 – 2mf – 9 – COR-330/1 – ne IDC [334]
LENINGRADSKAIA PRAVDA – Leningrad, USSR. 1924-1926 – 1 – us Res Libr [072]
LENINGRADSKAIA PROMKOOPERATSIIA V BOR'BE ZA SHIRPOTREB – M., L., 1932 – 1mf – 9 – COR-432/1 – ne IDC [334]
Leningradskoe obshchestvo bibliofilov *see* KHRONIKA LENINGRADSKOGO OBSHCHESTVA BIBLIOFILOV, 5 IANVARIA-20 IIUNIA 1930 G
LENINSKI SBORNIK – Moscow. v. 1-35. 1924-1945 and Index to v. 1-20 – 1 – us NY Public [335]
LENINSKII SBORNIK – Moscow. v1-35 + index; v1-20. 1924-45 – 5r – 1 – us Ross [335]
LENINSKOE ZNAMYA – Petrozavodsk, U.S.S.R. Leninskaya pravda. -d. Jan-Dec 1947; Jan 1950-Dec 1952; Jan 1954-Dec 1956. 14 reels – 1 – uk British Libr Newspaper [947]
Lennep, J D van *see*
- ETYMOLOGICUM LINGUAE GRAECAE, SIVE OBSERVATIONES AD SINGULAS VERBORUM NOMINUMQUE STIRPES
- PRAELECTIONES ACADEMICAE DE ANALOGIS LINGUAE GRAECAE, SIVE RATIONUM ANALOGICARUM LINGUAE GRAECAE EXPOSITIO

Lennep, M F van *see* DE HERVORMING IN SPANJE
LENNE-ZEITUNG – Altena, 1880-1907 – 1 – Dist. gw Mikrofilm – gw Misc Inst [943]
LENNOXVILLE MAGAZINE *see* THE STUDENT'S MONTHLY
THE LENNOXVILLE MAGAZINE – (Cont: The Student's Monthly) – Montreal: Dawson, [1868?-186-?] – 9 – cn C.I.H.M. [971]
Lenoir, W B *see* HISTORY OF SWEETWATER VALLEY
Lenormant, Charles F *see* J.J. ROUSSEAU, ARISTOCRATE
Lenormant, Francois *see*
- THE BEGINNINGS OF HISTORY ACCORDING TO THE BIBLE AND THE TRADITIONS OF ORIENTAL PEOPLES
- THE STUDENT'S MANUAL OF ORIENTAL HISTORY...THE ANCIENT HISTORY OF THE EAST TO THE COMMENCEMENT OF THE MEDIAN WARS

Lenormant, Frandcois *see* ETUDES CUNEIFORMES
LENOX 1756-1890 – (Mf 1-3: Birth Index 1767-1902. Mf 3-5: Marriage Index 1767-1902. Mf 5-6: Death Index 1767-1902. Mf 7-14: Vital Records 1831-1905. Mf 15-17: Vital Records 1756-1832. Mf 18-20: Vital Records 1843-54. Mf 21-27: Vital Records 1855-1902. Mf 18-19: Births 1843-54. Mf Mf 19: Marriages 1843-55. Mf 20: Deaths 1843-54. Mf 21-23: Births 1855-90. Mf 23-25: Marriages 1855-90. Mf 25-27: Deaths 1855-90. Mf 28-30: Vital Records 1891-1902) – (mf ed 1983) – 30mf – 9 – us Holbrook [920]
Lens, A *see* DE RECHTSTOESTAND IN NEDERLANDSCH-INDIE...
LENS RESEARCH – v1-. 1983- – 1,5,6,9 – us UMI [073]
Lenschau, Martha *see* GRIMMELSHAUSENS SPRICHWOERTER UND REDENSARTEN

Lensing, L *see* DER GROSSE BERGARBEITER-STREIK DES JAHRES 1889 IM RHEINISCH-WESTFAELISCHEN KOHLENREVIER

Lent, John A *see* THE JOHN A. LENT COLLECTION ON ASIAN MASS COMMUNICATIONS

Lentz, Andrea D *see*
- PAPERS
- THE WARREN G. HARDING PAPERS

Lentzen, Georg *see* STRUKTUR UND FUNKTION DES SIGNALERKENNUNGSPARTIKELS (SRP) AUS ESCHERICHIA COLI

LENZ ALS DRAMATIKER / Gluth, Oskar – (Includes bibliographical references) – Muenchen: H Sachs, 1912 – 1r – 1 – us U.W. Library [430]

Lenz, Eva-Maria *see* HUGO VON HOFMANNSTHALS MYTHOLOGISCHE OPER "DIE AEGYPTISCHE HELENA"

Lenz, Jakob Michael Reinhold *see*
- BRIEFE UEBER DIE MORALITAET DER LEIDEN DES JUNGEN WERTHERS
- J.M.R. LENZ UND SEINE SCHRIFTEN
- VERTHEIDIGUNG DES HERRN WIELAND GEGEN DIE WOLKEN
- DER WALDBRUDER

Lenz, Max *see* GESCHICHTSSCHREIBUNG UND GESCHICHTSAUFFASSUNG IM ELSASS ZUR ZEIT DER REFORMATION

Lenz, Oscar *see* TIMBOUCTOU, VOYAGE AU MAROC, AU SAHARA ET AU SOUDAN

LENZ UND GOETHE : MIT UNGEDRUCKTEN BRIEFEN VON LENZ, HERDER, LAVATER, ROEDERER, LUISE KOENIG / Froitzheim, Johann – Stuttgart: Deutsche Verlags-Anstalt, 1891 – 1r – 1 – us U.W. Library [430]

LENZ UND KLINGER : ZWEI DICHTER DER GENIEZEIT / Schmidt, Erich – Berlin: Weidmann, 1878 – 1r – 1 – us U.W. Library [430]

LENZBLUETHEN UND HERBSTBLAETTER : AUSGEWAEHLTE GEDICHTE / Thormaehlen, Anton – Milwaukee: Im Verlag des Verfassers, 1890 – 1r – 1 – us U.W. Library [810]

Lenzine, Hilke *see* DIE DEUTSCHE VOLKSGRUPPE IN DAENEMARK UND DAS NATIONAL-SOZIALISTISCHE DEUTSCHLAND 1933-1939

Leo *see* TRACTATUS

Leo 1, Pope *see* SAEMMTLICHE REDEN DES HL. LEO DES GROSSEN, PAPSTES UND KIRCHENLEHRERS

LEO 13. : SEINE WELTANSCHAUUNG UND SEINE WIRKSAMKEIT / Goetz, Leopold Karl – Gotha: Friedrich Andreas Perthes, 1899 – 1mf – 9 – 0-8370-8511-X – 1986-2511 – us A.T.L.A. [920]

LEO 13 AND ANGLICAN ORDERS / Halifax, Viscount – London; New York: Longmans, Green, 1912 – 2mf – us A.T.L.A. [240]

LEO 13 AND MODERN CIVILIZATION / Miller, John Bleecker – New York: Eskdale, c1897 – 1mf – 9 – 0-8370-8537-3 – 1986-2537 – us A.T.L.A. [240]

Leo 13, Pope *see* THE PRACTICE OF HUMILITY

Leo Baeck Institute, New York *see* GERMAN-JEWISH PERIODICALS

Leo, F *see*
- DER SATURNISCHE VERS
- VENANTI HONORI CLEMENTIANI FORTUNATI PRESBYTERI ITALICI OPERA POETICA (MGH 1: 4.BD. 1. TEIL)

Leo, John *see* A GEOGRAPHICAL HISTORIE OF AFRICA

Leo Magnus *see* TRACTATUS (CCSL 138-138A)

LEO THE GREAT / Gore, Charles – London: Society for Promoting Christian Knowledge; New York: E & J B Young, 1897 – 1mf – 9 – 0-8370-8512-8 – 1986-2512 – us A.T.L.A. [920]

LEO TOLSTOI UND DER SLAVISCHE ROMAN / Ernst, Paul – Berlin: Brachvogel und Banft, 1889 – 1r – 1 – us U.W. Library [460]

THE LEOFRIC COLLECTAR, VOL. 1 / Dewick, E S – 1914 – 9mf – 8 – ne Slangenburg [240]

THE LEOFRIC COLLECTAR, VOL. 2 / Frege, W H – 1921 – 8mf – 8 – ne Slangenburg [240]

THE LEOFRIC MISSAL / ed by Warren, F E – Oxford, 1883 – 14mf – 8 – Dfl49.00 – ne Slangenburg [240]

LEOMINSTER 1715-1900 – (Mf 1-6: Town Records 1740-99. Mf 7-8: Vital Records 1715-99. Mf 9-15: Town Records 1740-79. Mf 16-17: Vital Records 1715-99. Mf 18: Stray Animals 1740-90. Mf 19-21: Town Records 1756-98. Mf 21: Marriage & Ints 1778-96. Mf 22-29: Town Records 1799-1820. Mf 30-34: Town & Vitals 1786-1839. Mf 35-44: Town Records 1820-40. Mf 44-54: Town Records 1840-52. Mf 55-60: Vitals Index 1715-1886. Mf 61-67: Births & Deaths 1742-1844. Mf 68-71: Births & Deaths 1806-45. Mf 72-74: Marriages & Intents 1741-1885. Mf 75-78: Vital Records 1842-54. Mf 79-83: Deaths 1852-94. Mf 84-88: Marriages 1854-91. Mf 89-95: Births 1855-1900) – (mf ed 1992) – 95mf – 9 – 0-87623-156-3 – us Holbrook [920]

LEOMINSTER 1717-1849 – (Mf 1T: Marriage Intentions 1753-81. Mf 1T-2T: Births & Deaths 1717-99. Mf 3T: Marriages 1787-95; Intentions 1782-1809. Mf 4T: Intentions 1809-23; Marriages 1794-1818. Mf 5T: Marriages 1813-31; Intentions 1823-29. Mf 5T-10T: Births & Deaths 1759-1849. Mf 10T-11T: Births & Deaths 1828-44. Mf 11T-12T: Intentions & Marriages 1829-49. Mf 12T: Out-of-Town Marriages 1741-99. Mf 12T-13T: Births 1843-49. Mf 14T: Marriages 1844-49. Mf 15T-16T: Deaths 1843-49) – (mf ed 1997) – 16mf – 9 – 0-87623-277-2 – us Holbrook [920]

LEON 13, HOMME D'ETAT : DISCOURS PRONONCE PAR L'HONORABLE J. A. CHAPLEAU, LE 11 JANVIER 1888, LORS DE LA CELEBRATION DU JUBILE PONTIFICAL DE LEON 13, A L'UNIVERSITE LAVAL A MONTREAL / Chapleau, Joseph Adolphe – Montreal: l'Imprimerie generale, 1888. SEM16P124 – 1r – 5 – Can$9.00 – cn Bibl Nat [240]

LEON 13, HOMME D'ETAT: DISCOURS PRONONCE...LE 11 JANVIER, 1888 / Chapleau, Joseph Adolphe – Montreal: Imp. Generale, 1888. 02860. (Pre-1900 Canadiana) – 9 – cn C.I.H.M. [971]

LEON 13 INTIME / Narfon, Julien de – Paris: F Juven, [1902] – 1mf – 9 – 0-8370-8699-X – 1986-2699 – us A.T.L.A. [920]

Leon, A *see* PRACTICO DE MORBO GALICO, EN EL QUE SE CONTIENE EL ORIGEN Y CONOCIMIENTO DE ESTA ENFERMEDAD...

Leon, Antoine *see* HISTORY OF EDUCATION TODAY

Leon Gutierrez, Florencio *see*
- CONFERENCIAS MILITARES
- GLORIAS DE ASTURIAS
- HONOR Y PATRIA
- INFLUENCIA DE LA MATEMATICA...CARRERAS

Leon, Juan Manuel *see* SUPLEMENTO... GRAMATICA DE ANTONIO DE NEBRIJA

Leon L'Africain, Hasan ibm Mohammed al-Wassan al-Fasi (dit Jean) *see* HISTORIALE DESCRIPTION DE L'AFRIQUE, TIERCE PARTIE DU MONDE, CONTENANT SES ROYAUMES, REGIONS, VILLES, CITEZ

Leon, Luis de *see* DE LEGIBUS O TRATADO DE LEYES...

Leon, Nicolas *see* LAS CASTAS DEL MEXICO COLONIAL...1924

Leon, P *see* MADRID. ARCHIVO HISTORICO NACIONAL. SECCION DE CODICES. INVENTARIO DE LA SECCION DE CODICES

Leon, Pierre *see* LA NAISSANCE DE LA GRANDE INDUSTRIE EN DAUPHINE: FIN DE XVIIE SIECLE-1869

Leon, Ramon David *see* POR DONDE VAMOS...HISTORIA DE UN FETO POLITICO

Leon Tello, P *see* MADRID. ARCHIVO HISTORICO NACIONAL JUDAIZANTES EN...LA INQUISICION DE AMERICA

Leonard, Anne C *see* OCCUPATIONAL STRESS, EXERCISE, AND HEALTH

Leonard, Arthur Glyn *see* ISLAM, HER MORAL AND SPIRITUAL VALUE A RATIONAL AND PSYCHOLOGICAL STUDY.

Leonard, Arthur N *see* DER FLUCH DER SCHOENHEIT

Leonard Delavan Levant *see* A HUNDRED YEARS OF MISSIONS

LEONARD EULER. PEREPISKA. ANNOTIROVANNYI UKAZATEL / Euler, L – Leningrad, 1967. 391p. BR-10,950/1 – 9 – ne IDC [947]

Leonard, Hon. Joseph *see* HISTORY OF OLMSTED COUNTY

Leonard, Jacob C *see* CENTENNIAL HISTORY OF DAVIDSON COUNTY

Leonard, SW *see* THE CHRISTIAN PSALMIST

Leonard, William Ellery *see* THE POET OF GALILEE

LEONARDO ARETINO : ETHICA POLITICA – Seo de Urgel, SP. 1482 – 1,5 – sp Cultura [920]

LEONARDO: ART, SCIENCE AND TECHNOLOGY – v.1-. 1968- – 5,6,9 – us UMI [500]

LEONARDO DA VINCI. DAS BUCH VON DER MALEREI / Ludwig, Heinrich – O 517o. 1882 – 9 – ne IDC [760]

LEONARDO DRAWINGS / Royal Library. Windsor Castle – (Available in 3 binders) – 18 colour 1 bw mf – 15,9 – $530.00 set – 1-900853-11-6 – uk Mindata [740]

LEONARDO DRAWINGS *see*
- ANATOMICAL DRAWINGS
- HORSES AND OTHER ANIMALS
- NATURE STUDIES

Leonardo, Leo *see* OPERAS

Leonardo y Argensola, B J *see*
- CONQUISTA DE LAS ISLAS MALUCAS AL REY FELIPE 3
- HISTOIRE DE LA CONQUE'TE DES ISLES MOLUQUES...

Leoncavallo, Ruggiero *see*
- LA BOHEME
- MAIA

IL LEONE – Los Angeles, CA. 1971-1983 – 1r – 1 – $50.00 – C03297 – us Library Micro [071]

IL LEONE – San Francisco, CA. Mar 1929-1988 – 4r – 1 – us I.H.R.C. [071]

LEONE BATTISTA ALBERTI'S KLEINERE KUNSTTHEORETISCHE SCHRIFTEN / Janitschek, H – (Quellenschriften fuer Kunstgeschichte. v. 11. Wien. 1877). BO-517k 1 – 9 – ne IDC [700]

LEONE MEDIGOS LEHRE VOM WELTALL UND IHR VERHAELTNIS ZU GRIECHISCHEN UND ZEITGENOESSISCHEN ANSCHAUUNGEN / Appel, Ernst – Erlangen, 1906 – 1mf – DM48.00 – 3-8267-3046-1 – gw Hänsel [949]

Leonhard, C C von *see* TASCHENBUCH FUER DIE GESAMMTE MINERALOGIE

LEONHARD H. BALLARD, SENATE SERVICE 1947-1984 : INSPECTOR, U.S. CAPITOL POLICE – 4mf – 9 – $20.00 – us Scholarly Res [320]

LEONHARD KAISER : EIN EVANGELISCHER MAERTYRER AUS DEM INNVIERTEL / Roth, F – Halle: Verein fuer Reformationsgeschichte, 1900. ([Schriften des Vereins fuer Reformationsgeschichte; Bd. 66]) – 1mf – us A.T.L.A. [240]

Leonhard, Rudolf *see* HOELDERLIN

Leonid, Arkhimandrit *see*
- ISTORICHESKOE OPISANIE STAVROPIGIAL'NOGO VOSKRESENSKOGO, NOVYI IERUSALEM IMENUEMOGO MONASTYRIA
- OBOZRENIE RUKOPISEI I STAROPECHATNYKH KNIG V KNIGOKHRANILISHCHAKH MONASTYREI GORODSKIKH I SEL'SKIKH TSERKVEI KALUZHSKOI EPARKHII
- SISTEMATICHESKOE OPISANIE SLAVIANO-RUSSKIKH RUKOPISEI SOBRANIIA GRAFA A.S.UVAROVA
- SLAVIANSKIE RUKOPISI, KHRANISHCHIESIA RIZNITSE SVIATO-TROITSKOI SERGIE- VOI LAVRY
- SVEDENIE O SLAVIANSKIKH RUKOPISIAKH, POSTUPIVSHIKH IZ KNIGOKHRANILISHCHA SVIATO-TROITSKOI SERGIEVOI LAVRY V BIBLIOTEKU TROITSKOI DUKHOVNOI SEMINARII V 1747 G. (NYNE NAKHODIASHCHIKHSIA V BIBLIOTEKE MOSKOVSKOI DUKHOVNOI AKADEMII)

LEONORE : EINE ERZAEHLUNG / Heuschele, Otto – Stuttgart: J F Steinkopf, 1945 – 1r – 1 – us U.W. Library [830]

LEONORE OU L'AMOUR CONJUGAL / Bouilly, Jean Nicolas & Gaveaux – French Theatre Series. Paris. Barba, an VII. 1798 – 9 – fr Hachette [820]

Leonov, Ioann *see* SUZHDENIYA I TOLKI SHTUNDISTOV I OPROVERZHENIE IKH

Leonov, V *see* KRATKII KURS PO POTREBITEL'SKOI KOOPERATSII

LEON-PAMPHILE LE MAY ET SON OEUVRE / LeMay, Pamphile – SEM35P158 – 4r – 1 – Can$219.00 – cn Bibl Nat [440]

LEONTIUS VON BYZANZ 1. / Loofs, Friedrich – Leipzig, 1887 – 5mf – 9 – ne Slangenburg [240]

LEONTIUS VON BYZANZ UND DIE GLEICHNAMIGEN SCHRIFTSTELLER DER GRIECHISCHEN KIRCHE, ERSTES BUCH, DAS LEBEN UND DIE POLEMISCHEN WERKE DES LEONTIUS VON BYZANZ / Loofs, Friedrich – Leipzig: J.C. Hinrichs, 1887. (Texte und Untersuchungen zur Geschichte der altchristlichen Literatur; Bd. 3, Heft 1-2) – 1mf – us A.T.L.A. [240]

Leopard, J C et al *see* HISTORY OF DAVIESS AND GENTRY COUNTIES

LEOPOLD 2, FRANZ 2 UND CATHARINA : IHRE CORRESPONDENZ NEBST EINER EINLEITUNG ZUR GESCHICHTE DER POLITIK LEOPOLD'S / ed by Beer, A – Leipzig, 1874 – 3mf – 9 – ne IDC [920]

LEOPOLD F.G. VON GOECKINGK / Kasch, Fritz – (Includes bibliographical references) – Marburg a.L.: N G Elwert, 1909 – 1r – 1 – us U.W. Library [920]

LEOPOLD KOMPERTS SAEMTLICHE WERKE IN ZEHN BAENDEN / Kompert, Leopold – Leipzig: Max Hesse, [1906] – 1 – us U.W. Library [800]

O LEOPOLDINENSE : FOLHA COMERCIAL, AGRICOLA E NOTICIOSA – Leopoldina, 7 Nov 1880; Feb, Apr-Dec 1881; Jan 1882-Jul 1883; Nov 1890; Jan, Mar-Apr 1891; Sept, Nov-Dec 1894; Jan-Dec 1895; Jan, 22-29 Mar 1896 – 1,5,6 – bl Biblioteca [072]

LEOPOLDO DE MATTOS – Manaos, Amazonas. 11 Dez 1912 – 1,5,6 – bl Biblioteca [072]

Leotaud, A *see* OISEAUX DE L'ILE DE LA TRINIDAD (ANTILLES)

Lepage *see* SOUMISSION DES TRIBUS MUSULMANES DU TURKESTAN PAR LA CHINE (1757-1759) (APPENDICE TROIS LETTRES DE L'EMPEREUR K'IEN-LONG AU KHAN DE BADAKCHAN)

Lepage, Auguste *see* LA VIE D'UN ARTISTE

Lepage, Henri *see*
- LE DEPARTEMENT DE LA MEURTHE: STATISTIQUE, HISTORIQUE ET ADMINISTRATIVE
- DICTIONNAIRE TOPOGRAPHIQUE DU DEPARTEMENT DE LA MEURTHE

Lepan, E M J *see* VIE POLITIQUE, LITTERAIRE ET MORALE DE VOLTAIRE

Lepe de la Camara, Jose Maria *see*
- COMUNICACION SOBRE LA ESCULTURA DE JUAN MARTINEZ MONTANES, "SAN JERONIMO PENITENTE" EXISTENTE EN EL CONVENTO DE CLARISAS DE LLERENA
- NOTAS PARA UN CATALOGO ARTISTICO DE LLERENA
- LA PIEDAD (DOLOROSA A ANGUSTIAS). GRUPO ESCULTORICO EXISTENTE EN LA IGLESIA DE NUESTRA SENORA DE LA GRANADA, DE LLERENA

THE LEPER QUARTERLY – v2-11. 1933-37 (complete) – 1r – 1 – ATLA S0703C – us A.T.L.A. [073]

LEPERS: THIRTY-SIX YEARS' WORK AMONG THEM...IN INDIA AND THE EAST, 1874-1910 / Jackson, John – London: Marshall, 1910. xvi,208p. 1 fiche – 9 – us A.T.L.A. [240]

Lepicie, B *see*
- CATALOGUE RAISONNE DES TABLEAUX DU ROY, AVEC UNE ABREGE DE LA VIE DES PEINTRES
- VIES DES PREMIERS-PEINTRES DU ROI, DEPUIS M. LE BRUN, JUSQU'A PRESENT

Lepicier, Alexius Maria *see* TRACTATUS DE BEATISSIMA VIRGINE MARIA MATRE DEI

LEPIDOPTERA BRITTANICA, 1803-(1828) / Haworth, A H – 2152 2. 1932 – 8 – ne IDC [590]

LEPIDOPTERA INDICA / Moore, F & Swinhoe, C – Z-284 2. 10 v. 1890-1913 – 8 – ne IDC [590]

THE LEPIDOPTERA OF CEYLON / Moore, F – 2479 2. 3 v. 1880-1887 – 8 – ne IDC [590]

THE LEPIDOPTERA OF THE BRITISH ISLANDS / Barrett, CG – London, 1893-1907. 11v.Index of plates. Z-1046/2 – 8 – ne IDC [590]

DIE LEPIDOPTEREN DER SCHWEIZ / Frey, H – Leipzig, 1880. xxvi,454p. Z/1259/2 – 8 – ne IDC [590]

LES LEPIDOPTERES DE LA BELGIQUE, LEURS CHENILLES ET LEURS CHRYSALIDES, DECRITS ET FIGURES D'APRES NATURE / Dubois, CF & Dubois, A – Bruxelles, etc., 1859- 1874-84. 3v. Z/1202/2 – 8 – ne IDC [590]

LEPIDOPTEROLOGISCHE ERGEBNISSE EINER REISE IN PERSIEN IN...1858-1859 / Bienert, T – Leipzig, 1869. 56p. Z-1067/2 – 8 – ne IDC [590]

LEPIDOPTEROLOGISCHE FAUNA VON ESTLAND, LIVLAND AND KURLAND : N.S. ARBEITEN NATURFORSCHER VEREINS / Nolcken, J H W von – Riga. 2-4pt. 1868-1871 – 15mf – 9 – ne IDC [580]

LEPIDOPTERORUM EUROPAEORUM CATALOGUS METHODICUS / Heydenreich, G H – Leipzig, 1851. 130p. Z/1349/2 – 9 – ne IDC [590]

THE LEPIDOPTEROUS FAUNA OF LANCASHIRE AND CHESHIRE / Ellis, J W – Leeds, 1890. 136p (Reprinted from The Naturalist, 1885-90). Z/1214/2 – 8 – ne IDC [590]

LEPIDOTTERI ITALIANI / Griffini, A – Milano, 1895. viii,238p. Z/1312/2 – 8 – ne IDC [590]

Lepine, de *see* LE DIEU MALGRE LUI OU LE CLUB SOUS UN CLOCHER

Leppa, Karl Franz *see*
- ANDREAS OSANG
- BRUNNENRAUSCHEN

Leppmann, Franz *see* GOTTFRIED KELLERS "GRUENER HEINRICH" VON 1854/5 UND 1879/80

Leproserie du Village Segregation d'Akata-Palime, Togo *see* JOURNAL

LEPROSY MISSIONS DIGEST – (Some original pgs damaged. Cont and filmed with: Song After Sorrow) – v1-11. 1948-58 – 1r – 1 – ATLA S0722A – us A.T.L.A. [073]

LEPROSY MISSIONS DIGEST *see* SONG AFTER SORROW

LEPROSY REVIEW – London. v1-16. 1930-45 – 5,9 – Dfl480.00; Dfl30.00v – ne Swets [616]

Lepsius, C R *see* DENKMAELER AUS AEGYPTEN UND AETHIOPIEN

Lepsius, Richard *see* STANDARD ALPHABET FOR REDUCING UNWRITTEN LANGUAGES AND FOREIGN GRAPHIC SYSTEMS TO A UNIFORM ORTHOGRAPHY IN EUROPEAN LETTERS

Lepszy, K *see* DZIEJE FLOTY POLSKIEJ

LEQUE – Itacoatiara, Amazonas. 16-30 Jul 1916 – 1,5,6 – bl Biblioteca [072]

Lequinio de Kerblay, Joseph M *see* VOYAGE DANS LE JURA

LER – Lisbon. Portugal. -m. Sep 1952-Oct 1953. (1 reel) – 1 – uk British Libr Newspaper [072]

EL LER GOBIERNO PERONISTA / Gambini, Hugo – [Buenos Aires: Centro Editor de America Latina, c1971] – 1 – CSUXAHZ2054-B – us Hoover Inst Photo [320]

Lerbs, Karl *see* DER GRIFF INS ALL

LERCHENSANG UND SCHWERTERKLANG : LIEDER UND GEDICHTE / Germanus – New York: [s.n.], 1902 – 1r – 1 – us U.W. Library [810]

Lereda, S P *see* KUSTARNAIA PROMYSHLENNOST' SSSR

LERGODS, ADELMETALLER OCH VAVNADER – 1953 – 1 – us I.U. Libraries [390]

Leriche, Albert *see* TERMINOLOGIE GEOGRAPHIQUE MAURE

LERIDA. ARCHIVO HISTORICO PROVINCIAL INVENTARIO DE PROTOCOLOS NOTARIALES / Uson, C & Susin, M – Lerida, 1983 – 4mf – 9 – sp Cultura [025]

Lerida, Felipe *see* ELOGIO DE LOS PADRES Y HERMANOS DE LA COMPANIA DE JESUS, MUERTOS POR CRISTO EN ESPANA, 1936-39

Lerius, Th van *see* DE LIGGEREN EN ANDERE HISTORISCHE ARCHIEVEN DER ANTWERPSCHE SINT LUCAS GILDE

LERMONTOV POET SVERKHCHELOVECH-ESTVA / Merezhkovskii, Dimitrii – Gogol' tvorchestvo zhizn', religiia. Spb. 1911. BR-770 2 – 8 – ne IDC [460]

LERMONTOV POET SVERKHCHELOVECH-ESTVA / Merezhkovskii, Dimitrii – Spb. 1909. BR-769 2 – 8 – ne IDC [460]

LERMONTOVU / Venok, M Iu – Iubileinyi Sbornik. Moscow, St. Petersburg, 1914. 384p. B-1546/2 – 8 – ne IDC [460]

Lerner, Bart S *see* THE EFFECTS OF GOAL SETTING AND IMAGERY TRAINING PROGRAMS ON THE FREE-THROW PERFORMANCE OF FEMALE BASKETBALL PLAYERS

Lerner, D *see* LES "SCIENCES DE LA POLITIQUE" AUX ETATS-UNIS

Lerner, IY *see* THEORY OF CURRICULUM CONTENT IN THE USSR

Lerner, N O *see* TRUDY I DNI PUSHKINA

Lerner, R E *see* THE HERESY OF THE FREE SPIRIT IN THE LATER MIDDLE AGES

Lernet-Holenia, Alexander *see* DIE STANDARTE

LERNZIEL ANARCHIE / Mackay Gesellschaft – No. 1-8. 388 S. Together with: Anarchismus einmal ganz anders, 68 S., by K. H. Z. Solneman. 3 fiches (24x) – 9 – 1.00f – at Libertarian Micro [320]

Leroi-Gourhan, A *see* MECANIQUE VIVANTE. LE CRANE DES VERTEBRES DU POISSON A L'HOMME

Leroquais, Victor *see*
- BIBLIOTHEQUES PUBLIQUES. LES PONTIFICAUX MANUSCRITS
- LES BREVIAIRES
- LES BREVIAIRES MANUSCRITS DES BIBLIOTHEQUES PUBLIQUES DE FRANCE
- LES LIVRES D'HEURES, MANUSCRITS DE LA BIBLIOTHEQUE NATIONALE
- LES PONTIFICAUX. MANUSCRITS DES BIBLIOTHEQUES PUBLIQUES DE FRANCE
- LES PSAUTIERS
- LES PSAUTIERS, MANUSCRITS LATINS DES BIBLIOTHEQUES PUBLIQUES DE FRANCE
- SUPPLEMENT AUX LIVRES D'HEURES

Leroux de Lincy, A JV *see* LE LIVRE DES PROVERBES FRANCAIS

Leroux, Ernest *see* ETUDES SUR LES LANGUES DU HAUT-ZAMBEZE

Leroux, J M *see* ESSAI DE DICTIONNAIRE FRANCAIS-HAOUSSA ET HAOUSSA-FRANCAIS, PRECEDE D'UN ESSAI DE GRAMMAIRE DE LA LANGUE HAOUSSA, MAGNA N HAOUSSA, PALE PAR LES NEGRES DU SOUDAN

Leroux, Jules *see* LE PROLETAIRE ET LE BOURGEOIS, DIALOGUE SUR LA QUESTION DES SALAIRES

Leroy de Bosroger *see* PRINCIPES DE L'ART DE LA GUERRE, DEVELOPPES D'APRES LES MEILLEURS EXEMPLES

Leroy, J P *see* REPARTITION GEOGRAPHIQUE DES GISEMENTS DU PERIGORDIEN SUPERIEUR A BURINS DE NOAILLES EN FRANCE

Leroy, Maxime *see* LES TRANSFORMATIONS DE LA PUISSANCE PUBLIQUE. LES SYNDICATS DE FONCTIONNAIRES

Leroy-Beaulieu, Anatole *see*
- ISRAEL AMONG THE NATIONS
- PAPACY, SOCIALISM AND DEMOCRACY

Leroy-Beaulieu, P *see* LE TRAVAIL DES FEMMES AU XIXE SIECLE

Lersch, Heinrich *see*
- DEUTSCHLAND MUSS LEBEN!
- HAMMERSCHLAEGE

LERUMS TIDNING – Alingsas, Sweden. 1982- – 1 – sw Kungliga [072]

LERUMS TIDNING *see* ALINGSAS TIDNING

LERWICK TIMES – 1872-1874 – 1. 121 – £42.00r – uk Scot News [072]

LESA SEVERA I ELEKTRIFIKATSIIA LESNOGO KHOZIA ISTVA / Atsenko, I I – Petrograd: Gos. izdvo, 1921 – 1 – CSUX91-B2557 – us Hoover Inst Photo [634]

Lesage, Alano Renato *see*
- ADICION A LAS AVENTURAS DE GIL BLAS. TOMO 6
- ADICION A LAS AVENTURAS DE GIL BLAS. TOMO 7
- AVENTURAS DE GIL BLAS DE SANTILLANA. TOMO 1
- AVENTURAS DE GIL BLAS DE SANTILLANA. TOMO 2
- AVENTURAS DE GIL BLAS DE SANTILLANA. TOMO 3
- AVENTURAS DE GIL BLAS DE SANTILLANA. TOMO 4
- AVENTURAS DE GIL BLAS DE SANTILLANA. TOMO 5

Lesage, Jean *see* LESAGE S'ENGAGE

Lesage, Jules S *see* THEORIE DU "MERVEILLEUX" DANS LA LITTERATURE FRANCAISE ET CANADIENNE

LESAGE S'ENGAGE : LIBERALISME QUEBECOIS D'AUJOURD'HUI, JALON DE DOCTRINE / Lesage, Jean – Montreal: Editions politiques du Quebec, 1959. SEM16P169 – 1r – 5 – Can$9.00 – cn Bibl Nat [323]

Lesbazeilles, Eugene *see* TABLEAUX ET SCENES DE LA VIE DES ANIMAUX

LESBIAN AND GAY STUDIES NEWSLETTER *see* GSN

LESBIAN NEWS – No.1-. Aug 1975-. -m. Imprint varies – 1 – us U.W. Library [305]

LESBIAN TIDE – Los Angeles, CA. 1977-1980 – 1r – 1 – $50.00 – R04061 – us Library Micro [071]

Lescarbot, Marc *see*
- HISTOIRE DE LA NOUVELLE FRANCE CONTENANT LES NAVIGATIONS, DECOURVERTES, ET HABITATIONS FAITES PAR LES FRANCOIS ES INDES OCCIDENTAL ET NOUVELLE FRANCE..
- HISTOIRE DE LA NOUVELLE-FRANCE
- LES MUSES DE LA NOUVELLE FRANCE
- NOVA-FRANCIA

THE LESCHETIZKY METHOD: AN EXPOSITION OF HIS PERSONAL VIEWS / Bree, M – New York: The University Society Inc, [1913] – 1 – us Sibley [780]

Lesclache, L de *see*
- TRAITE DE L'ORTHOGRAPHE
- LES VERITABLES REGLES DE L'ORTHOGRAPHE FRANCEZE

Lesconvel, Pierre de *see* RELATION DU VOYAGE DU PRINCE DE MONTMERAUD DANS L'ILE DE NAUDELY

DIE LESE- UND SCHREIBFEHLER IM ALTEN TESTAMENT, NEBST DEN DEM SCHRIFTTEXTE EINVERLEIBTEN RANDNOTEN KLASSIFIZIERT / Delitzsch, Franz – Berlin, Leipzig. 1920. BJ-412-4 1 – 9 – ne IDC [220]

LESELINYANA LA LESOTHO – (Issues for nov 1863-1882 filmed with: The Little Light of Basotholand) – Morija, Basutoland: [A Mabillel], nov 3 1863; feb 1 1865; [1883-sep 18 1913]; [1915-32]; [1948-65]; mar 10, apr 7 1962; [jan 16 1965-dec 17 1976] – us Res Libr [072]

LESELINYANA LA LESOTHO – Morija, Lesotho. 1863-1882 – 1 – sa State Libr [072]

Leseman, Paul *see* EARLY INTERVENTION AND CULTURE PREPARATION FOR LITERACY

LESHONENU – v. 1-38. Jerusalem. 1928-74. Lacking: 1957, v. 21. BJ-100-167 1 – 9 – ne IDC [956]

Lesko, Stephen J *see* PERCEIVED COMPETENCE AND INTRINSIC MOTIVATION AMONG JUNIOR TENNIS PLAYERS

Leslau, W *see* BIBLIOGRAPHY OF THE SEMITIC LANGUAGES OF ETHIOPIA

Leslie, Charles Robert *see* AUTOBIOGRAPHICAL RECOLLECTIONS

LESLIE'S ILLUSTRATED WEEKLY NEWSPAPER – 1855-1922 – 1 – us UMI [073]

LESLIE'S MONTHLY MAGAZINE *see* AMERICAN MAGAZINE

LESNAIA KOOPERATSIIA – (Missing: 1922 n1-13. 1923 n14) – Moscow, 1922-32 n1 – 76mf – 9 – COR-649/1 – ne IDC [334]

LESNAIA PROMYSHLENNOST' – Moscow. U.S.S.R. 1961- – 1 – us UMI [330]

Lesne, Emile *see* L'ORIGINE DES MENSES DANS LE TEMPOREL DES EGLISES ET DES MONASTERES DE FRANCE AU 19E SIECLE

LESNOE DELO *see* LI ESNOE DI ELO

LESNOE KHOZI A ISTVO I LESNAI A PROMYSHLENNOST : EZHEMESI ACHNY I ZHURNAL IZDAVAEMY I LESPROMOM VSNKH RSFSR – (Library has: May 1930) – Leningrad: Lesprom VSNKh RSFSR, 1928-1931. 4v – 1 – CSUX89-S559 – us Hoover Inst Photo [947]

LESNOE KHOZI A ISTVO (MOSCOW, R.S.F.S.R.: 1928) – (Library has: 1931, no. 1-12) – Moskva: Soi uzlesprom VSNKh SSSR, 1928-1931. 3v – 1 – CSUX89-S808 – us Hoover Inst Photo [947]

LESNOE ZAKONODATEL'STVO UKRAINY / ed by Chumalo, F S – Kharkov, 1926. 730p. Texts of Ukrainian forestry legislation and departmental regulations. BR-9593/1 – 9 – ne IDC [340]

LESOPROMYSHLENNOE DELO : [ORGAN SOVETA LESNO I I DEREVOOBRABATYVAI USHCHE I PROMYSHLENNOSTI I TORGOVLI I T SENTRALNOGO LESO EKSPORTNOGO BI URO (VSNKH SSSR I NKT)] – (Includes c.1: Jan. 1926-Dec. 1929; March, May/June-Sept./Oct. 1930; Jan., June, Aug./Sept. 1931, Jan.-May 1932) – Moskva: Izd.T SUP VSNKh SSSR, 1922-1934. 13v – 1 – CSUX89-S850 – us Hoover Inst Photo [947]

Lesotho *see* FIVE YEAR DEVELOPMENT PLAN 1967-1972

Lesotho. Bureau of Statistics *see*
- 1966 POPULATION CENSUS REPORT
- EDUCATION STATISTICS 1977-1986

Lesotho. Central Planning and Development Office *see* FIRST FIVE-YEAR DEVELOPMENT PLAN, 1970/71-1974/75

LESOTHO (FORMERLY BASUTOLAND) : ANNUAL STATISTICAL BULLETIN 1963-1973 / Lesotho (formerly Basutoland). Bureau of Statistics – (Coll title: African Official Statistical Serials, 1867-1982) – 12mf – 9 – £100.00 – uk Chadwyck [960]

Lesotho (formerly Basutoland). Bureau of Statistics *see* LESOTHO (FORMERLY BASUTOLAND)

Lesotho. Ministry of Education *see* PRIMARY EDUCATION NEWS 1988-1989

Lesotho. National Assembly *see* OFFICIAL REPORTS

Lesourd, Paul *see* L'ANNEE MISSIONAIRE, 1931

Lesseps, Ferdinand de *see* RECOLLECTIONS OF FORTY YEARS

THE LESSER EASTERN CHURCHES / Fortescue, Adrian – London: Catholic Truth Society, 1913 – 2mf – us A.T.L.A. [240]

LESSING : AUSGEWAEHLTE PROSA UND BRIEFE / ed by White, Horatio Stevens – (Includes bibliographical references) – New York: G P Putnam's Sons, c1888 – 1 – us U.W. Library [800]

LESSING : DAS ERWACHEN DES DEUTSCHEN GEISTES / Wagner, Albert Malte – (Includes bibliographical references) – Leipzig, Berlin: Horen-Verlag, 1931 – 1r – 1 – us U.W. Library [430]

LESSING : GESCHICHTE SEINES LEBENS UND SEINER SCHRIFTEN / Schmidt, Erich – (Includes bibliographical references and index) – 2. veraend. Aufl. Berlin: Weidmann, 1899 – 1r – 1 – us U.W. Library [920]

LESSING ALS FREIMAURER – Hamburg, 1880 – 1mf – ne IDC [360]

LESSING ALS PHILOSOPH / Schrempf, Christof – Stuttgart: Frommann (E Hauff), 1906 – 1r – 1 – us U.W. Library [100]

Lessing, C F *see* SYNOPSIS GENERUM COMPOSITARUM

Lessing, Carl Robert *see* DIE GESCHICHTE DER FAMILIE LESSING

Lessing, G C *see* JOHANN FAUST

Lessing, Gotthold Ephraim *see*
- EMILIA GALOTTI
- DIE ERZIEHUNG DES MENSCHENGESCHLECHTS
- FABLES ALLEMANDES ET CONTES FRANCAIS EN VERS, AVEC UN ESSAI SUR LA FABLE
- G. E. LESSINGS UEBERSETZUNGEN AUS DEM FRANZOESISCHEN FRIEDRICHS DES GROSSEN UND VOLTAIRES
- GOTTHOLD EPHRAIM LESSINGS SAEMTLICHE SCHRIFTEN
- LESSINGS WERKE
- LICHTSTRAHLEN AUS SEINEN SCHRIFTEN UND BRIEFEN
- MINNA VON BARNHELM, ODER, DAS SOLDATENGLUECK
- MISS SARA SAMPSON
- NATHAN DER WEISE
- PHILOTAS
- POETISCHE UND DRAMATISCHE WERKE
- SELECTED PROSE WORKS
- WERKE
- WIE DIE ALTEN DEN TOD GEBILDET
- ZUR ERINNERUNG AN GOTTHOLD EPHRAIM LESSING

Lessing, Gotthold Ephraim et al *see* BRIEFE DIE NEUESTE LITTERATUR BETREFFEND

THE LESSING LEGEND = LESSING-LEGENDE / Mehring, Franz – (Includes bibliographical references) – New York: Critics Group Press, 1938 – 1r – 1 – us U.W. Library [430]

Lessing, Otto Eduard *see* MASTERS IN MODERN GERMAN LITERATURE

LESSING UND DIE ERZIEHUNG DES MENSCHENGESCHLECHTS : ZUGLEICH EINE AUSEINANDERSETZUNG MIT DER THAERLEGENDE / Krieck, Ernst – (Includes bibliographical references) – Heidelberg: C Winter, 1913 – 1r – 1 – us U.W. Library [430]

LESSING-GALERIE : CHARAKTERE AUS LESSING'S WERKEN / Fecht, Friedrich – Leipzig: Brockhaus, 1868 – 1r – 1 – us U.W. Library [430]

LESSING'S ARISTOTELISCHE STUDIEN UND DER EINFLUSS DERSELBEN AUF SEINE WERKE / Gotschlich, Emil – Berlin: F Vahlen, 1876 – 1r – 1 – us U.W. Library [430]

LESSINGS DRAMEN IN FRANKREICH / Kinkel, Hans – (Includes bibliographical references) – Darmstadt: G Otto, 1908 – 1r – 1 – us U.W. Library [430]

LESSINGS EMILIA GALOTTI : NEBST EINEM ANHANGE: DIE DREIACTIGE BEARBEITUNG / Werner, Richard Maria – Berlin: W Herz, 1882 – 1r – 1 – us U.W. Library [430]

LESSINGS FRAGMENTENSTREIT / Brandl, Benedict – Pilsen, 1908. 45p – 1 – us U.W. Library [430]

LESSINGS LAOKOON : ABSCHNITT 1-15, [16-25] DEM GEDANKENGANGE NACH DARGESTELLT / Brachvogel, Albert Emil – Stargard: E Timm, 1900-01 – 1r – 1 – us U.W. Library [430]

LESSINGS MINNA VON BARNHELM / Boehme, Walther – Berlin: Weidmann, 1890 – 1r – 1 – us U.W. Library [430]

LESSINGS MINNA VON BARNHELM / Stoffel, J – 2., verb. Aufl. Langensalza: H Beyer, 1898 – 1r – 1 – us U.W. Library [430]

LESSINGS "MINNA VON BARNHELM" UND GOLDONIS LUSTSPIEL "UN CURIOSO ACCIDENTE" / Wihan, Josef – Prag: Haase, 1903 – 1r – 1 – us U.W. Library [430]

LESSING'S NATHAN DER WEISE / Trosien, E – Berlin: C Habel, 1876 – 1r – 1 – us U.W. Library [410]

LESSINGS NATHAN DER WEISE : DURCH EINE HISTORISCH-KRITISCHE EINLEITUNG UND EINEN FORTLAUFENDEN KOMMENTAR BESONDERS ZUM GEBRAUCHE AUF HOEHEREN LEHRANSTALTEN / Niemeyer, Eduard – 2. Aufl. Leipzig: Siegismund, 1887 – 1r – 1 – us U.W. Library [430]

LESSINGS "PHILOTAS" UND SEINE PRODUKTIVE REZEPTION BEI BODMER UND GLEIM : ANALYSIERT MIT BEZUG AUF DIE ZEITGENOESSISCHE DRAMENTHEORETISCHE DISKUSSION / Pagel, Bjoern – 1992 – 144p – 9 – DM98.00 – 3-89349-606-8 – gw Hänsel [430]

LESSINGS RELIGIONSPHILOSOPHISCHE ANSICHTEN BIS ZUM JAHRE 1770 IN IHREM HISTORISCHEN ZUSAMMENHANG UND IN IHREN HISTORISCHEN BEZIEHUNGEN : NEBST ANHANG: GRUNDZUEGE VON LESSINGS RELIGIONSPHILOSOPHIE / Nieten, Otto – 1995 – 2mf – 9 – DM62.00 – 3-8267-3123-9 – gw Hänsel [430]

LESSINGS SEELENWANDERUNGSGEDANKE KRITISCH BELEUCHTET / Arnsperger, Walther – (Includes bibliographical references) – Heidelberg: J Hoerning, 1893 – 1r – 1 – us U.W. Library [430]

LESSINGS SPRACHLICHE REVISION SEINER JUGENDDRAMEN / Tyrol, Fritz – 1995 – 1mf – 9 – DM48.00 – 3-8267-3127-1 – gw Hänsel [430]

LESSINGS STELLUNG ZUM CHRISTENTUM / Loofs, Friedrich – (Includes bibliographical references) – Halle a.S.: Waisenhaus, 1910 – 1 – us U.W. Library [430]

LESSINGS VERHAELTNIS ZUR ALTROEMISCHEN KOMOEDIE : EINE LITTERATURHISTORISCHE UNTERSUCHUNG / Seldner, K – (Includes bibliographical references) – Mannheim: W Beutel, 1881 – 1r – 1 – us U.W. Library [430]

LESSINGS WERKE / Lessing, Gotthold Ephraim; ed by Petersen, Julius & Olshausen, Waldemar von – (Includes bibliographical references and indexes) – Berlin: Deutsches Verlagshaus Bong, [1926?] – 1 – us U.W. Library [800]

Lesson, A *see* VOYAGES DE LA CORVETTE "L'ASTROLABE"

THE LESSON OF LOVE / Miller, James Russell – New York: Thomas Y Crowell, c1903 – 1mf – 9 – 0-8370-7244-1 – 1986-1244 – us A.T.L.A. [240]

Lesson, R P *see*
- HISTOIRE NATURELLE DES OISEAUX DE PARADIS
- MANUEL D'ORNITHOLOGIE, OU DESCRIPTION DES GENRES ET DES PRINCIPALES ESPECES D'OISEAUX
- LES TROCHILIDEES, OU LES COLIBRIS

LESSON SHEETS ON CRIMINAL LAW / Sprague, William Cyrus – Detroit, Sprague 1896 12 numb. iln. LL-896 – 1 – us L of C Photodup [340]

LESSONS AND EXERCISES OUT OF CICERO AD ATTICUM / Webbe, Joseph – 1627. 290p. (English Linguistics Series 1500-1800) – 9 – us UMI [450]

LESSONS AND RECORDS OF THE SUNDAY SCHOOL *see* THE CHILD'S BIBLE EXPOSITOR, OR, LESSONS AND RECORDS OF THE SUNDAY SCHOOL

LESSONS FOR THE HARPSICHORD, INTERMIX'D WITH ITALIAN AND ENGLISH SONGS, OPERA 2 / Gambarini, Elizabeth – ca.1748 – 9 – us Sibley [780]

LESSONS FROM THE LIFE OF SAINT PETER : SIX ESSAYS / Lipscomb, Andrew Adgate – Macon, GA: John W Burke, 1882 – 1mf – 9 – 0-8370-4142-2 – 1985-2142 – us A.T.L.A. [920]

LESSONS FROM THE LIVES OF THREE GREAT FATHERS : WITH APPENDICES / Bright, William – London; New York: Lognmans, Green, 1890 – 1mf – us A.T.L.A. [240]

LESSONS ON AGENCY / Sprague, William Cyrus – Detroit, 1894 19 numb. iln. LL-883 – 1 – us L of C Photodup [340]

LESSONS ON PARTNERSHIP / Sprague, William Cyrus – Detroit. 1904 19 numb. iln. LL-881 – 1 – us L of C Photodup [340]

LESSONS ON SALES / Sprague, William Cyrus – Detroit, Sprague 1895 17 numb. iln. LL-880 – 1 – us L of C Photodup [340]

LESSONS ON THE GOSPEL OF LUKE WITH A COMMENTARY / Spaulding, Henry George – 2nd ed. Boston: Unitarian Sunday-School Society, 1890. x,210p – 1 – us U.W. Library [240]

LESSONS ON THE LIFE OF JESUS / Scrymgeour, William – (Includes bibliographical references and index) – Edinburgh: T & T Clark; New York: Scribner and Welford [distributor], 1883 – 1mf – 9 – 0-8370-5200-9 – 1985-3200 – us A.T.L.A. [240]

LESSONS ON THE PARABLES OF THE SAVIOUR / Huntington, Frederic Dan – 1847 – 9 – us A.T.L.A. [240]

Lester, Albert Jeffrey *see* THE REVISED UNIFORM LIFE INSURANCE ACT OF THE PROVINCES OF CANADA (EXCEPT QUEBEC)

Lester, W W *see* A DIGEST OF THE MILITARY AND NAVAL LAWS OF THE CONFEDERATE STATES

Lester, William W *see* DECISIONS OF THE INTERIOR DEPARTMENT IN PUBLIC LAND CASES AND LAND LAWS PASSED, 1838-1870

Lesterpt de Beauvais, Henri *see* DU DROIT DE CITE A ROME

Lestiboudois, T G *see*
- BOTANOGRAPHIE BELGIQUE
- ESSAI SUR LA FAMILLE DES CYPERACEES
- OBSERVATIONS PHYTOLOGIQUES

Lestiboudois, Themistocle *see* RAPPORT GENERAL SUR L'EPIDEMIE DU CHOLERA QUI A REGNE A LILLE EN 1832

L'Estoille, Antoine de *see* NOS PAYSANNES

LESTONENU – v. 1-38. Jerusalem. 1928-74. BJ-100-167 1 – 9 – ne IDC [073]

LESTORIE DES ENGLES SOLUM LA TRANSLACION MAISTRE GEFFREI GAIMAR (RS91) / Geoffrey Gaimar; ed by Hardy, T D & Martin, C T – (v1 1888 Dfl30.00. v2 1889 Dfl25.00) – ne Slangenburg [240]

L'Estourbeillon de la Garnache, Regis *see* LEGENDES BRETONNES DU PAYS D'AVESSAC

Lesuire, Robert Martin *see* LE NOUVEAU MONDE: POEME

Lesur *see*
- DES PROGRES DE LA PUISSANCE RUSSE DEPUIS SON ORIGINE JUSQU'AU COMMENCEMENT DU 19E SIECLE
- HISTOIRE DES KOSAQUES, PRECEDEE D'UNE INTRODUCTION, OU COUP D'OEIL SUR LES PEUPLES QUI ONT HABITE LE PAYS DES KOSAQUES, AVANT L'INVASION DES TARTARES

Leszczyc-Suminski, J *see* ZUR ENTWICKLUNGSGESCHICHTE DER FARRNKRAEUTER

LET FREEDOM PAY ITS WAY / Zube, John – A study paper on the financing of a libertarian party. 2nd ed. 1 fiche (24X) – 9 – 1.00f – at Libertarian Micro [320]

LET FREEDOM REIGN / Read, Leonard E – 1969. 167p. 1 fiche (24x) – 9 – 1.00f – at Libertarian Micro [320]

LET US BECOME THE VEHICLE OF HISTORY / Sukarno, Pres. Indonesia – SE 11,577 1. Address on Aug. 17, 1953 – 9 – ne IDC [324]

LETAIUSHCHII PROLETARII / Maiakovskii, Vladimir – M. 1925. BR-979 2 – 8 – ne IDC [305]

Letchmajee, Lingum *see* AN INTRODUCTION TO THE GRAMMAR OF THE KUI OR KANDH LANGUAGE

LETCHWORTH AND BALDOCK CITIZEN *see* CITIZEN GARDEN CITY RECORD AND ADVERTISING JOURNAL

LETCHWORTH AND BALDOCK CITIZEN GAZETTE – London. -w. 1980-81. 8 reels – 1 – uk British Libr Newspaper [072]

LETCHWORTH AND BALDOCK CITIZEN GAZETTE *see* CITIZEN GARDEN CITY RECORD AND ADVERTISING JOURNAL

Letellier, Albert *see* LES PRISONS DE FEMMES

Lethaby, W R *see* THE CHURCH OF SANCTA SOPHIA CONSTANTINOPLE

LETHAEA ROSSICA, OU PALEONTOLOGIE DE LA RUSSIE / ed by Eichwald, C E von – Stuttgart 1852-68. 3v – 80mf – 8 – ne IDC [560]

LETHAIA – (1981-. 1,5,6,9) – v1-. 1968- – 1 – us UMI [500]

LETHBRIDGE HERALD – (1993.-12r; 1905-1982.-581r) – Lethbridge, 1983-1992 – 127r – 1 – cn Preston [971]

LETHBRIDGE NEWS – Lethbridge, Canada. 1885-1900 – 8r – 1 – $520.00 – cn Library Assoc [971]

LETHBRIDGE TELEGRAM – Lethbridge, Alberta, CN. 1915-1918 – 2r – 1 – cn Commonwealth Micro [072]

LE/THE LIBERAL – Quebec, Canada. 17 jun-20 nov 1837 – 1r – 1 – Can$50.00 – cn Can Microfilming [072]

LE/THE VOYAGEUR DE LAVAL – Ville de Laval. v- n-. 17 dec 1953, 18 mar 1954, 25 mar 1954 – 1r – 1 – Can$25.00 – cn Can Microfilming [072]

Lethem, Gordan James et al *see* COLLOQUIAL ARABIC; SHUWA DIALECT OF BORNU, NIGERIA, AND OF THE REGION OF THE CHAD

Leto, Giulio Pomponio *see* COMPENDIO DEL'HISTORIA ROMANA..

LE-TOLEDOT ADAT HA-MAGRABIM BI-YRUSHALAYIM / Elmaleh, A – v. 14. Luah Erez-Yisra'el. 1909. BJ-27-40 1 – 9 – ne IDC [956]

LE-TOLEDOT BATTE HA-MIDRASH BI-YERUSHALAYIM BA-MEAH HA-17 / Benayahu, M – (Hebrew Union College Annual). v. 21. 1948. BJ-27-15 2 – 8 – ne IDC [270]

LE-TOLEDOT HA-YEHASIM SHEL YEHUDEI HAMBURG LE-EREZ-YISRA'EL / Brilling, D – v3. Yerushalayim. 1950. BJ-27-74 1 – 9 – ne IDC [956]

LE-TOLEDOT YISSUD BEIT HA-SEFER "LAEMEL" BI-YERUSHALAYIM / Gelber, N M – v. 1. Yerushalayim. 1948. BJ-27-79 1 – 9 – ne IDC [370]

Letonnelier, G *see* L'ABBAYE EXEMPTE DE CLUNY ET LE SAINT-SIEGE

LETOPIS' / Dom Literatorov. Leningrad – Leningrad. n1-9. 1921-22 – 1r – 1 – us Ross [460]

LETOPIS' – Dvukhnedel'nyi khudozhestvenyyi istoriko-literaturnyi zhurnal. nr. 1-4. M. 1913. BR-4130 2 – 8 – ne IDC [073]

LETOPIS' – Ezhemesiachnyi, literaturnyi, nauchnyi i politicheskii zhurnal. Spb. 1915-17. B-1194 2 – 8 – ne IDC [073]

LETOPIS' DOMA LITERATOROV – Literaturno-issledovatel'-sk kii i kritiko-bibliograficheskii zhurnal. nr. 1-9. Spb. 1921-22. B-2281 2 – 8 – ne IDC [460]

LETOPIS' DOMA LITERATOROV – St Petersburg. no. 1-9. Nov 1 1921-Feb 25 1922 – 1 – us NY Public [460]

LETOPIS' EKATERINOSLAVSKOI UCHENOI ARKHIVNOI KOMMISSII – (Available: 1912 v8. 1915 v10) – Ekaterinoslav, 1904-1915 – 16mf – 9 – ne IDC [947]

LETOPIS EZHEMESIACHNYI LITERATURNYI NAUCHNYI I POLITICHESKI ZHURNAL – Leningrad, 1916-17 – 2r – 1 – us Ross [460]

LETOPIS' FAKULTETOV NA 1835 G – Spb. 1835. BR-3372 2 – 8 – ne IDC [370]

LETOPIS' GAZETNYKH STATEI – Moscow: Knizhnaia palata, 1936- – 80mf – 9 – $169.00y – us East View [460]

LETOPIS' GAZETNYKH STATEI – Organ gos. bibliografii SSSR. Vykhodit ezhenedel'no do 1960 g. s 1960 g. ezhemesiachno (vspomogatel'nye ukazateli). M. 1936-73. Lacking: 1936-1955; 1957 (41-43); 1969 (4). BR-10,415 1 – 9 – ne IDC [010]

LETOPIS' ISTORIKO-RODOSLOVNAGO OBSHCHESTVA V MOSKVE – NR. 1-11. M., Orel. 1905-15. Ukazatel' za 1905-1909 gg. nr. 4. M. 1912. BR-3371 2 – 8 – ne IDC [947]

LETOPIS' LITERATURNOI ZHIZNI KARELII – Petrozavodsk: Karelkoe knizhnoe izd-vo, 1917-61 (mf ed 1963); 1962-66 (mf ed 1968) – us Res Libr [947]

LETOPIS RETSENZII / Vsesoiuznaia Knizhnaia Palata – Moscow, 1934-65 – 5r – 1 – us Ross [460]

LETOPIS' RETSENZII – za 1934; 1935; 1936; 1938 gg. M. 1935-36, 1938. BR-5624 2 – 8 – ne IDC [947]

LETOPIS' RETZENZII – Moscow. 1934-1965 – 1 – us NY Public [073]

LETOPIS' REVOLIUTSII – (Istoricheskii zhurnal). v. 1. Berlin. 1923. BR-3370 2 – 8 – ne IDC [073]

LETOPIS' REVOLIUTSII – Kharkov: Gos. izd-vo Ukrainy. n1(6)-4(9) 1924; n3(12), 5/6(14/15) 1925; n3/4(18/19)-6(21) 1926; n1(22)-5/6(26/27) 1927 – us Res Libr [947]

LETOPIS' RUSSKAGO TEATRA / Arapov, P – Spb. 1861. BR-5976 2 – 8 – ne IDC [460]

LETOPIS' VOINY – v. 1-132. Petrograd. 1914-17. BR-3369 2 – 8 – ne IDC [073]

LETOPIS' VOINY S IAPONIEI – St. Petersburg. 1904, nos. 1-40 – 1 – 35.00r – us Hoover Inst Photo [073]

LETOPIS' ZANIATII ARKHEOGRAFICHESKOI KOMISSII ZA 1861-ZA 1927-1928 GG – St. Petersburg, Leningrad, 1862-1929. v1-35. B-1296- – 8 – ne IDC [025]

LETOPIS' ZHURNAL'NYKH STATEI – Moscow: Knizhnaia palata, 1926- – 125mf – 9 – $499.95y – us East View [460]

LETOPISI MARKSIZMA – Moscow. n1-13. 1926-30 – 1r – 1 – us Ross [335]

LETOPISI MARKSIZMA – Moscow. v. 1-13. 1926-1930 – 1 – us NY Public [335]

LETOPISI RUSSKOI LITERATURY I DREVNOSTI. – Moscow, 1859-63.v1-5. BR-7648/2 – 8 – ne IDC [460]

UN LETRADO DEL SIGLO 18, EL DCOTOR JOSE PERFECTO DE SALAS. BUENOS AIRES, 1963 / Donoso, Ricardo – Madrid: Graf. Calleja, 1969 – 1 – sp Bibl Santa Ana [946]

LETRADOS Y POLITICOS / Vega, Fernando de la; ed by Bayle, Constantino – Madrid: Razon y Fe, 1927 – 1 – sp Bibl Santa Ana [320]

LETRAS E ARTES – (Suppl to: A Manha) – Rio de Janeiro, 3 Feb-Apr, Jun-Dec 1946; Jan-Nov 1947; Jan 1948-24 Aug 1954 – 1,5,6 – bl Biblioteca [072]

LET'S SAVE ANTARCTICA / Barnes, James N – A review of his book with a note by J. Zube on the Let's Save the XYZ Mania.1p – 9 – 1.00f – at Libertarian Micro [335]

LETSTE NAAYES – Israel, 1979- – 1 – $210.00y – us Ross [072]

Lettenhove, J Kervijn de *see* CODEX DUNENSIS

Lettenmair, Josef Guenther *see* ASKA WEINT

A LETTER / Shipler, Guy Emery – N. Y., 1938. Fiche W1160. (Blodgett Collection of Spanish Civil War Pamphlets) – 9 – us H.U. College Libr [946]

LETTER / Ford Foundation – (v6- 1975- 5,6 v7- 1976- 9) – v1- 1970- – 1 – us UMI [370]

A LETTER ADDRESSED TO MINISTERS OF STATE, BISHOPS, MAGISTRATES AND OTHERS RESPECTING THE BODY OF MEN GENERALLY TERMED METHODIST PREACHERS,... / Greaves, A B – Sheffield, 1799 – 1mf – 9 – MP-595/1 – ne IDC [240]

LETTER AND STATEMENT TO HENRY MEULEN ON THEIR DIFFERENCES/MONETARY FREEDOM / Beckerath, Ulrich von – 5fiches (24x) – 9 – 1.00f – at Libertarian Micro [320]

LETTER BOOK OF THE ARKANSAS TRADING HOUSE, 1805-10 / U.S. Bureau of Indian Affairs – 1roll. M142 – 1 – us Nat'l Archives [324]

THE LETTER BOOK OF THE COMPANY FOR PROPAGATION OF THE GOSPEL IN NEW ENGLAND, 1688-1761 – (With printed guide) – 1r – 1 – $85.00 – D3187 – us Scholarly Res [240]

LETTER BOOKS / Perry, Matthew C – 1843-45. 1 roll. M206 – 1 – us Nat'l Archives [324]

LETTER BOOKS, 1847-8 / Berkeley, G H F 4 fiche – 9 – sa SA Libr [960]

A LETTER BY MAR JACOB, BISHOP OF EDESSA, ON SYRIAC ORTHOGRAPHY / Jacob of Edessa – (Discussion and translation in English; texts in Syriac) – London: Williams and Norgate, 1869 – 1mf – 9 – 0-8370-9794-0 – 1986-3794 – us A.T.L.A. [470]

A LETTER, CONTAINING A MOST BRIEFE DISCOURSE APOLOGETICALL.. / Dee, John – London: Peter Short, 1603. illus. 12 leaves – 1 – us U.W. Library [920]

A LETTER FROM A CLERGYMAN TO ONE OF HIS PARISHIONERS WHO WAS INCLINED TO TURN METHODIST;... / Hardy, R – London, 1763 – 2mf – 9 – MP-424/1 – ne IDC [240]

A LETTER FROM A GENTLEMAN IN THE COUNTRY TO HIS FRIEND IN EDINBURGH CONCERNING MR. WH—F—D, WHEREIN HIS MISSION, DOCTRINE AND CHARACTER ARE IMPARTIALLY ENQUIRED INTO AND EXAMINED – Edinburgh, 1741 – 1mf – 9 – MP-293/1 – ne IDC [240]

A LETTER FROM GERMANY TO THE PRINCESS ROYAL OF ENGLAND / Croft, Herbert – 1797. 113p. (English Linguistics Series 1500-1800) – 9 – us UMI [400]

LETTER FROM HON. WILLIAM ANNAND TO THE ELECTORS OF HANTS / Annand, William – Halifax: Morning Chronicle, 1869. 05827. (Pre-1900 Canadiana) – 9 – cn C.I.H.M. [971]

LETTER FROM TAIZE – 1978-90 (complete) – Inquire – 1 – ATLA S0346 – us A.T.L.A. [240]

LETTER FROM THE PRESIDENT, PONTIAC PACIFIC JUNCTION RAILWAY CO., OTTAWA, DEC. 15TH, 1893 / Beemer, J J – Ottawa: 1893. 03302. (Pre-1900 Canadiana) – 9 – cn C.I.H.M. [380]

A LETTER FROM THE RIGHT HON. LORD BROUGHAM TO THE RIGHT HON. SIR JAMES GRAHAM, BT., M.P., ON THE MAKING AND DIGESTING OF THE LAW / Brougham, Henry Peter & Vaux – 2nd ed. London, Ridgway, 1849. 46 p. LL-104 – 1 – us L of C Photodup [340]

A LETTER FROM THE...MINISTER OF WESTBURY-UPON-TRYM TO THE OCCASIONAL PREACHERS AT PORTLAND CHAPEL, LATELY OPENED IN THAT PARISH / Edwards, WE – Bristol, 1792 – 1mf – 9 – MP-579/1 – ne IDC [240]

LETTER LEAFLET OF THE WOMAN'S AUXILIARY TO THE BOARD OF DOMESTIC AND FOREIGN MISSIONS OF THE CHURCH OF ENGLAND IN CANADA – (Cont: Monthly Letter Leaflet. Cont by: Living Message) – [Toronto]: The Auxiliary, [1893?-19–] (Toronto: Timms) – 9 – cn C.I.H.M. [240]

A LETTER OF ADVICE FROM A FATHER TO HIS SON, JUST ENTERING INTO HOLY ORDERS / Hill, Richard – London, 1762 – 1mf – 9 – MP-414/1 – ne IDC [240]

THE LETTER OF AN OLD BOLSHEVIK: A KEY TO THE MOSCOW TRIALS – London: G. Allen & Unwin, 1938. 79p. Signed Y.Z – 1 – us U.W. Library [335]

LETTER OF JOHN MCDONOGH ON AFRICA : ADDRESSED TO THE EDITORS OF THE NEW ORLEANS COMMERCIAL BULLETIN – New Orleans: Printed at the Tropic Office, 1842 – us Res Libr [960]

LETTER OF THE HON. EDWARD BLAKE TO THE WEST DURHAM REFORM CONVENTION: TO WHICH IS APPENDED CORRESPONDENCE AS TO THE INVERARY MEETING / Blake, Edward – Toronto: Budget Print. and Pub. Co., 1891. 00162. (Pre-1900 Canadiana) – 9 – cn C.I.H.M. [971]

A LETTER ON THE VALIDITY AND CONSTITUTIONALITY OF THE LEGAL TENDER ACT / Nichols, Effingham H – Washington: Gibson, 1869. 8p. LL-1215 – 1 – us L of C Photodup [340]

LETTER PRESS VOLUMES FROM THE COLLECTION OF THE KANSAS TOWN AND LAND CO., INC. (JULY 27, 1887) / Kansas Town and Land Company – 1888-1905. In Kansas State Historical Society. Guide – 1 – us KS Hist [978]

A LETTER TO A FRIEND ON THE SUBJECT OF METHODISM – London, 1775 – 1mf – 9 – MP-500/1 – ne IDC [240]

LETTER TO ELIZA – 1869. 06130. (Pre-1900 Canadiana) – 9 – cn C.I.H.M. [360]

LETTER TO E.T. SMYTH, BENTON COUNTY, AL, 1854 / Johnston, William – Also a letter to Dr. Davis C. Woolley from Davis C. Cooper – 1 – 5.00 – us Baptist [240]

LETTER TO FRIENDS *see* MINISTERS' LETTERS

LETTER TO H. DUNDAS AND TO THE COURT OF DIRECTORS OF THE EAST INDIA COMPANY, ON THE MODE OF IMPROVING THE NAVY OF GREAT BRITAIN / Snodgrass, Gabriel – 1797 – 9 – uk Libr Preservation [941]

A LETTER TO LA DEPECHE / Fabregon, Louis – n.p., n.d. Fiche W 867. (Blodgett Collection of Spanish Civil War Pamphlets) – 9 – us H.U. College Libr [946]

A LETTER TO ROBERT SEAGRAVE, M.A., OCCASIONED BY HIS TWO LATE PERFORMANCES,... / Scrub, T – London, 1739 – 1mf – 9 – MP-253/1 – ne IDC [240]

A LETTER TO SIR SAMUEL ROMILLY,KNT. ON THE REVISION OF THE BANKRUPT LAW / Evans, William David – London, Reed, 1810. 101 p. LL-1680 – 1 – us L of C Photodup [340]

A LETTER TO THE FOLLOWERS OF ELIAS HICKS : IN THE CITY OF BALTIMORE, AND ITS VICINITY / Gurney, Joseph John – Baltimore: Woods and Crane, 1839 – 1mf – us A.T.L.A. [240]

LETTER TO THE FRIENDS OF DEMOCRACY / Paddock, Robert Louis – N.Y., 1936. Fiche W1095. (Blodgett Collection of Spanish Civil War Pamphlets) – 9 – us H.U. College Libr [946]

LETTER TO THE HON. WILLIAM H. SEWARD, SECRETARY OF STATE: IN ANSWER TO ONE FROM HIM ON THE RESOLUTION OF THE SENATE AS TO THE RELATIONS OF THE UNITED STATES WITH THE BRITISH PROVINCES: AND THE ACTUAL CONDITION OF THE QUESTION OF THE FISHERIES / Derby, Elias Hasket – Washington, D.C.: s.n., 1867. 02643. (Pre-1900 Canadiana) – 9 – cn C.I.H.M. [971]

LETTER TO THE MERCHANTS AND TRADESMEN OF GT. BRITAIN, PARTICULARLY TO THOSE OF LONDON AND BRISTOL, CONCERNING THEIR SUCCESSFUL OPPOSITION TO THE EXTENSION OF THE EXCISE LAWS 1733 / Budgell, E A – 1 – uk Microform Academic [941]

LETTER TO THE PRESIDENT OF THE AMERICA SIC SOCIETY FOR THE ADVANCEMENT OF SCIENCE: ON THE SUBJECT OF STANDARD TIME FOR THE UNITED STATES OF AMERICA, CANADA AND MEXICO / Fleming, Sandford – s.l.: s.n., 1882?. 00044. (Pre-1900 Canadiana) – 9 – cn C.I.H.M. [971]

A LETTER TO THE REV. J. BUTLER / Quinby, Hosea – Containing a review of his friendly letters to a lady, together with a general outline of the Doctrine of the Freewill Baptists. 1832 – 1 – 5.74 – us Baptist [240]

A LETTER TO THE REV MR. JOHN WESLEY, CONCERNING HIS INCONSISTENCY WITH HIMSELF, OCCASIONED BY THE PUBLICATION OF HIS SERMON ENTITLED 'THE LORD OUR RIGHTEOUSNESS' / Parker, W – London, 1766 – 1mf – 9 – MP-436/1 – ne IDC [240]

A LETTER TO THE REV. MR. JOHN WESLEY IN ANSWER TO HIS LATE PAMPHLET ENTITLED 'FREE THOUGHTS ON THE PRESENT STATE OF PUBLIC AFFAIRS' / Towers, J – London, 1771 – 1mf – 9 – MP-474/1 – ne IDC [240]

A LETTER TO THE REV. MR. JOHN WESLEY RELATIVE TO HIS PRETENDED ABRIDGMENT OF ZANCHIUS ON PREDESTINATION / Toplady, Augustus Montague – London, 1770 – 1mf – 9 – MP-464/1 – ne IDC [240]

A LETTER TO THE REV. MR. M–RE B–K–R CONCERNING THE METHODIST / Evans, William – Dublin, 1752 – 1mf – 9 – MP-356/1 – ne IDC [240]

A LETTER TO THE REV. MR. WHITEFIELD, DESIGNED TO CORRECT HIS MISTAKEN ACCOUNT OF REGENERATION, OR THE NEW BIRTH;... / Land, T – London, 1739 – 1mf – 9 – MP-250/1 – ne IDC [240]

A LETTER TO THE REV. ROBERT HAWKER, D.D., VICAR OF THE PARISH OF CHARLES, PLYMOUTH, OCCASIONED BY HIS LATE EXPEDITION INTO CORNWALL / Polwhele, R – London, 1799 – 1mf – 9 – MP-596/1 – ne IDC [240]

A LETTER TO THE REV. SAMUEL DAVIDSON, D.D., LL. D : IN ANSWER TO HIS ESSAY AGAINST THE JOHANNINE AUTHORSHIP OF THE FOURTH GOSPEL / Bache, Kentish – 3rd ed. Oxford: Parker, 1886 – 1mf – 9 – 0-8370-2133-2 – 1985-0133 – us A.T.L.A. [220]

LETTER TO THE REV. SAMUEL DAVIDSON: IN ANSWER TO HIS ESSAY AGAINST THE JOHANNINE AUTHOR / Bache, Kent – Oxford: Parker, 1886. 1 fiche – 9 – us A.T.L.A. [240]

A LETTER TO THE REVD. MR. JOHN WESLEY, OCCASIONED BY HIS 'ADDRESS TO THE CLERGY', FEBRUARY 6, 1756 / Fleming, Caleb – London, 1756 – 1mf – 9 – MP-369/1 – ne IDC [240]

A LETTER TO THE REVEREND DR. DURELL, VICE-CHANCELLOR OF THE UNIVERSITY OF OXFORD, OCCASIONED BY A LATE EXPULSION OF SIX STUDENTS FROM EDMUND HALL / Whitefield, George – London, 1768 – 1mf – 9 – MP-449/1 – ne IDC [240]

A LETTER TO THE REVEREND MR. GEORGE WHITEFIELD, OCCASIONED BY HIS REMARKS UPON A PAMPHLET ENTITLED 'THE ENTHUSIASM OF METHODISTS AND PAPISTS COMPARED' – London, 1750 – 1mf – 9 – MP-340/1 – ne IDC [240]

A LETTER TO THE REVEREND MR. JOHN WESLEY, IN ANSWER TO HIS SERMON ENTITULED 'FREE-GRACE' / Whitefield, George – London, 1741 – 1mf – 9 – MP-284/1 – ne IDC [240]

A LETTER TO THE REVEREND MR. JOHN WESTLY, OCCASION'D BY HIS SERMON AGAINST PREDESTINATION;... / Christianus – London, 1740 – 1mf – 9 – MP-277/1 – ne IDC [240]

LETTER TO THE RIGHT HON. DAVID BOYLE, LORD PRESIDENT OF THE COURT OF SESSION, REGARDING ABUSES PRACTISED BY JUDICIAL FACTORS ON THE ESTATES OF MINORS. – Dalkeith Scot. Lyle 1852. 17 p. LL-2247 – 1 – us L of C Photodup [340]

A LETTER TO THE RIGHT HON. LORD MANNERS, &C. &C. &C. ON THE EXPEDIENCY OF AN IMMEDIATE AND SEPARATE RECORD COMMISSION, TO INVESTIGATE, ILLUSTRATE, AND ARRANGE THE RECORDS OF IRELAND. / Duhigg, Barthelomew Thomas – Dublin, Colles, 1810. 40, 37 p. LL-2300 – 1 – us L of C Photodup [340]

A LETTER TO THE RIGHT HON. LORD VISCOUNT GODERICH / Viger, Denis Benjamin – London [England]: Cunningham and Salmon, 1831. SEM105P1366 – 1mf – 9 – Can$2.25 – cn Bibl Nat [971]

A LETTER TO THE RIGHT HON. ROBERT POOL, ON THE COURTS OF LAW IN SCOTLAND / Bridges, James – Edinburgh, Constable, 1823. 75 p. LL-2289 – 1 – us L of C Photodup [340]

LETTER TO WILLIAM JOHNSTON FROM E.T. SMYTH, BENTON COUNTY, ALABAMA, 1854 / Smyth, E T – Includes letter to Dr. Davis C. Woolley from David S. Cooper. 3p – 1 – $5.00 – us Baptist [240]

A LETTER: WHEARIN, PART OF THE ENTERTAINMENT UNTOO THE QUEENZ MAIESTY AT KILLINGWOORTH CASTLE IZ SIGNIFIED / Laneham, Robert – 1575. 92p. (English Linguistics Series 1500-1800) – 9 – us UMI [941]

LETTERA DI FABRITIO GUASTAFERRI AL SIG. GIO. FRANCESCO SALITTI.. / Guastaferri, Fabritio – Roma: G. Dragonelli, 1663. 56p.First ed. Woodcut vignette on title, on vellum – 1 – us U.W. Library [530]

LA LETTERA DI SAN PAOLO AI COLOSSESI: STUDI / Luzzi, Giovanni – Torino: Ermanno Loescher, 1892. 1 fiche – 9 – us A.T.L.A. [240]

LETTERBOOK / Bacot, Thomas W – 1811-18.5 fiches – 9 – us South Carolina Historical [978]

LETTERBOOK / Manigault, Peter – 1750-54, 1758, 1773-75. 5 fiches – 9 – us South Carolina Historical [025]

LETTERBOOK / Manigault, Peter – 1763-73.4 fiches – 9 – us South Carolina Historical [978]

LETTERBOOK / Planters and Mechanics Bank. Charleston, South Carolina – 1839-47. 5 fiches – 9 – us South Carolina Historical [336]

LETTERBOOK / Porter, James Gray – 1878-79. 8 fiches – 9 – us South Carolina Historical [025]

LETTER-BOOK, 1748-1754, AND SERMONS / Bennet, J – (Coll title: The People Called Methodists, Phase 2: Primary Sources 1738-1800) – 4mf – 9 – MP-615/1 – ne IDC [240]

LETTERBOOK OF GEORGE WOOLSEY AND GEORGE SALMON / Woolsey, George – 1774-84 – 1 – 18.00 – us L of C Photodup [920]

LETTERBOOK OF THE NATCHITOCHES-SULPHUR FORK FACTORY, 1809-21 / U.S. Bureau of Indian Affairs – 1roll. T1029 – 1 – us Nat'l Archives [324]

LETTERBOOKS / Fison, Lorimer – v1-7. 1867-1883 – 4r – 1 – at Pacific Mss [980]

LETTERBOOKS / Gibbes, James Shoolbred – 1855-83. 15 fiches – 9 – us South Carolina Historical [025]

LETTERBOOKS, 1882-9, 1894-7 / Bokwe, J K – 18 fiche – 9 – sa SA Libr [960]

LETTERBOOKS AND JOURNALS / Shoolbred, James – 1786-96.44 fiches – 9 – us South Carolina Historical [025]

THE LETTERBOOKS OF THE PRESIDENTS OF THE AMERICAN FEDERATION OF LABOR – 341r – 1 – $11,935.00 – Dist. us Scholarly Res – us L of C Photodup [331]

LETTERE DEL GRAN MAHVMETO IMPERADORE DE' TVRCHI: SCRITTE A DIVERSI RE, PRENCIPI, SIGNORI, E REPVBLICHE – Vinegia, 1563 – 3mf – 9 – H-8161/1 – ne IDC [956]

LE LETTERE DI SANTA CATERINA DE'RICCI = CORRESPONDENCE. SELECTIONS : FIORENTINA RELIGIOSA DOMENICANA IN S. VINCENZIO DI PRATO: ALLA FAMIGLIA / De'Ricci, Caterina, Saint; ed by Gherardi, Alessandro – (In Italian. Includes bibliographical references) – Firenze: Mariano Ricci, 1890 – 1mf – 9 – 0-8370-6896-7 – 1986-0896 – us A.T.L.A. [860]

LETTERE DI UN PRETE MODERNISTA / Murri, R & Loisy, A – Roma: Libreria editrice Romana, 1908 – 1mf – 9 – 0-8370-8853-4 – 1986-2853 – us A.T.L.A. [240]

LETTERE, ET ORAZIONI...SCRITTE A PRINCIPI D'ITALIA INTORNO AL COLLE GARSI, ET IMPRENDER GUERRA CONTRO AL TURCO / Ressarion, Cardinal – Firenze, 1594 – 2mf – 9 – H-8379/1 – ne IDC [956]

Letteris, M H *see*
- BEN ABUYAH
- ZIKKARON BE-SEFER

LETTERPRESS COPY BOOKS / Callbreath, Grant & Callbreath, Cook – 1878-98. Correspondence of the Wrangell, Alaska Merchant Firm. University of Washington Libraries. Guide – 1 – $24.00 – us U.W. Libraries [978]

LETTERPRESS COPYBOOKS OF SAMUEL GOMPERS AND WILLIAM GREEN, PRESIDENTS – 1883-1925 – 1 – $9,517.00 – us L of C Photodup [330]

LETTERS – 1 – us KS Hist [978]

LETTERS / Aichel, Margaret Hurkamp – 1877-81.7 fiches – 9 – us South Carolina Historical [978]

LETTERS / Brown, John – 1 reel – 1 – us UMI [920]

LETTERS / Bryant Family – 1841-67 – 1 – us KS Hist [025]

LETTERS / Burckmeyer – 1863-65.19 fiches. Originals of the letters publ. by Charlotte R. Holmes, comp., the Burckmeyer Letters.(Columbia, 1926) – 9 – us South Carolina Historical [025]

LETTERS / Burt, Armistead – 1847-48. 1 fiche – 9 – us South Carolina Historical [025]

LETTERS / Calhoun, John C – 1824, 1831, 1844-50. 2 fiches – 9 – us South Carolina Historical [975]

LETTERS / Carney, Thomas – 1863-64 – 1 – us KS Hist [978]

LETTERS / Cummings, John N – 1863-64.3 fiches – 9 – us South Carolina Historical [976]

LETTERS / Curry, J L M – 1848-1939. 1,224p – 1 – 42.84 – us Baptist [240]

LETTERS / Dawson, Francis Warrington – 1881-89. 4 fiches – 9 – us South Carolina Historical [978]

LETTERS / Day, Warren & Day, Mary A – 1857, 1862-65, 1878 – 1 – us KS Hist [920]

LETTERS / Dougherty, Peter – 1838-1870; Andrew Porter. Letters. 1848-1871 – 1 – $100.00 – us Presbyterian [240]

LETTERS / Elliott, R G – 1849-66 – 1 – us KS Hist [920]

LETTERS / Floyd, John – 1775-76; 1784; 1786. 1 fiche – 9 – us South Carolina Historical [025]

LETTERS / Holcomb Family – 1815-1918 – 1 – us KS Hist [920]

LETTERS / Holmes, Daniel B – 1858-62 – 1 – us KS Hist [920]

LETTERS / Honnell, T C – 1861-65 – 1 – us KS Hist [920]

LETTERS / Hooper, William Hope – 1889-94 – 1 – us KS Hist [920]

LETTERS / Isely, Christian H – 1863 – 1 – us KS Hist [920]

LETTERS / Martin, John Alexander – 1857, 1861-64 – 1 – us KS Hist [978]

LETTERS / Nettleton, Lucy – 1863-64 – 1 – us KS Hist [978]

LETTERS / Porter, Andrew – 1848-1871; Peter Doughtery. Letters. 1838-1870 – 1 – $100.00 – us Presbyterian [920]

LETTERS / Powers, Otero, Lowe and Company. Kansas – 1869 – 1 – us KS Hist [978]

LETTERS / Priestley, Joseph – 1766-1803; 1789-1803. BRRAM – 1 – uk Microform Academic [920]

LETTERS / Quaque, Philip – 1766-1811. From Archives of United Society for Propagation of the Gospel (USPG) – 1 – uk Microform Academic [240]

LETTERS / Ramsay, David – 1786-1808. 1 fiche – 9 – us South Carolina Historical [025]

LETTERS / Reichart, Hally M – 1945-1946, Letters to Virginia Reichart and Gilman Gazette, Dec. 1945 thru Jan. 1946 – 1 – us KS Hist [920]

LETTERS / Riley, James D – 1867-79 – 1 – us KS Hist [978]

LETTERS / Rutledge, John – 1780-82. 3 fiches – 9 – us South Carolina Historical [025]

LETTERS / Sheldon, Charles Monroe – 1889-1934 – 1 – us KS Hist [978]

LETTERS / Smythe, Sarah Annie & Dunlap, Susan – 1867-68. 3 fiches – 9 – us South Carolina Historical [025]

LETTERS / Talbot, Theodore – 9 Jun-16 Aug 1845 – 1 – us KS Hist [978]

LETTERS / Trueblood, Alva Curtis – 1862-64. Diary, 1861-62 – 1 – us KS Hist [978]

LETTERS / U.S. Army. 2nd Cavalry Regiment. Company C – 1870-74 – 1 – us KS Hist [324]

LETTERS / Ward Family – 1828-1926 – 1 – us KS Hist [978]

LETTERS / Washington, George – 1781-98. 2 fiches – 9 – us South Carolina Historical [975]

LETTERS.. / Ibsen, Henrik – Trans. by John Nilsen Laurvik and Mary Morison. New York: Fox, Duffield and Co., 1905.463p – 1 – us U.W. Library [920]

LETTERS.. / Snow, Susan Eliza – 1888-89 – 1 – us KS Hist [978]

LETTERS, 1812-46 / Harvey, Jacob – From the National Library of Ireland. BRRAM – 1 – uk Microform Academic [920]

LETTERS AND CLIPPINGS / Holliday, Cyrus Kurtz – (Papers. 1854-96. 1. Papers of his estate. 1900-08. 1) – 1864-83 – 1 – us KS Hist [920]

LETTERS AND CORRESPONDENCE OF JOHN HENRY NEWMAN DURING HIS LIFE IN THE ENGLISH CHURCH, WITH A BRIEF AUTOBIOGRAPHY / Newman, John Henry – Ed. at Cardinal Newman's request, by Anne Mozley. London, New York: Longmans, Green, 1890.2v – 1 – us U.W. Library [240]

LETTERS AND DOCUMENTS IN THE ENOCH PRATT FREE LIBRARY / Poe, Edgar Allen – 9 – 10.00 – us Scholars' Facs [860]

LETTERS AND FAMILY PAPERS, MS 1381 / Vallandigham, Clement Laird – 1793-1871. Correspondence, speeches, writings, financial and legal documents. 1 reel – 1 – us Western Res [920]

THE LETTERS AND INSCRIPTIONS OF HAMMURABI, KING OF BABYLON / King, L W – v. 2-3. London. 1900. BNE-20,054 1 – 9 – ne IDC [930]

LETTERS AND LETTER BOOKS, 1887-1903 / Walker, Robert H – London: Kodak Ltd, Recordak Div, 1967 – us Res Libr [860]

LETTERS AND NOTEBOOKS / Remington, Frederic – 1888-1906 – 1 – us KS Hist [978]

LETTERS AND OPINIONS OF THE MASONIC INSTITUTION / Adams, John Quincy – Cincinnati: Lorenzo Stratton, 1851 – 4mf – 9 – $6.00 – LLMC 91-501 – us L.L.M.C. [360]

LETTERS AND OTHER MANUSCRIPTS / Rice, Luther – 1812-29.Materials from Gelman Library, George Washington University – 1 – 45.22 – us Baptist [240]

LETTERS AND OTHER PAPERS / Lykins, Johnston – undated, Physician, missionary, and Indian agent – 1 – us KS Hist [920]

LETTERS AND OTHER PAPERS OF JOSEPH BELLAMY / Bellamy, Joseph – 1739-1787 – 1 – $50.00 – us Presbyterian [240]

LETTERS AND PAPERS / Nightingale, Florence – 1 – uk Microform Academic [920]

LETTERS AND PAPERS ILLUSTRATIVE OF THE REIGN OF RICHARD 3 AND HENRY 7 (RS24) / ed by Gairdner, J – (v1 1861 Dfl35.00. v2 1863 Dfl35.00) – 2v – ne Slangenburg [941]

LETTERS AND PAPERS ILLUSTRATIVE OF THE WARS OF THE ENGLISH IN FRANCE DURING THE REIGN OF HENRY 6 (RS22) / ed by Stevenson, J – (v1 1861 Dfl39.00. v2,1 1864 Dfl30.00. v2,2 1864 Dfl35.00) – 2v – ne Slangenburg [941]

THE LETTERS AND PAPERS OF RICHARD RUSH / Rush, Richard; ed by Brescia, Anthony M – (With printed guide) – 1980 – 29r – 1 – $2,465.00 – S1621 – us Scholarly Res [920]

LETTERS AND PAPERS OF ROBERT BOYLE / Boyle, Robert – $1,760.00 – 1-55655-170-3 – us UPA [920]

LETTERS AND PAPERS OF ROBERT BOYLE : A GUIDE TO THE MANUSCRIPTS AND MICROFILM / Royal Society – $75.00 – 1-55655-217-3 – us UPA [920]

LETTERS AND PAPERS OF ROGER WILLIAMS / Williams, Roger – 1629-82. 368p – 1 – $12.88 – us Baptist [240]

LETTERS AND PAPERS OF SIR JOHN HERSCHEL : A GUIDE TO THE MANUSCRIPTS AND MICROFILM / Herschel, Sir John – $75.00 – 1-55655-218-1 – us UPA [920]

LETTERS AND PAPERS OF SIR JOHN HERSCHEL / Herschel, Sir John – $3,080.00 – 1-55655-169-X – us UPA [920]

LETTERS AND PAPERS ON AGRICULTURE, PLANTING, & C. SELECTED FROM THE CORRESPONDENCE OF THE BATH AND WEST OF ENGLAND SOCIETY, FOR THE ENCOURAGEMENT OF AGRICULTURE, ARTS, MANUFACTURERS, AND COMMERCE / Bath and West and Southern Counties Society – Bath, 1791-1816 – 3 – us Readex [630]

LETTERS AND SCRAPBOOK / Elder Family – 1 – us KS Hist [978]

LETTERS AND SKETCHES FROM NORTHERN NIGERIA / Kisch, M S – London. 1910. BA-325 2 – 8 – ne IDC [960]

LETTERS AND SOCIAL AIMS / Emerson, Ralph Waldo – Boston: James R. Osgood, 1876, c 1875 – 1mf – us A.T.L.A. [140]

LETTERS AND SPEECHES / Capper, Arthur – 1904-51 – 1 – us KS Hist [978]

LETTERS AND TELEGRAMS SENT BY THE CONFEDERATE ADJUTANT AND INSPECTOR GENERAL, 1861-65 / U.S. War Department. Confederate Records – 6rolls. M627. Printed guide – 1 – us Nat'l Archives [324]

LETTERS AND TELEGRAMS SENT BY THE CONFEDERATE QUARTERMASTER GENERAL / Confederate States of America – 1861-65. 8 rolls. M900 – 1 – us Nat'l Archives [324]

LETTERS AND TELEGRAMS SENT BY THE ENGINEER BUREAU OF THE CONFEDERATE WAR DEPT., 1861-64 / U.S. War Department. Confederate Records – 5 rolls. M628. Printed guide – 1 – us Nat'l Archives [324]

LETTERS BY HISTORICUS ON SOME QUESTIONS OF INTERNATIONAL LAW / [Harcourt, W G G Y V] – London, Cambridge, 1863 – 3mf – 1 – ILM-916/1 – ne IDC [327]

LETTERS CONCERNING THE PRESENT STATE OF POLAND: TOGETHER WITH THE MANIFESTO OF THE COURTS OF VIENNA, PETERSBURGH, AND BERLIN, AND THE LETTERS PATENT OF THE KING OF PRUSSIA / Lind, John – London, 1773. Includes bibliographical references – 1 – us U.W. Library [943]

LETTERS FROM ALASKA AND THE PACIFIC COAST / Briggs, Horace – 1889 – 1 – $50.00 – us Presbyterian [978]

LETTERS FROM AND OPINIONS OF THE ATTORNEYS GENERAL, 1791-1811 / U. S. Attorney General – 1roll. T326 – 1 – us Nat'l Archives [324]

LETTERS FROM DELIBES, ERLANGER, GODARD, MASSENET, MEYERBEER, REBER, STRAUSS, REMENYI, PLANQUETTE, PIERNE, DA PONTE, AUBER – 9 – us Sibley [780]

'LETTERS FROM FIJI, 1933-34' / Thompson, Laura – 1r – 1 – at Pacific Mss [980]

LETTERS FROM HONORABLE P. FORTIN, M.P. ON THE TELEGRAPH AND SIGNAL SERVICE SYSTEM IN THE GULF OF ST LAWRENCE, ON THE UNITED STATES SIGNAL SERVICE AND ON THE NORWEGIAN TELEGRAPH SYSTEM / Fortin, Pierre – Ottawa?: s.n., 1881 (Ottawa: Maclean, Roger). 05587. (Pre-1900 Canadiana) – 9 – cn C.I.H.M. [971]

LETTERS FROM INDIA / Eden, Emily – Ed. by her niece, Eleanor Eden. London: Bentley, 1872. 2v – 1 – us U.W. Library [390]

LETTERS FROM INDIA AND KASHMIR – London, 1874. 252 pp., ills. BI-1136 1 – 9 – ne IDC [950]

LETTERS FROM JOSEPH RITSON, ESQ. TO MR. GEORGE PATON / Ritson, Joseph – 1829 – 1 – us I.U. Libraries [390]

LETTERS FROM SWITZERLAND / Prime, Samuel Irenaeus – New York: Sheldon; Boston: Gould & Lincoln, 1860 – 1mf – us A.T.L.A. [240]

LETTERS FROM THE BATTLE-FIELDS OF PARAGUAY / Burton, Richard Francis – London: Tinsley Brothers, 1870. xix,491p. fold. map – 1 – us U.W. Library [972]

LETTERS FROM THE HONORABLE DENIS B. VIGER, TO THE HONORABLE LOUIS JOSEPH PAPINEAU, SPEAKER OF THE ASSEMBLY OF LOWER CANADA – s.l., s.n. SEM105P401 – 1mf – 9 – Can$2.25 – cn Bibl Nat [323]

LETTERS IN HEAT AND MASS TRANSFER *see* INTERNATIONAL COMMUNICATIONS IN HEAT AND MASS TRANSFER

LETTERS IN MATHEMATICAL PHYSICS – (v8-. 1984-. 5,6,9) – v1-. Dec 1975- – 1 – us UMI [073]

LETTERS, MANUSCRIPTS, ARTICLES, ETC / Brown, John – 1832-1964. Collected by Mrs. Velma West Sykes – 1 – us KS Hist [920]

LETTERS, MS 2150 / Pike, Zebulon Montgomery – 1801-11. General and personal letters – 1 – us Western Res [920]

LETTERS, MS 3263 / Swaim, David G – 1861-74. 1 reel – 1 – us Western Res [920]

LETTERS, MS 3947 / Huntington, Samuel – 1801-17. 1 reel – 1 – us Western Res [920]

LETTERS, MS P.P. / Chapman, Harlan P – 1862-64. 1 reel – 1 – us Western Res [920]

LETTERS OF AN ALTRURIAN TRAVELLER / Howells, William Dean – 1893-94 – 9 – 10.00 – us Scholars' Facs [910]

LETTERS OF APPLICATION AND RECOMMENDATION DURING THE ADMINISTRATION OF ANDREW JACKSON, 1829-37 / U.S. Department of State – (Printed guide) – M639 – 27r – 1 – us Nat'l Archives [324]

LETTERS OF APPLICATION AND RECOMMENDATION DURING THE ADMINISTRATION OF JAMES MADISON, 1809-17 / U.S. Department of State – 8rolls. M438. Printed guide – 1 – us Nat'l Archives [324]

LETTERS OF APPLICATION AND RECOMMENDATION DURING THE ADMINISTRATION OF JAMES MONROE, 1817-25 / U.S. Department of State – 19 rolls. M439. Printed guide – 1 – us Nat'l Archives [324]

LETTERS OF APPLICATION AND RECOMMENDATION DURING THE ADMINISTRATION OF JAMES POLK, ZACHARY TAYLOR, AND MILLARD FILLMORE / U.S. Department of State – 1845-53. 98 rolls. M873 – 1 – us Nat'l Archives [978]

LETTERS OF APPLICATION AND RECOMMENDATION DURING THE ADMINISTRATION OF JOHN ADAMS, 1797-1801 / U.S. Department of State – 3rolls. M406. Printed Guide – 1 – us Nat'l Archives [324]

LETTERS OF APPLICATION AND RECOMMENDATION DURING THE ADMINISTRATION OF JOHN QUINCY ADAMS, 1825-29 / U.S. Department of State – 8rolls. M531. Printed guide – 1 – us Nat'l Archives [324]

LETTERS OF APPLICATION AND RECOMMENDATION DURING THE ADMINISTRATION OF THOMAS JEFFERSON, 1801-09 / U.S. Department of State – 12 rolls. M418. Printed guide – 1 – us Nat'l Archives [975]

LETTERS OF APPLICATION AND RECOMMENDATION DURING THE ADMINISTRATIONS OF ABRAHAM LINCOLN AND ANDREW JOHNSON, 1861-69 / U.S. Department of State – (Printed guide) – M650 – 52r – 1 – us Nat'l Archives [324]

LETTERS OF APPLICATION AND RECOMMENDATION DURING THE ADMINISTRATIONS OF FRANKLIN PIERCE AND JAMES BUCHANAN / U.S. Department of State – 1853-61. M967 – 50r – 1 – us Nat'l Archives [324]

LETTERS OF APPLICATION AND RECOMMENDATION DURING THE ADMINISTRATIONS OF MARTIN VAN BUREN, WILLIAM HENRY HARRISON, AND JOHN TYLER, 1837-45 / U.S. Department of State – 35 rolls. M687. Printed guide – 1 – us Nat'l Archives [324]

LETTERS OF APPLICATION AND RECOMMENDATION DURING THE ADMINISTRATIONS OF ULYSSES S. GRANT / U.S. Department of State – 1869-77. M968 – 69r – 1 – us Nat'l Archives [324]

THE LETTERS OF ARCHBISHOP ALLEN / Westminster Cathedral. Archives – 1 – uk Microform Academic [240]

LETTERS OF BENJAMIN DIAS FERNANDEZ ON THE EVIDENCES OF CHRISTIANITY / Fernandez, Benjamin Dias – (Includes appendix on the life of Christ) – Cincinnati: Bloch, 1869 – 1mf – 9 – 0-8370-2923-6 – 1985-0923 – us A.T.L.A. [270]

THE LETTERS OF CHARLES LAMB : WITH A SKETCH OF HIS LIFE / Lamb, Charles – London: Edward Moxon, 1837 – 1 roll – 1 – 1-55879-083-7 – uk Libr Preservation [860]

LETTERS OF DANTE GABRIEL ROSSETTI TO WILLIAM ALLINGHAM, 1854-1870 / Rossetti, Dante Gabriel – London: T.F. Unwin, 1897 – 1 roll – 1 – 1-55879-536-7 – uk Libr Preservation [860]

LETTERS OF DOROTHEA, PRINCESS LIEVEN, DURING HER RESIDENCE IN LONDON, 1812-1834 / Lieven, Daria Khristoforovna – Ed. by Lionel G. Robinson. London, New York: Longmans, 1902. xx,414p – 1 – us U.W. Library [941]

LETTERS OF EDWARD JOHN TRELAWNY. EDITED WITH A BRIEF INTRODUCTION AND NOTES BY H. BUXTON FORMAN, C.B. / Trelawny, Edward John; ed by Forman, H Buxton – London, New York [etc.]: H. Frowde, Oxford university press, 1910 – 1 roll – 1 – 1-55879-688-6 – uk Libr Preservation [860]

LETTERS OF EDWARD LEAR : TO CHICHESTER FORTESCUE, LORD CARLINGFORD AND FRANCES, COUNTESS WALDEGRAVE / Lear, Edward – London: T. Fisher Unwin, 1907 – 1 roll – 1 – 1-55879-375-5 – uk Libr Preservation [860]

LETTERS OF HON. WILLIAM ATKINSON: AND OTHER CORRESPONDENTS RELATIVE TO THE CARRABASSETT AND CANADIAN RAILWAY – North Anson, ME: Advocate Job Print, 1890. 00845. (Pre-1900 Canadiana) – 9 – cn C.I.H.M. [971]

THE LETTERS OF JOHN HUS / Huss, John; ed by Workman, Herbert Brook & Pope, R Martin – London: Hodder and Stoughton, 1904 – 1mf – us A.T.L.A. [240]

LETTERS OF JOHN KEATS TO FANNY BRAWNE / Keats, John – London: Reeves & Turner, 2nd rev enl ed 1889 – 1 roll – 1 – 1-55879-869-2 – uk Libr Preservation [860]

LETTERS OF MARQUE / Kipling, Rudyard – Allahabad: A.H. Wheeler, 1891. ii,154p – 1 – us U.W. Library [390]

LETTERS OF MARQUE 1777-1783; DECLARATIONS AGAINST AMERICA / Great Britain. Public Record Office – 1 – uk Microform Academic [324]

THE LETTERS OF MARTIN LUTHER / Currie, Margaret A – London; New York: Macmillan, 1908 – 2mf – us A.T.L.A. [240]

LETTERS OF MATTHEW ARNOLD, 1848-1888 / Russell, George W E – London, New York: Macmillan, 1895 – 2mf – us A.T.L.A. [240]

LETTERS OF TENCH COXE, COMM. OF THE REVENUE, RELATING TO THE PROCUREMENT OF MILITARY, NAVAL, AND INDIAN SUPPLIES, 1794-96 / U.S. Bureau of Indian Affairs – 1roll. M74 – 1 – us Nat'l Archives [324]

LETTERS OF THE LATE EDWARD BULWER, LORD LYTTON, TO HIS WIFE... / Bulwer Lytton, Edward – London: W. Swan Sonnenschein, 1884 – 1 roll – 1 – 1-55879-327-5 – uk Libr Preservation [860]

LETTERS OF THE REV. DR. BEECHER AND REV. MR. NETTLETON ON THE "NEW MEASURES" IN CONDUCTING REVIVALS OF RELIGION : WITH A REVIEW OF A SERMON / Beecher, Lyman – New York: G. & C. Carvill, 1828 – 1mf – us A.T.L.A. [240]

LETTERS OF WILLIAM 3 AND LOUIS 14 AND THEIR MINISTERS / William 3, King; ed by Grimblot, Paul – London: Printed for Longman, Brown, Green, and Longmans, 1848. 2v. With appendix of treaties and documents – 1 – us U.W. Library [941]

LETTERS ON LITERATURE / Lang, Andrew – London, New York: Longmans, Green, 3rd ed 1889 – 1 roll – 1 – 1-55879-479-4 – uk Libr Preservation [420]

LETTERS ON NATURAL HISTORY AND MEDICINE TO CARL LINNAEUS FROM ABOUT 1728-1783, ARRANGED IN ALPHABETICAL ORDER / Linnaeus, Carl – Zug, 1968. London, Linnean Society. 16v. 1v suppl – 446mf – 9 – ne IDC [610]

LETTERS ON RELIGIOUS RETIREMENT, MELANCHOLY AND ENTHUSIASM / Langhorne, J – London, 1762 – 1mf – 9 – MP-413/1 – ne IDC [240]

LETTERS ON REVIVALS OF RELIGION : ADDRESSED TO MINISTERS OF THE GOSPEL / Finney, Charles Grandison – Manchester: W Bremner, [1861?] – 1mf – 9 – 0-8370-4719-6 – 1985-2719 – us A.T.L.A. [240]

LETTERS ON ROMANISM : IN REPLY TO MR. NEWMAN'S ESSAY ON DEVELOPMENT / Butler, William Archer; ed by Woodward, Thomas – Cambridge: Macmillan, 1858 – 1mf – us A.T.L.A. [240]

LETTERS ON THE DIVINE TRINITY : ADDRESSED TO HENRY WARD BEECHER / Barrett, Benjamin Fiske – New York:Mason Bros., 1860 – 1mf – 9 – 0-8370-2544-3 – 1985-0544 – us A.T.L.A. [270]

LETTERS ON THE ENGLISH NATION / Angeloni, B [ps. of J Shebbeare] – London, 2nd ed 1756. 2v – 8mf – 9 – ne IDC [320]

LETTERS ON THE LOGOS / Upham, Charles W – Boston: Bowles and Dearborn, 1828 – 1mf – us A.T.L.A. [240]

LETTERS ON THE MORAL AND RELIGIOUS STATE OF SOUTH AMERICA / Thomson, James – 1827 – 1 – $50.00 – us Presbyterian [240]

LETTERS ON THE ORIGIN AND PROGRESS OF THE NEW HAVEN THEOLOGY : FROM A NEW ENGLAND MINISTER TO ONE AT THE SOUTH / Tyler, Bennet – New York: R. Carter and E. Collier, 1837 – 1mf – us A.T.L.A. [240]

LETTERS ON THE SLAVE-TRADE AND THE STATE OF THE NATIVES IN THOSE PARTS OF AFRICA WHICH ARE CONTIGUOUS TO FORT ST LOUIS AND GOREE. / Clarkson, Thomas – London. 1791 – 1 – us Res Libr [960]

LETTERS ON THERON AND ASPASIO: ADDRESSED TO THE AUTHOR OF THAT WORK: WITH TWO PREFACES, AND TWO APPENDIXES,. / Sandeman, Robert – 4th ed. London: J. Chater, 1768. 2v – 1 – us U.W. Library [420]

LETTERS ON VARIOUS INTERESTING AND IMPORTANT SUBJECTS / Freneau, Philip – 1799 – 9 – 10.00 – us Scholars' Facs [860]

LETTERS, ORDERS FOR PAY, ACCOUNTS, RECEIPTS, AND OTHER SUPPLY RECORDS CONCERNING WEAPONS AND MILITARY STORES / U.S. Office of the Quartermaster General – 1776-1801. 1 roll. M927 – 1 – us Nat'l Archives [324]

LETTERS RECEIVED / Koeneke, Irene Aniata – 1931-1949, Koeneke lived in Halstead, KS – 1 – us KS Hist [920]

LETTERS RECEIVED..., 1805-21 / U.S. War Department. Adjutant General's Office – 144 rolls. M566. Printed guide – 1 – us Nat'l Archives [324]

LETTERS RECEIVED BY HEADQUARTERS, DISTRICT OF NEW MEXICO / New Mexico. (District) – Sept 1865 – Aug 1890. 65 rolls. M1088 – 1 – us Nat'l Archives [324]

LETTERS RECEIVED BY JOHN WESLEY POWELL, DIRECTOR OF THE GEOGRAPHICAL AND GEOLOGICAL SURVEY OF THE ROCKY MOUNTAIN REGION, 1869-79 / U. S. Geological Survey – 10 rolls. M156. Printed guide – 1 – us Nat'l Archives [550]

LETTERS RECEIVED BY THE ATTORNEY GENERAL, 1809-1870 : WESTERN LAW AND ORDER / ed by Calhoun, Frederick S – (Coll title: Research Collections in American Legal History. With printed guides) – 11r – 1 – $1,375.00 – 1-55655-634-9 – us UPA [340]

LETTERS RECEIVED BY THE ATTORNEY GENERAL, 1871-1884 : WESTERN LAW AND ORDER / ed by Calhoun, Frederick S – (Coll title: Research Collections in American Legal History. With printed guide) – 1997 – 63r – 1 – $8,270.00 – us UPA [340]

LETTERS RECEIVED BY THE BUREAU OF ENTOMOLOGY FROM W.D. HUNTER / Hunter, W D – 5 May 1902-23 Nov 1908. 3 rolls. M864 – 1 – us Nat'l Archives [324]

LETTERS RECEIVED BY THE COMMISSION BRANCH OF THE ADJUTANT GENERAL'S OFFICE / U.S. War Department. Adjutant General's Office – 1863-70. 527 rolls. M1064 – 1 – us Nat'l Archives [324]

LETTERS RECEIVED BY THE CONFEDERATE ADJUTANT AND INSPECTOR GENERAL, 1861-65 / U.S. War Department. Confederate Records – 164 rolls. M474. Printed guide – 1 – us Nat'l Archives [324]

LETTERS RECEIVED BY THE CONFEDERATE QUARTERMASTER GENERAL, 1861-65 / U.S. War Department. Confederate Records – 14 rolls. M469. Printed guide – 1 – us Nat'l Archives [324]

LETTERS RECEIVED BY THE CONFEDERATE SECRETARY..., 1861-65 / Confederate States of America. Secretary of the Treasury – 57 rolls. M499. Printed guide – 1 – us Nat'l Archives [324]

LETTERS RECEIVED BY THE CONFEDERATE SECRETARY OF WAR, 1861-65 / U.S. War Department. Confederate Records – 151 rolls. M437. Printed guide – 1 – us Nat'l Archives [324]

LETTERS RECEIVED BY THE DEPARTMENT OF JUSTICE FROM MISSISSIPPI / U.S. Department of Justice – 1871-84. 4 rolls. M970 – 1 – us Nat'l Archives [340]

LETTERS RECEIVED BY THE DEPARTMENT OF JUSTICE FROM SOUTH CAROLINA / U.S. Department of Justice – 1871-84. 9 rolls. M947 – 1 – us Nat'l Archives [340]

LETTERS RECEIVED BY THE DEPARTMENT OF JUSTICE FROM THE STATE OF ALABAMA, 1871-1884 – 7r – 1 – M1356 – us Nat'l Archives [340]

LETTERS RECEIVED BY THE DEPARTMENT OF JUSTICE FROM THE STATE OF ARKANSAS, 1871-1884 – 5r – 1 – M1418 – us Nat'l Archives [340]

LETTERS RECEIVED BY THE DEPARTMENT OF JUSTICE FROM THE STATE OF FLORIDA, 1871-1884 – 2r – 1 – M1327 – us Nat'l Archives [340]

LETTERS RECEIVED BY THE DEPARTMENT OF JUSTICE FROM THE STATE OF GEORGIA / U.S. Department of Justice – 1871-84 – 5r – 1 – M996 – us Nat'l Archives [340]

LETTERS RECEIVED BY THE DEPARTMENT OF JUSTICE FROM THE STATE OF KENTUCKY, 1871-1884 – 2r – 1 – M1362 – us Nat'l Archives [340]

LETTERS RECEIVED BY THE DEPARTMENT OF JUSTICE FROM THE STATE OF LOUISIANA / U.S. Department of Justice – 1871-84. 6 rolls. M940 – 1 – us Nat'l Archives [340]

LETTERS RECEIVED BY THE DEPARTMENT OF JUSTICE FROM THE STATE OF MARYLAND, 1871-1884 – 2r – 1 – M1352 – us Nat'l Archives [340]

LETTERS RECEIVED BY THE DEPARTMENT OF JUSTICE FROM THE STATE OF NORTH CAROLINA, 1871-1884 – 3r – 1 – M1345 – us Nat'l Archives [340]

LETTERS RECEIVED BY THE DEPARTMENT OF JUSTICE FROM THE STATE OF TENNESSEE, 1871-1884 – 4r – 1 – M1471 – us Nat'l Archives [340]

LETTERS RECEIVED BY THE DEPARTMENT OF JUSTICE FROM THE STATE OF TEXAS, 1871-1884 – 7r – 1 – M1449 – us Nat'l Archives [340]

LETTERS RECEIVED BY THE DEPARTMENT OF JUSTICE FROM THE STATE OF VIRGINIA, 1871-1884 – 4r – 1 – M1250 – us Nat'l Archives [340]

LETTERS RECEIVED BY THE DEPARTMENT OF JUSTICE FROM THE TERITORY OF DAKOTA, 1871-1884 – 3r – 1 – M1535 – us Nat'l Archives [340]

LETTERS RECEIVED BY THE EAST INDIA COMPANY, FROM ITS SERVANTS IN THE EAST, 1602-1617 / ed by Foster, W – London. v1-6. 1896-1902 – 44mf – 9 – ne IDC [950]

LETTERS RECEIVED BY THE NATIONAL BOARD OF HEALTH / U.S. National Board of Health – 1879-84. And related register, 1879-82. 59 rolls. M753 – 1 – us Nat'l Archives [324]

LETTERS RECEIVED BY THE OFFICE OF INDIAN AFFAIRS, 1824-81 / U.S. Bureau of Indian Affairs – 962 rolls. M234. Printed guide – 1 – us Nat'l Archives [324]

LETTERS RECEIVED BY THE OFFICE OF THE SECTY. OF WAR RELATING TO INDIAN AFFAIRS, 1800-23 / U.S. Bureau of Indian Affairs – 4rolls. M271 – 1 – us Nat'l Archives [324]

LETTERS RECEIVED BY THE OFFICE...(MAIN SERIES) / U.S. War Department. Adjutant General's Office – (1822-60. 636 rolls. M567. 1861-70. 828 rolls. M619. Printed guide. 1871-80. 593 rolls. M666. Printed guide. 1881-89. 740 rolls. M689. Printed guide) – 1 – us Nat'l Archives [324]

LETTERS RECEIVED BY THE PATENTS AND MISCELLANEOUS DIVISION OF THE OFFICE OF THE SECRETARY OF THE INTERIOR RELATING TO CUBA, THE PHILIPPINE ISLANDS, AND PUERTO RICO / U.S. Department of the Interior – 1898-1907. 2 rolls. M824 – 1 – us Nat'l Archives [324]

LETTERS RECEIVED BY THE SECRETARY..., IRREGULAR SERIES, 1861-66 / U.S. War Department. Office of the Secretary – 36 rolls. M492. Printed guide – 1 – us Nat'l Archives [324]

LETTERS RECEIVED BY THE SECRETARY OF THE NAVY: CAPTAINS' LETTERS, 1805-61; 1866-85 / U.S. Navy. Office of Naval Records and Library – 413 rolls. M125 – 1 – us Nat'l Archives [324]

LETTERS RECEIVED BY THE SECRETARY OF THE NAVY FROM: / U.S. Navy. Office of Naval Records and Library – (chiefs of navy bureaus, 1842-85. 33 rolls. M518. Printed guide. commanders, 1804-86. 124 rolls. M147. Printed guide. commanding officers of squadrons, 1841-86. 300 rolls. M89. Printed guide. navy agents and naval storekeepers, 1843-65. 12 rolls. M528. Printed guide. officers below the rank of commander, 1802-84. 518 rolls. M148. Printed guide. the president and executive agencies, 1837-86. 49 rolls. M517. Printed guide) – 1 – us Nat'l Archives [324]

LETTERS RECEIVED BY THE SECRETARY OF THE NAVY FROM THE ATTORNEY GENERAL OF THE UNITED STATES CONTAINING LEGAL OPINIONS AND ADVICE / U.S. Department of State – Jun 1807 – Nov 1825. 1 roll. M1029 – 1 – us Nat'l Archives [324]

LETTERS RECEIVED BY THE SECRETARY OF THE NAVY: MISCELLANEOUS LETTERS, 1801-84 / U.S. Navy. Office of Naval Records and Library – 647 rolls. M124 – 1 – us Nat'l Archives [324]

LETTERS RECEIVED BY THE SECRETARY OF THE TREASURY FROM SPECIAL AGENTS, 1854-61 / U.S. Bureau of the Customs – 3rolls. M177. Printed guide – 1 – us Nat'l Archives [324]

LETTERS RECEIVED BY THE SECRETARY..., REGISTERED SERIES, 1801-70 / U.S. War Department. Office of the Secretary – 317 rolls. M221. Printed guide – 1 – us Nat'l Archives [324]

LETTERS RECEIVED BY THE SECRETARY..., UNREGISTERED SERIES, 1789-1861 / U.S. War Department. Office of the Secretary – 34 rolls. M222. Printed guide – 1 – us Nat'l Archives [324]

LETTERS RECEIVED BY THE SECRETARY... FROM COLLECTORS OF CUSTOMS, 1833-69 / U.S. Treasury Department – 226 rolls. Printed guide. M174 – 1 – us Nat'l Archives [336]

LETTERS RECEIVED BY THE SECRETARY... FROM COLLECTORS OF CUSTOMS AT PORT TOWNSEND, WASHINGTON, RELATING TO NOMINATIONS FOR OFFICE, 1865-1910 / U.S. Treasury Department – 14 rolls. M188. Printed guide – 1 – us Nat'l Archives [324]

LETTERS RECEIVED BY THE SECRETARY...FROM THE PRESIDENT, EXECUTIVE DEPARTMENTS, AND WAR DEPARTMENT BUREAUS, 1862-70 / U.S. War Department. Office of the Secretary – 117 rolls. M494. Printed guide – 1 – us Nat'l Archives [324]

LETTERS RECEIVED BY THE SECRETARY... RELATING TO PUBLIC LANDS, (N SERIES) 1831-49 / U.S. Treasury Department – 23 rolls. M726 – 1 – us Nat'l Archives [336]

LETTERS RECEIVED BY THE SECRETARY...RELATING TO THE SUBTREASURY SYSTEM (U SERIES), 1846-60 / U.S. Treasury Department – 23 rolls. M736. Printed guide – 1 – us Nat'l Archives [336]

LETTERS RECEIVED BY THE SECTY. OF THE TREASURY AND THE COMM. OF THE GENERAL LAND OFFICE FROM THE SURVEYOR GENERAL OF THE TERRITORY NORTHWEST OF THE RIVER OHIO, 1797-1849 / U.S. Bureau of Land Management – 10 rolls. M478. Printed guide – 1 – us Nat'l Archives [324]

LETTERS RECEIVED BY THE SUPERINTENDENT OF THE U.S. NAVAL ACADEMY / U.S. Naval Academy – 1845-87. M949 – 11r – 1 – us Nat'l Archives [355]

LETTERS RECEIVED BY THE SUPT. OF INDIAN TRADE, 1806-24 / U.S. Bureau of Indian Affairs – 1roll. T58 – 1 – us Nat'l Archives [324]

LETTERS RECEIVED BY THE SURVEYOR GENERAL OF THE TERRITORY NORTHWEST OF THE RIVER OHIO, 1796-1856 / U.S. Bureau of Land Management – 43 rolls. M479. Printed guide – 1 – us Nat'l Archives [324]

LETTERS RECEIVED BY THE TOPOGRAPHICAL BUREAU..., 1824-65 / U.S. War Department. Office of the Chief of Engineers – 86 rolls. M506. Printed guide – 1 – us Nat'l Archives [355]

LETTERS RECEIVED BY THE U.S. GEOLOGICAL SURVEY, 1879-1901 / U. S. Geological Survey – 118 rolls. M590. Printed guide – 1 – us Nat'l Archives [550]

LETTERS RECEIVED FROM PROMINENT INDIVIDUALS / Docking, Virginia – 1955-60 – 1 – us KS Hist [025]

LETTERS RECEIVED IN THE OFFICE OF THE SECRETARY...RELATING TO CLAIMS, 1864-87 / U.S. Treasury Department – 91 rolls. M503. Printed guide – 1 – us Nat'l Archives [336]

LETTERS RECEIVED...FROM THE AGENT FOR RED RIVER AFFAIRS, CANADA, 1867-1870 / U.S. Department of State – 1r – 1 – T23 – us Nat'l Archives [971]

LETTERS, RETURNS, ACCOUNTS, AND ESTIMATES OF THE QUARTERMASTER GENERAL'S DEPARTMENT / U.S. Army. Office of the Quartermaster General – 1776-83. In the War Depatment Collection of Revolutionary War Records. 1 roll. M926 – 1 – us Nat'l Archives [324]

LETTERS SENT..., 1829-70 / U.S. War Department. Office of the Chief of Engineers – 37 rolls. M66. Printed guide – 1 – us Nat'l Archives [355]

LETTERS SENT..., 1893-1929 / U.S. Department of Agriculture. Office of the Secretary – 563 rolls. M440. Printed guide – 1 – us Nat'l Archives [324]

LETTERS SENT BY HEADQUARTERS, DEPARTMENT OF TEXAS, 1870-1898 / U.S. Army. Continental Commands – RG 393. M1114. 10 rolls – 1 – us Nat'l Archives [355]

LETTERS SENT BY LIEUT. COLONEL G.H. HILL, COMMANDER OF THE CONFEDERATE ORDNANCE WORKS AT TYLER, TEXAS, 1864-65 / U.S. War Department. Confederate Records – 1 roll. M119 – 1 – us Nat'l Archives [324]

LETTERS SENT BY THE AS SECTY. OF AGRICULTURE, 1889-94 / U.S. Department of Agriculture. Office of the Secretary – 16 rolls. M122 – 1 – us Nat'l Archives [324]

LETTERS SENT BY THE CHIEF OF ENGINEERS, 1812-1869 / U.S. Office of the Chief of Engineers – RG 77. M1113 – 8r – 1 – us Nat'l Archives [355]

LETTERS SENT BY THE COMMISSIONER OF EDUCATION, 1870-1909 / U.S. Department of Health, Education and Welfare – 71 rolls. M635. Printed guide – 1 – us Nat'l Archives [324]

LETTERS SENT BY THE COMMISSIONER OF THE REVENUE AND THE REVENUE OFFICE, 1792-1807 / U.S. Internal Revenue Service – 3rolls. M414. Printed guide – 1 – us Nat'l Archives [324]

LETTERS SENT BY THE CONFEDERATE SECRETARY..., 1861, 1864-65 / Confederate States of America. Secretary of the Treasury – 1roll. M500. Printed guide – 1 – us Nat'l Archives [324]

LETTERS SENT BY THE CONFEDERATE SECRETARY OF WAR, 1861-65 / U.S. War Department. Confederate Records – 10 rolls. M522. Printed guide – 1 – us Nat'l Archives [324]

LETTERS SENT BY THE CONFEDERATE SECRETARY OF WAR TO THE PRESIDENT, 1861-65 / U.S. War Department. Confederate Records – 2rolls. M523. Printed guide – 1 – us Nat'l Archives [324]

LETTERS SENT BY THE DEPARTMENT OF FLORIDA AND SUCCESSOR COMMANDS, APRIL 18, 1861-JANUARY 1869 / U.S. Army. Continental Commands – RG 393. M1096. 2 rolls – 1 – us Nat'l Archives [355]

LETTERS SENT BY THE DEPARTMENT OF TEXAS AND THE FIFTH MILITARY DISTRICT, 1856-58 AND 1865-1870 / U.S. Army. Continental Commands – RG 393. M1165. 3 rolls – 1 – us Nat'l Archives [355]

LETTERS SENT BY THE DEPT. OF JUSTICE TO EXECUTIVE OFFICERS AND MEMBERS OF CONGRESS, 1871-1904 / U.S. Department of Justice – 91 rolls. M702. Printed guide – 1 – us Nat'l Archives [340]

LETTERS SENT BY THE DIRECTOR OF THE U.S. MINT AT PHILADELPHIA, 1795-1817 / U.S. Bureau of the Mint – 1roll. M64 – 1 – us Nat'l Archives [324]

LETTERS SENT BY THE GENERAL LAND OFFICE TO THE SURVEYOR GENERAL, 1796-1901 / U.S. Bureau of Land Management – 31 rolls. M27. Printed guide – 1 – us Nat'l Archives [324]

LETTERS SENT BY THE GOVERNORS AND THE SECRETARY OF STATE OF CALIFORNIA, 1847-48 / U.S. War Department. Adjutant General's Office – 1roll. M182. Printed guide – 1 – us Nat'l Archives [324]

LETTERS SENT BY THE HEADQUARTERS OF THE ARMY / U.S. Army – 1828-1903. Main Series. 15 rolls. M857 – 1 – us Nat'l Archives [324]

LETTERS SENT BY THE INDIAN DIVISION..., 1849-1903 / U.S. Department of the Interior. Office of the Secretary – 127 rolls. M606. Printed guide – 1 – us Nat'l Archives [324]

LETTERS SENT BY THE LANDS AND RAILROADS DIVISION..., 1849-1904 / U.S. Department of the Interior. Office of the Secretary – 310 rolls. M620. Printed guide – 1 – us Nat'l Archives [324]

LETTERS SENT BY THE NINTH MILITARY DEPARTMENT, DEPARTMENT OF NEW MEXICO, AND DISTRICT OF NEW MEXICO / New Mexico. (District) – 1849-90. 7 rolls. M1072 – 1 – us Nat'l Archives [324]

LETTERS SENT BY THE OFFICE OF INDIAN AFFAIRS, 1824-81 / U.S. Bureau of Indian Affairs – 166 rolls. M21. Printed guide – 1 – us Nat'l Archives [324]

LETTERS SENT BY THE OFFICE OF THE QUARTERMASTER GENERAL, MAIN SERIES / U.S. Office of the Quartermaster General – 1818-70. 61 rolls. M745 – 1 – us Nat'l Archives [324]

LETTERS SENT BY THE OFFICE...RELATING TO INTERNAL IMPROVEMENTS, 1824-30 / U.S. War Department. Office of the Chief of Engineers – 3 rolls. M65 – 1 – us Nat'l Archives [355]

LETTERS SENT BY THE POST COMMANDER AT FORT BAYARD, NEW MEXICO, 1888-97 / U.S. Army – 3 rolls.T320 – 1 – us Nat'l Archives [324]

LETTERS SENT BY THE POSTMASTER GENERAL, 1789-1836 / U.S. Post Office Department. Records – 50 rolls. M601. Printed guide – 1 – us Nat'l Archives [380]

LETTERS SENT BY THE SECRETARY OF THE NAVY TO: / U.S. Navy. Office of Naval Records and Library – (chiefs of navy bureaus, 1842-86. 3 rolls. M480. Printed guide. commandants and navy agents, 1808-65. 5 rolls. M441. Printed guide. officers, 1798-1868. 86 rolls. M149. Printed guide. the president and executive agencies, 1821-86. 20 rolls. M472. Printed guide) – 1 – us Nat'l Archives [324]

LETTERS SENT BY THE SECRETARY...RELATING TO MILITARY AFFAIRS, 1800-89 / U.S. War Department. Office of the Secretary – 110 rolls. M6. Printed guide – 1 – us Nat'l Archives [324]

LETTERS SENT BY THE SECRETARY...RELATING TO PUBLIC LANDS (N SERIES), 1801-78 / U.S. Treasury Department – 4 rolls. M733 – 1 – us Nat'l Archives [333]

LETTERS SENT BY THE SECRETARY...RELATING TO RESTRICTED COMMERCIAL INTERCOURSE, 1861-87 / U.S. Treasury Department – 8 rolls. M513. Printed guide – 1 – us Nat'l Archives [336]

LETTERS SENT BY THE SECRETARY...RELATING TO THE SUBTREASURY SYSTEM (U SERIES), 1840-78 / U.S. Treasury Department – 7rolls. M737 – 1 – us Nat'l Archives [336]

LETTERS SENT BY THE SECRETARY...TO COLLECTORS AT PACIFIC PORTS, 1850-78 / U.S. Treasury Department – 10 rolls. M176. Printed guide – 1 – us Nat'l Archives [336]

LETTERS SENT BY THE SECRETARY...TO THE PRESIDENT AND EXECUTIVE DEPARTMENTS, 1863-70 / U.S. War Department. Office of the Secretary – 5rolls. M421. Printed guide – 1 – us Nat'l Archives [324]

LETTERS SENT BY THE SECTY. OF WAR RELATING TO INDIAN AFFAIRS, 1800-24 / U.S. Bureau of Indian Affairs – 6 rolls. M15 – 1 – us Nat'l Archives [324]

LETTERS SENT BY THE SUPERINTENDENT OF THE U.S. NAVAL ACADEMY / U.S. Naval Academy – 1845-65. M945 – 3r – 1 – us Nat'l Archives [355]

LETTERS SENT BY THE SUPERINTENDENT OF THE U.S. NAVAL ACADEMY / U.S. Naval Academy – 1865-1907. Main Series. M994 – 53r – 1 – us Nat'l Archives [355]

LETTERS SENT BY THE SUPT. OF INDIAN TRADE, 1807-23 / U.S. Bureau of Indian Affairs – 6 rolls. M16 – 1 – us Nat'l Archives [324]

LETTERS SENT BY THE SURVEYOR GENERAL OF THE TERRITORY NORTHWEST OF THE RIVER OHIO, 1797-1854 / U.S. Bureau of Land Management – 10 rolls. M477 – 1 – us Nat'l Archives [324]

LETTERS SENT BY THE U.S. GEOLOGICAL SURVEY, 1879-95 / U. S. Geological Survey – 29 rolls. M152. Printed guide – 1 – us Nat'l Archives [550]

LETTERS SENT BY THE WAR DEPARTMENT RELATING TO NAVAL MATTERS / U.S. War Department – Jan 3 1794 – Jun 14 1798. M739 – 1r – 1 – us Nat'l Archives [355]

LETTERS SENT, FORT MOJAVE, ARIZONA TERRITORY, 1859-90 / U.S. Army – 2rolls. T838 – 1 – us Nat'l Archives [324]

LETTERS SENT...: GENERAL AND MISCELLANEOUS, 1818-1904 / U.S. Department of Justice – 81 rolls. M699. Printed guide – 1 – us Nat'l Archives [340]

LETTERS SENT, REGISTERS OF LETTERS RECEIVED, AND LETTERS RECEIVED BY HEADQUARTERS, TROOPS IN FLORIDA, AND HEADQUARTERS, DEPARTMENT OF FLORIDA / Florida – 1850-58. 10 rolls. M1084 – 1 – us Nat'l Archives [324]

LETTERS SENT TO THE OFFICE OF INDIAN AFFAIRS BY THE PINE RIDGE AGENCY, 1875-1914 – 52r – 1 – M1282 – us Nat'l Archives [350]

LETTERS SENT TO THE PRESIDENT BY THE SECRETARY..., 1800-63 / U.S. War Department. Office of the Secretary – 6rolls. M127 – 1 – us Nat'l Archives [324]

LETTERS SENT TO THE PRESIDENT BY THE SECRETARY OF THE TREASURY, 1833-78 / U.S. Treasury Department – 1roll. M415 – 1 – us Nat'l Archives [336]

LETTERS SENT...CONCERNING JUDICIARY EXPENSES, 1849-84 / U.S. Department of Justice – 24 rolls. M700. Printed guide – 1 – us Nat'l Archives [340]

LETTERS SENT...:INSTRUCTIONS TO U.S. ATTORNEYS AND MARSHALS, 1867-1904 / U.S. Department of Justice – 212 rolls. M701. Printed guide – 1 – us Nat'l Archives [340]

LETTERS SENT...(MAIN SERIES), 1800-90 / U.S. War Department. Adjutant General's Office – 63 rolls. M565. Printed guide – 1 – us Nat'l Archives [324]

LETTERS SENT...RELATING TO CAPTURED AND ABANDONED PROPERTY, 1868-75 / U.S. Commissioner of Customs – 1r – 1 – M498 – us Nat'l Archives [340]

LETTERS SENT...RELATING TO SMUGGLING, 1865-69 / U.S. Commissioner of Customs – 1r – 1 – M497 – us Nat'l Archives [340]

LETTERS SENT...TO JUDGES AND CLERKS, 1874-1904 / U.S. Department of Justice – 34 rolls. M703. Printed guide – 1 – us Nat'l Archives [340]

LETTERS SENT...TO THE COLLECTORS OF CUSTOMS AT BALTIMORE, BOSTON, NEW ORLEANS, AND PHILADELPHIA ("I" SERIES), 1847-78 / U.S. Treasury Department. Office of the Secretary – 19 rolls. T1257 – 1 – us Nat'l Archives [336]

LETTERS SENT...TO THE COLLECTORS OF CUSTOMS AT NEW YORK ("H" SERIES), 1847-78 / U.S. Treasury Department. Office of the Secretary – 30 rolls. T1258 – 1 – us Nat'l Archives [336]

LETTERS, TESTIMONIAL (1842-1856) FOR JOHN CARTER BY HIS COLLEAGUES, PUPILS, CLERGY, AND OTHER ASSOCIATES – 33 LETTERS – 9 – us Sibley [780]

LETTERS TO A GODSON: HOW TO READ THE OLD TESTAMENT IN THE LIGHT OF THE NEW / Bickersteth, M Cyril – Oxford: A.R. Mowbray, 1908. 1 fiche – 9 – us A.T.L.A. [220]

LETTERS TO A LAW STUDENT / Burke, Junius Jessel – Toronto: Carswell, 1887. 00339. (Pre-1900 Canadiana) – 9 – cn C.I.H.M. [340]

LETTERS TO A LAW STUDENT / Burke, Junius Jessel – Toronto, Carswell, 1887. 77 p. LL-2243 – 1 – us L of C Photodup [340]

LETTERS TO A MEMBER OF THE WESLEYAN METHODIST CHURCH: IN WHICH CERTAIN REFLECTIONS AGAINST PROTESTANTISM, AND VARIOUS ASSUMPTIONS IN FAVOUR OF ROMANISM, PUT FORWARD BY AN ECCLESIASTIC OF ROME, ARE EXAMINED AND REFUTED / Borland, John – Montreal, Witness Print. House, 1873. 00185. (Pre-1900 Canadiana) – 9 – cn C.I.H.M. [240]

LETTERS TO A REFORMER, ALIAS CAMPBELLITE / Waller, John L – 1835 – 1 – 5.00 – us Baptist [240]

LETTERS TO A SISTER, OR, WOMAN'S MISSION / Alcott, William A – To accompany the letters to young men. 1850 – 9 – us A.T.L.A. [240]

LETTERS TO A YOUNG LAWYER / Harris, Arthur Merton – St. Paul: West, 1912. 193p. LL-455 – 1 – us L of C Photodup [340]

LETTERS TO AN UNIVERSALIST / Morris, J W – Containing a review of the controversy between Mr. Vidler and Mr. Fuller on the Doctrine of Universal Salvation. 1802 – 1 – 6.37 – us Baptist [240]

LETTERS TO BLANCHE C. MATTHIAS FROM MARGERY LATIMER AND JEAN TOOMER : AND TO HENRY CHESTER TRACY FROM MARGERY LATIMER / Matthias, Blanche C – 1921-1934 – 1r – 1 – us U.W. Library [920]

LETTERS TO BOYS AND GIRLS ABOUT THE HOLY LAND AND THE FIRST CHRISTMAS AT BETHLEHEM / Appel, Theodore – Reading, PA: Daniel Miller, 1886 – 1mf – 9 – 0-8370-2108-1 – 1985-0108 – us A.T.L.A. [910]

LETTERS TO CATHERINE E. BEECHER / Grimke, Angelina Emily – 1838 – 9 – us A.T.L.A. [240]

LETTERS TO DAN CASEMENT / White, William Allen – 1927-43 – 1 – us KS Hist [978]

LETTERS TO EDMOND FLEGG / Bloch, Ernest – 1901-47 – 1 – 69.00 – us L of C Photodup [780]

LETTERS TO ELIZABETH CADY STANTON / Robinson, Charles – 1867 – 1 – us KS Hist [360]

LETTERS TO GARDNER COLBY, 1846-49 / Judson, Adoniram – 52p – 1 – 5.00 – us Baptist [240]

LETTERS TO HIS HOLINESS POPE PIUS 10 / Sullivan, William – 2nd ed. Chicago: Open Court; London: Kegan Paul, Trench, Truebner [distributor], 1911 – 1mf – 9 – 0-8370-8552-7 – 1986-2552 – us A.T.L.A. [240]

LETTERS TO HIS SON ON RELIGION / Selborne, Roundell Palmer – London, New York: Macmillan, 1898 – 1mf – 9 – 0-8370-5329-3 – 1985-3329 – us A.T.L.A. [230]

LETTERS TO MISSIONARY FRIENDS / Small, Annie H – Edinburgh: Macniven & Wallace, 1908 – 1mf – 9 – 0-8370-7266-2 – 1986-1266 – us A.T.L.A. [240]

LETTERS TO MOLLY / Love, James E – 1862 – 1 – us KS Hist [976]

LETTERS TO SALMON PORTLAND CHASE / Wood, Samuel Newitt – 1857-70 – 1 – us KS Hist [978]

LETTERS TO T. L. HOLCOMB UPON RETIREMENT AS EXECUTIVE SECRETARY OF THE BAPTIST SUNDAY SCHOOL BOARD, 1953 – 263p – 1 – 9.20 – us Baptist [240]

LETTERS TO T. W. COKE, FROM DR. SAMUEL PARR, ETC / Coke, Thomas William – 1754-1842. Holkham mss. 747, 767. Holkham Hall, Norfolk, England – 1 – uk Microform Academic [920]

LETTERS TO THE ANONYMOUS AUTHOR OF REMARKS ON MICHAELIS / Marsh, Herbert – 1802 – 9 – us A.T.L.A. [240]

LETTERS TO THE HON. JOHN CARLING, MINISTER OF AGRICULTURE, ONTARIO, CANADA, ON EMIGRATION / Lynch, James – 1868. 02295. (Pre-1900 Canadiana) – 9 – cn C.I.H.M. [971]

LETTERS TO THE JONESES / Titcomb, Timothy – (p185-199 discuss legal ethics, particularly the ethics of a lawyer rerpresenting clients who may be guilty) – New York: Charles Scribner, 1863 – 4mf – 9 – $6.00 – LLMC 91-506 – us L.L.M.C. [170]

LETTERS TO THE PAMPHLETEER / Baptist, Edward – 1830. 78p – 1 – 5.00 – us Baptist [240]

LETTERS TO THE REV. WM. E. CHANNING, CONTAINING REMARKS ON HIS SERMON RECENTLY PREACHED AND PUBLISHED AT BALTIMORE / Stuart, Moses – 1819 – 9 – us A.T.L.A. [240]

LETTERS TO THE REVEREND MR. JOHN WESTLEY, AGAINST PERFECTION AS NOT ATTAINABLE IN THIS LIFE / Dutton, A – London, 1743 – 1mf – 9 – MP-299/1 – ne IDC [240]

LETTERS TO THE RIGHT HONOURABLE LORD HAWKESBURY AND THE RIGHT HONOURABLE HENRI ADDINGTON... / Cobbet, W – Ed 2. London, 1802 – 4mf – 1 – ILM-2574/1 – ne IDC [327]

LETTERS TO THOMAS WILIAM COKE / Roscoe, William – 1814-30. Holkham ms. 768. Holkham Hall, Norfolk, England – 1 – uk Microform Academic [920]

LETTERS TO WM. JOHNSTON FROM E. T. SMYTH, BENTON CITY, ALA., 1854; D. C. WOOLLEY FROM O. C. COOPER – 3p – 1 – us Baptist [240]

LETTERS TO YOUNG MINISTERS OF THE GOSPEL / Bangs, Nathan – 1826 – 9 – us A.T.L.A. [240]

LETTERS, TRANSCRIPTS AND PAPERS / Mary, Queen of Scots – Forster Collection, Victoria and Albert Museum, London – 1 – uk Microform Academic [920]

LETTERS WRITTEN DURING THE PRESIDENT'S TOUR 'DOWN EAST' / Smith, S – 1833 – 1 – $50.00 – us Presbyterian [320]

LETTERS...TO COLLECTORS OF CUSTOMS AT ALL PORTS (1789-1847) AND AT SMALL PORTS (1847-78) / U.S. Treasury Department – 43 rolls. M175. Printed guide – 1 – us Nat'l Archives [336]

A LETTER...TO THE REVEREND AUTHOR OF THE 'REMARKS, CRITICAL AND CHRISTIAN, ON "THE MINOR"' / Foote, S – London, 1760 – 1mf – 9 – MP-399/1 – ne IDC [240]

LETTISCHE GRAMMATIK : (INDOGERMANISCHE BIBLIOTHEK) / Endzelin, J – Heidelberg. v1(1). 1923 – 16mf – 9 – ne IDC [460]

LETTLANDS OKONOMIST – (Library has: 1929-1930) – Riga: Ausg. des Finanzministeriums, 1928- – 1 – CSUX89-S971 – us Hoover Inst Photo [360]

DE LETTRA DE CAMBIO... / De Veiga Beirao, F A – Lisboa, 1886 – 1mf – 1 – ILM-3548/1 – ne IDC [327]

LA LETTRE – Bulletin personnel d'opinion et d'information de Maurice Lemaitre. no. 1-18. Paris. oct 1962-mai 1964 – 1 – fr A.C.R.P.P. [073]

LETTRE... : LETTRES EDIFIANTES ET CURIEUSES... / Jartoux, P – (Letters, dated Peking, 1712, containing a note on ginseng: Illustration of the plant) – Paris, 1780-1783 – 1mf – 9 – ne IDC [615]

LETTRE A M. ROUSSEAU, AU SUJET DE SA LETTRE A M. D'ALEMBERT / Bastide, Jean Francois de – Amsterdam, 1758.42p – 1 – us U.W. Library [860]

LETTRE A MESSIEURS LES DISCIPLES DE SAINT-SIMON SUR QUELQUES POINTS DE LEUR DOCTRINE / Holland, Henri – Paris, Delaunay, s.d., 34 p. Les Saint-Simoniens, 1825-1834. 6982 – 9 – fr Hachette [335]

LETTRE. A MR LE MARQUIS DE CONDORCET / Bonneville, Nicolas de – Londres. Robinson. 1787 – 9 – fr Hachette [321]

LETTRE A SES ANCIENS CONSTITUANTS DU COMTE DE LAVAL / Bellerose, Joseph Hyacinthe – 1883. 00112. (Pre-1900 Canadiana) – 9 – cn C.I.H.M. [971]

LETTRE A UN DOCTEUR DE SORBONNE SUR LE SUJET DE PLUSIEURS ESCRITS COMPOSEZ DE LA VIE ET DE L'ETAT DE MARIE DES VALES, DU DIOCESE DE COUTANCES / Dufour, Charles – 9 – fr Hachette [360]

LETTRE A UN LIBERAL / Laurent, Paul-Mathieu – Paris, s. d. 18 p. Les Saint-Simoniens, 1825-1834. 6858 – 9 – fr Hachette [335]

LETTRE A UNE DAME D'UN CERTAIN AGE, SUR L'ETAT PRESENT DE L'OPERA / Holbach, Paul-Thiry d' – (D'Holbach series). 1752 – 9 – fr Hachette [780]

LETTRE AU MAIRE DU QUEBEC / Baillairge, Charles – 1884. 00059. (Pre-1900 Canadiana) – 9 – cn C.I.H.M. [971]

LETTRE AU ROI, ECRITE SOUS L'IMPRESSION DES EVENEMENTS DES 5 ET 6 JUIN 1832 / Veret, Jeanne-Desiree – (Paris, s.d.), 3 p. Aux femmes priviligees, Jeanne-Desiree, proletaire, Saint-Simonienne. S.1.n.d., 3 p. Les Saint-Simoniens, 1825-1834. 6907 – 9 – fr Hachette [305]

LETTRE AUX BAILLIAGES DE FRANCE / Condorcet, Marie Jean Antoine Nicolas de – Reprod. d'une edition s.l., s.n., 1789. 6p. 1 fiche. (Political Science Collection) – 9 – 6.00 – fr Bibl Nationale [323]

LETTRE AUX PREDICATEURS DE LA DOCTRINE DITE SAINTE-SIMONIENNE (MISSION DE L'EST) – Paris, Bricon, Dijon, Popelain, 1831, 63 p. Les Saint-Simoniens, 1825-1834. 6990 – 9 – fr Hachette [335]

LETTRE COLLECTIVE DES EVEQUES ESPAGNOLS A CEUX DU MONDE ENTIER A PROPOS DE LA GUERRE EN ESPAGNE – Paris, 1937. Fiche W996. (Blodgett Collection of Spanish Civil War Pamphlets) – 9 – us H.U. College Libr [946]

LETTRE CRITIQUE SUR L'EDUCATION / La Condamine, Charles-Marie de – Paris. Prault. 1751. 6766 – 9 – fr Hachette [370]

LETTRE DE CLEMENT MAROT A MONSIEUR DE. TOUCHANT CE QUI S'EST PASSE A L'ARRIVEE DE JEAN BAPTISTE DE LULLI, AUX CHAMPS ELISEES / Cenecay, A B de – Cologne. 1688. BP-663 1 – 9 – ne IDC [780]

LA LETTRE DE LA NATION – Paris. Dir., Pierre Charpy. no.1-2688.2 sept 1974-1993 – 1 – fr A.C.R.P.P. [073]

LETTRE DE M. AUGUSTIN LE GOAZRE DE KERVELEGAN, SENECHAL DE QUIMPER-CORENTIN, A M. BALAIS SUBDELEGUE...(17 NOV. 1788) / Legoazre de Kervelegan, Augustin – (Reflexions d'un philosophe breton a ses concitoyens sur les affaires presentes (20 dec. 1788); Extrait du proces-verbal des seances de la senechaussee de Quimper...des 21, 22 et 23 avril 1789, presidees par M. Le Goazre de Kervelegan...; Quimper: Derrien, 1789) – 1 – F75.90 – fr Armell [100]

LETTRE DE M. DE MAIRAN, SECRETAIRE PERPETUEL DE L'ACADEMIE ROYALE DES SCIENCES, &C. A MADAME: SUR LA QUESTION DES FORCES VIVES: EN REPONSE AUX OBJECTIONS QU'ELLE LUI FAIT SUR CE SUJET DANS SES INSTITUTIONS DE PHYSIQUE / Mairan, Jean Jacques Dortous de – Paris: C.-A. Jombert, 1741 – 1 – us U.W. Library [530]

LETTRE DE M. DE T A UN DE SES AMIS, EN REPONSE D'UN MEMOIRE DE M. GEOFFROY, SUR LES SELS ESSENTIELS DE M. LE COMTE DE LA GARAYE. ON Y A JOINT AUSSI UNE DISSERTATION DE M. GROSSE SUR LES MEME SELS – Paris, 1743 – 1 – us U.W. Library [540]

LETTRE DE M. L'EVEQUE DE LUCON A M.M. LES ELECTEURS DE LA VENDEE / Mercy, Marie-Ch.-l de – (Microf. avec Reponse de Monsieur Merci, eveque de Lucon, a la lettre de Monsieur Servan du Vivier, nomme eveque de la Vendee...[1791]) – [1791] – 1 – F50.00 – fr Armell [944]

LETTRE DE MYLORD BOLINBROKE, SERVANT D'INTRODUCTION A SES LETTRES PHILOSOPHIQUES A M. POPE – (D'Holbach series) – 9 – fr Hachette [190]

LETTRE DE N. A SES AMIS SUR CE QUI S'EST PASSE A LOUDUN – 1634 – 9 – fr Hachette [360]

LETTRE DE THRASIBULE A LEUCIPPE / Freret, Nicolas – (D'Holbach series). 1766 – 9 – fr Hachette [180]

LETTRE DES AMIS – 1984-1992 (complete) – 1r – 1 – ATLA S0917 – us A.T.L.A. [073]

LETTRE DU P. D'ENTRECOLLES AU PERE DUHALDE. A PEKIN, CE 12 MAI 1726. PEKIN, 1726 = LETTER TO DU HALDE ON INOCULATION BY THE CHINESE : MARTIN, L.A. LETTRES EDIFIANTES ET CURIEUSES... / Entrecolles, FX. – Paris, 1838-1843 – 1mf – 9 – ne IDC [614]

LETTRE DU PERE A CHARLES DUVEYRIER SUR LA VIE ETERNELLE / Enfantin, BP – juin 1830. Paris, Carpentier, Mericourt, 1834, 34 p. Les Saint-Simoniens, 1825-1834. 6892 – 9 – fr Hachette [120]

LETTRE DU PERE ENFANTIN A CHARLES DUVEYRIER. LETTRE DU PERE ENFANTIN A FRANCOIS ET A PEIFFER. LE PRETRE, L'HOMME ET LA FEMME / Enfantin, BP – Paris, Everat, 1831, 22 p. Les Saint-Simoniens, 1825-1834. 6867 – 9 – fr Hachette [920]

LETTRE D'UN AMI A L'AUTHEUR DES REFLEXIONS SUR LE FACTUM DE MARIE BUCAILLE, ET LE MEMOIRE FAIT CONTR'ELLE – Rouen, 1699 – 9 – fr Hachette [360]

LETTRE D'UN PATRIOTE SUR LA TOLERANCE CIVILE DES PROTESTANTS DE FRANCE ET SUR LES AVANTAGES QUI EN RESULTERAIENT POUR LE ROYAUME / Court, Antoine – Reprod. de 1756.119p. 2 fiches. (Politial Science Collection). (Religion Series) – 9 – 6.00 – fr Bibl Nationale [323]

LETTRE ESCRITE A MONSIEUR L'EVESQUE DE POICTIERS PAR UN DES PERES JESUITES QUI EXORCISENT A LOUDON / Surin, P Jean J Le – Paris. 1635 – 9 – fr Hachette [360]

LETTRE INEDITE DU P. PREMARE SUR LE MONOTHEISME DES CHINOIS / Premare, J H – Paris, 1861 – 1mf – 9 – HTM-231/1 – ne IDC [210]

LETTRE MISSIVE CONTENANT LA DESCRIPTION DU ROYAUME DE POULOGNE – N.p., 1573 – 1mf – 9 – H-8196/1 – ne IDC [956]

LETTRE MISSIVE D'UN GENTILHOMME A UN SIEN COMPAGNON: CONTENANTE LES CAUSES DU MESCONTENTEMENT DE LA NOBLESSE DE FRANCE – s.l.: s.n., 1567 – 1 – us U.W. Library [944]

LETTRE MISSIVE ENVOYEE DE ROME, PAR VN CHEVALIER DE MALTE, A VN SIEN AMY AUSSI CHEUALIER EN FRANCE: OU EST DECLARE LES DISCORDES QUI EST ENTRE LE GRAND TURC, ET LE SOPHY ROY DE PERSE – Paris, 1589 – 1mf – 9 – H-8207/1 – ne IDC [956]

LETTRE OUVERTE A SON EMINENCE, LE CARDINAL VERDIER, ARCHEVEQUE DE PARIS – n.p. 1937. Fiche W997. (Blodgett Collection of Spanish Civil War Pamphlets) – 9 – us H.U. College Libr [946]

LETTRE PHILOSOPHIQUE, MORALE ET LITTERAIRE DE VOLTAIRE AUX FRANCAIS / Voltaire, Francois Marie Arouet de – Paris. Delaunay. 1818 – 9 – fr Hachette [190]

LETTRE SUR J.J. ROUSSEAU / Bruny, Chevalier de – A Geneve, et se trouve a Paris: Thomas Brunet..., 1780. Publ. anonymously – 1 – us U.W. Library [920]

LETTRE SUR LA MUSIQUE FRANCOISE / Rousseau, Jean-Jacques – Ed. 2. 1753. BP-455 1 – 9 – ne IDC [780]

LETTRE SUR LE MECHANISME DE L'OPERA ITALIEN.. / Villeneuve, Josse de – 1756 – 9 – us Sibley [780]

LETTRE SUR L'EDUCATION PUBLIQUE AU SUJET DES EXERCICES DE L'ABBAYE ROYALE DE SOREZE / Le Roy, Chretien – Bruxelles. 1777. 6769 – 9 – fr Hachette [944]

LETTRE SUR L'HEREDITE, A MESSIEURS LES DISCIPLES DE SAINT-SIMON / Massias, Nicolas – Paris, F. Didot, 1831, 22 p. Les Saint-Simoniens, 1825-1834. 6984 – 9 – fr Hachette [335]

LETTRE...A PEKIN, LE 11 MAI 1726 : LETTRES EDIFIANTES ET CURIEUSES... / Entrecolles, FX. – Paris, 1780-1783 – 1mf – 9 – ne IDC [616]

LETTRES A ANGELE / Gide, Andre Paul Guillaume – Paris, 1900 – 1 – us U.W. Library [860]

LETTRES A BASILE: A PROPOS DES CAUSERIES DU DIMANCHE DE M. A. B. ROUTHIER / Frechette, Louis-Honore – Quebec: s.n., 1872 (Quebec: L'Evenement). 03235. (Pre-1900 Canadiana) – 9 – cn C.I.H.M. [971]

LETTRES A EUGENIE OU PRESERVATIF CONTRE LES PREJUGES / Holbach, Paul-Thiry d' – (D'Holbach series). 1768 – 9 – fr Hachette [190]

LETTRES A L'ACADEMIE / Fenelon – 1v. in 16. 1899 – 9 – fr I.C.S. [860]

LETTRES A M. LEON DE ROSNY SUR L'ARCHIPEL JAPONAIS ET LA TARTARIE ORIENTALE / Furet, Auguste T – Deuxieme ed. Paris: Maisonneuve. 1861 – 9 – 5.00 – fr Orientalistes [950]

LETTRES A SOPHIE – (D'Holbach series) – 9 – fr Hachette [830]

LETTRES AMERICAINES: 1798-1807 / Humboldt, Alexander von – Paris, 1905. xxxix,309p. (Historical Studies Series) – 9 – 12.00 – fr Bibl Nationale [900]

LETTRES AMERICAINES, DANS LESQUELLES ON EXAMINE L'ORIGINE, L'ETAT CIVIL, POLITIQUE, MILITAIRE ET RELIGIEUX, LES ARTS, L'INDUSTRIE, LES SCIENCES, LES MOEURS, LES USAGES DES ANCIENS HABITANTS DE L'AMERIQUE. POUR SERVIR DE SUITE AUX MEMOIRES DE D. ULLOA / Carli, Gian Rinaldo – Boston et se trouve a Paris: Buisson. 2v. 1788. SEM16P9 – 1r – 5 – Can$12.00 – cn Bibl Nat [970]

LETTRES AU CHEVALIER DE LEVIS...PUBLIEES SOUS LA DIRECTION DE L'ABBE H. R. CASGRAIN / Bourlamaque, Francois Charles de – Quebec: L. Demers, 1891. 00213. (Pre-1900 Canadiana) – 9 – cn C.I.H.M. [971]

LETTRES AU PEUPLE: PREMIER SERIE / Canadien-francais – Montreal: La Minerve, 1873. 02581. (Pre-1900 Canadiana) – 9 – cn C.I.H.M. [971]

LETTRES CHAMPENOISES – ou Correspondance politique, morale et litteraire. Paris. 1817-25 – 1 – fr A.C.R.P.P. [073]

LES LETTRES CHAMPENOISES, OU CORRESPONDENCE POLITIQUE, MORALE ET LITTERAIRE – Paris. 2v. 1817-1818 – 8mf – 9 – ne IDC [860]

LETTRES CRITIQUES ET POLITIQUES SUR LES COLONIES ET LE COMMERCE DES VILLES MARITIMES DE FRANCE / Buisson, Paul Ulric du – Adressees a G.T. Raynal. Geneve et Paris: s.n., 1785. (Political Science Collection) – 3mf – 9 – 8.00 – fr Bibl Nationale [320]

LETTRES CURIEUSES – Paris, 1730. Ms. more than one hand. Dated July 3, 1730-Octobre 29, 1730 – 1 – us U.W. Library [860]

LETTRES DE FERNAND CORTES A CHARLES QUINT SUR LA DECOUVERTE ET LA CONQUETE DU MEXIQUE / Cortes, Fernando – Paris. Hachette. 1896. (Strategy of War Series) – 9 – fr Hachette [355]

LETTRES DE FERNAND CORTES A CHARLES V / Cortes, Hernando – 1879 – 9 – $1.50f – sp Bibl Santa Ana [946]

LETTRES DE FEU: M. DE HALLER CONTRE M. DE VOLTAIRE / Haller, Albrecht von – Berne. Lausanne. Societe Typographique. 1780. XIII – 9 – fr Hachette [190]

LETTRES DE FRANCE ET D'ITALIE (1847-1852) / Herzen, Aleksandr I – (Russia – 19th C. series). 1871 – 9 – fr Hachette [360]

LETTRES DE GEORGES CUVIER A C.M. PFAFF SUR L'HISTOIRE NATURELLE, LA POLITIQUE ET LA LITTERATURE, 1788-1792 / Cuvier, Georges – Trad. de l'allemand par Louis Marchant. Paris: Victor Maison, 1888. 4 fiches. (Science Collection) – 9 – 10.00 – fr Bibl Nationale [574]

LETTRES DE JEAN CHAPELAIN, DE L'ACADEMIE FRANCAISE / Chapelain, Jean – Paris: Ph. Tamizey de Larroque, 1880-83.2v – 1 – us U.W. Library [860]

LETTRES DE LA DUCHESSE DE BROGLIE: 1814-1838 / Broglie, Albertine IG de Stael-Holstein, Duchesse de – Paris: Calmann-Levy, 1896. 338p. 4 fiches. (Literature Collection) – 9 – 10.00 – fr Bibl Nationale [920]

LETTRES DE L'INTENDANT BIGOT AU CHEVALIER DE LEVIS, PUBLIEES SOUS LA DIRECTION DE H. R. CASGRAIN / Bigot, Francois – Quebec?, 1895. 00832. (Pre-1900 Canadiana) – 9 – cn C.I.H.M. [971]

LETTRES DE M. DE VOLTAIRE ET DE SA CELEBRE AMIE / Voltaire, Francois Marie Arouet de – Suivies d'une parallele entre Voltaire et J.J. Rousseau. Geneve, Paris: Cailleau, 1782 – 9 – fr Hachette [920]

LETTRES DE PHYLLARQUE A ARISTE / Goulu, Le P J – 1627-28 – 9 – fr I.C.S. [440]

LETTRES DE RATIFICATION DU ROI...PASSES ENTRE LE CARDINAL DE RICHELIEU ET LE SIEUR BERRUYER POUR LA CONCESSION DE NOUVEAUX PRIVILEGES EN FAVEUR DE LA COMPAGNIE DES ISLES DE L'AMERIQUE – Paris: s.n, 1642. SEM105P444 – 1mf – 9 – Can$2.25 – cn Bibl Nat [944]

LETTRES DE VOYAGE: FRANCE, ITALIE, SICILE, MALTE, TUNISIE, ALGERIE, ESPAGNE / Beaugrand, Honore – Montreal: La Patrie, 1889. 03032. (Pre-1900 Canadiana) – 9 – cn C.I.H.M. [910]

LETTRES DU COMTE ET DE LA COMTESSE DE FICQUELMONT A LA COMTESSE TIESENHAUSEN / Sonis, F de – Paris, 1911 – 6mf – 9 – ne IDC [943]

LETTRES DU P. F. X. DUPLESSIS DE LA COMPAGNIE DE JESUS: ACCOMPAGNEES D'UNE NOTICE BIOGRAPHIQUE ET D'ANNOTATIONS / Duplessis, Francois-Xavier – Par J.-Edmond Roy. Levis Quebec: Mercier, 1892. 02802. (Pre-1900 Canadiana) – 9 – cn C.I.H.M. [971]

LETTRES D'UN MAMELUCK, OU TABLEAU MORAL ET CRITIQUE...DES MOEURS DE PARIS / Lavallee, Joseph – Paris: Capelle, 1803 – 1 – F184.07 – fr Armell [944]

LETTRES ECRITES DE NOUVELLE-CALEDONIE A SON PERE / Leenhardt, Maurice – 1902-20 – 9 – F360.00 – fr Ethnologie [025]

LETTRES ECRITES SUR UNE DISSERTATION D'UN VOYAGE DE GRECE; PUBLIE PAR MR. SPON AVEC DES REMARQUES SELON LES NOUVELLES DECOUVERTES DE L'ANTIQUAIRE / Guillet de Saint-George, Georges – Paris, E. Michallet, 1679, cviii-288 p. French Voyagers in the Mediterranean 16th to 18th Centuries. 5975 – 9 – fr Hachette [944]

LETTRES EDIFIANTES ET CURIEUSES, ECRITES DES MISSIONS ETRANGERES : NOUVELLE EDITION – Paris, 1780-1783. 26v – 146mf – 9 – ne IDC [240]

LETTRES EDIFIANTES ET CURIEUSES, ECRITES DES MISSIONS ETRANGERES PAR QUELQUES MISSIONNAIRES DE LA COMPAGNIE DE JESUS – Paris, 1702-1708. v1-5 – 15mf – 9 – ne IDC [240]

LETTRES ENVOYEES DE ROME – Paris, 1561 – 1mf – 9 – H-8159/1 – ne IDC [956]

LETTRES ET COPIES DE LETTRES – ROYAL INSTITUTION (1820-1849) / McGill University. Archives – Montreal, Canada – 6r – 1 – Can$50.00r – cn Can Microfilming [025]

LES LETTRES ET LES ARTS – Revue illustree. Dir. A. France. Paris. 1886-89 – 1 – fr A.C.R.P.P. [073]

LETTRES ET PAPIERS DU CHANCELIER COMTE DE NESSELRODE 1760-1850 / ed by Nesselrode, A de – Paris. 5v. [1904-1912] – 22mf – 9 – ne IDC [943]

LES LETTRES FRANCAISES – Arts. Spectacles. Dir. Aragon. Paris. sept 1944-11 17 oct 1972 – 1 – fr A.C.R.P.P. [073]

LES LETTRES GRECQUES EN OCCIDENT, DE MACROBE A CASSIODORE / Courcelle, P – Paris, 1948 – 12mf – 8 – ne Slangenburg [240]

LETTRES INEDITES / Retif de la Bretonne, Nicolas – Nantes: V. Forest et E. Grimand, 1883. 64p. 1 fiche. (Literature Collection) – 9 – 6.00 – fr Bibl Nationale [860]

LETTRES INEDITES ADRESSEES DE 1686 A 1737 A J.-A. TURRETTINI / ed by Bude, Eugene Guillaume Theodore de – 3v. 1887 – 1 – us A.T.L.A. [240]

LETTRES INEDITES DE RESTIF DE LABRETONE POUR FAIRE SUITE A LA COLLECTION DE SES OEUVRES / Retif de la Bretonne, Nicolas – Nantes: V. Forest, E. Grimaud, 1883 – fr Armell [860]

LETTRES, INSTRUCTIONS ET MEMOIRES DE COLBERT PUBLIES... / ed by Clement, P – Paris. 7v. 1861-1862 – 118mf – 9 – ne IDC [320]

LETTRES INSTRUCTIVES ET CURIEUSES SUR L'EDUCATION DE LA JEUNESSE / Martin, Gregoire – 1760. 6771 – 9 – fr Hachette [360]

LETTRES INTIMES DE MARIA EDGEWORTH PENDANT SES VOYAGES / Edgeworth, Maria – Paris: Guillaumin, 1896. xxxv,231p. (Les Femmes Collection). (Literature Collection) – 3mf – 9 – $8.00 – fr Bibl Nationale [860]

LETTRES JUIVES, OU CORRESPONDANCE PHILOSOPHIQUE, HISTORIQUE ET CRITIQUE ENTRE UN JUIF VOIAGEUR EN DIFFERENTS ETATS DE L'EUROPE ET SES CORRESPONDANS EN DIVERS ENDROITS – La Haye, chez Pierre Paupie. 6v. 1738 – 19mf – 9 – ne IDC [944]

LETTRES NORMANDES – ou Petit tableau moral, politique et litteraire puis ou Correspondance politique et litteraire. Paris. sept 1817-sept 1820 (I-XI) – 1 – fr A.C.R.P.P. [073]

LETTRES PHILOSOPHIQUES SUR L'ORIGINE DES PREJUGES DU DOGME DE L'IMMORTALITE DE L'AME, DE L'IDOLATRIE ET DE LA SUPERSTITION; SUR LE SYSTEME DE SPINOZA ET SUR L'ORIGINE DU MOUVEMENT DANS LA MATIERE /

Toland, John – (D'Holbach series). 1768 – 9 – fr Hachette [190]

LETTRES SPIRITUELLES = THE SPIRITUAL LETTERS OF ARCHBISHOP FENELON : LETTERS TO MEN / Fenelon, Francois de Salignac de la Mothe – (In English) – London; New York: Longmans, Green, 1898 – 1mf – 9 – 0-8370-7217-4 – 1986-1217 – us A.T.L.A. [240]

LETTRES SUR LA GRECE: POUR SERVIR DE SUITE A CELLES SUR L'EGYPTE / Savary, Claude – Nouvelle edition, Paris, Bleuet jeune, an VII 1798, 382 p., carte, illustr. French Voyagers in the Mediterranean 16th to 18th Centuries. 5989 – 9 – fr Hachette [949]

LETTRES SUR LA MOREE, HYDRA ET ZANTE / Castellan, Antoine L – Paris, H. Agasse, 1802, 2 t. en 1 v., 112-156 p. French Voyagers in the Mediterranean 16th to 18th Centuries. 6002 – 9 – fr Hachette [944]

LETTRES SUR LA RELIGION ET LA POLITIQUE, 1829, SUIVI DE L'EDUCATION DU GENRE HUMAIN, TRADUIT DE L'ALLEMAND, DE LESSING / Rodrigues, Eugene – Paris, Everat. 1831. 181 p. Les Saint-Simoniens, 1825-1834. 6851 – 9 – fr Hachette [190]

LETTRES SUR LA RUSSIE, LA FINLANDE ET LA POLOGNE / Marmier, Xavier – (Russia 19 C.). 1851 – 9 – fr Hachette [947]

LETTRES SUR L'EDUCATION / Pesselier, Charles-Etienne – Paris. C. J.-B. Bauche. 1762. 6779 – 9 – fr Hachette [370]

LETTRES SUR LES CONFESSIONS DE J.J. ROUSSEAU / Guinguene, Pierre-Louis – Paris, Barois. 1791 – 9 – fr Hachette [190]

LETTRES SUR LES DRAMES-OPERA / Du Roullet, Francois L – 1776 – 9 – us Sibley [780]

LETTRES SUR LES OCCUPATIONS DE L'ACADEMIE / Fenelon – 1897 – 9 – fr I.C.S. [860]

LETTRES SUR LES OUVRAGES ET LA CARACTERE DE J.J. ROUSSEAU / Stael – 1788 – 9 – fr Hachette [190]

LETTURE DI FILOSOFIA... / ed by Bayle, Constantino – Madrid: Razon y Fe – 1 – sp Bibl Santa Ana [100]

LETTY : AN ORIGINAL DRAMA, IN FOUR ACTS AND AN EPILOGUE / Pinero, Arthur Wing – [London: Chiswick Press, Charles Whittingham and Co.] – 1 roll – 1 – 1-55879-559-6 – uk Libr Preservation [820]

LETTY M. RUSSELL AS PASTORAL THEOLOGIAN / Bertolino-Green, Dianne Lyn – 1982 – 1 – 5.28 – us Baptist [240]

LETUCHIE LISTKI, IZDAVAEMYE FONDOM RUSSKOI VOL'NOIPRESSY V LONDONE – v. 1-46. London. 1893-99. BR-3368 2 – 8 – ne IDC [941]

Leturia, Pedro S *see*
- ANTONIO LEILA DE FERMO Y LA CONDENACION DEL INDIANUM JURE...
- BOLIVAR Y LEON 12
- PREVISION Y REFUTACION DEL ATEISMO COMUNISTA EN LOS ULTIMOS ESCRITOS DE JUAN DONOSO CORTES
- TORIBIO ALFONSO DE MOGROVEJO, SEGUNDO ARZOBISPO DE LIMA...

Leturia, Rafael *see* LO QUE SE VA. MADRID, 1928

DER LETZ – (New York). 1908 – 1 – us A.J.P.C. [073]

LETZEBURGER JOURNAL – Luxemburg. 1972- – 1 – gw Mikrofilm [949]

LETZEBURGER JOURNAL – Luxemburg, jul 2 1956-63 – 25r – 1 – us Res Libr [073]

D'LETZEBURGER LAND – Luxembourg. Feb 1954-Dec 1960 – 7r – 1 – uk British Libr Newspaper [072]

DIE LETZTE AM SCHAFOTT : NOVELLE / Le Fort, Gertrud – Muenchen: J Koesel & F Pustet, 1931 – 1r – 1 – us U.W. Library [830]

DER LETZTE CHRISTOFFELSTRUNK : UND ANDERE ERZAEHLUNGEN / Schworm, Karl – Kaiserlautern: Westpfalz-Verlag, 1938 – 1r – 1 – us U.W. Library [430]

LETZTE DORFGAENGE : KALENDERGESCHICHTEN UND SKIZZEN AUS DEM NACHLASS / Anzengruber, Ludwig – Stuttgart: J G Cotta, 1894 – 1r – 1 – us U.W. Library [800]

LETZTE GEDICHTE / Wildenbruch, Ernst von – Berlin: G Grote, 1909 – 1r – 1 – us U.W. Library [810]

LETZTE GEDICHTE UND GEDANKEN : AUS DEM NACHLASSE DES DICHTERS ZUM ERSTEN MALE VEROEFFENTLICHT / Heine, Heinrich; ed by Strodtmann, Adolf – (Unauthorized reprint of the original edition published in Hamburg 1869 as a supplement to Strodtmann's edition of Heine's saemmtliche Werke, 1861-63. Includes bibliographical references) – Hamburg: Hoffmann und Campe, 1869 – 1 – us U.W. Library [800]

DIE LETZTE KUGEL : ERZAEHLUNG / Hoerner, Herbert von – Stuttgart: Engelhornverlag A Spemann, c1937 – r – 1 – us U.W. Library [830]

LETZTE NEYES – Tel Aviv. 1949- Available: 1965-76. BJ-92-1 3 – 1. ; 1.; 10.00 – 2370.00; 063-932-0y – ne IDC [956]

DIE LETZTE PARTIE : ZWEI ERZAEHLUNGEN / Wildenbruch, Ernst von – Berlin: G Grote, 1909 – 1r – 1 – us U.W. Library [830]

DAS LETZTE UND DAS NAECHSTE ALLGEMEINE CONCIL / Fessler, Joseph – (Includes bibliographical references) – Freiburg i.B.: Herder, 1869 – 1mf – 9 – 0-8370-8738-4 – 1986-2738 – us A.T.L.A. [240]

DIE LETZTEN DINGE : UNTER BESONDERER BERUECKSICHTIGUNG DER ESCHATOLOGIE SCHLEIERMACHERS: NACH DER LEHRE DER HEILIGEN SCHRIFT / Gerlach, Hermann – Berlin: W. Hertz, 1869 – 1mf – us A.T.L.A. [240]

DIE LETZTEN HUMANISTEN : HISTORISCHER ROMAN / Stern, Adolf – Leipzig: Bernhard Schlicke (B. Elischer), 1881 – 1r – 1 – us U.W. Library [830]

DIE LETZTEN PHILOSOPHEN / Hess, Moses – 1845, 1961. 16p. Together with: INDIVIDUALISTISCHER ANARCHISMUS, eine Autorenauswahl, 1978, 66p.; and MEET KROPOTKIN, 73p. 1 fiche (24x) – 9 – 1.00f – at Libertarian Micro [320]

DIE LETZTEN TAGE VON KOLBERG / Voelker, Johannes – (Includes bibliographical references) – Wuerzburg: Holzner-Verlag, 1959 – 1 – us U.W. Library [943]

Leu, Hans Jakob *see* ALLGEMEINES, HELVETISCHES, EYDGENOESSISCHES ODER SCHWEIZERISCHES LEXICON UND SUPPLEMENT ZUM ALLGEMEINEN HELVETISCH-EIDGENOESSISCHEN LEXICON HERRN BUERGERMEISTERS LEU HERAUSGEGEBEN VON HANS JACOB HOLZHALB (AEL, ABT.1;8)

Leuchtenburg, William E *see* PRESIDENT FRANKLIN D. ROOSEVELT'S OFFICE FILES, 1933-1945

LEUCHTENDES LAND : ROMAN / Trenker, Luis – 9. Aufl. Muenchen: F Eher, 1942 – 1r – 1 – us U.W. Library [830]

LEUCHTENDES LEBEN : VOM WERDEN, WIRKEN UND WESEN PETER ROSEGGERS / Katterfeld, Anna – (Includes bibliographical references) – Stuttgart: Im Quell-Verlag, 1949 – 1r – 1 – us U.W. Library [920]

LEUCHTTUERMEN : VON HOELDERLIN ZU CELAN: WIRKUNG UND VERGLEICH: STUDIEN / Boeschenstein, Bernhard – Frankfurt am Main: Insel Verlag, c1977 – 1r – 1 – us U.W. Library [430]

LEUKEMIA AND LYMPHOMA / ed by Armitage, James O et al – 9,5,1 – us Harwood [616]

LEUKEMIA RESEARCH – v.1- 1977- – 5,6,9 – us UMI [073]

Leuliette, Victor *see* PROTESTANTISME LIBERAL

Leuman Ziur Orelau. Seud. de Benigno Lopez *see* LO QUE PUEDE LA PERRA-CHICA

Leunclavius, J *see*
- ANNALES SVLTANORVM OTHMANIDARVM, A TVRCIS SVA LINGVA SCRIPTI
- HISTORIAE MVSVLMANAE TVRCORVM, DE MONVMENTIS IPSORVM EXSCRIPTAE, LIBRI 18

Leunemann, Gottlieb *see* KRITISCH EXEGETISCHES HANDBUCH UEBER DIE BRIEFE AN DIE THESSALONICHER

Leuret, Francois *see* DU TRAITEMENT MORAL DE LA FOLIE

DIE LEUTE AUS DER MOHRENAPOTHEKE : ROMAN / Penzoldt, Ernst – Berlin: S Fischer, 1938 – 1r – 1 – us U.W. Library [830]

Leutelt, Gustav *see*
- GLASMACHER
- DIE KOENIGHAEUSER
- SCHICKSAL

Leutholtz, Brian C *see* THE EFFECTS OF EXERCISE TRAINING AND SEVERE CALORIC RESTRICTION ON LEAN-BODY MASS IN THE OBESE

Leutner, Karl *see* DENKWUERDIGKEITEN DES EIGENEN LEBENS

Leutwein, Theodor *see* ELF JAHRE GOUVERNEUR IN DEUTSCH-SUEDWESTAFRIKA

Leuve, R van *see* DOORLUGTE VOORBEELDEN DER OUDEN

Leuwer, Martin *see* BEFINDLICHKEITSVERAEN-DERUNGEN DURCH MUSIK

Leuwis, D de, de Rickel *see* CONTRA ALCHORANUM ET SECTAM MACHOMENTICAM LIBRI QUINQUE

LEV TOV – Prague. 1620. BJ-43-40 1 – 9 – ne IDC [270]

Levaillant, Francois *see*
- HISTOIRE NATURELLE DES OISEAUX D'AFRIQUE
- HISTOIRE NATURELLE DES PERROQUETS
- HISTOIRE NATURELLE D'UNE PARTIE D'OISEAUX NOUVEAUX ET RARES DE L'AMERIQUE ET DES INDES

Levanon, Jacob *see* THREE-DIMENSIONAL KINEMATIC AND KINETIC ANALYSIS OF TWO COMMON KICKING TECHNIQUES IN SOCCER

LEVANT HERALD – (Constantinople Messenger Eastern Express). Istanbul. Turkey. -d. 3 Jan 1873-30 May, 15 Jul-31 Oct 1878, 9-11 Mar, 19 Nov 1880-22 Jun 1881, 13 Jul 1881-27 Mar, 25-29 Apr 1882, 20 May 1882-6 Feb 1886, 19 20 Apr 1886-5 Apr 1913, 18 Oct 1913-25 Apr 1914. (117 reels) – 1 – uk British Libr Newspaper [949]

LEVANT HERALD-WEEKLY BUDGET – Istanbul, Turkey. 16 Nov 1880-5 Apr 1913 (imperfect).-w. 18 reels – 1 – uk British Libr Newspaper [072]

LEVANT TIMES AND SHIPPING GAZETTE – Istanbul. Turkey. -w. nov 1868-10 Aug 1874. Wanting Jul-Dec 1874. 9 reels – 1 – uk British Libr Newspaper [949]

Levanto y Vivaldo, Francisco *see* ORACION PANEGIRICA...IGLESIA METROPOLITANA... ENEMIGOS

Levasseur, Carmelle *see* BIBLIOGRAPHIE ANALYTIQUE DE REINE MALOUIN, MEMBRE DE LA SOCIETE DES ECRIVAINS CANADIENS, DIRECTRICE DE LA SOCIETE DES POETES DU CANADA ET SOCIETAIRE DE L'ACADEMIE DE LA BALLADE FRANCAISE

Levasseur, Georgette *see* BIO-BIBLIOGRAPHIE CANADIENNE DES OEUVRES DE MGR EMILE CHARTIER, P.D., 1938-1962

Levavasseur, Charles *see* ESCLAVAGE DE LA RACE NOIRE AUX COLONIES FRANCAISES

Levchenko, M V *see* AGAFII

Leveille, H *see* FLORE DU KOUY-TCHEOU

THE LEVEL OF COLLEGIATE ATHLETIC PARTICIPATION AND ITS EFFECTS ON SUICIDAL IDEATION, DEPRESSIVE SYMPTOMS, PSYCHOLOGICAL DISTRESS, AND HOPELESSNESS / McKenzie, J W – 1992 – 1mf – 9 – $4.00 – us Microform Publ [150]

THE LEVEL OF PROFESSIONALISM AMONG THERAPEUTIC RECREATION PRACTITIONERS IN ALBERTA, CANADA / Kelland, Jill – 1992 – 3mf – $12.00 – us Microform Publ [615]

THE LEVEL PLAN FOR CHURCH UNION / Brown, William Montgomery – New York: T. Whittaker, 1910 – 2mf – us A.T.L.A. [240]

LEVELS OF PARK SATISFACTION AMONG FLORIDA STATE PARK VISITORS AND THEIR RELATIONSHIPS TO SELECTED VISITOR CHARACTERISTICS / Bradle, T A – 1991 – 1mf – 9 – $4.00 – us Microform Publ [790]

HET LEVEN – (Some missing vols) – Amsterdam. v1-35. 1906-1940 – 642mf – 9 – ne IDC [072]

Leven de Templery, J *see* NOUVELLES REMARQUES SUR LA LANGUE FRANCOISE

LEVEN VAN SINTE GODELIEVE = VIE DE SAINTE GODELI EVE DE GHISTELLES / Claeys, Hector – (In French) – Pitthem: J Veys, 1901 – 1mf – 9 – 0-8370-6810-X – 1986-0810 – us A.T.L.A. [920]

LEVENDAS TAUMATINGICAS REFERIDAS A LOS PEQUENOS. BARCELONA, 1933 / Serra Boldu, Valerio – Madrid: Razon y Fe, 1934 – 1 – sp Bibl Santa Ana [946]

LEVENDIGE HERTS-THEOLOGIE, DAT ZIJN AENDACHTIGE BETRACHTINGEN, HOE JESUS IN DER GELOOVIGEN HERTEN WIL WOONEN, WERKEN EN LEVEN, EN HAAR WIL ZIJN ALLES IN ALLEN : MET SCHOONE, EN NETTE PRINT-VERBEELDINGE, TER SAKE DIENENDE, VERCIERT: NEVENS VERSEN, SUCHTINGEN, EN ALLEEN-SPRAKEN / Hoburg, Christiano – 1st ed. Amsterdam, 1686 – 3mf – 9 – O-3084/1 – ne IDC [760]

DE LEVENSBESCHRYVINGEN DER NEDERLANDSCHE KONST-SCHILDERS EN KONST-SCHILDERESSEN... / Weyerman, J C – 's-Gravenhage. 4v. 1729-1769 – 25mf – ne IDC [700]

Leveque, Isabella *see* BIO-BIBLIOGRAPHIE DE MONSIEUR GERARD FILION, JOURNALISTE, CONFERENCIER, ECRIVAIN

LEVER – Chicago. Ill. 1890-1899 – 1 – us UMI [071]

Lever, Charles James *see*
- THE CONFESSIONS OF HARRY LORREQUER
- DAVENPORT DUNN
- OUR MESS

Lever, R J A W *see* PESTS OF THE COCONUT PALM

Lever, Ralph *see* THE ARTE OF REASON

Lever, W H *see*
- HISTORY OF SANPETE AND EMERY COUNTIES
- HISTORY OF WHITMAN COUNTY

LEVERETT 1736-1890 – 10mf – 9 – us Holbrook [920]

THE LEVERING LECTURES *see* WHAT SHALL WE THINK OF CHRISTIANITY?

Leverkuehn, A *see* INHALT UND AUSLEGUNG DES HOHEN LIEDES

LEVERKUSENER ANZEIGER : BA DES KOELNER STADT-ANZEIGERS – Leverkusen, West Germany. 1992- – 1 – gw Mikrofilm [072]

Levers Pacific Plantations Pty Ltd / Lever Solomons Ltd *see* ARCHIVES

Levesque, D *see* L'ACTUALITE

Levesque de la Ravaliere, P-A *see* REVOLUTIONS DE LA LANGUE FRANCAISE DEPUIS CHARLEMAGNE JUSQU'A SAINT LOUIS. LEBER, [J.M.] C. COLLECTION DES MEILLEURES DISSERTATIONS, NOTICES ET TRAITES PARTICULIERS RELATIFS A L'HISTORE DE FRANCE

Levesque, Ginette *see* BIBLIOGRAPHIE DE L'OEUVRE DE LOUIS BERUBE...

Levesque, P C *see*
- DICTIONNAIRE DES ARTS DE PEINTURE, SCULPTURE ET GRAVURE

Levi, Camille *see* LA DEFENSE NATIONALE DANS LE NORD EN 1870-1871

Levi, Gerson Baruch *see* GNOMIC LITERATURE IN BIBLE AND APOCYRPHA

Levi, Israel *see* THE HEBREW TEXT OF THE BOOK OF ECCLESIASTICUS

Levi, Michel *see* TRAITE D'HYGIENE PUBLIQUE ET PRIVEE

Levi, S *see*
- L'ITINERAIRE D' OU-K'ONG (751-790)
- NEPAL, ETUDE HISTORIQUE D'UN ROYAUME HINDOU
- LE "TOKHARIEN B", LANGUE DE KOUTCHA

LEVI WOODBURY PAPERS / Woodbury, Levi – 44r – 1 – $1,540.00 – Dist. us Scholarly Res – us L of C Photodup [975]

LEVI WRIGHT DIARY *see* WRIGHT, LEVI, DIARY, MS P.P.

Levi-Alvares, D *see* LES OMNIBUS DU LANGAGE

LEVIATHAN – Santa Cruz, Calif., v1, no. 1 (Nov. 1972)-v1, no. 2 (Mar. 1973); v6, no. 1 (Feb. 1978)-v10, no. 1 (Fall 1981); v12, no. 1 (1984)-v15, no. 2 (Winter 1987) – us A.J.P.C. [270]

LEVIATHAN *see* VIET REPORT

THE LEVIATHAN – Santa Cruz, CA. 1972-1973 (Scats) – 1r – 1 – $50.00 – B03515 – us Library Micro [071]

LEVIATHAN COLLECTION OF INSTRUMENTAL MUSIC / Howe, Elias – containing over 500 pieces of music, consisting of polkas, schottisches, waltzes, quicksteps, marches, hornpipes, contra dances, &c. with 20 setts of quadrilles or cotillions, (including waltz and polka) with figures or callings, for the flute, violin, clarionet, &c. New York: S. T. Gordon & Son, 1858. Includes: "Hail Columbia," "Hail to the Chief," "Star-Spangled Banner," and "Yankee Doodle." MUSIC 1989, Item 3 – 1 – us L of C Photodup [780]

LE-VIKKORET IGGAROT YERUSHALMIYYOT MIN HA-MEAH HA-15 VE-HA-16 / Prawer, J – v. 1. Yerushalayim. 1948. BJ-27-63 1 – 9 – ne IDC [956]
Levillier, Roberto *see* DON FRANCISCO DE TOLEDO, SUPREMO ORGANIZADOR DEL PERU. 1515-1585. MADRID, 1935
Levi(-Morenos), D *see* L'ALGARUM ZANARDINI. WITH BIOGRAPHY OF G. A. M. ZANARDINI BY G. MENEGHINI
Levin, H *see*
- LAWYERS AND LAWMAKERS OF KENTUCKY
- THE LAWYERS AND LAWMAKERS OF KENTUCKY

Levin, I L (Pseudonym Yahalal) *see* KETAVIM NIVHARIM
Levin, LA *see*
- BIBLIOGRAFIIA OBSHCHESTVENNOI-POLITICHESKOI LITERATURY
- IZDANIIA PROIZVEDENIIA KLASSIKOV MARKSIZMA-LENINIZMA V SSSR

Levin, Leo *see* JUDICIAL DISCIPLINE AND REMOVAL IN THE U.S.
Levin, Robert *see* SUMMARY OF THE LAW OF NEGOTIABLE INSTRUMENTS
Levinas, Emmanuel *see*
- QUATRES LECTURES TALMUDIQUES
- LA THEORIE DE L'INTUITION DANS...DE HUSSERL

Levine, Israel *see* THE UNCONSCIOUS; AN INTRODUCTION TO FREUDIAN PSYCHOLOGY
Levins, Peter *see* MANIPULUS VOCABULORUM:A DICTIONARIE OF ENGLISH AND LATINE WORDES
Levinskii, V D *see* UKAZATEL'MATERIALOV PO ISTORII POCHT V ROSSII
Levinsohn, I B *see*
- BET YEHUDAH
- BIKKUREI RIVAL
- EFES DAMIM
- ESHKOL HA-SOFER
- TE'UDAH BE-YISRAEL
- ZERUBABEL

Levinson, A *see* IA. GUMILEV
Levinstein, Kurt *see*
- CHRISTIAN WEISE UND MOLIERE

LE LEVIS-DIMANCHE – Levis, Canada. v1 n1. 1 jan 1921 – 1r – 1 – Can$25.00 – cn Can Microfilming [072]
LE LEVISIEN : JOURNAL HEBDO, POLITIQUE ET LITTERAIRE – Levis, Canada. 3 nov 1924 – 1r – 1 – Can$25.00 – cn Can Microfilming [072]
Levison, W *see*
- PASSIONES VITAEQUE SANCTORUM AEVI MEROVINGICI (MGH 2: 5.BD)
- PASSIONES VITAEQUE SANCTORUM AEVI MEROVINGICI (MGH 2: 6.BD)
- PASSIONES VITAEQUE SANCTORUM AEVI MEROVINGICI (MGH 2: 7.BD)

Levita, E *see* SEFER METURGEMAN. LEXICON CHALDAICVM
Levita, Iohannes Isaac *see* DEFENSIO VERITATIS HEBRAICAE SACRARUM SCRIPTURARUM
Levitas, I *see* VLKSM I KOOPERATSIIA
Levitas, I et al *see* KOMSOMOL I KOOPERATSIIA
THE LEVITICAL PRIESTS : A CONTRIBUTION TO THE CRITICISM OF THE PENTATEUCH / Curtiss, Samuel Ives – (Includes appendixes & indexes) – Edinburgh: T & T Clark, 1877 – 1mf – 9 – 0-8370-2797-7 – 1985-0797 – us A.T.L.A. [220]
LEVITICUS / Bertholet, Alfred – Tuebingen: J.C.B. Mohr, 1901. 1 fiche – 9 – us A.T.L.A. [220]
LEVITICUS 17-26 UND HEZEKIEL : EINE BEITRAG ZUR PENTATEUCHKRITIK / Horst, L – Colmar: Eugen Barth, 1881 – 1mf – 9 – 0-8370-3658-5 – 1985-1658 – us A.T.L.A. [220]
Levitt, Albert *see* THE ALBERT LEVITT PAPERS
LEVITTOWN ADVANCE – Levittown, PA. -w 1952-1953 – 13 – $25.00r – us I.M.R. [071]
LEVITTOWN TIMES – Levittown, PA. -w 1953-1954 – 13 – $25.00r – us I.M.R. [071]
LEVITTOWN TW. PRESS – Levittown, PA., 1952-1953 – 13 – $25.00r – us I.M.R. [071]
Levizac, Abbe de *see* L'ART DE PARLER ET D'ECRIRE CORRECTEMENT
LEVOLDI DE NORTHOF CHRONICA COMITUM DE MARKA (MGH 6: 6.BD) / ed by Zschaeck, F – 1929 – Dfl19.00 – ne Slangenburg [240]
Levonevskii, D *see* OSNOVNYE MATERIALY DLIA CHTENIIA PO POEZII 20 VEKA
Levshin, B V *see* AKADEMICHESKIE ARKHIVY SSSR ZA 50 LET SOVETSKOI VLASTI (TRUDY 1-GO SOVESHCHANIIA ARKHIVISTOV AKADEMII NAUK SSSR I AKADEMII NAUK SOIUZNYKH RESPUBLIK, 17-23 MAIA 1967 G.)
Levstik, Frank R *see* SLAVE NARRATIVES, OHIO 1937 (INTERVIEWS)
Levy, Antoine *see* DIE EXEGESE BEI DEN FRANZOESISCHEN ISRAELITEN VOM 10. BIS 14. JAHRHUNDERT
Levy, Armand *see*
- LES EMEUTIERS
- LA RUSSIE SUR LE DANUBE, AVEC LA PROTESTATION DES ROUMAINS CONTRE L'INVASION DE LEUR PATRIE

LEVY COUNTY JOURNAL – Bronson. Fl. -w. 1946- – 1 – us P.K. Yonge [071]
Levy, J *see*
- CHALDAEISCHEN WOERTERBUCH UEBER DIE TARGUMIM UND EINEN GROSSEN THEIL DES RABBINISCHEN SCHRIFTTHUMS
- CHALDAEISCHES WOERTERBUCH UEBER DIE TARGUMIM
- CHALDAEISCHES WOERTERBUCH UEBER DIE TARGUMIM UND EINEN GROSSEN THEIL DES RABBINISCHEN SCHRIFTTHUMS
- CHALDAEISCHES WOETERBUCH UEBER DIE TARGUM UND EINEN GROSSEN THEIL DES RABBINISCHEN SCHRIFTTHUMS
- NEUHEBRAEISCHES UND CHALDAEISCHES WOERTERBUCH UEBER DIE TALMUDIM UND MIDRASCHIM

Levy, J H *see*
- POLITICS AND DISEASE
- SOCIALISM AND INDIVIDUALISM

Levy, Joseph Hiam *see* THE GOD OF ISRAEL
Levy, Joseph Leonard *see* A BOOK OF PRAYER
Levy, Louis Edward *see* THE AMERICAN JEW AS PATRIOT, SOLDIER AND CITIZEN
Levy, M *see* PARTICLE WORLD
Levy, Marvin R *see*
- DENTAL HYGIENISTS' KNOWLEDGE, ATTITUDES AND INFECTION CONTROL PRACTICES IN RELATION TO AIDS AND AIDS PATIENTS
- THE EFFECT OF YOGA AND RELAXATION TECHNIQUES ON OUTCOME VARIABLES ASSOCIATED WITH OSTEOARTHRITIS OF THE HANDS AND FINGER JOINTS

Levy, Michel *see* TRAITE D'HYGIENE PUBLIQUE ET PRIVEE
Levy, Moritz Abraham *see*
- DAS MESA-DENKMAL UND SEINE SCHRIFT
- PHOENIZISCHES WOERTERBUCH

Levy-Beaulieu, Victor *see* L'ILLETTRE
Lew, M S *see* STUDIES IN JEWISH THEOLOGY
Lewal, Jules Louis *see* ETUDES DE GUERRE
Lewanika, Godwin A M *see*
- ENGLISH-BEMBA PHRASE BOOK
- ENGLISH-LOZI PHRASE BOOK

Lewanika, Godwin Mbikusita *see* REGLES ET TRADITIONS, PROVERBES ET CONTES DU ZAMBEZE
Lewcock, Ronald *see*
- OLD WALLED CITY OF SAN'A'
- WADI HADRAMAWT AND THE WALLED CITY OF SHIBAM

Lewellen, Emerson Calvin *see*
- SCRAPBOOK

LEWELLEN GAZETTE – Lewellen, NE. -w. Jun 1911-Feb 1912; Sept 1914-Dec 1917 – 1 – us NE Hist [071]
LEWELLEN OPTIMIST – Lewellen, NE. -w. Mar 1917-Aug 1918; Dec 1918; Jun 1919-Apr 1923 – 1 – us NE Hist [071]
LEWELLEN TIMES – Lewellen, NE. -w. Dec 1937-Oct 1943 – 1 – us NE Hist [071]
Lewenstein, T *see* PROLEGOMENA ZU MOSES IBN ESRA'S BUCH DER 'TEGNIS.' PT. 1. HALLE. 1893. BJ-421-49/1
Lewes, George Henry *see*
- COMTE'S PHILOSOPHY OF THE SCIENCES
- ON ACTORS AND THE ART OF ACTING
- RANTHORPE
- SEA-SIDE STUDIES AT ILFRACOMBE, TENBY, THE SCILLY ISLES, AND JERSEY

Lewes. Presbytery (Pres. Ch. in the U.S.A.) *see* MINUTES, 1758-1810
LEWI BEN GERSON ALS RELIGIONSPHILOSOPH / Joel, M – Breslau. 1862. BJ-33-27 1 – 9 – ne IDC [180]
Lewin, B M *see*
- RAV SHERIRA GA'ON
- SEFER HA-YOVEL LE B. M. LEWIN

Lewin, Boleslao *see* EL JUDIO EN LA EPOCA COLONIAL; UN ASPECTO DE LA HISTORIA RIOPLATENSE
Lewin, Julius *see* THE NATIVE IN SOUTH AFRICA
Lewin, L *see* DIE PFEILGIFTE
Lewin, Malcolm *see* HAS OUDE BEEN WORSE GOVERNED BY ITS NATIVE PRINCES THAN OUR INDIAN TERRITORIES BY LEADENHALL STREET?
Lewin, Moses *see* ARAMAEISCHE SPRICHWOERTER UND VOLKSSPRUECHE
Lewin, Raphael de Cordova *see* WHAT IS JUDAISM?
Lewin, Thomas *see* FASTI SACRI
Lewinsky, Abraham *see* BEITRAEGE ZUR KENNTNIS DER RELIGIONSPHILOSOPHISCHEN ANSCHAUUNGEN DES FLAVIUS JOSEPHUS
Lewis *see*
- HISTORY OF KENTUCKY
- PAST AND PRESENT OF ADAMS COUNTY

Lewis, A S *see* THE PALESTINIAN SYRIAC LECTIONARY OF THE GOSPELS
Lewis, Abram Herbert *see*
- SPIRITUAL SABBATHISM
- SUNDAY LEGISLATION

Lewis, Agnes Smith *see*
- THE FORTY MARTYRS OF THE SINAI DESERT
- THE PALESTINIAN SYRIAC LECTIONARY OF THE GOSPELS
- STUDIA SINAITICA 11

LEWIS AND CLARK EXPEDITION – 1 – us Ross [910]
Lewis and Dunbar, Publishers *see* BIOGRAPHICAL HISTORY OF PAGE COUNTY
Lewis and Stackelbeck *see* BENCH AND BAR OF COLORADO
Lewis, Arthur *see* THE LIFE AND WORK OF THE REV. E.J. PECK AMONG THE ESKIMOS
Lewis, B *see* AREI EREZ-YISRA'EL BA-MEAH HA-16 ALPI TE'UDOT ME-HA-ARKHIYYON HA-OTHMANI
THE LEWIS CARROLL PICTURE BOOK : A SELECTION FROM THE UNPUBLISHED WRITINGS AND DRAWINGS OF LEWIS CARROLL, TOGETHER WITH REPRINTS FROM SCARCE AND UNACKNOWLEDGED WORK / Carroll, Lewis; ed by Collingwood, Stuart Dodgson – London: T. Fisher Unwin, 1899 – 1 roll – 1 – 1-55879-505-7 – uk Libr Preservation [740]
Lewis, Debra A *see* THE EFFECTS OF COPING SKILLS ON PHYSIOLOGICAL AND COGNITIVE ADAPTATION TO A HIGH RISK ACTIVITY
Lewis, Frank Grant *see* THE IRENAEUS TESTIMONY TO THE FOURTH GOSPEL; ITS EXTENT, MEANING, AND VALUE
Lewis, G *see* HISTORY OF PATRICK AND HENRY COUNTIES
Lewis, Gavin Llewellyn Mackenzie *see* THE BONDELSWARTS REBELLION OF 1922
Lewis, George *see* THE BIBLE, THE MISSAL, AND THE BREVIARY, OR, RITUALISM SELF-ILLUSTRATED
Lewis, George Cornewall *see* AN ESSAY ON THE ORIGIN AND FORMATION OF THE ROMANCE LANGUAGES
Lewis, Gertrud Jaron *see* BY WOMEN, FOR WOMEN, ABOUT WOMEN
Lewis, Harold *see* JOURNAL OF TEACHING IN SOCIAL WORK
Lewis, Henry *see* MODERN RATIONALISM AS SEEN AT WORK IN ITS BIOGRAPHIES
Lewis, Howell Elvet *see*
- BY THE RIVER CHEBAR: SOME APPLICATIONS OF EZEKIEL'S VISIONS
- NONCONFORMITY IN WALES
- SWEET SINGERS OF WALES

Lewis, John *see*
- AMERICAN RAILROAD AND CORPORATION REPORTS (OR REPORTER)
- A TREATISE ON THE LAW OF EMINENT DOMAIN IN THE UNITED STATES

Lewis, John L *see* PAPERS OF JOHN L. LEWIS, 1879-1969
Lewis, K E *see* JOHN MUIR PAPERS, 1858-1957
Lewis, Kathryn *see* THE EFFECTS OF AUDITORY BIOFEEDBACK ON THE ACCURACY OF THE TENNIS VOLLEY
Lewis, Norman *see* SAMPLES, DEMONSTRATIONS AND PACKAGING, THEIR USE IN ADVERTISING
Lewis, O T *see* HISTORY OF BRITISH RELATIONS WITH ZANZIBAR, 1800-86
Lewis, Robert E Jr *see* TRANSGENICS
Lewis, S Thompson *see* BIOGRAPHICAL AND GENEALOGICAL HISTORY OF APPANOOSE AND MONROE COUNTIES
Lewis, Samuel *see*
- TOPOGRAPHICAL DICTIONARY OF IRELAND
- A TOPOGRAPHICAL DICTIONARY OF IRELAND

Lewis, Seth *see* STRICTURES ON DR. LIVINGSTON'S SYSTEM OF PENAL LAWS, PREPARED FOR THE STATE OF LOUISIANA
Lewis, Sulwyn *see* MUSEUMS, IMAGINATION AND EDUCATION
Lewis, T W *see* ZANESVILLE AND MUSKINGHAM COUNTY
Lewis, Tayler *see*
- THE DIVINE HUMAN IN THE SCRIPTURES
- "THE LIGHT BY WHICH WE SEE LIGHT"

Lewis, Taylor *see* THE LIGHT BY WHICH WE SEE LIGHT, OR, NATURE AND THE SCRIPTURES: A COURSE OF LECTURES
Lewis, Theodore G *see* HISTORY OF WATERBURY
Lewis, W D *see* GREAT AMERICAN LAWYERS
Lewis, William Draper *see*
- CASES ON EQUITY JURISDICTION; RESTRAINT OF INFRINGEMENT OF INCORPOREAL RIGHTS. PART 1. A COLLECTION OF CASES WITH NOTES
- THE FEDERAL POWER OVER COMMERCE AND ITS EFFECT ON STATE ACTION

Lewis, William H *see* CHRISTIAN UNION AND THE PROTESTANT EPISCOPAL CHURCH IN ITS RELATIONS TO CHURCH UNITIY
LEWISBURG CHRONICLE – Lewisburg, PA., 1847-1912 – 13 – $25.00r – us I.M.R. [071]
LEWISBURG JOURNAL – Lewisburg, PA., 1865-1946 – 13 – $25.00r – us I.M.R. [071]
LEWISBURG SATURDAY NEWS – Lewisburg, PA., 1925-1952 – 13 – $25.00r – us I.M.R. [071]
LEWISHAM AND LEE HERALD – London. -w. Nov 1893-Jan 1896. (2 reels) – 1 – uk British Libr Newspaper [072]
LEWISHAM INDEPENDENT – (The Borough News Lewisham Borough News). London. -w. 1892-1975. (75 reels) – 1 – uk British Libr Newspaper [072]
LEWISHAM MERCURY – London, England. -w. April-Dec 1981. 2 reels – 1 – uk British Libr Newspaper [072]
LEWISIANA; OR THE LEWIS LETTER – 17v. 1887-June 1907 – 1 – $25.00 – us L of C Photodup [920]
LEWIS'S TOPOGRAPHICAL DICTIONARY OF ENGLAND – (Contains details descriptions of places from small hamlets to towns and cities. Wales, the Channel Islands and Isle of Man included) – England, 1845 – 21mf – 9 – NZ$68.00 – 0-908797-68-0 – nz BAB [941]
LEWISTON AND NEZ PERCE COUNTY DIRECTORY, 1908-1909 / R.L. Polk and Co – Spokane, 1908. v4. Idaho Reel 3. The Cox Library Collection – 5 – us Americana [978]
LEWISTON AND NEZ PERCE COUNTY, IDAHO DIRECTORY – 1908-09.V145-0003 – 5 – us A.G.L.L. [978]
LEWISTON POST – Lewiston, NE. -w. Apr 1913-Jun 1921 – 1 – us NE Hist [071]
Lewy, Ernst *see* ZUR SPRACHE DES ALTEN GOETHE
Lewy, Heinrich *see* DIE SEMITISCHEN FREMDWOERTER IM GRIECHISCHEN
Lewy, I *see* TIFERET YISRA'EL, FESTSCHRIFT. ISRAEL LEWY
Lewy, Y *see* SEFER YOHANAN LEWY
LEX BAIUWARIORUM (MGH LEGES 2A: 4.BD. PARS 2A) – 1926 – Dfl32.00 – ne Slangenburg [240]
LEX CREDENDI : A SEQUEL TO LEX ORANDI / Tyrrell, George – London; New York: Longmans, Green, 1907 – 1mf – 9 – 0-8370-8556-X – 1986-2556 – us A.T.L.A. [240]
LEX MAXIMES GENERALES DU DROICT FRANCOIS : DIUSIEES EN TROIS LIVRES / Delommeau, P – Rouen, 1612 – 12mf – 1 – ILM-1301/2 – ne IDC [327]
LEX MUNDI / Vincent, Alexander – London: Elliot Stock, 1892 – 2mf – 9 – $3.00 – LLMC 95-208 – us L.L.M.C. [340]
LEX ORANDI : OR, PRAYER AND CREED / Tyrrell, George – London; New York: Longmans, Green, 1904 – 1mf – 9 – 0-8370-8477-6 – 1986-2477 – us A.T.L.A. [240]
LEX RIBUARIA ET LEX FRANCORUM CHAMAVORUM (MGH LEGES 4: 6.BD) – 1883 – Dfl13.00 – ne Slangenburg [240]
LEX RIBVARIA (MGH LEGES 2A: 3.BD. PARS 2A) – 1954 – Dfl35.00 – ne Slangenburg [240]

LEX SALICA (MGH LEGES 2A: 4.BD. PARS 2A) – 1969 – Dfl32.00 – ne Slangenburg [240]
DER LEX VON GUTENHAG / Rosegger, Peter; ed by Morgan, Bayard Quincy – (German text with introd etc in English) – Boston: D C Heath, 1911 – 1r – 1 – us U.W. Library [430]
Lexa, F *see*
- GRAMMAIRE DEMOTIQUE
- LES RAPPORTS ENTRE LES LANGUES HAMITIQUES, SEMITIQUES ET LA LANGUE EGYPTIENNE

Lexarza, J de *see* NOVORUM VEGETABILIUM DESCRIPTIONES
LEXIC : SCHOLASTIC. PHIL. THEOL... B. JOANNE DUNS SCOTO / Garcia, Fernandez – Quaracchi, 1910 – 23mf – 8 – ne Slangenburg [290]
EL LEXICO DE LA HERRERIA EN BADAJOZ / Martinez Gonzalez, Antonio – Badajoz: Dip. Provincial, 1975 – 1 – sp Bibl Santa Ana [946]
A LEXICOGRAPHICAL AND HISTORICAL STUDY OF DIATHEKE : FROM THE EARLIEST TIMES TO THE END OF THE CLASSICAL PERIOD / Norton, Frederick Owen – Chicago: University of Chicago Press, 1908 – 1mf – 9 – 0-8370-9301-5 – 1986-3301 – us A.T.L.A. [450]
...LEXICON AETHIOPICO-LATINUM. / Ludolf, Hiob – Frankfort. 1699 – 1 – us Res Libr [470]
LEXICON AETHIOPICO-LATINUM... / Ludolf, J – Francofurti ad Moenum, 1699 – 7mf – ne IDC [470]
...LEXICON AMHARICO-LATINUM. / Ludolf, Hiob – Frankfort. 1698 – 1 – us Res Libr [470]
LEXICON ARISTOPHANEUM : HANDSCHRIFTLICHES SPEZIALWOERTERBUCH ZU DEN KOMOEDIEN DES ARISTOPHANES / ed by Wuest, Ernst – 1984 – 37 fiches (1:24) – 9 – silver DM1,280.00 – 3-598-30460-9 – gw Saur [450]
LEXICON BONAVENTURIANUM / Vicetia, A M & Rubino, J A – Venetiis, 1880 – 8mf – 8 – ne Slangenburg [240]
LEXICON COMMODIANEUM. DISS / Katwijk, AF van – Amstelodami, 1934 – 3mf – 9 – ne IDC [240]
LEXICON DER SCHLESWIG-HOLSTEIN-LAUENBURGISCHEN UND EUTINISCHEN SCHRIFTSTELLER VON 1796 BIS 1828 / Luebker, Detlev Lorenz & Schroeder, Hans – Altona, 1829-30. Schleswig, 1831. Hildesheim, 1983 – 12mf – 9 – DM120.00 diazo DM150.00 silver – gw Olms [430]
LEXICON DER SEIT DEM 15. JAHRHUNDERT VERSTORBENEN UND JETZT LEBENDEN OBERLAUSITZISCHEN SCHRIFTSTELLER UND KUENSTLER / Otto, Gottlieb Friedrich – Goerlitz, 1800-03. Hildesheim, 1983 – 27mf – 9 – DM220.00 diazo DM290.00 silver – gw Olms [430]
LEXICON ECCLESIASTICUM...CONCILIS / Jimenez Arias, Diego – 1618 – 9 – 1.50f – sp Bibl Santa Ana [240]
LEXICON ENTOMOLOGICUM, ODER ENTOMOLOGISCHES WOERTERBUCH... / Moeller, C H – Erfurt, 1795 – 12mf – ne IDC [590]
LEXICON GRAECOLATINUM / Gessner, C – Basileae: In officina Ioan. Walderi, 1537 – 10mf – 9 – H-2532/1 – ne IDC [054]
LEXICON GRAECOLATINUM... / Aleander, H – Lutetie Parisiorum, 1512 – 16mf – 9 – HB-495/1 – ne IDC [054]
LEXICON GRAECOLATINUM... / Gessner, C – Basileae: Ex officina Hieronymi Curionis, 1545 – 1mf – 9 – H-2534/1 – ne IDC [054]
LEXICON GRAECOLATINUM... / Gessner, C – Basileae: Per Hieronymum Curionem, 1543 – 1mf – 9 – H-2533/1 – ne IDC [450]
LEXICON GRAECOLATINUM DENUO IMPRESSUM..., NOVISSIME PER ADRIANUM IUNIUM... LOCUPLETATUM... / Gessner, C – Basileae: Heinrich Petri, 1548 – 12mf – 9 – PBU-508/1 – ne IDC [054]
LEXICON GRAECOLATINVM... – Parisiis, [1530] – 11mf – ne IDC [450]
LEXICON HIEROGLYPHICUM SACRO-PROFANUM, OF WOORDBOEK VAN GEWYDE EN ONGEWYDE VOOR- EN ZINNEBEELDEN : WAARIN PERSOONEN, DADEN, TYDEN, PLAATSEN, DIEREN, BOOMEN, PLANTEN, KRUIDEN, VISSCHEN, VOGELEN, ... / Koning, M – Sole ed. Dordrecht, Amsterdam, 1722-1727 – 58mf – 9 – O-3100/1 – ne IDC [760]
LEXICON IN 70 ET RELIQUOS INTERPRETES.. VET. TESTAMENTI / Schleusner, J F – Lipsiae v1-5 1820-1821 – 54mf – 8 – ne Slangenburg [220]
LEXICON LINGUAE AETHIOPICAE : CUM INDICE LATINO / Dillmann, August – (Includes Latin index) – Lipsiae [Leipzig]: T O Weigel, 1865 – 2mf – 9 – 0-8370-2918-X – 1985-0918 – us A.T.L.A. [470]
LEXICON MAGNUM LATINO-SINICUM... / Goncalves, J A – Macai, 1841 – 14mf – ne IDC [450]
LEXICON MANUALE LATINO-SINICUM... / Goncalves, J A – Macai, 1839 – 6mf – ne IDC [220]
A LEXICON OF FREEMASONRY;... / Mackey, A G – Charleston, 1845 – 4mf – ne IDC [360]
LEXICON PALAEOSLOVENICO-GRAECO-LATINUM / Miklosich, F – Vindobonae, 1862-1865 – 13mf – 9 – H-2950/1 – ne IDC [460]
LEXICON PHILOLOGICUM... / Martini, M – Amstelodami. 5v. 1701 – 40mf – ne IDC [400]
LEXICON REI HERBARIAE TRILINGUAE,... / Gessner, C (D Kyber) – (Available: p467-548) – Argentinae: V. Rihelius, 1553 – 1mf – ne IDC [580]
LEXICON...ADICIONES DE JUAN DE LAMA ESCUDERO / Jimenez Arias, Diego – 1750 – 9 – $1.50f – sp Bibl Santa Ana [240]
LEXICON...DIVORUM VITIS / Jimenez Arias, Diego – (1722. 1.50f; 9. 1728. 1.50f; BSA; 9) – 1713 – 9 – 1.50f – sp Bibl Santa Ana [240]
LEXICUM FRANTZOESISCH UND TEUTSCH (AEL, ABT 2;14) / Hessen, Moritz von – Franckfurt am Meyn: In Verlegung Johannis Ammonii, 1631 (mf ed 1995) – 8mf – 9 – DM320.00 – 3-89131-197-4 – gw Fischer [040]
LEXIKOLOGISCHE UNTERSUCHUNGEN ZUM FACHWORTSCHATZ DER OEKOLOGIE UND DES UMWELTSCHUTZES IM NEUGRIECHISCHEN / Goy, Ina – 1994 – 1mf – DM60.00 – 3-8267-2042-3 – gw Hänsel [574]
LEXIKON – A Pallas Nagy Lexikona (J. Koetet comp.). v. 1-18 Suppl. 1900. Budapest. 1893-1904. BR-5246 2 – 8 – ne IDC [040]
LEXIKON DER ENTOMOLOGISCHEN WELT / Gistl, J von N FX. – Stuttgart, 1846.326p – 8 – ne IDC [590]
LEXIKON DER HAMBURGISCHEN SCHRIFTSTELLER BIS ZUR GEGENWART / Schroeder, Hans et al – Hamburg, 1851-83. Hildesheim, 1983 – 52mf – 9 – DM370.00 diazo DM420.00 silver – gw Olms [430]
LEXIKON DER SCHLESWIG-HOLSTEIN-LAUENBURGISCHEN UND EUTINISCHEN SCHRIFTSTELLER VON 1829-1882 / Alberti, Eduard – Kiel, 1867-86. Hildesheim, 1983 – 24mf – 9 – DM175.00 diazo DM210.00 silver – gw Olms [430]
LEXIKON DEUTSCHER FRAUEN DER FEDER / Pataky, Sophie – Berlin, 1898. Hildesheim, 1983 – 13mf – 9 – DM130.00 diazo DM160.00 silver – gw Olms [430]
LEXIKON DEUTSCHSPRACHIGER SCHRIFTSTELLER VON DEN ANFAENGEN BIS ZUR GEGENWART / Albrecht, Guenter et al – (First published in 1960 under title: Deutsches Schriftsteller-Lexikon. Includes bibliographical references) – Leipzig: VEB Bibliographisches Institut, 1967-68 – 1 – us U.W. Library [430]
LEXIKON SLAVENO-ROSSKII – Kuteino, 1653. 324p. BR-8383/2 – 8 – ne IDC [460]
LEXIKON VERSTORBENER BAIERISCHER SCHRIFTSTELLER DES 18. UND 19. JAHRHUNDERTS / Baader, Clemens Alois – Augsburg und Leipzig, 1824-25. Hildesheim, 1983. – 14mf – 9 – DM110.00 diazo DM130.00 silver – gw Olms [430]
LEXINGTON BAPTIST CHURCH. LEXINGTON COUNTY. SOUTH CAROLINA : CHURCH RECORDS – 1950-1975 – 1 – 16.20 – us Baptist [240]
LEXINGTON CLIPPER – Lexington, NE. -w. (-sw 1910-30; -tw 1930-31). Jun 1892; Oct 1895-Mar 1899, scattered issues missing; Jun 1899 to date – 1 – us NE Hist [071]
Lexington County. South Carolina. Laurel Baptist Church *see* MISCELLANEOUS ITEMS
LEXINGTON FIRST BAPTIST CHURCH. LEXINGTON, NORTH CAROLINA : CHURCH RECORDS – 1881-1958 – 1 – 75.51 – us Baptist [240]
LEXINGTON INTELLIGENCER – 7 Jan 1834-4 Oct 1839 – 2 – $120.00 – us OmniSys [071]
Lexington, Mississippi *see* MISCELLANEOUS EARLY NEWSPAPERS
LEXINGTON NEWS – Lexington, NE. -w. Oct 1897-Aug 1899 – 1 – us NE Hist [071]
Lexington. Ohio. First United Presbyterian Church *see* RECORDS
LEXINGTON PARK BAPTIST CHURCH. LEXINGTON, LOUISIANA : CHURCH RECORDS – 1963-80 – 1 – 47.60 – us Baptist [240]
LEXINGTON PARK BAPTIST CHURCH. LEXINGTON PARK, MARYLAND : CHURCH RECORDS – 1946-1980 – 1 – 99.63 – us Baptist [240]
LEXINGTON PUBLIC ADVERTISER – 5 Jan 1820-30 Dec 1820 – 1 – $60.00 – us OmniSys [071]
LEXINGTON WEEKLY BUDGET – Lexington, OR. 14 Nov 1889-25 Aug 1890. 1 roll – 1 – us U.O. Library [071]
LEXINGTON WHEATFIELD – Lexington, OR. -w. 25 Sept 1905-19 Sept 1907. 1 roll – 1 – us U.O. Library [071]
LEXIQUE COMPARE DE LA LANGUE DE CORNEILLE, ET DE LA LANGUE DU XVIIE / Godefroy, FE – En General. 1862 – 9 – fr I.C.S. [440]
LEXIQUE DE LA LANGUE ALGONQUINE / Cuoq, Jean A – Montreal: J. Chapleau and fils, 1886. SEM16P283 – 1r – 5 – Can$9.00 – cn Bibl Nat [040]
LEXIQUE DE LA LANGUE DE BONAVENTURE DES PERIERS / Cheneviere, A & Frank, F – 1888 – 9 – fr I.C.S. [440]
LEXIQUE DE LA LANGUE DE MOLIERE / Livet, C L – 1895-97 – 9 – fr I.C.S. [440]
LEXIQUE ESPAGNOL-KI-CHE ET KI-CHE-ESPAGNOL / Demyk, M – (Avec notes morphologiques) – 9 – F30.00 – fr Ethnologie [040]
LEXIQUE ET CONCORDANCES DE CHRETIEN DE TROYES D'APRES LA COPIE GUIOT / ed by Ollier, Marie-Louise – (With introduction, index and rhyme analysis) – rev ed 1989 – 38mf – 9 – Can$80.00 – 0-88844-534-2 – cn Pontif [440]
LEXIQUE FAN-FRANCAIS / Martrou, L – Paris – 9 – $5.00 – fr Orientalistes [040]
LEXIQUE FRANCAIS-PEUL ET PEUL-FRANCAIS / Dauzats, Andre – Albi: Impr Albigeoise, [1939?] – us Res Libr [040]
Lexova, Irena *see* ANCIENT EGYPTIAN DANCES.
Lexow, Friedrich *see* GEDICHTE
LEXTON SHIRE MINUTES – 1987-1992 – 1mf – 9r – at Corangamite [350]
LEY DE 15 DE JULIO DE 1952 SOBRE EXPLOTACIONES AGRARIAS / Espana, Leyes, Decretos... – Caceres: Tip. El Noticiero, 1952 – 1 – sp Bibl Santa Ana [630]
LEY DE AGUAS VIGENTE EN LA ISLA DE PURTO RICO : (WATER LAW) – San Juan: Tip "La Primavera", 1908 – 1mf – 9 – $1.50 – LLMC 92-319 – us L.L.M.C. [327]
LA LEY ELECTORAL / Donoso Cortes, Juan Francisco – 1635 – 9 – 1.50f – sp Bibl Santa Ana [340]
LEY HIPOTECARIA PARA LA PROVINCIA DE PUERTO-RICO, 1878 : MORTGAGE LAW – EDICION OFICIAL – Madrid: Imprenta Nacional, 1878 – 2mf – 9 – $3.00 – LLMC 92-315A – us L.L.M.C. [340]
Ley, Julius *see*
- HISTORISCHE ERKLAERUNG DES ZWEITEN TEILS DES JESAIA, CAPITEL 40 BIS CAPITEL 66
- LEITFADEN DER METRIK DER HEBRAEISCHEN POESIE: NEBST DEM ERSTEN BUCHE DER PSALMEN

LA LEY MERCANTIL... / Alvarez del Manzano y Alvarez Rivera, F – Madrid, 1911 – 1mf – 9 – ILM-3758/1 – ne IDC [340]
LEY Y REGLAMENTO SOBRE EL PLAN DE OBRAS Y COLONIZACION, INDUSTRIALIZACION Y ELECTRIFICACION DE LA PROVINCIA DE BADAJOZ / Instituto Nacional de Industria. Secretaria Gestora del Plan – Madrid: Secretaria Gestora del Plan, 1952 – sp Bibl Santa Ana [946]
LEYDEN 1776-1890 – 21mf – 9 – us Holbrook [920]
Leyden, John *see* HISTOIRE COMPLETE DES VOYAGES ET DECOUVERTES EN AFRIQUE. ACCOMPAGNEE D'UN PRECIS GEOGRAPHIQUE SUR CE CONTINENT
Leydet, Dominique *see* LE PROBLEME DE LA SCISSION ET SON DEPASSEMENT DANS L'OEUVRE DU JEUNE HEGEL (1785-1802)
Leyen, Friedrich von der *see*
- DAS MAERCHEN IN DEN GOETTERSAGEN DER EDDA
- WERKE UND BRIEFE

LAS LEYENDAS DE WAGNER EN LA LITERATURA ESPANOLA : CON UN APENDICE SOBRE EL SANTO GRIAL EN EL "LANZAROTE DEL LAGO" CASTELLANO / Bonilla y San Martin, Adolfo – (Includes bibliographical references) – Madrid: Imprenta clasica espanola, 1913 – 1 – us U.W. Library [440]
LAS LEYENDAS DE WAGNER EN LA LITERATURA ESPANOLA : CON UN APENDICE SOBRE EL SANTO GRIAL EN EL "LANZAROTE DEL LAGO" CASTELLANO / Bonilla y San Martin, Adolfo – (Includes bibliographical references. The "Lanzarote" is preserved in ms. 9611 of the Biblioteca nacional) – Madrid: Imprenta clasica espanola, 1913 – 1 – us U.W. Library [790]
LAS LEYENDAS GEOGRAFICAS DEL PERU DE LOS INCAS / Cuneo-Vidal, Romulo – Madrid: Rev. Arch. Biblioteca y Museos, 1925 – 1 – sp Bibl Santa Ana [972]
LEYENDAS MARIANAS RECOPILADAS... / Corredor, Antonio – Madrid: Archivo Ibero Americano, 1964 – 1 – sp Bibl Santa Ana [946]
LEYES EXPEDIDAS POR LA CONVENCION NACIONAL CONSTITUYENTE DE LA REPUBLICA DE PANAMA EN 1904 / Panama. Laws, Statutes, etc – Panama: Nacional, 1912. 238,xvip. LL-2356 – 1 – us L of C Photodup [340]
LEYES NACIONALES SANCIONADAS EN EL PERIODO LEJISLATIVO DE 1883- / Argentine Republic. Laws, Statutes, etc – 1883-1942 – 1 – 101.00 – us L of C Photodup [324]
LAS LEYES OBRERAS Y EL 'PARTIDO COLORADO'. / Narancio, Attilio – Montevideo. 1917 – 1 – us Res Libr [972]
LEYES ORDENACIONES DE LA...SAN FRANCISCO...CINCO MARTIRES DE LA BELALCAZAR – 1751? – 9 – 1.50f – sp Bibl Santa Ana [340]
LEYES Y DECRETOS / Colombia. Laws, Statutes, etc – On film: 1845-47. LL-0222 – 1 – 23.00 – us L of C Photodup [340]
Leynaud, E *see* ASPECT RELIGIEUX DE LA DANSE DANS LES CIVILISATIONS ARCHAIQUES DE L'AFRIQUE DU SUD-EST
Leyret, Henry *see* EN PLEIN FAUBOURG (MOEURS OUVRIERES)
Leys, Franz Jacob *see*
- DIZZIONARIO ITALIANO-TEDESCO
- LE LIVRE INSTRUCTIF, OU NOUVEAU DICTIONNAIRE FRANCOIS-ESPAGNOL 1721 (AEL, ABT 2;9)

Leys, N *see* KENYA
Leyser, J *see* JOACHIM HEINRICH CAMPE. EIN LEBENSBILD AUS DEM ZEITALTER DER AUFKLAERUNG
Leysser, F W von *see* FLORA HALENSIS
LEYTON AND LEYTONSTONE INDEPENDENT – London, England. Leytonstone Express & Independent – Leyton. Leytonstone, Waltham Forest Express & Independent. -w. 10 March 1877-9 June 1972. 123 reels – 1 – uk British Libr Newspaper [072]
Lezhnev, A *see* LITERATURA REVOLIUTSIONNOGO DESIATILETIIA 1917-1927
Lezin, B A *see*
- VOPROSY TEORII I PSIKHOLOGII TVORCHESTVA

LEZIONI DI STORIA DELLA CHIESA / Comba, Emilio – Firenze: Tipografia Claudiana, 1889 – 1mf – us A.T.L.A. [240]
Lezius, Martin *see* KLIMATGEBIETE DER SACHSENGAENGER IN BRANDENBURG, POSEN UND SCHLESIEN
L.H. Everts and Co *see*
- HISTORY OF JEFFERSON COUNTY
- HISTORY OF OAKLAND COUNTY
- HISTORY OF OSWEGO COUNTY
- HISTORY OF ST. LAWRENCE COUNTY

L.H. Watkins and Co *see* HISTORY OF NOBLE COUNTY
LHASA BKA'-'GYUR – 2,466mf – $1,200.00 – us I.A.S.W.R. [280]
LHASA BKA'-'GYUR – 101v. 2,466 fiches – 9 – $1,200.00 – us I.A.S.W.R. [280]
Lhomond, Charles F *see*
- DE VIRIS ILLUSTRIBUS URBIS ROMAE, A ROMULO AD AUGUSTUM: AD USUM SEXTAE SCHOLAE
- ELEMENS DE LA GRAMMAIRE FRANCAISE
- ELEMENS DE LA GRAMMAIRE LATINE

- ELEMENS DE LA GRAMMAIRE LATINE, A L'USAGE DES COLLEGES
- EPITOME HISTORIAE SACRAE

Lhoste, P *see* TRYPANOTOLERANT LIVESTOCK IN WEST AND CENTRAL AFRICA

Lhotsky, A *see*
- CHRONICA AUSTRIAE (MGH 6: 13.BD)
- EIN OESTERREICHISCHER GESCHICHTSSCHREIBER, THEOLOGE UND DIPLOMAT DES 15. JAHRHUNDERTS 1957 (MGH SCHRIFTEN..: 15.BD)

Lhotzky, Heinrich *see* RELIGION, ODER, REICH GOTTES: EINE GESCHICHTE

Lhuyd, Edward *see* ARCHAEOLOGIA BRITANNICA

Li, Chung-t'an *see* LIFE OF LI SHU-CH'ING (CCC215)

LI ESNOE DI ELO : NAUCHNO-OBSHCHESTVENNY I ZHURNAL, IZDAVAEMY I KOOPERATIVNYM TOVARISHCHESTVOM "LI ESNOE DI ELO" – (Library has: Nov. 1, Dec. 15 1918; May 15, May 31 1919) – Moskva: t-vo, 1918-1919. 2v – 1 – CSUX89-S670 – us Hoover Inst Photo [947]

Li, Gladys S *see* SELF-PERCEPTIONS OF FEMALE DANCERS, ATHLETES, EXERCISERS, AND NON-EXERCISERS

Li Hsing-Tao *see* HOEI-LAN-KI (HISTOIRE DU CERCLE DE CRAIE)

Li, J *see* THE EFFECT OF SHORT TERM EMG BIOFEEDBACK ON NECK MUSCLE RELAXATION FOR ROTARY PURSUIT PERFORMANCE

LI JUI. MAO TSE-TUNG T'UNG-CHIH TI CH'U-CH'I KOMING HUO-TUNG – Mao Tse-tung's Early Revolutionary Activities. 1957. BCH-851 2 – 8 – ne IDC [950]

Li, Jui-fang *see* CHU JIH YUAN LIU (CCC272)

Li, Kuan-shen *see* A CHANGED EXCHANGE BROKER (CCC213)

Li, Sheng-hua *see* THE DISCOVERY OF CHINA'S EARLIEST STORY OF JESUS CHRIST (CCC214)

Li, Shu-ch'ing *see* LIFE OF LI SHU-CH'ING (CCC215)

LI TRAVASO *see* JOURNAUX DIVERS

LI UDI-VREDITELI, SHAKHTINSKOE DELO / Agranovski i, Abram Davidovich et al – Moskva: Gos. izd-vo, 1928 – 1 – CSUX88-B8912 – us Hoover Inst Photo [999]

Li, Yin *see* UNTERSUCHUNGEN ZUR REPRODUZIERBARKEIT VON LAKTAT-SCHWELLEN, RESPIRATORISCHEN SCHWELLEN UND KATECHOLAMINSCHWELLEN UND ZU IHREM VERHAELTNIS UNTEREINANDER

Li, Yung-fang *see* A GUIDE TO THE STUDY OF THE OLD TESTAMENT (CCC216)

LIABILITY OF PUBLIC OFFICERS TO PRIVATE ACTIONS FOR NEGLECT OF OFFICIAL DUTY / Cooley, Thomas McIntyre – St. Louis, Jones, 1877. 24 p. LL-257 – 1 – us L of C Photodup [340]

Liaeno, Heinrich St A von *see* THE CHURCH OF GOD AND THE BISHOPS

LIAISON : REVUE – Montreal, jan 1947-jun 1949 – 1r – 1 – Can$50.00 – cn Can Microfilming [073]

LIAN YU ZHUZANG ZOUGAO – Resident official Lian Yu's memorials from Tibet to the emperor. Comp. by Wu Fengpei.3 fiches. F-H189 – 9 – $21.00 – cc Microforms [950]

Liang Gie *see*
- PENGERTIAN, KEDUDUKAN DAN PERINTJIAN ILMU ADMINISTRASI
- TJARA BEKERDJA EFISIEN

Liang, Hsiao-ch'u *see*
- CHI TU T'U SHENGHUO TI P'EI YANG (CCC218)
- CHRISTIAN INTERPRETATION OF HISTORY (CCC217)

Liano, Antonia *see* PINCELADAS EN CUADROS DE AYER, DE HOY Y DESIEMPRE

Liano, Heinrich St A von *see*
- DOGMA UND SCHULMEINUNG
- DIE KIRCHE GOTTES UND DIE BISCHOEFE

Liano, Manuela *see* INQUIETUD

Liao, An-jen *see* WHY WE ARE CHRISTIANS (CCC219)

Liao, Chien-yue *see* SANJAK-SANJAK INDONESIA

LIAONING DAXUE XUEBAO – (Zhexue Shehui Kexue Ban). Journal of Liaonina University, Philosophy and Social Science. In Chinese but Table of Contents in English in each issue. F p216 – 9 – $4.50f – cc Microforms [073]

LIAO-NING JIH-PAO – Shenyang, Liaoning. Liaoning Daily. Sept 1954-Dec 1963. 17 reels – 1 – 446.00 – us Chinese Res [072]

LIAONING JINGJI BAO – China. Liaoning Economic Weekly. 1986-. M-D108 – 1 – $28.00r – cc Microforms [330]

LIAONING RIBAO – Liaoning Daily. China. In Chinese. Current Subscription. Annual Delivery. 1981- , 1r/y. M D24 – 1 – $55.00r – cc Microforms [072]

Liapunov, S *see*
- 3EME MAZURKA, OP. 17
- 4EME MAZURKA, OP. 19
- 12 ETUDES, OP. 11. VOL 1
- 12 STUDES, OP. 11. VOL 2
- NOVELETTE, OP. 18
- VALSE PENSIVE, OP. 20

Liardet, Francis *see* PROFESSIONAL RECOLLECTIONS ON POINTS OF SEAMANSHIP, DISCIPLINE, ETC

THE LIARS : AN ORIGINAL COMEDY IN FOUR ACTS / Jones, Henry Arthur – New York: Macmillan, 1901 – 1 roll – 1 – 1-55879-465-4 – uk Libr Preservation [820]

Lias, John James *see*
- ARE MIRACLES CREDIBLE?
- THE AUGUSTINIAN REVOLUTION IN THEOLOGY
- THE BOOK OF JUDGES: WITH MAPS, NOTES, AND INTRODUCTION
- THE DOCTRINAL SYSTEM OF ST JOHN...AS EVIDENCE FOR THE DATE OF HIS GOSPEL
- THE FIRST EPISTLE TO THE CORINTHIANS: WITH NOTES, MAP AND INTRODUCTION
- PRINCIPLES OF BIBLICAL CRITICISM
- THE SECOND EPISTLE TO THE CORINTHIANS: WITH NOTES, MAP AND INTRODUCTION

LIBAILIU = SATURDAY – Jun 1904-Feb 1913. 13 reels. M-C28 – 1 – $585.00 – cc Microforms [073]

LIBANON – Amsterdam. 1-7(3). 1908-1914 – 14mf – 9 – ne IDC [956]

LIBANON – (New York). 1876-77 – 1 – us A.J.P.C. [073]

DER LIBANON UND SEINE ALPENFLORA / Kotschy, T – Wien. 1864. B-1044 2 – 8 – ne IDC [580]

LIBAUSCHE ZEITUNG – Libau, Latvija. (Liepaja, USSR). 2 Oct 1922-22 Jun 1939 – 19r – 1 – gw Mikrofilm [943]

LIBELLI FRATRIS MICHAELIS DE CESENA – Lugduni per Jo. Trechsel, 1495 – Dfl9.00 – ne Slangenburg [240]

LIBELLUS DE COMPOSITIONE CANTUS IOANNIS GALLICULI / Gallicus, Johann – Vitebergae: Apud Georgium Rhau, Anno M.D. 38 – 1 – us Sibley [780]

LIBELLUS ORTHOGRAPHICUS / Hunt, Thomas – 1661. 147p. (English Linguistics Series 1500-1800) – 9 – us UMI [400]

LIBELLUS SODALITATIS : HOC EST CHRISTIANARUM INSTITUTIONUM, LIBRI QUINQUE, IN GRATIAM SODALITATIS B. VIRGINIS MARIAE / Coster, F – Ingolstadii, 1588 – 9mf – 9 – CA-48/1 – ne IDC [240]

LIBELLVS VERE CHRISTIANA... / Bartholomaeus, G – Romae, 1552 – 2mf – 9 – H-8284/1 – ne IDC [240]

LIBER AGENDARUM ECCLESIE ET DIOCESIS SLESZWICENSIS / Freisen, J – Paderborn, 1898 – Dfl19.00 – ne Slangenburg [240]

LIBER ALBUS CIVITATIS OXONIENSIS : ABSTRACT OF THE WILLS, DEEDS AND ENROLMENTS CONTAINED IN THE WHITE BOOK OF THE CITY OF OXFORD / Ellis, William Patterson – [Oxford]: The Oxford Chronicle Company, Ltd., 1909 – 1r – 1 – us U.W. Library [920]

THE LIBER ALBUS OR WHITE BOOK, 1301-1446 / Worcester Monastery – 1 – uk Microform Academic [240]

LIBER COMICUS MAREDSOLI / Morin, C – 1893 – 10mf – 8 – Dfl35.00 – ne Slangenburg [240]

LIBER CRONICARUM CUM FIGURIS ET YMAGINIBUS AB INICIO MUNDI / Schedel, H – O 1019 1. 1497 – 9 – ne IDC [760]

LIBER DE AFFECTIONIBUS PUERORUM... / Perez Cascales, F – Madrid, 1611 – 5mf – 9 – sp Cultura [610]

LIBER DE ARTE DISTILLANDI DE COMPOSITIS. DAS BUCH DER WAREN KUNST ZU DISTILLIEREN DIE COMPOSITA UND SIMPLICIA UND DAS BUCH THESAURUS PAUPERUM / Brunschwig, Hieronymus – Strassburg, 1512 – 1 – us U.W. Library [430]

LIBER DE DIFFERENTIA VULGARIUM LINGUARUM / Bovelles, Ch. de – 1533 – 9 – fr I.C.S. [440]

LIBER DE ILLUSTRIBUS HENRICIS (RS7) / Capgrave, John; ed by Hingeston, F C – 1858 – Dfl28.00 – ne Slangenburg [240]

LIBER DE PESTE, DE SIGNIS FEBRIUM ET DE DIEBUS CRITICIS / Cartagena, A – Venecia, 1530 – 5mf – 9 – sp Cultura [616]

LIBER DE PROFECTU RELIGIOSORUM / Buenaventura, San – 1546 – 9 – 1.50f – sp Bibl Santa Ana [240]

LIBER DE VERIS ET FALSIS ADIAPHORIS, IN QUO INTEGRE PROPEMODUM ADIAPHORICA CONTROUERSIA EXPLICATUR / Flacius Illyricus d.A E, M – Magdeburgi, 1549 – 2mf – 9 – ne IDC [240]

LIBER DE VITA ET MIRACLES / Diacono, Paulo – 1638 – 9 – 1.50f – sp Bibl Santa Ana [240]

LIBER FEUDORUM MAIOR Y LIBER FEUDORUM CERITANIAE (SIECLE 12) – Barcelona – 1r – 5,6 – sp Cultura [946]

LIBER FIDEI...TOMO 1. BRAGA, 1965 / Costa, Avelino de Jesus da – Madrid: Graf. Calleja, 1967 – 1 – sp Bibl Santa Ana [946]

LIBER FLORIDUS : MITTELLATEINISCHE STUDIEN PAUL LEHMANN ZUM 65.GEBURTSTAG AM 13.7.1949 – St. Ottilien, 1950 – Dfl28.00 – ne Slangenburg [240]

LIBER GENERATIONIS ET REGENERATIONIS ADAE SIVE DE HISTORIA / Arias Montano, Benito – 1593 – 9 – 1.50f – sp Bibl Santa Ana [450]

LIBER HYMNORUM *see* TROPI CARMINUM : LIBER HYMNORUM

LIBER IN PARTIBUS DONATI / Smaragdus – 1986 – 5mf – 9 – Bf1,350.00 – 2-503-63682-9 – be Brepols [240]

LIBER INSULARUM ARCHIPELAGI / Buondelmonti, Christophorus – 1429. Holkham ms. 475. Holkham Hall, Norfolk, England – 1. 22.50; ; 14 – uk Microform Academic [910]

LIBER LIBRORUM : ITS STRUCTURE, LIMITATIONS AND PURPOSE: A FRIENDLY COMMUNICATION TO A RELUCTANT SCEPTIC / Dunn, Henry – (In English) – New York: Charles Scribner, 1867 – 1mf – 9 – 0-8370-3003-X – 1985-1003 – us A.T.L.A. [220]

LIBER MEMORIALIS VON REMIREMONT (MGH ANTIQUITATES 3: 1.BD) – 1970 – Dfl53.00 – ne Slangenburg [240]

LIBER MONASTERII DE HYDA (RS45) : COMPRISING A CHRONICLE OF THE AFFAIRS OF ENGLAND FROM THE SETTLEMENT OF THE SAXONS TO THE REIGN OF KING CNUT, AND A CHARTULARY OF THE ABBEY OF HYDE, HAMPSHIRE / ed by Edwards, E – 1866 – Dfl39.00 – ne Slangenburg [240]

LE LIBER MOZARABICUS SACRAMENTORUM ET LES MANUSCRITS MOZARABES / Ferotin, M – Paris, 1912 – 37mf – 8 – Dfl130.00 – ne Slangenburg [240]

DER LIBER ORDINARIUS DES LUETTICHER ST JAKOBSKLOSTERS / Volk, P – Muenster, 1923 – 4mf – 8 – Dfl19.00 – ne Slangenburg [240]

LIBER ORDINIS S. VICTORIS PARISIENSIS – 1984 – 6mf – 9 – Bf1,050.00 – 2-503-60612-1 – be Brepols [240]

LIBER ORDINIS SANCTI VICTORIS PARISIENSIS – 10mf – 8 – ne Slangenburg [240]

LE LIBER ORDINUM DANS L'EGLISE WISIGOTH. ET MOZAR. D'ESPAGNE, DU 5E-19THS / Ferotin, M – Paris, 1904 – 15mf – 8 – Dfl53.00 – ne Slangenburg [240]

LE LIBER PONTIFICALIS / Duchesne, Louis – H.P.23. 2 v. 1886-1892 – 9 – ne IDC [240]

LIBER PONTIFICALIS / ed by Duchesne, Louis – Paris. v1-3. 1886-1957 – 62mf – 8 – Dfl217.00 – ne Slangenburg [240]

LIBER PONTIFICALIS CHR. BAINBRIDGE ARCHIEPISCOPI EBORACENSIS / Henderson, W – Edinburg, 1875 – 8mf – 8 – Dfl30.00 – ne Slangenburg [240]

LIBER PONTIFICALIS ECCLESIAE GRAECAE / Habertus, I Apxiepatikon – Parisis, 1667 – 34mf – 8 – Dfl119.00 – ne Slangenburg [240]

LIBER PONTIFICALIS OF EDMUND LACY, BISHOP OF EXETER / ed by Barnes, Ralph – Exeter, 1847 – 6mf – 8 – Dfl25.00 – ne Slangenburg [240]

LIBER PONTIFICALIS, PARS PRIOR (MGH 4: 1.BD) / ed by Mommsen, Theodor – 1898 – Dfl39.00 – ne Slangenburg [240]

LIBER QUARE – 1983 – 6mf – 9 – Bf975.00 – 2-503-63602-0 – be Brepols [240]

LIBER QUI DICITUR FLORES HISTORIARUM AB A. D. 1154 ANNOQUE HENRICI ANGLORUM REGIS SECUNDI PRIMO (RS84) / Roger Of Wendover; ed by Hewlett, H G – (v1 1886 Dfl25.00. v2 1887 Dfl28.00. v3 1889 Dfl22.00) – ne Slangenburg [240]

LIBER REGIS CAPELLE / Ullman, W – 1961 – 2mf – 8 – ne Slangenburg [240]

LIBER SACRAMENTORUM AUGUSTODUNENSIS – 1984 – 9mf – 9 – Bf1,050.00 – 2-503-61594-5 – be Brepols [240]

LIBER SACRAMENTORUM ENGOLISMENSIS – 1987 – 8mf – 9 – Bf1,550.00 – 2-503-61595-3 – be Brepols [240]

LIBER SCAE MARIAE RIEVALL – c.1100. York Minster Library. Ms. xvi 1-8 – 1 – uk Microform Academic [240]

LIBER SECUNDUS MUTETARUM QUINQUE VOCUM / Phinot, Dominique – 1555 – 9 – us Sibley [780]

LIBER TESTAMENTORUM...(ANNO 1066-). RESCRIPTA ET INSTRUMENTA...(ANNO 1091-) – Barcelona – 1r – 5,6 – sp Cultura [946]

LIBER USUALIS – 1963. SE-10,900 1 – 9 – ne IDC [240]

LIBER USUALIS – Untuk Misa besar; kitab njanjian greforian (menurut Liber usualis). Tjet.3. Ende Indonesia. Arnoldus 1963. 136pp. Latin words. Number notation. SEM-9576-9577 – 9 – ne IDC [240]

LIBERA PAROLA – (In Italian and English) – Philadelphia, PA. 1927-42; 1945-51; 1953-55; 1957-69 – 12r – 1 – $1,020.00 – D3391 – us Scholarly Res [071]

LIBERACION – (c.1: v.5:no.48 1947:July 15-v.6:no.53 (1948:Sept.)) – Buenos Aires, 1947-48 – 1 – CSUXAJA8135-S – us Hoover Inst Photo [978]

LIBERACION – (Includes c.1: v.1:no.2 1953:Oct) – Buenos Aires, 1953 – 1 – CSUXAJA8142-S – us Hoover Inst Photo [073]

LIBERACION – Malmo, Sweden. 1981- – 1 – sw Kungliga [072]

EL LIBERAL – Plasencia, 1903 y 1904 – 5 – sp Bibl Santa Ana [073]

EL LIBERAL – Trujillo, 1884 y 1885 – 5 – sp Bibl Santa Ana [073]

LIBERAL – Spain. 1884-85.No. sueltos – 9 – 1.50f – sp Bibl Santa Ana [072]

LIBERAL – Valley Falls. Kan. 1880-83 – 1 – us UMI [071]

O LIBERAL – Rio Branco, Acre. 15 Set, Nov-Dez 1957; Mar, Maio, Set-Out 1958; Nov 1961; 29 Maio 1963 – 1,5,6 – bl Biblioteca [072]

O LIBERAL – San Luiz, 25 Jul-Aug, Oct 1870. Jan, Apr 1871. Jun, Aug, Dec 1872. Jun 1873. May 1866-22 Apr 1887 – 1,5,6 – bl Biblioteca [072]

O LIBERAL – Sao Sebastiao do Paraiso, 30 Sep 1945 – 1,5,6 – bl Biblioteca [072]

THE LIBERAL – Detroit. Dec. 1921-Sept. 1926 – 1 – us NY Public [071]

THE LIBERAL – Richmond Hill, Ont., Canada. 1930- – 1 – cn Commonwealth Micro [072]

O LIBERAL 1090 ORGAO DO PARTIDO LIBERAL DAS ALAGOAS – (Cont by: Estado de Alagoas) – Maceio, Alagoas. 24 Maio 1869; Jun 1875; Ago, Nov 1876; Jul 1877; Nov 1878; Set 1880; Out 1881; Fev-Abr 1884; 23 Maio 1889 – 1,5,6 – bl Biblioteca [072]

THE LIBERAL AND CATHOLIC ELUCIDATOR – (Includes v4 index 20 sep 1843-19 sep 1844) – Hamilton, Ontario. v4 n32. 1 mai 1844-v4 n52. 18 sep 1844 – 1r – 1 – Can$35.00 – cn Can Microfilming [072]

LIBERAL CHRISTIAN – v. 1. January 11, 1823-March 6, 1824 – 1 – us UMI [240]

LIBERAL CHRISTIAN *see* THE INQUIRER

Liberal Conservative Association of the Eastern Townships *see* CONSTITUTION AND BY-LAWS...1891

LE LIBERAL DE LA MAYENNE – Laval, May 1882 – Jan. 1893 – 2r – fr Armell [320]

O LIBERAL DE MINAS – Ouro Preto, 2 Apr-Aug 1868; Sep 1869; 21 Apr 1870 – 1,5,6 – bl Biblioteca [072]

LIBERAL DEMOCRACY: PROBLEMS AND CHALLENGES / Cooray, L J M – 1979. 46p – 9 – 1.00f – at Libertarian Micro [335]

LIBERAL DO NORTE : ORGAO DO DIRECTIORIO LIBERAL – Diamantina, 18 Sep, Dec 1887; 4 Mar 1888 – 1,5,6 – bl Biblioteca [072]
LIBERAL EDUCATION – v1- 1915- 1; v55- 5,6; v61- 9 – us UMI [370]
EL LIBERAL EXTREMENO – Badajoz, 1898 – 5 – sp Bibl Santa Ana [073]
THE LIBERAL MAGAZINE *see* ARCHIVES OF THE BRITISH LIBERAL PARTY
LIBERAL MINEIRO – Ouro Preto, 5 Jan 1882-Dec 1886; Nov 1887; Jan, Mar-Apr 1888; 15 Jan 1889 – 1,5,6 – bl Biblioteca [072]
LIBERAL ORTHODOXY : A HISTORICAL SURVEY / Clark, Henry W – London: Chapman and Hall, 1914. (The Great Christian theologies) – 1mf – us A.T.L.A. [240]
Liberal Party. Great Britain *see* ARCHIVES OF THE BRITISH LIBERAL PARTY
LIBERAL RELIGIOUS THOUGHT AT THE BEGINNING OF THE TWENTIETH CENTURY : ADDRESSES AND PAPERS AT THE INTERNATIONAL COUNCIL OF UNITARIAN AND OTHER LIBERAL RELIGIOUS THINKERS AND WORKERS, HELD IN LONDON, MAY, 1901 / ed by Bowie, W Copeland – London: Philip Green, 1901 – 1mf – 9 – 0-8370-8751-1 – 1986-2751 – us A.T.L.A. [240]
LIBERAL REPUBLICAN – Dallas, OR. -w. 24 Aug 1872-18 Apr 1874. – 1 – us U.O. Library [071]
LIBERAL REVIEW – v1-3, no. 9 (monthly: all publ). 1904-06 – 1 reel – 1 – $115.00 – us UPA [360]
LIBERAL THEOLOGY AND THE GROUND OF FAITH:...A CONSERVATIVE... APOLOGETIC / Egerton, Hakluyt – New York: E.P. Dutton, 19–. 1 fiche – 9 – us A.T.L.A. [240]
LIBERAL-DEMOKRATISCHE ZEITUNG – Halle, 6 Mar-26 Oct 1946; 1947 – 1r – 1 – DM75.00 – gw Mikro Press [072]
LIBERAL-DEMOKRATISCHE ZEITUNG – Halle Saale, East Germany. 6 Mar 1946-47 (incomplete); 3 Aug 1954-Jun 1990 – 70r – 1 – gw Mikrofilm [072]
LIBERALE STUDENTENZEITUNG – Bonn, 1956-69 – 1 – Inquire at Mikrofilmarchiv for details – gw Misc Inst [320]
LIBERALE STUDENTENZEITUNG – Bonn, West Germany. 1956-69 – 1 – gw Mikrofilm [072]
LIBERALES JUDENTUM : MONATSCHRIFT FUER DIE RELIGIOSEN INTERESSEN DES JUDENTUMS – Frankfurt. v1-13. 1908-21 – 1r – 1 – us Ross [270]
LIBERALISM AND COMMUNISM; THE BACKGOUND OF THE SPANISH CIVIL WAR / Maranon, Gregorio – London, 1938? Fiche W 1020. (Blodgett Collection of Spanish Civil War Pamphlets) – 9 – us H.U. College Libr [946]
LIBERALISME DAN RASIONALISME BARAT DAN ISLAM / Lubis, M A – SE-814 1. 1950 – 9 – ne IDC [300]
LE LIBERALISME DE LAURIER / Rinfret, Fernand – [Montreal ?]: [s.n.], [1919 ?]. SEM105P1443 – 1mf – 9 – Can$2.25 – cn Bibl Nat [320]
LIBERALISME, TRADITIONALISME, DECENTRALISATION : CONTRIBUTION A L'HISTOIRE DES IDEES POLITIQUES / Pelloux, R – F50.00 – fr Ethnologie [320]
EL LIBERALISMO EL SOCIALISMO Y LA SOLUCION NACIONALSINDICALISTA / Gomez Ballesteros, Francisco – Caceres: Tip. El Noticiero, 1950 – sp Bibl Santa Ana [335]
LIBERALISMO ES PECADO = DER LIBERALISMUS IST SUENDE : BRENNENDE FRAGEN / Sardaa y Salvany, Felix – Salzburg: Matthias Mittermueller, 1889 – 1mf – 9 – 0-8370-8469-5 – 1986-2469 – us A.T.L.A. [240]
LIBERALISMO Y COMUNISMO; REFLEXIONES SOBRE LA REVOLUCION ESPANOLA – Buenos Aires, 1938. Fiche W1021. (Blodgett Collection of Spanish Civil War Pamphlets) – 9 – us H.U. College Libr [946]
LIBERALISMUS UND STAATSUMFANG : ZU DEN GRENZEN DER FREIHEIT IN DEN MODERNEN VERTRAGSTHEORIEN / Fischer, Uwe – 1995 – 3mf – 9 – DM98.00 – 3-8267-2259-0 – gw Hänsel [320]
LE LIBERAL-NATIONAL – Sorel, Canada. 26 jul 1890 – 1r – 1 – Can$25.00 – cn Can Microfilming [072]
LIBERALUL – Bucharest. Rumania. -d. 7 Jul 1946-27 Nov 1947. (Imperfect). (2 reels) – 1 – uk British Libr Newspaper [949]
LA LIBERATION : MENSUEL INDEPENDANT – Montreal, Canada. v1 n2. 10 nov 1958 – 1r – 1 – Can$25.00 – cn Can Microfilming [072]
LIBERATION – 1956-77 1; 1971-77 5,6; 1976-77 9 – us UMI [976]
LIBERATION – 1974-1994 – 1 – sz Infoprint [072]
LIBERATION – 1988-1993 – 3 times per yr – 6 – F4,400.00 – sz Infoprint [072]
LIBERATION – 1994 – 6 times per yr – 6 – F6,000.00 – sz Infoprint [072]
LIBERATION – 1995 – 12 times per yr – 1 – F6,200.00 – sz Infoprint [072]
LIBERATION – 1995 – 6 times per yr – 6 – F4,800.00 – sz Infoprint [072]
LIBERATION – (Also available on 35mm and CD-ROM) – France. 1988-1995 – 3r per y – 5,6 – Sfr1,176.00 – sz Infoprint [944]
LIBERATION – (Also available on CD-ROM) – 1973, 1974, 1975 – 1r per y – 5,6 – Sfr936.00 – sz Infoprint [072]
LIBERATION – (Also available on CD-ROM) – 1976-1977 – 2r per y – 5,6 – Sfr588.00 – sz Infoprint [072]
LIBERATION – (Also available on CD-ROM) – 1978-1980 – 4r per y – 5,6 – Sfr748.00 – sz Infoprint [072]
LIBERATION – (Also available on CD-ROM) – 1981-1987 – 4r per y – 5,6 – Sfr1,069.00 – sz Infoprint [072]
LIBERATION : COLONIAL FREEDOM NEWS – v13-14. 1969-70 – 9 – $5.00f – us Ross [975]
LIBERATION – Johannesburg. 1953-59. A journal of Democratic Discussion – 1 – uk Microform Academic [960]
LIBERATION : MAOISTE – Montreal. avr 1971-jul/aut 1977 – 1r – 1 – Can$60.00 – cn Can Microfilming [072]
LIBERATION – Montreal. v1-7. 1971-77. SEM35P200 – 1r – 1 – Can$34.00 – cn Bibl Nat [073]
LIBERATION – Paris. 21 aout 1944-nov 1964 – 1 – fr A.C.R.P.P. [073]
LIBERATION – Paris. Aug. 1944-Dec. 1948. Missing: 5 scattered issues – 1 – 35.00r – us Hoover Inst Photo [073]
LIBERATION – (Yrly reel count varies) – 1973- – 1 – inquire – us Ross [072]
LIBERATION MOVEMENTS IN LUSOPHONE AFRICA : SERIALS FROM THE COLLECTION OF IMMANUEL WALLERSTEIN / Wallerstein, Immanuel Maurice – New Haven, CT: Yale Uni Library, Photodup Service, 1976 – us Res Libr [960]
LIBERATION-CHAMPAGNE – Dir. Bernard Pieds. Troyes. janv-oct 1966 – 1 – fr A.C.R.P.P. [073]
LIBERATOR – A Journal of Revolutionary Progress. (Eastman). New York. v. 1-7, no. 10. Mar 1918-Oct 1924 – 1 – us NY Public [335]
LIBERATOR / ed by Garrison, W L – Boston. v1-35. 1831-65 – 11r – 1 – us Ross [975]
LIBERATOR – New York. v1-3. 1925-32 – 1r – 1 – us Ross [071]
LIBERATOR – v. 1-35. 1831-1865 – 1 – us UMI [976]
Liberator *see* LES FONDATEURS DE L'UNION NATIONALE / [LIBERATOR]
THE LIBERATOR / American Negro Labor Congress – New York. v. 1, no. 34-3, no. 46. Dec 7 1929-Dec 15 1932 – 1 – us NY Public [331]
THE LIBERATOR – Ballyshannon. Ireland. -w. 22 Jan-12 Nov 1839. (27 ft) – 1 – uk British Libr Newspaper [072]
THE LIBERATOR – Boston. (W. Lloyd Garrison). Jan 1831-Dec 1865 – 1 – us NY Public [073]
THE LIBERATOR – (Includes index by Shirley Maul) – New York. v1-7. 1918-24 – 2r – 1 – us Ross [335]
THE LIBERATOR – Tralee, Ireland. 1914-39 – 1 – ie Microforms [072]
THE LIBERATOR AND IRISH TRADE UNIONIST – Ireland.23 Aug-22 Nov 1913 – 1 – ie Microforms [072]
LES LIBERAUX ET LE TARIF : PREFERENCE SANS RECIPROCITE: LES INTERETS DES PRODUCTEURS CANADIENS SACRIFIES – [s.l.]: [s.n.], [1900 ?]. SEM105P59 – 1mf – 9 – Can$2.25 – cn Bibl Nat [338]
A LIBERDADE – Sabara, 1 Jan 1896 – 1,5,6 – bl Biblioteca [072]
LIBERIA / Great Britain. Foreign Office. Historical Section – London. 1920. (Handbooks. no. 130). Peace handbook. v. XX, no. 9. (App., p. 52-54). (Extr. from Treaties Relating to Liberia). BA-573 2 – 8 – ne IDC [960]
LIBERIA / Johnston, H H – With an appendix on the flora. by Dr. O. Stapf. 2 v. London. 1906. BA-320 2 – 8 – ne IDC [574]
LIBERIA / Johnston, Harry Hamilton – (With an appendix on the flora of Liberia by Dr Otto Stapf) – London. 2v. 1906 – 1r – 1 – us Ross [960]
Liberia *see* NATIONAL DEVELOPMENT PLAN, 1967-1970
LIBERIA CHRISTIAN ADVOCATE – v.1, no.5, Aug. 10, 1859. Monrovia, Liberia: F. Burns, S. J. Mathews and J. W. Roberts, for the Liberia Conference of the M.E. Church. With: New York Colonization Journal, and Colonization Herald – 1 – us U.W. Library [073]
Liberia. Dept. of Planning and Economic Affairs *see* DRAFT NATIONAL DEVELOPMENT PLAN, 1967-1970
LIBERIA IN WORLD POLITICS / Azikiwe, Nnamdi – London: A H Stockwell, 1934 [i.e. 1935] – us Res Libr [960]
LA LIBERIA INTIME / Lelong, M H – A-580 2. 1946 – 8 – ne IDC [960]
Liberia. Laws, Statutes, etc *see*
– REVISED STATUTES OF THE REPUBLIC OF LIBERIA; BEING A REVISION OF THE STATUTES FROM THE ORGANIZATION OF THE GOVERNMENT IN 1848 TO AND INCLUDING THE ACTS OF THE LEGISLATURE OF 1910-1911.
– STATUTE LAWS OF THE COMMONWEALTH OF LIBERIA, AND PLAN OF CIVIL GOVERNMENT
Liberia. National Planning Council *see* FOUR YEAR PLAN FOR ECONOMIC AND SOCIAL DEVELOPMENT, 1967-1970
Liberia. National Public Health Service *see* TEN YEAR NATIONAL HEALTH PLAN, 1967-1976
LIBERIA OFFICIAL GAZETTE – Monrovia. v1-111. 1905-70 – 7r – 1 – us Ross [324]
LIBERIAN AGE – (Issues filmed as pt of: St Clair Drake Collection) – Monrovia, Liberia, jun 22 1954-jun 17 1963 – us Res Libr [072]
THE LIBERIAN AGE – Monrovia, 1973-1977 – $99.00y – us African Imprint [960]
LIBERIAN EDUCATION / Henries, A Doris B – 1r – 1 – $49.50 – us African Imprint [960]
LIBERIAN KNIGHT – New York. v. 1, no. 1-2. Sep-Oct 1931 – 1 – us NY Public [073]
LIBERIAN STAR – Monrovia, Liberia, 1973-76 – 1 – $148.50y – us African Imprint [072]
Liberio, Silvio *see* CONVERSACIONES FAMILIARES ENTRE EL CENSOR, EL APOLOGISTA
LIBERO ANDREOTTI / Galleria Pesaro. Milan – 1921 – 9 – $4.90 – uk Chadwyck [700]
LA LIBERTA – New York, NY, 1902 – 2mf or 1r – 1,9 – us I.H.R.C. [978]
LA LIBERTA – Paris, France. -w. 1 May 1927-3 May 1934. 3 reels – 1 – uk British Libr Newspaper [072]
LA LIBERTA – Providence. R.I. 1902-1909 – 1 – us UMI [071]
LA LIBERTAD – Badajoz, 1927 y 1929 – 5 – sp Bibl Santa Ana [073]
LA LIBERTAD / Estrella Estralla, Jose Emilio – Barcelona: Graficas Ampurias, 1966 – sp Bibl Santa Ana [946]
LIBERTAD – Valladolid. Spain. -d. 2 Mar 1943-22 May 1945. (Imperfect). (10 reels) – 1 – uk British Libr Newspaper [072]
LA LIBERTAD A TRAVES DEL PENSAMIENTO DE PERON / Peron, Juan Domingo – Buenos Aires: Presidencia de la Nacion, Secretaria de Prensa y Difusion, 1955 – 1 – CSUXAHZ5207-B – us Hoover Inst Photo [320]
LA LIBERTAD MORAL... / Nieto y Serrano, M – Madrid, 1869 – 2mf – 9 – sp Cultura [170]
EL LIBERTADO O'HIGGINS Y EL GENERAL DE LA CRUZ / Orrego Vicuna, Eugenio – Santiago de Chile. 1946 – 1 – us Res Libr [920]
O LIBERTADOR : PERIODICO CRITICO E LITTERARIO – Aracaju, 19 Oct-Dec 1882; Jan-Jun, Dec 1883; Jan, 27 May 1884 – 1,5,6 – bl Biblioteca [072]
LE LIBERTAIRE – Paris. 16 nov 1895-juin 1914, 1919-aout 1939, 21 dec 1944-14 juil 1956, 1968-nov 1971 – 1 – fr A.C.R.P.P. [073]
LIBERTARIAN BOOKLISTS AND BOOK SOURCES – A preliminary listing. 5 fiches – 9 – 1.00f – at Libertarian Micro [320]
THE LIBERTARIAN CHALLENGE / Botsford, David – LA Political Notes, No.23, 2p – 9 – 1.00f – at Libertarian Micro [335]
THE LIBERTARIAN DIGEST – v.1-. 1981- – 9 – 1.00f – at Libertarian Micro [320]
LIBERTARIAN INTERNATIONAL: SOME LEAFLETS AND LETTERS – 1fiche (29x) – 9 – 1.00f – at Libertarian Micro [320]
LIBERTARIAN REVIEW – (v.8-. 1979- 5,6,9) – 1974-. Continues Books for Libertarians – 1 – us UMI [073]
IL LIBERTARIO – La Spezia, Italy, 1903-July 30 – 3r – 1 – us I.H.R.C. [945]
LIBERTAS – Brooklyn, NY. 1927-? – us I.H.R.C. [073]
LIBERTAS – S. Sebastiao do Paraiso, 21 Jul 1912; 5 Aug 1915 – 1,5,6 – bl Biblioteca [072]
LIBERTATEA – Bucharest, Romania. Aug 1944-May 1949 – 8r – 1 – us L of C Photodup [949]
LIBERTATEA – Madrid. Spain. -m. Jul 1951-Sep 1958. (17 ft) – 1 – uk British Libr Newspaper [072]
LIBERTATEA – Vrsac, Yugoslavia. -w. 27 Dec 1959-26 Feb 1967. 7 reels – 1 – uk British Libr Newspaper [949]
LIBERTATEA *see* INFORMATIA BUCURESTIULUI
LA LIBERTE – 1988- – 6r per y – 5 – inquire – us Ross [072]
LA LIBERTE – Bruxelles. No.1-180, 18 avr-21 oct 1871 – 1 – fr A.C.R.P.P. [073]
LA LIBERTE : DIEU ET MON DROIT – St-Boniface, Manitoba. 20 mai 1913-v7 n52. 8 jun 1920 – 3r – 1 – Can$50.00r – cn Can Microfilming [072]
LA LIBERTE – Fitchburg, MA. v30 n43. 15 jun 1939; v30 n49. 27 jul 1939 – 1r – 1 – Can$25.00 – cn Can Microfilming [071]
LA LIBERTE : HEBDO ANGLAIS/FRANCAIS – Montreal, Canada. 1,8 avr 1876 – 1r – 1 – Can$25.00 – cn Can Microfilming [072]
LA LIBERTE – Paris. 16 juil 1865-19 mai 1939, 2 mars-11 juin 1940 – 1 – fr A.C.R.P.P. [073]
LA LIBERTE – Paris. 2 mars 1848-16 juin 1850 – 1 – fr A.C.R.P.P. [073]
LA LIBERTE – Trois-Rivieres, Canada. 1 oct 1884-v2 n236. 15 nov 1886 – 2r – 1 – Can$45.00r – cn Can Microfilming [072]
LA LIBERTE *see* L'ECHO DES DEUX MONTAGNES
LIBERTE – Alger. juil 1943-sept 1955 – 1 – fr A.C.R.P.P. [073]
LA LIBERTE (CH) – (Also available on CD-ROM) – Switzerland. 1988-1993 – 6r per yr – 5,6 – Sfr1,176.00 – sz Infoprint [949]
LA LIBERTE DE CONSCIENCE EN FRANCE DEPUIS L'EDIT DE NANTES JUSQU'A LA SEPARATION (1598-1905) / Bonet-Maury, Gaston – Paris: Felix Alcan, 1909 – 1mf – us A.T.L.A. [944]
LIBERTE DE LA LANGUE FRANCOISE / Dupleix, Scipion – 1651 – 9 – fr I.C.S. [440]
LIBERTE DE L'ESPRIT – no. 1-41. Paris. fevr 1949-juin juil 1953 – 1 – fr A.C.R.P.P. [073]
LA LIBERTE DE PRESSE / Quebec. (Province). Assemblee nationale. Commission parlementaire speciale sur les Problemes de la Liberte de Presse – Quebec: La Commission. 5v. 1972-73. SEM16P308 – 1r – 5 – Can$12.00 – cn Bibl Nat [070]
LA LIBERTE DES MERS / C-S – Turin, 1807 – 1mf – 1 – ILM-1194/1 – ne IDC [327]
LIBERTE (LA) – 1994-1995 – 12 times per yr – 1 – F5,000.00 – sz Infoprint [072]
LA LIBERTE RELIGIEUSE – no. 1-7, 11-12, 16-23. Paris. 16 mars-1er juin 1848 – 1 – fr A.C.R.P.P. [073]
LIBERTY – A journal of Anarchist communism. London. -m. Jan 1894-Dec 1896. (28 ft) – 1 – uk British Libr Newspaper [073]
LIBERTY – A Journal of Anarchist Communism. London. v1-3, no. 12. (all publ). 1894-1896 – 1 reel – 1 – $65.00 – us UPA [335]
LIBERTY – Bangkok. Thailand. -d. Jan 1946-Apr 1948. (6 reels) – 1 – uk British Libr Newspaper [072]
LIBERTY – Boston. Ed. by B.R. Tucker. Nos.1-403. 1881-1908. Complete. Includes German issue of yLiberty-Libertas. Nos.1-8, & issue by issue index – 9 – 1.00f – at Libertarian Micro [320]

LIBERTY – (Lacking: 1928-1929, V.1-2(1-9); 1929-1930, V.2-3(11-24); 1930-1931, V.3-4((26-36); 1931-1932, V.4-5(38-56); 1932-1936, V.5-9(58-98); 1936-1938, V.9-11(100-122); 1938-1939, V.11-12(124-134); 1939, V.12(136); 1939-1946, V.12-15(139-165); 1946, V.15(168-181); 1946-1948, V.15-17(184-216); 1948, V.17(218-231)) – Malang, April 1928-1948, v1-17(1-232) – 22mf – 9 – ne IDC [073]
LIBERTY – London, UK. 1883. -w. 3 feet – 1 – uk British Libr Newspaper [072]
LIBERTY – (Some missing vols) – Surabaja, 1928-1971 – 351mf – 9 – ne IDC [950]
LIBERTY / Tucker, B R – (What's to Be Done, N. G. Tchernychewsky. (Liberty No. 42). A Politician in Sight of Heaven, by Auberon Herbert. (Liberty No. 47). A Vindication of Natural Society, by Edmund Burke. (Liberty No. 53). A Letter to Grover Cleveland, by Lysander Spooner. (Liberty No. 63). Ireland, by Georges Sauton. (Liberty No. 69). The Political Theology of Mazzini, by Michael Bakunin. (Liberty No. 87). The Science of Society, by Stephen Pearl Andrews. (Liberty No. 88). The Rag-Picker of Paris, by Felix Pyat. (Liberty No. 120). Love, Marriage and Divorce, and the Sovereignty of the Individual, by Yarros, Greeley and Andrews. (Liberty No. 119). Cranky Notions, by Joseph A. Labadie. (Liberty No. 117). Free Political Institutions: Their Nature, Essence and Maintenance; An Abridgement and Rearrangement of L. Spooner's "Trial By Jury", both by Victor Yarros. (Liberty No. 146). Problems of Anarchism, by William Bailie. (Liberty No. 253)) – Boston, Nos. 1-403. Also: Libertas, the German issue, Nos. 1-8. c3700p. 27 fiches. (29x). Contains the following works: – 9 – 1.00f – at Libertarian Micro [320]
LIBERTY- A PATH TO ITS RECOVERY / Harper, F A – 1949. 150p. 1 fiche (24x) – 9 – 1.00f – at Libertarian Micro [320]
LIBERTY AND LIFE : DISCOURSES / Powell, Edward Payson – Chicago: Charles H Kerr, 1889 – 1mf – 9 – 0-8370-8852-6 – 1986-2852 – us A.T.L.A. [240]
LIBERTY AND OTHER SERMONS / Brent, Charles H – New York: Longmans, Green, 1906 – 1mf – us A.T.L.A. [240]
LIBERTY AND PROGRESS – Melbourne, Australia. -w. 25 June 1914-25 Dec 1921. 2 reels – 1 – uk British Libr Newspaper [072]
LIBERTY AND THE GREAT LIBERTARIANS / Sprading, Charles – An anthology on Liberty, a handbook of freedom.1913. 549p. 1 fiche (24x) – 9 – 1.00f – at Libertarian Micro [320]
LIBERTY AVENUE BAPTIST CHURCH. BEREA, TENNESSEE : CHURCH RECORDS – 1949-79. 658p – 1 – 29.61 – us Baptist [240]
LIBERTY AVENUE BAPTIST CHURCH. TATE'S CREEK BAPTIST ASSOCIATION. BEREA, KENTUCKY : CHURCH RECORDS – 1949-Jul 1987 – 1 – 45.23 – us Baptist [240]
LIBERTY BAPTIST CHURCH. APPOMATTOX, VIRGINIA : CHURCH RECORDS – 1834-73 – 1 – 7.97 – us Baptist [240]
LIBERTY BAPTIST CHURCH. CALDWELL COUNTY. NORTH CAROLINA : CHURCH RECORDS – 1849-56 – 1 – 5.22 – us Baptist [240]
LIBERTY BAPTIST CHURCH. JACKSON, MISSISSIPPI : CHURCH RECORDS – 1840-1957 – 1 – 25.65 – us Baptist [240]
LIBERTY BAPTIST CHURCH. LIBERTY ASSOCIATION. DAVIDSON COUNTY. NORTH CAROLINA : CHURCH RECORDS – 1829-83 – 1 – 7.83 – us Baptist [240]
LIBERTY BAPTIST CHURCH. MADISONVILLE, KENTUCKY : CHURCH RECORDS – 1893-Mar 1964. History on first reel – 1 – 24.03 – us Baptist [240]
LIBERTY BAPTIST CHURCH. NOLACHUCKY BAPTIST ASSOCIATION. TENNESSEE : CHURCH RECORDS – Oct 1842-Dec 1876. New County Line Baptist Church. Church records. 1876-1941 – 1 – 18.45 – us Baptist [240]
LIBERTY BOOKS FOR SALE – Liberty Bookstore, The Alternative Bookshop, Laissez Faire Books and some other sources. 410p. 3 fiches (29x) – 9 – 1.00f – at Libertarian Micro [320]
LIBERTY BUCKS PROVE SUCCESSFUL / Dehn, Joe – 1p – 9 – 1.00f – at Libertarian Micro [332]
LIBERTY COUNTY FARMER – Joplin. Mont. 1936-1937 – 1 – us UMI [071]
LIBERTY COUNTY TIMES – Chester. Mont. 1938-1949; 1956-1957; 1959; 1966- – 1 – us UMI [071]
LIBERTY, EQUALITY AND UNHAPPINESS / Chipman, Lauchlan – 2fiches (29x) – 9 – 1.00f – at Libertarian Micro [320]
LIBERTY HERALD : WEEKLY ABOLITIONIST/ LIBERTY PARTY NEWSPAPER – Warren, OH. 14 Sept 1843-21 Feb 1846 – 1r – 1 – us Western Res [071]
LIBERTY JOURNAL – Liberty, NE. -w. Jan 1887-Jul 1907, scattered issues missing; Aug 1908-Aug 1916; Feb-Nov 1925; Jan 1926-Sept 1929; Apr 1930-Nov 1931, scattered issues missing; Jan 1932-Apr 1934; Aug-Dec 1934 – 1 – us NE Hist [071]
LIBERTY, JUSTICE AND THE MARKET / Chipman, Lauchlan – 1981, 14p – 9 – 1.00f – at Libertarian Micro [335]
LIBERTY: LEGACY OF TRUTH / Read, Leonard E – 1978. 206p. Together with: Deeper Than You Think. 1967. 129p. 1 fiche (24x) – 9 – 1.00f – at Libertarian Micro [320]
LIBERTY LETTER – 1960-75 1; 1970-75 5,6 – us UMI [073]
LIBERTY, LIFE AND FAMILY : AN INTERDISCIPLINARY JOURNAL OF PUBLIC POLICY – (Supersedes: Journal of Christian Jurisprudence. Subject: Family Law) – Regent University: v1-2. 1994-95 – 9 – $10.00 set – us Hein [340]
LIBERTY, LIFE AND FAMILY *see* JOURNAL OF CHRISTIAN JURISPRUDENCE
LIBERTY MAGAZINE – v1-27. 10 May 1924-Jul 1950 – 1 – us Primary [073]
LIBERTY NEWS – Niles. Ohio. 1967- – 1 – us UMI [071]
LIBERTY; NOT THE DAUGHTER BUT THE MOTHER OF ORDER – 1-17 2+1 (all publ). 1881-1908 – 4r – 1 – $460.00 – us UPA [335]
THE LIBERTY OF PROPHESYING : WITH ITS JUST LIMITS AND TEMPER CONSIDERED WITH REFERENCE TO THE CIRCUMSTANCES OF THE MODERN CHURCH... / Henson, H Hensley – New Haven, Conn.: Yale University Press, 1910, c1909 – 1mf – us A.T.L.A. [240]
LIBERTY PRESS – Liberty Center, Ohio, 1894-1992 – 24r – 1 – us Archival [978]
LIBERTY SECOND BAPTIST CHURCH. LIBERTY, MISSOURI : CHURCH RECORDS – 1869-1969 – 1 – 182.88 – us Baptist [240]
LIBERTY'S CATALOGUES : FASHION, DESIGN, FURNISHING 1881-1949 – (Reproduces coll of Liberty's catalogues in the V&A. Over 10,000 pages) – 142mf – 9 – $725.00 – 0-907006-34-5 – uk Mindata [740]
Libes, Antoine *see* LECONS DE PHYSIQUE-CHIMIQUE: OU, APPLICATION DE LA CHIMIE MODERN A LA PHYSIQUE
Libonati, Joseph R *see* EFFECT OF EXERCISE TRAINING ON THE FUNCTION OF THE RAT MYOCARDIUM DURING REPERFUSION FOLLOWING GLOBAL ISCHEMIA
Libor, Reinhard Maria *see* ARS CISTERCIENSI
Librairie Beauchemin *see* ALBUM HENRI JULIEN
LIBRARIAN *see* BOOK BITS
Librarians of Institutes and Schools of Education (LISE) *see*
– BETI CUMULATION 4
– BRITISH EDUCATION THESES INDEX, NEW SERIES 2, 1984-89
LIBRARIES – 1896-1931 – 1 – us UMI [020]
THE LIBRARIES OF PATRU AND BOILEAU / ed by Atkinson, David – 7mf – 9 – $50.00 – us UMI [010]
Libraries of the Royal Shakespeare Theatre and the Shakespeare Birthplace Trust *see*
– SHAKESPEARE AT STRATFORD-UPON-AVON
LIBRARY – v15- 1960- 1; v26- 5,6; v31- 9 – us UMI [020]
LIBRARY ACQUISITIONS; PRACTICE AND THEORY – v.1- 1977- – 5,6,9 – us UMI [073]
LIBRARY ADMINISTRATOR'S DIGEST *see* ADMINISTRATOR'S DIGEST
LIBRARY AND ARCHIVAL SECURITY / ed by Shuman, Bruce A – v1- 1975- – 1, 9 ($115.00 in US $161.00 outside hardcopy subsc) – us Haworth [020]
LIBRARY AND INFORMATION SCIENCE ABSTRACTS – 1985- – 1,5,6,9 – us UMI [020]
Library Association. China *see*
– BULLETIN
– CHUNG-HUA T'U-SHU-KUAN HSIEH-HUI HUI-PAO. BULLETIN
LIBRARY BINDER – 1952-71 – 1 – us UMI [073]
LIBRARY BULLETIN ... OF THE LITERARY AND HISTORICAL SOCIETY OF QUEBEC *see* BULLETIN/[LITERARY AND HISTORICAL SOCIETY OF QUEBEC]
LIBRARY BULLETIN...OF THE LITERARY AND HISTORICAL SOCIETY OF QUEBEC / Literary and Historical Society of Quebec – (Cont: Literary and Historical Society of Quebec. Bulletin) – [S.l.: The Soiety?, 1906-19–] – 9 – cn C.I.H.M. [360]
LIBRARY CATALOG / Metropolitan Museum of Art. New York – (Second Supplement, 1985.-50,000 cards 4 reels. $660.00 ISBN: 0-8161-1508-7; Third Supplement, 1987.-18,000 cards 3 reels. $660.00 ISBN: 0-8161-1560-5) – 2nd rev. ed., 1980.-761,000 cards 48 reels.-ISBN: 0-8161-1470-6 – 1 – $5320.00 – uk Hall [700]
LIBRARY CATALOG / Smythe, Augustus T – ca.1890. Largest private library in South Carolina in late 19th cent. 8 fiches – 9 – us South Carolina Historical [010]
LIBRARY CATALOG OF THE CONSERVATION CENTER / New York University. Institute of Fine Arts – 1980. 16,500 cards. 1 reel. ISBN 0-8161-1481-1; or 27mf. ISBN 0-8161-1776-4 – 1,9 – $110.00 – uk Hall [700]
LIBRARY CATALOG OF THE INTERNATIONAL MUSEUM OF PHOTOGRAPHY AT GEORGE EASTMAN HOUSE / International Museum of Photography at George Eastman House – (Also available on 66mf. $365.00 export $440.00. ISBN 0-8161-1733-0) – 1982. 47,293 cards on 4 reels – 1 – $365.00 export $440.00 – 0-8161-1445-5 – uk Hall [770]
LIBRARY CATALOG OF THE METROPOLITAN MUSEUM OF ART. SECOND EDITION : SECOND SUPPLEMENT / Metropolitan Museum of Art. New York – 1985. 50,000 cards on 4 reels – 1 – $600.00 export $725.00 – 0-8161-1508-7 – uk Hall [700]
LIBRARY CATALOG OF THE METROPOLITAN MUSEUM OF ART. SECOND EDITION : THIRD SUPPLEMENT / Metropolitan Museum of Art. New York – 1987 – 3r – 1 – $600.00 export $720.00 – 0-8161-1560-5 – uk Hall [700]
LIBRARY CATALOG OF THE METROPOLITAN MUSEUM OF ART. SECOND EDITION. REVISED / Metropolitan Museum of Art. New York – 1980. 761,000 cards on 48 reels – 1 – $4,835.00 export $5,850.00 – 0-8161-1470-6 – uk Hall [700]
LIBRARY CATALOG OF THE NEW YORK STATE SCHOOL OF INDUSTRIAL AND LABOR RELATIONS : FIFTH SUPPLEMENT / Cornell University. New York State School of Industrial and Labor Relations. Martin P. Catherwood Library – (Available on microfilm by request) – 1972. 18,100 cards – 9 – $125.00 export $150.00 – uk Hall [331]
LIBRARY CATALOG OF THE NEW YORK STATE SCHOOL OF INDUSTRIAL AND LABOR RELATIONS : FIRST SUPPLEMENT / Cornell University. New York State School of Industrial and Labor Relations. Martin P. Catherwood Library – (Available on microfilm by request.) – 1967. 18,300 cards – 9 – $115.00 export $140.00 – uk Hall [331]
LIBRARY CATALOG OF THE NEW YORK STATE SCHOOL OF INDUSTRIAL AND LABOR RELATIONS : FOURTH SUPPLEMENT / Cornell University. New York State School of Industrial and Labor Relations. Martin P. Catherwood Library – (Available on microfilm by request) – 1970. 18,400 cards – 9 – $125.00 export $150.00 – uk Hall [331]
LIBRARY CATALOG OF THE NEW YORK STATE SCHOOL OF INDUSTRIAL AND LABOR RELATIONS : FOURTH SUPPLEMENT TO THE CUMULATION / Cornell University. New York State School of Industrial and Labor Relations. Martin P. Catherwood Library – (Available on microfilm by request) – 1980. 23,625 cards – 9 – $275.00 export $330.00 – uk Hall [331]
LIBRARY CATALOG OF THE NEW YORK STATE SCHOOL OF INDUSTRIAL AND LABOR RELATIONS : SECOND SUPPLEMENT / Cornell University. New York State School of Industrial and Labor Relations. Martin P. Catherwood Library – (Available on microfilm by request) – 1968. 18,300 cards – 9 – $125.00 export $150.00 – uk Hall [331]
LIBRARY CATALOG OF THE NEW YORK STATE SCHOOL OF INDUSTRIAL AND LABOR RELATIONS : SEVENTH SUPPLEMENT / Cornell University. New York State School of Industrial and Labor Relations. Martin P. Catherwood Library – (Available on microfilm by request) – 1974. 18,100 cards – 9 – $125.00 export $150.00 – uk Hall [331]
LIBRARY CATALOG OF THE NEW YORK STATE SCHOOL OF INDUSTRIAL AND LABOR RELATIONS : SIXTH SUPPLEMENT / Cornell University. New York State School of Industrial and Labor Relations. Martin P. Catherwood Library – (Available on microfilm by request) – 1973. 18,200 cards – 9 – $125.00 export $150.00 – uk Hall [331]
LIBRARY CATALOG OF THE NEW YORK STATE SCHOOL OF INDUSTRIAL AND LABOR RELATIONS : THIRD SUPPLEMENT / Cornell University. New York State School of Industrial and Labor Relations. Martin P. Catherwood Library – (Available on microfilm by request) – 1969. 19,100 cards – 9 – $125.00 export $150.00 – uk Hall [331]
THE LIBRARY CATALOGS OF THE HOOVER INSTITUTION ON WAR, REVOLUTION, AND PEACE : CATALOG OF THE CHINESE COLLECTION / Stanford University. Hoover Institution on War, Revolution, and Peace – (Available on microfilm by request) – 1969 – 201,000 cards – 1 – $1,640.00 – 0-8161-0168-X – uk Hall [320]
THE LIBRARY CATALOGS OF THE HOOVER INSTITUTION ON WAR, REVOLUTION, AND PEACE : CATALOG OF THE CHINESE COLLECTION. FIRST SUPPLEMENT / Stanford University. Hoover Institution on War, Revolution, and Peace – 1972. – 4r – 1 – $355.00 – 0-8161-1318-1 – uk Hall [320]
THE LIBRARY CATALOGS OF THE HOOVER INSTITUTION ON WAR, REVOLUTION, AND PEACE : CATALOG OF THE CHINESE COLLECTION. SECOND SUPPLEMENT / Stanford University. Hoover Institution on War, Revolution, and Peace – 1977 – 4r – 1 – $330.00 – 0-8161-1341-6 – uk Hall [320]
THE LIBRARY CATALOGS OF THE HOOVER INSTITUTION ON WAR, REVOLUTION, AND PEACE : CATALOG OF THE JAPANESE COLLECITON. SECOND SUPPLEMENT / Stanford University. Hoover Institution on War, Revolution, and Peace – 1977 – 1r – 1 – $170.00 – 0-8161-1414-5 – uk Hall [320]
THE LIBRARY CATALOGS OF THE HOOVER INSTITUTION ON WAR, REVOLUTION, AND PEACE : CATALOG OF THE JAPANESE COLLECTION / Stanford University. Hoover Institution on War, Revolution, and Peace – 7r – 1 – $840.00 – 0-8161-1547-8 – uk Hall [320]
THE LIBRARY CATALOGS OF THE HOOVER INSTITUTION ON WAR, REVOLUTION, AND PEACE : CATALOG OF THE JAPANESE COLLECTION. FIRST SUPPLEMENT / Stanford University. Hoover Institution on War, Revolution, and Peace – 1972 – 1r – 1 – $150.00 – 0-8161-1413-7 – uk Hall [320]
THE LIBRARY CATALOGS OF THE HOOVER INSTITUTION ON WAR, REVOLUTION, AND PEACE : CATALOG OF THE WESTERN LANGUAGE COLLECTIONS / Stanford University. Hoover Institution on War, Revolution, and Peace – 63r – 1 – $7,530.00 – uk Hall [320]
THE LIBRARY CATALOGS OF THE HOOVER INSTITUTION ON WAR, REVOLUTION, AND PEACE : CATALOG OF THE WESTERN LANGUAGE COLLECTIONS. FIRST SUPPLEMENT, 1972 / Stanford University. Hoover Institution on War, Revolution, and Peace – 10r – 1 – $885.00 – 0-8161-1280-0 – uk Hall [320]
THE LIBRARY CATALOGS OF THE HOOVER INSTITUTION ON WAR, REVOLUTION, AND PEACE : CATALOG OF THE WESTERN LANGUAGE COLLECTIONS. SECOND SUPPLEMENT, 1977 / Stanford University. Hoover Institution on War, Revolution, and Peace – 6r – 1 – $1,015.00 – 0-8161-1431-5 – uk Hall [320]
THE LIBRARY CATALOGS OF THE HOOVER INSTITUTION ON WAR, REVOLUTION, AND PEACE : CATALOGS OF THE WESTERN LANGUAGE SERIALS AND NEWSPAPER COLLECTIONS / Stanford University. Hoover Institution on War, Revolution, and Peace –

3r – 1 – $365.00 – 0-8161-1494-3 – uk Hall [320]

LIBRARY CATALOGUE / University of London. School of Oriental and African Studies – (Second Suppl., 1973.-223,000 cards 27 reels. $1925.00 ISBN: 0-8161-1296-7) – 1963.-554,000 cards 50 reels.-ISBN: 0-8161-1225-8 – 1 – $2930.00 – uk Hall [950]

LIBRARY CATALOGUE, 5TH SUPPLEMENT 1978-1989 / School of Oriental and African Studies, London – (This suppl integrates 4th suppl and ca 230,000 new cards, subdivided into 5pts) – 695mf – 9 – A-1925/1 – ne IDC [020]

LIBRARY CATALOGUE OF THE INSTITUTION OF MECHANICAL ENGINEERS / Institution of Mechanical Engineers, London – (Over 25,000 catalogue cards reproduced) – 1984 – 335mf – 9 – $1,785.00 – 1-900853-60-4 – uk Mindata [621]

LIBRARY CATALOGUE OF THE MUSEUM OF MANKIND / Museum of Mankind (British Museum, Dept. of Ethnography). London – (Combines catalogues of British Museum Dept of Ethnography and the Royal Anthropological Society. A Tribal Index with over 17,000 references. Periodicals Index comprises over 170,000 references to articles in over 1,000 periodicals from 1963-89. Both titles also listed separately) – 1990 – 763mf – $4,000.00 set – 0-907006-99-X – uk Mindata [305]

LIBRARY CATALOGUE OF THE MUSEUM OF MANKIND *see*
- PERIODICALS CATALOGUE
- SUBJECT AND TRIBAL INDEXES

LIBRARY CATALOGUE OF THE SCHOOL OF ORIENTAL AND AFRICAN STUDIES / University of London. School of Oriental and African Studies – (Second Supplement, 1973. 223,000 cards on 27 reels. $1,750.00 export $2120.00. – ISBN 0-8161-1296-7) – 1963. 554,000 cards on 50 reels – $2,665.00 export $3,225.00 – 0-8161-1225-8 – uk Hall [950]

LIBRARY CHARGE BOOK / Monroe County. Mich, Bedford Township. Board of Education – 1880-1898 – 1r – 1 – $32.50r – us Archival [324]

LIBRARY CHRONICLE – v1-5 1884-1888. All pub – 1,5,6 – us Princeton Micro [020]

LIBRARY INDEX – West Liberty. Iowa. 1942-1951 – 1 – us UMI [020]

LIBRARY JOURNAL – (1969- 5,6. 1970- 9) – 1- 1876- – 1 – us UMI [020]

LIBRARY JOURNAL – v. 1-88. 1876-1963 – 1,5,6 – us Princeton Micro [020]

LIBRARY MATERIALS ON AFRICA – v1-10, 1967-72. London. Newsletter of the Standing Conference of Library Materials on Africa (SCOLMA) with printed index and finding list – 10mf – 9 – £40.00 – uk Altair [073]

LIBRARY OF AMERICAN LAW AND PRACTICE – Chicago. v. 1-12. 1912 – 1 – 65.00 – us L of C Photodup [340]

LIBRARY OF AMERICAN LAW AND PRACTICE; A GENERAL REFERENCE WORK ON CRIMINAL LAW, DOMESTIC RELATIONS, MERCANTILE LAW, TORTS, PROPERTY. – Chicago, American School of Correspondence, 1912. 12 v. LL-1634 – 1 – us L of C Photodup [340]

Library of Congress *see*
- CATALOG OF BRAZILIAN ACQUISITIONS OF THE LIBRARY OF CONGRESS, 1964-1974
- CHRONOLOGICAL BIBLIOGRAPHY OF ENGLISH LANGUAGE FICTION IN THE LIBRARY OF CONGRESS THROUGH 1950
- PAMPHLETS COLLECTED BY THE HOUSE COMMITTEE ON UN-AMERICAN ACTIVITIES

THE LIBRARY OF CONGRESS : A DOCUMENTARY HISTORY / ed by Cole, John Y – Foreward by Daniel Boorstin. Includes biogs. of each Librarian of Congress, annual reports, published book catalogs and collection guides, Congressional testimony, and correspondence. With printed guide – 549 fiches – 9 – $2,065.00 – us UPA [020]

LIBRARY OF CONGRESS ANNUAL REPORTS / U.S. Library of Congress – (Updates planned) – Washington: GPO, 1907-91 – 277mf – 9 – $415.00 – LLMC 79-426 – us L.L.M.C. [020]

LIBRARY OF CONGRESS CLASSIFICATION SCHEDULES : A CUMULATION OF ADDITIONS AND CHANGES THROUGH 1989 / U.S. Library of Congress; ed by Runchock, Rita & Droste, Kathy – (Covers every schedule (except B-BJ, DT-DX, KJ-KKZ, and PT, part 1). 42 cumulations; available individually) – 9 – $1570.00 – 0-8103-5150-1 – us Gale [020]

LIBRARY OF CONGRESS CLASSIFICATION SCHEDULES, COMBINED WITH ADDITIONS AND CHANGES THROUGH 1989 / U.S. Library of Congress; ed by Runchock, Rita & Droste, Kathy – Updated annually. Each vol. combines in one sequence the current edition of every schedule (except Q, PN-PZ, and PJ-PK) of the LCCS. Individual schedules available on request – 9 – $2935.00 – 0-8103-5244-3 – us Gale [020]

LIBRARY OF CONGRESS CLASSIFICATION SCHEDULES THROUGH 1993 : C AUXILLIARY SCI MFH / US Library of Congress; ed by Runchock-Droste, Rita & Droste, Kristy – 9 – us Gale [020]

LIBRARY OF CONGRESS CLASSIFICATION SCHEDULES THROUGH 1993 : KJ-KKZ MFH / US Library of Congress; ed by Runchock-Droste, Rita & Droste, Kristy – 9 – us Gale [020]

LIBRARY OF CONGRESS CLASSIFICATION SCHEDULES THROUGH 1993 : KJV-KJW LAW OF FRANCE / US Library of Congress; ed by Runchock-Droste, Rita & Droste, Kristy – 9 – us Gale [020]

LIBRARY OF CONGRESS CLASSIFICATION SCHEDULES THROUGH 1993 : KL-KW MFH / US Library of Congress; ed by Runchock-Droste, Rita & Droste, Kristy – 9 – us Gale [020]

LIBRARY OF CONGRESS CLASSIFICATION SCHEDULES THROUGH 1993 : MICROFICHE / US Library of Congress; ed by Runchock-Droste, Rita & Droste, Kristy – 9 – us Gale [020]

LIBRARY OF CONGRESS CLASSIFICATION SCHEDULES THROUGH 1993 : PT DUTCH AND SCANDINAVIAN, NO 2 / US Library of Congress; ed by Runchock-Droste, Rita & Droste, Kristy – 9 – us Gale [020]

LIBRARY OF CONGRESS CLASSIFICATION SCHEDULES WITH ADDITIONS AND CHANGES THROUGH 1992 : D-DJ MICROFICHE MFH / US Library of Congress – 9 – us Gale [020]

Library of Congress. Orientalia Division *see*
SOUTHEAST ASIA SUBJECT CATALOG

LIBRARY OF CONGRESS SHELFLIST – (6.8 million catalog cards. Subject segments available separately) – 3306mf – 9 – $6490.00 – us UMI [010]

LIBRARY OF CONGRESS SUBJECT HEADINGS IN MICROFORM / U.S. Library of Congress – ISSN: 0361-5243. Item Code: 8370300 – ca 31mf including children's headings – 9 – $115.00 – us L of C Cataloging [020]

THE LIBRARY OF H.E. SIR GEORGE GREY : PHILOLOGY / Bleek, W H I – (v1 pt1: South Africa; pt 2: The African Languages) – London, 1858 – 8 – BA-242 2 – ne IDC [020]

THE LIBRARY OF JEREMIAH SMITH / Dartmouth College. Library – (With printed guide) – 1759-1842 – 10mf – 9 – $17.50 – us Dartmouth [020]

Library of Jews' College. London *see*
MONTEFIORE COLLECTION OF HEBREW MANUSCRIPTS

THE LIBRARY OF MEDICAL HISTORY ON MICROFICHE / ed by Grooss, K S – (Some titles listed separately) – 1994 – ca. 19,000mf – 9 – ne IDC [610]

LIBRARY OF THE PEKING UNION MEDICAL COLLEGE : SELECTED CHINESE MEDICAL BOOKS – (In Chinese and Japanese) – 305r – 1 – $10,675.00 in US $40.00r outside – L9300067 – Dist. us Scholarly Res – us L of C Photodup [610]

Library of the Society of Friends, London *see*
- THE GREAT BOOK OF SUFFERINGS
- LONDON TWO WEEK MEETING
- QUAKER DIGEST REGISTERS OF BIRTHS, MARRIAGES AND BURIALS FOR ENGLAND AND WALES

THE LIBRARY OF WIT AND HUMOR, PROSE AND POETRY / ed by Spofford, A R & Shapley, Rufus E – Philadelphia: Classic Publ Co, 1910 – 5mf – 9 – $7.50 – LLMC 92-130 – us L.L.M.C. [870]

THE LIBRARY OF WORLD PEACE STUDIES / ed by Kuehl, W F – (24 titles, also available individually) – 9 – $4,485.00 – us UPA [327]

LIBRARY QUARTERLY – v1- 1931- 1; v39- 5,6; v47- 1977- 9 – us UMI [020]

LIBRARY QUARTERLY – v14-56. 1944-86 – 1 – us Princeton Micro [073]

LIBRARY RESOURCES AND TECHNICAL SERVICES – v1- 1957- 1; v15- 5,6; v19- 9 – us UMI [020]

LIBRARY SERVICE TO SCHOOLS AND CHILDREN / Ray, Colin – 1979 – 137p – 9 – 92-3-101640-7 – fr UNESCO [020]

LIBRARY SOCIETY COLLECTION / Charleston Library Society. Charleston, South Carolina – 1195 fiches. Titles listed and available individually – 9 – 848.25 – us South Carolina Historical [080]

LIBRARY SOFTWARE REVIEW: SR – v3-. 1984- – 1,5,6,9 – us UMI [020]

LIBRARY TRENDS – v20- 1971- 1; v1- 5,6; v24- 9 – us UMI [020]

LIBRARY TRENDS – Oct 1956 – 1 – uk Microform Academic [020]

LE LIBRE – no. 1-5. Paris. dec 1897-mai juin 1898 – 1 – fr A.C.R.P.P. [073]

LE LIBRE ARBITRE ETUDE PHILOSOPHIQUE / Naville, Jules Ernest – Paris: Librairie Fischbacher, 1890 – 338p – 1 – us U.W. Library [100]

LA LIBRE BELGIQUE – 1955- – 12r per y – 1 – inquire – us Ross [072]

LA LIBRE BELGIQUE – Brussels, Belgium. -d. 11 Feb-12 Aug 1919; 12 Sept 1944-9 Aug 1946; 1 Jan-30 March 1947; 1 Oct 1962-30 June 1964; 1 Oct 1964-31 March 1969. 84 reels – 1 – uk British Libr Newspaper [949]

LIBRE NATION / ed by Dupont, Jacques – Trois Rivieres, Canada. jan 1962-mai 1963 – 1r – 1 – Can$30.00 – cn Can Microfilming [072]

LA LIBRE PAROLE – de Paris. La France aux Francais. I, no. 1-7; II, no. 1-13. Paris puis Fontainebleau. sept 1928-15 juil 1929 – 1 – fr A.C.R.P.P. [073]

LA LIBRE PAROLE / ed by Huart, A & Leduc, R – Quebec, Canada. 17 jun 1905-21 dec 1912 – 1r – 1 – Can$40.00 – cn Can Microfilming [072]

LA LIBRE PAROLE – III, no. 10-11. Paris puis Alger, Paris. 20 25 juin-1er juil 1932. suivi de: La Libre parole populaire. Brunoy puis Paris. aout 1933-nov 1934. suivi de: Libres paroles. no. 1, 4. Paris. dec 1934-avr 1935. suivi de: La Libre parole. Paris puis Alger, Paris. 7 sept 1935-5 avr 1939, 25 oct-11 dec 1943, 20 juil, 1944 – 1 – fr A.C.R.P.P. [073]

LA LIBRE PAROLE – Montreal, Canada. 11 mar-13 mai 1893 – 1r – 1 – Can$25.00 – cn Can Microfilming [072]

LA LIBRE PAROLE – Paris. 20 avr 1892-7 juin 1924 – 1 – fr A.C.R.P.P. [073]

LA LIBRE PAROLE – Paris: Grande Impr, apr 20 1892-1916 – 52r – 1 – us Res Libr [072]

LA LIBRE PAROLE ILLUSTREE : CARICATURES – Montreal, Canada. 22 aut 1896-14 nov 1896 – 1r – 1 – Can$30.00 – cn Can Microfilming [072]

LA LIBRE PAROLE ILLUSTREE – Paris. juil 1893-95 – 1 – fr A.C.R.P.P. [073]

LIBRE SERVICE ACTUALITE – France. 1988-1995 – 3r per y – 5,6 – Sfr936.00 – sz Infoprint [944]

LIBRE VERMEY. DE PRIVILEGIOS DE MENORCA (SIECLE 14-15, Y SIECLE 599-18) – Ciudadela – 1r – 5,6 – sp Cultura [946]

LA LIBRE-PENSEE ET LE CATHOLICISME / Perraud, Charles-Alexis – (Includes bibliographical references) – Paris: Jules Gervais, 1887 – 1mf – 9 – 0-8370-8929-8 – 1986-2929 – us A.T.L.A. [210]

LIBRE-PENSEE ET PROTESTANTISME LIBERAL / Buisson, Ferdinand – Paris: Librairie Fischbacher, 1903. 1 fiche – 9 – us A.T.L.A. [240]

LA LIBRERIA DE JUAN DE HERRERA / Sanchez Canton, Francisco Javier – Madrid: Consejo Superior de investigaciones Cientificas Instituto Diego e Velazquez, 1941 – 1 – sp Bibl Santa Ana [940]

LIBRES ENTRETIENS / L'Union pour la Verite – Paris. nov 1904-12, nov. 1918-avr 1919 – 1 – fr A.C.R.P.P. [335]

LIBRES PROPOS – (Journal d'Alain). Nimes. avr 1921-oct 1924, mars 1927-36 – 1 – fr A.C.R.P.P. [073]

LIBRES PROPOS – v2-4, 7-9. 1922-24, 1933-35. Nimes: La Laborieuse, 1921-35. Imprint varies – 1 – us U.W. Library [073]

LIBRESENS – nos1-30. 1991-1993 (complete) – 1r – 1 – ATLA S0924 – us A.T.L.A. [073]

LIBRES-PENSEURS RELIGIEUX : ETUDES DIVERSES: L'IDEE DE DIEU DANS LES TEMPS MODERNES / Paris, Emilien – Paris: Librairie Fischbacher, 1905 – 1mf – 9 – 0-8370-4665-3 – 1985-2665 – us A.T.L.A. [210]

LIBRETTI IN DEUTSCHEN BIBLIOTHEKEN : KATALOG DER GEDRUCKTEN TEXTE ZU OPERN, ORATORIEN; KANTATEN, SCHULDRAMEN, BALLETTEN; GELEGENHEITSKOMPOSITIONEN VON DEN ANFAENGEN BIS ZUR MITTE DES 19. JAHRHUNDERTS / ed by Repertoire International des Sources Musicales (RISM) & Arbeitsgruppe Deutschland – 1992 – 107 fiches (1:24) – 9 – diazo DM4,980.00 – 3-598-30660-1 – gw Saur [780]

LIBREVILLE : LA VILLE ET SA REGION (GABON, A.E.F.). ETUDE DE GEOGRAPHIE HUMAINE / Lasserre, G – F60.00 – fr Ethnologie [307]

LIBRI 4 : SENTENTIARUM / Lombardus, Petrus – Florence 1916 – 24mf – 8 – ne Slangenburg [290]

LIBRI CAROLINI (MGH LEGES 2C: 2.BD) : SUPPLEMENTUM – 1924 – Dfl25.00 – ne Slangenburg [240]

LIBRI CONFRATERNITATUM SANCTI GALLI, AUGIENSIS, FABARIENSIS (MGH ANTIQUITATES 2: 6.BD) – 1884 – Dfl49.00 – ne Slangenburg [240]

LIBRI DE PISCIBUS MARINIS, IN QUIBUS VERAE PISCIUM EFFIGIES EXPR. SUNT... / Rondelet, G – (Volume 2 is entitled: "Universae Aquatilium historiae pars altera") – Lugduni, 1554-1555. 2v – 23mf – 9 – ne IDC [590]

LIBRI DUO DE CEREMONIIS AULAE BYZANTINAE (CBH 33) / Porphyrogenneti, Constantini; ed by Leich, J & Reiske, J – Lipsiae, 1751-1754 – Dfl98.00 – ne Slangenburg [930]

LIBRI LITURGICI BIBLIOTHECAE APOSTOLICAE VATICANAE MANU SCRIPTI / Ehrensberger, H – Freiburg i. Brsg., 1897 – 16mf – 8 – Dfl56.00 – ne Slangenburg [240]

LIBRI MIRACULORUM ALIAQUE OPERA MINORA / Turonensis, Gregorius; ed by Bordier, H L – Paris. Tomi 1-4. 1857-1864 – 31mf – 8 – Dfl109.00 – ne Slangenburg [240]

LIBRI SAMUELIS / Schloegl, Nivardus – Vienna: Mayer et Sociis, 1905. 1 fiche – 9 – us A.T.L.A. [240]

LIBRI STATUTORUM COMMUNITATIS FLORENTIAE / Florence – 15th cent. Holkham ms. 567. Holkham Hall, Norfolk, England – 1 – uk Microform Academic [324]

LIBRI TRES DE INSTITUTIONE HARMONICA.. / Aron, Pietro – 1516 – 9 – us Sibley [780]

LIBRI TRES DE RATIONE COGNOSCENDI CAUSAS ET SIGNA TAM IN PROSPERA QUAM ADVERSA VALITUDINE, URINARIUM / Diez Daza, A – Sevilla, 1577 – 6mf – 9 – sp Cultura [610]

LIBRO ANTIGUO DE ORDENANZAS MUNICIPALES (SIECLE 14-16) – Alcira – 1r – 5,6 – sp Cultura [350]

LIBRO CEREMONIAL DEL AYUNTAMIENTO DE CORDOBA (SIECLE 1800) – Cordoba – 1r – 5,6 – sp Cultura [946]

LIBRO DE ACTAS DEL AYUNTAMIENTO DE ARAN (ANNO 1820-1936) – Barcelona – 1r – 5,6 – sp Cultura [946]

LIBRO DE ALBAYTERIADE / Calvo Abeytar, Fernando – 1647 – 9 – 1.50f – sp Bibl Santa Ana [810]

LIBRO DE ALBEITERIA / Diez, M – Zaragoza, S.F. – 4mf – 9 – sp Cultura [630]

LIBRO DE ALBEYTERIA... / Reyna, Francisco de la – Mondonedo, 1552 – 3mf – 9 – sp Cultura [630]

LIBRO DE ALBEYTERIA...FERNANDO CALVO / Reyna, Francisco de la – 1647 – 9 – 1.50f – sp Bibl Santa Ana [890]

EL LIBRO DE BETTY: PARA LOS NINOS DE PRIMERA COMUNION / Martindale, Cyril Charlie – Trans. by J.F. de Correa y Rivero. Barcelona: Editorial Poliglota, 1920. 31p. illus. to be colored in – 1 – us U.W. Library [240]

LIBRO DE CIFRA NUEVA PARA TECLA, ARPA Y VIHUELA / Venegas de Henestrosa – Alcala de Henares, 1557 – 3mf – 9 – sp Cultura [780]

LIBRO DE CONOCIMIENTO...DEL GARROTILLO / Soto, J – Granada, 1616 – 6mf – 9 – sp Cultura [610]

LIBRO DE EXPERIENCIAS DE MEDICINA Y MUY APROBADO POR SUS EFFECTOS, ANSI EN ESTA ESPANA COMO FUERA DELLA / Lobera de Avila, L – Toledo, 1544 – 2mf – 9 – sp Cultura [610]

LIBRO DE HORAS (SIECLE 15-16) – Cordoba – 1r – 5,6 – sp Cultura [946]

LIBRO DE INSTRUMENTOS NUEVOS DE GEOMETRIA / Cespedes, A – Madrid, 1606 – 3mf – 9 – sp Cultura [510]

EL LIBRO DE JEREZ DE LOS CABALLEROS / Martinez Martinez, Matias Ramon – 1892 – 9 – 1.50f – sp Bibl Santa Ana [830]

LIBRO DE LA DESCENSION...TOLEDO Y VIDA DE SAN ILDEFONSO / Portocarrero, Francisco – 1616 – 9 – $1.50f – sp Bibl Santa Ana [240]

LIBRO DE LA MELANCOLIA... / Velazquez, A – Sevilla, 1585 – 3mf – 9 – sp Cultura [616]

LIBRO DE LAS CALIDADES Y EFFECTOS DE LA ALOXA / Figueroa, F – Lima, 1616 – 2mf – 9 – sp Cultura [615]

LIBRO DE LAS CLARAS E VIRTUOSAS MUGERES (SIC) POR... / Luna, Alvaro de – Madrid: Tip. Rafael G. Menor, 1909 – 1 – sp Bibl Santa Ana [946]

LIBRO DE LAS ENFERMEDADES MALIGNAS Y PESTILENTES, CAUSAS, PRONOSTICOS, CURACION... / Bocangelino, N – Madrid, 1600 – 3mf – 9 – sp Cultura [616]

LIBRO DE LAS QUATRO ENFERMEDADES CORTESANAS QUE SON CATARRO, GOTA ARTHETICA SCIATICA, MACDE PIEDRA... / Lobera de Avila, L – Toledo, 1544 – 3mf – 9 – sp Cultura [616]

LIBRO DE LAS VIDAS DE DOZE PRINCIPES DE LA MEDICINA / Villa, E de – Burgos, 1647 – 5mf – 9 – sp Cultura [610]

LIBRO DE LOS FUEROS DE CASTIELLA – Madrid: Razon y Fe, 1926 – 1 – sp Bibl Santa Ana [946]

LIBRO DE LOS PRIMITIVOS PRIVILEGIOS CONCEDIDOS POR ALFONSO 10 (SIECLE 14) – Alicante – 1r – 5,6 – sp Cultura [946]

LIBRO DE LOS PROVECHOS Y DANOS...POR BEBIDA DEL AGUA... / Diaz Daza, A – Sevilla, 1576 – 5mf – 9 – sp Cultura [616]

LIBRO DE LOS SECRETOS DE AGRICULTURA, CASA DE CAMPO PASTORIL / Agustin, M – Madrid, 1731 – 9mf – 9 – sp Cultura [630]

LIBRO DE LOS TRATADOS DE.. / Portillo, Rodrigo de – 1630 – 9 – 1.50f – sp Bibl Santa Ana [340]

LIBRO DE MUSICA DE VIHUELA AGORA NUEUMENTE COMPUESTO POR DIEGO PISADOR / Pisador, Diego – Salamanca: Diego Pisador, 1552 – 1 – us Sibley [780]

LIBRO DE ORO DEL PARTIDO NACIONAL HONDURENO, 1939-40 / Partido nacional. Honduras – 1 – us U.W. Library [972]

LIBRO DE PESTILENCIA, CURATIVO Y PRESERVATIVO... / Lobera de Avila, L – SL, SA: 1542? – 2mf – 9 – sp Cultura [614]

LIBRO DE POEMAS (1918-1921) : MANUSCRITO / Garcia Lorca, Federico – 9 – sp Cultura [810]

LIBRO DE THERIACA... / Perez, I – Toledo, 1575 – 8mf – 9 – sp Cultura [610]

EL LIBRO DEL JURADO / Garcia Romero de Tejada, Jose – 1894 – 9 – 1.50f – sp Bibl Santa Ana [340]

EL LIBRO DEL JURADO, 2ND PARTE / Garcia y Romero de Tejada, Jose – Jerez: Imp. El Guadalete, 1897 – 1 – sp Bibl Santa Ana [360]

LIBRO DEL MAESTRO. DIOS ES NUESTRO PADRE / Carmona Guillen, Juan – Badajoz: Secretariado Catequistico diocesano, 1967 – sp Bibl Santa Ana [240]

LIBRO DEL MAL USO DEL TABACO – 7mf – 9 – sp Cultura [580]

LIBRO DEL NUEVO COMETA... / Munoz, J – Valencia, 1573 – 2mf – 9 – sp Cultura [130]

EL LIBRO DEL PUEBLO / Henao y Munoz, Manuel – 1872. 2 tomos – 9 – 1.50f – sp Bibl Santa Ana [830]

EL LIBRO DEL TRABAJO / Maillo, Adolfo – Barcelona: Graficas Bobes, s.a., 1935 – 1 – sp Bibl Santa Ana [331]

LIBRO DELLA GVERRA DE GHOTTI COMPOSTO DA MISSER LEONARDO ARETINO / Bruni, LA – Firenze, 1526 – 2mf – 9 – H-8234/1 – ne IDC [945]

LIBRO DORADO. RECOPILACION DE REALES PROVISIONES. 3T (SIECLE 1700) – Cordoba – 1r – 5,6 – sp Cultura [946]

LIBRO EN QUE TRATA CON CLARIDAD LA NATURALEZA, CAUSAS, PROVIDENCIA Y MODO DE CURAR LA ENFERMEDAD VULGAR, PESTE / Mercado, L – Madrid, 1599 – 9 – sp Cultura [610]

IL LIBRO ETIOPICO DEL MIRACOLO DI MARIA E LE SUE FONTI NELLE LETTERATURE DEL MEDIO EVO LATINO / Cerulli, Enrico – Rome, 1943 – 1 – us Res Libr [240]

EL LIBRO GRIS / Gazul, Arturo – 1888 – 9 – 1.50f – sp Bibl Santa Ana [810]

EL LIBRO JAPONES / Mouton, Eugenio – Valencia: Editorial Castalia, 1948 – sp Bibl Santa Ana [946]

EL LIBRO, LA IMPRENTA EL PERIODISMO EN AMERICA DURANTE LA DOMINACION ESPANOLA / Revello, Jose Torre – Madrid: Razon y Fe, 1941 – sp Bibl Santa Ana [946]

LIBRO LLAMADO, ARTE DE TANER FANTASIA. Y APROVADO POR EL EMINENTE MUSICO DE SU MAGESTAD ANTONIO DE CABECON, Y POR JUAN DE CABECON, SU HERMANO / Santa Maria, Tomas de – pt. 1-2. 1565 – 9 – us Sibley [780]

UN LIBRO MAS DE CANTARES / Sanchez-Arjona, Vicente – Portada de Hohenleiter. Sevilla: Imp. Carlos Acuna.s.a. – 1 – sp Bibl Santa Ana [810]

LIBRO MEMORIA. JULIO-AGOSTO 1936-37. SANTISIMA VIRGEN DE LA PIEDAD. PATRONA DE ALMENDRALEJO – 1 – sp Bibl Santa Ana [240]

LIBRO NEGRO DE LA SEGUNDA TIRANIA / Argentine Republic. Comision Nacional de Investigaciones – Buenos Aires, 1958 – 1 – CSUXADP4977-B – us Hoover Inst Photo [320]

LIBRO PRIMERO DE ARCHITECTURA / Paladio, A – Madrid, 1616 – 5mf – 9 – sp Cultura [720]

LIBRO PRIMERO DE ARCHITECTURA / Paladio, A – Valladolid, 1625 – 2mf – 9 – sp Cultura [720]

LIBRO PRIMERO DE CABILDOS DE LA VILLA DE SAN MIGUEL DE IBARRA 1606-1617 / Bayle, Constantino – Quito, 1937; Burgos: Razon y Fe, 1938; Razon y Fe, 1938 – 1 – sp Bibl Santa Ana [946]

LIBRO PRIMERO DE LA ARITMETICA EN EL CUAL SE CONTIENEN LAS SIETE ESPECIES PRINCIPALES / Jeronimo de Santa Cruz, M – 9mf – 9 – sp Cultura [510]

LIBRO PRIMERO. METODO SIMULTANEO DE LECTURA Y DIBUJO / Conde Berron, Felix – Zafra: Industrias Tip. Extremenas, 1970 – sp Bibl Santa Ana [946]

LIBRO QUE TRATA DE LA ENFERMEDAD DE LAS BUBAS / Torres, P – Madrid, 1600 – 3mf – 9 – sp Cultura [616]

LIBRO REGISTRO DE PRIVILEGIOS (SIECLE 13-14) – Alcira – 1r – 5,6 – sp Cultura [946]

EL LIBRO ROJO DE PERON; CITAS / Peron, Juan Domingo – [Buenos Aires]: A. Pena Lillo, [1973] – 1 – CSUXADP8470-B – us Hoover Inst Photo [320]

LIBRO SEGUNDO DE CIFRAS SOBRE LA GUITARRA ESPANOLA, CON ARTE NUEVO PARA APRENDER A TANERLA SIN MAESTRO, CON GRAN FACILIDAD / Sanz, Gasper – Zaragoca. BP-755 1 – 9 – ne IDC [780]

LIBRO TERCERO DE MUSICA / Sanz, Gasper – De Cifras sobre la Gvitarra Espanola. Zaragoca. BP-756 1 – 9 – ne IDC [780]

LIBRO VIEJO DE LA FUNDACION DE GUATEMALA Y PAPELES RELATIVOS A D. PEDRO DE ALVARADO – Guatemala: Imp. Tip. Nacional, 1934 – sp Bibl Santa Ana [972]

EL LIBRO Y EL PUEBLO – v1-15. Mar 1922-Nov 1950; n.s.v16-. Jan 1954-; series 3, no.1, 1959-; series 4, May 1963-. Publicada por el Departamento de Bibliotecas de la Secretaria de Educacion Publica, 1922-. ill.-q – 1 – us U.W. Library [073]

LIBRO...DELLA ORIGINE DE TVRCHI ET IMPERIO DELLI OTTOMANNI / Cambini, A – Firenze, 1529 – 2mf – 9 – H-8237/1 – ne IDC [956]

LIBRO...EN QUE SE PRUEBA...CON CLARIDAD EL MAL...QUE CORRE POR ESPANA...SER NUEVO / Andosilla Salazar, V – Pamplona, 1661 – 5mf – 9 – sp Cultura [610]

LIBRO...FR. ANDRES DE GUADALUPE / Luengo, Juan – 1680 – 9 – 1.50f – sp Bibl Santa Ana [240]

LIBRO...PARA CURAR...DE PESTILENCIA... / Ficino, M – Pamplona, 1598 – 5mf – 9 – sp Cultura [614]

LIBRORUM ET MANUSCRIPTORUM ANGLIAE ET HIBERNIAE, CATALOGUE – 1697 – 1 – uk Microform Academic [025]

LIBROS CATOLICOS DE ESPANA... / Barrado Manzano, Arcangel – Madrid: Archivo Ibero Americano, 1965 – 1 – sp Bibl Santa Ana [240]

LIBROS DE ACUERDOS DEL HONRADO CONCEJO DE LA MESTA (ANNO 1499-1839) – Madrid – 27r – 5,6 – sp Cultura [946]

LIBROS DE BAUTISMOS (ANNO 1759) – Calahorra – 1r – 5,6 – sp Cultura [946]

LIBROS DE BAUTISMOS (ANNO 1688-1717) – Calahorra – 1r – 5,6 – sp Cultura [946]

LIBROS DE CUENTAS DEL HONRADO CONCEJO DE LA MESTA (ANNO 1510-1781) – Madrid – 10r – 5,6 – sp Cultura [946]

LIBROS DE MATRIMONIOS (ANNO 1584-1639) – Calahorra – 1r – 5,6 – sp Cultura [946]

LIBROS DE MATRIMONIOS (ANNO 1687-1768) – Calahorra – 1r – 5,6 – sp Cultura [946]

LOS LIBROS DEL CABILDO DE QUITO / Bayle, Constantino – Madrid: Razon y Fe, 1936 – 1 – sp Bibl Santa Ana [946]

Librovich, S F *see* ISTORIIA KNIGI V ROSSII

LIBYA : STATISTICAL ABSTRACT 1958-1974 / Libya. Census and Statistical Department – (Coll title: African Official Statistical Serials, 1867-1982) – 55mf – 9 – £405.00 – uk Chadwyck [960]

Libya *see*
- AL-JARIDAH AL-RASMIYAH
- CONSTITUTION OF THE KINGDOM OF LIBYA, AS MODIFIED BY LAW NR. 1 OF 1963
- CONSTRUCTION AND HOUSING
- COUNTRY PROGRAMMING DOCUMENT IN THE FORM OF A BACKGROUND PAPER (GENERAL STUDY) ON LIBYA
- DEVELOPMENT REPORT
- FIELD CROP PRODUCTION AND IMPROVEMENT
- FINANCING OF DEVELOPMENT PROGRAMMES: A REPORT ON DEVELOPMENT EXPENDITURES PLANNED AND MADE, 1952/1953-1957/1958
- GENERAL ECONOMIC BACKGROUND INFORMATION
- MONTHLY MAXIMUM OF FAMILY EXPENDITURE FOR TRIPOLI CITY
- PRELIMINARY NATIONAL ACCOUNTS OF LIBYA. 1962-1968
- PRIMO CENSIMENTO GENERALE DELIE AZIENDE AGRARIE METROPOLITANE DELLA LIBIA AL 21 APRILE 1937 XV
- REPORT OF THE ANNUAL SURVEY: LARGE CONSTRUCTION
- REPORT OF THE EVALUATION OF SPECIAL PROPOSALS CONCERNING THE EXPANSION OF THE PRODUCTION OF THE OLIVE OIL INDUSTRY
- REPORT OF THE SURVEY OF LICENSED CONSTRUCTION UNITS
- A REPORT ON THE INDUSTRIAL POSITION IN LIBYA, 1964-1966
- RESULTS OF WHEAT AND BARLEY TRIALS IN TRIPOLITANIA, 1966-1967
- SOME THOUGHTS ON LIBYAN AGRICULTURAL PROGRAMS FOR 1959-1960
- TECHNICAL PROBLEMS IN FORECASTING THE POPULATION OF LIBYA

Libya. Administration of Tripolitania *see*
- COMPULSORY STANDARDS FOR THE EXPORT OF EDIBLE PEANUTS
- REPORT ON TOBACCO VARIETY TRIALS AT SIDI MESRI TRIPOLI

Libya. Administration of Tripolitania. Dept. of Agriculture *see* ANNUAL DEMONSTRATION OF CROP IMPROVEMENT TRIALS, 1956

Libya. Advisor on Housing and Town Planning *see* COMMENTS ON DOXIADIS REPORT "HOUSING IN LIBYA"

Libya. Agricultural Information and Publicity Committee. Administration of Agriculture *see* RICE TRIALS IN TAURGA

LIBYA ANTIQUA – 1986 – 265p – 9 – 92-3-102376-4 – fr UNESCO [960]

Libya. Bank of Libya *see*
- DEVELOPMENT OF PUBLIC FINANCE IN LIBRARY, 1944-1963
- ECONOMIC DEVELOPMENT IN THE LIBYAN ARAB REPUBLIC, 1968-1971
- ECONOMIC MONTHLY REVIEW

Libya. Census and Statistical Department *see*
- LIBYA
- STATISTICAL DATA RESULTING FROM A SURVEY OF FAMILY BUDGETS OF FAMILIES OF LOWER INCOME GROUPS IN THE URBAN AREA OF TRIPOLI DURING THE YEAR 1962

Libya. Census and Statistical Department. National Accounts Section *see* PRELIMINARY COMPILATION OF STATISTICAL DATA ON NATIONAL ACCOUNTING IN LIBYA IN THE PERIOD FROM 1962 TO 1968

Libya. Central Statistics Office. Ministry of National Economy *see*
- BALANCE OF PAYMENTS
- NATIONAL INCOME ESTIMATES

Libya. Centre d'Etudes et de Documentation Economiques, Financieres et Sociales. Beirut *see* RESULTATS DE L'ENQUETE ANNUELLE SUR L'INDUSTRIE PETROLIERE. ETUDE MENSUELLE SUR L'ECONOMIE ET LES FINANCES DES PAYS ARABES

Libya. Centre d'Etudes et de Documentation Economiques. Financieres et Sociales S.A.L. Beyrouth-Damas *see* ETUDE MENSUELLE SUR L'ECONOMIE ET LES FINANCES DES PAYS ARABES

Libya. Direction de la Documentation *see* GENERAL STUDY OF LIBYA

Libya. Directorate General of Economic and Social Planning *see* ESTIMATES OF PRIVATE FINAL CONSUMPTION EXPENDITURE OF THE LIBYAN ARAB REPUBLIC, 1962-1969

Libya. Diwan of Audit *see* REPORT ON THE ACCOUNTS OF THE KINGDOM OF LIBYA FOR THE YEARS: 1963/1964; 1964/1965; 1965/1966; 1966/1967

Libya. Economic Social Development (incl. Planning, Literacy) *see*
- DEVELOPMENT BUDGET, 1965/1966-1968/1969
- GENERAL POPULATION CENSUS OF LIBYA, 1954. REPORT AND TABLES

Libya. Embassy of the Arab Republic in Libya. Press Counsellor's Office *see* LIBYAN ARAB REPUBLIC NEWS

Libya. Federation of Libya *see* TRADE UNIONS IN CYRENAICA

Libya. Industrial Planning Section *see*
- COMMENTS ON THE DECISION TO ESTABLISH A PERMANENT CONSULTATIVE COMMITTEE TO PROMOTE ECONOMIC COORDINATION AMONG THE MAGHRIB COUNTRIES AND TO SET UP A CENTRE FOR INDUSTRIAL STUDIES IN TRIPOLI
- COMMENTS ON THE POLSERVICE REPORT ON SUGAR BEET PLANT

Libya. London Embassy. Press Counsellor's Office *see* LIBYAN NEWS

Libya. Ministere de l'Economique Nationale. Administration de statistique et de recensement *see* STATISTIQUES DES BUDGETS FAMILIAUX DANS LA VILLE DE TRIPOLI

Libya. Ministry of Agriculture *see* AGRICULTURAL STATISTICS IN LIBYA

Libya. Ministry of Agriculture and Animal Wealth. Agricultural Planning and Economics Department. Statistics Division *see*
- MEAT PRODUCTION IN LIBYA
- RETAIL PRICES OF AGRICULTURAL COMMODITIES IN LIBYA IN 1965
- SOME DATA ON AGRICULTURAL STATISTICS IN LIBYA
- YEARLY BULLETIN OF PRICE STATISTICS, 1964

Libya. Ministry of Agriculture and Animal Wealth. Department of Planning and Agricultural Economics. Statistics Division *see* THE USE OF FERTILIZERS IN 1966

Libya. Ministry of Agriculture and Livestock *see*
- AGRICULTURE IN WESTERN TRIPOLITANIA
- THE CULTIVATION OF PISTACHIO IN LIBYA
- INFORMATION ABOUT THE FORESTS
- YEARBOOK OF THE MINISTRY'S ACHIEVEMENTS, 1964

Libya. Ministry of Agriculture. Census of Agriculture *see* REPORT AND TABLES

Libya. Ministry of Agriculture. Experimental Section *see* REPORT ON SUGAR BEET TRIALS FOR THE FALL OF 1962-1963

Libya. Ministry of Economy and Commerce. Census and Statistical Department *see*
- ANALYSIS OF THE RESULTS OF THE GENERAL POPULATION CENSUS 1964: THE SUPPLY OF LABOUR IN LIBYA
- ANALYSIS OF THE RESULTS OF THE GENERAL POPULATION CENSUS OF 1964: THE DISABLED CITIZENS IN LIBYA

Libya. Ministry of Economy and Trade. Census and Statistical Department *see*
- ANALYSIS OF THE RESULTS OF THE GENERAL POPULATION CENSUS 1964: TEACHING IN LIBYA
- AN ANALYSIS OF THE VALUE OF IMPORTS OF THE KINGDOM OF LIBYA, 1955-1966
- EMPLOYMENT IN THE PETROLEUM MINING INDUSTRY IN LIBYA, 1964
- EXTERNAL TRADE STATISTICS
- GENERAL POPULATION CENSUS 1964
- THE LABOUR FORCE OF LIBYA
- POPULATION CENSUS PAPER NR.(1): LITERACY IN LIBYA
- REPORT AND PRELIMINARY SURVEY OF FIVE IMPORTANT SERVICE TRADES IN TRIPOLI TOWN
- REPORT OF THE INDUSTRIAL CENSUS, 1964
- REPORT OF THE PRELIMINARY SURVEY OF WHOLESALE AND RETAIL TRADE IN TRIPOLI TOWN
- STATISTICAL ABSTRACT
- SUMMARY OF EXTERNAL TRADE STATISTICS

Libya. Ministry of Economy. Insurance Department *see* REPORT ON INSURANCE ACTIVITIES IN THE LIBYAN ARAB REPUBLIC, 1967/1969-

Libya. Ministry of Finance *see* BUDGET ESTIMATES, 1959/1960, 1965/1966, 1966/1967-1968/1969

Libya. Ministry of Industry *see*
- JEFREN AND ABU GHALAY SILICA SAND
- PHOSPHATE DEPOSITS OF TRIPOLITANIA, LIBYA

Libya. Ministry of Industry. Industrial Training and Service Department *see* THE LEATHER INDUSTRY IN LIBYA

Libya. Ministry of Information and Culture *see*
- CONFERENCE PAPER COMPRISING A ROYAL STATEMENT BEFORE PARLIAMENT ON GOVERNMENT POLICY
- THE NEW LIBYA. A GEOGRAPHICAL, SOCIAL, ECONOMIC AND POLITICAL STUDY

Libya. Ministry of Information and Culture. Public Relations Department *see*
- ACHIEVEMENTS OF THE FIRST OF SEPTEMBER REVOLUTION
- THE LIBYAN DIGEST
- THE LIBYAN REVIEW: A MONTHLY MAGAZINE

Libya. Ministry of Interior *see* REPORT ABOUT THE LOCAL ADMINISTRATION AND THEIR ROLE TOWARDS THE RE- SETTLEMENT OF NOMADS

Libya. Ministry of Labour and Social Affairs *see*
- EMPLOYMENT MARKET REPORT
- LIBYA'S MANPOWER RESOURCES AND EDUCATIONAL AND TRAINING NEEDS 1964-1971; A STUDY WITH REFERENCE TO THE SECOND FIVE YEAR ECONOMIC DEVELOPMENT PLAN
- REPORT ON THE TRAINING OF MANPOWER IN LIBYA DURING 1965-1966

Libya. Ministry of National Economy *see*
- BALANCE OF PAYMENTS FOR THE YEAR 1962, 1964-1968
- FAMILY BUDGET SURVEY IN TRIPOLI TOWN
- THE FIRST RESULTS OF THE GENERAL POPULATION CENSUS 1964
- FOOD BALANCE SHEET FOR LIBYA 1959
- MONTHLY COST OF LIVING INDEX FOR TRIPOLI TOWN
- PRELIMINARY RESULT OF THE GENERAL POPULATION CENSUS 1964
- PRELIMINARY RESULTS OF THE GENERAL POPULATION CENSUS 1964
- STATISTICAL ABSTRACT OF LIBYA 1958-1962

Libya. Ministry of Planning and Development *see*
- ARCHITECTURAL PLANNING PARTNERSHIP
- THE EVOLUTION OF PLANNING IN LIBYA
- FIVE-YEAR ECONOMIC AND SOCIAL DEVELOPMENT PLAN, 1963-1968
- A GENERAL SURVEY AND STUDY OF THE MEANS OF COMMUNICATIONS. TRANSPORT IN LIBYA
- KHUTTAT EL TANMEYA EL IQTISADEYA WA EL IJTIMAEYA LIL-SANAWAT EL KHAMS, 1963-1968
- LIBYA'S MONETARY INFLATION: CAUSES, CONSEQUENCES AND REMEDIES
- SUMMARY OF THE EVOLUTION OF PLANNING INSTITUTIONS ON LIBYA
- TRIPOLI INVENTORY REPORT

Libya. Ministry of Planning and Development. Census and Statistical Department *see*
- EXTERNAL TRADE INDICES, 1962-1966
- TRENDS IN LIBYAN IMPORTS AND EXPORTS, 1962-1968
- WHOLESALE PRICES IN TRIPOLI TOWN

Libya. Ministry of Planning and Development. Doxiadis Associates *see*
- BRIEF COMMENT ON "HOUSING IN LIBYA"
- EASTERN MUHAFADAT INVENTORY
- HOUSING IN LIBYA

Libya. Ministry of Planning and Development. El Khums and Misratah *see* INVENTORY REPORTS

Libya. Ministry of Planning and Development. Kingdom of Libya. Fezzan *see* FEZZAN INVENTORY REPORT

Libya. Ministry of Planning and Development. Legislation. Economic Administration *see* LAW NR. 5 FOR THE ORGANIZATION OF PLANNING AND DEVELOPMENT AFFAIRS, AND THE REGULATIONS AND DECISIONS ISSUED THEREUNDER

Libya. Ministry of Planning and Documentation. Doxiadis Associates *see* HOUSING IN LIBYA

Libya. Ministry of Planning. Census and Statistical Department *see*
- MONTHLY RETAIL PRICES IN TRIPOLI TOWN
- REPORT OF THE FIRST PHASE OF THE HOUSEHOLD SAMPLE SURVEY. REPORT ON THE SECOND PHASE OF HOUSEHOLD SAMPLE SURVEY

Libya. Ministry of Planning. Development Plans. 1972-1975 *see* THREE YEAR DEVELOPMENT PLANS, 1972-1975. FIRST YEAR DEVELOPMENT BUDGET, 1972-1973

Libya. Ministry of Trade and Economy, Planning and Development. Census and Statistical Department *see* REPORT OF THE ANNUAL SURVEY OF LARGE MANUFACTURING ESTABLISHMENTS

Libya. National Accounts Section *see* NATIONAL ACCOUNTS OF THE LIBYAN ARAB REPUBLIC, 1962-1969

Libya. National Bank of Libya *see* ANNUAL REPORT OF THE BOARD OF DIRECTORS

Libya. National Social Insurance Institution *see* TEXT OF LABOUR LEGISLATION AMENDMENTS ENACTED IN 1972 CONCERNING THE COMPULSORY SOCIAL PROTECTION OF WORKERS IN LIBYA

Libya. Provincial Government of Cyrenaica. Statistics Division *see*
- AGRICULTURAL STATISTICS FOR CYRENAICA, 1959
- LAND UTILIZATION AND CROP PRODUCTION ESTIMATES FOR CYRENAICA 1956/1957

Libya. Public Development and Stabilization Agency. Economic Social Development (incl. Planning, Literacy) *see* ANNUAL REPORT

Libya. Public Services Section *see* LIBYAN WATER RESOURCES PORTION OF LIBYAN DEVELOPMENT PLAN

Libya. Secretariat General du Gouvernement *see* NOTES ET ETUDES DOCUMENTAIRES

Libya. Technical Planning Body. Census and Statistical Department *see*
- IMPORTS BY OIL COMPANIES, 1969-1970
- MONTHLY STATISTICS OF PRODUCTION AND EMPLOYMENT IN SELECTED LARGE MANUFACTURING ESTABLISHMENTS

Libya. Technical Planning Body. Census and Statistical Department. *see* QUARTERLY BULLETIN OF STATISTICS

LIBYA TREATY / Italy – 15.12.1950. BNE-507 1 – 9 – ne IDC [945]

Libya. UNO. United Nations Mission in Libya *see* THE PROBLEM OF INFLATION

LIBYAN ARAB REPUBLIC NEWS / Libya. Embassy of the Arab Republic in Libya. Press Counsellor's Office – no. 1. London. Oct 1969? BNE-534 1 – 9 – ne IDC [956]

THE LIBYAN DIGEST / Libya. Ministry of Information and Culture. Public Relations Department – A Fortnightly News Bulletin. v. 1-3, 5, 8. 15 Apr 1968-Sep 1968. BNE-532 1 – 9 – ne IDC [956]

LIBYAN FARMER MAGAZINE (MAJALLET ALFALLAH ALLIBI).1962. BNE-1026/1 – 9 – ne IDC [630]

LIBYAN NEWS / Libya. London Embassy. Press Counsellor's Office – Monthly. no. 6. Dec 1968; no. 5. Jan 1969; no. 11. Aug 1969. BNE-535 1 – 9 – ne IDC [956]

THE LIBYAN REVIEW: A MONTHLY MAGAZINE / Libya. Ministry of Information and Culture. Public Relations Department – Jul 1966 (no. 7); Apr 1968 (v. 3, no. 4); Jun and Dec 1968. 1969. Jan-Jul. BNE-533 1 – 9 – ne IDC [956]

LIBYAN WATER RESOURCES PORTION OF LIBYAN DEVELOPMENT PLAN / Libya. Public Services Section – Aug 1964. Rupp, M. F. General Policy Proposals. BNE-801 1 – 9 – ne IDC [333]

LIBYA'S MANPOWER RESOURCES AND EDUCATIONAL AND TRAINING NEEDS 1964-1971; A STUDY WITH REFERENCE TO THE SECOND FIVE YEAR ECONOMIC DEVELOPMENT PLAN / Libya. Ministry of Labour and Social Affairs – Tripoli. 1967. Nair, A. N. K. BNE-909 1 – 9 – ne IDC [331]

LIBYA'S MONETARY INFLATION: CAUSES, CONSEQUENCES AND REMEDIES / Libya. Ministry of Planning and Development – 1966. BNE-627 1 – 9 – ne IDC [332]

A LICA : POLITICO E NOTICIOSO – Cuiaba, 8 Mar-Jul, Sep-11 Oct 1885 – 1,5,6 – bl Biblioteca [072]

LICENSE RECORDS / Huron County. Ohio. Common Pleas. Civil Division – 1818-1851 – 1r – 1 – $32.50r – us Archival [324]

THE LICENSED VICTUALLERS' GAZETTE – Montreal: Licensed Victuallers' Gazette Co, [1897-189- or 19–] – 9 – cn C.I.H.M. [640]

LICHENAEA AFRICANA / Stizenberger, E – St. Gallen. 1890-95. B-731 2 – 8 – ne IDC [580]

DIE LICHENEN-FLORA BAYERNS / Krempelhuber, A von – (Denkschriften der Kon. Bayer. Bot. Gesellschaft. v. 4). Regensburg. 1861. B-522 2 – 8 – ne IDC [580]

LICHENES AMERICANI QUOS PARTIM IN FLORA INDIAE OCCIDENTALIS DESCRIPSIT / Schwartz, O – fasc. 1. Norimbergae. 1811. B-5311 2 – 8 – ne IDC [580]

LICHENES ARCTOI EUROPAE GROENLANDIAEQUE / Fries, T M – (Nova Acta Regiae Societatis Scientiarum Upsaliensis, S. 3, v. 3. 1861). Uppsala. 1860. B-1262 2 – 8 – ne IDC [580]

LICHENES BRITANNICI / Crombie, J M – London. 1870. B-571 2 – 8 – ne IDC [580]

LICHENES. EXTRA-EUROPAEI A PLURIBUS COLLECTORIBUS AD MUSEUM PARISIENSE MISSI / Hue, A M – (Nouvelles Arch. Mus. Hist. Nat. S. 3, v. 10. Paris. 1898). B-1509 2 – 8 – ne IDC [580]

LICHENES FUEGIAE ET PATAGONIAE / Nylander, W – Paris. 1888. B-5390 2 – 8 – ne IDC [580]

LICHENES HELVETICI EORUMQUE STATIONES ET DISTRIBUTIO / Stizenberger, E – Bericht ueber die Thaetigkeit der St. Gallischen natuerwissenschaftlichen Gesellschaft, 1880-1881. p155-522. B-5216 2 – 8 – ne IDC [580]

LICHENES IN REGIONIBUS EXOTICIS QUIBUSDAM VIGENTES / Nylander, W – (Ann. Sc. Nat. v. 4., v. 11, 1859). B-553 – 8 – ne IDC [580]

LICHENES. IN: TRIANA, J. E. PLANCHON. PRODROMUS FLORAE NOVO-GRANATENSIS / Nylander, W – (Ann. Sc. Nat. s. 4, v. 19, 1863). B-552 2 – 8 – ne IDC [580]

LICHENES INSULARUM GUINEENSIUM / Nylander, W – (San Thome do Principe, das Cabras). Parisiis. 1889. B-1578 2 – 8 – ne IDC [580]

LICHENES INSULARUM PHILIPPINARUM 2 / Wainio, E A – Helsingforsiae. 1920. B-7644 2 – 8 – ne IDC [580]

LICHENES JAPONIAE. ACCEDUNT OBSERVATIONIBUS LICHENES INSULAE LABUAN / Nylander, W – Paris. 1890. B-504 2 – 8 – ne IDC [580]

LICHENES KNIGHTIANI IN NOVA ZELANDIA LECTI ADDITIS NONNULLIS ALIIS EJUSDEM REGIONES, QUOS EXPONIT / Mueller, J A – Bruxelles, 1892. 21 pp. (Bull. Soc. Roy. Bot. Belgique, v. 30, pt. 2. Compt. Rend.). B-5392 2 – 8 – ne IDC [580]

LICHENES LAPPONIAE ORIENTALIS / Nylander, W – Helsingfors. 1867. B-479 2 – 8 – ne IDC [580]

LICHENES NOVAE-ZELANDIAE / Nylander, W – Parisiis. 1888. B-1003 2 – 8 – ne IDC [580]

LICHENES PYRENAEORUM ORIENTALIUM OBSERVATIS NOVIS / Nylander, W – Parisiis. 1891. B-1281 2 – 8 – ne IDC [580]

LICHENES SCANDINAVIAE / Nylander, W – Helsingforsiae. 1861. B-478 2 – 8 – ne IDC [580]

THE LICHEN-FLORA OF GREAT-BRITAIN, IRELAND AND THE CHANNEL ISLANDS / Leighton, W A – Shrewsbury. 1871. B-6221 2 – 8 – ne IDC [580]

LICHENOGRAPHIA EUROPAEA REFORMATA / Fries, E M – Lund. 1831. B-1080 2 – 8 – ne IDC [580]

LICHENOGRAPHIA SCANDINAVICA / Fries, T M – Upsaliae. 1871-74. B-6222 2 – 8 – ne IDC [580]

LICHENOGRAPHIA UNIVERSALIS / Acharius, E – Goettingen. 1810. B-515 2 – 8 – ne IDC [580]

LICHENOGRAPHIAE GERMANICAE SPECIMEN PARMELIACEARUM FAMILIAM CONTINENS / Koerber, G W – Bratislava. 1846. B-581 2 – 8 – ne IDC [580]

LICHENOGRAPHIAE SUECICAE PRODROMUS / Acharius, E – Lincopiae. 1798. B-1076 2 – 8 – ne IDC [580]

LICHENOLOGISCHE AUSFLUEGE IN TIROL / Arnold, F C G – Wien. 1868-97. B-1292 2 – 8 – ne IDC [580]

LICHENOLOGISCHE BEITRAEGE / Mueller, J A – Collected papers published in "Flora," 1874-1891. pts. 1-35. B-609 2 – 8 – ne IDC [580]

LICHENS DE FRANCE. CATALOGUE SYSTEMATIQUE ET DESCRIPTIF, EPINAL- PARIS, 1905 / Harmand, J – Pars 1-3. Paris. 1905; Pars 4. Paris. 1909; Pars 5. Paris. 1913. B-7096 2 – 8 – ne IDC [580]

THE LICHENS OF CEYLON / Leighton, W A – Collected by G. H. K. Thwaites. (Trans. Linn. Soc. London, v. 27 1869). B-551 2 – 8 – ne IDC [580]

LICHENS PARAGUAYENSES / Mueller, J A – (Revue Mycologique, 1888, v. 10, p. 53-68, 113-120, 177-184). B-481 2 – 8 – ne IDC [580]

LICHENUM DIANOME NOVA / Fries, E M – Lundae. 1817. B-575 2 – 8 – ne IDC [580]

LICHENUM HELVETICORUM SPICILEGIUM / Schaerer, L E – Bernae. 1823-42. B-589 2 – 8 – ne IDC [580]

LICHENUM IN BOHEMIA OBSERVATORUM DISPOSITIO SUCCINCTAQUE DESCRIPTIO / Mann, W – Prague, 1825. 110 pp. B-583 2 – 8 – ne IDC [580]

Lichfield and South Staffordshire Archaeological and Historical Society *see* TRANSACTIONS

Lichfield Archaeological and Historical Society *see* TRANSACTIONS

LICHFIELD MERCURY – England. 28 Sep 1877-Dec 1898; 1911; 1917-21; 1944-45; 1965 (missing 1897). -w. 26mqn reels – 1 – uk British Libr Newspaper [072]

Lichnowsky, Mechtilde *see* DAS RENDEZVOUS IM ZOO

LICHNYE ARKHIVNYE FONDY V GOSUDARSTVENNYKH KHRANILISHCHAKH SSSR – Ikazatel'. Moscow, 1962-63. 2v. 470p, 502p. BR-10,655/1 – 9 – ne IDC [947]

LICHOEKOLOGISCHE UNTERSUCHUNGEN DER CHLOROPLASTENFARBSTOFFE PHOTOSTABILER UND PHOTOLABILER PFLANZEN (1952) / Zahn, Richard – 1992 – 74p – 9 – DM98.00 – 3-89349-422-7 – gw Hänsel [540]

DAS LICHT = THE LIGHT – (In German) – Berlin, DE. v1 no1 1920-no4 1924 – 1r – 1 – $30.00 – cn Can Microfilming [072]

DAS LICHT UND DIE FARBEN : IN NATUR, GEIST UND LEBEN / Claassen, Johannes – Guetersloh: C. Bertelsmann, 1896 – 1mf – us A.T.L.A. [210]

LICHT UND LEBEN : EVANGELISCHES WOCHENBLATT – (Lacking some pgs) – v31-45. 1919-33; 1987-91 – 17r – 1 – ATLA 80050 – us A.T.L.A. [073]

LICHT UND RECHT / Oncken, Johann Gerhard – 1901 – 1 – 9.73 – us Baptist [240]

LICHTBILD-BUEHNE *see* FILM-EXPRESS

LICHTBILDBUEHNE – (1932-1939, 9 Rollen DM675.00) – Berlin, 1925-1927 – 5r – 1 – DM375.00 – gw Mikro Press [790]

LICHTBILDBUEHNE – Berlin, 1911-24, oct 17 1927-31 – 60r – 1 – gw Mikrofilm [790]

LICHTBILDBUEHNE – Berlin, 1911-39 – 1 – Dist. gw Mikrofilm – gw Mikrofilm [790]

DER LICHTBILDKUENSTLER – Dresden. 1898-1906 – 1r – 1 – gw Mikrofilm [770]

DAS LICHTBILD-THEATER – Berlin. jul 6, 1911-aug 1, 1914 – 6r – 1 – gw Mikrofilm [790]

DAS LICHTBILD-THEATER – Wien, aug 3-dec 28 1911 – 1r – 1 – gw Mikrofilm [790]

DER LICHTBILDTHEATERBESITZER – Berlin. jan 21, 1922-jun 30, 1923 – 2r – 1 – gw Mikrofilm [790]

LICHTBILDVORTRAEGE UND FILME – Berlin. fal 1919 – 1 – gw Mikrofilm [790]

LICHTBLICKE UND ERLEBNISSE AUS DER WELT UND DEM PRIESTERLEBEN : GESAMMELT IN DEN JAHREN 1815-1833 / Hohenlohe-Waldenburg-Schillingsfuerst, Alexander Fuerst von – 1995 – 4mf – DM90.00 – 3-8267-3157-3 – gw Hänsel [240]
DIE LICHTEN STUNDEN : ERZAEHLUNGEN / Kochanowski, Bodo – Berlin: West-Ost-Verlag, [1944?] – 1r – 1 – us U.W. Library [830]
LICHTENBERG : ZUM PROBLEM DER DEUTSCHEN APHORISTIK / Requadt, Paul – (Includes bibliographical references & index) – Hameln: Fritz Seifert, 1948 – 1 – us U.W. Library [430]
Lichtenberg, Georg Christoph *see*
– G.C. LICHTENBERG'S BRIEFE AN DIETERICH, 1770-1798
– TAG UND DAEMMERUNG
LICHTENBERG IM SPIEGEL SEINER KRITISCHEN AEUSSERUNGEN UEBER KLOPSTOCK / Schlimbach, Alice – (Includes bibliographical references) – [New York, NY]: New York University, 1944 – 1r – 1 – us U.W. Library [430]
Lichtenberger, Andre *see* EINE ABENTEUERLICHE REISE
Lichtenberger, Frederic *see*
– DES ELEMENTS CONSTITUTIFS DE LA SCIENCE DOGMATIQUE
– ETUDE SUR LE PRINCIPE DU PROTESTANTISME D'APRES LA THEOLOGIE ALLEMANDE CONTEMPORAINE
– HISTORY OF GERMAN THEOLOGY IN THE NINETEENTH CENTURY
LICHTENBERGS BRIEFE AN JOHANN FRIEDRICH BLUMENBACH / ed by Leitzmann, Albert – (Includes bibliographical references) – Leipzig: Dieterich, 1921 – 1r – 1 – us U.W. Library [920]
Lichtenstein, Hinrich *see* TRAVELS IN SOUTHERN AFRICA IN THE YEARS 1803, 1804, 1805 AND 1806
Lichtenstein, J *see* DER VULGAERE RATIONALISMUS, ODER, DAS MODERNE HEIDENTHUM...CHRISTLICHEN KIRCHE
Lichtenstein, MH C *see* NOMENCLATOR AVIUM MUSEI ZOOLOGICI BEROLINENSIS
Lichtenthal, J David *see* JOURNAL OF BUSINESS-TO-BUSINESS MARKETING
Lichtfoot, J *see* THE APOSTOLIC FATHERS, PART 1
Lichtheim, R *see* REVISION DER ZIONISTISCHEN POLITIK
DIE LICHTSPIEL-BUEHNE – Sigmaringen, jun 15, jul 15, aug 1, aug 15, sep 1, nov 15 1917. feb 15, mar 1, mar 15 1918 – 1 – gw Mikrofilm [790]
DIE LICHTSPIELBUEHNE – Aussig, jan 1921; dec 1923 – 1 – gw Mikrofilm [790]
DIE LICHTSPIELKUNST – Storkow, apr? 1912-aug 1 1914 – 1 – gw Mikrofilm [790]
LICHTSPIEL-ZEITUNG – Berlin. oct 12, 1912. feb 14, mar 7, 1913 – 1 – gw Mikrofilm [790]
LICHTSTRAHLEN – Berlin, 1913-16, 1918-21 – 1 – Dist. gw Mikrofilm – gw Misc Inst [072]
LICHTSTRAHLEN – Berlin. Monatliches Bildungsorgan fuer denkende Arbeiter. From Nov 1918, called Zeitschrift fuer wissenschaftlichen Kommunismus. Subtitles vary – 1 – $35.00r – us Hoover Inst Photo [335]
LICHTSTRAHLEN : ZEITSCHRIFT FUER WISSENSCHAFTLICHEN KOMMUNISMUS – Berlin. v1-6. 1913-21 – 1 – us Ross [335]
LICHTSTRAHLEN AUS SEINEN SCHRIFTEN UND BRIEFEN / Lessing, Gotthold Ephraim – Leipzig: F A Brockhaus, 1869 – 1r – 1 – us U.W. Library [800]
LICKING VALLEY REGISTER – Covington. Ky. 1841-47 – 1 – us UMI [071]
Lickl, G *see*
– TROIS GRAND QUATUOR CONCERTANS POUR DEUX VIOLONS, ALTO ET BASSE
– TROIS TRIOS CONCERTANTES POUR VIOLON, ALTO ET VIOLONCELLE
LID MONTHLY / League for Industrial Democracy – 1-10 2+8. 1922-32 – 12mf – 9 – $75.00 – us UPA [335]
LID OYF DER MEGILE *see* BIBLE. O.T. ESTHER
LIDADOR : LITTERARIO, NOTICIOSO, AGRICOLA, COMMERCIAL E INDUSTRIAL – Pilar, Alagoas. 15 Abr 1883; 21 Jan 1885 – 1,5,6 – bl Biblioteca [072]
O LIDADOR : ORGAO IMPARCIAL – Pouso Alto, 28 Feb, 8 Jun 1897 – 1,5,6 – bl Biblioteca [072]
O LIDADOR : PERIODICO ARTISTICO, LITTERARIO E NOTICIOSO – Maceio, Alagoas. 7 Set 1880 – 1,5,6 – bl Biblioteca [072]
LIDAI RENWU NIANLI BEIZHUAN ZONGBIAO – General table of biographical records of historical figures. Comp. by Jiang Liangfu.9 fiches. F-J24 – 9 – 4.00f – cc Microforms [920]
Lidarti, C *see* TRIO-SONATAS, 2 VIOLINS AND CONTINUO
Lidderdale, D W S *see* LA PROCEDURE PARLEMENTAIRE EN EUROPE
Liddon, H P *see* DELLE CINQUE PIAGHE DELLA SANTA CHIESA
Liddon, Henry Parry *see*
– EXPLANATORY ANALYSIS OF ST PAUL'S EPISTLE TO THE ROMANS
– SOME ELEMENTS OF RELIGION: LENT LECTURES, 1870
Lidel, A *see* A SECOND SET OF SIX QUARTETTOS..
LIDER MAGAZIN = SONGSTER – (In Yiddish) – New York City, NY. v16 1893 – 1r – 1 – $25.00 – cn Can Microfilming [071]
Lidgerwood Collection of Morristown National Historical Park *see* HESSIAN DOCUMENTS OF THE AMERICAN REVOLUTION, 1776-1783
LIDINGO TIDNING – Stockholm, Sweden. 1910-87 – 1 – sw Kungliga [072]
LIDINGOE KOMMUNALBLAD – Lidingoe, Stockholm. 1928-35 – 9 – sw Kungliga [072]
LIDINGOE TIDNING – Norrtaelje, 1994- – 9 – sw Kungliga [072]
LIDINGOEBLADET – Lidingoe, 1926-28 – 9 – sw Kungliga [072]
LIDINGOEPOSTEN – Lidingoe, 1987-93 – 9 – sw Kungliga [072]
LIDKOPINGS TIDNING – Lidkoping, Sweden. 1842-72 – 8r – 1 – sw Kungliga [072]
LIDOVA DEMOKRACIE – Prague, Czechoslovakia. 1962-93 – 66r – 1 – us L of C Photodup [072]
LIDOVE NOVIGNY – De 1988 a 1990 – 4r – 1 – Sfr480.00 – sz Infoprint [947]
LIDOVE NOVIGNY – (Standing order available from De 1994 +. 6r per year. Sfr675.00y) – 1991-1995 – 6r – 1 – Sfr720.00 – sz Infoprint [947]
LIDOVE NOVIGNY SUPPLEMENT – 1992-1995 – 2 times per yr – 1 – F1,397.00 – sz Infoprint [072]
LIDOVE NOVINY – (1988-90 4r $340. 1991-98 6r per y $510y) – Prague: Norman Ross Pub, 1996- – 6r per y – 1 – $480.00y standing order – us Ross [073]
LIDOVE NOVINY – Brno and Prague. Czechoslovakia. -d. 10 Feb-22 Jul 1919, 1 Jan 1938-31 May 1940, 1 May 1941-3 Jun 1942, 9 May 1948-8 Feb 1952. (27 reels) – 1 – uk British Libr Newspaper [072]
LIDOVE NOVINY – (Some issues missing) – Brno, Czechoslovakia. Dec 1924; Apr 1942 – 1r – 1 – us L of C Photodup [072]
Lie, Tek Tjeng *see* SOME REMARKS ON THE PROBLEMS AND DIFFICULTIES BESETTING PRESENT-DAY INDONESIAN-JAPANESE RELATIONS
Liebana, Beatus a *see* IN APOCALYPSIN COMMENTARIUS
Liebanensis, Beatus *see* ADVERSUS ELIPANDUM
LIEBE : EINE TRAGOEDIE / Wildgans, Anton – Leipzig: L Staackmann, 1922, c1916 – 1r – 1 – us U.W. Library [820]
DIE LIEBE IN DER FRUEHROMANTIK MIT BESONDERER BERUECKSICHTIGUNG DES ROMANS / Schier, Alfred – (Includes bibliographical references and Index) – Marburg a.L.: N G Elwert, 1913 – 1r – 1 – us U.W. Library [430]
"LIEBE IN VERKLAERUNG" : AUSZUG AUS EINEM VORTRAG / Plattensteiner, Richard – Wien: Lese-Gemeinde Plattensteiner'scher Werke, 1951-1952 – 1 – us U.W. Library [080]
LIEBE IST EWIG : ROMAN EINER KUENSTLERIN / Polenz, Wilhelm von – [Bayreuth]: Gauverlag Bayreuth, 1944 – 1r – 1 – us U.W. Library [830]
LIEBE MUTTER : NOVELLE / Klucke, Walther Gottfried – Berlin: Bong, 1941 – 1r – 1 – us U.W. Library [830]
LIEBE UND TOD : EIN TRAUERSPIEL DES HERZENS: GEDICHTE / Leineweber, Clemens Heinrich – Milwaukee: Gutenberg, c1936 – 1r – 1 – us U.W. Library [810]
"LIEBE VON FREMD ZU FREMD..." : MENSCHLICHKEIT DES MENSCHEN UND GOETTLICHKEIT GOTTES BEI EMMANUEL LEVINAS UND KARL BARTH / Tippelskirch, Dorothee C von – 1995 – 5mf – 9 – DM118.00 – 3-8267-2194-2 – gw Hänsel [270]
LIEBE WAS DU LIEBEN DARFST : SCHAUSPIEL IN DREI AUFZUEGEN / Jordan, Wilhelm – Frankfurt a.M.: W Jordan, 1892 – 1r – 1 – us U.W. Library [820]
Liebegg, Rudolfus de *see* PASTORALE NOVELLUM
Lieber, Gabriele v. *see* FRAUEN-ZUKUNFT, 1.1910-3.1913 (HQ, 21)
Lieberman, Lauren J *see* THE EFFECT OF TRAINED HEARING PEER TUTORS ON THE PHYSICAL ACTIVITY LEVELS OF DEAF STUDENTS IN INCLUSIVE ELEMENTARY SCHOOL PHYSICAL EDUCATION CLASSES
Lieberman, S *see*
– AL HA-YERUSHALMI
– HA-YERUSHALMI KI-FESHUTO
– TALMUDAH SHEL KEISARIN: YERUSHALMI, MASSEKHET NEZIKIN
LIEBESFRUEHLING / Rueckert, Friedrich – Leipzig: H Seemann, [19–?] – 1r – 1 – us U.W. Library [810]
DIE LIEBESGESCHICHTE DES HIMMELS : UNTERSUCHUNGEN ZUR INDOGERMANISCHEN SAGENKUNDE / Siecke, Ernst – Straßburg, 1892 – 2mf – DM62.00 – 3-8267-3019-4 – gw Hänsel [430]
DIE LIEBESSCHAUKEL : ROMAN / Andres, Stefan Paul – Muenchen: R Piper, c1951 – 1 – us U.W. Library [830]
DIE LIEBESSCHAUKEL *see* DER GEFRORENE DIONYSUS
LIEBESZAUBER IM ALTEN ORIENT / Ebeling, Erich – Mitteilungen der altorientalischen Gesellschaft. v1, pt1. Leipzig. 1925. BNE-20,100 1 – 9 – ne IDC [290]
LIEBIGS ANNALEN DER CHEMIE : ORGANIC AND BIOORGANIC CHEMISTRY – v1-766. And 1973-1993; 1832-1993 – 1,5,6,13 – us V.C.H. [540]
Liebknecht, Wilhelm *see*
– GEGEN DEN MILITARISMUS UND GEGEN DIE NEUEN STEUERN
– NO COMPROMISE, NO POLITICAL TRADING
– WAS ICH IM BERLINER REICHSTAG SAGTE
– ZUR GRUND- UND BODENFRAGE
Lieblein, J D C *see* DICTIONNAIRE DE NOMS HIEROGLYPHIQUES EN ORDRE GENEALOGIQUE ET ALPHABETIQUE
Liebman, Lance *see* DISABILITY APPEALS IN SOCIAL SECURITY PROGRAMS
Liebmann, Otto *see* UEBER DEN INDIVIDUELLEN BEWEIS FUER DIE FREIHEIT DES WILLENS
Liebsch, G *see* SYNTAX DER WENDISCHEN SPRACHE IN DER OBERLAUSITZ
Liechtenhan, R *see* DIE GOETTLICHE VORHERBESTIMMUNG BEI PAULUS UND IN DER POSIDONIANISCHEN PHILOSOPHIE
Liechtenstern, Joseph Freiherr von *see* ALLGEMEINES DEUTSCHES SACH-WOERTERBUCH ALLER MENSCHLICHEN KENNTNISSE UND FERTIGKEITEN (AEL, ABT 1;22)
DAS LIED DER LIEDEREN, WELCHES IST SOLOMONS / Ephrata Community – Manuscript, ca.1750. MUSIC 1154, Reel 1 – 1 – us L of C Photodup [780]
DAS LIED MOSES: DEUT. 32:1-43 / Kamphausen, Adolf – Leipzig: F.A. Brockhaus, 1862. 1 fiche – 9 – us A.T.L.A. [220]
DAS LIED VOM ALTEN EISENHUTH : FUENF ERZAEHLUNGEN / Utermann, Wilhelm – 2. Aufl. Muenchen: F Eher, 1944 – 1 – us U.W. Library [430]
DAS LIED VON DER GLOCKE / Schiller, Friedrich von; ed by Teetz, Ferdinand – (Includes bibliographical references) – 3., verm. Aufl. Leipzig: W Engelmann, 1906 – 1r – 1 – us U.W. Library [430]
LIEDEBOECK (HET TWEEDE), VAN VELE DIUERSCHE LIEDEKENS – Amstelredam, Nic. Biestkens van Diest. 1583. BME-344 1 – 9 – ne IDC [240]
LIEDEKEN (EEN NIEU) VAN TWEE VRIENDEN OPGHE-OFFERT TOT LONNEN IN ENGHELANT AN. 1575 – 1579. BME-205 1 – 9 – ne IDC [240]
LIEDEKEN (EEN), TRACTERENDE VAN SOMMIGHE OPGHEOFFERDE KINDEREN GODS, VAN DEN JARE 62 TOT DEN JARE 69, BINNEN GENT OPGEOFFERT – 1577. BME-207 1 – 9 – ne IDC [240]
LIEDEKENS (SOMMIGE ANDACHTIGHE ENDE LEERACHTIGE GHEESTELICKE) ENDE PSALMEN DAVIDS – Met noch twee Christelicke Sentbrieven. geschreven ende ghesonden aen de Ghemeente Godes in Pruyssen. Amstelredam, Nic. Biestkens. 1597. BME-352 2 – 8 – ne IDC [240]
LIEDEKENS (VEELDERHANDE), GHEMAECKT WT DEN O. ENDE N.T – Met veel andere, die noyt in druc en zijn geweest, ende zijn in ordeninge vanden A.B.C. gestelt. 1569. BME-345 2 – 8 – ne IDC [240]
LIEDEKENS (VEELDERHANDE), GHEMAECT WT DEN O. ENDE N.T., DIE VOORTIJTS IN DRUCK ZIJN WTGHEGAEN – Amstelredam, Corn. Claesz. 1593. BME-348 1 – 9 – ne IDC [240]
LIEDEKENS (VEELDERHANDE), GHEMAECT WT DEN O. ENDE N.T., DIE VOORTIJTS IN DRUCK ZIJN WTGHEGAEN, ELCK OP SIGN LETTER VAN A, B, C GESTELT – BME-346 2 – 8 – ne IDC [240]
LIEDEKENS (VEELDERHANDE), GHEMAECT WT DEN O. ENDE N.T., DIE VOORTIJTS IN DRUCK ZIJN WTGHEGAEN, ENDE ZIJN IN ORDENINGHE VANDEN A.B.C. BIJDEN ANDEREN GEUOECHT – 1580. BME-347 2 – 8 – ne IDC [240]
LIEDEKENS (VEELDERHANDE SCHRIFTUERLIJCKE NIEUWE), VERMANINGEN – By malcanderen vergadert door L(enaert) K(lock). Utrecht. Reynder Wylicks. 1593. BME-351 2 – 8 – ne IDC [240]
LIEDENBOECK (EEN NIEU), VAN ALLE NIEUWE GHEDICHTE LIEDEKENS, DIE NOYT IN DRUCK EN ZIJN GHEWEEST – 1562. BME-343 1 – 9 – ne IDC [240]
LIEDER AUS STILLE UND STUERMEN : ERINNERUNGEN AN RUEGEN / Anacker, Heinrich – Muenchen: F Eher, 1938 – 1r – 1 – us U.W. Library [780]
LIEDER DER LAPPEN – 1876 – 1 – us I.U. Libraries [780]
LIEDER, DER LIEBE UND EINSAMKEIT. VOICE AND PIANO / Reichardt, Johann F – Pre-1850 – 1 – us Sibley [780]
LIEDER DER SEHNSUCHT NACH DEN ALPEN / Pyrker, Johann Ladislav – Stuttgart: J G Cotta, 1845 – 1r – 1 – us U.W. Library [780]
LIEDER EINES GEFANGENEN – Wien: Wodianer & Waizner, 1874 – 1r – 1 – us U.W. Library [780]
DIE LIEDER IN DEN HISTORISCHEN BUECHERN DES ALTEN TESTAMENTES / Palm, August – Freiburg i.B.: J.C.B. Mohr, 1883. 1 fiche – 9 – us A.T.L.A. [240]
LIEDER MIT MELODIEN. ZWEITE AUFLAGE / Kirnberger, Johann P – Berlin: Arnold Wever, 1774 – 1 – us Sibley [780]
LIEDER UND BALLADEN / Wildenbruch, Ernst von – 7. Aufl. Berlin: G Grote, 1900 – 1r – 1 – us U.W. Library [780]
LIEDER UND BILDER / Wilbrandt, Adolf von – Stuttgart: J G Cotta, 1907 – 1r – 1 – us U.W. Library [700]
LIEDER UND GEDICHTE : NEBST EINER ABHANDLUNG UEBER DEUTSCHES FAMILIENLEBEN IN AMERIKA / Widenmann, Pauline – Allentown, PA: Trexler und Haertzell, 1892 – 1 – us U.W. Library [780]
DIE LIEDER VOM KRIEG / Schumann, Gerhard – Muenchen: A Langen/G Mueller, 1944, c1941 – 1r – 1 – us U.W. Library [810]
LIEDERBUCH FUR JEANETTE LEITER VON AUFHAUSEN – Ms copy by Mrs. Edward Kirstein, Rochester, NY, 185- – 1 – us Sibley [780]
LIEDEREN (VIJF GEESTLICKE) – Twee vande Gheboorte Christi, Het derde den Lofsanck Marie. Leyden, Jan Theunisz. 1600. BME-354 2 – 8 – ne IDC [240]
LIEDERHANDSCHRIFT B / Wolkenstein, Oswald von – 41p + 4 color mf – DM410.00 – 3-89219-008-9 – gw Lengenfelder [780]
[LIEDERKREIS VON EICHENDORFF] OP. 39, 1842 / Schumann, Robert – (Title page and p1-4 missing. Engraved, corrections in pencil by Schumann for later edition) – Wien: Haslinger, 1842 – 1 – us Sibley [780]
Liederwald, Carl *see* DER BEGRIFF "EDEL" BEI GOETHE
Liefeld, Friedrich Wilhelm Albert *see* ERINNERUNGEN AUS DER SUEDAFRIKANISCHEN MISSION
Liefering, Max *see* DAS RHEINISCH-WESTFAELISCHE KOHLENSYNDIKAT UND SEIN EINFLUSS AUF DIE KOHLENPREISE UND DIE LAGE DER BERGARBEITER

EEN LIEFFELIJCKE VERMANINGE OFTE ONDERWIJSINGE WT GODS WOORT / Simons, Menno – 1541, 1561? BME-284 1 – 9 – ne IDC [240]
EEN LIEFLICKE VERMANINGHE WT DES HEEREN WOORT, INDEN WELCKEN / Philips, Dirk – 1558. BME-307 1 – 9 – ne IDC [240]
LIEGNITZER KREISBLATT – Liegnitz (Legnica), Poland. 1916-18, 1921-23 – 6r – 1 – gw Mikrofilm [943]
LIEGNITZER STADTBLATT – Liegnitz, Germany. 1854; 1859; 1914-1915 (incomplete); 1919 (incomplete); 1936 (incomplete) – 8r – 1 – gw Mikrofilm [072]
LIEKKI; CANADAN SUOMALAISTEN KAUNOKIRJALLINEN VIKKOLEHTI – Sudbury. 1958 74 – 1 – 1625.00 – cn McLaren [073]
Liem, Khiam Soen *see* KEDOEDOEKAN BANGSA TIONGHOA DI INDONESIA; DE POSITIE DER CHINEEZEN IN INDONESIE
Liem, Twan Djie *see* THE DISTRIBUTIVE INTERMEDIATE TRADE OF THE CHINESE ON JAVA
LIEN LAW OF THE STATE OF NEW YORK / Snyder, William Lamartine – 5th ed. New York, Baker, Voorhis, 1909. 613 p. LL-1415 – 1 – us L of C Photodup [340]
Lienard, Felix *see* DICTIONNAIRE TOPOGRAPHIQUE DU DEPARTEMENT DE LA MEUSE: COMPRENANT LES NOMS DE LIEU ANCIENS ET MODERNES
LIEN-CHOU CHIH – 1870, 12. BCH-644 2 – 8 – ne IDC [950]
LIEN-CHOU FU-CHIH – 1833, 26, 1. BCH-633 2 – 8 – ne IDC [950]
Lienert, Otto Hellmut *see* 'S GUELTETRUEKLI
Lienhard, Friedrich *see*
- ODYSSEUS AUF ITHAKA
- THUERINGER TAGEBUCH
- TILL EULENSPIEGEL
- DIE VORHERRSCHAFT BERLINS

LIEN-SHAN SUI-YAO T'ING-CHIH – 1837. BCH-645 2 – 8 – ne IDC [950]
LIEPAJA BAPTISTU PAVILA DRAUDZES, PARSKATS, 1934 = PAVILA BAPTIST CHURCH OF LIEPAJA, REPORT. 1934 – 1934. Publ. No. 6346,no. 5. One of sic items on reel. Total Pages 152 – 1 – us Baptist [240]
Lierow, Ralf *see* DER TRANSFORMATIONSPROZEß IN DER EHEMALIGEN SOWJETUNION
LIETBOECK INHOUDENDE SCHRIFTUERLIJCKE VERMAEN LIEDEREN, CLAECH LIEDEREN, GEBEDEN, DANCK LIEDEREN, LOFSANGHEN, PSALMEN / Ries, H de – Rotterdam, D. Mullem. 1582. BME-349 2 – 8 – ne IDC [240]
LIETUVA – Kaunas, 1925-28 (all publ) – 4r – 1 – us Ross [460]
LIETUVISKAI-VOKISKAS ZODYNAS: LITAUISCH-DEUTSCHES WOERTERBUCH / Paskevicius, Juozas – Augsburg: Sudavija, 1947. viii,734p – 1 – us U.W. Library [430]
LIETUVISKI ZODZIAI SENOSIOS LIETUVOS RASTINIU KALBOJE / Jablonskis, K – Kaunas, 1941 – 11mf – 9 – ne IDC [947]
LIETUVIU BIBLIOGRAFIIA / Birziska, V – Kaunas, 1924-1939 – 56mf – 9 – ne IDC [947]
LIETUVIU KALBOS ZODYNAS / ed by Balcikonis, J – Vilnius, 1941-1947. v1(A-B) – 2(C-F) – 33mf – 9 – 1090/2 – ne IDC [460]
LIETUVOS AIDAS – (Backfile through 1995 $75r) – 1996- – 2r per y – 1 – inquire – us Ross [072]
LIETUVOS AIDAS – (Backfile through 1998 $85r) – Lithuania, 1999- – 2r per y – 6 – $160.00 standing order – us Ross [072]
LIETUVOS AIDAS – De 1991 a 1993 – 1 – Sfr240.00 – sz Infoprint [947]
LIETUVOS AIDAS – Kaunas, Lithuania, 1928-36 – 10r – 1 – us Ross [07?]
LIETUVOS AIDAS – Kaunus, U.S.S.R. -d. 3 Jan 1938-27 April 1940. 19 reels – 1 – uk British Libr Newspaper [947]
LIETUVOS RYTAS – (Backfile 1990-1998 $85r) – Lithuania, 1999- – 12r per y – 1 – $800.00 standing order – us Ross [072]
LIETUVOS UKININKAS – Kaunas. June 27 1913-Aug 1 1940. Incomplete – 1 – us NY Public [073]
Lietz, Uwe *see*
- MUSIK UND BEWEGUNGSSCHULUNG BEI SCHUELERN DER SEKUNDARSTUFE 1
- MUSIKPAEDAGOGISCHE ZIELVORSTELLUNGEN VON EMILE JAQUES-DALCROZE

Lietzmann, Hans *see*
- BYZANTINISCHE LEGENDEN
- KLEINE SCHRIFTEN 1
- KLEINE SCHRIFTEN 2
- KLEINE SCHRIFTEN 3
- DAS LEBEN DES HEILIGEN SYMEON STYLITES (T.U.U. 3-32/4)
- DER WELTHEILAND: EINE JENAER ROSENVORLESUNG MIT ANMERKUNGEN
- WIE WURDEN DIE BUECHER DES NEUEN TESTAMENTS HEILIGE SCHRIFT?: FUENF VORTRAEGE

LIEUT. ZEBULON PIKE'S NOTEBOOK OF MAPS, TRAVERSE TABLES, AND METEOROLOGICAL OBSERVATIONS, 1805-7 / U.S. War Department. Adjutant General's Office – T36 – 1r – 1 – us Nat'l Archives [975]
Lieutenant S *see* OUR JOURNAL IN THE PACIFIC
LIEUX D'EAU. L'EAU ET L'HOMME DANS LE COMARCA DU RIPOLLES (PYRENEES CATALANES) / Porcell, G – 9 – F70.00 – fr Ethnologie [306]
Lieven, Daria Khristoforovna *see* LETTERS OF DOROTHEA, PRINCESS LIEVEN, DURING HER RESIDENCE IN LONDON, 1812-1834
LIFE – 1883-1936 – 1 – us UMI [073]
LIFE – (1966-72. 5,6. 1970-72. 9) – v. 1-73. 1936-72 – 1 – us UMI [073]
LIFE – Black and White Edition. v. 1-. 1978- – 1,5,6,9 – us UMI [073]
LIFE – Las Vegas, NV. 1946-1967 – 1r – 1 – $50.00 – U04911 – us Library Micro [071]
LIFE – New York. v1-103. 1883-1936 – 29r – 1 – us Ross [073]
LIFE – Toronto: Nichol & Caiger, [1888-18–] – 9 – cn C.I.H.M. [072]
LIFE – Watch Hill. R.I. 1899-1901 – 1 – us UMI [071]
THE LIFE AND ACTIONS OF ALEXANDER THE GREAT / Williams, John – London: J. Murray, 1829.vi,402p. fold. map – 1 – us U.W. Library [920]
LIFE AND ADMINISTRATION OF EDWARD, FIRST EARL OF CLARENDON; WITH ORIGINAL CORRESPONDENCE, AND AUTHENTIC PAPERS NEVER BEFORE PUBLISHED / Lister, Thomas Henry – (v.1-2. The life of Clarendon, 1838. v.3. Letters and papers, 1837) – London: Longman, Orme, Borwn, Green, and Longmans, 1837-1838. 3v – 1 – us U.W. Library [920]
THE LIFE AND ADVENTURES OF JAMES P. BECKWOURTH: MOUNTAINEER, SCOUT, PIONEER, AND CHIEF OF THE CROW NATION OF INDIANS: WRITTEN FROM HIS OWN DICTATION / Beckwourth, James P – New ed. London: T. Unwin, 1892.03538.(Pre-1900 Canadiana) – 9 – cn C.I.H.M. [920]
THE LIFE AND ADVENTURES OF MATTHEW BISHIP OF DEDDINGTON IN OXFORDSHIRE / Bishop, Matthew – London: Printed for J Brindley; G Hawkins; R Dodsley; J Millan, 1744. SEM105P408 – 4mf – 9 – Can$9.00 – cn Bibl Nat [920]
LIFE AND ADVENTURES OF WILSON BENSON / Benson, Wilson – Toronto: Hunter, Rose & Co., 1876. 02314. (Pre-1900 Canadiana) – 9 – cn C.I.H.M. [920]
THE LIFE AND CHARACTER OF ERASMUS / Pennington, Arthur Robert – London: Seeley, Jackson & Halliday, 1875 – 1mf – us A.T.L.A. [140]
THE LIFE AND CORRESPONDENCE OF ADMIRAL SIR CHARLES NAPIER, FROM PERSONAL RECOLLECTIONS, LETTERS, AND OFFICIAL DOCUMENTS / Napier, Edward Hungerford Delaval Elers – 2v 1862 – 9 – $60.00 – uk Libr Preservation [355]
THE LIFE AND CORRESPONDENCE OF GEORGE CALIXTUS : LUTHERAN ABBOT OF KOENIGSLUTTER, AND PROFESSOR PRIMARIUS IN THE UNIVERSITY OF HELMSTADT / Dowding, W C – Oxford: J. Henry and J. Parker, 1863 – 1mf – us A.T.L.A. [240]
LIFE AND CORRESPONDENCE OF JOHN, EARL OF ST VINCENT, G.C.B., ADMIRAL OF THE FLEET, ETC / Brenton, Edward Pelham – London, 1838. 2v. Map, port – 1 – us U.W. Library [920]
THE LIFE AND CORRESPONDENCE OF ROBERT BURNS / Cunningham, Allan – London: James Cochrane & Co., 1836 – 1 roll – 1 – 1-55879-855-2 – uk Libr Preservation [420]
LIFE AND CORRESPONDENCE OF SAMUEL JOHNSON, D.D. : MISSIONARY OF THE CHURCH OF ENGLAND IN CONNECTICUT, AND FIRST PRESIDENT OF KING'S COLLEGE, NEW YORK / Beardsley, E Edwards – New York: Hurd & Houghton; London: Rivingtons, 1874, c1873 – 1mf – us A.T.L.A. [240]
LIFE AND CORRESPONDENCE OF SIR WILLIAM SIDNEY SMITH / Barrow, John – 2v. 1848 – 9 – 80.00 – uk Libr Preservation [920]
THE LIFE AND CORRESPONDENCE OF THE RIGHT HONOURABLE HENRY ADDINGTON, FIRST VISCOUNT SIDMOUTH / Pellew, George – London: J. Murray, 1847.3v – 1 – us U.W. Library [920]
THE LIFE AND CORRESPONDENCE OF THOMAS VALPY FRENCH : FIRST BISHOP OF LAHORE / Birks, Herbert – London: John Murray, 1895 – 2mf – us A.T.L.A. [240]
THE LIFE AND DEATH OF AN AMERICAN HEROE; THE STORY OF DAVE DORAN / Starobin, Joseph Robert – N.Y., 1938. Fiche W1499. (Blodgett Collection of Spanish Civil War Pamphlets) – 9 – us H.U. College Libr [946]
THE LIFE AND DEATH OF THE SUBLIME SOCIETY OF BEEF STEAKS / Arnold, Walter – London: Bradbury, Evans & Co: 1871 – 2mf – 9 – $3.00 – LLMC 92-111 – us L.L.M.C. [360]
THE LIFE AND EPISTLES OF SAINT PAUL : HARMONIZED AND CHRONOLOGICALLY ARRANGED IN SCRIPTURE LANGUAGE / Pratt, Samuel Wheeler – (Includes index) – New York: Anson D F Randolph, 1895 – 1mf – 9 – 0-8370-4792-7 – 1985-2792 – us A.T.L.A. [920]
LIFE AND FATE OF THE ANCIENT LIBRARY OF ALEXANDRIA / El-Abbadi, Mostafa – 2nd rev ed 1992 – 250p – 9 – 92-3-102632-1 – fr UNESCO [930]
LIFE AND HABIT / Butler, Samuel – London: Trbner, 1878 – 1 roll – 1 – 1-55879-792-0 – uk Libr Preservation [840]
LIFE AND LABOR – v1-11 no 8 (all publ) 1911-21 – 3r – 1 – $320.00 – us UPA [360]
LIFE AND LABORS OF FRANCIS ASBURY : BISHOP OF THE METHODIST EPISCOPAL CHURCH IN AMERICA / Smith, George G – Nashville, Tenn.: Publishing House M.E. Church, South, 1896 – 1mf – us A.T.L.A. [240]
THE LIFE AND LABORS OF JOHN SEYBERT : FIRST BISHOP OF THE EVANGELICAL ASSOCIATION / Spreng, S P – Cleveland, O[hio]: Published for the Evangelical Association by Lauer & Mattill, Agents, 1888 – 1mf – us A.T.L.A. [240]
THE LIFE AND LABORS OF MAJOR W.E. PENN, THE TEXAS EVANGELIST / Penn, WE – 1896 – 1 – $12.95 – us Baptist [240]
THE LIFE AND LABORS OF THE REV. CHRISTIAN FREDERICK SCHWARTZ : THE GREAT LUTHERAN MISSIONARY TO INDIA / Price, Wm H – Columbus, OH: Lutheran Book Concern, 1895 – 1mf – 9 – 0-8370-7323-5 – 1986-1323 – us A.T.L.A. [920]
LIFE AND LABOUR IN SHANGHAI. A DECADE OF LABOUR AND SOCIAL ADMINISTRATION IN INTERNATIONAL SETTLEMENT / Hinder, E M – CH-986 2. 1944 – 8 – ne IDC [380]
LIFE AND LABOUR OF THE PEOPLE OF LONDON – (Pt 1: Mss. notebooks on industry, workhouse and asylum inmates, and the police. Pt 2: Industry, interviews and questionnaires. Pt 3: The Poverty Series, School Board Enquiry and House to House Visits; Pt 4: Poverty, Welfare and Religion in London, District by District; Pt 5: Poverty by District; Pt 6: Poverty by District) – Charles Booth Collection, 1885-1905, from British Library of Political and Economic Science, London – 1 – us Primary [320]
THE LIFE AND LABOURS OF SAINT THOMAS OF AQUIN / Vaughan, Roger William Bede; ed by Canon Vaughan – Abridged and London: Burns and Oates – 1 – us U.W. Library [240]
THE LIFE AND LABOURS OF THE REV. DANIEL BAKER, D.D. : PASTOR AND EVANGELIST / Baker, William Mumford – Philadelphia: William S & Alfred Martien, 1858 – 2mf – 9 – 0-8370-7362-6 – 1986-1362 – us A.T.L.A. [920]
THE LIFE AND LEGEND OF ST. PATRICK / Bieler, L – Dublin, 1948 – Dfl19.00 – ne Slangenburg [920]
LIFE AND LETTERS – Girard. Kansas. v. 1-3. Sept 1922-Mar 1925. Incomplete – 1 – us NY Public [920]
LIFE AND LETTERS – Girard, KS. v1-3. 1922-25 – 1r – 1 – us Ross [335]
LIFE AND LETTERS. / Cartwright, Richard – Toronto: Belford Bros., 1876. 02550. (Pre-1900 Canadiana) – 9 – cn C.I.H.M. [971]
LIFE AND LETTERS IN THE FOURTH CENTURY / Glover, Terrot Reaveley – Cambridge: University Press; New York: Macmillan [distributor], 1901 – 1mf – us A.T.L.A. [240]
THE LIFE AND LETTERS OF BENJAMIN MORGAN PALMER / Johnson, Thomas Cary – Richmond, Va.: Presbyterian Committee of Publication, c1906 – 2mf – us A.T.L.A. [240]
LIFE AND LETTERS OF CHARLES BUTLER / Stoddard, Francis H – 1903 – 1 – $50.00 – us Presbyterian [920]
THE LIFE AND LETTERS OF ELIZABETH PRENTISS, AUTHOR OF STEPPING HEAVENWARD / Prentiss, Elizabeth Payson – 1882 – 9 – us A.T.L.A. [240]
LIFE AND LETTERS OF ERASMUS : LECTURES / Froude, James Anthony – London: Longmans, Green, 1894 – 2mf – us A.T.L.A. [190]
THE LIFE AND LETTERS OF FATHER JOHN MORRIS, OF THE SOCIETY OF JESUS, 1826-1893 / Pollen, John Hungerford – London: Burns and Oates; New York: Benziger, 1896 – 1mf – us A.T.L.A. [240]
LIFE AND LETTERS OF FENTON JOHN ANTHONY HORT / Hort, Fenton John Anthony – 2v. 1896 – 1 – us A.T.L.A. [240]
LIFE AND LETTERS OF HENRY PARRY LIDDON, D.D., D.C.L., LL.D., CANON OF ST PAUL'S CATHEDRAL, AND SOMETIME IRELAND PROFESSOR OF EXEGESIS IN THE UNIVERSITY OF OXFORD / Johnston, John Octavius – London; New York: Longmans, Green, 1904 – 1mf – us A.T.L.A. [240]
THE LIFE AND LETTERS OF HERBERT SPENCER / Duncan, David – London: Methuen, 1908.xiii,621p. illus – 1 – us U.W. Library [920]
THE LIFE AND LETTERS OF JOHN ANGELL JAMES : INCLUDING AN UNFINISHED AUTOBIOGRAPHY / ed by Dale, Robert William – London: J. Nisbet, 1861 – 2mf – us A.T.L.A. [240]
LIFE AND LETTERS OF JOHN CAIRNS, D.D., LL.D. / MacEwen, Alexander R – London: Hodder and Stoughton, 1898 – 2mf – us A.T.L.A. [240]
THE LIFE AND LETTERS OF JOHN GIBSON LOCKHART FROM ABBOTSFORD AND MILTON LOCKHART AND OTHER ORIGINAL SOURCES / Lang, Andrew – London: John C. Nimmo; New York: Charles Scribner, 1897 – 1 roll – 1 – 1-55879-206-6 – uk Libr Preservation [420]
LIFE AND LETTERS OF JOSEPH HARDY NEESIMA / Hardy, A S – Boston, New York, 1892. KHT-58-1 – 9 – ne IDC [920]
LIFE AND LETTERS OF MANDELL CREIGHTON : D.D. OXON. AND CAM., SOMETIME BISHOP OF LONDON... / Creighton, Louise – London; New York: Longmans, Green, 1904 – 3mf – us A.T.L.A. [240]
LIFE AND LETTERS OF PAUL SEIGNERET = PAUL SEIGNERET, SEMINARISTE DE SAINT-SULPICE : SEMINARIST OF SAINT SULPICE – New York: P O'Shea, 1875 – 1mf – 9 – 0-8370-7058-9 – 1986-1058 – us A.T.L.A. [920]
LIFE AND LETTERS OF PAUL THE APOSTLE / Abbott, Lyman – Boston: Houghton, Mifflin, 1898.1 fiche – 9 – us A.T.L.A. [240]
LIFE AND LETTERS OF R.C. SCONCE, FORMERLY SECRETARY TO ADMIRAL SIR JOHN THOMAS DUCKWORTH / Sconce, Robert Clement; ed by Bunbury, Sarah S – 2v. 1861 – 9 – uk Libr Preservation [920]
THE LIFE AND LETTERS OF ROBERT LEWIS DABNEY / Johnson, Thomas Cary – Richmond, Va.: Presbyterian Committee of Publication, c1903 – 2mf – us A.T.L.A. [240]
LIFE AND LETTERS OF SAMUEL NORVELL LAPSLEY : MISSIONARY TO THE CONGO VALLEY / Lapsley, Samuel Norvell – Richmond, VA: Whittet & Shepperson, 1893 – 1mf – 9 – 0-8370-6204-7 – 1986-0204 – us A.T.L.A. [920]

LIFE AND LETTERS OF THE LATE ADMIRAL SIR B.J. SULIVAN, K.C.B., 1810-90 / ed by Sulivan, Henry North – With an introduction by Sir G.H. Edwards. 1896 – 9 – uk Libr Preservation [920]

LIFE AND LETTERS OF THE RIGHT HONOURABLE ROBERT LOWE, VISCOUNT SHERBROOKE...WITH A MEMOIR OF SIR JOHN COAPE SHERBROOKE, G.C.B., BY A. PATCHETT MARTIN / Martin, Arthur Patchett – London, New York: Longmans, Green and Co., 1893.2v. 6 port. facsim., geneal. tables – 1 – us U.W. Library [920]

LIFE AND LETTERS OF THOMAS CAMPBELL / Beattie, William; ed by Beattie, William – London: Hall, Virtue and Co., 2nd ed 1850 – 2 rolls – 1 – 1-55879-024-1 – uk Libr Preservation [920]

LIFE AND LETTERS OF THOMAS CROMWELL / Merriman, Roger Bigelow – Oxford: Clarendon Press; New York: H. Frowde [distributor], 1902 – 2mf – us A.T.L.A. [240]

THE LIFE AND LETTERS OF WALTER FARQUHAR HOOK.. / Stephens, William Richard Wood – 6th ed. London: R. Bentley & Son, 1881.x,626p – 1 – us U.W. Library [920]

THE LIFE AND LIFE-WORK OF POPE LEO 13 : VICAR OF JESUS CHRIST AND BISHOP OF ROME, SUCCESSOR OF ST. PETER PRINCE OF THE APOSTLES / McGovern, James Joseph – Author's ed. Chicago: Monarch, c1903 – 2mf – 9 – 0-8370-7002-3 – 1986-1002 – us A.T.L.A. [920]

THE LIFE AND LIGHT OF MEN : EXPOSITIONS OF JOHN 1-12 / Meyer, Frederick Brotherton – New York:Fleming H. Revell, [1892] – 1mf – 9 – 0-8370-4411-1 – 1985-2411 – us A.T.L.A. [220]

LIFE AND LITERATURE OF THE ANCIENT HEBREWS / Abbott, Lyman – Boston: Houghton, Mifflin, 1901. 1 fiche – 9 – us A.T.L.A. [270]

THE LIFE AND LITERATURE OF THE ANCIENT HEBREWS : IHR LEBEN UND WIRKEN AUS IHREN SCHRIFTEN / Abbott, Lyman – (Includes indexes) – Boston: Houghton, Mifflin, 1901 – 1mf – 9 – 0-8370-2026-3 – 1985-0026 – us A.T.L.A. [220]

LIFE AND MINISTRY OF JESUS: ACCORDING TO THE HISTORICAL AND CRITICAL METHOD / Otto, Rudolf – Chicago: Open Court, 1908. 1 fiche – 9 – us A.T.L.A. [240]

THE LIFE AND MISFORTUNES AND THE MILITARY CAREER OF BRIGADE GENERAL SIR JOHN JOHNSON, BART / DePeyster, John Watts – ("Anchor") New York?: s.n., 1882 (New York: C. Ludwig). 02642. (Pre-1900 Canadiana) – 9 – cn C.I.H.M. [971]

LIFE AND RECOLLECTIONS / Reinhart, Herman Francis – 1 – us KS Hist [978]

THE LIFE AND REIGN OF EDWARD 1 BY THE AUTHOR OF "THE GREATEST OF THE PLANTAGENETS" / Seeley, Robert Benton – London: Seeley, 1872. 352p. With: veld trails xC.S. Stokes – 1 – us U.W. Library [941]

THE LIFE AND SERVICES OF CAPTAIN PHILIP BEAVER / Smyth, William Henry – 1829 – 9 – uk Libr Preservation [920]

THE LIFE AND SERVICES OF HORATIO VISCOUNT NELSON / Clarke, James Stanier & MacArthur, John – 3v. 1840 – 9 – $120.00 – uk Libr Preservation [355]

THE LIFE AND SERVICES OF JOHN E. DAWSON / Dawson, John E – 1872 – 1 – $5.53 – us Baptist [240]

THE LIFE AND SPEECHES OF THE HON. HENRY CLAY / Mallory, Daniel – NY: Robert P Bixby & Co. 2v. 1843 – 14mf – 9 – $21.00 – LLMC 96-037 – us L.L.M.C. [920]

LIFE AND STORY OF JOSEPH STORY / Story, William Wetmore – Boston: Charles C Little & James Brown. 2v. 1851 – 15mf – 9 – $22.50 – LLMC 91-007 – us L.L.M.C. [340]

THE LIFE AND TEACHINGS OF JESUS / Rogers, Arthur Kenyon – New York: G.P. Putnam, 1894. 1 fiche – 9 – us A.T.L.A. [240]

THE LIFE AND TEACHINGS OF JESUS (CCC318) = YEH SUE TI SHENG-PING CHIAO HSUN / ed by Wang, Tzu-chung & Blakney, Raymond B – (In Chinese) – Hong Kong: Council on Christian Literature for Overseas Chinese, 1954 – 1r – 1 – 1984-6657 – us A.T.L.A. [240]

LIFE AND THE WAY THROUGH / Meyer, Frederick Brotherton – New York: Funk & Wagnalls, 1913 – 1mf – 9 – 0-8370-6282-9 – 1986-0282 – us A.T.L.A. [240]

LIFE AND TIMES – (Some issues missing) – v1 1977; v7-9. 1983-85 – 1r – 1 – ATLA S0859 – us A.T.L.A. [073]

LIFE AND TIMES OF ALFRED THE GREAT / Plummer, Charles – H 1172 2. 1902 – 8 – ne IDC [941]

THE LIFE AND TIMES OF ALFRED THE GREAT : BEING THE FORD LECTURES FOR 1901 / Plummer, Charles – Oxford: Clarendon Press, 1902 – 1mf – us A.T.L.A. [941]

THE LIFE AND TIMES OF BISHOP CHALLONER (1691-1781) / Burton, Edwin H – London, New York: Longmans, Green, 1909 – 2mf – us A.T.L.A. [240]

THE LIFE AND TIMES OF CARDINAL WISEMAN / Ward, Wilfrid Philip – London, New York: Longmans, Green, 1898 – 2mf – us A.T.L.A. [240]

THE LIFE AND TIMES OF CAREY, MARSHMAN, AND WARD : EMBRACING THE HISTORY OF THE SERAMPORE MISSION / Marshman, John Clark – London: Longman, Brown, Green, Longmans, & Roberts, 1859 – 3mf – us A.T.L.A. [240]

THE LIFE AND TIMES OF CLEOPATRA / Franzero, Charles Marie – New York: Philosophical Library, 1957. 299p. illus – 1 – us U.W. Library [920]

THE LIFE AND TIMES OF DANIEL O'CONNELL / Luby, Thomas Clarke – Glasgow, London: Cameron & Ferguson, 187?. ix,538p – 1 – us U.W. Library [920]

THE LIFE AND TIMES OF HENRY COOKE / Porter, Josias Leslie – 1871 – 9 – us A.T.L.A. [920]

THE LIFE AND TIMES OF HENRY, LORD BROUGHAM, WRITTEN BY HIMSELF / Brougham, Henry Peter – New York, Harper, 1871-72. 3 v. LL-1449 – 1 – us L of C Photodup [340]

LIFE AND TIMES OF HENRY MELCHIOR MUEHLENBERG / Mann, William J – Philadelphia: G.W. Frederick, 1888, c1887 – 2mf – us A.T.L.A. [240]

THE LIFE AND TIMES OF HUMAYUN / Prasad, Ishwari – Bombay: Orient Longmans, (1956).416p. ill.,maps – 1 – us U.W. Library [920]

THE LIFE AND TIMES OF JOSEPH IN THE LIGHT OF EGYPTIAN LORE / Tomkins, Henry George – (Includes bibliographical references and indexes) – [London?]: Religious Tract Society, 1891 – 1mf – 9 – 0-8370-9832-7 – 1986-3832 – us A.T.L.A. [220]

THE LIFE AND TIMES OF MASTERS JOHN HUS / Luetzow, Franz H H V von – London: J.M. Dent; New York: E.P.Dutton, 1909 – 1mf – us A.T.L.A. [240]

LIFE AND TIMES OF NATHAN BANGS, D.D. / Stevens, Abel – New York: Catlton & Porter, c1863 – 1mf – us A.T.L.A. [240]

THE LIFE AND TIMES OF REV. GEORGE PECK / Peck, George – 1874 – 9 – us A.T.L.A. [240]

LIFE AND TIMES OF REV. S.S. SCHMUCKER / Anstadt, P – York, Pa.: P. Anstadt, 1896 – 1mf – us A.T.L.A. [240]

THE LIFE AND TIMES OF ROBERT GROSSETESTE, BISHOP OF LINCOLN / Perry, George G – London: Society for Promoting Christian Knowledge, 1871 – 1mf – us A.T.L.A. [240]

THE LIFE AND TIMES OF RODRIGO BORGIA, POPE ALEXANDER 6 / Mathew, Arnold H – London: S. Paul, [1912?] – 2mf – us A.T.L.A. [240]

THE LIFE AND TIMES OF ST. BERNARD / Neander, Augustus – London: Rivington, 1843 – 1mf – us A.T.L.A. [240]

THE LIFE AND TIMES OF SAINT BERNARD, ABBOT OF CLAIRVAUX, A.D. 1091-1153 / Morison, James C – New ed., rev., 1968 – 1 – us A.T.L.A. [920]

THE LIFE AND TIMES OF SIR LEONARD TILLEY: BEING A POLITICAL HISTORY OF NEW BRUNSWICK FOR THE PAST SEVENTY YEARS / Hannay, James – St. John, N.B., 1897. 05354. (Pre-1900 Canadiana) – 9 – cn C.I.H.M. [971]

THE LIFE AND TIMES OF SIR RICHARD SOUTHEY / Wilmot, Alexander – London: S Low, Marston, 1904 – us Res Libr [920]

THE LIFE AND TIMES OF THE HON. ALGERNON SYDNEY, 1622-1683 / Ewald, Alexander Charles – London: Tinsley, 1873. 2v. fold. geneal. table – 1 – us U.W. Library [920]

LIFE AND TIMES OF THE HON. JOSEPH HOWE, THE GREAT NOVA SCOTIAN AND EX-LIEUT. GOVERNOR: WITH BRIEF REFERENCES TO SOME OF HIS PROMINENT CONTEMPORARIES / Fenety, George Edward – St. John, N.B.: E. Carter, 1896. 03082. (Pre-1900 Canadiana) – 9 – cn C.I.H.M. [971]

THE LIFE AND TIMES OF THE MOST REV. JOHN MACHALE : ARCHBISHOP OF TUAM AND METROPOLITAN / Bourke, Ulick Joseph – 3rd ed. New York: P J Kenedy, c1882 – 1mf – 9 – 0-8370-6804-5 – 1986-0804 – us A.T.L.A. [920]

THE LIFE AND TIMES OF THE REV. JOHN SKINNER : M.A., OF LINSHART, LONGSIDE, DEAN OF ABERDEEN, AUTHOR OF "TULLOCHGORUM", ETC. / Walker, William – London: W. Skeffington, 1883 – 1mf – us A.T.L.A. [240]

LIFE AND TIMES OF THE RIGHT HONOURABLE SIR JOHN A. MACDONALD, K.C.B., D.C.L., ETC., PREMIER OF THE DOMINION OF CANADA / Collins, Joseph Edmund – Toronto: Rose, 1883. 00716. (Pre-1900 Canadiana) – 9 – cn C.I.H.M. [320]

THE LIFE AND TIMES OF ULRIC ZWINGLI / Hottinger, J J – Harrisburg: Theo. F. Scheffer, 1856 – 1mf – us A.T.L.A. [240]

LIFE AND TRAVELS OF JAMES FISHER: AN AUTOBIOGRAPHY / Fisher, James – Toronto: Copp, Clark, 1890. 03108. (Pre-1900 Canadiana) – 9 – cn C.I.H.M. [971]

LIFE AND WORK – (Lacking: 1916-29. 1933-46) – 1901-91 – 25r – 1 – ATLA S0370 – us A.T.L.A. [073]

LIFE AND WORK OF HENRY IRVING / ed by Fitzgerald, Percy Hetherington – (22v) – Garrick Club Collections – 11r – $565.00 – us UMI [790]

LIFE AND WORK OF HENRY IRVING : THEATER LIFE IN 19TH CENTURY ENGLAND – 11r – 1 – us UMI [790]

THE LIFE AND WORK OF MARY CARPENTER / Carpenter, J Estlin – London: Macmillan, 1879 – 2mf – us A.T.L.A. [920]

THE LIFE AND WORK OF MARY LOUISA WHATELY / Whately, E J – London: Religious Tract Society, [1890?] – 1mf – us A.T.L.A. [240]

THE LIFE AND WORK OF ST. PAUL / Farrar, Frederic William – (Includes bibliographical references and index) – New York: E P Dutton, 1902 – 2mf – 9 – 0-8370-9383-X – 1986-3383 – us A.T.L.A. [220]

THE LIFE AND WORK OF ST. PAUL PRACTICALLY CONSIDERED AND APPLIED / Roberts, Alexander – London: James Blackwood, 1867 – 1mf – 9 – 0-8370-4916-4 – 1985-2916 – us A.T.L.A. [920]

LIFE AND WORK OF THE MINISTER (CCC280) / Shen, Tzu-kao – (In Chinese) – Hong Kong: Bible Book and Tract Depot for Council on Christian Literature for Overseas Chinese, 1953 – 1r – 1 – 1984-6619 – us A.T.L.A. [240]

THE LIFE AND WORK OF THE REV. E.J. PECK AMONG THE ESKIMOS / Lewis, Arthur – New York: A C Armstrong, 1904 – 1mf – 9 – 0-8370-6207-1 – 1986-0207 – us A.T.L.A. [920]

LIFE AND WORK OF THE REV. T.T. CARTER : HON. CANON OF CHRISTCHURCH, OXFORD, AND WARDEN OF THE HOUSE OF MERCY, CLEWER / Carter, J F M – London; New York: Longmans, Green, 1911 – 1mf – us A.T.L.A. [240]

THE LIFE AND WORK OF THE SEVENTH EARL OF SHAFTESBURY, K.G. / Hodder, Edwin – London; New York: Cassell, 1886-1887 – 4mf – us A.T.L.A. [240]

THE LIFE AND WORK OF WILLIAM AUGUSTUS MUHLENBERG / Ayres, Anne – New York: Harper, 1880 – 2mf – us A.T.L.A. [240]

THE LIFE AND WORKS OF JOHN ARBUTHNOT, M.D., FELLOW OF THE ROYAL COLLEGE OF PHYSICIANS / Aitken, George Atherton – Oxford: Clarendon Press, 1892. x,516p. Geneal. tab – 1 – us U.W. Library [920]

LIFE AND WRITINGS.. / Mazzini, Giuseppe – London. 6v. 1864-70 – 1 – 23.00r – us L of C Photodup [920]

THE LIFE AND WRITINGS OF HON. VINCENT L. BRADFORD / Dwight, Henry Edwin – Philadelphia, Times Printing House, 1885. 297 p. LL-348 – 1 – us L of C Photodup [340]

THE LIFE AND WRITINGS OF PHILIP, LATE DUKE OF WHARTON – London. 4v. 1731-1732 – 10mf – ne IDC [941]

THE LIFE AND WRITINGS OF ST JOHN / Macdonald, James Madison – New York: Scribner, Armstrong, 1877. 1 fiche – 9 – us A.T.L.A. [240]

LIFE ASSOCIATION NEWS – v.75-. 1980- – 1,5,6,9 – us UMI [073]

LIFE AT RIDEAU HALL – 1882?. 05610. (Pre-1900 Canadiana) – 9 – cn C.I.H.M. [971]

LIFE AT THE SPRINGS AND VISITORS' LIST – Caledonia Springs, Ontario. v6 n9. 7 jul 1846 – 1r – 1 – Can$30.00 – cn Can Microfilming [072]

THE LIFE BOAT – Montreal, Canada. 4 jan-v7 n50. 13 dec 1861 – 1r – 1 – Can$30.00 – cn Can Microfilming [072]

THE LIFE BOAT – Montreal: F W Campbell, [1852-18– or 19–] – 9 – cn C.I.H.M. [971]

LIFE, BY HIMSELF / Bennet, J – (Coll title: The People Called Methodists, Phase 2: Primary Sources 1738-1800) – 1mf – 9 – MP-616/1 – ne IDC [240]

LIFE CHEMISTRY REPORTS / ed by Bannister, J V – 1983- – 1,5,9 – us Harwood [540]

LIFE ECHOES – Hamilton, Ont: Canada Life Assurance Company, [1893-189- or 19–] – 9 – cn C.I.H.M. [360]

LIFE ED. CHICAGO – 1936-1994 – 1 – sz Infoprint [071]

LIFE ED. NEW YORK – 1883-1936 – 1 – sz Infoprint [071]

THE LIFE EVERLASTING / Corelli, Marie – British Fiction Archive: Unit 1 – 9 – uk Bell [830]

A LIFE FOR AFRICA : REV ADOLPHUS CLEMENS GOOD, AMERICAN MISSIONARY / Parsons, Ellen C – New York: Fleming H Revell, 1897 – 1mf – 9 – 0-8370-6296-9 – 1985-0296 – us A.T.L.A. [920]

LIFE FOR GOD EXEMPLIFIED IN THE CHARACTER AND WORK OF NEHEMIAH / Ritchie, William – Edinburgh:Andrew Elliot; London:Hamilton, Adams, 1861 – 1mf – 9 – 0-8370-4912-1 – 1985-2912 – us A.T.L.A. [220]

A LIFE FOR GOD IN INDIA : MEMORIALS OF MRS. JEANNIE FULLER OF AKOLA AND BOMBAY / Dyer, Helen S – (Includes appendix) – New York: Fleming H Revell, [1903] – 1mf – 9 – 0-8370-6489-9 – 1986-0489 – us A.T.L.A. [920]

LIFE IN A LOOK / Baldwin, Maurice Scollard – Montreal: Dawson, 1879. 03972. (Pre-1900 Canadiana) – 9 – cn C.I.H.M. [240]

LIFE IN A MODERN MONASTERY / McCabe, Joseph – London: G. Richards, 1898 – 1mf – us A.T.L.A. [240]

LIFE IN ALGOMA, OR, THREE YEARS OF A CLERGYMAN'S LIFE AND CHURCH WORK IN THE DIOCESE / Burden, Harold Nelson – London: Society for Promoting Christian Knowledge, 1894. 02010. (Pre-1900 Canadiana) – 9 – cn C.I.H.M. [240]

LIFE IN HAWAII : AN AUTOBIOGRAPHIC SKETCH OF MISSION LIFE AND LABORS (1835-1881) / Coan, Titus – (Includes index) – New York: Anson D F Randolph, c1882 – 1mf – 9 – 0-8370-6036-2 – 1986-0036 – us A.T.L.A. [920]

LIFE IN JAPAN : AS SEEN THROUGH A MISSIONARY'S SPECTACLES IN THE TWILIGHT OF THE 19TH CENTURY / Gardner, Ella – Nashville, TE: Cumberland Presbyterian Pub House, c1900 – 1mf – 9 – 0-8370-7139-9 – 1986-1139 – us A.T.L.A. [950]

LIFE IN JAVA : WITH SKETCHES OF THE JAVANESE / Almeida, W B d' – London. 2v. 1864 – 8mf – 9 – ne IDC [950]

LIFE IN THE ENGLISH CHURCH (1660-1714) / Overton, John H – London: Longmans, Green, 1885 – 1mf – us A.T.L.A. [240]

LIFE IN THE MEDIEVAL UNIVERSITY / Rait, Robert Sangster – Cambridge: University Press; New York: Putnam, 1912 – 1mf – us A.T.L.A. [370]

LIFE IN THE NIGER : OR, THE JOURNAL OF AN AFRICAN TRADER / Cole, William – London: Saunders, Otley, 1862 – us Res Libr [920]

LIFE IN THE SPIRIT : A MEMORIAL OF THE REV. ALEX. ANDERSON, M.A. / Walker, Norman Lockhart – London: J. Nisbet, 1859 – 1mf – us A.T.L.A. [240]

LIFE IN THE WEST – Sigourney. Iowa. 1856-1859 – 1 – us UMI [071]

LIFE INSIDE THE CHURCH OF ROME / Cusack, Mary – M. Francis Clare Cusack, "The Nun of Kenmare". Toronto: W. Briggs, 1889. 02250. (Pre-1900 Canadiana) – 9 – cn C.I.H.M. [971]

THE LIFE INSURANCE ACT / Garrett, Herbert G – Victoria, B.C., 1925. 63p. LL-2221 – 1 – us L of C Photodup [340]

THE LIFE INSURANCE COMPANY / Alexander, William – New York: D Appleton & Co, 1905 – 4mf – 9 – $6.00 – LLMC 92-155 – us L.L.M.C. [360]

LIFE INSURANCE FUNDAMENTALS / Lovelace, Griffin M – rev ed. NY/London: Harper & Bros, 1925? – 3mf – 9 – $4.50 – LLMC 96-054 – us L.L.M.C. [360]

LIFE INSURANCE IDEAS – (1979- 5,6,9) – 1966- – 1 – us UMI [073]

LIFE INSURANCE REPORT – v.1-2. 1905-06. Continued by yUnderwriters' Report of California – 1 – us UMI [073]

THE LIFE, LABOURS, AND WRITINGS OF CAESAR MALAN : MINISTER OF THE GOSPEL IN THE CHURCH OF GENEVA, DOCTOR OF DIVINITY, AND PASTOR OF "L'EGLISE DU TEMOIGNAGE" – London: James Nisbet, 1859 – 2mf – us A.T.L.A. [240]

LIFE LESSONS FROM THE BOOK OF PROVERBS / Perry, William Stevens – New York: T. Whittaker, 1872. 1 fiche – 9 – us A.T.L.A. [240]

LIFE, LETTERS, AND DIARIES OF SIR STAFFORD NORTHCOTE, FIRST EARL OF IDDESLEIGH / Lang, Andrew – Edinburgh: W. Blackwood, 1890. 2v in 1.Illus.1 reel. 1268 – 1 – us U.W. Library [920]

LIFE, LETTERS AND JOURNALS OF GEORGE TICKNOR / Ticknor, George – London: Sampson Low, Marston, Searle, & Rivington, 2nd ed 1876 – 1 roll – 1 – 1-55879-210-4 – uk Libr Preservation [920]

THE LIFE, LETTERS, AND JOURNALS OF THE REV. AND HON. PETER PARKER, M.D. : MISSIONARY, PHYSICIAN, AND DIPLOMATIST: THE FATHER OF MEDICAL MISSIONS AND FOUNDER OF THE OPHTHALMIC HOSPITAL IN CANTON / Stevens, George Barker & Markwick, William Fisher – (Includes index) – Boston: Congregational Sunday-School and Pub Society, c1896 – 1mf – 9 – 0-8370-6338-8 – 1986-0338 – us A.T.L.A. [920]

THE LIFE OF A CHEMIST / Ipatieff, Vladimir N – Memoirs of V. N. Ipatieff ed. by Xenia Joukoff Eudin, Helen Dwight Fisher and Harold H. Fisher. 1946. 658p – 1 – 35.00r – us Hoover Inst Photo [920]

THE LIFE OF A SIMPLE MAN / Guillaumin, Emile – Margaret Holden, trans. Foreward by Edward Garnett. New York: Frederick A. Stokes Co., (1920). xvi,271p. Printed in Great Britain – 1 – us U.W. Library [920]

LIFE OF ABRAHAM LINCOLN / Crosby, Frank – (Part of series: A Library of Universal Literature, Pt 2, Biography) – NY: P F Collier & Son, 1900 – 6mf – 9 – $9.00 – LLMC 96-047 – us L.L.M.C. [975]

THE LIFE OF ADMIRAL OF THE FLEET SIR WILLIAM PARKER, BART / Phillimore, Augustus – 3v. 1876-80 – 9 – $120.00 – uk Libr Preservation [920]

THE LIFE OF ADMIRAL SIR ISAAC COFFIN, BARONET: HIS ENGLISH AND AMERICAN ANCESTORS / Amory, Thomas Coffin – Boston: Cupples, Upham, 1886. 06578. (Pre-1900 Canadiana) – 9 – cn C.I.H.M. [920]

LIFE OF ADMIRAL SIR W.R. MENDS, G.C.B / Mends, Bowen Stilon – 1899 – 9 – $20.00 – uk Libr Preservation [920]

THE LIFE OF ADONIRAM JUDSON / Judson, Edward – Philadelphia, American Baptist Pub Society, c1883 – 2mf – 9 – 0-8370-6672-7 – 1986-0672 – us A.T.L.A. [920]

THE LIFE OF ADONIRAM JUDSON : MISSIONARY TO BURMAH, 1813-50 / Johnston, Julia Harriette – Chicago: Woman's Presbyterian Board of Missions of the Northwest, c1887 – 1mf – 9 – 0-8370-6505-4 – 1986-0505 – us A.T.L.A. [920]

THE LIFE OF ALEXANDER DUFF / Vermilye, Elizabeth B – Chicago: Woman's Presbyterian Board of Missions of the Northwest, c1890 – 1mf – 9 – 0-8370-6534-8 – 1986-0534 – us A.T.L.A. [920]

THE LIFE OF ALEXANDER DUFF, D.D, LL.D / Smith, George – (Includes index) – New York: A C Armstrong; Toronto: James Campbell, [1879?] – 4mf – 1 – 0-8370-6519-4 – 1986-0519 – us A.T.L.A. [920]

THE LIFE OF ALEXANDER POPE, INCLUDING EXTRACTS FROM HIS CORRESPONDENCE / Carruthers, Robert – 2nd ed., rev. and enl. London: Bohn, 1857. 490p. illus – 1 – us U.W. Library [920]

LIFE OF ALEXANDER VON HUMBOLDT / ed by Bruhns, Carl – Comp. in commemoration of the centenary of his birth by J. Loewenberg, Robert Ave-Lallemant and Alfred Dove. Trans. from the German by Jane and Caroline Lassell. London: Longmans, Green and Co., 1873. 2v – 1 – us U.W. Library [574]

THE LIFE OF ALI PACHA, OF JANNINA, LATE VIZIER OF EPIRUS, SURNAMED ASLAN, OR THE LION / Beauchamp, A de – Includes compendious history of modern Greece. London, 1823. xll,368p. maps – 1 – us U.W. Library [920]

THE LIFE OF ANDREW MARTIN FAIRBAIRN : D.D., D. LITT., LL.D., F.B.A., ETC, FIRST PRINCIPAL OF MANSFIELD COLLEGE, OXFORD / Selbie, W B – London, New York: Hodder and Stoughton, 1914 – 2mf – us A.T.L.A. [240]

LIFE OF ANDREW MELVILLE : CONTAINING ILLUSTRATIONS OF THE ECCLESIASTICAL AND LITERARY HISTORY OF SCOTLAND DURING THE LATTER PART OF THE SIXTEENTH AND BEGINNING OF THE SEVENTEENTH CENTURY: WITH AN APPENDIX CONSISTING OF ORIGINAL PAPERS / M'Crie, Thomas – Edinburgh: William Blackwood, 1856 (The works of Thomas M'Crie; v2) – 2mf – us A.T.L.A. [240]

THE LIFE OF ANTHONY A WOOD, WRITTEN BY HIMSELF / Wood, Anthony A – Ed. by Philip Bliss. Oxford: T. Coombe, 1848. 412p – 1 – us U.W. Library [920]

THE LIFE OF ARCHIBALD ALEXANDER, D.D. : FIRST PROFESSOR IN THE THEOLOGICAL SEMINARY, AT PRINCETON, NEW JERSEY / Alexander, James W – New York: C. Scribner, 1854 – 2mf – us A.T.L.A. [240]

THE LIFE OF ARTHUR MURPHY, ESQ. / Foot, Jesse – London: Printed for J. Faulder by John Nichols and Son, 1811 – 1 roll – 1 – 1-55879-669-X – uk Libr Preservation [920]

THE LIFE OF ARTHUR TAPPAN / Tappan, Lewis – New York: Hurd and Houghton, 1870 – 1mf – us A.T.L.A. [240]

THE LIFE OF ASHBEL GREEN, V.D.M. : BEGUN TO BE WRITTEN BY HIMSELF IN HIS EIGHTY-SECOND YEAR AND CONTINUED TO HIS EIGHTY-FOURTH / Green, Ashbel – New York: R. Carter, 1849 – 2mf – us A.T.L.A. [240]

THE LIFE OF B. CELLINI / Cellini, Benvento – O-969 1. 2 v. 1771 – 9 – ne IDC [920]

THE LIFE OF BARON FREDERICK TRENCK: CONTAINING HIS ADVENTURES, AND ALSO HIS EXCESSIVE SUFFERINGS DURING TEN YEARS IMPRISONMENT / Trenck, Friedrich von der – Trans. from the French by Thomas Holcroft. Albany: J. Munsell, 1853 – 1 – us U.W. Library [920]

THE LIFE OF BENEDICT ARNOLD: HIS PATRIOTISM AND HIS TREASON / Arnold, Isaac Newton – Chicago: Jansen, McClurg, 1880. 03320. (Pre-1900 Canadiana) – 9 – cn C.I.H.M. [975]

THE LIFE OF BENJAMIN WEST / Galt, John – 1816-1820 – 9 – $25.00 – us Scholars' Facs [760]

THE LIFE OF BENOYENDRA NATH SEN / Dutt, Surendra Nath – Calcutta: Nababidhan Trust, 1928 – us Res Libr [920]

LIFE OF BISHOP JOHN WORDSWORTH / Watson, Edward William – London, New York: Longmans, Green, 1915 – 1mf – us A.T.L.A. [240]

THE LIFE OF BRIGADIER-GENERAL SIR SAMUEL BENTHAM / Bentham, Maria Sophia – 1862 – 9 – uk Libr Preservation [941]

THE LIFE OF CARDINAL XIMENEZ / Hefele, Karl Joseph von – London: Catholic Pub. & Bookselling, 1860 – 2mf – us A.T.L.A. [240]

THE LIFE OF CATHERINE BOOTH : THE MOTHER OF THE SALVATION ARMY / Booth, Tucker & Latour, Frederick St. George de – v1-2 c.1892 – 9 – us A.T.L.A. [240]

LIFE OF CHARLES DICKENS / Marzials, Frank Thomas – London: W. Scott, 1887 – 1 roll – 1 – 1-55879-624-X – uk Libr Preservation [420]

THE LIFE OF CHARLES HADDON SPURGEON / Ray, Charles – London: Isbister & Co; Passmore and Alabaster, 1903. xxiv,506p. illus.Includes index – 1 – us U.W. Library [240]

THE LIFE OF CHARLES HODGE, D.D. : PROFESSOR IN THE THEOLOGICAL SEMINARY, PRINCETON, N.J. / Hodge, Archibald Alexander – (Includes index) – New York: Charles Scribner, c1880 – 2mf – 9 – 0-8370-9790-8 – 1986-3790 – us A.T.L.A. [920]

LIFE OF CHARLES SUMNER / Chaplin, J – With an intro. by William Claflin. Boston: D. Lothrop; Dover: G. T. Day, 1874. 02121. (Pre-1900 Canadiana) – 9 – cn C.I.H.M. [920]

LIFE OF CHARLOTTE BRONTE / Birrell, Augustine – London: Walter Scott, 1887 – 1 roll – 1 – 1-55879-632-0 – uk Libr Preservation [420]

THE LIFE OF CHARLOTTE BRONTE / Gaskell, Elizabeth Cleghorn – Edinburgh: John Grant, 1905 – 1 roll – 1 – 1-55879-652-5 – uk Libr Preservation [420]

LIFE OF CHRIST / Duggan, J – London: Kegan Paul, Trench, 1897. 1 fiche – 9 – us A.T.L.A. [240]

THE LIFE OF CHRIST : AN AID TO HISTORICAL STUDY AND A CONDENSED COMMENTARY ON THE GOSPELS / Burton, Ernest De Witt & Mathews, Shailer – (Includes bibliographies and indexes) – Chicago, IL: University of Chicago Press, 1901, c1900 – 1mf – 9 – 0-8370-9368-6 – 1986-3368 – us A.T.L.A. [240]

THE LIFE OF CHRIST / Stewart, Alexander Morris – London: J.M. Dent, 1907. 1 fiche – 9 – us A.T.L.A. [240]

LIFE OF CHRIST ACCORDING TO ST MARK / Bennett, William Henry – New York: A.C. Armstrong, 1907. 1 fiche – 9 – us A.T.L.A. [240]

THE LIFE OF CHRIST IN RECENT RESEARCH / Sanday, William – (Includes index) – New York: Oxford University Press, 1907 – 1mf – 9 – 0-8370-6365-5 – 1986-0365 – us A.T.L.A. [240]

THE LIFE OF COUNTESS EMILY PLATER / Plater, Emily – Trans. by J.K. Salomonski. New York: J. Linen, 1843. 285p – 1 – us U.W. Library [920]

LIFE OF DANTE GABRIEL ROSSETTI / Knight, Joseph – London: Walter Scott, 1887 – 1 roll – 1 – 1-55879-553-7 – uk Libr Preservation [420]

THE LIFE OF DAVID LIVINGSTONE / Worcester, John Hopkins (Mrs) – Chicago: Woman's Presbyterian Board of Missions of the Northwest, c1888 – 1mf – 9 – 0-8370-6544-5 – 1986-0544 – us A.T.L.A. [920]

THE LIFE OF EDUARD JENNER / Bacon, J – London. 2v. 1838 – 14mf – ne IDC [610]

THE LIFE OF EDWARD IRVING, MINISTER OF THE SCOTCH CHURCH, LONDON : ILLUSTRATED BY HIS JOURNALS AND CORRESPONDENCE / Oliphant, Margaret – Fifth ed. Hurst and Blackett – 9 – $15.00 – us I.R.C. [240]

THE LIFE OF EDWARD JENNER / Baron, J – London, 1832. 2v. M-440/1 – 9 – ne IDC [576]

THE LIFE OF EDWARD WHITE BENSON : SOMETIME ARCHBISHOP OF CANTERBURY / Benson, Arthur Christopher – London; New York: Macmillan, 1899 – 4mf – us A.T.L.A. [240]

THE LIFE OF ELDER BENJAMIN RANDAL / Buzzell, John M G – 1827 – 1 – $10.92 – us Baptist [240]

THE LIFE OF EMMELINE PANKHURST; THE SUFFRAGETTE STRUGGLE FOR WOMEN'S CITIZENSHIP / Pankhurst, Estelle Sylvia – Boston: Houghton, Mifflin, 1936.179p – 1 – us U.W. Library [320]

THE LIFE OF F. M., H. R. H. EDWARD, DUKE OF KENT: ILLUSTRATED BY HIS CORRESPONDENCE WITH THE DE SALABERRY FAMILY, NEVER BEFORE PUBLISHED, EXTENDING FROM 1791 TO 1814 / Anderson, William James – Ottawa: Toronto: hUnter, Rose & Co., 1870. 00800. (Pre-1900 Canadiana) – 9 – cn C.I.H.M. [920]

THE LIFE OF FATHER DE SMET, S.J., 1801-1873 / Laveille, E – New York: P.J. Kenedy, 1915 – 1mf – us A.T.L.A. [240]

LIFE OF FATHER GOREH / Gardner, C E; ed by Benson, Richard Meux – London; New York: Longmans, Green, 1900 – 1mf – us A.T.L.A. [240]

LIFE OF FATHER IGNATIUS OF ST. PAUL, PASSIONIST (THE HON. AND REV. GEORGE SPENCER) / Pius, Father – Dublin: James Duffy, 1866 – 2mf – 9 – 0-8370-7107-0 – 1986-1107 – us A.T.L.A. [920]

THE LIFE OF FREDERICK DENISON MAURICE, CHIEFLY TOLD IN HIS OWN LETTERS / Maurice, Frederick Denison – 1 – us A.T.L.A. [920]

LIFE OF FREDERICK DOUGLASS / Douglass, Frederick – London: R. Yorke Clarke & Co., 1847 – 1 reel – 1 – us Western Res [920]

LIFE OF GENERAL GORDON / Hope, Eva – London: Walter Scott, 1885. viii,369p – 1 – us U.W. Library [920]

THE LIFE OF GEORGE BORROW / Jenkins, Herbert – New York: G.P. Putnam; London: J. Murray, 1912 – 2mf – us A.T.L.A. [240]

THE LIFE OF GEORGE GRENFELL : CONGO MISSIONARY AND EXPLORER / Hawker, George – (Includes index) – 2nd ed. London: Religious Tract Society, 1909 – 2mf – 9 – 0-8370-6261-6 – 1986-0261 – us A.T.L.A. [920]

THE LIFE OF GEORGE MATHESON, D.D., LL.D., F.R.S.E. / Macmillan, D – London: Hodder and Stoughton, 1907 – 1mf – us A.T.L.A. [240]

THE LIFE OF GEORGE STEPHENSON, RAILWAY ENGINEER / Smiles, Samuel – From the 4th London ed. Boston: Ticknor and Fields, 1859. 463p. illus – 1 – us U.W. Library [380]

THE LIFE OF HAFIZ OOL-MOOLK, HAFIZ REHMUT KHAN / Mustajab Khan – 1831. Royal Asiatic Society – 1 – uk Microform Academic [950]

THE LIFE OF HENRY DRUMMOND / Smith, George Adam – Toronto: Fleming H. Revell; London: Hodder and Stoughton, 1899 – 2mf – us A.T.L.A. [971]

LIFE OF HENRY DUNSTER / Chaplin, J – 1872 – 1 – 12.39 – us Baptist [240]

LIFE OF HENRY MARTYN : MISSIONARY TO INDIA AND PERSIA, 1781-1812 / Rhea, Sarah J – Chicago: Woman's Presbyterian Board of Foreign Missions of the Northwest, c1888 – 1mf – 9 – 0-8370-6510-0 – 1986-0510 – us A.T.L.A. [920]

THE LIFE OF H.L. ZIA (CCC176) / Woo, Y K – (In Chinese) – 1st ed. Shanghai: Association Press of China, 1917 – 1r – 1 – 1984-B500 – us A.T.L.A. [920]

LIFE OF HOWELL HARRIS, THE WELSH REFORMER / Hughes, Hugh J – Newport, Mon., [Wales]: W. Jones, 1892 – 1mf – us A.T.L.A. [941]

THE LIFE OF HUGH PRICE HUGHES / Hughes, Dorothea Price – New York: A.C. Armstrong; London: Hodder and Stoughton, 1904 – 2mf – us A.T.L.A. [240]

THE LIFE OF HUGO GROTIUS... / Butler, C – London, 1826 – 3mf – 1 – ILM-147/1 – ne IDC [327]

THE LIFE OF... HUGO GROTIUS / Burigny, M de – London, 1754 – 5mf – Dfl 39 – ILM 720/1 – ne IDC [340]

LIFE OF J.A. HARDING; TWO OLDEST LIVING COLLEGES; CHURCH OF CHRIST / Srygley, F D – 1 – $5.00 – us Baptist [240]

THE LIFE OF JABEZ BUNTING, D.D. : WITH NOTICES OF CONTEMPORARY PERSONS AND EVENTS / Bunting, Thomas Percival – London: Longman, Brown, Green, Longmans, & Roberts; Edinburgh: A. and C. Black, 1859-1887 – 2mf – us A.T.L.A. [240]

THE LIFE OF JACOB GRUBER / Strickland, William Peter – New York: Carlton and Porter, 1860 – 1mf – us A.T.L.A. [240]

THE LIFE OF JAMES ARMINIUS / Bangs, Nathan – 1843 – 9 – us A.T.L.A. [240]

LIFE OF JAMES HEPBURN, EARL OF BOTHWELL / Schiern, Frederik Eginhard Amadeus – Trans. from Danish by Rev. David Berry. Edinburgh: D. Douglas, 1880. xvii,448p – 1 – us U.W. Library [920]

LIFE OF JEAN PAUL FREDERIC RICHTER / Lee, Eliza Buckminster – 3rd ed. Boston: Ticknor & Fields, 1864 – 1r – 1 – us U.W. Library [920]

THE LIFE OF JEDIDIAH MORSE, D.D. / Sprague, William Buell – (Includes index) – New York: Anson D F Randolph, c1874 – 1mf – 9 – 0-8370-9826-2 – 1986-3826 – us A.T.L.A. [920]

THE LIFE OF JEHOSHUA, THE PROPHET OF NAZARETH : AN OCCULT STUDY AND A KEY TO THE BIBLE / Hartmann, Franz – London: Kegan Paul, Trench, Truebner, 1909 – 1mf – 9 – 0-8370-3510-4 – 1985-1510 – us A.T.L.A. [230]

LIFE OF JEHUDI ASHMUN WITH AN APPENDIX CONTAINING A BRIEF SKETCH OF THE LIFE OF REV. LOTT CARY / Gurley, Ralph R – 1835 – 1 – 5.60 – us Baptist [240]

LIFE OF JESUS: A MANUAL FOR ACADEMIC STUDY / Hase, Karl – Boston: Walker, Wise, 1860. 1 fiche – 9 – us A.T.L.A. [240]

THE LIFE OF JESUS ACCORDING TO EXTRA-CANONICAL SOURCES / Pick, Bernhard – New York: John B. Alden, 1887. 1 fiche – 9 – us A.T.L.A. [240]

LIFE OF JESUS (CCC82) / Chao, Tzu-ch'en – (In Chinese) – 1st ed. Shanghai: Association Press of China, 1935 – 1r – 1 – 1984-B500 – us A.T.L.A. [240]

THE LIFE OF JESUS CHRIST / Ewald, Heinrich – Cambridge: Deighton, Bell, 1865.1 fiche – 9 – us A.T.L.A. [240]

THE LIFE OF JESUS CHRIST / Stalker, James – New York: American Tract Society, 1891. 1 fiche – 9 – us A.T.L.A. [240]

THE LIFE OF JESUS CRITICALLY EXAMINED / Strauss, David Friedrich – Trans. from 4th German ed. by George Eliot, with an introduction by Otto Pfleiderer. Stereotyped ed. 1898 – 1 – us A.T.L.A. [240]

LIFE OF JESUS FOR YOUNG PEOPLE / Brown, Howard Nicholson – Boston: Unitarian Sun.-Sch. Soc., 1908. 1 fiche – 9 – us A.T.L.A. [240]

THE LIFE OF JESUS OF NAZARETH : A STUDY / Rhees, Rush – (Includes bibliographies and indexes) – New York:Charles Scribner, 1900 – 1mf – 9 – 0-8370-4886-9 – 1985-2886 – us A.T.L.A. [240]

THE LIFE OF JESUS: OUTLINE STUDIES FOR SHOP BIBLE CLASSES – Cleveland: Y.M.C.A., 1904. 1 fiche – 9 – us A.T.L.A. [240]

LIFE OF JESUS THE CHRIST / Beecher, Henry Ward – New York: Bromfield, 1891. 3 fiches – 9 – us A.T.L.A. [240]

THE LIFE OF JESUS THE CHRIST / Beecher, Henry Ward – (Includes indexes in both vols. Includes appendixes) – Completed ed. New York: Bromfield, 1891 – 3mf – 9 – 0-8370-2237-1 – 1985-0237 – us A.T.L.A. [240]

THE LIFE OF J.M.W. TURNER, R.A. : FOUNDED ON LETTERS AND PAPERS FURNISHED BY HIS FRIENDS AND FELLOW ACADEMICIANS / Thornbury, Walter – New York: Holt, 2nd ed 1877 – 1 roll – 1 – 1-55879-734-3 – uk Libr Preservation [750]

THE LIFE OF JOHN ARNDT : AUTHOR OF THE WORK ON "TRUE CHRISTIANITY" / Morris, John G – Baltimore: T.N. Kurtz, 1853 – 1mf – us A.T.L.A. [240]

THE LIFE OF JOHN BRAINERD : THE BROTHER OF DAVID BRAINERD, AND HIS SUCCESSOR AS MISSIONARY TO THE INDIANS OF NEW JERSEY / Brainerd, Thomas – (Includes bibliographical references and index) – Philadelphia: Presbyterian Publ Committee, c1865 – 2mf – 9 – 0-8370-6650-6 – 1986-0650 – us A.T.L.A. [920]

THE LIFE OF JOHN GOODWIN / Jackson, Thomas – 2d ed. 1872 – 1 – us A.T.L.A. [920]

THE LIFE OF JOHN HENRY, CARDINAL NEWMAN : BASED ON HIS PRIVATE JOURNALS AND CORRESPONDENCE / Ward, Wilfrid Philip – New York: Longmans, Green, 1912 – 3mf – us A.T.L.A. [240]

THE LIFE OF JOHN HUNTER F.R.S. (1728-93) AND JOHN HUNTER'S 'DIRECTIONS FOR PRESERVING ANIMALS AND PARTS OF ANIMALS FOR EXAMINATION.' / Foot, Jesse – 1 – uk Microform Academic [636]

THE LIFE OF JOHN JEBB, D.D., F.R.S., BISHOP OF LIMERICK, ARDFERT, AND AGHADOE / Forster, Charles – London: R. Bentley, 1851 – 1mf – us A.T.L.A. [240]

LIFE OF JOHN KEATS / Rossetti, William Michael – London: W. Scott, 1887 – 1 roll – 1 – 1-55879-595-2 – uk Libr Preservation [420]

LIFE OF JOHN KNOX : CONTAINING ILLUSTRATIONS OF THE HISTORY OF THE REFORMATION IN SCOTLAND, WITH BIOGRAPHICAL NOTICES OF THE PRINCIPAL REFORMERS...AND AN APPENDIX CONSISTING OF ORIGINAL PAPERS / M'Crie, Thomas – Edinburgh: William Blackwood, 1855 (The works of Thomas M'Crie; v1) – 2mf – us A.T.L.A. [240]

THE LIFE OF JOHN LIVINGSTON NEVIUS : FOR FORTY YEARS A MISSIONARY IN CHINA / Nevius, Helen Sanford Coan – New York: Fleming H Revell, c1895 – 2mf – 9 – 0-8370-6589-5 – 1986-0589 – us A.T.L.A. [920]

LIFE OF JOHN, LORD CAMPBELL, LORD HIGH CHANCELLOR OF GREAT BRITAIN; CONSISTING OF A SELECTION FROM HIS AUTOBIOGRAPHY, DIARY, AND LETTERS / Campbell, John – Ed. by his daughter, Hon. Mrs. Hardcastle. London: J. Murray, 1881. 2v – 1 – us U.W. Library [941]

THE LIFE OF JOHN MARSHALL / Beveridge, Albert J – Boston/New York: Houghton, Mifflin. 4v. 1919 – 29mf – 9 – $43.50 – LLMC 92-191 – us L.L.M.C. [340]

THE LIFE OF JOHN MOCKETT CRAMP, D.D., 1796-1881, LATE PRESIDENT OF ACADIA COLLEGE.. / Higgins, Thomas Alfred – Montreal: W. Drysdale, 1887. 05563. (Pre-1900 Canadiana) – 9 – cn C.I.H.M. [370]

THE LIFE OF JOHN MURDOCH, LL.D. : THE LITERARY EVANGELIST OF INDIA / Morris, Henry – London: Christian Literature Society for India, 1906 – 1mf – us A.T.L.A. [240]

LIFE OF JOHN ROBERT MONAGHAN : THE HERO OF SAMOA / McCulloch, H L – n.p, 1906? – 5mf – 9 – $7.50 – LLMC 82-100C Title 23 – us L.L.M.C. [920]

LIFE OF JOHN RUSKIN / Wingate, Ashmore Kyle Paterson – London, Felling-on-Tyne, New York: Walter Scott Publishing, 1910 – 1 roll – 1 – 1-55879-483-2 – uk Libr Preservation [110]

THE LIFE OF JOHN STERLING / Carlyle, Thomas – London: Chapman and Hall, 1851 – 1mf – us A.T.L.A. [920]

THE LIFE OF JOHN WESLEY / Winchester, C T – New York: Macmillan, 1906 – 1mf – us A.T.L.A. [941]

THE LIFE OF JOHN WILKINSON : THE JEWISH MISSIONARY / Wilkinson, Samuel Hinds – (Includes index) – London: Morgan & Scott, 1908 – 1mf – 9 – 0-8370-6717-0 – 1986-0717 – us A.T.L.A. [920]

THE LIFE OF JOHN WILLIAM COLENSO, D.D. : BISHOP OF NATAL / Cox, George W – London: W. Ridgway, 1888 – 4mf – us A.T.L.A. [240]

THE LIFE OF JOHN WILSON, D.D. F.R.S. : FOR FIFTY YEARS PHILANTHROPIST AND SCHOLAR IN THE EAST / Smith, George – (Includes bibliographical references and index) – London: John Murray, 1878 – 2mf – 9 – 0-8370-6520-8 – 1986-0520 – us A.T.L.A. [920]

THE LIFE OF JOSEPH ADDISON ALEXANDER / Alexander, Henry Carrington – 2v in 1. 1875 – 9 – us A.T.L.A. [240]

LIFE OF LADY CATHERINE DE SOYSA / Abeyesooriya, Samson – Colombo: Lord Kitchener Press, [n.d.] – us Res Libr [920]

LIFE OF LAL BEHARI DAY : CONVERT, PASTOR, PROFESSOR, AND AUTHOR / Macpherson, G – Edinburgh: T.& T. Clark, 1900 – 1mf – us A.T.L.A. [240]

THE LIFE OF LAS CASAS, "THE APOSTLE OF THE INDIES" / Helps, Sir Arthur – New York: J.B. Lippincott, 1868 – 1mf – us A.T.L.A. [240]

LIFE OF LEUNG FAAT (CCC212) = CHUNG-HUA TSUI TSAO TI PU TAO CHE / McNeur, G H – (In Chinese. With: Good words exhorting mankind (ch'uan fu ch'uan shih liang yen) by Leung Faat) – 1st ed. Hong Kong: Council on Christian Literature for Overseas Chinese, 1955 – 1r – 1 – 1984-B500 – us A.T.L.A. [920]

LIFE OF LI SHU-CH'ING (CCC215) / Li, Shu-ch'ing; ed by Li, Chung-t'an – (In Chinese) – Shanghai: Christian Literature Society, 1934 – 1r – 1 – 1984-B500 – us A.T.L.A. [920]

LIFE OF LISZT / Nohl, Ludwig – Chicago: Jansen, McClurg & Co., 1884 – 1 – us Sibley [780]

LIFE OF LORD BYRON / Noel, Roden Berkeley Wriothesley – London: W. Scott, 1890 – 1 roll – 1 – 1-55879-315-1 – uk Libr Preservation [420]

THE LIFE OF LUISA DE CARVAJAL / Fullerton, Georgiana – 1881 – 9 – $1.50f – sp Bibl Santa Ana [920]

LIFE OF LUTHER / Koestlin, Julius – London: Longmans, Green, 1883 – 2mf – us A.T.L.A. [240]

THE LIFE OF LUTHER / Luther, Martin – Written by himself; collected and arranged by M. Michelet; trans. by William Hazlitt. 1846 – 1 – $17.43 – us Baptist [240]

LIFE OF MARGARET BEAUFORT...MOTHER OF KING HENRY THE SEVENTH / Halsted, Caroline Amelia – London: Smith, Elder and Co., 1845. xiii,262p – 1 – us U.W. Library [940]

THE LIFE OF MARY LYON / Gilchrist, Beth Bradford – Boston: Houghton, Mifflin, 1910 – 2mf – us A.T.L.A. [240]

THE LIFE OF MOTHER DUCHESNE : RELIGIOUS OF THE SOCIETY OF THE SACRED HEART OFJESUS, AND FOUNDRESS OF THE FIRST HOUSES OF THAT SOCIETY IN AMERICA / Baunard, Louis, Abbe – [S.l.: s.n.], 1879 (Roehampton: James Stanley) – 2mf – 9 – 0-8370-7042-2 – 1986-1042 – us A.T.L.A. [920]

THE LIFE OF MRS. MARY D. JAMES / James, Joseph H – c.1886 – 9 – us A.T.L.A. [240]

THE LIFE OF MRS. MARY FLETCHER: CONSORT AND RELICT OF THE REV. JOHN FLETCHER, VICAR OF MADELEY, SALOP / Moore, Henry – 1837 – 9 – us A.T.L.A. [240]

THE LIFE OF NELSON, THE EMBODIMENT OF THE SEA POWER OF GREAT BRITAIN / Mahan, Alfred Thayer – 2nd ed., rev. 1899 – 9 – $20.00 – uk Libr Preservation [920]

THE LIFE OF PAUL / Taylor, David Henry – Boston: D Lothrop, 1884 – Includes index – 9 – 0-8370-5481-8 – 1985-3481 – us A.T.L.A. [920]

THE LIFE OF PETER VAN SCHAACK. / Schaack, Henry Cruger Van – New York, Appleton, 1842. 490 p. LL-846 – 1 – us L of C Photodup [340]

THE LIFE OF PHILANDER CHASE : FIRST BISHOP OF OHIO AND ILLINOIS, FOUNDER OF KENYON AND JUBILEE COLLEGES / Smith, Laura Chase – New York: E.P. Dutton, 1903 – 1mf – us A.T.L.A. [370]

LIFE OF PHILIP DODDRIDGE, D.D.; WITH NOTICES OF SOME OF HIS CONTEMPORARIES AND SPECIMENS OF HIS STYLE / Harsha, David A – 1864 – 9 – us A.T.L.A. [240]

LIFE OF PHILIP MELANCHTHON / Stump, Joseph – Reading, Pa.: Pilger Publishing House, 1897 – 1mf – us A.T.L.A. [240]

THE LIFE OF PHILIP MELANCHTHON / Ledderhose, Karl Friedrich – Philadelphia: Lindsay & Blakiston, 1855, c1854 – 1mf – us A.T.L.A. [240]

A LIFE OF PIUS 9TH / O'Reilly, Bernard – 14th ed. New York: P F Collier, 1878, c1877 – 2mf – 9 – 0-8370-6827-4 – 1986-0827 – us A.T.L.A. [920]

LIFE OF POPE PIUS IX, AND THE GREAT EVENTS IN THE HISTORY OF THE CHURCH DURING HIS PONTIFICATE / Shea, John Dawson Gilmary – 1878? – 1 – us A.T.L.A. [240]

THE LIFE OF RAMON MONSALVATGE : A CONVERTED SPANISH MONK OF THE ORDER OF THE CAPUCHINS / Monsalvatge, Ramon – New York: J.F. Trow, 1845 – 1mf – us A.T.L.A. [240]

LIFE OF REV. BENJAMIN SCHNEIDER, D.D. : A MISSIONARY OF THE REFORMED CHURCH IN THE UNITED STATES THROUGH THE AMERICAN BOARD AT BROOSA AND AINTAB, TURKEY, 1834-1877 / Good, James I – Philadelphia, Pa.: Board of Foreign Missions, Reformed Church in the United States, [19..] – 1mf – us A.T.L.A. [240]

THE LIFE OF REV. CHARLES NERINCKY : WITH A CHAPTER ON THE EARLY CATHOLIC MISSIONS OF KENTUCKY, COPIOUS NOTES ON THE PROGRESS OF CATHOLICITY IN THE UNITED STATES / Maes, Camillus Paul – Cincinnati: Robert Clarke, 1880 – 2mf – us A.T.L.A. [240]

LIFE OF REV. GEORGE WHITEFIELD / Harsha, David A – 1866 – 9 – us A.T.L.A. [920]

THE LIFE OF REV. JAMES O'KELLY : AND THE EARLY HISTORY OF THE CHRISTIAN CHURCH IN THE SOUTH / MacClenny, WE – Raleigh, N. C.: Edwards & Broughton, 1910 – 1mf – us A.T.L.A. [240]

LIFE OF REV. JAMES RICHARDSON : A BISHOP OF THE METHODIST EPISCOPAL CHURCH IN CANADA / Webster, Thomas – Toronto: J.B. Magurn, 1876 – us A.T.L.A. [240]

THE LIFE OF REV. JOEL HAWES, D.D., TENTH PASTOR OF THE FIRST CHURCH, HARTFORD, CONN / Lawrence, Edward Alexander – 1873 – 1 – us A.T.L.A. [240]

THE LIFE OF REV. JOHN MURRAY, PREACHER OF UNIVERSAL SALVATION / Murray, John – Boston: Universalist Publishing House, 1869 – 1mf – us A.T.L.A. [240]

THE LIFE OF REV. JOHN WESLEY,...FOUNDER OF THE METHODIST SOCIETIES / Watson, Richard – 1st American official ed. Trans. and notes by John Emory. New York: J. Emory and B. Waugh, for the Methodist Episcopal Church, 1832. 323p – 1 – us U.W. Library [240]

LIFE OF REV. JUSTIN PERKINS, D.D. : PIONEER MISSIONARY TO PERSIA / Perkins, Henry Martyn – Chicago: Woman's Presbyterian Board of Missions of the Northwest, c1887 – 1mf – 9 – 0-8370-6509-7 – 1986-0509 – us A.T.L.A. [920]

THE LIFE OF REV. MICHAEL SCHLATTER : WITH A FULL ACCOUNT OF HIS TRAVELS AND LABORS AMONG THE GERMANS IN PENNSYLVANIA, NEW JERSEY, MARYLAND AND VIRGINIA... / Harbaugh, Henry – Philadelphia: Lindsay & Blakiston, 1857 – 1mf – us A.T.L.A. [240]

THE LIFE OF REV. MORRIS OFFICER, A.M. / Imhoff, Alexander Jesse – Dayton, OH: United Brethren Pub House, 1876 – 2mf – 9 – 0-8370-6579-8 – 1986-0579 – us A.T.L.A. [920]

THE LIFE OF REV. PHILIP WILLIAM OTTERBEIN : FOUNDER OF THE CHURCH OF THE UNITED BRETHREN IN CHRIST / Drury, A W – Dayton, Ohio: United Brethren Publishing House, 1884 – 1mf – us A.T.L.A. [240]

LIFE OF REV. WILLIAM KEELE / Ewell, John D – A minister of the primitive Baptist church in Rutherford County, Tenn., organized the Duck River Association of Baptists in 1826 – 1 – $8.68 – us Baptist [240]

THE LIFE OF REV. WILLIAM M'KENDREE : ONE OF THE BISHOPS OF THE METHODIST EPISCOPAL CHURCH / Fry, Benjamin St. James – New York: Carlton & Porter, c1852 – 1mf – us A.T.L.A. [240]

THE LIFE OF REVEREND ENOCH GEORGE : ONE OF THE BISHOPS OF THE METHODIST EPISCOPAL CHURCH / Fry, Benjamin St. James – New York: Carlton & Porter, [1856?] – 1mf – us A.T.L.A. [920]

THE LIFE OF RICHARD COBDEN / Morley, John – The story of a successful libertarian. 10 fiches (24x) – 9 – $1.00f – at Libertarian Micro [320]

THE LIFE OF RICHARD EARL HOWE, K.G., ADMIRAL OF THE FLEET AND GENERAL OF MARINES / Barrow, John – 1838 – 9 – 20.00 – uk Libr Preservation [941]

LIFE OF RIGHT REV. JOHN N. NEUMANN, D.D. = LEBEN UND WIRKEN DES HOCHSELIGEN JOHANNES NEP. NEUMANN : OF THE CONGREGATION OF THE MOST HOLY REDEEMER, FOURTH BISHOP OF PHILADELPHIA / Berger, Johann – (In English) – 2nd ed. New York: Benziger, 1884 – 2mf – 9 – 0-8370-6566-6 – 1986-0566 – us A.T.L.A. [920]

LIFE OF ROBERT BROWNING / Sharp, William – London: W. Scott, 1890 – 1 roll – 1 – 1-55879-321-6 – uk Libr Preservation [420]

LIFE OF ROBERT GRAY, BISHOP OF CAPE TOWN AND METROPOLITAN OF AFRICA / Lear, Henrietta Louisa Farrer – 2v. 1876 – 1 – us A.T.L.A. [240]

LIFE OF ROBERT R. MCBURNEY / Doggett, L L – Cleveland, [Ohio]: F.M. Barton, c1902 – 1mf – us A.T.L.A. [240]

THE LIFE OF S. THOMAS A BECKET OF CANTERBURY / Hope, Anne Fulton – London: Burns, Oates, [1868?] – 1mf – us A.T.L.A. [240]

THE LIFE OF ST. ANSELM : ARCHBISHOP OF CANTERBURY: A CONTRIBUTION TO A KNOWLEDGE OF THE MORAL, ECCLESIASTICAL, AND LITERARY LIFE OF THE ELEVENTH AND TWELFTH CENTURIES / Moehler, Johann Adam – London: T. Jones, 1842 – 1mf – us A.T.L.A. [240]

THE LIFE OF SAINT BONIFACE : ARCHBISHOP OF MAYENCE AND APOSTLE OF GERMANY / Cox, George W – London: Joseph Masters,1853 – 1mf – us A.T.L.A. [240]

THE LIFE OF SAINT DOMINICK : PRECEDED BY A MEMORIAL TO THE FRENCH PEOPLE FOR THE RESTORATION OF THE ORDER OF PREACHERS IN FRANCE / Lacordaire, Henri Dominique – Dublin: J. Duffy, 1851 – 1mf – us A.T.L.A. [240]

LIFE OF SAINT ELIZABETH OF HUNGARY : DUCHESS OF THURINGIA / Montalembert, Charles Forbes – New York: Longmans, Green, 1904 – 2mf – us A.T.L.A. [240]

LIFE OF ST FRANCIS OF ASSISI / Sabatier, Paul – London: Hodder and Stoughton, 1899 – 2mf – us A.T.L.A. [240]

THE LIFE OF SAINT MARY MAGDALEN – (Transl fr Italian) – London, New York: John Lane, 1904 – 1mf – 9 – 0-8370-4122-8 – 1985-2122 – us A.T.L.A. [230]

THE LIFE OF ST PAUL / Stalker, James – Edinburgh: T & T Clark; New York: Charles Scribner, [c1888] – 1mf – 9 – 0-8370-5537-7 – 1985-3537 – us A.T.L.A. [240]

THE LIFE OF ST. PAUL (CCC79) / Chao, Tzu-ch'en – (In Chinese) – 1st ed. Hong Kong: Council on Christian Literature for Overseas Chinese, 1956 – 1r – 1 – 1984-B500 – us A.T.L.A. [240]

THE LIFE OF SAMUEL JOHNSON / Boswell, James – 5v. 1831 – 1r – 1 – us Ross [920]

LIFE OF SIMON DE MONTFORT : EARL OF LEICESTER / Creighton, Mandell – London: Rivingtons, 1876. (Historical biographies) – 1mf – us A.T.L.A. [240]

THE LIFE OF SIR GEORGE WILLIAMS : FOUNDER OF THE YOUNG MEN'S CHRISTIAN ASSOCIATION / Hodder-Williams, J E – Cincinnati: Jennings & Graham; New York: Eaton & Mains, 1906 – 1mf – us A.T.L.A. [360]

THE LIFE OF SIR JAMES FITZJAMES STEPHEN, BART., K.C.S.I. : A JUDGE OF THE HIGH COURT OF JUSTICE... / Stephen, Leslie – London: Smith, Elder & Co., 2nd ed 1895 – 1 roll – 1 – 1-55879-945-1 – uk Libr Preservation [340]

LIFE OF SIR JOHN HAWLEY GLOVER / Glover, Elizabeth Rosetta Scott – ed. by Richard Temple. London: Smith,Elder, 1897. 03454. (Pre-1900 Canadiana) – 9 – cn C.I.H.M. [920]

LIFE OF SIR JOHN HAWLEY GLOVER / Glover, Elizabeth Rosetta Scott; ed by Temple, Richard – London: Smith, Elder, 1897 – us Res Libr [920]

THE LIFE OF SIR PHILIP SYDNEY / Brooke – 1907 – 1 – uk Microform Academic [920]

LIFE OF SIR ROBERT PEEL / Montague, Francis Charles – Philadelphia: J.B. Lippincott, 1889. xii,225p – 1 – us U.W. Library [920]

LIFE OF SIR WALTER RALEIGH: FOUNDED ON AUTHENTIC AND ORIGINAL DOCUMENTS, SOME OF THEM NEVER BEFORE PUBLISHED:. / Tytler, Patrick Fraser – Edinburgh: Oliver & Boyd, 1833. 468p. illus – 1 – us U.W. Library [910]

THE LIFE OF SPIRIT IN THE MODERN ENGLISH POETS / Scudder, Vida Dutton – Boston: Houghton, Mifflin, 1895 – 1mf – us A.T.L.A. [420]

THE LIFE OF ST. FRANCIS BORGIA OF THE SOCIETY OF JESUS / Clarke, A M – (Includes index) – London: Burns and Oates, 1894 – 2mf – 9 – 0-8370-6659-X – 1906-0659 – us A.T.L.A. [920]

THE LIFE OF ST HUGH OF AVALON : BISHOP OF LINCOLN: WITH SOME ACCOUNT OF HIS PREDECESSORS IN THE SEE OF LINCOLN / Perry, George G – London: J. Murray, 1879 – 1mf – us A.T.L.A. [240]

THE LIFE OF ST PATRICK AND HIS PLACE IN HISTORY / Bury, J B – London; New York: Macmillan, 1905 – 1mf – us A.T.L.A. [240]

A LIFE OF ST PETER: FOR THE YOUNG / Weed, George Ludington – Philadelphia: George W. Jacobs, 1901. 1 fiche. 8370-5736-1 – 9 – us A.T.L.A. [240]

THE LIFE OF TAKLA HAYMANOT... AND THE MIRACLES OF TAKLA HAYMANOT, IN THE VERSION OF DABRA LIBANOS, AND THE BOOK OF THE RICHES OF KINGS / Budge, E A W – London. 2v. 1906 – 29mf – 9 – ne IDC [930]

THE LIFE OF THE BLESSED MARY ANN OF JESUS, DE PAREDES Y FLORES : AN AMERICAN VIRGIN CALLED THE LILY OF QUITO / Boero, Joseph – Philadelphia: Peter F Cunningham, 1863, c1855 – 1mf – 9 – 0-8370-7044-9 – 1986-1044 – us A.T.L.A. [920]

THE LIFE OF THE CHEVALIER BAYARD; THE GOOD KNIGHT, SAN PEUR ET SANS REPROCHE / Simms, William Gilmore – New York: Harpers, 1847 – 1 – us U.W. Library [920]

THE LIFE OF THE COPPER ESKIMOS / Jenness, D – BN 268 2. 1922 – 8 – ne IDC [306]

LIFE OF THE EARL OF MAYO, FOURTH VICEROY OF INDIA / Hunter, William Wilson – London: Smith, Elder, 1875. 2v – 1 – us U.W. Library [941]

THE LIFE OF THE EARLY CHURCH (CCC95) = CH'U CH'I TI CHIAO HUI / Cheng, Andrew C Y – (In Chinese) – Shanghai: Christian Literature Society, 1939 – 1r – 1 – 1984-B500 – us A.T.L.A. [240]

THE LIFE OF THE LAW, OR, UNIVERSAL PRINCIPLES OF LAW / Howard, Overton – Richmond, Va.: Randolph & English, 1889. 114p. LL-211 – 1 – us L of C Photodup [340]

THE LIFE OF THE MASTER / Maclaren, Ian – New York: McClure, Phillips, 1901. 1 fiche. 8370-5724-8 – 9 – us A.T.L.A. [240]

A LIFE OF THE POPE (LEO THE THIRTEENTH) / Hall, Arthur D – New York: Street & Smith, c1899 – 1mf – 9 – 0-8370-8517-9 – 1986-2517 – us A.T.L.A. [920]

THE LIFE OF THE RENOWNED DOCTOR PRESTON / Ball, Thomas – Oxford: Parker, 1885 – 1mf – 9 – 0-8370-9762-2 – 1986-3762 – us A.T.L.A. [920]

LIFE OF THE REV. HENRY HARBAUGH, D.D. / Harbaugh, Linn – Philadelphia: Reformed Church Publication Board, Sunday-School Board of the Reformed Church, c1900 – 1mf – us A.T.L.A. [240]

LIFE OF THE REV. JAMES HERVEY / Harsha, David A – 1865 – 9 – us A.T.L.A. [240]

THE LIFE OF THE REV. JAMES IRELAND / Ireland, James – 236p – 1 – $8.26 – us Baptist [240]

THE LIFE OF THE REV. ROBERT BAIRD, D.D. / Baird, Henry Martyn – New York: A.D.F. Randolph, 1866, c1865 – 1mf – us A.T.L.A. [240]

THE LIFE OF THE RIGHT REVEREND ALEXANDER JOLLY, D.D. : BISHOP OF MORAY / Walker, William – Edinburgh: D. Douglas, 1878 – 1mf – us A.T.L.A. [240]

LIFE OF THE RIGHT REVEREND SAMUEL WILBERFORCE : D.D., LORD BISHOP OF OXFORD AND AFTERWARDS OF WINCHESTER, WITH SELECTIONS FROM HIS DIARIES AND CORRESPONDENCE / Ashwell, A R – London: John Murray, 1880-82 – 4mf – us A.T.L.A. [240]

THE LIFE OF THE RT. HON. SPENCER PERCEVAL, INCLUDING HIS CORRESPONDENCE WITH NUMEROUS DISTINGUISHED PERSONS / Walpole, Spencer – London: Hurst and Blackett, 1874. 2v – 1 – us U.W. Library [340]

THE LIFE OF THE SPIRIT : AN INTRODUCTION TO PHILOSOPHY / Eucken, Rudolf – New York: Putnam, 1909 – 1mf – us A.T.L.A. [100]

LIFE OF ULRICH ZWINGLI : THE SWISS PATRIOT AND REFORMER / Simpson, Samuel – New York: Baker & Taylor, 1902 – 1mf – us A.T.L.A. [240]

THE LIFE OF VICE-ADMIRAL EDMUND, LORD LYONS : WITH AN ACCOUNT OF NAVAL OPERATIONS IN THE BLACK SEA AND THE SEA OF AZOFF, 1854-56 / Wilmot, Sydney Marow Eardley – 1898 – 9 – uk Libr Preservation [941]

LIFE OF VICE-ADMIRAL SIR GEORGE TRYON, K.C.B / Fitzgerald, Charles Cooper Penrose – 1897 – 9 – $20.00 – uk Libr Preservation [355]

THE LIFE OF WALTER PATER / Wright, Thomas – London: Everett & Co., 1907 – 1 roll – 1 – 1-55879-232-5 – uk Libr Preservation [420]

THE LIFE OF WILLIAM CAREY / Farwell, Mary E – Chicago: Woman's Presbyterian Board of Missions of the Northwest, c1888 – 1mf – 9 – 0-8370-6492-9 – 1986-0492 – us A.T.L.A. [920]

LIFE OF WILLIAM CUNNINGHAM, D.D. : PRINCIPAL AND PROFESSOR OF THEOLOGY AND CHURCH HISTORY, NEW COLLEGE, EDINBURGH / Rainy, Robert & Mackenzie, James – London, New York: T. Nelson, 1871 – 2mf – us A.T.L.A. [370]

LIFE OF WILLIAM EDWARD COLLINS : BISHOP OF GIBRALTAR / Mason, Arthur James – London; New York: Longmans, Green, 1912 – 1mf – us A.T.L.A. [240]

THE LIFE OF...JOHN BAPTI..NEW YORK, 1925 / Fox, M A S Columba – Madrid: Razon y Fe, 1930 – 1 – sp Bibl Santa Ana [240]

LIFE PICTURES OF JOHN CALVIN : FOR YOUNG AND OLD / Good, James I & Richards, G W – Philadelphia: Presbyterian Board of Publication, 1909 – 1mf – us A.T.L.A. [240]

LIFE PICTURES OF THE PRODIGAL SON : A GIFT-BOOK FOR THE MILLION / Heisler, Daniel Yost – Philadelphia: s.n., 1878, c1877 – 1mf – 9 – 0-8370-3554-6 – 1985-1554 – us A.T.L.A. [220]

LIFE, POETRY, AND LETTERS OF EBENEZER ELLIOTT, THE CORN-LAW RHYMER : WITH AN ABSTRACT OF HIS POLITICS / Watkins, John – London: J. Mortimer, 1850 – 1 roll – 1 – 1-55879-623-1 – uk Libr Preservation [800]

LIFE SCIENCES – (Back issues of journal available from UMI) – 52 issues/y. v52-53. 1993 – 1,5,9 – £1,112.00y – uk Elsevier Sci [574]

LIFE SCIENCES – v1- 1962- – 5,6,9 – us UMI [574]

LIFE SKETCHES: BEING NARRATIONS OF SCENES OCCURRING IN THE LABOURS OF ALMIRA LOSEE / Losee, Almira – 1877 – 9 – us A.T.L.A. [240]

LIFE SKETCHES OF EMINENT LAWYERS : AMERICAN, ENGLISH AND CANADIAN, TO WHICH IS ADDED THOUGHTS, FACTS AND FACETIAE / Clark, Gilbert J – Kansas City: Mo. Lawyers' International Publ Co. 2v. 1895 – 10mf – 9 – $15.00 – LLMC 95-160 – us L.L.M.C. [340]

LIFE, SPORT AND DRAMA – Johannesburg, South Africa. 26 Mar-25 Jun 1921.1 reel – 1, 16 diazo available at reduced price – sa SA Libr [072]

THE LIFE STORY OF HENRY CLAY TRUMBULL : MISSIONARY, ARMY CHAPLAIN, EDITOR, AND AUTHOR / Howard, Philip E – Philadelphia: Sunday School Times, 1905 – 2mf – us A.T.L.A. [240]

THE LIFE STORY OF L. R. MILLICAN / Force, Fred P – 1956 – 1 – $5.18 – us Baptist [240]

LIFE STRESS AND ITS EFFECTS ON INJURY AND PERFORMANCE AMONG COLLEGIATE SOCCER PLAYERS / O'Connor, Kimberly A – 1989 – 131p 2mf – 9 – $8.00 – us Microform Publ [150]

LIFE STRESS AND SOCIAL SUPPORT AS PREDICTORS OF ATHLETIC INJURY / Kirsanoff, Mary T – 1987 – 101p 2mf – 9 – $8.00 – us Microform Publ [150]

LIFE SUPPORT SYSTEMS: THE JOURNAL OF THE EUROPEAN SOCIETY FOR ARTIFICIAL ORGANS – (1985-. 5,6,9) – v1-. 1983- – 1 – us UMI [610]

THE LIFE, TIMES AND CORRESPONDENCE OF THE RIGHT REV. DR. DOYLE, BISHOP OF KILDARE AND LEIGHLIN / Fitzpatrick, William John – Dublin: J. Duffy, 1861. 2v. front – 1 – us U.W. Library [920]

THE LIFE, TIMES, AND CORRESPONDENCE OF THE RIGHT REV. DR. DOYLE, BISHOP OF KILDARE AND LEIGHLIN / Fitzpatrick, William John – Boston: Patrick Donahoe. 2v. 1862 – 4mf – 9 – 0-8370-6663-8 – 1986-0663 – us A.T.L.A. [920]

THE LIFE, TRAVELS, LABORS, AND HELPERS OF MRS. AMANDA SMITH: THE FAMOUS NEGRO MISSIONARY EVANGELIST / Taylor, Marshall William – c1886 – 9 – us A.T.L.A. [240]

LIFE, WANDERINGS AND LABOURS IN EASTERN AFRICA.. / New, Charles – 1873 – 1 – us A.T.L.A. [960]

LIFEBOAT – 1852- 1; 1977- 5,6,9 – us UMI [790]

THE LIFEBOAT AND OTHER POEMS / Andrews, William – Toronto: W. Briggs, 189?. 00017. (Pre-1900 Canadiana) – 9 – cn C.I.H.M. [810]

LIFELINE – Miami, FL. Nov/Dec 1981-1983. Continues: Newsletter (South Florida Conference on Soviet Jewry). Ceased publication – 1 – us A.J.P.C. [071]

LIFELONG EDUCATION AND UNIVERSITY RESOURCES – 1978 – 193p – 9 – 92-3-101397-1 – fr UNESCO [370]

LIFELONG LEARNING *see*
- ADULT LEADERSHIP
- ADULT LEARNING

LIFELONG LEARNING: THE ADULT YEARS – v. 1-. 1977- – 1,5,6,9 – us UMI [370]

LIFE-POWER : OR, CHARACTER, CULTURE AND CONDUCT / Pierson, Arthur Tappan – New York: Fleming H Revell, c1895 – 1mf – 9 – 0-8370-9410-0 – 1986-3410 – us A.T.L.A. [200]

LIFE'S BASIS AND LIFE'S IDEAL : THE FUNDAMENTALS OF A NEW PHILOSOPHY OF LIFE / Eucken, Rudolf & Widgery, Alban G – London: A. and C. Black, 1912 – 1mf – us A.T.L.A. [190]

LIFE'S BYWAYS AND WAYSIDES / Miller, James Russell – Philadelphia: Presbyterian Board of Publ and Sabbath-School Work, 1895 – 1mf – 9 – 0-8370-7245-X – 1986-1245 – us A.T.L.A. [240]

LIFE'S EXPERIENCES (CCC64) / Chao, Hsia-yun – (In Chinese) – Shanghai: Christian Literature Society, 1932 – 1r – 1 – 1984-6403 – us A.T.L.A. [240]

LIFE'S HANDICAP : BEING STORIES OF MINE OWN PEOPLE / Kipling, Rudyard – London, New York: Macmillan, 1891 – 1 roll – 1 – 1-55879-912-5 – uk Libr Preservation [420]

LIFE'S LITTLE IRONIES : A SET OF TALES, WITH SOME COLLOQUIAL SKETCHES ENTITLED A FEW CRUSTED CHARACTERS / Hardy, Thomas – London: James R. Osgood, McIlvaine, [1894] – 1 roll – 1 – 1-55879-785-8 – uk Libr Preservation [830]

LIFE'S PROBLEMS, HERE AND HEREAFTER : AN AUTOBIOGRAPHY – Boston: Cupples and Hurd, 1887 – 1mf – 9 – 0-8370-4304-2 – 1985-2304 – us A.T.L.A. [230]

A LIFE'S SECRET / Wood, Ellen – British Fiction Archive: Unit 1 – 9 – uk Bell [830]

THE LIFE-STORY OF INSECTS / Carpenter, G H – Cambridge, 1913.iv,134p. 1 pl. Z-1122/2 – 8 – ne IDC [590]

LIFESTYLES *see* ALTERNATIVE LIFESTYLES

LIFE-THREATENING BEHAVIOR – (See also: Suicide) – v1-4. 1971-74 – 1 – us UMI [150]

Lifshiz, Y *see* ZIKHRON YA'AKOV

LIFT HER UP, TENDERLY / Lefevre, Robert – 1976. 3 fiches (24x) – 9 – 1.00f – at Libertarian Micro [320]

LIFT THE EMBARGO AGAINST SPAIN; A SURVEY OF THE FACTS, A CALL TO ACTION / Medical Bureau and North American Committee to Aid Spanish Democracy – N.Y., 1938? Fiche W 998. (Blodgett Collection of Spanish Civil War Pamphlets) – 9 – us H.U. College Libr [946]

A LIGA : ORGAM NOTICIOSO, LITTERARIO E DOS INTERESSES GERAES – Sao Francisco, 10 Apr 1921 – 1,5,6 – bl Biblioteca [072]

LIGA VOOR MENSENRECHTEN = LEAGUE FOR THE PROTECTION OF HUMAN RIGHTS – Gent. 97 docs. 1980-1991 – 49mf – 9 – ne IDC [320]

THE LIGAND QUARTERLY – v1-5. 1978-82 – 1 – us UMI [073]

Ligarides, Paisius *see* HISTORY OF THE CONDEMNATION OF THE PATRIARCH NICON

Lige, B *see* KOGUTAD JUTLUSI

Liger, Sieur *see* LA NOUVELLE MAISON RUSTIQUE

LIGERAS E INSIGNIFICANTES OBSERVACIONES SOBRE ALGUNOS PUNTOS CUESTIONABLES Y DUDOSOS EN LA HISTORIA DE MERIDA / Fadon Sanchez, Antonio – Merida: Joaquin Soler, 1906 – 1 – sp Bibl Santa Ana [946]

LIGERO APUNTE DE LA LOCALIDAD CACERENA DE PESCUEZA / Gutierrez Macias, Valeriano – Badajoz: Dip. Provincial, 1970. Sep. REE – 1 – sp Bibl Santa Ana [946]

DE LIGGEREN EN ANDERE HISTORISCHE ARCHIEVEN DER ANTWERPSCHE SINT LUCAS GILDE / ed by Rombouts, Ph & Lerius, Th van – Antwerpen, 1872-1876 – 2 vols – 9 – ne IDC [700]

Liggins, John *see* THE GREAT VALUE AND SUCCESS OF FOREIGN MISSIONS

LIGHT – 1948-79. Not published 1953-58. Reel includes Christian Life Bulletin, 1955-58. 406p – 1 – 14.21 – us Baptist [240]

LIGHT – San Antonio. Tex. 1882- – 1 – us UMI [071]

LIGHT AND DARKNESS (CCC336) = HEI AN YU KUANG MING / Wu, Yao-tsung – (In Chinese) – Shanghai: Association Press of China, 1949 – 1r – 1 – 1984-6675 – us A.T.L.A. [240]

LIGHT AND LEAVEN : HISTORICAL AND SOCIAL SERMONS TO GENERAL CONGREGATIONS / Henson, H Hensley – London: Methuen, 1897 – 1mf – us A.T.L.A. [240]

LIGHT AND LIFE – 1934-39 (incomplete) – 1r – 1 – ATLA S0706A – us A.T.L.A. [073]

LIGHT AND LIFE – (Title varies: The Free Methodist, 1868-1970) – 1868-1976 (complete) – 51r – 1 – ATLA S0322 – us A.T.L.A. [073]

LIGHT AND LIGHTING AND ENVIRONMENTAL DESIGN – v. 6-64. 1913-71 – 1,5,6 – us Princeton Micro [621]

THE LIGHT BEARER – Reno, NV. 1994 – 1+ r – 1 – $50.00 ($50.00y) – U04880 – us Library Micro [071]

LIGHT BREAKING THROUGH / Hayward, Mildred – 1937 – 1r – 1 – us Ross [810]

"THE LIGHT BY WHICH WE SEE LIGHT" : OR, NATURE AND THE SCRIPTURES: A COURSE OF LECTURES DELIVERED BEFORE THE THEOLOGICAL SEMINARY AND RUTGERS COLLEGE / Lewis, Tayler – NY: Board of Publication of the RCA, 1875 – 1mf – 9 – 0-8370-4101-5 – 1985-2101 – us A.T.L.A. [210]

THE LIGHT BY WHICH WE SEE LIGHT, OR, NATURE AND THE SCRIPTURES: A COURSE OF LECTURES / Lewis, Taylor – New York: Pub. Bd. of R.C.A., 1875. 1 fiche – 9 – us A.T.L.A. [240]

A LIGHT FROM THE ANCIENT EAST / Deissmann, Gustav Adolf – 1910 – 9 – us I.R.C. [950]

LIGHT FROM THE EAST, OR THE WITNESS OF THE MONUMENTS / Hall, C J – 1899 – 9 – $15.00 – us I.R.C. [930]

LIGHT IN AUGUST – Concordance to the novel – 12mf – 9 – us UMI [420]

LIGHT IN THE DARKNESS, OR, CHRISTIANITY AND PAGANISM...AROUND THE GLOBE / Birkeland, Knut Bergesen – Minneapolis: Minnehaha Publ., 1900. 669p. 2 fiches – 9 – us A.T.L.A. [240]

THE LIGHT INVISIBLE / Benson, Robert Hugh – New York: Benziger, 1903 – 1mf – 9 – 0-8370-7122-4 – 1986-1122 – us A.T.L.A. [240]

THE LIGHT OF ALL AGES / Carlyle, Gavin – London:Strahan, 1873 – 1mf – 9 – 0-8370-3182-6 – 1985-1182 – us A.T.L.A. [240]

THE LIGHT OF ASIA, OR, THE GREAT RENUNCIATION (MAHBHINISHKRAMANA)... / Arnold, Edwin – London: Trbner, 1879 – 1 roll – 1 – 1-55879-584-7 – uk Libr Preservation [280]

LIGHT OF HOPE – Portland, OR. Mar 1966-Dec 1970. – 1 – us U.O. Library [071]

THE LIGHT OF THE OCEAN = YUNG KUANG – (In Chinese) – nos 4-236. 1955-68 (complete) – 2r – 1 – ATLA S0321 – us A.T.L.A. [073]

LIGHT OF THE SUN AS REVEALED IN THE BOOK OF GENESIS / Cyrus, Enoch – Providence: Sun Publishing, 1908. 1 fiche – 9 – us A.T.L.A. [240]

THE LIGHT OF THE SUN AS REVEALED IN THE BOOK OF GENESIS / Cyrus, Enoch – Providence, RI: Sun Publishing Co., c1908 – 1mf – 9 – 0-8370-2800-0 – 1985-0800 – us A.T.L.A. [220]

LIGHT ON INDONESIA / Lim, Ek Cheang – SE-11,982 1. 1949 – 9 – ne IDC [360]

LIGHT ON LIFE'S DUTIES / Meyer, Frederick Brotherton – New York: Fleming H Revell, c1895 – 1mf – 9 – 0-8370-6336-1 – 1986-0336 – us A.T.L.A. [240]

LIGHT ON MASONRY : A COLLECTION OF ALL THE MOST IMPORTANT DOCUMENTS / Bernard, David – Utica, NY: William Williams, 1829 – 7mf – 9 – $10.50 – LLMC 91-508 – us L.L.M.C. [360]

LIGHT ON THE DARK RIVER : OR, MEMORIALS OF MRS. HENRIETTA A.L. HAMLIN: MISSIONARY IN TURKEY / Lawrence, Margarette Woods – 3rd ed. Boston: Ticknor, Reed, and Fields, 1854, c1853 – 1mf – 9 – 0-8370-6576-3 – 1986-0576 – us A.T.L.A. [920]

A LIGHT TO LILIE / Danes, John – 1637. 143p. (English Linguistics Series 1500-1800) – 9 – us UMI [420]

THE LIGHT WITHIN; THE STORY OF MARIA MONTESSORI / Smaridge, Norah – Illus. by Janet and Alex d'Amato. New York: Hawthorn Books, 1965. 172p. illus – 1 – us U.W. Library [370]

LIGHTBEARER – v1- – 1 – uk World [240]

THE LIGHT-BEARERS – HOME MISSION HEROES *see* AMERICAN PRESBYTERIANA 1

Lightfoot, J *see*
- FLORA SCOTICA

Lightfoot, Joseph B *see*
- THE APOSTOLIC FATHERS
- THE CHRISTIAN MINISTRY
- DISSERTATIONS ON THE APOSTOLIC AGE
- HISTORICAL ESSAYS
- LEADERS IN THE NORTHERN CHURCH
- ST. PAUL'S EPISTLE TO THE PHILIPPIANS
- SAINT PAUL'S EPISTLE TO THE PHILIPPIANS: A REVISED TEXT
- SAINT PAUL'S EPISTLES TO THE COLOSSIANS AND TO PHILEMON

Lightfoot, Joseph B et al *see* REVISION OF THE ENGLISH VERSION OF THE NEW TESTAMENT

Lightfoot, Joseph Barber *see*
- BIBLICAL ESSAYS
- ON A FRESH REVISION OF THE ENGLISH NEW TESTAMENT
- SAINT PAUL'S EPISTLE TO THE GALATIANS

LIGHTHOUSE = TENG T'A – (In Chinese) – v1-138. 1956-67 (complete) – 3r – 1 – ATLA S0315 – us A.T.L.A. [073]

LIGHTHOUSE DEEDS AND CONTRACTS, 1790-1853 / U.S. Coast Guard – M94 – 2r – 1 – us Nat'l Archives [975]

LIGHTHOUSE LETTERS, 1792-1809 / U.S. Coast Guard – M63 – 3r – 1 – us Nat'l Archives [977]

LIGHTING DIMENSIONS – v. 1-. 1977- – 1,5,6,9 – us UMI [621]

LIGHTING RESEARCH AND TECHNOLOGY – v1- 1969- 1; v7- 5,6; v8- 9 – us UMI [621]

LIGHTNING FLASHES AND THUNDERBOLTS / Jones, Samuel Porter – 1912 – 9 – us A.T.L.A. [240]

LIGHTS AND SHADES OF MISSIONARY LIFE... IN THE REGION OF LAKE SUPERIOR / Pitezel, John H – Cincinnati: Western Book Concern, 1861. 431p. 1 fiche – 9 – us A.T.L.A. [240]

LIGHTS AND SHADOWS OF AMERICAN LIFE / Dixon, A C – New York: Fleming H. Revell, c1898 – 1mf – us A.T.L.A. [306]

LIGHTS AND SHADOWS OF CHURCH HISTORY : FROM THE APOSTOLIC TIMES TO THE PRESENT DAY: A SERIES OF SHORT SERMONS / Hardman, William – 2nd ed. New York: James Pott, 1889 – 1mf – 9 – 0-8370-7154-2 – 1986-1154 – us A.T.L.A. [240]

LIGHTS AND SHADOWS OF CHURCH-LIFE IN AUSTRALIA : INCLUDING THOUGHTS ON SOME THINGS AT HOME / Binney, T – London: Jackson & Walford, 1860 – 1mf – us A.T.L.A. [240]

LIGHTS AND SHADOWS OF CLERICAL LIFE / Cheetham, William – Montreal: Lovell, 1879. 00596. (Pre-1900 Canadiana) – 9 – cn C.I.H.M. [240]

LIGHTS AND SHADOWS OF MISSION WORK IN THE FAR EAST : BEING THE RECORD OF OBSERVATIONS MADE DURING A VISIT TO THE SOUTHERN PRESBYTERIAN MISSIONS IN JAPAN, CHINA, AND KOREA IN THE YEAR 1897 / Chester, Samuel Hall – Richmond, VA: Presbyterian Committee of Publ, c1899 – 1mf – 9 – 0-8370-6034-6 – 1986-0034 – us A.T.L.A. [240]

LIGHTS AND SHADOWS OF NEW YORK CITY LIFE / McCabe, James D – (The work gives a lot of coverage to the political corruption of the Tammy Ring, crime, police and courts of the period) – Philadelphia, Chicago, St Louis: National Publ Co, 1879 – 9mf – 9 – $13.50 – LLMC 92-176 – us L.L.M.C. [910]

Lightwood, John M *see* THE NATURE OF POSITIVE LAW

LES LIGNES DE FORCE DU PLAN 1971-1975 / Belgium. Bureau de Programmation Economique – D-953 1 – 9 – ne IDC [338]

LIGONIER AMERICAN – Ligonier, PA., 1913-1936 – 13 – $25.00r – us I.M.R. [071]

LIGONIER ECHO – Ligonier, PA. -w 1977-1988 – 13 – $25.00r – us I.M.R. [071]

Ligot, Maurice *see* LAICISME ET LAICITE...

Ligue de defense des libertes publiques (Haiti) *see* BULLETIN

LIGUE DES DROITS DE L'HOMME = LEAGUE FOR HUMAN RIGHTS – Paris. 87 docs. 1982-1991 – 28mf – 9 – ne IDC [320]

La Ligue Syndicale pour la Defense des Interets du Travail, de l'Industrie et du Commerce *see* LA REVENDICATION

LIGUE TUNISIENNE POUR LA DEFENSE DES DROITS DE L'HOMME (LTDH) = TUNISIAN LEAGUE FOR HUMAN RIGHTS – Tunis. 9 docs. 1982-1990 – 6mf – 9 – ne IDC [320]

LIIKETALOUDELLINEN AIKAKAUSKIRJA = FINNISH JOURNAL OF BUSINESS ECONOMICS – v1- 1952- 1; v26- 1977- 5,6,9 – us UMI [338]

Lijftocht, F *see* VOOR-WINCKEL VAN PATIENTIE IN DEN DROEVEN TEGENSPOEDT

LIJST DER NEDERLANDSCHE HANDSCHRIFTEN IN DE KEIZERLIJKE BIBLIOTHEEK TE ST PETERSBURG / Welter, W L – Leiden, 1856 – 1mf – 9 – ne IDC [090]

LIJST DER NEDERLANDSCHE HANDSCHRIFTEN IN DE KEIZERLIJKE BIBLIOTHEEK TE ST PETERSBURG / Welter, W L – Leiden. 1856. List of manuscripts from the Netherlands (15-18th cents. in the Saltykov-Shchedrin Library (GPB). BR-9896 1 – 9 – ne IDC [010]

LIKE ALL THE NATIONS? JERUSALEM. 1930. BJ-28-17/1 / Magnes, J L – 9 – ne IDC [956]

LIKE AND UNLIKE / Braddon, Mary Elizabeth – British Fiction Archive: Unit 5 – 9 – uk Bell [830]

Likert, R *see* SOME APPLICATIONS OF BEHAVIOURAL RESEARCH

Likhachev, D S *see* KUL'TURA RUSI EPOKHI OBRAZOVANIIA RUSSKOGO NATSIONAL' NOGO GOSUDARSTVA (KONETS 14-NACHALO 16 V.)

Likhachev, N P *see*
- BIBLIOTEKA I ARKHIV MOSKOVSKIKH GOSUDAREI V 16 STOLETII
- BUMAGA I DREVNEISHIIA BUMAZHNYIA MEL'NITSY V MOSKOVSKOM GOSUDARSTVE
- IZ LEKTSII PO DIPLOMATIKE, CHITANNOI V SPB. ARKHEOLOGICHESKOM INSTITUTE
- KHOZHDENIE SV. APOSTOLA I EVANGELISTA IOANNA BOGOSLOVA
- LITSEVOE ZHITIE SVIATYKH BLAGOVERNYKH KNIAZEI RUSSKIKH BORISA I GLEBA
- RAZRIADNYE DIAKI 16 VEKA; OPYT ISTORIKO-IURIDICHESKAGO IZSLEDOVANIIA
- SBORNIK AKTOV SOBRANYKH V ARKHIVAKH I BIBLIOTEKAKH

LI-KHEVOD HA-TORAH VE-LI-KHEVOD LOMEDEHA – (Havazzelet, Jerusalem, 16th Tammuz, 5647). 1887. BJ-27-212 1 – 9 – ne IDC [270]

LIKKUTIM LA-PERUSH AL HA-TORAH / Malkhi, R M – pt. 1. Jerusalem. 1923. BJ-27-16 1 – 9 – ne IDC [470]

LILBURN FIRST BAPTIST CHURCH. LILBURN, GEORGIA : CHURCH RECORDS – 1840-1965. Membership Roll, 1891-1968. 1352p – 2r – 1 – $60.84 – us Baptist [240]

Lile, William Minor *see* NOTES TO V. 1 MINOR'S INSTITUTES

Lileev, M I *see* OPISANIE RUKOPISEI KHRANIASHCHIKHSIA V BIBLIOTEKE CHERNIGOVSKOI DUKHOVNOI SEMINARII

LES LILIACEES / Redoute, P J – (Les Roses. 1 reel. 1) – Different varieties of lilies printed in color, retouched by hand, with list of synonyms, detailed descriptions and observations on their history and cultivation. 3 reels.(Collections of the Department of Prints and Photographs) – 1 – fr Bibl Nationale [580]

LES LILIACEES / Redoute, P J – Paris. 1802-08. B-7356 1 – 9 – ne IDC [580]

LILIAN'S RETROSPECT / Bartley, E T – Toronto: Hunter, Rose, 1877. 03499. (Pre-1900 Canadiana) – 9 – cn C.I.H.M. [830]

Lilienblum, M L *see* KOL KITVEI

LILIENCRON / Leip, Hans – 1.-5. Tausend. Stuttgart: Cotta, 1938 – 1r – 1 – us U.W. Library [920]

Liliencron, Detlev, Freiherr von *see* GEDICHTE

Lilienfeld, Karl *see* ARENT DE GELDER, SEIN LEBEN UND SEINE KUNST

LILIENTHALER-KURIER : BEILAGE ZUM BREMER WESER-KURIER – Lilienthal, Germany. 12 Apr 1972- – 1 – gw Mikrofilm [072]

LILIIA I SERP. TRET'IA KNIGA STIKHOV / Baltrushaitis, Iu – YMCA-Press. Paris. 1948. BR-558 2 – 8 – ne IDC [460]

Liljencrantz, John *see* SPIRITISM AND RELIGION.

LILLA EDET-POSTEN – Lilla Edet, Trollhaettan. 1928-68 – 9 – sw Kungliga [072]

LILLA EDET-POSTEN *see*
- TROLLHATTAN
- TROLLHATTANS TIDNING

LILLA EDETS TIDNING – Goteborg, Sweden. 1889-92 – 1 reel – 1 – sw Kungliga [072]

Lille, Abraham J van *see* THE NATIVE COUNCIL SYSTEM WITH SPECIAL REFERENCE TO THE TRANSVAAL LOCAL COUNCILS.

Lille, Alain de *see* THE COMPLAINT OF NATURE

Lille, Jean *see* L'ENSEIGNEMENT QU'ON APPELLE AGRICOLE ET L'EVOLUTION DES ESPACES SOCIAUX A TRAVERS L'EXEMPLE DE LA BASSE-NORMANDIE

LILLE NORGE AVISEN – Toronto. 1944-45 – 1 – 85.00 – cn McLaren [948]

Lilley, Alfred Leslie *see* MODERNISM

Lilley, James Philip *see*
- THE PASTORAL EPISTLES: A NEW TRANSLATION
- THE PRINCIPLES OF PROTESTANTISM
- THE VICTORY OF THE GOSPEL

THE LILLIAN WALD PAPERS – from Columbia University, New York, 1895-1936 – us Primary [360]

Lilljeborg, W *see* SVERIGES OCH NORGES FISKARNE FAUNA

Lillo y Herrero, G *see* INSTRUCTIO MEDICORUM APPOLLINEAM AGGREDIENTIBUS VALDE UTILIS

Lilly, William Samuel *see*
- ANCIENT RELIGION AND MODERN THOUGHT
- THE CLAIMS OF CHRISTIANITY
- ESSAYS AND SPEECHES
- THE GREAT ENIGMA

LILY – v1-8 (all publ). 1849-1856 – 1 reel – 1 – $115.00 – us UPA [360]

LILY AMONG THE THORNS: A STUDY OF THE BIBLICAL DRAMA ENTITLED THE SONG OF SONGS / Griffis, William Elliot – Boston: Houghton, Mifflin, 1890.1 fiche – 9 – us A.T.L.A. [240]

THE LILY AMONG THORNS : A STUDY OF THE BIBLICAL DRAMA ENTITLED THE SONG OF SONGS / Griffis, William Elliot – Boston:Houghton, Mifflin, 1890, c1889 – 1mf – 9 – 0-8370-3394-2 – 1985-1394 – us A.T.L.A. [220]

THE LILY AND THE CROSS: A TALE OF ACADIA / De Mille, James – Boston: Lee and Shepard, 1874. 02632. (Pre-1900 Canadiana) – 9 – cn C.I.H.M. [830]

Lily, William *see*
- A SHORTE INTRODUCTION OF GRAMMAR

LILYDALE EXPRESS – 1921-1956/1965 – 14r – 1 – at Corangamite [072]

LILYDALE MAIL – 1929 – 1r – 1 – at Corangamite [072]

Lim, Ek Cheang *see* LIGHT ON INDONESIA

Lim, Kwi Tie N *see* PELADJARAN BAHASA TIONGHWA, DENGAN KAMOES HARIAN INDONESIA-TIONGHWA, PERKATAAN BIASA DAN SADERHANA. TJETAKAN 1

Lim, Mija *see* ZUR SYNTAX DES KOREANISCHEN

LIMA ANTIGUA. ESTUDIO BIOGRAFICO DEL AUTOR POR EVARISTO SAN CRISTOVAL. LIMA, 1935 / Patron, Pablo – Madrid: Razon y Fe, 1936 – 1 – sp Bibl Santa Ana [920]

Lima, Araujo *see* AMAZONIA. A TERRA E O HOMEM

Lima. (City). Consejo Provincal *see* BOLETIN MUNICIPAL

LIMA COURIER – Lima, Ohio. 1877-1916 – 5r – 1 – $32.50r – us Archival [071]

LIMA DAILY NEWS – Lima, Ohio. 1901-1919 – 8r – 1 – $32.50r – us Archival [071]

Lima, M A *see* L'ART RUPESTRE DE LA LAPA DO VEADO, JANUARIA, MONTALVANIA, BRESIL

Lima, Ohio *see* MISCELLANEOUS EARLY NEWSPAPERS

Lima. Ohio. Trinity United Methodist Church *see* RECORDS

LIMA TIMES-DEMOCRAT – Lima, Ohio. 1905-1920 – 16r – 1 – $32.50r – us Archival [071]

Limbaugh, R H *see* JOHN MUIR PAPERS, 1858-1957

Limborch, P van *see* PHILIPPUS VAN LIMBORCHS VRIENDELIJKE ONDERHANDELING MET EEN GELEERDEN JOOD,. URIELS ACOSTAAS VOORBEELD VAN 'T MENSCHELIJK LEVEN

DIE LIMBURGER CHRONIK DES TILEMANN ELHEN VON WOLFHAGEN (MGH 8: 4.BD. 1.ABT) – (2. Abt: Die Kreuzfahrt Des Landgrafen Ludwigs Des Frommen Von Thueringen, 1923) – 1883 – Dfl32.00 – ne Slangenburg [240]

LA LIME – Quebec, Canada. 18 nov 1863-23 jan 1864 – 1r – 1 – Can$40.00 – cn Can Microfilming [072]

LIMELIGHT – Big Bear Lake. Calif. -w. 1948-58 – 1 – us UMI [071]

LIMERICK AND CLARE EXAMINER – Ireland.1846-Jun 1855.-w. 9 1/2 reels – 1 – uk British Libr Newspaper [072]

LIMERICK CHRONICLE – Ireland. -sw. 13 Oct 1768-2 Aug 1800; 1832-68; 1879-1975. 158 reels – 1 – uk British Libr Newspaper [072]

LIMERICK CHRONICLE – Ireland.1 reel – 1 – ie Microforms [072]

LIMERICK EVENING POST – Limerick. Ireland. -tw. 1 Jan-26 Feb 1828, 14 Mar 1828-6 Apr 1832, 23 Oct 1832-29 Mar 1833, 2 Aug-17 Dec 1833. (5 reels) – 1 – uk British Libr Newspaper [072]

LIMERICK GUARDIAN – Limerick. Ireland. -w. 12 Oct-23 Nov 1833. (7 ft) – 1 – uk British Libr Newspaper [072]

LIMERICK HERALD – (Limerick Evening Herald). Limerick. Ireland. -sw. 18 Apr 1831-14 Apr 1835. (Wanting 1834). (3 reels) – 1 – uk British Libr Newspaper [072]

LIMERICK LEADER – Ireland. Jun 1893-Dec 1904.-w. 11mqn reels – 1 – uk British Libr Newspaper [072]

LIMERICK OBSERVER ETC – Ireland.19 Apr 1856-25 Jul 1857. -w. 1 reel – 1 – uk British Libr Newspaper [072]

LIMERICK REPORTER – Limerick. Ireland. -sw. 12 Jul 1839-Dec 1855. (16 reels) – 1 – uk British Libr Newspaper [072]

LIMERICK STANDARD – Limerick. Ireland. -sw. 10 Mar 1837-30 Dec 1841. (5 reels) – 1 – uk British Libr Newspaper [072]

LIMERICK STAR AND EVENING POST – Limerick. Ireland. -w. 7 Feb 1834-11 May 1838. (4 reels) – 1 – uk British Libr Newspaper [072]

LIMERICK TIMES – Limerick. Ireland. -sw. 30 Jun 1834-13 Feb 1837. (2 reels) – 1 – uk British Libr Newspaper [072]

LIMERICK, TIPPARARY AND WATERFORD EXAMINER *see* TIPPERARY EXAMINER ETC

THE LIMES TRIPOLITANUS IN THE LIGHT OF RECENT DISCOVERIES / Goodchild, R G – (Journal of Roman Studies). v. 39. 1949; v. 40. 1950. BA-652 2 – 8 – ne IDC [930]

LIMESTONE DEMOCRAT – Athens, AL. 1937; 1941-44; 1947-49 – 1 – us UMI [071]

LIMESTONE SPRINGS BAPTIST CHURCH. GHEROKEE COUNTY. GAFFNEY, SOUTH CAROLINA : CHURCH RECORDS – 1886-1920; 1967-77. Treasurer's Reports, 1926-57. Formerly called Ephesus Baptist Church, Lime's Spring Baptist Church and Limestone – 1 – 22.95 – us Baptist [240]

LIMITATION OF SHIPOWNER'S LIABILITY AND ... / Bisschop, W R – London, 1927 – 1mf – 9 – ILM-3347/1 – ne IDC [327]

LIMITATIONS OF ACTIONS AGAINST TRUSTEES AND RELIEF FROM LIABILITY FOR TECHNICAL BREACHES OF TRU / Anglin, Francis Alexander – Toronto: Canada Law Book Co., 1900. 02404. (Pre-1900 Canadiana) – 9 – cn C.I.H.M. [340]

LIMITATIONS OF POWER OF SUPREME COURT TO DECLARE ACTS OF CONGRESS UNCONSTITUTIONAL / Johnsen, Julia Emily – New York, Wilson Co., 1936. 276 p. LL-1438 – 1 – us L of C Photodup [340]

LIMITATIONS ON THE TREATY-MAKING POWER UNDER THE CONSTITUTION OF THE UNITED STATES / Tucker, Henry George – Boston: Little, Brown, 1915. 444p LL-1342 – 1 – us L of C Photodup [340]

LIMITES ENTRE LAS REPUBLICAS DEL ECUADOR Y DEL PERU / Canalejas y Mendez, J – Madrid, 1905 – 1mf – 9 – ILM-2381/1 – ne IDC [327]

LES LIMITES ET LES DIVISIONS TERRITORIALES DE LA FRANCE EN 1789 / Brette, Armand – Paris: E. Cornely, 1907.vii,120p. 2 fiches. (Statistics Series: Topography) – 9 – 6.00 – fr Bibl Nationale [944]

THE LIMITS OF RELIGIOUS THOUGHT...EIGHT LECTURES / Mansel, Henry Longueville – London: John Murray, 1867. 1 fiche – 9 – us A.T.L.A. [240]

THE LIMITS OF THE EFFECTIVENESS OF THE STATE / Humboldt, Wilhelm, Freiherr von – 1792. 220p. 1 fiche (24x) – 9 – 1.00f – at Libertarian Micro [320]

Limmer, Rupert *see* DER TOTE GAST

Limminghe, A de *see* FLORE MYCOLOGIQUE DE GENTINNES

LIMNOLOGICAL BIBLIOGRAPHY OF MALAWI – 1986 – 82p – it F.A.O. [550]

Limochel, F *see* LA FRANCE DEMANDANT SES COLONIES, OU RECLAMATIONS DE L'AGRICULTURE, DU COMMERCE, DES MANUFACTURES, DES ARTISTES ET DES OUVRIERS DE TOUS LES DEPARTEMENTS ADRESSEES AU CORPS LEGISLATIF...

Lin, Chih-szu *see* CATECHISM (CCC158)

Lin, Han-ying *see* PEACE ON EARTH (CCC220)

Lin, Pu-chi *see* AN INTRODUCTION TO THE CREEDS (CCC221)

LINACRE QUARTERLY – v1- 1932- 1; v38-5,6; v43- 9 – us UMI [073]

Linacre, Thomas *see*
- DE EMENDATA STRUCTURA LATINI SERMONIS LIBRI SEX
- RUDIMENTA GRAMMATICES

UN LINAJE EXTREMENOS, LOS MORENO DE DON BENITO / Moreno, Joaquin & Nieto, Manuel – Badajoz: (Imp. Diputacion Provincial), 1975. Sep. E. Est. Extremenos – 1 – sp Bibl Santa Ana [920]

Linares de Sapir, Olga *see* CULTURAL CHRONOLOGY OF THE GULF OF CHIRIQUI, PANAMA

LINCHAN HUAXUE YU GONGYE – Chemistry and Industry of Forest Products. 1981-86. F/P 277 – 9 – $4.50f – cc Microforms [073]

Lincke, Karl F A *see* SAMARIA UND SEINE PROPHETEN: EIN RELIGIONSGESCHICHTLICHER VERSUCH

Linckenheld, Emil *see* DER HEXAMETER BEI KLOPSTOCK UND VOSS

LINCOLN – Maceio, Alagoas. 24 Jul, Out-Nov 1884; Jul, Set 1885; Mar 1887; Abr, 17 Maio 1888 – 1,5,6 – bl Biblioteca [072]

Lincoln *see* THE HISTORY OF NEW IPSWICH

Lincoln, Abraham *see*
- COLLECTED PAPERS, MS 3031
- PAPERS
- ROBERT TODD LINCOLN COLLECTION OF PAPERS OF A. LINCOLN

LINCOLN AND SALEM / Onstot, T G – Pioneers of Menard and Mason Counties. Forest City: 1902. Illinois Reel 42. (The Cox Library Collection) – 5 – us Americana [978]

Lincoln, Benjamin *see* BENJAMIN LINCOLN PAPERS, 1635-1964

Lincoln Cathedral. Library *see*
- THE MEDIAEVAL MANUSCRIPT COLLECTION
- MUSIC COLLECTION: 15TH-19TH CENTURIES
- SEVENTEENTH CENTURY PAMPHLETS

LINCOLN CLARION – Jefferson City. Mo. v. 10, no. 1-v. 22, no. 4. 23 Oct 1942-15 Oct 1954 – 1 – us NY Public [071]

LINCOLN CLARION. LINCOLN UNIV – Jefferson City. Mo. 1963-65 – 1 – us UMI [071]

LINCOLN COUNTY HERALD – Toledo OR. Sep 30 1926 – 1 – us U.O. Library [071]

LINCOLN COUNTY INDEPENDENT – Pioche, NV. 1938-41 (incomplete) – 2r – 1 – $100.00 – U04642 – us Library Micro [071]

LINCOLN COUNTY JOURNAL – North Platte, NE. -w. Jul-Dec 1905; Apr-May 1907 – 1 – us NE Hist [071]

LINCOLN COUNTY LEADER – Toledo. Or. -w. 1904-63 – 1 – us UMI [071]

LINCOLN COUNTY LEADER – Toledo, OR. -w. 1904-63 – 1 – 504.00 – us Oregon Hist [071]

LINCOLN COUNTY LEADER – Toledo, OR. -w. 9 Mar 1893-25 Nov 1904, 2 rolls; 2 Jan 1964-. – 1 – us U.O. Library [071]

LINCOLN COUNTY PRESS – Oceanlake, OR. -w. 10 Oct 1929-6 Aug 1931. 1 roll – 1 – us U.O. Library [071]

LINCOLN COUNTY RECORD – Caliente, NV. 1900-1905; 1926-1931; 1968 – 27+ r – 1 – $1,350.00 ($50.00y) – UN04663 – us Library Micro [071]

LINCOLN COUNTY RECORD – Newport OR. Aug 27 1895 – 1 – us U.O. Library [071]

LINCOLN COUNTY RECORD *see* RECORD

LINCOLN COUNTY SENTINEL – Toledo OR. Oct 31 1913 – 1 – us U.O. Library [071]

LINCOLN COUNTY TIMES – Brookhaven. Miss. 1902-1937 – 1 – us UMI [071]

LINCOLN COUNTY TIMES – Waldport, OR. -w. 4 Dec 1941-28 Oct 1965. 10 rolls – 1 – us U.O. Library [071]

LINCOLN COUNTY TRIBUNE – North Platte, NE. -w. Sept 1885-Jan 1887, scattered issues missing; Mar 1887-Sept 1888; Dec 1888-Apr 1894, scattered issues missing; Dec 1894-May 1898; Jul 1899-Dec 1902; May 1908-Feb 1963 – 1 – us NE Hist [071]

LINCOLN DAILY GLOBE – Lincoln, NE. Jul 1876-May 1881, scattered issues missing – 1 – us NE Hist [071]

LINCOLN DAILY POST – Lincoln, NE. Aug 1896-Jan 1900; May 1900-Jan 1905, scattered issues missing – 1 – us NE Hist [071]

LINCOLN DAILY SUN – Lincoln, NE. Feb-Sept 1892 – 1 – us NE Hist [071]

LINCOLN EVENING CALL – Lincoln, NE. -d. Jun 1879-Jan 1885, scattered issues missing; Oct 1885-Nov 1886; Jan 1887-Jul 1898 – 1 – us NE Hist [071]

LINCOLN EVENING JOURNAL – Lincoln, NE. -d. Sept 1881-Sept 1887; Apr 1888 to date – 1 – us NE Hist [071]

LINCOLN FARM AND HOME NEWS – Lincoln, NE. -w. Jan 1911-Nov 1937; Feb-Apr 1938; Sept 1938-Mar 1953 – 1 – us NE Hist [071]

LINCOLN FREIE PRESSE – Lincoln, NE. -w, 3 Sep 1891-14 Apr 1925 – 1 – us NE Hist [071]

LINCOLN GAZETTE – England. Lincoln, Boston & Newark Tuesday's Gazette Lincoln, Boston, Gainsborough & Newark Gazette. -w. 2 Jan 1835 12 Oct 1841. 2 1 2 reels – 1 – uk British Libr Newspaper [072]

LINCOLN GAZETTE – Lincoln, NE. -m. May 1972 to date – 1 – us NE Hist [071]

LINCOLN HEIGHTS BULLETIN-NEWS – Los Angeles. Calif. -bw. 1919-64 – 1 – us UMI [071]

LINCOLN HERALD – Lincoln, NE. -w. Mar 1890-Nov 1894; Jun 1895-Dec 1899, scattered issues missing; Nov 1904-Jan 1936 – 1 – us NE Hist [071]

LINCOLN INDEPENDENT – Lincoln, NE. -w. Aug 1895-Jan 1896 – 1 – us NE Hist [071]

LINCOLN LAW REVIEW – Buffalo. v1-6. 1927-32 – 1 – $40.00 – us Hein [073]

LINCOLN LAW REVIEW – v. 11-. 1979- – 1,5,6,9 – us UMI [340]

LINCOLN LAW REVIEW – (v1-15 1965-84 on reel $129.00. v16-21 1945-93 on mf $74.00) – v1-21. 1965-93 – 5,6,9 – $203.00 set – us Hein [340]

A LINCOLN LEARNER'S ORIGINAL / ed by Cathey, James H et al – [S.l.: s.n, 199-?] – 35mf – 9 – us Schnappsburg [976]

LINCOLN MONITOR – Hamlin. West Virginia. 1909-1917 – 1 – us UMI [071]

Lincoln, Nebraska Unicameral Legislature *see* NEBRASKA

LINCOLN PARKER – Wyandotte. Mich. 1952-1954 – 1 – us UMI [071]

LINCOLN RECORD SOCIETY – (Coll title: Publications of the English Record Societies, 1835-1972...) – v1-50. 1911-56 – 209mf – 9 – £1,316.00 – uk Chadwyck [941]

LINCOLN REPUBLICAN – Hamlin. West Virginia. 1910-1957; 1959-1962 – 1 – us UMI [071]

LINCOLN RETAILER – Lincoln, NE. -w. Feb 1933-Oct 1935 – 1 – us NE Hist [071]

LINCOLN SHOPPING NEWS – Lincoln, NE. -w. Feb 1954-Jul 1958 – 1 – us NE Hist [071]

LINCOLN STAATS ANZEIGER – Lincoln, NE. -w. Nov 1883; Aug 1885; Sept 1891-Mar 1901 – 1 – us NE Hist [071]

LINCOLN STAR – Lincoln, NE. -d. Oct 1902 to date – 1 – us NE Hist [071]

LINCOLN STREET BAPTIST CHURCH. PORTLAND, OREGON : CHURCH RECORDS – 1924-63 – 1 – 68.67 – us Baptist [240]

LINCOLN SVENSKA TRIBUN – Lincoln, NE. -w. Apr 1901-Jan 1902; Apr-May 1902; Jul 1902-Mar 1904 – 1 – us NE Hist [071]

LINCOLN THE CAPITOL CITY AND LANCASTER COUNTY / Sawyer, Andrew J – Chicago: S.J. Clarke Publ. Co., 1916. v1, Nebraska Reel 10. v2, Nebraska Reel 11. (The Cox Library Collection) – 5 – us Americana [978]

LINCOLN TRIBUNE – Lincoln, NE. -w. Nov-Dec 1918; Jan-Oct 1920 – 1 – us NE Hist [071]

LINCOLN WEEKLY CALL – Lincoln, NE. Apr 1889-Oct 1890; Dec 1891-Jul 1898 – 1 – us NE Hist [071]

LINCOLN WEEKLY GLOBE – Lincoln, NE. Jul 1877; Mar 1878; Jun-Dec 1880; Sept 1881 – 1 – us NE Hist [071]

LINCOLN WEEKLY STAR – Lincoln, NE. Apr 1911-Mar 1912 – 1 – us NE Hist [071]

Lincoln, William *see*
- LECTURES ON THE EPISTLE TO THE HEBREWS
- LECTURES ON THE EPISTLES OF ST JOHN
- NOTES OF LECTURES ON THE EPISTLE TO THE HEBREWS

LINCOLN-DOUGLAS DEBATES – 1 – us Ross [976]

LINCOLNIANA ESSENTIALS – 35mf – $150.00 – us Schnappsburg [976]

LINCOLNLAND SUN – Bennet, NE. -w. Jan. 1911-Sep. 1922; Nov. 1922-Jan. 1923. Incomplete; Feb. 1923- – 1 – us NE Hist [071]

LINCOLN'S INN : ITS ANCIENT AND MODERN BUILDINGS / Spillsbury, William H – 2nd ed. London: Reeves & Turner, 1873 – 3mf – 9 – $4.50 – LLMC 84 314 – us L.L.M.C. [720]

LINCOLN'S INN : THE RECORDS AND BLACK BOOKS / Lincoln's Inn. London; ed by Baildon, W P – v1-5. 1897-1968 (all publ) – 28mf – 9 – $42.00 – LLMC 84-303 – us L.L.M.C. [340]

LINCOLN'S INN : STAGE 2 – 2903mf – 9 – H-1785-1788/1 – ne IDC [340]

LINCOLN'S INN; ITS ANCIENT AND MODERN BUILDINGS, WITH AN ACCOUNT OF THE LIBRARY / Spilsbury, William Holden – London: W. Pickering, 1850. xvi,324p. illus – 1 – us U.W. Library [720]

Lincoln's Inn. London *see* LINCOLN'S INN

LINCOLNSHIRE, 1822 : BRITISH ISLES CENSUS DIRECTORIES PROJECT, ENGLAND – (In prep) – at Vine [941]

LINCOLNSHIRE, 1830 : BRITISH ISLES CENSUS DIRECTORIES PROJECT, ENGLAND. VOL 69 – 1mf – 9 – A$9.00 – at Vine [941]

LINCOLNSHIRE, 1841 : BRITISH ISLES CENSUS DIRECTORIES PROJECT, ENGLAND. VOL 235 – 1mf – 9 – A$9.00 – at Vine [941]

LINCOLNSHIRE, 1850 : BRITISH ISLES CENSUS DIRECTORIES PROJECT, ENGLAND – at Vine [941]

LINCOLNSHIRE, 1856 : BRITISH ISLES CENSUS DIRECTORIES PROJECT, ENGLAND. VOL 4 – 6mf – 9 – A$39.00 – at Vine [941]

LINCOLNSHIRE, 1865 : BRITISH ISLES CENSUS DIRECTORIES PROJECT, ENGLAND. VOL 128 – 4mf – 9 – A$27.00 – at Vine [941]

LINCOLNSHIRE, 1876 : BRITISH ISLES CENSUS DIRECTORIES PROJECT, ENGLAND – at Vine [941]

LINCOLNSHIRE, 1889 : BRITISH ISLES CENSUS DIRECTORIES PROJECT, ENGLAND – at Vine [941]

LINCOLNSHIRE, 1922 : BRITISH ISLES CENSUS DIRECTORIES PROJECT, ENGLAND – (In prep) – at Vine [941]

LINCOLNSHIRE BOSTON AND SPALDING FREE PRESS *see* SPALDING FREE PRESS ETC

LINCOLNSHIRE (BOSTON, LINCOLN, GAINSBOROUGH AND STAMFORD), 1805 : BRITISH ISLES CENSUS DIRECTORIES PROJECT, ENGLAND. VOL 166 – 1mf – 9 – A$9.00 – at Vine [941]

LINCOLNSHIRE CHRONICLE AND GENERAL ADVERTISER – Lincoln, England. 1906-07.-w. 2 reels – 1 – uk British Libr Newspaper [072]

LINCOLNSHIRE FREE PRESS *see* SPALDING FREE PRESS ETC

LINCOLNSHIRE STANDARD (ALFORD AND COAST) – (Also known as: Mablethorpe, Alford and Sutton-on-Sea Standard) – 1987-92; Jan-Feb, Mar 5-Jun 25, Jul 1993-96 – 37 1/2r – 1 – uk British Libr Newspaper [072]

LINCOLNSHIRE STANDARD (HORNCASTLE EDN) *see* HORNCASTLE STANDARD

LINCOLNSHIRE STANDARD (LOUTH EDN) *see* LOUTH STANDARD

LINCOLNSHIRE STANDARD (SKEGNESS ED) – (Also known as: Skegness Standard) – 1986-96 – 38r – 1 – uk British Libr Newspaper [072]

LINCOLNSHIRE STANDARD (SLEAFORD ED) *see* SLEAFORD STANDARD

LINCOLNSHIRE STANDARD (SPILSBY ED) – (Also known as: Spilsby Standard) – 1987-92; Jan-Jun 1993 (Friday Ed); Jul 1993-96 – 39 1/2r – 1 – uk British Libr Newspaper [072]

Lind af Hageby, Louise *see* LA FONCTION DE LA FEMME DANS L'EVOLUTION SOCIALE

Lind, Allan *see* A REEVALUATION OF THE CIVIL APPEALS MANAGEMENT PLAN
Lind, E Allan *see*
- EVALUATION OF COURT-ANNEXED ARBITRATION IN THREE FEDERAL DISTRICT COURTS

Lind, J *see*
- AN ESSAY ON THE MOST EFFECTUAL MEANS OF PRESERVING THE HEALTH OF SEAMEN IN THE ROYAL NAVY
- A TREATISE OF THE SCURVY

Lind, John *see*
- LETTERS CONCERNING THE PRESENT STATE OF POLAND: TOGETHER WITH THE MANIFESTO OF THE COURTS OF VIENNA, PETERSBURGH, AND BERLIN, AND THE LETTERS PATENT OF THE KING OF PRUSSIA
- MEXICAN MISSION PAPERS

THE LIND & VISITOR *see* THE CANADIAN MISSIONARY LINK
LINDA TRESSEL / Trollope, Anthony – Edinburgh, London: W. Blackwood, 1868 – 1 roll – 1 – 1-55879-967-2 – uk Libr Preservation [830]
Lindau, B *see* RESHIT LIMMUDIM
Lindau, G *see* THESAURUS LITERATURAE MYCOLOGICAE ET LICHENOLOGICAE
Lindau, Paul *see*
- DER AGENT
- DER KOENIG VON SIDON

Lindau, Rudolf *see* MORGENLAND UND ABENDLAND
LINDAUER ZEITUNG *see*
- SCHWAEBISCHE ZEITUNG

Lindberg, S O *see* EUROPAS OCH NORD AMERIKAS HVITMOSSOR (SPHAGNA)
Lindblad, A *see* QUINTETT FUR 2 VIOLINER, 2 ALTAR OCH VIOLONCELL
Lindblom, Johannes *see* MICHA
Linde, Antonius van der *see*
- MICHAEL SERVET
- DE STRIJENDE GEREFORMEERDE KERK

Linde, Ernst *see* GUDES ERLAEUTERUNGEN DEUTSCHER DICHTUNGEN
Lindeboom, Johannes *see* ERASMUS
Lindeborn, J *see* HISTORIA SIVE NOTITIA EPISCOPATUS DAVENTRIENSIS
Lindell, CG *see* THE CONCEPT OF MISSION IN THE ROMAN CATHOLIC CHURCH IN LIGHT OF VATICAN 2
THE LINDEN HERALD – Linden, CA. 1959-81 – 16r – 1 – $800.00 ($50.00y) – B02343 – us Library Micro [071]
Linden, J J *see* TROISIEME VOYAGE DE J. LINDEN
LINDEN LANE – Princeton, NJ. 1982-1988 – 1r – 1 – $50.00 – R04148 – us Library Micro [071]
Linden, Walther *see*
- GESCHICHTE DER DEUTSCHEN LITERATUR VON DEN ANFAENGEN BIS ZUR GEGENWART
- GOETHE UND DIE DEUTSCHE GEGENWART

Lindenberg, J B W *see*
- SPECIES HEPATHICARUM
- SYNOPSIS HEPATICARUM EUROPAEARUM

Lindenblatt, Joerg *see* UNTERSUCHUNGEN ZUR FUNKTION UND BETEILIGUNG EINES GTP-BINDENDEN PROTEINS AM INTRAZELLULAEREN TRANSPORT IN NEURONALEM GEWEBE
Lindenbrogius, E *see* SCRIPTORES RERUM GERMANICARUM SEPTENTRIONALIUM
LINDENIA : INCONOGRAPHIE DES ORCHIDEES – Gand. v1-17. 1885-1901 – 119mf – 9 – ne IDC [700]
LINDENMAIER/MOEHRING (1950-1980) : NACHSCHLAGEWERK DER RECHTSPRECHUNG DES BUNDESGERICHTSHOFES – 126mf – 9 – ca DM1,800.00 – 3-406-09250-0 – gw Beck [340]
Lindenmeyer, Julius *see*
- ERKLAERUNG DER BRIEFE PETRI
- ERKLAERUNG DER OFFENBARUNG JOHANNES, CAP. 1-12
- ERKLAERUNG DER PROPHETEN MICHA UND JOEL
- ERKLARUNG DER PROPHETEN NAHUM UND ZEPHANJA
- DIE ETHISCHE ERSCHEINUNG DES CHRISTLICHEN LEBENS
- DIE GENETISCHE ANLAGE DES CHRISTLICHEN LEBENS
- DAS GOETTLICHE REICH ALS WELTREICH: NACH DER HEILIGEN SCHRIFT
- DIE PAEDAGOGISCHE ENTWICKLUNG DES CHRISTLICHEN LEBENS
- VORLESUNGEN UEBER CHRISTLICHE GLAUBENSLEHRE

Lindenstruth, Stefan *see* BREMSSTRAHLUNG NIEDERENERGETISCHER ELEKTRONEN
Linder, Usher F *see* REMINISCENCES OF THE EARLY BENCH AND BAR OF ILLINOIS
Linderbauer, BS *see*
- BENEDICTI REGULA MONACHORUM
- SANCTI BENEDICTI REGULA MONASTERIORUM
- SANCTI BENEDICTI REGULA MONASTERIORUM, PHILOLOGISCH ERKLAERT

Linderholm, Emanuel *see* SVEN ROS'EN OCH HANS INSATS I FRIHETS- TIDENS RADIKALA PIETISM
Linderman, J K *see* GLUCOREGULATION AND WORK PERFORMANCE IN GLUCONEOGENESIS-INHIBITED IRON DEFICIENT RATS
Lindermayer, A *see* DIE VOEGEL GRIECHENLANDS
Lindh, Gunnar *see* SOCIO-ECONOMIC ASPECTS URBAN HYDROLOGY
LINDISFARNE GOSPELS – 7th Century. British Museum Ms – 14 – uk Microform Academic [240]
Lindl, Ernest *see* DIE OKTATEUCHCATENE DES PROKOP VON GAZA UND DIE SEPTUAGINTAFORSCHUNG
Lindley *see* MEDICAL PROFESSION OF SOUTHERN CALIFORNIA
Lindley, J *see*
- APPENDIX TO THE FIRST 23 VOLUMES OF EDWARD'S BOTANICAL REGISTER
- COLLECTANEA BOTANICA
- FOLIA ORCHIDACEA
- THE GENERA AND SPECIES OF ORCHIDACEOUS PLANTS
- AN INTRODUCTION TO THE NATURAL SYSTEM OF BOTANY
- A NATURAL SYSTEM OF BOTANY
- NIXUS PLANTARUM
- OBSERVATIONS ON THE NATURAL GROUP OF PLANTS CALLED POMACEAE
- ORCHID HERBARIUM
- ORCHIDEARUM SCELETOS
- SERTUM ORCHIDACEUM
- THE VEGETABLE KINGDOM

Lindley, Nathaniel Lindley *see* A TREATISE ON THE LAW OF PARTNERSHIP
Lindov, G *see* BOL'SHEVIKI, MEN'SHEVIKI I REVOLIUTSIONNAIA SOTSIAL-DEMOKRATIIA
Lindov, G D *see* RABOCHIE KOOPERATIVY I PROFESSIONAL'NYE SOIUZY
Lindow, H *see* BLANDT ESKIMOERNE I LABRADOR
Lindqvist, Axel *see* EPIGRAMME
LINDSAY : A RAILWAY TOWN – Lindsay – 1r – 1 – cn Preston [971]
Lindsay, Alexander Wm. C, Earl *see* SCEPTICISM: A RETROGRESSIVE MOVEMENT IN THEOLOGY AND PHILOSOPHY
Lindsay, Anna Robertson Brown *see* GLORIA CHRISTI
LINDSAY CITY DIRECTORY – Tulare Co, CA. 1936 – 1r – 1 – $50.00 – D103 – us Library Micro [910]
LINDSAY DAILY POST – (1989-1992.-39r; 1993.-12r; 1900-Part.-1r) – Lindsay, 1920-1988 – 223r – 1 – cn Preston [971]
LINDSAY GAZETTE – Lindsay, CA. 1904-07; 1931- – 70+ r – 1 – $3,500.00 ($90.00y) – C02344 – us Library Micro [071]
Lindsay, Greg *see* OCCUPATIONAL REGULATION AND THE PUBLIC INTEREST, COMPETITION OR MONOPOLY
Lindsay, James *see* THE PROGRESSIVENESS OF MODERN CHRISTIAN THOUGHT
Lindsay, Margaret I *see* LINDSAYS OF AMERICA
LINDSAY NEWS – Lindsay, CA. 1944-56 – 7r – 1 – $350.00 – C03610 – us Library Micro [071]
LINDSAY POST – Lindsay, NE. -w. May 1908-Apr 1911; Nov 1936; Sep 1940 – 1 – us NE Hist [071]
Lindsay, Thomas M *see*
- COLLEGE ADDRESSES AND SERMONS
- THE GOSPEL ACCORDING TO ST LUKE
- LUTHER AND THE GERMAN REFORMATION

LINDSAY THURSDAY POST – Lindsay, 1933-1949 – 10r – 1 – cn Preston [971]
Lindsay, Wallace Martin *see* EARLY WELSH SCRIPT
LINDSAYS OF AMERICA / Lindsay, Margaret I – Albany, N.Y.: John Munsell's Sons, 1889 – 1 reel – 1 – us Western Res [920]
Lindsborg. Kansas. Bethany Lutheran Church *see* RECORDS
Lindsey, Charles *see* ROME IN CANADA
Lindsey. Ohio. Emmanuel Lutheran Church *see* RECORDS
Lindsey, Wilford Daniel *see* A FIVE-YEAR PLAN OF MINISTRY FOR THE FIRST BAPTIST CHURCH, MADISON, ILLINOIS
Lindsley, Philip *see* GREATER DALLAS AND VICINITY
Lindt, Peter M *see* SCHRIFTSTELLER IM EXIL; ZWEI JAHRE DEUTSCHE LITERARISCHE SENDUNG AM RUNDFUNK IN NEW YORK
LINE BASKETBALL, OR BASKETBALL FOR WOMEN / ed by Berenson, Senda – 1899 – 2mf – 9 – $6.00 – us Microform Publ [790]
LINE STREET BAPTIST CHURCH. LEXINGTON COUNTY. SOUTH CAROLINA : CHURCH RECORDS – 1955-57 – 1 – 5.00 – us Baptist [240]
LINEA (BUENOS AIRES, ARGENTINA: 1983) – (Includes c.1: v.8:no.91 1987:Sept.-v.9:no.104 (1988:Dec.)) – [Buenos Aires: Editorial de la Doctrina Nacional, 1983- – 1 – CSUXADP4647-S – us Hoover Inst Photo [972]
LINEAGE BOOK OF THE NATIONAL SOCIETY / Daughters of the American Revolution – v154-66, 1937-38. Indexed. V300-0076,77,78 – 1 – us A.G.L.L. [920]
LINEAMIENTOS FUNDAMENTALES DEL PLAN INTEGRAL DE TRANSFORMACION Y DESARROLLO 1973-1977 / Ecuador. Junta Nacional de Planificacion y Coordinacion Economica – (Fundamental outline for integral plan of change and development 1973-1977). Quito. 1973 – 9 – ne IDC [338]
LINEAR ALGEBRA AND ITS APPLICATIONS – v1-63. 1968-84 – 1,5,6,13 – sz Elsevier [073]
LINEAR AND MULTILINEAR ALGEBRA / ed by Watkins, W – 1,5,9 – us Gordon [510]
LINEAR PHONOGRAPHY: A NATURAL SYSTEM OF SHORT-HAND, FOR GENERAL USE, WITH AN EASY STENOGRAPHY FOR REPORTING PURPOSES / Armstrong, Robert – St. John, N.B.: McKillop & Johnston, 1876. 02468. (Pre-1900 Canadiana) – 9 – cn C.I.H.M. [380]
LINEAS DE AUTOBUSES / Comunicaciones – Badajoz: Industrias Graficas, 1963 – sp Bibl Santa Ana [380]
Linebarger, Paul Myron *see* ES ESPANA OTRA CHINA?
LINEMENTI DEL PROGRAMMA DI SVILUPPO DELL'OCCUPAZIONE E DEL REDDITO IN ITALIA (1955-1964) / Italy. Comitato interministeriale per la recostruzione. Segreteria per il programma di sviluppo economico – (Outline of the program for the development of employment and income in Italy). Roma. 1956 – 9 – ne IDC [338]
LINEN AND COTTON BROADWARE WEAVERS APOLOGY – 1758 – 7 – uk Microform Academic [650]
LINES FROM MY LOG-BOOKS / Hay, John Charles Dalrymple – 1898 – 9 – $20.00 – uk Libr Preservation [920]
LINES OF DEFENCE OF THE BIBLICAL REVELATION / Margoliouth, David Samuel – (Includes bibliographical references & indexes) – New York: Edwin S Gorham; London: Hodder & Stoughton, [ca 1900] – 1mf – 9 – 0-8370-6216-0 – 1986-0216 – us A.T.L.A. [220]
Ling, CS *see* BOEKOE PELADJARAN HOEROEF KANJI (PERMOELAAN)
Ling, James *see* THE CATECHISM FOR THE METHODIST CHURCH MEMBERS (CCC157)
LE LINGALA VEHICULAIRE / Anciaux, Leon – Anvers, 1955 – 1 – us Res Libr [960]
Lingelbach, W E *see* THE MERCHANT ADVENTURERS OF ENGLAND
Lingen, B *see* CURSUS PHILOSOPHICUS...
LA LINGERIE ET LES LINGERES / Bouvier, Jeanne – Paris. 1928. (La Condition Ouvriere. Part Two.) – 9 – 12.50 – fr Bibl Nationale [360]
Lingg, Hermann *see*
- LYRISCHES
- VATERLAENDISCHE BALLADEN UND GESAENGE

Ling-hung-hsun *see* SELF-EDITED CHRONICLE OF LING-HUNG-HSUN
Lingken, G Fr *see* DIE SITZE DER MUSICALISCHEN HAUPT-SAETZE IN EINER HARTEN UND WEICHEN TONART. IN ZWO TABELLEN ENTWORFFEN, ERKLAERT UND MIT EXEMPELN ERLAEUTERT VON GEORGE FRIEDRICH LINGKEN
LING-NAM : OR, INTERIOR VIEWS OF SOUTHERN CHINA / Henry, Benjamin Couch – 1886 – 1 – $50.00 – us Presbyterian [950]
LE LINGOT – Arvida, Canada. 5 fev 1943-20 dec 1991 – 29r – 1 – cn Can Microfilming [072]
LE LINGOT *see* LA SENTINELLE
LINGUA – v1-64. 1947-84 – 1,5,6,13 – sz Elsevier [400]
LINGUA AEGYPTIACA RESTITUTA OPUS TRIPARTITUM / Kircher, A – Romae, 1643 – 11mf – 8 – ne Slangenburg [470]
LA LINGUA DEGLI AFAR; VOCABOLARIO ITALIANO-DANKALO E DANKALO-ITALIANO / Capomazza, Ilario – Macerata, 1907 – 1 – us Res Libr [470]
LINGUA LINGUARUM:THE NATURALL LANGUAGE OF LANGUAGES / Edmundson, Henry – 1655. 200p. (English Linguistics Series 1500-1800) – 9 – us UMI [400]
LA LINGUA SOMALA; STRUMENTO D'INSEGNAMENTO PROFESSIONALE / Maino, Mario – Allessandria, Italy. 1953 – 1 – us Res Libr [470]
LINGUAE BRITANNICAE VERA PRONUNCATIO: OR, A NEW ENGLISH DICTIONARY / Buchanan, James – 1757. 509p. (English Linguistics Series 1500-1800) – 9 – us UMI [420]
LINGUAE KSANKA (KOOTENAI) ELEMENTA GRAMMATICAE / Canestrelli, Philip – Santa Clara, Calif.: N. H. Downing, 1894. 02443. (Pre-1900 Canadiana) – 9 – cn C.I.H.M. [490]
LINGUAE SYRIACAE : GRAMMATICA ET CHRESTOMATHIA CUM GLOSSARIO: SCHOLIS ACCOMMODATA / Gismondi, Enrico – (In Latin and Syriac) – 2 ed. Berythi Phoeniciorum: Typographia PP Soc Jesu, 1900 – 1mf – 9 – 0-8370-8576-4 – 1986-2576 – us A.T.L.A. [470]
LINGUARUM 12 CHARACTERIBUS DIFFERENTIUM INTRODUCTIO AC LEGENDI METHODUS / Postel, G – In French. (Linguistic series). 1538 – 9 – fr Hachette [400]
LINGUARUM VETT / Hickes, George – 1703. 2 v. 787; 405p. (English Linguistics Series 1500-1800) – 9 – us UMI [400]
Linguet, Simon N H *see* EXAMEN DES OUVRAGES DE M. DE VOLTAIRE
LINGUISTIC ATLAS OF THE GULF STATES / ed by Pederson, Lee – (Covers Alabama, Arkansas, Florida, Georgia, Louisiana, Mississippi, Tennessee, and Texas. Protocols 126,000p (phonetic transcriptions of 1118 field interviews) on 54r; LAGS Concordance 154mf $365) – 54r, 1200mf – 1,9 – $5820.00 complete collection film and fiche; $3540.00 fiche only – us UMI [420]
LINGUISTIC ATLAS OF THE GULF STATES AND CONCORDANCE – 54r, 1,200mf – 1,9 – us UMI [400]
A LINGUISTIC BIBLIOGRAPHY OF EAST AFRICA / Whiteley, W H & Gutkind, A E – Kampala, 1958 – 4mf – 9 – ne IDC [470]
LINGUISTIC MATERIAL AND CORRESPONDENCE ON LOCAL CUSTOMS, 1880-1894 / Fison, Lorimer – 1r – 1 – at Pacific Mss [306]
Linguistic Society of America *see* LSA BULLETIN
Linguistic Society of Japan *see* GENQO KENKYU
LINGUISTIC SURVEY OF INDIA / ed by Grierson, G A – Calcutta. 1903-28. 11 v. in 20 pts. – 341mf – 8 – ne IDC [490]
LINGUISTICS – (1982-. 1,5,6,9) – v1-. 1963- – 1 – us UMI [400]
LINGUISTICS – The Hague. No1-184. 1963-76 – 5,9 – Dfl9,200.00; Dfl50.00v – ne Swets [400]
LINGUISTICS AND PHILOSOPHY – (v7- 1984-5,6,9) – v1- 1977- – 1 – us UMI [400]
THE LINGUISTICS REVIEW – 1984-. -q – 1 – us UMI [400]
LINGUISTICS SPECIALIST COLLECTION / British Library; ed by Alston, R C – 5,023mf – 9 – £15,500.00 – uk Chadwyck [400]
LINGUISTIQUE – (Adelung, J. Chr. Bezauzee, N. Bibbesworth, Walter de. Bibliander. Bougeant, R.P.G.H. Brosses, Ch. de. Buffier, R.P. Cl. Burnet, James, Lord Monboddo. Caninius (A. Canini). Chesneau du Marsais, C. Condillac, E.B. de. Court de Gebelin, A. Dante Allighieri. Estienne, H. Favre de Vaugelas, Cl. Frain du Tremblay. Gessner, Conrad. Gyarmathy, S. Harris, James. Herber, J.G. Hervas y Panduro, L. Jenish, Daniel. Lamy, B. Lancelot, G. and Arnauld, A. Megister, J. Postel, G. Sacy, L. Sylvestre de. Sanchez de Las Brozas, F. (Sanctius). Scaliger, Julius Cesar. Smith, Adam. Snorre Sturleson (Sturlusen). Ten Kate, Lambert. Valckenaer, L.C. Lennep, J.D. van. Vico,

Giambattista. Wilkins, John) – (Series). Rare books of major writings on language dating from 1200 through the 18th C. In French (mostly). Titles also available individually: inquire. Following authors from this series are also listed individually in the Directory. – 9 – fr Hachette [400]

LINGVAJ PROBLEMOJ KAJ LINGVO-PLANADO/ LANGUAGE PROBLEMS AND LANGUAGE PLANNING – v.1-3. 1977-79 – 1 – us UMI [400]

LINGVARUM DUODECIM CHARACTERIBVS DIFFERENTIVM ALPHABETVM, INTRODVCTIO, AC LEGENDI MODUS LONGE FACILIMUS / Postel, G – Parisiis, 1538 – 1mf – 9 – AR-1487/1 – ne IDC [400]

Linhart Family *see* PHILIP LINHART FAMILY HISTORY

THE LINK / Communist Party. Great Britain – The Journal of the C.P.G.B. Women's Movement. 1973-87. Continued annually – 1 – uk World [360]

THE LINK The organ of the Law and Liberty League. London. -w. 4 Feb-1 Dec 1888. (14 ft) – 1 – uk British Libr Newspaper [073]

LINK AND LINK COMMUNITY – Alberta, CN. 1918-19, 1923 – 1r – 1 – cn Commonwealth Micro [072]

Link, J H F *see*
- ENUMERATIO PLANTARUM HORTI REGII BOTANICI BEROLINENSIS ALTERA
- FILICUM SPECIES IN HORTO REGIO BOTANICO BEROLINENSI CULTAE
- FLORAE GOETTINGENSIS SPECIMEN
- FLORE PORTUGAISE
- HANDBUCH ZUR ERKENNUNG DER NUTZBARSTEN AM HAEUFTIGSTEN VORKOMMENDEN GEWAECHSE
- HORTUS REGIUS BOTANICUS BEROLINENSIS
- ICONES PLANTARUM RARIORUM HORTI REGII BOTANICI BEROLINENSIS
- ICONES PLANTARUM SELECTARUM HORTI REGII BOTANICI BEROLINENSIS
- KRITISCHE BEMERKUNGEN UND ZUSAETZE ZU KURT SPRENGEL'S WERK: UEBER DEN BAU UND DIE NATUR DER GEWAECHSE

Linke, Johannes *see*
- DAS REICH
- DER WALD UND SEINE KINDER

Linker, Wilhelm *see* SPIEL IN FLANDERN

LINKING GIRLS' EXPERIENCES IN PHYSICAL ACTIVITY TO SCHOOL CULTURE AND SOCIAL AND POLITICAL CONTEXTS : ELEMENTS OF AN EXEMPLARY MODEL / Fenton, Jennifer M – University of British Columbia, 1996 – 2mf – 9 – $8.00 – PSY 1884 – us Microform Publ [150]

LINKOPINGSOSTGOTEN *see* OSTGOTEN

DIE LINKSKURVE – Berlin. v. 1, no. 1-v. 4, no. 12. Aug 1929-Dec 1932 – 1 – us NY Public [335]

LINKSKURVE – v1-4. 1929-32 – 1r – 1 – us Ross [335]

LINKVILLE WEEKLY STAR – Linkville OR. May 10 1884 – 1 – us U.O. Library [071]

LINL *see* NEW MEXICO JEWISH COMMUNITY LINK

Linley, T *see* [THE DUENNA] HAD I A HEART. IRISH AIR OF GRAMACHRE

LINLITHGOW GAZETTE – 1 – £42.00r – uk Scot News [072]

LINLITHGOWSHIRE, 1837 : BRITISH ISLES CENSUS DIRECTORIES PROJECT, SCOTLAND. VOL 45 – 1mf – 9 – A$9.00 – at Vine [941]

LINLITHGOWSHIRE GAZETTE – 1967-1968 – 1. 188 – £42.00r – uk Scot News [072]

LINN COUNTY ADVOCATE – Lebanon, OR. -w. 11 Jan 1912-28 Nov 1912. 1 roll – 1 – us U.O. Library [071]

Linn, John Blair *see*
- HISTORY OF CENTRE AND CLINTON COUNTIES
- VALERIAN, A NARRATIVE POEM

LINNAEA : EIN JOURNAL FUER DIE BOTANIK / ed by Schlechtendal, D F L von – Berlin, Halle, 1826-1882. 43v. – 589mf – 8 – ne IDC [580]

Linnaea, E C *see* OM INDIANSKA KRASSENS BLICKANDE

LINNAEA ENTOMOLOGICA – Berlin, Posen und Bromberg, 1846-66. v1-16 – 3 – us Readex [073]

LINNAEA ENTOMOLOGICA / ed by Entomologischer Verein in Stettin – Berlin etc. v1-16. 1846-1866 – 129mf – 9 – ne IDC [590]

Linnaeus, Carl *see*
- AMOENITATES ACADEMICAE
- BERAETTELSE OM DE INHEMSKA VAEXTER, SOM I BRIST AF SAD KUNNA ANVAENDAS TILL BROED-OCH MATREDNING
- BIBLIOTHECA BOTANICA...
- CLASSES PLANTARUM
- CLAVIS MEDICINAE DUPLEX, EXTERIOR AND INTERIOR
- DE NUPTIIS ET SEXU PLANTARUM
- DECAS PRIMA ET SECUNDA. PLANTARUM RARIORUM HORTI UPPSALIENSIS
- FAUNA SVECICA
- FLORA LAPPONICA
- FLORA SVECICA
- FLORA ZEYLANICA
- FUNDAMENTA BOTANICA
- FUNDAMENTORUM BOTANICORUM
- GENERA MORBORUM
- GENERA PLANTARUM
- HERBARIUM
- HORTUS CLIFFORTIANUS
- HORTUS UPSALIENSIS
- ITER AD FODINAS 1733
- ITER LAPPONICUM
- LETTERS ON NATURAL HISTORY AND MEDICINE TO CARL LINNAEUS FROM ABOUT 1728-1783, ARRANGED IN ALPHABETICAL ORDER
- MATERIA MEDICA. LIBER I. DE PLANTIS
- MUSA CLIFFORTIANA FLORENS HARTECAMPI
- MUSEUM LUDOVICAE ULRICAE REGINAE
- MUSEUM S. R. M. ADOLPHI FREDERICI REGIS SUECORUM
- OBSERVATIONES IN MATERIAM MEDICAM
- OPERA VARIA, IN QUIBUS CONTINENTUR FUNDAMENTA BOTANICA, SPONSALIA PLANTARUM, ET SYSTEMA NATURAE
- PHILOSOPHIA BOTANICA
- PLANTAE RARIORES AFRICANAE
- SKANSKA RESA
- SPECIES PLANTARUM
- SPECIES PLANTARUM: CURANTE C. L. WILLDENOW
- SPECIES PLANTARUM: CUSANTE C. L. WILLDENOW
- SUPPLEMENTUM PLANTARUM SYSTEMATIS VEGETABILIUM
- SYSTEMA, GENERA, SPECIES PLANTARUM UNO VOLUMINE. EDITIO CRITICA
- SYSTEMA NATURAE
- SYSTEMA NATURAE, EDITIO DUODECIMA, 12 REFORMATA
- SYSTEMA NATURAE. LUGDUNI BATAVORUM
- SYSTEMA PLANTARUM SECUNDUM CLASSES, ORDINES, GENERA SPECIES CUM CHARACTERIBUS
- SYSTEMA VEGETABILIUM
- SYSTEMA VEGETABILIUM. CURANTE C. SPRENGEL

LINNAEUS CORRESPONDENCE / Linnean Society, London – (Includes a paper reprint of Aehrling's catalogue "Carl von Linne's Brefvexling" Stockholm, 1885) – 446mf – 9 – ne IDC [500]

Linne, Karsten *see* DER "NUERNBERGER AERZTEPROZESS" 1946/47

Linnean Society *see*
- CATALOGUE OF THE LIBRARY
- JOURNAL

Linnean Society, London *see*
- LINNAEUS CORRESPONDENCE
- TRANSACTIONS
- TRANSACTIONS. 2D SER. BOTANY
- TRANSACTIONS. 2D SER. ZOOLOGY

THE LINNEAN SYSTEM OF CONCHOLOGY, DESCRIBING ORDERS, GENERA, AND SPECIES OF SHELLS / Mawe, J – 5606 2. 1823 – 8 – ne IDC [590]

LINNE'S NATUERLICHE PFLANZENKLASSE TRICOCCAE DES BERLINER HERBARIUM'S / Klotzsch, J F – (Abhandelungen der Koenigl. Akad. der Wiss. Berlin, 1859). Berlin. 1860. B-8327 1 – 9 – ne IDC [580]

LINNET: A ROMANCE / Allen, Grant – 2nd ed. London: G. Richards, 1899. 05049. (Pre-1900 Canadiana) – 9 – cn C.I.H.M. [830]

LINNTON LEADER – (Set incl. Linnton Live Wire) – Linnton, OR. -w. 8 Jan 1914-7 Jan 1915. – 1r – 1 – us U.O. Library [071]

LINNTON LIVE WIRE – Linnton OR. Dec 31 1910-Jan 7 1915 – 1 – us U.O. Library [071]

Linschoten, J H van *see*
- HIS DISCOURS OF VOYAGES INTO Y[E] EASTE AND WEST INDIES
- HISTOIRE DE LA NAVIGATION DE J.H. DE LINSCOT ET DE SON VOYAGE DES INDES ORIENTALES, A QUOI SONT AJOUTEES QUELQUES AUTRES DESCRIPTIONS TANT DU PAYS DE GUINEE ET AUTRES COTES D'ETHIOPIE, QUE DES NAVIGATIONS DES HOLLANDAIS VERS LE NORD

Linsenbardt, S *see* THE EFFECT OF BREATHING TECHNIQUE ON BLOOD PRESSURE RESPONSE TO WEIGHT LIFTING

Linsenmann, Franz Xaver *see* MICHAEL BAIUS UND DIE GRUNDLEGUNG DES JANSENISMUS

Linsenmayer, A *see* DIE BEKAEMPFUNG DES CHRISTENTUMS DURCH DEN ROEMISCHEN STAAT

LINSHI ZHENGFU GONGBAO, I-IV – Bulletins of the provisional government, v1-4. Comp. by the Second Chinese Archive of History. 1 reel. M-H116 – 5 – $40.00 – cc Microforms [950]

Linstead, Stephen G *see* THE LAW OF CROWN PRIVILEGE IN CANADA AND ELSEWHERE

L'Institut Francais d'Afrique Noire *see* BULLETIN

L'Institut francais de sociologie *see* BULLETIN

LINTASAN REPOLUSI / Djakasuria – SE-4409 1. 1955 – 9 – ne IDC [950]

L'Internationale Situationniste *see* INTERNATIONALE SITUATIONNISTE

Linton, Elizabeth Lynn *see*
- GRASP YOUR NETTLE
- MY LITERARY LIFE

Linton, W J *see* POEMS AND TRANSLATIONS

LINUS AUSTIN JOURNAL *see* AUSTIN, LINUS, JOURNAL, MS P.P.

LINYE KEXUE – (1979-82 $4.50f; 1983-84 $3.50f) – Scientia Silva Sinica. In Chinese but English abstracts to the main articles. F p57 – 9 – cc Microforms [073]

LION – 1-4 (all publ). 1828-1829 – 36mf – 9 – $120.00 – us UPA [290]

THE LION = LE LION – DEFENSE OUVRIERE : LABOR DEFENSE – (In English and French) – Montreal, Canada. 7 oct 1933 – 1r – 1 – Can$25.00 – cn Can Microfilming [331]

LE LION BLESSE – Red. en chef Alph. Cotelle. Paris. 8-10 nov. 1970 – 1 – fr A.C.R.P.P. [073]

Lionardi, Allesandro *see* DIALOGI DI MESSER DELLA INVENTIONE POETICA

Lioni, O *see* RITRATTI DI ALCUNI CELEBRI PITTORI DEL SECOLO 17. CON LE VITE DE'MEDESIMI

LIPA – v1-3, 1918-20 – 1 – us I.U. Libraries [073]

Lipenius, Martin *see* BIBLIOTHECA REALIS PHILOSOPHICA

LIPIDS – v1- 1966- 1; v5- 5,6; v11- 9 – us UMI [073]

Lipinski, Richard *see* FRIEDE AUF ERDEN!

Lipman, Arthur G *see* JOURNAL OF PHARMACEUTICAL CARE IN PAIN AND SYMPTOM CONTROL

Lipner, M E *see*
- AFRICAN ANIMAL GENETIC RESOURCES
- LIVESTOCK AND RESOURCE MANAGEMENT POLICY

Lipovskii, A L *see* OCHERKI PO ISTORII RUSSKOI LITERATURY OT EPOKHI PETRA VELIKOGO DO PUSHKINA

Lipp, F J *see* ENCHIRIDION BOTANICUM

Lippe, Karpel *see* DAS EVANGELIUM MATTHAEI VOR DEM FORUM DER BIBEL UND DES TALMUD

Lippe, R *see*
- MISSALE ROMANUM MEDIOLANI 1474, VOL 1
- MISSALE ROMANUM MEDIOLANI 1474, VOL 2

Lippens-Giguere, Magdeleine *see* BIO-BIBLIOGRAPHIE DU FRERE ROBERT, E.C., PROFESSEUR AU MONT-SAINT-LOUIS

Lippert, Gunther *see* ELEKTRISCHE MESSUNGEN AN GESTAEUBTEN $MOSI_2$-SCHICHTEN

Lippert, Julius *see*
- DIE RELIGIONEN DER EUROPAEISCHEN CULTURVOELKER, DER LITAUER, SLAVEN, GERMANEN, GRIECHEN, UND ROEMER, IN IHREM GESCHICHTLICHEN URSPRUNGE
- DER SEELENCULT IN SEINEN BEZIEHUNGEN ZUR ALTHEBRAEISCHEN RELIGION
- WIE DIE MENSCHEN KOCHEN LERNTEN
- ZIELE UND MITTEL DER VOLKSBILDUNG

Lippert, W *see* KAISERIN MARIA THERESIA UND KURFUERSTIN MARIA ANTONIA VON SACHSEN

Lipphartdt, W *see* DIE GESCHICHTE DES MEHRSTIMMIGEN PROPRIUM MISSAE

LIPPISCHE BERGWARTE *see* BLOMBERGER ANZEIGER

LIPPISCHE INTELLIGENZBLAETTER – (Cont by: Fuerstlich Lippisches Intelligenzblatt, 1830. Fuerstlich Lippisches Regierungs- und Anzeigeblatt, jan 7, 1843. Lippische Landes-Zeitung, 1878. Publ in Lemgo until 1842) – Detmold. 1976 – 1 – gw Mikrofilm [072]

LIPPISCHE LANDESKIRCHE : GESETZ- UND VERORDNUNGSBLATT – 1971-79; 1985-87 (complete) – 2r – 1 – ATLA S0347 – us A.T.L.A. [240]

LIPPISCHE LANDES-ZEITUNG – Detmold, West Germany. 1992- – 9r per yr – 1 – gw Mikrofilm [072]

LIPPISCHE LANDES-ZEITUNG *see* LIPPISCHE INTELLIGENZBLAETTER

Lippius, J *see* SYNOPSIS MUSICAE NOVAE. OMNINO VERAE ATQUE METHODICAE UNIVERSAE

Lippmann, Alphonse *see* GUERRIERS ET SORCIERS EN SOMALIE

Lippmann, F *see* ENGRAVINGS AND WOODCUTS BY OLD MASTERS (SEC 15-19) REPRODUCED IN FACSIMILE UNDER THE DIRECTION OF DR. FRIEDRICH LIPPMANN

Lipps, Theodor *see* DIE ETHISCHEN GRUNDFRAGEN

Liprandi, I P *see* OPYT KATALOGA VSEM OTDEL'NYM SOCHINENIIAM PO 1872 GOD OB OTECHESTVENNOI VOINE 1812 GODA

Lipscomb, Andrew Adgate *see*
- CHRISTIAN HEROISM: ILLUSTRATED IN THE LIFE AND CHARACTER OF ST PAUL
- LESSONS FROM THE LIFE OF SAINT PETER
- STUDIES IN THE FORTY DAYS BETWEEN CHRIST'S RESURRECTION AND ASCENSION

Lipscomb-Griffin *see* THE GALLATIN DEBATE

Lipset, SM *see* ELITES Y DESARROLLO EN AMERICA LATINA

Lipsio, Justo *see* LAS BIBLIOTECAS DE LA ANTIGUEDAD ESTUDIO, TRADUCCION PROLOGO Y NOTAS POR JOSE LOPEZ DE TORO

Lipsius, Karl Heinrich Adelbert *see* GRAMMATISCHE UNTERSUCHUNGEN UEBER DIE BIBLISCHE GRAECITAET

Lipsius, Richard Adelbert *see*
- DIE APOKRYPHEN APOSTELGESCHICHTEN UND APOSTELLEGENDEN
- CHRONOLOGIE DER ROEMISCHEN BISCHOEFE
- DIE EDESSENISCHE ABGAR-SAGE
- PHILOSOPHIE UND RELIGION: NEUE BEITRAEGE ZUR...GRUNDLEGUNG DER DOGMATIK
- DIE QUELLEN DER AELTESTEN KETZERGESCHICHTE
- DIE QUELLEN DER ROEMISCHEN PETRUS-SAGE
- UEBER DAS VERHAELTNIS DES TEXTES DER DREI SYRISCHEN BRIEFE DES IGNATIOS ZU DEN UEBRIGEN RECENSIONEN DER IGNATIANISCHEN LITERATUR
- ZUR QUELLENKRITIK DES EPIPHANIOS

THE LIQUEFACTION OF THE BLOOD OF ST. JANUARIUS, AT NAPLES : AN HISTORICAL AND CRITICAL EXAMINATION OF THE MIRACLE – New York: Catholic Publ Society, c1871 – 1mf – 9 – 0-8370-7306-5 – 1986-1306 – us A.T.L.A. [390]

LIQUID FUELS TECHNOLOGY – v1- 1983- – 1,5,6,9 – us UMI [660]

LIQUIDACION DEL PRESUPUESTO DE 1914, DEUDORES Y ACREEDORES PARA RESULTAS / Caceres – Caceres: Tip. La Minerva – 1 – sp Bibl Santa Ana [946]

LIQUIDATION DE LA COMPAGNIE DE PANAMA / Bressolles, P – Paris, 1894 – 2mf – 1 – ILM-1865/1 – ne IDC [327]

LIQUOR BLACKLISTS / Van Wert County. Ohio. Pleasant Township. Township Clerk – 1875-1887 – 1r – 1 – $32.50r – us Archival [324]

LIQUOR LEGISLATION IN THE UNITED STATES AND CANADA: REPORT OF A NON-PARTISAN INQUIRY ON THE SPOT INTO THE LAWS AND THEIR OPERATION / Fanshawe, Evelyn Leighton – Undertaken at the request of W. Rathbone. London: Cassell, 1893?. 02947. (Pre-1900 Canadiana) – 9 – cn C.I.H.M. [971]

THE LIQUOR LICENSE LAWS OF 1887. / Monaghan, James – Philadelphia: Johnson, 1887. 32p. LL-499 – 1 – us L of C Photodup [340]

LIQUOR NOTICE RECORD / Erie County. Ohio. Vermilion Township. Township Clerk – 1896-1898 – 1r – 1 – $32.50r – us Archival [324]

LIRA PROVINCIA. POESIA / Monterrey, Manuel – Badajoz: Tip. de Vicente Rodriguez, 1910 – 1 – sp Bibl Santa Ana [810]

LIRA SACRO-HISPANA – Madrid. 1869. 10v – 1 – 46.00 – us L of C Photodup [780]

Lirgg, Cathy D *see* EFFECTS OF SAME-SEX AND COEDUCATIONAL PHYSICAL EDUCATION ON PERCEPTIONS OF SELF-CONFIDENCE AND CLASS ENVIRONMENT

LIRICA POPULAR DE LA ALTA EXTREMADURA / Garcia Matos, Manuel – Dibujos de F Lancho, Madrid: Union Musical Espanola, s.a. – sp Bibl Santa Ana [780]

LIRIKA KAK OSOBYI VID TVORCHESTVA / Ovsianiko-Kulikovskii, D N – Voprosy teorii i psikhologii tvorchestva. v. 2 (2). 1910. BR-3287 2 – 8 – ne IDC [150]

LIRISMOS : LIBRO 1° / Moreno Torrado, Luis – Badajoz: Tip. y Lib. de A.Arqueros, 1915 – 1 – sp Bibl Santa Ana [946]

Liron, D *see* OBSERVATIONS SUR L'ORGINE DE LA LANGUE FRANCAISE VULGAIRE LEBER, [J.M.]C. COLLECTION DES MEILLEURES DISSERTATIONS, NOTICES ET TRAITES PARTICULIERS RELATIFS A L'HISTOIRE DE FRANCE

Lirou, J -F E de *see* EXPLICATION DU SYSTEME DE L'HARMONIE

LE LIS REFLEURI : ABREGE DE LA VIE ET DES REVELATIONS DE STE. MARGUERITE DE CORTONE: PENITENTE DU TIERS-ORDRE DE ST. FRANCOIS, 1247-97 / Hiral, Ange-Marie – Candiac, Quebec: Maison Ste-Marguerite, [1907?] – 1mf – 9 – 0-8370-6906-8 – 1986-0906 – us A.T.L.A. [920]

LISAN AD-DIN – Dir. Mustapha Hafid. no. 1-12. Alger. 1923 – 1 – fr A.C.R.P.P. [073]

LISAN-I OSMANI / Ekrem, Ali – Istanbul: 1332 [1916] – $10.00 – us MEDOC [470]

LISBON BAPTIST CHURCH. EASTERN ASSOCIATION. NORTH CAROLINA : CHURCH RECORDS – 1849-1925 – 1 – 15.75 – us Baptist [240]

Lisburn. Northern Ireland. Cathedral Church Yard *see* REGISTER OF BURIALS

LISBURN STANDARD – Ireland. Jan 1878-May1959.-w. 59men reels – 1 – uk British Libr Newspaper [072]

LISCIO E BUSSO : LANGUE ITALIENNE – Montreal, Canada. v1 n3. 18 nov 1974 – 1r – 1 – Can$25.00 – cn Can Microfilming [072]

LISCO TRIBUNE – Lisco, NE. -w. Jul 1912-Jul 1922 – 1 – us NE Hist [071]

LISES, VERSOS / Munoz de San Pedro, Miguel – Caceres: Imprenta Moderna, 1952. Cud. Alcant – 1 – sp Bibl Santa Ana [946]

LISES (VERSOS Y PROSAS) / Munoz de San Pedro, Miguel – Madrid: Ediciones Cuadernos Alcantara, 2nd ed 1963 – 1 – sp Bibl Santa Ana [440]

LISEZ LA CONDAMNATION DU REGIME LAURIER-TANE / Cook, Herman Henry – par un ancien depute liberal, M. Cook. s.l.: s.n., 1900?. 03434. (Pre-1900 Canadiana) – 9 – cn C.I.H.M. [971]

LISHI DANGAN – Historical Archives Quarterly. In Chinese, but Table of Contents in English in each issue. F p17 – 9 – $4.50f – cc Microforms [073]

LISHI YANJIU – (1982-83 $3.50f; 1981, 1984 $4.50f) – Historical Research. In Chinese but Table of Contents in English in each issue. F p14 – 9 – cc Microforms [073]

LI-SHIH CHENG-CHIH HSEUH-PA – (Journal of History and Political Science). v. 1-2. Canton. 1947. BCH-799 2 – 8 – ne IDC [900]

LI-SHIH CHIAO-HSUEH – (Teaching History). Tientsin. 1956-59. Lacking: 1956; 1957. BCH-924 2 – 8 – ne IDC [900]

LI-SHIH YEN-CHIU – (Historical studies). Peking. 1954-66. BCH-925 2 – 8 – ne IDC [900]

LI-SHIH YU K'AO-KU – (History and Archaeology). v. 1. Shenyang. 1946. BCH-800 2 – 8 – ne IDC [930]

Lisle de la Drevetiere, Louis-Francois de *see* ARLEQUIN SAUVAGE

Lisle du Dreneuc, Pitre de *see* HISTORIQUE DU CERCLE LOUIS 16TH

Lisle, William McIntire *see* THE EVOLUTION OF SPIRITUAL MAN

LISMORE ADVERTISER – 1910 – 1r – 1 – at Corangamite [072]

LISMORE PAPERS: INDEX AND CALENDAR, 1396-1774 – From Archives of Duke of Devonshire, Chatsworth, Derbys – 1 – uk Microform Academic [025]

Lisovskii, N M *see*
- BIBLIOGRAFIIA
- KRATKII OCHERK STOLETNEI DEIATEL NOSTI TIPOGRAFII GLAZUNOVYKH V SVIAZI S RAZVITIEMIKH KNIGOIZDATELSTVA 1803-1903
- OBOZRENIE LITERATURY PO TEATRU I MUZVKE 1889-1891 GG
- RUSSKAIA PERIODICHESKAIA PECHAT' 1703-1900
- SPISOK UKAZATELEI K RUSSKIM PERIODICHESKIM IZDANIIAM 17-19 ST

LISSAER TAGBLATT : DEUTSCH-POLNISCHE GRENZZEITUNG – Lissa (Leszno), Poland. 7 May 1922-1934 – 14r – 1 – gw Mikrofilm [943]

Lissauer, Abraham *see* ALBRECHT VON HALLER UND SEINE BEDEUTUNG FUER DIE DEUTSCHE CULTUR

Lissauer, Ernst *see*
- ECKERMANN
- FLAMMEN UND WINDE
- DER STROM
- VON DER SENDUNG DES DICHTERS
- YORCK

LISSEWEGHE, SON EGLISE ET SON ABBAYE / Hollebeke, L van – Bruges, 1863 – Dfl46.00 – ne Slangenburg [240]

LIST – v1-. 1983- – 1,5,6,9 – us UMI [073]

List, Friedrich *see*
- FRIEDERIKE BRION
- DER JUNGE GOETHE ALS SOZIALERZIEHER

List, Guido *see* ALRAUNENMAEREN

A LIST OF ALL THE METHODIST PREACHERS WHO HAVE LABOURED IN CONNEXION WITH THE LATE REV. JOHN WESLEY... / Myles, W – Bristol. [1801] – 1mf – 9 – ne IDC [240]

LIST OF ANCIENT MONUMENTS IN BURMA. MANDALAY DIVISION / Burma. Lists of Monuments – Rangoon, 1910. BI-736 2 – 8 – ne IDC [324]

LIST OF ANCIENT MONUMENTS SELECTED FOR CONSERVATION IN THE MADRAS PRESIDENCY / India; ed by Rae, A – Madras, 1891. BI-742 2 – 8 – ne IDC [930]

LIST OF ANNUAL OR SESSIONAL REPORTS OR RETURNS TO BE MADE TO THE LEGISLATURE OF CANADA, BY PUBLIC OFFICERS, COMMISSIONERS, OR PRIVATE CORPORATIONS... – Quebec: printed for the contractors by Hunter, Rose and Co., 1862. SEM105P1756 – 1mf – 9 – Can$2.25 – cn Bibl Nat [350]

LIST OF ARCHITECTURAL AND ARCHAEOLOGICAL REMAINS IN COORG / India – A. Rea, Comp. Madras, 1894. (Survey of India, N. Imp. Series, v. 17). BI-717 2 – 8 – ne IDC [324]

LIST OF ARCHIVES OF THE NEW HEBRIDES BRITISH SERVICE AND RELATED RECORDS / Western Pacific Archives – 1979 – 2r – 1 – PMB 1129 – at Pacific Mss [025]

A LIST OF BRITISH BIRDS / Wharton, H T – 2118 2. 1877 – 8 – ne IDC [590]

A LIST OF BRITISH DIPTERA / Verrall, G H – Z 1685 2. Lacking: Pt. 2-3. 1888 – 8 – ne IDC [590]

LIST OF BUILDINGS OF AT AND SF RR AND LEASED LINES / Atchison, Topeka and Santa Fe Railroad Company – undated, Goebel Collection, 176 – 1 – us KS Hist [380]

LIST OF CHIEFS AND LEADING FAMILIES / India. Central Provinces – (Filmed with: India, Imperial Record Dept: List of the Heads of Administrations in India and of the India Office in England) – Calcutta: Central Publ Branch, 1926 – us Res Libr [920]

LIST OF COMMODITIES AND COUNTRIES FOR THE IMPORT AND EXPORT STATISTICS OF INDONESIA / Indonesia. Biro Pusat Statistik – Indonesian, Dutch and English. SE-8557 1. 1968 – 9 – ne IDC [310]

LIST OF EMIGRANTS TO AMERICA FROM LIVERPOOL – 1697-1707. 1931. Item K. Indexed, 55p. SW16-0010 – 5 – us A.G.L.L. [920]

LIST OF EMIGRANTS TO AMERICA FROM LIVERPOOL, 1697-1707 – Item E. Reprint from The New England Historical & Genealogical Register, v64,65, 1913. Indexed, 48p.SW16-0151 – 5 – us A.G.L.L. [920]

LIST OF FINANCE DEPARTMENT RECORDS IN THE IMPERIAL RECORD OFFICE, CALCUTTA, 1805-1908 / India. Imperial Record Office – Calcutta. 1909. – 5mf – 8 – ne IDC [336]

LIST OF FOREIGN DEPARTMENT RECORDS IN THE IMPERIAL RECORD OFFICE, CALCUTTA, 1756-1859 / India. Imperial Record Office – 2v. Calcutta. 1906-07. BI-317 2 – 8 – ne IDC [950]

LIST OF FOREIGN DEPARTMENT RECORDS IN THE IMPERIAL RECORD OFFICE, CALCUTTA, PART 3 / India. Imperial Record Office – Persian Records from 1759-1878. Calcutta, 1909. BI-318 2 – 8 – ne IDC [950]

LIST OF HOME DEPARTMENT RECORDS IN THE IMPERIAL RECORD OFFICE, CALCUTTA, 1749-1892 / India. Imperial Record Office – 2v., Suppl. Contents: v. 1, 1749-1859; v. 2, 1859-1892. Calcutta. 1904-05. BI-314 2 – 8 – ne IDC [324]

LIST OF HOTELS AND LODGEMENTS IN INDONESIA / Indonesia. Dewan Tourisme – SE-3249 1. 1958 – 9 – ne IDC [950]

LIST OF INDIA OFFICE RECORDS / Great Britain. India Office – London. 1899. v1-17 – 179mf – 8 – ne IDC [941]

LIST OF INDIA OFFICE RECORDS – London. v1-17. 1899 – 179mf – 9 – ne IDC [324]

LIST OF INDIANA LAWYERS, JUDGES AND PROSECUTORS / Brown, Robert Allen – Indianapolis, Burford, 1899. 177 p. LL-1095 – 1 – us L of C Photodup [340]

LIST OF INSCRIPTIONS : CHRONOLOGICAL LIST OF INSCRIPTIONS OF THE PUDUKKOTTAI STATE, ARRANGED ACCORDING TO DYNASTIES – Pudukkottai, 1929 – 8mf – 9 – ne IDC [950]

A LIST OF INSCRIPTIONS ON CHRISTIAN TOMBS OR MONUMENTS IN THE PUNJAB, NORTH-WEST FRONTIER PROVINCE, KASHMIR AND AFGHANISTAN; POSSESSING HISTORICAL OR ARCH. INTEREST / Irving, M – With a historical introduction (Indian Mon. Inscriptions, v3, pt 1). Lahore, 1910. BI-704 2 – 8 – ne IDC [410]

LIST OF INSCRIPTIONS ON TOMBS OR MONUMENTS IN H.E.H. THE NIZAM'S DOMINIONS / Crofton, A S – Hyderabad, Deccan, 1941. 192 pp., index. BI-650 2 – 8 – ne IDC [410]

LIST OF INSCRIPTIONS ON TOMBS OR MONUMENTS IN MADRAS POSSESSING HISTORICAL OR ARCHAEOLOGICAL INTEREST / Cotton, J J – Madras, 1905. BI-706 – 8 – ne IDC [410]

LIST OF JUDGES OF ELECTION / Erie County. Ohio. Vermilion Township. Township Clerk – 1877 – 1 reel – 1 – us Archival [324]

LIST OF LANDS GRANTED BY THE CROWN IN THE PROVINCE OF QUEBEC, FROM 1763 TO 31ST DECEMBER 1890 – Charles-Francois Langlois..., 1891. SEM105P468 – 21mf – 9 – Can$47.25 – cn Bibl Nat [971]

A LIST OF LEGAL FEES, FOR THE USE OF PROBATE COURTS, WITHIN THE STATE OF CONNECTICUT / Brown, John T – Norwich, Bulletin Co., 1881. 57 p. LL-602 – 1 – us L of C Photodup [340]

LIST OF MALAYAN BIRDS COLLECTED BY T. CANTOR / Moore, F – (Proc. Zool. Soc. London, v. 22). London. 1854. BZ-1861 2 – 8 – ne IDC [590]

LIST OF MATERIAL AND PERSONAL OUTRAGES AND INJURIES PERPETRATED AGAINST INDONESIANS BY DUTCH SOLDIERY IN THE CITY OF DJAKARTA (OCT.-DEC. 1945) / Indonesia. Kementerian Luar Negeri – SE-11,903 1. 1946 – 9 – ne IDC [950]

LIST OF MEMBERS / Fine Art Trade Guild – 1,7 – uk Microform Academic [700]

LIST OF MEMBERS OF THE CIVIL SERVICE LODGE, A.F. & A.M., NO.148, G.R.C., OTTAWA, CONSTITUTED 14TH MAY, A. L. 5861 – Ottawa?: s.n., 1897 (Ottawa: Paynter & Abbott). 05615. (Pre-1900 Canadiana) – 9 – cn C.I.H.M. [350]

LIST OF MEN ABSENT FROM REGIMENT, QUEENSLAND DEFENCE FORCE, CHRONOLOGICAL SERIES, 1901-1902 / Chief Secretary's Office, Queensland – 4r – 1 – CRS B5173 – at Archives [920]

LIST OF MERCHANT SEAFARERS AND MEMBER OF CIVIL AIR CREWS CONVICTED OF NARCOTIC OFFENCES / United Nations. Commission on Narcotic Drugs – 1953-1957 – E.27 F.27 – 9 (E/NM) – us U.N. Pubs [360]

A LIST OF MICMAC NAMES OF PLACES, RIVERS, ETC., IN NOVA SCOTIA / Frame, Elizabeth – Cambridge Mass.: J. Wilson, 1892. 03165. (Pre-1900 Canadiana) – 9 – cn C.I.H.M. [910]

LIST OF MILITARY DEPARTMENT RECORDS IN THE IMPERIAL RECORD OFFICE, CALCUTTA / India. Imperial Record Office – 3v. Contents: v. 1. Military Records, 1774-1858; v. 2. Military Records, 1859-1901; v. 3. Military Board Records, 1775-1858. Calcutta. 1908. BI-321 2 – 8 – ne IDC [324]

LIST OF MONUMENTS : LISTS OF THE ANTIQUARIAN REMAINS IN THE BOMBAY PRESIDENCY WITH AN APPENDIX OF INSCRIPTIONS FROM GUJARAT / Burgess, J – Bombay, 1885 – 8mf – 9 – ne IDC [930]

LIST OF MUNICIPALITIES IN THE PROVINCE OF QUEBEC – C.E. Deschamps, comp. Levis: Mercier, 1886. 02680. (Pre-1900 Canadiana) – 9 – cn C.I.H.M. [971]

LIST OF NAMES OF THOSE TO WHOM INSURANCE HAS BEEN PAID IN RESPECT OF THE DEATH OF MEMBERS OF THE FIRST FOUR QUEENSLAND CONTINGENTS, QUEENSLAND DEFENCE FORCE, 1900-1902 / Chief Secretary's Office, Queensland – 1 reel – 1 – CRS B5159 – at Archives [920]

A LIST OF NORTH AMERICAN LEPIDOPTERA AND KEY TO THE LITERATURE OF THIS ORDER OF INSECTS / Dyar, H G – (United States Nat. Museum Bulletin, no.52, 1902.) xix,723p. Z/1211/2 – 8 – ne IDC [590]

LIST OF NORTH CAROLINA LAND GRANTS IN TENNESSEE, 1778-91 / U.S. Bureau of Land Management – 1 rolls.M68 – 1 – us Nat'l Archives [324]

LIST OF OBJECTS OF ANTIQUARIAN AND ARCHAEOLOGICAL INTEREST IN BRITISH BURMA / Burma. Lists of Monuments – Rangoon, 1884. BI-733 2 – 8 – ne IDC [324]

LIST OF OBJECTS OF ANTIQUARIAN AND ARCHAEOLOGICAL INTEREST IN UPPER BURMA / Burma. Lists of Monuments – Rangoon, 1901. BI-735 2 – 8 – ne IDC [324]

LIST OF OFFICERS OF THE BENGAL ARMY, 1758-1834 / Hodson, V C P – 4v. London. 1927-47. BI-344 2 – 8 – ne IDC [920]

LIST OF OFFICERS OF THE SEDENTARY MILITIA OF LOWER CANADA, 1862 / Canada. Departement de la Milice – Quebec: Printed by Stewart Derbishire and Georges Desbarats, 1863. SEM105P312 – 3mf – 9 – Can$6.75 – cn Bibl Nat [355]

LIST OF OFFICIAL DOCUMENTS, EXPLANATORY OF THE RELATIONS BETWEEN THE COLONISTS OF THE CAPE OF GOOD HOPE AND THE INDEPENDENT NATIVE TRIBES – 1836 – 1 – us Res Libr [960]

A LIST OF OUR CHURCHES CLASSFIED IN ALPHABETICAL ORDER IN CIRCUITS / United Methodist Church – repr ed 1987 – 1mf – 9 – ne IDC [240]

LIST OF PARLIAMENTARY COLLECTIONS IN INDIA, WITH INDEX / India – Ed. 3. London. 1913. BI-347 2 – 2mf – 8 – ne IDC [324]

LIST OF PAYMENTS MADE TO TEACHERS OF SCHOOLS UNDER SUNDRY ACTS OF THE PROVINCIAL PARLIAMENT, SINCE THE ACCOUNTS RENDERED TO THE LEGISLATURE DURING THE LAST SESSION IN 1831 – [Quebec]: [s.n.], [1831?]. SEM105P1147 – 1mf – 9 – Can$2.25 – cn Bibl Nat [336]

LIST OF PLANTS FROM ARMENIA AND TREBIZOND / Holmboe, J – Berger. 1907. B-640 2 – 8 – ne IDC [580]

LIST OF PLANTS USED IN NATIVE MEDICINE IN NIGERIA / Ainslie, J R – Oxford, 1937 – 3mf – ne IDC [580]

LIST OF PRINCIPAL RECOMMENDATIONS FOR AGRICULTURAL DEVELOPMENT IN LIBYA / Lalevic, D et al – BNE-1014 1 – 9 – ne IDC [630]

LIST OF REPTILES AND BATRACHIANS COLLECTED BY THE SWEDISH ZOOLOGICAL EXPEDITION TO EGYPT, THE SUDAN AND THE SINAITIC PENINSULA / Andersson, L G – Uppsala, 1904 – 1mf – ne IDC [590]

LIST OF RESIDENT AND NON-RESIDENT MEMBERS: MONDAY, 6 P.M., AUGUST 16, 1897 / British Association for the Advancement of Science. Canada – Toronto, 1897. 02522. (Pre-1900 Canadiana) – 9 – cn C.I.H.M. [971]

LIST OF ROGER WILLIAMS' WRITINGS / Chapin, Howard M – 1918 – 1 – $5.00 – us Baptist [240]

LIST OF RULING PRINCES AND CHIEFS IN POLITICAL RELATIONS WITH THE GOVERNMENT OF BOMBAY AND THEIR LEADING OFFICIALS, NOBLES AND PERSONAGES – Calcutta: Govt of India, Centarl Publ Branch, 1931 – us Res Libr [950]

LIST OF SCHOOLS HAVING LOWER / UPPER FORM 6 LEADING TO THE ADVANCED LEVEL EXAMINATION OF THE UNIVERSITY OF HONG KONG / Hong Kong. Education Department – Hong Kong, 1972 – 1mf – 9 – DE-173/1 – ne IDC [370]

LIST OF SELECTED DOMESTIC AND FOREIGN ATTORNEYS, AND A TELEGRAPHIC CODE. / The Attorneys' Mutual Association – Detroit, 1899. LL-808 – 1 – us L of C Photodup [340]

LIST OF SHIPS INTERFERED WITH, ATTACKED OR SUNK DURING THE WAR IN SPAIN, JULY 1936-JUNE 1938 – London, 1938? Fiche W1000. (Blodgett Collection of Spanish Civil War Pamphlets) – 9 – us H.U. College Libr [946]

A LIST OF SOUTH AFRICAN INDIGENOUS PLANTS USED AS REMEDIES BY THE COLONISTS OF THE CAPE OF GOOD HOPE – (Filmed with: The South African Quarterly Journal) – Cape Town: Printed by G J Pike, 1847 – us Res Libr [615]

LIST OF STOCKHOLDERS...OF 31ST MAY, 1897 / Bank of Montreal – Montreal, 1897. 01059. (Pre-1900 Canadiana) – 9 – cn C.I.H.M. [332]

LIST OF SUBSCRIBERS FOR REBUILDING OF CHURCH, 1837 / Charleston. South Carolina. Cumberland St. Methodist Episcopal Church – 1 fiche – 9 – us South Carolina Historical [978]

LIST OF THE BRITISH MACRO-LEPIDOPTERA / Browne, A M – Birmingham, 1871. 28p. Z-1099 2 – 8 – ne IDC [590]

LIST OF THE CLERGY, FOR THE YEAR OF OUR LORD *see* DUNIGAN'S AMERICAN CATHOLIC ALMANAC AND LIST OF THE CLERGY, FOR THE YEAR OF OUR LORD...

LIST OF THE COLEOPTERA OF SOUTHERN CALIFORNIA, WITH NOTES ON HABITS AND DISTRIBUTION AND DESCRIPTIONS OF NEW SPECIES / Fall, H C – California Academy of Sciences, Occasional Papers, v8, 1901, 282p. Z/1234/2 – 8 – ne IDC [590]

A LIST OF THE FERNS OF THE MALAY PENINSULA / Ridley, H N – 7251. 1907 – 9 – ne IDC [580]

A LIST OF THE FLOWERING PLANTS AND FERNS OF THE CAPE PENINSULA / Bolus, H & Wolley-Dod, A H – (Trans. South African Phil. Soc., v. 14, pt. 3). Cape Town. 1904. B-7163 1 – 9 – ne IDC [580]

A LIST OF THE FLOWERING PLANTS, FERNS AND MOSSES OF ANDOVER / Clarke, C B – Calcutta. 1866. B-5117 2 – 8 – ne IDC [580]

A LIST OF THE GENERA OF BIRDS / Gray, G R – London, 1840; Ed. 2, rev.,augm. with index, London, 1841; App. London, 1842. Z/1784/2 – 8 – ne IDC [590]

LIST OF THE HEADS OF ADMINISTRATION IN INDIA AND OF THE INDIA OFFICE IN ENGLAND / India. Imperial Record Department – Delhi, 1938 – us Res Libr [950]

LIST OF THE LEPIDOPTERA OF BOREAL AMERICA / ed by Smith, J B – Philadelphia, 1891 – 124p – 8 – ne IDC [590]

LIST OF THE LEPIDOPTERA OF NORTH AMERICA / Grote, Augustus Radcliffe – Philadelphia: American Entomological Society, 1868. 04389. (Pre-1900 Canadiana) – 9 – cn C.I.H.M. [590]

LIST OF THE PHOTOGRAPHS AND PHOTOG. NEGATIVES RELATING TO THE WAR FOR THE UNION / U.S. War Department. General and Special Staffs – War Dept. Subj. Cat. 5, 1897. 1 roll. T251 – 1 – us Nat'l Archives [324]

LIST OF THE TREES, SHRUBS AND LARGE CLIMBERS FOUND IN THE DARJEELING DISTRICT / Gamble, J S – Bengal. Calcutta. 1878. B-758 2 – 8 – ne IDC [580]

LIST OF THE VERTEBRATED ANIMALS EXHIBITED...1828-1927 / Zoological Society of London. Gardens – 10th ed.3v. London, 1929 – 1 – us U.W. Library [590]

LIST OF TOMBS AND MONUMENTS ERECTED IN MADRAS / India – Madras, 1898. BI-740 2 – 8 – ne IDC [720]

LISTA DE ABOGADOS DEL ILUSTRE COLEGIO DE BADAJOZ. ANO DE 1930 / Colegio de Abogados de Badajoz – Badajoz: Tip. Espanola, 1930 – sp Bibl Santa Ana [946]

LISTA DE ABOGADOS DEL ILUSTRE COLEGIO DE CACERES – 1843 – 9 – $1.50f – sp Bibl Santa Ana [340]

LISTA DE ALGUNAS PLANTAS MEDICINALES... / Paccard, E – Montevideo, 1905 – 2mf – 9 – ne IDC [615]

LISTA DE FARMACEUTICOS COLEGIADOS ANO 1943 / Colegio Oficial de Farmaceuticos. Caceres – Caceres: Tip. El Noticiero, S.A. 1943 – 1 – sp Bibl Santa Ana [060]

LISTA DE FARMACEUTICOS COLEGIADOS, ANO 1945 / Colegio Oficial de Farmaceuticos. Caceres – Caceres: Imp. Garcia Floriano, s.a. 1945 – 1 – sp Bibl Santa Ana [060]

LISTA DE LOS ABOGADOS DEL ILUSTRE COLEGIO DE CADERES EN ESTE ANO DE 1873 / Colegio de Abogados de Caceres – Caceres: Imp. de Fdez. y Cia, 1873 – 1 – sp Bibl Santa Ana [370]

LISTA DE LOS ABOGADOS...CACERES – (1865-1900. 1.50f; 9) – 1830 – 9 – 1.50f – sp Bibl Santa Ana [340]

LISTA DE LOS SENORES NOTARIOS QUE SE HALLAN EJERCIENDO EN EL TERRITORIO DE LA AUDIENCIA DE CACERES. ANO DE 1865 – (Tambien Anos) – Caceres: Imp. de Nicolas Maria Jimenez, 1865 – sp Bibl Santa Ana [946]

LISTA DE SENORES COLEGIADOS POR PARTIDOS JUDICIALES Y POR ORDEN DE INCORPORACION A ESTE COLEGIO PROVINCIAL / Colegio Oficial de Medicos de la Provincia de Caceres – Caceres: Imp. Garcia Floriano, 1939 – sp Bibl Santa Ana [340]

LISTA DE SRES. MEDICOS COLEGIADOS 1969 / Colegio Oficial de Medicos de la Provincia de Badajoz – Badajoz: Graf. Extremena, 1969 – sp Bibl Santa Ana [610]

LISTA OFICIAL DE LOS SENORES ABOGADOS DEL ILUSTRE COLEGIO PROVINCIAL DE CACERES Y GUIA JUDICIAL DE LOS TRIBUNALES DE DICHA CIUDAD PARA EL ANO 1956 / Colegio Provincial de Abogados de Caceres – Caceres: El Noticiero, 1956 – sp Bibl Santa Ana [340]

LISTA OFICIAL DE LOS SENORES ABOGADOS DEL ILUSTRE COLEGIO PROVINCIAL DE CACERES Y GUIA JUDICIAL DE LOS TRIBUNALES DE DICHA CIUDAD PARA EL ANO 1959 / Colegio Provincial de Abogados de Caceres – Caceres: El Noticiero, 1959 – sp Bibl Santa Ana [340]

LISTA OFICIAL DE LOS SENORES ABOGADOS DEL ILUSTRE COLEGIO PROVINCIAL DE CACERES Y GUIA JUDICIAL DE LOS TRIBUNALES DE DICHA CIUDAD PARA EL ANO 1960 / Colegio Provincial de Abogados de Caceres – Caceres: Tip. El Noticiero, 1960 – sp Bibl Santa Ana [340]

LISTA OFICIAL DE LOS SENORES ABOGADOS Y PROCURADORES Y GUIA JUDICIAL / Colegio Provincial de Abogados – Caceres: Tip. Tomas Rodriguez Santano, 1974 – 1 – sp Bibl Santa Ana [350]

LISTA OFICIAL DE LOS SENORES ABOGADOS Y PROCURADORES Y GUIA JUDICIAL. ANO 1967 / Colegio Provincial de Abogados – Caceres: El Noticiero, 1967 – 1 – sp Bibl Santa Ana [350]

LISTA OFICIAL DE LOS SENORES ABOGADOS Y PROCURADORES Y GUIA JUDICIAL DE LA PROVINCIA. ANO 1958 / Colegio Oficial de Abogados de Badajoz – Badajoz: Tipografia Clasica, 1958 – sp Bibl Santa Ana [340]

LISTA OFICIAL DE LOS SENORES ABOGADOS Y PROCURADORES Y GUIA JUDICIAL DE LA PROVINCIA. ANO DE 1953 / Colegio Provincial de Abogados de Badajoz – Badajoz: Tipografia Clasica, 1953 – sp Bibl Santa Ana [340]

LISTA OFICIAL DE LOS SENORES ABOGADOS Y PROCURADORES Y GUIA JUDICIAL DE LA PROVINCIA. ANO DE 1957 / Colegio Provincial de Abogados de Badajoz – Badajoz: Tipografia Clasica, 1957 – sp Bibl Santa Ana [340]

LISTA OFICIAL DE LOS SENORES COLEGIADOS Y GUIA JUDICIAL DE LOS TRIBUNALES DE LA CIUDAD. ANO 1961 / Colegio Provincial de Abogados de Caceres – Caceres: Tip. El Noticiero, 1961 – sp Bibl Santa Ana [340]

LISTA OFICIAL DE LOS SRES. ABOGADOS Y PROCURADORES Y GUIA JUDICIAL DE LA PROVINCIA. ANO DE 1959 / Colegio Provincial de Abogados de Badajoz – Badajoz: Tip. Clasica, 1959 – sp Bibl Santa Ana [340]

LISTA OFICIAL DE LOS SRES. ABOGADOS Y PROCURADORES Y GUIA JUDICIAL DE LA PROVINCIA. ANO DE 1960 / Colegio Provincial de Abogados de Badajoz – Badajoz: Tip. Clasica, 1960 – sp Bibl Santa Ana [340]

LISTA OFICIAL DE LOS SRES. ABOGADOS Y PROCURADORES Y GUIA JUDICIAL DE LA PROVINCIA. ANO DE 1961 / Colegio Provincial de Abogados de Badajoz – Badajoz: Tip. Clasica, 1961 – sp Bibl Santa Ana [340]

LISTA OFICIAL DE LOS SRES. ABOGADOS Y PROCURADORES Y GUIA JUDICIAL DE LA PROVINCIA. ANO DE 1962 / Colegio Provincial de Abogados de Badajoz – Badajoz: Tip. Clasica, 1962 – sp Bibl Santa Ana [340]

LISTA OFICIAL DE LOS SRES. ABOGADOS Y PROCURADORES Y GUIA JUDICIAL DE LA PROVINCIA. ANO DE 1965 / Colegio Oficial de Abogados de Badajoz – Badajoz: Tip. Clasica, 1965 – sp Bibl Santa Ana [340]

LISTA OFICIAL DE LOS SRES. COLEGIADOS, DE LOS SRES. PROCURADORES Y GUIA JUDICIAL DE LA PROVINCIA. ANO DE 1968 / Colegio Provincial de Abogados de Badajoz – Badajoz: Tip. Clasica, 1968 – sp Bibl Santa Ana [340]

LISTA OFICIAL DE LOS SRES. COLEGIADOS, DE LOS SRES. PROCURADORES Y GUIA JUDICIAL DE LA PROVINCIA. ANO DE 1971 / Colegio Provincial de Abogados de Badajoz – Badajoz: Tip. Clasica, 1971 – sp Bibl Santa Ana [340]

LISTA PRELIMINAR DE LAS PLANTAS DE EL SALVADOR / Standley, P C & Calderon, S – San Salvador, 1925. 274 pp. B-5259 2 – 8 – ne IDC [580]

LISTE ANNOTEE DES LEPIDOPTERES ENVOYES A LA SOCIETE D'HISTOIRE NATURELLE D'AUTUN / Constant, A – Autun, 1892. 69p. (Bull. Soc. Hist. Nat. Autun, v5). Z-1146/2 – 8 – ne IDC [590]

LISTE AUSGEWAEHLTER KEILSCHRIFTZEICHEN : ZUM GEBRAUCHE FUER ANFAENGER / Winckler, Hugo – Leipzig: Eduard Pfeiffer, 1893 – 1mf – 9 – 0-8370-8636-1 – 1986-2636 – us A.T.L.A. [470]

LISTE DE BENEFICIAIRES DE CITATIONS / France. Journal officiel – (CITATIONS GUERRE. 1941-43, 1946. 1. MINISTRE ET CITATIONS AIR. 1941-44. 1) – fr A.C.R.P.P. [944]

LISTE DE MESSIEURS LES ELECTEURS DES NEUF DISTRICTS DU DEPARTEMENT DE LA LOIRE-INFERIEURE... / Elections, Loire-Inferieure – Nantes: Malassis, 1790 – 1 – F50.00 – fr Armell [320]

LISTE DER BOERSEN-HALLE *see* PRIVILIGIRTE LISTE DER BOERSENHALLE

LISTE DES ALGUES MARINES DE CHERBOURG / Le Jolis, A F – (Mem. Soc. Sci. Nat. Cherbourg. v. 10. 1864). Cherbourg. 1864. B-5250 2 – 8 – ne IDC [580]

LISTE DES LIVRES OFFERTS EN DON A L'UNIVERSITE DE HARVARD PAR LE MARQUIS DE OLIVART – Madrid, 1912 – 1mf – ILM-2295/1 – ne IDC [340]

LISTE DES MUNICIPALITES DANS LA PROVINCE DE QUEBEC = LIST OF MUNICIPALITIES IN THE PROVINCE OF QUEBEC / Deschamps, Clement E – (10mf SEM105P51 Can$22.50) – Levis: Mercier, 1886. SEM35P62 – 1r – 1 – Can$25.00 – cn Bibl Nat [971]

LISTE DES PAPPORTS SIC OU ETATS ANNUELS OU SESSIONNELS QUI DOIVENT ETRE PRESENTES A LA LEGISLATURE DU CANADA. – Quebec: Des presses a vapeur de John Lovell, 1854. SEM105P424 – 1mf – 9 – Can$2.25 – cn Bibl Nat [323]

LISTE DES SOCIETES DE LA PAIX AU 30 OCTOBRE 1912 / Bureau International permanent de la Paix – N.p., [1913] – 2mf – 1 – ILM-4080/1 – ne IDC [327]

LISTE DES TERRAINS CONCEDES PAR LA COURONNE DANS LA PROVINCE DE QUEBEC DE 1763 AU 31 DECEMBRE 1890 – Quebec: Charles Francois Langlois, 1891. SEM105P249 – 21mf – 9 – Can$47.25 – cn Bibl Nat [971]

LISTE DES TERRES CONCEDEES PAR LA COURONNE DE 1763 A 1890 – Quebec, Canada. 1v. 1891 – 1r – 1 – Can$35.00 – cn Can Microfilming [971]

LISTE DES TRAVAUX DE M. BROSSET...LE 22 AOUT (3 SEPTEMBRE) 1880 / [Brosset, M] – Melanges Asiatiques. v9 (p. 1-53). 1880-1888 – 1mf – 9 – ne IDC [950]

LISTE OFFICIELLE D'ENNEMIS / France. Supplement au Journal officiel – mai 1944-fevr 1946 – 1 – fr A.C.R.P.P. [323]

LISTED ORDINATES OF THE "GUNACA" AEROFOILS A REVISION OF THE NACA 6 SERIES OF LOW-DRAG SECTIONS / Nonweiler, T R F – 1972 – 9 – uk Microform Academic [600]

LISTEN – v1- 1948- 1; v28- 5,6; v29- 9 – us UMI [300]

LISTENER – v105, no.2287. 3-9 Dec 1983-. -w. Broadcasting Corporation of New Zealand. Running title: NZ Listener – 1 – us U.W. Library [073]

THE LISTENER – Monrovia. Liberia. feb. 15-19, 1955 – 1 – us NY Public [071]

THE LISTENER, 1929-91 – (v1-102 1929-79 65r 1. v103-125 1980-91 330mf 9) – v1-125 – 1,9 – £4,820.00 – uk Chadwyck [073]

THE LISTENER-NEWS – New York. Oct. 29, 1938; Oct. 7, Dec. 23, 1939; Mar. 30, 1940 – 1 – us NY Public [071]

LISTENING – (v.15-. 1980- 5,6,9) – v.1-. 1966- – 1 – us UMI [073]

Listenius, Nicolaus *see*
- MUSICA NICOLAI LISTENII, AB AUTHORE DENUO RECOGNITA, MULTISQUE NOVIS REGULIS ET EXEMPLIS ADAUCTA
- MUSICA NICOLAUS LISTENII, AB AUTHORE DENUO RECOGNITA, MULTISQ NOUIS REGULIS ET EXEMPLIS ADAUCTA
- RUDIMENTA MUSICAE IN GRATIAM STUDIOSAE IUVENTUTIS DILIGENTER COMPORTATA

Lister, J B *see* HOW TO SUCCEED

Lister, M *see*
- HISTORIA SIVE SYNOPSIS METHODICA CONCHYLIORUM
- HISTORIAE SIVE SYNOPSIS METHODICAE CONCHYLIORUM

Lister, Thomas Henry *see* LIFE AND ADMINISTRATION OF EDWARD, FIRST EARL OF CLARENDON; WITH ORIGINAL CORRESPONDENCE, AND AUTHENTIC PAPERS NEVER BEFORE PUBLISHED

LISTES DE SOUSCRIPTION / Commission Internationale pour l'Aide aux Refugies Espanols – Paris, 1939. Fiche W 811. (Blodgett Collection of Spanish Civil War Pamphlets) – 9 – us H.U. College Libr [946]

LISTI UNDOL'SKOGO, OTRYVOK KIRILLOVSKOGO EVANGELIJA XI V. FOTOTIPICHESKOE VOSPROIZVEDINIE TEKSTA I ISSLEDOVANIE PIS'MA I IAZYKA / Karskii, E F – Saint Petersburg, 1904. BR-10,335/1 – 9 – ne IDC [460]

LISTIN DIARIA – Dominican Republic. 1910- – 1 – us UMI [072]

LISTING OF AMENDMENTS PROPOSED TO H.R. 6767, THE PROPOSED TRADE REFORM ACT OF 1973 / U.S. Congress. House. Committee on Ways and Means – Washington, Govt. Print. Off., 1973. 36 p. LL-2241 – 1 – us L of C Photodup [340]

LISTKI "KHLEB I VOLIA" – London. Mar. 15-Apr. 15, May 1, 1907 – 1 – 35.00r – us Hoover Inst Photo [073]

LISTOK – Uzhhorod, Sep. 14, 1885-Dec. 15, 1903 – 8r – 1 – us I.H.R.C. [073]

LISTOK DLIA SVETSKIKH LIUDEI – Ezhenedel'nik s karikaturami. v. 1-48. Spb. 1843-44. BR-3365 2 – 8 – ne IDC [073]

LISTOK KNIZHNIKH OB IAVLENII – Spb, 1903 – 8 – BR-4319 2 – ne IDC [947]

LISTON PAPERS 1796-1800 – November 1990, M.A.P. West Yorkshire – 4r – 1 – uk Microform Academic [975]

Liston, WG *see* A MONOGRAPH OF THE ANOPHELES MOSQUITOES OF INDIA

LISTS AND GUIDES TO OFFICIAL INDIAN PUBLICATIONS / India – 1892-1917 – 1 – us Res Libr [020]

LISTS OF ANCIENT MONUMENTS IN BENGAL / India – Revised and corrected up to 31st Aug 1895. Calcutta, 1896. BI-722 2 – 8 – ne IDC [930]

LISTS OF ANTIQUARIAN REMAINS IN HIS HIGHNESS THE NIZAM'S TERRITORIES / India; ed by Cousens, H – Calcutta, 1900. v31. BI-719 2 – 8 – ne IDC [950]

LISTS OF CHINESE APPLYING FOR ADMISSION TO THE UNITED STATES THROUGH THE PORT OF SAN FRANCISCO, 1903-1947 – 27r – 1 – M1476 – us Nat'l Archives [340]

LISTS OF CHINESE PASSENGER ARRIVALS AT SAN FRANCISCO, 1882-1914 – 32r – 1 – M1414 – us Nat'l Archives [340]

LISTS OF CHINESE PASSENGERS ARRIVING AT SEATTLE (PORT TOWNSEND), WASHINGTON, 1882-1916 – 10r – 1 – M1364 – us Nat'l Archives [340]

LISTS OF CHRISTIAN TOMBS AND MONUMENTS OF ARCHAEOLOGICAL AND HISTORICAL INTEREST AND THEIR INSCRIPTIONS IN THE N.W. PROV. AND OUDH / India; ed by Fuehrer, A – Allahabad, 1896. Index, Allahabad, 1899. BI-737 2 – 8 – ne IDC [720]

LISTS OF EMIGRANTS TO AMERICA – By John Camden Hotten 1880. English emigrants to America, 1600-1700. Item F. Indexed, 580p. SW16-0079 – 5 – us A.G.L.L. [920]

LISTS OF INSCRIPTIONS AND A SKETCH OF THE DYNASTIES OF SOUTHERN INDIA / India; ed by Sewell, R – Madras, 1883. BI-699 2 – 8 – ne IDC [410]

LISTS OF LANDS GRANTED BY THE CROWN IN THE PROVINCE OF QUEBEC, FROM 1763 TO 31 DECEMBER 1890 – Quebec: Charles Francois Langlois..., 1891. SEM105P468 – 21mf – 9 – Can$47.25 – cn Bibl Nat [971]

LISTS OF MEDALS AND CLASPS NEW SOUTH WALES DEFENCE FORCE, 1899-1902 – 6r – 1 – CRS B5197 – at Archives [920]

LISTS OF MONUMENTS / India; ed by Burgess, J – Lists of the antiquarian remains in the Bombay Presidency, with an appendix of inscriptions from Gujarat. Bombay. 1885. BI-715 2 – 8 – ne IDC [720]

LISTS OF MONUMENTS : LIST OF SOME ANCIENT AND NATIVE ARCHITECTURAL BUILDINGS IN INDIA – Simla, 1880 – 1mf – 9 – ne IDC [720]

LISTS OF PUBLIC WORKS DEPARTMENT RECORDS IN THE IMPERIAL RECORD OFFICE, CALCUTTA, 1880-1894 / India. Imperial Record Office – Calcutta. 1910. BI-325 2 – 8 – ne IDC [336]

LISTS OF SANSKRIT, JAINA AND HINDI MSS, PURCHASED BY ORDER OF GOVERNMENT AND DEPOSITED IN THE SANSKRIT COLLEGE, BENARES DURING 1902-1918/1919 – (Missing: 1907-1908. 1913/14-1914/15) – Allahabad, 1904-1919 – 6mf – 9 – ne IDC [490]

LISTS OF SANSKRIT MSS IN PRIVATE LIBRARIES OF SOUTHERN INDIA / Oppert, G – Madras. 2v. 1880-1885 – 15mf – 9 – ne IDC [490]

LISTS OF STATUES, MONUMENTS, AND BUSTS ERECTED IN MADRAS IN HONOUR OF DISTINGUISHED SERVANTS OF THE STATE / India – Madras, 1898. BI-739 2 – 8 – ne IDC [730]

LISTS OF STATUES, MONUMENTS AND BUSTS IN CALCUTTA OF HISTORICAL INTEREST / Bengal. India (State). Public Works Department – Calcutta, 1902. BI-732 2 – 8 – ne IDC [730]

LISTS OF THE ADJUTANT GENERAL'S OFFICE FOR CARDED RECORDS OF MILITARY ORGANIZATIONS : REVOLUTIONARY WAR THROUGH PHILIPPINE INSURRECTION ("THE AINSWORTH LIST") – 112r – 1 – T817 – us Nat'l Archives [355]

LISTS OF U.S. CITIZENS ARRIVING AT SAN FRANCISCO, 1930-1949 – 50r – 1 – M1439 – us Nat'l Archives [340]

LISTS OF U.S. CONSULAR OFFICERS, 1789-1939 / U.S. Department of State – 21 rolls. M587. Printed guide – 1 – us Nat'l Archives [975]

LISTS OF U.S. DIPLOMATIC OFFICERS, 1789-1939 / U.S. Department of State – 3rolls. M586. Printed guide – 1 – us Nat'l Archives [975]

LISTS OF U.S. POST OFFICES / U.S. Post Office – Official and semi-official lists or tables of post offices in the United States between 1797 and 1873. Some years lacking – 1 – 302.00 – us L of C Photodup [380]

LISTY / Slowacki, J – v. 1-3. Lwow. 1899-1915. BR-8021 2 – 8 – ne IDC [460]

LISTY PRATELUM – London, UK. Apr, Jul 1944 – 1 – uk British Libr Newspaper [072]

LISTY Z PODROZY: WYBOR / Odyniec, Antoni Edward – Lwow, 1900? 487p – 1 – us U.W. Library [460]

Liszt, F *see*
– ANNEES DE PELERINAGE

Liszt, Franz *see*
– ANNEES DE PELERINAGE
– FRANZ LISZT'S BRIEFE

LIT : LITERATURE INTERPRETATION THEORY / ed by Jacobus, Lee A & Barreca, Regina – 9,5,1 – us Gordon [400]

LITAFI NA TATSUNIYOYI NA HAUSA / Edgar, Frank – Belfast: W E Mayne, 1911-13 – us Res Libr [470]

LI-TAI-PE : NACHDICHTUNGEN / Klabund – Leipzig: Insel, [1915] – 1r – 1 – us U.W. Library [480]

LITAUISCHE RUNDSCHAU – Kauen (Kaunas), Lietuva.(Kowno, USSR). 20 Jul 1920-22 Jul 1921; 11 Jun 1924-29 Jun 1929 – 6r – 1 – gw Mikrofilm [947]

Litch, Josiah *see* A COMPLETE HARMONY OF DANIEL AND THE APOCALYPSE

Litchfield County. Connecticut *see*
– BURYING GROUND OF SHARON, CONNECTICUT & ANEMIA & NORTH EAST NEW YORK
– THE HISTORY OF THE TOWN OF LITCHFIELD, CONNECTICUT, 1720-1920
– RURAL LIFE IN LITCHFIELD COUNTY
– SHARON, CONNECTICUT BIRTHS, MARRIAGES AND DEATHS FROM 1721-1870

LITCHFIELD JOURNAL – Litchfield, Conn. 1818. Sold with yNew London Summary – 1,3 – us Readex [071]

Litchfield Law School *see* CATALOGUE... FROM 1793 TO 1827 INCLUSIVE

Litchfield, Maine. First Baptist Church *see* RECORDS

LITCHFIELD MONITOR – Litchfield, NE. -w. Oct 1886-88 (scattered issues missing); Mar 1892; Jun 1892; Dec 1895-May 1898; Oct 1902; Dec 1904; Dec 1907; Sept 1908-Sept 1911; Jun 1914-May 1955 – 1 – us NE Hist [071]

LITCHFIELD REPUBLICAN – Litchfield, Conn. 1819-21. Sold with New London Summary – 1,3 – us Readex [071]

LITCHI CULTIVATION – 1989 – 143p – it F.A.O. [634]

LITERACY 1972-1976 : PROGRESS ACHIEVED IN LITERACY THROUGHOUT THE WORLD – 1980 – 84p – 9 – 92-3-101731-4 – fr UNESCO [370]

LITERACY DISCUSSION – v1- 1970- 1; v6- 1975- 5,6,9 – us UMI [370]

LITERACY FOR RURAL WOMEN IN THE THIRD WORLD / Chlebowska, Krystyna – 1990 – 146p – 9 – 92-3-102710-7 – fr UNESCO [370]

LITERACY REVIEW – v.1-. 1980- – 1,5,6,9 – us UMI [073]

LITERACY SITUATION IN THAILAND : A NATIONAL STUDY / Thailand. Ministry of Education. Department of Non-Formal Education – Bangkok, 1983 – 2mf – 9 – DE-601/1 – ne IDC [370]

LITERACY STATISTICS AT A GLANCE / India. Directorate of Adult Education – New Delhi, 1979 – 4mf – 9 – DE-541/1 – ne IDC [370]

LITERACY WORK – 1971- 1; 1975- 5,6,9 – us UMI [370]

LITERAE CANTUARIENSES (RS85) = THE LETTER BOOKS OF THE MONASTERY OF CHRIST CHURCH, CANTERBURY / Canterbury. Christ Church Priory; ed by Sheppard, J B – (v1 1887 Dfl39.00. v2 1888 Dfl35.00. v3 1889 Dfl32.00) – ne Slangenburg [240]

LITERAE SVLTANI SVLEMANNI... – Patavii, [1563] – 1mf – 9 – H-8163/1 – ne IDC [956]

EN LITERAIR ANMELDELSE : TO TIDSALDRE, NOVELLE AF FORFATTEREN TIL "EN HVERDAGS-HISTORIE", UDGIVEN AF J.L. HEIBERG, KBHV., REITZEL, 1845 / Kierkegaard, Soren – Kjobenhavn: C.A. Reitzel, 1846 – 1mf – us A.T.L.A. [190]

DIE LITERARHISTORISCHE GESELLSCHAFT BONN IM ERSTEN DRITTEL DES 20. JAHRHUNDERTS : DARGESTELLT AM BRIEFNACHLASS VON CARL ENDERS / Horstmann, Christina – (Includes bibliographical references) – Bonn: Bouvier, 1987 – 1 – us U.W. Library [430]

DIE LITERARISCHE KRITIK IN DER MITTELHOCHDEUTSCHEN DICHTUNG UND IHR WESEN / Mueller, Karl Friedrich – (Includes bibliographical references) – Frankfurt am Main: M Diesterweg, 1933 – 1 – us U.W. Library [430]

LITERARISCHE UTOPIE-ENTWUERFE / ed by Gnueg, Hiltrud – (Inlcudes bibliographical references) – Frankfurt am Main: Suhrkamp, 1982 – 1r – 1 – us U.W. Library [430]

LITERARISCHE WELT – Berlin, 1931-34 – 1 – Dist. gw Mikrofilm – gw Misc Inst [430]

LITERARISCHE ZEITUNG – Berlin, 1842-43 – 1r – 1 – Dist. gw Mikrofilm – gw Misc Inst [430]

LITERARISCHER HANDWEISER ZUNAECHST FUER ALLE KATHOLIKEN DEUTSCHER ZUNGE – Muenster, Theissing. Jahrg. 1-67; 1862-1931. 1862-1903 numbered Nr. 1-788. Jahrg. numbering begins with Jahrg. 12, 1873. Includes index to Nr. 0-50 (1862-66) and Nr. 51-110 (1867-71). Film Mas C 613 – 1 – us H.U. Library [073]

LITERARISCHES CENTRALBLATT FUER DEUTSCHLAND, 1. 1850-95. 1944 : MIT: JAHRESBERICHTE DES LITERARISCHEN ZENTRALBLATTES, 1. 1924/25 – 18. 1941/42; DAS DEUTSCHE WISSENSCHAFTLICHE SCHRIFTTUM, 19. 1942/43; DIE SCHOENE LITERATUR, 3. 1902 – 31. 1930; DIE NEUE LITERATUR 32. 1931 – 44. 1943; DIE JAHRESERNTE 1. 1923 – 9. 1931 – 1850-1944 (mf ed 1997) – 999mf – 9 – DM7,900.00 – 3-89131-239-3 – gw Fischer [430]

LITERARISCHES WOCHENBLATT, 1818-1820 / ed by Kotzebue, August von – 1818-20 (mf ed 1997) – 31mf – 9 – DM420.00 – 3-89131-235-0 – gw Fischer [305]

LITERARISCHES ZENTRALBLATT FUER DEUTSCHLAND 1850-1945 : UNIVERSALWISSENSCHAFTLICHE ZEITSCHRIFT UND BIBLIOGRAPHISCHER ANZEIGER / ed by Zarncke, Friedrich – (Beilage: DIE SCHOENE LITERATUR, 1900-25, seit 1923 als selbstaendiges Rezensionsorgan herausgegeben von Will Vesper. Fortgefuehrt unter dem Titel DIE NEUE LITERATUR, 1931-43) – Leipzig, 1850-1944 – 400mf – subsc: DM2,200.00 diazo DM2,900.00 silver – gw Olms [430]

LITERARISHE MONATSHRIFTEN = LITERARY MONTHLY – (In Yiddish) – Vilnius, LT. no1. Feb 1908 – 1r – 1 – $25.00 – cn Can Microfilming [072]

LITERARKRITISCHE UNTERSUCHUNG ZUR ORIENTALISCH-APOKRYPHEN EVANGELIEN LITERATUR / Haase, Felix – Leipzig, 1913 – 2mf – 9 – ne IDC [240]

LITERARKRITISCHE UNTERSUCHUNGEN ZUR ORIENTALISCH-APOKRYPHEN EVANGELIENLITERATUR / Haase, Felix – Leipzig: J.C. Hinrichs, 1913 – 1mf – us A.T.L.A. [240]

LITERARNI LISTY – Kralovske Vinohrady, Prague, Czechoslovakia. 1923-24 – 1 – us I.U. Libraries [073]

LITERARNI LISTY – Prague, Czechoslovakia. 1865 – 1 – us I.U. Libraries [073]

LITERARNI LISTY – Prague. Czechoslovakia. -w. 4 Mar-15 Sep 1968. (1 reel) – 1 – uk British Libr Newspaper [072]

LITERARNI LISTY – Velke Mezirici, Czechoslovakia. v6-12,14. 1885-91, 1893 – 1 – us I.U. Libraries [073]

LITERARNI NOVIGNY – (Standing order available from De 1994 +. 2r per year. Sfr225.00y) – De 1992 a 1993 – 2r – 1 – Sfr240.00 – sz Infoprint [460]

LITERARNI NOVINY – (1992-1995 2r per y $170y. 1997-98 1r per y $85y) – Czech Republic, 1999- – 1r per y – 1 – $170.00 standing order – us Ross [460]

LITERARNY TYZDENNIK – (Backfile through 1998 $85r) – Slovakia, 1999- – 1r per y – 1 – $80.00 standing order – us Ross [072]

LITERARY AND EVANGELICAL MAGAZINE – v. 1-11. January 1818-December 1828 – 1 – us UMI [240]

LITERARY AND HISTORICAL ESSAYS / Davis, Thomas Osborne – Dublin: Published by James Duffy, 1846 – 1 roll – 1 – 1-55879-647-9 – uk Libr Preservation [840]

Literary and Historical Society of Quebec *see*
– BULLETIN/[LITERARY AND HISTORICAL SOCIETY OF QUEBEC]
– HISTORICAL DOCUMENTS
– LIBRARY BULLETIN...OF THE LITERARY AND HISTORICAL SOCIETY OF QUEBEC
– TRANSACTIONS

LITERARY AND HISTORICAL SOCIETY OF QUEBEC. BULLETIN *see* LIBRARY BULLETIN...OF THE LITERARY AND HISTORICAL SOCIETY OF QUEBEC

LITERARY AND MUSICAL MAGAZINE – v. 1-4. July 5, 1817-June 9, 1820 – 1 – us UMI [780]

LITERARY AND PHILOSOPHICAL REPERTORY – v1-2 Apr 1812-May 1817 – 1 – us UMI [100]

LITERARY AND PSYCHOLOGICAL ASPECTS OF THE HEBREW PROPHETS / Widengren, George – 9 – $10.00 – us I.R.C. [220]

LITERARY AND SCIENTIFIC REPOSITORY, AND CRITICAL REVIEW – v. 1-4. June 1820-May 1822 – 1 – us UMI [410]

LITERARY AND SOCIAL JUDGMENTS / Greg, William Rathbone – London: Trbner, 4th enl ed 1877 – 1 roll – 1 – 1-55879-205-8 – uk Libr Preservation [420]

LITERARY ANECDOTES AND CONTEMPORARY REMINISCENCES OF PROFESSOR PORSON AND OTHERS / Barker, Edmund Henry – From the mss. papers of the late E.H. Barker. London: J.R. Smith, 1852. 2v – 1 – us U.W. Library [420]

LITERARY ANECDOTES OF THE NINETEENTH CENTURY : CONTRIBUTIONS TOWARDS A LITERARY HISTORY OF THE PERIOD / Nicoll, William Robertson; ed by Nicoll, W Robertson & Wise, Thomas J – London: Hodder and Stoughton, 1895-1896 – 2 rolls – 1 – 1-55879-973-7 – uk Libr Preservation [420]

LITERARY CABINET – v. 1. November 15, 1806-October 31, 1807 – 1 – us UMI [073]

LITERARY CABINET AND WESTERN OLIVE BRANCH – N.S. 1. February 16, 1833-February 8, 1834 – 1 – us UMI [073]

LITERARY CASKET: DEVOTED TO LITERATURE, THE ARTS AND SCIENCE – v. 1. March 4, 1826-February 3, 1827 – 1 – us UMI [073]

LITERARY CAVALCADE – 1948- 1; 1971- 5,6; 1976- 4 x 6 in. 9 – us UMI [800]

LITERARY CHRONICLE AND WEEKLY REVIEW – v. 1-N.S. v. 1. May 22, 1819-July 26, 1828 – 1 – us UMI [410]

LITERARY COMPANION – v. 1. June 16-September 8, 1821 – 1 – us UMI [073]

LITERARY DIGEST – v. 1-51. 1890-1922 – 1 – us UMI [073]

LITERARY DIGEST – v.11-125. 1895-1938 – 1 – 221934.00 – us Princeton Micro [410]

LITERARY ECHO – Westerly. R.I. 1852-1853; 1873-1885 – 1 – us UMI [071]

THE LITERARY ECHO – Charlottetown, PEJ: Ross Sisters, [1874-18– or 19–] – 9 – cn C.I.H.M. [420]

LITERARY EXAMINER, CONSISTING OF THE INDICATOR, A REVIEW OF BOOKS, AND MISCELLANEOUS PIECES IN PROSE AND VERSE – v1 July 5-December 27, 1823 – 1 – us UMI [800]

LITERARY FOCUS – v. 1. June 1827-May 1828 – 1 – us UMI [410]

LITERARY GARLAND – v1-4. Dec 1838-Dec 1851 – 1 – cn Precision [800]

THE LITERARY GARLAND – Montreal, Canada. ns: v1 n2. fev 1843-v4 n12. dec 1846 – 1r – 1 – Can$50.00 – cn Can Microfilming [073]

LITERARY GAZETTE – London. 1817-50 – 1,5,6 – us Princeton Micro [800]

LITERARY GAZETTE – London. Jan 25 1817-Apr 26 1862. Incomplete – 1 – us NY Public [800]

LITERARY GAZETTE – v. 1-2. 1834-1835 – 1 – us UMI [073]

LITERARY GAZETTE : A WEEKLY JOURNAL OF LITERATURE, SCIENCE AND THE FINE ARTS – London. v1-42; ns: v1-8. 1817-62 – 15r – 1 – us Ross [073]

LITERARY GAZETTE: OR, JOURNAL OF CRITICISM, SCIENCE AND THE ARTS: BEING A COLLECTION OF ORIGINAL AND SELECTED ESSAYS – v. 1. January 6-December 29, 1821 – 1 – us UMI [073]

LITERARY GEMINAE – v. 1. June 1839-May 1840 – 1 – us UMI [073]

LITERARY GUARDIAN, AND SPECTATOR OF BOOKS, SCIENCE, FINE ARTS, THE DRAMA – v. 1-2. October 1, 1831-1832 – 1 – us UMI [073]

A LITERARY HISTORY OF EARLY CHRISTIANITY : INCLUDING THE FATHERS AND THE CHIEF HERETICAL WRITERS OF THE ANTE-NICENE PERIOD / Cruttwell, Charles Thomas – London: C. Griffin, 1893 – 2mf – us A.T.L.A. [240]

THE LITERARY HISTORY OF THE MIDDLE AGES : COMPREHENDING AN ACCOUNT OF THE STATE OF LEARNING FROM THE CLOSE OF THE REIGN OF AUGUSTUS, TO ITS REVIVAL IN THE FIFTEENTH CENTURY / Berington, Joseph – London: D. Bogue, 1846 – 2mf – us A.T.L.A. [400]

LITERARY JOURNAL: A REPOSITORY OF POLITE LITERATURE AND FINE ARTS – v. 1. November 1834-June 1835 – 1 – us UMI [073]
LITERARY JOURNAL: A REVIEW OF LITERATURE, SCIENCE, MANNERS, POLITICS – v. 1-N.S. v. 2. 1802-1806 – 1 – us UMI [073]
LITERARY JOURNAL AND GENERAL MISCELLANY OF SCIENCE, ART, HISTORY, POLITICS, ETC – v. 1-2. March 29, 1818-May 8, 1819 – 1 – us UMI [073]
THE LITERARY LIFE AND CORRESPONDENCE OF THE COUNTESS OF BLESSINGTON / Madden, Richard Robert – London: T.C. Newby, 1855 – 3 rolls – 1 – 1-55879-057-8 – uk Libr Preservation [420]
LITERARY MAGAZINE – v. 1. January 1835 – 1 – us UMI [073]
LITERARY MAGAZINE, AND AMERICAN REGISTER – v. 1-8. October 1803-December 1807 – 1 – us UMI [073]
LITERARY MAGAZINE: OR, THE HISTORY OF THE WORKS OF THE LEARNED – v. 1-2. January 1735-December 1736 – 1 – us UMI [410]
LITERARY MAGAZINE: OR, UNIVERSAL REVIEW – v. 1-3. April 15 May 14, 1756-July 1758 – 1 – us UMI [073]
LITERARY MAGAZINES OF THE IRISH RENAISSANCE – 1904-57 – 9 – ie Microforms [420]
LITERARY MAGNET; OR MONTHLY JOURNAL OF THE BELLES LETTRES – v. 1-N.S. v. 5. 1824-1828 – 1 – us UMI [073]
LITERARY MIRROR – v. 1. February 20, 1808-February 11, 1809 – 1 – us UMI [073]
LITERARY MISCELLANY, CONTAINING ELEGANT SELECTIONS OF THE MOST ADMIRED FUGITIVE PIECES AND EXTRACTS FROM WORKS OF THE GREATEST MERIT, WITH ORIGINALS – v. 1. 1795 – 1 – us UMI [800]
LITERARY MISCELLANY; OR MONTHLY REVIEW, A PERIODICAL WORK – v. 1. May-August 1811 – 1 – us UMI [073]
LITERARY MUSEUM – January-June 1797 – 1 – us UMI [073]
THE LITERARY NEWS – Victoria, BC: B C Stationery Co, [1880?-18– or 19–] – 9 – cn C.I.H.M. [420]
LITERARY PAMPHLETEER – containing some observations on the best mode of promoting the cause of literature in the State of Kentucky. v. 1-6. 1823- – 1 – us UMI [073]
LITERARY REGISTER AND SPECIAL ADVERTISER – Halifax, NS: W H Hagarty, [1857-18–] – 9 – cn C.I.H.M. [070]
LITERARY REMAINS OF THE UNITED IRISHMEN OF 1798. / Madden, Richard Robert – Dublin: J. Duffy, 1887. xix,360p – 1 – us U.W. Library [420]
LITERARY REVIEW – v1- 1957- 1; v15- 5,6; v20- 9 – us UMI [073]
LITERARY SHEAVES, OR LA LITTERATURE AU CANADA FRANCAIS: THE DRAMA, HISTORY, ROMANCE, POETRY, LECTURES, SKETCHES, ETC / Bender, Prosper – Montreal: Dawson Bros., 1881. 00120. (Pre-1900 Canadiana) – 9 – cn C.I.H.M. [800]
LITERARY SOUVENIR – 1825-35 – 52mf – 9 – £385.00 – uk Chadwyck [800]
LITERARY SPECULUM – v. 1-3. November 1821-January 1823 – 1 – us UMI [073]
LITERARY STUDIES / Whibley, Charles – London: Macmillan and Co., 1919 – 1 roll – 1 – 1-55879-518-9 – uk Libr Preservation [420]
THE LITERARY STUDY OF THE BIBLE : AN ACCOUNT OF THE LEADING FORMS OF LITERATURE REPRESENTED IN THE SACRED WRITINGS: INTENDED FOR ENGLISH READERS / Moulton, Richard Green – (Includes index) – Boston: D C Heath; London: Isbister, 1899 – 2mf – 9 – 0-8370-9807-6 – 1986-3807 – us A.T.L.A. [220]
LITERARY SUBALTERN – Providence. R.I. 1829-1833 – 1 – us UMI [071]
LITERARY TABLET – v. 1-2. 1833-March 29, 1834 – 1 – us UMI [073]
THE LITERARY TRANSCRIPT AND GENERAL INTELLEGENCER *see* THE QUEBEC TRANSCRIPT AND GENERAL ADVERTISER
THE LITERARY TRANSCRIPT AND GENERAL INTELLIGENCER – (Cont by: The Quebec Transcript and General Advertiser) – [Quebec?: s.n., 1838-1839] (Quebec: J T Donahue) – 9 – cn C.I.H.M. [072]
LITERARY UNION – NSv. 1-2 April 7, 1847-July 1850 – 1 – us UMI [073]
THE LITERARY WORKSHOP – New York. v. 1, no. 1-4. 1934-Jan 1935 – 1 – us NY Public [800]
LITERARY WORLD – v. 1-13. February 6, 1847-December 31, 1853 – 1 – us UMI [073]
LITERARY YEAR-BOOK 1897-1923 – 197mf – 9 – £745.00 – uk Chadwyck [400]
LITERATOS CACERENSES / Figueroa y Melgar, Alfonso de – Badajoz: Dip. Provincial, 1908. Sep. REE – sp Bibl Santa Ana [946]
LITERATUR DER MUSIK, ODER SYSTEMATISCHE ANLEITUNG ZUR KENNTNIS DER VORZUEGLICHEN MUSIKALISCHEN BUECHER,.. / Gruber, J S – Frankfurt, Leipzig, 1792 – 1mf – ne IDC [780]
LITERATUR, KUNST UND KINO – Magdeburg, 1919 n1-5 (incomplete) – 1 – gw Mikrofilm [790]
DIE LITERATUR; MONATSSCHRIFT FUER LITERATURFREUNDE – Berlin. v. 1-44. 1898-1942 – 1 – 323.00 – us L of C Photodup [073]
DIE LITERATUR OESTERREICHISCHER AUTOREN IN DER ERSTEN REPUBLIK, 1918-1938 : EINE STANDORTBESTIMMUNG / Boehner, Claus-Peter – 1992 – 9 – DM98.00 – 3-89349-488-X – gw Hänsel [430]
LITERATURA / Akademiia Nauk. SSSR. Institut Russkoi Literatury – Leningrad. v1. 1931 – 1r – 1 – us Ross [460]
LA LITERATURA COLONIAL DE COLOMBIA / Otero Munoz, Gustavo – 1928 – 1 – us I.U. Libraries [390]
LITERATURA DOLGOSROCHNAGO KREDITA – Bibliograficheskii ukazatel' sochinenii otdel'no izdannykh i statei pomeshchennykh v povremennykh izdaniiakh. Spb. 1901. BR-7136 2 – 8 – ne IDC [460]
LITERATURA ECLESIASTICA, CRONICA DE LA SEMANA PRO SEMINARIO CELEBRADA EN TOLEDO LOS D'IAS 4-10 DE NOVIEMBRE DE 1935... / Bayle, Constantino – Burgos: Razon y Fe, 1939 – 1 – sp Bibl Santa Ana [240]
LITERATURA I ISKUSSTVO, 1942-1944 *see* SOVETSKOE ISKUSSTVO
LITERATURA I ISKUSSTVO UZBEKISTANA – 1937-40. Available: 1938, v. 3-6. BU-111 2 – 8 – ne IDC [460]
LITERATURA I MASTATSZTVA – Minsk, U.S.S.R. -sw. 1957-70. 14 reels – 1 – uk British Libr Newspaper [460]
LITERATURA I OBSHCHESTVENNOST' / Ivanov-Razumnik, R I – no. 3. Zavety. 1914. BR-3270 2 – 8 – ne IDC [460]
LITERATURA I REVOLIUTSIIA / Trotskii, L – 2nd ed. Moscow, 1924 – 1 – 35.00r – us Hoover Inst Photo [335]
LITERATURA I ZHIZHN' : EZHEMESIACHNYI ZHURNAL O RUSSKIKH PISATELIAKH I RUSSKOI KNIGE ZA RUBEZHOM – Riga. v1. 1928 – 1mf – 9 – ne IDC [460]
LITERATURA I ZHIZN – Moscow. U.S.S.R. 1970 – 1 – us UMI [460]
LITERATURA I ZHIZN. (LITERATURNAYA ROSSIYA) – Moscow. 6 Apr 1958-Dec 1969. tw & w. 16 reels – 1 – uk British Libr Newspaper [460]
LITERATURA IR MENAS – (Backfile 1945-1998 $85r) – Lithuania, 1999- – 1r per y – 1 – $80.00 standing order – us Ross [072]
LITERATURA ISTORII I OBLICHENIYA RUSSKAGO = THE LITERATURE OF THE HISTORY AND EXPOSURE OF RUSSIAN DISSENT / Sakharov, F K – Tambov, 1887; St. Petersburg, 1892, 1900. 804p – 1 – us Baptist [240]
LITERATURA ISTORII I OBLITSENIIA RUSSKAGO RASKOLA. SISTEMATICHESKII UKAZATEL' KNIG, BROSHIUR I STATEI O RASKOLE. 1-3 / Sakharov, F K – Tambov, Spb. 1887-1900. BR-7245 2 – 8 – ne IDC [460]
LITERATURA MILITAR ESPANOLA / Barado, Francisco – 1890 – 9 – 1.50f – sp Bibl Santa Ana [946]
LITERATURA PO RUSSKOMU POCHVOVEDENIIU S 1765 PO 1896 G / Ototskii, P V – Spb. 1898. BR-7202 2 – 8 – ne IDC [460]
LITERATURA REVOLIUTSIONNOGO DESIATILETIIA 1917-1927 / Lezhnev, A & Gorbov, D – "Proletarii". Khar'kov. 1929. BR-1365 2 – 8 – ne IDC [335]
LITERATURA RUSSKAGO LESOVODSTVA / Verekha, P & Rudzkii, A – 1. Sistematicheskii ukazatel' otdel'nykh knig, izdannykh na russkom iazyke do 1878 goda. Spb. 1878. BR-7035 2 – 8 – ne IDC [460]
LITERATURA RUSSKOI BIBLIOGRAFII / Gennadi, G – Opis' bibliograficheskikh knig i statei izdannykh v Rossii. Spb. 1858. BR-4664 2 – 8 – ne IDC [460]
LITERATURA RUSSKOI GEOGRAFII, STATISTIKI I ETNOGRAFII ZA 1864-1880 G / Mezhov, VI – Spb., 1865-1883 – 63mf – 9 – R-7158/2 – ne IDC [947]
LITERATURA RUSSKOI GEOGRAFII, STATISTIKI I ETNOGRAFII ZA 1864-1880 G / Mezhov, VI – Spb., 1865-1883 – 63mf – 9 – ne IDC [947]
LITERATURA RUSSKOI ISTORII ZA 1859-1864 G / Mezhov, VI – VKL. 1. Spb. 1866. BR-7159 2 – 8 – ne IDC [947]
LITERATURA SUBLIME E HISTORIA GLORIOSA Y TRAGICA. COPIADA LA PRIMERA Y RELATADA LA SEGUNDA EN ARTICULOS / Ibarrola, Jose – Caceres: Imprenta Moderna, 1927 – 1 – sp Bibl Santa Ana [440]
LITERATURA UKRAINOVEDENIIA ZA 1912 / Doroshenko, V V – Ottisk iz izd. "Obozrenie trudov po slavianovedeniiu". Spb. 1914. BR-4340 2 – 8 – ne IDC [460]
LITERATURA UN MAKSLA – (1992-1998 1r per y $85y) – Latvia, 1999- – 1r per y – 1 – $80.00 standing order – us Ross [072]
LITERATURA VELIKOGO DESIATILETIIA / Kogan, P – M. 1927. BR-1340 2 – 8 – ne IDC [460]
LITERATURA VELIKOGO DESIATILETIIA (1917-1927) / Vladislavlev, I V – Khudozhestvennaia literatura-kritika-istoriia literaturnaia-teoriia i metodologiia. GIZ. I. M., L. 1928. B-1133 2 – 8 – ne IDC [460]
LITERATURA Y SUBDESARROLLO; NOTAS PARA UN ANALISIS DE LA LITERATURA ARGENTINA / Prieto, Adolfo – Rosario, Argentina: Editorial Biblioteca, c1968. 192p. Bibliog – 1 – us U.W. Library [440]
LITERATURAS AVIZE – Riga, De 1940 a 1941 – 1 reel – 1 – Sfr120.00 – sz Infoprint [460]
LITERATURAS AVIZE – Riga, Latvia, 1940-41 – 1r – 1 – $75.00 – us Ross [072]
LITERATURBERICHTE ZUR FLORA ODER ALLGEMEINE BOT. ZEITUNG – Regensburg. v1 (1-19). 1831; v2 (1-18) 1832 – 17mf – ne IDC [580]
LITERATURBILDER : DARSTELLUNGEN DEUTSCHER LITERATUR AUS DEN WERKEN DER VORZUEGLICHSTEN LITERARHISTORIKE: ZUR BELEBUNG DES UNTERRICHTS UND ZUR PRIVATLECTUERE / ed by Schaefer, Johann Wilhelm – Leipzig: F Brandstetter, 1861 – 1r – 1 – us U.W. Library [430]
LITERATURBLATT FUER GERMANISCHE UND ROMANISCHE PHILOLOGIE – Heilbronn, 1880-1920 – 281mf – 9 – ne IDC [430]
LITERATUR-BLATT FUER ORIENTALISCHE PHILOLOGIE – Unter Mitwirkung von dr. Johannes Klatt in Berlin, hrsg. von prof. dr. Ernst Kuhn in Muenchen. Leipzig, O. Schulze. 1.-4. Bd.; Oct. 1883-Oct. 1888. Film Mas 9226 – 1 – us H.U. Library [400]
LITERATURBLATT FUER ORIENTALISCHE PHILOLOGIE – Leipzig. v1-4. 1883-1888 – 18mf – 9 – ne IDC [480]
LITERATURE, 1897-1902 – Predecessor to the Times Literary Supplement – 1 – us Primary [420]
THE LITERATURE AND CURIOSITIES OF DREAMS; A COMMONPLACE BOOK OF SPECULATIONS CONCERNING THE MYSTERY OF DREAMS AND VISIONS / Seafield, Frank – London: Chapman and Hall, 1865. 2v – 1 – us U.W. Library [150]
LITERATURE AND DOGMA : AN ESSAY TOWARDS A BETTER APPREHENSION OF THE BIBLE / Arnold, Matthew – London: Smith, Elder, 1873 – 1 roll – 1 – 1-55879-196-5 – uk Libr Preservation [840]
LITERATURE AND MEDICINE – (1985-. 5,6,9) – 1982- – 1 – us UMI [610]
LITERATURE AND POETRY : STUDIES ON THE ENGLISH LANGUAGE, THE POETRY OF THE BIBLE... / Schaff, Philip – (Includes index) – New York:Scribner's, 1890 – 2mf – 9 – 0-8370-5070-7 – 1985-3070 – us A.T.L.A. [420]
LITERATURE AND PSYCHOLOGY – v1-31 1951-81 1; v21-31 5,6; v26-31 9 – us UMI [150]
LITERATURE CATEGORY / The NewsBank Review of the Arts – 1975-. Monthly index with cumulations – 9 – us NewsBank [800]
LITERATURE COLLECTION / Bibliotheque Nationale – 135 diverse titles on 1115 fiches. Titles available separately – 9 – 2760.00 – fr Bibl Nationale [410]
O LITERATURE I ISKUSSTVE / Lenin, Vladimir Ilyich – Sostavila Krutikova. Ed. 2. M. 1960. Index. BR-1362 2 – 8 – ne IDC [335]
LITERATURE IN THE CENTURY / De Mille, Alban Bertram – London: Toronto: Linscott Pub. Co., 1900. 03758. (Pre-1900 Canadiana) – 9 – cn C.I.H.M. [410]
LITERATURE LIST AND RESEARCH PROGRAMME / Research Centre for Monetary and Financial Freedom – 9 – 1.00f – at Libertarian Micro [320]
LITERATURE, MUSIC AND ART: THE ANNOTATED SALE CATALOGUES OF PUTTICK AND SIMPSON, 1846-1871 – Pt 1: 1846-56. Pt 2: 1856-63. Pt 3: 1864-67. Pt 4: 1867-71 – 1 – us Primary [780]
LITERATURE OF FOLKLORE – (Based on Literaturverzeichnis of Handwoerterbuch des deutschen Aberglaubens and other Handbuecher) – 902r – 1 – $54,500.00 – us OmniSys [390]
LITERATURE OF THE DOCTRINE OF A FUTURE LIFE / Abbot, Ezra – New York: W.J. Widdleton, 1871. 1 fiche – 9 – us A.T.L.A. [240]
THE LITERATURE OF THE DOCTRINE OF A FUTURE LIFE : OR, A CATALOGUE OF WORKS RELATING TO THE NATURE, ORIGIN, AND DESTINY OF THE SOUL / Abbot, Ezra – (Includes index) – New York: W J Widdleton, 1871 – 1mf – 9 – 0-8370-2007-7 – 1985-0007 – us A.T.L.A. [210]
THE LITERATURE OF THE EIGHTEENTH CENTURY – Literature titles selected from The Eighteenth Century Collection – 1 – us Primary [800]
THE LITERATURE OF THE SECOND CENTURY : SHORT STUDIES IN CHRISTIAN EVIDENCES / Wynne, F R et al – New York: James Pott, 1892. 1 fiche – 9 – us A.T.L.A. [240]
LITERATURE OF THEOLOGY : A CLASSIFIED BIBLIOGRAPHY OF THEOLOGICAL AND GENERAL RELIGIOUS LITERATURE / Hurst, John F – New York: Hunt & Eaton; Cincinnati: Cranston & Curts, 1896, c1895 – 2mf – us A.T.L.A. [240]
LITERATURE OF THEOLOGY AND CHURCH HISTORY: A BASIC LIBRARY OF BRITISH THEOLOGICAL STUDIES – 19th-century works selected from The New Cambridge Bibliography of English Literature – 9 – us Primary [240]
LITERATURE OF THEOLOGY AND CHURCH HISTORY IN THE UNITED STATES AND CANADA – History of religious thought in America from the colonial period – 9 – us Primary [240]
LITERATURE/FILM QUARTERLY – 1973- 1; 1975- 5,6; 1977- 4 x 6 in. 9 – us UMI [073]
LITERATUREN FORUM – (Cont: Literaturen Front) – 1977- – 1r per y – 1 – us Ross [072]
LITERATUREN FORUM *see* LITERATURENFRONT
LITERATUREN FRONT – Bulgarien. 1976-80 – 1 – DM280.00 – gw Mikro Press [949]
LITERATUREN FRONT – Sofia, Bulgaria. Jun 1945-4 Jan 1994 (incomplete) – 20r – 1 – us L of C Photodup [949]
LITERATUREN FRONT – Sofia, Bulgaria. -w. 1948-70. 8 reels – 1 – uk British Libr Newspaper [460]
LITERATUREN FRONT *see* LITERATUREN FORUM
LITERATURENFRONT – (Cont as: Literaturen Forum 1990) – 1977-1991ff – 15r – 1 – DM1,125.00 – gw Mikro Press [947]
LITERATURGESCHICHTE DES DEUTSCHEN SPRACHRAUMES / Lechner, Hermann – (Includes index) – Innsbruck: Tyrolia-Verlag, 1956 – 1r – 1 – us U.W. Library [430]
LITERATURGESCHICHTE DES DEUTSCHEN VOLKES : DICHTUNG UND SCHRIFTTUM DER DEUTSCHEN STAEMME UND LANDSCHAFTEN / Nadler, Josef – (Includes bibliographical references and index) – Berlin: Im Propylaen-Verlag [1938-1941] – 1 – us U.W. Library [430]
LITERATURNA UKRAINA – (Backfile 1927-1998 $85r) – Ukarine, 1999- – 1r per y – 1 – $80.00 standing order – us Ross [072]
LITERATURNA UKRANIA – Kiev. U.S.S.R. 1961- – 1 – us UMI [460]
LITERATURNAIA BIBLIOTEKA – Spb. 1866-68 (1). Lacking: 1866 (1-9). B-1772 2 – 8 – ne IDC [460]
LITERATURNAIA ENTSIKLOPEDIIA – M., 1929-1939. v1-9, 11 – 114mf – 9 – 1124/2 – ne IDC [460]

LITERATURNAIA ENTSIKLOPEDIIA – M., L., 1925. 2 vols – 8mf – 9 – R-15449/1 – ne IDC [460]
LITERATURNAIA GAZETA – (1990-1995 2r per y $170y. 1996-98 1r per y $85r. Backfile 1944-89 $85r) – Russia, 1999- – 1r per y – 1 – $80.00 standing order – us Ross [072]
LITERATURNAIA GAZETA – Moscow. Apr 22 1929-1960. Incomplete – 1 – us NY Public [460]
LITERATURNAIA GAZETA – Moscow: Literaturnaia gazeta, 1929- – 1mf – 9 – $99.95y – us East View [460]
LITERATURNAIA GAZETA – Moscow. U.S.S.R. 1955- – 1 – us UMI [460]
LITERATURNAIA GAZETA – v. 1-3. Spb. 1830-31. B-1195 – 8 – ne IDC [073]
LITERATURNAIA MOSKVA / Belousov, I A – (Vospominaniia. 1880-1928). Pisateli iz naroda. Pisateli-na-rodniki. 1929. BR-9055 1 – 9 – ne IDC [460]
LITERATURNAIA MYSL' : AL'MANAKH – Leningrad. v1-3. 1922-25 – 1 – us Ross [460]
LITERATURNAIA MYSL' – Petrograd. v. 1-3. 1922-1925 – 1 – us NY Public [460]
LITERATURNAIA MYSL' – Zhurnal (sbornik). Vyp. I-III. Izd. Mysl'. Spb. 1922. Available: Vyp. I, 1922. BR-3323 2 – 8 – ne IDC [073]
LITERATURNAIA RECH'. TOLKOVYI SLOVAR SOVREMENNOI OBSHCHELITERATURNOI FRAZEOLOGII / Ovsiannikov, VZ – M., 1933 – 8mf – 9 – 1355/2 – ne IDC [460]
LITERATURNAIA ROSSIIA – 1963-64 – 1 – 374.00 – us L of C Photodup [460]
LITERATURNAIA ROSSIIA – (1967-1995 2r per y $170y. 1996-98 1r per y $170y) – Russia, 1999- – 1r per y – 1 – $80.00 standing order – us Ross [460]
LITERATURNAIA ROSSLIA – 1 – sz Infoprint [460]
LITERATURNAYA GAZETA – Moscow, U.S.S.R. -w. April-Dec 1929; July-Sept 1930; July-Oct 1932; Jan 1933-Oct 1941; Nov 1944-Dec 1968. 35 reels – 1 – uk British Libr Newspaper [460]
LITERATURNOE NASLEDSTVO – Moscow, 1931-73. v1-84. v66 not published. B-1174/2 – 8 – ne IDC [460]
LITERATURNOE OBOZRENIE – (Missing: 1896-1901. v2-7) – Spb., 1895-1902. v1-9 – 18mf – 9 – 1399/1 – ne IDC [460]
LITERATURNO-KHUDOZHESTVENNYE AL' MANAKHI I SBORNIKI / Golubeva, O D – Bibliograficheskii ukazatel'. 1-4. M. 1957-60. BR-1267 2 – 8 – ne IDC [460]
LITERATURNO-KHUDOZHESTVENNYE AL'MANAKHI I SBORNIKI – Vsesoiuznaia Knizhnaia Palata. v. 1-3. 1957, 1958. BR-3566 2 – 8 – ne IDC [073]
LITERATURNO-KHUDOZHESTVENNYE AL'-MANAKHI I SBORNIKI. TOM VTOROI 1912-1917. VSESOIUZNAIA KNIZHNAIA PALATA / Rogozhin, N – M. 1958. BR-3291 2 – 8 – ne IDC [460]
LITERATURNO-KHUDOZHESTVENNYE AL'MANAKHI IZDATEL'STVA "SHIPOVNIK" – v. 1-23. Spb. 1907-14. BR-1870 2 – 8 – ne IDC [073]
LITERATURNO-KRITICHESKIE OCHERKI / Abramovich, N Ia – v. 1-2. Spb. 1909-11. BR-3245 2 – 8 – ne IDC [460]
LITERATURNY I LENINGRAD – (Library has no. 16-64 (Apr. 8-Dec 26, 1934)[Missing no. 17-19, 22-24, 31, 47-48]) – Leningrad: Gos. tip. "Len. pravda", 193u – 1 – CSUX88-S462 – us Hoover Inst Photo [947]
LITERATURNYE LISTKI – Spb. 1823-24. B-1414 2 – 8 – ne IDC [073]
LITERATURNYE OCHERKI / Otsup, N – Paris. 1961. BR-1216 2 – 8 – ne IDC [460]
LITERATURNYE OTKLIKI / Kranikhfel'd, V – 80 tysiah verst vokrug sebia. nr. 4. Sovremennyi mir. 1913. BR-3565 2 – 8 – ne IDC [460]
LITERATURNYE PORTRETY / Voronskii, A K – Izd. Federatsiia. v. 1. M. 1928. BR-2218 2 – 8 – ne IDC [460]
LITERATURNYE PORTRETY, PISATELI KUZNITSY / Akubovskii, Georgii – Moskva: Gos. izdvo, 1926 – 1 – CSUX89-B1535 – us Hoover Inst Photo [460]
LITERATURNYE STUDII ROSS. KOMM. SOI UZA MOLODEZHI, IKH T SELI I ZADACHI / Granin, A – Peterburg: Gos. izd-vo, 1920 – 1 – CSUX89-B5461 – us Hoover Inst Photo [460]
LITERATURNYE VOSPOMINANIIA 1890-1902 / Pertsov, P – M., Leningrad. 1933. BR-1483 2 – 8 – ne IDC [460]
LITERATURNYE ZAPISKI : LITERATURNO-OBSHCHESTVENNYI I KRITIKO-BIBLIOGRAFICHESKII ZHURNAL – St Petersburg. n1-3. 1922 – 1r – 1 – us Ross [460]
LITERATURNYE ZAPISKI – v. 1-3. Spb. 1922. B-2253 2 – 8 – ne IDC [460]
LITERATURNYI ARKHIV – Dvomisiachnik literaturoznavstva. (Institut Shevchenka). v1-2. Kharkiv. 1930-31. BR-5743 2 – 8 – ne IDC [460]
LITERATURNYI ARKHIV – Kharkov. v. 1-2. 1930-1931 – 1 – us NY Public [460]
LITERATURNYI ARKHIV – Kharkov. v1-2. 1930-31 – 1 – us Ross [460]
LITERATURNYI ARKHIV – Pis'ma osveshchaiushchie zhizn' i deiatel'nost' izvestnykh pisatelei kontsa XIX – nachala XX v. Pod. red. K. A. Muratovoi. Akademiia nauk SSSR. Institut russkoi literatury. v. 5. M. L. 1960. BR-1371 2 – 8 – ne IDC [460]
LITERATURNYI ARKHIV – v. 1-4. M., L. 1938-53. Lacking: v. 2. BR-1769 2 – 8 – ne IDC [460]
LITERATURNYI DNEVNIK / Gippius, Z N – Spb. 1908, 1899-1907. BR-714 2 – 8 – ne IDC [460]
LITERATURNYI DNEVNIK. STAT'I 1921-1923 G / Shaginian, M – ed. 2. Krug. M., Spb. 1923. BR-2107 2 – 8 – ne IDC [460]
LITERATURNYI KRITIK – Ezhemesiachnyi zhurnal literaturnoi teorii, kritiki i istorii literatury. v. 1. M. 1933. BR-159 2 – 8 – ne IDC [460]
LITERATURNYI KRITIK – Moscow. June 1933-Nov 1939; Feb-Dec 1940 – 1 – us NY Public [460]
LITERATURNYI KRITIK – Moscow. v1-8. 1933-40 – 7r – 1 – us Ross [460]
LITERATURNYI OBRAZY I MNENIIA 1903 G / Anichkov, E – St. Petersburg, 1904. BR-1966 2 – 8 – ne IDC [460]
LITERATURNYI RASPAD – Kriticheskii sbornik. v. 1-2. Spb. 1908-09. BR-1372 2 – 8 – ne IDC [460]
LITERATURNYI UZBEKISTAN – Tashkent. 1935-37. Available: 1937, v. 2. BU-113 2 – 8 – ne IDC [490]
LITERATURNYI VESTNIK – Izd. russkago bibliologicheskago obshchestva. v. 1-8. Spb. 1901-04. B-1774 2 – 8 – ne IDC [460]
LITERATURNYI ZHURNAL – v. 1-3. Spb. 1881. B-1775 2 – 8 – ne IDC [460]
LITERATURNYIA KHARAKTERISTIKI / Vengerova, Z – St. Petersburg, 1897-1905. v1-2. BR-2191/2 – 8 – ne IDC [460]
LITERATURSOZIOLOGISCHE UNTERSUCHUNGEN ZU DER WESTSAECHSISCHEN STADT SCHNEEBERG AN DER WENDE VOM 17. ZUM 18. JAHRHUNDERT / Hofmann, Adelheid – 1995 – 3mf – 9 – DM98.00 – 3-8267-2144-6 – gw Hänsel [430]
Lithard, Victor *see* CURSO DE TEOLOGIA PASTORAL. BARCELONA, 1933
LITHOGRAMS OF THE FERNS OF QUEENSLAND / Bailey, F M – Brisbane. 1892 – 8 – ne IDC [760]
LITHOGRAPHER'S BULLETIN, 1901-1904 : OFFICIAL PUBLICATION OF THE LITHOGRAPHER'S INTERNATIONAL PROTECTIVE AND BENEFICIAL ASSOCIATION, 1910-1913 : THE LITHOGRAPHER'S JOURNAL, 1918-1955 / Amalgamated Lithographers of America – (Coll title: Labor Union Periodicals, Pt 2) – 15r – $2,025.00 – 1-55655-308-0 – us UPA [680]
THE LITHOGRAPHER'S JOURNAL *see* LITHOGRAPHER'S BULLETIN, 1901-1904 : OFFICIAL PUBLICATION OF THE LITHOGRAPHER'S INTERNATIONAL PROTECTIVE AND BENEFICIAL ASSOCIATION, 1910-1913 : THE LITHOGRAPHER'S JOURNAL, 1918-1955
LITHOGRAPHIC VIEWS OF MILITARY OPERATIONS IN CANADA UNDER HIS EXCELLENCY SIR JOHN COLBORNE...DURING THE LATE INSURRECTION / Beauclerk, Charles – London: A Flint, 1840. SEM105P890 – 1mf – 9 – Can$2.25 – cn Bibl Nat [355]
LITHOLOGY AND MINERAL RESOURCES – v1-29. 1966-94 – 1,5 – $80.00v – us UMI [550]
LITHONIA BAPTIST CHURCH. LITHONIA, GEORGIA : CHURCH RECORDS – 31 Dec 1847-Jan 1903. WMS. 1921-67 – 1 – 52.65 – us Baptist [240]
LITHOS – (1981-. 1,5,6,9) – v1-. 1968- – 1 – us UMI [500]
LITHOS – v1-17. 1968-84 – 1,5,6,13 – sz Elsevier [550]
LITHUANIAN AMERICAN COMMUNITY OF THE USA – Philadelphia. 89 docs. 1980-1991 – 40mf – 9 – ne IDC [320]
LITHUANIAN CATHOLIC RELIGIOUS AID AND LITHUANIAN INFORMATION CENTER – Brooklyn. 171 docs. 1980-1990 – 39mf – 9 – ne IDC [320]
LITHUANIAN MATHEMATICAL JOURNAL – v13-34. 1973-94 – 1,5 – $60.00v – us UMI [510]
LITIGATION (ABA) – (v1-11 1975-85 on reel $135.00. v12-21 1985-95 on mf $181.00) – v1-21. 1975-95 – 5,6,9 – $316.00 set – us Hein [340]
LITIGATION. RELEASE NUMBER 1-5713, AUG. 5, 1942-JAN. 24, 1973 / U.S. Securities and Exchange Commission – Release No. 5711 is in the SEC Docket, vol. 1, no. 1. The series will continue in subsequent issues – 9 – us UMI [336]
LITIGATION RELEASES / U.S. Securities and Exchange Commission – nos 1-5713. 5 Aug 1942-24 Jan 1973 (all publ) – 140mf – 9 – $210.00 – LLMC 84-364 – us L.L.M.C. [340]
LITOPIS REVOLIUTSII – Kharkov. 1923, no. 3-4-1933, no. 1-2 gaps – 1 – 35.00r – us Hoover Inst Photo [947]
LITORALIA – v1-. 1984- – 1,5,6,9 – us UMI [574]
Litoshenko, LN *see*
- KREST'IANSKII BIUDZHET V 1922-23 GODU. IZD
- SNABZHENIE MOLOKOM KRUPNYKH GORODOV I MOLOCHNAIA KOOPERATSIIA
- SNABZHENIE MOSKVY I DRUGIKH BOL'SHIKH GORODOV MOLOKOM
- SOTSIALIZATSIIA ZEMLI

LITOU – The Plough. Aug-Dec 1926. 1 reel. M/C 88 – 1 – $45.00 – cc Microforms [073]
LITSEI – Periodicheskoe izdanie. v. 1-4. Spb. 1806. BR-3367 2 – 8 – ne IDC [073]
LITSEVOE ZHITIE SVIATYKH BLAGOVERNYKH KNIAZEI RUSSKIKH BORISA I GLEBA / Likhachev, N P – St. Petersburg, 1907. BR/10,037/2 – 8 – ne IDC [460]
Litteljohn, AN *see* THE CHRISTIAN MINISTRY AT THE CLOSE OF THE NINETEENTH CENTURY
LITTERA DE RAGUZIA DE GLI ORRIBILI SEGNI APPARSI IN BOSSINA ET APPRESSO A BEL GRADO – Deragugia, 1531 – 1mf – 9 – H-8141/1 – ne IDC [956]
DIE LITTERARISCHEN UND PERSOENLICHEN BEZIEHUNGEN SIR WALTER SCOTT'S ZU GOETHE : EIN BEITRAG ZU STUDIEN UEBER DAS VERHAELTNIS DER DEUTSCHEN LITTERATUR ZUR ENGLISCHEN AM ENDE DES 18. UND ZU BEGINN DES 19. JAHRHUNDERTS / Roesel, Ludwig Karl – (Includes bibliographical references) – Leipzig: J G Findel, 1901 – 1 – us U.W. Library [430]
LITTERARISCHES WOCHENBLATT / ed by Kotzebue, August von – Weimar. 6v. 1818-20 – 34mf – 9 – subsc: DM270.00 diazo DM300.00 silver – gw Olms [430]
LE LITTERATEUR CANADIEN – Quebec, Canada. 28 jun 1860-6 jul 1861 – 1r – 1 – Can$35.00 – cn Can Microfilming [073]
LITTERATUR DER AELTEREN REISEBESCHREIBUNGEN... / Beckmann, Johann – Goettingen. 2v. 1807-1810 – 24mf – 9 – U-764/2 – ne IDC [910]
LITTERATUR DER LANDES- UND VOLKSKUNDE DES DEUTSCHEN REICHS / Richter, P E – Leipzig, 1896 – 9mf – 9 – ne IDC [430]
LITTERATUR DER MUSIK, ODER SYSTEMATISCHE ANLEITUNG ZUR KENNTNISS DER VORZUEGLICHEN MUSIKALISCHEN BUECHER / Gruber, J S – Frankfurt und Leipzig. 1792. BP-690 1 – 9 – ne IDC [780]
DIE LITTERATUR DES ALTEN TESTAMENTS NACH DER ZEITFOLGE IHRER ENTSTEHUNG = LETTERKUNDE DES OUDEN VERBONDS NAAR DE TIJDSORDE VAN HAAR ONTSTAAN / Wildeboer, Gerrit – (Includes bibliographical references and indexes) – Goettingen: Vandenhoeck und Ruprecht, 1895 – 2mf – 9 – 0-8370-9753-3 – 1986-3753 – us A.T.L.A. [220]
LITTERATUR DES GESAMMTEN SOWOHL NATUERLICHEN ALS POSITIVEN VOELKERRECHTS / Ompteda, DH L & Kampf, C A von – Regensburg, Berlin. 3v. 1785, 1817 – 17mf – ne IDC [270]
LA LITTERATURE AU CANADA EN 1890 / Baillairge, Frederic Alexandre – 1891. 00081. (Pre-1900 Canadiana) – 9 – cn C.I.H.M. [971]
LA LITTERATURE BULGARE DU 14E SIECLE ET SA DIFFUSION DANS LES PAYS ROUMAINS / Turdeanu, E – Paris, 1947 – 4mf – 9 – ne IDC [460]
LA LITTERATURE DE LA REVOLUTION MONDIALE / L'Union Internationale des Ecrivains Revolutionnaires – Organe central. no. 1-5 et 2 no. speciaux. Moscou, Leningrad. juil-oct 1931. devenu: La Litterature internationale voir a ce titre – 1 – fr A.C.R.P.P. [335]
LITTERATURE ET CRITIQUE – Revue mensuelle. mars-aout 1892. devenu: La Revue. Litterature et critique. sept oct 1892-sept 1893. devenu: La Revue parisienne. OCT 1893-MARS 1894. Paris – 1 – fr A.C.R.P.P. [073]
LITTERATURE ET HISTOIRE DES TEXTES BYZANTINS. (1950-1965) / Darrouzes, J – London, 1972 – 9mf – 8 – ne Slangenburg [240]
LA LITTERATURE FEMININE DEFINIE PAR LES FEMMES ECRIVAINS / Moroy, Elie – Geneve: Semaine de Geneve, 1931. 138p. (Les Femmes Collection) – 2mf – 9 – $6.00 – fr Bibl Nationale [410]
LA LITTERATURE GRECQUE / Batiffol, Pierre – Paris: V. Lecoffre, 1897 – 1mf – us A.T.L.A. [450]
LA LITTERATURE INTERNATIONALE / L'Union Internationale des Ecrivains Revolutionnaires – Organe central. Moscou. 1933-39, 1942 – 1 – fr A.C.R.P.P. [335]
LITTERATURE LATINE AU MOYEN AGE / Ghellinck, J de – (T. 1: Depuis les origines jusqu'a la fin de la renaissance carolingienne 3mf; T. 2: De la Renaissance carolingienne a Saint Anselme 3mf) – Bruxelles, 1938 – 3mf – 8 – ne Slangenburg [450]
LA LITTERATURE QUODLIBETIQUE 2 / Glorieux, P – Bibliotheque Thomiste 21, Paris, 1935 – 8mf – 8 – ne Slangenburg [100]
LA LITTERATURE QUODLIBETIQUE DE 1260 A 1320 / Glorieux, P – Bibliotheque Thomiste 5, 1925 – 8mf – 8 – ne Slangenburg [100]
LA LITTERATURE SYRIAQUE / Duval, Rubens – Paris: V. Lecoffre, 1907 – 2mf – us A.T.L.A. [240]
LITTERATURHISTORIE – 1943-53 – 1 – us I.U. Libraries [410]
LITTERATUR-ZEITUNG – Erlangen, 1799-1802 (mf ed 1986) – 50mf – 9 – DM350.00 – 3-89131-030-7 – gw Fischer [430]
Little *see* COMPENDIUM OF HISTORY AND BIOGRAPHY OF KALAMAZOO COUNTY
Little, A.D., Inc. *see*
- FACTORS INFLUENCING INVESTMENT IN EGYPT
- ORGANIZATION AND OPERATION OF THE INDUSTRIAL BANK OF EGYPT
- SUMMARY OF EGYPTIAN STUDIES; FINAL REPORT TO U.S. GOVERNMENT INTERNATIONAL COOPERATION ADMINISTRATION

Little, Arthur Wilde *see* REASONS FOR BEING A CHURCHMAN
LITTLE BETHEL BAPTIST CHURCH. MARION COUNTY. SOUTH CAROLINA : CHURCH RECORDS – 1874-1925, 1929-1942, 1953-1954, 1958-1961; 1964-March 1973 – 1 – 33.03 – us Baptist [240]
LITTLE BLUE – Jenkins Mills, NE. -w. Aug 1869-Mar 1870; Nov 1870 – 1 – us NE Hist [071]
LITTLE BRIAR CREEK BAPTIST CHURCH. WARRENTON, GEORGIA : CHURCH RECORDS – Dec 1920-Jan 1989. 638p – 1 – 28.71 – us Baptist [240]
THE LITTLE BRONZED ANGEL – 1954-74. (American Indian Periodicals in the Princeton University Library). 1 fiche – 9 – $50.00 – us UPA [305]
LITTLE CONETOE BAPTIST CHURCH. PRIMITIVE BAPTIST ASSOCIATION. NORTH CAROLINA : CHURCH RECORDS – 1822-84 – 1 – 9.36 – us Baptist [240]
LITTLE FORT PORCUPINE – Waukegan. Ill. 1845-47 – 1 – us UMI [071]
Little, George T *see* GENEALOGICAL AND FAMILY HISTORY OF THE STATE OF MAINE
Little, Henry William *see* MADAGASCAR
"LITTLE KNOWN OR EXTINCT TOWNS OF KANSAS" / Montgomery, Mary Emma (Milner) – undated – 1 – us KS Hist [978]

LITTLE LAKE HERALD – Little Lake, CA. May 1901-Nov 1910 – 3r – 1 – $150.00 – B02346 – us Library Micro [071]

LITTLE LAKE HERALD – Willits, CA. May 1901-Nov 1910 – 3r – 1 – $150.00 – B03102 – us Library Micro [071]

THE LITTLE LIGHT OF BASOTHOLAND *see* LESELINYANA LA LESOTHO

LITTLE LORD FAUNTLEROY / Burnett, Frances Hodgson – New York: Charles Scribner's Sons, 1886 – 1 roll – 1 – 1-55879-382-8 – uk Libr Preservation [830]

LITTLE MAGAZINE – 1965- 1; 1971- 5,6; 1977- 4 x 6 in. 9 – us UMI [420]

LITTLE MAGAZINES (COLLECTION) – (Alcestis – a poetry quarterly: v1 1934-35 New York (all publ). American Spectator – a literary newspaper: v1-4 1932-37 n1-48 (all publ) New York (note: suspended apr-may 1935). Artists' and Writers' Chapbook: n1-2 1933-35 New York (all publ). Laughing Horse: n1-21 1922-39 Berkeley, Santa Fe, NM (all publ)) – reel 1 – 1 – us Ross [420]

LITTLE MAGAZINES (COLLECTION) – (All publ. Blues – a magazine of new rhythms: v1-2 (i.e. n1-9) 1929-30 Columbus, MS. Magazine – a journal of contemporary writing: v1-2 1933-35 (jun 1934 never publ) Beverly Hills, CA. Pagany: v1-3 1930-33 Boston) – reel 4 – 1 – us Ross [420]

LITTLE MAGAZINES (COLLECTION) – (All publ. Earth: v1-3 n6 1930-32 Wheaton, IL (note: suspended publ jul 1931-jan 1932). Literary Workshop: (Writers Laboratory Guild, Inc) v1 1934-35 New York. Symposium – a critical review v1-4 n4 1930-33 Concord, NH) – reel 3 – 1 – us Ross [420]

LITTLE MAGAZINES (COLLECTION) – (All publ. Others – a magazine of the new verse: v1-5 n6 1915-19 Grantwood, NJ. Poetry Journal: v1-8 1912-18 Boston. Poetry Review of America: v1-2 1916-17 Cambridge, MA. Soil – a Magazine of Art: v1 1916-17 New York. "391": v1 1915-16 New York. Cont: "291") – reel 2 – 1 – us Ross [420]

LITTLE MAGAZINES (COLLECTION) – (All publ. Phoenix – a magazine of individuality: v1-6 1914-16 South Norwalk, CT. Seven Arts: v1-2 1916-17 New York) – reel 3 – 1 – us Ross [420]

LITTLE MAGAZINES (COLLECTION) – (All's Well – or, the mirror repolished: v1-13 n5 1920-35 Fayetteville, AR (all publ). Cont: Reedy's Mirror. Blast – a magazine of proletarian fiction: v1 1933-34 New York (all publ). Caravel – an American Magazine Published in Majorca: n1-5 1934-36 Majorca (all publ). Greenwich Villager: v1-2 n1-15 1933-34 New York (all publ)) – reel 2 – 1 – us Ross [420]

LITTLE MAGAZINES (COLLECTION) – (Blast – Review of the great English vortex: v1-2 1914-15 London (all publ). Blue Review – literature, drama, art, music: v1 1913 London (all publ). Cont: Rhythm – Poetry and Drama: v1-2 1913-14 London (all publ). Cont by: Chapbook) – 1 – us Ross [420]

LITTLE MAGAZINES (COLLECTION) – (Briarcliff Quarterly: v1-3 n1-12 (all publ) College Park, MD. Briarcliff Manor, NY 1944-47. Cont: Old Line. Cont by: Golden Goose Poetry Chap-Book: v1-11 1942-53 New York (all publ) VVV. Poetry, Plastic Arts, Anthropology, Sociology, Psychology: n1-4 1942-44 New York (all publ) Note: Text in French & English) – reel 1 – 1 – us Ross [420]

LITTLE MAGAZINES (COLLECTION) – (Broom – an International Magazine of the Arts: v1-6 n1 (all publ) mar 1922, apr-jul 1923 never publ Rome; Berlin; New York, 1921-24. Exile (Ezra Pound): n1-4 1927-28 Chicago; Dijon (all publ). Fugitive – a journal of poetry: v1-4 1922-25 Nashville (all publ)) – reel 2 – 1 – us Ross [420]

LITTLE MAGAZINES (COLLECTION) – (Bruno Chap Books: v1-3 n5 1915-16 New York (all publ). Bruno's Weekly: v1-3 1915-16 New York (all publ. Lacks 2 issues). Cont by: Bruno's Glebe: v1-2 1913-14 New York (all publ)) – reel 1 – 1 – us Ross [420]

LITTLE MAGAZINES (COLLECTION) – (Calendar – an anthology of poetry: v1-3 1940-42 Prairie City, IL. Diogenes: v1 1940-41 Madison, WI (all publ). New Horizons: v1-3 1938-41 Chicago (all publ). Cont: Creative Writing – Palisade – The magazine of poetry: v1-2 1942-43 Indianola, IA (all publ). Cont: Poetry Palisade – Retort, a quarterly of social Philosophy: v1-5 n1 1942-51 Bearsville, NY) – reel 2 – 1 – us Ross [420]

LITTLE MAGAZINES (COLLECTION) – (Front: v1 1930-31 The Hague (all publ). London Bulletin (Surrealist Group in England): n1-18,20 1938-40 London (all publ). Cont: London Gallery Bulletin, Tambour: n1-8 1929-30 Paris (all publ)) – 1 – us Ross [420]

LITTLE MAGAZINES (COLLECTION) – (Measure – a journal of poetry: n1-64 1921-26 New York (all publ). Modern Review: v1-2 1922-24 Winchester, MA (all publ). Saturnian – a journal of art and literature: v1 1921-22 Cleveland (all publ)) – reel 1 – 1 – us Ross [420]

LITTLE MAGAZINES (COLLECTION) – (Secession: n1-8 1922-24 Vienna (all publ). Transatlantic Review: v1-2 1924 Paris (all publ)) – 1 – us Ross [420]

"LITTLE MAGAZINES" SERIES 1889-1972 – (Series 2: 1889-1972 £1,550 1) – Selected complete short-run cinema periodicals. With printed index – 1 – £695.00 – uk World [420]

LITTLE NOBODY: A FAIRY TALE FOR FAIRY PEOPLE / Dixon, Frederick Augustus – Toronto: Adam Stevenson, 1875. 02722. (Pre-1900 Canadiana) – 9 – cn C.I.H.M. [971]

THE LITTLE OFFICE OF OUR LADY : A TREATISE THEORETICAL, PRACTICAL, AND EXEGETICAL / Taunton, Ethelred Luke – (In English and Latin) – London: John Bale; New York: F Pustet, 1903 – 2mf – 9 – 0-8370-6843-6 – 1986-0843 – us A.T.L.A. [230]

LITTLE RIVER BAPTIST CHURCH. ABBEVILLE COUNTY. SOUTH CAROLINA : CHURCH RECORDS – 1791-1980. 1462p – 1 – 65.79 – us Baptist [978]

LITTLE RIVER BAPTIST CHURCH. FAIRFIELD COUNTY. SOUTH CAROLINA : CHURCH RECORDS – 1794-1820 – 1 – 5.00 – us Baptist [240]

LITTLE ROCK BAPTIST CHURCH. DILLON COUNTY. SOUTH CAROLINA : CHURCH RECORDS – (728p) – Minutes and Membership Rolls. Dec 1885-Sept 1988 – 1 reel – 1 – $32.76 – us Baptist [240]

THE LITTLE SCHOOLMASTER / Shorthouse, Joseph Henry – British Fiction Archive: Unit 1 – 9 – uk Bell [830]

THE LITTLE SERAPH / Graves, J R – Hymn book for church and Sunday Schools. Memphis. 1890 – 1 – 6.05 – us Baptist [240]

LITTLE SKETCHES OF BIG FOLKS, MINNESOTA 1907 / R.L. Polk and Co – Alphabetical list of representative men of Minnesota with biographical sketches. Minneapolis, Duluth, 1907. Minnesota Reel 2. The Cox Library Collection – 5 – us Americana [978]

LITTLE STEVENS BAPTIST CHURCH. EDGEFIELD, SOUTH CAROLINA : CHURCH RECORDS – (658p) – 1833-1928 – 1 reel – 1 – $29.61 – us Baptist [240]

LITTLE UNION BAPTIST CHURCH. TAYLORSVILLE, KENTUCKY : CHURCH RECORDS – 1811-1955 – 1 – 83.97 – us Baptist [240]

THE LITTLE WHALER; OR, THE ADVENTURES OF CHARLES HOLLBERG / Gerstaecker, Friedrich – Illus. by Harrison Weir.Transl. of Der Kleine Wallfischerfaenger. London, New York: G. Routledge, 1857. 343p. illus. With: Histoire Poetique du Quinzieme Siecle by P. Champion. 1 reel. 1261 – 1 – us U.W. Library [830]

THE LITTLE WHITE BIRD / Barrie, James Matthew – London: Hodder and Stoughton, 1902 – 1 roll – 1 – 1-55879-810-2 – uk Libr Preservation [830]

Little, William *see* THE EASY INSTRUCTOR

Littleberry, J Haley *see* DIARY, 1832-1917

Littlehales, H *see*
- THE OLD SERVICE-BOOKS OF THE ENGLISH CHURCH

LITTLEHAMPTON GAZETTE – England, 1977-81 – 50+ r – 1 – uk British Libr Newspaper [072]

Littlejohn, John *see* JOURNAL OF, 1773-1832

Littler, F M *see* A HANDBOOK TO THE BIRDS OF TASMANIA

LITTLETON AND BLATCHLEY'S DIGEST OF FIRE INSURANCE DECISIONS : GREAT BRITAIN AND NORTH AMERICA / Littleton, H A & Blatchley, J S – Dubuque: Daily Times Book & Job Printing Co. 1v. 1862 (all publ) – 9 – LLMC 95-132 – us L.L.M.C. [340]

Littleton, H A *see* LITTLETON AND BLATCHLEY'S DIGEST OF FIRE INSURANCE DECISIONS

Littlewoods Ltd. Liverpool *see* LITTLEWOODS MAIL-ORDER CATALOGUES 1932-1980

LITTLEWOODS MAIL-ORDER CATALOGUES 1932-1980 / Littlewoods Ltd. Liverpool – (With printed index) – 1986 – 584 colour mf – 15 – $8,130.00 – 0-907716-42-3 – uk Mindata [380]

Littmann, Enno *see* UEBER DIE ABFASSUNGSZEIT DES TRITOJESAIA

Litton, Edward Arthur *see* MIRACLES

IL LITTORIO DALMATICO – Zadar, Yugoslavia. 1924-31 – 3r – 1 – us L of C Photodup [949]

Littre, E *see*
- ETUDES ET GLANURES
- HISTOIRE DE LA LANGUE FRANCAISE

Littrow-Bischoff, Auguste von *see* AUS DEM PERSOENLICHEN VERKEHRE MIT FRANZ GRILLPARZER

LES LITUANIENS D'AMERIQUE / Bartuska, V – 1918 – 1r – 1 – us I.H.R.C. [305]

LITUANUS QUARTERLY JOURNAL – 1954- 1; 1971- 5,6; 1976- 4 x 6 in. 9 – us UMI [947]

LITURATURULI SAKARTVELO – Tbilisi, USSR. Apr 15 1988-May 1990 – 3r – 1 – us L of C Photodup [072]

LITURGIA ELEMENTAL 4TH EDICION / Secretariado Catequistico de la Diocesis de Plasencia – Plasencia: Tip. La Victoria, 1960 – 1 – sp Bibl Santa Ana [240]

LITURGIA ET POTESTAS IN RE LITURGICA / Gordon, I – Rome, 1966 – 3mf – 8 – Dfl13.00 – ne Slangenburg [240]

LA LITURGIA GALLICANA NEI PRIMI OTTO SECOLI / Marchesi, L – Roma. v1-2. 1867 – 11mf – 8 – Dfl39.00 – ne Slangenburg [240]

LITURGIA ROMANA VETUS / Muratori, Lodovico A – Neapolis. v1-2. 1776 – 25mf – 8 – Dfl88.00 – ne Slangenburg [240]

LITURGIAE PRACTICAE COMPENDIUM : SIVE, SACRORUM RITUUM RUBRICARUMQUE MISSALIS BREVIARII ET RITUALIS ROMANI COMPENDIOSA ELUCIDATIO / Falise, Jean Baptiste – (Includes indexes) – Ratisbonae [Regensburg]: Georgius Josephus Manz, 1876 – 2mf – 9 – 0-8370-7381-2 – 1986-1381 – us A.T.L.A. [240]

THE LITURGICAL HOMILIES OF NARSAI / Connolly, R H – 1909 – 5mf – 9 – Dfl22.00 – ne Slangenburg [240]

THE LITURGICAL POETRY OF ADAM OF ST VICTOR / Adam, de Saint Victor – London: K. Paul, Trench, 1881 – 2mf – us A.T.L.A. [240]

LA LITURGIE CAMBRESIENNE AU 18E SIECLE ET LE PROJET DE BREVIAIRE POUR TOUS LES DIOCESES DES PAYS-BAS / Hautcoeur, E – Louvain, 1882 – 2mf – 8 – Dfl9.00 – ne Slangenburg [240]

LA LITURGIE DE PREMONTRE / Lefevre, F – Louvain, 1957 – 4mf – 8 – Dfl19.00 – ne Slangenburg [240]

LITURGIE DER DREI ERSTEN CHRISTLICHEN JAHRHUNDERTE / Probst, Ferdinand – Tuebingen: H. Laupp, 1870 – 1mf – us A.T.L.A. [240]

DIE LITURGIE DER KATHOLISCHE ARMENIER / ed by Steck, Franz Xaver – (Aus dem Armenischen uebersetzt) – Tuebingen, 1845 – 2mf – 8 – Dfl9.00 – ne Slangenburg [240]

LITURGIE DES EGLISES REFORMEES DE FRANCE : PROJET DE REVISION PREPARE PAR LA COMMISSION SYNODALE DE LA LITURGIE – Paris, 1893 – 4mf – 8 – Dfl19.00 – ne Slangenburg [240]

LITURGIE DES VIERTEN JAHRHUNDERTS UND DEREN REFORM / Probst, Ferdinand – Muenster i.W.: Aschendorff, 1893 – 2mf – us A.T.L.A. [240]

LITURGIE, EGLISE REFORMEE DE FRANCE – Paris, 1963 – 12mf – 8 – Dfl42.00 – ne Slangenburg [240]

LITURGIE IN GEBRUIK BIJ DE VRIJE KATHOLIEKE KERK – Batavia, 1924 – 5mf – 8 – Dfl22.00 – ne Slangenburg [240]

LITURGIE UND GEISTLICHE DICHTUNG ZWISCHEN 1050 UND 1300 : MIT BESONDERER BERUECKSICHTIGUNG DER MESS- UND TAGZEITENLITURGIE / Stroppel, Robert – (Includes bibliographical references and index) – Frankfurt am Main: M Diesterweg, 1927 – 1r – 1 – us U.W. Library [240]

LITURGIE ZUM TAUF-FEST DER AETHIOPISCHEN KIRCHE / Arnhard, C von – Muenchen, 1886 – 2mf – 8 – Dfl9.00 – ne Slangenburg [240]

LITURGIES EASTERN AND WESTERN : 1. EASTERN LITURGIES / Brightman, FE – Oxford, 1896 – 9mf – 8 – Dfl32.00 – ne Slangenburg [240]

LITURGIES, EASTERN AND WESTERN : BEING A REPRINT OF THE TEXTS, ORIGINAL OR TRANSLATED, OF THE PRINCIPAL LITURGIES OF THE CHURCH, FROM VARIOUS SOURCES / ed by Hammond, C E – Oxford: Clarendon Press, 1878 – 2mf – us A.T.L.A. [240]

LITURGIES, EASTERN AND WESTERN : BEING THE TEXTS, ORIGINAL OR TRANSLATED, OF THE PRINCIPAL LITURGIES OF THE CHURCH / Brightman, FE – Oxford: Clarendon Press; New York: Macmillan [distributor], 1896 – 2mf – us A.T.L.A. [240]

LITURGIES OF CHRISTIAN CHURCHES (CCC248) = CHIAO-HUI LI-WEN – (In Chinese) – [s.l: s.n, 1891] – 1r – 1 – 1984-6548 – us A.T.L.A. [240]

LITURGIIA KRASOTY. STIKHIINYE GIMNY / Bal'mont, K D – M. 1905. BR-523 2 – 8 – ne IDC [460]

DE LITURGISCHE BOEKEN VAN DE KOLLEGIALE KERK VAN O.L. VROUW VAN TONGEREN VOOR HET CONCILIE VAN TRENTE / Corswarem, P de – Gent, 1923 – 4mf – 8 – Dfl19.00 – ne Slangenburg [240]

DIE LITURGISCHE GEWANDUNG IN OCCIDENT UND ORIENT / Braun, J – Freiburg i.Br., 1907 – 21mf – 8 – Dfl74.00 – ne Slangenburg [240]

DER LITURGISCHE PAPYRUS VON DER-BALYZEH : EINE ABENDMAHLSLITURGIE DES OSTERMORGENS (T.U.U. 3-36/1B) / Schermann, Theodor – Leipzig, 1910 – 1mf – 9 – ne Slangenburg [240]

DIE LITURGISCHE PARAMENTE IN GEGENWART UND VERGANGENHEIT / Braun, J – Freiburg i. Brsg., 1924 – 7mf – 8 – Dfl28.00 – ne Slangenburg [240]

DIE LITURGISCHEN ANSCHAUUNGEN DES VITUS ANTON WINTER / Vierbach, A – Muenchen, 1929 – 5mf – 8 – Dfl22.00 – ne Slangenburg [240]

LITURGY – v1- . 1980- – 1,5,6,9 – us UMI [073]

LITURGY AND RITUAL, GRADUAL – (Dominican gradual, including Scripture lessons, some offices. Some missing leaves at beginning and end) – French illuminated ms, between 1253 and 1262? – 1 – us Sibley [780]

THE LITURGY AND RITUAL OF THE ANTE-NICENE CHURCH / Warren, F E – London: S.P.C.K.; New York: E.S. Gorham, 1912 – 1mf – us A.T.L.A. [240]

THE LITURGY AND RITUAL OF THE CELTIC CHURCH / Warren, F E – Oxford, 1881 – 6mf – 8 – Dfl25.00 – ne Slangenburg [240]

LITURGY AND WORSHIP : A COMPANION TO THE PRAYER BOOKS OF THE ANGLICAN COMMISSION / ed by Clarke, W K Lowther – London, 1932 – 15mf – 8 – Dfl53.00 – ne Slangenburg [240]

LITURGY FOR THE LAITY, OR, AN EXPLANATION OF SACRED OBJECTS CONNECTED WITH DIVINE WORSHIP / O'Donnell, James H – New York: P O'Shea, 1889, c1888 – 1mf – 9 – 0-8370-7493-2 – 1986-1493 – us A.T.L.A. [240]

THE LITURGY OF THE EVANGELICAL LUTHERAN CHURCH / Evangelical Lutheran Church in the United States of America. General Synod. Liturgy and ritual – 1881 – 1 – us A.T.L.A. [240]

Litzmann, Berthold *see*
- DETLEV VON LILIENCRON
- ERNST VON WILDENBRUCH
- FRIEDRICH LUDWIG SCHROEDER
- GEDICHTE
- GESAMMELTE WERKE
- HOELDERLINS GESAMMELTE DICHTUNGEN
- IM ALTEN DEUTSCHLAND

LITZMANNSTADTER ZEITUNG – Lodz, Poland. 30 Jul 1940; 17,20 Oct 1941; 10-14 Jan 1945 – 1r – 1 – us L of C Photodup [943]

LITZMANNSTAEDTER ZEITUNG – Lodz, Poland. 1 Aug 1943-17 Jan 1945 – 5r – 1 – uk British Libr Newspaper [947]

LITZMANNSTAEDTER ZEITUNG *see* LODSCHER ZEITUNG

Liu, Chiao-fei *see* A BALLAD OF FOUR RELIGIONS (CCC222)
Liu, Ch'u-t'ang *see* THE DISCOVERY OF CHINA'S EARLIEST STORY OF JESUS CHRIST (CCC214)
LIU HONGSHENG QIYE SHILIAO (SHANGHAI ZIBEN ZHUYI DIANXING QIYE SHILIAO) – Historical materials on typical bourgeois enterprises in Shanghai: Materials on enterprises owned by Liu Hongsheng. Comp. by the Institute of Economics, Shanghai Academy of Social Sciences. 1 reel. M-H174 – 5 – $40.00 – cc Microforms [950]
LIU KUNYI YIJI (ZHONGGUO JINDAISHI ZILIAO CONGSHU) – Historical materials of modern China series: Posthumous manuscripts of Liu Kunyi. Comp. by the Institute of History, Chinese Academy of Social Sciences. 2 reels. M-H187 – 5 – $80.00 – cc Microforms [950]
Liu, Liang-mou *see*
– CHI TU CHIAO YU SHIH CHIEH HO P'ING (CCC223)
– CHRISTIAN YOUTH AT THE FRONT (CCC224)
Liu, Mary *see*
– THE CHRISTIAN FAMILY (CCC225)
– PRAYERS FOR THE DAILY TASK (CCC226)
Liu, Qi et al *see* THE RELATIONSHIP BETWEEN BODY ROLL AND HANDPATH DURING THE PULL PHASE IN FREESTYLE SWIMMING
Liu, X. *see* THE EFFECTS OF RETROACTIVE INHIBITION AND CONTEXTUAL INTERFERENCE ON LEARNING A MOTOR TASK
Liu, Yu-chen *see* NEW PARENTS (CCC227)
Liu, Yueh-sheng *see* HSIANG KANG CHI TU CHIAO HUI SHIH (CCC228)
Liu, Z *see* A CROSS-CULTURAL ANALYSIS OF CHILDREN'S ATTITUDES TOWARD PHYSICAL ACTIVITY AND PATTERNS OF PARTICIPATION
Liubetskii, S N *see* OTGOLOSKI STARINY
Liubimov, IE *see* DVA GODA RABOTY POTREBITEL'SKOI KOOPERATSII
Liubimov, N A *see* MOI VKLAD
Liublinskaia, A D *see*
– BASTILIIA I EE ARKHIV
– ZAPADNOEVROPEISKIE RUKOPISI, KHRANIASHCHIESIA V SSSR
Liublinskii, VS *see* ISTOCHNIKI PO ISTORII SKANDINAVSKIKH STRAN V LENINGRADSKOM OTDELENII INSTITUTA ISTORII AN SSSR
Liubomirov, P G *see* OCHERKII PO ISTORII RUSSKOI PROMYSHLENNOSTI 17, 18 I NACHALA 19 VEKA
Liubopytnyi, P *see*
– ISTORICHESKII SLOVAR' 86 OTSTEV I KATALOG ILI BIBLIOTEKA STAROVERCHESKOI TSERKVI
– RASKOL'NICHESKAIA BIBLIOGRAFIIA
LIUBOV BEZ LIUBVI / Ionev, R – 1925 – 9 – BR-10 541 1 – ne IDC [150]
LIUBOV' K TREM APELSINAM – Moscow, 1914-16 – 20mf – 9 – $140.00 – us Ross [790]
LIUBOV' SILNEE SMERTI / Merezhkovskii, Dimitrii – Ital'ianskaia novella XV veka. Ed. 2. Spb. 1904. BR-771 2 – 8 – ne IDC [460]
LIUBOV' SILNEE SMERTI / Merezhkovskii, Dimitrii – Nauka liubvi. Michel-Angelo. Sviatoi Satir. M. 1902. BR-772 2 – 8 – ne IDC [700]
LIUBOV'K TREM APEL'SINAM – Zhurnal doktora Apertutto. Petrograd. 1914-16. BR-3362 2 – 8 – ne IDC [073]
LIUBOVNAIA LIRIKA 18 VEKA / Veselovskii, A A – (k voprosu o vzaimootnoshenii narodnoi i khudozhestvennoi liriki 18 veka). Spb. 1909. BR-7948 2 – 8 – ne IDC [460]
Liubumov, L *see* NA CHUZHBINE (OB EMIGRANTSKOI LITERATURE)
LIUDI, GODY, ZHIZN' / Erenburg, I – Kniga 1-2. M. 1961. BR-2059 2 – 8 – ne IDC [460]
LIUDI I KNIGI / Chukovskii, K – "Goslitizdat". Ed. 2. M. 1960. BR-2032 2 – 8 – ne IDC [460]
LIUDI STARAGO VEKA / Esipov, G V – Spb. 1880. BR-6027 2 – 8 – ne IDC [460]
LIUDPRANDI OPERA (MGH 7: 41.BD) – Ed 3a. 1915 – Dfl22.00 – ne Slangenburg [240]
LIU-HO TS'UNG-T'AN – (General Miscellany). v. 1-13. Shanghai. 1857. BCH-801 2 – 8 – ne IDC [080]
LIU-SHIH NIEN-LAI CHUNG-KUO YU JIH-PEN – Sixty years Relationship between China and Japan. Bu Wang Yun-sheng. 7 v. 1932-34. BCH-843 2 – 8 – ne IDC [950]
Liuzza, Roy M *see* ANGLO-SAXON GOSPELS
Livanova, T *see* RUSSKAIA MUZYKAL'NAIA KUL'TURA XVIII VEKA V EE SVIAZIAKH S LITERATUROI, TEATROM I BYTOM
LIVE OAK TIMES – Live Oak, CA. Jul 1979-1981 – 3r – 1 – $150.00 – B02347 – us Library Micro [071]
LIVE WIRE – Pendleton, OR. -sw, w, d. 1910-14 – 1 – 89.00 – us Oregon Hist [071]
THE LIVE WIRE – Portland. Or. 1911-1913 – 1 – us UMI [071]
Liveing, E *see* ON MEGRIM, SICKHEADACHE AND SOME ALLIED DISORDERS
LE LIVERE DE REIS DE BRITTANIE E LE LIVERE DE REIS DE ENGLETERRE (RS42) : (FROM BRUTUS TO 1274, WITH TWO CONTINUATIONS TO 1326 AND A TRANSLATION) / Peter Of Ickham; ed by Glover, J – 1865 – Dfl30.00 – ne Slangenburg [941]
Livermore *see* HISTORY OF THE TOWN OF WILTON
LIVERMORE ECHO – Livermore, CA. 1905; 1914-17 (broken file) – 1r – 1 – $50.00 – B02349 – us Library Micro [071]
Livermore, Harriet *see*
– THE HARP OF ISRAEL: TO MEET THE LOUD ECHO IN THE WILDS OF AMERICA
– A NARRATION OF RELIGIOUS EXPERIENCE: IN TWELVE LETTERS
LIVERMORE HERALD *see* HERALD NEWS
Livermore, Mary Ashton Rice *see* WHAT SHALL WE DO WITH OUR DAUGHTERS?; SUPERFLUOUS WOMEN, AND OTHER LECTURES
Liverpool *see* PLANTATION REGISTERS
Liverpool Bibliographical Society. University of Liverpool *see* THE BOOK TRADE IN LIVERPOOL FROM 1806 TO 1850
Liverpool. City Libraries *see* HOLT AND GREGSON PAPERS 1778-1830
LIVERPOOL CUSTOMS REGISTERS OF SHIPPING, 1786-1823 – 38v of Customs Registers of Shipping for the Port of Liverpool, covering the period 1786-1823 plus printed finding list – ca 20r – 1 – ca £750.00 – uk Altair [380]
LIVERPOOL DAILY POST – England, Sep-Dec 1894 – 1r – 1 – uk British Libr Newspaper [072]
LIVERPOOL ECHO – England. 1986-Jun 1987 – 18r – 1 – uk British Libr Newspaper [072]
LIVERPOOL JOURNAL OF COMMERCE – England, 1863; 1868; 1873; 1878; 1883; 1888; 1893; 1958; 1962 – 30 1/2r – 1 – uk British Libr Newspaper [072]
LIVERPOOL MAIL – England. -d. 1860-65. (12 reels) – 1 – uk British Libr Newspaper [072]
LIVERPOOL MERCURY – England. -w. 1818-22. 2 1 2 reels – 1 – uk British Libr Newspaper [072]
Liverpool Papers *see* AMERICAN MATERIAL IN THE LIVERPOOL PAPERS
Liverpool. Record Office *see* TARLETON PAPERS: AMERICAN MATERIAL
LIVERPOOL STEAMSHIP OWNERS' ASSOCIATION: MINUTE BOOKS, 1858-1964 – Plus printed finding list – ca 60r – 1 – ca £2,500.00 – uk Altair [380]
LIVERPOOL SUN – Liverpool, PA. -w 1881-1910; 1921-24. 7 rolls – 13 – $25.00r – us I.M.R. [071]
LIVERPOOL TELEGRAPH AND SHIPPING GAZETTE – England. Liverpool Shipping Telegraph & Daily Commercial Advertiser. -d. 16 May 1846-29 April 1899. Lacking 1898. 117 reels – 1 – uk British Libr Newspaper [072]
LIVERPOOL TRADE LIST – England.26 Jul 1798-5 Jan 1800. -w. 1/2 reel – 1 – uk British Libr Newspaper [072]
THE LIVES AND BLOODY EXPLOITS OF THE MOST NOTED PIRATES, THEIR TRIALS AND EXECUTIONS, INCLUDING CORRECT ACCOUNTS OF THE LATE PIRACIES, COMMITTED IN THE WEST INDIAS. – Hartford, CT: E. Strong, 1836 1835. 298p. illus. plates – 1 – us U.W. Library [970]
LIVES AND EXPLOITS OF THE MOST NOTED HIGHWAYMEN : ROBBERS AND MURDERERS OF ALL NATIONS – Hartford: Silas Andrus & Son, n.d. – 3mf – 9 – $4.50 – LLMC 92-160 – us L.L.M.C. [920]
LIVES AND LABORS OF EMINENT DIVINES / Nason, Elias & Beale, J F – 1895 – 1 – 12.67 – us Baptist [240]
THE LIVES AND OPINIONS OF EMINENT PHILOSOPHERS / Diogenes, Laertius – Literally trans. by C.D. Yonge. London: George Bell & Sons, 1895. viii,488p – 1 – us U.W. Library [180]
THE LIVES OF ALCHEMYSTICAL PHILOSOPHERS : WITH A CRITICAL CATALOGUE OF BOOKS IN OCCULT CHEMISTRY,... / Barrett, F – London, 1815 – 5mf – 9 – VR-35.9/1 – ne IDC [130]
THE LIVES OF EARLY METHODIST PREACHERS, CHIEFLY WRITTEN BY THEMSELVES,... / ed by Jackson, T – London. 6v. 1865-1866 – 24mf – 9 – ne IDC [240]
LIVES OF EDWARD THE CONFESSOR (RS3) / ed by Luard, H R – 1858 – Dfl32.00 – ne Slangenburg [920]
LIVES OF EMINENT AND ILLUSTRIOUS ENGLISHMEN: FROM ALFRED THE GREAT TO THE LATEST TIMES, ON AN ORIGINAL PLAN. / ed by Cunningham, George Godfrey – Glasgow: A. Fullarton, 1836-37. 8v. illus – 1 – us U.W. Library [920]
THE LIVES OF EMINENT METHODIST MINISTERS : CONTAINING BIOGRAPHICAL SKETCHES, INCIDENTS, ANECDOTES, RECORDS OF TRAVEL, REFLECTIONS,... / Gorrie, P Douglas – Auburn, 1852 – 5mf – 9 – ne IDC [240]
THE LIVES OF EMINENT METHODIST MINISTERS : CONTAINING BIOGRAPHICAL SKETCHES, INCIDENTS, ANECDOTES, RECORDS OF TRAVEL, REFLECTIONS, ETC., ETC. / Gorrie, P Douglass – Auburn: Derby and Miller, 1852 – 1mf – us A.T.L.A. [240]
THE LIVES OF EMINENT METHODIST MINISTERS; CONTAINING BIOGRAPHICAL SKETCHES, INCIDENTS, ANECDOTES, RECORDS OF TRAVEL, REFLECTIONS,... / Gorrie, P Douglas – Auburn, 1852. 408p – 5mf – 9 – ne IDC [240]
THE LIVES OF JOHN SELDEN, AND ARCHBISHOP USHER... / Aikin, J – London, 1812 – 5mf – 9 – ILM-793/1 – ne IDC [340]
THE LIVES OF MABA' SYON AND GABRA KRESTOS / Budge, E A W – London, 1898 – 12mf – 9 – ne IDC [930]
LIVES OF MEN OF LETTERS OF THE TIME OF GEORGE 3 / Brougham, Henry – London: R. Griffin, 1855. 438p – 1 – us U.W. Library [920]
LIVES OF PROMINENT CHINESE PASTORS (CCC174) / Hsieh, Hung-lai – (In Chinese) – Shanghai: Association Press of China, 1916 – 1r – 1 – 1984-B500 – us A.T.L.A. [240]
LIVES OF S. NINIAN AND S. KENTIGERN : COMPILED IN THE TWELFTH CENTURY / Aelred of Rievaulx, Saint; ed by Forbes, Alexander Penrose – Edinburgh: Edmonston and Douglas, 1874 – 2mf – us A.T.L.A. [240]
THE LIVES OF ST. JOSEPH CALASANCTIUS, FOUNDER OF THE PIOUS SCHOOLS : AND OF THE BLESSED IPPOLITO GALANTINI, FOUNDER OF THE CONGREGATION OF CHRISTIAN DOCTRINE – London: Thomas Richardson, 1850 – 2mf – 9 – 0-8370-7020-1 – 1986-1020 – us A.T.L.A. [920]
THE LIVES OF THE BLESSED LEONARD OF PORT MAURICE AND OF THE BLESSED NICHOLAS FATTORE / Giuseppe, Maria & Alapont, Giuseppe – London: Richardson, 1852 – 2mf – 9 – 0-8370-6979-3 – 1986-0979 – us A.T.L.A. [920]
LIVES OF THE CHIEF JUSTICES OF ENGLAND – New York: Cockcroft. v1-6. 1874 (all publ) – 27mf – 9 – $40.50 – LLMC 81-402A – us L.L.M.C. [920]
LIVES OF THE EARLY POPES / Meyrick, Thomas – London: R Washbourne. 2v. 1878-80 – 2mf – 9 – 0-8370-6822-3 – 1986-0822 – us A.T.L.A. [920]
LIVES OF THE EMINENT DEAD AND BIOGRAPHICAL NOTICES OF LIVING CITIZENS / Auge, M – Norristown, 1879. Pennsylvania Reel 32. (The Cox Library Collection) – 5 – us Americana [978]
LIVES OF THE EMINENT MEN OF ABERDEEN / Bruce, James – Aberdeen: L Smith, 1841 – us Res Libr [920]
LIVES OF THE EMINENT MEN OF FIFE / Bruce, James – Edinburgh: M Macphail, 1846 – us Res Libr [920]
LIVES OF THE ENGLISH CARDINALS; INCLUDING HISTORICAL NOTICES OF THE PAPAL COURT, FROM NICHOLAS BREAKSPEAR (POPE ADRIAN 4) TO THOMAS WOLSEY, CARDINAL LEGATE / Williams, Robert Folkestone – London: W.H. Allen, 1868. 2v – 1 – us U.W. Library [920]
LIVES OF THE FATHERS : SKETCHES OF CHURCH HISTORY IN BIOGRAPHY / Farrar, Frederic William – Edinburgh: A.& C. Black, 1889 – 4mf – us A.T.L.A. [240]
LIVES OF THE LORD CHANCELLORS / Campbell, John – 5th ed. London: J Murray. v1-10. 1868 (all publ) – 49mf – 9 – $73.00 – LLMC 81-402B – us L.L.M.C. [920]
THE LIVES OF THE MOST FAMOUS ENGLISH POETS / Winstanley, William – 1687 – 9 – 15.00 – us Scholars' Facs [920]
LIVES OF THE NECROMANCERS... / Godwin, William – London: Frederick J. Mason, 1834 – 1 roll – 1 – 1-55879-653-3 – uk Libr Preservation [130]
LIVES OF THE NECROMANCERS: OR, AN ACCOUNT OF THE MOST EMINENT PERSONS IN SUCCESSIVE AGES WHO HAVE CLAIMED...OR TO WHOM HAS BEEN IMPUTED...THE EXERCISE OF MAGICAL POWER / Godwin, William – London: Chatto and Windus, 1876.xvi,282p – 1 – us U.W. Library [920]
THE LIVES OF THE NOVELISTS / Scott, Walter – London: J.M. Dent; New York: Dutton, [19–?] – 1 roll – 1 – 1-55879-665-7 – uk Libr Preservation [420]
LIVES OF THE PRIMITIVE FATHERS : BEING A FAITHFUL HISTORY OF THE ACTS AND SUFFERINGS OF THOSE EMINENT MEN WHO LIVED IN THE EARLY AGES OF THE CHRISTIAN CHURCH : WITH COPIOUS LISTS OF THEIR WRITINGS... / Blakey, Robert – London: J. Edwards, 1842 – 1mf – us A.T.L.A. [240]
LIVES OF THE PRIMITIVE FATHERS / Lupton – 1640 – 1 – uk Microform Academic [240]
THE LIVES OF THE ROMAN EMPERORS AND THEIR ASSOCIATES FROM JULIUS CAESAR (BC 100) TO AUGUSTULUS (AD 476) / ed by Reed, J Eugene – Trans. from original text of Suetonius, Tacitus, Mongez, Visconte, Crevier and others. Philadelphia: Gebbie & co., 1885.5v. illus – 1 – us U.W. Library [930]
LIVES OF THE TWELVE APOSTLES: TO WHICH IS PREFIXED A LIFE OF JOHN THE BAPTIST / Greenwood, Francis Wm. P – Boston: American Unitarian Assoc., 1874.1 fiche – 9 – us A.T.L.A. [240]
LIVES OF TWELVE GOOD MEN / Burgon, John William – London: J. Murray, 1891 – 2mf – us A.T.L.A. [240]
LIVES OF VICE ADMIRAL SIR C.V. PENROSE AND CAPTAIN J. TREVENEN / Penrose, John – 1850 – 9 – $20.00 – uk Libr Preservation [355]
LIVESTOCK AND MEAT MKTNG. INFO / Kentucky. Agricultural Extension Service – v. 1-14. 1964-68 – 1,5,6 – us Spaulding [636]
LIVESTOCK AND RESOURCE MANAGEMENT POLICY : ISSUES AND PRIORITIES FOR RESEARCH. PROCEEDINGS OF THE RESEARCH PLANNING WORKSHOP HELD AT ILCA, ADDIS ABABA, ETHIOPIA, 24-27 MARCH 1992 / ed by Ehui, S & Lipner, M E – 1993 – 9 – $13.00 – 92-9053-242-4 – et ILRI [636]
LIVESTOCK BREEDS OF CHINA – 1985 – 239p – it F.A.O. [636]
LIVESTOCK INTERNATIONAL – 1973- 1; 1976-5,6,9 – us UMI [073]
LIVESTOCK INTERNATIONAL *see* AGRICULTURE INTERNATIONAL
LIVESTOCK LEAFLET / Clemson University. Agricultural Extension Division – No.13-29. 1970-82. 1 reel – 1,5 – us Spaulding [636]
LIVESTOCK PRODUCERS DAY / Louisiana State University. Agricultural Experiment Station. Animal Science Department – No.11-25. 1971-84 – 1,5 – us Spaulding [636]
LIVESTOCK PRODUCTION IN CENTRAL MALI = LA PRODUCTION ANIMALE AU MALI CENTRAL: ETUDES A LONG TERME SUR LES BOVINS ET LES PETITS RUMINANTS DANS LE SYSTEME AGROPASTORAL : LONG-TERM STUDIES ON CATTLE AND SMALL RUMINANTS IN THE AGROPASTORAL SYSTEM / Wilson, R T – 1986 – 9 – $14.00 – 92-9053-118-5 – et ILRI [636]

LIVESTOCK PRODUCTION IN THE SUBHUMID ZONE OF WEST AFRICA = LA PRODUCTION ANIMALE DANS LA ZONE SUBHUMIDE DE L'AFRIQUE DE L'OUEST: UNE ETUDE REGIONALE : A REGIONAL VIEW / ILCA – 1979 – 9 – $10.00 – 92-9053-122-3 – et ILRI [630]
LIVESTOCK PRODUCTION SCIENCE – v1-11. 1974-84 – 1,5,6,13 – sz Elsevier [073]
LIVESTOCK RESEARCH ROUNDUP / North Dakota. Agricultural Experiment Station. Dickinson – 1951-75 – 1,5,6 – us Spaulding [636]
LIVESTOCK SYSTEMS RESEARCH IN NIGERIA'S SUBHUMID ZONE : PROCEEDINGS OF THE SECOND ILCA/NAPRI SYMPOSIUM HELD IN KADUNA, NIGERIA, 29TH OCTOBER-2ND NOVEMBER 1984 / ed by Kaufmann, R von et al – 1986 – 9 – $56.00 – 92-9053-140-1 – et ILRI [630]
LIVESTOCK SYSTEMS RESEARCH MANUAL : VOLUME 1 / ILCA – 1990 – 9 – 92-9053-221-1 – et ILRI [630]
LIVESTOCK SYSTEMS RESEARCH MANUAL : VOLUME 2 / ILCA – 1990 – 9 – 92-9053-222-X – et ILRI [630]
LIVESTOCK WATER NEEDS IN PASTORAL AFRICA IN RELATION TO CLIMATE AND FORAGE = INFLUENCE DU CLIMAT ET DE L'ALIMENTATION SUR LES BESOINS EN EAU DE BETAIL EN AFRIQUE TROPICALE / King, J M – 1983 – 9 – $18.00 – 92-9053-111-8 – et ILRI [636]
Livet, C L *see*
– LA GRAMMAIRE FRANCAISE ET LES GRAMMAIRIENS DU XVIE SIECLE
– LEXIQUE DE LA LANGUE DE MOLIERE
LIVETS HOGTIDER – 1944? – 1 – us I.U. Libraries [390]
LIVING AGE – (Boston) (Published as: Littell's Living Age 1844-1896). v. 1-360. 1844-1941 – 1,5,6 – us Princeton Micro [073]
LIVING AGE – v. 1-360. 1844-1941 – 1 – us UMI [073]
LIVING ARTS – London, 1963-64 – 1r – 1 – £60.00 – uk Chadwyck [700]
LIVING BY LIFE / Dodge, Jim – Some bioregional theory and practice. 2-p excerpt – 9 – 1.00f – at Libertarian Micro [335]
LIVING CHRIST AND THE FOUR GOSPELS / Dale, Robert William – New York: A.C. Armstrong, 1890. 1 fiche – 9 – us A.T.L.A. [240]
THE LIVING CHURCH – (Lacking: v7 nos 7,13) – v1-10. 1878-88 – 7r – 1 – ATLA S0822 – us A.T.L.A. [073]
THE LIVING DIALECT OF CARDINGTON, SHROPSHIRE / Jones, C – 7 – uk Microform Academic [420]
THE LIVING GOD : HIS WILL AND HIS WORK: AS GATHERED FROM HIS WORD / Williams, Nathan Witter – Providence: J A & R A Reid, 1877 – 1mf – 9 – 0-8370-5753-1 – 1985-3753 – us A.T.L.A. [210]
LIVING ISSUES – Salt Lake City. Utah. 1897-1900 – 1 – us UMI [071]
THE LIVING LABORER – London, Ont: Harvey, Smith and Co, [1870?-187- or 19–] – 9 – cn C.I.H.M. [971]
LIVING LIFE, OR, AUTOBIOGRAPHY OF REV. EMERSON ANDREWS : A.B., A.M., EVANGELIST / Andrews, Emerson – Boston: J.H. Earle, 1872 – 1mf – us A.T.L.A. [240]
LIVING LIGHT – 1964- 1; 1970- 5,6; 1976- 4 x 6 in. 9 – us UMI [073]
LIVING MARINE RESOURCES OF THE SOUTHEAST ATLANTIC – 1977 rev ed 1986 – 126p – it F.A.O. [333]
LIVING MESSAGE *see* LETTER LEAFLET OF THE WOMAN'S AUXILIARY TO THE BOARD OF DOMESTIC AND FOREIGN MISSIONS OF THE CHURCH OF ENGLAND IN CANADA
LIVING PRAYER – v19,no.3- . Sept 1986- – 1,5,6,9 – us UMI [073]
LIVING RESOURCES OF THE SOUTHERN OCEAN – 1977 – 160p – it F.A.O. [333]
THE LIVING THOUGHTS OF MACHIAVELLI / Machiavelli, Niccolo – By Count Carlo Sforza. New York: Fawcett World Library, 1958. 159p – 1 – us U.W. Library [920]
THE LIVING U.S. CONSTITUTION. / U. S. Constitution – New York, Praeger 1953 176 p. LL-1038 – 1 – us L of C Photodup [340]
THE LIVING WAY / Palmer, Byron – Cincinnati: Jennings and Graham, c1908 – 1mf – 9 – 0-8370-3963-0 – 1985-1963 – us A.T.L.A. [230]
LIVING WILDERNESS – (v.36-46. 1972-82. 9) – v.1-46. 1935-82 – 1,5,6 – us UMI [639]
LIVING WITH CHILDREN – 1957-61 – 1 – 32.34 – us Baptist [240]
LIVINGSTON COUNTY DIRECTORY 1873-1874 / Keating & Pawling – Ann Arbor, 1873. Michigan Reel 18. The Cox Library Collection – 5 – us Americana [978]
Livingston, Edward *see* A CODE OF REFORM AND PRISON DISCIPLINE.
THE LIVINGSTON HALL PAPERS / Hall, Livingston – (Guide only $100.00) – 1 – $4,405.00 – 0-89093-806-7 – us UPA [340]
Livingston, William *see*
– PAPERS OF WILLIAM LIVINGSTON, 1771-1790
– WILLIAM LIVINGSTON PAPERS, 1695-1839
LIVINGSTONE AND THE EXPLORATION OF CENTRAL AFRICA / Johnston, H H – London: G. Philipp, 1891. (The World's great explorers and explorations) – 1mf – us A.T.L.A. [910]
Livingstone, Charles *see* EXPLORATIONS DU ZAMBESE ET DE SES AFFLUENTS ET DECOUVERTE DES LACS CHIROUA ET NYASSA. 1858-1864
Livingstone, David *see*
– EXPLORATIONS DU ZAMBESE ET DE SES AFFLUENTS ET DECOUVERTE DES LACS CHIROUA ET NYASSA. 1858-1864
– MISSIONARY TRAVELS AND RESEARCHES IN SOUTH AFRICA: INCLUDING A SKETCH OF SIXTEEN YEARS' RESIDENCE IN THE INTERIOR OF AFRICA, AND A JOURNEY FROM THE CAPE OF GOOD HOPE...TO THE EASTERN OCEAN
– MISSIONARY TRAVELS AND RESEARCHES IN SOUTH AFRICA: NARRATIVE OF AN EXPEDITION TO THE ZAMBEZI AND ITS TRIBUTARIES
Livingstone, E A *see*
– STUDIA EVANGELICA
– STUDIA PATRISTICA, VOL. 12 (T.U.U. BAND 5-115)
– STUDIA PATRISTICA, VOL. 13 (T.U.U. BAND 5-116)
– STUDIA PATRISTICA, VOL. 14 (T.U.U. BAND 5-117)
LIVINGSTONE MAIL – Zambia. -w. Jan 1941-March 1966. Lacking Feb-Sept 1952. 21 reels – 1 – uk British Libr Newspaper [072]
LIVINGSTONE'S AND STANLEY'S TRAVELS IN AFRICA.. / Jones, Charles Henry – 1881 – 1 – us A.T.L.A. [960]
LIVINGSTON'S JUDICIAL OPINIONS / New York. (State) – 1v. 1802 (all publ) – 2mf – 9 – $3.00 – LLMC 80-026 – us L.L.M.C. [340]
LIVINGSTON'S MONTHLY LAW MAGAZINE – New York. v1-4 no 1. 1853-56 (all publ) – 30mf – 9 – $45.00 – LLMC 82-941 – us L.L.M.C. [073]
Livius, Thomas *see* THE BLESSED VIRGIN IN THE FATHERS OF THE FIRST SIX CENTURIES
LIVLAENDISCHE BEITRAEGE ZUR VERBREITUNG GRUENDLICHER KUNDE VON DER PROTESTANTISCHEN LANDESKIRCHE... – Berlin. v1-3. 1867-1871. Suppl. – 51mf – 9 – ne IDC [240]
LIVLANDISCHE BEITRAEGE – Berlin etc. Bd. 1-2; neue Folge Bd. 1; 1867-71. Vol 2 of first series includes Index to v. 1-2. Film Mas 9277 – 1 – us H.U. Library [073]
LIVONIA BAPTIST CHURCH. CAMPBELLSVILLE, INDIANA : CHURCH RECORDS – Jul 1866-16 Nov 1960 – 1 – 35.28 – us Baptist [240]
Livotova, O E *see* OSNOVNAIA LITERATURA OB AZIATSKOM MUSEE-INSTITUTE VOSTOKOVEDENIIA AKADEMII NAUK SSSR (1776-1954)
Livotova, O E et al *see* VOSTOKOVEDENIE V IZDANIIAKH AKADEMII NAUK 1726-1917. BIBLIOGRAFIIA
LE LIVRE CANADIEN *see* NOS LIVRES
LE LIVRE D'AMOS / Touzard, Jules – Paris: Librairie Bloud, 1909. 1 fiche – 9 – us A.T.L.A. [240]
LIVRE D'ARCHITECTURE / Androuet du Cerceau, Jacques – Paris, 1559. 30p., 50 pl. (Architecture Series) – 9 – fr Hachette [720]
LIVRE D'ARCHITECTURE / Androuet du Cerceau, Jacques – Paris, 1615. 26ff. (Architecture Series) – 9 – fr Hachette [720]
LIVRE D'ARCHITECTURE D'AUTELS ET DE CHEMINEES / Barbet, I – O-1166 1. 1641 – 9 – ne IDC [720]
LIVRE D'ARCHITECTURE, D'AUTELS ET DE CHEMINEES. / Barbet, Jean – Paris, M. Tavernier, 1633. 20 pl. (Architecture Series) – 9 – fr Hachette [720]
LIVRE DE COMPTE OU JOURNAL D'UN MARCHAND DE VILLE-MARIE, JEAN-ALEXIS LEMOINE MONIERE, DU 27 JUIN 1739 AU 8 JANVIER 1751 / Lemoine Moniere, Jean A – Montreal: Bibliotheque nationale du Quebec, 1972. SEM35P52 – 1r – 1 – Can$39.00 – cn Bibl Nat [380]
LIVRE DE FAMILLE : DOCUMENTS, BIOGRAPHIES, ANECDOTES, SOUVENIRS DIVERS RECUEILLIS ET COLLATIONNES DE 1920 A 1930 / Roze, Louis – [1930?] – 1 – F119.55 – fr Armell [920]
LE LIVRE DE FORTUNE / Cousin, Jean – O-953. 1883 – 9 – ne IDC [760]
LIVRE DE LA VIE ET DOCTRINE SPIRITUELLE DE SAINT ESTIENNE DE MURET... / Brunet, Pierre – 1617 – 1 – F235.60 – fr Armell [240]
LIVRE DE LECTURE COURANTE : COURS ELEMENTAIRE / Freres du Sacre-Coeur – Levis: Mercier & cie, imprimeurs, editeurs, libraires et relieurs, [1896?]. SEM105P1615 – 2mf – 9 – Can$4.50 – cn Bibl Nat [440]
LE LIVRE DES FEMMES DE BIEN: 1. LA MERE / Le Nordez, Albert Leon M – Paris: Lelarge, 1900. 289p. (Les Femmes Collection) – 4mf – 9 – $10.00 – fr Bibl Nationale [400]
LE LIVRE DES JUGES / Lagrange, Marie Joseph – (Includes bibliographical references) – Paris: Victor Lecoffre, 1903 – 1mf – 9 – 0-8370-7400-2 – 1986-1400 – us A.T.L.A. [220]
LE LIVRE DES PEINTRES ET GRAVEURS / Marolles, M de; ed by Duplessis, G – Paris, 1855 – 2mf – ne IDC [750]
LE LIVRE DES PROVERBES FRANCAIS / Leroux de Lincy, A JV – 1859 – 9 – fr I.C.S. [880]
LE LIVRE DES RECOMPENSES ET DES PEINES / Remusat, J P A – Paris. 1816. BCH-827 2 – 8 – ne IDC [340]
LIVRE DES RECOMPENSES ET DES PEINES / Lao Tzu – 1835 – 1 – uk Microform Academic [480]
LE LIVRE D'HENOCH: FRAGMENTS GRECS DECOUVERTS A AKHMIM (HAUTE-EGYPTE) / Lods, Adolphe – Paris: Ernest Leroux, 1892. 1 fiche – 9 – us A.T.L.A. [240]
LE LIVRE D'HERACLIDE DE DAMAS / Nestorius – Paris, 1910 – 12mf – 8 – ne Slangenburg [240]
LE LIVRE D'HERACLIDE DE DAMAS / Nestorius, Patriarch of Constantinople; ed by Bedjan, Paul – Paris: O. Harrassowitz, 1910 – 2mf – us A.T.L.A. [240]
LIVRE D'HEURES, AVEC CALENDRIER EN LATIN = BOOK OF HOURS WITH CALENDAR IN LATIN LANGUAGE – 15th cent – 1 – F149.91 – fr Armell [944]
LE LIVRE D'ISAIE: TRADUCTION CRITIQUE AVEC NOTES ET COMMENTAIRES / Condamin, Albert – Paris: Victor Lecoffre, 1905. 1 fiche – 9 – us A.T.L.A. [220]
LE LIVRE DU PAYS NOIR; ANTHOLOGIE DE LITTERATURE AFRICAINE / Lebel, Roland – Paris. 1928 – 1 – us Res Libr [800]
LE LIVRE INSTRUCTIF, OU NOUVEAU DICTIONNAIRE FRANCOIS-ESPAGNOL 1721 (AEL, ABT 2;9) / Leys, Franz Jacob – Handschrift aus der Universitaetsbibliothek Erlangen-Nuernberg (mf ed 1993) – 87mf – 9 – DM1,620.00 – gw Fischer [040]
LE LIVRE JOB. ETB / Dhorme, P – Paris, 1926 – Dfl49.00 – ne Slangenburg [220]
LIVRE NOUVEAU...D'ARCHITECTURE / Vignole, Barozzio de – Paris, France. 1v. 1767 – 1r – 1 – cn Can Microfilming [720]
LE LIVRE ROUGE – Journal politique. no. 1-10. Paris. oct-dec 1877 – 1 – fr A.C.R.P.P. [073]
LIVRES DE COMPTES DE KAY AND PATERSON (1774) ET DE ARTHUR WEBSTER (1820-1830) – Montreal, Canada – 1r – 1 – Can$40.00 – cn Can Microfilming [920]
LIVRES DE COMPTES DE LYMAN – Montreal, 1817-20 – 1r – 1 – Can$40.00 – cn Can Microfilming [090]
LIVRES DE PRIERES ET SELECTIONS DE FRAGMENTS DE L'ANCIEN TESTAMENT AVEC COMMENTAIRES, ETC / Archives de la Bibliotheque Juive – 15r – 1 – cn Can Microfilming [090]
LES LIVRES DES MACCABEES (ETB) / Abel, F M – Paris, 1949 – Dfl70.00 – ne Slangenburg [220]
LES LIVRES D'HEURES, MANUSCRITS DE LA BIBLIOTHEQUE NATIONALE / ed by Leroquais, Victor – (Suppl Paros, 1943) – Paris. 2v. 1927 – 28mf – 9 – O-483/1 – ne IDC [090]
LES LIVRES D'HEURES(MSS. DE LA BIBLIOTHEQUE NATIONALE). O-483/1. 2 V. PLUS ATLAS. 1927. SUPPL. AUX LIVRES 1943 – 9 – ne IDC [240]
LES LIVRES D'ICI... – Montreal: Societe de promotion du livre, c1975-. SEM35P266 – 2r – 1 – Can$107.00 – cn Bibl Nat [072]
LES LIVRES DISPONIBLES – (Auteurs-Titres: F3,330.02. Sujets: F2,023.22) – Paris, avr, sep, dec (3 issues per yr) – 163mf – 9 – F4,805.97 – fr Electre [010]
LIVRES ET ALBUMS ILLUSTRES DU JAPON / Duret, Theodore – Paris. 1900 – 9 – 7.50 – fr Orientalistes [070]
LIVRES ET AUTEURS CANADIENS...: PANORAMA DE LA PRODUCTION LITTERAIRE DE L'ANNEE – 1961-68. SEM105P427 – 19mf – 9 – Can$42.75 – cn Bibl Nat [420]
LIVRES ET AUTRES QUEBECOIS...: REVUE CRITIQUE DE L'ANNEE LITTERAIRE – 1969-1982. SEM105P428 – 64mf – 9 – Can$144.00 – cn Bibl Nat [440]
LES LIVRES IMPRIMES ARMENIENS DE LA BIBLIOTHEQUE DE L'UNIVERSITE D'AMSTERDAM / Macler, F – Paris, 1926 – 2mf – 9 – ne IDC [460]
LIVRES SUR LES BEAUX-ARTS, L'ARCHITECTURE, LA DANSE, LE DESSIN, LA MUSIQUE, LA NUMISMATIQUE, ET LA PEINTURE, PUBLIES AU CANADA DE 1750 A 1899... / Cote, Paul – 1958. SEM105P4 – 1mf – 9 – cn Bibl Nat [700]
LE LIVRET C'EST LE SERVAGE, PUBLIE PAR LA DEMOCRATIE PACIFIQUE – Paris. 1847. (La Condition Ouvriere. Part Two.) – 9 – 2.50 – fr Bibl Nationale [360]
LES LIVRETS DU MANDARIN – Paris. fevr 1931-62 – 1 – fr A.C.R.P.P. [073]
LIVRO DO POVO : PERIODICO LITTERARIO, COMMERCIAL E NOTICIOSO – Pouso Alegre, 12 Dec 1881; 18 Nov 1883 – 1,5,6 – bl Biblioteca [072]
LIVROS IMPRESSOS NO SECULO 16 EXISTENTES...EVORA / Nobre de Guzman, Armando – Madrid: Archivo Ibero-Americano, 1960 – 1 – sp Bibl Santa Ana [240]
LIVROS RAROS E CURIOSOS DE HISTORIA E LITERATURA A VENDA NA LIVRARIA PEREIRA DA SILVA AND CA. ARCHIVO DO BIBLIOPHILO / Pereira da Silva and Ca., Lisboa – Lisboa, 1908 – 10mf – 9 – CIDOC-674/1 – ne IDC [010]
Livshich, B *see* POLUTORAGLAZYI STRELETS
Livy *see*
– AB URBE CONDITA LIBRI 1,2,21,22: ADIUNCTAE SUNT PARTES E SELECTAE EX LIBRIS 3,4,5,6,7,26,29
– BOOKS 1-10
– BOOKS 1-10 AND 21-22
– BOOKS 1-10 AND 21-32: ILLUMINATIONS
– BOOKS 21-30
– BOOKS 31-40
– BOOKS 31-40, ETC
Li-wei-yuan *see* A COLLECTION OF POETRY OF THE SOAK COTTAGE
LIXUE XUEBAO – Acta Mechanica Sinica. In Chinese but English abstracts to the main articles. F p61 – 9 – 4.00f – cc Microforms [073]
Lizondo Borda, Manuel *see* HISTORIA DE LA GOBERNACION DEL TUCUMAN (SIGLO 16). BUENOS AIRES, 1928
Lizotte, Marguerite *see* BIBLIOGRAPHIE DE L'OEUVRE DE GEORGES DUHAMEL DE L'ACADEMIE FRANCAISE, PRESIDENT DE L'ALLIANCE FRANCAISE UNIVERSELLE...
LJUBLJANSKI DNEVNIK – Ljubljana. Yugoslavia. Jul 1951-Oct 1952; Jul 1954-Jun 1956; Nov-Dec 1958 – 7r – 1 – us L of C Photodup [949]
LJUDSKA PRAVICA – Ljubljana. Yugoslavia. -w and d. 15 May-16 Dec 1944, 3 Mar 1945-31 Dec 1949. (Imperfect). (19 reels) – 1 – uk British Libr Newspaper [949]
LJUNGBYTIDNINGEN SMALANNINGEN – Ljungby, Sweden. 1979-80 – 1 – sw Kungliga [072]
LJUSDALSPOSTEN – Ljusdal, Sweden. 1979- – 1 – sw Kungliga [072]
LJUSNAN – Bollnas, Sweden. 1912-78 – 302r – 1 – sw Kungliga [072]
LJUSNAN – Bollnas, Sweden. 1979- – 1 – sw Kungliga [072]

Llaguno Amirola, Eugenio *see*
- CRONICA DE DON PEDRO NINO
- CRONICA DE LOS REYES DE CASTILLA. TOMO 1
- CRONICA DE LOS REYES DE CASTILLA. TOMO 2

LLAIS Y WLAD – Bangor, Wales. -w. Feb 1874-Aug 1884. 10 reels – 1 – uk British Libr Newspaper [072]

EL LLAMADO DE LAS ARMAS, 17 DE OCTUBRE DE 1945 / Fares, Raimundo – Buenos Aires: Ediciones Matepha: [distribuidor Hispano Argentina Libros], c1966 – 1 – CSUXADP3942-B – us Hoover Inst Photo [972]

EL LLAMADO "SOCIALISMO NACIONAL" ?ES SOCIALISMO? / Laborde, Julio et al – Buenos Aires: Ediciones Centro de Estudios, [1974] – 1 – CSUXADQ1418-B – us Hoover Inst Photo [320]

LLAMARADA *see* SPARK

Llamas, Jose *see* MARTIRES AGUSTINOS DE EL ESCORIAL

Llanes Garcia, Enrique *see* CATECISMO DE LA DOCTRINA CRISTIANA Y NOCIONES DE URBANIDAD

LLANGOLLEN ADVERTISER – Wales. -w. 16 July 1869-Dec 1896. Lacking 1873, 1887, 1888. 12 reels – 1 – uk British Libr Newspaper [072]

Llano, Pedro N *see* COMPENDIO...ANTONIO GOMEZ...TORO

Llano y Persi, Manuel de *see* GARCIA DE PAREDES

Llanos y Torrigua, Felix de *see* UNOS AUTOGRAFOS DE DON BARTOLOME JOSE GALLARDO

LLANTOS FUNEBRES A LA SENTIDA, LAMENTABLE,...DONA MA REINA DE PORTUGAL / Chaves Masa, Pedro – Lisboa: Bernardo de Costa, 1699 – 1 – sp Bibl Santa Ana [943]

Llave, P de la *see* NOVORUM VEGETABILIUM DESCRIPTIONES

LLEN CYMRU – Cardiff. Wales. – 1950- 1; 1976- 5,6,9 – us UMI [490]

Llerena *see*
- FERIA Y FIESTAS DE 1946
- NOVENA A...DE LA GRANADA

LLERENA, SU PASADO Y SU PRESENTE / Sabido y Martinez, Antonio – 1888 – 9 – 1.50f – sp Bibl Santa Ana [946]

Llerena.(Spain). Ayuntamiento *see* ORDENANZAS

Llewellyn, Karl N *see*
- CASES AND MATERIALS ON THE LAW OF SALES
- KARL LLEWELLYN PAPERS, SECTION F
- KARL LLEWELLYN PAPERS, SECTION G
- KARL LLEWELLYN PAPERS, SECTION I
- KARL LLEWELLYN PAPERS, SECTION J
- KARL LLEWELLYN PAPERS, SECTION R

Llinas Estevez, Jeronimo *see* APUNTES DE MATEMATICAS

LLMC CANON LAW CATALOGS ON FICHE *see*
- CANON LAW

THE LLMC CIVIL LAW 1 CATALOGS ON FICHE *see*
- CIVIL LAW 1

THE LLMC CIVIL LAW 2 CATALOGS ON FICHE *see*
- CIVIL LAW 2

Llorca, Bernardino *see* DIE SPANISCHE INQUISITION UND DIE ALUMBRADOS. BERLIN-BONN, 1934

Llorens y Masdevall, F *see* FORMULAE MEDICAE

Llorente, Ignacio *see* EL VOTO PERONISTA

Llorente, J A *see* COLECCION DE LAS OBRAS

Lloret y Marti, F *see* LA CALENTURA MESENTERICA...

Lloyd, Alfred Henry *see* CITIZENSHIP AND SALVATION, OR, GREEK AND JEW

Lloyd, Arthur Selden *see* CHRISTIANITY AND THE RELIGIONS

Lloyd, Augustus Parlett *see* A TREATISE ON THE LAW OF BUILDING AND BUILDINGS.

Lloyd, Benjamin *see* THE PRIMITIVE HYMNS

Lloyd, C G 1500 Cincinnati (Ohio). v1-7. 1898-1923 *see* MYCOLOGICAL NOTES

Lloyd, Evan *see* THE METHODIST

Lloyd, Gareth *see*
- CATALOGUE OF THE CHARLES WESLEY PAPERS, V1
- CATALOGUE OF THE CHARLES WESLEY PAPERS, V2
- CATALOGUE OF THE HUGH BOURNE AND WILLIAM CLOWES PAPERS
- CATALOGUE OF THE THOMAS COKE PAPERS
- CATALOGUE OF THE WESLEY FAMILY MANUSCRIPTS, V1
- CATALOGUE OF THE WESLEY FAMILY PAPERS, V2
- CATALOGUE OF THE WESLEY FAMILY PAPERS, V3
HANDLIST OF HARTLEY-VICTORIA COLLEGE COLLECTION
- THE PAPERS OF DR. ADAM CLARKE
- THE PAPERS OF JOSEPH BENSON

Lloyd George, David *see* SPAIN AND BRITAIN

Lloyd, Gregory S *see* AN EXAMINATION OF THE RELATIONSHIP BETWEEN ANGLER SPECIALIZATION AND CONSTRAINTS TO TROUT FISHING

Lloyd, Henry *see* MEMOIRES MILITAIRES ET POLITIQUES, SERVANT D'INTRODUCTION A L'HISTOIRE DE LA GUERRE EN ALLEMAGNE EN 1756.

Lloyd, Henry Demarest *see*
- MAN, THE SOCIAL CREATOR
- PAPERS OF HENRY DEMAREST LLOYD, 1840-1937

Lloyd, Julius *see*
- THE GALLICAN CHURCH
- THE NORTH AFRICAN CHURCH
- SKETCHES OF CHURCH HISTORY IN SCOTLAND

Lloyd, Malcolm *see* THE PRINCIPLES OF THE LAW RELATING TO CORPORATE LIABILITY FOR ACTS OF PROMOTERS

Lloyd, Morgan *see* A TREATISE ON THE LAW OF PROHIBITION.

THE LLOYD PAPERS / ed by Arnold, Gary J – (With printed guide) – 1974 – 41r – 1 – $3,485.00 – S1617 – us Scholarly Res [920]

Lloyd, Seton *see*
- TELL HASSUNA
- TELL UQAIR

Lloyd. (Ship) *see* JOURNALS OF THE SHIP LLOYD, 1767-72

Lloyd, William Henry *see* CASES ON CERTAIN EQUITABLE DOCTRINES AND REMEDIES

LLOYDMINISTER TIMES – (Apr 1907-19 4r. 1921-42 8r) – Saskatchewan, CN. Apr 1907-19; 1921-42 – 12r – 1 – cn Commonwealth Micro [072]

LLOYDMINSTER TIMES – Lloydminster, Saskatchewan. 25 avr 1905; v51. 20 jul 1955 – 1r – 1 – Can$25.00 – cn Can Microfilming [072]

LLOYDS CAPTAINS REGISTERS – 1851-1947. From the Guildhall Library (London). Mss. 18567-71 – 1,14 – £4,500.00 – uk World [920]

LLOYD'S LAW REPORTS (1919-1989) – (Set includes printed cumulative indexes) – 962mf – 9 – $4,800.00 – us UNIFO [340]

LLOYD'S LIST – 1976-1994 – 1 – F3,667.00 – sz Infoprint [072]

LLOYD'S LIST – London. 1976- – 1 – us Primary [072]

LLOYD'S LIST – London. -d. 1827-50; 1914-69. (430mqn reels) – 1 – uk British Libr Newspaper [332]

LLOYD'S LIST – Subscription – 1 – F2,707.00 – sz Infoprint [072]

LLOYDS LISTS IN THE FIRST AND SECOND WORLD WARS / Lloyds of London – £470.00 – uk World [355]

LLOYD'S MARITIME AND COMMERCIAL LAW QUARTERLY – (1974-84 on reel $242.00. 1985-95 on mf $453.50) – 1974-95 – 5,6,9 – $695.00 set – us Hein [340]

Lloyds of London *see* LLOYDS LISTS IN THE FIRST AND SECOND WORLD WARS

Lloyd's Register of Shipping *see* ANNALS OF LLOYD'S REGISTER: BEING A SKETCH OF THE ORIGIN, CONSTITUTION, AND PROGRESS OF LLOYD'S REGISTER OF BRITISH & FOREIGN SHIPPING

LLUNDEINWR – London, UK. 10-31 May 1884 – 1 – uk British Libr Newspaper [072]

LLUVIA MENUDA / Sanchez-Arjona, Vicente – Sevilla: Graficas Tirvia, Tomo 3. 1954 – 1 – sp Bibl Santa Ana [810]

LLUVIA MENUDA / Sanchez-Arjona, Vicente – Sevilla: Imp. Carlos Acuna, Tomo 1. 1954 – 1 – sp Bibl Santa Ana [810]

LLUVIA MENUDA (PENSAMIENTOS INTRASCENDENTES) / Sanchez-Arjona, Vicente – Sevilla: Graficas Tirvia, Tomo 2. 1954 – 1 – sp Bibl Santa Ana [810]

LN – (Literaturni novini). Sofia. Bulgaria. -w. Jan 1962-Feb 1964. (1 reel) – 1 – uk British Libr Newspaper [949]

LO *see* HIGIENE ANTICOLERICA RAZONADA

Lo Gatto, E *see* STORIA DELLA LETTERATURA RUSSA CONTEMPORANEA

Lo, Yun-yen *see*
- CHRISTIANITY AND NEW CHINA (CCC229)
- SELECTED CHRISTIAN ESSAYS (CCC230)
- THE SPIRIT OF CHRISTIANITY (CCC231)

LOA – Titre francais: Le Porte-voix. Hanoi. fevr 1934-nov 1935, fevr 1936 – 1 – fr A.C.R.P.P. [073]

Loaisel-Treogate *see* LA FORET PERILLEUSE OU LES BRIGANDS DE LA CALABRE

LOAN AGREEMENT BETWEEN JORDAN AND THE KUWAIT FUND / Kuwait. Kuwait Fund for Arab Economic Development – 3Apr 1962. BNE-9798 1 – 9 – ne IDC [338]

LOAN AGREEMENT BETWEEN THE REPUBLIC OF SUDAN AND THE KUWAIT FUND FOR ARAB ECONOMIC DEVELOPMENT. DATED 25 MAR 1962. BNE-7658/1 / Kuwait. Kuwait Fund for Arab Economic Development – 9 – ne IDC [338]

LOAN AGREEMENT (ELECTRIC POWER AND IRRIGATION PROJECTS) BETWEEN IBRD AND LITANI RIVER AUTHORITY / Lebanon. International Bank for Reconstruction and Development – 25 Aug 1955. BNE-9663 1 – 9 – ne IDC [338]

LOAN AGREEMENT (HAOUD EL HAMRA-ARZEW OIL PIPELINE PROJECT) BETWEEN THE DEMOCRATIC AND POPULAR REPUBLIC OF ALGERIA AND KUWAIT FUND FOR ARAB ECONOMIC DEVELOPMENT / Kuwait. Kuwait Fund for Arab Economic Development – Dated 23 Jun 1964. 1964. BNE-8655 – 9 – ne IDC [338]

LOAN AGREEMENT (JERUSALEM POWER PROJECT) BETWEEN JORDAN AND KUWAIT FUND / Jordan. Kuwait fund for Arab Economic Development – 5Feb 1964. BNE-9799 1 – 9 – ne IDC [332]

A LOAN APPLICATION FOR THE PURCHASE OF ROLLING STOCK / USAHA Industri Indonesia – SE 10,741 1. 1960 – 9 – ne IDC [025]

LOAN TABLES / Cherriman, John Bradford – Hamilton, Ont.: A. Lawson, 1879. 02989. (Pre-1900 Canadiana) – 9 – cn C.I.H.M. [310]

Loat, Christopher E R *see* COMPARISON OF THE LACTATE AND VENTILATORY THRESHOLDS DURING PROLONGED WORK

Loat, W L S *see* PRE-DYNASTIC CEMETERY AT AL MAHASNA (MEES VOL 31)

Loat, W LS *see* THE CEMETERIES OF ABYDOS (MEES VOL 35)

LOB LIE-BY-THE-FIRE / Ewing, Juliana Horatia – British Fiction Archive: Unit 1 – 9 – uk Bell [830]

Loba, Jean Frederick *see* "REMINISCENCES OF JEAN FREDERICK LOBA"

Lobe, J C *see*
- CONSONANZEN UND DISSONANZEN
- FLIEGENDE BLAETTER FUER MUSIK
- MISUKALISCHE BRIEFE

Lobelius, M *see*
- KRUYDTBOECK OFT BESCHRIJVINGHE VAN ALLERLEYE GHEWASSEN, KRUYDEREN, HESTEREN, ENDE GHEBOOMTEN
- PLANTARUM SEU STIRPIUM ICONES

Lober, Cesar *see* DE LA MORTALITE DES NOUVEAU-NES ET DES MOYENS DE DIMINUER

Lobera de Avila, L *see*
- BANQUETE DE CAVALLEROS Y ORDEN DE VIVIR, ANSI EN TIEMPO DE LA SANIDAD COMO EN...
- BANQUETE DE NOBLES CABALLEROS...E MODO DE BIVIR DESDE QUE SE LEVANTAN HASTA QUE SE ACUESTAN E TRAYA DEL REGIMIENTO CURATIVO Y PRESERVATIVO DE LAS FIEBRES PESTILENCIALES E DE LA PESTILENCIA
- LIBRO DE EXPERIENCIAS DE MEDICINA Y MUY APROBADO POR SUS EFFECTOS, ANSI EN ESTA ESPANA COMO FUERA DELLA
- LIBRO DE LAS QUATRO ENFERMEDADES CORTESANAS QUE SON CATARRO, GOTA ARTHETICA SCIATICA, MACDE PIEDRA...
- LIBRO DE PESTILENCIA, CURATIVO Y PRESERVATIVO...
- REMEDIO DE CUERPOS HUMANOS Y SILVA DE LA EXPERIENCIAS Y OTRAS COSAS UTILISSIMAS

Lobinger, CS *see* EXTRATERRITORIAL CASES

LO-BLADET – Kobenhavn: Landsorganisationen i Danmark. 3 Jan 1973- -biw. Continues: Lon og Virke – 1 – us U.W. Library [073]

Lobo, Jerome *see* RELATION HISTORIQUE D'ABISSINIE TRADUITE DU PORTUGAIS, CONTINUEE ET AUGMENTEE DE PLUSIEURS DISSERTATIONS, LETTRES ET MEMOIRES

Lobo, Leocadio *see* PRIMATE AND PRIEST

Lobo, Miguel *see* EL EMPERADOR CARLOS V...YUSTE

Lobon. Ayuntamiento *see* ORDENANZAS MUNICIPALES

Lobov, GZ *see* KRATKII KURS KOOPERATSII

Lobry, J-B *see*
- HOMELIES POPULAIRES SUR LES EVANGILES DE CHAQUE DIMANCHE DE L'ANNEE
- INSTRUCTIONS POPULAIRES SUR LA PRIERE
- INSTRUCTIONS POPULAIRES SUR LE SYMBOLE DES APAOTRES
- INSTRUCTIONS POPULAIRES SUR LES SACREMENTS
- INSTRUCTIONS POUR DEUX CAR EMES ET UN MOIS DE MARIE

Lobstein, Paul *see*
- COLLECTED WORKS
- ESSAI D'UNE INTRODUCTION A LA DOGMATIQUE PROTESTANTE
- AN INTRODUCTION TO PROTESTANT DOGMATICS
- DIE LEHRE VON DER UEBERNATUERLICHEN GEBURT CHRISTI: CHRISTOLOGISCHE STUDIE
- THE VIRGIN BIRTH OF CHRIST: AN HISTORICAL AND CRITICAL ESSAY
- WAHRHEIT UND DICHTUNG IN UNSERER RELIGION

LA LOCA DEL SACRAMENTO / ed by Bayle, Constantino – Madrid: Razon y Fe, 1926 – 1 – sp Bibl Santa Ana [240]

LOCAL – Sandusky. Ohio. -w. 1882-86 – 1 – us UMI [071]

LOCAL 599 HEADLIGHT – Flint. Mich. 1941-1949; 1964-1969 – 1 – us UMI [331]

LOCAL ADMINISTRATION BULLETIN IN SOVIET RUSSIA / Moscow Soviet of Workers and Red Army Delegates – Moscow, USSR. 1918-19. In Russian – 1 – £35.00r – uk Altair [947]

LOCAL AGENT – v1-41, n. 8. 1931-1969. Continued as: American Agent and Broker – 1 – us UMI [336]

LOCAL AGENT *see* AMERICAN AGENT AND BROKER

LOCAL AND TRADITIONAL COSTUME / Victoria and Albert Museum. London – (Contains over 4,000 illustrations of traditional costumes from around the world. Includes printed catalogue included) – 1987 – 47 colour 4 b/w mf – 15,9 – $904.00 – 0-907696-25-2 – uk Emmett [390]

LOCAL AND TRADITIONAL COSTUMES IN THE VICTORIA AND ALBERT MUSEUM – (Printed index and list of sources. Available in the U.S. and Canada only) – 1989. 47 color, 4 black-and-white mf – $1,050.00 – 0-8161-1758-6 – uk Hall [390]

THE LOCAL COURTS' AND MUNICIPAL GAZETTE – (Cont: Upper Canada Law Journal) – Toronto: W C Chewett, 1865-1872 – 9 – cn C.I.H.M. [340]

THE LOCAL. (EDGWARE LOCAL.-EDGWARE & DISTRICT PO-EDGWARE PO-BOREHAMWOOD, ELSTREE AND EDGWARE POST) – London. 1946-81. -w. 60 reels – 1 – uk British Libr Newspaper [072]

LOCAL ENTERPRISE – Alamitos Bay, CA. 1964-1965 – 1r – 1 – $50.00 – H04000 – us Library Micro [071]

LOCAL ENTERPRISE – Belmont Shore, CA. 1960 – 1r – 1 – $50.00 – H04004 – us Library Micro [071]

LOCAL ENTERPRISE – Los Altos, CA. 1959-1967 – 16r – 1 – $800.00 – H04024 – us Library Micro [071]

LOCAL GOVERNMENT ADMINISTRATION : AN ORGAN OF THE INTERNATIONAL UNION OF LOCAL AUTHORITIES – London. v1-5. 1935-39 (all publ) – 16mf – 9 – $24.00 – LLMC 84-582 – us L.L.M.C. [073]

LOCAL GOVERNMENT FINANCIAL STATISTICS / Pennsylvania. Dept. of Community Affairs – 1955-77. 147 fiches. (Harvard Law School Library Collection.) – 9 – 1.50f – us H.U. Law [336]

LOCAL GOVERNMENT IN PALESTINE / Vaad Leumi General Council – Memorandum submitted to U.N.S.C.O.P. on behalf of the Vaad Leumi General Council of the Jewish Community of Palestine. Jerusalem. 1947. BJ-28-157 1 – 9 – ne IDC [956]

LOCAL HISTORY INDEX – 18mf – 9 – A$120.00 – at State Libr Vic [910]

LOCAL MESSENGER – Pioche, NV. Jun-Dec 1898 – 1r – 1 – $50.00 – U04644 – us Library Micro [071]

LOCAL MIRROR – Carlisle, PA., 1875 – 13 – $25.00r – us I.M.R. [071]

LOCAL OPINION – Grahamstown, South Africa. 5 Aug 1911-25 Jul 1914. 1 reel – 1, 16 diazo available at reduced price – sa SA Libr [072]
LOCAL, PERSONAL, AND PRIVATE ACTS / Great Britain. Laws, Statutes, etc – 1798-1977 – 1 – 7567.00 – us L of C Photodup [324]
LOCAL POPULATION STUDIES – v1- 1968- 1; v16- 5,6,9 – us UMI [073]
LOCAL PREACHERS' MAGAZINE : LOCAL PREACHERS' MAGAZINE, 1851-1930 [AN INDEX OF BIOGRAPHICAL REFERENCES] – N.p., n.d. – 2mf – 9 – ne IDC [240]
LOCAL PROBLEMS: LIBERTARIAN SOLUTIONS / Burt, William D – c1978. With: How to Start a Local Taxpayer Group. Together, 196p. 2 fiches (24x) – 9 – 1.00f – at Libertarian Micro [320]
LOCAL REVIEW – Decatur. Ill. 1873-76 – 1 – us UMI [071]
LOCAL SELF-GOVERNMENT AND CENTRALIZATION / Toulmin Smith, J – 5fiches. (24X) – 9 – 1.00f – at Libertarian Micro [320]
LOCAL SELF-GOVERNMENT FOR IRELAND: SPEECH DELIVERED IN THE HOUSE OF COMMONS OF CANADA, THURSDAY, APRIL 20, 1882 / Costigan, John – Ottawa: Citizen, 1882. 04179. (Pre-1900 Candiana) – 9 – cn C.I.H.M. [971]
LOCALIZACION DE LA RELIQUIA DE LA CABEZA DE SANTA EULALIA / Alvarez Saenz de Buruaga, Jose – Badajoz: Dip. Provincial, 1975. Se. REE – 1 – sp Bibl Santa Ana [946]
LOCALIZED IRRIGATION : DESIGN, INSTALLATION, OPERATION, EVALUATION – 1980 – 221p – it F.A.O. [627]
[LA LOCANDA] TUTTO DA VOI DISPENDE / Paisiello, G – (Full score) – London: Skillern/Goulding, 1791 – 1 – us Sibley [780]
Locard, A *see*
– CONCHYLIOLOGIE FRANCAISE. LES COQUILLES DES EAUX DOUCES ET SAUMATRES DE FRANCE
– CONCHYLIOLOGIE FRANCAISE. LES COQUILLES TERRESTRES DE FRANCE
– LES COQUILLES MARINES DES COTES DE FRANCE. DESCRIPTION DES FAMILLES, GENRES ET ESPECES
Locatelli, Pietro *see* 6 SONATE A TRE, DUE VIOLINI E FLAUTI E BASSO
LE LOCATEUR – devenu: Gazette des travaux publics. devenu: Journal des travaux publics. Paris. juil 1833-dec 1834 janv 1835 – 1 – fr A.C.R.P.P. [073]
LOCATION SCIENCE – 1,5,69 – us UMI [550]
LOCH ARD CEMETERY REGISTER – 1893-1895 – 1mf – 9 – at Corangamite [920]
LO-CH'ANG HSIEN-CHIH – 1871, 12, 1. BCH-602 2 – 8 – ne IDC [950]
Lochmiller, Charles *see* ISOLATION AND PURIFICATION
Lochner, G W R *see*
– JOHANN NEUDOERFER'S NACHRICHTEN VON KUENSTLERN UND WERKLEUTEN IN NUERNBERG
LOCI THEOLOGICI... / Chemnitz, Martin – Francoforti ad Moenvm, 1591 – 22mf – 9 – ne IDC [240]
Lock, Gerhard *see* DER HOEFISCH-GALANTE ROMAN DES 17. JAHRHUNDERTS BEI EBERHARD WERNER HAPPEL
LOCK HAVEN REVIEW – Series 1. v. 1-14. 1959-73 – 1 – us UMI [370]
Lock, Walter *see* JOHN KEBLE
Locke, Alain LeRoy *see* FOUR NEGRO POETS
Locke, Alison B *see* EFFECT OF A SOFTSHELL PROPHYLACTIC ANKLE STABILIZER ON PERFORMANCE IN EVENTS INVOLVING SPEED, AGILITY, AND VERTICAL JUMP DURING LONG-TERM USE
Locke, Clinton *see* THE AGE OF THE GREAT WESTERN SCHISM
Locke, David Ross *see* EASTERN FRUIT ON WESTERN DISHES; THE MORALS OF ABOU BEN ADHEM
Locke, John *see*
– CONDUCT OF THE UNDERSTANDING
– AN ESSAY CONCERNING HUMANE UNDERSTANDING
– OF THE CONDUCT OF THE UNDERSTANDING
– PHILOSOPHICAL WORKS
Locke, M *see* THE ENGLISH OPERA, OR THE VOCAL MUSICK IN PSYCHE...TO WHICH HAS BEEN ADJOYNED THE INSTRUMENTAL MUSICK IN THE TEMPEST
Locke, R *see* JOURNAL OF MUSICOLOGICAL RESEARCH
LOCKELAND BAPTIST CHURCH. NASHVILLE, TENNESSEE : CHURCH RECORDS – 1903-73 – 1 – 131.58 – us Baptist [240]
LOCKELAND BAPTIST CHURCH. NASHVILLE, TENNESSEE : CHURCH RECORDS – 1940-41 – 1 – 16.65 – us Baptist [240]
Locker, B *see* WHAT IS POALE ZIONISM?
Locker-Lampson, Frederick *see* LONDON LYRICS
Lockett, BL *see* DIARY, 1911-20
Lockhart, Aileene *see* DIFFERENTIATION OF ETHNIC CULTURE REGIONS USING LABAN MOVEMENT ANALYSIS
Lockhart, Arthur John *see* THE PAPERS OF PASTOR FELIX
Lockhart, Clinton *see* PRINCIPLES OF INTERPRETATION
Lockhart, JG *see* THE BALLANTYNE-HUMBUG HANDLED
Lockhart, John Gibson *see* PETER'S LETTERS TO HIS KINSFOLK
Lockhart, W P *see* THE GOSPEL WALL, OR, LESSONS FROM NEHEMIAH
Lockhart, William *see*
– CARDINAL NEWMAN
– THE CHURCH OF SCOTLAND IN THE THIRTEENTH CENTURY
Lockley, Fred *see* HISTORY OF COLUMBIA RIVER VALLEY
Lockley, G Lindsay *see* LOCKLEY PAPERS
LOCKLEY PAPERS : TRANSCRIPTS AND RESEARCH FILES RELATING TO THE LONDON MISSIONARY SOCIETY AND CONGREGATIONALISM IN THE PACIFIC AND AUSTRALIA / Lockley, G Lindsay – 4r – 1 – PMB1087 – at Pacific Mss [240]
LOCKPORT UNION – N.Y. 1866-1912 – 1 – us UMI [071]
Lockton, W *see* THE TREATMENT OF THE REMAINS AT THE EUCHARIST AFTER HOLY COMMUNION AND THE TIME OF THE ABLUTIONS
Lockwell, Huguette *see* BIBLIOGRAPHIE DE MADAME EMMA BOIVIN-VAILLANCOURT
Lockwood Expedition *see* JOURNAL OF THE LOCKWOOD EXPEDITION ON THE NORTH COAST OF GREENLAND
Lockwood, J P *see* MEMORIALS OF THE LIFE OF PETER BOEHLER
Lockwood, John P *see* THE WESTERN PIONEERS, OR, MEMORIALS OF THE LIVES AND LABOURS OF THE REV. RICHARD BOARDMAN AND THE REV. JOSEPH PILMOOR
Lockwood, Luke A *see* MASONIC LAW AND PRACTICE
LOCOMOTIEF – Semarang, 1864-1940, 1947-1956 – 387r – 9 – ne IDC [072]
A LOCOMOTIVA : ORGAO DOS INTERESSES LOCAES – Cuiaba, 14 Jan-Dec 1882; Jan, Jul, 27 Oct 1883 – 1,5,6 – bl Biblioteca [072]
A LOCOMOTIVA : PERIODICO HUMORISTICO E LITTERARIO – Sao Joao d'el-Rei, 17 May 1891 – 1,5,6 – bl Biblioteca [072]
A LOCOMOTIVA – Piranhas, Alagoas. 1 Jun-Nov 1880; Abr, Jun-Ago, Out-Dez 1881; Abr, 16 Dez 1882 – 1,5,6 – bl Biblioteca [072]
DIE LOCOMOTIVE – Halle, Berlin. jul-dec 1843, apr 1 1848-jan 9 1849 – 1r – 1 – Dist. gw Mikrofilm – gw Misc Inst [072]
LOCOMOTIVE – Indianapolis. Ind. 1846-1860 – 1 – us UMI [071]
LOCOS, ENANOS, NEGROS Y NINOS PALACIEGOS.. / Moreno Villa, Jose – Mexico, 1939. 157p – 1 – us U.W. Library [360]
AN LOCRANN – Tralee, Cork. Feb, Mar 1913; May 1916-Dec 1920 – 49ft – 1 – uk British Libr Newspaper [072]
LOCRANN *see* AN LOCRANN
LOCUPLETISSIMI RERUM NATURALIUM THESAURI ACCURATA DESCRIPTIO ET ICONIBUS / Seba, A – 4v. Amstelaedami. 1734-65. B-2592 2 – 8 – ne IDC [580]
LOCUST GROVE BAPTIST CHURCH. MURRAY, KUNTUCKY : CHURCH RECORDS – 1841-1948 – 1 – 43.29 – us Baptist [240]
LOCUST HILL BAPTIST CHURCH. GREENVILLE COUNTY. SOUTH CAROLINA : CHURCH RECORDS – (416p) – Oct 1921-Apr 1974 – 1 reel – 1 – $18.72 – us Baptist [240]
LES LOCUTIONS NANTAISES / Eudel, Paul – Nantes: Morel, 1884 – 1 – F125.24 – fr Armell [910]
Loddiges, C *see* BOTANICAL CABINET...
LODE – Delamar, NV. 1892-96; 1898-1900; 1901-06 – 5r – 1 – $250.00 – U04488 – us Library Micro [071]
THE LODE – Pinecone, NV. Mar-Dec 1893 – 1r – 1 – $50.00 – U04640 – us Library Micro [071]
THE LODE – Pioche, NV. Mar-Dec 1893 – 1r – 1 – $50.00 – U04645 – us Library Micro [071]
LODE-EXPRESS – Caliente, NV. 1905; 1906-08 – 1r – 1 – $50.00 – U04431 – us Library Micro [071]
Lodge, Henry Cabot *see*
– DANIEL WEBSTER
– THE FEDERALIST
Lodge, Oliver *see*
– MAN AND THE UNIVERSE
– SCIENCE AND IMMORTALITY
– THE SUBSTANCE OF FAITH ALLIED WITH SCIENCE
LODGE RECORDS / Elsmore Council. Kansas – 1867-75 – 1 – us KS Hist [978]
LODGEPOLE EXPRESS – Lodgepole, NE. -w. Jun 1892; Nov 1895-Apr 1897; Jul 1897-May 1898; Apr 1899-Dec 1949 – 1 – us NE Hist [071]
LODGEPOLE NEBRASKAN – Lodgepole, NE. -w. Apr 1957-May 1964 – 1 – us NE Hist [071]
LODI NEWS-SENTINEL – (Also known as: Lodi Sentinel) – Lodi, CA. 1881-87; 1901- – 380+ r – 1 – $19,000.00 ($300.00y) – B02360 – us Library Micro [071]
LODI SENTINEL *see* LODI NEWS-SENTINEL
LODI/GALT – 1926-44; 1992- – 21+ r – 1 – $1,050.00 – P00046 – us Library Micro [910]
LODOISKA: A MUSICAL ROMANCE IN THREE ACTS. / Storace, Stephen – (Vocal score). 1794 – 9 – us Sibley [780]
Lodores, Baltasar de *see* LOS FRANCISCANOS CAPUCHINOS EN VENEZUELA
Lodowyck, Francis *see*
– A COMMON WRITING
– THE GROUND-WORK OF FOUNDATION LAID... FOR THE FRAMING OF A NEW PERFECT LANGUAGE
Lods, Adolphe *see*
– JEAN ASTRUC ET LA CRITIQUE BIBLIQUE AUX 18E SIECLE
– LE LIVRE D'HENOCH: FRAGMENTS GRECS DECOUVERTS A AKHMIM (HAUTE-EGYPTE)
LODSCHER ZEITUNG – (Also known as: Litzmannstaedter Zeitung) – Lodz (Litzmannstadt), Poland. Aug 1943-17 Jan 1945 – 5r – 1 – gw Mikrofilm [943]
LODZER FREIE PRESSE – (Title change: Freie Presse) – Lodz, Poland. Jul 1920-22, Feb-27 Apr 1923 19 May-Jun 1923, 19 Oct-23 Sept 1939 – 5r – 1 – gw Mikrofilm [072]
LODZER TAGEBLAT = LODZE DAILY – (In Yiddish) – Lodz, PL. no102 5 May 1919-no191 15 Aug 1926 – 1r – 1 – $25.00 – cn Can Microfilming [072]
LODZER VOLKSZEITUNG – Lodz, Poland. Oct 1923-Dec 1938; Jan-Mar 1939; 18 May-Aug 1939 – 26r – 1 – gw Mikrofilm [943]
LODZKI EXPRESS ILUSTROWANY – Lodz, Poland. Sept 1953-Nov 1956 – 5r – 1 – us L of C Photodup [943]
Loe, Ping Kian *see* STARLING'S LAW OF THE HEART: ITS SIGNIFICANCE IN CHRONIC CONGESTIVE HEART FAILURE
Loebell, Richard *see* DER ANTI-NECKER J.H. MERCKS UND DER MINISTER FR. K. V. MOSER
Loeber, E G *see* INTERNATIONAL HISTORY OF PAPER AND PAPER MAKING
Loeber, J *see* HERDERBUCH
Loeff, Friedel *see* GELIEBETER JAN
Loeffler, Fritz *see* THEODOR KOERNER
Loefgren, O *see* DIE BEIDEN GEWOEHNLICHEN AETHIOPISCHEN GREGORIUS-ANAPHOREN
Loefling, P *see* ITER HISPANICUM
Loefstedt, E *see* PHILOLOGISCHER KOMMENTAR ZUR PEREGRINATIO AETHERIAE
Loehe, Wilhelm *see*
– THREE BOOKS CONCERNING THE CHURCH
– ZURUF AUS DER HEIMAT AN DIE DEUTSCH-LUTHERISCHE KIRCHE NORDAMERICAS
Loehr, Max *see*
– DIE KLAGELIEDER DES JEREMIAS
– SOZIALISMUS UND INDIVIDUALISMUS IM ALTEN TESTAMENT
– DIE STELLUNG DES WEIBES ZU JAHWE-RELIGION UND -KULT
– UNTERSUCHUNGEN ZUM BUCH AMOS
Loennemark, H *see* MULTIFARM USE OF AGRICULTURAL MACHINERY
Loens, Hermann *see* DER KLEINE ROSENGARTEN
LOENS-BREVIER / Kutscher, Artur – (Includes bibliographical references) – Muenchen: Zinnen-Verlag, c1943 – 1r – 1 – us U.W. Library [430]
Loesche, Georg *see*
– GESCHICHTE DES PROTESTANTISMUS IN OESTERREICH
– JOHANNES MATHESIUS
– LUTHER, MELANTHON UND CALVIN IN OESTERREICH-UNGARN
– ZUR GEGENREFORMATION IN SCHLESIEN
Loesche, Martin *see* GEDANKEN GOETHES IN DER NEUZEITLICHEN BIOLOGIE
Loeschke, Gerhard *see* DIE VATERUNSER-ERKLAERUNG DES THEOPHILUS VON ANTIOCHIEN
DIE LOESING VON OESTERREICHISCHEN, ... EHEN IN UNGARN / Biragh, J – Wien, 1918 – 1mf – 9 – ILM-3706/1 – ne IDC [327]
Loeske, L *see* MOOSFLORA DES HARZES
Loest, H W *see* HEINRICH LOEST UEBER E.T.A. HOFFMANN
Loew, C *see* WAS DER GOTTLOSE UND FALSCHE PROPHET MAHOMET FUER EIN FALSCHE VERFUEHRISCHE KETZEREY VND LEHR ERDACHT DURCH WELCHE ER IN GROSSES ANSEHEN BEY ALLERLEY VOELCKER KOMMEN VND JHM EIN GEWALTIGEN ANHANG GEMACHT...
Loew, E *see* DE CASUARINEARUM
Loew, I *see* MAZKERET IMMANUEL
Loew, L *see*
– ARMAEISCHE PFLANZENNAMEN
– GESAMMELTE SCHRIFTEN VON L. LOEW
– GRAPHISCHE REQUISITEN UND ERZEUGNISSE BEI DEN JUDEN
Loew, Leopold *see* BEN-CHANANJA
Loew, Wilhelm *see* GOETHE ALS RELIGIOESER CHARAKTER
Loewe, G *see* CORPUS GLOSSARIORUM LATINORUM
Loewe, H *see* A RABBINIC ANTHOLOGY
Loewen, Harry *see* LUTHER AND THE RADICALS
THE LOEWENBERG COLLECTION OF GERMAN DRAMA – (Each instalment supplied with short-title listing. Coll contains German plays dating from 1880-1930 as well as German translations of important foreign works that influenced, or were influenced by German productions) – 1995- – annual instalments of 325mf – 9 – ne IDC [790]
Loewenberg, Jakob *see*
– AELFRIDA
– UEBER OTWAY'S UND SCHILLER'S DON CARLOS
Loewenthal, Erich *see* STURM UND DRANG
LOF DER REINSTER VROWEN : DAS RHEINISCHE MARIENLOB: EINE DEUTSCHE DICHTUNG DES 13. JAHRHUNDERTS / ed by Bach, Adolf – Leipzig: K W Hiersemann, 1934 – 1 – us U.W. Library [810]
LOF-SANCK VAN IESUS CHRISTUS DEN EENIGEN ENDE EEUWIGEN SONE GODES : ENDE ZYNE ANDERE NEDERDUYTSE POEMATA / Heinsius, D – Amsterdam, 1622 – 4mf – 9 – O-3077/1 – ne IDC [760]
Lofthouse, J *see* A TRIP ON THE THA-ANNE RIVER, HUDSON BAY
Lofthouse, William Frederick *see*
– ETHICS AND ATONEMENT
– EZEKIEL
Loftie, William J *see* THE INNS OF COURT AND CHANCERY
Lofton, George A *see*
– THE BAPTISMAL REMISSION THEORY
– DEFENSE OF THE JESSEY RECORDS AND KIFFIN MANUSCRIPT WITH A REVIEW OF DR. JOHN T. CHRISTIAN'S WORK ENTITLED: "BAPTIST HISTORY VINDICATED"
– ENGLISH BAPTIST REFORMATION
– A REVIEW OF THE QUESTION
LOFTUS ADVERTISER – England. 5 Apr 1879-28 Dec 1906; 16 Apr 1909-25 Aug 1916 (missing 1896, 1898).-w. 30mqn reels – 1 – uk British Libr Newspaper [072]
Loftus, Augustus William Frederick Spencer, Lord *see* THE DIPLOMATIC REMINISCENCES OF LORD AUGUSTUS LOFTUS...1837-62
Loftus, W K *see* TRAVELS AND RESEARCHES IN CHALDAEA AND SUSIANA
LOG / Grimball, John – 1864-65. 7 fiches – 9 – us South Carolina Historical [910]

THE LOG – 1965-74. (American Indian Periodicals in the Princeton University Library). 1 fiche – 9 – $45.00 – us UPA [305]

THE LOG AND JOURNAL / The Black Prince. (Ship) – 1762-64 – 1 – uk Microform Academic [910]

LOG AND JOURNAL OF HIS JOURNEY ROUND THE WORLD IN THE BARK "ENDEAVOUR" / Cook, James – 1768-71. British Library Add Ms 8959 – 1 – uk Microform Academic [910]

LOG CABIN DEMOCRAT – Conway. Arkansas. 1959- – 1 – us UMI [071]

LOG CABIN LIBRARY – 1889-97. 197 issues – 1 – $84.00 – us L of C Photodup [830]

THE LOG OF A SEA-WAIF: BEING RECOLLECTIONS OF THE FIRST FOUR YEARS OF MY SEA LIFE / Bullen, Frank Thomas – Toronto: Methodist Book and Pub. House, 1899. 00323. (Pre-1900 Canadiana) – 9 – cn C.I.H.M. [920]

LOG OF ARCTIC STEAMER JEANETTE / U.S. Navy. Office of Naval Records and Library – 1roll. T297 – 1 – us Nat'l Archives [910]

LOG OF THE U.S.S. NAUTILUS, AUG. 1-31, 1958 / U.S. Navy. Office of Naval Records and Library – 1roll. T319 – 1 – us Nat'l Archives [910]

Logan, Algernon Sydney *see* JESUS IN MODERN LIFE

LOGAN COUNTY PIONEER – Gandy, NE. -w. Jan 1886-Jan 1896, scattered issues missing; May 1896-Jul 1898; Mar 1899-Dec 1900; Mar 1901-Aug 1925; Oct 1925-Dec 1936 – 1 – us NE Hist [071]

Logan, John R *see* SKETCHES, HISTORICAL AND BIOGRAPHICAL OF THE BROAD RIVER AND KINGS MOUNTAIN BAPTIST ASSOCIATION

LOGAN VALLEY MIRROR – Lyons. Neb. 1884-1893 – 1 – us UMI [071]

Logan, WE *see* ESQUISSE GEOLOGIQUE DU CANADA POUR SERVIR A L'INTELLIGENCE DE LA CARTE GEOLOGIQUE ET DE LA COLLECTION DES MINERAUX ECONOMIQUES ENVOYEES A L'EXPOSITION UNIVERSELLE DE PARIS, 1855

Logan, William Hugh *see* DRAMATISIS OF THE RESTORATION

LOGAT NIPPON – Djakarta, Gunseikanbu Kokumin Toshokyoku, 2605. 304p – 103-106mf – 9 – ne IDC [950]

LOGBERG – (In Icelandic. Some issues missing) – Canada, 1888-1959 – 25r – 1 – cn Commonwealth Micro [072]

LOGBERG-HEIMSKRINGLA – (In Icelandic) – Canada, 1959-1973 – 5r – 1 – cn Commonwealth Micro [072]

LOGBIRTINGABLAD – 1942-70 – 6r – 1 – us Ross [072]

LOGBOOKS AND JOURNALS / U.S.S. Constitution – 1798-1934. M1030 – 16r – 1 – us Nat'l Archives [355]

LOGBOOKS OF PT 109 (PRESIDENT KENNEDY) – T576 – 1r – 1 – us Nat'l Archives [977]

Logerstedt, David S *see* THE VALIDITY OF THE TEEM 100 METABOLIC ANALYSIS SYSTEM

LOGGING AND LOG TRANSPORT IN TROPICAL HIGH FOREST : A MANUAL ON PRODUCTION AND COSTS – 1977 – 90p – it F.A.O. [338]

LOGGING AND SAWMILLING JOURNAL – (1985- . 5,6,9) – v13- . 1982- – 1 – us UMI [073]

LOGGING AND SAWMILLING JOURNAL – (Cont: Woodlands ed of Canadian Pulp and Paper Industry at v13 1982) – Toronto. v13-24. 1982-1993/94 – 9 – Can$28.00y – cn Micromedia [634]

LOGGING AND SAWMILLING JOURNAL *see*
- CANADIAN PULP AND PAPER INDUSTRY
- SILVICULTURE

LOGGING AND TRANSPORT IN STEEP TERRAIN : REPORT OF THE 4TH FAO/ AUSTRIA TRAINING COURSE ON MOUNTAIN FOREST ROADS AND HARVESTING. OSSIACH AND ORT, AUSTRIA, 1983 – 1985 – 344p – it F.A.O. [634]

LOGGING OF MOUNTAIN FORESTS – 1982 – 297p – it F.A.O. [634]

LOGGING OPERATIONS : REPORT OF THE FAO/NORWAY TRAINING COURSE; SRI LANKA, SEPTEMBER – OCTOBER 1979 – 1979 – 118p – it F.A.O. [634]

DIE LOGIA JESU : NACH DEM GRIECHISCHEN UND HEBRAEISCHEN TEXT WIEDERHERGESTELLT: EIN VERSUCH / Resch, Alfred – (Includes bibliographical references & indexes) – Leipzig: J C Hinrichs, 1898 – 1mf – 9 – 0-8370-4881-8 – 1985-2881 – us A.T.L.A. [220]

THE LOGIC OF CHRISTIAN EVIDENCES / Wright, George Frederick – Andover: Warren F. Draper, 1890.1 fiche – 9 – us A.T.L.A. [240]

LOGICA INSTITUTIONIBUS PRAEVIIS QUAESTIONIBUS CONTEXTA / Aversa, R – Roma, 1623 – 9mf – 9 – CA-3/1 – ne IDC [100]

LOGICA MODERNA O ARTE DE HALLAR LA VERDAD... / Piquer, Andres – Valencia, 1747 – 4mf – 9 – sp Cultura [160]

LOGICA WESLEIENSIS : OR, THE FARRAGO DOUBLE DISTILLED, WITH AN HEROIC POEM IN PRAISE OF MR. JOHN WESLEY / Hill, Richard – London, 1773 – 1mf – 9 – MP-485/1 – ne IDC [240]

LOGICA Y ETICA / Pacios Lopez, Arsenio – Caceres: Tip. El Noticiero, 1948 – 1 – sp Bibl Santa Ana [170]

LA LOGIQUE DE LEIBNIZ D'APRES DES DOCUMENTS INEDITES / Couturat, Louis – Paris: F. Alcan, 1901. xiv,608p. 7 fiches. (Philosophy Collection) – 9 – 17.00 – fr Bibl Nationale [160]

LOGIQUE ET PRINCIPES DE GRAMMAIRE / Du Marsais, C – 1769 – 9 – fr I.C.S. [400]

LOGIQUE ET PRINCIPES DE GRAMMAIRE (NOUVELLE EDITION PLUS TRAITE D'INVERSION) / Chesneau du Marsais, C – (Linguistics series). 2 v. 1792 – 9 – fr Hachette [400]

LA LOGIQUE OU L'ART DE PENSER / Arnauld, Antoine & Lancelot, Claude – 1662 – 9 – fr I.C.S. [160]

LOGISTICAL SUPPORT TO PRISONERS OF WAR, JUL 1951-JUL 1953 / U.S. Army. Forces in the Far East – 1955? – 1 – 26.00 – us L of C Photodup [950]

LE LOGOGRAPHE, JOURNAL NATIONAL – Redige par Le Hodey d'apres le travail des membres de la Societe logographique. Paris. avr 1791-aout 1792 – 1 – fr A.C.R.P.P. [073]

LOGONOMIA ANGLICA / Gil, Alexander – 1621. 172p. (English Linguistics Series 1500-1800) – 9 – us UMI [420]

LOGOPANDECTEISION, OR AN INTRODUCTION TO THE UNIVERSAL LANGUAGE / Urquhart, Thomas – 1653. 53p. (English Linguistics Series 1500-1800) – 9 – us UMI [400]

LOGOS – Tuebingen. 1910-33. v1-22 – 112mf – 8 – ne IDC [100]

LOGOS – v11-25. 1970-86 (complete) – 4r – 1 – ATLA S0855 – us A.T.L.A. [073]

LOGOS SOTERIAS PROS TEN PARTHENON (DE VIRGINITATE) : EINE ECHTE SCHRIFT DES ATHENASIUS (T.U.U. 2-29/2A) / Goltz, Eduard von der – Leipzig, 1905 – 3mf – 9 – ne Slangenburg [240]

LOGOS SOTERIAS PROS TEN PARTHENON – DE VIRGINITATE : EINE ECHTE SCHRIFT DES ATHANASIUS / Goltz, Eduard von der – Leipzig: J.C. Hinrichs, 1905. (Texte und Untersuchungen zur Geschichte der altchristlichen Literatur; der ganzen Reihe 29, Bd. 2, Heft: n.F., 14. Bd., Heft 2a) – 1mf – us A.T.L.A. [240]

DIE LOGOSLEHRE DES HL. ATHANASIUS : IHRE GEGNER UND UNMITTELBAREN VORLAEUFER / Atzberger, Leonhard – Muenchen: E. Stahl, 1880 – 1mf – us A.T.L.A. [240]

LE LOGOTACHIGRAPHE – Journal de la Convention nationale de France, par le citoyen F.-E. Guiraut et d'apres ses procedes. no. 1-129; prosp. de dec. 1792. Paris. janv-mai 1793 – 1 – fr A.C.R.P.P. [073]

Logrosan. Ayuntamiento *see*
- FIESTAS PATRONALES EN HONOR DE NTRA. SRA. DEL CONSUELO 1971
- GRANDES FERIAS DE GANADO DE TODAS CLASES...LOS DIAS 18, 19, 20 DE JUNIO... 1960
- GRANDES FERIAS DE GANADOS DE TODAS CLASES EN...JUNIO 1959
- GRANDES FIESTAS PATRONALES EN HONOR DE NTRA. SRA. DEL CONSUELO. 1972

Logrosan, Juan de *see* EXPLICACION...REGLA DE SAN AGUSTIN

LOHARANO *see* NY LOHARANO

Lohde, Michael *see*
- DER OPTATIV-VOLUNTATIVE MODALITAETSTYP UND DIE ASPEKTVERHAELTNISSE DES PRAEDIKATIVEN INFINITIVS IM BEREICH DER AFFIRMATION UND NEGATION
- DIE VERWENDUNGSPOTENZEN DER AUSDRUCKSMITTEL FUNKTIONAL-SEMANTISCHER FELDER BEI DER SPRACHLICHEN REALISIERUNG VON HANDLUNGSTYPEN/ KOMMUNIKATIONSVERFAHREN

Lohe, Elisabeth *see* RHETORIK DER FRANZOESISCHEN REVOLUTION

LOHENGRIN : ROMANTISCHE OPER IN DREI AKTEN / Wagner, Richard – (With: Tristan und Isolde) – Leipzig: Breitkopf und Haertel, [18–?] – 1 – us U.W. Library [790]

Lohenstein, Daniel Casper von *see*
- AFRIKANISCHE TRAUERSPIELE
- ROEMISCHE TRAUERSPIELE
- TUERKISCHE TRAUERSPIELE

Lohlker, Ruediger *see* URKUNDEN UEBER LANDVERGABE AUS DER FATIMIDEN- UND BUJIDENZEIT

Lohmann Villena, Guillermo *see*
- EL ARTE DRAMATICO EN LIMA DURANTE EL VIRREINATO. MADRID, 1945
- LA ASCENDENCIA ESPANOLA EL INCA GARCILASO DE LA VEGA PRECISIONES GENEALOGICAS

LOHN- UND TARIFPOLITIK IN DER METALLINDUSTRIE 1918 BIS 1933 : EIN VERGLEICH ZWISCHEN RHEINISCH-WESTFAELISCHER EISEN- UND STAHLINDUSTRIE UND SUEDWESTDEUTSCHER METALLINDUSTRIE / Buckner, Heike – 1992 – 365p – 9 – DM98.00 – 3-89349-618-1 – gw Hänsel [331]

DIE LOHN- UND WIRTSCHAFTSVERHALTNISSE IN MASUREN IN DEN LETZTEN JAHRZEHNTEN / Pohl, Ernst – Koenigsberg, 1908 – 1 – DM30.00 – gw Mikro Press [943]

LOHNARBEIT UND KAPITAL / Marx, Karl – Breslau, 1881 – 1 – DM30.00 – gw Mikro Press [335]

Lohner, Wolfgang *see* BEWAEHRUNGS- UND ENTLASSENENHILFE IN EINEM WIEDERVEREINIGTEN DEUTSCHLAND

Lohnes, J C *see* SKETCH OF J. C. LOHNES AND HIS SETTLING ON PAWNEE CREEK

LOHONTAN DAILY NEWS – (Cont by: Lahontan Valley News) – Fallon, NV. 1974-1979 – 7r – 1 – $350.00 – N03705 – us Library Micro [071]

LOHRER ZEITUNG – (Title change: Ba der Main-Post, Wuerzburg; 1 Sep 1933) – Lohr, West Germany. 1981- – 4r per yr – 1 – gw Mikrofilm [072]

Lohrke, Eugene *see* JUNGLE GODS

LA LOI / At, Jean Antoine – Quebec: Imprimerie de l'Evenement, 1910. SEM105P1653 – 1mf – 9 – Can$2.25 – cn Bibl Nat [971]

LA LOI – Journal judiciarie. Paris. dec 1880-81, juil-dec 1883, 1891, 1893, 1898 – 1 – fr A.C.R.P.P. [073]

LA LOI DE CONCILIATION : GUIDE DU CONCILIATEUR: EXPLICATION DETAILLEE AVEC FORMULES USUELLES DE LA LOI 62 VICTORIA, CHAP. 54, ENTREE EN VIGUEUR LE 10 MAI 1899 / Sauvalle, Marc; ed by Theoret, C – Montreal: librairie de droit et de jurisprudence, 1899. SEM105P1507 – 2mf – 9 – Can$4.50 – cn Bibl Nat [971]

LA LOI DE FAILLITE / Beausoleil, Cleophas – Montreal: J. Plinguet. 04361. (Pre-1900 Canadiana) – 9 – cn C.I.H.M. [971]

LOI DE FONDATION ET STATUTS / Syria. Industrial bank in the Syrian region – Damascus. 1959 – 9 – ne IDC [330]

LOI DE LA BIBLIOTHEQUE NATIONALE DU QUEBEC = QUEBEC NATIONAL LIBRARY ACT : BILL 91 / Quebec. (Province). Laws, Statutes, etc – Quebec: Imprimeur de la Reine, 1967. SEM35P55 – 1r – 1 – Can$15.00 – cn Bibl Nat [323]

LOI DE TERIIMAEVARUE ET DE SES CHEFS, DE SES CITOYENS ET DE TOUS LES HABITANTS DU GOUVERNEMENT DE BORA BORA ET MAUPITI, ILES DU PACIFIQUE – 9 – F20.00 – fr Ethnologie [306]

LOI DES MINES DE QUEBEC : ACTE DE 1892, 55-56 VICTORIA, CHAP. 20 / Quebec. (Province). Canada – Quebec: Impr. generale A Cote, 1893. SEM105P626 – 1mf – 9 – Can$2.25 – cn Bibl Nat [622]

LA LOI DES NATIONS / Duplessix, E – Paris, 1906 – 3mf – 1 – ILM-871/1 – ne IDC [327]

LA LOI DU PAVILLON / Eynard, J – Paris, Aix-en-Provence, 1926 – 3mf – 1 – ILM-3223/1 – ne IDC [327]

LA LOI ET L'AVORTEMENT / Nast, Albert Andre – Paris. 1911. (La Condition Ouvriere. Part Two.) – 9 – 5.00 – fr Bibl Nationale [360]

LA LOI FALLOUX: 4 JANVIER 1849-15 MARS 1850 / Michel, Henry – Paris: Hachette, 1906. ii,524p.6 fiches. (Law Collection) – 9 – 15.00 – fr Bibl Nationale [340]

LA LOI FEDERALE DU 3 JUILLET 1876 SUR LA NATURALISATION... / Estoppey, A – Lausanne, 1888 – 2mf – 1 – ILM-3151/1 – ne IDC [327]

LOI FEDERALE SUR L'ORGANISATION JUDICIAIRE FEDERALE / Switzerland. Laws, Statutes, etc – (Du 27 juin 1874.) Berne, 1874 16 p. LL-4025 – 1 – us L of C Photodup [324]

LA LOI MUNICIPALE. / Morgand, Leon Francois Theophile – 8th ed. Paris: Berger-Levrault, 1911. 2v. LL-4111 – 1 – us L of C Photodup [340]

LA LOI MUNICIPALE DU 5 AVRIL 1884 ET L'ALGERIE / Abbas, Ahmed – 2mf – 9 – 10338 – fr Atelier National [340]

LOI PORTANT APPROBATION DU PLAN TRIENNAL DE DEVELOPPEMENT ECONOMIQUE ET SOCIAL (1960-1962) / Mauritania – (Journal officiel (Saint-Louis). 7 Sep 1960 – 9 – ne IDC [338]

LA LOI SUR LE PLAN BIENNAL, 1949-1950 / Albania – Tirana. 1949. BD-643 1 – 9 – ne IDC [324]

LOI-PLAN DE DEV. ECONOMIQUE SOCIAL ET CULTUREL POUR LES ANNEES 1967, 1968, 1969 ET 1970 (LOI NO. 67-302) / Ivory Coast – Journal Officiel (Abidjan). 23 Aug 1967 – 9 – ne IDC [338]

LA LOI-PROGRAMME TRIENNALE. POUR 1975-1976-1977 / Ivory Coast – Summary in French. Bulletin de l'Afrique Noire. numero special 3rd. ed. Paris. 1975. BD-1864 1 – 9 – ne IDC [338]

LA LOIRE ILLUSTREE : ET SON COMPLEMENT GAZETTA DO FERON – (9 missing numbers) – Hebd., Saint-Etienne (Loire), oct. 1887-mai 1895 (9 no. manq.) – 9r – 1 – F486,73 – fr Armell [073]

LA LOIRE REPUBLICAINE – no. 21096-21289. 31 dec 1943-20 aout 1944. suivi de: La Republique du soir. no. 1-12. 21 aout-2 sept 1944. suivi de: Le Cri du peuple. no. 1-98. 4 sept-dec 1944. Saint-Etienne – 1 – fr A.C.R.P.P. [073]

LOIS DE FINANCES. (RABAT IMPR. OFFICEILLE) / Morocco – 1965-72. BNE-3086 1 – 9 – ne IDC [336]

LES LOIS DE LA GUERRE ET LES DEUX CONFERENCES DE LA HAYE (1899-1907) / Boidin, P – Paris, 1908 – 3mf – 9 – ILM-4072/1 – ne IDC [327]

LOIS, DECRETS, ARRETES / France. Commission des Annales des Ponts et Chaussees – v71-111. 1901-41 – 12r – 1 – us Ross [624]

LOIS D'EDUCATION, B. C / Canada. Laws, Statutes, etc – Toronto: Imprime par S Derbishire & G Desbarats, 1856. SEM105P203 – 1mf – 9 – Can$2.25 – cn Bibl Nat [370]

LOIS ET DECRETS / France – (1869-1900 F6,000.00; 1901-1920 F7,000.00; 1921-1940 10,000.00; 1941-1960 F10,000.00; 1961-1970 F7,000.00; 1971-1980 F7,000.00;) – 1869-1980 – F43,000.00 – fr Journal Officiel [944]

LOIS ET DECRETS / France – 1981- – F880.00y – fr Journal Officiel [944]

LOIS ET DECRETS *see* LE JOURNAL OFFICIEL

LOIS ET DECRETS ASSOCIATIONS / France – 1985- – 52mf per year – F280.00y – fr Journal Officiel [340]

LOIS PRINCIPALES DU MOUVEMENT DE LA POPULATION DANS LA VILLE ET DANS L'ARRONDISSEMENT DE TOUL: STATISTIQUE MEDICALE ET HYGIENE / Husson, Pere Camille – Pont-a-Mousson: P. Toussaint, 1861. 110p. 2 fiches. (Statistics Series: Demography) – 9 – 6.00 – fr Bibl Nationale [310]

Loiseleur-Deslongchamps, J L A *see*
- HERBIER GENERALE DE L'AMATEUR
- NOTICE SUR LES PLANTES A AJOUTER A LA FLORE DE FRANCE
- NOUVEL HERBIER DE L'AMATEUR

LES LOISIRS DES JEUNES A CHATILLON-SUR-SEINE; REGARDS SUR LA DANSE POPULAIRE EN CHATILLONAIS / Chatillonais, R.C.P.Vignet-Zunz, J.Lancelot, F. – 9 – F20.00 – fr Ethnologie [390]
LOISIRS ET SPORTS – (Included Loisirs-presse, Bulletin-loisirs and Loisirs plus) – Montreal: Ed. Loisir-plus, 1979-81. SEM16P295 – 1r – 5 – Can$84.00 – cn Bibl Nat [790]
LOISIRS PLUS *see* LOISIRS QUEBEC (1984)
LOISIRS QUEBEC – Montreal: le Regroupement. v1 no 1 oct 1980-oct 81. SEM105P560 – 1mf – 9 – Can$2.25 – cn Bibl Nat [073]
LOISIRS QUEBEC (1984) – Montreal: Service des communications du Regroupment. v1-1984-. SEM35P26 – 1r – 1 – Can$15.00 – cn Bibl Nat [072]
LOISIRS-PRESSE – Montreal: le Regroupement. v1-3. 1982-84. SEM35P189 – 1r – 1 – Can$39.00 – cn Bibl Nat [073]
Loisson, H M *see* SUPPLEMENT AUX ERREURS DE VOLTAIRE OU REFUTATION COMPLETE DE SON TRAITE SUR LA TOLERANCE
Loisy, A *see*
- LES ACTES DES APOTRES
- LETTERE DI UN PRETE MODERNISTA

Loisy, Alfred Firmin *see*
- L'APOCALYPSE DE JEAN
- ETUDES BIBLIQUES
- QUELQUES LETTRES SUR DES QUESTIONS ACTUELLES ET SUR DES EVENEMENTS RECENTS

LOIX ET CONSTITUTIONS DES COLONIES FRANCOISES DE L'AMERIQUE SOUS LE VENT / Moreau de Saint-Mery, Mederic Louis Elie (1750-1819) – Paris: chez l'auteur. 6v. 1784-1790. SEM16P318 – 2r – 5 – Can$77.00 – cn Bibl Nat [971]
Lojacono, M *see* FLORA SICULA, O DESCRIZIONE DELLE PIANTE IN SICILIA
LOK THA – Rangoon, Burma. Nov 1963-May 1968 – 24r – 1 – us L of C Photodup [072]
LOKAL-ANZEIGER – Prigrevica, Yugoslavia. May 1941-1942 – 1r – 1 – us L of C Photodup [949]
LOKAL-ANZEIGER FUER STANISIC UND GAKOVO – Prigrevica, Yugoslavia. Jan-Mar 1941 – 1r – 1 – us L of C Photodup [949]
DER LOKAL-BOTE – Breslau, 1907-08, 1910 (incomplete), 1915, 1917 (incomplete) – 7r – 1 – Inquire at Mikrofilmarchiv for details – gw Misc Inst [072]
DER LOKAL-BOTE – Breslau (Wroclaw), Poland. 1907-08, 1910, 1915, 1917 – 7r – 1 – gw Mikrofilm [943]
LOKALTIDNINGEN DANDERYD – Stockholm, Sweden. 1987- – 1 – sw Kungliga [072]
LOKALTIDNINGEN FINNVEDEN – Stockholm, 1990, 1992 – 1 – sw Kungliga [072]
LOKALTIDNINGEN FINNVEDEN – Vaernamo, 1992- – 9 – sw Kungliga [072]
LOKALTIDNINGEN JAERFAELLA – Stockholm, 1990-92, 1994- – 9 – sw Kungliga [072]
LOKALTIDNINGEN JARFALLA/UPPLANDS-BRO – Stockholm, 1987-90, 1993-94 – 1 – sw Kungliga [072]
LOKALTIDNINGEN NORRA JARVA – Stockholm, Sweden. 1987- – 1 – sw Kungliga [072]
LOKALTIDNINGEN NYA HANINGE – Haninge, Sweden. 1988-89 – 1 – sw Kungliga [072]
LOKALTIDNINGEN OESTBO – Vaernamo, 1991 – 9 – sw Kungliga [072]
LOKALTIDNINGEN SIGTUNA/MAERSTA – Stockholm, 1993-94 – 9 – sw Kungliga [072]
LOKALTIDNINGEN SOEDRA JAERVA – Stockholm, Sweden. 1989- – 1 – sw Kungliga [072]
LOKALTIDNINGEN SOEDRA ROSLAGEN – Stockholm, 1994- – 9 – sw Kungliga [072]
LOKALTIDNINGEN SOLLENTUNA – Stockholm, Sweden. 1987- – 1 – sw Kungliga [072]
LOKALTIDNINGEN SOLNA/SUNDBYBERG – Stockholm, Sweden. 1989 – 1 – sw Kungliga [072]
LOKALTIDNINGEN SST – Stockholm, Sweden. 1989- – 1 – sw Kungliga [072]
LOKALTIDNINGEN TABY – Stockholm, Sweden. 1987- – 1 – sw Kungliga [072]
LOKALTIDNINGEN UPPLANDS-BRO/BALSTA – Stockholm, 1990-92, 1994- – 9 – sw Kungliga [072]
LOKALTIDNINGEN VAESTBO – Gislaved, 1991 – 9 – sw Kungliga [072]
LOKALTIDNINGEN VAESTERORT/BROMMA/MAELAROEARNA – Stockholm, 1993- – 9 – sw Kungliga [072]
LOKALTIDNINGEN VALLENTUNA – Stockholm, Sweden. 1987- – 1 – sw Kungliga [072]
LOKALTIDNINGEN VASBY – Stockholm, Sweden. 1987- – 1 – sw Kungliga [072]
LOKALTIDNINGEN VASTERORT – Stockholm, 1987-92 – 1 – sw Kungliga [072]
LOKALTIDNINGEN VAXHOLM/OSTERAKER – Stockholm, 1987-94 – 1 – sw Kungliga [072]
LOKAMANYA – Bombay, India. Dec 1950-1957 – 14r – 1 – us L of C Photodup [072]
LOKASATTA – Bombay, India. Jul 1966-Jun 1971 – 20r – 1 – us L of C Photodup [072]
LOKAYAN – Delhi. 28 docs. 1985-1991 – 33mf – 9 – ne IDC [320]
DIE LOKOMOTIVE – Halle-Berlin, Germany. Jul-Dec 1843; 1 Apr 1848-9 Jan 1849 – 1r – 1 – gw Mikrofilm [072]
Lokot, T V *see*
- PERVAIA DUMA
- POLITICHESKIE PARTII I GRUPPY V GOSUDARSTVENNOI DUME

THE LOLLARD; A STORY OF THE WICLIFITES / Davis, Minnie K – 1887 – 1 – us A.T.L.A. [240]
THE LOLLARDS OF THE CHILTERN HILLS : GLIMPSES OF ENGLISH DISSENT IN THE MIDDLE AGES / Summers, W H – London: F. Griffiths, 1906 – 1mf – us A.T.L.A. [941]
LOLLARDY AND THE REFORMATION IN ENGLAND : AN HISTORICAL SURVEY / Gairdner, James – London; New York: Macmillan,1908-1913 – 5mf – us A.T.L.A. [240]
Lollett, C C M *see* REPERTORIO DE LA BIBLIOGRAFIA VENEZOLANA ECONOMICA Y SOCIAL
LOLO SARNOFF – 1971. 4p., 1 illus. 1 fiche. Fiche no. 1041 – 9 – $2.50 – us Corning Mus [700]
Loma Linda University Heritage Room *see* BABY FAE COLLECTION
Loma Literacy Center *see* 132 PUBLICATIONS IN THE LOMA LANGUAGE
LOMAI OF LENAKEL : A HERO OF THE NEW HEBRIDES: A FRESH CHAPTER IN THE TRIUMPH OF THE GOSPEL / Paton, Frank Hume Lyall – New York: Fleming H Revell, c1903 – 1mf – 9 – 0-8370-6593-3 – 1986-0593 – us A.T.L.A. [240]
Lomami-Tshioamba, Paul *see* NGANDO
Loman, A D *see* LUTHER, 1483-1883
LOMAX, DEUK V. LA ORDEN DE SANTIAGO, 1,170-1,275. MADRID, 1965 / Pazos, Manuel R – Madrid: Graf. Calleja, 1966 – 1 – sp Bibl Santa Ana [240]
Lomazzo, G P *see*
- IDEA DEL TEMPIO DELLA PITTURA
- RIME DIVISE IN SETTE LIBRI, NELLE QUALI AD IMITATIONE DEI GROTTESCHI USATI DA' PITTORI, HA CANTATO LE LODI DI DIO
- A TRACTE CONTAINING THE ARTES OF CURIOUS PAINTINGE CARUINGE BUILDINGE
- TRATTATO DELL' ARTE DE LA PITTURA, SCOLTURA ET ARCHITETTURA

Lombard De Langres *see* LE JOURNALISTE OU L'AMI DES MOEURS
Lombard, Patricia A *see* A VALIDATION AND COMPARATIVE EVALUATION OF FOUR PREDICTIVE DEVICES FOR CLASSIFYING FEDERAL PROBATION CASELOADS
LOMBARD STREET : A DESCRIPTION OF THE MONEY MARKET / Bagehot, Walter – London: Henry S. King, 1873 – 1 roll – 1 – 1-55879-985-0 – uk Libr Preservation [332]
Lombardus, Petrus *see*
- LIBRI 4
- TEXTUS SENTENTIALE CUM CONCLUSIONIBUS MAGISTRI HENRICI GORICHEM

Lombogia, D *see* BUKU STATISTIK BARANG2 IMPOR; DISUSUN MENURUT NOMOR URUT 10 S/D 11660 DAN DIBAHAGI DALAM 15 KELOMPOK
Lombroso, Cesare *see*
- L'ANTHROPOLOGIE CRIMINELLE ET SES RECENTS PROGRES
- ETUDES DE SOCIOLOGIE: LES ANARCHISTES
- L'UOMO BIANCO E L'UOMO DE COLORE: LETTURE SU L'ORIGINE E LA VARIETA DELLA RAZZE UMANE

Lomeni, L *see* GALERIE DES CONTEMPORAINS ILLUSTRES, PAR UN HOMME DE RIEN. 3E LIVRAISON (3E DU 10E VOL.) M. SPONTINI
Lomier, Eugene *see* LES PICARDS AU CANADA
LOMITA NEWS – Lomita, CA. 1972-1980 – 9r – 1 – $450.00 – H04021 – us Library Micro [071]
Lommatzsch, C H E *see* OPERA OMNIA
Lomonosov, Mikhail V *see* POLNOE SOBRANIE SOCHINENII
Lonchamps, A *see* LA NOVISSIMA GRAMMATICA DELLE TRE LINGUA ITALIANA, FRANZESE E SPAGNUOLA
LONDENSCHE BEURSSTEMMING – London, UK. 23 May-7 Jun 1911 – 1 – uk British Libr Newspaper [072]
LONDON – Institute of Civil Engineers. London. v7-33. 1937-50. 946/2 – 8 – ne IDC [624]
LONDON, 1772 : BRITISH ISLES CENSUS DIRECTORIES PROJECT, ENGLAND – (In prep) – at Vine [941]
LONDON, 1814 : BRITISH ISLES CENSUS DIRECTORIES PROJECT, ENGLAND. VOL 144 – 4mf – 9 – A$27.00 – at Vine [941]
LONDON, 1817 : BRITISH ISLES CENSUS DIRECTORIES PROJECT, ENGLAND – at Vine [941]
LONDON, 1821 : BRITISH ISLES CENSUS DIRECTORIES PROJECT, ENGLAND. VOL 78 – 3mf – 9 – A$21.00 – at Vine [941]
LONDON, 1822 : BRITISH ISLES CENSUS DIRECTORIES PROJECT, ENGLAND – (In prep) – at Vine [941]
LONDON, 1823 : BRITISH ISLES CENSUS DIRECTORIES PROJECT, ENGLAND. VOL 208 – 4mf – 9 – A$27.00 – at Vine [941]
LONDON, 1824 : BRITISH ISLES CENSUS DIRECTORIES PROJECT, ENGLAND – (In prep) – at Vine [941]
LONDON, 1831 : BRITISH ISLES CENSUS DIRECTORIES PROJECT, ENGLAND – at Vine [941]
LONDON, 1833 : BRITISH ISLES CENSUS DIRECTORIES PROJECT, ENGLAND. VOL 207 – 6mf – 9 – A$39.00 – at Vine [941]
LONDON, 1834 : BRITISH ISLES CENSUS DIRECTORIES PROJECT, ENGLAND. VOL 49 – 5mf – 9 – A$33.00 – at Vine [941]
LONDON, 1842 : BRITISH ISLES CENSUS DIRECTORIES PROJECT, ENGLAND. VOL 114 – 9mf – 9 – A$57.00 – at Vine [941]
LONDON, 1846 : BRITISH ISLES CENSUS DIRECTORIES PROJECT, ENGLAND. VOL 239 – 23mf – 9 – A$99.00 – at Vine [941]
LONDON, 1850 : BRITISH ISLES CENSUS DIRECTORIES PROJECT, ENGLAND. VOL 94 – 13mf – 9 – A$81.00 – at Vine [941]
LONDON, 1862 : BRITISH ISLES CENSUS DIRECTORIES PROJECT, ENGLAND. VOL 125 – 44mf – 9 – A$267.00 – at Vine [941]
LONDON, 1874 : BRITISH ISLES CENSUS DIRECTORIES PROJECT, ENGLAND. VOL 135 – 49mf – 9 – A$297.00 – at Vine [941]
LONDON, 1880 : BRITISH ISLES CENSUS DIRECTORIES PROJECT, ENGLAND. VOL 140 – 33mf – 9 – A$189.00 – at Vine [941]
LONDON, 1896 : BRITISH ISLES CENSUS DIRECTORIES PROJECT, ENGLAND – at Vine [941]
LONDON, 1909 : BRITISH ISLES CENSUS DIRECTORIES PROJECT, ENGLAND. VOL 129 – 48mf – 9 – A$288.00 – at Vine [941]
LONDON, 1934 : BRITISH ISLES CENSUS DIRECTORIES PROJECT, ENGLAND – (In prep) – at Vine [941]
LONDON ADVERTISER – London, Canada. 1864-85 – 33r – 1 – $2,145.00 – cn Library Assoc [971]
LONDON ADVERTISER – London. Jan 1886-Jan 1887.-d. 6 reels – 1 – uk British Libr Newspaper [072]
London. All-Hallows. (London Wall) *see* PARISH REGISTERS
THE LONDON AMERICAN – May 1860-Mar 1863; Apr 1895-Oct 1901 – 1 – uk World [941]
LONDON AMUSEMENT GUIDE AND THEATRICAL REPORTER – London. -w. Jul 1835-Aug 1836. (1 reel) – 1 – uk British Libr Newspaper [790]
LONDON AND CHINA TELEGRAPH – (Missing: 1861-1863 v1-5(1-123)) – London. v1-63. 1861-1921 – 1783mf – 9 – ne IDC [072]
London and Middlesex Archaeological Society *see* TRANSACTIONS
London Anti-Slavery Society. Committee *see* NEGRO APPRENTICESHIP IN THE BRITISH COLONIES
LONDON BAPTIST ASSOCIATION / Baptist Missionary Society. Archives. London – Minutes, Reports and Letters, 1834-56. 2200p – 1 – $77.00 – us Baptist [240]
LONDON BILLS OF MORTALITY, 1701-1829 – Ed. by Paul Laxton. Weekly mortality returns from the City of London parishes, Guildhall Library, British Library, and the Bodleian Library – 258mf – 9 – £1,150.00 – uk Chadwyck [941]
London. Botanical Museum *see* ANNALES MUSEI BOTANICI LUGDUNO BATAVI
LONDON BULLETIN – London, 1938-40 – 1r – 1 – £60.00 – uk Chadwyck [760]
LONDON BULLETIN – London. no. 1-18 20. Apr 1938-June 1940 – 1 – us NY Public [800]
THE LONDON CHARTERHOUSE, ITS MONKS AND ITS MARTYRS. / Hendriks, Lawrence – London: K. Paul, Trench & Co., 1889. xv,390p. illus. plates – 1 – us U.W. Library [240]
LONDON CHRONICLE – London. 1757-1823 – 1 – uk Microform Academic [072]
THE LONDON CHRONICLE OR UNIVERSAL EVENING POST – London, England. v6 n392. 30 jun 1759-29 dec 1759 – 1r – 1 – Can$50.00 – cn Can Microfilming [072]
LONDON COLLEGE OF FASHION DESIGNER FILES – (Over 18,000 pages from international fashion journals. Arranged in alphabetical order by designer) – 309mf – 9 – $1,840.00 – 0-907006-93-0 – uk Mindata [740]
LONDON COMPUTER GROUP BULLETIN – 1957 – 1 – us UMI [073]
LONDON CO-OPERATIVE MAGAZINE – 1-4 2+3 (all publ). 1826-1830 – 15mf – 9 – $65.00 – us UPA [335]
LONDON CORPORATION *see* MUNIMENTA GILDHALLAE LONDONIENSIS (RS12)
London. Corporation of London *see* MEMORIALS OF LONDON AND LONDON LIFE, IN THE 13TH, 14TH, AND 15TH CENTURIES
London Corresponding Society *see* PAPERS
LONDON DAILY ADVERTISER – London, UK. 1731-1795 – 57r – 1 – us L of C Photodup [072]
LONDON DIRECTORIES / London. Guildhall Library – 1677-1899 – 1 – uk Microform Academic [941]
THE LONDON DIRECTORIES / Goss, CW F – 1677-1855 – 7 – uk Microform Academic [941]
LONDON DIRECTORIES FROM THE GUILDHALL LIBRARY, 1677-1855 – 1 – us Primary [941]
LONDON DISPATCH – London. -w. Sep 1836-Oct 1839. (5 reels) – 1 – uk British Libr Newspaper [072]
London Electrical Society *see*
- PROCEEDINGS OF THE LONDON ELECTRICAL SOCIETY, DURING THE SESSIONS 1841-2 AND 1842-3
- THE TRANSACTIONS AND PROCEEDINGS... FROM 1837 TO 1840

LONDON, ENGLAND. MILL YARD SEVENTH DAY BAPTIST CHURCH – Church Records – Other Countries, 1673-1964. 1,666p – 1 – $74.97 – us Baptist [240]
LONDON, ENGLAND. PINNER'S HALL SEVENTH DAY BAPTIST CHURCH – Church Records – Other Countries, 1686-1863. Also filed as Seventh Day Baptist Materials. 262p – 1 – $11.79 – us Baptist [240]
LONDON ENTR'ACTE – (London and Provincial Entr'acte The Entr'acte). London. -w. Jan 1870-Mar 1907. (33 reels) – 1 – uk British Libr Newspaper [790]
LONDON ESSAYS IN GEOGRAPHY / Stamp, D L & Wooldridge, S W – 1751 – 1 – uk Microform Academic [910]
LONDON FINANCIAL GUIDE – (Financial Times). London. -d. Jan 1888-Dec 1895. 17 reels – 1 – uk British Libr Newspaper [073]
LONDON FREE PRESS – (1849-1992.-1560r) – London, 1993 – 24r – 1 – cn Preston [971]
London Gallery *see* THE WALLACE COLLECTION
LONDON GAZETTE / Great Britain – London, Great Britain. 1665-1800 – 1 – uk Microform Academic [324]
LONDON GAZETTE – n1-15. 1665-1800 – 29r – 1 – us Ross [072]
THE LONDON GEOLOGICAL JOURNAL, AND RECORD OF DISCOVERIES IN FOREIGN PALEONTOLOGY – London, 1846-47 – 3 – us Readex [550]

London. Guildhall Library *see*
- INDEX TO THE LONDON DIRECTORIES
- LONDON DIRECTORIES

London. Guildhall Library. Parish Registers *see* HOLY TRINITY MINORIES

LONDON INVESTIGATOR – London, UK. 1857; 1859 – 1r – 1 – uk British Libr Newspaper [072]

London, Jack *see* SMOKE BELLEW

London. Sir John Soane's Museum *see*
- THE DRAWINGS OF ROBERT AND JAMES ADAM IN SIR JOHN SOANE'S MUSEUM
- SIR JOHN SOANE'S MUSEUM
- SIR JOHN SOANE'S MUSUEM

LONDON JOURNAL OF B0TANY / ed by Hooker, W J – London. 7v. 1842-1848 – 91mf – 9 – ne IDC [580]

LONDON JOURNAL OF BOTANY / Hooker, W J – v. 4 and 7. 1845 and 1848 – 7 – uk Microform Academic [580]

THE LONDON JOURNAL OF BOTANY – 1842-48 – 3 – us Readex [580]

LONDON LYRICS : WITH INTRODUCTION AND NOTES BY AUSTIN DOBSON / Locker-Lampson, Frederick – London, New York: Macmillan, 1904 – 1 roll – 1 – uk Libr Preservation [810]

LONDON MAGAZINE – (Absorbs: Ontario Living at v1 no 1 March 1991) – London. v1-3. 1991/92-1993/94 – 9 – Can$28.00y – cn Micromedia [073]

LONDON MAGAZINE – v. 1-osv. 3. January 1820-June 1829 – 1 – us UMI [073]

LONDON MAGAZINE *see* ONTARIO LIVING

LONDON MAGAZINE; OR GENTLEMEN'S MONTHLY INTELLIGENCER – v. 1-N.S. v. 4. April 1732-June 1785 – 1 – us UMI [073]

London Mathematical Society *see*
- JOURNAL
- PROCEEDINGS

LONDON MERCURY – London. -w. Sep 1836-Sep 1837. (1 reel) – 1 – uk British Libr Newspaper [072]

London Missionary Society *see*
- AUSTRALIA AND NEW ZEALAND BULLETIN
- CATALOGUE OF BOOKS CONTAINED IN THE LOCKHART LIBRARY AND IN THE GENERAL LIBRARY
- CHRONICLE
- MINISTERS' LETTERS
- A REGISTER OF MISSIONARIES, DEPUTATIONS, ETC. FROM 1796 TO 1923

LONDON MONTHLY TRADE REPORT AND CHEESE AND DAIRY RECORD – London, Ont: Matthews & Riddle, [1891-189- or 19–] – 9 – cn C.I.H.M. [630]

London. Museum of Practical Geology *see* HANDBOOK TO A COLLECTION OF THE MINERALS OF THE BRITISH ISLES:...FROM THE LUDLAM COLLECTION..

LONDON NEWS – London, England. -w. 8 May-13 Nov 1858. 43 ft – 1 – uk British Libr Newspaper [072]

LONDON (PART 1), 1805 : BRITISH ISLES CENSUS DIRECTORIES PROJECT, ENGLAND. VOL 205 – 4mf – 9 – A$27.00 – at Vine [941]

LONDON (PART 2), 1805 : BRITISH ISLES CENSUS DIRECTORIES PROJECT, ENGLAND. VOL 163 – 2mf – 9 – A$15.00 – at Vine [941]

LONDON PHALANX – 1-69 (all publ). 1831-1843 – 17mf – 9 – $65.00 – us UPA [335]

LONDON PHALANX – London. n1-69. 1841-43 – 1r – 1 – us Ross [073]

THE LONDON PHALANX – Monthly Magazine. London. v. 1. Apr 3 1841-Apr 30 1842; n.s. no. 1-12. June 1842-May 1843 – 1 – us NY Public [800]

THE LONDON PHYSIOLOGICAL JOURNAL, OR MONTHLY RECORD OF OBSERVATIONS ON ANIMAL AND VEGETABLE ANATOMY AND PHYSIOLOGY – London, 1843-44. v. 1, n.1-5 – 3 – us Readex [574]

THE LONDON POLYTECHNIC MAGAZINE, AND JOURNAL OF SCIENCE, LITERATURE, AND THE FINE ARTS – London, 1844 – 3 – us Readex [700]

LONDON PRICE CURRENT – (British and Foreign Price Current London, British and Foreign Price Current). London. -w. Jan 1822-Jan 1832. (4 reels) – 1 – uk British Libr Newspaper [332]

LONDON PRIDE, OR WHEN THE WORLD WAS YOUNGER / Braddon, Mary Elizabeth – British Fiction Archive: Unit 5 – 9 – uk Bell [830]

London. -Public Record Office *see* HANDLIST OF BAPTISMAL REGISTERS HELD AT THE RECORD OFFICE OF THE REGISTRAR GENERAL BY WILLIAM LEARY

LONDON QUARTERLY AND HOLBORN REVIEW – v1-180. 1853-1955 (complete) – 51r – 1 – ATLA S0060 – us A.T.L.A. [073]

LONDON REVIEW – v. 1-2. February 1809-November 1809 – 1 – us UMI [073]

LONDON REVIEW OF BOOKS – London, UK. 1979-1981 – 2r – $100.00 – R04210 – us Library Micro [073]

LONDON REVIEW OF BOOKS – v.1-. 1979- – 1 – us UMI [410]

London. St. Anne, Blackfriars *see* PARISH REGISTERS

London. St. Bartholomew, Exchange *see* PARISH REGISTERS

London. St. Botolph, Aldgate *see* PARISH REGISTERS

London. St. Christopher Le Stocks *see* PARISH REGISTERS

London. St. Lawrence, Pountney *see* PARISH REGISTERS

London. St. Martin's, Ironmonger Lane *see* PARISH REGISTERS

London. St. Mary Abchurch *see* PARISH REGISTERS

London. St. Mary Bothaw, Bowgate *see* PARISH REGISTERS

London. St. Mary, Colechurch *see* PARISH REGISTERS

London. St. Mildred, Poultry *see* PARISH REGISTERS

London. St. Olav, Jewry *see* PARISH REGISTERS

London. St. Stephen, Coleman Street *see* PARISH REGISTERS

London. St. Swithin, London Stone *see* PARISH REGISTERS

LONDON SCHOOL OF HYGIENE AND TROPICAL MEDICINE LIBRARY : FIRST SUPPLEMENT / University of London. London School of Hygiene and Tropical Medicine – (Available on microfilm by request) – 1971. 20,200 cards – 9 – $110.00 export $135.00 – uk Hall [610]

LONDON SOCIETY, A MONTHLY MAGAZINE OF LIGHT AND AMUSING LITERATURE FOR THE HOURS OF RELAXATION – v. 1-74. February 1862-December 1898 – 1 – us UMI [800]

LONDON SPY – v. 1-2. November 1698-April 1700 – 1 – us UMI [941]

London. St. Andrew by the Wardrobe *see* PARISH REGISTERS

LONDON STOCK EXCHANGE : MINUTES OF THE GENERAL PURPOSES COMMITTEE – 1798-1914 – 45r – 1 – $3310.00 – us UMI [941]

LONDON STOCK MARKET REPORT – London, UK. 12 Jun 1906-26 Oct 1907 – 1 – uk British Libr Newspaper [332]

LONDON THEATRES – 1818-20 – 2r – 1 – us Ross [790]

LONDON TIMES EDUCATIONAL SUPPLEMENT – London, UK. 1954-1974 – 44r – $2,200.00 – R63606 – us Library Micro [370]

The London Trades Council *see* MINUTES AND PAPERS

LONDON TRADESMAN – London, UK. 4 Jan-22 Mar 1889. -m. 1 foot – 1 – uk British Libr Newspaper [072]

London. Transport Board *see* ANNUAL REPORT AND STATEMENT OF ACCOUNTS

LONDON TWO WEEK MEETING / Library of the Society of Friends, London – 1672-1789. 6 reels with printed guide. Quaker Marriage Authorisation records – £350.00 – uk World [240]

LONDON VOLUNTARIES : THE SONG OF THE SWORD AND OTHER VERSES / Henley, William Ernest – London: D. Nutt, 2nd rev ed 1893 – 1 roll – 1 – 1-55879-690-8 – uk Libr Preservation [810]

LONDON WEEKLY TIMES *see* WEEKLY TIMES

London. -Wesley's Chapel *see* JOHN WESLEY'S LIBRARY, HOUSED IN WESLEY'S HOUSE, 49 CITY ROAD, LONDON, E.C.1

LONDONAS AVIZE – -w – 1 – us U.W. Library [073]

LONDONDERRY CHRONICLE – Londonderry. Ireland. -w. 18 Feb-7 Oct 1829. (24 ft) – 1 – uk British Libr Newspaper [072]

LONDONDERRY GUARDIAN – Ireland, 30 Sep 1857-1860; 1862-27 Sep 1871 – 4 1/2r – 1 – uk British Libr Newspaper [072]

LONDONDERRY JOURNAL – Ireland.7 reels – 1 – ie Microforms [072]

LONDONDERRY JOURNAL – (Lacking: Aug-Dec 1869. Jan-June 1926. 1969) – Ireland, 15 Mar 1825; Jan 1835- – 313+ r – 1 – uk British Libr Newspaper [072]

Londonderry. Presbytery (Assoc. Ref. Ch.) *see* MINUTES, 1783-1809

LONDONDERRY SENTINEL – Ireland, Sep 1928-Oct 1854; 1856- – 246+ r – 1 – uk British Libr Newspaper [072]

THE LONDONDERRY SIFTER – South Londonderry, VT. v31 n34. 24 jul 1914 – 1r – 1 – Can$25.00 – cn Can Microfilming [071]

LONDONDERRY STANDARD – (Derry Standard, 2 Jan 1950-) – Ireland, 1851-52; 1854-59; 1861-76; 1878-81; 1883-96; 1952; 1985-87 – 57r – 1 – uk British Libr Newspaper [072]

LONDONER ARBEITER-ZEITUNG – (Londoner Freie Presse: 8 Oct 1887-28 Jun 1890) – London, UK. 25 Nov 1886-1 Oct 1887 – 1 – uk British Libr Newspaper [072]

LONDONER ARBEITSKREIS DES FREIHEITSBUNDES DEUTSCHER SOZIALISTEN *see* FREIHEITSBUND DEUTSCHER SOZIALISTEN

LONDONER COURIER – London, UK. 23 Jan-25 Jul 1884 – 1 – uk British Libr Newspaper [072]

LONDONER FIGARO-CHRONIK *see* LANDSTREICHER

LONDONER FREIE PRESSE *see* LONDONER ARBEITER-ZEITUNG

LONDONER GENERAL-ANZEIGER *see* LANDSTREICHER

LONDONER JOURNAL – London, UK. 14 Feb 1878-12 Nov 1891 – 1 – uk British Libr Newspaper [072]

DER LONDONER MEDIZISCHE PAPYRUS UND DER PAPYRUS HEARST / Wreszinski, W – (Die Medizin der alten Aegypter, v2) – Leipzig, 1912 – 5mf – 9 – ne IDC [930]

LONDONER PLAUDEREIEN – London, UK. Herausgegeben von Haberlins Deutsche Buchhandlung. 1 Jul 1908-6 Jan 1909 – 1 – uk British Libr Newspaper [072]

LONDONER SONNTAGSBLATT – London, UK. 18 Mar 1883 – 1 – uk British Libr Newspaper [072]

LONDONER VOLKS-ZEITUNG – London, UK. 23 Oct 1909-2 Jul 1910 – 1 – uk British Libr Newspaper [072]

LONDONER VOLKS-ZEITUNG – London, UK. 3 Oct 1891-20 Feb 1892 – 1 – uk British Libr Newspaper [072]

LONDONER WOCHENPOST – London, UK. 12, 15, 19/25 Apr; 7/13, 14/20 Jun; 13/20 Sept 1936 – 1 – uk British Libr Newspaper [072]

LONDONER ZEITUNG – London, UK. Feb 1954-1955 – 1 – uk British Libr Newspaper [072]

LONDONSKI I SPRAVOCHNY I LISTOK – (Library has no. 1-65 (Dec. 20, 1930-July 1, 1934)[missing no. 64]) – London: Izdaetsi a Londonskim kruzhkom okonchivshikh russkii a vysshii a uchebnyi a zavedenii a, 1930- – 1 – CSUX88-S511 – us Hoover Inst Photo [947]

LONDRES ET PARIS : LA SAISON – (Courrier de Londres et Paris. 9 Mar-24 Aug 1844) – London, UK. 2 Mar 1844 – 1 – uk British Libr Newspaper [072]

LONDRES HEBDOMADAIRE – London, UK. Organ du Coin de France et des Interets francais en Angleterre. 10 Jun 1916-12 Mar 1921 – 1 – uk British Libr Newspaper [072]

LONE GRAVES OF THE NORTHERN TERRITORY 1839-1976. INDEX OF N.T. JUSTICE OF THE PEACE SPECIAL MAGISTRATES, BARRISTERS AND SOLICITORS PRACTITIONERS AND NOTARIES 1839-1965 – 9 – A$5.00 – 0-949124-20-6 – item 3 – at G.S.N.T. [920]

LONE HAND – Sydney, 1907-21 – 18r – 1 – A$558.00 silver A$486.00 visicular – at Pascoe [072]

LONE STAR BAPTIST CHURCH. OKLAHOMA CITY, OKLAHOMA : CHURCH RECORDS – 1956-70 – 1 – 11.07 – us Baptist [240]

LONE STAR REVIEW – v1-3. 1979-80 – 1 – us UMI [073]

THE LONE STAR, THE HISTORY OF THE TELUGU MISSION OF THE AMERICAN BAPTIST MISSIONARY UNION / Downie, David – Philadelpha: American Baptist Publications Society, (c1893). 232p – 1 – us U.W. Library [240]

LONE TREE SENTINEL – Lone Tree, NE. -w. May-Oct 1873 – 1 – us NE Hist [071]

A LONE WOMAN IN AFRICA : SIX YEARS ON THE KROO COAST / McAllister, Agnes – Chicago: Mission Campaign Library, c1896 – 1mf – 9 – 0-8370-6277-2 – 1986-0277 – us A.T.L.A. [920]

THE LONELY ISLAND, OR, THE REFUGE OF THE MUTINEERS / Ballantyne, Robert Michael – Ottawa: J. Durie, 1880?.07474.(Pre-1900 Canadiana) – 9 – cn C.I.H.M. [830]

Lonergan, David *see* BEHAVIORAL AND SOCIAL SCIENCES LIBRARIAN

LONESOME DOVE BAPTIST CHURCH. TARRANT COUNTY. TEXAS : CHURCH RECORDS – 1846-Jun 1875 – 1 – 8.01 – us Baptist [240]

AN LONG – Ireland.4 Oct 1922 – 1 – ie Microforms [072]

Long, A H *see* NAVAL YARNS

LONG BEACH – 1975-76; 1978-84 – 9r – 1 – $450.00 – P00047 – us Library Micro [910]

LONG BEACH AND VICINITY / Case, Walter H – Chicago: S.J. Clarke Publ. Co., 1927. 2v. California Reel 18. (The Cox Library Collection) – 5 – us Americana [978]

LONG BEACH BAR ASSOCIATION BULLETIN – (Lacking: v1,2,4) – v1-22. 1956-76 – 21mf – 9 – $94.00 – LLMC 84-584 – us L.L.M.C. [073]

LONG BEACH DAILY TELEGRAM – Long Beach, CA. 1905-1923 – 67r – 1 – $3,350.00 – R04048 – us Library Micro [071]

LONG BEACH EVENING TRIBUNE – Long Beach, CA. 1900-1907 – 19r – 1 – $950.00 – R04049 – us Library Micro [071]

LONG BEACH LABOR NEWS – Long Beach, CA. 1943-48 – 4r – 1 – $200.00 – C02363 – us Library Micro [331]

LONG BEACH PACIFIC WEEKLY – Long Beach, CA. 1900-1904 – 2r – 1 – $100.00 – R04050 – us Library Micro [071]

LONG BEACH PRESS – Long Beach, CA. 1901-1924 – 121r – 1 – $6,050,00 – R04051 – us Library Micro [071]

LONG BEACH TELEGRAM – Long Beach, CA. 1923-1924 – 15r – 1 – $750.00 – R04052 – us Library Micro [071]

LONG BRANCH BAPTIST CHURCH. SALINE ASSOCIATION. GALATIA, ILLINOIS : CHURCH RECORDS – 1860-1925 – 1 – 25.28 – us Baptist [240]

Long, Charles Edward *see* A REPLY TO THE...MILITARY REPUTATION

Long, Chester I *see* PAPERS

LONG CREEK BAPTIST CHURCH. WARREN COUNTY. GEORGIA : CHURCH RECORDS – 1786-1951 – 1 – 64.80 – us Baptist [240]

LONG CREEK EAGLE – Long Creek, OR. -w. 1 May 1891-21 Dec 1894. – 1 – us U.O. Library [071]

LONG CREEK LIGHT – Long Creek OR. Aug 14 1903 – 1 – us U.O. Library [071]

LONG CREEK RANGER – Long Creek OR. Jan 5 1928-Mar 1 1930 – 1 – us U.O. Library [071]

THE LONG DAY; THE STORY OF A NEW YORK WORKING GIRL, AS TOLD BY HERSELF / (Richardson, Dorothy) – New York: The Century Co., 1905.viii,303p – 1 – us U.W. Library [920]

LONG EATON ADVERTISER – Aug 5 1882-83; 1888-90; 1893-98; 1901; 1903; 1910; 1913; 1930-Jun 19 1959; Aug 14 1959-Dec 20 1984; 1985-Dec 19 1986; 1987-96 – 104r – 9 – uk British Libr Newspaper [072]

Long, Edward *see* THE HISTORY OF JAMAICA

LONG GIAN DOC LAP – Dir. Khan-Son. no. 3-86. Saigon. 8 nov 1930-5 sept 1931. mq no. 31, 78; 2e s., no. 1-14. 11 mai-13 sept 1934; 3e s., no. 1. 4 5 dec 1934 – 1 – fr A.C.R.P.P. [073]

LONG ISLAND JEWISH WORLD – Brooklyn, NY. 1976-86 – 1 – us A.J.P.C. [071]

LONG ISLAND NEWS LETTER – Port Jefferson, N.Y. Sept. 27, 1884-Mar. 12, 1887 – 1 – us NY Public [071]

Long Island. Presbytery (Pres. Ch. in the U.S.A.) *see* MINUTES, 1790-1811

LONG ISLAND PRESS – Jamaica. N.Y. 1945-77 – 1 – us UMI [071]

THE LONG ISLAND STAR – Jamaica. N.Y. Oct. 12-Dec. 21, 1953; Jan. 4-May 12, 1954. Scattered issues – 1 – us NY Public [071]

Long Island. Synod (Pres. Ch. in the U.S.A.) *see* MINUTES, 1870-1881

Long, J le *see* BIBLIOTHEQUE HISTORIQUE DE LA FRANCE

Long, James *see* HAND-BOOK OF BENGAL MISSIONS, IN CONNEXION WITH THE CHURCH OF ENGLAND

Long, Joseph Ragland *see* OUTLINE OF THE JURISDICTION AND PROCEDURE OF THE FEDERAL COURTS

THE LONG LABRADOR TRAIL / Wallace, David Duncan – BN 445 2. 1907 – 8 – ne IDC [910]

LONG LASTING TRAINING EFFECTS : THE COMPARISON OF TWO STRENGTH TRAINING PROGRAMS / Pinque, Tracey E – University of North Carolina at Chapel Hill, 1993 – 2mf – 9 – $8.00 – PH1471 – us Microform Publ [611]

LONG MARCH DISAMPING KETUA MAU TJE-TUNG / Ch'en, Ch'ang-feng – SE-10,261 1. 1963 – 9 – ne IDC [950]

LONG PINE JOURNAL – Long Pine, NE. -w. May 1883-Apr 1884, scattered issues missing; Oct 1895-May 1898; Jan 1899-Aug 1943 – 1 – us NE Hist [071]

THE LONG PURSUIT / Cleary, Jon – SE-5968 1. 1967 – 9 – ne IDC [950]

LONG RANGE PLANNING – (Back issues of journal available from UMI) – 6 issues/y. v26. 1993 – 9 – £276.00y – uk Elsevier Sci [338]

LONG RANGE PLANNING – v1- 1968- – 5,6,9 – us UMI [073]

LONG RANGE PLANNING IN THE FACE OF CHANGE / Goodwin, John Albert Reed – 1982 – 1 – 5.00 – us Baptist [240]

THE LONG ROLL / Johnston, Mary – Illus. by N.C. Wyeth. Boston, New York: Houghton, Mifflin, 1911. x,683p – 1 – us U.W. Library [976]

LONG TIME COMING – Montreal, v1-3, no 4, July 1973-Apr/May 1976 – 1 reel – 1 – Can$85.00 – cn McLaren [302]

Long, William Henry *see*
– MEDALS OF THE BRITISH NAVY AND HOW THEY WERE WON. WITH A LIST OF THOSE OFFICERS WHO FOR THEIR GALLANT CONDUCT WERE GRANTED HONORARY SWORDS AND PLATE BY THE COMMITTEE OF THE PATRIOTIC FUND
– NAVAL YARNS

Longchamp, S G *see* MEMOIRES SUR VOLTAIRE ET SUR SES OUVRAGES PAR LONGCHAMP ET WAGNIERE SES SECRETAIRES

Longchamps *see* MATANTE AURORE OU LE ROMAN IMPROMPTU

LONGER EPISTLES OF PAUL: ROMANS, 1 CORINTHIANS, 2 CORINTHIANS / Cowles, Henry – New York: Appleton, 1880. 1 fiche – 9 – us A.T.L.A. [240]

THE LONGER POEMS OF VELIMIR KHLEBNIKOV / Markov, V – Berkeley, Los Angeles. 1962. BR-1411 – 8 – ne IDC [460]

Longere, J *see* [SUMMA DE CONFESSIONE]

THE LONGEST REVOLUTION – San Diego, CA. 1977-83 – 4r – 1 – $200.00 – R027823 – us Library Micro [071]

Longfellow, Henry Wadsworth *see* EVANGELINE

LONGFIELD BAPTIST CHURCH (ORIG. CALLED CLEAR BRANCH). ANDERSON COUNTY. TENNESSEE : CHURCH RECORDS – 1831-1930. 870p – 1 – 39.15 – us Baptist [240]

Longfield, George *see* AN INTRODUCTION TO THE STUDY OF THE CHALDEE LANGUAGE

LONGFORD INDEPENDENT, ETC – England.Sept 1868-1894; 1915-16. -w. 10 reels – 1 – uk British Libr Newspaper [072]

LONGFORD JOURNAL – Ireland.1851-52; 1854-74; 1876-8 Mar 1890. -w. 13 reels – 1 – uk British Libr Newspaper [072]

LONGFORD LEADER – Ireland. -sw. 27 April 1907-30 July 1910. 2 reels – 1 – uk British Libr Newspaper [072]

LONGFORD MESSENGER – Longford. Ireland. -w. 6 Jan-14 Apr 1837. (10 ft) – 1 – uk British Libr Newspaper [072]

Longhurst, A H *see* HAMPI RUINS, DESCRIBED AND ILLUSTRATED

Longinov, M N *see*
– NOVIKOV I MOSKOVSKIE MARTINISTY
– SOCHINENIIA

LONGMEADOW 1784-1895 – 19mf – 9 – us Holbrook [920]

Longo, Joseph *see* LAURENCE STERNE UND JOHANN GEORG JACOBI

Longpre, E *see* QUAESTIONES DISPUTATAE DU B. GAUTHIER DE BRUGES

LONGQING CHAOYANG XIAN ZHI, 1572 / Guangdong Province. China – Records of Chaoyang County in the reign of Longqing, 15 vols. Comp. by Lin Huochun. (Rare Local Records in Chinese...1420-1507). F A94 – 9 – $36.00 – cc Microforms [950]

LONGQING HAIZHOU ZHI, 1572 / Jiangsu Province. China – Records of Haizhou in the reign of Longqing. 10 vols. Comp. by Zhang Feng. F A17. (Rare Local Records in Chinese...1420-1507) – 9 – $22.50 – cc Microforms [950]

LONGQING LINJIANG FU ZHI, 1572 / Jiangxi Province. China – Records of Linjiang Prefecture in the reign of Longqing. 14 vols. Comp. by Liu Song. F A47. (Rare Local Records in Chinese...1420-1507) – 9 – $49.50 – cc Microforms [950]

LONGQING RUICHANG XIAN ZHI, 1567 / Jiangxi Province. China – Records of Ruichang County in the reign of Longqing. 8 vols. Comp. by Liu Chu. F A51. (Rare Local Records in Chinese...1420-1507) – 9 – $18.00 – cc Microforms [950]

LONGQING YIZHEN XIAN ZHI, 1567 / Jiangsu Province. China – Records of Yizhen County in the reign of Longqing. 14 vols. Comp. by Shen Jiarui. F A18. (Rare Local Records in Chinese...1420-1507) – 9 – $31.50 – cc Microforms [950]

LONGQING YUEZHOU FU ZHI, 1572 / Hunan Province. China – Records of Yuezhou Prefecture in the reign of Longqing. 18 vols. Comp. by Zhong Chongwen. (Rare Local Records in Chinese...1420-1507). F A87 – 9 – $54.00 – cc Microforms [950]

LONGQING ZHAOZHOU ZHI, 1566 / Hebei Province. China – Records of Zhaozhou in the reign of Longqing. Comp. by Cai Maozhao. F A5. (Rare Local Records in Chinese...1420-1507) – 9 – $22.50 – cc Microforms [950]

LONGRANGE (1971-80) ECONOMIC DEVELOPMENT PLAN FOR TAIWAN AREA. / China. Republic. Council for International Economic Cooperation and Development – Taipei, 1972. 38p. BD-1636/1 – 9 – ne IDC [338]

"LONG-RANGE ECONOMIC DEVELOPMENT PLAN" D-1316/1. 1966 / Guam. Federal-Territorial Commission – 9 – ne IDC [338]

LONG-RANGE ECONOMIC PLAN (1971-1985?) / Denmark – D-1036 1. 1971 – 9 – ne IDC [338]

LONG-RANGE PLANNING FOR CIRCUIT COUNCILS : SPEECHES PRESENTED AT THE MEETING OF THE JUDICIAL COUNCIL OF THE NINTH CIRCUIT, MAY 1992 – Washington: FJC, 1992 – 1mf – 9 – $1.50 – LLMC 95-365 – us L.L.M.C. [340]

Longren, Albin K *see* PAPERS OF ALBIN K. LONGREN

THE LONG-TERM PROGRAM OF DENMARK / Denmark – Copenhagen. 1949. BD-361 1 – 9 – ne IDC [338]

LONG-TERM-PROGRAMM / Austria. Bundesministerium fuer Land-und Forstwirtschaft – Der Oesterreichischen Landwirtschaft fuer die Zeit von 1949 50-1952 53 (4-Jahresprogramm). Wien. 1949 – 9 – ne IDC [338]

Longue, LP de *see* RAISONNEMENTS HASARDEZ SUR LA POESIE FRANCOISE

Lonicerus, P *see*
– CHRONICORUM TURCICORUM
– CHRONICORVM TVRCICORVM, ...

Loofs, Friedrich *see*
– ANTI-HAECKEL: EINE REPLIK NEBST BEILAGEN
– EUSTATHIUS VON SEBASTE UND DIE CHRONOLOGIE DER BASILIUS-BRIEFE
– GRUNDLINIEN DER KIRCHENGESCHICHTE
– LEITFADEN ZUM STUDIUM DER DOGMENGESCHICHTE
– LEONTIUS VON BYZANZ 1.
– LEONTIUS VON BYZANZ UND DIE GLEICHNAMIGEN SCHRIFTSTELLER DER GRIECHISCHEN KIRCHE, ERSTES BUCH, DAS LEBEN UND DIE POLEMISCHEN WERKE DES LEONTIUS VON BYZANZ
– LESSINGS STELLUNG ZUM CHRISTENTUM
– NESTORIANA
– NESTORIUS AND HIS PLACE IN THE HISTORY OF CHRISTIAN DOCTRINE
– PAULUS VON SAMOSATA (T.U.U. 3-44/5)
– PREDIGT BEI DER FUENFTEN HAUPT-VERSAMMLUNG DES VEREINS FUER REFORMATIONSGESCHICHTE
– STUDIEN UEBER DIE DEM JOHANNES VON DAMASKUS ZUGESCHRIEBENEN PARALLELEN
– SYMBOLIK, ODER, CHRISTLICHE KONFESSIONSKUNDE
– THEOPHILUS VON ANTIOCHIEN ADVERSUS MARCIONEM (T.U.U. 4-46/2)

LOOK – v. 1-. 1979- – 1,5,6,9 – us UMI [073]

LOOK – (v. 30-35. 1966-71. 5,6. v. 34-35. 1970-71. 9) – (Black White). v. 1-35. 1937-71 – 1 – us UMI [073]

Look *see* A GUIDE TO THE RELIGIONS OF AMERICA; THE FAMOUS LOOK MAGAZINE SERIES ON RELIGION, PLUS FACTS, FIGURES, TABLES, CHARTS, ARTICLES.

A LOOK INTO THE PAST / Bolling, Helmuth – A history of the First Baptist Church of Schulenburg, Texas, 1873-1973 – 1 – 5.00 – us Baptist [240]

A LOOK ROUND LITERATURE / Buchanan, Robert Williams – London: Ward and Downey, 1887 – 1 roll – 1 – 1-55879-777-7 – uk Libr Preservation [420]

THE LOOKER ON – Port Elizabeth, South Africa. 1 Sept 1894-29 May 1903. 14 reels – 1, 16 diazo available at reduced price – sa SA Libr [072]

LOOKING AT AND EVALUATING DANCE : THE ADJUDICATION PROCESS / Williams, Holly – Texas Woman's University, 1994 – 1mf – 9 – PE 3678 – us Microform Publ [790]

LOOKING GLASS – Monroe, NE. -w. Mar 1890; Jun 1892; Dec 1892; Jul 1894; Oct 1895-Dec 1913 – 1 – us NE Hist [071]

A LOOKING GLASS FOR LADIES / Hawes, Joel – An address delivered at Hartford on 24 Aug 1845.1845 – 9 – us A.T.L.A. [240]

THE LOOKOUT – Providence. R.I. 1924-1946 – 1 – us UMI [071]

Loomis, Augustus Ward *see*
– CONFUCIUS AND THE CHINESE CLASSICS: OR, READINGS IN CHINESE LITERATURE
– CORRESPONDENCE AND REPORTS ON MISSIONS TO THE CHINESE IN CALIFORNIA

Loomis, Benjamin Bloomfield *see* STUDIES IN THE ACTS OF THE APOSTLES

Loomis, Elihu G *see* BUSINESS AND LAW, OR THE CAREFUL MAN'S GUIDE

Loomis, Francis B *see* PAPERS OF FRANCIS B. LOOMIS

Loomis, Henry *see* MAY WOMEN SPEAK IN A PROMISCUOUS RELIGIOUS ASSEMBLY

LOOMIS MUSICAL JOURNAL – v1-34. Aug 1867-1900 – 1 – 660.00 – us Opus [073]

LOOMIS' MUSICAL JOURNAL – New Haven. v1-34. 1867-1900 – 8r – 1 – £435.00 – uk Chadwyck [780]

Loomis, Samuel Lane *see* MODERN CITIES AND THEIR RELIGIOUS PROBLEMS

LOOMIS SENTINEL – Loomis, NE. -w. Sep 1913-Dec 1923; Jan 1926-Apr 1938 – 1 – us NE Hist [071]

LOOMIS SENTINEL – Loomis, Nebraska, 1910-1913 weekly – 1 – $35.00r – us NE Hist [071]

Loosli, J K *see* NONPROTEIN NITROGEN IN THE NUTRITION OF RUMINANTS

Loparev, Kh.M *see* OPISANIE RUKOPISEI OBSHCHESTVA LIUBITELEI DREVNEI PIS'MENNOSTI

Lopatin, L M *see*
– KNIAZ' S.N. TRUBETSKOI I EGO OBSHCHEE FILOSOFSKOE MIROSOZERTSANIE
– KURS PSIKHOLOGII

Lopatinsky, O *see*
– LES TEDDA DU TIBESTI ET LE PROBLEME DE SURVIE
– VETEMENT, PARURE, PARFUMS ET COIFFURE CHEZ LES TEDDA DU TIBESTI

Lopes de Castanneda, F *see* HISTORIA DELL' INDIE ORIENTALI, ...

Lopes, Duarte *see* A REPORT OF THE KINGDOM OF CONGO, AND OF THE SURROUNDING COUNTRIES..

Lopez Agurleta, Jose *see* BULLARIUM EQUESTRIS...IACOBI DE SPATHA

Lopez, Atanasio *see*
– EN NOTAS DE BIBLIOGRAFIA FRANCISCANA
– (FRANCISCANO DE LA PROVINCIA DE SAN MIGUEL) EN NOTAS DE BIBLIOGRAFIA FRANCISCANA
– (NATURAL DE FUENTE DE CANTOS) EN NOTAS DE BIBLIOGRAFIA FRANCISCANA

Lopez Aydillo, Eugenio *see* EL OBISPO DE ORENSE EN LA REGENCIA DEL ANO 1810

Lopez, Benigno *see* EN EL N° 2 CENTENARIO DEL NACIMIENTO DEL PRINCIPE DE LA PAZ (1767-1967). BADAJOZ Y SU HIJO GODOY, EL MAS ILUSTRE Y CALUMNIADO DE LOS 302 ILUSTRES BADAJOCENSES

Lopez Bravo, Mateo *see* DE REGE ET REGENDI RATIONE

Lopez Bustos, Carlos *see* CLIMA, PAISAJE Y NATURALEZA EN LA OBRA DE GABRIEL Y GALAN

Lopez, Cecilio *see*
– COMPARISON OF TAGALOG AND ILOKO
– A COMPARISON OF TAGALOG AND MALAY LEXICOGRAPHIES (ON PHONETIC-SEMANTIC BASIS)

Lopez Cornejo, A *see* GALENO ILUSTRADO, AVICENA EXPLICADO Y DOCTORES DEFENDIDOS

Lopez Coronel, P *see* DISCURSO SOBRE ALGUNAS PROPOSICIONES DEL DOCTOR LUYS DE MERCADO

Lopez Cruz, Lorenzo *see*
– DE LA TIERRA Y EL CIELO. POESIAS LIRICAS Y RELIGIOSAS. CACERES, 1925
– NOVENA EN HONOR DEL GLORIOSO PENITENTE SAN PEDRO DE ALCANTARA...
– RELIGION Y PATRIOTISMO. POESIAS LIRICAS Y RELIGIOSAS

Lopez de Araujo, B *see* HISTORIA DE LA DISPUTA QUE SOBRE LA ENFERMEDAD QUE QUITO LA VIDA A MANUEL RODRIGUEZ...

Lopez de Ayala, Adelardo *see*
– EL AGENTE DE MATRIMONIOS
– COLECCION DE ESCRITORES CASTELLANOS
– CONDE DE CASTRALLA
– CONSUELO
– LOS DOS ARTISTAS
– LOS DOS GUZMANES
– ESTUDIO FILOSOFICO...A. LOPEZ DE AYALA
– UN HOMBRE DE ESTADO
– LA MEJOR CORONA
– EL NUEVO DON JUAN
– OBRAS
– OBRAS COMPLETAS
– OBRAS DE D....TEATRO 6. CASTIGO Y PERDON. EL NUEVO DON JUAN
– OBRAS. EL TEJADO DE VIDRIO
– OBRAS. POESIAS
– RIOJA
– EL TEJADO DE VIDRIO

Lopez de Ayala, Ignacio *see*
– EPICEDIO EN LA MUERTE DE ISABEL DE FARNESIO
– HISTORIA DE GIBRALTAR
– THERMAE ARCHINCAE (CARMEN)

Lopez de Ayala, Pedro *see* CRONICAS DEL REY DON PEDRO Y DE DON ENRIQUE 2

Lopez de Berges, Miguel *see* UN RECUERDO HISTORICO

Lopez de Corella, A *see*
– DE ARTE CURATIVA LIBRI QUATOR QUIBUS SANANDI MORBOS BRENIS TRADITUR SATIS...
– DE MORBO POSTULATO SIVE CENTICVLARI

Lopez de Gomara, Francisco *see*
– ANNALS OF THE EMPEROR CHARLES 5TH
– CONQUISTA DE MEJICO
– HISTORIA DE LA CONQUISTA DE MEXICO
– HISTORIA DE MEJICO...HERNANDO CORTES
– HISTORIA DELA CONQUISTA DE MEXICO
– HISTORIA...INDIE...OCCIDENTALI

Lopez de Haro, Alonso *see* ARBOL DE LAS VERAS

Lopez de la Viesca, Evaristo *see* SOMBRA, PENUMBRA Y LUZ EN LA EXTREMADURA

Lopez de Leon, P *see* PRACTICA Y TEORICA DE LAS APOSTEMAS...CUESTIONES Y PRACTICAS DE CIRUGIA...

Lopez de Meneses, Amada *see*
– UN COMPANERO DE HERNANDO CORTES, JUAN CANO DE SAAVEDRA, VERNO DE MOCTEZUMA (CACERES, ?1501? SEVILLA, 2 DE SEPTIEMBRE DE 1572)
– NOTAS Y DOCUMENTOS ACERCA DE LA DESCENDENCIA DE MOCTEZUMA 3RD
– EL PRIMER REGRESO DE HERNAN CORTES A ESPANA
– TECNICH POCHTZIN, HIJA DE MOTECZUMA (?1510?-1550)

Lopez de Sosoaga y Borinaga, Benigno *see* DOCTRINA CRISTIANA CANTADA Y AMENIZADA, DEDICADA A CORTIJOS, ESCUELAS RURALES, BARRIADAS, ETC

Lopez de Toro, Jose *see*
– ARIAS MONTANO ESCRIBE A JUSTO LIPSIO Y A JUAN MORETO
– BENITO ARIAS MONTANO, "POETA LAUREATUS"
– FRAY LUIS DE LEON Y BENITO ARIAS MONTANO
– UN POEMA INEDITO SOBRE HERNAN CORTES

Lopez de Tovar, Gregorio *see*
– CODICE SIETE PARTIDAS DE ALFONSO X
– LOS CODIGOS ESPANOLES
– LA GLOSA QUE...CODIGO...PARTIDAS
– INDEX MATERIARUM QUAE IN SINGULIS...
– INDEX SEU REPERTORIUM...SEPTEM PARTITARUM
– INDICE DE LAS LEYES Y GLOSAS DE LAS SIETE PARTIDAS

- INDICE DE LAS LEYES Y GLOSAS DE LAS SIETE PARTIDAS DEL REY DON ALFONSO EL SABIO, POR EL LICENCIADO GREGORIO LOPEZ
- JUDEX MATERARUM...INSINGULIS
- OMNES FERE TITULI TAM IURIS CIVILIS...
- OMNES FERE...LEGUNTUR
- PARTIDAS 3 Y 4
- REPERTORIO MUY COPIOSO DEL TEXTO Y LEYES DE LAS SIETE PARTIDAS,...VA POR SU ABECEDARIO
- REPERTORIO...TEXTO DE...PARTIDAS
- LAS SIETE PARTIDAS DE ALFONSO 10

Lopez de Tovar, Gregorio et al *see* SIETE PARTIDAS. LAS...NUEVAMENTE GLOSADAS POR EL LICENCIADO

Lopez, Diego *see*
- COMMENTO EN DEFENSA DEL LIBRO 4...NEBRIJA
- CONSTRUCCION Y EXPLICACION DE LAS REGLAS DE LOS GENEROS Y PRETERITOS, CONFORME AL ARTE DE ANTONIO, MUY UTIL Y PROVECHOSA PARA LOS QUE COMIENZAN A ESTUDIAR
- DECLARACION MAGISTRAL SOBRE LOS EMBLEMAS DE ANDRES ALCIATO.
- DECLARACION...EMBLEMAS DE ANDRES ALCIATO
- DECLARACION...SATIRAS DE IUVENAL
- LOS NUEVE LIBROS DE LOS EXEMPLOS MORALES DE VALERIO MAXIMO TRADUCIDOS POR DIEGO LOPEZ
- LAS OBRAS DE PUBLIO V. MARON
- LAS OBRAS DE PUBLIO VIRGILIO MORAN. TRADUCIDO EN PROSA CASTELLANA POR... NATURAL...
- LAS OBRAS DE VIRGILIO MARON, TRADUCIDO EN PROSA CASTELLANA...
- VIRGILIO MARON. PUBLIO. LAS OBRAS

Lopez e Sosoaga y Borinaga, Benigno *see* CALLEJERO Y GUIA HISTORICA DE BADAJOZ

Lopez Fernandez, Antonio et al *see* DEFENSA DE MADRID. RELATO HISTORICO

Lopez, Francisco, Fr *see* GRAMATICA ILOCANA

Lopez, Honorio *see* MGA KATUIRAN NG FILIPINO: MAICLING KASAYSAYANG

Lopez, Jose Maria et al *see* BIOGRAFIA DOCUMENTADA

Lopez, Juan *see* CONCEPTO DEL FEDERALISMO EN LA GUERRA Y EN LA REVOLUCION; CONFERENCIA PRONUNCIADA EN EL CINE COLISEUM DE BARCELONA, EL DIA 7 DE FEBRERO DE 1937

Lopez Ledesma, Jose *see* SUENO REALIZADO. POESIAS

Lopez Lobo, Juan *see*
- MEMORIAL AJUSTADO
- MEMORIAL AJUSTADO HECHO EN VIRTUD DE DECRETO DEL CONSEJO

Lopez Martinez, Antonio *see*
- FELIPE 3 EN MERIDA DE PASO PARA PORTUGAL
- GITANOS, GITANERIAS. CANTOS, BAILES Y COSAS DE LOS GITANOS DE ESPANA

Lopez Medina, Emilio *see* FUNDAMENTOS DE UNA LOGICA SIMBOLICA DE LA CONTRADICCION

Lopez Ortiz de Leon, Angel *see* ARPEGIOS

Lopez Prudencio, Jose *see*
- EXTREMADURA Y ESPANA. CONFERENCIAS FAMILIARES SOBRE LA RAZA DE LOS CONQUISTADORES
- EL GENIO LITERARIO DE EXTREMADURA. APUNTES DE LITERATURA REGIONAL
- NOTAS LITERARIAS DE EXTREMADURA
- SAN MASONA. ARZOBISPO DE MERIDA

LOPEZ REGA / Cernadas Lamadrid, Juan Carlos & Halac, Ricardo – Buenos Aires, Argentina: Editorial Perfil, c1986 – 1 – CSUXADJ2749-B – us Hoover Inst Photo [920]

Lopez Sanchez, Ernesto *see* ENFERMEDADES ROJAS DEL CERDO

Lopez Sanchez, Eulogio *see* CATALOGO... BIBLIOTECA INSTITUTO...CACERES

Lopez Santamaria, Francisco *see* COLONIZACION Y PARCELACIONES

Lopez Santamaria, Luis *see* 4 CONSEJO ECONOMICO SINDICAL 11TH PROV. COMISION. SANIDAD Y ASISTENCIA SOCIAL

Lopez Sedano, Juan Jose *see*
- PARNASO ESPANOL. TOMO 1
- PARNASO ESPANOL. TOMO 2
- PARNASO ESPANOL. TOMO 3
- PARNASO ESPANOL. TOMO 4
- PARNASO ESPANOL. TOMO 5
- PARNASO ESPANOL. TOMO 6
- PARNASO ESPANOL. TOMO 7
- PARNASO ESPANOL. TOMO 8
- PARNASO ESPANOL. TOMO 9

Lopez Serrano, Mathilde *see*
- INCUNABLES DESCONOCIDOS
- INCUNABLES ESPANOLES
- INCUNABLES ESPANOLES DESCONOCIDOS

Lopez y Fuentes, Gregorio *see* LOS PEREGRINOS INMOVILES, NOVELA

Lopez y Zaragoza, Gregorio Mª. *see*
- CARTA PASTORAL QUE...DIRIGE A SUS DIOCESANOS EN SU PONTIFICADO EN MARZO DE 1864
- PASTORAL AL...PONTIFICADO

Lopukhin, I V *see* MASONSKIE TRUDY

Loquin, A *see* NOTIONS ELEMENTAIRES D'HARMONIE MODERNE...

Lorain *see* TABLEAU DE L'INSTRUCTION PRIMAIRE EN FRANCE, D'APRES LES RAPPORTS DES 490 INSPECTEURS CHARGES DE VISITER TOUTES LES ECOLES DE FRANCE EN 1833

LORAIN COUNTY TIMES – Lorain, Ohio. 24 Mar 1971-30 Sept 1976 – 4r – 1 – us Western Res [071]

Loraine, Nevison *see* THE SCEPTIC'S CREED

Lorain-Elyria, Ohio *see* MISCELLANEOUS EARLY NEWSPAPERS

Loranger, Thomas Jean Jacques *see*
- MEMOIRE COMPOSE DE LA PLAIDOIRIE.
- SUITE DU MEMOIRE DE M. LORANGER, CONTENANT SA REPLIQUE DEVANT LA COUR SEIGNEURIALE

Lorca, B *see* LOS ALUMBRADOS ESPANOLES DE LOS SIGLOS 16 Y 17

Lorcin, Louis *see* ETUDE SUR LA MORTALITE ET LA MORBIDITE DANS LA CLASSE OUVRIERE A PARIS

LORD APOSTOLI V BOL'SHOM PETERSBURGSKOM SVETE = THE LORD APOSTLE IN PETERSBURG HIGH SOCIETY / Meshcherskii, Vladimir P – St. Petersburg, 1876. 652p – 1 – 26.08 – us Baptist [240]

LORD BATEMAN'S PLEA FOR LIMITED PROTECTION OR FOR RECIPROCITY IN FREE TRADE / Bateman, William – With a preface by the author. London: W. Ridgway; Philadelphia: H. Baird: 1878. 03002. (Pre-1900 Canadiana) – 9 – cn C.I.H.M. [380]

LORD BEACONSFIELD : A STUDY / Brandes, Georg M – London: R. Bentley, 1880 – 1 roll – 1 – 1-55879-365-8 – uk Libr Preservation [920]

LORD BYRON : A BIOGRAPHY WITH A CRITICAL ESSAY ON HIS PLACE IN LITERATURE. TRANSLATED WITH THE AUTHOR'S SANCTION, AND EDITED WITH NOTES / Elze, Karl – London: John Murray, 1872 – 1 roll – 1 – 1-55879-723-8 – uk Libr Preservation [420]

LORD BYRON ALS UEBERSETZER / Maychrzak, Franz – 1995 – 1mf – 9 – DM48.00 – 3-8267-3144-1 – gw Hänsel [420]

LORD BYRON JUGE PAR LES TEMOINS DE SA VIE : MY RECOLLECTIONS OF LORD BYRON; AND THOSE OF EYE-WITNESSES OF HIS LIFE / Guiccioli, Teresa – New York: Harper and Brothers, 1869 – 1 roll – 1 – 1-55879-335-6 – uk Libr Preservation [420]

LORD BYRON UND DIE POLITIK / Josenhans, Walther – Tuebingen, 1919 – 1mf – DM48.00 – 3-8267-3034-8 – gw Hänsel [420]

Lord, Eleazar *see*
- ANALYSIS OF THE BOOK OF ISAIAH
- ANALYSIS OF THE BOOK OF ISAIAH: PART FIRST: INTRODUCTION

Lord, George de Forest *see*
- CASES ON THE LAW OF ADMIRALTY

LORD GLENELG'S DESPATCHES TO SIR F.B. HEAD, BART. DURING HIS ADMINISTRATION OF THE GOVERNMENT OF UPPER CANADA / Glenelg, Lord – London: James Ridgway and Sons, 1839. SEM105P364 – 3mf – 9 – Can$6.75 – cn Bibl Nat [323]

THE LORD GUIDETH : STUDIES ON PRIMITIVE ISLAM / Birkeland, Harris – Oslo, 1956 – 4mf – 8 – ne Slangenburg [260]

LORD HALIFAX'S GHOST BOOK; A COLLECTION OF STORIES OF HAUNTED HOUSES, APPARITIONS AND SUPERNATURAL OCCURRENCES / Halifax, Charles Lindley Wood – With introd. by Viscount Halifax, K.G. London: G. Bles, (1939). x,412p – 1 – us U.W. Library [830]

LORD HERBERT OF -. : AUTOBIOGRAPHY / Cherbury, Edward – 1764 u.oe / 2 rev ed London, 1906 – 3mf – 8 – ne Slangenburg [920]

Lord, Marcel A *see* BIBLIOGRAPHIE DU ROCHER DE GRAND-MERE

Lord, Marie-Paule *see* CHARLES-E. HARPE, PRESIDENT DE LA SOCIETE DES POETES CANADIENS-FRANCAIS, MEMBRE DE LA SOCIETE DES ECRIVAINS CANADIENS, 1909-1952

LORD MILNER AND SOUTH AFRICA / Iwan-Mueller, Ernest Bruce – London: Heinemann, 1902 – us Res Libr [960]

LORD OAKBURN'S DAUGHTERS / Wood, Ellen – British Fiction Archive: Unit 1 – 9 – uk Bell [830]

THE LORD OF GLORY / Warfield, Benjamin Breckinridge – New York: American Tract Soc., 1907. 1 fiche – 9 – us A.T.L.A. [240]

THE LORD OF THE ISLES : A POEM / Scott, Walter – Edinburgh: A. Constable and Company; London: Longman, Hurst, Rees, Orme, and Brown (Edinburgh: James Ballantyne), 1815 – 1 roll – 1 – 1-55879-288-0 – uk Libr Preservation [810]

LORD PALMERSTON / Trollope, Anthony – London: W. Isbister, 1882 – 1 roll – 1 – 1-55879-908-7 – uk Libr Preservation [941]

Lord, R H *see* THE SECOND PARTITION OF POLAND

LORD, TEACH US TO PRAY (CCC242) / McNeur, George H – (In Chinese) – 1st ed. Hong Kong: Bible Book and Tract Depot for the Council on Christian Literature for Overseas Chinese, 1953 – 1r – 1 – 1984-6581 – us A.T.L.A. [240]

LORDAGSKVALLEN HALLANDS NYHETERS VECKOBILAGA – Falkenberg, Sweden. 1922 – 1 reel – 1 – sw Kungliga [073]

LORDAGSPOSTEN *see* HJO TIDNING

LORD'S DAY LEADER – v1-55,no.3. 1915-69. Continued by: Sunday: The Magazine for the Lord's Day – 1 – us UMI [073]

THE LORD'S PRAYER / Gladden, Washington – 1881 – 1 – us A.T.L.A. [240]

THE LORD'S PRAYER AND ORIENTALISM (CCC113) = T'IEN FU CHEN CHING / Tsu, P N – (In Chinese) – Shanghai: Christian Literature Society, 1931 – 1r – 1 – 1984-B500 – us A.T.L.A. [240]

THE LORD'S PRAYER IN THE EARLY CHURCH / Chase, Frederic Henry – 1891 – 4mf – 9 – ne Slangenburg [240]

THE LORD'S PRAYER IN THE PRINCIPAL LANGUAGES, DIALECTS AND VERSIONS OF THE WORLD, PRINTED IN THE TYPE AND VERNACULARS OF THE DIFFERENT NATIONS / ed by Bergholtz, Gustav Fredric – Chicago, IL: Bergholtz, 1884 – 1mf – 9 – 0-8370-8402-4 – 1986-2402 – us A.T.L.A. [220]

THE LORD'S SUPPER : UNINSPIRED TEACHING / Hebert, Charles – London: Seeley, Jackson and Halliday, 1879 – 4mf – us A.T.L.A. [240]

THE LORD'S SUPPER IN BAPTIST CHURCHES / Adams, R J – 1871. 18p – 1 – 5.00 – us Baptist [240]

LORE AND LEGEND OF THE ENGLISH CHURCH / Tyack, G S – London: W. Andrews, 1899 – 1mf – us A.T.L.A. [240]

Lorei, Madlen *see* STUERMISCHER SEPTEMBER

Lorente, Sebastian *see*
- HISTORIA DE PERU...AUSTRIACA
- HISTORIA DEL PERU

Lorentz, P G *see* MOOSSTUDIEN

Lorentz, Th *see* BEITRAG ZUR KENNTNISS DER ORNITHOLOGISCHEN FAUNA AN DER NORDSEITE DES KAUKASUS

Lorenz, Friedrich *see* GOETHES LEBEN

Lorenz, Gerhard *see* UNRAST

Lorenz, Guenther *see* ZUR KONZEPTION EINER "SOCIALLY USEFUL ECONOMY"

LORENZ UND ELISABETH : EINE SCHATTIGE GESCHICHTE FUER DIE JUGEND / Schaumann, Ruth – Muenchen: Josef Koesel & Friedrich Pustet, 1936 – 1r – 1 – us U.W. Library [830]

Lorenzana y Molina, Manuel *see* INFORME... FERROCARRILES

Lorenzo de San Nicolas, Fray *see*
- ARTE Y USO DE ARCHITECTURA...
- ARTE Y USO DE LA ARQUITECTURA. CON EL PRIMER LIBRO DE EUCLIDES...
- SEGUNDA PARTE DEL USO DE LA ARCHITECTURA...CON LAS ORDENANZAS DE LA IMPERIAL CIUDAD DE TOLEDO

Lorenzo Fraguas, Francisco *see* SISTEMA RACIONALIZADO DE LIQUIDACION Y RECAUDACIOM EN LAS HACIENDAS LOCALES

Lorenzo, Pedro de *see*
- EXTREMADURA, LA FANTASIA HEROICA
- VIAJE DE LOS RIOS DE ESPANA
- ...Y AL OESTE PORTUGAL

Lorenzo, Sabine *see* BIOGRAPHICAL SKETCHES OF LOYALISTS OF THE AMERICAN REVOLUTION

Lorenzoni, A *see* SAGGIO PER BEN SONARE IL FLAUTO TRAVERSO

LORE'S LEIDEN : EINE AUSFUEHRLICHE GESCHICHTE DES HEINE-DENKMALS VON ANBEGINN BIS ZUR SCHLIESSLICHEN ENTHUELLUNG / Pabst, Curt – [S.l.: s.n.], 1899 (New York, N.Y.: Druck von I Goldmann) – 1r – 1 – us U.W. Library [730]

Lorimer, George Claude *see* THE GREAT CONFLICT

Lorimer, James *see* THE INSTITUTES OF LAW

Lorimer, Peter *see*
- JOHN KNOX AND THE CHURCH OF ENGLAND
- PATRICK HAMILTON, THE FIRST PREACHER AND MARTYR OF THE SCOTTISH REFORMATION
- THE SCOTTISH REFORMATION

Lorin, Henri *see*
- BIBLIOGRAPHIE GEOGRAPHIQUE DE L'EGYPTE
- LE COMTE DE FRONTENAC

Loring, Augustus Peabody *see* A TRUSTEE'S HANDBOOK

Loring, James Spear *see* THE HUNDRED BOSTON ORATORS APPOINTED BY THE MUNICIPAL AUTHORITIES AND OTHER PUBLIC BODIES, FROM 1770 TO 1852.

Lorinus, Ioan. *see*
- IN ACTA APOSTOLORUM COMMENTARIA
- IN CATHOLICAS BB. IACOBI ET IUDAE APOSTOLORUM EPISTOLAS COMMENTARII
- IN CATHOLICAS TRES B. JOANNIS, ET DUAS B. PETRI EPISTOLAS COMMENTARII

Loris, D *see* LE THRESOR DES PARTERRES DE L'UNIVERS

LORIS FIRST BAPTIST CHURCH. LORIS, SOUTH CAROLINA : CHURCH RECORDS – 1881-1904, 1938-76, 1973-1984 – 1 – $30.74 – us Baptist [240]

Lorm, Hieronymus *see*
- DIE ALTEN UND DIE JUNGEN
- DAS FORSTHAUS

LORNA DOONE / Blackmore, Richard Doddridge – British Fiction Archive: Unit 3 – 9 – uk Bell [830]

Lorrain, Jean *see* MONSIEUR DE PHOCAS: ASTARTE

LA LORRAINE ARTISTE – Nancy. 1889-nov 1904 – 1 – fr A.C.R.P.P. [073]

LA LORRAINE OUVRIERE ET PAYSANNE / Parti Communiste (S F IC) – Organe regional. Nancy. dec 1926-juil 1932 – 1 – fr A.C.R.P.P. [335]

LA LORRAINE SOCIALE / Syndicats Independants et des Oeuvres Sociales de Meurthe-et-Moselle – Organe. Nancy. fevr 1922-juil 1939 – 1 – fr A.C.R.P.P. [331]

Lorthe, Gabriel A de *see* ELOGE DE J.J. ROUSSEAU MIS AU CONCOURS DE 1790

Lort-Serignam, Arthur M T (pseud Arthur de Ganniers) *see* LES ILES SAMOA OU DES NAVIGATEURS

Lory, Carl *see* NIETZSCHE ALS GESCHICHTSPHILOSOPH

LOS ALTOS/LOS ALTOS HILLS – 1992- – 5+ r – 1 – $250.00 – P00048 – us Library Micro [910]

LOS ANGELES AND ENVIRONS, V2 – Biographical Sketches. California Reel 16. (The Cox Library Collection) – 5 – us Americana [978]

LOS ANGELES AND SOUTHERN CALIFORNIA / Burdette, Robert J – Chicago: Lewis Publ Co, 1906. California Reel 16. (The Cox Library Collection) – 5 – us Americana [978]

LOS ANGELES AREA TELEPHONE DIRECTORIES – (Individual fiches available) – 1900-51 – 1,300mf – 9 – 1300.00 – uk Libr Preservation [380]

LOS ANGELES BAR ASSOCIATION BULLETIN – v1- 1925- – 9 – LLMC 84-585 – us L.L.M.C. [073]

LOS ANGELES BAR JOURNAL – (Superseded by Los Angeles Lawyer) – v1-53. 1925-79 – 9 – $530.00 set – us Hein [340]

LOS ANGELES BUSINESS AND ECONOMICS – (v4-. 1978- 5,6,9) – v1-. 1975- – 1 – us UMI [338]

LOS ANGELES: BUSINESS-TO-BUSINESS – 1986; 1989; 1991- – 14+ r – 1 – $700.00 – P00051 – us Library Micro [910]

LOS ANGELES: CENTRAL – 1975- – 21+ r – 1 – $1,050.00 – P00052 – us Library Micro [910]

LOS ANGELES CHAMBER OF COMMERCE BULLETIN – Los Angeles, CA. 1913-1939 – 3r – 1 – $150.00 – R03304 – us Library Micro [071]

LOS ANGELES CITIZEN – Los Angeles, CA. 1943-48; 1953-1983 – 15r – 1 – $750.00 – RC02389 – us Library Micro [071]

LOS ANGELES COUNTY INCLUDES LOS ANGELES CITY – Los Angeles Co, CA. 1872; 1875; 1881-1888 – 8r – 1 – $400.00 – D050 – us Library Micro [910]

LOS ANGELES DAILY HERALD – Los Angeles, CA. 1873-1889 – 45r – 1 – $2,250.00 – R03305 – us Library Micro [071]

LOS ANGELES DAILY JOURNAL (LEGAL) – Los Angeles, CA. 1888- – 300+ r – 1 – $1,150.00 ($800.00y) – HC02392 – us Library Micro [071]

LOS ANGELES DAILY JOURNAL OF COMMERCE – (Cont: Journal of Commerce Review) – Los Angeles, CA. 1980 – 1r – 1 – $50.00 – R03306 – us Library Micro [071]

LOS ANGELES DAILY NEWS – Los Angeles, CA. 1869-1871 – 3r – 1 – $150.00 – R04062 – us Library Micro [071]

LOS ANGELES DOWNTOWNER – Los Angeles, CA. 1968-1970 – 1r – 1 – $50.00 – H04025 – us Library Micro [071]

LOS ANGELES: EAST – 1987-89 – 3r – 1 – $150.00 – P00053 – us Library Micro [910]

LOS ANGELES ENTERPRISE – Los Angeles, CA. 1950-1965 – 1r – 1 – $50.00 – H04026 – us Library Micro [071]

LOS ANGELES EVENING EXPRESS – Los Angeles, CA. 1874-1931 – 325r – 1 – $16,250.00 – RC02380 – us Library Micro [071]

LOS ANGELES EVENING HERALD – Los Angeles, CA. 1906-31 – 301r – 1 – $15,050.00 – R02381 – us Library Micro [071]

LOS ANGELES EVENING HERALD AND EXPRESS – Los Angeles, CA. 1931-45 – 157r – 1 – $7,850.00 – R02383 – us Library Micro [071]

LOS ANGELES EVENING TELEGRAM – Los Angeles, CA. 1882-1902 – 3r – 1 – $150.00 – R03307 – us Library Micro [071]

LOS ANGELES EXPRESS – Los Angeles, CA. 975-77 – 22r – 1 – $1,100.00 – R02382 – us Library Micro [071]

LOS ANGELES: EXTENDED – 1936-46 – 10r – 1 – $500.00 – P00049 – us Library Micro [910]

LOS ANGELES FREE PRESS – Los Angeles, CA. May-Jun 1956; 1966-78 – 20r – 1 – $1,000.00 – RC02391 – us Library Micro [071]

LOS ANGELES FROM THE MOUNTAINS TO THE SEA / McGroarty, John S – Chicago: American Historical Society, 1921. 3v. California Reel 16. (The Cox Library Collection) – 5 – us Americana [978]

LOS ANGELES: GREATER – 1884-85; 1904-37; 1939-42; 1946; 1948-50; 1952; 1954- – 227+ r – 1 – $11,350.00 – P00050 – us Library Micro [910]

LOS ANGELES HERALD EXAMINER – Los Angeles, CA – 1 – us UMI [071]

LOS ANGELES JEWISH CENTER – Los Angeles, CA. 1944 – 1 – us A.J.P.C. [071]

LOS ANGELES JEWISH COMMUNITY COUNCIL – Los Angeles, CA. Junior Division. 1943 – 1 – us A.J.P.C. [071]

LOS ANGELES LABOR PRESS – Los Angeles, CA. Jan-Apr 1916 – 1r – 1 – $50.00 – C02393 – us Library Micro [331]

LOS ANGELES LAWYER – v1-. 1978- – 1,5,6,9 – us UMI [073]

LOS ANGELES LAWYER – v1-18. 1978-96 – 9 – $340.00 set – us Hein [340]

LOS ANGELES LAWYER *see* LOS ANGELES BAR JOURNAL

LOS ANGELES MAPS 1 : THE CITY – 1888-1900. 540 maps. 6v. of Sanborn Company Fire Insurance Maps – 1 – $68.00r – us Shkurkin [910]

LOS ANGELES MAPS 2 : THE SUBURBS – 1885-1907. 700 maps. 31 towns. Sanborn Company Fire Insurance Maps – 1 – $80.00r – us Shkurkin [910]

LOS ANGELES, MONTEREY, SAN BENITO, SAN DIEGO, SAN LUIS OBISPO, SANTA BARABARA, SANTA CRUZ AND VENTURA COUNTIES – San Diego Co, CA. 1884-1885 – 1r – 1 – $50.00 – D052 – us Library Micro [978]

LOS ANGELES, MONTEREY, SAN BENITO, SAN DIEGO, SAN LUIS OBISPO, SANTA BARBARA, SANTA CRUZ AND VENTURA COUNTIES – Los Angeles Co, CA. 1884-1885 – 1r – 1 – $50.00 – D052 – us Library Micro [978]

LOS ANGELES, MONTEREY, SAN BENITO, SAN DIEGO, SAN LUIS OBISPO, SANTA BARBARA, SANTA CRUZ AND VENTURA COUNTIES – Monterey Co, CA. 1884-1885 – 1r – 1 – $50.00 – D052 – us Library Micro [978]

LOS ANGELES, MONTEREY, SAN BENITO, SAN DIEGO, SAN LUIS OBISPO, SANTA BARBARA, SANTA CRUZ AND VENTURA COUNTIES – San Benito Co, CA. 1884-1885 – 1r – 1 – $50.00 – D052 – us Library Micro [978]

LOS ANGELES, MONTEREY, SAN BENITO, SAN DIEGO, SAN LUIS OBISPO, SANTA BARBARA, SANTA CRUZ AND VENTURA COUNTIES – San Luis Obispo Co, CA. 1884-1885 – 1r – 1 – $50.00 – D052 – us Library Micro [978]

LOS ANGELES, MONTEREY, SAN BENITO, SAN DIEGO, SAN LUIS OBISPO, SANTA BARBARA, SANTA CRUZ AND VENTURA COUNTIES – Santa Barbara Co, CA. 1884-1885 – 1r – 1 – $50.00 – D052 – us Library Micro [978]

LOS ANGELES, MONTEREY, SAN BENITO, SAN DIEGO, SAN LUIS OBISPO, SANTA BARBARA, SANTA CRUZ AND VENTURA COUNTIES – Santa Cruz Co, CA. 1884-1885 – 1r – 1 – $50.00 – D052 – us Library Micro [978]

LOS ANGELES, MONTEREY, SAN BENITO, SAN DIEGO, SAN LUIS OBISPO, SANTA BARBARA, SANTA CRUZ AND VENTURA COUNTIES – Ventura Co, CA. 1884-1885 – 1r – 1 – $50.00 – D052 – us Library Micro [978]

LOS ANGELES: NORTHEASTERN – 1976-79; 1982-87; 1989-92 – 15r – 1 – $750.00 – P00054 – us Library Micro [910]

LOS ANGELES: NORTHWESTERN – 1948-71; 1975-87; 1989- – 100+ r – 1 – $5,000.00 – P00059 – us Library Micro [910]

LOS ANGELES POST RECORD – Los Angeles, CA. 1896-1936 – 52r – 1 – $2,600.00 – R03308 – us Library Micro [071]

LOS ANGELES READER – (1981-. 1,5,6,9) – v1-. 1978- – 1 – us UMI [073]

LOS ANGELES READER – Los Angeles, CA. 1978-1984 – 8r – 1 – $400.00 – R03309 – us Library Micro [071]

LOS ANGELES RECORD – Los Angeles, CA. 1898 – 4r – 1 – $200.00 – R03310 – us Library Micro [071]

LOS ANGELES SEMI-WEEKLY SOUTHERN NEWS – Los Angeles, CA. 1860-1862 – 2r – 1 – $100.00 – RC03311 – us Library Micro [071]

LOS ANGELES SENTINEL – Los Angeles, CA. 1934-68 – 56r – 1 – $2,800.00 – CH02397 – us Library Micro [071]

LOS ANGELES: SOUTH – 1947-66 – 36r – 1 – $1,800.00 – P00055 – us Library Micro [910]

LOS ANGELES: SOUTHEASTERN – 1987-90; 1992 – 7+ r – 1 – $350.00 – P00056 – us Library Micro [910]

LOS ANGELES: SOUTHWESTERN – 1987; 1989-90; 1992- – 11+ r – 1 – $550.00 – P00057 – us Library Micro [910]

LOS ANGELES: SPANISH – 1992- – 3+ r – 1 – $150.00 – P00060 – us Library Micro [910]

LOS ANGELES TIMES – Los Angeles, CA. 1881- – 1 – us UMI [071]

LOS ANGELES TIMES INDEX – 1972- – 1 – us UMI [071]

LOS ANGELES TRIBUNE – Los Angeles, CA. 1886-1917; 1946-56 – 94r – 1 – $4,700.00 – RC02401 – us Library Micro [071]

LOS ANGELES TRI-WEEKLY NEWS – Los Angeles, CA. 1863-1864 – 1r – 1 – $50.00 – RC03312 – us Library Micro [071]

LOS ANGELES WEEKLY – Los Angeles, CA. 1978- – 102+ r – 1 – $5,100.00 ($320.00y) – R02396 – us Library Micro [071]

LOS ANGELES: WEST – 1947-71; 1975-85 – 49r – 1 – $2,450.00 – P00058 – us Library Micro [910]

LOS BANOS CITY DIRECTORIES – Merced Co, CA. 1941; 1946; 1948 – 3r – 1 – $150.00 – D060 – us Library Micro [910]

LOS BANOS ENTERPRISE – Los Banos, CA. 1955- – 53+ r – 1 – $2,650.00 ($90.00y) – B02404 – us Library Micro [071]

LOS GATOS – No.1-54, Aug 1889-27 Jun 1893; 2. ser., no.1, 10 Aug 1893-no.3, 25 Jan 1894. Porto: A. Aranha & Ca., 1889-1894. 57v. -irr.Imprint varies – 1 – us U.W. Library [946]

LOS GATOS MAIL NEWS *see* MAIL

LOS GATOS STAR – Los Gatos, CA. 1923-1929 – 3r – 1 – $150.00 – B02408 – us Library Micro [071]

LOS GATOS WEEKLY *see* LOS GATOS WEEKLY TIMES

LOS GATOS WEEKLY TIMES – (Also known as: Los Gatos Weekly) – Los Gatos, CA. Mar 1982- – 17+ r – 1 – $850.00 ($100.00y) – B02410 – us Library Micro [071]

Los, J *see* POCZATKI PISMIENNICTWA POLSKIEGO

Los Santos de Maimona. Ayuntamiento *see* ORDENANZAS MUNICIPALES

LOSA SEPULCRAL DE SOLANA DE CABANAS EN EL PARTIDO DE LOGROSAN (CACERES) / Roso de Luna, Mario – Madrid: Est. Tip. Fortanet, 1898. B.R.A.H. 32, 1898, pp. 179-182 – 1 – sp Bibl Santa Ana [946]

Losada, M *see* CRITICA Y COMPENDIO ESPECULATIVO-PRACTICO DE LA ARQUITECTURA CIVIL...

L.A. IDISHER BULETIN – Los Angeles, CA.1927-28 – 1 – us A.J.P.C. [071]

L.A. JEWISH LIFE – Malibu, CA. Jan 1985. Ceased publication – 1 – us A.J.P.C. [071]

LOSE BLAETTER IM INTERESSE DER FRAUENFRAGE – Dresden, Germany. 1894-95 – 1 – gw Mikrofilm [072]

Lose, George William *see* LUTHERAN FOREIGN MISSIONS

Losee, Almira *see* LIFE SKETCHES: BEING NARRATIONS OF SCENES OCCURRING IN THE LABOURS OF ALMIRA LOSEE

Loserth, Johann *see*
- DOCTOR BALTHASAR HUBMAIER UND DIE ANFAENGE DER WIEDERTAUFE IN MAEHREN
- WICLIF AND HUS

Loseth, Eilert *see* LE ROMAN EN PROSE DE TRISTAN, LE ROMAN DE PALAMEDE, ET LA COMPILATION DE RUSTICIEN DE PISE; ANALYSE CRITIQUE..

Losh, James *see* THE DIARY

LOSHAD' KAK LOSHAD'. TER'IA KNIGA LIRIKI / Shershenevich, V – M. 1920. BR-1084 2 – 8 – ne IDC [460]

LOSS AND GAIN / Newman, John Henry – London: J. Burns, 1848 – 1 roll – 1 – 1-55879-517-0 – uk Libr Preservation [240]

LOSS, GRIEF AND CARE : A JOURNAL OF PROFESSIONAL PRACTICE / ed by Kutscher, Austin H – v1- 1986- – 1, 9 ($150.00 in US $210.00 outside hardcopy subscr) – us Haworth [360]

Loss, Louis *see* "FRAUD" AND CIVIL LIABILITY UNDER THE FEDERAL SECURITIES LAWS

LOSS OF CITIZENSHIP, DENATURALIZATION, THE ALIEN IN WARTIME / Cable, John Levi – Washington, DC: National Law Book Co., 1943. 149p. LL-1607 – 1 – us L of C Photodup [340]

Losseau, Leon *see* DE LA REPARATION DES ACCIDENTS DE TRAVAIL (RESPONSABILITE, GARANTIE, ASSURANCE). BIBLIOGRAPHIE DES TRAVAUX EN LANGUE FRANCAISE

Lossen, Max *see* BRIEFE VON ANDREAS MASIUS UND SEINEN FREUNDE 1538-1573 (PGRG 2)

Lossius, L *see*
- ACTA APOSTOLORVM. ANNOTATIONUM LUCAE LOSSIJ, IN NOVUM TESTAMENTUM IESU CHRISTI NAZARAENI,...DUODECIM CAPITUM ACTORUM APOSTOLICORUM
- ANNOTATIONVM SCHOLASTICARVM LVCAE LOSSII LVNEBVRGENSIS IN NOVVM TESTAMENTVM IESV CHRISTI NAZARENI,...
- CATECHISMVS, HOC EST, CHRISTIANAE DOCTRINAE METHODVS. ITEM, OBIECTIONES IN EVNDEM,...
- EROTEMATA MUSICAE PRACTICAE, EXPROBATISSIMIS QUIBUSQUE HUIUS DIUINAE ET DULCISSIMAE ARTIS SCRIPTORIBUS
- NOVI TESTAMENTI..., ANNOTATIONIBUS ERUDITIS AND PIJS IAM PRIMUM EXPLICATI AND ILLUSTRATI,...LVCAS AND IOANNES
- NOVVM TESTAMENTVM...ANNOTATIONIBUS ERUDITIS AND PIJS IAM PRIMUM EXPLICATUM AND ILLUSTRATUM,...MATTHAEUVS AND MARCVS
- PSALMODIA, HOC EST, CANTICA SACRA VETERIS ECCLESIAE SELECTA
- QVAESTIONES LVCAE LOSSII IN EVANGELIA DOMINICALIA ET PRAECIPUORUM FESTORUM...EXPRAELECTIONIBUS ET SCRIPTIS PHILIP. MELANTHONIS,...
- QVESTIVNCVLAE METHODICAE DE CHRISTIANO CATECHISMO, IN FORMAM DIALOGI...
- TOMVS QVARTVS ANNOTATIONVM LUCAE LOSSII, IN NOVVM TESTAMENTUM IESV CHRISTI NAZARENI,...CONTINENS NARRATIONEM ACTORUM APOSTOLICORUM...A CAPITE TERTIODECIMO USQUE AD FINEM...

THE LOST AND FOUND, OR, LIFE AMONG THE POOR / Halliday, Samuel B – New York: Blakeman & Mason, 1859 – 1mf – us A.T.L.A. [360]

A LOST EDEN / Braddon, Mary Elizabeth – British Fiction Archive: Unit 5 – 9 – uk Bell [830]

LOST FOR LOVE / Braddon, Mary Elizabeth – British Fiction Archive: Unit 5 – 9 – uk Bell [830]

LOST LINKS IN THE INDIAN MUTINY / Malet, Hugh Poyntz – London: T.C. Newby, 1867. 314p – 1 – us U.W. Library [390]

THE LOST TEN TRIBES, AND 1882 / Wild, Joseph – 2nd ed. London, Ontario: J O Robinson, 1879 – 1mf – 9 – 0-8370-5842-2 – 1985-3842 – us A.T.L.A. [270]

LOST TRACK OF A DAY: A STRICTURE ON SEVENTH DAY TEACHING AND SABBATH DESECRATION / Dezell, Robert – Owen Sound Ont.: A. Rutherford, 1899. 02654. (Pre-1900 Canadiana) – 9 – cn C.I.H.M. [971]

THE LOST TRIBES: A REFUTATION OF THE THEORIES OF MESSRS. WILSON, HINE AND OTHER WRITERS WHO HAVE IDENTIFIED THEM WITH THE ENGLISH NATION: A LECTURE DELIVERED UNDER THE AUSPICES OF THE YOUNG MEN'S SOCIETY OF ERSKINE CHURCH, MONTREAL ON 17TH DECEMBER, 1877 / Campbell, John – Montreal: The Society, 1878. 00379. (Pre-1900 Canadiana) – 9 – cn C.I.H.M. [000]

LOSTINE REPORTER – Lostine, OR. -w. 1 Mar 1917-26 Jul 1917. 1 roll – 1 – us U.O. Library [071]

Lostorf, Edmund Willi *see* DER BEGRIFF DES BETRIEBES

LOSVEGLIARINO – Seattle, WA. Aug 1947-1961 – 1r – 1 – us I.H.R.C. [071]

LOSVEGLIARINO *see* NORTHWEST ITALIEN NEWS

LOT RECORD BOOK / Burlingame Cemetery – ca1865-1980 – 1 – us KS Hist [025]

LOT RECORD CARDS / Rochester Cemetery, Topeka, KS – undated – 1 – us KS Hist [920]

Lotar, L *see*
- LA GRANDE CHRONIQUE DE BOMU
- LA GRANDE CHRONIQUE DE L'UBANGI

LE LOTBINIERE – (Filmed with: L'Echo de Lotbiniere v2 n1 4 nov 1938-28 oct 1966) – Montmagny, Canada. v1 n1. 3 avr 1931-1 avr 1932 – 6r – 1 – Can$45.00r – cn Can Microfilming [072]

LOTHARINGIEN UND DAS REICH AN DER SCHWELLE DER DEUTSCHEN GESCHICHTE (MGH SCHRIFTEN..: 21.BD) / Hlawitschka, E – 1968 – Dfl25.00 – ne Slangenburg [240]

LOTHIAN COURIER – 1 – £42.00r – uk Scot News [072]

Lothian, Maurice *see*
- THE WORD AND WORKS OF GOD
- THE WORD AND WORKS OF GOD: A COURSE OF ADDRESSES TO YOUNG MEN

Lothrop, J S *see* CHAMPAIGN COUNTY DIRECTORY 1870-1871

Lothrop, Thortoin K *see* WILLIAM HENRY SEWARD

LOTOS, ZEITSCHRIFT FUER NATURWISSENSCHAFTEN – Prag. v1-88. 1851-1942 – 249mf – 9 – ne IDC [500]

LOT'S WIFE – 1964-1990 – 10r – 1 – at Corangamite [980]

Lotsch, Fritz *see* UEBER ZOLA'S SPRACHGEBRAUCH

Lotsy, J P *see* PROGRESSUS REI BOTANICAE

Lott, Bernard *see* STYLE AND LINGUISTICS; AN INAUGURAL LECTURE DELIVERED IN THE UNIV. OF INDONESIA ON 31STOCT. 1959

LOTT FIRST BAPTIST CHURCH. LOTT, TEXAS : CHURCH RECORDS – 1890-1902, 1925-77 – 1 – 40.95 – us Baptist [240]
LOTTA CONTINUA – 1977-1980 – 1 – sz Infoprint [072]
LOTTA CONTINUA – Italy, 1977-1980 – 14r – 1 – inquire – us Ross [945]
LOTTA CONTINUA (ROME, ITALY) – (Includes c.1: 1977:Jan.4-1980:Dec.24) – 1 – CSUXAMH8836-S – us Hoover Inst Photo [947]
LOTTA DI CLASSE : GIORNALE DEI LAVORATORI ITALIANI – (See also series: Important Periodicals of Italian and International Socialism, 1868-1917) – Milan. v1,no1-v6,no12. Jul 1892-97. Principal source for the history of the Italian Socialist Party. 1 reel – 1 – $80.00 – us UPA [335]
LOTTA SCHMIDT : AND OTHER STORIES / Trollope, Anthony – London: Alexander Strahan, 1867 – 1 roll – 1 – 1-55879-892-7 – uk Libr Preservation [830]
Lotter, Johann Gottfried *see* BEYTRAEGE ZUR CRITISCHEN HISTORIE DER DEUTSCHEN SPRACHE, POESIE UND BEREDSAMKEIT
Lottin, O *see*
- PSYCHOLOGIE ET MORALE AUX 12 ET 13 SIECLKE
- LE QUODLIBET 15 ET TROIS QUESTIONS ORDINAIRES DE GODEFROID DE FONTAINE

LOTUS – (Monthy Asian Indian newspaper) – Cleveland, Cuyahoga, OH. Dec 1967-Feb 1995 – 1r – 1 – us Western Res [071]
LOTUS – v1-. 1985- – 1,5,6,9 – us UMI [510]
LOTUS *see* PC WORLD
Lotz, Wilhelm *see*
- DIE BIBLISCHE URGESCHICHTE
- GESCHICHTE UND OFFENBARUNG IM ALTEN TESTAMENT

LOU SALOME : INSPIRATRICE ET INTERPRETE DE NIETZSCHE, RILKE ET FREUD / Mackey, Ilonka Schmidt – (Includes bibliographical references and index) – Paris: Librairie A G Nizet, 1956 – 1r – 1 – us U.W. Library [430]
Louail-Fouillou-de Joncoux *see* HISTOIRE ABREGEE DU JANSENISME ET REMARQUES SUR L'ORDONNANCE DE M. L'ARCHEVEQUE DE PARIS
Loubere, S de La *see* A NEW HISTORICAL RELATION OF THE KINGDOM OF SIAM
Loud, Gordon *see*
- KHORSABAD, PT 1
- MEGIDDO, VOL 2

LOUD SPEAKER – Reading, PA., 1931 – 13 – $25.00r – us I.M.R. [071]
Loud, Thomas *see* THE ORGAN STUDY: BEING AN INTRODUCTION TO THE PRACTICE OF THE ORGAN; TOGETHER WITH A COLLECTION OF VOLUNTARIES, PRELUDES AND INTERLUDES
Loudon, David L *see* JOURNAL OF MINISTRY MARKETING AND MANAGEMENT
Loudon, J C *see*
- GARDENER'S MAGAZINE
- HORTUS BRITANNICUS. A CATALOGUE OF ALL THE PLANTS INDIGENOUS, CULTIVATED IN OR INTRODUCED TO BRITAIN

LOUDOUN TIMES-MIRROR – Leesburg. Va. -w. 1936- – 1 – us UMI [071]
Loudun, Ursulines *see* HISTOIRE DE LA POSSESSION DE LA MERE JEANNE DES ANGES..., SUPERIEURE DES RELIGIEUSES URSULINES DE LOUDUN
Lough, Loretta K *see* THE EFFECTS OF FIXED AND HINGED ANKLE FOOT ORTHOSES ON GAIT MYOELECTRIC ACTIVITY AND STANDING JOINT ALIGNMENT IN CHILDREN WITH CEREBRAL PALSY
LOUGHBORO' ADVERTISER – England. -w. 30 Sept-28 Oct 1882; 23 June, 17 Nov 1883-30 Sept 1884. 55 ft – 1 – uk British Libr Newspaper [072]
LOUGHBOROUGH ADVERTISER – England. -w. 4 Jan 1872-31 Aug 1882. 11 reels – 1 – uk British Libr Newspaper [072]
LOUGHBOROUGH ECHO – England, Jan 1912-Dec 1919; 1950; 1952; 1985- – 52+ r – 1 – uk British Libr Newspaper [072]
LOUGHBOROUGH HERALD – England, Jan 1883-Dec 1890 – 6 1/2r – 1 – uk British Libr Newspaper [072]
LOUGHBOROUGH HOME NEWS – England, 13 Oct-29 Dec 1876 – 24ft – 1 – uk British Libr Newspaper [072]
Loughborough, J N *see* RISE AND PROGRESS OF THE SEVENTH-DAY ADVENTISTS
LOUGHBOROUGH MONITOR – England, 20 Jan 1859-Dec 1867 – 7 1/2r – 1 – uk British Libr Newspaper [072]
LOUGHBOROUGH TELEGRAPH – England. Leicestershire, Nottinghamshire & Derbyshire Telegraph. -w. 6 Jan 1837-28 Dec 1839. 1 reel – 1 – uk British Libr Newspaper [072]
Loughran, Frank E *see* SELECTED QUESTIONS FOR NEW JERSEY LAW STUDENTS.
LOUGHREA NATIONALIST – Ballinasloe. Ireland. -w. 19 Jan-24 Aug 1905. (11 ft) – 1 – uk British Libr Newspaper [072]
Louie, L H *see* A FACTOR ANALYSIS OF SELECTED BADMINTON SKILLS TESTS FOR COLLEGE STUDENTS
LOUIS 15 ET ROCAILLE / Reunion des musees nationaux. Paris – 1950. 16 illus. 1 fiche – 9 – fr Réunion [700]
LOUIS 16 ET LA REVOLUTION / Souriau, Maurice Anatole – Paris: May & Motteroz, 1893. 316p. ill. (Bibliotheque d'Histoire illustree) – 1 – us U.W. Library [944]
LOUIS 17 VENGE: OU, LE DERNIER MOT DE L'HISTOIRE SUR LE VRAI DAUPHIN (BARON DE RICHEMONT). / Stenay, Victor de – Vendome: Collin La Herte, 1875. 304p. Includes bibliog – 1 – us U.W. Library [944]
LOUIS BLAND'S MONTHLY REVIEW – London, UK. 1849. -irr. 11 feet – 1 – uk British Libr Newspaper [072]
LOUIS BOURDAGES ET SON TEMPS: CONFERENCE FAITE DANS LES SALLES DE LA "PATRIE", VENDREDI, LE 22 JANVIER 1886 / Bruneau, Arthur – 1886. 03738. (Pre-1900 Canadiana) – 9 – cn C.I.H.M. [971]
THE LOUIS D. BRANDIES PAPERS / Brandeis, Louis Dembitz – (Pt 1: US Supreme Court October Terms, 1916-31. 60r ISBN 0-89093-801-6 $6,600.00; Pt 2: 1932-39. 34r ISBN 0-89093-808-3 $3,740.00; Guide only $150.00) – 1 – us UPA [920]
LOUIS HARMS ALS MISSIONSMANN : MISSIONSGEDANKEN UND MISSIONSTATEN DES BEGRUENDERS DER HERMANNSBURGER MISSION / Wendebourg, W – Hermannsburg: Druck und Verlag der Missionshandlung, 1910 – 2mf – us A.T.L.A. [240]
LOUIS HEBERT, PREMIER COLON CANADIEN ET SA FAMILLE / Couillard-Despres, Azarie – 2e ed. Montreal: Impr. de l'Institution des sourdsmuets, 1918. SEM16P128 – 1r – 5 – Can$9.00 – cn Bibl Nat [971]
THE LOUIS NICHOLS OFFICIAL AND CONFIDENTIAL FILE AND THE CLYDE TOLSON PERSONAL FILE / ed by Theoharis, Athan – 12r – 1 – $1,360.00 – 1-55655-163-0 – us UPA [324]
Louis, P C A *see*
- RECHERCHES ANTOMICO-PATHOLOGIQUES SUR LA PHTHISIE
- RECHERCHES...SUR LA MALADIE CONNUE SOUS LES NOMS DE GASTRO-ENTERITE,...

Louis, Paul *see*
- HISTOIRE DE LA CLASSE OUVRIERE EN FRANCE DE LA REVOLUTION A NOS JOURS; LA CONDITION MATERIELLE DES TRAVAILLEURS, LES SALAIRES ET LE COUT DE LA VIE
- LE SYNDICALISME CONTRE L'ETAT

LOUIS RENAULT. SA VIE – SON OEUVRE / Fauchille, P – Paris, 1918 – 3mf – 9 – Dfl 27 – ILM-168/1 – ne IDC [340]
LOUIS RIEL, MARTYR DU NORD-OUEST SA VIE, SON PROCES, SA MORT – 2e ed. Montreal: Imprimerie generale, 1885. SEM16P67 – 1r – 5 – Can$9.00 – cn Bibl Nat [920]
LOUIS RIEL, MARTYR DU NORD-OUEST SA VIE, SON PROCES, SA MORT – Montreal: Imprimerie generale, 1885. SEM16P68 – 1r – 5 – Can$9.00 – cn Bibl Nat [920]
Louis-Bernard, Soeur *see* BIBLIOGRAPHIE DE L'OEUVRE DU REVEREND PERE GASTON CARRIERE, O.M.I., PROFESSEUR DE PHILOSOPHIE A L'UNIVERSITE D'OTTAWA ET HISTORIEN DE LA CONGREGATION
LOUISBOURG: AN HISTORICAL SKETCH: READ BEFORE THE NOVA SCOTIA HISTORICAL SOCIETY, 27TH NOVEMBER, 1894 / Edwards, Joseph Plimsoll – Halifax, N.S.?: s.n., 1895 (Halifax, N.S.: Nova Scotia Print. Co.). 05221. (Pre-1900 Canadiana) – 9 – cn C.I.H.M. [971]
LOUISBOURG PAPERS, 1744-1758 – (5v relating to Cape Breton Expedition, 1745-46) – Massachusetts Historical Society – 1r – 1 – $85.00 – us UMI [976]
LOUISBURG BAPTIST CHURCH. TAR RIVER ASSOCIATION. NORTH CAROLINA : CHURCH RECORDS – 1854-77 – 1 – 5.31 – us Baptist [240]
Louis-Ernest, Soeur *see* BIBLIOGRAPHIE ANALYTIQUE DE L'OEUVRE D'UN GRAND CHRONIQUEUR LOUIS-PHILIPPE AUDET, DR PED., MEMBRE DE LA SOCIETE DES ECRIVAINS CANADIENS...
LOUISIANA – 6r – 1 – $480.00 – us Scholarly Res [370]
LOUISIANA : SESSION LAWS OF AMERICAN STATES AND TERRITORIES – 1804-1995 – 9 – $2,026.00 set – us Hein [340]
LOUISIANA : WEST'S LOUISIANA STATUTES ANNOTATED – St Paul: West Pub Co, 1951-Mar 1996 update – 9 – $2,683.50 set – us Hein [340]
Louisiana *see*
- GUNBY'S CIRCUIT COURT OF APPEALS REPORTS
- MCGLOIN'S APPEALS CASES
- REPORTS AND OPINIONS (A-G)
- REPORTS, POST-NRS
- REPORTS, PRE-NRS

LOUISIANA AGRICULTURE / Louisiana State University. Agricultural Experiment Station – v13,no.2-v27,no.2. 1969/70-1983/84. 1 reel – 1,5 – us Spaulding [630]
Louisiana and the Floridas. (Diocese) *see* RECORDS
LOUISIANA BAPTIST – 1859-69 (complete) – 1r – 1 – ATLA R0139 – us A.T.L.A. [073]
THE LOUISIANA BAR – v1-11. 1942-52 (all publ) – 9 – LLMC 84-589 – us L.L.M.C. [073]
LOUISIANA BAR ASSOCIATION PROCEEDINGS – (Lacking: 29th, 32nd, 35th meetings) – 1st to 44th annual meetings. 1899-1941 (all publ) – 9 – $138.00 – LLMC 84-586 – us L.L.M.C. [073]
LOUISIANA BAR JOURNAL – v1-42. 1953-95 – 9 – $360.00 set – us Hein [340]
LOUISIANA DEMOCRAT – Alexandria. La. 1865-1891; 1895-1897 – 1 – us UMI [071]
LOUISIANA LAW JOURNAL – New Orleans. nos1-4. 1841-42 – 1 – $40.00 – us Hein [073]
THE LOUISIANA LAW JOURNAL : DEVOTED TO THE THEORY AND PRACTICE OF THE LAW – (Also known as: Schmidt's Law Journal) – 1v. May 1841-Apr 1842 (all publ) – 7mf – 9 – $10.50 – LLMC 86-358 – us L.L.M.C. [073]
LOUISIANA LAW REVIEW – (v1-45 1938-85 on reel or mf $860.00. v46-55 1986-95 on mf $281.00) – v1-55. 1938-95 – 1,5,6,9,13 – $1,141.00 set – us Hein [340]
Louisiana library association *see* BULLETIN
THE LOUISIANA MAGISTRATE, AND PARISH OFFICERS' GUIDE. / Olcott, Edward Rufus – 2d ed. Parish of Plaquemines: Empire Parish Register, 1870. 295p. LL-927 – 1 – us L of C Photodup [340]
LOUISIANA MISCELLANY – 5r – 1 – $175.00 – Dist. us Scholarly Res – us L of C Photodup [978]
Louisiana. Orleans Court of Appeals *see* PARISH OF ORLEANS REPORTS
LOUISIANA PURCHASE – 1 – us Ross [975]
THE LOUISIANA PURCHASE AND OUR TITLE WEST OF THE ROCKY MOUNTAINS: WITH A REVIEW OF ANNEXATION BY THE UNITED STATES / Hermann, Binger – Washington: GPO, 1898. 05553. (Pre-1900 Canadiana) – 9 – cn C.I.H.M. [975]
LOUISIANA RURAL ECONOMIST / Louisiana State University. Agricultural Extension Service. Department of Agricultural Economics and Agribusiness – No.1-4. 1982. 1 reel – 1,5 – us Spaulding [330]
LOUISIANA SCRAPBOOK, CHURCH MUSIC DEPARTMENT, ALEXANDRIA, 1948-65 – 496p – 1 – 17.36 – us Baptist [240]
Louisiana. State Bar Association *see* PROCEEDINGS
LOUISIANA STATE BAR ASSOCIATION REPORTS – v1-10. 1941-52 (all publ) – 17mf – 9 – $25.50 – LLMC 84-588 – us L.L.M.C. [340]
Louisiana State University. Agricultural Experiment Station *see*
- BULLETIN
- CIRCULAR
- LOUISIANA AGRICULTURE
- REPORT OF PROJECTS FOR DEPARTMENT OF AGRONOMY
- TECHNICAL BULLETIN

Louisiana State University. Agricultural Experiment Station. Animal Science Department *see* LIVESTOCK PRODUCERS DAY
Louisiana State University. Agricultural Experiment Station. Dairy Science Club *see* BAYOU DAIRYMAN
Louisiana State University. Agricultural Experiment Station. Department of Agricultural Engineering *see* RESEARCH REPORT
Louisiana State University. Agricultural Experiment Station. Department of Agronomy *see* AGRONOMY RESEARCH REPORT
Louisiana State University. Agricultural Experiment Station. Department of Dairy Science *see* REPORT
Louisiana State University. Agricultural Experiment Station. Department of Horticulture *see* REPORT OF HORTICULTURE RESEARCH PROJECTS
Louisiana State University. Agricultural Experiment Station. Department of Plant Pathology and Crop Physiology *see* ANNUAL RESEARCH REPORT
Louisiana State University. Agricultural Experiment Station. Hill Farm Experiment Station *see* MIMEO REPORTS
Louisiana State University. Agricultural Experiment Station. Hill Farm Experiment Station, Homer *see* RESEARCH REPORT.DAIRY
Louisiana State University. Agricultural Experiment Station. Iberia Livestock Experiment Station. Jeanerette *see* REPORT
Louisiana State University. Agricultural Experiment Station. Livestock Show Open and Juniors *see* REPORT
Louisiana State University. Agricultural Experiment Station. North Louisiana Experiment Station, Calhoun *see*
- DAIRY PROGRESS REPORT
- HORTICULTURAL PROGRESS REPORT
- POULTRY PROGRESS REPORT

Louisiana State University. Agricultural Experiment Station. North Louisiana Hill Farm Experiment Station *see* HILL FARM FACTS.FORESTRY
Louisiana State University. Agricultural Experiment Station. Northeast Experiment Station *see* ANNUAL PROGRESS REPORT
Louisiana State University. Agricultural Experiment Station. Red River Valley Experiment Station, Bossier City *see* ANNUAL RESEARCH REPORT
Louisiana State University. Agricultural Experiment Station. Rice Experiment Station *see* ANNUAL PROGRESS REPORT. ..BI- NO.62-74. 1970-82
Louisiana State University. Agricultural Experiment Station. School of Forestry and Wildlife Management *see*
- ALUMNI NEWSLETTER
- ANNUAL FORESTRY SYMPOSIUM
- ANNUAL RING

Louisiana State University. Agricultural Experiment Station. School of Forestry and Wildlike Management *see* LSU FORESTRY NOTES
Louisiana State University. Agricultural Experiment Station. Southeast Louisiana Dairy and Pasture Experiment Station, Franklinton *see* PROGRESS REPORT
Louisiana State University. Agricultural Experiment Station. Southern Cooperative Series *see* BULLETIN
Louisiana State University. Agricultural Experiment Station. Sweet Potato Research Center *see* PROGRESS REPORT
Louisiana State University. Agricultural Experiment Station. West Louisiana Experiment Station, Rosepine *see* PROGRESS REPORT
Louisiana State University. Agricultural Extension Service. Department of Agricultural Economics and Agribusiness *see*
- AEA INFORMATION SERIES
- DAE RESEARCH REPORT
- LOUISIANA RURAL ECONOMIST

Louisiana State University. Agricultural Extension Service. Dixie Jubilee Horse Show Division *see* OFFICIAL PREMIUM LIST
Louisiana State University. Agricultural Extension Service. Junior Livestock Show *see* PREMIUM LIST CATALOG
Louisiana State University. Agricultural Extension Service. National Quarterhorse Show *see* PREMIUM LIST CATALOG
Louisiana State University. Agricultural Extension Service. Open Livestock Show *see* PREMIUM LIST CATALOG

Louisiana State University. Cooperative Extension Service *see*
- 4-H SHORT COURSE
- LOUISIANA SUMMARY: AGRICULTURE AND NATURAL RESOURCES
- PERSONNEL LIST
- PUBLICATION

Louisiana State University. Paul M. Herbert Law Center. Library *see* CHECKLIST OF INNS OF COURT HOLDINGS

LOUISIANA STUDIES: LITERATURE, CUSTOMS AND DIALECTS, HISTORY AND EDUCATION / Fortier, Alcee – New Orleans, La.: F. Hansell, c1894. 03156. (Pre-1900 Canadiana) – 9 – cn C.I.H.M. [971]

LOUISIANA SUMMARY: AGRICULTURE AND NATURAL RESOURCES / Louisiana State University. Cooperative Extension Service – 1979-81.1 reel – 1,5 – us Spaulding [333]

Louisiana. Supreme Court *see*
- LOUISIANA SUPREME COURT REPORTS
- MANNING'S CASES
- MCGLOIN'S COURT OF APPEALS REPORTS

LOUISIANA SUPREME COURT REPORTS / Louisiana. Supreme Court – (Pre-NRS: v1-103 1830-87 286mf $1,287.00. Official run includes: Martin's Reports v1-12 and ns: v1-8. Louisiana Reports v1-19. Robinson's Louisiana Reports v1-12. Louisiana Annual Reports v1-52. Updates planned) – v1-126. 1809-1920 – 352mf (1:42) 91mf (1:24) – 9 – $1,720.00 – LLMC 84-140 – us L.L.M.C. [340]

LOUISIANA SUPREME COURT REPORTS *see*
- GUNBY'S CIRCUIT COURT OF APPEALS REPORTS
- MANNING'S CASES
- MCGLOIN'S COURT OF APPEALS REPORTS
- PARISH OF ORLEANS REPORTS

LOUISIANA TODAY / ed by Thomson, James H – The Louisiana Society, 1939. Louisiana Reel 1. (The Cox Library Collection) – 5 – us Americana [978]

LOUISIANA WEEKLY – New Orleans. La. 1950- – 1 – us UMI [071]

LOUISVILLE COURIER – Louisville, NE. -w. Feb 1886; Jan 1887; Apr 1892-Mar 1902; Sep 1902-Feb 1903, scattered issues missing; May 1903-Nov 1905; Mar 1907-Jan 1970 – 1 – us NE Hist [071]

LOUISVILLE FIRST BAPTIST CHURCH. LOUISVILLE, MISSISSIPPI : CHURCH RECORDS – 1835-53 – 1 – 10.89 – us Baptist [240]

LOUISVILLE JOURNAL OF MEDICINE AND SURGERY – v. 1. January-April 1838 – 1 – us UMI [616]

Louisville. Kentucky. Davis Memorial Baptist Church *see* UNIVERSAL CHURCH RECORD BOOK

LOUISVILLE LAWYER – v1-9. 1979-88 (all publ) – 9 – $40.00 set – us Hein [340]

THE LOUISVILLE LEADER – Louisville. Ky. june 24, July 22, 29, 1939; May 11, 25, June 1, 15, Aug. 24, Dec. 7, 1940; Jan. 11, 1941; Feb. 5, 12, 1944 – 1 – us NY Public [071]

LOUISVILLE MEDICAL NEWS – v. 1-20. January 1,1876-December 26,1885 – 1 – us UMI [616]

LOUISVILLE MESSENGER – Louisville, NE. -w. Feb 1975 to date – 1 – us NE Hist [071]

LOUISVILLE WEEKLY KICKER – Louisville, NE. Jun 1899-Jun 1900 – 1 – us NE Hist [071]

LOUISVILLE'S FIRST FAMILIES / Jennings, Kathleen – A series of genealogical sketches. Louisville: Standard Printing Co., 1920. Kentucky Reel 7. (The Cox Library Collection) – 5 – us Americana [920]

Louit, Ch *see* LA PECHE A SAINT JEAN DE LUZ

THE LOUNGER – Ottawa: Lounger Pub. Co, [1896-19–?] – 9 – cn C.I.H.M. [971]

Lounsberry, Clement A *see* NORTH DAKOTA HISTORY AND PEOPLE

THE LOUNSBOURY WILL / Lounsbury, Charles – (2 versions: 1 by William Fish 12p n.d. and another 12p distributed by the Marble Hill Press. Both are reprints of the original which appeared in Harper's Weekly Sep 3 1898) – 1mf – 9 – $1.50 – LLMC 91-074 – us L.L.M.C. [340]

Lounsbury, Charles *see* THE LOUNSBOURY WILL

Lounsbury, Thomas Raynesford *see* ENGLISH SPELLING AND SPELLING REFORM

LOUP CITY LEADER – Loup City, NE. -w. Jan 1925-Dec 1937 – 1 – us NE Hist [071]

LOUP CITY NORTHWESTERN – Loup City, NE. -w. May-Jun 1892; Sep 1895-Sep 1917 – 1 – us NE Hist [071]

LOUP COUNTY NEWS – Taylor, NE. -w. Dec 1901-Dec 1902; Oct 1908-Oct 1910 – 1 – us NE Hist [071]

LE LOUP-GAROU : HUMORISTIQUE – Montreal, Canada. 4 jun 1921-20 aut 1921 – 1r – 1 – Can$25.00 – cn Can Microfilming [072]

LE LOUP-GAROU – Montreal, Canada. 5 sep 1861 – 1r – 1 – Can$25.00 – cn Can Microfilming [072]

LOURDES: CONFERENCE PAR LOUIS FRECHETTE LE 12 DECEMBRE 1895, A L'INSTITUT CANADIEN DE QUEBEC / Frechette, Louis-Honore – Quebec: C. Darveau, 1896. 03236. (Pre-1900 Canadiana) – 9 – cn C.I.H.M. [971]

LOURDES ET SES TENANCIERS / Bonnefon, Jean de – Paris: L. Michaud, 190?. xxiii, 279p – 1 – us U.W. Library [240]

Loureiro, J de *see*
- FLORA COCHINCHINENSIS
- HERBARIUM

LOURENCO MARQUES GUARDIAN – Mozambique. -d. 2 June 1913-13 Dec 1915; 24 Nov 1919-10 Sept 1920; 12 May-1 Sept 1921; 6 April 1922-8 Dec 1923. Imperfect. 7 reels – 1 – uk British Libr Newspaper [072]

LOUSIANA ATTORNEY GENERAL REPORTS AND OPINIONS – (6 1854-1969 $420.00. 9 1970-19931 $160.00) – 1854-1993 – 6,9 – $580.00 set – us Hein [340]

Loustaunau, Joseph *see* ETUDE SUR L'ADULTERE AU POINT DE VUE PENAL EN DROIT ROMAN ET EN DROIT FRANCAIS

LOUTH AND DOWN PILOT – Newry, Ireland. -w. 30 Oct 1852-10 March 1855. 1 reel – 1 – uk British Libr Newspaper [072]

LOUTH FREE PRESS – Dundalk. Ireland. -sw. 18 Mar 1829-21 Aug 1830. (1 reel) – 1 – uk British Libr Newspaper [072]

LOUTH STANDARD – (Also known as: Lincolnshire Standard (Louth Edn)) – Aug 22 1922-50; 1951-63 (Town and District Ed); 1964-Jun 1991; Jul 5-Dec 26 1991; 1992-96 – 173r – 1 – uk British Libr Newspaper [072]

Louttit, Chauncey McKinley *see* HANDBOOK OF PSYCHOLOGICAL LITERATURE

THE LOUVAIN AMERICAN COLLEGE, 1857-1907 / Heyden, J van der – Louvain: Printed by Fr.& R. Ceuterick, 1909 – 1mf – us A.T.L.A. [370]

Louvet, Jehan *see* RECIT VERITABLE DE TOUT CE QUI EST ADVENU DIGNE DE MEMOIRE, TANT EN LA VILLE D'ANGERS, PAIS D'ANJOU ET AUTRES LIEUX CONTENUS AU PRESENT MANUSCRIPT...

Louvet, Louis Eugene *see* LA COCHINCHINE RELIGIEUSE

Louw, C S *see* A MANUAL OF THE CHIKARANGA LANGUAGE

Louwers, O *see*
- LE PROBLEME COLONIAL DU POINT DE VUE INTERNATIONAL
- LE PROBLEME FINANCIER ET LE PROBLEME ECONOMIQUE AU CONGO BELGE EN 1932

THE LOVE AFFAIRS OF THE VATICAN, OR THE FAVOURITES OF THE POPES / Rappoport, Angelo Solomon – London: Stanley Paul, [1912?] – 1mf – us A.T.L.A. [240]

LOVE AND LAW IN RELIGION : A SIMPLE PHILOSOPHY OF SIN AND SALVATION ACCORDING TO THE SCRIPTURES / Ingersoll, William Halsey – Brooklyn, NY: Thos F Larkin, 1890 – 1mf – 9 – 0-8370-4605-X – 1985-2605 – us A.T.L.A. [220]

LOVE AND MARRIAGE: BEING MONTAIGNE'S ESSAY SUR DES VERS DE VIRGIL / Montaigne, Michel de – Trans. by Constance Vera Norman; woodcuts by Bruno Bramanti. Florence: Guintina, 19–? 87p. ill – 1 – us U.W. Library [840]

LOVE AND MR. LEWISHAM / Wells, H G – London, New York: Harper & Brothers, 1900 – 1 roll – 1 – 1-55879-709-2 – uk Libr Preservation [830]

LOVE AND THE PHILOSOPHER / Corelli, Marie – British Fiction Archive: Unit 1 – 9 – uk Bell [830]

LOVE FOR LOVE : A COMEDY / Congreve, W – London, 1720 – 2mf – 9 – ne IDC [820]

LOVE FOR SOULS / Scribner, William – New York: Charles Scribner, 1882 – 1mf – 9 – 0-8370-6370-1 – 1986-0370 – us A.T.L.A. [240]

LOVE INSURANCE / Biggers, Earl Derr – New York: Grosset & Dunlap, c1914. 4, leaf, 402p. Illus. by Frank Snapp – 1 – us U.W. Library [830]

Love, James E *see* LETTERS TO MOLLY

Love, James Franklin *see* THE MISSION OF OUR NATION

LOVE, MARRIAGE AND HOME (CCC238) / Ma, John K C et al – (In Chinese) – 1st ed. Hong Kong: Council on Christian Literature for Overseas Chinese, 1959 – 1r – 1 – 1984-6577 – us A.T.L.A. [640]

LOVE ME LITTLE / Reade, Charles L – British Fiction Archive: Unit 2 – 9 – uk Bell [830]

LOVE OF COUNTRY: A LECTURE DELIVERED BEFORE THE BENEVOLENT IRISH SOCIETY, CHARLOTTETOWN, PRINCE EDWARD ISLAND, ON MONDAY EVENING, FEBRUARY 23, 1885 / Ferguson, Donald – s.l.: s.n., 1885? (Charlottetown, P.E.I.: J. Mitchell). 03088. (Pre-1900 Canadiana) – 9 – cn C.I.H.M. [971]

THE LOVE OF GOD / Bell, William Melvin – Dayton, OH: United Brethren Publ. House, 1902 – 1mf – 9 – 0-8370-2609-1 – 1985-0609 – us A.T.L.A. [210]

THE LOVE OF LIBERTY / Read, Leonard E – 1975. 190p. 1 fiche (24x) – 9 – 1.00f – at Libertarian Micro [320]

THE LOVE OF LONG AGO / Corelli, Marie – British Fiction Archive: Unit 1 – 9 – uk Bell [830]

LOVE OR MARRIAGE? A NOVEL / Black, William – British Fiction Archive: Unit 4 – 9 – uk Bell [830]

LOVE OTHERS AS YOURSELF (CCC286) / Surdam, T Janet – (In Chinese) – 1st ed. Hong Kong: Council on Christian Literature for Overseas Chinese, 1958 – 1r – 1 – 1984-6625 – us A.T.L.A. [240]

LOVE SONNETS OF A CAVE MAN, AND OTHER VERSES / Marquis, Don – Drawings by Stuart Hay. Garden City, NY: Doubleday, Doran & Co., 1928. vii,151p incl. plates – 1 – us U.W. Library [810]

THE LOVE SONNETS OF PROTEUS / Blunt, Wilfrid Scawen – London: C. Kegan Paul, 1881 – 1 roll – 1 – 1-55879-401-8 – uk Libr Preservation [810]

Love, William Deloss *see*
- ST. PAUL AND WOMAN
- SAMSON OCCOM AND THE CHRISTIAN INDIANS OF NEW ENGLAND

LOVED I NOT HONOUR MORE / Rothwell, Annie – Toronto: Rose, 1887. 00636. (Pre-1900 Canadiana) – 9 – cn C.I.H.M. [830]

LOVEDALE, SOUTH AFRICA, 1824-1955 / Shepherd, Robert Henry Wishart – Alice: Lovedale Press, 1971 – 1 – us U.W. Library [960]

THE LOVE-FEAST : A POEM / Combe, William – London, 1778 – 1mf – 9 – MP-533/1 – ne IDC [810]

Lovejoy, Charles H *see* DIARIES AND PAPERS OF JULIA AND CHARLES LOVEJOY

Lovejoy, Evelyn M Wood *see* HISTORY OF ROYALTON

Lovejoy, Joseph C *see* MEMOIR OF THE REV. ELIJAH P. LOVEJOY

Lovejoy, Julia L *see* DIARIES AND PAPERS OF JULIA AND CHARLES LOVEJOY

Lovejoy, Owen *see* MEMOIR OF THE REV. ELIJAH P. LOVEJOY

Lovekin, Arthur A *see* GLOSSOLALIA

LOVEL THE WIDOWER / Thackeray, William Makepeace – London: Smith, Elder, 1861 – 1 roll – 1 – 1-55879-613-4 – uk Libr Preservation [830]

Lovelace, Griffin M *see* LIFE INSURANCE FUNDAMENTALS

Loveland, Franklin Olds *see* A TREATISE ON THE LAW AND PROCEEDINGS IN BANKRUPTCY

Lovell, Colin Rhys *see* HERTZOG AND THE SOUTH AFRICAN NATIONALIST PARTY

Lovell, John *see* THE CANADA DIRECTORY FOR 1857-1858

Lovell, MS *see* THE EDIBLE MOLLUSCA OF GREAT BRITAIN AND IRELAND

Lovell, William Stanhope *see* PERSONAL NARRATIVE OF EVENTS FROM 1799 TO 1815

LOVELL'S ANNUAIRE DE VILLE POUR MONTREAL = LOVELL'S MONTREAL CITY DIRECTORY – 134e ed. Montreal: John Lovell & Son, 1842/1843-1976. SEM16P257 – 82r – 5 – Can$2,938.00 – cn Bibl Nat [910]

LOVELL'S ANNUAL COMPENDIUM FOR.... *see*
- LOVELL'S COMPENDIUM FOR...1907-1908
- LOVELL'S LEGAL COMPENDIUM FOR...1904

LOVELL'S ANNUAL COMPENDIUM FOR...1905 – (Contd by: Lovell's Legal Compendium For....Cont of: Lovell's Compendium For....) – Montreal: John Lovell & Son Ltd, 1905-. SEM105P826 – 9 – Can$15.75 – cn Bibl Nat [380]

LOVELL'S BUSINESS PROFESSIONAL AND CLASSIFIE (SIC) TRADES DIRECTORY OF THE PROVINCE OF QUEBEC – Montreal: John Lovell & Son Ltd, 1910-11. SEM105P816 – 17mf – 9 – Can$38.25 – cn Bibl Nat [380]

LOVELL'S CLASSIFIED BUSINESS DIRECTORY FOR... : CONTAINING THE NAMES, BUSINESS AND ADDRESS OF EVERY FIRM OR PERSON DOING BUSINESS IN MONTREAL.. – Montreal: Lovell Printing & Publ Co, 1877, 1907, 1913 eds. SEM105P824 – 24mf – 9 – Can$54.00 – cn Bibl Nat [380]

LOVELL'S COMMERCIAL ANNUAL FOR... 1914-17 – Montreal: John Lovell & Son Ltd, 1914-. SEM105P817 – 8mf – 9 – Can$18.00 – cn Bibl Nat [380]

LOVELL'S COMMERCIAL COMPENDIUM FOR...1909 – Montreal: John Lovell & Son, [c189-?]-1909. SEM105P818 – 26mf – 9 – Can$58.50 – cn Bibl Nat [380]

LOVELL'S COMPENDIUM FOR... *see* LOVELL'S ANNUAL COMPENDIUM FOR...1905

LOVELL'S COMPENDIUM FOR.... *see* LOVELL'S LAW ANNUAL FOR...1909

LOVELL'S COMPENDIUM FOR...1907-1908 – (Only 1 issue publ. Contd by: Lovell's Annual Compendium for... Cont of: Lovell's Law Annual for...) – Montreal: John Lovell & Son Ltd. SEM105P815 – 12mf – 9 – Can$27.00 – cn Bibl Nat [380]

LOVELL'S GAZETTEER OF BRITISH NORTH AMERICA : CONTAINING THE LATEST AND MOST AUTHENTIC DESCRIPTIONS OF OVER SIX THOUSAND CITIES, TOWNS AND VILLAGES IN THE PROVINCES OF.. – Montreal: John Lovell; Rouse's Point: John Lovell & Sons, 1873-95. SEM105P820 – 43mf – 9 – Can$96.75 – cn Bibl Nat [910]

LOVELL'S GAZETTEER OF THE DOMINION OF CANADA : CONTAINING THE LATEST AND MOST AUTHENTIC DESCRIPTIONS OF OVER 14,850 CITIES, TOWNS, VILLAGES AND PLACES IN THE PROVINCES OF.. – Montreal: John Lovell & Son Ltd, 1908. SEM105P819 – 12mf – 9 – Can$27.00 – cn Bibl Nat [910]

LOVELL'S LAW ANNUAL FOR.... *see* LOVELL'S COMPENDIUM FOR...1907-1908

LOVELL'S LAW ANNUAL FOR...1909 – (Contd by: Lovell's Compendium for...) – Montreal: John Lovell & Son Ltd. SEM105P827 – 41mf – 9 – Can$92.25 – cn Bibl Nat [340]

LOVELL'S LEGAL COMPENDIUM FOR... *see* LOVELL'S ANNUAL COMPENDIUM FOR...1905

LOVELL'S LEGAL COMPENDIUM FOR...1904 – (Cont of: Lovell's Annual Compendium for....) – Montreal: John Lovell & Son, [c1901]-1904. SEM105P825 – 26mf – 9 – Can$58.50 – cn Bibl Nat [340]

LOVELL'S MONTREAL AND QUEBEC CLASSIFIED BUSINESS DIRECTORY FOR... : CONTAINING AN INDEX TO STREETS, NAMES, BUSINESS AND ADDRESS OF EVERY FIRM OR PERSON DOING BUSINESS IN THE CITIES OF MONTREAL AND QUEBEC – Montreal: John Lovell & Son Ltd, 1905. SEM105P823 – 9 – Can$11.25 – cn Bibl Nat [380]

LOVELOCK REVIEW-MINER – Lovelock, NV. 1987 – 2+ r – 1 – $100.00 ($90.00y) – N03708 – us Library Micro [622]

THE LOVELS OF ARDEN / Braddon, Mary Elizabeth – British Fiction Archive: Unit 5 – 9 – uk Bell [830]

Loven, S L *see*
- INDEX MOLLUSCORUM LITORA
- OM UTVECKLINGEN AF MOLLUSCA ACEPHALA

Lover, Samuel *see* HANDY ANDY

LOVERS THREE THOUSAND YEARS AGO: AS INDICATED BY THE SONG OF SOLOMON / Goodwin, Thomas A – Chicago: Open Court, 1895. 1 fiche – 9 – us A.T.L.A. [240]

LOVE'S MEINIE : LECTURES ON GREEK AND ENGLISH BIRDS, VOLUME 1 / Ruskin, John – Sunnyside, Orpington, Kent: G. Allen, 1881 – 1 roll – 1 – 1-55879-917-6 – uk Libr Preservation [590]

THE LOVES OF THE ANGELS : A POEM / Moore, Thomas – London: Longman, Hurst, Rees, Orme, and Brown, 1823 – 1 roll – 1 – 1-55879-845-5 – uk Libr Preservation [810]
Lovett, Richard *see*
- THE HISTORY OF THE LONDON MISSIONARY SOCIETY
- JAMES GILMOUR OF MONGOLIA
- THE PRINTED ENGLISH BIBLE, 1525-1885

Lovett, Robert Morss *see* THE HISTORY OF THE NOVEL IN ENGLAND
LOVING SERVICE : A RECORD OF THE LIFE OF MARTHA BRAITHWAITE / Emmott, Elizabeth B – London: Headley Brothers, 1896 – 1mf – us A.T.L.A. [240]
Lovins, Susan *see* THE RELATIONSHIP BETWEEN ATTITUDE AND IMPLEMENTATION OF AN ENVIRONMENTAL EDUCATION CURRICULUM IN PENNSYLVANIA PUBLIC ELEMENTARY SCHOOLS
Low, A P *see*
- REPORT ON EXPLORATIONS IN THE LABRADOR PENINSULA
- REPORT ON THE DOMINION GOVERNMENT EXPEDITION TO HUDSON BAY AND THE ARCTIC ISLANDS ON BOARD D.G.S. NEPTUNE, 1903-04

LOW DOWN *see* THE HIGH VIEW
Low, E M *see* THE MARKETING OF GROUNDNUTS IN THE SUDAN
LOW LEVEL AERIAL SURVEY TECHNIQUES = ENQUETES A BASSE ALTITUDE / ed by Grimsdell, J R & Westley, S – 1981 – 9 – $10.00 – 92-9053-128-2 – et ILRI [520]
LOW TEMPERATURE PHYSICS – 1,5,6,9 – us A.I.P. [530]
LOW TIDE ON GRAND PRE: A BOOK OF LYRICS / Carman, Bliss – New York: C. Webster, 1893. 00490. (Pre-1900 Canadiana) – 9 – cn C.I.H.M. [810]
Lowack, Alfred *see* DIE MUNDARTEN IM HOCHDEUTSCHEN DRAMA BIS GEGEN DAS ENDE DES ACHTZEHNTEN JAHRHUNDERTS
Lowder, CF *see* TWENTY-ONE YEARS IN S. GEORGE'S MISSION
LOWE ART MUSEUM CATALOGUE. CORAL GABLES – (Individual titles not listed separately) – uk Chadwyck [700]
Lowe, E A *see*
- THE BOBBIO MISSAL, VOL. 1
- THE BOBBIO MISSAL, VOL. 2

Lowe, E J *see*
- FERN GROWING. FIFTY YEARS' EXPERIENCE IN CROSSING AND CULTIVATION
- FERNS, BRITISH AND EXOTIC
- A NATURAL HISTORY OF NEW AND RARE FERNS
- OUR NATIVE FERNS; OR A HISTORY OF THE BRITISH SPECIES AND THEIR VARIETIES

Lowe, F *see* WENJAMINOW UEBER DIE ALEUTISCHEN INSELN UND DEREN BEWOHNER
Lowe, Hudson *see* DER STERBENDE NAPOLEON. UNVEROEFFENTLICHTES TAGEBUCH
Lowe, J *see* DZEN-HSI
Lowe, John *see* MEDICAL MISSIONS
Lowe, John C *see* CLINICAL BULLETIN OF MYOFASCIAL THERAPY
Lowe, P *see* A DISCOURSE OF THE WHOLE ART OF CHYRURGERIE
Lowe, R T *see* A HISTORY OF THE FISHES OF MADEIRA
Lowe, Solomon *see*
- THE CRITICAL SPELLING-BOOK
- A CRITIQUE ON THE ETYMOLOGY OF THE WESTMINSTER GRAMMAR
- A PROPOSAL FOR PERFECTING A LATIN GRAMMAR

Lowe, William Henry *see*
- A HEBREW GRAMMAR
- THE HEBREW STUDENT'S COMMENTARY ON ZECHARIAH

Lowell Hebrew Club *see* THE BOOK OF ESTHER: A NEW TRANSLATION
Lowell, J *see* LOWELL'S JUDGEMENTS IN THE U.S. COURT FOR THE DISTRICT OF MASSACHUSETTS, 1865-1877
Lowell, John *see* SKETCH OF AN ACT TO ESTABLISH A UNIFORM SYSTEM OF BANKRUPTCY THROUGHOUT THE UNITED STATES
THE LOWELL LECTURES ON THE ASCENT OF MAN / Drummond, Henry – New York: J. Pott, 1894 – 1mf – us A.T.L.A. [210]
LOWELL OFFERING – nsv. 1-5. October 1840-1845 – 1 – us UMI [073]
LOWELL OFFERING – Series 1: no. 1-4. 1840-1841. Series 2: v1-5 (all publ). 1841-45. -m – 20mf – 9 – $80.00 – us UPA [360]
Lowell, Percival *see* OCCULT JAPAN; OR, THE WAY OF THE GODS; AN ESOTERIC STUDY OF JAPANESE PERSONALITY AND POSSESSION
LOWELL REGISTER – Lowell, NE. -w. Dec 1875-Nov 1877, scattered issues missing – 1 – us NE Hist [071]
LOWELL'S JUDGEMENTS IN THE U.S. COURT FOR THE DISTRICT OF MASSACHUSETTS, 1865-1877 / Lowell, J – Boston: Little-Brown. v1-2. 1872-77 (all publ) – 14mf – 9 – $21.00 – LLMC 81-458 – us L.L.M.C. [340]
Lowensteyn, I *see* DIFFERENCES IN PEAK BLOOD LACTATE VALUES IN LONG COURSE VERSUS SHORT COURSE SWIMMING
LOWER CANADA : COPIES OR EXTRACTS OF CORRESPONDENCE RELATIVE TO THE AFFAIRS OF LOWER CANADA / Grant, Charles Baron Glenelg – [s.l.]: The House of Commons, 1837. SEM105P118 – 2mf – 9 – Can$4.50 – cn Bibl Nat [324]
LOWER CANADA : COPY OF ANY INFORMATION RECEIVED FROM THE EARL OF GOSFORD RESPECTING THE DEBT DUE BY SIR J. CALDWELL TO THE PROVINCE OF LOWER CANADA.. – s.l: House of Commons, 1837. SEM105P389 – 1mf – 9 – Can$2.25 – cn Bibl Nat [971]
LOWER CANADA : COPY OF THE MINUTES OF THE EVIDENCE TAKEN BEFORE THE SELECT COMMITTEE APPOINTED IN THE YEAR 1834 ON THE AFFAIRS OF LOWER CANADA / Grande-Bretagne. Parliament. House of Commons. Select Committee Appointed in the Year 1834 on the Affairs of Lower Canada – [s.l.]: The House of Commons, 1837. SEM105P117 – 3mf – 9 – Can$6.75 – cn Bibl Nat [971]
LOWER CANADA : FURTHER PAPERS RELATIVE TO THE AFFAIRS OF LOWER CANADA / Acheson, Archibald Earl of Gosford – [s.l.]: House of Commons, 1837. SEM105P405 – 1mf – 9 – Can$2.25 – cn Bibl Nat [971]
LOWER CANADA : REPORTS AND CORRESPONDENCE ON THE SUBJECT OF THE CHARGES PREFERRED AGAINST MR. CHISHOLME AND JUDGE FLETCHER – [s.l.]: House of commons, 1837. SEM105P409 – 2mf – 9 – Can$4.50 – cn Bibl Nat [971]
LOWER CANADA : RETURNS OF REVENUES RECEIVED IN RESPECT OF CASUAL AND TERRITORIAL REVENUE DUTIES AND LICENSES, AND OF THE PUBLIC EXPENDITURE OF THE PROVINCE OF LOWER CANADA, 1833 TO 1838 – s.l: House of Commons, 1839. SEM105P407 – 1mf – 9 – Can$2.25 – cn Bibl Nat [971]
LOWER CANADA AGRICULTURIST, MANUFACTURING, COMMERCIAL, AND COLONIZATION INTELLIGENCER – (Cont: Board of Agriculture of Lower Canada, The Farmers' Journal and Transaction of the Board of Agriculture of Lower Canada. Cont by: Canadian Agriculturist) – Montreal: Office of the Provincial Agricultural Depot, [1861-1867] – 9 – cn C.I.H.M. [630]
LOWER CANADA AGRICULTURIST, MANUFACTURING, COMMERCIAL, AND COLONIZATION INTELLIGENCER *see* REVUE AGRICOLE, MANUFACTURIERE, COMMERCIALE ET DE COLONISATION
LOWER CANADA AND UPPER CANADA : FURTHER COPIES OR EXTRACTS OF CORRESPONDENCE RELATIVE TO THE AFFAIRS OF LOWER CANADA AND UPPER CANADA – s.l: House of Commons, 1838. SEM105P109 – 3mf – 9 – Can$6.75 – cn Bibl Nat [324]
LOWER CANADA JURIST / Canada. Quebec – v1-35. 1845-91 (all publ) – 144mf – 9 – $216.00 – LLMC 81-074 – us L.L.M.C. [340]
LOWER CANADA LAW JOURNAL / Canada. Quebec – (v3-4 also known as: Canada Law Journal: A Magazine of Jurisprudence) – v1-4. 1865-68 (all publ) – 10mf – 9 – $15.00 – LLMC 81-017 – us L.L.M.C. [073]
THE LOWER CANADA LAW JOURNAL – (Cont by: The Canada Law Journal) – Montreal: Dawson Bros, [1865-1867] – 9 – cn C.I.H.M. [340]
THE LOWER CANADA LAW JOURNAL *see* THE CANADA LAW JOURNAL
THE LOWER CANADA MUNICIPAL ACT OF 1860 / Canada. Laws, Statutes, etc – Quebec: Printed by Stewart Derbishire & George Desbarats, 1860. SEM105P194 – 2mf – 9 – Can$4.50 – cn Bibl Nat [340]
LOWER CANADA MUNICIPAL AND ROAD ACT OF 1855...THE PARLIAMENTARY REPRESENTATION ACTS...AND THE SEIGNIORIAL ACTS. / Canada. Laws, Statutes, etc – Quebec: Printed by Stewart Derbishire and George Desbarats, 1855. SEM105P193 – 3mf – 9 – Can$6.75 – cn Bibl Nat [324]
THE LOWER CANADA MUNICIPAL AND ROAD AMENDMENT ACT OF 1856 / Canada. Laws, Statutes, etc – Toronto: Printed by Stewart Derbishire and George Desbarats, 1856. SEM105P186 – 1mf – 9 – Can$2.25 – cn Bibl Nat [380]
THE LOWER CANADA MUNICIPAL AND ROAD AMENDMENT ACT OF 1857 / Canada. Laws, Statutes, etc – Toronto: Printed by Stewart Derbishire & George Desbarats, 1857. SEM105P188 – 1mf – 9 – Can$2.25 – cn Bibl Nat [380]
LOWER CANADA REPORTS / Canada. Quebec – v1-17. 1850-67 (all publ) – 102mf – 9 – $153.00 – LLMC 81-075 – us L.L.M.C. [340]
LOWER CANADA REPORTS : SEIGNIORIAL QUESTIONS / Canada. Quebec – 2v. (A & B) (all publ) – 12mf – 9 – $18.00 – LLMC 81-086 – us L.L.M.C. [340]
LOWER FAIRFOREST BAPTIST CHURCH. UNION COUNTY. SOUTH CAROLINA : CHURCH RECORDS – 1890-1925, 1934-46 – 1 – 24.57 – us Baptist [240]
LOWER KIEWA WATER BOARD MINUTES – 1986-1989. LKWB2 – 1r – 5 – at Corangamite [910]
LOWER LAKE BULLETIN – Lower Lake, CA. 1894-1896 – 1r – 1 – $50.00 – B03331 – us Library Micro [071]
LOWER LIGHT – Portland OR. Issue Nos 2-11 – 1 – us U.O. Library [071]
LOWER SAXONY : PAMPHLET COLLECTION – 1987? – 9 – us Hoover Inst Photo [943]
THE LOWER ST LAWRENCE: ITS SCENERY, NAVIGATION AND COMMERCE, FORMING A COMPLETE TOURIST'S GUIDE / Anderson, William James – Quebec: 1872. 04057. (Pre-1900 Canadiana) – 9 – cn C.I.H.M. [910]
Lowery, Woodbury *see* INDEX-DIGEST ON PATENT CASES IN THE SUPREME COURT OF THE U.S
THE LOWEST RUNG / Cholmondeley, Mary – British Fiction Archive: Unit 3 – 9 – uk Bell [830]
LOWESTOFT WEEKLY JOURNAL. (LOWESTOFT JOURNAL.-LOWESTOFT JOURNAL & MERCURY) – England. 1873-1944, 1963-68, 1978-81. -w – 1 – uk British Libr Newspaper [072]
Lowey, George *see* CHINA (1949-1979), DOCUMENTS ON CONTEMPORARY
Lowing, M J *see* CASEBOOK OF METHODS FOR COMPUTING HYDROLOGICAL PARAMETERS FOR WATER PROJECTS
Lowndes County.Georgia *see* HISTORY.
LOWNDE'S DIRECTORY, 1773/ROBSON'S DIRECTORY, 1831 – 1 – uk Microform Academic [941]
Lowndes, E E K *see* EVERY-DAY LIFE IN SOUTH AFRICA
Lowndes, Mary E *see* THE NUNS OF PORT ROYAL
Lowndes, Richard *see* RENE DESCARTES
Lowndes, William Thomas *see*
- COMMONPLACE BOOK
- WILLIAM LOWNDES PAPERS

Lowrey, Asbury *see* BISHOP ASBURY
Lowrie, John Cameron *see* MISSIONARY PAPERS
Lowrie, Walter *see*
- THE DOCTRINE OF SAINT JOHN: AN ESSAY IN BIBLICAL THEOLOGY
- MEMOIRS OF THE HON. WALTER LOWRIE
- MONUMENTS OF THE EARLY CHURCH

Lowry, Malcolm *see* MALCOLM LOWRY'S SHAKESPEARE
Lowry, R E *see* HISTORY OF PREBLE COUNTY
Lowth, Robert *see*
- DE SACRA POESI HEBRAEORUM
- A SHORT INTRODUCTION TO ENGLISH GRAMMAR

Lowther, MK *see* HISTORY OF RITCHIE COUNTY
LOWVELD CHRONICLE – Nelspruit. South Africa. 1935-47 – 1 – sa State Libr [072]
LOWVELD LEADER – Barberton. South Africa. 1947-57 – 1 – sa State Libr [072]
LOWVELDER-LAEVELDER – Nelspruit, South Africa. 1958-81 – 1 – sa State Libr [072]
Loy, M *see*
- THE AUGSBURG CONFESSION
- THE DISTINCTIVE DOCTRINES AND USAGES OF THE GENERAL BODIES OF THE EVANGELICAL LUTHERAN CHURCH IN THE UNITED STATES
- STORY OF MY LIFE

THE LOYAL MOUNTAINEERS OF TENNESSEE / Humes, Thomas W – Knoxville: Ogden Brothers and Co., 1888. Tennessee Reel 1. (The Cox Library Collection) – 5 – us Americana [978]
LOYALTY: A LETTER TO MCGILL STUDENTS FROM THE PRINCIPAL / Dawson, John William – Montreal?: s.n., 18–. 03669. (Pre-1900 Canadiana) – 9 – cn C.I.H.M. [971]
LOYALTY: AN ADDRESS DELIVERED TO THE TORONTO YOUNG MEN'S LIBERAL CLUB, JANUARY 19TH, 1885 / Edgar, James David – Toronto?: s.n., 1885? (Toronto: Grip Print. and Pub. Co. 02881. (Pre-1900 Canadiana) – 9 – cn C.I.H.M. [971]
Loyd *see* HISTORY OF GREENE COUNTY
Loyer, Godefroy *see* RELATION DU VOYAGE DU ROYAUME D'ISSIGNY, COTE D'OR, PAYS DE GUINEE, EN AFRIQUE. LA DESCRIPTION DU PAYS, LES INCLINATIONS, LES MOEURS ET LA RELIGION DES HABITANTS; AVEC CE QUI S'EST PASSE DE PLUS REMARQUABLE DANS L'ETABLISSEMENT QUE LES FRANCAIS Y ONT FAIT
LOYOLA AND JESUITISM IN ITS RUDIMENTS / Taylor, Isaac – London: Printed for Longman, Brown, Green, and Longmans, 1849 – 1mf – us A.T.L.A. [240]
LOYOLA: AND JESUITISM IN ITS RUDIMENTS / Taylor, Isaac – London: Longman, Brown, Green, and Longmans, 1849. viii,374p – 1 – us U.W. Library [240]
LOYOLA CONSUMER LAW REPORTER – v1-7. 1988-95 – 9 – $81.00 set – us Hein [340]
Loyola, Ignatius, Saint *see* EXERCITITIA SPIRITUALIA
Loyola, Mary, Mother *see* THE SOLDIER OF CHRIST, OR, TALKS BEFORE CONFIRMATION
LOYOLA OF LOS ANGELES INTERNATIONAL AND COMPARATIVE LAW ANNUAL *see* LOYOLA OF LOS ANGELES INTERNATIONAL AND COMPARATIVE LAW JOURNAL
LOYOLA OF LOS ANGELES INTERNATIONAL AND COMPARATIVE LAW JOURNAL – (Title varies: v1-3 1978-80 as Loyola of Los Angeles International and Comparative Law Annual) – v1-17. 1978-95 – 9 – $250.00 set – us Hein [340]
LOYOLA OF LOS ANGELES LAW REVIEW – (v1-17 1968-84 on reel $325.00. v18-28 1985-95 on mf $259.00. Title varies: v1-4 1968-71 as University of Los Angeles Law Review) – v1-28. 1968-95 – 5,6,9 – $584.00 set – us Hein [340]
LOYOLA OF LOS ANGELES LAW REVIEW – v1-28. 1968-95 – 1,5,6 – $765.00 – us Hein [073]
Lozano, Antonio *see* DECLARACION FUNEBRE...CLERIGOS
Lozano, Francisco Franco *see* GRAMATICA ELEMENTAL DE LA LENGUA LATINA Y CASTELLANA
Lozano, Miguel *see* TEORIA DE LA SOCIEDAD SEGUN DE BONALD Y DONOSO CORTES
Lozano Pino, Manuel *see*
- PLAN EXPERIMENTAL DE EDUCACION FISICO-DEPORTIVA ESCOLAR

Lozano Ponce de Leon, Pablo *see* TRATADO...TISIS...HIGIENE
Lozano, Raymundo *see* CURSOS DE LENGUA PANAYANA
Lozano Rubio, Tirso *see*
- DE HISTORIA DE BADAJOZ
- HISTORIA...MONTACHEZ

Lozano Velilla, Arminda *see* LA ESCLAVITUD EN ASIA MENOR HELENISTICA
Lozinskii, M *see* GORNYI KLIUCH
Lozovoi, A *see* LENIN I KOOPERATSIIA
Lozovyi, A *see*
- SEL'SKOKHOZIAISTVENNAIA KOOPERATSIIA I ZNACHENIE EE V SOVREMENNYKH USLOVIIAKH
- VIDY I ZADACHI KOOPERATSII

LP/GAS – (1981-. 5,6,9) – Dec 1941- – 1 – us UMI [600]
LP-GAS MERCHANDISING – Feb 1941-Nov 1941 – 1 – us UMI [600]
LPV – Havana, Cuba. -w. May 1962-Nov 1964. 3 reels – 1 – uk British Libr Newspaper [072]

LRA : RADIO DEL ESTADO – (Includes c.1: 1953:June-1954:Dec) – Buenos Aires: Ministerio de Comunicaciones, Direcci on de Radiodifusion, 19uu – 1 – CSUXAJA7934-S – us Hoover Inst Photo [380]

LRA DESKBOOK : COMPLETE INDEX TO ALL L.R.A. NOTES – (Covers both series) – New York: Lawyers' Co-op. 1v. 1919 (all publ) – 15mf – 9 – $22.50 – LLMC 78-046B – us L.L.M.C. [340]

LSA BULLETIN / Linguistic Society of America – v1-84. 1926-79 – 7r – 9 – us Ross [400]

THE L.S.D., INDONESIA'S VOLUNTARY VILLAGE LEVEL SELF-HELP PROGRAM / Brigham, Thomas M – SE-4515 1. 1962 – 9 – ne IDC [360]

LSU FORESTRY NOTES / Louisiana State University. Agricultural Experiment Station. School of Forestry and Wildlike Management – n87-138. 1970-82 – 1r – 1,5 – us Spaulding [634]

L.T. PATTERSON STRATEGY LETTER – 1975-1; 1978- 5,6,9 – us UMI [320]

LU DANS LA PRESSE UNIVERSELLE – Paris. 1932-avr 1937. Absorbe par: Vu.Voir a ce titre – 1 – fr A.C.R.P.P. [073]

Lu, Junling *see* YUANREN WENJI PIANMU FENLEI SUOYIN

LU OU CHOU K'AN – La Garenne-Colombes et Tours. No.1-93. nov 1919-aout 1921 – 1 – fr A.C.R.P.P. [073]

Lu, Shao-fei *see* YIN-TU-NI-HSI-YA HUA CH'IAO MEI KUNG T'UAN TSO P'IN HSUAN CHI

Lu, Shih-Chiang *see* THE ORIGIN AND CAUSE OF THE ANTI-CHRISTIAN MOVEMENT BY CHINESE OFFICIALS AND GENTRY, 1860-1874 (CCC233)

Lu, Szu-wei *see* NATIONAL CULTURE AND THE DEVELOPMENT OF THE INDIVIDUAL (CCC232)

LUAH AHI'ASAF – 13 v. Warsaw. 1893-1903 04. BJ-291-15 1 – 9 – ne IDC [900]

LUAH EREZ-YISRA'EL – Ed. by A. M. Luncz. 21 v. Jerusalem. 1895-1916. Lacking: 1899, v. 5. BJ-100-108 1 – 9 – ne IDC [956]

LUAH EREZ-YISRA'EL – v. 5. BJ-27-242 1 – 9 – ne IDC [956]

LUAH HA-DIKDUK (EM HA-YELED) – Cracow. 1598. BJ-43-44 1 – 9 – ne IDC [956]

Luard, H R *see*
- ANNALES MONASTICI (RS36)
- CHRONICA MAJORA (RS57)
- FLORES HISTORIARUM (RS95)
- HISTORIA ANGLICANA (A.D. 449-1298) (RS16)
- LIVES OF EDWARD THE CONFESSOR (RS3)
- ROBERTI GROSSETESTE EPISCOPI QUONDAM LINCOLNIENSI EPISTOLAE (RS25)

Luard, Henry Richards *see* THE CORRESPONDENCE OF RICHARD PORSON, M.A. FORMERLY REGIUS PROFESSOR OF GREEK IN THE UNIVERSITY OF CAMBRIDGE

LUAT HOC = LEGAL STUDY – 1973-75 – 15mf – 9 SEL-125/1 – ne IDC [340]

LUAT LE NUOC VIET NAM DAN CHU CONG HOA = LAWS AND REGULATIONS OF THE DEMOCRATIC REPUBLIC OF VIETNAM / The People's Supreme Procuracy – 14mf – 9 SEL-105/1 – ne IDC [340]

LUAT LE VE TU PHAP = LAWS AND REGULATIONS ON THE JUDICIAL SYSTEM / The People's Supreme Court – (Lacking: v1, 3) – v1-5. 1945-67 – 21mf – 9 SEL-104/1 – ne IDC [340]

LUAT NGHIA VU QUAN SU = LAWS ON MILITARY SERVICE / Ha Tinh Province's Military Service Commission – 1962 – 1mf – 9 SEL-111/1 – ne IDC [340]

LUAT TO CHUC. VIEN KIEM SAT NHAN DAN – 1962 – 1mf – 9 SEL-116/1 – ne IDC [340]

LUBA DOCUMENTS / Reefe, Thomas – Shaba Region, Zaire. Originals in the Archives de la Zone de Kamina. 1907-67 – 1 – us Res Libr [960]

THE LUBAVITCH DIGEST – St. Paul, MN. 1977, 1983 – 1 – us A.J.P.C. [071]

Lubbock, J *see* MONOGRAPH OF THE COLLEMBOLA AND THYSANURA

Lubbock, John *see* PEACE AND HAPPINESS

Lube, Denis George *see* AN ANALYSIS OF THE PRINCIPLES OF EQUITY PLEADING.

LUBECK : PAMPHLET COLLECTION – 1920-1927? – 1 – us Hoover Inst Photo [943]

Lubertino, Jose *see* LA TRAGEDIA DE LAS DICTADURAS LATINOAMERICANAS Y CUATRO PROBLEMAS ARGENTINOS

Lubianovskii, F P *see* VOSPOMINANIIA, 1777-1834

Lubis, Anwarman *see* BERTJOTJOK TANAM SETJARA BIOLOGIS. (BIOLOGISCHE CULTURMETHODE)

Lubis, Darul Asjhar *see* THE IMPORTANCE OF DEDAKPADI IN LIVESTOCK FEEDING IN INDONESIA

Lubis, Harun *see* ETNOLOGY (ILMU BANGSA-BANGSA)

Lubis, M A *see* LIBERALISME DAN RASIONALISME BARAT DAN ISLAM

LUBLINER TOGBLAT – (Yiddish daily) – Lublin, PL. v1 no32 22 Feb 1918-v10 no234 10 Oct 1927 – 1r – 1 – $25.00 – cn Can Microfilming [072]

Lublink-Weddik, W F *see* ADATDELICTENRECHT IN DE RAPAT-MARGA-RECHTSPRAAK VAN PALEMBANG

LUBOK – Pt. 1: Russkaia pesnia. Moscow, 1939. 273p. BR-10,701/1 – 9 – ne IDC [025]

Lubos, Arno *see* DIE SCHLESISCHE ROMANTIK

LUBRECHT SERIES / Montana. Forest and Conservation Experiment Station. Missoula – no.1. 1968 – 1,5,6 – us Spaulding [630]

LUBRICATION – 1911- 1; 1970- 5,6; 1976- 4 x 6 in. 9 – us UMI [621]

LUBRICATION ENGINEERING – v1-27. 1945-71 – 1,5,6 – us Princeton Micro [073]

Luby, Thomas Clarke *see* THE LIFE AND TIMES OF DANIEL O'CONNELL

Luc, Jean Andre de *see* IDEES SUR LA METEROLOGIE

LE LUC VAN TIEN CA DIEN – Poeme annamite. 1883 – 9 – fr Orientalistes [810]

Lucand, J L *see* FIGURES PEINTES DES CHAMPIGNONS DE LA FRANCE. 1881-1893. SUITES A L'ICONOGRAPHIE DE BULLIARD. B-5101/1

Lucas *see* BENCH AND BAR OF ILLINOIS – 1920

LUCAS AVENUE BAPTIST CHURCH. LAURENS COUNTY. SOUTH CAROLINA : CHURCH RECORDS – 1927-72 – 1 – 22.59 – us Baptist [240]

Lucas, Bernard *see*
- CHRIST FOR INDIA
- CONVERSATIONS WITH CHRIST
- THE EMPIRE OF CHRIST

Lucas, Colin *see*
- FRENCH REVOLUTION RESEARCH COLLECTION
- THE FRENCH REVOLUTION RESEARCH COLLECTION AND VIDEODISK

Lucas County. Ohio. Board of County Commissioners *see*
- COUNTY HOME JOURNAL
- JOURNALS

Lucas County. Ohio. Common Pleas. Civil Division *see*
- JOURNALS
- NATURALIZATION RECORDS
- NATURALIZATION RECORDS/DECLARATION

Lucas County. Ohio. Engineer *see*
- BRIDGE AND CULVERT REPORTS
- COUNTY-TOWNSHIP ROAD INVENTORY
- DITCH CARDS
- DRAFT MAPS
- FIELD BOOKS
- ROAD FILES
- ROAD INDEX CARD FILES
- ROAD MAPS, TOWNSHIPS

Lucas County, Ohio. Maumee, City. City Council *see*
- MINUTES
- ORDINANCE AND RESOLUTION

Lucas County. Ohio. Planning Commission *see* RECORD OF PROCEEDINGS

Lucas County. Ohio. Probate Court *see*
- INDEX TO BIRTH CERTIFICATES
- INDEX TO BIRTH RECORDS
- NATURALIZATION – MINORS
- NATURALIZATION RECORDS – LOOSE

Lucas County. Ohio. Providence Township. Board of Trustees *see* MINUTES

Lucas County. Ohio. Supreme Court *see* APPEARANCE DOCKET

Lucas County, Ohio. Sylvania Township Township Clerk *see*
- ABSTRACTS OF ROAD TAXES
- ENUMERATION, SCHOOL AGE YOUTH
- POLL BOOKS AND TALLY SHEETS

Lucas County. Ohio. Toledo, City Board of Education *see*
- ANNUAL REPORTS
- MINUTES
- PRESIDENTS' REPORTS

Lucas County. Ohio. Toledo, City Board of Police Commissioners *see* MINUTES

Lucas County. Ohio. Toledo, City Board of Public Safety *see* MINUTES

Lucas County. Ohio. Toledo, City Board of Public Service *see*
- CEMETERY DEED RECORDS
- MINUTES

Lucas County. Ohio. Toledo, City Industrial Peace Board *see* MINUTES

Lucas County. Ohio. Toledo, City Park Commission *see*
- MINUTES
- RECEIPTS AND EXPENDITURES RECORD

Lucas County. Ohio. Toledo, City Planning Commission *see* CITY PLAT MAPS

Lucas County. Ohio. Toledo, City Police Department *see*
- JAIL REGISTERS
- JAIL REGISTERS (WOMEN)

Lucas County, Ohio. Toledo Metropolitan Park District *see* BOARD OF PARK COMMISSIONS

Lucas County, Ohio. Waterville Township. Justice of the Peace *see* CRIMINAL DOCKET

Lucas County. Ohio. Whitehouse, Village. Fire Department *see* MINUTES

Lucas, Edward Verrall *see*
- CHARLES LAMB AND THE LLOYDS

Lucas Family *see* PAPERS

LUCAS GROVE BAPTIST CHURCH. UPTON, KENTUCKY : CHURCH RECORDS – Aug 1896-Jul 1978. Lacks Aug 1924-Nov 1940. 456p – 1 – 20.52 – us Baptist [240]

Lucas, Hans Guenter *see* GIPS ALS HISTORISCHER AUSSENBAUSTOFF IN DER WINDSHEIMER BUCHT

Lucas, James Joseph *see* MEMOIR OF REV. ROBERT STEWART FULLERTON

Lucas, Jason *see* THE EFFECTS OF A STRENGTH TRAINING PROGRAM ON THE BODY IMAGE, SELF-CONCEPT, AND DYNAMIC STRENGTH OF SEVENTH GRADE GIRLS

Lucas, Martha M *see* COLLABORATIVE ADULT LEARNING PRINCIPLES IN BACCALAUREATE COMMUNITY HEALTH EDUCATION CURRICULA

Lucas, Paul *see* VOYAGE DU SIEUR PAUL LUCAS EN LEVANT: ON Y TROUVERA ENTR'AUTRE UNE DESCRIPTION DE LA HAUTE EGYPTE, SUIVANT LE COURS DU NIL. (TOME SECOND): ON Y VERRA LE RECIT DE L'ENTREPRISE VIOLENTE DU PACHAT DE BABYLONE

Lucas, Prosper *see* TRAITE PHILOSOPHIQUE ET PHYSIOLOGIQUE DE L'HEREDITE NATURELLE DANS LES ETATS DE SANTE ET DE MALADIE DU SYSTEME NERVEUX

Lucas Verdu, Antonio *see* PREGON DE LA SEMANA SANTA CACERENA. MARZO 1972

Lucas, W J *see*
- THE AQUATIC (NAIAD) STAGE OF THE BRITISH DRAGONFLIES
- A MONOGRAPH OF THE BRITISH ORTHOPTERA

Lucas, Wilhelm *see* DAS ADJEKTIV BEI ULRICH VON LICHTENSTEIN

Lucay, Jean Baptiste C L *see* DESCRIPTION DU DEPARTEMENT DU CHER

Luccock *see* NATURE AND PROPERTIES OF WOOL

LA LUCE – (Lacking: nos 28-35 9 Jul-10 Sep 1976) – Italy. v66-67. 1976-77 – 1r – 1 – ATLA S0578 – us A.T.L.A. [073]

LA LUCE; 335 – Utica, NY, Nov. 16, 1901-Jan. 29, 1921 – 5r – 1 – us I.H.R.C. [978]

Luce de Lancival *see* HECTOR

Luce, H K *see* THE GOSPEL ACCORDING TO LUKE

Luce, H W *see*
- AIDS TO THE STUDY OF ACTS (CCC236)
- HARMONY OF THE GOSPELS (CCC234)
- HISTORICAL STUDY OF THE ACTS AND THE EPISTLES (CCC235)

Luce, Morton *see* A HANDBOOK TO THE WORKS OF WILLIAM SHAKESPEARE

LUCEAFARUL – 1976- – 1r per y – 1 – us Ross [072]

LUCEAFARUL – Bucharest, Romania. -w. 1958-70. 9 reels – 1 – uk British Libr Newspaper [949]

LUCEAFARUL – Bucuresti, 1976-1992ff – 17r – 1 – DM1,275.00 – gw Mikro Press [949]

LUCERNAS ROMANAS DECORADAS DEL MUSEO EMERITENSE / Gil Farres, Octavio – Barcelona, 1948 – 1 – sp Bibl Santa Ana [946]

LUCERNE VALLEY LEADER – Lucerne Valley, CA. 1955 – 23+ r – 1 – $1,150.00 ($50.00y) – R04067 – us Library Micro [071]

LUCH DUKHOVNYI / Remizov, A – St. Petersburg, 1907. BR-826 2 – 8 – ne IDC [460]

LUCH (MUROM, R.S.F.S.R.) – (Includes c.1: 1921:Nov.7) – Murom: [s.n.], 191u – 1 – CSUXADQ2087-S – us Hoover Inst Photo [947]

LA LUCHA – Havana. Apr 22 1898-Dec 31 1912. Incomplete – 1 – us NY Public [072]

LA LUCHA ANTIPANEIDICA EN LA PROVINCIA DE CACERES / Campo Cardona, Antonio del – Madrid: Grafica Universal, 1940 – sp Bibl Santa Ana [946]

LUCHA DE ALAS / Barreda, Ernesto Maria – Buenos Aires. 1920 – 1 – us Res Libr [830]

LA LUCHA DE CLASES Y EL SENTIDO NACIONAL Y SOCIAL DEL NUEVO ESTADO / Urbina, Antonio – Barcelona, 1939. Fiche W1504. (Blodgett Collection of Spanish Civil War Pamphlets) – 9 – us H.U. College Libr [946]

LA LUCHA POR LA LIBERACION NACIONAL : EL RETORNO DE PERON; LA REVOLUCION Y EL PERONISMO / Cooke, John William – [Buenos Aires]: Ediciones Papiro, [1971] – 1 – CSUXADQ6395-B – us Hoover Inst Photo [320]

Luchaire, Achille *see*
- INNOCENT 3: LES ROYAUTES VASSALES DU SAINTE-SIEGE
- SOCIAL FRANCE AT THE TIME OF PHILIP AUGUSTUS

Luchaire, J *see* ESSAI SUR L'EVOLUTION INTELLECTUELLE DE L'ITALIE DE 1815-1930

LUCHAR POR LA PAZ Y LA SOLIDARIDAD ENTRE TODOS LOS PUEBLOS / Spain. Ministerio de Estado – Barcelona, n.d. Fiche W1509. (Blodgett Collection of Spanish Civil War Pamphlets) – 9 – us H.U. College Libr [946]

LAS LUCHAS DEL SIGLO 6 / Munoz Garcia, Juan – Bejar: Francisco Munoz, 1929 – 1 – sp Bibl Santa Ana [946]

LAS LUCHAS NACIONALES CONTRA LA DEPENDENCIA / Cardenas, Gonzalo Horacio – Buenos Aires: Editorial Galerna, 1969 – 1 – CSUXADP4628-B – us Hoover Inst Photo [320]

Luchet, Jean-Pierre-Louis de la Roche Du Maine, Mis de *see* LA REINE DE NENNI, NOUVELLE HISTORIQUE

LU-CHOU CHIH-LI CHOU-CHIH – 1882, 12. BCH-775 2 – 8 – ne IDC [950]

LUCIA DE FATIMA DICE... / Corredor Garcia, Antonio – Caceres: Edic. Cruzada Mariana, 1956 – 1 – sp Bibl Santa Ana [946]

LUCIA IN LONDON. LEIPZIG 1928 / Benson, E F; ed by Bayle, Constantino – Madrid: Razon y Fe, 1928 – 9 – sp Bibl Santa Ana [920]

Lucian *see* DIALOGOS MORALES DE LUCIANO

Lucian of Samosato *see* SELECTIONS FROM LUCIAN

LUCIANS EINFLUSS AUF WIELAND / Steinberger, Julius – (Includes bibliographical references) – Goettingen: Univ.-Buchdruckerei, 1902 – 1r – 1 – us U.W. Library [430]

Lucidus, Joannes *see* OPVSCVLVM DE EMENDATIONIBUS TERMPORUM AB ORBE CONDITIO ADVSQUE HANC AETATEM NOSTRAM

LUCIDUS ORDO... : AN ANALYTICAL COURSE OF STUDIES ON THE SEVERAL BRANCHES OF MUSICAL SCIENCE... / Relfe, J – London: Relfe, 1821 – 1 – us Sibley [780]

LUCIFER – Valley Falls. Kan. 1883-1907 – 1 – us UMI [071]

LUCIFER *see* THEOSOPHICAL REVIEW

LUCIFER, BISCHOF VON CALARIS UND DAS SCHISMA DER LUCIFERIANER / Krueger, Gustav – Leipzig: Breitkopf & Haertel, 1886 – 1mf – us A.T.L.A. [240]

LUCIFER THE LIGHT-BEARER – (New series: v3, no. 1-13 (incomplete). 1885. Series 3: v1, no. 10,13,15,16,18,19,28,42 (incomplete). 1897. v3, no. 1-13 (incomplete). 1899. v5, no. 26-29, 33-43, 45-52 (incomplete). 1901-1902. v6, no. 1-23 (incomplete). 1902. v7, no. 1-51 (incomplete). 1903. v8, no. 1-7 (incomplete). 1904. Series 4: Whole nos. 1035, 1038, 1042-1055. 1905 (incomplete). Whole nos. 1056, 1058-1074 (incomplete). 1906. -w. 1885-1906) – 1 reel – 1 – $90.00 – us UPA [360]

LUCIFERIANISM OR SATANISM IN ENGLISH FREEMASONRY, AN ESSAY. PART 1 / Fouquet, Leon – Montreal: Cadieux & Derome, 1898. 05661. (Pre-1900 Canadiana) – 9 – cn C.I.H.M. [971]
LUCIFERIANISM OR SATANISM IN ENGLISH FREEMASONRY, AN ESSAY. PART 2 / Fouquet, Leon – Montreal: Cadieux & Derome, 1898. 05662. (Pre-1900 Canadiana) – 9 – cn C.I.H.M. [971]
LUCILII CARMINUM RELIQUIAE / Marx, F – v. 1-2. Lipsiae. 1904-05. B-357 2 – 8 – ne IDC [450]
LUCINDE : EIN ROMAN / Schlegel, Friedrich von – Leipzig: P Reclam, [187-?] – 1r – 1 – us U.W. Library [830]
Lucinge, Rene de *see* LA MANIERE DE LIRE L'HISTORIE
LUCIO VERO. [OPERA IN TRE ATTI DI APOSTOLO ZENO. MUSICA] / Sacchini, A M – Copy of manuscript, unpublished, [1766?] – 1 – us Sibley [780]
LUCIUS DAVOREN, OR PUBLICANS AND SINNERS / Braddon, Mary Elizabeth – British Fiction Archive: Unit 5 – 9 – uk Bell [830]
Lucius, Paul Ernst *see*
– DIE ANFAENGE DES HEILIGENKULTS IN DER CHRISTLICHEN KIRCHE
– DER ESSENISMUS IN SEINEM VERHAELTNISS ZUM JUDENTHUM
– DIE THERAPEUTEN...IHRE STELLUNG IN DER GESCHICHTE DER ASKESE...DE VITA CONTEMPLATIVA
Lucius von Ballhausen, Freiherr Robert Sigmund Maria Joseph *see* BISMARCK-ERINNERUNGEN DES STAATSMINISTERS
Lucka, Emil *see* ISOLDE WEISSHAND
Luckin, Kristen A *see* A BIOCHEMICAL ANALYSIS OF THE EXERCISE-INDUCED DYSFUNCTION OF THE RAT GASTROCNEMIUS SARCO-PLASMIC RETICULUM CA2+-ATPASE PROTEIN
Luckock, Herbert Mortimer *see*
– THE BISHOPS IN THE TOWER
– THE CHURCH IN SCOTLAND
LUCKY BOY MINING RECORD – Lucky Boy, NV. Jun-Sep 1909 (scats) – 1r – 1 – $50.00 – U04627 – us Library Micro [071]
LUCKY BOY POST – Hawthorne, NV. May-Oct 1909 – 1r – 1 – $50.00 – U04578 – us Library Micro [071]
Lucques, Jacques *see* LE QUEBEC LIBRE
LUCRECIA / Fernandez de Moratin, Nicolas – s.a. – 1mf – 9 – Pta1,000.00 – 84-7848-148-6 – sp Pentalfa [820]
LUCRETIA BORGIA : ACCORDING TO ORIGINAL DOCUMENTS AND CORRESPONDENCE OF HER DAY / Gregorovius, Ferdinand – New York: D. Appleton, 1908 – 1mf – us A.T.L.A. [945]
Lucretius Carus, Titus *see* TITI LUCRETI CARI, PHILOSOPHI ET..
A LUCTA – Cidade de Prados, 9 May-5 Sep 1914 – 1,5,6 – bl Biblioteca [072]
A LUCTA : FOLHA CONSAGRADA AOS INTERESSES DA ZONA OESTE – Oliveira, 4 Aug 1918; Apr 1919; 5 Sep 1920 – 1,5,6 – bl Biblioteca [072]
A LUCTA – Itapecerica, 1 Jan-Feb, 8 Jun 1899 – 1,5,6 – bl Biblioteca [072]
A LUCTA – Lisbon, Portugal. 30 Dec 1916-5 Aug 1919 – 4r – 1 – uk British Libr Newspaper [072]
A LUCTA : ORGAM LITTERARIO E RECREATIVO – Uberaba, 10 May 1896 – 1,5,6 – bl Biblioteca [072]
A LUCTA : ORGAO DO PARTIDO REPUBLICANO – Queluz de Minas, 12 Mar-Aug, Oct-3 Nov 1912 – 1,5,6 – bl Biblioteca [072]
A LUCTA / POLITICA, DIREITO E LITTE-RATURA – Oliveira, 18 Dec 1894 – 1,5,6 – bl Biblioteca [072]
A LUCTA SOCIAL : ORGAM OPERARIO-LIVRE – Manaus, Amazonas. 29 Mar-Set, 1 Nov 1914 – 1,5,6 – bl Biblioteca [072]
O LUCTADOR : JORNAL IMPARCIAL, NOTICIOSO, AGRICOLA E COMMERCIAL – Pirapetinga, 6 Mar 1887 – 1,5,6 – bl Biblioteca [072]
O LUCTADOR – Penedo, Alagoas. 15 Jan 1903; 27 Mar 1908 – 1,5,6 – bl Biblioteca [072]
LUC-TINH TAN VAN – Saigon. avr 1910-sept 1944 – 1 – fr A.C.R.P.P. [073]
LUD – Jego Zwyczaje, Sposoa1b Zycia, Mowa, Podania, Przyslaowia Obrzedy, Guslaa, Zabawy, Piea1sni, Murzyka i Taa1nce. Cracow. ser. 8, 11, 16, 18, 20-23. 1875, 1877, 1883, 1885, 1887-1890 – 1 – us NY Public [073]
LUD : ORGAN STRANY SLOVENSKY OBRODY – (Coll title: Czech/Slovakian Periodicals. Cont. as: Lud. Organ Demokraticky Strany. 1989(Dec 11-30). Missing: 1987(Oct)-1988(March). In Slovak) – Praha, 1971-1989 – 1078mf – 9 – R-15376/1 – ne IDC [320]
LUD POLSKI – Paris. France. -w. 1 Dec 1946-8 Feb 1948. (1 reel) – 1 – uk British Libr Newspaper [943]
THE LUDDITE PAPERS / Radcliffe, Joseph – 1812-13 – 1 – uk Microform Academic [331]
Ludi Printing Co *see* HISTORY OF BURT COUNTY 1803-1929
Ludkiewicx, Zdzislaw *see* KWESTJA ROLNA W GALICJI
LUDLOW 1774-1855 – 5mf – 9 – us Holbrook [920]
Ludlow, J M *see* WOMAN'S WORK IN THE CHURCH: HISTORICAL NOTES ON DEACONESSES AND SISTERHOODS
Ludolf, Hiob *see*
– ...GRAMMATICA LINGUAE AMHARICAE.
– ...LEXICON AETHIOPICO-LATINUM.
– ...LEXICON AMHARICO-LATINUM.
– NOUVELLE HISTOIRE D'ABISSINIE OU D'ETHIOPIE, TIREE DE L'HISTOIRE LATINE DE M. LUDOLF
– SEU LEXICON AMHARICO-LATINUM...
Ludolf, J *see* LEXICON AETHIOPICO-LATINUM...
Ludolfi, Iobi *see* RELATIO NOVA DE HODIERNO HABESSINIAE STATU, EX INDIA NUPER ALLATA
Ludolfi, Iobi (alias Leut-holf) *see* HISTORIA AETHIOPICA
Ludolfi, Iobi (alias Leutholf dicti) *see* AD SUAM HISTORIAM AETHIOPICAM ANTEHAC EDITAM COMMENTARIUS.
Ludolfo, Iobo *see* GRAMMATICA LINGUAE AMHARICAE
LUDOUICI HELIANI VERCELLENSIS CHRSITANISSIMI FRANCO REGIS SENATORIS / Helianus, L – Auguste Vindelicor, 1510 – 1mf – 9 – H-8223/1 – ne IDC [956]
LUDOVE NOVINY – Skalice, Slovakia, 1906-1909 – 2r – 1 – us I.H.R.C. [947]
LUDOVE ZVESTI = PEOPLES NEWS – (In Czech) – Canada, 1914- – 1 – cn Commonwealth Micro [072]
Ludovici, Jacob Friedrich *see* EINLEITUNG ZUM KRIEGS-PROCESS
LUDU – Mandalay, Burma. 1957-Mar 12 1959; May 1960-Jun 1966 – 31r – 1 – us L of C Photodup [072]
LUDUS LITERARIUS: OR, THE GRAMMAR SCHOOLE / Brinsley, John – 1612. 394p. (English linguistics series 1500-1800) – 9 – us UMI [420]
LUDVIKA TIDNING – Borlange, 1979-93 – 1 – sw Kungliga [072]
LUDWIG ACHIM VON ARNIM ALS DRAMATIKER / Hartmann, Max – (Includes bibliographical references) – Breslau: F Hirt, 1911 – 1 – us U.W. Library [430]
Ludwig, Alfred Josef *see* DER KLASSISCHE WIENER FRANZ GRILLPARZER
LUDWIG ANZENGRUBER / Friedmann, Sigismund – Leipzig: H Seemann, 1902 – 1r – 1 – us U.W. Library [430]
LUDWIG ANZENGRUBER : EIN LEBENSBILD / Kleinberg, Alfred – Stuttgart: Cotta, 1921 – 1r – 1 – us U.W. Library [430]
LUDWIG ANZENGRUBER : DER MANN, SEIN WERK, SEINE WELTANSCHAUUNG / Bettelheim, Anton – Dresden: L Ehlermann, 1891 – 1r – 1 – us U.W. Library [430]
LUDWIG ANZENGRUBER / Neumann, Carl Wilhelm – (Includes index) – Leipzig: Reclam, 1920 – 1r – 1 – us U.W. Library [430]
LUDWIG BOERNE : EINE BIOGRAPHISCH-LITERARISCHE STUDIE ZUR FEIER SEINES HUNDERTJAEHRIGEN GEBURTSTAGS / Alberti, Conrad – (Includes bibliographical references) – Leipzig: O Wigand, 1886 – 1 – us U.W. Library [430]
LUDWIG BOERNE : SEIN LEBEN UND SEIN WIRKEN, NACH DEN QUELLEN DARGESTELLT / Holzmann, Michael – (Includes bibliographical references) – Berlin: R Oppenheim, 1888 – 1 – us U.W. Library [430]
LUDWIG BOERNES EINFLUSS AUF HEINRICH HEINE / Santkin, Paul – Bonn, 1913 – 1mf – DM48.00 – 3-8267-3101-8 – gw Hänsel [430]
LUDWIG BOERNES GESAMMELTE SCHRIFTEN / Boerne, Ludwig – Vollstaendige. Ausg. in sechs Baenden nebst Anhand: Nachgelassene Schriften in zwei Baenden. Mit Boernes Portraet, einem Briefe in Faksimile und einer biographisch-kritischen Einleitung von Alfred Klaar. Leipzig, M. Hesse 1899 8 v. in 3. Film Mas 8493 – 1 – us H.U. Library [080]
Ludwig, C G *see*
– DEFINITIONES GENERUM PLANTARUM
– DEFINITIONES GENERUM PLANTARUM IN USUM AUDITORUM
– INSTITUTIONES HISTORICO-PHYSICAE REGNI VEGETABILIS
Ludwig, Christian *see* A DICTIONARY ENGLISH, GERMAN AND FRENCH UND TEUTSCH-ENGLISCHES LEXICON (AEL, ABT.2;4)
Ludwig, Ella A *see* HISTORY OF THE HARBOR DISTRICT OF LOS ANGELES
Ludwig, Guenther *see* STUDIEN ZU EINER MONOGRAPHIE UEBER DEN BAROCKBILDHAUER MICHAEL ZUERN D.J.
Ludwig, Heinrich *see* LEONARDO DA VINCI. DAS BUCH VON DER MALEREI
LUDWIG HEINRICH CHRISTOPH HOELTY : SEIN LEBEN UND DICHTEN / Ruete, Hermann – (Includes bibliographical references) – Guben: E Berger, 1883 – 1r – 1 – us U.W. Library [920]
LUDWIG JACOBOWSKI : WERK, ENTWICKLUNG UND VERHAELTNIS ZUR MODERNE / Reuter, Otto – (Includes bibliographical references) – Berlin: S Calvary, 1900 – 1r – 1 – us U.W. Library [430]
LUDWIG NICOLOVIUS : ROKOKO, REFORM, RESTAURATION / Fischer, Fritz – Stuttgart, 1939 – xix/467p – 9 – DM48.00 – 3-89349-078-7 – gw Hänsel [720]
Ludwig, Otto *see* ZWISCHEN HIMMEL UND ERDE
Ludwig, Roland *see* DIE NEW MODEL ARMY UND DIE LEVELLERS (1647/48)
LUDWIG TIECK ALS UEBERSETZER MITTELHOCHDEUTSCHER DICHTUNG : EINE KRITIK / Brueggemann, Joseph – (Includes bibliographical references) – Trier: J Lintz, 1908 – 1 – us U.W. Library [430]
LUDWIG TIECK AND ENGLAND : A STUDY IN THE LITERARY RELATIONS OF GERMANY AND ENGLAND DURING THE EARLY NINETEENTH CENTURY / Zeydel, Edwin Hermann – (Includes bibliographical references) – Princeton, N.J.: Princeton University Press for the University of Cincinnati, 1931 – 1 – us U.W. Library [410]
LUDWIG TIECK UND DAS ALTE ENGLISCHE THEATER : EIN BEITRAG ZUR GESCHICHTE DER ROMANTIK / Luedeke, Henry – (Includes biliographical references) – Frankfurt am Main: M Diesterweg, 1922 – 1r – 1 – us U.W. Library [410]
LUDWIG TIECKS AUSGEWAEHLTE WERKE IN VIER BAENDEN / ed by Witkowski, Georg – Leipzig: Max Hesse, [1905?] – 1 – us U.W. Library [430]
LUDWIG TIECKS BEZIEHUNGEN ZUR DEUTSCHEN LITERATUR DES 17. JAHRHUNDERTS / Riederer, Frank – (Includes bibliographical references) – Greifswald: J Abel, 1915 – 1r – 1 – us U.W. Library [430]
LUDWIG UHLAND : DER DICHTER UND DER PATRIOT / Hoenes, Christian – Hamburg: J F Richter, 1887 – 1r – 1 – us U.W. Library [430]
LUDWIG UHLAND : SEIN LEBEN UND SEINE DICHTUNGEN: MIT ZAHLREICHEN UNGEDRUCKTEN POESIEN AUS DESSEN NACHLASS UND EINER AUSWAHL VON BRIEFEN / Notter, Friedrich – Stuttgart: J B Metzler, 1863 – 1r – 1 – us U.W. Library [430]
LUDWIG UHLAND : SEINE DARSTELLUNG DER VOLKSDICHTUNG UND DAS VOLKSTUEMLICHE IN SEINEN GEDICHTEN / Hassenstein, Georg – (Includes bibliographical references) – Leipzig: C Reissner, 1887 – 1r – 1 – us U.W. Library [430]
LUDWIG UHLAND : VORTRAG GEHALTEN BEI DER UHLANDFEIER IN BONN AM 11. FEBRUAR 1863 : MIT LITERARHISTORISCHEN BEILAGEN / Jahn, Otto – Bonn: M Cohen, 1863 – 1r – 1 – us U.W. Library [430]
LUDWIG UHLAND ALS DICHTER UND PATRIOT / Dederich, Hermann – (Includes bibliographical references) – Gotha: F A Perthes, 1886 – 1 – us U.W. Library [430]
LUDWIG UHLANDS LEBEN : AUS DESSEN NACHLASS UND AUS EIGENER ERINNERUNG ZUSAMMENGESTELLT / Uhland, Emilie Vischer – Stuttgart: J G Cotta, 1874 – 1r – 1 – us U.W. Library [430]
LUDWIG UHLANDS POLITISCHE BETAETIGUNGEN UDN ANSCHAUUNGEN / Bernhardt, Wilhelm – (Includes bibliographical references) – [s.l: s.n.] 1910: (Rochlitz: Druck von K Meltzer) – 1r – 1 – us U.W. Library [943]
LUDWIG UND ANNEMARIE : ERZAEHLUNG AUS DEM RIES / Meyr, Melchior – Bayreuth: Gauverlag Bayreuth, 1944 – 1r – 1 – us U.W. Library [430]
Ludwig, Werner *see* UNTERSUCHUNGEN UEBER DEN ENTWICKLUNGSGANG UND DIE FUNKTION DES DIALOGS IN DER ISLAENDISCHEN SAGA
LUDWIGSBURGER KREISZEITUNG – (Title changes: Ludwigsburger Wochenblatt, 1818; Ludwigsburger Tagblatt, 1846; Ludwigsburger Zeitung, 1873-1945) – Ludwigsburg, West Germany. 1969- – ca 8r per yr – 1 – gw Mikrofilm [072]
LUDWIGSBURGER TAGBLATT *see* LUDWIGSBURGER KREISZEITUNG
LUDWIGSBURGER WOCHENBLATT *see* LUDWIGSBURGER KREISZEITUNG
LUDWIGSBURGER ZEITUNG *see* LUDWIGSBURGER KREISZEITUNG
Luebbing, Wendel *see* UNTERNEHEMENSZUSAMMENSCHLUSSE NACH 23 GWB UND ART 66 MUV
LUEBECKER BEOBACHTER – Luebeck, may 31 1929-aug 31 1931, 1932-may 31 1933 – 9r – 1 – gw Mikrofilm [072]
LUEBECKER BUERGERFREUND – (Cont by: Luebecker Correspondent, apr 2 1848. Luebecker Volksfreund, aug 6 1848. Der Volksbote, jul 4 1849) – Luebeck, oct 8 1843-nov 16 1848, jul 4 1849-65 – 15r – 1 – gw Mikrofilm [943]
LUEBECKER CORRESPONDENT *see* LUEBECKER BUERGERFREUND
LUEBECKER GENERALANZEIGER *see* GENERALANZEIGER
LUEBECKER NACHRICHTEN / ed by Lauenburgische Nachrichten – Ratzeburg, West Germany. 1977- – ca 9r per yr – 1 – gw Mikrofilm [072]
LUEBECKER NACHRICHTEN – Luebeck, Apr 1946-Dec 1949 – 4r – 1 – DM300.00 – gw Mikro Press [072]
LUEBECKER NACHRICHTEN / ed by Ostholsteiner Nachrichten – Oldenburg, Holstein, West Germany. 1977- – ca 9r per yr – 1 – gw Mikrofilm [072]
LUEBECKER NACHRICHTEN *see*
– EISENBAHN-ZEITUNG
– LUEBECKER NACHRICHTEN-BLATT
LUEBECKER NACHRICHTEN-BLATT – Luebeck, May 1945-Mar 1946 – 1r – 1 – DM75.00 – gw Mikro Press [072]
LUEBECKER NACHRICHTEN-BLATT – (Title change: Luebecker Nachrichten, 3 Apr 1946) – Luebeck, West Germany. 1968- – ca 8r per yr – 1 – gw Mikrofilm [072]
LUEBECKER NEUESTE NACHRICHTEN *see* EISENBAHN-ZEITUNG
LUEBECKER POST – Luebeck, Jul 1945-Mar 1946 – 1r – 1 – DM75.00 – gw Mikro Press [072]
LUEBECKER POST – Luebeck, West Germany. 25 Jul 1945-30 Mar 1946 – 1r – 1 – gw Mikrofilm [072]
LUEBECKER VOLKSFREUND *see* LUEBECKER BUERGERFREUND
LUEBECKER VORSTADT-ZEITUNG *see* EISENBAHN-ZEITUNG
LUEBECKER ZEITUNG – Luebeck, apr 2 1942-may 1, 1945 – 7r – 1 – gw Mikrofilm [943]
LUEBECKER ZEITUNG – Luebeck, mar 16 1849-jun 30 1866 – 18r – 1 – gw Mikrofilm [943]
LUEBECKER ZEITUNG – Luebeck, oct 1 1872-sep 20 1890 – 26r – 1 – gw Mikrofilm [943]
LUEBECKISCHE ANZEIGEN – Luebeck, 1751-jun 1795, 1796-1933 – 260r – 1 – gw Mikrofilm [943]
Luebke, William F *see* EKKEHARD
Luebker, Detlev Lorenz *see* LEXICON DER SCHLESWIG-HOLSTEIN-LAUENBURGISCHEN UND EUTINISCHEN SCHRIFTSTELLER VON 1796 BIS 1828
Luebs, Johann *see* LUEBS'EN SIN RIEMELS
LUEBS'EN SIN RIEMELS : DICHTUNGEN / Luebs, Johann – Buetzow i. Mecklbg.: M Keuer, 1913 – 1r – 1 – us U.W. Library [810]

Lueddecke, Theodor *see* SCHWERTLILIEN
Luedeke, Hans-Peter *see* UNTERSUCHUNG VON SCHALTNETZTEILEN MIT KONTINUIERLICHEN RESONANZSCHWINGUNGEN
Luedeke, Henry *see* LUDWIG TIECK UND DAS ALTE ENGLISCHE THEATER
Luedemann, Hermann *see* DIE ANTHROPOLOGIE DES APOSTELS PAULUS UND IHRE STELLUNG INNERHALB SEINER HEILSLEHRE
LUEDEMANNSCHE ZEITUNG *see* HILDESHEIMER RELATIONS-COURIER
LUEDENSCHEIDER NACHRICHTEN – Luedenscheid, West Germany. 1992- – 8r per yr – 1 – gw Mikrofilm [072]
Lueder, Fritz *see* DIE EPISCHEN WERKE OTTO LUDWIGS UND IHR VERHAELTNIS ZU CHARLES DICKENS
LUEDERITZBUCHTER ZEITUNG – Luederitzbucht, South West Africa. 1909-37 – 1 – sa State Libr [072]
Lueders, H *see* ZUR GESCHICHTE UND GEOGRAPHIE OSTTURKESTANS
Luedtke, G *see* MINERVA-HANDBUECHER
Luehmann, Johann *see* JOHANN BALTHASAR SCHUPP
Luelmann, Christian *see* DAS BILD DES CHRISTENTUMS BEI DEN GROSSEN DEUTSCHEN IDEALISTEN
LUENEBURGER ZEITUNG – Lueneburg, jan 2-apr 16 1945 – 1r – 1 – gw Mikrofilm [943]
LUENEBURGSCHE ANZEIGEN – Lueneburg-Celle, Germany. 1848-1849 – 1r – 1 – gw Mikrofilm [072]
Luenemann, Gottlieb *see* CRITICAL AND EXEGETICAL HANDBOOK TO...EPISTLES OF ST PAUL TO... THESSALONIANS
Luengo, Juan *see*
- AL SINDICATO DE LA COMUNIDAD DE LABRADORES (PROYECTO DE COOPERATIVA VITICO-ALCOHOLERA EN ALMENDRALEJO)
- LIBRO...FR. ANDRES DE GUADALUPE

Luerssen, C *see*
- BEITRAEGE ZUR ENTWICKLUNGS-GESCHICHTE DER FARN-SPORANGIEN
- BIBLIOTHECA BOTANICA

Luetcke, Heinrich *see* FRIEDRICH GOTTLIEB KLOPSTOCK
LUETFIYE-I VEHBI / Vehbi – Istanbul: 1252 [1836] – $10.00 – us MEDOC [470]
Luetgert, Wilhelm *see* DAS REICH GOTTES: NACH DEN SYNOPTISCHEN EVANGELIEN
Lueth, Oliver Andreas *see* OPTIMIERUNG VON ROBOTERBAHNEN MIT KOLLISIONSVERMEIDUNG MITTELS DER POTENTIALFELDMETHODE
Luetjohann, CH *see* GAI SOLLII APOLLINARIS SIDONII EPISTULAE ET CARMINA (MGH 1: 8.BD)
Luetteken, Anton *see* DIE DRESDENER ROMANTIK UND HEINRICH VON KLEIST
Luettge, Willy *see*
- DIE RECHTFERTIGUNGSLEHRE CALVINS
- RELIGION UND DOGMA
- DIE TRENNUNG VON STAAT UND KIRCHE IN FRANKREICH UND DER FRANZOESISCHE PROTESTANTISMUS

Luetzkendorf, Felix *see* WIEDERGEBURT
Luetzow, Franz H H V von *see*
- A HISTORY OF BOHEMIAN LITERATURE
- THE HUSSITE WARS
- THE LIFE AND TIMES OF MASTERS JOHN HUS

LUETZOWS LAGER : EIN VATERLAENDISCHES VOLKSSCHAUSPIEL / Oels, Friedrich – Berlin-Friedenau: K Fischer, [1913?] – 1r – 1 – us U.W. Library [820]
LUFKIN NEWS – Lufkin. Texas. 1913- – 1 – us UMI [071]
DIE LUFTFLOTTE / German Aviation Society – Berlin. Amtliche Zeitschrift des Deutschen Luftflottenvereins. v. 1, no. 1-v. 11, no. 12. Oct. 1908-Feb. Mar. 1919 – 1 – 35.00r – us Hoover Inst Photo [073]
DAS LUFTSCHIFF IN VOELKERRECHTLICHER UND STRAFRECHTLICHER BEZIEHUNG / Gruenwald, F – Hannover, 1908 – 1mf – 1 – ILM-1627/1 – ne IDC [327]
DIE LUFTSCHIFFAHRT... / Daus, E – Erlangen, 1908 – 1mf – 1 – ILM-1628/1 – ne IDC [327]
LUFTSTREITKRAEFTE; NACHRICHTENBLATT – Germany. Mar. 14-Oct. 31, 1918 – 1 – 35.00r – us Hoover Inst Photo [629]
LUG ZELENYI. KNIGA STATEI / Belyi, A – 1910. BR-569 2 – 8 – ne IDC [460]
Lugard, F L *see* A TROPICAL DEPENDENCY
Lugard, Frederick John Dealtry *see*
- THE RISE OF OUR EAST AFRICAN EMPIRE
- THE RISE OF OUR EAST AFRICAN EMPIRE: EARLY EFFORTS IN NYASALAND AND UGANDA
- THE STORY OF THE UGANDA PROTECTORATE

LUGARES DE EXTREMADURA : EMERITA AUGUSTA / Sanches Loro, Domingo – Caceres, 1947 – 1 – sp Bibl Santa Ana [946]
LUGARES DE EXTREMADURA, EMERITA AUGUSTA. 1ST PARTE : HISTORIA Y MONUMENTOS / Sanchez Loro, Domingo – Caceres: Imp. Floriano, 1947 – 1 – sp Bibl Santa Ana [946]
LUGH : EMPORIO COMMERCIALE DEL GUIBA / Ferrandi, Ugo – Roma:Societa geografica italiana, 1903 – us Res Libr [960]
LUGHATNAMAH / ed by Dihkhuda, Ali Akbar – Tihran: Danishgah-i-Tihran, 1946-1983 – 382mf – 9 – $350.00 – us MEDOC [470]
Luginin, V F *see* SEL'SKIE SSUDNYE TOVARICHESTVA
Lugnier, S *see* HUIPILS TZOTZILS ET LEURS DECORS
Lugo, A M *see* SPORT SOCIALIZATION OF CEREBRAL PALSIED ADOLESCENTS
LUHAIJUN DAYUANSHUAI DABENYING GONGBAO XUANBIAN, 2, 1923-24 – A selection of bulletins of the Generalissimo's Headquarters, Feb 1923-Apr 1924.Comp. by Du Yongzheng.5 fiches. F-H117 – 9 – $27.00 – cc Microforms [950]
LU-HSING TSA-CHIH – "China Traveler". 28 v. Shanghai. 1927-54. monthly. Lacking: v. 6 (8) 1932; v. 10 (9) 1936; v. 11 (9-12) 1937; v. 12 (1-3, 5-12) 1938; v. 13 (1, 2, 4, 5, 7-9) 1939; v. 15 (1, 10, 11) 1941; v. 17 (9, 11, 12) 1943; v. 18 (1-11) 1944; v. 19 (1-12) 1945; v. 20 (1, 2, 6-9) 1946; v. 21 (4, 10, 11) 1947; v. 24 (12) 1950; v. 25 (4, 6, 9) 1951; v. 26 (1, 3, 5-12) 1952. BCH-312 1 – 9 – ne IDC [073]
LU-HSUN FENG – (Lacking: Pt 2) – Lu-hsun Winds, 1939 – 8 – BCH-973 2 – ne IDC [920]
LUI HO, SIVE VOCABULARIUM SINENSE IN KORAIANUM CONVERSUM... / Siebold, P F von – Lugduni Batavorum, 1838 – 1mf – ne IDC [480]
Luigi *see* M. L'ABBE SAX ET SES SOUFFLEURS OU REFUTATION DES ERREURS CONTENUES DANS LE MANIFESTE LIBERAL QUEBECQUOIS
Luiken, J *see*
- BESCHOUWING DER WERELD
- DE BYKORF DES GEMOEDS
- JESUS EN DE ZIEL. EEN GEESTELIJCKE SPIEGEL VOOR 'T GEMOED
- JESUS EN DE ZIEL. EEN GEESTELIJKE SPIEGEL VOOR 'T GEMOED
- HET LEERZAAM HUISRAAD
- HET LEERZAAM HUISRAED
- DES MENSCHEN BEGIN, MIDDEN EN EINDE
- DE ONWAARDIGE WERELD
- HET OVERVLOEIJEND HERTE
- SCHOUWTOONEEL DER MARTELAREN
- SPIEGEL VAN HET MENSELIJK BEDRYF
- VONCKEN DER LIEFDE JESU, VAN HET GODT-BEGERENDE ZIELEN-VUUR
- VONKEN DER LIEFDE JEZUS, VAN HET GOD-BEGEERENDE ZIELEN-VUUR
- DE ZEDELYKE EN STICHTELYKE GEZANGEN

Luiken, K *see* SPIEGEL VAN HET MENSELIJK BEDRYF
LUIS DE MORALES, EL DIVINO / Juez Nieto, Antonio – Badajoz: Tip.nuevo diario, 1925 – 1 – sp Bibl Santa Ana [946]
LUIS DE MORALES EN ARROYO DE LA LUZ / Criado Valcarcel, Vicente – Apuntes historicos Badajoz: Imp. Diputacion Provincial, 1963. Sep.Rev.Estudios Extremenos – 1 – sp Bibl Santa Ana [910]
Luis de Santa Maria, Fray *see* OCTAVA SAGRADAMENTE CULTA...UNICO MILAGRO DE SAN LORENZO DEL ESCORIAL
Luis, Werner *see* DAS BAUERNTUM IM GRENZ- UND VOLKSDEUTSCHEN ROMAN DER GEGENWART
LUISIANA – Sevilla – 5r – 5,6 – sp Cultura [977]
LUISIANA. CARGOS, DATAS, CUENTAS (ANNO 1762-1819) – Sevilla – 87r – 5,6 – sp Cultura [977]
DE LUITENANT-GENERAAL J. VAN SWIETEN CONTRA DEN LUITENANT-GENERAAL G. M. VERSPYCK / Swieten, Jan van – Zalt-Bommel: J. Noman, 1880 – 1 – us U.W. Library [949]
Lujan, Francisco *see*
- ITINERARIO DE UN VIAGE (SIC)
- MEMORIA...EXPOSICION...LONDRES

Lujan Garcia, Jose *see* BENITO ARIAS MONTANO. DATOS BIOGRAFICOS
Lujan Suarez, Pedro de *see*
- HISTORIA DE LOS ESTABLECIMIENTOS ULTRAMARINOS. TOMO 1
- HISTORIA DE LOS ESTABLECIMIENTOS ULTRAMARINOS. TOMO 2
- HISTORIA DE LOS ESTABLECIMIENTOS ULTRAMARINOS. TOMO 3
- HISTORIA DE LOS ESTABLECIMIENTOS ULTRAMARINOS. TOMO 4
- HISTORIA DE LOS ESTABLECIMIENTOS ULTRAMARINOS. TOMO 5

Lukach, H C *see* A BIBLIOGRAPHY OF SIERRA LEONE, PRECEDED BY AN ESSAY ON THE ORIGIN, CHARACTER AND PEOPLES OF THE COLONY AND PROTECTORATE
Lukachevdkii, Aleksandr Timofeevich (Emelyan Yaroslavdkii) *see* SEKTANTSTVO PREZHDE I TEPER'
LUKARDIS : SCHAUSPIEL IN DREI AKTEN / Wassermann, Jakob – Berlin: S Fischer, 1932, c1931 – 1r – 1 – us U.W. Library [820]
LUKAS DER ARZT DER VERFASSER DES DRITTEN EVANGELIUMS UND DER APOSTELGESCHICHTE / Harnack, Adolf von – Leipzig, 1906 – 3mf – 8 – ne Slangenburg [220]
LUKAS HOCHSTRASSERS HAUS : EIN ROMAN / Zahn, Ernst – Stuttgart: Deutsche Verlags-Anstalt, 1908 – 1r – 1 – us U.W. Library [830]
DAS LUKASEVANGELIUM UND DIE APOSTELGESCHICHTE : WERKE DESSELBEN VERFASSERS / Friedrich, Johann – Halle a. S: C A Kaemmerer, 1890 – 1mf – 9 – 0-8370-3205-9 – 1985-1205 – us A.T.L.A. [220]
DIE LUKASKATENE DES NIKETAS VON HERAKLEIA (T.U.U. 2-22/4) / Sickenberger, J – Leipzig, 1902 – 2mf – 9 – ne Slangenburg [240]
LUKIAN VON SAMOSATA UND DAS NEUE TESTAMENT : RELIGIONS-GESCHICHTLICHE UND PARAENETISCHE PARALLELEN (T.U.U. 5-76) / Betz, H D: – Berlin, 1961 – 5mf – 9 – ne Slangenburg [240]
Lukiewski, Mary A *see* ROMAN CATHOLIC PRIESTS' ATTITUDES AND BEHAVIORS REGARDING SELECTED SEXUALITY ISSUES
Lukin, A P *see* SKROMNYI NABLIUDATEL'
Lukin, Vl *see* SOCHINENIIA I PEREVODY
Lukman, Karmani *see* TELUK GONG
Lulle, Raymond *see*
- ARS BREVIS
- ARS GENERALIS ULTIMA
- OPERA LATINA 134
- OPERA LATINA 76-81
- OPERA LATINA 114-117
- OPERA LATINA 123-127
- OPERA LATINA 135-141
- OPERA LATINA 190-200
- OPERA LATINA 201-207
- OPERA LATINA 208-212
- OPERA LATINA SIVE IN LINGUAM LATINAM TRANSLATA 86-91

Lulli, Jean-B *see* ACIS ET GALATEE, PAROLES DE CAMPISTRON, MUSIQUE DE LULLI
Lully, Jean-Baptiste *see*
- ACIS ET GALATEE: PASTORALE HEROIQUE...
- [AMADIS. SELECTIONS]
- ROLAND
- THESEE

THE LUMBERJACK – (Also known as: H.S.T.C. Hooter) – Arcata, CA. 1929-1993 – 19r – 1 – $950.00 – B03141 – us Library Micro [071]
LUMBERLOGUE – Klamath Falls OR. Sep 23 1925 – 1 – us U.O. Library [071]
LUMBERMAN – Stevens Point. Wis. 1863-66 – 1 – us UMI [071]
Lumbreras Valiente, Pedro *see*
- LOS CAMPAMENTOS DE QUINTO CECILIO METELO PIO
- EL CUMPLIMIENTO DE LAS OGLIGACIONES
- LAS MUNICIPALIDADES HISPANO-PORTUGUESAS SU ORIGEN Y DESARROLLO HASTA EL SIGLO 15

Lumby, J R *see* CHRONICON HENRICI KNIGHTON, VEL CNITTHON, MONACHI LEYCESTRENSIS (RS92)
Lumby, J R (v3-9) *see* POLYCHRONICON RANULPHI HIGDEN MONACHI CESTRENSIS (RS41)
Lumby, Joseph Rawson *see*
- THE ACTS OF THE APOSTLES
- EPISTLES OF ST PETER
- THE FIRST BOOK OF KINGS: WITH MAPS, INTRODUCTION AND NOTES
- GREEK LEARNING IN THE WESTERN CHURCH DURING THE SEVENTH AND EIGHTH CENTURIES, A.D.
- A POPULAR INTRODUCTION TO THE NEW TESTAMENT
- THE SECOND BOOK OF THE KINGS: WITH INTRODUCTION AND NOTES

LUMEM : ORGAO DA FEDERACAO ESPIRITA ALAGOANA – Maceio, Alagoas. Out, Dez 1908; Jan 1909 – 1,5,6 – bl Biblioteca [072]
LUMEN AMAZONENSE : ORGAM DA SOCIEDADE LITTERARIA E SPORTIVA ESTUDANTINA – Manaos, Amazonas. 11 Maio 1912 – 1,5,6 – bl Biblioteca [072]
LUMEN VITAE – 14(1959) – 14mf – 9 – Dfl49.00 – ne Slangenburg [073]
LUMI NOSIDADES / Manas Marquecho, Jose Luis – Puente Genil. Tip. La Ideal, 1944 – 1 – sp Bibl Santa Ana [810]
LA LUMIERE – Hebdomadaire d'education civique et d'action republicaine puis Le grand hebdomadaire des gauches. Paris. mai 1927-juin 1940 – 1 – fr A.C.R.P.P. [073]
LA LUMIERE – Journal non politique. Beaux-arts, heliographie, science puis REVUE DE LA PHOTOGRAPHIE. Paris. Fev 1851-mars 1867 – 1 – fr A.C.R.P.P. [073]
LA LUMIERE – Notre Dame de Levis, Canada. 17 nov 1913-1 jan 1921 – 1r – 1 – Can$50.00 – cn Can Microfilming [072]
LA LUMIERE – Quebec, Canada. v1 n6. 2 fev 1924 – 1r – 1 – Can$25.00 – cn Can Microfilming [072]
LA LUMIERE A BON MARCHE – Montreal, Canada. 31 jan 1904 – 1r – 1 – Can$25.00 – cn Can Microfilming [072]
LA LUMIERE DE L'OUVRIER – Montreal, Canada. v1 n4. 16 mar 1878-v1 n8. 11 mai 1878 – 1r – 1 – Can$25.00 – cn Can Microfilming [072]
LUMIERE ET VIE – 1951-91 (complete) – Inquire – 1 – ATLA S0569 – us A.T.L.A. [073]
LA LUMO – (Livret en Esperanto) – Montreal, Canada. 1 jan 1902-aut 1903 – 1r – 1 – Can$25.00 – cn Can Microfilming [072]
Lumper, G *see* HISTORIA THEOLOGICA-CRITICA DE VITA
Lumsden, Carlos B *see* THE DAWN OF MODERN ENGLAND
LUN TAO (CCC104) / Chin, Yo-Lin – (In Chinese) – [s.l: s.n, 1940] – 1r – 1 – 1984-B500 – us A.T.L.A. [240]
Luna, Alvaro de *see* LIBRO DE LAS CLARAS E VIRTUOSAS MUGERES (SIC) POR...
Luna, Francisco *see* SAGRADAS DECLAMACIONES FUNEBRES PANEQYRICAS, EN LAS SOLEMNES EXEQUIAS...A LOS GLORIOSAS E INMORTALES...
Luna Gomez, Sergio *see* NOCIONES DE ARITMETICA Y GEOMETRIA
Luna, Juan *see* SAGRADAS DECLAMACIONES FUNEBRES PANEQYRICAS, EN LAS SOLEMNES EXEQUIAS...A LOS GLORIOSAS E INMORTALES...
Luna Rancel, Felipe *see* ESPANA ANTES Y DESPUES DE LA VENIDA DEL DIRECTORIO
Luna Vega, J *see*
- APOLOGIA DEL DOCTOR...
- APRENDIZ DE LA EXERCITATION 36
- EXERCITATION 36...EL LETARGO...
- EXERCITATION 37. CENSURA AL DISCURSO...
- EXERCUTATIO 31...VERSATUR IUSTA...GALENI DOCTRINAM...

Luna y Gomez, Sergio *see*
- ELEMENTOS DE TRIGONOMETRIA RECTILINEA
- PROBLEMAS DE ARITMETICA
- TRATADO ELEMENTAL DE ARITMETICA

Lunacharskii, A V *see*
- KRITICHESKIE ETIUDY
- RUSSKAIA LITERATURA POD RED. BELCHIKOVA

THE LUNACY OF SUPERMAN & OTHER PLAYS / Arrigoni, Enrico – 1977. 598p. 1 fiche (42x) – 9 – 1.00f – at Libertarian Micro [320]
Lunan, J *see* HORTUS JAMAICENSIS
Luncz, A M *see*
- HA-ME'AMMER
- YERUSHALAYIM, LE-ZEKHER AVRAHAM MOSHEH LUNCZ

Lund, Chr. *see* RELATION TIL KONG FREDERIK 3 OM DAVID DANELLS TRE REJSER TIL GRONLAND 1652-54
LUNDA FOR BEGINNERS / Fisher, M K – Mutshatsha: La Garenganze Evangelical Mission, 1951 – us Res Libr [490]
Lundberg, E *see* ZAPISKI PISATELIA
Lundberg, P *see* LA TYPOLOGIE BAPTISMALE DANS L'ANCIENNE EGLISE
Lundegren, Herberta M *see*
– HOW LEISURE BELIEFS RELATE TO ATTITUDES TOWARD THE NORMALIZATION PRINCIPLE AS PERCEIVED BY SERVICE PROVIDERS FOR PEOPLE WITH MENTAL RETARDATION
– THE LEISURE ACTIVITY SELECTION PROCESS
– LEISURE BEHAVIOR OF LESBIANS IN RELATION TO ALCOHOL CONSUMPTION
Lundell, Lynda *see* NUTRITIONAL KNOWLEDGE, ATTITUDES, AND PRACTICES AND THE ACTUAL DIETARY INTAKES OF FEMALE COLLEGE ATHLETES
Lundgreen, Friedrich *see* DIE BENUTZUNG DER PFLANZENWELT IN DER ALTTESTAMENTLICHEN RELIGION
LUNDS DAGBLAD – Lund, Sweden. 1897-1960 – 1 – sw Kungliga [072]
LUNDS VECKOBLAD – Lund, Sweden. 1961-70 – 1 – sw Kungliga [072]
LUNDS WECKOBLAD NYTT OCH GAMMALT – Lund, Sweden. 1775-1897 – 48r – 1 – sw Kungliga [072]
LUNDSKA POSTTIJENDER – Lund, Sweden. 1717-18 – 1 – sw Kungliga [072]
Lundy-Ekman, Laurie *see* SOFT NEUROLOGICAL SIGNS IN CLUMSY CHILDREN
Lundy's Lane Historical Society *see* ANNUAL REPORT
LA LUNE – Paraissant toutes les nouvelles lunes puis Semaine comique illustree. no. 1-98. Paris. oct 1865-janv 1868 – 1 – fr A.C.R.P.P. [073]
Luneau, R *see* LE MARIAGE COUTUMIER DANS LA SOCIETE BAMBARA
LUNENBURG 1707-1900 – (Mf 1-3: Marrs, Intents 1727-97. Mf 3-5: Births 1707-96. Mf 5,12: Deaths 1707-90. Mf 6: Out-of-Town Marr 1730-98. Mf 7-9: Town Records 1728-63. Mf 9-10, 12: Intentions 1747-85. Mf 10-12: Birth & Death 1707-91. Mf 11-12: Marriages 1730-95. Mf 12: Marks & Strays 1759-94. Mf 13-16: Town Records 1763-96. Mf 16-22: Vitals 1764-1895. Mf 23-27: Vitals 1764-1849. Mf 28-34: Proprietors 1729-1833. Mf 35-42: Town Records 1728-96. Mf 43-44: Treasurer 1745-1836. Mf 45-50: Selectmen 1765-1814. Mf 51-57: Town Records 1797-1828. Mf 58-62: Town Records 1828-48. Mf 61: Deaths 1841-43. Mf 63-64: Church Vital 1805-60. Mf 65-66: Births 1843-72. Mf 66: Marrs & Deaths 1843-54. Mf 67-68: Deaths 1855-91. Mf 69-70: Marriages 1854-91. Mf 71: Births 1873-91. Mf 72-74: Vitals 1892-1900) – (mf ed 1993) – 74mf – 9 – us Holbrook [920]
LES LUNETTES DES PRINCES / Meschinot, Jean – [Paris]: Jean du Pre, [ca 1492] – 1 – F87.92 – fr Armell [440]
LES LUNETTES DES PRINCES : VINGT-CINQ BALLADES / Meschinot, Jean – 15-16th cent – 1 – F75.90 – fr Armell [780]
Luney, Kenneth Dean *see* MR. JUSTICE BRANDEIS AND THE PROBLEMS OF LABOR
LUNG – v. 101-158. 1947-80 – 1,5,9 – 5699.00 – us UMI [073]
LUNG-CHOU CHI-LUEH – 1803, 2. BCH-657a 2 – 8 – ne IDC [950]
LUNG-CH'UAN HSIEN-CHIH – 1818, 40. BCH-612 2 – 8 – ne IDC [950]
LUNG-MEN HSIEN-CHIH – 1851, 16. BCH-595 2 – 8 – ne IDC [950]
LUNG-T'U KUNG-AN – A detective novel. BCH-945 2 – 8 – ne IDC [830]
Lunier, Jules Joseph Ludger *see*
– DE LA PRODUCTION ET DE LA CONSOMMATION DES BOISSONS ALCOOLIQUES EN FRANCE
– DE L'INFLUENCE DES GRANDES COMMOTIONS POLITIQUES ET SOCIALES SUR LE DEVELOPPEMENT DES MALADIES MENTALES: MOUVEMENT DE L'ALIENATION MENTALE EN FRANCE PENDANT LES ANNEES 1869 A 1873
– RAPPORT GENERAL A M. LE MINISTRE DE L'INTERIEUR SUR LE SERVICE DES ALIENES EN 1874 PAR LES INSPECTEURS GENERAUX DU SERVICE
L'Union Communiste *see* L'INTERNATIONALE
L'Union Departementale des Syndicats Unitaires d'Oran *see* LE REVEIL OUVRIER
L'Union des Femmes d'Algerie *see* FEMMES D'ALGERIE
L'Union Internationale des Ecrivains Revolutionnaires *see*
– LA LITTERATURE DE LA REVOLUTION MONDIALE
– LA LITTERATURE INTERNATIONALE
L'Union pour la Verite *see* LIBRES ENTRETIENS
Lunn, Arnold *see*
– SPAIN AND THE CHRISTIAN FRONT: UBI CRUX IBI PATRIA
– SPAIN, THE UNPOPULAR FRONT
LUNNYE MURAV'I, SHESTAIA KNIGA RAZSKAZOV / Gippius, Z N – izd. Al'Tsiona. M. 1912. BR-715 2 – 8 – ne IDC [460]
Lunsford, Isaac *see* JOURNAL
LUNTANDANYA – Kitwe, Zambia. -f. 1959-62. 1 reel – 1 – uk British Libr Newspaper [072]
Lunts, L *see* BERTRAN-DE-BORN
Lunts, L A *see* DENEZHNOE OBIAZATEL'STVO V GRAZHDANSKOM I KOLLIZIONNOM PRAVE KAPITALISTICHESKIKH STAN. M
LUN-YU PAN-YUEH-K'AN – The analects fortnightly. Shangahi. 1932-49. Available: (nrs. 1-116) 1932-37. BCH-311 2 – 8 – ne IDC [480]
Lupis-Vucic, Ivo F *see* PAPERS
IL LUPO – Omaha, Nebraska. 1925-1926 – us I.H.R.C. [073]
Luppov, S P *see*
– ISTORIIA BIBLIOTEKI AKADEMII NAUK SSSR, 1714-1964
– MEL'TS, M.IA. RUSSKII FOL'KLOR
– RUSSKII FOLKLOR
LUPTA CFR – Bucharest, Romania. -w. 1969-70. 2 reels – 1 – uk British Libr Newspaper [949]
Lupton *see* LIVES OF THE PRIMITIVE FATHERS
Lupton, J H *see* ARCHBISHOP WAKE AND THE PROJECT OF UNION (1717-1720) BETWEEN THE GALLICAN AND ANGLICAN CHURCHES
Luque, C *see* APOLINEO CADUCEO...CONCORDIA ENTRE OPINIONES...SOBRE CONSULTAS DE LOS MEDICOS...
Luquet, Georges-H *see* L'ART PRIMITIF
Lur'e, A *see* DETSKII RAI
Lur'e, E S *see* TSENTRAL'NYI OBLASTNOI KOOPERATIVNYI BANK
Lur'e, Gl *see*
– SOVETSKOE KOOPERATIVNOE ZAKONODATEL'STVO
– ZAKONY O FINANSAKH POTREBITEL'SKOI KOOPERATSII
Lur'e, Ia. S *see* IDEOLOGICHESKAIA BOR'BA V RUSSKOI PUBLITSISTIKE
Lur'e, ML *see*
– OCHERKI KREDITNOI KOOPERATSII V SSSR
– OSNOVY SEL'SKOI KREDITNOI KOOPERATSII
LURE OF GOLD – 1845-60 – 1 – us Ross [976]
LURGAN MAIL – Dec 18 1897-1901; Jan 4-Dec 27 1902; 1903-38; Jan 7 1939-Jun 1977; Jul 7-Dec 29 1977; 1978-82; Jan 6 1983-84; 1986-Jun 1991; Jul 4-Dec 24 1991; 1992-96 – 124 1/2r – 1 – uk British Libr Newspaper [072]
Luscinius, Ottmar *see*
– MUSICAE INSTITUTIONES OTHAMARI NACHTGALL ARGENTINI A NEMINE UN QUA PRIUS PARI FACILITATE TENTATE STUDIOSO, QUI AMOUSOI ESSE NOLINT NO MEDIPCRITER CONDUCIBILES
– MUSURGIA SEU PRAXIS MUSICAE
– MUSURGIA SEU PRAXIS MUSICAE ILLIUS PRIMO QUAE INSTRUMENTIS AGITUR CERTA RATIO
Luscombe, David K *see* APPLIED THERAPEUTICS
Luserke, Martin *see*
– DIE FAHRT NACH LETZTESAND
– DIE LEGENDE VON DEM ERZWUNGENEN BRUDER
Lusignan, Alphonse *see* L'ECHO DE LA GATINEAU
Lusignan de Cypre, E de *see* LES GENEALOGIES DE SOIXANTE ET SEPT TRES-NOBLES ET TRES-ILLUSTRES MAISONS, PARTIE DE FRANCE, PARTIE ESTRAGERES...
Lusignano, S di *see*
– DESCRIPTION DE TOVTE L'ISLE DE CYPRE, ET DES ROYS, PRINCES, ET SEIGNEURS, TANT PAYENS QUE CHRESTIENS, ...
– LES DROICTS, AVTORITEZ ET PREROGATIVES QVE PRETENDENT AU ROYAVME DE HIERUSALEM
– LES GENEALOGIES DE SOIXANTE ET SEPT TRES NOBLES ET TRES ILLUSTRES MAISONS, PARTIE DE FRANCE, PARTIE ESTRAGERES, YSSUES DE MEROUEE
– HISTOIRE CONTENANT VNE SOMMAIRE DESCRIPTION DES GENEALOGIES, ALLIANCES, ET GESTES DE TOUS LES PRINCES ET GRANS SEIGNEURS
LA LUSITANIA CELTIBERICA / Arenas Lopez, Anselmo – 1897 – 9 – 1.50f – sp Bibl Santa Ana [946]
Lusk, D W *see*
– EIGHTY YEARS OF ILLINOIS POLITICS AND POLITICIANS 1809-1889
– HISTORY OF MCDONOUGH COUNTY
Lust, John *see* WESTERN BOOKS ON CHINA PUBLISHED UP TO 1850
Lustig, Jacob Willem *see* INLIEDIG TOT DE MUZYKKUNDE...
Lustig, Johann Wilhelm *see*
– INLEIDING TOT DE MUZIEKKUNDE
– MUZYKALE SPRAAKKONST
– TWAALF REDENEERINGEN OVER NUTTIGE MUZIKAALE ONDERWERPEN. MET 20 CIERLYCKE OP KOPER GESNEDENE NOOTEN-PLATEN EN MET EEN VOLLEDIG REGISTER
LUSTIGE BLAETTER – Berlin, 1889-91, 1895-1902, 1904-06, 1908, 1910, 1915-16, 1918, 1922-25, jan 1927, 1932, 1941 – 21r – 1 – Dist. gw Mikrofilm – gw Misc Inst [072]
LUSTIGE BLETER = JOLLY LEAVES – (In Yiddish) – New York City, NY. v1 no1 27 Jan 1910-v1 no3 Mar 1910 – 1r – 1 – $30.00 – cn Can Microfilming [071]
LUSTIGE REYSS-BESCHREIBUNG AUS SALTZBURG IN VERSCHIEDENE LAENDER / Stranitzky, Joseph Anton; ed by Werner, R M – Wien: C Konegen, 1883 – 1r – 1 – us U.W. Library [943]
DER LUSTIGE SCHUSTER, ODER DER TEUFEL IST LOS, ZWEYTER THEIL / Hiller, Johann Adam – Eine comische Oper in drey Aufzuegen. (The music, originally composed by Johann Standfuss, was revised by Johann Adam Hiller, who also partly composed the text anew). 1771 – 9 – us Sibley [780]
A LUTA – Curitiba, 26 May 188; Jun-28 Sept 1887 – 1,5,6 – bl Biblioteca [072]
A LUTA – Lisbon. No.1-793. 25 Aug 1975-14 Apr 1978. Incomplete. (Portuguese Revolution of 1974. Newspapers from Portugal publ. from 21 Feb 1971 to 15 Feb 1980, collected and filmed by University of Wisconsin-Madison libraries.) – 1 – us U.W. Library [072]
A LUTA – Pirapora, 10 Jan-Jun 1934; Apr-Jun, Sep, Nov-Dec 1935; Jan-Feb, Apr, Jun 1936; 23 Oct 1937 – 1,5,6 – bl Biblioteca [072]
LU-TA JEN-MIN JIH-PAO – Dairen, China. Lu-ta Peoples Daily. Feb-May 1952; Mar-Apr, Jun-Jul, Oct-Dec 1955. 2 reels – 1 – 54.00 – us Chinese Res [072]
LU-TA JEN-MIN JIH-PAO = LU-TA PEOPLE'S DAILY – Dairen, China. Feb-May 1952; Mar-Apr, Jun-Jul, Oct-Dec 1955 – 2r – 1 – $54.00 – us Chinese Res [072]
LU-TA JIH-PAO – Dairen, China. Lu-ta Daily. 1956-60. 10 reels – 1 – 275.00 – us Chinese Res [072]
A LUTA (NEW YORK) – (Library has: v.28,no.23-v.29,no.18,21-v.32,no.11,13-v.39,no.11; Dec. 9, 1964-June 11, 1975) – New York: A luta, 19??- – 1 – CSUX86-S214 – us Hoover Inst Photo [978]
LU-TA PEOPLE'S DAILY *see* LU-TA JEN-MIN JIH-PAO
O LUTADOR : SEMANARIO CATHOLICO – Manhumirim, 26 Nov 1933; Feb 1939; Jul 1942; Apr-May, Jul, Nov 1952; Feb 1953; Feb 1955; Nov 1956; Jun, 25 Aug 1957 – 1,5,6 – bl Biblioteca [072]
Lute, Linda K *see* LEISURE BEHAVIOR OF LESBIANS IN RELATION TO ALCOHOL CONSUMPTION
Lutfi, Vak'anuevis Ahmed *see* DIVANCE
Luthardt, Christoph Ernst *see*
– APOLOGETIC LECTURES ON THE FUNDAMENTAL TRUTHS OF CHRISTIANITY
– APOLOGETIC LECTURES ON THE MORAL TRUTHS OF CHRISTIANITY
– APOLOGETIC LECTURES ON THE SAVING TRUTHS OF CHRISTIANITY
– APOLOGETISCHE VORTRAEGE UEBER DIE GRUNDWAHRHEITEN DES CHRISTENTHUMS
– APOLOGIE DES CHRISTENTHUMS
– DIE CHRISTLICHE GLAUBENSLEHRE
– THE CHURCH
– HISTORY OF CHRISTIAN ETHICS BEFORE THE REFORMATION
– DAS JOHANNEISCHE EVANGELIUM NACH SEINER EIGENTHUEMLICHKEIT GESCHILDERT UND ERKLAERT
– DIE JOHANNEISCHE URSPRUNG DES VIERTEN EVANGELIUMS
– ZUR EINFUEHRUNG IN DAS AKADEMISCHE LEBEN UND STUDIUM DES THEOLOGEN
LUTHER / Anderson, William Henry – (Includes bibliographical references) – London: Burns and Oates, [185-?] – 1mf – 9 – 0-8370-6720-0 – 1986-0720 – us A.T.L.A. [240]
LUTHER : AN HISTORICAL PORTRAIT / Verres, J – London: Burns & Oates; New York: Catholic Publ Society, 1884 – 1mf – 9 – 0-8370-7033-3 – 1986-1033 – us A.T.L.A. [920]
LUTHER : EIN KIRCHLICHES FESTSPIEL ZUR FEIER DES 400JAEHRIGEN GEBURTSTAGES MARTIN LUTHERS IN WORMS / Herrig, Hans – 13. Aufl. Berlin: F Luckhardt, 1889 – 1r – 1 – us U.W. Library [790]
LUTHER : A SHORT BIOGRAPHY / Froude, James Anthony – London: Longmans, Green 1883 – 1mf – us A.T.L.A. [240]
LUTHER, 1483-1883 : GEDACHTEN EN BESCHOUWINGEN NAAR AANLEIDING VAN HET VIERDE EEUWFEEST VAN DES HERVORMERS GEBOORTE / Loman, A D – Amsterdam: J.C. Loman, Jr., [1883] – 1mf – us A.T.L.A. [240]
LUTHER ALS KIRCHENHISTORIKER : EIN BEITRAG ZUR GESCHICHTE DER WISSENSCHAFT / Schaefer, Ernst – Guetersloh: C. Bertelsmann, 1897 – 2mf – us A.T.L.A. [240]
LUTHER AND CROMWELL / Headley, J T – New York: J.S. Taylor, 1852, c1850 – 1mf – us A.T.L.A. [940]
LUTHER AND OTHER LEADERS OF THE REFORMATION / Tulloch, John – Edinburgh: W. Blackwood, 1883 – 2mf – us A.T.L.A. [940]
LUTHER AND THE GERMAN REFORMATION / Lindsay, Thomas M – Edinburgh: T.& T. Clark, 1900 (The world's epoch-makers) – 1mf – us A.T.L.A. [943]
LUTHER AND THE RADICALS : ANOTHER LOOK AT SOME ASPECTS OF THE STRUGGLE BETWEEN LUTHER AND THE RADICAL REFORMERS / Loewen, Harry – 1974 – 208p – $18.00 – 0-88920-044-0 – cn W.L.U. Press [240]
LUTHER AND THE SWISS : A LECTURE / Uhlhorn, Gerhard – Philadelphia: Lutheran Book Store, 1876 – 1mf – us A.T.L.A. [240]
Luther, Bernhard *see* HEINRICH V. KLEIST – KANT UND WIELAND
LUTHER COLLEGE VISITOR – Wahoo, NE. 15 Dec 1904- – 1 – us NE Hist [071]
LUTHER D. GRISWOLD PAPERS, MS P.P. / Griswold, Luther D – 1862-65. 1 reel – 1 – us Western Res [920]
LUTHER HALSEY GULICK : MISSIONARY IN HAWAII, MICRONESIA, JAPAN, AND CHINA / Jewett, Frances Gulick – Boston: Congregational Sunday-School Publ Society, 1895 – 1mf – 9 – 0-8370-6192-X – 1986-0192 – us A.T.L.A. [920]
LUTHER IM KLOSTER, 1505-1525 : ZUM VERSTAENDNIS UND ZUR ABWEHR / Benrath, Karl – Halle a.d.S.: Im Kommissionsverlag von R. Haupt, 1905. (Schriften des Vereins fuer Reformationsgeschichte; 23.Jahrg., Schrift 87) – 1mf – us A.T.L.A. [240]
LUTHER IM LICHTE DER NEUEREN FORSCHUNG : EIN KRITISCHER BERICHT / Boehmer, Heinrich – Leipzig: B.G. Teubner, 1906. (Aus Natur und Geisteswelt; 113. Bdchn.) – 1mf – us A.T.L.A. [240]
LUTHER IM NEUESTEN ROEMISCHEN GERICHT / Walther, Wilhelm – Halle: Verein fuer Reformationsgeschichte, 1884. ([Schriften des Vereins fuer Reformationsgeschichte; Bd. 7]) – 1mf – us A.T.L.A. [240]
LUTHER IM VERHAELTNIS ZUR WISSENSCHAFT UND IHRER LEHRE : REDE BEI DER FEIER DER KOENIGL. FRIEDRICH-WILHELMS-UNIVERSITAET ZU BERLIN ZUM... / Kleinert, Paul – Berlin: Buchdruckerei der Koenigl. Akademie der Wissenschaft, 1883 – 1mf – us A.T.L.A. [370]
LUTHER IN DEN WANDLUNGEN SEINER KIRCHE / Stephan, Horst – Giessen: A. Toepelmann, 1907 – 1mf – us A.T.L.A. [240]

LUTHER IN KATHOLISCHER BELEUCHTUNG : GLOSSEN ZU H. GRISARS LUTHER / Kawerau, Gustav – Leipzig: Verein fuer Reformationsgeschichte, 1911. (Schriften des Vereins fuer Reformationsgeschichte; Jahrg. 29, 1. Stueck, Nr. 105) – 1mf – us A.T.L.A. [240]

LUTHER IN RATIONALISTISCHER UND CHRISTLICHER BELEUCHTUNG : PRINZIPIELLE AUSEINANDERSETZUNG MIT A. HARNACK UND R. SEEBERG / Denifle, Heinrich – Mainz: Kirchheim, 1904 – 1mf – us A.T.L.A. [240]

Luther, Martin *see*
- AN DEN CHRISTLICHEN ADEL DEUTSCHER NATION VON DES CHRISTLICHEN STANDES BESSERUNG
- BARBURGER, BOLSTANDIGES
- THE LIFE OF LUTHER
- EIN SENDBRIEFF WIDER ETLICHER ROTTENGEISTER
- SHORTER CATECHISM
- VON DER WIDERTAUFFE AN ZWEN PFARHERRN EIN BRIEF
- VON ER LERNHARD KEISER DES EUANGELI WILLEN VERBRANDT
- DAS WELTLICHE OBERKEITT DEN WIDERTAUFFEREN MIT LEIBLICHER STRAFF
- WORKS

LUTHER, MELANTHON UND CALVIN IN OESTERREICH-UNGARN : ZU CALVINS VIERTER JAHRHUNDERTFEIER: MIT ARCHIVALISCHEN BEILAGEN / Loesche, Georg – Tuebingen: J.C.B. Mohr, 1909 – 1mf – us A.T.L.A. [940]

LUTHER RICE / Baptist Association. Louisiana – 1951-87 – 1 – $69.84 – us Baptist [240]

LUTHER RICE, PIONEER IN MISSIONS AND EDUCATION / Pollard, Edward B – Philadelphia: Judson Press. 1928. 158p – 1 – $5.53 – us Baptist [240]

LUTHER UND ARISTOTELE : FESTSCHRIFT ZUM VIERHUNDERTJAEHRIGEN GEBURTSTAGE LUTHER'S / Nitzsch, Friedrich – Kiel: Universitaets-Buchhandlung, 1883 – 1mf – us A.T.L.A. [240]

LUTHER UND DAS LANDESHERRLICHE KIRCHENREGIMENT / Holl, Karl – Tuebingen: J.C.B. Mohr, 1911 – 1mf – us A.T.L.A. [943]

LUTHER UND DER REICHSTAG ZU WORMS, 1521 / Kolde, T – Halle: Verein fuer Reformationsgeschichte, 1883. ([Schriften des Vereins fUEr Reformationsgeschichte; Bd. 1]) – 1mf – us A.T.L.A. [240]

LUTHER UND DIE AUGSBURGISCHE CONFESSION : EINE PRUEFUNG DER HISTORISCHEN UNTERSUCHUNGEN RUECKERT'S UND HEPPE'S UEBER LETZTERE / Calinich, Hermann Julius Robert – (Includes bibliographical references) – Leipzig: Ernst Bredt, 1861 – 1mf – 9 – 0-8370-8565-9 – 1986-2565 – us A.T.L.A. [240]

LUTHER UND DIE GEWISSENSFREIHEIT / Paulus, Nikolaus – Muenchen: Muenchener Volksschriftenverlag, 1905 – 1mf – us A.T.L.A. [240]

LUTHER UND DIE KIRCHENBILDER SEINER ZEIT / Rogge, Christian – Leipzig: Verein fuer Reformationsgeschichte, 1912. (Schriften des Vereins fuer Reformationsgeschichte; Jahrg. 29, 4. Stueck, Nr. 108) – 1mf – us A.T.L.A. [240]

LUTHER UND DIE KIRCHENGESCHICHTE : NACH SEINEN SCHRIFTEN ZUNAECHST BIS 1521 / Koehler, V – Erlangen: F. Junge, 1900 – 1mf – us A.T.L.A. [240]

LUTHER UND DIE LUEGE / Koehler, Walther E – Leipzig: Verein fuer Reformationsgeschichte, 1912. (Schriften des Vereins fuer Reformationsgeschichte; 30. Jahrg., 1. u. 2. Stueck, Nr. 109/110) – 1mf – us A.T.L.A. [240]

LUTHER UND J. JANSSEN : DER DEUTSCHE REFORMATOR UND EIN ULTRAMONTANER HISTORIKER / Koestlin, Julius – Halle: m. Niemeyer, 1883 – 1mf – us A.T.L.A. [240]

LUTHER UND LUTHERTUM IN DER ERSTEN ENTWICKELUNG : QUELLENMAESSIG DARGESTELLT / Denifle, Heinrich – (Includes 2 suppl) – 2. durchgearb. Aufl. Mainz: F Kirchheim, 1904-09 – 1r – 1 – us U.W. Library [240]

LUTHER UND SEINE BEZIEHUNGEN ZUR SCHLESIEN, INSBESONDERE ZU BRESLAU / Erdmann, D – Halle: Verein fuer Reformationsgeschichte, 1887. ([Schriften des Vereins fuer Reformationsgeschichte; Bd. 19]) – 1mf – us A.T.L.A. [240]

LUTHER UND SEINE KAMPFGENOSSEN : EINE BELEUCHTUNG DES LUTHER-DENKMALS IN WORMS IM LICHTE UNSERER ZEIT / Schekel, Daniel – Lahr: J.H. Geiger, 1868 – 1mf – us A.T.L.A. [240]

LUTHER UND SEINE ZEIT : VOLKSSCHAUSPIEL / Truempelmann, August – Gotha: F A Perthes, 1889 – 1r – 1 – us U.W. Library [430]

LUTHER, ZINZENDORF, WESLEY : AN ACCOUNT OF JOHN WESLEY'S CONVERSION THROUGH HEARING LUTHER'S PREFACE TO THE EPISTLE TO THE ROMANS READ IN A MORAVIAN PRAYER MEETING IN LONDON, ENGLAND / Anstadt, P – York, Pa.: P. Anstadt, [18–?] – 1mf – us A.T.L.A. [240]

THE LUTHERAN – Australia. v1-24. 1967-90 (complete) – 10r – 1 – ATLA S0372 – us A.T.L.A. [073]

THE LUTHERAN – (Title and vol nos vary) – 1861-1962 – 107r – 1 – ATLA S0099 – us A.T.L.A. [073]

LUTHERAN AND HOME JOURNAL : DEVOTED TO THE INTERESTS OF THE EVANGELICAL LUTHERAN CHURCH – v1-2. 6 Jul 1860-11 Oct 1861 (complete) – 1r – 1 – ATLA S0101 – us A.T.L.A. [073]

LUTHERAN AND MISSIONARY *see* LUTHERAN HOME JOURNAL

LUTHERAN CHURCH IN AMERICA : MINUTES. BIENNIAL CONVENTION – (Lacking: 1983-85) – Philadelphia. v1-14. 1962-82; 1984; 1986-87 – 8r – 1 – ATLA S0441 – us A.T.L.A. [240]

LUTHERAN CHURCH IN AMERICA – New England Synod. 1962-79 – 1 – us A.T.L.A. [073]

LUTHERAN CHURCH IN AMERICA : NEW ENGLAND SYNOD. MINUTES – 1962-86 (complete) – 4r – 1 – ATLA S0412 – us A.T.L.A. [240]

LUTHERAN CHURCH IN AMERICA : YEARBOOK – 1963-87 (complete) – 9r – 1 – ATLA S0440 – us A.T.L.A. [240]

LUTHERAN CHURCH IN AMERICA. CANADA SECTION : MINUTES OF THE CONVENTION – 1963-83 (complete) – 1r – 1 – ATLA S0563 – us A.T.L.A. [240]

LUTHERAN CHURCH IN AMERICA. CENTRAL CANADA SYNOD : MINUTES – 1962-85 (complete) – Inquire – 1 – ATLA S0672 – us A.T.L.A. [240]

LUTHERAN CHURCH IN AMERICA. EASTERN PENNSYLVANIA SYNOD : MINUTES – 1962-68 (complete) – 1r – 1 – ATLA S0611 – us A.T.L.A. [240]

LUTHERAN CHURCH IN AMERICA. MARYLAND SYNOD : PROCEEDINGS – 1962-87 (complete) – Inquire – 1 – ATLA S0561 – us A.T.L.A. [240]

LUTHERAN CHURCH IN AMERICA. METROPOLITAN NEW YORK SYNOD : MINUTES – 1966-87 (complete) – 5r – 1 – ATLA S0564 – us A.T.L.A. [240]

LUTHERAN CHURCH IN AMERICA. NEW YORK SYNOD : MINUTES OF THE CONVENTION – 1962-66 (complete) – 2r – 1 – ATLA S0565 – us A.T.L.A. [240]

LUTHERAN CHURCH IN AMERICA. NORTHEAST PENNSYLVANIA SYNOD : MINUTES – 1968-87 (complete) – 3r – 1 – ATLA S0612 – us A.T.L.A. [240]

LUTHERAN CHURCH MESSENGER *see* THE CHURCH MESSENGER

LUTHERAN CHURCH – MISSOURI SYNOD : CONVENTION PROCEEDINGS – 1950-83 – Inquire – 1 – ATLA S0939 – us A.T.L.A. [073]

LUTHERAN CHURCH – MISSOURI SYNOD : PROCEEDINGS – 1950-75 – Inquire – 1 – ATLA S0938 – us A.T.L.A. [073]

LUTHERAN CHURCH – MISSOURI SYNOD : REPORTS OF DISTRICT PRESIDENTS / Lutheran Church. Missouri Synod – 1976-91 (complete) – Inquire – 1 – ATLA S0352A – us A.T.L.A. [240]

LUTHERAN CHURCH – MISSOURI SYNOD : STATISTICAL YEARBOOK – (Lacks: 1914-15) – 1884-1991 – Inquire – 1 – ATLA S0352B – us A.T.L.A. [240]

Lutheran Church. Missouri Synod *see* LUTHERAN CHURCH – MISSOURI SYNOD

LUTHERAN CHURCH – MISSOURI SYNOD. ATLANTIC DISTRICT : PROCEEDINGS – v1-45. 1907-76 (complete) – 3r – 1 – ATLA S0557 – us A.T.L.A. [073]

LUTHERAN CHURCH OF AUSTRALIA : YEARBOOK – 1918-93 (complete) – Inquire – 1 – ATLA S0762 – us A.T.L.A. [240]

LUTHERAN CHURCH QUARTERLY – Gettysburg, PA. v1-22. 1928-49 (complete) – 8r – 1 – ATLA S0020 – us A.T.L.A. [073]

LUTHERAN CHURCH REVIEW – (Includes index) – v1-46. 1882-1927 (complete) – 19r – 1 – ATLA S0019 – us A.T.L.A. [073]

LUTHERAN CHURCH REVIEW – v. 1-40. 1882-1921 – 1,5,6 – us Princeton Micro [240]

LUTHERAN CHURCH VISITOR – (Lacks: v1-2 and some pgs) – v3-6. 25 Apr 1907-30 Jun 1910 – 3r – 1 – ATLA S0122 – us A.T.L.A. [073]

LUTHERAN CHURCH WORK *see*
- LUTHERAN CHURCH WORK AND OBSERVER
- LUTHERAN OBSERVER

LUTHERAN CHURCH WORK AND OBSERVER – (Some pgs missing. Merged title) – v1-5. 1908-12; v5-7. 1912-19 – 9r – 1 – ATLA S0114 – us A.T.L.A. [073]

Lutheran Church.Book of Concord *see* DIE SYMBOLISCHEN BUECHER DER EVANGELISCH-LUTHERISCHEN KIRCHE, DEUTSCH UND LATEINISCH

LUTHERAN CHURCHES IN CANADA : DIRECTORY – 1970-91 (complete) – Inquire – 1 – ATLA S0505 – us A.T.L.A. [240]

LUTHERAN COMPANION – (Numbering combined with: Augustana) – v1-57; v95-108. 1892-1962 (complete) – 55r – 1 – ATLA S0107 – us A.T.L.A. [073]

LUTHERAN COUNCIL IN U.S.A : MINUTES AND REPORTS – 1968-87 (complete) – 4r – 1 – ATLA S0511 – us A.T.L.A. [240]

THE LUTHERAN CYCLOPEDIA / ed by Jacobs, Henry Eyster – New York: Scribner, 1899 – 2mf – us A.T.L.A. [240]

LUTHERAN EDUCATION – 1865- 1; 1970- 5,6; 1976- 4 x 6 in. 9 – us UMI [240]

LUTHERAN FOREIGN MISSIONS / Lose, George William – Columbus, OH: Lutheran Book Concern, [1897?] – 1mf – 9 – 0-8370-7304-9 – 1986-1304 – us A.T.L.A. [240]

LUTHERAN FORUM *see* AMERICAN LUTHERAN

LUTHERAN HERALD / Evangelical Lutheran Church – (Lacking some pgs. Some original pgs damaged. Several mergers) – v1-44. 5 Jul 1917-1960 – 45r – 1 – ATLA S0135 – us A.T.L.A. [073]

LUTHERAN HERALD : A RELIGIOUS WEEKLY – v1-12. 1906-28 Jun 1917 (complete) – 12r – 1 – ATLA S0248 – us A.T.L.A. [073]

LUTHERAN HERALD – v1-22. 1909-30 (complete) – 6r – 1 – ATLA S0263 – us A.T.L.A. [073]

LUTHERAN HERALD *see*
- ANSGAR LUTHERAN
- LUTHERAN STANDARD

LUTHERAN HISTORICAL CONFERENCE : NEWSLETTER – v1-24. 1963-83 (complete) – 1r – 1 – ATLA S0831 – us A.T.L.A. [073]

LUTHERAN HOME JOURNAL – (Several mergers) – v1-6. 1856-Jun 1860 (complete) – 2r – 1 – ATLA S0098 – us A.T.L.A. [073]

LUTHERAN HOME MISSIONS : A CALL TO THE HOME CHURCH / Hunt, J R E – Rock Island, Ill.: Augustana Book Concern, 1913 – 1mf – us A.T.L.A. [240]

LUTHERAN JOURNAL – (Lacks some issues. 1965 not publ) – 1961-86 – 2r – 1 – ATLA S0832 – us A.T.L.A. [073]

LUTHERAN LANDMARKS AND PIONEERS IN AMERICA : A SERIES OF SKETCHES OF COLONIAL TIMES / Finck, William J – Philadelphia: General Council Publication House, 1913 – 1mf – us A.T.L.A. [240]

LUTHERAN LITURGICAL ASSOCIATION : MEMOIRS – v1-7. 1906 (complete) – 1r – 1 – ATLA B0033 – us A.T.L.A. [240]

LUTHERAN MAGAZINE : WESTERN CONFERENCE OF LUTHERAN MINISTERS – v1-4. 1827-30 (complete) – 1r – 1 – ATLA B0524B – us A.T.L.A. [073]

LUTHERAN MISSIONARY JOURNAL – (Some pgs missing) – v1-28. 1880-1907 – 6r – 1 – ATLA S0109 – us A.T.L.A. [073]

THE LUTHERAN MOVEMENT IN ENGLAND DURING THE REIGNS OF HENRY 8TH AND EDWARD 6TH AND ITS LITERARY MONUMENTS / Jacobs, Henry Eyster – Philadelphia: General Council Publication House, 1908, c1890 – 1mf – us A.T.L.A. [240]

LUTHERAN OBSERVER – (Lacks: v20 1833. Cont by: Lutheran Church Work) – v1-83. Aug 1831-1915 – 51r – 1 – ATLA S0088 – us A.T.L.A. [073]

LUTHERAN PREACHER : AND PASTORAL MESSENGER – v1-2. 1833-34 (complete) – 1r – 1 – ATLA B0524D – us A.T.L.A. [073]

LUTHERAN PULPIT : AND MONTHLY RELIGIOUS MAGAZINE – v1-2. 1837-38 (complete) – 1r – 1 – ATLA B0524C – us A.T.L.A. [073]

LUTHERAN QUARTERLY – July 1849-1906 – 1 – us UMI [240]

LUTHERAN QUARTERLY – v1-57. 1871-1927 (complete) – 22r – 1 – ATLA S0018 – us A.T.L.A. [073]

THE LUTHERAN QUARTERLY – (Lacking: 20(1978)-21(1979)) – 1(1949)-24(1972) – 9 – Dfl585.00 – ne Slangenburg [073]

THE LUTHERAN QUARTERLY – (Missing: v20-21 1968-1969) – Gettysburg. v1-24. 1949-1972 – 167mf – 9 – ne IDC [240]

THE LUTHERAN REFORMATION, SOURCES 1500-1650 / ed by Maltby, William S – (Major sections: Germany, Scandinavia, The Eastern Habsburg Lands, The Netherlands, Southern Europe) – 1,644mf – 9 – ne IDC [240]

LUTHERAN SCHOLAR *see* ACADEMY

LUTHERAN SENTINEL – (Lacks: v35 and some pgs) – v13-34. 1930-51; v36-73. 1953-90 – 12r – 1 – ATLA S0872 – us A.T.L.A. [073]

THE LUTHERAN SPOKESMAN – v1-36. 1858-94 – 6r – 1 – ATLA S0459 – us A.T.L.A. [073]

LUTHERAN STANDARD – (With index. Merger and cont of: Lutheran Herald, and Ansgar Lutheran) – 1842-1987 (complete) – 86r – 1 – ATLA S0119 – us A.T.L.A. [073]

LUTHERAN STANDARD *see* ANSGAR LUTHERAN

LUTHERAN SYNOD QUARTERLY – (Some pgs lacking) – v1-31. Sep 1960-1991 – Inquire – 1 – ATLA S0806 – us A.T.L.A. [073]

LUTHERAN THEOLOGICAL JOURNAL – (1985-. 5,6,9) – v1-. 1967- – 1 – us UMI [240]

Lutheran Theological Seminary *see*
- BOUND MSS IN THE A.R. WENTZ LIBRARY. (MIMEO)
- INVENTORY OF SEMINARY-RELATED MSS IN THE A.R. WENTZ LIBRARY. (MIMEO)
- MSS COLLECTION IN THE A.R. WENTZ LIBRARY. (MIMEO)
- PRELIMINARY INVENTORY OF NON-SEMINARY-RELATED MSS IN THE A.R. WENTZ LIBRARY. (MIMEO.)

LUTHERAN THEOLOGICAL SEMINARY BULLETIN – (1985-. 5,6,9) – v60-. 1980- – 1 – us UMI [240]

LUTHERAN THEOLOGICAL SEMINARY BULLETIN / Lutheran Theological Seminary. Gettysburg, PA – v1-5. 1921-26 – 1 – us UMI [240]

Lutheran Theological Seminary. Gettysburg, PA *see*
- BULLETIN
- GETTYSBURG SEMINARY BULLETIN
- LUTHERAN THEOLOGICAL SEMINARY BULLETIN

LUTHERAN TIDINGS – (Some original pgs damaged) – Aug 1934-1962 – 9r – 1 – ATLA S0230 – us A.T.L.A. [073]

LUTHERAN TIDINGS *see* UNGDOM

LUTHERAN VISITOR – (Title varies. Several mergers) – v1-36 no 3. 1866-1904 (complete) – 20r – 1 – ATLA S0094 – us A.T.L.A. [073]

LUTHERAN WOMAN TODAY – v1-5. 1988-92 (complete) – Inquire – 1 – ATLA S0892 – us A.T.L.A. [073]

LUTHERAN WOMEN – (Lacks: v19-21 nos 2-12 1980) – v1-25. 1963-87 – 9r – 1 – ATLA S0400 – us A.T.L.A. [073]

LUTHERAN WORLD : A PAPER FOR THE HOME – v1-20 no 46. 3 Mar 1892-28 Feb 1912 (complete) – 19r – 1 – ATLA S0100 – us A.T.L.A. [073]

LUTHERAN WORLD FEDERATION : INFORMATION – 1968-91 (complete) – 15r – 1 – ATLA S0354 – us A.T.L.A. [073]

LUTHERAN WORLD FEDERATION : MARXISM AND CHINA STUDY. INFORMATION LETTER – (Ceased publ with v39) – v1-39. Sep 1972-Mar 1985 – 1r – 1 – ATLA S0466 – us A.T.L.A. [073]

LUTHERAN WORLD FEDERATION SERVICE TO REFUGEES – 1947-1949. v1,2 – 1r – 1 – us I.H.R.C. [360]

LUTHERANEN OG BIBEL-BUDET / Nor. Evang. Luth. Kirke i Amerika – v1-24, no.32. Jul 1866-69, Oct 1890. Lacks: v5:10, p151-54. 5 reels – 1 – us A.T.L.A. [073]

LUTHERANEREN – (Lacking: v5 no 10 p151-54) – Minneapolis. v1-24. 1866-90 – 5r – 1 – ATLA S0244 – us A.T.L.A. [073]
LUTHERANEREN – (Lacks some issues. Merger of: Budbaereren, and Ev. Luth. Kirk.) – v1-23. Jul 1895-27 Jun 1917 – 22r – 1 – ATLA S0250 – us A.T.L.A. [073]
LUTHERANEREN – (Several mergers) – v1-40. 4 Jul 1917-1 Aug 1956 (complete) – 31r – 1 – ATLA S0235 – us A.T.L.A. [073]
LUTHERANISM IN AMERICA : AN ESSAY ON THE PRESENT CONDITION OF THE LUTHERAN CHURCH IN THE UNITED STATES / Mann, William J – Philadelphia: Lindsay & Blakiston, 1857 – 1mf – us A.T.L.A. [240]
LUTHERANS ALERT-NATIONAL – v1-24. 1966-89 (complete) – 4r – 1 – ATLA S0383 – us A.T.L.A. [073]
THE LUTHERANS IN AMERICA : A STORY OF STRUGGLE, PROGRESS, INFLUENCE AND MARVELOUS GROWTH / Wolf, Edmund Jacob – New York: J.A. Hill, 1889 – 2mf – us A.T.L.A. [240]
LE LUTHERIEN – 1967-89 (complete) – 2r – 1 – ATLA S0348 – us A.T.L.A. [073]
LUTHERISCHE KIRCHENZEITUNG – (Some pgs missing) – v1-71. 1860-1930 – 40r – 1 – ATLA S0153 – us A.T.L.A. [073]
LUTHERISCHE METAPHYSIK : EIN VERSUCH, DIE PHILOSOPHISCHEN GRUNDLAGEN DES CHRISTENTUMS DARZUSTELLEN / Grohmann, Wilhelm – Leipzig: A Deichert, 1904 – 1mf – 9 – 0-8370-3403-5 – 1985-1403 – us A.T.L.A. [240]
LUTHERISCHE RUNDSCHAU – 1(1951)-21(1971) – 181mf – 9 – Dfl634.00 – ne Slangenburg [073]
LUTHERISCHES DIENST – v1-20. 1965-84 (complete) – 1r – 1 – ATLA S0813 – us A.T.L.A. [073]
LUTHER'S 95 THESEN UND IHRE DOGMENHISTORISCHEN VORAUSSETZUNGEN / Bratke, Eduard – Goettingen: Vandenhoeck & Ruprecht, 1884 – 1mf – us A.T.L.A. [240]
LUTHERS AUFFASSUNG DER GOTTHEIT CHRISTI / Kuegelgen, Constantin von – Leipzig: R. Woepke, 1901 – 1mf – us A.T.L.A. [240]
LUTHERS BERUF / Walther, Wilhelm – Halle: Verein fuer Reformationsgeschichte, 1890. ([Schriften des Vereins fuer Reformationsgeschichte; Bd. 31]) (Luther im neuesten roemischen Gericht / von Wilh. Walther; 3. Heft) – 1mf – us A.T.L.A. [240]
LUTHERS GLAUBENSGEWISSHEIT / Walther, Wilhelm – Halle: Verein fuer Reformationsgeschichte, 1892. ([Schriften des Vereins fuer Reformationsgeschichte; Bd. 35]) (Luther im neuesten roemischen Gericht / von Wilh. Walther; 4. Heft) – 1mf – us A.T.L.A. [240]
LUTHERS KATECHISMEN / Albrecht, Otto – Leipzig: Verein fuer Reformationsgeschichte, 1915. (Schriften des Vereins fuer Reformationsgeschichte; Jahrg. 33, 1. u. 2. Stueck, Nr. 121/122) – 1mf – us A.T.L.A. [240]
LUTHERS LAERA OM STATEN I DESS SAMBAND MED HANS REFORMATORISKA GRUNDTANKAR OCH MED TIDIGARE KYRKLIGA LAEROR : AKADEMISK AFHANDLING / Billing, Einar – Uppsala: Almqvist & Wiksell, 1900 – 1mf – us A.T.L.A. [240]
LUTHERS LEHRE IN IHRER ERSTEN GESTALT / Dieckhoff, A W – Rostock: Stiller, 1887 – 1mf – us A.T.L.A. [240]
LUTHERS NEUPLATONISMUS IN DER PSALMENVORLESUNG VON 1513-1516 / Hunzinger, A W – Leipzig: A. Deichert, 1906 – 1mf – us A.T.L.A. [240]
LUTHERS ROMFAHRT / Boehmer, Heinrich – Leipzig: A. Deichert, 1914 – 1mf – us A.T.L.A. [240]
LUTHERS SCHRIFT AN DEN CHRISTLICHEN ADEL DEUTSCHER NATION : IM SPIEGEL DER KULTUR- UND ZEITGESCHICHTE : EIN BEITRAG ZUM VERSTAENDNIS DIESER SCHRIFT LUTHERS / Koehler, Walther E – Halle a.S.: M. Niemeyer, 1895 – 1mf – us A.T.L.A. [240]
LUTHERS STELLUNG ZU DEN OECUMENISCHEN SYMBOLEN : FESTSCHRIFT DER GROSSHERZOGLICH HESSISCHEN LUDEWIGS-UNIVERSITAET ZUR FEIER DES VIERHUNDERTJAEHRIGEN GEBURTSTAGES MARTIN LUTHERS 10. NOVEMBER 1883 / Kattenbusch, Ferdinand – Giessen: Wenzel, 1883 – 1mf – us A.T.L.A. [240]
LUTHER'S TABLE TALK : A CRITICAL STUDY / Smith, Henry Preserved – New York: Columbia University Press, 1907 – 1mf – us A.T.L.A. [240]
LUTHERS THEOLOGIE : MIT BESONDERER BEZIEHUNG AUF SEINE VERSOEHNUNGS- UND ERLOESUNGSLEHRE / Harnack, T – Erlangen: T. Blaesing, 1862-1886 – 3mf – us A.T.L.A. [240]
LUTHERS WAFFEN / Walther, Wilhelm – Halle: Verein fuer Reformationsgeschichte, 1886. ([Schriften des Vereins fuer Reformationsgeschichte; Bd. 13]) (Luther im neuesten roemischen Gericht / von Wilh. Walther; 2. Heft) – 1mf – us A.T.L.A. [240]
LUTHERS WERKE : KRITISCHE GESAMTAUSGABE / ed by Boehlaus, H – (Missing: v55) – Weimar. v1-57. 1834-1939 – 1040mf – 9 – ne IDC [240]
LUTHERSK KIRKE – (Some missing issues) – v39-43. 1989-93 – Inquire – 1 – ATLA S0930 – us A.T.L.A. [073]
LUTHERSK KIRKEBLAD UDG. AF DEN FORENEDE NORSK LUTHERSKE KIRKE I AMERIKA – v1-5. 1890-Aug 1895 (complete) – 4r – 1 – ATLA S0238 – us A.T.L.A. [073]
LUTHERSK KIRKETIDENDE – (Lacking: v73-92 and some issues) – v1-125. 1863-1990 – Inquire – 1 – ATLA S0339 – us A.T.L.A. [073]
LUTHERSK UGEBLAD – (Lacks some pgs) – Blair, NE. v1-40. 1921-60 – 21r – 1 – ATLA S0286 – us A.T.L.A. [073]
LUTHERSKE VIDNESBYRD; GAMLE OG NYE – (Some pgs missing) – v1-9. 1882-90 – 3r – 1 – ATLA S0246 – us A.T.L.A. [073]
LE LUTIN : HUMORISTIQUE / ed by Guimond, E-L – Montreal, Canada. v1 n2. 2 mai 1896 – 1r – 1 – Can$25.00 – cn Can Microfilming [072]
LE LUTIN : HUMORISTIQUE / ed by Veritas, Armand – Quebec, Canada. 7 jun 1884 – 1r – 1 – Can$25.00 – cn Can Microfilming [072]
LE LUTIN – Montreal, Canada. 11 fev 1897-v1 n6. 18 mar 1897 – 1r – 1 – Can$25.00 – cn Can Microfilming [072]
LUTON ADVERTISER – England. -w. 1869-73. (2 reels) – 1 – uk British Libr Newspaper [072]
LUTON REPORTER – England. -w. 1879-86. (8 reels) – 1 – uk British Libr Newspaper [072]
LUTON TIMES ETC – (Bedfordshire Advertiser. 1894-25 Feb 1916) – England. 1859-60; 2 Mar 1861-20 Sept 1862; 1866-68; 1885; 1892-95; 1898-1910; 1912-14. -w – 24r – 1 – uk British Libr Newspaper [072]
LA LUTTE – Gerant Edgard Ganofsky puis Le-van-Thu. Saigon. avr 1933-sept 1938 – 1 – fr A.C.R.P.P. [073]
LA LUTTE DE CLASSE – no. 1-56. Paris. 25 mai 1913-20 27 juin 1914 – 1 – fr A.C.R.P.P. [073]
LA LUTTE DE CLASSE – Paris. 5 mai 1922-20 avr 1923. Absorbe par: L' Internationale syndicale rouge – 1 – fr A.C.R.P.P. [073]
LA LUTTE DE CLASSES – no. 1-5; N.S., no. 1. Oran. avr 1928-mai 1929, avr 1932 – 1 – fr A.C.R.P.P. [073]
LA LUTTE DE CLASSES – Paris. fevr mars 1928-janv fevr 1933, janv-avr juin 1935. suite de: Clarte voir a ce titre – 1 – fr A.C.R.P.P. [073]
LA LUTTE DE CLASSES – Paris. Nov 1921-Jan 1928 – 1 – us NY Public [305]
LA LUTTE DES JEUNES – no. 1-18. Paris. fevr-juil 1934 – 1 – fr A.C.R.P.P. [073]
LA LUTTE OUVRIERE – Montreal, Canada. nov 1964-1971 – 1r – 1 – Can$60.00 – cn Can Microfilming [072]
LA LUTTE OUVRIERE / Parti Ouvrier Internationaliste – Paris. juin 1936-juil 1939 – 1 – fr A.C.R.P.P. [073]
LUTTE OUVRIERE – (Includes: L'Internationaliste jan/mar 1991-aut/jun 1992f) – Montreal, 28 sep 1977 – 2r – 1 – Can$70.00 – cn Can Microfilming [072]
LUTTE OUVRI'ERE (PARIS, FRANCE: 1936) – (Includes c.1: v.1:no.1 (1936:June 19) – v.1:no.18(1936:Oct.30), v.1:no.20(1936:Nov.14) – v.2:No.64(1938:Jan.6), v.2:no.66(1938:Feb.3) – v.4:no.1(1939:July 10)) – Paris: Parti Ouvrier Internationaliste, 1936-1938. 64v – 1 – CSUXAMK7700-S – us Hoover Inst Photo [944]
LA LUTTE SOCIALE / Parti Socialiste (S.F.I.O.) et des Syndicats d'Oran – Journal hebdomadaire. Oran puis Alger. dec 1907-sept 1912, avr 1919-aout 1939. suivi de: Algerie-nouvelle voir a ce titre – 1 – fr A.C.R.P.P. [335]
LA LUTTE SOCIALE / Union Federative du Centre – I, no. 1-9. Paris. 17 mars-12 19 mai 1900; 2e s., no. 1-11. 5 mars-22 mai 1904 – 1 – fr A.C.R.P.P. [331]
Lutter, Candice D *see* THE CONSTRUCTION AND INITIAL VALIDATION OF THE PHYSIQUE ANXIETY SCALE
Lutteroth, Henri *see* LE RECENSEMENT DE QUIRINIUS EN JUDEE
LUTTERWORTH GUARDIAN ETC – England.Sept 1923-Feb 1928. -w – 1 – uk British Libr Newspaper [072]
LUTTERWORTH MERCURY ETC – England.22 Jul, 19 Aug, 2 Sept-23 Dec 1869. -w. 16 feet – 1 – uk British Libr Newspaper [072]
LUTTERWORTH NEWS ETC – (Hinckley Times & Lutterworth News etc. 25 Feb-6 May 1871) – England, Jul 1870-May 1871 – 1r – 1 – uk British Libr Newspaper [072]
LES LUTTES POLITIQUES ET DOCTRINALES AUX 17E ET 18E SIECLES (19) – Paris, 1955 – Dfl39.00 – ne Slangenburg [240]
Lutz, Gabriele K *see* AETIOPATHOGENETISCHE VORSTELLUNG DES LUMBAGO-ISCHIALGIE-SYNDROMS IN DER DEUTSCHEN MEDIZINISCHEN WOCHENSCHRIFT VON 1900 BIS 1991
Lutz, Johann Georg *see* CHRISTI WORTE UEBER VOLLENDUNG DER WEGE GOTTES
Lutz, Joseph Maria *see* DER GOETZENDIENST GOETHE
Lutz, Karen L *see* DIETARY ADEQUACY AND CHANGES IN THE NUTRITIONAL STATUS OF APPALACHIAN TRAIL THROUGH-HIKERS
Lutz, Markus *see* VOLLSTAENDIGE BESCHREIBUNG DES SCHWEIZERLANDES ODER GEOGRAPHISCH-STATISTISCHES HAND-LEXIKON UEBER ALLE IN GESAMMTER EIDSGENOSSENSCHAFT BEFINDLICHER KANTONE, BEZIRKE, KREISE, AEMTER (AEL, ABT 1;30)
Lutz, Ralph H *see* THE TREATY OF ST GERMAIN
LUTZKI CATALOG OF BIBLICAL MANUSCRIPTS : HEBREW MANUSCRIPT CATALOG / Jewish Theological Seminary; ed by Lutzki, Morris – 16 fiches – 9 – $80.00 – us UPA [270]
Lutzki, Morris *see* LUTZKI CATALOG OF BIBLICAL MANUSCRIPTS
LUULETUSED JA AUTOBIOGRAAFIA = POEMS AND AUTOBIOGRAPHY / Tetterman, Andres – New York, 1927. 204p – 1 – 8.16 – us Baptist [240]
LUX – London, UK. 6 Aug 1892-13 Jul 1895. -w. 3 reels – 1 – uk British Libr Newspaper [072]
LUX CHRISTI : AN OUTLINE STUDY OF INDIA: A TWILIGHT LAND / Mason, Caroline Atwater – (Includes appendix and index) – New York: Macmillan, 1902 – 1mf – 9 – 0-8370-6585-2 – 1986-0585 – us A.T.L.A. [950]
LUX EVANGELICA SUB VELUM SACRORUM EMBLEMATUM RECONDITA / Engelgrave, H – O 605. (Pt. 1). 1648 – 9 – ne IDC [240]
LUX EVANGELICA SUB VELUM SACRORUM EMBLEMATUM RECONDITA / Engelgrave, H – O-245 1. 2 pts. 1655 – 9 – ne IDC [240]
LUX EVANGELICA SUB VELUM SACRORUM EMBLEMATUM RECONDITA... / Engelgrave, H – Koeln, Amsterdam, 1655, 1659 – 24mf – 9 – ne IDC [700]
Lux, Hanns Maria *see*
- DAS GROSSE SIGNAL
- DER SCHWERE GANG
- DIE VERSCHWOERUNG DER 47 SAMURAI

Lux, Konrad *see* JOHANN KASPAR FRIEDRICH MANSO
LUX MUNDI : A SERIES OF STUDIES IN THE RELIGION OF THE INCARNATION – (Includes bibliographical references) – 4th ed. London: John Murray, 1890 – 2mf – 9 – 0-8370-4818-4 – 1985-2818 – us A.T.L.A. [230]
LE LUXE DE NOTRE EPOQUE : CONFERENCE DONNEE AU CONSEIL DES CHEVALIERS DE COLOMB DE SAINT-JEROME, LE 15 FEBRIER 1925 / Grignon, Joseph-Jerome – Saint-Jerome: Imprimerie de l'Avenir du Nord, [1925 ?]. SEM105P1745 – 1mf – 9 – Can$2.25 – cn Bibl Nat [100]
Luxembourg. (Grand Duchy) *see* MEMORIAL-RECUEIL SPECIAL
Luxembourg. (Grand Duchy). Service de la Publications. Geologique *see* PUBLICATIONS
LE LUXEMBOURGEOIS – Paris. 1917-janv 1920 – 1 – fr A.C.R.P.P. [073]
Luxemburg, Dionysius von *see* LEGENDE DER HEILIGEN
LUXEMBURGER WORT – Luxemburg, 1964-feb 1976 (131r); mar 1976-80 (58r) – 189r – 1 – us Res Libr [072]
LUXEMBURGER WORT – Luxemburg. 1972; 1977- – 1 – gw Mikrofilm [949]
Luxton, Clarence T J *see* DIARIES, CORRESPONDENCE AND RELATED PAPERS, 1945-1947
Luyken, C *see*
- AFBEELDING DER MENSCHELYKE BEZIGHEDEN, BESTAANDE IN HONDERT ONDERSCHEIDEN PRINTVERBEELDINGEN, VERTONENDE ALLERHANDE STANTSPERSONEN, ...
- MENSCHELYKE BEEZIGHEEDEN BESTAANDE IN REGEERING, KONSTEN EN AMBACHTEN, NA ORDE VAN HET A.B.C, IN HONDERD FIGUUREN, ZINRIJK UITGEBEELD
- HET MENSELYK BEDRYF VERTOOND, IN. 100. VERBEELDINGEN

Luyken, J *see*
- AFBEELDING DER MENSCHELYKE BEZIGHEDEN, BESTAANDE IN HONDERT ONDERSCHEIDEN PRINTVERBEELDINGEN, VERTONENDE ALLERHANDE STANTSPERSONEN, ...
- DUITSCHE LIER, DRAAYENDE VEEL VAN DE NIEUWSTE, DEFTIGE, EN DERTELENDE TOONEN
- DUYTSE LIER, DRAAYENDE VEEL VAN DE NIEUWSTE, DEFTIGE, EN DARTELENDE TOONEN, BEVAT IN TIEN VERDEELINGEN, EN VERCIERT MET KOPERE PLATEN
- DUYTSE LIER, DRAYENDE VEEL VAN DE NIEUWSTE, DEFTIGE, EN DARTELENDE TOONEN, BEVAD IN TIEN VERDEELINGEN, EN VERCIERT MET KOPERE PLATEN
- DUYTSE LIER, DRAYENDE VEEL VAN DE NIEUWSTE, DEFTIGE, EN DARTELENDE TOONEN, BEVAT IN TIEN VERDEELINGEN, EN VERCIERT MET KOPERE PLATEN
- EENIGE BYBELSE FIGUUREN GELYKENISSEN EN ZINNEBEELDEN
- GODDELYKE LIEFDE-VLAMMEN OF VERVOLG VAN JESUS EN DE ZIELE, HANDELENDE VAN EEN BOETVAERDIGE, GEHEILIGDE, LIEFHEBBENDE, EN HAAR ZELFSTERVENDE ZIELE, IN DRIE DEELEN, MET KOOPERE AFBEELDINGEN VERCIERT
- GODDELYKE LIEFDE-VLAMMEN, VAN EEN BOETVAARDIGE, GEHEILIGDE, LIEFHEBBENDE, EN AAN HAAR SELFS-STERVENDE ZIELE, IN DRIE DEELEN VERDEELT
- JESUS EN DE ZIEL
- JEZUS EN DE ZIEL
- MENSCHELYKE BEEZIGHEEDEN BESTAANDE IN REGEERING, KONSTEN EN AMBACHTEN, NA ORDE VAN HET A.B.C, IN HONDERD FIGUUREN, ZINRIJK UITGEBEELD
- HET MENSELYK BEDRYF VERTOOND, IN. 100. VERBEELDINGEN
- VONCKEN DER LIEFDE JESU, VAN HET GODTBEGERENDE ZIELENVIER

Luykx, B *see* ESSAI SUR LES SOURCES DE L'ORDO-MISSAE PREMONTRE
LUYOU BAO *see* ZHONGGUO LUYOU BAO
A LUZ : LIBERDADE IGUALDADE E FRATERNIDADE – ORGAO DA AUG. E REP. LOJ. MAC. LUZ DOS. FRANCISCO – Penedo, Alagoas. 23 Out 1902; Jan, 12 Jul 1903 – 1,5,6 – bl Biblioteca [072]
A LUZ : ORGAM DE PROPAGANDA ESPIRITA – Maceio, Alagoas. 1 Ago 1901 – 1,5,6 – bl Biblioteca [072]
A LUZ : ORGAO CRITICO, LITTERARIO E NOTICIOSO – Maceio, Alagoas. 8 Nov 1896 – 1,5,6 – bl Biblioteca [072]
A LUZ : PERIODICO LITTERARIO E NOTICIOSO – Juiz de Fora, 6 Apr-4 May 1879 – 1,5,6 – bl Biblioteca [072]
A LUZ : PROPRIEDADE E ORGAO DO PARTIDO LIBERAL DO 5. DISTRITO DAS ALAGOAS – Penedo, Alagoas. 6 Maio 1882 – 1,5,6 – bl Biblioteca [072]
LA LUZ – Madrid, Spain. -d. 7 Jan-31 Dec 1932. 5 reels – 1 – uk British Libr Newspaper [072]
A LUZ BAHIANA – '(s.l.')-Bahia, Brazil. 27 Oct 1837 – 1,5,6 – bl Biblioteca [072]
LUZ BRASILEIRA – Rio de Janeiro, 11 Sep 1829-30 Mar 1831 – 1,5,6 – bl Biblioteca [072]

LUZ DE MEDICINA... / Morato Roma, F – Lisboa, 1672 – 8mf – 9 – sp Cultura [610]
LUZ DE MEDICINA Y RESPUESTA A LAS OBJECIONES PUESTAS A LA UNIVERSAL / Aldrete y Soto, L – S.L., S.F. – 1mf – 9 – sp Cultura [610]
LUZ DEL ALMA CRISTIANA / Meneses, Felipe de – 1594 – 9 – 1.50f – sp Bibl Santa Ana [240]
LA LUZ DEL VATICANO / Hernandez Valbuena, Ramiro – 1888 – 9 – 1.50f – sp Bibl Santa Ana [240]
LUZ EN LA TIERRA : ENTRE LA RELIGION Y LA CIENCIA NO PUEDEN EXISTIR CONFLICTOS / Paz Sanchez, Abdon de – 1882. Libros en Microficha no 14 – 1mf – 9 – Pta1,000.00 – 84-85422-41-4 – sp Pentalfa [240]
LUZ MATINAL : PERIODICO LITTERARIO, CHISTOSO E NOTICIOSO – Aracaju, 1 Jun-26 Jul 1882 – 1,5,6 – bl Biblioteca [072]
LA LUZ NO VIENE DEL SOL / Mendoza, Luis de – 1866 – 9 – 1.50f – sp Bibl Santa Ana [830]
LUZ Y CONSUELO DEL ALMA. TAGALOG / Rodrigo, Valerio – Maynila: J. Martinez, 1918. 935p – 1 – us U.W. Library [240]
O LUZEIRO : ORGAM LITTERARIO, SCIENTIFICO E NOTICIOSO – Maceio, Alagoas. 3 Maio 1903 – 1,5,6 – bl Biblioteca [072]
LUZERNER KANTONSBLATT – 1951-68 – 10r – 1 – us Ross [324]
EL LUZERO – (New York). 1926-27 – 1 – us A.J.P.C. [073]
EL LUZERO SEFARDI – New York. v. 1 no. 1-12. Sept 1926-Aug 1927 – 1 – us NY Public [270]
O LUZIR – Santa Rita do Jacutinga, Brazil. Sept 1939-Jan 1947. Widely scattered issues – 1 – bl Biblioteca [072]
Luzon de Millares, A *see* IDEA POLITICA VERI CHRISTIANI, SIVE ARS OBLIVIONIS
Luzvic, S *see* HET GODTVRUCHTICH HERTE
Luzzati, D *see* RECHERCHES SUR LA STRUCTURE DU DISCOURS ORAL SPONTANE
Luzzatto, E *see* ELEH BENEI HA-NE'URIM
Luzzatto, P *see* NOTICE SUR ABOU-IOUSOUF HASDAI' IBN-SCHAPROUT
Luzzatto, S D *see*
- BETULAT BAT YEHUDAH
- DIWAN R. YEHUDAH HA-LEVI
- GEDENKBUCH
- KINNOR NA'IM
- TAL OROT
Luzzatto, Samuel David *see*
- ELEMENTI GRAMMATICALI DEL CALDEO BIBLICO E DEL DIALETTO TALMUDICO BABILONESE
- GRAMMATIK DER BIBLISCH-CHALDAEISCHEN SPRACHE UND DES IDIOMS DES THALMUD BABLI
Luzzatto, SD *see* HOTAM TOKHNIT
Luzzi, Giovanni *see* LA LETTERA DI SAN PAOLO AI COLOSSESI: STUDI
L'vovich, A *see* PARTII I KREST'IANSTVO V GOSUDARSTVENNOI DUME
LVOVSKI I VI ESTNIK – (Includes c.1: 1915:May 28-29) – Lvov: Upravlenie voennago general-gubernatorstva Galit sii, 1915 – 1 – CSUXAHZ7582-S – us Hoover Inst Photo [947]
LVS, Y NORTE MVSICAL PARA CAMINAR POR LAS CIFRAS DE LA GUITARRA ESPANOLA, Y ARPA TANER, Y CANTAR A COMPAS POR CANTO DE ORGANO; Y BREVE EXPLICACION DEL ARTE, CON PRECEPTOS FACILES, INDUBITABLES, Y EXPLICADOS CON CLARAS REGLAS POR TEORICA, Y PRACTICA / Ruiz de Ribayaz, Lucas – Madrid: M Alvarez, 1677 – 1 – us Sibley [780]
LWOW I WILNO – London, UK. 10 Nov 1946-4 Nov 1950 – 1 – uk British Libr Newspaper [072]
Ly, Amadou *see* L'EPOPEE DE SAMBA GUELADIEGUI
Lyall, Alfred Comyn *see* VERSES WRITTEN IN INDIA
UN LYCEE DE JEUNES FILLES, PROFESSEURS-FEMMES / Reval, Gabrielle – Paris: Ollendorff, 1901. 340p. (Les Femmes Collection) – 4mf – 9 – $10.00 – fr Bibl Nationale [360]
LE LYCEE FRANCAIS – ou Melanges de litterature et de critique. Paris. juil 1819-sept 1820 (I-V) – 1 – fr A.C.R.P.P. [073]
LE LYCEE FRANCAIS OU MELANGES DE LITTERATURE ET DE CRITIQUE – Paris. v1. 1819 – 8mf – 9 – ne IDC [440]
LES LYCEENS, CONTRIBUTION A L'ETUDE DU MILIEU SCOLAIRE / Vincent G – F150.00 – fr Ethnologie [370]
Lycett, J *see* A MONOGRAPH OF THE BRITISH FOSSIL TRIGONIAE
THE LYCEUM "FAUST" / Hatton, Joseph – (Description of Henry Irving's dramatic representation of Goethe's Faust) – London: J S Virtue, [188-?] – 1r – 1 – us U.W. Library [790]
LYCEUM LATERANENSE : ILLUSTRIUM SCRIPTORUM SACRI APOSTOLICI ORDINIS CLERICORUM CANONICORUM REGULARIUM SALVATORIS LATERANENSIS ELOGIA / Rosinis, C de – Caesenae. v1-2. 1649 – Dfl144.00 – ne Slangenburg [240]
THE LYCEUM WEEKLY OF KENESETH ISRAEL – Philadelphia, PA. 1894 – 1 – us A.J.P.C. [071]
LYCOMING CHRONICLE – Williamsport, PA., 1829 – 13 – $25.00r – us I.M.R. [071]
LYCOMING RECORDER – Williamsport, PA., 1887-1888 – 13 – $25.00r – us I.M.R. [071]
Lydekker, R *see* THE SHEEP AND ITS COUSINS
DE LYDENDE SIELE GHESCHONCKEN VOOR EEN NIEUW-IAER TOT TROOST VAN ALLE BEDRUCKTE / Smidt, A de – Antwerpen, 1665 – 1mf – 9 – ne IDC [700]
Lydgate, Chaucer et al *see* POEMS
Lydus, Ioannes *see* CORPUS SCRIPTORUM HISTORIAE BYZANTINAE (CSHB 31)
Lye, Thomas *see*
- THE CHILDS DELIGHT
- A NEW SPELLING BOOK
Lyell, Charles *see*
- THE GEOLOGICAL EVIDENCES OF THE ANTIQUITY OF MAN
- PRINCIPLES OF GEOLOGY, BEING AN ATTEMPT TO EXPLAIN THE FORMER CHANGES OF THE EARTH'S SURFACE, BY REFERENCE TO CAUSES NOW IN OPERATION
Lyell, D D *see* CENTRAL AFRICAN GAME AND ITS SPOOR
Lyell, G *see* THE BUTTERFLIES OF AUSTRALIA; A MONOGRAPH OF THE AUSTRALIAN RHOPALOCERA
Lyell, K M *see* A GEOGRAPHICAL HANDBOOK OF ALL THE KNOWN FERNS, WITH TABLES TO SHOW THEIR DISTRIBUTION
Lyford, James O *see* HISTORY OF THE TOWN OF CANTERBURY 1727-1912
LYKENS REGISTER – Lykens, PA. -w 1872-1903 – 13 – $25.00r – us I.M.R. [071]
LYKENS STANDARD – Lykens, PA., 1905-1972 – 13 – $25.00r – us I.M.R. [071]
LYKENS STANDARD AND REGISTER – Lykens, PA., 1874-1905 – 13 – $25.00r – us I.M.R. [071]
Lykins, Johnston *see* LETTERS AND OTHER PAPERS
Lyman, Albert Josiah *see* A PLAIN MAN'S WORKING VIEW OF BIBLICAL INSPIRATION
LYMAN BEECHER / Hayward, Edward F – Boston: Pilgrim Press, c1904 – 1mf – us A.T.L.A. [240]
LYMAN FAMILY PAPERS, 1785-1956 – Massachusetts Historical Society – 28r – 1 – $2105.00 – us UMI [920]
Lyman, Frank H *see* HISTORY OF CITY OF KENOSHA AND KENOSHA COUNTY
Lyman, Hannah Willard *see* THE MARTYR OF SUMATRA
Lyman, John *see* OEUVRE
LYMAN NEBRASKA LEADER – Lyman, NE. -w. May 1927-Jan 1937; Apr 1937-Dec 1947; Jan 1949-Dec 1958 – 1 – us NE Hist [071]
Lyman, W D *see* HISTORY OF WALLA WALLA COUNTY
O LYNCE : PERIODICO CRITICO E LITTERARIO – Sabara, 18 May 1890 – 1,5,6 – bl Biblioteca [072]
Lynch, Alice Clare *see* THE KENNEDY CLAN AND TIERRA REDONDA
Lynch, Elizabeth C *see* LYNCH RECORD
Lynch, Frederick *see* THE PEACE PROBLEM
LYNCH HERALD-ENTERPRISE – Lynch, NE. -w. Apr 1919-Nov 1933; Jan 1934-Sep 1974 – 1 – us NE Hist [071]
Lynch, James *see* LETTERS TO THE HON. JOHN CARLING, MINISTER OF AGRICULTURE, ONTARIO, CANADA, ON EMIGRATION
Lynch, James D *see* BENCH AND BAR OF TEXAS
LYNCH JOURNAL – Lynch, NE. -w. Jun 1897-Oct 1902; Mar 1908-Jul 1918 – 1 – us NE Hist [071]
Lynch, R I *see* THE BOOK OF THE IRIS
LYNCH RECORD : CONTAINING BIOGRAPHICAL RECORDS OF MEN OF THE NAME LYNCH / Lynch, Elizabeth C – New York, N.Y.: William Hirten Co., 1925 – 1 reel – 1 – us Western Res [920]
LYNCHBURG PRESS – Lynchburg, VA. 1814-22 – 1 – us UMI [071]
LYNCH-LAW : AN INVESTIGATION INTO THE HISTORY OF LYNCHING IN THE U.S. / Cutler, James E – (Originally publ in 1905) – Montclair, N.J.: Patterson Smith, 1969 – 4mf – 9 – $6.00 – LLMC 92-140 – us L.L.M.C. [340]
LYNCH'S READY GUIDE – (Cont by: Lynch's Ready Guide to Victoria and British Columbia) – Victoria, BC: J H A Lynch, [1892] – 9 – cn C.I.H.M. [910]
LYNCH'S READY GUIDE *see* LYNCH'S READY GUIDE TO VICTORIA AND BRITISH COLUMBIA
LYNCH'S READY GUIDE TO VICTORIA AND BRITISH COLUMBIA – (Cont: Lynch's Ready Guide) – Victoria, BC: J H A Lynch, [1892-189- or 19–] – 9 – cn C.I.H.M. [910]
LYNCH'S READY GUIDE TO VICTORIA AND BRITISH COLUMBIA *see* LYNCH'S READY GUIDE
Lynd, SW *see* SECOND ADVENT OF CHRIST
LYNDHURST SHIRE CHRONICLE – Blayney – at Pascoe [980]
THE LYNDON B. JOHNSON NATIONAL SECURITY FILES, 1963-69 – (Series: National Security Files. Africa $1,270.00 Index $245.00. Asia and the Pacific $1,740.00 Index $355.00. 1st suppl $1,500.00 Index $265.00. Israel (with index) $320.00. Latin America $1,500.00 Index $320.00. The Middle East $930.00 Index $205.00. The United Nations $810.00 Index $170.00. USSR and Eastern Europe $120.00 Index $50.00. Vietnam $1,965.00 Index $355.00. 1st suppl $2,250.00 Index $360.00 Vietnam Special Subjects $4,165.00 Index $440.00. Western Europe $1,160.00 Index $245.00. Agency File 34r ISBN 1-55655-470-2 $4,255.00. Committee File 12r ISBN 1-55655-471-0 $1,500.00. Name and Speech Files 10r ISBN 1-55655-427-9 $1,250.00) – us UPA [324]
Lyndon. Kansas. First Presbyterian Church *see* RECORDS
LYNDON-"US" AND OUR NEIGHBORS / Green, C R – A historical genealogical directory about Lyndon, Osage County, Kansas. Lyndon, 1901. Kansas Reel 10.(The Cox Library Collection) – 5 – us Americana [978]
Lynes, Liliana K *see* THE EFFECT OF RESISTANCE TRAINING ON RESTING BLOOD PRESSURE IN HYPERTENSIVE WOMEN
Lyngbye, H C *see*
- TENTAMEN HYDROPHYOLOGIAE DENICAW
- TENTAMEN HYDROPHYTOLOGIAE DANICAE
LYNN ADVERTISER. (LYNN NEWS & ADVERTISER) – King's Lynn, England. 1842-1963. -w. 141 reels – 1 – uk British Libr Newspaper [072]
LYNN ASSOCIATION. SONORA, KENTUCKY : CHURCH RECORDS – 1856-Aug 1987 – 1 – $63.09 – us Baptist [240]
LYON CHIRURGICAL – v.1-18. 1908-21 – 1,5,6 – 22124.00 – us Princeton Micro [610]
LYON COLONIAL / L'Association des Anciens Eleves de l'enseignement Colonial. Chambre de Commerce. Lyon – Bulletin trimestriel. Lyon. 1912-mars 1914, sept 1919-43 – 1 – fr A.C.R.P.P. [073]
LYON COUNTRY MONITOR – Yerington, NV. 1900-02 – 1r – 1 – $50.00 – U04824 – us Library Micro [071]
LYON COUNTY TIMES – Dayton, NV. Jan 1889; May 1891; Oct 1897-Apr 1902 – 2r – 1 – $100.00 – U04484 – us Library Micro [071]
LYON COUNTY TIMES – Silver City, NV. 1874-88; 1891-97; 1902-07 – 10r – 1 – $500.00 – U04738 – us Library Micro [071]
LYON COUNTY TIMES – Yerington, NV. 1902 – 1r – 1 – $50.00 – U04805 – us Library Micro [071]
LYON COUNTY WASP – Yerington, NV. 1912-13 – 1r – 1 – $50.00 – U04825 – us Library Micro [071]
Lyon, D Willard *see* A BRIEF HISTORY OF THE FIRST 25 YEARS' HISTORY OF THE YMCA'S IN CHINA (CCC237)
Lyon, David Gordon *see* AN ASSYRIAN MANUAL
Lyon, David Willard *see* SKETCH OF THE HISTORY OF PROTESTANT MISSIONS IN CHINA
Lyon, G F *see*
- L'AFRIQUE, OU HISTOIRE, MOEURS, USAGES ET COUTUMES DES AFRICAINS: FEZZAN
- A BRIEF NARRATIVE OF AN UNSUCCESSFUL ATTEMPT TO REACH REPULSE BAY
- THE PRIVATE JOURNAL OF H.M.S. HECLA
Lyon, George A *see* OBSEQUIES, REV. G.W. LYON
Lyon, James *see*
- URANIA, OR A CHOICE COLLECTION OF PSALM TUNES, ANTHEMS, AND HYMNS
- URANIA, OR A CHOICE COLLECTION OF PSALM TUNES, ANTHEMS, AND HYMNS: TO WHICH ARE PREFIX'D THE PLAINEST, AND MOST NECESSARY RULES OF PSALMODY...
Lyon, John *see* LANCASTER, HARRISBURG, LEBANON AND YORK GOPSILL'S DIRECTORY 1863/64
Lyon, Newell *see* COMMERCIAL LAW
Lyon, Otto *see* GOETHES VERHAELTNIS ZU KLOPSTOCK
Lyons. France *see* BULLETIN MUNICIPAL OFFICIEL
Lyons. France. Conseil Municipal *see* PROCESS VERBAUX DES SEANCES
Lyons, I *see* FASCICULUS PLANTARUM CIRCA CANTABRIGIAM NASCENTIUM
Lyons, Joseph A *see* SILVER JUBILEE OF THE UNIVERSITY OF NOTRE DAME, JUNE 23RD, 1869
Lyons, Louis S *see* WHO'S WHO AMONG WOMEN OF CALIFORNIA
LYONS MIRROR-SUN – Lyons, NE. -w. May 1884; Aug 1890-Dec 1916; Jan 1918 to date – 1 – us NE Hist [071]
Lyons. Ohio. East Chesterfield Church of Christ Disciples *see* RECORDS
Lyons, P A *see* CARTULARIUM MONASTERII DE RAMESEIA (RS79)
LYONS SUN – Lyons, NE. -w. Jan-Mar 1891; Aug-Dec 1892; Nov-Dec 1895; Feb 1896-Dec 1898; 1899-Jun 1915. Scattered issues missing – 1 – us NE Hist [071]
LYRA AMERICANA, OR, VERSES OF PRAISE AND FAITH FROM AMERICAN POETS / Rider, George T – New York: D. Appleton, 1865, c1864 – 1mf – us A.T.L.A. [240]
LYRA GERMANICA. SECOND SERIES, THE CHRISTIAN LIFE / Winkworth, Catherine – London: Longman, Brown, Green, Longmans, and Roberts, 1858 – 1mf – us A.T.L.A. [240]
LYRA HISPANA... / Gomez Bravo, Vicente – (Tambien 6 ed 1946) – Madrid: Razon y Fe, 1942 – 1 – sp Bibl Santa Ana [440]
LYRA HISPANA. CUESTOMATIA ESCOLAR PARA LECTURA Y ANALISIS LITERARIO / Gomez Bravo, Vicente – 7th ed. Madrid: Razon y Fe, 1948 – 1 – sp Bibl Santa Ana [440]
LYRA HISPANA. CUESTOMATIA ESCOLAR PARA LECTURA Y ANALISIS LITERARIO / Gomez Bravo, Vicente – Octava edicion. Madrid: Edit. Razon y Fe, 1953 – 1 – sp Bibl Santa Ana [440]
LYRA HISPANA. PROSA SELECTA / Gomez Bravo, Vicente – Madrid: Ediciones Studium, 1955 – 1 – sp Bibl Santa Ana [810]
LYRA HISPANA. PROSA SELECTA. SILVA DRAMATICA / Gomez Bravo, Vicente – Madrid: Graficas Nebrija, S.A., 1955 – 1 – sp Bibl Santa Ana [810]
Lyra, Nicolaus de *see*
- BIBLIA SACRA CUM GLOSSA ET EXPOSITIONIBUS
- BIBLIA SACRA CUM GLOSSA ORDINARIA ET EXPOSITIONIBUS
- BIBLIA SACRA CUM GLOSSA ORDINARIA ET POSTILLA
- BIBLIA SACRA CUM GLOSSIS, INTERLINEARI ET ORDINARIA
LYRA SACRA AMERICANA, OR, GEMS FROM AMERICAN SACRED POETRY : SELECTED AND ARRANGED, WITH NOTES AND BIOGRAPHICAL SKETCHES / Cleveland, Charles Dexter – New York: Scribner; London: Sampson Low, Son, and Marston, 1868 – 1mf – us A.T.L.A. [240]
LA LYRE D'OR – Ottawa, Ontario. v1 n3. 1 mar 1888-v1n8/9. aut?sep 1888 – 1r – 1 – Can$25.00 – cn Can Microfilming [072]
LA LYRE D'OR – Ottawa: S Drapeau, 1888-1889 – 9 – cn C.I.H.M. [440]
LYRICAL ECHOES / Clark, Katherine A – Toronto: W. Briggs, 1899. 00668. (Pre-1900 Canadiana) – 9 – cn C.I.H.M. [810]

LYRICS, IDYLS AND FRAGMENTS / Armstrong, Joseph H – New York: Publishers' Print Co., 1892. 06175. (Pre-1900 Canadiana) – 9 – cn C.I.H.M. [810]
LYRICS ON FREEDOM, LOVE AND DEATH / Cameron, George Frederick – Ed. by his brother, Charles J. Cameron. Kingston, Ont.: L. Shannon; Boston: A. Moore, 1887. 03224. (Pre-1900 Canadiana) – 9 – cn C.I.H.M. [810]
LYRICS, SONGS AND SONNETS / Chandler, Amos Henry – Toronto: Hunter, Rose, 1880. 00553. (Pre-1900 Canadiana) – 9 – cn C.I.H.M. [810]
DIE LYRIK HOELDERLINS : EINE ANALYTISCHE UNTERSUCHUNG / Vietor, Karl – (Includes bibliographical references) – Frankfurt am Main: M Diesterweg, 1921 – 1r – 1 – us U.W. Library [430]
O LYRIO : DEDICADO AO BELLO SEXO – Jaragua, Alagoas. 23 Fev-9 Mar 1902 – 1,5,6 – bl Biblioteca [072]
DIE LYRISCHE EINLAGE BEI THEODOR STORM : IHR KUENSTLISCHER SINN IM AUFBAU DER NOVELLE / Lenhartz, Rolf – (Includes bibliographical references) – Bonn a. Rh.: L Roehrscheid, 1933 – 1r – 1 – us U.W. Library [430]
LYRISCHE GEDICHTE, BALLADEN UND ERZAEHLUNGEN / Vogl, Johann Nepomuk – Wien: Karl Konegen, 1902 – 1r – 1 – us U.W. Library [810]
LYRISCHE KLAENGE / Samuely, N – Lemberg. 1868. BJ-422-72 1 – 9 – ne IDC [810]
LYRISCHES : NEUE GEDICHTE / Lingg, Hermann – Wien: Karl Prochaska, [1885?] – 1r – 1 – us U.W. Library [810]
Lys, Marie-des *see* BIBLIOGRAPHIE ANALYTIQUE DE ERNEST PALLASCIO-MORIN, JOURNALISTE, AUTEUR DRAMATIQUE, CONFERENCIER
LYSEKILS BADTIDNING – Uddevalla, Sweden. 1882-83 – 1 reel – 1 – sw Kungliga [073]
LYSEKILS TIDNING – Uddevalla, Sweden. 1884-85, 1889 – 1 reel – 1 – sw Kungliga [073]
LYSEKILSBLADET – Uddevalla, Sweden. 1881-83 – 3r – 1 – sw Kungliga [073]
LYSEKILSKURIREN – Lysekil, Sweden. 1901-21 – 12r – 1 – sw Kungliga [072]
LYSEKILSPOSTEN – Grebbestad, 1895-97 – 9 – sw Kungliga [072]
LYSEKILSPOSTEN – Lysekil, Sweden. 1979- – 1 – sw Kungliga [072]
LYSIMETERS – 1982 – 74p – it F.A.O. [540]
LYSISTRATA OU LES ATHENIENNES / Hoffmann – (French Theatre Series). Paris. Huet et Charon, an X. 1801 – 9 – fr Hachette [820]
Lysogorskii, N V *see* MOSKOVSKII MITROPOLIT PLATON LEVSHIN KAK PROTIVORASKOL'NICHII DEIATEL
Lyttelton, Edward *see* STUDIES IN THE SERMON ON THE MOUNT
Lyttleton, Alfred *see* THE LAW OF TRADE COMBINATION
Lytton, Edward Robert Bulwer Lytton *see* SERBSKI PESME, OR, NATIONAL SONGS OF SERBIA
M – New York, 1983- – 1 – $175.00y – us Fairchild Micro [390]
M. CHAUVEAU ET L'IDEE NATIONALE: CONFERENCE FAITE DEVANT L'ASSOCIATION DES INSTITUTEURS DE LA CIRCONSCRIPTION DE L'ECOLE NORMALE JACQUES CARTIER, A L'OCCASION DE SA CENTIEME CONFERENCE, LE 24 JANVIER, 1895 / Bourassa, Gustave – Montreal: C. Beauchemin, 1895? 00210. (Pre-1900 Canadiana) – 9 – cn C.I.H.M. [370]
M: CIVILIZED MAN – 1986- – 1,5,6,9 – us UMI [390]
M ENS, A *see* OORSPRONG EN BETEKENIS VAN DE NEDERLANDSE BEGIJNEN
M. ERNEST RENAN ET LA CHAIRE D'HEBREU AU COLLEGE DE FRANCE : LEDCON D'OUVERTURE FAITE AU COLLEGE DE FRANCE LE 9 DEC 1893 / Berger, Philippe – Paris: Ernest Leroux, 1894 – 1mf – 9 – 0-8370-9443-7 – 1986-3443 – us A.T.L.A. [370]
M. FAILLON, PRETREDE ST SULPICE: SA VIE ET SES OEUVRES / Desmazures, Adam Charles Gustave – Montreal: Bibliotheque Paroissiale, 1879. 02663. (Pre-1900 Canadiana) – 9 – cn C.I.H.M. [971]
M. FLAVIEN MARTINEAU, PRETRE DE ST SULPICE: ESQUISSE BIOGRAPHIQUE / Desmazures, Adam Charles Gustave – Montreal: s.n., 1889 (Montreal: J. Lovell). 02664. (Pre-1900 Canadiana) – 9 – cn C.I.H.M. [971]
M. JEAN LE SUEUR: ANCIEN CURE DE SAINT-SAUVEUR-DE-THURY, PREMIER PRETRE SECULIER DU CANADA, 1634-68 / Gosselin, Auguste – Evreux: Impr. de l'Eure, 1894. 03477. (Pre-1900 Canadiana) – 9 – cn C.I.H.M. [240]
M. L'ABBE LOUIS-EUGENE OTIS : BIBLIOGRAPHIE / Plourde, Marthe – 1964. SEM105P4 – 1mf – 9 – cn Bibl Nat [240]
M. L'ABBE SAX ET SES SOUFFLEURS / Pelletier, Alexis – Quebec, 1875. SEM16P234 – 1r – 5 – Can$9.00 – cn Bibl Nat [971]
M. L'ABBE SAX ET SES SOUFFLEURS OU REFUTATION DES ERREURS CONTENUES DANS LE MANIFESTE LIBERAL QUEBECQUOIS / Luigi – Quebec: [s.n.], 1875. SEM16P234 – 1r – Can$9.00 – cn Bibl Nat [320]
M. MERCIER JUGE PAR LES LIBERAUX: M. MERCIER EXECUTE PAR M. TARTE: M. MERCIER EXECUTE PAR LA PATRIE: M. MERCIER REPUDIE PAR LES HONNETES LIBERAUX – 1891?. 03194. (Pre-1900 Canadiana) – 9 – cn C.I.H.M. [971]
M. OPITZ, P. RONSARD UND D. HEINSIUS / Beckherrn, Richard – (Includes bibliographical references) – Koenigsberg in Pr.: R Leupold, 1888 – 1r – 1 – us U.W. Library [430]
M5V MAGAZINE – (Cont: Impulse. Cont by: Work 1994) – Toronto, 1991 – 9 – Can$20.00y – cn Micromedia [073]
M5V MAGAZINE *see*
– IMPULSE
– WORK
MA : EIN PORTRAET / Andreas-Salome, Lou – Stuttgart: J G Cotta, 1904 – 1r – 1 – us U.W. Library [943]
MA / Virginia. Polytechnic Institute. Extension Division – n.1-99. 1961-69 – 1,5 – us Spaulding [630]
MA CAPTIVITE EN ABYSSINIE SOUS L'EMPEREUR THEODOROS / Blanc, Henry – (African Library). Paris. Societe des traites religieux. 1870 – 9 – fr Hachette [960]
MA GASPESIE – Black Cape, Canada. v2 n1. 1 mai 1953-v8 n51. 9 jul 1960 – 1r – 1 – Can$55.00 – cn Can Microfilming [072]
Ma, I-yu *see* CHUNG-KUO HUI CHIAO SHIH CHIEN (CCC239)
Ma, John *see* VAN GULIK COLLECTION
Ma, John K C et al *see* LOVE, MARRIAGE AND HOME (CCC238)
M.A. Leeson and Co *see* HISTORY OF MACOMB COUNTY
MA YIN CHU YEN-CHIANG CHI / Ma Yin-Ch'u – (Lectures on Current Economic Problems in China). Shanghai, 1926-29. 4 v. 1 reel – 1 – 24.00 – us Chinese Res [950]
Ma Yin-Ch'u *see*
– CHUNG-KUO CHING-CHI KAI-TSAO
– MA YIN CHU YEN-CHIANG CHI
MAAA1SIR UL-UMARA / Nawab Samsamud$Dowla, Shah Hawaz Khan – Calcutta, 1888-1891. (Bibliotheca Indica, v. 112). 3 vols. BI-748 2 – 8 – ne IDC [490]
MA-AASAMIRU-L-UMARA / Nawab, Samsamu-D-Daula & Haqq, Abdul – H. Beveridge, Transl. Calcutta, 1913. (Bibliotheca Indica, v. 202). BI-751 2 – 8 – ne IDC [490]
MA'AGAL TOV HA-SHALEM / Azulai, H J D – Jerusalem. 1934. BJ-27-20 1 – 9 – ne IDC [550]
MAAL OG MINNE – 1909-70 – 1 – us I.U. Libraries [390]
MAAL OG VAEGT – 1936 – 1 – us I.U. Libraries [390]
MA'AMAR HA-MELEKH – v. 4. (Luah Yerushalayim, v. 4). 1892. BJ-27-235 1 – 9 – ne IDC [270]
MA'AMARIM / Smolenskin, P – Jerusalem. 4 v. 1925-26. BJ-422-88 1 – 9 – ne IDC [470]
MA'AMARIM LE-ZIKHRON R. ZEVI PEREZ CHAJES / Chajes, H P – 2v. (The first volume in German). Vienna. 1933. BJ-100-73 – 9 – ne IDC [956]
MAANDBLAD DER CENTRALE ORGANISATIE VOOR DE RELIGIEUSE EN MOREELE VERHEFFING DER JODEN – Amsterdam. v1-6(1,2). 1911-1920 – 10mf – 9 – ne IDC [270]
MAANDBLAD DER CULTURELE JOODSE CLUB – Amsterdam. Nos 1-2. 1938 – 1mf – 9 – ne IDC [305]
MAANDBLAD DER VEREENIGING VAN INSPECTEURS VAN FINANCIEN – Weltevreden. 1926-1947. Lacking: 1940, v15(3); 1941-45, v16-17 – 107mf – 9 – ne IDC [332]
MAANDBLAD VAN DEN JOODSCHEN VROUWENRAAD – Amsterdam. v1-6. 1923-1928 – 20mf – 9 – ne IDC [270]
MAAND-STATISTIEK VAN DEN UITVOER VAN SUMATRA'S OOSTKUST EN LANGSA NAAR HET BUITENLAND – Medan, 1925 (1-6); 1926 (1-12) – 3mf – 9 – ne IDC [332]
Maar, A et al *see* FISH CULTURE IN CENTRAL EAST AFRICA
MAARAHOT / Israel. Zahal. Israel Defence Forces – Military journal. Tel$Aviv. 1939-. 8 issues a year. Text in Hebrew – 9 – 320.00; 8.00y – is I.T.T.I. [324]
MA'ARIF – Sene 1-5, nos 1-204; n.s. nos 1-35 (1307-1312) – 64mf – 9 – $105.00 – us MEDOC [949]
MAARIFA – Zanzibar, Tanzania. -w. 1 Jan 1959-19 Dec 1963. 3 reels – 1 – uk British Libr Newspaper [072]
MA'ARIV – Israel, 1979- – 24r per y – 1 – $660.00y – us Ross [072]
MA'ARIV – Tel Aviv. 1948-70. BJ-91-100 3 – 1 – ne IDC [956]
Maas, Otto *see*
– MISIONES DE NUEVO MEJICO. TOMO 1
– LAS ORDENES RELIGIOSAS DE ESPANA Y LA COLONIZACION DE AMERICA EN LA SEGUNDA PARTE DEL SIGLO 18
MAASAI HERDING : AN ANALYSIS OF THE LIVESTOCK PRODUCTION SYSTEM OF MAASAI PASTORALISTS IN EASTERN KAJIADO DISTRICT, KENYA / ed by Bekure, Solomon et al – 1991 – 9 – $37.00 – et ILRI [630]
MA'ASE FUN DRAY VAYBERN – Prague? c.1650? BJ-43-47 1 – 9 – ne IDC [430]
MA'ASEH – Groningen. Nos 1-3. 1932-1933 – 1mf – 9 – ne IDC [949]
MAASIR I' ALAMGIRI / Muhammad Saqi – (Bibliotheca Indica Series: Persian). Calcutta. 1870-73. BI-765 2 – 8 – ne IDC [490]
MA'ASIR I RAHIMI / Abd Al-Baqi Niha Vandi – (Bibliotheca Indica series: Persian). Calcutta. 1924-31. BI-763 2 – 8 – ne IDC [890]
Maassen, Carl Georg von *see* HERRMANN UND ULRIKE
Maat, R H *see* TANJA DJAWAB: ANGKATAN 45
MAATSCHAPPIJ TOT EXPLOITATIE VAN STAATSSPOORWEGEN – Verslag. Utrecht etc. 1863 64-1937 – 1 – us NY Public [073]
Mabbs, G *see* CATALOGUE OF BOOKS CONTAINED IN THE LOCKHART LIBRARY AND IN THE GENERAL LIBRARY
Mabbutt, J A *see*
– CASE STUDIES ON DESERTIFICATION
– KHARTOUM WORKSHOP ON ARID LANDS MANAGEMENT
Mabey, Charles R *see* THE UTAH BATTERIES: A HISTORY
Mabie, Henry Clay *see*
– THE DIVINE RIGHT OF MISSIONS
– HOW DOES THE DEATH OF CHRIST SAVE US?
– THE MEANING AND MESSAGE OF THE CROSS
– THE TASK WORTH WHILE
Mabillon, D J *see* DE RE DIPLOMATICA LIBRI
Mabillon, J *see* ACTA SANCTORUM O.S.B.
Mabillon, Jean *see*
– ACTA SANCTORUM ORDINIS ST BENEDICTI
– ACTA SANCTORUM O.S.B.
– ANNALES ORDINIS S. BENEDICTI
– DE LITURGIA GALLICANA LIBRI 3
– OUVRAGES POSTHUMES DE D. JEAN MABILLON ET DE D. THIERRI RUINART
– REFLEXIONS SUR LA REPONSE DE M. L'ABBE DE LA TRAPPE
THE MABINOGION (MABINOGION. ENGLISH AND WELSH) – 1849 – 1 – us I.U. Libraries [390]
MABLETHORPE, ALFORD AND SUTTON-ON-SEA STANDARD *see* LINCOLNSHIRE STANDARD (ALFORD AND COAST)
Mabry, J C *see* A LEGAL VIEW OF THE TRIAL OF CHRIST
MAC: NEWSLETTER OF THE MIDWEST ARCHIVES CONFERENCE – (v.7-. 1979- 5,6,9) – v.1-. 1973- – 1 – us UMI [025]
O MACACO BRASILEIRO – Rio de Janeiro, Brazil. 1822 – 1 – bl Biblioteca [072]
McAdam, David *see*
– INDIVIDUAL, CORPORATE AND FIRM NAMES
– LAW DAYS; OR, DIES JURIDICI, COMMONLY CALLED "TERMS OF COURT," THEIR APPLICATION TO COURTS IN GENERAL, AND PARTICULARLY TO THE MARINE COURT OF THE CITY OF NEW YORK
– THE MARINE COURT OF THE CITY OF NEW YORK: ITS ORGANIZATION, JURISDICTION AND PRACTICE
– THE RIGHTS, DUTIES, REMEDIES AND INCIDENTS BELONGING TO AND GROWING OUT OF THE RELATION OF LANDLORD AND TENANT.
McAdams, F M *see* EVERYDAY SOLDIER LIFE
McAdams, MrS Harry K *see* KENTUCKY PIONEER AND COURT RECORDS
Macaire, Georges *see* HISTOIRE DE L'EGLISE D'ALEXANDRIE
Macalhaes, Basilio de *see* EXPANSAO GEOGRAPHICA DO BRASIL COLONIAL
Macalister, R A S *see*
– ECCLESIASTICAL VESTMENTS
– THE EXCAVATION OF GEZER
– EXCAVATIONS OF THE HILL OF OPHEL
McAll, Mrs. Robert Whitaker *see* ROBERT WHITAKER MCALL
McAll, Robert Whitaker *see* A CRY FROM THE LAND OF CALVIN AND VOLTAIRE
McAllister, Agnes *see* A LONE WOMAN IN AFRICA
McAllister, C *see* MACALLISTER'S REPORTS OF CASES IN THE NINTH CIRCUIT, 1855-1859
MACALLISTER'S REPORTS OF CASES IN THE NINTH CIRCUIT, 1855-1859 / McAllister, C – New York: Voorhis. 1v. 1859 (all publ) – 6mf – 9 – $9.00 – LLMC 81-459 – us L.L.M.C. [340]
McAndrews, M R *see* DEVELOPMENTAL AND SITUATIONAL FACTORS AFFECTING LITTLE LEAGUE PARTICIPATION
Macao *see*
– BOLETIM OFICIAL AND SUPPLEMENTS
– BOLETIM OFICIAL DE MACAU
Macao. (Portugal). Ministerios da Economia e do Ultramar *see* PLANO DE FOMENTO 1953-1958
Macao. (Portugal). Presidencia do Conselho *see* PLANO INTERCALAR DE FOMENTO PARA 1965-1967
AN MACAOMH – 1909-13.4 pts.4 fiches – 9 – Ir£5.00 – ie Microforms [073]
MACAOMH 1909-1913 – 4 mf – Ir£5.00 – ie Microforms [420]
MacArthur, A *see*
– MACARTHUR AND MACKEY'S REPORTS OF CASES IN THE DISTRICT OF COLUMBIA, 1879-1880
– MACARTHUR'S REPORTS OF CASES IN THE DISTRICT OF COLUMBIA, 1873-1879
MACARTHUR AND MACKEY'S REPORTS OF CASES IN THE DISTRICT OF COLUMBIA, 1879-1880 / MacArthur, A & Mackey, F H – Baltimore: Curlander. 1v. 1884 (all publ) – 6mf – 9 – $9.00 – LLMC 90-381 – us L.L.M.C. [340]
MacArthur, Arthur *see* THE RICH MAN AND LAZARUS
MacArthur, Frank *see*
– MACARTHUR'S D.C. PATENT CASES
– REPORTS OF CASES ARISING UPON APPLICATIONS FOR LETTERS-PATENT FOR INVENTIONS DETERMINED IN THE CIRCUIT AND SUPREME COURTS OF THE DISTRICT OF COLUMBIA.
MacArthur, John *see* THE LIFE AND SERVICES OF HORATIO VISCOUNT NELSON
McArthur, John *see* PRINCIPLES AND PRACTICE OF NAVAL AND MILITARY COURTS-MARTIAL
Macarthur, John Robertson *see* BIBLICAL LITERATURE AND ITS BACKGROUNDS
MacArthur, Robert Stuart *see*
– THE ATTRACTIVE CHRIST
– BIBLE DIFFICULTIES AND THEIR ALLEVIATIVE INTERPRETATION
MACARTHUR'S D.C. PATENT CASES / MacArthur, Frank – (Reports of cases arising upon applications for letters-patent for inventions determined in the Circuit and Supreme Courts of the District of Columbia) – Washington: Morrison. 1v. 1841-59 (all publ) – 9mf – 9 – $13.50 – LLMC 84-328 – us L.L.M.C. [340]
MACARTHUR'S REPORTS OF CASES IN THE DISTRICT OF COLUMBIA, 1873-1879 / MacArthur, A – Washington: W H & O H Morrison. v1-3. 1874?-1881 (all publ) – 22mf – 9 – $33.00 – LLMC 90-380 – us L.L.M.C. [340]
Macartney, G M *see* HOUSEHOLD ACCOUNTBOOK. 1797-98
Macassey, James *see* MACASSEY'S REPORTS OF CASES ARGUED AND DETERMINED IN THE SUPREME COURT OF NEW ZEALAND

McDermott, John T *see* OPERATION OF THE FEDERAL JUDICIAL COUNCILS
McDiarmid, Errett Weir *see*
– A MIDWEST COOPERATIVE LIBRARY PROGRAM
– A MIDWEST INTER-LIBRARY PROGRAM
MacDonald, Ch *see* OBJETS DES PHILIPPINES (MINDORO, PALAWAN)
McDonald, D *see* AGRICULTURAL WRITERS
McDonald, David *see* A TREATISE ON THE POWERS AND DUTIES OF JUSTICES OF THE PEACE, MAYORS, MARSHALS, AND CONSTABLES IN THE STATE OF INDIANA.
MacDonald, Dugald *see* ANCIENT SCIENCE, OR, SECRETS OF PYRAMIDS, WALLS AND TEMPLES
Macdonald, Eugene Montague *see* COL. ROBERT G. INGERSOLL, AS HE IS: A COMPLETE REFUTATION OF HIS CLERICAL ENEMIES' MALICIOUS SLANDERS..
MacDonald, George *see*
– THE HISTORY OF GUTTA-PERCHA WILLIE: THE WORKING GENIUS
– THE MIRACLES OF OUR LORD
McDonald, Isaac Burkhalter *see* DEVELOPING A PROGRAM OF FAMILY MINISTRY BY THE DEACONS OF FIRST BAPTIST CHURCH, HODGENVILLE, KENTUCKY
McDonald, IW *see* NONPROTEIN NITROGEN IN THE NUTRITION OF RUMINANTS
Macdonald, J A *see* FROM FAR FORMOSA
Macdonald, James Madison *see* THE LIFE AND WRITINGS OF ST JOHN
MacDonald, John *see* A TREATISE EXPLANATORY OF THE PRINCIPLES CONSTITUTING THE PRACTICE AND THEORY OF THE VIOLONCELLO...
McDonald, Kimberley D *see* THE RELATIONSHIP BETWEEN PRECOMPETITIVE ANXIETY AND TEAM COHESION
MacDonald, M *see* REPORT ON THE PROPOSED EXTENSION OF IRRIGATION IN THE JORDAN VALLEY
Macdonald, Neil W *see* RANDOM AND DETERMINISTIC (NONRANDOM) ASPECTS OF ATHLETIC BEHAVIOR WITH SPECIAL REFERENCE TO THE NATIONAL HOCKEY LEAGUE
McDonald, Susan A *see* PSYCHOLOGICAL AFFECT OF THE INJURED ATHLETE
McDonald, Walter *see* THE PRINCIPLES OF MORAL SCIENCE
MacDonald, William *see* A NEW CONSTITUTION FOR A NEW AMERICA
McDonel, Mary *see* AUSTRALIAN ANNUAL REPORT FILE 1993
MacDonnell, John *see* ENGLISH STATE TRIALS, 1163-1858
McDonnold, B W *see* HISTORY OF THE CUMBERLAND PRESBYTERIAN CHURCH
MacDougall, Donald *see* THE CONVERSION OF THE MAORIS
McDougall, John R *see* WORLD WIDE
MacDowell, Alexander B *see* FACTS ABOUT IRELAND; A CURVE-HISTORY OF RECENT YEARS
MacDowell, E *see*
– SONATA NO. 1, G MINOR, OP. 45, "SONATA TRAGICA"
– SONATA NO. 2, G MINOR, OP. 50, "SONATA EROICA"
– SONATA NO. 3, OP. 57, "NORSE"
– SONATA NO. 4, OP. 59, "KELTIC"
McDowell, William Fraser *see* THE PICKET LINE OF MISSIONS
McDowell, William Fraser et al *see* THE REVIVAL
McDudd *see* AN ILLUSTRATED HISTORY OF LINCOLN COUNTY AND HER PEOPLE
Macduff, John Ross *see*
– THE FOOTSTEPS OF ST PAUL
– THE HART AND THE WATER-BROOKS: A PRACTICAL EXPOSITION OF THE 42ND PSALM
– MEMORIES OF GENNESARET
– MEMORIES OF OLIVET
– MEMORIES OF PATMOS, OR, SOME OF THE GREAT WORDS AND VISIONS OF THE APOCALYPSE
– SUNSETS ON THE HEBREW MOUNTAINS
Mace, A C *see* EL ANRAH AND ABYDOS (MEES VOL 23)
Mace de Gastines, Edith *see* CHRONIQUE D'UN ANONYME DE BETHUNE, HISTOIRE DES DUCS DE NORMANDIE ET DES ROIS D'ANGLETERRE JUSQU'EN 1220
Mace de Lepinay, Jules Charles Antoine *see* FRANGES D'INTERFERENCE ET LEURS APPLICATIONS METROLOGIQUES
Mace, G *see* FEMMES CRIMINELLES
Mace, Thomas *see*
– MUSICK'S MONUMENT
– MUSICK'S MONUMENT; OR A REMEMBRANCER OF THE BEST PRACTICAL MUSICK
LA MACEDOINE – Geneva, Sofia, Bulgaria. -f. 13 June 1927-6 May 1934; Aug 1938. 2 reels – 1 – uk British Libr Newspaper [949]
LA MACEDOINE: ETUDES ETHNOGRAPHIQUES ET POLITIQUES / Belic, Aleksandar – Paris: Bloud & Gay, 1919. 278p. maps. With: Les Croates sous le joug Magyar par H. Hinkovitch. Paris: Plon-Nourrit, 1915 – 1 – us U.W. Library [949]
MACEDONIA : A PERIODICAL FOR REPORTING AND INTERPRETING BALKAN EVENTS – (Library has: May 1949-Oct. 1958. Many issues missing) – Indianapolis, Ind.: Central Committee of the Macedonian Political Organization of the United States and Canada, 1949- – 1 – CSUX86-S205 – us Hoover Inst Photo [947]
MACEDONIA BAPTIST CHURCH. CHEROKEE COUNTY. SOUTH CAROLINA : CHURCH RECORDS – (1,062p) – 1872-Oct. 1978 – 1 reel – 1 – $47.79 – us Baptist [240]
MACEDONIA BAPTIST CHURCH. CHESTERFIELD COUNTY. SOUTH CAROLINA : CHURCH RECORDS – 1832-1972 – 1 – 37.17 – us Baptist [240]
MACEDONIA BAPTIST CHURCH. LINCOLNTON, NORTH CAROLINA : CHURCH RECORDS – 1888-1938 – 1 – 28.80 – us Baptist [240]
MACEDONIAN *see* HELPING HAND
MACEDONIAN AND HELPING HAND *see* HELPING HAND
MACEDONIAN AND RECORD *see* HELPING HAND
MACEIO : ORGAO NOTICIOSO, LITTERARIO, ARTISTICO, COMMERCIAL E RELIGIOSO – Maceio, Alagoas. 8 Set-24 Dez 1897 – 1,5,6 – bl Biblioteca [072]
MACEIO ESTATISTICO E CULTURAL – Maceio, Alagoas. Set 1940 – 1,5,6 – bl Biblioteca [072]
Macel, O *see* AVANT-GARDE AND ARCHITECTURE IN CZECHOSLOVAKIA 1909-1938
McElroy *see* BIOGRAPHICAL ANNALS OF OHIO – A HANDBOOK OF THE GOVERNMENT AND INSTITUTIONS OF THE STATE OF OHIO
McElroy, Robert M *see* KENTUCKY IN THE NATION'S HISTORY
McErlane, Daniel *see* THE CHURCH OF CHRIST THE SAME FOREVER
McEwan *see* AIRS, MARCHES, MINUETTS...
McEwan, Thomas *see* THE BOOK OF ESTHER
MacEwen, Alexander R *see*
– ANTOINETTE BOURIGNON, QUIETIST
– THE ERSKINES
– LIFE AND LETTERS OF JOHN CAIRNS, D.D., LL.D.
Macfadden, Bernarr Adolphus *see* THE POWER AND BEAUTY OF SUPERB WOMANHOOD.
MacFadyen, J *see* THE FLORA OF JAMAICA
McFadyen, John Edgar *see*
– INTRODUCTION TO THE OLD TESTAMENT
– THE MESSAGES OF THE PROPHETIC AND PRIESTLY HISTORIANS
– THE MESSAGES OF THE PSALMISTS
Macfarland, Charles S *see*
– THE CHRISTIAN MINISTRY AND THE SOCIAL ORDER
– CHRISTIAN SERVICE AND THE MODERN WORLD
– CHRISTIAN UNITY AT WORK
Macfarland, Charles Stedman *see* THE INFINITE AFFECTION
McFarland, George Bradley *see*
– HISTORICAL SKETCH OF PROTESTANT MISSIONS IN SIAM, 1828-1928
McFarland, Joseph F *see* 20TH CENTURY HISTORY OF WASHINGTON COUNTY AND CITY
Macfarlane, Alan et al *see* RECORDS OF AN ENGLISH VILLAGE
McFarlane, Samuel *see* AMONG THE CANNIBALS OF NEW GUINEA
MacFarren, G *see* SIX LECTURES ON HARMONY
M'FINGAL : AN EPIC POEM / Trumbull, John – (Although there is very little of law in this satirical poem, it is the most famous work of its author, a well known patroit in the Revolutionary War, lawyer-poet, and judge on the Connecticut Supreme Court of Erros) – New York: American Book Exchange, 1881 – 4mf – 9 – $6.00 – LLMC 91-016 – us L.L.M.C. [810]
McGarvey, John William *see* THE AUTHORSHIP OF THE BOOK OF DEUTERONOMY
McGee, Joseph F *see* HISTORY OF BUTTE COUNTY, OROVILLE, CALIFORNIA
McGee, T D'Arcy *see* NEW ERA
McGee, Thomas D'Arcy *see* A HISTORY OF THE ATTEMPTS TO ESTABLISH THE PROTESTANT REFORMATION IN IRELAND
McGhee, J C *see* STALCUP'S STALL REVIEWED
McGiffert, Arthur Cushman *see*
– THE APOSTLES' CREED
– MARTIN LUTHER
– PRIMITIVE AND CATHOLIC CHRISTIANITY
– PROTESTANT THOUGHT BEFORE KANT
– THE RISE OF MODERN RELIGIOUS IDEAS
McGill University. Archives *see* LETTRES ET COPIES DE LETTRES – ROYAL INSTITUTION (1820-1849)
McGill University. Library *see* A CATALOGUE OF BOOKS ON ART AND ARCHITECTURE IN MCGILL UNIVERSITY LIBRARY AND THE GORDON HOME BLACKADER LIBRARY OF ARCHITECTURE
MacGillivray, D *see*
– A CENTURY OF PROTESTANT MISSIONS IN CHINA (1807-1907)
– THE TRIBULATIONS OF THE CHURCH IN CHINA, A.D. 1900 (CCC240)
MacGillivray, P H *see* A CATALOGUE OF THE FLOWERING PLANTS AND FERNS GROWING IN THE NEIGHBOURHOOD OF ABERDEEN
MacGillivray, W *see* A HISTORY OF BRITISH BIRDS, INDIGENOUS AND MIGRATORY
McGilvary, Daniel *see* A HALF CENTURY AMONG THE SIAMESE AND THE LAO
McGirt, James Ephraim *see* SOME SIMPLE SONGS AND A FEW MORE AMBITIOUS ATTEMPTS
McGlothlin, William Joseph *see*
– BAPTIST CONFESSIONS OF FAITH
– DIE BERNER TAEUFER BIS 1532
– A GUIDE TO THE STUDY OF CHURCH HISTORY
– PAPERS OF W.J. MCGLOTHLIN, 1930-32
McGlumphy, W H S *see* HISTORY OF CLINTON AND CLADWELL COUNTIES
M'Govern, Chauncey *see* PREPARING FOR TRIALS INVOLVING FORGERY.
McGovern, James Joseph *see* THE LIFE AND LIFE-WORK OF POPE LEO 13
McGovern, John *see*
– TERROR IN SPAIN: HOW THE COMMUNIST INTERNATIONAL HAS DESTROYED WORKING CLASS UNITY, UNDERMINED THE FIGHT AGAINST FRANCO, AND SUPPRESSED THE SOCIAL REVOLUTION
– WHY BISHOPS BACK FRANCO; REPORT OF VISIT OF INVESTIGATION TO SPAIN
McGovern, Thomas F *see* ALCOHOLISM TREATMENT QUARTERLY
MacGowan, John *see*
– ENGLISH AND CHINESE DICTIONARY OF THE AMOY DIALECT
– THE FOUNDRY BUDGET OPENED
– A FURTHER DEFENCE OF PRIESTCRAFT
– PRIESTCRAFT DEFENDED
MacGrail, Joseph F *see* THE CURSE OF ROME
McGrath, John W *see* MCGRATH'S MANDAMUS CASES
McGrath, Robert Hunter, jr *see* THE DOCTRINE OF CY PRES AS APPLIED TO CHARITIES
Macgregor, Duncan Campbell *see* GEORGE H.C. MACGREGOR, M. A., A BIOGRAPHY
Macgregor, George Hogarth Carnaby *see* A HOLY LIFE AND HOW TO LIVE IT
MACGREGOR HERALD – Manitoba, CN. 1976-87 – 20r – 1 – cn Commonwealth Micro [072]
Macgregor, James *see*
– THE APOLOGY OF THE CHRISTIAN RELIGION
– THE EPISTLE OF PAUL TO THE CHURCHES OF GALATIA: WITH INTRODUCTION AND NOTES
– THE REVELATION AND THE RECORD
– STUDIES IN THE HISTORY OF CHRISTIAN APOLOGETICS: NEW TESTAMENT AND POST-APOSTOLIC
McGregor, Malcolm *see* BIOGRAPHICAL RECORD OF JASPER COUNTY
MacGregor, Morris J *see* BLACKS IN THE U.S. ARMED FROCES
McGrew, Clarence A *see* CITY OF SAN DIEGO AND SAN DIEGO COUNTY
McGrew, W L *see* AMERICAN SAMOA, HOPE AND DESPAIR, 1947-1952
McGroarty, John S *see*
– HISTORY OF LOS ANGELES COUNTY
– LOS ANGELES FROM THE MOUNTAINS TO THE SEA
McGuigan, J J *see*
– LAWS OF THE CANAL ZONE, ISTHMUS OF PANAMA, 1904-1914
– TREATIES AND ACTS OF CONGRESS RELATING TO THE PANAMA CANAL
MacGuinness, Joannes *see* COMMENTARII DE RELIGIONE REVELATA EJUSQUE FONTIBUS AC DE ECCLESIA CHRISTI
McGuire, Mrs. C P et al *see* RECORDS OF PICKENS COUNTY, ALABAMA
McGuire, Don *see* A COMPARISON OF THE TENSILE STRENGTH OF THE UMBILICAL CORD OF BABIES OF SMOKING AND NON-SMOKING MOTHERS
McGuire, John R *see* AN EXAMINATION OF ENVIRONMENTAL ATTITUDES AMONG COLLEGE STUDENTS
McGuire, Thomas Horace *see* A HANDBOOK FOR MAGISTRATES, IN RELATION TO SUMMARY CONVICTIONS AND ORDERS AND INDICTABLE OFFENCES
Mach, Richard von *see* THE BULGARIAN EXARCHATE
Machado Alvarez, Antonio *see* LA BIBLIOTECA DE TRADICIONES POPULARES
Machado, Cristobal *see* RECREACIONES GEOGRAFICAS...GEOGRAFIA
Machado, Joaquim Jose *see*
– MAPUTO – LOURENCO MARQUES – MOSSAMEDES
– QUESTOES AFRICANAS
Machado, Jose E *see* EL DIA HISTORICO. CARACAS, 1929
MacHale, John *see*
– THE EVIDENCES AND DOCTRINES OF THE CATHOLIC CHURCH
– SERMONS AND DISCOURSES
MacHale, Thomas *see* SERMONS AND DISCOURSES
MACHANEI JISROEIL – Antwerpen. v1-2. 1929-1930 – 2mf – 9 – ne IDC [949]
Machat, J *see* LES RIVIERES DU SUD ET LE FOUTA DIALLON (GUINEE FRANCAISE)
MACHBERETH – Amsterdam, 1939(1-2) – 1mf – 9 – ne IDC [949]
MACHE – Athens, Greece. 6-28 Feb, 24-31 Mar, 11 May-30 Jun, 14 Jul-2 Dec 1946; 6 Jan-2 Jun, 8 Dec 1947-31 Dec 1967.-w. 14mqn reels – 1 – uk British Libr Newspaper [072]
Machen, Arthur Webster *see* A TREATISE ON THE FEDERAL CORPORATION TAX LAW OF 1909.
EL MACHETE – Mexico. no. 1-481. Mar 1924-June 20 1937. Incomplete – 1 – us NY Public [073]
MACHETE : PERIODICO OBRERO Y CAMPESINO – (Lacks some issues) – Mexico City. n1-481. 1924-37 – 1r – 1 – us Ross [330]
Machfudz, Shiddig *see* K.H. PEDOMAN TABLIGH
THE MACHIAS UNION – Machias, ME: Yates & Furbush, may 24 1853-jul 1 1920 – us Res Libr [071]
Machiavelli, Niccolo *see* THE LIVING THOUGHTS OF MACHIAVELLI
LOS MACHIGUENGAS. LIMA, 1944 / Cenitagoya, Vicente – Madrid: Razon y Fe, 1947 – 1 – sp Bibl Santa Ana [946]
MACHINE AND TOOL BLUE BOOK – 1906- 1; 1973- 5,6; 1977- 9 – us UMI [621]
MACHINE DESIGN – (1965- 5,6. 1970- 9) – 1-1929- – 1 – us UMI [621]
MACHINE-MEDITATED LEARNING – v1-. 1982- – 1,5,6,9 – us UMI [073]
MACHINERY – 1-79 1894-1973 1; 1964-73 5,6 – us UMI [621]
MACHINERY MOLDERS JOURNAL, 1888-1892 : VULCAN RECORD, 1868-1875 / Brotherhood of Machinery MoldersUnited Sons of Vulcan – (Coll title: Labor Union Periodicals, Pt 1) – 1r – 1 – $135.00 – 1-55655-240-8 – us UPA [331]
MACHINERY SERVICING ORGANIZATIONS – 1977 repr 1983 – 103p – it F.A.O. [060]
MACHINE-TRACTOR STATION *see* MASHINNO-TRAKTORNAI A STANT SII A
THE MACHINIST : 1946-1955 / International Association of Machinists – (Coll title: Labor Union Periodicals, Pt 1) – 3r – 1 – $405.00 – 1-55655-241-6 – us UPA [331]
MACHINISTS AND BLACKSMITHS' MONTHLY JOURNAL, 1870-1875 : THE BRASS WORKER, 1895-1896 : OFFICIAL JOURNAL, 1902-1904 – (Coll title: Labor Union Periodicals, Pt 1) – 1r – 1 – $135.00 – 1-55655-242-4 – us UPA [331]

Machold, Johann *see* COMPENDIUM GERMANICO-LATINUM MUSICES PRACTICAE...MUSICA DEUTSCH UND LATEINISCH..
MACHT DER HEIMAT : ROMAN / Zahn, Ernst – Stuttgart: Deutsche Verlags-Anstalt, c1947 – 1r – 1 – us U.W. Library [830]
"MACHT RUHESTAND KRANK?" : MORBIDITAET BEI 60JAEHRIGEN MAENNERN NACH AUSSCHEIDEN AUS DEM ERWERBSLEBEN DURCH ERREICHEN DER ALTERSGRENZE. KLINISCHE STUDIE UNTER BERUECKSICHTIGUNG PSYCHOSOMATISCHER UND PSYCHOSOZIALER ASPEKTE / Tillmann-Nonnenkamp, Tilke – 1995 – 2mf – 9 – DM80.00 – 3-8267-2119-5 – gw Hänsel [618]
Macias Laso, Pedro *see* APORTACION AL ESTUDIO DE LOS COMPUESTOS NITROGENADOS EN MOSTOS Y VINOS DE TIERRA DE BARROS
Macias Lorenzo, Angel *see* TODO POR CRISTO Y CRISTO POR TODOS
Macias, Maximiliano *see*
- EXCAVACIONES DE MERIDA. MEMORIA DE LOS TRABAJOS PRACTICADOS EN 1926 Y 1927
- LA POSTESCENA DEL TEATRO ROMANO DE MERIDA

Maciejewska, W *see* POLSKI SLOWNIK ARCHIWALNY
Maciines, John *see* THE BLACK ISLE 1851 CENSUS INDEX
McIlroy, Malcom S *see* HISTORY OF THE MIT RADAR SCHOOL IN RELATION TO ARMY TRAINING FROM JUNE 23, 1941 TO JUNE 30, 1945
McIlvain, J W *see* EARLY PRESBYTERIANISM IN MARYLAND
McIlvaine, C P et al *see* REVIVALS
McIlvaine, Charles Pettit *see*
- THE EVIDENCES OF CHRISTIANITY
- DIE WAHRHEIT DES CHRISTENTHUMS

McIlvaine, James Hall *see* THE WISDOM OF THE APOCALYPSE
McIlwaine, Henry R *see* THE STRUGGLE OF PROTESTANT DISSENTERS FOR RELIGIOUS TOLERATION IN VIRGINIA
McIlwaine, Henry Read *see* JOURNALS OF THE HOUSE OF BURGESSES OF VIRGINIA, 1619-1776
MacInnes, George *see* THE DEATH OF THE VERBAL THEORY AND THE UNVEILING OF CHRIST
Macinnes, John *see*
- CENTRAL INVERNESS 1851 CENSUS INDEX
- COUNTY OF BUTE 1851 CENSUS INDEX
- DINGWALL AND SURROUNDS 1851 CENSUS INDEX
- DISTRICT OF INVERNESS 1851 CENSUS INDEX
- ISLE OF ISLAY 1851 CENSUS INDEX
- ISLE OF SKYE (NORTH) 1851 CENSUS INDEX
- ISLE OF SKYE (SOUTH) AND THE SMALL ISLES 1851 CENSUS INDEX
- SPEYSIDE INVERNESS 1851 CENSUS INDEX
- TAIN AND SURROUNDS 1851 CENSUS INDEX
- WESTER ROSS PART 2 1851 CENSUS INDEX
- WESTERN INVERNESS 1851 CENSUS INDEX

McIntosh, Charles H *see* NOTES ON THE BOOK OF GENESIS
Macintosh, Douglas Clyde *see* IS THERE A GOD?
McIntosh, Patricia *see* BUTTE COUNTY HISTORICAL SOCIETY "DIGGIN'S"
McIntosh, W C *see* A MONOGRAPH OF THE BRITISH ANNELIDS
McIntyre, David *see*
- THE DIVINE AUTHORITY OF THE SCRIPTURES OF THE OLD TESTAMENT
- THE SPIRIT IN THE WORD

Macintyre, James J *see* THE INFLUENCE OF ARISTOCRACIES ON THE REVOLUTIONS OF NATIONS; CONSIDERED IN RELATION TO THE PRESENT CIRCUMSTANCES OF THE BRITISH EMPIRE
McIntyre, James Lewis *see* GIORDANO BRUNO
McIntyre, W E *see*
- A MANUAL OF BIBLIOGRAPHY, 1500-1914
- ON THE PLAINS IN 1867-68

McIver, Colin *see* THE SOUTHERN PREACHER
Mack, Ian McCallum *see* NEW BRITAIN PATROL REPORTS, 1926-1931
Mack, Joseph *see* KRITIK DER FREIHEITSTHEORIEN
Mack, Rana L *see* THE EFFICACY OF TOPICAL IBUPROFEN IN AN INFLAMMATORY MODEL
Mack, William *see*
- ENCYCLOPAEDIA OF FORMS AND PRECEDENTS
- MACK'S DIGEST OF CASES IN VOLS 1-24 OF THE AMERICAN STATE REPORTS
- RAPALJE AND MACK'S DIGEST OF RAILROAD DECISIONS

Mack, William et al *see* CYCLOPEDIA OF LAW AND PROCEDURE
Mackay *see* INVESTIGATION OF MINERAL DEPOSITS IN THE HASHEMITE KINGDOM OF JORDAN
Mackay, Alexander *see* A COMPENDIUM OF OFFICIAL DOCUMENTS RELATIVE TO NATIVE AFFAIRS IN THE SOUTH ISLAND
Mackay, Alexander Murdoch *see* A.M. MACKAY
Mackay, Andrew *see*
- THE COMPLETE NAVIGATOR
- THE THEORY AND PRACTICE OF FINDING THE LONGITUDE AT SEA OR LAND. TO WHICH ARE ADDED VARIOUS METHODS OF DETERMINING THE LATITUDE OF A PLACE AND VARIATION OF THE COMPASS, WITH NEW TABLES

Mackay, Charles *see* THE POETICAL WORKS OF CHARLES MACKAY
McKay, Charles L *see* THE CALL OF THE HARVEST
McKay, Claude *see* EXHIBIT MATERIAL
McKay, Donald *see* JOURNAL
Mackay, George Leslie *see* FROM FAR FORMOSA
Mackay Gesellschaft *see* LERNZIEL ANARCHIE
MacKay, J T *see* FLORA HIBERNICA
Mackay, James Hutton *see* RELIGOUS THOUGHT IN HOLLAND DURING THE NINETEENTH CENTURY
Mackay, John *see* THE CHURCH IN THE HIGHLANDS, OR, THE PROGRESS OF EVANGELICAL RELIGION IN GAELIC SCOTLAND, 563-1843
MacKay, John Henry *see*
- ABRECHNUNG-RANDBEMERKUNGEN ZU LEBEN UND ARBEIT
- THE ANARCHISTS
- DER FREIHEITSSUCHER
- GESAMMELTE WERKE
- MAX STIRNER, SEIN LEBEN UND SEIN WERK

Mackay, R W *see* THE TUEBINGEN SCHOOL AND ITS ANTECEDENTS: A REVIEW OF THE HISTORY AND PRESENT CONDITION OF MODERN THEOLOGY
MACKAY STANDARD (DAILY STANDARD) – Australia. -w, -d. 1884-1913. 33 reels – 1 – uk British Libr Newspaper [072]
Mackay, T *see* A PLEA FOR LIBERTY
Mackay, Thomas *see* A POLICY OF FREE EXCHANGE
Mackean, W H *see* CHRISTIAN MONASTICISM IN EGYPT TO THE CLOSE OF THE FOURTH CENTURY
McKearin, Helen *see* THE STORY OF AMERICAN HISTORICAL FLASKS
McKechnie, Archie *see* DIARY
Mckee, Patrick J *see* THE EFFECTS OF A TREATMENT PROGRAM FOR CHRONIC PAIN PATIENTS USING ENJOYABLE IMAGERY WITH BIOFEEDBACK INDUCED RELAXATION
MacKee, Seumas *see* I WAS A FRANCO SOLDIER
McKee, William *see* HISTORY OF THE ORIGIN AND DEVELOPMENT AND CONDITION OF MISSIONS AMONG THE SHERBRO AND MENDI TRIBES IN WESTERN AFRICA
McKeen, Silas *see* HISTORY OF BRADFORD
McKelvey, A T *see* CENTENNIAL HISTORY OF BELMONT COUNTY
McKelvey, John Jay *see* HANDBOOK OF THE LAW OF EVIDENCE
McKelway, Clair *see* MEDICAL AND OTHER EXPERTS
McKenna, J M *see* INDUSTRIAL DEMOCRACY
McKenna, Maurice *see* PAST AND PRESENT OF FOND DU LAC COUNTY
Mackensen, Lutz *see*
- BALTISCHE TEXTE DER FRUHZEIT
- ZUR DEUTSCHEN LITERATUR ALTLIVLANDS

MacKenzie, Alexander *see* VOYAGES FROM MONTREAL TO THE PACIFIC, 1789-1793
McKenzie, Alexander *see*
- CHRIST HIMSELF
- THE DIVINE FORCE IN THE LIFE OF THE WORLD
- SABBATH ESSAYS

MacKenzie, C S *see* A TREATISE ON THE MANAGEMENT OF DISEASE IN SHEEP
McKenzie, Charles *see*
- THE SPOKESMAN
- LA VOIX DE DRUMMOND

McKenzie, Donald C *see*
- ARTERIAL HYPOXEMIA AND PERFORMANCE DURING INTENSE EXERCISE
- THE EFFECT OF SALBUTAMOL ON PERFORMANCE IN ELITE NON-ASTHMATIC ATHLETES
- EFFECTS OF THE MENSTRUAL CYCLE AND ORAL CONTRACEPTIVES ON ATHLETIC PERFORMANCE
- OXYGEN CONSUMPTION DURING KAYAK PADDLING

Mackenzie, Duncan *see* EXCAVATIONS AT AIN SHEMS
Mackenzie, G *see* A MANUAL OF THE KISTNA DISTRICT OF THE PRESIDENCY OF MADRAS
Mackenzie, H *see*
- THE MAN OF FEELING, AND JULIA DE ROUBIGNE
- THE MAN OF THE WORLD

McKenzie, J W *see* THE LEVEL OF COLLEGIATE ATHLETIC PARTICIPATION AND ITS EFFECTS ON SUICIDAL IDEATION, DEPRESSIVE SYMPTOMS, PSYCHOLOGICAL DISTRESS, AND HOPELESSNESS
Mackenzie, James *see* LIFE OF WILLIAM CUNNINGHAM, D.D.
Mackenzie, John Stuart *see* A MANUAL OF ETHICS
MacKenzie, Norman *see* OPEN LEARNING
MacKenzie, W Lyon *see* MACKENZIE'S GAZETTE
Mackenzie, William Douglas *see*
- CHRISTIANITY AND THE PROGESS OF MAN
- JOHN MACKENZIE
- SOUTH AFRICA; ITS HISTORY, HEROES AND WARS

MACKENZIE'S GAZETTE / ed by MacKenzie, W Lyon – New York City, Rochester, NY. 12 may 1838-v1 n93. 22 feb 1840 – 1r – 1 – Can$55.00 – cn Can Microfilming [071]
MACKENZIE'S GAZETTE – New York and Rochester. 1838-40 – 1 reel – 1 – $68.00 – cn Library Assoc [971]
MACKENZIE'S WEEKLY MESSAGE – Toronto, 25 dec 1852 (Prospectus) – 1r – 1 – Can$25.00 – cn Can Microfilming [072]
MACKENZIE'S WEEKLY MESSAGE – Toronto, Canada. 1852-60 – 2r – 1 – $136.00 – cn Library Assoc [971]
M'Keown, Robert L *see* IN THE LAND OF THE OIL RIVERS
Mackey, A G *see* A LEXICON OF FREEMASONRY;...
Mackey, Albert Gallatin *see* THE HISTORY OF FREEMASONRY
Mackey, F H *see* MACARTHUR AND MACKEY'S REPORTS OF CASES IN THE DISTRICT OF COLUMBIA, 1879-1880
Mackey, Ilonka Schmidt *see* LOU SALOME
Mackey, James L *see* A GRAMMAR OF THE BENGA LANGUAGE
Mackey, Marcia J *see* AQUAPRENEURSHIP
Mackey, William F *see* EDUCATION AND BILINGUALISM
Mackie, Charles *see* THE CASTLES, PALACES AND PRISONS OF MARY OF SCOTLAND
Mackie, George M *see* BIBLE MANNERS AND CUSTOMS
Mackie, Sedley J *see* AN ACCOUNT OF THE CONQUEST OF GUATEMALA IN 1524
McKim, Randolph Harrison *see*
- CHRIST AND MODERN UNBELIEF
- PRESENT-DAY PROBLEMS OF CHRISTIAN THOUGHT
- THE PROBLEM OF THE PENTATEUCH... RESULTS OF THE HIGHER CRITICISM

MACKINAC AND LAKE STORIES / Catherwood, Mary Hartwell – With illus. New York: Harper & Bros., 1899. 0070I. (Pre-1900 Canadiana) – 9 – cn C.I.H.M. [830]
MACKINAC, FORMERLY MICHILIMACKINAC / Bailey, John Read – Lansing, Mich.: D. D. Thorp, 1895. 00082. (Pre-1900 Canadiana) – 9 – cn C.I.H.M. [971]
Mackinlay, J B *see* SAINT EDMUND, KING AND MARTYR
McKinley, William *see*
- PAPERS
- SCRAPBOOK COLLECTION

McKinney, BB *see*
- THE PUBLISHED WORKS
- PUBLISHED WORKS

McKinney, Edmund *see* PAPERS
McKinney, Gordon *see* THE PAPERS OF ZEBULON VANCE
McKinney, James C *see* MASTERING MUSIC READING
McKinney, William M *see*
- ENCYCLOPAEDIA OF PLEADING AND PRACTICE
- THE FEDERAL STATUTES ANNOTATED...1789-1903
- RULING CASELAW

MacKinnon, Albert Glenthorne *see* TANGIBLE TESTS FOR A YOUNG MAN'S FAITH
McKinnon, Edna R *see* REPORT TO THE PATHFINDER FUND
Mackinnon, James *see* NINIAN UND SEIN EINFLUSS AUF DIE AUSBREITUNG DES CHRISTENTHUMS IN NORD-BRITANNIEN
Mackinnon, Lauchlan Bellingham *see* STEAM WARFARE IN THE PARANA
Mackinnon, William *see* PERSONAL AND BUSINESS PAPERS
McKinstrey, Jay P *see* RISK MANAGEMENT BEHAVIORS OF NCAA DIVISION 3 HEAD FOOTBALL COACHES
MacKintosh, Catherine Winkworth *see*
- COILLARD OF THE ZAMBESI
- YETA 3

Mackintosh, Charles Henry *see* NOTES ON THE BOOK OF LEVITICUS
Mackintosh, Duncan *see* A PLAIN, RATIONAL ESSAY ON ENGLISH GRAMMAR
Mackintosh, Hugh Ross *see* TYPES OF MODERN THEOLOGY; SCHLEIERMACHER TO BARTH
Mackintosh, James *see* MEMOIRS OF THE LIFE.
Mackintosh, Robert *see* CHRIST AND THE JEWISH LAW
Macklin, J M *see* CUESTIONES ACTUALES DE DOCTRINA Y PRACTICA. BUENOS AIRES, 1927
MacKnight, Alexander *see* AN OUTLINE OF THE HISTORICAL EVIDENCE OF THE TRUTH OF THE CHRISTIAN RELIGION
Macknight, Thomas *see* THE RIGHT HONOURABLE BENJAMIN DISRAELI, M.P. A LITERARY AND POLITICAL BIOGRAPHY
McKnight, William J *see* JEFFERSON COUNTY-HER PIONEERS AND PEOPLE
Mackow, Jerzy *see* DIE ENTSTEHUNG DER DRITTEN POLNISCHEN REPUBLIK, 1989-1991
MACK'S DIGEST OF CASES IN VOLS 1-24 OF THE AMERICAN STATE REPORTS / Mack, William – San Francisco: Bancroft-Whitney (all publ) – 14mf – 9 – $21.00 – LLMC 78-038G – us L.L.M.C. [340]
Macksey, Charles *see* CATHOLIC EDUCATIONAL CONDITIONS IN THE UNITED STATES
MacKune-Karrer, Betty *see* JOURNAL OF FEMINIST FAMILY THERAPY
Mackworth of Gnoll (Neath), Humphrey *see* PAPERS AND BOOKS RELATING TO 1698-1763
MacLachlan, James Angell *see* CASES ON THE FEDERAL ANTI-TRUST LAWS OF THE UNITED STATES
Maclaren, Alexander *see*
- THE EPISTLES OF ST PAUL TO THE COLOSSIANS AND PHILEMON
- THE GOSPEL OF ST. LUKE
- THE PSALMS
- THE SECRET OF POWER

Maclaren, Ian *see*
- THE DOCTRINES OF GRACE
- GOD'S MESSAGE TO THE HUMAN SOUL... THE BIBLE IN THE LIGHT OF THE NEW KNOWLEDGE
- THE LIFE OF THE MASTER

McLaren, William Edward *see* CATHOLIC DOGMA: THE ANTIDOTE OF DOUBT
McLario, David J *see* THE CONTRIBUTION OF FORCE AND VELOCITY IN THE DEVELOPMENT OF PEAK POWER OUTPUT
Maclauchlan, Thomas *see* THE EARLY SCOTTISH CHURCH
Mclaughin, T P *see* LE TRES ANCIEN DROIT MONASTIQUE DE L'OCCIDENT
MacLaughlin, John *see* INDIFFERENTISM
McLaughlin, S *see* THE PHOTOGRAPHIC PORTFOLIO
Maclay, Edgar Stanton *see* A HISTORY OF AMERICAN PRIVATEERS
Maclay, Walker *see* HENRY SATER
LE MACLEAN – 1961-Aug 1976 – 9 – cn Micromedia [073]
McLean, Archibald *see*
- EPOCH MAKERS OF MODERN MISSIONS
- WHERE THE BIBLE SPEAKS, OR, MISSION STUDIES IN THE BIBLE
- WHERE THE BOOK SPEAKS

Maclean, Arthur John *see* THE CATHOLICOS OF THE EAST AND HIS PEOPLE

MacLean, Christopher L *see* ECCENTRIC KINETIC CHAIN EXERCISE AS A CONSERVATIVE MEANS OF FUNCTIONALLY REHABILITATING CHRONIC ISOLATED POSTERIOR CRUCIATE LIGAMENT INSUFFICIENCY
McLean County Historical Society *see* TRANSACTIONS OF THE MCLEAN COUNTY HISTORICAL SOCIETY
M'Lean, Daniel *see* THE GOSPEL IN THE PSALMS
McLean, John M *see*
- MCLEAN'S REPORTS OF CASES IN THE SEVENTH CIRCUIT, 1839-1855
- PAPERS

MacLean, John Patterson *see* INTRODUCTION TO THE STUDY OF THE GOSPEL OF ST LUKE
Maclean, Paul *see* HISTORY OF CARROLL COUNTY
MacLean y Estenos, Percy *see* LEGISLACION Y JURISPRUDENCIA PENAL EN AMERICA DEL SUR
Macleane, Douglas *see* REASON, THOUGHT, AND LANGUAGE
MACLEAN'S – (v.88-. 1975-. 5,6,9) – v.21-. 1911- – 1 – us UMI [073]
MACLEAN'S MAGAZINE – (Numbering starts with v101 1988) – Toronto, 1905-95 – 1,9 – Can$175.00y – cn Micromedia [073]
MACLEAN'S MAGAZINE – Toronto, Canada. -w. Jan 1916-Nov 1923. 11 1 2 reels – 1 – uk British Libr Newspaper [073]
Maclear, George Frederick *see*
- APOSTLES OF MEDIAEVAL EUROPE
- THE BOOK OF JOSHUA: WITH NOTES, MAPS, AND INTRODUCTION
- THE CELTS
- CHILDREN'S TREASURY OF BIBLE STORIES
- THE ENGLISH
- THE GOSPEL ACCORDING TO ST. MARK
- A HISTORY OF CHRISTIAN MISSIONS DURING THE MIDDLE AGES
- AN INTRODUCTION TO THE ARTICLES OF THE CHURCH OF ENGLAND
- AN INTRODUCTION TO THE CREEDS
- THE NORTHMEN
- SHILLING BOOK...NEW TESTAMENT HISTORY FOR NATIONAL AND ELEMENTARY SCHOOLS
- THE SLAVS

Maclear, George Frederick et al *see* HISTORICAL EVIDENCES OF THE NEW TESTAMENT
MACLEAY CHRONICLE (KEMPSEY) – Jan 5 1899-Dec 24 1919 – 9 – at Pascoe [072]
Macleay, W S *see*
- ANNULUSA JAVANICA, OR AN ATTEMPT TO ILLUSTRATE THE NATURAL AFFINITIES AND ANALOGIES OF THE INSECTS COLLECTED IN JAVA BY T. HORSFIELD...
- ANNULUSA JAVANICA, OU DESCRIPTION DES INSECTES DE JAVA...

Macleod, Donald *see* MEMOIR OF NORMAN MACLEOD
MACLEOD GAZETTE – Fort MacLeod, Canada. 1882-1906 – 10r – 1 – $650.00 – cn Library Assoc [971]
Macleod, John *see* L'AFRIQUE, OU HISTOIRE, MOEURS, USAGES ET COUTUMES DES AFRICAINS: DAHOMEY (GUINEE)
McLeod, Malcolm James *see* THE CULTURE OF SIMPLICITY
Macleod, Norman *see*
- PARISH PAPERS
- SIMPLE TRUTH FOR EARNEST MINDS

MACLEOD OF DARE: A NOVEL / Black, William – British Fiction Archive: Unit 4 – 9 – uk Bell [830]
MacLeod, Roy M *see*
- ARCHIVES OF BRITISH MEN OF SCIENCE
- JOHN TYNDALL, NATURAL PHILOSOPHER, 1820-1893: CATALOGUE OF CORRESPONDENCE, JOURNALS AND COLLECTED PAPERS

Macleod, William B *see* THE AFFLICTIONS OF THE RIGHTEOUS
Macler, F *see*
- LES LIVRES IMPRIMES ARMENIENS DE LA BIBLIOTHEQUE DE L'UNIVERSITE D'AMSTERDAM
- NOTICES DE MANUSCRITS ARMENIENS VUS DANS QUELQUES BIBLIOTHEQUES DE L'EUROPE CENTRALE

MacLise, Daniel *see* THE MACLISE PORTRAIT-GALLERY OF ILLUSTRIOUS LITERARY CHARACTERS, WITH MEMOIRS BIOGRAPHICAL, CRITICAL, BIBLIOGRAPHICAL & ANECDOTAL...ILLUSTRATIVE OF THE LITERATURE OF THE FORMER HALF OF THE PRESENT CENTURY
THE MACLISE PORTRAIT-GALLERY OF ILLUSTRIOUS LITERARY CHARACTERS, WITH MEMOIRS BIOGRAPHICAL, CRITICAL, BIBLIOGRAPHICAL & ANECDOTAL...ILLUSTRATIVE OF THE FORMER HALF OF THE LITERATURE OF THE PRESENT CENTURY / MacLise, Daniel – By William Bates, B.A. London: Chatto & Windus, 1883. xv,540p.With 85 portraits – 1 – us U.W. Library [920]
M'LLE – New York. v. 1, no. 1-v. 2, no. 3. Aug 1895-Dec 1898. Incomplete – 1 – us NY Public [073]
M'LLE – New York. v1; ns: v2. 1895-96; 1898 – 1r – 1 – us Ross [390]
MacLoughlin, P F M *see* RESEARCH FOR AGRICULTURAL DEVELOPMENT IN THE NORTHERN SUDAN TO 1967
THE MACLURE COLLECTION OF FRENCH REVOLUTIONARY MATERIALS – University of Pennsylvania – 1 – us Primary [944]
McMahil, Richard B *see* FEDERAL TRADE COMMISSION
McMahon, T A *see* METHODS OF COMPUTATION OF LOW STREAMFLOW
McMahon, Walter W *see* EFFICIENCY-BASED MANAGEMENT INFORMATION SYSTEM
McManis, BG *see* COMPARISON OF THE NUMBER OF CLASSIFICATION TRIALS FOR VARIOUS CRITERION-REFERENCED TESTING METHODS
MacMaster, Erasmus D *see* SERMONS, 1842-66
McMaster, J S *see* MCMASTER'S COMMERCIAL DECISIONS AFFECTING THE BANKER AND MERCHANT
McMaster, James Smith *see* SUMMARY OF SPECIAL COMMERCIAL DECISIONS AFFECTING THE BANKER, FROM THE REPORTS OF THE HIGHEST COURTS OF THE SEVERAL STATES
McMaster, John B *see* A HISTORY OF THE PEOPLE OF THE UNITED STATES
McMaster, Robert Bach *see* AN ACT TO PROVIDE FOR THE ORGANIZATION AND REGULATION OF CERTAIN BUSINESS CORPORATIONS
MacMechan, Archibald *see* SARTOR RESARTUS
Macmichael, H A *see* A HISTORY OF THE ARABS IN THE SUDAN
Macmichael, W *see* THE GOLDHEADED CANE
McMillan, Alexander Guy *see* NEW MANUAL OF THE COSTS, FORMS AND RULES, IN THE COMMON LAW COURTS OF UPPER CANADA
Macmillan, D *see*
- THE ABERDEEN DOCTORS
- JOHN KNOX
- THE LIFE OF GEORGE MATHESON, D.D., LL.D., F.R.S.E.

MacMillan, DB *see*
- ETAH AND BEYOND
- FOUR YEARS IN THE WHITE NORTH

MacMillan, Hugh *see*
- GLEANINGS IN HOLY FIELDS
- THE MIDDLE WAY

Macmillan, Hugh *see*
- BIBLE TEACHINGS IN NATURE
- THE MARRIAGE IN CANA OF GALILEE
- OUR LORD'S THREE RAISINGS FROM THE DEAD
- THE TRUE VINE
- TWO WORLDS ARE OURS

McMillan, Monique C *see* DIFFERENCES IN MOVEMENT SPEED BETWEEN SIX YEAR OLD CHILDREN AND ADULTS ON THREE MOTOR TASKS
Macmillan, Somerled *see* THE MACMILLANS AND THEIR SEPTS
McMillan, Thomas *see* AN EPISCOPALIAN DEMAND FOR CHRISTIAN SCHOOLS
THE MACMILLANS AND THEIR SEPTS / Macmillan, Somerled – Glasgow: K. and R. Davidson, 1952 – 1 – us U.W. Library [920]
MACMILLAN'S MAGAZINE – 1885-1907 – 1 – uk Microform Academic [800]
McMillen, Wayne *see* THIS IS OUR CONCERN; A STATEMENT TO AMERICAN SOCIAL WORKERS ON THEIR STAKE IN THE CIVIL WAR IN SPAIN
MacMunn, George Fletcher *see* THE UNDERWORLD OF INDIA
McMurray, Robert G *see*
- CAFFEINE, CARBOHYDRATE LOADING, AND PHYSICAL PERFORMANCE
- THE USE OF PROXY REPORTS AS PREDICTORS OF MAXIMAL AEROBIC POWER IN CHILDREN

McMurry, Richard *see* THE PAPERS OF ZEBULON VANCE
McMurtie, Richard Coxe *see* A READING ON ARTICLE 16, SECTION 7, OF THE CONSTITUTION OF PENNSYLVANIA
Macnab, Frances *see* BRITISH COLUMBIA FOR SETTLERS: ITS MINES, TRADE AND AGRICULTURE
McNabb, Vincent *see* INFALLIBILITY
M'Naghten, Captain *see* ANNOTATIONS ON THE MUTINY ACT...
McNamara, Catherine M *see* DIFFERENCES IN COMPETITIVE ANXIETY AND PERCEIVED COMPETENCE FOR HIGH AND LOW LEVEL COMPETITIVE YOUTH SWIMMERS
McNamara, Michael J *see* VALIDATION OF A CYCLE ERGOMETER VO2MAX PREDICTION EQUATION FOR NONSEDENTARY COLLEGE-AGE WOMEN
MacNaughtan, W *see* INDIVIDUAL EVANGELISM (CCC241)
McNaughton, A *see* DESCENDENTS OF THE LATE QUEEN VICTORIA
Macnaughton-Jones, Henry *see* AMBIDEXTERITY AND MENTAL CULTURE
McNeil, Barbara *see* BIO-BASE 1990: MASTER CUMULATION
MacNeil, John *see* THE SPIRIT-FILLED LIFE
McNeile, Alan Hugh *see*
- THE BOOK OF NUMBERS
- THE GOSPEL ACCORDING TO MATTHEW
- AN INTRODUCTION TO ECCLESIASTES

MacNeill, John *see* EARLY IRISH LAWS AND INSTITUTIONS
McNeill-Moss, Geoffrey *see* THE LEGEND OF BADAJOZ, BEING AN EXTRACT FROM "THE SIEGE OF ALCAZAR."
McNeilly, James Hugh *see* RELIGION AND SLAVERY
McNemar, Richard *see* THE KENTUCKY REVIVAL
McNeur, G H *see* LIFE OF LEUNG FAAT (CCC212)
McNeur, George H *see*
- HANDBOOK ON PASTORAL THEOLOGY (CCC244)
- HOMILETICS (CCC243)
- LORD, TEACH US TO PRAY (CCC242)

McNitt, William *see* THE DETROIT URBAN LEAGUE PAPERS
McNutt, Minnie Morrow *see* 1880, ALABAMA CENSUS
O MACOENSE : ORGAM LITTERARIO E NOTICIOSO – Manaos, Amazonas. 23 Jun-21 Jul 1901 – 1,5,6 – bl Biblioteca [072]
MACOMB COUNTY LEGAL NEWS – Mount Clemens. Mich. -w. 1957- – 1 – us UMI [071]
MACOMB DAILY – Mount Clemens. Mich. City Ed. 1964- – 1 – us UMI [071]
MACOMB DAILY – Mount Clemens. Mich. Home final ed. 1967-1968 – 1 – us UMI [071]
THE MACON GEORGIA TELEGRAPH – Macon, GA. v17 n26. 28 mar 1843 – 1r – 1 – Can$25.00 – cn Can Microfilming [071]
Macon, Mississippi *see* MISCELLANEOUS EARLY NEWSPAPERS
Maconachie, Robert *see* THE MISSIONS OF THE CHURCH MISSIONARY SOCIETY AND THE CHURCH OF ENGLAND ZENANA MISSIONARY SOCIETY IN THE PUNJAB AND SINDH
Maconochie, Alexander *see*
- CRIME AND PUNISHMENT. THE MARK SYSTEM
- EMIGRATION.
- NORFOLK ISLAND
- SECONDARY PUNISHMENT. THE MARK SYSTEM

LES MACONS DE LA CREUSE / Bandy de Naleche, Louis – Paris: E. Dentu, 1859. 96p. 1 fiche. (Economics Collection) – 9 – 6.00 – fr Bibl Nationale [330]
Macoun, J M *see* CATALOGUE OF CANADIAN PLANTS
Macphail, W M *see* THE PRESBYTERIAN CHURCH
Macpherson, G *see*
- LIFE OF LAL BEHARI DAY
- MEMOIRS OF THE LIFE OF ANNA JAMESON

Macpherson, Hector Carsewell *see* THOMAS CARLYLE
Macpherson, Hector Carswell *see*
- THE INTELLECTUAL DEVELOPMENT OF SCOTLAND
- SCOTLAND'S BATTLES FOR SPIRITUAL INDEPENDENCE
- SCOTLAND'S DEBT TO PROTESTANTISM
- THE SCOTTISH CHURCH CRISIS

MacPherson, J *see* THE HISTORY OF THE PRIMITIVE METHODIST CONNEXION, FROM ITS ORIGIN TO THE CONFERENCE OF 1860, THE FIRST JUBILEE YEAR OF THE CONNEXION
Macpherson, James *see* FINGAL, AN ANCIENT EPIC POEM
MacPherson, John *see* A HISTORY OF THE CHURCH IN SCOTLAND
Macpherson, John *see* WESTMINSTER CONFESSION OF FAITH
Macpherson, Kevin *see* EFFECTS OF A SEMIRIGID AND A SOFTSHELL PROPHYLACTIC ANKLE STABILIZER ON PERFORMANCE
McPherson, M B *see* RESEARCH ON URBAN HYDROLOGY
Macpherson, Norman *see* THE APPELLATE JURISDICTION OF THE HOUSE OF LORDS IN SCOTCH CAUSES, ILLUSTRATED BY THE LITIGATION RELATING TO THE CUSTODY OF THE MARQUIS OF BUTE
McPhersonville. South Carolina.Prince William (Episcopal) Parish Church *see* REGISTER
McQuaid, James *see* INDEX TO AMERICAN PHOTOGRAPHIC COLLECTIONS
Macquart, P J M *see* DIPTERES EXOTIQUES NOUVEAUX OU PEU CONNUS
MacQueary, Howard *see* THE EVOLUTION OF MAN AND CHRISTIANITY
McQueary, Lela O *see* COLORADO CEMETERY INSCRIPTIONS
Macqueen, John Fraser *see* A PRACTICAL TREATISE ON THE LAW OF MARRIAGE, DIVORCE, AND LEGITIMACY, AS ADMINISTERED IN THE DIVORCE COURT AND IN THE HOUSE OF LORDS
McQueen, Judy *see* DOCUMENT DELIVERY IN THE UNITED STATES: A REPORT
Macquer, Pierre Joseph *see* ELEMENS DE CHYMIE-PRATIQUE, CONTENANT LA DESCRIPTION DES OPERATIONS FONDAMENTALES DE LA CHYMIE, AVEC DES EXPLICATIONS ET DES REMARQUES SUR CHAQUE OPERATION
McQuillin, Eugene *see*
- MISSOURI PLEADING AND PRACTICE IN ACTIONS AT LAW AND IN EQUITY.
- A TREATISE ON THE LAW OF INSTRUCTIONS TO JURIES IN CIVIL CASES.

MacQuisten, P *see* REPORT OF THE CHIEF ENGINEER OF THE MEGANTIC JUNCTION RAILWAY, TO THE PROVISIONAL COMMITTEE
Macray, W D *see*
- CHARTERS AND DOCUMENTS ILLUSTRATING THE HISTORY OF THE CATHEDRAL, CITY AND DIOCESE OF SALISBURY, IN THE TWELFTH AND THIRTEENTH CENTURIES (RS97)
- CHRONICON ABBATIAE DE EVESHAM AD ANNUM 1418 (RS29)
- CHRONICON ABBATIAE RAMESIENSIS (RS83)

MACRO CONTROLS ON PUBLIC SPENDING / Craig, Jon D – 1986, 24p. CIS – 9 – 1.00f – at Libertarian Micro [336]
Macrobius *see* EYSSENHARDT ITERUM RECOGNOVIT
DIE MACROLEPIDOPTERENFAUNA DER ROEMISCHEN CAMPAGNA UND DER ANGRENZENDEN PROVINZEN MITTEL-ITALIENS / Calberla, H – Dresden, 1884-88. Z-1116/2 – 8 – ne IDC [590]
MACROMOLECULES – v1- 1968- – 1,5,6,9 – us A.C.S. [073]
McSherry, James *see* HISTORY OF MARYLAND
MacSwinney, Robert Forster *see* THE LAW OF MINES, QUARRIES, AND MINERALS
McTaggart, John McTaggart Ellis *see* SOME DOGMAS OF RELIGION
MAC-TALLA – Sydney, Nova Scotia. v9 n34. 22 feb 1901 – 1r – 1 – Can$25.00 – cn Can Microfilming [072]
McTigue, Thomas *see* THE POLICEMAN'S POCKET LAWBOOK
McTyeire, Holland N *see*
- A CATECHISM ON CHURCH GOVERNMENT
- A HISTORY OF METHODISM
- A MANUAL OF THE DISCIPLINE OF THE METHODIST EPISCOPAL CHURCH, SOUTH

McVean *see*
- HISTORY OF LINCOLN, ONEIDA AND VILAS COUNTIES
- HISTORY OF WOOD COUNTY

Macvicar, Neil *see* SIDE LIGHTS UPON SUPERSTITION
Macvicar, S M *see*
- A REVISED KEY TO HEPATICS OF THE BRITISH ISLANDS
- STUDENT'S HANDBOOK OF BRITISH HEPATICS

McVickar, John *see* THE EARLY YEARS OF THE LATE BISHOP HOBART
McWatters, George S *see* KNOTS UNTIED 1090 OR WAYS AND BY-WAYS IN THE HIDDEN LIFE OF AMERICAN DETECTIVES
McWhinny, Edward *see* UNITED NATIONS LAWMAKING
McWhorter, George Cumming *see* A POPULAR HAND-BOOK OF THE NEW TESTAMENT
McWhorter, Julian H *see* REPORT ON A STUDY OF THE PRINTING INDUSTRY OF INDONESIA, INCLUDING THE R.I. GOVERNMENT PRINTING OFFICE AND RELATED RECOMMENDATIONS
MACWORLD: THE MACINTOSH MAGAZINE – v1-. Feb 1984- – 1,5,6,9 – us UMI [073]
Macy, John W Jr. *see* THE FIRST DECADE OF THE CIRCUIT COURT EXECUTIVE
MAD – Tehran: shumarah-i 1 (Shahrivar 1325 [Aug 1945]) – 1 reel – 1 – $65.00 – us MEDOC [950]
MAD CREEK KICKER – v1-2. 1904-06 – 1r – 1 – us Ross [073]
THE MAD MULLAH OF SOMALILAND / Jardine, Douglas James – London: H Jenkins, 1923 – us Res Libr [920]
MADAGASCAR / Campbell, Belle McPherson – Chicago: Woman's Presbyterian Board of Missions of the Northwest, c1889 – 1mf – 9 – 0-8370-6481-3 – 1986-0481 – us A.T.L.A. [960]
MADAGASCAR / Castonnet des Fosses, Henri Louis – Paris: Libraire de la Societe bibliographique, 1884 – us Res Libr [960]
MADAGASCAR / Duignan, Peter – (The Malagasy Republic). A list of materials in the African Collections of Stanford University and the Hoover Institution. 1962. 25p – 1 – 35.00r – us Hoover Inst Photo [960]
MADAGASCAR : ITS HISTORY AND PEOPLE / Little, Henry William – Edinburgh: W Blackwood, 1884 – us Res Libr [960]
MADAGASCAR : ITS MISSIONARIES AND MARTYRS / Townsend, William John – New York: F.H. Revell, [1892?] – 1mf – us A.T.L.A. [240]
Madagascar *see*
- BULLETIN ECONOMIQUE
- PLAN DE DEVELOPPEMENT ECONOMIQUE ET SOCIAL RAPPORT D'EXECUTION, 1 JUILLET 1954-30 JUIN 1955
- PLAN DE DEVELOPPEMENT ECONOMIQUE ET SOCIAL RAPPORT D'EXECUTION, 1ER JUILLET 1955-30 JUIN 1956
- PLAN DECENNAL D'EQUIPEMENT ECONOMIQUE ET SOCIAL RAPPORT D'EXECUTION, 1 JUILLET 1950-30 JUIN 1951
- PLAN DECENNAL D'EQUIPEMENT ECONOMIQUE ET SOCIAL RAPPORT D'EXECUTION, 1 JUILLET 1952-30 JUIN 1953
- PLAN DECENNAL D'EQUIPEMENT ECONOMIQUE ET SOCIAL RAPPORT D'EXECUTION 1ER JUILLET 1947-30 JUIN 1950
- PLAN DECENNAL D'EQUIPEMENT ECONOMIQUE ET SOCIAL RAPPORT D'EXECUTION, 1ER JUILLET 1951-30 JUIN 1952
- PLAN DECENNAL D'EQUIPEMENT ECONOMIQUE ET SOCIAL RAPPORT D'EXECUTION 1ER JUILLET 1953-30 JUIN 1954

A MADAGASCAR BIBLIOGRAPHY : IN TWO PARTS...TO WHICH IS ADDED A LIST OF PUBLICATIONS IN THE MALAGASY LANGUAGE, AND A LIST OF MAPS OF MADAGASCAR / Sibree, James – (Pt 1 – arranged alphabetically according to authors' names. Pt 2 arranged chronologically according to subjects treated of) – Antananarive: London Missionary Society; London: Trubner, 1885 – us Res Libr [960]
MADAGASCAR, CREATION FRANCAISE / Leblond, Marius-Ary – Paris: Plon, [1934] – us Res Libr [960]
MADAGASCAR ET LA COTE DES SOMALIS SAINTE-MARIE ET LES SEYCHELLES : LEUR ROLE ET LEUR AVENIR / Guilloteaux, Erique – Paris: Perrin et Cie, 1922 – us Res Libr [960]
MADAGASCAR ET LES COMORES / Saron, Gilbert – Paris: P Hartmann, [1953] – us Res Libr [960]
MADAGASCAR ET LES HOVA : DESCRIPTION, ORGANISATION, HISTOIRE / Pioloet, Jean Baptiste – Paris: C Delagrave, 1895 – us Res Libr [960]
MADAGASCAR ILLUSTRE: GEOGRAPHIE, CLIMATOLOGIE, FAUNE ET FLORE, POPULATION, CHRISTIANISME MALGACHE / Eynard, Samuel – 1900 – 1 – us A.T.L.A. [240]
MADAGASCAR OF TO-DAY : AN ACCOUNT OF THE ISLAND, ITS PEOPLE, RESOURCES AND DEVELOPMENT / Shaw, George A – London: Religious Tract Society, 1886 – 1mf – 9 – 0-8370-7191-7 – 1986-1191 – us A.T.L.A. [960]
MADAGASCAR, PAST AND PRESENT : WITH CONSIDERATIONS AS TO THE COMMERCIAL INTERESTS OF GREAT BRITAIN AND FRANCE; AND AS TO THE PROGRESS OF THE CHRISTIAN CIVILIZATION – London: R Bentley, 1847 – us Res Libr [960]
MADAGASCAR RECORDS, 1866-1900 / United Society for the Propagation of the Gospel in Foreign Parts – 1 – uk Microform Academic [240]
MADAGASCAR-BIBLIOGRAPHY *see* BIBLIOGRAPHIE DE MADAGASCAR 1904-1933
MADAME ADONIS / Vallette, Marguerite Eymery – Paris: Monnier, 1888. xxxi,296p. (Les Femmes Collection) – 4mf – 9 – $10.00 – fr Bibl Nationale [640]
MADAME ANGOT AU SERAIL DE CONSTANTINOPLE / Aude, Joseph – (French Theatre Series). Paris. "Au Theatre de l'Ambigue," an VIII. 1800 – 9 – fr Hachette [820]
MADAME ANGOT OU LA POSSARDE PARVENUE / Eve – (French Theatre Series). Paris. Barba, an V. 1796 – 9 – fr Hachette [820]
MADAME AUBERTS GOVERNESS AND SCHOOL LIST – London, UK. Jul-Sept 1906. -irr. 7 feet – 1 – uk British Libr Newspaper [072]
MADAME BOVARY / Flaubert, Gustave – Introd. by Carl Van Doren. New York: The Literary Guild of America, 1932? – 1 – us U.W. Library [830]
MADAME DE MAINTENON, HER LIFE AND TIMES 1635-1719 / Dyson, C C – London, New York: J. Lane, 1910.316p. illus – 1 – us U.W. Library [944]
MADAME DE SEVIGNE / Bouilly, Jean Nicolas – (French Theatre Series). Paris. Barba, an XIV. 1805 – 9 – fr Hachette [820]
MADAME LOUISE DE FRANCE / La Briere, Leon de – (In English) – New York: Benziger, 1907 – 1mf – 9 – 0-8370-7075-9 – 1986-1075 – us A.T.L.A. [920]
Madan, Arthur Cornwallis *see*
- SENGA HANDBOOK
- WISA HANDBOOK

Madan, M *see* A SCRIPTURAL COMMENT UPON THE THIRTY-NINE ARTICLES OF THE CHURCH OF ENGLAND, WITH AN OCCASIONAL PREFACE AND APPENDIX
Madariaga, Salvador *see*
- EL AUGE DEL IMPERIO ESPANOL EN AMERICA
- HERNANDO CORTES
- HERNANDO CORTES. CONQUEROR OF MEXICO

LE MADAWASKA – Edmunston, New Brunswick. v50 n1. 3 jan 1963-v50 n52. 26 dec 1963 – 1r – 1 – Can$35.00r – cn Can Microfilming [072]
MADCAP VIOLET: A NOVEL / Black, William – British Fiction Archive: Unit 4 – 9 – uk Bell [830]
MADDEN BALLADS – Compilation of 30,000 18th- and 19th-century songs and ballads from Cambridge University Library, UK – 1 – us Primary [780]
Madden, F *see* HISTORIA ANGLORUM, SIVE, UT VULGO DICITUR, HISTORIA MINOR (RS44)
Madden, Frederick *see* DIARIES
Madden, Richard Robert *see*
- HISTORICAL NOTICE OF PENAL LAWS AGAINST CATHOLICS...
- HISTORICAL NOTICE OF PENAL LAWS AGAINST ROMAN CATHOLICS
- THE HISTORY OF THE PENAL LAWS ENACTED AGAINST ROMAN CATHOLICS
- THE LITERARY LIFE AND CORRESPONDENCE OF THE COUNTESS OF BLESSINGTON
- LITERARY REMAINS OF THE UNITED IRISHMEN OF 1798.
- THE SHRINES AND SEPULCHRES OF THE OLD AND NEW WORLD; RECORDS OF PILGRIMAGES IN MANY LANDS.

O MADEIRENSE : ORGAO DOS INTERESSES DO MUNICIPIO – Humayta, Amazonas. 1 Mar-Jul, Set-Nov 1918; Fev-22 Jun 1919 – 1,5,6 – bl Biblioteca [072]
Madelaine, Philipon de la *see* AGRICOL VIALA OU LE JEUNE HEROS DE LA DURANCE
Madelin, Louis *see* PIE 6 ET LA PRIMIERE COALITION
LE MADELINOT – Cap-Aux-Meules, Canada. 15 jul 1965; v1 n5. 25 oct 1965-30 dec 1976 – 2r – 1 – Can$55.00r – cn Can Microfilming [072]
MADEMOISELLE – (1968- 5,6. 1969- 9) – 1-1935- – 1 – us UMI [073]
MADEMOISELLE DE GUISE, OPERA-COMIQUE EN TROIS ACTES / Solie, J – Paris: Barba, 1808 – 1 – us Sibley [780]
MADEMOISELLE MATHILDE / Kingsley, Henry – British Fiction Archive: Unit 2 – 9 – uk Bell [830]
MADERA CITY, MADERA COUNTY AND ATWATER – Madera Co, CA. 1914; 1920; 1924-1956 – 11r – 1 – $550.00 – D055 – us Library Micro [978]
MADERA MERCURY – Madera, CA. 1901-1925 – 15r – 1 – $750.00 – C03332 – us Library Micro [071]
MADERA NEWS-TRIBUNE *see* MADERA TRIBUNE
MADERA TRIBUNE – (Also known as: Madera News-Tribune) – Madera, CA. 1945-48; 1954- – 252+ r – 1 – $12,600.00 ($300.00y) – B02415 – us Library Micro [071]
MADERA TRIBUNE – Madera, CA. 1925-1944 – 51r – 1 – $2,550.00 – C03333 – us Library Micro [071]
MADHYA PRADESH CHRONICLE – Bhopal, India. 1962-94 – 115r – 1 – us L of C Photodup [072]
MADILOG: MATERIALISM-DISLEKTIKA-LOGIKA / Tan Malaka – SE 12,137 1. 1951 – 9 – ne IDC [335]
MADINAH – Bijnor, India. 1912-25; 1927-Jul 1974 – 52r – 1 – us L of C Photodup [072]
MADISON CHRONICLE – Madison, NE. -w. (-sw 1902-10). Jan 1874-Jan 1877; Dec 1878-Dec 1880; Feb 1881-Jul 1883; Sep 1884-Aug 1888, scattered issues missing; Jan 1892-Apr 1921 – 1 – us NE Hist [071]
Madison County. Arkansas *see* INVENTORY OF THE COUNTY ARCHIVES OF ARKANSAS: MADISON
MADISON COUNTY COURIER – Edwardsville. Ill. -w. 1865-86 – 1 – us UMI [071]
MADISON COUNTY HERALD – Canton. Miss. 1915-1926; 1952- – 1 – us UMI [071]
MADISON COUNTY NEWSWEEK – Richmond. Ky. 1970- – 1 – us UMI [071]
MADISON COUNTY TIMES – Chittenango. N.Y. -w. 1964-67 – 1 – us UMI [071]
Madison First Presbyterian Church, Madison, KS *see* RECORDS
Madison, James *see*
- THE DEBATES IN THE FEDERAL CONVENTION OF 1789
- NOTES OF DEBATES IN THE FEDERAL CONVENTION OF 1787
- PAPERS

MADISON MAIL – Madison, NE. -w. Jan 1902-Feb 1903 – 1 – us NE Hist [071]
MADISON NEWS – Madison, NE. -w. Jan 1927-Jul 1933 – 1 – us NE Hist [071]
Madison. Presbytery (Pres. Ch. in the U.S.A.) *see* MINUTES, 1826-42
MADISON SHOPPER – Oneida. N.Y. 1956-1962 – 1 – us UMI [071]
MADISON STAR-MAIL – Madison, NE. -w. (-sw 1927). Jun 1896-Aug 1897; Jan 1898-Nov 1903, scattered issues missing; Apr 1905 to date – 1 – us NE Hist [071]
THE MADISONIAN – Virginia City. Mont. 1934-1954; 1956-1959; 1966- – 1 – us UMI [071]
Madison.Presbytery (Presbyterian Church in the U.S.A., New School) *see* MINUTES, 1838-1857
MADISONVILLE FIRST BAPTIST CHURCH. MADISONVILLE, KENTUCKY : CHURCH RECORDS – 1870-1978. 10 books. 3752p. 2 reels – 1 – 168.84 – us Baptist [240]
MADJALAH / Akademi Angkatan Bersendjata Republik Indonesia – (Irregular. Missing:[1970] no 11; 1971 no 15) – Djakarta, 1967-1972 – 17mf – 9 – SE-1303/1 – ne IDC [350]
MADJALAH ANGKATAN DARAT – Djakarta. Incomplete. SE-589 1. 1950-1959 – 9 – ne IDC [073]
MADJALAH BANK NEGARA INDONESIA – Djakarta. Incomplete. SE-298 1. 1959-1970 – 9 – ne IDC [336]
"MADJALAH BULANAN AKSI KATOLIK."SE-5413/1 / Penggalang rohani. Medan – 9 – ne IDC [240]
MADJALAH EKONOMI – Bandung. SE-300 1. 1959, 1960 – 9 – ne IDC [330]
MADJALAH ILMIAH ANGKATAN LAUT – Djakarta. Incomplete. SE-772 1. 1964-197- – 9 – ne IDC [073]
MADJALAH ILMU ALAM UNTUK INDONESIA (INDONESIAN JOURNAL OF NATURAL SCIENCE) – Djakarta. 1951-1957. v107-113. – 589mf – 9 – ne IDC [500]
MADJALAH KEDOKTERAN INDONESIA – Djakarta. 1951-71. Lacking: 1952, v2(5,p.161-204); 1962, v12(7,p.194-236); 1970,v20(12-?); 1971,v.21(1,p1-54) – 267mf – 9 – ne IDC [073]
MADJALAH NASIONAL – Djakarta. Incomplete. SE-914 1. 1950-1960 – 9 – ne IDC [073]
MADJALAH PERTANIAN – Djakarta. Incomplete. SE-831 1. 1950-1965 – 9 – ne IDC [073]
MADJALAH SARI PENGETAHUAN MILITER – Bandung. Incomplete. SE-590 1. 1961-1971 – 9 – ne IDC [073]
MADJALAH SEDJARAH MILITER ANGKATAN DARAT – Bandung. SE-593 1. Lacking: v. 1-4;9;14;23. 1954-1966 – 9 – ne IDC [073]
MADJALAH UNIVERSITAS HASANUDDIN – Makassar. SE-490 1. 1960-1965 – 9 – ne IDC [073]
MADJALLAH BOELANAN BERGAMBAR : MEDAN / Minami – (Lacking: 1942 v1(2-3). 1943 v2(8-12). 1944 v3(3-4, 9-12)) – Syonan Sinbun Kai, Medan Sibu, 1942-1945(3). 4v – 337-374mf – 9 – ne IDC [950]
MADJALLAH HOEKOEM : ISTILLAH HOEKOEM – Pemerintah, 1947. 23p – 1mf – 9 – ne IDC [950]
MADJALLAH TENTARA REPOEBLIK INDONESIA – (Lacking: 1946, V.1(2)) – Jogjakarta, 1946 – 4mf – 9 – ne IDC [950]
Madjelis Ilmu Pengetahuan Indonesia *see*
- BULLETIN
- INDEX OF INDONESIAN LEARNED PERIODICALS
- SCIENTIFIC PUBLICATIONS PUBLISHED IN INDONESIA

MADJULAH INTELIGENSIA INDONESIA, BERKERUMUN DISEKITAR MANIPOL / Adjitorop, Jusuf – SE-4778 1. 1962 – 9 – ne IDC [950]
Madlena, Troy A *see* RELATIONSHIP BETWEEN PERCEIVED EXERTION AND REPETITIONS PERFORMED TO EXHAUSTION AT SELECTED PERCENTAGES OF ONE-REPETITION MAXIMUM IN APPARENTLY HEALTHY ADULTS
MADOC / Southey, Robert – London: Printed for Longman, Hurst, Rees, and Orme, and A. Constable and Co.; Edinburgh, 1805 – 1 roll – 1 – 1-55879-875-7 – uk Libr Preservation [810]
THE MADONNA IN LEGEND AND HISTORY / Vincent, Elizabeth Carter – New York: Thomas Whittaker, c1899 – 1mf – 9 – 0-8370-8796-1 – 1986-2796 – us A.T.L.A. [240]
DER MADONNENMALER FRANZ ITTENBACH (1813-1879) / Finke, Heinrich – Koeln, 1898 – 9 – DM48.00 – 3-89349-266-6 – gw Hänsel [750]
Madox, Thomas *see* HISTORY AND ANTIQUITIES OF THE EXCHEQUER OF THE KINGS OF ENGLAND
MADRAS / Madras. India. Census Office – Madras: Supt Govt Press. pt 4. 1901 – us Res Libr [310]
Madras *see*
- LEGISLATIVE COUNCIL DEBATES
- SOUTH-INDIAN TEMPLE INSCRIPTIONS

MADRAS CHRISTIAN COLLEGE MAGAZINE 1883-1990 – 28r – 1 – £1,150.00 – 1-897955-14-6 – uk Academic [240]
MADRAS COURIER – India. -w. 22 Sept 1791-8 Nov 1793. 2 reels – 1 – uk British Libr Newspaper [072]
MADRAS DISTRICT GAZETTEER / Innes, C A & Evans, Frank B – I-745 2. 1908 – 8 – ne IDC [072]
Madras. Home Department (Education) *see*
- PROGRESS REPORT ON EPIGRAPHICAL WORK, ACCOMPLISHED FROM 1887 TO 1917
- PROGRESS REPORT ON EPIGRAPHICAL WORK, FOR THE YEARS 1918/1919-1922

Madras. India. Census Office *see*
- MADRAS
- VILLAGE STATISTICS

Madras. India. Legislative Assembly *see* DEBATES

Madras. (India: State). Record Office *see*
- GUIDE TO THE RECORDS OF THE GUNTUR DISTRICT, 1795-1835
- GUIDE TO THE RECORDS OF THE MASULIPATAM DISTRICT, 1682 TO 1835
- GUIDE TO THE RECORDS OF THE NELLORE DISTRICT, 1801 TO 1835
- GUIDE TO THE RECORDS OF THE TINNEVELLY DISTRICT, 1796 TO 1835

MADRAS JOURNAL OF LITERATURE AND SCIENCE – (Lacks: v13; 1878-81; 1886-94) – Madras: Madra Literary Society & Auxiliary of the RAS, Old College, Nungumbaukum. v1-ser 3 n2. oct 1833-1866 – us Res Libr [073]

MADRAS JOURNAL OF LITERATURE AND SCIENCE – Madras. 1833-89. Lacking: 1840-1847 – 204mf – 8 – ne IDC [400]

MADRAS MAIL – India. -d. March 1871-Dec 1889. 77 reels – 1 – uk British Libr Newspaper [072]

MADRAS, MYSORE, AND THE SOUTH OF INDIA, OR, A PERSONAL NARRATIVE OF A MISSION TO THOSE COUNTRIES FROM MDCCCXX TO MDCCCXXVII. / Hoole, Elijah – 2nd ed. London: Longman, Brown, Green, and Longmans, 1844. xlvii,443p. ill – 1 – us U.W. Library [950]

Madras Native Association *see* REPORT OF THE PROCEEDINGS...PRESENTATION TO JOHN CRUCE NORTON

MADRAS PIONEER – Madras, OR. -w. 25 Aug 1904-. – 1 – us U.O. Library [071]

Madras. Presidency *see* FORT ST GEORGE GAZETTE

MADRAS STANDARD – India. -w. 1877-1889. 26 reels – 1 – uk British Libr Newspaper [072]

MADRAS TIMES – India. -d. Aug 1858-Dec 1914. 429 reels – 1 – uk British Libr Newspaper [072]

MADRAS TIMES OVERLAND EDITION – India. -w. Jan-Dec 1890. 3 reels – 1 – uk British Libr Newspaper [072]

Madras. University *see* ANNALS OF ORIENTAL RESEARCH

Madrazo, Pedro de *see* HISTORIAS DE MERIDA

Madre, A de *see* DES OUVRIERS ET DES MOYENS D'AMELIORER LEUR CONDITION DANS LES VILLES

LA MADRE CELESTINA – Mexico. 16 Oct-21 Dec 1861.-w. 13 ft – 1 – uk British Libr Newspaper [072]

MADRE, YA TENEMOS BANDERA / Fernandez Pascual, Alfonso – Zaragoza. 1937? Fiche W 881. (Blodgett Collection of Spanish Civil War Pamphlets) – 9 – us H.U. College Libr [946]

Madres Capuchinas *see* MONTE DE LA MYRRA Y COLLADO DEL INCIENSO TRASLADADOS POR LA IMITACION AL SERAFICO MONASTERIO DE...Y CHRONICA DE LA FUNDACION DEL Y DE LAS VENERABLES RELIGIOSAS...

MADRES CAPUCHINAS...MONTE DE LA MYRRA Y COLLADO – 1718 – 9 – 1.50f – sp Bibl Santa Ana [240]

MADRES DE PLAZA DE MAYO = MOTHERS OF THE PLAZA DE MAYO – Capital Federal. 106 docs. 1980-1990 – 53mf – 9 – ne IDC [320]

MADRID – Madrid. Spain. -d. 1 Mar 1943-21 Apr 1944, 16 May-20 Jun 1 Aug 1944-28 May 1945. (Imperfect). (10 reels) – 1 – uk British Libr Newspaper [072]

Madrid. Academia de la Historia *see* MEMORIAL HISTORICO ESPANOL

Madrid. Archivo Historico Nacional *see* INDICE DE LAS PRUEBAJ DE CABALLEROS DE LA ORDEN DE SANTIAGO

MADRID. ARCHIVO HISTORICO NACIONAL. EXTRACTO DEL CATALOGO DE DOCUMENTOS DEL CONSEJO DE INDIAS... / Gonzalez Palencia, A – Madrid, 1920 – 1mf – 9 – sp Cultura [946]

MADRID. ARCHIVO HISTORICO NACIONAL JUDAIZANTES EN...LA INQUISICION DE AMERICA / Leon Tello, P – Madrid, 1958 – 9 – sp Cultura [970]

MADRID. ARCHIVO HISTORICO NACIONAL. SEC. DIVERSOS. DOCUMENTOS DE INDIAS / Pescador del Hoyo, C – Madrid, 1954 – 6mf – 9 – sp Cultura [970]

MADRID. ARCHIVO HISTORICO NACIONAL. SECCION DE CLERO. INVENTARIO DE LIBROS – (TOMO 1 (Alava-Ciudad Real). TOMO 2 (Cordoba-Jaen). TOMO 3 (Leon-Lugo). TOMO 4 (Madrid-Orense). TOMO 5 (Oviedo-Salamanca). TOMO 6 (Santander-Segovia). TOMO 7 (Sevilla-Toledo). TOMO 8 (Valencia-Valladolid). TOMO 9 (Vizcaya-Zaragoza)) – 30mf – 9 – sp Cultura [025]

MADRID. ARCHIVO HISTORICO NACIONAL. SECCION DE CLERO. INVENTARIO DE PERGAMINOS – (TOMO 1, (Alava-Huelva); TOMO 2, (Huesca-Logrono); TOMO 3, (Lugo); TOMO 4, (Madrid-Palencia); TOMO 5, (Pontevedra-Soria); TOMO 6, (Tarragona); TOMO 7, (Tarragona); TOMO 8, (Teruel-Toledo); TOMO 9, (Valencia-Valladolid); TOMO 10, (Zamora-Zaragoza)) – 55mf – 9 – sp Cultura [025]

MADRID. ARCHIVO HISTORICO NACIONAL. SECCION DE CODICES. INVENTARIO DE LA SECCION DE CODICES / Leon, P & Pena, MT – Madrid, 1952 – 9 – sp Cultura [340]

MADRID. ARCHIVO HISTORICO NACIONAL. SECCION DE CONSEJOS. CATALOGO ALFABETICO DE TITULOS DEL REINO Y GRANDEZAS DE ESPANA, TOMO 1-3 – Madrid, 1951-1953 – 41mf – 9 – sp Cultura [025]

MADRID. ARCHIVO HISTORICO NACIONAL. SECCION DE CONSEJOS. CATALOGO ALFABETICO DE TITULOS Y GRANDEZAS DE REINO CONSERVADOS... – Madrid, 1919 – 13mf – 9 – sp Cultura [025]

MADRID. ARCHIVO HISTORICO NACIONAL. SECCION DE CONSEJOS. INVENTARIO GENERAL. TOMO 1-2 – 26mf – 9 – sp Cultura [946]

MADRID. ARCHIVO HISTORICO NACIONAL. SECCION DE DIVERSOS. CONCEJOS Y CIUDADES. INVENTARIO DEL ARCHIVO DE RUEDA – 1mf – 9 – sp Cultura [946]

MADRID. ARCHIVO HISTORICO NACIONAL. SECCION DE DIVERSOS. TITULOS Y FAMILIAS. ARCHIVOS NOBILIARIOS: CONDE DE PENALVER, BARON DE LAS CUATRO TORRES : CONDE DE PENALVER, BARON DE LAS CUATRO TORRES – 1mf – 9 – sp Cultura [946]

MADRID. ARCHIVO HISTORICO NACIONAL. SECCION DE DIVERSOS. TITULOS Y FAMILIAS. CATALOGO DEL ARCHIVO DE LA FAMILIA CORONEL – 4mf – 9 – sp Cultura [946]

MADRID. ARCHIVO HISTORICO NACIONAL. SECCION DE DIVERSOS. TITULOS Y FAMILIAS. CATALOGOS DE LEOPOLDO MATOS – 5mf – 9 – sp Cultura [946]

MADRID. ARCHIVO HISTORICO NACIONAL. SECCION DE DIVERSOS. TITULOS Y FAMILIAS. INVENTARIO DEL ARCHIVO DE MARGARITA NELKEN – 1894-1968 – 3mf – 9 – sp Cultura [946]

MADRID. ARCHIVO HISTORICO NACIONAL. SECCION DE DIVERSOS. TITULOS Y FAMILIAS. INVENTARIO DEL ARCHIVO DEL GENERAL WEYLER Y NICOLAU – 2mf – 9 – sp Cultura [946]

MADRID. ARCHIVO HISTORICO NACIONAL. SECCION DE ENTINTA SIGILOGRAFIA. SELLOS MUNICIPALES – 331mf – 9 – sp Cultura [350]

MADRID. ARCHIVO HISTORICO NACIONAL. SECCION DE ESTADO. CATALOGO DE CORRESPONDENCIA DE LOS CAPITANES GENERALES DE CUBA Y PUERTO RICO – 3mf – 9 – sp Cultura [320]

MADRID. ARCHIVO HISTORICO NACIONAL SECCION DE ESTADO. INVENTARIO DE LIBROS – Madrid, 1973 – 2mf – 9 – sp Cultura [010]

MADRID. ARCHIVO HISTORICO NACIONAL. SECCION DE FONDOS CONTEMPORANEOS. AUDIENCIA TERRITORIAL DE MADRID (1900-1942) – 1900-1942 – 1mf – 9 – sp Cultura [360]

MADRID. ARCHIVO HISTORICO NACIONAL. SECCION DE FONDOS CONTEMPORANEOS. CAUSA GENERAL ACTAS DEL TRIBUNAL DE RESPONSABILIDAD CIVIL – 1937 – 5mf – 9 – sp Cultura [324]

MADRID. ARCHIVO HISTORICO NACIONAL. SECCION DE FONDOS CONTEMPORANEOS. CAUSA GENERAL CATALOGO : CATALUNA DURANTE LA GUERRA CIVIL – 3mf – 9 – sp Cultura [355]

MADRID. ARCHIVO HISTORICO NACIONAL. SECCION DE FONDOS CONTEMPORANEOS. CAUSA GENERAL. INVENTARIO EXPEDIENTES JUDICIALES DE MADRID 1936-1939 – 33mf – 9 – sp Cultura [360]

MADRID. ARCHIVO HISTORICO NACIONAL. SECCION DE FONDOS CONTEMPORANEOS. CAUSA GENERAL INVENTARIOS ADMINISTRACION DE JUSTICIA 1936-1939 – 1mf – 9 – sp Cultura [946]

MADRID. ARCHIVO HISTORICO NACIONAL. SECCION DE FONDOS CONTEMPORANEOS. CAUSA GENERAL. INVENTARIOS DOCUMENTOS – 3mf – 9 – sp Cultura [946]

MADRID. ARCHIVO HISTORICO NACIONAL. SECCION DE FONDOS CONTEMPORANEOS. DELEGACION DE HACIENDA. INVENTARIO DE LIBROS. CATALOGO DE LEGAJOS – 1mf – 9 – sp Cultura [025]

MADRID. ARCHIVO HISTORICO NACIONAL. SECCION DE FONDOS CONTEMPORANEOS. GUIA DE LA SECCION – 1988 – 2mf – 9 – sp Cultura [025]

MADRID. ARCHIVO HISTORICO NACIONAL. SECCION DE FONDOS CONTEMPORANEOS. GUIA DE LIBROS PROCEDENTES DEL MINISTERIO DE HACIENDA (1609-1957) – 1609-1957 – 4mf – 9 – sp Cultura [025]

MADRID. ARCHIVO HISTORICO NACIONAL. SECCION DE FONDOS CONTEMPORANEOS. HACIENDA. INDICE DE EXPEDIENTES DE FUNCIONARIOS JUBILADOS 1800-1870 – 6mf – 9 – sp Cultura [025]

MADRID. ARCHIVO HISTORICO NACIONAL. SECCION DE FONDOS CONTEMPORANEOS. HACIENDA. INVENTARIO DE LOS FONDOS DE ORDENES MILITARES 1578-1870 – 2mf – 9 – sp Cultura [025]

MADRID. ARCHIVO HISTORICO NACIONAL. SECCION DE FONDOS CONTEMPORANEOS. INVENTARIO DE LA DIRECCION GENERAL DE PROPIEDADES DEL ESTADO 1850-1952 – 9mf – 9 – sp Cultura [025]

MADRID. ARCHIVO HISTORICO NACIONAL. SECCION DE FONDOS CONTEMPORANEOS. INVENTARIO DE LIBROS DE LAS MINAS DE ALMADEN 1735-1962 – 1735-1962 – 2mf – 9 – sp Cultura [025]

MADRID. ARCHIVO HISTORICO NACIONAL. SECCION DE FONDOS CONTEMPORANEOS. INVENTARIO DE LIBROS Y LEGAJOS DE LA FABRICA DE MONEDA Y TIMBRE 1719-1935 – 1mf – 9 – sp Cultura [025]

MADRID. ARCHIVO HISTORICO NACIONAL. SECCION DE FONDOS CONTEMPORANEOS. INVENTARIO DE REGISTRADORES 1871-1931 – 2mf – 9 – sp Cultura [025]

MADRID. ARCHIVO HISTORICO NACIONAL. SECCION DE FONDOS CONTEMPORANEOS. MINISTERIO DE JUSTICIA. INVENTARIO DE JUECES Y MAGISTRADOS. S. 19 – 5mf – 9 – sp Cultura [350]

MADRID. ARCHIVO HISTORICO NACIONAL. SECCION DE FONDOS CONTEMPORANEOS. MINISTERIO DE LA GOBERNACION. INVENTARIO SERIA A 1872-1936 – 1mf – 9 – sp Cultura [025]

MADRID. ARCHIVO HISTORICO NACIONAL. SECCION DE FONDOS CONTEMPORANEOS. MINISTERIO DE LA GOBERNACION. NUEVAS POBLACIONES 1748-1865 – 1mf – 9 – sp Cultura [350]

MADRID. ARCHIVO HISTORICO NACIONAL. SECCION DE INQUISICION. CATALOGO DE LAS CAUSAS DE FE...DE LA INQUISICION DE TOLEDO – Madrid, 1903 – 12mf – 9 – sp Cultura [240]

MADRID. ARCHIVO HISTORICO NACIONAL. SECCION DE INQUISICION. GUIA DE LA SECCION – 1mf – 9 – sp Cultura [240]

MADRID. ARCHIVO HISTORICO NACIONAL. SECCION DE ORDENES MILITARES. INVENTARIO DEL ARCHIVO DE UCLES. INDICES ONOMASTICO Y TOPONIMICO – 8mf – 9 – sp Cultura [025]

MADRID. ARCHIVO HISTORICO NACIONAL. SECCION DE ORDENES MILITARES. INVENTARIO DEL ARCHIVO DE UCLES, TOMO 1-3 / Fernandez, Juan Antonio – 32mf – 9 – sp Cultura [025]

MADRID. ARCHIVO HISTORICO NACIONAL. SECCION DE ORDENES MILITARES. INVENTARIOS ANTIGUOS. SAN JUAN DE JERUSALEN. LENGUA DE ARAGON – 60mf – 9 – sp Cultura [025]

MADRID. ARCHIVO HISTORICO NACIONAL. SECCION DE ORDENES MILITARES. INVENTARIOS ANTIGUOS. SAN JUAN DE JERUSALEN. LENGUA DE CASTILLA – 59mf – 9 – sp Cultura [240]

MADRID. ARCHIVO HISTORICO NACIONAL. SECCION DE OSUNA, ENCABEZAMIENTOS DEL INDICE DE REFERENCIA, TOMOS 1 Y 2 – 10mf – 9 – sp Cultura [946]

MADRID. ARCHIVO HISTORICO NACIONAL. SECCION DE SIGILOGRAFIA. CATALOGO DE SELLOS. 1-3 / Guglieri Navarro, A – Madrid, 1974 – 36mf – sp Cultura [240]

MADRID. ARCHIVO HISTORICO NACIONAL. SECCION DE UNIVERSIDADES. LA SECCION DE UNIVERSIDADES / Gutierrez del Arroyo, C – Madrid, 1952 – 9 – sp Cultura [370]

MADRID. ARCHIVO HISTORICO NACIONAL. SECCION DIVERSOS. PAPELES DE LUIS ARAQUISTAIN / Pena Marazuela, T de la – Madrid, 1983 – 4mf – 9 – sp Cultura [025]

MADRID. ARCHIVO HISTORICO NATIONAL. SECCION DE ORDENES MILITARES. GUIA DE LA SECCION DE ORDENES MILITARES / Javierre, A & Gutierrez, C – Madrid, S.A. – 6mf – 9 – sp Cultura [025]

Madrid. Ayuntamiento *see*
- BOLETIN DEL AVUNTAMIENTO DE MADRID
- BOLETIN DEL AYUNTAMIENTO

MADRID. BIBLIOTECA NACIONAL. CATALOGO DE INCUNABLES / Garcia Rojo, D & Ortiz, G – Madrid, 1945 – 11mf – 9 – sp Cultura [020]

MADRID. BIBLIOTECA NACIONAL. CATALOGO DE LOS MANUSCRITOS DE AMERICA / Paz, J – Madrid, 1933 – 13mf – 9 – sp Cultura [972]

MADRID. BIBLIOTECA NACIONAL. CATALOGO DE OBRAS DE IBEROAMERICA Y FILIPINAS / Cuesta, M – Madrid; 1935 – 6mf – 9 – sp Cultura [410]

MADRID EN RUINAS – Madrid in Ruins. n.p. 1936. Fiche W1015. (Blodgett Collection of Spanish Civil War Pamphlets) – 9 – us H.U. College Libr [946]

MADRID ERA – Madrid, NE. -w. Jun 1911-Feb 1918 – 1 – us NE Hist [071]

MADRID HERALD – Madrid, NE. -w. Jan 1920-Jun 1943; Jan 1946-Dec 1964 – 1 – us NE Hist [071]

MADRID. MUSEO ARQUEOLOGICO NACIONAL INVENTARIO DE LA SECCION DE ETNOGRAFIA / Janer, F – 9mf – 9 – sp Cultura [930]

MADRID NEWS – Madrid, NE. -w. Dec 1892; Dec 1895-Jul 1896; Feb 1897 – 1 – us NE Hist [071]

MADRID, THE "MILITARY" ATROCITIES OF THE REBELS: A RECORD OF MASSACRE, MURDER, MUTILATION / Labour Party. Great Britain – London, 1937. Fiche W 982. (Blodgett Collection of Spanish Civil War Pamphlets) – 9 – us H.U. College Libr [946]

MADRIGAL / Martinez Sierra, Gregorio – Madrid. 1925 – 1 – us Res Libr [830]

O MADRIGAL : ORGAO DA SOCIEDADE LITTERARIA TAVARES BASTOS – Maceio, Alagoas. 5 Nov-8 Dez 1899 – 1,5,6 – bl Biblioteca [072]

O MADRIGAL : ORGAO LITTERARIO COLLEGIAL – Uniao, Alagoas. 10 Set-8 Out 1893 – 1,5,6 – bl Biblioteca [072]

Madrigal, Alfonso de *see*
- EL TOSTADO. OPERA OMNIA...(ANNO 1596)

MADRIGAL SOCIETY: THE HISTORY AND AIMS – 1 – uk Microform Academic [780]

Madrigalejo. Mercado de Abastos *see* REGLAMENTO

MADRIGALI A CINQUE VOCI...LIBRO PRIMO / Quartieri, Pietro Paolo – 1592 – 9 – us Sibley [780]

MADRIGALI DEL S. MICHEL'ANGELO ROSSI : LIBRI DUE / Rossi, Michelangelo – [ca 1626-ca 1629]. SEM105P1335 – 4mf – 9 – Can$9.00 – cn Bibl Nat [780]

MADRIGALS / Monteverdi, Claudio – (Venetia). 1638. York Minster Library – 1 – uk Microform Academic [780]

[MADRIGALS, 5 VOICES, BOOK 1] / Scaramella, B – (5 parts book) – In Venetia: appresso Giacomo Vincenti, [1591] – 1 – us Sibley [780]

MADRONA 90 / California Botanical Society – Berkeley. 1916-1941. v1-6 – 24mf – 1 – ne IDC [580]

Madronera, Ayuntamiento *see* ORDENANZAS MUNICIPALES

Madronera. Ayuntamiento *see*
- ALA SANTISIMA VIRGEN DEL ROSARIO. ACTOS Y FESTEJOS EN SU HONOR, 1946
- FIESTAS DE LA JUVENTUD. 1974
- FIESTAS EN HONOR DE NTRA. SRA. DE SOTERRANA (VIRGEN DE LAS NIEVES). 1971

Maduabuchi, A *see* HEALTH BEHAVIORS AND ATTITUDES OF SELECTED NIGERIAN AND AMERICAN UNIVERSITY STUDENTS

A M.(ADULT MUSIC) – Dec 1979- – 1,5,6,9 – us UMI [073]

MADURA COUNTRY / Nelson, J H – (A manual). I-744 2. 1868 – 8 – ne IDC [950]

Madvig, Johan Nicolai *see* DIE VERFASSUNG UND VERWALTUNG DES ROEMISCHEN STAATES

MAECHDEN-PLICHT OFTE AMPT DER IONCK-VROUWEN / Cats, J – O 195. 1618 – 9 – ne IDC [760]

DAS MAEDCHEN VON BYZANZ : TRAUERSPIEL IN FUENF AUFZUEGEN / Kruse, Heinrich – Leipzig: S Hirzel, 1877 – 1r – 1 – us U.W. Library [820]

DAS MAEDCHEN VON TREPPI / Heyse, Paul – (Italienische Liebesgeschichten) – Berlin: Buchverlag der Morgen, 1965 – 1 – us U.W. Library [830]

MAEGDEN-PLICHT OFTE AMPT DER IONGHVROUWEN, IN EERBAER LIEFDE, AANGEWESEN DOOR SINNE-BEELDEN / Cats, J – N.p., n.d. – 4mf – 9 – ne IDC [700]

Maehly, Jakob *see* SEBASTIAN CASTELLIO

"DAS MAEHRCHEN" : EINE NEU AUFGESCHLOSSENE URKUNDE ZU GOETHES WELTANSCHAUUNG / Schneider, Hermann – 2. Aufl. Leipzig: J C Hinrich, 1912 – 1r – 1 – us U.W. Library [430]

Maehrische Gesellschaft zur Befoerderung der Landwirtschaft, der Natur- und Landeskunde. Historisch-Statistische Section *see* SCHRIFTEN

MAEHRISCHER GRENZBOTE – Iglau (Jihlava), Czechoslovakia. 5 May 1930-1942 – 1 – gw Mikrofilm [072]

MAEHRISCH-SCHLESISCHE PRESSE – Freiwaldau (Jesenik), Czechoslovakia. 31 Oct 1928-38 – 1 – gw Mikrofilm [072]

MAELCHO : A SIXTEENTH-CENTURY NARRATIVE / Lawless, Emily – British Fiction Archive: Unit 4 – 9 – uk Bell [830]

MAELESTUSI ELUTEELT JA TOEOEMAALT = MEMOIRS FROM MY LIFE AND MINISTRY / Laks, Johannes – Toronto Vabakoguduse Kirjastus, 1965. Publ. No. 6295c. One of four items on a reel. Total pages, 504 – 1 – us Baptist [240]

Maemecke, Thomas *see* DAS VERSTAENDNIS DER SUENDE IN ROEMER 7

MAENNER, DIE NAHRUNG SCHUFEN / Keune, O – Hannover, 1952 – 1 – DM30.00 – gw Mikro Press [920]

Maenss, Johannes *see* FRANZ VON SICKINGEN

DIE MAERCHEN DES PAPYRUS WESTCAR / Erman, A – (Mitt. Orient. Sammlungen, Koen. Mus. heft 5. Berlin, 1890). BNE-372 1 – 9 – ne IDC [390]

DAS MAERCHEN IN DEN GOETTERSAGEN DER EDDA / Leyen, Friedrich von der – 1899 – 1 – us I.U. Libraries [390]

Maercker, Friedrich *see* EINLADUNGSSCHRIFT DES GYMNASIUM BERNHARDINUM IN MEININGEN

MAERKISCHE BLAETTER – Hattingen, Ruhr, Germany. 2 Jan 1850-21 Jan 1852; 30 Jun-25 Sep 1852; 12-29 Jan 1853; 3 Jan-29 Dec 1855; 26 Jan-28 Dec 1859; 1 Jan-4 Dec 1861; 3 Jan-18 Nov 1863; 2 Jan-29 Jun 1864; 7 Jan-16 Dec 1865 – 3r – 1 – gw Mikrofilm [072]

MAERKISCHE FORSCHUNGEN – Berlin. Bd. 13-20; 1876-87. Film Mas C 306 – 1 – us H.U. Library [073]

MAERKISCHE ODERZEITUNG *see*
– NEUER TAG

MAERKISCHE UNION – Potsdam, DE. Aug 1954-Sept 1961; Apr-Sept 1963; Apr 1964-Feb 1990 – 59r – 1 – gw Mikrofilm [072]

MAERKISCHE VOLKSSTIMME – (Also Bereichsausgaben available (nur Kreisseiten): BELZIG, apr 1 1958-oct 31 1961, mar 3 1966-jul 31 1969 (incomplete); BRANDENBURG, apr 3 1958-oct 31 1961, 1965-may 22 1969 (incomplete), jul 20 1983-88; BRANDENBURG-LAND, apr 2 1958-oct 31 1961, jun 2 1988-sep 25 1990; GRANSEE, feb 7 1958-oct 31 1961; JUETERBOG, apr 3 1958-oct 7 1964 (incomplete); KOENIGS WUSTERHAUSEN, apr 2 1958-sep 21 1977, mar 1 1979-sep 26 1990 (all incomplete); KYRITZ, apr 2 1958-oct 31 1961, apr 18 1963-jul 28 1964 (incomplete); LUCKENWALDE, apr 3 1958-oct 31 1961, jan 5 1963-sep 28 1968 (incomplete); NAUEN, apr 3 1958-aug 26 1969 (incomplete), sep 29 1985-sep 28 1990; NEURUPPIN, apr 2 1958-aug 7 1968, jan 30 1984-dec 19 1986 (all incomplete); ORANIENBURG, apr 1 1958-oct 31 1961, feb 16 1963-nov 30 1966 (incomplete), jul 3 1984-apr 30 1985; POTSDAM-LAND, apr 2 1958-sep 2 1962 (incomplete), jan 12-jul 31 1977; PRITZWALK, apr 2 1958-oct 31 1961, jan 24 1963-oct 22 1966 (incomplete); RATHENOW, apr 3 1958-oct 31 1961, feb 13 1962-jul 20 1968 (incomplete); WITTSTOCK, apr 2 1958-nov 2 1966 (incomplete); ZOSSEN, apr 3 1958-oct 16 1963 (incomplete), feb 23 1965-jul 5 1967 (incomplete), 1974-mar 22 1975, sep 21 1985-sep 29 1990) – Potsdam, apr 20 1946-sep 29 1990 – 1 – Inquire at Mikrofilmarchiv for details – gw Misc Inst [072]

MAERKISCHE VOLKSSTIMME – Berlin, Potsdam. 2 Jul 1946-47 – 1r – 1 – DM75.00 – gw Mikro Press [072]

MAERKISCHE VOLKSSTIMME – Potsdam, East Germany. 2 Jul 1946-47; 1952-29 Sep 1990 1981 – 78r – 1 – gw Mikrofilm [072]

MAERKISCHER SPEICHER *see* BOCHUMER KREISBLATT

Maerten, Lu *see* BERGARBEITER

Maerz, Lothar *see* UEBERPRUEFUNG EINES SOFTWAREPROGRAMMES IM HINBLICK AUF SEINEN EINSATZ ALS PLANUNGS- UND STEUERUNGSINSTRUMENT

Maes, Bonifacius *see* MYSTICKE THEOLOGIE-SERAPHINSCHE PRACTYCKE-OPRRECHTE DEVOTIE-BRANT DER LIEFDE

Maes, Camillus Paul *see* THE LIFE OF REV. CHARLES NERINCKY

Maestracci, Noel *see* LE MAROC CONTEMPORAIN.

Maestre de San Juan, Lucas *see*
– DE LEYTE DE CAVALLEROS...CAVALLOS
– DELEYTE DE CAVALLEROS Y PLACER DE LOS CAVALLOS

Maestre, Vicente *see* MEMORIA...MARIA DOLORES CABRERA...BIENES...FUNDACIONES

EL MAESTRO...ORACION FUNEBRE / Vazquez de Cilleros, Francisco – 1734 – 9 – 1.50f – sp Bibl Santa Ana [850]

Maestu, Luisa Maria *see* PROVINCIA DE SAN FRANCISCO SOLANO Y SUS MISIONES...

MAETEN-GAITLINK : GEDICHTE IN MUENSTERLAENDER MUNDART / Wibbelt, Augustin – Essen-Ruhr: Fredebeul und Koenen, [1909?] – 1r – 1 – us U.W. Library [390]

MAETEN-GAITLINK : GEDICHTE IN MUENSTERLAENDISCHER MUNDART / Wibbelt, Augustin – 1. Aufl. Essen (Ruhr): Fredebeul & Koenen, [1909?] – 1 – us U.W. Library [810]

Maetzing, Ortwin *see* BUEROKRATIE ALS LERNENDE ORGANISATION

Maeztu, Ramiro de *see* DEFENSA DE LA HISPANIDAD

MAFEKING MAIL – Mafeking, South Africa. 20 May 1899-31 Dec 1917. 37 reels. Title varies: Mafeking Mail and Protectorate Guardian, 1900-66; Mafeking Mail and Botswana Guardian, 1966-80 – 1, 16 diazo available at reduced price – sa SA Libr [072]

MAFEKING MAIL AND BOTSWANA GUARDIAN – Mafeking, South Africa: Mafeking Mail Ltd, 1967-78 – 9r – 1 – us Res Libr [072]

THE MAFEKING MAIL AND PROTECTORATE GUARDIAN – Mafeking, South Africa: Townshend & Son, jan 12 1945-sep 23 1966 – 10r – 1 – us Res Libr [072]

MAFES RESEARCH HIGHLIGHTS / Mississippi State University. Agricultural Experiment Station. Agricultural and Forestry Experiment Station – No.36-45. 1973-82. 1 reel – 1,5 – us Spaulding [630]

Maffei, G P *see*
– HISTORIARUM INDICARUM LIBRI 16
– LE HISTORIE DELLE INDIE ORIENTALI

Maffei, P A *see* RACCOLTA DI STATUE ANTICHE E MODERNE DATA IN LUCE SOTTO I GLORIOSI AUSPICJ, DELLA SANTITA DI N.S. PAPA CLEMENTE 11...

Mafoud, P *see* JOSEPH S. ASSEMANI ET LA CELEBRATION DU CONCILE LIBANAIS MARONITE DE 1736

MAFTEAH LI-TESHUVOT HA-GE'ONIM / Mueller, J – v. 1. Berlin. 1891. BJ-32-41 1 – 9 – ne IDC [900]

Magagno, G B *see* FROTOLA...PER LA VITTUORIA DE I NUOSTRI SEGNORE CONTRA I TURCHI

Magalhaes, Couto de *see* VIAGEM AO ARAGUAYA

Magalhaes, F *see* CANTUM ECCLESIASTICUM PRAECIBUS APUD DEUM ANIMAS JUVANDI, CORPOR RAQUE HUMAND...

[Magalhaes, G de] *see* A NEW HISTORY OF THE EMPIRE OF CHINA,...

MAGALLANES EN 1925...POR MANUEL ZORRILLA / Bayle, Constantino – Madrid: Razon y Fe, 1926 – 1 – sp Bibl Santa Ana [946]

MAGANJOGI DONTVENYTAR. / Hungary. Kuria – Budapest. On film: v1-27; 1907-35. LL-0248 – 1 – us L of C Photodup [340]

Maganza, G B *see* HERCVLANA, IN LINGVA VENETIANA, NELLA VITTORIA DELL' ARMATA CHRISTIANA CONTRA TURCHI

LE MAGASIN DE LIBRAIRIE – Litterature, histoire, philosophie, voyages. Paris. nov 1858-oct 1860 (I-XII) – 1 – fr A.C.R.P.P. [073]

LE MAGASIN DU BAS-CANADA – Montreal, Canada. 1 jan-dec 1832 – 1r – 1 – Can$30.00 – cn Can Microfilming [073]

MAGASIN ENCYCLOPEDIQUE *see* REVUE ENCYCLOPEDIQUE

MAGASIN ENCYCLOPEDIQUE, OU JOURNAL DES SCIENCES, DES LETTRES, ET DES ARTS – Paris, 1792-1816. Table generale, 1819 – 3 – us Readex [500]

DAS MAGAZIN : MONATSSCRIFT FUER LITERATUR, KUNST UND KULTUR – v1-84. 1915-32 – 1 – $556.00 – us L of C Photodup [410]

MAGAZIN ALLER NEUEN ERFINDUNGEN – (Cont by: Neues Magazin [...], 1809. Magazin der Neuesten Erfindungen, 1816) – Leipzig, 1797-1826 – 4r – 1 – gw Mikrofilm [600]

MAGAZIN DER AESTHETISCHEN BOTANIK / ed by Reichenbach, Heinrich G L – Leipzig. 1821, 1822-24, 1826. 2v. – 8mf – 9 – ne IDC [580]

MAGAZIN DER ENTOMOLOGIE / ed by Germar, E F – Halle, 1813-1821 – 31mf – 9 – ne IDC [400]

MAGAZIN DER INSEKTENKUNDE / ed by Illiger, K – Braunschweig. v1-6. 1801-1807 – 38mf – 9 – ne IDC [590]

MAGAZIN DER MUSIK / Cramer, Carl F – Erster Jahrgang. Erste-Zweyte Haelfte. 1783 – 9 – us Sibley [780]

MAGAZIN DER NEUESTEN ERFINDUNGEN *see* MAGAZIN ALLER NEUEN ERFINDUNGEN

MAGAZIN ENCYCLOPEDIQUE – ou Journal des sciences, des lettres et des arts. Paris. 1804-mai 1816 – 1 – fr A.C.R.P.P. [073]

MAGAZIN FOR NATURVIDENSKABERNE – Christiania (Oslo). v1-10. 1823-28 – 3 – us Readex [574]

MAGAZIN FUER DAS NEUESTE AUS DER PHYSIK UND NATURGESCHICHTE – Gotha, 1781-99. 1785-88, v. 1-12 – 3 – us Readex [500]

MAGAZIN FUER DIE BERGBAUKUNDE – Dresden, 1785-99 – 3 – us Readex [622]

MAGAZIN FUER DIE BOTANIK / ed by Roemer, J J & Usteri, P – (Cont. as: Roemer, J.J. Neues Magazin fuer die Botanik. Zuerich, 1794) – Zuerich, 1787-1790 – 48mf – 8 – ne IDC [580]

MAGAZIN FUER DIE BOTANIK – Zurich, 1787-90 – 3 – us Readex [580]

MAGAZIN FUER DIE GEOGRAPHIE UND STATISTIK DER KOENIGLICH-PREUSSISCHEN STAATEN – Berlin, 1791 (very incomplete) – 1mf – 9 – Dist. gw Mikrofilm – gw Misc Inst [310]

MAGAZIN FUER DIE GESAMMTE HEILKUNDE, 1.1816-66.1848 – 1816-1848 (mf ed 1995) – 9 – DM4,400.00 – 3-89131-222-9 – gw Fischer [610]

MAGAZIN FUER DIE LIEBHABER DER ENTOMOLOGIE / ed by Fuessly, J C – (Cont as: Neues Magazin fuer die Liebhaber der Entomologie, Zuerich, Winterthur v1-3 1782-1787) – Zuerich, Winterthur. v1-2. 1778-1779 – 27mf – 9 – ne IDC [400]

MAGAZIN FUER DIE LIEBHABER DER ENTOMOLOGIE – Zurich und Winterthur. 1778-79. v. 1-2 – 3 – us Readex [590]

MAGAZIN FUER DIE LITERATUR DES AUSLANDES *see* DAS MAGAZIN

MAGAZIN FUER DIE NATURGESCHICHTE DES MENSCHEN – Zittau und Leipzig, 1788-91 – 3 – us Readex [910]

MAGAZIN FUER DIE NATURKUNDE HELVETIENS – Zurich, 1787-89 – 3 – us Readex [500]

MAGAZIN FUER DIE ORYKTOGRAPHIE VON SACHSEN – Freyberg, 1828-48 – 3 – us Readex [550]

MAGAZIN FUER DIE WISSENSCHAFT DES JUDENTHUMS – Berlin. v. 1-20. 1874-1893 – 1 – us NY Public [270]

MAGAZIN INOSTRANNOI LITERATURY – Spb. 1873-74. Lacking: 1874 (11-12). B-1777 2 – 8 – ne IDC [073]

MAGAZIN VOR AERZTE, 1775-1778 NEUES MAGAZIN FUER AERZTE, 1.1779-20.1798 – 1775-1798 (mf ed 1995) – 80mf – 9 – DM1,570.00 – 3-89131-223-7 – gw Fischer [610]

MAGAZIN ZUR VERBREITUNG GEMEINNUETZIGER KENNTNISSE *see* DAS HELLER-BLATT

MAGAZIN ZUR VERVOLLKOMMNUNG DER THEORETISCHEN UND PRAKTISCHEN HEILKUNDE, 10 BAENDE 1799-1807 / ed by Roeschlaub, Andreas – Frankfurt, 1799-1807 (mf ed 1994) – 23mf – 9 – DM980.00 – 3-89131-188-5 – gw Fischer [615]

MAGAZINE – Beverly Hills. v. 1-2, no. 6. Dec 1933-June 1935 – 1 – us NY Public [073]

MAGAZINE – San Francisco, 1963-85; 1987-89 – 22r – 1 – $1,100.00 – B02840 – us Library Micro [073]

MAGAZINE ABOUT SMALL BUSINESS *see* SMALL BUSINESS

MAGAZINE AND NEWSPAPER ADVERTISEMENTS AND ARTICLES AND OTHER PUBLICITY / Great Northern Railway Company. Advertising and Publicity Dept – 1884-1970 – 7r – 1 – $210.00; $35.00r – us M.H.S. [380]

MAGAZINE ANTIQUES – (1969- 5,6. 1970-9) – v. 1- 1922- – 1 – us UMI [930]

MAGAZINE INDEX – Monthly cumulative index of over 400 of the most frequently cited periodicals cover-to-cover – 5,17 – us I.A.C. [073]

MAGAZINE OF AMERICAN HISTORY, WITH NOTES AND QUERIES – 1-30. 1877-Sep 1893 – 1 – us UMI [970]

MAGAZINE OF ART – 42-46. 1949-1953 – 1 – us UMI [700]

THE MAGAZINE OF ART – 1878-1904 – 178mf – 9 – £800.00 – uk Chadwyck [700]

MAGAZINE OF BOTANY / ed by Paxton, J – London. v1-16. 1834-1849 – 132mf – 9 – ne IDC [580]

MAGAZINE OF CONCRETE RESEARCH – v38-. 1986- – 1,5,6,9 – us UMI [073]

MAGAZINE OF FANTASY AND SCIENCE FICTION *see* FANTASY AND SCIENCE FICTION

MAGAZINE OF KNOWLEDGE – Newark. N.J. 1894 – 1 – us A.J.P.C. [071]

MAGAZINE OF MASONRY CONSTRUCTION *see* ABERDEEN'S MAGAZINE OF MASONRY CONSTRUCTION

THE MAGAZINE OF NATURAL HISTORY – London, 1829-40 – 3 – us Readex [574]

MAGAZINE OF NATURAL HISTORY AND JOURNAL OF ZOOLOGY, BOTANY, MINERALOGY, GEOLOGY AND METEOROLOGY – London. v1-9 1829-1836; N.S. v1-4 1837-1840 – 145mf – 9 – ne IDC [500]

THE MAGAZINE OF NATURAL PHILOSOPHY...A POPULAR HISTORY OF SCIENCE – London, 1855-56. v.1, pts. 1-5 – 3 – us Readex [500]

MAGAZINE OF WALL STREET – 1- 1907- 1; 1969- 5,6; 1977- 9 – us UMI [336]

MAGAZINE OF ZOOLOGY AND BOTANY – (Cont as: Annals of Natural History; or, Magazine of Zoology, Botany and Geology. London v1-5 1838-1840; Cont as: The Annals and Magazine of Natural History, including Zoology, Botany and Geology. London, 1841-1937) – Edinburgh. v1-2. 1837-1838 – 2095mf – 9 – ne IDC [590]

MAGAZINE OF ZOOLOGY AND BOTANY – Edinburgh, 1837-38 – 3 – us Readex [580]

MAGAZINE OF ZOOLOGY, BOTANY AND GEOLOGY *see* MAGAZINE OF ZOOLOGY AND BOTANY

MAGAZINE, OR, ANIMADVERSIONS ON THE ENGLISH SPELLING – 1703. 40p. (English Linguistics Series 1500-1800) – 9 – us UMI [420]

MAGAZINE QUEBEC : MAGAZINE ILLUSTRE – Quebec, Canada. jun 1909-v1 n5. 25 nov 1909 – 1r – 1 – Can$25.00 – cn Can Microfilming [073]

MAGAZINET WESTERVIKS EXTRA – 1993-94 – 9 – sw Kungliga [072]

MAGAZYN POLSKI – Warsaw. 1957-1963 – 1 – us NY Public [073]

MAGDALENA : POESIAS / Sanchez-Arjona, Vicente – Sevilla: Imp. Zambrano, 1958 – 1 – sp Bibl Santa Ana [810]

Magdaleno, R *see* VALLADOLID. ARCHIVO GENERAL DESIMANCAS. DIRECCION GENERAL DEL TESORO. TITULOS DE INDIAS

Magdeburg, J *see*
- DIALOGVS ODER. EIN GESPRECHE EINES ESELS VND BERGKNECHTS...DEM SYNODO AUIUM ZU LIEB GESCHRIEBEN
- EYNE SCHOENE ARTZNEY, DADURCH DER LEIDENDEN CHRISTEN SORGE UND TRUBNUS GELINDERT...WERDEN

MAGDEBURGER VOLKSSTIMME *see* VOLKSSTIMME

MAGDEBURGISCHE PRIVILEGIRTE ZEITUNG *see* MAGDEBURGISCHE ZEITUNG

MAGDEBURGISCHE ZEITUNG – (Cont: Magdeburgische privilegirte Zeitung, 1731?. Koeniglich privilegirte Magdeburgische Zeitung, jan 3 1788. Actual title since nov 13 1806) – Magdeburg, feb 19 1954-sep 4 1956 – 1r – 1 – gw Mikrofilm [072]

MAGDEBURGISCHE ZEITUNG – Germany. -d. April 1916-July 1919. Imperfect. 18 reels – 1 – uk British Libr Newspaper [072]

MAGDEBURGISCHE ZEITUNG – Magdeburg, Germany. 1914-8 Nov 1925; 11 Jan-31 Oct 1926; 1927-31 May 1930; 1 Sep-31 May 1930; 1 Sep 1930-31 Jan 1935, Sep 1939-Aug 1944 – 127r – 1 – gw Mikrofilm [072]

Mage, Abdon Eugene *see*
- VOYAGE DANS LE SOUDAN OCCIDENTAL
- VOYAGE DANS LE SOUDAN OCCIDENTAL (SENEGAMBIE-NIGER) 1863-1866

Mage, M E *see*
- VOYAGE DANS LE SOUDAN OCCIDENTAL. 1863-1866
- VOYAGE DANS LE SOUDAN OCCIDENTAL (SENEGAMBIE, NIGER) 1863-1866

Magee, E D *see* MAGEE'S DIGEST OF CASES IN VOLS 49-72 OF THE AMERICAN STATE REPORTS

Magee, W C *see* SPEECHES AND ADDRESSES

MAGEEN DAVID – Amersfoort. v1-3(7). 1937-1940 – 4mf – 9 – ne IDC [999]

MAGEE'S CREEK BAPTIST CHURCH. JAYESS, MISSISSIPPI : CHURCH RECORDS – 1838-1916 – 1 – 31.68 – us Baptist [240]

MAGEE'S DIGEST OF CASES IN VOLS 49-72 OF THE AMERICAN STATE REPORTS / Magee, E D – San Francisco: Bancroft-Whitney, 1900 (all publ) – 16mf – 9 – $24.00 – LLMC 78-038I – us L.L.M.C. [340]

MAGEE'S WEEKLY PACKET – Dublin. Ireland. -w. 21 Jun 1777-26 Mar 1785, 31 Mar, 5, 26 May 1787, 26 Apr 1788, 11 Jul, 10 Oct 1789, 3 Jul, 7 Aug 1790, 4 Aug, 10 Nov 1792, 2 Mar, 10 Aug 1793. (3 reels) – 1 – uk British Libr Newspaper [072]

Magelang Indonesia. Akademi Militer Nasional *see* ACADEMIC CURRICULUM, OFFICER'S GENERAL EDUCATION OF THE A.M.N

Magelhaes, Couto de *see* O SELVAGEM

MAGELLAN TIMES – Punta Arenas. Chile. -d. Jul 1914-Dec 1921, Apr 1923-Dec 1932. (24 reels) – 1 – uk British Libr Newspaper [072]

MAGEN AVRAHAM – Lublin. 1624. BJ-43-50 1 – 9 – ne IDC [956]

Maggi, Girolamo *see* DE TINTINNABULIS LIBER POSTVMVS

MAGGID EMET / Ginzburg, M A – Leipzig. 1843. BJ-290-9 1 – 9 – ne IDC [940]

Maggid-Steinschneider, H N *see* IR VILNAH

MAGGIE, A GIRL OF THE STREETS / Crane, Stephen – 1893 – 9 – $10.00 – us Scholars' Facs [830]

Maggs Bros. London *see* BIBLIOTHECA AMERICANA ET PHILIPPINA

Maggs, Joseph Thomas Lawrence *see* OLD TESTAMENT WORD STUDIES

Magherini *see* TRIOS, SIX, FOR VIOLINS OR GERMAN FLUTES AND A BASS.

LE MAGHREB ET LA COMMUNAUTE ECONOMIQUE EUROPEENNE / D'Yvoire, J – F50.00 – fr Ethnologie [330]

MAGHREB-MACHREK – 1992-1995 – 8 times per yr – 9 – F1,280.00 – sz Infoprint [072]

THE MAGI AND THEIR GIFTS – 1961. 2p., 1 illus. 1 fiche. Fiche No. 1028 – 9 – $2.50 – us Corning Mus [700]

MAGIA NATURALIS: DAS IST KUNST UND WUNDERBUCH DARINNE BEGRIFFEN WUNDERBAHRE SECRETA / Hildebrand, Wolfgang – Buch 1-4 in 1 vol.. Erffurdt, Johann Birckners, Buchhaendler, 1645-1650. Film Mas 8447 – 1 – us H.U. Library [150]

MAGIC CITY HOOF AND HORN – Omaha, NE. -w. Jan 1899-Nov 1902 – 1 – us NE Hist [071]

THE MAGIC DOCUMENTS : SUMMARIES AND TRANSCRIPTS OF THE TOP-SECRET DIPLOMATIC COMMUNICATIONS OF JAPAN, 1938-45 / ed by Kesaris, Paul – (Subject and name index only, 0-89093-242-5. $70.00) – 1983. U.S.-produced summaries and transcripts of intercepted and deciphered messages between the Japanese Foreign Office and its key personnel and allies. Printed calendar of documents – 1 – $1,350.00 – 0-89093-244-1 – us UPA [950]

THE MAGIC INK; AND OTHER TALES / Black, William – British Fiction Archive: Unit 4 – 9 – uk Bell [830]

THE MAGIC LANTERN – Montreal, Canada. 1 mar-15 sep 1848 – 1r – 1 – Can$50.00 – cn Can Microfilming [072]

THE MAGIC OF THE MIDDLE AGES / Rydberg, Viktor – Trans. from the Swedish by August Hjalmar Edgren. New York: H. Holt and Co., 1879. 231p – 1 – us U.W. Library [150]

THE MAGICIAN ANNUAL – 1906-16 – 1r – 1 – us Ross [790]

THE MAGICIAN MONTHLY – v1-35. 1904-39 – 4r – 1 – us Ross [790]

Magii, G *see* HIERONYMI MAGII DE TINTINNABULIS LIBE POSTUMUS

Maginn, William *see*
- THE FRASERIAN PAPERS OF THE LATE WILLIAM MAGINN, LL.D.
- MISCELLANIES
- SHAKSPEARE PAPERS

Maginot, M A *see* [COMPTE-RENDU] INSTITUEE

Magirus, Johann *see* ARTIS MUSICAE LEGIBUS LOGICIS METHODICE INFORMATAE LIBRI DUO...REVISI ET RECOGNITI, MULTISQUE IN LOCIS EMENDATI ET CORRECTI, AB AUCTORE..

DER MAGISCHE IDEALISMUS IN NOVALIS' MAERCHENTHEORIE UND MAERCHENDICHTUNG / Albrecht, Luitgard – (Includes bibliographical references) – Hamburg: Hansischer Gildenverlag, 1948 – 1r – 1 – us U.W. Library [430]

LE MAGISTER : LE SEUL MAGAZINE AU CANADA DEDIE A TOUS LES NIVEAUX D'ENSEIGNEMENTS – St. Nicolas: les Presses du Magister. v1-20. 1965-85. SEM35P25 – 2r – 1 – Can$94.00 – cn Bibl Nat [072]

MAGISTER JOHANNES HUS UND DER ABZUG DER DEUTSCHEN PROFESSOREN UND STUDENTEN AUS PRAG, 1409 / Hoefler, Karl Adolf Constantin, Ritter von – Prag: F. Tempsky, 1864 – 1mf – us A.T.L.A. [943]

O MAGISTERIO : ORGAO DO INSTITUTO DOS PROFESSORES PRIMARIOS – Maceio, Alagoas. 15 Jul, Out 1887; Fev, Ago, Out 1888; 30 Mar 1889 – 1,5,6 – bl Biblioteca [072]

MAGISTERIO DE AMOR FRAY JUAN DE LOS ANGELES (1536-1610) / Gomis, Juan B – Barcelona: Edit. Tip. Casals, s.a., 1946 – 1 – sp Bibl Santa Ana [920]

EL MAGISTERIO EXTREMENO – Badajoz, 1873-1883 y 1892-1897 – 5 – sp Bibl Santa Ana [072]

EL MAGISTERIO EXTREMENO-ONUBENSE – Badajoz, 1886-1891 – 5 – sp Bibl Santa Ana [072]

MAGISTRATE – 1921- 1; 1975- 5,6,9 – us UMI [340]

THE MAGISTRATE : BULLETIN OF THE MAGISTRATES' ASSOCIATION – (Lacking: v1 p1-16,46-64,113-128,209-224. v2 p369-384) – London. v1-41. 1921-85 – 118mf – 9 – $177.00 – LLMC 84-592 – us L.L.M.C. [073]

THE MAGISTRATE – London. 1v. 1825 (all publ) – 9 – LLMC 84-590 – us L.L.M.C. [073]

THE MAGISTRATE – NY Association of Magistrates. os: v1-15. 1942-83. ns: v1-23. 1984-Jul 1985 (all publ) – 56mf – 9 – $84.00 – LLMC 84-593 – us L.L.M.C. [073]

THE MAGISTRATE AND MUNICIPAL AND PAROCHIAL LAWYER – London. v1-5. 1848-53 (all publ) – 9 – LLMC 84-591 – us L.L.M.C. [073]

MAGISTRATE'S HAND-BOOK / Dempsey, Richard – Toronto, Rowsell and Ellis, 1860. 82 p. LL-2228 – 1 – us L of C Photodup [340]

THE MAGISTRATE'S MANUAL...4TH ED / Toone, William – London, Butterworth, 1828. 2 p. iln., vii viii, 16 p. LL-131 – 1 – us L of C Photodup [340]

MAGISTRI ADAM BREMENSIS GESTA HAMBURGENSIS ECCLESIAE PONTIFICUM (MGH 7: 2.BD) – Ed 3a. 1917 – Dfl25.00 – ne Slangenburg [240]

Magius, H *see*
- DE TINTINNABULIS
- DE TINTINNABULIS LIBER POSTUMUS

Magloire, Frere *see* BIO-BIBLIOGRAPHIE DU COLONEL G.E. MARQUIS, CONSERVATEUR DE LA BIBLIOTHEQUE DE LA LEGISLATURE DU QUEBEC

MAGNA CHARTA AND STATUTA / Holkham Hall. Norfolk. England – Holkham MS. 229. 15th cent – 1 – uk Microform Academic [340]

THE MAGNA CHARTA BARONS & THEIR AMERICAN DESCENDANTS. / Browning, Charles H – 1969. Orig. publ., 1898. Indexed. 7 fiches.F-1594 – 9 – us A.G.L.L. [920]

MAGNA CHARTA BARONS & THEIR DESCENDANTS, WITH THE STORY OF THE GREAT CHARTER OF KING JOHN. / Browning, Charles H – 1969. Orig. publ., 1915. Indexed. 6 fiches.F-1595 – 9 – us A.G.L.L. [920]

THE MAGNA CHARTA OF THE KINGDOM OF GOD : PLAIN STUDIES OF OUR LORD'S SERMON ON THE MOUNT / Genung, George Frederick – Philadelphia: American Baptist Publ Society, 1900 – 1mf – 9 – 0-8370-3252-0 – 1985-1252 – us A.T.L.A. [220]

MAGNA CHARTA, PART 8 – By John S. Wurts. Item I. 2392-3062p. Main families listed in T.O.C.Indexed. SW16-0080 – 5 – us A.G.L.L. [920]

MAGNA VITA S. HUGONIS, EPISCOPI LINCOLNIENSIS (RS37) : FROM MSS IN THE BODLEIAN LIBRARY, OXFORD, AND THE IMPERIAL LIBRARY, PARIS / Adam Of Evesham; ed by Dimock, J F – 1864 – Dfl32.00 – ne Slangenburg [240]

Magnan, C-J *see* L'INSTRUCTION PUBLIQUE DANS LA PROVINCE DE QUEBEC...

Magnan, Hormidas *see* DICTIONNAIRE HISTORIQUE ET GEOGRAPHIQUE DES PAROISSES, MISSIONS ET MUNICIPALITES DE LA PROVINCE DE QUEBEC

Magne, Emile *see* FEMMES GALANTES DU XVIIE SIECLE: MME. DE VILLEDIEU (1632-1692)

Magnes, J L *see*
- LIKE ALL THE NATIONS? JERUSALEM. 1930. BJ-28-17/1
- SEFER MAGNES
- WHAT ZIONISM HAS GIVEN THE JEWS

MAGNES SIVE DE ARTE MAGNETICA OPUS TRIPARTITUM / Kircher, Athanasius – 1641 – 9 – us Sibley [780]

MAGNESS MEMORIAL BAPTIST CHURCH. MCMINNVILLE, TENNESSEE : CHURCH RECORDS – 1838-1915 – 1 – 17.28 – us Baptist [240]

MAGNET – (Atlanta). 1894 – 1 – us A.J.P.C. [073]

MAGNET – Big Rapids. Mich. 1874-1876 – 1 – us UMI [071]

MAGNET / New Orleans Baptist Seminary – 1925-46. (Includes The B.B. Eye. Sep 1944-May 1946) – 1 – 59.64 – us Baptist [240]

MAGNET – Sparks, NV. 5 Feb 1910 – 1r – 1 – $50.00 – U04745 – us Library Micro [071]

THE MAGNET – Manhattan, NV. 1917-22 – 1r – 1 – $50.00 – U04629 – us Library Micro [071]

MAGNET MAIL – Magnet, NE. -w. Aug 1909-Mar 1911; Dec 1911-Oct 1914 – 1 – us NE Hist [071]

MAGNETIC AND ELECTRICAL SEPARATION / ed by Svoboda, Jan & Friedlaender, F J – 1,5,9 – us Gordon [621]

MAGNETIC RESONANCE IMAGING – (Includes Reviews of Magnetic Resonance in Medicine) – v1- 1983- – 5,6,9 – us UMI [621]

MAGNETIC RESONANCE IN MEDICINE – v29-36. 1993-1996 – 1,5,6,9 – $110.00r – us Williams [616]

MAGNETIC RESONANCE REVIEW / ed by Jameson, C – 1,5,9 – us Gordon [621]

MAGNETISCHES MAGAZIN FUER NIEDERDEUTSCHLAND – Bremen, 1787-89. Pts. 1-8 – 3 – us Readex [530]

MAGNETISER'S MAGAZINE AND ANNALS OF ANIMAL MAGNETISM – London, 1816 – 3 – us Readex [530]

MAGNETISM / Haidemenakis, E D – 1,5,9 – 70.50; 41.50v – us Gordon [530]

MAGNETISM LETTERS – 1976- – 1,5,9 – us Gordon [530]

THE MAGNETISM OF CHRIST : A STUDY OF OUR LORD'S MISSIONARY METHODS / Smith, John – New York: A C Armstrong; London: Hodder & Stoughton, 1904 – 1mf – 9 – 0-8370-5294-7 – 1985-3294 – us A.T.L.A. [240]

MAGNETOHYDRODYNAMICS – v1-30. 1965-94 – 1,5 – $65.00v – us UMI [600]

MAGNI FELICIS ENNODI OPERA (MGH 1: 7.BD) / ed by Vogel, F – 1885 – Dfl46.00 – ne Slangenburg [240]

MAGNIFICAT AND NUNC DIMITTIS [SATB ORGAN] / VanLaer, C – (Magnificat is unfinished and Nunc dimittis is lacking) – Autograph ms, [1901] – 1 – us Sibley [780]

MAGNISA – Manisa, 1909-19? – 9 – $10.00 – us MEDOC [956]

Magno, C *see* TRIONFO DI CHRISTO PER LA VITTORIA CONTRA TVRCHI...

Magnol, P *see*
- BOTANICUM MONSPELIENSI, SIVE PLANTARUM CIRCA MONSPELIUM NASCENTIUM
- HORTUS REGIUS MONSPELIENSIS

MAGNOLIA BAPTIST CHURCH. CLAIBORNE COUNTY. MISSISSIPPI : CHURCH RECORDS – 1852-Jun 1875 – 1 – 9.45 – us Baptist [240]

MAGNOLIA BAPTIST CHURCH. SEVERNS VALLEY ASSOCIATION. KENTUCKY : CHURCH RECORDS – 1893-1968 – 1 – 35.91 – us Baptist [240]

MAGNUM BULLARIUM ROMANUM – 459mf – 9 – $975.00 – us OmniSys [240]

MAGNUM OECUMENICUM CONSTANTIENSE CONCILIUM. / Council of Constance – Edited By Hermann von der Hardt. 7 v. 1697-1700, 1742 – 1 – us A.T.L.A. [240]

Magnus Gothus, O *see* HISTORIA DE GENTIBUS SEPTENTRIONALIBUS

MAGNUS IN ORTU: MAXIMUS IN MERIDIE: MAJOR IN OCCASU SEMPERQUE SERENISSIMUS PRINCIPUM SOL MAXIMILIANUS EMANUEL / Khuen, Joseph Cajetan – O 321. 1727 – 9 – ne IDC [320]

Magnusson, A H *see* STUDIES IN THE LECIDEA RIVULOSA GROUP

Magnusson, Eiriker *see* THOMAS BECKET (RS65)

EL MAGO DE LOGROSAN. VIDA Y MILAGROS DE UN RARO MORTAL, TEOSOFO Y ATENEISTA / Canetti y Alvarez de Gades, Liborio – Madrid: Vda. de Pueyo, 1917 – 1 – sp Bibl Santa Ana [240]

MAGODANG AEK, MARALI TAPIAN / Siagian, Abu Arab – SE 4689 1. 1955 – 9 – ne IDC [950]

MAGOG ENTERPRISE – Magog, Canada. 10 jan 1895-25 dec 1924 – 1r – 1 – Can$45.00 – cn Can Microfilming [072]

THE MAGOG NEWS – Magog, Canada. v1 n51. 25 mar 1886-v70 n18. 30 mai 1918 – 1r – 1 – Can$35.00 – cn Can Microfilming [072]

Magon, Leopold *see* DIE ENTWICKLUNG FRIEDRICH RUECKERTS BIS 1810 UND SEINE DICHTERISCHEN ANFAENGE

Magone, Clifford Richard *see* CORONERS GUIDE AND THE CORONERS ACT, R. S. O. 1927, CHAPTER 123, AS AMENDED BY 1931, CHAPTER 31.

Magoun, George F *see* ASA TURNER

MAGRIB *see* AL-MAGRIB

MAGRIB AL-ARABI *see* AL-MAGRIB AL-ARABI

MAGRIB EL-MAGHRIB *see* AL-MAGRIB EL-MAGHRIB

Magruder, Herman B *see* A MANUAL OF THE LAW RELATING TO MARRIAGE AND DIVORCE AS DETERMINED BY THE SUPREME COURT OF LOUISIANA

MAGUEY – El Cerrito, CA. n1-5. 1968-71 – 7mf – 9 – $5.00f – us Ross [410]

Maguire, John MacArthur *see* CASES ON THE LAW OF TAXATION: PARTS 1, 2 AND 3...4 AND 5

MAGYAR ALLAMPOLGARSAGI JOG / Ferenc, F – Gyoma, 1928 – 3mf – 1 – ILM-3630/1 – ne IDC [327]

MAGYAR BANYASZLAP – New York: M Himler. [v5 n49-v10] dec 1917-1922 (5r); [v11-39 n9] 1923-feb 1952 (19r) – 24r – 1 – us Res Libr [071]

MAGYAR BOTANIKAI LAPOK – Ungarische botanische Blaetter. v. 1-33. Budapest. 1902-34. B-7477 1 – 9 – ne IDC [580]

A MAGYAR BUNVADI ELJARASI JOG VAZLATA. 3. KIAD / Bursics, Zoltan – Budapest, Grill K., 1947. 338 p. LL-4059 – 1 – us L of C Photodup [340]

A MAGYAR DRAMAIRODALOM TOERTENETE / Bayer, J – v. 1-2. Budapest. 1897. BR-5428 2 – 8 – ne IDC [490]
MAGYAR ELET – (In Hungarian) – Canada, 1957- – 1 – cn Commonwealth Micro [072]
A MAGYAR ES MAGYARORSZAGI IDOESZAKI SAJTO IDOERENDI ATTEKINTESE, 1705-1867 / Kereszty, L – Budapest. 1916. BR-5241 2 – 8 – ne IDC [940]
MAGYAR FOELDTANI TARSULAT – 1. Jelentes a Magyarhoni foeldtani tarsulatrol.1v. Pesten, 1852 – 3 – us Readex [550]
MAGYAR HIRADO – Pittsburgh: B T Tarkanyi, dec 13 1917-1921 (4r); 1922-jun 1925 (3r) – 7r – 1 – us Res Libr [071]
MAGYAR HIRLAP = HUNGARIAN NEWS – Detroit, MI: F Antal, nov 9 1917-1924 (8r); 1925-jul 6 1933 (8r) – 16r – 1 – us Res Libr [071]
MAGYAR HIRLAP – Ungarn, 1980-81 – 6r – 1 – DM450.00 – gw Mikro Press [943]
MAGYAR HIRLAP – (Backfile 6r per y $85r) – Hungary, 1999- – 6r per y standing order – 1 – us Ross [072]
MAGYAR HIRMONDO : WEEKLY HUNGARIAN LANGUAGE NEWSPAPER – Cleveland, Ohio. Apr 5-Dec 27 1900 – 1r – 1 – us Western Res [071]
MAGYAR IFJUSAG – Budapest. 1957- – 1 – $23.00r – us L of C Photodup [640]
A MAGYAR KIR. CURIA FELULVIZSGALATI TANACSA ALTAL A SOMMAS ELJARASROL SZOLO TORVENY (1893: XVIII. TCZ.) ALAPJAN HOZOTT HATAROZATOKNAK GYUJTEMENYE. / Hungary. Kuria. Felulvizsgalati tanacs – Budapest. On film: v1-20; 1897-1917. Index, v1-10; 1900-06. LL-0247 – 1 – us L of C Photodup [340]
MAGYAR KOEZLOENY – (Supplement: 1989(1)-1990(2). 87mf. Dfl531.00) – Budapest, 1973-90(2). Missing parts: 1982(1); 1986; 1988. BH-1109/1 – 524mf – 9 – ne IDC [943]
MAGYAR MYTHOLOGIA / Kandra, K – Eger. 1897. BR-5383 2 – 8 – ne IDC [390]
MAGYAR NAPILAP : DAILY HUNGARIAN LANGUAGE DEMOCRATIC NEWSPAPER – Cleveland, Oh. Jul 1-Dec 31 1908 – 2r – 1 – us Western Res [071]
MAGYAR NEMZET – Budapest: Athenaeum, mar 30 1949-55 – 26r – 1 – us Res Libr [072]
MAGYAR NEMZET – Budapest, Hungary. 1962-76 – 30r – 1 – us L of C Photodup [072]
MAGYAR NEMZET – Budapest, Hungary. -w. 2 Jan 1906-27 July 1913. 36 reels – 1 – uk British Libr Newspaper [072]
MAGYAR NEMZET – Ungarn, 1976-93ff – 61r – 1 – DM4,575.00 – gw Mikro Press [943]
MAGYAR NEMZET – (1996-98 12r per y. Backfile through 1995 $85r) – Hungary, 1999- – 12r per y standing order – 1 – us Ross [072]
MAGYAR NEPDAL / Bartok, Bela – German, Das Ungarische Volkslied. 1925 – 1 – us I.U. Libraries [390]
A MAGYAR NEPKOZTARSASAG HIVATALOS LAPJA / Hungary. Magyar Kozlony – Budapest, 1947-64 – 7r – 1 – us Ross [324]
MAGYAR NOEVENYTANI LAPOK – v. 1-13. Kolozsvart. 1877-90. B-7472 1 – 9 – ne IDC [073]
A MAGYAR NYELVJARASOK OSZTALYOZASA ES JELLEMZESE / Balassa, Jozsef – Budapest, 1891. 150p. Tabls. BR-5344 2 – 8 – ne IDC [943]
MAGYAR ORZAG TISZTI CIM-ES NEVTARA / Hungary. Kozponti Statisztikai Hivatal – v.2-50, 1875-1943 – 1 – 345.00 – us L of C Photodup [310]
A MAGYAR POLGARY PERJOG NEMZETKOEZI VONATKOZASAI / Geza, M – Budapest, 1902 – 2mf – 1 – ILM-2474/1 – ne IDC [327]
MAGYAR STATISZTIKAI EVKONYV / Hungary.Statisztikai Evkonyv – Budapest. 20v. 1872-91 – 1 – 299.00 – us L of C Photodup [310]
Magyar Statisztikai Tarsasag. Budapest *see* JOURNAL DE LA SOCIETE HONGROISE DE STATISTIQUE
MAGYAR SZABADSAG – Passaic, NJ. Hungarian Freedom. -w. 5 May 1963-15 Jan 1966. 1 reel – 1 – uk British Libr Newspaper [071]
MAGYAR SZO – Novi Sad, Yugoslavia. 1950-52; 1955-Aug 1989; 1991 (incomplete) – 155r – 1 – us L of C Photodup [949]
Magyar Szocial-Demokrata Part *see* NEPSZAVA
Magyar Tudomanyos Akademia *see* ACTA ORIENTALIA
MAGYAROK VASARNAPJA – (Weekly Hungarian language Roman Catholic newspaper; issues between dec 29, 1904 and jan 6, 1916 lacking) – Cleveland, OH. jan 8, 1903-dec 28, 1916 – 2r – 1 – us Western Res [071]
MAGYAROK VILAGPLAPJA – Budapest, July 1938 – 1r – 1 – us I.H.R.C. [947]
MAGYARORSZAG CSALADAI / Nagy, Ivan – Pest. 12 v. 1857-65 – 1 – 164.00 – us L of C Photodup [920]
MAGYARORSZAG EGYHAZI ES POLITIKAI OESSEKOETTETESEI A ROMAI SZENTSZEKKEL / Fraknoi, V – 3v. Budapest. 1901-03. BR-5401 2 – 8 – ne IDC [320]
MAGYARORSZAGI MELLEKLET – Budapest, Sep.-Oct. 1938 – 1r – 1 – us I.H.R.C. [947]
MAGYARORSZAGI SZT. ERZSEBET AMERIKAI HIRNOKE – Cleveland, OH -w. Dec 1894 – Nov 1895; Dec 1898 – Nov 1899. 1 reel – 1 – us Western Res [071]
MAGYAR-ZSIDO SZEMLE – v. 1-39. 1884-Jan Mar 1922 – 1 – 139.00 – us L of C Photodup [270]
MAHABHARATA – Indonesian. Bhagavadgita. Indonesian and Sanskrit in Latin script. SE-8489 1. 1967 – 9 – ne IDC [280]
MAHABHARATA – Indonesian. Bhagavat-Gita Interpreted; Dalam Bahasa Indonesia Sederhana. SE-5852 1. 1961? – 9 – ne IDC [280]
MAHABHARATA – Indonesian. Selections. Bharatayuda. SE-5853 1. 7 v. 1962-63 – 9 – ne IDC [800]
MAHABHARATA – Javanese. Selections. Bharata Yuddha, Babaranipun Ki Siswoharsojo. SE-6585 1. 3 v. in 1. 1962-65 – 9 – ne IDC [800]
MAHABHARATA – Javanese. Selections. Narasoma. SE-5484 1. 1932 – 9 – ne IDC [800]
MAHABHARATA – Javanese. Selections. Serat Baratajuda. SE-5855 1. v. 1 only. 1964 – 9 – ne IDC [800]
MAHABHARATA – Javanese. Selections. Serat Baratajuda. SE-6586 1. 3 v. 1954-56 – 9 – ne IDC [800]
MAHABHARATA – Sundanese. Mahabharata, Karangan Wyasa. SE-6741 1. 1955 – 9 – ne IDC [800]
MAHABHARATA – Sundanese. Selections. Loeloehoer Pendawa. SE-5857 1. 1930 – 9 – ne IDC [800]
MAHABHARATA – Sundanese. Selections. Pendawa Nagih Djangdji. SE-5858 1. 1932 – 9 – ne IDC [800]
MAHABHARATA AND THE BHAGVAT-GEETA – 1785 – 9 – $10.00 – us Scholars' Facs [490]
THE "MAHABHARATA" OF KRISHNA-DWAIPAYANA VYASA INTO ENGLISH PROSE / Ray, P C – Ed. 2. 18 v. Calcutta. 1889-96. Lacking: v. 7. BI-1071 1 – 9 – ne IDC [490]
MAHACHON – Bangkok, Thailand. 1947-48 – 1r – 1 – us L of C Photodup [072]
Mahadi *see* SOAL DEWASA
Mahalingam, T V *see* SOUTH INDIAN POLITY
Mahamane, Tandina Ousmane *see* UNE EPOPEE ZARMA
Mahan, Alfred Thayer *see*
– THE INFLUENCE OF SEA POWER UPON THE FRENCH REVOLUTION AND EMPIRE, 1793-1815
– THE LIFE OF NELSON, THE EMBODIMENT OF THE SEA POWER OF GREAT BRITAIN
– SEA POWER IN ITS RELATIONS TO THE WAR OF 1812
Mahan, Asa *see*
– THE BAPTISM OF THE HOLY GHOST
– THE SCIENCE OF NATURAL THEOLOGY
Mahan, Milo *see* PALMONI, OR, THE NUMERALS OF SCRIPTURE, A PROOF OF INSPIRATION
MAHANAYIM – v. 1-22. Tel Aviv. 1948-72. BJ-91-59 1 – 9 – ne IDC [956]
MAHANOY TRI-WEEKLY RECORD – Mahanoy City, PA. 1889-1894 – 13 – $25.00r – us I.M.R. [071]
THE MAHAPARINIBBANA SUTTANTA / ed by Mueller, Friedrich Max – (1. The Dhamma-kakka-ppvattana Sutta. 3. The Tevigga Suttanta; 4. The Akkankheyya Sutta; 5. The Ketokhila Sutta. The Maha-sudassana Suttanta; 7. The Sabbasava Sutta) – 1881 – 7mf – 8 – ne Slangenburg [280]
Mahar, E P *see* LEGISLATIVE HISTORY OF THE SECURITIES ACT OF 1933 AND SECURITIES EXCHANGE ACT OF 1934
Mahar, Matthew T *see*
– COMPARISON OF ACUTE HEART RATE AND BLOOD PRESSURE RESPONSES AMONG ISOMETRIC, ISOTONIC, AND ISOKINETIC EXERCISE
– GENDER DIFFERENCES IN RUNNING ECONOMY
– HEALTH-RELATED FITNESS LEVELS IN BAHAMIAN ELEMENTARY SCHOOL AGE CHILDREN
– INFLUENCE OF AGE AND CAFFEINE ON RESTING METABOLIC RATE, BLOOD PRESSURE, AND MOOD STATE IN YOUNGER AND OLDER INDIVIDUALS
Maharadja, Habib Sutan *see* ILMU BUMI PROPINSI SUMATERA BARAT DENGAN RIWAJAT PENDEK MINANGKABAU
MAHARASHTRA – Nagpur, India. May-Dec 1945 – 1r – 1 – us L of C Photodup [072]
THE MAHARASHTRA GOVERNMENT GAZETTE / Maharashtra. India – Bombay. 1960-66. For earlier file see: Bombay.Government Gazette – 1 – us NY Public [950]
Maharashtra. India *see* THE MAHARASHTRA GOVERNMENT GAZETTE
MAHARASHTRA TAIMSA (TIMES) – Bombay, India. Jul 1977-1988 – 42r – 1 – us L of C Photodup [072]
MAHASIN – (Sahib-i Imtiyaz: Asif Muammer, Mueduer ve Sermuharriri: Mehmed Rauf. No. 6 (Subat 1324[1909])) – Istanbul: Derziyan Matbaasi, Hilal Matbaasi, 1908-1909 – 2mf – 9 – $30.00 – us MEDOC [949]
MAHAVYUTPATTI – Sanskrit-Tibetan-English. An edition and translation of the MahavyutpattiBY Alexander Csmona de Koros. (Mem. Asiatic Soc. of Bengal). v. 4 (1-2). Calcutta. 1910, 1916. BI-1075 1 – 9 – ne IDC [800]
MAHAZOT / Hirschbein, P – Warsaw. 1923. BJ-422-32 1 – 9 – ne IDC [470]
Mahdi, Muhsin *see* IBN KHALDUN'S PHILOSOPHY OF HISTORY: A STUDY IN THE PHILOSOPHIC FOUNDATION OF THE SCIENCE OF CULTURE
Mahend Betind, P *see* LE SYMBOLISME DU NOM ET L'ART DE DONNER DES NOMS AUX HOMMES
Maher, Charles A *see* SPECIAL SERVICES IN THE SCHOOLS
Maher, William *see* GUIDE TO THE UNIVERSITY OF ILLINOIS ARCHIVES
Maheux, Laura *see* BIBLIOGRAPHIE ANALYTIQUE DE L'OEUVRE DE MONSIEUR RENE POMERLEAU, DOCTEUR ES SCIENCES DE LA SOCIETE ROYALE DU CANADA, PATHOLOGISTE FORESTIER, LABORATOIRE DES RECHERCHES FORESTIERES, GOUVERNEMENT DU CANADA, QUEBEC
MAHFEL – Sene 1-6, nos. 1-68 (1338-1344) – 23mf – 9 – $175.00 – us MEDOC [949]
Mahias, M C *see* DELIVRANCE ET CONVIVIALITE
Mahiels, E *see* LE DROIT CRIMINEL BELGE...
Mahieu, L *see* DOMINIQUE DE FLANDRE
Mahilla Santos, Juan *see* SISTEMA RACIONALIZADO DE LIQUIDACION Y RECAUDACIOM EN LAS HACIENDAS LOCALES
Mahillo Santos, Juan *see* ESTUDIO SOBRE EL FUERO DE BAYLIO
Mahillo Santos, Julio *see* ORGANIZACION Y METODOS DE LOS SERVICIOS ECONOMICOS DE LAS CORPORACIONES LOCALES...
MAHITAP / Boztepe, Halil Nihad – Istanbul: Yeni Matbaa, 1924 – $18.00 – us MEDOC [470]
Mahizflor *see* LOS CUATRO CAMINOS DEL TOREO
Mahizflor. Museo Taurino. Aceuchal *see* CATALOGO-GUIA 1950
Mahlck, Lars O *see* FROM DATA TO ACTION
DER MAHLER DER SITTEN / ed by Bodmer, Johann Jakob & Breitinger, Johann Jakob – Zuerich, 1746. Hildesheim, 1977 – 15mf – 9 – DM150.00 diazo DM180.00 silver – gw Olms [430]
Mahler, Eduard *see* BIBLISCHE CHRONOLOGIE UND ZEITRECHNUNG DER HEBRAEER
Mahler, Erik B *see* CROSS-EDUCATION FOLLOWING SINGLE-LIMB ECCENTRIC AND CONCENTRIC TRAINING ON THE BIODEX ISOKINETIC DYNAMOMETER
MAHMUD AL-KASA7GHARIS DARSTELLUNG DES TURKISCHEN VERBALBAUS / Brockelmann, C – Keleti Szemle. Budapest, 1918-1919. p. 29-49. BU-353 1 – 9 – ne IDC [490]
Mahmud, Syed *see* CORRESPONDENCE WITH KAISAR BAGH 1914-1917
MAHNRUF – Berlin, 1929-33 – 1r – 1 – Dist. gw Mikrofilm – gw Misc Inst [072]
MAHOMET 2 / Baour-Lormian – (French Theatre Series). Paris. Latour. 1811 – 9 – fr Hachette [820]
Mahoning County. Ohio. Canfield Township *see* MINUTES, MS 1250
MAHONING COURIER – Youngstown. Ohio. 1865-1869 – 1 – us UMI [071]
MAHONING FREE DEMOCRAT – Youngstown. Ohio. 1853-55 – 1 – us UMI [071]
MAHONING INDEX : WEEKLY DEMOCRATIC NEWSPAPER – (Weekly Democratic newspaper) – Mahoning, OH. 3 Jun 1846-10 Oct 1851 – 1r – 1 – us Western Res [071]
MAHONING INDEX – Youngstown. Ohio. 1846-1848 – 1 – us UMI [071]
MAHONING SENTINEL – Youngstown. Ohio. 1860-64 – 1 – us UMI [071]
Mahoning Valley Historical Society *see*
– HISTORICAL COLLECTIONS OF THE MAHONING VALLEY
MAHONING VALLEY REVIEW : WEEKLY INDEPENDENT NEWSPAPER – Warren, OH. 24 Apr 1889-28 July 1892 – 1r – 1 – us Western Res [071]
MAHONING VINDICATOR – Youngstown. Ohio. 1869-77 – 1 – us UMI [071]
Mahrenholtz, Richard *see* FRANZ GRILLPARZER
MA'HUAN TERKENAL DENGAN SUNAN AMPEL KETUA WALI SANGA / Sukirno, Adhy – SE 4650 1. 1962 – 9 – ne IDC [950]
MAHZIQEY HA-DAT – (Missing: Several numbers) – Lemberg (L'vov), 1879-1913 – 6r – 1 – J-91-111/3 – ne IDC [072]
Mai, A *see* SPICILEGIUM ROMANUM
MAI AK (HARBIN, CHINA) – (Library has June 1930) – Kharbin: Russko-kita iski i prii ut uchilishche, 1930- – 1 – CSUX88-S444 – us Hoover Inst Photo [950]
MAI AK KOMMUNY – (Library has Dec. 21, 1922 and Jan. 4, 1923) – Sevastopol: Sevastopolski i ispolkom i okrkom, 1920-1942 – 1 – CSUX88-S438 – us Hoover Inst Photo [947]
Mai, Angelo *see* NOVA PATRUM BIBLIOTHECA
Mai Than-trong *see* VIETNAMESE COLLECTION OF THE ANU LIBRARY
MAIA : DRAMA LYRIQUE EN TROIS ACTES... PARTITION CHANT ET PIANO TRANSCRITE PAR L'AUTEUR / Leoncavallo, Ruggiero – Paris: Choidens, ca 1908 – 1 – us Sibley [780]
MAIAK SOVREMENNOGO PROSVESHCHENIIA I OBRAZOVANNOSTI : TRUDY UCHENYKH I LITERATOROV RUSSKIKH I INOSTRANNYKH / ed by Korsakov, P & Burachek, S – (Missing: 1844(27-28) v14(p1-8). 1844(29-30) v15(p61-..; 1-16). 1844(31-32) v16(p1-32). 1845(39-40) v20(p85-86)) – Spb. v1-24. 1840(1)-1845(47) – 205mf – 9 – ne IDC [947]
MAIAK SOVREMENNOGO PROSVESHCHENIIA I OBRAZOVANNOSTI : TRUDY UCHENYKH I LITERATOROV RUSSKIKH I INOSTRANNYKH / ed by Korsakov, P & Burachek, S – (Missing: 1844(27-28), v14(p1-8); 1844(29-30), v15(p61-...; 1-16); 1844(31-32), v16(p1-32); 1845(39-40), v20(p85-86)) – Spb. v1-24. 1840(1)-1845(47) – 205mf – 9 – RET-7/1 – ne IDC [947]
MAIAKOVSKII / Katanian, V A – Literaturnaia khronika. Ed. 2. Leningrad. 1948. BR-1327 2 – 8 – ne IDC [920]
MAIAKOVSKII / Katanian, V A – Literaturnaia khronika. Ed. 4. M. 1961. BR-1328 2 – 8 – ne IDC [920]
MAIAKOVSKII / Katanian, V A – Literaturnaia khronika. M. 1945. BR-1326 2 – 8 – ne IDC [920]
MAIAKOVSKII / Maslin, N – Ocherki tvorchestva. M. 1956. BR-1415 2 – 8 – ne IDC [920]
MAIAKOVSKII / Pertsov, V – Zhizn' i tvorchestvo. 2 v. M. 1957-58. BR-1488 2 – 8 – ne IDC [920]
MAIAKOVSKII / Petsov, V – Zhizn' i tvorchestvo. M. 1951. BR-1484 2 – 8 – ne IDC [920]
MAIAKOVSKII I EGO SPUTNIKI / Spasskii, S – L., "Sovetskii pisatel". 1940. BR-2144 2 – 8 – ne IDC [460]
MAIAKOVSKII I TEATR / Rostotskii, B – M. 1952. BR-2092 2 – 8 – ne IDC [790]
Maiakovskii, IL *see* OCHERKI PO ISTORII ARKHIVNOGO DELA V SSSR

MAIAKOVSKII, MATERIALI I ISSLEDOVANIIA – (V. O. Pertsova, I. I. Serebrianskogo, Red.). M., Akademiia nauk SSSR. 1940. BR-1396 2 – 8 – ne IDC [460]
MAIAKOVSKII ULYBAETSIA. MAIAKOVSKII SMEETSIA. MAIAKOVSKII IZDEVAETSIA / Maiakovskii, Vladimir – M. 1936. BR-981 2 – 8 – ne IDC [460]
MAIAKOVSKII V AZERBAIDZHANE / Babaev, G V – Baku, 1960. 196,(2)p. BR-1980 2 – 8 – ne IDC [910]
MAIAKOVSKII V BOR'BE ZA KOMMUNIZM / Koloskov, A – M. 1958. BR-1342 2 – 8 – ne IDC [335]
MAIAKOVSKII V PERVYE GODY SOVETSKOI VLASTI / Naumov, E – (1917-1922). M. 1950. BR-1450 2 – 8 – ne IDC [460]
MAIAKOVSKII V PERVYE GODY SOVETSKOI VLASTI / Naumov, E – Ed. 2. M. 1955. BR-1452 2 – 8 – ne IDC [460]
Maiakovskii, Vladimir *see*
- 8 MARTA
- 150,000.000
- ANTIRELIGIOZNYE STIKHI
- FUTURIZM
- GROZNYI SMEKH
- IZBRANNOE
- IZBRANNYE PROIZVEDENIIA
- IZBRANNYE PROIZVEDENIIA V DVUKH TOMAKH
- IZBRANNYE STIKHI
- KAK DELAT' STIKHI
- KHOROSHO
- KOMSOMOL'SKIE STIKHI
- LETAIUSHCHII PROLETARII
- MAIAKOVSKII ULYBAETSIA. MAIAKOVSKII SMEETSIA. MAIAKOVSKII IZDEVAETSIA
- MAIAKOVSKII'S NAMI
- MINISTERIIA-BUFF
- MOE OTKRYTIE AMERIKI
- NEPOBEDIMOE ORUZHIE
- NO.S
- OBORONNYE STIKHI
- OPISANIE DOKUMENTAL'NYKH MATERIALOV
- OTKRYTIE AMERIKI
- POLNOE SOBRANIE SOCHINENII TOM 4, CHAST'I
- POLNOE SOBRANIE SOCHINENII V 13 TOMAKH
- PROSTOE KAK MYCHANIE
- SBORNIK I. POD
- SOBRANIE SOCHINENII V 4-KH TOMAKH
- SOBRANIE SOCHINENII V ODNOM TOME
- SOBRANIE STIKHOTVORENII V DVUKH TOMAKH
- SOCHINENIIA V ODNOM TOME
- SOLNTSE V GOSTIAKH U MAIAKOVSKOGO
- STIKCHI I POEMY
- STIKHI O ZAGRANITSE
- STIKHI, POEMY, PROZA
- STIKHOTVORENIIA
- TEATR I KINO
- TUDA I OBRATNO
- UMER BLOK
- V POVESTKU DNIA
- VLADIMIR IL'ICH LENIN
- VLADIMIR MAIAKOVSKII
- VOINA I MIR

MAIAKOVSKII-DRAMATURG / Fevral'skii, A – M., L. 1940. BR-1256 2 – 8 – ne IDC [460]
MAIAKOVSKII'S NAMI / Maiakovskii, Vladimir – Izbrannye proizvedeniia. M., L. 1942. BR-980 2 – 8 – ne IDC [460]
MAIAKOVSKII-SAM / Kassil, L – Ocherki zhizni i raboty poeta. M. 1960. BR-1325 2 – 8 – ne IDC [460]
O MAIAKOVSKOM / Shklovskii, V – "Sovetskii pisatel'". M. 1940. Izd. BR-2132 2 – 8 – ne IDC [460]
THE MAID OF KILLEENA; AND OTHER STORIES / Black, William – With The Marriage of Moira Fergus. British Fiction Archive: Unit 4 – 9 – uk Bell [830]
THE MAID OF ORLEANS, TRANSLATED FROM THE GERMAN BY ANNA SWANWICK / Schiller, Friedrich von – New York: Arthur Hinds & Co., n.d. 109p – 1 – us U.W. Library [820]
THE MAID OF SKER / Blackmore, Richard Doddridge – British Fiction Archive: Unit 3 – 9 – uk Bell [830]
Maiden, J H *see*
- THE FLOWERING PLANTS AND FERNS OF NEW SOUTH WALES
- THE USEFUL NATIVE PLANTS OF AUSTRALIA (INCLUDING TASMANIA)

MAIDEN MONA THE MERMAID: A FAIRY PLAY FOR FAIRY PEOPLE / Dixon, Frederick Augustus – Toronto: Belford Bros., 1877. 02723. (Pre-1900 Canadiana) – 9 – cn C.I.H.M. [971]
MAIDENHEAD ADVERTISER – England, Apr 1870-Oct 1897; 1898-1911; Mar-Oct 1912; 1913-54; 1967-72; 1980- – 201+ r – 1 – uk British Libr Newspaper [072]
MAIDENHEAD ARGUS – England, 8 Dec 1900-26 Dec 1903 – 2r – 1 – uk British Libr Newspaper [072]
EIN MAIDENSOMMER / Sellschopp, Herta – Braunschweig: G Westermann, c1941 – 1r – 1 – us U.W. Library [830]
Maidment, James *see* DRAMATIS OF THE RESTORATION
MAIDSTONE AND KENTISH JOURNAL *see* MAIDSTONE JOURNAL
MAIDSTONE GAZETTE – England, 1830-51 – 12r – 1 – uk British Libr Newspaper [072]
MAIDSTONE JOURNAL – (Lacking: 1897) – England, 5 Jan 1830-30 Dec 1911 – 78r – 1 – uk British Libr Newspaper [072]
Maier, Dieter *see* KANTS FORMBEGRIFF UND SYSTEMENTWUERFE
Maier, Georg *see*
- MORPHOLOGISCHE UNTERSUCHUNGEN AN SCHMELZKRISTALLISIERTEM PLOYAETHYLEN UND POLYAMID
- UNTERSUCHUNGEN UEBER DEN EINFLUSS DER FERTIGUNGSBEDINGUNGEN BEIM SPRITZGIESSEN AUF DIE FESTIGKEITSEIGENSCHAFTEN VON PROBESTAEBEN AUS POLYAETHYLEN

Maier, Lothar August *see* BUENDNISPOLITIK UND REVOLUTIONAERE KRISE
Maigne, W *see* NOUVEAU MANUEL COMPLET DU MARQUETEUR DU TABLETIER ET DE L'IVOIRIER
Maignen, Charles *see* STUDIES IN AMERICANISM
Maignen, Maurice *see* SCENES ET CROQUIS DE LA VIE OUVRIERE
MAIK DAN MADJU : BUKU BATJAAN ILMU BUMI UNTUK SEKOLAH-SEKOLAH DI NIEUW-GUINEA / Groot, L de – 1956 – 9 – SE-4255 1 – ne IDC [370]
Maikov, L N *see*
- MATERIALY DLIA BIOGRAFII KN
- OCHERKI IZ ISTORII RUSSKOI LITERATURY 17 I 18 STOLETII

MAIL – (Also known as: Los Gatos Mail News) – Los Gatos, CA. 1893-1953 – 35r – 1 – $1,750.00 – BC02406 – us Library Micro [071]
MAIL – Camden. N.J. 1834-1845 – 1 – us UMI [071]
MAIL – Charleroi. Pa. 1905-1921; 1924-1954; 1957-1960 – 1 – us UMI [071]
MAIL – Charleston. West Virginia. 1897-1905; 1914- – 1 – us UMI [071]
MAIL – Granby, Canada. 1896-1901 – 3r – 1 – $204.00 – cn Library Assoc [971]
MAIL – Hagerstown. Md. 1828-1830; 1835-1842; 1890- – 1 – us UMI [071]
MAIL – Ireland.1851-80; 1885-96. -d.74 1/2 reels – 1 – uk British Libr Newspaper [072]
MAIL – Magnet. Neb. 1909-1914 – 1 – us UMI [071]
MAIL – Manhasset. N.Y. 1927-1962 – 1 – us UMI [071]
MAIL – Manhattan, NV. 1909-11 – 1r – 1 – $50.00 – U04630 – us Library Micro [071]
MAIL – Middletown. Ohio. and Farmer. -W. 1839-40 – 1 – us UMI [071]
MAIL – Mountain City, NV. 1938-39 – 1r – 1 – $50.00 – U04630 – us Library Micro [071]
MAIL – Myrtle Creek, OR. -w. 1 Jan 1953-30 June 1982 – 1 – us U.O. Library [071]
MAIL – Philipsburg. Mont. 1951- – 1 – us UMI [071]
MAIL – Sheldon. Iowa. -w. 1951- – 1 – us UMI [071]
MAIL – Topeka. KS. Also, Breeze and preds. 1882-1903 – 1 – us UMI [071]
THE MAIL – (Cont by: The Granby Mail. The Granby Leader Mail) – Granby, Canada. 2 sep 1896-30 sep 1899 – 1r – 1 – Can$60.00 – cn Can Microfilming [072]
THE MAIL – Hagerstown. Md. -w. 1828-1842; 1861-1917 – 1 – us UMI [071]
THE MAIL – Madras, India. -d. Jan 1951-Dec 1975. 138 reels – 1 – uk British Libr Newspaper [072]
THE MAIL – South Sioux City. Dakota County, Nebraska. Jul 18, 1919-May 11, 1928 – 1 – us NE Hist [071]
MAIL AND EMPIRE – Toronto, Canada. 1895-1900 – 32r – 1 – $2,080.00 – cn Library Assoc [971]
MAIL (HARTLEPOOL) *see* NORTHERN EVENING MAIL
MAIL NEWS – Los Gatos. Calif. -w. 1944-53 – 1 – us UMI [071]
MAIL OF WOODLAND – Woodland, CA. 1920-1937 – 34r – 1 – $1,700.00 – C03696 – us Library Micro [071]
MAIL ON SUNDAY (LONDON) – 1986-Oct 1991; Nov 3 1991-Jun 28 1992; Jul 1992-93; Jan 2-9, 16-30, Feb-May 15, May 22-29, Jun-Sep, Oct 2-16, 23-30, Nov 6-13, 20-27, Dec 4-18 1994; Jan 1-15, 22-29, Feb-Apr 16, Apr 23-Jun, Jul 2-16, 23-Oct, Nov 5-26, Dec 3-17, 24-31 1995; Jan-Mar 17, 24-31, Apr 7-Dec 1996 – 121 1/2r – 1 – uk British Libr Newspaper [072]
MAIL ORDER CATALOGUES / T. Eaton Co. Ltd – 1884-1976 – 58r – 1 – $3,770.00 – cn Library Assoc [971]
MAIL & WATERFORD DAILY EXPRESS – Ireland.13 Jul 1855-30 Jun 1860. -d. 6 reels – 1 – uk British Libr Newspaper [072]
Maillett, Benoit de *see* TELHAMED OU ENTRETIENS D'UN PHILOSOPHE INDIEN AVEC UN MISSIONAIRE FRANCAIS SUR LA DIMINUTION DE LA MER, LA FORMATION DE LA TERRE, L'ORIGINE DE L'HOMME
Maillard, Emile *see*
- L'ART A NANTES AU 19E SIECLE...
- NANTES ET LE DEPARTEMENT AU 19E SIECLE...

Maillard, O *see*
- QUADRAGESIMALE...
- SERMONES DE ADVENTU

Maille, Joseph *see* MAILLE'S DIVORCE LAWS OF THE STATE OF LOUISIANA WITH COMMENTARIES AND A SYNOPTICAL HISTORY OF THE LAWS OF DIVORCE
MAILLE'S DIVORCE LAWS OF THE STATE OF LOUISIANA WITH COMMENTARIES AND A SYNOPTICAL HISTORY OF THE LAWS OF DIVORCE / Maille, Joseph – New Orleans: Mueller, 1884. 107p. LL-321 – 1 – us L of C Photodup [340]
Mailles, Jacques de *see* THE VERY JOYOUS, PLEASANT AND REFRESHING HISTORY OF THE FEATS, EXPLOITS, TRIUMPHS AND ACHIEVEMENTS OF THE GOOD KNIGHT WITHOUT FEAR AND WITHOUT REPROACH, THE GENTLE LORD DE BAYARD
Maillet, Benoit de *see* TELLIAMED, OU ENTRETIENS D'UN PHILOSOPHE INDIEN AVEC UN MISSIONAIRE FRANCAIS SUR LA DIMINUTION DE LA MER, LA FORMATION DE LA TERRE, L'ORIGINE DE L'HOMME
Maillet, Eugene *see* DE L'ESSENCE DES PASSIONS. ETUDE PSYCHOLOGIQUE ET MORALE
Maillet, Roger *see* LE MATIN
Maillet, Roger et al *see* LE PETIT JOURNAL
Maillo, Adolfo *see*
- APUNTES DE PEDAGOGIA
- EL LIBRO DEL TRABAJO

MAILRAPPORT 1885 – No. 642a: Bewegingen Preanger regentschappen (Tjiandjur). BSD-101/1 – 1mf – 9 – ne IDC [950]
MAILRAPPORT 1885 – No. 647c: Woelingen Preanger Regentschappen. Tjiandjur. BSD-101/1 – 2mf – ne IDC [950]
MAILRAPPORT 1885 – No. 807b: Verwijdering Said Achmad bin Mohamad al Sagaf uit de Preanger regentschappen (Sukabumi). BSD-101/1 – 3mf – 9 – ne IDC [950]
MAILRAPPORT 1886 – No. 262: Godsdienstige bewegingen Preanger regentschappen. BSD-101/1 – 4mf – 9 – ne IDC [950]
MAILRAPPORT 1889 – No. 41: Mohammedaanse Secten in de Residentie Banjumas. BSD-101/1 – 5mf – 9 – ne IDC [950]
MAILRAPPORTEN/MAIL REPORTS FROM THE NETHERLANDS EAST INDIES, 1869-1940 [1945] – ne MMF Publ [324]
THE MAIL-STAR – Halifax, Nova Scotia, CN. 1894- – 24r per yr – 1 – Can$53.00r – cn Commonwealth Micro [072]
Maimbourg, L *see*
- HISTOIRE DU CALVINISME
- HISTOIRE DU LUTHERANISME

Maimon. (Fishman, J L) *see* SEFER HA-YOVEL LI-YEHUDAH LEIB HA-KOHEN FISHMAN
MAIMONIDES : A PAPER... / Grossmann, Louis – New York: G P Putnam, 1890 – 1mf – 9 – 0-8370-3411-6 – 1985-1411 – us A.T.L.A. [270]
Maimonides, Moses *see* SIRAEJ. HALLAH
MAIN CATALOG OF THE LIBRARY OF CONGRESS 1898-1980 – 1984-1989 – 8,926mf (1:48) – diazo DM39,980.00 silver DM45,800.00 (silver DM45,800.00 ISBN: 3-598-41061-1) – 3-598-41041-7 – gw Saur [010]
MAIN CURRENTS IN MODERN THOUGHT – 1940-75 1; 1971-75 5,6 – us UMI [073]
MAIN CURRENTS OF MODERN THOUGHT : A STUDY OF THE SPIRITUAL AND INTELLECTUAL MOVEMENTS OF THE PRESENT DAY / Eucken, Rudolf – New York: Scribner, 1912 – 2mf – us A.T.L.A. [190]
MAIN GROUP CHEMISTRY NEWS / ed by Holmes, Robert R – 9,5,1 – us Gordon [540]
Main, John *see* RELIGIOUS CHASTITY
MAIN LINE TIMES – Ardmore. Pa. 1952- – 1 – us UMI [071]
LA MAIN, L'OUTIL ET LA MACHINE / Aynard, Joseph – Paris. 1942. (La Condition Ouvriere. Part Two.) – 9 – 6.00 – fr Bibl Nationale [360]
MAIN MISE – Montreal, jan 1971-jul/aut 1978 – 5r – 1 – Can$75.00 – cn Can Microfilming [072]
MAIN STREET – (Cont: Journal of Community Development v2 1988. Ceased v2 no 3 1988) – v2. 1988 – 9 – Can$20.00y – cn Micromedia [360]
MAIN STREET *see* JOURNAL OF COMMUNITY DEVELOPMENT
Mainardi, Arlotto *see* DIE SCHWAENKE UND SCHNURREN DES PFARRERS ARLOTTO
MAINE : RESOURCES, ATTRACTIONS AND ITS PEOPLE / ed by Coe, Harrie B – New York: The Lewis Historical Publ. Co., Inc., 1928. v1-4. Maine Reel 1. The Cox Library Collection – 5 – us Americana [978]
MAINE : REVISED STATUTES ANNOTATED – St Paul: West Pub Co, 1964-Mar 1996 update – 9 – $961.50 set – us Hein [340]
MAINE : SESSION LAWS OF AMERICAN STATES AND TERRITORIES – 1820-1995 – 9 – $1,818.00 set – us Hein [340]
Maine *see*
- REPORTS AND OPINIONS (A-G)
- REPORTS, POST-NRS
- REPORTS, PRE-NRS
- STATE LABOR REPORTS
- STATE WATER RESOURCES REPORTS

Maine. Agricultural Experiment Station *see*
- ANNUAL REPORT AND BULLETIN
- BULLETIN
- MISCELLANEOUS PUBLICATIONS
- MISCELLANEOUS REPORT
- OFFICIAL INSPECTIONS
- RESEARCH IN LIFE SCIENCES
- TECHNICAL BULLETIN

MAINE ANTIQUE DIGEST – (1982-. 1,5,6,9) – v1-. 1973- – 1 – us UMI [073]
MAINE ATTORNEY GENERAL REPORTS AND OPINIONS – (6 1840-1972 $140.00. 9 1973-1994 $238.00) – 1840-1994 – 6,9 – $378.00set – us Hein [340]
Maine Baptist Educational Society *see* MINUTES
Maine Baptist Historical Society *see* RECORDS
MAINE BAPTIST MESSENGER – Waterville/Augusta. United Baptist Convention of Maine.1920-64. Incomplete. Single reels available – 1 – 190.30 – us A.B.H.S. [073]
Maine Baptist Missionary Society *see*
- RECORDS

MAINE BAR ASSOCIATION REPORTS – v1-57. 1892-1968 (all publ) – 117mf – 9 – $175.00 – LLMC 84-594 – us L.L.M.C. [340]
MAINE BAR BULLETIN – (Lacking: v17 no 1) – v1-19. 1967-85 – 57mf – 9 – $85.00 – LLMC 84-595 – us L.L.M.C. [073]
MAINE BAR BULLETIN – (Superseded by Maine Bar Journal) – v1-19. 1967-85 – 9 – $220.00 set – us Hein [340]
MAINE BAR BULLETIN *see* MAINE BAR JOURNAL
MAINE BAR JOURNAL – (Supersedes Maine Bar Bulletin) – v1-9. 1986-94 – 9 – $110.00 set – us Hein [340]
MAINE BAR JOURNAL *see* MAINE BAR BULLETIN
THE MAINE CAMPUS – Orono. Maine. 1913-1936 – 1 – us UMI [071]
MAINE COAST FISHERMAN – Bangor, Maine. 1962-74 – 1 – us UMI [071]
MAINE COAST FISHERMAN – v.9-15 no. 3, Aug 1954-Oct 1960 – 1 – us Res Libr [639]
MAINE CORPORATION LAW / Dyer, Isaac Watson – 5th ed. Portland, Loring, Short & Harmon, 1901. 251 p. LL-616 – 1 – us L of C Photodup [340]
MAINE ERLEBNISSE IN DER WISSMANN-TRUPP / Richelmann, G – Magdeburg. 1892 – 1 – us Res Libr [920]

MAINE FARMER – 1-68. 21 Jan 1833-1900 – 1 – us UMI [630]
MAINE FREE PRESS – Hallowell, ME: Herrick & Farwell, jul 29 1831-jul 19 1833 – 1r – 1 – us Res Libr [071]
Maine, Henry James Sumner *see* VILLAGE-COMMUNITIES IN THE EAST AND WEST
Maine, Henry S *see* LECTURES ON THE EARLY HISTORY OF INSTITUTIONS
MAINE LAW REVIEW – 1908- 1; 1971- 5,6 – us UMI [340]
MAINE LAW REVIEW – (In 1962, the University of Maine Law School revived the original Maine Law Review, continuing its original numbering system. So v19 is dated 1962. This and subsequent vols are too deeply into copyright to be offered) – v1-18. 1908-1919/20 – 50mf – 9 – $75.00 – LLMC 84-596 – us L.L.M.C. [073]
MAINE LAW REVIEW – (v1-36 1908-84 on reel $300.00. v37-47 1985-95 on mf $183.00. Suspended 1920-62) – v1-47. 1908-95 – 5,6,9 – $483.00 set – us Hein [340]
THE MAINE LIQUOR LAW : AN ADDRESS DELIVERED AT THE ANNUAL MEETING OF THE QUEBEC TEMPERANCE AND PROHIBITORY LEAGUE, FEB 20, 1873 / Burns, R F – [Montreal ?: s.n., 1873 ?]. SEM105P1550 – 1mf – 9 – Can$2.25 – cn Bibl Nat [340]
Maine. State Bar Association *see* PROCEEDINGS
MAINE STATE LABOR NEWS – Augusta, ME: Maine Fed of Labor [etc]. v8 n10-v30. jul 1940-1962 – us Res Libr [331]
Maine. Superior Court. Cumberland County *see* RULES AND ORDERS OF THE SUPERIOR COURT OF CUMBERLAND COUNTY, IN THE STATE OF MAINE
Maine. Supreme Court *see* MAINE SUPREME COURT REPORTS
MAINE SUPREME COURT REPORTS / Maine. Supreme Court – (Pre-NRS: v1-77 1820-85 517mf $775.00. Updates planned) – v1-118. 1820-1920 – 810mf – 9 – $1,215.00 – LLMC 81-802 – us L.L.M.C. [340]
MAINE TIMES – Topsham, ME. v1-18. 1968-86 – 32r – 1 – us Ross [071]
MAINE TOWNSMAN – [Augusta, etc: Maine Municipal Association], 1948-56 – 2r – 1 – us Res Libr [978]
MAINE WORKING MAN'S ADVOCATE – Belfast, ME: John Dorr, nov 3 1830-jun 19 1833 – us Res Libr [331]
MAIN-ECHO – Aschaffenburg, 1969- – ca 10r per yr – 1 – Dist. gw Mikrofilm – gw Misc Inst [072]
Mainguy, Louise *see* BIO-BIBLIOGRAPHIE ANALYTIQUE DE JEAN SIMARD
Maini, P L *see* THE INDIAN PROBLEM IN KENYA
MAINICHI – Tokyo: Manichi Newspapers, jun 1951-may 9 1960 – us Res Libr [072]
THE MAINICHI *see* OSAKA MAINICHI
MAINICHI DAILY NEWS – 1922- – 1 – us UMI [072]
MAINICHI DAILY NEWS / ed by Mainichi Newspapers, Osaka and Tokyo – Apr 12 1922-Dec 31 1994 – 569r – 1 – Y3,926,100 – ja Yushodo [950]
MAINICHI NEWS DAILY – Tokyo, JA. 1955-1969 – 1r – $50.00 – R04212 – us Library Micro [072]
Mainichi Newspapers, Osaka and Tokyo *see* MAINICHI DAILY NEWS
MAINICHI SHIMBUN : TOKYO EDITION – (1990- 36r per year.Y309,600) – February 1872-December 1989 – 1,295r – 1 – Y14,226,500.00 – ja Japan Micro [950]
MAINICHI SHIMBUN – (Yrly reel count varies) – Tokyo, 1872- – 1 – inquire – us Ross [072]
MAINICHI SHOUGAKUSEI SHIMBUN – 1937-1985 – 141r – 1 – ja Japan Micro [950]
MAINICHI SHOUGAKUSEI SHIMBUN – Japan, 1937-85 – 141r – 1 – inquire – us Ross [072]
MAINLAND GUARDIAN – Canada. -w. Aug 1869-July 1871. Imperfect. 1 reel – 1 – uk British Libr Newspaper [073]
MAINLAND GUARDIAN – New Westminster, Canada. 1870-89 – 7r – 1 – $455.00 – cn Library Assoc [971]
MAINLAND SOUTH-EAST ASIA – (Titles listed separately) – 8,155mf – 9 – ne IDC [950]
MAINLINER DISPATCH – Gallitzin, PA. 1971. 1 roll – 13 – $25.00r – us I.M.R. [071]
Maino, Mario *see*
– LA LINGUA SOMALA; STRUMENTO D'INSEGNAMENTO PROFESSIONALE
– TERMINOLOGIA MEDICA E SUE VOCI NELLA LINGUA SOMALA
MAIN-POST – Wuerzburg, West Germany. 1 Jul 1968- – ca 10r per yr – 1 – gw Mikrofilm [072]
MAIN-SPITZE – Ruesselsheim, Germany. 1 Jun 1983- – ca 8r per yr – 1 – gw Mikrofilm [072]
MAINTENANCE ENGINEERING IN PLANTS, MILLS AND FACTORIES *see* FACTORY
MAINTENANCE MANAGEMENT INTERNATIONAL – v1-5. 1979-84. Continues: Terotechnical – 1,5,6,13 – sz Elsevier [650]
MAINTENANCE SYSTEM FOR THE DAIRY PLANT – 1984 – 80p – it F.A.O. [636]
MAINTENANT – Montreal: Ed Maintenant. no 1-141. 1962-74. SEM16P280 – 2r – 5 – Can$82.00 – cn Bibl Nat [073]
MAINTENANT – Recueil international illustre de litterature et d'art. Dir. Henry Poulaille. Cahiors no. 1-10. Paris. nov 1945-48 – 1 – fr A.C.R.P.P. [073]
MAINTENANT – Revue litteraire. Dir. Arthur Cravan. no. 1-5. Paris. avr 1912-avr 1915 – 1 – fr A.C.R.P.P. [073]
Mainwaring, J *see*
– GEORG FRIDERICH HAENDELS LEBENSBESCHREIBUNG
– MEMOIRS OF THE LIFE OF THE LATE GEORGE FREDERIC HANDEL
MAINZER JOURNAL – Mainz, Germany. 6 Jun 1848-1849 – 3r – 1 – gw Mikrofilm [072]
MAINZER ZEITUNG – Mainz, Germany. 1848-49 – 3r – 1 – gw Mikrofilm [072]
Maio, Angelo *see* SCRIPTORUM VETERUM NOVA COLLECTIO E VATICANIS CODICIBUS
Mair, Alexander *see* STUDIES IN THE CHRISTIAN EVIDENCES: BEING APOLOGETICS FOR THE TIMES
Mair, L P *see* NATIVE POLICIES IN AFRICA
Mair, Robert H *see* DEBRETT'S BARONETAGE AND KNIGHTAGE,...INFORMATION RESPECTING THE IMMEDIATE FAMILY CONNECTIONS OF BARONETS
Mairan, Jean Jacques Dortous de *see* LETTRE DE M. DE MAIRAN, SECRETAIRE PERPETUEL DE L'ACADEMIE ROYALE DES SCIENCES, &C. A MADAME: SUR LA QUESTION DES FORCES VIVES: EN REPONSE AUX OBJECTIONS QU'ELLE LUI FAIT SUR CE SUJET DANS SES INSTITUTIONS DE PHYSIQUE
Maire, R *see* RECHERCHES CYTOLOGIQUES ET TAXONOMIQUES SUR LES BASIDIOMYCEA6TES
Mairs, Clara Gardner *see* PAPERS
Mais, Clara Maria *see* BERUFSAUSLESE UND ANPASSUNG EINER FABRIKARBEITERINNENGRUPPE
LA MAISON A VENDRE / Dalayrac, N – Mayence: Zulehner, 1800? – 1 – us Sibley [780]
Maison de France *see* COURRIER ROYAL
La Maison de la Culture de Marseille *see* PEUPLE ET CULTURE
LA MAISON DIEU – 1(1945)-100(1970) – 292mf – 9 – Dfl1,022.00 – ne Slangenburg [073]
LA MAISON JOHN BULL & CIE.: LES GRANDES SUCCURSALES, LE CANADA, L'AUSTRALIE, LA NOUVELLE-ZELANDE, L'AFRIQUE DU SUD / O'Rell, Max – Paris: C. Levy, 1894. 03746. (Pre-1900 Canadiana) – 9 – cn C.I.H.M. [321]
LA MAISON MODERNE – Montreal, Canada. 13 mai 1905-v5. n4 mai 1908 – 1r – 1 – Can$25.00 – cn Can Microfilming [640]
MAISON POUR DAMES / Duval, Paul Alexandre Martin – Paris: P. Ollendorff, 1908. 280p. 3 fiches. (Literature Collection) – 9 – 8.00 – fr Bibl Nationale [830]
MAISON RUSTIQUE A L'USAGE DES HABITANS DE LA PARTIE DE LA FRANCE EQUINOXIALE CONNUE SOUS LE NOM DE CAYENNE / Prefontaine, Chevalier de – Paris: C.J.B. Bauche, 1763. ii,211p. 3 fiches.(Economics Collection) – 9 – 8.00 – fr Bibl Nationale [330]
LA MAISON SALUBRE ET LA MAISON INSALUBRE / Havard, Louis – Paris, Noblet, 1890. 31p. (Architecture Series) – 9 – fr Hachette [720]
MAISON-DIEU – Paris, v1-100 – 292mf – 9 – ne IDC [240]
LA MAISONNEE – Montreal. v2 n10. 20 oct 1953-v9 n48. 24 mar 1960 – 1r – 1 – Can$60.00 – cn Can Microfilming [072]
MAISONS HISTORIQUES DE GASCOGNE ET DE GUYENNE / Noulens – Paris, 1865. 2v – 3mf – 9 – F90.00 – fr F.F.G. [720]
Maistre, C *see* A TRAVERS L'AFRIQUE CENTRALE DE CONGO AU NIGER: 1892-1893
LE MAISTRE D'ESCOLE ANGLOIS. THE ENGLISHE SCHOLEMAISTER / Bellot, James – 1580. 133p. (English Linguistics Series 1500-1800) – 9 – us UMI [420]
Maistre, Joseph de *see* VOM PAPSTE
Maistre, Joseph Marie, Comte de *see* THE POPE
DER MAISTREIK 1924 IM RUHRBERGBAU / Spethmann, H – Essen – 1 – DM30.00 – gw Mikro Press [331]
MAITLAND ADVERTISING MEDIUM – Jan 5 1875-Oct 10 1877 – 9 – at Pascoe [072]
Maitland, Brownlow *see*
– THE ARGUMENT FROM PROPHECY
– THEISM OR AGNOSTICISM: AN ESSAY ON THE GROUNDS OF BELIEF IN GOD
Maitland, Charles *see* THE CHURCH IN THE CATACOMBS
MAITLAND DAILY MERCURY – Australia. 1 Jan 1894-30 Jun 1922. -d. 97mqn reels – 1 – uk British Libr Newspaper [072]
MAITLAND ENSIGN – Jan 2 1861-Dec 31 1862;Sept 21 1864-Apr 1865 – 9 – at Pascoe [072]
Maitland, F W *see*
– THE HISTORY OF ENGLISH LAW BEFORE THE TIME OF EDWARD I
– RECORDS OF THE PARLIAMENT HOLDEN AT WESTMINSTER, 28 FEBRUARY IN THE 33RD YEAR OF THE REIGN OF EDWARD 1 (1305) (RS98)
Maitland, Frank *see* SEARCHLIGHT ON THE DUCHESS OF ATHOLL
Maitland, Frederic William *see* DOMESDAY BOOK AND BEYOND
Maitland, Frederick Lewis *see* THE SURRENDER OF NAPOLEON; BEING THE NARRATIVE OF THE SURRENDER OF BUONAPARTE AND OF HIS RESIDENCE ON BOARD H.M.S. BELLEROPHON
Maitland, Frederick William *see*
– COLLECTED PAPERS
– DOMESDAY BOOK AND BEYOND
– ROMAN CANON LAW IN THE CHURCH OF ENGLAND
– A SKETCH OF ENGLISH LEGAL HISTORY
– TOWNSHIP AND BOROUGH
MAITLAND MERCURY – Jan 1 1926-Dec 31 1940 – 9 – at Pascoe [072]
Maitland, S R *see* ESSAYS ON SUBJECTS CONNECTED WITH THE REFORMATION IN ENGLAND
MAITLAND WEEKLY POST – Jan 30 1878-Nov 17 1880 – 9 – at Pascoe [072]
Maitland, William *see* THE COMING INDUSTRIAL STRUGGLE
LE MAITRE DE CLAVECIN POUR L'ACCOMPAGNEMENT, METHODE THEORIQUE ET PRATIQUE / Corrette, M – 1753 – 9 – us Sibley [780]
LE MAITRE DE FRANCAIS – Montreal: L Tesson, [1893-1894] – 9 – cn C.I.H.M. [440]
LE MAITRE EN DROIT. OPERA BOUFFON EN DEUX ACRES / Monsigny, P-A – Paris: Bailleux, [1760?] – 1 – us Sibley [780]
Maitre, L *see* LES ECOLES EPISCOPALES ET MONASTIQUES EN OCCIDENT
Maitre, Leon *see* LES VILLES DISPARUES DE LA LOIRE-INFERIEURE
Maitrejean, Auguste *see* HUIT MOIS AU CONGO
DES MAITRES DE COLOGNE A ALBERT DURER. PRIMITIFS DE L'ECOLE ALLEMANDE / Reunion des musees nationaux. Paris – 1950. 36 illus. 2 fiches – 9 – fr Réunion [700]
LES MAITRES DE L'AFFICHE – Paris, 1896-1900 – 1r – 14 – £105.00 – uk Chadwyck [760]
MAITRES ET DOMESTIQUES FIN-DE-SIECLE – Paris. 1898. (La Condition Ouvriere. Part Two.) – 9 – 5.00 – fr Bibl Nationale [360]
Maitron, Jean *see* LE SYNDICALISME REVOLUTIONNAIRE: PAUL DELESALLE
Maittaire, Michael *see* THE ENGLISH GRAMMAR
Maiuri, Amedeo *see* POMPEII
MAIZE IN HUMAN NUTRITION – 1992 – 168p – it F.A.O. [640]
Maize Week Exhibition, 1964 *see* INTERNATIONAL CORN RECIPES
Majallah Ilmiyah Adabiyah Akhlaqiyah Ijtima iyah. Saydun, Lebanon *see* AL-IRFAN
Majallah shahriyah ta ni bi-Shu"un al-Adab wa-al-Fann wa-al-Fikr *see* AL SHARQ
MAJALLAH-'I ADABI – (Missing issue: shumarah-i 1-2. Sal-i 3, shumarah-i 1-2[begins May, 1920]) – Sal-i 1, shumarah-i 1-7 (begins February, 1918]. Sali 2, shumarah-i 8, 9, 3, 4, 5 [1919] – 1 reel – 1 – $75.00 – us MEDOC [950]
MAJALLAH-I ULUM-I MALIYAH VA IQTISAD – Tehran: shumarah-i 1-4 [1923?] – 1 reel – 1 – $125.00 – us MEDOC [950]
MAJALLAH-I USUL-I TA'LIMAT (USUL-I TA'LIIM) – Sal-i 1, shumarah-i 1-6, Hamal 1297-? [March-April 1918-?]; sal-i 2, shumarah-i 1-6, 15 Hamal 1299-? [4 April 1920] – 1 reel – 1 – $140.00 – us MEDOC [950]
Majeke, Nosipho *see* THE ROLE OF THE MISSIONARIES IN CONQUEST
Majer, J F B C *see*
– NEU-EROEFFNETER THEORETISCH- UND PRACKTISCHER MUSIC-SAAL
– NEU-EROEFFNETER THEORETISCH-UND PRACKTISCHER MUSIC-SAAL
Majerczak, R *see* RENSEIGNEMENTS HISTORIQUES SUR LES KAZAKS OU KIRGHIZES-KAZAKS, DEPUIS LA FORMATION DE LA HORDE KAZAKE JUSQU' A-LA FIN DU 19E
Majewski, W *see* PREDICTING EFFECTS OF POWER PLANT ONCE-THROUGH COOLING ON AQUATIC SYSTEMS
MAJLIS – Kuala Lumpur, Malaysia. May 1949-Mar 1951; Sept 1953-Nov 1954; May-Sept 1955 – 6r – 1 – us L of C Photodup [072]
MAJMU'AH SALYANAH / Iran. Laws, Statutes, etc – Tehran. 1312, 1315; 1933-34, 1936-37. LL-019 – 1 – us L of C Photodup [340]
MAJMU'AH-'I QAVANIN – Tehran. Vol. 1-15. (14 Jumadi al-sani 1324 (A.H.)-6 Murdad 1328 [5 Aug 1906-29 Jul 1949]) – 3r – 1 – $75.00 – us MEDOC [950]
MAJMU'AT AL-ANZIMAH / Israel – (1974-. approx.50.00y; 1) – 1970-73 – 1 – 184.00 – us L of C Photodup [324]
MAJMU'AT AL-NASHARAT / Israel – (1977-. approx.50.00y; 1) – 1970-76 – 1 – 322.00 – us L of C Photodup [324]
MAJOR COUNCIL MEETINGS OF AMERICAN INDIAN TRIBES : PART ONE, SECTION 1 / U.S. Bureau of Indian Affairs – 1914-56. Navaho, Five Civilized Tribes, Ute, Pueblo, Cheyenne and Arapahoe. 1982 – 13r with printed guide – 1 – $1,250.00 – 0-89093-406-1 – us UPA [305]
MAJOR COUNCIL MEETINGS OF AMERICAN INDIAN TRIBES : PART ONE, SECTION 2 / U.S. Bureau of Indian Affairs – 1911-56. Sioux (Standing Rock, Rosebud, Pine Ridge and Cheyenne River), Chippewa and Klamath. 1982 – 13r with printed guide – 1 – $1,250.00 – 0-89093-407-X – us UPA [305]
MAJOR COUNCIL MEETINGS OF AMERICAN INDIAN TRIBES : PART TWO, SECTION 1 / U.S. Bureau of Indian Affairs – 1957-71. Navaho, Five Civilized Tribes, Ute, Pueblo, Cheyenne and Arapahoe. 1982 – 14r with printed guide – 1 – $1,350.00 – 0-89093-408-8 – us UPA [305]
MAJOR COUNCIL MEETINGS OF AMERICAN INDIAN TRIBES : PART TWO, SECTION 2 / U.S. Bureau of Indian Affairs – 1957-71. Sioux (Standing Rock, Rosebud, Pine Ridge, and Cheyenne River), Chippewa and Klamath – 12r with printed guide – 1 – $1,150.00 – 0-89093-409-6 – us UPA [360]
Major, Elbert Franklin *see* A MINISTRY TO PRESCHOOL CHILDREN AND THEIR PARENTS IN FIRST BAPTIST CHURCH, POOLER, GEORGIA
MAJOR FILM PERIODICALS FOR MEDIA RESEARCH, SERIES 1 – (Part One: Wid's Film and Film Folk, 1915-16; Wid's Independent Review of Feature Films, 1916-18; Wid's Daily, 1918-21; Film Daily, 1922-27. Part Two: Film Daily, 1928-37. Part Three: 1938-48. Part Four: 1945-59; Part Five: 1960-1990) – Film Daily and predecessors, 1915-70 – 1 – us Primary [790]
MAJOR FILM PERIODICALS FOR MEDIA RESEARCH, SERIES 2 – Film Daily Yearbook and Predecessors, 1918-1969 – 1 – us Primary [790]
Major, G *see*
– AUSLEGUNG DER EPISTEL S. PAULI AN DIE EPHESER IN ZEHEN PREDIGT DEN DOERFFPFARHERRN VND HAUSVETERN ZU DIENST EINFELTIGLICH VERFASSEL
– BEKENTNIS D. GEORGIJ MAIORIS VON DEM ARTICKEL DER IUSTIFICATION...
– CHRISTLICHES BEDENCKEN DES MINISTERIJ DER KIRCHEN ZU BRUNSCHWIG. AUFF D. MAIORS REPITITION VND ENDTLICHE ERKLERUNG. GELANGEND DEN STREIT, OB GUTE WERCKE ZUR SELIGKEIT NOETIG

SIND, ALSO, DAS ES VNMUEGLICH SEY, OHNE GUTE WERCKE SELIG ZUWERDEN
- COMMONEFACTIO HISTORICA DE STATV EIVS TEMPORIS,...CUI INSERTA EST BREUITER CONFESSIO...DE DOCTRINA IUSTIFICATIONIS AND BONORUM OPERUM,..
- DE ORIGINE ET AVTORITATE UERBI DEI, AND QUAE PONTIFICUM, PATRUM AND CONCILIORUM...ADMONITIO HOC TEMPORE, QUO DE CONCILIO CONGREGANDO AGITUR, UALDE NECESSARIA
- ENARRATIO EPISTOLAE PAVLI, SCRIPTAE AD PHILIPPENSES
- ENARRATIO PSALMI SEXAGESIMI OCTAVI,...
- VITA SANCTI PAVLI APOSTOLI,...
- VITAE PATRVM, IN VSUM MINISTRORUM VERBI, QUO AD EIUS FIERI POTUIT REPURGATAE
- ZWO PREDIGTEN VON ZWEIERLEY GERECHTIGKEIT, DES GESETZES UND DES EUANGELIJ...

MAJOR GENERAL EDWARD BRADDOCK'S ORDERLY BOOKS: FROM FEBRUARY 26 TO JUNE 17, 1755 / Braddock, Edward – Cumberland, MD: W. Lowdermilk, 1878. 00982. (Pre-1900 Canadiana) – 9 – cn C.I.H.M. [975]

MAJOR GENERAL FREDERICK FUNSTON ("1948") / Eckdall, Ella – 1927-1973 – 1 – us KS Hist [920]

Major, Henry Dewsbury Alves *see* THE SCIENCE OF RELIGION AND ITS BEARING UPON CHRISTIAN CLAIMS

MAJOR IRRIGATION PROJECTS / Iraq. Development Board and Ministry of Development – 1956. BD-1789 1 – 9 – ne IDC [956]

MAJOR ISSUES IN IMMIGRATION LAW / Martin, David A – Washington: FJC, 1987 – 2mf – 9 – $3.00 – LLMC 95-376 – us L.L.M.C. [340]

MAJOR ISSUES IN THE FEDERAL LAW OF EMPLOYMENT DISCRIMINATION / Rutherglen, George – 2nd ed. Washington: FJC, 1987 – 2mf – 9 – $3.00 – LLMC 95-363 – us L.L.M.C. [340]

MAJOR ISSUES IN THE FEDERAL LAW OF EMPLOYMENT DISCRIMINATION / Rutherglen, George – (Plus Suppls 1 and 2 issued in 1985) – Washington: FJC, Sept 1983 – 5mf – 9 – $7.50 – LLMC 95-806 – us L.L.M.C. [340]

Major, J F *see* TABLEAU D'UN COLLEGE EN ACTIVITE

MAJOR LAWRENCE, FLS / Lawless, Emily – British Fiction Archive: Unit 4 – 9 – uk Bell [830]

LE MAJOR PALMER / Pigault-Lebrun & Bruni – French Theatre Series. Paris. Huet, an V. 1797 – 9 – fr Hachette [820]

Major, R H *see*
- A HISTORY OF TRAVAILLE INTO VIRGINIA
- NOTES UPON RUSSIA AND KINGDOMS LYING THAT WAY

MAJOR STUDIES AND ISSUE BRIEFS OF THE CONGRESSIONAL RESEARCH SERVICE : QUARTERLY INDEX AND MICROFICHE SERVICE – (Backfiles: 1995 ca 665mf ISBN 1-55655-551-2 $2,135. 1994 785mf ISBN 1-55655-506-7 $2,135. 1993 619mf ISBN 1-55655-458-3 $2,135. 1992 779mf ISBN 1-55655-445-1 $2,290.00. 1991 827mf ISBN 1-55655-388-9 $2,135. Guides available for $395.00 ea) – 1996 – 1 – $ 2,135.00 – 1-55655-606-3 – us UPA [324]

MAJOR STUDIES AND ISSUE BRIEFS OF THE LEGISLATIVE REFERENCE SERVICE/ RESEARCH SERVICE: 1916-74 / U.S. Library of Congress. Legislative Reference Service Congressional Research Service – (Supplements: 1975-76 6r $770.00 ISBN 0-89093-144-5. 1976-78 13r $1,660.00 ISBN 0-89093-208-5. 1978-79 11r $1,405.00 ISBN 0-89093-209-3. 1979-80 10r $1,275.00 ISBN 0-89093-313-8. 1980-81 11r $1,405.00 ISBN 0-89093-405 -3. 1981-82 11r $1,405.00 ISBN 0-89093-490-8. 1982-83 12r $1,525.00 ISBN 0-89093-544-0. 1983-84 13r $1,660.00 ISBN 0-89093-644-7. 1984-85 13r $1,660.00 ISBN 0-89093-743-5. 1985-86 13r $1,660.00 ISBN 0-89093-774-5. 1986-87 13r $1,660.00 ISBN 0-89093-455-X. 1987-88 14r $1,780.00 ISBN 1-55655-045-6. 1988-89 14r $1,780.00 ISBN 1-55655- 098-7, Guide only $395.00. 1989-90 14r $1,780.00 ISBN 1-55655-168-1, Guide only $395.00. 1990 13r $1,660.00 ISBN 1-55655-292-0, Guide only $395.00. 1991 14r $1,780.00 ISBN 1-55655-389-7, Guide only $395.00. 1992 15r $1,910.00 ISBN 1-55655-456-7, Guide only $395.00. 1993 14r $1,780.00 ISBN 1-55655-505-9, Guide only $395.00. 1994 14r $1,780.00 ISBN 1-55655-552-0. Guide only $395.00. 1995 14r $1,780.00 ISBN 1-55655-607-1, Guide only $395.00) – 1975 – 17r – 1 – $2,160.00 – 0-89093-001-5 – us UPA [324]

MAJOR TRENDS IN EDUCATION 1976-1978 / Malawi. Ministry of Education – Zomba – 1mf – 9 – DE-446/1 – ne IDC [370]

MAJOR WEEDS OF THE NEAR EAST – 1991 – 312p – it F.A.O. [631]

MAJOR-GENERAL RICHARD MONTGOMERY / Cullum, George Washington – s.l.: s.n., 1884?. 02231. (Pre-1900 Canadiana) – 9 – cn C.I.H.M. [971]

MAJORICARUM (ANNO 1416-1458) / Alfonso 4 – Barcelona – 1r – 5,6 – sp Cultura [946]

MAJORITY AND MINORITY STATE SENATE REPORTS OF THE SPECIAL JOINT COMMITTEE ON THE MENDOCINO WAR – Sacramento, CA. 1860 – 1r – 5 – $50.00 – B50529 – us Library Micro [324]

MAKAMAT / Hariri – 1850 – 1 – uk Microform Academic [470]

Makarenko, Anton Semenovich *see* OPIS' DOKUMENTAL'NYKH MATERIALOV FONDA NO.332

Makarewicz, Tadeusz *see* EMIGRACJA AMERYKANSKA A MACIERZYSLA GRUPA PARAFIALNA

Makarov, N P *see*
- KREST'IANSKOE KHOZIAISTVO I EGO INTERESY
- KREST'IANSKOE KOOPERATIVNOE DVIZHENIE V ZAPADNOI SIBIRI
- NOVAIA KOOPERATSIIA V SEL'SKOM KHOZIAISTVE I KARTOFELEKRAKHMAL'NOE PROIZVODSTVO
- OCHERK KOOPERATIVNOGO SBYTA ZERNA
- ORGANIZATSIIA SEL'SKOGO KHOZIAISTVA

MAKASSAARSCHE CHRESTOMATHIE : OORSPRONKELIJKE MAKASSAARSCHE GESCHRIFTEN, IN PROZA EN POEZY UITGEGEVEN, VAN AANTEEKENINGEN VOORZIEN EN TEN DEELE VERTAALD / Matthes, B F – Ed. 2. 's-Gravenhage, 1883 – 8mf – 9 – ne IDC [490]

MAKASSAR. SULSELRA, ITS CULTURE, ARTS AND BEAUTY / Jajasan, Karya Pariwisata – SE-4433 1 – 9 – ne IDC [700]

Makaweczky *see* DUO CONCERTANT POUR COR ET VIOLA

MAKE THEIR "CASTLES IN SPAIN" COME TRUE / Medical Bureau and North American Committee to Aid Spanish Democracy – N.Y., 1939? Fiche W 1036. (Blodgett Collection of Spanish Civil War Pamphlets) – 9 – us H.U. College Libr [946]

MAKE WAY FOR THE KING / Brobst, Flavius J – Boston: Lee and Shepard, 1895. 1 fiche – 9 – us A.T.L.A. [240]

MAKEDONIYA – Sofia, Bulgaria. -d. 28 Dec 1926-18 Aug 1934. Imperfect. 9 reels – 1 – uk British Libr Newspaper [949]

A MAKER OF THE NEW ORIENT : SAMUEL ROBBINS BROWN: PIONEER EDUCATOR IN CHINA, AMERICA, AND JAPAN: THE STORY OF HIS LIFE AND WORK / Griffis, William Elliot – (Includes index) – New York: Fleming H Revell, c1902 – 1mf – 9 – 0-8370-6187-3 – 1986-0187 – us A.T.L.A. [920]

Makerova, N Ia. *see* POTREBITEL'SKAIA KOOPERATSIIA ZA 10 LET SOVETSKOI VLASTI

MAKERS OF AMERICAN / Caldwell, A B – Historical and biographical sketches. Atlanta, Florida Historical Society, 1909. Vols. 1-4. Florida Reel 1. (The Cox Library Collection) – 5 – us Americana [978]

Makhnovets, L E *see* UKRAJINS'KI PYS'MENNYKY

Makhnovets, V *see* MIASNOE DELO V POTREBITEL'NYKH OBSHCHESTVAKH

MAKHNOVSHCHYNA : DRAMATYCHNYI ETI UD NA L DII U: ZHIDNO Z POSTANOVOI U VYSHCHOI NAUKOVO-REPERTUARNOI RADI PRI HOLOVPOLITOSVITY N.K.O.U.S.R.R. VID 9/11-1927 R. PI ESA DO VYSTAVY DOZVOLENA ZA CH 2713 / Bohoslavskyi, Mykola – Kharkiv: Sklad vyd. Derzh. vyd-vo Ukrainy, 1927 – 1 – CSUX88-B5104 – us Hoover Inst Photo [947]

Makhov, V N *see*
- INSTRUKTAZH SEL'SKOKHOZIAISTVENNOI KOOPERATSII I EGO OSNOVNYE PROBLEMY
- KOOPERATIVNYI INSTRUKTAZH I EGO METODY
- PO KOOPERATIVNOMU PUTI
- POTREBITEL'SKAIA KOOPERATSIIA V SIBIRI V PROTSESSE EE RAZVITIIA
- REVIZIIA SOSTOIANIIA SREDSTV I OBOROTOV KOOPERATIVA

MAKHOVIK : ORGAN PETROGRADSKOGO GUBERNSKOGO SOVETA PROFESSIONALNYKH SOI UZOV – (Includes c.1: 1921:Nov.16) – Petrograd: 14-i a gos. tip., 1921 – 1 – CSUXANR9395-S – us Hoover Inst Photo [947]

Makinen, Antti *see* VAPAAKIRKOLLINEN LIIKE SUOMESSA (THE FREE CHURCH MOVEMENT IN FINLAND)

MAKING A WILL, BY WHOM, WHEN AND HOW; KINDS OF WILLS, WHY AND WHY NOT, AND IF NOT; SPECIMENS / Hall, J Eugene – Beverly Hills, Calif., 1933 38 p. LL-1373 – 1 – us L of C Photodup [340]

MAKING GOOD IN THE LOCAL CHURCH / Elliott, Ernest Eugene – New York: Fleming H. Revell, c1913 – 1mf – us A.T.L.A. [240]

THE MAKING OF A CHRISTIAN / Jarvis, Robert Edward Lee – Topeka, KS: Crane, 1903 – 1mf – 9 – 0-8370-3774-3 – 1985-1774 – us A.T.L.A. [230]

THE MAKING OF A CONTRACT / Lawson, John Davison – Columbia, Mo., Stephens, 1901; 57 p. LL-221 – 1 – us L of C Photodup [340]

THE MAKING OF MODERN LONDON – (Part 1: 1495-1599. Part 2: 1599-1649. Part 3: 1649-92) – Series 1: The Repertories of the Court of Aldermen, 1495-1835, from the Corporation of London Records Office – 1 – us Primary [941]

THE MAKING OF RHODESIA / Hole, Hugh Marshall – London: Macmillan and Co. Ltd., 1926. xi,415p. Maps, plates. 1 reel. 1258 – 1 – us U.W. Library [960]

THE MAKING OF THE ENGLISH BIBLE / McComb, Samuel – New York: Moffat, Yard, 1909. 1 fiche – 9 – us A.T.L.A. [240]

THE MAKING OF THE ENGLISH BIBLE / McComb, Samuel – New York: Moffat, Yard and Company, 1909. xiv,187p. fold. tables – 1 – us U.W. Library [220]

THE MAKING OF THE GREAT WEST, 1512-1883 / Drake, Samuel Adams – New York. C. Scribner's, 1887. 02756. (Pre-1900 Canadiana) – 9 – cn C.I.H.M. [971]

THE MAKING OF THE SCOTTISH PRAYER BOOK OF 1637 / Donaldson, G – Edinburgh, 1954 – 7mf – 8 – Dfl28.00 – ne Slangenburg [941]

MAKING THE MOST OF ONESELF : TALKS TO YOUNG MEN ON THE LIFE WORTH LIVING / Gumbart, A S – Boston: United Society of Christian Endeavor, c1899 – 1mf – 9 – 0-8370-7384-7 – 1986-1384 – us A.T.L.A. [240]

DIE MAKKABAEER : EINE UNTERSUCHUNG DES TRAUERSPIELS UND SEINER UNGEDRUCKTEN VORARBEITEN NEBST EINEM AUSBLICK AUF ZACHARIAS WERNERS "MUTTER DER MAKKABAEER" / Schmidt-Oberloessnitz, Wilhelm – Leipzig: Dieterich, 1908 – 1r – 1 – us U.W. Library [430]

Makogonenko, E P *see* RUSSKAIA PROZA 18 VEKA

Makogonenko, G P *see*
- NIKOLAI NOVIKOV I RUSSKOE PROSVESHCHENIE 18 VEKA
- RADISHCHEV I EGO VREMIA

MAKOV TSVET / Gippius, Z N – Drama v 4 deistviiakh. Spb. 1908. BR-716 2 – 8 – ne IDC [460]

Makovskii, S K *see*
- NA PARNASE SEREBRIANOGO VEKA
- PORTRETY SOVREMENNIKOV

Makower, Felix *see* THE CONSTITUTIONAL HISTORY AND CONSTITUTION OF THE CHURCH OF ENGLAND

MAKROMOLEKULARE CHEMIE – Basel. v1-28. 1947-58.201/2 – 8 – ne IDC [073]

Maksakov, V V *see* ISTORIIA I ORGANIZATSIIA ARKHIVNOGO DELA V SSSR (1917-1945 GG.)

Maksimov, D *see*
- IZ PROSHLOGO RUSSKOI ZHURANLISTIKI
- IZ PROSHLOGO RUSSKOI ZHURNALISTIKI
- MATERIALY K BIBLIOGRAFII A. BLOKA ZA 1928-1957 GODY
- POEZIIA VALERIIA BRIUSOVA

Maksimovich, L *see* NOVYI I POLNYI GEOGRAFICHESKII SLOVAR' ROSSIISKOGO GOSUDARSTVA

Maksimov-Slobozhanin, E D *see* O METODIKE ORGANIZATSII KOOPERATIVOV

MAKTAB – (Purchase with Azarbaycan) – Baku, nos. 1-4 (25 Zi'l-hijjah 1329-29 Muharram 1339 [29 Nov 1911-1 Jan 1912]) – 9 – us MEDOC [949]

MAKTUL SEHZADELER / Zeki [Pakalin], Mehmet – Istanbul: Sems Matbaasi, 1336 [1920] – $42.00 – us MEDOC [956]

MAL DE LA ROSA / Casal, G – Manou, 1936 – 1mf – 9 – sp Cultura [610]

MALABAR HERALD – Cochin, India. 1962-Nov 1975 – 14r – 1 – us L of C Photodup [072]

MALABOCH : OR, NOTES FROM MY DIARY ON THE BOER CAMPAIGN OF 1894 AGAINST THE CHIEF MALABOCH OF BLAAUWBERG, DISTRICT ZOUTPANSBERG, SOUTH AFRICAN REPUBLIC / Rae, Colin – London: S Low, Marston, 1898 – us Res Libr [960]

MALACCA GUARDIAN – Malaysia. -w. 2 Jan 1928-30 Dec 1940. (16 reels) – 1 – uk British Libr Newspaper [072]

MALACCA OBSERVER – Malaysia. -w. 3 Nov 1924-26 Dec 1927. (3 reels) – 1 – uk British Libr Newspaper [072]

MALACHI : WITH NOTES AND INTRODUCTION / Barnes, William Emery – (Includes bibliographical references and indexes) – Cambridge: University Press, 1917 – 1mf – 9 – 0-8370-6086-9 – 1986-0086 – us A.T.L.A. [220]

Malachi, E R *see*
- HERZL VE-HA-YISHUV HA-YASHAN BI-YERUSHALAYIM
- IGGROT DAVID FRISCHMANN

MALACOGRAPHIA MADERENSIS / Albers, J C – Z-381 2. 1854 – 8 – ne IDC [590]

MALACOLOGIA MONENSIS / Forbes, E A – Z-531 2. 1838 – 8 – ne IDC [999]

MALACOLOGIA VERONESE / Menegazzi, L – Z-650 2. 1855 – 8 – ne IDC [590]

MALACOLOGIE D'AIX-LES-BAINS / Bourguignat, J R – Z-420 2. 1864 – 8 – ne IDC [580]

MALACOLOGIE DE LA GRANDE CHARTREUSE / Bourguignat, J R – Z-422 2. 1864 – 8 – ne IDC [580]

MALACOLOGIE MEDITERRANEENNE ET LITTORALE / Cantraine, F J – Z-465 2. 1841 – 9 – ne IDC [590]

MALACOLOGIE TERRESTRE ET FLUVIATILE DE LA BRETAGNE / Bourguignat, J R – Z-413 2. 1860 – 8 – ne IDC [580]

Malaga Garcia, Eduardo *see*
- LENGUA ESPANOLA. TOMO 1. ORTOGRAFIA, PROSODIA, MORFOLOGIA, ANALISIS
- LENGUA ESPANOLA. TOMO 2
- PEDAGOGIA GENERAL

Malagasy Republic *see*
- ECONOMIE ET PLAN DE DEVELOPPEMENT
- JOURNAL OFFICIEL
- JOURNAL OFFICIEL DE MADAGASCAR
- PLAN DE DEVELOPPEMENT ECONOMIQUE ET SOCIAL RAPPORT D'EXECUTION, 1ER JUILLET 1958-30 JUIN 1959

Malagasy Republic. Commissariat General au Plan *see*
- DEUXIEME RAPPORT SUR L'EXECUTION DU PLAN QUINQUENNAL, 1964-1968
- PLAN QUIQUENNAL, 1964-1968
- RAPPORT SUR LE DEVELOPPEMENT DE MADAGASCAR

MALAGASY REPUBLIC (MADAGASCAR) : ANNUAIRE STATISTIQUE DE MADAGASCAR 1938-1951 / Malagasy Republic (Madagascar). Service de Statistique Generale – (Coll title: African Official Statistical Serials, 1867-1982) – 2mf – 9 – £17.00 – uk Chadwyck [960]

Malagasy Republic (Madagascar). Service de Statistique Generale *see* MALAGASY REPUBLIC (MADAGASCAR)

Malagasy Republic. Ministere de l'Industrie et du Plan *see* PROGRAMME TRIENNAL DE DEVELOPPEMENT ECONOMIQUE ET SOCIAL, 1959-1962

Malagon. Ayuntamiento *see* FERIAS Y FIESTAS, MALAGON 1961

Malagon (Ciudad Real). Ayuntamiento *see* FERIA Y FIESTAS...1960

Malagon, Joan *see*
- HA DE NUESTRA SRA. DE GUADALUPE
- HISTORIA...GUADALUPE

A MALAGUETA – Rio de Janeiro, 18 Dec 1821-Mar 1832 – 1,5,6 – bl Biblioteca [072]

A MALAGUETA EXTRAORDINARIA – Rio de Janeiro, 31 Jul 1822-10 Jul 1824 – 1,5,6 – bl Biblioteca [072]

A MALAGUETA MARANHENSE – '(s.l.')-Sao Luiz, Brazil. 30 Jun-Jul 1844; 19 Aug 1848 – 1,5,6 – bl Biblioteca [072]

MALAHAT REVIEW – Victoria. nos 90-109. 1990-94 – 9 – Can$28.00y – cn Micromedia [420]

Malak, o. Henryk Maria *see* APOSTOLKA MILOSIERDZIA Z CHICAGO

DER MAL'AKH JAHWE / Rybinski, J – Paderborn, 1930 – 3mf – 8 – ne Slangenburg [200]
Malakhov, S *see*
- CHTO TAKOE FUTURIZM?
- RUSSKII FUTURIZM POSLE REVOLIUTSII
MALAKOZOOLOGISCHE BLAETTER – Cassel. v1-25 1854-1878; N.S. v1-11 1879-1891 – 163mf – 9 – ne IDC [590]
Malalae, Joannis Antiocheni *see*
- CHRONOGRAPHIA (CSHB 15)
- HISTORIA CHRONICA
- HISTORIA CHRONICA (CBH 30,3)
MALAM SUNJI; KUMPULAN SADJAK / Ukur, Fridolin – SE 4499 1. 1961 – 9 – ne IDC [950]
Malan, C H *see* RIDES IN THE MISSION FIELD OF SOUTH AFRICA
MALANDRO – Carajas, Amazonas. 5 Abr 1909 – 1,5,6 – bl Biblioteca [072]
MALARIA : RECIT DE LA BROUSSE MALGACHE / Vally, Georges – Paris: J Renard, [1944] – us Res Libr [616]
MALAROARNAS NYHETER *see* VASTERORT
Malassis, Louis *see* RURAL WORLD
Malato de Corne, Charles A *see* LA GRANDE GREVE
Malawi *see*
- DEVELOPMENT PLAN, 1965-1969
- DEVELOPMENT PROGRAMME 1970-1972/73
Malawi. Economic Planning Division *see* STATEMENT OF DEVELOPMENT POLICIES 1971-1980
MALAWI (FORMERLY NYASALAND) : COMPENDIUM OF STATISTICS 1965-1970 / Malawi (formerly Nyasaland). National Statistical Office – (1967-69 not publ. Coll title: African Official Statistical Serials, 1867-1982) – 9 – £7.00f (set £150.00 18mf) – uk Chadwyck [960]
MALAWI (FORMERLY NYASALAND) : MALAWI STATISTICAL YEARBOOK 1972-1974 / Malawi (formerly Nyasaland). National Statistical Office – (Coll title: African Official Statistical Serials, 1867-1982) – 14mf – 9 – £7.00f (set £150.00 18mf) – uk Chadwyck [960]
Malawi (formerly Nyasaland). National Statistical Office *see*
- MALAWI (FORMERLY NYASALAND)
Malawi. Ministry of Economic Affairs *see* DEVELOPMENT PROGRAMME, 1968-70
Malawi. Ministry of Education *see*
- EDUCATION PLAN OF MALAWI 1973-1980
- MAJOR TRENDS IN EDUCATION 1976-1978
- TEN YEARS OF DEVELOPMENT AND PROGRESS IN EDUCATION 1966-1976
Malawi. Ministry of Education and Culture. Planning Unit *see* EDUCATION STATISTICS 1981-1989
Malawi. Ministry of Natural Resources *see* DEVELOPMENT POLICIES AND PLANS
Malawi. Office of the President and Cabinet. Economic Planning Div *see* STATE OF DEVELOPMENT POLICIES 1971-1980
MALAY DAILY CHRONICLE – Ipoh. Malaysia. 19 Aug 1912-7 Aug 1914. (12 reels) – 1 – uk British Libr Newspaper [072]
MALAY MAGIC / Skeat, W W – London, 1900 – 8mf – 9 – ne IDC [390]
MALAY MAIL – Kuala Lumpur. Malaysia.1955-64 – 1 – us UMI [072]
Malay States. Federated *see* MALAYA, STATEMENT OF POLICY FOR THE FUTURE CONSTITUTION OF THE MALAYAN UNION AND THE COLONY OF SINGAPORE
Malaya *see*
- DRAFT DEVELOPMENT PLAN OF THE FEDERATION OF MALAYA
- SECOND FIVE-YEAR PLAN, 1961-1965
MALAYA CATHOLIC LEADER – Singapore. -w. 5 Jan 1935-27 Sep 1941. (6 reels) – 1 – uk British Libr Newspaper [072]
Malaya. Economic Secretariat *see* A PLAN OF DEVELOPMENT FOR MALAYA 1956-60
Malaya (Federation) *see* AN ACT TO AMEND AND CONSOLIDATE THE LAW RELATING TO EDUCATION
Malaya (Federation) Education Review Committee *see* REPORT 1960
THE MALAYA MAIL – (1962-1967 35r. Sept 1970-1992 76r) – Kuala Lumpur, Malaysia. Sept 1945-1954 – 33r – 1 – us L of C Photodup [072]
MALAYA, STATEMENT OF POLICY FOR THE FUTURE CONSTITUTION OF THE MALAYAN UNION AND THE COLONY OF SINGAPORE / Malay States. Federated – Singapore, 194?. 4p – 1 – us U.W. Library [950]
THE MALAYA TRIBUNE – Singapore, Apr 1927-28; Nov 1945-Jan 1951 – 20r – 1 – us L of C Photodup [072]
MALAYALA MANORAMA – Kottayam,India. Jan-18 Oct 1959; 1962-1991 – 121r – 1 – us L of C Photodup [072]
MALAYAN CEYLONESE CHRONICLE – George Town. Malaysia. -m. Feb-May 1941. (6 ft) – 1 – uk British Libr Newspaper [072]
MALAYAN DAILY NEWS – Kuala Lumpur. Malaysia. -d. 20 Oct 1945-31 Jul 1947. (3 reels) – 1 – uk British Libr Newspaper [072]
MALAYAN FAMILY MEMOIRS BY THEMSELVES – 1830 – 1 – uk Microform Academic [920]
MALAYAN FERNS / Alderwerelt van Rosenburgh, C R W K van – Batavia, 1908 – 11mf – 9 – ne IDC [580]
MALAYAN FERNS ALLIES / Alderwerelt van Rosenburgh, C R W K van – Batavia, 1915 – 3mf – 9 – ne IDC [580]
MALAYAN FERNS AND FERN ALLIES : SUPPLEMENT 1 / Alderwerelt van Rosenburgh, C R W K van – Batavia, 1916 – 8mf – 9 – ne IDC [580]
MALAYAN OBSERVER – Ipoh. Malaysia. -d. 30 Sep-30 Dec 1922. (1 reel) – 1 – uk British Libr Newspaper [072]
MALAYAN OBSERVER – Kuala Lumpur. Malaysia. -w. 28 Apr-20 Oct 1946. (1 reel) – 1 – uk British Libr Newspaper [072]
MALAYAN SATURDAY REVIEW – Singapore. -w. 16 Sep 1933-28 Apr 1934. (1 reel) – 1 – uk British Libr Newspaper [072]
Malaysia *see*
- EDUCATION (AMENDMENT) ACT 1972
- FIRST MALAYSIA PLAN, 1966-1970
- HIS MAJESTY'S GOVERNMENT GAZETTE
- INTERIM REVIEW OF DEVELOPMENT IN MALAYA UNDER THE SECOND FIVE-YEAR PLAN
- MID-TERM REVIEW OF THE FIRST MALAYSIA PLAN 1966-1970
- MID-TERM REVIEW OF THE SECOND MALAYSIA PLAN, 1971-1975
- SECOND FIVE-YEAR PLAN, 1971-1975
- SECOND MALAYSIAN PLAN, 1971-1975
Malaysia. Dept. of Information *see* INDONESIAN INTENTIONS TOWARDS MALAYSIA
Malaysia. (Federation). Kelantan *see* GOVERNMENT GAZETTE
Malaysia. (Federation). Pahang *see* GOVERNMENT GAZETTE
Malaysia. (Federation). Penang *see* GOVERNMENT GAZETTE
Malaysia. (Federation). Perlis *see* GOVERNMENT GAZETTE
Malaysia. Higher Education Planning Committee *see* REPORT
MALAYSIA. HISTORICAL DOCUMENTS AND MANUSCRIPTS *see* HISTORICAL DOCUMENTS AND MANUSCRIPTS
THE MALAYSIA ISSUE; BACKGROUND AND DOCUMENTS / Indonesia. Departemen Luar Negeri – SE-11,656 1. 1964 – 9 – ne IDC [324]
Malaysia. Malaysian Association for Education *see* ISUE-ISUE DI-DALAM RIWAYAT PELAJARAN MALAYSIA
Malaysia. Ministry of Education *see*
- EDUCATION IN MALAYSIA
- EDUCATION IN MALAYSIA 1974
- EDUCATIONAL STATISTICS OF MALAYSIA 1938 TO 1967
- EDUCATIONAL STATISTICS OF MALAYSIA 1980
- EDUCATIONAL STATISTICS OF MALAYSIA 1974/75
- EDUCATIONAL STATISTICS OF MALAYSIA 1976-1979
- KAJIAN KECICIRAN
- NATIONAL SEMINAR ON CURRICULUM DEVELOPMENT IN TEACHER EDUCATION PENANG 1970
- NATIONAL WORKSHOP ON POPULATION EDUCATION, 4-16 OCTOBER 1971 KUALA LUMPUR
- REPORT ON THE IMPLEMENTATION OF THE RECOMMENDATIONS OF THE EDUCATION REVIEW COMMITTEE 1960
Malaysia. Ministry of Education. Educational Planning and Research Division *see* EDUCATION IN MALAYSIA 1980
Malaysia. Royal Commission on the Teaching Services *see* REVISED REPORT
Malaysia. University of Penang. Centre for Educational Services *see* PROPOSED DEVELOPMENTAL PLAN FOR THE PERIOD 1971-1975
MALAYSIAN SERIALS : NON-GOVERNMENT / Razia Begum Mukhtar – 1983 – A$10.00 – 0-86758-133-6 – at BISA [010]
MALAYSIA-SINGAPORE-BRUNEI STUDIES GROUP OF THE SOUTHEAST ASIA COUNCIL, ASSOCIATION FOR ASIAN STUDIES (ASA) – Philadelphia. 30 docs. 1980-1990 – 13mf – 9 – ne IDC [320]
Malbim, ML *see* MASHAL U-MELIZAH
MALBOROUGH TIMES ETC – England.24 Sept 1859-29 Dec 1860; 1880-1962. -w. 75 1/2 reels – 1 – uk British Libr Newspaper [072]
Malcolm, A *see* A TREATISE OF MUSICK, SPECULATIVE, PRACTICAL, AND HISTORICAL
Malcolm, John *see* THE HISTORY OF PERSIA, FROM THE MOST EARLY PERIOD TO THE PRESENT TIME; CONTAINING AN ACCOUNT OF THE RELIGION, GOVERNMENT, USAGES, AND CHARACTER OF THE INHABITANTS OF THAT KINGDOM
MALCOLM LOWRY'S SHAKESPEARE / Shakespeare, William & Lowry, Malcolm; ed by Collier, J Payne – (Annotated by novelist Malcolm Lowry) – New York: F M Lupton Publishing Co, [1855?] – 1r – 1 – Can$100.00r – cn U.B.C. Preserve [420]
MALCOLM MESSENGER – Malcolm, NE. -w. Jan-May 1896; Aug 1896-Dec 1898; Mar 1908-Apr 1934 – 1 – us NE Hist [071]
MALCOLM X: FBI SURVEILLANCE FILE *see* FBI FILE ON MALCOLM X
Malcom, H *see* TRAVELS IN SOUTH-EASTERN ASIA, EMBRACING HINDUSTAN, MALAYA, SIAM, AND CHINA
EL MALCRIADITO – Los Angeles, CA. 1975-1976 – 1r – 1 – $50.00 – R03291 – us Library Micro [071]
EL MALCRIADO – Delano, CA. 1971 – 1r – 1 – $50.00 – R02167 – us Library Micro [071]
EL MALCRIADO – [Delano, CA]: Asociacion de Trabajadores Campesinos, dec 19 1964-jun 23 1972 – us Res Libr [071]
MALDEN 1677-1849 – (Mf 1T-2T: Marriages/ Intentions 1677-1781. Mf 2T-7T: Births 1677-1809. Mf 4T-5T: Deaths 1693-1810. Mf 7T-8T: Marriages/Intentions 1770-1820. Mf 8T-9T: Births 1771-1849. Mf 9T-10T: Deaths 1811-42. Mf 10T-12T: Marriages/Intentions 1820-42. Mf 12T: Births 1812-47; Marriage Intentions 1842-50. Mf 12T-13T: Deaths 1834-43. Mf 13T-14T: Marriages 1841-51; Births 1843-51. Mf 15T: Deaths 1843-51) – (mf ed 1997) – 15mf – 9 – 0-87623-283-7 – us Holbrook [920]
Malden, Richard Henry *see* FOREIGN MISSIONS
Maldives. Ministry of Education *see*
- BASIC DATA ON STUDENT ENROLMENT IN MALDIVES, FEBRUARY 1990
- BASIC EDUCATION AND LITERACY PROGRAMME
- DEVELOPMENT OF EDUCATION 1988-1990. MALDIVES COUNTRY REPORT
Maldonado, Juan *see*
- COMENTARII IN QUATOR EVANGELISTAS
- COMMENTARI IN PROPHETAS. JEREMIAN EZECHIELEM
Maldonado, Juan de *see* S. MATTHEW'S GOSPEL
Maldonado y Cocat, Jose Ramon *see* ORIGENES Y ARMAS DE LA CASA DE MARQUEZ DE PRADO
Maldonatus, Ioan. *see* COMMENTARII IN QUATTUOR EVANGELISTAS
EL MALEFICIO DE LA MARIPOSA / Garcia Lorca, Federico – MS DE 1920 – 1mf – 9 – sp Cultura [830]
Malegue, H *see* ELEMENTS DE STATISTIQUE GENERALE DU DEPARTEMENT DE LA HAUTE-OIRE ET DICTIONNAIRE DES LIEUX HABITES
Maleki-Ardebili, Mansour *see* NUMERISCHE SIMULATION DER PARTIKELBEWEGUNG IN EINEM INSTATIONAEREN STROEMUNGSFELD
Malekoff, Andrew *see* SOCIAL WORK WITH GROUPS
Malen, J H *see* DIE OPKONS VAN'N REPUBLIEK
Malendez Valdes, Juan *see*
- COLECCION DE POESIAS
- DISCURSOS FORENSES
- POESIAS
- POESIAS ESCOGIDAS
MALEN'KAIA KHRESTOMATIIA DLIA VZROSLYKH. MNENIIA RUSSKIKH O SAMIKH SEBE. ED. 3 / Skal'kovskii, K A – Spb, 1905 – 8 – BR-10 262 2 – ne IDC [947]
MALEN'KIE KOMEDII / Mariengof, A – Leningrad, M. 1957. BR-1079 2 – 8 – ne IDC [460]
DIE MALER : LUSTSPIEL IN DREI AUFZUEGEN / Wilbrandt, Adolf von – 2. Aufl. Stuttgart: J G Cotta, 1901 – 1r – 1 – us U.W. Library [820]
Maler, J *see* DIE TEUETSCH SPRAACH
MALER MUELLER : NEUWERTUNG SEINES SCHAFFENS / Oeser, Willy – (Includes bibliographical references) – Mannheim: J Gremm, 1928 – 1r – 1 – us U.W. Library [700]
MALER MUELLERS JUGENDSPRACHE / Lange, Carl Friedrich August – (Includes bibliographical references) – Ann Arbor, Mich.: G Wahr, 1904 – 1r – 1 – us U.W. Library [430]
DIE MALEREIEN DER KATAKOMBEN ROMS : TEXT UND TAFELN / Wilpert, J – Freiburg im Breisgau, 1903 – 37mf – 8 – Dfl103.00 – ne Slangenburg [240]
Malet, Hugh Poyntz *see* LOST LINKS IN THE INDIAN MUTINY
MALEVICH ARCHIVE / Stedelijk Museum, Amsterdam – 46mf – 9 – ne IDC [110]
Malfilatre, J C L de *see* LE GENIE DE VIRGILE
Malherbe, A *see* FAUNA ORNITHOLOGIQUE DE LA SICILE
Malherbe, Ernst Gideon *see* THE BILINGUAL SCHOOL
Malherbe, G *see*
- LE CHANT LITURGIQUE COLLECTIF A L'EPOQUE PATRISTIQUE
- LE MANUALE PASTORUM DE TOURNAI
- LE PASTORALE DE MALINES
- LES RITUELS LIEGEOIS
O MALHETE : ORGAM DE PROPAGANDA E DEFEZA MACONICA – Maceio, Alagoas. 16 Maio-Jul, Out 1899; 12 Jul 1901 – 1,5,6 – bl Biblioteca [072]
MALHEUR ENTERPRISE – Vale, OR. -w. 1929-33, 1938-52 – 1 – 216.00 – us Oregon Hist [071]
MALHEUR ENTERPRISE – Vale, OR. -w. 20 Nov 1909-17 Aug 1929, 5 rolls; 4 Jan 1934-26 Dec 1935, 1 roll; 1 Jan 1953-. – 1 – us U.O. Library [071]
MALHEUR GAZETTE – Vale, OR. -w. 18 Jan 1900-5 Nov 1908. 2 rolls – 1 – us U.O. Library [071]
Mali *see*
- ECONOMIE ET PLAN ET DEVELOPPEMENT
- JOURNAL OFFICIEL DE LA REPUBLIC DU MALI
- LE PLAN QUINQUENNAL 1974-1978 DE DEVELOPPEMENT
Mali. Direction Generale du Plan et de la Statistique *see* PROGRAMME TRIENNAL DE REDRESSEMENT ECONOMIQUE ET FINANCIER 1970-1972
MALI (FORMERLY FRENCH SUDAN) : ANNUAIRE STATISTIQUE DE LA REPUBLIQUE DU MALI 1963-1973 / Mali (formerly French Sudan). Service de la Statistique Generale de la Comptabilite Nationale et de la Mecanographie – (1967 not publ. Coll title: African Official Statistical Serials, 1867-1982) – 25mf – 9 – £210.00 – uk Chadwyck [960]
Mali (formerly French Sudan). Service de la Statistique Generale de la Comptabilite Nationale et de la Mecanographie *see* MALI (FORMERLY FRENCH SUDAN)
Mali. Ministere du Plan et de l'Economie Rurale *see* RAPPORT SUR LE PLAN QUINQUENNAL DE DEVELOPPEMENT ECONOMIQUE ET SOCIAL DE LA REPUBLIQUE DU MALI, 1961-1965
Maliakovskogo, Vladimira *see* GEROI I ZHERTVY REVOLIUTSII
MALIBU-TOPANGA NEWS – Santa Monica, CA. 1957-1977 – 1r – 1 – $50.00 – R03521 – us Library Micro [071]
Malik, Adam *see* RIWAJAT DAN PERDJUANGAN SEKITAR PROKLAMASI KEMERDEKAAN INDONESIA 17 AUGUSTUS 1945
MALIKI LAW : BEING A SUMMARY FROM FRENCH TRANSLATIONS OF MUKHTASAR OP SIDI KHALIL / Ishaq al-Jundi, Khalil ibn – London: Luzac, 1916 – us Res Libr [260]
MALIN ENTERPRISE – Malin, OR. -w. 29 Mar 1934-23 Aug 1934. 1 roll – 1 – us U.O. Library [071]
Malin, James C *see* HISTORY OF THE RECENT AGRICULTURAL POLICY OF THE UNITED STATES
MALIN PROGRESS – Malin OR. May 13 1926-Feb 9 1928 – 1 – us U.O. Library [071]

Malingoudis, Phaedon *see* DIE NACHRICHTEN DES NIKETAS CHONIATES UEBER DIE ENTSTEHUNG DES ZWEITEN BULGARISCHEN STAATES

Malinin, D I *see* CHTO CHITAT' PO RUSSKOI LITERATURE 19 VEKA?

MALINO CONFERENCE *see*
- CONFERENTIE? PERMOESJAWARATAN MALINO, 15-24 JULY 1946
- KESIMPOELAN2 DAN KEPOETOESAN2 MOETAMAR DI MALINO

Malinowski, Bronislaw *see* THE SEXUAL LIFE OF SAVAGES IN NORTHWESTERN MELANESIA; AN ETHNOGRAPHIC ACCOUNT OF COURTSHIP, MARRIAGE, AND FAMILY LIFE AMOUNG THE NATIVES OF THE TROBRIAND ISLANDS, BRITISH NEW GUINEA

MALINOWSKI'S SOCIOLOGICAL THEORIES / Gluckman, M – 7 – uk Microform Academic [960]

Malissen, M *see* INVESTISSEMENT ET FINANCEMENT

Malitskogo, AL *see* GRAZHDANSKII KODEKS SOVETSKIKH RESPUBLIK

Malitz, Bruno *see* STADT IM STURM

Maliye, Nezareti *see* TAHSILAT-I 'UMUMIYEYI NATIK IHSAIYAT-I MALIYE MECMUASI

Malkhi, R M *see* LIKKUTIM LA-PERUSH AL HA-TORAH

Malkins, S E *see*
- SBORNIK VAZHNEISHIKH POSTANOVLENII PO TRUDU

Mall, E *see* HARROWING OF HELL

Mallada, DL *see* MEMORIAS DE LA COMISION DEL MAPA GEOLOGICO DE ESPANA. MEMORIA GEOLOGICA-MINERA DE LA PROVINCIA DE CACERES

Mallakh, R. El *see* THE ECONOMICS OF RAPID GROWTH. MIDDLE EAST JOURNAL

Mallalieu, W F *see* THE HISTORY OF CHRISTIANITY

Mallemans de Messanges, Cl *see* REPONSE A UNE CRITIQUE SATYRIQUE (CONTRE L'ACADEMIE)

Mallery *see* DIRECTORY AND REFERENCE BOOK OF SCHOHARIE COUNTY

Malleson, George Bruce *see* AMBUSHES AND SURPRISES: BEING A DESCRIPTION OF SOME OF THE MOST FAMOUS INSTANCES OF THE LEADING INTO AMBUSH AND THE SURPRISE OF ARMIES, FROM THE TIME OF HANNIBAL TO THE PERIOD OF THE INDIAN MUTINY

Mallet, A *see* LES TRAVAUX DE MARS

Mallet, Bernard *see* THE PRINCIPLE OF PROGRESSION IN TAXATION

Mallie, Augusto S *see*
- ACUERDOS DEL EXTINGUIDO CABILDO DE BUENOS AIRES
- ACUERDOS DEL EXTINGUIDO CABILDO DE BUENOS AIRES...
- ACUERDOS DEL EXTINGUIDO CABILDO DE BUENOS AIRES. SERIE 2, TOMO 4 (1719 A 1722). BUENOS AIRES, 1927
- ACUERDOS DEL EXTINGUIDO CABILDO DE BUENOS AIRES. SERIE 2, TOMO 6 1729-1733; SERIE 3, TOMO 5 1774-76; SERIE 4, TOMO 5 1812-1813. BUENOS AIRES, 1918-1928

Mallmann, Jacob E *see* HISTORICAL PAPERS ON SHELTER ISLAND

Malloch, D Macleod *see*
- LAW AND LAUGHTER

Mallock, William Hurrell *see*
- THE RECONSTRUCTION OF RELIGIOUS BELIEF
- RELIGION AS A CREDIBLE DOCTRINE: A STUDY OF THE FUNDAMENTAL DIFFICULTY

Mallory, Daniel *see* THE LIFE AND SPEECHES OF THE HON. HENRY CLAY

Mallory, John *see* QUARE IMPEDIT. IN TWO PARTS

Malloy, William M et al *see* MALLOY'S TREATIES

MALLOY'S TREATIES : CONVENTIONS, INTERNATIONAL ACTS, PROTOCOLS, AND AGREEMENTS BETWEEN THE U.S. AND OTHER POWERS, 1776-1937 / Malloy, William M et al – 4v (all publ) – 61mf – 9 – $91.00 – LLMC 80-917 – us L.L.M.C. [975]

MALMBERGET – Lulea, Sweden. 1884-97 – 7r – 1 – sw Kungliga [072]

Malmesbury Abbey *see* REGISTRUM MALMESBURIENSE (RS72)

MALMFALTENS TIDNINGAR – Lulea, Sweden. 1901-04 – 1 reel – 1 – sw Kungliga [072]

MALMFALTSBLADET – Lulea, Sweden. 1905-06 – 1 reel – 1 – sw Kungliga [072]

MALMO ALLEHANDA – (Allehanda, 1827-28; Malmo Nya Allehanda, 1840-93) – Malmo, Sweden. 1828-39 – 35r – 1 – sw Kungliga [072]

MALMO NYA ALLEHANDA *see* MALMO ALLEHANDA

MALMOEHUS LAENS TIDNING – Lund, Sweden. 1897-98 – 1 – sw Kungliga [072]

MALMOTIDNINGEN – (Suppl: Solglimten 1899-1907) – Malmo, Sweden. 1895-1907 – 27r – 1 – sw Kungliga [072]

Malmusi, Giuseppe *see* ANALISI DEL QUARESIMALE DEL PADRE PAOLO SEGNERI

MALNUTRITION AND INFECTION IN THE CLASSROOM / Pollitt, Ernesto – 1990 – 211p – 9 – 92-3-102662-3 – fr UNESCO [360]

Malo, J-H *see*
- LE BOUQUET
- L'IMPARTIAL

Malombra, B *see* NVOVA CANZONE NELLA FELICISSIMA VITTORIA CONTRA INFEDELI

Malon, Benoit *see* LE SOCIALISME INTEGRAL

Malone, Edward *see* THE MONK AND THE MARTYR

Malone, KN *see* THE EFFECT OF BODY POSITION ON SPINAL CORD INJURED SWIMMERS

Maloney, John Philip *see* CASES AND MATERIALS ON SECURITY TRANSACTIONS

Malonga, Jean *see* LA LEGENDE DE M'PHOUMOU MA MAZONO

MALOROSIYA V GODU 1767 / Avsieenko, Vasilii G E – 1864 – 1r – 1 – us Ross [947]

Malot, Hector Henri *see* SANS FAMILLE

Malou, J B *see* CHRONICON MONASTERII ALDENBURGENSIS

Malouet, Pierre-Victor *see* MEMOIRE SUR L'ESCLAVAGE DES NEGRES DANS LEQUEL ON DISCUTE LES MOTIFS PROPOSES POUR LEUR AFFRANCHISSEMENT, CEUX QUI S'Y OPPOSENT ET LES MOYENS PRATICABLES POUR AMELIORER LEUR SORT

Malouin, Paul J *see* DESCRIPTION ET DETAILS DES ARTS DU MEUNIER, DU VERMICELIER ET DU BOULANGER

MALOZNACHITEL'NOE PRESTUPLENIE I TOVARISHCHESKII SUD / Chugaev, A P – Kazan, 1966. 298p. Considers the role of comrades' courts in dealing with petty crimes: by a Tatar jurist. BR-8436- – 9 – ne IDC [340]

Malpartida de Caceres. Ayuntamiento *see*
- EXPOSICION DE LA OBRA GRAFICA ORIGINAL MIRO EN EXTREMADURA
- FERIAS Y FIESTAS 1973

Malpartida de Plasencia. Ayuntamiento *see*
- FERIAS DE GANADOS DURANTE...SEPTIEMBRE 1962
- FERIAS Y FIESTAS DE 1974
- FERIAS Y FIESTAS DE JUNIO. 1963
- FERIAS Y FIESTAS LOS DIAS...1960
- ORDENANZAS MUNICIPALES

MALPARTIDA LA SU CELESTIAL PATRONA LA SANTISIMA VIRGEN DE LA LUZ. ANO 1973 – Plasencia: Imp. La Victoria, 1973 – 1 – sp Bibl Santa Ana [946]

Malpiere, DB de *see* LA CHINE, MOEURS, USAGES, COSTUMES...

Malpighi, M *see*
- DE VISCERUM STRUCTURA EXERCITATIO ANATOMICA
- DISSERTATIO EPISTOLICA DE FORMATIONE PULLI...
- OPERA OMNIA

MALPIGHIA / Rassegna mensuale di botanica – Messina et al. v1-28. 1887-1917/1920 – 216mf – 9 – ne IDC [580]

Malpuss, Samuel *see* DAYBOOK AND ACCOUNTS

Malraux, Andre *see* THE FASCIST THREAT TO CULTURE; A SPEECH DELIVERED ON MARCH 8, 1937, IN THE NEW LECTURE HALL, HARVARD UNIVERSITY

Malta *see*
- DEVELOPMENT PLAN FOR THE MALTESE ISLANDS, 1959-64
- DEVELOPMENT PLAN FOR THE MALTESE ISLANDS, 1964-69
- GOVERNMENT GAZETTE
- REVIEW OF DEVELOPMENT PLAN FOR THE MALTESE ISLANDS, 1959-64

MALTA GOVERNMENT GAZETTE – 1950-70 – 37r – 1 – us Ross [324]

Malta. Office of the Prime Minister *see*
- DEVELOPMENT PLAN FOR MALTA, 1973-1980
- OUTLINE OF DEVELOPMENT PLAN FOR MALTA. 1973-1980
- THIRD DEVELOPMENT PLAN FOR MALTESE ISLANDS 1969-74

MALTBY GENEALOGY MSS / Verill, D – 9 – $15.00 – us Godfrey [920]

Maltby, T J *see* THE GENJAM DISTRICT MANUAL

Maltby, William S *see* THE LUTHERAN REFORMATION, SOURCES 1500-1650

Malte-Brun, Conrad *see* UNIVERSAL GEOGRAPHY

Malte-Brun, Victor Adolphe *see* LES DERNIERES EXPLORATIONS DU DOCTEUR ALFRED PENEY DANS LA REGION DU HAUT FLEUVE BLANC

THE MALTESE JOURNAL – New York. v. 1-12. 1935-46 – 1 – 80.00 – cn McLaren [977]

MALTESE MANUSCRIPTS AND ARCHIVES MICROFILMED FOR HMML – (not for bulk or commercial purchase or resale) – One printed vol. Handlist of CEM Archives available from HMML – 1 – $35.00r + $10.00 per owning library – us H.M.M.L. [090]

MALTHE OU LISLE-ADAM: DERNIER GRAND-MAITRE DE RHODES ET PREMIER GRAND-MAITRE DE MALTHE: POEME / Privat de Fontanilles – Paris: Huart et Moreau fils, Durand, 1749. xxiv,199p. 3 fiches. (Literature Collection) – 9 – 8.00 – fr Bibl Nationale [810]

Malthus, Thomas Robert *see* AN ESSAY ON THE PRINCIPLE OF POPULATION: OR, A VIEW OF ITS PAST AND PRESENT EFFECTS ON HUMAN HAPPINESS.

Maltitz, Gotthilf August, Freiherr von *see* VERMISCHTE SCHRIFTEN

Maltret, C L *see*
- ARCANA HISTORIA (CBH 3,3)
- DE AEDIFICIIS DN. IUSTINIANI LIBRI 6 (CBH 3,2)
- HISTORIARUM SUI TEMPORIS LIBRI 8 (CBH 3,1)

Maltz, Albert *see* THE WAY THINGS ARE AND OTHER STORIES

Maltzahn, Wendelin von *see*
- SCHILLER'S BRIEFWECHSEL MIT SEINER SCHWESTER CHRISTOPHINE UND SEINEM SCHWAGER REINWALD
- SCHILLER'S UND GOETHE'S XENIEN-MANUSCRIPT

MALUM PASA – (Followed Merhumpasa in the Markopasa set) – Nos. 1-6 (1947) – 1mf – 9 – $10.50 – us MEDOC [949]

MALVACEAE, BUETTNERIACEAE. TILIACEAE / Kunth, C S – Paris. 1822. B-5992 2 – 8 – ne IDC [580]

MALVAS Y ORTIGAS – Caceres, 1904 – 5 – sp Bibl Santa Ana [073]

LAS MALVINAS HANSIDO, SON Y SER AN ARGENTINAS : PUBLICACI ON DISPUESTA POR EL HONORABLE SENADO EL 23 DE JUNIO DE 1950 / Argentina. Congreso de la Nacion. Senado de la Nacion – Buenos Aires: Impr. del Congreso de la Nacion, 1951 – 1 – CSUXADJ1297-B – us Hoover Inst Photo [320]

Malykhih, P *see*
- VORONEZHSKII LITERATURNYI SBORNIK

Malyshev, VI *see* UST'-TSILEMSKIE RUKOPISNYE SBORNIKI 16-20 VV

Malzac, R P *see* DICTIONNAIRE FRANCAIS-MALGACHE

Malzac, V *see* HISTOIRE DU ROYAUME HOVA

MAMA KOMMT! : HUMORESKE / Bluethgen, Viktor – Leipzig: M Hesse, [18–?] – 1 – us U.W. Library [870]

MAMBO LEO – Dar-es-Salaam, Tanzania. -m. Jan 1948-Aug 1958; Feb 1959-April 1962. 3 reels – 1 – uk British Libr Newspaper [072]

Mame, Alfred et fils *see* A TRAVERS LE ZANZIBAR, VOYAGE DANS L'OUDOE, L'OUZIGOUA, L'OUKWERE, L'OUKAMI ET L'OUSAGARA

Mameev, S N *see* MATERIALY DLIA BIBLIOGRAFII SIBIRI

Mamin-Sibiriak, D N *see* D. N. MAMIN-SIBIRIAK. RUKOPISI I PEREPISKA

MAMMA / Broughton, Rhoda – British Fiction Archive: Unit 4 – 9 – uk Bell [830]

MAMMALIA FAUNA JAPONICAE / Siebold, P F von – 2065 2. 1850 – 8 – ne IDC [590]

MAMMALS IN THE SEAS – it F.A.O. [590]

THE MAMMALS OF AUSTRALIA / Gould, J – 2060 2. 3 v. (1845)-1863 – 8 – ne IDC [590]

THE MAMMALS OF INDIA / Jerdon, T C – Z-278 2. 1867 – 8 – ne IDC [590]

THE MAMMILLARIA HANDBOOK / Craig, R T – 1945 – 1. 36.00; ; 7 – uk Microform Academic [590]

MA'MOER – (Lacking: 1946, V.1(4, pp. 121-162)) – Djakarta, 1945-1946 – 12mf – 9 – ne IDC [950]

Mamontov, I I *see*
- UKAZATEL' IZDANII BYVSHAGO MINISTERSTVA ZEMLEDELIIA I GOSUDARSTVENNYKH IMUSHCHESTV PO SEL'SKOKHOZIAISTENNOI I LESNOI CHASTI VYSHEDSHIKH ZA 1903 GOD
- UKAZATEL' IZDANII MINISTERSTVA ZEMLEDELIIA I GOSUDARSTVENNYKH IMUSHCHESTV PO SEL'SKOKHOZIAISTVENNOI I LESNOI CHASTI VYSHEDSIKH SO VREMENINUCHREZHDENIIA ETOGO VEDOMSTVA (1894-1900)
- UKAZATEL' IZDANII MINISTERSTVA ZEMLEDELIIA I GOSUDARSTVENNYKH IMUSHCHESTV PO SEL'SKOKHOZIAISTVENNOI I LESNOI CHASTI VYSHEDSKIKH ZA 1901 GOD

MAMTIK SOD / Kaempf, Saul Isaac – Prague. 1861. BJ-32-5 1 – 9 – ne IDC [800]

MA'MURET'UEL-AZIZ – (No. 1789 (8 Subat 1338[1922])) – Elazig: Vilayet Matbaasi. Yayimliyan: Ma'muret'uel-aziz Vilayeti, 1883-? – 1mf – 9 – $10.00 – us MEDOC [949]

MAN – A Journal of the Anarchist Ideal and Movement. San Francisco. v. 1, no. 1-v. 8, no. 4. Jan 1933-Apr 1940 – 1 – us NY Public [073]

MAN – (Cont: Dominion Sanitary Journal. Cont by: Canada Health Journal (Ottawa, Ont: 1886)) – Ottawa: Man, [1885-1886] (Ottawa: Citizen Print. and Pub. Co.) – 9 – cn C.I.H.M. [614]

MAN : A JOURNAL OF THE ANARCHIST IDEAL AND MOVEMENT – San Francisco. v1-8. 1933-40 – 1r – 1 – us Ross [320]

MAN – London, UK. 1833. -irr. 15 feet – 1 – uk British Libr Newspaper [072]

MAN : A REVELATION OF GOD / Ackerman, George Everett – [2nd ed]. NY: Phillips & Hunt, 1888 – 1mf – 9 – 0-8370-2038-7 – 1985-0038 – us A.T.L.A. [301]

MAN *see* THE CANADA HEALTH JOURNAL

MAN! : A JOURNAL OF THE ANARCHIST IDEAL AND MOVEMENT – 1-8 2+4 (all publ). 1933-40 – 1 reel – 1 – $115.00 – us UPA [335]

MAN, A REVELATION OF GOD / Ackerman, George Everett – New York: Phillips & Hunt, 1888.1 fiche – 9 – us A.T.L.A. [240]

MAN AND BEAST, HERE AND HEREAFTER / Wood, J G – New York: George Routledge, n.d.484p – 1 – us U.W. Library [150]

MAN AND HIS SUPERSTITIONS / Read, Carveth – 2nd ed. Cambridge: The University Press, 1925. xvi,278p – 1 – us U.W. Library [390]

MAN AND MEDICINE; AN INTRODUCTION TO MEDICAL KNOWLEDGE / Sigerist, Henry Ernest – Introd. by William H. Welch. Margaret Galt Boise, trans. New York: W.W. Norton Co., (c1932). x,340p – 1 – us U.W. Library [610]

THE MAN AND THE MASTER / Freeman, James Edward – New York:Thomas Whittaker, c1906 – 1mf – 9 – 0-8370-3187-7 – 1985-1187 – us A.T.L.A. [240]

MAN AND THE UNIVERSE / Lodge, Oliver – London: Methuen, 1909 – 1mf – 9 – us A.T.L.A. [240]

MAN AND WOMAN : A STUDY OF HUMAN SECONDARY SEXUAL CHARACTERS / Ellis, Havelock – London: W. Scott; New York: Charles Scribner's Sons – 1 roll – 1 – 1-55879-550-2 – uk Libr Preservation [150]

MAN AND WOMAN: OR THE LAW OF HONOR APPLIED TO THE SOLUTION OF THE PROBLEM, WHY ARE SO MANY MORE WOMEN THAN MEN CHRISTIANS? / Slaughter, Philip – 1860 – 9 – us A.T.L.A. [240]

THE MAN IN A TRANCE : REV. WM. TENNENT / Boudinot, Elias – 1837 – 1 – $50.00 – us Presbyterian [240]

MAN IN ARID LANDS : NOMADS IN TRANSITION – (English and French) – 9 – 92-3-001952-6 – fr UNESCO [304]

MAN IN GENESIS AND IN GEOLOGY : OR, THE BIBLICAL ACCOUNT OF MAN'S CREATION / Thompson, Joseph Parrish – (Includes bibliographical references) – New York: Samuel R Wells, 1870 – 1mf – 9 – 0-8370-5521-0 – 1985-3521 – us A.T.L.A. [210]

MAN IN INDIA – Ranchi. 1921-64. v1-44. Lacking: 1963, v. 43. – 269mf – 8 – ne IDC [073]

MAN IN THE PRESENT JAVANESE MYSTICISM / Hadiwijono, Harun – SE-6283 1. 1967 – 9 – ne IDC [290]

THE MAN OF FEELING, AND JULIA DE ROUBIGNE / Mackenzie, H – Chiswick, 1822 – 4mf – 9 – ne IDC [830]

THE MAN OF GALILEE / Haygood, Atticus Greene – New York: Hunt & Eaton, 1890, c1889 – 1mf – 9 – 0-8370-3540-6 – 1985-1540 – us A.T.L.A. [240]
THE MAN OF THE WORLD / Mackenzie, H – Dresden, 1792. 2v – 5mf – 9 – ne IDC [830]
MAN, THE SOCIAL CREATOR / Lloyd, Henry Demarest – New York: Doubleday, Page, 1906 – 1mf – us A.T.L.A. [300]
MAN TO MAN, THE STORY OF INDUSTRIAL DEMOCRACY / Leitch, John – 1920. 280p. 1 fiche. (24x) – 9 – 1.00f – at Libertarian Micro [320]
THE MAN VERSUS THE STATE / Spencer, Herbert – 1881. With: A Bibliography of Herbert Spencer, by J. Rumney. 1 fiche (24x) – 9 – 1.00f – at Libertarian Micro [320]
THE MAN WHO KNEW; HOW HE BROUGHT THE GOOD NEWS THAT THE KINGDOM OF GOD IS WITHIN US, AND THAT WE MAY PUT OURSELVES IN TUNE WITH THE CENTRE OF LIFE / Trine, Ralph Waldo – Indianapolis, New York: The Bobbs-Merrill Co., c1936. 204p – 1 – us U.W. Library [240]
MANAGEMENT – v.1-. Sep. 1979- – 1,5,6,9 – us UMI [650]
MANAGEMENT ABSTRACTS – 1961-73 – 9 – uk Microform Academic [650]
MANAGEMENT ACCOUNTING – 1965- – 1; 1978- 5,6,9 – us UMI [650]
MANAGEMENT ACCOUNTING – New York, 1964-86 – 16r – 1 – us Ross [650]
MANAGEMENT ACCOUNTING – (See also: Cost Accountant) – v1- 1919- 1; v57- 6; v58- 1976- 9 – us UMI [650]
MANAGEMENT ADVISOR – v1-11 1964-74 1; v8-11 1971-74 5,6 – us UMI [650]
MANAGEMENT AND UTILIZATION OF PASTURES, EAST AFRICA – 1978 – 3pts 142p – it F.A.O. [636]
MANAGEMENT BEHAVIORS OF WOMEN DIRECTORS IN LEISURE SERVICES AGENCIES IN THE UNITED STATES / Vanderveer, Beth – 1989 – 148p 2mf – 9 – $8.00 – us Microform Publ [650]
MANAGEMENT BY TASK FORCES: A MANUAL ON THE OPERATION OF INTERDISCIPLINARY TEAMS / Bass, Lawrence W – 1975. 197p. ISBN: 0-912338-10-5 – 9 – 9.50 – us Lomond [650]
MANAGEMENT: CONCEPTS AND PRACTICE / Brown, Fred R – 1977. 200p – 9 – 0-912338-16-4 – us Lomond [650]
MANAGEMENT CONCEPTS FOR SMALL-SCALE FISHERIES : ECONOMIC AND SOCIAL ASPECTS – 1988 – 58p – it F.A.O. [650]
MANAGEMENT DATA LIST (ML), ML-MARINE CORPS / U.S. National Technical Information Service – Quarterly. Cumulative listing of National Stock Numbers – 9 – us N.T.I.S. [350]
MANAGEMENT DATA LIST (ML), ML-NAVY / U.S. National Technical Information Service – Quarterly. Cumulative listing of National Stock Numbers – 9 – us N.T.I.S. [350]
MANAGEMENT FOR FRESHWATER FISH CULTURE : FARMS AND FISH STOCKS – it F.A.O. [639]
MANAGEMENT FOR FRESHWATER FISH CULTURE : PONDS AND WATER PRACTICES – it F.A.O. [639]
MANAGEMENT IN PRACTICE – 1970-77 – 1 – us UMI [650]
MANAGEMENT INTERNATIONAL REVIEW – v1- 1961- 1; v11- 5,6; v15- 9 – us UMI [650]
MANAGEMENT JAPAN – v11-. 1978- – 1 – us UMI [650]
MANAGEMENT OF AGRICULTURAL SCHOOLS AND COLLEGES : A MANUAL FOR PRACTICAL USE – 1985 – 99p – it F.A.O. [370]
MANAGEMENT OF COASTAL LAGOON FISHERIES – 1984 – 2v 797p – it F.A.O. [338]
MANAGEMENT OF COASTAL LAGOON FISHERIES AND AQUACULTURE IN ITALY – 1988 – 110p – it F.A.O. [639]
MANAGEMENT OF CROCODILES IN CAPTIVITY – 1989 – 69p – it F.A.O. [590]
MANAGEMENT OF CYPRUS FISHERIES – 1986 – 46p – it F.A.O. [639]
MANAGEMENT OF DISTANCE LEARNING SYSTEMS / Rumble, Greville – 1992 – 120p – 9 – 92-803-1145-X – fr UNESCO [370]
MANAGEMENT OF FOREST INDUSTRIES – 1986 – 316p – it F.A.O. [650]
MANAGEMENT OF GLOBAL ANIMAL GENETIC RESOURCES – 1992 – 314p – it F.A.O. [636]
MANAGEMENT OF GROUP FEEDING PROGRAMMES – 1982 – 163p – it F.A.O. [640]
MANAGEMENT OF GYPSIFEROUS SOILS – 1990 – 89p – it F.A.O. [631]
MANAGEMENT OF LIVING RESOURCES IN THE MEDITERRANEAN COASTAL AREA – 1981 – 356p – it F.A.O. [333]
MANAGEMENT OF MULTISPECIES RESOURCES AND MULTI-GEAR FISHERIES : EXPERIENCE IN COASTAL WATERS AROUND JAPAN – 1989 – 77p – it F.A.O. [636]
MANAGEMENT OF NATURAL RESOURCES IN AFRICA : TRADITIONAL STRATEGIES AND MODERN DECISION-MAKING – 1978 – 81p – 9 – 92-3-101587-7 – fr UNESCO [333]
MANAGEMENT OF TROPICAL MOIST FORESTS IN AFRICA – 1989 – 172p – it F.A.O. [634]
MANAGEMENT OF UPLAND WATERSHEDS : PARTICIPATION OF THE MOUNTAIN COMMUNITIES – 1983 2nd print 1986 – 216p – it F.A.O. [631]
MANAGEMENT OF VERTISOLS IN SUB-SAHARAN AFRICA : PROCEEDINGS OF A CONFERENCE HELD AT ILCA, ADDIS ABABA, ETHIOPIA, 31 AUGUST-4 SEPTEMBER 1987 / ed by Jutzi, S C et al – 1988 – 9 – $31.00 – 92-9053-143-6 – et ILRI [631]
MANAGEMENT OF VICUNA : ITS CONTRIBUTION TO RURAL DEVELOPMENT IN THE HIGH ANDES OF PERU – 1985 – 43p – it F.A.O. [630]
MANAGEMENT OF WORLD WASTES – v26-. 1983- – 1,5,6,9 – us UMI [628]
MANAGEMENT PERSONALIA / Manullang, Manginar – Includes legislation. SE-5100 1. 1964 – 9 – ne IDC [650]
MANAGEMENT PERSONALIA / Manullang, Manginar – Includes legislation. SE-6074 1. 1967 – 9 – ne IDC [650]
MANAGEMENT PROPERTIES OF FERRASOLS – 1979 – 120p – it F.A.O. [550]
MANAGEMENT REVIEW – (v. 58- 1969- 5,6. v. 64- 1975- 9) – v. 1- 1914- – 1 – us UMI [600]
MANAGEMENT SCIENCE – v1- 1954- 1; v17- 5,6; v22- 9 – us UMI [650]
MANAGEMENT SERVICES – v. 20-. 1976- – 1,5,6,9 – us UMI [650]
MANAGEMENT STRATEGIES FOR INLAND FISHERIES IN THE SAHEL : SUMMARY OF THE PAPERS PRESENTED AT THE SEMINAR ON FISHERIES PLANNING AND MANAGEMENT IN THE CONVENTIONAL BASIN OF LAKE CHAD, N'DJAMENA, 1990... – 1991 – 158p – it F.A.O. [338]
MANAGEMENT; SUATU PENGANTAR / Panglaykim, J – SE-10,181 1. 1960 – 9 – ne IDC [650]
MANAGEMENT SYSTEMS FOR RIVERINE FISHERIES – 1985 – 92p – it F.A.O. [650]
MANAGEMENT WORLD – v1- 1972- 1; v5- 5,6,9 – us UMI [650]
MANAGEMENT'S HIDDEN ENEMY-AND WHAT YOU CAN DO ABOUT IT / Brown, David S – 1987. 123p. ISBN:0-912338-60-1 – 9 – 12.50 – us Lomond [650]
THE MANAGER – 1950-66.Continues: Industry – 1 – uk Microform Academic [650]
MANAGERIAL AND DECISION ECONOMICS: MDE – (1982-. 1,5,6,9) – v1-. 1980- – 1 – us UMI [650]
MANAGERIAL PLANNING – v1- 1952- 1; v19- 5,6; v24- 9 – us UMI [650]
MANAGER-MAGAZINE – (1971-1992 DM4,188.00 set DM215.00y; Index, 1971-1992 DM875.00 set DM40.00y; Index, 1993 DM42.00y) – 1993 – 9 – DM224.00y – gw IOS [650]
THE MANAGIL EXTENSION / Sudan. Ministry of Social Affairs – The achievement of the Republic of Sudan. 1957? BNE-7675 1 – 9 – ne IDC [360]
THE MANAGIL SOUTH-WESTERN EXTENSION; AN EXTENSION TO THE GESIRA SCHEME; AN EXAMPLE OF AN IRRIGATION DEVELOPMENT PROJECT IN THE REPUBLIC OF THE SUDAN / Shaw, D J – 1965. BNE-7684 1 – 9 – ne IDC [631]
MANAGING – v.1-. 1979- – 1,5,6,9 – us UMI [650]
MANAGING APPEALS IN FEDERAL COURTS – Washington: GPO, 1988 – 9mf – 9 – $13.50 – LLMC 95-341 – us L.L.M.C. [340]
MANAGING COMPLEXITY / Stephens, James C – Work, technology, resources and human relations.1v. Rev. ed. 1977. ISBN: 0-912338-14-8 – 9 – 9.50 – us Lomond [650]
MANAGING EMPLOYEE INVOLVEMENT / Meldrum, Bill – Based on New Zealand case studies. 3 fiches (29x) – 9 – 1.00f – at Libertarian Micro [320]
MANAGING THE FARM / Wisconsin. College of Agricultural and Life Sciences. Dept. of Agricultural Economics – Feb. 1957-Jun 20, 1968 – 1,5 – us Spaulding [650]
MANAGING THE LARGE ORGANIZATION: ISSUES, IDEAS, PRECEPTS, INNOVATIONS / Brown, David S – 1982. 300p. ISBN: 0-912338-34-2 – 9 – 19.50 – us Lomond [650]
MANAGING THE OCEAN: RESOURCES, RESEARCH, LAW / ed by Richardson, Jacques – 1985. 407p. ISBN:0-912338-50-4 – 9 – 19.50 – us Lomond [333]
Manalastas Laraya, Consorcia *see* BATAYANG AKLAT SA WIKA
EL MANANA : SEMI-WEEKLY EDITION – Mexico City, Mexico. June 15 1911-Feb 28 1913 – 1r – 1 – us L of C Photodup [072]
UNA MANANA GRIS / Cerezo Moreno, Antonio – Madrid: Rivadeneyra, S.A. 1963 – sp Bibl Santa Ana [946]
MANAOS : ORGAO DE TODAS AS CLASSES – Manaos, Amazonas. 1 Nov 1887 – 1,5,6 – bl Biblioteca [072]
MANAOS : ORGAO DO PARTIDO REPUBLICANO – Manaos, Amazonas. 20 Fev 1900 – 1,5,6 – bl Biblioteca [072]
MANAOS NATAL : ARTTES E LETRAS – Manaos, Amazonas. 25 Dez 1903 – 1,5,6 – bl Biblioteca [072]
MANARO MERCURY (COOMA) – Feb 16 1869-Nov 6 1886 – 9 – at Pascoe [072]
Manas Marquecho, Jose Luis *see* LUMI NOSIDADES
Manassis, Constantini *see*
– BREVIARIUM HISTORIAE METRICUM (CSHB 29)
– BREVIARIUM HISTORICUM (CBH 12,1)
MANATREE RIVER JOURNAL-HERALD – Bradenton. Fl. 1918-Apr 1926 – 1 – us P.K. Yonge [071]
MANAWATU DAILY EVENING TIMES – Palmerston North. New Zealand. -d. 22 Jun 1899-Dec 1901. (5 reels) – 1 – uk British Libr Newspaper [072]
Manby, G W *see* JOURNAL OF A VOYAGE TO GREENLAND, IN YEAR 1821
Mancebo, Samuel T *see* ELEMENTS OF THE STRUCTURE OF AGRICULTURAL EDUCATION IN THE PHILIPPINES
MANCHERLEY FORM ZU PREDIGEN VON DEN FUERNEMBSTEN STUECKEN SO IN DER CHRISTLICHEN KIRCHEN TEGLICH GELERT VND GETRIEBEN SOLLEN WERDEN / Huberinus, Caspar – Nuernberg: J. vom Berg & U. Neuber, 157. [G.F.: 22.3] – 5mf – 9 – HUB-80/1 – ne IDC [240]
MANCHESTER 1624-1892 – (mf ed 1989) – 77mf – 9 – 0-87623-098-2 – us Holbrook [920]
MANCHESTER 1661-1849 – (Mf 1T-2T: Vital Records 1661-1745. Mf 1T-4T: Births 1715-94. Mf 4T-6T: Marriages & Intentions 1746-1811. Mf 5T: Deaths 1760-1809. Mf 6T-7T: Births 1769-1843. Mf 7T-8T: Publishments 1811-49. Mf 8T-10T: Marriages 1686-1844. Mf 9T: Births 1719-40. Mf 9T-10T: Deaths 1792-1844. Mf 10T: Births 1843-49; Marriages 1844-49. Mf 11T: Deaths 1844-49) – (mf ed 1997) – 11mf – 9 – 0-87623-284-5 – us Holbrook [920]
MANCHESTER AND SALFORD STREET DIRECTORIES – 1818-1969 – 1 – uk Manchester Libr [380]
Manchester Center, Vermont. First Baptist Church and Society *see* RECORDS
Manchester Chamber of Commerce and Industry. Archives *see* AFRICAN SECTIONAL COMMITTEE RECORDS
MANCHESTER CITY NEWS – Manchester: Manchester City News Co Ltd, jan 7-un 24 1899 – 1r – 1 – us Res Libr [072]
MANCHESTER COURIER – Manchester, Great Britain. 1825-1916 – 1 – uk Manchester Libr [072]
MANCHESTER DAILY EXAMINER AND TIMES – England. -d. Jan 1861-Dec 1862. (8 reels) – 1 – uk British Libr Newspaper [072]
Manchester, Diane L *see* EFFECTS OF AGE, VELOCITY, AND ADDED MASS ON POSTURAL ADJUSTMENTS ASSOCIATED WITH A RAPID ARMRAISING MOVEMENT
MANCHESTER EVENING NEWS TO DATE – 1 – uk Manchester Libr [072]
MANCHESTER FIRST BAPTIST CHURCH. MANCHESTER, VERMONT : CHURCH RECORDS – 1781-1900. 1314p – 1 – us Baptist [240]
MANCHESTER GAZETTE AND WEEKLY ADVERTISER – Manchester, Great Britain. 1796-1829 – 1 – uk Manchester Libr [072]
MANCHESTER GUARDIAN – Manchester, 1938-1952 – 18r – 1 – cn Preston [971]
MANCHESTER GUARDIAN – Manchester, Great Britain. 1821-1952 – 1 – uk Manchester Libr [072]
MANCHESTER GUARDIAN WEEKLY – July 1919 – 1 – uk Manchester Libr [072]
MANCHESTER HERALD – England.1792-93. -w. 1/2 reel – 1 – uk British Libr Newspaper [072]
MANCHESTER JEWISH TELEGRAPH – Manchester, UK. 30 May-30 Sept 1908 – 1 – uk British Libr Newspaper [072]
MANCHESTER, LANCASHIRE AND CHESHIRE PARISH REGISTERS – 1665-1972 – 1 – uk Manchester Libr [941]
Manchester Literary and Philosophical Society. Manchester *see* MEMOIRS AND PROCEEDINGS
MANCHESTER MAGAZINE – Manchester, Great Britain. 1737-1760 – 1 – uk Manchester Libr [072]
MANCHESTER MERCURY – Manchester. 1752-1830 – 1 – uk Microform Academic [072]
MANCHESTER MERCURY – Manchester, Great Britain. 1752-1830 – 1 – 2480.00 – uk Manchester Libr [072]
Manchester, New Hampshire. Peoples Baptist Church *see* RECORDS
Manchester, New Hampshire. Pine Street Baptist church *see* RECORDS
MANCHESTER NEWS LETTER – Manchester, Great Britain. 1724-1725 – 1 – uk Manchester Libr [072]
MANCHESTER OBSERVER – England. -w. 3 Jan 1818-30 Dec 1820. (1 reel) – 1 – uk British Libr Newspaper [072]
MANCHESTER REVIEW OF POLITICS, LITERATURE AND NEWS – England. -w. Jan-Dec 1861. (1 reel) – 1 – uk British Libr Newspaper [072]
The Manchester Statistical Society. Transactions *see* ECONOMIC AND SOCIAL INVESTIGATIONS IN ENGLAND SINCE 1833
MANCHESTER WEEKLY EXPRESS AND REVIEW – (Weekly Express). England. -w. Jan-Dec 1862. (69 ft) – 1 – uk British Libr Newspaper [072]
MANCHESTER WEEKLY TIMES – 1841-1921 – 1 – uk Manchester Libr [072]
MANCHURIA DAILY NEWS – (Including supplements entitled "Manchuria"). Dairen. China. -d. 19 Oct 1912-May 1940. (63 reels) – 1 – uk British Libr Newspaper [072]
MAN'CHZHURSKAIA KHRESTOMATIIA / Ivanovskii, A O – 2v. Spb. 1893-95. BU-487 2 – 8 – ne IDC [947]
MAN'CHZHURY, IKH IAZYKH I PIS'MENNOST' / Grebenshchikov, A V – (Izvestiia Vostochnago instituta, v. 45). 1912. BU-471 2 – 8 – ne IDC [460]
Mancinus, Thomas *see* PASSIO DOMINI NOSTRI JESU CHRISTI: DAS LEYDEN UND STERBEN UNSERS HERRN JESU CHRISTI.....
Manconumidad Internacional de la Vera *see* ESTATUROS DE LA VE...ANO 1977
Mancourt, C *see* QUATUOR BRILLIANT, TROISIEME, POUR DEUX VIOLONS, ALTO ET VIOLONCELLE
MANDADT NUW UND ORDNUNG VON SCHULTHEISSEN DER WIDERTOEUFFEREN WEGEN – 1597. BME-13 1 – 9 – ne IDC [240]
DIE MANDAEISCHE RELIGION : IHRE ENTWICKLUNG UND GESCHICHTLICHE BEDEUTUNG / Brandt, A J H Wilhelm – Leipzig: J.C. Hinrichs, 1889 – 1mf – us A.T.L.A. [930]
MANDAEISCHE SCHRIFTEN / Brandt, W – Goettingen: Vandenhoeck und Ruprecht, 1893 – 1mf – us A.T.L.A. [930]
THE MANDAING – Rangoon, Burma. May 1961-Jul 1962 – 1 – $98.00 – us L of C Photodup [072]
MANDAING DAILY – Hangoon, Burma. May 1958-Jul 1962 – 18r – 1 – us L of C Photodup [072]
MANDALA AND THE MEN'S MOVEMENT(S) IN THE LIGHT OF FEMINISM / Smith, Clyde – University of North Carolina of Greensboro, 1995 – 1mf – 9 – PE 3670 – us Microform Publ [790]

Mandala, M *see* LA PROTESIS DELLA LITURGIA NEL RITO BIZANTINO-GRECO
MANDALAY AND OTHER CITIES OF THE PAST IN BURMA / O'Conner, V C Scott – London, 1907. 430 pp., pls., maps, plans. BI-1047 2 – 8 – ne IDC [950]
LE MANDAT COLONIAL / Alcandre, J – Paris, 1935 – 2mf – 9 – ILM-1969/1 – ne IDC [340]
EIN MANDAT ETC / Herman, N – Strassburg, Schwan. 1524. BME-39 1 – 9 – ne IDC [240]
LE MANDAT FRANCAIS EN SYRIE ET AU LIBAN / Burckhard, C – Nimes, 1925 – 3mf – 1 – ILM-2154/1 – ne IDC [327]
EYN MANDAT JESU CHRISTI / Herman, N – 1524 – 9 – BME-40 1 – ne IDC [240]
MANDAT JESU CHRISTI *see* EYN MANDAT JESU CHRISTI
EIN MANDAT JESU CHRISTI. AUS DEM ORIGINALI, MIT PRAEFATION AN TAG GEGEBEN DURCH C. PAWLER / Herman, N – Freybergk i. Meissen, G. Hoffmann. 1613. BME-46 1 – 9 – ne IDC [240]
AIN MANDAT JHESU CHRISTI / Herman, N – 1524. BME-41 1 – 9 – ne IDC [240]
EYN MANDAT JHESU CHRISTI, AN ALLE SEYNE GETREWEN / Herman, N – 1524 – 9 – ne IDC [240]
LE MANDAT SUR LA PALESTINE / Baumkoller, A – Paris, 1931 – 3mf – 9 – ILM-2223/1 – ne IDC [327]
MANDATE FOR PALESTINE : LETTER FROM THE SECRETARY TO THE SECRETARY-GENERAL OF THE LEAGUE OF NATIONS OF JULY 1, 1922, IN REPLY TO CARDINAL GASPARRI'S LETTER OF MAY 15, 1922 / Great Britain. Cabinet Secretariat – London, 1922 – 9 – BJ-2865/1 – ne IDC [956]
MANDATE FOR PALESTINE : SOME OBJECTIONS ANSWERED / Zionist Organization. London – 1922 – 9 – BJ-28-128/1 – ne IDC [956]
THE MANDATES SYSTEM / Bentwich, N – London, New York, 1930 – 3mf – 9 – ILM-1903/1 – ne IDC [327]
EL MANDATO DE PERON / Campora, Hector Jose – [s.l.]: Ediciones Quehacer Nacional, c1975 – 1 – CSUXADQ6389-B – us Hoover Inst Photo [320]
MANDATS ET SOUVERAINETE / Comisetti, L – Paris, n.d. – 2mf – 1 – ILM-2104/1 – ne IDC [327]
LES MANDATS INTERNATIONAUX / Boutant, C A – Paris, 1936 – 3mf – 9 – ILM-1961/1 – ne IDC [327]
LES MANDATS INTERNATIONAUX / Cioriceanu, G – Paris, n.d. – 2mf – 1 – ILM-1919/1 – ne IDC [327]
LES MANDATS ORIENTAUX / Ayoub, C – Paris, 1924 – 2mf – 9 – ILM-2379/1 – ne IDC [340]
Mandela, Nelson *see* STATE VS. NELSON MANDELA, OCT. 1962
Mandelkern, S *see*
– SHIREI SEFAT EVER
– VET. TE CONCORDANTIAE HEBR
– VETERIS TESTAMENTI CONCORDANTIAE HEBRAICAE
Mandell, Ross A *see* THE INFLUENCE OF ROLE STATUS, SELF-EFFICACY AND SOCCER PERFORMANCE
O MANDEL'SHTAM, SHUM VREMENI / Mirskii, D S – 'Sovremennye Zapiski' no 25 1925. BR-3681 2 – 8 – ne IDC [460]
Mandelstam, Osip E *see*
– KAMEN'
– SOBRANIE SOCHINENII POD. RED. G. P. STRUVE. IZD. IMENI CHEKHOVA
– STIKHI
– TRISTIA
Mandelstamm, B *see* HAZOB LE-MO'ED
MANDEMENT DE CLAUDE FAUCHET, EVEQUE DU CALVADOS, DEPUTE A L'ASSEMBLEE NATIONALE / Fauchet, Claude – Paris. Imp. du Cercle Social. s.d – 9 – fr Hachette [321]
MANDEMENTS, LETTRES PASTORALES ET CIRCULAIRES DES EVEQUES DE QUEBEC / Tetu, Henri – Quebec: A Cote. 6v. 1887-90. SEM16P88 – 2r – 5 – Can$59.00 – cn Bibl Nat [240]
Mander, Carel van *see* HET SCHILDER-BOECK
LES MANDING ET LEUR LANGUE / Labouret, Henri – Paris. 1934 – 1 – us Res Libr [306]
MANDINGAS DA GUINE PORTUGUESA / Carreira, A – (Centro de Estudos da Guine Portuguesa no. 4). 1957. BA-395 2 – 8 – ne IDC [305]
Mandonnet, P *see*
– SIGER DE BRABANT ET L'AVERROISME LATIN AU 13E SIECLE. ETUDE CRITIQUE
– SIGER DE BRABANT ET L'AVERROISME LATIN AU 13E SIECLE. TEXTES INEDITS
MANDOS POLITICOS Y REPRESENTATIVOS / Organizacion Sindical – Badajoz: Graficas Jimenez, 1961 – sp Bibl Santa Ana [320]
MANDSCHUSINESISCHE GRAMMATIK NACH DEM SAN-HO-PIAN-LAN / Gabelentz, H. C. von der – (Zeitschrift Kunde des Morgenlandes), v. 3. Goettinghen. 1840. BU-479 2 – 8 – ne IDC [480]
MANDSHU-MONGOLISCHE GRAMMATIK, AUS DEM SAN-HO-PIANLAN UEBERSETZT / Gabelentz, H. C. von der – (Zeitschr. fuer die Kunde des Morgenlandes). Goettingen. 1837. BU-478 2 – 8 – ne IDC [490]
Mane, Ignacio Rubio *see* LOS PIRATAS LOFITTE...
Manenti, F *see*
– L'ABRI TOCA DO CALDEIRAO DOS RODRIGUEZ 2, SITE DU STYLE VARZEA GRANDE, SUD-OUEST DU PIAUI, BRESIL
– L'ABRI TOCA DO CALDEIRAO DOS RODRIGUEZ I, SITE DU STYLE VARZEA GRANDE, SUD-EST DU PIAUI, BRESIL
Manepaard, C H J *see* REPORT TO THE GOVERNMENT ON AGRICULTURAL DEVELOPMENT
Maner, Salvador *see*
– ANTI-TEATRO CRITICO. TOMO 1
– ANTI-TEATRO CRITICO. TOMO 2
– ANTI-TEATRO CRITICO. TOMO 3
Manera de Rezar *see* COMENDADORES... ALCANTARA
MANERA DE REZAR SUS HORAS CANONICAS LOS COMENDADORES Y CAVALLEROS DE LA ORDEN DE ALCANTARA – Madrid: Diego Diaz de la Carrera, 1663 – 1 – sp Bibl Santa Ana [240]
Manesson-Mallet, Allain *see* DESCRIPTION DE L'UNIVERS CONTENANT LES DIFFERENTS SYSTEMS DU MONDE, LES CARTES GENERALES ET PARTICULIERES DE LA GEOGRAPHIE ANCIENNE ET MODERNE
MANET, 1832-1883 / Reunion des musees nationaux. Paris – 1932. 49 illus. 2 fiches – 9 – fr Réunion [700]
Manez, E *see* THESES PHYSICO-MEDICAS DISPUTATIONI PROPONIT IN PETITIONE BOTANICAE CATHEDRAE
Manfredini *see* REGOLE ARMONICHE
Mangabeira, Joao *see* RUI, O ESTADISTA DA REPUBLICA
Mangan, James Clarence *see* POEMS
Manganyi, M C *see* GOD'S OTHER CHILDREN AND OTHER SKETCHES
Manganyi, N C *see* BEING-BLACK-IN-THE-WORLD
Mangarriello, Ma Esther *see* TRADICION Y...
Mangeot, C *see* TISSAGE QUECHUA CONTEMPORAIN, REGION DE CUZCO, PEROU
Manget, Jean Jacques *see* DIE "BIBLIOTHECAE" DES JEAN JACQUES MANGET (AEL, ABT 3;20)
MANGLE – Bogor, Badan Penerbit Mangle. Incomplete. SE-921 1. 1957-1971 – 9 – ne IDC [999]
MANGO BUNKEN-SHU = TENRI COLLECTION OF THE MANCHU-BOOKS IN MANCHU-CHARACTERS. SERIES 1: DICTIONARIES, GRAMMARS AND READERS : GOGAKUHEN – In the custody of the Tenri Central Library, Nara Pref. 30 items. 314 parts. 43,580p – 52r – 1 – Y396,000.00 – ja Yushodo [480]
THE MANGO IN PORTO RICO / Collins, G N – 931 2. 1903 – 8 – ne IDC [972]
MANGOE-NAGARAN. ANALYSE VAN EEN JAVAANSCH VORSTENDOM / Metz, T M – Ed. 2. Rotterdam, 1939 – 3mf – 9 – ne IDC [950]
"MANGOENHARDJO", VEREENIGING VAN INLANDSCHE AMBTENAREN TE SEMARANG. (MEDEDEELING NO. 1-4) – Semarang, 1911-1915. 4v – 5mf – 9 – ne IDC [950]
Mangoenkoesomo, Tjipto *see* IK BESCHULDIG...
Mangold, Wilhelm *see* DER ROEMERBRIEF UND SEINE GESCHICHTLICHEN VORAUSSETZUNGEN
MANGROVE ECOSYSTEMS : RESEARCH METHODS – 1984 – 251p – 9 – 92-3-102181-8 – fr UNESCO [574]
MANGROVE MANAGEMENT IN THAILAND, MALAYSIA AND INDONESIA – 1985 – 72p – it F.A.O. [630]
MANGUABA – Pilar, Alagoas. 8 Jun 1887; 8 Set 1888 – 1,5,6 – bl Biblioteca [072]
MANGYUAN = WASTELAND – Semimonthly. v1-2. 1926-27. 1 reel. M-C71 – 1 – $80.00 – cc Microforms [073]
A MANHA – Lisbon, Portugal. 1 Jul 1917-8 Aug 1919 (imperfect) – 4r – 1 – uk British Libr Newspaper [072]
A MANHA – Rio de Janeiro, 29 Dec 1925-Dec 1926; Jan-Oct, Dec 1927; Jan 1928-Dec 1929; May-Aug 1935; Aug 1941-7 Jun 1953 – 1,5,6 – bl Biblioteca [072]
A MANHA *see*
– AUTORES E LIVROS
– CIENCIA PARA TODOS
– LETRAS E ARTES
– VIDA POLITICA
MANHATTAN ADVERTISER – Toledo. Ohio. 1838-1841 – 1 – us UMI [071]
MANHATTAN ENGINEER DISTRICT HISTORY / U.S. Army. Corps of Engineers – New York, NY. 14 rolls. A1218 – 1 – us Nat'l Archives [355]
MANHATTAN INC – v1-. Sept 1984- – 1,5,6,9 – us UMI [073]
Manhattan. Kansas. First Baptist Church *see* RECORDS
MANHATTAN PROJECT : OFFICIAL HISTORY AND DOCUMENTS / ed by Kesaris, Paul – (With printed guide) – 1977 – 12r – 1 – $1,210.00 – 0-89093-199-2 – us UPA [324]
Manhattan Town Association. Manhattan, Kansas *see* RECORDS
O MANHUASSU : ORGAM DESTINADO A DEFESA DOS INTERESSES DO MUNICIPIO – Manhuassu, 4 Jul 1897; 19 Oct 1902 – 1,5,6 – bl Biblioteca [072]
MANHUMIRIM : ORGAM DO PARTIDO REPUBLICANO MINEIRO E DA CAMARA MUNICIPAL DE MANHUMIRIM – Villa Manhumirim, 20 Feb-Mar 1927; 16 Dec 1928 – 1,5,6 – bl Biblioteca [072]
MANICA : COMMUNECADO E PROPOSTA DO SOCIO / Paiva d'Andrada, Joachim Carlos – (Filmed with: Barahona e Costa, Henrique Cesar da Silva. Apontamentos para a historia de guerra de Zambezia 1871-75, and others) – Lisboa: Sociedade de Geographia, 1882 – us Res Libr [960]
MANICA POST – Umtali, Rhodesia. 1 Jun 1950- . Formerly 'Umtali Post' – 85r – 1 – sa Microfile [960]
Manicacci, Jean *see* L'ARCHIPEL DES COMORES
DAS MANICHAEISCHE RELIGIONSSYSTEM / Baur, Ferdinand Christian – Tuebingen: C.F. Osiander, 1831 – 2mf – us A.T.L.A. [180]
O MANICORE – Manicore, Amazonas. 7 Set-Out 1907; 15 Mar 1908 – 1,5,6 – bl Biblioteca [072]
O MANICORE : ORGAO DO COMMERCIO – Manicore, Amazonas. 10 Dez 1899-3 Jun 1900 – 1,5,6 – bl Biblioteca [072]
MANIERE DE BIEN BASTIR POUR TOUTES SORTES DE PERSONNES. / Le Muet, Pierre – Paris. F. Jollain, 1681, 2v. in 1, illus. (Architecture Series) – 9 – fr Hachette [720]
LA MANIERE DE BIEN TRADUIRE / Dolet, E – 1540 – 9 – fr I.C.S. [440]
LA MANIERE DE FAIRE DES VERS EN FRANCOIS / La Taille, J de – 1573 – 9 – fr I.C.S. [440]
LA MANIERE DE LIRE L'HISTORIE / Lucinge, Rene de – Paris, 1614 – 1 – us U.W. Library [900]
MANIERE DE PARLER LA LANGUE FRANCOISE / Renaud, A – 1697 – 9 – fr I.C.S. [440]
MANIFES PARTAI KOMUNIS / Marx, Karl – Translation of Manifest Der Kommunistischen Partei. SE-3269 1. 1959 – 9 – ne IDC [335]
MANIFEST 17 OKTIABRIA 1905 G. I POLITICHESKOE DVIZHENIE, EGO VYZVAVSHEE / Alekseev, S A – M., 1915. 26p – 1mf – 9 – ne IDC [320]
DAS MANIFEST DER FREINHEIT UND DES FRIEDENS / Solneman, K H Z – 1977. 350p. 1 fiche (29x) – 9 – 1.00f – at Libertarian Micro [320]
MANIFEST FUTURISTOV / Larionov, M, Zdanevich, I – Pochemu my raskrashivaemsia. nr. 12. Argus. 1913. BR-3604 2 – 8 – ne IDC [700]
MANIFEST OF PASSENGERS ARRIVING IN THE ST ALBANS, VERMONT DISTRICT THROUGH CANADIAN PACIFIC AND ATLANTIC PORTS, 1895-1954 CANADIAN PACIFIC AND ATLANTIC PORTS, 1895-1954 – 639r – 1 – M1464 – us Nat'l Archives [340]
MANIFESTACION DE LAS RAZONES Y FUNDAMENTOS QUE TUVO EL DR. ANDRES PIQUER...PARA INZGAR Y DE CLARA SU HETICO VICENTE NAVARRO / Piquer, Andres – Valencia, 1746 – 1mf – 9 – sp Cultura [610]
MANIFESTACION HECHA POR EL SINDICO / Suarez, Gabriel – 1854 – 9 – $1.50f – sp Bibl Santa Ana [946]
MANIFESTACION...AYUNTAMIENTO...BADAJOZ / Suarez, Gabriel – 1854 – 9 – 1.50f – sp Bibl Santa Ana [946]
THE MANIFESTATION OF AGES / Kluh, John M – Chicago: J.M. Kluh, 1898. 1 fiche – 9 – us A.T.L.A. [240]
MANIFESTATIONS OF THE RISEN JESUS / Doane, William Croswell – Oxford: University Press, 1898. 1 fiche – 9 – us A.T.L.A. [240]
LE MANIFESTE – Port-au-Prince. Haiti. 1841-1844 – 1 – us UMI [072]
MANIFESTE POLITIQUE ADRESSE AUX ELECTEURS DU COMTE DE DORCHESTER / Caron, Adolphe – 18?? 02820. (Pre-1900 Canadiana) – 9 – cn C.I.H.M. [971]
IL MANIFESTO – 1987- – 4r per y – 5 – inquire – us Ross [072]
IL MANIFESTO – (Also available on CD-ROM) – 1987-1995 – 3r per y – 5,6 – Sfr962.00 – sz Infoprint [072]
IL MANIFESTO – Italy, 1976-80 – 7r – 1 – inquire – us Ross [072]
MANIFESTO – 1976-1980 – Cumul – 1 – L600,000 – sz Infoprint [072]
MANIFESTO – Surabaja. Indonesia. 1964-1965 – 1 – us UMI [072]
THE MANIFESTO – (Title varies: The Shaker. Shaker and Shakeress Monthly. The Shaker Manifesto) – v1-29. 1871-99 (complete) – 7r – 1 – ATLA S0104 – us A.T.L.A. [073]
THE MANIFESTO CHURCH / Boston. Brattle square church – Records of the church in Brattle square, Boston, with lists of communicants, baptisms, marriages, and funerals, 1699-1872. 1902 – 1 – us A.T.L.A. [240]
MANIFESTO OF CATALAN INTELLECTUALS – Barcelona, 1936. Fiche W1018. (Blodgett Collection of Spanish Civil War Pamphlets) – 9 – us H.U. College Libr [946]
MANIFESTO OF MARHAENISM / Partai Nasional Indonesia – SE-2215 1 – 9 – ne IDC [320]
MANIFESTO POLITIK / Sukarno, Pres. Indonesia – By Bung Karno. Ulasan Tiga Tahun Bermanipol,BY Achmad Notosoetardjo. SE 3747 1. 1961? – 9 – ne IDC [324]
MANIFESTS OF PASSENGERS ARRIVING IN THE ST ALBANS, VERMONT, DISTRICT THROUGH CANADIAN PACIFIC PORTS, 1929-1949 – 25r – 1 – M1465 – us Nat'l Archives [340]
MANIFIESTO QUE PRESENTA A EUROPA... EXTREMADURA / Garcia de la Cuesta, Gregorio – 1811 – 9 – 1.50f – sp Bibl Santa Ana [946]
MANIFIESTO...ARANJUEZ, MADRID Y BAYONA / Godoy, Manuel – 1808 – 9 – 1.50f – sp Bibl Santa Ana [946]
MANIFIESTO...ORENSE A LA.. / Quevedo y Quintano, Pedro – 1814 – 9 – 1.50f – sp Bibl Santa Ana [440]
MANIFOLD WITNESS FOR CHRIST / Barry, Alfred – New York: E.P. Dutton, 1880. 1 fiche – 9 – us A.T.L.A. [240]
Manigault, Charles Izard *see* TRAVEL NOTES
Manigault, Peter *see*
– LETTERBOOK
Manigault-Burnet *see* PAPERS OF MANIGAULT-BURNET
Manikam, Rajah B *see* THE CHRISTIAN FAMILY IN CHANGING EAST ASIA (CCC246)
MANIKKOTI – Madras: Navayuka Piracuralayam limitet. v[4-8 n8]. apr 1936-39? – us Res Libr [072]
MANILA BULLETIN – (Yrly reel count varies) – 1973- – 1 – us Ross [072]
MANILA CHRONICLE – Manila. Philippines. 1959- – 1 – us UMI [072]
MANILA CHRONICLE – (Yrly reel count varies) – 1986- – 1 – us Ross [072]
MANILA TIMES – (Yrly reel count varies) – 1986- – 1 – us Ross [072]
THE MANILA TIMES – Manila: Manila Times Pub Co, 1956-sep 22 1972 – 60r – 1 – us Res Libr [072]
Manilli, J *see* VILLA BORGHESE FUORI DI PORTA PINCIANA

LE MANIOC CHEZ LES INDIENS WAYANA ET WAYAPI DE GUYANE FRANCAISE ET DU BRESIL / Grenand, F – 9 – F20.00 – fr Ethnologie [306]
MANION FORUM – v1-1294 1954-79 1; v795-1294 5,6; v1161-1294 9 – us UMI [073]
MANION FORUM – South Bend. Ind. 1962-1968 – 1 – us UMI [071]
MANIPOL (MANIFESTO POLITIK REPUBLIK INDONESIA), U.U.D. '45, USDEK (INTI SARI DARIPADA MANIFESTO POLITIK) DAN DJAREK (DJALANNJA REVOLUSI KITA) – SE-3911 1. 1962? – 9 – ne IDC [324]
MANIPOL-USDEK DAN ISLAM / Nasution, Amir Taat – SE-5106 1. 1963 – 9 – ne IDC [320]
MANIPUELO DE FLORES DEL MAESTRO FR. FRANCISCO DE VITORIA / Getino, Luis A – Madrid, 1933; Madrid: Razon y Fe, 1934 – 1 – sp Bibl Santa Ana [240]
MANIPULUS VOCABULORUM:A DICTIONARIE OF ENGLISH AND LATINE WORDES / Levins, Peter – 1570. 161p. (English Linguistics Series 1500-1800) – 9 – us UMI [420]
MANIPUR GAZETTE / Manipur. India – 1963-1966 – 1 – us NY Public [950]
Manipur. India *see* MANIPUR GAZETTE
Maniscalco, Ignatius A *see* EXCESS POSTEXERCISE OXYGEN CONSUMPTION AND ENERGY EXPENDITURE OF ENDURANCE TRAINED AND UNTRAINED WOMEN
Manitius, M *see* GESCHICHTE DER LATEINISCHEN LITERATUR DES MITTELALTERS
LE MANITOBA – (Also as Metis) – St Boniface, Canada. 1871-1900 – 9r – 1 – $585.00 – cn Library Assoc [971]
LE MANITOBA *see* LE METIS
MANITOBA – 4th ed 1994 – 9 – cn Communication [971]
Manitoba *see* LEGISLATIVE ASSEMBLY JOURNALS
MANITOBA AND NORTH WEST ILLUSTRATED QUARTERLY – Winnipeg: Bishop Engraving and Print. Co, [1883-18–] – 9 – cn C.I.H.M. [910]
MANITOBA ARTS REVIEW – v1-17. 1938-1965. Missing v7 – 1 – cn Precision [700]
MANITOBA BUSINESS – Winnipeg. v1-16. 1976-94 – 9 – Can$28.00y – cn Micromedia [380]
Manitoba. Canada *see*
- CAREY'S MANITOBA REPORTS
- MANITOBA LAW REPORTS
- MANITOBA REPORTS TEMPORE WOOD
- MANITOBA STATUTES, SESSION LAWS AND REVISIONS
- WESTERN LAW TIMES AND REPORTS

MANITOBA COLONIST *see* THE COLONIST
MANITOBA GAZETTE – (v99-111 1970-82 Can$105.00 5. v112- 1983- 9) – Winnipeg. v86- 1957- – 1,5,9 – Price varies – cn Micromedia [073]
MANITOBA GAZETTE – Winnepeg, 1957-69 – 11r – 1 – us Ross [072]
THE MANITOBA GOOD TEMPLAR / Independent Order of Good Templars. Grand Lodge of Manitoba and N.W.T. – Winnipeg: Independent Order of Good Templars, Grand Lodge of Manitoba and N.W.T., [1897-189- or 19–] – 9 – cn C.I.H.M. [240]
MANITOBA INDIAN AND METIS CONFERENCE REPORT – Winnipeg, 1954-69 – 5 – Can$100.00 – cn Micromedia [306]
MANITOBA JOURNAL OF EDUCATION – (v 1-9 1965-74, 10-15 1975-81 Can$100.00. v16-17 1981-83 $50.00y.Ceased v17) – Winnipeg. v1-17. 1965-1982/83 – 5 – Price varies – cn Micromedia [370]
MANITOBA LAW JOURNAL – (v1-14 1962-85 on reel $200.00. v15-25 1988-95 on mf $184.00) – v1-23. 1962-95 – 5,6,9 – $384.00 set – us Hein [340]
MANITOBA LAW REPORTS / Manitoba. Canada – (Cont by 2nd series. Not offered by LLMC) – 1st series: v1-67. 1883-1961 (all publ) – 471mf – 9 – $706.00 – LLMC 81-022 – us L.L.M.C. [340]
THE MANITOBA LIBERAL – Portage La Prairie, Manitoba. v18 n10. 8 apr 1900 – 1r – 1 – Can$25.00 – cn Can Microfilming [072]
MANITOBA LIBRARY ASSOCIATION BULLETIN – 1952-67 – 1r – 1 – $68.00 – cn Library Assoc [020]
MANITOBA MEDICINE – (Cont: University of Manitoba Medical Journal at v57 1987. Incorporated in: Prairie Medical Journal at v64 1994) – Winnipeg. v57-63. 1987-93 – 9 – Can$20.00y – cn Micromedia [610]
MANITOBA MEDICINE *see* UNIVERSITY OF MANITOBA MEDICAL JOURNAL
THE MANITOBA MESSENGER – Winnipeg: The Union, [1893-19–?] – 9 – cn C.I.H.M. [240]
MANITOBA REPORTS TEMPORE WOOD / Manitoba. Canada – 1v. 1875-83 (all publ) – 5mf – 9 – $7.50 – LLMC 81-023 – us L.L.M.C. [340]
MANITOBA STATUTES, SESSION LAWS AND REVISIONS / Manitoba. Canada – (Updates planned) – 1st Parliament-1945 Parliament 5th sess. 1871-1945 – 607mf – 9 – $910.00 – LLMC 90-130 – us L.L.M.C. [340]
MANITOBA TEACHER – (v 39-52 1960-74 Can$100.00v. v53 1975-75 Can$60.00. v 54-59 1975-1981 Can$1 15.00. v 60-62 1981-84 Can$85.00. v 63-72 1984-94 Can$20.00y) – Winnipeg, v39-72. 1960-1993/94 – 5,1,9 – Price varies – cn Micromedia [370]
MANITOBAN – Winnipeg. v1-2. 1891-93 – 5 – Can$100.00 – cn Micromedia [073]
MANITOBA-PICTORIAL AND BIOGRAPHICAL – (v2. Canada Reel 5) – Winnipeg, Vancouver, Montreal, 1913. v1. Canada Reel 4. The Cox Library Collection – 5 – us Americana [971]
MANITOULIN, OR, FIVE YEARS OF CHURCH WORK AMONG OJIBWAY INDIANS AND LUMBERMEN, RESIDENT UPON THAT ISLAND OR IN ITS VICINITY / Burden, Harold Nelson – London: Simpkin, Marshall, Hamilton, Kent, 1895. 00333. (Pre-1900 Canadiana) – 9 – cn C.I.H.M. [240]
MANKATO: ITS FIRST FIFTY YEARS 1852-1902 / Free Press Printing Co – Biographical sketches. Mankato, 1903. Minnesota Reel 4. (The Cox Library Collection) – 5 – us Americana [978]
Mankevich, A I *see* SPRAVOCHNIK. ESTESTVENNYE I FIZIKOMATEMATICHESKIE NAUKI
MANKIND – (1975-. 1,5,6,9) – v1-6. 1967-81 – 1,5,6 – us UMI [301]
MANKIND AND THE CHURCH : BEING AN ATTEMPT TO ESTIMATE THE CONTRIBUTION OF GREAT RACES TO THE FULNESS OF THE CHURCH OF GOD / ed by Montgomery, H H – London; New York: Longmans, Green, 1907 – 1mf – us A.T.L.A. [240]
Manko, Mandane *see* FIGUREN- UND KONFLIKTDARSTELLUNG BEI FRIEDRICH SPIELHAGEN, THEODOR FONTANE, FERDINAND VON SAAR, EDUARD VON KEYSERLING
Mankowni, N L *see*
- ERKOW AP'E TSAP'E
- HATS'I HAMAR

THE MANLINESS OF CHRIST / Hughes, Thomas – Boston: Houghton, Osgood, 1880 – 1mf – 9 – 0-8370-3689-5 – 1985-1689 – us A.T.L.A. [920]
Manly, Basil *see* BIBLE DOCTRINE OF INSPIRATION EXPLAINED
Manly, Basil Jr. *see*
- THE BAPTIST PSALMODY
- PAPERS OF BASIL MANLY, JR.

Manly, Basil Sr. *see*
- THE BAPTIST PSALMODY
- MANUSCRIPT, SERMONS AND NOTES

Manly Family *see*
- CORRESPONDENCE, 1829-92
- PAPERS OF THE MANLY FAMILY

MANMA ALIN – Rangoon, Burma. 1945-Sept 1988 (incomplete) – 58r – 1 – us L of C Photodup [072]
MAN-MADE LANDSCAPE – 1977 – 178p – 9 – 92-3-101455-2 – fr UNESCO [710]
MAN-MADE TEXTILES – (See also: Textile Month) – v1-44. 1924-67 – 1 – us UMI [670]
Mann, Betty J *see*
- EXERCISE ADOPTION AND ADHERENCE OF COLLEGE WOMEN
- THE INFLUENCE OF GOAL SETTING ON INDIVIDUAL ENDURANCE SWIMMING PERFORMANCE

DER MANN DER NACH SYRAKUS SPAZIERENGING : DAS ABENTEUERLICHE LEBEN DES JOHANN GOTTFRIED SEUME / Heine, Gerhard – Weimar: Gustav Kiepenheuer, 1961 – 1r – 1 – us U.W. Library [920]
Mann, Enos R *see* THE BENCH AND BAR OF SARATOGA COUNTY.
Mann, Gerald H *see* FALKLAND / MALVINAS
Mann, Heinrich *see*
- KUNSTERNOVELLEN
- MUTTER MARIE
- THE ROYAL WOMAN

Mann, Horace *see*
- LECTURES ON EDUCATION
- TWELVE SERMONS

Mann, I *see* ANIMAL BY-PRODUCTS
DER MANN IN DER FLASCHE : LUSTSPIEL IN 4 AKTEN / Rosen, Julius – Berlin: Felix Bloch, 1880 – 1r – 1 – us U.W. Library [820]
MANN IN DER ZEIT – (Cont by: Weltbild, nov 1 1968. Also available: Ausgabe B, jul 1-dec 15 1967, 1r) – Augsburg, nov 1959-96 – 55r – 1 – Dist. gw Mikrofilm – gw Misc Inst [072]
Mann, J *see*
- HITYASHEVUT HA-MEKUBBAL RABBI AVRAHAM ROVIGO VA-HAVURATO BI-YERUSHALAYIM
- MASSA'AM SHEL RABBI HAYYIM BEN ATTAR VA-HAVURATO LE-EREZ-YISRA'EL

Mann, K H *see* MATHEMATICAL MODELS IN BIOLOGICAL OCEANOGRAPHY
EIN MANN NAMENS SCHMITZ : NOVELLE / Schaefer, Wilhelm – Muenchen: A Langen, G Mueller, 1942, c1933 – 1r – 1 – us U.W. Library [830]
DER MANN OHNE HERZ : ROMAN / Zierer, Otto – Nuernberg: J L Schrag, c1944 – 1r – 1 – us U.W. Library [830]
Mann, Thomas *see*
- GOETHE ALS REPRAESENTANT DES BUERGERLICHEN ZEITALTERS
- GOETHE AND DEMOCRACY
- GOETHE UND TOLSTOI
- GOETHES LAUFBAHN ALS SCHRIFTSTELLER
- HERR UND HUND
- MARIO UND DER ZAUBERER
- DAS PROBLEM DER FREIHEIT
- SELECTIONS FROM HIS WORKS
- TONIO KROEGER

DER MANN UND DAS WEIB. DIE HERRSCHAFT DER DIFFERENZ. ZUR BEWUSSTSEINSGESCHICHTE VON NATUR UND GESCHLECHT / Mueller, Hannelore – 1995 – 6mf – 9 – DM125.00 – 3-8267-2098-9 – gw Hänsel [100]
Mann, W *see* LICHENUM IN BOHEMIA OBSERVATORUM DISPOSITIO SUCCINCTAQUE DESCRIPTIO
Mann, William J *see*
- LIFE AND TIMES OF HENRY MELCHIOR MUEHLENBERG
- LUTHERANISM IN AMERICA
- A PLEA FOR THE AUGSBURG CONFESSION

Manna, J E *see* MORCEAUX CHOISIS DE LITTERATURE ARAMEENNE
THE MANNER OF CORONATION OF KING CHARLES 1 OF ENGLAND AT WESTMINISTER, 2 FEBR. 1626 / Wordworth, C – 1892 – 4mf – 8 – Dfl19.00 – ne Slangenburg [390]
THE MANNER OF PRAYER / Walford, William – 1836 – 1 – 11.06 – us Baptist [240]
Manners, N *see*
- A FULL CONFUTATION OF THE REV. JOHN FLETCHER'S APPEAL,...
- A FULL CONFUTATION OF THE REV. MR. JOHN FLETCHER'S APPEAL TO MATTER OF FACT AND COMMON SENSE
- PREACHERS DESCRIBED AND THE PEOPLE ADVISED
- REMARKS ON THE WRITINGS OF THE REV. J.W.

Mannes, Ulrich *see* ERNST VON WILDENBRUCHS DRAMATISCHE TECHNIK
MANNHAFFTER KUNST-SPIEGEL / Furttenbach, J – O-1158 1. 1663 – 9 – ne IDC [700]
MANNHEIMER ABENDZEITUNG – (Cont as: Badischer Merkur 1849-) – Mannheim, 1842-1849 – 9r – 1 – DM990.00 – gw Mikro Press [072]
MANNHEIMER ABENDZEITUNG – (Title change: Badischer Merkur, 1 Jul 1849) – Mannheim, Germany. Jul 1842-Jun 1849 – 14r – 1 – gw Mikrofilm [072]
MANNHEIMER GENERAL-ANZEIGER *see* WOECHENTLICHES FRAG- UND KUNDSCHAFFTS-BLATH
MANNHEIMER INTELLIGENZBLATT *see* WOECHENTLICHES FRAG- UND KUNDSCHAFFTS-BLATH
MANNHEIMER JOURNAL – Mannheim, 1850-1871 – 23r – 1 – DM1,840.00 – gw Mikro Press [072]
MANNHEIMER JOURNAL *see* WOECHENTLICHES FRAG- UND KUNDSCHAFFTS-BLATH
DER MANNHEIMER MORGEN *see* DER MORGEN
MANNHEIMER MORGEN – Mannheim, Germany. Jul 1967-1969; Apr 1971-May 1991 – 274r – 1 – us L of C Photodup [072]
MANNHEIMER MORGEN *see* DER MORGEN
MANNHEIMER MORGENBLATT – (Title change: Badische Zeitung, 1 Nov 1848) – Mannheim, Germany. 1848-Jun 1849 – 1r – 1 – gw Mikrofilm [072]
MANNHEIMER TAGBLATT – Mannheim, Germany. 8 Oct 1867-68 – 2r – 1 – gw Mikrofilm [072]
MANNHEIMER TAGEBLAETTER *see* WOECHENTLICHES FRAG- UND KUNDSCHAFFTS-BLATH
MANNHEIMER TAGEBLATT – Mannheim, 1867-68 – 2r – 1 – DM150.00 – gw Mikro Press [072]
MANNHEIMER TAGEBLATT *see* WOECHENTLICHES FRAG- UND KUNDSCHAFFTS-BLATH
MANNING F. FORCE PAPERS / Force, Manning F – 1835-85. University of Washington Libraries. Guide – 1 – $60.00 – us U.W. Libraries [920]
Manning, Harold Ernest *see* THE CANADIAN LAW OF FIXTURES
Manning, Henry Edward *see*
- THE CENTENARY OF SAINT PETER AND THE GENERAL COUNCIL
- ENGLAND AND CHRISTENDOM
- THE ETERNAL PRIESTHOOD
- THE GROUNDS OF FAITH
- THE INDEPENDENCE OF THE HOLY SEE
- THE OECUMENICAL COUNCIL AND THE INFALLIBILITY OF THE ROMAN PONTIFF
- THE TRUE STORY OF THE VATICAN COUNCIL
- THE VATICAN COUNCIL AND ITS DEFINITIONS

Manning, Jacob Merrill *see*
- HALF TRUTHS AND THE TRUTH...UNBELIEF... IN RELATION TO...THE CHRISTIAN SYSTEM
- NOT OF MAN BUT OF GOD

Manning, Keitha D *see* DANCE HISTORY AND COMPUTER COURSEWARE
Manning, Mark, M *see* PRAGMATIC AND ADMINISTRATIVE FACTORS RELATED TO A SUCCESSFUL WRESTLING PROGRAM
MANNING RIVER TIMES (TAREE) – Jan 1 1898-Dec 28 1907; Jan 11 1913 -Dec 24 1913; Jan 8 1921-Dec 24 1921; Jan 7 1925-Dec 24 1930; Jan 6 1932-Dec 23 1933; Jul 3 1935-Nov 17 1951 – 9 – at Pascoe [072]
Manning, Robert *see* THE SHORTEST WAY TO END DISPUTES ABOUT RELIGION
MANNING THE NAVY; A STATEMENT, IN WHICH THE EVILS AND LOSSES ARISING FROM THE PRESENT SYSTEM ARE SET FORTH, AND A REMEDY IS PROPOSED, WHEREBY A PERMANENT NAVY MAY BE ESTABLISHED, AND THE CONDITION OF THE BRITISH SEAMAN IMPROVED / Wilmot, Arthur Parry Eardley – 1849 – 9 – uk Libr Preservation [941]
Manning, William M Manning *see* NEVILE AND MANNING'S REPORTS
MANNING'S CASES : UNREPORTED / Louisiana. Supreme Court – (A Pre-NRS title) – 1v. 1877-80 (all publ) – 6mf – 9 – $9.00 – LLMC 84-142 – us L.L.M.C. [340]
Mannock, John *see*
- MANUEL ABREGE DE CONTREVERSE, OU CONTREVERSE DES PAUVRES
- THE POOR MAN'S CATECHISM

EINE MANNSCHAFT / Laar, Clemens – Berlin: Traditions-Verlag Kolk, c1942 – 1r – 1 – us U.W. Library [830]
Manobens, Enrique *see* CRONICAS DE LA GUERRA
Manolesso, E M *see* HISTORIA NOVA, NELLA QVALE SI CONTENGONO TUTTI I SUCCESSI DELLA GUERRA TURCHESCA, LA CONGIURA DEL DUCA DE NORTSOLCH CONTRA LA REGINA D'INGHILTERRA; ...
MANORIAL COURT ROLLS AND VILLAGE SURVEYS / King's College, Cambridge – 13th-16th centuries – 1 – uk Microform Academic [941]
THE MANORS OF SUFFOLK; NOTES ON THEIR HISTORY AND DEVOLUTION, WITH SOME ILLUSTRATIONS OF THE OLD MANOR HOUSES / Copinger, Walter Arthur – London: T.F. Unwin, 1905-11. 7v. illus., plates, maps, geneal. tables – 1 – us U.W. Library [941]
MANOSCRITTI ETIOPICA : BIBLIOGRAFIA ETIOPICA / Zanutto, A – Rome. 2v. 1929-1932 – 4mf – 9 – ne IDC [090]
MANPOWER ADMINISTRATION RESEARCH AND DEVELOPMENT FINDINGS – Washington: GPO. nos1-15. 1967-73 (all publ) – 25mf – 9 – $37.50 – LLMC 95-001 – us L.L.M.C. [340]

MANPOWER SITUATION IN CONTEMPORARY BANGLADESH : FINDINGS OF THE BANGLADESH MANPOWER SURVEY OF 1980 / Bangladesh. Bureau of Statistics – Dacca, 1982 – 2mf – 9 – DE-529/1 – ne IDC [370]

Manrique, Angel *see*
- ANNALES CISTERCIENSIUM
- LAUREA EVANGELICA DE..

Manrique, Manuel *see* MEJORAS...ALMA

Manry, Robert A *see* PAPERS, MS 3479

MAN'S ESTATE : AN INTERPRETATION OF GENESIS 2. 4-4.26 / Coggin, Frederick Ernest – (Includes indexes) – London: John Murray, 1905 – 1mf – 9 – 0-8370-2701-2 – 1985-0701 – us A.T.L.A. [220]

MAN'S INFLUENCE ON THE HYDROLOGICAL CYCLE – 1976 – 78p – it F.A.O. [550]

MAN'S KNOWLEDGE OF GOD / Armstrong, Richard Acland – London:Simpkin, Marshall, [1886?] – 1mf – 9 – 0-8370-2514-1 – 1985-0514 – us A.T.L.A. [210]

MAN'S MORAL NATURE: AN ESSAY / Bucke, Richard Maurice – New York: G. Putnam; Toronto: Willing & Williamson, 1879. 00324. (Pre-1900 Canadiana) – 9 – cn C.I.H.M. [170]

Mans, P Raphael du *see* L'ESTAT DE LA PERSE

Mansel, Henry Longueville *see*
- THE LIMITS OF RELIGIOUS THOUGHT...EIGHT LECTURES
- METAPHYSICS; OR, THE PHILOSOPHY OF CONSCIOUSNESS, PHENOMENAL AND REAL

Mansfeld, Alfred *see* URWALD-DOCUMENTE

Mansfeld'sche Kupferschieferbauende Gewerkschaft *see*
- STATUT..
- VORLAGEN...AM 27 MAI 1867

MANSFIELD 1703-1895 – (Mf 1-5: Vital Records 1771-1844. Mf 6-11: Vital Records 1771-1840. Mf 12: Out-of-Town Marrs 1703-96. Mf 13-19: Town Records 1731-91. Mf 20-21: Accounts 1783-1809. Mf 22-29: Town Records 1791-1838. Mf 30-33: Town Records 1838-57. Mf 34-35: School Records 1830-82. Mf 36: Intents Index 1849-62. Mf 37-41: Marriages 1839-78. Mf 42-47: Marriages 1839-86. Mf 48-51: Vitals Index 1844-95. Mf 52-53: Vital Records 1844-50. Mf 54-58: Births 1851-95. Mf 59-62: Marriages 1851-95. Mf 63-66: Deaths 1851-95) – (mf ed 1991) – 66mf – 9 – us Holbrook [920]

MANSFIELD 1730-1849 – (Mf 1T-2T: Births 1844-49. Mf 2T: Marriages 1844-49. Mf 2T-3T: Deaths 1844-49. Mf 3T: Marriage Intentions 1771-83. Mf 3T-6T: Vital Records 1750-1861. Mf 6T-9T: Marriages/Intents 1783-1840. Mf 9T-10T: Births & Deaths 1730-1842. Mf 10T: Marriages 1839-44, 1775-76. Mf 10T-11T: Marriage Intents 1840-49) – (mf ed 1997) – 11mf – 9 – 0-87623-285-3 – us Holbrook [920]

MANSFIELD ADVERTISER – Mansfield, PA. -w 1873-1962; 1962-1973 – 13 – $25.00r – us I.M.R. [071]

MANSFIELD AND NORTH NOTTS. ADVERTISER – Nottinghamshire.1871-1952 – 1 – uk Microform Academic [072]

MANSFIELD AND NORTH NOTTS. CHRONICLE ADVERTISER – Nottinghamshire. 1952 to date – 1 – uk Microform Academic [072]

MANSFIELD AND SUTTON RECORDER – (Recorder (Mansfield and Sutton Edition), Jul 1983-) – England, 31 Dec 1981; 25 Feb 1982; 4 Mar-24 Jun, Jul-Dec 1982; 6 Jan 1983-1984 – 6reels – 1 – uk British Libr Newspaper [072]

MANSFIELD CHRONICLE – Nottinghamshire. 1895-1952 – 1 – uk Microform Academic [072]

Mansfield. Connecticut *see* BIRTHS, BAPTISMS, MARRIAGES & DEATHS, 1703-1850

MANSFIELD GAP BAPTIST CHURCH. JEFFERSON COUNTY ASSOCIATION. JEFFERSON CITY, TENNESSEE = MANSFIELD GAP BAPTIST CHURCH RECORDS, 1911-67 : CHURCH RECORDS, 1911-67 – 708p – 1 – 31.86 – us Baptist [240]

Mansfield, George C *see*
- HISTORY OF BUTTE COUNTY
- HISTORY OF BUTTE COUNTY, CALIFORNIA
- WHAT BUTTE COUNTY OFFERS THE HOME-SEEKER

Mansfield, Lewis William *see* TRACES OF THE PLAN OF OUR BEING

Mansfield. Ohio. First United Methodist Church *see* RECORDS

MANSFIELD REPORTER – England. -w. 1871-93; 1913-27; 1937. 39 reels – 1 – uk British Libr Newspaper [072]

THE MANSFIELDIAN – Mansfield, PA., 1942 – 13 – $25.00r – us I.M.R. [071]

MANSHU KEIZAI JUNEN SHI / Manshukoku Tsushin Sha – Chang-chun. Manchukuo economic policy and economic relations with Japan. 506 p. 1942. (J 333 Ma47) – 1 – 35.00r – us Hoover Inst Photo [950]

MANSHU KENKOKU SOKUMEN SHI – Tokyo. A collection of articles on various aspects of the history of Manchukuo, with much emphasis on the economic. 417 p. 1942. (J 222.5 Ma47m) – 1 – 35.00r – us Hoover Inst Photo [950]

MANSHUKOKU SEIFU KOHO = MANCHUKUO EMPIRE, OFFICIAL GAZETTE: FROM THE FOUNDATION TO THE DESTRUCTION – No1-3329, April 1, 1932-July 26, 1945. 52,798p – 120r – 1 – Y990,000 – ja Yushodo [950]

Manshukoku Tsushin Sha *see* MANSHU KEIZAI JUNEN SHI

Mansi, J D *see*
- BIBLIOTHECA LATINA MEDIAE ET INFIMAE AETATIS
- NOVA ET AMPLISSIMA COLLECTIO CONCILIORUM
- SACRORUM CONCILIORUM NOVA ET AMPLISSIMA COLLECTIO

Mansikka, V *see* ZHITIE ALEKSANDRA NEVSKAGO

Manso Mangou-Eyi, J M *see* TRADITIONS ET MUTATIONS DANS UN VILLAGE IVOIRIEN DE PALMERAIE

MAN/SOCIETY/TECHNOLOGY – v1- 1942- 1; 1971- 5,6; 1975- 4 x 6 in. 9 – us UMI [370]

Manson, T W *see* THE TEACHING OF JESUS

Manssen, W J *see* ADOLF FRIEDRICH GRAF VON SCHACK

Mansur, Kamil *see* ISRAIL FI AL-ISTIRATIJIYAH AL-AMIRIKIYAH FI AL-THAMANINAT

MANTECA NEWS – Manteca, CA. 1983 – 2r – 1 – $100.00 – B03334 – us Library Micro [071]

Mantecon Movellan, T Antonio *see* LAS COFRADIAS RELIGIOSAS DEL VALLE DEL RIO MIERA SIGLOS 17 Y 18

Mantegazza, Vico *see* IL BENADIR

DER MANTEL DER TRAEUME : CHINESISCHE NOVELLEN / Balazs, Bela – Muenchen: D & R Bischoff, 1922 – 1 – us U.W. Library [830]

MANTELTARIFVERTRAG FUER DAS SCHUHMACHERHANDWERK VOM 18 APR 1931: UND BEZIRKSTARIFVERTRAG SACHSEN-ANHALT VOM 27 AUG 1931 – 28p. (Serial publications of German trade unions in the Memorial Library, University of Wisconsin-Madison.) – 1 – us U.W. Library [331]

MANTETSU CHOSA GEPPO = MONTHLY REPORTS OF THE RESEARCH INSTITUTE OF SOUTH MANCHURIAN RAILWAY – In Japanese. v1-24, 1919-1944 – 37r – 1 – Y300,000.00 – ja Yushodo [380]

Manteuffel, T *see* ARCHIVES DE L'ETAT EN POLOGNE

Manthey-Zorn, Otto *see* JOHANN GEORG JACOBIS IRIS

MANTIQUE BABYLONIENNE ET MANTIQUE HITTITE / Boissier, A – Paris. 1935. BNE-441 1 – 9 – ne IDC [290]

MANTISSA MUSCORUM AD FLORAM PEDEMONTANAM / Notaris, G de – (Mem. Acad. Sc., v. 39, Torino 1836). B-5233 2 – 8 – ne IDC [580]

MANTISSA PLANTARUM FLORAE ALPIUM APUANARUM / Bertoloni, A – Bononiae. 1832. B-5114 2 – 8 – ne IDC [580]

MANTISSAE INSECTORUM ICONIBUS ILLUSTRATAE SPECIES NOVAS / Reich, G C – Norimbergae, 1797. 16p.1 pl. Z-1573/2 – 8 – ne IDC [590]

Mantuanus Spagnuoli, Baptista *see* THE ECLOGUES OF MANTUAN, 1448-1516

MANTUIREA – (In Romanian and Hebrew) – Bucarest, RM. v4 no41. 8 Jul 1945 – 1r – 1 – $25.00 – cn Can Microfilming [072]

MANU / ed by Mueller, Friedrich Max – (Translated by Georg Buehler) – 1886 – 13mf – 8 – ne Slangenburg [280]

MANUA OF UNIVERSAL CHURCH HISTORY / Alzog, John – Cincinnati, Ohio: R. Clarke, 1874-1878 – 7mf – us A.T.L.A. [240]

MANUAL / Israel. Ministry of Health. Chronic Diseases and Rehabilitation. Israel Cancer Registry – By Ruth Steinitz, Corina Costin, Leah Katz, et al. July 1975. 91 p – 9 – 2.00 – is I.T.T.I. [324]

Manual *see* MANUAL DE LA COCINERA EXTREMENA

MANUAL AND ACCOUNT BOOK FOR ADMINISTRATORS AND EXECUTORS IN THE STATE OF OHIO. – Columbus: Siebert & Lilley, 1886. 52, 36p. LL-701 – 1 – us L of C Photodup [340]

MANUAL DE APLICACION Y CORRECION DE LA BATERIA "C" / Gessa – Plasencia: Imp. E.S.R., S.A., 1972 – 1 – sp Bibl Santa Ana [946]

MANUAL DE FISIOLOGIA EXPERIMENTAL / Diaz Villar Martinez, Juan Manuel – Madrid: Establecimiento tipografico de los hijos de R. Alvarez, 1907.-v1 – 1 – sp Bibl Santa Ana [550]

MANUAL DE FISIOLOGIA EXPERIMENTAL / Diaz Villar y Martinez, Juan M – Madrid: Establecimiento Tipografico de los Hijos de R. Alvarez, 1913 – 1 – sp Bibl Santa Ana [550]

MANUAL DE HERALDICA ESPANOLA / Riquer, Martin de – Barcelona: Apolo, 1942 – 1 – us U.W. Library [920]

MANUAL DE HISTORIA DE LA ORDEN DE LA MERCED. TOMO 1. (1218-1574) / Marquez Nunez, Guillermo – Toledo, 1931; Madrid: Razon y Fe, 1932 – 1 – sp Bibl Santa Ana [240]

MANUAL DE HISTORIA DE LAS MISIONES / Montalban, Francisco J – Burgos: Razon y Fe, 1939 – 1 – sp Bibl Santa Ana [240]

MANUAL DE LA BATERIA DE TEST GESAR / Gabinete Psicopedagogico Sanchez Rodrigo – Plasencia: Edit. Sanchez Rodrigo, 1971 – 1 – sp Bibl Santa Ana [350]

MANUAL DE LA COCINERA EXTREMENA / Manual – Villanueva de la Serena: Imprenta de J. Morcillo Tena, 3rd ed 1945 – 1 – sp Bibl Santa Ana [946]

MANUAL DE LA GUARDIA DE HONOR DEL INMACULADO CORAZON DE MARIA – Caceres: Ediciones Cruzada Mariana, 1960 – 1 – sp Bibl Santa Ana [240]

MANUAL DE LA LEGISLATION COLOMBIANA / Borges, Milo Adrian – Bogota. 3v. 1948-49 – 1 – 23.00r – us L of C Photodup [340]

MANUAL DE LA MILITANCIA POLITICA / Astesano, Eduardo – [Buenos Aires]: Editorial Relevo, [1973] – 1 – CSUXAGP8747-B – us Hoover Inst Photo [320]

MANUAL DE LAS CUARENTA HORAS... / Arratibel, Juan – Madrid: Razon y Fe, 1927 – 1 – sp Bibl Santa Ana [610]

MANUAL DE L'EMPRUNTEUR SUR WARRANTS COMMERCIAUX ET SUR WARRANTS AGRICOLES / Beyne, Pierre – (Supplement. Paris, Marchal & Godde, 1914. 97 p) – Paris, Marchal et Billard, 1898. 109 p. LL-4029 – 1 – us L of C Photodup [340]

MANUAL DE MISIONOLOGIA. VITORIA, 1933 / Mondragones, Pio Ma. de & Escalante, Gumersindo – Madrid: Razon y Fe, 1934 – 1 – sp Bibl Santa Ana [946]

MANUAL DE TEOSOFIA O BREVE ESTUDIO CRITICO DE LAS DOCTRINAS TEOSOFICAS. MEJICO, 1929 / Busnelli, Juan – Madrid: Razon y Fe, 1930 – 1 – sp Bibl Santa Ana [240]

MANUAL DEL CATEQUISTA. TRAD. DEL ITALIANO POR D. FELIX MERINO REVUELTA. BARCELONA, 1943 / Marquez, Gabino & Francisco, Tonolo – Madrid: Razon y Fe, 1945 – 1 – sp Bibl Santa Ana [240]

MANUAL DEL EJERCITO AZUL DE MARIA – Caceres – 5 – sp Bibl Santa Ana [073]

MANUAL ECLESIASTICO Y REGULAR PARA LOS RELIGIOSES DE LA SANTA PROVINCIA DE SAN GABRIEL... / Santano de Membrio, Juan – Salamanca: Francisco Garcia Onorato y San Miguel, 1719 – 1 – sp Bibl Santa Ana [240]

MANUAL ETIMOLOGICO GRECOLATINO / Moran Triana, Eduardo – Badajoz: Tip. El Noticiero, 1905 – 1 – sp Bibl Santa Ana [590]

MANUAL FOR ADMINISTRATIVE LAW JUDGES / Ruhlen, Merritt – 1st ed 1974. Washington: GPO, 1974 (all publ) – 2mf – 9 – $3.00 – LLMC 94-337A – us L.L.M.C. [340]

MANUAL FOR ADMINISTRATIVE LAW JUDGES / Ruhlen, Merritt – 2nd ed 1982. Washington: GPO, 1982 (all publ) – 2mf – 9 – $3.00 – LLMC 94-337B – us L.L.M.C. [340]

MANUAL FOR ANIMAL HEALTH AUXILIARY PERSONNEL – 1983 2nd print 1984 – 392p – it F.A.O. [636]

MANUAL FOR CLASSIFICATION OF CORRESPONDENCE, DEPT. OF STATE (4TH ED., 1938) / U.S. Department of State – 1r – 1 – M600 – us Nat'l Archives [350]

MANUAL FOR COURTS-MARTIAL, 1951 : EFFECTIVE 31 MAY 1951 – n.p., n.d. – 7mf – 9 – $10.50 – LLMC 96-099 – us L.L.M.C. [340]

A MANUAL FOR EXECUTORS, ADMINISTRATORS AND GUARDIANS, EMBRACING ALL THE STATUTES IN FORCE IN THE STATE OF INDIANA RELATING TO THE SETTLEMENT OF DECENDENTS' ESTATES. / Howland, John D – Indianapolis: Merrill, Hubbard, 1879. 419p. LL-641 – 1 – us L of C Photodup [340]

A MANUAL FOR GUARDIANS AND TRUSTEES OF MINORS, INSANE PERSONS, IMBECILES, IDIOTS, DRUNKARDS, AND FOR GUARDIANS AD LITEM, RESIDENT AND NON-RESIDENT, AFFECTED BY THE LAWS OF OHIO / Giauque, Florien – 4th ed. Cincinnati: Clarke, 1894. 380p. LL-658 – 1 – us L of C Photodup [340]

MANUAL FOR INTERIOR SOULS = MANUEL DES AMES INTERIEURES : A COLLECTION OF UNPUBLISHED WRITINGS / Grou, Jean Nicholas – (In English) – London: S Anselm's Society, 1891 – 1mf – 9 – 0-8370-7148-8 – 1986-1148 – us A.T.L.A. [230]

MANUAL FOR LAW STUDENTS – Columbus, OH: Students' 1885 16p. LL-412 – 1 – us L of C Photodup [340]

A MANUAL FOR NOTARIES PUBLIC, GENERAL CONVEYANCERS, COMMISSIONERS, JUSTICES, MAYORS, CONSULS. / Giauque, Florien – Cincinnati: Clarke, 1888. 388p. LL-527 – 1 – us L of C Photodup [340]

A MANUAL FOR NOTARIES PUBLIC, JUSTICES OF THE PEACE, AND THEIR EMPLOYERS IN MASSACHUSETTS / Keen, James T – Boston: Little, Brown & Co, 1903 – 3mf – 9 – $4.50 – LLMC 92-152 – us L.L.M.C. [340]

MANUAL FOR SURVEYING NATIONAL SCIENTIFIC AND TECHNOLOGICAL POTENTIAL – 2nd rev ed 1990 – 197p – 9 – 92-3-102435-3 – fr UNESCO [500]

MANUAL FOR THE PRODUCTION OF ANTHRAX AND BLACKLEG VACCINES – 1991 – 133p – it F.A.O. [636]

MANUAL FOR THE PRODUCTION OF MAREK'S DISEASE, GUMBORO DISEASE AND INACTIVATED NEWCASTLE DISEASE VACCINES – 1991 – 97p – it F.A.O. [636]

MANUAL FOR THE SLAUGHTER OF SMALL RUMINANTS IN DEVELOPING COUNTRIES – 1985 – 50p – it F.A.O. [636]

MANUAL FOR THE USE OF MISSIONARIES / Presbyterian Church in the U.S.A. Board of Foreign Missions – 1840, 1862, 1873, 1881, 1882, 1889, 1894, 1904 – 1 – $50.00 – us Presbyterian [240]

A MANUAL FOR THE USE OF NOTARIES PUBLIC AND BANKERS. / Roelker, Bernard – (4th ed. New-York: Bankers', 1864. 368p. LL-1487) – New-York: Bankers', 1857. 244p. LL-1488 – 1 – us L of C Photodup [340]

MANUAL FOR THE USE OF ROAD & RURAL INSPECTORS & POUND-KEEPERS: CONTAINING ALSO A MONTHLY CALENDAR OF DUTIES COMPILED FROM THE LATEST EDITION OF THE MUNICIPAL CODE (1888) WITH DECISIONS OF THE TRIBUNALS QUOTED / Colfer, George W – Quebec: E. Vincent, 1888. 04155. (Pre-1900 Canadiana) – 9 – cn C.I.H.M. [380]

MANUAL FOR THE USE OF THE LEGISLATURE OF THE STATE OF NEW YORK / Cook, Frederick – Albany: Weed, Parsons and Co., 1888. New York Reel 2. The Cox Library Collection – 5 – us Americana [978]

MANUAL OF ADMINISTRATION OF THE TRUST TERRITORY OF THE PACIFIC ISLANDS / Trust Territory of the Pacific Islands. (U.S.) – Saipan: Office of the High Commissioner. 2v. 28 Sept 1964 – 20mf – 9 – $30.00 – LLMC 82-100F Title 6 – us L.L.M.C. [324]

MANUAL OF AMERICAN COLLEGES AND THEOLOGICAL SEMINARIES / Freeman, Z – 1856 – 1 – $50.00 – us Presbyterian [290]

A MANUAL OF AMERICAN MINING LAW / Ricketts, Alfred Herbert – San Francisco: Scientific, 1911. LL-1059 – 1 – us L of C Photodup [622]

A MANUAL OF BIBLIOGRAPHY, 1500-1914 / McIntyre, W E – v1-5, manuscript – 1 – $86.86 – us Baptist [240]

A MANUAL OF BRITISH BUTTERFLIES AND MOTHS / ed by Stainton, H T – London, [1856-]1857-1859 – 2 vols – 8 – ne IDC [590]

A MANUAL OF BRITISH COLEOPTERA, OR BEETLES... / Stephens, J F – London, 1839 – XII, 443p – 8 – ne IDC [590]

A MANUAL OF BRITISH LICHENS / Mudd, W – Darlington, 1861. 309, pp., 5 pls. B-587 2 – 8 – ne IDC [580]

MANUAL OF BUSINESS AND PROCEDURE. : PREPARED IN THE LEGISLATIVE ASSEMBLY DEPARTMENT OF THE GOVERNMENT OF INDIA FOR THE USE OF MEMBERS OF THE ASSEMBLY / India. Legislature. Legislative Assembly – 5th ed. Delhi, 1938 – us Res Libr [324]

A MANUAL OF CHRISTIAN DOCTRINE / Banks, John Shaw – London: Charles H. Kelly, 1891. 1 fiche – 9 – us A.T.L.A. [240]

A MANUAL OF CHRISTIAN EVIDENCES / Row, Charles Adolphus – New York: Thomas Whittaker, 1888. 1 fiche. 8370-4986-5 – 9 – us A.T.L.A. [240]

MANUAL OF CHRISTIAN EVIDENCES / Fisher, George Park – Meadville: Flood & Vincent, 1892. 1 fiche – 9 – us A.T.L.A. [240]

MANUAL OF CHRISTIAN THEOLOGY ON THE INDUCTIVE METHOD / Burwash, Nathaniel – (Vol. 2. London: H. Marshall, 1900. 05502. (Pre-1900 Canadiana)) – Vol. 1. London: H. Marshall, 1900. 05501. (Pre-1900 Canadiana) – 9 – cn C.I.H.M. [240]

A MANUAL OF CHURCH HISTORY / Funk, Franz Xaver; ed by Kent, W H – London: Burns & Oates, 1914 – 2mf – us A.T.L.A. [240]

A MANUAL OF CHURCH HISTORY / Guericke, Henry E F – Andover: W.F. Draper, 1874-1882, c1857-c1870 – 2mf – us A.T.L.A. [240]

MANUAL OF COLLECTIONS OF TREATIES... / Myers, DP – Cambridge, 1922 – 8mf – 9 – ILM-817/1 – ne IDC [270]

MANUAL OF CONCHOLOGY / ed by Tryon, G W A & Pilsbry, H A – Philadelphia. v1-17 1879-1898; S.2 v1-28 1885-1927 – 374mf – 9 – ne IDC [590]

A MANUAL OF CONGREGATIONAL PRINCIPLES / Dale, Robert William – (Includes bibliographical references) – 9th ed. London: Congregational Union of England and Wales, 1902 – 1mf – 9 – 0-8370-8806-2 – 1986-2806 – us A.T.L.A. [240]

A MANUAL OF COUNCILS OF THE HOLY CATHOLIC CHURCH / Landon, Edward H – London: Griffith Faran, [1893?] (The Westminster library) – 2mf – us A.T.L.A. [240]

A MANUAL OF CRIMINAL LAW AND CRIMINAL PROCEDURE FOR POLICE / Puttkammer, Ernst Wilfred – Chicago: The University of Chicago Press, 1931 93,1p. LL-1375 – 1 – us L of C Photodup [340]

A MANUAL OF CRIMINAL LAW, AS ESTABLISHED IN THE STATE OF MARYLAND / Hocheimer, Lewis – Baltimore: Scrimger, 1889. 200p. LL-756 – 1 – us L of C Photodup [340]

A MANUAL OF CRIMINAL LAW, INCLUDING THE MODE OF PROCEDURE BY WHICH IT IS ENFORCED / Washburn, Emory – 3d ed. Chicago, Callaghan, 1900. 278 p. LL-1499 – 1 – us L of C Photodup [340]

MANUAL OF EARLY ECCLESIASTICAL HISTORY TO 476 A.D. / Wells, Charles Luke – Sewanee, Tenn.: University Press at the University of the South, c1912 – 1mf – us A.T.L.A. [240]

MANUAL OF ECCLESIASTICAL ARCHITECTURE : COMPRISING A STUDY OF ITS VARIOUS STYLES, THE CHRONOLOGICAL ARRANGEMENTS OF ITS ELEMENTS, AND ITS RELATION TO CHRISTIAN WORSHIP / Martin, William Wallace – Cincinnati: Curts & Jennings; New York: Eaton & Mains, 1897 – 2mf – us A.T.L.A. [720]

A MANUAL OF ELEMENTARY PHONETICS / Burt, A W – Toronto: Copp, Clark, 1898. 00355. (Pre-1900 Canadiana) – 9 – cn C.I.H.M. [400]

A MANUAL OF ENTOMOLOGY / Burmeister, C H C – London, 1836 – XII, 654p, 33pls – 8 – ne IDC [590]

A MANUAL OF EQUITY JURISPRUDENCE, FOR PRACTITIONERS AND STUDENTS, FOUNDED ON THE WORKS OF STORY, SPENCE, AND OTHER WRITERS. / Smith, Josiah William – 2d Amer. ed.....From the 12th London ed. Washington City: Morrison, 1878. 530p. LL-1075 – 1 – us L of C Photodup [340]

A MANUAL OF ETHICS / Mackenzie, John Stuart – (Includes bibliographical references and index) – 3rd enl ed. [S.l.]: University Correspondence College Press; New York: Hinds & Noble, 1897 – 2mf – 9 – 0-8370-7308-1 – 1986-1308 – us A.T.L.A. [170]

A MANUAL OF EUROPEAN BUTTERFLIES / Kirby, W F – London, Edinburgh, 1862.xii,153p. 1 pl. Z-1391/2 – 8 – ne IDC [590]

MANUAL OF FOOD QUALITY CONTROL – it F.A.O. [660]

MANUAL OF FOREST INVENTORY WITH SPECIAL REFERENCE TO MIXED TROPICAL FORESTS – 1981 – 208p – it F.A.O. [634]

MANUAL OF FUMIGATION FOR INSECT CONTROL / Monro, H AU – 2nd rev ed 1975 – 381p – it F.A.O. [660]

A MANUAL OF INDIAN BOTANY / Bose, J C A – London, Glasgow. 1920. B-5305 2 – 8 – ne IDC [580]

A MANUAL OF INDIAN TIMBERS / Gamble, J S – An account of the structure, growth, distribution and qualities of Indian woods, Calcutta. 1881. B-2336 2 – 8 – ne IDC [580]

A MANUAL OF INJURIOUS INSECTS / Collinge, WE – Birmingham, 1912. xx,268p. Z-1140/2 – 8 – ne IDC [590]

A MANUAL OF INJURIOUS INSECTS / Ormerod, E A – Z-1515 2. 1881 – 8 – ne IDC [590]

MANUAL OF INTERNATIONAL LAW... / Ferguson, J H – London, 1884 – 14mf – 1 – ILM-169/1 – ne IDC [327]

MANUAL OF LAWS RELATING TO PRIVATE CLAIMS AGAINST THE STATE OF NEW YORK.. / Holbrook, Edwin M – Albany: Argus, 1884. 72p. LL-777 – 1 – us L of C Photodup [340]

A MANUAL OF LOGIC / Smart, Benjamin Humphrey – London: Longman, Brown, Green, and Longmans, 1849 – xii/268p – 1 – us U.W. Library [160]

A MANUAL OF METHODISM AND OF WESLEYAN POLITY / Burton, H R – London, 1881 – 1mf – 9 – ne IDC [240]

MANUAL OF METHODS FOR FISH STOCK ASSESSMENT, PART 1 : FISH POPULATION ANALYSIS / Gulland, J A – 1976 – 154p – it F.A.O. [639]

MANUAL OF METHODS FOR FISHERIES RESOURCE SURVEY AND APPRAISAL, PART 2 : THE USE OF ACOUSTIC INSTRUMENTS FOR FISH DETECTION AND ABUNDANCE ESTIMATION / ed by Forbes, S T & Nakken, O – 1975 – 138p – it F.A.O. [639]

MANUAL OF METHODS IN AQUATIC ENVIRONMENT RESEARCH. PART 10 : SHORT-TERM STATIC BIOASSAYS – 1987 – 72p – it F.A.O. [639]

MANUAL OF METHODS IN AQUATIC ENVIRONMENT RESEARCH, PART 11 : BIOLOGICAL ASSESSMENT OF MARINE POLLUTION – WITH PARTICULAR REFERENCE TO BENTHOS – 1992 – 56p – it F.A.O. [360]

A MANUAL OF NATURAL AND REVEALED THEOLOGY : DESIGNED, ESPECIALLY, FOR LOCAL PREACHERS AND SUNDAY-SCHOOL TEACHERS / Williams, Henry Wilkinson – (Includes index) – 2nd ed. London: T Woolmer, 1883 – 1mf – 9 – 0-8370-5755-8 – 1985-3755 – us A.T.L.A. [240]

MANUAL OF NATURAL THEOLOGY / Fisher, George Park – New York: Scribner, 1893. 1 fiche – 9 – us A.T.L.A. [240]

A MANUAL OF NORTH AMERICAN BIRDS / Ridgway, R – Z 1887 2. 1887 – 8 – ne IDC [590]

MANUAL OF PARLIAMENTARY PRACTICE : RULES OF PROCEEDINGS AND DEBATE IN DELIBERATIVE ASSEMBLIES / Cushing, Luther Stearns – Boston: Brown & Taggard, 1862 – 2mf – 9 – $9.00 – LLMC 92-166 – us L.L.M.C. [340]

MANUAL OF PATENT LAW / Simonds, William Edgar – Hartford, 1874. 256p. LL-1686 – 1 – us L of C Photodup [340]

A MANUAL OF PATROLOGY : BEING A CONCISE ACCOUNT OF THE CHIEF PERSONS, SECTS, ORDERS, ETC., IN CHRISTIAN HISTORY FROM THE FIRST CENTURY TO THE PERIOD OF THE REFORMATION. WITH SELECT BIBLIOGRAPHICAL REFERENCES / Stearns, Wallace Nelson – New York: Scribner,1899 – 1mf – us A.T.L.A. [240]

MANUAL OF PEST CONTROL FOR FOOD SECURITY RESERVE GRAIN STOCKS – 1985 – 208p – it F.A.O. [630]

A MANUAL OF PRACTICE IN THE COURTS OF THE UNITED STATES / Desty, Robert – (2nd ed., San Francisco, Whitney, 1876. 477 p. LL-1656. 5th issue, San Francisco, Whitney, 1881. 447 p. LL-1694. 6th ed., San Francisco, Bancroft-Whitney, 1887. 934 p. LL-165. 7th ed., San Francisco, Bancroft-Whitney, 1889. LL-73. 8th ed., San Francisco, Bancroft-Whitney, 1893. 2 v. LL-72) – San Francisco, Whitney, 1875. 447 p. LL-74 – 1 – us L of C Photodup [340]

MANUAL OF PROCEDURES FOR PARTICIPATING LIBRARIES / Midwest Inter-Library Center. Chicago – Rev. 1957 – 1 – us Res Libr [020]

A MANUAL OF RELIGION AND OF THE HISTORY OF THE CHRISTIAN CHURCH : FOR THE USE OF UPPER CLASSES IN PUBLIC SCHOOLS IN GERMANY AND FOR ALL EDUCATED MEN IN GENERAL / Bretschneider, Karl Gottlieb – London: N. Truebner, [1857?] – 1mf – us A.T.L.A. [240]

MANUAL OF REVIVALS : PRACTICAL HINTS AND SUGGESTIONS FROM HISTORIES OF REVIVALS AND BIOGRAPHIES OF REVIVALISTS / Hervey, George Winfred – (Includes indexes) – New York: Funk & Wagnalls, c1884 – 1mf – 9 – 0-8370-6502-X – 1986-0502 – us A.T.L.A. [240]

A MANUAL OF STATUTES AND FORMS, AND A COMMENTARY UPON THE RIGHTS, DUTIES AND POWERS OF EXECUTORS AND ADMINISTRATORS OF THE STATE OF KANSAS / Spalding, Hugh Mortimer – Topeka, Crane, 1881. 318 p. LL-1690 – 1 – us L of C Photodup [340]

A MANUAL OF STATUTORY CORPORATION LAW / Overland, Martha Uboe – Interleaved ed. of 1909. New York: Ronald, 1909. 508p. LL-1141 – 1 – us L of C Photodup [340]

A MANUAL OF TELUGU GRAMMAR : CHIEFLY INTENDED FOR MIDDLE AND ELEMENTARY NORMAL SCHOOLS / Sastri, T Anjaneya – 4th rev ed. Guntur: A E L Mission Press, 1906 – us Res Libr [490]

A MANUAL OF THE ARAMAIC LANGUAGE OF THE BABYLONIAN TALMUD / Margolis, Max Leopold – Muenchen. 1910. BJ-32-52 1 – 9 – ne IDC [470]

MANUAL OF THE BELLARY DISTRICT / Kelsall, J – Madras. 1872. BI-150-11 2 – 8 – ne IDC [950]

A MANUAL OF THE BOTANY OF THE NORTHERN UNITED STATES / Gray, A – 7546 1. 1848 – 9 – ne IDC [580]

MANUAL OF THE BOTANY OF THE ROCKY MOUNTAIN REGION / Coulter, J M – 7522 2. 1885 – 8 – ne IDC [580]

A MANUAL OF THE CATHOLIC RELIGION FOR CATECHISTS, TEACHERS AND SELFINSTRUCTION / Weninger, Francis Xavier – 3rd ed. New York: D & J Sadlier, c1861 – 1mf – 9 – 0-8370-6460-0 – 1986-0460 – us A.T.L.A. [240]

A MANUAL OF THE CHIKARANGA LANGUAGE : WITH GRAMMAR, EXERCISES, USEFUL CONVERSATIONAL SENTENCES AND VOCABULARY: ENGLISH-CHIKARANGA AND CHIKARANGA-ENGLISH / Louw, C S – Bulawayo [Rhodesia]: Philpott & Collins, 1915 – us Res Libr [470]

A MANUAL OF THE CONSTITUTIONAL HISTORY OF CANADA FROM THE EARLIEST PERIOD TO THE YEAR 1888: INCLUDING THE BRITISH NORTH AMERICA ACT, 1867, AND A DIGEST OF JUDICIAL DECISIONS ON QUESTIONS OF LEGISLATIVE JURISDICTION / Bourinot, John George – Montreal: Dawson Bros., 1888. 00199. (Pre-1900 Canadiana) – 9 – cn C.I.H.M. [971]

A MANUAL OF THE DISCIPLINE OF THE METHODIST EPISCOPAL CHURCH, SOUTH : INCLUDING THE DECISIONS OF THE COLLEGE OF BISHOPS AND RULES OF ORDER APPLICABLE TO ECCLESIASTICAL COURTS AND CONFERENCES / McTyeire, Holland N – Nashville, Tenn.: Publishing House of the Methodist Episcopal Church, South, 1870 – 1mf – us A.T.L.A. [240]

A MANUAL OF THE DISTRICT OF CUDDAPAH IN THE PRESIDENCY OF MADRAS / Gribble, J D B – Madras. 1875. BI-150-12 2 – 8 – ne IDC [950]

A MANUAL OF THE DISTRICT OF TANJORE / Row, T Venkaswami – I-150-16 2. 1883 – 8 – ne IDC [950]

A MANUAL OF THE DISTRICT OF VIZAGAPATAM / Carmichael, D F – Madras. 1869. BI-150-2 2 – 8 – ne IDC [950]

MANUAL OF THE DUTIES OF ROAD AND RURAL INSPECTORS, UNDER THE MUNICIPAL CODE OF THE PROVINCE OF QUEBEC / Belanger, Louis Charles – Sherbrooke, Quebec: Pionnier Job Office, 1872. 03548. (Pre-1900 Canadiana) – 9 – cn C.I.H.M. [971]

MANUAL OF THE FLORA OF THE NORTHERN STATES AND CANADA / Britton, N L – 7513 2. 1901 – 8 – ne IDC [580]

A MANUAL OF THE GEOLOGY OF INDIA / Medlicott, H B & Blanford, WT – G-161 2. 4 v. 1877-1887 – 8 – ne IDC [550]

A MANUAL OF THE KISTNA DISTRICT OF THE PRESIDENCY OF MADRAS / Mackenzie, G – Madras. 1883. BI-150-9 – 8 – ne IDC [950]

A MANUAL OF THE KURNOOL DISTRICT IN THE PRESIDENCY OF MADRAS / Chetty, N G – Madras. 1886. BI-150-13 2 – 8 – ne IDC [950]

A MANUAL OF THE LAND AND FRESHWATER SHELLS OF THE BRITISH ISLANDS / Turton W – Z 843 2. 1831 – 8 – ne IDC [580]

A MANUAL OF THE LAW OF FIXTURES / Hill, John Ward – 2d ed. New York: Baker, Voorhis, 1871. 91p. LL-276 – 1 – us L of C Photodup [340]

A MANUAL OF THE LAW OF PLEADING / Parks, James Giddings – Knoxville, Tenn., 1894. 217p. LL-949 – 1 – us L of C Photodup [340]

A MANUAL OF THE LAW OF PRINCIPAL AND AGENT / Petgrave, Ezekiel Charles – London: Stevens and Norton, 1857. 264p. LL-123 – 1 – us L of C Photodup [340]

A MANUAL OF THE LAW RELATING TO MARRIAGE AND DIVORCE AS DETERMINED BY THE SUPREME COURT OF LOUISIANA / Magruder, Herman B – New Orleans: Brandao, 1884. 154p. LL-562 – 1 – us L of C Photodup [340]

MANUAL OF THE LAWS AND COURTS OF THE UNITED STATES. / Andrews, Horace – New York, Andrews, Gibson and Bateman, 1873. 443 p. LL-705 – 1 – us L of C Photodup [340]

MANUAL OF THE LAWS OF MARYLAND, DISTRICT OF COLUMBIA, VIRGINIA AND WEST VIRGINIA RELATIVE TO RELIGIOUS CORPORATIONS, CHARITABLE USES. / Richardson, Charles Herbert – Washington, D.C.: Wilson, 1887. 62p. LL-1200 – 1 – us L of C Photodup [340]

MANUAL OF THE LEADING MUHAMMADAN OBJECTIONS TO CHRISTIANITY / Clair-Tisdall, W St. – London, 1911 – Dfl13.00 – ne Slangenburg [260]

MANUAL OF THE MEDICAL BOTANY OF THE UNITED STATES / Rafinesque-Schmaltz, Constantine S – Philadelphia, 1841 – 5mf – 9 – ne IDC [615]

A MANUAL OF THE MOLLUSCA OR RUDIMENTARY TREATISE OF RECENT AND FOSSIL SHELLS / Woodward, S P – Z 886 2. 1851-1856 – 8 – ne IDC [560]

A MANUAL OF THE NELLORE DISTRICT / Boswell, J A C – Madras. 1873. BI-150-14 2 – 8 – ne IDC [950]

A MANUAL OF THE NILGIRI DISTRICT IN THE PRESIDENCY OF MADRAS / Grigg, H B – Madras. 1880. BI-150-4 2 – 8 – ne IDC [950]

A MANUAL OF THE NORTH ARCOTT DISTRICT IN THE PRESIDENCY OF MADRAS / Cox, A F – 2v. 1895. BI-150-1 2 – 8 – ne IDC [950]

MANUAL OF THE ORDER OF CITIZENSHIP / Ku Klux Klan of Canada – 1927? – 9 – $15.00 – cn McLaren [360]

MANUAL OF THE REVISED STATUTES OF THE STATE OF NEW YORK. – Glen's Falls: Smith, 1831. 412p. LL-464 – 1 – us L of C Photodup [340]

THE MANUAL OF THE SACRED CHOIR / Ball, Eli – 1849 – 1 – 5.28 – us Baptist [240]

A MANUAL OF THE SALEM DISTRICT / Le Fanu, J H – I-150-7 2. 2 v. 1883 – 8 – ne IDC [978]

A MANUAL OF THE SOUTH ARCOTT DISTRICT / Garstin, J H – Madras Presidency. Madras. 1878. BI-150-18 2 – 8 – ne IDC [950]

A MANUAL OF THE TRICHINOPOLY DISTRICT / Moore, L – Madras. 1878. BI-150-10 2 – 8 – ne IDC [950]

MANUAL OF THE U.S. BANKRUPTCY ACT, 1867. / Rice, Clinton – Washington, D.C.: Philip & Solomons, 1867. 442p. LL-1056 – 1 – us L of C Photodup [340]

A MANUAL OF THEOLOGY / Strong, Thomas Banks – (Includes bibliographical references & index) – 2nd rev enl ed. London: Adam & Charles Black, 1903 – 1mf – 9 – 0-8370-5548-2 – 1985-3548 – us A.T.L.A. [240]
A MANUAL OF TRADEMARK CASES / Cox, Rowland – Boston, Houghton, Mifflin, 1881. 478 p. LL-69 – 1 – us L of C Photodup [340]
A MANUAL OF TRANSLATION FROM TAMIL INTO ENGLISH : BASED ON THE ANALYSIS OF SENTENCES WITH NUMEROUS EXERCISES / Venkatarama Aiyar, K – 2nd. ed. Kumbakonam: Hindu Educational Trading Co, 1902 – us Res Libr [490]
MANUAL ON AGRICULTURAL PRICE INDEX NUMBERS – 1988 – 45p – it F.A.O. [650]
MANUAL ON DRAINAGE IN URBANIZED AREAS / ed by Zuidema, Floris C et al – 9 – fr UNESCO [627]
MANUAL ON EMPLOYMENT DISCRIMINATION LAW AND CIVIL RIGHTS ACTIONS / Richey, Charles R – Washington: FJC, 1988 – 10mf – 9 – $15.00 – LLMC 95-342 – us L.L.M.C. [340]
MANUAL ON EVALUATION OF POPULATION COMMUNICATION PROGRAMMES / Gillespie, R – 1981 – 128p – 9 – 92-3-101559-1 – fr UNESCO [380]
MANUAL ON FERTILIZER DISTRIBUTION – 1985 – 124p – it F.A.O. [631]
MANUAL ON FERTILIZER STATISTICS – 1991 – 52p – it F.A.O. [631]
MANUAL ON FISH CANNING – 1988 – 77p – it F.A.O. [660]
MANUAL ON FOOD AND NUTRITION POLICY – 4th printing 1978 – 95p – it F.A.O. [338]
MANUAL ON HOUSEHOLD FOOD CONSUMPTION SURVEYS / Reh, E – 4th printing 1976 – 96p – it F.A.O. [338]
MANUAL ON HOW TO DO A DIVORCE CASE IN THE MARSHALL ISLANDS TOGETHER WITH FORMS : INCLUDES SEPARATION AND ANNULMENT / Lanham, John C – Nov 9 1983 – 6mf – 9 – $9.00 – LLMC 82-100l Title 20 – us L.L.M.C. [340]
MANUAL ON MEAT COLD STORE OPERATION AND MANAGEMENT – 1991 – 128p – it F.A.O. [660]
MANUAL ON MUSHROOM CULTIVATION – 1983 2nd print 1985 – 75p – it F.A.O. [631]
MANUAL ON RECURRING PROBLEMS IN CRIMINAL TRIALS : 1985 REVISION / Voorhees, Donald S – Washington: FJC, 1985 – 2mf – 9 – $3.00 – LLMC 95-394 – us L.L.M.C. [340]
MANUAL ON RECURRING PROBLEMS IN CRIMINAL TRIALS / Voorhees, Donald S – 3rd ed. Washington: FJC, 1990 – 2mf – 9 – $3.00 – LLMC 95-368 – us L.L.M.C. [340]
MANUAL ON SAWMILL OPERATIONAL MAINTENANCE – 1990 – 69p – it F.A.O. [670]
MANUAL ON SIMPLE METHODS OF MEAT PRESERVATION – 1990 – 99p – it F.A.O. [660]
MANUAL ON SYSTEMS OF INVENTORYING IMMOVABLE CULTURAL PROPERTY / Sykes, Meredith H – 1984 – 180p – 9 – 92-3-102080-3 – fr UNESCO [306]
MANUAL ON THE DEVELOPMENT AND USE OF FAO SPECIFICATIONS FOR PLANT PROTECTION PRODUCTS – 3rd rev ed 1987 – 128p – it F.A.O. [630]
MANUAL ON THE DIAGNOSIS OF RINDERPEST / Scott, G R et al – 1986 – 187p – it F.A.O. [636]
MANUAL ON THE ESTABLISHMENT, OPERATIONS AND MANAGEMENT OF CEREAL BANKS – 1985 – 117p – it F.A.O. [338]
MANUAL ON THE NATIONAL BUDGETING OF SCIENTIFIC AND TECHNOLOGICAL ACTIVITIES : INTEGRATION OF THE 'SCIENCE AND TECHNOLOGY' FUNCTION IN THE GENERAL STATE BUDGET – 1984 – 233p – 9 – 92-3-101927-9 – fr UNESCO [350]
MANUAL SHOWING THE PRIVATE BILL PRACTICE OF THE PARLIAMENT OF CANADA / Hartney, Edward P – Ottawa: MacLean, Roger, 1882. 03017. (Pre-1900 Canadiana) – 9 – cn C.I.H.M. [971]
EL MANUAL TOLENDANO PARA LA ADMINISTRATION DE SACRAMENTOS A TRAVERS DE LOS SIGLOS / Garcia, Alf. I – 1958 – 2mf – 8 – Dfl9.00 – ne Slangenburg [240]
A MANUAL UPON THE SEARCHING OF RECORDS AND THE PREPARATION OF ABSTRACTS OF TITLE TO REAL PROPERTY / Curwen, Maskell E – (2nd? ed.. Cincinnati, Clarke, 1883. 264 p. LL-281) – Cincinnati, Clarke, 1865. 191 p. LL-282 – 1 – us L of C Photodup [340]
Manuale *see* MANUSCRIPT IN RED AND BLACK
MANUALE AD USUM PER CELEBRIS ECCL. SARISBURIENSIS / Collins, A Jefferies – 1960 – 4mf – 8 – ne Slangenburg [240]
MANUALE DEGLI INVITATORI CO'SUOI SALMI.. / Coferati, Matteo – Seconda edizione. 1718 – 2 – us Sibley [780]
MANUALE DI COMPUTO...DI VERONA... / Meersseman-Adda – Madrid: Graf. Calleja, 1967 – 1 – sp Bibl Santa Ana [946]
MANUALE ET PROCESSIONALE AD USUM INSIGNIS ECCLESIAE EBORACENSIS / Henderson, W – Edinburgh, 1874 – 8mf – 8 – Dfl30.00 – ne Slangenburg [240]
MANUALE HISTORIAE MISSIONUM. SHANGAI, 1935 / Montalban, Francisco J – Madrid: Razon y Fe, 1935 – 1 – sp Bibl Santa Ana [240]
LE MANUALE PASTORUM DE TOURNAI / Malherbe, G – 1933 – 1mf – 8 – Dfl6.00 – ne Slangenburg [240]
MANUALE PASTORUM DIOECENSIS BUSCODUCENSIS – 1572 – 1mf – 8 – Dfl6.00 – ne Slangenburg [240]
MANUALE THOMISTARUM SEU BREVIS THEOLOGIAE CURSUS... / Gonet, J B – Biterris. 6v. 1680 – 42mf – 9 – CA-50/1 – ne IDC [240]
MANUAL+INSTALLATION SOFTWARE – it F.A.O. [000]
MANUDUCTIO AD ORGANUM.. / Samber, Johann B – 1704 – 2 – us Sibley [780]
MANUEL A L'USAGE DES ADMINISTRATEURS ET DU PERSONNEL DES AFFAIRES INDIGENES DE LA COLONIE DU SENEGAL ET DES COLONIES RELEVANT DU GOUVERNEMENT GENERAL DE L'AFRIQUE OCCIDENTALE FRANCAISE / Roux, Emile – Paris: A Challamel, 1911 – us Res Libr [350]
MANUEL ABREGE DE CONTREVERSE, OU CONTREVERSE DES PAUVRES / Mannock, John – Quebec: Nouvelle Imprimerie, 1806. SEM16P69 – 1r – 5 – Can$9.00 – cn Bibl Nat [830]
MANUEL BREVIARIOS DEL PENSAMIENTO ESPANOL... / Ballesteros, Gaibrois – Burgos: Razon y Fe, 1939 – 1 – sp Bibl Santa Ana [946]
Manuel, Carlos *see*
– BIBLIOGRAFIA CUBANA DE LES SIGLOS 17 Y 18
– BIBLIOTECA HISTORICA CUBANA
MANUEL CONMIGO, ILUSTRACIONES DE ENRIQUE SOPENA SCAPARDINI / Carande, Bernardo Victor – Sevilla: Imp. Flores, 1953 – 1 – sp Bibl Santa Ana [740]
MANUEL DAHOMEEN GRAMMAIRE-CHRESTOMATHIE / Delafosse, Maurice – Dictionnaire francais-dahomeen et dahomeen-francais. Paris, Ernest Leroux. 1894 – 9 – $12.50 – fr Orientalistes [490]
MANUEL D'ARCHITECTURE OU PRINCIPES DES OPERATIONS PRIMITIVES DE CET ART / Seguin, Charles – Paris. Didot, 1786. 8 fol. xvi, 304p., tab., ill. (Architecture Series) – 9 – fr Hachette [720]
LE MANUEL D'ARTISANAT AU FOYER – [Quebec Province: s.n., 194-?]. SEM105P1531 – 1mf – 9 – Can$2.25 – cn Bibl Nat [690]
MANUEL DE BOTANIQUE / Duchesne, Antoine Nicolas – Paris. 1764. B-82 2 – 8 – ne IDC [580]
MANUEL DE CUISINE RAISONNEE – 2e ed. Quebec: l'Action sociale, limitee, 1926. SEM105P1811 – 6mf – 9 – Can$13.50 – cn Bibl Nat [600]
MANUEL DE DIPLOMATIQUE / Giry, A – Paris, 1894 – Dfl70.00 – ne Slangenburg [240]
MANUEL DE DIPLOMATIQUE (DONNE LES CONCORDANCES DE DATES ANCIEN STYLE ET NOUVEAN STYLE) / Giry, A – Paris, 1894 – 3mf – 9 – F90.00 – fr F.F.G. [327]
MANUEL DE DROIT ... / Bonfils, H – Paris, 1894 – 10mf – 9 – ILM-103/1 – ne IDC [327]
MANUEL DE DROIT PUBLIC ET ADMINISTRATIF DE L'EMPIRE OTTOMAN / Heidborn, A – Vienne, 1909-1912. 2v – 9mf – 9 – NE-20.147/1 – ne IDC [350]
MANUEL DE LA LANGUE MALGACHE (DIALECTE MERINA) / Berthier, Hugues Jean – Tananarive: Impr de la Mission norvegienne, 1922 – us Res Libr [470]
MANUEL DE LA LANGUE TOULE / Grimal de Guiraudon, T – Paris, Leipzig, H. Welter. 1894 – 9 – $5.00 – fr Orientalistes [490]
MANUEL DE LA PROHIBITION D'APRES LA LOI DE TEMPERANCE DU CANADA, LES ARRETES EN CONSEIL FEDERAUX DU TEMPS DE GUERRE, ETC. – Quebec: Editions de l'Action sociale catholique, 1918. SEM105P1674 – 1mf – 9 – Can$2.25 – cn Bibl Nat [340]
MANUEL DE LA PURETE DU LANGAGE / Blondin, J N – 1823 – 9 – fr I.C.S. [440]
MANUEL DE L'HISTOIRE NATURELLE, DES MOLLUSQUES ET DE LEURS COQUILLES / Rang, PKS L – Z 738 2. 1829 – 8 – ne IDC [590]
MANUEL DE LIBRAIRE ET DE L'AMATEUR DE LIVRES / Brunet, Jacques Charles – 5e ed Paris Tome 1-6; Supplement Tome 1-2 1869 – 174mf – 8 – ne Slangenburg [020]
MANUEL DE LINGALA : TENANT COMPTE DU LANGAGE PARLE ET DU LANGAGE LITTERAIRE / Boeck, L B de – Bruxelles: Scheut, 1952 – us Res Libr [490]
MANUEL DE L'INSTITUTEUR CATHOLIQUE DE LA PROVINCE DE QUEBEC / Cazes, Paul de – (Quebec: Darveau), 1900. 02564. (Pre-1900 Canadiana) – 9 – cn C.I.H.M. [370]
MANUEL DE PALEOGRAPHIE LATINE ET FRANCAISE / Prou, M – Paris, 1889 – Dfl25.00 – ne Slangenburg [410]
MANUEL DE PIETE A L'USAGE DES CONGREGANISTES. / Congregation de la Sainte-Vierge de Ville-Marie. Montreal, Quebec – 5e ed. Montreal: J. B. Rolland, 1890. 05408. (Pre-1900 Canadiana) – 9 – cn C.I.H.M. [240]
MANUEL DE TSHILUBA (KASAYI, CONGO BELGE) / Burssens, Amaat – Anvers: de Sikkel, 1946 – us Res Libr [470]
MANUEL DES AMATEURS DE LA LANGUE FRANCAISE / Boniface, A – 2e ed. 1825 – 9 – fr I.C.S. [440]
MANUEL DES ANTIQUITES ROMAINES / Marquardt, Karl – 19 V. 1888-1907 – 1 – 78.00 – us L of C Photodup [930]
MANUEL DES ARTISTES ET DES AMATEURS, OU / Petity, L'Abbe Jean-Raymond de – O-397 1. 4 v. 1770 – 9 – ne IDC [700]
MANUEL DES ARTISTES ET DES AMATEURS, OU... / Petity, L'Abbe Jean-Raymond de – Paris. 4v. 1770 – 30mf – ne IDC [700]
MANUEL DES DIALECTES MALGACHES, COMPRENANT SEPT DIALECTES : HOVA, BETSILEO, TANKARANA, BETSIMISARAKA, TAIMORANA, TANOSY, SAKALAVA (MAHAFALY) ET LE SOAHELY / Jully, Antony – Paris: J Andre, 1901 – us Res Libr [470]
MANUEL DES EXPRESSIONS VICIEUSES LES PLUS FREQUENTES / Gingras, Jules Fabien – Ottawa: Imp. MacLean, Roger & Cie, 1880. SEM105P456 – 1mf – 9 – Can$2.25 – cn Bibl Nat [440]
LE MANUEL DES INQUISITEURS A 'USAGE DES INQUISITIONS D'ESPAGNE ET DU PORTUGAL. OU ABREGE DE L'OUVRAGE INTITULE: DIRECTORIUM INQUISITORUM / Morellet, Andre – (D'Holbach series). 1762 – 9 – fr Hachette [240]
MANUEL DES LOCUTIONS VICIEUSES / Pomier, M – 1835 – 9 – fr I.C.S. [440]
MANUEL DES MALADIES DES FEMMES: LECONS CLINIQUES / Atthill, Lombe – Paris: H. Lauwereyns, 1882. 07894. (Pre-1900 Canadiana) – 9 – cn C.I.H.M. [618]
MANUEL D'HERMENEUTIQUE BIBLIQUE = BIBLICAL HERMENEUTICS / Cellerier, Jacob Elisee – (In English. Includes index) – New York: Anson D F Randolph, c1881 – 1mf – 9 – 0-8370-2615-6 – 1985-0615 – us A.T.L.A. [220]
MANUEL D'HISTOIRE DU DROIT FRANCAIS (SOURCES, DROIT PUBLIC, DROIT PRIVE) A L'USAGE DES ETUDIANTS EN LICENCE ET EN DOCTORAT / Brissaud, Jean Baptiste – Paris, Fontemoing, 1898-1904. 1892 p. LL-4066 – 1 – us L of C Photodup [340]
MANUEL D'ORNITHOLOGIE, OU DESCRIPTION DES GENRES ET DES PRINCIPALES ESPECES D'OISEAUX / Lesson, R P – 2100 2. 2 v. 1828 – 8 – ne IDC [590]
MANUEL DRAMATIQUE: A L'USAGE DES AUTEURS ET DES ACTEURS, ET NECESSAIRE AUX GENS DU MONDE QUI AIMENT LES IDEES TOUTES TROUVEES, ET LES JUGEMENS TOUT FAITS / Geoffroy, Julien Louis – Paris: Painparre, 1822 – 1 – us U.W. Library [790]
MANUEL DU CODE CHINOIS / China. Laws, Statutes, etc – Par Gui Boulais.2v. 1923-24 – 1 – us A.T.L.A. [950]
MANUEL DU JUGE DE PAIX: COMPRENANT LA NATURE DES FONCTIONS DU JUGE DE PAIX, LA PROCEDURE REGULIERE AT LA PROCEDURE SOMMAIRE, LA RESPONSABILITE DES JUGES DE PAIX...ETC. : AVEC RENVOIS AUX AUTEURS CANADIENS ET ANGLAIS / Dandurand, Raoul & Lanctot, Charles – Montreal: C. Beauchemin, 1891. 02261. (Pre-1900 Canadiana) – 9 – cn C.I.H.M. [971]
MANUEL DU LECTEUR, D'UN AUTEUR INCONNU : PUBLIE D'APRAES UN MANUCRIT VENU DU YEMEN ET ACCOMPAGNE DE NOTES / Derenbourg, Joseph – (Includes bibliographical references and index) – Paris: Imprimerie nationale, 1871 – 1mf – 9 – 0-8370-6177-6 – 1986-0177 – us A.T.L.A. [470]
MANUEL DU MISSIONNAIRE SECULIER OU REGULIER : ET DU PASTEUR ORDINAIRE APPELE A COOPERER A L'OEUVRE DES MISSIONS ET DES RETRAITES / Nampon, Adrien – 3e rev corr augm ed. Lyon: Girard et Josserand, 1861 – 2mf – 9 – 0-8370-6688-3 – 1986-0688 – us A.T.L.A. [240]
MANUEL DU PROVENCAL / Gabrielli, C de – 1836 – 9 – fr I.C.S. [440]
MANUEL D'UTILISATION DU SYSTEME BIP / Vollering, Andre – Quebec: La Direction, 1984. SEM105P483 – 1mf – 9 – Can$2.25 – cn Bibl Nat [510]
MANUEL ELEMENTAIRE ... / Bourdon-Viane, G – Paris, 1897 – 4mf – 9 – ILM-436/1 – ne IDC [327]
MANUEL ENTOMOLOGIQUE. GENERA DES COLEOPTERES D'EUROPE / Jacquelin du Val, L P N C – 2487 2. 4 v. 1857-1868 – 8 – ne IDC [590]
MANUEL FRANCAIS-DAHOMEEN / Joulord – Lyon, Imprimerie Mme Vve Paquet. 1907 – 9 – $7.50 – fr Orientalistes [490]
MANUEL GENERAL DE L'INSTRUCTION PRIMAIRE – Paris. 1863-1915 – 1 – fr A.C.R.P.P. [073]
MANUEL GENERAL DES PLANTES, ARBRES, ARBUSTES / Jacques, A & Herinco, F – v. 1-4. Paris. 1847-57. B-7398 1 – 9 – ne IDC [580]
MANUEL GERCIA GARRIDO : !EH TU! / Garcia Garcia, A – Madrid: Archivo Ibero Americano, 1959 – 1 – sp Bibl Santa Ana [946]
MANUEL JIMENEZ FERNANDEZ... / Bayle, Constantino – Madrid: Razon y Fe, 1941 – sp Bibl Santa Ana [920]
MANUEL LEXIQUE DES MOTS FRANCAIS / Prevost, Abbe – 1750 – 9 – fr I.C.S. [440]
MANUEL MEDICAL ET USUEL DES PLANTES,... / Buchoz, P J – Paris, 1770. 2v – 11mf – 9 – ne IDC [615]
MANUEL PRACTIQUE DES SOCIETES ANONYMES ETRANGERES / Adolph, L – Paris, 1913 – 3mf – 9 – ILM-3290/1 – ne IDC [340]
MANUEL PRATIQUE DE LA LANGUE HAOUSSA / Dirr, A – Paris, Ernest Leroux. 1895 – 9 – $5.00 – fr Orientalistes [470]
MANUEL PRATIQUE DE LA LOI DU 12 JANVIER 1895 SUR LA SAISIE-ARRET AVEC UN FORMULAIRE COMPLET A L'USAGE DES JUGES DE PAIX, GREFFIERS, HUISSIERS, ET AUSSI DES PATRONS, EMPLOYES ET OUVRIERS / Le Pelletier, Emile – Nouv. ed., Paris, Marchal & Godde, 1913. 108 p. LL-4043 – 1 – us L of C Photodup [340]
MANUEL VICENTE VILLARAN, EX RECTOR DE LA UNIVERSIDAD. LA UNIVERSIDAD DE SAN MARCOS, DE LIMA... / Bayle, Constantino – Madrid: Razon y Fe, 1940 – sp Bibl Santa Ana [946]
THE MANUFACTURE, CONSUMPTION AND PRODUCTION OF IRON, STEEL, AND COAL IN THE DOMINION OF CANADA: WITH SOME NOTES OF THE MANUFACTURE OF IRON, AND ON THE IRON TRADE, IN OTHER COUNTRIES / Bartlett, James Herbert – Montreal: Dawson, 1885. 03006. (Pre-1900 Canadiana) – 9 – cn C.I.H.M. [670]

THE MANUFACTURE OF IRON IN CANADA / Bartlett, James Herbert – 1885?. 02971. (Pre-1900 Canadiana) – 9 – cn C.I.H.M. [670]

MANUFACTURE OF NARCOTIC DRUGS AND PSYCHOTROPIC SUBSTANCES / United Nations. Commission on Narcotic Drugs – 1947-1982 – E.30 F.20 – 9 (E/NF) – us U.N. Pubs [615]

THE MANUFACTURER *see* CANADIAN MANUFACTURER

MANUFACTURERS MUTUAL FIRE INSURANCE SITE MAPS, 1894-1954 – (With guide £35) – 232mf – 9 – £1,020.00 – uk Chadwyck [978]

MANUFACTURING AND PROCESS AUTOMATION – (Cont: Automation Systems at v8 1993/94) – v8. 1993/94 – 1 – Can$60.00y – cn Micromedia [670]

MANUFACTURING AND PROCESS AUTOMATION *see* AUTOMATION SYSTEMS

MANUFACTURING CHEMIST AND AEROSOL NEWS – v29- 1958- 1; v46- 5,6; v47- 9 – us UMI [660]

MANUFACTURING ENGINEERING – (See also: Manufacturing Engineering and Management) – v75- 1975- – 1,5,6 – us UMI [620]

MANUFACTURING ENGINEERING AND MANAGEMENT – (See now: Manufacturing Engineering) – v1-75 1932-75 1; 1968-75 5,6 – us UMI [600]

MANUFACTURING INDUSTRIAL CENSUS, 1967 / Jordan. Department of Statistics – 1968. BNE-9771 1 – 9 – ne IDC [310]

MANUFACTURING INDUSTRY IN JORDAN: REPORT ON THE INDUSTRIAL CENSUS OF 1959 / Jordan. Department of Statistics – BNE-9773 1 – 9 – ne IDC [310]

MANUFACTURING SOFTWARE DIRECTORY – 1985- – 1 – us UMI [000]

MANUFACTURING SYSTEMS – (1985- . 5,6,9) – v1- . 1983- – 1 – us UMI [620]

Manuilov, A A *see* KURSY PO KOOPERATSII

MANUKAU NEWS – Auckland. New Zealand. -w. 14 May 1914-7 Apr 1915. (1 reel) – 1 – uk British Libr Newspaper [072]

Manullang, Manginar *see*
– MANAGEMENT PERSONALIA

Manusama, A T *see* BEKNOPTE GESCHIEDENIS VAN DE VEREENIGING "AMBONSCH STUDIEFONDS" (1909-1917) MET EEN KORTE TOESPRAAK TOT HET AMBONSCHE VOLK

MANUSCRIPT BOOK WRITTEN ON THREE STAVES, TWO TREBLE AND ONE BASS; INSTRUMENTATION UNSPECIFIED. ON THE COVER: THE PROPERTY OF BELLAMY BAND, JUNE 1799. INCLUDES: PRESIDENTS MARCH; WASHINGTON'S MARCH; AND YANKEE DOODLE. MUSIC-539 – Manuscript book written on three staves, two treble and one bass; instrumentation unspecified. On the cover: "The Property of the Bellamy Band, June, 1799." Includes: "Presidents March," "Washingtons March," and "Yankee Doodle." MUSIC 539 – 1 – us L of C Photodup [780]

MANUSCRIPT CATALOG OF THE AMERICAN JEWISH ARCHIVES / American Jewish Archives. Cincinnati – (First Supplement.-1978.-26,100 cards on 2r.-ISBN 0-8161-1436-6.$105.00 export $125.00; Second Supplement on Microfiche.-1991.-50mf.-9.-ISBN 0-8161-0158-9.$350.00 export $395.00) – 1971 – 82,600 cards on 4r – 1 – $440.00 export $530.00 – 0-8161-1430-7 – uk Hall [010]

MANUSCRIPT COLLECTION / Korn, Victor Emanuel – Collected by V. E. Korn during the course of his career which he ended in Indonesia as Resident from 1912-1939 and his period as Professor of Adatrecht in Leiden from 1939-1958. A printed inventory list prepared by F. G. P. Jaquet comes with the microfiche collection. BSE-20.105 1 – 1594mf – 9 – ne IDC [950]

MANUSCRIPT COLLECTION / Winchester Cathedral – With printed index – 1 – £575.00 – uk World [240]

MANUSCRIPT COLLECTION OF MARCHES, DANCES, ETC / Morse, Samuel – Inscribed on the first page is "Samuel Morse Newburyport April 29th, 1811," followed by an index of the collection. Some solos for various instruments; some scored for 2 horns, 2 clarinets, and bassoon; trios, 3 songs and a catch. MUSIC 1993 – 1 – us L of C Photodup [780]

MANUSCRIPT COLLECTION OF PIANOFORTE MUSIC / Carr, Benjamin – Compiler's manuscript, not dated. One composition may be by Carr. MUSIC 1972, Item 1 – 1 – us L of C Photodup [780]

MANUSCRIPT COLLECTION OF TUNES FOR TREBLE INSTRUMENT / Murphey, Edward – In the front is written: Newport Edward Murphey October 26, 1790. Includes: General Washingtons March, Presidents New March, and Yankee Doodle. Music-3060 – 1 – us L of C Photodup [780]

MANUSCRIPT COLLECTION OF VOCAL MUSIC / Carr, Benjamin – Composer's manuscript, not dated. Contains duets with piano accomp.: "Unless with Amada" by Storace, seven nursery songs by Carr, and "Duetto: tytto da voi di pende del Sigr. Paisiello nella Locandiera". MUSIC 1972, Item 2 – 1 – us L of C Photodup [780]

MANUSCRIPT COLLECTIONS FROM THE SCHOMBURG CENTER FOR RESEARCH IN BLACK CULTURE *see* THE PAUL ROBESON COLLECTION

MANUSCRIPT COLLECTIONS FROM THE SCHOMBURG CENTRE FOR RESEARCH IN BLACK CULTURE *see* THE ARTHUR A. SCHOMBURG PAPERS, 1724-1938

MANUSCRIPT COLLECTIONS ON THE EARLY AMERICAN LABOR MOVEMENT, 1862-1908 / American Bureau of Industrial Research – (With printed guide) – 12r – 1 – $1,170.00 – us UPA [331]

MANUSCRIPT HISTORIES / Keene, New Hampshire. Keene Baptist Church – 1873, 1885 – 1 – 15.50 – us A.B.H.S. [240]

MANUSCRIPT IN RED AND BLACK / Manuale – 1481 – 1 – us Sibley [780]

MANUSCRIPT JOURNAL OF COOK'S SECOND VOYAGE, 1772-75 / Cook, James – 5 – Ir£25.00 – ie Microforms [980]

MANUSCRIPT LETTERS / Dickens, Charles – From Dickens House. London – 1 – uk Microform Academic [920]

MANUSCRIPT LETTERS BY AND CONCERNING VOLTAIRE AT THE VOLTAIRE FOUNDATION – Oxford. 1986 – 9 – $72.00 – uk Voltaire [440]

MANUSCRIPT LISTINGS FOR THE AUTHORED WORKS OF THE PALAEOLOGAN PERIOD / Sinkewicz, Robert E & Hayes, Walter M – 1989 – 3mf – Can$6.00 – 0-88844-852-X – cn Pontif [930]

MANUSCRIPT LISTINGS FOR THE AUTHORS OF CLASSICAL AND LATE ANTIQUITY / Sinkewicz, Robert E – 1990 – 6mf – 9 – Can$20.00 – 0-88844-853-8 – cn Pontif [090]

MANUSCRIPT LISTINGS FOR THE AUTHORS OF THE PATRISTIC AND BYZANTINE PERIODS / Sinkewicz, Robert E – 1992 – 17mf – 9 – Can$50.00 – 0-88844-854-6 – cn Pontif [930]

MANUSCRIPT MATERIAL / Keats, John – 1 – uk Microform Academic [810]

MANUSCRIPT MINUTES / Baptist Associations, Pennsylvania. Beaver Baptist Association – 1809-69 – 1 – 15.50 – us A.B.H.S. [240]

MANUSCRIPT MINUTES / Baptist Associations, Pennsylvania. Redstone Baptist Association – 1776-1854 – 1 – 15.50 – us A.B.H.S. [240]

MANUSCRIPT MINUTES / Flat River Association. North Carolina – 1828-59 – 1 – $7.44 – us Baptist [240]

MANUSCRIPT NOTES OF SERMONS, 1838-1957 / Howell, Robert Boyte C – v3 – 1 – 99.82 – us Baptist [240]

THE MANUSCRIPT OF 'GREAT EXPECTATIONS' / Dickens, Charles – 1v with index – 14 – 2450.00 – us UMI [830]

MANUSCRIPT OF HIS CHRONICOS LAGEANAS / Cleary, Reuben – 4v. An enlarged and rev. version of his earlier MS. entitled Brazil under the Monarchy. 1865-85 – 1 – 35.00 – us L of C Photodup [920]

MANUSCRIPT OF MILITARY MARCHES / Cavalerie Signale – 1866 – 1 – us Sibley [780]

MANUSCRIPT OF THE ECHO OF THE FREE CHINA-TAIWAN TO "CHINA SPRING." – Taipei, 1983. 200p – 9 – 15.00 – ch Transmission [950]

MANUSCRIPT OF THE INFORMATION DATA / China. Republic. Government Information Office. Executive Yuan – (Hsin-wen tzu-liao te-kao). no.1-150. Nov 3 1968-11 Jul 1978. 660p. 1 reel – 1 – 32.50 – ch Transmission [950]

MANUSCRIPT OF THE TAIWAN VISIT OF THE ALEXANDR SOLZHENITSYN – Taipei, 1983. 2v. 500p. (So-j'en-ni-hsin fang-t'ai-chi-w'en) – 9 – 25.00 – ch Transmission [950]

MANUSCRIPT PROCEEDINGS / Southern Baptist Convention – 1845-63. 206p – 1 – 6.00 – us Baptist [240]

MANUSCRIPT SERMONS / Edwards, Morgan – 15 vols. 2,697p – 1 – 94.39 – us Baptist [240]

MANUSCRIPT SERMONS / Renfroe, J J D – (Chaplain of the 10th Alabama Regiment of the Army of Va.), 1863-64. 746p – 1 – 26.11 – us Baptist [240]

MANUSCRIPT SERMONS, 1710-1723, 1730-1734 / Wesley, Samuel – (Coll title: The People Called Methodists, Phase 2: Primary Sources 1738-1800) – 10mf – 9 – MP-660/1 – ne IDC [240]

MANUSCRIPT, SERMONS AND NOTES / Manly, Basil Sr. – 1823-65 – 1 – 186.97 – us Baptist [240]

MANUSCRIPT SOURCES OF THE HISTORY OF IRISH CIVILIZATION / Ireland. National Library; ed by Hayes, Richard J – 1965.-310,000 cards 22 reels.-ISBN: 0-8161-1383-1; or 254mf.-ISBN: 0-8161-1751-9 – 1,9 – $1200.00 – uk Hall [941]

MANUSCRIPT VAN TH. G. TH. PIGEAUD BETREFFENDE JAVAANSE BESCHAVINGSGESCHIEDENIS – Jogjakarta, 1943. 3v. KITLV,H 717(a-c). BSD-105/1 mf. 1-19 – 9 – ne IDC [950]

MANUSCRIPTA MATHEMATICA – v. 1-33. 1969-80 – 1,5,9 – 1980.00 – us UMI [073]

MANUSCRIPTS – 14th cent. Holkham ms. 2. Holkham Hall, Norfolk, England – 1 – uk Microform Academic [220]

MANUSCRIPTS / American Museum in Britain – BRRAM – 1 – uk Microform Academic [970]

MANUSCRIPTS / Caisse Nationale des Monuments Historiques et des Sites. Paris – (Illuminated and other from National and Provincial Museums and Libraries. Over 3500 reproductions) – 60mf – 9 – $390.00 – 0-907006-90-6 – uk Mindata [700]

MANUSCRIPTS / Draper Collection – Vol. I. A series of letters concerning American pioneers in Illinois, with a few original papers of Capt. James Piggott. This material furnished to Drapper, 1842-68, by J. M. Peck, Isaac Newton Piggott, John Reynolds, Pierre Menard, Benjamin Scott, James Lemen, John T. and George Lusk. 364p – 1 – 12.74 – us Baptist [240]

MANUSCRIPTS – New York. n1-5. 1922-23 – 1r – 1 – us Ross [073]

MANUSCRIPTS – New York. no. 1-5. Feb 1922-Mar 1923? – 1 – us NY Public [073]

MANUSCRIPTS / Seabury, Samuel – From the General Theological Seminary – 1 – us A.T.L.A. [240]

MANUSCRIPTS: ALIENATED ESTATES; HILLESDEN AND FARNHAM ROYAL, BUCKS / Holkham Hall. Norfolk. England – From the 16th century – 1 – uk Microform Academic [025]

MANUSCRIPTS AND EARLY PRINTED WORKS / Inner Temple. London. Library – (Sections are available seperately) – The Petyt collection; the Barrington collection; Records of the Inner Temple; The Mitford Collection of Legal Manuscripts; Misc. Mss. With printed index – 1 – £8,995.00 – uk World [025]

MANUSCRIPTS AND LETTERS / Mendelssohn, Felix – 1 – 9 – us Sibley [780]

MANUSCRIPTS AND PAMPHLETS / Grime, Elder J H – 742p – 1 – 25.97 – us Baptist [240]

MANUSCRIPTS AND PAPERS FROM THE COLLECTION IN NORTHAMPTON CENTRAL LIBRARY / Clare, John – 1 – uk Microform Academic [810]

MANUSCRIPTS AND SKETCHES / Handel, George Frederic – (Fitzwilliam Museum, Cambridge). MSS 251-265 – 1 – uk Microform Academic [780]

MANUSCRIPTS: COLLECTION INFORMATION FORMS / Minnesota Historic Resources Survey – 1973-79 – 7r – 5 – $30.00r – us M.H.S. [978]

MANUSCRIPTS FROM THE COLLECTION IN PETERBOROUGH MUSEUM / Clare, John – 1 – uk Microform Academic [810]

MANUSCRIPTS IN AUSTRIAN MONASTERIES – Printed catalog available – 1 – us UMI [090]

MANUSCRIPTS OF 19 SERMONS DELIVERED AT FIRST BAPTIST CHURCH, CHICAGO, 1891 / Henson, P S – 275p – 1 – 9.62 – us Baptist [240]

MANUSCRIPTS OF THE HOUSE OF LORDS, 1678-1693 / Historical Manuscripts Commission – London, 1887-1894 – 37mf – ne IDC [090]

MANUSCRIPTS OF THE IRISH LITERARY RENAISSANCE, SERIES ONE : DIARIES OF JOSEPH HOLLOWAY 1895-1944, FROM THE NATIONAL LIBRARY OF IRELAND, DUBLIN – Part 1: 1895-1911; Part 2: 1912-1917; Part 3: 1918-1924; Part 4: 1925-1929 – 1 – us Primary [420]

MANUSCRIPTS OF THE IRISH LITERARY RENAISSANCE, SERIES THREE : THE J.M. SYNGE MANUSCRIPTS FROM THE LIBRARY OF TRINITY COLLEGE, DUBLIN – Part 1: Manuscripts and typescript plays, notebooks, diaries and other material; Part 2: Stephen/ Synge Collection, including the unpublished Synge biography – 1 – us Primary [820]

MANUSCRIPTS OF THE IRISH LITERARY RENAISSANCE, SERIES TWO : THE ABBEY THEATRE AND CULTURAL LIFE – Part 1: W.A. Henderson Scrapbooks, 1899-1911 – 1 – us Primary [820]

MANUSCRIPTS ON THE HISTORY AND LEGENDS OF MANGAREVA IN HIS POSSESSION / Uebe, Auguste – n.d – 1r – 1 – PMB1083 – at Pacific Mss [090]

MANUSCRIPTS, PERSONAL PAPERS, PASTORAL RECORDS, PUBLISHED ARTICLES, ETC / Cox, Norman W – 15,673p – 1 – $548.55 – us Baptist [240]

MANUSCRIPTS RELATING TO PAPUA NEW GUINEA, (1943) / Douglas, Kenneth C & Noss, James – ca 1970s – 1r – 1 – PMB1055 – at Pacific Mss [980]

MANUSCRIT ANTIMORONA ARABICO-MALGACHE – 9 – F80.00 – fr Ethnologie [800]

UN MANUSCRIT DEL LIBRE DEL CONSOLAT DE MAR... / Broca, G de – Barcelona, 1917 – 1mf – 1 – ILM-1647/1 – ne IDC [327]

MANUSCRIT JURIDIC – Seo de Urgel, SP. S.14 – 1,5 – sp Cultura [340]

MANUSCRIT MERINA DIT MANUSCRIT HOVA – 9 – F220.00 – fr Ethnologie [470]

MANUSCRITO CHINO – Madrid – 1r – 5,6 – sp Cultura [090]

UN MANUSCRITO DE PEDRO DE VALENCIA QUE LLEVA POR TITULO EN SU PORTADA : "UNA GRAN PARTE DE LA ESTORIA APOSTOLICA EN LOS ACTOS... / Fernandez, Juan – Badajoz: Dip. Provincial, 1975. Sep. REE – 1 – sp Bibl Santa Ana [240]

EL MANUSCRITO DELAS REVELACIONES SOBRE LA FUNDACION DEL CONVENTO DE SERRADILLA / Munoz de San Pedro, Miguel – (Isabel de la Madre de Dios). Badajoz: (Imprenta de la Diputacion Prov.), 1968. Sep. de la Revista de Estudios Extremenos – 1 – sp Bibl Santa Ana [240]

UN MANUSCRITO INEDITO DE JUAN LEANDRO JIMENEZ / Manzano de Garias, Antonio – 1 – sp Bibl Santa Ana [946]

MANUSCRITOS FRANCISCANOS DE LA BIBLIOTECA DE VICENTE BARRANTES / Barrado Manzano, Arcangel – Madrid: Archivo Ibero Americano, 1949 – 1 – sp Bibl Santa Ana [240]

LOS MANUSCRITOS JURIDICOS MEDIEVALES DE... / Garcia y Garcia, Antonio – Madrid: Archivo Ibero Americano, 1964 – 1 – sp Bibl Santa Ana [340]

MANUSCRITOS MUSICALES – Madrid – 1r – 5,6 – sp Cultura [780]

LES MANUSCRITS ARABES DE L'ESCURIAL / Derenbourg, Hartwig – 1884, 1903 – 9 – fr Orientalistes [470]

MANUSCRITS ARMENIENS ILLUSTRES DES 12E, 13E ET 14E SIECLES DE LA BIBLIOTHEQUE DES PERES MEKHITARISTES DE VENISE / Der Nersessian, S – Paris. 2v. 1936-1937 – 7mf – 9 – ne IDC [460]

MANUSCRITS COPTES DUMUSEE D'ANTIQUITES DES PAYS-BAS A LEYDE / Pleyte, W & Boeser, P A A – Leiden, 1897 – 21mf – 9 – ne Slangenburg [240]

LES MANUSCRITS DE DIDEROT CONSERVES EN RUSSIE. CATALOGUE / Tourneux, M – Paris, 1885. BR-10,869/1 – 9 – ne IDC [190]

MANUSCRITS ET PEINTURES DE TOUEN-HOUANG / Reunion des musees nationaux. Paris – 1947. 1 fiche – 9 – fr Réunion [700]

MANUSCRITS FRANCAIS DU MOYEN AGE CONSERVES A LENINGRAD / Brayer, E – Bulletin d'information de l'Institut de recherches et d'histoire des textes, 1958, no.7, p22-23. French mss. in the GPB library. BR-10,863/1 – 9 – ne IDC [010]
MANUSCRITS HEBREUX DE L'ORATOIRE A LA BIBLIOTHEQUE NATIONALE DE PARIS : NOTICES INEDITES / Munk, S – Francfort-sur-le-Mein, 1911 – 1mf – ne IDC [470]
MANUSCRITS LEGUES PAR MLLE. DE LESPINASSE – A reproduction of the commonplace books of Jeanne-Julie-Eleonore de Lespinasse at the Voltaire Foundation. Oxford. 1986 – 9 – $100.00 – 0-7294-0357-2 – uk Voltaire [880]
MANUSHI – New Delhi. 64 docs. 1979-1991 – 47mf – 9 – ne IDC [950]
MANUSIA DAN MASJARAKAT BARU INDONESIA (CIVICS) / ed by Supardo – SE 4386 1. 1962 – 9 – ne IDC [320]
MANUSIA: KEDJADIAN, PERTUMBUHAN, PERKEMBANGAN DJASMANI (DAN) ROHANI / Beck, Lester Ford – Translation of human growth. SE-11,014 1. 1962 – 9 – ne IDC [950]
MANUSIA SOSIALIS INDONESIA / Surjo Untoro, S – SE 4489 1. 1962 – 9 – ne IDC [300]
Manuzio, Aldo *see*
– PHRASES LINGUAE LATINAE
– VIAGGI FATTI DA VINETIA, ALLA TANA, IN PERSIA, IN INDIA, ET IN CONSTANTINOPOLI
Manwaring, Edward *see* INSTITUTES OF LEARNING TAKEN FROM ARISTOTLE, PLUTARCH, LONGINUS—AND MANY OTHER WRITERS BOTH ANCIENT AND MODERN
Manwayring, Henry *see* THE SEA-MANS DICTIONARY
MAN-WHENCE AND WHITHER? / Westbrook, Richard Brodhead – Philadelphia: J.B. Lippincott, 1884. xxiii,226p – 1 – us U.W. Library [240]
MANX FAIRY TALES / Morrison, Sophia – London: D. Nutt, 1911. viii,185p – 1 – us U.W. Library [390]
MANX INDEPENDENT (TUES AND FRI EDITIONS) – May 19-Aug 28, Sep 1987-Sep 24, Oct 1993-96 – 45r – 1 – uk British Libr Newspaper [072]
MANX SOCIETY – (Coll title: Publications of the English Record Societies, 1835-1972...) – v1-3. 1859-82 – 92mf – 9 – £680.00 – uk Chadwyck [941]
THE MANY ADVANTAGES OF A GOOD LANGUAGE TO ANY NATION – Anon. 1724. 103p. (English Linguistics Series 1500-1800) – 9 – us UMI [400]
MANY FIRST BAPTIST CHURCH. MANY, LOUISIANA : CHURCH RECORDS – 1908-76.988p – 1 – 39.52 – us Baptist [240]
MANY INFALLIBLE PROOFS,...OR, THE WRITTEN AND LIVING WORD OF GOD / Pierson, Arthur Tappan – New York: Fleming H. Revell, 1886. 1 fiche. 8370-4753-6 – 9 – us A.T.L.A. [240]
MANY NATIONS – (Lacks: v42,44-48. Cont and filmed with: Slavic and Baltic Chronicle) – v1-49. 1962-74 – 1r – 1 – ATLA S0723A – us A.T.L.A. [073]
MANY NATIONS *see* THE SLAVIC AND BALTIC CHRONICLE
MANY SMOKES – 1966-79. (American Indian Periodicals in the Princeton University Library). 14 fiches – 9 – $65.00 – us UPA [305]
MANY VOICES / Tollemache, Marguerite – London: Kegan Paul, Trench, 1883 – 1mf – us A.T.L.A. [240]
MANY VOICES, ONE WORLD : COMMUNICATION AND SOCIETY, TODAY AND TOMORROW / MacBride, Sean et al – repr 1988 – 9 – 92-3-101802-7 – fr UNESCO [301]
Manz, Gustav *see* DER TROMPETER VON SAEKKINGEN
Manzanares, Blas de *see* EPITOME DE... MILAGROS...PEDRO DE ALCANTARA
Manzanares, Luis Angel *see* VISION HISTORICA DE ESPANA DESDE LA ABDICACION DE CARLOS 5TH EN BRUSELAS
Manzanilla, Yanurario *see* RECUERDOS DE LA CAMPANA DE LOS REPUBLICANOS CONTRA EL IMPERIO, EN EL ESTADO DE YUCATAN
Manzano de Garias, Antonio *see*
– DEL PAIS DE LA QUIMERA. HISTORIAS Y PAISAJES
– UN MANUSCRITO INEDITO DE JUAN LEANDRO JIMENEZ
– PEDRO DE VALDIVIA. INTERROGANTES PARA SU BIOGRAFIA
Manzano Garias, A *see* NUESTRA SENORA DE LA ESTRELLA
Manzano Manzano, Juan *see* LAS "NOTAS A LAS LEYES DE INDIAS" DE MANUEL JOSE DE AYALA. MADRID, 1935
Manzo, Luis G *see* PSYCHOMETRIC ASSESSMENT OF THE CAROLINA SPORT CONFIDENCE INVENTORY
Manzoni, Alejandro *see*
– LOS NOVIOS
– IL PROMESSI SPOSI (LOS NOVIOS)
Manzoni, G *see* ANNALI TIPOGRAFICI DEI SONCINO; PARTE SECONDA... NEL SECOLO 16...
Mao, Tse-tung *see*
– MELAWAN KARJA GAJADELAPAN DIDALAM PARTAI, ON 2 FEB., 1942
– MENGAPA KEKUASAAN POLITIK MERAH TIONGKOK DAPAT BERDIRI?
– TENTANG SENI DAN SASTERA
MAOMETTO II / Rossini, G – Milano: Ricordi, [1820] – 1 – us Sibley [780]
MAORI LAND CLAIMS IN THE AJHR AND LC 1855-1923 – (A chronological listing of petitions tabled in Parliament. Contains yr, name(s) of claimants, description of claim, notes and source) – 3mf – 9 – NZ$17.00 – 0-908797-41-9 – nz BAB [980]
Mao-tun *see* CHINESE CHRISTIAN MONOGRAPH (CCC247)
MAP AND TOURIST GUIDE DJAWA-BALI / Latif, Isom – SE-4154 1 – 9 – ne IDC [950]
THE MAP OF EUROPE BY TREATY... / Hertslet, E – London, 1814-91 – 40mf – 1 – ILM-2464/1 – ne IDC [327]
THE MAP OF LIFE, CONDUCT, AND CHARACTER / Lecky, William Edward Hartpole – London, New York: Longmans, Green, 1899 – 1mf – 9 – 0-8370-6138-5 – 1986-0138 – us A.T.L.A. [240]
MAP OF THE ISLAND OF JAVA,... / Horsfield, T – London, 1852 – 1mf – 9 – ne IDC [910]
MAP ROOM ARMY AND NAVY MESSAGES OF PRESIDENT ROOSEVELT, DECEMBER 1941-MAY 1942 – (Includes printed guide) – 10r – 1 – $1,150.00 – 1-55655-269-6 – us UPA [320]
MAP ROOM CONFERENCE AND SPECIAL FILES OF PRESIDENT ROOSEVELT, 1942-45 – (Includes printed guide) – 11r – 1 – $1,210.00 – 1-55655-268-8 – us UPA [320]
MAP ROOM GROUND OPERATIONS FILES, 1941-45 : FILES OF PRESIDENT ROOSEVELT – 28r – 1 – $3,335.00 – 1-55655-513-X – us UPA [355]
MAP ROOM MESSAGES OF PRESIDENT ROOSEVELT (1939-45) / Roosevelt, Franklin D – 1980 – 9r – 1 – $990.00 – 0-89093-351-0 – us UPA [977]
MAP ROOM MESSAGES OF PRESIDENT TRUMAN (1945-1946) – (With printed guide) – 1980 – 5r – 1 – $555.00 – 0-89093-352-9 – us UPA [324]
MAP ROOM MILITARY SUBJECT FILES OF PRESIDENT ROOSEVELT, 1941-45 – (Includes printed guide) – 26r – 1 – $2,860.00 – 1-55655-270-X – us UPA [320]
MAP ROOM NAVAL OPERATIONS FILES, 1942-45 : FILES OF PRESIDENT ROOSEVELT – Includes printed guide – 21r – 1 – $2,500.00 – 1-55655-514-8 – us UPA [355]
MAPA GEOLOGICO DE ESPANA : EXPLICACION DE LA HOJA N° 701. VALENCIA DE ALCANTARA (CACERES) / Instituto Geologico y Minero de Espana – Madrid: Tip. Lit. Coullaut, 1951 – 1 – sp Bibl Santa Ana [550]
MAPA GEOLOGICO DE ESPANA. ESCALA 1:50000 : EXPLICACION DE LA HOJA N° 753. MIAJADAS (POR ISMAEL ROSO DE LUNA Y FRANCISCO HERNANDEZ PACHECO / Instituto GeologicoMinero de Espana Madrid – Madrid: Tip. Collant, 1946 – 1 – sp Bibl Santa Ana [550]
MAPAS PROVINCIALES DE CARRETERAS. BADAJOZ – Madrid: Edit. Hernado, S.A. 1969 – 1 – sp Bibl Santa Ana [910]
MAPAS TURISTICOS PROVINCIALES : BADAJOZ – Madrid: Ed. Hernando S.A., s.a. – sp Bibl Santa Ana [910]
MAPAS TURISTICOS PROVINCIALES : CACERES – Madrid: Ed. Hernando S.A., s.a. – sp Bibl Santa Ana [910]
Mapes, Orlo *see* PHYSICIAN'S RECORDS: OTTAWA COUNTY, OHIO
Maple *see* MISSOURI BAPTIST BIOGRAPHY
MAPLE BAPTIST CHURCH. HORRY COUNTY. SOUTH CAROLINA : CHURCH RECORDS – 1955-88 – 1 – $36.36 – us Baptist [240]
MAPLE GROVE BAPTIST CHURCH. PERKS, ILLINOIS : CHURCH RECORDS – 1896-1985. Lacking: 1902-07, 1925-41. 806p – 1 – us Baptist [240]
MAPLE GROVE BURIAL RECORDS / Hancock County. Ohio. Findlay, City Board of Cemetery Trustees – 1850-1917 – 2r – 1 – $32.50r – us Archival [324]
MAPLE HEIGHTS PRESS : WEEKLY CLEVELAND SUBURBAN NEWSPAPER – Maple Heights, Oh. 8 Jun 1972-24 Nov 1988 – 14r – 1 – us Western Res [071]
MAPLE LEAF – 1944-46. United Kingdom – 5r – 1 – $325.00 – cn Library Assoc [971]
MAPLE LEAF – (Printed in Belgium for Forces Overseas) – Brussels, Belgium. 27 jul 1944; 10 apr 1945; v3 n39. 9 may 1945 – 1r – 1 – Can$25.00 – cn Can Microfilming [072]
THE MAPLE LEAF – [Montreal?]: Publ for E H Lay by J C Becket, [1852-1854?] – 9 – cn C.I.H.M. [971]
MAPLE LEAVES / D, Susie – London, Ont.: s.n., 1871 (London, Ont.: Daily Free Press). 02778. (Pre-1900 Canadiana) – 9 – cn C.I.H.M. [971]
MAPLE LEAVES AND HEMLOCK BRANCHES: A COLLECTION OF POEMS / Butler, Martin – Fredericton, N.B.: "Gleaner," 1889. 00365. (Pre-1900 Canadiana) – 9 – cn C.I.H.M. [810]
Maple, William H *see*
– NO "BEGINNING", OR, THE FUNDAMENTAL FALLACY: A COMMON-SENSE DEMONSTRATION OF THE NON-EXISTENCE OF A "FIRST CAUSE", THEREBY IDENTIFYING GOD WITH NATURE
– NO BEGINNING, OR, THE FUNDAMENTAL FALLACY:...IDENTIFYING GOD WITH NATURE
MAPLETON BEE – Mapleton OR. Oct 5-Dec 21 1934 – 1 – us U.O. Library [071]
MAPS / Sanborn Map Company, Topeka, KS – 1950-1970 – 1 – us KS Hist [910]
MAPS / U.S. Central Intelligence Agency – 1970-86.Not complete – 9 – 900.00 – us Updata [910]
MAPS AND DRAWINGS OF THE NETHERLANDS : PART 1: DUTCH DOMESTIC MAPS AND DRAWINGS, 16TH-19TH CENTURIES – 1995 – 1,830mf – 9 – Dfl10,698.00 – ne MMF Publ [623]
MAPS AND DRAWINGS OF THE NETHERLANDS, 16TH-20TH CENTURIES, PART 2: COLLECTIONS OF THE CORPS OF ENGINEERS (GENIE) : PART 2A: PLANS OF BUILDINGS, 17TH-20TH CENTURIES – (Pt 2b: Situation plans of forts and fortified towns 165mf Dfl968.00; Pt 2c: Plans of forts and fortified towns in prep) – 1995 – 1,511mf – 9 – Dfl9,359.00 – ne MMF Publ [720]
MAPS FROM THE UNITED KINGDOM : PREMIER SERIES – STREET MAPS / British Ordnance Survey – (Birmingham. 2mf. $14.25; Bradford. 2mf. $14.25; Bristol. 2mf. $14.25; Bournemouth. 1mf. $11.25; Cardiff. 1mf. $11.25; Leeds. 2mf. $14.25; Liverpool. 2mf. $14.25; London. 2mf. $14.25; Manchester. 2mf. $14.25; Newcastle upon Tyne. 2mf. $14.25; Nottingham. 1mf. $11.25; Portsmouth. 1mf. $11.25; Sheffield. 2mf. $14.25; Southhampton. 1mf. $11.25) – 1994 – 23mf – 15 – $175.00 set – us Comics [910]
MAPUTO – LOURENCO MARQUES – MOSSAMEDES : COMMUNICADO A SOCIEDADE GEOGRAPHICA DE LISBOA, 1 APR 1889 / Machado, Joaquim Jose – (Filmed with: Apontamentos para a historia de guerra de Zambezia 1871-75, and others) – Lisboa, 1889 – us Res Libr [960]
Maqqari *see* A HISTORY OF THE MOHAMMEDAN DYNASTIES IN SPAIN
Maqrizi *see* HISTOIRE DES SULTANS MAMLOUKS DE L'EGYPTE
MA'QUL VA MANQUL – Tehran: Adad 1-8, Farvardin 1314-Tir 1317 [Mar 1935-Jun 1938] – 1 reel – 1 – $175.00 – us MEDOC [950]
MAR DE FONFO / Rebollo Parras, Francisco – 1888 – 9 – 1.50f – sp Bibl Santa Ana [830]
O MAR DE HESPANHA : ORGAO DO PARTIDO REPUBLICANO – Mar de Hespanha, 24 Mar 1898 – 1,5,6 – bl Biblioteca [072]
EL MAR TERRITORIAL / Bustamante y Sirven, A S de – Habana, 1930 – 4mf – 1 – ILM-2324/1 – ne IDC [327]
MARAE MARAE TA'ATA / Garanger, J – 9 – F30.00 – fr Ethnologie [306]
Marais, Marin *see*
– PIECES A UNE ET A DEUX VIOLES..
– PIECES DE VIOLES..
Maramis, A A *see* NO MORE LEGAL POWER OF THE NETHERLANDS IN INDONESIA
Maran, Rene *see* UN HOMME PAREIL AUX AUTRES: ROMAN
Maranca, S *see* ABRI TOCA DO PINGA DO BOI, SITE TYPIQUE DE LA VARIETE SERRA BRANCA, STYLE VARZEA GRANDE, BRESIL
Marangoni, G *see* DELLE COSE GENTILESCHE E PROFANE TRASPORTATE AD USO ET ADORNAMENTO DELLE CHIESE
Maranon, Gregorio *see*
– LIBERALISM AND COMMUNISM; THE BACKGOUND OF THE SPANISH CIVIL WAR
– LA REVOLUCION ESPANOLA
– SURVEYING THE SPANISH WAR; LIBERALISM AND COMMUNISM
MARANON'S BETRAYAL / Bergamin, Jose – n.p. 193? Fiche W 752. (Blodgett Collection of Spanish Civil War Pamphlets) – 9 – us H.U. College Libr [946]
MARAROSHER JEWISH CENTER – Cleveland, OH, 1911-1966 – 1r – 1 – us I.H.R.C. [270]
Marat, Jean-Paul *see* DECOUVERTES SUR LE FEU, L'ELECTRICITE ET LA LUMIERE CONSTATEES PAR UNE SUITE D'EXPERIENCES NOUVELLES QUI VIENNENT D'ETRE VERIFEES PAR MM. LES COMMISSAIRES DE L'ACAD. DES SC
MARATHON MERCURY – 1948-1956 – cn Commonwealth Micro [072]
MARATHON PERFORMANCE TIME IN RELATION TO AGE, PHYSICAL CHARACTERISTICS, PREVIOUS RUNNING EXPERIENCE, AND VARIOUS TRAINING INDICES OF FEMALE DISTANCE RUNNERS / Hamm, Tracy M – University of Wisconsin-La Crosse, 1995 – 1mf – 9 – PE 3649 – us Microform Publ [617]
MARATHON WORLD – 1964- 1; 1977- 5,6,9 – us UMI [790]
Maratti, G F *see* FLORA ROMANA
MARAVILLAS / Sanchez-Arjona, Vicente – Sevilla: Imp. Alvarez, 1955 – 1 – sp Bibl Santa Ana [810]
Marbach, C *see* CARMINA SCRIPTURARUM
Marbach, J *see*
– CHRISTLICHER UNDERRICHT UND WARHAFFTIGE ERWEISZUNG...DAS JHESUS CHRISTUS...DURCH D. PERSONL. VEREINIGUNG D. GOTTL. U. VLEUESCHL. NATUREN...IN ALLE GOETTLICHE HERRLICHKEYT...GESETZT SEYE
– CHRISTLICHER VND WARHAFFTIGER UNDERRICHT VON DEN WORTEN DER EINSATZUNG DES HEYLIGEN ABENDTMALS JHESU CHRISTI...
Marbe, K *see* EXPERIMENTELL-PSYCHOLOGISCHE UNTERSUCHUNGEN UEBER DAS URTEILH-526/2. 1901
Marbeau, J BF *see*
– DES CRECHES OU MOYEN DE DIMINUER LA MISERE EN AUGMENTANT LA POPULATION
– DU PAUPERISME EN FRANCE ET DES MOYENS D'Y REMEDIER, OU PRINCIPES D'ECONOMIE CHARITABLE
Marbeck, J *see* THE BOOK OF COMMON PRAYER WITH MUSICAL NOTES
Marbille, P *see* HISTOIRE NATURELLE DES LEPIDOPTERES. 1885-1886
MARBLE ISLAND AND THE NORTH-WEST COAST OF HUDSON'S BAY / Bell, Robert – Toronto: Copp, Clark Co., 1887. 00902. (Pre-1900 Canadiana) – 9 – cn C.I.H.M. [910]
MARBLEHEAD 1654-1849 – (Mf 1T: Births & Deaths 1670-1737. Mf 2T: B,M,D 1654-1775. Mf 3T-6T: Marriages 1721-1843. Mf 6T-9T: Births & Deaths 1726-1849. Mf 10T: Deaths 1837-44; Marriages, Births 1842-44. Mf 11T-12T: Births 1843-49. Mf 12T-13T: Marriages 18474-50. Mf 14T-15T: Deaths 1844-49. Mf 15T-23T: Marriages & Intentions 1764-1849. Mf 24T: Out-of-Town Marriages 1693-1800) – (mf ed 1997) – 24mf – 9 – 0-87623-286-1 – us Holbrook [920]
Marburg, Theodore *see* THE WAR WITH SPAIN. II.THE VENEZUELAN DISPUTE
MARBURGER INDEX. INVENTAR DER KUNST IN DEUTSCHLAND : PHOTOGRAPHIC DOCUMENTATION OF ART IN GERMANY / ed by Bildarchiv Foto Marburg im Kunstgeschichtlichen Institut der Philipps Universitaet Marburg – (Lfg 1-20: Foto-Inventar 1977-1982 4800 fiches DM13,980; Lfg 21-30: Foto- Inventar 1983-1987 3000 fiches DM12,980; Lfg 31-38: Foto-Inventar 1988-1990 1350 fiches DM8,980; Lfg 39-58:

Foto-Inventar 1991-1998 ca 3800 fiches je Lfg DM1,680; Lfg 1-5: Text-Inventar und Register 1983-1987 600 fiches DM4,980; Lfg 6-8: Text-Inventar und Register 1988-1991 877 fiches DM3,380; Gebrauchsanleitung von Lutz Heusinger 2. Aufl 1985 132 Seiten Broschiert DM20.00 (fuer Bez. d. Gesamted. kostenlos): Users' Manual by Lutz Heusinger 2nd ed 1985 127p sb DM20.00 (free of charge for subscribers to the Marburger Index)) – 1977-1998 – ca 14,427 mf (1:24) – 9,17 – silver DM38,000.00 – 3-598-30700-4 – gw Saur [700]

Marburger, Lorri K *see* EFFECTS OF LOW-INTENSITY, PAIN-FREE EXERCISE ON MUSCLE METABOLISM IN PATIENTS WITH PERIPHERAL VASCULAR DISEASE EVALUATED BY 31P-NMR SPECTROSCOPY

MARBURGER PRESSE *see* OBERHESSISCHER ANZEIGER

MARBURGER-INDEX : OEESTERREICH SUPPLEMENT. BILDDOKUMENTATION ZUR KUNST IN OESTERREICH / ed by Bildarchiv Foto Marburg – Deutsches Dokumentationszentrum fuer Kunstgeschichte Philipps-Universitaet Marburg – (Lfg 1 103 silver mf DM1,800.00 ISBN: 3-598-33217-3. Lfg 2 141 silver mf DM1,800.00 ISBN: 3-598-33218-1. Subsc to Marburger Index DM1,680.00 ea) – 1996 – 244 silver mf (1:24) – 9 – DM3,600.00 set – 3-598-33199-1 – gw Saur [700]

Marbury, Edward *see* A COMMENTARY OR EXPOSITION UPON THE PROPHECY OF HABAKKUK

Marc, Charles Chretien Henri *see* DE LA FOLIE CONSIDEREE DANS SES RAPPORTS AVEC LES QUESTIONS MEDICO-JUDICIARIES

Marc, L *see* LE PAYS MOSSI

Marc, S *see* HISTOIRE DE L'EGLISE D'ALEXANDRIE

Marcanti, Ruth *see* THE 1919-20 BREASTED EXPEDITION TO THE NEAR EAST

Marcel, J *see*
- LE TRIOMPHE DE LA FOY CATHOLIQUE
- LA VIE DU R.P. CESAR DE BUS

MARCELLA / Ward, Mary Augusta – British Fiction Archive: Unit 2 – 9 – uk Bell [830]

MARCELLA: EPISODE DRAMATIQUE / Feige, L – Montreal: E. Senecal, 1887. 03080. (Pre-1900 Canadiana) – 9 – cn C.I.H.M. [820]

Marcello, Benedetto *see* IL TEATRO ALLA MODA

MARCFICHE – Library of Congress cataloging – 9 – us MARC Applied [020]

MARCH AIR FORCE BASE BEACON – Riverside, CA. 1990 – 2+ r – 1 – $100.00 ($50.00) – R04094 – us Library Micro [071]

March, Francis Andrew *see* THE SPELLING REFORM

March, Jose *see* LA EXCLUSIVA DADA POR ESPANA CONTRA EL CARDENAL CIUSTINIANI EN EL CONCLAVE DE 1830-1831, SEGUN LOS DESPACHOS DIPLOMATICOS

March, N H *see* PHYSICS AND CHEMISTRY OF LIQUIDS

MARCH OF OUR REVOLUTION / Sukarno, Pres. Indonesia – SE 5651 1. Address on 17 Augustus 1960 – 9 – ne IDC [324]

MARCHA – Monteviedeo, UY – 1r – $50.00 – R04232 – us Library Micro [072]

MARCHA – v1-. 1939-. -w – 1 – us U.W. Library [073]

LA MARCHA DE LA CARRONA / Vera, Emilio – Madrid, Barcelona: Alfaguara, 1907 – sp Bibl Santa Ana [946]

EN MARCHA HACIA LA VICTORIA / Carrillo, Santiago – Valencia? 1937. Fiche W 775. (Blodgett Collection of Spanish Civil War Pamphlets) – 9 – us H.U. College Libr [946]

Marchal, J *see* LE "DROIT D'OBLAT"

Marchand, Clement *see* LE MAURICIEN

LE MARCHAND DE SMYRNE / Bossi, C – London: Goulding, Phipps & D'Almaine, 1799 – 1 – us Sibley [780]

Marchand, Felix-Gabriel *see*
- LES FAUX BRILLANTS COMEDIE EN CINQ ACTES ET EN VERS
- LE FRANCO-CANADIEN
- LE TEMPS

MARCHAND L'AFRICAIN / Castellani, Charles Jules – Paris: E Flammarion, [189-?] – us Res Libr [960]

Marchand, Leon *see* L'EVANGELISATION DES INDIGENES PAR LES INDIGENES DANS LES ILES CENTRALES DU PACIFIQUE (DE TAHITI A LA NOUVELLE CALEDONIE)

Marchand, PR *see* DU PAUPERISME

Marchant, LR *see* A GUIDE TO THE ARCHIVES AND RECORDS OF PROTESTANT CHRISTIAN MISSIONS FROM THE BRITISH ISLES TO CHINA 1796-1914

Marche, Alfred *see* TROIS VOYAGES DANS L'AFRIQUE OCCIDENTALE

MARCHE DE L'OPERA D'ACHILLE : MUSIQUE DE PAER. VARIEE PAR GELINEK / Gelinek, J – Paris: Pacini, 1810 – 1 – us Sibley [780]

MARCHE DES ANCIENS COMTES DE ROSS...MARCHE POUR PIANO A QUATRE MAINS....MARCHE ECOSSAISE / Debussy, Claude – 189-? – 9 – us Sibley [780]

MARCHE DES BRAVES / Fontaine, Pierre – Quebec: Lavigueur & Hutchison, 1916. SEM105P911 – 1mf – 9 – Can$2.25 – cn Bibl Nat [780]

LA MARCHE DU 150IEME, 1815-1965 – Drummondville, Canada. nov 1964 (numero special de "La Parole" – 150ieme anniversaire de la fondation de Drummondville) – 1r – 1 – Can$25.00 – cn Can Microfilming [971]

LE MARCHE MAROCAIN / France. Centre national du commmerce exterieur – Paris. 1961. BNE-3053 1 – 9 – ne IDC [380]

DES MARCHES A TERME SUR DEVISES ETRANGERES / Berland, R – Paris, 1923 – 2mf – 9 – ILM-3188/1 – ne IDC [327]

MARCHES AND MINUETTS, 16 IN EIGHT PARTS FOR 2 VIOLINS, 2 HAUTBOYS OR GERMAN FLUTES, 2 FRENCH HORNS, TENOR, AND BASS. OP. 8 / Valentine, J – (Flauto and hautboy primo part only) – Leicester?: Author, 1785? – 1 – us Sibley [780]

LES MARCHES DE LA VILLE DES TROIS-RIVIERES / Sulte, Benjamin – Trois-Rivieres: L A Bergeron, 1868. SEM16P208 – 1r – 5 – Can$9.00 – cn Bibl Nat [910]

LES MARCHES DU PAYS BAOULE DE LA ZONE DENSE / Michotte, J – (v1.Typologie, Organisation et Fonctionnement. v2.Annexes cartographiques) – 1970. 2v. (Africa Series) – 9 – fr Hachette [550]

MARCHES POUR PIANOFORTE... NOS 1-5 / Mozart, Wolfgang Amadeus – (In process) – Offenbach: chez Jean Andre, [1805-6] – 1 – us Sibley [780]

MARCHES TROPICAUX ET MEDITERRANEENS – France. 1988-1995 – 3r per y – 5,6 – Sfr1,216.00 – sz Infoprint [073]

[IL MARCHESE TULIPANO] OVERTURE, AIR, AND TRIO; ARRANGED PIANO WITH AD LIB VIOLIN / Paisiello, G – (Piano part only) – Paris: Boyer, 179- – 1 – us Sibley [780]

Marchese, V *see* DELLE BENEMERENZE DI S. TOMMASO D'AQUINO VERSO LE ARTI BELLE

Marchesi, L *see* LA LITURGIA GALLICANA NEI PRIMI OTTO SECOLI

MARCHING IN HARMONY = HSEIH CHIN – (Lacking: 1932-42. In Chinese) – 1930-54 – 1r – 1 – ATLA S0306 – us A.T.L.A. [073]

"MARCHING RULE" : A PERSONAL MEMOIR, C. 1970-80, CONCERNING THE MASINA RULE MOVEMENT, 1944-1947 / Davies, Roy – 1r – 1 – PMB1076 – at Pacific Mss [920]

Marchione, Margherita *see* THE COMPREHENSIVE MICROFORM EDITION OF HIS PAPERS, 1730-1816

Marchiori, M *see* STICK DANCE. ESSAIS SUR LA FETE DES MORTS DES INDIENS KOYUKONS DE L'ALASKA

Marcia et Faenes, G *see* THEOREMATA PHYSICO-THEORICA MEDICO-PRACTICA, CHIRURGICO-MECHANICA...

MARCION : DAS EVANGELIUM VOM FREMDEN GOTT (T.U.U. 3-45) / Harnack, Adolf von – Leipzig, 1924 – 11mf – 9 – ne Slangenburg [240]

IL MARCO POLO : "A BULLETIN FOR THE PROMOTION OF THE ITALO-INDONESIAN TRADE AND CULTURAL RELATIONS." – (in English) – Italian Embassy – 7mf – 9 – ne IDC [324]

MARCO POLO/IL MILIONE / Benedetto, LF; ed by Benedetto, L F – Firenze. 1928. BU-676 2 – 8 – ne IDC [920]

Marco Pons, Alejandro *see* EXCAVACIONES DE RUINAS DE EPOCA VISIGODA EN LA ALDEA DE SAN PEDRO DE MERIDA

Marco Rintro, Diego *see* POESIAS VARIAS

Marco, S A *see* ESTATUTOS DE...CACERES

MARCONIGRAPH – v. 1-2. 1911-13 – 1 – us UMI [621]

Marcora, C *see* IL MESSALE DI CIVATE

Marcos Calleja, Leopoldo *see* EL SEGURO DE ENFERMEDAD EN EL MUNDO Y EN NUESTRA PATRIA

Marcos y Navas, Francisco *see* ARTE, O COMPENDIO GENERAL DEL CANTO-LLANO..

Marcos-Garcia, Miguel Angel *see*
- COLECCION NUMISMATICA ANTIGUA DEL MUSEO MUNICIPAL BB.AA. DE SANTANDER
- ESTUDIO DE MATERIALES ARQUEOLOGICOS DEL YACIMIENTO DE CELADA MARLANTES

MARCOTICS CONTROL DIGEST *see* WASHINGTON CRIME NEWS SERVICES' NARCOTICS DEMAND REDUCTION DIGEST

Marcotte, Beatrice *see* BIBLIOGRAPHIE ANALYTIQUE DE L'OEUVRE DU R.P. MARCEL DUBOIS, C.SS.R.

Marcoux, Lucile *see* BIBLIOGRAPHIE ANALYTIQUE DE L'AMIANTE DU CANADA

Marcum, Billy Darrell *see* IMPROVING AND EVALUATING THE CHILD'S WORSHIP AT THE FIRST BAPTIST CHURCH

Marcu-Pandrea, A *see* CONTRIBUTION A L'ETUDE ETHNOLOGIQUE DE LA TERMINOLOGIE DE LA PARENTE AU "PAYS" DE LOVISTEA, ROUMANIE

Marcus, Adalbert Friedrich *see* JAHRBUECHER DER MEDIZIN ALS WISSENSCHAFT

MARCUS AND MIRIAM : A STORY OF JESUS / Springer, Rebecca Ruter – Elgin, IL:David C Cook, [c1908] – 1mf – 9 – 0-8370-5349-8 – 1985-3349 – us A.T.L.A. [830]

MARCUS AURELIUS AND THE LATER STOICS / Bussell, FW – New York: Scribner, 1910 – 1mf – us A.T.L.A. [930]

Marcus Aurelius, Emperor of Rome *see*
- THE THOUGHTS OF THE EMPEROR

MARCUS EREMITA : EIN NEUER ZEUGE FUER DAS ALTKIRCHLICHE TAUFBEKENNTNIS / Kunze, Johannes – Leipzig: Doerffling & Francke, 1895 – 1mf – us A.T.L.A. [240]

MARCUS GARVEY : FBI INVESTIGATION FILE / U.S. Federal Bureau of Investigation – 1979 – 1r – 1 – $85.00 – S1756 – us Scholarly Res [360]

MARCUS TULLIUS CICERO : RECUEIL D'OEUVRES RELIEES ET MICROFILMEES ENSEMBLE, ENRICHIES DE NOMBREUSES NOTES MANUSCRITES / Cicero, Marcus Tullius – 1 – F320.69 – fr Armell [100]

Marcuse, Max *see* SEXUAL-PROBLEME (HQ 7)

Marczali, H *see*
- UNGARISCHE VERFASSUNGSGESCHICHTE
- UNGARISCHES VERFASSUNGSRECHT

MARD – London, UK. 1897-1900. -w. 1 reel – 1 – uk British Libr Newspaper [072]

Mardones Zabalandi Koetxea, Francisco G *see* LES OUVRIERS CHRETIENS SOUS LE GOUVERNEMENT DE FRANCO

MARDUM – (Dawrah-'i 5; shumarah-'i 1-98 (10 Farvardin 1338-1 Isfand 1343[30 Mar 1959-20 Feb 1964]; dawrah-'i 6: shumarah-'i 1-74 (Farvardin 1344-Aban 1350[Mar 1965-Oct 1971]; dawrah-'i 7: shumarah-'i 1-sal-i 2, shumarah-'i 530 (23 Isfand 1358-17 Isfand 1360[14 Mar 1980-10 Mar 1982]). Missing issues: dawrah-'i 5: 4-10, 15-19, 21, 34, 38, 43-44, 50-51, 71; dawrah-'i 6: 3, 7, 10, 17, 31, 36, 40-41, 44-49, 59, 64-75) – [Tehran] Hizb-i Tudah-'i Iran – 1 reel – 1 – $250.00 – us MEDOC [950]

MARDUM-I IRAN – (Shumarah-'i 0-117 (23 Isfand 1357-18 Tir 1360[14 Mar 1979-9 Jul 1981]). Missing issues: 103, 110-113, 116) – Tehran – 1 reel – 1 – $35.00 – us MEDOC [950]

MARE LIBERUM SIVE DE JURE QUOD BATAVIS... / Grotius, H – Leiden, 1609 – 1mf – 1 – ILM-187/1 – ne IDC [327]

IL MARE TERRITORIALE... / Baldoni, C – Padova, 1934 – 3mf – 9 – ILM-2315/1 – ne IDC [340]

LE MARECHAL DE CAMP DESANDROUINS, 1729-1792: GUERRE DU CANADA 1756-1760: GUERRE DE L'INDEPENDANCE AMERICAINE 1780-1782 / Gabriel, Charles Nicolas – Verdun: Renve-Lallemant, 1887. 03273. (Pre-1900 Canadiana) – 9 – cn C.I.H.M. [971]

Marechal, Pierre-Sylvain *see* CORRECTIF A LA REVOLUTION

Marechal, Sylvain *see* LE JUGEMENT DERNIER DES ROIS

Marechal, Sylvain et Gretry *see* LA FETE DE LA RAISON

Marek, Miroslav et al *see* CULTURAL POLICY IN CZECHOSLOVAKIA

Maresca, Giovanni *see* JUAN DONOSO CORTES E LA NOBILTA

Marescalchi, L *see* SEI TRIO E UNA SERENATA PER DUE VIOLINI E VIOLONCELLO OBBLIGATO, CON UNA PARTE DI PIU DA ESEGUIRSI CON LA VIOLA IN VOCE DEL VIOLONCELLO

Mareschal, Andre *see* LA CHRYSOLITE OU LE SECRET DES ROMANS

Marescot, Michel *see* DISCOURS VERITABLE SUR LA FAICT DE MARTHE BROSSIER DE ROMORANTIN

Maret, H *see* ELOGE HISTORIQUE DE M. RAMEAU

Marett, R R *see* ANTHROPOLOGY AND THE CLASSICS

MAREVO / Bal'mont, K D – Paris. 1922. BR-524 2 – 8 – ne IDC [460]

Marey, Etienne J *see* LA CHRONOPHOTOGRAPHIE

MARFA POSADNITSA NOVGORODSKAIA / Pogodin, M P – Tragediia v 5-i deistviiakh. M. 1830. BR-8312 2 – 8 – ne IDC [460]

Marfin, J P *see* BIOLOGIE DE L'ATHERINE: ATHERINA BOYERI RISSO, 1810 (POISSON-TELEOSTEEN) DANS TROIS MILIEUX SAUMATRES DU ROUSSILLON (LEUCATE, CANET, BOURDIGOU)

THE MARGARET CROSS NORTON WORKING PAPERS, 1924-1958 / ed by Bailey, Robert E & Evans, Elaine Shemoney – (Includes an inventory and index on 7 com mf) – Springfield: Illinois State Archives, 1993 – 8r – 1 – $50.00 SAA members $60.00 nonmembers – us IL Archives [920]

MARGARET FULLER (MARCHESA OSSOLI) / Howe, Julia Ward – Boston: Roberts Brothers, 1883 (Famous women) – 1mf – us A.T.L.A. [240]

MARGARET OGILVY / Barrie, James Matthew – London: Hodder and Stoughton, 1896 – 1 roll – 1 – 1-55879-199-X – uk Libr Preservation [830]

THE MARGARET SANGER PAPERS : COLLECTED DOCUMENTS – 1996 – ca 18r – 1 – $2,125.00 – 1-55655-635-7 – us UPA [305]

THE MARGARET SANGER PAPERS : THE SMITH COLLEGE COLLECTIONS – (With printed guide) – 83r – 1 – $10,380.00 – 1-55655-529-6 – us UPA [305]

Margarinos, Santiago *see* HERNANDO CORTES, ESTAMPAS DE SU VIDA

Margarinus, G *see* BULLARIUM CASINENSE SEU CONSTITUTIONES

LA MARGARITA ESCONDIDA / Una Religiosa Concepcionista – 3rd Edicion. Sevila, Imp. San Antonio, 1949 – 1 – sp Bibl Santa Ana [240]

LES MARGES – Paris. nov 1903-oct 1936, juin 1937 – 1 – fr A.C.R.P.P. [073]

Marggraf, Andreas Siegismund *see* CHYMISCHER SCHRIFTEN. ERSTER - ZWEYTER THEIL. NEUE VERBESSERTE AUFLAGE

MARGINALIA TO THE HISTORIES OF THE NORTHERN DYNASTIES / Boodberg, P A – (Harvard Journal of Asiatic Studies). v. 3. 1938. BU-552 2 – 8 – ne IDC [950]

MARGINALIEN ZU GOETHES BRIEFEN AN CHARLOTTE VON STEIN / Fraenkel, Jonas – (Includes bibliographical references) – Jena: E Diederichs, 1909 – 1r – 1 – us U.W. Library [430]

LES MARGINAUX: BEGGARS, THIEVES, AND PROSTITUTES – 9 – fr Hachette [360]

Margolin, I *see* PAMIATI MANDEL'SHTAMA

Margoliouth, D S *see* A COMMENTARY ON THE BOOK OF DANIEL

Margoliouth, David Samuel *see*
- AN ESSAY ON THE PLACE OF ECCLESIASTICUS IN SEMITIC LITERATURE
- JEPHET INB ALI THE KARAITE
- LINES OF DEFENCE OF THE BIBLICAL REVELATION

Margoliouth, G *see* DESCRIPTIVE LIST OF THE HEBREW AND SAMARITAN MSS IN THE BRITISH MUSEUM

Margolis, A *see* GESHIKTE FUN IDN IN RUSLAND

Margolis, A J *see* PAPERS AND CORRESPONDENCE

Margolis, Max Leopold *see*
- THE COLUMBIA COLLEGE MSS OF MEGHILLA (BABYLONIAN TALMUD)
- COMMENTARIUS ISAACIDIS QUATENUS AD TEXTUM TALMUDIS...POSSIT TRACTATU ERUBHIN
- A MANUAL OF THE ARAMAIC LANGUAGE OF THE BABYLONIAN TALMUD
- MICAH
- THE THEOLOGICAL ASPECT OF REFORMED JUDAISM

MARGOWIRJO. SERAT MARGAWIRJA...KA-ETAP INGKANG KAPING 2 / Djajadiningrati, Raden Mas Arja – Soerakarta, 1908 – 1mf – 9 – ne IDC [950]

MARGUERITE D'ANGOULEME, QUEEN OF NAVARRE, 1492-1549 / ed by Frank, Felix – Les Marguerites de la Marguerite des Princesses: texte de l'edition de 1547. With introd., notes and glossary by Felix Frank. Paris: Librairie des Bibliophiles, 1873. 4v. port. With reprod. of original title page – 1 – us U.W. Library [810]
Marguerite, Queen of Navarre *see*
- THE HEPTAMERON; OR TALES AND NOVELS OF MARGUERITE, QUEEN OF NAVARRE
- MEMOIRS OF MARGARET DE VALOIS, QUEEN OF NAVARRE

Marguerite-Marie, Soeur OSU *see* FAMILLE ALEXIS REAU
Margulies, H S *see* DUBNO RABBATI
MARHAEN DAN PROLETAR / Sukarno, Pres. Indonesia – Also under title: "Shaping and reshaping" Indonesia. SE 1218 1 – 9 – ne IDC [324]
MARHAENISME; ADJARAN BAPAK MARHAENISME BUNG KARNO / Sukarno, Pres. Indonesia – SE 5654 1. 1965 – 9 – ne IDC [324]
MARHAENISME PERDJUANGKAN DAN AMALKAN DITENGAHTENGAH MARHAEN / Sukarno, Pres. Indonesia – SE 5274 1. 1964 – 9 – ne IDC [324]
LE MARI AMBITEUX OU L'HOMME QUI VEUT FAIRE SON CHEMIN / Picard – (French Theatre Series). Paris. Huet, Ravinet et Charon, an XI. 1802 – 9 – fr Hachette [820]
Mari, G *see* GRANDEZZE DELLA CITA DI ROMA
MARIA / Santos Alvarez, Miguel de los – 1840 – 9 – 1.50f – sp Bibl Santa Ana [830]
Maria Antonia Walpurgis *see*
- TALESTRI, REGINA DELLE AMAZZONI
- IL TRIONFO DELLA FEDELTA..

MARIA CALLEJA'S GOZO : A LIFE HISTORY / ed by Galley, Micheline – 1994 – 246p – 9 – 92-3-102977-0 – Co-publ with Utah State University Press/UNESCO Publishing – fr UNESCO [940]
MARIA CHAPDELAINE / Hemon, Louis – Paris: Mornay, 1933. SEM16P147 – 1r – 5 – Can$9.00 – cn Bibl Nat [390]
Maria Paula, Sister *see* DER SELIGE JOHANNES VON TRIORA, EIN MAERTYRER CHINAS ZU ANFANG DES NEUNZEHNTEN JAHRHUNDERTS..
MARIA STUART : TRAUERSPIEL IN FUENF AUFZUEGEN / Schiller, Friedrich von – Berlin: M Matthiesen, [19–] – 1r – 1 – us U.W. Library [820]
MARIA STUART IM DRAMA DER WELTLITERATUR : VORNEHMLICH DES 17. UND 18. JAHRHUNDERTS: EIN BEITRAG ZUR VERGLEICHENDEN LITERATURGESCHICHTE / Kipka, Karl – (Includes bibliographical references (" Bibliographische Zeittafel der Maria Stuartdramen") – Leipzig: M Hesse, 1907 – 1 – us U.W. Library [410]
MARIA THERESIA UND JOSEPH 2 : IHRE CORRESPONDENZ SAMMT BRIEFEN JOSEPH'S AN SEINEN BRUDER LEOPOLD / ed by Arneth, A von – Wien. 3v. 1867-1868 – 15mf – 9 – ne IDC [943]
MARIA THERESIAS STAATS- UND LEBENSANSCHAUUNG / Dorschel, Gotthold – Gotha, 1908 – 9 – DM48.00 – 3-89349-275-5 – gw Hänsel [240]
LE MARIAGE CHINOIS AU POINT DE VUE LEGALE / Hoang, P – Chang-hai. 1898 – 7mf – 9 – CH-932/2 – ne IDC [306]
LE MARIAGE COUTUMIER DANS LA SOCIETE BAMBARA / Luneau, R – Les traditions du village de Beleko (Mali) – 9 – F60.00 – fr Ethnologie [306]
LE MARIAGE DE LA MUSIQUE AVEC LA DANCE / Du Manoir, G – 1664 – 9 – us Sibley [780]
LE MARIAGE DES NKUNDO / Hulstaert, G – Brussels. 1938 – 1 – us Res Libr [306]
LE MARIAGE EN FRANCE / Cadet, Ernest – Paris: Guillaumin, 1870. xiv,249p. (Les Femmes Collection) – 3mf – 9 – $8.00 – fr Bibl Nationale [306]
MARIAGE ET FIANCAILLES DANS LE HAUT-BOCAGE VENDEEN (XXE SIECLE): LES MARIES DE CHAMBRETAUD / Herault, L – 9 – F50.00 – fr Ethnologie [306]
LE MARIAGE: HIER ET AUJOURD'HUI / Bordeaux, Henry – Paris: E. Flammarion, 1921. (Les Femmes Collection) – 4mf – 9 – $10.00 – fr Bibl Nationale [306]
LE MARIAGE MEXICAIN, DIVERTISSEMENT BALLET / Egville, J d' – (Piano score) – London: Monzani & Cimador, 1800 – 1 – us Sibley [780]
MARIAGE PARISIEN / Lagros de Langeron, Gabriel – Paris: Cocuaud, 1908. 126p. (Les Femmes Collection) – 2mf – 9 – $6.00 – fr Bibl Nationale [306]
LE MARIAGE...ET LA CONFERENCE DE LA HAYE / Guillaume – Bruxelles, 1894 – 6mf – 1 – ILM-3686/1 – ne IDC [327]
MARIAH – v. 1-3. 1976-79 – 1,5,6,9 – us UMI [790]
THE MARIAN REACTION IN ITS RELATION TO THE ENGLISH CLERGY : A STUDY OF THE EPISCOPAL REGISTERS / Frere, Walter H – London: S.P.C.K.; New York: E.& J.B. Young, 1896. (Church Historical Society; 18) – 1mf – us A.T.L.A. [240]
Mariana Islands. Spanish *see* RECORDS
Mariana, Juan de *see* HISTORIAE DE REBUS HISPANIAE LIBRI TRIGINTA. ACCENDUNT JOSEPHI EMMANUELIS MINIANAE..
MARIANA PINEDA / Garcia Lorca, Federico – MS DE 1925 – 2mf – 9 – sp Cultura [830]
MARIANA PINEDA, FRAGMENTO MANUSCRITO / Garcia Lorca, Federico – 1925 – 1mf – 9 – sp Cultura [830]
MARIANNE – Paris. 26 oct 1932-28 aout 1940 – 1 – fr A.C.R.P.P. [073]
O MARIANNENSE : COMPLETA NEUTRALIDADE POLITICA – DEFENDE OS INTERESSES DA RELIGIAO, LAVOURA E COMMERCIO – Marianna, 23 Sep 1888 – 1,5,6 – bl Biblioteca [072]
MARIA'S HEERLIJKHEID IN EGYPTE : EEN STUDIE DER KOPTISCHE MARIA-LITTERATUUR / Muyser, J – Utrecht. Deel 1. 1935 – 6mf – 8 – ne Slangenburg [240]
Mariatmo, L *see* ANTHROPOLOGY KEBUDAJAAN UNTUK PENGADJARAN MENEGAH TINGKAT ATAS
MARIBORER ZEITUNG – (Cont: Marburger Zeitung) – Maribor, Yugoslavia. Oct 1925-Oct 1927; Mar 1929-Aug 1934; Mar 1935-Jun 1940 – 21r – 1 – us L of C Photodup [949]
MARIBORER ZEITUNG – Maribor (Marburg), Germany. 21 Mar 1928-13 Dec 1940 (incomplete) – 1 – gw Mikrofilm [072]
Maridos de Coral, Montemor *see* LA PASION DE UNA RELIGIOSA, BENITEZ DE CASTRO, CUARTO GALEON, IRIGAROY DE BUZO A GENERAL, TOMAS LECCION DE AMOR SIN PALABRAS Y PEREZ Y PEREZ, CABEZA DE ESTOPA
MARIE ANTOINETTE, ARCHIDUCHESSE, DAUPHINE ET REINE / Reunion des musees nationaux. Paris – 1955. 33 illus. 4mf – 9 – fr Réunion [700]
Marie, C L *see* LES OMNIBUS DU LANGAGE
MARIE DE BRETAGNE : ABBESSE DE FONTEVRAULT (1424-1477) / Fonssagrives, E – Vannes, 1923 – Dfl6.00 – ne Slangenburg [920]
Marie, de France *see* POESIES DE MARIE DE FRANCE, POETE ANGLO-NORMAND DU XIIIE SIECLE.
Marie de l'Incarnation, Mere *see* LA VIE DE LA VENERABLE MERE MARIE DE L'INCARNATION, PREMIERE SUPERIEURE DES URSULINES DE LA NOUVELLE-FRANCE
Marie de St-Thomas d'Aquin *see* VIE SPIRITUELLE
Marie Gemma, Soeur *see* BIBLIOGRAPHIE ANALYTIQUE DE L'OEUVRE DU DOCTEUR MARCEL LANGLOIS, PROFESSEUR TITULAIRE A L'UNIVERSITE LAVAL, CERTIFIE DU COLLEGE ROYAL EN PEDIATRIE...
Marie Simeon, Soeur *see* BIBLIOGRAPHIE DE M. JEAN-PAUL GELINAS, B.A., M.D.
MARIE VERWAHNEN : ROMAN / Lauff, Joseph von – Berlin, Wien: Ullstein, [1910?] – 1r – 1 – us U.W. Library [830]
Marie-Antoinette, Mere FCS P *see* NOTES HISTORIQUES
MARIE-CLAIRE BLAIS : BIBLIOGRAPHIE ANALYTIQUE / Dufour, Helene – 1964. SEM105P4 – 1mf – 9 – cn Bibl Nat [010]
Marie-Clement, Frere *see* ESSAI DE BIO-BIBLIOGRAPHIE ANNOTEE DU REVEREND FRERE MARC, S.C.
Marie-de-la-Charite, Soeur *see* BIBLIOGRAPHIE ANALYTIQUE DE L'OEUVRE DE MADEMOISELLE GERTIE KATHLEEN HART, DIPLOMEE DE L'UNIVERSITE LAVAL, DE L'UNIVERSITE D'OXFORD, DE LA FACULTE DES LETTRES DE LA SORBONNE
Marie-de-la-Croix, Soeur *see* BIBLIOGRAPHIE DE MONSIEUR L'ABBE J.-ALFRED TREMBLAY
Marie-de-la-Portectin, Soeur *see* BIBLIOGRAPHIE DES BIOGRAPHIES DES RELIGIEUSES AUGUSTINES HOSPITALIERES DE LA MISERICORDE DE JESUS
Marie-Elie, Frere *see* BIBLIOGRAPHIE DU REVEREND FRERE ROBERT, E.C., D.SC.
Marie-Francoise, Soeur *see* LE REVEREND PERE FRANCOIS DELAPLACE DE LA CONGREGATION DES PERES DU SAINT-ESPRIT...
Marie-Helene-de Rome, Soeur *see* BIBLIOGRAPHIE ANALYTIQUE DE L'OEUVRE DU REVEREND PERE JEAN BOUSQUET, O.P., LECTEUR EN THEOLOGIE
Marie-Irene, Soeur *see* BIO-BIBLIOGRAPHIE DE MONSEIGNEUR LOUIS-JOSEPH-ARTHUR MELANSON, PREMIER ARCHEVEQUE DE MONCTON, N.-B., 1879-1941
Marie-Liberatrice, Soeur *see* BIBLIOGRAPHIE ANALYTIQUE DE L'OEUVRE DE MONSEIGNEUR VICTORIN GERMAIN, P.D., D.TH., L.PH., O.B.E., DIRECTEUR-ADMINISTRATEUR DE LA SAUVEGARDE DE L'ENFANCE
Marie-Libermann, Soeur *see* LES INSTITUTS FAMILIAUX DE NOTRE PROVINCE
MARIENBADER ZEITUNG – Marienbad (Marianske Lazne), Germany. 19 Nov 1928-1933; 1938 – 7r – 1 – gw Mikrofilm [072]
Mariengof, A *see*
- BRITYI CHELOVEK
- MALEN'KIE KOMEDII
- ROMAN BEZ VRAN'IA
- TSINIKI

MARIENKIND : FUER DIE MAERCHENSPIELE DER KUENSTLERISCHEN VOLKSBUEHNE NACH DEM GLEICHNAMIGEN MAERCHEN DER GEBRUEDER GRIMM IN HANDLUNG UND REIM GEBRACHT / Guembel-Seiling, Max – Leipzig: Breitkopf & Haertel, 1918 – 1r – 1 – us U.W. Library [820]
MARIENVERORDNUNGSBLATT – Berlin, Germany. 1876 – 1r – 1 – gw Mikrofilm [073]
Marie-Patricia, Soeur *see* BIBLIOGRAPHIE ANALYTIQUE SUR L'HYGIENE MENTALE PREVENTIVE DES JEUNES DE LA PROVINCE DE QUEBEC, 1925-1955
Marie-Paul, Frere *see* BIBLIOGRAPHIE SUR LA METHODOLOGIE DE LA LECTURE
MARIESTADS WECKOBLAD – (Tidning for Skaraborgs Lan 1884-91; Lanstidningen Tidning for Skaraborgs Lan, 1892-1923) – Mariestad, Sweden. 1817-84 – 46r – 1 – sw Kungliga [072]
MARIESTADSTIDNINGEN – Mariestad, Sweden. 1924-25, 1971-78 – 50r – 1 – sw Kungliga [072]
MARIESTADSTIDNINGEN – Mariestad, Sweden. 1926-70, 1979- – 1 – sw Kungliga [072]
Marie-Stella, Soeur *see* GUY LAVIOLETTE (MICHEL-HENRI GINGRAS), EN RELIGION, LE REVEREND FRERE ACHILLE DES FRERES DE L'INSTRUCTION CHRETIENNE, AUTEUR DE "GLOIRES NATIONALES"
Mariette, A *see*
- CATALOGUE GENERAL DES MONUMENTS D'ABYDOS DECOUVERTS PENDANT LES FOUILLES DE CETTE VILLE
- DENDERAH. DESCRIPTION GENERALE DU GRAND TEMPLE DE CETTE VILLE
- KARNAK. ETUDE TOPOGRAPHIQUE ET ARCHEOLOGIQUE AVEC UN APPENDICE COMPRENANT LES PRINCIPAUX TEXTES HIEROGLYPHIQUES
- LES MASTABAS DE L'ANCIEN EMPIRE FRAGMENT DU DERNIER OUVRAGE
- LES PAPYRUS EGYPTIENS DU MUSEE DE BOULAQ PUBLIES EN FAC-SIMILE SOUS LES AUSPICES DE S. A. ISMAIL-PACHAK, KHEDIVE D'EGYPTE

MARIJUANA AND DRUG ABUSE COMMISSION : "SHAFER COMMISSION" FIRST AND SECOND REPORTS WITH TECHNICAL PAPERS – Washington: GPO, 1972-73 (all publ) – 63mf – 9 – $94.00 – LLMC 80-526 – us L.L.M.C. [324]
MARILAH MEMBELA TANAH AIR KITA, DENGAN DARAH DAGING KITA! : KITAB PENOENTOEN PEMBELAAN TANAH AIR OENTOEK OEMOEM – N.p., 2604. ii/188p – 107-109mf – 9 – ne IDC [950]
MARIN AND SAN ANSELMO HERALD – San Anselmo. Calif. 1921-1929 – 1 – us UMI [071]
THE MARIN AND SAN ANSELMO HERALD – San Anselmo, CA. 1912-13; 1915-31; 1933-37; 1938; 1940-46 – 28r – 1 CB02759 – $1,400.00 – us Library Micro [071]
MARIN COUNTY – 1904-34; 1992- – 34+ r – 1 – $1,700.00 – P00061 – us Library Micro [910]
MARIN COUNTY INCLUDING SAN RAFAEL – Marin Co, CA. 1825; 1905-1906; 1925, 1946-1947 – 4r – 1 – $200.00 – D057 – us Library Micro [978]
MARIN COUNTY TOCSIN – San Rafael, CA. 1890-1918 – 13r – 1 – $650.00 – C02930 – us Library Micro [071]
MARIN INDEPENDENT JOURNAL – San Rafael, CA. 1949- – 781+ r – 1 – $39,050.00 ($975.00y) – R02927 – us Library Micro [073]
MARIN INDEPENDENT JOURNAL *see* INDEPENDENT
MARIN JOURNAL – San Rafael, CA. 1861-99; 1902-36; 1938-49 – 68r – 1 BC02928 – $3,400.00 – us Library Micro [073]
MARIN JOURNAL – San Rafael. Calif. -w. 1861-1937, 1938-49 – 1 – us UMI [071]
Marin, Marre-de *see* GRAMMAIRE MALGACHE FONDEE SUR LES PRINCIPES DE LA GRAMMAIRE JAVANAISE, SUIVIE D'EXERCICES ET D'UN RECUEIL DE CENT ET UN PROVERBES
Marin Mendoza, Joaquin *see* HISTORIA DE LA MILICIA ESPANOLA
MARIN NEWS – Sausalito, CA. 1961-66 – 3r – 1 – $150.00 – B02985 – us Library Micro [071]
MARIN NEWS *see* SAUSALITO NEWS
Marin, P *see* NOUVELLE METODE POUR APPRENDRE LES PRINCIPES ET L'USAGE DES LANGUES FRANCOISE ET HOLLANDOISE
MARIN SCOPE – Sausalito, CA. Apr 1971- – 16+ r – 1 – $800.00 ($90.00y) – B02986 – us Library Micro [071]
MARIN THIS MONTH – Marin Co, July 1959-Jun 1961 – 1r – 1 – $50.00 – B40229 – us Library Micro [978]
MARINA / Sanchez-Arjona, Vicente – Sevilla: Imp. Alvarez, 1959 – 1 – sp Bibl Santa Ana [810]
MARINE ALGAE OF NEW ENGLAND AND ADJACENT COAST / Farlow, WG – Washington, 1881 – 210p, 15pls – 8 – ne IDC [580]
THE MARINE ALGAE OF THE DANISH WEST INDIES, PT I-II. CHOLOROPHYCAEA-PHAEOPHYCEAE / Boergesen, FC E – Dansk Botanisk Arkiv, 1913, v1, nr. 4, p 1-160, 1map, 1914, v2, nr. 2, p 1-68 – 8 – ne IDC [580]
LA MARINE AU CANADA: RAPPORT DE MISSION / Delevaque, Charles – Paris: E. Lacroix, 1874?. 02288. (Pre-1900 Canadiana) – 9 – cn C.I.H.M. [910]
MARINE BEHAVIOUR AND PHYSIOLOGY – 1,5,9 – us Gordon [574]
The Marine Biological Association *see* JOURNAL
MARINE BIOLOGY – v. 1-62. 1967-80 – 1,5,9 – 7068.00 – us UMI [574]
MARINE BIOLOGY LETTERS – v1-6. 1979-84 – 1,5,6,13 – sz Elsevier [574]
LA MARINE BRETONNE AUX 15E ET 16E SIECLES / Nicolliere Teijeiro, Stephane Praude de la – Nantes. 1885. 107p. (Historical Studies Series) – 9 – $6.00 – fr Bibl Nationale [623]
MARINE CASUALTIES ON THE GREAT LAKES, 1863-73 / U.S. Coast Guard – T729 – 1r – 1 – us Nat'l Archives [623]
MARINE CHEMISTRY – v1-15. 1972-84 – 1,5,6,13 – sz Elsevier [073]
THE MARINE CORP GAZETTE – v1-47. 1916-63. Wanting Jan-May 1925 – 1 – $589.00 – us L of C Photodup [355]
MARINE CORPS GAZETTE – 1916- 1; 1971-5,6; 1976- 4 x 6 in. 9 – us UMI [355]
THE MARINE COURT OF THE CITY OF NEW YORK: ITS ORGANIZATION, JURISDICTION AND PRACTICE / McAdam, David – (2nd ed. New York, Diossy, 1872. 336p. LL-1348 1) – New York, McAdam & Vannett, 1868. 164p. LL-1401 – 1 – us L of C Photodup [340]
MARINE ENVIRONMENTAL RESEARCH – v1-13. 1978-84 – 1,5,6,13 – sz Elsevier [574]
MARINE FISHERIES REVIEW / U.S. National Marine Fisheries Service (NOAA) – Includes predecessors: Commercial Fisheries Review and Fisheries Market News. 1939-86. v1-48:1. 684 fiches – 9 – 1050.00 – us Updata [324]
MARINE GEODESY – v. 1-. 1977- – 1,5,6,9 – us UMI [550]
MARINE GEOLOGY – v1-61. 1964-84 – 1,5,6,13 – sz Elsevier [550]
MARINE GEOPHYSICAL RESEARCHES – (v6-. 1984-. 5,6,9) – v1-. Aug 1970- – 1 – us UMI [550]
MARINE GEOTECHNOLOGY – v. 1- 1975- – 1,5,6,9 – us UMI [550]
MARINE GUIDE – Portland, OR. and Seattle, Wash. 1941-56 – 1 – 456.00 – us Oregon Hist [071]

MARINE (ILLUSTRE BELGE MENSUEL) – London, UK. Sept 1941-May 1945 – 1 – uk British Libr Newspaper [073]

MARINE LOBSTERS OF THE WORLD : AN ANNOTATED AND ILLUSTRATED CATALOGUE OF SPECIES OF INTEREST TO FISHERIES KNOWN TO DATE – 1991 – 300p – it F.A.O. [590]

THE MARINE MAMMALS OF THE NORTH-WESTERN COAST OF NORTH AMERICA / Scammon, C M – 2062 2. 1874 – 8 – ne IDC [590]

MARINE MICROPALAEONTOLOGY – v1-9. 1976-84 – 1,5,6,13 – sz Elsevier [560]

MARINE MINING – v1- 1977- – 1,5,6,9 – us UMI [622]

MARINE NEWS WITH INDEX – 1947-1976 – 9 – uk Manchester Libr [623]

MARINE POLLUTION BULLETIN – v1- 1970- – 5,6,9 – us UMI [360]

MARINE RECORD – Cleveland, Ohio. 1883-90 – 4r – 1 – $32.50r – us Archival [071]

MARINE RESOURCE MAPPING : AN INTRODUCTORY MANUAL 1907 – 277p – it F.A.O. [333]

MARINE RUNDSCHAU – Berlin. Wissenschaftliche Zeitschrift fur Marinefragen. Jan 1900-Jul 1914 – 1 – 35.00r – us Hoover Inst Photo [550]

MARINE SCIENCE EDUCATION – v1-5. 1975-79 – 1 – us UMI [073]

MARINE SHELLS OF SOUTH AFRICA / Sowerby, G B – Z 801 2. 1892 – 8 – ne IDC [590]

Marine Society *see*
- THE BYE-LAWS AND REGULATIONS OF THE MARINE SOCIETY

MARINE TERMINAL OPERATIONS; ORGANIZATION, METHODS, FACILITIES,BY C. L. SAUERBIER. SE 11,627/1. 1964 / U.S. Agency for International Development – 9 – ne IDC [324]

MARINE WEEK – v. 1-. 1974- – 1,5,6,9 – us UMI [550]

MARINE WORKER / Amalgemated Marine Workers' Union. London, England – Feb 1922-Jun 1926. -m. 1 reel – 1 – uk British Libr Newspaper [331]

Marinello, Juan *see*
- CULTURA EN LA ESPANA REPUBLICANA
- DOS DISCURSOS AL SERVICIO DE LA CAUSA POPULAR

Marineo Siculo, Lucio *see* DE REBUS HISPANIAE MEMORABILI

A MARINER OF ENGLAND: AN ACCOUNT OF THE CAREER OF WILLIAM RICHARDSON... 1780-1819, AS TOLD BY HIMSELF / Richardson, William; ed by Childers, Spencer – 1908 – 9 – $20.00 – uk Libr Preservation [920]

THE MARINER'S HAND BOOK OF MARINE LAW – Cleveland, OH: Marine Record Publishing Co. 1881 88p. LL-188 – 1 – us L of C Photodup [340]

The Mariners Museum. Newport News, Virginia *see* DICTIONARY CATALOG OF THE LIBRARY, THE MARINERS MUSEUM

MARINETTE TRIBUNEN – Marinette, Wisconsin. 1894-1908 – 3r – 1 – sw Kungliga [071]

MARINEVERORDNUNGSBLATT – Berlin, 1875-76 – 1r – 1 – Dist. gw Mikrofilm – gw Misc Inst [355]

MARINI MERSENNI ORD. S. FRANCISCI A PAULA, HARMONICORUM LIBRI / Mersenne, Marin – P 725. 1635 – 9 – ne IDC [780]

Marinin, V S *see* ISSLEDOVANIIA TERMODINAMICHESKIKH SVOISTV ZHIDKOGO VODORODA

Marino de Lovera, Pedro *see*
- COLECCION DE HISTORIADORES DE CHILE Y DOCUMENTOS RELATIVOS A LA HISTORIA NACIONAL
- COLECCION HISTORIADORES DE CHILE-DOCUMENTO

MARINO FALIERO : TRAUERSPIEL IN FUENF AUFZUEGEN / Kruse, Heinrich – Leipzig: S Hirzel, 1876 – 1r – 1 – us U.W. Library [820]

MARINO FALIERO, DOGE OF VENICE : AN HISTORICAL TRAGED, IN FIVE ACTS; WITH NOTES. THE PROPHECY OF DANTE: A POEM / Byron, George Gordon Byron – London: John Murray, 1821 – 1 roll – 1 – 1-55879-328-3 – uk Libr Preservation [820]

Marino, Giambattista *see* HRN. B.H. BROCKES...VERTEUTSCHTER BETHLEHEMITISCHER KINDER-MORD DES RITTERS MARINO

MARINO MERCANTE, RAZA DE HEROES, SALUD – Valencia, 193? Fiche W 1026. (Blodgett Collection of Spanish Civil War Pamphlets) – 9 – us H.U. College Libr [946]

MARINOS EXTREMENOS / Fernandes Gaytan, J – Madrid: Talleres Graficas del Ministerio de Marina, 1963 – 1 – sp Bibl Santa Ana [355]

MARINOS EXTREMNOS / Solar y Taboada, Antonio & Ciadoncha, Marques de – Badajoz: Tip. Vda. de A. Arqueros – 1 – sp Bibl Santa Ana [946]

Marinus, Marcus *see* ARCA NOE. THESAURUS LINGUAE SANCTAE NOVUS

MARIO UND DER ZAUBERER : EIN TRAGISCHES REISEERLEBNIS / Mann, Thomas – Berlin: S Fischer [1930] – 1r – us U.W. Library [830]

MARIOLATRY, NEW PHASES OF AN OLD FALLACY / Ganss, Henry George – (Includes bibliography and index) – Notre Dame, IN: Ave Maria, c1897 – 1mf – 9 – 0-8370-8343-5 – 1986-2343 – us A.T.L.A. [230]

MARION CITIZEN – Marion, NE. -w. Jul 1909-Mar 1910 – 1 – us NE Hist [071]

MARION COUNTY RECORD – (Set incl. Marion County Record (Aumsville)) – Silverton, OR. -w. 11 May 1894-25 Dec 1896. – 1 – us U.O. Library [071]

MARION COUNTY RECORD – Silverton OR. May 11 1894-Dec 25 1895 – 1 – us U.O. Library [071]

MARION ENTERPRISE – Marion, NE. -w. Mar 1910-Sep 1922 – 1 – us NE Hist [071]

MARION FIRST BAPTIST CHURCH. MARION COUNTY. SOUTH CAROLINA : CHURCH RECORDS – (Also, Financial Records/Budgets, 1956-1984; Newsletters, 1960-1961, 1984-1986, incomplete. 1,690p) – 1885-1915, 1920-1941 – 1 reel – 1 – $76.05 – us Baptist [240]

MARION FIRST BAPTIST CHURCH. MARION, ILLINOIS : CHURCH RECORDS – 1865-1980 – 1 – 127.08 – us Baptist [240]

Marion. Presbytery (Pres. Ch. in the U.S.A.) *see* MINUTES, 1836-1870

Marion. South Carolina.First United Methodist Church *see* REGISTERS

MARIONETTE – Florence. v1. 1918 – 1r – 1 – us Ross [790]

MARIPOSA COUNTY, 1938; 1955-1956 – 3r – 1 – $150.00 – D058 – us Library Micro [978]

MARIPOSA FREE PRESS – Mariposa, CA. 1864-66; 1870-72 – 3r – 1 – $150.00 – C02418 – us Library Micro [071]

MARIPOSA GAZETTE *see* MARIPOSA WEEKLY GAZETTE AND MINER

MARIPOSA WEEKLY GAZETTE AND MINER – (Also known as: Mariposa Gazette) – Mariposa, CA. 1864- – 45+ r – 1 BC02419 – $2,250.00 ($50.00y) – us Library Micro [071]

Maris, A J *see* LEEN-, KEURMEDIGE EN TYNSGOEDEREN

Maris, Bartolomeus *see* ANALYSE DER FETALEN HERZFREQUENZ MIT METHODEN DER CHAOSTHEORIE

LE MARIS GARCONS. OPERA COMIQUE EN UN ACTE / Berton, H – Paris: Duhan et Co, 1806 – 1 – us Sibley [780]

MARIS LIBERI VINDICIAE:... / Graswinckel, T J F – Hagae Comitum, 1652 – 4mf – 1 – ILM-947/1 – ne IDC [327]

EL MARISCAL DE BERWICK / Berwick y de Alba, Duque de; ed by Baylo, Constantino – Madrid: Razon y Fe, 1926 – 1 – sp Bibl Santa Ana [946]

Marischi, Vicente *see* CONSCIENCIA Y OGANIZACION EN EL MUNDO SINDICAL

Maritain, Jacques *see* LOS REBELDES ESPANOLES NO HACEN UNA "GUERRA SANTA."

THE MARITIME AGRICULTURIST – Sackville, NB: R J Gilbert, [1889-1891] – 9 – cn C.I.H.M. [630]

MARITIME ART – 1940-43 – 1 – $85.00 – cn McLaren [700]

Maritime Baptist Historical Collection, in the Library of Acadia University *see* A CATALOGUE (MIMEO.)

Maritime Law Association of the United States *see* DOCUMENTS 1-701

MARITIME LAWYER *see* TULANE MARITIME LAW JOURNAL

MARITIME LIBRARY ASSOCIATION BULLETIN – 1936-57 – 1r – 1 – $68.00 – cn Library Assoc [020]

THE MARITIME MERCHANT – Halifax and St. John, N.B. 1893-1920 – 30r – 1 – $1950.00 – cn Library Assoc [380]

THE MARITIME MINING RECORD – Stellarton, NS: R Drummond, [1898-1926?] – 9 – cn C.I.H.M. [622]

MARITIME MONTHLY – Saint John. v1-5. 1873-75 – 5 – Can$100.00 – cn Micromedia [623]

MARITIME NOTES AND QUERIES – London. v1-14. 1873-1900 – 1 – $47.50 – us Hein [073]

MARITIME NOTES AND QUERIES : A RECORD OF SHIPPING LAWS AND USAGE – London. v1-14. 1873-1901 (all publ) – 40mf – 9 – $60.00 – LLMC 84-597 – us L.L.M.C. [073]

THE MARITIME PHILATELIST – Yarmouth, NS: J Wallis, [1891] – 9 – cn C.I.H.M. [760]

THE MARITIME PRESBYTERIAN – [New Glasgow, NS: E Scott, 1881-1891] – 9 – cn C.I.H.M. [240]

MARITIME SUBSIDY BOARD, MARITIME ADMINISTRATION AND DEPARTMENT OF COMMERCE DECISIONS / U. S. Dept of Commerce – v1-5. Aug 1961-Jul 1981 (all publ) – 51mf – 9 – $76.00 – LLMC 81-228 – us L.L.M.C. [324]

MARITIME TRADE REVIEW – (Is absorbed by: Trade Review) – Saint John, NB: F L Jones, [1874?-1875?] – 9 – cn C.I.H.M. [380]

MARITIME TRANSPORT STUDY/RESULTS OF THE MARITIME TRANSPORT STUDY *see* INTERNATIONAL SEA-BORNE TRADE STATISTICS YEARBOOK (MARINE TRANSPORT)

MARITIME WARFARE / Bowles, T G – London, 1878 – 2mf – 1 – ILM 343/1 – ne IDC [327]

MARITIME WARFARE / Gibson Bowles, T – London, 1877 – 2mf – 1 – ILM-931/1 – ne IDC [327]

O MARITIMO : ORGAO DA LIGA NAVAL DA AMAZONIA – Manaos, Amazonas. 27 Abr-16 Maio 1911 – 1,5,6 – bl Biblioteca [072]

MARITZBURG ADVERTISER – Pietermaritzburg, South Africa. 1905-06 – 1 – sa State Libr [072]

MARIU A ENSE : PERIODICO NOTICIOSO, COMMERCIAL E LITTERARIO – Barcellos, Amazonas. 28 Mar 1897-7 Mar 1898 – 1,5,6 – bl Biblioteca [072]

O MARIUA : PERIODICO NOTICIOSO, COMMERCIAL E LITTERARIO – [s.l.] – 1,5,6 – bl Biblioteca [072]

Marius, Emanuel *see* DIE PERSOENLICHKEIT JESU CHRISTI: MIT...MYTHOLOGIEN UND MYSTERIEN DER ALTEN VOELKER

MARIUS THE EPICUREAN : HIS SENSATIONS AND IDEAS / Pater, Walter – London, New York: Macmillan and Co., 1891 – 1 roll – 1 – 1-55879-409-3 – uk Libr Preservation [450]

MARIUS VICTORINUS UND DIE ENTWICKLUNG DER ABENDLAENDISCHEN WILLENSMETAPHYSIK / Benz, E – Stuttgart, 1932 – 8mf – 8 – ne Slangenburg [110]

Marivaux, Pierre C *see*
- L'ISLE DE LA RAISON OU LES PETITS HOMMES. COMEDIE EN TROIS ACTES
- L'ISLE DES ESCLAVES. COMEDIE EN UN ACTE, REPRESENTEE POUR LA PREMIERE FOIS PAR LES COMEDIENS ITALIENS DU ROI, LE LUNDI 5 MARS 1725

Marjolaine *see*
- AU COIN DU FEU
- AUX BAMBINS CANADIENS
- AUX FILLETTES CANADIENNES
- CONTES POUR ENFANTS CANADIENS

Marjoto *see* KITAB UNDANG2 HUKUM DISIPLIN TENTARA (K.U.H.D.T.) SERTA KOMENTAR-KOMENTARNJA LENGKAP PASAL DEMI PASAL

Mark, Charles C *see* STUDY OF CULTURAL POLICY IN THE UNITED STATES

MARK LANE EXPRESS AND AGRICULTURAL JOURNAL – London, UK. 1854-55. -w. 2 reels – 1 – uk British Libr Newspaper [630]

MARK ROTHKO / Reunion des musees nationaux. Paris – 1972. 21 illus. 1 fiche – 9 – fr Réunion [700]

MARK TWAIN JOURNAL – 1951- 1; 1970- 5,6; 1977- 4 x 6 in. 9 – us UMI [420]

MARKERS OF MUSCLE DAMAGE FOLLOWING PROLONGED SWIMMING, CYCLING, AND RUNNING AND A TRIATHLON COMPETITION / Hinson, BT – 1991 – 1mf – 9 – $4.00 – us Microform Publ [613]

MARKET BULLETIN – Charleston. West Virginia. 1960-1970 – 1 – us UMI [071]

MARKET HARBOROUGH ADVERTISER – (Also known as: Harborough Mail) – Aug 3-Dec 28 1869; Jan 24 1870-Dec 22 1894; 1895-Dec 22 1900; 1901-03; 1905-Jun 1912; 1913-15; Jan 4 1916-Dec 25 1917; 1918-59; Jan 2-Dec 24 1969; 1970-Nov 1994; 1995-96 – 132 1/2r – 1 – uk British Libr Newspaper [072]

MARKET INFORMATION SERVICES – 1983 – 88p – it F.A.O. [360]

MARKET RASEN MAIL *see* MARKET RASEN WEEKLY MAIL

MARKET RASEN WEEKLY MAIL – (Also known as: Market Rasen Mail) – Jan 3-Nov 7 1857; 1862; 1875-77; 1879; 1889; 1896; 1912; 1986-96 – 31 3/4r – 1 – uk British Libr Newspaper [072]

MARKET REVIEW OF PEEP AND MOO / Virginia. Polytechnic Institute. Extension Division – May 1950-Jun 1960 – 1,5 – us Spaulding [636]

MARKET THEORY: WHICH ONE? / Moldofsky, Naomi – 1fiche (29x) – 9 – 1.00f – at Libertarian Micro [320]

MARKETABLE TITLE TO REAL ESTATE. / Maupin, Chapman White – (2nd ed. New York: Baker, Voorhis, 1907. 910p. LL-794. 3rd ed. New York: Baker, Voorhis, 1921. 997p. LL-791) – New York: Baker, Voorhis, 1896. 850p. LL-1020 – 1 – us L of C Photodup [340]

MARKETING – 1907- – 1 – us UMI [380]

MARKETING – (v99-100 1995 Can$115.00y) – Toronto. v1-100. 1896-95 – 1 – Can$85.00y – cn Micromedia [650]

MARKETING BULLETINS / U.S. Department of Agriculture – Nos. 1-74. 1959-86. 73 fiches – 9 – $100.00 – us Updata [380]

MARKETING COMMUNICATIONS – (v.5-. 1980- 5,6,9) – v.1-. 1976- – 1 – us UMI [073]

MARKETING COMPUTERS *see* ADWEEK'S COMPUTER AND ELECTRONICS MARKETING

MARKETING EFFECTIVENESS AND PROMOTIONAL STRATEGIES IN NATIONAL COLLEGIATE ATHLETIC ASSOCIATION DIVISION 1 BASKETBALL PROGRAMS / Gundogan, Nese – Temple University, 1996 – 2mf – 9 – $8.00 – PE 3648 – us Microform Publ [790]

MARKETING EGGS AND POULTRY / Stewart, G F & Abbott, J C – 4th printing 1978 – 194p – it F.A.O. [380]

MARKETING FRUITS AND VEGETABLES / ed by Abbott, J C – 2nd rev ed 1974 – 181p – it F.A.O. [380]

MARKETING IMPROVEMENT IN THE DEVELOPING WORLD : WHAT HAPPENS AND WHAT WE HAVE LEARNED / Abbott, J C – 1986 – 237p – it F.A.O. [650]

MARKETING IN EUROPE – 1962-92. Continued annually – 1 – uk World [650]

MARKETING INFORMATION GUIDE – v. 15-17. 1968-1970 – 1,5,6 – us Princeton Micro [380]

MARKETING LIVESTOCK AND MEAT / Fenn, MG – 2nd ed 1977 – 198p – it F.A.O. [380]

MARKETING OF FISHERIES PRODUCTS BY MUNICIPAL FISHERMEN IN PANGUIL BAY, PHILLIPPINES / Auburn University. Agricultural Experiment Station – 1976. 1 reel – 1, 5 – us Spaulding [636]

THE MARKETING OF GROUNDNUTS IN THE SUDAN / Low, E M – 1967. BNE-7660 1 – 9 – ne IDC [380]

MARKETING OF TROPICAL WOOD, PART B : WOOD SPECIES FROM SOUTH AMERICAN TROPICAL MOIST FORESTS – 1976 – 67p – it F.A.O. [380]

MARKETING RESEARCH REPORTS / U.S. Department of Agriculture – Nos. 1-1147. 1952-86. 1303 fiches – 9 – 1900.00 – us Updata [324]

MARKETING SCIENCE: MARKETING JOURNAL OF TIMS-ORSA – (1985-. 5,6,9) – v1-. 1982- – 1 – us UMI [380]

MARKETING STRUCTURES, ACTIVITIES AND OUTCOMES AMONGST SELECTED NATIONAL SPORT ORGANIZATIONS / Gage, Sandra L & Danylchuk, Karen – 1992 – 2mf – $8.00 – us Microform Publ [650]

MARKETING THE PRODUCTS OF AQUACULTURE – 1986 – 116p – it F.A.O. [650]

MARKETING-COMMUNICATIONS – New York. v1-253. 1888-1955. Continues: Printers Ink – 1,5,6 – us Princeton Micro [073]

MARKETING/COMMUNICATIONS – (v. 297-300. 1969-72. 5,6. v. 298-300. 1970-72. 9) – v. 1-300. 1888-1972 – 1 – us UMI [380]

MARKETS FOR FISH AND FISHERY PRODUCTS IN EASTERN EUROPE – 1983 – 28p – it F.A.O. [650]
MARKETS FOR THE PRIME MEDITERRANEAN SPECIES – SEA BASS, SEA BREAM, MULLETS AND EEL – AND THEIR LINKS WITH INVESTMENT – 1987 – 49p – it F.A.O. [650]
Markham, A H *see* A WHALING CRUISE TO BAFFIN'S BAY AND THE GULF OF BOOTHIA
Markham, C R *see* THE CINCHONA SPECIES OF NEW GRANADA
Markham, Clements R *see* A HISTORY OF THE ABYSSINIAN EXPEDITION
MARKHAM ECONOMIST AND SUN – Ontario, CN. 1942- – 4r per yr – 1 – Can$55.00r – cn Commonwealth Micro [072]
MARKHAM TRIBUNE – Harvey. Ill. 1960- – 1 – us UMI [071]
Markham, Violet Rosa *see* THE NEW ERA IN SOUTH AFRICA
MARKOPASA – (See also Bizimpasa, Huer Markopasa, Lalapasa, Malumpasa, and Merhumpasa) – Series 1-2 (1946, 1948-1949) – 5mf – 9 – $25.00 – us MEDOC [949]
Markov, V *see*
- THE LONGER POEMS OF VELIMIR KHLEBNIKOV
- MYSLI O RUSSKOM FUTURIZME
- O POEZII GEORGIIA IVANOVA

Marks, Bayly Ellen *see*
- THE DAVID BAILIE WARDEN PAPERS
- THE ROBERT GOODLOE HARPER PAPERS

Marks, Constant R *see* PAST AND PRESENT OF SIOUX CITY AND WOODBURY COUNTY
Marks, Jacob *see* TRIAL BY JURY. ADDRESSES OF MR. JACOB MARKS.
Marks, K *see* K EVREISKOMU VOPROSU
Marks, Melissa A *see* DEMOGRAPHICS, EMPLOYMENT STATUS, AND EMPLOYMENT SATISFACTION OF GRADUATES FROM NATA APPROVED UNDERGRADUATE ATHLETIC TRAINING PROGRAMS IN THE STATE OF PENNSYLVANIA
MARKTBERICHT VON KLEINWORT & CO – London, UK. Ueber Getreide, Butter & Co. Nov 1852-Nov 1853 – 1 – uk British Libr Newspaper [072]
MARKTINFORMATIONEN FUER DEN AUSSENHANDEL – Berlin, mar 4 1957-sep 17 1973 – 17r – 1 – Dist. gw Mikrofilm – gw Misc Inst [380]
MARKTREDWITZER TAGBLATT : BA DER FRANKENPOST – Marktredwitz, West Germany. 1977- – ca 7r per yr – 1 – gw Mikrofilm [072]
MARK-UP – 1977-86 (complete) – 1r – 1 – ATLA S0852 – us A.T.L.A. [073]
DAS MARKUSEVANGELIUM: NACH SEINEM QUELLENWERTHE FUER DIE EVANGELISCHE GESCHICHTE / Klostermann, August – Goettingen: Vandenhoeck & Rup., 1867. 1 fiche – 9 – us A.T.L.A. [240]
MARKUS-STUDIEN / Chajes, Hirsch Perez – Berlin: C A Schwetschke, 1899 – 1mf – 9 – 0-8370-2623-7 – 1985-0623 – us A.T.L.A. [220]
Markwick, William Fisher *see* THE LIFE, LETTERS, AND JOURNALS OF THE REV. AND HON. PETER PARKER, M.D.
MARLBORO DEMOCRAT – Bennettsville. S.C. 1885-1908 – 1 – us UMI [071]
MARLBOROUGH 1652-1849 – (Mf 1T-8T: Births 1652-1826. Mf 7T-8T: Marriages 1664-1817. Mf 8T-10T: Deaths 1663-1837. Mf 10T: Marriages 1834-37. Mf 10T-12T: Births 1774-1846. Mf 12T-13T: Marriages 1817-43. Mf 13T-14T: Intentions 1845-49. Mf 14T: Deaths 1838-47; Births 1812-51. Mf 14T-16T: Births 1843-49. Mf 16T: Marriages 1843-49. Mf 17T: Deaths 1843-49) – (mf ed 1997) – 17mf – 9 – 0-87623-287-X – us Holbrook [920]
Marley, K L *see* ELU JA SONAGE
MARLIN DAILY DEMOCRAT – Marlin. Texas. 1978- – 1 – us UMI [071]
Marlow, H Carleton *see* BIBLIOGRAPHY OF AMERICAN WOMEN
Marlow, Isaac *see*
- BRIEF DISCOURSE CONCERNING SINGING IN PUBLIC WORSHIP
- CONTROVERSIE OF SINGING BROUGHT TO AN END

Marmier, Xavier *see* LETTRES SUR LA RUSSIE, LA FINLANDE ET LA POLOGNE
Marmol (y Carvajal) *see* L'AFRIQUE DE MARMOL
Marmont, AF L de *see* ESPRIT DES INSTITUTIONS MILITAIRES
Marmontel, Jean Francois *see* POETIQUE FRANCOISE
Marmontel, M *see*
- LES INCAS OU LA DESTRUCTION DE L'EMPIRE DU PEROU
- LES INCAS...EMPIRE DU PEROU

Marmorstein, Arthur *see*
- THE DOCTRINE OF MERITS IN OLD RABBINICAL LITERATURE
- THE OLD RABBINIC DOCTRINE OF GOD
- STUDIES IN JEWISH THEOLOGY

MARMOTA FLUMINENSE *see* A MARMOTA NA CORTE
A MARMOTA MARANHENSE : FOLHA LITTERARIA E RECREATIVO – '(s.l.')-Sao Luiz, Brazil. 20 Nov 1850; Jan-16 May 1851 – 1,5,6 – bl Biblioteca [072]
A MARMOTA NA CORTE – (Cont of: Marmota Fluminense) – Rio de Janeiro, 7 Sep 1849-30 Apr 1852 – 1,5,6 – bl Biblioteca [072]
A MARMOTINHA : JORNAL JOCO-SERIO, LITTERARIO E RECREATIVO – '(s.l.')-Sao Luis, Brazil. 13 Oct 1852-12 Feb 1853 – 1,5,6 – bl Biblioteca [072]
Marnas, Francisque *see* LA RELIGION DE JESUS (IASO JA-KYO) RESSUSCITEE AU JAPON DANS LA SECONDE MOITIE DU 19E SIECLE
LE MAROC AU TRAVAIL / Morocco. Ministere du Travail et des Affaires Sociales – 1968. BNE-3083 1 – 9 – ne IDC [331]
MAROC CINQ ANS DE REALISATION DU PROGRAMME D'EQUIPEMENT, 1949-1953 / Morocco. Division du Commerce et de la Marine Marchande – Rabat. 1954 – 9 – ne IDC [380]
LE MAROC CONTEMPORAIN. / Maestracci, Noel – Paris. 1928 – 1 – us Res Libr [960]
LE MAROC DANS LES PREMIERES ANNEES DU 16E SIECLE... / Massignon, Louis F-J – Alger: Jourdan, 1906 – 1 – F154.65 – fr Armell [960]
LE MAROC DE 1631 A 1812 – Texte arabe et traduction par O. Houdas. 1886 – 9 – fr Orientalistes [470]
LE MAROC DE DEMAIN / Marty, Paul-N – Paris. 1925 – 1 – us Res Libr [960]
LE MAROC INCONNU... / Moulieras, Auguste – (T.1: Paris: Andre, 1895; T.2: Paris: Challamel, 1899) – 1 – F511.40 – fr Armell [306]
LE MAROC: MONOGRAPHIE ECONOMIQUE / Belgium. Office Belge du Commerce Exterieur – 1965. BNE-3016 1 – 9 – ne IDC [330]
MAROC SOIR – Casablanca: Societe "Maroc soir-Le matin", 1973-81 – us Res Libr [072]
MAROC-PRESSE – Casablanca, jan-apr 1956 – 2r – 1 – us Res Libr [072]
O MAROINENSE – Maroim, Brazil. 16 May 1886; 10 Apr 1892 – 1 – bl Biblioteca [072]
Marolles, M de *see* LE LIVRE DES PEINTRES ET GRAVEURS
Maron, Ida Bagus Putu *see* BALI-TATUA; WRITINGS ON BALINESE HISTORY AND TRADITIONS
Maronier, J H *see*
- HET INWENDIG WOORD
- JACOBUS ARMINIUS
- DE ORDE DER JEZUIETEN

Marostica, V *see* VENETIA TRIONFANTE
MARPLE'S BUSINESS NEWSLETTER – 1975- – 1,5,6,9 – us UMI [650]
MARPLE'S BUSINESS ROUNDUP – (See also: Marple's Business Newsletter) – 1974 – 1 – us UMI [650]
MARPOLE RICHMOND REVIEW – Richmond, British Columbia, CN. Apr 1932-1964 – 11r – 1 – cn Commonwealth Micro [072]
Marprelate, Martin *see* HAY ANY WORKE FOR COOPER
Marpug, Friedrich Wilhelm *see* DES CRITISCHEN MUSICUS AN DER SPREE ESTER BAND
Marpurg, E W *see* ZWEYTER VERSUCH IN FIGUTIRTEN CHORAELEN SOWOHL FUER DIE ORGEL, ALS FUER DAS CLAVICHORD
Marpurg, Friedrich Wilhelm *see*
- ABHANDLUNG VON DER FUGE
- ABHANDLUNG VON DER FUGE NACH DEM GRUNDSAETZEN UND EXEMPELN DER BESTEN DEUTSCHEN UND AUSLAENDISCHEN MEISTER ENTWORFEN VON FRIEDRICH WILHELM MARPURG
- ANFANGSGRUENDE DER THEORETISCHEN MUSIK
- ANHANG ZUM HANDBUCHE BEY DEM GENERALBASSE UND DER COMPOSITION
- ANLEITUNG ZUM CLAVIERSPIELEN DER SCHOENERN AUSUEBUNG DER HEUTIGEN ZEIT GEMAESZ
- ANLEITUNG ZUR MUSIK UEBERHAUPT
- ANLEITUNG ZUR SINGCOMPOSITION
- FUGHE E CAPRICCJ
- HANDBUCH BEY DEM GENERALBASSE UND DER COMPOSITION
- HISTORISCH-KRITISCHE BEYTRAEGE ZUR AUFNAHME DER MUSIK
- KRITISCHE BRIEFE UEBER DIE TONKUN.
- KRITISCHE BRIEFE UEBER DIE TONKUNST MIT KLEINEN CLAVIERSTUECKEN UND SINGODEN
- KRITISCHE EINLEITUNG IN DIE GESCHICHTE UND LEHRSAETZE DER ALTEN UND NEUEN MUSIK
- DIE KUNST DAS CLAVIER ZU SPIELEN. DRITTE, VERBESSERTE UND VERMEHRTE AUFLAGE
- LEGENDE EINIGER MUSIKHEILGEN
- NEUE LIEDER ZUM SINGEN BEYM CLAVIER
- NEUE METHODE, ALLERLEY ARTEN VON TEMPERATUREN DEM CLAVIERE AUFS BEQUEMSTE MITZUTHEILEN
- VERSUCH IN FIGURIRTEN CHORAELEN: SOWOHL FUER DIE ORGEL, ALS FUER DAS CLAVICHORD...
- VERSUCH UEBER DIE MUSIKALISCHE TEMPERATUR NEBST EINEM ANHANG
- VERSUCH UEBER DIE MUSIKALISCHE TEMPERATUR, NEBST EINEM ANHANG UEBER DEN RAMEAU- UND KIRNBERGERSCHEN GRUNDBASZ

Marquard, Leopold *see* THE NATIVE IN SOUTH AFRICA
Marquardt, Janis R *see* STRENGTH GAINS CONSEQUENT TO TEN WEEKS OF UNIVERSAL OR BOWFLEX TRAINING
Marquardt, Karl *see* MANUEL DES ANTIQUITES ROMAINES
Marquart, J *see*
- ERANSAHR NACH DER GEOGRAPHIE DES PS. MOSES XORENAC'I
- GUWAINI'S BERICHT UEBER DIE BEKEHRUNG DER UIGUREN
- OSTEUROPAEISCHE UND OSTASIATISCHE STREIFZUEGE
- SKIZZEN ZUR GESCHICHTLICHEN VOELKERKUNDE VON MITTELASIEN UND SIBIRIEN
- UEBER DAS VOLKSTUM DER KOMANEN

Marquerie, Alfredo *see* FRANCISCO PIZARRO, LARGO EN VIDA Y EN HAZANAS
Marques, A *see* ILES SAMOA
EL MARQUES DE MONSALUD ES SUSTITUIDO POR D. ADOLFO BONILLA / Fita, Fidel & Fernandez de Bethencourt, Francisco – Madrid: Fortanet, 1910. B.R.A.H. 56, 1910, p. 339 – sp Bibl Santa Ana [946]
EL MARQUES DE MONSALUD MIEMBRO DEL INSTITUTO ARQUEOLOGICO DE BERLIN / Fita, Fidel – Madrid: Fortanet. B.R.A.H. 57, 1910, p. 256 – sp Bibl Santa Ana [930]
MARQUES DE TORRES CABRERA. NARRACIONES Y POESIAS / Torres Gonzalez de la Laguna, Miguel – Lit. y Encuad. de Uceda Hnos. 1907 – 1 – sp Bibl Santa Ana [810]
EL MARQUES DE USTARIZ / Spain. Laws, Statutes, etc – 1789 – 9 – 1.50f – sp Bibl Santa Ana [324]
Marques Esparteiro, Antonio *see* O FAMOSO BOTAO DE ANCORA (1600-1895)
Marques, Lourenco *see* O EMANCIPADOR
MARQUESADO DE AGUILAFUENTE, EL / Cobos de Belchite, Baron de – Madrid, s.i., 1956 – 1 – sp Bibl Santa Ana [946]
Marquet, Francois-Nicolas *see* NOUVELLE METHODE FACILE ET CURIEUSE POUR APPRENDRE.
Marquet, J *see* EMIGRANTS SAISONNIERS ESPAGNOLS EN FRANCE
MARQUETTE INDEPENDENT – Marquette, NE. -w. Jan 1884-Feb 1885 – 1 – us NE Hist [071]
MARQUETTE LAW REVIEW – (v1-68 1916-85 on reel $646.00. v69-78 1985-95 on mf $200.00) – v1-78. 1916-95 – 5,6,9 – $846.00 set – us Hein [340]
Marquette, Michigan *see* MISCELLANEOUS EARLY NEWSPAPERS
MARQUETTE NEWS – Marquette, NE. -w. Jun 1937-Feb 1938 – 1 – us NE Hist [071]
Marquez de Medina, Marcos *see* EL ARTE EXPLICADO Y GRAMATICO
Marquez, Gabino *see*
- COMISION CATEQUISTICA DE ZARAGOZA. RELIGION Y CULTURA, UN GRAFICO Y EJEMPLOS ZARAGOZA, 1940
- COMPENDIO DE FILOSOFIA ESCOLASTICA. TOMO 1
- COMPENDIO DE FILOSOFIA ESCOLASTICA. TOMO 2. FILOSOFIA MORAL
- DIEZ BLANCO, ALEJANDRO EVOLUCION DEL PENSAMIENTO FILOSOFICO. TOMO 1
- DOCTRINA DE LA IGLESIA SOBRE EL DERECHO DE ENSENAR
- DON ANDRES MANJON Y LA LIBERTAD DE ENSENANZA
- DON ANDRES MANJON Y LA LIBERTAD DE ENSENANZA (CONCLUSION)
- ELIAS DE TEJADA SPINOLA, FRANCISCO. LA TRADICION GALLEGA. PROLOGO DE R. OTERO PEDRAYO. MADRID, 1944
- LAS ENCICLICAS
- ERRORES ACTUALES QUE SE HALLAN EXTENDIDOS EN ESPANA CAUSANDO GRAVISIMOS ESTRAGOS EN EL PUEBLO CATOLICO...
- ERRORES MODERNOS, EXPUESTOS Y REFUTADOS POR...CON UN APENDICE SOBRE LA NUEVA BULA DE LA SANTA CRUZADA
- ETICA
- EXPLICACION LITERAL DEL CATECISMO DEL PADRE ASTETE CON UNA EXPOSICION Y REFUTACION DE LOS ERORES MODERNOS Y LA EXPLICACION DE LA BULA DE LA SANTA CRUZADA
- FILOSOFIA MORAL
- FILOSOFIA MORAL. TOMO 2. LA MORALIDAD EN PARTICULAR, O SEA, EL DERECHO NATURAL
- FUNDAMENTOS DE RELIGION
- GARCIA GARCES, NARCISO. EXPOSICION DEL DOGMA CATOLICO
- MANUAL DEL CATEQUISTA. TRAD. DEL ITALIANO POR D. FELIX MERINO REVUELTA. BARCELONA, 1943
- LA OBRA DE DON ANDRES MANJON
- SARABIA, REDENTORISTA. RAMON. SACERDOTES, NINOS Y CATEQUISTAS. TOMO 1. MADRID, 1942
- SEMBLANZA DE DON ANDRES MANJON
- TEXTOS DE FILOSOFIA (PRIMER CURSO). INTRODUCCION A LA FILOSOFIA
- VIGNA, LUIS. BREVIARIO DE DOCTRINA CATOLICA. BARCELONA, 1943
- VIVE TU VIDA

MARQUEZ, GABINO. LAS ENCICLICAS "RERUM NOVARUM", "QUADRAGESIMO ANNO" Y "DIVINI REDEMPTORIO" CONTRA EL COMUNISMO, AL ALCANCE DE TODOS. TOLEDO, 1938 / Azpiazu, J – Burgos: Razon y Fe, 1938 – 1 – sp Bibl Santa Ana [946]
Marquez Nunez, Guillermo *see* MANUAL DE HISTORIA DE LA ORDEN DE LA MERCED. TOMO 1. (1218-1574)
Marquis, Albert N *see*
- THE BOOK OF DETROITERS
- THE BOOK OF MINNESOTANS

Marquis, D G *see*
- PSYCHOLOGIE

Marquis, Don *see*
- ARCHY'S LIFE OF MEHITABEL
- LOVE SONNETS OF A CAVE MAN, AND OTHER VERSES

Marquis, Gerard *see* LA SENTINELLE
Marquis, Jean J *see* MEMOIRE STATISTIQUE DU DEPARTEMENT DE LA MEURTHE
Marquis, Maurice *see*
- LE COURRIER DE MONTMAGNY
- LE COURRIER DU NORD
- LE GASPESIEN
- LA SENTINELLE

LA MARQUISE DE SADE / Vallette, Marguerite Eymery – Paris: Monnier, 1887. 287p. (Les Femmes Collection) – 5mf – 9 – $12.00 – fr Bibl Nationale [920]
DIE MARQUISE VON O– : DIE DICHTUNG UND IHRE QUELLEN / Kleist, Heinrich von; ed by Klaar, Alfred – (German and French text) – Berlin: Propylaeen-Verlag, [1922?] – 1 – us U.W. Library [830]
LES MARQUISIENS / Clavel, Charles – Paris: Doin, 1885 – 1 – F99.62 – fr Armell [305]
Marr, N Ia *see* SPISOK RUKOPISEI SEVANSKAGO MONASTYRIA
Marranca, Harriett A *see* EFFECT OF AGE ON REACTION AND MOVEMENT TIMES IN GIRLS AND WOMEN
Marrant, John *see* A SELECTION OF WORKS BY AND ABOUT JOHN MARRANT
Marre, Aristide *see*
- GRAMMAIRE MALGACHE FONDEE SUR LES PRINCIPES DE LA GRAMMAIRE JAVANAISE SUIVIE D'EXERCICES ET D'UN RECUEIL DE CENT ET UN PROVERBES
- VOCABULAIRE DES PRINCIPALES RACINES MALAISES ET JAVANAISES DE LA LANGUE MALGACHE

Marre-de Marin *see* GRAMMAIRE MALGACHE FONDEE SUR LES PRINCIPES DE LA GRAMMAIRE JAVANAISE

A MARRETA – Manaos, Amazonas. 22 Set 1912-Fev 1913; Fev-Set 1915; Jul-Dez 1918 – 1,5,6 – bl Biblioteca [072]
A MARRETA : SEMANARIO CRITICO E NOTICIOSO – Manaos, Amazonas. 1 Abr-Maio 1917; Mar-Jul 1918; Jan 1919 – 1,5,6 – bl Biblioteca [072]
MARRIAGE – (See now: Marriage and Family Living) – 1919-73 1; 1971-73 5,6 – us UMI [306]
THE MARRIAGE AID – Hamilton, Ont: Mutual Marriage Aid Association of Canada, [1882?-18– or 19–] – 9 – cn C.I.H.M. [360]
MARRIAGE AND DIVORCE TODAY – (v5-1979- 5,6,9) – v3- 1977- – 1 – us UMI [306]
MARRIAGE AND FAMILY LIVING – (See also: Marriage) – v56- 1974- 1,5,6; 1975- 9 – us UMI [306]
MARRIAGE AND FAMILY REVIEW / ed by Sussman, Marvin B – v1- 1978- – 1,9 ($250.00 in US $350.00 outside hardcopy subsc) – us Haworth [306]
MARRIAGE AND MORALS / Russell, Bertrand – (This work ranges broadly over the subjects of ethics and the right of the state to mandate individual conduct) – NY: Horace Liveright, 1929 – 4mf – 9 – $6.00 – LLMC 96-051 – us L.L.M.C. [170]
MARRIAGE BONDS / South Carolina. Probate Court – 1743-44. 3 fiches – 9 – us South Carolina Historical [340]
MARRIAGE CONSIDERED FROM LEGAL AND ECCLESIASTICAL VIEWPOINTS, IN CONNECTION WITH THE RECENT NE TEMERE DECREE OF THE ROMAN CATHOLIC CHURCH / Stockton, Lewis – Buffalo: Huebner-Bleistein Patents Co., 1912. 113p – 1 – us U.W. Library [306]
MARRIAGE, DIVORCE AND THE FAMILY NEWSLETTER – (1985- 5,6,9) – 1978- – 1 – us UMI [306]
MARRIAGE, DIVORCE, AND THE FAMILY NEWSLETTER – v1-3 1974-77 Continued by: Marriage and Divorce Today – 1 – us UMI [306]
MARRIAGE FEES / Defiance County, Ohio. Probate Court – 1852-1856 – 1r – 1 – $32.50r – us Archival [324]
THE MARRIAGE IN CANA OF GALILEE / Macmillan, Hugh – London:Macmillan, 1882 – 1mf – 9 – 0-8370-4246-1 – 1985-2246 – us A.T.L.A. [220]
MARRIAGE IN CHURCH AND STATE / Lacey, T A – London: R. Scott, 1912. (Library of historic theology) – 1mf – us A.T.L.A. [306]
MARRIAGE IN EARLY ISLAM / Stern, G H – 1939 – 1 – uk Microform Academic [260]
THE MARRIAGE LAWS / Goudy, H – London, 1901 – 1mf – 1 – ILM-3882/1 – ne IDC [327]
THE MARRIAGE LAWS OF NEW YORK STATE / Johnston, Graydon – New York? 1884. 13 p. LL-980 – 1 – us L of C Photodup [340]
A MARRIAGE OF SHADOWS AND OTHER POEMS. WITH BIOGRAPHICAL PREFACE BY LESLIE STEPHEN / Veley, Margaret – London: Smith, Elder, 1888 – 1 roll – 1 – 1-55879-486-7 – uk Libr Preservation [810]
THE MARRIAGE OF WILLIAM ASHE / Ward, Mary Augusta – British Fiction Archive: Unit 2 – 9 – uk Bell [830]
MARRIAGE PARTNERSHIP *see* PARTNERSHIP
MARRIAGE RECORDS / Crawford County. Ohio. Probate Court – 1879-1885 – 1r – 1 – $32.50r – us Archival [324]
MARRIAGE RECORDS / Cuyahoga County. Ohio. Probate Court – 1810-1949; Indexes 1810-1973 – 137r – 1 – us Western Res [920]
MARRIAGE RECORDS / Defiance County, Ohio. Probate Court – 1885-1892 – 14r – 1 – $32.50r – us Archival [324]
MARRIAGE RECORDS / Ottawa County. Ohio. Probate Court – 1840-1952 – 5r – 1 – $32.50r – us Archival [920]
MARRIAGE RECORDS / Putnam County. Ohio. Common Pleas. Probate Division – 1837-1850 – 1r – 1 – $32.50r – us Archival [324]
MARRIAGE RECORDS / Putnam County. Ohio. Common Pleas. Probate Division – 1837-1850 – 1r – 1 – $32.50r – us Archival [324]
MARRIAGE RECORDS / Van Wert County. Ohio. Probate Court – 1840-1951 – 10r – 1 – $32.50r – us Archival [324]
MARRIAGE RECORDS / Wyandot County. Ohio. Probate Court – 1904-1919 – 2r – 1 – $32.50r – us Archival [324]
MARRIAGE REGISTER AND ACCOUNT BOOK / Clelland, Thomas – 1813-1857 – 1 – $50.00 – us Presbyterian [920]
MARRICKVILLE EXPRESS – Jan 7 1899-Mar 21 1903 – 9 – at Pascoe [072]
Marrier, D Martin *see* BIBLIOTHECA CLUNIACENSIS
Marriott, Wharton B *see*
- THE TESTIMONY OF THE CATACOMBS AND OF OTHER MONUMENTS OF CHRISTIAN ART
- VESTIARIUM CHRISTIANUM

Marrodan, Mario Angel *see* LA RAZON CONTEMPLATIVA
Marrou, H -I *see* SAINT AUGUSTIN ET LA FIN DE LA CULTURE ANTIQUE
THE MARROW OF MODERN DIVINITY : IN TWO PARTS 1645, 1649 / Fisher, Edward; ed by M'Crie, C G – Glasgow: D. Bryce, 1902 – 1mf – us A.T.L.A. [240]
Marryat, Frederick *see* THE NAVAL OFFICER
LE MARS FRANCAIS OU LA GUERRE DE FRANCE / Jansenius, Corneil Jansen dit – s.l., s.n. 1637. Parts lacking. 453p. (Strategy of War Series) – 9 – fr Hachette [355]
MARS HILL BAPTIST CHURCH. SUMMIT, MISSISSIPPI : CHURCH RECORDS – 1855-1949 – 1 – 42.39 – us Baptist [240]
Mars, Zoe *see* COMMUNITY DEVELOPMENT
Marsack, C C *see* SAMOAN LAND TITLES
Marsaudon, Yves *see* SOUVENIRS ET REFLEXIONS: UN HAUT DIGNITAIRE DE LA FRANCMACONNERIE DE TRADITION REVELE DES SECRETS
Marschan, Joachim Hans *see* DAS MITLEID BEI GERHART HAUPTMANN
MARSCHENBUCH : LAND- UND VOLKSBILDER AUS DEN MARSCHEN DER WESER UND ELBE / Allmers, Hermann – Oldenburg, Leipzig: Schulz, 1891 – 1r – 1 – us U.W. Library [910]
Marschner, H *see* BILDER DES ORIENTS VON H. STEIGLITZ FUR EIN SINGSTIMME MIT BEGLEITUNG DES PIANOFORTE. OP. 140 HEFT 3
Marsden, G *see* ACCOUNT, 1801-1838, V3-6, 8
Marsden, J B *see* THE HISTORY OF THE EARLY PURITANS
Marsden, John Buxton *see* THE HISTORY OF THE EARLY PURITANS: FROM THE REFORMATION TO THE OPENING OF THE CIVIL WAR IN 1642
Marsden, K *see* REPORT TO THE GOVERNMENT OF LIBYA ON THE ROLE OF HANDICRAFTS IN A RAPIDLY DEVELOPING ECONOMY
Marsden, R G *see* SELECT PLEAS IN THE COURT OF ADMIRALITY
Marsden, W *see* THE HISTORY OF SUMATRA
LA MARSEILLAISE – Dir. Valentin Simond. Paris. 11 juil-dec 1880 – 1 – fr A.C.R.P.P. [073]
LA MARSEILLAISE – Red. en chef Henri Rochefort. Paris. 19 dec 1869-5 juil 1870 – 1 – fr A.C.R.P.P. [073]
MARSEILLAISE – London, UK. L'Hebdomadaire de la France au combat. 14 Jun 1942-3 Jul 1943 – 1 – uk British Libr Newspaper [072]
Marseille *see* BULLETIN MUNICIPAL OFFICIEL
Marseul, S A de *see* ABEILLE
Marsh, Gideon William Barker *see* THE RESURRECTION OF CHRIST, IS IT A FACT?
Marsh, Gregory D *see* 31-PHOSPHOROUS, NUCLEAR MAGNETIC RESONANCE SPECTROSCOPY STUDIES OF EXERCISING HUMAN MUSCLE
Marsh, Herbert *see* LETTERS TO THE ANONYMOUS AUTHOR OF REMARKS ON MICHAELIS
Marsh, Howard Franklin *see* THE CONSTABLE'S GUIDE AND FORM BOOK
Marsh, John W *see* THE STORY OF COMMANDER ALLEN GARDINER, R.N.,WITH SKETCHES OF MISSIONARY WORK IN SOUTH AMERICA
Marsh, John William *see* NARRATIVE OF THE ORIGIN AND PROGRESS OF THE SOUTH AMERICAN MISSION
Marsh, M C *see* THE FISHES OF PORTO RICO
Marsh, Richard *see* JUSTICE SUSPENDED
Marsh, W H H *see* THE NEW TESTAMENT CHURCH
Marshall, A P *see* A GUIDE TO NEGRO PERIODICAL LITERATURE
Marshall, C H T *see*
- THE GAME BIRDS OF INDIA, BURMA AND CEYLON
- THE GAME BIRDS OF INDIA, BURMAH AND CEYLON

MARSHALL COUNTY NEWS – Marysville. Kansas. 1872-1930 – 1 – us UMI [071]
MARSHALL COUNTY REPUBLICAN – Holly Springs. Miss. and Trade Advocate. 1838-39 – 1 – us UMI [071]
Marshall, Edward P *see* A TREATISE UPON BAPTIST CHURCH JURISPRUDENCE
Marshall, G FL *see* THE BUTTERFLIES OF INDIA, BURMAH AND CEYLON
Marshall, G W *see* THE GENEALOGIST'S GUIDE
Marshall, Gabez P *see* MEMOIRS OF THE LATE REV. ABRAHAM MARSHALL
Marshall, George C *see* COMPLETE RECORDS OF THE MISSION OF GENERAL GEORGE C. MARSHALL TO CHINA, DEC 1945-JAN 1947
Marshall Islands *see*
- CONSTITUTION OF THE MARSHALL ISLANDS, 1979
- DRAFT ANALYSIS OF THE U.S. JOINT RESOLUTION FOR APPROVAL OF THE COMPACT OF FREE ASSOCIATION
- MARSHALL ISLANDS REVISED CODE, 1988

Marshall Islands High Court *see* RULES OF APPELLATE PROCEDURE, 1983
MARSHALL ISLANDS REVISED CODE, 1988 / Marshall Islands – Majuro: the Nitejela. 2v. 1988 – 15mf – 9 – $22.50 – LLMC 82-1001 Title 2 – us L.L.M.C. [324]
Marshall, J *see*
- MOHENJO-DARO AND THE INDUS CIVILISATION
- THE MONUMENTS OF SANCHI

Marshall, John *see*
- THE CENTENNIAL ANNIVERSARY OF THE ELEVATION OF JOHN MARSHALL TO THE OFFICE OF CHIEF JUSTICE OF THE SUPREME COURT OF THE UNITED STATES OF AMERICA.
- KANSAS TRIAL BRIEF.
- ROYAL NAVAL BIOGRAPHY

Marshall, John Albert *see* DISEASES OF THE TEETH: THEIR DIAGNOSES AND TREATMENT
Marshall, Katharine R *see* THE EFFECTS OF PARTICIPATION IN A LEISURE EDUCATION PROGRAM UPON THE LESIURE BEHAVIOR OF MENTALLY RETARDED ADULTS
Marshall, Kristin R *see* EXCESS POSTEXERCISE OXYGEN CONSUMPTION AND ENERGY EXPENDITURE OF ENDURANCE TRAINED AND UNTRAINED WOMEN
Marshall, Newton Herbert *see* THEOLOGY AND TRUTH
Marshall, Prentice H *see* PATTERN CRIMINAL JURY INSTRUCTIONS
Marshall, Samuel *see* TREATISE ON THE LAW OF INSURANCE
Marshall, Samuel Lyman Atwood *see* MEN AGAINST FIRE
Marshall, T W *see* MY CLERICAL FRIENDS AND THEIR RELATIONS TO MODERN THOUGHT
Marshall, T W M *see* CHRISTIAN MISSIONS
Marshall, Thomas Alexander *see* AN INTRODUCTORY ADDRESS, DELIVERED BEFORE THE LAW CLASS OF TRANSYLVANIA UNIVERSITY, ON THE 9TH OF NOV. 1839
Marshall, Thomas William *see* CHURCH DEFENSE
MARSHALL/LOVETT MEMORANDUMS TO PRESIDENT TRUMAN, 1947-1948 / U.S. Department of State – RG 59. M1135. 3 rolls – 1 – us Nat'l Archives [977]
MARSHALL'S CHRISTMAS BOX – 1831-32 – 6mf – 9 – £50.00 – uk Chadwyck [800]
MARSHALL'S GENEALOGISTS' GUIDE : 1903 – 10mf – 9 – A$60.00 – at State Libr Vic [920]
Marshalovas, N V *see* SOVETSKOE UGOLOVNOE PRAVO: BIBLIOGRAFIIA (1917-60)
MARSHFIELD 1631-1890 – 67mf – 9 – us Holbrook [920]
MARSHLANDS – Amherst, NS: [s.n., 1895-189- or 19–] – 9 – cn C.I.H.M. [971]
Marshman, J R *see* CARRINGTON AND MARSHMAN'S REPORTS
Marshman, John Clark *see* THE LIFE AND TIMES OF CAREY, MARSHMAN, AND WARD
Marsigny, Jean Charle de *see* TRAITTE DES ELEMENS CHYMIQUES, OV EST DONNE AVX CVRIEVX DE L'ART, LA CONNAISANCE DES SELS, DISSOLUANS, MENSTRUES, FONDANS ET PRECIPITANS
Marsil, Tancrede *see* LE REVEIL
Marsili, S *see* GIOVANNI CASSIANO ED EVAGRIO PONTICO
MARSILIUS VON PADUA (MGH LEGES 4: 7.BD) : DEFENSOR PACIS – 1932 – Dfl46.00 – ne Slangenburg [240]
Marsollier et Dalayrac *see* CAMILLE OU LE SOUTERRAIN
Marston, Bruce Steven *see* A PROCEDURE FOR DETERMINING AND MEETING THE FACILITY NEEDS OF BROOKS BAPTIST CHURCH
Marston-on-Dove.Staffordshire *see* PARISH REGISTERS
MARSTRANDS ANNONSBLAD – Goeteborg, 1879-84 – 9 – sw Kungliga [072]
MARSTRANDS TIDNING – Goeteborg, 1877 – 9 – sw Kungliga [072]
MARSTRANDS TIDNING – Marstrand, 1867-68 – 9 – sw Kungliga [072]
MARSTRANDSPOSTEN – Marstrand, 1868 – 9 – sw Kungliga [072]
Marsudi, Djojodipuro *see* HIMPUNAN KULIAH-KULIAH PENGANTAR ILMU EKONOMI; JANG DIKULIAHKAN PADA FAKULTAS HUKUM DAN PENGETAHUAN MASJARAKAT UNIVERSITAS INDONESIA DI DJAKARTA
Martainville *see*
- LES ASSEMBLEES PRIMAIRES OU LES ELECTIONS
- LE PIED DE MOUTON
- RODERIC ET CUNEGONDE OU L'HERMITE DE MONTMARTRE OU LA FORTERESSE DE MOULINOS OU LE REVENANT DE LA GALERIE DE L'OUEST

Marteau, Eugen Henrik *see* BEWAEHRUNG
Martel, C *see* CURSO DE MATEMATICAS
Martel, Louise *see* JOSEPH COSTISELLA
O MARTELLO : CRITICO E RECREATIVO – Manaos, Amazonas. 5 Jul-13 Ago 1911 – 1,5,6 – bl Biblioteca [072]
MARTELL-SPRAGUE LEADER – Martell, NE. -w. May 1914-Apr 1934 – 1 – us NE Hist [071]
Martene, Dom E *see*
- HISTOIRE DE LA CONGREGATION DE SAINT-MAUR
- LA VIE DES JUSTES

Martene, E *see* HISTOIRE DE LA CONGREGATION DE SAINT-MAUR
Martene, Edmond *see*
- DE ANTIQUIS ECCLESIAE RITIBUS
- DE ANTIQUIS MONACHORUM RITIBUS
- THESAURUS NOVUS ANECDOTORUM
- VETERUM SCRIPTORUM ET MONUMENTORUM HISTORICORUM, DOGMATICORUM, MORALIUM AMPLISSIMA COLLECTIO
- LA VIE DU VENERABLE PERE DOM CLAUDE MARTIN, RELIGIEUX BENEDICTIN DE LA CONGREGATION DE S. MAUR...

Martens, Alfred *see* UNTERSUCHUNGEN UEBER WIELAND'S DON SYLVIO
Martens, F F *see* RECUEIL DES TRAITES ET CONVENTIONS CONCLUS PAR LA RUSSIE AVEC LES PUISSANCES ETRANGERES
Martens, George F *see* COLLECTION OF UPPER VOLTA POLITICAL AND OTHER EPHEMERA
Martens, M *see* MEMOIRES SUR LES FOUGERES DE MEXIQUE
Martens, Wilhelm *see* DIE BESETZUNG DES PAEPSTLICHEN STUHLS UNTER DEN KAISERN HEINRICH 3. UND HEINRICH 4.
Martensen, Hans Lassen *see* BRIEFWECHSEL ZWISCHEN H. L. MARTENSEN UND J. A. DORNER, 1839-1881..
THE MARTHAS; OR, THE VARIETIES OF FEMALE PIETY / Philip, Robert – In The Christian Library: a reprint of popular religious works. 1836 – 9 – us A.T.L.A. [240]
Marti, Jose Julian *see* OBRAS COMPLETAS, ORDENADAS Y PROLOGADAS POR ALBERTO GHIRALDO
Marti, Karl *see*
- DAS DODEKAPROPHETON
- GESCHICHTE DER ISRAELITISCHEN RELIGION
- KURZGEFASSTE GRAMMATIK DER BIBLISCHARAMAEISCHE SPRACHE
- RELIGION OF THE OLD TESTAMENT

Marti Mayor, Jose *see* EL CONVENTO DE SANTA MARIA DE JESUS...
MARTIAL LAW / Nicholas, Samuel Smith – Philadelphia: Campbell, 1862. 31p. LL-1213 – 1 – us L of C Photodup [340]
Martigny *see* VOYAGE D'ALCIMEDON, OU NAUFRAGE QUI CONDUIT AU PORT. HISTOIRE PLUS VRAIE QUE VRAISEMBLABLE MAIS QUI PEUT ENCOURAGER A LA RECHERCHE DE TERRES INCONNUES
Marti-Ibanez, Felix *see* GRANDEZAS Y MISERIAS DE LA REVOLUCION SOCIAL ESPANOLA

THE MARTILOGE IN ENGLYSSHE AFTER THE USE OF THE CHURCH OF SALISBURY AND AS IT REDDE IN SYON. WITH ADDICYONS / Procter, F & Dewick, E S – (Printed by Wynkyn De Worde in 1526) – 1893 – 6mf – 8 – Dfl25.00 – ne Slangenburg [240]
Martin, Alfred Wilhelm von *see*
– THE REAL JESUS: A SERIES OF CONSTRUCTIVE DISCOURSES
– ROMANTISCHER "KATHOLIZISMUS" UND KATHOLISCHE "ROMANTIK"
Martin, Arthur Patchett *see* LIFE AND LETTERS OF THE RIGHT HONOURABLE ROBERT LOWE, VISCOUNT SHERBROOKE...WITH A MEMOIR OF SIR JOHN COAPE SHERBROOKE, G.C.B., BY A. PATCHETT MARTIN
Martin, Benjamin *see* INSTITUTIONS OF LANGUAGE
Martin, Benjamin Ellis *see* IN THE FOOTPRINTS OF CHARLES LAMB
MARTIN BUBER ARCHIVE / Jewish National and University Library. Jerusalem – (Card catalogue also available separately 22mf Dfl176.00) – 797mf – 9 – ne IDC [270]
MARTIN BUCER / Anrich, Gustav – Strassburg: Karl J. Truebner, 1914 – 1mf – us A.T.L.A. [240]
MARTIN BUCER'S LITURGICAL IDEAS / Poll, G Jv.d. – Assen, 1954 – 4mf – 8 – Dfl19.00 – ne Slangenburg [240]
MARTIN BUCKER IN ENGLAND / Harvey, A Edward – Marburg a.L.: Heinrich Bauer, 1906 – 1mf – us A.T.L.A. [240]
Martin, C T *see*
– LESTORIE DES ENGLES SOLUM LA TRANSLACION MAISTRE GEFFREI GAIMAR (RS91)
– REGISTRUM EPISTOLARUM FRATRIS JOHANNIS PECKHAM (RS77)
– REGISTRUM MALMESBURIENSE (RS72)
Martin Carnes Moreno, Rafael *see* PLAN... FUNCIONES A LA...FREGENAL...REMEDIOS
Martin, Chalmers *see* APOSTOLIC AND MODERN MISSIONS
Martin, Charles *see*
– LES PROTESTANTS ANGLAIS REFUGIES A GENEVE AU TEMPS DE CALVIN 1555-1560
– LA VIE DE LA VENERABLE MERE MARIE DE L'INCARNATION
Martin, Charles Hynes *see* A DIRECTORY TREATISE
Martin, Charles I *see* HISTORY OF DOOR COUNTY
Martin, Daniel Strobel *see* CHRISTIAN EVOLUTIONISM AND ITS INFLUENCE ON RELIGIOUS THOUGHT
Martin, David A *see* MAJOR ISSUES IN IMMIGRATION LAW
Martin de Caceres y Cruz, Emilio *see* POEMAS DE JUVENTUD (ANTOLOGIA 1913-1922)
MARTIN DE SESSE Y LACASTA, 1751-1808 AND JOSE MARIANO MOCINO, 1757-1820 / Royal Botanical Garden, Madrid – 275mf – 9 – ne IDC [580]
Martin Echevarria, L *see* GEOGRAFIA DE ESPANA...
Martin, Edward James *see* A HISTORY OF THE ICONOCLASTIC CONTROVERSY
Martin, Edward Osborn *see* THE GODS OF INDIA; A BRIEF DESCRIPTION OF THEIR HISTORY, CHARACTER & WORSHIP
MARTIN EL HUMANO (ANNO 1396-1410) – Barcelona – 1r – 5,6 – sp Cultura [946]
Martin, Elizabeth (Hosack) Ayres *see* PERPETUAL DIARY
Martin, Ernest *see* HISTOIRE DES MONSTRES DEPUIS L'ANTIQUITE JUSQU'A NOS JOURS
Martin, Felix *see* LE JAPON VRAI
Martin, Frances *see* ANGELIQUE ARNAULD
Martin, Francisco et al *see* EL PLEITO DE "LA ESPERANZA DE LAS HURDES" FOLLETO HISTORICO-DOCUMENTADO QUE DEDICAN A LOS SOCIOS PROTECTORES DE LA MISMA, LOS INDIVIDUOS DE LA JUNTA DIRECTIVA...
Martin, Francois *see* TEXTES RELIGIEUX ASSYRIENS ET BABYLONIENS
Martin, Frank M *see* THE COUNTY OF NOBLE
Martin, G *see* LA FACE DE L'EGLISE PRIMITIVE
Martin, G H *see* HUSTING ROLLS OF DEEDS AND WILLS 1252-1485
Martin Galindo, Jose Luis *see* ARCAISMO Y MODERNIDAD EN LA EXPLOTACION AGRARIA DE VALDEBURON (LEON)
Martin, Gaston *see* L'ABOLITION DE L'ESCLAVAGE (27 AVRIL 1848)
Martin, George *see* DIARY
Martin, George Currie *see*
– EPHESIANS, COLOSSIANS, PHILEMON, AND PHILIPPIANS
– FOREIGN MISSIONS
Martin, George J *see* MARTIN'S NUMERICAL TABLE OF CASES IN THE TRINITY SERIES
Martin, Germain *see* CONTRIBUTION A L'HISTOIRE DES CLASSES RURALES EN FRANCE AU 19E SIECLE: LA COTE D'OR
Martin Gil, Thomas *see*
– EL ARTE EXTREMENO ACTUAL
– MOTIVOS EXTREMENO
Martin Gil, Tomas *see*
– UNA PINTURA DE VELAZQUEZ (EL LOBO DE CORIA)
– TESTAMENTO DE D. RODRIGO PEREZ, ARCEDIANO EN 1550 DE LA ARCHIDIOCESIS DE LIMA
Martin Gonzalez, Angel *see* MELENAS Y FALDAS CORTAS
Martin, Gregoire *see* LETTRES INSTRUCTIVES ET CURIEUSES SUR L'EDUCATION DE LA JEUNESSE
Martin, Guillaume *see* VOYAGE A CONSTANTINOPLE FAIT A L'OCCASION DE L'AMBASSADE DE M. LE COMTE DE CHOISEUL-GOUFFIER A LA PORTE OTTOMANE
Martin, H S *see* THE NEW YORK STOCK EXCHANGE
Martin, Henri *see* LA RUSSIE ET L'EUROPE
Martin, Hugh *see* THE PROPHET JONAH: HIS CHARACTER AND MISSION TO NINEVEH
Martin, J *see* STUDIEN UND BEITRAEGE ZUR ERKLAERUNG UND ZEITBESTIMMUNG COMMODIANS (T.U.U. 3-39/4A)
Martin, J G *see* POLITICAL AND SOCIAL CHANGES IN CATALONIA DURING THE REVOLUTION, JULY 19-DECEMBER 31, 1936
Martin, J Lemuel *see* THE VOICE OF THE SEVEN THUNDERS, OR, LECTURES ON THE APOCALYPSE
Martin, James *see* ORIGIN AND HISTORY OF THE NEW TESTAMENT
Martin, James L *see*
– ANTI-EVOLUTION: GIRARDEAU VS WOODROW
– DR. GIRARDEAU'S ANTI-EVOLUTION: THE LOGIC OF HIS REPLY
Martin, Jeffrey J *see* AN INVESTIGATION OF SELF-EFFICACY AND CONTROL THEORY WITH ELITE DISTANCE RUNNERS
Martin, John Alexander *see* LETTERS
Martin, John H *see*
– THE CORNING FLOOD: MUSEUM UNDER WATER
– SCIENTIFIC RESEARCH IN EARLY CHINESE GLASS
THE MARTIN KLING TARGETED READING COLLECTION / ed by Svobodny, Dolly – 8500 titles. 900mf – 9 – us A.T.B.I. [370]
Martin, Konrad *see*
– DIE ARBEITEN DES VATIKANISCHEN CONCILS
– LEHRBUCH DER KATHOLISCHEN GLAUBENS- UND SITTENLEHRE FUER DIE OBEREN KLASSEN DER HOEHEREN LEHRANSTALTEN OESTERREICHS
Martin Lobo, Manuel *see*
– REALIDAD Y PERSPECTIVA DE LA PLANIFICACION REGIONAL EN ESPANA
– LA REPOBLACION FORESTAL Y LOS GRUPOS SINDICALES DE COLONIZACION
MARTIN LUTHER : AND OTHER ESSAYS / Hedge, Frederic Henry – Boston: Roberts, 1888 – 1mf – 9 – 0-8370-4903-2 – 1985-2903 – us A.T.L.A. [240]
MARTIN LUTHER / Freytag, Gustav – Chicago: Open Court, 1897, c1896 – 1mf – us A.T.L.A. [240]
MARTIN LUTHER : THE HERO OF THE REFORMATION, 1483-1546 / Jacobs, Henry Eyster – New York: Putnam, 1899, c1898 (Heroes of the Reformation; [v. 1]) – 2mf – us A.T.L.A. [240]
MARTIN LUTHER : HIS LIFE AND WORK / Bayne, Peter – London; New York: Cassell, 1887 – 3mf – us A.T.L.A. [240]
MARTIN LUTHER : KIRCHENGESCHICHTLICHES LEBENSBILD AUS DEM ERSTEN ZEHNTEL DER REFORMATION / Wildenhahn, August – 2. Aufl. Leipzig: Gebhardt & Reisland, 1853 – 1r – 1 – us U.W. Library [240]
MARTIN LUTHER : THE MAN AND HIS WORK / McGiffert, Arthur Cushman – New York: Century, 1911 – 2mf – us A.T.L.A. [240]
MARTIN LUTHER : REFORMATIONSDRAMA IN FUENF AKTEN UND EINEM VORSPIEL / Henzen, Wilhelm – Leipzig: C Reissner, 1883 – 1r – 1 – us U.W. Library [820]
MARTIN LUTHER : A STUDY OF REFORMATION / Mead, Edwin Doak – Boston: G.H. Ellis, 1884, c1883 – 1mf – us A.T.L.A. [240]
MARTIN LUTHER AND THE REFORMATION IN GERMANY : UNTIL THE CLOSE OF THE DIET OF WORMS / Beard, Charles; ed by Smith, J Frederick – London: K. Paul, Trench, 1889 – 2mf – us A.T.L.A. [240]
MARTIN LUTHER, HIS LIFE AND WORK / Bayne, Peter – London: Cassell, 1887. 2v – 1 – us U.W. Library [240]
MARTIN LUTHER KING, JR. : FBI ASSASSINATION FILE / U.S. Federal Bureau of Investigation – 1978 – 25r – 1 – $2,125.00 – S1757 – us Scholarly Res [320]
THE MARTIN LUTHER KING, JR. FBI FILE / U.S. Federal Bureau of Investigation – Part 1. 16 reels with printed guide – 1 – $1,760.00 – 0-89093-678-1 – us UPA [360]
THE MARTIN LUTHER KING, JR. FBI FILE / U.S. Federal Bureau of Investigation – Part 2: The King-Levison File. 9 reels with printed guide – 1 – $990.00 – 0-89093-937-3 – us UPA [360]
MARTIN LUTHER, THE PROPHET OF GERMANY / Banks, John Shaw – London: Wesleyan Conference Office, [1887?] – 1mf – us A.T.L.A. [240]
MARTIN LUTHERS ROMFAHRT : NACH EINEM GLEICHZEITIGEN PILGERBUCHE / Hausrath, Adolf – Berlin: G. Grote, 1894 – 1mf – us A.T.L.A. [240]
Martin, Lyn Elizabeth M *see* INTERNET REFERENCE SERVICES QUARTERLY
MARTIN, MARY B., SCRAPBOOK, MS 4047 – 1905-1962 – 1 reel – 1 – us Western Res [370]
Martin Mateos, N *see* VEINTE Y SEIS CARTAS AL...VALDEGAMAS...ENSAYO SOBRE EL LIBERALISMO
Martin, Melanie M *see* STRENGTH GAINS THROUGH AQUATIC EXERCISE
Martin Moreno, Rafael *see* HISTORIA DE LA ANTIQUISIMA E ILUSTRE VILLA DE FREGENAL
Martin Moreno, Saturnino *see* MEMORIA LEIDA POR SOBRE LA ACCION DEL PARA PRODUCIR ENERGIA MECANICA Y SOBRE SI POR LA LUZ...
MARTIN OPITZ / Gundolf, Friedrich – Muenchen: Duncker & Humbolt, 1923 – 1r – 1 – us U.W. Library [430]
MARTIN OPITZ : EINE MONOGRAPHIE / Strehlke, Friedrich – (Includes bibliographical references) – Leipzig: F A Brockhaus, 1856 – 1r – 1 – us U.W. Library [430]
MARTIN OPITZ VON BOBERFELD : EIN VORTRAG IN DER HARMONIE ZU KIEL AM 15. FEBRUAR 1862 GEHALTEN / Weinhold, Karl – (Includes bibliographical references) – Kiel: E Homann, 1862 – 1r – 1 – us U.W. Library [430]
MARTIN OPITZ VON BOBERFELD : ZWEI BEITRAEGE ZUR LEBENSGESCHICHTE DES DICHTERS: 1. MARTIN OPITZ ALS AGENT SCHLESISCHER HERZOGE BEI DEN SCHWEDEN. 2. MARTIN OPITZ UND JANUS GRUTER / Palm, Hermann – Breslau: E Morgenstern, 1862 – 1r – 1 – us U.W. Library [430]
MARTIN OPITZEN'S BUCH VON DER DEUTSCHEN POETEREI : EIN KRITISCHER VERSUCH / Fritsch, Otto – (Includes bibliographical references) – Halle: E Karras, 1884 – 1r – 1 – us U.W. Library [430]
Martin, Orem F *see* HISTORY OF PENDLETON COUNTY
Martin, Raymond A *see* THE EXEGETICAL METHOD OF THE AUTHOR OF HEBREWS
Martin Santivanez, Romualdo *see* HISTORIA... CRUZ DEL CASAR DE PALOMERO
Martin, Theodore *see* THE BOOK OF BALLADS
Martin, Thomas H *see* ATLANTA AND ITS BUILDERS, A COMPREHENSIVE HISTORY OF THE GATE CITY OF THE SOUTH
Martin, V *see*
– LA CHRETIENTE AFRICAINE DE DAKAR
– HISTOIRE DE L'EGLISE DEPUIS LES ORIGINES JUSQUA NOS JOURS
Martin, W *see* WOMEN'S STUDIES
Martin, W C *see* HISTORY OF WARREN COUNTY
Martin, W Donald *see* KEY TRENDS AND ISSUES IMPACTING LOCAL GOVERNMENT RECREATION AND PARK ADMINISTRATION IN THE 1990S
Martin, William A P *see* THE PEIHO AND PEKING
Martin, William Wallace *see*
– THE LAW AND COVENANT: BEING THE RESTORATION OF TWO OF THE BOOKS OF MOSES
– MANUAL OF ECCLESIASTICAL ARCHITECTURE
– THE TORA OF MOSES: BEING A CRITICAL STUDY OF DEUTERONOMY
Martin y Bueso, Tomas *see* LOS 14 EL AUXILIAR DEL QUINIELISTA POR CACERES
Martin y Castro, Florencio *see*
– NOCIONES ELEMENTALES...QUIMICA
– PINAUD, MR. PROGRAMA...FISICA
– PROGRAMA DE UN CURSO ELEMENTALDE FISICA. TRADUCIDO DE A MARTA EDICION FRANCESA POR DON FLORENCIO MARTIN Y CASTRO
Martin y Solar, V *see*
– L'ALBERO DI DIANA
– L'ARBORE DI DIANE. DER BAUM DER DIANA. EINE COMISCHE OPER IN 2 ACTEN...
– LA COSA RARA. OVERTURE, ARR. PIANO AND VIOLIN BY FERDINND STAES
Martin-Chauffier, Louis *see* CATHOLICISME ET REBELLION
Martindale *see* A HISTORY OF THE TOWNSHIPS OF BYBERRY AND MORELAND IN PHILADELPHIA
Martindale, Cyril Charlie *see* EL LIBRO DE BETTY: PARA LOS NINOS DE PRIMERA COMUNION
Martindale, Frederick C *see* MICHIGAN OFFICIAL DIRECTORY AND LEGISLATIVE MANUAL FOR YEARS 1913-14
Martindale, John *see* EVOLUTIONARY STUDIES ON SOME AUSTRALIAN HONEYEATERS
Martindell-Jensen, Jane *see* A COMPARISON OF THE POLITICAL ATTITUDES OF FEMALE AND MALE ATHLETES
Martine, George *see* ESSAYS MEDICAL AND PHILOSOPHICAL
Martineau, Harriet *see* BIOGRAPHICAL SKETCHES, 1852-1875
Martineau, Harriett *see* HISTORY OF ENGLAND, A.D. 1800-1815; BEING AN INTRODUCTION TO THE HISTORY OF THE PEACE
Martineau, James *see*
– A STUDY OF SPINOZA
– TYPES OF ETHICAL THEORY
MARTINEAU & SMITH'S MONTHLY CIRCULAR – Birmingham, England. Martineau & Smith's Hardware Trade Circular Martineau & Smith's Hardware Trade Journal. -m. Jan 1874-Dec 1882. Lacking Dec 1876-Dec 1877. 10 reels – 1 – uk British Libr Newspaper [072]
MARTINEAU: THE COLLECTED WRITINGS OF HARRIET MARTINEAU (1802-1876) – Marlborough: Adam Matthew Publications, 1996 – 20r – 1 – $2,400.00 – uk Matthew [300]
Martinelli, V *see* L'AMATEUR, OU NOUVELLE PIECES ET DISSERTATIONS FRANCOISES ET ETRANGERES
Martinengo, N *see* L'INTIERO RAGGVAGLIO DEL SVCCESSO DI FAMACOSTA
Martinengo-Cesaresco, Evelyn Lilian Hazeldine *see* ESSAYS IN THE STUDY OF FOLK-SONGS
Martinet *see* EMBLESMES ROYALES A LOUIS LE GRAND
Martinez Abeytia, Mateo *see*
– EL CERCO DE ZAMORA
– COMPOSICIONES...DONA ISABEL 2
– POESIAS
Martinez Barrio, Diego *see*
– UN INFORME, UNA OPINION Y UNA ORIENTACION
– PAGINAS PARA LA HISTORIA DEL FRENTE POPULAR
Martinez Cosio, Leopoldo *see* LOS CABALLEROS DE LAS ORDENES MILITARES EN MEXICO
MARTINEZ DAILY STANDARD – Martinez, CA. 1911-1930 – 38r – 1 – $1,900.00 – C03335 – us Library Micro [071]
Martinez de Carnero y Diaz, Rafael *see* LA CIMBARRA
Martinez de Castrillo, F *see* TRATADO BREVE Y COMPENDIOSO SOBRE LA MARAVILLOSA OBRA DE LA BOCA Y DENTADURA
Martinez de Escobar, T *see* CRONICA DE ISIDORO PACENSE
Martinez de Santa Maria, Juan *see* CONTESTACION...VECINO DE BURGUILLOS...VENTA DE ARBOLADA
Martinez de Zuniga, J *see* AN HISTORICAL VIEW OF THE PHILIPPINE ISLANDS

Martinez del Rio, Manual A *see* SERMON... ZAFRA...LIBERTAD DE...SENOR

Martinez del Rio, Pablo *see* POR LA VENTANA DE LA PREHISTORIA...

Martinez Diez, Gonzalo *see* LA COLECCION CANONICA HISPANA 1. ESTUDIO POR... MADRID, 1966

Martinez Escobar, Jose *see* NOCIONES DE INDUSTRIA Y COMERCIO

Martinez Fernando, J E *see* GUIA DEL ARCHIVO DE LA CORONA DE ARAGON

Martinez Garcia, Ramon *see* CURIOSIDADES GRAMATICALES, GRAMATICA AMPLIADA DEL IDIOMA ESPANOL Y SUS DIALECTOS

Martinez Gonzalez, Antonio *see* EL LEXICO DE LA HERRERIA EN BADAJOZ

Martinez Gracida, Manuel *see* COLECCION DE "CUADROS SINOPTICOS" DE LOS PUEBLOS, HACIENDAD Y RANCHOS DEL ESTADO LIBRE Y SOBERANO DE OAXACA: ANEXO NUMERO 50 A LA MEMORIA ADMINISTRATIVA PRESENTADA AL H. CONGRESO DEL MISMO EL 17 DE SETIEMBRE DE 1883

MARTINEZ HERALD – Martinez, CA. 1931-1934; 1935-1937; 1939 – 17r – 1 – $850.00 – B03614 – us Library Micro [071]

Martinez, Ildefonso *see* ASI MURIO EL INSIGNE BIBLIOGRAFO DON BARTOLOME J. GALLARDO

Martinez la Rios, Jose *see* SERMON DE DEDICACION DE UN RETABLO

Martinez, M *see* LAS PLANTAS MEDICINALES DE MEXICO

Martinez, Mariano *see* INDUSTRIAS SANTIAGUINAS

Martinez Martinez, Matias Ramon *see*
- APUNTES PARA...TOPOGRAFICO...BURGUILLOS
- BASILICA DEL SIGLO 7 EN BURGUILLOS
- BURGUILLOS, ALDEA Y BASILICA DEL SIGLO 17
- HISTORIA DEL REINO DE BADAJOZ DURANTE LA DOMINACION MUSULMANA
- HISTORIA DEL REINO DE BADAJOZ DURANTE LA DOMINACION MUSULMANA. NOTICIA
- INSCRIPCIONES ROMANAS DE BURGUILLOS
- EL LIBRO DE JEREZ DE LOS CABALLEROS

Martinez Mediero, Manuel *see* EL ULTIMO GALLINERO DE CON CANCIONES ESPIRITUALES DE JESUS DELGADO VALHOMDO, EN FESTIVAL DE TEATRO DE SITGES

Martinez Montero, Emilio *see* DIECISIETE MESES DE ALCALDIA

Martinez Morales, Maria *see* LEGISLACION LATINO-AMERICANA SOBRE PROPIEDAD INDUSTRIAL

MARTINEZ NEWS-GAZETTE – Martinez, CA. 1949- – 148+ r – 1 – $7,400.00 ($135.00y) – C02424 – us Library Micro [071]

Martinez Perez, Eloy *see* EL COMERCIO Y LA BANCA

Martinez Quesada, Juan *see*
- DOCUMENTACION DE LA CAPELLANIA Y ENTERRAMIENTO DEL PRESIDENTE DON JUAN DE OVANDO
- NOTAS DOCUMENTALES SOBRE ARTISTAS Y ARTESANOS DE EXTREMADURA
- PLASENCIA DURANTE LA INVASION NAPOLEONICA. CATALOGO DE DOCUMENTOS QUE SE CONSERVAN EN EL ARCHIVO HISTORICO DE CACERES

Martinez Sanchez-Arjona, Jose Maria *see* INFORME POLITICO DEL GOBIERNO AL CONSEJO NACIONAL DEL MOVIMIENTO SOBRE POLITICA DE VIVIENDA, URBANISMO Y ARQUITECTURA

Martinez Serrano, Francisco *see* INVESTIGACIONES...BANOS DE MONTEMAYOR Y BEJAR

Martinez Sierra, Gregorio *see*
- MADRIGAL
- EL PALACIO TRISTE

Martinez Siliceo, Juan *see*
- DE DIVINO...JESUS...ORATIONEM
- DECLARACIONES DEL PATER NOSTER Y AVE MARIA
- DECLARACIONES...NOSTER

Martinez Zarate, Jose de Jesus *see* JESUCRISTO A TRAVES DE LAS EDADES. INSTRUCCION PASTORAL DIRIGIDA A SUS DIOCESANOS CON MOTIVO DEL 19TH CENTENARIO DE LA REDENCION DEL GENERO HUMANO...

Martini, F H W *see* SYSTEMATISCHES CONCHYLIEN-CABINET

Martini, G *see*
- ESEMPLARE O SIA SAGGIO FONDAMENTALE PRATICO DI CONTRAPPUNTO SOPRA IL CANTO FERMO
- STORIA DELLA MUSICA

Martini, J -P *see* [HENRY IV] OUVERTURE ET ENTR'ACTE D'. ARR. CLAVECIN OU LE PIANO-FORTE AVEC ACCOMPAGNEMANET DE VIOLON PAR M. CESAR

Martini, M *see* LEXICON PHILOLOGICUM...

Martiniere, G *see* LE BRESIL ET L'AFRIQUE

MARTINIQUE : ANNUAIRE STATISTIQUE DE LA MARTINIQUE 1952-1969/72 / France. Institut National de la Statistique et des Etudes Economiques – (Coll title: Latin American and Caribbean Official Statistical Serials, 1821-1982) – 13mf – 9 – £110.00 – uk Chadwyck [972]

Martinique. French West Indies *see*
- JOURNAL OFFICIEL
- JOURNAL OFFICIEL DE LA MARTINIQUE
- RECUEIL DES ACTS ET ADMINISTRATIFS

Martinique. French West Indies. Archives Departementales *see* CARD CATALOG

Martinique. French West Indies. Commission locale du plan *see* CINQUIEME PLAN

Martinius *see* CAPELLA LIPSIAE

Martinius, Petrus *see* THE KEY OF THE HOLY TONGUE

Martino, Giacomo de *see* LA SOMALIA ITALIANA NEI TRE ANNI DEL MIO GOVERNO.

Martinow, J *see* ANNUS ECCLESIASTICUS GRAECORUM-SLAVICUS 1863

MARTIN'S HOME AND FARM – Sydney, Australia. Home & Farm. -m. Dec 1893-May 1908 – 4r – 1 – uk British Libr Newspaper [640]

MARTIN'S MINING CASES / British Columbia. Canada – v1-2. 1867-1907 (all publ) – 17mf – 9 – $25.50 – LLMC 81-020 – us L.L.M.C. [340]

MARTIN'S NUMERICAL TABLE OF CASES IN THE TRINITY SERIES / Martin, George J – 4th ed. San Francisco: Bancroft-Whitney. 1v. 1905 (all publ) – 5mf – 9 – $7.50 – LLMC 78-038E – us L.L.M.C. [340]

MARTIN'S OIL AND GAS LEGAL SERVICE – Dallas. v1-2. 1919-21 (all publ) – 15mf – 9 – $22.50 – LLMC 84-598 – us L.L.M.C. [073]

Martinson, F A *see* UKAZATEL' K KATALOGU KHRANIASHCHAGOSIA V IMP. PUBLICHNOI BIBLIOTEKE SOBRANIIA SLAVIANO-RUSSKIKH RUKOPISEI P. D. BOGDANOVA

MARTINSVILLE FIRST BAPTIST CHURCH. MARTINSVILLE, ILLINOIS : CHURCH RECORDS – 1879-1909, 1970-1989. 2339p – 1 – 105.26 – us Baptist [240]

Martinus ab azpilcueta Navarrus *see* ENCHIRIDION SIVE MANUALE CONFESSARIORUM ET POENITENTIUM

UNA MARTIR DEL SIGLO 19TH. HELENA PETROUNA BLAVATSKY / Roso de Luna, Mario – Madrid: Editorial Pueyo, 1924 – 1 – sp Bibl Santa Ana [946]

MARTIRES AGUSTINOS DE EL ESCORIAL / Llamas, Jose – El Escorial, 1940. Fiche W1001. (Blodgett Collection of Spanish Civil War Pamphlets) – 9 – us H.U. College Libr [946]

LOS MARTIRES DE LAS MISIONES DEL PARAGUAY. BILBAO, 1934. MADRID, 1934 / Gonzales Pintado, Gaspar – Madrid: Razon y Fe, 1936 – 1 – sp Bibl Santa Ana [972]

MARTIRES Y VERDUGOS / Ferla, Salvador – Buenos Aires: Ediciones Revelacion, 3rd ed 1972 – 1 – CSUXADJ3731-B – us Hoover Inst Photo [972]

MARTIROLOGIO DE LA COMPANIA DE JESUS / Sanchez Ruiz, Valentin M – Madrid: Apostolado de la Prensa, S.A. 1949 – 1 – sp Bibl Santa Ana [240]

MARTIROLOGIO ROMANO / Sanchez Ruiz, Valentin M – Madrid: Apostolado de la Prensa, S.A. 1949 – 1 – sp Bibl Santa Ana [240]

Martius, CF P von *see* BEITRAG ZUR FLORA BRASILIENS

Martius, Friedrich Philipp von *see* HISTORIA NATURALIS PALMARUM

Martius, J G *see* HISTORIA DAVIDIS GEORGI EJUSQUE ASSECLARUM

Martius, Karl Friedrich Philipp von *see*
- BEITRAEGE ZUR KENNTNIS DER GATTUNG ERYTHROXYLON
- FLORA BRASILIENSIS
- FLORA BRASILIENSIS, SEU ENUMERATIO PLANTARUM IN BRASILIA
- FLORA CRYPTOGAMICA ERLANGENSIS
- HISTORIA NATURALIS PALMARUM
- HORTUS BOTANICUS R. ACADEMIAE MONACENSIS, SEU HORTI BOTANICI, QUI MONACHII FLORET, HISTORIA BREVITER ENARRATA, ET PRAESENS CONDITIO DESCRIPTA
- ICONES SELECTAE PLANTARUM CRYPTOGAMICARUM QUAS IN ITINERE PER BRASILIAM ANNIS 1817-1820 INSTITUTO COLLEGIT ET DESCRIPSIT
- NOVA GENERA ET SPECIES PLANTARUM
- PALMARUM FAMILIA EJUSQUE GENERA DENUO ILLUSTRATA
- PALMETUM ORBIGNIANUM
- PLANTARUM HORTI ACADEMICI ERLANGENSIS
- PRODROMUS FLORAE MOSQUENSIS
- SYSTEMA MATERIAE MEDICAE VEGETABILIS BRASILIENSIS

THE MARTLET – (Cont by: The McGill Martlet) – Montreal: Students of McGill University, [1908-1909 or 1910] – 9 – cn C.I.H.M. [370]

THE MARTLET *see* THE MCGILL MARTLET

Martorell y Pena, M *see* CATALOGOMETODICO Y RAZONADO DE LOS COLEOPTEROS OBSERVADOS IN CATALUNA

Martov, L *see*
- OBSHCHESTVENNYE I UMSTVENNYE TECHENIIA V ROSSII, 1870-1905
- POLITICHESKIE PARTII V ROSSII

Martov, N *see* GALLEREIA RUSSKIKH PISATELEI I KHUDOZHNIKOV S PUSHKINSKOI EPOKHI DO NASKIKH DNEI

Martrou, L *see* LEXIQUE FAN-FRANCAIS

THE MARTURION – [Listowel Ont?: s.n, 1866? Listowel, Ont?]: Listowel Banner – 9 – cn C.I.H.M. [240]

Marty, Paul *see*
- L'EMIRAT DES TRARZAS
- L'ISLAM EN GUINEE
- L'ISLAM ET LES TRIBUS DANS LA COLONIE DU NIGER

Marty, Paul-N *see*
- ETUDES SUR L'ISLAM ET LES TRIBUS MAURES
- LE MAROC DE DEMAIN

Marty-Laveaux, Charles Joseph *see*
- ETUDES DE LANGUE FRANCAISE (XVIE ET XVIIE SIECLES)
- LA PLEIADE FRANCOISE. LA LANGUE DE LA PLEIADE

Martyn, Carlos *see*
- JOHN B. GOUGH
- WENDELL PHILLIPS
- WILLIAM E. DODGE

Martyn, Henry *see* MEMOIR OF THE REV. HENRY MARTYN, B.D.

Martyn, J *see* HISTORIA PLANTARUM RARIORUM

Martyn, James L *see* HISTORY AND THEOLOGY IN THE FOURTH GOSPEL

Martyn, T *see* PLANTAE CANTABRIGIENSES

Martyn, W Carlos *see* THE PILGRIM FATHERS OF NEW ENGLAND

Martynov, N G *see* KATALOG RUSSKIKH KNIG

THE MARTYR CHURCH / Ellis, William – A narrative of the introduction, progress and triumph of Christianity in Madagascar. 1870 – 1 – us A.T.L.A. [240]

THE MARTYR OF ERROMANGA, OR, THE PHILOSOPHY OF MISSIONS, ILLUSTRATED FROM THE LABOURS, DEATH, AND CHARACTER OF THE LATE REV. JOHN WILLIAMS / Campbell, John – London: J. Snow, 1842 – 2mf – us A.T.L.A. [240]

THE MARTYR OF SUMATRA : A MEMOIR OF HENRY LYMAN / Lyman, Hannah Willard – New York: Robert Carter, 1856 – 1mf – 9 – 0-8370-6754-5 – 1986-0754 – us A.T.L.A. [920]

THE MARTYRDOM OF MAN / Reade, William Winwood – London: Trbner & Co, 1872 – 1r – 1 – 1-55879-761-0 – uk Libr Preservation [200]

LE MARTYRE DE MADRID, TEMOIGNAGES INEDITS / Delapree, Louis – Madrid, 1937. Fiche W 826. (Blodgett Collection of Spanish Civil War Pamphlets) – 9 – us H.U. College Libr [946]

MARTYRED MISSIONARIES OF THE CHINA INLAND MISSION : WITH A RECORD OF THE PERILS AND SUFFERINGS OF SOME WHO ESCAPED / ed by Broomhall, Marshall – New York: Fleming H Revell, [1901?] – 1mf – 9 – 0-8370-6027-3 – 1986-0027 – us A.T.L.A. [920]

DAS MARTYRIUM DER CHARLOTTE VON STEIN : VERSUCH IHRER RECHTFERTIGUNG / Boy-Ed, Ida – Stuttgart: J G Cotta, 1920 – 1r – 1 – us U.W. Library [430]

DAS MARTYRIUM DES HEILIGEN ABO VON TIFLIS (T.U.U. 2-28/4B) / Schultze, K – Leipzig, 1905 – 1mf – 9 – ne Slangenburg [240]

DAS MARTYRIUM VON MADRID; EIN UNVEROEFFENTLICHTES ZEUGNIS / Delapree, Louis – n.p. 1937. Fiche W 827. (Blodgett Collection of Spanish Civil War Pamphlets) – 9 – us H.U. College Libr [946]

MARTYROLOGE COLONIAL, NO. 1-3 – Tableau De l'Esclavage Aux Colonies Francaises. (Slave Trade and Abolitionism in France series). 1848 – 9 – fr Hachette [305]

LE MARTYROLOGE NATIONAL – Ouvrage patriotique, dedie a tous les martyrs par un heureux de la Revolution. Par Suleau, Bertin d'Antilly et autres. no. 1-24. Paris. mars-juil 1790 – 1 – fr A.C.R.P.P. [073]

DIE MARTYROLOGIEN : IHRE GESCHICHTE UND IHR WERT / Achelis, Hans – Berlin: Weidmann, 1900. (Abhandlungen der Koeniglichen Gesellschaft der Wissenschaften zu Goettingen. Philologisch-historische Klasse; n.F., Bd. 3, Nr. 3) – 1mf – us A.T.L.A. [240]

EIN MARTYROLOGIUM DER CHRISTLICHEN GEMEINDE ZU ROM (T.U.U. 2-21/3) / Urbain, A – Leipzig, 1901 – 4mf – 9 – ne Slangenburg [240]

DAS MARTYROLOGIUM DES NUERNBERGER MEMORBUCHES / ed by Salfeld, Siegmund – Berlin, 1898 – 6mf – ne IDC [270]

THE MARTYROLOGY OF GORMAN / Stokes, W – 1895 – 8mf – 8 – Dfl30.00 – ne Slangenburg [240]

THE MARTYROLOGY OF OENGUS THE CULDEE / Stokes, W – 1905 – 8mf – 8 – ne Slangenburg [200]

A MARTYROLOGY OF THE CHURCHES OF CHRIST / Van Braght, T J – Ed. for Hanserd Knolly's Society by Edward B. Underhill. v. 1 and 2. 1524-68 – 1 – 33.81 – us Baptist [240]

A MARTYROLOGY OF THE CHURCHES OF CHRIST, 1524-52 / ed by Underhill, Edward B – v1-2. Ed. for the Hansard Knollys Society – 1 – 33.81 – us Baptist [240]

A MARTYROLOGY OF THE CHURCHES OF CHRIST COMMONLY CALLED BAPTISTS *see* PUBLICATIONS

MARTYRS AND SAINTS OF THE FIRST TWELVE CENTURIES : STUDIES FROM THE LIVES OF THE BLACK LETTER SAINTS OF THE ENGLISH CALENDAR / Schoenberg-Cotta, Family – London: S.P.C.K.; New York: E. & J.B. Young, 1893 – 2mf – us A.T.L.A. [240]

MARTYRS DE GORCUM = DE MARTELAREN VAN GORCUM / Meuffels, Hubert – (In Dutch) – Leiden: J W van Leeuwen, [1909?] – 1mf – 9 – 0-8370-6760-X – 1986-0760 – us A.T.L.A. [920]

THE MARTYRS OF SCIENCE. LIVES OF GALILEO, TYCHO BRAHE, AND KEPLER / Brewster, David – new ed, with portraits. London: Chatto & Windus, 1874. xii,248p. 3 ports – 1 – us U.W. Library [500]

THE MARTYRS OF THE EARLY CHURCH / Workman, Herbert Brook – London: C.H. Kelly, 1912 – 1mf – us A.T.L.A. [240]

MARTYRS OMITTED BY FOXE : BEING RECORDS OF RELIGIOUS PERSECUTIONS IN THE SIXTEENTH AND SEVENTEENTH CENTURIES / Caufeild, Miss. – London: J. Hodges, 1870 – 1mf – us A.T.L.A. [240]

MARTYRS TO THE TRACT CAUSE : A CONTRIBUTION TO THE HISTORY OF THE REFORMATION / Hurst, John F – New York: Nelson & Phillips; Cincinnati: Hitchcock & Walden,1872 – 1mf – us A.T.L.A. [240]

Martzolff, Clement L *see* HISTORY OF PERRY COUNTY, OHIO

Marucchi, Orazio *see* LE CATACOMBE ROMANE

Ma-Ruf, Anas *see* MODERN INDONESIAN LITERATURE

Marufke, Willy *see* DER AELTESTE ENGLISCHE MARIENHYMNUS "ON GOD UREISUN OF URE LEFDI"

MARUKUSU SHUGI = MARXISM – Japan, 1924-29 – 6r – 1 – inquire – us Ross [335]

Marure, Alejandro *see* BOSQUEJO HISTORICO DE LAS REVOLUCIONES DE CENTRO-AMERICA. DESDE 1811 HASTA 1834

MARVEL MYSTERY – (Includes Marvel Comics No. 1) – Issue Nos. 1-5 Oct-Nov 1939-March 40 – 5mf – 15 – $31,95 – us Comics [760]

MARVEL MYSTERY – Issue Nos. 11-15 Sept 1940-Jan 1941 – 5mf – 15 – $31,95 – us Comics [760]
MARVEL MYSTERY – Issue Nos. 16-20 Feb 1941-June 1941 – 5mf – 15 – $31,95 – us Comics [760]
MARVEL MYSTERY – Issue Nos. 21-25 July 1941-Nov 1941 – 5mf – 15 – $31,95 – us Comics [760]
MARVEL MYSTERY – Issue Nos. 26-30 Dec 1941-Apr 1942 – 5mf – 15 – $31,95 – us Comics [760]
MARVEL MYSTERY – Issue Nos. 31-35 May 1942-Sept 1942 – 5mf – 15 – $31,95 – us Comics [760]
MARVEL MYSTERY – Issue Nos. 36-40 Oct 1942-Feb 1943 – 5mf – 15 – $31,95 – us Comics [760]
MARVEL MYSTERY – Issue Nos. 41-45 Mar 1943-July 1943 – 5mf – 15 – $31,95 – us Comics [760]
MARVEL MYSTERY – Issue Nos. 46-50 Aug 1943-Dec 1943 – 5mf – 15 – $31,95 – us Comics [760]
MARVEL MYSTERY – Issue Nos. 6-10 Apr 1940-Aug 1940 – 5mf – 15 – $31,95 – us Comics [760]
MARVELS OF THE NEW WEST / Thayer, William M – 1887 – 9 – 75.00 – us Opus [910]
Marvin, Abijah Perkins *see* THREE ERAS OF REVIVALS IN THE UNITED STATES
Marvin, Frederic R *see* CONSECRATED WOMANHOOD: A SERMON PREACHED IN FIRST CONGREGATIONAL CHURCH, PORTLAND, OREGON
Marwick, B A *see* THE SWAZI
Marx, A B *see*
- ALLGEMEINE MUSIKLEHRE
- THEORY AND PRACTICE OF MUSICAL COMPOSITION

Marx, Alexander *see*
- ALEXANDER MARX JUBILEE VOLUME
- SEFER HA-YOVEL LI-KHEVOD ALEXANDER MARX

MARX AND JESUS / Conway, Jim – 1973 – 1 – us A.T.L.A. [240]
Marx, F *see* LUCILII CARMINUM RELIQUIAE
Marx, Jakob *see* LEHRBUCH DER KIRCHENGESCHICHTE
Marx, Karl *see*
- ASAL USUL KAPITALIS INDUSTRI. BAB 31 "KAPITAL" DJILIK I KARL MARX
- DIE FRUHSCHRIFTEN
- LOHNARBEIT UND KAPITAL
- MANIFES PARTAI KOMUNIS

Marx Memorial Library. London *see* CATALOGUE OF THE MARX MEMORIAL LIBRARY
Marx, Moses *see* HISTORY AND ANNALS OF HEBREW PRINTING IN THE FIFTEENTH AND SIXTEENTH CENTURIES
Marx, Olga *see* CARLYLE'S TRANSLATION OF WILHELM MEISTER
Marx-Aveling, Eleonore *see* DIE ARBEITERCLASSEN-BEWEGUNG IN ENGLAND
MARXIAN – 1-2 (all publ). 1921 – 2mf – 9 – $35.00 – us UPA [335]
MARXISM QUARTERLY – London. 1954-57 – 1 – uk World [073]
MARXISM TODAY – London, 1957-91. Continued annually – 1 – uk World [073]
MARXISM TODAY *see* NEW TIMES
MARXISME DAN AGAMA / Hashem, O – Incl. Bibliography. SE-11,039 1. 1961 – 9 – ne IDC [335]
MARXIST / Workers' Educational Institute – 1-4 (all publ). 1925-27 – 6mf – 9 – $45.00 – us UPA [335]
MARXIST IDEOLOGY IN THE CONTEMPORARY WORLD: ITS APPEALS AND PARADOXES / ed by Drachkovitch, M M – 1 – 35.00r – us Hoover Inst Photo [335]
MARXIST PERSPECTIVES – v. 1-. 1978- – 1,5,6,9 – us UMI [335]
MARXIST QUARTERLY – 1-3 (all publ). 1937 – 6mf – 9 – $45.00 – us UPA [335]
THE MARXIST QUARTERLY – 1962-66 – 9 – 55.50 – cn McLaren [073]
MARXIST QUARTERLY. 1954-57 / Communist Party. Great Britain – 1 – uk World [073]
MARXIST REVIEW / Marxist Workers' Party – 1-3 (all publ). 1937-1940 – 6mf – 9 – $45.00 – us UPA [335]
MARXIST REVIEW / Marxist Workers' Party – v1-3. 1937-40 – 1r – 1 – us Ross [335]
Marxist Workers' Party *see*
- MARXIST REVIEW

MARXISTISCHE TRIBUENE : DISKUSSIONSBLAETTER DER SAP – Paris. Nov 1935-Nov, Dec 1937 – 1r – 1 – gw Mikrofilm [073]
Marxuach, Teofilo *see* EL LENGUAJE CASTELLANO EN PUERTO RICO
MARY / Braddon, Mary Elizabeth – British Fiction Archive: Unit 5 – 9 – uk Bell [830]
MARY : A FICTION / Wollstonecraft, Mary – London: J. Johnson, 1788 – 1 roll – 1 – 1-55879-671-1 – uk Libr Preservation [830]
MARY ALL-MERCIFUL : OUR LADY OF PELLEVOISIN – Montreal, 1898. SEM105P528 – 1mf – 9 – Can$2.25 – cn Bibl Nat [240]
MARY AND I : FORTY YEARS WITH THE SIOUX / Riggs, Stephen R – Boston: Congregational Sunday-School and Pub Society, c1887 – 1mf – 9 – 0-8370-6608-5 – 1986-0608 – us A.T.L.A. [920]
MARY ANERLEY / Blackmore, Richard Doddridge – British Fiction Archive: Unit 3 – 9 – uk Bell [830]
MARY B. GROSSMAN PAPERS *see* GROSSMAN, MARY B, PAPERS, MS 3660
MARY B. MARTIN SCRAPBOOK *see* MARTIN, MARY B., SCRAPBOOK, MS 4047
"MARY HAMILTON", EINE KRITISCHE UNTERSUCHUNG DER VARIANTEN / Grasedieck, Brunhild – Marburg, 1933 – 1mf – DM48.00 – 3-8267-3035-6 – gw Hänsel [420]
MARY, HELP OF CHRISTIANS : AND THE FOURTEEN SAINTS INVOKED AS HOLY HELPERS: INSTRUCTIONS, LEGENDS, NOVENAS AND PRAYERS / Hammer, Bonaventure – New York: Benziger, c1909 – 2mf – 9 – 0-8370-6980-7 – 1986-0980 – us A.T.L.A. [240]
MARY IMMACULATE, MOTHER OF GOD : OR, DEVOTIONS IN HONOUR OF THE BLESSED VIRGIN MARY / Kinane, Thomas H – (Includes bibliographical references) – 7th ed. Dublin: M H Gill, 1878 – 1mf – 9 – 0-8370-8355-9 – 1986-2355 – us A.T.L.A. [240]
MARY LAMB / Gilchrist, Anne Burrows – London: W.H. Allen & Co., 1883 – 1r – 1 – 1-55879-333-X – uk Libr Preservation [420]
MARY MCLEOD BETHUNE PAPERS : THE BETHUNE FOUNDATION COLLECTION, PART 1: WRITINGS, DIARIES, SCRAPBOOKS, BIOGRAPHICAL MATERIALS, AND FILES ON THE NATIONAL YOUTH ADMINISTRATION AND WOMEN'S ORGANIZATIONS, 1918-1955 – (With printed guide) – 1996 – ca 18r – 1 – ca $2,250.00 – 1-55655-636-5 – us UPA [370]
MARY MCLEOD BETHUNE PAPERS / Bethune, Mary McLeod – 1875-1955 – 1 – $36.00 – us Amistad [920]
MARY MCLEOD BETHUNE PAPERS : THE BETHUNE-COOKMAN COLLEGE COLLLECTION, 1922-1955 – (With printed guide) – 13r – 1 – $1,625.00 – 1-55655-554-7 – us UPA [370]
MARY QUEEN OF SCOTS : FROM HER BIRTH TO HER FLIGHT INTO ENGLAND : A BRIEF BIOGRAPHY / Fleming, David Hay – London: Hodder and Stoughton, 1898 – 2mf – us A.T.L.A. [240]
Mary, Queen of Scots *see* LETTERS, TRANSCRIPTS AND PAPERS
MARY QUEEN OF SCOTS, 1542-1587 : EXTRACTS FROM THE ENGLISH, SPANISH, AND VENETIAN STATE PAPERS, BUCHANAN, KNOX, LESLEY, MELVILLE, THE "DIURNAL OF OCCURRENTS", NAU, &C. &C. / Rait, Robert Sangster – London: D. Nutt, 1900 – 1mf – us A.T.L.A. [941]
MARY REED : MISSIONARY TO THE LEPERS / Jackson, John – New York: Fleming H Revell, [1900?] – 1mf – 9 – 0-8370-6267-5 – 1986-0267 – us A.T.L.A. [920]
MARY THE VIRGIN : AS COMMEMORATED IN THE CHURCH OF CHRIST / Seabury, Samuel – (Includes bibliographical references) – New York:Pott & Amery, 1868 – 1mf – 9 – 0-8370-5201-7 – 1985-3201 – us A.T.L.A. [240]
MARY WEBB AND THE MOTHER SOCIETY / Vail, Albert L – Philadelphia: American Baptist Publication Society, 1914 – 1 – 5.04 – us Baptist [240]
MARY WOLLSTONECRAFT / Jebb, Camilla – London, 1912 – 1 – us U.W. Library [920]
MARY WOLLSTONECRAFT JOURNAL – v. 2. 1974 – 1 – us UMI [420]
MARY WOLLSTONECRAFT NEWSLETTER – v. 1-2. 1972-73 – 1 – us UMI [420]
Maryanov, Gerald Seymour *see* POLITICAL POWER AND POLITICAL CULTURE IN INDONESIA
MARYBOROUGH ADVERTISER – 1929-1963. 1949-53 on reels A1-5, Advertiser (Maryborough). MA1-28 – 33r – 1 – at Corangamite [072]
MARYBOROUGH AND DUNOLLY ADVERTISER – 1901-1929. MDA1-41 – 41r – 1 – at Corangamite [072]
MARYBOROUGH & DUNOLLY ADVERTISER – Australia. Jan 1873-Jul 1879.-w. 6mqn reels – 1 – uk British Libr Newspaper [072]
MARYLAND : ANNOTATED CODE OF MARYLAND – Charlottesville: Michie Company, 1957-Apr 1996 update – 9 – $3,011.00 set – us Hein [340]
MARYLAND : SESSION LAWS OF AMERICAN STATES AND TERRITORIES – 1777-1995 – 9 – $3,365.00 set – us Hein [340]
Maryland *see*
- ARCHIVES
- MISCELLANEOUS NEWSPAPERS
- REPORTS AND OPINIONS (A-G)
- REPORTS, POST-NRS
- REPORTS, PRE-NRS
- STATE LABOR REPORTS

MARYLAND ATTORNEY GENERAL REPORTS AND OPINIONS – (6 1916-1979 $ 455.00. 9 1980-1989 + indexes $175.00) – 1916-1989 + indexes – 6,9 – $630.00set – us Hein [340]
Maryland. Bank Commissioner *see* REPORTS
MARYLAND BAPTIST – 1902-07 – 1 – 41.00 – us A.B.H.S. [073]
THE MARYLAND BAPTIST – Baltimore. 1902-03, 1905-07. 1248p – 1 – 62.40 – us Baptist [240]
MARYLAND BAPTIST CHURCH LIFE/MARYLAND BAPTIST – 1917-62.Maryland Baptist Union Assoc., Baptist Convention of Maryland. Single reels available – 1 – 233.50 – us A.B.H.S. [073]
MARYLAND BAR ASSOCIATION RECORD – 1895-end of copyright – 9 – LLMC 84-599 – us L.L.M.C. [073]
MARYLAND BAR JOURNAL – v1-28. 1968-95 – 9 – $327.00 set – us Hein [340]
Maryland. Bureau of Industrial Statistics and Information *see* REPORTS
Maryland. Bureau of Statistics and Information *see* REPORTS
MARYLAND CHANCERY REPORTS / Maryland. Court of Appeals – v1-4. 1847-1854 (all publ) – 21mf – 9 – $31.50 – LLMC 90-302 – us L.L.M.C. [340]
Maryland. Commissioner of Labor and Statistics *see* REPORTS
Maryland. Court of Appeals *see*
- GILL AND JOHNSON'S LAW REPORTS
- GILL'S LAW REPORTS
- HARRIS AND GILL'S LAW REPORTS
- HARRIS AND JOHNSON'S LAW REPORTS
- HARRIS AND MCHENRY'S LAW REPORTS
- MARYLAND CHANCERY REPORTS
- RAYMOND'S DIGESTED CHANCERY CASES

THE MARYLAND DIRECTORY, 1880 / J. Frank Lewis and Co – Baltimore, MD. Maryland Reel 1. The Cox Library Collection – 5 – us Americana [978]
Maryland. Division of Labor and Industry *see* REPORTS
THE MARYLAND GAZETTE, 1745-1839 / Annapolis, Maryland – 1973 – 14r – 1 – $1,190.00 – S1724 – us Scholarly Res [978]
MARYLAND HERALD – Hagerstown. Md. and Hagerstown Weekly Advertiser. 1802-26 – 1 – us UMI [071]
Maryland. Insurance Division *see* REPORTS OF THE INSURANCE COMMISSIONER
MARYLAND JOURNAL – Towson, Maryland. 1865-1896 – 1 – us MD Archives [071]
MARYLAND JOURNAL OF INTERNATIONAL LAW AND TRADE – (Cont: International Trade Law Journal) – v1-16. 1975-92 – 1,5,6 – $225.00 – us Hein [073]
MARYLAND LAW FORUM – v1-11. 1970-88 – 1,5,6 – $90.00 – us Hein [073]
MARYLAND LAW RECORD – Baltimore. On film: v1-16; 1878-86. LL-076 – 1 – us L of C Photodup [340]
MARYLAND LAW REVIEW – (1971- . 5,6. 1976- . 9) – 1936- – 1 – us UMI [340]
MARYLAND LAW REVIEW – Baltimore. v1-2. 1901-03 – 1 – $40.00 – us Hein [073]
MARYLAND LAW REVIEW – v1-2. 1901-1903 (all publ) – 3mf – $4.50 – LLMC 90-325 – us L.L.M.C. [073]
Maryland. Laws, Statutes, etc *see* MAYER'S DIGEST OF DECISIONS CONSTRUING MARYLAND STATUTES
MARYLAND MANUAL 1923 / Perlman, Philip B – A compendium of legal historical and statistical information relating to the state of Maryland. Baltimore, 20th Century Printing Co., 1923. Maryland Reel 2. The Cox Library Collection – 5 – us Americana [978]
MARYLAND MESSENGER – Baltimore, MD. Maryland Baptist Union Assoc. 1910-Oct 1914 – 1 – 36.00 – us A.B.H.S. [073]
MARYLAND PRACTICE / Evans, Hugh – 2d ed. Baltimore, Cushings & Bailey, 1867. 726 p. LL-571 – 1 – us L of C Photodup [340]
Maryland. Public Service Commission *see* REPORTS
Maryland. State Bar Association *see* PROCEEDINGS
Maryland. State Dept. of Assessments and Taxation *see* REPORTS
Maryland. Supreme Court *see*
- BALTIMORE CITY REPORTS
- MARYLAND SUPREME COURT REPORTS

MARYLAND SUPREME COURT REPORTS / Maryland. Supreme Court – (Pre-NRS: v1-63 1851-85 471mf $706.00. Add vols planned. This court is known officially as: Maryland Court of Appeals) – v1-135. 1851-1919 – 1095mf – 9 – $1,642.00 – LLMC 80-808 – us L.L.M.C. [340]
MARYLAND SUPREME COURT REPORTS *see*
- BALTIMORE CITY REPORTS
- BLAND'S CHANCERY REPORTS
- GILL AND JOHNSON'S LAW REPORTS
- GILL'S LAW REPORTS
- HARRIS AND GILL'S LAW REPORTS
- HARRIS AND JOHNSON'S LAW REPORTS
- HARRIS AND MCHENRY'S LAW REPORTS
- MARYLAND CHANCERY REPORTS
- MAYER'S DIGEST OF DECISIONS CONSTRUING MARYLAND STATUTES
- RAYMOND'S DIGESTED CHANCERY CASES
- STEIN'S DECISIONS

Maryland. Ten Hour Law Bureau *see* REPORTS
MARYLEBONE MERCURY – Aug 22 1857-Dec 13 1859; 1860-Dec 18 1909; 1910-49; Jan 13-Dec 29 1950; 1951; Jan 4-Dec 19 1952; Jan 2-Dec 18 1953; 1954-67; Jan 12-Apr 26, May 1968-Jun, Jul 5-Dec 20 1990; Jan-Jun, Jul 4-Dec 19 1991; 1992-96 – 163r – 1 – uk British Libr Newspaper [072]
O MARYRANA – [s.l.] 1899 – 1,5,6 – bl Biblioteca [072]
THE MARYROLOGY OF TALLAGHT / Best, R & Lawlor, H – 1931 – 5mf – 8 – ne Slangenburg [240]
MARY'S MEADOW / Ewing, Juliana Horatia – British Fiction Archive: Unit 1 – 9 – uk Bell [830]
THE MARYS; OR, THE BEAUTY OF FEMALE HOLINESS / Philip, Robert – In The Christian Library: a reprint of popular religious works. 1835 – 9 – us A.T.L.A. [240]
MARYSVILLE APPEAL-DEMOCRAT – Marysville, CA. 1922-59 – 165r – 1 BC02425 – $8,250.00 – us Library Micro [071]
MARYSVILLE DAILY APPEAL INDEX – Marysville, CA. 1854-1967 – 12r – 1 – $600.00 – B06002 – us Library Micro [071]
MARYSVILLE DEMOCRAT *see* EVENING DEMOCRAT
MARYSVILLE SEMI-WEEKLY APPEAL – Marysville, CA. 1895-1920 – 20r – 1 – $1,000.00 – C03616 – us Library Micro [071]
MARYSVILLE WEEKLY APPEAL – Marysville, CA. 1875-1895 – 5r – 1 – $250.00 – C03615 – us Library Micro [071]
MARYVILLE FIRST BAPTIST CHURCH. MARYVILLE, MISSOURI : CHURCH RECORDS – Through 1987. Alphabetical and chronological rolls – 1 – 15.35 – us Baptist [240]
Marzi, D *see* LA QUESTIONE DELLA RIFORMA DEL CALENDARIO NEL QUINTO CONCILIO LATERANENSE
Marzials, Frank Thomas *see* LIFE OF CHARLES DICKENS
Marzilli, L G *see* COMMENTS ON INORGANIC CHEMISTRY
Marzluf, Arnulf *see* SELBSTBEWUSSTSEIN ALS BILDKATEGORIE
IL MARZOCCO – Florence, Italy. -w. 2 Jan 1921-25 Dec 1932. 5 reels – 1 – uk British Libr Newspaper [072]

MAS ALL A DE LA REVOLUCION : [POLEMICA RADICAL-SOCIALISTA SOBRE REPRESENTACION PROPORCIONAL: LA REFORMA CONSTITUCIONAL] / Ghioldi, Americo – Buenos Aires: [Ediciones La Izquierda], 1957 – 1 – CSUXADH4013-B – us Hoover Inst Photo [320]
MAS SOBRE MEJICO – Madrid: Razon y Fe, 1926 – 1 – sp Bibl Santa Ana [972]
MAS SONETOS...TODAVIA? / Sanchez-Arjona, Vicente – Sevilla: Imp. Alvarez, Tomo 1,2. 1959 – 1 – sp Bibl Santa Ana [810]
MAS SONETOS...TODAVIA? / Sanchez-Arjona, Vicente – Sevilla: Imp. Alvarez, Tomo 3,4. 1959 – 1 – sp Bibl Santa Ana [810]
Masa Campos, A *see* ORDENACION DE LA ECONOMIA PORCINA
Masa Campos, Antonio *see* 1ST CONGRESO SINDICAL AGRARIO DE EXTREMADURA. PONENCIA 4 SERVICIOS ECONOMICOS DE LAS HERMANDADES
Masa Godoy, Jose *see* 4 CONSEJO ECONOMICO SINDICAL 14TH PROV. COMISION. TRADAJO
DIE MASAI / Merker, Mertiz – [Nairobi, 196-?] – us Res Libr [305]
MASAKA AU RWANDA. CONTRIBUTION A L'ETUDE DE LA COLONISATION DES TERRES NEUVES EN AFRIQUE / Silvestre, V – 9 – F160.00 – fr Ethnologie [306]
MASAKAN INDONESIA, ASIA, BROPAH / Suryati – SE 6773 1. 1959? – 9 – ne IDC [950]
MASAKAN INDONESIA MODERN / Suryati – SE 6602 1. 1959 – 9 – ne IDC [950]
MASAKO, SINGE D'AFRIQUE; ROMAN / Gregoire, Herman – Paris. 1921 – 1 – us Res Libr [830]
MASALAH SEPATU MILITER / Dam, Z Antonist – SE-4407 1. 1961.n – 9 – ne IDC [950]
MASALAH TUBERCULOSA DI PERUSAHAAN / Kapitan, J C – SE-10,113 1. 1958 – 9 – ne IDC [610]
Masanawa, I *see*
– ADULT EDUCATION MEMORANDA
Masani, Rustom Pestonji *see* [CORRESPONDENCE WITH REED STANLEY AND DRAFTS OF TWO ARTICLES, 1915-1933?]
Masanov, I F *see*
– BIBLIOGRAFIIA SOCHINENII A. P. CHEKHOVA
– BIBLIOGRAFIIA VLADIMIRSKOI GUBERNII
– RUSSKIE SATIRO-IUMORISTICHESKIE ZHURNALY
Masar, Ilhami *see* THE IRRIGATION OF THE JORDAN VALLEY
Masara *see* MOTEZUMA
A MASCARA : ORGAO DA RAPAZIADA CHIC DO WHIT CLUB – [s.l.] 15 Jun 1910 – 1,5,6 – bl Biblioteca [072]
A MASCARA : PUBLICACAO TEMPORARIA – Manaos, Amazonas. 17 Fev 1910 – 1,5,6 – bl Biblioteca [072]
LA MASCARADE – Quebec, Canada. 14 nov-10 dec 1863 – 1r – 1 – Can$25.00 – cn Can Microfilming [072]
O MASCARADO – Curitiba, 30 Nov 1861 – 1,5,6 – bl Biblioteca [072]
Mascarenas, Geronimo *see* CAMPANA DE PORTUGAL...EXTREMADURA
MASCARENE FAMILY PAPERS, 1687-1839 – Massachusetts Historical Society – 1r – 1 – $85.00 – us UMI [920]
DER MASCHINENBAUER – Leipzig, Germany.Jan 1893-Sep 1900.-m. 2men reels – 1 – uk British Libr Newspaper [073]
MASCHINENBAUTECHNIK – (v24- . 1975- . 5,6,9) – v. 1-. 1952- – 1 – us UMI [621]
Masclef, A *see* ATLAS DES PLANTES DE FRANCE...
THE MASCOT – Sisson, CA. 1891-95 – 1r – 1 – $50.00 – B02955 – us Library Micro [071]
LA MASCOTTE : JOURNAL "SPORTIQUE" – Montreal, Canada. 6 mai 1900 – 1r – 1 – Can$25.00 – cn Can Microfilming [790]
Masduki, W *see* REPORT ON DOCKYARD MAKASAR
Maseres, Francis *see* MEMOIRE A LA DEFENSE D'UN PLAN D'ACTE DE PARLEMENT POUR L'ETABLISSEMENT DES LOIX DE LA PROVINCE DE QUEBEC, CONTRE LES OBJECTIONS DE MR. FRANCOIS JOSEPH CUGNET..
MASHAL U-MELIZAH / Malbim, ML – Warsaw. 1877. BJ-422-57 1 – 9 – ne IDC [470]
Mashbits-Verov, I *see* POEMY MAIAKOVSKOGO KUIBYSHEV, 1960
MASHINNO-TRAKTORNAI A STANT SII A – (Library has: July-Aug. 1950, June 1956) – Moskva: Izd-vo. Narkomzema SSSR, 1945-1958. 14v – 1 – CSUX89-S602 – us Hoover Inst Photo [947]
MASHINOSTROENIE – Moscow, USSR. Oct 1937-1940; Jan 1-Feb 16, May 27/29-June 3/10 1941 – 5r – 1 – us L of C Photodup [072]
Mashkovich, A G *see* DEIATELNOST PRODOVOLSTVENNOI ORGANIZATSII
MASHPIE 1834-1899 – 3mf – 9 – us Holbrook [920]
MASHROU' AL ITAR AL'AM LIL KHITTA AL INMAIYYA AL KHAMSIYYA LIL SANAWAT 1990/91-1994/95 / Kuwait. Central Statistical Office – Kuwait, 1990 – 4mf – 9 – ne IDC [338]
MASHRU'AT AL-QAWANIN / Israel – (1978-. approx.25.00y; 1) – 1970-77 – 1 – 46.00 – us L of C Photodup [324]
Mashukovs, V A *see* KHRONOLOGICHESKII PERECHEN' ZAKONOV SOIUZA SSR PO SOSTOIANIIA NA 1 IIULIA 1935 G
Masides Rosado, Severiano *see* LA ESTELA DE UN CAMPESINO. MUESTRARIO DE ACCION, IDEAS Y SENTIMIENTOS
Masini, Eleonora *see* WOMEN, HOUSEHOLDS AND CHANGE
Masius, A *see* JOSUAE IMPERATORIS HISTORIA ILLUSTRATA ATQUE EXPLICATA
THE MASK: AND OTHER STORIES / Chambers, Robert William – Racine: Whitman Pub. Co., c1929.126p – 1 – us U.W. Library [830]
THE MASK OF ANARCHY : WRITTEN ON THE OCCASION OF THE MASSACRE AT MANCHESTER / Shelley, Percy Bysshe – London: Pub. for the Shelley Society by Reeves and Turner, 1887 – 1 roll – 1 – 1-55879-854-4 – uk Libr Preservation [810]
Maskell, W *see* MONUMENTA RITUALIA ECCLESIAE ANGLICANAE OR OCCASIONAL OFFICES OF THE CHURCH OF ENGLAND ACCORDING TO THE ANCIENT USE OF SALISBURY THE PRYMER IN ENGLISH
DIE MASKEN ERWIN REINERS : ROMAN / Wassermann, Jakob – 9. Aufl. Berlin: S Fischer, 1917, c1910 – 1r – 1 – us U.W. Library [830]
HET MASKER VAN DE WERELD : AFGETROKKEN / Poirters, Adrianus – Antwerpen, 1827 – 4mf – 9 – O-3253/1 – ne IDC [760]
HET MASKER VAN DE WERELD, AFGETROKKEN : EN DEEZE AAN HAARE BEMINNAAREN, OP EEN GODVRUCHTIGE EN VROLYKE WYZE IN HAAR EIGEN GEDAANTE VOORGESTELD / Poirters, Adrianus – Amsterdam, 1767 – 5mf – 9 – O-3252/1 – ne IDC [760]
HET MASKER VANDE WERELDT AFGETROCKEN / Poirters, Adrianus – Den 13 druck. Antwerpen, [c1694] – 5mf – 9 – O-3153/1 – ne IDC [760]
HET MASKER VANDE WERELDT AFGETROCKEN / Poiters, A – Den 7. druck. Antwerpen [1741] – 5mf – 9 – O-3154/1 – ne IDC [760]
HET MASKER VANDE WERELDT AFGETROCKEN DOOR P. ADRIANUS POIRTERS S.I. / Poirters, Adrianus – Antwerpen, 1688 – 5mf – 9 – ne IDC [700]
HET MASKER VANDE WERELDT AFGHETROCKEN DOOR P. ADRIANUS POIRTERS S.I. / Poirters, Adrianus – 1st ed. Antwerpen, 1646 – 4mf – 9 – ne IDC [700]
MASKI – Ezhemesiachnik iskusstva i teatra. M. 1912-14. BR-3360 2 – 8 – ne IDC [460]
LE MASKOUTAIN – St-Hyacinthe, Canada. 2 oct 1952-v1 n41. 30 jul 1953 – 1r – 1 – Can$45.00 – cn Can Microfilming [072]
Maslin, N *see*
– MAIAKOVSKII
– VLADIMIR MAIAKOVSKII
Masliyah, Nesim *see* OSMANLI PARLAMENTOSU BEYNELMILEL SULH HEYETI
MASLODEL'NYE ARTELI V VOLOGODSKOI GUBERNII / Bogdanov, B & Vorovskii, V – Vologda, 1915 – 6mf – 9 – COR-9/1 – ne IDC [334]
Maslov, P P *see* OSNOVY KOOPERATSII V USLOVIIAKH NAKOPLENIIA KOOPERATIVNOGO KAPITALA
Maslov, S I *see*
– BIBLIOTEKA STEFANA IAVORSKAGO
– OPISANIE RUKOPISEI ISTORICHESKAGO OBSHCHESTVA NESTORA LETOPISTSA
Maslov, S L *see*
– KOOPERATIVNAIA ARENDA ZEMLI
– KREST'IANSKOE KHOZIAISTVO
– KREST'IANSKOE KHOZIAISTVO I SEL'SKOKHOZIAISTVENNAIA KOOPERATSIIA
– SEL'SKOKHOZIAISTVENNAIA KOOPERATSIIA, EE FORMY, ZNACHENIE I ZADACHI
– SOVREMENNYE VOPROSY ORGANIZATSII I PRAKTIKI SEL'SKOKHOZIAISTVENNOI KOOPERATSII
– ZEMSTVO I KOOPERATSIIA
Maslovskii, S D *see* SISTEMATICHESKII UKAZATEL' KNIG (1832-1910) BIBLIOTEKI IMP. NIKOLAEVSKOI VOENNOI AKADEMII
Maslow, Abraham S *see* THE CREATIVE ATTITUDE
Masnata, F *see* LE PARTI SOCIALISTE ET LA TRADITION DEMOCRATIQUE EN SUISSE
MASOANDRO *see* NY MASOANDRO
Mason, Arthur James *see*
– THE CHURCH OF ENGLAND AND EPISCOPACY
– THE CONDITIONS OF OUR LORD'S LIFE ON EARTH
– LECTURES ON COLET, FISHER, AND MORE, AT ST PAUL'S CATHEDRAL, 1894
– LIFE OF WILLIAM EDWARD COLLINS
– THE MISSION OF ST AUGUSTINE TO ENGLAND ACCORDING TO THE ORIGINAL DOCUMENTS
– THE PERSECUTION OF DIOCLETIAN
– THE PRINCIPLES OF ECCLESIASTICAL UNITY
– THOMAS CRANMER
Mason, Caroline Atwater *see* LUX CHRISTI
MASON CITY STAR – Mason City, NE. -w. Jun 1903-Nov 1904; Jul 1907; Jan 1908-Mar 1910 – 1 – us NE Hist [071]
MASON CITY TRANSCRIPT – Mason City, NE. -w. Aug 1892; Oct 1895-Dec 1899; Feb 1900-Sep 1902; Apr-Jul 1910; Sep 1911-Mar 1943; Feb 1952-Dec 1954 – 1 – us NE Hist [071]
MASON COUNTY JOURNAL – Point Pleasant. West Virginia. 1867-1872 – 1 – us UMI [071]
MASON COUNTY NEWS – Point Pleasant. West Virginia. 1959-1967 – 1 – us UMI [071]
MASON COUNTY RECORD – Ludington. Mich. 1879-1880 – 1 – us UMI [071]
Mason, George *see* GRAMMAIRE ANGLOISE
Mason IL *see* TRYPANOTOLERANT LIVESTOCK IN WEST AND CENTRAL AFRICA
Mason, John *see*
– AN ESSAY ON ELOCUTION
– AN ESSAY ON THE POWER AND HARMONY OF PROSAIC NUMBERS
– AN ESSAY ON THE POWER OF NUMBERS
Mason, John Brown *see* HITLER'S FIRST FOES; A STUDY IN RELIGION AND POLITICS
Mason, John Mitchell *see* CHRISTIAN MOURNING: A SERMON, OCCASIONED BY THE DEATH OF MRS. ISABELLA GRAHAM, AND PREACHED ON THE EVENING OF SABBATH, THE 14TH AUG. 1814
Mason, Joseph *see*
– PRACTICE AND PLEADING IN CIVIL ACTIONS AND PROCEEDINGS AT LAW IN ALL COURTS OF MASSACHUSETTS
– THE PRACTICE IN CIVIL ACTIONS AND PROCEEDINGS AT LAW IN THE COMMON LAW COURTS OF THE NEW ENGLAND STATES
Mason, New Hampshire. Mason Baptist Church *see* RECORDS
Mason, Otis Tufton *see*
– ABORIGINAL AMERICAN HARPOONS
– POINTED BARK CANOES OF THE KUTENAI AND AMUR
– THE ULU, OR WOMAN'S KNIFE OF THE ESKIMO
– WOMAN'S SHARE IN PRIMITIVE CULTURE
Mason, Rufus Osgood *see* HYPNOTISM AND SUGGESTION IN THERAPEUTICS, EDUCATION, AND REFORM
MASON VALLEY NEWS – Yerington. Nev. -w. 1949- – 1 – us UMI [071]
MASON VALLEY NEWS – Yerington, NV. 1909-49 (broken series); 1949- – 74+ r – 1 – $3,700.00 ($180.00y) – UN04827 – us Library Micro [071]
MASON VALLEY TIDINGS – Yerington, NV. 1893-94 – 1r – 1 – $50.00 – U04571 – us Library Micro [071]
Mason, William *see*
– COLLECTION OF 42 HOLOGRAPH MANUSCRIPTS
– MASON'S REPORTS OF CASES IN THE FIRST CIRCUIT, 1816-1830
– METHODISM DISPLAYED AND ENTHUSIASM DETECTED;...
– THE SCRIPTURE-DOCTRINE OF IMPUTED RIGHTEOUSNESS ASSERTED AND MAINTAINED BY THE REV. MR. JOHN WESLEY, M.A., LATE FELLOW OF LINCOLN COLLEGE, OXFORD...
– A SEASONABLE ANTIDOTE AGAINST RELIGIOUS DELUSION;...
– A SPIRITUAL TREASURY FOR THE CHILDREN OF GOD
THE MASONIC INSTRUCTOR : COMPRISING THE FIRST, SECOND, AND THIRD DEGREES OF FREEMASONRY – Toronto: Society Publishing Syndicate, 1899. 03244. (Pre-1900 Canadiana) – 9 – cn C.I.H.M. [360]
MASONIC LAW AND PRACTICE : WITH FORMS / Lockwood, Luke A – New York: Macoy Publishing & Masonic Supply Co, 1905 – 2mf – 9 – $3.00 – LLMC 91-502 – us L.L.M.C. [360]
MASONIC MIRROR AND KEYSTONE – v1-9 1852-60 – 1 – $69.00 – us L of C Photodup [360]
THE MASONIC MIRROR AND PYTHIAN HERALD – St. John, NB: Day's Print., [1870?-18-?] – 9 – cn C.I.H.M. [360]
THE MASONIC MUSEUM, CONTAINING SONGS... LIST OF LODGES : DEDICATED TO HIS ROYAL HIGHNESS THE PRINCE OF WALES. GRAND MASTER – London, 1799 – 1mf – ne IDC [360]
MASON'S REPORTS OF CASES IN THE FIRST CIRCUIT, 1816-1830 / Mason, William – 2nd ed. Boston: Wells-Lilly. v1-5. 1819-31 (all publ) – 32mf – 9 – $48.00 – LLMC 81-462 – us L.L.M.C. [340]
MASONSKIE TRUDY / Lopukhin, I V – M. 1913. BR-7663 – 8 – ne IDC [999]
MASONSTVO V EGO PROSHLOM I NASTOIASHCHEM / ed by Mel'gunov, S P & Sidorov, N P – 2v. M. 1914-15. BR-7693 2 – 8 – ne IDC [460]
DER MASORAHTEXT DES KOHELETH: KRITISCH UNTERSUCHT / Euringer, Sebastian – Leipzig: J.C. Hinrichs, 1890. 1 fiche – 9 – us A.T.L.A. [240]
Maspero, Gaston *see*
– THE DAWN OF CIVILIZATION; EGYPT AND CHALDAEA
– HISTORY OF EGYPT, CHALDEA, SYRIA, BABYLONIA, AND ASSYRIA
– THE PASSING OF THE EMPIRES, 850 BC TO 330 BC
Maspero, J *see* HISTOIRE DES PATRIARCHES D'ALEXANDRIE DEPUIS LA MORT DE L'EMPEREUR ANASTASE JUSQU'A LA RECONCILIATION DES EGLISES JACOBITES (518-616)
LE MASQUE / Reunion des musees nationaux. Paris – 1959. 32 illus. 2 fiches – 9 – fr Réunion [700]
MASQUES DOGONS / Griaule, M – 9 – F240.00 – fr Ethnologie [740]
THE MASS AND FUNERAL SERVICE OF THE LATE RT. HON. SIR WILFRID LAURIER, P.C., G.C.M.G., AT THE BASILICA, OTTAWA, 22ND FEBRUARY 1919 – [S.l.]: [s.n.], [1919 ?]. SEM105P1442 – 1mf – 9 – Can$2.25 – cn Bibl Nat [320]
MASS EDUCATION IN INDONESIA / Indonesia. Djawatan Pendidikan Masjarakat – SE-2017 1. 1953? – 9 – ne IDC [370]
MASS HIGH TECHNOLOGY – (1985-. 1,5,6) – v3-. 1984- – 9 – us UMI [600]
THE MASS IN SWEDEN, ITS DEVELOPMENT FROM THE LATIN RITE, FROM 1531-1917 / Yelvertone, E – 1920 – 4mf – 8 – ne Slangenburg [240]
MASS MEDIA : THE IMAGE, ROLE AND SOCIAL CONDITIONS OF WOMEN / Ceulemans, Mieke & Fauconnier, G – 1979 – 9 – 92-3-101648-2 – fr UNESCO [302]
MASS MEDIA CODES OF ETHICS AND COUNCILS : A COMPARATIVE INTERNATIONAL STUDY ON PROFESSIONAL STANDARDS / Jones, Clement J – 1980 – 9 – 92-3-101715-2 – fr UNESCO [170]
MASS MEDIA MINISTRIES – (See also: Mass Media Newsletter) – Bi-weekly Newsletter. v1-11. 1963-1974 – 1 – us UMI [370]
MASS MEDIA NEWSLETTER – (See also: Mass Media Ministries) – v12-. 1975- – 1,5,6,9 – us UMI [370]
MASS PRODUCTION – 1945-58 – 7 – uk Microform Academic [338]
MASS SPECTROMETRY REVIEWS – v1-. 1982- – 1,5,6,9 – us UMI [073]
MASS SPECTROMETRY REVIEWS – v1-5. 1982-86 – 1,5,6 – us Princeton Micro [073]
MASS TRANSIT – (1983-. 1,5,6,9) – v1-. 1974- – 1 – us UMI [073]

MASS UND WERK – Zuerich. Zweimonatschrift fuer freie deutsche Kultur. Nov. Dec. 1937-Sept. Nov. 1940 (complete) – 1 – 35.00r – us Hoover Inst Photo [073]

MASS UND WERT : ZWEIMONATSSCHRIFT FUER FREIE DEUTSCHE KULTUR – Zuerich. Sept 1937-Nov 1940 – 2r – 1 – gw Mikrofilm [949]

MASSA EREZ YISRA'EL. SPB., 1896-1897 / Derenbourg, J – BJ-32-62 1 – 9 – ne IDC [900]

MASSA MESHULLAM MI-VOLTERRA BE-EREZ-YISRA'EL BI-SHENAT 5241 / ed by Yaari, A – Jerusalem. 1949. BJ-27-8 1 – 9 – ne IDC [550]

MASSA'AM SHEL RABBI HAYYIM BEN ATTAR VA-HAVURATO LE-EREZ-YISRA'EL / Mann, J – v. 7. Tarbiz. 1936. BJ-27-22 1 – 9 – ne IDC [270]

MASSACHUSETTS : GENERAL LAWS ANNOTATED – St Paul: West Pub Co, 1958-Apr 1996 update – 9 – $1,615.00 set – us Hein [340]

MASSACHUSETTS : ITS HISTORIANS AND ITS HISTORY : AN OBJECT LESSON / Adams, Charles Francis – Boston: Houghton, Mifflin, 1894, c1893 – 1mf – us A.T.L.A. [976]

MASSACHUSETTS : SESSION LAWS OF AMERICAN STATES AND TERRITORIES – 1775-1994 – 9 – $2,739.00 set – us Hein [340]

Massachusetts *see*
- MASSACHUSETTS APPELLATE DIVISION REPORTS
- MASSACHUSETTS SUPREME COURT REPORTS
- REPORTS AND OPINIONS (A-G)
- REPORTS, POST-NRS
- REPORTS, PRE-NRS
- STATE LABOR REPORTS
- STATE WATER RESOURCES REPORTS

Massachusetts. Agricultural Experiment Station *see*
- ANNUAL REPORT
- BULLETIN
- CIRCULAR
- CONTROL SERIES BULLETIN
- METEOROLOGICAL SERIES BULLETIN
- PROGRESS REPORT
- RESEARCH IN REVIEW
- SPECIAL BULLETIN UNNUMBERED
- TECHNICAL BULLETIN

Massachusetts. Agricultural Extension Service *see*
- BULLETIN
- PUBLICATION

Massachusetts Anti-Slavery Society *see* ANNUAL REPORT AND PROCEEDINGS

MASSACHUSETTS APPELLATE DIVISION REPORTS : BOSTON MUNICIPAL COURT / Massachusetts – 1v. 1935 (all publ) – 5mf – 9 – $7.50 – LLMC 84-159 – us L.L.M.C. [340]

MASSACHUSETTS ASSOCIATION OF BOARDS OF HEALTH JOURNAL *see* AMERICAN JOURNAL OF PUBLIC HYGIENE

MASSACHUSETTS ATTORNEY GENERAL REPORTS AND OPINIONS – (6 1832-1977 $315.00. 9 1977-1993 $97.50) – 1832-1993 – 6,9 – $412.50set – us Hein [340]

MASSACHUSETTS BAPTIST MISSIONARY MAGAZINE – 1-4. September 1803-December 1816 – 1 – us UMI [240]

MASSACHUSETTS BAPTIST MISSIONARY MAGAZINE – Boston. Sept 1803-1816 – 1 – 43.00 – us A.B.H.S. [071]

MASSACHUSETTS BAR ASSOCIATION REPORTS – 1st to 5th annual meetings. 1911-15 (all publ) – 5mf – 9 – $7.50 – LLMC 84-600 – us L.L.M.C. [073]

MASSACHUSETTS BIBLE SOCIETY : ANNUAL REPORT – 1812-1976 (complete) – 3r – 1 – ATLA S0413 – us A.T.L.A. [240]

MASSACHUSETTS BIRTH INDEX 1841-1895 – (mf ed 1988) – 417mf – 9 – 0-87623-061-3 – us Holbrook [920]

Massachusetts. Board of Conciliation and Arbitration *see*
- REPORTS

Massachusetts. Board of Gas and Electric Light Commissioners *see* REPORTS

Massachusetts. Board of Railroad Commissioners *see* REPORTS

MASSACHUSETTS CEMETERY RECORDS *see* QUABBIN PARK 1741-1984

MASSACHUSETTS CHARITABLE FIRE SOCIETY PAPERS, 1792-1970 – Massachusetts Historical Society – 5r – 1 – $380.00 – us UMI [978]

MASSACHUSETTS CHURCH RECORDS – Scituate Church Records 1695-1871 (19mf) and Warren Church Records 1791-1866 (5mf) – 9 – us Holbrook [920]

MASSACHUSETTS CHURCH RECORDS *see* WARREN 1791-1869

MASSACHUSETTS COLLECTION OF MARTIAL MUSICK. / Robinson, Alvan – Second edition, corrected, improved and enlarged. Exeter, N.H.: Alvan Robinson, 1820. MUSIC 3080, Item 2 – 1 – us L of C Photodup [780]

MASSACHUSETTS COLLECTION OF MARTIAL MUSICK, CONTAINING A PLAIN, EASY AND CONCISE INTRODUCTION TO THE GROUNDS OF MARTIAL MUSICK. / Robinson, Alvan – Designed principally for the benefit of the militia of the United States. Hallowell, Maine: E. Goodale, 1818. MUSIC 3080, Item 1 – 1 – us L of C Photodup [780]

Massachusetts. College of Agriculture. Holdsworth Natural Resources Center *see* PLANNING AND RESOURCE DEVELOPMENT SERIES

Massachusetts. (Colony) *see* RECORDS OF THE GOVERNOR AND COMPANY OF THE MASSACHUSETTS BAY IN NEW ENGLAND

Massachusetts. Commission Against Discrimination *see* REPORTS

Massachusetts. Commission on Economy and Efficiency *see* REPORTS

Massachusetts. Comptroller's Division *see*
- ABSTRACTS OF THE FINANCIAL REPORTS
- FINANCIAL REPORTS
- TAX REFERENCE MANUALS

MASSACHUSETTS CONTESTED ELECTION CASES / Massachusetts. Supreme Court – v1-2. 1903-42 (all publ) – 7mf – 9 – $10.50 – LLMC 84-157 – us L.L.M.C. [340]

MASSACHUSETTS DEATH INDEX 1841-1895 – (mf ed 1988) – 310mf – 9 – 0-87623-063-X – us Holbrook [920]

Massachusetts. Dept. of Banking and Insurance. Division of Banks and Loan Agencies *see*
- REPORTS OF THE COMMISSIONER OF BANKS
- REPORTS OF THE MASSACHUSETTS' COMMISSIONER OF BANKS RELATING TO LICENSED SMALL LOAN LENDERS

Massachusetts. Dept. of Banking and Insurance. Division of Insurance *see* REPORTS OF THE COMMISSIONER OF INSURANCE

Massachusetts. Dept. of Corporations and Taxation *see*
- AGGREGATES OF POLLS, PROPERTY AND TAXES
- REPORTS

Massachusetts. Dept. of Corporations and Taxation. Bureau of Accounts *see*
- MUNICIPAL BULLETIN
- REPORT ON THE STATISTICS OF MUNICIPAL FINANCES

Massachusetts. Dept. of Labor and Industries. Division of Employment Security *see* REPORTS

Massachusetts. Dept. of Labor and Industries. Division of Minimum Wage *see* REPORTS

Massachusetts. Dept. of Labor and Industries. Division of Statistics *see*
- DIRECTORY OF LABOR ORGANIZATIONS
- REPORT ON THE STATISTICS OF LABOR

Massachusetts. Dept. of Public Utilities *see* REPORTS

MASSACHUSETTS ECCLESIASTICAL LAW / Buck, Edward – Boston: Gould & Lincoln, 1866 – 4mf – 9 – $6.00 – LLMC 92-119 – us L.L.M.C. [340]

Massachusetts. General Court. Committee on Railways and Canals *see* REPORTS OF THE RAILROAD CORPORATIONS IN THE STATE OF MASSACHUSETTS

Massachusetts Historical Society *see* PROCEEDINGS OF THE MASSACHUSETTS HISTORICAL SOCIETY

Massachusetts Horticultural Society. Boston *see* DICTIONARY CATALOG OF THE LIBRARY OF THE MASSACHUSETTS HORTICULTURAL SOCIETY

Massachusetts Horticultural Society. Library *see* DICTIONARY CATALOG

Massachusetts Institute of Technology. Center for International Studies *see* THE EMERGING NATIONS

Massachusetts. Insurance Dept *see* REPORTS OF THE LOAN FUND ASSOCIATIONS, BY THE INSURANCE COMMISSIONERS

MASSACHUSETTS LAW / Simpson, Frank Leslie – 4th ed. Boston: Boston University, 1926. 694p. LL-1040 – 1 – us L of C Photodup [340]

THE MASSACHUSETTS LAW OF LANDLORD AND TENANT. INCLUDING THE CASES IN VOL. 170 OF THE REPORTS, AND THE LEGISLATION OF 1898 / Hall, Prescott Farnsworth – (Supplement. Boston, 1903. 47 p. LL-1668) – Boston, Reed, 1899. 534 p. LL-1668 – 1 – us L of C Photodup [340]

MASSACHUSETTS LAW QUARTERLY – (Add vols as copyright expires) – v1-5. 1915-1920 – 38mf – $57.00 – LLMC 90-326 – us L.L.M.C. [073]

MASSACHUSETTS LAW QUARTERLY *see* MASSACHUSETTS LAW REVIEW

MASSACHUSETTS LAW REVIEW – (v1-69 1915-84 on reel or mf $665.00. v70-80 1985-95 on mf $176.00. Title varies: v1-62 1915-77 as Massachusetts Law Quarterly) – v1-80. 1915-95 – 5,6,9 – $841.00 set – us Hein [340]

Massachusetts. Laws, Statutes, etc *see* A COMPILATION OF MASSACHUSETTS LAW RELATING TO PRIVACY AND PERSONAL DATA

MASSACHUSETTS MAGAZINE – v. 1-8. January 1789-December 1796 – 1 – us UMI [073]

MASSACHUSETTS MARRIAGE INDEX 1841-1895 – (mf ed 1988) – 327mf – 9 – 0-87623-062-1 – us Holbrook [920]

MASSACHUSETTS MERCURY – Boston. Mass. 1793-1803. New England Palladium. 1803-1820. Sold as one unit – 3 – us Readex [071]

Massachusetts. Minimum Wage Commission *see* REPORTS

MASSACHUSETTS MUSICAL JOURNAL – Boston. v1-2 n20. 1885-57 – 1r – 1 – £60.00 – uk Chadwyck [780]

MASSACHUSETTS MUSICAL JOURNAL – v1-2. May 1855-Feb 1857 – 1 – 175.00 – us Opus [073]

THE MASSACHUSETTS PEACE OFFICER / Williams, Gorham Deane – Boston, Reed, 1891. 276 p. LL-1563 – 1 – us L of C Photodup [340]

Massachusetts. Public Service Commission *see* REPORTS

MASSACHUSETTS REGISTER – (1982-. 1,5,6,9) – 1976- – 1 – us UMI [073]

MASSACHUSETTS REVIEW – 1959- 1; 1971- 5,6; 1976- 4 x 6 in. 9 – us UMI [071]

Massachusetts. Secretary of the Commonwealth *see*
- MASSACHUSETTS SOLDIERS AND SAILORS OF THE REVOLUTIONARY WAR
- RETURNS OF THE RAILROAD CORPORATIONS IN MASSACHUSETTS

MASSACHUSETTS SOLDIERS AND SAILORS OF THE REVOLUTIONARY WAR / Massachusetts. Secretary of the Commonwealth – 1-17 V. 1896-1908 – 1 – 139.00 – us L of C Photodup [975]

THE MASSACHUSETTS SPY – Worcester. Mass. 1775-1820 – 1,3 – us Readex [071]

Massachusetts. State Bar Association *see* PROCEEDINGS

Massachusetts. State Tax Commission *see* REPORT SUBMITTING AN EQUALIZATION AND APPORTIONMENT UPON THE SEVERAL CITIES AND TOWNS

Massachusetts. Supervisor of Administration *see* REPORTS

Massachusetts. Supreme Court *see*
- CUSHING'S ELECTION CASES
- DAVIS' LAND COURT CASES
- MASSACHUSETTS CONTESTED ELECTION CASES
- QUINCY'S REPORTS
- RULES AND ORDERS
- RULES OF PROBATE COURTS
- RUSSELL'S ELECTION CASES
- THACHER'S CRIMINAL CASES

MASSACHUSETTS SUPREME COURT REPORTS / Massachusetts – (Pre-NRS: v1-138 1804-85 955mf $1,432.00. Updates planned) – v1-233. 1804-1919 – 1733mf – 9 – $2,599.00 – LLMC 80-810 – us L.L.M.C. [340]

MASSACHUSETTS SUPREME COURT REPORTS *see*
- CUSHING'S ELECTION CASES
- DAVIS' LAND COURT CASES
- MASSACHUSETTS CONTESTED ELECTION CASES
- QUINCY'S REPORTS
- RULES AND ORDERS
- RULES OF PROBATE COURTS
- RUSSELL'S ELECTION CASES
- THACHER'S CRIMINAL CASES

Massachusetts. Supreme Judicial Court *see*
- A CHARGE DELIVERED TO THE GRAND JURY FOR THE COUNTY OF ESSEX...HELD AT IPSWICH. MAY TERM, 1832
- THE RIGHTS OF JURORS IN CRIMINAL CASES. OPINION BY HON. B. F. THOMAS.

MASSACHUSETTS VITAL RECORD TRANSCRIPTS TO 1850 – Boston: Thomas W. Baldwin, 1917 – 1mf – 9 – us Holbrook [920]

MASSACHUSETTS VITAL RECORD TRANSCRIPTS TO 1850 *see*
- ABINGTON 1691-1849
- ACTON 1734-1849
- ALFORD 1759-1849
- AMESBURY 1685-1849
- ANDOVER 1647-1849
- ARLINGTON 1754-1849
- ASHBURNHAM 1752-1849
- ASHFIELD 1740-1849
- ATHOL 1737-1849
- ATTLEBORO 1692-1849
- BARRE 1718-1849
- BECKETT 1753-1849
- BEDFORD 1693-1849
- BELLINGHAM 1698-1849
- BEVERLY 1650-1849
- BILLERICA 1627-1849
- BOLTON 1728-1849
- BOXBOROUGH 1767-1849
- BOXFORD 1666-1849
- BRADFORD 1669-1849
- BRIDGEWATER 1608-1849
- BRIMFIELD 1696-1849
- BROCKTON 1795-1849
- BROOKFIELD 1696-1849
- BROOKLINE 1655-1849
- BUCKLAND 1841-1849
- BURLINGTON 1752-1849
- CAMBRIDGE 1635-1849
- CARLISLE 1732-1849
- CARVER 1748-1849
- CHARLEMONT 1719-1849
- CHELMSFORD 1645-1849
- CHELSEA 1655-1849
- CHESTER 1762-1849
- CHILMARK 1673-1849
- COHASSET 1737-1849
- COLRAIN 1740-1849
- CONWAY 1750-1849
- DALTON 1772-1849
- DANA 1801-1849
- DANVERS 1652-1849
- DARTMOUTH 1650-1849
- DEERFIELD 1676-1849
- DOUGLAS 1724-1849
- DOVER 1753-1849
- DRACUT 1687-1849
- DUDLEY 1725-1849
- DUNSTABLE 1681-1849
- DUXBURY 1681-1849
- EAST BRIDGEWATER 1769-1849
- EDGARTOWN 1656-1849
- ESSEX 1708-1849
- FOXBOROUGH 1720-1849
- FRAMINGHAM 1687-1849
- GARDNER 1737-1849
- GEORGETOWN 1779-1849
- GILL 1719-1849
- GLOUCESTER 1641-1849
- GRAFTON 1693-1849
- GRANVILLE 1735-1849
- GREAT BARRINGTON 1741-1849
- GREENFIELD 1709-1849
- GROTON 1648-1849
- HAMILTON 1750-1849
- HANSON 1779-1849
- HARDWICK 1670-1849
- HARVARD 1723-1849
- HAVERHILL 1641-1849
- HEATH 1737-1849
- HINSDALE 1784-1849
- HOLDEN 1739-1849
- HOLLISTON 1720-1849
- HOPKINTON 1705-1849
- HUBBARDSTON 1746-1849
- HULL 1630-1849
- IPSWICH 1648-1849
- KINGSTON 1683-1849
- LAWRENCE 1847-1849
- LEE 1738-1849
- LEICESTER 1738-1849
- LEOMINSTER 1717-1849
- MALDEN 1677-1849
- MANCHESTER 1661-1849
- MANSFIELD 1730-1849
- MARBLEHEAD 1654-1849
- MARLBOROUGH 1652-1849
- MEDFIELD 1651-1849
- MEDFORD 1673-1849
- MEDWAY 1650-1849
- MENDON 1665-1849

- METHUEN 1714-1849
- MIDDLEFIELD 1758-1849
- MIDDLETON 1703-1849
- MILFORD 1732-1849
- MILLBURY 1761-1849
- MONTAGUE 1737-1849
- MONTGOMERY 1698-1851
- NANTUCKET 1662-1849
- NATICK 1718-1849
- NEW ASHFORD 1755-1859
- NEW BEDFORD 1650-1849
- NEWBURY 1635-1849
- NEWBURYPORT 1740-1849
- NEWTON 1621-1849
- NORTHBRIDGE 1748-1849
- NORTON 1688-1849
- OAKHAM 1739-1849
- OTIS 1764-1849
- OXFORD 1713-1849
- PALMER 1727-1849
- PELHAM 1709-1849
- PEMBROKE 1692-1849
- PERU 1742-1849
- PETERSHAM 1739-1849
- PHILLIPSTON 1762-1849
- PLYMPTON 1679-1849
- PRINCETON 1742-1849

MASSACHUSETTS VITAL RECORDS *see*
- ABINGTON 1691-1892
- ACUSHNET 1860-1900
- ADAMS 1878-1894
- AGAWAM 1855-1892
- ALFORD 1759-1906
- AMHERST 1747-1891
- ANDOVER 1647-1905
- ASHBURNHAM 1735-1900
- ASHBY 1754-1891
- ASHFIELD 1750-1895
- ASHLAND 1840-1895
- ATTLEBORO 1694-1890
- AUBURN 1704-1900
- AYER 1871-1900
- BARNSTABLE 1643-1892
- BARRE 1718-1895
- BECKET 1765-1900
- BELCHERTOWN 1765-1893
- BERKLEY 1670-1900
- BERNARDSTON 1735-1897
- BEVERLY 1653-1907
- BLACKSTONE 1844-1903
- BLANDFORD 1737-1860
- BOLTON 1726-1905
- BOSTON BIRTHS 1849-1881
- BOSTON BIRTHS 1882-1895
- BOSTON DEATHS 1849-1890
- BOSTON MARRIAGES 1849-1890
- BOSTON-OUT-OF-TOWN MARRIAGES 1858-1895
- BOXBOROUGH 1767-1905
- BOYLSTON 1742-1905
- BREWSTER 1745-1900
- BRIDGEWATER 1641-1900
- BRIGHTON 1771-1873
- BRIMFIELD 1696-1893
- BROOKFIELD 1700-1895
- BUCKLAND 1873-1895
- CARVER 1733-1900
- CHARLEMONT 1765-1899
- CHARLESTOWN 1692-1874
- CHARLTON 1742-1890
- CHATHAM 1693-1900
- CHELMSFORD 1653-1900
- CHESHIRE 1793-1892
- CHESTER 1793-1892
- CHESTERFIELD 1762-1892
- CHICOPEE 1848-1890
- CHILMARK 1674-1900
- CLARKSBURG 1798-1915
- CLINTON 1850-1900
- COHASSET 1717-1900
- COLRAIN 1741-1895
- CONWAY 1749-1892
- CUMMINGTON 1751-1902
- DANA 1801-1890
- DARTMOUTH 1650-1900
- DEERFIELD 1675-1898
- DENNIS 1710-1890
- DIGHTON 1695-1890
- DORCHESTER 1631-1869
- DOUGLAS 1718-1890
- DRACUT 1697-1900
- DUDLEY 1725-1891
- DUNSTABLE 1679-1900
- EAST BRIDGEWATER 1754-1900
- EASTHAMPTON 1785-1892
- EASTON 1693-1900
- EDGARTOWN 1651-1900
- EGREMONT 1838-1897
- ENFIELD 1770-1890
- ERVING 1844-1906
- ESSEX 1819-1892
- FALL RIVER 1803-1889
- FALMOUTH 1688-1892
- FITCHBURG 1751-1895
- FLORIDA 1781-1900
- FOXBOROUGH 1720-1897
- FREETOWN 1686-1890
- GARDNER 1762-1892
- GEORGETOWN 1639-1905
- GILL 1754-1895
- GLOUCESTER 1634-1895
- GOSHEN 1781-1898
- GRAFTON 1693-1900
- GRANBY 1710-1900
- GRANVILLE 1732-1902
- GREAT BARRINGTON 1745-1903
- GREENFIELD 1750-1891
- GREENWICH 1741-1890
- GROTON 1640-1900
- HALIFAX 1703-1902
- HAMILTON 1714-1897
- HAMPDEN 1878-1895
- HANCOCK 1767-1896
- HANOVER 1712-1895
- HANSON 1820-1900
- HARDWICK 1735-1895
- HARVARD 1723-1900
- HARWICH 1673-1895
- HAWLEY 1727-1892
- HEATH 1763-1899
- HINGHAM 1635-1900
- HINSDALE 1860-1893
- HOLBROOK 1872-1900
- HOLLAND 1771-1890
- HOLYOKE 1850-1895
- HUBBARDSTON 1747-1900
- HUDSON 1866-1900
- HULL 1630-1900
- HYDE PARK 1868-1892
- IPSWICH 1634-1892
- KINGSTON 1683-1900
- LAKEVILLE 1853-1902
- LANCASTER 1647-1905
- LANESBORO 1765-1895
- LAWRENCE 1847-1905
- LEE 1844-1892
- LEICESTER 1706-1891
- LENOX 1756-1890
- LEOMINSTER 1715-1900
- LEVERETT 1736-1890
- LEYDEN 1776-1890
- LONGMEADOW 1784-1895
- LUDLOW 1774-1855
- LUNENBURG 1707-1900
- MANCHESTER 1624-1892
- MANSFIELD 1703-1895
- MARSHFIELD 1631-1890
- MASHPIE 1834-1899
- MEDWAY 1712-1900
- MIDDLEBOROUGH 1658-1900
- MIDDLEFIELD 1774-1899
- MIDDLETON 1704-1905
- MILFORD 1732-1900
- MILLBURY 1761-1899
- MONROE 1777-1896
- MONTAGUE 1731-1891
- MONTEREY 1825-1895
- MONTGOMERY 1739-1899
- MOUNT WASHINGTON 1745-1903
- NANTUCKET 1662-1900
- NEEDHAM 1711-1858
- NEW ASHFORD 1844-1920
- NEW BRAINTREE 1751-1913
- NEW MARLBORO 1734-1890
- NEW SALEM 1742-1894
- NORTH ANDOVER 1854-1905
- NORTH BROOKFIELD 1841-1890
- NORTHAMPTON 1650-1893
- NORTHBOROUGH 1716-1892
- NORTHBRIDGE 1748-1900
- NORTHFIELD 1717-1902
- NORTON 1688-1900
- NORWELL 1633-1900
- OAKHAM 1750-1895
- ORANGE 1767-1891
- ORLEANS 1637-1892
- OTIS 1764-1892
- OXFORD 1690-1905
- PALMER 1731-1904
- PAXTON 1749-1890
- PEABODY 1855-1905
- PELHAM 1738-1895
- PEMBROKE 1662-1897
- PEPPERELL 1699-1891
- PERU 1771-1894
- PETERSHAM 1743-1893
- PHILLIPSTON 1762-1900
- PITTSFIELD 1761-1899
- PLAINFIELD 1785-1863
- PLYMOUTH 1663-1890
- PLYMPTON 1649-1900
- PRESCOTT 1795-1890
- PRINCETON 1676-1900
- PROVINCETOWN 1620-1890
- QUINCY 1792-1889
- RANDOLPH 1731-1890
- RAYNHAM 1699-1895
- RICHMOND 1791-1901
- ROCHESTER 1646-1900
- ROCKPORT 1840-1900
- ROWE 1774-1848
- ROWLEY 1639-1900
- ROXBURY 1630-1867
- ROYALSTON 1772-1895
- RUSSELL 1776-1896
- RUTLAND 1719-1894
- SANDISFIELD 1762-1894
- SANDWICH 1651-1900
- SAVOY 1736-1854
- SCITUATE 1633-1900
- SEEKONK 1760-1900
- SHARON 1727-1900
- SHEFFIELD 1726-1897
- SHELBURNE 1756-1895
- SHIRLEY 1729-1892
- SHREWSBURY 1717-1890
- SHUTESBURY 1746-1890
- SOMERSET 1680-1892
- SOUTH HADLEY 1730-1890
- SOUTHAMPTON 1758-1890
- SOUTHBRIDGE 1816-1889
- SOUTHWICK 1771-1890
- SPENCER 1744-1890
- SPRINGFIELD 1640-1894
- STERLING 1740-1900
- STOCKBRIDGE 1737-1887
- STOUGHTON 1709-1900
- STOW 1669-1905
- STURBRIDGE 1723-1891
- SUNDERLAND 1778-1908
- SUTTON 1720-1825
- TEMPLETON 1760-1895
- TISBURY 1669-1900
- TOLLAND 1843-1900
- TOPSFIELD 1645-1905
- TOWNSEND 1726-1890
- TRURO 1702-1890
- TYRINGHAM 1759-1898
- UXBRIDGE 1702-1900
- WARE 1735-1890
- WAREHAM 1719-1892
- WARREN 1727-1893
- WARWICK 1739-1890
- WASHINGTON 1755-1907
- WAYLAND 1638-1905
- WEBSTER 1832-1905
- WELLFLEET 1723-1890
- WENDELL 1763-1893
- WENHAM 1642-1900
- WEST BOYLSTON 1843-1899
- WEST BRIDGEWATER 1762-1900
- WEST BROOKFIELD 1848-1891
- WEST NEWBURY 1804-1905
- WEST ROXBURY 1712-1873
- WEST STOCKBRIDGE 1774-1902
- WESTBOROUGH 1717-1900
- WESTFIELD 1669-1895
- WESTFORD 1726-1902
- WESTHAMPTON 1778-1893
- WESTMINSTER 1728-1905
- WESTPORT 1717-1900
- WEYMOUTH 1633-1900
- WHATELY 1771-1895
- WILBRAHAM 1762-1895
- WILLIAMSBURG 1771-1899
- WILLIAMSTOWN 1757-1900
- WINCHENDON 1763-1891
- WINDSOR 1778-1908
- WORCESTER 1719-1890
- WORTHINGTON 1763-1895
- YARMOUTH 1665-1890

MASSACHUSETTS VITAL RECORDS 1620-1905 : MANUSCRIPTS ON MICROFICHES – (Individual listings available. With a 3mf-bibliography $3) – 22,000mf coll ca 100mf per mth – 9 – us Holbrook [920]

MASSACHUSETTS VITAL RECORDS TO 1850 – (Towns "A" through "P" now available. Remainder to be processed on an irregular basis. Inquire) – 2304mf complete coll – 9 – us Holbrook [920]

MASSACHUSETTS VITALS INDEXES 1841-1895 – 9 – us Holbrook [920]

"MASSACRE BY INDIANS...." / Bishop, L C – 1865 – 1 – us KS Hist [978]

Massalongo, A B *see*
- ALCUNI GENERI DI LICHENI NUOVAMENTE LIMITATI E DESCRITTI
- MEMORIE LICHENOGRAFICHE CON UN' APPENDICE ALLE RICERCHE SULL' AUTONOMIA DEI LICHENI CROSTOSI
- RICHERCHE SULL' AUTONOMIA DEI LICHENI CROSTOSI
- SYMMICTA LICHENUM NOVORUM VEL MINUS COGNITORUM

MASSA'OT EREZ-YISRA'EL LE-RABBI MOSHEH BASOLA / ed by Ben-Zvi, I – Jerusalem 1938. BJ-27-9 1 – 9 – ne IDC [956]

Massaquoi-Fahnbulleh, Fatima *see* WRITINGS AND PAPERS OF FATIMA MASSAQUOI-FAHNBULLEH

THE MASSARENES / Ouida – British Fiction Archive: Unit 3 – 9 – uk Bell [830]

LA MASSE : FRONT DE LIBERATION POPULAIRE – Montreal, Canada. mai 1968-mar 1970 – 1r – 1 – Can$25.00 – cn Can Microfilming [072]

Masse, Daniel *see* AU DAHOMEY, 1892

Massebieau, L *see* LES COLLOQUES SCOLAIRES DU XVIE SIECLE

Massenbach, Eugen Freiherr von *see* DIE MORGEN STUNDEN EINES KOENIGES AN SEINEN BRUDER SOHN 1766

Massenet, J *see* HERODINDE

MASSES – 1932-34 – 1 – 55.00 – cn McLaren [971]

MASSES / Jamaica Labour Movement – Kingston, Jamaica. v4-6. 1944-46 – 1r – 1 – us Ross [331]

MASSES : A MONTHLY MAGAZINE DEVOTED TO THE INTERESTS OF THE WORKING PEOPLE – New York. v1-10. 1911-17 – 1r – 1 – us Ross [331]

MASSES – New York. v. 1-10, no. 2. 1911-1917 – 1 – us NY Public [073]

MASSES – Revue mensuelle d'action proletarienne puis Bulletin mensuel d'information des groupes d'etudes; Socialisme et liberte. Dir. Rene Lefeuvre. Paris. avr 1931-avr 1932, 1933-juil 1934, janv 1939, 1946-oct nov 1947 – 1 – fr A.C.R.P.P. [073]

MASSES OF INDIA – Paris, 1925-28 – 1r – 1 – us Ross [073]

MASSES, VESPERS, LITANIES, HYMNS, PSALMS, ANTHEMS & MOTETS / Carr, Benjamin – Composed, selected, and arranged for the use of Catholic churches in the United States of America. A new ed. with an appendix. Baltimore: J. Carr 181?. MUSIC 3082, Item 3 – 1 – us L of C Photodup [780]

Massey, Isabella *see* TEXT- UND QUELLENSTUDIEN ZU DEM ANONYMEN MITTELDEUTSCHEN GEDICHT VON DEN SIEBEN WEISEN MEISTERN

Massey, MS *see* THE DEVELOPMENT OF A CRITERION-REFERENCED HEALTH KNOWLEDGE INSTRUMENT FOR GRADES FOUR, FIVE, AND SIX

MASSEY-HARRIS ILLUSTRATED – Toronto: Massey Press, [188- or 189–19–] – 9 – cn C.I.H.M. [971]

MASSEY'S ILLUSTRATED – n.s., v. 1-7. 1888-95 – 1 – 185.00 – cn McLaren [073]

MASSEY'S ILLUSTRATED – v. 1. 1882-84 – 1 – 65.00 – cn McLaren [073]

MASSEY'S MAGAZINE – v1-3. Jan 1896-Jun 1897 – 1 – cn Precision [073]

Massiah, Joycelin *see* WOMEN IN DEVELOPING ECONOMIES

Massias, Nicolas *see* LETTRE SUR L'HEREDITE, A MESSIEURS LES DISCIPLES DE SAINT-SIMON

Massicotte, Edmond-Joseph *see* TABLEAUX DE EDMOND-J. MASSICOTTE

Massicotte, Edouard-Zotique *see* COLLECTION

Massie, John *see* CORINTHIANS

Massie, M D *see* PAST AND PRESENT OF PIKE COUNTY

Massie, Nathaniel *see* NATHANIEL MASSIE PAPERS, MS 3282

Massie, R H *see* THE NATIVE TRIBES OF THE TRANSVAAL

Massignon, Louis F-J *see* LE MAROC DANS LES PREMIERES ANNEES DU 16E SIECLE...

Massion, A *see* LES POTIERS DE GRES. PERMANENCES ET CHANGEMENTS TECHNO-ECONOMIQUES DANS UNE COMMUNAUTE ARTISANALE RURALE

Masslp, J M *see*
- CONTRIBUTION A L'INVENTAIRE DES RESSOURCES DU TIBESTI
- NOMADES ET NOMADISME EN ENNEDI

Masson, CF Ph *see* MEMOIRES SECRETS SUR LA RUSSIE ET PARTICULIEREMENT SUR LA FIN DU REGNE DE CATHERINE 2 ET SUR CELUI DE PAULLER

Masson, David *see*
- BRITISH NOVELISTS AND THEIR STYLES
- CARLYLE, PERSONALLY AND IN HIS WRITINGS
- EDINBURGH SKETCHES AND MEMORIES
- MEMORIES OF LONDON IN THE 'FORTIES'

Masson de Saint-Amand, Amand N *see* MEMOIRE STATISTIQUE DU DEPARTEMENT DE L'EURE

Masson, F *see* STAPELIAE NOVAE: OR A COLLECTION OF SEVERAL NEW SPECIES OF THAT GENUS
Masson, Lorenzo *see* ACTION LIBERALE
Masson, V M *see* HISTORY OF CIVILIZATIONS OF CENTRAL ASIA
THE MASSORETIC TEXT AND THE ANCIENT VERSIONS OF THE BOOK OF MICAH / Taylor, John – London: Williams & Norgate, 1890. 1 fiche – 9 – us A.T.L.A. [240]
MASSOT U-MEHKARIM, LE-ZEKHER LINDA R. MILLER / Miller, L R – New York. 1938. BJ-100-75 1 – 9 – ne IDC [900]
MASSOVAIA POLITICHESKAIA STACHKA I SOTSIALDEMOKRATIIA / Bebel, Auguste – Peterburg: Utro, 1906 – 1 – us U.W. Library [330]
Massow, VH von *see* DAIRY IMPORTS INTO SUB-SAHARAN AFRICA
MAST JOURNAL – (v 1-98 1896-1993 Can$20.00y) – Winnipeg. v15-21. 1988-94 – 9 – Can$115.00y – cn Micromedia [073]
Masta, Henry Lorne *see* ABENAKI INDIAN LEGENDS, GRAMMAR AND PLACE NAMES
DIE MASTABA DES SEMNI-KAI IM VEREIN MIT A.E.P / ed by Bissing, F W von – 2v. Weigall. 1905-11. BNE-389 1 – 9 – ne IDC [930]
LES MASTABAS DE L'ANCIEN EMPIRE FRAGMENT DU DERNIER OUVRAGE / Mariette, A – Paris. 1889. BNE-363 1 – 9 – ne IDC [930]
Masten, Arthur H *see* MEMORIAL OF FRANCIS M. SCOTT.
MASTER BUILDER – Portland OR. Dec 24 1924, Mar 15-Apr 15 June 3 24 1925, Feb 17 24 Mar 3 Apr 15 1926 – 1 – us U.O. Library [071]
MASTER FREQUENCY DATA BASE (SERVICE GROUP CODE SEQUENCE) / U.S. National Technical Information Service – Quarterly. Contains non-government frequency assignments – 9 – us N.T.I.S. [000]
MASTER INTERNATIONAL FREQUENCY LIST *see* INTERNATIONAL FREQUENCY LIST
THE MASTER METHOD: AN ENQUIRY INTO THE LIQUOR PROBLEM IN AMERICA / Hayler, Guy – Introd. by G.W. Kitchin. 1st ed. Newcastle-on-Tyne: Temperance Institute, 1901. 120p. illus. fold. col. map – 1 – us U.W. Library [360]
MASTER NAMES FILE GAZETTEER – 9 – A$37.00 – at A.U.S.L.I.G. [920]
THE MASTER OF BALLANTRAE : A WINTER'S TALE / Stevenson, Robert Louis – London, New York: Cassell, 1889 – 1 roll – 1 – 1-55879-676-2 – uk Libr Preservation [830]
THE MASTER OF GREYLANDS / Wood, Ellen – British Fiction Archive: Unit 1 – 9 – uk Bell [830]
A MASTER OF MYSTERIES / Smith, Elizabeth Thomasina Meade (1854-1914) & Smith, Robert Eustace (pseud) – Illus. by J. Ambrose Walton. London: Ward, Lock & Co., (1898). 279p. 6 leaves of plates. 1 reel. 1260 – 1 – us U.W. Library [830]
Master of the Rolls *see* RERUM BRITANNICARUM MEDII AEVI SCRIPTORES
MASTER PLAN REPORT OF SURVEY / Singapore – Singapore. 1955. BD-578 1 – 9 – ne IDC [338]
Master Plumbers Association. Canada *see* THE MONTREAL BUILDER
Master, Ronald R *see* DRUG USAGE BY ATHLETES RELATED TO PERFORMANCE
MASTER WORSLEY'S BOOK ON THE HISTORY AND CONSTITUTION OF THE MIDDLE TEMPLE / Worsley, Charles; ed by Ingpen, Arthur R – London: Chiswick Press, 1910 – 5mf – 9 – $7.50 – LLMC 84-319 – us L.L.M.C. [340]
THE MASTER-CHRISTIAN / Corelli, Marie – British Fiction Archive: Unit 1 – 9 – uk Bell [830]
MASTERING MUSIC READING / McKinney, James C – Orig. manuscript, typed copy – 1 – 11.62 – us Baptist [240]
Masterman, Charles FG *see*
– FREDERICK DENISON MAURICE
– TENNYSON AS A RELIGIOUS TEACHER
MASTER-MISSIONARIES : CHAPTERS IN PIONEER EFFORT THROUGHOUT THE WORLD / Japp, Alexander Hay – (Includes bibliographical references) – New York: Robert Carter, 1881 – 1mf – 9 – 0-8370-6067-2 – 1986-0067 – us A.T.L.A. [240]
MASTERS ABSTRACTS – 1962- 1; 1970- 5,6; 1976- 4 x 6 in. 9 – us UMI [010]
Masters, Frank M *see* A HISTORY OF THE BETHEL BAPTIST ASSOCIATION IN KENTUCKY, 1807-1944
THE MASTER'S FRIENDSHIPS / Miller, James Russell – New York:Thomas Y Crowell, 1909 – 1mf – 9 – 0-8370-4431-6 – 1985-2431 – us A.T.L.A. [240]
MASTERS IN ART – v. 1-10. no. 2. 1900-February 1909 – 1 – us UMI [700]
MASTERS IN ENGLISH THEOLOGY : BEING THE KING'S COLLEGE LECTURES FOR 1877 / ed by Barry, Alfred – New York: E.P. Dutton, 1877 – 1mf – us A.T.L.A. [240]
MASTERS IN MODERN GERMAN LITERATURE / Lessing, Otto Eduard – Dresden: Carl Reissner, 1912. 196p. 1 reel. 1261 – 1 – us U.W. Library [430]
Masters, M T *see*
– VEGETABLE TERATOLOGY
– VEGETABLE TERATOLOGY AN ACCOUNT OF THE PRINCIPAL DEVIATIONS FROM THE USUAL STRUCTURE OF PLANTS
Masters, Victor I *see* THE HOME MISSION TASK
Masters, William Gallio *see* PAPERS
THE MASTER-SINGERS OF NUREMBERG = DIE MEISTERSINGER VON NUERNBERG : OPERA IN THREE ACTS / Wagner, Richard – (English and German in parallel columns. Includes musical selections from the opera, for voice) – Philadelphia: O Ditson, 1889 – 1 – us U.W. Library [790]
THE MASTER-SINGERS OF NUREMBERG : OPERA IN THREE ACTS; WITH GERMAN AND ENGLISH WORDS, AND THE MUSIC OF THE PRINCIPAL AIRS / Wagner, Richard – (Includes musical selections from the opera, for voice) – Philadelphia: O Ditson, 1889 – 1 – us U.W. Library [780]
O MASTERSTVE MAIAKOVSKOGO / Papernyi, Z – M. 1953. BR-1480 2 – 8 – ne IDC [920]
MASTERSTVO DERZHAVINA / Zapadov, A V – M. 1958. BR-7979 2 – 8 – ne IDC [460]
MASTERSTVO GOGOLIA / Belyi, A – Issledovanie. 1934. B-1278 2 – 8 – ne IDC [460]
THE MASTODEN GIGANTEUS OF NORTH AMERICA / Warren, J C – 2563 2. 1855 – 8 – ne IDC [590]
Mastrius, B *see* THEOLOGIA MORALIS AD MENTEM DD
MASTRO PAOLO – Philadelphia, PA, 1903 – 1mf or 1r – 1,9 – us I.H.R.C. [978]
Masuhr, Andreas *see* HAEMODYNAMISCHE UND METABOLISCHE REAKTIONEN IM TENNISSPORT – UNTER BERUECKSICHTIGUNG DES HOEHEREN LEBENSALTERS
MAT I DITIA V SOVETSKOI ROSSII / Arbore-Ralli, Ekaterina Zamfirevna – Moskva: Gos. izd-vo, 1920 – 1 – CSUX89-B1541 – us Hoover Inst Photo [306]
Mata Jimeno, Amador *see* PRONTUARIO DE LEGISLACION Y PRACTICA LABORAL
MATA PELADJARAN KEWARGAAN NEGARA (CIVICS) / Sakti, Slamet S – SE 4295 1. 1962? – 9 – ne IDC [950]
Matagrin, Amedee *see* HISTOIRE DE LA TOLERANCE RELIGIEUSE
MATANTE AURORE OU LE ROMAN IMPROMPTU / Longchamps & Boieldieu – French Theatre Series. Paris. Barba, an XI. 1803 – 9 – fr Hachette [410]
LE MATCH – Hull, Canada. 9 aut 1957-v1 n43. 7 jun 1958 – 1r – 1 – Can$45.00 – cn Can Microfilming [072]
MATCHBOX – New York, NY. 1978-83 – 8r – 1 – $400.00 – R04913 – us Library Micro [073]
MATCHBOX – -q. v.1, no.1, Spring Summer 1974. Palo Alto, Calif.: Western Regional Office, Amnesty International in the U.S., 1974- – 1 – us U.W. Library [073]
THE MATE OF THE DAYLIGHT, AND FRIENDS ASHORE / Jewett, Sarah Orne – Boston: Houghton, Mifflin and Co., 1884.254p – 1 – us U.W. Library [830]
Mateer, Samuel *see* NATIVE LIFE IN TRAVANCORE
Matenko, Percy *see* TIECK AND SOLGER
Mateos, Francisco *see*
– ASI ERA EL HERMANO AGUSTIN. UN JESUITA DESCONOCIDO. CINCUENTA ANOS DE HEROISMO CORONADOS POR EL MOCTIVIO. VIDA HEROICA DE AGUSTIN MARIA DIAZ ZAPATA...1869-1936
– DEMETRIO RAMOS PEREZ. EL TRATADO DE LIMITES DE 1750 Y LA EXPEDICIONS DE ITURIAGA AL ORINOCO...
– HISTORIA DE LA FUNDACION DEL CONVENTO DE RELIGIOSAS CARMELITAS DE BADAJOZ
– EL PADRE CONSTANTINO BAYLE (1882-1953)
Mateos, J *see*
– DE ORTHO SEU MATUTINO BYZANTINO
– DOCUMENTA HISTORICA
Mateos, Nicomedes *see* VEINTE Y SEIS CARTAS...VALDEGAMAS...ENSAYO...LIBERALISMO
Mateos Rodrigo, Gonzalo *see* TRATADO DE ARITMETICA Y ALGEBRA
Mateos, S F *see* FUNDACION DEL COLEGIO DE COYOACAN HERNAN Y MARTIN CORTES
MATER ADMIRABILIS : A HAND-BOOK OF INSTRUCTION ON THE POWER AND PREROGATIVES OF OUR BLESSED LADY / O'Brien, Cornelius – Montreal: D & J Sadlier, 1882 – 1mf – 9 – 0-8370-8366-4 – 1986-2366 – us A.T.L.A. [240]
MATER ADMIRABILIS : OR, FIRST FIFTEEN YEARS OF MARY IMMACULATE / Monnin, Alfred – New York: James B Kirker, 1865 – 2mf – 9 – 0-8370-7411-8 – 1986-1411 – us A.T.L.A. [240]
MATER ECCLESIA : AN INQUIRY INTO THE CONCEPT OF THE CHURCH AS MOTHER IN EARLY CHRISTIANITY / Plumpe, J C – 1943 – 4mf – 9 – ne Slangenburg [240]
MATER IALY DLIA ISTORII VYSSHAGO SUDA I NADZORA V PERVUIU POLOVINU.. / Gribovskii, Viacheslav Mikhailovich – St. Petersburg: Tip. Trud, 1901.vi,259p – 1 – us U.W. Library [947]
MATERIA INDICA / Ainslie, W – 2v. London. 1826. B-918 2 – 8 – ne IDC [580]
MATERIA MEDICA AMERICANA... / Schoepf, J D – Erlangae, 1787 – 2mf – 9 – ne IDC [615]
MATERIA MEDICA. LIBER I. DE PLANTIS / Linnaeus, Carl – 170. 1749 – 9 – ne IDC [615]
MATERIAL – Pattee, University Park, PA. 1983 – 203p 5mf – 9 – $0.50f – us Lawrence Pub [720]
MATERIAL 2 – Pattee, University Park, PA. 1984 – 38p 7mf – 9 – $0.50f – us Lawrence Pub [720]
MATERIAL CULTURE OF THE IGLULIK ESKIMOS / Mathiassen, T – BN 314 2. 1928 – 8 – ne IDC [306]
MATERIAL HANDLING ENGINEERING – v1-1945- 1; v26- 5,6; v32- 9 – us UMI [670]
MATERIAL HANDLING ILLUSTRATED *see* HANDLING AND SHIPPING
MATERIAL RE-CREATION IN THE APOSTOLIC FATHERS (T.U.U. 5-100) / O'Hagan, A P – Berlin, 1968 – 3mf – 9 – ne Slangenburg [220]
MATERIAL RELATING TO AMERICA / Great Britain. Parliament. House of Lords – 1702-1920. BRRAM – 1 – uk Microform Academic [970]
MATERIAL RELATING TO CANADA / United Society for the Propagation of the Gospel. Archives – 1 – uk Microform Academic [025]
MATERIAL REMAINS OF THE MEGIDDO CULT : WITH A CHAPTER BY ROBERT M. ENGBERG / May, Herbert Gordon – 1935 – 9 – $5.00f – 0-226-51177-4 – us U.C. Orient [930]
THE MATERIAL RESPONSE OF THE POLAR ESKIMO TO THEIR FAR ARCTIC ENVIRONMENT / Ekblaw, W E – BN-199 2. 1928 – 8 – ne IDC [306]
MATERIAL TESTING LABORATORIES / Gillemot, LF – 1970 – 38p – 9 – 92-3-100826-9 – fr UNESCO [620]
DAS MATERIALANGEBOT – Berlin, Die Wirtschaft. biweekly. 1973-77 – 1 – us U.W. Library [331]
MATERIALDIENST – (Lacks: v19-24 1956-61) – v14-55. 1951-92 – Inquire – 1 – ATLA S0774 – us A.T.L.A. [073]
MATERIALDIENST DES KONFESSIONSKUNDLICHEN INSTITUTS – v1-41. 1950-90 (complete) – 5r – 1 – ATLA S0380 – us A.T.L.A. [240]
MATERIALI PER SERVIRE ALLA COMPILAZIONE DELLE FAUNA ENTOMOLOGICA ITALIANA / Ghiliani, V – Torino, 1852. 119p. Z/1282/2 – 8 – ne IDC [590]
MATERIALIEN ZU AKZEPTANZPROBLEMEN BEIM EINSATZ INNOVATIVER INFORMATIONSTECHNOLOGIE IM BUERO- UND VERWALTUNGSBEREICH ANALYSIERT AM BEISPIEL EINES INDUSTRIEBETRIEBES / Wagner, Albert – Nuernberg, 1981 – 2mf – DM38.00 – 3-89349-903-2 – gw Hänsel [650]
MATERIALIEN ZUR ENTWICKLUNG DER ALTJUEDISCHEN ZEITRECHNUNG IM TALMUD / Zuckermann, Benedict – (Includes bibliographical references) – Breslau: S Schottlaender, 1882 – 1mf – 9 – 0-8370-6557-7 – 1986-0557 – us A.T.L.A. [270]
MATERIALIEN ZUR KUNDE DES AELTEREN ENGLISCHEN DRAMAS / ed by Bang, W – Louvain. 1902-14. 44v. – 243mf – 8 – ne IDC [420]
MATERIALIEN ZUR MEDIENTHEORIE / Boll, Uwe – 1992 – 120p – 9 – DM98.00 – 3-89349-470-7 – gw Hänsel [380]
MATERIALISM: ITS HISTORY AND INFLUENCE ON SOCIETY / Buechner, Ludwig – Trans. by Alexander Loos. New York: Asa K. Butts & Co., c1873. 28p – 1 – us U.W. Library [140]
THE MATERIALISM OF THE PRESENT TIME : A CRITIQUE OF DR. BUCHNER'S SYSTEM / Janet, Paul – Trans. from French by Gustave Masson. London: H. Bailliere, 1866 – xii/202p – 1 – us U.W. Library [190]
MATERIALISME DIALEKTIK DAN HISTORI (SEPT. 1938) / Stalin, Iosif – SE 2760 1. 1955 – 9 – ne IDC [321]
MATERIALLY STRUCTURED SPACE – Pattee, University Park, PA. 1989 – 15p 1mf – 9 – $0.50f – us Lawrence Pub [720]
MATERIALO PO ARKHEOLOGII ROSSII – v. 3-37. Spb. 1888-1918. BR-3358 2 – 8 – ne IDC [073]
MATERIALS / Blount, George A – Diaries, sermon outlines, clippings, records of marriage, service with Home Mission Board, records of baptism. c1874-1924. 1136p – 1 – 39.76 – us Baptist [240]
MATERIALS / Broadus, John A – Diary, sermons, addresses, essays, and lectures. 1845-46. 1462p – 1 – 51.17 – us Baptist [920]
MATERIALS / Kehukee Baptist Association. North Carolina – (1. Strictures on the Sentiments of the Kehukee Baptist Association by Nehemia, 1829. 2. Review of the History of Kehukee Baptist Association to Which Are Added the Comparative Claims of Missionary Baptists and Anti-Missionary Baptists by Rev. Mark Bennett, 1854) – 1 – 5.00 – us Baptist [240]
MATERIALS / National Baptist Publication Board – Miscellaneous printed materials related to the 1915 division in the National Baptist Convention, Annual Reports of the Publication Board, 1916, 1920, 1929-61, etc.). National Baptist Convention of America, Nashville, Tenn – 1 – 38.92 – us Baptist [240]
MATERIALS / Newman, Albert Henry – 2212p – 1 – 77.42 – us Baptist [240]
MATERIALS / Oklahoma Baptist State Convention – 1914-47 – 1 – 22.82 – us Baptist [240]
MATERIALS / Woman's Christian Temperance Union – undated, Official records of this temperance organization – 1 – us KS Hist [240]
MATERIALS AND CORROSION = WERKSTOFFE UND KORROSION : WITH INTERNATIONAL CORROSION ABSTRACTS – v11-32. 1960-81; v35-47. 1984-96 – 1,5,6,13 – us V.C.H. [540]
MATERIALS AND MANUFACTURING PROCESSES *see* ADVANCED MATERIALS AND MANUFACTURING
MATERIALS AND METHODS FOR TAGGING TUNA AND BILLFISHES, RECOVERING THE TAGS AND HANDLING THE RECAPTURE DATA – 1986 – 41p – it F.A.O. [639]
MATERIALS (BIOGRAPHICAL AND GENEALOGICAL) / Whitsett, James – Incl. data on W. H. Whitsett. 176p – 1 – 6.16 – us Baptist [920]
MATERIALS CHEMISTRY – v1-7. 1976-82 – 1,5,6 – sz Elsevier [073]
MATERIALS CHEMISTRY AND PHYSICS – v1-11. 1976-84 – 1,5,6,13 – sz Elsevier [073]
MATERIALS ENGINEERING – v1- 1929- 1; v61-5,6; v83- 9 – us UMI [621]
MATERIALS FOR A HISTORY OF FIRST BAPTIST CHURCH. JEFFERSON CITY, TENNESSEE : CHURCH RECORDS – 1841-1941 – 1 – 5.00 – us Baptist [240]
MATERIALS FOR A HISTORY OF OIL PAINTING / Eastlake, Charles L – O-982 1. 2 v. 1847-1869 – 9 – ne IDC [750]

MATERIALS FOR A HISTORY OF THE REIGN OF HENRY 7 (RS60) : FROM ORIGINAL DOCUMENTS RESERVED IN THE PUBLIC RECORD OFFICE / ed by Cambell, W – (v1 1873 Dfl46.00. v2 1877 Dfl42.00) – ne Slangenburg [941]

MATERIALS FOR THE HISTORY OF THOMAS BECKET (RS67) / ed by Robertson, J C & Sheppart, J P – (v1 1875 Dfl39.00. v2 1876 Dfl35.00. v3 1877 Dfl39.00. v4 1879 Dfl32.00. v5 1881 Dfl39.00. v6 1882 Dfl46.00. v7 1885 Dfl42.00) – ne Slangenburg [240]

MATERIALS FOR THE STUDY OF OLD ENGLISH DRAMA / ed by Vocht, H de – Louvain. 1911-39. – 110mf – 8 – ne IDC [420]

MATERIALS FROM THE SCRAPBOOK OF THE ASHCRAFT FAMILY / Ashcraft Family – 1920. 15p – 1 – 5.00 – us Baptist [240]

MATERIALS HANDLING IN CANADA – v.4-15. 1959-Feb 1970. Continued as Materials management and distribution – 1 – us UMI [650]

MATERIALS HANDLING IN CANADIAN INDUSTRY – v.1-3. Oct 1955-58. Continued as Materials Handling in Canada – 1 – us UMI [650]

MATERIALS HANDLING NEWS – v1- 1956- 1; 1976- 5,6,9 – us UMI [621]

MATERIALS MANAGEMENT AND DISTRIBUTION – (Incorporates: Bar Code Quarterly. v1-34 1956-89 Can$37.00y) – Toronto. v1-39. 1956-94 – 9 – Can$28.00y – cn Micromedia [650]

MATERIALS MANAGEMENT AND DISTRIBUTION – (v.24-. Jan 1979- 5,6,9) – v.15-. Mar 1970- – 1 – us UMI [380]

MATERIALS MANAGEMENT AND DISTRIBUTION *see* BAR CODE QUARTERLY

MATERIALS OF THE SIXTH NATIONAL CONGRESS OF THE COMMUNIST PARTY OF INDONESIA / Communist Party. Indonesia. Kongres Nasional – SE-1248 1. 1959 – 9 – ne IDC [950]

MATERIALS ON THE COMPACT OF FREE ASSOCIATION FOR MICRONESIA, PALAU AND THE MARSHALLS : MATERIALS FROM THE CONGRESSIONAL RECORD AND OTHER SOURCES / Hawaiian/Pacific Collection of the Uni of Hawaii Library – Honolulu: Uni of Hawaii Library. 2v. 1985 – 8mf – 9 – $12.00 – LLMC 82-100F, Title 64 – us L.L.M.C. [980]

MATERIALS ON THE COMPACT OF FREE ASSOCIATION FOR MICRONESIA, PALAU AND THE MARSHALLS : MATERIALS FROM THE CONGRESSIONAL RECORD AND OTHER SOURCES / Hawaiian/Pacific Collection of the Uni of Hawaii Library – Honolulu: Uni of Hawaii Library. 3v. 1980 – 8mf – 9 – $12.00 – LLMC 82-100F, Title 61 – us L.L.M.C. [323]

MATERIALS ON THE EARLY EDUCATIONAL LIFE OF THE ENGLISH BAPTISTS / British Museum – 11,766p – 1 – us Baptist [240]

MATERIALS ON THE EARLY EDUCATIONAL LIFE OF THE ENGLISH BAPTISTS / Regent's Park College – 3106p – 1 – us Baptist [240]

MATERIALS RELATING TO THE APPEALS OF ROBERT M SOBUKWE AND SHANTAVOTHIE NAIDOO, AND THE MINISTER OF JUSTICE (RESPONDENT) TO THE END OF OBTAINING EXIT PERMITS FROM THE REPUBLIC OF SOUTH AFRICA / Sobukwe, Robert Mangaliso – Johannesburg: Microfile, [19–?] – us Res Libr [340]

MATERIALS RESEARCH AND STANDARDS *see* ASTM BULLETIN

MATERIALS SCIENCE – (Cont: Soviet Materials Science) – v1-29. 1965-93 – 1,5 – $80.00v – us UMI [620]

MATERIALS SCIENCE AND ENGINEERING – v1-67 1966-84 – 1,5,6,13 – sz Elsevier [620]

MATERIALS SCIENCE AND TECHNOLOGY : MST: A PUBLICATION OF THE INSTITUTE OF METALS – v1- 1985- – 1,5,6,9 – us UMI [620]

MATERIALS TOWARD A HISTORY OF BAPTISTS IN PROV. OF PENN., R.I., N.J., DEL., MD., VA., N.C., S.C., AND GEORGIA / Edwards, Morgan – (Mss. in Crozer Theological Seminary. Text varies from Mss. at Furman Univ.) 663p – 1 – 23.20 – us Baptist [240]

MATERIALS USED AT THE EMBALMING OF KING TUT-ANKH-AMUN / Winlock, H E – 1941 – 9 – $10.00 – us I.R.C. [930]

MATERIALS-BOOKS, CLIPPINGS, PAMPHLETS, PROGRAMS, 1909-45 / Ridgecrest. North Carolina. Ridgecrest Baptist Assembly – 3628p – 1 – 126.98 – us Baptist [240]

MATERIALWISSENSCHAFT UND WERKSTOFFTECHNIK : ENTWICKLUNG, FERTIGUNG, PRUEFUNG, EIGENSCHAFTEN UND ANWENDUNG TECHNISCHER WERKSTOFFE – v15-27. 1984-96 – 1,5,6,13 – us V.C.H. [600]

MATERIALY ARKHIVA G.V. PLEKHANOVA / Kurbatova, IN – Voprosy filosofii, 1964, No.2, p138-144.BR-10,908/1 – 9 – ne IDC [100]

MATERIALY DLI A IZUCHENII A MIROVOGO KHOZI A ISTVA = DIE WELTWIRTSCHAFT; ECONOMIE MONDIALE – (Includes c.1: 1924:Sept./Oct.-Nov./Dec) – Berlin: Torgovoe predstavitelstvo SSSR v Germanii, 19uu – 1 – CSUXAKZ0168-S – us Hoover Inst Photo [330]

MATERIALY DLIA BIBLIOGRAFII RABOT O PERSIDSKIKH RUKOPISIAKH / Akimushkin, O F & Borshchevskii, I E – Bibliog. of publ. catalogs and descriptions of Persian mss. in the USSR. BR-10,669/1 – 9 – ne IDC [010]

MATERIALY DLIA BIBLIOGRAFII SIBIRI / Mameev, S N – Ukazatel' izdanii, vyshedshikh v 1892 i 1893 g. Tobol' sk. 1892-93. BR-7140 2 – 8 – ne IDC [460]

MATERIALY DLIA BIOGRAFICHESKAGO SLOVARIA DIE ISTVITELNYKH CHLENOV IMPERATORSKO I AKADEMII NAUK / Imperatorskaia akademiia nauk – Petrograd: Imperatorskaia akademiia nauk, 3-e izd. 1915-1917 – 1 – CSUX89-B4513 – us Hoover Inst Photo [920]

MATERIALY DLIA BIOGRAFII KN / Maikov, L N – A. D. Kantemira. Spb. 1903. BR-7673 2 – 8 – ne IDC [920]

MATERIALY DLIA FLORY KAVKAZA. FLORA CAUCASICA CRITICA / Kusnetsov, N & Bus, N & Fomin, A – v. 1 (1), v. 2 (1, 4), v. 3 (3, 4, 7, 8, 9), v. 4 (1, 2, 6). Jur'ev. 1901-13. B-5556 2 – 8 – ne IDC [580]

MATERIALY DLIA ISTORII ANTIEVREISKIKH PROGROMOV V ROSSII – v. 1. Petrograd. 1919. B-1529 2 – 8 – ne IDC [947]

MATERIALY DLIA ISTORII IMP. AKADEMII NAUK – 10v. Spb. 1885-1900. BR-7687 2 – 8 – ne IDC [947]

MATERIALY DLIA ISTORII NARODNAGO PROSVESHCHENIIA V ROSSII / Mezhov, VI – Literatura russkoi pedagogiki, metodiki i didaktiki s 1866-1872. v. 3. Spb. 1874. BR-7160 2 – 8 – ne IDC [370]

MATERIALY DLIA ISTORII PROSVESHCHENIIA V ROSSII / Keppen, P – v. 1-3. Spb. 1819-27. BR-4352 2 – 8 – ne IDC [947]

MATERIALY DLIA ISTORII RUSSKOI LITERATURY / ed by Efremov, P A – Spb. 1867. BR-6023 2 – 8 – ne IDC [460]

MATERIALY DLIA ISTORII RUSSKOI LITERATURY I DLIA SLOVARIA PISATELEI EPOKHI EKATERINY 2 / Semennikov, V P – Spb. 1914. BR-7845 2 – 8 – ne IDC [073]

MATERIALY DLIA OB IASNITEL'-NOGO OBLASTNOGO SLOVARIA VIATSKOGO GOVORA / Vasnetsov, N M – Viatka, 1907 – 7mf – 9 – 1377/2 – ne IDC [460]

MATERIALY DLIA RUSSKOI BIBLIOGRAFII. KHRONOLOGICHESKOE OBOZRENIE REDKIKH I ZAMECHATEL'NYKH KNIG XVIII...1725-1800 / Guberti, Nikolai V – Moscow, 1878-91.BR/4674/2 – 8 – ne IDC [947]

MATERIALY DLIA SLOVARIA / Sreznevskii, 2 – (Materials for an Old Russian dictionary). 3 v. 1890-1912 – 3 – us Readex [460]

MATERIALY DLIA SLOVARIA DREVNE-RUSSKAGO IAZYKA PO PISMENNYM PAMIATNIKAM – St. Petersburg. (Materials for a Dictionary of Early Russian). 3 v. 1890-1912 – 3 – us Readex [490]

MATERIALY DLIA SLOVARIA DREVNERUSSKOGO IAZYKA / Diuvernua, A – Moscow, 1894. BR-10,493/1 – 3mf – 9 – ne IDC [947]

MATERIALY DLIA SLOVARIA DREVNERUSSKOGO IAZYKA PO PIS'MENNYM PAMIATNIKAM / Sreznevskii, 2 – Spb., 1893-1912. 3 vols – 86mf – 9 – R-8283/2 – ne IDC [460]

MATERIALY DLIA SLOVARIA PRAVOVYKH I BYTOVYKH DREVNOSTEI PO RUSSKOI PRAVDE / Mrochek-Drozdovskii, P N – 1910. BR-9523/1 – 3mf – 9 – ne IDC [340]

MATERIALY DLIA TERMINOLOGICHESKOGO SLOVARIA DREVNEI RUSI / Kochin, GE – M., 1937 – 13mf – 9 – 925/2 – ne IDC [460]

MATERIALY DLIA VEDENIA PRAKTICHESKIKH ZANIATII NA KURSAKH PO SCHETOVODSTVU POTREBITEL'NYKH OBSHCHESTV : PO AMERIKANSKOI DVOINOI SISTEME / Shalov, I S – M., 1916 – 2mf – 9 – COR-141/1 – ne IDC [334]

MATERIALY DLYA ISTORII RUSSKAGO FLOTA / Russia. Morskoe Ministerstvo – Chast. 1. St. Petersburg. 1865-1904 – 1 – us NY Public [947]

MATERIALY DO UKRAINS'KOIKO-RUS'KOI ETNOL'OHII : NAUKOVE TOVARYSTVO IM. SHEVCHENKA – L'viv. v1-20. 1899-1919 – 95mf – 9 – 1255/2 – ne IDC [947]

MATERIALY DO UKRAJINS'KOJI BIBLIOGRAFIJI – v. 1-7. L'viv. 1909-37. Lacking: 5 (2), 1924. BR-1772 2 – 8 – ne IDC [460]

MATERIALY I ISSLEDOVANIIA PO ISTORII RUSSKAGO LITERATURNOGO IAZYKA – v. 1. M., L. 1949. BR-7689 2 – 8 – ne IDC [460]

MATERIALY I SOOBSHCHENIIA PO FONDAM OTDELA RUKOPISNOI I REDKOI KNIGI BIBLIOTEKI AKADEMII NAUK SSSR – Moscow, Leningrad, 1966. 207p. BR-10,956/1 – 9 – ne IDC [015]

MATERIALY K BIBLIOGRAFII A. BLOKA ZA 1928-1957 GODY / Kolpakova, E & Kuprhanovskii, P & Maksimov, D – Uchenye zapiski Vil'niusskogo pedinstituta. v. 6. 1959. BR-1344 2 – 8 – ne IDC [460]

MATERIALY K BIBLIOGRAFII. OPISANIE RUKOPISEI / Stasov, Vladimir Vasil'evich – Moscow, 1956. 283p. BR-10,913/1 – 9 – ne IDC [010]

MATERIALY K ISTORII RUSSKOGO TEATRA V GOSUDARSTVENNYKH ARKHIVAKH SSSR / ed by Petrovskaia, I F – Obzory dokumentov. 17 vek-1917 g. Moscow, 1966. 285p. BR-10,737/1 – 9 – ne IDC [790]

MATERIALY K ISTORII RUSSKOI KONTRREVOLIUTSII : VOL 1: POGROMY PO OFFICIAL'NYM DOKUMENTAM – Spb., 1908. 451p – 8mf – 9 – ne IDC [320]

MATERIALY KOMISSII EKSPEDITSIONNYKH ISSLEDOVANII – v. 1-30. L. 1928-30. Lacking: 1930 (25-27, 29-30). BR-3359 2 – 8 – ne IDC [073]

MATERIALY NARODNOGO KOMISSARIATA I USTIT SII / Russian S.F.S.R. Narodny i komissariat i ustit sii – (Library has: Vol. 1-15; missing vol. 14) – Moskva: Komissariat, 1918-1922. 18v – 1 – CSUX89-S568 – us Hoover Inst Photo [947]

MATERIALY O MONGOLAKH, KALMYKAKH I BURIATAKH V ARKHIVAKH LENINGRADA / Iorish, II – Istoriia, pravo, ekonomika. Moscow, 1966. 206p BR-10,668/1 – 9 – ne IDC [947]

MATERIALY PIATILETNEGO PLANA RAZVITIIA KUSTARNO-PROMYSLOVOI KOOPERATSII RSFSR : 1928/29-1932/33 GG – M., 1930 – 3mf – 9 – COR-434/1 – ne IDC [334]

MATERIALY PO ETNOGRAFI – Leningrad. v. 1-5. 1933-1934, 1936, 1939 – 1 – us NY Public [305]

MATERIALY PO ISTORII LENINGRADSKOGO UNIVERSITETA, 1819-1917 – Obzor arkhivnykh dokumentov. Leningrad, 1961. 123p. BR-10,945/1 – 9 – ne IDC [947]

MATERIALY PO ISTORII PROFESSIONAL'NOGO DVIZHENIYA V ROSSII – Sbornik. Moscow. v. 1-5. 1924-1927 – 1 – us NY Public [370]

MATERIALY PO ISTORII SVIAZI V ROSSII 18-NACHALA 20 VV – Obzor dokumental'nykh materialov. Leningrad, 1966. 335p. BR-10,735/1 – 9 – ne IDC [947]

MATERIALY PO KITAISKOMU VOPROSU – Moscow. 1927-1928 – 1 – 35.00r – us Hoover Inst Photo [073]

MATERIALY PO KOOPERATSII NOVGORODSKOI GUBERNII – (Missing: v9-10. 1920) – Novgorod. v1-24. 1919-21 – 7mf – 9 – COR-726/1 – ne IDC [334]

MATERIALY PO NOVOMU KOOPRATIVNOMU STROITEL'STVU V PORIADKE DEKRETOV SOVETA NARODNYKH KOMISSAROV RSFSR OT 7 APRELIA 1921 G. I USSR OF 13 APRELIA 1921 GODA – Odessa, v4. 1922 – 2mf – 9 – COR-727/1 – ne IDC [334]

MATERIALY PO OBSLEDOVANIIU KOOPERATSII SEVERO-ZAPADNOI OBLASTI ZA 1924 G – L., 1925 – 3mf – 9 – COR-728/1 – ne IDC [310]

MATERIALY PO STATISTIKE TORGOVLI TEKSTILNO I SINDIT SIROVANNO I PROMYSHLENNOSTI ZA... : VSESOI UZNY I TEKSTILNY I SINDIKAT – (Includes c.1: 1924/1925) – Moskva, Leningrad: T Sentr. upr. pechati VSNKh SSSR, 1924 – 1 – CSUXAKY5321-S – us Hoover Inst Photo [947]

MATERIALY PO STATISTIKE TRUDA : T SENTRALNOE BI URO STATISTIKI TRUDA V.T S.S.P.S., T S.S.U. I N.K.T. – (Includes c.1: v.11 1921) – Moskva: [Bi uro], 19uu – 1 – CSUXAKZ2119-S – us Hoover Inst Photo [947]

MATERIALY PO STATISTIKE TRUDA NA UKRAINE : UPRAVLENIE UPOLNOMOCHENNOGO NARKOMTRUDA R.S.F.S.R. PRI SOVNARKOME U.S.S.R., OTDEL STATISTIKI – (Includes c.1: v.1 1920, v.3 (1922)) – [Kharkov]: Otdel, 1920- – 1 – CSUXAKZ1516-S – us Hoover Inst Photo [947]

MATERIALY PO TEKUSHCHE I SELSKOKHOZI A ISTVENNO I STATISTIKE...GG : T SENTRALNOE STATISTICHESKOE UPRAVLENIE SSSR I RSFSR, SEKTOR SELSKOKHOZI A ISTVENNO I STATISTIKI – (Includes c.1: 1923-1925) – Moskva: Upravlenie, 1929- – 1 – CSUXAKY9918-S – us Hoover Inst Photo [947]

MATERIALY PO VOPROSAM ORGANIZATSII PRODOVOL'STVENNOGO DELA / Chaianov, A V – (Missing: Pt 5) – M., 6pts. 1916-17 – 9mf – 9 – COR-70/1 – ne IDC [334]

MATERIALY PO VOPROSAM PROMYSLOVOI KOOPERATSII – M., 1925 – 1mf – 9 – COR-433/1 – ne IDC [334]

MATERIALY PO VOPROSU O VYVOZE IZ Z. SIBIRI PISHCHEVYKH PRODUKTOV : (KHLEB, MIASNYE TOVARY I SKOT, MASLO) I ZHIVOTNOGO SYRIA (KOZHEVENNYE TOVARY I SHERST) I POLOZHENIE ZAPADNO-SIBIRSKOGO RAIONA PO OTNOSHENIIU K OBSHCHERUSSKOMU I MIROVOMU RYNKAM ETIKH PRODUKTOV / Berezin, N I – Moskva: VSNKh, Otdel red.-izd., 1921 – 1 – CSUX91-B45 – us Hoover Inst Photo [380]

MATERIALY POISTORII OTPADENII A ZAKAVKAZI A OT ROSSII / Arkomed, S T – Tiflis: Krasnai a kniga, 1923 – 1 – CSUX88-B1981 – us Hoover Inst Photo [320]

MATERIALY SAMIZDATA – (Includes a printed guide) – 238mf – 9 – Gld1,437.00 – ne IDC [947]

MATERIALY...VERKHOVNOGO SOVETA SSSR... / Soviet Union, Verkhovnyi Sovet – (Includes c.1: 1962:Dec.10-13; 1963:Dec.16-19; 1964:Dec.9-11) – Moskva: Izdvo politicheskoi literatury – 1 – CSUXAKY5598-S – us Hoover Inst Photo [320]

MATERIAUX POUR LA FLORE MEDICALE DE MONTPELLIER... / Planchon, [F]G – Montpellier, 1868 – 1mf – 9 – ne IDC [615]

MATERIAUX POUR L'ETUDE DES HABITATIONS PROTO-HISTORIQUES A TAHITI / Orliac, C – 9 – F120.00 – fr Ethnologie [306]

MATERIAUX POUR UNE FLORE LICHENOLOGIQUE DU BRESIL / Fee, A L A – (Bull. Soc. Bot. France. v. 20. 1873; v. 21. 1874). B-942 2 – 8 – ne IDC [580]

DIE MATERIELLE KULTUR DER INGESSANA (REP. SUDAN) / Langenbahn, Hans-Juergen – 1993 – 5mf – 9 – DM118.00 – 3-89349-748-X – gw Hänsel [306]

MATERJALY DO SPISU INSTYTUCY I TOWARZYSTW NAUKOWYCH W POLSCE – v7. Nauka Polska. Warszawa. 1927; Suppl. v12. Nauka Polska. Warszawa. 1930. BR-9825 1 – 9 – ne IDC [943]

MATERNAL AND CHILD HEALTH SURVEY IN INDONESIA (JAVA, BALI AND SUMATRA) / Haas, J H de – SE-3336 1. 1955? – 9 – ne IDC [610]

MATERNAL AND FETAL RESPONSES TO MAXIMAL EXERCISE DURING SWIMMING AND CYCLING / Gall, M M – 1990 – 2mf – 9 – $8.00 – us Microform Publ [612]

MATERNIDAD, GENERACION, CRIANZA... / Ruiz-Contreras, Jose – Madrid: Razon y Fe, 1926 – 1 – sp Bibl Santa Ana [618]

LA MATERNITE, LA NAISSANCE ET LEURS RITUELS EN BIRMANIE : CONTRIBUTION A L'ETUDE DE LA MATERNITE EN ASIE DU SUD-EST / Delachet-Guillon, C – 9 – F90.00 – fr Ethnologie [306]

MATERNITY : A POPULAR TREATISE FOR YOUNG WIVES AND MOTHERS / Verdi, Tullio Suzzara – New York: J B Ford, 1870 – us Res Libr [618]

MATERYIALY DO UKRAJINS'KO-RUS'KOI ETNOL'OGIJI – (Naukove Tovarystvo im. Shevchenka). v. 1-20. Lemberg. 1899-1919. B-1255 2 – 8 – ne IDC [306]

Mates, Bartolome *see* GRAMATICA LATINA (I. 1468)
Matheis, Juergen *see* SCHWERBEHINDERTE IM BETRIEB
MATHEMATICAE COLLECTIONES A FEDERICO COMMANDINO IN LATINVM CONVERSAE ET COMMENTARIIS ILLVSTRATAE / Pappus of Alexandria – Pisauri, 1588 – 1 – us U.W. Library [510]
MATHEMATICAL AND COMPUTER MODELLING – 1,5,69 – us UMI [510]
MATHEMATICAL BIOSCIENCES – v1-72. 1967-84 – 1,5,6,13 – sz Elsevier [574]
MATHEMATICAL CORRESPONDENT – v. 1-2. 1804-1807 – 1 – us UMI [510]
MATHEMATICAL GAZETTE – v. 1- 1894- – 1. ; 5,6. ; 9 – apply; v.52-; v.60- – us UMI [510]
MATHEMATICAL GEOLOGY – v1-26. 1969-94 – 1,5 – $120.00v – us UMI [550]
THE MATHEMATICAL INTELLIGENCER – v.1-4, 1978-81. ISSN: 0343-6993 – 1,5,6,9,13 – 21.00v – us UMI [073]
MATHEMATICAL MODELLING OF LIVESTOCK PRODUCTION SYSTEMS = MODELISATION METHEMATIQUE DES SYSTEMES DE PRODUCTION ANIMALE: APPLICATION AU BOTSWANA DU MODELE DE PRODUCTION BOVINE DE LA TEXAS A & M UNIVERSITY : APPLICATION OF THE TEXAS A & M UNIVERSITY BEEF CATTLE PRODUCTION MODEL TO BOTSWANA / ILCA – 1978 – 9 – $8.00 – 92-9053-121-5 – et ILRI [630]
MATHEMATICAL MODELS IN BIOLOGICAL OCEANOGRAPHY / ed by Platt, T & Mann, K H & Ulanowicz, R E – 1982 – 157p – 9 – 92-3-101922-8 – fr UNESCO [510]
MATHEMATICAL MODELS IN HYDROLOGY – 1973 repr 1984 – 292p – it F.A.O. [550]
MATHEMATICAL NOTES – (Continues: Mathematical Notes of the USSR) – v1-56. 1967-94 – 1,5 – $80.00v – us UMI [510]
MATHEMATICAL PHYSICS REVIEWS / ed by Novikov, S P – 9,5,1 – us Harwood [530]
MATHEMATICAL POPULATION STUDIES : AN INTERNATIONAL JOURNAL OF MATHEMATICAL DEMOGRAPHY / ed by Bonneuil, Noel et al – 9,5,1 – us Gordon [304]
MATHEMATICAL PROGRAMMING – v1-30. 1971-84 – 1,5,6,13 – sz Elsevier [073]
MATHEMATICAL PROGRAMMING STUDIES – v1-24. 1974-84 – 1,5,6,13 – sz Elsevier [073]
THE MATHEMATICAL PSYCHOLOGY OF GRATRY AND BOOLE TRANSLATED FROM THE LANGUAGE OF THE HIGHER CALCULUS INTO THAT OF ELEMENTARY GEOMETRY / Boole, Mary Everest – London: Swan Sonnenschein & Co., 1897. 116p – 1 – us U.W. Library [150]
MATHEMATICAL REPORTS – 1983- – 1,5,9 – us Harwood [510]
MATHEMATICAL REVIEWS – (1982-. 1,5,6,9) – v1-. 1940- – 1 – us UMI [073]
MATHEMATICAL SCIENCES – v63-81 1959-77 1; v75-81 5,6; v80-81 9 – us UMI [510]
MATHEMATICAL SOCIAL SCIENCES – v1-8. 1981-84 – 1,5,6,13 – sz Elsevier [073]
Mathematical Society of Japan *see* JOURNAL
MATHEMATICAL SYSTEMS THEORY – v. 1-13. 1966-80 – 1,5,9 – 780.00 – us UMI [073]
MATHEMATICAL TABLES AND OTHER AIDS TO COMPUTATION – v1-13. 1943-59 – 1 – us UMI [073]
MATHEMATICHESKII SBORNIK – Moscow. N.s.1-83; v43-125. 1936-70 – 1,5,6 – us Princeton Micro [073]
MATHEMATICS AND COMPUTERS IN SIMULATION – v1-26. 1959-84 – 1,5,6,13 – sz Elsevier [073]
MATHEMATICS IN SCHOOL – v1- 1971- 1; v5- 5,6,9 – us UMI [370]
MATHEMATICS IN THE ALTERNATIVE SET THEORY / Vopenka, Petr – Leipzig: B. G. Teubner. c1979. 120 p. Summary in French, German, and Russian – 1 – us U.W. Library [510]
MATHEMATICS OF COMPUTATION – (1982-. 1,5,6,9) – v14-. 1960- – 1 – us UMI [073]
MATHEMATICS OF COMPUTATION – v1-15. 1943-61.Continues: Mathematical Tables and other Aids to Computation – 1,5,6 – us Princeton Micro [510]
MATHEMATICS OF OPERATIONS RESEARCH – (1985-. 5,6,9) – v1-. 1976- – 1 – us UMI [510]
MATHEMATICS OF THE USSR: IZVESTIJA – (1982-. 1,5,6,9) – v1-. 1967- – 1 – us UMI [073]
MATHEMATICS OF THE USSR: SBORNIK – (1982-. 1,5,6,9) – v1-. 1967- – 1 – us UMI [073]
MATHEMATICS TEACHER – (v. 63- 1970- 5,6. v. 66- 1973- 9) – v. 1- 1908- – 1 – us UMI [510]
MATHEMATICS TEACHER – (v.63- 1970- 5,6. v.66- 1973- 9) – v.1- 1908- – 1 – us UMI [510]
MATHEMATICS TEACHING – v1- 1955- 1; v74-1976- 5,6,9 – us UMI [370]
MATHEMATISCHE ANNALEN – v. 81-254. 1920-80 – 1,5,9 – 30,537.00 – us UMI [073]
MATHEMATISCHE ANNALEN – v1-129. 1869-1955 – 1,5,6 – us Princeton Micro [510]
MATHEMATISCHE VERFAHREN ZUR BEWERTUNG VON STANDORT- UND AUSLIEFERUNGSALTERNATIVEN IM HANDEL / Baumann, Johannes – 1992 – 234p – 9 – DM98.00 – 3-89349-572-X – gw Hänsel [510]
MATHEMATISCHE ZEITSCHRIFT – v. 1-175. 1918-80 – 1,5,9 – 30,975.00 – us UMI [073]
MATHEMATISCHE ZEITSCHRIFT – v1-63. 1918-55 – 1,5,6 – us Princeton Micro [510]
MATHEMATISCHES WOERTERBUCH / Kluegel, Georg Simon et al – Leipzig. 7v. 1803-36 – 75mf – 9 – subsc: DM450.00 diazo DM540.00 silver – gw Olms [510]
MATHEMATISCH-NATURWISSENSCHAFTLICHE KLASSE ABHANDLUNGEN / Akademie der Wissenschaften. Berlin – 1908-1949 – 1 – us Schnase [500]
MATHEMATISCH-NATURWISSENSCHAFTLICHE KLASSE SITZUNGSBERICHTE / Akademie der Wissenschaften. Berlin – 1922-1949 – 1 – us Schnase [500]
MATHEMATISCH-NATURWISSENSCHAFTLICHE KLASSE: SITZUNGSBERICHTE / Akademie der Wissenschaften. Vienna – Series 1, v. 115-155. 1906-1946 – 1,5,6 – us Princeton Micro [510]
MATHEMATISCH-NATURWISSENSCHAFTLICHE KLASSE: SITZUNGSBERICHTE / Akademie der Wissenschaften. Vienna – Series 2A, v. 81-155. 1880-1946 – 1,5,6 – us Princeton Micro [510]
MATHEMATISCH-NATURWISSENSCHAFTLICHE KLASSE: SITZUNGSBERICHTE / Akademie der Wissenschaften. Vienna – Series 2B, v. 97-156. 1888-1947 – 1,5,6 – us Princeton Micro [510]
Mather *see* BIOGRAPHICAL REVIEW OF CALHOUN COUNTY
Mather, A *see* OUT-LETTERS, 1769-1799
Mather, Cotton *see* THE ECCLESIASTICAL HISTORY OF NEW ENGLAND
Mather, James S *see* WILLIAM MATHER
MATHER PAPERS – (Pt 1 Papers of Cotton Mather: diaries, sermons, letters, essays, tracts, MS bibliography on Mathers by William S. Piper, 19r $1465; Pt 2 biographical material on Increase Mather and Mather family history, 4r $305) – Massachusetts Historical Society – 23r – 1 – $1770.00 complete collection – us UMI [920]
MATHER, S. LIVINGSTON, PAPERS, MS 4613 – 1850-1960 – 7r – 1 – us Western Res [978]
MATHER, WILLIAM G., PAPERS, MS 4578 – 1702-1957 – 3r – 1 – us Western Res [338]
Mathern, V *see* VYPOVED OBVINENEHO A SVEDKA V KONANI PRED SUDOM
Mathesius, Johannes *see*
- AUSSLEGUNG DER EUANGELIEN VON DEN FUERNEMBSTEN FESTEN VOM ADVENT BISS AUFF OSTERN. [3 AND 4]
- BEKANTNUSS VOM HEYLIGEN ABENDMAL...IN SECHTZEHEN PREDIGT GETHEYLET
- CATECHISMUS, DAS IST: TROSTREICHE VND NUETZLICHE AUSLEGUNG VBER DIE FUENFF HEUBTSTUECK DER CHRISTLICHE LEHRE
- CHRISTLICHE...AUSSLEGUNG IN DAS ERSTE CAPITEL DES EUANGELISTEN S. JOHANNIS...
- EHESPIEGEL MATHESIJ...
- ETLICHE FRAGSTUECK VON DER BEICHT, ABSOLUTION, VND VOM HOCHWIRDIGEN SACRAMENTS DES ALTARS, FUER DIE CHRISTLICHE JUGENT...
- HOCHZEITPREDIGTEN. VOM EHESTAND VND HAUSSWESEN...
- HOMILIAE MATHESII. DAS IST: AUSSLEGUNG...DER ERSTEN UND ANDERN EPISTELN...AN DIE CORINTHIER
- KURTZE AUSSLEGUNG DER SONTAGS EUANGELIEN VNND CATECHISMI
- POSTILLA ODER AUSSLEGUNG DER SONTAGS EUANGELIEN UBER DAS GANTZE JAR

Matheson, George *see*
- AIDS TO THE STUDY OF GERMAN THEOLOGY
- CAN THE OLD FAITH LIVE WITH THE NEW?
- LANDMARKS OF NEW TESTAMENT MORALITY
- MOMENTS ON THE MOUNT
- NATURAL ELEMENTS OF REVEALED THEOLOGY
- THE PSALMIST AND THE SCIENTIST, OR, MODERN VALUE OF THE RELIGIOUS SENTIMENT
- THE REPRESENTATIVE MEN OF THE BIBLE
- REPRESENTATIVE MEN OF THE BIBLE: ADAM TO JOB
- REPRESENTATIVE MEN OF THE BIBLE: ISHMAEL TO DANIEL
- THE REPRESENTATIVE MEN OF THE NEW TESTAMENT
- REPRESENTATIVE MEN OF THE NEW TESTAMENT
- THE REPRESENTATIVE WOMEN OF THE BIBLE
- REPRESENTATIVE WOMEN OF THE BIBLE
- SEARCHINGS IN THE SILENCE
- SIDELIGHTS FROM PATMOS BY GEORGE MATHESON
- SPIRITUAL DEVELOPMENT OF ST. PAUL
- STUDIES OF THE PORTRAIT OF CHRIST
- VOICES OF THE SPIRIT

Matheson, George et al *see* CHRISTIANITY AND EVOLUTION
Matheson, H E *see* COHESION OF COACTING AND INTERACTING FEMALE INTERCOLLEGIATE ATHLETES
Matheson, James *see* A NARRATIVE OF THE VISIT TO THE AMERICAN CHURCHES BY THE DEPUTATION FROM THE CONGREGATIONAL UNION OF ENGLAND AND WALES
Mathew, Arnold H *see* THE LIFE AND TIMES OF RODRIGO BORGIA, POPE ALEXANDER 6
Mathew, Toby *see* THE DIARY AND JOURNAL OF HIS GRACE, THE ARCHBISHOP OF YORK
MATHEWS BAPTIST CHURCH. HUDGINS, VIRGINIA : CHURCH RECORDS – 1932-1976 – 1 – 108.90 – us Baptist [240]
Mathews, E *see* FACTS FOR BAPTIST CHURCHES
Mathews, G M *see* AUSTRAL AVIAN RECORD
MATHEWS GAZETTE-JOURNAL – Gloucester. Va. -w. 1938- – 1 – us UMI [071]
Mathews, H J *see* COMMENTARY ON EZRA AND NEHEMIAH
Mathews, James McFarlane *see* THE BIBLE AND MEN OF LEARNING
Mathews, M M *see* TEN YEARS IN NEVADA: OR, LIFE ON THE PACIFIC COAST
Mathews, Shailer *see*
- THE FRENCH REVOLUTION
- THE LIFE OF CHRIST
- THE MESSIANIC HOPE IN THE NEW TESTAMENT
- SELECT MEDIAEVAL DOCUMENTS
- THE SUFFICIENCY OF THE GOSPEL FOR THE SALVATION OF SOCIETY

Mathews, Thomas *see* THE EARLY CHURCHES OF CONSTANTINOPEL
Mathey, Michel *see* LA TRAITE DES BLANCS; ROMANS DE MOEURS COLONIALES
Mathias, KE *see* A COMPARISON OF THE EFFECTIVENESS OF INTERACTIVE VIDEO IN TEACHING THE ABILITY TO ANALYZE TWO MOTOR SKILLS IN SWIMMING
Mathias, principal du college de Langres *see* DE L'ENSEIGNEMENT PUBLIC
Mathiassen, T *see*
- ARCHAEOLOGY OF THE CENTRAL ESKIMOS
- MATERIAL CULTURE OF THE IGLULIK ESKIMOS

Mathieson, J E *see* THE SUPREMACY AND SUFFICIENCY OF JESUS CHRIST OUR LORD...IN...THE EPISTLE TO THE HEBREWS
Mathieson, William Law *see*
- THE AWAKENING OF SCOTLAND
- THE AWAKENING OF SCOTLAND, A HISTORY FROM 1747 TO 1797
- CHURCH AND REFORM IN SCOTLAND; A HISTORY FROM 1797 TO 1843
- POLITICS AND RELIGION; A STUDY IN SCOTTISH HISTORY FROM THE REFORMATION TO THE REVOLUTION
- SCOTLAND AND THE UNION

Mathieu, F D *see* LE CONCORDAT DE 1801. SES ORIGINES SON HISTOIRE
Mathiopoulos, Elsie *see* ZUR TYPOLOGIE DER GOETTIN ATHENA
Mathiot, A *see* LE REGIME POLITIQUE BRITANNIQUE
Mathorez, Jules *see* 5 BROCHURES MICROFILMEES ENSEMBLE
MATHRUBHUMI – Kozhikode, India. 27 Apr 1944-1960 – 31r – 1 – us L of C Photodup [072]
MATHRUBHUMI ILLUSTRATED WEEKLY – Calcutta, India. 1947-Nov 1950 – 4r – 1 – us L of C Photodup [072]
MATHURIN J. BOULLAULT : 18 OEUVRES MICROFILMEES ENSEMBLE / Boullault, Mathurin-J – (Le Bon savetier: traite historique mele de vaudeville; Dithyrambe sur l'attentat du 14 janvier 1858; Elegie sur ma cecite[suivie de] Au Prince imperial, le 16 mars 1863 etc) – 1 – F324.49 – fr Armell [910]
Matias Gil, Alejandro *see*
- LAS SIETE CENTURIAS...ALFONSO 8
- LAS SIETE CENTURIAS...DE PLASENCIA... (PROSPECTO)

Matic, Tioslav *see* TOTENKULT BEI DEN SERBEN
MATICA SLOVENSKA – Martin, Slovakia, 1890-1940 – 2r – 1 – us I.H.R.C. [947]
MATICA SLOVENSKA – Martin, Slovakia, 1935 – 1 reel – 1 – us I.H.R.C. [947]
Matijaschtschuk, Evelyn *see* INTERAKTIONSHANDLUNGEN IM RUSSISCHUNTERRICHT
LE MATIN – 1879-1949 – 2r per y – 5,6 – Sfr962.00 – sz Infoprint [949]
LE MATIN – 1950-1995 – 3r per y – 5,6 – Sfr1,123.00 – sz Infoprint [949]
LE MATIN – Grand journal d'information. Paris. 26 fevr 1884-17 aout 1944 – 1 – fr A.C.R.P.P. [072]
LE MATIN – Istanbul. Turkey. -d. 21 Apr-26 Jul 1879. (Included in microfilm of "Stamboul") – 1 – uk British Libr Newspaper [949]
LE MATIN – Journal hebdomadaire. no. 1-8. Paris. juin-aout 1862 – 1 – fr A.C.R.P.P. [073]
LE MATIN – Journal quotidien de renseignements et d'annonces. Haiti. May 1898-Apr 1899 – 1 – us UMI [072]
LE MATIN – Journal republicain. Paris. 17 juin 1882-1er mars 1883 – 1 – fr A.C.R.P.P. [073]
LE MATIN / ed by Maillet, Roger – (Cont by: Le Matin 4 fev 1922-6 jan 1923 and by: Le Petit Journal 1926) – Montreal, Canada. v1 n23. 15 jul 1920-v3 n52. 29 dec 1923 – 1r – 1 – Can$45.00 – cn Can Microfilming [072]
LE MATIN – Montreal, 6 fev 1987-31 mar 1987f – 1r – 1 – Can$70.00 – cn Can Microfilming [072]
LE MATIN : OPPOSE A MERCIER / ed by Rouillard, Eugene – Quebec, Canada. 13 jan-19 sep 1892 – 1r – 1 – Can$35.00 – cn Can Microfilming [072]
LE MATIN – (Yrly reel count varies) – 1879- – 5 – inquire – us Ross [072]
LE MATIN *see* LE MATIN
MATIN DE PARIS – v.1-. 1977- – 1 – us UMI [073]
LE MATIN FRANCAIS – Paris. 2 aout-22 oct 1884 – 1 – fr A.C.R.P.P. [073]
LA MATINEE D'UNE JOLIE FEMME / Vigee – (French Theatre Series). Paris. Prault. 1793 – 9 – fr Hachette [820]
THE MATING OF LYDIA / Ward, Mary Augusta – British Fiction Archive: Unit 2 – 9 – uk Bell [830]
Matlack, Lucius C *see*
- THE ANTI-SLAVERY STRUGGLE AND TRIUMPH IN THE METHODIST EPISCOPAL CHURCH
- THE HISTORY OF AMERICAN SLAVERY AND METHODISM FROM 1780 TO 1849; AND, HISTORY OF THE WESLEYAN METHODIST CONNECTION OF AMERICA

Matlock, Guy E *see* WHO'S WHO IN ALABAMA 1939-1940
MATLOCK MERCURY AND WEST DERBYSHIRE NEWS – 1986-96 – 29r – 1 – uk British Libr Newspaper [072]
Matorina, R P *see* OPISANIE AVTOGRAFOV I.S. TURGENEVA
Matos Sequeira, Rocha *see* OLIVENCA
Matota, H *see* INFLUENCE DES MEMBRES MASCULINS DE LA FAMILLE SUR L'ENFANT MUKONGO
A MATRACA : ORGAO NOTICIOSO HUMORISTICO E CRITICO – Manaos, Amazonas. 5 Out 1913 – 1,5,6 – bl Biblioteca [072]

DIE MATRATZENGRUFT : ERINNERUNGEN AN HEINRICH HEINE / Meissner, Alfred – Stuttgart: R Lutz, 1921 – 1 – us U.W. Library [430]

DIE MATRIKEL DER UNIVERSITAET HEIDELBERG VON 1386 BIS 1662 / Toepke, G – Heidelberg. v1-3. 1881-93 – 40mf – 8 – Dfl140.00 – ne Slangenburg [240]

DIE MATRIKEL DER UNIVERSITAET KOELN 1389 BIS 1559 (PGRG 4) / ed by Keussen, H – Bonn, 1892 – Dfl42.00 – ne Slangenburg [240]

MATRIMONIAL POST – London, UK. 1912. -f. 12 feet – 1 – uk British Libr Newspaper [306]

MATRIMONIO CELEBRATO DAVANTI L'AGENTE DIPLOMATICO DA CITTADINI ITALIANI RESIDENTI ALL'ESTERO:... / Fiore, P – Castello, 1902 – 1mf – 1 – ILM-3665/1 – ne IDC [327]

IL MATRIMONIO DELLO STRANIERO / Cimbali, E – Torino, 1898 – 3mf – 1 – ILM-3638/1 – ne IDC [327]

IL MATRIMONIO DINANZI AGLI AGENTI DIPLOMATICI / Cimbali, E – Roma, 1901 – 1mf – 1 – ILM-3185/1 – ne IDC [327]

EL MATRIMONIO SECRETO / Hurtado, Antonio – 1869 – 9 – 1.50f – sp Bibl Santa Ana [830]

MATRIMONIOS ROTOS / Aradillas Agudo, Antonio – Barcelona: Mundo Actual de Ediciones, S.A., 1976 – 1 – sp Bibl Santa Ana [306]

EN LOS MATRIMONIOS ROTOS QUE HACEMOS CON LOS HIJOS? / Aradillas Agudo, Antonio – Madrid: Ediciones Maisal, S.A., 1977 – 1 – sp Bibl Santa Ana [306]

MATRIX – 1974-87 (complete) – 1r – 1 – ATLA S0847 – us A.T.L.A. [073]

MATRIX – nos. 1-107/108 (all publ). Jul 1954-Dec 1975. (Jazz Periodicals) – 2r – 1 – $190.00 – us UPA [780]

MATRIX – Ste-Anne-de-Bellevue. nos 11-44. 1980-94 – 9 – Can$20.00y – cn Micromedia [420]

MATRONS' MONTHLY REPORTS / Huron County. Ohio. Children's Services Board – 1900-1910 – 1r – 1 – $32.50r – us Archival [324]

MATRUBHUMI – Calicut, India. Jan 1961-Jun 1967; Ernakulam, Jul 1967-31 Dec 1967; Cochin, Jan 1968-31 Dec 1994 – 138r – 1 – us L of C Photodup [072]

MATRUBHUMI – (Oriya language) – Cuttack, India. 1962-Sept 1966 – 10r – 1 – us L of C Photodup [072]

Matschoss, Conrad *see* BEITRAEGE ZUR GESCHICHTE DER TECHNIK UND INDUSTRIE

Matson, N *see* REMINISCENCES OF BUREAU COUNTY

Matsougata, Masayochi *see* MEMOIRE SUR L'IMPOT FONCIER AU JAPON

MATSQUI NEWS *see* ABBOTSFORD SUMAS AND MATSQUI NEWS

Matsuev, N I *see* KHUDOZHESTVENNAIA LITERATURA RUSSKAIA I PEREVODNAIA 1917-1925 GG. UKAZATEL' STATEI I RETSENZII

MATSUMOTO COLLECTION OF THE CHINESE PRESS CUTTINGS OF POLITICS AND ECONOMY IN THE 20TH CENTURY – 1908-23. 10 classifications – 10r – 1 – Y103,000.00 – ja Yushodo [950]

Matsumura, J *see* ICONES PLANTARUM KOISIKAVENSES

A MATTA : ORGAO REGIONAL – Cidade de Palma, 12 Jul 1908; 25 Jul 1909 – 1,5,6 – bl Biblioteca [072]

MATTA'EI KEDEM / Ha-Cohen, S – Frankfort on the Main. 1807. BJ-422-78 1 – 9 – ne IDC [470]

Matteis, N *see* LE FALSE CONSONANSE DELLA MUSICA..

Matteo, Johan *see* DEMOCRACY OR REVOLUTION IN SPAIN?

MATTER, FORCE, AND SPIRIT, OR, SCIENTIFIC EVIDENCE OF A SUPREME INTELLIGENCE / Lazelle, Henry Martyn – New York: G.P. Putnam, 1895. 1 fiche – 9 – us A.T.L.A. [210]

Matthaei Parisiensis *see*
- CHRONICA MAJORA (RS57)
- HISTORIA ANGLORUM, SIVE, UT VULGO DICITUR, HISTORIA MINOR (RS44)

Matthaesius, Friedrich *see* DIE ENDLOSE STRASSE

Matthaeus, C *see* KURTZER/DOCH AUSFUEHRLICHER BERICHT/VON DEN MODIS MUSICIS, WELCHEN AUS DEN BESTEN/ AELTESTEN/BERUEHMTESTEN UND

DAS MATTHAEUSEVANGELIUM UND SEINE LUCAS-PARALLELEN / Weiss, Bernhard – (Commentary in German; text in Greek. Includes bibliographical references) – Halle: Buchh des Waisenhauses, 1876 – 2mf – 9 – 0-8370-9667-7 – 1986-3667 – us A.T.L.A. [220]

MATTHAEUS-KOMMENTARE AUS DER GRIECHISCHEN KIRCHE (T.U.U. 5-61) / Reuss, J – Berlin, 1957 – 9mf – 9 – ne Slangenburg [240]

Matthaey, Heinrich *see* DEUTSCHE LIEDER

Matthes, B F *see*
- BOEGINEESCH-HOLLANDSCH WOORDENBOEK, MET HOLLANDSCH-BOEGINESCHE WOORDENLIJST, EN VERKLARING VAN EEN TOT OPHELDERING BIJGEVOEGDEN ETHNOGRAPHISCHEN ATLAS. SUPPLEMENT
- BOEGINEESCH-HOLLANDSCH WOORDENBOEK, MET HOLLANDSCH-BOEGINESCHE WOORDENLIJST, EN VERKLARING VAN EEN TOT OPHELDERING BIJGEVOIEGDEN ETHNOGRAPHISCHEN ATLAS
- BOEGINESCHE CHRESTOMATHIE
- MAKASSAARSCHE CHRESTOMATHIE

Mattheson, J *see*
- BEHAUPTUNG DER HIMMLISCHEN MUSIK AUS DEN GRUENDEN DER VERNUNFT, KIRCHEN-LEHRE UND HEILGEN SCHRIFT
- DAS BESCHUETZTE ORCHESTRE, ODER DESSELBEN ZWEYTE EROEFFNUNG
- CRITICA MUSICA
- CRITICA MUSICA, D.I. GRUNDRICHTIGE UNTERSUCHUNG UND BEURTHEILUNG
- EXEMPLARISCHE ORGANISTEN-PROBE IM ARTIKEL VOM GENERAL-BASS..
- DAS FORSCHENDE ORCHESTRE, ODER DESSELBEN DRITTE EROEFFNUNG
- GEORG FRIEDRICH HAENDELS LEBENSBESCHREIBUNG, NEBST EINEM VERZEICHNISSE SEINER AUSUEBUNGSWERKE UND DEREN BEURTEILUNG...
- GROSSE GENERAL-BASS-SCHULE..
- GROSSE GENERAL-BASS-SCHULE. ODER: DER EXEMPLARISCHEN ORGANISTEN-PROBE
- GRUNDLAGE EINER EHREN-PFORTE
- KERN MELODISCHER WISSENSCHAFFT
- KLEINE GENERAL-BASS-SCHULE
- MATTHESONS PHILOLOGISCHES TRESEPIEL, ALS EIN KLEINER BEYTRAG ZUR KRITISCHEN GESCHICHTE DER DEUTSCHEN SPRACHE
- DER MUSICALISCHE PATRIOT, WELCHER SEINE GRUENDLICHE BETRACHTUNGEN UEBER GEIST- UND WELTL. HARMONIEN
- DER MUSICALISCHE PATRIOT WELCHER SEINE GRUENDLICHE BETRACHTUNGEN, UEBER GEIST-UND WELTL. HARMONIEN
- DER NEUE GOETTINGISCHE ABER VIEL SCHLECHTER
- DIE NEUESTE UNTERSUCHUNG DER SINGSPIELE
- PLUS ULTRA...ERSTER ZWEETER VORRATH....1754-55
- DER VOLLKOMMENE CAPELLMEISTER

MATTHESONS PHILOLOGISCHES TRESEPIEL, ALS EIN KLEINER BEYTRAG ZUR KRITISCHEN GESCHICHTE DER DEUTSCHEN SPRACHE / Mattheson, J – 1752 – 9 – us Sibley [780]

MATTHEW AND MARK : WITH NOTES, CRITICAL, EXPLANATORY, AND PRACTICAL... / Cowles, Henry – (Includes chapters on myth in the Gospels and on the Inspiration of the Bible) – New York: D Appleton, 1881 – 1mf – 9 – 0-8370-2755-1 – 1985-0755 – us A.T.L.A. [220]

THE MATTHEW B. BRADY COLLECTION OF CIVIL WAR PHOTOGRAPHS / U.S. Army. Office of the Chief Signal Officer – 4 rolls. T252 – 1 – us Nat'l Archives [355]

Matthew, C G *see* NOTES ON THE FERNS OF HONG KONG AND THE ADJACENT MAINLAND

Matthew Of Westminster *see* FLORES HISTORIARUM (RS95)

Matthews *see* HISTORY OF LEHIGH AND CARBON COUNTIES

Matthews, Alfred *see* FIRE CONSIDERED AS THE SEAMAN'S SCOURGE

MATTHEWS AND BANGS' CIRCUIT COURT REPORTS / Illinois – v1-3. 1866-1912 – 21mf – 9 – $31.50 – LLMC 90-300 – us L.L.M.C. [340]

MATTHEWS BAPTIST CHURCH. MECKLENBURG COUNTY. NORTH CAROLINA : CHURCH RECORDS – 1877-1942 – 1 – 32.76 – us Baptist [240]

Matthews, Brander *see* A STUDY OF THE DRAMA

MATTHEW'S GOSPEL / Worcester, John – Boston: Mass. New-Church Un., 1898. 1 fiche – 9 – us A.T.L.A. [240]

Matthews, James Muscoe *see*
- DIGEST OF THE LAWS OF VIRGINIA OF A CIVIL NATURE
- DIGEST OF THE LAWS OF VIRGINIA, OF A CRIMINAL NATURE
- A GUIDE TO COMMISSIONERS IN CHANCERY.

Matthews, John *see*
- VOYAGE A LA RIVIERE DE SIERRA-LEONE, SUR LA COTE D'AFRIQUE
- VOYAGE TO THE RIVER SIERRA LEONE

Matthews, Margaret *see* THE NATURE AND STATUS OF HEALTH-PROMOTION PROGRAMS IN NOVA SCOTIAN GOODS-PRODUCING INDUSTRIES

Matthews, Stanley *see*
- THE JUDICIAL POWER OF THE UNITED STATES IN SOME OF ITS ASPECTS.
- THE RELATION OF THE STATE TO RELIGIOUS EDUCATION

Matthews, Warren L *see* "JESSE CHISHOLM"

Matthews, William Baynham *see*
- A DIGEST OF THE DECISIONS OF THE DEPARTMENT OF THE INTERIOR AND THE GENERAL LAND OFFICE IN CASES RELATING TO THE PUBLIC LANDS, FROM JULY, 1881 TO DECEMBER, 1887
- FORMS OF PLEADINGS IN CIVIL AND CRIMINAL CASES.

MATTHIAE FLACIJ ILLYRICI, DE VOCE AND RE FIDEI, QUODQUE SOLA FIDE IUSTIFICEMUR, CONTRA PHARISAICUM HIPOCRITARUM FERMENTUM... / Flacius Illyricus d.A E, M – [Basel], 1563 – 3mf – 9 – ne IDC [240]

Matthias, Adolf *see* UNTERSUCHUNGEN UEBER DIE DEUTSCHE UEBERSETZUNG DES ALTEN TESTAMENTS

Matthias, Blanche C *see* LETTERS TO BLANCHE C. MATTHIAS FROM MARGERY LATIMER AND JEAN TOOMER

MATTHIAS CLAUDIUS, DER WANDSBECKER BOTE : EINE EINFUEHRUNG IN DEN SINN SEINES SCHAFFENS / Pfeiffer, Johannes – Dessau: K Rauch, 1941 – 1 – us U.W. Library [430]

MATTHIAS FLACIUS ILLYRICUS : EINE VORLESUNG / Twesten, A – Berlin: G. Bethge, 1844 – 1mf – us A.T.L.A. [240]

Matthieu, A *see* DEVIS DE LA LANGUE FRANCOYSE

IL MATTINO – 1989-1995 – 6r per y – 5,6 – Sfr1,123.00 – sz Infoprint [945]

MATTINO – 1987-1988 – 4 times per yr – 6 – F4,000.00 – sz Infoprint [072]

Mattison, Hiram *see*
- THE ABDUCTION OF MARY ANN SMITH BY THE ROMAN CATHOLICS
- THE IMMORTALITY OF THE SOUL
- POPULAR AMUSEMENTS
- THE RESURRECTION OF THE DEAD
- ROMANISM
- SPIRIT-RAPPING UNVEILED

O MATTO-GRASSO – Cuiaba, 5 Jan 1890-Feb 1892; Feb 1893-Nov 1894; Jan-Mar, Aug-Sep, Dec 1895; Feb, May, Jul-Dec 1897; Jan-Mar, May 1898; Mar-Aug, Oct 1904; Mar-Sep 1905; Sept 1911-Dec 1920; Oct 1921; Jul-Dec 1922; Jan 1928-Jul 1933; Aug, Nov 1935; May 1936-6 Mar 1937 – 1,5,6 – bl Biblioteca [072]

Mattoon, C H *see* BAPTIST ANNALS OF OREGON

Mattsperger, M *see* GEISTLICHE HERZENS EINBILDUNGEN INN ZWEIHUNDERT UND FUENFZIG BIBLISCHEN FIGURSPRUECHEN ANGEDEUTET

Matull, Wilhelm *see*
- OSTDEUTSCHLANDS ARBEITERBEWEGUNG
- OSTPREUSSENS ARBEITERBEWEGUNG

Maturin, C R *see* BERTRAM; OR, THE CASTLE OF ST ALDOBRAND

MATURITAS – v1-6. 1978-84 – 1,5,6,13 – sz Elsevier [073]

MATUTINO – Panama City, Panama. Jan, Apr 1975-1983 – 54r – 1 – us L of C Photodup [072]

O MATUTO : FOLHA DOMINIGUEIRA – Pilar, Alagoas. 7 Maio 1899; 19 Jul 1900 – 1,5,6 – bl Biblioteca [072]

Matveev-Bodryi, N N *see* KOMSOMOLETS NA KOOPERATIVNUIU UCHEBU

Maty, M *see* JOURNAL BRITANNIQUE

Maty, P H *see* PHILOSOPHICAL TRANSACTIONS OF THE ROYAL SOCIETY OF LONDON

Mau, Robert E *see* DIFFERENCES OF CO-DEPENDENCY AND SELF-ESTEEM IN COLLEGE AGE MALE AND FEMALE ATHLETES AND NONATHLETES

Maubach, Jos *see* DIE KARDINAELE UND IHRE POLITIK UM DIE MITTE DES 13. JAHRHUNDERTS

Maubert De Gouvest, Jean-Henri *see* LE TEMPS PERDU OU LES ECOLES PUBLIQUES, CONSIDERATIONS D'UN PATRIOTE SUR L'EDUCATION DE LA PREMIERE JEUNESSE EN FRANCE AVEC L'IDEE D'UN NOUVEAU COLLEGE ET LE PRECIS DE L'INSTRUCTION QUI Y SERAIT DONNEE

Maubert de Gouvest, Jean-Henri *see* LE TEMPS PERDU, OU LES ECOLES PUBLIQUES

MAUCH CHUNK COAL GAZETTE – Mauch Chunk, PA. -sw 1871-1912 – 13 – $25.00r – us I.M.R. [071]

THE MAUCH CHUNK COURIER – Mauch Chunk, PA. 1829-1842. Also incl. Democrat & Argus (Mauch Chunk), 1836-41; The Mauch Chunk Courier, 1840-42. 1 roll – 13 – $25.00r – us I.M.R. [071]

MAUCH CHUNK DEMOCRAT – Mauch Chunk, PA. -w 1870-1910 – 13 – $25.00r – us I.M.R. [071]

MAUCH CHUNK GAZETTE – Mauch Chunk, PA., 1853-1870 – 13 – $25.00r – us I.M.R. [071]

MAUCH CHUNK TIMES NEWS – Mauch Chunk, PA. -d 1912-1953; 1953-1954 – 13 – $25.00r – us I.M.R. [071]

Mauclerc, Julien *see* TRAITE DE L'ARCHITECTURE SUIVANT VITRUVE

Mauconduit, De *see* TRAITE DE L'ORTHOGRAPHE

MAUD : AND OTHER POEMS / Tennyson, Alfred, Lord – London: E. Moxon, 1855 – 1 roll – 1 – 1-55879-557-X – uk Libr Preservation [810]

Maude, Henry Evans *see*
- PAPERS RELATING TO THE GILBERT ISLANDS, 1942-1970
- RESEARCH NOTES ON THE GILBERT ISLANDS, C. 1952-62

Maude, J H *see* THE FOUNDATIONS OF THE ENGLISH CHURCH

LA MAUDITE / Mie d'Aghonne, J LA P – Paris: E. Dentu, 1896. 249p. 3 fiches.(Literature Collection) – 9 – 8.00 – fr Bibl Nationale [830]

Maudsley, Henry *see* BODY AND MIND: AN INQUIRY INTO THEIR CONNECTION AND MUTUAL INFLUENCE, SPECIALLY IN REFERENCE TO MENTAL DISORDERS: AN ENLARGED AND REVISED EDITION

Mauduit, I *see* THE CASE OF THE DISSENTING MINISTERS

Maue, August *see* HISTORY OF WILL COUNTY

Mauger, Cl *see* FRENCH GRAMMAR, WITH ADDITIONS

Mauger, Nicolas *see* LES HOTTETERRE, CELEBRES JOUERS ET FACTEURS DE FLUTES, HAUTBOIS, BASSONS ET MUSETTES DES 17E ET 18E SIECLES; NOUVELLES RECERCES PAR N. MAUGER

Maulde La Claviere, Marie Alphonse Rene de *see* LES MILLE ET UNE NUITS D'UNE AMBASSADRICE DE LOUIS XIV

MAULMAIN CHRONICLE – Burma. -w. 15 April 1837-28 Feb 1844. 2 reels – 1 – uk British Libr Newspaper [072]

MAUMEE ADVANCE-ERA – Maumee, Ohio. 1910-45 – 14r – 1 – $32.50r – us Archival [071]

Maumee. Ohio. First Presbyterian Church *see* RECORDS

MAUMEE VALLEY HERALD – Maumee, Ohio. 1978- – 3r – 1 – $32.50r – us Archival [071]

MAUMEE VALLEY NEWS – Maumee, Ohio. 1925-78 – 26r – 1 – $32.50r – us Archival [071]

Maumus, Vicente *see* LA REPUBLICA Y LA POLITICA DE LA IGLESIA

Maund, B *see* THE BOTANIC GARDEN...

Maupas, Ch *see* GRAMMAIRE ET SYNTAXE FRANCOISE

Maupas du Tour, H de *see* LA VIE DE LA VENERABLE MERE JEANNE FRANCOISE FREMIOT

Maupate, Leon *see* RECHERCHES D'ANTHROPOLOGIE CRIMINELLE CHEZ L'ENFANT. CRIMINALITE ET DEGENERESCENCE

Maxwell-Lefroy, H *see*
- INDIAN INSECT LIFE
- INDIAN INSECT PESTS

MAXWELL'S TALISMAN : THE HOMECROFT MAGAZINE – Chicago [etc]: Guild of the Talisman. v n1-5 mar-jul 1906; v8 n3 5 sep, nov 1907; v9 n2-v10 n6 feb-dec 1908; v12-13 n2 jul 1912-frb 1913 – us Res Libr [073]

MAY DAY WITH THE MUSES / Bloomfield, Robert – London: Printed for the author and for Baldwin, Cradock, and Joy, 1822 – 1 roll – 1 – 1-55879-750-5 – uk Libr Preservation [810]

May, Geoffrey *see* DIVORCE LAW IN OHIO

May, Herbert Gordon *see* MATERIAL REMAINS OF THE MEGIDDO CULT

May, John Wilder *see*
- INSIDE THE BAR AND OTHER OCCASIONAL POEMS
- THE LAW OF INSURANCE, AS APPLIED TO FIRE, LIFE, ACCIDENT, GUARANTEE, AND OTHER NON-MARITIME RISKS

May, Joseph *see* THE MIRACLES AND MYTHS OF THE NEW TESTAMENT

May, Kurt *see* DAS WELTBILD IN GELLERTS DICHTUNG

May, Leon Pamphile Le *see* OEUVRE

May, Werner *see* BUCHHAENDLER PALM

MAY WOMEN SPEAK? A BIBLE STUDY BY A PRESBYTERIAN MINISTER / Hays, George P – 1889 – 9 – us A.T.L.A. [240]

MAY WOMEN SPEAK IN A PROMISCUOUS RELIGIOUS ASSEMBLY / Loomis, Henry – (The Congregational Quarterly, v., April 1874, p. 264-278) – 9 – us A.T.L.A. [240]

LA MAYA / Hurtado, Antonio – 1869 – 9 – 1.50f – sp Bibl Santa Ana [830]

MAYAN CIVILIZATION – 1993 – 36p – 9 – 92-3-102589-9 – fr UNESCO [930]

Mayans y Siscar, Gregorio *see*
- CARTAS MORALES, MILITARES, CIVILES Y LITERARIAS, TOMO 1
- CARTAS MORALES, MILITARES, CIVILES Y LITERARIAS, TOMO 2
- CARTAS MORALES, MILITARES, CIVILES Y LITERARIAS, TOMO 3
- CARTAS MORALES, MILITARES, CIVILES Y LITERARIAS, TOMO 4
- CARTAS MORALES, MILITARES, CIVILES Y LITERARIAS, TOMO 5
- EL ORADOR CRISTIANO
- RETORICA. TOMO 1
- RETORICA. TOMO 2

Maybaum, S *see* FESTSCHRIFT

Maybaum, Siegmund *see*
- DIE ENTWICKELUNG DES ALTISRAELITISCHEN PRIESTERTHUMS
- DIE ENTWICKELUNG DES ISRAELITISCHEN PROPHETENTHUMS

Maybury, Robert *see* VIOLENT FORCES OF NATURE

Maychrzak, Franz *see* LORD BYRON ALS UEBERSETZER

Maycock *see* FLORA BARBEDENSIS. 1830

MAYDAN *see* AL-MAYDAN

LA MAYENNE AGRICOLE – Laval, Nov. 1937 – Apr. 1941 – 1r – fr Armell [630]

Mayer, Gottlob *see* ZUR GESCHICHTE DES RELIGIOESEN ERKENNTNISPROBLEMS. ERSTER TEIL

Mayer, Gustav *see* ERINNERUNGEN. VOM JOURNALISTEN ZUM HISTORIKER DER DEUTSCHEN ARBEITERBEWEGUNG

Mayer, H E *see* DAS ITENERARIUM PEREGRINORUM (MGH SCHRIFTEN..: 18.BD)

Mayer, Hans *see*
- DEUTSCHE LITERATURKRITIK IM ZWANZIGSTEN JAHRHUNDERT
- MEISTERWERKE DEUTSCHER LITERATURKRITIK

Mayer, J *see* CANDID ANIMADVERSIONS ON THE REV. THOMAS WHITAKER'S FOUR LETTERS

Mayer, Johann Tobias *see* PHYSICALISCH-MATHEMATISCHE ABHANDLUNG..

Mayer, Max, Ritter von *see* DIE PAPSTWAHL INNOCENZ 13

Mayer, P H S *see* BENEDIKTINISCHES ORDENSRECHT

Mayer, Peter M *see* PSYCHOLOGICAL DESCRIPTORS OF PREDICTED ROS EXPERIENCES

Mayer, Philip *see* GUSII BRIDEWEALTH LAW AND CUSTOM

Mayer, Renate *see* HAEUSLICHE ALTENPFLEGE

Mayer, Th. et al *see* KAISERTUM UND HERZOGSGEWALT IM ZEITALTER FRIEDRICHS 1 (MGH SCHRIFTEN..: 9.BD)

MAYER-QUASTEN-NEUNHEUSER : VOM CHRISTLICHEN MYSTERIUM: GESAMMELTE ARBEITEN ZUM GEDAECHTNIS VON ODO CASEL – Duesseldorf, 1951 – 7mf – 8 – Dfl28.00 – ne Slangenburg [240]

MAYER'S DIGEST OF DECISIONS CONSTRUING MARYLAND STATUTES / Maryland. Laws, Statutes, etc – 1v (all publ) – 9 – $12.00 – LLMC 84-151 – us L.L.M.C. [340]

Mayes, Edward *see* RIBS OF THE LAW.

Mayeur de Saint Paul, Francois Marie *see* LE DESOEUVRE OU L'ESPOIN DU BOULEVARD DU TEMPLE: CHRONIQUE SCANDALEUSE DES PETITS THEATRES... AU XVIIIE SIECLE

MAYFAIR BAPTIST CHURCH. JACKSONVILLE, FLORIDA : CHURCH RECORDS – 15 May 1948-Mar 1968 – 1 – 213.66 – us Baptist [240]

MAYFIELD FIRST BAPTIST CHURCH. MAYFIELD, KENTUCKY : CHURCH RECORDS – 1864-Jan 1982. Lacks 1880-86. 6386p – 1 – 287.37 – us Baptist [240]

MAYFIELD NEWS – Palo Alto, CA. 1924-35 – 8r – 1 – $400.00 – B02596 – us Library Micro [071]

MAYFIELD RD. HERALD *see* THE BEACON

THE MAYFLOWER – 1851-52. Also: Ladies' Acadian Newspaper – 1 – $75.00 – cn McLaren [640]

THE MAYFLOWER DESCENDANT – v8,9,12,13,14. 1906-12.Indexed. SW16-0229/0123 – 5 – us A.G.L.L. [978]

THE MAYFLOWER DESCENDANT 1620-1937 : PILGRIM GENEALOGY AND HISTORY / Bowman, George Ernest – (For vital records of SE Massachusetts, including Plymouth Colony & Cape Cod. Includes Mayflower Descendant cemetery & church records. Contains autographs, Bible records, depositions etc and lists of Plymouth people in 1623 & 1627, along with many other documents from the archives of Amsterdam and Leyden, Holland) – Boston: The Massachusetts Society of Mayflower Descendants, 1899-1937 (mf ed 1994) – 35mf – 9 – 0-87623-192-X – us Holbrook [920]

MAYFLOWER DESCENDANTS & THEIR MARRIAGES, FOR TWO GENERATIONS AFTER THE LANDING – Item O. Includes A Short History of the Church of the Pilgrim Founders of New England. 37p. SW16-0080 – 5 – us A.G.L.L. [978]

MAYFLOWER INDEX – (v2, Item D.SW16-0226) – v1, comp. & ed. by William Alexander McAuslan, 1932. Item L. Names of the persons they married & the parents working number.618p. SW16-0010 – 5 – us A.G.L.L. [920]

EL "MAYISMO" AL DESNUDO : UNA REGIMEN DE IMPUDICIA POLITICA, DE SUBVERSION INSTITUCIONAL Y DE TRAICION AL PERONISMO / Asiain, Niceforo – Santa Fe: "Irarkola"], 1st ed 1949 – 1 – CSUXADH9754-B – us Hoover Inst Photo [320]

MAYN SHUL KHAVER = MY SCHOOL MATE – (In Yiddish. Monthly) – Buenos Aires, AG. v2 no8. Jan 1936 – 1r – 1 – $25.00 – cn Can Microfilming [072]

Maynar Marino, Juan *see*
- APORTACION AL ESTUDIO DE LOS VINOS DE LA ZONA DE "TIERRA DE BARROS" (BADAJOZ)
- CONTRIBUCION AL ESTUDIO DE LA COMPOSICION ACOMATICA DE LOS VINOS Y DERIVADOS VINICOS DE TIERRA DE BARROS

Maynard, D N *see* DECISIONS OF THE APPELLAT SPORTS, AND FACILITIES OF THE STATE OF WASHINGTON

Maynard, Jerry A *see* THE EFFECT OF A LIFETIME OF PHYSICAL ACTIVITY ON THE QUANTITY OF BONE IN THE CANINE

Maynarde, Thomas *see* SIR FRANCIS DRAKE, HIS VOYAGE, 1595

MAYNARDS YEARBOOKS: EDWARD 1 TO HENRY 8, 1273-1536 – 7 – uk Microform Academic [941]

Maync, Harry Wilhelm *see*
- GESCHICHTE DER DEUTSCHEN GOETHE-BIOGRAPHIE
- GOTTFRIED KELLER

Mayne, John Dawson *see* MAYNE'S TREATISE ON DAMAGES

MAYNE ZIKHROYNES / Kotik, J – 2v. Berlin. 1922. BJ-290-27 1 – 9 – no IDC [940]

MAYNE'S TREATISE ON DAMAGES / Mayne, John Dawson – 3d ed. London: Stevens and Haynes, 1877. 561p. LL-1450 – 1 – us L of C Photodup [340]

MAYO – 1983- – 52mf per y – 9 – $300.00y – us Ross [072]

Mayo, A D *see* SOUTHERN WOMEN IN THE RECENT EDUCATIONAL MOVEMENT IN THE SOUTH

Mayo Clinic *see*
- PROCEEDINGS

MAYO CONSTITUTION – Castlebar, Ireland. -w. 3 Jan 1828-18 Nov 1871. 21 reels – 1 – uk British Libr Newspaper [072]

MAYO DOCUMENTAL, ADVERTENCIA Y PROLOGO DE R. CAILLET-BOIS. 12 TOMOS. BUENOS AIRES. 1961-1966 / Barrado Manzano, Arcangel – Madrid: Graf. Calleja, 1968 – 1 – sp Bibl Santa Ana [946]

MAYO EN LA BIBLIOGRAFIA. BUENOS AIRES, 1961 / Caffese, Maria E & Lafuente, Carlos F – Madrid: Graf. Calleja, 1968 – 1 – sp Bibl Santa Ana [019]

Mayo, Joseph *see* A GUIDE TO MAGISTRATES, WITH PRACTICAL FORMS FOR THE DISCHARGE OF THEIR DUTIES OUT OF COURT

MAYO MERCURY AND CONNAUGHT ADVERTISER – Castlebar. Ireland. -w. 25 Jan 1840-6 Mar 1841. (37 ft) – 1 – uk British Libr Newspaper [072]

MAYO NEWS – Westport, Ireland. 7 Jan 1893-Dec 1976.-w. 64 reels – 1 – uk British Libr Newspaper [072]

Mayor, Federico *see* NEW PAGE

Mayor, J E B *see* RICARDI DE CIRENCESTRIA SPECULUM HISTORIALE DE GESTIS REGUM ANGLIAE (RS30)

Mayor, Joseph Bickersteth *see*
- THE EPISTLE OF ST. JAMES
- THE EPISTLE OF ST JUDE AND THE SECOND EPISTLE OF ST PETER

EL MAYORAZGO DE BLASCO MUNOZ. FUNDACION VINCULAR DE PRINCIPIOS DEL S. 16 / Munoz de San Pedro, Miguel – Badajoz: Diputacion Provincial de Badajoz, 1948. Sep.Rev, Estu. Extrem. – 1 – sp Bibl Santa Ana [946]

MAYORAZGO DEL CONDE DON ENRIQUE DE ALBA LISTE – 1612? – 9 – $1.50f – sp Bibl Santa Ana [350]

MAYOREZGO DE HERNANDO CORTES / Olozaga, Juan de – Madrid, 1954 – 1 – sp Bibl Santa Ana [946]

Mayorga y Guzman, D *see* SEGUNDO MANIFIESTO...CONTRA EL DOCTOR IVAN BERNES

MAYOR'S COURT, NEW YORK CITY : SELECT CASES / New York. (City). Mayor's Court – (v2 of American Legal Records) – 1v. 1674-1784 (all publ) – 9mf – 9 – $13.50 – LLMC 80-047 – us L.L.M.C. [340]

Mayow, J *see*
- TRACTATUS DUO
- TRACTATUS QUINQUE MEDICO-PHYSICI

Mayr, Aloys *see* WORTE ZUR VERSTAENDIGUNG IM STREITE UEBER DIE PAEPSTLICHE UNFEHLBARKEIT

Mayr, H *see* MONOGRAPHIE DER ABIETINEEN DES JAPANISCHEN REICHES

Mayr, Richard *see* BEITRAEGE ZUR BEURTHEILUNG G E LESSING'S

Mayrhofer, Otto *see* GUSTAV FREYTAG UND DAS JUNGE DEUTSCHLAND

Mays, Benjamin Elijah *see* THE NEGRO'S CHURCH

Mayser, Frederick Peter *see* SHALL WOMEN VOTE IN THE CHURCH?

MAYU – Cairo, Egypt. March 1981-1992 – 14r – 1 – us L of C Photodup [072]

Mayvogel, J C *see* GULDEN SPIEGEL, OFTE OPWECKINGE TOT CHRISTELIJCKE DEUGHDEN

Mazaev D I *see* VSEMIRNYI KONGRESS" BAPTISTOV" V" LONDONE V" 1905 GODU

Mazaev, MN *see* OPYT SLOVARIA PSEVDONIMOV RUSSKIKH PISATELEI

Mazarakii, V V *see* UKAZATEL' SOOBSHCHENII, SDELANNYKH NA OBSHCHIKH SOBRANIIAKH RUSSKAGO ENTOMOLOGICHESKAGO OBSHCHESTVA ZA 35 LET EGO SUSHCHESTVOVANIIA (1859-1894)

MAZAVA *see* NY MAZAVA

MAZDAZNAN – v1-5. 1902-6 – 1r – 1 – us Ross [100]

Maze, Frederick *see* PAPERS RELATING TO THE CHINESE MARITIME CUSTOMS SERVICE

MAZEPPA. OPERA EN 5 ACTES ET 6 TABLEAUX... / Grandval, M F – (Vocal score) – Paris: Choudensfils, c1892 – 5 – us Sibley [780]

Mazhar, Mehmed Fevzi Elhac Kureyszade *see* DABER-I SAHIH

MAZKERET IMMANUEL / Loew, I – Semitic Studies in memory of I. Loew. Budapest. 1947. BJ-100-74 1 – 9 – ne IDC [270]

Mazloum, S *see* LE PROBLEME DE L'EAU EN SYRIE ET AU LIBAN. LECON DONNEE A LA 3. SEMAINE SOCIALE DE BEYROUTH EN 1942

Mazure, F A J *see* VIE DE VOLTAIRE

MAZURKA, OP. 46, NO. 2 / Moszkowski, M – Breslau: Hainauer, 188- – 1 – us Sibley [780]

MAZZAV AHEINU BENEI YISRA'EL YOSHEVEI AREZOT HA-MIZRAH – (Ha-Levanon, 12th Iyyar 5629). 1869. BJ-27-229 1 – 9 – ne IDC [370]

Mazzei, Philip *see* THE COMPREHENSIVE MICROFORM EDITION OF HIS PAPERS, 1730-1816

Mazzinghi *see* [IDALIDE] AH CHE NEL PETTO LO SENTO

Mazzinghi, J *see*
- L'ALBERO DI DIANA (VON V. MARTIN). CHE BEL SPASSETTO
- LES DELASSEMENTS MILITARIES. THE FAVORITE DIVERTISMENT COMPOSED BY MON. GALLET AS DANCED AT THE KING'S THEATRE
- PIZARRE. THE FAVORITE GRAND BALLET PERFORMED AT THE KING'S THEATRE HAYMARKET COMPOSED BY MON. GATLET
- SAPHO ET PHAON, THE GRAND BALLET, AS PERFORMED AT THE KING'S THEATRE HAYMARKET, COMPOSED BY MONR. DIDELOT
- THREE SONATAS FOR THE PIANOFORTE WITH OR WITHOUT THE ADDITIONAL KEYS AND AN ACCOMPANYMENT FOR A FLUTE OR A VIOLIN
- TURNPIKE GATE. COMIC OPERA IN 2 ACTS

Mazzini, Giuseppe *see* LIFE AND WRITINGS..

Mazzocca, Augustus D *see* THE EFFECT OF A CIRCUIT WEIGHT TRAINING PROGRAM FOLLOWED BY A DETRAINING PERIOD ON SALIVA CORTISOL AND TESTOSTERONE IN MALES

MB / Virginia. Polytechnic Institute. Extension Division – May 1966-Oct 1969.n.1-99 – 1,5 – us Spaulding [630]

Mbah-Onana, J *see* LA VISION DE LA FEMME A TRAVERS LES CONTES BETI. ETUDE ETHNOLINGUISTIQUE

Mbodj, M *see* UN EXEMPLE D'ECONOMIE COLONIALE, LE SINE-SALOUM, SENEGAL, DE 1887 A 1940

M.C. ESCHER DRAWINGS – (Includes a printed guide and plastic binder) – 106mf – 9 – ne IDC [740]

MCBRIDE'S MAGAZINE – 1-97. January 1868-April 1916 – 1 – us UMI [073]

MCBRIDE'S MAGAZINE – (Also known as: Lippincott's Magazine.) v. 1-95. 1868-1915 – 1 – us Princeton Micro [073]

MCCAHON'S TERRITORY REPORTS / Kansas. Supreme Court – (A Pre-NRS title) – 1v. 1858-63 (all publ) – 4mf – 9 – $6.00 – LLMC 84-137 – us L.L.M.C. [340]

MCCALL'S MAGAZINE – v21- 1894- 1; v98-5,6,9 – us UMI [073]

MCCALL'S NEEDLEWORK & CRAFTS – (v29-1984- 5,6,9) – v1- 1956- – 1 – us UMI [740]

MCCALL'S WORKING MOTHER – v1-4 1978-81 – 1 – us UMI [640]

MCCARTHY ERA BLACKLISTING OF SCHOOL TEACHERS, COLLEGE PROFESSORS, AND OTHER PUBLIC EMPLOYEES : THE FBI RESPONSIBILITIES PROGRAM FILE AND THE DISSEMINATION OF INFORMATION POLICY FILE / ed by O'Reilly, Kenneth – 8r – 1 – $880.00 – 1-55655-121-5 – us UPA [324]

MCCARTY'S CIVIL PROCEDURE REPORTS / New York. (State) – 1v. 1882 (all publ) – 6mf – 9 – $9.00 – LLMC 80-029 – us L.L.M.C. [340]

MCCLOUD RIVER PIONEER – Bartle, CA. 1889-93 – 1r – 1 – $50.00 – B02049 – us Library Micro [071]

MCCLURE PRESS – McClure, Ohio. 1950-60 – 2r – 1 – $32.50r – us Archival [071]

MCCONE COMMISSION REPORT / California. Governor's Commission on the Los Angeles Riots, 1965 – (Index $5.00) – 18v – 6r – 1 – $150.00 – us Microfilm [360]

MCCOOK DAILY – McCook, NE. Jan 1925 to date – 1 – us NE Hist [071]

MCCOOK REPUBLICAN – McCook, NE. -w. Jun 1885-Jan 1900; Mar 1900-Jan 1901; Apr 1901-Jul 1943 – 1 – us NE Hist [071]

MCCOOK TRIBUNE – McCook, NE. -w. (-tw 1924-36). Sep 1883-May 1887; Jun 1888-May 1889; Oct 1889; May 1890-Aug 1891; May 1892-Dec 1924; Jan 1926-Jun 1936 – 1 – us NE Hist [071]

MCCOOL JUNCTION RECORD – McCool, NE. -w. May 1887-Nov 1894; Jul-Sep 1896 – 1 – us NE Hist [071]

MCCRARY'S REPORTS OF CASES IN THE EIGHTH CIRCUIT, 1877-1883 / McCrary, George Washington – Chicago: Callaghan. v1-5. 1881-84 (all publ) – 40mf – 9 – $60.00 – LLMC 81-460 – us L.L.M.C. [340]

MCDOUALL'S CHARTIST JOURNAL AND TRADES' ADVOCATE – 1-27 (all publ). 1841 – 3mf – 9 – $55.00 – us UPA [941]

MCDOWELL RECORDER – Welch. West Virginia. 1916; 1929-1930 – 1 – us UMI [071]

MCFARLAND, ISABELLE AND HELEN, DIARIES – (Diaries of these two sisters, which record daily and social activities, church and Sunday School attendence, travel in northeast Ohio, and the family life of Irish immigrants) – South Euclid, Cuyahoga, OH. 1874-89 – 1 – us Western Res [920]

MCFARLAND NEWS – McFarland, CA. 1928-45 – 5r – 1 – $250.00 – C02438 – us Library Micro [071]

MCFARLAND PRESS – McFarland, CA. 1948-51 – 3r – 1 – $150.00 – C02439 – us Library Micro [071]

MCGILL FORTNIGHTLY – (Cont by: McGill Outlook) – Montreal: [Students of the University, 1892-1898] – 9 – cn C.I.H.M. [370]

MCGILL FORTNIGHTLY *see* MCGILL OUTLOOK

MCGILL JOURNAL OF EDUCATION – (v21-29 1986-94 Can$20.00y 9) – Montreal. v1-29. 1966-94 – 5,9 – Price varies – cn Micromedia [370]

MCGILL LAW JOURNAL – v1-36. 1952-91 – 1,5,6 – $540.00 – us Hein [073]

THE MCGILL MARTLET – (Cont: The Martlet) – Montreal: [Students of McGill University, 1909 or 1910-1911?] – 9 – cn C.I.H.M. [370]

THE MCGILL MARTLET *see* THE MARTLET

MCGILL OBSTETRIC NOTE BOOK / Cameron, James Chalmers – Montreal: E. Renouf, 1896. 02285. (Pre-1900 Canadiana) – 9 – cn C.I.H.M. [618]

MCGILL OUTLOOK – (Cont: McGill Fortnightly) – Montreal: Students of McGill University, [1898-1900] – 9 – cn C.I.H.M. [370]

MCGILL OUTLOOK *see* MCGILL FORTNIGHTLY

MCGILL UNIVERSITY: ANNUAL UNIVERSITY LECTURE OF THE SESSION 1884-5 / Dawson, John William – Montreal?: s.n., 1884?. 03670. (Pre-1900 Canadiana) – 9 – cn C.I.H.M. [971]

MCGLOIN'S APPEALS CASES / Louisiana – v1-2. 1881-84 (all publ) – 10mf – 9 – $15.00 – LLMC 84-143 – us L.L.M.C. [340]

MCGLOIN'S COURT OF APPEALS REPORTS / Louisiana. Supreme Court – (A Pre-NRS title) – v1-2. 1880-1884 (all publ) – 31mf – 9 – $46.50 – LLMC 91-026 – us L.L.M.C. [340]

MCGRATH'S MANDAMUS CASES / McGrath, John W – 1v. 1891-97 (all publ) – 8mf – 9 – $12.00 – LLMC 81-303 – us L.L.M.C. [340]

MCGRAW-HILL PUBLICATIONS COMPANY ECONOMIC REPORTS – (1979- 5,6,9) – 1948- – 1 – us UMI [380]

MCGRAW-HILL'S MEDICAL UTILIZATION REVIEW *see* PSRO LETTER

MCGRAW-HILL'S MEDICINE AND HEALTH *see* FAULKNER AND GRAY'S MEDICINE AND HEALTH

MCGRAW-HILL'S WASHINGTON REPORT ON MEDICINE AND HEALTH *see* FAULKNER AND GRAY'S MEDICINE AND HEALTH

MCGUFFEY READERS – 1849-1936 – 2r – 1 – us Ross [370]

MC-JT TIMES NEWS – Mauch Chunk, PA., 1954 – 13 – $25.00r – us I.M.R. [071]

MCKEAN COUNTY DEMOCRAT – Smethport. Pa. -w. 1859-65, 1890- – 1 – us UMI [071]

MCKEAN COUNTY MINER – Smithport, PA. -w 1900-1932 – 13 – $25.00r – us I.M.R. [071]

MCKEAN ORBIT – Bradford. Pa. 1849-58 – 1 – us UMI [071]

MCKENNEY'S BUSINESS DIRECTORY OF PRINCIPAL TOWNS OF CALIFORNIA, NEVADA, UTAH, WYOMING, COLORADO AND NEBRASKA – West Coast. 1882 – 2r – 1 – $100.00 – D129 – us Library Micro [380]

MCKENNEY'S BUSINESS DIRECTORY OF PRINCIPAL TOWNS OF SOUTHERN CALIFORNIA, ARIZONA, NEW MEXICO, COLORADO AND KANSAS – West Coast. 1882-1883 – 1r – 1 – $50.00 – D130 – us Library Micro [978]

MCKENNEY'S CENTRAL PACIFIC RAILROAD DIRECTORY – West Coast, 1872 – 1r – 1 – $50.00 – D125 – us Library Micro [380]

MCKENZIE RIVER REFLECTIONS – Leaburg OR. Jan 6 1984 + – 1 – us U.O. Library [071]

MCKIM'S DIRECTORY OF CANADIAN PUBLICATIONS: A COMPLETE LIST OF NEWSPAPERS AND PERIODICALS PUBLISHED IN THE DOMINION OF CANADA AND NEWFOUNDLAND – 1892-1942 – 1 – 325.00 – cn McLaren [072]

MCKINLEYVILLE JOURNAL – (Combined with: Arcata Union Jun 1972) – McKinleyville, CA. 1971-72 – 1r – 1 – $50.00 – B02440 – us Library Micro [073]

MCKINLEYVILLE NEWS – McKinleyville, CA. 1967-1970 – 1r – 1 – $50.00 – B02441 – us Library Micro [071]

MCLEAN BAPTIST CHURCH. MEMPHIS, TENNESSEE : CHURCH RECORDS – 1926-55 – 1 – 35.73 – us Baptist [240]

MCLEAN'S REPORTS OF CASES IN THE SEVENTH CIRCUIT, 1839-1855 / McLean, John M – Cincinnati: Derry. v1-6. 1840-56 – 44mf – 9 – $66.00 – LLMC 81-461 – us L.L.M.C. [340]

MCLEMORESVILLE BAPTIST CHURCH. MCLEMORESVILLE, TENNESSEE : CHURCH RECORDS – 1836-Aug 1954 – 1 – 33.39 – us Baptist [240]

MCMAHAN'S WASP – Salem OR. May 19 1894-Jan 29 1895 – 1 – us U.O. Library [071]

THE MCMASTER MONTHLY *see* THE MCMASTER UNIVERSITY MONTHLY

MCMASTER UNIVERSITY MONTHLY *see* THE WOODSTOCK COLLEGE MONTHLY

THE MCMASTER UNIVERSITY MONTHLY – (Cont: Woodstock College Monthly. Cont by: The McMaster Monthly) – [Toronto?: s.n, 1891-1930?] (Toronto: Dudley & Burns) – 9 – cn C.I.H.M. [370]

MCMASTER'S COMMERCIAL CASES FOR THE BANKER, TREASURER AND CREDIT MAN... *see* MCMASTER'S COMMERCIAL DECISIONS AFFECTING THE BANKER AND MERCHANT

MCMASTER'S COMMERCIAL DECISIONS AFFECTING THE BANKER AND MERCHANT / McMaster, J S – (Title changes to: McMaster's Commercial Cases for the Banker, Treasurer and Credit Man – Current Business Law with v17 1914) – New York: The Commercial Book Co. v1-29. 1879-1920 (all publ) – 9 – LLMC 95-127 – us L.L.M.C. [340]

MCMINNVILLE NEWS – McMinnville OR. Jan 15 1902 – 1 – us U.O. Library [071]

MCMINNVILLE TELEPHONE REGISTER – McMinnville OR. Feb 8-Nov 15 1889 – 1 – us U.O. Library [071]

MCMULLAN'S CASES IN EQUITY / South Carolina. Supreme Court – (A Pre-NRS title) – 1v. 1840-1842 (all publ) – 6mf – 9 – $9.00 – LLMC 94-034 – us L.L.M.C. [340]

MCMULLAN'S LAW REPORTS / South Carolina. Supreme Court – (A Pre-NRS title) – v1-2. 1840-1842 (all publ) – 12mf – 9 – $18.00 – LLMC 94-022 – us L.L.M.C. [340]

MCN: THE AMERICAN JOURNAL OF MATERNAL CHILD NURSING – v. 1-. 1976- – 1,5,6,9 – us UMI [618]

MCORD'S CASES IN EQUITY / South Carolina. Supreme Court – (A Pre-NRS title) – v1-2. 1825-1827 (all publ) – 8mf – 9 – $12.00 – LLMC 94-028 – us L.L.M.C. [340]

MCORD'S LAW REPORTS / South Carolina. Supreme Court – (A Pre-NRS title) – v1-4. 1821-1828 (all publ) – 17mf – 9 – $25.50 – LLMC 94-014 – us L.L.M.C. [340]

MCPHERSON COUNTY TIMES – Omega, NE. -w. Jul 1896-Dec 1896 – 1 – us NE Hist [071]

MCPHUN'S AUSTRALIAN NEWS – Glasgow. Scotland. -m. Jan 1853-Jul 1855. (29 ft) – 1 – uk British Libr Newspaper [072]

MD. (MEDICAL DOCTOR) – (v.23-. 1979- 5,6,9) – v.1-. 1957- – 1 – us UMI [073]

MDE. MANAGERIAL AND DECISIONS ECONOMICS – (1982-. 1,5,6,9) – v1-. 1980- – 1 – us UMI [650]

MDT : MOTORCYCLE DEALER AND TRADE – Toronto. v12-17. 1989-94 – 1 – Can$60.00y – cn Micromedia [380]

ME / Virginia. Polytechnic Institute. Extension Division – n.1-53. Feb 1952-Feb 1969 – 1,5 – us Spaulding [630]

ME CALLAGH, CAPTAIN FRANCIS...LONDON, 1928 / Me Callagh, Francis – Madrid: Razon y Fe, 1929 – 1 – sp Bibl Santa Ana [946]

Me Callagh, Francis *see* ME CALLAGH, CAPTAIN FRANCIS...LONDON, 1928

Meachum, John B *see* AN ADDRESS TO ALL THE COLORED CITIZENS OF THE UNITED STATES

MEAD ADVOCATE – Mead, NE. -w. Apr 1893; Nov 1895-Oct 1898, scattered issues missing; Dec 1897-Jul 1911; Jan 1912-Jan 1913; Apr-Jul 1913; Oct 1914-Feb 1917 – 1 – us NE Hist [071]

Mead, Charles Marsh *see* CHRIST AND CRITICISM...THE RELATION OF CHRISTIAN FAITH TO BIBLICAL CRITICISM

Mead, Chauncey W *see* CHAUNCEY W. MEAD PAPERS, MS 3602

Mead, Edwin Doak *see*
- MARTIN LUTHER
- THE PAPERS OF EDWIN DOAK MEAD AND LUCIA AMES MEAD, 1876-1936

Mead Lucia Ames *see* THE PAPERS OF EDWIN DOAK MEAD AND LUCIA AMES MEAD, 1876-1936

Mead, Matthew *see* THE ALMOST CHRISTIAN DISCOVERED

Mead, Willis W *see* THE APOCALYPSE OF JESUS CHRIST: AN EXPOSITION

MEADOW BRANCH BAPTIST CHURCH. UNION ASSOCIATION. NORTH CAROLINA : CHURCH RECORDS – 1810-46 – 1 – 5.00 – us Baptist [240]

MEADOW GROVE NEWS – Meadow Grove, NE. -w. May 1919 to date – 1 – us NE Hist [071]

MEADOW GROVE TRIBUNE – Meadow Grove, NE. -w. Aug 1895; Nov 1895; Mar 1897-May 1898 – 1 – us NE Hist [071]

Meadow, H Lee *see* JOURNAL OF AMBULATORY CARE MARKETING

MEADOWS OF GOLD AND MINES OF GEMS / El Masudi – 1841 – 1 – uk Microform Academic [950]

MEADVILLE GAZETTE – Meadville, PA. -w 1891-1907. 8 rolls – 13 – $25.00r – us I.M.R. [071]

Meadville. Presbytery (Pres. Ch. in the U.S.A. New School) *see* MINUTES, 1843-1870

MEAGHER COUNTY NEWS – White Sulphur Springs. Mont. 1968-1959; 1966- – 1 – us UMI [071]

Meagher, James Luke *see* CHRIST'S KINGDOM ON EARTH

Meagher, R F *see* PUBLIC INTERNATIONAL DEVELOPMENT FINANCING IN SUDAN

Meakin, Budgett *see* MODEL FACTORIES AND VILLAGES: IDEAL CONDITIONS OF LABOUR AND HOUSING

Meakin, Frederick *see* NATURE AND DEITY

THE MEANING AND MESSAGE OF THE CROSS : A CONTRIBUTION TO MISSIONARY APOLOGETICS / Mabie, Henry Clay – 2nd ed. New York: Fleming H Revell, c1906 – 1mf – 9 – 0-8370-4279-8 – 1985-2279 – us A.T.L.A. [230]

MEANING AND METHOD OF LIFE: A SEARCH FOR RELIGION / Gould, George M – New York: G.P. Putnam, 1893 – 9 – us A.T.L.A. [240]

MEANING AND SURVIVAL : DANCE IN THE CONCENTRATION CAMPS / Filips, Teri L – Texas Woman's University, 1994 – 1mf – 9 – PE 3638 – us Microform Publ [790]

THE MEANING OF HOMOOUSIOS IN THE "CONSTANTINOPOLITAN" CREED / Bethune-Baker, James Franklin – Cambridge: University Press, 1901 – 1mf – us A.T.L.A. [240]

THE MEANING OF HOMOOUSIOS IN THE 'CONSTANTINOPOLITAN CREED' / Bethune-Baker, James Franklin – 1901 – 2mf – 9 – ne Slangenburg [240]

THE MEANING OF LEISURE FROM THE PERSPECTIVE OF WIFE CAREGIVERS OF OLDER HUSBANDS / Rogers, Nancy B – Indiana University, 1995 – 3mf – 9 – $12.00 – RC494 – us Microform Publ [306]

THE MEANING OF PRAYER / Fosdick, Harry Emerson – New York: Association Press, 1915 – 1mf – us A.T.L.A. [240]

THE MEANING OF SANCTIFICATION IN TWENTIETH CENTURY SOUTHERN BAPTIST THOUGHT / Hollon, D Leslie – 1981 – 1 – 5.00 – us Baptist [240]

THE MEANING OF THE CHURCH (CCC67) = CHI TU CHIAO CHIAO HUI TI I I / Chao, Tzu-ch'en – (In Chinese) – Shanghai: Association Press of China, 1948 – 1r – 1 – 1984-B500 – us A.T.L.A. [240]

Means, Stewart *see* SAINT PAUL AND THE ANTE-NICENE CHURCH

Meares, J *see* VOYAGES FROM CHINA TO THE NORTHWEST COAST OF AMERICA, 1788 AND 1789, AND FROM BENGAL 1786

ME-ARKHIYYONO SHEL HE-HAKHAM BASHI / Dinur, B – v. 1. Ziyyon. 1926. BJ-27-75 1 – 9 – ne IDC [290]

Mearns, James *see*
- THE CANTICLES OF THE CHRISTIAN CHURCH
- EARLY LATIN HYMNARIES

MEARNS LEADER – (Leader May 1927-Mar 1930. Mearns Leader & Kincardineshire Mail Apr 1930-) – Stonehaven, Scotland, UK. 1913-81 – 53r – 1 – uk British Libr Newspaper [072]

MEARNS LEADER AND KINCARDINESHIRE MAIL *see* MEARNS LEADER

Mearns, Peter *see* CHRISTIAN TRUTH VIEWED IN RELATION TO PLYMOUTHISM

Mears, David Otis *see*
- DEATHLESS BOOK
- INSPIRED THROUGH SUFFERING

Mears, James *see* PLANT TAXONOMIC LITERATURE

Mears, John *see* THE BEGGARS OF HOLLAND AND THE GRANDEES OF SPAIN

Mears, John W *see*
- HEROES OF BOHEMIA
- THE STORY OF MADAGASCAR

Mears, Leon A *see*
- CARBOHYDRATE FOODS IN THE INDONESIAN DIET
- ECONOMIC ESSAYS ON THE SOCIALIST(SIC) ECONOMY OF INDONESIA
- ECONOMIC PAPERS PRESENTED AT SECOND NATIONAL SCIENTIFIC CONGRESS OF INDONESIA BY ECONOMIC FACULTY, UNIV. OF INDONESIA
- FOOD GRAIN CONSUMPTION TRENDS AND THEIR EFFECTS ON FOOD GRAIN MARKETING IN INDONESIA
- READINGS IN BUSINESS ADMINISTRATION AND ECONOMICS
- RICE MARKETING IN THE REPUBLIC OF INDONESIA

ME'ASSEF / ed by Rabinovich, L – 2v. St. Petersburg. 1902. BJ-422-70 1 – 9 – ne IDC [470]

ME'ASSEF LE-SIFRUT YAFAH U-LE-VIKKORET – Odessa. 1919. BJ-422-59 1 – 9 – ne IDC [470]

THE MEASURE – A Journal of Poetry. New York. no. 1-64. Mar 1921-June 1926 – 1 – us NY Public [410]

MEASURE BOOK / Rugheimer, John – 1870-90. Charleston, SC tailor. 24 fiches – 9 – us South Carolina Historical [740]

MEASURE FOR MEASURE – Battle Mountain, NV. Mar-Oct 1875 – 1r – 1 – $50.00 – U04410 – us Library Micro [071]

MEASUREMENT AND INSPECTION TECHNOLOGY – v.1-5. 1979-83 – 1,5,6,9 – us UMI [073]

THE MEASUREMENT OF ATHLETIC POWER / McCloy, Charles H – 1932 – 5mf – 9 – $15.00 – us Microform Publ [790]

THE MEASUREMENT OF PERCEIVED-SELF AND PERCEIVED-PARENTAL GENDER-ROLE ORIENTATION / Grogan, Jennifer – 1988 – 148p 2mf – 9 – $8.00 – us Microform Publ [150]

MEASUREMENT OF STROKE VOLUME DURING EXERCISE, RECOVERY FROM EXERCISE, AND CALCIUM CHANNEL BLOCKADE USING ELECTROCARDIOGRAPHY / Rock James A – 1994 – 2mf – $8.00 – us Microform Publ [612]

MEASUREMENT SCIENCE AND TECHNOLOGY – v1-. 1990- – 1,5,6,9 – £360.00 – uk I.O.P. [530]

MEASUREMENT TECHNIQUES – v1-36. 1958-93 – 1,5 – $180.00v – us UMI [620]

MEASURES OF PROTECTION : METHODOLOGY, ECONOMIC INTERPRETATION AND POLICY RELEVANCE – 1989 – 96p – it F.A.O. [330]

MEASURING MOTOR ABILITY / Brace, David K – 1930 – 3mf – 9 – $9.00 – us Microform Publ [790]

MEAT AND MEAT PRODUCTS IN HUMAN NUTRITION IN DEVELOPING COUNTRIES – 1992 – 100p – it F.A.O. [640]

MEAT OF IT, 1945-1966 : INTERNATIONAL MEAT WORKER, 1946-1948 / United Packinghouse Workers of AmericaPan-American Committee of Meat Workers – (Coll title: Labor Union Periodicals, Pt 3) – 1996 – 1r – 1 – $135.00 – 1-55655-628-4 – us UPA [331]

MEAT PRODUCTION IN LIBYA / Libya. Ministry of Agriculture and Animal Wealth. Agricultural Planning and Economics Department. Statistics Division – 1966. BNE-1018 1 – 9 – ne IDC [338]

MEAT SCIENCE – v1-11 1977-84 – 1,5,6,13 – sz Elsevier [660]

MEAT WORKER : 1946-1948 – (Coll title: Labour Union Periodicals, Part 3) – 1996 – 1r – 1 – $135.00 – 1-55655-626-8 – us UPA [331]

MEATH CHRONICLE – Meath, Ireland. -d. 1904-78. 87 reels – 1 – PS27.50r – ie European Micro [072]

MEATH HERALD – Ireland.15 Feb 1845-1853; 1857-69; 1871-87; 1889-94. -w. 17 reels – 1 – uk British Libr Newspaper [072]

MEATH HERALD – Ireland.1895-96. -w. 1 reel – 1 – uk British Libr Newspaper [072]

MEATH PEOPLE – Navan, Ireland. -w. 1 Aug 1857-28 Nov 1863. 6 reels – 1 – uk British Libr Newspaper [072]

MECANIQUE ANALYTIQUE / Lagrange, Joseph Louis de – Paris, 1788, xii, 512 p. Histoire des Sciences XVIIe-XIXe Siecles. 7984 – 9 – fr Hachette [530]

LA MECANIQUE DES LANGUES ET L'ART DE LES ENSEIGNER / Pluche, N A – 1751 – 9 – fr I.C.S. [370]

MECANIQUE VIVANTE. LE CRANE DES VERTEBRES DU POISSON A L'HOMME / Leroi-Gourhan, A – 9 – F70.00 – fr Ethnologie [574]

LE MECANISME DU FLUTEUR AUTOMATE / Vaucanson, J de – 1738 – 9 – us Sibley [780]

MECANO – Theo van DoesBurg. No.1-4/5. Leiden, Paris. 1922 – 1 – fr A.C.R.P.P. [073]

MECCA OIL BULLETIN – (Weekly newsletter serving the petroleum industry) – Warren, OH. nov 24, 1860 – 1r – 1 – us Western Res [071]

MECCA OIL COMMERCIAL : TRADE JOURNAL FOR THE TRUMBULL CO OIL INDUSTRY – Warren, OH. 13 April 1861 – 1r – 1 – us Western Res [073]

MECELLE-I AHKAMN ADLIYE / Cevdet, Ahmet – 3d ed. Istanbul: Matbaayi Osmaniye 1892. 633p. LL-12016 – 1 – us L of C Photodup [340]

MECH – Warsaw. May 1934-Aug. 1939, nos. 1-272. Missing: no. 33, 1934 – 1 – 35.00r – us Hoover Inst Photo [073]

MECH' DUKHOVNYI V" OGRAZHDENIE OT" SEKTANTSKIKH" = THE SPIRITUAL SWORD IN PROTECTION FROM SECTARIAN HERESIES / Smolin, Ioann – St. Petersburg, 2nd ed 1911 – 1r – 1 – $27.80 – us Baptist [240]

MECH GEDEONA = THE SWORD OF GIDEON – (Publ. No. 3481-7b. One of a four-part item) – Harbin, Manchuria, China, 1929-1940 (incomplete). A non-denominational evangelical periodical. 2,308p – 1 – $124.80 – us Baptist [240]

Mechan, Charles M *see* A HISTORY OF CHRISTIAN COUNTY

MECHANIC – Bangor. Maine. and Farmer. -W. 1838-39 – 1 – us UMI [071]

THE MECHANIC – Fall River, MA: [v1 n1-46. apr 27 1844-apr 1 1845] – us Res Libr [071]

MECHANIC AND FARMER *see* THE BEE

Mechanic Falls, Maine. Mechanic Falls Baptist Church *see* RECORDS

MECHANICAL AND MUSCLE ACTIVATION CHARACTERISTICS DURING CROUCH STANCE BALANCE IN CHILDREN WITH SPASTIC CEREBRAL PALSY / Burtner, Patricia A – University of Oregon, 1996 – 2mf – 9 – $8.00 – PE 3633 – us Microform Publ [612]

MECHANICAL AND PHYSIOLOGICAL DIFFERENCES BETWEEN RUNNING AND WALKING AT VARIOUS VELOCITIES / Falvo, Lisa A & Scheuchenzeuber, H Joseph – 1992 – 1mf – 9 – $4.00 – us Microform Publ [612]

MECHANICAL ENERGY ANALYSIS OF WALKING IN ELDERLY MEN / Duranczyk, Denise M – 1989 – 145p 2mf – 9 – $8.00 – us Microform Publ [612]

MECHANICAL ENGINEERING – v28- 1906- 1; v87- 5,6; v98- 9 – us UMI [621]

MECHANICAL ENGINEERING – New York. v28-77. 1906-55 – 1,5,6 – us Princeton Micro [621]

MECHANICAL ENGINEERING BULLETIN – (1981-. 1,5,6,9) – 1974- – 1 – us UMI [073]

MECHANICAL ENGINEERING NEWS – (1983-. 1,5,6,9) – 1973- – 1 – us UMI [073]

MECHANICAL HANDLING INTERNATIONAL – NS 61-63. 1974-76 – 1 – us UMI [621]

MECHANICAL LABOR ESTIMATING GUIDE – Covers 19 years of models – 9 – $139.00; $185.00 in Canada – us Mitchell Int'l [629]

MECHANICS AND FAITH: A STUDY OF SPIRITUAL TRUTH IN NATURE / Porter, Charles Talbot – New York: G. Putnam, 1888. 1 fiche. 8370-4780-3 – 9 – us A.T.L.A. [240]

THE MECHANIC'S FREE PRESS, 1829-1831 / Philadelphia, Pennsylvania – 1972 – 1r – 1 – $85.00 – S1712 – us Scholarly Res [978]

THE MECHANICS' LIEN ACTS; BEING THE REVISED STATUTE OF ONTARIO, CHAPTER 120, AND 41 VICTORIAE, CHAPTER 17, WITH ANNOTATIONS / Holmested, George Smith – Toronto: Rowsell & Hutchison, 1878. 77 1p. LL-2218 – 1 – us L of C Photodup [340]

THE MECHANICS' LIEN LAW FOR THE STATE OF CALIFORNIA / Montgomery, Zachariah – San Diego: Stenhouse, 1891. 36p LL-597 – 1 – us L of C Photodup [340]

THE MECHANICS' LIEN LAW OF ILLINOIS, AS AMENDED BY ACT OF 1887. / Cooper, Charles William – Chicago: Building, 1887. 52p. LL-64 – 1 – us L of C Photodup [340]

THE MECHANIC'S LIEN LAW OF THE STATE OF ILLINOIS / Coleman, Julius Archer – Chicago 1895. 114 p. LL-13 – 1 – us L of C Photodup [340]

MECHANICS' LIEN LAW OF THE STATE OF NEW JERSEY AND BUILDERS' GUIDE. / Cloughly, Alfred – Newark: Baker, 1887. 128p. LL-62 – 1 – us L of C Photodup [340]

MECHANICS' LIENS IN NORTH CAROLINA / Mordecai, Samuel Fox – Raleigh: Edwards & Broughton, 1897. 150p. LL-892 – 1 – us L of C Photodup [340]

MECHANICS' MAGAZINE, AND JOURNAL OF THE MECHANICS' INSTITUTE – v. 1-10. January 1833-August 1837 – 1 – us UMI [621]

MECHANICS OF COMPOSITE MATERIALS – v1-30. 1965-94 – 1,5 – $80.00v – us UMI [620]

MECHANICS OF NORMAL AND PATHOLOGICAL LOCOMOTION IN MAN / Steindler, Arthur – 1935 – 9mf – 9 – $27.00 – us Microform Publ [612]

MECHANICS RESEARCH COMMUNICATIONS – v1- 1974- – 5,6,9 – us UMI [621]

MECHANICSBURG FREE PRESS – Mechanicsburg, PA. -w 1884-1899; 1900-1902. 2 rolls – 13 – $25.00r – us I.M.R. [071]

MECHANICSBURG WEEKLY GAZETTE – Mechanicsburg, PA. -w 1856-58. 2 rolls – 13 – $25.00r – us I.M.R. [071]

DIE MECHANISIERUNG DES LEBENS IM WERK JOHANN GOTTFRIED HERDERS / Birkner, Siegfried – Frankfurt a.M., 1957 – 2mf – 9 – DM62.00 – 3-89349-379-4 – gw Hänsel [120]

MECHANISIERUNG DES LEBENS UND MODERNE LYRIK / Jost, Theodor – (Includes bibliographical references) – Bonn a. Rh.: L Roehrscheid, 1934 – 1r – 1 – us U.W. Library [400]

MECHANISM AND MACHINE THEORY – v1-1966- – 5,6,9 – us UMI [621]

MECHANISM IN THOUGHT AND MORALS : AN ADDRESS DELIVERED BEFORE THE PHI BETA KAPPA SOCIETY OF HARVARD UNIVERSITY, 29 JUN 1870, WITH NOTES AND AFTERTHOUGHTS / Holmes, Oliver Wendell, Jr – Boston: J.R. Osgood & Co., 1871 – 101p – 1 – us U.W. Library [170]

MECHANISMS OF AGING AND DEVELOPMENT – v1-27. 1972-84 – 1,5,6,13 – sz Elsevier [073]

MECHANISMUS DER PERMISSIVEN WIRKUNG DES GLUCOCORTICOIDS DEXAMETHASEN AUF DIE GLUCAGON-ABHAENGIGE AKTIVIERUNG DES PHOSPHOENOLPYRUVAT CARBOXYKINASE GENS IM KULTIVIERTEN RATTENHEPATOCYTEN / Runge, Dieter – 1995 – 2mf – 9 – DM80.00 – 3-8267-2139-X – gw Hänsel [574]

DER MECHANISMUS DER VATIKANISCHEN RELIGION : NACH DEM FAKULTAETENBUCH DER REDEMPTORISTEN / Friedrich, Johann – Bonn: P. Neusser, 1876 – 1mf – us A.T.L.A. [240]

THE MECHANISTIC PRINCIPLE AND THE NON-MECHANICAL : AN INQUIRY INTO FUNDAMENTALS, WITH EXTRACTS FROM REPRESENTATIVES OF EITHER SIDE / Carus, Paul – Chicago: Open Court, 1913 – 1mf – us A.T.L.A. [100]

MECHANIX ILLUSTRATED – (v. 66- 1970- 5,6. v. 67- 1971- 9) – v. 1- 1928- – 1 – us UMI [621]

MECHANIZATION OF IRRIGATED CROP PRODUCTION – 1977 repr 1979 – 413p – it F.A.O. [631]

THE MECHANIZATION OF SMALL-SCALE INDUSTRIES / Mulia, Wanda – Second Report. SE 3429 1. 1957 – 9 – ne IDC [621]

MECHANIZED SPRINKLER IRRIGATION – 1982 – 438p – it F.A.O. [631]

UNE MECHANTE FEMME / Moreton de Chabrillan, Elizabeth Celeste Venard de – Paris: Leroy, 1877. 280p. (Les Femmes Collection) – 3mf – 9 – $8.00 – fr Bibl Nationale [830]

MECHATRONICS – 1,5,69 – us UMI [620]

Mechel, Kurt *see* DIE "HISTORIE VON VIER KAUFMAENNERN" UND DEREN DRAMATISCHE BEARBEITUNGEN IN DER DEUTSCHEN LITERATUR DES 16. UND 17. JAHRHUNDERTS

Mechelen, Lucas van *see* HET BOEK DER GEESTELIJKE GEZANGEN

Mechem, Floyd Russell *see*
- CASES ON DAMAGES SELECTED FROM DECISIONS OF ENGLISH AND AMERICAN COURTS
- CASES ON THE LAW OF PARTNERSHIP
- CASES ON THE LAW OF SUCCESSION TO PROPERTY AFTER THE DEATH OF THE OWNER.
- ELEMENTS OF THE LAW OF PARTNERSHIP
- OUTLINES OF THE LAW AGENCY
- A TREATISE ON THE LAW OF SALE OF PERSONAL PROPERTY

MECHITHAR'S DES MEISTERARTZES AUS HER "TROST BEI FIEBERN" / Seidel, E – Leipzig, 1908 – 6mf – 9 – ne IDC [610]

Mechow, Karl Benno von *see* REITER IM KRIEG

MECHROUTIETTE – Paris, France. Le Constitionnel. -m. 15 Oct 1909-April 1914. 4 reels – 1 – uk British Libr Newspaper [072]

MECHTILDE DE MAGDEBOURG (1207-1282) : ETUDE DE PSYCHOLOGIE RELIGIEUSE / Ancelet-Hustache, J – Paris, 1926 – 11mf – 8 – ne Slangenburg [290]

Meckel, Eberhard *see* WIEDERSEHEN MIT DER JUGEND

Meckel, J F *see* ADDITAMENTA AD HISTORIAM MOLLUSCORUM, PISCIUM ET AMPHIBIORUM

EIN MECKLENBURGER : ROMAN / Wilbrandt, Adolf von – Stuttgart: J G Cotta, 1901 – 1r – 1 – us U.W. Library [830]

MECKLENBURGISCHES URKUNDENBUCH – Schwerin. Bd. 1-25; 1863-1913. Published by Verein fuer Mecklenburgische Geschichte und Altertumskunde. Film Mas C 632 – 1 – us H.U. Library [073]

Mecklenburg-Schwerin. Statistisches Landesamt *see* BEITRAEGE ZUR STATISTIK MECKLENBURGS

MECMUA-I EBUEZZIYA – Istanbul, cilt 1-15, cuez 1-159 (15 Ramadan 1297-2 Ramadan 1330 [21 Aug 1880-15 Aug 1912]) – 76mf – 9 – $700.00 – us MEDOC [949]

MECMU'A-I ES'AR-I RE'FET – Istanbul, 1289 – 1mf – 9 – $6.00 – us MEDOC [949]

MECMU'A-I 'IRFAN PASA – Istanbul, 1287 – 2mf – 9 – $12.00 – us MEDOC [949]

MECMUA-I MUALLIM – (Muallim Naci, ed. 1.-2. sene, nos 1-58 (24 Muharrem 1305-i Rebiuelevvel 1306 H[30 Eyluel 1303-3 Tesrinisani 1304 M. 12 Oct 1887-5 Nov 1888])) – Istanbul: Mihran Matbaasi – 9mf – 9 $250.00 – us MEDOC [949]

MECMU'A-I MUENSEAT-I SELATIN / Bey, Feridun – 1848 Istanbul edition, vols 1-2. – 23mf. $52.50; 1858 Istanbul edition, vols 1-2. – 14mf. $52.50 – 9 – us MEDOC [260]

MECMU'AT UEL-KAVANIN – Beirut, 1928-1932 – 7v 55mf – 9 – $105.00 – us MEDOC [949]

MECOSTA COUNTY PIONEER – Big Rapids. Mich. -w. 1862-74 – 1 – us UMI [071]

LES MEDAILLES DECERNEES AUX INDIENS : ETUDE HISTORIQUE ET NUMISMATIQUE DES COLONISATIONS EUROPEENNES EN AMERIQUE / Morin, Victor – Ottawa, 1916. SEM105P776 – 2mf – 9 – Can$4.50 – cn Bibl Nat [730]

MEDAL ROLLS AND CLASPS OF THE QUEENSLAND DEFENSE FORCE, 1902-1903 / Chief Secretary's Office, Queensland – 4r – 1 – CRS B5167 – at Archives [920]

MEDALLA BATIDA POR LA VILLA DE ALCANTARA, EN HONOR DEL CORONEL MAINE / Azuar, Antonio – Caceres: Tip. Enc. y Lib. Jimenez, 1907 – 1 – sp Bibl Santa Ana [946]

MEDALLAS DE LAS COLONIAS. TOMO 1 / Florez Setien, Enrique – 1757 – 2mf – 9 – Pta1,500.00 – 84-7848-046-3 – sp Pentalfa [946]

MEDALLAS DE LAS COLONIAS. TOMO 2 / Florez Setien, Enrique – 1758 – 1mf – 9 – Pta1,000.00 – 84-7848-047-1 – sp Pentalfa [946]

MEDALLAS DE LAS COLONIAS. TOMO 3 / Florez Setien, Enrique – 1773 – 1mf – 9 – Pta1,000.00 – 84-7848-048-X – sp Pentalfa [946]

MEDALLONES EXTREMENOS / Monterrey, Manuel – Badajoz: Tip. A. Arqueros, 1945 – 1 – sp Bibl Santa Ana [946]

MEDALLONES EXTREMENOS : POESIAS / Monterrey, Manuel – Badajoz: Tip. V.Arqueros, 1945 – 1 – sp Bibl Santa Ana [810]

MEDALLONES EXTREMENOS 2 / Monterrey, Manuel – Badajoz: Tip.Vda. de A.Arqueros, 1949 – 1 – sp Bibl Santa Ana [946]

MEDAL'ONY. SONETY / Severianin, I – Belgrad. 1934. BR-1030 2 – 8 – ne IDC [460]

MEDALS OF THE BRITISH NAVY AND HOW THEY WERE WON. WITH A LIST OF THOSE OFFICERS WHO FOR THEIR GALLANT CONDUCT WERE GRANTED HONORARY SWORDS AND PLATE BY THE COMMITTEE OF THE PATRIOTIC FUND / Long, William Henry – 1895 – 9 – 20.00 – uk Libr Preservation [941]

MEDAN POST : ALGEMEEN TIJDSCHRIFT VOOR SUMATRA'S OOSTKUST – Medan, 1931, v3 (10-13); 1932, v3 (14-38); v4 (1-9, 27-33) – 9mf – 9 – ne IDC [072]

MEDAN PRESS SUMMARY / U.S. Information Service – Djakarta. Indonesia. 1961-1967 – 1 – us UMI [072]

Medard, J F *see* COMMUNAUTE LOCALE ET ORGANISATION COMMUNAUTAIRE AUX ETATS-UNIS

MEDBORGAREN – Stockholm, Sweden. 1829-32 – 2r – 1 – sw Kungliga [072]

Meddybemps, Maine. Meddybemps Baptist Church *see* RECORDS

MEDDYGON MIDDFAL *see* THE PHYSICIANS OF MYDDVAL; MEDDYGON MIDDFAL

MEDEA : ER SOLL DEIN HERR SEIN: ZWEI NOVELLEN / Heyse, Paul – Stuttgart: C Krabbe, [189-?] – 1 – us U.W. Library [830]

MEDECINE MODERNE DU CANADA *see* MODERN MEDICINE OF CANADA

LES MEDECINS AU THEATRE DE L'ANTIQUITE AUX DIX-SEPTIEME SIECLE / Witkowski, Gustave Jules A – 1905 – 1 – us Res Libr [410]

MEDEDEELINGEN VAN "DE HANDELSVEREENIGING TE MEDAN" – Medan. 1930-39, v16-25(1-20); 1940,v26(1-3). – 21mf – 9 – ne IDC [380]

MEDEDEELINGEN VAN WEGE HET NEDERLANDSCH ZENDE LINGGENOOTSCHAP – Tijdschrift voor zendingswetenschap. -q. Title varies slightly. 1857-1919 – 1 – us U.W. Library [240]

MEDEDEELINGEN VAN'S RIJKS HERBARIUM – Leiden, 1919-33. Nos. 1-70. – 65mf – 8 – ne IDC [580]

MEDEDELINGEN VAN DE DIENST VOOR DE ZEEVISSERIJ – Batavia, 1947 – 4mf – 9 – ne IDC [950]

MEDEDELINGEN VAN HET ALGEMEEN PROEFSTATION DER A.V.R.O.S. (SUMATRA PLANTERS ASSOCIATION) – Batavia, 1948 – 1mf – 9 – ne IDC [631]

MEDELA MEDICINAE / Needham, M – London, 1665 – 10mf – 9 – ne IDC [610]

Medellin. Colombia. Ayuntamiento *see* ORDENANZAS MUNICIPALES

MEDELLIN, RUTA DE TURISMO / Garcia Sanchez, Francisco – Don Benito: Sanchez Trejo, Impresor, 1968 – 1 – sp Bibl Santa Ana [338]

LE MEDERIC : JOURNAL DE MEDERIC MARTIN, MAIRE DE MONTREAL – Montreal, Canada. 14 avr 1927-v1 n3. 28 avr 1928 – 1r – 1 – Can$25.00 – cn Can Microfilming [073]

MEDFIELD 1651-1849 – (Mf 1T-6T: Births 1651-1819. Mf 6T-8T: Marriages 1653-1819. Mf 8T-9T: Intentions 1774-1815. Mf 9T-11T: Deaths 1652-1819. Mf 12T: Births 1813-44. Mf 12T-13T: Intentions 1820-45. Mf 13T: Marriages 1820-43; Deaths 1820-44. Mf 14T: Vital Records 1844-49) – (mf ed 1997) – 14mf – 9 – 0-87623-288-8 – us Holbrook [920]

Medfield, Massachusetts.Medfield Baptist Church *see* RECORDS

MEDFORD 1673-1849 – (Mf 1T-2T: Vital Records 1673-1764. Mf 3T: Births 1764-1809. Mf 3T-6T: Marriages 1745-1843. Mf 4T-5T: Deaths 1742-1813. Mf 5T-7T: Births 1781-1852. Mf 5T: Out-of-Town Marriages 1692-1799. Mf 7T: Deaths 1802-48; Marriages 1840-49. Mf 7T-8T: Births 1796-1849. Mf 7T-9T: Intentions 1812-49. Mf 11T: Marriages 1844-49. Mf 12T-13T: Deaths 1843-49) – (mf ed 1997) – 13mf – 9 – 0-87623-289-6 – us Holbrook [920]

MEDFORD DAILY TRIBUNE – Medford OR. Mar 22 1906-Oct 31 1909 – 1 – us U.O. Library [071]

MEDFORD DISTRICT NEWS – Medford OR. May 1 June 1 July 1 1935, Nov 1 Dec 1 1935, Feb 1 Mar 1 1936, Jan 1 Mar 1 Apr 1 1937 – 1 – us U.O. Library [071]

MEDFORD ENQUIRER – Medford, OR. -w. 9 Feb 1900-3 Jul 1903. 1 roll – 1 – us U.O. Library [071]

MEDFORD MAIL – Medford, OR. -w. 7 Jan 1892-22 Oct 1909. 6 rolls – 1 – us U.O. Library [071]

MEDFORD MAIL TRIBUNE – Medford, OR. -w. 4 Nov 1909-30 Dec 1920. 4 rolls – 1 – us U.O. Library [071]

MEDFORD MORNING MAIL – Medford OR. May 24 Sep 17 Dec 1-31 1908, Feb 28 Apr 20 1909 – 1 – us U.O. Library [071]

MEDFORD NEWS – Medford, OR. -d,-sw. 28 Oct 1926-24 May 1951. 19 rolls – 1 – us U.O. Library [071]

MEDFORD REPORTER – Medford OR. Feb 26 Apr 1 15 29 1932, May 6 13 June 3 10 1932, Sep 2 30 Oct 7 21 1932, Nov 4 18 Dec 9 1932 – 1 – us U.O. Library [071]

MEDFORD SUCCESS – Medford, OR. -sw. 31 Oct 1902-28 Apr 1903. 1 roll – 1 – us U.O. Library [071]

MEDFORD SUN – Medford, OR. -d. 15 Nov 1910-27 Dec 1925. 14 rolls – 1 – us U.O. Library [071]

Medhurst, W H *see*
- CHINA
- CHINESE AND ENGLISH DICTIONARY
- THE CHINESE MISCELLANY;...
- A DICTIONARY OF THE HOK-KEEN DIALECT OF THE CHINESE LANGUAGE

MEDIA – (Incorporating: Bulletin (CAJ), content) – v1- 1994- – 9 – Can$20.00y – cn Micromedia [070]

MEDIA *see* CONTENT

MEDIA AND METHODS – 1964- 1; 1971- 5,6; 1975- 4 x 6 in. 9 – us UMI [370]

MEDIA COVERAGE OF WOMEN'S NCAA VARSITY SPORTS AS A FUNCTION OF THE STRUCTURE OF THE SPORTS INFORMATION OFFICE / Winslow, Jan D & West, Charlotte – 1993 – 2mf – $8.00 – us Microform Publ [790]

MEDIA DIGEST – (See also: Sneak Preview) – v5- 1975- – 1. ; 5,6,9 – apply; v.7- – us UMI [370]

MEDIA EDUCATION – 1984 – 432p – 9 – 92-3-102204-0 – fr UNESCO [370]

MEDIA GENERAL FINANCIAL WEEKLY – 1971- – 1 – us UMI [073]

MEDIA PROJECT / Black-Jewish Information Center – New York, NY. 1977-83 – 1 – us A.J.P.C. [071]

MEDIA STUDIES IN EDUCATION – 1977 – 9 – 92-3-101446-3 – fr UNESCO [370]

MEDIA WATCH – v. 1-. 1976- – 1. – apply; v.7-; 5,6,9 – us UMI [380]

MEDIA WAVE – (Cont: Media West at v10 no 2 1994) – v10- 1994/95- – 9 – Can$20.00y – cn Micromedia [070]

MEDIA WAVE *see* MEDIA WEST

MEDIA WEST – (Cont by: Media Wave at v10 no 2 1994) – West Vancouver. v6-9. 1990/91-1993/94 – 9 – Can$20.00y – cn Micromedia [380]

MEDIA WEST *see* MEDIA WAVE

LA MEDIACION : CARTILLA PARA AGENCIAS GUBERNAMENTALES / Colosi, Thomas R & Colosi, Christopher B – Acus: np. nd. (all publ) – 1mf – 9 – $1.50 – LLMC 94-340S – us L.L.M.C. [340]

O MEDIADOR – Leopoldina, 28 Jan-Dec 1896 – 1,5,6 – bl Biblioteca [072]

MEDIAEVAL AND RENAISSANCE MANUSCRIPT COLLECTIONS AT OXFORD COLLEGES – With printed indexes. The complete manuscript collections of six colleges: Balliol, Christ Church, Corpus Christi, Magdalen, Merton, New College. Organized by subject areas: I, Biblical Texts and Studies; II, Illuminated Mss; III, Theology-General and Patristics; IV, Law; V, Medical and Natural Sciences; VI, Humanistic Studies; VII, Classics – 1,14 – uk World [025]

MEDIAEVAL AND RENAISSANCE STUDIES – The Warburg Institute, London. H 789. v1-6 1943-68. Lacking v2 – 9 – ne IDC [940]

MEDIAEVAL ART : SUBJECT COLLECTIONS – (Individual titles not listed separately) – 24 catalogues on 46mf – 9 – £386.00 – uk Chadwyck [700]

THE MEDIAEVAL CHURCH AND THE PAPACY / Jennings, Arthur C – London: Methuen, 1909: (Handbooks of English church history; 3) – 1mf – us A.T.L.A. [240]

MEDIAEVAL EUROPE (814-1300) / Emerton, Ephraim – Boston, U.S.A.: Ginn, 1894 – 2mf – us A.T.L.A. [940]

THE MEDIAEVAL HOSPITALS OF ENGLAND / Clay, Rotha Mary – London: Methuen, 1909. (The Antiquary's books) – 2mf – us A.T.L.A. [360]

MEDIAEVAL ITALY FROM CHARLEMAGNE TO HENRY 7 / Villari, Pasquale – London: T. Fisher Unwin, 1910 – 1mf – us A.T.L.A. [945]

MEDIAEVAL MANUSCRIPT COLLECTION / Queens' College. Cambridge – With printed index – 1 – £495.00 – uk World [025]

MEDIAEVAL MANUSCRIPT COLLECTION / Winchester College. Warden and Fellows' Library – 1382-1600. With printed index – 1,14 – £750.00 – uk World [025]

THE MEDIAEVAL MANUSCRIPT COLLECTION / Lambeth Palace Library – (Section 1: Old English, French, etc. Mss. 1. Section 2: Law mss. 1. Section 3: Illuminated mss. 1. Section 4: Humanistic Studies. 1. Section 5: Theology. 1. Section 6: Biblical Studies. 1. Section 7: Liturgy. 1. Section 8: Patristic Studies. 1. James' Catalogue. 1) – With printed indexes. Catalogue available – 1,14 – £7,500.00 – uk World [025]

THE MEDIAEVAL MANUSCRIPT COLLECTION / Lincoln Cathedral. Library – (Section 1: Illuminated mss, 14; Section 2: Law and Administration, 1; Section 3: Secular mss, 1; Section 4: Theology, 1; Section 5: Biblical Studies, 1; Section 6: Sermons, Homilies, Liturgy, Saints' Lives, 1; Catalogue of the Lincoln Cathedral Chapter Library, by Dr. R.M. Woolley, London, 1927, 1,9) – Manuscripts previously unpublished. Printed index. The collection is divided into sections arranged by subject area – 1 – £3,600.00 – uk World [090]

THE MEDIAEVAL MANUSCRIPTS / Trinity College. Cambridge – Complete collection. With illus. printed brochure – 1,14 – uk World [090]

THE MEDIAEVAL MANUSCRIPTS, SECTION 1 / Trinity College. Cambridge – Law Manuscripts. With printed index – 1 – £895.00 – uk World [025]

THE MEDIAEVAL MANUSCRIPTS, SECTION 2 / Trinity College. Cambridge – Medica – 1 – £1,395.00 – uk World [025]

THE MEDIAEVAL MANUSCRIPTS, SECTION 3 / Trinity College. Cambridge – Mathematica – 1 – £675.00 – uk World [025]

THE MEDIAEVAL MANUSCRIPTS, SECTION 4 / Trinity College. Cambridge – Illuminated Manuscripts – 14 – £3,750.00 – uk World [025]

MEDIAEVAL MANUSCRIPTS, SECTION 5 / Trinity College. Cambridge – (Part A: General. £1,450.00; 1. Part B: Greek and Latin Classics. £1,425.00; WMP; 1) – Literature – uk World [025]

MEDIAEVAL MANUSCRIPTS, SECTION 6 / Trinity College. Cambridge – (Part A: General. £2,350.00; 1. Part B: History, etc. £1,450.00; WMP; 1) – Secular manuscripts – uk World [025]

THE MEDIAEVAL MANUSCRIPTS, SECTION 7 / Trinity College. Cambridge – (Part A: Biblical Texts. £1,100.00; 1. Part B: Biblical Studies. £1,650.00; WMP; 1) – The Bible – uk World [025]

THE MEDIAEVAL MANUSCRIPTS, SECTION 8 / Trinity College. Cambridge – (Part A: General. £2,325.00; 1. Part B: Patristics. £2,300.00; WMP; 1) – Theology – uk World [025]

MEDIAEVAL MISSIONS / Smith, Thomas – Edinburgh: T & T Clark, 1880 – 1mf – 9 – 0-8370-6409-0 – 1986-0409 – us A.T.L.A. [240]

MEDIAEVAL ROME : FROM HILDEBRAND TO CLEMENT 8, 1073-1600 / Miller, William – New York: Putnam, 1902 – 1mf – us A.T.L.A. [945]

MEDIAEVALIA (MGH SCHRIFTEN..: 17.BD) : AUFSAETZE, NACHRUFE, BESPRECHUNGEN / Baethgen, Friedrich – 2 Teile. 1960 – Dfl46.00 – ne Slangenburg [240]

MEDIA-PERSPEKTIVEN – Frankfurt/Main, DE. 1963-1985; 1992; 1993 – 1 – gw Mikrofilm [072]

MEDIATION : A PRIMER FOR FEDERAL AGENCIES / Colosi, Thomas R & Colosi, Christopher B – Acus: np. nd. (all publ) – 1mf – 9 – $1.50 – LLMC 94-340 – us L.L.M.C. [340]

MEDIATION IN THE WESTERN DISTRICT OF WASHINGTON / Tegland, Karl – Washington: FJC, Sept 1984 – 1mf – 9 – $1.50 – LLMC 95-834 – us L.L.M.C. [340]

MEDIATION, INVESTIGATION AND ARBITRATION IN INDUSTRIAL DISPUTES / Barnett, George E & McCabe, David A – NY/London: D Appleton & Co, 1916 – 3mf – 9 – $4.50 – LLMC 96-060 – us L.L.M.C. [331]

MEDIATOR – Omaha, NE. -w. Feb 1916; Jul 1919-Aug 1926 – 1 – us NE Hist [071]

Mediavilla, Victor Herrero *see* AUSTRALASIAN BIOGRAPHICAL ARCHIVE (ANZO-BA)

MEDICA CONTROVERSIA...SE AYA DE SANGRAR DEL BRAZO Y VENA PROXIMOS AL DOLOR... / Perez Merino, I – Malaga, 1636 – 1mf – 9 – sp Cultura [610]

MEDICAL AND BIOLOGICAL ENGINEERING – v.1-9. 1963-71 – 5,6,9 – us UMI [610]

MEDICAL AND OTHER EXPERTS / McKelway, Clair – n.p. 1898. 12p LL-771 – 1 – us L of C Photodup [340]

MEDICAL AND VETERINARY ENTOMOLOGY – v1- . 1987- – 1,5,6,9 – us UMI [073]

MEDICAL ANTHROPOLOGY : CROSS-CULTURAL STUDIES IN HEALTH AND ILLNESS / ed by Brown, Peter J – 9,5,1 – us Gordon [306]

MEDICAL ANTHROPOLOGY – v. 1-. 1977- – 1,5,6,9 – us UMI [573]

MEDICAL BIOLOGY *see*
- ANNALS OF CLINICAL RESEARCH
- ANNALS OF MEDICINE

Medical Bureau and North American Committee to Aid Spanish Democracy *see*
- BOMBS OVER BARCELONA
- CHILDREN IN CONCENTRATION CAMPS
- LIFT THE EMBARGO AGAINST SPAIN; A SURVEY OF THE FACTS, A CALL TO ACTION
- MAKE THEIR "CASTLES IN SPAIN" COME TRUE
- ONE YEAR IN SPAIN; A PICTURE STORY OF AMERICAN DOCTORS AND NURSES
- RELIEF FOR SPANISH TRADE UNION REFUGEES
- TWO YEARS OF AMERICAN AID TO SPAIN
- WHERE IS THE CONSCIENCE OF THE WORLD?

Medical Bureau to Aid Spanish Democracy. New York *see* SPAIN IN TORMENT

MEDICAL CARE REVIEW – (v41-. 1984-. 5,6,9) – v24-. 1967- – 1 – us UMI [616]

MEDICAL CASEBOOK / Moore, Norman – 22 v. 1869-97 – 1 – uk Microform Academic [616]

MEDICAL CHALLENGE – v. 5-11. 1973-79 – 1,5,6,9 – us UMI [610]

MEDICAL CHALLENGE *see* A AND C MEDICAL CHALLENGE

MEDICAL CLASSIC – v. 1-5. 1936-1940 – 1 – us Princeton Micro [610]

MEDICAL CLINICS OF NORTH AMERICA – 1916- 1; 1967- 5,6; 1975- 4 x 6 in. 9 – us UMI [616]

MEDICAL CLINICS OF NORTH AMERICA – v1-39. 1917-55 – 1,5,6 – us Princeton Micro [610]

MEDICAL COMPUTER JOURNAL – v.1-. 1979- – 1,5,6,9 – us UMI [610]

MEDICAL CRITICISM / Edwards, David, fl. 1882 – (Merged with: Pulpit Criticism. Merged to become: The Critic) – Toronto: [s.n., 1882-1883] – 9 – cn C.I.H.M. [170]

MEDICAL CRITICISM *see*
- THE CRITIC
- PULPIT CRITICISM

A MEDICAL DICTIONARY, INCLUDING PHYSIC, SURGERY, ANATOMY, CHIMISTRY AND BOTANY (AEL, ABT 3;3.1) / James, Robert – London. 3v. 1743-1745 (mf ed 1994) – 37mf – 9 – DM460.00 – 3-89131-152-4 – gw Fischer [610]

MEDICAL DIGEST – (See also: Journal of Continuing Education in Family Medicine) – v1-22 1955-76 1; 1975-76 5,6,9 – us UMI [616]

MEDICAL DOSIMETRY – 1,5,69 – us UMI [616]

MEDICAL ECONOMICS – 1- 1923- 1; 1970- 5,6,9 – us UMI [610]

MEDICAL ENQUIRER : A QUARTERLY JOURNAL AND REVIEW; THE ORGAN OF THE NATIONAL MEDICAL ASSOCIATION FOR THE ABOLITION OF THE STATE REGULATION OF PROSTITUTION – Liverpool, 1875-1883 – 28mf – 9 – ne IDC [610]

MEDICAL FACTS AND EXPERIMENTS / Home, F – M 138. 1759 – 9 – ne IDC [610]

MEDICAL FLORA... / Rafinesque-Schmaltz, Constantine S – Philadelphia, 1828-1830. 2v – 12mf – 9 – ne IDC [615]

MEDICAL HERITAGE – v1-. 1985- – 1,5,6,9 – us UMI [073]

MEDICAL HISTORY SHEETS OF MEMBERS OF THE 6TH QUEENSLAND CONTINGENT RETURNING BY TSS "DEVON" 1902-1902 / Chief Secretary's Office, Queensland – 1 reel Major Turnbridge – Private Hudson Ernst A by rank – 1 – CRS B5155 – at Archives [920]

MEDICAL HYPOTHESES – (1982-. 1,5,6,9) – v1-. 1975- – 1 – us UMI [616]

MEDICAL INQUIRIES AND OBSERVATIONS UPON THE DISEASES OF THE MIND / Rush, B – M 127. 1812 – 9 – ne IDC [150]

MEDICAL INSTRUMENT CATALOGUES : CATALOGUES FROM MUSEUM BOERHAAVE, LEIDEN AND THE THACKERAY MEDICAL MUSEUM IN LEEDS – (Two printed guides with indexes) – 2,146mf – 9 (Dfl1,950.00 per installment) – ne IDC [610]

MEDICAL JOURNAL OF AUSTRALIA – 1927-83 – 1,5,6 – us Princeton Micro [610]

MEDICAL JOURNAL OF AUSTRALIA – (1970- . 5,6. 1976- . 9) – 1914- – 1 – us UMI [610]

MEDICAL JURISPRUDENCE, FORENSIC MEDICINE AND TOXICOLOGY / Witthaus, Rudolph August – 2d ed. New York, 1906-11. 4 v. LL-1429 – 1 – us L of C Photodup [340]

THE MEDICAL JURISPRUDENCE OF INEBRIETY / Medico-Legal Society. New York – New York: Medico-Legal Journal Association, 1888. 183p. LL-1239 – 1 – us L of C Photodup [340]

MEDICAL JURISPRUDENCE OF INSANITY; OR, FORENSIC PSYCHIATRY / Clevenger, Shobal Vail – Rochester, NY: The Lawyers' Co-Operative Publishing Co., 1898. 2v. LL-905 – 1 – us L of C Photodup [340]

MEDICAL LAB – (v13- . 5,6,9) – v. 1-. 1968- – 1 – us UMI [615]

Medical library association *see* BULLETIN

MEDICAL MICROBIOLOGY AND IMMUNOLOGY *see* ZEITSCHRIFT FUER MEDIZINISCHE MIKROBIOLOGIE UND IMMUNOLOGIE

MEDICAL MICROBIOLOGY AND IMMUNOLOGY MMI – v. 127-170. 1947-80 – 1,5,9 – 3399.00 – us UMI [073]

THE MEDICAL MISSION : ITS PLACE, POWER AND APPEAL / Wanless, William James – Philadelphia: Westminster Press, 1908, c1898 – 1mf – 9 – 0-8370-6787-1 – 1986-0787 – us A.T.L.A. [610]

THE MEDICAL MISSIONARY – Toronto: Missionary Board of the Medical Students' YMCA, [1891-189- or 19–] – 9 – cn C.I.H.M. [360]

THE MEDICAL MISSIONARY SOCIETY IN CHINA / Colledge, T R – (Missing: Title page) – Philadelphia, 1838 – 1mf – 9 – ne IDC [610]
THE MEDICAL MISSIONARY SOCIETY IN CHINA. ADDRESS, WITH MINUTES OF PROCEEDINGS – Canton, 1838 – 1mf – 9 – ne IDC [610]
MEDICAL MISSIONS : THEIR PLACE AND POWER / Lowe, John – (Includes index) – 3rd ed. New York: Fleming H Revell, [188-] – 1mf – 9 – 0-8370-6679-4 – 1986-0679 – us A.T.L.A. [610]
MEDICAL NEWS – v. 1-87. 1843-1905 – 1 – us UMI [610]
MEDICAL NEWS-PAPER – v. 1. 1 Jan 1822-15 Feb 1824 – 1 – us UMI [610]
MEDICAL NOTES ON CHINA / Wilson, J – London, 1846 – 4mf – 9 – ne IDC [610]
MEDICAL OFFICER OF HEALTH ANNUAL REPORTS FROM CIRCA 1895 TO 1950 : LOCAL GOVERNMENT ANNUAL REPORTS – (Part 1: Scotland, Northern Ireland and North of England; Part 2: Midlands, Eastanglia and Wales; Part 3: Southern England and Eire) – ca 50r – 1 – ca £2,000.00 – uk Altair [614]
MEDICAL PHYSICS – v1-. 1974- – 1,5,6,9 – us A.I.P. [530]
MEDICAL PORTRAIT GALLERY / Pettigrew, T J – (Missing: 1840. v3-4) – London, [1838]-1840 – 10mf – ne IDC [610]
MEDICAL POST – Sep. 1965 – 1 – us UMI [073]
MEDICAL POST – Toronto. v1-31. 1965-95 – 1 – Can$100.00y – cn Micromedia [610]
MEDICAL PRINCIPLES AND PRACTICE – v4-. 1993- – 1,5,9 – us UMI [610]
MEDICAL PROCEEDINGS – 1955-73 – 1. 1970-73.; ; 5,6 – us UMI [610]
MEDICAL PRODUCTS SALESMAN – (v.10-. Jan. 1979- 5,6,9) – v.1-. Jan. 1970- – 1 – us UMI [380]
MEDICAL PROFESSION OF SOUTHERN CALIFORNIA / Kress & Lindley – Los Angeles: Times-Mirror Printing and Binding House. 1910. California Reel 38. (Cox Library Collection) – 5 – us Americana [978]
MEDICAL PROGRESS THROUGH TECHNOLOGY – v. 1-7. 1972-80 – 1,5,9 – 483.00 – us UMI [073]
MEDICAL RECORD – 1949-60 – 1 – uk Microform Academic [616]
MEDICAL RECORDS / Fabrique, Andrew Hinsdale – Births, 1871-76; visiting list, 1889 – 1 – us KS Hist [025]
MEDICAL RECORDS OF THE QUEENSLAND DEFENCE FORCE, LEXICOGRAPHICAL SERIES, 1900-1901 / Chief Secretary's Office, Queensland – 3r – 1 – CRS B5166 – at Archives [920]
MEDICAL REFERENCE SERVICES QUARTERLY / ed by Wood, M Sandra – v1- 1982- – 1, 9 ($125.00 in US $175.00 outside hardcopy subsc) – us Haworth [020]
MEDICAL REFORMER – v.1. Jan1823 – 1 – us UMI [073]
MEDICAL REPOSITORY – v. 1-n.s. v. 8. 1797-1824 – 1 – us UMI [610]
MEDICAL SCIENCE DIGEST – (1979- 5,6,9) – 1950- – 1 – us UMI [073]
MEDICAL SELF-CARE – (1983-. 5,6,9) – Summer 1976- – 1 – us UMI [613]
Medical Society of London *see*
- PROCEEDINGS
- TRANSACTIONS

MEDICAL STAFF NEWS – v14, no.3-. Mar 1985- – 1,5,6,9 – us UMI [073]
MEDICAL TEACHER – 1979- 15v – 9 – £188.50 – 0142-159X – uk Carfax [370]
MEDICAL TECHNOLOGIST AND SCIENTIST – v. 5-11. 1975-81 – 1 – us UMI [610]
MEDICAL TECHNOLOGY *see* AMERICAN JOURNAL OF MEDICAL TECHNOLOGY
MEDICAL TIMES – v1- 1873- 1; 1971- 5,6; 1976- 4 x 6 in. 9 – us UMI [610]
MEDICAL TRIAL TECHNIQUE QUARTERLY – (v1-30 1955-84 on reel $329.00. v31-41 1985-95 and index on mf $340.00) – v1-41. 1955-95 – 5,6,9 – $634.00 set – us Hein [340]
MEDICAL ULTRASOUND – v. 1-. 1977- – 1,5,6,9 – us UMI [616]
MEDICAL WORK OF THE WOMAN'S FOREIGN MISSIONARY SOCIETY / Gracey, Annie Ryder – 1888 – 9 – us A.T.L.A. [240]
MEDICAL WORLD – Incorporates Journal of Hospital PharmacyAND Medical World Newsletter – v1- 1913- 1; v114- 5,6,9 – us UMI [616]
MEDICAL WORLD NEWS – 1- 1960- 1; 1970- 5,6; 1976- 4 x 6 in. 9 – us UMI [610]
MEDICAL WORLD NEWS FOR OBSTETRICIANS, GYNECOLOGISTS, UROLOGISTS – v1-. 1985- – 1,5,6,9 – us UMI [073]
MEDICAMENTOS DE ACTUALIDAD. (DRUGS OF TODAY) – Barcelona. v. 7-9. 1971-73 – 1,5,6 – us Princeton Micro [610]
MEDICI BOOK OF HOURS – 15th cent. Holkham ms. 41. Holkham Hall, Norfolk, England – 14 – uk Microform Academic [240]
THE MEDICI POPES : LEO 10 AND CLEMENT 7 / Vaughan, Herbert Millingchamp – (Includes index) – London: Methuen, 1908 – 1mf – 9 – 0-8370-8718-X – 1986-2718 – us A.T.L.A. [920]
DIE MEDICIN IN WIEN WAEHREND DER LETZTEN 100 JAHRE / Puschmann, Theodor – Vienne: M. Perles, 1884.ii,327p. 4 fiches. (Statistics Series: Medical Studies) – 9 – 10.00 – fr Bibl Nationale [310]
MEDICINA – 1- 1939- 1; v30- 5,6; v36- 9 – us UMI [610]
MEDICINA DELLO SPORT – 1938- 1; 1975- 5,6,9 – us UMI [790]
MEDICINA DOMESTICA...DEL MEDICO CARITATIVO... / Borbon, F – Zaragoza, 1685 – 7mf – 9 – sp Cultura [610]
LA MEDICINA EN EL SIGLO 19 / Miguel y Guerra, Regino de – 1885 – 9 – 1.50f – sp Bibl Santa Ana [610]
MEDICINA ESPANOLA...PROVECHOSA / Sorapan de Rieros, Juan – 1616 – 9 – 1.50f – sp Bibl Santa Ana [610]
MEDICINA ET PHARMACOLOGIA *see* MEDICINA EXPERIMENTALIS
MEDICINA EXPERIMENTALIS – v14-19. 1966-69 – 1 – us UMI [610]
MEDICINA GYMNASTICA / Fuller, Francis – 1705 – 4mf – 9 – $12.00 – us Microform Publ [615]
MEDICINA MUSICA / Browne, R – or A Mechanical Essay on the Effects of Singing, Musick and Dancing on Human Bodies. London. 1729. BP-648 1 – 9 – ne IDC [780]
MEDICINA SOCIALE – 1951- 1; 1975- 5,6,9 – us UMI [610]
MEDICINA VETUS ET NOVA...CONTINENS PHARMACIAM GALENICO-CHIMICAM / Piquer, Andres – Valencia, 1735 – 6mf – 9 – sp Cultura [615]
LA MEDICINA Y LAS MISIONES / Bayle, Constantino – Madrid: Missionalia Hispanica, 1944 – 1 – sp Bibl Santa Ana [240]
MEDICINA...GUADALUPE / Sanz de Dios y Guadalupe, Francisco – 1756 – 9 – 1.50f – sp Bibl Santa Ana [610]
MEDICINAL COUNCELS / Turquet de Mayerne, T – M 378. 1677 – 9 – ne IDC [610]
MEDICINAL EXPERIMENTS / Boyle, R – Ed. 2. 2 v. M-309. 1693 – 9 – ne IDC [610]
MEDICINAL PLANTS / Bentley & Trimen – 1839-45 – 5 – uk Microform Academic [580]
THE MEDICINAL PLANTS OF THE PHILIPPINES / Pardo de Tavra, T H J – Philadelphia, 1901 – 3mf – 9 – ne IDC [615]
MEDICINAL RESEARCH REVIEWS – v1-. 1981- – 1,5,6,9 – us UMI [073]
MEDICINAL RESEARCH REVIEWS – v1-4. 1981-84 – 1,5,6 – us Princeton Micro [616]
THE MEDICINAL VALUE OF FRENCH BRANDY / Jackson, George H – Montreal: printed by Therien freres, limitee, cop. 1928. SEM105P1669 – 4mf – 9 – Can$9.00 – cn Bibl Nat [615]
DIE MEDICINAL-PFLANZEN DER OESTERREICHISCHEN PHARMAKOPOEE / Endlicher, S L – Wien, 1842 – 7mf – 9 – ne IDC [615]
MEDICINE – v1-75. 1922-96 – 1,5,6,9 – $90.00r – us Williams [610]
MEDICINE AND SCIENCE IN SPORTS – v1-11. 1969-79 – 1 – us UMI [073]
MEDICINE AND SCIENCE IN SPORTS AND EXERCISE – v12-. 1980- – 1,5,6,9 – us UMI [073]
MEDICINE AND SCIENCE IN SPORTS AND EXERCISE – v21-28. 1989-96 – 8r – 1,5,6,9 – $85.00r – us Williams [613]
MEDICINE AND WAR – v1-. 1985- – 1,5,6,9 – us UMI [610]
MEDICINE HAT NEWS – Medicine Hat, Alberta, CN. 1889- – 12r per yr – 1 – Can$53.00r – cn Commonwealth Micro [072]
MEDICINE HAT WEEKLY NEWS – Medicine Hat, Alberta, CN. 1890-1949 – 38r – 1 – cn Commonwealth Micro [072]
MEDICINISCH-CHIRURGISCHE ENCYKLOPAEDIE FUER PRAKTISCHE AERZTE (AEL, ABT.3;7) / ed by Prosch, Heinrich & Ploss, H – Leipzig, 1854-1856, 1863 (mf ed 1993) – 25mf – 9 – DM340.00 – 3-89131-156-7 – gw Fischer [617]
MEDICINISCHES AUS DER AELTESTEN KIRCHENGESCHICHTE (T.U.U. 1-8/4B) / Harnack, Adolf von – Leipzig, 1892 – 2mf – 9 – ne Slangenburg [240]
MEDICNISCHES SCHRIFTSTELLER-LEXIKON DER JETZT LEBENDEN AERZTE, WUNDAERZTE UND GEBURTSHELFER, APOTHEKER UND NATURFORSCHER ALLER GEBILDETEN VOELKER (AEL, ABT 3;17) / Callisen, Adolph Peter – Kopenhagen, 1830-1845 (mf ed 1994) – 67mf – 9 – DM1,720.00 – 3-89131-186-9 – gw Fischer [610]
EL MEDICO A PALOS / Fernandez de Moratin, Leandro – 1814 – 1mf – 9 – Pta1,000.00 – 84-7848-188-5 – sp Pentalfa [610]
EL MEDICO DE CAMARA / Hurtado, Antonio – 1853 – 9 – 1.50f – sp Bibl Santa Ana [830]
MEDICO DE GUIJO DE SANTA BARBARA. TRATAMIENTO DE LA NEURALGIA CIATICA POR LA CAUTERIZACION DEL HELIX / Gonzalez Castro, Jose – Madrid: Revista de medicina y Cirugia practicas, 1898 – 1 – sp Bibl Santa Ana [610]
MEDICO EN LAS HURDES / Reizabal, Luis – Madrid: Tip. Aldus, 1976 – sp Bibl Santa Ana [610]
EL MEDICO RURAL / Trigo, Felipe – Madrid: Renacimiento, 1921 – sp Bibl Santa Ana [910]
MEDICO-LEGAL BULLETIN – (v.28-. 1979- 5,6,9) – 1951- – 1 – us UMI [340]
MEDICO-LEGAL JOURNAL – New York, 1883-1933 – 11r – 1 – $650.00 – us Trans-Media [340]
THE MEDICOLEGAL JOURNAL – v1-50. 1884-1933 (all publ) – 255mf – 9 – $382.00 – LLMC 84-601 – us L.L.M.C. [073]
MEDICOLEGAL NEWS – (v.7-. 1979- 5,6,9) – v.1-. 1973- – 1 – us UMI [340]
MEDICOLEGAL NEWS *see* JOURNAL OF LAW MEDICINE AND ETHICS
Medico-Legal Society. New York *see* THE MEDICAL JURISPRUDENCE OF INEBRIETY
MEDICOLEGAL SOCIETY TRANSACTIONS – London. v1-26. 1902-32 (all publ) – 25mf – 9 – $112.00 – LLMC 84-602 – us L.L.M.C. [073]
MEDIDAS DEL ROMANO, NECESARIAS A LOS OFICIALES QUE QUIEREN SEGUIR LAS FORMACIONES... / Sagredo, D – Toledo, 1526 – 2mf – 9 – sp Cultura [720]
MEDIENFIGUREN IM ALLTAG VON KINDERN AM BEISPIEL DER TURTLES / Ehmke, Jochen – 1994 – 3mf – 9 – DM98.00 – 3-8267-2064-4 – gw Hänsel [640]
MEDIEVAL AND RENAISSANCE LITERARY MANUSCRIPTS FROM THE JOHN RYLANDS UNIVERSITY LIBRARY OF MANCHESTER, PART 1 : ENGLISH, FRENCH, ITALIAN AND SPANISH MANUSCRIPTS – (Part 2: Latin Manuscripts. ca 19 reels. $2,250.00) – Marlborough: Adam Matthew Publications, 1996 – 21r – 1 – $2,500.00 – uk Matthew [090]
MEDIEVAL AND RENAISSANCE MANUSCRIPTS FROM THE SOCIETY OF ANTIQUARIES, LONDON – (Part One: Literary Manuscripts. Part Two: Manuscripts Relating to History and Art History) – 1 – us Primary [090]
THE MEDIEVAL AND RENAISSANCE MANUSCRIPTS OF ST JOHN'S COLLEGE, OXFORD – 1 – us Primary [090]
MEDIEVAL ARCHAEOLOGY – H-808 2. v. 1-12. 1957-1968 – 8 – ne IDC [930]
MEDIEVAL BACKGROUND / Holkham Hall. Norfolk. England – A selection of miniatures and Mss. illustrations – 14 – uk Microform Academic [025]
THE MEDIEVAL CHURCH IN SCOTLAND : ITS CONSTITUTION, ORGANISATION AND LAW / Dowden, John – Glasgow: J. Maclehose; New York: Macmillan [distributor], 1910. (The Rhind lectures for 1901, revised and greatly enlarged) – 1mf – us A.T.L.A. [240]
THE MEDIEVAL EMPIRE / Fisher, Herbert – London; New York: Macmillan, 1898 – 2mf – us A.T.L.A. [240]
MEDIEVAL FAITH AND FABLE / MacCulloch, John Arnott – Forward by Sir J.G. Frazer. London: George G. Harrap & Co., (1932) – 1 – us U.W. Library [240]
A MEDIEVAL GARNER : HUMAN DOCUMENTS FROM THE FOUR CENTURIES PRECEDING THE REFORMATION / ed by Coulton, G G – London: Constable, 1910 – 2mf – us A.T.L.A. [240]
MEDIEVAL JEWISH CHRONICLES, VOL 2 / ed by Neubauer, A – Oxford. v1-pt6. 1895 – Dfl35.00 – ne Slangenburg [270]
THE MEDIEVAL LIBRARY / Westfall Thompson, J – New York, 1957 – 15mf – 8 – Dfl53.00 – ne Slangenburg [240]
MEDIEVAL, LITERARY AND HISTORICAL MANUSCRIPTS IN THE COTTON COLLECTION, BRITISH LIBRARY, LONDON – Seven-part collection – 1 – us Primary [025]
MEDIEVAL MANUSCRIPT LIBRARY OF PEMBROKE COLLEGE, CAMBRIDGE – (Part 1: Manuscripts 1-56; Part 2: Manuscripts 57-120; Part 3: Manuscripts 121-175; Part 4: Manuscripts 176-240; Part 5: Manuscripts 241-308) – 1 – us Primary [900]
THE MEDIEVAL MANUSCRIPTS OF CAROLINA REDIVIVA : C – COLLECTION OF THE UNIVERSITY OF UPPSALA LIBRARY – (Includes 2/3 of the entire manuscript collection) – Univ of Uppsala, Sweden, 1970 – 242r – 1 – $21,500.00 – us OmniSys [240]
THE MEDIEVAL MOSAICS OF SAN MARCO, VENICE : A COLOR ARCHIVE / Demus, Otto – (60p accompanying text) – 1986 – 18 color mf – 15 – $600.00f – 0-226-68975-1 – us Chicago [730]
THE MEDIEVAL PAPACY : AND OTHER ESSAYS / Beet, William Ernest – London: C.M. Kelly, 1914 – 1mf – us A.T.L.A. [240]
THE MEDIEVAL SCIENCE OF WEIGHTS (SCIENTIA DE PONDERIBUS); TREATISES ASCRIBED TO EUCLID, ARCHIMEDES, THABIT IBN QURRA, JORDANUS DE NEMORE, AND BLASIUS OF PARMA / ed by Moody, Ernest Addison – Madison: University of Wisconsin Press, (c1952). x,438p. illus – 1 – us U.W. Library [380]
MEDIHA HANIM'IN SERGUEZESTI VE FECI HATIMA-I HAYATI – S.A. [Istanbul]: Kadr Matbaasi, 1337 [1921] – $45.00 – us MEDOC [956]
Medikus, F K *see*
- BEITRAEGE ZUR KULTUR EXOTISCHER GEWAECHSE
- BEITRAEGE ZUR PFLANZENANATOMIE, PFLANZENPHYSIOLOGIE UND EINER NEUEN CHARAKTERISTIK DER BAEUME UND STRAEUCHER
- BEITRAEGE ZUR SCHOENEN GARTENKUNST
- BESCHREIBUNG DER LAGERSTROEMIA INDICA
- BEYTRAEGE ZUR PFLANZEN-ANATOMIE, PFLANZEN-PHYSIOLOGIE
- BOTANISCHE BEOBACHTUNGEN
- BOTANISCHE BEOBACHTUNGEN DES JAHRES 1782
- BOTANISCHE BEOBACHTUNGEN DES JAHRES 1783
- GESCHICHTE DER BOTANIK UNSERER ZEITEN
- INDEX PLANTARUM HORTI ELECTORALIS MANHEMIENSIS
- KRITISCHE BEMERKUNGEN UA5BER GEGENSTAA5NDE AUS DEM PFLANZENREICHE
- KURZER UMRISS EINER SYSTEMATISCHEN BESCHREIBUNG DER MANNIGFALTIGEN UMHUELLUNGEN DER SAAMEN
- OBSERVATIONES BOTANICAE
- PFLANZEN-GATTUNGEN NACH DEM INBEGRIFFE SAEMMTLICHER FRUKTIFIKATIONS-THEILE GEBILDET
- PFLANZEN-PHYSIOLOGISCHE ABHANDLUNGEN
- PHILOSOPHISCHE BOTANIK
- THEODORA SPECIOSA, IN NEUES PFLANZENGESCHLACHT
- UEBER EINIGE KUENSTLICHE GESCHLECHTER DER MALVENFAMILIE, DER KLASSE DER MONADELPHIEN
- UEBER NORDAMERIKANISCHE BAEUME UND STRAEUCHER
- UNAECHTER ACACIEN-BAUM. ZUR ERMUNTERUNG DES ALLGEMEINEN ANBAUES DIESER IN IHREN ART
- VERSUCH EINER NEUEN LEHRART DIE PFLANZEN NACH ZWEI METHODEN ZUGLEICH
- VON DEM BAUE DER SUESEN POMERANZANSTAUDE
- VON DER NEIGUNG DER PFLANZEN ZICH ZU BEGATTEN

MEDINA COUNTY GAZETTE – Medina. Ohio. 1969- – 1 – us UMI [071]

MEDINA COUNTY GAZETTE – Medina. Ohio. and News. 1890-99 – 1 – us UMI [071]

Medina de Las Torres. Ayuntamiento *see* ORDENANZAS MUNICIPALES

Medina, Harold Raymond *see*
- CASES ON FEDERAL JURISDICTION AND PROCEDURE.
- SUMMARY OF THE LAW OF PLEADING, PRACTICE AND EVIDENCE IN THE STATE OF NEW YORK.

Medina, Ioannes *see*
- DE POENITENTIA
- DE RESTITUTIONE ET CONTRACTIBUS

Medina, Jose Toribio *see*
- BIBLIOGRAFIA DE LA LENGUA GUARANI. BUENOS AIRES, 1930
- BIBLIOGRAPHIES BY MEDINA RELATING TO LATIN AMERICA AND THE PHILIPPINES
- BIBLIOTECA HISPANO-AMERICANA (1493-1810)
- COLECCION DE DOCUMENTOS INEDITOS PARA LA HISTORIA DE CHILE
- COLECCION DOCUMENTOS...CHILE

Medina, Pedro de *see*
- L'ARTE DEL NAVEGAR
- L'ARTE DEL NAVEGAR, IN LAQVAL SI CONTENGONO LE REGOLE, DECHIARATIONI, SECRETI, AND AUISI, ALLA BONA NAUEGATION NECESSARIJ
- PRIMERA Y...GRANDEZAS...ESPANA

Medinaceli, Duquesa de *see* INFORMACION EN DERECHO...JUAN SANTOS CUENDA...LOS JUICIOS

MEDINA'S BIBLIOTECA HISPANA-AMERICANA – 185r – 1 – $12,500 $825.00y – us OmniSys [972]

O MEDIO AMAZONAS : O JORNAL DA INTEGRACAO – Parintins, Amazonas. 24 Dez 1979; Fev, Maio-Dez 1980; Jan-Fev, Jun-17 Ago 1981 – 1,5,6 – bl Biblioteca [072]

MEDIOCRE ET RAMPANT OU LE MOYEN DE PARVENIR / Picard – (French Theatre Series). Paris. Huet, an V. 1797 – 9 – fr Hachette [820]

MEDIODIA – Havana. no. 49-70. 27 Dec 1937-30 May 1938 – 1 – us NY Public [073]

MEDISCH MAANDBLAD – (Continues as: Madjalah Kedokteran Indonesia) – Djakarta, 1946-1950 – 28mf – 9 – ne IDC [072]

MEDITACIONES DE LA VIDA DE CRISTO... / Buenaventura, San; ed by Bayle, Constantino – Madrid: Razon y Fe, 1928 – 9 – sp Bibl Santa Ana [240]

MEDITACIONES DE UN LECTOR CON MOTIVO DE LA FIESTA DEL LIBRO / Romero Mendoza, Pedro – Caceres: Dip. Prov. de Caceres, Servicio Culturales, 1955 – 1 – sp Bibl Santa Ana [946]

MEDITACIONES LIRICAS / Montaner, Joaquin – Barcelona, 1918 – 1 – sp Bibl Santa Ana [810]

MEDITACIONES PERUANAS. LIMA, 1933 / Belaunde, Victor Andres – Madrid: Razon y Fe, 1934 – 1 – sp Bibl Santa Ana [972]

MEDITATIO PAUPERIS IN SOLITUDINE AUCTORE ANONYMO SAEC. 13, EDIDIT P. FERDINANDUS M. DELORME – 1929 – 1 – us A.T.L.A. [240]

THE MEDITATIONS / Aurelius, Marcus – Trans. by John Jackson. Introd. by Charles Bigg. Oxford: The Clarendon Press, 1906. (Oxford Library of Translations). 239,(1)p 1 reel. 1261 – 1 – us U.W. Library [930]

MEDITATIONS AND MAXIMS OF KOHOLETH / Finlayson, Thomas Campbell – London: T. Fisher Unwin, 1887. 1 fiche – 9 – us A.T.L.A. [240]

MEDITATIONS ON THE ESSENCE OF CHRISTIANITY / Collier, Robert Laird – Boston: Roberts Bros, 1876 – 1mf – 9 – 0-8370-2715-2 – 1985-0715 – us A.T.L.A. [240]

MEDITATIONS ON THE LORD'S PRAYER (CCC162) = CHU TAO WEN MO HSIANG LU / Holth, Sverre – (In Chinese) – 1st ed. Hong Kong: Council on Christian Literature for Overseas Chinese, 1955 – 1r – 1 – 1984-B500 – us A.T.L.A. [240]

MEDITATIONS ON THE MIRACLES OF CHRIST / Howson, John Saul – London: Religious Tract Society, [ca 1877] – 1mf – 9 – 0-8370-3683-6 – 1985-1683 – us A.T.L.A. [240]

MEDITATIONS SERAPHIQUES SUR LA PASSION DE JESUS: EN FORME DE CHEMIN DE CROIX / Franciscain de Montreal – Quebec: Impr. franciscaine missionaire, 1896?. 02201. (Pre-1900 Canadiana) – 9 – cn C.I.H.M. [971]

MEDITATIONS SUR LA VIE DE L'APOTRE SAINT-PIERRE / Werner, Eugene – Geneve: F. Richard, 1872. 1 fiche – 9 – us A.T.L.A. [240]

MEDITATIONS SUR L'ESSENCE DE LA RELIGION CHRETIENNE = MEDITATIONS ON THE ESSENCE OF CHRISTIANITY AND ON THE RELIGIOUS QUESTIONS OF THE DAY / Guizot, M Francois – (In English. Includes bibliographical references) – New York: Charles Scribner, 1867 – 1mf – 9 – 0-8370-4777-3 – 1985-2777 – us A.T.L.A. [240]

MEDITATIONS SUR L'ETAT ACTUEL DE LA RELIGION CHRETIENNE / Guizot, M Francois – (Includes bibliographical references) – Paris: Michel Levy, 1866 – 1mf – 9 – 0-8370-4770-6 – 1985-2770 – us A.T.L.A. [230]

MEDITATIONS SUR L'ETAT ACTUEL DE LA RELIGION CHRETIENNE = MEDITATIONS ON THE ACTUAL STATE OF CHRISTIANITY AND ON THE ATTACKS WHICH ARE NOW BEING MADE UPON IT / Guizot, M Francois – (In English. Includes bibliographical references) – New York: Charles Scribner, [c1866] – 1mf – 9 – 0-8370-4783-8 – 1985-2783 – us A.T.L.A. [230]

MEDITATOR – Cape Town, South Africa. 3 Jan 1837-25 Jun 1839. 1 reel. Title varies: The Moderator, or Cape of Good Hope Impartial Observer, Jan-Jul 1837 – 1, 16 diazo available at reduced price – sa SA Libr [072]

MEDITERRANEAN DEVELOPMENT PROJECT: UNITED ARAB REPUBLIC, SYRIAN REGION, COUNTRY REPORT / Syria – 1959. BNE-9701 1 – 9 – ne IDC [338]

MEDITERRANEAN FORESTS AND MAQUIS : ECOLOGY, CONSERVATION AND MANAGEMENT – 1977 – 9 – 92-3-101388-2 – fr UNESCO [634]

MEDITERRANEAN PASSES / Great Britain. Public Record Office – 1662-1784. BRRAM – 1 – uk Microform Academic [025]

MEDITSINSKII SOVREMENNIK 1911 G – Tekushchaia meditsiuskaia literatura. Stat' i i referaty po razlichnym otdelam nauchnoi i prakticheskoi meditsiny. Spb. 1912. BR-7149 2 – 8 – ne IDC [610]

MEDITSINSKY GAZETA – Moscow. U.S.S.R. 1961- – 1 – us UMI [073]

MEDIUM – Communication surrealiste. no. 1-8; n.s., no. 1-4. Paris. 1952-janv 1955 – 1 – fr A.C.R.P.P. [073]

MEDIUM-TERM ECONOMIC PLAN 1964-1968 / Japan. Economic Planning Agency – D-1348 1. 1965 – 9 – ne IDC [338]

MEDIUS DECANI, PART BOOKS – York Minster ms. music 13 – 1 – uk Microform Academic [240]

MEDIZINISCHE WELT – 1968-79 – 1,5,6 – us Princeton Micro [616]

MEDIZINISCHES REALWOERTERBUCH ZUM HANDGEBRAUCH PRACTISCHER AERZTE UND WUNDAERZTE..(AEL, ABT.3;6) / ed by Pierer, Johann Friedrich – Leipzig, Altenburg, 1816-1829 (mf ed 1993) – 80mf – 9 – DM790.00 – 3-89131-155-9 – gw Fischer [610]

THE MEDJELLE OR OTTOMAN CIVIL LAW / Turkey. Laws, Statutes, etc – London, Stevens, 1895. 433 p. LL-12033 – 1 – us L of C Photodup [340]

MEDJUNARODNO MEDJUPOKRAJINSKO (INTERLOKALNO) I MEDJUVJERSKO... / Eisner, B – Zagrebu, 1935 – 3mf – 1 – ILM-3794/1 – ne IDC [327]

MEDLEY; OR, MONTHLY MISCELLANY – v. 1. Jan-Dec 1803 – 1 – us UMI [073]

Medlicott, H B *see*
- A MANUAL OF THE GEOLOGY OF INDIA
- SKETCH OF THE GEOLOGY OF THE PUNJAB

Medlycott, A E *see* INDIA AND THE APOSTLE THOMAS

Medonius, B *see* EXCERPTA DE ANTIQUITATIBUS CONSTANTINOPOLITANIS (CBH 12,2)

Medovogo, A I *see* GONKONG V SISTEME MIROVYKH EKONOMICHESKIKH SVIAZEI

Medrano, Trifon *see* HOMBRES NUEVOS Y NUEVOS CUADROS; INFORME PRONUNCIADO EN LA QUINTA SESION DE LA CONFERENCIA EL DIA 16 DE ENERO

MEDULA DE LA MUSICA THEORICA.. / Cruz Brocarte, Antonio de la – 1707 – 2 – us Sibley [780]

MEDULLA FUNDAMENTALIS THEOLOGIAE MORALIS / Stang, William – Neo-Eboraci [New York]: Benziger, 1907 – 1mf – 9 – 0-8370-6414-7 – 1986-0414 – us A.T.L.A. [230]

MEDULLAE THEOLOGIAE PATRUM SYNTAGMA.. / Scultetus, Abraham – 1634 – 1 – us A.T.L.A. [240]

Meduna, B *see* DIALOGO SOPRA LA MIRACOLOSA VITTORIA OTTENVTA DALL' ARMATA DELLA SANTISSIMA LEGA CHRISTIANA, CONTRA LA TURCHESCA

MEDUNARODNI UGOVORI I DRUGI SPORAZUMI / Yugoslavia. Treaties, etc – 1954-1969 – 1 – us NY Public [949]

MEDUNARODNI UGOVORI I DRUGI SPORAZUMI *see* SLUZBENI LIST SOCIJALISTICKE FEDERATIVNE REPUBLIKE JUGOSLAVIJE

MEDURA OR PENNY POLITICIAN – London, UK. 1819-20. -irr. 18 feet – 1 – uk British Libr Newspaper [072]

MEDUSA'S MIRROR : STUDIES IN GERMAN LITERATURE / Closs, August – (Includes bibliographical references and index) – London: Cresset Press, 1957 – 1r – 1 – us U.W. Library [430]

Medvedev, P *see*
- DRAMY I POEMY ALEKSANDRA BLOKA
- V LABORATORII PISATELIA

Medvedev, V V *see* KOOPERATSIIA

MEDWAY 1650-1849 – (Mf 1T: Marriage Intentions 1740. Mf 1T-2T: Births 1713-34. Mf 2T: Marriages 1712-33. Mf 2T-3T: Deaths 1714-1811. Mf 3T-14T: Births 1712-1848. Mf 14T-20T: Marriages 1712-1836. Mf 20T-29T: Marriage Intentions 1740-1850. Mf 29T-30T: Marriages 1836-43. Mf 30T: Out-of-Town Marriages 1706-99. Mf 31T-34T: Deaths 1714-1845. Mf 34T-36T: Vitals 1843-49) – (mf ed 1997) – 36mf – 9 – 0-87623-290-X – us Holbrook [920]

MEDWAY 1712-1900 – (Mf 1: Deaths 1714-1845. Mf 2-5,7: Births 1713-1848. Mf 6-7: Marriages 1712-1843. Mf 7: Out-of-Town Marrs 1714-99. Mf 8-9: Vitals Index 1713-1848. Mf 10-12: Intentions 1740-1850. Mf 13-15: Births 1733-1825. Mf 14-15: Intentions 1755-1826. Mf 15-16: Marriages 1733-1823. Mf 17: Deaths 1733-1825. Mf 18: Intentions 1744-1813. Mf 19-23: Town Records 1765-85. Mf 24-30: Town Records 1785-1812. Mf 31-35: Town Records 1812-34. Mf 36-37: Birth Index 1850-97. Mf 38-39: Marr Index 1850-97. Mf 40-41: Death Index 1850-97. Mf 42-45: Births 1843-1897; 46-50: Marriages 1843-1897; 50-53: Deaths 1843-97. Mf 57: Intentions 1850-87. Mf 58: Intentions 1892-1905) – (mf ed 1993) – 58mf – 9 – us Holbrook [920]

Medwin, Thomas *see* MEMOIR OF PERCY BYSSHE SHELLEY

Medynskii, E *see* SISTEMATICHESKII UKAZATEL' KNIG I STATEI PO VNESHKOL'NOMU OBRAZOVANIIU

Meehan, T *see* THE NATIVE FLOWERS AND FERNS OF THE UNITED STATES

MEEHAN'S MONTHLY – Germantown, Philadelphia. v1-3. 1891-1893 – 10mf – 9 – ne IDC [978]

Meek, Basil *see* 20TH CENTURY HISTORY OF SANDUSKY COUNTY AND REPRESENTATIVE CITIZENS

Meek, Charles Kingsley *see*
- A SUDANESE KINGDOM
- TRIBAL STUDIES IN NORTHERN NIGERIA

Meeker Family *see* MEEKER FAMILY CORRESPONDENCE AND PAPERS

MEEKER FAMILY CORRESPONDENCE AND PAPERS / Meeker Family – 1825-68 – 1 – us KS Hist [920]

Meeker, Jotham *see*
- JOTHAM MEEKER PAPERS
- JOURNAL

Meerburgh, N *see*
- AFBEELDINGEN VAN ZELDZAME GEWASSEN
- PLANTAE RARIORES VIVIS COLORIBUS DEPICTAE
- PLANTARUM SELECTARUM ICONES PICTAE

DES MEERES UND DER LIEBE WELLEN : TRAUERSPIEL IN FUENF AUFZUEGEN / Grillparzer, Franz – Leipzig: Hesse & Becker, [19-?] – 1r – 1 – us U.W. Library [430]

Meersseman, G G *see* DOSSIER DEL ORDRE DE LA PENITENCE...

Meersseman-Adda *see* MANUALE DI COMPUTO...DI VERONA...

MEESON AND WELSBY'S REPORTS : REPORTS OF CASES ARGUED AND DETERMINED IN THE COURTS OF EXCHEQUER AND EXCHEQUER CHAMBER... / Meeson, R & Welsby, WN – v1-16 + index vol. 1836-47. London: Sweet, Stevens & Maxwell, 1837-49 (all publ) – 156mf – 9 – $234.00 – LLMC 95-297 – us L.L.M.C. [324]

Meeson, R *see* MEESON AND WELSBY'S REPORTS

Meester, Placidus de *see*
- DE MONACHICO STATU IUXTA DICIPLINAM BYZANTINAM
- STUDI SUI SACRAMENTI AMMINISTRATI SECONDO IL RITO BIZANTINO

MEET B. H. CARROLL / Burroughs, P E – 1 – 5.04 – us Baptist [240]

MEET THE PRESS – New York, 1956-71 – 288mf – 9 – $5.00f – us Ross [070]

MEET THE PRESS, 1957-1986 – (Transcripts of the NBC News interviews with public figures) – 9 – $1790.00 – us UMI [920]

MEETING OF THE EASTERN AFRICAN SUB-COMMITTEE FOR SOIL CORRELATION AND LAND EVALUATION (2, 1976, ADDIS ABABA) – 1976 – 131p – it F.A.O. [631]

MEETING OF THE EDINBURGH MEDICAL MISSIONARY SOCIETY, HELD 13TH JANUARY 1846... – Edinburgh, 1846 – 1mf – 9 – ne IDC [610]

MEETING OF THE WEST AFRICAN SUB-COMMITTEE FOR SOIL CORRELATION AND LAND EVALUATION (4, 1979, BANJUL, GAMBIA) – 1981 – 127p – it F.A.O. [333]

MEETING PAPERS / American Institute of Chemical Engineers – New York: American Institute of Chemical Engineers: ca 70mf per meeting – 9 – $6.00f non-members $4.00f AICHE members – us AIChE [660]

MEETING TECHNICAL PAPERS OF THE AMERICAN CONGRESS ON SURVEYING AND MAPPING *see* ANNUAL MEETING ACSM

MEETING TECHNICAL PAPERS OF THE ANNUAL MEETING ACSM *see* ANNUAL MEETING OF THE AMERICAN CONGRESS ON SURVEYING AND MAPPING

MEETINGS / American Electro-Chemical Society – v1-99. 1902-51. Continued as: Electrochemical Society – 1 – us UMI [073]

MEETINGS / Electrochemical Society – v100-130. 1951-66. Continues: American Electro-chemical Society – 1 – us UMI [073]

MEETINGS AND CONVENTIONS – 1966- 1; v10- 5,6,9 – us UMI [999]

MEETINGS AND INCENTIVE TRAVEL – Toronto. v1-23. 1972-94 – 9 – Can$20.00y – cn Micromedia [073]

Meeuszlin, W *see* EEN CLAERE ENDE SCHRIFTELICKE ONDERRICHTINGHE VANDEN EEDT. WAER TOEGHEDAEN IS EEN CLEIN ANHANCKSEL, DEN SELUEN HANDEL ANGAENDE

Meeuwisse, Willem H *see* THE EFFECT OF SALBUTAMOL ON PERFORMANCE IN ELITE NON-ASTHMATIC ATHLETES

Meffert, Franz *see* DER HEILIGE ALFONS VON LIGUORI

MEGALITHGRAEBER IN YAMATO AUS DREI PERIODEN DER KOFUN-ZEIT / Wittig, Hildja Yukino – 1994 – 3mf – DM98.00 – 3-8267-2070-9 – gw Hänsel [930]

Megally, S *see* THE WATER WHEEL OF LOVE

Megally, Shafik *see*
- AN ANTHOLOGY OF MODERN ARABIC POETRY
- EGYPTIAN POETRY, FROM ITS RENAISSANCE TO THE PRESENT TIME
- KEAT'S GREAT ODES; A RECONSIDERATION OF THE FIVE ODES WHICH REDEEM ROMANTICISM

LE MEGANTIC : HEBDO / ed by Adams, Cleophas – Thetford, Canada. 25 sep 1925-v9 n45. 3 jan 1935 – 2r – 1 – Can$50.00r – cn Can Microfilming [072]

Mege, Joseph *see* COMMENTAIRE SUR LA REGLE DE S. BENOIT

Mege, P *see* SOUVENIRS DE LA LANGUE D'AUVERGNE

THE MEGHADUTA KALIDASA / ed by Hultzch, E – 1911 – 1 – uk Microform Academic [280]

MEGIDDO MESSAGE – v41- 1954- 1; v62- 5,6; v63- 9 – us UMI [073]

MEGIDDO, VOL 2 : SEASONS OF 1935-1939 / Loud, Gordon – (Texts and plates on separate fiche) – 1948 – 9 – $10.00f – 0-226-49386-5 – us U.C. Orient [930]

MEGILLAT ESTER – Cracow. 1589. BJ-43-52 1 – 9 – ne IDC [220]

Meginnes, John F *see* HISTORY OF LYCOMING COUNTY
Megister, J *see* THESAURUS POLYGLOTTUS
Meglin, Joellen A *see* REPRESENTATIONS AND REALITIES
MEHASIN – Mueduer: Mehmed Rauf; Istanbul: Derziyan Matbaasi, Hilal Matbaasi. Sene 1-2, sayi 1-12 (1324-1325 [1908-1909]) – 16mf – 9 – $100.00 – us MEDOC [949]
MEHASIN UEL-AS-AR VE HAKA'IK UEL-AHBAR (VASIF TARIHI) / Vasif, Ahmed – Istanbul, 1219 – 2v 14 mf – 9 – $47.25 – us MEDOC [949]
MEHERRIN BAPTIST CHURCH. MURFREESBORO, NORTH CAROLINA : CHURCH RECORDS – 1833-74 – 1 – 8.46 – us Baptist [240]
MEHKARIM BE-MIKRA VA-TALMUD UVE-SIFRUT RABBANIT / Kaminka, A I – Tel Aviv. 1938. BJ-100-14 1 – 9 – ne IDC [270]
Mehlhorn, Paul *see* DIE WIEDERKUNFTSWEISSAGUNG JESU CHRISTI
Mehmed 'Ali Hilmi Dede, Baba *see* DIVAN
Mehmed Emin, Iffet *see* DIVAN
Mehmed, Mehmed ibn *see* NUHBET UEL-TEVARIH VE'L AHBAR
Mehmed, Sebateddin *see* DIVAN
Mehmet Sureyya *see* SICILL-I OSMANI YAHUT TEZKERE-I MESAHIR I OSMANIYE ISTANBUL
Mehmet Tahir, Bursali *see* OSMANLI MUELLIFERI, IATANBUL. MATBAA-I AMIRE-SUKRU MATBASSI, 1333-1342
Mehnert, K *see* DIE SOVET-UNION 1917-1932
Mehring, Franz *see*
– AUFSAETZE ZUR DEUTSCHEN LITERATURGESCHICHTE
– DIE DEUTSCHE KLASSIK UND DIE FRANZOESISCHE REVOLUTION
– DIE DEUTSCHE LITERATUR UND DIE REVOLUTION VON 1848
– LEGENDA O LESSINGE
– THE LESSING LEGEND
– MEHRING WERKAUSWAHL
– SCHILLER
– ZUR PHILOSOPHIE UND POESIE DES KAPITALISMUS
Mehring, Walter *see* NEUBESTELLTES ABENTEUERLICHES TIERHAUS; EIN ZOOLOGIE DES ABERGLAUBENS, DER MYSTIK UND MYTHOLOGIE VOM MITTELALTER BIS AUF UNSERE ZEIT, VON WATER MEHRING
MEHRING WERKAUSWAHL = SELECTIONS, 1974 / Mehring, Franz; ed by Raddatz, Fritz J – (Includes bibliographical references and indexes) – Darmstadt: Luchterhand, 1974- – 1 – us U.W. Library [430]
Mehringer, Hartmut *see* WIDERSTAND ALS "HOCHVERRAT" 1933-1945
"MEI ERICH" : AUS OTTO ERICHS LEBEN / Hartleben, Selma – Berlin: S Fischer, 1910 – 1r – 1 – us U.W. Library [920]
Mei, G *see* [DE NOMI CORDE DEL MONOCHORDO]
MEI JIH HSIN WEN – Swatow, China. Feb 4 1956-March 31 1957 – 1r – 1 – us L of C Photodup [072]
MEI SHU – Reproductions of art work and critical articles.1954-80. 188 ill. ARIf – 9 – 630.00 – cc Globe [073]
MEI ZHOU PING LUN – Dec 1918-Aug 1919. 2 ill. DL15f – 9 – 30.00 – cc Globe [073]
Meibomius, M *see*
– ANTIQUAE MUSICAE AUCTORES SEPTEM. GRAECE ET LATINE
– ANTIQUAE MUSICAE AUCTORES SEPTEM, GRAECE ET LATINE, MARCUS MEIBOMIUS RESTITUIT AC NOTIS EXPLICAVIT
MEI-CHOU CHUNG-YAO SHU-PAO MU-LU SO-YIN – (Weekly Index of Important Publications). 6 v. Shanghai. 1931-37. Lacking: v. 1 (1-27, 44, 46) 1931-32; v. 3 (5-6) 1933; v. 6 (27-52) 1936-37. BCH-313 1 – 9 – ne IDC [073]
Meidinger-Geise, Inge *see* PERSPEKTIVEN DEUTSCHER DICHTUNG
MEIE ELU – (In Estonian) – Canada, Mar 1950-1976 – 26r – 1 – cn Commonwealth Micro [072]
Meier, August *see*
– THE PAPERS OF A. PHILIP RANDOLPH
– PAPERS OF THE NAACP
– PAPERS OF THE NAACP, PART 1
– PAPERS OF THE NAACP, PART 2
– PAPERS OF THE NAACP, PART 3
– PAPERS OF THE NAACP, PART 4
– PAPERS OF THE NAACP, PART 5
– PAPERS OF THE NAACP, PART 6
– PAPERS OF THE NAACP, PART 8
– PAPERS OF THE NAACP, PART 10
– PAPERS OF THE NAACP, PART 11
– PAPERS OF THE NAACP, PART 12
– PAPERS OF THE NAACP, PART 13
– PAPERS OF THE NAACP, PART 14
– PAPERS OF THE NAACP, PART 15
– PAPERS OF THE NAACP, PART 23
– RECORDS OF THE AMERICAN COMMITTEE ON AFRICA
Meier, D I *see* RUSSKOE GRAZHDANSKOE PRAVO
Meier, G *see*
– DIE ASSYRISCHE BESCHWOERUNGSSAMM-LUNG MAQLU
– DE CAPTA CONSTANTINOPOLI, ANNO 1453
MEIER HELMBRECHT : TRAGOEDIE IN DREI AKTEN UND EINEM VORSPIEL / Ortner, Eugen – Muenchen: Die Wende Verlag, 1928 – 1r – 1 – us U.W. Library [820]
Meier, Mark F *see* REMOTE SENSING OF SNOW AND ICE
Meier, P Gabriel *see* AUSGEWAEHLTE SCHRIFTEN VON COLUMBAN, ALKUIN, DODANA, JONAS, HRABANUS MAURUS, NOTKER BALBULUS, HUGO VON SANKT VIKTOR UND PERALDUS. EINL. U. UEBERS. P. GABRIEL MEIER
Meierhoefer, Barbara S *see*
– THE CASELOAD EXPERIENCES OF THE DISTRICT COURTS FROM 1972 TO 1983
– COURT-ANNEXED ARBITRATION IN TEN DISTRICT COURTS
– THE GENERAL EFFECT OF MANDATORY MINIMUM PRISON TERMS
– HOME CONFINEMENT
– IN-COURT ORIENTATION PROGRAMS IN THE FEDERAL DISTRICT COURTS
Meighan, John M *see* MOTOR BUS LAWS AND REGULATIONS
Meigret, Louis *see*
– DEFENSES DE LOUIS MEIGRET
– LA RESPONSE A L'APOLOGIE DE JACQUES PELETIER
– RESPONSE DE LOUIS MEIGRET
– TRAITE TOUCHANT LE COMMUN USAGE DE L'ESCRITURE FRANCOISE
– LE TRETTE DE LA GRAMMERE FRANCOEZE
MEIGS CREEK BAPTIST ASSOCIATION, MS 880 – (Minutes of 11 annual meetings, including reports on the contributions of member churches, and on other church activities held in various counties in Southeastern Ohio) – Ohio, 1826-36 – 1r – 1 – us Western Res [240]
Meigs, Montgomery C. *see* PAPERS
Meigs, Return J *see* PAPERS
Meigs, William M *see* THE GROWTH OF THE CONSTITUTION IN THE FEDERAL CONVENTION OF 1787
MEIGUO QINHUA SHILIAO – Historical materials on American aggression in China. Comp. by the Chinese People's Committee for the Defense of World Peace, Beijing branch. 4 fiches. F-H201 – 9 – $28.00 – cc Microforms [950]
Meijboom, Louisa Susan Pedro *see* RAADSELACHTIGE VERHALEN UIT HET OUDE EN HET NIEUWE VERBOND
Meijer, Hilda *see* SLAVIC PALAEOGRAPHY
MEIJI ERA BOOKS COLLECTION – Japan, 1868-1912 – 15,536r – 1 – Y180,000,000.00 set – Dist. ja Maruzen – ja Nat'l Diet [080]
MEIJI KYOIKU TOKEI SHIRYO = EDUCATIONAL STATISTICS OF THE RESPECTIVE PREFECTURES OF JAPAN IN THE MEIJI ERA / Japan. Prefectures – 1882-1912 – 80r – 1 – Y475,000.00 – ja Yushodo [370]
MEIJI NENKAN FUKEN TOKEISHO SHUSEI = COMPLETE COLLECTION OF THE STATISTICAL ANNUALS OF THE RESPECTIVE PREFECTURES OF JAPAN IN THE MEIJI ERA, 1873-1912 – All of the annual statistical reports of the 47 prefectures, totaling 2,030v, 800,000p – 504r – 1 – Y3,478,000.00 – ja Yushodo [950]
MEIJI ZENKI KYOIKU SHIRYO SHUSEI = COMPILATION OF DOCUMENTS ON THE DEVELOPMENT OF EDUCATION IN THE EARLY MEIJI ERA – 1870-92. Documents, reports, histories from various libraries in Japan. 100,000p. Table of contents, index by Dr. Hajime Yaguchi – 60r – 1 – Y475,000.00 – ja Yushodo [370]
MEIJI-KI KANKO-BUTSU SHUSEI = JAPAN MEIJI SHORT TITLE CATALOGUE: SEGMENT 1: LITERATURE AND LINGUISTICS – (94 units. Available by unit or title. Ca 450-500fiche per unit) – All books publ. in Meiji Era (1868-1912) – 45,466mf – 9 – Y481,500.00 per unit – ja Yushodo [480]
Meiklejohn Civil Liberties Institute *see*
– THE ANGELA DAVIS TRIAL WITH INDEX
– THE PENTAGON PAPERS TRIAL WITH INDEX
Meilakh, B *see*
– LENIN I PROBLEMY RUSSKOI LITERATURY KONTSA 19 NACHALA 20 V. ISSLEDOVANIIA I OCHERKI
– LENIN I PROBLEMY RUSSKOI LITERATURY KONTSA 19 NACHALA 20 VV. ISSLEDOVANIIA I OCHERKI
Meilakh, B S *see* DEKABRISTY I IKH VREMIA. MATERIALY I SOOBSHCHENIIA
Meilakii, B *see* VOPROSY LITERATURNYI I ESTETIKI
LE MEILLEUR JOURNAL – (Cont by: Le Meilleur Journal le Nordic, Port-Cartier et Sept-Iles v8 n21 26 mai 1971-24 mar 1984. Cont by: Promo-Services Le Nordic, Port-Cartier et Sept-Iles 31 mar 1984-8 mar 1985) – Port-Cartier, Canada. v9 n1. 7 jan 1970-12 mai 1971 – 21r – 1 – Can$75.00r – cn Can Microfilming [072]
LE MEILLEUR JOURNAL LE NORDIC *see* LE MEILLEUR JOURNAL
MEIN BERNSTEINLAND UND MEINE STADT / Miegel, Agnes – (In verse) – Koenigsberg Pr.: Graefe und Unzer, 1944 – 1r – 1 – us U.W. Library [910]
MEIN ERSTES ABENTEUER : UND ANDERE NOVELLEN / Wolzogen, Ernst von – Berlin: Ullstein & Co., [1910?] – 1r – 1 – us U.W. Library [830]
MEIN ERSTES ABENTEUER UND ANDERE GESCHICHTEN / Hopfen, Hans – Stuttgart: J Engelhorn, 1886 – 1r – 1 – us U.W. Library [830]
MEIN FILM – Wien, 1926-dec 8 1939, oct 26 1945-jul 4 1957 – 23r – 1 – gw Mikrofilm [790]
MEIN HERZ, MEIN LAND : AUSGEWAEHLTE GEDICHTE / Schickele, Rene – Berlin: P Cassirer, 1919 – 1r – 1 – us U.W. Library [810]
MEIN LEBEN / Hohlbaum, Robert – (Includes bibliographical references) – Berlin: Junker und Duennhaupt, 1936 – 1r – 1 – us U.W. Library [920]
MEIN LEBEN / Huch, Rudolf – (Includes bibliographical references) – Berlin: Junker und Duennhaupt, 1935 – 1r – 1 – us U.W. Library [920]
MEIN LEBEN : NATUR UND KUNST / Paulsen, Rudolf – (Includes bibliographical references) – Berlin: Junker und Duennhaupt, 1936 – 1r – 1 – us U.W. Library [920]
MEIN LEBEN : VON DER KRAFT DER LANDSCHAFT / Griese, Friedrich – (Includes bibliographical references) – Berlin: Junker und Duennhaupt, 1934 – 1r – 1 – us U.W. Library [920]
MEIN LEBEN / Wehner, Josef Magnus – (Includes bibliographical references) – Berlin: Junker und Duennhaupt, 1934 – 1r – 1 – us U.W. Library [920]
MEIN LEBEN / Weismantel, Leo – (Includes bibliographical references) – Berlin: Junker und Duennhaupt, 1936 – 1 – us U.W. Library [920]
MEIN LEBENSABEND / Altenberg, Peter – Berlin: S Fischer, 1919 – 1r – 1 – us U.W. Library [943]
MEIN LEBENSGANG. GEDICHTE AUS FUNF JAHRZEHNTEN / Otto, Louise – Leipzig: Moritz Schafer, 1893. With: Der Genius der Menscheit; Schloss und Fabrik – 1 – us U.W. Library [810]
MEIN SILBERGRAUER WEGGEFAEHRTE : ROMAN / Strohmeyer, Curt – Berlin: Safari-Verlag, c1943 – 1r – 1 – us U.W. Library [830]
MEIN TAGEWERK / Reinke, J – Freiburg im Breisgau, 1925 – 6mf – ne IDC [580]
MEIN WEG ALS DEUTSCHER UND JUDE / Wassermann, Jakob – Berlin: S. Fischer, 1921. 125p – 1 – us U.W. Library [943]
Meinck, Ernst *see*
– FRIEDRICH HEBBELS UND RICHARD WAGNERS NIBELUNGEN-TRILOGIEN
– RICHARD WAGNERS DICHTUNG DER RING DES NIBELUNGEN AUS DER SAGE NEU ERLAEUTERT
MEINE BEREISUNG VON DEUTSCH-OSTAFRICA / Trotha, Oberst von – Berlin: B Brigl, 1897 – us Res Libr [960]
MEINE FERIEN / Rosegger, Peter – Wien: A Hartleben, 1883 – 1r – 1 – us U.W. Library [430]
MEINE GUTACHTEN VOR GERICHT IN SACHEN DER LIGUORISCHEN MORAL : DER GRASSMANNSCHEN ANKLAGE DARAUS UND DES VERTEIDIGUNGSVERSUCHES SR. K.H. DES PRINZEN MAX VON SACHSEN / Nippold, Friedrich – Halle a.S.: H.W. Schmidt, 1904 – 1mf – us A.T.L.A. [340]
Meinecke, Friedrich *see* ERLEBTES, 1862-1901
Meiners, Earlet P *see* THE EFFECT OF TOE AND PLANTAR FLEXOR STRENGTH TRAINING ON VERTICAL JUMP PERFORMANCE OF FOLK DANCERS
Meinertz, M *see* JESUS UND DIE HEIDENMISSION
MEINERZHAGENER ZEITUNG – Meinerzhagen, Germany. 1 Jun 1992- – 7r per yr – 1 – gw Mikrofilm [072]
Meinhold, Johannes *see*
– BEITRAEGE ZUR ERKLAERUNG DES BUCHES DANIEL HEFT I, DAN. 2-6
– DIE BIBLISCHE URGESCHICHTE I. MOSE 1-12 GEMEINVERSTAENDLICH DARGESTELLT
– DIE COMPOSITION DES BUCHES DANIEL
– JESAJA UND SEINE ZEIT
– DIE JESAJAERZAEHLUNGEN: JESAJA 36-39
– JESUS UND DAS ALTE TESTAMENT: EIN... WORT AN DIE EVANGELISCHEN CHRISTEN
– DIE LADE JAHVES
Meinsma, KO *see* SPINOZA EN ZIJN KRING
Meisami, Julie *see* EDEBIYAT
Meisel, M *see* A BIBLIOGRAPHY OF AMERICAN NATURAL HISTORY
Meisel, W A *see*
– PRINZ UND DERWISCH
– DER PRUEFSTEIN
Meisen, A *see* NIKOLAUSKULT UND NIKOLAUSBRAUCH IM ABENDLANDE (FVK HFT 9-12)
Meisenburg, Friedrich *see* DER DEUTSCHE REICHSTAG WAEHREND DES OESTERREICHISCHEN ERBFOLGEKRIEGES (1740-1748)
MEISHU YANJIU – Studies in the Fine Arts. In Chinese but Table of Contents in English in each issue. F p30 – 9 – 4.00f – cc Microforms [073]
Meisl, J *see* ELLEH TOLEDOT KEREN MOSHEH MONTEFIORE
Meisner, C F *see*
– MONOGRAPHIAE GENERIS POLYGONI PRODROMUS
– PLANTARUM VASCULARIUM GENERA SECUNDUM ORDINES NATURALES
Meisner, Oskar *see* DER DEKALOG: EINE KRITISCHE STUDIE: TEIL I: DER DEKALOG IM HEXATEUCH
Meissas, G *see* LES GRANDS VOYAGEURS CONTEMPORAINS
Meissner, Alfred *see*
– GEDICHTE
– GESAMMELTE SCHRIFTEN
– DIE GRABESSCHULD
– DIE MATRATZENGRUFT
– ZIZKA
Meissner, B *see*
– ALTORIENTALISCHEN STUDIEN
– SUPPLEMENT ZU DEN ASSYRISCHEN WOERTERBUECHERN
Meissner, Bruno *see*
– ALEXANDER UND GILGAMOS
– KURZGEFASSTE ASSYRISCHE GRAMMATIK
Meissner, Heinrich *see* ORGELTOENE
Meissonnier, Casimir *see* CONSIDERATIONS SUR LE CHOLERA D'ARLES.
MEISTER – v. 1-8. 1888-95 – 1 – us UMI [073]
MEISTER DER SCHWEIZERISCHEN DICHTUNG DES NEUNZEHNTEN JAHRHUNDERTS / Saitschick, Robert – Freuenfeld: J Huber, 1894 – 1r – 1 – us U.W. Library [430]
MEISTER DIETRICH, SEIN LEBEN, SEINE WERKE, SEINE WISSENSCHAFT : BGPHMA 5/5-6 / Krebs, E – Muenster, 1906 – 7mf – 9 – ne Slangenburg [240]
MEISTER ECKEHART : DAS SYSTEM SEINER RELIGIOESEN LEHRE UND LEBENSWEISHEIT / Karrer, O – Muenchen, 1926 – 6mf – 8 – ne Slangenburg [290]
Meister, Jacques-Henri *see* DE L'ORIGINE DES PRINCIPES RELIGIEUX
MEISTER LUKAS : EIN BILD AUS DER VORZEIT DER SIEBENBUERGER SACHSEN / Schuller, Gustav – Hermannstadt: Michaelis & Seraphin, 1888 – 1r – 1 – us U.W. Library [810]
MEISTER MARTIN DER KUEFNER UND SEINE GESELLEN / Hoffmann, Ernst Theordor Amadeus; ed by Gerz, Alfred – Potsdam: Ruetten & Loening, [19-?] – 1r – 1 – us U.W. Library [830]
DER MEISTER VON PALMYRA : DRAMATISCHE DICHTUNG IN FUENF AUFZUEGEN / Wilbrandt, Adolf von – 8. Aufl. Stuttgart: J G Cotta, 1899 – 1r – 1 – us U.W. Library [820]
MEISTERDRAMEN / Laube, Heinrich – Leipzig: M Hesse, [1908?] – 1 – us U.W. Library [820]

DIE MEISTERSINGER VON NUERNBERG : OPER IN DREI AKTEN / Wagner, Richard – Mainz: B Schott's Soehne, [1880?] – 1r – 1 – us U.W. Library [790]
DIE MEISTERSINGER VON NUERNBERG / Wagner, Richard – New York: American Book Company, c1904 – 1r – 1 – us U.W. Library [790]
MEISTERWERKE DEUTSCHER LITERATURKRITIK : AUFKLAERUNG, KLASSIK, ROMANTIK / Mayer, Hans – (Includes bibliographical references and index) – Stuttgart: Govert, 1962 – 1r – 1 – us U.W. Library [430]
MEISTERWERKE DEUTSCHER LITERATURKRITIK / Mayer, Hans; ed by Mayer, Hans – (Cont by the author's Deutsche Literaturkritik im zwanzigsten Jahrhundert. Includes bibliographical references and indexes) – Berlin: Ruetten und Loening, 1954-1956 – 1 – us U.W. Library [430]
MEISTERWERKE DEUTSCHER LITERATURKRITIK *see* DEUTSCHE LITERATURKRITIK IM ZWANZIGSTEN JAHRHUNDERT
MEISTERWERKEN : MUHAMMEDANISCHER KUNST – (Reproduction of 3-volume portfolio illustrating and describing the Islamic Art exhibition held in Munich in 1910) – Munich – 1r – 1 – $95.00 – 0-907006-43-4 – uk Mindata [700]
MEITAN KEXOE JISHU – Coal Science and Technology. In Chinese, with English abstracts to the main articles – 9 – $4.00f – cc Microforms [622]
MEITAN XUEBAO – Journal of China Coal Society. In Chinese, with English abstracts to the main articles – 9 – $4.00f – cc Microforms [622]
Meixner, Esther Chilstrom *see* THE JOHN ERICSSON COLLECTION OF THE AMERICAN SWEDISH HISTORICAL FOUNDATION
MEIZHOU PINGLUN – The Weekly Review. 22 Dec 1918-30 Aug 1919. F C1. In Chinese – 9 – $13.50 – cc Microforms [073]
Mejer, Otto *see*
- DIE GRUNDLAGEN DES LUTHERISCHEN KIRCHENREGIMENTES
- LEHRBUCH DES DEUTSCHEN KIRCHENRECHTES
- DIE PROPAGANDA
- DIE PROPAGANDA IN ENGLAND

Mejia Valera, M *see* FUENTES PARA LA HISTORIA DE LA FILOSOFIA EL EN PERU
Mejias, Lola *see* HASTA LLEGAR A DIOS
MEJICO.-LA ERA DE LOS MARTIRES / ed by Bayle, Constantino – Madrid: Razon y Fe, 1926 – 1 – sp Bibl Santa Ana [240]
LA MEJOR CORONA / Lopez de Ayala, Adelardo – 1868 – 9 – 1.50f – sp Bibl Santa Ana [820]
EL MEJOR GUZMAN DE LOS BUENOS / Gil de Godoy, Juan – 3v. 1674, 1690, 1717 – 9 – 1.50f – sp Bibl Santa Ana [946]
MEJORAS...ALMA / Manrique, Manuel – 1738 – 9 – 1.50f – sp Bibl Santa Ana [890]
LAS MEJORES TRADICIONES PERUANAS / Palma, Ricardo – Barcelona: Maucci, 1918?. 351p – 1 – us U.W. Library [972]
Mekar Bunga Indonesia *see* INDONESIAN POPULAR MELODIES AND SIGHTSEEINGS
MEKARIM'UEL-AHLAK – 1. sene, 1-30 (1324-1325) – 5mf – 9 – $55.00 – us MEDOC [949]
MEKEEL'S WEEKLY STAMP NEWS – St-Louis, MO. v1 n25. 24 jun 1891-v1 n52. 30 dec 1891 – 1r – 1 – Can$30.00 – cn Can Microfilming [071]
DER MEKHABEL : HUMORISTISH – (Yiddish weekly) – Warsaw, PL. v1 no2 22 May 1919-v1 no8 Jul 1919 – 1r – 1 – $25.00 – cn Can Microfilming [072]
MEKHANIZAT SII A I MOTORIZAT SII A RKKA – (Library has: Jan.-Aug. 1936) – [Moskva]: Gos. voennoe izd-vo, 1932-1936. 5v – 1 – CSUX89-S600 – us Hoover Inst Photo [947]
Mekler, I L *see* PILEGESH BE-GIVAH
MEKTEB – (Sahib-i Imtiyaz: Kitabci Karabet, Mueduerue: Ebuel-Feyyaz Hakki, Sermuharriri: Ismail Hakki. III. sene, nos. 1-15 (30 Kanuniewel 1309-28 Temmuz 1310[1893-1894])) – Istanbul: Mahmud Bey Matbaasi, 1891-1897 – 12mf – 9 – $200.00 – us MEDOC [949]
MEKTEBLI – Samsun. Sahib-i Imtiyaz: Hayreddin Nadi. Mueduer-i Umur: Hueseyin Huesni. No. 5 (20 Subat 1338 [1922]) – 9 – $20.00 – us MEDOC [956]
Mel, Marian Louise *see* PRIVATE EMPLOYMENT AGENCIES; LAWS RELATING TO THEIR REGULATION AS OF SEPTEMBER 1, 1943
Mela, Pomponius *see* COSMOGRAPHIA, ETC
Melagan, Edward *see* THE JESUITS AND THE GREAT MOGUL
MELANCHOLIE : GEDICHTE / Morgenstern, Christian – Berlin: B Cassirer, 1921 – 1r – 1 – us U.W. Library [810]
Melanchthon, Phil *see*
- VERLEGUNG ETLICHER VNCHRISTLICHER ARTIKEL WELCHE DIE WIDERTEUFFER FURGEBEN

Melanchthon, Philip *see*
- ADVERSVS ANABAPTISTAS. IUDICIUM
- COLLECTED WORKS
- ETLICHE PROPOSITIONES WIDER DIE LEHR DER WIDERTEUFFER
- VERLEGUNG ETLICHER VNCHRISTLICHER ARTIKEL WELCHE DIE WIDERTEUFFER FURGEBEN
- VNDERRICHT WIDER DIE LERE DER WIDERTEUFFER AUSZ DEM LATEIN VERDEUTSCHET DURCH JU JONAS

Melanchton, P *see* OPERA OMNIA
Melanesian Mission *see* EXECUTIVE COMMITTEE MINUTES, 21 APR 1921-5 MAR 1925, AND FINANCE BOARD MINUTES, 25 MAR 1925-31 JUL 1934
MELANESIAN NIUS / THE KIOKIO NIUS – n1-10. jan-mar 1977 – Pt of 1r – 1 – PMB Doc416 – at Pacific Mss [072]
MELANESIANS AND POLYNESIANS : THEIR LIFE-HISTORIES DESCRIBED AND COMPARED / Brown, George – London; New York: Macmillan, 1910 – 2mf – us A.T.L.A. [950]
MELANGES / Derenboug, H – Paris. 1909. BJ-100-27 1 – 9 – ne IDC [305]
MELANGES ASIATIQUES / Remusat, J P A – ou Choix de Morceaux critiques. 2 v. Paris. 1825-26. BCH-828 2 – 8 – ne IDC [950]
MELANGES ASIATIQUES TIRES DE BULLETIN HISTORICO-PHILOSOPHIQUE DE L'ACADEMIE IMPERIALE DES SCIENCES DE ST PETERSBOURG / Academie Imperiale des Sciences. St. Petersburg – Spb. 1849 52-1894. v1-10 – 128mf – 8 – ne IDC [950]
MELANGES ASIATIQUES, TIRES DE L'ACADEMIE IMPERIALE DES SCIENCES DE ST. PETERSBOURG / L'Academie Imperiale des Sciences. St. Petersbourg – 1849. 52-1894 – 1 – $152.00 – us L of C Photodup [950]
MELANGES D'ARCHEOLOGIE ET D'HISTOIRE – Paris, Rome. 1881-1920. v1-38 – 349mf – 9 – ne IDC [930]
MELANGES DE CRITIQUE RELIGIEUSE / Scherer, Edmond Henri Adolphe – Paris: J. Cherbuliez, 1860 – 2mf – us A.T.L.A. [240]
MELANGES DE CRITIQUE RELIGIEUSE / Vernes, Maurice – Paris: Sandoz & Fischbacher, 1880 – 1mf – 9 – 0-8370-2911-2 – 1985-0911 – us A.T.L.A. [220]
MELANGES DE SCIENCE RELIGIEUSE – 1(1944)-27(1970) – 135mf – 9 – Dfl473.00 – ne Slangenburg [073]
MELANGES DE SCIENCE RELIGIEUSE – Lille. v1-27. 1944-1970 – 135mf – 9 – ne IDC [210]
MELANGES D'EPIGRAPHIE ET D'ARCHEOLOGIE SEMITIQUES / Halevy, Joseph – (Includes bibliographical references) – Paris: Imprimerie nationale, 1874 – 1mf – 9 – 0-8370-8430-X – 1986-2430 – us A.T.L.A. [470]
MELANGES EN L'HONNEUR DE MGR. M. ANDRIEU – Straszbourg, 1956 – 9mf – 8 – Dfl32.00 – ne Slangenburg [240]
MELANGES ET DOCUMENTS: 2E CENTENAIRE DE LA MORT DE LA MABILLON – Archives de la France Monastique. V. 1908 – 9mf – 8 – ne Slangenburg [240]
MELANGES HENRI LICHTENBERGER : HOMMAGE DE SES ELEVES ET DE SES AMIS, JUIN 1934 – (Includes bibliographical references. Includes a biographical sketch of Lichtenberger and a list of his publications) – Paris: Stock (Delamain et Boutelleau), c1934 – 1 – us U.W. Library [430]
MELANGES HISTORIQUES ET RELIGIEUX / Chastel, Etienne Louis – Paris: G. Fischbacher; Geneve: A. Cherbuliez, 1888 – 2mf – us A.T.L.A. [240]
MELANGES JAPONAIS – Serie d'articles sur le Japon. Tokyo. 1904, 1905 – 9 – 25.00 – fr Orientalistes [950]
MELANGES OFFERTS A ME. RAYMOND COSSETTE / Cossette, Raymond – Quebec: Chambre des notaires de la province de Quebec, 1968. 483p. LL-2336 – 1 – us L of C Photodup [340]
MELANGES ORIENTAUX – Textes et traductions publies par les professeurs de l'Ecole des langues. Congres de Leyde. 1883 – 9 – fr Orientalistes [480]
MELANGES RELIGIEUX – Montreal, Canada. 14 dec 1840-16 jul 1852 – 6r – 1 – Can$40.00r – cn Can Microfilming [240]
MELANGES: TROIS CONFERENCES / Beaugrand, Honore – Montreal: La Patrie, 1888. 03524. (Pre-1900 Canadiana) – 9 – cn C.I.H.M. [971]
MELANGES. UN VOYAGE AU JAPON; LES PRINCIPALES FABRIQUES; LES PRINCIPALES FABRIQUES DE PORCELAINE AU JAPON – Paris. 1874-1875-76 – 9 – 5.00 – fr Orientalistes [910]
Melani, Gaudezio *see* LA POVERTA A CURA DI...ASSISI, 1967
MELANIPPA-FILOSOF. TRAGEDIIA / Annenskii, I F – Spb. 1901. BR-505 2 – 8 – ne IDC [460]
Melara Berrocal, Isidro *see* ARMONIA
MELAWAN KARJA GAJADELAPAN DIDALAM PARTAI, ON 2 FEB., 1942 / Mao, Tse-tung – SE-10,496 1. 1962 – 9 – ne IDC [324]
MELBOURNE BULLETIN – 1880-1886 – 5mf – 9 – at Corangamite [980]
MELBOURNE DAILY LAW LIST – Australia. 22 Apr 1856-22 Dec 1860.-d. 3 reels – 1 – uk British Libr Newspaper [340]
MELBOURNE DAILY NEWS – Australia. -d. Jan 1849-Dec 1851. Lacking June 1849-June 1850. 7 reels – 1 – uk British Libr Newspaper [072]
MELBOURNE LEADER. (THE LEADER) – Australia. 4 Jan 1862-31 Dec 1869; 7 Jan 1871-24 Apr 1880;o 3 Jan 1885-29 Jun 1940.-w. 149mqn reels – 1 – uk British Libr Newspaper [072]
THE MELBOURNE PAPERS / Lamb, William – 19th century. From Royal Archives, Windsor Castle – 1 – uk Microform Academic [920]
MELBOURNE PUNCH. (PUNCH.-NEW PUNCH) – Australia. 2 Aug 1855-28 Dec 1871; 16 Jan 1873-26 Dec 1878; 1 Jun 1899-29 Jun 1922.-w. 56 reels – 1 – uk British Libr Newspaper [072]
MELBOURNE UNIVERSITY LAW REVIEW – (v.12-. 1979- 5,6,9) – v.1-. 1957- – 1 – us UMI [370]
Melcher, Kurt *see* FRIEDRICH GRIESE
MELCHIOR VON DIEPENBROCK ALS UEBERSETZER SPANISCHER DICHTUNGEN / Horsthemke, Johannes – Muenster, 1915 – 102p – 9 – DM48.00 – 3-89349-001-9 – gw Hänsel [440]
MELCHIOR'S DREAM / Ewing, Juliana Horatia – British Fiction Archive: Unit 1 – 9 – uk Bell [830]
Meldrum, Bill *see* MANAGING EMPLOYEE INVOLVEMENT
MELEKH : KATALOG BIBLIOTEKI VILENSKOGO VOENNOGO SOBRANIIA – Ed. 2. Vil'na. 1908 – 12mf – 9 – ne IDC [947]
MELEKHET HA-SHIR / Neubauer, A – Frankfurt am Main. 1865. BJ-421-85 1 – 9 – ne IDC [270]
Melekii *see* KATALOG BIBLIOTEKI VILENSKAGO VOENNAGO SOBRANIIA
MELENAS Y FALDAS CORTAS / Martin Gonzalez, Angel – El breve Alcalde de Almendralejo. Don Francisco Montero de Espinosa y de la Barrera. Almendralejo: Imp. de Juan Bote, 1927 – 1 – sp Bibl Santa Ana [640]
Melendez Valdes, Juan *see*
- BATILO. EGLOGA
- CORRESPONDANCE RELATIVE A LA REUNION DES HOPITAUX D'AVILA. TEXTES EN PROSE INEDITS PUBLIES...PAR GEORGES DEMERSON
- POESIAS

Melero Ximenez, M *see* EXAMEN...DE LA ALEGACION APOLOGETICA MEDICO-PHYSECA
MELETEMATA BOTANICA / Schott, H W & Endlicher, S L – Vindobonae. 1832. B-722 2 – 8 – ne IDC [580]
Melgares, Marin, Julio *see* PROCEDIMIENTOS DE LA INQUISICION
Mel'gunov, S P *see*
- MASONSTVO V EGO PROSHLOM I NASTOIASHCHEM
- RELIGIOZNO-OBSHCHESTVENNYE DVIZHENIIA 17-18 VV. V ROSSII

Melia, Pius *see* WORDS OF A BELIEVER ON THE WAYS OF PROVIDENCE TOWARDS MAN HERE AND HEREAFTER
Melia, Raphael *see* THE WOMAN BLESSED BY ALL GENERATIONS, OR, MARY
Melichar, G A *see* HEALTH RELATED MOTIVATIONAL DETERMINANTS AMONG PARTICIPANTS IN A WORKSITE WEIGHT MANAGEMENT INTERVENTION
Melichar, L *see* HOMOPTEREN-FAUNA VON CEYLON
Melida, Jose Ramon *see*
- ALFAR MORUNO DE BADAJOZ
- EL ANFITEATRO ROMANO DE MERIDA. MEMORIA (1916 A 1918)
- EL ANFITEATRO Y EL CIRCO ROMANOS DE MERIDA. MEMORIA
- CATALOGO MONUMENTAL DE ESPANA
- CATALOGO MONUMENTAL DE ESPANA. PROVINCIA DE BADAJOZ. TEXTO 2
- CATALOGO MONUMENTAL DE ESPANA. PROVINCIA DE CACERES. (1914-1916)
- CATALOGO MONUMENTAL DE ESPANA. PROVINCIA DE CACERES. TEXTO 1
- EL CIRCO ROMANO DE MERIDA. MEMORIA DE LAS EXCAVACIONES PRACTICADAS DE 1920 A 1925
- CULTOS EMERITENSES DE SERAPIS Y DE MITHRAS
- DON JUAN DECADENTE
- EL EX CONVENTO E SAN BENITO DE ALCANTARA EN LA PROVINCIA DE CACERES
- EXCAVACIONES ARQUEOLOGICAS EN LA CIUDAD DE MERIDA
- LAS EXCAVACIONES DE MERIDA
- EXCAVACIONES DE MERIDA. LAS. ULTIMOS HALLAZGOS
- EXCAVACIONES DE MERIDA. MEMORIA DE LOS TRABAJOS PRACTICADOS EN 1926 Y 1927
- EXCAVACIONES EN MERIDA. MEMORIA
- LES FOUILLES DE MERIDA
- GRUPO DE DOLMENES EN TERMINO DE BARCARROTA, PROVINCIA DE BADAJOZ
- INSCRIPCIONES ROMANAS DE MERIDA Y REINA
- MEMORIA DE LOS TRABAJOS PRACTICADOS. UNA CASA-BASILICA ROMANO-CRISTIANA
- MERIDA
- MERIDA. 4 CONGRES INTERNATIONAL D'ARCHEOLOGIA
- MONUMENTOS ROMANOS DE LA ANTIGUA AUGUSTOBRIGA, HOY TALAVERA LA VIEJA, EN LA PROVINCIA DE CACERES
- MOSAICO EMERITENSE
- MUSEO ARQUEOLOGICO NACIONAL. ADQUISICIONES EN 1920. NOTAS DESCRIPTIVAS
- LAS NAVAS DEL MARQUES
- NOTICIA SOBRE SAN GERMAN Y SAN SERVAN
- LA POSTESCENA DEL TEATRO ROMANO DE MERIDA
- EL PUENTE DE ALCANTARA
- SANTA EULALIA DE MERIDA
- DER SCHATZ VON ALISEDA
- EL TEATRO ROMANO DE MERIDA
- TESORO DE ALISEDA
- TESORO DE LA ALISEDA

MELIORA – A quart rev. of social sci. in its ethical, economical, political and ameliorative aspects. v. 1-12. 1858-69 – 1 – us UMI [300]
MELIORA: AN ORATION BEFORE THE ALUMNI OF THE MOUNT ALLISON WESLEYAN COLLEGE, SACKVILLE, ON THE 1ST OF JUNE, 1880 / Elder, William – Sackville?: s.n., 1880?. 05223. (Pre-1900 Canadiana) – 9 – cn C.I.H.M. [971]
Melioranskii, P M *see* ARAB FILOLOG O TURETSKOM IAZYKE
Melissander, Friedrich *see* EIN BLICK AUF RUSSLAND
MELIZ EHAD MINNI ALEF / ed by Zederbaum, A – St. Petersburg. 1884. BJ-422-100 1 – 9 – ne IDC [470]
MELKAIA PROMYSHLENNOST'I EE ROL'V VOSSTANOVLENII RUSSKOGO NARODNOGO KHOZIAISTVA / Rybnikov, A A – M., 1922 – 1mf – 9 – COR-442/1 – ne IDC [334]
MELKII BES / Sologub, F – Roman. Izd. "Shipovnik". Spb. 1907. BR-866 2 – 8 – ne IDC [460]
MELKII BES / Sologub, F – Roman. Izd. Z.J. Grzhebina. Berlin. 1923. BR-867 2 – 8 – ne IDC [460]
MELKII ZEMEL'NYI KREDIT V ROSSII / Vasil'chikov, A I & Iakovlev, A V – Spb., 1876 – 2mf – 9 – COR-14/1 – ne IDC [334]

MELKOE KHOZIAISTVO I KOOPERATSIIA : POSOBIE DLIA MESTNYKH KOOPERATIVNYKH KURSOV / Kablukov, N A – M., 1917 – 1mf – 9 – COR-39/1 – ne IDC [334]
Mell, Max *see* DAS SPIEL VON DEN DEUTSCHEN AHNEN
Mell, Patrick H *see* CORRECTIVE CHURCH DISCIPLINE
Mellanby, I *see* ENVIRONMENTAL BIOLOGY AND MEDICINE
Mellema, E *see* DICTIONAIRE FRANCOIS-FLAMENG
Meller, V L *see* KREST'IANSKOE DVIZHENIE V 1917 GODU
MELLERSTA SKANE – Horby, Sweden. 1968-70, 1978 – 27r – 1 – sw Kungliga [072]
MELLERSTA SKANE – Kristianstad, Sweden. 1986 – 1 – sw Kungliga [072]
MELLERSTA SKANE *see* KRISTIANSTADSBLADET
MELLIAND TEXTILBERICHTE – v. 1-40. 1920-59 – 1,5,6 – us Princeton Micro [540]
Mellichamp, Joseph H *see* CORRESPONDENCE
Mellinet, Camille *see*
- LA COMMUNE ET LA MILICE DE NANTES
- DE LA MUSIQUE A NANTES, DEPUIS LES TEMPS LES PLUS RECULES JUSQU'A NOS JOURS

MELLOR'S MUSICAL MIRROR – Pittsburgh. v1 n1-12. 1868-69 – 1r – 1 – £60.00 – uk Chadwyck [780]
Melman, Seymour *see* THE IMPACT OF THE PATENT SYSTEM ON RESEARCH
Mel'nikov, N P *see* ISTORIIA, STATISTIKA, LITERATURA PISCHEBUMAZHNAGO PROIZVODSTVA
Mel'nikov, P *see* KNIAZHNA TARAKANOVA I PRINTSESSA VLADIMIRSKAIA
Mel'nikov, P N *see* ISTORIIA, STATISTIKA, LITERATURA PISCHEBUMAZHNAGO PROIZVODSTVA
Melo, Alberto *see* EXPERIMENTS IN POPULAR EDUCATION IN PORTUGAL 1974-1976
MELOCHE UN ERDARBET BEIYIDDIN : "O.R.T." – (In Yiddish) – Berlin, DE. no15. Mar 1925 – 1r – 1 – $25.00 – cn Can Microfilming [072]
MELOCHI IZ ZAPASA MOEI PAMIATI / Dmitriev, M A – Ed. 2. M. 1869. BR-6015 2 – 8 – ne IDC [947]
THE MELODEON – A collection of songs... adapted to sacred and moral words. 1842? – 9 – us Sibley [780]
LA MELODIA: GIORNALE MUSICALE LETTERARIO / ed by Gasparini, L – no.1-12, 1869 – 9 – us Sibley [073]
DIE MELODIE NACH IHREM WESEN SOWOHL. ALS NACH IHREN EIGENSCHAFTEN, VON CHRISTOPH NICHELMANN / Nichelmann, C – 1755 – 9 – us Sibley [780]
MELODIE UND RHYTHMUS – 1966-1975, 1977-1983 – 264mf – 1 – DM1,504.80 – gw Mikro Press [780]
MELODIES POETIQUES / Ferland, Albert – Montreal: P. J. Bedard, 1893. 03090. (Pre-1900 Canadiana) – 9 – cn C.I.H.M. [971]
MELODIK UND RHYTHMIK DER 'ZUEIGNUNG' GOETHES / Saran, Franz – (Includes bibliographical references) – Halle a.S.: M Niemeyer, 1903 – 1r – 1 – us U.W. Library [430]
MELODOI KOMMUNIST = YOUNG COMMUNIST – Moscow. U.S.S.R. 1961- – 1 – us UMI [335]
MELODY MAKER – 1926- 1; 1976- 5,6,9 – us UMI [780]
MELODY MAKER – London. 1926-76. 36 reels – 1 – 685.00 – us L of C Photodup [780]
MELODY OF GOD'S LOVE : A NEW UNFOLDING OF THE TWENTY-THIRD PSALM / Huckel, Oliver – New York: Thomas Y Crowell, c1905 – 1mf – 9 – 0-8370-3684-4 – 1985-1684 – us A.T.L.A. [220]
THE MELODY OF SPEAKING DELINEATED; OR, ELOCUTION TAUGHT LIKE MUSIC / Walker, John – 1787. 83p. (English Linguistics Series 1500-1800) – 9 – us UMI [400]
MELODYEN GESANGBUCH DARINN D. LUTHERS... – Gedruckt zu Hamburg, durch Samuel Rudinger, 1604 – 1 – us Sibley [780]
EL MELOPEO Y MAESTRO. TRACTADO DE MUSICA THEORICA Y PRACTICA: EN QUE SE PONE POR EXTENSO / Cerone, Pedro – P 664. 1613 – 9 – ne IDC [780]
EL MELOPEO Y MAESTRO. TRACTADO DE MUSICA THEORICA Y PRATICA / Cerone, Pedro – 1613 – 9 – us Sibley [780]
MELOS – v. 1-13. 1920-1934 – 1 – us Schnase [073]
Melser, Allen S *see* INTELLECTUAL PROPERTY LAW
Melsheimer, Rudolph Eyre *see* THE LAW AND CUSTOMS OF THE STOCK EXCHANGE
MELTON MOWBRAY TIMES – Aug 16 1856-Nov 10 1860; Mar 19 1887-1910; 1912-Mar, Jul 1990-Jun 1997 – 147 1/2r – 1 – uk British Libr Newspaper [072]
Mel'ts, M Ia *see* RUSSKII FOLKLOR
MEL'TS, M.IA. RUSSKII FOL'KLOR : BIBLIOGRAFICHESKII UKAZATEL' / ed by Astakhova, A M & Luppov, S P – (v1: 1917-1944. L., 1966. 683p; v2: 1945-1959. L., 1961. 402p; v3: 1960-1965. L., 1967. 539p) – L. 3v. 1961-1967. [PKG-A-58] – 19mf – 9 – ne IDC [390]
Meltzer, Milton *see* THE COLLECTED CORRESPONDENCE OF LYDIA MARIA CHILD, 1817-1880
Meltzer, Otto *see* GESCHICHTE DER KARTAGER
Melun, Armand de *see* DE L'INTERVENTION DE LA SOCIETE POUR PREVENIR ET SOULAGER LA MISERE
MELUSINE : RECUEIL DE MYTHOLOGIE, LITTERATURE POPULAIRE, TRADITIONS ET USAGES – (Index included) – Paris, 1878-1912 – 67mf – 9 – ne IDC [390]
MELUSINE – Revue puis Recueil de mythologie, litterature populaire, traditions et usages. Paris. 1878, avr 1884-1901 – 1 – fr A.C.R.P.P. [073]
MELVILLE AVENUE BAPTIST CHURCH. DANVILLE, VIRGINIA : CHURCH RECORDS – 16 Oct 1949-4 May 1960 – 1 – 9.63 – us Baptist [240]
Melville, L G *see* REPORT ON ORGANIZATION AND MANAGEMENT PROBLEMS IN ECONOMIC AND SOCIAL PLANNING IN SYRIA
Melville, William *see* BATTLE-PIECES AND ASPECTS OF THE WAR
Mely, Fernand de *see* LES PRIMITIFS ET LEURS SIGNATURES
Melzer, Ernst *see* GOETHES ETHISCHE ANSICHTEN
Melzian, H J *see* THE KPELLE LANGUAGE IN LIBERIA: GRAMATICAL OUTLINE, COLLOQUIAL SENTENCES AND VOCABULARY
MEMALIK-I OSMANIYE CEP ATLASI / Hilmi, Tueccarzade Ibrahim – Istanbul: Kitabhane-i Islam ve Askeri, 1323 [1907] – $45.00 – us MEDOC [956]
MEMALIK-I OSMANIYENIN 1325, 1326, 1327 SENELERINE MAHSUS MAADIN ISTATISTIKIDIR – Istanbul: Matbaa-yi Osmaniye, 1330 [1914] – 9 – $85.00 – us MEDOC [350]
MEMALIK-I OSMANIYE'NIN COGRAFYA-I TICARISI – Istanbul: Kagatiyan Matbaasi, 1302 [1887] – $12.00 – us MEDOC [380]
MEMBAKAR MATAHARI : KISAH PERDJOANGAN DIBAWAH TANAH DIDAERAH MALAYSIA SEMASA KONFRONTASI / Basuki, Sulistyo – 1966 – 9 – SE-5794 1 – ne IDC [950]
MEMBANGUN DESA, TJEPAT, SERENTAK, PRAKTIS; PEDOMAN BAGI SETIAP WARGA-NEGARA / Sindhupramana, S – SE 4478 1. 1961 – 9 – ne IDC [950]
MEMBERSHIP RECORD / Overbrook. Kansas. Bethel Methodist Church – ca1920-ca1959 – 1 – us KS Hist [920]
MEMBERSHIP REGISTER / First United Methodist Church, Wellington, KS – 1953-1970 – 1 – us KS Hist [240]
MEMBERSHIP, SPEECH AND NEWSPAPER FILES / National Nonpartisan League – 1916-28 – 19r – 5 – $570.00; $35.00r – us M.H.S. [025]
MEMBRANE BIOCHEMISTRY – v. 1- 1978- – 1,5,6,9 – us UMI [540]
Membrio. Ayuntamiento *see* FERIAS Y FIESTAS EN HONOR DE NTRA. SRA. DE GRACIA. 1974
MEMBUAT ICE CREAM, COCKTAIL, PUDDING / Kwee, H – SE-11,071 1. 1964 – 9 – ne IDC [640]
Memduh, Mehmed *see*
- ES'AR
- MER'AT-I SUUNAT

MEMELER ALLGEMEINE ZEITUNG – (Title change: Memeler Neueste Nachrichten, 15 Jan 1933) – Memel (Klaipeda, U.S.S.R.). 1-17 Dec 1927; Jan 1928-15 Feb 1934 – 9r – 1 – gw Mikrofilm [943]
MEMELER NEUESTE NACHRICHTEN *see* MEMELER ALLGEMEINE ZEITUNG
MEMELER VOLKSSTIMME – Memel (Klaipeda, U.S.S.R.). 1923-Sept 1925; Jan-9 Jun 1926 – 4r – 1 – gw Mikrofilm [943]
MEMELLAENDISCHE RUNDSCHAU – Heydekrug (Silutje, U.S.S.R.). Oct 1922-28 Jul 1934 – 22r – 1 – gw Mikrofilm [943]
MEMELLAENDISCHE VOLKSZEITUNG – Kauen, (Kaunas, Kowno, U.S.S.R.). 4 Jan 1930-1 Jun 1933 – 1r – 1 – gw Mikrofilm [943]
MEMEL-ZEITUNG – Memel (Klaipeda, U.S.S.R.). 17 Jan 1924-25 – 3r – 1 – gw Mikrofilm [943]
MEMENTO PRATIQUE DE L'ECONOMIE AGRICOLE MAROCAINE / Morocco. Ministere de l'Agriculture – 1960. BNE-3064 1 – 9 – ne IDC [630]
Memminger, Christopher G *see* PAPERS
MEMMINGER ZEITUNG : BA DER ALLGAEUER ZEITUNG – Memmingen, West Germany. 1 Sept 1978- – ca 9r per yr – 1 – gw Mikrofilm [072]
A MEMOIR / Badger, Joseph – 1851 – 1 – $50.00 – us Presbyterian [920]
MEMOIR / Fullerton, Robert Stewart – 1928 – 1 – $50.00 – us Presbyterian [920]
MEMOIR AND LETTERS OF FRANCIS W. NEWMAN / Sieveking, I Giberne – London: K. Paul, Trench, Truebner, 1909 – 2mf – us A.T.L.A. [240]
MEMOIR AND LETTERS OF FREDERIC DAN HUNTINGTON, FIRST BISHOP OF CENTRAL NEW YORK / Huntington, Arria – 1906 – 9 – us A.T.L.A. [920]
MEMOIR BY ANTHONY MOOYART, COMMANDER OF JAFFNAPATAM, FOR THE INFORMATION AND GUIDANCE OF HIS SUCCESSOR, NOEL ANTHONY LEBECK, 1766 / Mooyaart, A – Trans. by S. Pieters. Colombo. 1910. BI-953 2 – 8 – ne IDC [950]
MEMOIR LEFT BY G.W. BARON VAN IMHOFF, GOVERNOR AND DIRECTOR OF CEYLON TO HIS SUCCESSOR W.M. BRUYNINK / Imhoff, G W van – I-950. 1911 – 9 – ne IDC [950]
MEMOIR LEFT BY PIELAT TO HIS SUCCESSOR, DIEDERIK VAN DOMBURG, 1734 / Pielat, J Ch – Trans. by S. Pieters. I 949. 1905 – 9 – ne IDC [025]
MEMOIR OF A FRENCH NEW TESTAMENT, IN WHICH THE MASS AND PURGATORY ARE FOUND IN THE SACRED TEXT... / Cotton, Henry – 2nd enl ed. London:Bell & Daldy, 1863 – 1mf – 9 – 0-8370-2748-9 – 1985-0748 – us A.T.L.A. [220]
MEMOIR OF A MAP OF THE COUNTRIES COMPREHENDED BETWEEN THE BLACK SEA AND THE CASPIAN : WITH AN ACCOUNT OF THE CAUCASIAN NATIONS AND VOCABULARIES OF THEIR LANGUAGES / Ellis, G – London, 1788 – 2mf – ne IDC [460]
MEMOIR OF A MISSION TO GIBRALTAR AND SPAIN : WITH COLLATERAL NOTICES OF EVENTS FAVOURING RELIGIOUS LIBERTY, AND OF THE DECLINE OF ROMISH POWER IN THAT COUNTRY, FROM THE BEGINNING OF THIS CENTURY TO THE YEAR 1842 / Rule, William Harris – London: J. Mason, 1844 – 1mf – us A.T.L.A. [240]
MEMOIR OF ADMIRAL SIR GRAHAM MOORE / Gardiner, Robert William – 1844 – 9 – $20.00 – uk Libr Preservation [920]
MEMOIR OF ANN H. JUDSON: MISSIONARY TO BURMA / Knowles, James Davis – 1846 – 9 – us A.T.L.A. [240]
A MEMOIR OF BARON BUNSEN : LATE MINISTER PLENIPOTENTIARY AND ENVOY EXTRAORDINARY OF HIS MAJESTY FREDERIC WILLIAM 4. AT THE COURT OF ST. JAMES / Bunsen, Frances – London: Longmans, Green, 1868 – 3mf – us A.T.L.A. [920]
MEMOIR OF CAPTAIN EDWARD PELHAM BRENTON, WITH SKETCHES OF HIS PROFESSIONAL LIFE, OBSERVATIONS UPON HIS NAVAL HISTORY, AND LIFE OF THE EARL OF SAINT VINCENT / Brenton, Jahleel – 1842 – 9 – $20.00 – uk Libr Preservation [920]
MEMOIR OF CORNELIS JEAN SIMONS, GOVERNOR AND DIRECTOR OF CEYLON, FOR HIS SUCCESSOR HENDRICK BECKER, 1707 / Simons, C J – Trans. by Sophia Anthonisz, with an introduction and notes by the Government Archivist. Colombo. 1914. BI-948 1 – 9 – ne IDC [920]
A MEMOIR OF EDWARD STEERE, D.D., LL.D. : THIRD MISSIONARY BISHOP IN CENTRAL AFRICA / Heanley, R M – London: G. Bell, 1890 – 2mf – us A.T.L.A. [240]
MEMOIR OF ELIZABETH NEWPORT / Townsend, Ann Albertson – 1878 – 9 – us A.T.L.A. [240]
A MEMOIR OF GENERAL JAMES OGLETHORPE : ONE OF THE EARLIEST REFORMERS OF PRISON DISCIPLINE IN ENGLAND AND THE FOUNDER OF GEORGIA IN AMERICA / Wright, Robert – London: Chapman and Hall, 1867 – 1mf – us A.T.L.A. [975]
MEMOIR OF HENDRICK ZWAARDECROON, COMMANDEUR OF JAFFNAPATAM, 1697 / Zwaardecroon, Hendrick – Trans. by S. Pieters. Colombo. 1911. BI 947 2 – 8 – ne IDC [920]
A MEMOIR OF HENRY BRADSHAW, FELLOW OF KING'S COLLEGE / Prothero, George Walter – London: K. Paul, Trench & Co., 1888. vii,447p. illus. Appendix – 1 – us U.W. Library [941]
MEMOIR OF JAMES PETIGRU BOYCE, D.D., LL.D. : LATE PRESIDENT OF THE SOUTHERN BAPTIST THEOLOCIGAL SEMINARY, LOUISVILLE, KY. / Broadus, John A – New York: A.C. Armstrong, 1893 – 1mf – us A.T.L.A. [240]
A MEMOIR OF JOHN ARMSTRONG, D.D. : LATE LORD BISHOP OF GRAHAMSTOWN / Carter, T T – Oxford: John Henry & James Parker, 1857 – 2mf – us A.T.L.A. [240]
MEMOIR OF JOSHUA WATSON / ed by Churton, Edward – Oxford: J.H. and J. Parker, 1861 – 2mf – us A.T.L.A. [240]
MEMOIR OF JULIUS CHARLES RIEU / Monod, Frederic – Philadelphia: French & Perkins, 1833 – 1mf – us A.T.L.A. [240]
A MEMOIR OF MADAME FELLER : WITH AN ACCOUNT OF THE ORIGIN AND PROGRESS OF THE GRANDE LIGNE MISSION / Cramp, John Mockett – London: E. Stock, [1876?] – 1mf – us A.T.L.A. [920]
A MEMOIR OF MADAME FELLER: WITH AN ACCOUNT OF THE ORIGIN AND PROGRESS OF THE GRANDE LIGNE MISSION / Cramp, John Mockett – London: E. Stock; Montreal: Grafton and Drysdale; Toronto: Baptist Book Rooms and J. Campbell, 1876. 00275. (Pre-1900 Canadiana) – 9 – cn C.I.H.M. [971]
MEMOIR OF MARGARET, COUNTESS OF RICHMOND AND DERBY / Cooper, Charles Henry – Cambridge: University Press, 1874. xiv,319p. port – 1 – us U.W. Library [920]
MEMOIR OF MRS. BARBAULD : INCLUDING LETTERS AND NOTICES OF HER FAMILY AND FRIENDS BY HER GREAT NIECE, ANNA LETITIA LE BRETON / Le Breton, Anna Letitia Aikin – London: George Bell, 1874 – 1 roll – 1 – 1-55879-485-9 – uk Libr Preservation [420]
MEMOIR OF MRS. SARAH L. HUNTINGTON SMITH: LATE OF THE AMERICAN MISSION IN SYRIA / Hooker, Edward William – 1845 – 9 – us A.T.L.A. [920]
MEMOIR OF NICHOLAS HILL, A MEMBER OF THE BAR OF NEW YORK, WHO DIED IN THE CITY OF ALBANY, ON THE 1ST OF MAY, 1859 / New York. Bar of the City of New York – New York 1859. 60p. LL-1106 – 1 – us L of C Photodup [340]
MEMOIR OF NORMAN MACLEOD : D.D., MINISTER OF BARONY PARISH, GLASCOW, ONE OF HER MAJESTY'S CHAPLAINS, DEAN OF THE CHAPEL ROYAL, DEAN OF THE MOST ANCIENT AND MOST NOBLE ORDER OF THE THISTLE / Macleod, Donald – New York: Scribner, Armstrong, 1876 – 2mf – us A.T.L.A. [240]
MEMOIR OF OTIS ALLEN. / Allen, Otis – Albany, Bar, Munsell, 1865. 54p. LL-366 – 1 – us L of C Photodup [340]
MEMOIR OF PERCY BYSSHE SHELLEY : INCLUDING ORIGINAL POEMS AND PAPERS BY PERCY BYSSHE SHELLEY, NOW FIRST COLLECTED / Medwin, Thomas – London: Whittaker, Treacher, 1833 – 1 roll – 1 – 1-55879-434-4 – uk Libr Preservation [420]
A MEMOIR OF RALPH WALDO EMERSON / Cabot, James Elliot – Boston: Houghton Mifflin, 1888, c1887 – 2mf – us A.T.L.A. [420]
MEMOIR OF RECONNAISSANCES WITH MAPS DURING THE FLORIDA CAMPAIGN – Apr 1854 – Feb 1858. 1 roll. M1090 – 1 – us Nat'l Archives [324]
MEMOIR OF REV. DAVID TAPPAN STODDARD : MISSIONARY TO THE NESTORIANS / Thompson, Joseph Parrish – New York: Sheldon, Blakeman, 1858 – 1mf – us A.T.L.A. [240]

MEMOIR OF REV. HENRY LOBDELL, M.D., LATE MISSIONARY OF THE AMERICAN BOARD AT MOSUL : INCLUDING THE EARLY HISTORY OF THE ASSYRIAN MISSION / Tyler, William Seymour – Boston: American Tract Society, c1859 – 1mf – 9 – 0-8370-6432-5 – 1986-0432 – us A.T.L.A. [920]

A MEMOIR OF REV. JOSEPH BADGER : CONTAINING AN AUTOBIOGRAPHY, AND SELECTIONS FROM HIS PRIVATE JOURNAL AND CORRESPONDENCE / Badger, Joseph – Hudson, Ohio: Sawyer, Ingersoll, 1851 – 1mf – us A.T.L.A. [240]

MEMOIR OF REV. LUTHER RICE, ONE OF THE FIRST AMERICAN MISSIONARIES TO THE EAST / Taylor, James B – Baltimore: Armstrong and Berry, 1840. 350p – 1 – $12.25 – us Baptist [240]

MEMOIR OF REV. ROBERT STEWART FULLERTON / Lucas, James Joseph – 1928 – 1 – $50.00 – us Presbyterian [240]

A MEMOIR OF RICHARD WILLIAMS, SURGEON : CATECHIST TO THE PATAGONIAN MISSIONARY SOCIETY IN TIERRA DEL FUEGO / Hamilton, James – New York: Carlton & Phillips, 1855 – 1mf – 9 – 0-8370-7150-X – 1986-1150 – us A.T.L.A. [920]

MEMOIR OF ROBERT MOFFAT : MISSIONARY TO SOUTH AFRICA, 1817-1870 / Wilder, Martha L – Chicago: Woman's Presbyterian Board of Missions of the Northwest, c1887 – 1mf – 9 – 0-8370-6540-2 – 1986-0540 – us A.T.L.A. [920]

MEMOIR OF SAMUEL JOHN MILLS / Spring, Gardiner – Boston: Perkins & Marvin; New York: J. Leavitt and J.P. Haven, 1829 – 1mf – us A.T.L.A. [240]

MEMOIR OF SARAH B. JUDSON: MEMBER OF THE AMERICAN MISSION TO BURMAH / Judson, Emily C – 1849 – 9 – us A.T.L.A. [920]

A MEMOIR OF SIR BENJAMIN HEYWOOD, BARONET. WITH TWO CHAPTERS OF DOMESTIC LIFE AND LETTERS, 1840-65 / Heywood, Thomas – Manchester: Printed for private circulation by T. Fargie, (1888). 339p. illus – 1 – us U.W. Library [920]

MEMOIR OF THE ABBE LACORDAIRE / Montalembert, Charles Forbes – [London?]: R. Bentley, 1863 – 1mf – us A.T.L.A. [240]

MEMOIR OF THE EARLY LIFE OF WILLIAM COPWER, ESQ. WRITTEN BY HIMSELF, AND NEVER BEFORE PUBLISHED... / Cowper, William – London: Printed for R. Edwards, 1816 – 1 roll – 1 – 1-55879-318-6 – uk Libr Preservation [420]

A MEMOIR OF THE LATE TIMOTHY DWIGHT : WITH THE SERMON DELIVERED ON THE OCCASION OF HIS DEATH / Thompson, Joseph Parrish – New Haven: J.H. Benham, 1844 – 1mf – us A.T.L.A. [240]

MEMOIR OF THE LIFE AND EPISCOPATE OF EDWARD FIELD : D.D., BISHOP OF NEWFOUNDLAND, 1844-1876 / Tucker, H W – London: W. Wells Gardner, [1876?] – 1mf – us A.T.L.A. [240]

A MEMOIR OF THE LIFE AND LABORS OF THE REV. ADONIRAM JUDSON, D.D. / Wayland, Francis – Boston: Phillips, Sampson. 2v. 1853 – 4mf – 9 – 0-8370-6713-8 – 1986-0713 – us A.T.L.A. [920]

MEMOIR OF THE LIFE AND SERVICES OF ADMIRAL SIR WILLIAM HARGOOD, ETC / Allen, Joseph Antisell – 1841 – 9 – 20.00 – uk Libr Preservation [920]

A MEMOIR OF THE LIFE AND TIMES OF THE REV. ISAAC BACKUS, A.M / Hovey, Alvah – 1859 – 1 – 13.02 – us Baptist [240]

MEMOIR OF THE LIFE OF ADMIRAL SIR EDWARD CODRINGTON, WITH SELECTIONS FROM HIS PUBLIC AND PRIVATE CORRESPONDENCE / Codrington, Edward; ed by Bourchier, Lady – 2v. 1873 – 9 – $80.00 – uk Libr Preservation [920]

MEMOIR OF THE LIFE OF DONALD CAMERON: WITH REMARKS BY HIS SON ARCHIBALD OF VELLORE, VAUGHAN TOWNSHIP, COUNTY OF YORK, ONTARIO / Cameron, Donald – (Printed at the Times office, 1893). 00388. (Pre-1900 Canadiana) – 9 – cn C.I.H.M. [920]

MEMOIR OF THE LIFE OF THE RIGHT REVEREND WILLIAM WHITE, D.D. : BISHOP OF THE PROTESTANT EPISCOPAL CHURCH IN THE STATE OF PENNSYLVANIA / Wilson, Bird – Philadelphia: James Kay, Jun.; Pittsburgh: C.H. Kay, 1839 – 1mf – us A.T.L.A. [240]

MEMOIR OF THE NAVAL LIFE AND SERVICES OF ADMIRAL SIR P.C.H.C. DURHAM / Murray, Alexander – 1846 – 9 – $20.00 – uk Libr Preservation [920]

MEMOIR OF THE NAVAL LIFE AND SERVICES OF ADMIRAL SIR P.C.H.C. DURHAM / Murray, Alexander – London, 1846 – 1mf – 1 – 1-55879-105-1 – uk Libr Preservation [355]

MEMOIR OF THE REV. ELIJAH P. LOVEJOY : MURDERED IN DEFENSE OF LIBERTY OF THE PRESS... / Lovejoy, Owen & Lovejoy, Joseph C – 4mf – 9 – $6.00 – LLMC 91-507 – us L.L.M.C. [920]

MEMOIR OF THE REV. HENRY MARTYN, B.D. / Martyn, Henry; ed by Sargent, John – New York: Protestant Episcopal Society for the Promotion of Evangelical Knowledge, 1858 – 1mf – 9 – 0-8370-6507-0 – 1986-0507 – us A.T.L.A. [920]

MEMOIR OF THE REV. JACOB J. JANEWAY / Janeway, Thomas Leiper – 1861 – 9 – us A.T.L.A. [920]

A MEMOIR OF THE REV. SYDNEY SMITH : BY HIS DAUGHTER, LADY HOLLAND; WITH A SELECTION FROM HIS LETTERS, EDITED BY MRS. AUSTIN / Smith, Sydney – London: Longman, Brown, Green, and Longmans, 3rd ed 1855 – 2 rolls – 1 – 1-55879-251-1 – uk Libr Preservation [240]

MEMOIR OF THE REV. WILLIAM SHAW, LATE GENERAL SUPERINTENDENT OF THE WESLEYAN MISSIONS IN SOUTH-EASTERN AFRICA / Shaw, William – 1874 – 1 – us A.T.L.A. [240]

MEMOIR OF THE RIGHT REVEREND JOHN STRACHAN, D.D., LL. D. : FIRST BISHOP OF TORONTO / Bethune, Alexander Neil – Toronto: H. Rowsell; London: Rivingtons, 1870 – 1mf – us A.T.L.A. [240]

MEMOIR OF THE RIGHT REVEREND JOHN STRACHAN, D.D.L., L.D.: FIRST BISHOP OF TORONTO / Bethune, Alexander Neil – Toronto: H. Roswell, 1870. 00095. (Pre-1900 Canadiana) – 9 – cn C.I.H.M. [971]

MEMOIR OF THEOPHILUS PARSONS, CHIEF JUSTICE OF THE SUPREME JUDICIAL COURT OF MASSACHUSETTS / Parsons, Theophilus – Boston: Ticknor and Fields, 1859. 476p. LL-317 – 1 – us L of C Photodup [340]

A MEMOIR OF THOMAS STERRY HUNT / Douglas, James – s.l.: s.n., 1898 (Philadelphia: MacCalla). 02746. (Pre-1900 Canadiana) – 9 – cn C.I.H.M. [971]

MEMOIR OF WILLIAM FOX, ESQ. FOUNDER OF THE SUNDAY SCHOOL SOCIETY / Ivimey, Joseph – 1831 – 1 – $5.00 – us Baptist [240]

A MEMOIR OF WILLIAM JACKSON ELMSLIE... , LATE MEDICAL MISSIONARY, C.M.S., KASHMIR / Thomson, W Burns – London, Ed.3 1881 – 4mf – 9 – ne IDC [610]

A MEMOIR OF WILLIAM WOLSELEY / Innes, Mary C – 1895 – 9 – $20.00 – uk Libr Preservation [920]

A MEMOIR OR DEFENCE OF HUGH PETERS / Felt, Joseph B – Boston: Printed by C.C.P. Moody, 1851 – 1mf – us A.T.L.A. [240]

MEMOIRE / Moreau, Jacob N – Paris: de l'Imprimerie Royale, 1756. SEM16P71 – 1r – 5 – Can$9.00 – cn Bibl Nat [944]

MEMOIRE / Moreau, Jacob N – Paris: de l'Imprimerie Royale, 1756. SEM35P74 – 1r – 1 – Can$15.00 – cn Bibl Nat [944]

MEMOIRE A LA DEFENSE D'UN PLAN D'ACTE DE PARLEMENT POUR L'ETABLISSEMENT DES LOIX DE LA PROVINCE DE QUEBEC, CONTRE LES OBJECTIONS DE MR. FRANCOIS JOSEPH CUGNET.. / Maseres, Francis – Londres: Imp. chez Edmund Allen, 1773. SEM105P372 – 2mf – 9 – Can$4.50 – cn Bibl Nat [971]

MEMOIRE ACCOMPAGNANT LA REQUETE PRESENTEE A LA CHAMBRE D'ASSEMBLEE PAR LE CLERGE CATHOLIQUE DU BAS-CANADA, CONTRE L'ADMISSION DES NOTABLES DANS LES ASSEMBLEES DE FABRIQUE / Lartigue, Jean J – Quebec: Imprime par Frechette, 1831? SEM16P182 – 1r – 5 – Can$9.00 – cn Bibl Nat [240]

MEMOIRE ADRESSE A CHARLES 10 / L'Hospital, Michel de – Paris. A. Boulland. 1824. p.171-216 des oeuvres completes. (Strategy of War Series) – 9 – fr Hachette [355]

MEMOIRE ADRESSE A L'ASSEMBLEE NATIONALE PAR PLUSIEURS CURES DU DEPARTEMENT DE LA VENDEE / Revolution Vendee – Les Sables d'Olonne: Ferre, 1790 – 1 – F50.00 – fr Armell [944]

MEMOIRE AU MINISTRE DE L'INTERIEUR SUR LA SITUATION DU DEPARTEMENT DES HAUTES-ALPES / Bonnaire, Felix – an IX – 9 – fr Hachette [944]

MEMOIRE COMPOSE DE LA PLAIDOIRIE. / Loranger, Thomas Jean Jacques – Montreal, La Minerve, 1855. 94 p. LL-2220 – 1 – us L of C Photodup [340]

MEMOIRE COMPOSE DE LA PLAIDOIRIE DE T.J.J. LORANGER, C.R., UN DES SUBSTITUTS DU PROCUREUR-GENERAL, DEVANT LA COUR SEIGNEURIALE – Montreal: Imp. de la Minerve, 1855. SEM105P270 – 2mf – 9 – Can$4.50 – cn Bibl Nat [971]

MEMOIRE CONTENANT LES FAITS EXTRAORDINAIRES RAPORTEZ DANS LE PROCES DE MARIE BUCAILLE – Rouen – 9 – fr Hachette [360]

MEMOIRE CONTENANT UN RESUME DU PLAIDOYER DE C.S. CHERRIER...SUR LES QUESTIONS SOUMISES PAR L'HONORABLE LEWIS THOMAS DRUMMOND,...EN VERTU DES DISPOSITIONS DE L'ACTE SEIGNEURIAL DE 1854 – Montreal: Imp. John Lovell, 1855. SEM105P266 – 2mf – 9 – Can$4.50 – cn Bibl Nat [971]

MEMOIRE DE LA LIGUE, CONTENANT LES EVENEMENTS LES PLUS REMARQUABLES DEPUIS 1576, JUSQU'A LA PAIX ACCORDEE ENTRE LE ROI DE FRANCE ET LE ROI D'ESPAGNE, EN 1598 / Goulart, Simon – Nouvelle ed. Amsterdam: Arkstee et Merkus. 6v. 1758. SEM16P285 – 2r – 5 – Can$59.00 – cn Bibl Nat [944]

MEMOIRE DE L'UNIVERSITE SUR LES MOYENS DE POURVOIR A L'INSTRUCTION DE LA JEUNESSE, ET DE LA PERFECTIONNER / Combalusier, Francois de P – S.1 – 9 – fr Hachette [370]

MEMOIRE DE' PITTORI PERUGINI DEL SEC. 28 / Orsini, B – Perugia. 1806. BO-972 1 – 9 – ne IDC [920]

MEMOIRE DES INTENDANTS SUR L'ETAT DES GENERALITES POUR L'INSTRUCTION DU DUC DE BOURGOGNE / Boislisle, Arthur Michel de – Paris, 1881. (Historical Studies Series) – 9 – 30.00 – fr Bibl Nationale [900]

MEMOIRE DU BUREAU SERVANT DE LA COMMUNAUTE DE RENNES, SUR LE NOUVEAU PLAN D'EDUCATION DEMANDE PAR ARRET DE LA COUR – Rennes. impr. G. Vatar. 1762. 6774 – 9 – fr Hachette [305]

MEMOIRE D'UN PREDICATEUR SAINT-SIMONIEN / Charton, E Th – Paris, Everat, 1832, 30 p. Les Saint-Simoniens, 1825-1834. 6952 – 9 – fr Hachette [335]

MEMOIRE HISTORIQUE ET PHYSIQUE SUR LES CHUTES DES PIERRES...EPOQUES / Bigot de Morogues, Pierre Marie Sebastien – Orelans, 1812 – 1 – us U.W. Library [920]

MEMOIRE HISTORIQUE SUR LA NEGOCIATION DE LA FRANCE ET DE L'ANGLETERRE, DEPUIS LE 26 MARS 1761 JUSQU'AU 20 SEPTEMBRE DE LA MEME ANNEE, AVEC LES PIECES JUSTIFICATIVES / Choiseul-Stainville, Etienne F – Paris: de l'imprimerie royale, 1761. SEM16P271 – 1r – 5 – Can$9.00 – cn Bibl Nat [941]

MEMOIRE JUSTIFICATIF POUR P. QUETINEAU, COMMANDANT EN CHEF LES TROUPES REUNIES A THOUARS / Quetineau, Pierre – Saumur: Degouy, [1826?] – 1 – F50.00 – fr Armell [355]

MEMOIRE POUR SERVIR A L'HISTOIRE DE QUELQUES INSECTES / ed by Smeathman, H – Paris, 1786 – 63p, 7pls – 8 – ne IDC [590]

MEMOIRE PRESENTE AU GOUVERNEMENT DE LA PROVINCE DE QUEBEC...AU SUJET DE L'ENQUETE TENUE PAR LA COMMISSION ROYALE SUR L'ADMINISTRATION DES DITS COMMISSAIRES CATHOLIQUES / Bureau des commissaires d'ecoles catholiques romains de Montreal – Montreal?, 188? 02057. (Pre-1900 Canadiana) – 9 – cn C.I.H.M. [370]

MEMOIRE QUATRIEME MEMOIRE SUR LA NECESSITE DE FONDER UNE ECOLE POUR FORMER DES MAITRES, SELON LE PLAN D'EDUCATION DONNE PAR LE PARLEMENT / Pellicier – 4parties en un vol. in 12. 1762-63. 6778 – 9 – fr Hachette [944]

MEMOIRE STATISTIQUE DU DEPARTEMENT DE LA LYS / Viry, Joseph M F J – an XII – 9 – fr Hachette [944]

MEMOIRE STATISTIQUE DU DEPARTEMENT DE LA MEURTHE / Marquis, Jean J – an XI – 9 – fr Hachette [944]

MEMOIRE STATISTIQUE DU DEPARTEMENT DE LA MOSELLE / Colchen – an XI – 9 – fr Hachette [944]

MEMOIRE STATISTIQUE DU DEPARTEMENT DE L'ESCAUT / Faypoult de Maisoncelle, Guillaume C – an XIII – 9 – fr Hachette [944]

MEMOIRE STATISTIQUE DU DEPARTEMENT DE L'EURE / Masson de Saint-Amand, Amand N – an XIII – 9 – fr Hachette [944]

MEMOIRE STATISTIQUE DU DEPARTEMENT DE L'INDRE / Alphonse, Francois J-B d' – an XII – 9 – fr Hachette [944]

MEMOIRE STATISTIQUE DU DEPARTEMENT DE RHIN-ET-MOSELLE / Boucqueau, Philippe – an XII – 9 – fr Hachette [944]

MEMOIRE STATISTIQUE DU DEPARTEMENT DES DEUX-SEVRES / Dupin, Claude FE – an XII – 9 – fr Hachette [944]

MEMOIRE STATISTIQUE DU DEPARTEMENT DU DOUBS / Bry, Jean A J – an XII – 9 – fr Hachette [944]

MEMOIRE STATISTIQUE SUR LE DEPARTEMENT DU VAUCLUSE / Seguin de Pazzis, Maxime – 1808 – 9 – fr Hachette [944]

MEMOIRE SUR LA COLONIE FRANCAISE DU SENEGAL : AVEC QUELQUES CONSIDERATIONS HISTORIQUES ET POLITIQUES SUR LA TRAITE DES NEGRES... – Paris: Panckoucke, [1800] – us Res Libr [920]

MEMOIRE SUR LA COLONIE FRANCAISE DU SENEGAL / Pelletan, Jean Gabriel – Vve Panckouke. 1801 – 9 – 5.00 – fr Orientalistes [960]

MEMOIRE SUR LA COLONIE FRANCAISE DU SENEGAL, AVEC QUELQUES CONSIDERATIONS HISTORIQUES ET POLITIQUES SUR LA TRAITE DES NEGRES, SUR LEUR CARACTERE, ET ...A LA PROSPERITE DE CETTE COLONIE / Pelletan, Jean-Gabriel – (Slave Trade and Abolitionism in France series). 1800 – 9 – fr Hachette [960]

MEMOIRE SUR LA DISTRIBUTION DE LA POPULATION FRANCAISE PAR SEXE ET PAR ETAT ET SUR LA NECESSITE DE PERFECTIONNER NOS TABLEAUX DE POPULATION ET DE MORTALITE / Villerme, Louis Rene – Reprod. d'un extrait des Annales d'Hygiene publique et de Medecine legale. 1837.p245-80. 1 fiche. (Statistics Series: Demography) – 9 – 6.00 – fr Bibl Nationale [310]

MEMOIRE SUR LA FAMILLE DES RHAMNEES / Brongniart, A T – (Ann. Nat.) v. 10. 1827. B-44 2 – 8 – ne IDC [580]

MEMOIRE SUR LA FAMILLE DES RUBIACEES / Richard, Achille – (Mem. Soc. Hist. Nat., v. 5, Paris, 1834). B-5672 2 – 8 – ne IDC [580]

MEMOIRE SUR LA LOI 43 ET 44 VICT., CH. 22, ETABLISSANT UN FONDS DE RETRAITE ET DE SECOURS EN FAVEUR DES FONCTIONNAIRES DE L'ENSEIGNEMENT PRIMAIRE / Archambault, Urgel Eugene – 1886? 04105. (Pre-1900 Canadiana) – 9 – cn C.I.H.M. [340]

MEMOIRE SUR LA MUSIQUE DES ANCIENS.. / Roussier, Pierre-Joseph – 1770 – 2 – us Sibley [780]

MEMOIRE SUR LA NAVIGATION AUX COTES OCCIDENTALES D'AFRIQUE DEPUIS LE CAP BOJADOR JUSQU'AU MONT SOUZOS / Roussin, Alb – Paris, Imprimerie Royale. 1827 – 9 – 5.00 – fr Orientalistes [910]

MEMOIRE SUR LA POPULATION: DANS LEQUEL ON INDIQUE LE MOYEN DE LA RETABLIR ET DE SE PROCURER UN CORPS MILITAIRE / Cerfvol, de – Londres, 1768. 115 p. 2 fiches. (Statistics Series: Demography) – 9 – 6.00 – fr Bibl Nationale [310]

MEMOIRE SUR LA POSSIBILITE ET L'UTILITE D'UNE THEORIE EXACTE DES PRINCIPES NATURELS DA LA MUSIQUE... / Villoteau, G – Paris: De L'Limprimerie imperiale, 1807 – 1 – us Sibley [780]

MEMOIRE SUR LA PROPAGATION DE LA CHALEUR / Biot, M – French text. Address at National Institute, France – 7 – uk Microform Academic [530]

MEMOIRE SUR LA PROPORTION DES NAISSANCES DES FILLES ET DES GARCONS / Poisson – Reprod. de l'extrait des Annales de Chimie et de Physique, 1829, p39-46. 1 fiche. (Statistics Series:

Medical Studies) – 9 – 6.00 – fr Bibl Nationale [310]
MEMOIRE SUR LA STATISTIQUE DE L'ARRONDISSEMENT DE SUZE, ADRESSE AU GENERAL JOURDAN / Jacquet – an X – 9 – fr Hachette [944]
MEMOIRE SUR LA STATISTIQUE DU DEPARTEMENT DE LA HAUTE-SAONE / Vergnes, Jacques P – an IX – 9 – fr Hachette [944]
MEMOIRE SUR LA TAILLE DE L'HOMME EN FRANCE / Villerme, Louis Rene – Reprod. d'un extrait des Annales d'Hygiene publique et de Medecine legale. v1, 1829. p351-95. 1 fiche.(Statistics Series: Medical Studies) – 9 – 6.00 – fr Bibl Nationale [310]
MEMOIRE SUR LA TOPOGRAPHIE MEDICALE DU 4 ARRONDISSEMENT DE LA VILLE DE PARIS / Bayard, Henri – Reprod. d'un extrait des "Annales d'Hygiene publique," 1842. p1-46, 241-310. 2 fiches. (Statistics: Medical Studies Series) – 9 – $6.00 – fr Bibl Nationale [310]
MEMOIRE SUR LE CHOLERA / Canada. Bureau d'Agriculture et de Statistiques – Ottawa: Imprime pour le Bureau d'Agriculture et de Statistiques, 1866. SEM105P236 – 1mf – 9 – Can$2.25 – cn Bibl Nat [610]
MEMOIRE SUR LE DEPARTEMENT DE LA CORREZE / Verneil-Puyraseau, Jean J – 9 – fr Hachette [944]
MEMOIRE SUR LE GROUPE DES RUTACEES / Jussieu, A H L de – (Mem. Mus. d'Hist. Nat. Paris, v. 12. 1825). B-1596 2 – 8 – ne IDC [580]
MEMOIRE SUR LE PAIS DES CAFRES ET LA TERRE DE NUYTS / Purry, Jean-Pierre – Amsterdam, Pierre Humbert. 1718 – 9 – 5.00 – fr Orientalistes [960]
MEMOIRE SUR LE PAUPERISME / Tocqueville, Alexis de – (Condition of 19th C. French working class series). 1915 – 9 – fr Hachette [360]
MEMOIRE SUR LE SENEGAL PAR M. LAMIRAL, DEPUTE DE LA COLONIE DU SENEGAL, PRES L'ASSEMBLEE NATIONALE / Lamiral, D H – (African Library series). 1791 – 9 – fr Hachette [960]
MEMOIRE SUR LE SOUDAN / Escayrac de Lauture, Pierre H S d' – Paris: A. Bertrand, 1856. (African Library) – 9 – fr Hachette [960]
MEMOIRE SUR L'EDUCATION NATIONALE FRANCAISE, SUIVI D'UN PROJET DE DECRET PAR M. L'ABBE AUDREIN / Audrein, Yves-Marie – Paris, Volland. 1791. 6731 – 9 – fr Hachette [944]
MEMOIRE SUR L'EDUCATION PUBLIQUE, AVEC LE PROSPECTUS D'UN COLLEGE, SUIVANT LES PRINCIPES DE CET OUVRAGE / Guyton de Morveau, Louis-Bernard – 1764. 6763 – 9 – fr Hachette [360]
MEMOIRE SUR LES CHEVAUX DE L'AMERIQUE DU NORD, ETATS-UNIS ET CANADA / Faverot de Kerbrech, Francois Nicholas Guy Napoleon – par Favarot i.e. Faverot de Kerbrech. Montreal: Imprimerie generale, 1885. 03078. (Pre-1900 Canadiana) – 9 – cn C.I.H.M. [971]
MEMOIRE SUR LES DIFFERENTES ESPECES, RACES ET VARIETES DE CHOUX ET DE RAIFORTS CULTIVES EN EUROPE / Candolle, A P de – Paris. 1822. B-6112 2 – 8 – ne IDC [580]
MEMOIRE SUR LES GENRES CONNARUS ET OMPHALOBIUM OU SUR LES CONNARACEES SARCOLOBEES / Candolle, A P de – (Mem. Soc. Hist. Nat.). v. 2. Paris. 1825. B-5875 2 – 8 – ne IDC [580]
MEMOIRE SUR LES LIVRES CHINOIS DE LA BIBLIOTHEQUE DU ROI;... / Remusat, J P A – Paris, 1818 – 1mf – 9 – ne IDC [950]
MEMOIRE SUR LES LOIS DES NAISSANCES ET DE LA MORTALITE A BRUXELLES / Quetelet, Adolphe Lambert Jacques – Reprod. de l'ed.: s.l.,s.d. p496-512. 1 fiche. Statistics Series: Medical Studies) – 9 – 6.00 – fr Bibl Nationale [310]
MEMOIRE SUR LES PRINCIPAUX OBJETS DE L'EDUCATION PUBLIQUE / Corbin, Le P – Paris. impr. Desaint. 1788. 6743 – 9 – fr Hachette [944]
MEMOIRE SUR L'ESCLAVAGE DES NEGRES DANS LEQUEL ON DISCUTE LES MOTIFS PROPOSES POUR LEUR AFFRANCHISSEMENT, CEUX QUI S'Y OPPOSENT ET LES MOYENS PRATICABLES POUR AMELIORER LEUR SORT / Malouet, Pierre-Victor – (Slave Trade and Abolitionism in France series). 1788 – 9 – fr Hachette [305]
MEMOIRE SUR L'ETAT DE LA POPULATION DANS LE PAYS DE VAUD. / Muret, Jean-Louis – Yverdon, 1766. 2 v. en 1. 130, 128 p. 3 fiches. (Statistics Series: Demography) – 9 – 8.00 – fr Bibl Nationale [310]
MEMOIRE SUR L'ETAT DU DEPARTEMENT DE L'INDRE / Gretre – an VIII – 9 – fr Hachette [944]
MEMOIRE SUR L'EXECUTION DU PLAN D'EQUIPEMENT EN AFRIQUE EQUATORIALE FRANCAISE. 1947-48 ET 48-49 / French Equatorial Africa – Brazzaville. 1950. BD-481 1 – 9 – ne IDC [338]
MEMOIRE SUR L'IMPOT FONCIER AU JAPON / Matsougata, Masayochi – Traduction du japonais, Paris, typographie G. Chamarot. 1878 – 9 – 5.00 – fr Orientalistes [336]
MEMOIRE SUR L'INTERIEUR DE L'AFRIQUE / Lalande, Jerome – (African Library) – 9 – fr Hachette [960]
MEMOIRE SUR L'INTERIEUR DE L'AFRIQUE / Lalande, Jerome – Paris, Imprimerie des administrations Nationales. 1795 – 9 – 5.00 – fr Orientalistes [960]
MEMOIRE SUR PLUSIEURS ESPECES DE COQUILLES NOUVELLES, OU PEU CONNUES / Grateloup, J P S de – Z-550 2. 1841 – 8 – ne IDC [580]
MEMOIRE SUR QUELQUES POINTS DE LA PHYSIOLOGIE DES ALGUES / Derbes, A & Solier, A J J – Paris. 1856 – 8 – ne IDC [580]
DIE MEMOIREN DER FRAU V. KRILWITZ : LUSTSPIEL IN 1 AKT / Winterfeld, Adolf Wilhelm Ernst von – Berlin: A W Hayn's Erben, 1874 – 1 – us U.W. Library [820]
MEMOIREN DER MARKGRAEFIN WILHELMINE VON BAYREUTH / Wilhelmine, Margravine – 2nd ed. Leipzig: Insel-Verlag, 1910. 2v – 1 – us U.W. Library [943]
MEMOIRES / Academie des Sciences, Inscriptions et Belles-Lettres de Toulouse – (Series 2-9, 1807-97. 3) – 1782-1790 – 3 – us Readex [500]
MEMOIRES. / Academie Nationale des Sciences, Arts et Belles-Lettres. Caen – 1877-1917 – 1,5,6 – us Princeton Micro [500]
MEMOIRES / Akademie der Wissenschaften. Berlin – 16v 1786-1804 – 1 – us Schnase [500]
MEMOIRES / Museum National d'Histoire Naturelle. Paris – 1815-32 – 3 – us Readex [580]
MEMOIRES / Societe d'histoire naturelle de Paris – Paris. 1823-34 – 3 – us Readex [580]
MEMOIRES / Societe Ethnologique de Paris – Paris. 1841-45 (I-II) – 1 – fr A.C.R.P.P. [306]
MEMOIRES = VERHANDELINGEN IN-80 : COLLECTION IN-80 / Bruxelles. Institut Royal Colonial Belge. Section des Sciences Morales et Politiques – Bruxelles: G van Campenhout. v1-9 n4. (1933-41) – us Res Libr [320]
MEMOIRES.. / Bouchette, Robert Shore Milnes – Montreal, 1903? SEM105P526 – 2mf – 9 – Can$4.50 – cn Bibl Nat [920]
MEMOIRES CONCERNANT L'ASIE ORIENTALE – Paris. v1-3. 1913-1919 – 26mf – 9 – ne IDC [950]
MEMOIRES CONCERNANT LE FONCTIONNEMENT DES LOIS QUI REGISSENT LES ECOLES DE REFORME ET D'INDUSTRIE / Bernier, Bernard – Presentes a l'Executif de la Province de Quebec, a sa seance du 29 mars 1893 au nom de l'Hospice Saint Charles de Quebec. Quebec?, 1893? 02310. (Pre-1900 Canadiana) – 9 – cn C.I.H.M. [971]
MEMOIRES CONCERNANT LES ECOLES NATIONALES / Thelis, Claude-Antoine de – Paris. Impr. Clousier. 1781-89 – 9 – fr Hachette [370]
MEMOIRES CONCERNANT L'HISTOIRE, LES SCIENCES, LES ARTS, LES MOEURS, LES USAGES, ETC. DES CHINOIS – Paris. v1-9. 1776-1783 – 101mf – 9 – ne IDC [880]
MEMOIRES CRITIQUES D'ARCHITECTURE. / Fremin – Paris, Saugrain, 1702. 14-12, 12, 368p. (Architecture Series) – 9 – fr Hachette [720]
LES MEMOIRES DE CAILLETTE ET AUTRES RECITS / Morin, Victor – Montreal: les Editions des Dix, 1955. SEM105P931 – 3mf – 9 – Can$6.75 – cn Bibl Nat [880]
LES MEMOIRES DE CAILLETTE ET AUTRES RECITS / Morin, Victor – Montreal: les Editions des Dix, 1956. SEM105P932 – 6mf – 9 – Can$13.50 – cn Bibl Nat [880]
MEMOIRES DE GAUDENTIO DI LUCCA, OU IL REND COMPTE AUX PERES DE L'INQUISITION DE BOLOGNE QUI L'ONT FAIT ARRETER, DE TOUT CE QUI LUI EST ARRIVE DE PLUS REMARQUABLE... / Berington, Simon – (Utopias in the Enlightenment series). 1746 – 9 – fr Hachette [830]
MEMOIRES DE LA CONGREGATION DE LA MISSION / ed by Perboyre, G – Paris. 9v 1863-1867 – 79mf – 9 – HTM-229/1 – ne IDC [240]
MEMOIRES DE LA SOCIETE D'HISTOIRE NATURELLE DE PARIS / Societe d'histoire naturelle de Paris – Paris, prairial an VII i.e.1799 – 3 – us Readex [580]
MEMOIRES DE LA SOCIETE ENTOMOLOGIQUE DE BELGIQUE – Brussels. v1-22. 1892-1920 – 100mf – 9 – ne IDC [400]
MEMOIRES DE LA SOCIETE ZOOLOGIQUE DE FRANCE – Paris. v1-29. 1888-1930 – 245mf – 9 – ne IDC [590]
MEMOIRES DE L'ACADEMIE DE DIJON / Academie de Dijon – Dijon. v1-2. 1769-74 – 3 – us Readex [500]
MEMOIRES DE L'ACADEMIE IMPERIALE DES SCIENCES DE ST PETERSBOURG – Spb., S.5, 1809-1830. V.1-11; S. 7, 1859-1897. V.1-42; Assemblees. Spb., 1831-1859. V.1-8 – 1,525mf – 9 – ne IDC [500]
MEMOIRES DE L'ACADEMIE ROYALE DES SCIENCES / Academie des Sciences. Paris – 1666-1699 – 3 – us Readex [500]
MEMOIRES DE L'ACADEMIE ROYALE DES SCIENCES : DEPUIS 1666 JUSQU'A 1699 – Paris. v3-11. 1729-1734 – 101mf – 9 – ne IDC [500]
MEMOIRES DE L'ACADEMIE ROYALE DES SCIENCES DE L'INSTITUT DE FRANCE – Paris. n.s. 2. 1816-1941. v1-64. – 788mf – 9 – ne IDC [500]
MEMOIRES DE L'ACADEMIE ROYALE DES SCIENCES ET BELLES-LETTRES DEPUIS L'AVENEMENT DE FREDERIC GUILLAUME 2 AU TRONE : AOUT 1786 JUSQU'A 1797. AVEC L'HISTOIRE POUR LE MEME TEMPS – Berlin, 1786-1800 – 160mf – 9 – ne IDC [500]
MEMOIRES DE L'ACADEMIE ROYALE DES SCIENCES ET BELLES-LETTRES DEPUIS L'AVENEMENT DE FREDERIC GUILLAUME 2 FREDERIC GUILLAUME 3 AU THRONE / Akademie der Wissenschaften. Berlin – 1792-1807 – 3 – us Readex [500]
MEMOIRES DE L'ACADEMIE ROYALE DES SCIENCES ET BELLES-LETTRES DEPUIS L'AVENEMENT DE FREDERIC GUILLAUME 3 AU TRONE : 1798-1803. AVEC L'HISTOIRE POUR LE MEME TEMPS – Berlin, 1801-1805 – 106mf – 9 – ne IDC [500]
MEMOIRES DE L'HERBIER BOISSIER – Geneve. v1-22. 1900. Suppl 1 – 15mf – 9 – ne IDC [580]
MEMOIRES DE L'HERBIER BOISSIER – Suite au Bulletin de l'herbier Boissier. Par Gustave Beauverd. no. 1-22. Geneve, Bale. 1900. mq no. 10 – 1 – fr A.C.R.P.P. [073]
MEMOIRES DE L'INSTITUT NATIONAL DES SCIENCES ET ARTS, POUR L'AN 4 DE LA REPUBLIQUE : SCIENCES. MATHEMATIQUES ET PHYSIQUES, 1795-1815 – Paris, 1798-1818 – 170mf – 9 – ne IDC [500]
MEMOIRES DE MATHEMATIQUE ET DE PHYSIQUE, PRESENTES A L'ACADEMIE ROYALE DES SCIENCES, PAR DIVERS SCAVANS, ET LUS DANS SES ASSEMBLEES / Academie des Sciences. Paris – 1750-1786 – 3 – us Readex [500]
MEMOIRES DE MESSIRE PHILIPPE DE MORNAY / Du Plessis, P – H-375 2. 3 v. 1624-1652 – 8 – ne IDC [920]
MEMOIRES DE MME. DUNOYER ECRITS PAR ELLE-MEME / Dunoyer, Anne Marguerite – London: Jean Nourse, 1739. 500p. (Les Femmes Collection) – 6mf – 9 – $15.00 – fr Bibl Nationale [920]
MEMOIRES DE MONTECUCCOLI, GENERALISSIME DES TROUPES DE L'EMPEREUR, DIVISES EN TROIS LIVRES / Montecuccoli, Raimondo – 1. De l'art militaire en general; 2. De la guerre contre le Turc; 3. Relation de la campagne de 1664. Amsterdam, Wotstein. 1752. xl, 520p. Portrait. (Strategy of War Series) – 9 – fr Hachette [355]
MEMOIRES DE RIVAROL / Rivarol, Antoine – Paris: Baudouin freres, 1824. xvi,386p – 1 – us U.W. Library [944]
MEMOIRES DE VIDOCQ / Vidocq – 1828-29 – 9 – fr I.C.S. [920]
MEMOIRES DES COMMISAIRES DU ROI ET DE SA MAJESTE BRITANNIQUE. PARIS IMPR. ROYALE / France. Sovereigns, etc., 1715-1774. Louis XV – 1755- – 1 – us UMI [920]
MEMOIRES DES COMMISSAIRES DU ROI ET DE CEUX DE SA MAJESTE BRITANIQUE SUR LES POSSESSIONS ET LES DROITS RESPECTIFS DES DEUX COURONNES EN AMERIQUE, AVEC LES ACTES PUBLICS ET PIECES JUSTIFICATIVES / France – Paris: Imprimerie Royale. 4v. 1755-57. SEM35P85 – 2r – 1 – Can$82.00 – cn Bibl Nat [944]
MEMOIRES, DOCUMENTS ET ECRITS DIVERS LAISSES PAR LE PRINCE DE METTERNICH CHANCELIER DE COUR ET D'ETAT / ed by Metternich, R de – Paris. 4v. 1880-1881 – 25mf – 9 – ne IDC [943]
MEMOIRES DU CAPITAINE LANDOLPHE, CONTENANT L'HISTOIRE DE SES VOYAGES PENDANT TRENTE-SIX ANS, AUX COTES D'AFRIQUE ET AUX DEUX AMERIQUES / Landolphe – (African Library). Paris. A. Bertrand. 1823 – 9 – fr Hachette [960]
MEMOIRES DU CAPITAINE PERON SUR SES VOYAGES AUX COTES D'AFRIQUE EN ARABIE, A L'ILE D'AMSTERDAM, AUX ILES D'ANJOUAN ET DE MAYOTTE / Peron – Paris. 1824 – 9 – $20.00 – fr Orientalistes [910]
MEMOIRES DU MUSEUM D'HISTOIRE NATURELLE – Paris. 20v. 1815-1832 – 348mf – 9 – ne IDC [500]
LES MEMOIRES DU R. P. DOM BERNARD AUDEBERT / Guilloreau, L – Paris, 1911 – Dfl28.00 – ne Slangenburg [240]
MEMOIRES DU REGNE DE BOSSA-AHADEE, ROI DE DAHOME / Norris, Robert – Traduction de l'anglais. Paris, Gattey. 1790 – 9 – 7.50 – fr Orientalistes [960]
MEMOIRES DU REGNE DE BOSSA-AHADEE ROI DU DAHOME, ETAT, SITUE DANS L'INTERIEUR DE LA GUINEE; ET VOYAGE DE L'AUTEUR A ABOME, QUI EN EST LA CAPITALE. OBSERVATIONS SUR LA TRAITE DES NEGRES ET DESCRIPTION DE QUELQUES ENDROITS DE LA COTE DE GUINEE / Norris, Robert – (African Library series) – 9 – fr Hachette [960]
MEMOIRES D'UN OUVRIER DE PARIS, 1871-1872 / Audiganne, A – (Condition of 19th C. French working class series). 1873 – 9 – fr Hachette [360]
MEMOIRES D'UN TOURISTE, T. 2 / Stendhal, M-Henri Beyle – Paris: Le Divan, 1929 – fr Armell [910]
MEMOIRES D'UNE PETROLEUSE / Teram, A – Paris, 1874. 251p. (Les Femmes Collection) – 3mf – 9 – $8.00 – fr Bibl Nationale [920]
MEMOIRES ENTOMOLOGIQUES.ETUDES SUR LES COLEOPTERES / Grouvelle, A – Paris, 1916-17. 2pts. Z/1317/2 – 8 – ne IDC [590]
MEMOIRES ET ANECDOTES, POUR SERVIR A L'HISTOIRE DE M. DE VOLTAIRE / Villette, Ch. de – Amsterdam. 1779 – 9 – fr Hachette [920]
MEMOIRES ET ANECDOTES POUR SERVIR A L'HISTOIRE DE VOLTAIRE – Depuis sa naissance jusqu'a sa mort. Au Temple de la gloire. 1780. VIII – 9 – fr Hachette [920]
MEMOIRES ET ANECDOTES SUR LA DYNASTIE REGNANTE DES DJOGOUNS – Traducteur by Isaac Titsingh. Traduction du japonais. Paris, Nepveu. 1820 – 9 – 10.00 – fr Orientalistes [950]
MEMOIRES ET CORRESPONDANCE. ET PRECEDES D'UNE NOTICE HISTORIQUE, REDIGEES SUR PIECES AUTHENTIQUES ET ORIGINALES / Favart, CS; ed by Dumoulard, H F – 3v 1808 – 9 – us Sibley [780]
MEMOIRES ET DOCUMENTS / France. Commission des Annales des Ponts et Chaussees – v71-104. 1901-34 – 13r – 1 – us Ross [624]
MEMOIRES ET DOCUMENTS RELATIFS A L'HISTOIRE DU CANADA / Societe Historique de Montreal – Montreal: imprime par Duvernay. v1-12. 1859-1921. SEM16P206 – 1r – 5 – Can$29.00 – cn Bibl Nat [971]

MEMOIRES: EXTRAIT DU TOME 2 D'HISTOIRE DE HENRI DE LA TOUR D'AUVERGNE / Turenne, Henri de la Tour d'Auvergne – Paris. Vve. Mazieres, 1735. clxxviip (Strategy of War Series) – 9 – fr Hachette [355]

MEMOIRES HISTORIQUES POUR LE SIECLE COURANT – Amsterdam. 1734 – 1 – fr A.C.R.P.P. [073]

MEMOIRES IN-80 = VERHANDELINGEN IN-80 / Bruxelles. Academie Royale des Sciences Coloniales. Classe des Sciences Morales et Politiques – Bruxelles: Editions J Duculot. n.s.: v1-4 n2 (1955-56) – us Res Libr [320]

MEMOIRES LITTERAIRES DE LA GRANDE-BRETAGNE – La Haye. 1720-24 (I-XVI) – 1 – fr A.C.R.P.P. [073]

MEMOIRES LUS DEVANT LA SOCIETE ROYALE DU CANADA 1882 & 1883 / Baillairge, Charles – 1884. 00900. (Pre-1900 Canadiana) – 9 – cn C.I.H.M. [971]

MEMOIRES MILITAIRES ET POLITIQUES, SERVANT D'INTRODUCTION A L'HISTOIRE DE LA GUERRE EN ALLEMAGNE EN 1756. / Lloyd, Henry – Paris. Magimel. 1801. xlviii, 354p. pl. (Strategy of War Series) – 9 – fr Hachette [355]

MEMOIRES OU ESSAIS SUR LA MUSIQUE / Gretry, Andre E M – P 303. 3 v. 1797 – 9 – ne IDC [780]

MEMOIRES OU ESSAIS SUR LA MUSIQUE.. / Gretry, Andre E M – 1789 – 2 – us Sibley [780]

"MEMOIRES OU RECUEIL DE DIPLOMES, CHARTES, NOTICES ET AUTRES ACTES AUTHENTIQUES POUR SERVIR A L'HISTOIRE DU POITOU ET PROVINCES VOISINES..." – 18th-19th c. – fr Armell [944]

MEMOIRES POUR L'HISTOIRE DES SCIENCES ET DES BEAUX-ARTS – Trevoux puis Lyon, Paris. 1701-67 (I-CCLXV) – 1 – fr A.C.R.P.P. [073]

MEMOIRES POUR SERVIR A L'HISTOIRE DE LA REVOLUTION OPEREE DANS LA MUSIQUE PAR M. LE CHEVALIER GLUCK / ed by Leblond, Gaspard-Michel – 1781 – 9 – us Sibley [780]

MEMOIRES POUR SERVIR A L'HISTOIRE DE M. DE VOLTAIRE / Servieres – Dans lesquels on trouvera divers ecrits de lui, peu connus, sur ses differents avec J.-B. Rousseau et d'autres gens de lettres; un grand nombre d'anecdotes et une notice critique de ses pieces de theatre. Amsterdam. 1785. VIII. IV – 9 – fr Hachette [920]

MEMOIRES POUR SERVIR A L'HISTOIRE DES INSECTES / ed by Geer, C de – Stockholm. 1752-78. 9v. – 122mf – 9 – ne IDC [590]

MEMOIRES POUR SERVIR A L'HISTOIRE ECCLESIASTIQUE DES SIX PREMIERS SIECLES / Lenain De Tillemont, LS – Venise. Tom 1-16. 1732 – Dfl1,253.00 – ne Slangenburg [240]

MEMOIRES POUR SERVIR L'HISTOIRE ANATOMIQUE ET PHYSIOLOGIQUE DES ANIMAUX ET DES VEGETAUX / Dutrochet, R J Henri – Paris, J. B. Balliere, 1837, t. I: 576 p.; t. II: 573 p. plus atlas de 36 p. et 30 pl. Histoire des Sciences XVIIe-XIXe Siecles. 7940 a 7942 – 9 – fr Hachette [580]

MEMOIRES RELATIFS A L'EMPRISONNEMENT DE L'HONORABLE D. B. VIGER / Viger, Denis Benjamin – Montreal: Imprime par F Cinq-Mars, 1840. SEM16P183 – 1r – 5 – Can$9.00 – cn Bibl Nat [971]

MEMOIRES SECRETS SUR LA RUSSIE ET PARTICULIEREMENT SUR LA FIN DU REGNE DE CATHERINE 2 ET SUR CELUI DE PAULLER / Masson, CF Ph – Formant Un Tableau Des Moeurs De Saint-Petersbourg A La Fin Du 18e Siecle. (Russia 19th C. series). 1800 – 9 – fr Hachette [947]

MEMOIRES SOUMIS A LA COMMISSION D'ENQUETE SUR LE TRANSPORT SCOLAIRE / Canada. Commission d'Enquete sur le Transport Scolaire – Montreal: Bibliotheque Nationale du Quebec, 1970. SEM35P54 – 1r – 1 – Can$18.00 – cn Bibl Nat [380]

MEMOIRES SUR LA CHALEUR / Rumford, Benjamin T – Paris, F. Didot, 1804, lxviii p., 166 p. Histoire des Sciences XVIIe-XIXe Siecles. 7995 – 9 – fr Hachette [530]

MEMOIRES SUR LA COALITION: ETUDE POLITIQUE – 1886. 02572. (Pre-1900 Canadiana) – 9 – cn C.I.H.M. [971]

MEMOIRES SUR LA FAMILLE DES FOUGERES / Fee, A L A – 1852 – 7 – uk Microform Academic [580]

MEMOIRES SUR LA FAMILLE DES FOUGERES / Fee, A L A – v. 4-11. Strasbourg, Paris. 1844-66. B-5206 2 – 8 – ne IDC [580]

MEMOIRES SUR LA FAMILLE DES FOUGERES. 5. GENERA FILICUM / Fee, A L A – Strasbourg, Paris. 1850-52. B-523 2 – 8 – ne IDC [580]

MEMOIRES SUR LA FAMILLE DES LEGUMINEUSES / Candolle, A P de – Paris. 1825-27. B-5017 2 – 8 – ne IDC [580]

MEMOIRES SUR LA GUERRE OU L'ON A RASSEMBLE LES MAXIMES LES PLUS NECESSAIRES DANS LES OPERATIONS DE L'ART MILITAIRE / Feuquieres, Antoine de Pas – Amsterdam F. Changuion. 1731. xxiv, 434p. (Strategy of War Series) – 9 – fr Hachette [355]

MEMOIRES SUR L'AMBASSADE DE FRANCE PRES LA PORTE OTTOMANE / Saint-Priest, – 1877 – 9 – fr Orientalistes [944]

MEMOIRES SUR LES CONTREES OCCIDENTALES / Hsuan-Tsang – (Si-yu-ki). 1857-58 – 1 – uk Microform Academic [900]

MEMOIRES SUR LES CONTREES OCCIDENTALES TRADUITS DU SANSCRIT EN CHINOIS EN L'AN 648 PAR HIOUEN-THSANG ET DU CHINOIS EN FRANCAIS / Julien, S – v. 1. Paris. 1857-58. BU-593 2 – 8 – ne IDC [900]

MEMOIRES SUR LES FOUGERES DE MEXIQUE / Martens, M & Galeotti, H G – (Nouveaux Mem. Ac. Royale Sci. Belgique, 1842, v. 15, 99 pp., 23 pls.). B-7224 1 – 9 – ne IDC [580]

MEMOIRES SUR LES HOPITAUX DE PARIS / Tenon, Jacques Rene – Paris: P.D. Pierres et Royez, 1788. 7 fiches. (Statistics Series: Medical Studies) – 9 – 17.00 – fr Bibl Nationale [310]

MEMOIRES SUR LES OBJETS LES PLUS IMPORTANTS DE L'ARCHITECTURE / Patte, Pierre – Paris. Rozet, 1769. 4 fol. 4, 375p., 27 pl., ill. (Architecture Series) – 9 – fr Hachette [720]

MEMOIRES SUR LES RELATIONS POLITIQUES DES PRINCES CHRETIENS ET PARTICULIEREMENT DES ROIS DE FRANCE, AVEC LES EMPEREURS MONGOLS / Abel-Remusat – Memoires...de l'Academie des inscriptions et belles-lettres. 1822. v6, p396-469; 1824. v7, p335-438. BU-704 2 – 8 – ne IDC [944]

MEMOIRES SUR LES RUTACEES / Jussieu, A H L de – Paris. 1825. B-5135 2 – 8 – ne IDC [580]

MEMOIRES SUR L'ORIGINE ET LES REVOLUTIONS DES LANGUES CELTIQUE ET FRANCAISE. LEBER. LEBER [J.M.] C. COLLECTION DES MEILEURES DISSERTATIONS, NOTICES ET TRAIT ES PARTICULIERS RELATIFS A L'HISTOIRE DE FRANCE / Duclos, C P – Paris. v14(p15-63). 1838 – 1mf – 9 – ne IDC [440]

MEMOIRES SUR VOLTAIRE ET SUR SES OUVRAGES PAR LONGCHAMP ET WAGNIERE SES SECRETAIRES : SUIVIS DE DIVERS ECRITS INEDITS TOUS RELATIFS A VOLTAIRE. / Longchamp, S G & Wagniere, J L – Paris: A. Andre, 1826 – 9 – fr Hachette [920]

MEMOIRES TOUCHANT LA VIE DE MONSIEUR DE S. CYRAN / Lancelot, M – Cologne. Tom 1-2. 1738 – Dfl46.00 – ne Slangenburg [920]

MEMOIRES...PRECEDES DE SON HISTOIRE. / Societe Linneenne de Paris – Paris. 1788-1822-(1827) (1828) – 3 – us Readex [580]

MEMOIRE...SUR LA QUESTION PROPOSEE EN CES TERMES "DETERMINER PAR L'OBSERVATION QUELLES SONT LES MALADIES QUI RESULTENT DES EMANATIONS DES EAUX STAGNANTES. / Baumes, Jean Baptiste Theodore – Nimes, C. Belle et Paris, Barrois et Mecquignon, 1789. 290 p. 4 fiches. (Statistics: Medical Studies Series) – 9 – 10.00 – fr Bibl Nationale [310]

MEMOIRS / American Academy of Arts and Sciences – $435.00 – us UPA [700]

MEMOIRS / Anthropological Society of London – (United with the Ethnological Society of London to form the Royal Anthropological Institute of Great Britain and Ireland.) v. 1-3. 1863-1869 – 1,5,6 – us Princeton Micro [306]

MEMOIRS / Botsford, Elder Edmund – 1832 – 1 – 8.96 – us Baptist [240]

MEMOIRS / Finney, Charles G – 1876 – 1 – $50.00 – us Presbyterian [240]

MEMOIRS / Gano, John – 1806 – 1 – 5.46 – us Baptist [240]

MEMOIRS / Montpensier, de – Paris: Bibliotheque Charpentier, n.d. Collations sur le manuscrit autographe. 560p. (Les Femmes Collection) – 6mf – 9 – $15.00 – fr Bibl Nationale [306]

MEMOIRS / Royal Astronomical Society – v69-77 1964-73 – 1,5,6 – 2235.00 – us Princeton Micro [520]

MEMOIRS / Sherman, William Tecumseh – New York. D. Appleton. 1875. 2v: 405p.; 409p. maps. (Strategy of War Series) – 9 – fr Hachette [355]

MEMOIRS / Society for American Archaeology – v. 1-31. 1941-76 – 1 – us UMI [930]

MEMOIRS / Strickland, Hugh Edwin – By Sir William Jardine, bart. London: J. Van Voorst, 1858. 441p. illus."Chronological list of writings" – 1 – us U.W. Library [580]

MEMOIRS / Texas Baptist Oral History Consortium – Jimmy Allen (1973); W. A. Criswell (1973); J. M. Dawson (1972); E. S. James (1973); E. N. Jones (1973); T. B. Maston (1973); A. C. Miller (1972); Blake Smith (1972); R. A. Springer (1972); W. R. White (1973). 2208p. 2 reels – 1 – us Baptist [240]

MEMOIRS / Wernerian Natural History Society. Edinburgh – 1811-39 – 3 – us Readex [580]

MEMOIRS. / Fanshawe, Anne Harrison – Ed. with introd. by Beatrice Marshall. London, New York: J. Lane, 1905 – 1 – us U.W. Library [946]

MEMOIRS AND CORRESPONDENCE [DESPATCHES, AND OTHER PAPERS,] OF VISCOUNT CASTLEREAGH, SECOND MARQUESS OF LONDONDERRY / ed by Vane, C W – London. 12v. 1850-1853 – 70mf – 9 – ne IDC [941]

MEMOIRS AND CORRESPONDENCE OF ADMIRAL LORD DE SAUMAREZ, FROM ORIGINAL PAPERS / Ross, John – 2v. 1838 – 9 – 80.00 – uk Libr Preservation [920]

MEMOIRS AND LETTERS OF CAPT. SIR W.H / Hoste, William – 1833. 2v – 9 – 40.00 – uk Libr Preservation [920]

MEMOIRS AND LETTERS OF JAMES KENT, LL.D., LATE CHANCELLOR OF THE STATE OF NEW YORK / Kent, William – Boston, Little, Brown, 1898. 341 p. LL-456 – 1 – us L of C Photodup [340]

THE MEMOIRS AND OBSERVATIONS,... (HARRIS, J. NAVIGANTIUM ATQUE ITINERANTIUM BIBLIOTHECA...) / LeComte, LD – London. v2. 1705 – 2mf – 9 – ne IDC [950]

MEMOIRS AND PROCEEDINGS / Manchester Literary and Philosophical Society. Manchester – Manchester Memoirs. London: 1785-1887; Manchester: 1888- – 3 – us Readex [100]

MEMOIRS AND PROCEEDINGS OF THE CHEMICAL SOCIETY OF LONDON FOR 1841-48 / Chemical Society. London – London, 1843-48 – 3 – us Readex [540]

MEMOIRS AND REMAINS OF THE REVEREND WALTER INGLIS, AFRICAN MISSIONARY AND CANADIAN PASTOR / Cochrane, William – Toronto: C. Blackett Robinson, 1887. 00692. (Pre-1900 Canadiana) – 9 – cn C.I.H.M. [920]

MEMOIRS AND SERVICES OF SIR SAMUEL BURDON ELLIS FROM HIS OWN MEMORANDA / Ellis, Samuel Burdon; ed by Ellis, Lady – 1866 – 9 – $20.00 – uk Libr Preservation [920]

MEMOIRS BY HIMSELF / Timur – 1830 – 1 – uk Microform Academic [920]

MEMOIRS FOR A NATURAL HISTORY OF ANIMALS / Perrault, C – M 380. 1688 – 9 – ne IDC [590]

MEMOIRS FOR THE CURIOUS – v. 1. 1701 – 1 – us UMI [000]

MEMOIRS FOR THE INGENIOUS – v. 1. Jan-Dec 1693 – 1 – us UMI [010]

MEMOIRS FOR THE NATURAL HISTORY OF HUMANE BLOOD, ESPECIALLY THE SPIRIT OF THAT LIQUOR / Boyle, R – 1683-84.M-189 – 9 – ne IDC [612]

LES MEMOIRS HISTORIQUES DE SE-MA TS'IEN / Chavannes, E – Paris. 1895-1905. BU-555 2 – 8 – ne IDC [930]

MEMOIRS OF ADIEL SHERWOOD / Sherwood, Julia L – Assisted by Rev. S. Boykin. 1884 – 1 – 14.63 – us Baptist [240]

MEMOIRS OF ADMIRAL THE RIGHT HON. SIR ASTLEY COOPER, K.G.C.B / Colomb, Philip Howard – 1898 – 9 – uk Libr Preservation [920]

MEMOIRS OF ALLEGHENY COUNTY / Northwestern Historical Association – Personal and genealogical. Madison, 1904. Vols. 1-2, Pennsylvania Reel 8. (The Cox Library Collection) – 5 – us Americana [978]

THE MEMOIRS OF CORDELL HULL / Hull, Cordell – New York: Macmillan Co., 1948. 2v – 1 – CSUXAGP9723-B – us Hoover Inst Photo [920]

MEMOIRS OF EDWARD AND CATHERINE STANLEY / ed by Stanley, Arthur Penrhyn – (Includes index) – 3rd ed. London: John Murray, 1880 – 1mf – 9 – 0-8370-5845-7 – 1985-3845 – us A.T.L.A. [920]

MEMOIRS OF EMINENTLY PIOUS WOMEN / Burder, Samuel – 1834 – 9 – us A.T.L.A. [240]

MEMOIRS OF EMINENTLY PIOUS WOMEN / Dana, Daniel – Abridged from the large work by Dr. Allibone. 1803 – 9 – us A.T.L.A. [240]

MEMOIRS OF GAUR AND PANDUA / Khan, Abid Ali; ed by Stapleton, H E – Calcutta, 1931. 190 pp., ills. BI-1007 2 – 8 – ne IDC [910]

MEMOIRS OF GEORGIA – 2v, 1895. Biog. sketches indexed. Hist. accounts of civil, military, industrial and professional interests.Indexes. F-0304, F-0305 – 9 – us A.G.L.L. [920]

MEMOIRS OF GREAT BRITAIN AND IRELAND : FROM CHARLES 2 TO THE SEA-BATTLE OF LA HOGUE / Dalrymple, J – (v2: Letters From The French Ambassadors to Their Court London, 1773) – Dfl67.00 – ne Slangenburg [941]

MEMOIRS OF HENRIETTA CARACCIOLO : OF THE PRINCESS OF FORINO: EX-BENEDICTINE NUN / Caracciolo, Henrietta – new ed. London: Richard Bentley, 1865 – 1mf – 9 – 0-8370-8726-0 – 1986-2726 – us A.T.L.A. [920]

MEMOIRS OF JAMES ROBERT HOPE-SCOTT OF ABBOTSFORD, D.C.L., Q.C. : WITH SELECTIONS FROM HIS CORRESPONDENCE / Ornsby, Robert – London: J. Murray, 1884 – 2mf – us A.T.L.A. [240]

MEMOIRS OF JOHN MASON PECK, D.D., 1864 / Babcock, Rufus – 1 – 13.02 – us Baptist [240]

MEMOIRS OF JOSEPH FOUCHE...MINISTER OF THE GENERAL POLICE OF FRANCE / Fouche, Joseph – Trans. from French. London: H.S. Nichols, 1896.2v. Reprint of 1825 translation – 1 – us U.W. Library [920]

MEMOIRS OF JOSEPH JOHN GURNEY : WITH SELECTIONS FROM HIS JOURNAL AND CORRESPONDENCE / Gurney, Joseph John; ed by Braithwaite, Joseph Bevan – London: Headley Brothers; New York: Friends' Book & Tract Committee, 1902 – 2mf – us A.T.L.A. [240]

MEMOIRS OF LENAWEE COUNTY / Bonner, Richard I – Genealogical and biographical records. Madison: Western Historical Asso., 1909. Vol. 1. Michigan Reel 17; Vol. 2. Michigan Reel 18. (The Cox Library Collection) – 5 – us Americana [978]

MEMOIRS OF LEONORA CHRISTINA, DAUGHTER OF CHRISTIAN 4 OF DENMARK : WRITTEN DURING HER IMPRISONMENT IN THE BLUE TOWER AT COPENHAGEN, 1663-8 / Ulfeldt, Grevinde Leonora Christina – Trans. by F.E. Bunnett. London: King, 1872. x/330p – 1 – us U.W. Library [920]

MEMOIRS OF LITERATURE – v. 1-4. 13 Mar 1710-6 Sep 1714 – 1 – us UMI [010]

MEMOIRS OF LUCAS COUNTY AND CITY OF TOLEDO / Scribner, Harvey – Genealogical and biographical records. Madison: Western Historical Assoc., 1910. Vol. 1. Ohio Reel 44; Vol. 2. Ohio Reel 45. (The Cox Library Collection) – 5 – us Americana [978]

MEMOIRS OF MARGARET DE VALOIS, QUEEN OF NAVARRE : CONTAINING THE SECRET HISTORY OF THE COURT OF FRANCE FOR SEVENTEEN YEARS, VIZ., FROM 1565 TO 1582, DURING THE REIGNS OF CHARLES 9. AND HENRY 3. / Marguerite, Queen of Navarre – London: H.S. Nichols, 1895 – 1mf – us A.T.L.A. [944]

MEMOIRS OF MARGARET FULLER OSSOLI / Ossoli, Margaret Fuller – By R.W. Emerson, W.H. Channing. and J.F. Clarke. v.1-2. 1881 – 9 – us A.T.L.A. [240]
MEMOIRS OF MILWAUKEE / Watrous, Jerome A – Madison: Western Historical Asso., 1909. Vols. 1-2. Wisconsin Reel 16. (The Cox Library Collection) – 5 – us Americana [978]
MEMOIRS OF PRETENDED PROPHETS WHO HAVE APPEARED IN DIFFERENT AGES OF THE WORLD, AND ESPECIALLY IN MODERN TIMES, POINTING OUT, FROM AUTHENTIC SOURCES, THEIR BLUNDERS AND THE PERNICIOUS CONSEQUENCES OF THEIR PRETENSIONS;... / Franks, James – London, 1795 – 1mf – 9 – MP-591/1 – ne IDC [240]
MEMOIRS OF REAR-ADMIRAL SIR W.E. PARRY / Parry, Edward – 1857 – 9 – $20.00 – uk Libr Preservation [920]
MEMOIRS OF REV. CHARLES G. FINNEY / Finney, Charles G – New York: A.S. Barnes, c1876 – 2mf – us A.T.L.A. [240]
MEMOIRS OF REV. JACOB GOERING, REV. GEORGE LOCHMAN, D.D., AND REV. BENJAMIN KURTZ, D.D., LL. D. / Hay, Charles A – Philadelphia: Lutheran Publication Society, c1887 – 1mf – us A.T.L.A. [240]
MEMOIRS OF REV. JOHN LEIGHTHON WILSON / DuBose, Hampden C – 1895 – 1 – $50.00 – us Presbyterian [920]
MEMOIRS OF SAMUEL M. JANNEY : LATE OF LINCOLN, LOUDOUN COUNTY, VA., A MINISTER IN THE RELIGIOUS SOCIETY OF FRIENDS / Janney, Samuel M – Philadelphia.: Friends' Book Association, 1881 – 1mf – us A.T.L.A. [240]
THE MEMOIRS OF SHERLOCK HOLMES / Doyle, Arthur Conan – London: George Newnes, 1894 – 1 roll – 1 – 1-55879-682-7 – uk Libr Preservation [830]
MEMOIRS OF SIR JOHN RERESBY: THE COMPLETE TEXT AND A SELECTION FROM HIS LETTERS / Reresby, John – Edited with introd. and notes by Andrew Browning. Glasgow: Jackson, Son & Co., 1936. xlv, 626p – 1 – us U.W. Library [920]
MEMOIRS OF SIR PHILIP FRANCIS, K.C.B., WITH CORRESPONDENCE AND JOURNALS / Parkes, Joseph – Completed and ed. by Herman Merivale. London: Longman's, Green, & Co., 1867. 2v – 1 – us U.W. Library [920]
MEMOIRS OF THE AMERICAN ACADEMY OF ARTS AND SCIENCES / American Academy of Arts and Sciences, Boston – (All that is currently available) – Boston. v1-4 1785-1818; ns1-12 1833-aug 1902 – 1 – D3916 – us UMI [073]
MEMOIRS OF THE ARCHAEOLOGICAL SOCIETY OF INDIA / Ceylon. Archaeological Survey – Colombo. 1924-46. v1-5. – 38mf – 8 – ne IDC [930]
MEMOIRS OF THE ARCHAEOLOGICAL SOCIETY OF INDIA / India. Archaeological Survey – Calcutta. 1919-55. v1-73 – 251mf – 8 – ne IDC [930]
MEMOIRS OF THE ASIATIC SOCIETY OF BENGAL / Asiatic Society of Bengal – Calcutta. 1905-34. v1-12. Lacking: v10(p503-end); v12(p.316-end) – 122mf – 9 – ne IDC [950]
MEMOIRS OF THE COUNT DE ROCHECHOUART, 1788-1822, IN FRANCE, SOUTHERN RUSSIA, IN THE NAPOLEONIC WARS, AND AS COMMANDANT OF PARIS / Rochechouart, Louis Victor Leon – Authorized trans. by Frances Jackson. London: J. Murray, 1920. xv,329p – 1 – us U.W. Library [944]
MEMOIRS OF THE CRUSADES / Villehardouin, Geoffroy de – London: J.M. Dent; New York: E.P. Dutton, [1908?] – 1mf – us A.T.L.A. [240]
MEMOIRS OF THE EGYPT EXPLORATION SOCIETY *see*
- THE 11TH DYNASTY TEMPLE AT DEIR EL-BAHARI (MEES VOL 28)
- THE 11TH DYNASTY TEMPLE AT DEIR EL-BAHARI (MEES VOL 30)
- THE 11TH DYNASTY TEMPLE AT DEIR EL-BAHARI (MEES VOL 32)
- ABYDOS (MEES VOL 22)
- ABYDOS (MEES VOL 24)
- ABYDOS (MEES VOL 25)
- AHNAS EL MEDINEH (MEES VOL 11)
- EL ANRAH AND ABYDOS (MEES VOL 23)
- BALABISH (MEES VOL 37)
BUBASTIS (MEES VOL 8)
- THE BUCHEUM (MEES VOL 41, 2)
- THE BUCHEUM (MEES VOL 41, 3)
- THE BUCHEUM (MEES VOL 41,1)
- THE CEMETERIES OF ABYDOS (MEES VOL 33)
- THE CEMETERIES OF ABYDOS (MEES VOL 34)
- THE CEMETERIES OF ABYDOS (MEES VOL 35)
- THE CITY OF AKHENATEN (MEES VOL 38)
- DENDEREH (MEES VOL 17)
- DESHASHEH (MEES VOL 15)
- DIOSPOLIS PARVA (MEES VOL 20)
- EHNASYA (MEES VOL 26)
- THE FESTIVAL-HALLOF CSORKON 2 IN THE GREAT TEMPLE OF BUBASTIS (MEES VOL 10)
GOSHEN AND THE SHRINE OF SAFT EL HENNEH (MEES VOL 4)
- THE MOUND OF THE JEW AND THE CITY OF ONIAS (MEES VOL 7)
- NAUKRATIS (MEES VOL 3)
- NAUKRATIS (MEES VOL 6)
- PRE-DYNASTIC CEMETERY AT AL MAHASNA (MEES VOL 31)
- THE ROYAL TOMBS OF THE EARLIEST DYNASTIES (MEES VOL 21)
- THE ROYAL TOMBS OF THE FIRST DYNASTY (MEES VOL 18)
- TANIS (MEES NO 2)
- TANIS (MEES VOL 5)
- THE TEMPLE OF DEIR EL BAHARI (MEES VOL 12)

MEMOIRS OF THE EGYPT EXPLORATION SOCIETY (MEES) – (Lacking: n9,13,14,16,19,27,29,36,39,40. Individual vols also listed separately) – 1(1885)-41(1934) – 249mf – 9 – Dfl872.00 – ne Slangenburg [910]
MEMOIRS OF THE EGYPT EXPOLRATION SOCIETY *see* THE STORY-CITY OF PITHOM AND THE ROUTE OF THE EXODUS (MEES NO 1)
MEMOIRS OF THE FIRST FORTY-FIVE YEARS OF THE LIFE OF JAMES LACKINGTON, THE PRESENT BOOKSELLER IN CHISWELL STREET, MOORFIELDS, LONDON, WRITTEN BY HIMSELF;... / Lackington, J – London, [1791] – 4mf – 9 – MP-577/1 – ne IDC [920]
MEMOIRS OF THE HON. WALTER LOWRIE / Lowrie, Walter – New York: Baker & Taylor, 1896. v,192p.1 fiche – 9 – us A.T.L.A. [240]
MEMOIRS OF THE INDIAN MUSEUM / Indian Museum; ed by Superintendant Indian Museum – Calcutta. 1907-42. v1-13. – 191mf – 8 – ne IDC [060]
MEMOIRS OF THE JACOBITES OF 1715 AND 1745 / Thomson, Katherine Byerley – London: R. Bentley, 1845-46. 3v – 1 – us U.W. Library [941]
MEMOIRS OF THE LATE REV. ABRAHAM MARSHALL / Marshall, Gabez P – Typed from the original copy by J. P. McGraw. 100p – 1 – 5.00 – us Baptist [240]
MEMOIRS OF THE LATE REV. JOHN WESLEY, A.M., WITH A REVIEW OF HIS LIFE AND WRITINGS AND A HISTORY OF METHODISM FROM ITS COMMENCEMENT IN 1729 TO THE PRESENT TIME / Hampson, J – Sunderland, 1791.-3v – 9mf – 9 – MP-578/1 – ne IDC [240]
MEMOIRS OF THE LIFE. / Mackintosh, James – Ed. by Robert James Mackintosh from the 2nd London ed. Boston: Little, Brown and Co., 1853. 2v – 1 – us U.W. Library [920]
MEMOIRS OF THE LIFE AND SERVICES OF REAR-ADMIRAL SIR WILLIAM SYMONDS, SURVEYER OF THE NAVY, FROM 1832 TO 1847 : WITH CORRESPONDENCE AND OTHER PAPERS DIRECTED TO BE PUBLISHED UNDER HIS WILL / ed by Sharp, James A – 1858 – 9 – uk Libr Preservation [920]
MEMOIRS OF THE LIFE AND SERVICES OF THE RT. REV. ALONZO POTTER, D.D., LL.D. : BISHOP OF THE PROTESTANT EPISCOPAL CHURCH IN THE DIOCESE OF PENNSYLVANIA / Howe, M A De Wolfe – Philadelphia: J.B. Lippincott, 1871, c1870 – 1mf – us A.T.L.A. [240]
MEMOIRS OF THE LIFE AND WRITINGS OF THE ABATE METASTASIO / Burney, Charles – v. 1-3. 1796 – 9 – us Sibley [780]
MEMOIRS OF THE LIFE AND WRITINGS OF THE REV. CLAUDIUS BUCHANAN / Pearson, H – Oxford, 1817. 2nd ed. 2 vols. BI-1012 1 – 9 – ne IDC [240]
MEMOIRS OF THE LIFE AND WRITINGS OF THE REVEREND ALEXANDER GEDDES, LL.D / Good, John Mason – London, 1803. xxiii,547p – 1 – us U.W. Library [240]
MEMOIRS OF THE LIFE OF ANNA JAMESON / Macpherson, G – Boston: Roberts, 1878 – 1mf – us A.T.L.A. [240]
MEMOIRS OF THE LIFE OF THAT LEARNED ANTIQUARY... / Ashmole, E – London, 1717 – 2mf – ne IDC [920]
MEMOIRS OF THE LIFE OF THE LATE GEORGE FREDERIC HANDEL / Mainwaring, J – 1760 – 9 – us Sibley [780]
MEMOIRS OF THE LOWER OHIO VALLEY / Federal Publishing Co – Personal and genealogical. Madison: 1905. Vols. 1-2. Mississippi Reel 8. (The Cox Library Collection) – 5 – us Americana [978]
MEMOIRS OF THE MARQUIS OF ROCKINGHAM AND HIS CONTEMPORARIES / Albemarle, George Thomas Keppel, Earl – London: Bentley, 1852. 2v – 1 – us U.W. Library [920]
MEMOIRS OF THE MIAMI VALLEY / Robert O. Law Co – Chicago, 1919. v1-3. Ohio Reel 9. The Cox Library Collection – 5 – us Americana [978]
MEMOIRS OF THE NEW YORK BOTANICAL GARDEN – New York (N.Y.) v1-6. 1900-1916 – 32mf – 9 – ne IDC [580]
MEMOIRS OF THE PRETENDERS AND THEIR ADHERENTS / Jesse, John Heneage – (Includes bibliographical references and index) – New ed. London: Bohn, 1860 – 1r – 1 – us U.W. Library [920]
MEMOIRS OF THE PRINCE DE TALLEYRAND / Talleyrand-Perigord, Charles Maurice de – Paris; Boston: The Napoleon Society, 1895 – 1 – us U.W. Library [944]
MEMOIRS OF THE PRINCIPAL HYMN-WRITERS AND COMPILERS OF THE 17TH, 18TH AND 19TH CENTURIES / Gadsby, John – 3rd ed. London. 1861 – 1 – 5.60 – us Baptist [240]
MEMOIRS OF THE QUEENS OF FRANCE / Bush, Annie Forbes – From the 2nd London ed. Philadelphia: John E. Potter and Co., n.d. 351p – 1 – us U.W. Library [920]
MEMOIRS OF THE RESEARCH DEPARTMENT OF THE TOYO BUNKO (THE ORIENTAL LIBRARY) – Tokyo. v1-25. 1926-1967 – 87mf – 9 – ne IDC [950]
MEMOIRS OF THE REV. NICHOLAS MURRAY, D.D. (KIRWAN) / Prime, Samuel Irenaeus – New York: Harper, 1862 – 1mf – us A.T.L.A. [240]
MEMOIRS OF THE SECRET SOCIETIES OF THE SOUTH OF ITALY, PARTICULARLY THE CARBONARI – Trans. from the original ms. London: J. Murray, 1821. Attributed to Bertoldi – 1 – us U.W. Library [945]
MEMOIRS OF THE SIEGE OF QUEBEC, CAPITAL OF ALL CANADA, AND OF THE RETREAT OF MONSIEUR DE BOURLEMAQUE, FROM CARILLON TO THE ISLE AUX NOIX IN LAKE CHAMPLAIN / Gardiner, Richard – London: R and J Dodsley, 1761. SEM105P888 – 1mf – 9 – Can$2.25 – cn Bibl Nat [971]
MEMOIRS OF THE WERNERIAN NATURAL HISTORY SOCIETY – Edinburgh, 1811-1838. 7v – 52mf – 9 – ne IDC [500]
MEMOIRS OF THOMAS PAPILLON, OF LONDON, MERCHANT.(1623-1702) / Papillon, Alexander Frederick William – By a lineal descendant. xx,442p. plates, ports., facsim – 1 – us U.W. Library [920]
MEMOIRS OF VERNON COUNTY / Rogers, Earl M – Madison: Western Historical Assoc., 1907. Wisconsin Reel 20. (The Cox Library Collection) – 5 – us Americana [978]
MEMOIRS OF VISCOUNTESS SUNDON, MISTRESS OF THE ROBES TO QUEEN CAROLINE, CONSORT OF GEORGE 2; INCLUDING LETTERS FROM THE MOST CELEBRATED PEOPLE. / ed by Thomson, A T – 2nd ed. London: H. Colburn. 1848. 2v – 1 – us U.W. Library [920]
MEMOIRS OF WAUKESHA COUNTY / Haight, Theron W – Madison: Western Historical Co., 1907. Wisconsin Reel 22. (The Cox Library Collection) – 5 – us Americana [978]
MEMOIRS OF WEST AFRICAN CELEBRITIES : EUROPE...1700-1850, WITH SPECIAL REFERENCE TO THE GOLD COAST / Ahuma, S R B Attoh – Liverpool: Marples, 1905 – us Res Libr [920]
MEMOIRS ON THE HISTORY, FOLK-LORE, AND DISTRIBUTION OF THE RACES OF THE NORTH WESTERN PROVINCES OF INDIA.. / Elliot, Henry Miers – Ed., rev. and re-arranged by John Beames. London: Truebner & Co., 1869. 2v. plates, maps – 1 – us U.W. Library [306]
MEMOIRS RELATING TO FOUCHE, MINISTER OF POLICE UNDER NAPOLEON 1 / Fouche, Joseph – Trans. from French by E. Jules Meras. New York: Sturgis & Walton, 1912. 315p. illus – 1 – us U.W. Library [944]
MEMOIRS...WRITTEN BY HERSELF / Staal, Marguarite Jeanne Cordier de – Trans. from the French by Selina Bathurst. London: R. Bentley, 1877. viii,350p. includes index – 1 – us U.W. Library [920]
MEMOIRS...WRITTEN BY HIMSELF. AND FRAGMENTA REGALIA: BEING A HISTORY OF QUEEN ELIZABETH'S FAVOURITES / Carey, Robert – by Sir Robert Naunton. London: John Murray, 1808. xxxviii,301p – 1 – us U.W. Library [920]
THE MEMORABLE SERMON ON THE LAW : DELIVERED AT THE REGULAR BAPTIST ASSOCIATION, ON CROSS CREEK, VIRGINIA IN 1816 / Campbell, Alexander – St Louis: Christian Pub Co, [1846?] – 1mf – 9 – 0-8370-9450-X – 1986-3450 – us A.T.L.A. [220]
MEMORABLE WOMEN OF IRISH METHODISM IN THE LAST CENTURY / Crookshank, C H – London. [4], 1882 – 3mf – 9 – ne IDC [240]
MEMORANDA : (CAB 24) / Great Britain. Cabinet Office – (Subject indexes, bibliographical chronological guide. Individual years available) – 1916-39 – 198r – 1 – us Ross [941]
MEMORANDA / Jewish Agency for Palestine – To the Secretary-General of the League of Nations for the information of the Permanent Mandates Commission. 18 v. 1922-39. In French and English. Lacking: 1923, v. 2. BJ-28-125 1 – 9 – ne IDC [305]
MEMORANDA AND NOTEBOOKS / Gilbert, David W – 1861-1865, Virginia, Tennessee, Kentucky, and Ohio – 1 – us KS Hist [920]
MEMORANDA AND STATEMENTS RELATING TO BENEFACTORS' EXEMPTIONS AND FREE TUITIONS TO THEOLOGICAL STUDENTS IN MCGILL UNIVERSITY / Dawson, John William – Prepared by the Principal. s.l.: s.n., 1892?. 03671. (Pre-1900 Canadiana) – 9 – cn C.I.H.M. [971]
MEMORANDA BOOKS, 1774-1815 / Bradburn, S – (Coll title: The People Called Methodists, Phase 2: Primary Sources 1738-1800) – 10mf – 9 – MP-623/1 – ne IDC [240]
MEMORANDA OF NATIVE STATES IN INDIA : TOGETHER WITH A LIST OF INDEPENDENT RULING CHIEFS... – Calcutta: Supt Govt Print, 1908- 1907, 1912 – us Res Libr [950]
MEMORANDA PREPARED BY THE GOVERNMENT OF PALESTINE FOR THE USE OF THE PALESTINE ROYAL COMMISSION / Palestine – 3v. Jerusalem. 1936. BJ-28-79 1 – 9 – ne IDC [956]
MEMORANDA RELATING TO COLEOPTEROUS INSECTS FOUND IN THE NEIGHBORHOOD OF SWANSEA / Dillwyn, L W – Swansea, 1829.75p. Z-1186/2 – 8 – ne IDC [590]
MEMORANDA SACRA / Harris, James Rendel – New York: A D F Randolph, 1893 – 1mf – 9 – 0-8370-5027-8 – 1985-3027 – us A.T.L.A. [240]
MEMORANDUM / Jewish Agency for Palestine – The Jewish Agency for Palestine to Sir John Hope Simpson, Jul 1930. London. 1930. BJ-28-133 1 – 9 – ne IDC [310]
MEMORANDUM BOOK / Brown, John – 1753-1797 – 1 – $50.00 – us Presbyterian [240]
MEMORANDUM CONCERNING THE MINISTRY OF EDUCATION / Indonesia. Ministry of Education – SE-2821 1. April 2, 1959 – 9 – ne IDC [370]
MEMORANDUM DE SON EXCELLENCE LE GOUVERNEUR GENERAL... RESUME DE CE QUI S'EST PASSE ENTRE MESSRS PAPINEAU ET CARON, DEPUIS LE 12 MARS AU 6 AVRIL 1847 – Quebec, 1847. SEM105P652 – 1mf – 9 – Can$2.25 – cn Bibl Nat [971]
MEMORANDUM FOR CONTRACTORS / Caughnawaga Ship Canal Company – Prepared by the directors. Ottawa?: A. S. Woodburn, 1873. 05712. (Pre-1900 Canadiana) – 9 – cn C.I.H.M. [380]

MEMORANDUM IN SUPPORT OF THE RETENTION OF THE SPANISH EMBARGO / Wright, Herbert Francis – Washington, DC. 1939. Fiche W1258. (Blodgett Collection of Spanish Civil War Pamphlets) – 9 – us H.U. College Libr [946]

MEMORANDUM OF INFORMATION ON FOREIGN AFFAIRS AND THE WORLD CRISIS – 1938-41. Continued as: Review of World Affairs – 1 – us UMI [327]

MEMORANDUM ON A PROPOSED SUDAN INDUSTRIAL DEVELOPMENT BANK AND RELATED MATTERS / Wood, R H & Ladd, W C – 1961. BNE-7698 1 – 9 – ne IDC [338]

MEMORANDUM ON ACTS OF ARAB AGGRESSION TO ALTER BY FORCE THE SETTLEMENT ON THE FUTURE GOVERNMENT OF PALESTINE / Jewish Agency for Palestine – Submitted to the United Nations Palestine Commission by the Jewish Agency for Palestine. 1948. BJ-28-159 1 – 9 – ne IDC [956]

MEMORANDUM ON BRITISH POLICY IN PALESTINE SINCE THE ADOPTION OF THE GENERAL ASSEMBLY'S PALESTINE RESOLUTION / Jewish Agency for Palestine – Submitted to the United Nations Palestine Commission by the Jewish Agency for Palestine. 1948. BJ-28-161 1 – 9 – ne IDC [956]

MEMORANDUM ON FIVE-YEAR DEVELOPMENT PLAN, 1952-1953 TO 1956-1957 – 1954? BNE-9602 1 – 9 – ne IDC [338]

MEMORANDUM ON THE BUDGET ESTIMATES OF THE REPUBLIC OF SUDAN / Sudan. Ministry of Finance and Economics – 1956-69. (lacking 1957, 1958, 1959, 1960). BNE-7669 1 – 9 – ne IDC [336]

MEMORANDUM ON THE DRAFT ESTIMATES OF REVENUE AND EXPENDITURE – 1957 1958. 1v. NE-9605 1 – 9 – ne IDC [956]

MEMORANDUM ON THE FILLING UP OF THE SCHOOL RETURNS – [S.l.] : [s.n.], [1831]. SEM105P1370 – 1mf – 9 – Can$2.25 – cn Bibl Nat [350]

MEMORANDUM ON THE FOURTH FIVE YEAR PLAN (1965/66-1970/71) / India. Planning Commission – D-1329 1. 1964 – 9 – ne IDC [330]

MEMORANDUM ON THE GENERAL PROGRESS OF DEVELOPMENT AND WELFARE SCHEMES. 1 NOV 1947 TO 31 OCT 1948 – (Sessional Paper No. 17 of 1948). 1948 – 9 – ne IDC [338]

MEMORANDUM ON THE GENERAL PROGRESS OF DEVELOPMENT AND WELFARE SCHEMES FOR THE PERIOD 1 APR 1946 TO 31 OCT 1947 – (Sessional Paper No. 17 of 1947). Zanzibar. 1947. BD-695 1 – 9 – ne IDC [360]

MEMORANDUM ON THE JEWISH AGENCY WITH APPENDIX OF DOCUMENTS / Jewish Agency for Palestine – (Issued for the use of the delegates to the Anglo-Jewish Conference on the Jewish Agency). London. 1929. BJ-28-35 1 – 9 – ne IDC [956]

MEMORANDUM ON THE LONG TERM ECONOMIC PROGRAMME OF THE NETHERLANDS DEPENDENT OVERSEAS TERRITORIES (INDONESIA) / Netherlands East Indies. (Netherlands). O.E.E.C – D-1384 1. v. 2. 1948 – 9 – ne IDC [338]

MEMORANDUM ON THE PENETRATION OF THE TRADES UNIONS BY ROMAN CATHOLIC GUILDS / Council for the Investigation of Vatican Influence and Censorship – London, 1938. Fiche W 1042. (Blodgett Collection of Spanish Civil War Pamphlets) – 9 – us H.U. College Libr [946]

MEMORANDUM ON THE POSITION OF THE JEWISH COMMUNITIES IN ORIENTAL COUNTRIES / Jewish Agency for Palestine. Jerusalem – Submitted to U.N.S.C.O.P. 1947. BJ-28-153 1 – 9 – ne IDC [956]

MEMORANDUM ON THE PROBLEM OF THE DISPLACED AND INSECURE JEWS IN EUROPE / Jewish Agency for Palestine. Jerusalem – Submitted to U.N.S.C.O.P. 1947. BJ-28-152 1 – 9 – ne IDC [956]

MEMORANDUM ON THE PROGRESS OF DEVELOPMENT AND WELFARE SCHEMES FOR THE PERIOD 1 OCT 1951 TO 30 SEP 1952 – (Sessional Paper No. 8 of 1952). 1952 – 9 – ne IDC [360]

MEMORANDUM ON THE PROGRESS OF DEVELOPMENT AND WELFARE SCHEMES FOR THE PERIOD 1 OCT 1952 TO 30 SEP 1953 – (Sessional Paper No. 9 of 1953). 1953 – 9 – ne IDC [360]

MEMORANDUM ON THE RECORDS IN THE FOREIGN DEPARTMENT / Wheeler, J T – Calcutta, 1864. 412, pp. Lists of proceedings, correspondence and indexes to 1756; 1756-1783; 1784-1858, annotated. BI-319 2 – 8 – ne IDC [025]

MEMORANDUM ON THE RECORDS OF THE HOME DEPARTMENT / Wheeler, J T – Calcutta. 1868. BI-316 2 – 8 – ne IDC [941]

MEMORANDUM ON THE "REPORT OF THE COMMISSION ON THE PALESTINE DISTURBANCES OF AUGUST 1929."MAY 1929. BJ-28-129/1 / Jewish Agency for Palestine. London – 9 – ne IDC [956]

MEMORANDUM ON TRUSTEESHIP FOR PALESTINE / Jewish Agency for Palestine. New York – Observations on a temporary Trusteeship for Palestine as proposed by the United States, 5 Apr 1948. Submitted to the General Assembly of the United Nations. New York. 1948. BJ-28-162 1 – 9 – ne IDC [956]

MEMORANDUM OUTLINING ACTS OF VIOLENCE AND INHUMANITY PREPETRATED BY INDONESIAN BANDS ON INNOCENT CHINESE BEFORE AND AFTER THE DUTCH POLICE ACTION WAS ENFORCED ON JULY 21, 1947 / Chung Hua Tsung Hui – Batavia.SE-11,780-1 – 9 – ne IDC [950]

MEMORANDUM SUBMITTED TO THE ANGLO-AMERICAN COMMITTEE OF INQUIRY / Jewish Agency for Palestine. Jerusalem – 1946. BJ-28-143 1 – 9 – ne IDC [956]

MEMORANDUM SUBMITTED TO THE PALESTINE ROYAL COMMISSION ON BEHALF OF THE JEWISH AGENCY FOR PALESTINE / Jewish Agency for Palestine. London – 1936. BJ-28-136 1 – 9 – ne IDC [956]

MEMORANDUM SUR LE PROGRAMME DE DEVELOPPEMENT ECONOMIQUE DE LA GRECE / Greece. Ministere de la Coordination – Athenes. 1962. BD-709 1 – 9 – ne IDC [338]

MEMORANDUM. THE WRITE OF CERTIORARI IN THE DISTRICT OF COLUMBIA IN RELATION TO THE INTERSTATE COMMERCE COMMISSION / Daish, John Broughton – Washington, Sudwarth, 1906 18 p. LL-604 – 1 – us L of C Photodup [340]

MEMORANDUM TO CONSIDER THE QUESTION OF A TRIGONOMETRICAL SURVEY OF THE DOMINION / Association of Dominion Land Surveyors – Prepared by a committee appointed at the fifth annual meeting of the Dominion Land Surveyors Association, held at Ottawa, March 15th and 16th, 1888. Montreal: J. Lovell, 1888. 02163. (Pre-1900 Canadiana) – 9 – cn C.I.H.M. [971]

MEMORANDUM TO THE GUAM COMMISSION ON SELF-DETERMINATION : PREPARED....AT THE REQUEST OF THE GUAM COMMISSION ON SELF-DETERMINATION TO RESPOND TO THE ZAFREN STUDY / Leibowitz, Arnold H – 3 Oct 1986 – 1mf – 9 – $1.50 – LLMC 82-100B Title 30 – us L.L.M.C. [324]

MEMORANDUM TO THE PERMANENT MANDATES COMMISSION AND TO THE SECRETARY OF STATE FOR THE COLONIES, 23 JUL 1937 / Arab Higher Committee – Jerusalem. 1937. BJ-28-137 1 – 9 – ne IDC [956]

MEMORANDUM TO UNITED NATIONS / Jewish Agency for Palestine – Jewish Agency Statement at San Francisco Conference. Tel Aviv. 1945. BJ-28-142 1 – 9 – ne IDC [956]

MEMORIA / Argentine Republic. Contaduria General de la Nacion – Buenos Aires. 1912-1947. Incomplete – 1 – us NY Public [073]

MEMORIA / Chile. Inspeccion Jeneral de Tierras i Colonizacion – 1903-20. 12v – 1 – 46.00 – us L of C Photodup [330]

MEMORIA / Chile. Ministerio de Justica – 1900-41. Incomplete – 1 – 92.00 – us L of C Photodup [340]

MEMORIA / Chile. Ministerio de Relaciones Exteriores – 1834-1960 – 1 – $460.00 – us L of C Photodup [972]

MEMORIA / Costa Rica. Secretaria de Educacion Publica – 74v. 1866 67-1951 – 1 – 184.00 – us L of C Photodup [370]

MEMORIA / Navarro Muzquiz, Fernando – Badajoz, 1934. Tip.La Ec.Alberto Merino – 1 – sp Bibl Santa Ana [946]

MEMORIA / Sociedad Economica Amigos del Pais – 1889 – 9 – $1.50f – sp Bibl Santa Ana [946]

MEMORIA / Uruguay. Ministerio de defense nacional.. – Montevideo. 1873-1927. (Wanting 1874-78, 1882-89, 1895-1914) – 1 – 88.00 – us L of C Photodup [972]

MEMORIA.. / Badajoz. Spain. Diputacion Provincial – 1882 – 9 – 1.50f – sp Bibl Santa Ana [946]

MEMORIA 1942 / Monte de Piedad y Caja General de Ahorros – Badajoz: Tip. Vda. de A. Arqueros, 1943 – 1 – sp Bibl Santa Ana [946]

MEMORIA 1957 / Caritas Diocesana – Caceres: Tip. La Minerva, 1958 – 1 – sp Bibl Santa Ana [240]

MEMORIA. 1958 / Caja de Ahorros y Monte de Piedad. Plasencia – Plasencia: Graf. Sandoval, 1959 – 1 – sp Bibl Santa Ana [946]

MEMORIA 1959 / Carta Diocesanas – Caceres: Tip. La Minerva, 1960 – 1 – sp Bibl Santa Ana [240]

MEMORIA, 1964 / Ministerio Obras Publicas – Badajoz: Doncel, I.G., 1965 – sp Bibl Santa Ana [946]

MEMORIA 1969. PRESUPUESTOS 1970 / Parroquia del Salvador – Plasencia: Imp. Padilla, 1970 – 1 – sp Bibl Santa Ana [946]

MEMORIA, 1970 / Cooperativa del campo Nuestra Senora de Botoa y de la Caja Rural de Badajoz – Badajoz: Graficas Tejado, 1970 – sp Bibl Santa Ana [240]

MEMORIA. 1970 / Mutua Cerealista de Caceres – (Tambien 1960, 1974) – Caceres: Imp. La Minerva, 1971 – 1 – sp Bibl Santa Ana [946]

MEMORIA 1970 Y CINCUENTA ANIVERSARIO DE SU PRECURSORA LA CAJA RURAL DE AHORROS Y PRESTAMOS DEL SINDICATO CATOLICO AGRARIO / Cooperativa del campo Nuestra Senora de Botoa y de la Caja Rural de Badajoz – Badajoz: Graf. Tejado, 1971 – sp Bibl Santa Ana [240]

MEMORIA 1971 / Terpresa – Caceres: Edit. Extremadura, 1971 – 1 – sp Bibl Santa Ana [946]

MEMORIA 1972 / Caja de Ahorros y Monte de Piedad. Plasencia – Plasencia: T. Sanguino, 1973 – 1 – sp Bibl Santa Ana [946]

MEMORIA 1972 / Cooperativa del campo Nuestra Senora de Botoa y de la Caja Rural de Badajoz – Badajoz: Imp. Vicente Campini, 1973 – sp Bibl Santa Ana [240]

MEMORIA 1972 / Terpresa – Caceres: Imp. La Minerva, 1973 – 1 – sp Bibl Santa Ana [946]

MEMORIA 1973 / Mutua Cerealista de Caceres – Caceres: Imp. La Minerva, 1974 – 1 – sp Bibl Santa Ana [946]

MEMORIA 1974 / Caceres. Terpresa – Aldea Moret (Caceres): Imp. Linea 21, 1975 – 1 – sp Bibl Santa Ana [946]

MEMORIA 1974 / Delegacion Provincial de Educacion y Ciencia – Caceres: Impreso en Linea XXI, 1975 – sp Bibl Santa Ana [370]

MEMORIA, 1974 / Delegacion de Mutualidades Laborales – Caceres: T. Extremadura, 1975 – 1 – sp Bibl Santa Ana [331]

MEMORIA 1975 / Caja Rural de Almendralejo – Almendralejo: Ventura Rodriguez, 1975 – sp Bibl Santa Ana [946]

MEMORIA 1976 / Mutua Cerealista de Caceres – Caceres: Tip. La Minerva, 1977 – 1 – sp Bibl Santa Ana [946]

MEMORIA, 1976 / Tecnicos Empresarios promotores de Empresas – Aldea-Moret: Imp. Linea 21, 1977 – sp Bibl Santa Ana [060]

MEMORIA 1977 / Camara Privada de Compensacion Bancaria de Caceres – Caceres: Imp. T. Rodriguez, 1978 – sp Bibl Santa Ana [946]

MEMORIA 1980 / Caceres. Hermandad de Donantes de Sangre. San Pedro de Alcantara – Caceres: Editorial Extremadura, 1981 – 1 – sp Bibl Santa Ana [946]

MEMORIA 1948-49 / Congregacion de la Inmaculada San Luis y San Estanislao – Madrid: Nuevas Graficas, s.a. – 1 – sp Bibl Santa Ana [946]

MEMORIA A LARGO PLAZO : PROCESOS DE RECUPERACION Y BUSQUEDA / Vallejo Seco, Guillermo – 3mf – 9 – Pta2,000.00 – 84-85422-45-7 – sp Pentalfa [999]

MEMORIA ACERCA DE LA NECESIDAD Y UTILIDAD DE UNA ASOCIACION GENERAL DE PROFESORES DE CIENCIAS MEDICAS / Nieto y Serrano, M – Madrid, 1840 – 1mf – 9 – sp Cultura [610]

MEMORIA ACERCA DEL ESTADO DEL INSTITUTO DE SEGUNDA ENSENANZA DE LA PROVINCIA DE BADAJOZ DURANTE EL CURSO DE 1872 A 1873 LEIDA...POR EL DIRECTOR DON... / Saa Maldonado, Manuel – Badajoz: Imp. Jose Santamaria, 1873 – 1 – sp Bibl Santa Ana [946]

MEMORIA ACERCA DEL MOVIMIENTO DE LOS NEGOCIOS EN LOS ANOS 1962-1963 / Camara Oficial de Comercio e Industria de Badajoz – Badajoz: Tip. Grafica Extremena, 1966 – sp Bibl Santa Ana [946]

MEMORIA ACERCA DEL MOVIMIENTO DE LOS NEGOCIOS EN LOS ANOS 1964-1965 / Camara Oficial de Comercio e Industria de Badajoz – Badajoz: Alfonso Mangas Cuenda, 1966 – sp Bibl Santa Ana [946]

MEMORIA ACERCA...INSTITUTO...SEGUNDA ENSENANZA DE BADAJOZ...1878 A 1879... CATEDRATICO Y DIRECTOR / Ordonez de Adrian, Valeriano – Badajoz: Tip. Vda. de Arteaga, 1880 – 1 – sp Bibl Santa Ana [946]

MEMORIA ACERCA...SOCIEDAD.. / Merino de Torres, Alberto – 1884 – 9 – 1.50f – sp Bibl Santa Ana [830]

MEMORIA, ANO 1937 / Circulo de Artesanos – (Caceres): Tip. El Noticiero, s.a. 1938 – sp Bibl Santa Ana [946]

MEMORIA, ANO 1938 / Circulo de Artesanos. – Caceres: Tip. La Minerva, . 1939? – sp Bibl Santa Ana [946]

MEMORIA, ANO 1946 / Union de Conductores Deautomoviles de la Provincia de Caceres – Tip. El Noticiero, s.a., 1947 – sp Bibl Santa Ana [946]

MEMORIA, ANO 1958 / Circulo de Artesanos – Caceres: Imp. Moderna, 1958 – 1 – sp Bibl Santa Ana [946]

MEMORIA, ANO 1959 / Coria-Caceres. Caritas Diocesana – Caceres: Tip. La Minerva, 1960 – sp Bibl Santa Ana [240]

MEMORIA, ANO 1967, 1968 / Consejo Superior de Investigaciones Cientificas – Badajoz: Consejo Superior de Investigaciones Cientificas. Centro de Investigaciones Agricolas, 1968 – 1 – sp Bibl Santa Ana [630]

MEMORIA, ANO 1976 / Hogar Extremeno en Paris. Paris – Plasencia: Imp. Garcilasso, 1977 – sp Bibl Santa Ana [946]

MEMORIA, ANO DE 1978 / Diputacion Provincial – Badajoz: Imp. Diputacion Provincial, 1978 – sp Bibl Santa Ana [946]

MEMORIA ANUAL DE LA SANTA INFANCIA. EJERCICIO 1966-67 / Santa Infancia – Badajoz: Tip. Clasica, 1968 – sp Bibl Santa Ana [240]

MEMORIA BIOGRAFICHE DEGLI SCULTORI, ARCHITETTI, PITTORI EC. NATIVI DI CARRARA E DI ALTRI LUOGHI DELLA PROVINCIA DI MASSA / Campori, G – Modena. 1873. BO-973 1 – 9 – ne IDC [920]

MEMORIA COMERCIAL Y ESTADISTICA RELATIVA AL ESTADO DE LOS NEGOCIOS EN LA PROVINCIA DE BADAJOZ / Camara Oficial de Comercio e Industria Badajoz – Badajoz: Graf. Iberia, 1960 – sp Bibl Santa Ana [946]

MEMORIA COMERCIAL Y ESTADISTICA RELATIVA AL ESTADO DE LOS NEGOCIOS EN LA PROVINCIA DE BADAJOZ / Camara Oficial de Comercio e Industria de Badajoz – Badajoz: Tip. A. Mangas, 1970 – sp Bibl Santa Ana [338]

MEMORIA CORRESPONDIENTE AL EJERCICIO DE 1948 / Monte de Piedad y Caja General de Ahorros – Badajoz: Tipografia Viuda de Antonio Arqueros, 1949 – 1 – sp Bibl Santa Ana [946]

MEMORIA CORRESPONDIENTE AL EJERCICIO DE 1961 / Caja de Ahorros y Monte de Piedad. Caceres – Caceres: Tip. Extremadura, 1962 – 1 – sp Bibl Santa Ana [946]

MEMORIA CORRESPONDIENTE AL EJERCICIO DE 1962 / Caja de Ahorros y Monte de Piedad. Caceres – Caceres: Tip. Extremadura, 1963 – 1 – sp Bibl Santa Ana [946]

MEMORIA CORRESPONDIENTE AL EJERCICIO DE 1963 / Caja de Ahorros y Monte de Piedad. Caceres – Caceres: Tip. Extremadura, 1964 – sp Bibl Santa Ana [946]

MEMORIA CORRESPONDIENTE AL EJERCICIO DE 1964 / Caja de Ahorros y Monte de Piedad. Caceres – Caceres: Tip. Edit. Extremadura, 1966 – sp Bibl Santa Ana [946]

MEMORIA CORRESPONDIENTE AL EJERCICIO DE 1967 APROBADA EN JUNTA GENERAL DE ACCIONISTAS CELEBRADA EL 18-2-1968 / Caja Rural de Ahorros y Prestamos de Almendralejo – Almendralejo: F. Rodriguez, 1968 – sp Bibl Santa Ana [946]

MEMORIA. CURSO 1957-58 / Instituto Laboral Garcia de Paredes – Caceres: Imprenta Moderna, 1959 – 1 – sp Bibl Santa Ana [946]

MEMORIA DE 1976 / Caja de Ahorros y Monte de Piedad. Caceres – Caceres: Tip. Extremadura, 1977 – 1 – sp Bibl Santa Ana [946]

MEMORIA DE ACTIVIDADES / Camara Oficial Sindical Agraria – Badajoz: Imp. Inca, 1965 – sp Bibl Santa Ana [630]

MEMORIA DE ACTIVIDADES / Camara Oficial Sindical Agraria – Badajoz: Imp. Inca, 1966 – sp Bibl Santa Ana [630]

MEMORIA DE ACTIVIDADES / Delegacion Provincial de Mutualidades Laborales (de Badajoz) – Ejercicio 1967. Badajoz: Tip. Manuel Barrena, 1968 – 1 – sp Bibl Santa Ana [946]

MEMORIA DE ACTIVIDADES, 1967 / Camara Oficial Sindical Agraria – Badajoz: Imprenta Inca, 1968 – sp Bibl Santa Ana [630]

MEMORIA DE ACTIVIDADES, 1968 / Camara Oficial Sindical Agraria – Badajoz: Imprenta Inca, 1969 – sp Bibl Santa Ana [630]

MEMORIA DE ACTIVIDADES 1975-76 / Club Taurino Emeritense – Plasencia: Graf. Sandoval, 1976 – 1 – sp Bibl Santa Ana [060]

MEMORIA DE LA ESCUELA ELEMENTAL DE TRABAJO DE MERIDA – Merida: A. Rodriguez, 1946 – 1 – sp Bibl Santa Ana [370]

MEMORIA DE LA ESCUELA MUNICIPAL DE ARTES Y OFICIOS DE BADAJOZ. LEIDA EN EL ACTO DE LA APERTURA DEL CURSO 1896-97 / Santos Redondo, Ignacio – Badajoz: Imp., Lit. y Enc. de Uceda Hermanos, 1897 – 1 – sp Bibl Santa Ana [946]

MEMORIA DE LAS ACTIVIDADES DESARROLLADAS POR LA JUNTA DIRECTIVA... / Caceres. Asociacion Nacional de Invalidos Civiles – Caceres: Tip. La Minerva, 1960 – sp Bibl Santa Ana [060]

MEMORIA DE LAS OBRAS DE RESTAURACION Y AMPLIACION DE LA IGLESIA PARROQUIAL DE NUESTRA SENORA DE LOS ANGELES DE FUENTES DE LEON. ANOS 1940-1943 / Corrales Lazaro, Juan Luis – Sevilla: Imp. La Gavidia, 1943 – 1 – sp Bibl Santa Ana [240]

MEMORIA DE LAS VIRTUDES Y USOS DE LA RAIZ DE LA PLANTA ILAMADA EN EL PERU BEJUCO E LA ESTRELLA / Ruiz Lopez, Hipolito – Madrid, 1805 – 1mf – 9 – ne IDC [580]

MEMORIA DE LAS VIRTUDES Y USOS DE LA RAIZ DE LA PLANTA ILAMADA YALLHOY EN EL PERU / Ruiz Lopez, Hipolito – Madrid, 1805 – 1mf – 9 – ne IDC [580]

MEMORIA DE LOS TRABAJOS EFECTUADOS POR LA MISMA DURANTE EL ANO 1889 / Sociedad Economica de Amigos del Pais de Badajoz – Badajoz: Tip. Lit. y enc. La Industria, 1890 – sp Bibl Santa Ana [331]

MEMORIA DE LOS TRABAJOS PRACTICADOS. UNA CASA-BASILICA ROMANO-CRISTIANA / Melida, Jose Ramon – Madrid: Tip.Rev.de Archivo, Bib. y Museos, 1917 – 1 – sp Bibl Santa Ana [946]

MEMORIA DE LOS TRABAJOS REALIZADOS / Instituto Geografico – Madrid, 1867 – 2mf – 9 – sp Cultura [910]

MEMORIA DE LOS TRABAJOS REALIZADOS DURANTE EL ANO 1940... / Camara Oficial de la Propiedad Urbana de la Provincia de Caceres – Caceres: Imp. El Noticiero, 1941 – 1 – sp Bibl Santa Ana [946]

MEMORIA DE LOS TRABAJOS REALIZADOS DURANTE EL ANO 1959... / Colegio Oficial de Agentes Comerciales – Caceres: Imp. Moderna, 1960 – 1 – sp Bibl Santa Ana [946]

MEMORIA DE LOS TRABAJOS REALIZADOS DURANTE EL ANO 1960 LEIDA Y APROBADA EN SESION DEL 25 DE MARZO DE 1961 / Colegio Oficial de Agentes Comerciales – Caceres: Imprenta Moderna, 1961 – 1 – sp Bibl Santa Ana [946]

MEMORIA DE LOS TRABAJOS REALIZADOS DURANTE EL EJERCICIO DE 1931, QUE SE ELEVA AL EXCMO. SR. MINISTRO DE TRABAJO Y PREVISION / Camara Oficial de la Propiedad Urbana – Badajoz: Tip. Artes Graficas, 1932 – 1 – sp Bibl Santa Ana [331]

MEMORIA DE...ANO 1979 / Olivenza. Escuelas Parroquiales Sagrado Corazon – Badajoz: Imp. Provincial, 1980 – 1 – sp Bibl Santa Ana [370]

MEMORIA DEL A.ESC.37-38 / Colegio de San Jose de Villafranca de los Barros (Badajoz) – Badajoz: Tip.Espanola, 1938 – 1 – sp Bibl Santa Ana [946]

MEMORIA DEL ANO 1945 / Union de Conductores de Automoviles de la Provincia de Caceres – Caceres: Tip. El Noticiero, s.a. 1946 – sp Bibl Santa Ana [946]

MEMORIA DEL ANO ESCOLAR 1932-1933 / Colegio de San Jose. Estremoz (Portugal) – Lisboa: Bertrand (Irmaos) L.D.A., 1933 – 1 – sp Bibl Santa Ana [946]

MEMORIA DEL ANO ESCOLAR 1933-34 / Colegio de San Jose. Estremoz (Portugal) – Lisboa: Bertraund (Irmaos), 1934 – 1 – sp Bibl Santa Ana [946]

MEMORIA DEL ANO ESCOLAR 1934-35 / Colegio de San Jose. Estremoz (Portugal) – Lisboa: Bertrand (IRMAS) LDA, 1935 – 1 – sp Bibl Santa Ana [946]

MEMORIA DEL ANO ESCOLAR 1935-36 / Colegio de San Jose. Estremoz (Portugal) – Lisboa: Betrand (Irmaos), 1936 – 1 – sp Bibl Santa Ana [946]

MEMORIA DEL ANO ESCOLAR 1936-37 / Colegio de San Jose de Villafranca (Badajoz) – Sevilla: Raimundo Blanco, 1937 – 1 – sp Bibl Santa Ana [946]

MEMORIA DEL ANO ESCOLAR 1938-39 / Colegio de San Jose de Villafranca (Badajoz) – Badajoz – 1 – sp Bibl Santa Ana [946]

MEMORIA DEL ANO ESCOLAR DE 1927 A 1928 / Colegio de San Jose de Villafranca (Badajoz) – Madrid: Tip. de Alberto Fontana, 1928 – 1 – sp Bibl Santa Ana [946]

MEMORIA DEL ANO ESCOLAR DE 1928 A 1929 / Colegio de San Jose de Villafranca (Badajoz) – Madrid: Tip. de A. Fontana, 1929 – 1 – sp Bibl Santa Ana [946]

MEMORIA DEL ANO ESCOLAR DE 1929 A 1930 / Colegio de San Jose de Villafranca (Badajoz) – Madrid: Tip. Catolica de A. Fontana, 1930 – 1 – sp Bibl Santa Ana [946]

MEMORIA DEL ANO ESCOLAR DE 1931-1932 / Colegio de San Jose de Villafranca (Badajoz) – Lisboa: Bertraund (Irmaos), 1932 – 1 – sp Bibl Santa Ana [946]

MEMORIA DEL CONGRESO NACIONAL / Sociedades Hispanas Confederadas de Ayuda a Espana – Celebrado durante los dias 6 y 7 de noviembre de 1937 en la ciudad de Pittsburgh, Pa., U.S.A. Brooklyn, NY, 1937. Fiche W1164. (Blodgett Collection of Spanish Civil War Pamphlets) – 9 – us H.U. College Libr [946]

MEMORIA DEL CURSO 1935 A 1936, 1936 A 1937 / Instituto Nacional de 2nd Ensenanza. Caceres – Caceres: Tip. La Minerva, S.A. – sp Bibl Santa Ana [946]

MEMORIA DEL CURSO 1966 / Escuela Diocesana de Catequetica – Badajoz: Graf. Nemesio Jimenez, 1966 – sp Bibl Santa Ana [240]

MEMORIA DEL CURSO 1959-60 / Instituto Laboral Garcia de Paredes – Caceres: Imp. Moderna, 1960 – 1 – sp Bibl Santa Ana [946]

MEMORIA DEL CURSO 1971-72 / Montanchez, Escuela Hogar Leon Leal – Caceres: Tip. Extremadura, 1972 – 1 – sp Bibl Santa Ana [370]

MEMORIA DEL CURSO ACADEMICO 1955-56 / Ministerio de Educacion Nacional. Centro de Ensenanza Media y Profesional de Azuaga – Azuaga: Tip. Domenech, 1956 – sp Bibl Santa Ana [370]

MEMORIA DEL CURSO ACADEMICO 1956-57 / Instituto Laboral General Moscardo – Azuaga: Tip. Domenech, 1957 – 1 – sp Bibl Santa Ana [370]

MEMORIA DEL CURSO ACADEMICO 1960-61, 1961-62 / Instituto Laboral Garcia de Paredes – Caceres: Imp. Moderna, 1963 – 1 – sp Bibl Santa Ana [370]

MEMORIA DEL CURSO DE 1934 A 1935 / Instituto Nacional de 2nd Ensenanza. Caceres – Caceres: Tip. La Minerva, s.a. – sp Bibl Santa Ana [946]

MEMORIA DEL EJERCICIO DE 1927 LERIDA... PRESUPUESTO ORDINARIO PARA 1928 / Villafranca de los Barros. Ayuntamiento – Villafranca de los Barros: Imprenta Ventura Rodriguez, 1928 – 1 – sp Bibl Santa Ana [946]

MEMORIA DEL EJERCICIO MISIONAL 1974 / Plasencia. Diocesis – Plasencia: Imp. Padilla, 1975 – 1 – sp Bibl Santa Ana [240]

MEMORIA DEL EJERCICIO MISIONAL 1976 / Plasencia. Diocesis – Plasencia: Imp. Padilla D. Merino, 1977 – sp Bibl Santa Ana [240]

MEMORIA DEL EJRCICIO MISIONAL DE 1968 / Diocesis – Caceres: Imp. La Victoria, 1969 – 1 – sp Bibl Santa Ana [240]

MEMORIA DEL INSTITUTO DE SEGUNDA ENSENANZA DE LA PROVINCIA DE BADAJOZ LEIDA EN LA APERTURA DEL CURSO...1867 A 1868 POR EL DOCTOR D...DIRECTOR / Ordonez de Adrian, Valeriano – Badajoz: Imp. Jose Santamaria, 1867 – 1 – sp Bibl Santa Ana [946]

MEMORIA DEL INSTITUTO...BADAJOZ / Ordonez de Adrian, Valeriano – (1880 ed.1.50f; 9) – 1863 – 9 – 1.50f – sp Bibl Santa Ana [440]

MEMORIA DEL JURADO...DONA ISABEL 2 / Belmonte, Francisco – 1861 – 9 – $1.50f – sp Bibl Santa Ana [946]

MEMORIA DEL MUSEO DE BELLAS ARTES DE CACERES / Sanguino y Michel, Juan – Caceres: Santos Floriano Gonzalez, 1919 – 1 – sp Bibl Santa Ana [700]

MEMORIA. EJERCICIO 1958 / Mutua Cerealista de Caceres – Caceres: Tip. La Minerva, 1959 – 1 – sp Bibl Santa Ana [946]

MEMORIA. EJERCICIO 1959 / Caceres. Mutua Cerealistica – Caceres: Tip. La Minerva, 1960 – sp Bibl Santa Ana [946]

MEMORIA. EJERCICIO 1960 / Caceres. Mutua Aseguradora de transportistas – Caceres: Tip. La Minerva, 1961 – 1 – sp Bibl Santa Ana [946]

MEMORIA. EJERCICIO 1962 / Mutua Aseguradora de Transportistas – Caceres: Imp. Moderna, 1963 – 1 – sp Bibl Santa Ana [380]

MEMORIA. EJERCICIO 1964 / Caceres. Mutua Aseguradora de Transportes – Caceres Imprenta Moderna, 1965 – 1 – sp Bibl Santa Ana [380]

MEMORIA. EJERCICIO 1968 / Mutua Aseguradora de Transportistas – Caceres: Imprenta Moderna, 1969 – 1 – sp Bibl Santa Ana [946]

MEMORIA. EJERCICIO 1969 / Mutua Aseguradora de Transportistas – Caceres: Imp. Moderna, 1970 – 1 – sp Bibl Santa Ana [946]

MEMORIA. EJERCICIO 1970 / Mutua Extremana de Vehiculos – Caceres: Imprenta Moderna, 1970 – 1 – sp Bibl Santa Ana [946]

MEMORIA EJERCICIO 1972 / Mutua Extremena de Vehiculos – Caceres: I. Moderna, 1973 – 1 – sp Bibl Santa Ana [946]

MEMORIA. EJERCICIO 1973 / Caceres. Mutua extremena de Vehiculos – Caceres: Imp. Moderna, 1974 – 1 – sp Bibl Santa Ana [946]

MEMORIA EJERCICIO 1975 / Tecnicos Empresarios promotores de Empresas – Caceres: Imp. Linea 21, 1976 – 1 – sp Bibl Santa Ana [946]

MEMORIA. EJERCICIO 1975 / Mutua Extremena de Seguros. Caceres – Plasencia: Imp. Sanchez Rodrigo, 1976 – 1 – sp Bibl Santa Ana [946]

MEMORIA EJERCICIO 1977 / Mutua Extremena de Seguros. Caceres – Plasencia: Imp. Sanchez Rodrigo, 1978 – sp Bibl Santa Ana [946]

MEMORIA EJERCICIO 1978 / Extremena de Seguros – (Tambien ano 1976) – Plasencia: Imp. Sanchez Rodrigo, S.A. 1979 – 1 – sp Bibl Santa Ana [946]

MEMORIA EJERCICIO 1979 / Mutua Extremena de Seguros. Caceres – Plasencia: Tip. Sanchez Rodrigo, 1980 – 1 – sp Bibl Santa Ana [946]

MEMORIA. EJERCICIO DE 1966 / Caja Rural de Ahorros y Prestamos Nuestra Senora de Botoa – Badajoz: Imp. Arqueros, 1967 – sp Bibl Santa Ana [240]

MEMORIA. EJERCICIOS DE 1956-57 / Caja Rural de Ahorros y Prestamos Nuestra Senora de Botoa – Badajoz: Arqueros, 1958 – sp Bibl Santa Ana [240]

MEMORIA ELEVADA AL CONSEJO DE MINISTROS / Instituto Geografico – Madrid, 1869 – 11mf – 9 – sp Cultura [910]

MEMORIA EN QUE SE REBATEN CALUMNIAS CONTRA LA JUNTA CENTRAL / Jovellanos, Melchor Gaspar de – 1811 – 1mf – 9 – Pta1,000.00 – 84-7848-121-4 – sp Pentalfa [946]

MEMORIA ESTADISTICA DE LA REPUBLICA DE GUATEMALA. ANO 1893 – Guatemala, 1895 – 16mf – 9 – sp Cultura [972]

MEMORIA ESTATISTICA SOBRE OS DOMINIOS PORTUGUEZES NA AFRICA ORIENTAL / Botelho, S X. – Lisboa. 1835. BA-281 2 – 8 – ne IDC [910]

MEMORIA GRAECA HERCULANENSIS : CUM TITULORUM AEGYPTI PAPYRORUM CODICUM DENIQUE TESTIMONIIS COMPARATAM / Croenert, Wilhelm – (In Latin and Greek. Includes bibliographical references and indexes) – Lipsiae: In Aedibus B G Teubneri, 1903 – 1mf – 9 – 0-8370-9218-3 – 1986-3218 – us A.T.L.A. [450]

MEMORIA HISTORICA...HISTORIA / Delgado, Antonio – 1849 – 9 – 1.50f – sp Bibl Santa Ana [900]

MEMORIA HISTORICA...PUBLICA...DON JAN BRAVO MURILLO / Perez de Anaya, Francisco – 1857 – 9 – 1.50f – sp Bibl Santa Ana [946]

MEMORIA HISTORICAS DE LA CIUDAD DE BARCELONA. TOMO 3 / Capmany Montpalau, Antonio – 1792 – 1mf – 9 – Pta1,000.00 – 84-7848-052-8 – sp Pentalfa [946]

MEMORIA INSTRUCTIVA DE LOS MEDIOS DE PRECAVER LOS MALES RESULTAS DE UN TEMPORAL EXCESIVA MENTE HUMEDO / Ased y Latorre, A – Zaragoza, 1784 – 1mf – 9 – sp Cultura [610]

MEMORIA LEIDA EL DIA 16 DE SEPTIEMBRE EN LA APERTURA DEL CURSO DE 1867 A 1868 EN EL INSTITUTO DE SEGUNDA ENSENANZA DE CACERES, POR... / Gomez de Santana, Indalecio – Caceres: Imp. El Eco de Extremadura, 1867 – 1 – sp Bibl Santa Ana [946]

MEMORIA LEIDA EN LA JUNTA GENERAL DE SOCIOS, CELEBRADA EL DIA 3 DE MARZO DE 1907 / Caja Rural de Ahorros y Prestamos de Fuente de Cantos – Badajoz: Tip. Uceda Hermanos, 1907 – sp Bibl Santa Ana [946]

MEMORIA LEIDA POR EL SECRETARIO DON NICOLAS SANCHEZ ASENSIO EN LA JUNTA GENERAL (16 DE) FEBRERO 1949 / Sanchez Asensio, Nicolas – Caceres: Imp. Moderna – sp Bibl Santa Ana [615]

MEMORIA LEIDA POR SOBRE LA ACCION DEL PARA PRODUCIR ENERGIA MECANICA Y SOBRE SI POR LA LUZ... / Martin Moreno, Saturnino – Barcelona: Nagsa, 1929 – 1 – sp Bibl Santa Ana [333]

MEMORIA PRACTICA SOBRE LAS CALENTURAS PUTRIDAS DEL AMPURDAN / Pons, F – Barcelona, 1790 – 4mf – 9 – sp Cultura [610]

MEMORIA PRESENTADA EN EL 14TH CONGRESO INTERNACIONAL DE MEDICINA POR... / Bejarano y Sanchez, Eloy – Madrid: Imprenta del Colegio Nacional de Sordomudos y de Ciegos, 1903 – 1 – sp Bibl Santa Ana [610]

MEMORIA PRESENTADA POR LA COMISION PROVINCIAL DE BADAJOZ EN LA SEGUNDA REUNION SEMESTRAL CORRESPONDIENTE AL ANO ECONOMICO DE 1882-1883 – Badajoz: La Minerva Extremena, 1883 – sp Bibl Santa Ana [946]

MEMORIA PRESENTADA POR LA JUNTA DIRECTIVA A LA ASAMBLEA GENERAL / Badajoz – 1898 – 9 – 1.50f – sp Bibl Santa Ana [946]

MEMORIA QUE LA COMISION PROVINCIAL PRESENTA A LA DIPUTACION PROVINCIAL DE BADAJOZ EN LA PRIMERA REUNION SEMESTRAL DEL ANO ECONOMICO DE 1886-1887 – Badajoz: La Minerva Extremena, 1886 – sp Bibl Santa Ana [946]

MEMORIA QUE SUSCRIBE EL ALCALDE-PRESIDENTE Y EL...PARA DAR A CONOCER CON DETTALE LA LABOR EXTRAORDINARIA...HASTA FINALES DE 1958 / Pedroso de Acin. Ayuntamiento – Caceres: Imprenta La Minerva, 1959 – 1 – sp Bibl Santa Ana [946]

MEMORIA QUINQUENIO 1940-1944 / Patronato Local de Formacion Profesional. Caceres – Caceres: Imp. Garcia Floriano, 1945 – sp Bibl Santa Ana [946]

MEMORIA REGLAMENTARIA DE SECRETARIA GENERAL 1967 / Badajoz – Badajoz: Graf. Tejado, 1968 – sp Bibl Santa Ana [946]

MEMORIA SOBRE LA ARNICA DE LOS MONTES LEIDA EN LA REAL ACADEMIA DE CIENCIAS NATURALES Y ARTES DE BARCELONA / Sala, A – Barcelona, 1786 – 1mf – 9 – sp Cultura [610]

MEMORIA SOBRE LA CALENTURA AMARILLA... QUE INVADIO A CADIZ Y SEVILLA / Cibat, A – Barcelona, 1804 – 2mf – 9 – sp Cultura [610]

MEMORIA SOBRE LA CRIA CABALLAR / Alvarez de Sotomayor, Agustin – 1851 – 9 – 1.50f – sp Bibl Santa Ana [946]

MEMORIA SOBRE LA ESTADISTICA GENERAL DE ESPANA / Instituto Geografico – Madrid, 1857 – 8mf – 9 – sp Cultura [946]

MEMORIA SOBRE LA LEGITIMA CALAGUALA Y OTRAS DOS RAICES QUE CON EL MISMO NOMBRE NOS VIENEN DE LA AMERICA MERIDIONAL / Ruiz Lopez, Hipolito – MADRID, 1805 – 1mf – 9 – ne IDC [580]

MEMORIA SOBRE LA NATURALEZA DEL CONTAGIO DE LA FIEBRE AMARILLA... / Cibat, A – Barcelona, 1805 – 3mf – 9 – sp Cultura [616]

MEMORIA SOBRE LAS PLANTAS BARRILLERAS DE ESPANA / Lagasca y Segura, M – Madrid. 1817. B-5558 2 – 8 – ne IDC [580]

MEMORIA SOBRE...GUADALUPE / Garcia de Atocha, Jose – 1838 – 9 – 1.50f – sp Bibl Santa Ana [972]

MEMORIA SOBRE...MONARQUIA / Donoso Cortes, Juan Francisco – 1832 – 9 – 1.50f – sp Bibl Santa Ana [946]

MEMORIA Y ACTAS DE LAS REUNIONES PRO-HISPANIDAD CELEBRADAS EN EL REAL MONASTERIO DE GUADALUPE...MAYO DE 1948 / Asociacion Amigos de Guadalupe – Caceres: Tip. Edit. Extremadura, 1948 – 1 – sp Bibl Santa Ana [946]

MEMORIA Y BALANCE DEL PRIMER EJERCICIO PARA DAR CUENTA EN LA JUNTA GENERAL QUE HA DE CELEBRARSE EL DIA 28 DE JULIO DE 1907 / Villafranca de los BarrosEl Credito Extremeno – Villafranca: Imp. Ventura Rodriguez, 1907 – 1 – sp Bibl Santa Ana [946]

MEMORIA Y BALANCE DEL TERCER EJERCICIO SOCIAL, LEIDA Y APROBADA EN LA JUNTA GENERAL DE SOCIOS...1909 / Caja Rural de Ahorros y Prestamos de Almendralejo – Badajoz: Tip. Uceda Hermanos, 1909 – sp Bibl Santa Ana [946]

MEMORIA Y BALANCE GENERAL EN 30 DE JUNIO DE 1938. 37 EJERCICIO SOCIAL. LEIDA Y APROBADA...1938 / Electrica berlanguena S.A. Berlanga, Badajoz – Llerena: Pap. y Lib. de Carmen Leon, 1938 – sp Bibl Santa Ana [946]

MEMORIA Y BALANCE PRESENTADO POR EL SINDICATO EN LA JUANTA GENERAL ORDINARIA DE 8 DE DICIEMBRE COMPLEMENTADA CON DATOS HASTA EL 31 DE DICIEMBRE DE 1918 / Villafranca de los Barros. Comunidad de Labradores – Villafranca de los Barros: Imp. Felix Rodriguez s.a.Tambien, 1919,1920, 1924,1925,1926,1927,1929 – 1 – sp Bibl Santa Ana [946]

MEMORIA Y BALANCES 1975 / Cooperativa y Caja Rural Comarcal del Campo Nuestra Senora de Piedraescrita. Espinaso – Trujillo: Imp. Gexme, 1976 – 1 – sp Bibl Santa Ana [240]

MEMORIA Y CUENTA / Venezuela. Ministerio de educacion nactional – Caracas. 1884-1929 30. (Wanting 1892-95, 1900-01 and scattered issues) – 1 – 470.00 – us L of C Photodup [972]

MEMORIA Y CUENTA GENERAL 1947-48 / Cofradia de Ntra. Sra. de la Montana, Real. Caceres – Caceres: Imp. Garcia Floriano, s.a., 1948 – sp Bibl Santa Ana [946]

MEMORIA Y CUENTA GENERAL QUE PRESENTA LA JUNTA DIRECTIVA DE LA COFRADIA A LA GENERAL DE HERMANOS. POR LA GESTION...1949 / Real Cofradia de Nuestra Senora de la Santisima Virgen de la Montana – Caceres: Imp. Vda. Garcia Floriano, 1949 – 1 – sp Bibl Santa Ana [946]

MEMORIA Y CUENTA GENERAL...ANO 1942 / Cofradia de Ntra. Sra. de la Montana, Real. Caceres – Caceres: Imp. Garcia Floriano, 1942 – sp Bibl Santa Ana [946]

MEMORIA Y CUENTA GENERAL...ANO 1949 / Cofradia de Ntra. Sra. de la Montana, Real. Caceres – Caceres: Imp. Vda. Garcia Floriano, 1950 – sp Bibl Santa Ana [946]

MEMORIA Y DATOS ESTADISTICOS CORRESPONDIENTES AL ANO 1934 / Monte de Piedad y Caja General de Ahorros – Badajoz: Tip. Vda. de A. Arqueros, 1935 – 1 – sp Bibl Santa Ana [946]

MEMORIA Y DATOS ESTADISTICOS CORRESPONDIENTES AL ANO 1936 / Monte de Piedad y Caja General de Ahorros de Badajoz – Badajoz: Tip. Vda. de A. Arqueros, 1937 – 1 – sp Bibl Santa Ana [946]

MEMORIA Y DATOS ESTADISTICOS CORRESPONDIENTES AL ANO 1952 / Caja de Ahorros y Monte de Piedad. Caceres – Caceres: Editorial Extremadura, s.a., 1953 – sp Bibl Santa Ana [946]

MEMORIA Y DATOS ESTADISTICOS CORRESPONDIENTES AL ANO 1954 / Caja Ahorros y Monte de Piedad de Caceres – Caceres: Tip. Extremadura, s.a., 1955 – sp Bibl Santa Ana [060]

MEMORIA Y DATOS ESTADISTICOS CORRESPONDIENTES AL ANO DE 1925 / Monte de Piedad y Caja General de Ahorros de Badajoz – Almendralejo: Imp. Lit. M. Soto, 1926 – 1 – sp Bibl Santa Ana [946]

MEMORIA Y DATOS ESTADISTICOS CORRESPONDIENTES AL ANO DE 1955 / Caja de Ahorros y Monte de Piedad. Caceres – Caceres: Tip. Editorial Extremadura, 1955 – 1 – sp Bibl Santa Ana [946]

MEMORIA Y DATOS ESTADISTICOS CORRESPONDIENTES AL EJERCICIO 1958 / Caja de Ahorros y Monte de Piedad – Salamanca: Cervantes, 1959 – 1 – sp Bibl Santa Ana [946]

MEMORIA Y DATOS ESTADISTICOS CORRESPONDIENTES AL EJERCICIO DE 1957 / Caja de Ahorros y Monte de Piedad – Caceres: Tip. Extremadura, 1958 – 1 – sp Bibl Santa Ana [946]

MEMORIA Y EJERCICIO DE 1961 / Caja Rural de Ahorros y Prestamos Nuestra Senora de Botoa – Badajoz: Imprenta Arqueros, 1962 – sp Bibl Santa Ana [240]

MEMORIA Y...EJERCITO DE ESTREMADURA (SIC) / Ramirez, Pedro – 1842 – 9 – 1.50f – sp Bibl Santa Ana [355]

MEMORIA...23 DE SEPTIEMBRE...DE 1867 A 1868...COLEGIO DE ISABEL 2... / Gomez de Santana, Indalecio – Caceres: Imp. El Eco de Extremadura, 1867 – 1 – sp Bibl Santa Ana [946]

MEMORIA...1916 DEL AYUNTAMIENTO DE DOS HERMANAS (SEVILLA)... / Rodriguez Monino, Rafael – Sevilla: Tip. La Exposicion, 1916 – sp Bibl Santa Ana [946]

MEMORIA...CACERES / Gomez de Santana, Indalecio – 1867 – 9 – 1.50f – sp Bibl Santa Ana [946]

MEMORIA...CLASE OBRERA...PLACENTINA / Pinto Sanchez, Evaristo – 1885 – 9 – 1.50f – sp Bibl Santa Ana [890]

MEMORIA...COMISION PROVINCIAL DE BADAJOZ...ECONOMICO – (1886. 1.50f; 9) – 1883 – 9 – 1.50f – sp Bibl Santa Ana [380]

MEMORIA...CONFERENCIAS DE PARIS..COMPARACION...TARIFAS ARANCELARIAS DE ESPANA Y FRANCIA / Navaro Reverter, J – Madrid, 1893 – 9 – sp Cultura [380]

MEMORIA...CURSO DE 1889 A 1890... / Gonzalez Cuadrado, Antonio – Badajoz: Tip. La Industria, 1890 – 1 – sp Bibl Santa Ana [946]

MEMORIA...DERECHO...DUQUES DE CADAVAL EN EL PLEITO – 1864 – 9 – 1.50f – sp Bibl Santa Ana [946]

MEMORIA-EJERCICIO 1961 / Mutua Aseguradora de Transportistas – Caceres: Imp. Moderna, 1962 – 1 – sp Bibl Santa Ana [946]

MEMORIA...EXPOSICION LONDRES / Montesino, Cipriano S – 1863 – 9 – 1.50f – sp Bibl Santa Ana [910]

MEMORIA...EXPOSICION...LONDRES / Lujan, Francisco – 1863 – 9 – $1.50f – sp Bibl Santa Ana [900]

MEMORIA...FERROCARRIL MERIDA-SEVILLA / Una Sarton, Juan – 1881 – 9 – 1.50f – sp Bibl Santa Ana [946]

MEMORIA-INDICE DE LOS TRABAJOS EFECTUADOS DURANTE LOS ANOS 1938-1944. INCLUSIVES / Junta Provincial de Fomento Pecuario – Badajoz: Junta Provincial de Fomento Pecuario – 1 – sp Bibl Santa Ana [331]

MEMORIA-INFORME 1970 / Diocesis – Plasencia: Imp. La Victoria, 1971 – 1 – sp Bibl Santa Ana [946]

MEMORIA-INFORME 1973. RECONCILIACION? SER JUSTO Y FRATERNAL CON TODOS / Caritas Diocesana – Plasencia: Imp. Gercilasso, 1974 – 1 – sp Bibl Santa Ana [240]

MEMORIA...INSTITUTO DE 2A ENSENANZA / Gomez de Santana, Indalecio – 1865 – 9 – 1.50f – sp Bibl Santa Ana [370]

MEMORIA...INSTITUTO DE BADAJOZ / Gonzalez Cuadrado, Antonio – (1882. 1.50f; 9. 1883. 1.50f; BSA; 9. 1884. 1.50f; BSA; 9. 1885. 1.50f; BSA; 9. 1887. 1.50f; BSA; 9. 1888. 1.50f; BSA; 9. 1890. 1.50f; BSA; 9. 1891. 1.50f; BSA; 9) – 1881 – 9 – 1.50f – sp Bibl Santa Ana [370]

MEMORIA...INSTITUTO DE BADAJOZ / Muntada y Andrade, Jose – 1861 – 9 – 1.50f – sp Bibl Santa Ana [440]

MEMORIA...INSTITUTO DE BADAJOZ / Suarez Quintero, Valentin – 1892-98 – 9 – 1.50f – sp Bibl Santa Ana [946]

LE MEMORIAL – 1939-20 aout 1944. suivi de: La Republique. 21 aout-3 sept 1944. suivi de: La Depeche democratique. 4 sept 1944-31 dec 1945 1er janv 1946. Saint-Etienne – 1 – fr A.C.R.P.P. [073]

LE MEMORIAL – ou Recueil historique, politique et litteraire, feuille de tous les jours. Par MM. de La Harpe, de Vauxcelles et Fontanes. no. 1-108. Paris. mai-sept 1797 – 1 – fr A.C.R.P.P. [073]

MEMORIAL / Browne, Chad – 1638-1888. Providence, Rhode Island. 280p – 1 – 9.80 – us Baptist [240]

MEMORIAL / Ulloa Gofin, Alvaro F – 1675 – 9 – 1.50f – sp Bibl Santa Ana [920]

MEMORIAL AJUSTADO / Lopez Lobo, Juan – 1771 – 9 – 1.50f – sp Bibl Santa Ana [890]

MEMORIAL AJUSTADO.. / Candido de Rivera, J – 1719 – 9 – 1.50f – sp Bibl Santa Ana [946]

MEMORIAL AJUSTADO AL EXPEDIENTE DE CONCORDIA...MESTA CON LA DIPUTACION PROVINCIAL...EXTREMADURA / Campomanes, Conde de – 1783 – 9 – 1.50f – sp Bibl Santa Ana [946]

MEMORIAL AJUSTADO DE LOS ACTOS ACREEDORES...IGLESIA COLEGIAL Y HOSPITAL DE ZAFRA / Coronel, Ambrosio – 1767 – 9 – sp Bibl Santa Ana [360]

MEMORIAL AJUSTADO ENTRE...JUAN HERRERA CON DON LUIS DE MENESES – 1724? – 9 – $1.50f – sp Bibl Santa Ana [946]

MEMORIAL AJUSTADO HECHO EN VIRTUD DE DECRETO DEL CONSEJO / Lopez Lobo, Juan – San Ildefonso, 1764 – 1 – sp Bibl Santa Ana [946]

MEMORIAL AJUSTADO...CONVENTO DEL AMPARO DE ALMENDRALEJO...DONA MARIANA GOLFIN...DUQUE DE VILLAHERMOSA Y D. GARCIA GOLFIN...VINCULO DE DONA JUANA... / Fernandez de Quesada, Juan Antonio – Madrid, 1787 – 1 – sp Bibl Santa Ana [946]

MEMORIAL AJUSTADO...DEL PLEYTO...DE LA ALISEDA...CON LA PROPIA VILLA, PUEBLOS DE SU SEXMERIA Y DEL SENOR FISCAL SOBRE EXCUSION DE SORTEOS, CONTRIBUCION DE SOLDADOS...Y QUE CACERES CON SU SEXMERIA ENTREGUE...A ALISEDA / Caballero y Tejerina, Antonio – 1777 – 9 – 1.50f – sp Bibl Santa Ana [946]

MEMORIAL AJUSTADO...JUAN SANTOS CUENDA...Y DUQUESA DE MEDINACELI – 9 – 1.50f – sp Bibl Santa Ana [946]

MEMORIAL AJUSTADO...MARQUES DE PERALES / Torres, Manuel de – 1795 – 9 – 1.50f – sp Bibl Santa Ana [946]

MEMORIAL AJUSTADO...MESTA CON LA DIPUTACION...EXTREMADURA – (Tomo II.1783. 1.50f; 9) – 1783. Tomo I – 9 – 1.50f – sp Bibl Santa Ana [946]

MEMORIAL AL REY PIDIENDOLE SE REMITA LA CAUSA AL NUNCIO Y A OTROS PRELADOS Y DA CUENTA DE SU VIDA / Caceres, Diego de – 1641 – 9 – $1.50f – sp Bibl Santa Ana [946]

MEMORIAL AND BIOGRAPHICAL HISTORY OF DALLAS COUNTY – Chicago, 1892. Texas Reel 10. (The Cox Library Collection) – 5 – us Americana [978]

MEMORIAL AND BIOGRAPHICAL HISTORY OF JOHNSON AND HILL COUNTIES – Chicago, 1892. Texas Reel 11. (The Cox Library Collection) – 5 – us Americana [920]

MEMORIAL AND BIOGRAPHICAL HISTORY OF MCLENNAN FALLS, BELL AND CORYELL COUNTIES – Chicago, 1893. Texas Reel 12. (The Cox Library Collection) – 5 – us Americana [978]

MEMORIAL AND BIOGRAPHICAL HISTORY OF NORTHERN CALIFORNIA – Chicago, 1891. California Reel 6. (The Cox Library Collection) – 5 – us Americana [978]

A MEMORIAL AND BIOGRAPHICAL HISTORY OF THE COAST COUNTIES OF CENTRAL CALIFORNIA / Barrows, H D & Ingersoll, LA – 1893 – 1r – 1 – $50.00 – B40038 – us Library Micro [978]

MEMORIAL AND BIOGRAPHICAL HISTORY OF THE COUNTIES OF FRESNO, TULARE AND KERN – Chicago, 1892. California Reel 9. (The Cox Library Collection) – 5 – us Americana [978]

MEMORIAL AND BIOGRAPHICAL HISTORY OF THE COUNTIES OF FRESNO, TULARE AND KERN, 1891 – Fresno Co, CA. 1891 – 1r – 1 – $50.00 – B40219 – us Library Micro [978]

A MEMORIAL AND BIOGRAPHICAL HISTORY OF THE COUNTIES OF MERCED, STANISLAUS, CALAVERAS, TUOLUMNE AND MARIPOSA – Lewis, CA. 1892 – 1r – 1 – $50.00 – B40212 – us Library Micro [978]

A MEMORIAL AND BIOGRAPHICAL HISTORY OF THE COUNTIES OF SANTA BARBARA, SAN LUIS OBISPO AND VENTURA, CALIFORNIA / Storke, Yda A – Chicago: Lewis Publ. Co., 1891. California Reel 31. (The Cox Library Collection) – 5 – us Americana [978]

MEMORIAL AND BIOGRAPHICAL RECORD / G.A. Ogle and Co – Compendium of Biography, Local and National. Chicago, 1897. South Dakota Reel 3. The Cox Library Collection – 5 – us Americana [978]

MEMORIAL AND BIOGRAPHICAL RECORD OF BUTLER, POLK, SEWARD, YORK AND FILLMORE COUNTIES / G.A. Ogle and Co – Chicago, 1899. Nebraska Reel 6. The Cox Library Collection – 5 – us Americana [978]

MEMORIAL AND BIOGRAPHICAL RECORD OF COLUMBIA, SAUK AND ADAMS COUNTIES / G.A. Ogle and Co – Chicago, 1901. Wisconsin Reel 7. The Cox Library Collection – 5 – us Americana [978]

A MEMORIAL AND BIOGRAPHICAL RECORD OF IOWA – Chicago: 1896. Iowa Reel 2. (The Cox Library Collection) – 5 – us Americana [978]

A MEMORIAL AND BIOGRAPHICAL RECORD OF KANSAS CITY AND JACKSON COUNTY – Chicago, 1896. Missouri Reel 20. (The Cox Library Collection) – 5 – us Americana [920]

MEMORIAL AND BIOGRAPHICAL RECORD OF SOUTH DAKOTA / G.A. Ogle and Co – Chicago, 1898. South Dakota Reel 4. The Cox Library Collection – 5 – us Americana [978]

MEMORIAL AND BIOGRAPHICAL REVIEW OF MERCED, STANISLAUS, CALAVERAS, TUOLUMNE, AND MARIPOSA COUNTIES – Chicago, 1892. California Reel 8. (The Cox Library Collection) – 5 – us Americana [978]

MEMORIAL AND BIOGRAPHICAL SKETCHES / Clarke, James Freeman – Boston: Houghton, Osgood, 1880, c1878 – 1mf – us A.T.L.A. [240]

MEMORIAL AND FAMILY HISTORY OF ERIE COUNTY / Genealogical Publishing Co – Biographical and genealogical. Buffalo, 1906-08. Vols. 1-2. New York Reel 15. (The Cox Library Collection) – 5 – us Americana [978]

MEMORIAL AND GENEALOGICAL RECORD OF DODGE AND JEFFERSON COUNTIES – Chicago: 1894. Wisconsin Reel 10. (The Cox Library Collection) – 5 – us Americana [978]

MEMORIAL BAPTIST CHURCH. COLUMBIA, MISSOURI : CHURCH RECORDS – Scrapbook and history. 1944-86 – 1 – 163.17 – us Baptist [240]

MEMORIAL BAPTIST CHURCH. MURRAY, KENTUCKY : CHURCH RECORDS – 1937-56. Roll book. 1942-56 – 1 – 32.22 – us Baptist [240]

MEMORIAL BAPTIST CHURCH. SAVANNAH, GEORGIA : CHURCH RECORDS – 1959-62 – 1 – 37.17 – us Baptist [240]

MEMORIAL BIOGRAPHIES OF THE NEW ENGLAND HISTORIC GENEALOGICAL SOCIETY – v3, 1883. Biog. of members of the society who died between 1856 & 1859. Indexed, 9 fiches. F-0339 – 9 – us A.G.L.L. [920]

LE MEMORIAL CATHOLIQUE – Ouvrage puis Recueil periodique. Par l'Abbe Gerbet, de Salinis, de Lamennais, etc. Paris. 1824-29 – 1 – fr A.C.R.P.P. [073]

MEMORIAL CATHOLIQUE – Paris: Bureau du Memorial catholique. v1-12. 1824-29. SEM16P246 – 1r – 5 – Can$20.00 – cn Bibl Nat [240]

MEMORIAL COLLECTION OF NEWSPAPERS ON MICROFILM CHRONICLING EVENTS OF THE ASSASSINATION / Kennedy, John F – 22-26 Nov 1963 – 1 – us UMI [977]

MEMORIAL COLLECTION OF SERMONS / Park, Edwards Amasa – Boston: Pilgrim Press, c1902 – 1mf – us A.T.L.A. [240]

MEMORIAL DE LA POLITICA NECESARIO Y UTIL RESTAURACION A LA REPUBLICA DE ESPANA / Gonzalez de Cellorigo, M – Valladolid, 1600 – 3mf – 9 – sp Cultura [320]

LE MEMORIAL DE L'ALLIER – Journal politique, litteraire, industriel, agricole et commercial. Annonces judiciaires et avis divers. Moulins. 12 mars 1848-49 – 1 – fr A.C.R.P.P. [073]

UN MEMORIAL DEL I. MARQUES DE LA CONQUISTA / Munoz de San Pedro, Miguel – (Juan Fernando Pizarro). Badajoz. (Imprenta de la Diput. Prov.), 1969. Sep. de la Rev. de Estudios Extremenos – 1 – sp Bibl Santa Ana [946]

MEMORIAL DES FAMILLES CASGRAIN, BABY ET PERRAULT DU CANADA / Casgrain, Philippe Baby – Quebec: C. Darveau, 1898. 00538. (Pre-1900 Canadiana) – 9 – cn C.I.H.M. [920]

MEMORIAL DES HONNEURS ETRANGERS CONFERES A DES CANADIENS OU DOMICILIES DE LA PUISSANCE DU CANADA / Bibaud, Francois Marie Uncas Maximilien – Montreal: Beauchemin and Valois, 1885. SEM16P5 – 1r – 5 – Can$9.00 – cn Bibl Nat [971]

MEMORIAL DES SEANCES – v.1-105. 1873-1977 – 1 – us A.T.L.A. [240]

LE MEMORIAL DES VICISSITUDES ET DES PROGRES DE LA LANGUE FRANCAISE EN CANADA / Bibaud, Francois Marie Uncas Maximilien – Montreal: J B Byette..., 1879. SEM105P459 – 2mf – 9 – Can$4.50 – cn Bibl Nat [971]

LE MEMORIAL DIPLOMATIQUE – Paris. -w. 17 May 1863-1 Sep 1870; 6 Jan 1872-25 Jan 1914. 50 reels – 1 – uk British Libr Newspaper [072]

MEMORIAL DU GRANDE-DUCHE DE LUXEMBOURG – 1958-70 – 24r – 1 – us Ross [324]

MEMORIAL HISTORICO ESPANA9OL / Academia de la Historia. Madrid – Madrid. v. 13-48. 1861-1918 – 1 – us NY Public [946]

MEMORIAL HISTORICO ESPANOL : COLLECCION DE DOCUMENTOS, OPUSCULOS Y ANTIGUEDADES / Academia de la Historia. Madrid – v1-48 1851-1918 – 1 – $230.00 – us L of C Photodup [946]

MEMORIAL HISTORICO ESPANOL / Madrid. Academia de la Historia – v13-48. 1861-1918 – 5r – 1 – us Ross [946]

THE MEMORIAL HISTORY OF HARTFORD COUNTY, CONNECTICUT, 1633-1884 / ed by Trumbull, J Hammond – Boston: Edw. L. Osgood, 1886. v1-2. Connecticut Reel 3. (The Cox Library Collection) – 5 – us Americana [978]

MEMORIAL HISTORY OF LOUISVILLE / Johnston, J Stoddard – Chicago: American Biographical Publishing Co., 1896. 2v. Kentucky Reel 7. (The Cox Library Collection) – 5 – us Americana [978]

MEMORIAL HISTORY OF UTICA / Bagg, M M – Syracuse, D. Mason and Co., 1892. New York Reel 24. (The Cox Library Collection) – 5 – us Americana [978]

MEMORIAL JUDICIAIRE DE LA LOIRE – 20 sept 1845-29 dec 1947. Suivi de: L'Avenir republicain. 1848-2/3 janv 1852. Suivi de: L'Industrie. 4 janv 1852-31 dec 1853. Suivi de: Memorial de la Loire. 1854-1919 – 1 – fr A.C.R.P.P. [073]

Memorial Lawn Cemeteries Association. Emporia, Kansas *see* RECORDS OF INTERMENTS

MEMORIAL OF AMBROSE SPENCER, FORMER CHIEF JUSTICE OF THE SUPREME COURT OF THE STATE OF NEW YORK. – Albany: Munsell, 1849. 78p. LL-364 – 1 – us L of C Photodup [340]

MEMORIAL OF FIRST BAPTIST CHURCH, NASHVILLE, TENN., 1820-63 / Howell, Robert Boyte C – 2014p – 1 – 70.49 – us Baptist [240]

MEMORIAL OF FRANCIS M. SCOTT. / Masten, Arthur H – New York? 1923? 9p. LL-418 – 1 – us L of C Photodup [340]

A MEMORIAL OF HORACE TRACY PITKIN / Speer, Robert Elliott – New York: Fleming H Revell, c1903 – 1mf – 9 – 0-8370-6617-4 – 1986-0617 – us A.T.L.A. [920]

A MEMORIAL OF JAMES M. HAWORTH : SUPERINTENDENT OF UNITED STATES INDIAN SCHOOLS / Vail, A L – Kansas City: H.N. Farey, 1886 – 1mf – us A.T.L.A. [370]

THE MEMORIAL OF MOSES ON MOUNT NEBO / Saller, Sylvester J – 3vols. 1941 – 9 – $30.00 – us I.R.C. [930]

MEMORIAL OF MR. DAVID L. DODGE : CONSISTING OF AN AUTOBIOGRAPHY / Dodge, David Low – Boston: Published only for the family by S.K. Whipple, 1854 – 1mf – us A.T.L.A. [240]

MEMORIAL OF NATHANIEL W. TAYLOR, D.D. : THREE SERMONS / Bacon, Leonard et al – New Haven: T.H. Pease, 1858 – 1mf – us A.T.L.A. [240]

MEMORIAL OF PATRICK HUES MELL *see* MISCELLANEOUS BOOKS AND PAMPHLETS

MEMORIAL OF THE DE FORSYTHS DE FRONSAC / Fronsac, Frederic Gregory Forsyth – Boston: s.n., 1897 (Boston: Rockwell and Churchill). 03261. (Pre-1900 Canadiana) – 9 – cn C.I.H.M. [971]

A MEMORIAL OF THE FUTTEHGURH MISSION : AND HER MARTYRED MISSIONARIES: WITH SOME REMARKS ON THE MUTINY IN INDIA / Walsh, John Johnston – Philadelphia: Joseph M Wilson; London: James Nisbet, 1859, c1858 – 1mf – 9 – 0-8370-6536-4 – 1986-0536 – us A.T.L.A. [950]

A MEMORIAL OF THE WESLEYAN METHODIST NEW CONNEXION; CONTAINING A SHORT ACCOUNT OF THE CIRCUIT PREACHERS WHO HAVE DIED... / Salt, W – Nottingham, 1823. ix/256p – 3mf – 9 – ne IDC [240]

MEMORIAL OLIVENTINO / Rincon Jimenez, Jesus – Badajoz: A.Arqueros, 1917 – 1 – sp Bibl Santa Ana [946]

MEMORIAL QUE DEDICAN A MONASTERIOS... RELIGION – 1726? – 9 – 1.50f – sp Bibl Santa Ana [240]

MEMORIAL QUE DEDICAN...MONASTERIOS DE...GUADALUPE...PARRAL...ESCORIAL Y OTROS...AL...NUNCIO... – s.l., s.i., s.a. 1691? – 1 – sp Bibl Santa Ana [240]

MEMORIAL QUE ELEVO A S.M. EN 1673 DON INIGO ANTONIO ARGUELLO CARVAJAL... / Solar y Taboada, Antonio – Madrid: Tip. de Archivos, 1932 – 1 – sp Bibl Santa Ana [920]

MEMORIAL RECORD OF ALABAMA / Brant, Fuller and Co – Concise account of the State's Political, Military, Professional and Industrial Progress. Madison: 1893. Vols. 1-2. Alabama Reel 1. (The Cox Library Collection) – 5 – us Americana [978]

MEMORIAL RECORD OF BUTLER COUNTY / Record Publishing Co – Biographical sketches. Chicago, 1894. Ohio Reel 16. (The Cox Library Collection) – 5 – us Americana [978]

MEMORIAL RECORD OF LICKING COUNTY / Record Publishing Co – Biographical sketches. Chicago: 1894. Ohio Reel 42. (The Cox Library Collection) – 5 – us Americana [978]

MEMORIAL RECORD OF THE COUNTIES OF DELAWARE, UNION AND MORROW – Chicago, 1895. Ohio Reel 29. The Cox Library Collection) – 5 – us Americana [978]

MEMORIAL RECORD OF THE COUNTIES OF FARIBAULT, MARTIN, WATONWAN AND JACKSON – Chicago, 1895. Minnesota Reel 5. (The Cox Library Collection) – 5 – us Americana [978]

MEMORIAL RECORD OF THE COUNTY OF CUYAHOGA AND THE CITY OF CLEVELAND – Chicago, 1894. Ohio Reel 25. (The Cox Library Collection) – 5 – us Americana [978]

MEMORIAL RECORD OF THE FATHERS OF WISCONSIN / Atwood & Tenney – Madison: David Atwood, 1880. Wisconsin Reel 2. (The Cox Library Collection) – 5 – us Americana [978]

A MEMORIAL RECORD OF THE NORTHERN PENINSULA OF MICHIGAN – Chicago, 1895. Michigan Reel 2. (The Cox Library Collection) – 5 – us Americana [978]

MEMORIAL RECORD OF WESTERN KENTUCKY – Chicago, 1904. 2v. Kentucky Reel 5. (The Cox Library Collection) – 5 – us Americana [978]

Memorial Sloan-Kettering Cancer Center *see* CLINICAL BULLETIN

MEMORIAL SOBRE LAS ANALOGIAS Y DIFERENCIAS...ENTRE EL GARROTILLO...Y LA ANGINA... / Iglesias, M – Madrid, 1862 – 1mf – 9 – sp Cultura [610]

A MEMORIAL TO CHARLES PAGE / U.S. Court of Appeals for the Ninth Circuit – San Francisco? 1912 47 p. LL-1105 – 1 – us L of C Photodup [340]

MEMORIAL VOLUME OF THE FIRST FIFTY YEARS OF THE AMERICAN BOARD OF COMMISSIONERS FOR FOREIGN MISSIONS – (Includes index) – Boston: The Board, 1861 – 2mf – 9 – 0-8370-6613-1 – 1986-0613 – us A.T.L.A. [240]

MEMORIAL VOLUME OF THE WESTMINSTER ASSEMBLY 1647-1897 : CONTAINING ELEVEN ADDRESSES DELIVERED BEFORE THE GENERAL ASSEMBLY OF THE PRESBYTERIAN CHURCH IN THE UNITED STATES, AT CHARLOTTE, N.C., IN MAY, 1897 – 3rd ed. Richmond, VA: Presbyterian Committee of Publ, c1897 – 1mf – 9 – 0-8370-8780-5 – 1986-2780 – us A.T.L.A. [240]

MEMORIAL...ANO DE 1633 / Chumacero y Carrillo, Juan – 1 – sp Bibl Santa Ana [946]

MEMORIAL...CONSEJO...VICENTO PAINO Y.. – 1771 – 9 – 1.50f – sp Bibl Santa Ana [946]

MEMORIAL...D. ISIDRO DE CARVAJAL / Fernandez Cortes, Gil – 1768 – 9 – 1.50f – sp Bibl Santa Ana [920]

IL MEMORIALE DELLA LINGUA / Pergamini, Giacomo – Venetia, 1602 (mf ed 1992) – 10mf – 9 – DM112.00 – 3-89131-058-7 – gw Fischer [440]

MEMORIALE FRATRIS WALTERI DE COVENTRIA (RS58) = THE HISTORICAL COLLECTIONS OF WALTER OF COVENTRY / Walter Of Colveltry; ed by Stubbs, W – v1 1872 v2 1873 – Dfl32.00v – ne Slangenburg [240]

MEMORIAL...JUAN PABLO DE AZLOR CON DON FERNANDO GOLFIN – 1830 – 9 – $1.50f – sp Bibl Santa Ana [946]

MEMORIAL...P. CACERES / Serena, Juan de la, et al – 1642 – 9 – 1.50f – sp Bibl Santa Ana [920]

MEMORIAL-RECUEIL SPECIAL / Luxembourg. (Grand Duchy) – Luxemburg. Index. 1958-1959 – 1 – us NY Public [324]

MEMORIALS : JOHN BOWEN / Bowen, John – Late Bishop of Sierra Leone. 1862 – 1 – us A.T.L.A. [240]

MEMORIALS / Ray, John – 1846 – 1 – uk Microform Academic [580]

MEMORIALS OF A TOUR ON THE CONTINENT, 1820 / Wordsworth, William – London: Longman, Hurst, Rees, Orme, and Brown, 1822 – 1 roll – 1 – 1-55879-304-6 – uk Libr Preservation [910]

MEMORIALS OF ACADIA COLLEGE AND HORTON ACADEMY FOR THE HALF-CENTURY 1828-1878 – Montreal: Dawson Bros., 1881. 00028. (Pre-1900 Canadiana) – 9 – cn C.I.H.M. [370]

MEMORIALS OF BAPTIST MARTYRS / Belcher, Joseph – Philadelphia: American Baptist Publication Society, c1854 – 1mf – us A.T.L.A. [240]

MEMORIALS OF CARDINAL MANNING / ed by Oldcastle, John – London: Burns & Oates; New York: Catholic Publ Society, 1892 – 1mf – 9 – 0-8370-6690-5 – 1986-0690 – us A.T.L.A. [920]

MEMORIALS OF CHRISTIAN LIFE IN THE EARLY AND MIDDLE AGES = DENKWUERDIGKEITEN AUS DER GESCHICHTE DES CHRISTENTHUMS UND DES CHRISTLICHEN LEBENS : INCLUDING HIS "LIGHT IN DARK PLACES" / Neander, August – (In English. Includes bibliographical references) – London: Henry G Bohn, 1852 – 2mf – 9 – 0-8370-6287-X – 1986-0287 – us A.T.L.A. [240]

MEMORIALS OF FOREIGN MISSIONARIES OF THE PRESBYTERIAN CHURCH USA / Rankin, William – (Includes index) – Philadelphia: Presbyterian Board of Publication and Sabbath-School Work, 1895 – 2mf – 9 – 0-8370-6604-2 – 1986-0604 – us A.T.L.A. [240]

MEMORIALS OF HENRY 7 (RS10) = HISTORIA REGIS HENRICI SEPTIMI : A BERNARDO ANDREA THOLOSATE CONSCRIPTA; NECNON ALIA QUAEDAM AD EUNDEM REGEM SPECTANTIA / ed by Gairdner, J – 1858 – Dfl35.00 – ne Slangenburg [941]

MEMORIALS OF HENRY THE FIFTH (RS11) : KING OF ENGLAND / ed by Cole, C A – (Contains: Vita Henrici 5: Roberto Redmanno Auctore- Versus Rhytmici In Laudem Regis Henrici – Elmhami's, Liber Metricus De Henrico 5) – 1858 – Dfl22.00 – ne Slangenburg [941]

MEMORIALS OF JAMES HENDERSON..., MEDICAL MISSIONARY TO CHINA / Henderson, J – London, Ed.5 1869 – 3mf – 9 – ne IDC [610]

MEMORIALS OF JAMES HOGG, THE ETTRICK SHEPHERD / Garden, Mary Gray Hogg – London: A. Gardner, 1885 – 1r – 1 – 1-55879-629-0 – uk Libr Preservation [920]

MEMORIALS OF JOHN MCLEOD CAMPELL, D.D. : BEING SELECTIONS FROM HIS CORRESPONDENCE / Jeens, C H; ed by Campbell, Donald – London: Macmillan, 1877 – 2mf – us A.T.L.A. [240]

MEMORIALS OF LONDON AND LONDON LIFE IN THE 13TH, 14TH, AND 15TH CENTURIES / Riley, H T – 1868. H 1302 2 – 8 – ne IDC [025]

MEMORIALS OF LONDON AND LONDON LIFE, IN THE 13TH, 14TH, AND 15TH CENTURIES / London. Corporation of London – Being a series of extracts, local, social, and political, from the early archives of the City of London, A.D.1276-1419.Selected, transl., and ed. by Henry Thomas Riley... London: Longmans, Green and Co., 1868. lxxviii,706p. Title in red and black – 1 – us U.W. Library [941]

MEMORIALS OF MISSIONARY LABOURS IN WESTERN AFRICA, THE WEST INDIES, AND AT THE CAPE OF GOOD HOPE.. / Moister, William – 3rd ed. 1866 – 1 – us A.T.L.A. [240]

MEMORIALS OF PRISON LIFE / Finley, James B – Cincinnati: L. Swormstedt & J.H. Power, 1851, c1850 – 1mf – us A.T.L.A. [360]

MEMORIALS OF R. HAROLD A. SCHOFIELD, FIRST MEDICAL MISSIONARY TO SHAN-SI, CHINA; CHIEFLY COMP. FROM HIS LETTERS AND DIARIES... / Schofield, A T – London, 1898 – 3mf – 9 – ne IDC [610]

MEMORIALS OF ST DUNSTAN, ARCHBISHOP OF CANTERBURY (RS63) / ed by Stubbs, W – 1874 – Dfl39.00 – ne Slangenburg [920]

MEMORIALS OF ST EDMUNDS ABBEY (RS96) / ed by Arnold, T – (v1 1890 v2 1892 Dfl30.00. v3 1896 Dfl32.00) – ne Slangenburg [240]

MEMORIALS OF SEVENTEENTH AND EIGHTEENTH CENTURY SOUTH CAROLINA LAND TITLES / South Carolina. Department of Archives and History – 12r. M-12 – 1 – $75.00r – Out-of-state orders: us Scholarly Res – us SC Archives [978]

MEMORIALS OF SEVENTEENTH- AND EIGHTEENTH- CENTURY SOUTH CAROLINA LAND TITLES – (5r index on 16 mm) – South Carolina Depratment of Archives and History, 1995 – 7r – 1 – $1,020.00 – D3319 – us Scholarly Res [975]

MEMORIALS OF THE EMPIRE OF JAPAN / Japan – Hakluyt Society. 16th and 17th centuries – 7 – uk Microform Academic [950]

MEMORIALS OF THE GRAND RIVER VALLEY / Everett, Franklin – Chicago: The Chicago Legal News Company, 1878. Michigan Reel 3.(The Cox Library Collection) – 5 – us Americana [978]

MEMORIALS OF THE HON. ION KEITH-FALCONER : LATE LORD ALMONER'S PROFESSOR OF ARABIC IN THE UNIVERSITY OF CAMBRIDGE, AND MISSIONARY TO THE MOHAMMEDANS OF SOUTHERN AFRICA / Sinker, Robert – (Includes index) – new ed. Cambridge: Deighton, Bell; London: George Bell, 1903 – 1mf – 9 – 0-8370-6517-8 – 1986-0517 – us A.T.L.A. [920]

MEMORIALS OF THE LIFE OF PETER BOEHLER : BISHOP OF THE CHURCH OF THE UNITED BRETHREN / Lockwood, J P – London: Wesleyan Conference Office, 1868 – 1mf – us A.T.L.A. [240]
MEMORIALS OF THE REIGN OF KING HENRY 6 (RS56) : OFFICIAL CORRESPONDENCE OF THOMAS BEKYNTON, SECRETARY TO HENRY 6 / Thomas Beckington; ed by Williams, G – (v1 1872 Dfl35.00. v2 1872 Dfl30.00) – ne Slangenburg [941]
MEMORIALS OF THE SOUTH SAXON SEE AND CATHEDRAL CHURCH OF CHICHESTER / Stephens, William Richard Wood – London: R. Bentley, 1876 – 1mf – us A.T.L.A. [240]
MEMORIALS OF TWO SISTERS : SUSANNA AND CATHERINE WINKWORTH / ed by Shaen, Margaret J – London, New York: Longmans, Green, 1908 – 1mf – us A.T.L.A. [240]
MEMORIALS OF WESLEYAN METHODIST MINISTERS : OR, THE YEARLY DEATH ROLL FROM 1777 TO 1840 / Hall, J – London, 1876 – 4mf – 9 – ne IDC [240]
MEMORIALS, PERSONAL AND HISTORICAL OF ADMIRAL LORD GAMBIER. WITH ORIGINAL LETTERS FROM WILLIAM PITT FIRST LORD CHATHAM, LORD NELSON, LORD CASTLEREAGH, LORD MULGRAVE, HENRY FOX FIRST LORD HOLLAND, THE RIGHT HON. GEORGE CANNING / Chatterton, Henrietta Georgiana Marcia – Ed., from family papers, by Lady Chatterton. 2v. 1861 – 9 – $20.00 – uk Libr Preservation [920]
MEMORIALS RESPECTING THE WORKING OF THE LAWS GOVERNING REFORMATORY AND INDUSTRIAL SCHOOLS / Bernier, Bernard – Submitted to the Executive of the Province of Quebec at its sitting of the 29th of March, 1892 in the name of the Hospice Saint Charles de Quebec. Quebec?, 1893? 03359. (Pre-1900 Canadiana) – 9 – cn C.I.H.M. [971]
MEMORIAL...SAN GABRIEL / Moles, Juan B – 1592 – 9 – 1.50f – sp Bibl Santa Ana [240]
MEMORIA...MARIA DOLORES CABRERA... BIENES...FUNDACIONES / Maestre, Vicente – 1848 – 9 – 1.50f – sp Bibl Santa Ana [946]
MEMORIA...MOLINO-PANADERIA...HABITANTES / Passot, Luis – 1881 – 9 – 1.50f – sp Bibl Santa Ana [946]
MEMORIAS / Academia das Sciencias de Lisboa – Lisboa. 1780-1856 – 3 – us Readex [500]
MEMORIAS / Godoy, Manuel – 1836 – 9 – 1.50f – sp Bibl Santa Ana [946]
MEMORIAS / Heine, Heinrich – Madrid: Calpe, 1920 – 1r – 1 – us U.W. Library [920]
MEMORIAS / Instituto Oswaldo Cruz – v. 1-53. 1909-1955 – 1,5,6 – us Princeton Micro [610]
MEMORIAS ACADEMICAS DE LA REAL SOCIEDAD DE MEDICINA... / Gonzalez y Centeno, V – Sevilla, 1788 – 10mf – 9 – sp Cultura [610]
MEMORIAS ANUALES, 1968. DOMUND JUSTICIA Y PAZ / Secretariado Diocesano de Misiones de Badajoz – Badajoz: Tip. clasica, 1968 – sp Bibl Santa Ana [240]
MEMORIAS DE ARQUITECTURA... / Blondel – Paris, SA – 3mf – 9 – sp Cultura [720]
MEMORIAS DE LA COMISION DEL MAPA GEOLOGICO DE ESPANA. MEMORIA GEOLOGICA-MINERA DE LA PROVINCIA DE CACERES / Egozcue, J & Mallada, DL – Madrid: Manuel Tello, 1876 – 1 – sp Bibl Santa Ana [550]
MEMORIAS DE LAS ENFERMEDADES EXPERIMENTADAS EN SEVILLA EN 1785 / Nieto de Pina, C – Sevilla, 1786 – 2mf – 9 – sp Cultura [610]
MEMORIAS DE LAS ENFERMEDADES EXPERIMENTADAS EN SEVILLA EN 1786 / Nieto de Pina, C – Sevilla, 1787 – 1mf – 9 – sp Cultura [610]
MEMORIAS DE LAS REINAS CATOLICAS. TOMO 1 / Florez Setien, Enrique – 1770, 2nd ed – 2mf – 9 – Pta1,500.00 – 84-7848-061-7 – sp Pentalfa [240]
MEMORIAS DE LAS REINAS CATOLICAS. TOMO 2 / Florez Setien, Enrique – 1770, 2nd ed – 2mf – 9 – Pta1,500.00 – 84-7848-062-5 – sp Pentalfa [240]
MEMORIAS DE LOS VIRREYES DEL PERU, MARQUES DE MANCERA Y CONDE DE SALVATIERRA – Lima: IMprenta del Estado, 1896 – us Res Libr [972]
MEMORIAS DE UN AMNISTIADO / Munoz-Epelde, Melchor – Badajoz: Tip. El Progreso, de Antonio Arqueros, 1901 – 1 – sp Bibl Santa Ana [320]
MEMORIAS DE UN LOCO / Carral Oviedo, Don Benigno – 1888. 1889 – 9 – 1.50f – sp Bibl Santa Ana [920]
MEMORIAS DEL GENERAL O'LEARY / O'Leary, Daniel F – Caracas. 1879-1914. 32 v – 1 – 140.00 – us L of C Photodup [920]
MEMORIAS DEL P. FLORIAN PAUCKE: 1748 A 1767 / Baucke, Florian – Buenos Aires: L. Mirau, 1900. 161p – 1 – us U.W. Library [240]
MEMORIAS DEL REY ALONSO EL NOBLE / Cerda Rico, Francisco – 1783 – 2mf – 9 – Pta1,500.00 – 84-7848-262-8 – sp Pentalfa [920]
MEMORIAS ESTUDANTIS – Nanuque, Brazil. Oct 1964; Auq 1965; Oct 1967 – 1 – bl Biblioteca [072]
MEMORIAS EXTERIORES, 1947-1964 / Areilza, Jose Maria de – Barcelona: Editorial Planeta, 1st ed 1984 – 1 – CSUXADQ2520-B – us Hoover Inst Photo [920]
MEMORIAS FISICAS SOBRE EL INFLUJO DELGES INDIOGENO EN LA ANESTITUCION DEL NOMBRE SOBRE EL OPIGENO... DEL AIRE ATMOSFERICO / Cibat, A – Barcelona, SA – 9mf – 9 – sp Cultura [500]
MEMORIAS HISTORIAS...CARLOTA JOAQUINA Y DONA MARIANA VICTORIAS / Herrera, Benardino – 1787 – 9 – $1.50f – sp Bibl Santa Ana [946]
MEMORIAS HISTORICAS DE LA CIUDAD DE BARCELONA. TOMO 1 / Capmany Montpalau, Antonio – 1779 – 2mf – 9 – Pta1,500.00 – 84-7848-050-1 – sp Pentalfa [946]
MEMORIAS HISTORICAS DE LA CIUDAD DE BARCELONA. TOMO 2 / Capmany Montpalau, Antonio – 1779 – 2mf – 9 – Pta1,500.00 – 84-7848-051-X – sp Pentalfa [946]
MEMORIAS HISTORICAS DE LA CIUDAD DE BARCELONA. TOMO 4 / Capmany Montpalau, Antonio – 1792 – 2mf – 9 – Pta1,500.00 – 84-7848-053-6 – sp Pentalfa [946]
MEMORIAS SOBRE EL CASTILLO DE BELLVER / Jovellanos, Melchor Gaspar de – 1813 – 1mf – 9 – Pta1,000.00 – 84-7848-124-9 – sp Pentalfa [920]
MEMORIAS SOBRE EL ESTADO POLITICO, GOBIERNO Y ADMINISTRACION DE LA ISLA DE CUBA / Habana, Jose Gutierrez de la Concha y de Irigoyen – Madrid: J. Trujillo, 1853 – 1 – us U.W. Library [972]
MEMORIAS. TOMO 1-12 / Instituto Geografico – Madrid, 1873-1903 – 157mf – 9 – sp Cultura [946]
MEMORIAS...ACADEMIA...LEGISLACION / Villanueva y Canedo, Luis – 1844 – 9 – 1.50f – sp Bibl Santa Ana [946]
MEMORIA...SOBRE LA LIBERTAD DE COMERCIO Y EL PUERTO DE CADIZ / Pita y Pizarro, P – Cadiz, 1834 – 17mf – 9 – sp Cultura [380]
MEMORIE BIOGRAFICHE DEGLI SCULTORI, ARCHITETTI, PITTORI ECC. NATIVI DI CARRARA E DI ALTRI LUOGHI DELLA PROVINCIA DI MASSA. / Campori, G – Modena, 1873 – 6mf – ne IDC [700]
MEMORIE LICHENOGRAFICHE CON UN' APPENDICE ALLE RICERCHE SULL' AUTONOMIA DEI LICHENI CROSTOSI / Massalongo, A B – Verona, 1853. 183 pp., 29 pls. B-1075 2 – 8 – ne IDC [580]
MEMORIE VAN OVERGAVE VAN BANJUMAS 1907 DOOR RESIDENT G.J. OUDEMANS – Arch. Kol. Mailrap. 481/1908. BSD-106/1 mf. 4-7 – 9 – ne IDC [950]
MEMORIE VAN OVERGAVE VAN BANTAM 1911 DOOR RESIDENT F.K. OVERDUYN – Arch. Kol. Mailrap. 1283/1911. BSD-106/1 mf. 15-19(2-2) – 9 – ne IDC [950]
MEMORIE VAN OVERGAVE VAN CHERIBON 1911 DOOR RESIDENT G.J. OUDEMANS – Arch. Kol. Mailrap 1362/1911. BSD-106/1 mf. 32-37 – 9 – ne IDC [950]
MEMORIE VAN OVERGAVE VAN DE PREANGER REGENT-SCHAPPEN 1912 DOOR RESIDENT G.J. OUDEMANS – Arch. Kol. Mailrap. 799/1913. BSD-106/1 mf. 64-49 – 9 – ne IDC [950]
MEMORIE VAN OVERGAVE VAN DE PREANGER REGENTSCHAPPEN 1922 DOOR RESIDENT L. DE STUERS – Arch. Kol. Mailrap. 182/1922. BSD106/1. mf 70-75 – 9 – ne IDC [950]
MEMORIE VAN OVERGAVE VAN MADIUN 1903-1907 DOOR RESIDENT W.T.L. BOISSEVAIN – Arch. Kol. Mailrap. 1637/1907. BSD-106/1 mf. 57-59 – 9 – ne IDC [950]
MEMORIE VAN OVERGAVE VAN SURAKARTA 1900-1914 DOOR RESIDENT G.F. VAN WIJK – Arch. Kol. Mailrap. 1338/1914. BSD106/1. mf 76-79 – 9 – ne IDC [950]
MEMORIE VAN OVERGAVE VAN SURAKARTA 1918-1922 DOOR RESIDENT A.J.W. HARLOFF – Arch. Kol. Mailrap. 763/1922. BSD-106/1 mf. 80-86 – 9 – ne IDC [950]
MEMORIES OF A MANAGER; REMINISCENCES OF THE OLD LYCEUM AND OF SOME PLAYERS OF THE LAST QUARTER CENTURY / Frohman, Daniel – Garden City, NY: Doubleday, Page & Co., 1911. xvii,235p – 1 – us U.W. Library [790]
MEMORIES OF CANADA AND SCOTLAND : SPEECHES AND VERSES / Argyll, John Douglas Sutherland Campbell, Duke of – Montreal: Dawson, 1884, c1883. 00045. (Pre-1900 Canadiana) – 9 – cn C.I.H.M. [810]
MEMORIES OF FRANKSTON – 7r – 9 – at Corangamite [910]
MEMORIES OF GENNESARET / Macduff, John Ross – New York: Robert Carter, 1875. 1 fiche – 9 – us A.T.L.A. [240]
MEMORIES OF GOSPEL TRIUMPHS AMONG THE JEWS DURING THE VICTORIAN ERA / ed by Dunlop, John – London: S W Partridge: John Snow, 1894 – 2mf – 9 – 0-8370-7136-4 – 1986-1136 – us A.T.L.A. [240]
MEMORIES OF LIFE AT OXFORD AND EXPERIENCES IN ITALY, GREECE, TURKEY, GERMANY, SPAIN, AND ELSEWHERE / Meyrick, Frederick – London: J. Murray, 1905 – 1mf – us A.T.L.A. [240]
MEMORIES OF LONDON IN THE 'FORTIES' : ARRANGED FOR PUBLICATION AND ANNOTATED BY HIS DAUGHTER FLORA MASSON / Masson, David – Edinburgh, London: William Blackwood, 1908 – 1 roll – 1 – 1-55879-902-8 – uk Libr Preservation [941]
MEMORIES OF MANY MEN AND OF SOME WOMEN: BEING PERSONAL RECOLLECTIONS OF EMPERORS, KINGS, QUEENS, PRINCES, PRESIDENTS, STATESMEN, AUTHORS. / Field, Maunsell Bradhurst – New York: Harper & Brothers, 1874 – 1 – us U.W. Library [920]
MEMORIES OF MY EXILE / Kossuth, Lajos – Trans. from the Hungarian by Ferencz Jausz. New York: D. Appleton, 1880. xxxii,446p – 1 – us U.W. Library [943]
MEMORIES OF ODD ADVENTURES, STRANGE DELIVERANCES, ETC. IN THE CAPTIVITY OF JOHN GILES, ESQ., COMMANDER OF THE GARRISON OF SAINT GEORGE RIVER, IN THE DISTRICT OF MAINE / Gyles, John – Cincinnati: Spiller & Gates, 1869. 04396. (Pre-1900 Canadiana) – 9 – cn C.I.H.M. [971]
MEMORIES OF OLIVET / Macduff, John Ross – New York: Robert Carter, 1868. 1 fiche – 9 – us A.T.L.A. [240]
MEMORIES OF PATMOS, OR, SOME OF THE GREAT WORDS AND VISIONS OF THE APOCALYPSE / Macduff, John Ross – New York: Robert Carter, 1871. 1 fiche – 9 – us A.T.L.A. [240]
MEMORIES OF STAMBOURNE / Spurgeon, Charles Haddon – 1891? – 1 – us A.T.L.A. [240]
MEMORIES OF THE TENNYSONS / Rawnsley, Hardwicke Drummond – Glasgow: J. MacLehose, 2nd ed 1912 – 1 roll – 1 – 1-55879-951-6 – uk Libr Preservation [420]
MEMORIES VAN OVERGAVE (MEMORANDA OF CONVEYANCE), DUTCH EAST INDIES, 1849-1962 – (Available separately; MMK series.-1199mf.Dfl8,250.00; KIT series.-1742mf.Dfl11,975; Subsections of both series available separately (Please inquire); Inventory included in cost of each set: Fiche also available separately for Dfl125.00) – 2941mf – 9 – Dfl17,325.00set – ne MMF Publ [949]
A MEMORY / Chapman, Edward John – Toronto: J. Lovell, 1874. 00622. (Pre-1900 Canadiana) – 9 – cn C.I.H.M. [971]
MEMORY AND COGNITION – v1- 1973- 1,5,6; v3- 9 – us UMI [150]
MEMORY AND MICROCOMPUTERS – 1,5,9 – in prep – us Gordon [073]
THE MEMORY OF LINCOLN; POEMS SELECTED WITH AN INTROD / Howe, M A De Wolfe – Boston: Small, Maynard & Co., 1899. xvii,65p – 1 – us U.W. Library [810]
[MEMOS] / South African Institute of Race Relations – Johannesburg, [1929?-66] – us Res Libr [305]
MEMOS OF THE SPECIAL ASSISTANT FOR NATIONAL SECURITY AFFAIRS : MCGEORGE BUNDY TO PRESIDENT JOHNSON, 1963-66 – (With printed guide) – 4r – 1 – $400.00 – 0-89093-748-6 – us UPA [977]
MEMPHIS / Petrie, William Matthew Flinders – 2v. 1909 – 9 – $12.00 – us I.R.C. [930]
THE MEMPHIS LAW JOURNAL – v1-2. 1878-79 (all publ) – 9mf – 9 – $13.50 – LLMC 82-942 – us L.L.M.C. [073]
MEMPHIS STATE UNIVERSITY LAW REVIEW – v1- 1970- 1; 1973- 5,6 – us UMI [340]
Memphis, Tennessee *see* MISCELLANEOUS EARLY NEWSPAPERS
LE MEMU – Montreal, Canada. 7 dec 1903 – 1r – 1 – Can$25.00 – cn Can Microfilming [072]
MEN AGAINST FIRE / Marshall, Samuel Lyman Atwood – In Indonesian. SE-11,401 1. 1963 – 9 – ne IDC [950]
MEN AND BOOKS / Phelps, Austin – 1892 – 9 – us A.T.L.A. [240]
MEN AND MISSIONS / Ellis, William Thomas – (Includes appendixes and index) – Philadelphia: Sunday School Times, 1909 – 1mf – 9 – 0-8370-6115-6 – 1986-0115 – us A.T.L.A. [240]
MEN AND THE MODERN MISSIONARY ENTERPRISE : HISTORY, CALL, ADDRESSES, DELIVERANCES, CONFERENCES AND DELIBERATIONS OF THE FIRST INTER-SYNODICAL FOREIGN MISSIONARY CONVENTION FOR MEN, HELD AT OMAHA, NEBRASKA, FEBRUARY 19-21, 1907 / Inter-synodical Foreign Missionary Convention for Men; ed by Bradt, Charles Edwin – (Includes index) – Chicago, IL: Winona, c1907 – 1mf – 9 – 0-8370-6330-2 – 1986-0330 – us A.T.L.A. [240]
MEN I HAVE KNOWN / Farrar, Frederic William – New York: T.Y. Crowell, c1897 – 1mf – us A.T.L.A. [240]
MEN IN THE RANKS; THE STORY OF 12 AMERICANS IN SPAIN / North, Joseph – N.Y., 1939. Fiche W 1081. (Blodgett Collection of Spanish Civil War Pamphlets) – 9 – us H.U. College Libr [946]
MEN, MYTHS, AND MOVEMENTS IN GERMAN LITERATURE : A VOLUME OF HISTORICAL AND CRITICAL PAPERS / Rose, William – (Includes bibliographical references and index) – New York: Macmillan, 1931 – 1r – 1 – us U.W. Library [430]
MEN OF HAWAII / ed by Nellist, George F – Hawaii: The Honolulu Star-Bulletin, 1935. v5. Hawaii reel 1. (Cox Library Collection) – 5 – us Americana [978]
MEN OF ILLINOIS / Witherspoon, Halliday – Chicago: 1902. Illinois Reel 6. (The Cox Library Collection) – 5 – us Americana [978]
MEN OF MARK : EMINENT, PROGRESSIVE AND RISING / Simmons, William J – Cleveland, 1887 – 1r – 1 – us Ross [920]
MEN OF MARK IN GEORGIA / Northen, W F – Historical and biographical sketches. Atlanta, A. B. Caldwell, 1907. Vols. 1-3. Georgia Reel 2; Vol. 4. Georgia Reel 3. (The Cox Library Collection) – 5 – us Americana [978]
MEN OF MARK IN SOUTH CAROLINA / Hemphill, J C – Washington, DC, Men of Mark Publishing Co., 1907. Vols. 1-4. South Carolina Reel 2. (The Cox Library Collection) – 5 – us Americana [978]
MEN OF MARK OF HARRISON AND ROCKINGHAM COUNTY / Wayland, John W – Biographical sketches of men and women. Staunton, McClure Co., 1943. Virginia Reel 4. (The Cox Library Collection) – 5 – us Americana [978]
MEN OF MIGHT IN INDIA MISSIONS : THE LEADERS AND THEIR EPOCHS, 1706-1899 / Holcomb, Helen Harriet – (Includes index) – New York: Fleming H Revell, 1901 – 1mf – 9 – 0-8370-6124-5 – 1986-0124 – us A.T.L.A. [920]
MEN OF MINNESOTA / Minnesota Historical Co – St. Paul, 1902. Minnesota Reel 2. (The Cox Library Collection) – 5 – us Americana [978]

MEN OF PROGRESS: BIOGRAPHICAL SKETCHES AND PORTRAITS OF LEADERS IN BUSINESS AND PROFESSIONAL LIFE IN AND OF THE STATE OF MAINE / Herndon, Richard – Boston, New England Magazine, 1897. Maine Reel 2. (The Cox Library Collection) – 5 – us Americana [978]
MEN OF PROGRESS IN WISCONSIN / Aikens & Proctor – Biographical sketches. Milwaukee: Evening Wisconsin Co., 1906. Wisconsin Reel 3. (The Cox Library Collection) – 5 – us Americana [978]
THE MEN OF THE NORTH AND THEIR PLACE IN HISTORY / Haliburton, R G – Montreal: John Lovell, 1869. SEM105P395 – 1mf – 9 – Can$2.25 – cn Bibl Nat [920]
MEN OF THE NORTHERN TERRITORY POLICE 1870-1914 – 1990 – 2mf – 9 – A$10.00 – 0-949124-61-3 – item 26 – at G.S.N.T. [920]
MEN OF VERMONT / Ullery, Jacob G – An illustrated biographical history of Vermonters and Sons of Vermont. Brattleboro Transcript Publishing Co., 1894. Vermont Reel 5. (The Cox Library Collection) – 5 – us Americana [978]
MEN OF WYOMING 1915 / Peterson, CS – Denver, 1915. Wyoming reel 2. (Cox Library Collection) – 5 – us Americana [978]
MEN VERSUS THE MAN / La Monte, R R & Mencken, H L – Correspondence on socialism. 1910. With "Liberty", by B. R. Tucker. Feb. 1906. Together, 388p. 1 fiche (24x) – 9 – 1.00f – at Libertarian Micro [320]
MEN WHO MADE TEXAS FREE / Dixon, Sam Houston – Houston: Texas Historical Publ. Co., n.d. Texas Reel 12. (The Cox Library Collection) – 5 – us Americana [978]
Mena, Anselmo *see* LOS TRIBUNALES DE MENORES EN LOS ESTADOS UNIDOS DE AMERICA
Mena, Juan de *see* OBRAS
Mena, Vicente *see*
- COMENTARIOS A LA VIDA DE PEDRO DE VALDIVIA
- VINETAS CASTUERANAS

MENACE – (Weekly anti-Catholic newspaper) – Aurora, MO. Jul 15 1911-Oct 23 1918 – 1r – 1 – us Western Res [071]
THE MENACE – Aurora, MO -w. 1911-18. 1 reel – 1 – us Western Res [071]
LE MENAGE DE MME. SYLVAIN, LIVRE DE LECTURE COURANTE A L'USAGE DES JEUNES FILLES / Halt, Marie Malezieux – Paris: P. Delaplaine, 1895. 372p. (Les Femmes Collection) – 4mf – 9 – $10.00 – fr Bibl Nationale [830]
Menage, G *see*
- DICTIONAIRE ETYMOLOGIQUE...
- DICTIONNAIRE ETYMOLOGIQUE
- DICTIONNAIRE ETYMOLOGIQUE DE LA LANGUE FRANCOISE
- OBSERVATIONS SUR LA LANGUE FRANCAISE
- LES ORIGINES DE LA LANGUE FRANCOISE
- LA REQUETE DES DICTIONNAIRES

Menagios, D de *see* REPERTOIRE DES TRAITES, CONVENTIONS, ET AUTRES ACTES PRINCIPAUX DE LA RUSSIE AVEC LES PUISSANCES ETRANGERES DEPUIS 1474 JUSQU'A NOS JOURS
MENAHEM BEN SARUK / Gross, S – Mit Beruechsichtigung seiner Vorgaenger und Nachfolger. Breslau. 1872. BJ-421-41 1 – 9 – ne IDC [920]
Menahem Mendell of Lublin *see* 2 MANUSCRIPTS IN CURSIVE HEBREW, BOUND, CONTAINING ESSAYS AND LETTERS SUPPOSEDLY BY
Menant, Delphine *see* THE PARSIS IN INDIA, BEING AN ENLARGED AND COPIOUSLY ANNOTATED UP TO DATE ENGLISH EDITION..
Menant, Joachim *see*
- LES LANGUES PERDUES DE LA PERSE ET DE L'ASSYRIE
- LECONS D'EPIGRAPHIE ASSYRIENNE
- LES NOMS PROPRES ASSYRIENS

MENARA : TIJDSCHRIFT VOOR DE CULTURELE SAMENWERKING – (Missing: 1955(14, 16)) – Djakarta, 1952-1956 – 19mf – 9 – ne IDC [306]
Menard, Adjutor *see*
- LE BAVARD
- LE GOGLU

Menard, Joseph *see* L'ECHO D'IBERVILLE
Menasje, A *see* CATALOGUS DER TENTOONSTELLING IN HET PORTUGEESCH ISREALIETISCH SEMINARIUM "ETS HAIM" TE AMSTERDAM...
MENASSE BEN ISRAEL, SEIN LEBEN UND WIRKEN / Kayserling, M – Berlin. 1861. BJ-262-30 1 – 9 – ne IDC [900]
MENASSEH BEN ISRAEL, MIQVEH ISRAEL – Esto es Esperanca de Israel. Amsterdam. 1650. BJ-262-37 1 – 9 – ne IDC [270]
Menavino, G A *see* TRATTATO DE COSTVMI ET VITA DE TURCHI, ...
Menayo Garcia, Alfonso *see* EL DESPIDO DE OBREROS Y LAS DEMAS CAUSAS DE DETERMINACION DEL CONTRATO DE TRABAJO
Mencke, Otto et al *see* ACTA ERUDITORUM; NOVA ACTA ERUDITORUM
Mencken, H L *see*
- MEN VERSUS THE MAN
- THE PHILOSOPHY OF FRIEDRICH NIETZSCHE

MENCKENIANA – v1- 1962- 1; v41- 4,6; v57- 9 – us UMI [410]
Menczer, Bela *see* METTERNICH Y DONOSO CORTES
Mende, Gottfried *see* RELIGIOESE BETRACHTUNGEN UEBER WERKE GERHART HAUPTMANNS
Mende, Traute *see* BESTIMMUNG DER RENALEN CLEARANCE IM RAHMEN DER NUKLEARMEDIZINISCHEN NIERENDIAGNOSTIK
Mendel, Herman *see* MUSIKALISCHES CONVERSATIONS-LEXIKON UND ERGAN ZUNGSBAND
Mendel, Menahem (b. Aaron of Kamenets) *see* KOROT HA-ITTIM
Mendels, I *see* DE JOODSE GEMEENTE TE GRONINGEN
Mendelssohn, Felix *see*
- FANTASIA, PIANO, OP. 16, E MAJOR
- GRAND TRIO POUR PIANO, VIOLON ET VIOLONCELLE, OEUVRE 49
- MANUSCRIPTS AND LETTERS
- EIN SOMMERNACHTSTRAUM, VON SHAKESPEARE. VIERHAENDIGER CLAVIERAUSZUG VON COMPONISTEN, OP.61
- WERKE

MENDELSSOHN UND LESSING : NEBST EINER GEDAECHNTISREDE AUF MOSES MENDELSSOHN ZU DESSEN HUNDERTJAEHRIGEM TODESTAGE / Ritter, Immanuel Heinrich – (Includes bibliographical references) – 2. Aufl. Berlin: L Steinthal, 1886 – 1r – 1 – us U.W. Library [430]
Mendelssohn-Bartholody, K *see* BRIEFE VON FRIEDRICH VON GENTZ AN BILAT
Mendenhall, J K *see* SCRAPBOOK
Mendenhall, James William *see*
- ECHOES FROM PALESTINE
- PLATO AND PAUL

Mendes, Catulle *see* LA DEMOISELLE EN OR
Mendes dos Remedios, J *see* OS JUDEUS PORTUGUESES EM AMSTERDAM
Mendes Pinto, F *see* THE VOYAGES AND ADVENTURES OF F. MENDEZ PINTO
Mendez Martinez, Gonzalo *see*
- APORTACION A UN INVENTARIO DE LA CARTOGRAFIA GEOGRAFICA EN GALICIA
- EVOLUCION DE LA MORFOLOGIA URBANA DE PONTEVEDRA HASTA 1900

Mendez Pereira, Octavio *see*
- NUNEZ DE BALBOA. EL TESORO DEL DABAIBE
- EL TESORO DE DOBAIDE

Mendheim, Max *see* DREI REDEN JAKOB GRIMMS
MENDIANTS ET VAGABONDS / Riviere, Louis – Paris. 1902. (La Condition Ouvriere. Part Two.) – 9 – 7.50 – fr Bibl Nationale [360]
Mendiburu, Manuel de *see*
- DICCIONARIO HISTORICO-BIOGRAFICO DEL PERU. 2ND ED. TOMOS 9, 10 Y 11. LIMA 1934-1935
- DICCIONARIO HISTORICO-BIOGRAFICO DEL PERU...2ND ED. PUBLICADA POR EVARISTO SANCRISTOVAL

Mendieta, E A *see* EUSTATHIUS
Mendieta, Geronimo *see*
- CODICE MENDIETA
- HISTORIA ECLESIASTICA INDIANA
- HISTORIA...INDIANA

Mendive, Jose *see* LA RELIGION CATOLICA VINDICADA DE LAS IMPOSTURAS RACIONALISTAS
MENDOCINO AND LAKE COUNTIES / Carpenter & Millberry – Los Angeles: Historic Record Co., 1914. California Reel 20. (The Cox Library Collection) – 5 – us Americana [978]
MENDOCINO BEACON – Mendocino, CA. 1878- – 80+ r – 1 – $4,000.00 ($90.00y) – C02442 – us Library Micro [071]
MENDOCINO DISPATCH DEMOCRAT – Ukiah, CA. 1881-99 – 4r – 1 – $200.00 – B03049 – us Library Micro [071]
MENDOCINO HERALD – Ukiah, CA. 1861-70 – 1r – 1 – $50.00 – B03050 – us Library Micro [071]
MENDOCINO/LAKE COUNTIES – 1992- – 3+ r – 1 – $150.00 – P00044 – us Library Micro [910]
MENDOCINO/LAKE/SONOMA COUNTIES – 1907-33 – 21r – 1 – $1,050.00 – P00128 – us Library Micro [910]
MENDON 1665-1849 – (Mf 1T-3T: Marriage Intentions 1744-68. Mf 1T,17T: Births & Deaths 1665-1751. Mf 1T,3T: Marriages 1712-46. Mf 2T-7T: Vital Records 1685-1795. Mf 7T-9T: Marriages/Intentions 1746-1806. Mf 9T-10T: Vital Records 1740-1828. Mf 11T-14T: Births & Deaths 1762-1844. Mf 14T-15T: Marriage Intentions 1807-35. Mf 14T-17T: Marriages 1805-44. Mf 17T: Out-of-Town Marriages 1710-98. Mf 17T-18T: Marriage Intentions 1835-49. Mf 18T-20T: Vital Records 1832-49) – (mf ed 1997) – 20mf – 9 – 0-87623-291-8 – us Holbrook [920]
Mendonca, Renato *see*
- UM DIPLOMATA NA CORTE DE INGLATERRA
- A INFLUENCIA AFRICANA NO PORTUGUES DO BRASIL

Mendoza, Antonio *see* EL JOVEN Y EL ZAPATERO
Mendoza, B *see* TEORICA Y PRACTICA DE GUERRA
MENDOZA COLLECTION : COLECCION DE DOCUMENTOS INEDITOS – Panama: Biblioteca Nacional de Panama – 1r – 1 – us Ross [972]
Mendoza Jordan, Lorenzo *see*
- POR DON LUIS PACHECO...CON DONA MARIANA DE CARDENAS
- POR DON LUIS PACHECO...DON CRISTOBAL DE PORTOCARRERO...MAYORAZGO

Mendoza, Luis de *see*
- LA FAMILIA SOBRE TODO
- LA LUZ NO VIENE DEL SOL
- PROYECTO DE PAZ UNIVERSAL
- REGLA DE LA ORDEN DE LA CABALLERIA DE SANTIAGO
- EL TALISMAN

Mendoza, Pedro *see* ORACION...APERTURA DE LA AUDIENCIA DE CACERES
Mendoza Ruiz, Manuel *see*
- HACIA UNA ESPANA SIN GANADO?
- HACIA UNA ORDENACION GANADERA

Mendoza y Gonzalez, Luis de *see*
- EL SACRIFICIO GLADATORIO
- TAICOLE O EL SACRIFICIO GLADIATORIO

Mendras, H *see*
- ETUDES DE SOCIOLOGIE RURALE
- LES PAYSANS ET LA POLITIQUE DANS LA FRANCE CONTEMPORAINE

Mends, Bowen Stilon *see* LIFE OF ADMIRAL SIR W.R. MENDS, G.C.B
MENE MENE TEKEL UPHARSIN : AN HISTORICAL STUDY OF THE FIFTH CHAPTER OF DANIEL / Prince, John Dyneley – (In English. Includes indexes) – Baltimore: [s.n.], 1893 – 1mf – 9 – 0-8370-4801-X – 1985-2801 – us A.T.L.A. [220]
Menefee, C A *see*
- HISTORICAL AND DESCRIPTIVE SKETCHBOOK OF NAPA, SONOMA, LAKE AND MENDOCINO
- SKETCH BOOK OF NAPA, SONOMA, LAKE AND MENDOCINO COUNTIES, 1873

Menegazzi, L *see* MALACOLOGIA VERONESE
Meneghini, G *see*
- ALGHE ITALIANE E DALMATICHE
- CENNI SULLA ORGANOGRAFIA E FISIOLOGIA DELLE ALGHE
- MONOGRAPHIA NOSTOCHINEARUM ITALICARUM ADDITO SPECIMINE DE RIVULARIIS

Menegoz, Eugene *see* LA THEOLOGIE DE L'EPITRE AUX HEBREUX
MENELIK : L'ITALIA E L'ETIOPIA / Montegazza, Vico – Milano: Libraria editrice milanese, 1910 – us Res Libr [960]
Menendez, Josefa, Sister *see* PESAN TJINTA DAN BELAS-KASIH
Menendez Pidal, Juan *see* DISCURSOS LEIDOS ANTE LA REAL ACADEMIA ESPANOLA EN LA RECEPCION PUBLICA DE....
Menendez Pidal Navascues, Fautismo *see* LOS GAUTES ESPANOLES. MADRID...1954
Menendez Pidal, Ramon *see* HISTORIA DE ESPANA DIRIGIDA POR...TOMOS 5, 14 Y 18, MADRID, 1965-1966
Menendez Reigada, A G *see* VIDA DE SAN ALBERTO MAGNO. DOCTOR DE LA IGLESIA
Menendez y Pelayo, Marcelino *see* LAS CIEN MEJORES POESIAS (LIRICAS) DE LA LENGUA CASTELLANA
Menendez-Reigada, Ignacio G *see* LA GUERRA NACIONAL ESPANOLA ANTE LA MORAL Y EL DERECHO
Meneses, Felipe de *see* LUZ DEL ALMA CRISTIANA
LE MENESTREL – Journal de musique puis Musique et theatres. Paris. dec 1833-sept 1914 – 1 – fr A.C.R.P.P. [073]
LE MENESTREL : LITTERATURE ET MUSIQUE – Quebec, Canada. avr 1844-16 jan 1845 – 1r – 1 – Can$30.00 – cn Can Microfilming [073]
LE MENESTREL; JOURNAL DU MONDE MUSICAL, MUSIQUE ET THEATRES – Paris. 1833-1940 – 1 – 897.00 – us L of C Photodup [073]
MENESTREL'. NOVEISIIA POEZY / Severianin, I – Berlin. 1921. BR-1031 2 – 8 – ne IDC [460]
Menestrier, Claude-Francois *see*
- L'ART DES EMBLEMES OU S'ENSEIGNE LA MORALE
- DES BALLETS ANCIENS ET MODERNES SELON LES REGLES DU THEATRE
- LA METHODE DU BLASON
- LA NOUVELLE METHODE RAISONNEE DU BLASON
- PHILOSOPHIA IMAGINUM
- LA PHILOSOPHIE DES IMAGES
- DES REPRESENTATIONS EN MUSIQUE ANCIENNES ET MODERNES

Menet, John *see* SHORT NOTES ON THE ACTS OF THE APOSTLES
Meng, Li-Chuen *see* PERDANA MENTERI PEREMPUAN DALAM PENJAMARAN (BENG LEE KOEN)
MENG TSANG WEI YUAN HUI KUNG PAO / China. Commission of Mongolian and Tibetan Affairs – Gazette. Nanking. Sep 1930-Mar 1931. v.11-14. 1 reel – 1 – 20.00 – us Chinese Res [950]
MENG TSANG YUEH PAO / China. Commission of Mongolian and Tibetan Affairs – Monthly bulletin. Nanking 1934-44. Available: v. 2 (1, 3) 1934; v. 2 (5) 1935; v. 14 (7-12) 1942; v. 15 (2-5) 1943; v. 15 (7-8) 1944. BCH-1076 1 – 9 – ne IDC [950]
MENGAMANKAN PANDJI-PANDJI REVOLUSI / Nasution, Abdul Haris – SE-4681 1. 1964 – 9 – ne IDC [335]
MENGAPA KEKUASAAN POLITIK MERAH TIONGKOK DAPAT BERDIRI? / Mao, Tse-tung – SE-5399 1. 1962 – 9 – ne IDC [324]
Menge, A *see*
- PREUSSISCHE SPINNEN. SCHRIFTEN NATURF
- UEBER DIE SCHEERENSPINNEN, CHERNETIDAE. NEUESTE SCHRIFTEN NATURF

MENGELINGEN VOOR ROOMSCH-CATHOLIJKEN – 2(1808)-5(1814) – 31mf – 9 – Dfl109.00 – ne Slangenburg [073]
MENGELZANGEN EN ZINNEBEELDEN / Sweerts, C – 1st ed. Amsterdam, 1694 – 2mf – 9 – O-3173/1 – ne IDC [760]
Menger, Anton *see* DIE ZULASSIGKEIT NEUEN THATSACHLICHEN VORBRINGENS IN DEN HOHEREN INSTANZEN; EINE CIVILPROCESSUALISCHE ABHANDLUNG
MENG-HUA CHIH-LI T'ING-CHIH – 1790; 1881, 6, 1. Lacking: ch. 6. BCH-685 2 – 8 – ne IDC [950]
MENG-HUA FU-CHIH – 1698; 1881, 6, 1. BCH-684 2 – 8 – ne IDC [950]
MENGISI "PANTJA WARDHANA," SISTIM PENDIDIKAN INDONESIA / Sumardi Atmaprawira – Inc. legislation. SE 5149 1. 1962 – 9 – ne IDC [950]
MENGOLAH KUE, PENGANAN DAN MINUMAN / Pramita, Sal – SE-4176 1. 1962? – 9 – ne IDC [950]
MENGO-UGANDA NOTES – 1900-21 – 1 – uk Microform Academic [960]
MENGYO KEIZAI SHIRYO = RECORDS OF THE JAPANESE COTTON INDUSTRIAL CIRCUMSTANCES – (Reference data of considerations on the cotton spinning industry of Japan. No1-75, 1903-40. Osaka; Monthly report of the Japanese Cotton Spinners' Assoc. No1-600, 1889-1942, Osaka. Lacks No12 and 162; Statistical annual of the Japan Cotton and Silk Fabrics Industry. 1927-37. Tokyo; Monthly Report of the Nippon Union of Cotton Textile Manufacturers' Assoc. No1-89, 1935-42. Tokyo; Monthly Statistical

Report of the Japan Cotton and Staple-Fiber Weavers' Assoc. No1-52, 1935-40. Tokyo) – 95,000p – 66r – 1 – Y621,000.00 – ja Yushodo [380]

Menhart, Ursula *see* NEUE ENTWICKLUNGEN IM MINDERHEITENSCHUTZ IN EUROPA

Meniaud, Jacques *see* LES PIONNIERS DU SOUDAN, AVANT, AVEC ET APRES ARCHINARD, 1879-1894

MENIFEE VALLEY NEWS – Sun City, CA. 1989 – 1r – 1 – $50.00 – R04125 – us Library Micro [071]

MENIFEE WEEK – Menifee, CA. 1990 – 1+ r – 1 – $50.00 ($50.00y) – R04068 – us Library Micro [071]

MENILMONTANT OU EXAMEN DE LA RELIGION SAINT-SIMONIENNE – Angers, impr. E. Le Sourd, 1833, 38 p. Les Saint-Simoniens, 1825-1834. 7003 – 9 – fr Hachette [335]

Menin, Abraham Isaac *see* HANDBOOK OF FORMS AND PRACTICE IN BANKRUPTCY

Menius, J *see*
- VON DEM GEIST DER WIDERTEUFFER. M. VORREDE (V.) M. LUTHER
- DER WIDDERTEUFFER LERE VND GEHEIMNIS. AUS HEILIGER SCHRIFFT WIDDERLEGT. MART. LUTH. VON DER WIDDERTAUFFE AN ZWEEN PFARHER, EIN BRIEFF. PHILIP MELANCHTON. VNTERRICHT WIDDER DIE LERE DER WIDERTOUFFER...

MENJINGKAP RAHASIA KEBAHAGIAAN / Al-Ghazzali, Iman – (Trans. of Kimyau's sa'adah.) SE-4907 1. 1963 – 9 – ne IDC [950]

Menke-Glueckert, Emil *see*
- DIE GESCHICHTSCHREIBUNG DER REFORMATION UND GEGENREFORMATION
- GOETHE ALS GESCHICHTSPHILOSOPH UND DIE GESCHICHTSPHILOSOPHISCHE BEWEGUNG SEINER ZEIT

Menkel, Peter *see* JOURNALS

MENLO ATHERTON RECORDER *see* RECORDER/MENLO ATHERTON RECORDER

Menne, Karl Johannes Joseph *see* GOETHES 'WERTHER' IN DER NIEDERLAENDISCHEN LITERATUR

MENNINGER CLINIC BULLETIN – v1- 1936- 1; v35- 1971- 5,6; v41- 9 – us UMI [616]

Menninger, Edwin A *see* "MIDWESTERN MAGNIFICENCE."

MENNINGER PERSPECTIVE – v1- 1970- 1; v4- 5,6; v7- 9 – us UMI [073]

MENNO SIMONS, HIS LIFE, LABORS, AND TEACHINGS / Horsch, John – 1916 – 1 – 11.76 – us Baptist [240]

MENNONITE – v1- 1885- 1; v87- 5,6; v91- 9 – us UMI [240]

THE MENNONITE – Hillsboro, KA. v51-65. 1936-50 (complete) – 5r – 1 – ATLA 1993-S015 – us A.T.L.A. [073]

THE MENNONITE – Philadelphia, PA. v1-48. 1885-1933 (complete) – 12r – 1 – ATLA 1993-S014 – us A.T.L.A. [073]

THE MENNONITE AND THE CHRISTIAN EVANGEL – v1-2. 1934-35 (complete) – 1r – 1 – ATLA 1993-S011 – us A.T.L.A. [073]

MENNONITE BOARD OF MISSIONS AND CHARITIES : REPORTS – 1940-91 (complete) – Inquire – 1 – ATLA S0606 – us A.T.L.A. [240]

MENNONITE CHURCH HISTORY / Hartzler, Jonas Smucker & Kauffman, Daniel – Scottdale, Pa.: Mennonite Book and Tract Society, 1905 – 1mf – us A.T.L.A. [240]

MENNONITE CHURCHES OF NORTH AMERICA : A STATISTICAL COMPILATION / Krehbiel, H P – Berne, Ind.: Mennonite Book Concern; Newton, Kan.: Herold Book & Publ., c1911 – 1mf – us A.T.L.A. [240]

MENNONITE FAMILY ALMANAC – 1870 (complete) – 1r – 1 – ATLA 1993-S001 – us A.T.L.A. [073]

MENNONITE HISTORICAL BULLETIN – v1- 1940- 1; v33- 5,6; v35- 9 – us UMI [240]

MENNONITE LIFE – (1985-. 5,6,9) – v1- – 1 – us UMI [240]

MENNONITE MISSIONARY MESSENGER – (lacks: no 3) – v1. 1901 – 1r – 1 – ATLA 1993-S009 – us A.T.L.A. [073]

MENNONITE REPORTER – (1985-. 5,6,9) – v2- – 1 – us UMI [240]

THE MENNONITE REPORTER – (v10-19 1980-89 Can$60.00y) – Waterloo. v10-24. 1980-94 – 1 – Can$85.00y – cn Micromedia [240]

THE MENNONITE REPORTER – v10-25. 1980-95 – 1 – Prices vary – cn Micromedia [073]

Mennonite Seminary Library. Amsterdam *see* SEVENTEENTH CENTURY DOCUMENTS RELATED TO BAPTISTS

MENNONITE SERIALS COLLECTION *see*
- ANGENEHME STUNDEN
- BEAMS OF LIGHT
- BOTSCHAFTER DER WAHRHEIT
- BOTSCHAFTER DES HEILS IN CHRISTO UND ZEICHEN DIESER ZEIT
- BRETHREN'S ALMANAC AND DIRECTORY
- BUNDESBOTE-KALENDER
- THE CHRISTIAN EVANGEL
- THE CHRISTIAN EXPONENT
- CHRISTIAN MONITOR
- DER CHRISTLICHE JUGEND-FREUND
- DAS CHRISTLICHE VOLKS-BLATT
- CHRISTLICHER BUNDES-BOTE
- CHRISTLICHER FAMILIEN-KALENDER
- THE COMPLETE MAN
- CORRESPONDENCE OF THE MENNONITE WOMAN'S MISSIONARY SOCIETY
- DIRECTORY OF THE BRETHREN IN CHRIST
- DIRECTORY OF THE CHURCH OF THE BRETHREN IN CHRIST
- DIRECTORY OF THE MEMBERS AND OFFICIALS OF THE BRETHREN IN CHRIST CHURCH
- DAS ECHO
- EVANGELICAL VISITOR
- DER EVANGELISATIONS-BOTE
- EVANGELISATIONSBOTE AND GOSPEL TIDINGS
- EVANGELIUMS PANIER
- EVENING AT HOME
- FAMILIEN-KALENDER
- FAMILY ALMANAC
- DIE GEMEINDE UNTERM KREUZ
- GENERAL CONFERENCE MENNONITE CHURCH
- GOSPEL BANNER
- THE GOSPEL BANNER
- GOSPEL HERALD
- THE GOSPEL TEACHER
- GOSPEL TIDINGS
- GOSPEL TRUTHS
- THE GOSPEL WITNESS
- HANDBOOK OF INFORMATION OF THE GENERAL CONFERENCE OF THE MENNONITE CHURCH OF N.A.
- DER HEILS-BOTE
- THE HERALD OF TRUTH
- HEROLD DER WAHRHEIT
- KINDER BOTE
- DER KINDERBOTE
- KINDER-BOTE AND JUNIOR-MESSENGER
- DIE KIRCHE UNTERM KREUZ
- DER KLEINE SAEMANN
- THE MENNONITE
- THE MENNONITE AND THE CHRISTIAN EVANGEL
- MENNONITE FAMILY ALMANAC
- MENNONITE MISSIONARY MESSENGER
- MENNONITE YEAR BOOK AND ALMANAC
- MENNONITE YOUNG PEOPLE'S BIBLE MEETING TOPICS
- MENNONITE YOUNG PEOPLE'S MEETING TOPICS
- DER MENNONITISCHE FRIEDENSBOTE
- MENNONITISCHER FAMILIEN-KALENDER
- MESSENGER OF TRUTH
- THE MISSION WORKER
- MONTHLY LETTER
- NACHRICHTEN AUS DER HEIDENWELT FUER ALT UND JUNG
- RELIGIOESER BOTSCHAFTER
- THE REVIEW
- SAEMANN
- DER SAEMANN
- THE SUNDAY SCHOOL BANNER
- DER WAHRHEITSFREUND
- THE WATCHFUL PILGRIM
- WELCOME TIDINGS
- WORDS OF CHEER
- YEAR BOOK OF THE GENERAL CONFERENCE OF THE MENNONITE CHURCH OF N.A.
- YOUNG PEOPLE'S BIBLE MEETING TOPICS
- YOUNG PEOPLE'S PAPER
- YOUTH'S MONITOR
- ZION'S TIDINGS
- ZUR HEIMATH

MENNONITE SOURCES UP TO 1600 – 773 titles – 9 – ne IDC [240]

MENNONITE YEAR BOOK AND ALMANAC – 1895-1930 (complete) – 1r – 1 – ATLA 1993-S005 – us A.T.L.A. [240]

MENNONITE YEARBOOK AND DIRECTORY – (Lacking: 1948-50) – 1947-84 – Inquire – 1 – ATLA S0647 – us A.T.L.A. [240]

MENNONITE YOUNG PEOPLE'S BIBLE MEETING TOPICS – 1913-14 (complete) – 1r – 1 – ATLA 1994-S001 – us A.T.L.A. [240]

MENNONITE YOUNG PEOPLE'S BIBLE MEETING TOPICS – 1939-1944 (complete) – 1r – 1 – ATLA 1994-S003 – us A.T.L.A. [240]

MENNONITE YOUNG PEOPLE'S MEETING TOPICS – 1915-18 (complete) – 1r – 1 – ATLA 1994-S002 – us A.T.L.A. [240]

THE MENNONITES IN IOWA / Gingerich, Melvin – (Iowa City: State Historical Society of Iowa, 1939). Iowa Reel 2. (The Cox Library Collection) – 5 – us Americana [240]

MENNONITISCHE BLAETTER – 1974-85 (complete) – Inquire – 1 – ATLA S0432 – us A.T.L.A. [073]

MENNONITISCHE BLAETTER – Danzig, (Gdansk). Jan 1854-Mai 1941 – 4r – 1 – gw Mikrofilm [240]

MENNONITISCHE BLAETTER – Danzig, Jan 1854-Mai 1941 – 4r – 1 – DM400.00 – gw Mikro Press [072]

DER MENNONITISCHE FRIEDENSBOTE – v11-26. 1867-81 (complete) – 3r – 1 – ATLA 1994-S009 – us A.T.L.A. [073]

MENNONITISCHE RUNDSCHAU : EIN CHRISTLICHES FAMILIENBLATT / ed by Der Konferenz der Mennoniten-Bruedergemeinde in Kanada – Winnipeg, Canada. 1972- – 1 – gw Mikrofilm [072]

MENNONITISCHE RUNDSCHAU – (v.102-. 1979-5,6,9) – v.1-. 1880- – 1 – us UMI [073]

MENNONITISCHER FAMILIEN-KALENDER – 1870 (complete) – 1r – 1 – ATLA 1993-S003 – us A.T.L.A. [073]

MENOLOGIUM BENEDICTINUM / Bucelini, Gabr. – Feldkirch, 1655 – 42mf – 8 – Dfl147.00 – ne Slangenburg [240]

MENOLOGIUM CISTERCIENSIS / Henriquez, Chrysostomus – Antwerpen, 1630 – 25mf – 8 – Dfl32.00 – ne Slangenburg [240]

Menominee Restoration Committee *see* AQUACHAMINE

Menon, C Narayana *see* SHAKESPEARE CRITICISM: AN ESSAY IN SYNTHESIS

Menon (pseud. Agostino Rava) *see* VETTUORIA INCONTRA EL TURCO, DE MENON

MENORAH : INDEPENDENT ORDER OF B'NAI B'RITH – New York. v1-42. 1886-1907 (all publ) – 8r – 1 – us Ross [270]

THE MENORAH – New York. N.Y. 1886-1907 – 1 – us A.J.P.C. [071]

MENORAH, JARHON MESEWAJER LEBET HA-JEHUDI : ILLUSTRIERTE MONATSSCHRIFT FUER DIE JUEDISCHE FAMILIE / ed by Hoffmann, Norbert – Wien, 1923-32 – 75mf – 9 – subsc: DM520.00 diazo DM600.00 silver – gw Olms [270]

MENORAH (TEHINNOT) – Prague. c.1650? BJ-43-55 1 – 9 – ne IDC [270]

Menovscikov, G A *see* ESKIMOSSKO RUSSKII SLOVAR'

Menovshchikov, G A *see* ESKIMOSSKO-RUSSKII SLOVAR'

MENS EN MAATSCHAPPIJ – (v.54-. 1979-5,6,9) – v.23-. 1948- – 1 – us UMI [073]

MENS EN ONDERNEMING – Mededelingen van het psychologisch Centrum van de Nederlandse Steenkolenmijnen. Haarlem. 1947-50. BH-1805 1 – 9 – ne IDC [150]

Mensaert, G P *see* LE PEINTRE AMATEUR ET CURIEUX

MENSAGEIRO : ORGAM DA PROPAGANDA SPIRITA – Manaos, Amazonas. 1-15 Jan, Maio, Ago-Set 1901; Maio-Jun, 1 Set 1902 – 1,5,6 – bl Biblioteca [072]

O MENSAGEIRO : REVISTA CATHOLICA, SOCIAL – Serro, 15 Oct 1891; Mar-Apr 1892; Mar, 9 Apr 1893 – 1,5,6 – bl Biblioteca [072]

O MENSAGEIRO DA BAHIA – Salvador, 20 Mar 1832 – 1,5,6 – bl Biblioteca [072]

MENSAGEIRO D'APPARECIDA – Tres Pontas, Brazil. May 1917 – 1 – bl Biblioteca [072]

MENSAGEIRO DO EVANGELHO : CASTELO FORTE – nos18-19. 1963-1964 (complete) – Inquire – 1 – ATLA S0894 – us A.T.L.A. [073]

MENSAGEIRO DO EVANGELHO – v18 nos6-7. 1963 (complete) – Inquire – 1 – ATLA S0893 – us A.T.L.A. [073]

MENSAGEM – Sete Lagoas, 27 Feb 1963 – 1,5,6 – bl Biblioteca [072]

MENSAGERO ARGENTINO – Buenos Aires. Argentina. -w. Nov 1825-Dec 1826. (1 reel) – 1 – uk British Libr Newspaper [072]

EL MENSAGERO SEMANAL – New York. v1-3. 1828-31 – 1r – 1 – us Ross [071]

MENSAJE DE AMISTAD A LA NACION MEXICANA / Becerra, Hasperue – Mexico: [s.n.], 1952 – 1 – CSUXADQ4909-B – us Hoover Inst Photo [320]

MENSAJE DE ARTESANIA, LO QUE TE DECIAN OBRERO / Sanz, Angel B – Delegacion Sindical Local de la Central Nacional-Sindicalista de Valencia de Alcantara. Caceres: Tip. El Noticiero, S.A., (1937) – 1 – sp Bibl Santa Ana [946]

MENSAJE DE EXTREMADURA / Munoz de San Pedro, Miguel – Barcelona, 1969 – 1 – sp Bibl Santa Ana [946]

MENSAJE DEL EXCELENTISIMO SENOR PRESIDENTE DE LA NACION, GRAL. EDELMIRO J. FARRELL, Y MEMORIA DEL SEGUNDO ANO DE LABOR : SECUNDO ANIVERSARIO DEL GOBIERNO DE LA REVOLUCION, 1943-4 DE JUNIO-1945 – [Buenos Aires?, 1945?] – 1 – CSUXADQ4406-B – us Hoover Inst Photo [320]

MENSAJE DEL GOBIERNO A ESPANA / Spain. Ministerio del Interior – n.p., 1938. Fiche W1045. (Blodgett Collection of Spanish Civil War Pamphlets) – 9 – us H.U. College Libr [946]

MENSAJE DEL PODER EJECUTIVO E INFORME DEL MINISTERIO DE HACIENDA : CUENTA DE INVERSION / Argentina. Ministerio de Hacienda de la Nacion – (Includes c.1: 1948-1950, 1952, 1954) – Buenos Aires: Ministerio de Hacienda, [19–]- – 1 – CSUXAJA7598-S – us Hoover Inst Photo [324]

MENSAJE DEL PRESIDENTE DE LA REPUBLICA TENIENTE GENERAL JUAN D. PERON : PRONUNCIADO EN LA ASAMBLEA LEGISLATIVA EL 1. DE MAYO DE 1974, Y RESENA DE LA OBRA DEL GOBIERNO DEL PUEBLO EXPUESTA POR LOS MINISTROS DEL PODER EJECUTIVO NACIONAL AL INAUGURAR EL 99. PERIODO DE SESIONES ORDINARIAS / Peron, Juan – [Buenos Aires]: Presidencia de la Nacion, Secretaria de Prensa y Difusion, 1974 – 1 – CSUXADM8832-B – us Hoover Inst Photo [320]

EL MENSAJERO JUVENIL – 1925. 332p – 1 – 11.62 – us Baptist [240]

MENSAJES DE SOL Y LUNA / Delgado Fernandez, Manuel – Madrid: Maribel, Artes Graficas, 1963 – 1 – sp Bibl Santa Ana [810]

MENSARIO DE ESTATISTICA : ORGAO DO SISTEMA REGIONAL – Manaus, Amazonas. Mar, Dez 1938; Jan, Jul 1939; Fev 1940 – 1,5,6 – bl Biblioteca [072]

"O MENSCH" : ROMAN / Bahr, Hermann – Wien: Druckerei der "Neuen Freien Presse", 1910 – 1r – 1 – us U.W. Library [830]

DER MENSCH AN DER WAGE / Paulsen, Rudolf – 2. Aufl. Leipzig: H Haessel, 1926 – 1r – 1 – us U.W. Library [430]

MENSCH AUS ERDE GEMACHT : EIN DRAMA IN 5 AUFZUEGEN UND EINEM VORSPIEL / Griese, Friedrich – 2., veraenderte Aufl. Berlin: Theater-Verlag A Langen/G Mueller, 1933 – 1r – 1 – us U.W. Library [820]

MENSCH EN LAND IN DE MIDDELEEUWEN / Slicher van Bath, B H – Assen. v1-2. 1944 – Dfl32.00 – ne Slangenburg [240]

MENSCH EN MAATSCHAPPIJ – v.1-22. May 1925-47. Continued as Mens en Maatschappij – 1 – us UMI [073]

DER MENSCH IM STANDE DER SCHULD NACH DEM BUCHE JESAJA / Gerlach, Martin von – Leipzig: Akademische Buchhandlung (W Faber), 1890 – 1mf – 9 – 0-8370-3256-3 – 1985-1256 – us A.T.L.A. [220]

MENSCH UND CHRIST: DREI ABHANDLUNGEN / Thum, Rudolf – Dortmund: Wilhelm Cruewell, 1867. 1 fiche – 9 – us A.T.L.A. [240]

MENSCHELYKE BEEZIGHEEDEN BESTAANDE IN REGEERING, KONSTEN EN AMBACHTEN, NA ORDE VAN HET A.B.C, IN HONDERD FIGUUREN, ZINRIJK UITGEBEELD : IN KOPER GEEST EN GESNEEDEN / Luyken, J & Luyken, C – 1st ed. Haarlem, 1695 – 2mf – 9 – O-3116/1 – ne IDC [760]

DES MENSCHEN BEGIN, MIDDEN EN EINDE / Luiken, J – O 349. 1712 – 9 – ne IDC [760]

MENSCHENBILDUNG UND KINDERARBEIT BEI PESTALOZZI UND OWEN : EINE ANALYSE DER ERZIEHUNGSWERKE PESTALOZZIS UND OWENS ALS BEITRAG ZUR IDEENGESCHICHTE DER ARBEITSSCHULE / Koneffke, Gernot – Heidelberg, 1961 –

3mf – DM76.00 – 3-89349-967-9 – gw Hänsel [370]
DER MENSCHENFEIND : SCHAUSPIEL IN 3 AKTEN, MIT BEIBEHALT DES GLEICHNAMIGEN SCHILLER'SCHEN FRAGMENTES / Bieleck, Rudolph – 1. Aufl. Wien: Im Selbstverlage des Verfassers, 1872 – 1 – us U.W. Library [820]
MENSCHENKINDER : NOVELLENSAMMLUNG / Andreas-Salome, Lou – Stuttgart: Cotta, 1902 – 1r – 1 – us U.W. Library [830]
HET MENSCHENOFFER IN ISRAEL / Oort, Henricus – Haarlem: A.C. Kruseman, 1865. 1 fiche – 9 – us A.T.L.A. [270]
MENSCHENOPFER BEI DEN ALTEN HEBRAEERN / Mommert, Carl – Leipzig: E. Haberland, 1905. 1 fiche – 9 – us A.T.L.A. [270]
DIE MENSCHENRECHTE / ed by Kuczynski, Juergen – Berlin, apr 1 1926-jun 3 1932 – 1r – 1 – Dist. gw Mikrofilm – gw Misc Inst [073]
DIE MENSCHENRECHTE – Organ der Deutschen Liga fuer Menschenrechte. Berlin. v1-7. 1926-1932. Lacking: v4, 1929. B675. (Leo Baeck Institute. German-Jewish Periodicals, Pt 1) – 1r – 1 – $75.00 – us UPA [270]
MENSCHENSCHICKSALE / Storm, Theodor; ed by Hoyer, Richard – Koeln: Atlas-Verlag, [19–] – 1r – 1 – us U.W. Library [830]
DAS MENSCHLICH ANZIEHENDE IN DER ERSCHEINUNG JESU CHRISTI / Zart, Gustav – Muenchen: C.H. Beck, 1898. 1 fiche – 9 – us A.T.L.A. [240]
DIE MENSCHLICHE WILLENSFREIHEIT IM LEHRSYSTEM DES THOMAS VON AQUIN UND JOHANNES DUNS SCOTUS / Auer, J – Muenchen, 1938 – 7mf – 8 – ne Slangenburg [190]
HET MENSELYK BEDRYF VERTOOND, IN. 100. VERBEELDINGEN : VAN: AMBACHTEN, KONSTEN, HANTEERINGEN EN BEDRYVEN: MET VERSEN / Luyken, J & Luyken, C – 1st ed. Amsterdam, 1694 – 2mf – 9 – O-3117/1 – ne IDC [760]
Men'shchikov, L *see* OKHRANA I REVOLIUTSIIA
Menshchikova, L *see* NE MOGU MOLCHAT
MENSHEVIK COLLECTION – 1903-19 PLUS INDEX – 1 – 35.00r – us Hoover Inst Photo [080]
MENSHEVIKI I ESERY V RUSSKOI REVOLIUTSII / Bystrianskii, Vadim – Peterburg: Gos. izd-vo, 1921 – 1 – CSUX88-B2155 – us Hoover Inst Photo [947]
MENSHEVIZM V PERIOD SOVETSKOI VLASTI / Dallin, David J – [S.l.: s.n., 195-?] – 1 – CSUX89-B6605 – us Hoover Inst Photo [947]
MENSTRUAL DYSFUNCTION IN RUNNERS / Triana, Beverly F – 1989 – 188p 2mf – 9 – $8.00 – us Microform Publ [612]
MENSUR SIIRLER / Usakligil, Halit Ziya – Izmir: Hidmet Matbaasi, 1307 [1890] – $30.00 – us MEDOC [470]
Men'sutin, A *see* POEZIIA PERVYKH LET REVOLIUTSII 1917-1920
THE MENTAL CHARACTERISTICS OF THE LORD JESUS CHRIST / Bernard, Henry Norris – New York:Thomas Whittaker, 1888 – 1mf – 9 – 0-8370-2647-4 – 1985-0647 – us A.T.L.A. [240]
MENTAL DISEASES: A SYNOPSIS OF TWELVE LECTURES DELIVERED AT THE HOSPITAL FOR THE INSANE, TORONTO, TO THE GRADUATING MEDICAL CLASSES / Clark, Daniel – Toronto: W. Briggs; Montreal: C. W. Coates; Halifax: S. F. Huestis, 1895?. 00661. (Pre-1900 Canadiana) – 9 – cn C.I.H.M. [616]
MENTAL HEALTH LEGISLATION IN CANADA, 1959 / Canada. Department of National Health and Welfare – Ottawa: Research and Statistics Division, Dept. of National Health and Welfare, 1960. 40p. LL-2399 – 1 – us L of C Photodup [324]
MENTAL RETARDATION – v1- 1963- 1; v9-5,6; v13- 9 – us UMI [616]
MENTAL RETARDATION ABSTRACTS – 1964-73 1; 1970-73 5,6 – us UMI [360]
MENTAL RETARDATION NEWS – v. 1- 1952- – 1 – us UMI [073]
MENTALLY ILL PERSONS RECORDS / Huron County. Ohio. Probate Court – 1855-1954 – 3r – 1 – $32.50r – us Archival [324]
LE MENTEUR : HUMORISTIQUE – Montreal, Canada. 17 oct 1878; 26 oct 1878 – 1r – 1 – Can$25.00 – cn Can Microfilming [072]
MENTJIPTAKAN UHUWWAH ISLAMIJAH / Usman el Muhammady, T. M – SE 5946 1 – 9 – ne IDC [260]
MENTON AND MONTE CARLO NEWS – (Riviera News). Menton. France. -w. 15 Nov 1913-Aug 1939, 31 May 1947-Jul 1948. (8 reels) – 1 – uk British Libr Newspaper [072]
Mentor Willoughby. Ohio. Baptist Church. (Ohio Plains Conference) *see* CHURCH RECORDS, MS 654
Mentrida, Alonso de *see* ARTE DE LA LENGUA HILIGUAYNA DE LA ISLA DE PANAY.
Mentzel, C *see* SYLLOGE MINUTIARUM LEXICI
Mentzel, Elisabeth Schippel *see* DER FRANKFURTER GOETHE
MENUDENCIAS / Pineda, Ramon – Badajoz: Imprenta Industrias Graficas, 1960 – sp Bibl Santa Ana [946]
MENUDJU PRIBADI JANG MULIA DAN TINGGI / Kasim Sulaiman – Medan, Saiful, 1950. 72p. SEM-676/1 – 9 – ne IDC [950]
MENUDJU REPUBLIK INDONESIA (KARJA 1924) / Tan Malaka – SE 5758 1. 1967 – 9 – ne IDC [320]
MENUS PROPOS D'UN CATHOLIQUE LIBERAL / Chaine, Leon – (Includes bibliographical references and index) – Paris: Librairie critique, 1908 – 1mf – 9 – 0-8370-8656-6 – 1986-2656 – us A.T.L.A. [240]
Menzel, Alfred *see* GOETHES WELT- UND LEBENSANSCHAUUNG
Menzel, G *see* VERSUCH EINER ERKLAERUNG VON EPHESER 5:31
Menzel, Herybert *see*
– DER GRENZMARK-RAPPE
– HERRN FIGULLAS SCHAUFENSTER
Menzel, Konrad *see* DENKWUERDIGKEITEN
Menzel, Roderich *see* DAS HEIMLICHE LEUCHTEN
Menzel, Wolfgang *see*
– DENKWUERDIGKEITEN
– DEUTSCHE DICHTUNG VON DER AELTESTEN BIS AUF DIE NEUESTE ZEIT
– DIE DEUTSCHE LITERATUR
Menzies, Allan *see*
– THE CHURCH HISTORY OF THE FIRST THREE CENTURIES
– THE EARLIEST GOSPEL: A HISTORICAL STUDY OF THE GOSPEL ACCORDING TO MARK
MEPPENER TAGESPOST : BA DER NEUEN OSNABRUECKER ZEITUNG – Meppen, West Germany. 1977- – ca 7r per yr – 1 – gw Mikrofilm [072]
O MEQUETREFE : PERIODICO LIVRE E ILLUSTRADO – Maceio, Alagoas. 12 Set-7 Nov 1886 – 1,5,6 – bl Biblioteca [072]
LA MER / Geouffre de la Pradelle, A de – Paris, 1934 – 7mf – 1 – ILM-1650/1 – ne IDC [327]
LA MER COTIERE / Godey, P – Paris, 1896 – 3mf – 1 – ILM-1834/1 – ne IDC [327]
MERAH PUTIH – Djakarta. Incomplete. SE-925 1. 1953-1968 – 9 – ne IDC [073]
MERAM – (Sahib-i Imtiyaz. Rafet Avni, Muedurue: OEmer Lutfi. Nos. 1-10 (30 Tesriniewel-29 Kanunisani 1324[1908])) – Istanbul: Selanik Matbaasi, 1908 – 5mf – 9 – $90.00 – us MEDOC [949]
MERASIM-I TESRIFATIYEYE TABI BULUNAN KABULLARDAN MAADA HUZUR-I HUEMAYUNDA HUSUSI SURETTE SEREF-I MUESULE NAILIYET HAKKINDA TALIMATNAMEDIR – Dersaadet: Tanin Matbassi, 1329? [1913] – $10.00 – us MEDOC [956]
MER'AT-I SUUNAT / Memduh, Mehmed – Izmir: Ahenk Matbaasi, 1328 [1912] – $42.00 – us MEDOC [956]
LE MERAVIGLIE DELL'ARTE... / Ridolfi, C – Venetia, 1648 – 9 – ne IDC [700]
MERBEIN IRRIGATIONIST – 1919-1920. Ml1 – 1r – 1 – at Corangamite [072]
Mercadier de Belesta, Jean-Baptiste *see* EBAUCHE D'UNE DESCRIPTION ABREGEE DU DEPARTEMENT DE L'ARIEGE
Mercado, L *see*
– INSTITUTIONES QUE SU MAGESTAD MANDO HACER A VIS MERCADO PARA EL EXAMEN DE LOS ALGEBRISTAS
– LIBRO EN QUE TRATA CON CLARIDAD LA NATURALEZA, CAUSAS, PROVIDENCIA Y MODO DE CURAR LA ENFERMEDAD VULGAR, PESTE
Mercado, Luys de *see* GONAECIERUM LIBRI 3. DE MORBIS MULIERUM COMMUNIBUS...
Mercado, M *see* INSTRUCCION SOBRE LA PESTE
Mercado, P *see* DE FEBRIUM DIFFERENTIIS...
MERCANTIL : JORNAL COMMERCIAL, NOTICIOSO, LITTERARIO E ECCLESIASTICO – Maceio, Alagoas. 1 Dez 1863; Out 1864; 23 Jan 1865 – 1,5,6 – bl Biblioteca [072]
O MERCANTIL – Rio de Janeiro, 16 Sep 1844-31 Dec 1847 – 1,5,6 – bl Biblioteca [072]
O MERCANTIL *see* CORREIO MERCANTIL
O MERCANTIL DO PILAR – Pilar, Alagoas. 19 Mar 1870 – 1,5,6 – bl Biblioteca [072]
EL MERCANTIL EXTREMENO – Badajoz, 1902-1904 – 5 – sp Bibl Santa Ana [073]
MERCANTILE ADVERTISER – New York, N.Y. 1798-1820 – 3 – 850.00 – us Readex [071]
THE MERCANTILE AND LEGAL RECORD FOR BRITISH COLUMBIA – Nelson [BC]: R G Dun, [1892?-19–] – 9 – cn C.I.H.M. [332]
MERCANTILE GAZETTE AND PRICES CURRENT – San Francisco, CA. Jun 1856-Jul 1864 – 1r – 1 – $50.00 – B02841 – us Library Micro [071]
MERCANTILE GUIDE AND CALIFORNIA, BUSINESS DIRECTORIES – State of California. v18. 1914-1915 – 2r – 1 – $100.00 – D114 – us Library Micro [380]
Mercantile Guide Co *see* MERCANTILE GUIDE TO CITIES AND SUBURBS OF THE UNITED STATES OF AMERICA, CALIFORNIA AND NORTHWEST EDITION
MERCANTILE GUIDE TO CITIES AND SUBURBS OF THE UNITED STATES OF AMERICA, CALIFORNIA AND NORTHWEST EDITION / Mercantile Guide Co – San Francisco, 1893. Calif. reel 38. (Cox Library Collection) – 5 – us Americana [978]
MERCANTILE JOURNAL / ed by Wright, G J – Quebec, Canada. 4 sep 1816 – 1r – 1 – Can$25.00 – cn Can Microfilming [072]
THE MERCANTILE REVIEW – Ottawa: F B Linden, [1887-18- or 19–] – 9 – cn C.I.H.M. [650]
THE MERCANTILE TEST AND LEGAL RECORD – Toronto: [s.n, 1871?-18– or 19–] – 9 – cn C.I.H.M. [650]
Mercati, Giovanni *see* UN ANTICO CATALOGO GRECO DE' ROMANI PONTEFICI INEDITO
MERCATOR – v. 1-181. 1 May 1713-20 Jul 1714 – 1 – us UMI [073]
LA MERCED (COMPENDIO HISTORICO EN 12 LECCIONES) / Guede, Lisardo – Olivenza: Tip. Martinez Rengifo, 1965 – sp Bibl Santa Ana [946]
MERCED COUNTY, MERCED CITY AND ATWATER – Merced Co, CA. 1914; 1920; 1924-1931; 1938-1948; 1955-1956 – 12r – 1 – $600.00 – D059 – us Library Micro [978]
MERCED COUNTY TIMES – Merced, CA. 1990 – 3+ r – 1 – $150.00 ($90.00y) – B06037 – us Library Micro [071]
MERCED MORNING STAR – (Cont by: Merced Sun-Star) – Merced, CA. 1921-Jun 1925 – 9r – 1 – $450.00 – B02451 – us Library Micro [071]
MERCED SUN-STAR – Merced, CA. 1880-83; 1891-92; 1900-06; 1925- – 335+ r – 1 BC02453 – $16,750.00 ($480.00y) – us Library Micro [071]
MERCED SUN-STAR *see* MERCED MORNING STAR
LOS MERCEDARIOS EN EL PERU EN EL SIGLO 16. DOCUMENTOS INEDITOS DEL ARCHIVO GENERAL DE INDIAS. TOMO 1. ROMA, 1933 / Barriga, Victor – Madrid: Razon y Fe, 1935 – 1 – sp Bibl Santa Ana [972]
MERCED/MARIPOSA – 1989 – 9+ r – 1 – $450.00 – P00062 – us Library Micro [910]
MERCER BEASLEY LAW REVIEW *see* RUTGERS LAW REVIEW
MERCER COUNTY STANDARD – (Weekly Democratic newspaper) – Celina, OH. 1870-76 – 2r – 1 – us Western Res [071]
Mercer, Jesse *see* THE CLUSTER OF SPIRITUAL SONGS, DIVINE HYMNS AND SACRED POEMS
MERCER LAW REVIEW – v. 26-. 1974- – 1,5,6,9 – us UMI [340]
MERCER LAW REVIEW – v1-46. 1949-95 – 9 – $849.00 set – us Hein [340]
Mercer, Samuel A B *see*
– THE ETHIOPIC LITURGY
– THE TELL EL-AMARNA TABLETS
Merchan Cantisan, Felisa *see* CAMINOS DEL ALMA
Merchan Merchan, Felipe *see* COLONIZACION Y PARCELACIONES
Merchan Vargas, Regina *see* DIVORCIAS? !LAGARTO!
MERCHANDISING – v. 1- 1976- (Supercedes Merchandising Week) – 1 – us UMI [380]
MERCHANDISING WEEK – v. 1-108. 1907-76 – 1 – us UMI [380]
Merchant *see* HARVESTER, FOR GATHERING THE RIPENED CROPS ON EVERY HOMESTEAD: LEAVING THE UNRIPE TO MATURE
THE MERCHANT ADVENTURES OF ENGLAND / Lingelbach, W E – H-1334 2. 1902 – 8 – ne IDC [941]
Merchant Ship Classification Society *see* REGISTRE MARITIME
THE MERCHANT SHIPPING CODE OF THE USSR (1968) / Russia. (1923-U.S.S.R.). Laws, Statutes, etc – Baltimore: Johns Hopkins, 1970. 169p. LL-4217 – 1 – us L of C Photodup [340]
THE MERCHANTMAN – Toronto: [s.n, 1873?-18– or 19–] – 9 – cn C.I.H.M. [380]
THE MERCHANTS' LAW BOOK; BEING A TREATISE ON THE LAW OF ACCOUNT RENDER, ATTACHMENT, BAILMENT, BILLS OF EXCHANGE AND PROMISSORY NOTES. / Grimshaw, William – Philadelphia: Hunt, 1831. 346p. LL-338 – 1 – us L of C Photodup [340]
MERCHANT'S MAGAZINE AND COMMERCIAL REVIEW – v. 1-63. Jul 1839-Dec 1870 – 1 – us UMI [380]
MERCHANTS MAGAZINE AND COMMERCIAL REVIEW – New York. v1-113. 1839-77 (all publ) – 9 – LLMC 84-603 – us L.L.M.C. [073]
THE MERCHANTS' MAGAZINE AND FINANCIAL REVIEW – [Montreal?]: F Weir, 1891 (Montreal: J Lovell) – 9 – cn C.I.H.M. [332]
Merci, J *see* PRESPEVKY K DEJINAM HNUTIA POLNOHOSPODARSKYCH ROBOTNIKOV
Mercier, Charles *see* LE PROPHETE OSEE
Mercier, Desire *see* LE MODERNISME
THE MERCIER GOVERNMENT BEFORE THE ELECTORS: A DISASTROUS REGIME – 1890. 00352. (Pre-1900 Canadiana) – 9 – cn C.I.H.M. [971]
Mercier, Honore *see*
– L'AVENIR DU CANADA: DISCOURS PRONONCE AU PARC SOHMER A MONTREAL, LE 4 AVRIL 1893
– DISCOURS DE L'HON. M. MERCIER, PREMIER MINISTRE DE LA PROVINCE DE QUEBEC DEVANT UNE ASSEMBLEE A LA SALLE BONSECOURS A MONTREAL, LE 9 FEVRIER, 1891
– LES PRINCIPES DE L'HON. M. MERCIER
Mercier, Jean (Mercerius, Joannes) *see* EMBLEMATA
Mercier, Jean-Jacques *see* LA VOIX POPULAIRE
Mercier, Jeanne Mance *see* BIO-BIBLIOGRAPHIE DE BEATRICE CLEMENT
Mercier, Louis S *see* DE J.J. ROUSSEAU, CONSIDERE COMME L'UN DES PREMIERS AUTEURS DE LA REVOLUTION
Mercier, Louis-Sebastien *see*
– L'AN DEUX MILLE QUATRE CENT QUARANTE, REVE S'IL EN FUT JAMAIS, SUIVI DE L'HOMME DE FER, SONGE
– L'HOMME SAUVAGE. HISTOIRE TRADUITE PAR M. MERCIER
Mercier, LS *see* LA NEOLOGIE OU VOCABULAIRE DES MOTS NOUVEAUX A RENOUVELER, AN- 9
Merck, C H *see* ETHNOGRAPHISCHE BEOBACHTUNGEN UEBER DIE VOELKER DES BERINGSMEERES 1789-91
Merck, Johann Heinrich *see*
– BRIEFE AN UND VON JOHANN HEINRICH MERCK
– FRANKFURTER GELEHRTE ANZEIGEN
MERCK'S JAHRESBERICHT – v. 39-70. 1925-1957 – 1,5,6 – us Princeton Micro [610]
MERCKWUERDIGE MISSIONS- UND REISE-BESCHREIBUNG NACH CONGO IN ETHIOPIEN / Zuchelli, A – Frankfurt. 1715. BA-108 2 – 8 – ne IDC [910]
MERCURE ARMORIAL, ENSEIGNANT LES PRINCIPES ET ELEMENS DU BLAZON DES ARMOIRIES / Segoing, Charles – Paris: chez Alexandre Lesselin..., 1649. SEM16P304 – 1r – 5 – Can$9.00 – cn Bibl Nat [321]
LE MERCURE DE FRANCE – Revue universelle de litterature et des beaux-arts. Paris. nov 1851-fevr 1853 – 1 – fr A.C.R.P.P. [073]
MERCURE DE FRANCE – Serie moderne. Paris. 1890-juil aout 1965. tb: 1890-1924 – 1 – fr A.C.R.P.P. [073]

MERCURE DE FRANCE – v. 1-1148. 1672-1810. Missing issues – 1 – 2,561.00 – us L of C Photodup [073]
LE MERCURE GALANT – Paris. mars 1672-1832 – 1 – fr A.C.R.P.P. [073]
Mercure, Henri *see* BIBLIOGRAPHIE ANALYTIQUE DE L'OEUVRE DE GERARD MORISSET, N.P., DE LA SOCIETE ROYALE DU CANADA...
MERCURE HISTORIQUE ET POLITIQUE – Paris. 1734 – 1 – fr A.C.R.P.P. [073]
LE MERCURE SEGUSIEN – Journal des arts et du commerce. no. 1-2684. Saint-Etienne. 29 oct 1825-7 juil 1848 – 1 – fr A.C.R.P.P. [073]
MERCURE UNIVERSEL – Paris. mars 1791-94 (I-XLVI) – 1 – fr A.C.R.P.P. [073]
MERCURIALIS OF WINTERGROEN / Abraham a Sancta Clara – O-533 1. 1763 – 9 – ne IDC [700]
MERCURIUS MUSICUS – 1699-1702 – 1 – us UMI [780]
MERCURY – (Also known as: Daily Mercury) – Oroville, CA. 1883-91; 1897-1903; 1904 (broken series); 1908-27; 1940-53 – 98r – 1 BC02574 – $4,900.00 – us Library Micro [071]
MERCURY – Charleston. S.C. 1822-1868 – 1 – us UMI [071]
MERCURY – (Current issues avail on subscription) – Hobart, 1854-1996 – 636r – 1 – at Pascoe [072]
MERCURY – Kinsley. Kan. -w. 1883-1965 – 1 – us UMI [071]
MERCURY – Manhattan. Kan. 1961- – 1 – us UMI [071]
MERCURY – Moline. Kan. 1882-1889 – 1 – us UMI [071]
MERCURY / Montague, Katherine & Montague, Peter – 1r – 5,9 – $50.00 – B70007 – us Library Micro [622]
MERCURY – New York. N.Y. 1753-1759; 1829 – 1 – us UMI [071]
MERCURY – Newport. R.I. 1822-1928 – 1 – us UMI [071]
MERCURY – Newport. R.I. and Weekly News. 1928-49 – 1 – us UMI [071]
MERCURY – Oroville. Calif. 1951-53 – 1 – us UMI [071]
MERCURY – Oroville. Calif. -w. 1875-87 – 1 – us UMI [071]
MERCURY – Pottstown. Pa. 1933- – 1 – us UMI [071]
THE MERCURY – Hobart, Australia. -d. Jan 1941-26 April 1957; 1 Jan 1968-31 Dec 1973. 276 reels – 1 – uk British Libr Newspaper [072]
THE MERCURY – Pittsburgh. Pa. 1812-1842 – 1 – us UMI [071]
THE MERCURY – Quebec, Canada. v1 n6. 11 mar 1933 – 1r – 1 – Can$25.00 – cn Can Microfilming [072]
THE MERCURY – Toronto. Syrian-Lebanese Newspaper. 1936-38 – 1 – 65.00 – cn McLaren [072]
MERCURY BEXLEY BOROUGH *see* SIDCUP AND BEXLEY MERCURY
MERCURY (DAILY) – San Jose, CA. 1861-62; 1869-70; 1872-79; 1880-1902 – 79r – 1 BC02880 – $3,950.00 – us Library Micro [071]
MERCURY (ENGLISH) – Quebec, 1862-1874 – 7r – 1 – cn Preston [971]
MERCURY GREENWICH BOROUGH – Jul 1995-Mar 1997 – 7r – 1 – uk British Libr Newspaper [072]
MERCURY HERALD – San Francisco. Calif. 1945-1947 – 1 – us UMI [071]
MERCURY HERALD – San Jose, CA. 1945-1947 – 43r – 1 – $2,150.00 – C02882 – us Library Micro [071]
MERCURY LEWISHAM BOROUGH *see* GREENWICH WOOLWICH AND DEPTFORD GAZETTE
MERCURY SERIES – Ottawa, 1972- – 9 – cn Micromedia [073]
MERCURY SERIES: ARCHAEOLOGICAL SURVEY / National Museum of Man – 1972- – 9 – cn Micromedia [930]
MERCURY SERIES: CANADIAN CENTRE FOR FOLK CULTURE STUDIES / National Museum of Man – 1972- – 9 – cn Micromedia [390]
MERCURY SERIES: CANADIAN WAR MUSEUM PAPERS / National Museum of Man – 1972-76 – 9 – cn Micromedia [971]
MERCURY SERIES: COMMUNICATIONS DIVISION / National Museum of Man – 1973-76 – 9 – cn Micromedia [380]
MERCURY SERIES: ETHNOLOGY DIVISION / National Museum of Man – 1972- – 9 – cn Micromedia [306]
MERCURY SERIES: HISTORY DIVISION / National Museum of Man – 1972- – 9 – cn Micromedia [900]
MERCURY (WEEKLY) – San Jose, CA. 1861-81; 1882-84; 1887 – 13r – 1 – $650.00 – B02881 – us Library Micro [071]
MERCURY-REGISTER – Oroville, CA. 1928-44; 1949-51; 1958-90 – 279r – 1 – $13,950.00 – B02575 – us Library Micro [071]
MERCURY'S CADUCEAN ROD: OR, THE GREAT AND WONDERFUL OFFICE OF THE UNIVERSAL MERCURY, OR GOD'S VICEGERENT, DISPLAYED.. / Conti, Luigi de – By Cleidophorus Mystagogus. London: Printed by W. Pearson, and sold by T. Northcott, 1702. Part with Title: "A philosophical epistle, discovering the unreavealed mystery of the three fires of the Sophi" separately paged. Filmed with Sanguis naturae. Madison, 1980 – 1 – us U.W. Library [500]
MERCY AND JUSTICE / Thorning, Joseph Francis – A reply to 450 Protestant bishops and clergymen, prepared at the suggestion and with the approval of Michael J. Curley, Archbishop of Baltimore. New York, 1939. Fiche W1226. (Blodgett Collection of Spanish Civil War Pamphlets) – 9 – us H.U. College Libr [946]
Mercy, Marie-Ch.-I de *see*
– LETTRE DE M. L'EVEQUE DE LUCON A M.M. LES ELECTEURS DE LA VENDEE
– REPONSE DE MONSIEUR MERCI, EVEQUE DE LUCON, A LA LETTRE DE MONSIEUR SERVAN DU VIVIER, NOMME EVEQUE DE LA VENDEE [...]
MERCY WARREN PAPERS, 1709-1841 / Warren, Mercy – (Correspondence with 35 figures prominent in the American War of Independence and 52 pages of her published poetry) – Massachusetts Historical Society – 2r – 1 – $155.00 – us UMI [920]
MERDEKA / Amrullah, Abdul Malik Karim – SE-6700 1. 1946 – 9 – ne IDC [950]
MERDEKA – Bombay. Incomplete. SE-560 1. 1947-1949 – 5mf – 9 – ne IDC [073]
MERDEKA – Djakarta. Indonesia. 1945-1951; 1954-1964 – 1 – us UMI [072]
MERDEKA – New Delhi. Incomplete. SE-561 1. 1948-1950 – 4mf – 9 – ne IDC [073]
MERDEKA EDISI MINGGU – Indonesia. Djakarta. 1955-1965 – 1 – us UMI [072]
MERDEKA, THE VOICE OF FREE INDONESIA – New York. 1948-1949. Lacking: 1949, v1(26-28) – 8mf – 9 – ne IDC [073]
"MERDEKA."SE-11,743/1. 1945 / Amrullah, Abdul Malik Karim – 9 – ne IDC [950]
MERDU; NJANJIAN2 UNTUK KL. 5 DAN 6 S.R / Kasim Sutan Mohammad Sjah – Djakarta, Pustaka Rakjat, 1952. v2 only. illus. SEM-3034/1 – 9 – ne IDC [950]
LA MERE DE DIEU: EPOPEE RELIGIEUSE ET HUMANITAIRE / Constant, Alphonse Louis – Paris. 1844. 389p. (Religion series) – 9 – 15.00 – fr Bibl Nationale [240]
LA MERE ET L'ENFANT – Montreal: S Lachapelle, [1890-1891?] – 9 – cn C.I.H.M. [640]
MERE MARIA DE JESUS EMILIE D'OULTREMONT = THE LIFE OF MOTHER MARY OF JESUS : EMILIA D'OULTREMONT BARONESS D'HOOGHVORST, 1818-78 / Suau, Pierre – (In English) – London: Burns & Oates, 1913 – 2mf – 9 – 0-8370-7026-0 – 1986-1026 – us A.T.L.A. [920]
Meredith, George *see*
– THE AMAZING MARRIAGE
– THE SHAVING OF SHAGPA
– THE WORKS OF GEORGE MEREDITH
Meredith, H *see* AN ACCOUNT OF THE GOLD COAST OF AFRICA
Meredith, New Hampshire.Meredith Baptist Church *see* RECORDS
MEREK PERUSAHAAN DAN PERNIAGAAN / Sugondo Sumodiredjo – SE 4483 1. 1963 – 9 – ne IDC [950]
Meres, Francis *see* PALLADIS TAMIA
Merezhkovskh, D *see* FRANTSISK ASSIZSKII
Merezhkovskii, Dmitrii *see*
– 14 DEKABRIA
– ALEKSANDR PERVYI
– ANTIKHRIST
– BOL'NAIA ROSSIIA
– BUDET RADOST'
– BYLO I BUDET
– DAFNIS I KHLOA
– DANTE
– DVE TAINY RUSSKOI POEZII
– ESHCHE SHAG GRIADUSHCHEGO KHAMA
– GOGOL'
– GOGOL' I CHORT
– GRIADUSHCHII KHAM
– IISUS NEIZVESTNYI
– KHRISTOS I ANTIKHRIST
– L. TOLSTOI I DOSTOEVSKII
– LERMONTOV POET SVERKHCHELOVECH-ESTVA
– LIUBOV' SILNEE SMERTI
– MESSIIA
– NAPOLEON
– NE MIR, NO MECH
– NE VOENNYI DNEVNIK
– NOVYIA STIKHOTVORENIIA
– PAVEL
– PAVEL I
– PERVENTSY SVOBODY
– POLNOE SOBRANIE SOCHINENII
– O PRICHINAKH UPADKA I O NOVYKH TECHENIIAKH SOVREMENNOI RUSSKOI LITERATURY
– PROROK RUSSKOI REVOLIUTSII
– ROMANTIKI
– ROZHDENIE BOGOV
– SIMVOLY
– SMERT' BOGOV
– SOBRANIE STIKHOV (1883-1903)
– STIKHOTVORENIIA (1883-1887)
– TAINA TREKH
– TAINA ZAPADA
– TSAREVICH ALEKSEI
– TSARSTVO ANTIKHRISTA
– VECHNYE SPUTNIKI
– VOSKRESSHIE BOGI
– ZHANNA D'ARK
Merezhkovskii, Dmitrii *see* JOSEPH PILSUDSKI
MERGERS AND ACQUISTIONS – (v.14-. 1979-5,6,9) – v.1-. 1965- – 1 – us UMI [073]
MERHUM PASA – (Followed Markopasa in the Markopasa set) – Nos. 1-4 (1947) – 1mf – 9 – $10.50 – us MEDOC [949]
Merian, Maria Sibylla *see*
– DER RAUPEN WUNDERBARE VERWANDELUNG, UND SONDERBARE BLEUMEN-NAHRUNG
– TODTEN-TANZ
MERIDA / Melida, Jose Ramon – 4th Internationalez Archacologischer Congress. Barcelona. 1929 – 1 – sp Bibl Santa Ana [930]
MERIDA – Merida, 1952-1955 – 5 – sp Bibl Santa Ana [073]
MERIDA / Subsecretariade Turismo – Badajoz: Subsecretaria de Turismo, 1965 – sp Bibl Santa Ana [910]
MERIDA. 4 CONGRES INTERNATIONAL D'ARCHEOLOGIA / Melida, Jose Ramon – Barcelona, 1929 – 1 – sp Bibl Santa Ana [930]
Merida. Ayuntamiento *see* ORDENANZAS MUNICIPALES
MERIDA DAS SPANISCHE ROM / Schulken, Adolf – 1 – sp Bibl Santa Ana [946]
MERIDA EN EL SIGLO 27 (CONTINUACION DE LA "HISTORIA DE LA CIUDAD DE MERIDA" DE MORENO DE VARGAS) / Alvarez Saenz de Buruaga, Jose – Badajoz: Dip. Provincial, 1971. Sep. REE – 1 – sp Bibl Santa Ana [946]
MERIDA. FERIAS Y FIESTAS – (1933, 1934, 1935, 1940, 1941, 1942, 1943, 1944, 1945, 1946, 1946 (hay dos publicaciones distintas), 1947, 1947 (id), 1948, 1950, 1952, 1953, 1955, 1956, 1957, 1958, 1960, 1961, 1962, 1963, 1964, 1965, 1966, 1967, 1968, 1969, 1970, 1921, 1922, 1929, 1971) – 1933- – 1 – sp Bibl Santa Ana [946]
MERIDA. GUIDE DE LA VILLE ET DE SES MONUMENTS / Almagro Basch, Martin – Merida: Direction Generale des Beaux Arts et Deputation Provinciale de Badajoz, 1959 – 1 – sp Bibl Santa Ana [910]
MERIDA, LA ROMA ESPANOLA / Schulken, Adolf – (Traduccion) – 1 – sp Bibl Santa Ana [946]
MERIDA REVISTA-PROGRAMA DE FERIA 1923 – Badajoz: Imp. Joaquin Sanchez, 1923 – 1 – sp Bibl Santa Ana [946]
MERIDA, ROMA DE OCCIDENTE. GUION LITERARIO PARA UN DOCUMENTAL CINEMATOGRAFICO / Jimenez Rodriguez, Fernando – 10p – 1 – sp Bibl Santa Ana [790]
MERIDA Y LOS VIAJEROS / Alvarez Saenz de Buruaga, Jose – Badajoz: Imp. Prov, 1950 – 1 – sp Bibl Santa Ana [946]
MERIDIAN BOOSTER – (1959-1992.-93r) – Lloydminster, 1993 – 6r – 1 – cn Preston [971]
MERIDIAN FIRST BAPTIST CHURCH. MERIDIAN, MISSISSIPPI : CHURCH RECORDS – 1912-53 – 1 – 68.40 – us Baptist [240]
Meridian, Mississippi *see* MISCELLANEOUS EARLY NEWSPAPERS
MERIDIAN STAR – Cozad, NE. -w. May 1896-Feb. 1897 – 1 – us NE Hist [071]
MERIDIENS – Cahiers mensuels de litterature et d'art. Dir. Rene Char. no. 1-3. L'Isle-sur-Sorgue (Vaucluse). avr-dec 1929 – 1 – fr A.C.R.P.P. [073]
MERIDION / Castro, Manuel de – Montevideo. 1946 – 1 – us Res Libr [810]
LE MERIDIONAL LA FRANCE – Marseille. Toutes eds. mai 1971-86 – 1 – fr A.C.R.P.P. [073]
Merimee, Prosper *see* NOTES D'UN VOYAGE DANS L'OUEST DE LA FRANCE
Merino, Alberto *see* EL OBRERO DEL CAMPO
Merino de Jesucristo, Andres *see*
– POEMA. LA MUJER FELIZ. TOMO 1
– POEMA. LA MUJER FELIZ. TOMO 2
– POEMA. LA MUJER FELIZ. TOMO 3
Merino de Torres, Alberto *see*
– APUNTES...HISTORIA...AMIGOS DEL PAIS DE BADAJOZ
– MEMORIA ACERCA...SOCIEDAD..
– EL OBRERO DEL CAMPO (ESTUDIO SOCIAL)
Merino, Eugenio *see* CURA Y MIL VECES CURA. BARCELONA, 1928
Merino Hompanera, Jose *see* ALGUNOS RASGOS SOBRE COMO DEBIERA ORGANIZARSE LA LUCHA ANTITUBERCULOSAS EN EL NUEVO ESTADO ESPANOL NACIONAL SINDICALISTA
Merino, M *see* EL PROTECTOR DE INDIOS
Merino Ortiz, Tomas *see* INFORME LEGAL POR D. FRANCISCO DE ULLOA Y FLORES... CON D. FRANCISCO JAVIER ESCOBAR Y TORRES...Y DONA MARIA LUISA FLORES CHAVES...SOBRE LA PROPIEDAD DE LOS MAYORAZGOS QUE FUNDARON D. JUAN DE LA HINOJOSA Y DONA TERESA CALDERON...
Merino, R P B *see* FLORA DESCRIPTIVA E ILLUSTRADA DE GALICIE
MERIP REPORTS – 1971- – 1 – 5,6. 9 – us UMI [956]
MERIT SYSTEMS PROTECTION BOARD DECISIONS – (Includes index for v1-2. Cont by: Merit Systems Protection Board Reporter publ by West Pub Co) – v1-13. 1979-83 (all publ) – 97mf – 9 – $145.00 – LLMC 83-500 – us L.L.M.C. [324]
MERIT SYSTEMS PROTECTION BOARD REPORTER *see* MERIT SYSTEMS PROTECTION BOARD DECISIONS
Merivale, Charles *see*
– AUTOBIOGRAPHY OF DEAN MERIVALE, WITH SELECTIONS FROM HIS CORRESPONDENCE
– THE CONTINENTAL TEUTONS
– THE CONVERSION OF THE NORTHERN NATIONS
– THE CONVERSION OF THE ROMAN EMPIRE
– ST. PAUL AT ROME
Merivale, Judith Anne *see* AUTOBIOGRAPHY OF DEAN MERIVALE
Merk, Conrad *see* EXCAVATIONS AT THE KESSLERLOCH NEAR THAYNGEN, SWITZERLAND. A CAVE OF THE REINDEER PERIOD
Merk, KJ *see* DAS BREVIER UND DER SAEKULARKLERUS
MERKAZI ITTILAAT – Delhi, India. 1941-Sept 1947; Feb 1948-Jun 1949 – 3r – 1 – us L of C Photodup [072]
Merkel, Bertha *see* DIE SPRACHE DER MUTTER GOETHES
Merkel, F *see* MOLLUSKENFAUNA VON SCHLESIEN
Merkel, Garlieb *see* THERSITES
DER MERKER – Oesterreichische Zeitschrift fuer Musik und Theater. Wien. Jahrg 1 no. 1-Jahrg 13 no. 5. Oct. 1909-Mar. 1922 – 1 – us NY Public [780]
Merker, Mertiz *see* DIE MASAI
DER MERKER; OESTERREICHISCHE ZEITSCHRIFT FUER MUSIK UND THEATER – v. 1-13. 1909-22 – 1 – 152.00 – us L of C Photodup [780]
Merker, Paul *see* REALLEXIKON DER DEUTSCHEN LITERATURGESCHICHTE
DIE MERKMALE DER ISRAELITISCHEN PROPHETIE NACH DER TRADITIONELLEN AUFFASSUNG DES TALMUD / Bass, E – Prag, 1917 – 1mf – 8 – ne Slangenburg [270]
MERKMALE VERSTEHENS- UND BEHALTENSFOERDERNDER KONTEXTUELLER BEDEUTUNGSERKLAERUNGEN / Kostrzewa, Frank – 1992 – 9 – DM98.00 – 3-89349-510-X – gw Hänsel [400]

Merkulov, A V *see*
- BRAT'IA LUGININY, PIONERY KREDITNOI KOOPERATSII I PERVYI KREDITNYI KOOPERATIV V ROSSII
- CHTO CHITAT' PO PROMYSLOVOI KOOPERATSII
- CHTO TAKOE TSENTROSOIUZ?
- IZDANIIA TSENTROSOIUZA ZA 25 LET (1898-1923)
- KAK ORGANIZOVAT'I VESTI POTREBITEL'SKOE OBSHCHESTVO
- KREDITNYE OPERATSII SEL'SKOKHOZIAISTVENNYKH TOVARISHCHESTV
- SISTEMATICHESKII UKAZATEL' RUSSKOI LITERATURY PO KOOPERATSII 1856-1924 GG
- VOPROSY KOOPERATIVNOGO DVIZHENIA V ROSSII

MERKUR : DEUTSCHE ZEITSCHRIFT FUER EUROPAEISCHES DENKEN – Stuttgart, 1947-56 – 5r – 1 – DM500.00 – gw Mikro Press [072]

MERKUR : DEUTSCHE ZEITSCHRIFT FUER EUROPAEISCHES DENKEN – Stuttgart, West Germany. 1947-1956 – 5r – 1 – gw Mikrofilm [073]

Merkx, P A H J *see* ZUR SYNTAX DER KASUS UND TEMPORA IN DEN TRAKTATEN DES HL. CYPRIAN

Merlet, L *see* CARTULAIRE DE L'ABBAYE DE NOTRE DAME DES VAUX DE GERNAY

Merlet, Lucien *see* DICTIONNAIRE TOPOGRAPHIQUE DU DEPARTEMENT D'EURE-ET-LOIR: COMPRENANT LES NOMS DE LIEU ANCIENS ET MODERNES

MERLIN (1827), TOGETHER WITH RECOLLECTIONS OF EDGAR A. POE / Wilmer, Lambert A – (1866) – 9 – $5.00 – us Scholars' Facs [830]

Mermet, Cl *see* LA PRACTIQUE DE L'ORTHOGRAPHE FRANCOISE

Merobaudes *see* CORPUS SCRIPTORUM HISTORIAE BYZANTINAE (CSHB 28)

Merola, J *see* REPUBLICA...ORIGINAL SACADA DEL CUERPO HUMANO...

MEROPE : A TRAGEDY / Arnold, Matthew – London: Longman, Brown, Green, Longmans, and Roberts, 1858 – 1 roll – 1 – 1-55879-197-3 – uk Libr Preservation [820]

MEROPRIIATIIA SOVETSKOI VLASTI V AZERBAIDZHANE V OBLASTI TRUDOVOGO PRAVA (1917-18) / Khalafov, MS – Baku, 1964. 83p. Discusses reforms in Azerbaidzhani labor law during the first year of Soviet power. BR-8475/1 – 9 – ne IDC [340]

LA MEROVEIDE OU LES CHAMPS CATALAUNIQUES: POEME / Lemercier, Nepomucene – Paris: F. Didot et Nepveu, 1818.xii,322p. 4 fiches. (Literature Collection) – 9 – 10.00 – fr Bibl Nationale [810]

DIE MEROVINGERZEIT / Friedrich, Johann – Bamberg: O. Reindl, 1869. (Kirchengeschichte Deutschland / von J. Friedrich; 2. T., 1. Haelfte) – 2mf – us A.T.L.A. [240]

Merriam, Ralph *see* CLAIMS BETWEEN SHIPPERS AND CARRIERS: A DIGEST OF THE AMERICAN DECISIONS

MERRICK COUNTY ITEM – Central City, NE. -w. Jan. 1880-Jan. 1881 – 1 – us NE Hist [071]

Merrick, George B *see*
- GENEALOGY OF THE MERRICK FAMILY
- STEAMBOATS AND STEAMBOATMEN OF THE UPPER MISSISSIPPI: DESCRIPTIVE, PERSONAL AND HISTORICAL

MERRICKVILLE STAR – Ontario, CN. 1899-1908 – 4r – 1 – cn Commonwealth Micro [072]

Merrill *see* ALLEGANY COUNTY AND ITS PEOPLE

Merrill, E D *see* AN ENUMERATION OF THE PLANTS OF GUAM

Merrill, George Edmunds *see*
- THE PARCHMENTS OF THE FAITH
- THE REASONABLE CHRIST: A SERIES OF STUDIES
- STORY OF THE MANUSCRIPTS

Merrill, Joanne *see* EXERCISE ADOPTION AND ADHERENCE OF COLLEGE WOMEN

Merrill, Samuel *see* NEWSPAPER LIBEL, A HANDBOOK FOR THE PRESS

Merrill, Selah *see* ANCIENT JERUSALEM

MERRILL TIMES – Merrill OR. June 1 1918 – 1 – us U.O. Library [071]

Merrill, Walter Alfred *see* THE WORKMEN'S COMPENSATION ACT OF QUEBEC & REPORTED DECISIONS (CASES REPORTED TO 1ST JANUARY, 1916)

MERRILL-PALMER QUARTERLY – 1,5,6,9 – us UMI [073]

MERRIMACK COLLECTION OF INSTRUMENTAL AND MARTIAL MUSICK: CONTAINING A LARGE VARIETY OF THE MOST APPROVED MARCHES, AIRS, MINUETS, WALTZES, &C. TOGETHER WITH COMPLETE SCALES FOR THE CLARIONET, FLUTE, VIOLIN, VIOLINCELLO SIC AND BASSOON : HARMONIZED WITH THREE PARTS / Moore, Henry E – v1. Concord: Jacob B. Moore, 1833. MUSIC 1982 – 1 – us L of C Photodup [780]

MERRIMACK MAGAZINE AND LADIES' LITERARY CABINET – v. 1. 17 Aug 1805-9 Aug 1806 – 1 – us UMI [073]

MERRIMACK MAGAZINE AND MONTHLY REGISTER OF POLITICS, AGRICULTURE, LITERATURE, AND RELIGION – v. 1. 1 Jan-Jul 1825 – 1 – us UMI [073]

MERRIMACK MISCELLANY – v. 1. 8 Jun-5 Oct 1805 – 1 – us UMI [073]

Merrimack Valley, New Hampshire.Merrimack Valley Free Will Baptist Mission Society *see* RECORDS

Merriman, Mansfield *see* A TEXT BOOK ON THE METHOD OF LEAST SQUARES

MERRIMAN MAVERICK – Merriman, NE. -w. Mar 1910-Dec 1928 – 1 – us NE Hist [071]

Merriman, Roger Bigelow *see*
- ANNALS OF THE EMPEROR CHARLES 5TH
- LIFE AND LETTERS OF THOMAS CROMWELL

Merriott, Thomas *see* GRAMMATICALL MISCELLANIES

THE MERRITT CRAWFORD PAPERS – 5 reels with printed guide – 1 – $480.00 – 0-89093-947-0 – us UPA [920]

Merritt, W W *see* HISTORY OF THE COUNTY OF MONTGOMERY

Merry del Val, Alfonso *see*
- THE CONFLICT IN SPAIN; COMMUNISTIC MISSTATEMENTS REFUTED
- SPAIN IS FIGHTING FOR CIVILIZATION

MERRY ENGLAND – v. 1-24. 1883-1895 – 1 – us UMI [073]

Merry, John F *see* HISTORY OF DELAWARE COUNTY AND ITS PEOPLE

THE MERRY MEN : AND OTHER TALES AND FABLES / Stevenson, Robert Louis – London: Chatto & Windus, 1887 – 1 roll – 1 – 1-55879-678-9 – uk Libr Preservation [830]

MERRYVILLE FIRST BAPTIST CHURCH. MERRYVILLE, LOUISIANA : CHURCH RECORDS – 1926-69 – 1 – 97.92 – us Baptist [240]

Mersenne, Marin *see*
- COGITATA PHYSICOMATHEMATICA, IN QUIBUS TAM NATURAE QUAM ARTIS EFFECTUS ADMIRANDI CERTISSIMIS DEMONSTRATIONIBUS EXPLICANTUR
- HARMONIE UNIVERSELLE
- HARMONIE UNIVERSELLE, CONTENANT LA THEORIE ET LA PRATIQUE DE LA MUSIQUE
- MARINI MERSENNI ORD. S. FRANCISCI A PAULA, HARMONICORUM LIBRI
- NOVARUM OBSERVATIONUM PHYSICO-MATHEMATICARUM F. MARINI MERSENNI MINIMI TOMUS 3, QUIBUS ACCESSIT ARISTARCHUS SAMIUS DE MUNDI SYSTEMATE
- OBSERVATIONES ET EMENDATIONES AD FRANCISCI GEORGII VENETI PROBLEMATA
- LES PRELUDES DE L'HARMONIE UNIVERSELLE
- QUAESTIONES CELEBERRIMAE IN GENESIM
- UNIVERSAE GEOMETRIAE MIXATEQUE MATHEMATICAE SYNOPSIS, ET BINI REFRACTIONUM DEMONSTRATARUM TRACTATUS

Merseyside Maritime Museum (National Museums and Galleries on Merseyside). Liverpool *see* NINETEENTH AND TWENTIETH CENTURY MARITIME AND TRADING RECORDS

MERSIN – Mersin. Sahib-i Imtiyaz: Mustafa Sakir. Mesul Mueduerue ve Sermuharriri: Hueseyin Sami. No. 89 (6 Kanuniewel 1923) – 9 – $20.00 – us MEDOC [956]

Mersky, Roy M *see* SUPREME COURT OF THE U.S. HEARINGS AND REPORTS ON SUCCESSFUL AND UNSUCCESSFUL NOMINATIONS OF SUPREME COURT JUSTICES BY THE SENATE JUDICIARY COMMITTEE

Mertens, Heinz *see* UNHELDENHAFTE UND HELDENHAFTE MENSCHEN

Mertens, Joseph *see* LES BA DE LA KAMTSHA

Mertens, Volker *see* GEWERKSCHAFTLICHE KOOPERATION AUF BETRIEBLICHER EBENE INNERHALB EINES MULTINATIONALEN KONZERNS

MERTHYR AND CARDIFF CHRONICLE ETC – Merthyr Tydfil, Wales, UK. 26 Aug-16 Dec 1837. -w. 1/4 reel – 1 – uk British Libr Newspaper [072]

MERTIJU STAR – Jogjakarta, Indonesia. 1966- – 1 – us UMI [072]

MERTJU; BUNGARAMPAI UNTUK SEKOLAH LANDJUTAN / Sastrowardojo, Samud – SE 3938 1. v. 2 only. 1951 – 9 – ne IDC [950]

Mertonegoro, KR T *see* SANITATION DI INDONESIA

MERVEILLES BIOGRAPHIQUES ET HISTORIQUES / al-Jabarti – v. 1-9. 1888-96 – 1 – 38.00 – us L of C Photodup [900]

MERVYN PEAKE REVIEW – v. 3- 1976- – 1,5,6,9 – us UMI [000]

Mervyn Peake Society *see* NEWSLETTER

Merwin, Elias *see* THE PRINCIPLES OF EQUITY AND EQUITY PLEADING

MERY'S BLOCK BOOK OF SAN FRANCISCO / California Block Book & Map Co – San Francisco, 1909. California Reel 29. (The Cox Library Collection) – 5 – us Americana [978]

Merz, A *see* NEUESTE SAMMLUNG JENER SCHRIFTEN, DIE VON EINIGEN JAHREN HER UEBER VERSCHIEDENE WICHTIGSTE GEGENSTAENDE ZUR STEUER DER WAHRHEIT IM DRUCK ERSCHIENEN SIND

MerzMacLellan (Consulting Engineers) *see* REPORT ON ELECTRIC POWER DEVELOPMENT IN SUDAN

MES AVENTURES AU SENEGAL. SOUVENIRS DE VOYAGE / Verneuil, Victor – (African Library). Paris. Librarie nouvelle. 1858 – 9 – fr Hachette [960]

MES CONTEMPORAINS / David, Laurent Olivier – Montreal?: s.n., 1894 (Montreal: E. Senecal). 02516. (Pre-1900 Canadiana) – 9 – cn C.I.H.M. [971]

MES DE MARIA O EL MES DE MAYO – 1857 – 9 – 1.50f – sp Bibl Santa Ana [240]

MES DE MAYO PARA NINOS / Vidal, Ceferino G – Plasencia: Sanchez Rodrigo, 2nd ed 1943 – 1 – sp Bibl Santa Ana [946]

MES GRANDES CHASSES DANS L'AFRIQUE CENTRALE / Foa, Edouard – 7e ed. Paris: Plon, 1911 – us Res Libr [960]

MES IMPRESSIONS SUR L'AFRIQUE OCCIDENTALE FRANCAISE : ETUDE DOCUMENTAIRE DU PAYS DE TAM-TAM / Lahille, Abel – Paris: A Picard, [n.d.] – us Res Libr [300]

MES INCONNUS CHEZ EUX / Cousturier, Lucie – Paris: F Rieder, 1925 – us Res Libr [960]

MES LOISIRS : POESIES / Frechette, Louis-Honore – Quebec: Typographie de Leger Brousseau..., 1863. SEM105P22 – 3mf – 9 – Can$6.75 – cn Bibl Nat [810]

MES PREMIERES LECONS DE REDACTION / Freres du Sacre-Coeur – Montreal: [freres du Sacre-Coeur, 1915?]. SEM105P1614 – 2mf – 9 – Can$4.50 – cn Bibl Nat [440]

MES PREMIERES LECONS DE REDATION : LIVRE DU MAITRE / Freres du Sacre-Coeur – Montreal: les freres du Sacre-Coeur, 1937 [Montreal: Imprimerie des sourds-muets], 1937. SEM105P1613 – 3mf – 9 – Can$6.75 – cn Bibl Nat [440]

MES REVERIES / Saxe, Hermann Maurice de – Amsterdam. Arkstee et Merkus. 1757. (Strategy of War Series) – 9 – fr Hachette [355]

MES TABLETTES 1820-1848 / Trudeau, Romuald – Montreal: Bibliotheque Nationale du Quebec, 1972. SEM16P220 – 1r – 5 – Can$21.00 – cn Bibl Nat [971]

MES VERS / Belanger, Jean Amable – 1882. 00904. (Pre-1900 Canadiana) – 9 – cn C.I.H.M. [810]

Mesa, Cristobal *see*
- LAS EGLOGAS Y GEORGICAS...VIRGILIO
- VALLE DE LAGRIMAS Y DIVERSAS RIMAS

MESA EDUCATOR *see* CARRIAGE AND WAGON WORKERS JOURNAL, 1899-1908 : OFFICIAL JOURNAL, 1912-1915 : MESA EDUCATOR, 1944-1951

MESA REVUELTA... / Savall, Domingo – Madrid: Arch. Ibero Americano, 1960 – 1 – sp Bibl Santa Ana [240]

MESA REVUELTA. REDACCIONES DE 6° Y PREU COGIDAS AL VUELO. 2 DE MAYO DE 1957 (PROMANUSCRIPTO). T.I. / Colegio de San Antonio. Caceres – Caceres: Tip. La Minerva, 1957 – 1 – sp Bibl Santa Ana [370]

MESA REVUELTA. REDACCIONES DE 6TH Y PREU. DIA DE SAN PEDRO DE ALCANTARA DE 1961 (PRO-MANUSCRITO) / Colegio de San Antonio. Caceres – Caceres: Imp. La Minerva, 1961 – 1 – sp Bibl Santa Ana [240]

MESA REVUELTA. REDACCIONES DE NO 6 Y PREN. T. 4-B. DIA DE LA ASUNCION 1961 / Colegio de San Antonio – Caceres: Imprenta la Minerva, 1961 – 1 – sp Bibl Santa Ana [946]

LA MESA SCOUT – La Mesa, CA. 1921-58 – 24r – 1 – $1,200.00 – C02337 – us Library Micro [071]

MESA TRIBUNE – Mesa, AZ. Jul 1972-81 – 81r – 1 – $4,050.00 – H04041 – us Library Micro [071]

DAS MESA-DENKMAL UND SEINE SCHRIFT / Levy, Moritz Abraham – Breslau: Schletter, 1871 – 1mf – 9 – 0-8370-7081-3 – 1986-1081 – us A.T.L.A. [470]

Mesaguer Fernandez, J *see* CRONICA EL EMPERADOR CARLOS 5TH. EDICION DE JUAN SANCHEZ MONTES. PROLOGO DE PETER RASOW. MADRID, 1964

MESALE – (Sahib ve Mueduer-i Mes'ul: Yusuf Ziya[Ortac]. Nos. 1-8 Temmuz-Tesriniewel 1928)) – Istanbul: Iktisat Matbaasi, 1928 – 4mf – 9 – $36.75 – us MEDOC [949]

LA MESANGERE – Parisian costumes, 1797-1839. Drawings by La Mesangere, Gavarni, Vernet, Baquoy and Lante; engraved by Gatine, Delvaux and Nargeot. 4 reels.(Collections of the Department of Prints and Photographs) – 1 – fr Bibl Nationale [740]

Mesanza, Andres *see*
- APUNTES Y DOCUMENTOS CONTRA LA ORDEN DOMINICANA EN COLOMBIA 1680-1930. CARACAS, 1936
- BIBLIOGRAFIA DE LA PROVINCIA DOMINICANA DE COLOMBIA
- CABOS SUELTOS PARA LA HISTORIA DE CHIGUINGUIRA
- EL CONVENTO DOMINICANO DE NUESTRA SRA. DEL ROSARIO EN SANTA FE Y SU UNIVERSIDAD
- CORONACION DE LA VIRGEN DE CHIGUINGUIRA

MESAYIHI OSMANIYEDEN SEKIZ ZATIN TERCEME-I AHVALT / Tahir, Bursali Mehmed – Istanbul: Kitabhane-i Islam, 1318 [1902] – $15.00 – us MEDOC [956]

LE MESCHACEBE : JOURNAL OFFICIEL DE SAINT-JEAN-BAPTISTE – St-Jean-Baptiste de la Nouvelle-Orleans, LA. v7 n323. 2 avr 1859-v54 n32. 11 aut 1906 – 1r – 1 – Can$25.00 – cn Can Microfilming [071]

Meschet, D Louis *see* LE VERITABLE GOUVERNEMENT DE L'ORDRE DE CISTEAUX

Meschinot, Jean *see*
- LES LUNETTES DES PRINCES

Meschke, Waltraut *see* GEDICHTE GOETHES VERANSCHAULICHT NACH FORM- UND STRUKTURWANDEL

Meschler, Moritz *see* NOVENE ZU UNSERER LIEBEN FRAU VON LOURDES

MESECHNI STATISTICHESKI IZVESTIIA / Bulgaria. Glavna Direktsiia na Statistikata – v.1-35. 1908-48 – 1 – 184.00 – us L of C Photodup [310]

Meseguer Fernandez, Juan *see*
- CACERES. IGLESIA DEL CONVENTO DE SAN FRANCISCO...
- COMENTO DE LOS MAJORETES, 1500
- ESTADISTICA DE LOS ALCANTARISTAS Y PASCUALISTAS HACIA 1567-1570. MEMORIA DE LAS CASAS DE LA PROVINCIA DE SANT JOSEPH
- FR. ALONSO DE LA CRUZ (ALONSO DE SOTOMAYOR) DOTA A SU HIJA FELIPA
- GUADALUPE EN LA AMERICA ANDINA. MADRID, 1969

Meseguer, Pedro *see*
- BIOGRAFIAS BAYLE
- GABINO MARQUEZ, S.J. DEBERES PATRIOTICOS

Meshcheriakova, N L *see*
- GRAZHDANSKAIA VOINA V SIBIRII SEVERNOI OBLASTI
- KOOPERATSIIA I SOTSIALIZM
- KOOPERATSIIA V SOVETSKOI ROSSII
- LENIN, V.I. O KOOPERATSII
- ZADACHI SOVREMENNOI KOOPERATSII

Meshcherskii, Vladimir P *see*
- LORD APOSTOLI V BOL'SHOM PETERSBURGSKOM SVETE
- PIS'MA OTTSA K SYNU (STARAGO PRAVOVEDA K NOVOMU) I SYNA (MINISTRA) K OTTSU (IZ PROSHLAGO)
- RECHI KONSERVATORA
- V ULIKU VREMENI

MESHECH WEARE PAPERS, 1776-1786 / Weare, Meshech – Massachusetts Historical Society – 1r – 1 – $85.00 – us UMI [920]

MESHIV DAVAR / Reifmann, J – Vienna, 1866 – 9 – BJ-32-38 1 – ne IDC [270]

Meshkovskii, V M *see* PARTIIA O PROMYSLOVOI KOOPERATSII I KUSTARNOI PROMYSHLENNOSTI

MESHOPPEN ENTERPRISE – Meshoppen, PA. -w 1897-1907; 1926-1941 – 13 – $25.00r – us I.M.R. [071]

MESI AT S RABOTY PRAVLENII A GOSUDARSTVENNOGO BANKA R.S.F.S.R. / Gosudarstvenny i bank RSFSR – Moskva: [s.n.], 1921 – 1 – CSUX90-B9609 – us Hoover Inst Photo [332]

Mesiatsev, P P *see* ZADACHI SEL'SKOKHOZIAISTVENNOI KREDITNOI KOOPERATSII V SSSR

MESICNI PREHLED ZAHRANICNIHO OBCHODU / Czechoslovakia. Statni Urad Statisticky – Prerov. 1921-1948. Incomplete – 1 – us NY Public [310]

MESIMVRINI – (Yrly reel count varies) – 1989- – 1 – inquire – us Ross [072]

MESMERISM, SPIRITUALISM, AND C.: HISTORICALLY AND SCIENTIFICALLY CONSIDERED : BEING TWO LECTURES / Carpenter, William B – New York: D. Appleton, 1877 – 1mf – us A.T.L.A. [140]

Mesnil, Jean Baptiste du *see* ADVERTISSEMENT SURLE FAICT DU CONCILE DE TRENTE: FAICT PAN MIL CING SENS SOIXANTE QUATRE

Mesnil-Durand *see* FRAGMENTS DE TACTIQUE

Mesonero Romanos, Manuel *see* GOYA, MORATIN, MELENDEZ VALDES Y DONOSO CORTES. RESENA HISTORICA DE LOS ANTERIORES ENTERRAMIENTOS Y TRASLACIONES DE SUS RESTOS MORTALES HASTA SU INHUMACION EN EL MAUSOLEO DEL CEMENTERIO DE SAN ISIDRO EL DIA 11 DE MAYO DE 1900

MESOPOTAMIA AND PERSIA UNDER THE MONGOLS IN THE 14TH CENTURY / Le Strange, G – century A.D., from the Nuzhat-al-Kulub of Hamd Allah, Mustawfi. 1903 – 1 – uk Microform Academic [900]

Mesplet, Fleury *see*
- GAZETTE DU COMMERCE ET LITTERAIRE
- MONTREAL GAZETTE

MESRUTIYET – Paris: Islahat-i Esasiyye Firkasi. Mueduer-i Siyasi: Serif Pasa, 1910-19? – 9 – $25.00 – us MEDOC [956]

MESRUTIYET UGRUNDA / Ziya, Ahmet – Istanbul: Yeni Osmanli Matbaa ve Kuetuephanesi, 1327 [1911] – $12.00 – us MEDOC [956]

MESSAGE : AYLMER, GOVERNOR IN CHIEF / Goderich, Frederick John Robinson, Viscount – [S.l.: s.n., 1832?]. SEM105P1381 – 1mf – 9 – Can$2.25 – cn Bibl Nat [324]

MESSAGE – Port Townsend. Wash. -w. 1867-69 – 1 – us UMI [071]

THE MESSAGE *see*
- DEACONESS ADVOCATE
- MONTHLY LEAFLET OF THE CANADA CONGREGATIONAL WOMAN'S BOARD OF MISSIONS
- MONTHLY LETTER

THE MESSAGE AND DEACONESS ADVOCATE *see* DEACONESS ADVOCATE

THE MESSAGE AND DEACONESS WORLD *see* DEACONESS ADVOCATE

MESSAGE AND MISSION / Nida, E – London, 1960 – 6mf – 8 – ne Slangenburg [240]

THE MESSAGE AND POSITION OF THE CHURCH OF ENGLAND : BEING AN ENQUIRY INTO THE CLAIMS OF THE MEDIAEVAL CHURCH / Galton, Arthur – London: Kegan Paul, Trench, Truebner, 1899 – 1mf – us A.T.L.A. [240]

THE MESSAGE BIRD – New York City. v1-25. 1849-60 – 7r – 1 – £380.00 – uk Chadwyck [780]

MESSAGE BROUGHT TO THE NEW YORK COLONIZATION SOCIETY / Pinney, John B – 1836 – 1 – 5.00 – us Baptist [240]

MESSAGE DE SON EXCELLENCE, LE GOUVERNEUR GENERAL, AVEC RAPPORTS SUR UNE EXPLORATION GEOLOGIQUE DE LA PROVINCE DE CANADA... / Canada. Exploration Geologique – Montreal: Imp. Lovell et Gibson, 1845. SEM105P343 – 2mf – 9 – Can$4.50 – cn Bibl Nat [550]

MESSAGE DU GOUVERNEUR-GENRAL, TRANSMETTANT COPIE DE LA CORRESPONDANCE RELATIVE A LA SENTENCE DE MORT PRONONCEE CONTRE AMBROISE LEPINE POUR LE MEURTRE DE THOMAS SCOTT, A FORT-GARRY – [Ottawa]: [s.n.], [1875]. SEM105P643 – 1mf – 9 – Can$2.25 – cn Bibl Nat [971]

MESSAGE, DUFFERIN. THE GOVERNOR GENERAL TRANSMITS FOR THE INFORMATION OF THE SENATE AND HOUSE OF COMMONS COPIES OF A CORRSPONDENCE... – [Ottawa]: [s.n.], [1875]. SEM105P642 – 1mf – 9 – Can$2.25 – cn Bibl Nat [971]

MESSAGE FROM HIS EXCELLENCY THE GOVERNOR GENERAL, WITH REPORTS ON A GEOLOGICAL SURVEY OF THE PROVINCE OF CANADA.. / Canada. Exploration Geologique – Montreal: Lovell and Gibson, 1845. SEM105P344 – 2mf – 9 – Can$4.50 – cn Bibl Nat [550]

MESSAGE FROM HIS EXCELLENCY THE GOVERNOR IN CHIEF, RELATING TO THE EXPULSION OF MR. CHRISTIE / Bas-Canada. Gouverneur – [Quebec ?: s.n., 1832 ?]. SEM105P1380 – 1mf – 9 – Can$2.25 – cn Bibl Nat [971]

MESSAGE FROM HIS EXCELLENCY THE GOVERNOR IN CHIEF, RELATING TO THE SUPPLY BILL FOR THE YEAR 1833. RECEIVED 13TH JANUARY, 1834 MESSAGE DE... / Bas-Canada. Gouverneur – [Quebec]: [s.n.], [1834]. SEM105P1228 – 1mf – 9 – Can$2.25 – cn Bibl Nat [324]

MESSAGE FROM THE TEAM OF CONSULTATION OF THE RELIGIOUS GROUPS IN INDONESIA / Indonesia. Religious groups – SE-4032 1. 1963 – 9 – ne IDC [290]

THE MESSAGE OF CHRISTIANITY TO OTHER RELIGIONS / Dennis, James Shepard – New York: Fleming H Revell, 1893 – 1mf – 9 – 0-8370-2892-2 – 1985-0892 – us A.T.L.A. [240]

MESSAGE OF GOOD-WILL TO MEN – Picton [Ont]: D Oliphant, [1845?-18–] – 9 – cn C.I.H.M. [240]

THE MESSAGE OF THE APOSTLES / Stevens, George Barker – New York: Charles Scribner, 1900. 1 fiche – 9 – us A.T.L.A. [240]

THE MESSAGE OF THE DISCIPLES FOR THE UNION OF THE CHURCH : INCLUDING THEIR ORIGIN AND HISTORY / Ainslie, Peter – New York: Fleming H. Revell, c1913 – 1mf – us A.T.L.A. [240]

THE MESSAGE OF THE SON OF MAN / Abbott, Edwin Abbott – (Includes appendix) – London: Adam & Charles Black, 1909 – 1mf – 9 – 0-8370-2015-8 – 1985-0015 – us A.T.L.A. [240]

MESSAGE TRANSMITTING DRAFT OF PROPOSED LEGISLATION TO APPROVE THE "COMPACT OF FREE ASSOCIATION" : BETWEEN THE U.S. AND THE GOVERNMENT OF PALAU, APR 9, 1986 / U.S. President – Washington: GPO, 1986 – 5mf – 9 – $7.50 – LLMC 82-100G, Title 7 – us L.L.M.C. [327]

MESSAGE TRANSMITTING HIS CERTIFICATION OF APPROVAL OF THE COMPACT OF FREE ASSOCIATION BETWEEN THE U.S. AND PALAU : PURSUANT TO P.L. 99-658, DEC 1, 1987, 100TH CONG, 1ST SESS / U.S. President – Washington: GPO, 1987 – 1mf – 9 – $1.50 – LLMC 82-100G, Title 35 – us L.L.M.C. [327]

MESSAGE TRANSMITTING PROPOSED LEGISLATION TO APPROVE THE COMPACT OF FREE ASSOCIATION WITH THE FEDERATED STATES OF MICRONESIA AND THE MARSHALL ISLANDS : HSE.DOC N99-29, 99TH CONG, 1ST SESS, FEB 20, 1985 / U.S. President – Washington: GPO, 1985 – 4mf – 9 – $6.00 – LLMC 82-100F, Title 19 – us L.L.M.C. [980]

LE MESSAGER – Lewiston, ME. v12 n11. 4 jun 1891-21 dec 1967 – 1r – 1 – Can$40.00 – cn Can Microfilming [071]

LE MESSAGER = THE MESSENGER – Verdun, Canada. v37 n1. 6 jan 1949-22 dec 1991 – 48r – 1 – Can$70.00r – cn Can Microfilming [072]

LE MESSAGER = THE MESSENGER – Ville LaSalle, Canada, v1 n16. 23 jun 1954; v5 n43. 30 dec 1958-22 dec 1991 – 51r – 1 – Can$70.00r – cn Can Microfilming [072]

LE MESSAGER : ORGANE DES PAROISSES ST-JACQUES ET ST-JEAN-BAPTISTE – New Orleans, LA. v8 n41. 26 aut 1853 – 1r – 1 – Can$25.00 – cn Can Microfilming [071]

LE MESSAGER – Saint Jovite, Canada. 26 mar 1974-21 fev 1984 – 8r – 1 – Can$70.00r – cn Can Microfilming [072]

LE MESSAGER CANADIAN DU COEUR DE JESUS *see* LE MESSAGER CANADIEN DU SACRE-COEUR DE JESUS

LE MESSAGER CANADIEN – Granby, Canada. v5 n8. 8 mar 1872-v8 n16. 4 jun 1875 – 1r – 1 – Can$25.00 – cn Can Microfilming [072]

LE MESSAGER CANADIEN DU SACRE-COEUR DE JESUS – (Fait suite a: Le Petit messager des Coeurs de Jesus et de Marie. Suivi de: Le Messager canadian du Coeur de Jesus. Autre ed. de lang: The Canadian Messenger) – Montreal: [s.n., 1892?-1902] – 9 – cn C.I.H.M. [240]

LE MESSAGER CANADIEN DU SACRE-COEUR DE JESUS *see* LE PETIT MESSAGER DES COEURS DE JESUS ET DE MARIE

LE MESSAGER COMIQUE – Ottawa: H Hardy, [1885?] – 9 – cn C.I.H.M. [072]

LE MESSAGER COMIQUE – Ottawa, Ontario. 6 nov 1885 – 1r – 1 – Can$25.00 – cn Can Microfilming [072]

LE MESSAGER D'ATHENES – Greece. -w. 5 June 1875-13 Feb 1886; 29 Dec 1915-18 Nov 1916; 22 April 1917-16 Jan 1919; 1 July 1926-30 June, 5 Oct-31 Dec 1940. Imperfect. 34 reels – 1 – uk British Libr Newspaper [949]

LE MESSAGER DE JOLIETTE – Joliette, Canada. 7 jul 1863-20 oct 1865 – 1r – 1 – Can$50.00 – cn Can Microfilming [072]

LE MESSAGER DE LA FOI ET DES BONNES OEUVRES – Montreal: E Senecal, 1873-1875 – 9 – cn C.I.H.M. [240]

LE MESSAGER DE LA RUE SAINTE-CATHERINE : JOURNAL LITTERAIRE ET COMMERCIAL – Montreal, Canada. v1 n3. avr 1882(?) – 1r – 1 – Can$25.00 – cn Can Microfilming [072]

LE MESSAGER DE LACHINE – Lachine, Canada. 2 mai 1929-23 dec 1991 – 52r – 1 – Can$70.00r – cn Can Microfilming [072]

LE MESSAGER DE L'ASSEMBLEE – Journal quotidien, politique et litteraire. Paris. 16 fevr-2 dec 1851 – 1 – fr A.C.R.P.P. [073]

LE MESSAGER DE NICOLET – Nicolet, Canada. 12 jan 1881-v4 n23. 19 jun 1884 – 1r – 1 – Can$45.00 – cn Can Microfilming [072]

LE MESSAGER DE PARIS – Paris. 31 mai-dec 1858, juil-dec 1899 – 1 – fr A.C.R.P.P. [073]

LE MESSAGER DE SAINT-ANTOINE – (Autre ed. de lang: St. Anthony's Canadian Messengers) – Chicoutimi, Quebec: Hotel-Dieu Saint-Vallier, [1895-19–] – 9 – cn C.I.H.M. [240]

LE MESSAGER DE SAINT-ANTOINE *see* ST. ANTHONY'S CANADIAN MESSENGER

LE MESSAGER DE SAINTE ANNE – (Fait suite a: Bulletin de Ste Anne de la Pointe-au-Pere) – Rimouski, Quebec: M P Sylvain, [1882-19–] – 9 – cn C.I.H.M. [240]

LE MESSAGER DE SOREL – Sorel, Canada. v1 n38. 10 jan 1872-v6 n14. 29 jul 1876 – 1r – 1 – Can$80.00 – cn Can Microfilming [072]

LE MESSAGER DE ST-RAPHAEL – Quebec. n3. 3 mai 1910 – 1r – 1 – Can$25.00 – cn Can Microfilming [072]

LE MESSAGER DES CHAMBRES – Journal des principes constitutionnels. Dir. A. Brindeau. Paris. janv-juin 1830, fevr-avr 1841 – 1 – fr A.C.R.P.P. [073]

LE MESSAGER DES FIDELES – 1(1884)-9(1892) – 93mf – 9 – Dfl326.00 – ne Slangenburg [073]

MESSAGER DES THEATRES ET DES ARTS – Paris. aout 1848-aout 1870 – 1 – fr A.C.R.P.P. [073]

LE MESSAGER DORVAL MESSENGER – Dorval, 20 aut 1980-23 sep 1981f – 1r – 1 – Can$50.00 – cn Can Microfilming [072]

MESSAGER DU SOIR – puis a partir du 2 oct 1815 Le Messager des Chambres. Journal du soir. no. 1-301. Paris. 4 juin 1815-31 mars 1816. mq no. 1, 4, 17, 36, 86, 245 – 1 – fr A.C.R.P.P. [073]

LE MESSAGER DU T.S. SACREMENT *see* LE PETIT MESSAGER DU TRES SAINT SACREMENT

LA MESSAGER EVANGELIQUE – 1905-13 (complete) – 1r – 1 – ATLA S0666C – us A.T.L.A. [073]

MESSAGER FINANCIER DE LONDRES – London, UK. 19 Mar-25 Jun 1902 – 1 – uk British Libr Newspaper [072]

LE MESSAGER FRANCO-AMERICAIN : JOURNAL QUOTIDIEN. POLITIQUE, COMMERCIAL ET LITTERAIRE – New York City, NY. v5 n39. 16 fev 1864-v24 n62. 3 mar 1883 – 4r – 1 – Can$75.00r – cn Can Microfilming [071]

MESSAGER ORTHODOXE. L'ACTION CHRETIENNE DES ETUDIANTS RUSSES – Paris. 1965-72. – 28mf – 9 – ne IDC [240]

IL MESSAGERO *see* JOURNAUX DIVERS

MESSAGES AND PAPERS OF THE PRESIDENTS – 1789-1897 – 3r – 1 – $150.00 – us Trans-Media [324]

MESSAGES AND PAPERS OF THE PRESIDENTS, 1789-1897 : A COMPILATION PUBLISHED BY AUTHORITY OF CONGRESS / Richardson, James D – Washington: GPO. v1-10 in 11 books. 1896-99 (all publ) – 88mf – 9 – $132.00 – LLMC 81-238 – us L.L.M.C. [324]

MESSAGES AND PAPERS OF THE PRESIDENTS, 1789-1914 / Richardson, James D – (Revision and expansion of earlier publ with the add of an encyclopedic index) – New York: Bureau of National Literature. 20v. 1908-14 – 116mf – 9 – $174.00 – LLMC 82-211 – us L.L.M.C. [324]

MESSAGES BETWEEN FRANKLIN D. ROOSEVELT AND WINSTON S. CHURCHILL / U. S. President – 1939-45 – 1 – us UMI [324]

THE MESSAGES BETWEEN FRANKLIN D. ROOSEVELT AND WINSTON S. CHURCHILL / Roosevelt, Franklin D – (MESSAGE AND RELATED MATERIALS. 6 rolls. 1) – 1939-45. 3 rolls – 1 – us Roosevelt [977]

MESSAGES FROM MARS (MACHINE-ASSISTED REFERENCE SECTION) – v.1-13. 1976-80. Continued by R A S D Update – 1 – us UMI [020]

THE MESSAGES OF ISRAEL'S LAWGIVERS : THE LAWS OF THE OLD TESTAMENT CODIFIED, ARRANGED IN ORDER OF GROWTH... / Kent, Charles Foster – (Includes bibliographical references & index) – New York: Charles Scribner, 1907 – 1mf – 9 – 0-8370-3887-1 – 1985-1887 – us A.T.L.A. [220]

THE MESSAGES OF JESUS ACCORDING TO THE GOSPEL OF JOHN : THE DISCOURSES OF JESUS IN THE FOURTH GOSPEL / Riggs, James Stevenson – New York: Charles Scribner, 1907 – 1mf – 9 – 0-8370-7329-4 – 1986-1329 – us A.T.L.A. [220]

THE MESSAGES OF THE EARLIER PROPHETS / Sanders, Frank Knight – Philadelphia: John D. Wattles, 1898. 1 fiche – 9 – us A.T.L.A. [240]

MESSAGES OF THE MEN AND RELIGION MOVEMENT : COMPLETE IN SEVEN VOLUMES, INCLUDING THE REVISED REPORTS OF THE COMISSIONS – New York: Association Press, c1912 – 4mf – us A.T.L.A. [240]

THE MESSAGES OF THE PROPHETIC AND PRIESTLY HISTORIANS / McFadyen, John Edgar – New York: Charles Scribner, 1901. 1 fiche – 9 – us A.T.L.A. [240]

THE MESSAGES OF THE PSALMISTS : THE PSALMS OF THE OLD TESTAMENT ARRANGED IN THEIR NATURAL GROUPING AND FREELY RENDERED IN PARAPHRASE / McFadyen, John Edgar – (Includes index) – New York:Charles Scribner, 1904 – 1mf – 9 – 0-8370-4353-0 – 1985-2353 – us A.T.L.A. [220]

MESSAGES TO WORKINGMEN / Stelzele, Charles – New York: F.H. Revell, c1906 – 1mf – us A.T.L.A. [240]

IL MESSAGGERE – Roma, 1935-49 – 3r – 1 – inquire – us Ross [945]

IL MESSAGGERO – (Also available on CD-ROM) – 1878-1885 – 1r per y – 5,6 – Sfr535.00 – sz Infoprint [072]

IL MESSAGGERO – (Also available on CD-ROM) – 1911 – 1r – 5,6 – Sfr615.00 – sz Infoprint [072]

IL MESSAGGERO – (Also available on CD-ROM) – 1912-1922 – 2r per y – 5,6 – Sfr695.00 – sz Infoprint [072]

IL MESSAGGERO – (Also available on CD-ROM) – 1957-1980 – 3r per y – 5,6 – Sfr1,069.00 – sz Infoprint [072]
IL MESSAGGERO – (Also available on CD-ROM) – Italy. 1981-1995 – 6r per y – 5,6 – Sfr1,176.00 – sz Infoprint [945]
IL MESSAGGERO – (Yrly reel count varies) – 1878- – 5 – inquire – us Ross [072]
MESSAGGERO – 1878-1885 – Once per yr – 6 – F2,000.00 – sz Infoprint [072]
IL MESSAGGIERO – v1-10. 1903-12 (complete) – 1r – 1 – ATLA R0129 – us A.T.L.A. [240]
IL MESSALE DI CIVATE / Marcora, C – Civate, 1958 – 3mf – 8 – Dfl13.00 – ne Slangenburg [240]
IL MESSALE GLAGOLITICO DI KIEW (SEC. 9) ED IL SUO PROTOTIPO ROMANO DEL SEC. 6-7 / Mohlberg, C – Roma, 1928 – 5mf – 8 – Dfl22.00 – ne Slangenburg [240]
Messance, receveur des tailles *see*
– NOUVELLES RECHERCHES SUR LA POPULATION DE LA FRANCE: AVEC DES REMARQUES IMPORTANTES SUR DIVERS OBJETS D'ADMINISTRATION
– RECHERCHES SUR LA POPULATION DES GENERALITES D'AUVERGNE, DE LYON, DE ROUEN, ET DE QUELQUES PROVINCES ET VILLES DU ROYAUME.
MESSE, A QUATTRO VOCI...LIBRO PRIMO... NUOVAMENTE DATI IN LUCE / Tresti, Flaminio – Parts. 1613 – 9 – us Sibley [780]
DIE MESSE IM DEUTSCHEN MITTELALTER / Franz, Albert – Freiburg i/Br., 1902 – 12mf – 8 – Dfl42.00 – ne Slangenburg [943]
DIE MESSE IM MITTELALTER UND IHRE GESANGLICHE AUSSTATTUNG / Wagner, P – s.d. – 1mf – 8 – Dfl6.00 – ne Slangenburg [240]
DIE MESSE IN DEN DEUTSCHEN DIOEZESAN-GESANG- UND GEBETBUECHERN / Hacker, J – Muenchen, 1950 – 3mf – 8 – Dfl13.00 – ne Slangenburg [943]
MESSE IN ES / Schubert, Franz – Leipzig: Breitkopf & Haertel, [19–] – 1 – us Sibley [780]
MESSE [IN F] / Schubert, Franz – Leipzig: Breitkopt & Haertel, [1887] – 1 – us Sibley [780]
MESSE QVATTRO. OPERA SECONDA : LA PRIMA A TRE, AND A QUATTRO VOCI, CON SINFONIA, OBLIGATA, A SECONDA CON SINFONIA, SE PIACE, LA TERZA A QUATTRO VOCI A CAPELLA, LA QUARTA MESSA PER LI DEFONTI. DEL PADRE GUISEPPE MARIA ANGELERI AGONSTINIANO / Angeleri, G M – Milan: F Vigone, 1691 – 1 – us Sibley [780]
MESSENGER – Athens. Ohio. -w. 1906- – 1 – us UMI [071]
MESSENGER – Battle Mountain, NV. 1881-84 – 1r – 1 – $50.00 – U04411 – us Library Micro [071]
MESSENGER – Beckley. West Virginia. 1910-17 – 1 – us UMI [071]
MESSENGER – Clio. Mich. 1932-1969 – 1 – us UMI [071]
MESSENGER – Ellsworth. Kan. 1891-1901 – 1 – us UMI [071]
MESSENGER – Fremont. Ohio. 1918-41 – 1 – us UMI [071]
MESSENGER – Greenville. Tex. 1894-1939 – 1 – us UMI [071]
MESSENGER – Hartsville. S.C. 1895- – 1 – us UMI [071]
MESSENGER – Louisville. Miss. 1842-1843 – 1 – us UMI [071]
MESSENGER – Madisonville. Ky. 1967- – 1 – us UMI [071]
MESSENGER – Marcus. Wash. 1910-1919 – 1 – us UMI [071]
MESSENGER – Montague, CA. 1909-19; 1924-33 – 6r – 1 – $300.00 – B02474 – us Library Micro [071]
MESSENGER – Morgantown. West Virginia. 1852-1854 – 1 – us UMI [071]
MESSENGER – Okolona. Miss. 1936-1951 – 1 – us UMI [071]
MESSENGER – Owensboro. Ky. 1879-1954 – 1 – us UMI [071]
MESSENGER – Owensboro. Ky. -w. 1877-1918 – 1 – us UMI [071]
MESSENGER – Owensville, IN. General Baptists. 1913-14. Incomplete – 1 – 15.50 – us A.B.H.S. [071]
MESSENGER – Perrysburg. Ohio. 1935- – 1 – us UMI [071]
MESSENGER – Pittsburg. Kan. 1893-1895 – 1 – us UMI [071]
MESSENGER – Plainfield. Ind. -sw. 1916- – 1 – us UMI [071]
MESSENGER – Schuyler. Neb. 1909-1920 – 1 – us UMI [071]
MESSENGER – South Haven. Mich. -w. 1881-1903 – 1 – us UMI [071]
MESSENGER – Springfield OR. Apr 8 22 May 20 Sep 30 1892, Oct 14 Nov 25 1892, Feb 24 Mar 24 1893 – 1 – us U.O. Library [071]
MESSENGER : WORLD'S GREATEST NEGRO MONTHLY – 1-10 2+5 (all publ). 1917-1928 – 33mf – 9 – $230.00 – us UPA [975]
MESSENGER : WORLD'S GREATEST NEGRO MONTHLY – New York. v1-10. 1917-28 – 1r – 1 – us Ross [071]
THE MESSENGER – Kansas City, 1926-1965 – 5r – 1 – us I.H.R.C. [978]
THE MESSENGER – Los Angeles. Calif. 1933-34 – 1 – us A.J.P.C. [071]
THE MESSENGER – The Only Radical Negro Magazine in America. New York. v. 1, no. 11-v. 10, no. 5. Nov. 1917-May June 1928. Incomplete – 1 – us NY Public [073]
THE MESSENGER – Toronto, Canada. v1 n1. (no date re Dr Chase's Nerve Food) – 1r – 1 – Can$25.00 – cn Can Microfilming [072]
THE MESSENGER – Utica, NY, Jan. 4, 1936-Oct. 30, 1948 – 3r – 1 – us I.H.R.C. [978]
MESSENGER AND CHRONICLE – Ft. Dodge. Iowa. 1966- – 1 – us UMI [071]
MESSENGER AND INQUIRER – Owensboro. Ky. (City edition). 1954-1968 – 1 – us UMI [071]
MESSENGER AND INQUIRER – Owensboro. Ky. (Home and City Editions). 1954- – 1 – us UMI [071]
MESSENGER AND INQUIRER – Owensboro. Ky. (Home edition). 1954- – 1 – us UMI [071]
MESSENGER OF OUR LADY OF AFRICA *see* AFRICA
MESSENGER OF PEACE – 1904-59 (complete) – 13r – 1 – ATLA R0146 – us A.T.L.A. [073]
MESSENGER OF PEACE – Macon. Mo. v. 3 and v. 11. 1877, 1884 – 1 – 9.03 – us Baptist [240]
MESSENGER OF PEACE, DEVOTED TO DOCTRINE, RELIGION AND MORALITY – v. 1. 13 Mar 1824-26 Feb 1825 – 1 – us UMI [073]
THE MESSENGER OF THE CIVIL COURTS – Montreal, Canada. v1 n48. 4 mai 1885-v2 n86. 23 Jun 1886 – 1r – 1 – Can$25.00 – cn Can Microfilming [340]
THE MESSENGER OF THE EVANGELICAL AND REFORMED CHURCH – Dec 1827-1958 (complete) – 101r – 1 – ATLA S0157 – us A.T.L.A. [073]
MESSENGER OF THE SACRED HEART – (Cont by: The Canadian Messenger. Other lang. ed: Le Petit messager des Coeurs de Jesus et de Marie) – Montreal: [League of the Sacred Heart, 1891?-1892] – 9 – cn C.I.H.M. [240]
MESSENGER OF THE SACRED HEART *see*
– THE CANADIAN MESSENGER
– LE PETIT MESSAGER DES COEURS DE JESUS ET DE MARIE
MESSENGER OF TRUTH – (gaps in: v12, v20-22, v24-27, v28-29, v39) – v1-52. 1906-53 – 5r – 1 – ATLA 1994-S031 – us A.T.L.A. [073]
Messenguer, E *see* THE SUNDAY EPISTLES SIMPLY EXPLAINED. FOREWORD BY... LONDON
Messer, August *see* ERLAEUTERUNGEN ZU NIETZSCHES ZARATHUSTRA
MESSER UND FEILE – Ludwigshafen, Germany. 1899-1912 (missing Sep-Dec 1904).-m. 7 reels – 1 – uk British Libr Newspaper [073]
Messerschmid, F *see* DIE GEMEINDEGESAENGE DER HEILIGEN MESSE
Messerschmid, Georg Friedrich *see* VOCABULARIUM, DAS IST
LA MESSIADE / Klopstock, Friedrich Gottlieb – Paris: Charpentier, 1857. 488p.6 fiches. (Literature Collection) – 9 – 15.00 – fr Bibl Nationale [810]
MESSIAH IDEA IN JEWISH HISTORY / Greenstone, Julius Hillel – Philadelphia: Jewish Publications Society, 1906 – 9 – us A.T.L.A. [270]
MESSIAH OF THE APOSTLES / Briggs, Charles Augustus – New York: Scribner's, 1895. 1 fiche – 9 – us A.T.L.A. [240]
MESSIAH OF THE GOSPELS / Briggs, Charles Augustus – New York: Scribner's, 1894. 1 fiche – 9 – us A.T.L.A. [240]
MESSIANIC EXPECTATIONS AND MODERN JUDAISM LECTURES / Schindler, Solomon – Boston: S E Cassino, 1886 – 1mf – 9 – 0-8370-5091-X – 1985-3091 – us A.T.L.A. [270]
THE MESSIANIC HOPE IN THE NEW TESTAMENT / Mathews, Shailer – Chicago: University of Chicago Press, 1905. 1 fiche – 9 – us A.T.L.A. [240]
MESSIANIC PROPHECIES / Gloag, Paton J – Edinburgh: T.&T. Clark, 1879 – 9 – us A.T.L.A. [240]
MESSIANIC PROPHECIES : LECTURES / Delitzsch, Franz – (Includes indexes) – Edinburgh:T. & T. Clark, 1880 – 1mf – 9 – 0-8370-2871-X – 1985-0871 – us A.T.L.A. [220]
MESSIANIC PROPHECY = MESSIANISCHE WEISSANGUNG : ITS ORIGIN, HISTORICAL GROWTH, AND RELATION TO NEW TESTAMENT FULFILMENT / Riehm, Eduard – (In English. Includes index) – New rev ed. Edinburgh: T & T Clark; New York: Charles Scribner [distributors], 1900 – 1mf – 9 – 0-8370-4899-0 – 1985-2899 – us A.T.L.A. [220]
MESSIANIC PROPHECY, AND THE LIFE OF CHRIST / Kennedy, William S – 2nd ed. 1860 – 1 – us A.T.L.A. [240]
MESSIANIC PROPHECY...A CRITICAL STUDY / Briggs, Charles Augustus – New York: Scribner's, 1886. 2 fiches – 9 – us A.T.L.A. [240]
DAS MESSIANISCHE BEWUSSTSEIN JESU / Volter, Daniel – Strassburg: J H Ed Heitz (Heitz & Muendel), 1907 – 1mf – 9 – 0-8370-6441-4 – 1986-0441 – us A.T.L.A. [240]
DAS MESSIANISCHE SELBSTBEWUSSTSEIN JESU CHRISTI / Schuerer, Emil – Goettingen: Dieterich, 1903. 1 fiche – 9 – us A.T.L.A. [240]
MESSIANISCHE WEISSAGUNGEN IN GESCHICHTLICHER FOLGE / Delitzsch, Franz – Leipzig: Akademie Buchhandlung, 1890 – 1mf – 9 – 0-8370-2872-8 – 1985-0872 – us A.T.L.A. [220]
DIE MESSIANISCHEN VORSTELLUNGEN DES JUEDISCHEN VOLKES IM ZEITALTER DER TANNAITEN : KRITISCH UNTERSUCHT UND IM RAHMEN DER ZEITGESCHICHTE DARGESTELLT / Klausner, Joseph – Krakau: J Klausner, 1903 – 1mf – 9 – 0-8370-3914-2 – 1985-1914 – us A.T.L.A. [270]
DIE MESSIANISCHEN WEISSAGUNGEN DES ALTEN TESTAMENTS : IN IHRER ENTSTEHUNG, ENTWICKLUNG UND AUSBILDUNG: MIT BERUECKSICHTIGUNG DER HAUPTSAECHLICHSTEN NEUTESTAMENTLICHEN CITATE / Staehelin, Johann Jakob – Berlin: G Reimer, 1847 – 1mf – 9 – 0-8370-9828-9 – 1986-3828 – us A.T.L.A. [220]
DIE MESSIANISCHEN WEISSAGUNGEN DES ALTEN TESTAMENTS NEBST DESSEN TYPEN / Schulte, Adalbert – Paderborn: Ferdinand Schoeningh, 1908. 1 fiche – 9 – us A.T.L.A. [240]
LE MESSIANISME CHEZ LES JUIFS (150 AV.J.C. A 200 AP.J.C.) / Lagrange, Marie Joseph – Paris: J. Gabalda, 1909.1 fiche – 9 – us A.T.L.A. [270]
LE MESSIANISME DANS LE TALMUD ET LES MIDRASCHIM / Rabinsohn, Marcus – (Includes bibliographical references) – Paris: A Reiff.-Heymann, 1907 – 1mf – 9 – 0-8370-4819-2 – 1985-2819 – us A.T.L.A. [270]
DER MESSIAS / Klopstock, Friedrich Gottlieb – Halle, im Magdeburgischen: Carl Herrmann Hemmerde. 4v. 1756-73 – 1 – us U.W. Library [830]
DER MESSIAS : TRAUERSPIEL / Gumppenberg, Hanns, Freiherr von – Muenchen: L Finsterlin, 1891 – 1r – 1 – us U.W. Library [820]
DER MESSIASBOTE *see* NATHANAEL
MESSIDOR – Dir. Gerault-Richard. Paris. 13 sept 1906-26 sept 1908 – 1 – fr A.C.R.P.P. [073]
MESSIDOR – Le grand magazine du peuple. Hebdomadaire de la democratie syndicale. Dir. Leon Jouhau. Paris. mars 1938-sept 1939 – 1 – fr A.C.R.P.P. [073]
LE MESSIE: POEME: SUIVI DE QUELQUES POESIES MELEES / Dubourg – Amsterdam et Paris: Musier, 1777. 215p.3 fiches. (Literature Collection) – 9 – 8.00 – fr Bibl Nationale [810]
Messier, Stephen P *see* RELATIONSHIPS AMONG SELECTED KINETIC PARAMETERS, BAT VELOCITIES, AND THREE METHODS OF STRIDING BY FEMALE SOFTBALL BATTERS
MESSIIA / Merezhkovskii, Dimitrii – 2v. Paris. n.d. BR-773 2 – 8 – ne IDC [240]
Messiter, A H *see* A HISTORY OF THE CHOIR AND MUSIC OF TRINITY CHURCH, NEW YORK, FROM ITS ORGANIZATION TO THE YEAR 1897
Messler, Abraham *see* FORTY YEARS AT RARITAN
MESSUNG DER DESINTEGRATIONSLEISTUNG DES HOLMIUM-YAG-LASERS IN HINBLICK AUF DEN EINSATZ IN DER LITHOTRIPSIE / Henke, Heinz-Werner – 1995 – 2mf – 9 – DM80.00 – 3-8267-2234-5 – gw Hänsel [612]
MESSUNG DER WIRKUNGSQUERSCHNITTE FUER DEPOLARISATION DES 6^3P_1 YB-ZUSTANDS DURCH EDELGASSTOESSE MIT HILFE DER QUANTUM-BEAT-METHODE UNTER VERWENDUNG EINES GEPULSTEN FARBSTOFFLASERS / Radloff, Hans-Henning – 1995 – 1mf – 9 – DM60.00 – 3-8267-2233-7 – gw Hänsel [530]
MESSUNG VON MUSKELANTWORTEN AUF UNTERSCHIEDLICHE MODULATIONSFORMEN BEI FUNKTIONELLER NEUROMUSKULAERER STIMULATION AN GESUNDEN UND QUERSCHNITTGELAEHMTEN / Winkler, Joerg – 1995 – 2mf – 9 – DM80.00 – 3-8267-2252-3 – gw Hänsel [612]
Mestas, Alberto de *see* AGUSTIN DE ITURBIDE
MESTNAI A PROMYSHLENNOST I KHUDOZHESTVENNYE PROMYSLY : [EZHEMESI ACHNY I PROIZVODSTVENNO-MASSOVY I ZHURNAL GOSUDARSTVENNOGO KOMITETA SOVETA MINISTROV RSFSR PO DELAM MESTNO I PROMYSHLENNOSTI I KHUDOZHESTVENNYKH PROMYSLOV I T SK PROFSOI UZA RABOCHIKH MESTNO I PROMYSHLENNOSTI I KOMMUNALNOGO KHOZI A ISTVA.] – (Library has: Oct. 1960-May 1963; missing Oct. 1962) – [Moskva]: Komitet, 1960-1963. 4v – 1 – CSUX89-S852 – us Hoover Inst Photo [947]
MESTO POTREBITEL'SKOI KOOPERATSII V SISTEME SOVETSKOGO KHOZIAISTVA I EE OCHEREDNYE ZADACHI NA 1924-25 KHOZIAISTVENNYI GOD – M., 1925 – 2mf – 9 – COR-336/1 – ne IDC [334]
Mestwerdt, P *see* DIE ANFAENGE DES ERASMUS
MESUAE MEDICI. CLARISSIMI OPERA... / Costa, J – Venecia, 1570 – 19mf – 9 – sp Cultura [610]
LE MESUREUR – Quebec, Canada. v2 n7. jul/aut 1953 – 1r – 1 – Can$25.00 – cn Can Microfilming [073]
META – v1- 1955- 1; v21- 5,6,9 – us UMI [971]
METABOLIC AND PEDIATRIC OPHTHAMOLOGY – v.1-. 1977- – 5,6,9 – us UMI [617]
METABOLIC BRAIN DISEASE – v1-9. 1986-94 – 1,5 – $65.00 – us UMI [616]
METABOLIC COST OF DOWNHILL SKI ERGOMETRY IN MALES / Audet, Diane – 1994 – 1mf – $4.00 – us Microform Publ [612]
METABOLIC RESPONSE TO ACUTE COLD AIR EXPOSURE AND TWO LEVELS OF BETA BLOCKADE IN MALES AND FEMALES / Moser, C Daniel & Paolone, Albert M – 1991 – 2mf – 9 – $8.00 – us Microform Publ [612]
METABOLIC RESPONSES TO GRADED DOWNHILL WALKING / Wanta, Daniel – 1989 – 41p 1mf – 9 – $4.00 – us Microform Publ [612]
METAFISICA DE LOS SEXOS HUMANOS / Caba, Pedro – Madrid: Indice, 1956 – sp Bibl Santa Ana [140]
LA METAFISICA DEL ESPACIO / Caba, Pedro – Cienloxias, 1957 – 1 – sp Bibl Santa Ana [946]
METAHYPSICES COMPENDIUM / Avicenna – Roma, 1926 – 4mf – 8 – ne Slangenburg [110]
METAL FINISHING – v1- 1903- 1; v69- 1971- 5,6; v73- 9 – us UMI [670]
METAL FINISHING JOURNAL – v1-20 1955-74 1; v17-20 5,6 – us UMI [670]
METAL POLISHER, BUFFER AND PLATER : 1897-1955 / Metal Polishers, Buffers, Platers and Helpers International Union – (Coll title: Labor Union Periodicals, Pt 1) – 13r – 1 – $1,755.00 – 1-55655-243-2 – us UPA [331]

Metal Polishers, Buffers, Platers and Helpers International Union *see* METAL POLISHER, BUFFER AND PLATER
METAL PRODUCTS MANUFACTURING *see* APPLIANCE
METAL PROGRESS – v18- 1930- 1; v87- 1965- 5,6; v107- 9 – us UMI [670]
METAL PROGRESS – v30-56 Jul 1936-1949 – 1,5,6 – us Princeton Micro [660]
METAL PROGRESS *see*
– ADVANCED MATERIALS AND PROCESSES
METAL SCIENCE AND HEAT TREATMENT – v1-36. 1959-94 – 1,5 – $100.00v – us UMI [660]
METAL STATISTICS – 1909. Annual – 1 – $75.00y – us Fairchild Micro [310]
THE METAL WORKER / The Engineering and Allied Trades Shop Stewards' National Council – Journal of the Engineering and Allied Trades Shop Stewards' National Council. 1946-63 – 1 – uk World [331]
METAL WORKERS BULLETIN, 1910-1914 : WELDORS' JOURNAL, 1938-1941 : 1910-1914 / Brotherhood of Metal WorkersUnited Brotherhood of Weldors, Cutters and Helpers of America – (Coll title: Labor Union Periodicals, Pt 1) – 1r – 1 – $135.00 – 1-55655-244-0 – us UPA [331]
METAL/CENTER NEWS – 1985- – 1,5,6,9 – us UMI [660]
DER METALLARBEITER – Berlin, Vienna. Jan 1884-Jul 1914 – 17r – 1 – uk British Libr Newspaper [670]
METALLARBEITER-ZEITUNG – Stuttgart? v24, no.11,17,26. 1906. (Serial publications of German trade unions in the Memorial Library, University of Wisconsin-Madison.) – 1 – us U.W. Library [331]
METALLARBEITER-ZEITUNG *see* DEUTSCHE METALLARBEITERZEITUNG
METALLINDUSTRIEPLAN / Austria. Bundesministerium fuer Vermoegenssicherung und Wirtschaftsplanung – Wien. 1948. BD-382 – 9 – ne IDC [338]
Metallinos, Eustathius *see* ANSWER OF THE GREAT CHURCH OF CONSTANTINOPLE TO THE PAPAL ENCYCLICAL ON UNION
METALLIST – St. Petersburg. no 1-8, 11-13, 15-16, 18, 20, 22-24, 27, 36-37. 1911-1913 – 1 – us NY Public [670]
METALLOGRAPHY – v1-17. 1968-84 – 1,5,6,13 – sz Elsevier [540]
METALLURGIA – v1-83 1929-71 1; v83- 5,6 – us UMI [660]
METALLURGIA AND METAL FORMING – v25- 1958- 1; v38- 5,6; v42- 9 – us UMI [660]
METALLURGICAL, AND PETROLEUM ENGINEERS TRANSACTIONS / American Institute of Mining – (Ceased publ. Cont: American Institute of Mining and Metallurgical Engineers transactions) – New York. v212-246. feb 1958-1969 – 1 – D1663 – us UMI [622]
METALLURGICAL REVIEWS – Institute of Metals, London. v1-5. 1956-60. 423/2 – 8 – ne IDC [660]
METALLURGICAL TRANSACTIONS : B: PROCESS METALLURGY – v6B- 1975- – 1,5,6,9 – us UMI [660]
METALLURGICAL TRANSACTIONS : A: PHYSICAL METALLURGY AND MATERIALS SCIENCE – v6A- 1975- – 1,5,6,9 – us UMI [660]
METALLURGICAL TRANSACTIONS – v1-5. 1970-74 – 1 – us UMI [660]
METALLURGIST – v1-12. 1925-1940 – 1 – us Princeton Micro [660]
METALLURGIST – v1-38. 1957-94 – 1,5 – $80.00v – us UMI [660]
THE METALLURGIST AND MATERIALS TECHNOLOGIST – v5- 1973- – 1,5,6,9 – us UMI [660]
METALLVERARBEITUNG – 1947- – 1; 1975- 5,6,9 – us UMI [670]
METALOGICON / Saresberiensis, Ioannes – 1991 – 6mf – 9 – Bf1,500.00 – 2-503-63982-8 – be Brepols [240]
METALOWIEC – Warsaw. Poland. -m and w. Jan 1952-Jun 1955. (1 reel) – 1 – uk British Libr Newspaper [947]
METALS – v. 25-31. 1954-61 – 1 – us UMI [332]
METALS AND MATERIALS: THE JOURNAL OF THE INSTITUTE OF METALS – v1-. 1985- – 1,5,6,9 – us UMI [660]
METALS FORUM – v1-. 1978- – 5,6,9 – us UMI [660]
METALS SOURCEBOOK – 1973-75 1,5,6; 1975 9 – us UMI [073]
METALS TECHNOLOGY – v1-15 1934-48 – 1,5,6 – us Princeton Micro [660]
METALS WEEK – v1- 1930- 1; v41- 5,6; v47- 9 – us UMI [660]
METALS WEEK PRICE HANDBOOK – (1985- . 5,6,9) – 1973- – 1 – us UMI [332]
METALWORK : ARCHITECTURE, APPLIED ARTS, STUDIO ARTS – (Individual titles not listed separately) – 35 catalogues on 44mf – 9 – £370.00 – uk Chadwyck [730]
METALWORK / Victoria and Albert Museum. London – (Over 8,000 reproductions) – 138mf – 9 – $740.00 – 0-907006-05-1 – uk Mindata [740]
METAL-WORKING – 1948-55 – 1 – us UMI [670]
METALWORKING – 1956-69 – 1 – us UMI [670]
METALWORKING ECONOMICS – v25-27 1969-71 – 1 – us UMI [670]
METALWORKING NEWS – New York, 1988- – 1 – $175.00y – us Fairchild Micro [670]
METAMEDICINE – v1-3. Feb 1980-Oct 1982 – 1 – us UMI [073]
Metamora Methodist Church (Metamora, Ohio) *see* RECORDS
LES METAMORPHOSES D'OVIDE, AVEC DES EXPLICATIONS A LA FIN DE CHAQUE FABLE / Ovid – Amsterdam: aux depens d'Etienne Roger..., 1716. SEM105P7 – 5mf – 9 – Can$11.25 – cn Bibl Nat [450]
METAMORPHOSES, ETC / Ovidius – 15th cent. Holkham ms. 324. Holkham Hall, Norfolk, England – 1,14 – uk Microform Academic [760]
METANOEO AND METAMELEI IN GREEK LITERATURE UNTIL 100 A.D. : INCLUDING DISCUSSION OF THEIR COGNATES AND OF THEIR HEBREW EQUIVALENTS / Thompson, Effie Freeman – Chicago: University of Chicago Press, 1908 – 1mf – 9 – 0-8370-9315-5 – 1986-3315 – us A.T.L.A. [450]
METANOIA – v1- 1969- 1; v6- 5,6; v7- 9 – us UMI [073]
METAPHILOSOPHY – (v8- 1977- 5,6,9) – v1- 1970- – 1 – us UMI [100]
METAPHISIQUE DES CAUSES D'APRES ST THOMAS ET ALB. LE GRAND / Regnon, T D – Paris, 1896 – 13mf – 8 – ne Slangenburg [240]
METAPHISIQUE DES CAUSES D'APRES ST THOMAS ET ALB. LE GRAND / Regnon, T D – Paris, 1896 – 13mf – 8 – ne Slangenburg [120]
METAPHORA MEDICINE ET CHIRURGIE... / Laredo, B – Sevilla, 1536 – 4mf – 9 – sp Cultura [617]
METAPHRASES ET ENARRATIONES PERPETUAE EPISTOLARUM D. PAULI APOSTOLI. TOMUS PRIMUS. IN EPISTOLAM AD ROMANOS. PER MARTINUM BUCERUM – 1536 – 1 – us A.T.L.A. [240]
METAPHYSICA SIVE PRIMA PHILOSOPHIA / Avicenna – Venetiis, 1495 – 3mf – 8 – ne Slangenburg [110]
THE METAPHYSICAL MIRACLES OF THE NEW TESTAMENT...WITH REFERENCE...TO... HUME / Smith, Thomas – London: William Skeffington, 1871. 1 fiche – 9 – us A.T.L.A. [240]
THE METAPHYSICAL SYSTEM OF HOBBES AS CONTAINED IN TWELVE CHAPTERS FROM HIS ELEMENTS OF PHILOSOPHY CONCERNING BODY...AND HUMAN NATURE... AND LEVIATHAN / Hobbes, Thomas; ed by Calkins, Mary Whiton – Chicago: Open Court Publishing Co., 1905 – xxv/187p – 1 – us U.W. Library [190]
METAPHYSICORUM LIBRICUM AVERROIS COMMENTARIIS ET EPITOME VENETIIS / Aristotle – 1552 – 12mf – 8 – ne Slangenburg [110]
METAPHYSICS / Bowne, Borden Parker – New York: Harper, 1898 – 1mf – us A.T.L.A. [110]
METAPHYSICS; OR, THE PHILOSOPHY OF CONSCIOUSNESS, PHENOMENAL AND REAL / Mansel, Henry Longueville – 1871 – 1 – us A.T.L.A. [110]
METAPHYSIK UND DOGMATIK...UNTER BESONDERER BEZIEHUNG AUF DIE RITSCHL'SCHE THEOLOGIE / Fricke, G – Leipzig: J.C. Hinrichs, 1882. 1 fiche – 9 – us A.T.L.A. [240]
METAS E BASES PARA ACAO DO GOVERNO / Brazil. Presidencia de Republica – D-1244 1. 1970-1980 – 9 – ne IDC [324]
Metcalf, Bryce *see* ORIGINAL MEMBERS AND OTHER OFFICERS ELIGIBLE TO THE SOCIETY OF THE CINCINNATI 1783-1938
Metcalf, Theron *see* PRINCIPLES OF THE LAW OF CONTRACTS, AS APPLIED BY COURTS OF LAW
Metcalf, Wilder S *see* SCRAPBOOKS
Metchenko, A *see*
– TVORCHESTVO MAIAKOVSKOGO 1917-1924 GG
– TVORCHESTVO MAIAKOVSKOGO 1925-1930 GG
Metchinikoff, Leon *see* L'EMPIRE JAPONAIS
Meteor Expedition *see* WISSENSCHAFTLICHE ERGEBNISSE DER DEUTSCHEN ATLANTISCHEN EXPEDITION AUF DEM FORSCHUNGS-UND VERMESSUNGSSCHIFF "METEOR", 1925-1927
A METEOR KING / Copland, John A – Harriston Ont.: Harriston Tribune, 1899, c1901. 00244. (Pre-1900 Canadiana) – 9 – cn C.I.H.M. [971]
METEORITICS – v1- 1953- 1; v11- 5,6,9 – us UMI [520]
METEORITO DE GUARENA / Calderon S & Quiroga, F – Badajoz, 1892 – 1 – sp Bibl Santa Ana [550]
EL METEORITO DE OLIVENZA (BADAJOZ) / Fernandez Navarro, Lucas – Madrid: Jose Molina, Impresor, 1925. Sep. Trabajos del Museo Nacional de Ciencias Naturales. Serie Geologica, no 35 – 1 – sp Bibl Santa Ana [550]
METEOROLOGIA PHILOSOPHICO-POLITICA / Reinzer, Franciscus – O 728. 1709 – 9 – ne IDC [190]
METEOROLOGICAL AND GEOASTROPHYSICAL ABSTRACTS – v1-17 1950-66 – 1,5,6 – us Princeton Micro [550]
METEOROLOGICAL MAGAZINE – 1886- 1; 1971- 5,6; 1976- 4 x 6 in. 9 – us UMI [550]
METEOROLOGICAL RECORDS / Glennie, Alexander – 1834-80 – 41mf – 9 – us South Carolina Historical [550]
METEOROLOGICAL RECORDS / Weston, Plowden Charles Jennett – 1829-33 – 2mf – 9 – us South Carolina Historical [550]
METEOROLOGICAL SERIES BULLETIN / Massachusetts. Agricultural Experiment Station – v1-930 1889-1966 – 1,5,6 – us Spaulding [550]
METEOROLOGIE DE MADAGASCAR / Poisson, C – 5936B 2. v. 3. 1930 – 8 – ne IDC [550]
METEOROLOGISCHE EPHEMERIDEN. / Akademie der Wissenschaften. Munich – Munich, 1783-89 – 3 – us Readex [550]
METHANREFORMIERUNG MIT CO2 BEI ENERGIEEINKOPPLUNG DURCH DIREKTBESTRAHLUNG DES KATALYSATORS / Huder, Karin – 1992 – 147p – 9 – DM98.00 – 3-89349-566-5 – gw Hänsel [540]
Methner, Wilhelm *see* UNTER DREI GOUVERNEUREN
METHOD FOR PRESERVATION OF SELECTIVE SERVICE RECORDS – 1944-45. 2 rolls. T1002 – 1 – us Nat'l Archives [324]
METHOD FOR PRIORITY DETERMINATION IN SCIENCE AND TECHNOLOGY – 1977 – 108p – 9 – 92-3-101485-4 – fr UNESCO [600]
METHOD OF ANALYSIS AND USE OF SYMBOLS IN BRIEF-MAKING. / Thompson, William Goodrich – Boston, Ellis Co., 1916. 65 p. LL-1191 – 1 – us L of C Photodup [340]
THE METHOD OF THE DIVINE GOVERNMENT : PHYSICAL AND MORAL / McCosh, James – (Includes appendixes and index) – New York: Robert Carter, [1867] – 2mf – 9 – 0-8370-6919-X – 1986-0919 – us A.T.L.A. [210]
THE METHOD OF THE DIVINE GOVERNMENT; PHYSICAL AND MORAL / McCosh, James – New York: Robert Carter & Bros., 1853. xiii,512p – 1 – us U.W. Library [240]
THE METHOD OF THEOLOGY: AND OTHER ESSAYS / Mignot, Eduoxe Irenee Edouard et al – London: Catholic Truth Society, 1901. 1 fiche – 9 – us A.T.L.A. [240]
METHODE CLAIRE, CERTAINE ET FACILE, POUR APPRENDRE A CHANTER LA MUSIQUE / Rousseau, Jean-Jacques – Quatrieme edition, revue, augmentee et mise dans un meilleur etat. 1700 – 9 – us Sibley [780]
METHODE DE CONSULTER ET DE PRESCRIRE LES FORMULES DE MEDICINE / Ettmueller, Michael – Lyon: Chez Thomas Amaulry, 1698 – 1 – us U.W. Library [610]
METHODE DE LECTURE : SYLLABAIRE / Freres du Sacre-Coeur – Montreal: [freres du Sacre-Coeur, 1897?]. SEM105P1616 – 1mf – 9 – Can$2.25 – cn Bibl Nat [370]
METHODE DE MUSIQUE.. / Demoz de la Salle – 1728 – 2 – us Sibley [780]
LA METHODE D'EDUCATION SUIVIE PAR JESUS D'APRES LES SYNOPTIQUES / Weber, Jules – Geneve: Schautz, 1901. 1 fiche – 9 – us A.T.L.A. [240]
DIE METHODE DES ANSCHAUUNGS-UNTERRICHTS AUF PSYCHOLOGISCHER GRUNDLAGE DURCHGEFUHRT AN DER BOTANIK / Schickhelm, Franz – Halle a.S., Buchhandlung des Waisenhauses, 1889.69p – 1 – us U.W. Library [580]
LA METHODE DU BLASON / Menestrier, Claude-Francois – Lyons: Thomas Amaulry, 1689. SEM105P949 – 5mf – 9 – $11.25 – cn Bibl Nat [920]
METHODE EPROUVEE AVEC LAQUELLE ON PARVIENT FACILEMENT, ET SANS MAITRE, A CONNAITRE LES PLANTES / Dubois, F N A – Ed. 2. Orleans. 1833. B-5475 1 – 9 – ne IDC [580]
METHODE ET REFLEXIONS SUR LES LECONS DE MUSIQUE / Bemetzrieder, A – Nouvelle ed. 1781 – 9 – us Sibley [780]
METHODE NOUVELLE OU PRINCIPES GENERAUX POUR APPRENDRE FACILEMENT LA MUSIQUE ET L'ART DE CHANTER / David, F – 1737 – 9 – us Sibley [780]
METHODE NOUVELLE POUR APPRENDRE L'ART DU BLASON / Feuille, D de la – O 823. 1695 – 9 – ne IDC [920]
METHODE NOUVELLE POUR APPRENDRE PARFAITEMENT LES REGLES DU PLAIN-CHANT.. / LaFeillee, Francois de – Troisieme edition. 1773 – 2 – us Sibley [780]
METHODE POUR APPRENDRE AISEMENT A JOUER DE LA FLUTE TRAVERSIERE / Corrette, M – 1753 – 9 – us Sibley [780]
METHODE POUR DECHIFFRER LES NOMS SANSCRITS DANS LES LIVRES CHINOIS / Julien, S – 1861 – 1 – uk Microform Academic [490]
METHODE POUR LA MUSETTE / Hotteterre, J – Oeuvre X. 1738 – 9 – us Sibley [780]
METHODE RAISONNEE, POUR APPRENDRE LA MUSIQUE D'UNE FACON PLUS CLAIRE ET PLUS PRECISE A LAQUELLE ON JOINT L'ETENDUE DE LA FLUTE TRAVERSIERE / Bordet – Paris. Lion. 1755. BP-647 1 – 9 – ne IDC [780]
METHODE, THEORIQUE ET PRATIQUE POUR APPRENDRE EN PEU DE TEMS LE VIOLONCELLE DANS SA PERFECTION / Corrette, M – XXIV Ouvrage. 1741 – 9 – us Sibley [780]
METHODE UND HERMENEUTIK / Petersen, Guenter – Heidelberg, 1973 – 2mf – 9 – DM62.00 – 3-89349-381-6 – gw Hänsel [100]
METHODEN ZUR BERECHNUNG OPTIMIERTER BRECHZAHLPROFILE VON MONOMODEFASERN FUER DIE UEBERTRAGUNG HOECHSTER DATENRATEN / Trommer, Gert F – 1995 – 2mf – 9 – DM80.00 – 3-8267-2160-8 – gw Hänsel [621]
LES METHODES SCIENTIFIQUES DANS L'ETUDE ET LA CONSERVATION DES OEUVRES D'ART / Godfrey, Carlos E – 5 – us Americana [700]
METHODI NATURALIS AVIUM DISPONENDARUM TENTAMEN / Sundevall, C J – Text in Swedish. Z 1941. 1872-1873 – 9 – ne IDC [590]
METHODI PRACTICAE SPECIMEN: AN ESSAY OF A PARCTICAL GRAMMAR / Wase, Christopher – 1660. 112p. (English Linguistics Series 1500-1800) – 9 – us UMI [420]
METHODICA EXPLICATIO PRAECIPVORVM CAPITVM DOCTRINAE COELESTIS... / Kirchner, T – Ienae, 1586 – 14mf – ne IDC [240]
A METHODICAL SYSTEM OF UNIVERSAL LAW : OR, THE LAWS OF NATURE AND NATIONS... / Heineck, J G – London. 2v. 1763 – 8mf – 1 – ILM-2601/1 – ne IDC [327]
METHODIK DER FLOW-OF-FUNDS-RECHNUNG FUER PROGNOSEN DES MONETAEREN SEKTORS IN ENTWICKLUNGSLAENDERN / Heuser, Ralph – 1993 – 4mf – 9 – DM112.00 – 3-89349-786-2 – gw Hänsel [332]
METHODISCHE UND SYSTEMATISCHE UNTER-SUCHUNGEN ERKENNTNISTHEORETISCH WICHTIGER SACHLICHER GRUNDPROBLEME IN DER PLATONISCHEN IDEENLEHRE : DARGESTELLT MIT BESONDERER BERUECKSICHTIGUNG DES PROBLEMS DER EINHEIT IDEALER UND REALER

STRUKTURMOMENTE IN DER ERKENNTNIS DES WIRKLICHEN / Karmann, Anton – Wuerzburg, 1936 – xiii/134p – 9 – DM48.00 – 3-89349-053-1 – gw Hänsel [180]
METHODISM / Brash, W B – London, 1928 – 3mf – 9 – ne IDC [240]
METHODISM / Workman, Herbert Brook – Cambridge: University Press; New York: Putnam, 1912 – 1mf – us A.T.L.A. [240]
METHODISM AND LITERATURE : A SERIES OF ARTICLES FROM SEVERAL WRITERS ON THE LITERARY ENTERPRISE AND ACHIEVEMENTS OF THE METHODIST EPISCOPAL CHURCH / ed by Archibald, F A – Cincinnati: Walden and Stowe; New York: Phillips & Hunt, 1883, c1882 – 1mf – us A.T.L.A. [240]
METHODISM AND POPERY DISSECTED AND COMPARED, AND THE DOCTRINES OF BOTH PROVED TO BE DERIVED FROM A PAGAN ORIGIN,... – London, 1779 – 1mf – 9 – MP-536/1 – ne IDC [240]
METHODISM DISPLAY'D : A FARCE OF ONE ACT, AS IT WAS INTENDED TO BE PERFORM'D AT THE MOOT HALL IN NEWCASTLE, NOV. 4, 1743... / Este, T – Newcastle upon Tyne, [1743] – 1mf – 9 – MP-300/1 – ne IDC [820]
METHODISM DISPLAYED : OR, REMARKS UPON MR. WHITEFIELDS, ANSWER TO THE BISHOP OF LONDON'S LAST PASTORAL LETTER / Bate, J – London, [1739] – 1mf – 9 – MP-265/1 – ne IDC [240]
METHODISM DISPLAYED AND ENTHUSIASM DETECTED;... / Mason, William – London, 1756 – 1mf – 9 – MP-372/1 – ne IDC [240]
METHODISM EXAMINED AND EXPOSED : OR, THE CLERGY'S DUTY OF GUARDING THEIR FLOCKS AGAINST FALSE TEACHERS:... / Downes, J – London, 1759 – 2mf – 9 – MP-384/1 – ne IDC [240]
METHODISM IN CANADA : ITS WORK AND ITS STORY: BEING THE THIRTY-THIRD FERNLEY LECTURE, DELIVERED IN PENZANCE, 31ST JULY, 1903 / Sutherland, Alexander – London: C.H. Kelly, 1903 – 1mf – us A.T.L.A. [240]
METHODISM SUCCESSFUL, AND THE INTERNAL CAUSES OF ITS SUCCESS.. / Tefft, Benjamin F – 1860 – 1 – us A.T.L.A. [240]
METHODISM TRIUMPHANT : OR, THE DECISIVE BATTLE BETWEEN THE OLD SERPENT AND THE MODERN SAINT / Lancaster, N – London, 1767 – 2mf – 9 – MP-443/1 – ne IDC [240]
THE METHODIST : A COMEDY, BEING A CONTINUATION AND COMPLETION OF THE PLAN OF 'THE MINOR', WRITTEN BY MR FOOTE... / Pottinger, I – London, 3rd ed [1760?] – 1mf – 9 – MP-400/1 – ne IDC [820]
THE METHODIST : A POEM / Lloyd, Evan – London, 1766 repr 1972 – 1mf – 9 – MP-438/1 – ne IDC [810]
METHODIST ADVOCATE – Sutton. West Virginia. 1896-1930 – 1 – us UMI [071]
METHODIST ARCHIVES CATALOGUES / John Rylands University Library, Manchester – (Special catalogue "The People Called Methodists" available free on request) – 121mf – 9 – MP-600/1 – ne IDC [025]
METHODIST CHALLENGE *see* THE BOB SHULER PERIODICALS, 1916-1960
METHODIST CHRISTIAN ADVOCATE – (Lacks: 1961, 1966. Title varies: Alabama Christian Advocate) – 25 May 1881-Jun 1981 – 72r – 1 – ATLA S0251 – us A.T.L.A. [073]
THE METHODIST CHURCH 1090 ITS ORIGIN, DIVISIONS AND REUNION / Harrison, A H W et al – London, 1932. 229p – 3mf – 9 – ne IDC [240]
THE METHODIST CHURCH AND MISSIONS IN CANADA AND NEWFOUNDLAND : A BRIEF ACCOUNT OF THE METHODIST CHURCH IN CANADA: WHAT IT IS AND WHAT IT HAS DONE / Sutherland, Alexander – Toronto, Ont.: Department of Missionary Literature of the Methodist Church, Canada, [1906?] – 1mf – us A.T.L.A. [240]
Methodist Church. -Archives and History Committee *see* SURVEY OF METHODIST RECORDS [...CONNEXIONAL COMMITTEES, RESIDENTIAL SCHOOLS AND COLLEGES,...
METHODIST CHURCH BUILDINGS:... / Methodist Church. -Department for Chapel Affairs – Manchester, [1947] – 4mf – 9 – ne IDC [240]
Methodist Church. China Central Conference *see* CHINA CHRISTIAN ADVOCATE
Methodist Church. -Department for Chapel Affairs *see* METHODIST CHURCH BUILDINGS:...
Methodist Church. (Indonesia). Conferences. Sumatra *see* MINUTES OF SIXTH SESSION OF SUMATRA PROVISIONAL ANNUAL CONFERENCE OF METHODIST CHURCH HELD IN MEDAN, SUMATRA, MAR. 17-20, 1949
METHODIST CHURCH OF AUSTRALASIA OVERSEAS MISSION – (Executive Committee minutes 1898-1939 (MOM 210-12,276) 3r. Mission District minutes 1855-1914 (MOM5-26, 174.81) 17r. Mission Board minutes 1865-97 (MOM 1-3) 1r. Sydney Synod minutes 1906 (MOM 4) Port Darwin Circuit quarterly minutes 1873-99 (MOM 27) 1r. Minutes of the Victorian Section of the General Conference, Tonga Committee 1888-92 (MOM 28)) – 22r – 1 – PMB1062 – at Pacific Mss [240]
METHODIST CHURCH OF AUSTRALASIA OVERSEAS MISSION : MINUTES OF MEETINGS OF THE MISSION BOARD, 1898-1934 AND MISSION DISTRICT, 1915-1943 – 36r – 1 – PMB1063 – at Pacific Mss [240]
Methodist Church. Singapore *see* METHODIST MESSAGE. OFFICIAL ORGAN OF THE METHODIST CHURCH IN SINGAPORE
METHODIST CHURCH (U.S.) GENERAL BOARD OF SOCIAL AND ECONOMIC RELATIONS : INTERRACIAL CONFERENCE REPORTS – 1955-59 (complete) – 2r – 1 – ATLA B0067 – us A.T.L.A. [240]
METHODIST CHURCH (U.S.) GENERAL CONFERENCE : PROCEEDINGS – 1939-68 (quadrennial) (complete) – 5r – 1 – ATLA S0042 – us A.T.L.A. [240]
METHODIST CHURCH (U.S.) GENERAL CONFERENCES : GENERAL MINUTES OF ANNUAL CONFERENCES – 1941-58 (complete) – 6r – 1 – ATLA S0037 – us A.T.L.A. [240]
METHODIST CHURCH (U.S.) UNITING CONFERENCE : JOURNAL – (Filmed with: Journal of the General Conference) – 1939-52 (complete) – 4r – 1 – ATLA S0035B – us A.T.L.A. [240]
THE METHODIST CHURCHES OF TORONTO: A HISTORY OF THE METHODIST DENOMINATION AND ITS CHURCHES IN YORK AND TORONTO, WITH BIOGRAPHICAL SKETCHES OF MANY OF THE CLERGY AND LAITY / ed by Champion, Thomas Edward – Toronto: G. Rose, 1899. 00651. (Pre-1900 Canadiana) – 9 – cn C.I.H.M. [240]
A METHODIST DISSECTED : OR, A DESCRIPTION OF THEIR ERRORS / Fletcher, N – York, 1749 – 1mf – 9 – MP-335/1 – ne IDC [240]
Methodist Episcopal Church *see* GENERAL MISSION CONVENTION
THE METHODIST EPISCOPAL CHURCH AND THE CIVIL WAR / Sweet, William Warren – Cincinnati: Methodist Book Concern Press, [1912?] – 1mf – us A.T.L.A. [240]
Methodist Episcopal Church. Bowling Green Circuit *see* RECORDS
METHODIST EPISCOPAL CHURCH. CONFERENCES : MINUTES OF THE ANNUAL CONFERENCES – 1773-1940 (complete) – 26r – 1 – ATLA S0038 – us A.T.L.A. [240]
METHODIST EPISCOPAL CHURCH. GENERAL CONFERENCE : DAILY CHRISTIAN ADVOCATE – v1-23. 1848-1936 (complete) – 8r – 1 – ATLA S0043 – us A.T.L.A. [240]
METHODIST EPISCOPAL CHURCH. GENERAL CONFERENCE : JOURNAL – 1792-1936 (complete) – 12r – 1 – ATLA S0036 – us A.T.L.A. [240]
Methodist Episcopal Church. Kansas *see* RECORDS OF THE METHODIST EPISCOPAL CHURCH IN KANSAS
Methodist Episcopal Church. Kansas Mission Conference *see* MINUTES
Methodist Episcopal Church. Missions. Nevada *see* MINUTES OF SESSIONS
Methodist Episcopal Church. Missouri Conference *see* JOURNAL..
METHODIST EPISCOPAL CHURCH, SOUTH. ANNUAL CONFERENCE : GENERAL MINUTES AND YEARBOOK – 1845-1941 (complete) – 12r – 1 – ATLA S0040 – us A.T.L.A. [240]
METHODIST EPISCOPAL CHURCH, SOUTH. GENERAL CONFERENCE : DAILY CHRISTIAN ADVOCATE – (Lacking some issues) – 1858-1938 – 3r – 1 – ATLA S0044 – us A.T.L.A. [240]
METHODIST EPISCOPAL CHURCH, SOUTH. GENERAL CONFERENCE : JOURNAL – 1846-1938 (complete) – 7r – 1 – ATLA S0039 – us A.T.L.A. [240]
Methodist Episcopal Church. Southwestern Conference *see* JOURNAL
METHODIST EPISCOPAL TIMES – Buckhannon. West Virginia. 1895-1903 – 1 – us UMI [071]
METHODIST HERALD AND WEST AFRICAN EDUCATIONAL TIMES – Freetown. Sierra Leone. -m. Oct 1882-Mar 1888. (1 reel) – 1 – uk British Libr Newspaper [072]
METHODIST LAYMAN – v1-24. 1941-Jun 1964 (complete) – 5r – 1 – ATLA S0240 – us A.T.L.A. [073]
METHODIST LOCAL PREACHERS' WHO'S WHO : A COMPLETE RECORD OF THE LIVES AND CAREERS OF METHODIST LOCAL PREACHERS – London, 1934 – 3mf – 9 – ne IDC [240]
METHODIST MAGAZINE – v. 1-2. Jan 1797-Dec 1798 – 1 – us UMI [240]
THE METHODIST MAGAZINE – (Cont: The Canadian Methodist Magazine. Merged to become: The Methodist Magazine and Review) – Toronto: W Briggs, 1889-[1895] – 9 – cn C.I.H.M. [240]
THE METHODIST MAGAZINE *see*
– THE CANADIAN METHODIST MAGAZINE
– THE METHODIST MAGAZINE AND REVIEW
METHODIST MAGAZINE AND REVIEW – v1-4. 1875-1906. Title varies – 1 – cn Precision [240]
METHODIST MAGAZINE AND REVIEW *see* THE CANADIAN METHODIST REVIEW
THE METHODIST MAGAZINE AND REVIEW – (Absorbed: The Canadian Methodist Review. Merger of: The Methodist Magazine) – Toronto: W Briggs, [1896?-1906] – 9 – cn C.I.H.M. [240]
THE METHODIST MAGAZINE AND REVIEW *see* THE METHODIST MAGAZINE
THE METHODIST MEMORIAL : BEING AN IMPARTIAL SKETCH OF THE LIVES AND CHARACTERS OF THE PREACHERS WHO HAVE DEPARTED THIS LIFE SINCE THE COMMENCEMENT OF THE WORK OF GOD AMONG THE PEOPLE CALLED METHODISTS... / Atmore, C – Bristol, 1801 – 7mf – 9 – ne IDC [240]
METHODIST MESSAGE. OFFICIAL ORGAN OF THE METHODIST CHURCH IN SINGAPORE / Methodist Church. Singapore – 1891-1988. Continued annually – 1 – uk World [073]
Methodist minister, Ohio. Caddy, Charles Chester *see* PAPERS
METHODIST MISSIONARY SOCIETY ARCHIVES 1791-1948 / School of Oriental and African Studies, London – (Includes printed guide) – 25,064mf – 9 – ne IDC [240]
METHODIST MISSIONARY SOCIETY WOMEN'S WORK *see* WOMEN'S MISSIONARY SERVICE
THE METHODIST MONTHLY – Brandfort, Ont: Young People's Literary Association of the Brant Avenue Methodist Church, [1882?-18– or 19–] – 9 – cn C.I.H.M. [240]
METHODIST NEW CONNEXION : CONFERENCE. MINUTES... – Leeds, Hanley. 1797-1851. Lacking: 1798-1800; 1802-03; 1805 – 31mf – 9 – ne IDC [240]
Methodist New Connexion *see* GENERAL RULES FOR THE GOVERNMENT OF THE NEW CONNEXION OF METHODISTS
METHODIST NEW CONNEXION CIRCUITS AND MINISTERS, 1797-1907 / Rose, E A – N.p, 1979 – 1mf – 9 – ne IDC [240]
METHODIST NEW CONNEXION COLLEGE, RANMOOR, SHEFFIELD : CATALOGUE OF THE HULME SECTION OF THE LIBRARY / Sheffield. -Ranmoor College – Sheffield, 1898 – 1mf – 9 – ne IDC [240]
METHODIST NEW CONNEXION MAGAZINE : THE METHODIST MAGAZINE; OR, EVANGELICAL REPOSITORY... – (Cont as: The New Methodist Magazine and Evangelical Repository...Hanley, 1812-1832. V.15-25; N.S., V.1-10: Cont as: The Methodist New Connexion Magazine and Evangelical Repository. Manchester, 1833-1850. S.III, V.1-18: Missing: 1816, V.19; 1841, V.9(p. 81-104)) – Leeds, 1798-1811. V.1-14 – 327mf – 9 – MP-348/1 – ne IDC [240]
METHODIST NEW CONNEXION MISSIONS : GLEANINGS IN HARVEST FIELDS, 1889-1907 – (Some missing vols) – 15mf – 9 – ne IDC [240]
THE METHODIST O[BSE]RVER – Bowmanville [Ont]: James' Publishing House, [1887?-18–] – 9 – cn C.I.H.M. [240]
A METHODIST PAGEANT : A SOUVENIR OF THE PRIMITIVE METHODIST CHURCH / Barber, B A – London, 1932. xv/317p – 4mf – 9 – ne IDC [240]
METHODIST PROTEST – (Some missing vols) – London, 1876-1883 – 23mf – 9 – ne IDC [240]
METHODIST PROTESTANT – (Lacking some pgs. Some original pgs damaged. Cont: Mutual Rights and Methodist Protestant. Merged with: Methodist Recorder) – v1-99. 1834-1929 – 67r – 1 – ATLA S0170 – us A.T.L.A. [240]
METHODIST PROTESTANT *see*
– THE METHODIST PROTESTANT RECORDER
– MUTUAL RIGHTS AND METHODIST PROTESTANT
THE METHODIST PROTESTANT RECORDER – (Some years lacking. Merger of: Methodist Recorder, and Methodist Protestant) – 1846-1940 – 78r – 1 – ATLA S0172 – us A.T.L.A. [073]
METHODIST QUARTERLY REVIEW – (Lacks some issues. Discontinued 1861. Resumed 1879) – v1-79 no 4. Jan 1847-Oct 1930 – 52r – 1 – ATLA S0045 – us A.T.L.A. [240]
METHODIST RECORDER – (Cont: Columbian Methodist Recorder. Cont by: Western Methodist Recorder) – Victoria, BC: British Columbia Conference of the Methodist Church, [1899] – 9 – cn C.I.H.M. [240]
METHODIST RECORDER : INDEX TO THE WINTER NUMBERS OF THE METHODIST RECORDER, 1892-1907 – N.p., n.d. – 1mf – 9 – ne IDC [240]
METHODIST RECORDER – v. 1. Aug 1824-Jul 1825 – 1 – us UMI [240]
METHODIST RECORDER *see*
– COLUMBIAN METHODIST RECORDER
– METHODIST PROTESTANT
– THE METHODIST PROTESTANT RECORDER
– WESTERN METHODIST RECORDER
THE METHODIST RECORDER – 1861-1992. Continued annually – 1 – £4,650.00 – uk World [073]
THE METHODIST RECORDER – (Yrly reel count varies) – 1861- – 1 – inquire – us Ross [072]
METHODIST REVIEW – (Some pgs lacking. v100 never publ) – v1-114 no 3. 1818-Jun 1931 – 48r – 1 – ATLA S0085 – us A.T.L.A. [240]
METHODIST REVIEW – v. 1-114. 1818-1931 – 1 – us UMI [240]
METHODIST WHO'S WHO, 1910 – London, 1910 – 2mf – 9 – ne IDC [240]
THE METHODIST WHO'S WHO, 1912 – London, 1912 – 3mf – 9 – ne IDC [240]
THE METHODIST WHO'S WHO, 1913 – London, 1913 – 4mf – 9 – ne IDC [240]
THE METHODIST WHO'S, WHO, 1914 – London, 1914 – 4mf – 9 – ne IDC [240]
METHODIST WORTHIES : CHARACTERISTIC SKETCHES OF METHODIST PREACHERS OF THE SEVERAL DENOMINATIONS, WITH HISTORICAL SKETCH OF EACH CONNEXION / Stevenson, George J – London, 1884-1886 – 14mf – 9 – ne IDC [240]
METHODISTICAL DECEIT : A SERMON PREACHED IN THE PARISH CHURCH OF ST. MATTHEW, BETHNAL GREEN, MIDDLESEX, ON THE 29TH. OF APRIL 1770 / Smith, H – London, 1770 – 1mf – 9 – MP-465/1 – ne IDC [240]
THE METHODISTS : AN HUMOROUS BURLESQUE POEM, ADDRESS'D TO THE REV. MR. WHITEFIELD AND HIS FOLLOWERS,... – London, 1739 – 1mf – 9 – MP-260/1 – ne IDC [240]
METHODO DE HACER LA AMPUTACION DEL MUSLO... / Jenty, C – Madrid, 1766 – 2mf – 9 – sp Cultura [617]
METHODO DE LA COLLECTION Y REPOSICION DE LAS MEDICINAS SIMPLES / Oviedo, L – Madrid, 1571 – 1mf – 9 – sp Cultura [610]
METHODO EXEMPLAR DEL DOCTOR MEJANO PARA EL ESTUDIO DE LA MEDICINA... / Arguello Castrillo, A – Malaga, 1765 – 1mf – 9 – sp Cultura [610]

METHODOLOGISCHE UNTERSUCHUNGEN ZUR ISOLIERUNG VON HIRNRINDENARTERIOLEN DES MEERSCHWEINCHENS UND KULTUR VON GEFAESSWANDZELLEN / Seidel, Matthias Frank – 1993 – 1mf – 9 – DM60.00 – 3-89349-776-5 – gw Hänsel [636]

METHODOLOGY AND GUIDELINES FOR FISHERIES DEVELOPMENT PLANNING, WITH SPECIAL REFERENCE TO THE DEVELOPING COUNTRIES IN THE AFRICA REGION – 1989 – 68p – it F.A.O. [338]

METHODOLOGY OF CONTEMPORARY AFRICAN HISTORY – 1984 – 218p – 9 – 92-3-102117-6 – fr UNESCO [960]

METHODOS – v. 1-15. 1949-63 – 1 – us UMI [380]

METHODS AND RESULTS OF RESCUE WORK / Flatbush, Adda M – 1899 – 9 – us A.T.L.A. [240]

METHODS AND TECHNIQUES IN POST-SECONDARY EDUCATION / Bligh, Donald A – 1980 – 138p – 9 – 92-3-101575-3 – fr UNESCO [370]

METHODS FOR DEVELOPMENT PLANNING : SCENARIOS, MODELS AND MICRO-STUDIES – 1981 – 269p – 9 – 92-3-101875-2 – fr UNESCO [338]

METHODS FOR THE EVALUATION OF THE IMPACT OF FOOD AND NUTRITION PROGRAMMES / ed by Sahn, David E et al – 1984 – 291p – microfiche – $10.00 – 92-808-0473-1 – ja U.N. Univ [360]

METHODS OF ANALYSIS FOR PROCESSED FRUITS AND VEGETABLES – it F.A.O. [660]

METHODS OF CENSUSING BIRDS IN AUSTRALIA / ed by Davies, S J J F – 1984 – 9 – A$15.00 – at R.A.O.U. [590]

METHODS OF CHURCH WORK : RELIGIOUS, SOCIAL AND FINANCIAL / Stall, Sylvanus – New York: Funk & Wagnalls, 1888, c1887 – 1mf – 9 – 0-8370-6412-0 – 1986-0412 – us A.T.L.A. [240]

METHODS OF COMMUNICATION PLANNING / ed by Middleton, John & Wedemeyer, Dan J – 1985 – 487p – 9 – 92-3-102112-5 – fr UNESCO [350]

METHODS OF COMPUTATION OF LOW STREAMFLOW / ed by McMahon, T A & Arenas, A Diaz – 1982 – 95p – 9 – 92-3-102013-7 – fr UNESCO [550]

METHODS OF COMPUTATION OF THE WATER BALANCE OF LARGE LAKES AND RESERVOIRS – 2v – 9 – fr UNESCO [550]

THE METHODS OF ETHICS / Sidgwick, Henry – (Includes index) – 5th ed. London: Macmillan, 1893 – 2mf – 1 – 0-8370-6378-7 – 1986-0378 – us A.T.L.A. [170]

THE METHODS OF ETHICS / Sidgwick, Henry – London: Macmillan and Co., 1874 – 1 roll – 1 – 1-55879-923-0 – uk Libr Preservation [170]

METHODS OF FARM MANAGEMENT INVESTIGATIONS FOR IMPROVING FARM PRODUCTIVITY / Yang, W Y – 1965 – 258p – it F.A.O. [338]

METHODS OF HYDROLOGICAL COMPUTATIONS FOR WATER PROJECTS / ed by Eichert, B S et al – 1982 – 122p – 9 – 92-3-102005-6 – fr UNESCO [627]

THE METHODS OF METHODISM : A MANUAL OF THE GOVERNMENT, FINANCE, TEACHING AND DEPARTMENTS OF THE WESLEYAN METHODIST CHURCH / Angus, J – London, [1908] – 2mf – 9 – ne IDC [240]

METHODS OF MIND-TRAINING; CONCENTRATED ATTENTION AND MEMORY / Aiken, Catharine – New York: Harper & Brothers, 1896. 110 p. plates. 1 reel – 1 – us U.W. Library [150]

METHODS OF MISSION WORK / Nevius, John Livingston – New York: Foreign Mission Library, [1895?] – 1mf – 9 – 0-8370-6826-6 – 1986-0826 – us A.T.L.A. [240]

METHODS OF NON-MILITARY ACCOUNTING IN ECONOMIC UNDERTAKINGS / Chayanov, A V – Moscow. 1921. (Russian text) – 1. 12.00; ; 7 – uk Microform Academic [650]

METHODS OF TEACHING PATRIOTISM IN THE PUBLIC SCHOOLS: BEING AN EXTRACT FROM AN ADDRESS...JUNE 28, 1889 / Balch, George Thacher – New York, 1890. xli,109p – 1 – us U.W. Library [370]

THE METHODS OF THEISM : AN ESSAY / Beattie, Francis Robert – Brantford, Ont.: Watt & Shenston, 1887 – 1mf – 9 – 0-8370-2224-X – 1985-0224 – us A.T.L.A. [210]

METHODS OF THEISM: AN ESSAY / Beattie, Francis Robert – Brantford: Watt & Shenston, 1887 – 1mf – 9 – us A.T.L.A. [240]

THE METHODS OF THEISM: AN ESSAY / Beattie, Francis Robert – Brantford, Ont.: Watt & Shenston, 1887.03513.(Pre-1900 Canadiana) – 9 – cn C.I.H.M. [240]

METHODUS COGNOSCENDI EXTIRPANDIQUE ECRESCENTES IN VESICAE COLLO CARUNCULAS... / Laguna, A de – SL, SA: 1551? – 1mf – 9 – sp Cultura [610]

METHODUS FOLIORUM, SEU PLANTAE MONSPELIENSES JUXTA FOLIORUM ORDINEM DIGESTAE / Sauvages, F B – La Haye. 1751. B-6195 2 – 8 – ne IDC [580]

METHODUS FUNGORUM EXHIBENS GENERA, SPECIES ET VARIETATES / Gleditsch, J G – Berolini. 1753. B-5931 2 – 8 – ne IDC [580]

METHODUS MEDENDI... / Valles de Covarrubias, F – SL, 1588 – 9mf – 9 – sp Cultura [610]

METHODUS MUSCORUM / Necker, N J de – Mannhemii, 1771. 296 pp., 1 pl. B-588 2 – 8 – ne IDC [580]

METHODUS MUSCORUM ILLUSTRATA / Swartz, O P – Upsaliae, 1781. 38 pp., 2 pls. B-6186 2 – 8 – ne IDC [580]

METHODUS PLANTARUM / Ray, J – Londini. 1703. B-5278 1 – 9 – ne IDC [580]

METHODUS PLANTARUM NOVA / Ray, J – London. 1682. BM-391 2 – 8 – ne IDC [580]

METHODUS PLANTAS HORTI BOTANICI ET AGRI MARBURGENSIS / Moench, C – Marburgi Cattorum, 1794. 780 pp. suppl. 1802, 328 pp. B-698 2 – 8 – ne IDC [580]

METHODUS QUA OMNES DETECTOS LICHENES SECUNDUM ORGANA / Acharius, E – Stockholmiae. 1803. B-1077 2 – 8 – ne IDC [580]

METHODVS CONCIONANDI... / Andreae d.A E, J – N.p., n.d. – 2mf – 9 – ne IDC [240]

METHODVS CONCIONANDI PRAECEPTIS ET EXEMPLIS DOMINICALIVM QVORVNDAM... / Hunnius, A – VVitebergae, 1595 – 10mf – ne IDC [240]

METHUEN 1714-1849 – (Mf 1T-6T: Vital Records 1714-1828. Mf 6T-9T: Births & Deaths 1775-1850. Mf 8T-9T: Marriages 1807-39. Mf 9T-12T: Marriage Intentions 1809-49. Mf 11T-12T: Marriages 1839-44. Mf 12T: Births 1800-49. Mf 12T-13T: Out-of-Town Marriages 1728-99. Mf 13T-14T: Births & Deaths 1744-1838. Mf 14T: Marriages 1784-99. Mf 15T-16T: Maariages/Intentions 1768-1809. Mf 16T-19T: Vital Records 1844-49) – (mf ed 1997) – 19mf – 9 – 0-87623-292-6 – us Holbrook [920]

LE METIS – (Also: Le Manitoba v11 n1 13 oct 1881-v5 n12 31 dec 1885) – St-Boniface, Manitoba. 27 mai 1871-29 sep 1881 – 3r – 1 – Can$50.00r – cn Can Microfilming [072]

LE METIS : ORGANE DES POPULATIONS DU NORD-OUEST – Montreal, Canada. 2,23 mai 1885 – 1r – 1 – Can$25.00 – cn Can Microfilming [072]

METIS *see* LE MANITOBA

LE METIS CANADIEN / Giraud, M – Son role dans l'histoire des provinces de l'Ouest – 9 – F330.00 – fr Ethnologie [971]

LES METIS CANADIENS-FRANCAIS / Derouet, Camille – s.l.: s.n., 1896?. 03770. (Pre-1900 Canadiana) – 9 – cn C.I.H.M. [305]

Metis, Eduard *see* KARL GUTZKOW ALS DRAMATIKER

METOD KONTURNOGO INTEGRALA E EGO PRIMENENIE L ISSLEDOVANIIU ZADACH DLIIA DIFFERENTSIALNYKH URAVENII / Rasulov, Medzhid L – Moskva: Nauka, 1964 – us Res Libr [330]

O METODIKE ORGANIZATSII KOOPERATIVOV / Maksimov-Slobozhanin, E D – L., 1925 – 1mf – 9 – COR-265/1 – ne IDC [334]

METODIST = METHODIST: BULLETIN OF THE SIBERIA/MANCHURIA MISSION OF THE METHODIST EPISTOPAL CHURCH, SOUTH : BYULLETIN SIBIR-MANCHZHURIYA MISSII METODISTSKOI EPISKOPAL'NOI TSERAVI, YUG – August 1925-July 1927. 394p – 1 – $15.76 – us Baptist [240]

METODO DE ENSENANZA DE LA LECTURA Y LA ESCULTURA / Rodriguez Alvarez, Angel – Plasencia: Editorial Sanchez Rodrigo, 2nd parte 1969 – 1 – sp Bibl Santa Ana [946]

METODO E FINE...DIRITTO INTERNATIONALE / Catellani, E L – Torino, 1884 – 1mf – 1 – ILM-1506/1 – ne IDC [327]

METODOLOGIA DEL DERECHO (ORDENACION CRITICA DE LAS PRINCIPALES DIRECCIONES METODOLOGICAS). MADRID, 1945 / Truyol, A & Hernandez Gil, Antonio – Madrid: Razon y Fe, 1947 – 1 – sp Bibl Santa Ana [946]

METODY KOLICHESTVENNOGO UCHETA EFFEKTA ZEMLEUSTROISTVA : SBORNIK STATEI / Chaianov, A V – M., 1925 – 2mf – 9 – COR-212/1 – ne IDC [334]

Metral, Antoine *see* LES ESCLAVES

METRIC MONITOR = MONITEUR METRIQUE – Ottawa. mar 1974-v4 n5. mai 1977 – 1r – 1 – Can$45.00 – cn Can Microfilming [072]

METRICAL CHRONICLE OF ROBERT OF GLOUCESTER (RS86) / Robert Of Gloucester; ed by Wright, W A – (v1 1887 Dfl35.00. v2 1887 Dfl32.00) – ne Slangenburg [941]

METRICAL LEGENDS OF NORTHUMBERLAND – 1834 – 1 – us I.U. Libraries [390]

METRICES BIBLICAE REGULAE EXEMPLIS ILLUSTRATAE / Bickell, Gustav – Oeniponte [Innsbruck]: Sumptibus Libr Wagnerianae, 1879 – 1mf – 9 – 0-8370-2336-X – 1985-0336 – us A.T.L.A. [470]

DIE METRIK DES BUCHES JOB / Vetter, Paul – Freiburg i.B.: Herder, 1897. 1 fiche – 9 – us A.T.L.A. [240]

METRIK UND RHYTHMIK IN TANNHAEUSERS GEDICHTEN / Siebert, Johannes – 1995 – 1mf – 9 – DM48.00 – 3-8267-3120-4 – gw Hänsel [430]

DIE METRISCHEN STUECKE DES BUCHES JEREMIA / Cornill, Carl Heinrich – Leipzig: J.C. Hinrichs, 1901. 1 fiche – 9 – us A.T.L.A. [220]

METRO – Bakersfield. Calif. 1960-1966 – 1 – us UMI [071]

METRO – Stockholm, 1995- – 9 – sw Kungliga [072]

METRO JOURNAL DU QUEBEC : ACTION SOCIALE POUR L'INDEPENDANCE DU QUEBEC – Montreal, Canada. v1 n3. avr 1961 – 1r – 1 – Can$25.00 – cn Can Microfilming [072]

METRO PM ET METRO MATIN – Montreal, v1 n3. 27 oct 1978-v1 n84. 9 mar 1979 – 1r – 1 – Can$35.00 – cn Can Microfilming [072]

METRO TORONTO B'NAI B'RITH NEWS – Toronto, Ont. Apr 1962.Ceased publication – 1 – us A.J.P.C. [072]

METRO-EAST JOURNAL – East St. Louis. IL. 1965- – 1 – us UMI [071]

METRO-EXPRESS : QUOTIDIEN / ed by Brillant, Jacques – Montreal, Canada. 21 jul 1964-14 sep 1966 – 14r – 1 – Can$60.00r – cn Can Microfilming [072]

METROLOGIA – v. 1-16. 1965-80 – 1,5,9 – 1212.00 – us UMI [073]

METRONOME – Boston. v1-3. 1871-74 – 1r – 1 – £60.00 – uk Chadwyck [780]

THE METRONOME: OR MUSIC-TEACHER'S ASSISTANT / Beecher, Charles – New York: M. H. Newman & Co., 1851. Proposes a numerical system of musical notation with hymns written in this notation. ymusic 932 – 1 – us L of C Photodup [780]

METROPOLIS – Miami. Fla. -w. 1897-1922 – 1 – us UMI [071]

METROPOLIT MOSKOVSKII PLATON LEVSHIN KAK PROPOVEDNIK / Nadezhin, A – Kazan'. 1882. BR-7721 2 – 8 – ne IDC [920]

METROPOLITAN – v62- 1966- 1; v67- 5,6 – us UMI [073]

METROPOLITAN – A Monthly Magazine, Devoted to Religion" Education, Literature, and General Information. v. 1-n.s.v. 1. Feb 1853-Jan 1859 – 1 – us UMI [073]

METROPOLITAN – Georgetown. D.C. 1820 – 3 – us Readex [071]

METROPOLITAN BAPTIST CHURCH. PORTLAND, OREGON : CHURCH RECORDS – 1949-73 – 1 – 39.51 – us Baptist [240]

Metropolitan Board of Works *see* MINUTES, 1853-88

THE METROPOLITAN CATHOLIC ALMANAC : AND LAITY'S DIRECTORY FOR THE YEAR OF OUR LORD... – Baltimore: Fielding Lucas, Jr., 1838-57 – 3r – 1 – $40.00r – us U.N.D. Archives [240]

THE METROPOLITAN CATHOLIC ALMANAC AND LAITY'S DIRECTORY FOR THE UNITED STATES – Baltimore: John Murphy and Co., 1859-61 – 1r – 1 – $40.00r – us U.N.D. Archives [240]

METROPOLITAN FASHIONS – Toronto: Delineator Pub. Co, [18–189- or 19–] – 9 – cn C.I.H.M. [640]

Metropolitan Life Insurance Company *see* STATISTICAL BULLETIN

METROPOLITAN MAGAZINE – v. 1-58. 1831-50 – 1 – us UMI [073]

THE METROPOLITAN MONTREAL – Montreal, Canada. v7 n46. 12 nov 1898; v8 n11. 18 mar 1899 – 1r – 1 – Can$25.00 – cn Can Microfilming [072]

METROPOLITAN (MONTREAL, QUEBEC) *see* MONTREAL LIFE

Metropolitan Museum of Art *see*
- BULLETIN
- PUBLICATIONS OF THE METROPOLITAN MUSEUM OF ART ON MICROFICHE, 1870 TO THE PRESENT
- PUBLICATIONS OF THE MUSEUM OF PRIMITIVE ART ON MICROFICHE, 1957-1975

Metropolitan Museum of Art. New York *see*
- CATALOG
- LIBRARY CATALOG
- LIBRARY CATALOG OF THE METROPOLITAN MUSEUM OF ART. SECOND EDITION
- LIBRARY CATALOG OF THE METROPOLITAN MUSEUM OF ART. SECOND EDITION. REVISED

METROPOLITAN RECORD : OFFICIAL ORGAN OF THE MOST REV ARCHBISHOP (ROMAN CATHOLIC) OF NEW YORK – New York, NY. Jan 7 1860-May 28 1864 – 5r – 1 – us Western Res [071]

METROPOLITAN RECORD AND NEW YORK VINDICATOR – (Roman Catholic newspaper for the Archdiocese of NY) – New York, Jun 4 1864-Dec 29 1868 – 5r – 1 – us Western Res [071]

METROPOLITAN STAR – New York, NY. 1975-82 – 1 – us A.J.P.C. [071]

METROPOLITAN TORONTO BUSINESS JOURNAL – (Cont by: Board of Trade of Metro Toronto Business Journal at v84 1994) – Toronto. v61-83. 1970-93 – 9 – Can$28.00y – cn Micromedia [380]

Metropolitan Toronto Central Library *see* VALENTINE CARD COLLECTION: A SELECTION

THE METROPOLITAN TRACT OF THE UNIVERSITY OF WASHINGTON / Washington. University – Seattle, University of Washington, 1961 259 p. LL-1608 – 1 – us L of C Photodup [340]

METROPOLITAN-VICKERS GAZETTE – v. 29-31. 1958-60 – 1 – us UMI [621]

Metrowich, F C *see* THE DEVELOPMENT OF HIGHER EDUCATION IN SOUTH AFRICA, 1873-1927

Mettenius, G H *see*
- FILICES HORTI BOTANICI LIPSIENSIS
- FILICES LECHLERIANAE, CHILENSES AC PERUANAE, CURA R. F. HOHENACKERI EDITAE
- UEBER EINIGE FARNGATTUNGEN

Metternich, R de *see* MEMOIRES, DOCUMENTS ET ECRITS DIVERS LAISSES PAR LE PRINCE DE METTERNICH CHANCELIER DE COUR ET D'ETAT

METTERNICH UND KUEBECK : EIN BRIEFWECHSEL / ed by Kuebeck, M von – Wien, 1910 – 3mf – 9 – ne IDC [943]

METTERNICH Y DONOSO CORTES / Menczer, Bela – Madrid: Arbor, 1949 – 1 – sp Bibl Santa Ana [320]

Metternich-Winneburg, R *see* OESTERREICHS THEILNAHME AN DEN BEFREIUNGSKRIEGEN

Metz, T M *see* MANGOE-NAGARAN. ANALYSE VAN EEN JAVAANSCH VORSTENDOM

Metze *see* METZE (CCC249)

METZE (CCC249) / Metze – (In Chinese) – [S.l: s.n. 2v. 1937] – 1r – 1 – 1984-6588 – us A.T.L.A. [920]

METZINGER URACHER VOLKSBLATT : BA DER SUED-WEST PRESSE – Metzingen-Ulm, Germany. 1980- – 1 – gw Mikrofilm [072]

Meuffels, Hubert *see* MARTYRS DE GORCUM

Meulen, Henry *see* THREE PAMPHLETS

Meulen, I P vander *see*
- DECLARATIO, OFT OPENBARE VERTOONINGE, ENDE NOOTELICKE VERCLARINGE, TEGHEN
- DEFENSIO, WT DE HEYLIGHE GODLIJCKE SCHRIFTUERE

Meulen, J P vander *see* SVCCESSIO APOSTOLICA. DAT IS, NAECOMINGHE, OFT DE NAETREDINGHE DER

Meunier, F J *see* LES TISSUS OSSEUX DES OSTEICHTHYENS: STRUCTURE, GENESE, CROISSANCE ET EVOLUTION

Meunier, Francis *see* ESSAI SUR LA VIE ET LES OUVRAGES DE NICOLE ORESME

Meurier, G *see*
- COLOQUES FAMILIERS
- CONJUGAISONS, REGLES ET INSTRUCTIONS POUR CEUX QUI DESIRENT APPRENDRE FRANCOIS, ITALIEN, ESPAGNOL ET FLAMENS

LE MEURTRE DU VODUN DAN / Saulnier, P – 9 – F70.00 – fr Ethnologie [300]

LA MEUSE – Quotidien belge d'information. Illustre. no. 120-134. Paris. 17-31 mai 1940 – 1 – fr A.C.R.P.P. [072]

Meusel, Johann G *see*
- MISCELLANEEN ARTISTISCHEN INHALTS. HERAUSGEGEBEN VON JOHANN GEORG MEUSEL
- MUSEUM FUER KUENSTLER UND FUER KUNSTLIEBHABER

Meusel, M *see* THOMAS HARDY UND DIE BIBEL. EIN BEITRAG ZUR ENGLISCHEN LITERATUR- UND KULTURGESCHICHTE

Meuszlin, W *see* AIN FRYDSAMS VNND CHRISTLICHS GESPRECH, AINS EUANGELISCHEN. VND AINS WIDERTEUFFERS

Mevil, Andre *see* AU PAYS DU SOLEIL ET DE L'OR

MEVO HA-YERUSHALMI / Frankel, Zacharias – Breslau. 1870. BJ-32-16 1 – 9 – ne IDC [900]

MEXBOROUGH & SWINTON TIMES – England. South Yorkshire Times. -w. 20 June 1877-Dec 1974. Lacking 1898. 135 reels – 1 – uk British Libr Newspaper [072]

MEXICAN ARCHIVES / New Mexico. State Records Center and Archives – (Comes with guide) – 1821-46 – 43r – 1 – $15.00r – us NM Archives [978]

MEXICAN CARTE-DE-VISITE ALBUM / U.S. Library of Congress. Prints and Photographs Division – 182 cartes-de-visite by photographers active in Mexico in 19th century. 1 reel. P&P3112 – 1 – 23.00r – us L of C Photodup [080]

MEXICAN FOLKWAYS – v. 1-8. 1925-33 – 1 – 25.00 – us L of C Photodup [390]

MEXICAN LIFE – v. 26-30. 1950-54 – 1 – us UMI [972]

MEXICAN MISSION PAPERS / Lind, John – (Research Note Cards. 1 roll including filmed inventory. 15.00; 1) – 1913-31 – 7r – 1 – $210.00; $35.00r – us M.H.S. [920]

MEXICAN STUDIES = ESTUDIOS MEXICANOS – v1- . 1985- – 1,5,6,9 – us UMI [073]

MEXICAN-AMERICAN REPORTS : REPORT OF THE MEXICAN-AMERICAN LABOR SITUATION IN THE IMPERIAL VALLEY, CALIFORNIA / Block, Louis – 1r – 1 – $50.00 – C63008 – us Library Micro [331]

EL MEXICANO – Tijuana, MX. 1959- – 728+ r – $36,400.00 ($1,150.00y) – R60715 – us Library Micro [072]

THE MEXICANS IN MINNESOTA / Minnesota State Govt – 1953 – 1r – 1 – $50.00 – C63010 – us Library Micro [305]

MEXICO : ANUARIO ESTADISTICO 1893-1968/69 / Mexico. Direccion General de Estadistica – (1908-22, 1925-29, 1931-37 not publ. 1905, 1923-24, 1946-50 not available. Coll title: Latin American and Caribbean Official Statistical Serials, 1821-1982) – 255mf – 9 – £1,340.00 – uk Chadwyck [972]

MEXICO : GENERAL CORRESPONDENCE, 1919-58 / Great Britain. Foreign Office – 1 – $14,085.00 – us UPA [324]

Mexico *see*
- DIARIO OFICIAL
- GACETA DE MEXICO, COMPENDIO DE NOTICIAS DE NUEVA ESPANA
- PLAN SEXENAL DEL PARTIDO NACIONAL REVOLUCIONARIO
- SEGUNDO PLAN SEXENAL, 1941-1946

MEXICO, 1919-41 : REPORTS / U.S. Military Intelligence – 9 reels with printed guide – 1 – $965.00 – 0-89093-661-7 – us UPA [324]

Mexico. Banco Nacional de Comercio Exterior *see*
- MEXICO: LA POLITICA ECONOMICA PARA 1972
- THE NEW GOVERNMENT'S ECONOMIC POLICY

Mexico (City). Radiodifusora XELA *see* BOLETIN

Mexico. Comision de reformas en el sistema postal *see* PROYECTO DE CODIGO POSTAL DE LOS ESTADOS UNIDOS-MEXICANOS.

Mexico. Comision Intersecretarial para formular Planes Nacionales de Desarrollo Economico y Social *see* DESARROLLO ECONOMICO Y SOCIAL DE MEXICO, 1966-1970. BORRADOR PARA DISUSION

Mexico. Convencion Nacional Bautista *see* ACTAS

Mexico. Direccion General de Estadistica *see* MEXICO

Mexico. Direccion general de estadistica *see* CENSO GENERAL DE LA REPUBLICA MEXICANA, 1895, 1900, 1910, 1921, 1930

MEXICO, EL PAIS DE LOS ALTARES ENSANGRENTADOS. DOCUMENTOS Y NOTAS DE EBER COLE BYAM / Kelley, Francis Clement – Madrid: Razon y Fe, 1943 – 1 – sp Bibl Santa Ana [972]

MEXICO EN LA CULTURA – Mexico City, MX. 1949-1968 – 8r – $400.00 – R04223 – us Library Micro [072]

Mexico. (Federal district) *see* GACETA OFICIAL

MEXICO IN TRANSITION : FROM THE POWER OF POLITICAL ROMANISM TO CIVIL AND RELIGIOUS LIBERTY / Butler, William – New York: Hunt & Eaton; Cincinnati: Cranston & Curts, c1892 – 1mf – us A.T.L.A. [972]

MEXICO: LA POLITICA ECONOMICA PARA 1972 / Mexico. Banco Nacional de Comercio Exterior – (Mexico: Economic Policy for 1972). Mexico City. May 1972. BD-1694 1 – 9 – ne IDC [330]

Mexico. Laws, Statutes, etc. *see* LEGISLACION MEXICANA

Mexico. Mexico Revolution Party *see* SECOND SIX-YEAR PLAN, 1941-1946

Mexico. Parral *see* ARCHIVES

Mexico. Secretaria de Educacion Publica *see* ACCION EDUCATIVA DEL GOBIERNO FEDERAL DEL...

Mexico. Secretaria de Hacienda y Credito Publico *see* INFORME SOBRE EL RAMO DE HACIENDA Y CREDITO PUBLICO

Mexico Secretaria de Recursos Hidraulicos *see* INFORME DE LABORES DE LA SECRETARIA DE RECURSOS HIDRAULICOS

Mexico. Secretaria de Relaciones Exteriores *see* CORRESPONDENCIA DIPLOMATICA CAMBIADA ENTRE EL GOBIERNO DE LOS ESTADOS UNIDOS MEXICANOS Y LOS DE VARIAS POTENCIAS EXTRANJERAS

Mexico. (State) *see* GACETA DEL GOBIERNO

MEXICO THIS MONTH – v1-17 1955-71 1; 1970-71 5,6 – us UMI [073]

MEXICO TO-DAY : SOCIAL, POLITICAL AND RELIGIOUS CONDITIONS / Winton, George B – New York: Missionary Education Movement of the United States and Canada, 1913 – 1mf – us A.T.L.A. [972]

LE MEXIQUE CONQUIS / Boesnier – Paris. 1752. (Historical Studies Series) – 9 – 18.00 – fr Bibl Nationale [900]

MEYDAN – (Continued by Meydan Selonika) – Selonika, 1 sene, nos 1-62/63 (9 Seban 1327-25 Mayis 1328 [4 Rebi' I 1330-20 Cumadi II 1330 (23 Subat 1912-7 Haziran 1912)]) – 6mf – 9 – $40.00 – us MEDOC [949]

MEYDUM AND MEMPHIS (3) / Petrie, William Matthew Flinders – BSA, 1910 – 9 – $10.00 – us I.R.C. [930]

Meyen, F J F *see*
- OBSERVATIONES BOTANICAS
- OUTLINES OF THE GEOGRAPHY OF PLANTS

Meyenburg, Erwin *see* QUELLENSTUDIEN ZU JOH. H. VOSS' ODEN

Meyer, A B *see*
- THE BIRDS OF CELEBES AND THE NEIGHBOURING ISLANDS
- INDEX ZU L. REICHENBACH'S ORNITHOLOISCHEN WERKEN
- UEBER NEUE UND UNGENUEGEND BEKANNTE VOEGEL VON NEU-CHINA

Meyer, Arnold *see*
- DIE AUFERSTEHUNG CHRISTI
- JESU MUTTERSPRACHE
- JESUS OR PAUL?
- DIE MODERNE FORSCHUNG UEBER DIE GESCHICHTE DES URCHRISTENTUMS
- DAS WEIHNACHTSFEST
- WER HAT DAS CHRISTENTUM BEGRUENDET, JESUS ODER PAULUS?
- WER HAT DAS CHRISTENTUM BEGRUENDET, JESUS ODER PAULUS

Meyer, Arnold Oskar *see* STUDIEN ZUR VORGESCHICHTE DER REFORMATION

Meyer, B *see* TASCHENBUCH DER DEUTSCHEN VOEGELKUNDE

Meyer, C A *see* VERZEICHNIS DER PFLANZEN, WELCHE WAEHREND DER 1829-1830 UNTERN. REISE IM CAUCASUS GEFUNDEN WORDEN SIND

Meyer, C A von *see*
- CATALOGUS HORTI IMPERIALIS PETROPOLITANI
- ENUMERATIO PLANTARUM NOVARUM A CL. SCHRENK LECTARUM
- INDEX SEMINUM, QUAE HORTUS BOTANICUS IMPERIALIS PETROPOLITANUS PRO MUTUA COMMUTATIONE OFFERT...
- SERTUM PETROPOLITANUM SEU ICONES ET DESCRIPTIONES PLANTARUM QUAE IN HORTO BOTANICO

Meyer, Conrad Ferdinand *see*
- L'AMULETTE
- ANGELA BORGIA
- CONRAD FERDINAND MEYER UND JULIUS RODENBERG
- ENGELBERG
- GEDICHTE
- GEORG ENACH
- DIE RICHTERIN
- DIE VERSUCHUNG DES PESCARA

Meyer, Curt *see* DIE ROMANE VON FRIEDRICH VON UECHTRITZ

Meyer, E H F *see*
- COMMENTARIORUM DE PLANTIS AFRICAE AUSTRALIORIS
- FLORA DER PROVINZ PREUSSEN
- GESCHICHTE DER BOTANIK
- SYNOPSIS JUNCORUM RITE COGNITORUM. AD INAUGURANDUM EIUSDEM PLANTARUM GENERIS MONOGRAPHIAM
- SYNOPSIS LUZULARUM

Meyer, Eduard *see* DER PAPYRUSFUND VON ELEPHANTINE

Meyer, Elard Hugo *see* INDOGERMANISCHE MYTHEN

Meyer, Frederick Brotherton *see*
- THE BELLS OF IS
- CHEER FOR LIFE'S PILGRIMAGE
- CHRIST IN ISAIAH
- CHRISTIAN LIVING
- THE DIRECTORY OF THE DEVOUT LIFE
- THE FUTURE TENSES OF THE BLESSED LIFE
- THE GLORIOUS LORD
- JEREMIAH
- JOHN THE BAPTIST
- JOSHUA AND THE LAND OF PROMISE
- THE LIFE AND LIGHT OF MEN
- LIFE AND THE WAY THROUGH
- LIGHT ON LIFE'S DUTIES
- PAUL
- THE PRESENT TENSES OF THE BLESSED LIFE
- THE PSALMS
- SAMUEL THE PROPHET
- THE SHEPHERD PSALM
- STEPS INTO THE BLESSED LIFE
- THE WAY INTO THE HOLIEST
- THE WIDENESS OF GOD'S MERCY

Meyer, G F W *see* PRIMITIAE ESSEQUEBOENSIS

Meyer, George Wilbur *see* WORDSWORTH'S FORMATIVE YEARS

Meyer, Gernot *see* FUNKTIONELLE MORPHOLOGIE UND CYTOCHEMIE OSTEOBLASTAERER RATTENOS-TEOSARKOMZELLEN UNTER EINWIRKUNG VON CALCIUM; PARATHORMON ODER ALUMINIUM

Meyer, H A W *see*
- KRITISCH EXEGETISCHES HANDBUCH UEBER DIE APOSTELGESCHICHTE

Meyer, H L *see* ILLUSTRATIONS OF BRITISH BIRDS

Meyer, Heinrich *see* PASTOR IN BUDAPEST

Meyer, Heinrich August Wilhelm *see* KRITISCH EXEGETISCHES HANDBUCH UEBER DIE EVANGELIEN DES MARKUS UND LUKAS

Meyer, Herbert *see* EDUARD MOERIKE

Meyer, Jane C *see* PERCEPTIONS OF AGENCIES THAT MARKET COLLEGIATE EMBLEMATIC MERCHANDISE TOWARD SELECTED FACTORS RELATED TO ROYALTY INCOME

Meyer, Johannes *see* EINFUEHRUNG IN DIE DEUTSCHE LITERATUR

Meyer, John R *see* VALUES EDUCATION

Meyer, Josef *see* DAS GROSSE CONVERSATIONSLEXIKON FUER GEBILDETE STAENDE (AEL, ABT.1;5)

Meyer, Juergen *see* DER CHORAL BEI JOHANN SEBASTIAN BACH

Meyer, K W *see* WELCHE REFORMEN ERSCHEINEN BEI DER JETZIGEN STELLUNG UND AUFGABE DES EVANGELISCHEN RELIGIONSUNTERRICHTS AUF GYMNASIEN NOTWENDIG?

Meyer, KH *see* ALTKIRCHENSLAVISCH-GRIECHISCHES WOERTERBUCH DES CODEX SUPRASLIENSIS

Meyer, Konrad *see* DER PROLOG DES JOHANNESEVANGELIUMS

Meyer, Lucy R *see* DEACONESSES: BIBLICAL, EARLY CHURCH, EUROPEAN, AMERICAN: WITH THE STORY OF THE CHICAGO TRAINING SCHOOL FOR CITY, HOME, AND FOREIGN MISSIONS AND THE CHICAGO DEACONESS HOME

Meyer, Maria *see* CARLYLES EINFLUSS AUF KINGSLEY IN SOZIALPOLITISCHER UND RELIGIOES-ETHISCHER HINSICHT

Meyer, Ralf I *see* EIN BEITRAG ZUR DREIDIMENSIONALEN FINITE-ELEMENTE-BERECHNUNG VON GESCHICHTETEN VERBUNDWERKSTOFFEN

Meyer, Richard M *see*
- GOETHE UND SEINE FREUNDE IM BRIEFWECHSEL
- JONATHAN SWIFT UND G. CH. LICHTENBERG

Meyer, Timothy A *see* VERGLEICHENDE UNTERSUCHUNGEN DER EXTRAZELLULAEREN KOHLEHYDRAT-KOMPONENTEN VON NOSTOC PUNCITFORME UND NOSTOC MUSCORUM

Meyer, Wilhelm *see* VITA ADAE ET EVAE

Meyerbeer, Giacomo *see* OPERAS

Meyer-Benfey, Heinrich *see* DAS DRAMA HEINRICH VON KLEISTS

Meyer-Berlin, Richard *see* KLEINE HIEROGLYPHEN-GRAMMATIK (AUSZUG) NACH DEM WERK H. PROF. HEINRICH BRUGSCH, BERLING, HANDSCHRIFT

Meyer-Foerster, Wilhelm *see*
- ALT-HEIDELBERG
- KARL HEINRICH

Meyer-Giesow, Helmut *see* STIMMVERBOTE IN DEN AKTIENRECHTEN DER EWG-STAATEN

MEYERS KONVERSATIONS-LEXIKON : EINE ENCYKLOPAEDIE DES ALLGEMEINEN WISSENS – (Einzelbezug der Baende ist moeglich (je DM 98.00)) – Leipzig, Wien, 4th ed 1890 – 17v ca 220mf – 9 – DM980.00 – 3-89349-705-6 – gw Hänsel [030]

MEYER'S MINUTES : SECRETARY TO THE BAR – New York. v1-4. 1930-34 (all publ) – 6mf – 9 – $9.00 – LLMC 84-604 – us L.L.M.C. [073]

MEYERSDALE COMMERCIAL – Meyersdale, PA. -w 1888-1912 – 13 – $25.00r – us I.M.R. [071]

MEYERSDALE REPUBLICAN – Meyersdale, PA., 1900-1978 – 13 – $25.00r – us I.M.R. [071]

Meyhoefer, Max *see*
- DER KREIS LOETZEN
- DIE LANDGEMEINDEN DES KREISES LOETZEN
- DIE LANDGEMEINDEN DES KREISES ORTELSBURG

Meynard, Barbier de *see* DICTIONNAIRE TURC-FRANCAIS

Meynaud, J *see*
- LES GROUPES DE PRESSION EN FRANCE
- INTRODUCTION A LA SCIENCE POLITIQUE
- NOUVELLES ETUDES SUR LES GROUPES DE PRESSION EN FRANCE

Meynaud, Jet al *see* LA DECISION POLITIQUE EN BELGIQUE

Meynell, Wilfrid *see* CARDINAL NEWMAN

Meynier, B *see*
- DE L'EDIT DE NANTES EXECUTE SELON...
- LA SAINCTE LIBERTE DES ENFANS DE DIEU

Meyr, Melchior *see*
- ENDE GUT, ALLES GUT
- GEORG
- GOTT UND SEIN REICH
- LUDWIG UND ANNEMARIE

Meyrelles de Souto, A *see* ARCEBISPO DE CANGRANOR

Meyrick, E *see* EXOTIC MICROLEPIDOPTERA

Meyrick, F *see* OLD ANGLICANISM AND MODERN RITUALISM

Meyrick, Frederick *see* MEMORIES OF LIFE AT OXFORD AND EXPERIENCES IN ITALY, GREECE, TURKEY, GERMANY, SPAIN, AND ELSEWHERE

Meyrick, Thomas *see* LIVES OF THE EARLY POPES

Meyrink, Gustav *see* DES DEUTSCHEN SPIESSERS WUNDERHORN

Meyster, E *see* DE KRUYS-LEER TER ZALIGHEYDT

MEYWAR, RAJPUTANA / India. Preservation of National Monuments; ed by Cole, H H – Calcutta, 1884. BI-685 2 – 8 – ne IDC [720]

Mez, Adam *see* L'ISLAM AU IVE-XE SIECLE
MEZELI – (Missing issues 2-3, some pages obscured by censor) – Baku. No. 1-41, (29 Sefer 1333-20 Zilhicce 1333 [3 Jan 1915-17 Oct 1914]) – 7mf – 9 – $50.00 – us MEDOC [949]
Mez'er, A V *see*
- RUSSKAIA SLOVESNOST'
- SLOVARNYI UKAZATEL' PO KNIGOVEDENIIU
- SOLVARNYI UKAZATEL'PO KNIGOVEDENIIU

Mezes, Sidney Edward *see* ETHICS: DESCRIPTIVE AND EXPLANATORY
MEZHDU DVUKH REVOLIUTSII / Belyi, A – 1934. BR-571 2 – 8 – ne IDC [460]
MEZHDU DVUMI A BOLSHEVIZMAMI / Argunov, Andrei Aleksandrovich – Paris: Impr. Union, 1919 – 1 – CSUX88-B9669 – us Hoover Inst Photo [335]
MEZHDU DVUMIA REVOLIUTSIIAMI : SB. STATEI / Kamenev, L B – 2nd ed. M., 1923. ii/632p – 7mf – 9 – ne IDC [320]
MEZHDUNARODNAIA KOOPERATSIIA *see* BIULLETEN' KOOPERATIVNOI SEKTSII KOMINTERNA
MEZHDUNARODNAIA MUZYKA : BULLETIN OF THE MEZHDUNARODNOE MUZYKAL'NOE BIURO – Moscow, 1933 – 3mf – 9 – us Ross [780]
MEZHDUNARODNAIA ZHIZN – U.S.S.R.1959- – 1 – us UMI [073]
MEZHDUNARODNAIA ZHIZN' – Moscow. Aug., Dec. 1954, Jan. 1955-Dec. 1970. Missing no. 2, 1965 – 1 – 35.00r – us Hoover Inst Photo [947]
MEZHDUNARODNOE POLOZHENIE I ZADACHI KOMINTERNA : OTCHETNYI DOKLAD ISPOLKOMA KOMINTERNA I ZAKLI UCHITELNOE SLOVO NA 6TH KONGRESSE KOMINTERNA / Bukharin, Nikolai Ivanovich – Moskva: Gos. izd.-vo, 1928 – 1 – CSUX89-B3036 – us Hoover Inst Photo [947]
MEZHDUNARODNOE PRAVO PO LEKTSIIAM / Kamarovskii, L A & Ul'ianitskii, V A – Moscow, 1908. 276p. Last ed. of author's lectures on international law. Suppl. by Ul'ianitskii – 9 – ne IDC [340]
MEZHDUNARODNOE PRAVO V 19 VEKE / Kamarovskii, L A – Moscow, 1901. 51p. Essay on the historical development and major trends of international law during the 19th century. BR-9149/1 – 9 – ne IDC [340]
MEZHDUNARODNOE RABOCHEE DVIZHENIE – Moscow. May-Aug. 1920, nos. 1-6; Jan.-Oct. 1921, nos. 1-7 – 1 – 35.00r – us Hoover Inst Photo [947]
O MEZHDUNARODNOM SUDE / Kamarovskii, L A – Moscow, 1881. 542p. Tsarist treatise on peaceful methods of dispute settlement with proposals for creating international tribunals. BR-9680/1 – 9 – ne IDC [340]
MEZHDUNARODNO-PRAVOVOI REZHIM TERRITORIAL'NYKH VOD / Ustal', A T – Tartu. 1958 – 2mf – 9 – ne IDC [340]
MEZHDUNARODNYE OTNOSHENIIA V EPOKHU IMPERIALIZMA / U.S.S.R. Komissiia po izdaniia dokumentov epokhi imperializma – 12v in 17. 1931-38 – 1 – $176.00 – us L of C Photodup [947]
MEZHDUNARODNYI KOOPERATIVNYI SOIUZ / Pazhitnov, K A – M., 1917 – 1mf – 9 – COR-88/1 – ne IDC [334]
MEZHEVYE AKTY I UKRIEPLENIE VOTCHINNYKH PRAV NA NEDVIZHIMYIA IMIENIIA. V DVUKH CHASTIAKH. I. S. IGNATOVSKAGO / Ignatovskii, I S – St. Petersburg, Tip. Pravitelstvuiushchago senata, 1896. 333 p. LL-4001 – 1 – us L of C Photodup [340]
Mezhov, V I *see* BIBLIOGRAFICHESKII UKAZATEL' KNIG I STATEI, OTNOSIASHCHIKHSIA DO OBSHCHESTV, OSNOVANNYKH NA NACHALAKH VZAIMNOSTI, ARTELEI, POLOZHENIIA RABOCHEGO SOSLOVIIA I MELKOI KUSTARNOI PROMYSHLENNOSTI V ROSSII
Mezhov, VI *see*
- BIBLIOGRAFICHESKII UKAZATEL' KNIG I STATEI I ZHIZNI I SOCHINENIIAKH EGO. 1816-1852
- BIBLIOGRAFICHESKII UKAZATEL' KNIG I ZAKLIUCHAIUSHCHIKHSIA V NIKH STATEI...
- BIBLIOGRAFICHESKII UKAZATEL' KNIG I ZAKLIUCHAIUSHCHIKHSIA V NIKH STATEI OBNIMAIUSHCHII DEIATEL'NOST' STATISTICHESKII KOMITETOV S SAMAGO NACHALA IKH UCHREZHDENII VPLOT' DO 1873 G
- BIBLIOGRAFICHESKII UKAZATEL' KNIG I ZAKLIUCHAIUSHCHIKHSIA V NIKH STATEI OBNIMAIUSHCHII DEIATEL'NOST' STATISTICHESKIKH KOMITETOV S SAMOGO NACHALA IKH UCHREZHDENIIA VPLOT' DO 1873 G
- BIBLIOGRAFIIA AZII, VSIA AZIIA, ISKLIUCHAIA SIBIRI UKAZATEL' KNIG I STATEI OB AZII NA RUSSKOM IAZYKE I ODNEKH TOL'KO KNIG NA INOSTRANNYKH IAZYKAKH, KASAIUSHCHIKHSIA OTNOSHENII ROSSII K AZIATSKIM GOSUDARSTVAM
- BIBLIOGRAFIIA ZA 1856 I 1857 GG. ILI UKAZATEL' KNIG, SOSTAVLENNYI NA OSNOVANII ISTOCHNIKOV, DOSTAVLENNYKH IZ IMP. PUBLICHNOI BIBLIOTEKI V.I.M
- BLAGOTVORITEL'NOST V ROSSII
- ISTORIIA RUSSKOI I VSEOBSCHEI
- ISTORIIA RUSSKOI I VSEOBSHCHEI SLOVESNOSTI
- IUBILEI PETRA VELIKAGO
- LITERATURA RUSSKOI GEOGRAFII, STATISTIKI I ETNOGRAFII ZA 1864-1880 G
- LITERATURA RUSSKOI ISTORII ZA 1859-1864 G
- MATERIALY DLIA ISTORII NARODNAGO PROSVESHCHENIIA V ROSSII
- OTKRYTIE PAMIATNIKA A. S. PUSHKINA V MOSKVE V 1880 GODU
- POVREMENNYIA IZDANIIA V ROSSII V 1860-M I 1861-GODAKH
- PROVREMENNYIA IZDANIIA V ROSSII V 1858-M GODU
- PUSCHKINIANA
- RUSSKAIA ISTORICHESKAIA BIBLIOGRAFIIA
- SIBIRSKAIA BIBLIOGRAFIIA
- SISTEMATICHESKII KATALOG RUSSKIKH KNIG ZA 1875 I 1876 GODY PRODAIUSHCHIKHSIA V KNIZHNOM MAGAZINE IA. A. ISAKOVA
- SISTEMATICHESKII KATALOG RUSSKIKH KNIG ZA 1877 I 1878 GODY
- SISTEMATICHESKII KATALOG RUSSKIM KNIGAM, PRODAIUSHCHIMSIA V KNIZHNOM MAGAZINE A. F. BAZUNOVA
- TRUDY TSENTRAL'NOGO I GUBERNSKIKH STATISTICHESKIKH KOMITETOV
- VKLAD PRAVITEL' STVA, UCHENYKH I DRUGIKH OBSHCHESTV NA POL'ZU RUSSKAGO PROSVESHCHENIIA

Mezier, A V *see* UKAZATEL' ISTORICHESKIKH ROMANOV ORIGINAL'NYKH PEREVODNYKH, RASZPOLOZHENNYKH PO STRANAM I EPOKHAM
Mezieres, Henri *see* L'ABEILLE CANADIENNE
MEZINARODNI POLITIKA – (Backfile through 1998 $85r) – 1999- – 1r per y – 1 – $80.00 standing order – us Ross [072]
MEZINARODNI POLITIKA – (Backfile through 1998 $85r) – Czech Republic, 1999- – 1r per y standing order – 1 – us Ross [072]
MEZINARODNI VZTAHY – Czech Republic, 1990-94 – 2r – 1 – $85.00r – us Ross [072]
MEZINARODNI VZTAHY – Czech Republic, 1990-94 – 2r – 1 – us Ross [072]
MEZRITSHER TRIBUNE = MIEDZYRZEC TRIBUNE – Miedzyrzec, PL. v1 no1 1928-v2 no4(no129) 1931 – 1r – 1 – $35.00 – cn Can Microfilming [072]
MEZRITSHER VOKHNBLAT – (Yiddish weekly) – Miedzyrzec, PL. v1 no1(no1) 20 Jul 1926-v4 no1 9 Jun 1930 – 1r – 1 – $50.00 – cn Can Microfilming [072]
MEZUDAH – v. 1-7. London. 1943-54. BJ-91-62 1 – 9 – ne IDC [270]
IL MEZZOGIORNO – Organo dei lavatori italiani in Francia. Politico, sindicale, cooperativo. no. 1-76. Toulouse. 10 oct 1925-26 mars 1927. mq no. 4-5, 11, 13, 16, 25, 27, 29, 39, 41, 75 – 1 – fr A.C.R.P.P. [073]
M.G. Tousley and Co *see*
- CENTENNIAL DIRECTORY OF FOND DU LAC COUNTY
- ILLINOIS LEGISLATIVE MANUAL FOR 30TH GENERAL ASSEMBLY-1877 AND 1878

MGA KATUIRAN NG FILIPINO: MAICLING KASAYSAYANG / Lopez, Honorio – Maynila: Santos at Bernal, 1905.26p – 1 – us U.W. Library [490]
MGA PAMARAAN SA PAGTUTURO NG WIKANG PILIPINO PARA SA KOLEHIYO / Tablan, Andrea Amor – Manila: Philippine Book Co., n.d. Title also in English: Methods of Teaching – 1 – us U.W. Library [370]
MGR. JOSEPH OCTAVE PLESIS: EVEQUE DE QUEBEC / Ferland, Jean Baptiste Antoine – l'abbe Ferland. Quebec: s.n., 1878 (Quebec: L. Brousseau). 03091. (Pre-1900 Canadiana) – 9 – cn C.I.H.M. [971]
MGR SEGHERS, L'APOTRE DE L'ALASKA / Baets, Maurice de – Paris: H. Oudin,1896. 00899. (Pre-1900 Canadiana) – 9 – cn C.I.H.M. [920]
MH (MECHANICAL HANDLING) – (See also: M H (Mechanical Handling) International) – v. 1-N.S. 60, no. 5. 1891-1973 – 1 – us UMI [621]
MH (MECHANICAL HANDLING) INTERNATIONAL – (See also: Materials Handling News; See now: Mechanical Handling International) – n.s. 60, no. 6-n.s. 61, no. 1. 1973-74 – 1 – us UMI [621]
MI CRUCERO A SPITZBURG. CACERES, 1935 / Sanchez Torres, Eloy – Madrid: Razon y Fe, 1936 – 1 – sp Bibl Santa Ana [946]
MI DESPEDIDA DE LA CURIA ROMANA / Villanueva, Joaquin Lorenzo – 1823 – 9 – 1.50f – sp Bibl Santa Ana [240]
MI ESHCHANSKOE DVIZHENIE 1906-1917 G.G. / Druzhinin, Nikolai Petrovich – I Aroslavl: Tip. t-va "Golos", 1917 – 1 – CSUX89-B776 – us Hoover Inst Photo [947]
MI HERMANA EVITA / Duarte, Erminda – Buenos Aires: Centro de Estudios Eva Peron, 3rd ed 1972 – 1 – CSUXAJA7495-B – us Hoover Inst Photo [920]
MI HISTORIA MILITAR Y POLITICA, 1810-1874; MEMORIAS INEDITAS / Santa Anna, Antonio Lopez de – Mexico: C. Pouret, 1905.viii,279p – 1 – us U.W. Library [972]
MI MAGAZINE (MILITARY INTELLIGENCE) – v.1-2. Apr 1974-Fall 1976. Continued as Military Intelligence – 1 – us UMI [073]
MI PATRIA Y MI DAMA / Cordero, Juan Luis – Barcelona: Mucci, 1910 – 1 – sp Bibl Santa Ana [946]
MI SEMINARIO / Plasencia. Seminario – Caceres: Imp. La Victoria, 1970 – 1 – sp Bibl Santa Ana [946]
MI TIA CAROLINA CORONADO / Gomez de la Serna, Ramon – Buenos Aires: Emece, 1942 – 1 – sp Bibl Santa Ana [946]
MI TORRE DE BABEL / Cordero, Juan Luis – Caceres: El Noticiero, 1908 – 1 – sp Bibl Santa Ana [810]
MI VOZ PARA TU RECUERDO / Rivero, Marciano – Caceres: Tip. Rodriguez, 1972 – 1 – sp Bibl Santa Ana [946]
Miajadas. Ayuntamiento *see*
- FERIAS Y FIESTAS DE MIAJADAS 1972
- GUIA OFICIAL DE LAS FERIAS Y FIESTAS DE MIAJADAS, AGOSTO 1971
- ORDENANZAS MUNICIPALES

Mialaret, G *see* INTRODUCTION TO THE EDUCATIONAL SCIENCES
Mialaret, Gaston *see* CHILD'S RIGHT TO EDUCATION
Miall, Edward *see*
- BASES OF BELIEF: AN EXAMINATION OF CHRISTIANITY AS A DIVINE REVELATION
- CITATIONS OF THE STATUTES OF ALBERTA AND SASKATCHEWAN (1886-1912)

MIAMI GAZETTE – Waynesville. Ohio. -w. 1865-83, 1898-1955 – 1 – us UMI [071]
MIAMI HELMET – Piqua. Ohio. 1874-1905 – 1 – us UMI [071]
MIAMI JEWISH TRIBUNE – (v2 No46; Oct 28 1988-v4 No51 (Nov 30-Dec 6 1990)) – Miami, FL – 2r – 1 – us A.J.P.C. [071]
MIAMI JEWISH TRIBUNE *see*
- BROWARD JEWISH WORLD
- PALM BEACH JEWISH WORLD

MIAMI LEADER – Piqua. Ohio. 1890-1893 – 1 – us UMI [071]
MIAMI OF THE LAKE – Perrysburg, Ohio. 1844-46 – 1r – 1 – $32.50r – us Archival [071]
Miami. Presbytery (Assoc. Pres. Ch. of N.A.) *see* MINUTES
Miami. Presbytery (Pres. Ch. in the U.S.A.) *see* MINUTES, 1810-1870
MIAMI SHORES BAPTIST CHURCH. MIAMI, FLORIDA : CHURCH RECORDS – 1947-59 – 1 – 6.84 – us Baptist [240]
MIAMI TIMES – Miami. Fl. 1948- – 1 – us P.K. Yonge [071]
Miami Trading Post *see* DAY BOOK
MIAMI UNION – Troy. Ohio. 1864-83; 1887-1952 – 1 – us UMI [071]
MIAMI VALLEY FARMER – Fairborn. Ohio. -w. 1947-56 – 1 – us UMI [071]
MIAMI VALLEY, OHIO: LOCAL HISTORY AND GENEALOGY, 1921-1939 – 2rolls 35mm set – 1 – us Ohio Hist [920]
MIAMI VISITOR – Waynesville. Ohio. -w. 1850-55 – 1 – us UMI [071]
Miansarov, M *see* BIBLIOGRAPHIA CAUCASICA ET TRANSCAUCASICA
MIASNOE DELO V POTREBITEL'NYKH OBSHCHESTVAKH / Makhnovets, V – M., 1923 – 2mf – 9 – COR-333/1 – ne IDC [334]
MIAU – Caceres, 1912 – 5 – sp Bibl Santa Ana [073]
MIBAYIT UMIHUZ / Dolitzki, M M – Vilna, 1891 – 3mf – 9 – ne IDC [305]
MICAH / Margolis, Max Leopold – (Includes indexes) – Philadelphia: Jewish Publ Society, 1908 – 1mf – 9 – 0-8370-6217-9 – 1986-0217 – us A.T.L.A. [220]
MICANOPY FIRST BAPTIST CHURCH. MICANOPY, FLORIDA : CHURCH RECORDS – 1854-Oct 1934; scattered Oct 1944-Jun 1950. 844p – 1 – 37.98 – us Baptist [240]
MICHA / Lindblom, Johannes – 1929 – 1 – us A.T.L.A. [220]
Michael, A D *see* BRITISH ORIBATIDAE
MICHAEL BAIUS UND DIE GRUNDLEGUNG DES JANSENISMUS : EINE DOGMENGESCHICHTLICHE MONOGRAPHIE / Linsenmann, Franz Xaver – (Includes bibliographical references and index) – Tuebingen: H Laupp, 1867 – 1mf – 9 – 0-8370-8761-9 – 1986-2761 – us A.T.L.A. [240]
Michael Baker Jr., Inc *see* YARMOUK-JORDAN VALLEY PROJECT, THE HASHEMITE KINGDOM OF JORDAN MASTER PLAN
MICHAEL BAKUNIN, EINE BIOGRAPHIE, 1814-1876 / Nettlau, Max – London, 1896-1900 – 1r – 1 – $70.00 – us UPA [320]
Michael, Emil *see* SALIMBENE UND SEINE CHRONIK
Michael, J F *see* AN EVALUATION OF STUDENT ATTITUDES, INTENTIONS, AND PERSONAL HEALTH BEHAVIORS AS A RESULT OF HAVING COMPLETED HEALTH EDUCATION 214 AT THE OHIO STATE UNIVERSITY DURING THE SPRING QUARTER OF 1990
Michael, James *see* PRIVACY AND HUMAN RIGHTS
Michael, Oscar S *see* THE SUNDAY-SCHOOL IN THE DEVELOPMENT OF THE AMERICAN CHURCH
Michael, P *see* A SANCTO AUGSTINO
MICHAEL SERVET : EEN BRANDOFFER DER GEREFORMEERDE INQUISITIE / Linde, Antonius van der – Groningen: P. Noordhoff, 1891 – 1mf – us A.T.L.A. [240]
Michael, William Henry *see* THE LAW RELATING TO GAS AND WATER.
Michaelis, C B *see* DE HEBRAEA ET ADFINIBVS ORIENTIS LINGVIS A GRAECA DERIVANDIS
MICHAELIS DE CESENA, FRATRIS, LIBELLI / Trechsel, Jo – 1495 – Dfl9.00 – ne Slangenburg [240]
Michaelis, Johann David *see*
- COMMENTARIES ON THE LAWS OF MOSES
- INTRODUCTION TO THE NEW TESTAMENT

MICHAEL'S CRAG / Allen, Grant – With over 350 illus. by Francis Carruthers Gould and Alec Carruthers Gould. Chicago: Rand, McNally, c1893. 05052. (Pre-1900 Canadiana) – 9 – cn C.I.H.M. [830]
Michalevitch, B *see* ZIKHROYNES FUN A IDISHN SOTSIALIST
Michaud *see* REPONSE D'UN SAINT-SIMONIEN AU "SPECTATEUR"
Michaud, Eugene *see*
- LES FAUX LIBERAUX DE L'EGLISE ROMAINE
- GUIGNOL ET LA REVOLUTION DANS L'EGLISE ROMAINE
- PLUTOT LA MORT QUE LE DESHONNEUR
- PROGRAMME DE REFORME DE L'EGLISE D'OCCIDENT

Michaud, Gustave *see* LE PEUPLE AVAIT-IL DES ECOLES AVANT 1789?
Michaud, L G *see* BIOGRAPHIE UNIVERSELLE
Michaud, M *see* BIBLIOTHEQUE DES CROISADES
Michaud, Peter *see* PERCEIVED BENEFITS OF STRENGTH TRAINING FOR YOUTH PARTICIPANTS AS DETERMINED BY ORTHOPEDIC SURGEONS
Michaud, Yves *see* LE HAUT-PARLEUR
Michaux, A *see*
- FLORA BOREALI AMERICAN
- FLORA BOREALI-AMERICANA
- HERBARIUM
- HISTOIRE DES CHEA4NES DE L'AMEA1RIQUE

Michaux, Francois Andre *see*
- HISTOIRE DES ARBRES FORESTIERS DE L'AMEA1RIQUE SEPTENTRIONALE
- THE NORTH AMERICAN SYLVA, OR A DESCRIPTION OF THE FOREST TREES OF THE UNITED STATES
- PERSIAN MANUSCRIPT

Michel, A *see* DIE SENTENZEN DES KARDINALS HUMBERT (MGH SCHRIFTEN..: 7.BD)
MICHEL BUCK ALS MUNDARTDICHTER / Schramm, Heinz-Eugen – (Includes bibliographical references) – Stuttgart: Verlag des Schwaebischen Albvereins, 1956 – 1 – us U.W. Library [430]
MICHEL DE L'HOPITAL ET LA LIBERTE DE CONSCIENCE AU XVIE SIECLE / Amphoux, Henri – Paris: Fischbacher, 1900 – 2mf – us A.T.L.A. [240]
Michel, Ernst *see*
- DIE TRAGIK DES ORPHISCHEN DICHTERS
- DER WEG ZUM MYTHOS
- WELTANSCHAUUNG UND NATURDEUTUNG

Michel, Henry *see* LA LOI FALLOUX: 4 JANVIER 1849-15 MARS 1850
Michel, J F *see* DICTIONNAIRE DES EXPRESSIONS VICIEUSES
Michel, Jean *see* WOMEN IN ENGINEERING EDUCATION
Michel, Louise *see*
- A TRAVERS LA VIE
- LA FILLE DU PEUPLE

Michel, P A *see* ANALYSE STYLISTIQUE DE QUELQUES OEUVRES DU PAYS DOGON SUIVIE D'UN ESSAI D'ANALYSE SEMANTIQUE
MICHEL UND DIE SCHWESTERN : ROMAN / Kunow, Hanns von – Berlin: Verlag "Die Wehrmacht", 1942 – 1r – 1 – us U.W. Library [830]
Michel, Wilhelm *see* FRIEDRICH HOELDERLIN
Michelangelo *see* THE SONNETS OF MICHAEL ANGELO BUONARROTI AND TOMMASO CAMPANELLA.
Michele Writ Maggiordomo, G *see* RAGGUAGLIO DELLA SOLENNE COMPARSA FATTA IN ROMA GLI OTTO DI GENNAIO MDCLXXXVII, DALL ILLUSTRISSIMO, ET ECCELLEMTISSIMO SIGNOR CONTE DI CASTELMAINE AMBASCIADORE...
Michelet, Jules *see*
- FRANCE BEFORE EUROPE
- LE PRETRE, LA FEMME ET LA FAMILLE: LES JESUITES

Michelet, Ludwig *see* DER GEDANKE, 1. 1861-9. 1884
Michelet, S *see*
- AMOS OVERSAT OG FORTOLKET
- AMOS: OVERSAT OG FORTOLKET

Micheli, P A *see*
- NOVA GENERA PLANTARUM
- NOVA PLANTARUM GENERA JUXTA TOURNEFORTII METHODUM DISPOSITA

MICHELIA : COMMENTARIUM MYCOLOGIAE ITALICAE / ed by Saccardo, P A – Patavii. 2v. [1877] 1879-1882 – 17mf – 9 – ne IDC [580]
Michelin, J L H *see* ICONOGRAPHIE ZOOPHYTOLOGIQUE
Michell, George *see* ISLAMIC HERITAGE OF BENGAL
Michell, W J *see* BRIEF BIOGRAPHICAL SKETCHES OF BIBLE CHRISTIAN MINISTERS AND LAYMEN
Michels, Gerd *see* FESTSCHRIFT FUER FRIEDRICH KEINECKER ZUM 60. GEBURTSTAG
MICHETO, EL PIRATA / Munarriz, Urtasun – Madrid, 1932; Madrid: Razon y Fe, 1933 – 1 – sp Bibl Santa Ana [830]
Micheva, P et al *see* ADULT EDUCATION IN THE PEOPLE'S REPUBLIC OF BULGARIA
Michie, Thomas J *see* BANKING CASES ANNOTATED
Michiels, A *see* L'ORIGINE DE L'EPISCOPAT
MICHIGAN : COMPILED LAWS ANNOTATED – St Paul: West Pub Co, 1967-Mar 1996 update – 9 – $2,053.00 set – us Hein [340]
MICHIGAN : SESSION LAWS OF AMERICAN STATES AND TERRITORIES – 1805-1994 – 9 – $1,960.00 set – us Hein [340]
Michigan *see*
- MICHIGAN CHANCERY REPORTS
- REPORTS AND OPINIONS (A-G)
- REPORTS, POST-NRS
- REPORTS, PRE-NRS
- SESSION LAWS, 1821-99
- STATE LABOR REPORTS

MICHIGAN APPELLATE REPORTS / Michigan. Intermediate Court of Appeals – (Bo Pre-NRS vols. Updates planned) – v1-205. 1965-94 – 1962mf – 9 – $2,943.00 – LLMC 79-436 – us L.L.M.C. [340]
MICHIGAN APPELLATE REPORTS *see*
- BROWN'S NISI PRIUS REPORTS
- HOWELL'S NISI PRIUS CASES
- MCGRATH'S MANDAMUS CASES
- MICHIGAN ATTORNEY GENERAL OPINIONS
- MICHIGAN CHANCERY REPORTS
- SESSION LAWS

Michigan. Attorney General *see* MICHIGAN ATTORNEY GENERAL OPINIONS
MICHIGAN ATTORNEY GENERAL OPINIONS / Michigan. Attorney General – (Includes 6 index vols covering 1913-79. 1991/92 issue part of a biennial report of the Attorney General's Office. Updates planned) – 1838-1992 – 439mf – 9 – $658.00 – LLMC 77-001 – us L.L.M.C. [340]
MICHIGAN ATTORNEY GENERAL REPORTS AND OPINIONS – (6 1890-1978 $385.00. 9 1977-1994 $197.50) – 1890-1994 – 6,9 – $582.50set – us Hein [340]
MICHIGAN BAPTIST – Lansing/East Lansing, MI. 1914-Oct 1970. Single reels available – 1 – 189.90 – us A.B.H.S. [073]
MICHIGAN BAPTIST ADVOCATE – Southfield, MI. 1986-1991. 922p – 1 – $45.36 – us Baptist [071]
Michigan Baptist Convention. Executive Board *see* MINUTES OF STATE CONVENTION, 1965-78
MICHIGAN BAR ASSOCIATION REPORTS AND PROCEEDINGS – 1st to 44th annual. 1891-1935 (all publ) – 102mf – 9 – $153.00 – LLMC 84-605 – us L.L.M.C. [073]
MICHIGAN BAR JOURNAL – 1979-. Continues: Michigan State Bar Journal – 1,5,6,9 – us UMI [073]
MICHIGAN BAR JOURNAL – (Title varies: v1-57 1921-78 as Michigan State Bar Journal) – v1-73. 1921-94 – 9 – $1,335.00 set – us Hein [340]
MICHIGAN BUSINESS LAW JOURNAL – (Title varies: v1-10 1976-87 as Corporation, Finance and Business Law Section Journal) – v1-16. 1976-95 – 9 – $176.00 set – us Hein [340]
MICHIGAN BUSINESS REVIEW – (See also: University of Michigan Business Review) – v1-26. 1949-74 – 1,1971-74.; ; 5,6 – us UMI [380]
MICHIGAN CHANCERY REPORTS / Michigan – v1-2. 1836-45 (all publ) – 13mf – 9 – $19.50 – LLMC 81-302 – us L.L.M.C. [340]
MICHIGAN CHRISTIAN HERALD – 1843-1910 (complete) – 16r – 1 – ATLA R0132 – us A.T.L.A. [073]
MICHIGAN CHRONICLE – Detroit. Mich. -w. 1943- – 1 – us UMI [071]
Michigan. Commissioner of Railroads *see* REPORTS
MICHIGAN: COUNTY AND REGIONAL HISTORIES AND ATLASES – 1 – us Primary [978]
THE MICHIGAN DAILY / Michigan. University – 1951- – 1 – us UMI [370]
Michigan. Dept. of Labor *see* REPORTS
Michigan. Dept. of Revenue *see* REPORTS
MICHIGAN EXPOSITOR – Adrian. Mich. -w. 1850-58 – 1 – us UMI [071]
MICHIGAN FARMER – v1-8. Feb 1843-Dec 1850 – 1 – us UMI [630]
MICHIGAN FARMER AND WESTERN HORTICULTURIST *see* MICHIGAN FARMER
Michigan. Financial Institutions Bureau *see* REPORTS
Michigan. Financial Institutions Bureau. Bank and Trust Division *see* REPORTS
MICHIGAN FLORA / Beal, William James & Wheeler, C F – 7509 2. 1892 – 8 – ne IDC [580]
MICHIGAN FREE PRESS – 1974-78 1; 1976-78 5,6,9 – us UMI [071]
The Michigan Historical Publishing Association *see* THE PAST AND PRESENT OF EATON COUNTY
Michigan Historical Publishing Co *see* PAST AND PRESENT OF SHIAWASSEE COUNTY
MICHIGAN HISTORY – v1- 1917- 1; v54- 5,6; v59- 9 – us UMI [978]
MICHIGAN HISTORY MAGAZINE – v. 1-43. 1917-1960 – 1,5,6 – us Princeton Micro [073]
MICHIGAN HOSPITALS – 1965- 1; 1974- 5,6; 1975- 4 x 6 in. 9 – us UMI [610]
Michigan. Insurance Bureau *see* STATISTICAL REPORT
Michigan. Intermediate Court of Appeals *see* MICHIGAN APPELLATE REPORTS
MICHIGAN JEWISH HISTORY – (v.20-. 1980- 5,6,9) – v.1-. 1960- – 1 – us UMI [270]
MICHIGAN JOURNAL OF GENDER AND THE LAW – v1-2. 1993-1994 – 9 – $19.00 set – us Hein [340]
MICHIGAN JOURNAL OF INTERNATIONAL LAW – (None published 1986. Title varies: v1-9 1979-88 as Michigan Yearbook of International Legal Studies) – v1-16. 1979-95 – 9 – $236.00 set – us Hein [340]
MICHIGAN LAW JOURNAL – Detroit. v1-7. 1892-98 – 1 – $40.00 – us Hein [073]
MICHIGAN LAW JOURNAL – (Lacking: 1898 nos 1-3) – v1-7. 1892-98 (all publ) – 13mf – 9 – $58.00 – LLMC 82-943 – us L.L.M.C. [073]
MICHIGAN LAW REVIEW – (Add vols as copyright expires) – v1-18. 1902-20 – 145mf – 9 – $217.00 – LLMC 84-606 – us L.L.M.C. [073]
MICHIGAN LAW REVIEW – (v1-83 1902-85 on reel or mf $1,681.00. v84-93 1985-95 on mf $359.00) – v1-93. 1902-95 – 5,6,9 – $2,040.00 set – us Hein [340]
Michigan. Laws, Statutes, etc *see* AN ABRIDGMENT OF THE COMPILED LAWS OF THE STATE OF MICHIGAN, 1897.
MICHIGAN LAWYER – Detroit. v1-4. 1875-79 – 1 – $40.00 – us Hein [073]
THE MICHIGAN LAWYER – v1-4. 1875-78 (all publ) – 9 – LLMC 82-944 – us L.L.M.C. [073]
Michigan Legislature *see*
- HOUSE JOURNALS
- THE REVISED STATUTES OF MICHIGAN AND MICHIGAN COMPILED LAWS
- SENATE JOURNALS
- SESSION LAWS

MICHIGAN LIBRARIAN – v1-46 1934-80 1; 1972-80 5,6; 1975-80 9 – us UMI [020]
MICHIGAN MATHEMATICAL JOURNAL – v. 1-9. 1952-1962 – 1,5,6 – us Princeton Micro [510]
MICHIGAN MEDICINE – v1- 1902- 1; 1970- 5,6; 1975- 9 – us UMI [610]
MICHIGAN MESSENGER – Adrian. Mich. -sw. 1890-1897 – 1 – us UMI [071]
MICHIGAN MUNICIPAL REVIEW – v1- 1928- 1; 1971- 5,6; 1977- 4 x 6 in. 9 – us UMI [323]
MICHIGAN OFFICIAL DIRECTORY AND LEGISLATIVE MANUAL FOR YEARS 1913-14 / Martindale, Frederick C – (The Cox Library Collection) – 5 – us Americana [978]
MICHIGAN PHARMACIST – 1970- 1; 1973- 5,6; 1975- 4 x 6 in. 9 – us UMI [615]
Michigan. Public Utilities Commission *see* REPORTS
MICHIGAN QUARTERLY REVIEW – v1- 1962- 1; 1971- 5,6; 1976- 4 x 6 in. 9 – us UMI [073]
Michigan. Railroad Commission *see* REPORTS
MICHIGAN ROADS AND CONSTRUCTION – 1905-80 1; 1971-80 5,6; 1975-80 9 – us UMI [625]
Michigan School Board *see* JOURNAL
Michigan. State Bar Association *see* PROCEEDINGS
MICHIGAN STATE BAR JOURNAL – Superseded by Michigan Bar Journal – v1-57 1921-78 1; v54-57 5,6,9 – us UMI [340]
MICHIGAN STATE BAR JOURNAL *see* MICHIGAN BAR JOURNAL
Michigan. State Board of Tax Administration *see* REPORTS
MICHIGAN STATE MEDICAL SOCIETY *see* MICHIGAN MEDICINE
Michigan. State Tax Commission *see*
- PROCEEDINGS...IN DETERMINING STATE EQUALIZED VALUATIONS
- REPORTS OF THE MICHIGAN STATE TAX COMMISSION AND THE STATE BOARD OF ASSESSORS

Michigan State University *see* MSU BUSINESS TOPICS
Michigan State University. Robert Vincent Voice Library *see* DICTIONARY CATALOG OF THE G. ROBERT VINCENT VOICE LIBRARY
Michigan. Supreme Court *see*
- BLUME'S UNREPORTED OPINIONS
- FULLER'S PRACTICE REPORTS
- MCGRATH'S MANDAMUS CASES
- MICHIGAN SUPREME COURT REPORTS

MICHIGAN SUPREME COURT REPORTS / Michigan. Supreme Court – (Includes 2 territorial vols by Douglas. Pre-NRS: v1-40 + 2 Douglas vols 1843-79 309mf $463.00. Updates planned) – v1-443. 1847-1993 – 3992MF – 9 – $5,988.00 – LLMC 77-003 – us L.L.M.C. [340]
MICHIGAN SUPREME COURT REPORTS *see*
- BLUME'S UNREPORTED OPINIONS
- FULLER'S PRACTICE REPORTS

MICHIGAN TECH LODE – Houghton, MI. 1921-71 – 1 – us UMI [071]
MICHIGAN TRIBUNE – Battle Creek. Mich. -w. 1872-74, 1877-82 – 1 – us UMI [071]
Michigan. University *see*
- CATALOGS OF THE ASIA LIBRARY
- THE MICHIGAN DAILY

Michigan. University. Museum of Art *see* ITALY THROUGH DUTCH EYES. DUTCH 17TH CENTURY LANDSCAPE ARTISTS IN ITALY
Michigan. University. Political Science Association *see* CONSTITUTIONAL HISTORY OF THE UNITED STATES AS SEEN IN THE DEVELOPMENT OF AMERICAN LAW.
Michigan. University. Robert Vincent Voice Library *see* DICTIONARY CATALOG
MICHIGAN YEARBOOK OF INTERNATIONAL LEGAL STUDIES *see* MICHIGAN JOURNAL OF INTERNATIONAL LAW
Michoacan. Mexico (State) *see* PERIODICO OFICIAL DEL GOBIERNO DEL ESTADO DE MICHOACAN DE OCAMPA
Michoff, N V *see* CONTRIBUTION A L'HISTOIRE DU COMMERCE BULGARE (DOCUMENTS OFFICIELS ET RAPPORTS CONSULAIRES)
Michotte, J *see*
- LA DIFFUSION DU COTON ALLEN DANS LA ZONE DENSE A L'OUEST DE BOUAKE
- ESSAI D'APPRECIATION DES EFFETS DES OPERATIONS DE DEVELOPPEMENT A PARTIR DE L'ETUDE D'UN GROUPE DE BUDGETS FAMILIAUX
- ETUDE D'UNE EXPERIENCE D'ANIMATION RURALE EN COTE D'IVOIRE
- GROUPE DE PRODUCTION ET NIVEAU DE REVENU DANS LA ZONE DENSE DE L'OUEST DE BOUAKE
- LES MARCHES DU PAYS BAOULE DE LA ZONE DENSE
- MOUVEMENTS MIGRATOIRES ET DEVELOPPEMENT ECONOMIQUE DANS LA ZONE DENSE A L'OUEST DE BOUAKE
- LES ZONES RURALES ET LES CENTRES SECONDAIRES DE LA REGION DE BOUAKE

Michoutouchkine, Nicolai *see* TRAVEL JOURNALS
Micka, E F *see* THE PROBLEM OF DIVINE ANGER IN ARNOBIUS AND LACTANTIUS
Mickelson, Connie L *see* EFFECTS OF HIGH SCHOOL CONCEPTS-BASED PHYSICAL EDUCATION ON STUDENT BEHAVIOR, KNOWLEDGE, AND MOTIVATION
Mickiewicz, Adam *see*
- CORRESPONDENCE
- LES SLAVES, HISTOIRE ET LITTERATURE DES NATIONS POLONAISE, BOHEME, SERBE ET RUSSE

THE MICMAC NEWS – Cape Breton, CN. 1971-77 – 1 – cn Commonwealth Micro [072]
Micon, F *see* ALIVIO DE LOS SEDIENTOS...
MICRO – (1980-. 5,6,9) – 1977- – 1 – us UMI [510]
MICRO AERO CHARTS / ed by Micro Aero Charts – (Also available in sets: Entire U.S. – 89mf. $529.50 with album. $489.50 without album; Eastern U.S. – 39mf. $234.50 with album. $214.50 without album; Western U.S. – 50mf. $295.00 with album. $275.00 without album) – Colorado Springs: Micro Aero Charts, 1989 – 89mf – 15 – $6.25.f – us Aero [550]
Micro Aero Charts *see* MICRO AERO CHARTS
MICRO COMMUNICATIONS – v1-. 1984- – 1,5,6,9 – us UMI [073]
MICRO ECONOMIC-DEMOGRAPHIC MODEL OF THE AGRICULTURAL HOUSEHOLD IN THE PHILIPPINES – 1983 – 35p – it F.A.O. [338]
LE MICROBE : HUMORISTIQUE – Montreal, Canada. 6 avr 1907 – 1r – 1 – Can$25.00 – cn Can Microfilming [072]
MICROBIAL ECOLOGY – v. 1-6. 1974-80 – 1,5,9 – 306.00 – us UMI [073]
MICROBIAL GENETICS – 1 – uk Microform Academic [610]
MICROBIOLOGICAL REVIEWS – (See also: Bacteriological Review) – v42-. 1978- – 1,5,6,9 – us UMI [576]
MICROBIOLOGICAL REVIEWS – v1-46. 1937-82.Continues: Bacteriological Reviews – 1,5,6 – us Princeton Micro [576]
MICROBIOLOGICAL REVIEWS *see* BACTERIOLOGICAL REVIEWS
MICROBIOLOGY – v31-63. 1962-94 – 1,5 – $80.00v – us UMI [576]
MICROBIOLOGY ABSTRACTS: SECTION A – Industrial and Applied Microbiology – 9 – us C.S.A. [576]
MICROBIOLOGY ABSTRACTS: SECTION B – Bacteriology – 9 – us C.S.A. [576]
MICROBIOLOGY ABSTRACTS: SECTION C – Algology, Mycology and Protozoology – 9 – us C.S.A. [576]

MICROCOMPUTER ASISTANCE FOR EDUCATORS IN PRESCRIBING ADAPTED PHYSICAL EDUCATION / Kelly, Luke E – 1981 – 2mf – 9 – $8.00 – us Microform Publ [790]
MICROCOMPUTING – v8, no.11-. Nov 1984- – 1,5,6,9 – us UMI [073]
MICROCOMPUTING INDUSTRY NEWSLETTER – (1978- 5,6,9) – 1977- – 1 – us UMI [380]
THE MICROCOSMIC MONTHLY – Toronto: Simpson Pub. Co, [1891?-189-] – 9 – cn C.I.H.M. [971]
MICROCOSMO – Pao de Assucar-Alagoas. 1 Jun, 30 Ago 1896 – 1,5,6 – bl Biblioteca [072]
Microeditions Hachette *see* CATALOGUES THEMATIQUES
MICROELECTRONICS AND RELIABILITY – v1- 1962- – 5,6,9 – us UMI [621]
A MICROFICHE CONCORDANCE TO OLD ENGLISH : THE HIGH-FREQUENCY WORDS / Venezky, Richard L & Butler, Sharon – (Includes 2 handbks) – 1985 – 253mf – 9 – Can$150.00 – 0-88844-902-X – cn Pontif [420]
A MICROFICHE CONCORDANCE TO OLD ENGLISH / Venezky, Richard L & Healey, Antonette DiPaolo – (Includes handbook) – 1980 – 418mf – 9 – Can$175.00 – 0-88844-901-1 – cn Pontif [420]
MICROFICHE EDITION OF THE SHEL DKAR MANUSCRIPT BKA"GYUR / British Library – 1996 – 6700mf – 9 – £2,750.00 – 0-7123-0425-8 – uk British Libr Humanities [480]
MICROFICHE LIBRARY OF GERONTOLOGY AND GERIATRICS – (Former title: Gerontology and Geriatrics Training Materials) – 1099mf – 9 – us UMI [618]
MICROFILM ACCESSIONS REGISTER, NOS 1-299 [-435] / Rhodesia. National Archives – [Salisbury]: National Archives of Rhodesia, [19-?] – us Res Libr [324]
MICROFILM CORPUS OF AMERICAN LUTHERANISM – (Individual titles also listed separately) – 6 serial titles and 233 monographs – 28r – 1 – ATLA B0524 – us A.T.L.A. [240]
MICROFILM CORPUS OF AMERICAN LUTHERANISM *see*
- EVANGELICAL LUTHERAN INTELLIGENCER
- DAS EVANGELISCHES MAGAZIN
- LUTHERAN MAGAZINE
- LUTHERAN PREACHER
- LUTHERAN PULPIT

MICROFILM NEWSLETTER – (See now: Micrographics Newsletter) – 1969-74 1; 1974 5,6 – us UMI [073]
A MICROFILM SUPPLEMENT TO THE TERRITORIAL PAPERS OF THE U.S.: WISCONSIN, 1836-48 / U.S. National Archives and Records Service – 122r – 1 – M236 – us Nat'l Archives [324]
MICROFILM TECHNIQUES – v1- 1971- 1; v5- 5,6,9 – us UMI [770]
MICROFILMED COLLECTION OF RARE BOOKS / British Architectural Library – (With printed index) – 35r – 1 – £1,380.00 – uk World [720]
MICROFILMED FINNISH-AMERICAN NEWSPAPERS – Helsinki: Helsinki University Library, 1994 – 669r – 1 – fi H.U. Libr [072]
MICROFILMS OF LATVIAN NEWSPAPERS – (Appendix to the catalogue of the microfilmed Latvian newspapers in the Helsinki University Library) – 327r – 1 – fi H.U. Libr [072]
THE MICROFORM JOURNAL ON THE HISTORY OF PLASTIC AND AESTHETIC-PLASTIC SURGERY – us Striker [617]
MICROFORM PUBLICATIONS IN HEALTH, PHYSICAL EDUCATION, RECREATION, AND ALLIED ARTS – A Health and Physical Education Microform Bulletin will be sent free of charge upon request – 9 – us Microform Publ [790]
MICROGRAPHIA / Hooke, Robert – M 205. 1665 – 9 – ne IDC [760]
MICROGRAPHIA : OR, SOME PHYSIOLOGICAL DESCRIPTIONS OF MINUTE BODIES MADE BY MAGNIFYING GLASSES / Hooke, Robert – 1665 – 1r – 1 – us Ross [500]
MICROGRAPHIA SUE ICONES FUNGERUM / Cooke, M A – 1875-79 – 1 – uk Microform Academic [580]
MICROGRAPHICS EDUCATION FOR LIBRARIANS / American Library Association – 1977 – 9 – 8.00 – us L of C Photodup [770]
MICROGRAPHICS NEWSLETTER – (See also: Microfilm Newsletter) – v7- 1975- – 1,5,6,9 – us UMI [770]
MICROGRAVITY QUARTERLY – 1,5,69 – us UMI [530]
MICROKOSMOGRAPHIA. A DESCRIPTION OF THE BODY OF MAN / Crooke, H – M 331. 1615 – 9 – ne IDC [611]
MICROLOG – (System of Canadian report literature. Subject, geographic and individual reports available. Index available separately) – 9 – cn Micromedia [971]
MICRON – (Incorporating: Microscopica Acta and Electron Microscopy Reviews) – v1- 1969- – 5,6,9 – us UMI [600]
Micron, M *see*
- EEN APOLOGIA OF VERANDTWOORDINGHE, OP 20. VERSHEYDEN ARTIKELEN DIE MENNO SYMONS TEGHEN HET DISPUTACY BOECXKEN VAN HET BESPRECK MET HEM OUER DE LEERE GEHOUDEN
- EEN APOLOGIE OF VERANDTWOORDINGHE, OP 20. VERSCHEYDEN ARTIKELEN DIE MENNO SYMONS TEGHEN HET DISPUTACY BOECXKEN VAN HET BESPRECK MET HEM OUER DE LEERE GEHOUDEN
- EEN WAERACHTIGH VERHAAL DER T'ZAMENSPREKINGHEN TUSSCHEN MENNO SIMONS ENDE MARTINUS MIKRON VAN DER MENSCHWERDINGHE JESU CHRISTI
- EEN WAERACHTIGH VERHAAL DER T'ZAMENSPREKINGHEN TUSSHEN MENNO SIMONS ENDE MARTINUS MIKRON VAN DER MENSCHWERDINGHE JESU CHRISTI

MICRONESIA COMPACT OF FREE ASSOCIATION : HEARING BEFORE THE HOUSE COMMITTEE ON FOREIGN AFFAIRS, 98TH CONG, 2ND SESS, SEP 18, 1984 / U.S. Congress – (Covers FSM and RMI) – Washington: GPO, 1984 – 2mf – 9 – $3.00 – LLMC 82-100F, Title 17 – us L.L.M.C. [323]
MICRONESIA: EVOLUTION TO SEPARATE POLITICAL ENTITIES *see*
- THE COMPACT OF FREE ASSOCIATION
- COMPACT OF FREE ASSOCIATION ACT OF 1985 (FSM AND MARSHALL ISLANDS)
- COMPACT OF FREE ASSOCIATION BETWEEN THE UNITED STATES AND THE GOVERNMENTS OF PALAU, THE MARSHALL ISLANDS AND THE FEDERATED STATES OF MICRONESIA
- THE COMPACT OF FREE ASSOCIATION, FOREIGN POLITICAL PROVISIONS
- DRAFT ENVIRONMENTAL IMPACT STATEMENT FOR THE COMPACT OF FREE ASSOCIATION
- ENVIRONMENTAL IMPACT STATEMENT RELATIVE TO PROPOSED COMPACT OF FREE ASSOCIATION
- FROM TRUSTEESHIP TO ... ?
- HEARING ON THE IMPLEMENTATION OF THE COMPACT OF FREE ASSOCIATION ACT IN THE MARSHALL ISLANDS AND THE FEDERATED STATES OF MICRONESIA
- HEARING ON THE MICRONESIAN COMPACT
- HEARINGS ON THE COMPACT OF FREE ASSOCIATION (MICRONESIA-WIDE)
- HOUSE REPORT APPROVING THE COMPACT OF FREE ASSOCIATION WITH THE MARSHALL ISLANDS AND THE FEDERATED STATES OF MICRONESIA, AND APPROVING CONDITIONALLY THE COMPACT OF FREE ASSOCIATION WITH PALAU
- MATERIALS ON THE COMPACT OF FREE ASSOCIATION FOR MICRONESIA, PALAU AND THE MARSHALLS
- MESSAGE TRANSMITTING PROPOSED LEGISLATION TO APPROVE THE COMPACT OF FREE ASSOCIATION WITH THE FEDERATED STATES OF MICRONESIA AND THE MARSHALL ISLANDS
- MICRONESIAN STATUS NEGOTIATIONS
- MICRONESIAN STATUS NEGOTIATIONS, 8TH ROUND
- ORDER N3027
- PROCLAMATION OF THE U.S. PRESIDENT PLACING INTO FULL FORCE AND EFFECT THE COVENANT WITH THE COMMONWEALTH OF THE NORTHERN MARIANA ISLANDS, AND THE COMPACTS OF FREE ASSOCIATION WITH THE FEDERATED STATES OF MICRONESIA AND THE REPUBLIC OF THE MARSHALL ISLANDS
- REPORT ON 8TH ROUND OF STATUS NEGOTIATIONS
- SENATE REPORT APPROVING THE COMPACT OF FREE ASSOCIATION
- SUMMARY RECORD OF THE U.S.-MICRONESIA ROUNDTABLE CONFERENCE ON THE FUTURE POLITICAL STATUS OF THE TRUST TERRITORY OF THE PACIFIC
- TRUSTEESHIP TERMINATION

MICRONESIA: EVOLUTION TO SEPARATE POLITIVCAL ENTITIES *see* SENATE REPORT APPROVING THE COMPACT OF FREE ASSOCIATION
MICRONESIA: EVOLUTION TO SEPERATE POLITICAL ENTITIES *see* MICRONESIA COMPACT OF FREE ASSOCIATION
MICRONESIA: INTERIM GOVERNANCE *see*
- HOUSE JOURNALS 1966-79
- JOURNAL OF THE GENERAL ASSEMBLY
- LAWS AND RESOLUTIONS
- PROCEEDINGS
- SENATE JOURNALS 1966-79

MICRONESIA: PRELUDE TO THE CONSTITUTIONAL CONVENTION *see*
- ANALYSIS OF THE DRAFT COMPACT OF ASSOCIATION
- DRAFT COMPACT OF FREE ASSOCIATION
- FOURTEEN QUESTIONS
- HEARINGS IN TRUK, PONAPE AND THE MARSHALL ISLANDS, JUL 1973
- HEARINGS IN YAP, PALAU AND THE MARIANAS, JUL 1973
- INTERIM REPORT TO THE CONGRESS OF MICRONESIA
- JOINT RESOLUTION REGARDING THE STATUS OF THE TTPI
- MICRONESIAN STATUS NEGOTIATIONS, 7TH ROUND
- OFFICIAL RECORDS OF THE 4TH ROUND OF MICRONESIAN FUTURE POLITICAL STATUS TALKS
- PAPERS OF THE 2ND MEETING
- PAPERS OF THE FUTURE POLITICAL STATUS NEGOTIATIONS
- POLITICAL STATUS DIGEST
- PROCEEDINGS OF THE 6TH ROUND OF FUTURE POLITICAL STATUS NEGOTIATIONS
- RECORDS OF THE 5TH ROUND OF MICRONESIAN FUTURE POLITICAL STATUS NEGOTIATIONS
- REPORT OF PRESIDENT'S PERSONAL REPRESENTATIVE ON THE STATUS NEGOTIATIONS [TTPI (U.S.)]
- REPORT ON 4TH ROUND OF STATUS NEGOTIATIONS
- REPORT ON 7TH ROUND OF STATUS NEGOTIATIONS
- REPORT ON THE 3RD ROUND OF STATUS NEGOTIATIONS
- REPORT TO THE 3RD CONGRESS
- REPORT TO THE 5TH CONGRESS OF MICRONESIA
- REPORT TO THE CONGRESS OF MICRONESIA
- SUMMARY OF FUTURE POLITICAL FUTURE STATUS TALKS

Micronesia Support Committee and the Pacific Concerns Research Center *see* FROM TRUSTEESHIP TO ... ?
Micronesia. (U.S.) *see*
- COMPACT OF FREE ASSOCIATION BETWEEN THE UNITED STATES AND THE GOVERNMENTS OF PALAU, THE MARSHALL ISLANDS AND THE FEDERATED STATES OF MICRONESIA
- DRAFT ENVIRONMENTAL IMPACT STATEMENT FOR THE COMPACT OF FREE ASSOCIATION
- ENVIRONMENTAL IMPACT STATEMENT RELATIVE TO PROPOSED COMPACT OF FREE ASSOCIATION

MICRONESIAN ADVOCATE : A LEGAL REVIEW – Kolonia, Ponape, Eastern Caroline Islands: The Ponapean District Bar Assoc. v1 no 2-v2 no 3. 1967-68 – 8mf – 9 – $12.00 – LLMC 82-100F Title 68 – us L.L.M.C. [340]
MICRONESIAN CONSTITUTIONAL CONVENTION, 1975 *see*
- ANALYSIS OF THE PROPOSED CONSTITUTION OF THE FEDERATED STATES OF MICRONESIA
- COMMITTEE REPORTS N1-67
- CONVENTION JOURNAL
- DELEGATE PROPOSALS
- DELEGATION DIRECTORY
- A GLOSSARY OF WORDS AND TERMS USED IN THE CONSTITUTION
- MINUTES OF THE COMMITTEE OF THE WHOLE
- ORGANIZATIONAL ACTIVITIES AND MATERIALS
- PRESS RELEASES N1-116

MICRONESIAN INDEPENDENT *see* MICRONITOR (1 FEB 1972) AND MICRONESIAN INDEPENDENT (25 JUN 1976-5 SEP 1980)
THE MICRONESIAN REPORTER / Trust Territory of the Pacific Islands (U.S.) – (Title is sometimes given as: Micronesian Reporter: The Journal of Micronesia) – v1-28. nov 1951-mar 31, 1980 (all publ?) – 72mf – 9 – $108.00 – LLMC 82-100F, Title 67 – us L.L.M.C. [980]
MICRONESIAN STATUS NEGOTIATIONS : OPENING STATEMENT, MAUI CONFERENCE, OCT 3, 1981 – (Various pagination) – n.p, n.d. – 1mf – 9 – $1.50 – LLMC 82-100F, Title 113 – us L.L.M.C. [323]
MICRONESIAN STATUS NEGOTIATIONS, 7TH ROUND : HELD IN WASHINGTON, D.C, NOV 1973 / Office for Micronesian Status Negotiations – Washington: Off for Micronesian Status Negotiations, n.d. – 1mf – 9 – $1.50 – LLMC 82-100F, Title 55 – us L.L.M.C. [323]
MICRONESIAN STATUS NEGOTIATIONS, 8TH ROUND : HELD IN SAIPAN, MAY-JUN 1976 / Office for Micronesian Status Negotiations – Washington: Off for Micronesian Status Negotiations, n.d. – 1mf – 9 – $1.50 – LLMC 82-100F, Title 57 – us L.L.M.C. [323]
MICRONITOR (1 FEB 1972) AND MICRONESIAN INDEPENDENT (25 JUN 1976-5 SEP 1980) – Majuro, Marshall Islands – 1r – 1 – PMB Doc404 – at Pacific Mss [073]
MICRONUTRIENTS – 1983 – 92p – it F.A.O. [631]
MICRONUTRIENTS AND THE NUTRIENT STATUS OF SOILS – 1982 – 458p – it F.A.O. [631]
MICRONUTRIENTS ASSESSMENT AT THE COUNTRY LEVEL : AN INTERNATIONAL STUDY – 1990 – 216p – it F.A.O. [631]
MICROPALEONTOLOGY – v1- 1955- 1; v22- 5,6,9 – us UMI [073]
MICROPOLITICS – v.1-. 1981- – 1,5,6,9 – us UMI [320]
MICROPROCESSING AND MICROPROGRAMMING – v1-14. 1975-84 – 1,5,6,13 – sz Elsevier [073]
MICROPROCESSORS – v1-2. 1976-78 – 1 – us UMI [073]
MICROPROCESSORS AND MICROSYSTEMS – (1982-. 1,5,6,9) – v2-. 1978- – 1 – us UMI [073]
MICROPROPAGATION OF SELECTED ROOTCROPS, PALMS, CITRUS AND ORNAMENTAL SPECIES : PROCEEDINGS OF THE FAO/NORWAY SYMPOSIUM. AS, NORWAY, 1984 – 1984 – 237p – it F.A.O. [634]
MICROPUBLISHING OF CURRENT PERIODICALS – v. 1-. 1977- – 5,6,9 – us UMI [070]
THE MICROSCOPE OF THE NEW TESTAMENT / Sewell, William; ed by Crichton, W J – (Includes index) – London: Rivingtons, 1878 – 2mf – 9 – 0-8370-5238-6 – 1985-3238 – us A.T.L.A. [220]
THE MICROSCOPIC JOURNAL, AND STRUCTURAL RECORD. – London, 1841-42 – 3 – us Readex [576]
MICROSCOPICA ACTA *see* MICRON
MICROSYSTEMS – (1982-. 1,5,6,9) – v1-. 1980- – 1 – us UMI [073]
MICROSYSTEMS – 1982-84 – 1 – us UMI [510]
MICROWAVE JOURNAL – v1- 1958- 1; v20- 5,6,9 – us UMI [621]
MICROWAVE LICENSES ISSUED / U.S. National Technical Information Service – Monthly.In ascending state/county sequence – 9 – us N.T.I.S. [000]
MICROWAVE SYSTEMS NEWS – v1- 1971- 1; v5- 5,6,9 – us UMI [621]
MICROWAVES – v1-21 1962-82 1; v10-21 5,6; v15-21 9 – us UMI [600]
MICROWAVES AND RF – v21-. 1982- – 1,5,6,9 – us UMI [073]
MID COUNTY ENTERPRISE – Parkrose OR. Oct 25-Nov 15 1962 – 1 – us U.O. Library [071]
MID OCEAN – Black Island. R.I. 1899-1906 – 1 – us UMI [071]
MID WEEK PICTORIAL – 1914-37 – 1 – us UMI [073]
MID-AMERICA – v1- 1918- 1; v53- 1971- 5,6; v58- 9 – us UMI [240]
MID-AMERICAN REVIEW OF SOCIOLOGY – v. v. 1- v. 1976- – 1,5,6,9 – us UMI [300]
Midang *see* EARLY LYRICS OF SO CHONG JU
MID-ATLANTIC COUNTRY – 1986- – 1,5,6,9 – us UMI [073]
MID-ATLANTIC GRAPHIC ARTS REVIEW – 1960- – 1. 1970-; ; 56 – us UMI [760]
MID-CHANNEL : A PLAY IN FOUR ACTS / Pinero, Arthur Wing – London: William Heinemann, 1911 [c1910] – 1 roll – 1 – 1-55879-560-X – uk Libr Preservation [820]

MID-CITIES : BELLFLOWER, CARSON, HOLLYDALE, LONG BEACH, PARAMOUNT, ETC. – 1975-85; 1987-92 – 28r – 1 – $1,400.00 – P00063 – us Library Micro [910]
MID-CITIES DAILY NEWS – Hurst. Tex. 1970- – 1 – us UMI [071]
MID-CONTINENT JEWELER – 1914-62 – 1 – us UMI [740]
MID-CONTINENT MAGAZINE – 1-6, no. 4. Aug 1892-Aug 1895 – 1 – us UMI [073]
MIDCONTINENT OIL AND GAS WORLD *see*
- HART'S OIL AND GAS WORLD
- PACIFIC OIL AND GAS WORLD
MID-CONTINENTAL JOURNAL OF ARCHAEOLOGY – v. 1- 1976- – 1,5,6,9 – us UMI [930]
MID-COUNTY POST – Capitola, CA. 1990-1994 – 5r – 1 – $250.00 – B02094 – us Library Micro [071]
THE MIDDELBURG GAZETTE – Middelburg (Cape), South Africa.4 Jan 1876-27 Dec 1881. 3 reels. Continued by: Middelburg Getuige – 1, 16 diazo available at reduced price – sa SA Libr [072]
MIDDELBURG GETUIGE, DE – Middelburg (Cape), South Africa. 7 Jan 1882-29 Dec 83. 1 reel – 1, 16 diazo available at reduced price – sa SA Libr [072]
MIDDELBURG OPMERKER, DE – Middelburg (Cape), South Africa. 13 Jun-24 Oct 1884. 1 reel – 1, 16 diazo available at reduced price – sa SA Libr [072]
MIDDELLANDSCHE AFRIKAANDER *see* DIE AFRIKANER
MIDDELLANDSCHE AFRIKAANDER, DE – (Title varies: Die Afrikaner, 1933-69; Continues as: De Cradock Afrikaner, 1884-98) – Cradock, South Africa. 6 Jan 1899-18 Dec 1936 – 26r – 1, 16 diazo available at reduced price – sa SA Libr [072]
Middendorff, A T von *see* BEITRAEGE ZU EINER MALACOZOOLOGIA ROSSICA
Middle Bass Club. Middle Bass, Ohio *see* RECORDS AND SCRAPBOOK
MIDDLE EAST – (v.50$. 1979- 5,6,9) – v.1-. 1974- – 1 – us UMI [073]
THE MIDDLE EAST / U.S. Office of Strategic Services – (1950-61 Suppl Pt 12 $320.00 ISBN 0-89093-247-6. Series: US State Department Intelligence and Research Reports) – 1977. Series: US State Department Intelligence and Research Reports, Pt 7 – 1 – $305.00 – 0-89093-123-2 – us UPA [956]
THE MIDDLE EAST, 1925-41 : CONFIDENTIAL U.S. DIPLOMATIC POST RECORDS – (Part 1: Iran. ISBN 0-89093-526-2. $4,290; Part 2: Iraq. ISBN 0-89093-527-0. $2,645.00; Part 3: Beirut. ISBN 0-89093-576-9. $2,310.00; Part 4: Jerusalem. ISBN 0-89093-577-7. $1,320.00; Part 5: Aden. ISBN 0-89093-575-0. $990.00. All with printed guides) – 1 – $10,980.00 set – us UPA [956]
THE MIDDLE EAST, 1942-44 : CONFIDENTIAL U.S. DIPLOMATIC POST RECORDS / U.S. Department of State – (Part 1: Iran. 15 reels. $1,655.00; Part 2: Iraq. 9 reels. $990.00; Part 3: Lebanon. 7 reels. $770.00. All with printed guides) – 1 – $3,240.00 set – us UPA [977]
THE MIDDLE EAST, 1946-76 / U.S. Central Intelligence Agency – 1982. Series: CIA Research Reports – 1 – $305.00 – 0-89093-421-5 – us UPA [956]
THE MIDDLE EAST, 1970-94 : SPECIAL STUDIES SERIES / ed by Kesaris, Paul – (1970-80: 18r $1,980.00 ISBN 0-89093-400-2; Supplements, 1980-82: 3r $330.00 ISBN 0-89093-433-9; 1982-85: 8r $880.00 ISBN 0-89093-374-X; 1985-88: 8r $880.00 ISBN 1-55655-110-X; 1989-91: 10r $1,105.00 ISBN 1-55655-425-7; 1992-94: 15r $1,785.00 ISBN 1-55655-538-5. With printed guides) – 1 – us UPA [320]
MIDDLE EAST AND ISLAM: A BIBLIOGRAPHICAL INTRODUCTION / Hopwood, D & Grimwood-Jones, Diana – NE-292 1. 1972 – 9 – ne IDC [956]
THE MIDDLE EAST AT WAR AND IN SEARCH OF PEACE – (1: The War of Independence November 1 1947-July 31 1949. 2: The Sinai Campaign October 1 1956-March 31 1957. 3: The Six-Day War April 1 1967-June 30 1967. 4: The War of Attrition October 1 1967-August 31 1970. 5: The Yom Kippur War October 1 1973-May 31 1974. 6: Intervention in Lebanon March 1 1978-June 30 1978. 7: The Egypt-Israel peace treaty. November 1 1977-March 31 1979) – 40r – 1 – ne IDC [355]
Middle East Centre, St. Antony's College, Oxford *see* JERUSALEM AND EAST MISSION ARCHIVE 1842-1976
MIDDLE EAST EDUCATION – v.1-. 1979- – 1,5,6,9 – us UMI [073]
MIDDLE EAST ELECTRICITY – 1976- – 1,5,6,9 – us UMI [621]
MIDDLE EAST GENERAL CATALOGUE – 1,466 monographs; 153 serials and sets – 9 – ne IDC [956]
The Middle East Institute. Washington, D.C *see* STATE AND SOCIETY IN INDEPENDENT NORTH AFRICA
MIDDLE EAST INTERNATIONAL – 1971- 1; 1974- 5,6; 1976- 4 x 6 in. 9 – us UMI [956]
MIDDLE EAST JOURNAL – v1- 1947- 1; v24-1970- 5,6; v30- 9 – us UMI [956]
MIDDLE EAST NEWSLETTER – (v.103-. 1979- 5,6,9) – 1975- – 1 – us UMI [073]
MIDDLE EAST PERSPECTIVE – New York, NY. Oct 1969-Mar 1985. Lacking many issues. Continues: Perspective (New York, 1968) – 1 – us A.J.P.C. [071]
MIDDLE EAST POLICY *see* AMERICAN-ARAB AFAIRS
MIDDLE EAST RESEARCH AND INFORMATION PROJECT – Washington D.C. 95 docs. 1980-1991 – 65mf – 9 – ne IDC [320]
MIDDLE EAST RESEARCH AND INFORMATION PROJECT *see* MERIP REPORTS
MIDDLE EAST REVIEW – v1- 1974- 1; v9- 5,6,9 – us UMI [956]
MIDDLE EAST REVIEW – 1985-. -q – 1 – us UMI [073]
THE MIDDLE EAST TIMES – v1-. 1983-. -w. Nicosia, Cyprus: Middle East Times Ltd., 1983- – 1 – us U.W. Library [073]
MIDDLE EAST TRANSPORT – (v.14-. 1979- 5,6,9) – v.1-. 1977- – 1 – us UMI [073]
MIDDLE EAST TRAVEL – (1979- 5,6,9) – 1977- – 1 – us UMI [910]
MIDDLE EAST WATCH – New York. 16 docs. 1989-1991 – 10mf – 9 – ne IDC [956]
MIDDLE EAST/NORTH AFRICA DEVELOPMENT DOCUMENTS / ed by Hopwood, Derek – 648 titles – 9 – ne IDC [956]
MIDDLE JR. HIGH SCIENCE BULLETIN – v1-5. 1978-82 – 1 – us UMI [500]
MIDDLE SCHOOL JOURNAL – v1- 1970- 1; v8- 5,6,9 – us UMI [370]
Middle States Association of Colleges and Secondary Schools *see* PROCEEDINGS
Middle Temple. London *see*
- MIDDLE TEMPLE RECORDS
- MIDDLE TEMPLE RULES AND ORDERS, 1596-1914
Middle Temple. London. Library *see* A CATALOG OF THE PRINTED BOOKS..
MIDDLE TEMPLE RECORDS / Middle Temple. London; ed by Hopwood, Charles H – London: Butterworth. 4v. 1904-05 – 19mf – 9 – $28.50 – LLMC 84-308 – us L.L.M.C. [340]
MIDDLE TEMPLE RULES AND ORDERS, 1596-1914 : FOR THE CONDUCT OF BUSINESS AT THEIR PARLIAMENTS AND COMMITTEES.. / Middle Temple. London – 3rd ed. London: Bonner, 1914 – 2mf – 9 – $3.00 – LLMC 84-309 – us L.L.M.C. [340]
MIDDLE TEMPLE TALK : WITH SOME TALK OF THE TABLE ITSELF / Thorpe, William G – London: Hutchinson & Co, 1895 – 5mf – 9 – $7.50 – LLMC 84-315 – us L.L.M.C. [340]
MIDDLE TYGER BAPTIST CHURCH. SPARTANBURG COUNTY. SOUTH CAROLINA : CHURCH RECORDS – 1875-Apr 1898 – 1 – 5.00 – us Baptist [240]
THE MIDDLE WAY / MacMillan, Hugh – 1 – uk Microform Academic [840]
THE MIDDLE WEST SIDE; A HISTORICAL SKETCH / Cartwright, Otho Grandford – New York: Survey Associates, 1914. xiii,67p. Fold. front, plates, diagr.(West Side Studies, v2,pt1). At head of title: Russell Sage Foundation – 1 – us U.W. Library [360]
MIDDLEBOROUGH 1658-1900 – (Mf 1-5: Birth Index 1670-1849. Mf 6-7: Death Index 1682-1846. Mf 8-13: Intents Index 1743-1854. Mf 14-15: Marr Index 1666-1850. Mf 16-54: Vital & Town 1658-1848. Mf 53-54: Vitals 1757-1850. Mf 55-60: Marriages 1837-1911. Mf 61-64: Selectmen 1736-89. Mf 65-85: Town & Vital 1746-1808. Mf 86-110: Town Record 1802-66. Mf 111-118: Accounts 1799-1823. Mf 119-127: School Rec 1837-1900. Mf 128-130: Rebellion 1861-64. Mf 131-140: Militia 1850-72. Mf 141-151: Sales 1832-62. Mf 152-157: Accounts 1795-1850. Mf 158: Pauper Burials 1829-1953. Mf 159-163: Paupers 1885-1900. 164-169: Birth Index 1847-1955; 170-175: Marr Index 1847-1955; 176-181: Death Index 1847-1955; 182-185: Vitals 1843-1861; 186-190: Births 1861-1891; 191-195: Marriages 1861-1898; 195-205: Deaths 1861-1915; 206-207: Births 1892-1900) – (mf ed 1992) – 207mf – 9 – us Holbrook [920]
MIDDLEBURY MERCURY – Middlebury, VT. 1801-1810 – 3 – us Readex [071]
MIDDLEFIELD 1758-1849 – (Mf 1T-2T: Births & Deaths 1758-1845. Mf 1T: Intentions & Marriages 1767-1808. Mf 1T,5T: Out-of-Town Marriages 1781-98. Mf 2T-3T: Intentions 1808-45. Mf 3T: Marriages & Intentions 1844-47; Marriages 1808-44. Mf 3T-4T: Deaths 1778-1844. Mf 4T: Births 1843-49. Mf 5T: Marriages 1843-50; Deaths 1843-49) – (mf ed 1997) – 5mf – 9 – 0-87623-293-4 – us Holbrook [920]
MIDDLEFIELD 1774-1899 – (mf ed 1988) – 10mf – 9 – 0-87623-084-2 – us Holbrook [920]
MIDDLEFIELD, OHIO, TAXES, MS V.F.O. – (List of the residents within the district of Middlefield, then Turnbull Co.) – 1801 – 1r – 1 – us Western Res [978]
MIDDLEMARCH : A STUDY OF PROVINCIAL LIFE / Eliot, George – Edinburgh: William Blackwood, 1871-72 – 2 rolls – 1 – 1-55879-220-1 – uk Libr Preservation [830]
Middlesboro, Kentucky *see* MISCELLANEOUS EARLY NEWSPAPERS
MIDDLESBRO' WEEKLY AND CLEVELAND ADVERTISER – England. Jul 1869-75. -w. 3mqn reels – 1 – uk British Libr Newspaper [072]
MIDDLESEX, 1823 : BRITISH ISLES CENSUS DIRECTORIES PROJECT, ENGLAND. VOL 209 – 1mf – 9 – A$9.00 – at Vine [941]
MIDDLESEX, 1839 : BRITISH ISLES CENSUS DIRECTORIES PROJECT, ENGLAND. VOL 66 – 1mf – 9 – A$9.00 – at Vine [941]
MIDDLESEX, 1846 : BRITISH ISLES CENSUS DIRECTORIES PROJECT, ENGLAND. VOL 157 – 7mf – 9 – A$45.00 – at Vine [941]
MIDDLESEX, 1855 : BRITISH ISLES CENSUS DIRECTORIES PROJECT, ENGLAND. VOL 252 – 8mf – 9 – A$51.00 – at Vine [941]
MIDDLESEX, 1899 : BRITISH ISLES CENSUS DIRECTORIES PROJECT, ENGLAND. – at Vine [941]
MIDDLESEX, 1908 : BRITISH ISLES CENSUS DIRECTORIES PROJECT, ENGLAND – at Vine [941]
MIDDLESEX ADVERTISER *see* BUCKINGHAMSHIRE AND ADJACENT COUNTIES ADVERTISER
MIDDLESEX AND BUCKINGHAMSHIRE ADVERTISER *see* BUCKINGHAMSHIRE AND ADJACENT COUNTIES ADVERTISER
MIDDLESEX AND SURREY GAZETTE – London, 15 Dec 1877-12 Jan 1878 – 9ft – 1 – uk British Libr Newspaper [072]
MIDDLESEX AND WESTMINSTER CALENDAR AND SESSIONS BOOK – 1638-1751 – 1 – uk Microform Academic [941]
MIDDLESEX COUNTY CHRONICLE/COUNTY OF MIDDLESEX CHRONICLE – London, UK. 1951. -w. 1 reel – 1 – uk British Libr Newspaper [072]
MIDDLESEX COUNTY RECORD SOCIETY – (Coll title: Publications of the English Record Societies, 1835-1972...) – v1-4. 1886-92 – 23mf – 9 – £195.00 – uk Chadwyck [941]
MIDDLESEX COUNTY TIMES – (Also known as: Ealing and Acton Gazette; Gazette Ealing Borough; Middlesex County Times; West Middlesex Gazette: Ealing Edition) – Sep 29, Oct 6, Nov 3 1866-1950; 1951 (Ealing Edn); 1952-54; 1957-73; Jan 18-Mar 1 1974; Mar 8-Jun 28 1974; Jul 5-Sep 27 1974; Oct 4-Dec 27 1974; 1975-78; Feb 14-Apr 27 1979; May 1979-96 – 214 3/4r – 1 – uk British Libr Newspaper [072]
MIDDLESEX COUNTY TIMES – London. Mid-week edition. -w. 1969-80. (14 reels) – 1 – uk British Libr Newspaper [072]
MIDDLESEX COUNTY TIMES *see* MIDDLESEX COUNTY TIMES
MIDDLESEX COUNTY TIMES AND WEST MIDDLESEX GAZETTE (GREENFORD AND NORTHOLT EDN) *see* GREENFORD AND NORTHOLT GAZETTE
MIDDLESEX COUNTY TIMES. EALING EDITION – (Ealing Gazette). London. -w. 1863-1954; 1957-81. (159mqn reels) – 1 – uk British Libr Newspaper [072]
MIDDLESEX COUNTY TIMES. GREENFORD AND NORTHOLT EDITION – (Greenford and Northolt Gazette). London. -w. 1974-81. (26 reels) – 1 – uk British Libr Newspaper [072]
MIDDLESEX COUNTY TIMES. SOUTHALL EDITION – Southall Gazette). London. -w. 1965-81. (51 reels) – 1 – uk British Libr Newspaper [072]
MIDDLESEX COURIER *see* HENDON COURIER
MIDDLESEX DEEDS REGISTRY: INDICES TO THE MEMORIALS, 1709-1837 – 1 – uk Microform Academic [920]
MIDDLESEX GAZETTE – Middletown. Conn. 1785-1820 – 1,3 – us Readex [071]
MIDDLESEX (PART), 1924 : BRITISH ISLES CENSUS DIRECTORIES PROJECT, ENGLAND – at Vine [941]
MIDDLESEX SESSIONS RECORDS – 1607-12 – 1 – uk Microform Academic [941]
MIDDLETON 1703-1849 – (Mf 1T: Deaths 1731-86. Mf 1T-4T: Births 1703-1848. Mf 2T: Marriages 1730-87. Mf 4T: Marriages 1730-1843; Out-of-Town Marriages 1730-98. Mf 4T-5T: Deaths 1732-1844. Mf 5T-6T: Marriage Intentions 1784-1849. Mf 6T: Births 1844-49; Marriages 1844-49; Deaths 1844-49) – (mf ed 1997) – 6mf – 9 – 0-87623-294-2 – us Holbrook [920]
MIDDLETON 1704-1905 – (Mf 1-10: Town Records 1728-88. Mf 10: Marriage Intentions 1784-1801. Mf 11-26: Town Records 1788-1848. Mf 24: Militia Lists 1845-48. Mf 26-45: Town Records 1849-1911. Mf 46-49: Tax Assessments 1729-53. Mf 50-53: Tax Assessments 1753-72. Mf 54-59: Tax Assessments1773-98. Mf 60-61: Property Valuations 1798. Mf 62-65: Tax Assessments 1799-1813. Mf 66: Tax Valuations 1827, 1846. Mf 67: Taxes & Military 1862-63. Mf 68-69: School Meetings 1808-67. Mf 70-74: Mortgages 1844-77. Mf 75-82: Church Records 1729-1855. Mf 82-83: Rebellion Records 1861-66. Mf 84-86: Marriage Intentions 1851-1905. Mf 86-88: Vital Records 1703-91. Mf 89-91: Vital Records 1702-1823. Mf 92-95: Vital Records 1703-1848. Mf 96: Births 1850-99. Mf 97: Birth Index 1844-1920. Mf 98: Marriage Index 1844-1920. Mf 99: Death Index 1844-1920. Mf 100-101: Vital Records 1844-74. Mf 102-105: Vital Records 1870-1905) – (mf ed 1998) – 105mf – 9 – 0-87623-401-5 – us Holbrook [920]
MIDDLETON ALBION – England. Middleton & Rochdale Albion. -w. 30 May 1857-13 July 1895. Lacking Dec 1858; 14 Dec 1867-17 July 1869; 15-29 Jan, 5 March 1890. 15 reels – 1 – uk British Libr Newspaper [072]
Middleton, Arthur *see* PAPERS OF ARTHUR MIDDLETON
Middleton, Evan P *see* HISTORY OF CHAMPAIGN COUNTY
MIDDLETON GUARDIAN – Lancashire. 1877 to date – 1 – uk Microform Academic [072]
Middleton, Henry Augustus *see* PLANTATION JOURNAL
Middleton, John *see*
- APPROACHES TO COMMUNICATION PLANNING
- METHODS OF COMMUNICATION PLANNING
Middleton, Margaret Simons *see* JEREMIAH THEUS
Middleton Place. Dorchester County. South Carolina *see* PAPERS
MIDDLETON TIMES STAR – Middleton, CA. 1976- – 17+ r – 1 – $850.00 ($90.00y) – B02456 – us Library Micro [071]
MIDDLETOWN BAPTIST CHURCH. MIDDLETOWN, VERMONT : CHURCH RECORDS – 1805-1847 – 1 – 5.00 – us Baptist [240]
MIDDLETOWN BAPTIST CHURCH (OLD FIRST). MIDDLETOWN, NEW JERSEY : CHURCH RECORDS – 1712-1922. 960p – 1 – 43.20 – us Baptist [240]
DEMIDELLANDSCHE AFRIKAANDER – Cradock, South Africa, jan 10-dec 21 1928 – us Res Libr [072]
MIDHAT PASA'NIN SURIYE LAYIHASI / Tosun, Hueseyin – Dersaadet: Cihan Matbaasi, 1324 [1908] – $25.00 – us MEDOC [956]
MIDI – Montreal, Canada. 22 fev 1954 – 1r – 1 – Can$25.00 – cn Can Microfilming [072]
MIDI MADAGASIKARA – Antananarivo, Madagascar. 1984-1990 – 28r – 1 – us L of C Photodup [072]
LE MIDI SOCIALISTE – Quotidien regional. Toulouse. 1922-25 – 1 – fr A.C.R.P.P. [073]

MIDI-LIBRE – Montpellier. Toutes eds. 1961-juil 1990 – 1 – fr A.C.R.P.P. [073]
MID-ISLAND HERALD – Hicksville. N.Y. -w. 1949- – 1 – us UMI [071]
MID-ISLAND TIMES. BETHPAGE NEWSGRAM. SYOSSET ADVANCE – Hicksville. N.Y. 1963- – 1 – us UMI [071]
MIDLAND – Iowa City. v. 1-20 no. 2 3. 1915-May June 1933 – 1 – us NY Public [978]
MIDLAND : A MAGAZINE OF THE MIDDLE WEST – v1-20. 1915-33 – 3r – 1 – us Ross [073]
THE MIDLAND – Fremont, NE. Midland College. 1890- . Bi-weekly during college year. Title varies. Incomplete – 1 – us NE Hist [071]
MIDLAND AND NORTHERN COAL & IRON TRADES GAZETTE, ADVERTISER AND DIRECTORY – Barnsley, England. 4 Aug 1875-13 Aug 1884; 3 Feb-10 Mar 1886.-w. 10 reels – 1 – uk British Libr Newspaper [072]
MIDLAND CHRONICLE AND WESTMEATH INDEPENDENT – Mullingar. Ireland. -w. 10 Jan-7 Nov 1827. (29 ft) – 1 – uk British Libr Newspaper [072]
MIDLAND COUNTIES EVENING EXPRESS – (Also known as: Evening Express and Star; Wolverhampton Express and Star) – 1876-77; 1880; 1885; 1889; Jul 1898-Jun 1899; Jul 8-Nov 20 1899; Jan-Jun 1901; Jul-Dec 1910; Jan 12-Jul 26 1911; Jul-Sep 1942; 1950; Jan 1962-Apr 1963; 1964-Nov 1974; Dec 1974 (wanting); Jan 17 1975-91; Jan-May 1992 (town final); Jun 1992-Jun 1997 – 485r – 1 – uk British Libr Newspaper [072]
MIDLAND COUNTIES ILLUMINATOR – Leicester. England. -w. 13 Feb-29 May 1841. (7 ft) – 1 – uk British Libr Newspaper [072]
MIDLAND DAILY TRIBUNE – (Also known as: Nuneaton Evening Tribune; Evening Tribune Nuneaton; Heartland Evening News; Nuneaton Evening News) – 1957-Jun 20 1959; Aug 6 1959-92; Jan 11-29 1993; Feb-Apr 1993; May 4-Jun 29 1993; Jul-Dec 1993; Jan 4-Apr 1994; May 3 1994-Jun 1997 – 208 3/4r – 1 – uk British Libr Newspaper [072]
MIDLAND MAIL – Bicester, England. South Midland Mail. -w. 9 June 1899-5 Oct 1900. 45 ft – 1 – uk British Libr Newspaper [072]
Midland, Michigan *see* MISCELLANEOUS EARLY NEWSPAPERS
MIDLAND MONTHLY MAGAZINE – v. 1-11. Jan 1894-Jun 1899 – 1 – us UMI [073]
MIDLAND NEWS – 1927- – 1 – us UMI [072]
MIDLAND NEWS *see* DIE AFRIKANER
MIDLAND NEWS AND KARROO FARMER – Cradock, South Africa. 8 Sept 1891-30 Apr 1929 – 114r – 1, 16 diazo available at reduced price – sa SA Libr [072]
THE MIDLAND NEWS AND KARROO FARMER – Cradock, South Africa: White & Boughton [etc], 1926-27; 1929-61 – us Res Libr [072]
MIDLAND REPRESENTATIVE AND BIRMINGHAM HERALD – Birmingham. England. -w. 23 Apr 1831-2 Jun 1832. (37 ft) – 1 – uk British Libr Newspaper [072]
MIDLAND TIMES AND RUGBY GAZETTE – England.1872-73. 1 reel – 1 – uk British Libr Newspaper [072]
MIDLAND TRIBUNE – Birr, Ireland. 15, 22 Sep 1881; 3 Aug 1882-Dec 1919.-w. 17 reels – 1 – uk British Libr Newspaper [072]
MIDLAND WORKMAN AND GENERAL ADVERTISER – Leicester, England. 1861-62. -w. 23 feet – 1 – uk British Libr Newspaper [072]
MIDLANDS OBSERVER – Que Que, Zimbabwe. -w. Nov 1959-Sept 1964. 4 reels – 1 – uk British Libr Newspaper [072]
MIDLOTHIAN, 1837 : BRITISH ISLES CENSUS DIRECTORIES PROJECT, SCOTLAND. VOL 25 – 2mf – 9 – A$15.00 – at Vine [941]
MIDLOTHIAN, 1852 : BRITISH ISLES CENSUS DIRECTORIES PROJECT, SCOTLAND. VOL 16 – 2mf – 9 – A$15.00 – at Vine [941]
MIDLOTHIAN (EDINBURGH AND LEITH), 1804 : BRITISH ISLES CENSUS DIRECTORIES PROJECT, SCOTLAND – at Vine [941]
MIDLOTHIAN (EDINBURGH AND LEITH), 1805 : BRITISH ISLES CENSUS DIRECTORIES PROJECT, SCOTLAND. VOL 24 – 1mf – 9 – A$9.00 – at Vine [941]
MIDLOTHIAN (EDINBURGH AND LEITH), 1814 : BRITISH ISLES CENSUS DIRECTORIES PROJECT, SCOTLAND. VOL 7 – 3mf – 9 – A$21.00 – at Vine [941]
MIDLOTHIAN (EDINBURGH AND LEITH), 1823 : BRITISH ISLES CENSUS DIRECTORIES PROJECT, SCOTLAND – at Vine [941]
MIDLOTHIAN (EDINBURGH AND LEITH), 1878 : BRITISH ISLES CENSUS DIRECTORIES PROJECT, SCOTLAND – at Vine [941]
MIDLOTHIAN (EDINBURGH AND LEITH), 1890 : BRITISH ISLES CENSUS DIRECTORIES PROJECT, SCOTLAND – at Vine [941]
MIDLOTHIAN (EDINBURGH DIST), 1833 : BRITISH ISLES CENSUS DIRECTORIES PROJECT, SCOTLAND. VOL 4 – 4mf – 9 – A$27.00 – at Vine [941]
MIDLOTHIAN (EDINBURGH, LEITH AND DALKEITH), 1820 : BRITISH ISLES CENSUS DIRECTORIES PROJECT, SCOTLAND. VOL 58 – 2mf – 9 – A$15.00 – at Vine [941]
MIDLOTHIAN JOURNAL – Portobello, Scotland, UK. 1888-89. -w.1 reel – 1 – uk British Libr Newspaper [072]
MIDNIGHT SOFTWARE GAZETTE – (1986-. 1,5,6) – 1984- – 9 – us UMI [510]
MIDNIGHT SUN – Oak Hill. West Virginia. and Times. 1929-30 – 1 – us UMI [071]
MID-OCEAN NEWS – Hamilton, Bermuda. July 16 1993-1995 – 9r – 1 – us L of C Photodup [072]
MID-PENINSULA NEWS *see* THE PALO ALTO NEWS
MID-PLAN REVIEW EVALUATION OF PROGRESS DURING THE FIRST THREE YEARS OF THE SECOND FIVE-YEAR PLAN / Pakistan. Planning Commission – Karachi. 1964 – 9 – ne IDC [338]
MID-PLAN REVIEW OF PROGRESS IN 1960/61-1961/62 UNDER THE SECOND FIVE-YEAR PLAN / Pakistan. Planning Commission – Karachi. 1963. BD-459 1 – 9 – ne IDC [338]
DER MIDRACH ZUM I. BUCHE SAMUELIS UND SEINE SPUREN BEI KIRCHENVAETERN UND IN DER ORIENTALISCHEN SAGE. / Kellermann, Benzion – Frankfurt a.M. 1896. BJ-32-36 1 – 9 – ne IDC [470]
MIDRASCH TEHILLIM, ODER HAGGADISCHE ERKLAERUNG DER PSALMEN / Buber, S – 2v. Trier. 1892-93. BNE-20,029 1 – 9 – ne IDC [260]
DER MIDRASCH ZUM I. BUCHE SAMUELIS UND SEINE SPUREN BEI KIRCHENVAETERN / Kellermann, Benzion – Frankfurt a.M.: M.R. Golde, 1896. 1 fiche – 9 – us A.T.L.A. [270]
Mid-South Sociological Association *see* SOCIOLOGICAL SPECTRUM
MID-STATE NEWS – St. Paul, NE. -w. Aug 1971-Dec 1974 – 1 – us NE Hist [071]
MID-STREAM – v1- 1961- 1; v16- 5,6,9 – us UMI [240]
MIDSTREAM – (New York). 1955-60 – 1 – us A.J.P.C. [073]
A MIDSUMMER HOLIDAY AND OTHER POEMS / Swinburne, Algernon Charles – London: Chatto and Windus, 1884 – 1 roll – 1 – 1-55879-555-3 – uk Libr Preservation [810]
MID-SURREY STANDARD AND WIMBLEDON TIMES – London, 11 Dec 1880-24 Sep 1881 – 26ft – 1 – uk British Libr Newspaper [072]
MID-SUSSEX TIMES – Haywards Heath, England. 1881-1900; 1912; 1939-45; 1952; 1977- – 111+ r – 1 – uk British Libr Newspaper [072]
MID-TERM REVIEW OF THE FIRST MALAYSIA PLAN 1966-1970 / Malaysia – Kuala Lumpur. 1969 – 9 – ne IDC [338]
MID-TERM REVIEW OF THE SECOND MALAYSIA PLAN, 1971-1975 / Malaysia – Kuala-Lumpur. 1973. BD-1857 1 – 9 – ne IDC [338]
MID-TYNE OBSERVER – South Shields, England. Apr 1937-May 1939 – 1 1/2r – 1 – uk British Libr Newspaper [072]
MID-ULSTER MAIL – Cookstown, Ireland. 7 Feb 1891-1916; 1918-19; 1922- – 138+ r – 1 – uk British Libr Newspaper [072]
MIDWAY – v. 1-11. 1960-70 – 1 – us UMI [073]
MIDWAY BAPTIST CHURCH. PHENIX, VIRGINIA : CHURCH RECORDS – 1833, 1857, Aug 1866-Jul 1867 – 1 – 26.16 – us Baptist [240]
MIDWAY BAPTIST CHURCH. THOMASVILLE, ALABAMA : CHURCH RECORDS – Nov 1885-Jul 1927 – 1 – 13.59 – us Baptist [240]
MIDWAY BAPTIST CHURCH. WILLIAMSBURG COUNTY. SOUTH CAROLINA : CHURCH RECORDS – 1954-72 – 1 – 5.40 – us Baptist [240]
MIDWAY DRILLER – Taft. Calif. -w. 1910-13 – 1 – us UMI [071]
Midway Stock Ranch, Osborne County, KS *see* RECORD BOOK
MIDWEEK *see* MIDWEEK ADVERTISER
MIDWEEK ADVERTISER – Luton, England. 1980-81 – 3r – 1 – uk British Libr Newspaper [072]
THE MIDWEEK SUN – (Con by: Contra Costa Sun) – Lafayette, CA. 1970-80 – 18r – 1 – $900.00 – B02329 – us Library Micro [071]
THE MIDWEEK WORKER *see* THE WORKER : THE MIDWEEK WORKER
MIDWEST CITY LEADER – Oklahoma City. Okl. 1948-56 – 1 – us UMI [071]
A MIDWEST COOPERATIVE LIBRARY PROGRAM / McDiarmid, Errett Weir – Preliminary draft no.1. 1948 – 1 – us Res Libr [020]
Mid-west Debate Bureau *see* SUPREME COURT AND CONGRESS
MIDWEST ENGINEER – v1- 1948- 1; v25- 5,6; v28- 9 – us UMI [620]
MIDWEST FOLKLORE – Journal of the Folklore Institute. -q. v1, no.1-v13, no.4. Apr 1951-Winter 1964. 3 reels – 1 – us I.U. Libraries [390]
MIDWEST FREE PRESS – v. 1-3. 1930-33 – 1 – us UMI [073]
Midwest Inter-Library Center. Chicago *see*
- INVENTORY OF HOLDINGS OF CERTAIN CLASSES OF MATERIALS
- MANUAL OF PROCEDURES FOR PARTICIPATING LIBRARIES
- NEWSLETTER

Midwest Inter-Library Center. Chicago. Advisory Committee of Librarians *see* MINUTES OF MEETINGS
Midwest Inter-Library Center. Chicago. Board of Directors *see* MINUTES OF MEETINGS
Midwest Inter-Library Center. Chicago. Board of Directors. Executive Committee *see* MINUTES OF MEETINGS
A MIDWEST INTER-LIBRARY PROGRAM / McDiarmid, Errett Weir – Final draft. 1948 – 1 – us Res Libr [020]
A MIDWEST INTER-LIBRARY PROGRAM / McDiarmid, Errett Weir – Preliminary draft. no.2. 1948 – 1 – us Res Libr [020]
MIDWEST JOURNAL OF POLITICAL SCIENCE – (Continued as: American Journal of Political Science) – v1-16 1957-72 1; v15-16 5,6 – us UMI [320]
MIDWEST JOURNAL OF POLITICAL SCIENCE *see* AMERICAN JOURNAL OF POLITICAL SCIENCE
MIDWEST MESSENGER – Tekamah, NE. -bw. Apr-Dec 1974; Feb 1975 to date – 1 – us NE Hist [071]
MIDWEST QUARTERLY – v1- 1959- 1; v13- 1971- 5,6; v17- 9 – us UMI [073]
MIDWEST SOCIOLOGISTS FOR WOMEN IN SOCIETY NEWSLETTER – Summer 1977-Winter 1978. 2v. Other title: M-SWS Newsheet, 1975. Filmed with M-SWS Newsheet. Continued by: Tapestries – 1 – us U.W. Library [305]
MIDWEST TEACHERS SERVICE REGULATIONS 1971 / Nigeria. Mid-Western State – Benin City, 1971 – 1mf – 9 – DE-112/1 – ne IDC [370]
MIDWESTERN ARCHIVIST – (v4-. 1979- 5,6,9) – v1-. 1976- – 1 – us UMI [073]
"MIDWESTERN MAGNIFICENCE." / Menninger, Edwin A – 1 – us KS Hist [978]
MID-WESTERN NIGERIA DEVELOPMENT PLAN, 1964-68 / Nigeria. Mid-Western. Ministry of Internal Affairs – Benin City. 1965. BD-602 1 – 9 – ne IDC [338]
MID-WESTERN NIGERIA GAZETTE – Benin City. v2-4. 1965-67 – 1r – 1 – us Ross [324]
MIDWIFE – 1-2. 16 Oct 1750-53 – 1 – us UMI [073]
MIDWIFERY – v1- . 1985- – 1,5,6,9 – us UMI [618]
MIDWIVES CHRONICLE – v1- 1887- 1; v90- 5,6,9 – us UMI [618]
Mie d'Aghonne, J LA P *see* LA MAUDITE
Miebach, Peter *see* DIE KATECHESE IN DER ERZDIOEZESE KOELN UNTER DEN KURFUERSTEN MAX HEINRICH BIS MAX FRANZ. 1650-1801
MIECZ I PLUG – (Filmed with: Barykada) – [Poland], 1940-44 – 1r – 1 – $85.00 – us Ross [072]
MIECZ I PLUG *see* BARYKADA
MIEDZYNARODOWE PRAWO ZEGLUGI RZECZNEJ / Gasiorowski, M – Warszawa, 1923 – 2mf – 1 – ILM-2509/1 – ne IDC [327]
Miedzynarodowej Socyjalno-Rewolucyjnej Partyi *see* WALKA KLAS
Miege, Guy *see*
- THE ENGLISH GRAMMAR
- THE GROUNDS OF THE FRENCH TONGUE
- A NEW DICTIONARY FRENCH AND ENGLISH
- NOUVELLE METHODE POUR APPRENDRE L'ANGLOIS

Miegel, Agnes *see*
- DEUTSCHE BALLADEN
- GEDICHTE
- HERBSTGESANG
- MEIN BERNSTEINLAND UND MEINE STADT

Mielke, Adolf *see* SCHILLERS DEMETRIUS
Mielke, Manfred *see* WILLST DU DEIN RECHT, SO HILF DIR SELBST
Mier, Santiago *see* ORACION FUNEBRE...DON JUAN BALTASAR DE LOAYSA
Mierlo, J van *see*
- EEN PARAPHRASE VAN DE BRIEVEN VAN HADEWYCH DOOR HENDRIK MANDE
- UIT DE GESCHIEDENIS VAN ONZE MIDDELEEUWSE LETTERKUNDE

Miers *see* CONTRIBUTIONS TO BOTANY
Miers, J *see*
- CONTRIBUTIONS TO BOTANY
- ILLUSTRATIONS OF SOUTH AMERICAN PLANTS

Mies, Theodor *see* DIE AUFNAHMEN DER ALKOHOLPSYCHOSEN AN DER UNIV.-NERVENKLINIK IN FRANKFURT/MAIN FUER DIE JAHRE 1922-1950
LES MIETTES: DISTRACTIONS POETIQUES / Casgrain, Henri-Raymond – Quebec: P. Delisle, 1869. 02544. (Pre-1900 Canadiana) – 9 – cn C.I.H.M. [810]
Mietzner, Franz *see* DER KREIS SCHLOSSBERG
MIFFLINBURG TELEGRAPH – Mifflinburg, PA., 1862-1912 – 13 – $25.00r – us I.M.R. [071]
MIFOHA I MADAGASCAR – puis Ny Mifoha. Antananarivo. 7 juin 1907-14 oct 1909 – 1 – fr A.C.R.P.P. [073]
Mifsud, Frank M *see* CUSTOMARY LAND LAW IN AFRICA
MIGDAL HA-LEVANON ZOFEH PENEI YERUSHALAYIM – (Ha-Levanon, 14th Tammuz 5626). 1866. BJ-27-222 – 9 – ne IDC [270]
MIGDAL HA-LEVANON ZOFEH PENEI YERUSHALAYIM – (Ha-Levanon, 16th Sivan 5626). 1866. BJ-27-225 1 – 9 – ne IDC [270]
A MIGHTY ARMY / Felder, Vada P – 118p – 1 – 5.00 – us Baptist [240]
THE MIGHTY ATOM / Corelli, Marie – British Fiction Archive: Unit 1 – 9 – uk Bell [830]
MI-GINZEI YERUSHALAYIM / Grajewski, A L – Jerusalem. 1937. BJ-27-78 1 – 9 – ne IDC [956]
Migliore, F L del *see* FIRENZE CITTA NOBILISSIMA ILLUSTRATA
Mignat, Johannes *see* DER KREIS GOLDAP
Migne *see*
- PATROLOGIA GRAECA, VOL 166
- PATROLOGIA LATINA, VOL 221

Migne, J P *see* PATROLOGIAE
Migne, Jacques-Paul *see*
- PATROLOGIAE
- PATROLOGIAE CURSUS COMPLETUS
- QUARTI SAECULI...JUVENCI...OPERA OMNIA
- QUARTI...AURELII PRUDENTII

Mignet *see* EL EMPERADOR CARLOS V... YUSTE
Mignet, F A *see* THE HISTORY OF MARY, QUEEN OF SCOTS
Mignet, Mr *see* EL EMPERADOR CARLOS V
MIGNON : ORGAO CRITICO SOCIAL – Itacoatiara, Amazonas. 23 Maio 1915 – 1,5,6 – bl Biblioteca [072]
Mignon, A *see*
- LES ORIGINES DE LA SCOLASTIQUE ET HUGUES DE SAINT-VICTOR

Mignot, Claude *see* FRENCH ARCHITECTURAL WRITINGS: 16TH-19TH CENTURIES
Mignot, Eduoxe Irenee Edouard et al *see* THE METHOD OF THEOLOGY: AND OTHER ESSAYS
MIGRACIONES EN LA ARGENTINA : ESTUDIO DE LA MIGRACIONES INTERNAS E INTERNACIONALES, BASADO EN DATOS CENSALES, 1869-1960 / Recchini de Lattes, Zulma L – [Buenos Aires]: Centro de Investigaciones Sociales, Instituto Torcuato di Tella, [1969] – 1 – CSUXADQ3358-B – us Hoover Inst Photo [304]
MIGRATION AND EDUCATION IN PAPUA NEW GUINEA / Papua New Guinea. Manpower Planning Unit – Waigani, 1978 – 2mf – 9 – DE-234/1 – ne IDC [370]

MIGRATION AND RURAL DEVELOPMENT : SELECTED TOPICS FOR TEACHING AND RESEARCH – 1978 – 69p – it F.A.O. [304]

MIGRATION TO THE ARAB WORLD : EXPERIENCE OF RETURNING MIGRANTS / ed by Gunatilleke, Godfrey – 9 – $14.00 – 92-808-0745-5 – ja U.N. Univ [331]

MIGRATION TODAY – v1- 1973- 1; v5- 1977- 5,6,9 – us UMI [310]

MIGRATION TODAY – Switzerland. 1961-87 (complete) – 2r – 1 – ATLA S0870 – us A.T.L.A. [073]

MIGRATIONS ET DEVELOPPEMENT AGRICOLE DANS LE NORD DU SENEGAL (GUUTA TOORO) : 1954-1980 / Toure, El Hadj Seydou N – 2mf – 9 – 10519 – fr Atelier National [307]

Miguel Romero, Antonio *see* POESIAS VARIAS

Miguel Sanchez *see* DISCURSO...AUDIENCIA... CACERES. .Bl.-1838

Miguel y Guerra, Regino de *see*
– DISCURSO..."EL TRATAMIENTO ANTIPARASITO DE LA TUBERCULOSIS Y LA LINFA DE KOCH"
– DISCURSO...TRATAMIENTO...TUBERCULOSIS
– LA MEDICINA EN EL SIGLO 19

Miguens, Jose Enrique *see* JUAN PERON AND THE RESHAPING OF ARGENTINA

Migueta, Juan *see* BREVIARIO DE CIUDADANIA...

MIGUIRTINIA / Vecchi, Bernardo Valentino – Torino: Fratelli Bocca, 1933 – us Res Libr [072]

Migulin, P P *see* NOVYI EKONOMIST

Mihajlovic, Velimir *see* ARCHIVSKI FONDOMI U VOJVODINI

Mihri *see* MUHARRERAT-I RESMIYYE VE GAYRI RESMIYYE

MIHRIGAN – (Some issues missing) – Tehran. Sal-i 2, shumarah-i 1-Shumarah-i 134 (Farvardin 1314-Urdibihisht 1320 [Mar 1935-May 1941]) – 9 – $250.00 – us MEDOC [956]

Mije, Antonio *see*
– EL PAPEL DE LOS SINDICATOS EN LOS MOMENTOS ACTUALES
– LOS REFUGIADOS REPUBLICANOS ESPANOLES EN FRANCIA Y LA SOLIDARIDAD AMERICANA
– UNIDAD DE COMBATE Y VICTORIA

MIK. AFRIKANSKAIA POEMA / Gumilev, Nikolai Sepanovich – Ed. 2. Petrograd. 1922. BR-1145 2 – 8 – ne IDC [460]

O MIKADO : PERIODICO INNOCENTE, SUGGESTIVO, ALEGRE E PICANTE – Manaos, Amazonas. 14 Set-17 Out 1905 – 1,5,6 – bl Biblioteca [072]

MIKE FLETCHER : A NOVEL / Moore, George – London: Ward and Downey, c1889 – 1 roll – 1 – 1-55879-941-9 – uk Libr Preservation [830]

Mikell, William Ephraim *see* CASES ON CRIMINAL LAW

Mikhail, Kyriakos *see* COPTS AND MOSLEMS UNDER BRITISH CONTROL

Mikhailov, M *see* SBORNIK ISTORICHESKIKH MATERIALOV I DOKUMENTOV, OTNOSIASHCHIKHSIA K NOVOI RUSSKOI ISTORIIA XVIII I XIX VEKA

Mikhailovskii, BV *see* AKMEIZM

Mikhailovskii, N K *see* POLNOE SOBRANIE SOCHINENII

Mikhailovskoi Artilleriiskoi Akademii *see* SISTEMATICHESKII KATALOG BIBLIOTEKI MIKHAILOVSKOI ARTILLERIISKOI AKADEMII I UCHILISHCHA

Mikhailowitch, N *see* LES RAPPORTS DIPLOMATIQUES DE LEBZELTERN, MINISTRE D'AUTRICHE... (1816-1826)

Mikhel'son, M I *see* RUSSKAIA MYSL' I RECH. SVOE I CHUZHOE. OPYT ROSSKOI FRAZEOLOGII

Mikhov, N V *see* BIBLIOGRAFSKI ISTOCHNITSI ZA ISTORIIATA NA TURTSIIA I BALGARIIA

MIKHTAV GALUY LE-AHAD HA-AM / Pines, Y M – (Havazzelet. Jerusalem. 8th Tevet 5655). 1895. BJ-27-211 1 – 9 – ne IDC [270]

MIKHTAV LI-VENEI ZIYYON BE-ROHATYN / Pines, Y M – (Havazzelet, Jerusalem, 5655). 1895. BJ-27-210 1 – 9 – ne IDC [270]

MIKHTAV ME-HEVRON – (Ha-Levanon, 29th Shevat 5630). 1870. BJ-27-224 1 – 9 – ne IDC [270]

MIKHTAV MI-HEIFAH – (Ha-Maggid, Lyck, 29th Tevet 5635). 1874-75. BJ-27-217 1 – 9 – ne IDC [305]

MIKHTAV MI-YERUSHALAYIM / Avi-Yizhak – (Ha-Levanon, 21st Shevat 5636). 1876. BJ-27-221 1 – 9 – ne IDC [956]

MIKHTAV MI-YERUSHALAYIM / Neumann – (Allgemeine Zeitung des Judentums. nr. 33. 1853. BJ-27-239 1 – 9 – ne IDC [270]

MIKHTAV MI-YERUSHALAYIM / Rivlin, J – (Ha-Levanon, 18th Tevet 5634). 1873-74. BJ-27-226 1 – 9 – ne IDC [270]

MIKHTAV MI-YERUSHALAYIM / Sachs, M – (Ha-Maggid, Lyck, 3rd Shevat 5630). 1870. BJ-27-219 1 – 9 – ne IDC [305]

MIKHTAV MI-ZAREFAT / Ben-Yehuda, E – (Havazzelet, Jerusalem, 19th Av. 5639). 1879. BJ-27-208 1 – 9 – ne IDC [470]

MIKLAT – v. 1-5. New York. 1919-20. BJ-91-63 – 9 – ne IDC [270]

Miklosich, F *see*
– LEXICON PALAEOSLOVENICO-GRAECO-LATINUM
– MONUMENTA LINGUAE PALEOSLOVENICAE E CODICE SUPRASLIENSI VINDOBONAE
– VERGLEICHENDE GRAMMATIK DER SLAVISCHEN SPRACHEN

Miklukho-Maklai, N D *see* OPISANIE TADZHIKSHIKH I PERSIDSKIKH RUKOPISEI INSTITUTA VOSTOKOVEDENIIA

Miko, Eugenie *see* BIO-BIBLIOGRAPHIE ANALYTIQUE DE ROGER CHARTIER, DIRECTEUR DU PERSONNEL A L'HYDRO-QUEBEC, PROFESSEUR A LA FACULTE DES SCIENCES SOCIALES DE L'UNIVERSITE LAVAL

Mikov, V *see* PROIZKHOD I ZNACHENIE NA IMENATA NA NASHITE GRADOVE I SELA, REKI, PLANINI I MESTA

MIKROCHIMICA ACTA – 1923-81. Title varies. ISSN: 0026-3672 – 1,5,6,9,13 – 184.00v – us UMI [073]

MIKRODATORN – (1985-. 5,6,9) – 1978- – 1 – us UMI [510]

MIKROGEOLOGIE / Ehrenberg, CG – G-104 2. 1854 – 8 – ne IDC [550]

MIKROKOSMOS PARVUS MUNDUS – Antwerpen, 1589 – 2mf – 9 – O-3123/1 – ne IDC [760]

MIKROSKOPISCHE ABBILDUNGEN UND BESCHREIBUNGEN DER SPOREN DER EUROPAEISCHEN LICHENEN / Hepp, P – Zuerich. 1833-67. B-714 2 – 8 – ne IDC [580]

MIKROSKOPISCHE PHYSIOGRAPHIE DER MINERALIEN UND GESTEINE / Rosenbuch, C H F – 2525 2. 2 v. Ed. 2. 1885-1887 – 8 – ne IDC [550]

DAS MIKROTUBULI-ASSOZIIERTE PROTEIN TYP 4 (MAP 4) DES HAUSHUHNS : EIN NEUES MITGLIED DER MAP 4 – FAMILIE / Stassen, Michael – 1995 – 1mf – 9 – DM60.00 – 3-8267-2210-8 – gw Hänsel [574]

MIKROVOE KHOZI A ISTVO I IMPERIALIZM : EKONOMICHESKI I OCHERK / Bukharin, Nikolai Ivanovich – Moskva: Moskovski i rabochi i, 1927 – 1 – CSUX89-B3131 – us Hoover Inst Photo [330]

MIL NEUF CENT TRENTE-TROIS – puis trente-quatre; trente-cinq. Le magazine d'aujourd'hui. no. 1-95. Paris. 11 oct 1933-31 juil 1935. mq no. 72 – 1 – fr A.C.R.P.P. [073]

MIL Y CUATRO SONETOS / Sanchez-Arjona, Vicente – Sevilla: Imp. Carlos Acuna, 1955 – 1 – sp Bibl Santa Ana [810]

MIL Y TRES SONETOS / Sanchez-Arjona, Vicente – Sevilla: Imp. Carlos Acuna, 1954 – 1 – sp Bibl Santa Ana [810]

MIL Y UN SONETOS / Sanchez-Arjona, Vicente – Sevilla: Imp. Carlos Acuna, 1951 – 1 – sp Bibl Santa Ana [810]

MILAGROS DE FATIMA / Corredor Garcia, Antonio – Caceres: Ed. Cruzada Mariana, 1955 – 1 – sp Bibl Santa Ana [946]

MILAGROS EUCARISTICOS Y FLORES... / Corredor Garcia, Antonio – Madrid: Arch. Ibero Americano, 1965 – 1 – sp Bibl Santa Ana [240]

LA MILAGROSA EN EXTREMADURA – Badajoz, 1925. 3 numeros – 5 – sp Bibl Santa Ana [073]

MILAGROS...GUADALUPE / San Jose, Francisco de – Tomo II.1766 – 9 – 1.50f – sp Bibl Santa Ana [972]

MILAN LEDGER – Milan, Ohio. 1892-1968 – 17r – 1 – $32.50r – us Archival [071]

Milan. Ohio. First Presbyterian Church *see* RECORDS

Milan Preparative Meeting of Friends (Erie County, Ohio) *see* RECORDS

Milanesi, G M *see* LE VITE DE PIU ECCELLENTI PITTORI, SCULTORI ED ARCHITETTORI

MILANO FINANZA – 1992-1995 – 2r por y – 5,6 – Sfr428.00 – sz Infoprint [945]

MILAP – New Delhi, India. Apr 1949-1962; 1964-Jul 1994 – 113r – 1 – us L of C Photodup [072]

MILBANK MEMORIAL FUND QUARTERLY – v1-50 1923-72 1; v49-50 1971-71 5,6 – us UMI [610]

MILBANK MEMORIAL FUND QUARTERLY: HEALTH AND SOCIETY – (v.57-. 1973- 9) – v.57-. 1973- – 1,5,6 – us UMI [073]

Milburn, Benjamin Arrell *see*
– CURIOUS CASES
– CURIOUS CASES; A COLLECTION OF AMERICAN AND ENGLISH DECISIONS, SELECTED FOR THEIR READABILITY

Milburn, W *see* ORIENTAL COMMERCE

Milburn, William Henry *see*
– THE PIONEERS, PREACHERS AND PEOPLE OF THE MISSISSIPPI VALLEY
– THE RIFLE, AXE, AND SADDLE-BAGS, AND OTHER LECTURES
– TEN YEARS OF PREACHER-LIFE

MILBURN'S MAGAZINE – Toronto: [s.n., 1895?-189- or 19–] – 9 – cn C.I.H.M. [072]

Milch, Werner *see* SOPHIE LA ROCHE

MILD IRON DEFICIENCY AND HORMONAL ALTERATIONS DURING REST AND EXHAUSTIVE EXERCISE / Zinker, B A – 1990 – 2mf – 9 – $8.00 – us Microform Publ [612]

Mildbread, J *see* DIE AFRIKANISCHE ARTEN DER GATTUNG FICUS LINN

Milde, J *see*
– BRYOLOGIA SILESIACA
– DE SPORARUM EQUISETORUM GERMINATIONE
– FILICES EUROPAE ET ATLANTIDIS, ASIAE MINORIS ET SIBIRIAE
– MONOGRAPHIA EQUISETORUM
– MONOGRAPHIA GENERIS OSMUNDAE

MILDMAY : OR, THE STORY OF THE FIRST DEACONESS INSTITUTION / Cooke, Harriette J – 1893 – 1 – $50.00 – us Presbyterian [240]

THE MILDMAY CONFERENCE, 1882 : REPORT OF THE ADDRESSES, CORRECTED BY THE SPEAKERS – London: John F Shaw, [1882?] – 1mf – 9 – 0-8370-6337-X – 1986-0337 – us A.T.L.A. [240]

MILDMAY, THE DIARY OF LADY GRACE... – 1 – uk Microform Academic [920]

MILDRED ARKELL / Wood, Ellen – British Fiction Archive: Unit 1 – 9 – uk Bell [830]

MILDURA AND MERBEIN SUN – 1921. MMS1 – 1r – 1 – at Corangamite [072]

MILDURA TELEGRAPH – 1913-1920. MT1-8 – 8r – 1 – at Corangamite [072]

MI-LE CHOU-CHIH – 1739, 10-24. BCH-681 2 – 8 – ne IDC [950]

Miles *see*
– ALPHABETICAL LIST OF THE BOMBAY CIVIL SERVANTS, 1798-1839
– ALPHABETICAL LIST OF THE MADRAS CIVIL SERVANTS, 1780-1838
– ALPHABETICAL LIST OF THE OFFICERS OF THE INDIAN ARMY, 1760-1837

Miles, Clement A *see* CHRISTMAS IN RITUAL AND TRADITION, CHRISTIAN AND PAGAN

Miles, Perry *see* TEN HUMAN RIGHTS POINTS FROM THEIR 1971 WORK, A CONSTITUTION FOR A MORAL GOVERNMENT

Miles, S Daniel *see* THE ECUMENICAL RECONSTRUCTION OF CHRISTIANITY: AN EXPOSITION AND EVALUATION OF THE CHRISTOLOGY OF JOHN HICK

MILES TRANSIENS INNOXIUS,... / Fritsch, A – Jena, 1674 – 1mf – 1 – ILM-1119/1 – ne IDC [327]

Miles-Casman, Cecil Frank *see* SOCIALISM FOR SOUTH AFRICA

MILESTONES / Connecticut. College of Agriculture – v. 1-13, no. 2. 1953-70 – 1,5,6 – us Spaulding [630]

MILESTONES: A COLLECTION OF VERSES / Bannerman, Frances – London: G. Richards, 1899. 03363. (Pre-1900 Canadiana) – 9 – cn C.I.H.M. [810]

MILESTONES IN THE HISTORY OF THE GOLD COAST : AUTOBIOGRAPHY OF NII KWABENA BONNE 3, OSU ALATA MANTSE, ALSO NANA OWUSU AKTENTEN 3, OYOKOHENE OF TECHIMAN, ASHANTI / Nii Kwabena Bonne 3 – [London]: Diplomatist Press, [1953] – us Res Libr [920]

MILFORD 1732-1849 – (Mf 1T-2T: Marriages & Intents 1780-1828. Mf 2T-4T: Births 1732-1814. Mf 4T: Deaths 1766-1837. Mf 4T-6T: Marriages 1826-44. Mf 5T: Marriage Intentions 1831-49. Mf 6T-7T: Births 1765-1844. Mf 7T-8T: Deaths 1805-44. Mf 8T-10T: Births 1821-49. Mf 10T: Marriages 1843-49. Mf 11T: Deaths 1843-49. Mf 11T-12T: Births 1791-1853. Mf 12T: Out-of-Town Marriages 1755-1800) – (mf ed 1997) – 12mf – 9 – 0-87623-295-0 – us Holbrook [920]

MILFORD 1732-1900 – (Mf 1: Births 1732-1845 A-H. Mf 2: Births 1732-1845 H-W. Mf 3: Deaths 1753-1844. Mf 4-5: Marriages 1780-1844. Mf 6-9: Town Records 1777-98. Mf 9: Intentions 1780. Mf 10-17: Town Records 1798-1825. Mf 18-33: Town Records 1826-45. Mf 34-43: Town Records 1844-61. Mf 44-52: Assessments 1784-1885. Mf 53-54: Births 1826-49. Mf 54: Marriages 1843-49. Mf 54: Deaths 1843-50. Mf 55-57: Vitals 1783-1853. Mf 58-62: Deaths 1854-69. Mf 63-67: Deaths 1869-91. Mf 68-70: Deaths 1892-1902. Mf 71-75: Marriages 1853-71. Mf 76-80: Marriages 1871-98. 81-85: Births 1793-1866; 86-90: Births 1867-1889; Mf 91-93: Births 1889-1900. Mf 94-99: Births Index 1849-1909. Mf 100-103: Marr Index 1843-98. Mf 104-107: Death Index 1843-1907. Mf 108-112: Ints Index 1780-1900) – (mf ed 1993) – 112mf – 9 – us Holbrook [920]

MILFORD AND PIKE COMPANY DISPATCH – Milford, PA., 1955-1962 – 13 – $25.00r – us I.M.R. [071]

MILFORD BAPTIST CHURCH. GREENVILLE COUNTY. SOUTH CAROLINA : CHURCH RECORDS – 1869-January 1976 – 1 – $71.19 – us Baptist [240]

MILFORD DISPATCH – Milford, PA., 1889-1971 – 13 – $25.00r – us I.M.R. [071]

MILFORD MONITOR – Milford, NE. -w. (-sw 1886-87). Feb 1884-Jan 1901; Apr 1901-May 1902; Aug-Sep 1902; Apr 1903-Sep 1905; Apr 1906-Dec 1909 – 1 – us NE Hist [071]

MILFORD REVIEW – Milford, NE. -w. Oct 1911-Nov 1956; Jun 1961-May 1968 – 1 – us NE Hist [071]

MILFORD TIMES – Milford, NE. -w. Jul 1957 to date – 1 – us NE Hist [071]

Milhaud, Edgar *see* GOLDBURGFRIEDE U. INTERNATIONALES CLEARING

MILHEMET HA-YEHUDIM BA-MISSION MI-SHENAT 5584 AD HA-YOM HA-ZEH / Grajewski, P – Jerusalem. 1935. BJ-27-54 1 – 9 – ne IDC [270]

MILICE ET DEFENSE DU CANADA: DISCOURS PRONONCE DANS LA CHAMBRE DES COMMUNES LE 10 AVRIL 1883 / Caron, Adolphe – Ottawa: Maclean, Roger, 1883. 02819. (Pre-1900 Canadiana) – 9 – cn C.I.H.M. [971]

LA MILICE FRANCAISE, CONTENANT PLUSIEURS BELLES ET NOTABLES INSTRUCTIONS SUR CE QUI DOIT ETRE OBSERVE A BIEN ORDONNER DES BATAILLES / Montgommery, Louis de – Paris. 1636. Corrozet, 147p., table. (Strategy of War Series) – 9 – fr Hachette [355]

EL MILICIANO REMIGIO / Munoz, Jimenez, Francisco – Badajoz: Imprenta Vda. de Antonio Arqueros, 1939 – 1 – sp Bibl Santa Ana [820]

THE MILINDAPANHO / Trenckner, V – (The Pali Text). 1928 – 1 – uk Microform Academic [280]

MILITAERGESCHICHTE – 1962-1989 – 473mf – 1 – DM2,696.10 – gw Mikro Press [350]

MILITAERISCHE SCHRIFTEN / Scharnhorst, Gerhard Johann David von – Berlin. F. Schneider. 1881. xxv, 340p. (Strategy of War Series) – 9 – fr Hachette [355]

MILITAERWESEN – 1957-1989 – 1,079mf – 1 – DM6,150.30 – gw Mikro Press [350]

MILITAER-WOCHENBLATT – Berlin. Germany. v. 76-102. Jan. 1891-Dec. 1917. Supplements: Militaer-Literatur zeitung. v. 72-V. 91, no. 22. Jan. 1891-Dec. 1913. Beihefte 1871-1914 – 1 – 35.00r – us Hoover Inst Photo [072]

MILITAIR TIJDSCHRIFT – (Continues as: Indisch Militair Tijdschrift. Batavia, 1878-1924. Index 1870-1903: Lacking: 1906(1)) – Batavia, 1870-1877 – 804mf – 9 – ne IDC [350]

LE MILITAIRE PHILOSOPHE OU DIFFICULTES SUR LA RELIGION PROPOSEES AU R.P. MALEBRANCHE, PRETRE DE L'ORATOIRE / Holbach, Paul-Thiry d' & Naigeon, Jacques-Andre – (D'Holbach series). 1768 – 9 – fr Hachette [190]

LE MILITANT – Organe de defense proletarienne et de combat marxiste. no. 1-16. Saigon. sept 1936-juin 1937 – 1 – fr A.C.R.P.P. [073]

MILITANT / Communist League of America – 1-7 2+48 (all publ). 1928-34 – 1 reel – 1 – $115.00 – us UPA [335]

MILITANT – NY City, NY. 1972-1981 – 18r – 1 – $900.00 – R04926 – us Library Micro [071]
THE MILITANT – New York. N.Y. 1959-1966 – 1 – us UMI [071]
THE MILITANT ATHEIST – (Library has: v.1, no.1-v.1, no.8 (Jan.-Aug. 1933)) – Girard, Kan.: Haldeman-Julius Publications, 1933- – 1 – CSUX89-S103 – us Hoover Inst Photo [210]
MILITANT TENDENCY *see* THE LEFT IN BRITAIN, PART 1
MILITARES EXTREMENOS / Solar y Taboada, Antonio – Badajoz: La Minerva – 1 – sp Bibl Santa Ana [350]
MILITARIS ORDINIS IOHANNITARVM RHODIORVM, AVT MELITENSIVM EQVITVM, ... / Pantaleon, H – Basilea, 1581 – 8mf – 9 – H-8360/1 – ne IDC [956]
MILITARREGIERUNG IN ARGENTINIEN : DAS POLITISCHE SYSTEM DER ARGENTINISCHEN REVOLUTION / Evers, Tilman Tonnies – Frankfurt am Main: In Kommission bei A. Metzner, 1972 – 1 – CSUXADH4125-B – us Hoover Inst Photo [320]
MILITARY (1776-79) TRANSACTIONS OF MAJOR, AFTERWARDS COLONEL, 8TH OR KING'S FOOT, ARENT SCHUYLER DE PEYSTER / De Peyster, John Watts – s.l.: s.n., 18??). 04051. (Pre-1900 Canadiana) – 9 – cn C.I.H.M. [971]
MILITARY AMUSEMENT – A collection of 24 of the most favorite marches.Adapted for one or two German flutes, fifes, or oboes, &c. Philadelphia: B. Carr, 1796. Music-123, Item 6; Music-1467, Item 2 – 1 – us L of C Photodup [780]
MILITARY AND NAVAL MAGAZINE OF THE UNITED STATES – v. 1-6. March 1833-February 1836 – 1 – us UMI [355]
MILITARY ANTIQUITIES OF THE ROMANS IN BRITAIN / Roy, W – H 1138 2. 1793 – 8 – ne IDC [941]
MILITARY ARCHITECTURE IN ENGLAND DURING THE MIDDLE AGES / Hamilton Thompson, A – H-1196 2. 1912 – 8 – ne IDC [355]
MILITARY BAND MUSIC / Stratton, John F – New York: John F. Stratton, 1866-1871. Music for brass band, 141 numbers in score, 12 in parts. Title list available on request. MUSIC 1981 – 1 – us L of C Photodup [780]
MILITARY CAMPAIGNS OF CHINA: 1924-1950 / U.S. Office of the Chief of Military History – 1966 – 1 – 18.00 – us L of C Photodup [950]
MILITARY CENSUS, 1861-1862 / Illinois. Military Records – List of all males 18 to 45 arranged by county. V124-0001 and 0002 – 1 – us A.G.L.L. [920]
MILITARY CENSUS, 1862-1863 / Illinois. Military Records – List of all males, 18 to 45 arranged by county. V124-0003 to 0021 – 1 – us A.G.L.L. [920]
MILITARY COLLECTOR AND HISTORIAN – v1-1949- 1; v22- 5,6; v28- 9 – us UMI [355]
MILITARY COMMISSIONS FOR THE TRIAL OF CITIZENS / James, John Henry – Cincinnati, Clarke, 1869. 16 p. LL-1703 – 1 – us L of C Photodup [340]
MILITARY DISCHARGE INDEX / Putnam County. Ohio. Recorder – 1945-1955 – 1r – 1 – $32.50r – us Archival [324]
THE MILITARY ENCYCLOPEDIA = VOENNAIA ENTSIKLOPEDIIA / ed by Velichko, K et al – Moscow: I Sytin Publ. v1-18. 1911-15 – 166mf 156 bw + 10 colour mf – 9,15 – $990.00 – us Ross [355]
MILITARY ENGINEER : JOURNAL OF THE SOCIETY OF AMERICAN MILITARY ENGINEERS / Society of American Military Engineers – v1-53 1909-61 – 1 – $765.00 – us L of C Photodup [623]
MILITARY ENGINEER : JOURNAL OF THE SOCIETY OF AMERICAN MILITARY ENGINEERS / Society of American Military Engineers – v34-39. 1942-1947 – 1,5,6 – us Princeton Micro [623]
MILITARY EXPEDITIONS 1695-1763 / Great Britain. State Papers – SP 87 – 21r – 1 – us Ross [355]
MILITARY GAZETTE = GAZETTE MILITAIRE – Quebec, Canada. n33. 29 aut 1857-v2 n35. 20 oct 1858 – 1r – 1 – Can$30.00 – cn Can Microfilming [072]
THE MILITARY GAZETTE – (1885-94 3r. 1895-1948 19r) – Canada, 1885-1948 – 22r – 1 – Can$65.00r – cn Commonwealth Micro [355]
MILITARY IMAGES MAGAZINE – v.1-. 1979- – 1,5,6,9 – us UMI [073]
MILITARY INTELLIGENCE – (v.5-. 1979-5,6,9) – v.3-. 1977- – 1 – us UMI [073]
MILITARY INTELLIGENCE IN THE PACIFIC, 1942-1946 : BULLETINS OF THE INTELLIGENCE CENTER, PACIFIC OCEAN AREA, AND THE JOINT INTELLIGENCE CENTER, PACIFIC OCEAN AREA – (Guide also sold separately: $10.00) – 1984 – 41 rolls – 9 – $3,075.00 – Dist. us Scholarly Res – Published in cooperation with the U.S. Naval Historical Center – us L of C Photodup [355]
MILITARY INTELLIGENCE IN THE PACIFIC, 1942-46 / U.S. Navy. Pacific Ocean Area. Intelligence Center – (With printed guide) – 1984 – 41r – 1 – $3,485.00 – S1661 – us Scholarly Res [355]
MILITARY JUSTICE : JOINT HEARINGS OF THE COMMITTEES ON THE JUDICIARY AND ARMED SERVICES, U.S. SENATE – (Pt 3 added to coll in 1996) – 89th Congress, 2nd session, Jan 18-19, 25-26 & Mar 1-3, 1966, Pt 3 Appendix B. Washington: GPO, 1966 – 3mf – 9 – $4.50 – LLMC 88-054B – us L.L.M.C. [340]
THE MILITARY JUSTICE ACT OF 1982 : HEARINGS BEFORE THE SUBCOMMITTEE ON MANPOWER AND PERSONNEL OF THE COMMITTEE ON ARMED SERVICES, SENATE. 97TH CONGRESS, 2ND SESSION, SEPTEMBER 9 AND 16 1982, ON S. 2521 TO AMEND (UCMJ) TO IMPROVE THE MILITARY JUSTICE SYSTEM... – Washington: GPO, 1983 – 3mf – 9 – $4.50 – LLMC 96-089 – us L.L.M.C. [340]
MILITARY JUSTICE ACT OF 1983 : REPORT FROM THE CHAIRMAN OF THE COMMITTEE ON ARMED SERVICES – 98th Congress, 1st session, House of Rep. report no 98-549. n.p. (Washington: GPO?) 1982? – 1mf – 9 – $1.50 – LLMC 96-081 – us L.L.M.C. [340]
MILITARY JUSTICE ACT OF 1983 : REPORT FROM THE CHAIRMAN OF THE COMMITTEE ON ARMED SERVICES – 98th Congress, 1st session, Senate report no 98-53. n.p. (Washington: GPO?) 1982? – 1mf – 9 – $1.50 – LLMC 96-082 – us L.L.M.C. [340]
MILITARY JUSTICE AMENDMENTS OF 1981 : REPORT FROM THE CHAIRMAN OF THE COMMITTEE ON ARMED SERVICES – 97th Congress, 1st session, House of Rep. report no 97-306. n.p. (Washington: GPO?) 1981? – 1mf – 9 – $1.50 – LLMC 96-083 – us L.L.M.C. [340]
MILITARY JUSTICE REPORTER *see* COURT-MARTIAL REPORTS
MILITARY LAW AUTHORITIES / Hough, William – Calcutta/London: Thacker & Co/ Allen & Co, 1839 – 3mf – 9 – $4.50 – LLMC 89-034 – us L.L.M.C. [340]
MILITARY LAW COLLECTION *see*
- THE ADVOCATE
- AIR FORCE LAW REVIEW
- AIR UNIVERSITY REVIEW
- THE ARMY LAWYER
- CONSCRIPTION NEWS
- THE JUDGE ADVOCATE JOURNAL
- MILITARY LAW REVIEW
- PENSION AND BOUNTY-LAND CLAIMS DECISIONS
- SEMIANNUAL REPORT OF THE DIRECTOR OF THE SELECTIVE SERVICE SYSTEM

THE MILITARY LAW OF ENGLAND : WITH ALL THE RPINCIPAL AUTHORITIES, ADAPTED TO THE GENERAL USE OF THE ARMY, IN ITS VARIOUS DUTIES AND RELATIONS, AND THE PRACTICE OF COURTS MARTIAL / Scott, Robert – (Index included) – London: T Goddard, 1810 – 5mf – 9 – $7.50 – LLMC 88-030 – us L.L.M.C. [340]
MILITARY LAW REVIEW – 1958- 1; v51- 5,6; v67- 9 – us UMI [355]
MILITARY LAW REVIEW / U.S. Army – (Offered as part of LLMC's Military Law Collection. Updates planned) – Dept of Defense. v1-146. 1958-Fall 1994 – 401mf – 9 – $601.00 – LLMC 80-020 – us L.L.M.C. [073]
MILITARY MAGAZINE – v. 1-3. Mar 1839-Jun 1842 – 1 – us UMI [073]
MILITARY MEDICINE – (v.144- 1979- 5,6,9) – v.116- 1955- – 1 – us UMI [610]
MILITARY MONITOR AND AMERICAN REGISTER – New York, NY. 1812-14. Also: The War, 1812-17.Sold as one unit – 3 – us Readex [975]
MILITARY MONITOR AND AMERICAN REGISTER – v. 1-2. 17 Aug 1812-2 Apr 1814 – 1 – us UMI [975]
MILITARY MONOGRAPH ON SIBERIA / U.S. War Department. General Staff – v. 1-2. 1918 – 1 – 26.00 – us L of C Photodup [947]
MILITARY OPERATIONS AT QUEBEC: FROM THE CAPITULATION BY DE RAMEZAY, ON THE 18TH SEPTEMBER, 1759 TO THE RAISING OF THE SIEGE BY DE LEVIS, BETWEEN THE NIGHT OF THE 17TH AND THE MORNING OF THE 18TH MAY, 1760 / Anderson, William James – Quebec: Middleton & Dawson. 00801. (Pre-1900 Canadiana) – 9 – cn C.I.H.M. [971]
MILITARY OPERATIONS OF THE CIVIL WAR: A GUIDE INDEX TO THE OFFICIAL RECORDS OF THE UNION AND CONFEDERATE ARMIES, 1861-1865, VOL. 1 / U.S. War Department – 1 – M1036 – us Nat'l Archives [324]
MILITARY POLICE LAW ENFORCEMENT JOURNAL – v1- 1973- 1; v3- 5,6,9 – us UMI [073]
MILITARY RECORDS / Confederate States of America. Army – 1861-65. 32 fiches – 9 – us South Carolina Historical [976]
MILITARY RECORDS / Inman, Henry – undated, Enlistment papers and military service records – 1 – us KS Hist [350]
MILITARY RECORDS OF SCHOHARIE COUNTY VETERANS OF FOUR WARS / Warner, George H – Albany: Weed, Parsons, and Co., 1891. New York Reel 33. (The Cox Library Collection) – 5 – us Americana [978]
MILITARY REGISTER – London. -w. 30 Mar 1814-11 Apr 1821. (6 reels) – 1 – uk British Libr Newspaper [072]
MILITARY RELIEF JOURNAL / Hardin County. Ohio. Pleasant Township. Board of Trustees – 1863-1867 – 1r – 1 – $32.50r – us Archival [324]
THE MILITARY RELIGIOUS ORDERS OF THE MIDDLE AGES : THE HOSPITALLERS, THE TEMPLARS, THE TEUTONIC KNIGHTS, AND OTHERS: WITH AN APPENDIX OF OTHER ORDERS OF KNIGHTHOOD: LEGENDARY, HONORARY, AND MODERN / Woodhouse, F C – London: S.P.C.K.; New York: Pott, Young, 1879 – 1mf – us A.T.L.A. [350]
MILITARY REMINISCENCES OF THE CIVIL WAR. VOL. 1. APRIL 1861-NOVEMBER 1863 / Cox, Jacob Dolson – New york: C. Scribner's, 1900. 05269. (Pre-1900 Canadiana) – 9 – cn C.I.H.M. [971]
MILITARY REMINISCENCES OF THE CIVIL WAR. VOL. 2. NOVEMBER 1863-JUNE 1865 / Cox, Jacob Dolson – New York: C. Scribner's, 1900. 05270. (Pre-1900 Canadiana) – 9 – cn C.I.H.M. [971]
MILITARY REPORT ON SOMALILAND, 1907 / Great Britain. War Office. Intelligence Division – London: HMSO. v1 [1907] – us Res Libr [355]
MILITARY REPORT ON THE GOLD COAST, ASHANTI AND THE NORTHERN TERRITORIES / Great Britain. War Office. General Staff – London: HMSO, 1912 – us Res Libr [355]
MILITARY REVIEW – 1922-63 – 1 – 563.00 – us L of C Photodup [355]
MILITARY REVIEW – (v. 51- 1971- 5,6. v. 55- 1975- 9) – v. 1- 1922- – 1 – us UMI [355]
MILITARY SERVICE AND THE LAW; A BIBLIOGRAPHY / McCarthy, Betty Anne – Sacramento, California State Library, Law Library, 1969. 5 p. LL-2283 – 1 – us L of C Photodup [340]
Military Service Institution of the United States *see* JOURNAL
THE MILITARY SITUATION IN SPAIN AFTER TERUEL / Charlton, Lionel Evelyn Oswald – London, 1938. Fiche W 792-793. (Blodgett Collection of Spanish Civil War Pamphlets) – 9 – us H.U. College Libr [946]
THE MILITARY SITUATION IN THE FAR EAST AND THE RELIEF OF GENERAL DOUGLAS MACARTHUR / U.S. Congress. Senate Joint Committee on Armed Services and Foreign Relations – v1-45. 1951 – 1 – $770.00 – 0-89093-103-8 – us UPA [950]
MILITARY SPACE ELECTRONICS DESIGN – v1-. 1984- – 1,5,6,9 – us UMI [073]
MILITARY SPECIFICATION LIBRARIES – (AN, AND, MS, NAS. One-year subscription service and monthly updates) – 9 – $650.00. Annual revision ca $405.00 – us Aircraft Tech [629]
MILITARY SURGEON – v.20-115. 1907-54. Continued by: Military Medicine – 1 – us UMI [610]
MILITARY TOPICS – Toronto: Military Pub. Co, [1900-19–] – 9 – cn C.I.H.M. [355]
Military-Scientific Directorate of the Soviet General Staff *see* BOEVOI SOSTAV SOVETSKOI ARMII
MILITARY/U.S. FEDERAL GOVERNMENT SPECIFICATIONS, STANDARDS AND REGULATIONS – 6,9 – us Info Handling [355]
MILITIA AND VOLUNTEER SERVICE GAZETTE – Quebec: R Davis, [1862?-18–?] – 9 – cn C.I.H.M. [355]
MILITIA CHRISTI : DIE CHRISTLICHE RELIGION UND DER SOLDATENSTAND IN DEN ERSTEN DREI JAHRHUNDERTEN / Harnack, Adolf von – Tuebingen: J.C.B. Mohr, 1905 – 1mf – us A.T.L.A. [240]
MILITIA CHRISTI – (Lacking: 1967. Cont by and filmed with: Kerk en Vrede) – v17-37. 1962-88 – Inquire – 1 – ATLA S0376 – us A.T.L.A. [073]
MILITIA CHRISTI *see* KERK EN VREDE
MILITIA RECORDS, MISCELLANEOUS / Ottawa County. Ohio. Auditor – 1862-1877 – 1r – 1 – $32.50r – us Archival [324]
MILITIA REPORTER – v. 1. 1810 – 1 – us UMI [355]
MILITIA ROLL / Wood County. Ohio. Auditor – 1864 – 1r – 1 – $32.50r – us Archival [324]
MILITIA ROLLS / Defiance County. Ohio. Auditor – 1845-1871 – 1r – 1 – $32.50 – us Archival [324]
MILITIA ROLLS / Fulton County. Ohio. Auditor – 1864 – 1r – 1 – $32.50r – us Archival [324]
MILITIA ROLLS / Hancock County. Ohio. Auditor – 1865 – 1r – 1 – $32.50r – us Archival [324]
MILITIA ROLLS AND ENUMERATIONS / Williams County. Ohio. Auditor – 1858-1877 – 2r – 1 – $32.50r – us Archival [324]
Miliukov, P N *see* GOSUDARSTVENNOE KHOZIAISTVO ROSSII V PERVOI CHETVERTI XVIII STOLETIIA I REFORMA PETRA VELIKOGO
Miliutin, V *see*
- BLIZHAISHIE EKONOMICHESKIE ZADACHI
- KOOPERATSIIA V DEREVNE

Miliutin, VP *see* SOVREMENNAIA KOOPERATSIIA I EE ZADACHI
MILJOEMAGASINET – Stockholm, 1992- – 9 – sw Kungliga [072]
MILK AND DAIRY PRODUCTS : PRODUCTION AND PROCESSING COSTS – 1988 – 120p – it F.A.O. [338]
MILK AND MILK PRODUCTS : TERMINOLOGY – 1980 – 127p – it F.A.O. [636]
MILK AND MILK PRODUCTS IN HUMAN NUTRITION / Kon, SK – 2nd rev ed 1972 repr 1975 – 80p – it F.A.O. [640]
MILK PROCESSING TECHNIQUES : SOUR MILK / O'Connor, C B & Tripathi, B R – 1992 – 9 – $6.00 – 92-9053-229-7 – et ILRI [630]
MILK RIVER REVIEW – Alberta, CN. 1948-61 – 2r – 1 – cn Commonwealth Micro [072]
MILKING, MILK PRODUCTION HYGIENE AND UDDER HEALTH – 1989 – 125p – it F.A.O. [636]
Milkowski, Zygmunt *see* "OPOWIADANIE Z WEDROWKI PO KOLONIACH POLSKICH W AMERYCE POLONCNEJ"
MILL CITY ENTERPRISE – Mill City, OR. -w. 25 Nov 1948-. – 1 – us U.O. Library [071]
MILL CITY LOGUE – Mill City, OR. -w. 26 Aug 1926-25 May 1933. 2 rolls – 1 – us U.O. Library [071]
MILL CREEK BAPTIST CHURCH. BEULAH ASSOCIATION. NORTH CAROLINA : CHURCH RECORDS – Beulah Association. Person County. North Carolina. Mill Creek Baptist Church – 1 – 31.50 – us Baptist [240]
MILL CREEK BAPTIST CHURCH. BRUNSWICK ASSOCIATION. NORTH CAROLINA : CHURCH RECORDS – 1818-48 – 1 – 5.00 – us Baptist [240]
MILL HILL – Roosendaal: St Joseph's Missiehuis. v46 n4-v48 n12. aug 1935-apr 1938 – us Res Libr [960]
Mill, James *see* ELEMENTS OF POLITICAL ECONOMY
Mill, John Stuart *see*
- INAUGURAL ADDRESS
- NATURE
- NATURE, THE UTILITY OF RELIGION, AND THEISM
- ON LIBERTY
- PRINCIPLES OF POLITICAL ECONOMY

- SOCIALISM
- A SYSTEM OF LOGIC, RATIOCINATIVE AND INDUCTIVE

MILL VALLEY HERALD – Mill Valley, CA. 1990 – 4+ r – 1 – $100.00 ($50.00y) – B06038 – us Library Micro [071]

Mill, William Hodge *see* OBSERVATIONS ON THE ATTEMPTED APPLICATION OF PANTHEISTIC PRINCIPLES... TO GOSPEL

Millar, Clive *see* THE CONTEMPORARY SOUTH AFRICAN SHORT STORY IN ENGLISH WITH SPECIAL REFERENCES TO THE WORK OF NADINE GORDIMER, DORIS LESSING, ALAN PATON, JACK COPE, UYS KRIGE AND DAN JACOBSON

Millard, Bailey *see* THE SAN FRANCISCO BAY REGION

Millard, Benjamin Albert *see* THE QUEST OF THE INFINITE

MILLARD COURIER – Millard, NE. -w. Oct 1897; Aug 1905; Jul 1914-Jul 1918 – 1 – us NE Hist [071]

MILLARD FILLMORE PAPERS / ed by Smith, Lester W – 68r – 1 – $1,500.00 set $25.00r – us Buffalo [977]

Millard, Linda *see*
- A COMPARISON OF VALUED OUTCOMES OF YOUTH SPORT PROGRAMS
- GENDER DIFFERENCES IN OVERT COACHING BEHAVIORS OF HIGH SCHOOL SOCCER COACHES

MILLARD MERCURY – Papillion, NE. -w. Nov 1951-Nov 1955 – 1 – us NE Hist [071]

MILLARD'S REVIEW 1917-1953 – 1993 – 30r – 1 – $1.800,00 – Dist. + cc China Nat'l, Shanghai – cc Haifu Micro [950]

MILLAT-I BIDAR – (Dawrah-'i 1, shumarah-'i 1-Dawrah-'i 4, shumarah-'i 12 (Mihr 1360-Azar 1365[Oct 1981-Nov/Dec 1986]). Missing issues: Dawrah-'i 1: shumarah-'i 9-12; Dawrah-'i 2: shumarah-'i 3, 6, 8-12; Dawrah-'i 3: shumarah-'i 1-5, 7; dawrah-'i 4: shumarah-'i 1-4, 6) – Beverly Hills, CA: Melli Publishing House, Inc. – 1 reel – 1 – $50.00 – us MEDOC [950]

MILLBRAE SUN – Millbrae, CA. 1961- – 41+ r – 1 – $2,050.00 ($90.00y) – B02457 – us Library Micro [071]

MILLBROOK BAPTIST CHURCH. AIKEN, SOUTH CAROLINA : CHURCH RECORDS – 1935-68 – 1 – 30.60 – us Baptist [240]

MILLBURY 1761-1849 – (Mf 1T: Births 1790-1843 A-N. Mf 2T: Births 1761-1843 M-W,C,S. Mf 2T-3T: Marriage Intents 1813-35. Mf 3T-4T: Marriages 1813-35. Mf 4T: Births 1826-45 W,C,S,G,H; Deaths 1796-1843 A-Y. Mf 5T: Marriages 1832-43. Mf 5T-6T: Marriage Intents 1835-49. Mf 7T: Births 1843-49. Mf 7T-8T: Marriages 1843-49. Mf 8T: Deaths 1843-49) – (mf ed 1997) – 8mf – 9 – 0-87623-296-9 – us Holbrook [920]

MILLBURY 1761-1899 – (Mf 1-6: Town Records 1813-35. Mf 7-15: Town Records 1836-62. Mf 16-17: School Recs 1813-36. Mf 18-23: Town Account 1840-89. Mf 24-25: Civil War 1861-65. Mf 26-28: GAR Sketches 1861-65. Mf 29-32: Vital Record 1761-1844. Mf 32-42: Intentions 1835-1917. Mf 43-46: Vital Record 1843-65. Mf 47-51: Births 1866-99. Mf 52-56: Marriages 1853-99. Mf 57-60: Deaths 1861-99. Mf 61-64: Death Index 1843-99. Mf 65-69: Marr Index 1843-99. Mf 70-75: Birth Index 1843-99) – (mf ed 1992) – 75mf – 9 – us Holbrook [920]

Millbury. Ohio.St. Peter's United Church of Christ *see* RECORDS

LES MILLE ET UNE NUITS D'UNE AMBASSADRICE DE LOUIS XIV / Maulde La Claviere, Marie Alphonse Rene de – Paris: Hachette, 1896. 252p. 3 fiches.(Les Femmes Collection). (Historical Studies Series) – 9 – $8.00 – fr Bibl Nationale [900]

MILLE HUIT-CENT TRENTE-TROIS – ou L'Annee de la Mere. Mission de l'Est. Redige par Collin, Roge, Marechal, et al. Toulon, impr. de Canquoin, 1833, 63 p. Les Saint-Simoniens, 1825-1834. 6940 – 9 – fr Hachette [335]

Mille, Pierre *see* AU CONGO BELGE

Mille y Suarez, E *see* CONGRESO INTERNACIONAL DE BRUSELAS (1888)

MILLEDGEVILLE REPUBLICAN – Milledgeville. Ga. 1816. and yReflector. 1817-19. Sold as one unit – 1,3 – us Readex [071]

MILLENIAL HARBINGER AND BIBLE ADVOCATE – 3sv. 1-27. 1844-1857 – 1 – us UMI [240]

MILLENIUM: A JOURNAL OF INTERNATIONAL STUDIES – 1971- – 1,5,6,9 – us UMI [320]

MILLENNIAL HARBINGER – Non-Baptist periodical. 1830-70 – 1 – $955.08 – us Baptist [240]

Miller *see*
- PAST AND PRESENT OF O'BRIEN AND OSCEOLA COUNTIES
- WEST VIRGINIA AND ITS PEOPLE

Miller, Andrew *see* THE PROBLEM OF THEOLOGY IN MODERN LIFE AND THOUGHT

Miller, Arthur R *see*
- ATTORNEYS' FEES IN CLASS ACTIONS
- THE AUGUST 1983 AMENDMENTS TO THE FEDERAL RULES OF CIVIL PROCEDURE

Miller Brothers Hardware Company, Onaga, KS *see* LEDGERS

Miller, Carol J *see* SELF-CONCEPT AS A PREDICTOR OF LEISURE BEHAVIOR

Miller, Charles C *see*
- HISTORY OF ALLEN COUNTY
- HISTORY OF FAIRFIELD COUNTY AND REPRESENTATIVE CITIZENS

MILLER, CHAS. G., SCRAPBOOKS, NO. 112 – 1907 – 2r – 1 – us Western Res [350]

Miller, D C *see* PREDICTING EFFECTS OF POWER PLANT ONCE-THROUGH COOLING ON AQUATIC SYSTEMS

Miller, David Hunter *see*
- THE ALASKA TREATY
- MILLER'S TREATIES

Miller, David L *see* COMPETITION, EXERCISE, PROVOCATION, AND VERBAL COMMENTS: INFLUENCES ON ATTRIBUTIONS AND AGGRESSION?

Miller, Edgar George, Jr *see* NOTES ON TITLES.

Miller, Edward *see* A SELECTION FROM THE PSALMS OF DAVID

Miller, Flora *see* AN INFORMAL RECORD OF MISSIONARY SERVICE IN THE ISLAND OF TONGOA AND THE SHEPHERD ISLANDS, 1941-1947

MILLER FORUM – Miller, NE. -w. Oct 1898-Aug 1911 – 1 – us NE Hist [071]

Miller, G S *see* THE FAMILIES AND GENERA OF BATS

Miller Gamble, WT *see* MONUMENTA GERMANIAE HISTORICA

MILLER GAZETTE – Miller, NE. -w. Dec 1897-Sep 1900 – 1 – us NE Hist [071]

Miller, George, Jr *see* THE TRIAL OF FRANK JAMES FOR MURDER

Miller, George Noyes *see* HOME-TALKS

Miller, J Graham *see* AN INFORMAL RECORD OF MISSIONARY SERVICE IN THE ISLAND OF TONGOA AND THE SHEPHERD ISLANDS, 1941-1947

Miller, J S *see* A NATURAL HISTORY OF THE CRINOIDEA

Miller, James H *see* HISTORY OF SUMMERS COUNTY

Miller, James R *see* WOMEN'S MINISTRY AND OTHER PAPERS

Miller, James Russell *see*
- THE BUILDING OF CHARACTER
- BY THE STILL WATERS
- THE EVERY DAY OF LIFE
- FINDING THE WAY
- FOR THE BEST THINGS
- THE JOY OF SERVICE
- THE LESSON OF LOVE
- LIFE'S BYWAYS AND WAYSIDES
- THE MASTER'S FRIENDSHIPS
- PERSONAL FRIENDSHIPS OF JESUS
- STRENGTH AND BEAUTY
- WEEK-DAY RELIGION
- WHEN THE SONG BEGINS
- YOUNG MEN

Miller, Joan Wilson *see* THE OZARK CULTURE REGION REVEALED BY TRADITIONAL MATERIALS

Miller, John *see*
- THE DIVINE AUTHORITY OF HOLY SCRIPTURE ASSERTED, FROM ITS ADAPTATION TO THE REAL STATE OF HUMAN NATURE IN EIGHT SERMONS PREACHED BEFORE THE UNIVERSITY OF OXFORD IN THE YEAR MDCCCXVII
- FETICH IN THEOLOGY, OR, DOCTRINALISM TWIN TO RITUALISM
- THEOLOGY
- THE TUTOR, OR A NEW ENGLISH AND BENGALEE WORK
- WAS CHRIST IN ADAM?

Miller, John Bleecker *see* LEO 13 AND MODERN CIVILIZATION

Miller, John et al *see* OPTIMIZATION OF THE VALGUS INTERTROCHANTERIC OSTEOTOMY

Miller, K A *see* THE CARDIOVASCULAR AND METABOLIC RESPONSES OF MEN WITH CARDIOVASCULAR DISEASE TO AQUA DYNAMIC EXERCISE

Miller, L R *see* MASSOT U-MEHKARIM, LE-ZEKHER LINDA R. MILLER

Miller, Lillian B *see*
- CHARLES FENDERICH
- THE COLLECTED PAPERS OF CHARLES WILLSON PEALE AND HIS FAMILY

Miller, Marilyn K *see* THE EFFECTIVENESS OF JOB SPECIFIC TRAINING ON THE WORK PERFORMANCE OF FEMALE STUDENT NURSES

Miller, MK *see* THE EFFECTIVENESS OF REPEATED SUBMAXIMAL CONCENTRIC EXERCISE AND HEATED WHIRLPOOL IN THE TREATMENT OF DELAYED ONSET MUSCULAR SORENESS

Miller, Nicholas Dubois *see* THE COMPETENCY OF WITNESSES IN CIVIL CAUSES IN PENNSYLVANIA.

Miller, Nyle and Esther (Pennock) Family *see* A PICTORIAL HISTORY OF THE FAMILY

Miller, OF *see*
- IL'IA MUROMETS I BOGATYRSTVO KIEVSKOE

Miller, P *see*
- CATALOGUS PLANTARUM BY A SOCIETY OF GARDENERS
- FIGURES OF THE MOST BEAUTIFUL, USEFUL AND UNCOMMON PLANTS DESCRIBED IN THE GARDENERS DICTIONARY
- GARDENERS DICTIONARY...
- GARDENERS DICTIONARY
- THE GARDENER'S DICTIONARY
- ORTHODOXY IN MASSACHUSETTS 1630-1650

Miller, Paul W *see* SEVEN MINOR EPICS OF THE ENGLISH RENAISSANCE

Miller, Perry *see* ORTHODOXY IN MASSACHUSETTS, 1630-1650

Miller, Rebecca D *see* INNER PASSAGES

Miller, Rev. J Graham *see* TONGOAN DICTIONARY AND OTHER VANUATU LANGUAGE MATERIAL

Miller, Russell King *see* THE SERVICE-HYMNAL: WITH AN INTRODUCTORY SERVICE

Miller, Samuel, DD *see* PRESBYTERIAN REUNION

Miller, Stephen Franks *see* THE BENCH AND BAR OF GEORGIA: MEMOIRS AND SKETCHES

Miller, Thelma B *see* HISTORY OF KERN COUNTY

Miller, Thomas B *see* ORIGINAL AND SELECTED THOUGHTS ON THE LIFE AND TIMES OF REV. THOMAS MILLER, AND REV. THOMAS WARBURTON

MILLER UNION – Miller, NE. -w. Jul-Aug 1890; Jul 1892; Oct-Nov 1895 – 1 – us NE Hist [071]

Miller, V F *see*
- EKSKURSY V OBLAST' RUSSKOGO NARODNOGO EPOSA
- EKSKURSY V OBLAST'RUSSKOGO NARODNOGO EPOSA
- OCHERKI RUSSKOI NARODNOI SLOVESNOSTI

Miller, Wayne C *see*
- DIETARY FAT AND CARBOHYDRATE IN RELATION TO BODY FATNESS IN LEAN AND OBESE MEN AND WOMEN
- PLASMA FREE FATTY ACIDS AT REST AND EXHAUSTION FOLLOWING THEOBROMINE INGESTION

Miller, William *see*
- THE LATINS IN THE LEVANT
- MEDIAEVAL ROME

Miller, William C *see* JOURNAL OF RELIGIOUS AND THEOLOGICAL INFORMATION

Miller, William G *see* THE DATA OF JURISPRUDENCE

Milleran, R *see* LES DEUX GRAMMAIRES FRANSAIZES

MILLERITES AND EARLY ADVENTISTS, 1840-1870 – (Cataloging available) – 60r – 1 – $6130.00 – us UMI [240]

MILLERS COVE BAPTIST CHURCH. CHILHOWEE ASSOCIATION. WALLAND, TENNESSEE : CHURCH RECORDS – 1813-1962 – 1 – 34.83 – us Baptist [240]

MILLER'S TREATIES : TREATIES AND OTHER INTERNATIONAL ACTS OF THE UNITED STATES, 1776-1863 / Miller, David Hunter – ('For this period it supersedes Malloy for scholarly purposes' Price-Bitner "Effective Legal Research" 3rd ed p45) – v1-8 (all publ) – 79mf – 9 – $118.00 – LLMC 80-916 – us L.L.M.C. [976]

MILLER'S VOKHENSHRIFT = MILLER'S WEEKLY – (In Yiddish) – New York City, NY. v1 no15. 30 Mar 1917 – 1r – 1 – $25.00 – cn Can Microfilming [071]

MILLERSBURG HERALD – Millersburg, PA., 1877-1909 – 13 – $25.00r – us I.M.R. [071]

MILLERSBURG HISTORICAL SOCIETY MINUTES – Millersburg, PA., 1850-1982 – 13 – $25.00r – us I.M.R. [071]

MILLERSBURG HISTORICAL SOCIETY ORDINANCES – Millersburg, PA., 1865-1982 – 13 – $25.00r – us I.M.R. [071]

MILLERSBURG SENTINEL – Millersburg, PA., 1884-1931 – 13 – $25.00r – us I.M.R. [071]

MILLERSTOWN GAZETTE – Millerstown, PA. -w 1857-60. 1 roll – 13 – $25.00r – us I.M.R. [071]

MILLERSTOWN LEDGER – Millerstown, PA., 1875-1878 – 13 – $25.00r – us I.M.R. [071]

Miller-Tait, Jennifer *see* NONVERBAL BEHAVIOR OF NATIONAL FIGURE SKATING COACHES

MILLES LIEUS DANS L'INCONNU : EN PLEIN FORET EQUATORIALE CHEZ LES FANG ANTHROPOPHAGES / Trilles, H – Bruges: Librarie de l'oeuvre St-Charles, [n.d.] – us Res Libr [960]

Millet, A F *see* REPORT ON THE SETTLEMENT OF THE LAND REVENUE OF THE FYZABAD DISTRICT

Millet, G *see* RECHERCHES SUR L'ICONOGRAPHIE DE L'EVANGILE, AUX 14E

MILLET YOLU – Bursa, 1920-19? – 9 – $10.00 – us MEDOC [956]

MILLI GAZETE : TUERKISCHE TAGESZEITUNG – Frankfurt/Main, Germany. 1 Jul 1980- – ca 3r per yr – 1 – gw Mikrofilm [072]

MILLI MECMUA – (Mueessis ve Mueduer-i Mes'ul: Mehmed Mesih[Akyigit]. Nos. 1-114 (1 Tesrinisani 1339[1923]-15 Tesrinisani 1928)) – Istanbul: Evkaf Matbaasi, Ikdam Matbaasi, 1923-1928 – 36mf – 9 – $525.00 – us MEDOC [949]

MILLI NEVSAL – (1338M. – 4mf. $70.00; 1339M. – 5mf. $75.00; 1340M. – 5mf. $75.00; 1341M. – 5mf. $75.00) – 9 – us MEDOC [949]

MILLI TETEBBULAR MECMUASI – (Vol. 1-5 (Mart-Kanunievvel 1331[1915])) – Istanbul: Matbaa-i Amire. Nesreden: Asar-i Islamiye ve Milliye Tetkik Encuemeni. Mueduer: Koeprueluezade Mehmed Fuad, 1915 – 17mf – 9 – $295.00 – us MEDOC [949]

Milligan, George *see*
- THE ENGLISH BIBLE
- ST. PAUL'S EPISTLES TO THE THESSALONIANS
- THE THEOLOGY OF THE EPISTLE TO THE HEBREWS

MILLIGAN JOURNAL – Milligan, NE. -w. Sep 1897-Jul 1901 – 1 – us NE Hist [071]

MILLIGAN REVIEW – Milligan, NE. -w. Mar 1933-Sep 1953 – 1 – us NE Hist [071]

MILLIGAN TIMES – Milligan, NE. -w. Mar 1901-Dec 1914; Jan 1917-Nov 1920 – 1 – us NE Hist [071]

Milligan, William *see*
- THE ASCENSION AND HEAVENLY PRIESTHOOD OF OUR LORD
- THE BOOK OF REVELATION
- BOOK OF REVELATION
- THE REVELATION OF ST. JOHN

MILLIKAN HIGH SCHOOL YEARBOOK – Aries, Long Beach, CA. 1958-93 – 14r – 1 – $700.00 – R60013 – us Library Micro [370]

Milliken, Charles F *see* HISTORY OF ONTARIO COUNTY AND ITS PEOPLE

MILLIKEN'S VENTURA HOMESEEKERS DIRECTORY – Ventura Co, CA. 1898 – 1r – 1 – $50.00 – D105 – us Library Micro [978]

Millin, Aubin-L *see* HISTOIRE METALLIQUE DE LA REVOLUTION FRANCAISE, OU RECUEIL DES MEDAILLES ET MONNAIES (...)

Millin, George Francis *see* EVIL AND EVOLUTION

MILLING PRODUCTION – v. 4-25. 1939-60 – 1 – us UMI [670]

A MILLIONAIRE'S COUSIN / Lawless, Emily – British Fiction Archive: Unit 4 – 9 – uk Bell [830]

MILLIONS: MONTHLY MAGAZINE OF THE CHINA INLAND MISSION OVERSEAS MISSIONARY FELLOWSHIP – 1952-61 – 1 – us UMI [240]

MILLIYET – 1980- – 6r per y – 1 – inquire – us Ross [072]

MILLIYET : TAGESZEITUNG FUER TUERKISCHE ARBEITNEHMER – Neu-Isenburg, Germany. 1 Sept 1978- – ca 5r per yr – 1 – gw Mikrofilm [072]

MILLKEN'S TOURIST DIRECTORY – West Coast, 1898-1899 – 1r – 1 – $50.00 – D132 – us Library Micro [030]

MILLON HIDDUSHEI RASHI / ed by Avinery, Y – Part I of Heikhal Rashi encyclopaedia in five volumes. Tel Aviv. 1940. BJ-412-1 1 – 9 – ne IDC [270]
MILLONARIO DE POBREZA (MECANOGRAFIADO) / Belloso Rodriguez, Pedro – 1 – sp Bibl Santa Ana [810]
Millot, Claude-Francois-Xavier *see* HISTOIRE PHILOSOPHIQUE DE L'HOMME
Mills and Co *see*
- HISTORY OF JASPER COUNTY
- HISTORY OF PIKE COUNTY

Mills, Benjamin Fay *see* GOD'S WORLD AND OTHER SERMONS
Mills, Brett D *see* CATASTROPHE MODEL OF ANXIETY AND PERFORMANCE
Mills, Christine *see* BEST IDEAS, A DIRECTORY OF SOCIAL INVENTIONS
MILLS' CONSTITUTIONAL ANNOTATIONS / Mills, Jared Warner – Chicago: Myers, 1890. 444p. LL-260 – 1 – us L of C Photodup [340]
MILL'S CONSTITUTIONAL REPORTS : 1817-18 / South Carolina. Supreme Court – (A Pre-NRS title) – new ed. 2v in 1. 1887 (all publ) – 5mf – 9 – $7.50 – LLMC 94-012 – us L.L.M.C. [340]
Mills, D L et al *see* COMMENTS ON CONDENSED MATTER PHYSICS
Mills, Elaine L *see* THE PAPERS OF JOHN PEABODY HARRINGTON IN THE SMITHSONIAN INSTITUTION
Mills, FW *see* AN INDEX TO THE GENERA AND SPECIES OF THE DIATOMACEAE...
Mills, Henry A *see* DIARY, MS P.P.
Mills, J P *see*
- TOUR DIARIES AND ARTICLES ON ASSAM
- TOUR NOTES BY J. P. MILLS

Mills, James C *see* HISTORY OF SAGINAW COUNTY
Mills, Jared Warner *see*
- MILLS' CONSTITUTIONAL ANNOTATIONS
- NEGOTIABLE INSTRUMENTS LAW

Mills, Lawrence *see* OKLAHOMA INDIAN LAND LAWS.
Mills, Robert *see*
- DRAWINGS AND SPECIFICATIONS
- PAPERS OF ROBERT MILLS
- THE PAPERS OF ROBERT MILLS, 1781-1855

Millstone, Maurice Shelly *see*
- THE LAW OF LANDLORD AND TENANT IN ONTARIO
- THE LAW OF REAL ESTATE MORTGAGES IN ONTARIO

MILLY AND OLLY / Ward, Mary Augusta – British Fiction Archive: Unit 2 – 9 – uk Bell [830]
MILLY DARRELL; AND OTHER TALES / Braddon, Mary Elizabeth – British Fiction Archive: Unit 5 – 9 – uk Bell [830]
Milman, Arthur *see* HENRY HART MILMAN, D.D.
Milman, Henry Hart *see*
- BELSHAZZAR
- THE FALL OF JERUSALEM
- THE HISTORY OF CHRISTIANITY
- HISTORY OF THE JEWS FROM THE EARLIEST PERIOD DOWN TO MODERN TIMES
- SAVONAROLA, ERASMUS AND OTHER ESSAYS
- SAVONAROLA, ERASMUS, AND OTHER ESSAYS

Milne, Robert *see* THE PROBLEM OF THE CHURCHLESS AND POOR IN OUR LARGE TOWNS
Milne-Edwards, Henri *see*
- A MONOGRAPH OF THE BRITISH FOSSIL CORALS
- RAPPORT SUR LES PROGRES RECENTS DES SCIENCES ZOOLOGIQUES EN FRANCE

Milne-Edwards, M et al *see* EXPEDITIONS SCIENTIFIQUES DU "TRAVAILLEUR" ET DU "TALISMAN" PENDANT LES ANNEES 1880, 1881, 1882, 1883
Milner, John *see* A PRACTICAL GRAMMAR OF THE LATIN TONGUE
MILNGAVIE AND BEARSDEN HERALD – 1 – £42.00r – uk Scot News [072]
MILNGAVIE HERALD. (MILNGAVIE & BEARSDEN HERALD) – Scotland. Sep 1901-Dec 1979. -w. 59mqn reels – 1 – uk British Libr Newspaper [072]
Milo, New York. Second Baptist Church *see* RECORDS
Milonova, U. *see*
- ISTORIIA RABOCHEGO I PROFESSIONALNOGO DVIZHENIIA DEREVOOBDELOCHNIKOV DO REVOLIUTSII 1917 GODA
- PROFESSIONALNOE DVIZHENIE V ROSSII V 1905-1907 GG

Miloradovich, L *see* ARTELI RABOCHIKH DLIA OSNOVANIIA FABRIK ILI MASTERSKIKH
Milot, A-D *see* LE COURRIER DE BERTHIERVILLE
Milov, V V *see* KOMSOMOL V STROITEL'STVE RABOCHEI KOOPERATSII
Milovidov, A I *see*
- IZ ISTORII VILENSKOI PUBLICHNOI BIBLIOTEKI
- OPISANIE SLAVIANORUSSKIKH STARO-PECHATNYKH KNIG VILENSKOI PUBLICHNOI BIBLIOTHEKI (1491-1800 GG.)

LA MILPA / Perez Toro, Augusto – Merida de Yucatan. 1942 – 1 – us Res Libr [830]
MILPITAS POST – Milpitas, CA. 1955-68; 1969- – 58+ r – 1 – $2,900.00 ($90.00y) – B02463 – us Library Micro [071]
MILTIADE A MARATHON / Guillard et Le Moine – (French Theatre Series). Paris. Lormel. s.d – 9 – fr Hachette [820]
MILTON / Brooke, Stopford Augustus – London: Macmillan, 1879 – 1mf – us A.T.L.A. [450]
MILTON EAGLE – Milton, OR. -w. 14 Oct 1887-20 Nov 1903; 6 Jan 1949-25 Jan 1951, – 1r – 1 – us U.O. Library [071]
MILTON EAGLE – Milton, OR. -w. 1901-48 – 1 – 346.00 – us Oregon Hist [071]
MILTON GAZETTE – (See also: Press Gazette. Milton, Fl) – Milton. Fl. -w. 1924-1937, 1938, 1939-1941, 1943-52 – 1 – us P.K. Yonge [071]
Milton, John *see*
- ACCEDENCE COMMENC'T GRAMMAR
- LE PARADIS PERDU
- PARADISE LOST, A POEM IN TWELVE BOOKS
- TRACTATE OF EDUCATION

MILTON JOURNAL – Milton, Ontario. v1 n52. 4 jul 1856 – 1r – 1 – Can$25.00 – cn Can Microfilming [072]
MILTON KEYNES CITIZEN – 1989; Jul 1990-96 – 76r – 1 – uk British Libr Newspaper [072]
MILTON KEYNES GAZETTE *see* BLETCHLEY GAZETTE
MILTON UND KLOPSTOCK : MIT BESONDERER BERUECKSICHTIGUNG DES "PARADISE LOST" UND DES "MESSIAS" / Huebler, Franz – (Includes bibliographical references) – Reichenberg: Selbstverlag der k. und k. Staatsmittelschule, 1893 – 1r – 1 – us U.W. Library [410]
MILTON-FREEWATER EAGLE TIMES – Milton$Freewater, OR. 2 Feb 1951 – 9 Jun 1960. 4 rolls – 1 – us U.O. Library [071]
MILTONIAN – Milton, PA. -w 1889-1912; 1918-1932 – 13 – $25.00r – us I.M.R. [071]
Milukas, Antanas *see*
- AMERIKOS LIETUVIAI 19. SIMTMETYJE, 1868-1900
- PIRMIEJI AMERIKOS LIETUVIU PROFESIJONALAI IR KRONIKA

MILVAKER IDISHE SHTIMME = MILWAUKEE JEWISH VOICE – Milwaukee, WI. 1930-31 – 1 – us A.J.P.C. [071]
Milwaukee Bar Association *see* GAVEL
MILWAUKEE BAR ASSOCIATION GAVEL *see* MILWAUKEE LAWYER
MILWAUKEE HEROLD – (Cont by: Amerika-Woche, Chicago) – Omaha, NE. 1972-1982 – 1 – gw Mikrofilm [071]
MILWAUKEE LAWYER – (Supersedes Milwaukee Bar Association Gavel) – v1-13. 1976-92 (all publ) – 9 – $105.00 set – us Hein [340]
THE MILWAUKEE LAWYER – v1-8. 1976-85 – 15mf – 9 – $22.50 – LLMC 84-608 – us L.L.M.C. [073]
MILWAUKEE PRESS – Milwaukee, OR. -w. 5 Oct 1916-5 Jul 1917. 1 roll – 1 – us U.O. Library [071]
MILWAUKEE PROFESSIONAL NURSE – v1-1963- 1; v11- 5,6; v14- 1976- 9 – us UMI [073]
MILWAUKER WOCHENBLAT – Milwaukee. Wis. 1917-59 – 1 – us A.J.P.C. [071]
MILWAUKIE NORTH CLACKAMAS REVIEW – Milwaukie OR. Sep 3 1975-Nov 15 1978 – 1 – us U.O. Library [071]
Mimande, Paul *see* L'HERITAGE DE BEHANZIN
MIMBAR INDONESIA – Djakarta. Incomplete. SE-563 1. 1947-1966 – 9 – ne IDC [073]
MIMBAR PEMERINTAH DAERAH DJAWA TENGAH / Central Java (Province) – (Irregular. Missing: 1966(1)) – Semarung, 1966(1-2) – 2mf – 9 – SE-1376/1 – ne IDC [950]
MIMBAR PENERANGAN – Djakarta. Incomplete. SE-564 1. 1950-1970 – 9 – ne IDC [073]
MIMBAR UMUM – (Some issues missing) – Medan, Indonesia. Sept 1948-Dec 1949; Jul 1963-Jun 1964; Jun 1966-Jun 1993 – 78r – 1 – us L of C Photodup [072]
MIMEO / Mississippi. Agricultural Experiment Station. State College – v. 1-16. 1935-38 – 1,5,6 – us Spaulding [630]
MIMEO AE (AGRICULTURAL ENGINEERING) / Purdue University. Cooperative Extension Service – 1944-80.1 reel – 1,5 – us Spaulding [630]
MIMEO AH AND AS (ANIMAL HUSBANDRY AND ANIMAL SCIENCE) / Purdue University. Cooperative Extension Service – No.1-430. 1942-79 – 1,5 – us Spaulding [636]
MIMEO AY (AGRONOMY) / Purdue University. Cooperative Extension Service – No.1-253. 1940-84 – 1,5 – us Spaulding [630]
MIMEO BP (BOTANY AND PLANT PATHOLOGY) / Purdue University. Cooperative Extension Service – No.1-1 – 11-17. 1943-62. 1 reel – 1,5 – us Spaulding [580]
MIMEO DH (DAIRY HUSBANDRY) / Purdue University. Cooperative Extension Service – No.3-128. 1963-83. 1 reel – 1,5 – us Spaulding [636]
MIMEO E (ENTOMOLOGY) / Purdue University. Cooperative Extension Service – No.1-91 – 1,5 – us Spaulding [630]
MIMEO EC (AGRICULTURAL ECONOMICS) / Purdue University. Cooperative Extension Service – No.1-611 – 1,5 – us Spaulding [330]
MIMEO F (FORESTRY) / Purdue University. Cooperative Extension Service – No.1-68.1951-76. 1 reel – 1,5 – us Spaulding [634]
MIMEO FH (4-H) / Purdue University. Cooperative Extension Service – No.1-660. 1955-84 – us Spaulding [630]
MIMEO HE (HOME ECONOMICS) / Purdue University. Cooperative Extension Service – Nos 1-581 1951-84 – 1,5 – us Spaulding [640]
MIMEO HO (HORTICULTURE) / Purdue University. Cooperative Extension Service – No.1-180 – 1,5 – us Spaulding [630]
MIMEO ID (INTERDEPARTMENTAL) / Purdue University. Cooperative Extension Service – No.1-162. 1955-84 – 1,5 – us Spaulding [630]
MIMEO PIH (PORK INDUSTRY HANDBOOK) / Purdue University. Cooperative Extension Service – No.1-95.1 reel – 1,5 – us Spaulding [630]
MIMEO REPORT / Minnesota. College of Agriculture. Dep't. of Agricultural and Applied Economics – nos.1-532 – 1,5,6 – us Spaulding [630]
MIMEO REPORTS / Louisiana State University. Agricultural Experiment Station. Hill Farm Experiment Station – No.43-51. 1977-81. 1 reel – 1,5 – us Spaulding [630]
MIMEO SERIES / Georgia. Experiment Station. Experiment – v. 1-72. 1949-54 – 1,5,6 – us Spaulding [630]
MIMEOGRAPH PAMPHLET / South Dakota. State University. Agricultural Experiment Station – nos.1-2. 1942 – 1,5,6 – us Spaulding [630]
MIMEOGRAPH PAPER / Georgia. Coastal Plain Experiment Station. Tifton – v. 1-85. 1941-54 – 1,5,6 – us Spaulding [630]
MIMEOGRAPH SERIES / Georgia. Agricultural Experiment Station. Athens – n.s. v. 1-263. 1951-69 – 1,5,6 – us Spaulding [630]
MIMEOGRAPHED CIRCULAR / South Dakota. Agricultural Extension Service. State College of Agriculture and Mechanic Arts – nos.100-600. 1935-69 – 1,5,6 – us Spaulding [630]
MIMEOGRAPHED REPORT / Mississippi. Agricultural Experiment Station. State College – v. 1-24. 1947-58 – 1,5,6 – us Spaulding [630]
MIMEOGRAPHED SERIES / Georgia. Agricultural Experiment Station. Athens – v. 1-2. 1952-54 – 1,5,6 – us Spaulding [630]
MIMESIS DER WIRKLICHKEIT IM ROMANWERK C.P. SNOWS : EIN BEITRAG ZUR ERKENNTNIS DES LITERARISCHEN REALISMUS / Nold, Guenter – Frankfurt a.M., 1973 – 2mf – 9 – DM62.00 – 3-89349-669-6 – gw Hänsel [420]
MI-MIKHTEVEI RABBI YEHOSEF SCHWARZ – (Der Orient). 1840. BJ-27-243 1 – 9 – ne IDC [956]
O MIMO : DEDICADO AO BELLO SEXO – Jaguary, 15 Sep 1897 – 1,5,6 – bl Biblioteca [072]
MIMOSES ET AUTRES PLANTES LEGUMINEUSES DU NOUVEAU CONTINENT / Kunth, C S – (Voyage aux regions equinoctiales, Humboldt e.a. Paris, 1823). v. 6, pt. 4. B-5991 2 – 8 – ne IDC [580]
MIMS AFRICA – Monthly Index of Medical Specialties. 1976- – 1,5,6,9 – us UMI [616]
MIMS MIDDLE EAST – Monthly Index of Medical Specialties. 1969- – 1; 1975- 5,6,9 – us UMI [610]
MIN LI PAO – Shanghai. 11 Oct 1910-Sep 1913 – 1 – 35.00r – us Hoover Inst Photo [072]
Minadoi, GT *see* HISTORIA DELLA GVERRA FRA TVRCHI, ET PERSIANI
Minami *see* MADJALLAH BOELANAN BERGAMBAR
Minami, Kazuo *see* FEUDAL GOVERNMENTAL GAZETTE
MINANG MODERN INDONESIA DAN MALAJA / Irama Baru – SE-10,276 1. 1962 – 9 – ne IDC [950]
MINANG MODERN; NEW SONG'S (MELODY) – (Songs with piano accompaniment). SE-10,326 1. 1961 – 9 – ne IDC [780]
Minard *see* ALLEGANY COUNTY AND ITS PEOPLE
MINARETE – Pindamonhangaba, Brazil. 1903-04; Jan-Nov 1905; 1906-08 – 1 – bl Biblioteca [072]
MINAS – Belo Horizonte, Brazil. May-Dec 1975; 1976-77. (Minas Tenis Club) – 1 – bl Biblioteca [072]
MINAS DO SUL : ORGAM OFFICIAL DO ESTADO – Campanha, 19 Feb 1892; Jan-29 Dec 1935 – 1,5,6 – bl Biblioteca [072]
MINAS DO SUL : ORGAO DO CLUB SEPARATISTA TRINTA E UM DE JANEIRO – Campanha, 4 May 1893 – 1,5,6 – bl Biblioteca [072]
MINAS GERAES : ORGAM OFICIAL DOS PODERES DO ESTADO – Ouro Preto, 16 Dec 1862; Apr 1892-Mar 1900 – 1,5,6 – bl Biblioteca [072]
MINAS GERAIS – Belo Horizonte, Brazil. Jun-Dec 1898; 1899-1978; Jan-Jun 1979 – 1 – bl Biblioteca [072]
Minas Gerais. Brazil *see*
- DIARIO DA JUSTICA
- ORGAO OFICIAL DOS PODERES DO ESTADO
- PLANO INTEGRADO DE DESENVOLVIMENTO, REGIAO NORDESTE

MINAS JORNAL – Conselheiro Lafaiete, 3 Mar 1938-Dec 1938; Apr-May Oct, Dec 1939; Jan-Jun 1940; Feb-May, Jul, Sep-Dec 1941; Jan 1942-12 Jul 1945 – 1,5,6 – bl Biblioteca [072]
MINAS LIVRE : ORGAM REPUBLICANO – Juiz de Fora, 26 Apr, Jul-Aug 1891; 29 May 1892 – 1,5,6 – bl Biblioteca [072]
O MINAS NOVAS – Minas Novas, 21 Apr 1902; Oct-Nov 1934; Jan-May, Jul, Sep-15 Oct 1935 – 1,5,6 – bl Biblioteca [072]
MINATARE FREE PRESS – Minatare, NE. -w. Mar-Oct 1908; Jan 1909-Nov 1964 – 1 – us NE Hist [071]
MINATARE REPORTER – Minatare, NE. -w. Sep 1914-Sep 1915 – 1 – us NE Hist [071]
MIN-CHIEN – (Among the People). 4 v. Peiping. 1934-37. Lacking: v. 4 (6-24) 1937. BCH-314 1 – 9 – ne IDC [950]
MIN-CHU SHENG-HUO – (Democratic Life). BCH-959 2 – 8 – ne IDC [320]
MIN-CH'UAN-SU TS'UI-PIEN – (Democratic Elements). Shanghai. 1914-16. BCH-802 2 – 8 – ne IDC [320]
Minckwitz, Johannes *see* DEUTSCHLANDS TRAUM, KAMPF UND SIEG
Minco, Marga *see* OTHER SIDE
Mincoff-Marriage, Elizabeth *see* BERGLIEDERBUECHLEIN
MIND – v1-83 1876-1974 1; v80-83 1971-74 5,6 – us UMI [100]
MIND : A QUARTERLY REVIEW OF PSYCHOLOGY AND PHILOSOPHY – n.s. v1-75 1892-1966 – 1 – us Princeton Micro [100]
MIND : A QUARTERLY REVIEW OF PSYCHOLOGY AND PHILOSOPHY – o.s. v1-16 1876-91 – 1 – us Princeton Micro [100]
MIND AND BRAIN : OR, THE CORRELATIONS OF CONSCIOUSNESS AND ORGANIZATION; SYSTEMATICALLY INVESTIGATED AND APPLIED TO PHILOSOPHY, MENTAL SCIENCE AND PRACTICE / Laycock, Thomas – 2nd ed. New York: Appleton, 1869. 2v. illus – 1 – us U.W. Library [190]

THE MIND AND FACE OF BOLSHEVISM: AN EXAMINATION OF CULTURAL LIFE IN SOVIET RUSSIA / Fueloep-Miller, Rene – Trans. from German by F.S. Flint and D.F. Tait. New York: A.A. Knopf, 1929. xvi,308p. Plates, ports, biliog – 1 – us U.W. Library [335]

MIND AND HEART IN RELIGION, OR, JUDAISM AND CHRISTIANITY : A HEART'S EXPERIENCE AND A POPULAR RESEARCH INTO THE TRUE RELIGION OF THE BIBLE / Jaeger, Abraham – New York: Goodspeed, 1873 – 1mf – 9 – 0-8370-3754-9 – 1985-1754 – us A.T.L.A. [230]

MIND IN MATTER : A SHORT ARGUMENT ON THEISM / Tait, James – London:Charles Griffin, [1884?] – 1mf – 9 – 0-8370-5477-X – 1985-3477 – us A.T.L.A. [210]

THE MIND OF CHRI..WHAT DID JESUS BELIEVE? / McClelland, Thomas Calvin – New York: Thomas Y. Crowell, 1909. 1 fiche – 9 – us A.T.L.A. [240]

THE MINDANAO CROSS – Catabato. Philippines. 1948-51 – 1 – us UMI [072]

MINDANAO TIMES – Davao City. Philippines. 1950-51 – 1 – us UMI [072]

MINDEN COURIER – Minden, NE. -w. Oct 1890 to date – 1 – us NE Hist [071]

MINDEN FIRST BAPTIST CHURCH. MINDEN, LOUISIANA : CHURCH RECORDS – 1844-1980 – 1 – 211.50 – us Baptist [240]

MINDEN NEWS – Minden, NE. -w. (-m 1896-98). Mar 1897-Sep 1922 – 1 – us NE Hist [071]

MINDENER TAGEBLATT – Minden, dec 1 1949-75 – 1 – gw Mikrofilm [072]

Minde-Pouet, Georg *see* HEINRICH VON KLEIST

MINDER OM DANSKE OG NORDMAENDENE I ENGLAND, SKOTLAND OG IRLAND / Worsaae, Jens Jakob Asmussen – Kjobenhavn, C.A. Reitzel, 1851. 444p. illus. maps – 1 – us U.W. Library [941]

MINDEUDGAVE / Rasmussen, Knud – v1-3. 1934-35 – 1 – us I.U. Libraries [390]

Mindlinu, Z L *see* EVREI V SSSR

MINE CITY BAPTIST CHURCH. DUCKTOWN, TENNESSEE : CHURCH RECORDS – 1868-1987 – 1 – 44.19 – us Baptist [978]

LA MINE ET LES MINEURS / Ghesquiere, Henri J – Lille. 1901. (La Condition Ouvriere. Part Two.) – 9 – 2.50 – fr Bibl Nationale [360]

MINE SAFETY AND HEALTH ADMINISTRATION PUBLICATIONS / U.S. Department of Labor – Collection, inception to 1977 – 460mf – 9 – $600.00 – us Updata [622]

Mine Ventilation Society of South Africa *see*
– JOURNAL
– MONTHLY BULLETIN

Minelli, Pablo M *see* EL PUEBLO ESPANOL EN ARMAS

MINE-MILL UNION : 1942-1955 / International Union of Mine, Mill and Smelter Workers – (Coll title: Labor Union Periodicals, Pt 1) – 3r – 1 – $405.00 – 1-55655-245-9 – us UPA [331]

MINER – Cherry Creek, NV. Apr 1903 – 1r – 1 – $50.00 – U04478 – us Library Micro [071]

MINER – Eureka. Nev. 1973- – 1 – us UMI [071]

MINER – Eureka, NV. 1971-1973 – 1r – 1 – $50.00 – N04513 – us Library Micro [622]

MINER – Galena. Kan. -w. 1877-81, 1888-89 – 1 – us UMI [071]

MINER – Gold Circle, NV. 11 Apr 1908 – 1r – 1 – $50.00 – U04545 – us Library Micro [071]

MINER – Jumbo, NV. Apr-Jul 1908 – 1r – 1 – $50.00 – U04591 – us Library Micro [071]

MINER – National, NV. 1910-13 – 1r – 1 – $50.00 – U04632 – us Library Micro [071]

MINER – Newport. Wash. 1908-1912 – 1 – us UMI [071]

MINER – Rawhide, NV. 1908 – 1r – 1 – $50.00 – U04653 – us Library Micro [622]

MINER – Rochester, NV. 1913-14 – 1r – 1 – $50.00 – U04733 – us Library Micro [071]

MINER – Tonopah, NV. 1903-21 – 7r – 1 – $350.00 – U04766 – us Library Micro [071]

THE MINER – Clancy. Mont. 1896-1899 – 1 – us UMI [071]

THE MINER / Miners' Federation of Great Britain – London. 4 Jun 1926-1 Nov 1930.-w. 2mqn reels – 1 – uk British Libr Newspaper [331]

THE MINER – Nelson, Canada. Nelson Weekly Miner. -w. April 1894-April 1902. 5 reels – 1 – uk British Libr Newspaper [072]

MINER AND WORKMAN'S ADVOCATE *see* BRITISH MINER AND GENERAL NEWSMAN

MINERAL AND ELECTROLYTE METABOLISM – v1-. 1978- – 1,5,9 – us UMI [612]

MINERAL COUNTY AND HAWTHORNE NEWS *see* MINERAL COUNTY INDEPENDENT NEWS

MINERAL COUNTY DEMOCRAT – Hawthorne, NV. Jan 1961 – 1r – 1 – $50.00 – U04579 – us Library Micro [071]

MINERAL COUNTY FORUM – Hawthorne, NV. Feb-Sep 1961 – 1r – 1 – $50.00 – U04580 – us Library Micro [071]

MINERAL COUNTY INDEPENDENT – Hawthorne. Nev. -w. 1947- – 1 – us UMI [071]

MINERAL COUNTY INDEPENDENT NEWS – (Also known as: Mineral County and Hawthorne News) – Hawthorne, NV. 1933-36 (scats); 1937- – 40+ r – 1 UN04581 – $2,000.00 ($60.00y) – us Library Micro [071]

MINERAL DAILY NEWS TRIBUNE – Keyser. West Virginia. 1943- – 1 – us UMI [071]

MINERAL INDEPENDENT – Superior. Mont. 1958-1959; 1966- – 1 – us UMI [071]

THE MINERAL INDICATOR: A PRACTICAL GUIDE TO THE DETERMINATION OF GENERALLY-OCCURRING MINERALS / Chapman, Edward John – Toronto: Copp, Clark, 1884. 00623. (Pre-1900 Canadiana) – 9 – cn C.I.H.M. [550]

MINERAL PROCESSING AND TECHNICAL REVIEWS / ed by Han, K N et al – 1983- – 1,5,9 – us Gordon [540]

MINERAL RESOURCES / U. S. Geological Survey – 1882-1931 – 1,5,6 – 22518.00 – us Princeton Micro [550]

MINERAL RESOURCES ACTIVITIES 1967-1970 / Saudi Arabia. Directorate General of Mineral Resources – 3v. BNE-6605 1 – 9 – ne IDC [550]

MINERAL RESOURCES DEVELOPMENT SERIES / United Nations – 255 mf – 9 – $480.00; $1.90f – uk UNIMICRO [622]

MINERAL RESOURCES DEVELOPMENT SERIES / United Nations – (No. 1. ST/ECAFE/5. E.5; Nos. 3; 6. ST/TAA/Ser.C/15;27. E.10; Nos. 2; 4-5; 7-41. E/CN/11/. E.186; Nos 42-55. E/ESCAP/. E.62) – 9 – us U.N. Pubs [333]

THE MINERAL RESOURCES OF THE HUDSON'S BAY TERRITORIES / Bell, Robert – 1886. 00104. (Pre-1900 Canadiana) – 9 – cn C.I.H.M. [550]

THE MINERAL RESOURCES OF THE PROVINCE OF NEW BRUNSWICK / Bailey, Loring Woart – Ottawa, 1898. 00913. (Pre-1900 Canadiana) – 9 – cn C.I.H.M. [550]

MINERAL RIDGE ECHO : WEEKLY REPUBLICAN NEWSPAPER – Mineral Ridge, OH. 6 and 13 Mar, 4 Dec 1891 – 1r – 1 – us Western Res [071]

MINERAL SPRINGS BAPTIST CHURCH. SANDY CREEK ASSOCIATION. NORTH CAROLINA : CHURCH RECORDS – 1835-1934 – 1 – 25.58 – us Baptist [240]

MINERAL STATISTICS – 1853/54-1881. In the British Library, London – 1 – uk Microform Academic [550]

MINERALIUM DEPOSITA – v. 1-15. 1966-80 – 1,5,9 – 1238.00 – us UMI [550]

MINERALOGIA ASTURIANA / Fuertes Acevedo, Maximo – 1880 – 9 – 1.50f – sp Bibl Santa Ana [660]

MINERALS ENGINEERING – 1,5,69 – us UMI [622]

MINERALS & METALLURGICAL PROCESSING – v1- May 1984- – 1,5,6,9 – us UMI [660]

MINERALS YEARBOOK / U.S. Bureau of Mines – 1955-79 – 1,5,6 – us Princeton Micro [622]

DER MINERALSTOFFHAUSHALT IN VISCUM ALBUM L. (WEISSBEERIGE MISTEL) / Goedings, Peter – 1995 – 3mf – 9 – DM98.00 – gw Hänsel [615]

LA MINERIA EN LA BAJA EXTREMADURA EN LA PRIMERA MITAD DEL SIGLO 29 / Guerra Guerra, Arcadio – Badajoz: Dip. Provincial, 1975 – 1 – sp Bibl Santa Ana [622]

MINERS' ADVOCATE AND RECORD – Middlesborough, England, 17 Jan 1873-31 Oct 1874 – 1r – 1 – uk British Libr Newspaper [072]

MINERS EXPRESS – Dubuque. Iowa. -d. 1851-52, 1854 – 1 – us UMI [071]

MINERS EXPRESS – Dubuque. Iowa. -w. 1847-54 – 1 – us UMI [071]

Miners' Federation of Great Britain *see* THE MINER

THE MINERS JOURNAL – Pottsville, PA. -d 1889-1906 – 13 – $25.00r – us I.M.R. [071]

A MINERVA : FOLHA POLITIVA, LITTERARIO E COMMERICAL – '(s.l.')-Sao Luiz, Brazil. 21 Aug 1828-5 Mar 1829 – 1,5,6 – bl Biblioteca [072]

MINERVA – Berlin, Hamburg. jan-jun 1792, 1793, jul 1794-jun 1795, jan-mar 1796, 1797, jul 1798-99, apr-jun 1800, 1801-05 – 10r – 1 – Dist. gw Mikrofilm – gw Misc Inst [072]

MINERVA – Budapest, 1922-42 – 2r – 1 – us Ross [460]

MINERVA – Budapest. v. 1-21. Jan Mar 1922-Dec 1942. Incomplete – 1 – us NY Public [073]

MINERVA / Sanchez de las Brozas, Francisco – 1587 – 9 – 1.50f – sp Bibl Santa Ana [810]

MINERVA / Sanchez de las Brozas, Francisco – 1761 – 9 – 1.50f – sp Bibl Santa Ana [810]

MINERVA ANESTESIOLOGICA – 1935- 1; v41-5,6,9 – us UMI [617]

MINERVA BRASILIENSE : JORNAL DE SCIENCIAS, LETTRAS E ARTES – Rio de Janeiro, 1 Nov 1843-15 Jun 1845 – 1,5,6 – bl Biblioteca [072]

MINERVA BRITANNA OR A GARDEN OF HEROICAL DEVISES / Peacham, Henry – O-710 1. 1612 – 9 – ne IDC [760]

MINERVA CARDIOANGLIOLOGICA – 1953- 1; 1975- 5,6,9 – us UMI [616]

MINERVA CHIRURGICA – v1- 1946- 1; v30-5,6,9 – us UMI [617]

MINERVA DIETOLOGICA E GASTROENTEROLOGICA – (See also: Minerva Gastroenterologica) – v23-. 1977- – 1,5,6,9 – us UMI [616]

Minerva Extremena *see* CATALOGO DE MODELACION IMPRESA 1958

MINERVA GASTROENTERLOGICA – 1955-1977 1; 1975-1977 5,6,9 – us UMI [616]

MINERVA GINECOLOGICA – 1949- 1; 1975-5,6,9 – us UMI [618]

MINERVA MEDICA – 1909- 1; 1975- 5,6,9 – us UMI [616]

MINERVA MEDICOLEGALE – 1880- 1; 1975-5,6,9 – us UMI [610]

MINERVA NEFROLOGICA – 1954- 1; 1975-5,6,9 – us UMI [616]

MINERVA OFTALMOLOGICA – 1959- 1; 1975-5,6,9 – us UMI [617]

MINERVA: PARTE SEGUNDA / Sanchez de las Brozas, Francisco – 1754 – 9 – 1.50f – sp Bibl Santa Ana [810]

MINERVA PEDIATRICA – 1949- 1; 1975- 5,6,9 – us UMI [616]

MINERVA PNEUMOLOGICA – 1962- 1; 1975-5,6,9 – us UMI [616]

MINERVA PSICHIATRICA E PSICOLOGICA – 1960- 1; 1975- 5,6,9 – us UMI [150]

MINERVA; REVUE DES LETTRES ET DES ARTS – Paris. v. 1-8. Mar 1902-May 1903 – 1 – us NY Public [073]

MINERVA, SIVE DE CAUSIS LINGUAE LATINAE / Sanchez de las Brozas, Francisco – In French. (Linguistic series). 1587 – 9 – fr Hachette [450]

MINERVA STOMATOLOGICA – 1952- 1; 1975-5,6,9 – us UMI [616]

MINERVA UROLOGICA – 1949- 1; 1975- 5,6,9 – us UMI [616]

MINERVA UROLOGICA E NEFROLOGICA – v36-. 1984- – 1,5,6,9 – us UMI [073]

MINERVA-HANDBUECHER / ed by Wentzeke, P & Luedtke, G – Pt. 1: Die Archive. v1: Deutsches Reich, Daenemark, Estland, Finnland, Lettland, Litauen, Luxemburg, Niederlande, Norwegen, Osterreich, Schweden, Schweiz. In 4 sections. Berlin, Leipzig. 1932. BR-9827 1 – 9 – ne IDC [025]

LA MINERVE / ed by Duvernay, Ludger et al – Montreal, Canada. 12 fev 1827-27 mai 1899 – 55r – 1 – Can$75.00r – cn Can Microfilming [072]

LA MINERVE – Montreal, Canada. 1826-37; 1842-54 – 15r – 1 – $975.00 – cn Library Assoc [971]

LA MINERVE / ed by Morin, Augustin-Norbert – Montreal, Canada. 9 nov-27 nov 1826 – 1r – 1 – Can$35.00 – cn Can Microfilming [072]

LA MINERVE / ed by Sauve, Arthur – Montreal, jun 1918-26 dec 1925 – 2r – 1 – Can$50.00r – cn Can Microfilming [073]

LA MINERVE FRANCAISE – Par B. Constant, etc. no. 1-113. Paris. fevr 1818-mars 1820. Remplace: Mercure de France – 1 – fr A.C.R.P.P. [073]

LA MINERVE FRANCAISE – Paris. 9v. 1818-1820 – 99mf – 9 – ne IDC [944]

LA MINERVE LITTERAIRE – Par E. Dupaty, A. Duval, etc. no. 1-24. nov 1820-avr 1821. devenu: L' Abeille. no. 25-71. avr 1821-mars 1822. Paris – 1 – fr A.C.R.P.P. [073]

Minervin, BM *see*
– ORGANIZATSIIA KONTROLIA V KREDITNOI KOOPERATSII
– REVIZIIA, ANALIZ BALANSA I OPREDELENIE KREDITOSPOSOBNOSTI KREDITNYKH KOOPERATOROV

LES MINES CANADIENNES / ed by Challen, G A – Montreal, Canada. v1 n9. 4 jan 1937; v1 n13. 1 fev 1937 – 1r – 1 – Can$25.00 – cn Can Microfilming [622]

MINES D'OR DE LA BEAUCE / Chapman, William – Quebec: Mercier, 1881. 00577. (Pre-1900 Canadiana) – 9 – cn C.I.H.M. [622]

LES MINES DU QUEBEC – Toronto. v1 n6. 12 avr 1946; v1 n10. 10 mai 1946 – 1r – 1 – Can$25.00 – cn Can Microfilming [072]

LE MINEUR / ed by Duguay, Camille – Thetford, Canada. 23 avr 1910-v5 n3. 3 jun 1915 – 1r – 1 – Can$40.00 – cn Can Microfilming [072]

LE MINEUR / La Federation de Syndicats Chretiens de Mineurs – no. 1-8. Lens. mai 1938-aout 1939 – 1 – fr A.C.R.P.P. [622]

LE MINEUR – Interprete des mines d'or de la Californie. Dir.-gerant Vachon jeune. no. 1-42. Paris. juin 1850-mars 1854 – 1 – fr A.C.R.P.P. [073]

LE MINEUR UNITAIRE / La Federation unitaire des Travailleurs du Sous-Sol et similaires – Organe mensuel. no. 4, 11-12, 27-29, 31-41. Paris. dec 1923-mars avr 1931 – 1 – fr A.C.R.P.P. [073]

LES MINEURS, OBSERVATIONS VECUES / Valdour, Jacques – Lille. 1919. (La Condition Ouvriere. Part Two.) – 9 – $12.50 – fr Bibl Nationale [360]

THE MINEWORKER – London, England. -w. 1 March 1924-4 Dec 1926. 30 ft – 1 – uk British Libr Newspaper [072]

MING BAO – China. 1916-29 – 9 – 215.00 – cc Globe [072]

Ming, John Joseph *see* THE DATA OF MODERN ETHICS EXAMINED

MING QING SUZHOU GONGSHANG YE BEIKEJI – Collection of tablet inscriptions of business circles in Suzhou during the Ming and Qing Dynasties. Comp. by the Suzhou Museum. 5 fiches. F-H197 – 9 – $22.50 – cc Microforms [950]

MING QING YILAI BEIJING GONGSHANG HUI GUAN BEIKE XUANBIAN – Selection of tablet inscriptions by business societies in Beijing dating from the Ming and Qing Dynasties. Comp. by Li Hua. 3 fiches.F-H195 – 9 – $13.50 – cc Microforms [950]

Mingana *see* SOURCES SYRIAQUES, VOL 1

Mingana, A *see* WOODBROOKE STUDIES

THE MINGANA COLLECTION – (Syriac Collection: 2,580mf Dfl15,950.00; Christian Arabic Collection: 735mf Dfl3,988.00; Islamic Arabic Collection: 6,281mf Dfl35,090.00. Catalogue (4 vols) available on mf and in printed form) – 9,596mf – 9 – ne IDC [080]

MING-CH'ING SHIH-LIAO – Collection of Documents of Ming and Ch'ing Dynasties. v. 1 (1-10). 1930-31; v. 2 (11-20) 1936; v. 3 (21-30); v. 4 (31-40) 1951. BCH-838 2 – 8 – ne IDC [950]

Minges, P *see*
– IST DUNS SCOTUS INDETERMINIST?

MINGGU PAGI – Jogjakarta, Indonesia. Feb 1 1969-89 – 20r – 1 – us L of C Photodup [072]

MINGGUAN HARAPAN – Bandung. Indonesia. 1956-1967 – 1 – us UMI [072]

MINHAGIM – Amsterdam. 1645. BJ-43-59 1 – 9 – ne IDC [270]

MINHAGIM – Venice. 1593. Illus. BJ-43-56 1 – 9 – ne IDC [270]

MINHAGIM – Venice. 1601. BJ-43-57 1 – 9 – ne IDC [270]

MINHAH LE-DAVID, SEFER HA-YOVEL LE DAVID YELLIN / Yellin, D – Jerusalem. 1935. BJ-100-44 1 – 9 – ne IDC [956]

MINHAMITE SHIRE MINUTE BOOKS – 1871-1969. SM1-6 – 9r – 1,5 – at Corangamite [910]

MINHAMITE SHIRE RATE BOOKS – 1871-1937 SOMR1-2 – 6r – 1 – at Corangamite [910]

MINIATURE SACRE E PROFANE DELL' ANNO 1023, ILLUSTRANTI L'ENCICLOPEDIA MEDIOEVALE DI RABANO MAURO / Amelli, A M – Montecassino. 1896. BO-119 1 – 9 – ne IDC [760]
MINIATUREN / Witkowski, Georg – Leipzig: E A Seemann, 1922 – 1 – us U.W. Library [890]
MINIATUREN / Witkowski, Georg – Leipzig: E A Seemann, 1922 – 1 – us U.W. Library [943]
MINIATURES : SUBJECT COLLECTIONS – (Individual titles not listed separately) – 17 catalogues on 28mf – 9 – £235.00 – uk Chadwyck [700]
MINIATURES DES PLUS ANCIENS MANUSCRITS GRECS... DU 6E AU 14E SIECLE... / Bibliotheque Nationale; ed by Omont, H – Paris, 1929 – 10mf – 9 – ne IDC [090]
Minier, A M *see* PAPERS
MINI-JORNAL – Brumadinho, Brazil. Oct. 1973; Apr-Jul 1974 – 1 – bl Biblioteca [072]
LE MINI-JOURNAL *see* LA VOIX DE WOLFE
MINIKES'S MONAT-BLATT UND YOM TOV BLETTER = MINIKE'S MONTHLY – New York, NY. 1902-03 – 1 – us A.J.P.C. [071]
MINIKES'S YOM TOV BLETER = MINIKE'S MAGAZINE – New York, NY. 1905-31 – 1 – us A.J.P.C. [071]
MINIM – v. 1-9. 1893-1902 – 1 – us UMI [073]
O MINIMO : ORGAM HUMORISTICO INOFFENSIVO – Manaos, Amazonas. 2 Maio-30 Nov 1918 – 1,5,6 – bl Biblioteca [072]
MINIMUM REQUIREMENTS FOR RECEIVING AND MAINTAINING TISSUE CULTURE PROPAGATING MATERIAL – 1985 – 39p – it F.A.O. [636]
Minin, A A *see* SEL'SKOKHOZIAISTVENNAIA KOOPERATSIIA SSSR
Minin, M *see* KOOPERATIVY
MINING AND ENGINEERING REVIEW *see* AUSTRALIAN MINING AND ENGINEERING REVIEW
MINING AND GENERAL ADVERTISER (YOUNG AND FORBES) – Feb 2 1861-Nov 26 1862 – 9 – at Pascoe [072]
MINING AND MINERALS ENGINEERING – (See also: Mine and Quarry) – v1-8 1964-72 – 1 – us UMI [622]
MINING CODE / Carpenter, Mason B – Denver: Richards, 1879. 116p. LL-158 – 1 – us L of C Photodup [340]
MINING CONGRESS JOURNAL – v1- 1915- 1; v61- 5,6,9 – us UMI [073]
MINING CONGRESS JOURNAL *see* AMC JOURNAL
MINING DECISIONS OF THE SECRETARY OF THE INTERIOR AND THE COMMISSIONER OF THE GENERAL LAND OFFICE / Copp, Henry Norris – San Francisco: Bancroft & Co, 1874 – 4mf – 9 – $6.00 – LLMC 84-113 – us L.L.M.C. [340]
MINING DIGEST – Reno, NV. 1 Dec 1908 – 1r – 1 – $50.00 – U04677 – us Library Micro [071]
MINING ENGINEERING – v1- 1949- 1; v22- 1970- 5,6; v27- 9 – us UMI [622]
MINING EQUIPMENT INTERNATIONAL – v1- 1977- – 1,5,6,9 – us UMI [622]
MINING EXPOSITOR – Ely, NV. Feb-Dec 1908; 1913-14 – 3r – 1 – $150.00 – U04504 – us Library Micro [071]
THE MINING GAZETTE – Kimberley, South Africa.26 Feb-23 Nov 1875. 1 reel – 1, 16 diazo available at reduced price – sa SA Libr [072]
MINING JOURNAL – 1835- 1; 1972- 5,6; 1976- 9 – us UMI [622]
MINING JOURNAL – Frostburg. Md. 1872-1910 – 1 – us UMI [071]
MINING JOURNAL – London. -w. 1835-94 – 73r – 1 – uk British Libr Newspaper [622]
MINING JOURNAL – Marquette. Mich. -w. 1868-1918 – 1 – us UMI [071]
MINING JOURNAL AND INVESTORS REVIEW – Perth, Australia. Jul 1896-Sep 1897. -d – 2r – 1 – uk British Libr Newspaper [622]
MINING MAGAZINE – v146- 1982- – 1,5,6,9 – us UMI [622]
MINING, MINERAL AND GEOLOGICAL LAW / Shamel, Charles Harmonas – London: Hill, 1907. 627p. LL-1112 – 1 – us L of C Photodup [622]
MINING NEWS – Montreal: H Bragg, [189-?-18– or 19–] – 9 – cn C.I.H.M. [622]
MINING NEWS – Ruby Hill, NV. 1883-84 – 1r – 1 – $50.00 – U04735 – us Library Micro [071]
THE MINING NEWS AND REGISTER OF THE STOCK AND REAL ESTATE MARKETS – Victoria, Vancouver Island [BC: s.n, 1864] – 9 – cn C.I.H.M. [332]
MINING NEWS OF CANADA – Montreal, Canada. v2 n33. 5 mai 1934 – 1r – 1 – Can$25.00 – cn Can Microfilming [622]
MINING RECORD – 1984- – 1,5,6,9 – us UMI [622]
MINING RECORD – (Also known as: Ely Record) – ELy, NV. 1905-11; 1916-79 – 39r – 1 UN04505 – $1,950.00 – us Library Micro [071]
THE MINING RECORD – (Cont by: British Columbia Mining and Engineering Record) – Vancouver: [s.n, 1895-1908?] – 9 – cn C.I.H.M. [622]
THE MINING RECORD *see* BRITISH COLUMBIA MINING RECORD
MINING REPORT – Ruby Hill, NV. 1879 – 1r – 1 – $50.00 – U04736 – us Library Micro [071]
MINING REPORTER – Tonopah, NV. 1921-29 – 3r – 1 – $150.00 – U04768 – us Library Micro [071]
THE MINING REVIEW – Rossland, BC: Mining Review, [1896-189- or 1900] – 9 – cn C.I.H.M. [622]
MINING RIGHTS IN THE WESTERN STATES AND TERRITORIES / Morrison, Robert Stewart – (10th ed. Denver: Smith-Brooks, 1900. 500p. LL-196) – 8th ed. Denver: Chain & Hardy, 1895. 457p. LL-197 – 1 – us L of C Photodup [622]
MINING RIGHTS ON THE PUBLIC DOMAIN / Morrison, Robert Stewart – (13th ed. Denver: Smith-Brooks, 1908. 587, 1p. LL-293) – 12th ed. Denver: Smith-Brooks, 1905. 549 1p. LL-225 – 1 – us L of C Photodup [622]
MINING SUN (UMTETELI WA BANTU) – Johannesburg, South Africa. 1920-30 – 1 – sa State Libr [072]
MINING TIT-BITS – (Cont: B.C. Mining Exchange and Investors' Guide. Cont by: B.C. Mining Exchange and Investors' Guide and Mining Tit-Bits) – Vancouver: [s.n, 1899] – 9 – cn C.I.H.M. [622]
MINING TIT-BITS *see*
– THE B.C. MINING EXCHANGE AND INVESTORS' GUIDE
– THE B.C. MINING EXCHANGE AND INVESTOR'S GUIDE AND MINING TIT-BITS
MINING TOPICS – Unionville, NV. 1921-22 – 1r – 1 – $50.00 – U04777 – us Library Micro [071]
MINING VOICE *see* AMC JOURNAL
MINING WORLD – v11-25 1949-63 – 1 – us UMI [622]
MINING WORLD NEWS – Reno, NV. 1994 – 2+ r – 1 – $100.00 ($90.00y) – U04881 – us Library Micro [071]
MINISTER AND CHURCH LISTS / United Methodist Church. Kansas West Conference – 1 – us KS Hist [978]
THE MINISTER AND THE SPIRITUAL LIFE / Gunsaulus, Frank Wakeley – New York: Fleming H. Revell, 1911. 397p. 1 fiche – 9 – us A.T.L.A. [240]
THE MINISTER OF BAPTISM : A HISTORY OF CHURCH OPINION FROM THE TIME OF THE APOSTLES, ESPECIALLY WITH REFERENCE TO HERETICAL, SCHISMATICAL AND LAY ADMINISTRATION / Elwin, Warwick – London: J. Murray, 1889 – 1mf – us A.T.L.A. [240]
MINISTERIAL BUDGET ESTIMATES: ESTIMATES OF EXPENDITURE AND DETAILS OF ESTABLISHMENTS / Arabian Gulf Emirates. Abu-Dhabi – 4v. in 2. 1970-73. BNE-10,002 1 – 9 – ne IDC [336]
THE MINISTERIAL DIRECTORY OF THE BAPTIST CHURCHES / Lasher, George – 834p – 1 – 29.19 – us Baptist [240]
MINISTERIAL ETHICS – A collection of 26 seminar papers submitted to Professor Henlee Barnette for his seminar on Ministerial Ethics.1976. 683p – 1 – $23.90 – us Baptist [170]
MINISTERIAL FORMATION – (1985-. 5,6,9) – Nos.1-.1978- – 1 – us UMI [240]
MINISTERIIA-BUFF / Maiakovskii, Vladimir – Ed. 2. M., Spb. n.d. BR-982 2 – 8 – ne IDC [460]
Ministerio de Educacion Nacional *see* INSTRUCCIONES PARA LA DEFENSA DE LOS CONJUNTOS HISTORICO-ARTISTICOS
Ministerio de Educacion Nacional. Centro de Ensenanza Media y Profesional de Azuaga *see* MEMORIA DEL CURSO ACADEMICO 1955-56
Ministerio de Educacion Nacional. Junta Nacional contra el analfabetismo *see* ACTIVIDADES DE EDUCACION FUNDAMENTAL EN LA PROVINCIA DE BADAJOZ
Ministerio de Education Nacional *see* INSTRUCCION PARA DEFENSA DE LOS CONJUNTOS HISTORICO-ARTISTICOS
Ministerio de la Vivienda. Delegacion Provincial de Badajoz *see* PRONTUARIO LEGISLATIVO DE VIVIENDAS SUBVENCIONADAS
Ministerio de Planificacion y Coordinacion... *see* EL SALVADOR
Ministerio de Planification Nacional y Politica Economica *see* COSTA RICA
Ministerio de Relaciones Exteriores *see* COLLECCION DE LOS TRATADOS...
Ministerio de Trabajo *see*
– CENSO DE LA POBLACION DE ESPANA. REGION DE EXTREMADURA. CUADERNO N° 8
– I CATALOGO DE LA BIBLIOTECA CIRCULANTE A UTILIZAR POR LOS ASEGURADOS Y BENEFICIARIOS INTERNADOS EN ESTE CENTRO SANITARIO, CONSTA DE UN TOTAL DE SEISCIENTOS VOLUMENES
MINISTERIO DE TRABAJO Y PREVISION. APORTACION DE LOS COLONIZADORES ESPANOLES A LA PROSPERIDAD DE AMERICA (1493-16...) / Bayle, Constantino – Madrid: Razon y Fe, 1930 – 1 – sp Bibl Santa Ana [331]
MINISTERIO DE TRABAJO Y PREVISION. CATALOGO PASAJEROS A INDIAS...VOL 1 (1509-1533) / Bayle, Constantino – Madrid: Razon y Fe, 1930 – 1 – sp Bibl Santa Ana [331]
MINISTERIO DE TRABAJO Y PREVISION. DISPOSICIONES COMPLEMENTARIAS DE LAS LEYES DE INDIAS. TRES TOMOS / Bayle, Constantino – Madrid: Razon y Fe, 1930 – 1 – sp Bibl Santa Ana [331]
MINISTERIO DE TRABAJO Y PREVISION. SELECCION DE LAS LEYES DE INDIAS... / Bayle, Constantino – Madrid: Razon y Fe, 1930 – 1 – sp Bibl Santa Ana [331]
Ministerio Obras Publicas *see* MEMORIA, 1964
MINISTERS' LETTERS : LATER, LETTER TO FRIENDS / London Missionary Society – Sydney, Dec 1946-Jan 1970 – 1r – 1 – PMB Doc412 – at Pacific Mss [920]
MINISTERS' QUARTERLY – (Some original pgs damaged) – v1-22. Feb 1945-winter 1966 (complete) – 2r – 1 – ATLA S0191 – us A.T.L.A. [073]
Ministerstvo inostrannykh del SSSR *see* DOKUMENTY VNESHNE I POLITIKI SSSR
Ministerstvo inostrannykh del SSSRMinisterstvo inostrannykh del GDR *see* ZA ANTIFASHISTSKUI U DEMOKRATICHESKUI U GERMANII U
Ministerstvo vneshne i torgovli, Glavnoe planovo- ekonomicheskoe upravlenie *see* VNESHNIAIA TORGOVLIA SSSR V...G
Ministerstvo vneshnikh ekonomicheskikh sviaze i SSSR, Glavnoe ekonomicheskoe upravlenie *see* VNESHNIE EKONOMICHESKIE SVIAZI SSSR V...G
MINISTERSTVO VNUTRENNICH DEL 1802-1902. ISTORICHESKII OCHERK – v. 1-2, suppl. Spb. 1901-02. BR-4253 2 – 8 – ne IDC [324]
Ministerstvo zdravookhraneniia Soiuza SSR *see* GIGIENA TRUDA I PROFESSIONALNYE ZABOLEVANIIA
LE MINISTRE ANGLAIS / Riboutte – (French Theatre Series). Paris. J. G. Dentu. 1812 – 9 – fr Hachette [820]
LES MINISTRES DE LA COURONNE DU QUEBEC, 1867-1964 / Belanger, Pauline – 1965. SEM105P4 – 3mf – 9 – cn Bibl Nat [971]
MINISTRIES: MAGAZINE FOR CHRISTIAN LEADERS – (1985-. 5,6,9) – v1-. 1983- – 1 – us UMI [240]
el Ministro Secretario de Estado en el Departamento del Interior y Relaciones Esteriores *see* ESPOSICION QUE PRESENTA AL CONGRESO CONSTITUCIONAL DE [...]
MINISTRY – (1985-. 5,6,9) – v1-. 1928- – 1 – us UMI [240]
MINISTRY AND SPECIAL INTEREST SALNAME : NEVSAL-I ASR – (1313[1895].-4mf. $36.75; 1314[1896].-4mf. $36.75) – 9 – us MEDOC [949]
MINISTRY AND SPECIAL INTEREST SALNAME : NEVSAL-I BAHRI – 1325 [1909] – 3mf – 9 – $60.00 – us MEDOC [949]
MINISTRY AND SPECIAL INTEREST SALNAME : NEVSAL-I MAARIF – 1306K/1268S [1889] – 4mf – 9 – $75.00 – us MEDOC [949]
MINISTRY AND SPECIAL INTEREST SALNAME : NEVSAL-I MARIFET – 1307/08K [1890] – 3mf – 9 – $125.00 – us MEDOC [949]
MINISTRY AND SPECIAL INTEREST SALNAME : NEVSAL-I MILLI – 1330 [1914] – 10mf – 9 – $47.25 – us MEDOC [949]
MINISTRY AND SPECIAL INTEREST SALNAME : NEVSAL-I RAGIP – 1324 [1908] – 6mf – 9 – $42.00 – us MEDOC [949]
MINISTRY AND SPECIAL INTEREST SALNAME : ORDU SALNAMESI – 1330 [1914] – 22mf – 9 – $52.50 – us MEDOC [949]
MINISTRY AND SPECIAL INTEREST SALNAME : OSMANLI HILAL-I AHMER CEMIYETI 1329-1331 SALNAMESI – 6mf – 9 – $50.00 – us MEDOC [949]
MINISTRY AND SPECIAL INTEREST SALNAME : OSMANLI HILAL-I AHMER CEMIYETI HANIMLAR HEYET-I MERKEZIYESI TAKVIM – (1332M[1916], no.2.-2mf $50.00; 1335M[1919], no.5.-2mf. $50.00) – 9 – us MEDOC [949]
MINISTRY AND SPECIAL INTEREST SALNAME : REBI-I MARIFET – 1302K [1885] – 2mf – 9 – $23.50 – us MEDOC [949]
MINISTRY AND SPECIAL INTEREST SALNAME : REBI-I MARIFET (TAKVIM-I EBUEZZIYA) – 1304K/1265S [1887], 7.sene – 2mf – 9 – $35.00 – us MEDOC [949]
MINISTRY AND SPECIAL INTEREST SALNAME : RESIMLI GAZETE SALNAMESI – [1927] – 2mf – 9 – $25.00 – us MEDOC [949]
MINISTRY AND SPECIAL INTEREST SALNAME : RUSUMAT SALNAMESI – 1330 [1912], 1. def'a – 5mf – 9 – $65.00 – us MEDOC [949]
MINISTRY AND SPECIAL INTEREST SALNAME : SALNAME-I ASKERI – (1286M[1869].-6mf. $75.00; 1306M[1890].-16mf. $80.00) – 9 – us MEDOC [949]
MINISTRY AND SPECIAL INTEREST SALNAME : SALNAME-I NEZARET-I MA'ARIF-I UMUMIYE – (1316[1898].-17mf. $200.00; 1317[1899].-15mf. $200.00; 1318[1900].-22mf. $200.00; 1319[1901].-14mf. $48.00; 1321[1903].-13mf. $52.50) – 9 – us MEDOC [949]
MINISTRY AND SPECIAL INTEREST SALNAME : SALNAME-I NEZARET-I UMUR-I HARICIYYE – (1306[1889].-10mf. $50.00; 1318[1900].-7mf. $42.00; 1320[1902].-4mf. $36.75) – 9 – us MEDOC [949]
MINISTRY AND SPECIAL INTEREST SALNAME : TAKVIM-I EBUEZZIYA – 1310 [1892], 1 sene – 3mf – 9 – $40.00 – us MEDOC [949]
MINISTRY AND SPECIAL INTEREST SALNAME : TAKVIM-I NUECUMI – 1322 (1309) [1904] – 3mf – 9 – $21.00 – us MEDOC [949]
MINISTRY AND SPECIAL INTEREST SALNAME : T.C. MALUL GAZILER BUEYUEK TICARET SALNAMESI – 1928 – 32mf – 9 – $45.00 – us MEDOC [949]
MINISTRY AND SPECIAL INTEREST SALNAME : T.C. MALUL GAZILER TICARET SALNAMESI – 1927 – 34mf – 9 – $45.00 – us MEDOC [949]
MINISTRY AND SPECIAL INTEREST SALNAME : TUERKIYE (FI) SENE 1290 / Suavi, Ali – [1873] – 2mf – 9 – $21.00 – us MEDOC [949]
THE MINISTRY (CCC284) / Slattery, Charles Lewis – (In Chinese) – [S.l.]: Church Literature Committee of the Chung Hua Sheng Kung Hui, 1924 – 1r – 1 – 1984-6623 – us A.T.L.A. [240]
A MINISTRY INVOLVING OLDER WIDOWS IN THE OAKHURST BAPTIST CHURCH, CLARKSDALE, MISSISSIPPI / Sullivan, C Glenn – 1982 – 1 – 5.20 – us Baptist [240]
Ministry of Agricultural Development Projects *see* MOT SO CHE DO, CHINH SACH CUA NHA NUOC TRONG TINH HINH MOI
MINISTRY OF AGRICULTURE AND WATER DURING ONE YEAR / Saudi Arabia. Ministry of Agriculture and Water – (title varies). 4 v. 1963-66. BNE-6608 1 – 9 – ne IDC [333]
THE MINISTRY OF ART / Cram, Ralph Adams – Boston: Houghton Mifflin, 1914 – 1mf – us A.T.L.A. [240]
MINISTRY OF EDUCATION THAILAND : NINETY-ONE YEARS OF EXPERIENCE / Thailand. Ministry of Education – Bangkok, 1983 – 2mf – 9 – DE-288/1 – ne IDC [370]

THE MINISTRY OF GRACE : STUDIES IN EARLY CHURCH HISTORY WITH REFERENCE TO PRESENT PROBLEMS / Wordsworth, John – London, New York: Longmans, Green, 1903 – 2mf – us A.T.L.A. [240]
Ministry of Justice *see* TAP LUAT LE VE TU PHAP, THEO CAC VAN DA CONG BO DEN NGAY 10/7/1957
Ministry of Justice, Tonga, Tongatapu Registry *see* BIRTHS AND DEATHS REGISTERS, 1867-1973 (GAPS – MAINLY 19TH CENTURY REGISTERS)
A MINISTRY OF MARRIAGE ENRICHMENT DESIGNED FOR CHURCH COUPLES / Lehrer, Harry Frederick – 1981 – 1 – 6.40 – us Baptist [240]
THE MINISTRY OF MERCY : 33 DEVOTIONAL STUDIES OF THE GOSPEL MIRACLES / Dover, Thomas Birkett – New York: James Pott, 1887 – 1mf – 9 – 0-8370-2960-0 – 1985-0960 – us A.T.L.A. [240]
THE MINISTRY OF RELIGIOUS AFFAIRS / Wahid Hasjim, Abdul – SE 12,169 1 – 9 – ne IDC [290]
THE MINISTRY OF THE LORD JESUS / Selby, Thomas Gunn – London: Charles H. Kelly, 1896. 1 fiche – 9 – us A.T.L.A. [240]
THE MINISTRY OF WOMEN / Gordon, Adoniram Judson – (The missionary review of the world, v. 17, Dec. 1894, p. 910-921) – 9 – us A.T.L.A. [240]
A MINISTRY TO PRESCHOOL CHILDREN AND THEIR PARENTS IN FIRST BAPTIST CHURCH, POOLER, GEORGIA / Major, Elbert Franklin – 1982 – 1 – 5.92 – us Baptist [240]
Mink, Randi S *see* A CONFIRMATORY FACTOR ANALYSIS OF THE CAROLINA SPORT CONFIDENCE INVENTORY
Minke, Pauline *see* CHINESE IN THE MOTHER LODE
Mink-van der Plas, Oetje de *see* BOTANY
MINN VON UNS, HERR... S. 101 = LITANEY VON MARTIN LUTHER UND JS BACH / Bach, Johann Sebastian – (Opening movement) – ed. A B Marx. Bonn: Simrock, 1830 – 1 – us Sibley [780]
MINNA VON BARNHELM, ODER, DAS SOLDATENGLUECK : LUSTSPIEL IN FUENF AUFZUEGEN / Lessing, Gotthold Ephraim – (German text with introd & notes in English. Includes bibliographical references) – rev ed. Boston [Mass.]: D C Heath, 1898, c1889 – 1 – us U.W. Library [820]
MINNA VON BARNHELM, ODER, DAS SOLDATENGLUECK : EIN LUSTSPIEL IN FUENF AUFZUEGEN / Lessing, Gotthold Ephraim – Leipzig: Max Hesse, [between 1904-1906?] – 1r – 1 – us U.W. Library [820]
MINNAH LI-YEHUDAH. YEHUDAH ZLOTNICK / Avida (Zlotnick), Yehuda L – Jerusalem. 1950. BJ-100-67 1 – 9 – ne IDC [999]
Minneapolis Institute of Arts *see* BULLETIN
MINNEAPOLIS STAR – Minneapolis, MN. 1920-82 – 1 – us UMI [071]
MINNEAPOLIS STAR AND TRIBUNE – Minneapolis, MN. 1982- – 1 – us UMI [071]
MINNEAPOLIS TRIBUNE – Minneapolis, MN. 1867-1982 – 1 – us UMI [071]
MINNESOTA – 1r – 1 – $80.00 – us Scholarly Res [370]
MINNESOTA : SESSION LAWS OF AMERICAN STATES AND TERRITORIES – 1849-1995 – 9 – $1,979.00 set – us Hein [340]
MINNESOTA : STATUTES ANNOTATED – 1946-Apr 1996 update – 9 – $2,095.00 set – us Hein [340]
Minnesota *see*
- INDEX TO THE POPULATION CENSUS SCHEDULES
- NONPOPULATION CENSUS SCHEDULES
- POPULATION CENSUS SCHEDULES
- REPORTS AND OPINIONS (A G)
- REPORTS, POST-NRS
- REPORTS, PRE-NRS
- SESSION LAWS

Minnesota. Agricultural Experiment Station. St. Paul. Northeast Experiment Station *see* REPORT
Minnesota. Agricultural Experiment Station. St. Paul. Northeast Experiment Station. Duluth *see*
- PUBLICATIONS
- REPORT

Minnesota. Agricultural Experiment Station. St. Paul. Northwest Experiment Station. Crookston *see* REPORT
Minnesota. Agricultural Experiment Station. St. Paul. Southeast Experiment Station. Waseca *see* REPORT
Minnesota. Agricultural Experiment Station. St. Paul. West Central Experiment Station *see* MORRIS REPORT
Minnesota. Agricultural Extension Service *see*
- EXTENSION BULLETIN
- MINNESOTA FARM BUSINESS NOTES
- RURAL SCHOOL AGRICULTURE
- SPECIAL REPORT

Minnesota. Agricultural Extension Service. Agricultural Extension Division *see* CIRCULAR
Minnesota. Agricultural Extension Service. Agricultural Extension Division. Minnesota Farmers' Library *see* EXTENSION BULLETIN
MINNESOTA AND ITS PEOPLE AND EARLY HISTORY OF MINNEAPOLIS / Stevens, John H – Minneapolis, 1890. Minnesota Reel 2. (The Cox Library Collection) – 5 – us Americana [978]
MINNESOTA ARCHAEOLOGIST – v1- 1935- 1; v36- 5,6,9 – us UMI [930]
MINNESOTA ARTISTS' PAPERS – Personal papers of seven 19th- and 20th- century artists, born and/or lived in Minnesota. Individual artist's papers available – 1 – us M.H.S. [920]
MINNESOTA ATTORNEY GENERAL REPORTS AND OPINIONS – (1858-1968 on reel $210.00. 1968-1994 $110.00 on mf) – 1858-1994 – 6,9 – $320.00set – us Hein [340]
MINNESOTA BAPTIST NEWS/LIFT – Minneapolis, MN.Minn. Board of Promotion/ Minn. Convention of American Baptist Churches. 1947-64. Single reels available – 1 – 66.10 – us A.B.H.S. [073]
MINNESOTA BEEF CATTLE FEEDERS DAY / Minnesota. College of Agriculture – 1953-69 – 1,5,6 – us Spaulding [636]
MINNESOTA CENSUS SCHEDULES FOR 1870 / U.S. Bureau of the Census – 13 rolls. T132 – 1 – us Nat'l Archives [310]
Minnesota Citizens Concerned for Life *see* NEWSPAPER CLIPPINGS
Minnesota. College of Agriculture *see*
- MINNESOTA BEEF CATTLE FEEDERS DAY
- MINNESOTA WILDLIFE DISEASE INVESTIGATION
- PROGRESS REPORT
- RURAL SCHOOL AGRICULTURAL BULLETIN
- SOIL SERIES

Minnesota. College of Agriculture. Chemical Products from Peat Project *see* PROGRESS REPORT
Minnesota. College of Agriculture. Cloquet Forest Research Center *see*
- CLIMATOLOGICAL OBSERVATIONS
- FOREST WILDLIFE INVESTIGATIONS

Minnesota. College of Agriculture. Department of Agricultural Engineering *see*
- AGRICULTURAL ENGINEERING NEWSLETTER
- REPORT

Minnesota. College of Agriculture. Dep't. of Agricultural and Applied Economics *see*
- ECONOMIC STUDY REPORT
- MIMEO REPORT
- MINNESOTA HIGHWAY RESEARCH PROJECT REPORT

Minnesota. College of Agriculture. Dept. of Agricultural and Applied Economics *see*
- ECONOMIC INFORMATION REPORT
- STAFF PAPERS

Minnesota. College of Agriculture. Institute of Agriculture *see*
- INTERNATIONAL AGRICULTURE SERIES
- SWINE FEEDERS' DAY

Minnesota. College of Agriculture. School of Forestry *see* MINNESOTA FORESTRY NOTES
MINNESOTA CONFERENSENS PROTOKOLL *see* AUGUSTANA EVANGELICAL LUTHERAN CHURCH
Minnesota. Dept. of Labor and Industry *see* STATE LABOR REPORTS
MINNESOTA FARM AND HOME SCIENCE / Minnesota. University. Agricultural Experiment Station. St. Paul – v.1-22. 1943-65 – 1,5,6 – us Spaulding [630]
MINNESOTA FARM BUSINESS NOTES / Minnesota. Agricultural Extension Service – nos.1-506. 1914-68 – 1,5,6 – us Spaulding [650]
MINNESOTA FORESTRY NOTES / Minnesota. College of Agriculture. School of Forestry – 15 Jul 1952-15 Oct 1970 – 1,5,6 – us Spaulding [634]
MINNESOTA HIGHWAY RESEARCH PROJECT REPORT / Minnesota. College of Agriculture. Dep't. of Agricultural and Applied Economics – 1958-63 – 1,5,6 – us Spaulding [630]
Minnesota. Historic Preservation Office Nomination Forms *see* MINNESOTA PROPERTIES LISTED ON THE NATIONAL REGISTER OF HISTORIC PLACES
Minnesota Historic Resources Survey *see* MANUSCRIPTS: COLLECTION INFORMATION FORMS
Minnesota Historical Co *see* MEN OF MINNESOTA
Minnesota Historical Society *see* COLLECTIONS
MINNESOTA IN THE CIVIL AND INDIAN WARS, 1861-1865 – (Index to Rosters, 488p. 1 reel. 10.00; 1) – 2v. 844+652p. v1 (1890), historical sketches and rosters of Minnesota organizations.v2 (1892), official reports and correspondence and lists of officers and rosters of soldiers in the Dakota War. 1 reel – 1 – 20.00 – us M.H.S. [978]
MINNESOTA INSECT LIFE / Minnesota. University. State Entomologist – v.1-4. 1910-17 – 1,5,6 – us Spaulding [590]
MINNESOTA: ITS STORY AND BIOGRAPHY / Castle, Henry A – Chicago: Lewis Publ. Co., 1915. 3v. Minnesota Reel 1. (The Cox Library Collection) – 5 – us Americana [978]
MINNESOTA LAW JOURNAL – St Paul. v1-5. 1893-97 – 1 – $40.00 – us Hein [073]
THE MINNESOTA LAW JOURNAL – v1-5. 1893-97 (all publ) – 16mf – 9 – $24.00 – LLMC 82-945 – us L.L.M.C. [073]
MINNESOTA LAW REVIEW – (Add vols as copyright expires) – v1-4. 1917-1919/20 – 24mf – $36.00 – LLMC 95-139 – us L.L.M.C. [073]
MINNESOTA LAW REVIEW – (v1-69 1917-85 on reel or mf $1,341.00. v70-79 1985-96 on mf $313.00) – v1-80. 1917-96 – 5,6,9 – $1,654.00 set – us Hein [340]
Minnesota. Laws, Statutes, etc *see* THE GENERAL STATUTES OF THE STATE OF MINNESOTA AS AMENDED BY SUBSEQUENT LEGISLATION.
MINNESOTA LAWYERS INTERNATIONAL HUMAN RIGHTS COMMITTEE – Minneapolis. 62 docs. 1986-1991 – 38mf – 9 – ne IDC [320]
MINNESOTA LIBRARIES – 1904- 1; 1970- 5,6; 1976- 4 x 6 in. 9 – us UMI [020]
MINNESOTA MEDICINE – v1- 1918- 1; v54- 5,6; v59- 9 – us UMI [616]
MINNESOTA NATURALIZATION RECORDS – 1 – $30.00r – us M.H.S. [323]
Minnesota. Presbytery (Pres. Ch. in the U.S.A.) *see* MINUTES
MINNESOTA PROPERTIES LISTED ON THE NATIONAL REGISTER OF HISTORIC PLACES / Minnesota. Historic Preservation Office Nomination Forms – 1969-82, arranged alphabetically by counties, alphabetically by historic name within each county. 4r including filmed inventory – 1 – $120.00; $30.00r – us M.H.S. [720]
MINNESOTA REVIEW – v1- 1960- 1,5,6; v9- 9 – us UMI [073]
MINNESOTA SCIENCE / Minnesota. University. Agricultural Experiment Station. St. Paul – v.23-31. 1966-75 – 1,5,6 – us Spaulding [630]
Minnesota. Secretary of State *see* ELECTION RETURNS, 1858-1962
Minnesota. State Bar Association *see* PROCEEDINGS
MINNESOTA STATE BAR ASSOCIATION REPORTS OF PROCEEDINGS – (Lacking: 1919, 1931, 1942) – 1st series: 1st annual meeting 1884; 2nd series: proceedings 1901-48 and 1943-49 Committee Reports (all publ) – 104mf – 9 – $156.00 – LLMC 84-609 – us L.L.M.C. [073]
Minnesota State Govt *see* THE MEXICANS IN MINNESOTA
Minnesota. Supreme Court *see*
- MINNESOTA SUPREME COURT REPORTS
- PROCEEDINGS IN MEMORY OF JUDGE EDWARD LEES

MINNESOTA SUPREME COURT REPORTS / Minnesota. Supreme Court – (Pre-NRS: v1-25 1851-79 148mf $222.00. Updates planned) – v1-145. 1851-1920 – 989mf – 9 – $1,483.00 – LLMC 80-811 – us L.L.M.C. [340]
Minnesota. Synod. (Pres. Ch. in the U.S.A.) *see* MINUTES
MINNESOTA TWINS SCRAPBOOKS – Primarily newspaper clippings (1938-81) documenting history of Minn. Twins baseball team, predecessor franchise, farm clubs, etc. 14r – 1 – $420.00; $30.00r – us M.H.S. [790]
Minnesota. University. Agricultural Experiment Station. St. Paul *see*
- ANNUAL REPORT
- BULLETIN
- CLASS BULLETINS
- MINNESOTA FARM AND HOME SCIENCE
- MINNESOTA SCIENCE
- MISCELLANEOUS REPORTS
- POSTWAR AGRICULTURE IN MINNESOTA
- PRESS BULLETINS
- TECHNICAL BULLETIN

Minnesota. University. State Entomologist *see*
- ANNUAL REPORT
- MINNESOTA INSECT LIFE

MINNESOTA WILDLIFE DISEASE INVESTIGATION / Minnesota. College of Agriculture – v.1-4. Jul 1933-Dec 1938 – 1,5,6 – us Spaulding [639]
Minnesota Woman Suffrage Association *see* RECORDS, 1894-1923
MINNESOTA-WISCONSIN SOUTHERN BAPTIST – Rochester, MN. 1986-1991. 378p – 1 – $17.60 – us Baptist [071]
MINNESOTIAN – Duluth. Minn. 1869-78; 1971- – 1 – us UMI [071]
MINNE-SPIEGEL ENDE WEG.WYSER.TER DEUGDEN / Krul, J H – (Contains: – Alcip en Amarillis. Bly-eynd-spel. – Faustina bly-eynd-spel. Op de spreuck: de leughen selden wel geluckt, hoe seer dy waerheyt onderdruckt. – Celion en Bellinde, pastorel, bly-eynd-spel. Ghetrocken uyt de Fransche Astrea. – Wegh-wyser ter deughden, tweede deel) – Amsterdam, [1640] – 7mf – 9 – O-3103/1 – ne IDC [760]
MINNE-SPIEGEL TER DEUGHDEN : BESTAENDE IN VERSCHEYDE MINNE BEELDEN, MINNE WETTEN, SOET GEVOYSDE LIEDTJENS, ENDE COMEDIEN / Krul, J H – Amsterdam, 1640 – 5mf – 9 – O-3104/1 – ne IDC [760]
A MINNIATURE OV INGLISH ORTHOGGRAPHY / Elphinston, James – 1795. 52p. (English Linguistics Series 1500-1800) – 9 – us UMI [420]
Minniear, T C *see* A STUDY OF MEASUREMENT AND EVALUATION PROCEDURES IN INDIANA ELEMENTARY PHYSICAL EDUCATION PROGRAMS
Minning, Arthur C *see* A TABULAR ANALYSIS OF THE LAW OF AGENCY
MINOBE YOJI MONJO = YOJI MINOBE COLLECTION OF MATERIALS CONCERNING WAR-TIME ECONOMIC POLICIES – Basic materials for the studies of economic policy and political history of Japan during the Second World War (1935-1945) – 114r – Y1,140,000.00 – ja Yushodo [950]
Minocchi, Salvatore *see*
- LA GENESI: CON DISCUSSIONI CRITICHE
- STORIA DEI SALMI E DELL'IDEA MESSIANICA

Minor, J *see* FRIEDRICH SCHLEGEL 1794-1802
Minor, Jacob *see*
- CHRISTIAN FELIX WEISSE UND SEINE BEZIEHUNGEN ZUR DEUTSCHEN LITERATUR DES ACHTZEHNTEN JAHRHUNDERTS
- JOHANN GEORG HAMANN IN SEINER BEDEUTUNG FUER DIE STURM- UND DRANGPERIODE
- REDE AUF GRILLPARZER

Minor, John Barbee *see* INSTITUTES OF COMMON AND STATUTE LAW
MINOR OIL CROPS – 1992 – 3pts 247p – it F.A.O. [630]
MINOR PROPHETS: WITH NOTES, CRITICAL, EXPLANATORY, AND PRACTICAL / Cowles, Henry – New York: D. Appleton, 1879. 1 fiche – 9 – us A.T.L.A. [220]
Minor, Raleigh Colston *see* THE LAW OF REAL PROPERTY (BASED ON MINOR'S INSTITUTES)
MINORICA ELUCIDATIVA RACIONABILIS SEPARATIONIS FRATRUM MINORUM DE OBSERVANTIA AB ALIIS FRATRIBUS EJUSDEM ORDINIS – Deventer, Jacob van Breda 1500 – Dfl9.00 – ne Slangenburg [240]
MINORITY AFFAIRS AND POLAND: AN INFORMATORY OUTLINE / ed by Paprocki, Stanislaw J – Warsaw: Nationality Research Institute, 1935. 184p – 1 – us U.W. Library [321]
MINORITY GROUPS IN ISRAEL, WITHIN THE GREEN LINE / Israel. Prime Minister's Office. Bureau of the Advisor on Arab Affairs – Jerusalem. 1973. 38 p – 9 – 2.00 – is I.T.T.I. [324]
MINORITY OF ONE – 1959-68 – 1 – us UMI [073]

MINORITY RIGHTS GROUP – London. 170 docs. 1980-1991 – 70mf – 9 – ne IDC [320]

THE MINOR-LAW-BOOKS : PART 1: NARADA, BRIHASPATI / ed by Mueller, Friedrich Max – (Translated by Julius Jolly) – 1889 – 8mf – 8 – ne Slangenburg [280]

MINOR'S REPORTS / Alabama. Supreme Court – (A Pre-NRS title) – Alabama. 1v. 1820-26 (all publ) – 5mf – 9 – $7.50 – LLMC 91-028 – us L.L.M.C. [340]

Minorsky, V *see* SHARAF-AL-ZAMAN TAHIR MARVAZI ON CHINA, THE TURKS AND INDIA

Minot, G *see* WOODBURY AND MINOT'S REPORTS OF CASES IN THE FIRST CIRCUIT, 1845-1847

LE MINOTAURE – Revue artistique et litteraire. no. 1-12 13. Paris. 1933-mai 1939 – 1 – fr A.C.R.P.P. [073]

MINQUANSU = THE ESSENCE OF DEMOCRACY – Apr 1914-Apr 1916. 4 reels. F-C34 – 1 – $180.00 – cc Microforms [073]

Minsheu, John *see* A DICTIONARIE IN SPANISH AND ENGLISH

MINSKAI A GAZETA – (Includes c.1: 1918:Dec.1-2) – Minsk: M. Dvorzhet s, 190u – 1 – CSUXANR9285-S – us Hoover Inst Photo [947]

MINSKER ZEITUNG – Minsk, USSR. April 15 1942-Jan 1 1944, Apr-June 1944 – 6r – 1 – us L of C Photodup [072]

MINSKI I GOLOS – (Includes c.1: 1918:Dec.1-2, 4) – Minsk: "Minski i golos", 190u – 1 – CSUXANR9254-S – us Hoover Inst Photo [947]

MINSKIE GUBERNSKIE VEDOMOSTI, 1838-1917 – 122r – 1 – $10,500.00 coll $100.00r – us Ross [072]

MINSKII A GUBERNSKII A VI EDOMOSTI – (Includes c.1: 181:Jan.17) – Minsk: Gub. tip – 1 – CSUXANR9306-S – us Hoover Inst Photo [947]

Minskii, N *see*
- AL'MA
- IZ MRAKA K SVETU
- KOGO ISHCHESH', (MISTERIIA)
- NA OBSHCHESTVENNYIA TEMY
- OT DANTE K BLOKU
- PRI SVETE SOVESTI
- RELIGIIA BUDUSHCHEGO (FILOSOFSKIE RAZGOVORY)
- STIKHOTVORENIIA

Minster Lovell. Oxfordshire *see* COURT ROLLS

THE MINSTRELSY OF THE ENGLISH BORDER – 1847 – 1 – us I.U. Libraries [810]

MINSU – Journal of Chinese Folk-Lore. 1928-43. 7 reels. M/C 82 – 1 – $385.00 – cc Microforms [073]

MIN-SU. JOURNAL OF CHINESE FOLKLORE – CH-316 2. v. 1-68, 71-99. 1928-30 – 8 – ne IDC [073]

Mintarum *see* 1958 ANNUAL REPORT KABUPATEN OF MALANG, EASTERN JAVA

Minter, William M *see* IMPERIAL NETWORK AND EXTERNAL DEPENDENCY

Minto, W *see* AUTOBIOGRAPHICAL NOTES ON THE LIFE OF WILLIAM BELL SCOTT

Minton, Henry Collin *see* THE COSMOS AND THE LOGOS

Mints, S V *see* ZAKONY O CHAST NOI PROMYSHLENNOSTI

Mintslof *see* PROGULKA PO S.-PETERBURGSKOI IMP. PUBLICHNOI BIBLIOTEKA

Mintslov, S R *see*
- OBZOR ZAPISOK, DNEVNIKOV, VOSPOMINANII, PISEM, PUTESHESTVII OTNOSIASHCHIKSIA K ISTORII ROSSII I NAPECHATNNYKH NA RUSSKOM IAZYKE
- REDCHAISHIIA KNIGI NAPECHATANNYIA V ROSSII NA RUSSKOM IAZYKE

MIN-TSU T'UAN-CHIEH / China. People's Republic – (National Unity). Peking. 1958-66. Lacking: v. 3-5, 7, 1958; v. 3, 1961; v. 8-12, 1966. BCH-926 2 – 8 – ne IDC [335]

MIN-TSU-HSUEH YEN-CHIU CHI-K'AN – (Ethnological studies). 6 v. Chungking. 1936-48. Lacking: v. 3, v. 5, 194? BCH-318 1 – 9 – ne IDC [306]

Mintz, I I *see*
- IAPONSKAIA INTERVENTSIIA 1918-1922 GG. V DOKUMENTAKH
- VELIKI OKTIABR'I NEPROLETARSKIE PARTII

Mintz, II *see* INTERVENTSIIA NA SEVERE V DOKUMENTAKH

Mintz, M *see* DIE NATIONALE AUTONOMIE... MINDERHEITSENRECHTS

MINUET IN A, TRANSCRIBED FOR THE ORGAN BY E.H. LEMARE / Boccherini, Luigi & Lemare, E H – 1 – us Sibley [780]

MINUETTI E CONTRIDANZE... / Duni, E – Londra, 1738 – 1 – us Sibley [780]

MINUTE – (Also available on CD-ROM) – France. 1989-1995 – 2r per y – 5,6 – Sfr535.00 – sz Infoprint [944]

MINUTE – Chicoutimi, 30 mar 1975-20 sep 1975f – 1r – 1 – Can$35.00 – cn Can Microfilming [072]

MINUTE BOOK / Osborne City Town Company, Osborne, KS – 1871-1872 – 1 – us KS Hist [978]

MINUTE BOOK / Patrons of Husbandry. Rose Grange No. 1384, Woodson County, KS – 1874-1877 – 1 – us KS Hist [920]

MINUTE BOOKS / Ancient Order of United Workmen. Delphos Lodge No. 129 – 1883-1899 – 1 – us KS Hist [978]

MINUTE BOOKS / Ilkley. Yorkshire. England. Urban District Council – 1864-87 – 1 – uk Microform Academic [941]

MINUTE BOOKS / Independent Labour Party. Great Britain – 1893 to 1906 – 1 – uk Microform Academic [335]

THE MINUTE BOOKS / American Chamber of Commerce. Liverpool. BRRAM – 1801-1908 – 1 – uk Microform Academic [970]

MINUTE BOOKS OF THE U.S. CIRCUIT COURT FOR WEST TENNESSEE / U.S. Circuit and District Courts. Tennessee – 1803-39. U.S. Circuit Court for the Middle District of Tennessee, 1839-64. 4 rolls – 1 – M1214 – us Nat'l Archives [324]

MINUTE BOOKS OF THE U.S. DISTRICT COURT FOR WEST TENNESSEE / U.S. Circuit and District Courts. Tennessee – 1797-1839. U.S. District Court for the Middle District of Tennessee, 1839-65. 1 roll – 1 – M1213 – us Nat'l Archives [324]

MINUTE BOOKS, U.S. CIRCUIT COURT, EASTERN DISTRICT OF NORTH CAROLINA, RALEIGH, 1791-1866 – 2r – 1 – M1428 – us Nat'l Archives [340]

MINUTE BOOKS, U.S. DISTRICT COURT, EASTERN DISTRICT OF NORTH CAROLINA, ALBEMARLE DIVISION AT EDENTON, 1807-70, AND AT ELIZABETH CITY, 1870-1914 – 1r – 1 – M1425 – us Nat'l Archives [340]

MINUTE BOOKS, U.S. DISTRICT COURT, EASTERN DISTRICT OF NORTH CAROLINA, CAPE FEAR DIVISION AT WILMINGTON, 1795-96 AND 1858-1911 – 2r – 1 – M1426 – us Nat'l Archives [340]

MINUTE BOOKS, U.S. DISTRICT COURT, EASTERN DISTRICT OF NORTH CAROLINA, PAMLICO DIVISION AT NEW BERN, 1858-1914 – 2r – 1 – M1427 – us Nat'l Archives [340]

MINUTES / Albany. Synod (Pres. Church in the U.S.A.) – 1803-1828, 1838-1881. (New School. 1838-1839; Old School. 1859-1869) – 1 – $50.00 – us Presbyterian [240]

MINUTES / Allen County. Ohio. Board of Elections – 1905-1950 – 2r – 1 – $32.50r – us Archival [324]

MINUTES / Allen County. Ohio. Board of Revision – 1888-1946 – 2r – 1 – $32.50r – us Archival [324]

MINUTES / Allen County. Ohio. Budget Commission – 1911-1913 – 2r – 1 – $32.50r – us Archival [324]

MINUTES / Allen County. Ohio. Trustees of the Sinking Fund – 1920-1930 – 1r – 1 – $32.50r – us Archival [324]

MINUTES / American Convention for Promoting the Abolition of Slavery, and Improving the Condition of the African Race – v1-8,11,13-15,20 – 1r – 1 – us Ross [976]

MINUTES / Austin. Texas. Highland Park Baptist Church – 1953-82 – 1 – us UMI [240]

MINUTES / Baptist Associations, Maine. Androscroggin Free Will Baptist and United Baptist Annual Meetings – 1916-63 – 1 – us A.B.H.S. [240]

MINUTES / Baptist Associations, Maine. Bowdoinham Free Will Baptist Quarterly Meeting – 1825-1917 – 1 – 48.25 – us A.B.H.S. [240]

MINUTES / Baptist Associations, Maine. Eastern Maine Baptist Association. Bible and Religious Tract Society – 1818-67 – 1 – 15.50 – us A.B.H.S. [240]

MINUTES / Baptist Associations, Maine. Kennebec Free Will Baptist Yearly Meeting – (Maine Central Free Will Baptist Yearly Meeting, Minutes, 1853-89) – 1853-89 – 1 – us A.B.H.S. [240]

MINUTES / Baptist Associations, Maine. Lincoln Baptist Association – 1835-1909. Includes Records of Lincoln Baptist Benevolent Society – 1 – us A.B.H.S. [240]

MINUTES / Baptist Associations, Maine. Maine Free Baptist Association. Annual Meeting – 1889-1944. Lacking: 1917 – 1 – 16.80 – us A.B.H.S. [240]

MINUTES / Baptist General Association. Kentucky. Executive Board – 1853-1956. 3330p – 1 – us Baptist [240]

MINUTES / Baptist Southern Convention – 1948-58 – 1 – $8.12 – us Baptist [240]

MINUTES / Baptist Triennial Convention. Board of Foreign Missions of the Baptist General Missionary Convention – 1814-47 – 1 – $27.75 – us Baptist [240]

MINUTES / Baptist Woman's Missionary Union. Spartan Woman's Missionary Union, Auxiliary to Spartan Baptist Association – 1912-19 – 1 – $6.16 – us Baptist [240]

MINUTES / Baptist World Alliance. Administrative and Executive Committees – 1940-79 – 1 – us A.B.H.S. [240]

MINUTES / Baptist World Alliance. Advisory Committee – 1920-29 – 1 – us A.B.H.S. [240]

MINUTES / Baptist World Alliance. Committee on Relief and Development – 1943-80 – 1 – us A.B.H.S. [240]

MINUTES / Baptist World Alliance. Continental Committee – 1904-40 – 1 – us A.B.H.S. [240]

MINUTES / Baptist World Alliance. North American Baptist Fellowship – 1966-79 – 1 – us A.B.H.S. [240]

MINUTES / Barnesville. Georgia. Mount Zion Baptist Church – Sept 1852-1916. Lacking: Dec 1852-Apr 1857 – 8 – ne IDC [240]

MINUTES / Bloom Center Literary Society (Wood County, Ohio) – 1875-76 – 1r – 1 – $32.50r – us Archival [978]

MINUTES / Boston. Presbytery – 1745-1755, 1769-1775; New England. Synod. Minutes. 1776-1782; Salem. Presbytery. Minutes. 1782-1791 – 1 – $50.00 – us Presbyterian [240]

MINUTES / Calvinistic Methodist Church in the U.S.A. General Assembly – 1869-1904, 1907-1920 – 1 – $50.00 – us Presbyterian [240]

MINUTES / Carlisle. Presbytery (Pres. Ch. in the U.S.A.) – 1765-1766, 1786-1794 – 1 – $50.00 – us Presbyterian [240]

MINUTES / Carolina Rifle Club. Charleston, South Carolina – 1869-82. 12 fiches – 9 – us South Carolina Historical [790]

MINUTES / Central New York. Synod. (Pres. Ch. in the U.S.A.) – 1873, 1875 – 1 – $50.00 – us Presbyterian [240]

MINUTES / Charleston County Democratic Executive Committee – 1876-80. 2 fiches – 9 – us South Carolina Historical [978]

MINUTES / Clionian Debating Society. Charleston, South Carolina – 1847-51. 3 fiches – 9 – us South Carolina Historical [978]

MINUTES / Conference on Co-operative Communities – 1982 – 9 – 1.00f – at Libertarian Micro [335]

MINUTES / Convention Evangelica Bautista. Argentine Baptist convention – 1933-73. 2012p – 1 – 70.42 – us Baptist [240]

MINUTES / Crawford County. Ohio. Galion – 1962-1979 – 1r – 1 – $32.50r – us Archival [324]

MINUTES / Defiance County, Ohio. County Home – 1868-1897 – 1r – 1 – $32.50r – us Archival [324]

MINUTES / Donegal. Presbytery (Pres. Ch. in the U.S.A.) – 1732-1750, 1759-1786; Lancaster. Presbytery (Pres. Ch. in the U.S.A.). Minutes. 1765-1766; Carlisle. Presbytery. (Pres. Ch. in the U.S.A.). Minutes. 1765-1777 – 1 – $100.00 – us Presbyterian [240]

MINUTES / Dorchester. South Carolina. Independent Congregational Church – 1794-1858. 5 fiches – 9 – us South Carolina Historical [240]

MINUTES / Enon, Pennsylvania. Enon Baptist Church – (Maple Creek Baptist Church Records, 1825-77. Amnon Baptist Church (West VA), Records, 1878-1934) – 1791-1823. Primitive Baptists, members of Redstone Baptist Assoc – 1 – 15.50 – us A.B.H.S. [240]

MINUTES / Erie County. Ohio. Huron, City City Council – 1937-1961 – 1r – 1 – $32.50r – us Archival [324]

MINUTES / Erie County. Ohio. Kelley's Island Twp Board of Trustees – 1883-1890 – 1r – 1 – $32.50r – us Archival [324]

MINUTES / Erie County. Ohio. Milan Township. Board of Trustees – 1821-1982 – 1 reel – 1 – us Archival [978]

MINUTES / Erie County, Ohio. Milan Township. Board of Trustees – 1821-1995 – 4r – 1 – $32.50r – us Archival [978]

MINUTES / Erie County. Ohio. Milan, Village. Village Council – 1876-1942 – 1r – 1 – $32.50r – us Archival [324]

MINUTES / Erie County. Ohio. Oxford Township. Board of Trustees – 1903-1986 – 2r – 1 – us Archival [978]

MINUTES / Erie County. Ohio. Oxford Township. Board of Trustees – 1903-96 – 3r – 1 – $32.50r – us Archival [978]

MINUTES / Erie County. Ohio. Vermilion. City Council – 1876-1909 – 1r – 1 – $32.50r – us Archival [324]

MINUTES / Erie County. Ohio. Vermilion. Depository Commission – 1932-1936 – 1r – 1 – $32.50r – us Archival [324]

MINUTES / Erie County. Ohio. Vermilion. Sinking Fund Trustees – 1908-1942 – 1r – 1 – $32.50r – us Archival [324]

MINUTES / Erie County. Ohio. Vermilion Township. Board of Education – 1853-1918 – 1r – 1 – $32.50r – us Archival [978]

MINUTES / Erie County. Ohio. Vermilion Township. Board of Health – 1893-1917 – 1r – 1 – $32.50r – us Archival [324]

MINUTES / Erie County, Ohio. Vermilion Township. Board of Trustees – 1837-1988 – 4r – 1 – $32.50r – us Archival [978]

MINUTES / Faith and Order Commission – 1910-49 and Minutes of its Executive Committee, 1910-27 and Correspondence of Robt. H. Gardiner, 1910-27, Correspondence of Ralph W. Brown. 1924-1932 – 1 – us A.T.L.A. [240]

MINUTES / Female Charitable Association. Charleston – 1824-1860. 2 fiches – 9 – us South Carolina Historical [360]

MINUTES / Fulton County. Ohio. Archbold. Village. Board of Public Affairs – 1915-1973 – 2r – 1 – $32.50r – us Archival [324]

MINUTES / Fulton County. Ohio. Archbold. Village. Fire Department – 1896-1965 – 2r – 1 – $32.50r – us Archival [324]

MINUTES / Fulton County. Ohio. Archbold. Village. Village Council – 1865-1976 – 5r – 1 – us Archival [978]

MINUTES / Fulton County. Ohio. Board of Revision – 1914-1947 – 1r – 1 – $32.50r – us Archival [324]

MINUTES / Fulton County. Ohio. Budget Commission – 1918-1950 – 1r – 1 – $32.50r – us Archival [324]

MINUTES / Fulton County. Ohio. County Home – 1874-1912 – 2r – 1 – $32.50r – us Archival [324]

MINUTES / Fulton County, Ohio. Franklin Township. Board of Education. SubDist.2 – 1853-1872 – 1r – 1 – $32.50r – us Archival [324]

MINUTES / Geneva. Presbytery (Pres. Ch. in the U.S.A.) – 1805-13, 1820-85 – 1 – $50.00 – us Presbyterian [240]

MINUTES / Georgia. Black Baptist Associations – 1873-1938. 3 reels – 1 – 124.30 – us A.B.H.S. [240]

MINUTES / Gold Coast. (Colony). Legislative Council – 1916 17-1945. 1930 31, 1931 32 wanting – 1 – 113.00 – us L of C Photodup [960]

MINUTES / Grand Army of the Republic. Post 332. White Cloud, Kansas – 1884-91 – 1 – us KS Hist [976]

MINUTES / Hampton, Iowa. First Baptist Church – (Annual Meeting Minutes, 1884-91, 1894-1960. Executive Board Minutes, 1982-85. Newsletters, Annual Reports, 1950-80. Correspondence) – 1865-94 – 1 – us A.B.H.S. [240]

MINUTES / Hancock County. Ohio. Biglick Township. Board of Education – 1856-1905 – 1r – 1 – $32.50r – us Archival [324]

MINUTES / Hancock County. Ohio. Biglick Township. Board of Health – 1894-1903 – 1r – 1 – $32.50r – us Archival [324]

MINUTES / Hancock County. Ohio. Biglick Township. Board of Trustees – 1838-1978 – 2r – 1 – us Archival [978]

MINUTES / Hancock County. Ohio. Biglick Township. Board of Trustees – 1838-1988 (gaps) – 3r – 1 – $32.50r – us Archival [978]

MINUTES / Hancock County. Ohio. Cass Township. Board of Education – 1909-1920 – 1r – 1 – $32.50r – us Archival [324]
MINUTES / Hancock County. Ohio. Eagle Township. Board of Trustees – 1840-1865 – 1r – 1 – $32.50r – us Archival [324]
MINUTES / Hancock County. Ohio. Marion Township. Board of Trustees – 1835-1983 – 1r – 1 – $32.50r – us Archival [324]
MINUTES / Huron County. Ohio. County Home – 1848-1926 – 1r – 1 – $32.50r – us Archival [324]
MINUTES / Huron County. Ohio. Plymouth. Village. Cemetery Trustees. – (Incomplete) – 1873-1965 – 1r – 1 – $32.50r – us Archival [324]
MINUTES / Huron. Presbytery (Pres. Ch. in the USA) – 1823-40; 1880-1919 – 1 – $50.00 – us Presbyterian [240]
MINUTES / Lucas County, Ohio. Maumee, City. City Council – 1839-1969 – 5r – 1 – $32.50r – us Archival [324]
MINUTES / Lucas County. Ohio. Providence Township. Board of Trustees – 1836-1984 – 2r – 1 – $32.50r – us Archival [324]
MINUTES / Lucas County. Ohio. Toledo, City Board of Education – 1849-1912 – 7r – 1 – $32.50r – us Archival [324]
MINUTES / Lucas County. Ohio. Toledo, City Board of Police Commissioners – 1867-1907 – 2r – 1 – $32.50r – us Archival [324]
MINUTES / Lucas County. Ohio. Toledo, City Board of Public Safety – 1908-1927 – 3r – 1 – $32.50r – us Archival [324]
MINUTES / Lucas County. Ohio. Toledo, City Board of Public Service – 1903-1937 – 8r – 1 – $32.50r – us Archival [324]
MINUTES / Lucas County. Ohio. Toledo, City Industrial Peace Board – 1939-1943 – 1r – 1 – $32.50r – us Archival [324]
MINUTES / Lucas County. Ohio. Toledo, City Park Commission – 1891-1921 – 2r – 1 – $32.50r – us Archival [324]
MINUTES / Lucas County. Ohio. Whitehouse, Village. Fire Department – 1896-1988 – 1r – 1 – $32.50r – us Archival [324]
MINUTES / Maine Baptist Educational Society – (Treasurer's Books, 1857-1915) – 1819-1915. Lacking: 1831-57 – 1 – 24.60 – us A.B.H.S. [240]
MINUTES / Methodist Episcopal Church. Kansas Mission Conference – 1855-61 – 1 – us KS Hist [240]
MINUTES / Miami. Presbytery (Assoc. Pres. Ch. of N.A.) – (Includes: Kentucky. Presbytery (Assoc. Pres. Ch. of N.A.), Minutes, 1798-1821) – v1-3. 1798-1858 – 1 – $50.00 – us Presbyterian [240]
MINUTES / Minnesota. Presbytery (Pres. Ch. in the U.S.A.) – 1850-69. (New School); St. Paul. Presbytery. Minutes. 1855-70. (Old School). 1870-84 – 1 – $50.00 – us Presbyterian [240]
MINUTES / Minnesota. Synod. (Pres. Ch. in the U.S.A.) – 1858-69 (New School); 1870-76; St. Paul. Synod. Minutes. 1860-69 (Old School) – 1 – $50.00 – us Presbyterian [240]
MINUTES / Missouri. Synod (Pres. Ch. in the U.S.A.) – 1832-34; 1841-86 – 1 – $50.00 – us Presbyterian [240]
MINUTES / Monroe County. Mich, Bedford Township. Board of Trustees – 1919-1975 – 2r – 1 – $32.50r – us Archival [324]
MINUTES / Musical Art Club. Charleston, South Carolina – 1923-39. 6 fiches – 9 – us South Carolina Historical [780]
MINUTES / National Free Will Baptist Bodies of the United States – 1942-65. (lacking 1946) – 1 – $57.54 – us Baptist [240]
MINUTES / New Castle. Presbytery (Pres. Ch. in the U.S.A.) – 1716-31, 1759-1814; Lancaster. Presbytery. Minutes. 1765-66 – 1 – $50.00 – us Presbyterian [240]
MINUTES / New Jersey. Synod (Pres. Ch. in the U.S.A.) – 1837-1838, 1865-1958 – 1 – $300.00 – us Presbyterian [240]
MINUTES / New York Baptist Convention. Executive Board – Apr 30, 1964-Oct 22, 1971. 278p – 1 – us Baptist [240]
MINUTES / New Zealand. Methodist Church. Overseas Mission Board – dec 1955-nov 1972 – 1r – 1 – PMB1110 – at Pacific Mss [240]
MINUTES / Oklahoma, Choctaw-Chickasaw Sunday School Convention – 1917-51 – 1 – 33.95 – us Baptist [240]
MINUTES / Ottawa County. Ohio. Carroll Township. Board of Trustees – 1877-1982 – 2r – 1 – $32.50r – us Archival [324]
MINUTES / Ottawa County. Ohio. Carroll Township. Fruit Commissioners – 1897 – 1r – 1 – $32.50r – us Archival [324]
MINUTES / Ottawa County. Ohio. County Home – 1872-1926 – 1r – 1 – $32.50r – us Archival [324]
MINUTES / Ottawa County. Ohio. Middle Bass Island Board of Education – 1900-1962 – 1r – 1 – $32.50r – us Archival [324]
MINUTES / Ottawa County. Ohio. Put-in-Bay. Village. Village Council – 1879-1954 – 2r – 1 – $32.50r – us Archival [324]
MINUTES / Ottawa County. Ohio. Soldiers Relief Commission – 1892-1903 – 2r – 1 – $32.50r – us Archival [324]
MINUTES / Paulding County. Ohio. Cecil Village Council – 1882-1887 – 1r – 1 – $32.50r – us Archival [324]
MINUTES / Paulding County, Ohio. Cecil Village Council – 1882-1887 – 1r – 1 – us Archival [324]
MINUTES / Pennsylvania. Presbytery (Cum. Pres. Ch.) – 1832-85; 1901-07 – 1 – $50.00 – us Presbyterian [240]
MINUTES / Philadelphia. Pennsylvania. Second Presbyterian Church Corporation – 1772-1805; 1810-15. Typed transcript of 1772-1805 minutes – 1 – $50.00 – us Presbyterian [240]
MINUTES / Philadelphia. Presbytery (Pres. Ch. in the U.S.A.) – 1706-1716, 1733-1746, 1758-1901 – 1 – $250.00 – us Presbyterian [240]
MINUTES / Poetry Society of South Carolina – 1922-23. 2 fiches – 9 – us South Carolina Historical [420]
MINUTES / Putnam County. Ohio. County Home – 1869-1907 – 1r – 1 – $32.50r – us Archival [324]
MINUTES / Reformed Dissenting Presbytery – 1801-45; 1847-50 – 1 – $50.00 – us Presbyterian [240]
MINUTES / Reformed Presbytery of America – 1798-1809, 1888 – 1 – $50.00 – us Presbyterian [240]
MINUTES / St. Paul. Presbytery (Pres. Ch. in the U.S.A.) – 1855-70 (Old School), 1870-84; Minnesota. Presbytery. Minutes. 1850-69 (New School) – 1 – $50.00 – us Presbyterian [240]
MINUTES / St. Paul. Synod. (Pres. Ch. in the U.S.A.) – 1860-69 (Old School); Minnesota. Synod. Minutes. 1858-69 (New School); 1870-76 – 1 – $50.00 – us Presbyterian [240]
MINUTES / Salem. Presbytery – 1782-1791; Boston. Presbytery. Minutes. 1745-1755, 1769-1775; New England. Synod. Minutes. 1776-1782 – 1 – $50.00 – us Presbyterian [240]
MINUTES / Sandusky County. Ohio. Woodville Township. Board of Trustees – 1856-1942 – 1r – 1 – $32.50r – us Archival [324]
MINUTES / Savannah & Charleston Railroad. Board of Directors, etc – 1869-78. 3 fiches – 9 – us South Carolina Historical [380]
MINUTES / Seneca County. Ohio. Bloom Township. Board of Trustees – 1838-1982 – 2r – 1 – $32.50r – us Archival [324]
MINUTES / Seneca County. Ohio. Fostoria, City. City Council – 1866-1950 – 5r – 1 – us Archival [324]
MINUTES / Seneca County. Ohio. Fostoria, City. City Council – 1866-1950 – 5r – 1 – $32.50r – us Archival [324]
MINUTES / Seneca County. Ohio. Liberty Township. Board of Education – 1857-1918 – 1r – 1 – $32.50r – us Archival [324]
MINUTES / Seneca County. Ohio. Liberty Township. Board of Trustees – 1865-1958 – 2r – 1 – $32.50r – us Archival [324]
MINUTES / Seneca County, Ohio. Tiffin, City. City Council – 1850-1990 – 11r – 1 – $32.50r – us Archival [324]
MINUTES / Sherman County. Kansas. Homesteaders Union Association. Lodge No. 3 – 1887-88 – 1 – us KS Hist [978]
MINUTES / Society of the Cincinnati of the State of South Carolina – 1862-1969. 70 fiches – 9 – us South Carolina Historical [978]
MINUTES / South Carolina. Militia. German Fusiliers – 1905-14.20 fiches – 9 – us South Carolina Historical [978]
MINUTES / Southern Baptist Association of Executives of Baptist Children's Homes – 19 Jan 1949-1 Jun 1954, 1955-Jan 1962. 406p – 1 – us Baptist [240]
MINUTES / Union. Presbytery (Cum. Pres. Ch.) – 1837-56, 1861-1907 – 1 – $50.00 – us Presbyterian [240]
MINUTES / Van Wert County. Ohio. Board of County Commissioners – 1973-1981 – 2r – 1 – $32.50rr – us Archival [324]
MINUTES / Van Wert County. Ohio. County Home – 1875-1902 – 1r – 1 – $32.50r – us Archival [324]
MINUTES / Van Wert County. Ohio. Pleasant Township. Board of Education – 1864-1894 – 1r – 1 – $32.50r – us Archival [324]
MINUTES / Wauseon Ministerial Association (Wauseon, Ohio) – 1880-1886 – 1r – 1 – $32.50r – us Archival [240]
MINUTES / Wayne, Pennsylvania. Central Baptist Church – (Membership Register, 1896-1948. Legal Papers, 1927-28; 1951) – 1896-1955 – 1 – 43.20 – us A.B.H.S. [240]
MINUTES / Williams County. Ohio. County Home – 1874-1900 – 1r – 1 – $32.50r – us Archival [324]
MINUTES / Wood County. Ohio. Bloom Township. Board of Trustees – 1844-1977 – 2r – 1 – $32.50r – us Archival [324]
MINUTES / Wood County. Ohio. Board of Education – 1914-1963 – 2r – 1 – $32.50r – us Archival [324]
MINUTES / Wood County. Ohio. Bowling Green City. Board of Education – 1900-1976 – 5r – 1 – $32.50r – us Archival [324]
MINUTES / Wood County. Ohio. Bowling Green, City. Board of Public Utilities – 1942-1982 – 7r – 1 – $32.50r – us Archival [324]
MINUTES / Wood County. Ohio. Bowling Green. City Council – 1855-1866 – 1r – 1 – $32.50r – us Archival [324]
MINUTES / Wood County. Ohio. Bradner, Village. Board of Education – 1876-1950 – 2r – 1 – $32.50r – us Archival [324]
MINUTES / Wood County. Ohio. Bradner. Village Council – 1890-1940 – 2r – 1 – $32.50r – us Archival [324]
MINUTES / Wood County. Ohio. Freedom Township. Board of Trustees – 1883-1985 – 2r – 1 – $32.50r – us Archival [324]
MINUTES / Wood County. Ohio. Pemberville, Village. Board of Public Affairs – 1929-1985 – 1r – 1 – $32.50r – us Archival [324]
MINUTES / Wood County. Ohio. Pemberville, Village. Village Council – 1876-1984 – 3r – 1 – $32.50r – us Archival [324]
MINUTES / Wood County. Ohio. Weston. Village Council – 1898-1975 – 2r – 1 – $32.50r – us Archival [324]
MINUTES / Wyandot County. Ohio. County Home – 1899-1909 – 1r – 1 – $32.50r – us Archival [324]
MINUTES / Wyandot County. Ohio. Upper Sandusky. City Council – 1857-1977 – 5r – 1 – $32.50r – us Archival [324]
MINUTES, 13 APRIL 1852-13 APRIL 1859 / Illinois. Second Presbytery (Associate Reformed Church) – 1 – $50.00 – us Presbyterian [240]
MINUTES, 1672-1700 / Laggan Presbytery. Ireland – 1 – $50.00 – us Presbyterian [240]
MINUTES, 1738-1798 / New Brunswick. Presbytery (Pres. Ch. in the U.S.A.) – 1 – $50.00 – us Presbyterian [240]
MINUTES, 1745-58 / New York. Synod – Also: New York and Philadelphia. Synod. Minutes, 1758-88 – 1 – $50.00 – us Presbyterian [240]
MINUTES, 1747-1789 / Suffolk. Presbytery (Pres. Ch. in the U.S.A.) – (Long Island. Presbytery. Minutes. 1790-1811) – 1 – $50.00 – us Presbyterian [240]
MINUTES, 1758-1810 / Lewes. Presbytery (Pres. Ch. in the U.S.A.) – 1 – $50.00 – us Presbyterian [240]
MINUTES, 1762-1795 / Dutchess. Presbytery (Pres. Ch. in the U.S.A.) – 1 – $50.00 – us Presbyterian [240]
MINUTES, 1762-1798 / Pennsylvania. Presbytery (Assoc. Ch.) – 1 – $50.00 – us Presbyterian [240]
MINUTES, 1765-66 / Lancaster. Presbytery (Pres. Ch. in the U.S.A.) – New Castle. Presbytery. Minutes, 1716-31, 1759-1814 – 1 – $50.00 – us Presbyterian [240]
MINUTES, 1766-75; PRESBYTERIAN CHURCH IN THE U.S.A., RECORDS, 1706-88 / General Convention for Religious Liberty – 1904 – 1 – $50.00 – us Presbyterian [240]
MINUTES, 1771-92 / Eastward. Presbytery (Pres. Ch. in the U.S.A.) – (With Londonderry. Presbytery (Assoc. Ref. Ch.) Minutes, 1783-1809) – 1 – $50.00 – us Presbyterian [240]
MINUTES, 1776-1782 / New England. Synod – (Salem. Presbytery. Minutes. 1782-1791; Boston. Presbytery. Minutes. 1745-1755, 1769-1775) – 1 – $50.00 – us Presbyterian [240]
MINUTES, 1781-1902 / Redstone. Presbytery (Pres. Ch. in the U.S.A.) – 1 – $100.00 – us Presbyterian [240]
MINUTES, 1782-1822 / Associate Reformed Church in North America. General Synod – 1 – $50.00 – us Presbyterian [240]
MINUTES, 1783-1809 / Londonderry. Presbytery (Assoc. Ref. Ch.) – (Also: Eastward. Presbytery (Pres. Ch. in the U.S.A.), Minutes, 1771-92) – 1 – $50.00 – us Presbyterian [240]
MINUTES, 1786-1906 / Baltimore. Presbytery (Pres. Ch. in the U.S.A.) – 1 – $200.00 – us Presbyterian [240]
MINUTES, 1788-1822 / New York and New Jersey. Synod (Pres. Ch. in the U.S.A.) – 1 – $100.00 – us Presbyterian [240]
MINUTES, 1790-1811 / Long Island. Presbytery (Pres. Ch. in the U.S.A.) – (Also: Suffolk. Presbytery. Minutes, 1747-89) – 1 – $50.00 – us Presbyterian [240]
MINUTES..., 1790-1842, AND INDEX TO PLAINTIFFS AND DEFENDANTS..., 1790-1860 / U.S. District Courts. Georgia – RG21. 3 rolls – 1 – M1184 – us Nat'l Archives [340]
MINUTES. 1790-1950 / U.S. Supreme Court – 41 rolls. M215. printed guide – 1 – us Nat'l Archives [340]
MINUTES, 1793-1802 / Pennsylvania. Second Presbytery. (Assoc. Ref. Ch. of NA) – (With: Monongahela. Presbytery (Assoc. Ref. Ch. of NA). Minutes, 1803-1858) – 1 – $50.00 – us Presbyterian [240]
MINUTES, 1795-1895 / Huntingdon. Presbytery – 1 – $100.00 – us Presbyterian [240]
MINUTES, 1799-1821 / Washington. Presbytery (Pres. Ch. in the U.S.A.) – 1 – $50.00 – us Presbyterian [240]
MINUTES, 1799-1948 / Union. Presbytery (Pres. Ch. in the U.S.A.) – 1 – $200.00 – us Presbyterian [240]
MINUTES, 1801-1809 / Reformed Presbyterian Church in North America. Presbytery – (General Synod. Minutes. 1809-53) – 1 – $50.00 – us Presbyterian [240]
MINUTES, 1801-1821 / Associate Synod of North America – 1 – $50.00 – us Presbyterian [240]
MINUTES, 1801-1861 / Philadelphia. Presbytery (Assoc. Ch.) – 1 – $50.00 – us Presbyterian [240]
MINUTES, 1802-1810 / Kentucky. Synod (Pres. Ch. in the U.S.A.) – 1 – $50.00 – us Presbyterian [240]
MINUTES, 1802-1924 / Erie. Presbytery (Pres. Ch. in the U.S.A.) – Old School: 1838-1869 – 1 – $150.00 – us Presbyterian [240]
MINUTES, 1803-1858 / Monongahela. Presbytery. (Assoc. Ref. Ch. of NA) – (With: Pennsylvania. Second Presbytery (Assoc. Ref. Ch. of NA). Minutes, 1793-1802) – 1 – $50.00 – us Presbyterian [240]
MINUTES, 1803-1901 / New York. Synod (Assoc. Ref. Ch.) – 1 – $100.00 – us Presbyterian [240]
MINUTES, 1805-1815 / Chartiers. Presbytery (Assoc. Pres. Ch. of No. Am.) – 1 – $50.00 – us Presbyterian [240]
MINUTES, 1808-1867 / Ohio. Presbytery (Assoc. ChurchUnited Pres. Ch. of No. Am.) – (With: Portage. Presbytery (Pres. Ch. in the U.S.A. New School). Minutes, 1843-63; Trumbull. Presbytery (Pres. Ch. in the U.S.A. New School). Minutes, 1827-70) – 1 – $50.00 – us Presbyterian [240]
MINUTES, 1810-13; CUMBERLAND. SYNOD / Cumberland. Presbytery (Cum. Pres. Ch.) – (Minutes, 1813-28; Cumberland Presbyterian Church. General Assembly. Minutes, 1829-55) – 1 – $50.00 – us Presbyterian [240]
MINUTES, 1810-1840 / New York. Presbytery (Pres. Ch. in the U.S.A.) – 1 – $50.00 – us Presbyterian [240]
MINUTES, 1810-1870 / Miami. Presbytery (Pres. Ch. in the U.S.A.) – 1 – $50.00 – us Presbyterian [240]
MINUTES, 1812-1881 / Geneva. Synod (Pres. Ch. in the U.S.A.) – New School: 1838-1869 – 1 – $50.00 – us Presbyterian [240]

MINUTES, 1815-1856 / Presbyterian Church in the U.S.A. Board of Missions – (Board of Domestic Missions. Minutes. 1857-73) – 1 – $50.00 – us Presbyterian [240]

MINUTES, 1817-1862 / Bath. Presbytery (Pres. Ch. in the U.S.A.) – 1 – $50.00 – us Presbyterian [240]

MINUTES, 1817-1900 / Newton. Presbytery (Pres. Ch. in the U.S.A.) – 1 – $150.00 – us Presbyterian [240]

MINUTES, 1819-1897 / Presbyterian Church in the U.S.A. Board of Education – 1 – $50.00 – us Presbyterian [240]

MINUTES, 1821-1870 / Genesee Synod. (Pres. Ch. in the U.S.A.) – New School: 1838-1869 – 1 – $50.00 – us Presbyterian [240]

MINUTES, 1822-1911 / Cincinnati. Presbytery (Presbyterian Church in the U.S.A.) – 1 – $250.00 – us Presbyterian [240]

MINUTES, 1823-1889 / New Jersey. Synod (Pres. Ch. in the U.S.A.) – 1 – $100.00 – us Presbyterian [240]

MINUTES, 1826-42 / Madison. Presbytery (Pres. Ch. in the U.S.A.) – 1 – $50.00 – us Presbyterian [240]

MINUTES, 1827-1870 / Trumbull. Presbytery (Pres. Ch. in the USA. New School) – (With Ohio Presbytery (Assoc. Ch.; United Pres. Ch. of No. Am./. Minutes. 1808-67; Portage. Presbytery (Pres. Ch. in the USA. New School). Minutes. 1843-63) – 1 – $50.00 – us Presbyterian [240]

MINUTES, 1828-1856 / Angelica. Presbytery (Pres. Ch. in the U.S.A.) – 1 – $50.00 – us Presbyterian [240]

MINUTES, 1829-1861 / The Lakes. Presbytery (Assoc. Ref. Ch.) – 1 – $50.00 – us Presbyterian [240]

MINUTES, 1830-1870 / Oxford. Presbytery (Pres. Ch. in the U.S.A.) – 1 – $50.00 – us Presbyterian [240]

MINUTES, 1830-1883 / Cleveland. Presbytery (Pres. Ch. in the U.S.A.) – 1 – $50.00 – us Presbyterian [240]

MINUTES, 1830-1920 / Blairsville. Presbytery (Pres. Ch. in the U.S.A.) – 1 – $150.00 – us Presbyterian [240]

MINUTES, 1831-1870 / New York. Third Presbytery (Pres. Ch. in the U.S.A.) – 1 – $200.00 – us Presbyterian [240]

MINUTES, 1832-1919 / New Brunswick & Nova Scotia. Presbytery (Ref. Pres. Ch. of N.A.) – 1 – $50.00 – us Presbyterian [240]

MINUTES, 1833-1841 / Steubenville. Presbytery (Pres. CH. in the U.S.A.) – 1 – $50.00 – us Presbyterian [240]

MINUTES, 1833-1870 / Beaver. Presbytery (Pres. Ch. in the U.S.A.) – (With Shenango. Presbytery (Presbyterian Church in the U.S.A.). Minutes. 1870-72) – 1 – $50.00 – us Presbyterian [240]

MINUTES, 1833-1924 / Presbyterian Church in the U.S.A. Board of Publication and Sabbath School Work – 1 – $50.00 – us Presbyterian [240]

MINUTES, 1836-1870 / Marion. Presbytery (Pres. Ch. in the U.S.A.) – 1 – $50.00 – us Presbyterian [240]

MINUTES, 1836-1870 / Philadelphia Third. Presbytery (Pres. Ch. in the U.S.A. New School) – 1 – $50.00 – us Presbyterian [240]

MINUTES, 1836-1894 / Chemung. Presbytery (Pres. Ch. in the U.S.A.) – 1 – $50.00 – us Presbyterian [240]

MINUTES, 1837-1870 / Presbyterian Church in the U.S.A. Board of Foreign Missions. Executive Committee – 1 – $50.00 – us Presbyterian [240]

MINUTES, 1837-1870 / Sidney. Presbytery (Pres. Ch. in the U.S.A. Old School) – 1 – $50.00 – us Presbyterian [240]

MINUTES, 1837-1906 / Texas. Presbytery (Cum. Pres. Ch.) – 1 – $50.00 – us Presbyterian [240]

MINUTES, 1837-1918 / Presbyterian Church in the U.S.A. Board of Foreign Missions – 1 – $450.00 – us Presbyterian [240]

MINUTES, 1838-1857 / Madison.Presbytery (Presbyterian Church in the U.S.A., New School) – 1 – $50.00 – us Presbyterian [240]

MINUTES, 1838-1859 / Shenango. Presbytery – 1 – $50.00 – us Presbyterian [240]

MINUTES, 1838-1870 / Erie. Presbytery (Pres. Ch. in the U.S.A. New School) – 1 – $50.00 – us Presbyterian [240]

MINUTES, 1839-1870 / Rockaway. Presbytery (Pres. Ch. in the U.S.A. New School) – 1 – $50.00 – us Presbyterian [240]

MINUTES, 1840-1869 / New York and New Jersey. Synod (Pres. Ch. in the U.S.A.) – 1 – $50.00 – us Presbyterian [240]

MINUTES, 1843-1863 / Portage. Presbytery (Pres. Ch. in the USA. New School) – (With Ohio. Presbytery (Assoc. Ch.; United Pres. Ch. of No. Am.). Minutes. 1808-67; Trumbull. Presbytery (Pres. Ch. in the USA. New School). Minutes. 1827-70) – 1 – $50.00 – us Presbyterian [240]

MINUTES, 1843-1870 / Buffalo. Synod (Pres. Ch. in the U.S.A. Old School) – 1 – $50.00 – us Presbyterian [240]

MINUTES, 1843-1870 / Donegal. Presbytery (Pres. Ch. in the U.S.A. Old School) – 1 – $50.00 – us Presbyterian [240]

MINUTES, 1843-1870 / Meadville. Presbytery (Pres. Ch. in the U.S.A. New School) – 1 – $50.00 – us Presbyterian [240]

MINUTES, 1844-83 / Zanesville. Presbytery (Pres. Ch. in the U.S.A.) – 1 – $100.00 – us Presbyterian [240]

MINUTES, 1845-1861 / Philadelphia. Presbytery (Assoc. Ref. Ch.) – 1 – $50.00 – us Presbyterian [240]

MINUTES, 1845-1870 / Philadelphia Fourth. Presbytery (Pres. Ch. in the U.S.A. New School) – 1 – $50.00 – us Presbyterian [240]

MINUTES, 1846-1870 / Franklin. Presbytery (Pres. Ch. in the U.S.A. New School) – 1 – $50.00 – us Presbyterian [240]

MINUTES, 1846-1870 / Hamilton. Presbytery (Pres. Ch. in the U.S.A. New School) – 1 – $50.00 – us Presbyterian [240]

MINUTES, 1848-1942 / Cumberland Presbyterian Church. General Assembly – 1 – $550.00 – us Presbyterian [240]

MINUTES, 1849-1887 / Brazos. Synod (Cum. Pres. Ch.) – (With Texas. Synod. (Cum. Pres. Ch.) Minutes, 1843-88; 1898; 1905) – 1 – $50.00 – us Presbyterian [240]

MINUTES, 1850-58 / Springfield. Presbytery (Assoc. Ref. Pres. Ch.) – (Also: Miami. Presbytery (Assoc. Pres. Ch. of N.A.). Minutes, 1821-58; Kentucky. Presbytery (Assoc. Pres. Ch. of N.A.). Minutes, 1798-1821) – 1 – $50.00 – us Presbyterian [240]

MINUTES, 1851-1892 / Winnebago. Presbytery (Presbyterian Church in the USA) – 1 – $50.00 – us Presbyterian [240]

MINUTES, 1852-1870 / Passaic. Presbytery (Pres. Ch. in the U.S.A. Old School) – 1 – $50.00 – us Presbyterian [240]

MINUTES, 1853-1869 / Susquehanna. Synod (Pres. Ch. in the U.S.A. New School) – 1 – $50.00 – us Presbyterian [240]

MINUTES, 1853-88 / Metropolitan Board of Works – 1 – uk World [941]

MINUTES, 1854-1887 / Colorado. Synod (Cum. Pres. Ch.) – (With Trinity. Synod (Cum. Pres. Ch.), Minutes, 1878-87) – 1 – $50.00 – us Presbyterian [240]

MINUTES, 1854-1907 / Athens. Presbytery (Cum. Pres. Ch.) – 1 – $50.00 – us Presbyterian [240]

MINUTES, 1855-1918 / Nassau. Presbytery (Pres. Ch. in the U.S.A.) – (Old Series: 1855-70) – 1 – $100.00 – us Presbyterian [240]

MINUTES, 1856-1870 / Presbyterian Church in the U.S.A. General Assembly. Permanent Committee on Education for the Ministry (New School) – 1 – $50.00 – us Presbyterian [240]

MINUTES, 1858-1886 / Genesee Valley. Presbytery. (Pres. Ch. in the U.S.A.) – 1 – $50.00 – us Presbyterian [240]

MINUTES, 1859-1922 / Philadelphia. Presbytery (United Pres. Ch. of No. Am.) – 1 – $50.00 – us Presbyterian [240]

MINUTES, 1860-1891 / Philadelphia Central. Presbytery (Pres. Ch. in the U.S.A.) – 1 – $100.00 – us Presbyterian [240]

MINUTES, 1869-1901 / Trinity. Presbytery (Cum. Pres. Ch.) – (San Jacinto. Presbytery, 1885-1906) – 1 – $50.00 – us Presbyterian [240]

MINUTES, 1870-1881 / Long Island. Synod (Pres. Ch. in the U.S.A.) – 1 – $50.00 – us Presbyterian [240]

MINUTES, 1870-1881 / Western New York. Synod (Pres. Ch. in the U.S.A.) – 1 – $50.00 – us Presbyterian [240]

MINUTES, 1870-1902 / Morris and Orange. Presbytery (Pres. Ch. in the U.S.A.) – 1 – $50.00 – us Presbyterian [240]

MINUTES, 1870-1907 / Philadelphia North. Presbytery (Pres. Ch. in the U.S.A.) – 1 – $50.00 – us Presbyterian [240]

MINUTES, 1870-1919 / Presbyterian Church in the U.S.A. Board of Home Missions – 1 – $500.00 – us Presbyterian [240]

MINUTES, 1870-1924 / Westminister. Presbytery (Pres. Ch. in the U.S.A.) – 1 – $100.00 – us Presbyterian [240]

MINUTES, 1870-1926 / Chester. Presbytery (Pres. Ch. in the U.S.A.) – 1 – $100.00 – us Presbyterian [240]

MINUTES, 1870-72 / Shenango. Presbytery – (With: Beaver. Presbytery (Pres. Ch. in the U.S.A.), Minutes, 1833-70) – 1 – $50.00 – us Presbyterian [240]

MINUTES, 1871-1908 / Utah. Presbytery (Pres. Ch. in the U.S.A.) – (Includes: Wyoming Presbytery Minutes. 1871-74) – 1 – $50.00 – us Presbyterian [240]

MINUTES, 1872-1902 / North Laos Mission. (Pres. Ch. in the U.S.A.) – 1 – $50.00 – us Presbyterian [240]

MINUTES, 1876-1918 / Presbyterian Church in the U.S.A. Board of Relief for Disabled Ministers and the Widows and Orphans of Deceased Ministers – (Includes: Presbyterian Church in the U.S.A. Ministerial Sustenation Fund, Minutes, 1908-18) – 1 – $100.00 – us Presbyterian [240]

MINUTES, 1878-1957 / Texas. Synod (Pres. Ch. in the U.S.A.) – 1 – $150.00 – us Presbyterian [240]

MINUTES, 1879-1936 / New York and Vermont. Synod (Welsh Cal. Meth.Pres. Ch. in the U.S.A.) – 1 – $50.00 – us Presbyterian [240]

MINUTES, 1880-1899 / Georgia. Presbytery (Cum. Pres. Ch.) – (Ocoee. Presbytery (Cum. Pres. Ch.). Minutes, 1887-89. Chattanooga. Presbytery (Cum. Pres. Ch.). Minutes, 1889-99) – 1 – $50.00 – us Presbyterian [240]

MINUTES, 1883-1870 / Philadelphia Second. Presbytery (Pres. Ch. in the U.S.A. New School) – 1 – $50.00 – us Presbyterian [240]

MINUTES, 1883-1916 / Presbyterian Church in the U.S.A. College Board – 1 – $50.00 – us Presbyterian [240]

MINUTES, 1885-1898 / Laos (North). Presbytery (Presbyterian Church in the USA) – 1 – $50.00 – us Presbyterian [240]

MINUTES, 1885-1906 / San Jacinto. Presbytery (Cum. Pres. Ch.) – (Trinity. Presbytery, 1869-1901) – 1 – $50.00 – us Presbyterian [240]

MINUTES, 1887-1889 / Ocoee. Presbytery (Cumberland Presbyterian Church) – (Includes: Chattanooga Presbytery (Cumberland Presbyterian Church), Minutes, 1889-99) – 1 – $50.00 – us Presbyterian [240]

MINUTES, 1887-1906 / Indian Territory. Synod (Pres. Ch. in the U.S.A.) – (With Oklahoma. Synod (Pres. Ch. in the U.S.A.). Minutes. 1907-57. and Oklahoma. Synod (United Pres. Ch. in the U.S.A.). Minutes. 1958-60) – 1 – $100.00 – us Presbyterian [240]

MINUTES, 1887-1913 / Catawba. Synod (Pres. Ch. in the U.S.A.) – 1 – $50.00 – us Presbyterian [240]

MINUTES, 1888-1906 / Arizona. Presbytery (Pres. Church in the U.S.A.) – 1 – $50.00 – us Presbyterian [240]

MINUTES, 1889-1902 / Oregon. Presbytery. (Cum. Pres. Ch.) – 1 – $50.00 – us Presbyterian [240]

MINUTES, 1898-1906 / Indianola. Synod (Cum. Pres. Ch.Pres. Ch. in the U.S.A.) – 1 – $50.00 – us Presbyterian [240]

MINUTES, 1899-1906 / Pittsburgh. Presbytery (Cum. Pres. Ch.) – 1 – $50.00 – us Presbyterian [240]

MINUTES, 1900-1911 / Utah. Synod. (Pres. Ch. in the U.S.A.) – 1 – $50.00 – us Presbyterian [240]

MINUTES, 1907-55 / Canadian Synod. (Pres. Ch. in the U.S.A.) – (With Oklahoma-Arkansas. Synod (United Pres. Ch. in the U.S.A.), Minutes, 1961-72) – 1 – $50.00 – us Presbyterian [240]

MINUTES, 1912-1958 / New England. Synod (Pres. Ch. in the U.S.A.) – (New England. Synod (United Pres. Ch. in the U.S.A.). Minutes. 1959-73) – 1 – $50.00 – us Presbyterian [240]

MINUTES, 1924-1934 / Yunnan Mission (Pres. Ch. in the U.S.A.) – 1 – $50.00 – us Presbyterian [240]

MINUTES, 1938-1955 / Bible Presbyterian Church. General Synod – 1 – $50.00 – us Presbyterian [240]

MINUTES, 1956-1960 / Bible Presbyterian Church. General Synod. Columbus – (Also: Evangelical Presbyterian Church, General Synod, Minutes, 1961-65) – 1 – $50.00 – us Presbyterian [240]

MINUTES, 1956-1985 / Bible Presbyterian Church. General Synod. Collingswood – 1 – $200.00 – us Presbyterian [240]

MINUTES, 1958-1972 / Board of National Missions (United Pres. Ch. in the U.S.A.) – 6r – 1 – $300.00 – us Presbyterian [240]

MINUTES, 1968-70 / Montana Inter-Tribal Policy Boards – 6 fiches. (American Indian Periodicals in the Princeton University Library) – 9 – $45.00 – us UPA [305]

MINUTES, 1972-1974 / The Sun. Synod (United Pres. Ch. in the U.S.A.) – 1 – $50.00 – us Presbyterian [240]

MINUTES, 1973-1974 / Southwest. Synod (United Pres. Ch. in the U.S.A.) – 1 – $50.00 – us Presbyterian [240]

MINUTES AND ACCOUNT BOOKS / Van Wert County. Ohio. Pleasant Township. Board of Trustees – 1839-1966 – 3r – 1 – $32.50r – us Archival [324]

MINUTES AND CORRESPONDENCE, ETC / Scottish Womens' Suffrage Movement – 1902-1933 – 1 – uk Microform Academic [941]

MINUTES AND CORRESPONDENCE OF THE ACADEMY OF NATURAL SCIENCES OF PHILADELPHIA, 1812-1924 – (With printed guide) – 1972 – 38r – 1 – $3,230.00 – D1841 – us Scholarly Res [500]

MINUTES AND DOCUMENTS / Canada. Colonial Conferences – 1887-1907 – 1 – cn Micromedia [324]

MINUTES AND DOCUMENTS / Canada. Privy Council. War Cabinet Committee – 1939-45 – 1 – cn Micromedia [971]

MINUTES AND DOCUMENTS OF THE CABINET MEETINGS OF PRESIDENT EISENHOWER, 1953-61 / Eisenhower, Dwight D – 1980. (Presidential Documents Series) – 1 – $965.00 – 0-89093-355-3 – us UPA [977]

MINUTES AND DOCUMENTS OF THE CABINET MEETINGS OF PRESIDENT LYNDON B. JOHNSON (1963-69) / Johnson, Lyndon B – 1982. (Presidential Documents Series) – 1 – $1,655.00 – 0-89093-387-1 – us UPA [977]

MINUTES AND LOT OWNERS / Sandusky County. Ohio. Woodville Township. Cemetery Association – 1849-1936 – 1r – 1 – $32.50r – us Archival [324]

MINUTES AND MEMBERS / Allenwood, Pennsylvania.White Deer Baptist Church – 1854-1912 – 1 – 15.50 – us A.B.H.S. [240]

MINUTES AND ORDINANCES / Ottawa County. Ohio. Carroll Township. Board of Health – 1893-1919 – 1r – 1 – $32.50r – us Archival [324]

MINUTES AND PAPERS / The London Trades Council – 1860-1953 – 1 – £440.00 – uk World [380]

MINUTES AND RECORDS / Gaboon and Corisco Mission. (Pres. Ch. in the U.S.A) – 1856-1902 – 1 – $50.00 – us Presbyterian [960]

MINUTES AND RECORDS / Ridgecrest. North Carolina. Ridgecrest Baptist Assembly – 4 Aug 1909-12 Aug 1931. 428p – 1 – 14.98 – us Baptist [240]

MINUTES AND REPORTS / Council on Education. Committee – 1839-99 – 1 – uk Microform Academic [025]

MINUTES AND REPORTS / Presbyterian Church in the U.S.A. General Assembly – 1789-1958 – 1 – $3,850.00 – us Presbyterian [240]

MINUTES AND REPORTS / United Presbyterian Church in the U.S.A. General Assembly – 1958-1983 – 1 – $1,250.00 – us Presbyterian [240]

MINUTES AND REPORTS / United Presbyterian Church of North America. General Assembly – 1859-1958 – 1 – $150.00 – us Presbyterian [240]

MINUTES AND REPORTS OF THE NATIONAL HOUSING AND TOWN PLANNING COUNCIL / National Housing and Town Planning Council. London, England – 1906-52. With printed Introduction and Finding List – 1 – £35.00r – uk Altair [710]

MINUTES AND ROLLS OF ATTORNEYS OF THE U.S. DISTRICT COURT FOR THE SOUTHERN DISTRICT OF NEW YORK / U.S. Circuit and District Courts. New York – 1789-1841. 9 rolls – 1 – M886 – us Nat'l Archives [324]

MINUTES AND ROSTER / Grand Army of the Republic. Post No. 69 (O.M. Mitchell), Osborne, KS – 1882-1927 – 1 – us KS Hist [350]

MINUTES AND TREASURER'S ACCOUNTS / The Russia Company – 1667-1955. With printed index – 1 – £425.00 – uk World [947]

MINUTES, APR 13-15, 1972 / Tennessee Baptist Church Library Convention – East Ridge Baptist Church. 58p – 1 – us Baptist [240]

MINUTES, CIRCUIT AND DISTRICT COURT..., 1789-1842, AND INDEX TO JUDGMENTS, CIRCUIT AND DISTRICT COURTS, 1792-1874 / U.S. District Courts. South Carolina – RG 21. 2 rolls – 1 – M1181 – us Nat'l Archives [340]

MINUTES, CORRESPONDENCE, REPORTS, ETC / Cooperative Women's Guild – 1888-1939 – 1 – uk Microform Academic [360]

MINUTES, ETC / Scottish Trades Union Congress – 1897-1951 – 1 – uk Microform Academic [338]

MINUTES, MISSION BOARD / Baptist State Conventions (American Baptist). Oregon. Baptist Convention of the North Pacific Coast and Oregon Baptist Convention – (Board of Managers and Executive Committee, Minutes, 1890-94. Board Meetings, Minutes, 1882-1913. Executive Committee and Board of Directors, Minutes, 1912-46) – 1882-90 – 1 – us A.B.H.S. [240]

MINUTES, MS 1250 / Mahoning County. Ohio. Canfield Township – 1805-9. Incomplete. 1 reel – 1 – us Western Res [978]

MINUTES OF ANNUAL MEETINGS, REPORTS AND WOMEN'S NETWORK FILES / Council of Pacific Teachers Organisations – 1984-94 – 2r – 1 – PMB1094 – at Pacific Mss [370]

MINUTES OF DITCH PROCEEDINGS / Ottawa County. Ohio. Carroll Township. Board of Trustees – 1941-1959 – 1r – 1 – $32.50r – us Archival [324]

MINUTES OF EVIDENCE / Kenya. Land Commission.Carter Commission – 1 – uk Microform Academic [960]

[MINUTES OF EVIDENCE AND EXHIBITS] : (NAMELY THE SHARPEVILLE LOCATION AND EVATON) AND VANDERBIJLPARK, IRANSVAAL, ON 21ST MARCH 1960 / South Africa. Commission of Inquiry into the Events in the District of Vereeniging – Vereeniging, 1960? – us Res Libr [960]

MINUTES OF EVIDENCE AND REPORT OF THE SPECIAL COMMITTEE OF THE HOUSE OF ASSEMBLY OF LOWER CANADA... / Bas-Canada. Parliament. House of Assembly – Quebec: Neilson & Cowan, 1829. SEM105P1557 – 1mf – 9 – Can$2.25 – cn Bibl Nat [323]

MINUTES OF EVIDENCE HEARD AT PUBLIC SESSIONS / Great Britain. Colonial Office. Palestine Royal Commission – London. 1937. Index. BJ-28-78 1 – 9 – ne IDC [956]

MINUTES OF MEETINGS / Kansas. State Board of Dental Examiners – 1901-45 – 1 – us KS Hist [617]

MINUTES OF MEETINGS / Midwest Inter-Library Center. Chicago. Advisory Committee of Librarians – 1 – us Res Libr [020]

MINUTES OF MEETINGS / Midwest Inter-Library Center. Chicago. Board of Directors – 1949-57 – 1 – us Res Libr [020]

MINUTES OF MEETINGS / Midwest Inter-Library Center. Chicago. Board of Directors. Executive Committee – Aug, Dec 1949 – 1 – us Res Libr [020]

MINUTES OF MEETINGS / New England Emigrant Aid Co. Trustees – 1854-55 – 1 – us KS Hist [978]

MINUTES OF MEETINGS / Ottawa Town Company – 1864-67, 1872-75 – 1 – us KS Hist [025]

MINUTES OF MEETINGS / Russell. Kansas. Free Public Library. Board of Directors – 1901-11 – 1 – us KS Hist [978]

MINUTES OF MEETINGS / Santa Fe and Los Angeles Harbor Railway Company – 1922-1943 – 1 – us KS Hist [380]

MINUTES OF MEETINGS OF HIS EXECUTORS / Coke, Edward – 1707-14.Holkham ms. 743. Holkham Hall, Norfolk, England – 1 – uk Microform Academic [941]

MINUTES OF MEETINGS OF THE COMMISSION, 1915-49 : RECORDS OF THE FEDERAL TRADE COMMISION, PART 1 / U.S. Federal Trade Commission – (Series A, 1915-32: 18r. ISBN 0-89093-882-2. $1,920.00; Series B, 1933-40: 25r. ISBN 0-89093-883-0. $2,750.00; Series C, 1941-49: 21r. ISBN 0-89093-884-9. $2,310.00. All with printed guides) – 1 – $6,635.00 set – us UPA [324]

MINUTES OF MEETINGS OF THE COMMITTEE ON WOMEN'S DEFENSE WORK – May 2, 1917 – Feb 12, 1919. Weekly and monthly reports of the Committee on Women's Defense Work, May 12, 1917 – Oct 15, 1918. 1 roll. M1074 – 1 – us Nat'l Archives [324]

MINUTES OF MEETINGS OF THE FEDERAL OPEN MARKET COMMITTEE, 1923-1975 / U. S. Federal Reserve System – Part Two of Papers of the Federal Reserve System Series. 1983 – 1 – $3,080.00 – 0-89093-510-6 – us UPA [336]

MINUTES OF MEETINGS OF THE INTERDIVISIONAL AREA COMMITTEE ON THE FAR EAST – 1943-46. T1197 – 1r – 1 – us Nat'l Archives [950]

MINUTES OF MEETINGS OF THE NATIONAL SECURITY COUNCIL : WITH SPECIAL ADVISORY REPORTS / U.S. National Security Council – (Series: Documents of the National Security Council. 1st suppl 5r $625.00 ISBN 0-89093-939-X. 2nd suppl 3r $375.00 ISBN 1-55655-162-2. 3rd suppl 7r $875.00 ISBN 1-55655-600-4. All with printed guides. Printed index to documents $475.00 ISBN 0-89093-994-2) – 1 – $375.00 – 0-89093-462-2 – us UPA [977]

MINUTES OF MEETINGS OF THE STATE-WAR-NAVY COORDINATING COMMITTEE (SWNCC), 1944-47 / U.S. War Department – 1 roll. T1194 – 1 – us Nat'l Archives [977]

MINUTES OF MEETINGS OF THE SUBCOMMITTEE FOR THE FAR EAST – 1945-47. T1198 – 1r – 1 – us Nat'l Archives [950]

MINUTES OF PROCEEDINGS / Institution of Civil Engineers. London – v1-240 1837-1935 – 1,5,6 – us Princeton Micro [624]

MINUTES OF PROCEEDINGS AND EVIDENCE / Canada. Parliament. House of Commons. Committees – 17th Parliament- 1934- – 9 – cn Micromedia [324]

MINUTES OF PROCEEDINGS AND EVIDENCE / Canada. Parliament. Senate. Committees – (Also available by year) – 17th Parliament-1934- – 9 – cn Micromedia [324]

MINUTES OF PROCEEDINGS AND VOTES AND PROCEEDINGS / Rhodesia. Southern. Legislative Council (later Legislative Assembly) – 1899-19 Mar 1965 – 1 – 309.00 – us L of C Photodup [960]

MINUTES OF SESSIONS / Methodist Episcopal Church. Missions. Nevada – N.P. 1887, 1890-1894, 1896-1908 – 1 – us NY Public [240]

MINUTES OF SIXTH SESSION OF SUMATRA PROVISIONAL ANNUAL CONFERENCE OF METHODIST CHURCH HELD IN MEDAN, SUMATRA, MAR. 17-20, 1949 / Methodist Church. (Indonesia). Conferences. Sumatra – SE-6514 1 – 9 – ne IDC [240]

MINUTES OF STATE CONVENTION, 1965-78 / Michigan Baptist Convention. Executive Board – 450p – 1 – us Baptist [240]

MINUTES OF THE AMERICAN FISHERIES SOCIETY *see* TRANSACTIONS

MINUTES OF THE ANNUAL CONFERENCES OF THE UNITED METHODIST CHURCH – London, 1932 – 10mf – 9 – ne IDC [240]

MINUTES OF THE ANNUAL MEETINGS OF THE BOARD OF TRUSTEES. 1861-70 / Atchison County. Kansas. School District 9 – 1 – us KS Hist [324]

MINUTES OF THE BOARDS OF SPECIAL INQUIRY AT THE SAN FRANCISCO IMMIGRATION OFFICE, 1899-1909 – 2r – 1 – M1387 – us Nat'l Archives [340]

MINUTES OF THE COMMITTEE OF THE WHOLE : MINUTES, JUL 22-NOV 6, 1975; RESOLUTIONS N1-38; AND PROPOSALS, PETITIONS AND MEMORIALS – Saipan, n.p, 1975 – 28mf – 9 – $42.00 – LLMC 82-100F, Title 92 – us L.L.M.C. [323]

MINUTES OF THE DIVISION STAFF MEETINGS OF THE U.S. GROUP COUNCIL FOR GERMANY AND THE OFFICE OF MILITARY GOVERNMENT FOR GERMANY (U.S.) (OMGUS) / U.S. Group Council for Germany – Nov 1944 – Aug 1949. 3 rolls. M1075 – 1 – us Nat'l Archives [324]

MINUTES OF THE EDUCATIONAL ALLIANCE, 1879-1980 – 9 – $610.00 – us UPA [370]

MINUTES OF THE EXECUTIVE BOARD OF THE CONGRESS OF INDUSTRIAL ORGANIZATIONS, 1935-1955 – (Comes with printed guide) – 18r – 1 – $2,140.00 – 1-55655-390-0 – us UPA [338]

MINUTES OF THE EXECUTIVE COUNCIL, JULY 11, 1933-NOV. 13, 1934 / U.S. Office of Government Reports – 1roll – 1 – T37 – us Nat'l Archives [324]

MINUTES OF THE EXECUTIVE COUNCIL OF THE AMERICAN FEDERATION OF LABOR PART 1 : 1893-1924. WITH VOTE BOOKS, 1892-1924 – (With printed guide) – 22r – 1 – $2,420.00 – 1-55655-377-3 – us UPA [331]

MINUTES OF THE EXECUTIVE COUNCIL OF THE AMERICAN FEDERATION OF LABOR, PART 2 : 1925-1955. WITH VOTE BOOKS, 1925-1954 – (With printed guide) – 19r – 1 – $2,090.00 – 1-55655-378-1 – us UPA [331]

MINUTES OF THE FEDERAL OPEN MARKET COMMITTEE, 1936-61, AND OF ITS EXECUTIVE COMMITTEE, 1936-55 / U. S. Federal Reserve System – 41 rolls. M591. Printed guide – 1 – us Nat'l Archives [324]

MINUTES OF THE GENERAL ASSEMBLY, 1861-1983 / Presbyterian Church in the United States – Atlanta, Gerogia, annually – 28r – 1 – $2,400.00 – us Presbyterian [240]

MINUTES OF THE GENERAL COMMITTEE / British and Foreign Bible Society. Archives – 1807-1914 – 1 – uk Microform Academic [240]

MINUTES OF THE GOVERNING BODY / International Labour Organisation – 1919-92. Continued annually – 9 – uk World [323]

MINUTES OF THE GOVERNING BODY / International Labour Organisation – Session 1- 1919-1993 – 9 – Sfr4000.00 – 92-2-109772-2 – sz I.L.O. [330]

MINUTES OF THE INDUSTRIAL COMMISSION, 1898-1902 / U.S. Department of Commerce. General Records – 1roll. T10 – 1 – us Nat'l Archives [324]

MINUTES OF THE MEETINGS OF THE COUNCIL OF NATIONAL DEFENSE / U.S. Council of National Defense – (Advisory Commission of the Council of National Defense, 1916-18. Interdepartmental Advisory Committee, 1917. Joint Weekly Conference, 1917-18. Interdepartmental Defense Board, 1919-20) – 1916-21. 1 roll. M1069 – 1 – us Nat'l Archives [324]

MINUTES OF THE PROCEEDINGS OF A CONVENTION OF CHURCHES THAT FORMED THE FREEDOM ASSOCIATION OF UNITED BAPTISTS / Story, Isaac A – 1898 – 1 – $6.09 – us Baptist [240]

MINUTES OF THE SERVICE COMMITTEE OF THE FOREST SERVICE / U.S. Forest Service – Mar 14, 1903 – Oct 16, 1935. 8 rolls. M1025 – 1 – us Nat'l Archives [324]

MINUTES OF THE TOWN AND COUNTRY PLANNING ASSOCIATION / Town and Country Planning Association. London, England – 1913-52. With printed Introduction and Finding List – 1 – £35.00r – uk Altair [710]

MINUTES OF THE TOWN PLANNING INSTITUTE / Town Planning Institute. London, England – (With printed introduction and finding list) – 1913-52 – 1 – £35.00r – uk Altair [710]

MINUTES OF THE TRIENNIAL CONVENTION / Baptist General Missionary Convention. Board of Foreign Missions – 1814-47. MS. 793p – 1 – us Baptist [240]

MINUTES OF THE U.S. CIRCUIT COURT FOR THE DISTRICT OF COLUMBIA / U.S. Circuit and District Courts. District of Columbia – 1801-63. 6 rolls – 1 – M1021 – us Nat'l Archives [324]

MINUTES OF THE U.S. CIRCUIT COURT FOR THE DISTRICT OF MARYLAND / U.S. Circuit and District Courts. Maryland – 1790-1911. 7 rolls – 1 – M931 – us Nat'l Archives [324]

MINUTES OF THE U.S. CIRCUIT COURT FOR THE EASTERN DISTRICT OF PENNSYLVANIA / U.S. Circuit and District Courts. Pennsylvania – 1790-1844. 2 rolls – 1 – M932 – us Nat'l Archives [324]

MINUTES OF THE U.S. SUPREME COURT, 1790-1950 – 41r – 1 – M215 – us Nat'l Archives [340]

MINUTES OF THE WESLEYAN METHODIST CONFERENCES FROM THE FIRST HELD IN LONDON IN THE YEAR 1744-1976 – London, 1862-1976 – 811mf – 9 – ne IDC [240]

MINUTES OF THE...SESSION OF THE AFRICAN ADVISORY COUNCIL / Bechuanaland Protectorate. African Advisory Council – Mateking: The Council. 29th-32nd, 34th, 36th-39th sess. 1948-52; 1954; 1956-60 – 1r – 1 – us Res Libr [324]

MINUTES OF TREATY CONFERENCES BETWEEN THE U.S. AND JAPANESE REPRESENTATIVES AND TREATY DRAFTS, 1872 / U.S. Department of State – T119 – 1r – 1 – us Nat'l Archives [950]

MINUTES OF TRIENNIAL CONVENTION / Baptist General Missionary Convention. Board of Foreign Missions – 1814-47. Manuscript. 793p – 1 – 27.75 – us Baptist [240]

MINUTES OF TRUSTEES OF THE POOR / ed by Coll, Blanche D – Baltimore, 1833-1935 – 2r – 1 – $170.00 – S1861 – us Scholarly Res [360]

MINUTES OF VOYAGE, 1830-1 / Harrison, W – 6 fiche – 9 – sa SA Libr [960]

MINUTES, REPORTS AND CORRESPONDENCE / Christian Life Commission. Advisory Council of Southern Baptist Work with Negroes – 1955-67 – 1 – $25.06 – us Baptist [240]

MINUTES, REPORTS, AND CORRESPONDENCE / Southern Baptist Convention. Advisory Council on Work with Negroes – 1955-1967 – 1 – 25.06 – us Baptist [240]

MINUTES, REPORTS, CORRESPONDENCE / Trades Council. Aberdeen – 1876-1951 – 1 – uk Microform Academic [330]

MINUTES, REPORTS, CORRESPONDENCE, ETC / Trades Council. Bradford. England – 1867-1951 – 1 – uk Microform Academic [330]

MINUTES, REPORTS, CORRESPONDENCE, ETC / Trades Council. Edinburgh – 1 – uk Microform Academic [330]

MINUTES, REPORTS, CORRESPONDENCE, ETC / Trades Council. Glasgow – 1858-1951 – 1 – uk Microform Academic [330]

MINUTES, REPORTS, CORRRESPONDENCE, ETC / Trades Council. Belfast – 1 – uk Microform Academic [941]

MINUTES, STATION CONFERENCE / Kansas. State University. Agricultural Experiment Station – 1954-75 – 1,5,6 – us Spaulding [630]

MINUTES, TRIAL NOTES, AND ROLL OF ATTORNEYS OF THE U.S. CIRCUIT COURT FOR THE SOUTHERN DISTRICT OF NEW YORK, 1790-1841 – 3r – 1 – M854 – us Nat'l Archives [340]

Minuth, Mark Torsten *see* UNTERSUCHUNGEN ZUR PRAKTISCHEN ANWENDBARKEIT WAESSRIGER ZWEIPHASENSYSTEME AUF DER BASIS NICHTIONISCHER TENSIDE ALS TECHNISCHE REINIGUNGSMETHODE FUER AMPHIPHILE PROTEINE

MINUVSHIE GODY – Leningrad. n1-12. 1908 – 2r – 1 – us Ross [947]

MINUVSHIE GODY – St Petersburg. Year 1 no. 1-12. 1908 – 1 – us NY Public [073]

MINYIP GOLF CLUB MINUTES – 1r – 5 – at Corangamite [360]

MINYIP GUARDIAN – 1921-1962. MG1-13 – 13r – 1 – at Corangamite [072]

MINZHU YU FAZHI = DEMOCRACY AND LEGAL SYSTEM – 1979-. F-P258 – 9 – $4.50f – cc Microforms [073]

MINZU YANJIU – Studies in Nationalities. In Chinese but Table of Contents in English in each issue. F p9 – 9 – $4.50f – cc Microforms [073]

IL MIO GARZONI IL PIFARO FROM "LA MOLINARA" / Paisiello, G – London: Goulding/Skillern, 1791 – 1 – us Sibley [780]

MIOCENA BALTISCHE FLORA / Heer, Oswald – Koenigsberg, 1869 – 2mf – 9 – ne IDC [580]

Mioni, Ugo *see* MOLLA HUSSEIN

MI-PENEI KOSHET / Klein, S W – Frankfurt a.M. 1861. BJ-32-7 1 – 9 – ne IDC [270]

Miquel, F A W *see*
- ANNALES MUSEI BOTANICI LUGDUNO-BATAVI
- FLORA INDIAE BATAVAE
- FLORA INDIAE BATAVAE...SUPPLEMENTUM PRIMUM. PRODROMUS FLORAE SUMATRANAE
- ILLUSTRATIONS DE LA FLORE DE L'ARCHIPEL INDIEN...
- JOURNAL DE BOTANIQUE NEA1ERLANDAISE
- OVER DE AFRIKAANSE VIJGE-BOOMEN
- PLANTAE JUNGHUHNIANAE

- SERTUM EXOTICUM
- SYSTEMA PIPERACEARUM
Miquelarena, Jacinto *see* UNIFICACION
MIR – Pueblo, CO, 1901-1903 – 5mf or 1r – 9,1 – us I.H.R.C. [975]
MIR – Sofia. Bulgaria. -d. Aug 1916-Jul 1919, Jan 1938-Dec 1944. (Very imperfect). (15 reels) – 1 – uk British Libr Newspaper [949]
Mir Abu Turab Vali *see* A HISTORY OF GUJARAT
MIR BOZHII – v. 1-15. 1892-1906 – 1 – 520.00 – us L of C Photodup [073]
MIR ISKUSSTVA – St Petersburg. 1899-1904 – 1 – us NY Public [700]
MIR ISKUSSTVA – Zhurnal. Spb. 1899-1904. B-1108 2 – 8 – ne IDC [073]
MIR ISLAMA – Izdanie Imperatorskago Obshchestva Vostokovedeniia. v. 1-2. Spb. 1912-13. BR-5824 2 – 8 – ne IDC [956]
Mir Khwand *see* HISTORY OF THE EARLY KINGS OF PERSIA
Mir, Miguel *see*
- ARMONIA ENTRE LA CIENCIA Y LA FE
- ZUSAMMENHANG ZWISCHEN WISSENSCHAFT UND GLAUBEN
MIR ZHENSHCHINY – Moscow, 1912 n1-3; 1913 n4-22; 1914 n1-24; 1915 n1-17; 1916 n1-10 – 43mf – 9 – $290.00 – us Ross [073]
MIRA SATIS, AC SINE OMNI PECCATO MARIAE SANCTISSIMA CONCEPTIO / Zoller, Josepho – O 469 1. 1712 – 9 – ne IDC [240]
Mirabal, A de *see* MIS CRONICAS
Mirabaud, Jean-Baptiste de *see*
- OPINION DES ANCIENS SUR LES JUIFS
- REFLEXIONS IMPARTIALES SUR L'EVANGILE
Mirabeau, Honore-Gabriel de Riqueti *see* TRAVAIL SUR L'EDUCATION PUBLIQUE, TROUVE DANS LES PAPIERS DE MIRABEAU L'AINE, PUBLIE PAR P. J. G. CABANIS
LE MIRABEL – Mirabel, Canada. 22 mai 1974; v1 n12. 23 oct 1974 – 1r – 1 – Can$25.00 – cn Can Microfilming [072]
Miraben, A *see* PRECIS DE DROIT ANNAMITE ET DE JURISPRUDENCE EN MATIERE INDIGENE
MIRACLE / Bettex, Frederic – Defiance: Handbook-Press, 1900. 1 fiche – 9 – us A.T.L.A. [240]
LE MIRACLE ET SES CONTREFACONS / Bonniot, Joseph de – (Includes bibliographical references) – Paris: Retaux-Bray, 1887 – 1mf – 9 – 0-8370-7365-0 – 1986-1365 – us A.T.L.A. [230]
THE MIRACLE OF OUR LORD IN RELATION TO MODERN CRITICISM / Steinmeyer, Franz Ludwig – Edinburgh: T. & T. Clark, 1875. 1 fiche – 9 – us A.T.L.A. [240]
MIRACLE STORIES – v1 (all publ). 1931 – 1 reel – 1 – $50.00 – us UPA [830]
MIRACLES : AN ARGUMENT AND A CHALLENGE / Cox, Samuel – London: Kegan Paul, Trench, 1884 – 1mf – 9 – 0-8370-2763-2 – 1985-0763 – us A.T.L.A. [210]
MIRACLES / Litton, Edward Arthur – London: S.P.C.K., 1868. 1 fiche – 9 – us A.T.L.A. [240]
MIRACLES: AN ARGUMENT AND A CHALLENGE / Cox, Samuel – London: Kegan Paul, Trench, 1884. 1 fiche – 9 – us A.T.L.A. [240]
THE MIRACLES AND MYTHS OF THE NEW TESTAMENT / May, Joseph – Boston: George H. Ellis, 1901. 1 fiche – 9 – us A.T.L.A. [240]
MIRACLES AND SUPERNATURAL RELIGION / Whiton, James Morris – (Includes bibliographical references) – New York: Macmillan, 1903 – 1mf – 9 – 0-8370-5830-9 – 1985-3830 – us A.T.L.A. [230]
THE MIRACLES: HELPS TO FAITH, NOT HINDRANCES / Taylor, William MacKergo – Edinburgh: William Oliphant, 1865. 1 fiche – 9 – us A.T.L.A. [240]
Miracles, Marie-des *see* BIBLIOGRAPHIE ANALYTIQUE DE L'OEUVRE DE MAITRE EUGENE L'HEUREUX, MEMBRE DE LA SOCIETE ROYALE DU CANADA ET DE L'ACADEMIE CANADIENNE, REDACTEUR EN CHEF DU PROGRES DU SAGUENAY ET DE L'ACTION CATHOLIQUE, 1929-1940
THE MIRACLES OF CHRIST : AS ATTESTED BY THE EVANGELISTS / Hovey, Alvah – (Includes bibliographical references) – Boston: Graves & Young, 1864; c1863 – 1mf – 9 – 0-8370-3678-X – 1985-1678 – us A.T.L.A. [240]
MIRACLES OF JESUS / Beth, Karl – New York: Eaton & Mains, 1907. 1 fiche – 9 – us A.T.L.A. [240]
THE MIRACLES OF JESUS AS MARKS ON THE WAY OF LIFE / Lang, Cosmo Gordon – new Am ed. New York: E P Dutton, 1918 – 1mf – 9 – 0-8370-4042-6 – 1985-2042 – us A.T.L.A. [240]
THE MIRACLES OF MISSIONS : THE MODERN MARVELS IN THE HISTORY OF MISSIONARY ENTERPRISE / Pierson, Arthur Tappan et al – (Includes bibliographical references) – New York: Funk & Wagnalls, 1895-1901 – 4mf – 9 – 0-8370-6600-X – 1986-0600 – us A.T.L.A. [240]
THE MIRACLES OF OUR LADY SAINT MARY : BROUGHT OUT OF DIVERS TONGUES AND NEWLY SET FORTH IN ENGLISH BY EVELYN UNDERHILL – New York: E P Dutton, 1906 – 1mf – 9 – 0-8370-8628-0 – 1986-2628 – us A.T.L.A. [240]
THE MIRACLES OF OUR LORD / MacDonald, George – New York: George Routledge, 1871. 1 fiche – 9 – us A.T.L.A. [240]
MIRACLES OF UNBELIEF / Ballard, Frank – Edinburgh: T. & T. Clark, 1900. 1 fiche – 9 – us A.T.L.A. [240]
THE MIRACLES OF UNBELIEF / Ballard, Frank – Edinburgh:T. & T. Clark, 1900 – 1mf – 9 – 0-8370-2173-1 – 1985-0173 – us A.T.L.A. [240]
THE MIRACULOUS ELEMENT IN THE GOSPELS : A COURSE OF LECTURES ON THE ELY FOUNDATION / Bruce, Alexander Balmain – (Includes index) – New York: A C Armstrong, 1892, c1886 – 1mf – 9 – 0-8370-2485-4 – 1985-0485 – us A.T.L.A. [240]
MIRACULUM NATURAE / Swammerdam, Jan – M 411. 1685 – 9 – ne IDC [574]
LA MIRADA LAMPLIGHTER – La Mirada, CA. 1955-1958; 1961; 1964 – 4r – 1 – $200.00 – H04017 – us Library Micro [071]
MIRADJ-NAMEH – Texte turc-oriental et traduction par Pavet de Courteille. 1882 – 9 – fr Orientalistes [800]
Miraeus A *see* DE ORTU ET PROGRESSU ORDINIS...DE MONTE CARMELO
Miraeus, A *see*
- CHRONICON CISTERCIENSIS
- CODEX REGULARUM ET CONSTITUTIONUM CLERICALIUM
- DE CONGREGATIONIBUS CLERICORUM IN COMMUNI VIVENTIUM
- DE STATU RELIGIONIS CHRISTIANAE
- DIPLOMATUM BELGICORUM NOVA COLLECTIO
- NOTITIA EPISCOPATUUM ORBIS CHRISTIANI SIVE CODEX PROVINCIALIS ROMANUS
- OPERA DIPLOMATICA ET HISTORICA
- ORDINIS PRAEMONSTRATENSIS CHRONICON
- ORIGINES BENEDICTINAE
- REGULAE ET CONSTITUTIONES CLERICORUM IN CONGREGATIONE VIVENTIUM
DIE MIRAG – (Cont by: Funk alle Tage, oct 15 1935) – Leipzig, 1926-35 – 20r – 1 – gw Mikrofilm [790]
A MIRAGEM : ORGAO LITTERARIO – Maceio, Alagoas. 20 Jul 1900 – 1,5,6 – bl Biblioteca [072]
Miramar, Aloys *see* HISTOIRE PITTORESQUE D'UNE FAMILLE DE PALESTINE. AKKINAI AU PAYS DE JESUS. PARIS, 1933
MIRAMICHI MERCURY – Chatham, Canada. 1826-29 – 2r – 1 – $136.00 – cn Library Assoc [971]
Miramon, Alberto *see* JOSE ASUNCION SILVA; ENSAYO BIOGRAFICO CON DOCUMENTOS INEDITOS
MIRANDA / Braddon, Mary Elizabeth – British Fiction Archive: Unit 5 – 9 – uk Bell [830]
Miranda, Luis de *see* COMEDIA PRODIGA
Miranda, Rui *see* ROLE DES LIGNEUX FOURRAGERS DANS LA NUTRITION DES RUMINANTS EN AFRIQUE SUBSAHARIENNE
Miranda. Venezuela *see* GACETA OFICIAL DEL ESTADO MIRANDA
MIR'AT AL-SHARQ – (Missing: V.1(32-33, 45); V.2(55, 83, 102, 106, 123-124); V.3(135, 143); 1922/23-1924/25, V.4-6; V.7(452); V.10/597, 605, 607, 626, 629); V.11(632); V.15(1074, 1076-1079, 1099, 1109-1110, 1112)) – Jerusalem, 1919-1938. V.1-19 – 5r – 1 – NE-1515/3 – ne IDC [072]
MIR'AT UEL-KA'INAT / Nisancizade, Mehmed b. Ahmed – Cairo: Bulak, 1257 [1841] – 2v 18mf – 9 – $47.25 – us MEDOC [949]
MIR'AT-I 'ALEM – [1300-?] Sene 1, ['aded 1] – nu. 23/24 – 4mf – 9 – $47.00 – us MEDOC [949]
Mirbt, Carl *see*
- GESCHICHTE DER KATHOLISCHEN KIRCHE
- DIE KATHOLISCH-THEOLOGISCHE FAKULTAET ZU MARBURG
- QUELLEN ZUR GESCHICHTE DES PAPSTTUMS
- QUELLEN ZUR GESCHICHTE DES PAPSTTUMS UND DES ROEMISCHEN KATHOLIZISMUS
- DIE STELLUNG AUGUSTINS IN DER PUBLICISTIK DER GREGORIANISCHEN KIRCHENSTREITS
MIRCEN: JOURNAL OF APPLIED MICROBIOLOGY AND BIOTECHNOLOGY – v1-. 1984- – 1,5,6,9 – us UMI [073]
LA MIRE – Donnacona, Canada. v1 n1. 17 dec 1957-v6 n7. 1 mai 1964 – 1r – 1 – Can$50.00 – cn Can Microfilming [072]
Mireur, Hippolyte *see* ETUDE HISTORIQUE ET PRATIQUE SUR LA PROPHYLAXIE ET LE TRAITEMENT DU CHOLERA, BASEE SUR LES OBSERVATIONS FOURNIES PAR L'EPIDEMIE DE MARSEILLE (1884)
Mirez Carvajal, C *see*
- ANTIPOLOGIA BREVE EN QUE SE PRUEBA EL VERDADERO TEMPERAMENTO QUE LA NIEVE POSEE...
- TRATADO DE LAS QUALIDADES QUE LA NIEVE TIENE A PREDOMINIO...
MIRIAM'S SCHOOLING AND OTHER PAPERS. EDITED BY [THE AUTHOR'S] FRIEND REUBEN SHAPCOTT / White, William Hale – London: Kegan Paul, Trench, Trbner, 1890 – 1 roll – 1 – 1-55879-509-X – uk Libr Preservation [860]
MIRIKH – Shumarah-'i 1-18 (5 Muharram 1296-16 Jumada al-Lani 1297 [30 December 1878-26 May 1880]) – 1 reel – 1 – $35.00 – us MEDOC [950]
MIRKEVET HA-MISHNEH – Sefer R. Anshel. Cracow. c.1534. BJ-43-60 1 – 9 – ne IDC [956]
MIRKO, DER KNECHT : ROMAN / Altrichter, Gertrud – Berlin: W Limpert, 1944- – 1r – 1 – us U.W. Library [830]
LA MIRLITON – Montreal: [s.n, 1897-189- ou 19–] – 9 – cn C.I.H.M. [440]
MIRNOE NASTUPLENIE / Ioffe, Adolf Abramovich – Peterburg: Gos. izdvo, 1921 – 1 – CSUX88-B7686 – us Hoover Inst Photo [947]
LE MIROIR / ed by Arcand, Adrien – Montreal, Canada. v1 n45. 1 mar 1930-19 mar 1933 – 2r – 1 – Can$50.00r – cn Can Microfilming [072]
LE MIROIR – Red. Beaulieu. Paris. mai 1796-sept 1797 – 1 – fr A.C.R.P.P. [073]
MIROIR DE PARIS – London, UK. 7 Mar-1 Oct 1898 – 1 – uk British Libr Newspaper [072]
LE MIROIR DES CARACTERES : ART DE JUGER LES HOMMES – Quebec: J N Duquet, 1885. SEM16P277 – 1r – 5 – Can$9.00 – cn Bibl Nat [150]
LE MIROIR DES FRANCOIS, COMPRIS EN TROIS LIVRES / Barnaud, Nicolas – Paris, 1582 – 1 – us U.W. Library [944]
LE MIROIR DES SPECTACLES, DES LETTRES, DES MOEURS ET DES ARTS – Paris. fevr 1821-juin 1823 – 1 – fr A.C.R.P.P. [073]
LE MIROIR DU PARLEMENT – (Suivi de: Thompson's Mirror of Parliament) – Quebec: S Thompson, [1860] – 9 – cn C.I.H.M. [320]
MIROIR DU QUEBEC / ed by Duceppe, Jean – Ville d'Anjou, Canada. 28 aut 1965-16 sep 1966 – 1r – 1 – Can$60.00 – cn Can Microfilming [072]
LE MIROIR JOUR ET NUIT – Montreal, aut 1974; v1 n2. sep 1974 – 1r – 1 – Can$25.00 – cn Can Microfilming [072]
Mironov, N D *see*
- KATALOG INDIISKIKH RUKOPISEI
- KATALOG INDIISKIKH RUKOPISEI ROSSIISSKOI PUBLICHNOI BIBLIOTEKI
LE MIROUER DE LA MORT – En Breton. Saint Francois de Cuburien, 1575. 2 fiches.(Literature Collection) – 9 – 6.00 – fr Bibl Nationale [400]
MIROVAIA VOINA 1914-1918 : ATLAS SKHEM K TRUDU A. ZA IONCHKOVSKOGO / De-Lazari, Aleksandr Nikolaevich – Moskva: Gos. voen. izd-vo, 1924 – 1 – CSUX88-B2685 – us Hoover Inst Photo [940]
MIROVAYA EKONOMIKA I MEZHDUNARODNIYE OTNOSHENIA – Moscow. U.S.S.R. 1961-. World Economics and International Relations – 1 – us UMI [337]
MIROVOI KHLEBNYI RYNOK I PERSPEKTIVY NASHE GO KHLEBNOGO EKSPORTA / Kondrat'ev, N D – M., 1923 – 1mf – 9 – COR-200/1 – ne IDC [334]
MIROVOZZRENIE M. V. LOMONOSOVA / Azarenko, E K – Minsk, 1959. 270p. BR-6080 2 – 8 – ne IDC [460]
MIRRELIIA. NOVYIA POEZY / Severianin, I – v. 7. M., Berlin. 1922. BR-1032 2 – 8 – ne IDC [460]
MIRROR – (Also known as: Mirror News) – Los Angeles, CA. 1948-59 – 144r – 1 – $7,200.00 – C02394 – us Library Micro [071]
MIRROR – Altoona. Pa. 1874-1878; 1888-1932; 1950- – 1 – us UMI [071]
MIRROR – Clinton. Iowa. 1896-1917 – 1 – us UMI [071]
MIRROR – Cranston. R.I. -w. 1961- – 1 – us UMI [071]
MIRROR : DON MILLS EDITION – Toronto, 1957-1982 – 71r – 1 – cn Preston [971]
MIRROR – Georgetown, Guyana. Evening edition. -d. 2 Sept 1963-31 March 1966. 3 reels – 1 – uk British Libr Newspaper [072]
MIRROR – Georgetown, Guyana. -w. 10 March 1963-27 March 1966. Imperfect. 2 reels – 1 – uk British Libr Newspaper [072]
MIRROR – Los Angeles. Calif. 1948-54; 1960-1962 – 1 – us UMI [071]
MIRROR – Lyons. Neb. 1893-1916; 1918-1948 – 1 – us UMI [071]
MIRROR – Maumee, Ohio. 1980-81 – 1r – 1 – $32.50r – us Archival [071]
MIRROR – Olathe. Kan. 1861-1869; 1872-1920 – 1 – us UMI [071]
MIRROR – Toronto. Sept 30, 1837-Dec 8, 1865 – 1 – 875.00 – cn McLaren [971]
MIRROR – Wesson. Miss. 1889-1893 – 1 – us UMI [071]
MIRROR : WESTON-DOWNSVIEW – Toronto, 1967-1979 – 36r – 1 – cn Preston [971]
MIRROR : WILLOWDALE EDITION – Toronto, 1970-1980 – 40r – 1 – cn Preston [971]
MIRROR *see* DAILY MIRROR
THE MIRROR – Lagos. Nigeria. -w. 17, 24 Dec 1887, 18, 25 Feb, 17 Mar, 26 May, 21 Jul, 3, 17, 24 Nov 1888. (7 ft) – 1 – uk British Libr Newspaper [072]
THE MIRROR – Port of Spain, Trinidad. 28 Jan 1898-5 Dec 1916 (imperfect).-d. 75 reels – 1 – uk British Libr Newspaper [072]
THE MIRROR – Stillwater, Minn. v. 1, no. 1; v. 18-57, no. 52. Aug 10 1877; July 21 1904-July 6 1944 – 1 – us NY Public [071]
MIRROR AND DAILY NEWS – Los Angeles. Calif. 1954-55 – 1 – us UMI [071]
MIRROR NEWS *see* MIRROR
THE MIRROR OF ARCHITECTURE: OR THE GROUND-RULES OF THE ART OF BUILDING / Scamozzi, V – 1708. O 1163 – 9 – ne IDC [720]
A MIRROR OF HANNIBAL / Green, C P – Complete and authentic history of the city. Hannibal, 1905. Missouri Reel 25. (The Cox Library Collection) – 5 – us Americana [978]
THE MIRROR OF LITERATURE – Prescott, UC [Ont]: Beckford and Bayley, [1835] – 9 – cn C.I.H.M. [420]
MIRROR OF LITERATURE, AMUSEMENT AND INSTRUCTION – v. 5-10. 1823-25 – 1 – us UMI [073]
MIRROR OF TASTE AND DRAMATIC CENSOR – v. 1-4. Jan 1810-Dec 1811 – 1 – us UMI [073]
MIRROR OF THE STAGE – 1-4. 1822-24 – 1 – us UMI [790]
MIRROR SUN – Lyons. Neb. 1948-1962 – 1 – us UMI [071]
MIRROR-NEWS – Los Angeles. Calif. 1955-1960 – 1 – us UMI [071]
MIRROUR – Concord. New Hampshire. 1792-99; New Star. Concord. New Hampshire. 1797; Republican Gazetteer. Concord, New Hampshire. 1796-99. Sold as one unit – 3 – us Readex [071]
THE MIRROUR OF MAIESTIE / Green, H & Croston, J – O-616. 1870 – 9 – ne IDC [810]
MIRSAD – Istanbul, 1. sene, nos. 1-24 (14 Mart 1307-19 Agustos 1307 [28 Mar 1892-2 Sep. 1892]) – 4mf – 9 – $45.00 – us MEDOC [949]
Mirskii, D S *see*
- O BRIUSOVE
- O MANDEL'SHTAM, SHUM VREMENI
- OB A. BLOKE
MIRSKOI VESTNIK – Narodnyi zhurnal. Spb. 1863-90. Lacking: (9) 1864; (7-12) 1876; 1881-90. BR-3353 2 – 8 – ne IDC [073]

MIRTA / Reyes Huertas, Antonio – Barcelona: Ediciones Hynsa, 1943 – 1 – sp Bibl Santa Ana [946]
MIS AMORES / Amores Gonzalez, Meliton – Astorga: Talleres Graficos, 1926 – 1 – sp Bibl Santa Ana [946]
MIS CANTARES / Gordo Moreno, Angel – Caceres: Tip. Luciano Jimenez, 1927 – sp Bibl Santa Ana [780]
MIS CRONICAS / Mirabal, A de – Badajoz: Tip. El Noticiero Extremeno, 1908 – 1 – sp Bibl Santa Ana [946]
MIS ESTUDIOS HISTORICOS.. / Barado, Francisco – 1893 – 9 – 1.50f – sp Bibl Santa Ana [946]
MIS PASATIEMPOS / Garcia Monge, Eduardo – 1884 – 9 – 1.50f – sp Bibl Santa Ana [920]
MIS WEEK – 1984- – 1,5,6,9 – us UMI [510]
MISA COMUNITARIA DE SAN PEDRO DE ALCANTARA PATRON DE EXTREMADURA / Sanchez Loro, Domingo – Caceres: Imprenta Moderna, 1964 – 1 – sp Bibl Santa Ana [240]
MISA DE SAN JUAN CRISOSTOMO / Morillo Trivino, Santiago – Granada: Tip. Ntra. Sra. de las Angustias, 1944 – 1 – sp Bibl Santa Ana [240]
MISA DIALOGADA / Secretariado Catequistico – Plasencia: Imp. y Libr. Montero, 1963 – 1 – sp Bibl Santa Ana [946]
MISA RECITADA Y CANTADA / Prieto, Ignacio – Colegio de S.Jose, Villafranca, 1942. Sevilla. Ed.de la Gavilla – 1 – sp Bibl Santa Ana [780]
MISAL DE SANTA EULALIA. DONADO POR EL OBISPO JUAN DE ARMENGOL (SIECLE 14) – Barcelona – 1r – 5,6 – sp Cultura [220]
MISAL DE SANTA EULALIA (SIECLE 14-15) – Barcelona – 1r – 5,6 – sp Cultura [220]
THE MISANTHROPE OF MOLIERE; DONE INTO ENGLISH BY WILLIAM F. GIESE / Moliere, Jean BP – Boston, New York: Houghton, Mifflin, 1928. vii,103p – 1 – us U.W. Library [820]
MISANTHROPIE ET REPENTIR / Kotzebue – (French Theatre Series). Paris. Chez le libraire "Au Theatre du Vaudeville." an VII. 1798 – 9 – fr Hachette [820]
MISAO – 1919- . Issues for v1-6, 23-24 not numbered consecutively. -irr – 1 – us U.W. Library [949]
MISAO – v1-41, 1919-33 – 1 – us I.U. Libraries [073]
MISBAH *see* AL-MISBAH
MISBOEK DER OUD-KATHOLIEKE KERK – Amsterdam, 1909 – 7mf – 8 – Dfl28.00 – ne Slangenburg [240]
MISC. ANNUALS / Baptist Associations – Bowdoinham, ME: 1792-93; Charleston, SC: 1774; Danbury, Ct: 1795; Shaftesbury, VT: 1790; Stonington, CT: 1793; Vermont, VT: 1790. 65p – 1 – us Baptist [240]
MISC. MANUSCRIPTS / Charleston Library Society. Charleston, South Carolina – ca. 1750 – ca. 1950 – 58mf – 9 – us South Carolina Historical [090]
MISC. MATERIALS / Backus, Isaac – 1752-1804. 50p – 1 – 5.00 – us Baptist [240]
MISC. NEW BULLETINS / Arkansas Central Baptist Association – The Associational Messenger, 1943-44; Central Baptist Association Bulletin, Mar 1947, 1952; Central Baptist News, Aug 1957-Aug 1978; Arkansas Baptist Special Edition for Central Baptist Assoc., Aug 1978-9 Apr 1981. 3116p – 1 – 109.06 – us Baptist [240]
MISC. PAMPHLETS AND PERIODICALS BY THE DEUTSCHE KOMMUNISTISCHE PARTEI, THE GRUPPE REVOLUTIONAERER KOMMUNISTEN (TROTZKISTEN), KOMMUNISTISCHE PARTEI DEUTSCHLANDS.. – German left-wing organizations, publ. 1964-72, 1983-84 – 1 – us U.W. Library [080]
MISC. PAPERS / Montana. Forest and Conservation Experiment Station. Missoula – no.4.1968 – 1,5,6 – us Spaulding [630]
MISC. PLAT BOOK / U.S. Land Office. Dodge City, Kansas – ca1876-78 – 1 – us KS Hist [324]
MISC. SCRAPBOOKS / Weber, Jaroy – 1972-78. 680p – 1 – 23.80 – us Baptist [240]
MISCELANEA – Llerena, 1979 – 5 – sp Bibl Santa Ana [073]
MISCELANEA EMERITENSE DEL S. 16 / Alvarez Saenz de Buruaga, Jose – Badajoz, 1958 – 1 – sp Bibl Santa Ana [946]
MISCELANEA O COLECCION DE VARIOS DISCURSOS / Foronda, Valentin de – 1787 – 1mf – 9 – Pta1,000.00 – 84-7848-144-3 – sp Pentalfa [440]
MISCELANEA SAGRADA DE VARIOS DISCURSOS PANEGIRICOS / Ambrosio de Montanchez – 1709 – 9 – 1.50f – sp Bibl Santa Ana [880]
MISCELLANEA / Ewing, Juliana Horatia – British Fiction Archive: Unit 1 – 9 – uk Bell [830]
MISCELLANEA AGOSTINIANA TESTI E STUDI, VOL 1 : SANCTI AUGUSTINI SERMONES POST MAURINOS REPERTI / ed by Morin, D G – 27mf – 8 – ne Slangenburg [240]
MISCELLANEA AGOSTINIANA TESTI E STUDI, VOL 2 : STUDI AGOSTINIANI – Romae, 1931 – 34mf – 8 – ne Slangenburg [240]
MISCELLANEA AUSTRIACA AD BOTANICAM, CHEMIAM ET HISTORIAM NATURALEM SPECTANTIA / Jacquin, N J von – 2v. Vindobonae. 1778-81. B-5976 2 – 8 – ne IDC [580]
MISCELLANEA BEROLINENSIA / Akademie der Wissenschaften. Berlin – 7v and suppl 1710-43 – 1 – us Schnase [500]
MISCELLANEA BEROLINENSIA AD INCREMENTUM SCIENTIARUM, EX SCRIPTIS SOCIETATI REGIAE SCIENTIARUM EXHIBITIS EDITA, CUM FIGVRIS AENEIS ET INDICE MATERIARUM / Akademie der Wissenschaften. Berlin – 1710-1744 – 3 – us Readex [500]
MISCELLANEA BEROLINENSIA AD INCREMENTUM SCIENTIARUM EX SCRIPTIS SOCIETATIS EDITA – Berlin. v1-7. 1710-1743 – 61mf – 9 – ne IDC [500]
MISCELLANEA BOTANICA / Bertoloni, A – 2v. Bononiae. 1842-63. B-707 2 – 8 – ne IDC [580]
MISCELLANEA CURIOSA / Deutsche Akademie der Naturforscher – Norimbergae, etc. 1670-1706 – 3 – us Readex [574]
MISCELLANEA CURIOSA MATHEMATICA: OR, THE LITERARY CORRESPONDENCE OF SOME EMINENT MATHEMATICIANS IN GREAT BRITAIN AND IRELAND – London, 1749-53 – 3 – us Readex [510]
MISCELLANEA CURIOSA SIVE EPHEMERIDUM MEDICO-PHYSICARUM GERMANICARUM ACADEMIAE NATURAE CURIOSORUM / Deutsche Akademie der Naturforscher – (Index. 1670-91) – Lipsiae, Jenae, Francofurti, etc. v. 1-10. 1670-1679; S. 2. v. 1-10. 1694-1706; S. 3. v. 1-10. – 385mf – 8 – ne IDC [580]
MISCELLANEA HISTORICA IN HONOREM ALBERTI DE MEYER – Lovanii. Tom 1-2. 1946 – Dfl130.00 – ne Slangenburg [240]
MISCELLANEA LITURGICA IN HONOREM L.C. MOHLBERG – Roma. v1-2. 1948 – 19mf – 8 – Dfl67.00 – ne Slangenburg [240]
MISCELLANEA LOMBARDIANA – Novara, 1957 – 14mf – 8 – ne Slangenburg [290]
MISCELLANEA MUSICALE / Berardi, A – 1689 – 9 – us Sibley [780]
MISCELLANEA: SERIES DE MORCEAUX POUR PIANO, OP. 16, NO. 1: LEGENDE / Paderewski, Ignace Jan – Berlin: Bote & Book, 188- – 1 – us Sibley [780]
MISCELLANEA: SERIES DE MORCEAUX POUR PIANO, OP. 16, NO. 2: MELODIE / Paderewski, Ignace Jan – Berlin: Bote & Book, 188- – 1 – us Sibley [780]
MISCELLANEA: SERIES DE MORCEAUX POUR PIANO, OP. 16, NO. 3: THEME VARIE / Paderewski, Ignace Jan – Berlin: Bote & Book, 188- – 1 – us Sibley [780]
MISCELLANEA: SERIES DE MORCEAUX POUR PIANO, OP. 16, NO. 4: NOCTURNE / Paderewski, Ignace Jan – Berlin: Bote & Book, 188- – 1 – us Sibley [780]
MISCELLANEA: SERIES DE MORCEAUX POUR PIANO, OP. 16, NO. 5 : LEGENDE NO. 2 / Paderewski, Ignace Jan – Berlin: Bote & Book, 188- – 1 – us Sibley [780]
MISCELLANEA: SERIES DE MORCEAUX POUR PIANO, OP. 16, NO. 7: MINUET / Paderewski, Ignace Jan – Berlin: Bote & Book, 188- – 1 – us Sibley [780]
MISCELLANEA ZOOLOGICA. / Pallas, Peter Simon – La Haye: P. Van Cleef, 1766. 3 fiches. (Science Collection) – 9 – 8.00 – fr Bibl Nationale [590]
MISCELLANEEN ARTISTISCHEN INHALTS. HERAUSGEGEBEN VON JOHANN GEORG MEUSEL / Meusel, Johann G – 1779-87 – 9 – us Sibley [700]
MISCELLANEORUM LIBRI 7, HOC EST COLLECTIO VETERUM MONUMENTORUM QUAE HACTENUS LATUERANT IN VARIIS CODICIBUS AC BIBLIOTHECIS / Baluzius, Stephanus – Parisiis, 1678-1715 – 72mf – 8 – Dfl252.00 – ne Slangenburg [240]
MISCELLANEOUS / Kentucky. Agricultural Extension Service – v. 1-202 – 402. 1953-72 – 1,5,6 – us Spaulding [630]
MISCELLANEOUS / UN Economic Commission for Europe (ECE) – E.16 – 9 – us U.N. Pubs [340]
MISCELLANEOUS AMERICAN MANUSCRIPTS / Lambeth Palace Library – 16th-18th Centuries. Printed Index – 1 – £225.00 – uk World [025]
MISCELLANEOUS ARCHIVES, 1948-1978 / Papua New Guinea National Fisheries Authority. Research Branch – reels 1-2 – 1 – PMB1118 – at Pacific Mss [639]
MISCELLANEOUS BABYLONIAN INSCRIPTIONS / Barton, G A – New Haven, 1918. BNE-20,006 – 9 – ne IDC [410]
MISCELLANEOUS BAPTIST PAPERS – (Arkansas Baptist, 1859-61; Baptist Champion, 1859-60; Baptist Correspondent, 1860; Baptist Herald, 1873, 1874; Baptist Messenger, 1850, 1859-61; Baptist Monthly, 1865, 1866, 1867; Baptist Watchman, 1855, 1856-58, 1871, 1873-75, 1879; Baptist Witness, 1866; Christian Herald, 1865-1866, 1867-69, 1871, 1872; Louisiana Baptist, 1856-1861, 1868-1869; Mississippi Baptist, 1857, 1858-60, 1861; Missouri Baptist, 1860; Missouri Baptist Journal, 1866, 1867, 1868; New Orleans Baptist Chronicle, 1853-54; Southern Baptist, 1883-84, 1887; Southwestern Baptist Chronicle, 1847, 1848, 1849-50; Texas Baptist, 1859-60; Virginia Baptist, 1859; Western Baptist, 1874-76; Western Watchman, 1856-57, 1858-60. 1) – 1853-79. (Index included) – 1 – $194.74 – us Baptist [240]
MISCELLANEOUS BAPTIST PAPERS – Baptist Watchman, Knoxville, Tennessee 1855-58, 1871, 1873-75, 1879. Baptist Witness, Nashville, Tennessee. 1866. 702p – 1 – 24.57 – us Baptist [240]
MISCELLANEOUS BAPTIST PAPERS – Christian Herald, Alabama, 1865-66, 1867-69, 1871, 1872. 659p – 1 – 23.06 – us Baptist [240]
MISCELLANEOUS BAPTIST PAPERS – (East Tennessee Baptist, 1869-70; The Christian Era, 1856-57; Pacific Evangel (San Francisco), Oct 1878-57 (sic)) – 87p – 1 – 5.00 – us Baptist [071]
MISCELLANEOUS BAPTIST PAPERS – (Georgia Baptist, 27 Feb, 17 Apr, 12 Jun 1902) – 20p – 1 – 5.00 – us Baptist [071]
MISCELLANEOUS BAPTIST PAPERS – (Richmond Christian Advocate. 13 May 1857. Old Faith Contender, California.Nov 1943. The Baptist Guardian, Virginia. 1 Aug 1848. Southern Baptist Record, Mississippi. 16 Oct 1890) – 25p – 1 – 5.00 – us Baptist [071]
MISCELLANEOUS BLACK BAPTIST MATERIALS – Assocs., conventions, papers and periodicals, books and pamphlets, addresses, programs, news clippings, catalogs, letters. 4 reels. 14,340p – 1 – 501.90 – us Baptist [240]
MISCELLANEOUS BOARD RECORDS / Hancock County. Ohio. Biglick Township. Board of Education – 1871-1902 – 1r – 1 – $32.50r – us Archival [324]
MISCELLANEOUS BOOKLETS – (Graves, James R. Individualism. Grime, J. H. Blood before water and Christ before the church. Phillips, Daniel W. Scrapbook. 1809-90. Reynolds, Mary C. Baptist missionary pioneers among Negroes. Smith, Charles S. Race question reviewed) – 1 – 13.72 – us Baptist [240]
MISCELLANEOUS BOOKS – (Heber, Reginald. Sermons preached in India. 1829. 1. Spilman, Leavell, Moore. Convention normal manual for Sunday School workers. 1909. 6.10; 1. Both sides. A full investigation of the charges preferred against Elder J. R. Graves by R. B. C. Howell and others. 1859. 6.15; SBC; 1) – 1 – 59.99 – us Baptist [240]
MISCELLANEOUS BOOKS AND PAMPHLETS – (Includes: Brown, Jesse. Highlights in Baptist History. 1946. Calhoun, H.H. Memorial of Patrick Hues Mell. 1850-1918. Crain, J.D. A Mountain Boy's Life Story. 1914. Crumpton, Ethel H. Religion for a Century. 1840-1940. Dill, J.S. Paper: "The Old Boykin Home". n.d. Haldeman, I.M. A History of the First Baptist Church, New York. 1745-1928. In Memoriam Broadman Hartwell Crumpton. 1840. Reports of the Commission on Reconstruction and Missionary Survey in Europe and the Near East. 1919) – 1 – $11.34 – us Baptist [240]
MISCELLANEOUS BOTANICAL WORKS / Brown, Robert – Ray Society. 1886-88 – 1. 148.00; ; 7 – uk Microform Academic [580]
THE MISCELLANEOUS BOTANICAL WORKS / Brown, Robert – 2v. London. 1867. B-697 2 – 8 – ne IDC [580]
MISCELLANEOUS BULLETINS / Tennessee. University. Agricultural Experiment Station – v1-4. 1889-1956 – 1,5 – us Spaulding [630]
MISCELLANEOUS CABINET – v. 1. 12 Jul 1823-3 Jan 1824 – 1 – us UMI [073]
MISCELLANEOUS CHURCH RECORDS / Charleston. South Carolina. St. James United Methodist Church – 1849-1916. 9 fiches – 9 – us South Carolina Historical [978]
MISCELLANEOUS COLLECTION OF 20 VOCAL AND INSTRUMENTAL COMPOSITIONS / Johnson, Francis – One composer's manuscript, the rest early printed editions. music 3085 – 1 – us L of C Photodup [780]
MISCELLANEOUS DISCOURSES AND EXPOSITIONS OF SCRIPTURE / Young, George Paxton – Edinburgh: Johnstone and Hunter; Hamilton, Canada West: D McLellan, 1854 – 1mf – 9 – 0-8370-7518-1 – 1986-1518 – us A.T.L.A. [240]
MISCELLANEOUS DOCUMENTS / Labour Party. South Africa – 1911-46 – 1 – us Res Libr [960]
MISCELLANEOUS DOCUMENTS / United Nations – 1970-1986 – E.168 F.123 R.5 S.32 – 9 (TD/STAT, UNCTAD/LDC, UNCTAD/ST/MD, UNCTAD/TAP, UNCTAD/TT) – us U.N. Pubs [320]
MISCELLANEOUS DOCUMENTS / War Veterans Torch Commando. (South Africa) – 1951-53 – 1 – us Res Libr [960]
MISCELLANEOUS DOCUMENTS AND PAPERS / Sierra Leone – 1887-1962 – 1r – 1 – $49.50 – us African Imprint [960]
MISCELLANEOUS DOCUMENTS FROM A LONDON-BASED IRANIAN TROTSKYITE ORGANIZATION – London, 1974-1978 – $50.00 – us MEDOC [060]
MISCELLANEOUS DOCUMENTS RELATING TO JAPAN'S ECONOMIC, INDUSTRIAL, MILITARY, AND DIPLOMATIC ACTIVITIES : USED AS BACKGROUND MATERIALS BY THE INTERNATIONAL PROSECUTING SECTION, 1929-45 – 7 rolls – 9 – $161.00 – Dist. us Scholarly Res – us L of C Photodup [355]
MISCELLANEOUS DOCUMENTS RELATING TO THE ATOMIC BOMBING OF JAPAN, ALLIED AND JAPANESE MILITARY OPERATIONS IN THE PACIFIC, AND JAPANESE REPORTS ON THE CHINESE COMMUNIST PARTY – 1993 – 8r – 1 – $184.00 set in US $30.00r outside – M1738 – us Nat'l Archives [355]
MISCELLANEOUS DOCUMENTS RELATING TO THE RECIPROCITY NEGOTIATIONS OF THE DEPT. OF STATE, 1848-54; 1884-85; 1891-92 / U.S. Department of State – 1roll. T493 – 1 – us Nat'l Archives [324]
MISCELLANEOUS EARLY NEWSPAPERS / Akron, Ohio – 1869-99; 1903-06 – 1 – us UMI [071]
MISCELLANEOUS EARLY NEWSPAPERS / Alexandria, Louisiana – 1883-1918 – 1 – us UMI [071]
MISCELLANEOUS EARLY NEWSPAPERS / Athens, Ohio – 1850-1903 – 1 – us UMI [071]
MISCELLANEOUS EARLY NEWSPAPERS / Bayonne, New Jersey – 1889-93 – 1 – us UMI [071]
MISCELLANEOUS EARLY NEWSPAPERS / Bluffton, Indiana – 1851-1878 – 1 – us UMI [071]
MISCELLANEOUS EARLY NEWSPAPERS / Canton, Mississippi – 1837-1863 – 1 – us UMI [071]
MISCELLANEOUS EARLY NEWSPAPERS / Carrollton, Mississippi – 1840-1847 – 1 – us UMI [071]
MISCELLANEOUS EARLY NEWSPAPERS / Charleston. South Carolina – 1732-82 – 1 – us UMI [071]
MISCELLANEOUS EARLY NEWSPAPERS / Clinton, Mississippi – 1835-1888 – 1 – us UMI [071]
MISCELLANEOUS EARLY NEWSPAPERS / Columbus, Mississippi – 1837-1882 – 1 – us UMI [071]

MISCELLANEOUS EARLY NEWSPAPERS / Crystal Springs, Mississippi – 1872-1892 – 1 – us UMI [071]

MISCELLANEOUS EARLY NEWSPAPERS / Cumberland, Maryland – 1845-1916 – 1 – us UMI [071]

MISCELLANEOUS EARLY NEWSPAPERS / Davenport, Iowa – 1856-1904 – 1 – us UMI [071]

MISCELLANEOUS EARLY NEWSPAPERS / Dubuque, Iowa – 1837-59 – 1 – us UMI [071]

MISCELLANEOUS EARLY NEWSPAPERS / Easton, Pennsylvania – 1799-1875 – 1 – us UMI [071]

MISCELLANEOUS EARLY NEWSPAPERS / Elizabeth, New Jersey – 1779-1876 – 1 – us UMI [071]

MISCELLANEOUS EARLY NEWSPAPERS / Elmira, New York – 1835-96; 1912-1920 – 1 – us UMI [071]

MISCELLANEOUS EARLY NEWSPAPERS / Elyria-Lorain, Ohio – 1829-1907 – 1 – us UMI [071]

MISCELLANEOUS EARLY NEWSPAPERS / Fort Adams, Mississippi – 1853-1855 – 1 – us UMI [071]

MISCELLANEOUS EARLY NEWSPAPERS / Frederick, Maryland – 1830-32; 1883-84 – 1 – us UMI [071]

MISCELLANEOUS EARLY NEWSPAPERS / Gallatin, Mississippi – 1838-1844 – 1 – us UMI [071]

MISCELLANEOUS EARLY NEWSPAPERS / Garden City, Kansas – 1882-1900 – 1 – us UMI [071]

MISCELLANEOUS EARLY NEWSPAPERS / Gary, Indiana – 1908-10; 1919-20; 1924-32 – 1 – us UMI [071]

MISCELLANEOUS EARLY NEWSPAPERS / Gettysburg, Pennsylvania – 1803-1854 – 1 – us UMI [071]

MISCELLANEOUS EARLY NEWSPAPERS / Gouverneur, New York – 1864-84 – 1 – us UMI [071]

MISCELLANEOUS EARLY NEWSPAPERS / Greenville, Pennsylvania – 1869-1899 – 1 – us UMI [071]

MISCELLANEOUS EARLY NEWSPAPERS / Grenada, Mississippi – 1838-1846 – 1 – us UMI [071]

MISCELLANEOUS EARLY NEWSPAPERS / Haverhill, Massachusetts – 1793-1821 – 1 – us UMI [071]

MISCELLANEOUS EARLY NEWSPAPERS / Hazelhurst, Mississippi – 1865-1895 – 1 – us UMI [071]

MISCELLANEOUS EARLY NEWSPAPERS / Hill City, Kansas – 1879-81, 1889-91 – 1 – us UMI [071]

MISCELLANEOUS EARLY NEWSPAPERS / Holly Springs, Mississippi – 1839-41 – 1 – us UMI [071]

MISCELLANEOUS EARLY NEWSPAPERS / Hudson, Ohio – 1833-1855 – 1 – us UMI [071]

MISCELLANEOUS EARLY NEWSPAPERS / Jackson, Mississippi – 1838-99. (scattered) – 1 – us UMI [071]

MISCELLANEOUS EARLY NEWSPAPERS / Johnstown, Pennsylvania – 1831-89 – 1 – us UMI [071]

MISCELLANEOUS EARLY NEWSPAPERS / Keokuk, Iowa – 1849-98 – 1 – us UMI [071]

MISCELLANEOUS EARLY NEWSPAPERS / Kittanning, Pennsylvania – 1872-87 – 1 – us UMI [071]

MISCELLANEOUS EARLY NEWSPAPERS / Kosciusko, Mississippi – 1838-1901. (scattered) – 1 – us UMI [071]

MISCELLANEOUS EARLY NEWSPAPERS / Lawrence, Kansas – 1869-95 – 1 – us UMI [071]

MISCELLANEOUS EARLY NEWSPAPERS / Lexington, Mississippi – 1838-43 – 1 – us UMI [071]

MISCELLANEOUS EARLY NEWSPAPERS / Lima, Ohio – 1846-1896 – 1 – us UMI [071]

MISCELLANEOUS EARLY NEWSPAPERS / Lorain-Elyria, Ohio – 1829-1907 – 1 – us UMI [071]

MISCELLANEOUS EARLY NEWSPAPERS / Macon, Mississippi – 1838-1842 – 1 – us UMI [071]

MISCELLANEOUS EARLY NEWSPAPERS / Marquette, Michigan – 1846-56 – 1 – us UMI [071]

MISCELLANEOUS EARLY NEWSPAPERS / Memphis, Tennessee – 1834-92 – 1 – us UMI [071]

MISCELLANEOUS EARLY NEWSPAPERS / Meridian, Mississippi – 1870-1916 – 1 – us UMI [071]

MISCELLANEOUS EARLY NEWSPAPERS / Middlesboro, Kentucky – 1911-24 – 1 – us UMI [071]

MISCELLANEOUS EARLY NEWSPAPERS / Midland, Michigan – 1870-75 – 1 – us UMI [071]

MISCELLANEOUS EARLY NEWSPAPERS / Mount Clemens, Michigan – 1926-31 – 1 – us UMI [071]

MISCELLANEOUS EARLY NEWSPAPERS / Muncie, Indiana – 1837-77; 1905-06 – 1 – us UMI [071]

MISCELLANEOUS EARLY NEWSPAPERS / Natchez, Mississippi – 1805-37 – 1 – us UMI [071]

MISCELLANEOUS EARLY NEWSPAPERS / Norfolk, Virginia – 1795-1798 – 1 – us UMI [071]

MISCELLANEOUS EARLY NEWSPAPERS / Oklahoma City, Oklahoma – 1893-1904 – 1 – us UMI [071]

MISCELLANEOUS EARLY NEWSPAPERS / Oswego, New York – 1830-49 – 1 – us UMI [071]

MISCELLANEOUS EARLY NEWSPAPERS / Owensboro, Kentucky – 1874-90 – 1 – us UMI [071]

MISCELLANEOUS EARLY NEWSPAPERS / Oxford, Mississippi – 1849-52 – 1 – us UMI [071]

MISCELLANEOUS EARLY NEWSPAPERS / Panola, Mississippi – 1843-57 – 1 – us UMI [071]

MISCELLANEOUS EARLY NEWSPAPERS / Paulding, Mississippi – 1845-61 – 1 – us UMI [071]

MISCELLANEOUS EARLY NEWSPAPERS / Pontotoc, Mississippi – 1838-46 – 1 – us UMI [071]

MISCELLANEOUS EARLY NEWSPAPERS / Port Gibson, Mississippi – 1852-59, 1890 – 1 – us UMI [071]

MISCELLANEOUS EARLY NEWSPAPERS / Poughkeepsie, New York – 1785-1860 – 1 – us UMI [071]

MISCELLANEOUS EARLY NEWSPAPERS / Raymond, Mississippi – 1837-79 – 1 – us UMI [071]

MISCELLANEOUS EARLY NEWSPAPERS / Ripley, Mississippi – 1837-38, 1843-46 – 1 – us UMI [071]

MISCELLANEOUS EARLY NEWSPAPERS / Rochester, New York – 1836-59 – 1 – us UMI [071]

MISCELLANEOUS EARLY NEWSPAPERS / Rodney, Mississippi – 1837-40 – 1 – us UMI [071]

MISCELLANEOUS EARLY NEWSPAPERS / St. Louis, Missouri – 1828-46 – 1 – us UMI [071]

MISCELLANEOUS EARLY NEWSPAPERS / Sault Sainte Marie, Michigan – 1887-1903 – 1 – us UMI [071]

MISCELLANEOUS EARLY NEWSPAPERS / Tulsa, Oklahoma – 1900-17 – 1 – us UMI [071]

MISCELLANEOUS EARLY NEWSPAPERS / Las Vegas, New Mexico – 1889-1919. Printed in Spanish – 1 – us UMI [071]

MISCELLANEOUS EARLY NEWSPAPERS / Xenia, Ohio – 1826-1880 – 1 – us UMI [071]

MISCELLANEOUS EARLY NEWSPAPERS / Yazoo City, Mississippi – 1839-56 – 1 – us UMI [071]

MISCELLANEOUS EARLY NEWSPAPERS / Yonkers, New York – 1864-93 – 1 – us UMI [071]

MISCELLANEOUS ESSAYS / Saintsbury, George – London: Percival and Co., 1892 – 1 roll – 1 – 1-55879-482-4 – uk Libr Preservation [840]

MISCELLANEOUS ESSAYS AND ADDRESSES / Sidgwick, Henry – London: Macmillan and Co., limited; New York: Macmillan Co., 1904 – 1 roll – 1 – 1-55879-570-7 – uk Libr Preservation [840]

MISCELLANEOUS ESSAYS AND REVIEWS / Barnes, Albert – New York: Ivison & Phinney, 1855, c1854 – 2mf – us A.T.L.A. [240]

MISCELLANEOUS EXTENSION PUBLICATION / Clemson University. Agricultural Extension Division – 1972. 2 fiches – 9 – us Spaulding [630]

MISCELLANEOUS EXTENSION PUBLICATIONS / North Carolina. State University. Raleigh. Agricultural Extension Service – v.1-51 – 1,5 – us Spaulding [630]

MISCELLANEOUS EXTENSION PUBLICATIONS / North Carolina State University.Agricultural Extension Service – No.52-162 – 1,5 – us Spaulding [630]

MISCELLANEOUS EXTENSION PUBLICATIONS / Wisconsin. Agricultural Extension Service – 1,5 – us Spaulding [630]

MISCELLANEOUS GERMAN RECORDS COLLECTION / Germany – 440r – 1 – T84 – us Nat'l Archives [324]

MISCELLANEOUS HUNGARIAN NEWSPAPERS-1956 REVOLT – 23 Oct-31 Dec 1956 – 1r – 1 – us L of C Photodup [072]

MISCELLANEOUS ISSUES OF EARLY NEWSPAPERS / Gatlinburg, Tennessee – 1882; 1883; 1886; 1905; 1930; 1935 – 1 – us UMI [071]

MISCELLANEOUS ITEMS / Lexington County. South Carolina. Laurel Baptist Church – 1962-68 – 1 – 5.00 – us Baptist [240]

MISCELLANEOUS LETTERS, GIVING AN ACCOUNT OF THE WORKS OF THE LEARNED – v1-2 17 Oct 1694-Mar 1696 – 1 – us UMI [800]

MISCELLANEOUS LETTERS OF THE DEPT. OF STATE, 1789-1906 / U.S. Department of State – 1,310 rolls. M179. Printed guide – 1 – us Nat'l Archives [324]

MISCELLANEOUS LETTERS SENT BY THE GENERAL LAND OFFICE, 1796-1889 / U.S. Bureau of Land Management – 228 rolls. M25. Printed guide – 1 – us Nat'l Archives [324]

MISCELLANEOUS LETTERS SENT BY THE PUEBLO INDIAN AGENCY / U.S. Bureau of Indian Affairs – 1874-91. 10 rolls. M941 – 1 – us Nat'l Archives [324]

MISCELLANEOUS LETTERS SENT BY THE SECRETARY..., 1800-09 / U.S. War Department. Office of the Secretary – 3rolls. M370. Printed guide – 1 – us Nat'l Archives [324]

MISCELLANEOUS LETTERS SENT BY THE SECRETARY..., 1870-87. AND BY THE ASSISTANT SECRETARY, 1876-93 / U.S. Treasury Department – 4rolls. M741. Printed guide – 1 – us Nat'l Archives [336]

MISCELLANEOUS LETTERS SENT BY THE SECRETARY OF THE NAVY, 1798-1886 / U.S. Navy. Office of Naval Records and Library – 43 rolls. M209. Printed guide – 1 – us Nat'l Archives [324]

MISCELLANEOUS MAGAZINE – v. 1. Jan-Dec 1824 – 1 – us UMI [073]

MISCELLANEOUS MANUSCRIPT WORKS / Burrows, H. Lansing – 236p – 1 – 8.26 – us Baptist [240]

MISCELLANEOUS MANUSCRIPTS / Royal Society – $965.00 – 0-89093-877-6 – us UPA [090]

MISCELLANEOUS MANUSCRIPTS, 1847-1977 / Cook Islands Library and Museum Society – Rarotonga – 1r – 1 – PMB1066 – at Pacific Mss [980]

MISCELLANEOUS MANUSCRIPTS, 1891-1973 / Cook Islands Library and Museum Society – Rarotonga – 1r – 1 – PMB1069 – at Pacific Mss [980]

MISCELLANEOUS MANUSCRIPTS, 1903-1939 / Cook Islands Library and Museum Society – Rarotonga – 1r – 1 – PMB1070 – at Pacific Mss [980]

MISCELLANEOUS MANUSCRIPTS, 1933-1970 / Cook Islands Library and Museum Society – Rarotonga – 1r – 1 – PMB1065 – at Pacific Mss [980]

MISCELLANEOUS MANUSCRIPTS, 1968-1983 / Darques, F Martin & Moniton, P Albert – 3r – 1 – PMB1081 – at Pacific Mss [980]

MISCELLANEOUS MANUSCRIPTS, BIOGRAPHICAL DATA, AND DOCUMENTS / Alison, Francis – 1 – $50.00 – us Presbyterian [240]

MISCELLANEOUS MANUSCRIPTS OF THE REVOLUTIONARY WAR ERA, 1771-1791 / Pennsylvania Historical and Museum Commission – (With printed guide) – 1r – 1 – $85.00 – D3290 – Dist. us Scholarly Res – us Penn Hist [975]

MISCELLANEOUS MATERIALS RELATED TO POLITICS AND ELECTIONS...1960'S-1970'S – Collection of German pamphlets. With: Pamphlets published by the Social Democratic Party of the Federal Republic of Germany for the Election in 1969 – 1 – us U.W. Library [080]

MISCELLANEOUS MATERIALS RELATING TO THE LIFE AND CAREER OF BENJAMIN FRANKLIN DAN / Secrest, William – 1 – us KS Hist [978]

MISCELLANEOUS MSS IN THE ARCHIVES OF THE MARQUESS OF BATH / Bath. Archives (Marquess). Longleat – nos. 5, 6, 10, 11, 13 and 15 – 1 – uk Microform Academic [025]

MISCELLANEOUS NEWSPAPERS / Australia – (Apply to publ for details) – 1 – at Pascoe [072]

MISCELLANEOUS NEWSPAPERS / Charleroi, Pennsylvania – 1904-1929 – 1 – us UMI [071]

MISCELLANEOUS NEWSPAPERS / Colton, California – 1967-70 – 1 – us UMI [071]

MISCELLANEOUS NEWSPAPERS / Decatur, Illinois – 1856-86 – 1 – us UMI [071]

MISCELLANEOUS NEWSPAPERS / Garden City, Michigan – 1941-1946 – 1 – us UMI [071]

MISCELLANEOUS NEWSPAPERS / Lecompton, Kansas – 1856-75 – 1 – us UMI [071]

MISCELLANEOUS NEWSPAPERS / Maryland – 3 – us Readex [071]

MISCELLANEOUS NEWSPAPERS / Oregon – 1 – us Oregon Hist [071]

MISCELLANEOUS NEWSPAPERS / Pennsylvania – 1732-1957 – 1 – us UMI [071]

MISCELLANEOUS NEWSPAPERS / Philadelphia, Pennsylvania – 3 – us Readex [071]

MISCELLANEOUS NEWSPAPERS / Virginia – 3 – us Readex [071]

MISCELLANEOUS NEWSPAPERS / Washington. (State) – 1 – us Oregon Hist [071]

MISCELLANEOUS NEWSPAPERS AND BROADSHEETS – Panama Canal Commission. Panama Canal Collection. 1880-1920 – 1r – 1 – us L of C Photodup [072]

MISCELLANEOUS NUMBERED RECORDS (THE MANUSCRIPT FILE) IN THE WAR DEPARTMENT COLLECTION OF REVOLUTIONARY WAR RECORDS / U.S. War Department. Collection of Revolutionary War Records – 1775-90's. 125 rolls. M859 – 1 – us Nat'l Archives [324]

MISCELLANEOUS ORDERS, APPOINTMENTS, ETC / Korea. (Territory under U.S. Occupation, 1945-1948). Military Governor – 1945-48.Title supplied by cataloger – 1 – us U.W. Library [950]

MISCELLANEOUS PAMPHLETS – By Fuller, Brawley, Vedder, Lorimer, Maddrey, Goodchild, Whitley, Bitting, Dodd, et al – 1 – $22.85 – us Baptist [240]

MISCELLANEOUS PAMPHLETS / North Carolina. State University. Raleigh. Agricultural Extension Service – v.1-215. 1930-Jan 1963 – 1,5 – us Spaulding [630]

MISCELLANEOUS PAMPHLETS AND PERIODICALS ON FREE THOUGHT AND ATHEISM – Publ. or ed. by Emanuel Haldeman-Julius.2 reels – 1 – us U.W. Library [210]

MISCELLANEOUS PAMPHLETS FROM GERMAN POLITICAL PARTIES AND GROUPS – s.l.: s.n., 1916-1950. Includes 60 pamphlets published between 1916 and 1950 on German labor-unions and political parties of the period – 1 – us U.W. Library [943]

MISCELLANEOUS PAMPHLETS IN ITALIAN ON OCCULT SCIENCES – 1580-c1640. 42 pieces. ill. Title supplied by cataloger – 1 – us U.W. Library [130]

MISCELLANEOUS PAMPHLETS, PERIODICALS, AND EPHEMERA BY GERMAN COUNTERCULTURAL AND LEFTIST GROUPS AND ORGANIZATIONS, PUBLISHED 1964-73, 1983 – Two reels – 1 – us U.W. Library [073]

MISCELLANEOUS PAMPHLETS, PERIODICALS, AND FLYERS BY THE SOZIALISTISCHER DEUTSCHER STUDENTENBUND, VERBAND DEUTSCHER STUDENTENSCHAFTEN...AT FREE UNIVERSITY OF BERLIN.. – Publ. between 1967 and 1970, and between 1983 and 1985 – 1 – us U.W. Library [080]

MISCELLANEOUS PAMPHLETS, PERIODICALS, AND FLYERS...1957-1969...BY THE COMMITTEE OF 100, FRIENDS PEACE COMMITTEE, NATIONAL COUNCIL FOR CIVIL LIBERTIES.. – Madison: University of Wisconsin, Madison Libraries, 1986 – 1 – us U.W. Library [080]

MISCELLANEOUS PAPERS / Georgia. Experiment Station. Experiment – 1955-58 – 1,5,6 – us Spaulding [630]

MISCELLANEOUS PAPERS : PHOTOGRAPHS OF THE PRESBYTERIAN MISSION AT WEST AMBRYM / Vanuatu. National Library – (Also includes: Final Report on Tropical Cyclone Uma 1987. Tavue: a coll of short stories from East Aoba (n.d.). Autobiography of Chief Silas Nari Leo Bulr of Labultamata

North Pentecost 1984) – 1913 – 1r – 1 – PMB 1128 – at Pacific Mss [980]
MISCELLANEOUS PAPERS / Priestley, Joseph & Aiken, John – ((From Warrington Library)) – 1 – uk Microform Academic [500]
MISCELLANEOUS PAPERS, 1774-89 / U.S. Continental Congress – 10 rolls. Printed Guide – 1 – M332 – us Nat'l Archives [324]
MISCELLANEOUS PAPERS AND THOROLD POST – Thorold, 1870-1955 – 26r – 1 – cn Preston [971]
MISCELLANEOUS PAPERS, AUTOBIOGRAPHICAL MEMOS, FAMILY CERTIFICATES AND "SOGERINUMU" MAGAZINE OF THE SOGERI HIGH SCHOOL, MAPS AND PHOTOGRAPHS, 1934-1990 / Johnston, Edgar Lisle (Ted) – 1r – at Pacific Mss [920]
MISCELLANEOUS PAPERS CONCERNING EDUCATION IN THE COOK ISLANDS, 1922-66 / Coppell, William George – 1r – 1 – at Pacific Mss [370]
MISCELLANEOUS PAPERS FOR THE PERIOD 1924-1965 / Stanley, G A V – 5r – at Pacific Mss [920]
MISCELLANEOUS PAPERS FROM THE FILES OF THE FEDERATION / South Africa. Federation of Mining Unions – Johannesburg: Microfile, [19–?] – us Res Libr [331]
MISCELLANEOUS POSTERS DISTRIBUTED BY THE INTER-UNIVERSITY JEWISH FEDERATION OF GREAT BRITAIN AND IRELAND AND... OTHER PRIMARILY LEFT-WING GROUPS... FROM 1965-1973? – Madison: University of Wisconsin-Madison Libraries, 1986 – 1 – us U.W. Library [080]
MISCELLANEOUS PRINTED PUBLICATIONS; ALSO SERMONS BY 38 OTHER NEW ENGLAND WRITERS, 1746-1800 / Backus, Isaac – 1 – 174.58 – us Baptist [240]
THE MISCELLANEOUS PROSE WORKS OF SIR WALTER SCOTT, BART / Scott, Walter – 30v. 1834-46 – 5r – 1 – us Ross [880]
MISCELLANEOUS PUBLICATION / Clemson University. Department of Horticulture – No.1-22.1962-79. 7 fiches – 9 – us Spaulding [630]
MISCELLANEOUS PUBLICATION / Connecticut. Agricultural Experiment Station. Storrs – v. 1-2. 1957 – 1,5,6 – us Spaulding [630]
MISCELLANEOUS PUBLICATION / Rhode Island. Agricultural Experiment Station – v. 1-62. 1938-66 – 1,5,6 – us Spaulding [630]
MISCELLANEOUS PUBLICATION / Washington. Agricultural Extension Service – nos.1-57. 1953-62 – 1,5,6 – us Spaulding [630]
MISCELLANEOUS PUBLICATION / Wisconsin. College of Agriculture. Dept. of Dairy Industry – 1,5 – us Spaulding [630]
MISCELLANEOUS PUBLICATIONS / Clemson University. Agricultural Extension Division – 1,5 – us Spaulding [630]
MISCELLANEOUS PUBLICATIONS / Kentucky. Agricultural Experiment Station – 1,5,6 – us Spaulding [630]
MISCELLANEOUS PUBLICATIONS / Maine. Agricultural Experiment Station – v. 1-677. 1903-66 – 1,5,6 – us Spaulding [630]
MISCELLANEOUS PUBLICATIONS / Montana. Agricultural Experiment Station – nos.1-15. Oct 1958-Aug 1975 – 1,5,6 – us Spaulding [630]
MISCELLANEOUS PUBLICATIONS / Nebraska. Agricultural Experiment Station. Lincoln – n.1-24. 1952-69 – 1,5 – us Spaulding [630]
MISCELLANEOUS PUBLICATIONS / New Mexico. Department of Agriculture – 1 reel – 1,5 – us Spaulding [630]
MISCELLANEOUS PUBLICATIONS / New Mexico State University. Agricultural Experiment Station – 1,5 – us Spaulding [630]
MISCELLANEOUS PUBLICATIONS / New Mexico State University. Cooperative Extension Service – 10 reels – 1,5 – us Spaulding [630]
MISCELLANEOUS PUBLICATIONS / New Mexico State University. Range Improvement Task Force – 1 reel – 1,5 – us Spaulding [630]
MISCELLANEOUS PUBLICATIONS / Oklahoma State University. Agricultural Experiment Station – MP83-MP113. 1970-82. 1 reel – 1,5 – us Spaulding [630]
MISCELLANEOUS PUBLICATIONS / South Carolina. Agricultural Experiment Station. Clemson – 1,5 – us Spaulding [630]
MISCELLANEOUS PUBLICATIONS / Texas A & M University. Agricultural Experiment Station – MP151-MP920 (revisions of pre-1970 publications); 1970-82. MP921, MP941-MP1525 – 1,5 – us Spaulding [630]
MISCELLANEOUS PUBLICATIONS / U.S. Department of Agriculture – Nos. 1-1446. 1927-86. 2178 fiches – 9 – $3,000.00 – us Updata [630]
MISCELLANEOUS PUBLICATIONS / University of Missouri. Agricultural Extension Service – No.1-540. 1966-82 – 1,5 – us Spaulding [630]
MISCELLANEOUS PUBLICATIONS / Vietnam – 1 – 202.00 – us L of C Photodup [950]
MISCELLANEOUS PUBLICATIONS / Virginia. Polytechnic Institute. Extension Division – v. 1-8. 1960-68 – 1,5,6 – us Spaulding [630]
MISCELLANEOUS PUBLICATIONS / Wisconsin. Agricultural Experiment Station – 1,5 – us Spaulding [630]
MISCELLANEOUS PUBLICATIONS / Wisconsin. College of Agricultural and Life Sciences. Dept. of Agricultural Engineering – 1,5 – us Spaulding [630]
MISCELLANEOUS PUBLICATIONS / Wisconsin. College of Agricultural and Life Sciences. Dept. of Forestry – 1,5 – us Spaulding [630]
MISCELLANEOUS PUBLICATIONS / Wisconsin. College of Agricultural and Life Sciences. Dept. of Rural Sociology – 1,5 – us Spaulding [630]
MISCELLANEOUS PUBLICATIONS / Wisconsin. College of Agriculture. Dept. of Agricultural and Extension Education – 1,5 – us Spaulding [630]
MISCELLANEOUS PUBLICATIONS / Wisconsin. College of Agriculture. Dept. of Agricultural Economics – 1,5 – us Spaulding [630]
MISCELLANEOUS PUBLICATIONS / Wisconsin. College of Agriculture. Dept. of Dairy and Food Industries – 1,5 – us Spaulding [630]
MISCELLANEOUS PUBLICATIONS / Wisconsin. College of Agriculture. Dept. of Soils – 1,5 – us Spaulding [630]
MISCELLANEOUS PUBLICATIONS / Wisconsin. College of Agriculture. School of Home Economics – 1,5 – us Spaulding [640]
[MISCELLANEOUS PUBLICATIONS] / New York. (State). Moreland Act Commission on Nursing Homes and Residential Facilities – New York: The Commission, 1975-76 – us Res Libr [324]
MISCELLANEOUS RECORD / Hancock County. Ohio. Biglick Township. Township Clerk – 1856-1877 – 1r – 1 – $32.50r – us Archival [324]
MISCELLANEOUS RECORDS / Drayton Family – 1733-c1850. 11 fiches – 9 – us South Carolina Historical [978]
MISCELLANEOUS RECORDS / Fulton County. Ohio. Swan Creek Township. Board of Trustees – 1852-1915 – 1r – 1 – $32.50r – us Archival [324]
MISCELLANEOUS RECORDS / Ottawa County. Ohio. Carroll Township. Board of Education – 1900-1920 – 1r – 1 – $32.50r – us Archival [324]
MISCELLANEOUS RECORDS / Ottawa County. Ohio. Carroll Township. Township Clerk – 1839-1918 – 1r – 1 – $32.50r – us Archival [324]
MISCELLANEOUS RECORDS / Putnam County. Ohio. Probate Court – 1885-1912 – 1r – 1 – $32.50r – us Archival [324]
MISCELLANEOUS RECORDS / Stevens County. Kansas – 1888-95 – 1 – us KS Hist [978]
MISCELLANEOUS RECORDS / Wyandot County. Ohio. Recorder – 1879-1937 – 1r – 1 – $32.50r – us Archival [324]
MISCELLANEOUS RECORDS, MS 1086 / Clermont County. Ohio – 1801-05, 1819, 1831, 1856-63. 1 reel – 1 – us Western Res [978]
MISCELLANEOUS REPORT / Maine. Agricultural Experiment Station – v. 1-144. 1948-72 – 1,5,6 – us Spaulding [630]
MISCELLANEOUS REPORTS / Minnesota. University. Agricultural Experiment Station. St. Paul – nos.1-90. 1939-69 – 1,5,6 – us Spaulding [630]
MISCELLANEOUS REPORTS AND PAMPHLETS / Progressive National Baptist Convention – 1962-74 – 1 – 99.05 – us Baptist [240]
MISCELLANEOUS RUSSIAN RECORDS COLLECTION – 4r – 1 – T88 – us Nat'l Archives [947]
MISCELLANEOUS SARATOGA NEWSPAPERS – (Saratoga Record 1915-1916; Saratoga Sentinal 1941-1942; Saratoga Standard 1893; The Los Gatos Mail (Saratoga Ed.) 1945; The Saratoga Observer 1948-1951) – 1r – 1 – $50.00 – B05061 – us Library Micro [071]
MISCELLANEOUS SCIENCE POLICY DOCUMENTS / Morehouse, Ward – New Delhi: Nehru Memorial Museum & Library, [19–?] – us Res Libr [500]
MISCELLANEOUS SELECTIONS / Bibliotheque Nationale – 20 titles on 131 fiches. Available separately – 9 – 324.00 – fr Bibl Nationale [080]
MISCELLANEOUS SLOVAK STATISTICAL DATA AND CORRESPONDENCE OF VARIOUS ORGANIZATIONS – 1800-1908, 1911-1913, 1920, 1923, 1950s – 1r – 1 – us I.H.R.C. [304]
MISCELLANEOUS SONNETS / Platen, August, Graf von – Ithaca, NY: Andrus & Church, 1921 – 1r – 1 – us U.W. Library [810]
MISCELLANEOUS SS RECORDS : THE EINWANDERERZENTRALSTELLE WAFFEN-SS UND SS-OBERABSCHNITTE – 680r – 1 – T354 – us Nat'l Archives [943]
MISCELLANEOUS STATISTICAL PAPERS / United Nations – E.329 – 9 (ST/STAT/Ser.M/1-55; ST/EAS/STAT/Ser.M/56-79) – us U.N. Pubs [310]
MISCELLANEOUS STATISTICS RELATING TO BRITISH INDIA – v. 1-4. Calcutta. 1876-80. Cont. as: Statistical Tables for British India. BI-481 2 – 8 – ne IDC [950]
MISCELLANEOUS STUDIES : A SERIES OF ESSAYS / Pater, Walter – New York, London: Macmillan and Co., 1895 – 1 roll – 1 – 1-55879-455-7 – uk Libr Preservation [840]
MISCELLANEOUS TITLES – (La Coalicion Boletin 1974; 1975; 1976; 1977; Libre Expresion v3, Issues 4 and 5 1976; La Lucha 1972; El Noticiero 1972 (Scats); El Tenaz 1971-1972 (Scats)) – Santa Cruz, CA – 1r – 1 – $50.00 – B03682 – us Library Micro [071]
MISCELLANEOUS TITLES – (Santa Cruz Times 1973-1975 (Broken Series); The Paper 1968-1996; The Capitolan 1973-1973; The Black Mountain Express 1965-1967 (Scats); The Aptos Voice 1973-1974; Index available for above 5 Titles) – Santa Cruz, CA – 1r – 1 – $50.00 – B03517 – us Library Micro [071]
MISCELLANEOUS TITLES – (The Cowell Rebel 1968-1969; The Crown Paper. The Crown Jeremiad v1-7 (Broken Series); The Pioneer 1965-1966; Stevenson Libre 1966-1971 (Broken Series)) – Santa Cruz, CA – 1r – 1 – $50.00 – B03516 – us Library Micro [071]
MISCELLANEOUS TITLES – Watsonville, CA. 1886-1935 (scats) – 1r – 1 – $50.00 – B03086 – us Library Micro [071]
MISCELLANEOUS TREASURY ACCOUNTS OF THE FIRST AUDITOR (FORMERLY THE AUDITOR). OF THE TREASURY DEPARTMENT, SEPT. 6, 1790-JULY 15, 1840 / U.S. Treasury Department. First Auditor's Office – 1170 rolls – 1 – M235 – us Nat'l Archives [336]
MISCELLANEOUS WHITBY NEWSPAPERS – Whitby, Mr1850-1941Au – 1r – 1 – cn Preston [971]
MISCELLANIES / Fitzgerald, Edward – London, New York: Macmillan, 1900 – 1r – 1 – 1-55879-804-8 – uk Libr Preservation [880]
MISCELLANIES / ed by Maginn, William – London: S. Low, Marston, Searle & Rivington, 1885 – 1 roll – 1 – 1-55879-244-9 – uk Libr Preservation [810]
MISCELLANIES / Stuart, Moses – 1857 – 9 – us A.T.L.A. [240]
MISCELLANIES, AESTHETIC AND LITERARY : TO WHICH IS ADDED THE THEORY OF LIFE / Coleridge, Samuel Taylor – London: George Bell and Sons, 1885 – 1 roll – 1 – 1-55879-654-1 – uk Libr Preservation [110]
MISCELLANIES IN VERSE AND PROSE / Cooper, John – 1678-9. Holkham Ms 687 – 1 – uk Microform Academic [810]
MISCELLANIES OVER CLARET – v1 1697 – 1 – us UMI [800]
A MISCELLANY – (Collection of important rare and esoteric works) – 106v – 9 – us Primary [920]
MISCELLANY / Berar. India (State). Superintendent of Census Operations – 1900-01 – 1 – us Res Libr [324]
MISCELLANY – v. 1. 10 Jun-2 Dec 1805 – 1 – us UMI [073]
MISCHMASCH / Scherr, Johannes – Berlin: R Lesser, [1867?] – 1r – 1 – us U.W. Library [800]
LA MISE EN PLACE DES INSTITUTIONS ALGERIENNES / Douence, J C – F50.00 – fr Ethnologie [350]
LA MISERE : ORGANE ANARCHISTE BI-MENSUEL – Brussels, Belgium. -f. Apr-Oct 1892. (14 ft) – 1 – uk British Libr Newspaper [072]
MISERERE, C. MINOR / Hasse, J A – (Manuscript) – 180- – 1 – us Sibley [780]
MISERIAS Y GRANDEZAS DE UN HABITO / Palacio y de Palacio, Jose Maria – Madrid, 1955-1956 – 1 – sp Bibl Santa Ana [946]
MISERY AGE MAYA / Demyk, M – Etude des conflits sociaux dans quatre villages des Altos guatemalteques, de la Conquete a nos jours – 9 – F180.00 – fr Ethnologie [972]
THE MISFORTUNES OF ELPHIN... / Peacock, Thomas Love – London: T. Hookham, 1829 – 1 roll – 1 – 1-55879-274-0 – uk Libr Preservation [830]
MISHBEZET HA-TARSHISH / Joseph, S A – London. 1926. BJ-421-46 1 – 9 – ne IDC [470]
Mishchenko, F *see* OBOZRENIE RUSSKOI LITERATURY PO GRECHESKOI FILOLIGII ZA 1882-1883 GODY
Mishev, D *see* THE BULGARIANS IN THE PAST, PAGES FROM BULGARIAN CULTURAL HISTORY
Mishimens, Isaac *see* ACCOUNT BOOK, MS 1627
MISHKAT AL-ANWAR / Al-Ghazzali – "The Niche for Lights". 1924 – 1 – uk Microform Academic [830]
THE MISHNA ON IDOLATRY ABODA ZARA / ed by Elmslie, W A L – 1911 – 3mf – 9 – ne Slangenburg [240]
THE MISHNAH / Danby, Herbert – 1938 – 9 – $27.00 – us I.R.C. [270]
MISHNAT R. YA'AKOV. MAVO AL HA-TOSEFTA / Schor, J – Warsaw. 1930. BJ-32-23 1 – 9 – ne IDC [270]
MISHPAT L'EKOLEI YAAKOV – 1838. BJ-27-47 1 – 9 – ne IDC [270]
MISION – v1-6. 1982-87 (complete) – 1r – 1 – ATLA S0871 – us A.T.L.A. [073]
UN MISIONERO Y MISIONOLOGO DESCONOCIDO / Bayle, Constantino – Madrid: Missionalia Hispanica, 1949 – 1 – sp Bibl Santa Ana [240]
MISIONES AUSTRALIANAS DE LOS BENDICTINOS ESPANOLES / Rios, Roman – Barcelona, 1931; Madrid: Razon y Fe, 1932 – 1 – sp Bibl Santa Ana [240]
MISIONES DE LOS PADRES CAPUCHINOS DE VENEZUELA / Rionegro, Friolan – Pontevedra, 1929; Madrid: Razon y Fe, 1933 – 1 – sp Bibl Santa Ana [240]
MISIONES DE MAINAS HACIA LA MITAD DEL SIGLO 16 / Bayle, Constantino – Madrid: Missionalia Hispanica, 1948 – 1 – sp Bibl Santa Ana [240]
MISIONES DE NUEVO MEJICO. TOMO 1 / Maas, Otto – Madrid, 1929; Madrid: Razon y Fe, 1933 – 1 – sp Bibl Santa Ana [240]
LAS MISIONES, DEFENSA DE LAS FRONTERAS MAINAS / Bayle, Constantino – Madrid: Missionalia Hispanica, 1951 – 1 – sp Bibl Santa Ana [240]
MISIONES EXTRANJERAS DEL CLERO SECULAR ESPANOL – (Cont by: ID) – nos I-13. 1929-36 (complete) – 1r – 1 – ATLA S0705B – us A.T.L.A. [073]
MISIONES EXTRANJERAS DEL CLERO SECULAR ESPANOL *see* ID
LAS MISIONES FRANCISCANAS EN CHINA. CARTAS, INFORMES Y RELACIONES DEL PADRE BUENAVENTURA IBANEZ (1650-1690) / Alcobendes, Severiano – Madrid, 1933; Madrid: Razon y Fe, 1933 – 1 – sp Bibl Santa Ana [240]
MISIONES MEXICANAS EN ARCHIVOS EUROPEOS / Carrera Stampa, M – Mexico D.F.: Instituto Panamericano de Geografia e Historia, 1949 – 2mf – 9 – ne IDC [972]
MISIONES...SAN MIGUEL...RECUERDOS – 1816 – 9 – 1.50f – sp Bibl Santa Ana [240]
MISJONSVENNEN – v32-49. 1934-50 (complete) – 1r – 1 – ATLA S0544 – us A.T.L.A. [240]
MISLEADING CASES IN THE COMMON LAW / Herbert, A P – 4th English ed. New York: G P Putnam's Sons, 1930 – 3mf – 9 – $4.50 – LLMC 95-167 – us L.L.M.C. [340]

MISLS: THE TRAINING HISTORY OF THE MILITARY INTELLIGENCE SERVICE LANGUAGE SCHOOLS / U.S. War Department. General Staff. G-2 Division – 17v. 1949 – 1 – 43.00 – us L of C Photodup [324]
Misra, Binayak *see* DYNASTIES OF MEDIAEVAL ORISSA
MISS ANGEL / Thackeray, Anne – British Fiction Archive: Unit 3 – 9 – uk Bell [830]
MISS BRETHERTON / Ward, Mary Augusta – British Fiction Archive: Unit 2 – 9 – uk Bell [830]
MISS CAYLEY'S ADVENTURES / Allen, Grant – New York: G. Putnam, 1899. 05053. (Pre-1900 Canadiana) – 9 – cn C.I.H.M. [830]
MISS DEXIE: A ROMANCE OF THE PROVINCES / Eveleth, Stanford – Toronto: W. Briggs, 1895. 02658. (Pre-1900 Canadiana) – 9 – cn C.I.H.M. [830]
MISS MCCREA / Hilliard-D'Auberteuil, Michel Rene de – 1784 – 9 – 10.00 – us Scholars' Facs [830]
MISS SARA SAMPSON : EIN TRAUERSPIEL IN FUENF AUFZUEGEN / Lessing, Gotthold Ephraim – Leipzig: P Reclam, [1930-?] – 1r – 1 – us U.W. Library [430]
MISS WILLIAMSON'S DIVAGATIONS / Thackeray, Anne – British Fiction Archive: Unit 3 – 9 – uk Bell [830]
MISSA SOLEMNIS, OP. 132. [SKETCHES OF PORTIONS OF "QUONIAM TU SOLUS SANCTUS" PARTICULARLY "IN GLORIA DEI PATRIS, AMEN." / Beethoven, Ludwig van – (Extracted from sketchbook, 46-47p) – Between 1819-1823 – 5 – us Sibley [780]
MISSAE QUATERNIS, 5. 6. ET 7 VOCIBUS... / Hassler, H L – Norimbergae: P Kaufmann, 1599 – 1 – us Sibley [780]
THE MISSAL OF ROBERT OF JUMIEGES / Wilson, H Austin – 1896 – 8mf – 8 – Dfl30.00 – ne Slangenburg [240]
THE MISSAL OF THE NEW MINISTER, WINCHESTER / Turner, D H – 1962 – 5mf – 8 – ne Slangenburg [240]
MISSALE – Missale Romanum.14th cent. Holkham ms. 35. Holkham Hall, Norfolk, England – 1 – uk Microform Academic [240]
MISSALE – Missale Romanum.15th cent. Milanese. Holkham ms. 34.Holkham Hall, Norfolk, England – 14 – uk Microform Academic [240]
MISSALE AD USUM ECCLESIAE WESTMONASTERIENSIS: FAC. 3 / Wickham Legg, J – 1897 – 8mf – 8 – Dfl30.00 – ne Slangenburg [240]
MISSALE AD USUM ECCLESIAE WESTMONASTERIENSIS: FACS. 2 : HENRY BRANDSHAW SOCIETY, VOL 5 / Wickham Legg, J – 1893 – 7mf – 8 – Dfl28.00 – ne Slangenburg [240]
MISSALE AD USUM ECCLESIAE WESTMONASTERIENSIS. FASC. 1 / Wickham Legg, J – 1891 – 5mf – 8 – Dfl22.00 – ne Slangenburg [240]
MISSALE AD USUM INSIGNIS ECCLESIAE EBORANCENSIS / Henderson, W – Edinburgh. v1-2. 1874 – 13mf – 8 – Dfl46.00 – ne Slangenburg [240]
MISSALE AD USUM INSIGNIS ECCLESIE SARISBURIENSIS / Church of England. Liturgy and Ritual. Missal – 1555 – 9 – us Sibley [240]
MISSALE AD USUM INSIGNIS ET PRAECLARAE ECCLESIAE SARUM / ed by Dickinson, F H – Burntisland, 1861-1883 – 14mf – 8 – Dfl49.00 – ne Slangenburg [240]
MISSALE AD USUM PERCELEBRIS ECCLESIAE HERFORDENSIS / Henderson, W – Leeds, 1874 – 9mf – 8 – Dfl32.00 – ne Slangenburg [240]
MISSALE FRANCORUM / ed by Mohlberg, C – Roma, 1957 – 3mf – 8 – Dfl13.00 – ne Slangenburg [240]
MISSALE GALLICANUM VETUS / ed by Mohlberg, C – Roma, 1958 – 5mf – 8 – Dfl22.00 – ne Slangenburg [240]
MISSALE GOTHICUM / Bannister, H – 2v. 1917-1919 – 6mf – 8 – ne Slangenburg [240]
EEN MISSALE LEODIENSE GEDRUKT DOOR JOH. DE WESTFALIA TE LEUVEN (OVERDRUCK) / Kruitwagen, E – 1910 – 1mf – 8 – Dfl6.00 – ne Slangenburg [240]
MISSALE PARISIENSE..CAROLI G.G. DE VINTIMILLE..PARISIENSIS ARCHIEPISCOPI..AUCTORITATE..EDITUM – Parisiis, 1776 – 27mf – 8 – Dfl95.00 – ne Slangenburg [240]
MISSALE ROMANUM MEDIOLANI 1474, VOL 1 : TEXT / Lippe, R – 1899 – 8mf – 8 – Dfl30.00 – ne Slangenburg [240]
MISSALE ROMANUM MEDIOLANI 1474, VOL 2 / Lippe, R – 1907 – 7mf – 8 – Dfl28.00 – ne Slangenburg [210]
HET MISSALE VAN DE KERK TE WIJK BIJ HEUSDEN / Beurden, AF van – 1906 – 1mf – 8 – Dfl6.00 – ne Slangenburg [240]
MISSARUM JOSQUIN LIBER PRIMUS / Depres, Josquin – (Superius and bassus parts only. Publication of Ottaviano Petrucci). 1516 – 9 – us Sibley [780]
MISSARUM JOSQUIN LIBER PRIMUS / Depres, Josquin – (Superius part only. Publication of Ottaviano Petrucci. Some leaves missing). 15–? – 9 – us Sibley [780]
MISSARUM JOSQUIN LIBER SECUNDUS / Depres, Josquin – (Superius and bassus parts only. Publication of Ottaviano Petrucci). 1515 – 9 – us Sibley [780]
MISSARUM JOSQUIN LIBER SECUNDUS / Depres, Josquin – (Superius part only. Publication of Ottaviano Petrucci. Some leaves missing). 1505 – 9 – us Sibley [780]
MISSARUM JOSQUIN LIBER TERTIUS / Depres, Josquin – (Superius and bassus parts only. Publication of Ottaviano Petrucci). 1514 – 9 – us Sibley [780]
MISSBRAUCHTE AUFKLAERUNG? : SCHRIFTEN ZUM PREUSSISCHEN RELIGIONSEDIKT VOM 9. JULI 1788 / ed by Kemper, Dirk – 190mf – 9 – subsc: DM1,250.00 diazo DM1,650.00 silver – gw Olms [200]
MISSCELLANEA: SERIES DE MORCEAUX POUR PIANO, OP. 16, NO. 6: UN MOMENT MUSCIAL / Paderewski, Ignace Jan – Berlin: Bote & Book, 188- – 1 – us Sibley [780]
MISSING / Ward, Mary Augusta – British Fiction Archive: Unit 2 – 9 – uk Bell [830]
MISSING AIR CREW REPORTS OF THE U.S. ARMY AIR FORCES, 1942-1947 – 5,990 cards – 9 – M1380 – us Nat'l Archives [350]
MISSING FRAGMENT OF THE LATIN TRANSLATION OF THE FOURTH BOOK OF EZRA / Bensley, Robert L – Cambridge: University Press, 1875. 1 fiche – 9 – us A.T.L.A. [220]
THE MISSING LINK : OR, BIBLE-WOMEN IN THE HOMES OF THE LONDON POOR – New York: Robert Carter, 1860 – 1mf – 9 – 0-8370-6135-0 – 1986-0135 – us A.T.L.A. [305]
Missinsch, J *see* LATWEESCHU RAKSTNEEZIBAS RAHDITAJS 1585-1925
MISSIOLOGY – v1- 1973- 1; v4- 5,6,9 – us UMI [240]
MISSION – International Missionary Council Archives, 1918-1965. Geneva – 63mf – 9 – ne IDC [073]
MISSION *see* AMERICAN BAPTIST
MISSION AND COMBAT REPORTS OF THE FIFTH FIGHTER COMMAND / U.S. Army. Air Force – 1942-45. 9 rolls. M1065 – 1 – us Nat'l Archives [324]
MISSION AND STATE IN THE CONGO / Lagergren, D – Uppsala, 1970 – 10mf – 8 – ne Slangenburg [240]
MISSION AND STATE IN THE CONGO / Lagergren, D – Uppsala, 1970 – 10mf – 8 – ne Slangenburg [960]
MISSION DES RAS-SHAMRA – (Individual vols also listed separately) – Paris. v1-9. 1936-1956 – 8 – Dfl336.00 set – ne Slangenburg [270]
MISSION DES RAS-SHAMRA, VOL 1 *see* LA LEGENDE PHENICIENNE DE DANEL
MISSION DES RAS-SHAMRA, VOL 2 *see* LA LEGENDE DE KERET
MISSION DES RAS-SHAMRA, VOL 3 *see* UGARITICA
MISSION DES RAS-SHAMRA, VOL 4 *see* LA DEESSE ANAT.
MISSION DES RAS-SHAMRA, VOL 5 *see* UGARITICA 2
MISSION DES RAS-SHAMRA, VOL 6 *see* LE PALAIS ROYAL D'UGARIT 1
MISSION DES RAS-SHAMRA, VOL 7 *see* LE PALAIS ROYAL D'UGARIT 2
MISSION DES RAS-SHAMRA, VOL 8 *see* UGARITICA 3
MISSION DES RAS-SHAMRA, VOL 9 *see* LE PALAIS ROYAL D'UGARIT 4
MISSION DIPLOMATIQUE DE LAURENT DE BRINDES...PADOUE, 1964 / Cormiguano de Brenta, Arthur – Madrid: Graf. Calleja, 1966 – 1 – sp Bibl Santa Ana [320]
LA MISSION DU PROPH ETE EZECHIEL / Gautier, Lucien – Lausanne: Georges Bridel, 1891 – 1mf – 9 – 0-8370-3235-0 – 1985-1235 – us A.T.L.A. [220]
UNE MISSION D'UN ANTHROPOLOGUE FRANCAIS EN AMERIQUE DU SUD / Vellard, J – 1931-33 – 9 – F120.00 – fr Ethnologie [306]
MISSION EVANGELICA AL REYNO DE CONGO POR LA SERAFICA RELIGION DE LOS CAPUCHINOS / Pellicer de Tovar, Joseph – Madrid. 1649. BA-101 2 – 8 – ne IDC [240]
MISSION EVANGELICA AL REYNO DE CONGO POR LA SERAFICA RELIGION DE LOS CAPUCINOS / Pellicer de Tovar, Joseph – Madrid. 1649 – 1 – us Res Libr [240]
THE MISSION FIELD – (Lacking some pgs and issues) – v11-32. 1898-1920 – 7r – 1 – ATLA S0745 – us A.T.L.A. [073]
MISSION FROM CAPE COAST CASTLE TO ASHANTEE / Bodwich, T E – London. 1819. BA-284 2 – 8 – ne IDC [240]
MISSION FROM CAPE COAST CASTLE TO ASHANTEE / Bowditch, Thomas Edward – 1819 – 7 – uk Microform Academic [240]
MISSION HERALD – 1907-15, 1917, 1919-73 – 1 – 509.46 – us Baptist [240]
DIE MISSION IN DER SCHULE : EIN HANDBUCH FUER DEN LEHRER / Warneck, Gustav – 5. verb Aufl. Guetersloh: C Bertelsmann, 1889 – 1mf – 9 – 0-8370-6628-X – 1986-0628 – us A.T.L.A. [370]
MISSION LIFE AMONG THE ZULU-KAFIRS.. / Robertson, Henrietta – 1875 – 1 – us A.T.L.A. [240]
MISSION MARCHAND : JOURNAL DE ROUTE DU DR J EMILY / Emily, Jules – Paris: Hatchette, 1913 – us Res Libr [920]
MISSION METHODS IN MANCHURIA / Ross, John – New York: Fleming H Revell, [1903?] – 1mf – 9 – 0-8370-6609-3 – 1986-0609 – us A.T.L.A. [240]
MISSION MONITOR – Omaha, NE. v2-6. 1895-1901 (complete) – 1r – 1 – ATLA B0504 – us A.T.L.A. [073]
MISSION NEWS – San Juan. Calif. -w. 1943-56 – 1 – us UMI [071]
THE MISSION OF APOLLO 12 – 13-25 Nov 1969 – 1 – us UMI [629]
THE MISSION OF HELP TO THE CHURCH IN SOUTH AFRICA : WHAT IT HAS DONE, AND WHAT IT HAS TAUGHT US / Robinson, Arthur W – London, New York: Longmans, Green, 1906 – 1mf – us A.T.L.A. [240]
THE MISSION OF METHODISM : BEING THE TWENTIETH FERNLEY LECTURE / Green, Richard – London: Wesleyan Methodist Book-room, 1890 – 1mf – us A.T.L.A. [240]
THE MISSION OF OUR NATION / Love, James Franklin – New York: F.H. Revell, c1912 – 1mf – us A.T.L.A. [240]
THE MISSION OF ST AUGUSTINE TO ENGLAND ACCORDING TO THE ORIGINAL DOCUMENTS : BEING A HANDBOOK FOR THE THIRTEENTH CENTENARY / ed by Mason, Arthur James – Cambridge: University Press; New York: Macmillan [distributor], 1897 – 1mf – us A.T.L.A. [240]
THE MISSION OF THE OLD MAGAZINE / Aberdeen Association – 1898? 02346. (Pre-1900 Canadiana) – 9 – cn C.I.H.M. [971]
THE MISSION OF THE PRESBYTERIAN CHURCH : A SERMON DELIVERED AT THE OPENING OF THE SECOND COUNCIL OF THE PRESBYTERIAN ALLIANCE, AT PHILADELPHIA, SEP 23, 1880 / Paxton, William Miller – New York: Anson D F Randolph, [1880?] – 1mf – 9 – 0-8370-8777-5 – 1986-2777 – us A.T.L.A. [240]
THE MISSION OF THE PROPHET / Gordon, George A – Boston: Pilgrim Press, c1912 – 1mf – us A.T.L.A. [240]
MISSION PROBLEMS AND MISSION METHODS IN SOUTH CHINA : LECTURES ON EVANGELISTIC THEOLOGY / Gibson, John Campbell – New York: Fleming H Revell, [1901?] – 1mf – 9 – 0-8370-6118-0 – 1986-0118 – us A.T.L.A. [240]
Mission Saint-Simonienne *see*
– AN ADDRESS TO THE BRITISH PUBLIC
– PROFESSION DE FOI DES SAINT-SIMONIENS
MISSION SAINT-SIMONIENNE. PROFESSION DE FOI DES SAINTS-SIMONIENS / Lechevalier, J – Besancon, impr. Ch. Deis, 1831, 8 p. Les Saint-Simoniens, 1825-1834. 6916 – 9 – fr Hachette [335]
Mission scientifique du Maroc *see* ARCHIVES MAROCAINES
MISSION STORIES OF MANY LANDS : A BOOK FOR YOUNG PEOPLE / ed by Strong, Elnathan Ellsworth – (Includes indexes) – Boston: American Board of Commissioners for Foreign Missions, 1894, c1885 – 1mf – 9 – 0-8370-7345-6 – 1986-1345 – us A.T.L.A. [240]
MISSION STUDIES : OUTLINES OF MISSIONARY PRINCIPLES AND PRACTICE: FOR STUDY IN SCHOOL, CHURCH AND HOME / Pfeiffer, Edward – (Includes index) – Columbus, OH: Lutheran Book Concern, 1908 – 1mf – 9 – 0-8370-6595-X – 1986-0595 – us A.T.L.A. [240]
A MISSION TO GELELE, KING OF DAHOMEY / Burton, Richard Francis – (V. III and IV of the Memorial Edition of Burton's Works). 2 v. London. 1893. BA-286 2 – 8 – ne IDC [910]
MISSION TO THE EAST COAST OF SUMATRA, IN 1823 / Anderson, J – London, 1826 – 6mf – 9 – ne IDC [950]
MISSION TO THE INTERIOR OF AFRICA / Park, Mungo – 1815 – 7 – uk Microform Academic [240]
MISSION UND EVANGELISATION IM ORIENT = A HISTORY OF PROTESTANT MISSIONS IN THE NEAR EAST / Richter, Julius – (In English. Includes index) – New York: Fleming H Revell, c1910 – 1mf – 9 – 0-8370-6345-0 – 1986-0345 – us A.T.L.A. [240]
MISSION WORK AMONG THE INDIAN TRIBES IN THE FORESTS OF GUIANA / Brett, W H – London: S.P.C.K.; New York: E. & J.B. Young, [1881?] – 1mf – us A.T.L.A. [240]
THE MISSION WORK OF THE PRESBYTERIAN CHURCH IN THE UNITED STATES IN CHINA, 1867-1952 / Bear, James E – 1963-73 – 1 – us A.T.L.A. [240]
THE MISSION WORKER – v1 nos2,4; v2 nos2, 4-5. 1907-08 (complete) – 1r – 1 – ATLA 1994-S013 – us A.T.L.A. [073]
MISSIONALIA – v1-19. 1973-91 (complete) – 7r – 1 – ATLA S0460 – us A.T.L.A. [073]
MISSIONAR CHRISTIAN FRIEDRICH SCHWARTZ : SEIN LEBEN UND WIRKEN AUS BRIEFEN DES HALLESCHEN MISSIONSARCHIVS / Germann, W – Erlangen: A. Deichert, 1870 – 1mf – us A.T.L.A. [240]
THE MISSIONARY : A PERIODICAL...AMERICAN LUTHERAN CHURCH – (Several mergers) – v1-8. ns: v1-6. Feb 1848-24 Oct 1861 (complete) – 3r – 1 – ATLA S0103 – us A.T.L.A. [073]
MISSIONARY ADDRESSES / Thoburn, James Mills – New York: Phillips & Hunt; Cincinnati: Cranston & Stowe, 1888 – 1mf – 9 – 0-8370-6421-X – 1986-0421 – us A.T.L.A. [240]
THE MISSIONARY, AN INDIAN TALE / Morgan, Sydney O – 3V. 1811 – 1 – us A.T.L.A. [830]
THE MISSIONARY AND HIS CRITICS / Barton, James Levi – (Includes indexes) – New York: Fleming H Revell, 1906 – 1mf – 9 – 0-8370-6008-7 – 1986-0008 – us A.T.L.A. [230]
THE MISSIONARY AND SABBATH SCHOOL RECORD – Montreal: Printed for the Canada Sunday School Union by J C Becket, [184–185-] – 9 – cn C.I.H.M. [240]
Missionary Archives. Council for World Mission, 1775-1940. London *see* DOCUMENTS ON ASIA, AFRICA, OCEANIA AND SOUTH AMERICA
MISSIONARY ARCHIVES FOR SOUTH AFRICA / United Society for the Propagation of the Gospel – c1819-1900 – 1 – uk Microform Academic [240]
MISSIONARY BAPTIST VOICE – Feb 1944-Sept 1950 – 1 – 21.35 – us Baptist [240]
MISSIONARY BROADCASTER – 1928-67 (complete) – 5r – 1 – ATLA S0709 – us A.T.L.A. [073]
MISSIONARY CAMPAIGNER – (Is absorbed by: Missionary Outlook) – Toronto: [s.n, 1896-1898] – 9 – cn C.I.H.M. [240]
MISSIONARY CHRONICLE – (Cont as: The Missionary Magazine and Chronicle; related chiefly to the missions of the London Missionary Society. London v1-23 1836/1837-1859; N.S. v24-30 1860-1866; Cont as: The Chronicle of the London Missionary Society. London, 1867-1891; N.S. v1-48 1892-1940; Missing: 1822(Feb); 1827-1835) – London, 1822-1835 – 399mf – 9 – ne IDC [240]
MISSIONARY CHRONICLE – New York, N.Y. v10-17. 1842-1849 – 1r – 1 – $50.00 – us Presbyterian [240]

MISSIONARY CORRESPONDENCE / American Baptist Foreign Mission Societies – (Burma. South India. Assam. China. Japan. Africa. Haiti. Germany. Spain. Sweden. Switzerland. France. Greece. Misc. Judson Papers and Correspondence) – 1800-1900. Single reels available – 5 – 13.50r – us A.B.H.S. [240]
THE MISSIONARY ECHO OF THE UNITED METHODIST FREE CHURCHES – London. v1-12 1894-1905; N.S. v1-39 1906-1932 – 124mf – 9 – ne IDC [240]
THE MISSIONARY ENTERPRISE : A CONCISE HISTORY OF ITS OBJECTS, METHODS AND EXTENSION / Bliss, Edwin Munsell – (Includes index) – New York: Fleming H Revell, c1908 – 1mf – 9 – 0-8370-6024-9 – 1986-0024 – us A.T.L.A. [240]
MISSIONARY ENTERPRISE AMONG THE COLORED PEOPLE OF THE MARITIME PROVINCES OF CANADA / African Methodist Episcopal Church of Nova Scotia – Halifax, N.S.?: 1899?. 05672. (Pre-1900 Canadiana) – 9 – cn C.I.H.M. [240]
MISSIONARY EXPANSION SINCE THE REFORMATION / Graham, John Anderson – (Includes index) – New York: Fleming H Revell, 1899 – 1mf – 9 – 0-8370-6057-5 – 1986-0057 – us A.T.L.A. [240]
MISSIONARY EXPLORERS AMONG THE AMERICAN INDIANS / ed by Humphreys, Mary Gay – New York: Scribner, 1913 – 1mf – us A.T.L.A. [975]
THE MISSIONARY GAZETTEER : COMPRISING A GEOGRAPHICAL AND STATISTICAL ACCOUNT OF THE VARIOUS STATIONS OF THE AMERICAN AND FOREIGN PROTESTANT MISSIONARY SOCIETIES OF... / Edwards, BB – Boston: W. Hyde, 1832 – 2mf – us A.T.L.A. [240]
MISSIONARY HERALD – 1-102. Jun 1805-Dec 1906 – 1 – us UMI [240]
MISSIONARY HERALD AT HOME AND ABROAD *see* MISSIONARY HERALD
MISSIONARY HISTORY OF THE PACIFIC NORTHWEST : CONTAINING THE WONDERFUL STORY OF JASON LEE / Hines, Harvey Kimball – Portland: H K Hines; San Francisco: J D Hammond, c1899 – 2mf – 9 – 0-8370-6123-7 – 1986-0123 – us A.T.L.A. [920]
MISSIONARY JUBILEE / The American Baptist Missionary Union – An account of the 50th Anniversary. 1864 – 1 – 18.06 – us Baptist [240]
THE MISSIONARY JUBILEE:...AMERICAN BAPTIST MISSIONARY UNION...1864 – New York: Sheldon, 1869.500p. 2 fiches – 9 – us A.T.L.A. [240]
MISSIONARY LEAFLET – (Cont by: Monthly Letter) – Toronto: Woman's Missionary Society of the Methodist Church, Canada, [1885?-1893] – 9 – cn C.I.H.M. [240]
MISSIONARY LEAFLET *see* MONTHLY LETTER
THE MISSIONARY LEAGUER – Toronto: [s.n, 1895-1896?] – 9 – cn C.I.H.M. [240]
MISSIONARY LIFE AMONG THE CANNIBALES : BEING THE LIFE OF THE REV. JOHN GEDDIE, D.D., FIRST MISSIONARY TO THE NEW HEBRIDES / Patterson, George – Toronto: J. Campbell, J. Bain, Hart, 1882 – 2mf – us A.T.L.A. [240]
MISSIONARY LIFE IN PERSIA : BEING GLIMPSES OF A QUARTER OF A CENTURY OF LABORS AMONG THE NESTORIAN CHRISTIANS / Perkins, Justin – Boston: American Tract Society, c1861 – 1mf – us A.T.L.A. [240]
MISSIONARY LIFE IN THE SOUTHERN SEAS / Hutton, J – 1874 – 1 – us A.T.L.A. [240]
MISSIONARY LUTHERAN – (Lacks: 1924-29, Feb-Mar 1930. Cont: The Colored Lutheran) – v1-39. 1923-61 – 3r – 1 – ATLA S0708 – us A.T.L.A. [073]
THE MISSIONARY MAGAZINE AND CHRONICLE *see* MISSIONARY CHRONICLE
THE MISSIONARY MANUAL : A HANDBOOK OF METHODS FOR MISSIONARY WORK IN YOUNG PEOPLE'S SOCIETIES / Wells, Amos Russell – Boston: United Society of Christian Endeavor, 1901, c1899 – 1mf – 9 – 0-8370-6788-X – 1986-0788 – us A.T.L.A. [240]
THE MISSIONARY MESSAGE IN RELATION TO NON-CHRISTIAN RELIGIONS : WITH SUPPLEMENT, PRESENTATION AND DISCUSSION OF THE REPORT IN THE CONFERENCE ON 18TH JUNE 1910 – (Includes indexes) – Edinburgh: Publ for the World Missionary Conference by Oliphant, Anderson & Ferrier; New York: Fleming H Revell, [1910?] – 1mf – 9 – 0-8370-6477-5 – 1986-0477 – us A.T.L.A. [240]
MISSIONARY MESSENGER *see*
- MONTHLY LEAFLET OF THE CANADA CONGREGATIONAL WOMAN'S BOARD OF MISSIONS
- MONTHLY LETTER

MISSIONARY METHODS FOR MISSIONARY COMMITTEES / Park, David – Chicago: Fleming H Revell, c1898 – 1mf – 9 – 0-8370-6829-0 – 1986-0829 – us A.T.L.A. [240]
MISSIONARY MONTHLY – v43-63. 1939-58 (complete) – 4r – 1 – ATLA S0484 – us A.T.L.A. [073]
MISSIONARY MONTHLY *see*
- MONTHLY LEAFLET OF THE CANADA CONGREGATIONAL WOMAN'S BOARD OF MISSIONS
- MONTHLY LETTER

MISSIONARY NEWS FROM BULGARIA – v1-54. 31 Jan 1885-7 Mar 1896 (complete) – 1r – 1 – ATLA S0083 – us A.T.L.A. [240]
MISSIONARY NOTICES OF THE METHODIST CHURCH OF CANADA – (Cont: Wesleyan Methodist Church in Canada. Missionary Society. Wesleyan Missionary Notices, Canada Conference) – Toronto: Mission Rooms, [1875?-1878?] – 9 – cn C.I.H.M. [240]
MISSIONARY NOTICES OF THE METHODIST CHURCH OF CANADA *see* WESLEYAN MISSIONARY NOTICES, CANADA CONFERENCE
MISSIONARY NOTICES, RELATING PRINCIPALLY TO THE FOREIGN MISSIONS, ESTABLISHED BY WESLEY AND COKE...THE METHODIST CONFERENCE – (Cont as: Wesleyan Missionary Notices. N.S. London, 1839-1904) – London. v1-9. 1816-1838 – 288mf – 9 – ne IDC [240]
THE MISSIONARY OFFERING – 1850 – 1 – us A.T.L.A. [240]
THE MISSIONARY OFFERING: A MEMORIAL OF CHRIST'S MESSENGERS IN HEATHEN LANDS – Auburn: Derby, Miller, 1850. xii,372p. 1 fiche – 9 – us A.T.L.A. [240]
MISSIONARY OUTLOOK *see*
- MISSIONARY CAMPAIGNER
- MONTHLY LEAFLET OF THE CANADA CONGREGATIONAL WOMAN'S BOARD OF MISSIONS
- MONTHLY LETTER

MISSIONARY PAPERS / Lowrie, John Cameron – (Includes index) – New York: Robert Carter, 1881 – 1mf – 9 – 0-8370-6680-8 – 1986-0680 – us A.T.L.A. [240]
THE MISSIONARY PASTOR : HELPS FOR DEVELOPING THE MISSIONARY LIFE IN HIS CHURCH / ed by Adams, James Edward – New York: Fleming H Revell, c1895 – 1mf – 9 – 0-8370-6080-X – 1986-0080 – us A.T.L.A. [240]
THE MISSIONARY PASTOR: HELPS FOR DEVELOPING THE MISSIONARY LIFE IN HIS CHURCH / Adams, James Edward – New York: Fleming H. Revell, 1895. 171p. 1 fiche – 9 – us A.T.L.A. [240]
MISSIONARY PERIODICALS FROM THE CHINA MAINLAND – See indiv. titles for prices: Anking Newsletter; China Christian Advocate; China Christian Yearbook; China Medical Journal; China Mission Advocate; Educational Review; Fenchow; Foochow Messenger; Four Streams; Hainan Newsletter; West China Missionary News – 35r – 1 – $3,625.00 – us UPA [240]
MISSIONARY POINTS AND PICTURES / Johnston, James – London: Religious Tract Society, 1892.127p. 1 fiche – 9 – us A.T.L.A. [240]
MISSIONARY PRINCIPLES AND PRACTICE : A DISCUSSION OF CHRISTIAN MISSIONS AND OF SOME CRITICISMS UPON THEM / Speer, Robert Elliott – (Includes index) – New York: Fleming H Revell, c1902 – 2mf – 9 – 0-8370-6391-4 – 1986-0391 – us A.T.L.A. [240]
THE MISSIONARY PROBLEM: CONTAINING A HISTORY OF PROTESTANT MISSIONS IN SOME OF THE PRINCIPAL FIELDS OF MISSIONARY ENTERPRISE: TOGETHER WITH A HISTORICAL AND STATISTICAL ACCOUNT OF THE RISE AND PROGRESS OF MISSIONARY SOCIETIES IN THE NINETEENTH CENTURY / Croil, James – Toronto: W. Briggs; Montreal: W. Drysdale; Halifax, N. S.: McGregor & Knight, 1883. 02130. (Pre-1900 Canadiana) – 9 – cn C.I.H.M. [971]
THE MISSIONARY PROSPECT / Robinson, Charles H – London: S.W. Partridge, [1912?] – 1mf – us A.T.L.A. [240]
THE MISSIONARY RECORD – Montreal, Canada. v7 n2. 4 jun 1848 – 1r – 1 – Can$25.00 – cn Can Microfilming [240]
THE MISSIONARY RECORD AND ECCLESIASTICAL INTELLIGENCER OF THE FREE CHURCH OF NOVA SCOTIA – (Cont by: The Ecclesiastical and Missionary Record of the Free Church of Nova Scotia) – Halifax, NS: The Committee of the Synod ot the Free Church of Nova Scotia, [1851-1853] – 9 – cn C.I.H.M. [240]
MISSIONARY RECORDER : A REPOSITORY OF INTELLIGENCE FROM EASTERN MISSIONS – (Cont by: Chinese Recorder) – v1. 1867 (complete) – 1r – 1 – ATLA S0074 – us A.T.L.A. [240]
MISSIONARY REGISTER OF THE PRESBYTERIAN CHURCH OF NOVA-SCOTIA – (Merged with: The Christian Instructor and Missionary Register of the Presbyterian Church of Nova Scotia. Merged with: The Ecclesiastical and Missionary Record of the Free Church of Nova Scotia. Merged to become: The Home and Foreign Record of the Presbyterian Church of the Lower Provinces of British North America) – [Pictou, NS: E M Macdonald, 1850?-1860] – 9 – cn C.I.H.M. [240]
MISSIONARY REPORTER AND EDUCATION REGISTER VOLS 1-3 (1829-1832) – (Includes: Missionary Intelligence (1811-13) on reel) – Philadelphia, Pa. – 1r – 1 – $50.00 – us Presbyterian [240]
Missionary Research Library. New York *see* DICTIONARY CATALOG
MISSIONARY REVIEW = CHUNG-HSI CHIAO-HUI PAO – (Lacking: nos 1-11, 13-36. In Chinese) – nos 12, 37-48. 1896-98 – 1r – 1 – ATLA S0302 – us A.T.L.A. [073]
THE MISSIONARY REVIEW *see* THE MISSIONARY REVIEW OF THE WORLD
MISSIONARY REVIEW OF THE WORLD – (Some original pgs damaged) – v1-62. 1878-1939 – 52r – 1 – ATLA S0178 – us A.T.L.A. [073]
MISSIONARY REVIEW OF THE WORLD *see* THE MISSIONARY REVIEW (OF THE WORLD)
THE MISSIONARY REVIEW (OF THE WORLD) – (Cont by: Missionary Review of the World) – 1878-1939 – 400mf – 9 – $1,000.00 – us Schnappsburg [240]
THE MISSIONARY REVIEW OF THE WORLD – (Cont: The Missionary Review) – Toronto: W Briggs, [1888?-1939] – 9 – cn C.I.H.M. [240]
MISSIONARY SCENES IN MANY LANDS / Barrass, Edward – Toronto: Methodist Mission Rooms, 1885. 03379. (Pre-1900 Canadiana) – 9 – cn C.I.H.M. [240]
MISSIONARY SKETCHES : A CONCISE HISTORY OF THE WORK OF THE AMERICAN BAPTIST MISSIONARY UNION / Smith, Samuel Francis – Boston: W G Corthell, 1879 – 1mf – 9 – 0-8370-6777-4 – 1986-0777 – us A.T.L.A. [240]
Missionary Society of Connecticut *see* PAPERS
MISSIONARY SOCIETY OF CONNECTICUT PAPERS, 1759-1948 – (Includes Connecticut Evangelical Magazine (1800-7) and Connecticut Evangelical Magazine and Religious Intelligencer (1808-15)) – 20r – 1 – $1485.00 – us UMI [240]
MISSIONARY STANDARD *see* OMS (ORIENTAL MISSIONARY STANDARD) OUTREACH
MISSIONARY TRAVELS AND RESEARCHES IN SOUTH AFRICA: INCLUDING A SKETCH OF SIXTEEN YEARS' RESIDENCE IN THE INTERIOR OF AFRICA, AND A JOURNEY FROM THE CAPE OF GOOD HOPE...TO THE EASTERN OCEAN / Livingstone, David – 25th ed.New York: Harper, 1872. xxiv,755p. illus., fold. map, index – 1 – us U.W. Library [240]
MISSIONARY TRAVELS AND RESEARCHES IN SOUTH AFRICA: NARRATIVE OF AN EXPEDITION TO THE ZAMBEZI AND ITS TRIBUTARIES / Livingstone, David – London. 1857. BA-157 2 – 8 – ne IDC [910]
MISSIONARY VISITOR – (Lacks: 1897-1901 (not publ)) – 1894-1930 (complete) – 13r – 1 – ATLA S0758 – us A.T.L.A. [073]
THE MISSIONARY'S WIFE, OR, A BRIEF ACCOUNT OF MRS. LOVELESS, OF MADRAS, THE FIRST MISSIONARY TO FOREIGN LANDS / Knill, Richard – c.1839 – 9 – us A.T.L.A. [920]
MISSIONE DI ASSISTENZA TECNICA ALL'EMIGRAZIONE NEL BRAZILE – Firenze: Stab. Tip. Vallecchi, 1952-53. 3v. illus., maps – 1 – us U.W. Library [330]
MISSIONERSKAYA BESEDA SO SHTUNDISTAMI O KRESTE I O KRESTNOM ANAMENII / Bogdanovich, Savva – Kiev. A missionary discussion with Stundists on the Cross and the Sign of the Cross. 4th ed.One of 13 titles on same reel – 1 – 86.44 – us Baptist [240]
MISSIONERSKII SPUTNIK = THE MISSIONARY GUIDE / Skvortsov, Vasilii M – St. Petersburg, 1904. 2nd enl. ed. One of 13 titles on reel – 1 – 86.44 – us Baptist [240]
MISSIONERSKOE OBOZRENIE – Mission periodical of Russian Orthodox Church. Contains numerous articles on Baptists & other evangelical sectarians. 1896-1916 – 1 – 2102.72 – us Baptist [240]
UN MISSIONNAIRE REPUBLICAN EN RUSSIE / Rohr, Jean-Geoffroy – (Russia 19th C. series). 1852 – 9 – fr Hachette [947]
Missionnaires de la Congregation du Saint-Esprit *see*
- DICTIONNAIRE FRANCAIS-PONGOUE
- DICTIONNAIRE FRANCAIS-WOLOF ET WOLOF-FRANCAIS
- DICTIONNAIRE PONGOUE-FRANCAIS PRECEDE DES PRINCIPES DE LA LANGUE PONGOUEE
- PRINCIPES DE LA LANGUE WOLOFE

LES MISSIONNAIRES FRANCAIS AU TONKIN / Launay, Adrien – Paris: Delhomme et Briguet, 1900 – 1mf – us A.T.L.A. [240]
MISSIONS, AMERICAN BAPTIST INTERNATIONAL MAGAZINE *see* AMERICAN BAPTIST
MISSIONS AND GOVERNMENTS : WITH SUPPLEMENT, PRESENTATION AND DISCUSSION OF THE REPORT IN THE CONFERENCE ON 20TH JUNE 1910 – (Includes indexes) – Edinburgh: Publ for the World Missionary Conference by Oliphant, Anderson & Ferrier; New York: Fleming H Revell, [1910?] – 1mf – 9 – 0-8370-6478-3 – 1986-0478 – us A.T.L.A. [230]
THE MISSIONS AND MISSIONAIRES OF CALIFORNIA...SANTA BARBARA, 1929 / Engelhardt, Zephyrin – Madrid: Razon y Fe, 1930 – 1 – sp Bibl Santa Ana [240]
MISSIONS AND MISSIONARY SOCIETY OF THE METHODIST EPISCOPAL CHURCH / Reid, John Morrison – rev enl ed. New York: Hunt & Eaton; Cincinnati: Cranston & Curts. 3v. c1895-1896 – 6mf – 9 – 0-8370-6605-0 – 1986-0605 – us A.T.L.A. [240]
MISSIONS AND MODERN HISTORY : A STUDY OF THE MISSIONARY ASPECTS OF SOME GREAT MOVEMENTS OF THE NINETEENTH CENTURY / Speer, Robert Elliott – (Includes bibliographical references and index) – Philadelphia: Westminster Press. 2v. c1904 – 2mf – 9 – 0-8370-6703-0 – 1986-0703 – us A.T.L.A. [900]
MISSIONS AND MODERN THOUGHT / Carver, William Owen – (Includes index) – New York: Macmillan, 1910 – 1mf – 9 – 0-8370-6092-3 – 1986-0092 – us A.T.L.A. [240]
MISSIONS AND POLITICS IN ASIA : STUDIES OF THE SPIRIT OF THE EASTERN PEOPLES, THE PRESENT MAKING OF HISTORY IN ASIA, AND THE PART THEREIN OF CHRISTIAN MISSIONS / Speer, Robert Elliott – (Includes bibliographical references) – New York: Fleming H Revell, 1898 – 1mf – 9 – 0-8370-6392-2 – 1986-0392 – us A.T.L.A. [240]
MISSIONS AND SOCIOLOGY / Slater, Thomas Ebenezer – London: Elliot Stock, 1908 – 1mf – 9 – 0-8370-7265-4 – 1986-1265 – us A.T.L.A. [240]
MISSIONS AT HOME AND ABROAD : PAPERS AND ADDRESSES PRESENTED AT THE WORLD'S CONGRESS OF MISSIONS, OCT 2-4, 1893 / Wherry, Elwood Morris – New York: American Tract Society, c1895 – 2mf – 9 – 0-8370-6799-5 – 1986-0799 – us A.T.L.A. [240]
MISSIONS AU SAHARA / Gautier, Emile Felix – Paris: A Colin, 1908-09 – us Res Libr [960]
MISSIONS CATHOLIQUES – Lyon. juin 1868-janv 1950 – 1 – fr A.C.R.P.P. [073]
MISSIONS DE GIRONCOURT EN AFRIQUE OCCIDENTALE, 1908/1909/1912 : DOCUMENTS SCIENTIFIQUES / Gironcourt, George R de – Paris: Societe de geographie, 1920 – us Res Libr [960]

MISSIONS DE LA CONGREGATION DES OBLATS DE MARIE IMMACULEE – Marseille: Typo veuve Marius Olive. n1-209. 1862-1967 – 24r – 1 – us Res Libr [240]

Missions de la Societe de Marie *see* ANNALES

MISSIONS FROM THE MODERN VIEW / Hume, Robert Allen – New York: Fleming H. Revell, 1905. 292p. 1 fiche – 9 – us A.T.L.A. [240]

MISSIONS IN HINDUSTAN : WITH A BRIEF DESCRIPTION OF THE COUNTRY AND OF THE MORAL AND SOCIAL CONDITION OF THE INHABITANTS / Campbell, James R – Philadelphia: Geo H Stuart, 1853, c1852 – 1mf – 9 – 0-8370-6168-7 – 1986-0168 – us A.T.L.A. [240]

MISSIONS IN SOUTH AMERICA : REPORT / Speer, Robert Elliott – New York: Board of Foreign Missions of the Presbyterian Church in the USA, [1909?] – 1mf – 9 – 0-8370-6393-0 – 1986-0393 – us A.T.L.A. [240]

MISSIONS IN THE PLAN OF THE AGES : BIBLE STUDIES IN MISSIONS / Carver, William Owen – (Includes index of biblical texts cited) – 3rd ed. New York: Fleming H Revell, c1909 – 1mf – 9 – 0-8370-6093-1 – 1986-0093 – us A.T.L.A. [240]

MISSIONS IN WESTERN POLYNESIA.. / Murray, A W – 1863 – 1 – us A.T.L.A. [240]

A MISSIONS INFORMATION CONFERENCE MANUAL FOR THE SOUTHERN BAPTIST FOREIGN MISSION BOARD, RICHMOND, VIRGINIA / Kruschwitz, William Albin – 1982 – 1 – 5.52 – us Baptist [240]

MISSIONS MAGAZINE – 1803-1953. (Various other names: Massachusetts Missionary Magazine, 1803-16; American Baptist Missionary Magazine, 1817-35; The Baptist Missionary Magazine, 1835-1909) – 1 – 2789.22 – us Baptist [240]

THE MISSIONS OF THE CHURCH MISSIONARY SOCIETY AND THE CHURCH OF ENGLAND ZENANA MISSIONARY SOCIETY IN THE PUNJAB AND SINDH / Clark, Robert; ed by Maconachie, Robert – London: Church Missionary Society, 1904 – 1mf – us A.T.L.A. [240]

DIE MISSIONS STUNDE – v21-31. 1933-43 (complete) – 1r – 1 – ATLA S0660 – us A.T.L.A. [073]

MISSIONS TO CHINESE IN CALIFORNIA / Presbyterian Church in the U.S.A. Board of Foreign Missions – Correspondence and reports. 1852-1858 – 1 – $50.00 – us Presbyterian [240]

MISSIONS TO THE WOMEN IN CHINA – Ed. by Miss Whately. 1866 – 9 – us A.T.L.A. [240]

MISSIONSARBEIT DER BRUEDERGEMEINDE IN AUSTRALIEN / Schneider, Hermann G – Gnadau: Verlag der Unitaets-Buchhandlung, 1882 – 1mf – us A.T.L.A. [240]

EIN MISSIONSBISCHOF AUS LAENGST VERGANGENER ZEIT / Buchmann, Jacob – Breslau [Wroclaw]: Fiedler & Hentschel, 1874 – 1mf – 9 – 0-8370-9129-2 – 1986-3129 – us A.T.L.A. [920]

MISSIONSBLATT DER EVANGELISCHE-TAUFGESTINNTEN – (Later called Missionsblatt der Gemeine Getaufter Christen). (German Baptist). 1844-78 – 1 – 224.21 – us Baptist [240]

MISSIONSFOERBUNDET – (Some issues lacking) – v14-57. 1896-1939 – 28r – 1 – ATLA S0214 – us A.T.L.A. [240]

MISSIONS-KINDERFREUND – Bremen, Germany. 1904-1922; 1924-1939 – 2r – 1 – gw Mikrofilm [072]

MISSIONS-KINDERFREUND – (Cont by: Das Missionsschiff, 1939) – Bremen, 1904-22, 1924-39 – 2r – 1 – Inquire at Mikrofilmarchiv for details – gw Misc Inst [240]

DAS MISSIONSSCHIFF *see* MISSIONS-KINDERFREUND

MISSIONSVAENNERNA I AMERIKA : EN ATERBLICK PA DERAS UPPKOMST OCH FOERSTA VERKSAMHETSTID / Bowman, CV – Minneapolis, Minn.: Minneapolis Veckoblad Pub. Co., 1908, c1907 – 1mf – us A.T.L.A. [240]

MISSIONSWANNEN – Chicago, IL. 1874-98; 1901-35; 1939-60 – 51r – 1 – sw Kungliga [071]

MISSIONSWISSENSCHAFT UND RELIGIONSWISSENSCHAFT – v1-4. 1947-49 (complete) – Inquire – 1 – ATLA 1993-S527 – us A.T.L.A. [073]

MISSISKOUI STANDARD – Frelighsburg, Canada. 1835-39 – 2r – 1 – $136.00 – cn Library Assoc [971]

MISSISKOUI STANDARD – Frelighsburg, Canada. 8 avr 1835-v4 n50. 23 avr 1839 – 2r – 1 – Can$35.00r – cn Can Microfilming [072]

MISSISQUOI – (Cont by: Le Missisquoi de Farnham, Farnham v10 n38. 19 jun 1968-20 mar 1974) – Beauharnois, Canada. v4 n22. 3 avr 1958 – 1r – 1 – Can$55.00 – cn Can Microfilming [072]

LE MISSISQUOI DE FARNHAM *see* MISSISQUOI

THE MISSISQUOI NEWS AND FRONTIER ADVOCATE – Philipsburg, Canada. v1 n47. 14 dec 1848 – 1r – 1 – Can$25.00 – cn Can Microfilming [072]

MISSISQUOI RECORD / ed by Corey, M D – Stanbridge, Canada. 5 jun 1885-v3 n49. 26 avr 1888 – 1r – 1 – Can$45.00 – cn Can Microfilming [072]

MISSISQUOI TIMES – Bedford, Canada. 16 jan 1874 – 1r – 1 – Can$25.00 – cn Can Microfilming [072]

MISSISSAUGA BUSINESS – 1982- – 1r per yr – 1 – cn Commonwealth Micro [073]

MISSISSAUGA NEWS – Ontario, CN. 1986- – 12r per yr – 1 – Can$55.00r – cn Commonwealth Micro [072]

MISSISSIPPI – 7r – 1 – $560.00 – us Scholarly Res [370]

MISSISSIPPI : SESSION LAWS OF AMERICAN STATES AND TERRITORIES – 1799-1995 – 9 – $1,972.00 set – us Hein [340]

MISSISSIPPI : STATUTES ANNOTATED – Superseded volumes 1972-Apr 1996 – 9 – $793.00 – us Hein [340]

Mississippi *see*
- REPORTS AND OPINIONS (A-G)
- REPORTS, POST-NRS
- REPORTS, PRE-NRS
- SESSION LAWS, 1799-

MISSISSIPPI 4H NEWS / Mississippi. State College. Agricultural Extension Service – v. 1-19. 1950-70 – 1,5,6 – us Spaulding [630]

Mississippi. Agricultural Experiment Station. State College *see*
- AEC MIMEOGRAPHED REPORT
- AEC STATISTICAL SERIES
- AEC TECHNICAL PUBLICATION
- AGRICULTURAL PRODUCTION IN MISSISSIPPI
- ANNUAL REPORT
- BULLETIN
- CIRCULAR
- INFORMATION SHEET
- MIMEO
- MIMEOGRAPHED REPORT
- MISSISSIPPI FARM RESEARCH
- PRESS CIRCULAR
- PROGRESS REPORT (ADMINISTRATIVE REPORTS)
- PROGRESS REPORTS
- SHORT COURSE FOR SEEDSMEN. PROCEEDINGS
- SMALL GRAIN VARIETY TESTS
- STONEVILLE SERVICE SHEETS
- TECHNICAL BULLETIN

MISSISSIPPI ATTORNEY GENERAL REPORTS AND OPINIONS – (6 1893-1967 $105.00. 9 1987-1995 $602.00. 1968-1986 not available) – 1893-1995 – 6,9 – $707.00set – us Hein [340]

THE MISSISSIPPI BAPTIST – 1857-60 (complete) – 1r – 1 – ATLA R0138 – us A.T.L.A. [240]

MISSISSIPPI BAPTIST CONVENTION. EXECUTIVE BOARD : CHURCH RECORDS – 1913-52. 1896p – 1 – us Baptist [240]

MISSISSIPPI COLLEGE LAW REVIEW – (v1-5 1978-85 on reel $60.00. v6-15 1985-95 on mf $146.00) – v1-15. 1978-95 – 5,6,9 – $206.00 set – us Hein [340]

MISSISSIPPI DEMONSTRATOR / Mississippi. State College. Agricultural Extension Service – v. 1-3. 1921-24 – 1,5,6 – us Spaulding [630]

MISSISSIPPI EDUCATIONAL ADVANCE – v1-1911- 1; v64- 5,6; v67- 9 – us UMI [073]

MISSISSIPPI ENTERPRISE – Jackson. Miss. 1939-1966 – 1 – us UMI [071]

MISSISSIPPI FARM RESEARCH / Mississippi. Agricultural Experiment Station. State College – v. 1-35. 1938-72 – 1,5,6 – us Spaulding [630]

MISSISSIPPI FREE LANCE – Jackson. Miss. 1923-1928 – 1 – us UMI [071]

MISSISSIPPI FREE TRADER – Natchez. Miss. and Natchez Gazette. -TW, SW. 1835-51 – 1 – us UMI [071]

MISSISSIPPI LAW JOURNAL – v1-64. 1928-95 – 1,5,6 – $945.00 – us Hein [073]

MISSISSIPPI LAWYER – v1-40. 1954-94 – 9 – $620.00 set – us Hein [340]

Mississippi Legislature *see* BANKING ACT OF 1809

MISSISSIPPI LIBRARIES – v.43-. 1979-. Continues: Mississippi Library News – 1,5,6,9 – us UMI [073]

MISSISSIPPI LIBRARY NEWS – v1-42 1936-78 1; v35-42 5,6; v40-42 9 – us UMI [020]

MISSISSIPPI MANUAL OF LEGAL AND BUSINESS FORMS. / Webb, George Franklin – Jackson, Miss., Clarion, 1869. 144 p. LL-1627 – 1 – us L of C Photodup [340]

MISSISSIPPI PALLADIUM – Holly Springs. Miss. 1851-1852 – 1 – us UMI [071]

MISSISSIPPI PRESS – Pascagoula. Miss. 1970- – 1 – us UMI [071]

MISSISSIPPI QUARTERLY – v1- 1948- 1; v24-5,6; v30- 9 – us UMI [073]

MISSISSIPPI RAG – no.1-. Nov. 1973- – 1 – us U.W. Library [073]

MISSISSIPPI REPUBLICAN – Natchez. Miss. 1813-1824 – 1 – us UMI [071]

THE MISSISSIPPI RIVER AND ITS SOURCE: A NARRATIVE AND CRITICAL HISTORY OF THE DISCOVERY OF THE RIVER AND ITS HEADWATERS, ACCOMPANIED BY THE RESULTS OF DETAILED HYDROGRAPHIC AND TOPOGRAPHIC SURVEYS / Brower, Jacob V – Minneapolis: Harrison & Smith, 1893. 00976. (Pre-1900 Canadiana) – 9 – cn C.I.H.M. [910]

The Mississippi Society for Baptist Missions *see* CIRCULAR ADDRESS

Mississippi. State Bar Association *see* PROCEEDINGS

MISSISSIPPI STATE BAR ASSOCIATION REPORTS – (Missing: ns 18th meeting 1923) – os: 1st-7th meetings 1886-92; ns: 1st-25th meetings 1906-30 (all publ) – 55mf – 9 – $82.00 – LLMC 84-610 – us L.L.M.C. [340]

Mississippi. State College. Agricultural Extension Service *see*
- AGRICULTURAL NEWS REPORT
- THE BRIEF
- BULLETIN
- EXTENSION CIRCULAR
- EXTENSION LEAFLET
- MISSISSIPPI 4H NEWS
- MISSISSIPPI DEMONSTRATOR

Mississippi. State College. Cooperative Extension Work in Agriculture and Home Economics *see* NEWS LETTER

Mississippi State University. Agricultural Experiment Station *see*
- ANNUAL REPORT
- BULLETIN
- CRIS PROGRESS REPORT
- INFORMATION SHEET
- PROGRESS REPORTS IN SOCIOLOGY AND RURAL LIFE

Mississippi State University. Agricultural Experiment Station. Agricultural and Forestry Experiment Station *see*
- AEC. M.R
- AEC TECHNICAL PUBLICATION
- BULLETIN
- INFORMATION BULLETIN
- MAFES RESEARCH HIGHLIGHTS
- RESEARCH REPORT
- SHORT COURSE FOR SEEDMEN; PROCEEDINGS
- TECHNICAL BULLETIN

Mississippi State University. Agricultural Experiment Station. Department of Agricultural Economics *see* STAFF PAPER SERIES

Mississippi State University. Cooperative Extension Service *see*
- 4-H REVIEW
- ANNUAL REPORT
- ANNUAL REPORT ON STATE-OWNED INSTITUTIONAL FARMS
- FINANCIAL REPORT
- INFORMATION SHEET
- PUBLICATION
- STATE OWNED INSTITUTIONAL FARMS; ANNUAL REPORT

Mississippi. State University. Cooperative Extension Service *see* PUBLICATION

Mississippi. State University. Division of Sociology and Rural Life *see*
- PROGRESS REPORT IN SOCIOLOGY AND RURAL LIFE
- SOCIOLOGY AND RURAL LIFE SERIES

MISSISSIPPI SUN – Charleston. Miss. 1920-21; 1936-1960 – 1 – us UMI [071]

Mississippi. Supreme Court *see*
- FREEMAN'S CHANCERY CASES
- HEMINGWAY AND MCDONALD'S REPORTS
- MISSISSIPPI SUPREME COURT REPORTS
- MORRIS' STATE CASES
- SMEDES AND MARSHALL'S CHANCERY CASES

MISSISSIPPI SUPREME COURT REPORTS / Mississippi. Supreme Court – (Pre-NRS: v1-63 1818-88 567mf $850.00. Updates planned) – v1-121. 1818-1920 – 1200mf – 9 – $1,800.00 – LLMC 81-803 – us L.L.M.C. [340]

MISSISSIPPI SUPREME COURT REPORTS *see*
- BANKING ACT OF 1809
- FREEMAN'S CHANCERY CASES
- HEMINGWAY AND MCDONALD'S REPORTS
- MORRIS' STATE CASES
- SMEDES AND MARSHALL'S CHANCERY CASES

Mississippi Valley Historical Association *see*
- PROCEEDINGS

MISSISSIPPI VALLEY HISTORICAL REVIEW *see* JOURNAL OF AMERICAN HISTORY

THE MISSISSIPPI VALLEY LUMBERMAN – (Individual reels available. v11 missing) – v1-10 v12-104 17 Aug 1876-Mar 1973 – 175r – 1 F-81-A – $5250.00 $30.00r – us M.H.S. [073]

Mississippi Valley Trading Company *see* PAPERS 1874-78

MISSISSIPPIAN – Carthage. Miss. 1908-1909 – 1 – us UMI [071]

MISSISSIPPIAN – Jackson. Miss. 1834-1856; 1859-1863 – 1 – us UMI [071]

MISSISSIPPIAN – Jackson. Miss. -sw. 1854-60 – 1 – us UMI [071]

THE MISSISSIPPIAN OCCUPATION OF THE RED WING AREA / Gibbon, Guy E – 1979. Guide. (ISBN 0-87351-137-9) – 9 – 12.50 – us M.H.S. [930]

MISSISSIPPI'S BUSINESS – v29- 1970- 1; v33-5,6; v34- 9 – us UMI [073]

MISSOES DOS JESUITAS NO ORIENTE NOS SECULOS 16 E 17 / Pinheiro d'Almeida da Camara Manuel, Jeronymo – Trabalho destinado a X Sessao de Congresso internacional dos Orientalistas.1894 – 1 – us A.T.L.A. [240]

MISSOULIAN – Missoula. Mont. 1892-1898; 1900- – 1 – us UMI [071]

MISSOULIAN – Missoula. Mont. -w. 1899-1900 – 1 – us UMI [071]

MISSOURI : SESSION LAWS OF AMERICAN STATES AND TERRITORIES – 1813-1994 – 9 – $1,121.00 set – us Hein [340]

MISSOURI : VERNON'S ANNOTATED MISSOURI STATUTES – 1951-Apr 1996 update – 9 – $1,229.00 set – us Hein [340]

Missouri *see*
- MISSOURI APPELLATE REPORTS
- REPORTS AND OPINIONS (A-G)
- REPORTS, POST-NRS
- REPORTS, PRE-NRS
- SESSION LAWS, 1813-
- STATE LABOR REPORTS

MISSOURI AND NEW MEXICO – 1r – 1 – $80.00 – us Scholarly Res [370]

MISSOURI APPELLATE REPORTS / Missouri – (Pre-NRS: v1-93 1876-1902 269mf $1,210.00. Updates planned) – v1-202. 1876-1919 – 515mf (1:42) 241mf (1:24) – 9 – $2,679.00 – LLMC 84-162 – us L.L.M.C. [340]

MISSOURI ARGUS – St. Louis. MO. 1835-40 – 1 – us UMI [071]

MISSOURI ATTORNEY GENERAL REPORTS AND OPINIONS – (6 1993-1975 + indexes $1,505.00. 9 v33-46 + digest 1976-1995 $100.00) – 1933-1995 – 6,9 – $1,605.50 set – us Hein [340]

MISSOURI BAPTIST BIOGRAPHY / Maple & Rider – Kansas City: Western Baptist Publ. Co., 1914. Missouri Reel 2. (The Cox Library Collection) – 5 – us Americana [978]

MISSOURI BAR ASSOCIATION REPORTS – 1st to 50th Meetings. 1880-1930 (all publ) – 133mf – $199.00 – LLMC 84-611 – us L.L.M.C. [073]

MISSOURI BAR JOURNAL – (Cont by: Journal of the Missouri Bar v1- 1944- which is not offered by LLMC) – v1-15. 1930-44 (all publ) – 18mf – 9 – $81.00 – LLMC 84-612 – us L.L.M.C. [073]

MISSOURI BAR JOURNAL – (Superseded by Journal of the Missouri Bar) – v1-15. 1930-44 – 9 – $100.00 set – us Hein [340]

MISSOURI BAR JOURNAL *see* JOURNAL OF THE MISSOURI BAR

Missouri Botanical Garden *see* ANNALS OF THE MISSOURI BOTANICAL GARDEN
MISSOURI CEMETRY INSCRIPTION SOURCES : PRINT AND MICROFORM / Kot, Elizabeth G & Thomson, Shirley P – 1995 – 9 – $55.00 – 0-9641213-3-6 – us Indices [920]
MISSOURI DEMOCRACY / Jackson, W Rufus – St. Louis: S.J. Clarke Publ. Co., 1935. 3v. Missouri Reel 3. (The Cox Library Collection) – 5 – us Americana [978]
Missouri Dental Association *see* JOURNAL
MISSOURI DENTAL JOURNAL: THE JOURNAL OF THE MISSOURI DENTAL ASSOCIATION – v65-. 1985- – 1,5,6,9 – us UMI [073]
MISSOURI ENVIRONMENTAL LAW AND POLICY REVIEW – v1-2. 1993-94 – 1,5,6,9 – $210.00 set – us Hein [340]
MISSOURI FORM BOOK AND LEGAL MANUAL FOR LAWYERS, COUNTY OFFICERS AND BUSINESS MEN / Pattison, Everett Wilson – 12th ed. St. Louis: Gilbert, 1890. 938p. LL-717 – 1 – us L of C Photodup [340]
MISSOURI GAZETTE – St. Louis. MO. Also, Public Advertiser. 1819-22 – 1 – us UMI [071]
MISSOURI GEOLOGICAL SURVEY / Keyes, C R – Paleontology of Missouri. v. 4 (1), v. 5 (2). Jefferson City. 1891. B-150 2 – 8 – ne IDC [550]
THE MISSOURI HARMONY / Carden, Allen D – 1838 – 1 – 8.40 – us Baptist [240]
THE MISSOURI HARMONY / ed by Carden, Allen D – 18th ed. 1846 – 9 – us Sibley [780]
MISSOURI HERALD – Jackson. Mo. 1819-1820 – 1 – us UMI [071]
Missouri Historical Co *see*
- HISTORY OF LAFAYETTE COUNTY
- HISTORY OF SALINE COUNTY
MISSOURI HISTORICAL REVIEW – v1- 1906- 1; 1976- 5,6,9 – us UMI [978]
Missouri Historical Society *see*
- BULLETIN
- COLLECTIONS
- PUBLICATIONS
MISSOURI IN PERSPECTIVE – (v. 7- 1979- 5,6,9) – v. 3-. 1973- – 1 – us UMI [978]
MISSOURI JOURNAL OF DISPUTE RESOLUTION *see* JOURNAL OF DISPUTE RESOLUTION
MISSOURI LAW REVIEW – (v1-49 1936-84 on reel $490.00. v50-60 1985-95 on mf $276.00. Index v1-30 1936-65) – v1-60. 1936-95 – 5,6,9 – $766.00 set – us Hein [340]
MISSOURI MEDICINE – (v.76-. 1979- 5,6,9) – v.50-. 1953- – 1 – us UMI [073]
MISSOURI PLEADING AND PRACTICE IN ACTIONS AT LAW AND IN EQUITY. / McQuillin, Eugene – St. Louis, Gilbert, 1892. 2v. LL-755 – 1 – us L of C Photodup [340]
Missouri Primitive Baptist Associations *see* ANNUALS
Missouri Publishing Company *see* LEAVENWORTH COUNTY PLAT BOOK
MISSOURI REPUBLICAN – St. Louis. MO. 1822-28 – 1 – us UMI [071]
THE MISSOURI SCHOOL DISTRICT COUNSELOR: A COMMENTARY ON THE SCHOOL LAW OF MISSOURI / Stevenson, R F – Jefferson City, Carter & Regan, 1880. 240, vi p. LL-1612 – 1 – us L of C Photodup [340]
MISSOURI SENTINEL – Columbia. Mo. -w. 1852-53 – 1 – us UMI [071]
Missouri. State Bar Association *see* PROCEEDINGS
MISSOURI STATE GAZET-COUNTY / R.L. Polk and Co – Biographical sketches. St. Louis, 1882. Missouri Reel 4. The Cox Library Collection – 5 – us Americana [978]
MISSOURI STATUTE ANNOTATIONS. / McCullock, Samuel Johnson – 2nd ed. Kansas City, Mo., 1902. 215 p. LL-707 – 1 – us L of C Photodup [340]
Missouri. Supreme Court *see*
- MISSOURI SUPREME COURT REPORTS
- REPORTS
MISSOURI SUPREME COURT REPORTS / Missouri. Supreme Court – (Pre-NRS: v1-88 1821-85 617mf $925.00. Updates planned) – v1-280. 1821-1919 – 2317mf – 9 – $3,475.00 – LLMC 82-983 – us L.L.M.C. [340]
Missouri. Synod (Pres. Ch. in the U.S.A.) *see* MINUTES
MISSOURI WEEKLY – Kennett. Mo. 1962- – 1 – us UMI [071]
MISSOURIAN – St. Charles. MO. 1820-22 – 1 – us UMI [071]
MISSOURI'S HALL OF FAME / Shoemaker, Floyd C – Columbia: The Missouri Book Co., 1923. Missouri Reel 2.(The Cox Library Collection) – 5 – us Americana [978]
MIST – St. Helens. OR.-w. 1913-33 – 1 – us UMI [071]
MISTAKES OF DR W.E.B. DUBOIS : BEING AN ANSWER TO DR W.E.B. DUBOIS'S ATTACK UPON THE HONORABLE MARCUS GARVEY / Sheppard, Wheeler – Pittsburgh. 2v. 1921 – 1r – 1 – us Ross [975]
MISTAKES OF INGERSOLL: AS SHOW BY REV. W.F. CRAFTS...AND OTHERS / ed by McClure, James Baird – Chicago: Rhodes & McClure, 1880.1 fiche – 9 – us A.T.L.A. [240]
MISTER HORN AND HIS FRIENDS / Pearse, Mark Guy – 18– – 9 – us A.T.L.A. [240]
LE MISTERE DU SIEGE D'ORLEANS, PUBLIE... – Paris: Imp. imperiale, 1862 – 1 – F454.00 – fr Armell [944]
MISTEREI PARIS / Schulman, K – Vilna. 4 v. 1857-60. BJ-422-74 1 – 9 – ne IDC [470]
EL MISTERIO DEL CRISTO MISTICO (LECCIONES DIVULGADORAS DE LA EPISTOLA DE SAN PABLO A LOS EFESIOS) BADAJOZ, 1944 / Fernandez y Fernandez, Juan – Madrid: Razon y Fe, 1947 – 1 – sp Bibl Santa Ana [240]
MISTERIO Y POESIA / Caba, Pedro – Santander: Artes Graficas de los Hermanos Bedia, 1951 – sp Bibl Santa Ana [810]
EL MISTERIOSO CORONEL POLACO (HISTORIA NOVELADA) / Munoz de la Pena, Arsenio – Badajoz: Imprenta de la Diputacion Provincial, 1963. Sep. Rev. Estudios Extremenos – 1 – sp Bibl Santa Ana [350]
LA MISTICA SOCIAL DE EVA PERON / Franco, Alberto – Buenos Aires: Presidencia de la Nacion, Subsecretaria de Informaciones, 1954 – 1 – CSUXAJA7273-B – us Hoover Inst Photo [320]
MISTICAS / Sanchez-Arjona, Vicente – Sevilla: Graficas Salesianas, Tomo 6. 1954 – 1 – sp Bibl Santa Ana [810]
MISTICAS / Sanchez-Arjona, Vicente – Sevilla: Imp. Carlos Acuna, Tomo 1. 1947 – 1 – sp Bibl Santa Ana [810]
MISTICAS / Sanchez-Arjona, Vicente – Sevilla: Imp. Carlos Acuna, Tomo 2. 1949 – 1 – sp Bibl Santa Ana [810]
MISTICAS / Sanchez-Arjona, Vicente – Sevilla: Imp. Carlos Acuna, Tomo 3. 1952 – 1 – sp Bibl Santa Ana [810]
MISTICAS / Sanchez-Arjona, Vicente – Sevilla: Imp. Carlos Acuna, Tomo 4. 1952 – 1 – sp Bibl Santa Ana [810]
MISTICAS / Sanchez-Arjona, Vicente – Sevilla: Imp. Carlos Acuna, Tomo 5. 1953 – 1 – sp Bibl Santa Ana [810]
LOS MISTICOS ESPANOLES: MALON DE CHAIDE, JUAN DE AVILA, LUIS DE GRANADA, LUIS DE LEON, SANTA TERESA, SAN JUAN DE LA CRUZ Y SU GROUPO / Rousselot, Paul – Barcelona: Imp. de Henrich, 1907. 2v – 1 – us U.W. Library [240]
Mistler, Jean *see* HOFFMANN LE FANTASTIQUE
MISTLETOE – v. 1. Jan-Mar 1849 – 1 – us UMI [071]
THE MISTLETOE – Athens, Ga. v. 1, no. 1-3. Jan-Mar 1849. Incomplete. Sold with Wheler's Southern Monthly Magazine – 1 – us NY Public [073]
MISTR KAMPANUS: HISTORICKY OBRAZ Z DOBY BELOHORSKE / Winter, Zikmund – Chicago: Slavie, 1915 – 1 – us U.W. Library [460]
MISTRESS AND MAID, AND MASTER AND MAN – London. -w. 8 Oct 1890-12 Oct 1892. (2 reels) – 1 – uk British Libr Newspaper [072]
MISUKALISCHE BRIEFE : WAHRHEIT UBER TONKUNST UND TONKUNSTLER / Lobe, J C – Leipzig: Baumgartner, 1852 – 1 – us Sibley [780]
MISUL' – Sofia, Bulgaria. v1-2, 4-7, 9-11, 13-14, 16-17. 1892-1897, 1899-1901, 1902-1904, 1906-1907 – 1 – us I.U. Libraries [073]
MISUSE AND ABUSE OF THE RIGHT OF PETITION FOR THE REMOVAL OF JUDICIAL OFFICERS / Essex Bar Association. Salem, Massachusetts – n.p. Essex and Middlesex bar associations, 1900. 4 p. LL-690 – 1 – us L of C Photodup [340]
MIT DERNBURG NACH OSTAFRIKA / Zimmermann, Adolph – Berlin: C A Schwetschte, 1908 – us Res Libr [960]
MIT GOETHE DURCH DIE SCHWEIZ : EIN WANDERBUCH MIT HANDZEICHNUNGEN GOETHES UND NOCH NICHT VEROEFFENTLICHTEN AQUARELLEN UND KUPFERSTICHEN AUS DER KUNSTSAMMLUNG DES MUSEUMS IN BASEL / Goethe, Johann Wolfgang von; ed by Benisch-Darlang, Eugenie – (Includes bibliographical references) – Wien: Gerlach und Wiedling, 1913 – 1 – us U.W. Library [910]
MIT LEIB UND LEBEN : GEDANKEN EINES FRONTSOLDATEN UNSERER TAGE / Wipper, Paul – Luxemburg: Verlagsanstalt Moselland, 1943 – 1r – 1 – us U.W. Library [810]
MIT UNSERER JUGEND: NEUE CONFIRMATIONS-REDEN FUER DEN BARMIZWA / Ehrentheil, Adolf – Frankfurt a.M.: J. Kauffmann, 1878. 1 fiche – 9 – us A.T.L.A. [270]
MIT VERGNUEGTEN SINNEN : KLEINE HAUSPOSTILLE / Steguweit, Heinz – Hamburg: Hanseatische Verlagsanstalt, 1938 – 1r – 1 – us U.W. Library [943]
MITAUER NACHRICHTEN – Mitau, Latvija. (Jelgava, U.S.S.R.). 4 Feb 1922-29 Dec 1923; 24 Mar (Nr.1) 1925; 2 Feb 1927-28; 1932-3 Jul 1934 – 2r – 1 – gw Mikrofilm [943]
MITBESTIMMUNG UND GERECHTER LOHN ALS ELEMENTE EINER NEUORDNUNG DER WIRTSCHAFT / Kuss, E – Duisburg, 1950 – 1 – DM30.00 – gw Mikro Press [330]
Mitchall, William A *see* HISTORY OF LINN COUNTY
Mitchel, Ormsby MacKnight *see*
- ASTRONOMY OF THE BIBLE
- THE ASTRONOMY OF THE BIBLE
MITCHELL ADVOCATE – 1978- – 1 – cn Commonwealth Micro [072]
Mitchell, Alexander F *see*
- CATECHISMS OF THE SECOND REFORMATION
- THE SCOTTISH REFORMATION
Mitchell, Bruce *see* INSTITUTIONAL ARRANGEMENTS FOR WATER MANAGEMENT
Mitchell, Caleb *see* BLACKSMITH'S ACCOUNT BOOK
MITCHELL COMMERCIAL TRIBUNE – Mitchell, NE. -w. Sep 1935-Sep 1938 – 1 – us NE Hist [071]
MITCHELL COUNTY PRESS – Osage. Iowa. 1951- – 1 – us UMI [071]
Mitchell, Donald Grant *see* REVERIES D'UN CELIBATAIRE
Mitchell, Hinckley Gilbert *see*
- AMOS: AN ESSAY IN EXEGESIS
- GENESIS
- ISAIAH: A STUDY OF CHAPTERS I-XII
MITCHELL INDEX – Mitchell, NE. -w. Mar-Dec 1896, scattered issues missing; Jan 1897-Jun 1899; Aug 1899-Jan 1901; Apr 1901 to date – 1 – us NE Hist [071]
Mitchell, James A *see* EFFECTS OF COCAINE ON GLUCAGON AND INSULIN IN EXERCISING RATS
Mitchell, James Coffield *see* THE TENNESSEE JUSTICE'S MANUAL AND CIVIL OFFICER'S GUIDE
Mitchell, John Murray *see* FOREIGN MISSIONS OF THE PROTESTANT CHURCHES
Mitchell, John N *see* JOHN MITCHELL PAPERS, 1885-1919
Mitchell, Kenneth R *see* PSYCHOLOGICAL AND THEOLOGICAL RELATIONSHIPS IN THE MULTIPLE STAFF MINISTRY
Mitchell Library. New South Wales *see*
- SYDNEY MAIL INDEX
- SYDNEY MORNING HERALD INDEX
Mitchell Library. Sydney, Australia *see* THE PUBLIC LIBRARY OF NEW SOUTH WALES: DICTIONARY CATALOG OF PRINTED BOOKS
MITCHELL LIBRARY SYDNEY MAIL INDEX / Bayley, WA – (Apply to publ for details) – 9 – at Pascoe [020]
MITCHELL LIBRARY TOWN AND COUNTRY INDEX / New South Wales; ed by Bayley, W A – Details on request – 9 – at Pascoe [073]
Mitchell, Robert McBurney *see* HEYSE AND HIS PREDECESSORS IN THE THEORY OF THE NOVELLE
Mitchell, S C *see* AFTER WHITSITT WHAT?
Mitchell, S H *see* THE INDIAN CHIEF JOURNEYCAKE
Mitchell, S W *see* INJURIES OF NERVES AND THEIR CONSEQUENCES
MITCHELL SENTINEL – Mitchell, OR. -w. 1915-25 – 1 – 48.00 – us Oregon Hist [071]
Mitchell, Stanley *see* TAX SAVINGS FOR CAR OWNERS
Mitchell, William Bell *see* HISTORY OF STEARNS COUNTY
MITCHELL'S MARITIME REGISTER – London. -w. 27 Sep 1856-Dec 1883 – 54r – 1 – uk British Libr Newspaper [380]
MITCHELL'S MORNING SHIPPING NEWS – London, England. -w. 1 Sept 1864-1 July 1869. 10 reels – 1 – uk British Libr Newspaper [072]
Mithat, Ahmet *see*
- OSMANLI TARIHI
- UESS-I INKILAB
MITHRIDATES ODER ALLGEMEINE SPRACHENKUNDE... / Adelung, J C – Berlin. 3v. 1806-1816 – 32mf – 9 – ne IDC [400]
MITHRIDATES, ODER ALLGEMEINE SPRACHENKUNDE / Adelung, J C – In French. (Linguistics series). 6v. 1806-1817 – 9 – fr Hachette [400]
MITHRIDATES, SIVE DE DIFFERENTIIS LINGUARUM / Gessner, Conrad – In French. (Linguistic series). 1555 – 9 – fr Hachette [400]
Miti, James Kibuka *see* A SHORT HISTORY OF BUGANDA, BUNYORO, BUSOGA, TORO AND ANKOLE...
DAS MITLEID BEI GERHART HAUPTMANN : PSYCHOLOGISCH-AESTHETISCHE BETRACHTUNGEN / Marschan, Joachim Hans – (Includes bibliographical references) – Dortmund: F W Ruhfus, 1919 – 1r – 1 – us U.W. Library [430]
EL MITO ALFONSINISTA : LIBERACION NACIONAL Y LUCHA DE CLASES EN LA ARGENTINA / Corbiere, Emilio J – Buenos Aires: Icaria Ediciones, 1985 – 1 – CSUXAJA7776-B – us Hoover Inst Photo [320]
EL MITO DE EVA DUARTE / Ghioldi, Americo – Montevideo, 1952 – 1 – CSUXADJ4144-B – us Hoover Inst Photo [920]
EL MITO DEL ORO EN LA CONQUISTA DE AMERICA. VALLADOLID, 1933 / Ferrandis Torres, Manuel – Madrid: Razon y Fe, 1934 – 1 – sp Bibl Santa Ana [946]
MITOLOGIA NORDICA / Mogak, Eugen – Barcelona, 1932; Madrid: Razon y Fe, 1934 – 1 – sp Bibl Santa Ana [390]
Mitra, H *see* CONTRIBUTION TO A BIBLIOGRAPHY OF INDIAN ART AND AESTHETICS
Mitra, Rajendralala, Raja *see* THE SANSKRIT BUDDHIST LITERATURE OF NEPAL
LA MITRAILLE : LA TERRE LIBRE AU COLON LIBRE – Quebec, Canada. 28 oct 1907 – 1r – 1 – Can$25.00 – cn Can Microfilming [072]
THE MITRE – (Merged with: Nue Vue: Merged to become: The New Mitre) – Lennoxville, Quebec: Students of Bishop's College and the Boys of Bishop's College School, [1893?-189- or 19–] – 9 – cn C.I.H.M. [370]
MITROPOLIT EVGENII KAK UCHENII. RANNIE GODY ZHIZNI 1767-1804 / Shmurlo, E F – Spb. 1888. BR-7884 2 – 8 – ne IDC [240]
Mitskevicha, S I *see* ALBOM PERVO I RUSSKO I REVOLIUTSII 1905-1907 G.G.
Mitsui Editorial Board *see* MITSUI-KE SHIRYO
MITSUI-KE SHIRYO = HISTORICAL MATERIALS OF THE HOUSE OF MITSUI, 1600-1900: CHRONOLOGICAL COLLECTION OF MITSUI DOCUMENTS / ed by Mitsui Editorial Board – Complete 92v in 89 and 5 supplementary vols, 94 in all. 34,800p with many plates. Limited to 30 sets. Printed from 1904 to 1911. Tokyo – 26r – 1 – Y300,000.00 – ja Yushodo [950]
MITT I BOTKYRKA – Huddinge, Sweden. 1988- – 1 – sw Kungliga [072]
MITT I HANINGE – Haninge, Sweden. 1989- – 1 – sw Kungliga [072]
MITT I HUDDINGE – Huddinge, Sweden. 1988- – 1 – sw Kungliga [072]
MITT I SOEDER OM SOEDER – Skaerholmen, Sweden. 1988- – 1 – sw Kungliga [072]
MITT I SOEDER OM SOEDER – Stockholm, 1988-91 – 9 – sw Kungliga [072]
MITT I SOEDER OM SOEDER OESTRA – Stockholm, 1991- – 9 – sw Kungliga [072]
MITT I SOEDER OM SOEDER VAESTRA – Stockholm, 1991- – 9 – sw Kungliga [072]
MITT I TYRESOE – Haninge, Sweden. 1989- – 1 – sw Kungliga [072]
MITTAGONG ARGUS – Jan 4 1902-Jun 11 1904 – 9 – at Pascoe [072]
MITTAGONG EXPRESS – Jan 3 1899-Mar 28 1902 – 9 – at Pascoe [072]

MITTAGONG STAR – Sept 7 1956-Oct 11 1960 – 9 – at Pascoe [072]

DIE MITTAGSGOETTIN : EIN ROMAN AUS DEM GEISTESKAMPFE DER GEGENWART / Boelsche, Wilhelm – 3. Aufl. Jena: E Diederichs, 1905 – 1r – 1 – us U.W. Library [830]

Mittarelli, J -B *see* RERUM FAVENTINARUM SCRIPTORES

Mittarelli, J B *see* ANNALES CAMALDULENSES O.S.B.

MITTEILUNGEN : [FILM] – Berlin. apr, jul, sep, dec 1915 – 1 – gw Mikrofilm [790]

MITTEILUNGEN / Geographische Gesellschaft. Munich – 1.-35. Bd.; 1904 06-1949 50. Supersedes: Geographische Gesellschaft in Mua5nchen. Jahresberichte. Film Mas C 463 – 1 – us H.U. Library [910]

MITTEILUNGEN / Geschichts- und Altertumforschender Verein. Eisenberg – Bd. 1-2 (Heft 1-15). 1886-1900. Includes index. Heft 1-10, 11-15. Film Mas 8054 – 1 – us H.U. Library [073]

MITTEILUNGEN / Gesellschaft fuer Salzburger Landeskunde – Salzburg. v.1-49. 1860-1909. Beginning with v. 20, indexed in every 10th vol. Film Mas C 692 – 1 – us H.U. Library [073]

MITTEILUNGEN / Hohenzollerischer Geschichtverein – Sigmaringen etc. Jahrg. 1-63; 1867 68-1932. Issued by the society under its earlier name: Verein fuer Geschichte und Altertumskunde in Hohensollern. Vol. 22 includes index, v. 1-20. Superseded by Hohensollerische Jahreshefte. Reel 4 includes index, 1867-1932. Film Mas C 375 – 1 – us H.U. Library [073]

MITTEILUNGEN / Kunsthistorisches Institut. Florenz – Berlin, Leipzig. v1-3. 1908-19 – 12mf – 9 – ne IDC [073]

MITTEILUNGEN / Nordboehmischer Verein fuer Heimatforschung und Wanderpflege – Leipa. Jahrg. 1-42, 44-46; 1872-1923. Reel 7 includes Hauptregister, Jahrg. 1-25 and Register, Jahrg. 11-15. 1878- issued under the earlier name of the Society: Nordboehmischer Excursions-Klub. Film Mas C 639 – 1 – us H.U. Library [910]

MITTEILUNGEN / Reichsverband der Juedischen Kulturbunde in Deutschland – Berlin-Charlottenburg. v1-14, 1937-38. Complete. B337. (Leo Baeck Institute. German-Jewish Periodicals, Pt 2) – 1r – 1 – $60.00 – us UPA [270]

MITTEILUNGEN / Verein fuer Geschichte der Duetschen in Boehmen – Prag. Jahrg. 43-80; 1905-43. 1939-43 issued under the later name of the Verein: Verein fuer Geschichte der Duetschen in den Sudeten laendern. Includes Inhaltsverzeichnis, Bd. 1-60. Film Mas C 669 – 1 – us H.U. Library [073]

MITTEILUNGEN / Verein fuer Geschichte der Stadt Nuernberg – Nuernberg. v1-17, 23-25, 39-47 1879-1906, 1919-24, 1944-56. Film Mas C 365 – 1 – us H.U. Library [943]

MITTEILUNGEN AUS DEM GEOGRAPHISCHEN INSTITUT DER SUN-YATSEN UNIVERSITAT, 1930-1931 / Kanton – v. 1 (1-2). BCH-1202 1 – 9 – ne IDC [910]

MITTEILUNGEN AUS DEM OSTERLANDE – 43v. 1837-1941. Altenburg, Thueringen, Naturforschenden Gesellschaft des Osterlande zu Altenburg. Some vols. have suppls – 1 – us U.W. Library [574]

MITTEILUNGEN AUS DEM VEREIN ZUR ABWEHR DES ANTISEMITISMUS – Berlin, 1891 (incomplete), 1892-1915 – 5r – 5 – Dist. gw Mikrofilm – gw Misc Inst [943]

MITTEILUNGEN AUS DEN DEUTSCHEN SCHUTZGEBIETEN – v. 20-36 (lacks 25,31), 1907-28 29. Ergaenzungsheft. v. 1-13, 1908-17 – 1 – us Res Libr [943]

MITTEILUNGEN AUS DEN TECHNISCHEN INSTITUTEN DER STAATLICHEN TUNG-CHI-UNIVERSITAET / Woosung – pt. 3, 5. 1931-32. BCH-1203 1 – 9 – ne IDC [370]

MITTEILUNGEN AUS DER HISTORISCHEN LITTERATUR / Historische Gesellschaft zu Berlin – Berlin. 1.-40. Jahrg. 1873-1912. Film Mas C 276 – 1 – us H.U. Library [430]

MITTEILUNGEN DER AUSLAND-HOCHSCHULE AN DER UNIVERSITAET BERLIN – Berlin. v39-42. 1936-39 – 2r – 1 – us Res Libr [370]

MITTEILUNGEN DER DEUTSCHEN DENDROLOGISCHEN GESELLSCHAFT – Ed 2 Bonn, Poppelsdorf 1892-1932 – 177mf – 9 – ne IDC [580]

MITTEILUNGEN DER DEUTSCHEN FREIHEITSBIBLIOTHEK – (Title change: Das freie Deutschland/Mitteilungen der..., 1936) – Paris. May 1935-Jan 1937 – 1 – gw Mikrofilm [073]

MITTEILUNGEN DER FDP IN BAYERN / F D P – (Cont by: Freie Deutsche Presse, Coburg) – Nuernberg, West Germany. 7 Aug 1946-May 1948 – 1 – gw Mikrofilm [073]

MITTEILUNGEN DER JUEDISCHEN REFORMGEMEINDE ZU BERLIN – (Cont by: Juedisches Gemeindeblatt, aug 1937) – Berlin, 1911-38 – 1 – Inquire at Mikrofilmarchiv for details – gw Misc Inst [270]

MITTEILUNGEN DER LIEBENZELLER MISSION – 1949-69 (complete) – 2r – 1 – ATLA S0488 – us A.T.L.A. [240]

MITTEILUNGEN DER POLLICHIA, EINES NATURWISSENSCHAFTLICHEN VEREINS DER RHEINPFALZ – 1888-1919. 31v.ill. Continues: Jahresbericht der Pollichia – 1 – us U.W. Library [500]

MITTEILUNGEN DER PREUSSISCHEN ARCHIVVERWALTUNG – Leipzig. 27v. 1900-39 – 43mf – 9 – subsc: DM220.00 – gw Olms [943]

MITTEILUNGEN DER ZENTRALVEREINIGUNG DEUTSCHER EMIGRANTEN – Amsterdam, feb 15-oct 1937 n1-5 – 1r – 1 – Dist. gw Mikrofilm – gw Misc Inst [943]

MITTEILUNGEN DES ALLGEMEINEN DEUTSCHEN VERBANDES *see* ALLDEUTSCHE BLAETTER

MITTEILUNGEN DES DEUTSCHEN ORIENT-VEREINS – Berlin, 1934-35 (incomplete) – 1 – Inquire at Mikrofilmarchiv for details – gw Misc Inst [956]

MITTEILUNGEN DES DEUTSCH-EVANGELISCHEN FRAUENBUNDES, 1. 1900/01 – 4. 1903/04; EVANGELISCHE FRAUENZEITUNG, 5. 1904/05 – 42. 1940/41 (HQ 25) : ORGAN DES DEUTSCH-EVANGELISCHEN FRAUENBUNDES / Mueller, Paula et al – Hannover, 1900-41 (mf ed 1997) – 101mf – 9 – DM980.00 – 3-89131-137-0 – gw Fischer [305]

MITTEILUNGEN DES GESAMTARCHIVS DER DEUTSCHEN JUDEN – Leipzig, Berlin. v1-6. 1908-14; 1926. Complete. B292. (Leo Baeck Institute. German-Jewish Periodicals, Pt 2) – 1r – 1 – $75.00 – us UPA [270]

MITTEILUNGEN DES GESAMTARCHIVS DER DEUTSCHEN JUDEN / ed by Taeubler, Eugen & Jacobsohn, Jacob – Leipzig, 1900-15. Berlin, 1926. Hildesheim, 1992 – 13mf – 9 – DM100.00 diazo DM130.00 silver – gw Olms [270]

MITTEILUNGEN DES KAMPFBUNDES FUER DEUTSCHE KULTUR – Muenchen, 1929-31 – 0,5r – 1 – gw Mikrofilm [073]

MITTEILUNGEN DES PARTEIVORSTANDES / ed by Sozialdemokratische Partei Deutschlands (Sopade) – Paris, Jun 1939-Apr 1940 – 1r – 1 – gw Mikrofilm [073]

MITTEILUNGEN DES REICHSVERBANDES DER JUEDISCHEN KULTURBUENDE IN DEUTSCHLAND – Berlin-Charlottenburg, 1937-38 – 1r – 1 – Inquire at Mikrofilmarchiv for details – gw Misc Inst [943]

MITTEILUNGEN DES SEMINARS FUER ORIENTALISCHE SPRACHEN AN DER FREIDRICH-WILHELMS-UNIVERSITAET ZU BERLIN – Berlin. v22-38. 1919-1935; suppl to v36 1933; suppl to v38 1935 – reels 16-17 – 1 – us Res Libr [410]

MITTEILUNGEN DES STATISITSCHEN STAATSAMTES DER CECHOSLOVAKISCHEN REPUBLIK / Czechoslovakia. Statni Urad Statisticky – v.1-18., 1920-37 – 1 – 276.00 – us L of C Photodup [310]

MITTEILUNGEN DES SYNDIKUS DES CENTRALVEREINS DEUTSCHER STAATSBUERGER JUEDISCHEN GLAUBENS – Berlin, 1919-22 (incomplete) – 1 – Inquire at Mikrofilmarchiv for details – gw Misc Inst [943]

MITTEILUNGEN DES VERBANDES DER JUEDISCHEN JUGENDVEREINE DEUTSCHLANDS – Berlin, sep 1 1912-21 n4 (incomplete) – 1r – 1 – Inquire at Mikrofilmarchiv for details – gw Misc Inst [943]

MITTEILUNGEN DES VEREINS ARBEITERPRESSE / Arbeiter Presse Verein – Berlin, Germany. Jun 1905-1 May 1933 – 3r – 1 – gw Mikrofilm [073]

MITTEILUNGEN DES VEREINS ARBEITERPRESSE – Berlin, 1905-may 1 1933 – 1 – Inquire at Mikrofilmarchiv for details – gw Misc Inst [070]

MITTEILUNGEN VOM DEUTSCH-ISRAELITISCHEN GEMEINDEBUNDE – Berlin, 1873 n1-1921 n94 (many issues missing) – 1 – Inquire at Mikrofilmarchiv for details – gw Misc Inst [270]

MITTEILUNGEN VON FORSCHUNGSREISENDEN UND GELEHRTEN AUS DEN DEUTSCHEN SCHUTZGEBIETEN : MIT BENUTZUNG AMTLICHER QUELLEN... – Berlin: U Usher. v6-13, 15-16 1893-1900, 1902-03; v17 n1-3 1904; v18 n4 1905; v19 1906 – us Res Libr [943]

MITTEILUNGEN ZUR JUEDISCHEN VOLKSKUNDE – Hamburg, Leipzig, Berlin, Vienna. v1-32. 1898-1929. Complete. B293. (Leo Baeck Institute. German-Jewish Periodicals, Pt 2) – 2r – 1 – $135.00 – us UPA [270]

MITTEILUNGSBLAETTER DER BEZIRKE-LANDESVERBAENDE / Sozialdemokratische Partei Deutschlands – 1946-68 – 1 – DM1,400.00 – gw Mikro Press [335]

MITTEILUNGSBLAETTER FUER SUDETENDEUTSCHE SOZIALDEMOKRATEN *see* BLAETTER FUER SUDETENDEUTSCHE SOZIALDEMOKRATEN

MITTEILUNGSBLATT *see* VOLKSSTIMME FUER WESTFALEN UND LIPPE

MITTEILUNGSBLATT DER ARBEITSGEMEINSCHAFT "DEMOKRATISCHES DEUTSCHLAND" – Basel, sep 1945-jan 2 1949 (incomplete) – 1r – 1 – Dist. gw Mikrofilm – gw Misc Inst [072]

MITTEILUNGSBLATT DER ARBEITSGEMEINSCHAFT FREIER ANGESTELLTENVERBAENDE – Berlin, Germany. 1919-1923 – 1 – gw Mikrofilm [073]

MITTEILUNGSBLATT DER ARBEITSGEMEINSCHAFT FREIER ANGESTELLTENVERBAENDE *see* AFA-BUNDESZEITUNG

MITTEILUNGSBLATT DER GESCHAEFTSKOMMISSION DER FREIEN VEREINIGUNG DEUTSCHER GEWERKSCHAFTEN – Berlin, Germany. 1914-1915 – 1 – gw Mikrofilm [072]

MITTEILUNGSBLATT DER GROSSBUERGERMEISTEREI BENSHEIM – Bensheim, aug 7-dec 31 1948 – 1 – Dist. gw Mikrofilm – gw Misc Inst [943]

MITTEILUNGSBLATT DER USPD – Berlin, apr 1917-18 – 1 – Inquire at Mikrofilmarchiv for details – gw Misc Inst [320]

MITTEILUNGSBLATT DER USPD – Berlin, Germany. Apr 1917-1918 – 1 – gw Mikrofilm [073]

MITTEILUNGSBLATT DES ALLGEMEINEN FREIEN ANGESTELLTENBUNDES *see* AFA-BUNDESZEITUNG

MITTEILUNGSBLATT DES SOZIALDEMOKRATISCHEN VEREINS DUISBURG – Duisburg, Jun 1916-Mar 1917 – 1r – 1 – DM75.00 – gw Mikro Press [072]

MITTEILUNGSBLATT DES SOZIALDEMOKRATISCHEN VEREINS DUISBURG / Der Sozialdemokratischer Verein. Duisburg, Germany – Duisburg. Jun 1916-Mar 1917 – 1r – 1 – gw Mikrofilm [073]

MITTEILUNGSBLATT DES VERBANDES DER SOZIALDEMOKRATISCHEN WAHLVEREINE BERLIN UND UMGEBUNG – Berlin, 1916-18 – 1r – 1 – DM90.00 – gw Mikro Press [072]

MITTEILUNGSBLATT DES VERBANDES DER SOZIALDEMOKRATISCHEN WAHLVEREINE BERLIN UND UMGEBUNG – Berlin, Germany. 1906-12 Mar 1913, 14 Apr 1915-8 Mar 1916 – 1r – 1 – gw Mikrofilm [072]

MITTEILUNGSBLATT DES VERBANDES DER SOZIALDEMOKRATISCHEN WAHLVEREINE BERLINS UND UMGEBUNG – Berlin, 1906-dec 29 1918 (incomplete) – 1 – Inquire at Mikrofilmarchiv for details – gw Misc Inst [320]

MITTEILUNGSBLATT DES VERBANDES NATIONALDEUTSCHER JUDEN – (Cont by: Der nationaldeutsche Jude, 1925) – Berlin, 1921-34 – 1r – 1 – Inquire at Mikrofilmarchiv for details – gw Misc Inst [320]

MITTEILUNGSBLATT DES ZENTRALVERBANDES DER SCHUMACHER – Zahlstelle Berlin. v2-3. 1929-30. (Serial publications of German trade unions in the Memorial Library, University of Wisconsin-Madison.) – 1 – us U.W. Library [331]

MITTELALTERLICH GEISTESLEBEN / Grabmann, M – Muenchen. 3 Bnd. 1926-1956 – 30mf – 8 – ne Slangenburg [240]

MITTELALTERLICHE SKULPTUREN IN BAROCKALTAEREN : UNTER BESONDERER BERUECKSICHTIGUNG DES UNMITTELBAREN DIOEZESANGEBIETES DES ERZBISTUMS SALZBURG VOR DER SAEKULARISIERUNG DES ERZSTIFTES / Beck, Herbert – Frankfurt a.M., 1968 – 1mf – 9 – DM48.00 – 3-89349-374-3 – gw Hänsel [730]

MITTELALTERLICHE STUDIEN : AUSGEWAEHLTE AUFSAETZE ZUR SCHRIFTKUNDE UND LITERATURGESCHICHTE / Bisschof, B – Stuttgart. 3 Bde. 1966 – Dfl105.00 – ne Slangenburg [240]

DIE MITTELALTERLICHEN HANDSCHRIFTEN DER ANHALTISCHEN LANDESBUECHEREI DESSAU – 119 Handschriften (mf ed 1995) – 462mf – 9 – DM15,500.00 – 3-89131-215-6 – gw Fischer [090]

MITTELBADISCHER BOTE *see* ACHER- UND BUEHLER BOTE

MITTELBAYERISCHE ZEITUNG – Regensburg, West Germany. Jul 1952- – ca 12r per yr – 1 – gw Mikrofilm [072]

MITTELBAYERISCHE ZEITUNG *see*
- ALTMUEHL-BOTE, KELHEIMER ZEITUNG
- REGENSBURGER POST
- REGENSBURGER UMSCHAU

Mittelbayerischen Zeitung, Regensburg *see* REGENSBURGER UMSCHAU

MITTELDEUTSCHE NEUESTE NACHRICHTEN – Leipzig, East Germany. 26 Oct 1956-30 Jun 1990 – 63r – 1 – gw Mikrofilm [072]

MITTELDEUTSCHE TAGESZEITUNG "FREIHEIT" *see* FREIHEIT

MITTELDEUTSCHE ZEITUNG – (Cont by: Mitteldeutschland – Bereichsausgabe von Mitteldeutschland-Saale-Zeitung, Halle, jan 2, 1934. Thueringer Gauzeitung-Der Nationalsozialist – Bereichsausgabe, Weimar, oct 2, 1939) – Erfurt. oct 2, 1939-jan 1, 1940. jul 1-sep 30, 1940. apr 1-sep 30, 1941 – 3r – 1 – gw Mikrofilm [072]

MITTELDEUTSCHE ZEITUNG *see*
- FREIHEIT

MITTELDEUTSCHLAND – BEREICHSAUSGABE VON MITTELDEUTSCHLAND-SAALE-ZEITUNG *see* MITTELDEUTSCHE ZEITUNG

MITTELFRAENKISCHE ZEITUNG FUER RECHT, FREIHEIT UND VATERLAND – Nuernberg, Germany. 1848-1849 – 3r – 1 – gw Mikrofilm [072]

EINE MITTELHOCHDEUTSCHE EVANGELIENSYNOPSE DER PASSION CHRISTI : UNTERSUCHUNG UND TEXT / Klemmt, Rolf – Heidelberg, 1964 – 4mf – 9 – DM90.00 – 3-89349-765-X – gw Hänsel [240]

MITTELHOCHDEUTSCHES LESEBUCH: MIT GRAMMATIK UND WOERTERBUCH / Bachmann, Albert – 9. and 10. Aufl.Zurich: Beer, 1927. xlii,318p – 1 – us U.W. Library [430]

MITTELRHEINISCHE LANDES-ZEITUNG *see* GODESBERGER VOLKSZEITUNG

MITTELRHEINISCHE LANDESZEITUNG *see*
- DEUTSCHE REICHSZEITUNG

MITTELRHEINISCHE ZEITUNG *see* ALLGEMEINE BADZEITUNG

MITTELSCHWAEBISCHE NACHRICHTEN – Augsburg, 1954-73 – 1 – Dist. gw Mikrofilm – gw Misc Inst [072]

Mittelstadt, SW *see* THE RELATIONSHIP BETWEEN SKELETAL MUSCLE BLOOD FLOW AND BLOOD LACTATE CONCENTRATIONS DURING EXERCISE IN RATS

MITTEN IM WELTKRIEG / Winckler, Josef – Jena: Eugen Diederichs, 1919 – 1r – 1 – us U.W. Library [943]

Mitten, W *see*
- MUSCI AUSTRO-AMERICANI
- MUSCI INDIAE ORIENTALIS

Mittenzwei, Peter *see* DAS KAIDOKI

Mitterer, R M *see* AMINO ACID AND PROTEIN GEOCHEMISTRY IN MOLLUSK SHELLS(DISS.). Z-225/2. 1966

MITTERNACHTSWALZER : EIN ROMAN VON LIEBE UND SCHAFFEN, LEBEN UND TOD DES ALT-WIENER WALZERKOENIGS JOSEF LANNER: IM GEDAECHTNISJAHR DER 100. WIEDERKEHR SEINES TODES: AUS FREIER PHANTASIE / Zampach, Della – Wien: Berglandverlag, 1943 – 1r – 1 – us U.W. Library [830]

Mitterpacher, L *see* ITER PER POSEGANAM SCLAVONIAE PROVINCIAM

DER MITTHEILER AN DER UNTER-WESER – Bremerhaven, Germany. 5 Jan-29 Jun 1859 – 1r – 1 – gw Mikrofilm [072]

DER MITTHEILER AN DER UNTERWESER – (Cont: Bremerleher woechentliche Anzeigen, oct 1842-apr 1846; Woechentliche Anzeigen fuer Lehe, Umgegend und Land Wursten, -1847. Cont by: Volksblatt an der Nordsee, dec 11 1860?; Volksblatt an der Weser, dec 1862) – Bremerhaven-Lehe, 1854-56, 1858-jun 27 1869 – 1 – Inquire at Mikrofilmarchiv for details – gw Misc Inst [943]

MITTHEILUNGEN / Berlin. Universitaet. Seminar fuer Orientalische Sprachen – Berlin, Stuttgart. 1898-1925. v1-41 – 508mf – 8 – ne IDC [480]

MITTHEILUNGEN / Deutscher Alpenverein – Frankfort a. M. v. 1-55, 1875-1929. V. 11- also numbered Neue Folge v. 1-. Issued 1875-Mar. 1, 1938 by the Society under its earlier name: Deutscher und Oesterreichischer Alpenverein. Film Mas C 497 – 1 – us H.U. Library [073]

MITTHEILUNGEN / Deutsches Archaeologisches Institut. Roemische Abteilung – Rom. 1886-1920. v1-35. – 230mf – 9 – ne IDC [930]

MITTHEILUNGEN AN DIE MITGLIEDER / Frankfurter Verein fuer Geschichte und Landeskunde – Frankfurt a. M. v1-7 1858-85. Film Mas C 340 – 1 – us H.U. Library [943]

MITTHEILUNGEN AUS DER KOENIGSBERGER UNIVERSITAETS-AUGENKLINIK 1877-1879 / Jacobson, J – Berlin, 1880 – 6mf – 9 – ne IDC [617]

MITTHEILUNGEN AUS DER PRAXIS DES DAMPFKESSEL-UND DAMPFMASCHINEN-BETRIEBES – Wroclaw, Poland. Zeitschrift fuer Dampfkessel und Maschinenbetrieb. -m. 28 Jan 1887-31 Dec 1909. 14 reels – 1 – uk British Libr Newspaper [073]

MITTHEILUNGEN DER SCHWEIZERISCHEN ENTOMOLOGISCHEN GESELLSCHAFT, 1862-1920 – Schaffhausen. v1-13. 1865-1927 – 127mf – 9 – ne IDC [590]

MITTHEILUNGEN DES INSTITUTS FUER OESTERREICHISCHE GESCHICHTSFORSCHUNG : 3. ERGAENZUNGSBAND – (4. Ergaenzungsband: Innsbruck 1893. 10mf) – Innsbruck, 1890-1894 – 9 – Dfl42.00 – ne Slangenburg [073]

MITTHEILUNGEN DES INSTITUTS FUER OESTERREICHISCHE GESCHICHTSFORSCHUNG – (Available: v25-28 1904-1907; v30-33 1909-1912. Kunstgeschichtliche Anzeigen. Beiblatt der Mittheilungen des Instituts fuer oesterreichische Geschichtsforschung. 1904-1907, 1909-1912. Index 1900-1909) – Innsbruck – 126mf – 9 – ne IDC [900]

MITTHEILUNGEN DES MUENCHNER ENTOMOLOGISCHEN VEREINS – Muenchen. v1-5. 1877-1881 – 18mf – 9 – ne IDC [590]

Mittler, Elmar *see* BIBLIOTHECA PALATINA

MITZPEH – College Park, Md., v2, no. 7 (3 Apr. 1985); v3, no. 2 (16 Oct. 1985)-v3, no. 5 (12 Feb. 1986); v3, no. 8 (7 May 1986)-v4, no. 5 (11 Feb. 1987) – us A.J.P.C. [270]

MITZVOT – San Jose, CA. Winter 1982-Fall 1987. Absorbed by: Jewish Community News (San Jose, CA). Ceased publication – 1 – us A.J.P.C. [071]

Mivart, St George Jackson *see* THE ORIGIN OF HUMAN REASON

MIVRAK = TELEGRAM – (In Hebrew. Evening newspaper) – Tel Aviv, IS. 15 May 1948 (Birth of Israel Issue) – 1r – 1 – $25.00 – cn Can Microfilming [072]

MIXED AND PURE FOREST PLANTATIONS IN THE TROPICS AND SUBTROPICS – 1992 – 158p – it F.A.O. [634]

MIXED ESSAYS / Arnold, Matthew – London: Smith, Elder, 1879 – 1 roll – 1 – 1-55879-187-6 – uk Libr Preservation [840]

Miyabe, K *see*
- FESTSCHRIFT, OR A COLLECTION OF BOTANICAL PAPERS PRESENTED TO PROF. KINGO MIYABE ON THE OCCASION OF THE TWENTY-FIFTH ANNIVERSARY OF HIS ACADEMIC SERVICE BY HIS FRIENDS AND PUPILS
- FLORA OF SAGHALIN

Miyake, T *see* FLORA OF SAGHALIN

MIYAKO SHIMBUN (KYO SHIMBUN) – September 1884-October 1942 (last no.) – 290r – 1 – Y2,900,000 – ja Japan Micro [950]

MIYAKO SHIMBUN KYO SHIMBUN – Japan, 1884-1942 – 331r – 1 – inquire – us Ross [072]

MIYAR *see* AL-MI'YAR

MIYAR-I SEDAT – Istanbul: Karabet ve Kasbar Matbaasi, 1303 [1886] – $35.00 – us MEDOC [470]

MIZAN : SECOND SERIES – Istanbul: Mahmud Bey Matbaasi, 1908-09 Muessis ve Sahib-i Imtiyaz ve Mueduer: Mehmed Murad. Nos. 1-135 (17 Temmuz 1324-11 Nisan 1325 [1908-1909]) – $70.00/10 – us MEDOC [073]

MIZAN – (Shumarah-'i 1-198 (16 Shahrivar 1359-17 Khurdad 1360[6 Sep 1980-7 Jun 1981]). Missing issues: 15, 75-90, 99-109, 111, 117-121, 124, 136-147, 163, 184, 190) – Tehran: Nahzat-i Azadi-i Iran, 1980- – 3r – 1 – $250.00 – us MEDOC [950]

MIZAN – v1-2, nos. 1-104 (1304-1306) – 21mf – 9 – $63.00 – us MEDOC [949]

Mizanci, Mehmed Murad *see* TURFANDA MI YOKSA TURFA MI?

MI-ZIKHRONOT ISH YERUSHALAYIM / Cohn-Reiss, E – Jerusalem. 1934. BJ-27-34 1 – 9 – ne IDC [360]

Mizler, L C *see*
- ANFANGS-GRUENDE DES GENERAL-BASSES
- MUSIKALISCHE BIBLIOTHEK, ODER GRUENDLICHE NACHRICHT NEBST UNPARTHEYISCHEM URTHEIL VON ALTEN UND
- MUSIKALISCHE BIBLIOTHEK ODER GRUENDLICHE NACHRICHT NEBST UNPARTHEYISCHEM URTHEIL VON ALTEN UND
- MUSIKALISCHER STAARSTECHER
- NEU EROEFFNETE MUSIKALISCHE BIBLIOTHEK ODER GRUENDLICHE NACHRICHT NEBST UNPARTHEYISCHEM URTHEIL VON MUSIKALISCHEN SCHRIFTEN UND BUECHERN
- NEU EROEFFNETE MUSIKALISCHE BIBLIOTHEK ODER GRUENDLICHE NACHRICHT NEBST UNPARTHEYISCHEM URTHEIL VON MUSIKALISCHEN SCRIFTEN UND BUECHERN

MIZMOR LE-TODAH – Amsterdam. 1644. Cowley. BJ-43-62 1 – 9 – ne IDC [270]

MIZPAH BAPTIST CHURCH. FLORENCE COUNTY. FLORENCE, SOUTH CAROLINA : CHURCH RECORDS – 1834-62 – 1 – 10.80 – us Baptist [240]

Mizrachi, E *see* JERUSALEM. INVENTORY TO THE FILES OF HERBERT LOUIS, FIRST VISCOUNT SAMUEL (FIRST HIGH COMMISSIONER FOR PALESTINE), 1914-1962

DER MIZRACHI VEG = THE MIZRACHI WAY – New York City, NY. v8 no6 Mar 1944-v9 no4 Jan 1945 – 1r – 1 – $30.00 – cn Can Microfilming [071]

MIZRACHIE – (Not published: v20(10-12) 1937) – Amsterdam. v1-23 1916-1940; v24-26(3) 1949-1951 – 94mf – 9 – ne IDC [999]

MIZRAH U-MA'ARAV – v. 1-5. Jerusalem. 1920-32. BJ-100-171 1 – 9 – ne IDC [270]

MIZROCHO – Amsterdam. v1-5(1). 1923-1927 – 7mf – 9 – ne IDC [999]

MIZUE – 50r – 1 – Y750,000 – ja Yushodo [700]

MIZVAT HA-NASHIM – Basle. 1602. BJ-43-63 1 – 9 – ne IDC [270]

MIZVAT NASHIM – Cracow. 1577. BJ-43-65 1 – 9 – ne IDC [270]

MIZVAT NASHIM – Hanau. 1627. BJ-43-68 1 – 9 – ne IDC [270]

MIZVAT NASHIM – Venice. 1552. BJ-43-64 1 – 9 – ne IDC [270]

MIZVAT NASHIM – Venice. 1588. BJ-43-67 1 – 9 – ne IDC [270]

Mizzi, L *see* PRECIS DE LA LANGUE MALTAISE

M.J. Minch Co *see* COMPLETE DIRECTORY OF HENRY COUNTY

MJOELBYPOSTEN – Mjoelby, 1892 – 9 – sw Kungliga [072]

MLA QUARTERLY – Missouri Library Association v. 1-30. 1940-69 – 1 – us UMI [410]

MLADA FRONTA – (Coll title: Czech/Slovakian Periodicals. Missing: 1970. In Czech) – Praha, 1970-1989 – 1378mf – 9 – R-15378/1 – ne IDC [320]

MLADA FRONTA – Prague, Czechoslovakia. -d. 17 July 1945-30 May 1947; 1 Oct 1951-Dec 1970. 55 reels – 1 – uk British Libr Newspaper [072]

MLADA FRONTA – Prague, Czechoslovakia. May 1945-1992 – 93r – 1 – us L of C Photodup [072]

MLADA FRONTA DNES – (1991-93 4r per y. 1994-98 12r per y $900y) – Czech Republic, 1999- – 12r per y – 1 – $800.00 standing order – us Ross [072]

MLADENCHESTVO / Ivanov, V – "Alkonost". Spb. 1918. BR-738 2 – 8 – ne IDC [460]

Mladenov, S *see* GESCHICHTE DER BULGARISCHEN SPRACHE

MLADEZ *see*
- FAKS
- NARODNA MLADEZ

MLADI BORAC – Belgrade, Yugoslavia. Apr 1945-Jul 1951 – 3r – 1 – us L of C Photodup [949]

MLADOROSSKI I BIULLETEN – (Library has: no. 2, 6-7 (1936-1937)) – San Francisco: 33- i Kaliforni iski i ochag, 1936-1937. 1v – 1 – CSUX89-S2 – us Hoover Inst Photo [947]

MLADOST – Belgrade, Yugoslavia. Oct 1956-1968 – 12r – 1 – us L of C Photodup [949]

MLADOST – Beograd, 1976- – 11r – 1 – DM825.00 – gw Mikro Press [949]

MLADY SVET – 1990-1992 – 2r – 1 – sz Infoprint [947]

MLADY SVET – (1990-92 2r per y $150y. 1993-95 4r per y $300y) – Czech Republic, 1999- – 4r per y – 1 – $280.00 standing order – us Ross [073]

MLADY SVET – (Standing order available from De 1994 +. 4r per year. Sfr450.00y) – 1993 – 4r – 1 – Sfr480.00 – sz Infoprint [947]

MLN (MODERN LANGUAGE NOTES.) – (v.84-1969- 5,6. v.91- 1976- 9) – v.1- 1886- – 1 – us UMI [400]

MLO: MEDICAL LABORATORY OBSERVER – (v.11-. 1979- 5,6,9) – v.1-. 1969- – 1 – us UMI [073]

MLODZI IDA – Lodz, Poland. May-Aug 1945 – 1r – 1 – us L of C Photodup [943]

Mlodzianowski, A *see* ICONES SYMBOLICAE VITAE ET MORTIS B. JOSAPHAT MARTYRIS ARCHIEPISCOPI POLOCENSIS EXPRESSAE...

MLODZIEZ – London, UK. Miesiecznik literacko-spoleczny. Mar-Nov 1953 – 1 – uk British Libr Newspaper [072]

MME. SARAH BERNHARDT / His Majesty's Theatre. Montreal – Montreal, 1916. SEM105P904 – 1mf – 9 – Can$2.25 – cn Bibl Nat [790]

MMWR: CDC SURVEILLANCE SUMMARIES: MORBIDITY AND MORTALITY WEEKLY REPORT – v32-. 1983- – 1,5,6,9 – us UMI [073]

MMWR: MORBIDITY AND MORTALITY WEEKLY REPORT – (v33-. 1984-. 5,6,9) – 25-. Mar 1976- – 1 – us UMI [073]

MMWR: SURVEILLANCE SUMMARIES: MORBIDITY AND MORTALITY WEEKLY REPORT – v32. 1983 – 1,5,6,9 – us UMI [073]

MNEMOSYNE : ARBEITEN ZUR ERFORSCHUNG VON SPRACHE UND DICHTUNG / ed by Walzel, Oskar Franz – Bonn a. Rh.: L Roehrscheid, 1929- – 1r – 1 – us U.W. Library [430]

MNEMOSYNE : BLAETTER DER ERINNERUNG AN GEFEIERTE NAMEN / Rogge, Friedrich Wilhelm – Minden i. Westf.: J.C.C. Brun, 1885 – 1r – 1 – us U.W. Library [430]

MNEMOSYNE – London, Ont: Western Normal Literary Society, [1900] – 9 – cn C.I.H.M. [370]

MNEMOSYNE; BIBLIOTHECA CLASSICA BATAVA – Leiden. Series 4, v1-43. 1948-90 – 5,9 – Dfl4,300.00; Dfl100.00v – ne Swets [000]

THE MOABITE STONE / DeCosta, Benjamin Franklin – (Includes bibliographical references) – New York: Anson D F Randolph, 1871 – 1mf – 9 – 0-8370-7291-3 – 1986-1291 – us A.T.L.A. [470]

THE MOABITE STONE : THE SUBSTANCE OF TWO LECTURES / Walsh, William Pakenham – Dublin: George Herbert, 1873 – 1mf – 9 – 0-8370-9338-4 – 1986-3338 – us A.T.L.A. [270]

MOABITER SONETTE / Haushofer, Albrecht – Berlin: L Blanvalet, 1946 – 1r – 1 – us U.W. Library [810]

Moahi, Kgomotso H *see*
- DEVINDEX BOTSWANA

Moak, S *see* THE LAST OF THE MILL CREEKS

MOAMA BORDER POST – Sept 4 1893-Dec 8 1893 – 9 – at Pascoe [072]

MOAPA VALLEY PROGRESS – Logandale, NV. 1993 – 1+ r – 1 – $50.00 ($50.00y) – U04868 – us Library Micro [071]

AL MOAYAD – Cairo, 1907-14 – 15r – 1 – us Ross [072]

LE MOBACHER – Alger. Texte francais. fevr 1849-oct 1851, 1861, mai 1863-nov 1864, 1866-aout 1870, aout 1873, juin 1876-1880, 1896-1910, 1912-26.Pour l'ed. arabe voir Al-Mubassir – 1 – fr A.C.R.P.P. [073]

Moberly, C A E *see* DULCE DOMUM

Moberly, C E *see* THE EARLY TUDORS

MOBILE DAILY REGISTER – Mobile, AL. Mar 11 1860 (damaged) – 1r – 1 – us Western Res [071]

MOBILE EVENING TELEGRAPH – (Daily Confederate newspaper) – Mobile, AL. Aug 19 1864 – 1r – 1 – us Western Res [071]

THE MOBILE PRESS – Mobile, Ala. 1970- – 1 – us UMI [071]

THE MOBILE REGISTER – Mobile, Ala. 1970- – 1 – us UMI [071]

Mobilier National. Paris *see* LES GOBELINS. 3 SIECLES DE TAPISSERIE

MOBILISATION / Agence de Presse Libre du Quebec – Montreal: [s.n.], 1969-76. SEM35P150 – 1r – 1 – Can$63.00 – cn Bibl Nat [073]

MOBILIZATION FOR TOTAL WAR : THE CANADIAN, AMERICAN AND BRITISH EXPERIENCE 1914-1918, 1939-1945 / ed by Dreisziger, N F – 1981 – xvi/115p – 9 – $15.00 – 0-88920-109-9 – cn W.L.U. Press [350]

Mobillon, Jean *see* TRAITE DES ETUDES MONASTIQUES

MOBIUS – v.1-. 1981- – 1,5,6,9 – us UMI [073]

MOBSTER TIMES – 1972 – 1 – us UMI [073]

Moby-Etia, P *see* LES PAYS DU BAS-MUNGO, BAS-WOURI

MOCCASIN TELEGRAPH – Dec 1961-Summer 1975 – 2r – 1 – $136.00 – cn Library Assoc [073]

MOCCASINS AND THEIR RELATION TO ARCTIC FOOTWEAR / Hatt, G – BN 241 2. 1916 – 8 – ne IDC [390]

LA MOCHILA DEL CORONEL / Durelli, Augusto J – Buenos Aires: Accion Democratica de Ingenieros, Agrimensores y Tecnicos, [3rd ed 1946] – 1 – CSUXADJ1897-B – us Hoover Inst Photo [320]

Mochul'skii, K *see*
- ALEKSANDR BLOK
- ANDREI BELYI
- IUNOST' VALERIIA BRIUSOVA
- KLASSITSIZM V SOVREMENNOI RUSSKOI POEZII
- O.E. MANDEL'SHTAM
- POETICHESKOE TVORCHESTVO ANNY AKHMATOVOI

MOCI – (Also available on CD-ROM) – 1988-1995 – 3r per y – 5,6 – Sfr1,069.00 – sz Infoprint [072]

A MOCIDADE : JORNAL LITTERARIO, CRITICO E NOTICIOSO – '(s.l.')-Sao Luiz, Brazil. 1 Aug 1875-24 Jun 1876 – 1,5,6 – bl Biblioteca [072]

MOCIDADE : REVISTA PARA A MOCIDADE ESTUDIOSA – Maceio, Alagoas. Out 1946-Jul 1949 – 1,5,6 – bl Biblioteca [072]

O MOCIDADE : ORGAM IMPARCIAL, DEDICADO AOS INTERESSES LOCAES – Ponte Nova, 22 Oct 1891 – 1,5,6 – bl Biblioteca [072]

Mocino, Jose Mariano *see*
- FLORA MEXICANA
- PLANTAE NOVAE HISPANIAE...

MOCION FORMULADA Y EXPUESTA A LA CONSIDERACION DEL EXCMO. AYUNTAMIENTO CONSTITUCIONAL DE BADAJOZ / Paez de la Cadena, Francisco – Badajoz: La Minerva Extremena, 1921 – 1 – sp Bibl Santa Ana [320]

MOCION PRESENTADA AL AYUNTAMIENTO DE OLIVENZA / Gomez Castanos, Marcial – Badajoz: Imp. La Economica, de Vicente Rodriguez, 1914 – 1 – sp Bibl Santa Ana [330]

THE MOCK-PREACHER : A SATYRICO-COMICAL-ALLEGORICAL FARCE,... – London, 1739 – 1mf – 9 – MP-259/1 – ne IDC [240]

MOCKSVILLE BAPTIST CHURCH. SOUTH YADKIN ASSOCIATION. NORTH CAROLINA : CHURCH RECORDS – 1876-1930. (Roll book) – 1 – 17.01 – us Baptist [240]

Mocquet, Jean *see*
- VOYAGES EN AFRIQUE, ASIE, INDES ORIENTALES ET OCCIDENTALES FAITS PAR JEAN MOCQUET, GARDE DU CABINET DES SINGULARITES DU ROI, AUX TUILERIES
- VOYAGES EN AFRIQUE, ASIE, INDES ORIENTALES & OCCIDENTALES

LAS MODAS Y EL LUJO, ANTE LA LEY CRISTIANA, LA SOCIEDAD Y EL ARTE. 3RD ED SAN SEBASTIAN, 1935 / Goma, Isidoro – Burgos: Razon y Fe, 1938 – 1 – sp Bibl Santa Ana [946]

LA MODE : REVUE DU MONDE ELEGANT – (Missing: 1838(2)) – Paris, 1839-1844 – 244mf – 9 – ne IDC [740]

A MODEL BILL TO PREVENT DISCRIMINATION ON GROUNDS OF SEX. / National Council for Civil Liberties. London – London, 1974. 25,15p. LL-2251 – 1 – us L of C Photodup [340]

MODEL CITIES REPORTS – (Cataloging and MARC tapes available) – 3465mf – 9 – $9460.00 – us UMI [360]

MODEL FACTORIES AND VILLAGES: IDEAL CONDITIONS OF LABOUR AND HOUSING / Meakin, Budgett – London: T.F. Unwin, 1905. 480p.illus.,plates, plans – 1 – us U.W. Library [310]

A MODEL FOR DEVELOPING EFFECTIVE DECISION-MAKING DURING GAME PARTICIPATION / Turner, A P – 1991 – 2mf – 9 – $8.00 – us Microform Publ [150]

A MODEL FOR MEN OF BUSINESS, OR, THE CHRISTIAN LAYMAN CONTEMPLATED / Stowell, Hugh – New York: Carlton & Phillips, 1855. 1 fiche – 9 – us A.T.L.A. [240]

MODEL PERSONAL WORK (CCC319) / Wang, Yuan-te – (In Chinese) – Shanghai: Association Press of China, 1931 – 1r – 1 – 1984-6658 – us A.T.L.A. [920]

THE MODEL PREACHER : COMPRISED IN A SERIES OF LETTERS ILLUSTRATING THE BEST MODE OF PREACHING THE GOSPEL / Taylor, William MacKergo – Cincinnati: Swormstedt & Poe, 1859 – 1mf – us A.T.L.A. [240]

A MODEL SUPERINTENDENT : A SKETCH OF THE LIFE, CHARACTER, AND METHODS OF WORK OF HENRY P. HAVEN OF THE INTERNATIONAL LESSON COMMITTEE / Trumbull, Henry Clay – Philadelphia: John D. Wattles, c1880 – 1mf – us A.T.L.A. [240]

A MODEL TO UNDERSTAND SPORT-CONFIDENCE AND SPORT COMPETITION ANXIETY OF COLLEGE VARSITY ATHLETES / Yoo, Seang L – Springfield College, 1994 – 3mf – 9 – $12.00 – PSY1876 – us Microform Publ [150]

MODELES CINETIQUES ET STRUCTURAUX EN DYNAMIQUE DES POPULATIONS EXPLOITEES: APPLICATION AUX SQUILLES; SQUILLA MANTIS (L.) (CRUSTACE STOMATOPODE) DU GOLFE DU LION / Do Chi, T – Montpellier. 1978 – 272p – 9 – F70.00 – fr Ethnologie [574]

MODELING AND MOTOR SEQUENCING STRATEGIES OF LEARNING DISABLED BOYS / Kowalski, Ellen M – 1989 – 332p 4mf – 9 – $16.00 – us Microform Publ [150]

MODELLBILDUNG VON MEHRWICKLUNGSTRANSFORMATOREN BEI QUASI-STATIONAEREN FELDSTAERKEVERTEILUNGEN / Heinemann, Lothar – 1994 – 2mf – DM80.00 – 3-8267-2036-9 – gw Hänsel [620]

MODELLING AND SIMULATION IN MATERIALS SCIENCE AND ENGINEERING – 1,5,6 – uk I.O.P. [620]

MODELLING AND SIMULATION IN MATERIALS SCIENCE AND ENGINEERING / ed by Baskes, M I – Bristol, UK: IOP Publishing – 1,5,6,9 – £153.00 – uk I.O.P. [621]

MODELLING OF EXTENSIVE LIVESTOCK PRODUCTION SYSTEMS : PROCEEDINGS OF THE ILCA/ARO/CABO WORKSHOP HELD AT ARO, BET DAGAN, ISRAEL, 5-9 FEBRUARY 1985 / ed by Ridder, N de et al – 1986 – 9 – $16.00 – 92-9053-139-8 – et ILRI [636]

EL MODELO EDUCATIVO COSTARRICENSE / Costa Rica. Asociacion Nacional de Fomento Economico – San Jose, 1985 – 4mf – 9 – DE-649/1 – ne IDC [370]

MODELS FOR ESTIMATING POTENTIAL FISH YIELDS OF AFRICAN INLAND WATERS – 1992 – 25p – it F.A.O. [639]

MODELS OF REALITY: SHAPING THOUGHT AND ACTION / ed by Richardson, Jacques – 1984. 328p. Index. ISBN: 0-912338-36-9 – 9 – 15.00 – us Lomond [650]

MODENG QINGNIAN = DER MOODERNE JUNGE – Dec 1929-Apr 1930. 6 fiches. F-C43 – 9 – $22.50 – cc Microforms [073]

DIE MODENWELT : VEREINIGT MIT DER PRAKTISCHEN BERLINERIN – Berlin. oct 1924-sep 1925 – 1r – 1 – gw Mikrofilm [640]

A MODERACAO – '(s.l.')-Sao Luiz, Brazil. 26 Mar 1857-Dec 1859; Feb 1860-17 Oct 1861 – 1,5,6 – bl Biblioteca [072]

O MODERADOR, NOVO CORREIO DO BRASIL : JORNAL POLITICO, COMMERCIAL E LITTERARIO – Rio de Janeiro, 10 Apr 1830-2 Apr 1831 – 1,5,6 – bl Biblioteca [072]

MODERATOR *see* MEDITATOR

MODERN AGE – v1- 1957- 1; 1971- 5,6; 1976- 4 x 6 in. 9 – us UMI [320]

MODERN AGE : A QUARTERLY REVIEW – v1-15. 1957-71 – 141mf – 9 – $5.00f – us Ross [073]

MODERN AMERICAN LAW / Blackstone Institute – 15v. 1914 – 9 – $320.00 – 0-89941-292-0 – us Hein [340]

MODERN AMERICAN SPIRITUALISM : A TWENTY YEARS RECORD OF THE COMMUNION BETWEEN EARTH AND THE WORLD OF SPIRITS / Hardinge, Emma – New York: The author, 1870 – 2mf – us A.T.L.A. [240]

MODERN APOSTLES OF MISSIONARY BYWAYS / Thompson, Augustus Charles et al – (Includes index) – New York: Student Volunteer Movt for Foreign Missions, c1899 – 1mf – 9 – 0-8370-6423-6 – 1986-0423 – us A.T.L.A. [920]

MODERN ARISTOCRACY, OR THE BARD'S RECEPTION : THE FRAGMENT OF A POEM, WRITTEN IN MARCH 1830 / Brydges, S E – Geneva, 1831 – 2mf – 9 – ne IDC [810]

MODERN ASIAN STUDIES – v1- 1967- 1; v10- 1976- 5,6,9 – us UMI [950]

MODERN AUSTRIAN LITERATURE – v1- 1968- 1; v4- 5,6; v9- 9 – us UMI [430]

MODERN BRITISH PAINTINGS DRAWINGS AND SCULPTURE – (Over 20,000 reproductions, 2,000 artists) – 213mf – $1,170.00 – 1-900853-01-9 – uk Mindata [750]

MODERN BUDDHISM = XIANDAI FOXUE – (In Chinese) – no 6. 1960 (complete) – 1r – 1 – ATLA S0296S – us A.T.L.A. [280]

A MODERN BUDGET SYSTEM FOR INDONESIA / Indonesia. Department of Finance – Part A: Budget Organization,BY Kroeger Griffenhagen, Inc. SE-6063 1. 1963 – 9 – ne IDC [324]

MODERN BUSINESS ADMINISTRATION / Radiks Purba – v. 1 ONLY. Contents: Balans Permanen Dan Rekeningstelsel. SE-4829 1. 1964 – 9 – ne IDC [650]

THE MODERN CALL OF MISSIONS : STUDIES IN SOME OF THE LARGER ASPECTS OF A GREAT ENTERPRISE / Dennis, James Shepard – New York: Fleming H. Revell, c1913 – 1mf – us A.T.L.A. [240]

MODERN CASTING – v1- 1938- 1; v59- 1971- 5,6; v67- 9 – us UMI [670]

MODERN CHINA – (1983-. 1,5,6,9) – v1-. 1975- – 1 – us UMI [073]

MODERN CHINA 1 – 34 titles divided into five categories: (1) Diplomatic Periodicals (2) Diplomatic Documents (3) Shanghai Foreign Settlements (4) Afro-Asian People's Solidarity Conference (5) Chinese Society. Write for complete list of titles and prices – 1 – $35.00r – us Hoover Inst Photo [950]

MODERN CHINESE PICTORIAL ART 1949-1979 : ALPHABETICAL CHRONOLOGICAL AND SUBJECT INDEXES / Heilesen, SB – N.p., n.d. – 3mf – 9 – ne IDC [960]

MODERN CHRISTIANITY : A CIVILIZED HEATHENISM / Pullen, Henry William – New York: R Worthington, 1880 – 1mf – 9 – 0-8370-3857-X – 1985-1857 – us A.T.L.A. [240]

MODERN CHURCH BROTHERHOODS : A SURVEY OF THE PRACTICAL ACTIVITIES OF THE CHURCHMEN'S CLUBS AND BROTHERHOODS / Patterson, William B – New York: F.H. Revell, c1911 – 1mf – us A.T.L.A. [240]

MODERN CHURCHMAN – v1- 1911- 1; v14- 5,6; v20- 9 – us UMI [240]

MODERN CITIES AND THEIR RELIGIOUS PROBLEMS / Loomis, Samuel Lane – New York: Baker & Taylor, c1887 – 1mf – us A.T.L.A. [900]

MODERN CONCEPTS OF CARDIOVASCULAR DISEASE – v1- 1932- 1; v39- 5,6; v45- 9 – us UMI [616]

MODERN CONCRETE – v1- 1937- 1; v38- 5,6,9 – us UMI [690]

MODERN CONSTITUTIONS IN OUTLINE : AN INTRODUCTORY STUDY IN POLITICAL SCIENCE / Alston, Leonard – London, New York: Longmans, Green & Co, 1909 – 1mf – 9 – $1.50 – LLMC 92-154 – us L.L.M.C. [323]

MODERN CRIMINOLOGY – v1 no 1 1907 (all publ) – 1mf – 9 – $1.50 – LLMC 84-265 – us L.L.M.C. [073]

MODERN CRITICISM AND THE PREACHING OF THE OLD TESTAMENT / Smith, George Adam – New York: A.C. Armstrong, 1901. 1 fiche – 9 – us A.T.L.A. [240]

MODERN CUBA MAGAZINE – Havana. v1-4. 1913-16 – 1r – 1 – us Ross [972]

MODERN DEMOCRACIES / Bryce, James – 2v. NY: The Macmillan Co, 1921 – 13mf – 9 – $19.50 – LLMC 96-043 – us L.L.M.C. [320]

MODERN DEVELOPMENTS IN METHODISM / Redfern, W – London, 1906. x/168p – 2mf – 9 – ne IDC [240]

MODERN DRAMA – Downsview. v1-37. 1958-94 – 9 – Can$28.00y – cn Micromedia [790]

MODERN DRAMA – (v.23-. 1980-. 5,6,9) – v.1-. 1958- – 1 – us UMI [073]

MODERN DRUMMER – (v.3-. 1979- 5,6,9) – v.1-. 1977- – 1 – us UMI [073]

MODERN ENGLISH : ITS GROWTH AND PRESENT USE / Krapp, George Philip – New York: Charles Scribner's, 1909 – 1 roll – 1 – 1-55879-830-7 – uk Libr Preservation [420]

MODERN ENTRIES, ADAPTED TO THE AMERICAN COURTS OF JUSTICE. / Harris, Thomas – Annapolis: Green, 1801. 2v. LL-866 – 1 – us L of C Photodup [340]

MODERN EUROPEAN DRAMA – (Lists 166 productions) – 177mf – 9 – £955.00 – uk Chadwyck [790]

MODERN FICTION STUDIES – (v15- 1969- 5,6 v17- 1971- 9) – v1- 1955- – 1 – us UMI [420]

MODERN FLOOR COVERINGS – 1986- – 1,5,6,9 – us UMI [690]

THE MODERN GENGHIS KHAN / Fedoseyev, Anatoly – Anti-Soviet Society publication.8p – 9 – $1.00f – at Libertarian Micro [335]

MODERN GEOLOGY / ed by Fraser, N C et al – 1970- – 1,5,9 – us Gordon [550]

MODERN GREECE : A NARRATIVE OF A RESIDENCE AND TRAVELS IN THAT COUNTRY, WITH OBSERVATIONS ON ITS ANTIQUITIES, LITERATURE, LANGUAGE, POLITICS, AND RELIGION / Baird, Henry M – New York: Harper, 1856 – 1mf – us A.T.L.A. [306]

THE MODERN GREEK : ITS PRONUNCIATION AND RELATIONS TO ANCIENT GREEK / Timayenis, Telemachus Thomas – (With an appendix on the rules of accentuation, etc) – New York: D Appleton; Springfield, MA: J D Gill, 1877 – 1mf – 9 – 0-8370-9318-X – 1986-3318 – us A.T.L.A. [450]

MODERN HEALTHCARE – (See also: Modern Healthcare/Short-Term Care Edition) – v7-. 1977- – 1,5,6,9 – us UMI [610]

MODERN HEALTHCARE/ LONG-TERM CARE EDITION – v1-6 1974-76 1,5,6; 1976- 9 – us UMI [610]

MODERN HEALTHCARE/SHORT-TERM CARE EDITION – v. 1-6. 1974-76 – 1,5,6,9 – us UMI [610]

MODERN HEBREW LITERATURE – v1- 1975- 1; v3- 5,6,9 – us UMI [470]

MODERN HEROES OF THE MISSION FIELD / Walsh, William Pakenham – (Originally printed in the Clergyman's magazine for 1881) – New York: T Whittaker, 1882 – 1mf – 9 – 0-8370-5813-9 – 1985-3813 – us A.T.L.A. [920]

MODERN HOSPITAL – (v104-122. 1965-74. 5,6. v114-122. 1970-74. 9. See now: Modern Healthcare) – 1-122. 1913-74 – 1 – us UMI [610]

MODERN IDEAS OF EVOLUTION AS RELATED TO REVELATION AND SCIENCE / Dawson, John William – London: Religious Tract Society, 1890. 02625. (Pre-1900 Canadiana) – 9 – cn C.I.H.M. [971]

MODERN INDONESIAN DRAMA : A SELECT BIBLIOGRAPHY / Widawan, Rosa – 1986 – A$10.00 – 0-86758-201-4 – at BISA [820]

MODERN INDONESIAN LITERATURE / Ma-Ruf, Anas – Speech delivered at 15th Sept. 1957 at Seoul National University. SE-6225 1. 1957 – 9 – ne IDC [490]

MODERN INDONESIAN SHORT STORIES / ed by Su, I – In Chinese. SE 5638 1. v. 1 only. 1962- – 9 – ne IDC [830]

MODERN INDUSTRY – Bristol, CT. v1-26. 1941-53 – 10r – 1 – us Ross [338]

MODERN INTERNATIONAL DRAMA – v1- 1967- 1; v10- 5,6,9 – us UMI [073]

MODERN ISLAM : THE SEARCH FOR CULTURAL IDENTITY / Gruenebaum, GE von – Berkeley, 1962 – 7mf – 8 – ne Slangenburg [260]

MODERN JEWELER – 1914-62 – 1 – us UMI [740]

MODERN JEWELER – (1984- 5,6,9) – 1981- – 1 – us UMI [740]

MODERN JEWELER – National Executive Ed. 1979-81 – 1 – us UMI [740]

MODERN JUDAISM – v.1-. 1981- – 1,5,6,9 – us UMI [270]

Modern Language Association of America *see* PUBLICATIONS (P.M.L.A.)

MODERN LANGUAGE FORUM – v. 1-42. 1915-57 – 1 – us UMI [400]

MODERN LANGUAGE JOURNAL – v1- 1916- 1; v53- 5,6; v59- 9 – us UMI [400]

MODERN LANGUAGE JOURNAL – v. 1-48. 1916-1964 – 1 – us Princeton Micro [370]

MODERN LANGUAGE NOTES – Baltimore. v1-30. 1886-1915 – 280mf – 9 – ne IDC [400]

MODERN LANGUAGE NOTES – v. 1-78. 1886-1963 – 1 – us Princeton Micro [400]

MODERN LANGUAGE QUARTERLY – v. 1-25. 1940-1964 – 1,5,6 – us Princeton Micro [400]

MODERN LANGUAGE REVIEW – v. 1-64. 1905-1969 – 1,5,6 – us Princeton Micro [400]

MODERN LANGUAGE REVIEW – (v. 1-65. Cum. ind. 1-60. 1905-70. London. $24610.00; v. 1-60. $249.00v. v. 61-65. $2415.00v; Cum. ind. 1-60. $2410.50v) – 9 – uk Dawson [400]

MODERN LANGUAGE STUDIES – (1983-. 1,5,6,9) – v1-. 1971- – 1 – us UMI [400]

MODERN LITHOGRAPHY – v1-42 1933-74 1; v38-42 5,6 – us UMI [760]

MODERN LITURGY – v. 3, no. 6$ 1976$ – 1,5,6,9 – us UMI [240]

MODERN MACHINE SHOP – v1- 1928- 1; v43- 5,6; v47- 9 – us UMI [621]

MODERN MANUFACTURING *see* – FACTORY

MODERN MATERIALS HANDLING – (1984-. 5,6,9) – 1946- – 1 – us UMI [600]

MODERN MATERIALS HANDLING *see* PALLETIZER

MODERN MEDICINE – v52-. 1984- – 1,5,6,9 – us UMI [073]

MODERN MEDICINE OF CANADA – (Cont: Modern Medicine of Canada/Medecine Moderne du Canada at v25 1970. Ceased v46 no 4 1991) – Don Mills. v25-46. 1970-91 – 9 – Price varieS – cn Micromedia [610]

MODERN MEDICINE OF CANADA = MEDECINE MODERNE DU CANADA – (Cont by: Modern Medicine of Canada at v25 1970) – Don Mills. v1-24. 1946-1969 – 5 – cn Micromedia [610]

MODERN MEDICINE OF CANADA *see* MODERN MEDICINE OF CANADA

MODERN MEDICINE OF GREAT BRITAIN – v16- 1971- 1,5,6; v20- 9 – us UMI [073]

MODERN METALS – 1984- – 1,5,6,9 – us UMI [670]

MODERN METHODS OF CHARITY : AN ACCOUNT OF THE SYSTEMS OF RELIEF, PUBLIC AND PRIVATE, IN THE PRINCIPAL COUNTRIES HAVING MODERN METHODS / Henderson, Charles Richmond – New York: Macmillan, 1904 – 2mf – us A.T.L.A. [360]

THE MODERN MISSION CENTURY...A REVIEW / Pierson, Arthur Tappan – New York: Baker & Taylor, 1901. x,517p.2 fiches – 9 – us A.T.L.A. [240]

THE MODERN MISSIONARY CHALLENGE : A STUDY OF THE PRESENT DAY WORLD MISSIONARY ENTERPRISE: ITS PROBLEMS AND RESULTS / Jones, John Peter – (Includes tables and index) – New York: Fleming H Revell, 1910 – 1mf – 9 – 0-8370-6130-X – 1986-0130 – us A.T.L.A. [240]

MODERN NURSING HOME – (See now: Modern Healthcare/Long-Term Edition) – v1-32 1947-74 1; v24-32 5,6 – us UMI [610]

MODERN OBJECTIONS AGAINST THE CATHOLIC CHURCH, THE POPE AND THE JESUITS ANSWERED : IN REPLY TO R.W. THOMPSON, SECRETARY OF THE NAVY / Weninger, Francis Xavier – (Previously publ under title: Reply to Hon. R.W. Thompson, Secretary of the Navy, addressed to the American people) – 9th ed. New York: P O'Shea, 1878 – 1mf – 9 – 0-8370-6792-8 – 1986-0792 – us A.T.L.A. [240]

MODERN OFFICE PROCEDURES – v1- 1956- 1; v16- 5,6; v20- 9 – us UMI [650]

MODERN OLIVE-GROWING – 1977 – 262p – it F.A.O. [634]

MODERN PACKAGING – v1- 1927- 1; v39- 5,6; v49- 9 – us UMI [680]

MODERN PACKAGING *see* PACKAGE ENGINEERING INCLUDING MODERN PACKAGING

MODERN PAINT AND COATINGS *see* PAINT AND VARNISH PRODUCTION

MODERN PAINTERS / Ruskin, John – London: Smith, Elder, and Co., 1843-60 – 3 rolls – 1 – 1-55879-234-1 – uk Libr Preservation [750]

MODERN PAINTERS / Ruskin, John – London: Smith, Elder and Co., 1873 – 3 rolls – 1 – 1-55879-235-X – uk Libr Preservation [750]

MODERN PASSENGER TRANSPORTATION – v. 3-56. 1907-59 – 1,5,6 – us Princeton Micro [380]

MODERN PATHOLOGY – (Vol 2 includes Abstracts) – v1-9. 1988-1996 – 9r – 1,5,6,9 – $95.00r – us Williams [616]

MODERN PHILOLOGY – v1- 1903- 1; v66- 1968- 5,6; v75- 1977- 9 – us UMI [400]

MODERN PHILOLOGY – Chicago. v1-37. 1903-1939/1940 – 378mf – 9 – ne IDC [400]

MODERN PHILOLOGY – v. 1-39. 1903-1942 – 1,5,6 – us Princeton Micro [400]

MODERN PHILOSOPHY : FROM DESCARTES TO SCHOPENHAUER AND HARTMANN / Bowen, Francis – New York: Scribner, Armstrong, 1877 – 2mf – us A.T.L.A. [190]

MODERN PHOTOGRAPHY – (v. 34- 1970- 5,6. v.35- 1971- 9) – v. 1- 1937- – 1 – us UMI [770]

MODERN PLASTICS – (v. 44- 1966- 5,6. v.47- 9) – v. 1- 1925- – 1 – us UMI [660]

MODERN PLASTICS INTERNATIONAL – v1- 1971- 1; v3- 5,6; v4- 9 – us UMI [073]

MODERN POWER AND ENGINEERING – v1- 1907- 1; v69- 5,6,9 – us UMI [620]

MODERN PRECEDENTS IN CONVEYANCING. / Barton, Charles – 3d ed. London, Hunter, 1821. 1 v. LL-134 – 1 – us L of C Photodup [340]

MODERN PROBATE OF WILLS, CONTAINING AN ANALYSIS OF THE MODERN LAW OF PROBATE IN ENGLAND AND AMERICA. – Boston: Little, Brown, 1846. 578p. LL-792 – 1 – us L of C Photodup [340]

MODERN PURCHASING – v1- 1959- 1; v17- 5,6,9 – us UMI [380]

MODERN PURCHASING – (v1-11 1959-69 Can$415.00 5) – Willowdale. v1-36. 1959-94 – 5,9 – Can$28.00y – cn Micromedia [650]

MODERN QUARTERLY – (1938-39. 1. 1945-53. 1) – Communist Party of Gt. Britain. 1938-39; 1945-53 – 1 – uk World [073]

MODERN QUARTERLY : A JOURNAL OF RADICAL OPINION – 1-11 2+7 (all publ). 1923-40 – 63mf – 9 – $250.00 – us UPA [335]

MODERN QUARTERLY : A JOURNAL OF RADICAL OPINION – Baltimore. v1-11. 1923-40 – 2r – 1 – us Ross [073]

THE MODERN QUARTERLY – Baltimore etc. v. 1-11, no. 7. 1923-Fall 1940 – 1 – us NY Public [073]

MODERN RATIONALISM / McCabe, Joseph – London: Watts & Co., 1897 – 163p – 1 – us U.W. Library [140]

MODERN RATIONALISM AS SEEN AT WORK IN ITS BIOGRAPHIES / Lewis, Henry – London: S.P.C.K.; New York: E.S. Gorham, 1913 – 1mf – us A.T.L.A. [140]

MODERN RECORDS CENTRE, UNIVERSITY OF WARWICK : ANNUAL REPORTS, BULLETINS AND OCCASIONAL PAPERS, 1973-1995 – 7mf – 9 – uk Microform Academic [331]

MODERN RELIGIOUS MOVEMENTS IN INDIA / Farquhar, J N – New York: Macmillan, 1915. (The Hartford-Lamson lectures on the religions of the world) – 2mf – us A.T.L.A. [200]

THE MODERN REPRESENTATIONS OF THE LIFE OF JESUS = MODERNEN DARSTELLUNGEN DES LEBENS JESU : FOUR DISCOURSES DELIVERED BEFORE THE EVANGELICAL UNION AT HANOVER / Uhlhorn, Gerhard – (In English. Includes bibliographical references) – Boston: Little, Brown, 1868 – 1mf – 9 – 0-8370-9322-8 – 1986-3322 – us A.T.L.A. [240]

MODERN RESEARCH AS ILLUSTRATING THE BIBLE / Driver, Samuel Rolles – (Includes bibliographical references and index) – London: Publ for the British Academy by Henry Frowde, Oxford University Press, 1909 – 1mf – 9 – 0-8370-9380-5 – 1986-3380 – us A.T.L.A. [220]

MODERN REVIEW – A quarterly magazine. v. 1-5. 1880-Oct 1884 – 1 – us UMI [073]

MODERN REVIEW / American Labor Conference on International Affairs – 1-3 2+2 (all publ). 1947-50 – 18mf – 9 – $105.00 – us UPA [320]

MODERN REVIEW – (Some missing vols) – Calcutta. v1-106. 1907-1959 – 1531mf – 9 – ne IDC [950]

MODERN REVIEW – Winchester, Mass. v. 1-2, no. 3. Autumn 1922-July 1924 – 1 – us NY Public [073]

THE MODERN REVIEW – v1-5. 1880-Oct 1884 (complete) – 3r – 1 – ATLA S0183 – us A.T.L.A. [073]

MODERN SCHOOLS – 1955-77 1; 1975-77 5,6,9 – us UMI [073]

MODERN SCIENCE AND ANARCHISM / Kropotkin, Petr Alekseevich – Trans....David A. Modell. Philadelphia. 1903 – 1 – us Res Libr [335]

MODERN SCIENCE AND THE ILLUSIONS OF PROFESSOR BERGSON / Elliot, S R – London, New York: Longmans, Green, 1912 – 1mf – us A.T.L.A. [140]

MODERN SCIENCE IN BIBLE LANDS / Dawson, John William – Montreal: Dawson, 1888. 02626. (Pre-1900 Canadiana) – 9 – cn C.I.H.M. [971]

MODERN SKEPTICISM IN ITS RELATIONS TO YOUNG MEN : AN ADDRESS / Hopkins, Mark – New York: Fleming H Revell, c1893 – 1mf – 9 – 0-8370-3653-4 – 1985-1653 – us A.T.L.A. [230]

MODERN SOCIALISM – 1-4 (all publ). 1941-42 – 3mf – 9 – $35.00 – us UPA [335]

MODERN SPECIFIC SETTLEMENTS... / Darby, W E – London, 1904 – 2mf – 9 – ILM-458/1 – ne IDC [971]

MODERN SPIRITUALISM : A HISTORY AND A CRITICISM / Podmore, Frank – London: Methuen, 1902 – 2mf – us A.T.L.A. [240]

THE MODERN STATE / Beaulieu, Paul Leroy – 1891. 215p – 9 – 1.00f – at Libertarian Micro [335]

MODERN SUBSTITUTES FOR TRADITIONAL CHRISTIANITY / McClure, Edmund – London: S.P.C.K.; New York: Gorham, 1914 – 1mf – us A.T.L.A. [240]

A MODERN SYMPOSIUM – Detroit: Rose-Belford Publ, 1878 – 1mf – 9 – 0-8370-4092-2 – 1985-2092 – us A.T.L.A. [230]

MODERN TEXTILES – v37- 1956- 1; v46- 1965- 5,6; v57- 9 – us UMI [670]

MODERN THEOLOGY AND THE PREACHING OF THE GOSPEL / Brown, William Adams – New York: Scribner, 1914 – 1mf – us A.T.L.A. [240]

MODERN THEORIES IN PHILOSOPHY AND RELIGION / Tulloch, John – Edinburgh: W. Blackwood, 1884 – 2mf – us A.T.L.A. [200]

MODERN THOUGHT AND THE CRISIS IN BELIEF / Wenley, Robert Mark – (Includes bibliographical references) – New York: Macmillan, 1909 – 1mf – 9 – 0-8370-2967-8 – 1985-0967 – us A.T.L.A. [240]

MODERN TIMES – v. 1-6. 1970-76 – 1 – us UMI [073]

MODERN TIRE DEALER – (v.61- 1980- 5,6,9) – 1959- – 1 – us UMI [380]

MODERN TRANSPORT – v. 1-100. 1919-68 – 1 – us UMI [380]

MODERN USES OF LOGIC IN LAW *see* JURIMETRICS

A MODERN UTOPIA / Wells, H G – London: Chapman & Hall, 1905 – 1 roll – 1 – 1-55879-949-4 – uk Libr Preservation [830]

MODERN VETERINARY PRACTICE – v.39-46. 1958-65. Continued by MVP: Modern veterinary practice – 1 – us UMI [073]

MODERN VETERINARY PRACTICE – (v.60-. 1979$ 5,6,9) – v.54-. 1973- – 1 – us UMI [073]

MODERN VIEW – St. Louis. Mo. 1913-40 – 1 – us A.J.P.C. [071]

MODERNE ANTIKEN : DER KOPF DES CRASSUS; OENONE; LYSANDERS MAEDCHEN / Widmann, Joseph Viktor – 2. Aufl. Frauenfeld: Huber, 1912 – 1r – 1 – us U.W. Library [450]

MODERNE BLOCKFLOETENTECHNIKEN UND IHRE VERMITTLUNG / Bocklenberg, Ute – 1995 – 2mf – 9 – DM80.00 – 3-8267-2161-6 – gw Hänsel [780]

MODERNE CHARAKTERISTIKEN / Laube, Heinrich – Mannheim: C Loewenthal, 1835 – 1r – 1 – us U.W. Library [830]

DER MODERNE DEUTSCHE BILDUNGSROMAN / Berger, Berta – Bern, 1937 – 1mf – DM48.00 – 3-8267-3044-5 – gw Hänsel [430]

MODERNE DICHTUNG – Leipzig, Germany. 1890 – 1 – gw Mikrofilm [072]

DIE MODERNE FORSCHUNG UEBER DIE GESCHICHTE DES URCHRISTENTUMS : VORTRAG / Meyer, Arnold – Freiburg i.B: J C B Mohr, 1898 – 1mf – 9 – 0-8370-4401-4 – 1985-2401 – us A.T.L.A. [240]

DIE MODERNE GEMEINSCHAFTSBEWEGUNG / Schian, Martin – Stuttgart: Greiner & Pfeiffer, 1909 – 1mf – us A.T.L.A. [240]

DIE MODERNE GESELLSCHAFT, IHRE GESELLIGKEIT UND IHRE MORAL / Pochhammer, Margarete Cauer & Erman, G – Kiel: Lipsius und Tischer, 1892 – 1r – 1 – us U.W. Library [170]

DAS MODERNE KRIEGSRECHT ... / Bluntschli, J K – Noerdlingen, 1874 – 2mf – 9 – ILM-132/1 – ne IDC [327]

MODERNE KUNST – Berlin, Leipzig, Stuttgart, Wien. 1897 n14-26 – 1r – 1 – Inquire at Mikrofilmarchiv for details – gw Misc Inst [700]

MODERNE REALISTISCHE LITTERATUR IM LICHTE DER ETHIK UND AESTHETHIK / ed by Allgemeinen Konferenz der Deutschen Sittlichkeitsvereine – (Running title: Die deutsche Litteratur und die Unsittlichkeit) – Berlin: Allgemeine Konferenz der Deutschen Sittlichkeitsvereine, [189-?] – 1 – us U.W. Library [430]

DE MODERNE RICHTING EN DE KRISTELIJKE KERK / Pierson, A – Arnhem: D.A. Thieme, 1866 – 1mf – us A.T.L.A. [240]

DIE MODERNE THEOLOGIE (DER MODERNISMUS) = MODERNISME : EINE FATA MORGANA AUF CHRISTLICHEM GEBIET / Kuyper, Abraham – (In German) – Zuerich:S. Hoehr, 1872 – 1mf – 9 – 0-8370-4483-9 – 1985-2483 – us A.T.L.A. [230]

DIE MODERNE UND DIE PRINZIPIEN DER THEOLOGIE / Beth, Karl – Berlin: Trowitzsch, 1907 – 1mf – 9 – 0-8370-2314-9 – 1985-0314 – us A.T.L.A. [200]

DAS MODERNE VOELKERRECHT ... / Bluntschli, J K – Noerdlingen, 1868 – 6mf – 9 – ILM-102/1 – ne IDC [327]

DIE MODERNEN DARSTELLUNGEN DES LEBENS JESU : VIER VORTRAEGE IM EVANGELISCHEN VEREIN ZU HANNOVER / Uhlhorn, Gerhard – (Includes bibliographical references) – Hannover: Carl Meyer, 1866 – 1mf – 9 – 0-8370-5597-0 – 1985-3597 – us A.T.L.A. [240]

LES MODERNES ENRICHIS / Pujoulx – (French Theatre Series). Paris. Migneret et Vente, an VI. 1798 – 9 – fr Hachette [820]

LA MODERNISATION DES INSTRUMENTS DE TRAVAIL ET DES METHODES DANS LES ADMINISTRATIONS PUBLIQUES / Puget, H et al – F30.00 – fr Ethnologie [350]

MODERNISM : A RECORD AND REVIEW / Lilley, Alfred Leslie – (Includes index) – New York: Charles Scribner, 1908 – 1mf – 9 – 0-8370-8759-7 – 1986-2759 – us A.T.L.A. [240]

MODERNISM IN ITALY : ITS ORIGIN, ITS INCENTIVE, ITS LEADERS AND ITS AIMS / Jordan, Louis Henry – (Includes bibliographical references) – London; New York: Oxford University Press, 1909 – 1mf – 9 – 0-8370-8752-X – 1986-2752 – us A.T.L.A. [240]

LE MODERNISME : SA POSITION VIS-A-VIS DE LA SCIENCE / Mercier, Desire – Bruxelles: Action catholique, [1908?] – 1mf – 9 – 0-8370-8533-0 – 1986-2533 – us A.T.L.A. [230]

MODERNISME ET TRADITION CATHOLIQUE EN FRANCE / Guignebert, Charles – (Includes bibliographical references) – Paris: Collection de la Grande Revue, [1908?] – 1mf – 9 – 0-8370-8904-2 – 1986-2904 – us A.T.L.A. [240]

IL MODERNISMO : E I RAPPORTI TRA RELIGIONE E FILOSOFIA : SAGGI / Gentile, Giovanni – Bari: Gius. Laterza & Figli, 1909 – 1mf – 9 – 0-8370-3356-X – 1985-1356 – us A.T.L.A. [240]

DER MODERNISMUS / Holl, Karl – Tuebingen: J.C.B. Mohr, 1908. (Religionsgeschichtliche Volksbuecher fuer die deutsche christliche Gegenwart; 4. Reihe, 7. Heft) – 1mf – us A.T.L.A. [240]

MODERNISTY I IKH PREDSHESTVENNIKI I KRITICHESKAIA LITERATURA O NIKH / Povesa & Kogan – Odessa. 1908. BR-3333 2 – 8 – ne IDC [460]

LA MODERNITE DES PROPHETES / Havet, Ernest – (Includes list of biblical citations) – Paris: Calmann Levy, 1891 – 1mf – 9 – 0-8370-3537-6 – 1985-1537 – us A.T.L.A. [220]

MODERNITY AND THE CHURCHES / Gardner, Percy – New York: G P Putnam; London: Williams and Norgate, 1909 – 1mf – 9 – 0-8370-4950-4 – 1985-2950 – us A.T.L.A. [240]

MODERNIZM V MUZYKE / Vol'fing, Emil' Medtner – 1907-10. "Musaget". M. 1912. BR-3308 2 – 8 – ne IDC [780]

LOS MODERNOS EVANGELIZADORES EN LA TIERRA DE LA SANTA CRUZ / Bayle, Constantino – Madrid: Razon y Fe, 1930 – 1 – sp Bibl Santa Ana [240]

A MODEST AND SERIOUS DEFENCE OF THE AUTHOR OF 'THE WHOLE DUTY OF MAN' FROM THE FALSE CHARGES AND GROSS MISREPRESENTATIONS OF MR. WHITEFIELD AND THE METHODISTS, HIS ADHERENTS – London, 1740 – 1mf – 9 – MP-279/1 – ne IDC [240]

Modeste, Victor *see* DU PAUPERISME EN FRANCE. ETAT ACTUEL CAUSES, REMEDES POSSIBLES

MODESTO – 1920-44 – 24r – 1 – $1,200.00 – P00064 – us Library Micro [910]

MODESTO BEE – (Cont by: Modesto Bee and News-Herald) – Modesto, CA. 1895- – 1172+ r – 1 RB02466 – $58,600.00 ($1,180.00y) – us Library Micro [071]

MODESTO BEE AND NEWS-HERALD *see* MODESTO BEE

Modick, Otto *see* GOETHES BEITRAEGE ZU DEN FRANKFURTER GELEHRTEN ANZEIGEN VON 1772

MODIFICATION AND REVISION OF THE LEADERSHIP SCALE FOR SPORT / Zhang, Jianhui & Jensen, Barbara E – 1993 – 5mf – $20.00 – us Microform Publ [790]

MODNYI KUR'ER – St Petersburg, 1899-1916 – 232mf – 9 – $1,490.00 – us Ross [073]

MODNYI SVET – St Petersburg, 1868-78; 1880-98; 1902-05; 1910-16 – 466mf – 9 – $2,490.00 – us Ross [073]

MODO DE EMBALSAMAR CUERPOS DIFUNTOS... / Perez Fadrique, J – Sevilla, 1666 – 3mf – 9 – sp Cultura [610]

MODOC BAPTIST CHURCH. EDGEFIELD COUNTY. SOUTH CAROLINA : CHURCH RECORDS – 1884-1901, 1904-19, 1948-82. Incomplete; Sunday School records 1897-1901. 378p – 1 – 17.01 – us Baptist [240]

MODOC COUNTY RECORD – Alturas. Calif. -w. 1953-57 – 1 – us UMI [071]

THE MODOC COUNTY RECORD – Alturas, CA. Feb 1937-87; 1988- – 44+ r – 1 – $2,200.00 ($90.00y) – B02007 – us Library Micro [071]

MODOC COUNTY REPUBLICAN – Alturas, CA. Apr 1906-Jul 1915 – 3r – 1 – $150.00 – B02012 – us Library Micro [071]

MODOC COUNTY TIMES – Alturas, CA. Aug 1928-May 1929 (incomplete); May 1929-Dec 1934 – 6r – 1 – $300.00 – B02008 – us Library Micro [071]

MODORUM SACRORUM SIVE CANTIONUM... / Erbach, C – (Parts) – Augustae Vindel: apud Ionnem Praetorium, 1604 – 1 – us Sibley [780]

Modrowski, K *see* CENT ANS DE SEDENTARISATION CHEZ LES MARAZIGUES DU SUD-TUNISIEN

MODULAR APPROACH IN TECHNICAL EDUCATION – 1989 – 63p – 9 – 92-3-102535-X – fr UNESCO [370]

MODUS FACIENDI CUM ORDINE MEDICANDI... / Laredo, B – Sevilla, S. XVI – 8mf – 9 – sp Cultura [610]

Modzalevskii, B L *see*
– CARD CATALOG OF RUSSIAN PERSONALITIES (B.L. MODZALEVSKII COLLECTION)

- SPISOK CHLENOV IMP. AKADEMII NAUK (1725-1907)
Moe, Frank R *see* MOUNTAIN ILLNESS SYMPTOMOLOGY ON MOUNT MCKINLEY, ALASKA
MOE OTKRYTIE AMERIKI / Maiakovskii, Vladimir – M. 1926. BR-983 2 – 8 – ne IDC [460]
MOE ZNAKOMSTVO S MANDEL'SHTAMOM; NOVYI ZHURNAL / Karpovich, M – v. 49. 1957. BR-3666 2 – 8 – ne IDC [460]
Moebius, Paul *see* THUERINGER RAETHSEL UND CHARADEN
Moebius, Paul Julius *see*
- UEBER DAS PATHOLOGISCHE BEI GOETHE
- UEBER SCHEFFELS KRANKHEIT
MOE-EI. ROSSIIA / Bal'mont, K D – Prague. 1924. BR-525 2 – 8 – ne IDC [460]
MOEGLICHKEITEN UND GRENZEN EINER ERHOEHUNG DER STAATSWIRTSCHAFTLICHEN PLANUNGSRATIONALITAET DURCH CUTBACK-MANAGEMENT-TECHNIKEN UND ERFOLGSKONTROLLEN / Grafenstein, Andreas – 1992 – 495p – 9 – DM125.00 – 3-89349-536-3 – gw Hänsel [338]
MOEGLICHKEITEN UND GRENZEN INDIVIDUELLER FREIHEIT : EINE UNTERSUCHUNG ZUM WERK MARIE VON EBNER-ESCHENBACHS / Kayser, Brigitte – Frankfurt a.M., 1974 – 3mf – 9 – DM76.00 – 3-89349-727-7 – gw Hänsel [430]
Moehlenkamp, Annegret *see* DIE KLOSTERKIRCHE SAN CARLO ALLE QUATTRO FONTANE VON FRANCESCO BORROMINI IN ROM
Moehler, Johann Adam *see*
- ATHANASIUS DER GROSSE UND DIE KIRCHE SEINER ZEIT
- DR. J.A. MOEHLER'S, ERNANNTEN DOMDECANS ZU WUERZBURG UND RITTERS, DES KGL. BAYER. ST MICHAEL-ORDENS, EHEDEM ORD. PROFESSORS DER THEOLOGIE AN DER UNIVERSITAET MUENCHEN, PATROLOGIE, ODER, CHRISTLICHE LITERAERGESCHICHTE
- THE LIFE OF ST. ANSELM
- NEUE UNTERSUCHUNGEN DER LEHRGEGENSAETZE ZWISCHEN DEN KATHOLIKEN UND PROTESTANTEN
- ON THE RELATION OF ISLAM TO THE GOSPEL
- SYMBOLIK
- SYMBOLISM; OR, EXPOSITION OF THE DOCTRINAL DIFFERENCES BETWEEN CATHOLICS AND PROTESTANTS, AS EVIDENCED BY THEIR SYMBOLICAL WRITINGS
Moehring, P H G *see* AVIUM GENERA
Moellendorff, PG von *see* LE DROIT DE FAMILLE CHINOIS
Moeller, A *see*
- LES GRANDES LIGNES DES MIGRATIONS DES BANTOUS DE LA PROVINCE ORIENTALE DU CONGO BELGE
- SHIPBUILDING AND SHIPREPAIRING INDUSTRY IN INDONESIA
Moeller, C H *see* LEXICON ENTOMOLOGICUM, ODER ENTOMOLOGISCHES WOERTERBUCH...
Moeller, E Wilhelm *see* GESCHICHTE DER KOSMOLOGIE IN DER GRIECHISCHEN KIRCHE BIS AUF ORIGINES
Moeller, Eberhard Wolfgang *see*
- DER ADMIRAL
- DAS BRUEDERLICHE JAHR
- ROTHSCHILD SIEGT BEI WATERLOO
- DER UNTERGANG KARTHAGOS
Moeller, G *see* HIERATISCHE PALAEOGRAPHIE. DIE AEGYPTISCHE BUCHSCHRIFT IN IHRER ENTWICKLUNG VON DER FUENFTEN DYNASTIE BIS ZUR ROEMISCHEN KAISERZEIT
Moeller, H P C *see* INDEX MOLLUSCORUM GROENLANDIAE
Moeller, Hans *see* HEBBEL ALS LYRIKER
Moeller, Hermann *see* VERGLEICHENDES INDOGERMANISCH-SEMITISCHES WOERTERBUCH
Moeller, Karl von *see*
- IM SCHATTEN DER EXZELLENZ
- SPAETSOMMER
Moeller, L *see* DEUTSCHE GARTENZEITUNG
Moellers, Martin *see*
- BUERGERNAEHE DER VERWALTUNG ALS THEMA DER AUSBILDUNG VON BEAMTEN DES GEHOBENEN NICHTTECHNISCHEN DIENSTES
- DAS POLITISCHE SYSTEM DER BUNDESREPUBLIK DEUTSCHLAND NACH DER WIEDERVEREINIGUNG
- PROJEKT
- DAS WESEN DES SACHENRECHTS IN GEGENUEBERSTELLUNG ZUM SCHULDRECHT UNTER DEM BESONDEREN ASPEKT EINER ERFASSUNG DES ABSTRAKTIONSPRINZIPS
Moeller-Witten, Hanns *see* GESCHICHTE DER RITTER DES ORDENS POUR LA MERITE IM WELTKRIEG
Moellmann, Margarete *see* SPRACHE, REGEL UND SPIEL
Moench, C *see* METHODUS PLANTAS HORTI BOTANICI ET AGRI MARBURGENSIS
DAS MOENCHSKLEID IM CHRISTLICHEN ALTERTUM / Oppenheim, Ph. – Freiburg i.Br., 1931 – 6mf – 8 – Dfl25.00 – ne Slangenburg [240]
DAS MOENCHTUM DES HEILIGEN AUGUSTINUS / Zumkeller, A – Wuerzburg, 1950 – 7mf – 9 – ne Slangenburg [240]
DAS MOENCHTUM, SEINE IDEALE UND SEINE GESCHICHTE / Harnack, Adolf von – 6. Auflage. Giessen, 1903 – Dfl9.00 – ne Slangenburg [240]
MOENCHTUM UND SARAPISKULT : EINE RELIGIONSGESCHICHTLICHE ABHANDLUNG / Preuschen, Erwin – 2e Ausgabe. Giessen, 1903 – Dfl9.00 – ne Slangenburg [240]
MOENCHTUM UND SARAPISKULT : EINE RELIGIONSGESCHICHTLICHE ABHANDLUNG / Preuschen, Erwin – Giessen: J. Ricker, 1903 – 1mf – us A.T.L.A. [240]
Moenckeberg, Carl *see* HERMANN SAMUEL REIMARUS UND JOHANN CHRISTIAN EDELMANN
Moerch, O A L *see* SYNOPSIS MOLLUSCORUM MARINORUM DANIAE
Moericke, Eduard Friedrich *see* GEDICHTE
MOERIKE / Goes, Albrecht – Stuttgart: J G Cotta, c1938 – 1r – 1 – us U.W. Library [430]
Moerike, Eduard Friedrich *see*
- MOZART AUF DER REISE NACH PRAG
MOERIKE-ALBUM / Schwind, Moritz von; ed by Windegg, Eggert – Muenchen: C Beck, 1922 – 1r – 1 – us U.W. Library [700]
MOERIKES MALER NOLTEN : IN SEINER ERSTEN UND ZWEITEN FASSUNG / Drawert, Ernst Arno – (Includes bilbiographical references (p. 86-87)) – Halle (Saale): E Klinz, 1935 – 1r – 1 – us U.W. Library [750]
Moerikofer, JC *see* ULRICH ZWINGLI NACH DEN URKUNDLICHEN QUELLEN
Moerman, J *see*
- APOLOGI CREATURARUM
- DE CLEYN WERELT
- IN EN OM DE CHINEESCHE KAMP
Moerzinger, Johann *see* PETRUS STIRBT NICHT!
Moesbach, Ernesto W de *see* VIDA Y COSTUMBRES DE LOS INDIGENAS ARAUCANOS...
Moeslimin Soematera Baroe *see* RAPAT BESAR KAOEM MOESLIMIN SOEMATERA BAROE DI MEDAN, PADA 20-6-2603
Moestue, Wilhelm *see* UHLANDS NORDISCHE STUDIEN
MOEURS, COUTUMES ET INSTITUTIONS DES INDIGENES DE L'ALGERIE / Villot, E-C-E – Alger: A. Jourdan, 1888 – fr Armell [306]
LES MOEURS DU JOUR OU L'ECOLE DES JEUNES FEMMES / Collin d'Harleville, Jean Francois – (French Theatre Series). Paris. Huet et Charon, an VIII. 1800 – 9 – fr Hachette [820]
MOEURS ET COUTUMES DES ESKIMO / Birket-Smith, K – BN-470 2. 1955 – 8 – ne IDC [306]
MOEURS ET COUTUMES DES NATURELS DE LA NOUVELLE-BRETAGNE / Glaumont, G – 9 – F30.00 – fr Ethnologie [306]
Moffat, James C *see*
- CHURCH HISTORY IN BRIEF
- THE CHURCH IN SCOTLAND
Moffatt, J *see* THE FIRST EPISTLE OF PAUL TO THE CORINTHIANS
Moffatt, James *see*
- THE HISTORICAL NEW TESTAMENT
- AN INTRODUCTION TO THE LITERATURE OF THE NEW TESTAMENT
Moffett, Jonas William *see* TEXAS CIVIL FORM BOOK.
Moffett, Thomas C *see* THE AMERICAN INDIAN ON THE NEW TRAIL
Moffitt, James W *see* A HISTORY OF EARLY BAPTIST MISSIONS AMONG THE FIVE CIVILIZED TRIBES
THE MOFUSSILITE – Calcutta, Meerut, Umballa, India. -w. Aug 1845-22 Nov 1845; Jan 1847-May 1876. 64 reels – 1 – uk British Libr Newspaper [072]
Mogak, Eugen *see* MITOLOGIA NORDICA
Moges *see* AMBASSADE EN CHINE ET AU JAPON
Moggridge, J T *see* HARVESTING ANTS AND TRAPDOOR SPIDERS
Moghabghab, Faddoul *see* THE SHEPHERD SONG ON THE HILLS OF LEBANON
Moghaddam, Abdollah Golijani *see* ALI AKBAR DIHHUDA (1879-1956)
MOGHREB AL-AKSA *see* AL-MOGHREB AL-AKSA
LA MOGIGATA / Fernandez de Moratin, Leandro – 1806 – 1mf – 9 – Pta1,000.00 – 84-7848-189-3 – sp Pentalfa [946]
Mogk, Eugen *see* GERMANISCHE MYTHOLOGIE
Mogollon, Antonio *see* LAMENTACIONES DE JEREMIAS
Mogroveio de Cerda, Ivan *see*
- ARBOL DE LAS VERAS Y...ELOGIOS
- ELOGIOS DE LOS CINCO PRINCIPIOS
Mohamed bin Abas *see* HAMKA
Mohammad ibn Omar al Tounisi ibn Solaiman *see*
- VOYAGE AU DARFOUR OU L'AIGUISEMENT DE L'ESPRIT, PAR LE VOYAGE AU SOUDAN ET PARMI LES ARABES DU CENTRE DE L'AFRIQUE
- VOYAGE AU DARFOUR PAR LE CHEYKH MOHAMMED EBN-OMAR EL-TOUNSY
MOHAMMED ET SAINT FRANCOIS... / Basetti-Sani, Julio – Madrid: Archivo Ibero Americano, 1959 – 1 – sp Bibl Santa Ana [240]
THE MOHAMMEDAN MISSIONARY PROBLEM / Jessup, Henry Harris – Philadelphia: Presbyterian Board of Publ, c1879 – 1mf – 9 – 0-8370-7159-3 – 1986-1159 – us A.T.L.A. [230]
MOHAMMEDANISH, WRITINGS ON *see* 4 (I.E EMPAT)
Mohan, R Dorsey *see* R. DORSEY MOHAN PAPERS, 1892-1913
MOHAWK LEADER – Sycamore, Ohio, 1975-1991 – 12r – 1 – $32.50r – us Archival [978]
MOHAWK LEADER – Sycamore, Ohio, 1975-1992 – 12r – 1 – us Archival [978]
MOHAWKS / Braddon, Mary Elizabeth – British Fiction Archive: Unit 5 – 9 – uk Bell [830]
MOHENJO-DARO AND THE INDUS CIVILISATION / ed by Marshall, J – 2v. text, 1 v. pls. London. 1931. B-641 2 – 8 – ne IDC [930]
Mohl, H von *see* BOTANISCHE ZEITUNG
MOHLABANI – Maseru: Moloti Information Bureau. v1 n4-v12 n11. mar 1955-sep 9 1967 – us Res Libr [960]
Mohlberg, C *see*
- IL MESSALE GLAGOLITICO DI KIEW (SEC. 9) ED IL SUO PROTOTIPO ROMANO DEL SEC. 6-7
- MISSALE FRANCORUM
- MISSALE GALLICANUM VETUS
- RADULPH DE RIVO DER LETZTE VERTRETER DER ALTROEMISCHEN LITURGIE
- SACRAMENTARIUM GELASIANUM
- SACRAMENTARIUM VERONENSE (LEONIANUM)
THE MOHONK ARBITRATION CONFERENCES, 1895-1903 – 1r – 1 – $60.00 – us Trans-Media [340]
Mohr, D M H *see*
- BOTANISCHES TASCHENBUCH AUF DAS JAHR 1807
- GROSSBRITANNIENS CONFERVEN
- OBSERVATIONES BOTANICAE
Mohr, E *see* WIR IM FERNEN VATERLAND GEBOREN...DIE CENTURIA THAELMANN
Mohrmann, Chr. *see* STUDIEN ZUR SYNTAX DER BRIEFE DES HL. CYPRIAN
MOI A MISSII A V ROSSII : VOSPOMINANII A DIPLOMATA / Buchanan, George Sir – Berlin: Obelisk, 1924. 2v – 1 – CSUX88-B3506 – us Hoover Inst Photo [320]
MOI PUT' / Esenin, Sergei – Paris. 1926. BR-1056 2 – 8 – ne IDC [460]
MOI VKLAD / Liubimov, N A – Stat'i, zapiski, chteniia, zametki. v. 1-2. M. 1881-87. BR-10,601 2 – 8 – ne IDC [460]
MOI VOSPOMINANIIA / Brusilov, Aleksei Alekseevich – Posmertnoe izd. Moskva: Gos. izd-vo, Otdel voenl. lit-ry, 1929 – 1 – CSUX88-B1390 – us Hoover Inst Photo [920]
MOI VSTRECHI S GR. RASPUTINYM / Dzhanumova, Elena F – Petrograd: "Petrograd", 1923 – 1 – CSUX89-B6834 – us Hoover Inst Photo [947]
MOI VYZOV PREDATELIAMI IKH ZASHCHITNIKAM / Burtsev, Vladimir Lvovich – [S.l.]: Izd. Russkago polit. kom-ta, [1919?] – 1 – CSUX88-B9821 – us Hoover Inst Photo [947]
LE MOINE / Cammaille Saint-Aubin – (French Theatre Series). Paris. Barba, an VI. 1797 – 9 – fr Hachette [820]
LE MOINE ET L'ANTIMOINE – (D'Holbach series). 1767 – 9 – fr Hachette [240]
Moineau, J *see* LA PETITE FEUILLE
LES MOINES DE L'AFRIQUE ROMAINE. (4TH ET 5TH SIECLE.) / Besse, Dom J M – Paris. 2v. 1903 – 2mf – 8 – Dfl19.00 – ne Slangenburg [240]
LES MOINES DE L'ANCIENNE FRANCE / Besse, Dom J M – 1906 – Dfl42.00 – ne Slangenburg [240]
LES MOINES DE SOLESMES : EXPULSIONS DU 6 NOVEMBRE 1880 ET DU 22 MARS 1882 – Le Mans: Edmond Monnoyer, 1882 – 1mf – 9 – 0-8370-6942-4 – 1986-0942 – us A.T.L.A. [944]
LES MOINES D'ORIENT ANTERIEURS AU CONCILE DE CHALCEDOINE (451) / Besse, Dom J M – Paris, 1900 – 15mf – 8 – Dfl53.00 – ne Slangenburg [240]
LES MOINES EYGPTIENS. VIE DE SCHNOUDI / Amelineau, E – Paris, 1889 – 5mf – 8 – ne Slangenburg [240]
MOIS – 1974- 1; 1977- 5,6,9 – us UMI [330]
LE MOIS D'AOAUT : CONSACRE AU SAINT COEUR DE MARIE – (In French and Latin) – 2e ed. Paris: H Casterman, 1870 – 1mf – 9 – 0-8370-8432-6 – 1986-2432 – us A.T.L.A. [240]
MOIS DU SACRE-COEUR / Lefebvre, Alexis – 7e ed. Paris: Librairie saint-germain des pres, [1869?] – 1mf – 9 – 0-8370-7078-3 – 1986-1078 – us A.T.L.A. [240]
LE MOISE HISTORIQUE ET LA REDACTION MOSAIQUE DU PENTATEUQUE CHARLES SCHOEBEL / Schoebel, Charles – (Includes bibliographical references) – Paris:Maisonneuve, 1875 – 1mf – 9 – 0-8370-5130-4 – 1985-3130 – us A.T.L.A. [220]
Moisson-Franckhauser, Suzanne *see* SERGE PROKOFIEV ET LES COURANTS ESTHETIQUES DE SON TEMPS
Moister, William *see*
- HERALDS OF SALVATION
- MEMORIALS OF MISSIONARY LABOURS IN WESTERN AFRICA, THE WEST INDIES, AND AT THE CAPE OF GOOD HOPE..
MOJAVE DESERT NEWS – Mojave. Calif. 1954-1967 – 1 – us UMI [071]
MOJAVE DESERT-UPPER – 1992- – 3+ r – 1 – $150.00 – P00065 – us Library Micro [910]
MOJAVE/RANDSBURG RECORD TIMES – Randsburg, CA. 1929-1932 – 2r – 1 – $100.00 – C03639 – us Library Micro [071]
Mokhtar Muhydin, H *see* HIMPUNAN ISTILAH DAN KIASAN BAHASA INGGERIS, ARTI DAN TUDJUANNJA
Mokler, Alfred J *see* HISTORY OF NATRONA COUNTY 1888-1922
Mola Y Vidal, Emilio *see* DOCTRINAL DE UN HEROE Y HOMBRE DE ESTADO
MOLALLA BULLETIN – Molalla, OR. 5 Jan 1977-15 Feb 1984 – 1 – us U.O. Library [071]
MOLALLA PIONEER – Molalla, OR. -w. 7 Mar 1913-. – 1 – us U.O. Library [071]
Molard, E *see*
- DICTIONNAIRE GRAMMATICAL DU MAUVAIS LANGAGE, AN 11
- LE MAUVAIS LANGAGE CORRIGE
MOLASSES UTILIZATION – 1975 repr 1983 – 41p – it F.A.O. [660]
MOLD AND DENBIGH CHRONICLE – Denbigh,Wales, UK. 8 May 1869-30 Dec 1870. -w.1 reel – 1 – uk British Libr Newspaper [072]
Moldenke, Alfred B *see* BABYLONIAN CONTRACT TABLETS IN THE METROPOLITAN MUSEUM OF ART
Moldofsky, Naomi *see* MARKET THEORY: WHICH ONE?
MOLDOVA SOCIALISTA – (Cont as: Moldova Suverana 1990) – UdSSR, 1976-1991 – 16r – 1 – DM1,200.00 – gw Mikro Press [949]
MOLDOVA SUVERANA *see* MOLDOVA SOCIALISTA
MOLECULAR AND BIOCHEMICAL PARASITOLOGY – v1-13. 1980-84 – 1,5,6,13 – sz Elsevier [574]
MOLECULAR AND CELLULAR BIOLOGY – v.1-. 1981- – 1,5,6,9 – us UMI [574]

MOLECULAR AND CELLULAR BIOLOGY – v1-3. 1981-83 – 1,5,6 – us Princeton Micro [540]
MOLECULAR AND CELLULAR ENDOCRINOLOGY – v1-38. 1974-84 – 1,5,6,13 – sz Elsevier [073]
MOLECULAR AND GENERAL GENETICS – v. 82-180. 1948-80 – 1,5,9 – 17,449.00 – us UMI [073]
MOLECULAR AND GENERAL GENETICS *see* ZEITSCHRIFT FUER VERERBUNGSLEHRE
MOLECULAR ASPECTS OF MEDICINE – v1- 1975- – 5,6,9 – us UMI [610]
MOLECULAR BIOLOGY – (v11-28 1977-94 $160.00v) – v1-10. 1967-76 – 1,5 – $80.00v – us UMI [574]
MOLECULAR BIOLOGY AND EVOLUTION – 1983- – 1,5,6,9 – us UMI [574]
MOLECULAR CRYSTALS AND LIQUID CRYSTALS / ed by Donovan, R J et al – 1966- – 1,5,9 – us Gordon [540]
MOLECULAR IMMUNOLOGY – v1- 1964- – 5,6,9 – us UMI [540]
MOLECULAR MATERIALS / ed by Bunov, L M – 1,5,9 – us Gordon [530]
MOLECULAR PHARMACOLOGY – v19-50. 1981-96 – 1,5,6,9 – $110.00r – us Williams [615]
MOLECULAR PHOTOCHEMISTRY – v.1-. 1969- – 1,5,6,9 – us UMI [540]
MOLECULAR PHYSICS – v.1-30 with index 1-20. 1958-75 – 9 – $24470.00; $2415.00v – uk Dawson [530]
MOLECULAR PHYSIOLOGY – v1-6. 1981-84 – 1,5,6,13 – sz Elsevier [073]
MOLECULAR SIMULATION / ed by Quirke, N & Gunsteren, W F van – 9,5,1 – us Gordon [540]
MOLEKULARE PHYLOGENIE UND EVOLUTION DER GATTUNG ECHIUM L. (BORAGINACEAE) / Boehle, Uta-Regina – 1995 – 2mf – 9 – DM80.00 – 3-8267-2124-1 – gw Hänsel [574]
Molema, S M *see* [COLLECTION OF EPHEMERA RELATED TO THE AFRICAN NATIONAL CONGRESS AND DR. S.M. MOLEMA
Molen, S. van der *see* BAHASA INDONESIA; AN ELEMENTARY TEXTBOOK OF THE INDONESIAN LANGUAGE, ADAPTED FOR THE USE OF ENGLISH SPEAKING STUDENTS
Molenes, Emile de *see* TORQUEMADA ET L'INQUISITION
Moles, Juan B *see* MEMORIAL...SAN GABRIEL
Moleti, Giuseppe *see* TABULAE GREGORIANAE MOTUUM OCTAUAE SPHAERAE AC LUMINARIUM AD USUM CALENDARIJ ECCLESIASTICI
Moleva, N *see* PEDAGOGICHESKAIA SISTEMA AKADEMII KHUDOZHESTV 18 VEKA
Moley, Raymond *see*
- THE INITIATION OF CRIMINAL PROSECUTIONS BY INDICTMENT OR INFORMATION
- AN OUTLINE OF THE CLEVELAND CRIME SURVEY

Molher, Edmond *see* SUR L'AMELIORATION DU SORT DES TRAVAILLEURS. DE L'ASSOCIATION DES OUVRIERS. NECESSITE D'UNE NOUVELLE ENQUETE INDUSTRIELLE ET MODELES DE STATUTS POUR UNE CAISSE DE SECOURS ET DE RETRAITES
Moliere, Jean BP *see* THE MISANTHROPE OF MOLIERE; DONE INTO ENGLISH BY WILLIAM F. GIESE
LE MOLIERISTE – Revue mensuelle. Dir. Georges Monval. no. 1-120. Paris. avr 1879-mars 1889 – 5 – fr A.C.R.P.P. [073]
Molina Cano, Juan A *see* DESCUBRIMIENTOS GEOMETRICOS
Molina, G J *see* ESSAI SUR L'HISTOIRE NATURELLE DU CHILI
Molina, Gaspar de *see* CARTA PASTORAL...A TODOS LOS PRELADOS Y RELIGIOSOS DE DICHA PROVINCIA...
Molinaeus, Car. *see* OPERA OMNIA
Molinari, Gustave de *see*
- ENTRETIENS SUR LE LOIS ECONOMIQUE ET DEFENCE DE LA PROPRIETE
- QUESTIONS D'ECONOMIQUE POLITIQUE ET DE DROIT PUBLIQUE,II
- RELIGION

Molinie, Louis *see* REPONSE AUX OBSERVATIONS DE M. H.D. SUR L'APPEL AU PEUPLE DU SIEUR VIDAL
Molinier, Auguste *see*
- LES SOURCES DE L'HISTOIRE DE FRANCE
- THE THOUGHT OF BLAISE PASCAL

Molins, Antonio Elias de *see* CATALOGO DEL MUSAO PROVINCIAL DE ANTIGUEDADES DE BARCELONA
Molitor, R *see* AUS DER RECHTSGESCHICHTE BENEDIKTINISCHER VERBAENDE
Molitva Gospodnia *see* OTCHE NASH, NABRANNAIA SHRIFTAMI TIPOGRAFII I SLOVOLITNI IMP. KAZANSKAGO UNIVERSITETA
Molk, J *see* ELEMENTS DE LA THEORIE DES FONCTIONS ELLIPTIQUES
Molkenboer *see* NEDERLANDSCH KRUIDKUNDIG ARCHIEF
Molkenboer, J H *see*
- BRYOLOGIA JAVANICA...
- MUSCI FRONDOSI INEDITI ARCHIPELAGI INDICI...
- MUSCORUM FRONDOSORUM NOVAE SPECIES EX ARCHIPELAGO INDICO ET JAPONICA
- NOVAE FUNGORUM SPECIES IN BELGIO SEPTENTRIONALI

Moll, Albert *see* HYPNOTISM
Moll, Carl Bernhard *see*
- BRIEF AN DIE HEBRAEER
- DER BRIEF AN DIE HEBRAEER

Moll, KE von *see* NATURHISTORISCHE BRIEFE UEBER OESTREICH, SALZBURG, PASSAU UND BERCHTESGADEN
MOLLA HUSSEIN / Mioni, Ugo – Torino, 1933; Madrid: Razon y Fe, 1933 – 1 – sp Bibl Santa Ana [999]
Molland, E *see* CHRISTENDOM
Mollat, G *see* VITAE PAPARUM AVENIONENSIUM
MOLLER AND CAPRON'S MONTHLY – Nos. 1-3. MUSIC 123, Item 10 – 1 – us L of C Photodup [780]
Moller, Heinrich *see* ENARRATIONIS PSALMORUM DAVIDIS
Molleson, Stanley Holcomb *see* SUMMARY OF SALES OF PERSONAL PROPERTY
Mollet, Andre *see* LE JARDIN DE PLASIR
Molleur, J E *see* LE COURRIER DE SAINT-JEAN
Mollien, Gaspard T *see*
- TRAVELS IN THE INTERIOR OF AFRICA
- VOYAGE DANS L'INTERIEUR DE L'AFRIQUE AUX SOURCES DU SENEGAL ET DE LA GAMBIE

Mollot *see* LE CONTRAT D'APPRENTISSAGE EXPLIQUE AUX MAITRES ET AUX APPRENTIS, SELON LES LOIS, REGLEMENTS ET USAGES ET LA JURISPRUDENCE DES CONSEILS DE PRUD'HOMMES
MOLLUSCA AND CRUSTACEA OF THE MIOCENE FORMATIONS OF NEW JERSEY / Whitfield, R P – Z 871 2. 1894 – 8 – ne IDC [590]
THE MOLLUSCA OF PORTO RICO / Dall, W H & Simpson, CT – Z-165 2. 1900 – 8 – ne IDC [590]
THE MOLLUSCA OF SOMERSET (LAND, FRESHWATER, ESTUARINE AND MARINE) / Swanton, E W – Z 826 2. 1912 – 8 – ne IDC [590]
MOLLUSCORUM BORUSSICORUM SYNOPSIS / Kleeberg, J A G – Z-598 2. 1828 – 8 – ne IDC [590]
MOLLUSCORUM SPECIES QUAS IN ITINERE PER ORIENTEM FACTO COMITES / Roth, J R – Z 756 2. 1839 – 8 – ne IDC [590]
MOLLUSCORUM SYSTEMA ET CATALOGUS / Paetel, F – Z-694 2. 1869 – 8 – ne IDC [590]
MOLLUSKENFAUNA VON SCHLESIEN / Merkel, F – Z-652 2. 1894 – 8 – ne IDC [580]
MOLLUSQUE VECTEUR ET SCHISTOSOMOSE INTESTINALE EN GUADELOUPE / Pointier, J P – 9 – F70.00 – fr Ethnologie [590]
MOLLUSQUES / Orbigny, Alcide d' – 5707G 2. 2 v. 1853 – 8 – ne IDC [590]
LES MOLLUSQUES MARINS DU ROUSILLON / Bucquoy, E et al – Z-458 2. 2v. 1882-1898 – 8 – ne IDC [590]
MOLLUSQUES MEDITERRANEENS / Verany, J B – Pt. 1: Cephalopodes. Genes. Z 846 2. 1851 – 8 – ne IDC [590]
MOLNDALSPOSTEN – Molndal, Sweden. 1949-56 – 5r – 1 – sw Kungliga [072]
MOLNDALSPOSTEN – Molndal, Sweden. 1979- – 1 – sw Kungliga [072]
Molo, Walter Ritter von *see*
- IM SCHRITT DER JAHRHUNDERTE
- ITALIEN

MOLOCHNOE KHOZIAISTVO – (Missing: 1930 n20) – M., 1925-31 n12 – 82mf – 9 – COR-651/1 – ne IDC [334]
MOLOCHNYE TOVARICHESTVA MOSKOVSKOI GUB. V 1914 GODU / Fridolin, S P – M., 1916 – 2mf – 9 – COR-76/1 – ne IDC [334]
MOLODAIA GVARDIA – Moscow, 1956-73.Lacking: 1956 (1-6); 1960 (7); 1967 (11). BR-10,424/1 – 9 – ne IDC [073]
MOLODAIA ROSSIIA : KONETS RUSSKAGO PROGRAMA / Delevsky, J & Volin, A – Berlin: Izd-vo V. Sii alski i i A. Kre ishman, [1923?] – 1 – CSUX88-B7089 – us Hoover Inst Photo [947]
MOLODAYA GUARIDIYA – Moscow. U.S.S.R. -m. 1968- – 1 – us UMI [072]
MOLODEZH ESTONII – (Library has: no. 4426-8172 (Jan. 1, 1970-Dec. 31, 1983)[missing 39 issues; some issues slightly mutilated]) – Tallin: Izd-vo T Sentr. Kom-ta Kommunistichesko i partii Estonii, 1950- – 1 – CSUX86-S150 – us Hoover Inst Photo [947]
Molodkin, V B *see* PHYSICS OF METALS
MOLODO I RABOCHI I : EZHEDNEVNAI A GAZETA RABOCHE I MOLODEZHI–ORGAN SIBIRKRA IKOMA, NOVOSIBIRSKOGO OKRUZHKOMA VLKSM I KRA ISOVPROFA – (Includes c.1: 1930:Mar.4, 15-16, 18, 22, 25-26) – Novosibirsk: "Sovetskai a Sibir", 192u – 1 – CSUXANR9362-S – us Hoover Inst Photo [947]
MOLODOE SLOVO – (Library has: no. 12-20 (Oct. 1932-Nov. 1933), 28-29 (Oct.-Nov. 1936)) – Sofiia: "Molodoe slovo", 1931- – 1 – CSUX88-S496 – us Hoover Inst Photo [947]
MOLODOI KOMMUNIST – Moscow, 1939-72.Lacking: 1939 (1-9,13-18,21,23-24); 1940 (1-4,7); 1946 (1-12); 1948 (1-3,12); 1953 (3,6); 1958 (6). Suspended from Jul 1941 to Mar 1946. BR-10,425/1 – 9 – ne IDC [073]
MOLODOI KOMMUNIST – Moscow. Feb. 1939-Dec. 1960 gaps – 1 – 35.00r – us Hoover Inst Photo [073]
MOLODOST' / Khodasevich, V – Stikhi. 1907 goda. M. 1908. BR-696 2 – 8 – ne IDC [460]
MOLODYE OPRICHNIKI BUZHUAZII = YOUTHFUL MEMBERS OF THE BOURGEOIS OPRICHINA / Azarenko, A – Moscow, Leningrad, 1930.One of 13 titles by Soviet authors on reel – 1 – 74.32 – us Baptist [240]
MOLODYE PORYVY – Zhurnal literaturno-obshchestvenny i nachno-populiarnyi. nr. 1-8. Rostov na Donu. 1908-09. BR-4132 2 – 8 – ne IDC [073]
Molotsky, E J *see* RELATIONSHIPS AMONG AGE, COMPETITIVE STRUCTURE, AND MOTIVE STRUCTURES FOR ENGAGING IN REGULAR EXERCISE
Moltke, H *see* GROANLAND, ILL, SKILDRING AF DEN DANSKE LITERAERE GROANL. EXP
Moltke, Helmuth Carl Bernhard *see* GEDANKEN
Moltke, Helmuth Carl Bernhard von *see* PAPERS
Moltke, Helmuth Karl Bernhard von *see* QUESTIONS DE TACTIQUE APPLIQUEE TRAITEES DE 1858 A 1882 AU GRAND ETAT-MAJOR ALLEMAND: THEMES, SOLUTIONS ET CRITIQUES DU MARECHAL
MOLTKES VERMAECHTISS / Schlichting – Munich. DIE ALLGEMEINE ZEITUNG. 1901. 103 p. (Strategy of War Series) – 9 – fr Hachette [355]
MOLUCCAS SPEECHES OF PRESIDENT SOEKARNO / Soekarno – Djakarta, 1959 – 1mf – 9 – SE-1602/1 – ne IDC [320]
MOM, GUESS WHAT? – Sacramento, CA. 1978-1989 – 2r – 1 – $100.00 – B05056 – us Library Micro [071]
Mombert, Alfred *see* DER HIMMLISCHE ZECHER
DER MOMENT – (Missing: Many vols) – Warsaw. v1-30. 1910-1938; Evening Supplement. v1-11. 1914-1924; Radio Supplement. v1-3. 192?-1926 – 62r – 1 – J-92-25/3 – ne IDC [072]
DER MOMENT = MORNING ISSUE – (Yiddish daily) – Warsaw, PL. v23 no241 10 Oct 1932-v23 no243 20 Oct 1932; v26 no142A 21 Jun 1935-v26 no 298A 25 Dec 1935; & 1910/1935 Jubilee Issue (25th Anniversary) – 1r – 1 – $35.00 – cn Can Microfilming [072]
MOMENT – v. 1-. 1975- – 1,5,6,9 – us UMI [290]
MOMENTI DI CULTURA TEDESCA / Bonfatti, E et al – (Includes bibliographical references and index) – Cremona: Libreria del Convegno, 1973 – 1r – 1 – us U.W. Library [430]
MOMENTO – (In Italian) – Philadelphia, PA. 1917-19 – 1r – 1 – $85.00 – D3372 – us Scholarly Res [071]
O MOMENTO – Diamantina, 7 Sept 1922; Jan, Dec 1923; 12 Apr 1925 – 1,5,6 – bl Biblioteca [072]
O MOMENTO – Januaria, Brazil. Aug 1927 – 1 – bl Biblioteca [072]
O MOMENTO – Maceio, Alagoas. 4 Jul 1893; 27 Jun 1894 – 1,5,6 – bl Biblioteca [072]
O MOMENTO : PROPUGNADOR PELOS INTERESSES DO MUNICIPIO – Conselheiro Pena, 6 Apr 1941 – 1,5,6 – bl Biblioteca [072]
MOMENTO SERA – 1991-1995 – 2r per y – 5,6 – Sfr936.00 – sz Infoprint [945]
LOS MOMENTOS DE LA RAZA : ROMANCES / Sanchez-Arjona, Vicente – Sevilla: Imp. Carlos Acuna, Tomo 2. 1942 – 1 – sp Bibl Santa Ana [810]
LOS MOMENTOS DE LA RAZA : ROMANCES / Sanchez-Arjona, Vicente – Sevilla: Imp. Carlos Acuna, Tomo 3. 1941 – 1 – sp Bibl Santa Ana [810]
MOMENTS OF VISION AND MISCELLANEOUS VERSES / Hardy, Thomas – London: Macmillan, 1917 – 1 roll – 1 – 1-55879-786-6 – uk Libr Preservation [810]
MOMENTS ON THE MOUNT : A SERIES OF DEVOTIONAL MEDITATIONS / Matheson, George – 2nd ed. New York: A C Armstrong, [1884?] – 1mf – 9 – 0-8370-7167-4 – 1986-1167 – us A.T.L.A. [240]
MOMENTUM – v1- 1970- 1; v3- 5,6; v7- 9 – us UMI [073]
Momerie, Alfred Williams *see*
- AGNOSTICISM: SERMONS
- BASIS OF RELIGION
- THE RELIGION OF THE FUTURE AND OTHER ESSAYS

MOM...GUESS WHAT – v1- 1978- Sacramento: Linda D. Birner, 1978-. -m – 1 – us U.W. Library [640]
Momigliano, A *see* THE CONFLICT BETWEEN PAGANISM AND CHRISTIANITY IN THE FOURTH CENTURY
Momigny, J-J *see* TROIS QUATUORS, OP.1
Mommert, Carl *see*
- MENSCHENOPFER BEI DEN ALTEN HEBRAEERN
- ZUR CHRONOLOGIE DES LEBENS JESU

Mommsen, Theodor *see*
- CASSIODORIS SENATORIS VARIAE (MGH 1: 12.BD)
- CHRONICA MINORA SAEC. 4, 5, 6, 7 (MGH 1: 11.BD)
- CHRONICA MINORA SAEC. 4, 5, 6, 7 (MGH 1: 13.BD)
- CHRONICA MINORA SAEC. 4, 5, 6,7 (MGH 1: 9.BD)
- GESAMMELTE SCHRIFTEN
- IORDANIS ROMANA ET GETICA (MGH 1: 5.BD. 1.TEIL)
- ITALIENISCHE ANALEKTEN ZUR REICHSGESCHICHTE DES 14. JAHRHUNDERTS (1310-1378) (MGH SCHRIFTEN..: 11.BD)
- LIBER PONTIFICALIS, PARS PRIOR (MGH 4: 1.BD)
- THE PROVINCES OF THE ROMAN EMPIRE FROM CAESAR TO DIOCLETIAN

IL MOMO – Philadelphia, PA. 1922 – us I.H.R.C. [073]
MOMO AND I / Hives, Frank – London: J Kane, 1934 – us Res Libr [920]
MON DROIT – Journal independant, paraissant le samedi. Satirique, politique, litteraire, illustre. no. 1-13, 17-19. Paris. 4 mars-15 juil 1899 – 1 – fr A.C.R.P.P. [073]
MON JOURNAL – Ville des Laurentides (St-Lin). v1 n1. aut 1979-24 dec 1988f – 1r – 1 – Can$60.00 – cn Can Microfilming [072]
MON JOURNAL DE BORD D'ANVERS A LEOPOLDVILLE PAR LE CHEMIN DES ECOLIERS / Monthaye – Paris: J Briguet, 1899 – us Res Libr [910]
MON JOURNAL DE CHAMBLY – Chambly. v20-22. 1987-1989. SEM35P290 – 4r – 1 – Can$252.00 – cn Bibl Nat [971]
MON JOURNAL DE VOYAGE EN RUSSIE / Frossard, LO – Articles parus dans l'Internationale entre. nov 1921 et janv 1922 – 1 – fr A.C.R.P.P. [910]
MON MAGAZIN / ed by Fortin, Edouard – Montreal. v1 n2. fev 1926-v5 n1. avr 1930 – 1r – 1 – Can$45.00 – cn Can Microfilming [072]
MON ROMAN AU NIGER : ROMAN D'AVENTURES / Nielle, Henri – Paris: C Offenstadt, 1902 – us Res Libr [910]

MON SEJOUR AUPRES DE VOLTAIRE ET LETTRES INEDITES QUE M'ECRIVIT CET HOMME CELEBRE JUSQU'A LA DERNIERE ANNEE DE SA VIE / Collini, Alexandre – Paris. L. Collin. 1807. XVI – 9 – fr Hachette [920]
MON VIEUX REAL : JOURNAL DES ETUDIANTS DU CEGEP DU VIEUX-MONTREAL – Montreal. v2- 1980-. SEM35P227 – 1 – Can$34.00 – cn Bibl Nat [910]
MON VOYAGE AU SOUDAN FRANCAIS / Petit, Andre – Paris: E LaRose, 1922 – us Res Libr [910]
LE MONACHISME CLUNISIEN DES ORIGINES AU 15E SIECLE / Valous, G de – Tome 1: L'Abbaye de Cluny. Les Monasteres Clunisiens, 1935 – Dfl35.00 – ne Slangenburg [240]
LE MONACHISME CLUNISIEN DES ORIGINES AU 15E SIECLE / Valous, G de – Tome 2: L'Ordre de Cluny, 1935 – Dfl28.00 – ne Slangenburg [240]
LE MONACHISME EN SAINTONGE ET EN AUNIS. (11 ET 12 SIECLES) / Bruhat, L – La Rochelle, 1907 – 8mf – 8 – Dfl30.00 – ne Slangenburg [240]
MONACHISME LAIQUE / Lemercier, G – s.l., 1959 – 1mf – 8 – Dfl6.00 – ne Slangenburg [240]
LE MONACO – Paris, France. -w. 20 Jan 1887-5 Jan 1893. 2 reels – 1 – uk British Libr Newspaper [072]
Monaco, Prince de *see* DU PAUPERISME EN FRANCE ET DES MOYENS DE LE DETRUITE
MONADELPHIAE CLASSIS DISSERTATIONES DECEM / Cavanilles, A J – Paris, Madrid. 1785-90 – 30mf – 9 – ne IDC [580]
LA MONADOLOGIE / Leibniz, Gottfried Wilhelm von – Paris: G. Bailliere, 1881. 245p. 3 fiches. (Philosophy Collection) – 9 – 8.00 – fr Bibl Nationale [190]
Monageng, Stella B *see*
– DEVINDEX BOTSWANA
Monaghan, James *see* THE LIQUOR LICENSE LAWS OF 1887.
Monaghan, James Patrick *see* A COMPLETE LEGAL ADVERTISING FORM BOOK.
MONAGHAN'S REPORTS : UNREPORTED / Pennsylvania. Superior Court – (A Pre-NRS title) – v1-2. 1888-90 (all publ) – 18mf – 9 – $27.00 – LLMC 84-204 – us L.L.M.C. [340]
MONANDRIAN PLANTS OF ORDER SCITAMINEAE, CHIEFLY DRAWN FROM LIVING SPECIMENS IN THE BOTANIC GARDEN AT LIVERPOOL / Roscoe, W – Liverpool. 1824-1828-29. B-5688 2 – 8 – ne IDC [580]
MONARCH NOTES – (Biographical, critical, bibliographical notes on literature) – 229mf – 9 – $675.00 – us UMI [410]
THE MONARCH OF MINCING LANE: A NOVEL / Black, William – British Fiction Archive: Unit 4 – 9 – uk Bell [830]
MONARCH TRIBUNE – Monarch, NV. 25 Aug 1906 – 1r – 1 – $50.00 – U04629 – us Library Micro [071]
MONARCHIANISCHE PROLOGE ZU DEN VIER EVANGELIEN (T.U.U. 1-15/1) / Corssen, P – Leipzig, 1896 – 3mf – 9 – ne Slangenburg [240]
Monardes, N *see* IOYFULL NEWES OUT OF THE NEW FOUND WORLD
LA MONARQUIA TRADICIONAL / Elias de Tejada Spinola, Francisco – Madrid: Ediciones Rialp S.A., 1954 – sp Bibl Santa Ana [946]
LA MONARQUIA Y LA RELIGION TRIUNFANTES DE LOS SOFISMAS / Amado, Manuel – 1829 – 9 – 1.50f – sp Bibl Santa Ana [240]
MONA'S HERALD – Isle of Man. 1833-1918 – 1 – uk Microform Academic [072]
MONASH UNIVERSITY LAW REVIEW – v1-18. 1975-1992 – 9 – us Hein [340]
Monash University Library. South-East Asia Pamphlet Collection *see* GRAVEL AND GOLD DUST
LES MONASTERES DU DIOCESE DE GRENOBLE A L'EPOQUE MEROVINGIENNE : SAINT-LAURENT DE GRENOBLE ET NOTRE-DAME DE VIZILLE / David, P – Grenoble, 1930 – Dfl6.00 – ne Slangenburg [240]
MONASTERIES AND RELIGIOUS HOUSES OF GREAT BRITAIN AND IRELAND : WITH AN APPENDIX ON THE RELIGIOUS HOUSES IN AMERICA / Steele, Francesca Maria – London: R & T Washbourne; New York: Benziger, 1903 – 1mf – 9 – 0-8370-7021-X – 1986-1021 – us A.T.L.A. [240]
THE MONASTERIES OF THE WADI'N NATRUN / White, Evelyn H G – New York, 1926-1933. 3v – 83mf – 8 – ne Slangenburg [240]
EL MONASTERIO DE GUADALUPE – 1917 – 5 – sp Bibl Santa Ana [073]
EL MONASTERIO DE GUADALUPE / Callejo, Carlos – Madrid: Editorial Plus Ultra, 1958 – 1 – sp Bibl Santa Ana [720]
EL MONASTERIO DE GUADALUPE – Madrid, 1918 – 5 – sp Bibl Santa Ana [240]
EL MONASTERIO DE GUADALUPE – Madrid, 1927 y 1930-1932 – 5 – sp Bibl Santa Ana [073]
EL MONASTERIO DE GUADALUPE / Puyol, Julio – Madrid: Tip. Rev. Archivos, Bibliotecas y Museos, 1927. B.R.A.H. 91, pp. 5-10 – sp Bibl Santa Ana [240]
MONASTERIO DE GUADALUPE / Puyol, Julio – Madrid: Tip La Revista de Archiv.y Biblioteca y Museos, 1927 – 1 – sp Bibl Santa Ana [240]
MONASTERIO DE GUADALUPE, EL – Revista. Ano 1. 1916 – 1 – sp Bibl Santa Ana [240]
EL MONASTERIO DE YUSTE Y LA RETIRADA DEL EMPERADOR CARLOS 5. JARAIZ DE LA VERA / Siguenza, Jose de et al – Imp. La Verata, 1975 – 1 – sp Bibl Santa Ana [240]
Monasterio, Rita A *see* POSTURAL ADJUSTMENT FOR VOLUNTARY LEG MOVEMENT IN DANCERS
MONASTERIOLOGIAE REGNI HUNGARIAE / Fuxhoffer, D, OSB & Czin r, M, OSB – (Tom. 1: Monasteria Ord. S. Benedicti Dfl42.00. Tom. 2: Sacrae Domus Canonicorum Regularium, Cisterciensium, Ordinum Equestrium et Eremitarum August. Dfl30.00) – Vindobonae, 1869 – ne Slangenburg [240]
MONASTERIOS DE JARANDILLA / Soria Sanchez, Valentin – Badajoz: Diputacion Provincial de Badajoz, 1976 – sp Bibl Santa Ana [946]
THE MONASTERY OF EPIPHANIUS AT THEBES / Winlock, H E & Crum, W E – New York. v1-2. 1936 – 46mf – 8 – Dfl161.00 – ne Slangenburg [240]
THE MONASTIC BREVIARY OF HYDE ABBEY / Tolhurst, J B L – (Vol 1.-4mf; Vol 2.-3mf; Vol 3.-2mf) – 1932-1934 – 8 – ne Slangenburg [240]
THE MONASTIC BREVIARY OF HYDE ABBEY, WINCHESTER, VOL 3, 4, 6 / Toletus, Franciscus – 1939, 1939, 1942 – 13mf – 8 – ne Slangenburg [240]
MONASTIC LIFE AT CLUNY, 910-1157 / Evans, J – London, 1931 – Dfl22.00 – ne Slangenburg [240]
THE MONASTIC ORDINALE OF ST VEDAST'S ABBEY ARRAS / Brou, L – 1957. 2v – 7mf – 8 – ne Slangenburg [240]
MONASTIC RULES IN MEROVINGIAN GAUL / O'Caroll, J – s.l., 1955 – 1mf – 8 – Dfl6.00 – ne Slangenburg [240]
MONASTIC STUDIES – 1963- 1; 1973- 5,6; 1976- 4 x 6 in. 9 – us UMI [073]
MONASTICISM = MOENCHTUM : ITS IDEALS AND HISTORY; AND, THE CONFESSIONS OF ST. AUGUSTINE / Harnack, Adolf von – London: Williams & Norgate, 1913 – 1mf – 9 – 0-8370-9478-X – 1986-3478 – us A.T.L.A. [240]
MONASTICISM, ANCIENT AND MODERN : ITS PRINCIPLES, ORIGIN, DEVELOPMENT, TRIUMPHS, DECADENCE AND SUPPRESSION: WITH AN ENQUIRY AS TO THE POSSIBILITY OF ITS REVIVAL / Woodhouse, F C – London: Gardner, Darton, 1896 – 1mf – us A.T.L.A. [240]
MONASTICON ANGLICANUM / ed by Caley, J & Ellis, H & Bandinel, B – London. 1846. 6v. Lacking: v3 – 233mf – 8 – ne IDC [073]
MONASTICON ANGLICANUM – New ed. London. v1-8. 1817-30 – 255mf – 8 – Dfl893.00 – ne Slangenburg [240]
MONASTICON AUGUSTINIANUM / Crusenius, N O E S A – 1361 2. 1623 – 8 – ne IDC [240]
MONASTICON DIOCOECIS EXONIENSIS : COUNTIES OF CORNWALL AND DEVON / Oliver, G – Exeter/London, 1846 – Dfl84.00 – ne Slangenburg [240]
MONASTICON GALLICANUM / Germain, Dom Michel OSB – Paris: M. Peigne-Delacourt, 1871 – Dfl60.00 – ne Slangenburg [240]
Monastier, Antoine *see* HISTOIRE DE L'EGLISE VAUDOISE
DER MONAT : BLAETTER FUER KRITIK UND AUFBAU – Paris. Apr-Jun 1936 – 1r – 1 – gw Mikrofilm [072]
DER MONAT MARIAE / Weninger, Francis Xavier – Cincinnati: Hermann Lehmann, 1850 – 1mf – 9 – 0-8370-6861-4 – 1986-0861 – us A.T.L.A. [240]
MONATLICHE BEITRAEGE ZUR NATURKUNDE – Berlin, 1752 – 3 – us Readex [574]
DER MONATLICHE BOTSCHAFTER – Bremen, n.d. [1872-93], n9-14, 16, 73-76, 99-100, 113, 121-129 – 1r – 1 – Inquire at Mikrofilmarchiv for details – gw Misc Inst [072]
MONATLICHE UNTERREDUNGEN EINIGER GUTEN FREUNDE VON ALLERHAND BUECHERN UND ANDERN ANNEHMLICHEN GESCHICHTEN / ed by Tentzel, Wilhelm Ernst – Leipzig. v1-10. 1689-1698 (mf ed 1993) – 46mf – 9 – DM1,100.00 – 3-89131-086-2 – gw Fischer [073]
MONATLICHER AUSZUG AUS ALLERHAND NEU HERAUSGEGEBENEN NUETZLICHEN UND ARTIGEN BUECHERN / ed by Eckhard, J G – Hannover. Teil1-3. 1700-1702 (mf ed 1993) – 36mf – 9 – DM380.00 – 3-89131-090-0 – gw Fischer [943]
MONATLICHER STAATS-SPIEGEL – Augsburg, may-sep 1698 – 1 – Dist. gw Mikrofilm – gw Misc Inst [943]
MONATSBERICHTE / Akademie der Wissenschaften. Berlin – 26v 1856-81 – 1 – us Schnase [500]
MONATSBLAETTER / Gesellschaft fuer Pommersche Geschichte, Altertumskunde und kunst – Stettin. v. 1-55, n. 1 3. 1887-1941. Includes Register, 1887-1906. Film Mas C 727 – 1 – us H.U. Library [073]
MONATSBLAETTER FUER DEUTSCHE LITTERATUR – (Available: v6 1901-1902; v9-10(1-9) 1904-1905) – Berlin – 31mf – 9 – ne IDC [430]
MONATSBLATT DER NORDDEUTSCHEN MISSIONSGESELLSCHAFT – Bremen, Germany. Mar 1851-Feb 1864; 1873; 1883-1887; 1891-Jun 1941 – 7r – 1 – gw Mikrofilm [073]
MONATSBLATT DER NORDDEUTSCHEN MISSIONSGESELLSCHAFT – (Partly with suppl and table of contents) – Bremen, mar 1851-feb 1864, 1873, 1883-87, 1891-jun 1941 – 7r – 1 – Inquire at Mikrofilmarchiv for details – gw Misc Inst [240]
MONATSCHRIFT FUER LITURGIE UND KIRCHENMUSIK – v1-45. 1876-1920 – 4r – 1 – us Ross [780]
DIE MONATSFEIER / ed by Schweitzer, Albert – Berlin. apr, may 1919 – 1 – gw Mikrofilm [073]
MONATSGESPRAECHE / ed by Thomasius, Christian – Halle, 1688-90. Hildesheim, 1979 – 46mf – 9 – DM350.00 diazo DM410.00 silver – gw Olms [430]
MONATSHEFTE: A JOURNAL DEVOTED TO THE STUDY OF GERMAN LANGUAGE AND LITERATURE – v1- 1899- 1; v63- 5,6; v69- 9 – us UMI [430]
MONATSHEFTE FUER CHEMIE – v. 1-74. 1880-1943 – 1 – us UMI [540]
MONATSHEFTE FUER CHEMIE – v.76-112. 1946-81. ISSN: 0026-9247 – 1,5,6,9,13 – 370.00v – us UMI [073]
MONATSHEFTE FUER CHEMIE UND VERWANDTE TEILE ANDERER WISSENSCHAFTEN – v1-86. 1880-1955 – 1,5,6 – us Princeton Micro [540]
MONATSHEFTE FUER DEUTSCHEN UNTERRICHT, DEUTSCHE SPRACHE UND LITERATUR – v. 1-32. 1899-1940 – 1 – us Princeton Micro [430]
MONATSHEFTE FUER KUNSTWISSENSCHAFT – Leipzig, 1908-1922 – 175mf – 9 – ne IDC [700]
MONATSHEFTE FUER MATHEMATIK – v. 1-45. 1890-1937 – 1,5,6 – us Princeton Micro [510]
MONATSHEFTE FUER MATHEMATIK – v.52-92, 1948-81. ISSN: 0026-9255 – 1,5,6,9,13 – 123.00v – us UMI [073]
MONATSHEFTE FUER MUSIK-GESCHICHTE / Gesellschaft fuer Musikforschung – (Beilagen, 1871; 1872; 1874; 1975; 1877; 1890; 1892; 1896-1898. Index 1869-1898) – Berlin, Leipzig, 1869-1905 – 118mf – 9 – ne IDC [780]
MONATSHEFTE FUER MUSIKGESCHICHTE (EITNER) – Supplements (33) – 1 – us Schnase [780]
MONATSSCHRIFT DES VEREINES ZUR BEFOERDERUNG DES GARTENBAUES... – Berlin. 9v. 1873-1881 – 62mf – 9 – ne IDC [710]
MONATSSCHRIFT F. KINDERHEILKUNDE – v. 96-128. 1948-80 – 1,5,9 – 3341.00 – us UMI [618]
MONATSSCHRIFT FUER DIE GESCHICHTE WESTDEUTSCHLANDS – Trier. Jahrg. 5-7; 1878-81. "Hrsg. von Richard Pick." Continues Monatsschrift fuer rheinisch-wesfaelische Geschichtsforschung und Alterthumskunde. Film Mas C 720 – 1 – us H.U. Library [073]
MONATSSCHRIFT FUER GESCHICHTE UND WISSENSCHAFT DES JUDENTHUMS / ed by Frankel, Zacharias et al – Dresden, Leipzig, Berlin, Breslau, 1851-1938. v46-82. Hildesheim, 1982 – 232mf – 9 – DM1,700.00 diazo DM2,100.00 silver – gw Olms [270]
MONATSSCHRIFT FUER GESCHICHTE UND WISSENSCHAFT DES JUDENTHUMS – Red. Prof. Dr. H. Graetz. Krotoschin. 1861-67, 1873-86 – 1 – fr A.C.R.P.P. [073]
MONATSSCHRIFT FUER GESCHICHTE UND WISSENSCHAFT DES JUDENTHUMS – v1-83. 1851-1939 (complete) – 21r – 1 – ATLA S0066 – us A.T.L.A. [270]
MONATSSCHRIFT FUER GESCHICHTE UND WISSENSCHAFT DES JUDENTUMS – Dresden, Leipzig, Breslau, Frankfurt a.M. 1852-1934. v1-78. – 521mf – 9 – ne IDC [073]
MONATSSCHRIFT FUER GOTTESDIENST UND KIRCHLICHE KUNST – v. 1-46. no. 5 6. 1896-1941 – 1 – us Schnase [780]
MONATSSCHRIFT FUER KAKTEENKUNDE – Berlin. v1-30. 1891-1920 – 100mf – 9 – ne IDC [580]
MONATSSCHRIFT FUER THEATER UND MUSIK – Wien. v1-11. 1855-1865 – 108mf – 9 – ne IDC [790]
Monceaux, P *see* HISTOIRE LITTERAIRE DE L'AFRIQUE CHRETIENNE DEPUIS LES ORIGINES JUSQU'A L'INVASION ARABE
Moncreiff, Henry Wellwood *see*
– CREEDS AND CHURCHES IN SCOTLAND
– THE FREE CHURCH PRINCIPLE
– HISTORY OF THE CASE OF PROFESSOR W. ROBERTSON SMITH
– A VINDICATION OF THE FREE CHURCH CLAIM OF RIGHT
Moncreiff, James Moncreiff *see* ADDRESSES ON THE ART OF PLEADING, DELIVERED TO THE GLASGOW LEGAL AND SPECULATIVE SOCIETY ON SEPTEMBER 29, 1860
Mond, R *see*
– THE BUCHEUM (MEES VOL 41, 2)
– THE BUCHEUM (MEES VOL 41, 3)
– THE BUCHEUM (MEES VOL 41,1)
Mondain, G *see* RAKETAKA
MONDAY BUDGET – Virginia City, NV. 1917-18; 1927-29 – 3r – 1 – $150.00 – UC04793 – us Library Micro [071]
Monday, Henry A *see* COLLECTION
MONDAY MORNING – v1-57. 1936-92 (complete) – Inquire – 1 – ATLA S0784 – us A.T.L.A. [073]
MONDAY REPUBLICAN *see* THE REPUBLICAN
LE MONDE – Dir. Eugene Taconet. Ed. semi-quotidienne. Paris. 1869-7 dec 1871 – 1 – fr A.C.R.P.P. [073]
LE MONDE – Dir. F.L. Pistor puis Lamennais. no. 1-165 avec un prosp. d'oct 1836. Paris. 16 nov 1836-30 avr 1837. mq no. 3-4 – 1 – fr A.C.R.P.P. [073]
LE MONDE – Paris. Dir., Eugene Taconet. 18 fevr 1860-mai 1865, 1866-67, juil 1868-30 sept 1870, 9 mars 1871-27 juil 1896 – 1 – fr A.C.R.P.P. [073]
LE MONDE – Paris, France. 1944- . Index available, 1944-51, 1965-68, 1987- – 1 – us Primary [072]
LE MONDE – Paris. v1 n1. 18 fev 1860-v1 n159. 30 dec 1860 – 1r – 1 – Can$35.00 – cn Can Microfilming [072]
LE MONDE *see* LE NOUVEAU MONDE
MONDE – 1 – F4,016.00 – sz Infoprint [072]
MONDE – 1944-1945 – 1 – F1,659.00 – sz Infoprint [072]
MONDE – 1946-1948 – 1 – F1,659.00 – sz Infoprint [072]
MONDE – 1949-1953 – 1 – F2,270.00 – sz Infoprint [072]
MONDE – 1954-1965 – 1 – F2,925.00 – sz Infoprint [072]
MONDE – 1966-1994 – 1 – F5,326.00 – sz Infoprint [072]

MONDE – Hebdomadaire d'information litteraire, artistique, scientifique, economique et sociale puis Hebdomadaire international. Dir. H. Barbusse. no. 1-353. Paris. juin 1928-oct 1935 – 1 – fr A.C.R.P.P. [073]
LE MONDE CANADIEN *see* LE NOUVEAU MONDE
LE MONDE DE DESCARTES : SITUATION ET ENJEUX DE LA FABLE DU MONDE / Cavaille, Jean Pierre – 2mf – 9 – 10061 – fr Atelier National [190]
MONDE DE LA REVOLUTION – 1 – F611.00 – sz Infoprint [072]
LE MONDE DE L'EDUCATION – Paris. France. 1974- – 1 – us Primary [072]
MONDE DE L'EDUCATION – 1 – F655.00 – sz Infoprint [072]
MONDE DE L'EDUCATION – 1974-1994 – 6,1 – F786.00 – sz Infoprint [072]
LE MONDE DE L'ESPRIT – DIE GEISTIGE WELT / Dilthey, Wilhelm – Trans. by M. Remy. Paris: Aubier, 1947. 2v – 1 – us U.W. Library [190]
LE MONDE DES AFFAIRES : BI-MENSUEL / ed by Peladeau, Pierre – Montreal, Canada. 20 jun 1966-v1 n12. 1 mai 1967 – 1r – 1 – Can$40.00 – cn Can Microfilming [072]
LE MONDE DIPLOMATIQUE – Paris. France. 1954- – 1 – us Primary [944]
LE MONDE DIPLOMATIQUE – (Paris): Le Monde. -m. May 1954- – 1 – us U.W. Library [327]
MONDE DIPLOMATIQUE – 1 – F698.00 – sz Infoprint [072]
MONDE DIPLOMATIQUE – 1954-1976 – Cumul – 1 – F6,810.00 – sz Infoprint [072]
MONDE DIPLOMATIQUE – 1977-1993 – 1 – F786.00 – sz Infoprint [072]
MONDE DOSSIERS AND DOCUMENTS – 1972-1977 – 9 – F1,353.00 – sz Infoprint [072]
LE MONDE DOSSIERS ET DOCUMENTS – Paris, France. 1972- – 9 – us Primary [944]
MONDE DOSSIERS ET DOCUMENTS – 9 – F1,004.00 – sz Infoprint [072]
MONDE DOSSIERS ET DOCUMENTS – 1978-1982 – 9 – F1,353.00 – sz Infoprint [072]
MONDE DOSSIERS ET DOCUMENTS – 1981-1982 – 9 – F1,353.00 – sz Infoprint [072]
MONDE DOSSIERS ET DOCUMENTS – 1983-1985 – 9 – F1,091.00 – sz Infoprint [072]
MONDE DOSSIERS ET DOCUMENTS – 1986-1990 – 9 – F742.00 – sz Infoprint [072]
MONDE DOSSIERS ET DOCUMENTS – 1991-1993 – 9 – F1,091.00 – sz Infoprint [072]
LE MONDE DRAMATIQUE – Revue des spectacles anciens et modernes. Paris. 1835-16 sept 1841 – 1 – fr A.C.R.P.P. [073]
LE MONDE ILLUSTRE – Journal Hebdomadaire. Paris. Dir., Pointel. 1867-69 – 1 – fr A.C.R.P.P. [073]
LE MONDE ILLUSTRE – Montreal, Canada. 10 mai 1884-12 avr 1902 – 9r – 1 – Can$60.00r – cn Can Microfilming [072]
LE MONDE ILLUSTRE – Paris. Annee 1-54. 1857-1910 – 1 – 799.00 – us L of C Photodup [073]
LE MONDE INFORMATIQUE – (1985-. 5,6,9) – 1981- – 1 – us UMI [510]
LE MONDE LITTERAIRE – Revue de la semaine. Litterature, beaux-arts, sciences, arts industriels. Red. en chef Hippolyte Babou. no. 1-6. Paris. 20 mars-24 avr 1858 – 1 – fr A.C.R.P.P. [073]
LE MONDE NOUVEAU – Revue mensuelle interalliee et internationale puis Revue de culture, de documentation et d'information internationales. Paris. mars 1919-juin 1932, 1934 – 1 – fr A.C.R.P.P. [073]
LE MONDE OUVRIER = THE LABOR WORLD – Montreal, Canada. 18 mar 1916-dec 1991 – 9r – 1 – Can$70.00r – cn Can Microfilming [072]
LE MONDE POETIQUE – Revue de poesie universelle. Paris. juin 1884-aout 1889 – 1 – fr A.C.R.P.P. [073]
LE MONDE PROFESSIONNEL – Montreal, Canada. v2 n16. 23 sep 1964 – 1r – 1 – Can$25.00 – cn Can Microfilming [073]
LE MONDE REPUBLICAIN – no. 1-86. Paris. 1er avr-25 juin 1848. mq no. 72, 85. Les no. 1-4: Le Monde de 1848 – 1 – fr A.C.R.P.P. [073]
LE MONDE RUSSE ET LA REVOLUTION, MEMOIRES / Herzen, Aleksandr I – (Russia – 19th C. series).m 1860-1862 – 9 – fr Hachette [947]
LE MONDE SLAVE – (Missing: 1919-1923; 1933(4)) – Paris, 1917-1938 – 483mf – 9 – ne IDC [947]
MONDO – 1976-1995 – 2r per y – 5,6 – Sfr615.00 – sz Infoprint [072]
MONDO ECONOMICO – 1987-1995 – 2 times per yr – 6 – F2,300.00 – sz Infoprint [072]
MONDO OPERAIO – 1987-1995 – 1r per y – 5,6 – Sfr401.00 – sz Infoprint [790]
Mondragones, Pio Ma. de *see* MANUAL DE MISIONOLOGIA. VITORIA, 1933
DIE MONDZUEGLER : EINE KOMOEDIE DER GEGENWART / Hoffmann, Heinrich – Frankfurt (Main): Jaeger, 1843 – 1 – us U.W. Library [820]
LA MONEDA EMERITENSE / Rey Trujillo, G del – Madrid: Editorial Dossat, S.A., 1962 – 1 – sp Bibl Santa Ana [730]
Monell, Claudius L *see* A TREATISE ON THE PRACTICE OF THE COURTS OF THE STATE OF NEW YORK.
Monesterio *see* ROMERIA DE SAN ISIDRO EN VENTAS DE CULEBRIN. 1971
Monet, P *see* INVANTAIRE DES DEUS LANGUES, FRANCOISE ET LATINE
MONETARY ASPECTS OF INDONESIA'S ECONOMIC REORGANIZATION IN 1959 / Anspach, Ralph – SE-3431 1. 1960 – 9 – ne IDC [332]
MONETARY TIMES – Toronto, Canada. 1867-1929 – 61r – 1 – $3,965.00 – cn Library Assoc [971]
MONETARY TIMES – Toronto, Canada. May 1955-Dec 1960.-m. 6 reels – 1 – uk British Libr Newspaper [072]
MONETARY TIMES – v59-136. 1917-1968 – 1 – cn Precision [332]
LE MONETE DEI PAPI DESCRITTE IN TAVOLLE SINOTTICHE / Cinagli, Ang. – Fermo, 1848 – Dfl74.00 – ne Slangenburg [240]
MONEY – 1- 1972- – 1,5,6,9 – us UMI [073]
MONEY. A JOURNAL OF BUSINESS AND FINANCE – London, UK. 17 Feb, 31 Mar, 26 May, 15 Sept 1906. -irr. 10 feet – 1 – uk British Libr Newspaper [073]
MONEY AND CREDIT – 1972- 1; 1975- 5,6,9 – us UMI [073]
MONEY AND PAPER CURRENCY: A STUDY FOR THE TIMES / Casey, George Elliott – Ottawa?: Maclean, Roger, 1880. 00510. (Pre-1900 Canadiana) – 9 – cn C.I.H.M. [332]
MONEY AND RISKS – Toronto: Money and Risks Print and Pub. Co, [1894?-189- or 19–] – 9 – cn C.I.H.M. [332]
MONEY AND THE MONEY QUESTION IN CANADA: AND SOME CONSIDERATIONS ARISING THEREFROM / Husbandman – Toronto: Hunter, Rose, 1897. 02748. (Pre-1900 Canadiana) – 9 – cn C.I.H.M. [336]
MONEY DIGEST – (Numbering starts with v5 1990) – Toronto, 1986-94 – 9 – Can$20.00y – cn Micromedia [332]
MONEY MAKER – v.1-. 1979- – 1,5,6,9 – us UMI [380]
MONEY OBSERVER, 1979-1993 – 148mf – 9 – uk Microform Academic [332]
THE MONEY QUESTION / Kitson, Arthur – Also: not worth a continental, xby P. Webster; the case for political and economic tolerance by Beckerath Zube. 3 fiches – 9 – 1.00f – at Libertarian Micro [320]
Money, Sharon M *see* BIOMECHANICAL COMPARISON OF SUPPORT PROVIDED BY THE AIRSTIRRUP ANKLE TRAINING BRACE™ PRE- AND POST-EXERCISE
MONEYSWORTH – v1- 1970- 1; v9- 5,6,9 – us UMI [073]
MONEYSWORTH – NY City, NY. 1970-1972 – 1r – 1 – $50.00 – R04927 – us Library Micro [071]
Monfalcon, J B *see* HISTOIRE DES ENFANTS TROUVES, NOUVELLE EDITION REVUE ET AUGMENTEE
EL MONGE DEL MONASTERIO DE YUSTE (ULTIMOS DIAS DEL EMPERADOR CARLOS 5) / Herrero, Leandro – Madrid: Apostolado de la Prensa, 1911 – 1 – sp Bibl Santa Ana [240]
Monge, Gaspard *see* DESCRIPTION DE L'ART DE FABRIQUER LES CANONS
MONGGO HAN SAI DA SEKIYEN / Haenisch, E – Die Mandschufassung von Secen Sagang's Mongolischer Geschichte. Leipzig. 1933. BU-491 2 – 8 – ne IDC [950]
MONGHYR SAMACHAR – Monghyr, India. Apr 1944-1947; 1949 – 1r – 1 – us L of C Photodup [072]
Mongolfier-Kouevi, C de *see* TENDANCES ET PERSPECTIVES DE L'AGRICULTURE ET DE L'ELEVAGE EN AFRIQUE SUB-SAHARIENNE
Mongolia. U.S.S.R *see*
- PLANIROVANIE NARODNOGO KHOZIAISTVA MONGOLII (SBORNIK MATERIALOV)
- SANKHUA5UA5-ZEELIN TALAARKHI KHULL'CHILSAN ARTUUDIN SISTEMCHILSEN EMKHTGEL

MONGOLIAN KANJUR / ed by Chandra, Lokesh – 1,564mf – $1,000.00 – us I.A.S.W.R. [090]
MONGOLISCHE MAERCHEN-SAMMLUNG. DIE NEUN MAERCHEN DES SIDDHI-KUER / Juelg, B – Innsbrueck. 1868. BU-423 2 – 8 – ne IDC [390]
MONGOLO-OIRATSKIE ZAKONY 1640 GODA, DOPOLNITEL'NYE GALDAN-KHUN-TAIDZHIIAI ZAKONYM SOSTAVLENNYE DLIA VOLZHSKIKH KALMYKOV PRI KALMYTSKOM KHANE DONDUK-DASHI / Golstunskii, K F – Spb. 1880. BU-723 2 – 8 – ne IDC [947]
LES MONGOLS ET LA PAPAUTE / Pelliot, P – (ROC. 1922, 1924, 1931). BU-703 2 – 8 – ne IDC [950]
MONGOL'SKIE BURIAT-MONGOL'SKIE I OIRATSKIE RUKOPISI I KSILOGRAFY INSTITUTA VOSTOKOVEDENIIA – Moscow, Leningrad, 1957.v1: Istoriia. Pravo. 277p. BR-9811/1 – 9 – ne IDC [010]
MONGOL'SKII SLOVAR' MUKADDIMAT AL-ADAB / Poppe, N N – M., 1938 – 12mf – 9 – U-434/2 – ne IDC [460]
LES MONIALES CISTERCIENNES DANS L'ANCIEN ROMAN-PAYS DU BRABANT : HISTOIRE DES ABBAYES D'AYWIERES, DE LA RAMEE, DE FLORIVAL, DE WAUTHIER-BRAINE / Ploegaerts, Th. – Bruxelles, 1925 – Dfl42.00 – ne Slangenburg [240]
Monier, P *see*
- HISTOIRE DES ARTS
- THE HISTORY OF PAINTING, SCULPTURE, ARCHITECTURE, GRAVING; AND OF THOSE WHO HAVE EXCELL'D IN THEM

Monier-Williams, Monier, Sir *see*
- SANSKRIT-ENGLISH DICTIONARY
- SANSKRIT-ENGLISH DICTIONARY, ETYMOLOGICALLY AND PHILOLOGICALLY ARRANGED

Monique-Madeleine, Soeur *see* BIBLIOGRAPHIE ANALYTIQUE "POUR MIEUX SERVIR", DE 1956 A 1960
MONISM AS CONNECTING RELIGION AND SCIENCE; THE CONFESSION OF FAITH OF A MAN OF SCIENCE / Haeckel, Ernst Heinrich Philipp August – Trans. from the German by J. Gilchrist. London: A. & C. Black, 1894. viii,117p – 1 – us U.W. Library [240]
MONITA AMORIS VIRGINEI, SIVE OFFICIUM PUELLARUM IN CASTIS AMORIBUS, EMBLEMATE EXPRESSUM / Cats, J – Amsterdam, 1622 – 2mf – 9 – ne IDC [700]
MONITA SECRETA SOCIETATIS JESU = THE SECRET INSTRUCTIONS OF THE JESUITS – New York: The Truth Seeker Co., 190-?.From the London ed. 60p – 1 – us U.W. Library [240]
LE MONITEUR – (Autre ed. de lang.: The Monitor) – [Quebec?: s.n., 1831-183-?] – 9 – cn C.I.H.M. [360]
LE MONITEUR : JOURNAL OFFICIEL DE LA REPUBLIQUE D'HAITI – Port-au-Prince, [Haiti]. v4-61. 1849-68 – 25r – 1 – us Ross [324]
LE MONITEUR = THE MONTHLY MONITOR – Montreal, Canada. v1 n4. mar 1854; v1 n6. mai 1854 – 1r – 1 – Can$25.00 – cn Can Microfilming [073]
LE MONITEUR : REVUE / ed by Goodwin, W L – (With Index des Sommaires) – Gardenvale, Canada. nov 1934-v5. mai 1939 – 1r – 1 – Can$50.00 – cn Can Microfilming [073]
LE MONITEUR *see* THE TEMPERANCE MONITOR
LE MONITEUR ACADIEN – Shediac, Canada. 1867-1926 – 26r – 1 – $1,690.00 – cn Library Assoc [971]
LE MONITEUR ACADIEN – Shediac, New Brunswick. v2 n17. 23 oct 1868; v41 n8. 22 aut 1907 – 1r – 1 – Can$25.00 – cn Can Microfilming [072]
MONITEUR ALGERIEN / Algeria – Journal officiel de la Colonie. 1832-38 – 1 – fr A.C.R.P.P. [960]
LE MONITEUR BELGE – 1830- – 300-400mf per y – 9 – inquire – us Ross [072]
LE MONITEUR BELGE – Belgium, 1845-1989 – 551r – 1 – inquire – us Ross [072]
MONITEUR BELGE / Belgium – Brussels. and Prix Courant. 1944-1952 – 1 – us NY Public [330]
MONITEUR BELGE – Brussels, 1953-70 – 94r – 1 – us Ross [072]
LE MONITEUR CANADIEN : HEBDOMADAIRE – Montreal, Canada. 1 sep 1849-v8 n49. 4 oct 1855 – 1r – 1 – Can$50.00 – cn Can Microfilming [072]
LE MONITEUR CANADIEN : PREMIER QUOTIDIEN – Montreal, Canada. 10 mai 1849-v2 n83. 6 jun 1850 – 1r – 1 – Can$50.00 – cn Can Microfilming [072]
LE MONITEUR CATHOLIQUE – 6fevr-15 juin 1850. suite de: Le Moniteur religieux. Paris ?. 19 juin 1849 – 1 – fr A.C.R.P.P. [073]
MONITEUR CONGOLAIS / Congo – Leopoldville. 1960-67. v1-8. – 163mf – 9 – ne IDC [960]
MONITEUR CONGOLAIS Zairo. v1 8. 1060 67 – 4r – 1 – us Ross [960]
LE MONITEUR DE LA FLOTTE – Organe des interets politiques, maritimes et commerciaux de la France et des colonies. Paris. janv-sept 1870 – 1 – fr A.C.R.P.P. [073]
LE MONITEUR DE LA GYMNASTIQUESCO-LAIRE, HYGIENIQUE, MEDICALE. DIR. EUG. PAZ. NO. 1-24. PARIS. DEC 1868-MAI 1873. N'A PAS PARU DE NOV. 1869 A OCT. 1872 – 1 – fr A.C.R.P.P. [073]
LE MONITEUR DE LA PHOTOGRAPHIE – Revue internationale et universelle des progres de la photographie et des arts qui s'y rattachent. Paris. mars 1861-fevr 1893, 1894-mars 1907, 1913-juin 1914 – 1 – fr A.C.R.P.P. [073]
MONITEUR DE L'ALGERIE – Journal politique. Dir. A. Bouyer. Alger. 1888 – 1 – fr A.C.R.P.P. [073]
LE MONITEUR DE L'ARMEE – Paris. 1842-2 fevr 1843, 5 avr-dec 1850 – 1 – fr A.C.R.P.P. [073]
MONITEUR DE L'ENTREPRISE ET DE L'INDUSTRIE / Chambres Syndicales de la Ville de Paris – devenu: L' Action du batiment. devenu par fusion: Batiment et travaux publics. Paris. 1905-juin 1921 – 1 – fr A.C.R.P.P. [073]
LE MONITEUR DE L'EPICERIE – spec. no. 1-104. Paris. 26 dec 1850-52 – 1 – fr A.C.R.P.P. [073]
LE MONITEUR DE LEVIS – Levis, Canada. 5 mai 1893-20 jun 1896 – 1r – 1 – Can$45.00 – cn Can Microfilming [072]
LE MONITEUR DE L'EXPOSITION DE 1789 : JANVIER 1885 A MAI 1889 – Paris, 1885-89 – 52mf – 9 – $109.00 – fr Bibl Nationale [944]
MONITEUR DES MINES – London, UK. 7 Mar-1 Oct 1898 – 1 – uk British Libr Newspaper [072]
LE MONITEUR DES PRODUITS CHEMIQUES – Paris, France. -m. 10 July 1870-10 April 1898. 10 reels – 1 – uk British Libr Newspaper [073]
LE MONITEUR DES TRAVAUX PUBLICS – puis et du batiment. Entreprise et industrie puis Journal des travaux publics reunis. Paris. sept 1902-17, 1919-22 – 1 – fr A.C.R.P.P. [073]
LE MONITEUR DU COMMERCE – Journal des interets commerciaux, industriels et agricoles. Paris. 4 janv-30 juin 1832, 2-25 janv, mars, 1 no., 2-4, 25 juin 1833 avec un prosp. du 14 mars 1833 – 1 – fr A.C.R.P.P. [073]
LE MONITEUR DU COMMERCE : REVUE DES MARCHES, DE LA FINANCE, DE L'INDUSTRIE ET DES ASSURANCES – (Avec Index semi-annuel des sujets et annonceurs: 4 jan 1918-11 oct 1929 10r Can$60.00) – Montreal, Canada. 25 fev 1881-11 jul 1913 – 34r – 1 – Can$60.00r – cn Can Microfilming [336]
MONITEUR DU PROTECTORAT DE L'ANNAM ET DU TONKIN / France. Annam – 1885-88 – 1 – fr A.C.R.P.P. [073]
LE MONITEUR DU PUY-DE-DOME – Quotidien republicain du Centre.Clermont-Ferrand. 3 mai 1856-juin 1870, 1871-98, mars 1899-27 aout 1944 – 1 – fr A.C.R.P.P. [073]
MONITEUR DU SUD-KASAI – (Cont as: Bulletin Provincial du Sud-Kasai. 1962(11)-1964(12)) – 1961-1962(10) – 21mf – 9 – ne IDC [960]
LE MONITEUR HAITIEN / Haiti – Journal officiel. Port-au-Prince. fevr 1845-nov 1849 – 1 – fr A.C.R.P.P. [073]
MONITEUR INDUSTRIEL – Paris, France. -w. 6 Jan 1856-9 June 1859. 1 reel – 1 – uk British Libr Newspaper [073]

LE MONITEUR INDUSTRIEL PUIS ET FINANCIER – Journal progressif. Paris. juil 1838-juin 1839, juil-dec 1841, 1845-46, juil 1847-1852, 1860-19 juil 1870 – 1 – fr A.C.R.P.P. [073]
LE MONITEUR JORNAL OFICIAL / Haiti – 1862-1957; 1970-72; 1975- – 1 – us L of C Photodup [340]
LE MONITEUR: JOURNAL OFFICIEL / Haiti – 1847-1867. (scattered issues), 1868-1950 – 1 – us UMI [324]
MONITEUR KATANGAIS / Congo – 1960-63. 4v. – 40mf – 9 – ne IDC [960]
MONITEUR KATANGAIS – Elisabethville. 8 Aug 1960-15 Jan 1963 gaps – 1 – 35.00r – us Hoover Inst Photo [072]
MONITEUR OFFICIEL DU GOUVERNEMENT GENERAL DE REIMS / Rheims – I, no. 1-15; II, no. 1-27. Reims. 10 oct 1870-12 mars 1871. mq II, no. 2, 8 – 1 – fr A.C.R.P.P. [073]
LE MONITEUR REPUBLICAIN – no. 1, 3, 6, 8. Paris. nov 1837-juil 1838 – 1 – fr A.C.R.P.P. [073]
LE MONITEUR UNIVERSEL – Fond. Ch.-J. Panckouke. 1811-juin 1901. suite de: Gazette nationale ou Le Moniteur universel. 24 nov 1789-1810 (comprend les no. retrospectifs a partir du 5 mai 1789 publies en 1795). Paris – 1 – fr A.C.R.P.P. [073]
LE MONITEUR UNIVERSEL – Paris. -d. 1850-1901. 172 reels – 1 – uk British Libr Newspaper [072]
LE MONITEUR UNIVERSEL – Paris. France. 1789, 1793, 1795-1804 and Tables 1799-1814 – 1 – us P.K. Yonge [072]
LE MONITEUR UNIVERSEL – Reimpression de l'Ancien Moniteur. Seule histoire authentique et inalteree de la Revolution francaise depuis la reunion des Etats generaux jusqu'au Consulat, avec des notes explicatives. Paris. mai 1789-nov 1799 (I-XXIX). tb: (XXX-XXXI) et Introduction – 1 – fr A.C.R.P.P. [073]
MONITEUR UNIVERSEL DU PARTI NATIONAL FRANCAIS / Parti National Francais – Paris. 26 sept 1901-25, mai dec 1928, 1929-34, avr juin 1936-40, avr-sept 1944. Se pretend la suite de: Moniteur universel 1811-juin 1901 – 1 – fr A.C.R.P.P. [073]
Moniton, P Albert *see* MISCELLANEOUS MANUSCRIPTS, 1968-1983
LE MONITOR = THE MONITOR – Rouyn-Noranda, Canada. v1 n12. 9 jul 1959; v8. 11 oct 1967-v13. 25 oct 1973 – 2r – 1 – Can$60.00r – cn Can Microfilming [072]
MONITOR – 1850-1851 – 1 – us UMI [240]
MONITOR – An Illustrated Dublin Magazine. v. 1-2. 1879 – 1 – us UMI [073]
MONITOR – Belfast, Ireland. Aug 1853-Apr 1855. -w. 1/2 reel – 1 – uk British Libr Newspaper [072]
MONITOR – Boulder. Mont. -w. 1917-19, 1923-26, 1951-54, 1956-59, 1966- – 1 – us UMI [071]
MONITOR – Charlottetown, Canada. 1862-64 – 1 reel – 1 – $68.00 – cn Library Assoc [971]
MONITOR – Clearfield. Pa. 1913-1915 – 1 – us UMI [071]
MONITOR – Concord. N.H. and Patriot. 1949- – 1 – us UMI [071]
MONITOR – Designed to Improve the Taste, the Understanding, and the Heart. v. 1-2. 1823-24 – 1 – us UMI [073]
MONITOR – Fort Scott. Kan. -w. 1867-69, 1876-1904 – 1 – us UMI [071]
MONITOR – Hampton. Va. 1905-1918 – 1 – us UMI [071]
MONITOR – Manning. Iowa. -w. 1951-60, 1962- – 1 – us UMI [071]
MONITOR – Mentor. Ohio. -w. 1939- – 1 – us UMI [071]
MONITOR – Moberly. Mo. 1876-1879; 1882-1916 – 1 – us UMI [071]
MONITOR – Moberly. Mo. -w. 1880-1916, 1922-32 – 1 – us UMI [071]
MONITOR – Mount Clemens. Mich. 1880-1921; 1926-42 – 1 – us UMI [071]
MONITOR – Owensboro. Ky. 1862-1867 – 1 – us UMI [071]
MONITOR : REVISTA DO INTERESSES PUBLICOS – San Luiz, 21 Apr-May, Aug 1870. Jul 1871 – 1,5,6 – bl Biblioteca [072]
MONITOR – San Francisco, CA. 1861-1984 – 112r – 1 – $5,600.00 – B02842 – us Library Micro [071]
MONITOR – San Francisco. Calif. -w. 1937-38, 1943-52 – 1 – us UMI [071]
MONITOR – Wellington. Kan. 1886-1892 – 1 – us UMI [071]
MONITOR *see* AEDS MONITOR
O MONITOR – Maceio, Alagoas. 10 Jun-Jul 1888; Fev, 29 Maio 1889 – 1,5,6 – bl Biblioteca [072]
O MONITOR – Manaos, Amazonas. 1 Ago 1901 – 1,5,6 – bl Biblioteca [072]
O MONITOR – Manaos, Amazonas. 3-14 Set 1901 – 1,5,6 – bl Biblioteca [072]
O MONITOR : ORGAM DA EGREIJA EVANGELICA AMAZONENSE – Manaos, Amazonas. 27 Maio, 18 Set 1912 – 1,5,6 – bl Biblioteca [072]
O MONITOR – Penedo, Alagoas. 4 Jan-28 Jun 1909 – 1,5,6 – bl Biblioteca [072]
THE MONITOR – London [Ont]: London Life Insurance Co, [1892-19–] – 9 – cn C.I.H.M. [360]
THE MONITOR – Montreal, Canada. v25 n38. 22 sep 1949; v42 n22. 1 jun 1967; v42 n23. 8 jun 1967 – 1r – 1 – Can$25.00 – cn Can Microfilming [072]
THE MONITOR – Montreal: Irvin Pub Co. v1-1925-. SEM35P129 – 40r – 1 – cn Bibl Nat [072]
THE MONITOR : SILVER ANNIVERSARY SUPPLEMENT / ed by Parsley, Al – Ville St-Laurent, 21 sep 1950 – 1r – 1 – Can$25.00 – cn Can Microfilming [072]
THE MONITOR – Sydney, Australia. Sydney Monitor. -w. May 1826-Nov 1839. Imperfect. 4 1 2 reels – 1 – uk British Libr Newspaper [072]
THE MONITOR *see* LE MONITEUR
O MONITOR CAMPISTA – (Cont of: O Monitor and Jornal Corrente) – Campos, 31 Mar 1840- – 1,5,6 – bl Biblioteca [072]
MONITOR DO NORTE : PERIODICO DEDICADO A INTERESSE MORAL E MATERIAL – Manaos, Amazonas. 24 Mar 1878 – 1,5,6 – bl Biblioteca [072]
MONITOR DO NORTE : PUBLICACAO SEMANAL LITTERARIA E NOTICIOSA – Diamantina, 18 Jun 1876 – 1,5,6 – bl Biblioteca [072]
MONITOR INDEX AND DEMOCRAT – Moberly. Mo. 1919- – 1 – us UMI [071]
MONITOR LEADER – Mount Clemens. Mich. 1942-1964 – 1 – us UMI [071]
MONITOR MINER – Medford OR. June 16 Oct 13 1898 – 1 – us U.O. Library [071]
MONITOR POLSKI : DZIENNIK URZEDOWY RZECHZYPOSPOLITEJ POLSKIEJ – Warsaw, 1951-70 – 10r – 1 – us Ross [943]
MONITOR POLSKI / Poland – (Supplement: 1988; 1990-91. 32mf. Dfl201.00) – Warszawa, 1973-91. Missing parts of 1985; 1987; 1989. BH-1108/1 – 160mf – 9 – ne IDC [943]
MONITOR POLSKI – Warsaw, Paris, Angers. Aug. 13-Dec. 1920; Sept. 25-Dec. 1939; Jan. 5-29, Feb. 22-May 20, 1940 – 1 – 35.00r – us Hoover Inst Photo [072]
MONITOR PRESS – Wellington. Kan. 1892-1931 – 1 – us UMI [071]
MONITOR SUL-MINEIRO : SEMANARIO DE LITTERATURA, INDUSTRIA E NOTICIAS – Campanha, 4 Dec 1892-Dec 1895; Jan-Jul, Oct 1896; Nov 1901; Oct 1903; 27 May 1917 – 1,5,6 – bl Biblioteca [072]
EL MONITOR/HAYDEN'S WEEKLY – Riverside, CA. 1933-1938 – 2r – 1 – $100.00 – R03412 – us Library Micro [071]
MONITORING AND EVALUATION OF PARTICIPATORY FORESTRY PROJECTS – 1985 2nd print 1988 – 138p – it F.A.O. [634]
MONITORING AND EVALUATION OF SOCIAL FORESTRY IN INDIA : AN OPERATIONAL GUIDE – 1986 – 231p – it F.A.O. [634]
MONITORING DIGEST OF NEWS FROM PEKING, VIETMINH, AND MOSCOW / Radio Singapore Special News Service – 1Sep 1950-30 Aug 1962 – 1 – 713.00 – us L of C Photodup [073]
MONITORING SYSTEMS FOR AGRICULTURAL AND RURAL DEVELOPMENT PROJECTS – 1989, 1983 – 2v 315p – it F.A.O. [307]
MONITORING UND GEOTECHNISCHE ANALYSE VON MASSENBEWEGUNGEN IN FLYSCH UND FALTEN-MOLASSE DES GUNZESRIEDER TALS (OBERALLGAEU) / Keller, Gabriele – 1993 – 2mf – 9 – DM80.00 – 3-89349-802-8 – gw Hänsel [550]
MONITORUL OFICIAL / Romania – Bucuresti. Nov. 9, 1894-July 7, 1944 – 1 – us NY Public [324]
MONITORUL OFICIAL AL ROMANIA / Romania – Bucharest. 1867, 1874, 1876, 1882-1949 – 1 – 12,420.00 – us L of C Photodup [340]
EL MONJE DEL MONASTERIO DE YUSTE / Herrero, Leandro – 1883 – 9 – 1.50f – sp Bibl Santa Ana [240]
THE MONK AND THE MARTYR / Malone, Edward – Washington, D.C., 1950 – 5mf – 8 – ne Slangenburg [240]
Monk, William H *see* HYMNS ANCIENT AND MODERN
Monmarche, M *see* THE CHATEAUX OF THE LOIRE
MONMOUTH DEMOCRAT – Monmouth OR. Mar 20 1890 + – 1 – us U.O. Library [071]
MONMOUTH, GLAMORGAN AND BRECON HERALD – (South Wales Times and Star of Gwent. 1889- . Star of Gwent and South Wales Times. 1854-) – Newport, Wales, UK. 1853-24 Jul 1903. -w. Missing: 1898 – 49r – 1 – uk British Libr Newspaper [072]
MONMOUTH HERALD – Monmouth, OR. -w. 4 Sept 1908-26 Jun 1969; 27 Dec 1918-10 Jan 1919. – 19r – 1 – us U.O. Library [071]
MONMOUTHSHIRE, 1822 : BRITISH ISLES CENSUS DIRECTORIES PROJECT, ENGLAND – (In prep) – at Vine [941]
MONMOUTHSHIRE, 1830 : BRITISH ISLES CENSUS DIRECTORIES PROJECT, ENGLAND – at Vine [941]
MONMOUTHSHIRE, 1835 : BRITISH ISLES CENSUS DIRECTORIES PROJECT, ENGLAND – at Vine [941]
MONMOUTHSHIRE, 1844 : BRITISH ISLES CENSUS DIRECTORIES PROJECT, ENGLAND – at Vine [941]
MONMOUTHSHIRE, 1850 : BRITISH ISLES CENSUS DIRECTORIES PROJECT, ENGLAND – at Vine [941]
MONMOUTHSHIRE, 1858 : BRITISH ISLES CENSUS DIRECTORIES PROJECT, ENGLAND. VOL 32 – 2mf – 9 – A$15.00 – at Vine [941]
MONMOUTHSHIRE, 1880 : BRITISH ISLES CENSUS DIRECTORIES PROJECT, ENGLAND. VOL 261 – 3mf – 9 – A$21.00 – at Vine [941]
MONMOUTHSHIRE, 1891 : BRITISH ISLES CENSUS DIRECTORIES PROJECT, ENGLAND – at Vine [941]
MONMOUTHSHIRE ADVERTISER ETC – Newport, Wales, UK. 25 Aug 1840-24 Jul 1841. -w. 1- – 1 – uk British Libr Newspaper [072]
MONMOUTHSHIRE BEACON ETC – Wales, UK. 14 Oct 1837-1908. -w. 63 1/2 reels. Missing: Jul-Dec 1873; 1896 – 1 – uk British Libr Newspaper [072]
Monneret de Villard, Ugo *see* LES COUVENTS PRES DE SCHAG
Monnet, Jean *see* LES ETATS-UNIS D'EUROPE ONT COMMENCE; LA COMMUNAUTE EUROPEENE DU CHARBON ET DE L'ACIER, DISCOURS ET ALLOCUTIONS, 1952-54
Monnin, Alfred *see* MATER ADMIRABILIS
MONOCHORDUM ANDREAE REINHARDI, NIVIMONTAMI / Reinhard, A M – Lipsiae. 1604. BP-445 – 9 – ne IDC [780]
O MONOCULO : LITTERARIO, HUMORISTICO E SPORTIVO – Manaos, Amazonas. 17 Set 1922 – 1,5,6 – bl Biblioteca [072]
O MONOCULO : ORGAO HUMORISTICO – Manaus, Amazonas. 7-12 Out 1899 – 1,5,6 – bl Biblioteca [072]
O MONOCULO : SEMANARIO NOTICIOSO E HUMORISTICO – Manaos, Amazonas. 14 Jun-5 Jul 1913 – 1,5,6 – bl Biblioteca [072]
Monod, Adolphe *see* SAINT PAUL: FIVE DISCOURSES
Monod, Adolphe et al *see* SELECT DISCOURSES
Monod, Frederic *see* MEMOIR OF JULIUS CHARLES RIEU
Monod, G *see* BIBLIOGRAPHIE DE L'HISTOIRE DE FRANCE
Monod, Henri Charles *see*
- LE CHOLERA (HISTOIRE D'UNE EPIDEMIE, FINISTERE 1885-1886)
- L'EPIDEMIE DE CHOLERA AU GUILVINEC EN 1886

Monod, Leopold *see* LE PROBLEME DE L'AUTORITE
Monod, T *see* CHECKLIST OF THE FISHES OF THE NORTH-EASTERN ATLANTIC AND OF THE MEDITERRANEAN (CLOFNAM)
Monod, Wilfred *see* LA FIN D'UN CHRISTIANISME
MONOGALIA FARMER – Morgantown. West Virginia. 1834 – 1 – us UMI [071]
MONOGATARI BUNGAKU SOKWAN = DAITOKYU COLLECTION OF TALES, ESSAYS, DIARIES AND ACCOUNT OF TRAVELS IN THE HEIAN, KAMAKURA AND MUROMACHI PERIODS / ed by Kawase, Kazuma – (In the Diatokyu Memorial Library, Tokyo. 95 manuscripts and printed books in 695 parts) – 80r – 1 – Y766,000 – ja Yushodo [480]
MONOGATARI BUNGAKUSHO SHUSEI = COLLECTION OF OLD TALES AND THE CRITICAL WORKS IN THE CUSTODY OF THE SEIKADO LIBRARY, TOKYO – Manuscripts and printed books, 938 items in 4,130v – 318r – 1 – Y3,080,000.00 – ja Yushodo [480]
MONOGRAFI OEFVER SVERIGES OCH NORGES CHARACEER / Wahlstedt, L J – Christianstad. 1875. B-6416 2 – 8 – ne IDC [580]
MONOGRAFIA DE S. VICENTE DE ALCANTARA / Estevez Verdejo, Ramiro – Badajoz: La Minerva Extremena, 1907 – 1 – sp Bibl Santa Ana [240]
MONOGRAFIA HISTORICO DEL CASTILLO DE JARNDILLA / Castelao, Fernanda – Badajoz: Tip. y Enc. La Alianza, 1936 – 1 – sp Bibl Santa Ana [946]
MONOGRAFIA HISTORICO-DESCRIPTIVA Y ESTUDIO CRITICO-HISTORICO SOBRE : EL CUERPO DE SANTA EULALIA ESTA EN MERIDA O EN OVIEDO? / Perez Valero, Jose – Zafra: E. Morsba, 1924 – 1 – sp Bibl Santa Ana [946]
MONOGRAFIA HISTORICO-...HORNACHOS / Munoz de Rivera, Antonio – 1895 – 9 – 1.50f – sp Bibl Santa Ana [946]
MONOGRAFIA...ALANGE / Villaescusa, Julian de – 1850 – 9 – 1.50f – sp Bibl Santa Ana [946]
MONOGRAFIA...VILLA DE AZUAGA / Rodriguez Diaz, Felix – 1894 – 9 – 1.50f – sp Bibl Santa Ana [300]
MONOGRAFIE DER REPRODUCTIVEN PHAENOMENE / Emoan, Max – Erlangen, 1912 – 1mf – DM48.00 – 3-8267-3069-0 – gw Hänsel [150]
MONOGRAFIE DER SOLOSCHE ENCLAVES PASARGEDE EN IMAGIRI / Bevervoorde, W F E van – Jogjakarta, 1905 – 13mf – 9 – ne IDC [950]
MONOGRAFIE HYDNACEI REPUBLIKY CESKOSLOVENSKE, FAUNA ET FLORA CECHOSLOVENICA / Cejp, K – Praza. 1928. B-5285 2 – 8 – ne IDC [580]
DIE MONOGRAMMISTEN UND DIEJENIGEN BEKANNTEN UND UNBEKANNTEN KUENSTLER ALLER SCHULEN / Nagler, Georg K – 5v. Muenchen. 1858-79. BO-378 1 – 9 – ne IDC [920]
MONOGRAPH – (v1-10 1950-59 Can$37.00. v11-32 1960-81 Can$100.00) – Hamilton. v1-45. 1950-94 – 9 – Can$20.00y – cn Micromedia [073]
A MONOGRAPH OF AUSTRALIAN LAND SHELLS / Cox, J C – Z-486 2. 1868 – 8 – ne IDC [590]
A MONOGRAPH OF BRITISH BELEMNITIDAE / Phillips, J – G-212 1. 5 pts. 1865-1903 – 9 – ne IDC [910]
A MONOGRAPH OF BRITISH DESMIDACEAE / West, W & West, G S – B7665 2. 4 v. 1904-1912 – 8 – ne IDC [580]
A MONOGRAPH OF BRITISH GRAPTOLITES / Elles, G L & Wood, E M R; ed by Lapworth, C – BG-185 2. 1901-1918 – 8 – ne IDC [550]
A MONOGRAPH OF BRITISH NUCLIBRANCHIATE MOLLUSCA / Alder, J & Hancock, A – 1910. Ray Society – 1 – uk Microform Academic [590]
MONOGRAPH OF NORTH AMERICAN CYPERACEAE / Torrey, J – 5301. 1836 – 9 – ne IDC [580]
A MONOGRAPH OF ODONTOGLOSSUM / Bateman, J – London. 1864-74. B-5836 2 – 8 – ne IDC [580]
A MONOGRAPH OF THE ANOPHELES MOSQUITOES OF INDIA / James, S P & Liston, WG – Z-274 2. 1904 – 8 – ne IDC [590]
A MONOGRAPH OF THE BAMBUSACEAE / Munro, W – Linnean Society. 1866 – 1 – uk Microform Academic [580]
A MONOGRAPH OF THE BRITISH ANNELIDS / McIntosh, W C – Ray Society. 1873 etc – 1. 252.00; ; 7 – uk Microform Academic [590]
A MONOGRAPH OF THE BRITISH APHIDES / Buckton, G B – Ray Society. 1876-9 – 1. 56.00; ; 7 – uk Microform Academic [590]

A MONOGRAPH OF THE BRITISH CAMBRIAN TRILOBITES / Lake, P - G-200 1. Pt. 1. 1906. 1946 - 9 - ne IDC [560]

A MONOGRAPH OF THE BRITISH DESMIDIACEAE / West, W & West, G S - 1904-23 - 1. 164.00; ; 7 - uk Microform Academic [580]

A MONOGRAPH OF THE BRITISH EOCENE FLORA / Gardiner, J S & Ettingshausen, C von - BG-187 2. 2 v. 1879-1886 - 8 - ne IDC [580]

A MONOGRAPH OF THE BRITISH FOSSIL CORALS / Duncan, P M - G-182 2. 1866-1891 - 8 - ne IDC [550]

A MONOGRAPH OF THE BRITISH FOSSIL CORALS / Milne-Edwards, Henri & Haime, J - London. 1850-54. BG-184 2 - 8 - ne IDC [560]

A MONOGRAPH OF THE BRITISH FOSSIL SPONGES / Hinde, G J - G 226 1. 1887-1912 - 9 - ne IDC [590]

A MONOGRAPH OF THE BRITISH FOSSIL TRIGONIAE / Lycett, J - G-202 1. 1872-1883 - 9 - ne IDC [560]

A MONOGRAPH OF THE BRITISH LICHENS / Smith, A L - 1358. 2 V. Ed. 2. 1918-1926 - 9 - ne IDC [580]

MONOGRAPH OF THE BRITISH NAKED-EYE MEDUSAE / Forbes, E A - Ray Society. v. 12. 1848 - 7 - uk Microform Academic [590]

A MONOGRAPH OF THE BRITISH ORTHOPTERA / Lucas, W J - Ray Society. 1920 - 1. 32.00; ; 7 - uk Microform Academic [590]

A MONOGRAPH OF THE BRITISH PHYTOPHAGOUS HYMENOPTERA / Cameron, P - Ray Society. 1885 and 1893 - 1. 88.00; ; 7 - uk Microform Academic [590]

A MONOGRAPH OF THE BRITISH PLEISTOCENE MAMMALIA / Dawkins, W B et al - G-181 1. v1; v2, pts. 1-4; v3, pts. 1-2. 1866-1912 - 9 - ne IDC [560]

A MONOGRAPH OF THE BRITISH SPONGIADAE / Bowerbank, J S - 1864-82 - 1. 36.00; ; 7 - uk Microform Academic [580]

MONOGRAPH OF THE COCCIDAE OF THE BRITISH ISLES / Newstead, R - 1901 and 1903 - 1. 68.00; ; 7 - uk Microform Academic [580]

MONOGRAPH OF THE COLLEMBOLA AND THYSANURA / Lubbock, J - Ray Society. 1873 - 7 - uk Microform Academic [580]

A MONOGRAPH OF THE CRETACEOUS LAMELLIBRANCHIA OF ENGLAND / Woods, H - G 221 1. 2 v. 1899-1903 - 9 - ne IDC [590]

A MONOGRAPH OF THE DEVONIAN FAUNA OF THE SOUTH OF ENGLAND / Whidborne, G F - 3v. London. 1889-1907. BG-228 2 - 8 - ne IDC [590]

A MONOGRAPH OF THE EAST AMERICAN SCAPHOPOD MOLLUSKS / Henderson, J B - Bull. U.S. Nat. Mus., 1920. Bulletin 3, pi-vi,1-177. Pls. 1-20. Z-2237/1 - 9 - ne IDC [590]

A MONOGRAPH OF THE ECHINOIDEA / Mortensen, Theodor - Copenhagen, etc. 1928-1951. 5v - 1 - us Res Libr [590]

A MONOGRAPH OF THE ENTOMOSTRACA OF THE CRETACEOUS FORMATION OF ENGLAND / Jones, T R - London. 1849. BG-191 1 - 9 - ne IDC [550]

A MONOGRAPH OF THE EOCENE BIVALVES OF ENGLAND / Wood, S V - London. 1861-77. Suppl. BG-220 2 - 8 - ne IDC [590]

A MONOGRAPH OF THE EOCENE CEPHALOPODA AND UNIVALVES OF ENGLAND / Edwards, FE & Wood, S V - London. 1849-77. BG-183 2 - 8 - ne IDC [590]

A MONOGRAPH OF THE ERYSIPHACEAE / Salmon, E S A - (Mem. Bot. Club, v. 9). New York. 1900. B-1344 2 - 8 - ne IDC [580]

A MONOGRAPH OF THE FISHES OF THE OLD RED SANDSTONE OF BRITAIN / Lankester, E R & Traquair, R H - 2pts. London. 1868-1914. BG-227 1 - 9 - ne IDC [560]

A MONOGRAPH OF THE FLUVIATILE BIVALVE SHELLS OF THE RIVER OHIO / Rafinesque-Schmaltz, Constantine S - Philadelphia, 1832 - 72p - 9 - ne IDC [590]

A MONOGRAPH OF THE FORAMINIFERA OF THE CRAG / Jones, T R et al - 4pts. London. 1866-1907. BG-198 1 - 9 - ne IDC [560]

A MONOGRAPH OF THE FOSSIL LEPADIDAE, OR PEDUNCULATED CIRRIPEDES OF GREAT BRITAIN / Darwin, Charles - Z-164 1. 1851 - 9 - ne IDC [560]

A MONOGRAPH OF THE FREE AND SEMI-PARASITIC COPEPODA OF THE BRITISH ISLANDS / Brady, G S - Ray Society. 1878 - 1 £35.00 7 £21.00 - uk Microform Academic [590]

A MONOGRAPH OF THE FRESH-WATER POLYZOA, INCLUDING ALL THE KNOWN SPECIES, BOTH BRITISH AND FOREIGN / Allman, G J - Ray Society. 1856 - 1 £35.00 7 £24.50 - uk Microform Academic [590]

A MONOGRAPH OF THE GENUS ALLIUM / Don, G - (Mem. Wernerian Nat. Hist. Soc.). v. 6. Edinburgh. 1832. B-5223 2 - 8 - ne IDC [580]

MONOGRAPH OF THE GENUS CROCUS / Maw - 1886 - 1 - uk Microform Academic [580]

A MONOGRAPH OF THE GENUS DRYOPTERIS / Christensen, C F A - Pt. I. The tropical American pinnatifidbipinnatifid species. (Det Kongelige Danske Videnskabernes Selskabs Skrifter). 1913. B-7174 1 - 9 - ne IDC [580]

A MONOGRAPH OF THE GENUS HERITIERA DRY (STERCULIACEAE). INC. ARGYRODENDRON F.V.M. AND TARRIETIA BL / Kostermans, Andre Joseph Guillaume Henri - SE-11,607 1. 1959 - 9 - ne IDC [580]

A MONOGRAPH OF THE GENUS LILIUM / Elwes, H J - Illustrated by H. W. Fitch. London. 1877-80. B-5920 2 - 8 - ne IDC [580]

A MONOGRAPH OF THE GENUS TERACOLUS / ed by Sharpe, E M B - London, 1898-1902 - 8 - ne IDC [590]

A MONOGRAPH OF THE GYMNOBLASTIC OR TUBULARIAN HYDROIDS / Allman, G J - 1871-72 - 7 - uk Microform Academic [590]

A MONOGRAPH OF THE JACAMARS AND PUFF-BIRDS / Sclater, P L - London. 1879-82. Z-1919 2 - 8 - ne IDC [590]

A MONOGRAPH OF THE MEMBRACIDAE / Buckton, G B - 2475 2. 1901-1903 - 8 - ne IDC [580]

A MONOGRAPH OF THE NORTH AMERICAN PROCTOTRYPIDAE / Ashmead, William Harris - Washington: G.P.O., 1893. 00965. (Pre-1900 Canadiana) - 9 - cn C.I.H.M. [580]

MONOGRAPH OF THE NORTH-AMERICAN SPECIES OF THE GENUS CAREX / Schweinitz, L D von - (Ann. Lyc. Nat. Hist. New York, v. 1, pt. II). New York. 1825. B-5161 2 - 8 - ne IDC [580]

A MONOGRAPH OF THE ODONTOPHORINAE / Gould, J - London, 1844-50.Z/1774/2 - 8 - ne IDC [590]

A MONOGRAPH OF THE PARADISE IDAE... / Elliot, Daniel Giraud - [London], 1873 - 32, [90]p, 37pls - 8 - ne IDC [590]

A MONOGRAPH OF THE PERMIAN FOSSILS OF ENGLAND / King, W - G-199 1. 1850 - 9 - ne IDC [560]

A MONOGRAPH OF THE PETRELS (ORDER TUBINARES) / Goldman, F du Cane - 2086 2. 2 v. 1907-1910 - 8 - ne IDC [590]

A MONOGRAPH OF THE PHASIANIDAE, OR FAMILY OF THE PHEASANTS / Elliot, Daniel Giraud - New York, (1870)-1872 - 2 vols - 8 - ne IDC [590]

A MONOGRAPH OF THE RAMPHASTIDAE, OR, FAMILY OF TOUCANS / Gould, J - London, 1834-35.Z/1770/2 - 8 - ne IDC [590]

A MONOGRAPH OF THE SUB-CLASS CIRRIPEDIA: THE BALANIDAE, THE VERRUEIDAE ETC / Darwin, Charles - Ray Society. 1854 - 1 £35.00 7 £59.50 - uk Microform Academic [590]

A MONOGRAPH OF THE SUB-CLASS CIRRIPEDIA: THE LAPADIDAE OR PODUNCULATED CIRRIPEDES / Darwin, Charles - Ray Society. 1851 - 1 £35.00 7 £35.00 - uk Microform Academic [590]

A MONOGRAPH OF THE TERRESTRIAL MOLLUSCA INHABITING THE UNITED STATES / Tryon, G WA - 2170 2. 1866 - 8 - ne IDC [580]

A MONOGRAPH OF THE TERTIARY ENTOMOSTRACA OF ENGLAND / Jones, T R - G-192 1. 1856 - 9 - ne IDC [580]

A MONOGRAPH OF THE TROCHILIDAE / Gould, J - London, 1849-61.5v. Suppl., London, 1880-87. Z/1776/2 - 8 - ne IDC [590]

A MONOGRAPH OF THE WEAVER-BIRDS / Bartlett, E - Maidstone, London. 1888. BZ-343 2 - 8 - ne IDC [590]

A MONOGRAPH OF WEST AMERICAN PYRAMIDELLID MOLLUSKS / Dall, W H & Bartsch, P - Z-490 2. 1909 - 8 - ne IDC [590]

MONOGRAPH ON THE BRITISH FOSSIL ECHINODERMATA OF THE OOLITIC FORMATIONS / Wright, T - 2v. London. 1857-80. BG-224 1 - 9 - ne IDC [560]

MONOGRAPH ON THE BRITISH FOSSIL ELEPHANTS / Adams, Andrew Leith - G-172 2. 1877-1881 - 9 - ne IDC [560]

A MONOGRAPH ON THE FOSSIL BALANIDAE AND VERRUCIDAE OF GREAT BRITAIN / Darwin, Charles - C-191 1. 1854 - 9 - ne IDC [560]

A MONOGRAPH ON THE FOSSIL REPTILIA OF THE MESOZOIC FORMATIONS / Owen, R - G-211 1. 1874-1889 - 9 - ne IDC [560]

MONOGRAPH ON THE LIAS AMMONITES OF THE BRITISH ISLANDS / Wright, T - G 225 1. 1878-1886 - 9 - ne IDC [590]

A MONOGRAPH ON THE STRUCTURE AND DEVELOPMENT OF THE SHOULDER-GIRDLE AND STERNUM IN THE VERTEBRATA / Parker, W K - Ray Society. 1868 - 1 £35.50 7 £52.50 - uk Microform Academic [612]

A MONOGRAPH ON THE SUBCLASS CIRRIPEDIAE: 1, THE BALANTIDAE; 2, THE VERRICIDAE / Darwin, Charles - Z-191 2. 1854 - 8 - ne IDC [590]

MONOGRAPH SERIES; HISTORICAL AND OPERATIONAL BACKGROUND OF THE SELEC. SERV. SYS. IN THE U.S / U.S. Selective Service System - 1947-56. 52 books. 80-521 - 9 - 120.00 - us L.L.M.C. [324]

MONOGRAPHIA ANOPLURORUM BRITANNIAE / Denny, H - London, 1842. xxiv,262p. 26 pls. Z-1183/2 - 8 - ne IDC [590]

MONOGRAPHIA CLADONIARUM UNIVERSALIS / Wainio, E A - (Acta Soc. pro Fauna et Flora Fennica. v. 4, 10, 14). 3 v. Helsingfors. 1887-97. B-512 2 - 8 - ne IDC [580]

MONOGRAPHIA COLEOPTERORUM MICROPTERORUM / Gravenhorst, J L C - Goettingae, 1806. xvi,236p. Z/1302/2 - 8 - ne IDC [590]

MONOGRAPHIA DE CERASTIO / Grenier, J C M - Vesontione. 1841. B-703 2 - 8 - ne IDC [580]

MONOGRAPHIA DE POTENTILLA / Nestler, C G - Parisiis, Argentorati, 1816. 80 pp., 12 pls. B-5482 2 - 8 - ne IDC [580]

MONOGRAPHIA EQUISETORUM / Milde, J - (Nova Acta Academia Caesarea Leopoldino Carolina, Dresden, 1865 -1867, v. 32, pt. 2, 605 pp., 35 pls.). B-7230 1 - 9 - ne IDC [580]

MONOGRAPHIA FESTUCARUM EUROPEARUM / Hackel, E - 1882 - 1 - uk Microform Academic [580]

MONOGRAPHIA GENERIS ACONITI / Reichenbach, Heinrich G L - Lipsiae. 1820. B-1179 2 - 8 - ne IDC [580]

MONOGRAPHIA GENERIS CAPSICI / Fingerhuth, K A - Duesseldorpii. 1832. B-6505 2 - 8 - ne IDC [580]

MONOGRAPHIA GENERIS OSMUNDAE / Milde, J - Vindobonae, 1868. 139 pp., 8 pls. B-5489 2 - 8 - ne IDC [580]

MONOGRAPHIA GENERIS POTENTILLARUM / Lehmann, J G C - Hamburgi, etc. 1820; suppl. Hamburgi. 1835. B-6012 2 - 8 - ne IDC [580]

MONOGRAPHIA GENERIS VERONICAE / Koch, K H E - Wirceburgi. 1833. B-951 - 8 - ne IDC [580]

MONOGRAPHIA GENERUM ALOES ET MESEMBRYANTHEMI / Salm-Reifferscheid-Dyck, J - Duesseldorf-Bonn. 1836-63. B-5710 2 - 8 - ne IDC [580]

MONOGRAPHIA LYCOPERDINEORUM AUGUSTAE TAURINORUM, 1842 / Vittadini, C - B-898 2 - 8 - ne IDC [580]

MONOGRAPHIA MYRTACEARUM XEROCARPICARUM. SECTIO I. CHAMAELAUCIERUM HUCUSQUE COGNITARUM GENERA ET SPECIES ILLUSTRANS / Schauer, J C - (Nova Acta Academiae Leopoldino-Carolinae Naturae Curiosorum, v. 19, suppl. 2, 1842). B-2302 2 - 8 - ne IDC [580]

MONOGRAPHIA NOSTOCHINEARUM ITALICARUM ADDITO SPECIMINE DE RIVULARIIS / Meneghini, G - Augustae Taurinorum, 1842. 143 pp., 17 pls. (Mem. R. Accad. Sci. Torino., s. 2, v. 5.). B-6382 1 - 9 - ne IDC [580]

MONOGRAPHIA POLYGALACEARUM / Chodat, R - Geneve. 1891 - 8 - ne IDC [580]

MONOGRAPHIA ROCCOLEORUM / Darbishire, O V - Ein Beitrag zur Flechtensystematik. (Bibliotheca Botanica. Heft 45). Stuttgart. 1898. B-677 2 - 8 - ne IDC [580]

MONOGRAPHIA STEREOCAULORUM ET PHILPHORUM / Fries, T M - (Nova Acta Kongl. Vetensk. Soc. S. 3, v. 2, nr. 9). Uppsala. 1858. B-941 2 - 8 - ne IDC [580]

MONOGRAPHIA TUBERACEARUM / Vittadini, C - Mediolani. 1831. B-5289 - 8 - ne IDC [580]

MONOGRAPHIA UREDINEARUM / Sydow, P & Sydow, H - Leipzig, 1902-1924. 4 vols. B-503 2 - 8 - ne IDC [580]

MONOGRAPHIAE GENERIS POLYGONI PRODROMUS / Meisner, C F - Genevae, 1826. 116 pp., 7 pls. B-5569 2 - 8 - ne IDC [580]

MONOGRAPHIAE PHANEROGAMARUM / Candolle, A P de - 1878-96 - 5 - uk Microform Academic [580]

MONOGRAPHIAE PHANEROGAMARUM / Candolle, A P de - v. 1-9. Paris. 1878-1896 - 8 - ne IDC [580]

MONOGRAPHIE DE LA FAMILLE DES ANONACEES / Dunal, M F - Paris. 1817. B-6128 1 - 9 - ne IDC [580]

MONOGRAPHIE DE LA FAMILLE DES HIRUDINEES / Moquin-Tandon, C H B A - Z-277 2. 1827 - 8 - ne IDC [306]

MONOGRAPHIE DE LA FAMILLE DES LYCOPODIACEES / Spring, F A - (Mem. Acad. Roy. Belgique, v. 15, 24). Bruxelles. 1842, 1850. B-7266 1 - 9 - ne IDC [580]

MONOGRAPHIE DE LA FAMILLE DES URTICEES / Weddell, H A - (Arch. Mus. Hist. Nat. Paris, v. 9, 1856-57). B-5804 2 - 8 - ne IDC [580]

MONOGRAPHIE DE QUELQUES GENRES DE COLEOPTERES HETEROMERES... / Breme, F de - Paris, 1842 - 25p, 1pl - 8 - ne IDC [590]

MONOGRAPHIE DER ABIETINEEN DES JAPANISCHEN REICHES / Mayr, H - Mua5nchen, 1890. 104 pp., 7 pls. B-7371 1 - 9 - ne IDC [580]

MONOGRAPHIE DER ALPINEN ERIGERON-ARTEN EUROPAS UND VORDERASIENS / Vierhapper, F - (Beih. Botan. Centralbl. Abt. 2, v. 19, 1906). B-1015 2 - 8 - ne IDC [580]

MONOGRAPHIE DER ARKTISCHEN ACARIDEN / Traegardh, I - 1904 - 8 - 1555-2 - ne IDC [990]

MONOGRAPHIE DER FAMILIEN DER PFLANZENLAEUSE / Kaltenbach, J H - Pt. 1 - Die Blatt- Und Erdlaeuse, Aphidina Et Hyponomeutes. 2155 2. 1843 - 8 - ne IDC [590]

MONOGRAPHIE DER GATTUNG EUPHRASIA / Wettstein, R von - Leipzig. 1896. B-355 2 - 8 - ne IDC [580]

MONOGRAPHIE DER NEMATODEN / Schneider, A F - 2337 2. 1866 - 8 - ne IDC [630]

MONOGRAPHIE DER PAPAGEIEN / Brehm, C L - Z-363 2. 1842-1854 - 8 - ne IDC [590]

MONOGRAPHIE DER SPINNEN / Hahn, C W - Z-2172 2. Pt. 1-8, 14. (1820-) and 1821-1836 - 8 - ne IDC [590]

MONOGRAPHIE DER TURBELLARIEN / Graff, L von - 2173 2. 2 v. 1882-1899 - 8 - ne IDC [580]

MONOGRAPHIE DES ANTIRRHINEES / Chavannes, E - Paris, Lausanne. 1833. B-5880 2 - 8 - ne IDC [580]

MONOGRAPHIE DES BETSILEO (MADAGASCAR) / Dubois, H M - 9 - F350.00 - fr Ethnologie [960]

MONOGRAPHIE DES CAMPANULEES / Candolle, A P de - Paris. 1830. B-435 2 - 8 - ne IDC [580]

MONOGRAPHIE DES CAULERPES / Weber-Van Bosse, A - (Ann. Jardin Bot. Buitenzorg, v. 15, 1898). B-5518 2 - 8 - ne IDC [580]

MONOGRAPHIE DES COLEOPTEREN-TRIBUS HYPERINI / Petri, K - Berlin, 1901. iv,210p, 3 pls.Z-1546/2 - 8 - ne IDC [590]

MONOGRAPHIE DES FOUGERES / Bommer, J E - (Bull. Soc. Roy. Bot.). v. 5. Belgique, Bruxelles. 1866. B-7164 1 - 9 - ne IDC [580]

MONOGRAPHIE DES ISOETEAE / Motelay, L & Vendryes, A – Bordeaux, 1882. 99 pp., 10 pls. Act. Soc. Linn. Bordeaux, v. 36. B-7237 1 – 9$2.00 – ne IDC [580]
MONOGRAPHIE DES MARATTIACEES / Vriese, W H de & Harting, P – Leide, Duesseldorf. 1853. B-7274 2 – 8 – ne IDC [580]
MONOGRAPHIE DES OSCILLARIES / Gomont, M – 1892 – 7 – uk Microform Academic [580]
MONOGRAPHIE DU DICTIONNAIRE DE L'ACADEMIE / Courtat, F T – 1880 – 9 – fr I.C.S. [440]
MONOGRAPHIE DU GENRE CHIODECTON / Fee, A L A – (Act. Soc. de Sci. de Lille, 1827-28). B-943 2 – 8 – ne IDC [580]
MONOGRAPHIE DU GENRE THALICTRUM / Lecoyer, J C – (Bull. Soc. Roy. Bot. Belg. v. 24, 1885). Bruxelles. 1885. B-1014 2 – 8 – ne IDC [580]
MONOGRAPHIE DU GENRE TRYPETHELIUM / Fee, A L A – (Ann. des Sc. Nat. v. 23, 1831). B-940 2 – 8 – ne IDC [580]
MONOGRAPHIE D'UN ARTISAN PARISIEN / Rostoker, J – 9 – F50.00 – fr Ethnologie [305]
MONOGRAPHIE POUR SERVIR A L'HISTOIRE NATURELLE ET BOTANIQUE DE LA FAMILLE DES PLANTES ETOILEES / Willemet, P R – Strasbourg. 1791. B-5816 2 – 8 – ne IDC [580]
MONOGRAPHIEEN AFRIKANISCHER PFLANZEN-FAMILIEN UND GATTUNGEN / Engler, H G A – 5v. Leipzig. 1898-1900. B-1259 2 – 8 – ne IDC [580]
MONOGRAPHIES COOPERATIVES: LE MOUVEMENT OUVRIER D'ASSOCIATION ET DE COOPERATION / Gaumont, Jean – Lyon. 1921. (La Condition Ouvriere. Part Two.) – 9 – 5.00 – fr Bibl Nationale [360]
MONOGRAPHIES: GOUVERNEURS, INTENDANTS ET EVEQUES DE LA NOUVELLE-FRANCE / Bechard, Auguste – Ottawa, Courrier Federal, 1888. 03314. (Pre-1900 Canadiana) – 9 – cn C.I.H.M. [971]
MONOGRAPHS / Connecticut. Agricultural Experiment Station. Storrs – v. 1-3. 1961-69 – 1,5,6 – us Spaulding [630]
MONOGRAPHS / Palaeontographical Society – 7, 9 – uk Microform Academic [910]
MONOGRAPHS OF THE UNITED STATES GEOLOGICAL SURVEY – (Missing: v32(1)) – Washington. v1-55. 1890-1929 – 956mf – 9 – ne IDC [550]
MONOGRAPHS PERSONAL AND SOCIAL / Houghton, Richard Monckton Milnes – London: J Murray, 1873 – 1r – 1 – 1-55879-834-X – uk Libr Preservation [880]
DER MONOLOG IM DRAMA DES STURM UND DRANG / Grußendorf, Hermann – Muenchen, 1914 – 2mf – DM62.00 – 3-8267-3103-4 – gw Hänsel [400]
DER MONOLOG IN DEN DRAMEN DES ANDREAS GRYPHIUS / Knueppelholz, Paul – (Includes bibliographical references) – Greifswald: H Adler, 1911 – 1r – 1 – us U.W. Library [430]
DIE MONOLOGE IN DEN DRAMEN HEBBELS : EIN BEITRAG ZUR DRAMATURGIE / Sprink, Walter – (Includes bibliographical references) – [S.l.: s.n.],. 1914 (Nakel: Buchdruckerei O Brewing) – 1r – 1 – us U.W. Library [430]
MONOLOGO EN PROSA. MUSICA DE DON JOAQUIN PEREZ / Asins, Manuel – Badajoz: Tip. La Moderna, 1906 – 1 – sp Bibl Santa Ana [780]
MONONGAHELA NEWS – Fairmont. West Virginia. 1961-1966 – 1 – us UMI [071]
Monongahela. Presbytery. (Assoc. Ref. Ch. of NA) *see* MINUTES, 1803-1858
Monongahela. Presbytery (United Pres. Ch. of N.A.) *see* RECORDS, 1855-1906
MONONGAHELA VALLEY REPUBLICAN – Monongahela, PA. -w 1851-1908 – 13 – $25.00r – us I.M.R. [071]
LE MONOPHYSISME SEVERIEN / Lebon, J – Lovanii, 1909 – 11mf – 8 – ne Slangenburg [240]
MONOPHYSITISCHE STREITIGKEITEN IM ZUSAMMENHANGE MIT DER REICHSPOLITIK / Krueger, Gustav – Jena: H. Pohle, 1884 – 1mf – us A.T.L.A. [943]
LOS MONOPOLIOS IMPERIALISTAS EN LA ARGENTINA : UNA OPINI ON DE LOS COMUNISTAS ARGENTINOS – Buenos Aires: Editorial Problemas, 1941 – 9 – us Hoover Inst Photo [320]
MONOPOLIOS O CUASI MONOPOLIOS / Munoz Casillas, Juan – (Separate do Tome 6.5th Seccao C. Sociales) – Lisboa, 1950 – 1 – sp Bibl Santa Ana [338]
MONOPOLY AND THE INDIVIDUAL / Hardy, George – 3fiches. (24x diazo) – 9 – 1.00f – at Libertarian Micro [320]
MONOPOLY STUDY RELEASES / U.S. Securities and Exchange Commission – (Also known as "S" series releases and sometimes cited under the U.S. Temporary Economic Committee) – nos S1-S23. 14 Jan 1939-9 Dec 1939 (all publ) – 1mf – 9 – LLMC 89-001 – us UMI [332]
MONOWI NEWS – Monowi, NE. -w. May 1908-Mar 1910 – 1 – us NE Hist [071]
Monrad, Hans Christian *see* BIDRAG TIL EN SKILDRING AF GUINEA-KYSTEN OG DENS INDBYGGERE
Monro, H AU *see* MANUAL OF FUMIGATION FOR INSECT CONTROL
MONROE 1777-1896 – 1990 – 20mf – 9 – 0-87623-115-6 – us Holbrook [920]
MONROE BOOSTER – Monroe, NE. -w. Oct 1946 to date – 1 – us NE Hist [071]
Monroe County. Mich, Bedford Township. Board of Education *see*
- BOARD RECORD
- GRADE SCHOOL REGISTER
- LIBRARY CHARGE BOOK
- SCHOOL DISTRICT RECORD
- TOWNSHIP SCHOOL RECORD

Monroe County. Mich, Bedford Township. Board of Elections *see* VOTER REGISTRATION RECORDS
Monroe County. Mich, Bedford Township. Board of Trustees *see*
- BIRTH RECORDS
- CEMETERY RECORDS
- DEATH RECORDS
- MINUTES
- ROAD RECORD

Monroe County. Mich, Bedford Township. Justice of the Peace *see* DOCKETS
Monroe County. Mich, Bedford Township. Township Treasurer *see*
- ACCOUNT RECORDS
- ASSESSMENT ROLLS
- BONDS AND OATHS
- CHATTEL MORTGAGE INDEX
- VOUCHER RECORD

MONROE COUNTY NEWS – Albia. Iowa. -w. 1951- – 1 – us UMI [071]
MONROE DEMOCRAT – Aberdeen. Miss. 1850-1852 – 1 – us UMI [071]
MONROE DEMOCRAT – Stroudsburg, PA. -w 1860-1863; 1864-1865; 1907-1910 – 13 – $25.00r – us I.M.R. [071]
MONROE DOCTRINE – 1 – us Ross [323]
Monroe, James *see* PAPERS
MONROE LEADER MONITOR – Monroe OR. Sep 21 1916-Jan 4 1917 – 1 – us U.O. Library [071]
Monroe, Lilla Day *see* COLLECTION OF PIONEER STORIES
Monroe, Lynn *see* BURBANK COMMUNITY BOOK
THE MONROE MISSION TO FRANCE 1794-96 / Bond, B – Baltimore, 1907 – 2mf – 9 – ILM-1147/1 – ne IDC [327]
MONROE MONITOR – (Set incl. Monroe Leader-Monitor) – Monroe, OR. -w. 21 Sept 1916-4 Apr 1918. 1 roll. – 1 – us U.O. Library [071]
MONROE NEWS – Monroe, NE. -w. Oct 1895-Feb 1896; Apr 1896-May 1898; Jan 1899-Mar 1925; May 1925-Jun 1942 – 1 – us NE Hist [071]
Monroe, Paul *see* THOMAS PLATTER AND THE EDUCATIONAL RENAISSANCE OF THE SIXTEENTH CENTURY
MONROE RECORD – Stroudsburg, PA. -w 1908-1914 – 13 – $25.00r – us I.M.R. [071]
MONROE WATCHMAN – Union. West Virginia. 1872-1959; 1961-1968 – 1 – us UMI [071]
MONROEVILLE SPECTATOR – Monroeville, Ohio, 1870-1986 – 24r – 1 – $32.50r – us Archival [978]
MONROISME?... / Capella y Pons, F – Paris, 1913 – 2mf – 1 – ILM-362/1 – ne IDC [327]
MONROVIA BLUE BOOK / Davis, Charles F – Monrovia: A.H. Cawston, 1943. California Reel 18. (The Cox Library Collection) – 5 – us Americana [978]
MONROVIA JOURNAL *see* MONROVIA-DURATE JOURNAL
MONROVIA MESSENGER – (Cont by: Monrovia News-Post) – Monrovia, CA. 1888-1891; 1907-1912 – 3r – 1 – $150.00 – H04028 – us Library Micro [071]
MONROVIA MESSENGER *see* MONROVIA PLANET
THE MONROVIA MESSENGER *see* MONROVIA NEWS-POST
MONROVIA NEWS-POST – (Cont: Monrovia Planet and The Monrovia Messenger) – Monrovia, CA. 1910-1920; 1922-1986 – 352r – 1 – $17,600.00 – H03341 – us Library Micro [071]
MONROVIA NEWS-POST *see* MONROVIA MESSENGER
MONROVIA PLANET – (Cont by: Monrovia Messenger) – Monrovia, CA. 1886-1888 – 1r – 1 – $50.00 – H04029 – us Library Micro [071]
MONROVIA PLANET *see* MONROVIA NEWS-POST
THE MONROVIA SPECTATOR – Monrovia. Liberia. Feb. 9, Mar. 16, 30; Apr. 22, 1907 – 1 – us NY Public [071]
MONROVIA-DURATE JOURNAL – (Also known as: Monrovia Journal) – Monrovia, CA. 1934-1937; 1963-1973; 1974-1975 – 26r – 1 – $1,300.00 – H04030 – us Library Micro [073]
Monroy. Ayuntamiento *see* FIESTAS EN MONROY DURANTE...SEPTIEMBRE 1962
Monroy, Jean Francois *see* TRAITE D'ARCHITECTURE PRATIQUE
Monsalud, Marques de *see*
- EL CAPITAN GENERAL MARQUES DE MONSALUD
- EL CASTILLO DE LOARRE (INFORME)
- CITANIAS EXTREMENAS
- EPIGRAFIA ROMANA DE EXTREMADURA
- EPIGRAFIA ROMANA DE EXTREMADURA. MARCAS DE ALFAREROS Y GRAFITOS (VILLAFRANCA DE LOS BARROS)
- EPIGRAFIA ROMANA DE MEDINA DE LAS TORRES Y FREGENAL DE LA SIERRA
- EPIGRAFIA ROMANA DE ZARAGOZA Y EXTREMADURA. ZARAGOZA, TARAZONA, ALMENDRALEJO, VALLE DE SANTA ANA, JEREZ DE LOS CABALLEROS
- EPIGRAFIA ROMANA, GRIEGA Y VISIGOTICA DE EXTREMADURA (MERIDA, SOLANA DE LOS BARROS E ITALICA)
- EPIGRAFIA ROMANA Y VISIGOTICA DE EXTREMADURA (MERIDA Y BARCARROTA)
- EPIGRAFIA ROMANA Y VISIGOTICA DE EXTREMADURA Y ANDALUCIA
- INFORME SOBRE LA DECLARACION DE MONUMENTO NACIONAL DE LA IGLESIA. PARROQUIAL DE SANTA EULALIA DE ALAMIA
- INFORME SOBRE LA INSTITUCION DE LA CRUZ-INSIGNIA DE LA REAL MAESTRANZA DE CABALLERIA DE ZARAGOZA
- LAPIDAS EXTREMENAS DE LA EDAD ROMANA Y VISIGOTICA (SALVALEON, MERIDA, ALANGE Y VILLAFRANCA DE LOS BARROS)
- LAS MURALLAS ROMANAS DE ZARAGOZA
- NUEVA LAPIDA ROMANA DE MERIDA
- NUEVAS INSCRIPCIONES CRISTIANAS DE EXTREMADURA Y ANDALUCIA (MERIDA, LA PUEBLA DEL PRIOR Y SEVILLA)
- NUEVAS INSCRIPCIONES DE EXTREMADURA (MERIDA Y TORREMEJIA)
- NUEVAS INSCRIPCIONES DE EXTREMADURA Y ANDALUCIA
- NUEVAS INSCRIPCIONES DE IBAHERNANDO
- NUEVAS INSCRIPCIONES ROMANAS
- NUEVAS INSCRIPCIONES ROMANAS DE EXTREMADURA
- NUEVAS INSCRIPCIONES ROMANAS DE EXTREMADURA. MALPARTIDA DE LA SERENA, ESPARRAGOSA DE LA SERENA, MERIDA
- NUEVAS INSCRIPCIONES ROMANAS DE EXTREMADURA. (MERIDA E IBAHERNANDO)
- NUEVAS INSCRIPCIONES ROMANAS DE EXTREMADURA (VILLAMIEL, MERIDA Y HORNACHOS)
- NUEVAS INSCRIPCIONES ROMANAS DE EXTREMADURA Y ANDALUCIA (MEDELLIN, VILLAFRANCA DE LOS BARROS E ITALICA
- NUEVAS INSCRIPCIONES ROMANAS DE MERIDA
- NUEVAS INSCRIPCIONES ROMANAS EN EXTREMADURA. (MERIDA Y ALANGE)
- NUEVAS INSCRIPCIONES ROMANAS Y VISIGOTICAS DE EXTREMADURA
- NUEVAS INSCRIPCIONES ROMANAS Y VISIGOTICAS DE EXTREMADURA (MERIDA, FERIA, Y SALVATIERRA DE LOS BARROS)
- NUEVAS INSCRIPCIONES ROMANAS Y VISIGOTICAS DE EXTREMADURA (MERIDA, SOLANA DE LOS BARROS, Y LA ALCONERA)
- NUEVAS INSCRIPCIONES ROMANAS Y VISIGOTICAS. MERIDA
- NUEVAS INSCRIPCIONES VISIGOTICAS DE EXTREMADURA (MERIDA Y ALANJE-SIC)
- NUEVAS INSCRIPTIONES ROMANAS DE EXTREMADURA
- NUEVAS LAPIDAS ROMANAS DE EXTREMADURA
- NUEVAS LAPIDAS ROMANAS DE EXTREMADURA (IBAHERNANDO, ARROYO DEL PUERCO Y ALISEDA)
- NUEVAS LAPIDAS VISIGOTICAS
- SANTA EULALIA DE ABAMIA (INFORME)
- LA SINAGOGA DE ZARAGOZA
- EL TEMPLO DE SANTA EULALIA DE MERIDA
- TOMA DE POSESION DE ACADEMICO. NOTICIA
- LAS TORRES DEL SALVADOR Y DE SAN MARTIN Y TECHUMBRE DE LA CATEDRAL DE TERUEL (INFORME)
- VIA ROMANA DE MERIDA A VILLAFRANCA DE LOS BARROS

Monsalvatge, Ramon *see* THE LIFE OF RAMON MONSALVATGE
Monsalvo, O *see* DE PASTILLIS VIPERINIS THERIACAE...
MONSANTO MAGAZINE – v. 51. 1973 – 1,5,6 – us UMI [073]
MONSEIGNEUR DE LAUBERIVIERE, CINQUIEME EVEQUE DE QUEBEC, 1739-1740 / Tanguay, Cyprien – Montreal: Librarie St. Joseph; Cadieux et Derome, 1885. SEM105P54 – 2mf – 9 – Can$4.50 – cn Bibl Nat [240]
MONSEIGNEUR DOMINIQUE RACINE, PREMIER EVEQUE DE CHICOUTIMI. / Huart, V Alphonse – Nouv. ed. Quebec: Drouin et frere..., 1889. SEM105P73 – 2mf – 9 – Can$4.50 – cn Bibl Nat [920]
Monselet, Charles *see* GASTRONOMIE
MONSIEUR BOTTE OU LE NEGOCIANT ANGLAIS / Serviere & Ernest – French Theatre Series – 9 – fr Hachette [820]
MONSIEUR DE PHOCAS: ASTARTE / Lorrain, Jean – Paris: A. Michel, 1929. 316p. 4 fiches. Roman. (Literature Collection) – 9 – 10.00 – fr Bibl Nationale [830]
MONSIEUR GUILLAUME OU LE VOYAGEUR INCONNUE / Barre, Radet, Desfontaines et Bourgueil – (French Theatre Series). Paris. Brunet, an VII. 1800 – 9 – fr Hachette [820]
Monsigny, P *see* LE ROY ET LE FERMIER. COMEDIE EN TROIS ACTES
Monsigny, P-A *see*
- LE DESERTEUR
- LE MAITRE EN DROIT. OPERA BOUFFON EN DEUX ACRES
- ROSE ET COLAS

Monstier, A du OF M *see* NEUSTRIA PIA SEU DE OMNIBUS ET SINGULIS ABBATIIS ET PRIORATIBUS TOTIUS NORMANDIAE
MONSTROSITATES COLEOPTERORUM... / Asmuss, H M – Rigae, Dorpati, 1835 – 2mf – 9 – ne IDC [947]
EL MONSTRUO HORRIBLE DE GRECIA MORTAL ENEMIGO DEL HOMBRE. LAS SANGRIAS / Bustos de Olmedilla, G – Valencia, 1669 – 5mf – 9 – sp Cultura [600]
MONT – 1936 – 1 – us I.U. Libraries [390]
DER MONTAG – Berlin, 1921-32 (incomplete) – 11r – 1 – Inquire at Mikrofilmarchiv for details – gw Misc Inst [943]
DER MONTAG-MORGEN : AUSGABE B – Berlin, 1924-33 (incomplete) – 1 – Inquire at Mikrofilmarchiv for details – gw Misc Inst [943]
LE MONTAGNARD / La Democratie Socialiste des Arrondissements de Saint-Claude (Jura) et de Nantua (Ain) – Organe bi-hebdomadaire. no. 1-144. Saint-Claude. 1893-94 – 1 – fr A.C.R.P.P. [073]
LE MONTAGNARD DU MIDI – Journal du peuple. no. 2-115. Montpellier. 11 mai 1849-1er mai 1850 – 1 – fr A.C.R.P.P. [073]
LA MONTAGNE – Quotidien regional des gauches puis Quotidien populaire independant. Clermont-Ferrand. mai 1940-44. mq 10-30 juin 1940 – 1 – fr A.C.R.P.P. [073]
Montagne, J P F C *see*
- DIAGNOSES PHYCOLOGICAE
- PLANTES CELLULAIRES
- PRODROMUS GENERUM, SPECIERUMQUE PHYCEARUM NOVARUM
- SYLLOGE GENERUM SPECIERUMQUE CRYPTOGAMARUM

Montagne, Lucien *see* ESSAI DE GRAMMAIRE MALGACHE
MONTAGS-ECHO *see* BERLINER MONTAGS-ECHO
MONTAGS-POST – Bremen, 1878-79 (incomplete) – 1r – 1 – Inquire at Mikrofilmarchiv for details – gw Misc Inst [072]
MONTAGS-POST – Bremen, Germany. 1878-1879 (incomplete) – 1r – 1 – gw Mikrofilm [073]

Montagu, Basil *see* A DIGEST OF THE LAW OF PARTNERSHIP.
Montagu, G *see*
- ORNITHOLOGICAL DICTIONARY
- ORNITHOLOGICAL DICTIONARY...

MONTAGUE 1731-1891 – (mf ed 1987) – 30mf – 9 – 0-87623-053-2 – us Holbrook [920]
MONTAGUE 1737-1849 – (Mf 1T: Births & Deaths 1737-1844. Mf 2T: Births 1845-49. Mf 2T-3T: Marriage Intentions 1767-1849. Mf 4T: Marriages 1767-1849; Out-of-Town Marriages 1760-1817. Mf 4T-5T: Deaths 1744-1849) – (mf ed 1997) – 5mf – 9 – 0-87623-297-7 – us Holbrook [920]
Montague Bell, H T *see* CHINA YEAR BOOK
Montague, E R *see* TALES FROM THE TALMUD
Montague, FC *see* CRITICAL AND HISTORICAL ESSAYS CONTRIBUTED TO THE EDINBURGH REVIEW
Montague, Francis Charles *see* LIFE OF SIR ROBERT PEEL
Montague, Katherine *see* MERCURY
Montague, Peter *see* MERCURY
Montaigne, Michel de *see*
- ESSAYS DE MESSIRE MICHEL SEIGNEUR DE MONTAIGNE, ...
- LOVE AND MARRIAGE: BEING MONTAIGNE'S ESSAY SUR DES VERS DE VIRGIL

Montalban, Francisco J *see*
- MANUAL DE HISTORIA DE LAS MISIONES
- MANUALE HISTORIAE MISSIONUM. SHANGAI, 1935

Montalembert, Charles Forbes *see*
- CATHOLIC INTERESTS IN THE NINETEENTH CENTURY
- LIFE OF SAINT ELIZABETH OF HUNGARY
- MEMOIR OF THE ABBE LACORDAIRE

Montalivet, J -P Bachasson *see*
- EXPOSE DE LA SITUATION DE L'EMPIRE PRESENTE AU CORPS LEGISLATIF. LE 12 DEC 1809
- EXPOSE DE LA SITUATION DE L'EMPIRE PRESENTE AU CORPS LEGISLATIF. LE 25 FEV 1813

Montalto, Nicholas V *see* THE INFLUENCE OF ETHNICITY UPON THE POLITICAL BEHAVIOUR OF THE NEW YORK CITY ITALIAN-AMERICAN COMMUNITY SINCE WW2
Montalvo, T *see* PRACTICA POLITICA Y ECONOMICA DE EXPOSITOS...
LA MONTANA – Caceres, 1925 y 1924 – 5 – sp Bibl Santa Ana [073]
MONTANA / American Historical Society – Chicago, 1921. Montana reel 4. (Cox Library Collection) – 5 – us Americana [978]
MONTANA : SESSION LAWS OF AMERICAN STATES AND TERRITORIES – 1864-1995 – 9 – $1,098.00 set – us Hein [340]
Montana *see*
- REPORTS AND OPINIONS (A-G)
- REPORTS, POST-NRS
- REPORTS, PRE-NRS
- SESSION LAWS, 1864-

Montana. Agricultural Experiment Station *see*
- BULLETIN
- CIRCULAR
- MISCELLANEOUS PUBLICATIONS

Montana. Agricultural Extension Service *see*
- AGRICULTURAL PLANNING SERIES
- BULLETIN
- CIRCULARS
- FOLDER
- LEAFLET
- MULTILITH BULLETIN
- MULTILITH CIRCULAR
- NOW
- SERIES B (PLANT DISEASE CIRCULAR)

MONTANA ATTORNEY GENERAL REPORTS AND OPINIONS – (6 1900-1976 $245.00. 9 1977-1990 $110.00) – 1900-1990 – 6,9 – $355.00set – us Hein [340]
MONTANA BAPTIST – Billings, Montana: Montana Southern Baptist Fellowship, 1988-1991 – 1 reel – 1 – $16.64 – us Baptist [240]
MONTANA BAR ASSOCIATION REPORTS – 1885-1914 (all publ) – 4mf – 9 – $18.00 – LLMC 84-615 – us L.L.M.C. [073]
MONTANA BAR ASSOCIATION REPORTS – 1921-47 (all publ) – 8mf – 9 – $36.00 – LLMC 84-616 – us L.L.M.C. [073]
Montana. Bureau of Agriculture, Labor and Industry *see* STATE LABOR REPORTS
MONTANA CATHOLIC REGISTER – Great Falls. Mont. 1954-1959; 1966- – 1 – us UMI [071]
MONTANA CATHOLIC REGISTER – Helena. Mont. Western Ed. 1966- – 1 – us UMI [071]
MONTANA EDUCATION – v1-53 1924-77 1; v47-53 5,6; v53 9 – us UMI [370]
MONTANA FARMER – v1-v34,no.17. 1913-1 May 1947 – 1 – us UMI [630]
MONTANA FARMER-STOCKMAN – Great Falls. Mont. 1950-1954; 1956-1957; 1966- – 1 – us UMI [071]
Montana. Forest and Conservation Experiment Station. Missoula *see*
- BULLETIN
- LUBRECHT SERIES
- MISC. PAPERS
- NOTES
- PROCEEDINGS
- SPECIAL

MONTANA FREE PRESS – Butte. Mont. 1928-1929 – 1 – us UMI [071]
MONTANA GRANGE NEWS – Kalispell. Mont. 1966- – 1 – us UMI [071]
Montana Inter-Tribal Policy Boards *see* MINUTES, 1968-70
MONTANA: ITS STORY AND BIOGRAPHY / Stout, Tom – (v3. Montana reel 3) – Chicago: American Historical Society, 1921. v1-2. Montana reel 2. (Cox Library Collection) – 5 – us Americana [978]
MONTANA KAIMAN – Missoula. Mont. 1901-1904; 1910-1918; 1921-1967 – 1 – us UMI [071]
MONTANA LABOR NEWS – Butte. Mont. 1946-1951 – 1 – us UMI [071]
MONTANA LAW NOTES – v1 no 1 1929 (all publ) – 1mf – 9 – $1.50 – LLMC 84-614 – us L.L.M.C. [073]
MONTANA LAW REVIEW – v1- 1940- 1; v36- 5,6,9 – us UMI [340]
MONTANA LAW REVIEW – (v1-45 1940-84 on reel $320.00. v46-55 1985-94 on mf $137.00) – v1-55. 1940-94 – 5,6,9 – $457.00 set – us Hein [340]
MONTANA LAWYER – v1-19. 1975-94 – 9 – $242.00 set – us Hein [340]
MONTANA LIBRARY QUARTERLY – 1955-63 – 1 – us UMI [020]
MONTANA MAGAZINE – 1985-. -bim – 1 – us UMI [073]
MONTANA MINERS' CODE. / Howell, Edward Beach – Butte, Mont.: Inter Mountain Publishing Co., 1896. 72p. LL-576 – 1 – us L of C Photodup [340]
MONTANA OIL JOURNAL – Billings. Mont. -w. 1947-54, 1956-59, 1966- – 1 – us UMI [071]
MONTANA SILVERITE – Missoula. Mont. 1894-1897 – 1 – us UMI [071]
MONTANA STANDARD – Butte. Mont. 1929- – 1 – us UMI [071]
Montana. State Bar Association *see* PROCEEDINGS
Montana. Supreme Court *see* MONTANA SUPREME COURT REPORTS
MONTANA SUPREME COURT REPORTS / Montana. Supreme Court – (Pre-NRS: v1-3 1868-83 8mf $36.00; 9. Updates planned) – v1-51. 1868-1919/20 – 123mf (1:42) 80mf (1:24) – 9 – $674.00 – LLMC 84-163 – us L.L.M.C. [340]
MONTANA, THE MAGAZINE OF WESTERN HISTORY – v1- 1951- 1; 1971- 5,6; 1977- 4 x 6 in. 9 – us UMI [978]
Montanchez, Ayuntamiento *see* ORDENANZAS MUNICIPALES
Montanchez. Ayuntamiento *see* PROGRAMA OFICIAL DE CULTOS Y FESTEJOS EN HONOR DE LA VIRGEN DE LA CONSOLACION DEL CASTILLO...1977
Montanchez, Enrique y *see* PROGRAMA... CASTELLANO
Montanchez, Escuela Hogar Leon Leal *see* MEMORIA DEL CURSO 1971-72
MONTANCHEZ. NUEVA INSCRIPCION ROMANA / Fita, Fidel – Madrid: Fortanet, 1902. B.R.A.H. 41. pp. 446-447 – 1 – sp Bibl Santa Ana [946]
Montanchez. Sociedad de Seguros de Ganados *see* REGLAMENTO DE...DENOMINADA "LA REALIDAD"
Montaner, Joaquin *see*
- MEDITACIONES LIRICAS
- POEMAS INMEDIATOS
- PRIMER LIBRO DE ODAS

Montang, E J *see* THE SIN OF THE ANGELS
Montanus, A *see* BIBLIA SACRA HEBRAICE, CHALDAICE, GRAECE, LATINE
MONTANUS REDIVIVUS : OR, MONTANISM REVIVED IN THE PRINCIPLES AND DISCIPLINE OF THE METHODISTS (COMMONLY CALLED SWADLERS),... / Clark, J – Dublin, 1760 – 2mf – 9 – MP-387/1 – ne IDC [240]
MONTAN-ZEITUNG FUER OESTERRECH UNGARN, UND DIE BALKANLAENDEN – Graz, Austria. -f. Jan 1897-Dec 1906. 5 reels – 1 – uk British Libr Newspaper [072]
Montauban *see* RELATION DU VOYAGE DU SIEUR DE MONTAUBAN EN L'ANNEE 1695. AVEC UNE DESCRIPTION DU ROYAUME DU CAP DE LOPEZ, DES MOEURS, DES COUTUMES, ET DE LA RELIGION DU PAYS
MONTAVILLA SUN – Portland OR. Mar 12-June 18 1915 – 1 – us U.O. Library [071]
MONTAVILLA TIMES – Portland OR. Feb 18 1926-Feb 15 1935 – 1 – us U.O. Library [071]
Montblanc, C de *see* LE JAPON SES INSTITUTIONS, SES PRODUITS, SES RELATIONS AVEC L'EUROPE
LE MONTCALM – Ste-Julienne, Canada. v2 n11. 17 nov 1888; v2 n12. 24 nov 1888 – 1r – 1 – Can$25.00 – cn Can Microfilming [072]
MONTCALM DEVANT LA POSTERITE: ETUDE HISTORIQUE / Falgairolle, Edmond – Paris: Challamel, 1886. 02944. (Pre-1900 Canadiana) – 9 – cn C.I.H.M. [971]
MONTCALM ET LE CANADA FRANCAIS: ESSAIS HISTORIQUE / Bonnechose, Charles de – Paris: Hachette, 1877. 00181. (Pre-1900 Canadiana) – 9 – cn C.I.H.M. [971]
MONTCALM ET LEVIS: LES FRANCAIS AU CANADA / Casgrain, Henri-Raymond – Tour: Mame, 1898?. 03312. (Pre-1900 Canadiana) – 9 – cn C.I.H.M. [971]
MONTCALM ET LEVIS: LES HEROS DE QUEBEC / Casgrain, Henri-Raymond – Tours, France: A. Mame, 1895? 02054. (Pre-1900 Canadiana) – 9 – cn C.I.H.M. [920]
Montciel, Marie-de *see* BIBLIOGRAPHIE ANALYTIQUE DE L'OEUVRE DU DOCTEUR JEAN-CHARLES MILLER, MEDECIN-PSYCHIATRE A L'ECOLE LA JEMMERAIS, 1898-1952
MONTCLAIR COURIER – Montclair, CA. 1973-83 – 11r – 1 – $550.00 – R02476 – us Library Micro [071]
THE MONTCLARION – Oakland, CA. 1971 – 27+ r – 1 – $1,350.00 ($90.00y) – B03365 – us Library Micro [071]
MONTE CARMELLO – Cidade de Monte Carmello, 26 Nov 1922; 24 Oct 1926 – 1,5,6 – bl Biblioteca [072]
MONTE CARMELLO : UM JORNAL A SERVICO DA REGIAO – Monte Carmelo, 12 May-12 Nov 1979 – 1,5,6 – bl Biblioteca [072]
MONTE DE LA MYRRA Y COLLADO DEL INCIENSO TRASLADADOS POR LA IMITACION AL SERAFICO MONASTERIO DE...Y CHRONICA DE LA FUNDACION DEL Y DE LAS VENERABLES RELIGIOSAS... / Madres Capuchinas – Madrid: Imp. de Miguel Gomez, 1718 – 1 – sp Bibl Santa Ana [240]
Monte de Piedad y Caja General de Ahorros *see*
- MEMORIA 1942
- MEMORIA CORRESPONDIENTE AL EJERCICIO DE 1948
- MEMORIA Y DATOS ESTADISTICOS CORRESPONDIENTES AL ANO 1934

MONTE DE PIEDAD Y CAJA GENERAL DE AHORROS DE BADAJOZ – Tip. Vda. de A. Arqueros, 1944 – 1 – sp Bibl Santa Ana [946]
Monte de Piedad y Caja General de Ahorros de Badajoz *see*
- MEMORIA Y DATOS ESTADISTICOS CORRESPONDIENTES AL ANO 1936
- MEMORIA Y DATOS ESTADISTICOS CORRESPONDIENTES AL ANO DE 1925
- REGLAMENTO DE SUCURSALES Y AGENCIAS ANO, 1940

MONTE DE PIEDAD Y CAJA GENERAL DE AHORROS DE BADAJOZ. MEMORIA DE 1945 – Badajoz: Tip. Arqueros, 1946 – 1 – sp Bibl Santa Ana [946]
MONTE DE PIEDAD Y CAJA GENERAL DE AHORROS DE BADAJOZ. MEMORIA DEL EJERCICIO DE 1938 – Sevilla: Imp. Arte, 1939 – 1 – sp Bibl Santa Ana [946]
MONTE DE PIEDAD Y CAJA GENERAL DE AHORROS. MEMORIA DE 1946 – Badajoz Arqueros, 1947 – 1 – sp Bibl Santa Ana [946]
UN MONTE DI PILATO IN ITALIA / Graf, Arturo – 1889 – 1 – us I.U. Libraries [390]
Monteclair, Michel P *see* PRINCIPES DE MUSIQUE..
Montecuccoli, Raimondo *see* MEMOIRES DE MONTECUCCOLI, GENERALISSIME DES TROUPES DE L'EMPEREUR, DIVISES EN TROIS LIVRES
Montefiore, CG *see* A RABBINIC ANTHOLOGY
Montefiore, Claude Goldsmid *see* LECTURES ON THE ORIGIN AND GROWTH OF RELIGION AS ILLUSTRATED BY THE RELIGION OF THE ANCIENT HEBREWS
MONTEFIORE COLLECTION OF HEBREW MANUSCRIPTS / Library of Jews' College. London – (589 Hebrew mss concerning a range of subjects. Coll also contains five censuses conducted between 1839-1875 which detail thousands of Jewish inhabitants of Palestine. With printed catalogue and contents list) – 1994 – 1250mf – 9 – $9,994.00 – 1-869934-64-4 – uk Emmett [090]
Montefiore, Joshua *see* COMMERCIAL AND NOTARIAL PRECEDENTS.
Montegazza, Vico *see*
- IL BENADIR
- MENELIK

Montegut, Maurice *see* LEMUR: MARS-AVRIL-MAI 1871
Monteil, Amans A *see* DESCRIPTION DU DEPARTEMENT DE L'AVEIRON
Monteil, Charles Victor *see* SOUDAN FRANCAIS
Monteil, Edgar *see* THE FREETHINKER'S CATECHISM
Monteil, P L *see*
- DE SAINT-LOUIS A TRIPOLI PAR LE LAC TCHAD
- DE SAINT-LOUIS A TRIPOLI PAR LE LAC TCHAD, VOYAGE AU TRAVERS DU SOUDAN ET DU SAHARA ACCOMPLI PENDANT LES ANNEES 1890-91-92

Monteil, Vincent *see* ESSAI SUR LE CHAMEAU AU SAHARA OCCIDENTAL
Monteiro, J J *see* ANGOLA AND THE RIVER CONGO
Monteiro, Mariana *see* LEGENDS AND POPULAR TALES OF THE BASQUE PEOPLE
Montejano *see* NOTAS PARA UNA BIBLIOGRAFIA GUADALUPANA
Monte-Lauduno, Guillermo de *see* SACRAMENTALE (SIECLE 14)
Monteleon, C de *see* SILUETA BIOGRAFICA DEDICADA AL EXCMO. SR. D. RAFAEL DURAN Y MARTINEZ. (MANUSCRITO)
Montella, G D *see* SETTIMO LIBRO DE MADRGALI, A CINQUE VOCI DI GIO. DOMENICO MONTELLA NAPOLITANO
MONTEMOLIN. HALLAZGOS EN SU TERMINO MUNICIPAL DE LA EPOCA ROMANA – Madrid: Fortanet, 1891. B.R.A.H. 18, pp. 468-470 – sp Bibl Santa Ana [946]
Montenay, G de *see*
- EMBLEMES, OU DEVISES CHRESTIENNES
- HONDERD CHRISTELIJKE ZINNEBEELDEN NAAR GEORGETTE DE MONTENAY, DOOR ANNA ROEMERS VISSCHER

Montenegro *see* SLUZBENI LIST
Montenegro, Abelardo Fernando *see* HISTORIA DO FANATISMO RELIGIOSO NO CEARA
Montenegro, Carlos *see* AVIONES SOBRE EL PUEBLO
Montengon, Pedro *see*
- EUSEBIO (NOVELA). TOMO 1
- EUSEBIO (NOVELA). TOMO 2
- EUSEBIO (NOVELA). TOMO 3
- EUSEBIO (NOVELA). TOMO 4

MONTEREY 1825-1895 – (mf ed 1988) – 8mf – 9 – 0-87623-091-5 – us Holbrook [920]
MONTEREY AMERICAN – Monterey, CA. 1913-1916 – 8r – 1 – $360.00 – B03618 – us Library Micro [071]
MONTEREY ARGUS – Monterey, CA. 1887-88 (broken series) – 1r – 1 – $50.00 – C02477 – us Library Micro [071]
MONTEREY COUNTY HERALD – Monterey, CA. 1952- – 690+ r – 1 – $34,500.00 ($650.00y) – 02484 – us Library Micro [071]
MONTEREY COUNTY INCLUDING CARMEL, DEL MONTE, PACIFIC GROVE, SEASIDE AND SALINAS – Monterey Co, CA. 1907; 1916-1917; 1926-1951 – 16r – 1 – $800.00 – D061 – us Library Micro [978]
MONTEREY COUNTY POST – Salinas, CA. 1929-1933 – 3r – 1 – $150.00 – C03445 – us Library Micro [071]
MONTEREY DEMOCRAT – Monterey, CA. 1870-1872 – 1r – 1 – $50.00 – C03619 – us Library Micro [071]
MONTEREY DEMOCRAT – Salinas, CA. 1888-89 – 1r – 1 – $50.00 – C02754 – us Library Micro [071]

MONTEREY FIRST BAPTIST CHURCH. MONTEREY, TENNESSEE : CHURCH RECORDS – 1927-61 – 1 – 42.93 – us Baptist [240]
MONTEREY PARK PROGRESS : AND MONTEREY PARK TRIBUNE UND COURIER – (Also known as: Ramona Acres Progress) – Monterey Park, CA. 1918-1924; 1927 – 82+ r – 1 – $4,100.00 ($60.00y) – H04031 – us Library Micro [071]
MONTEREY SENTINEL – Monterey, CA. 1855-56 – 1r – 1 – $50.00 – B02481 – us Library Micro [071]
MONTEREY TRADER – Monterey, CA. 1933-36; 1940-51 – 7r – 1 – $350.00 – C02486 – us Library Micro [071]
MONTEREY WEEKLY CYPRESS – Monterey, CA. 1889-91; 1896-1901 – 3r – 1 – $150.00 – C02479 – us Library Micro [071]
MONTEREYAN – Monterey. Calif. 1951-55 – 1 – us UMI [071]
THE MONTEREYAN – Monterey, CA. 1951-55 – 1r – 1 – $50.00 – C02482 – us Library Micro [071]
MONTEREY/SAN BENITO COUNTIES – 1909-34; 1992- – 22+ r – 1 – $1,100.00 – P00066 – us Library Micro [910]
Montero de Espinosa, Luis *see*
– ADMINISTRACION DE ESPANA EN EL REINADO DE LOS REYES CATOLICOS
– ADMINISTRACION...REYES CATOLICOS
Montero de Espinosa, Marques de *see* NUEVAS NOTAS SOBRE EL CONDADO DE LA GOMERA
Montero de Espinosa y de la Barrera, Francisco *see* UN TRAJE A MEDIDA DE LOS ALCALDES
Montero Diaz, Santiago *see*
– LA POLITICA SOCIAL EN LA ZONA MARXISTA
– LA REVOLUCION NACIONAL-SINDICALISTA Y LOS TRABAJADORES
Montero, Eloy *see* LO QUE VI EN RUSIA. MADRID, 1935
Montero Garcia, Feliciano *see* REFORMISMO CONSERVADOR...ESPANA DE LA RESTAURACION
UN MONTERO GENIAL / Segura Otano, Enrique – Madrid: Centro de Estudios Extremenos, 1939 – sp Bibl Santa Ana [946]
Montero Monago, Nemesio E *see* CANTOS EN NEGRO Y ESPERANZA
Montero y Santaren, Eulogio *see*
– ARITMETICA ELEMENTAL
– DIALOGO DE LA INFANCIA Y ADOLESCENCIA
Monterrey, Manuel *see*
– LIRA PROVINCIA. POESIA
– MEDALLONES EXTREMENOS
– MEDALLONES EXTREMENOS 2
– NOSTALGIAS
– PALABRAS LIRICAS
Monterrubio de la Serena, Ayuntamiento *see* FERIA Y FIESTAS SEPTIEMBRE 1970
Montes, Eugenio *see* LA HORA DE LA UNIDAD
Montes, J *see* TRATADO DE ENFERMEDADES ENDEMICAS EPIDEMICAS CONTAGIOSAS A TODA ESPECIE DE GANADO
Montes, Jose *see* FORMACION DE LAS FALANGES JUVENILES DE FRANCO
Montes, San Pedro de *see*
– HISTORIA DEL MONASTERIO (SIECLE 19)
– TUMBO ANTIGUO (SIECLE 13)
Montesino, Cipriano S *see*
– MEMORIA...EXPOSICION LONDRES
– ROMPIMIENTO DEL ISTMO DE SUEZ
Montet, Edouard Louis *see* ESSAI SUR LES ORIGINES DES PARTIS SADUCEEN ET PHARISIEN...
MONTEUR KLINKHAMMER : UND ANDERE BRUECKENBAUERGESCHICHTEN / Grisar, Erich – Bayreuth: Gauverlag Bayreuth, 1943 – 1 – us U.W. Library [830]
MONTEVALLO BAPTIST CHURCH. MONTEVALLO, ALABAMA : CHURCH RECORDS – 1856-1939 – 1 – 13.32 – us Baptist [240]
Monteverdi, Claudio *see*
– MADRIGALS
– SONATA SOPRA SANCTA MARIA ORA PRO NOBIS. ARRANGED FOR SOPRANO, STRING QUARTET, AND PIANO BY L. TORRI
Montevideo. Uruguay *see* DIARIO OFICIEL
Montezuma, Carlos *see* THE PAPERS OF CARLOS MONTEZUMA, M.D
Montfaucon, B de *see* BIBLIOTHECA BIBLIOTHECARUM MANUSCRIPTORUM NOVA
MONTFERRAND : DRAME CANADIEN EN 4 ACTES ET 9 TABLEAUX / Guyon, Louis – Montreal: Mercantile Printing, [1923?]. SEM105P1642 – 1mf – 9 – Can$2.25 – cn Bibl Nat [820]
Montfort, Charles *see* LE JOURNAL D'UNE SAPHISTE
MONTGOMERY 1698-1851 – (Mf 1T-2T: Vital Records 1698-1845. Mf 3T: Intents & Marriages 1781-1826. Mf 3T-4T: Births & Deaths 1798-1844. Mf 4T: Intentions 1825-50. Mf 4T-5T: Marriages 1823-50. Mf 5T: Births 1844-50; Deaths 1844- 50) – (mf ed 1997) – 5mf – 9 – 0-87623-298-5 – us Holbrook [920]
MONTGOMERY 1739-1899 – (mf ed 1988) – 9mf – 9 – 0-87623-085-0 – us Holbrook [920]
MONTGOMERY BAPTIST CHURCH. COLMAR, PENNSYLVANIA : CHURCH RECORDS – 1719-c1944 – 1 – 5.00 – us Baptist [240]
Montgomery, H H *see*
– MANKIND AND THE CHURCH
– SERVICE ABROAD
– VISIONS
– VISIONS. THIRD SERIES
Montgomery, Helen Barrett *see*
– CHRISTUS REDEMPTOR
– FOLLOWING THE SUNRISE
– WESTERN WOMEN IN EASTERN LANDS
Montgomery, James *see*
– ORIGINAL HYMNS FOR PUBLIC, PRIVATE AND SOCIAL DEVOTION
– SELECTED PAPERS
Montgomery, James A *see*
– ARABIA AND THE BIBLE
– THE SAMARITANS, THE EARLIEST JEWISH SECT; THEIR HISTORY, THEOLOGY, AND LITERATURE
Montgomery, John *see* HISTORY OF MAJOR JOHN MONTGOMERY WHO CAME FROM IRELAND ABOUT 1720 OR '24
THE MONTGOMERY JOURNAL – Montgomery, AL: [s.n.] jan-june 1920 – 2r – 1 – us Res Libr [071]
MONTGOMERY KANSAS MARRIAGES – Item H. News clippings of vital statistics orig. publ. in this newspaper. SW16-0028 – 5 – us A.G.L.L. [310]
MONTGOMERY LEDGER – Montgomery, PA. -w 1889-1910 – 13 – $25.00r – us I.M.R. [071]
Montgomery, Mary Emma (Milner) *see* "LITTLE KNOWN OR EXTINCT TOWNS OF KANSAS"
Montgomery. Maryland. Baptist Associations *see* ANNUALS
Montgomery, Morton L *see*
– HISTORICAL AND BIOGRAPHICAL ANNALS OF BERKS COUNTY
– HISTORY OF BERKS COUNTY
MONTGOMERY NEWS MESSENGER – Christiansburg. Va. 1950- – 1 – us UMI [071]
Montgomery, Robert *see*
– THE OMNIPRESENCE OF THE DEITY
– SATAN
Montgomery, Robert H *see* AUDITING THEORY AND PRACTICE
MONTGOMERY TRANSCRIPT – Boyertown, PA., 1951 – 13 – $25.00r – us I.M.R. [071]
Montgomery W *see* ST. AUGUSTINE
Montgomery Watt, W *see* FREE WILL AND PREDESTINATION IN EARLY ISLAM
Montgomery, Zachariah *see* THE MECHANICS' LIEN LAW FOR THE STATE OF CALIFORNIA
MONTGOMERY'S VINDICATOR – Sevierville. Tenn. 1897-1934 – 1 – us UMI [071]
Montgommery, Louis de *see* LA MILICE FRANCAISE, CONTENANT PLUSIEURS BELLES ET NOTABLES INSTRUCTIONS SUR CE QUI DOIT ETRE OBSERVE A BIEN ORDONNER DES BATAILLES
MONTH – 1864- 1; 1971- 5,6; 1977- 9 – us UMI [073]
"THE MONTH AT GOODSPEED'S", 1929-1969 – 5r – 1 – $65.00 set – us Dartmouth [090]
MONTH AT GOODSPEED'S, 1929-1969 / ed by Dodge, Norman – (Catalog of Goodspeed's rare book shop, Boston) – 5r – 1 – $370.00 – us UMI [090]
A MONTH IN THE UNITED STATES AND CANADA IN THE AUTUMN OF 1873 / Cameron, William – Greenock Scotland: Pollock and M'Cunn, 1874. 00924. (Pre-1900 Canadiana) – 9 – cn C.I.H.M. [910]
Monthaye *see* MON JOURNAL DE BORD D'ANVERS A LEOPOLDVILLE PAR LE CHEMIN DES ECOLIERS
Montherot, F de *see* OFFRANDE AUX SAINT-SIMONIENS. LE NAIN MYSTERIEUX, PROVERBE DRAMATIQUE
THE MONTHLY ADVOCATE – [Saint John, NB]: R A H Morrow, [1880-188-] – 9 – cn C.I.H.M. [240]
MONTHLY AMERICAN JOURNAL OF GEOLOGY AND NATURAL SCIENCE – v. 1-12. Jul 1831-Jun 1832 – 1 – us UMI [550]
MONTHLY ANTHOLOGY AND BOSTON REVIEW – v. 1-10. Nov 1803-Jun 1811 – 1 – us UMI [073]
MONTHLY BULLETIN – Federation of State Medical Boards of the United States. v.1-6. 1915-20. Continued as yFederation Bulletin – 1 – us UMI [073]
MONTHLY BULLETIN / Mine Ventilation Society of South Africa – v1-9 1948-1956 – 1 – us UMI [622]
MONTHLY BULLETIN / Washington. Western Washington Research and Extension Center. Puyallup. Agricultural Experiment Station – v.1-12. 1913-25 – 1,5,6 – us Spaulding [630]
MONTHLY BULLETIN OF STATISTICS – 1947- 1; 1971- 5,6; 1976- 4 x 6 in. 9 – us UMI [310]
THE MONTHLY BULLETIN OF THE OHIO MESSIANIC TESTIMONY – 1938-48 (complete) – 1r – 1 – ATLA S0530 – us A.T.L.A. [240]
MONTHLY CALENDAR OF THE CHURCH OF OUR LADY OF GOOD COUNSEL, ST MARY'S – [S.]: s.n., 18—189-?] – 9 – cn C.I.H.M. [240]
MONTHLY CATALOG OF UNITED STATES GOVERNMENT PUBLICATIONS – (1968- 5,6. 1970- 9) – 1895- – 1 – us UMI [010]
MONTHLY CATALOG OF UNITED STATES GOVERNMENT PUBLICATIONS / Government Printing Office, Superintendent of Documents – (Not to be issued in mf after 1995) – 1994-1995 – 9 – $41.00y in US $51.25y outside (1995 $47.00 in US $58.75 outside) – 0-16-011207-9 – us Gov't Printing [324]
MONTHLY CATALOG OF U.S. GOVERNMENT PUBLICATIONS / U.S. Superintendent of Documents – Nos. 367-1035. 1925-80 – 1,5,6 – us Princeton Micro [324]
MONTHLY CATALOGUE – v. 1-4. Mar 1723-30 – 1 – us UMI [010]
THE MONTHLY CHAPBOOK – London. v. 1-40. July 1919-1925 – 1 – us NY Public [800]
MONTHLY CHECKLIST OF STATE PUBLICATIONS / U.S. Library of Congress – (Final index vol to be available) – Washington: GPO. v1-85 no 12. 1910-94 (all publ) – 985mf – 9 – $1,477.00 – LLMC 81-409 – us L.L.M.C. [324]
MONTHLY CHRONICLE – A National Journal of Politics, Literature, Science, and Art. v. 1-7. Mar 1838-Jun 1841 – 1 – us UMI [073]
MONTHLY CHRONICLE, OF EVENTS, DISCOVERIES, IMPROVEMENTS, AND OPINIONS – v. 1-3. Apr 1840-42 – 1 – us UMI [073]
MONTHLY CHURCH REGISTER FOR THE DIOCESES OF QUEBEC, TORONTO, AND MONTREAL *see* THE CANADIAN ECCLESIASTICAL GAZETTE, OR, MONTHLY CHURCH REGISTER FOR THE DIOCESES OF QUEBEC, TORONTO, AND MONTREAL
THE MONTHLY CIRCULAR / Labour Research Department. London – 1917-30.Continued by: Labour Research – 1 – uk World [331]
MONTHLY COST OF LIVING INDEX FOR TRIPOLI TOWN / Libya. Ministry of National Economy – Tripoli Jul, Oct-Dec 1965, Jan-Aug 1966, Jan-Dec 1967, Jul-Sep 1968, Apr, Oct-Dec 1969, Jan-Sep 1970, Jul-Dec 1971, Jan-Dec 1972, Jan-Jun 1973. BNE-619 1 – 9 – ne IDC [339]
MONTHLY DETROIT – 1978- – 1,5,6,9 – us UMI [073]
MONTHLY DIGEST : AN ANALYTICAL DIGEST OF EQUITY, COMMON LAW, ETC – London. 1v. 1850 (all publ) – 9 – LLMC 84-617 – us L.L.M.C. [073]
THE MONTHLY ECHO – Englishtown, NS: J C McLean, [1883-1884] – 9 – cn C.I.H.M. [971]
MONTHLY ENERGY REVIEW – v4- 1978- – 1,5,6,9 – us UMI [621]
MONTHLY FILM BULLETIN – (Incorporated with Sight and Sound after 1991) – London, 1934-91 – 1 – £895.00 – uk World [790]
MONTHLY FREIGHT AND SHIPPING REPORT OF R.P. RITHET AND CO., LTD. FOR... – Victoria, BC: The Company, [18—189- or 19-] – 9 – cn C.I.H.M. [380]
THE MONTHLY ILLUSTRATOR – 1893-95 – 22mf – 9 – £120.00 – uk Chadwyck [740]
MONTHLY INTELLIGENCER – (New York). 1900-02 – 1 – us A.J.P.C. [073]
MONTHLY JOURNAL OF AGRICULTURE *see* AMERICAN FARMERS' MAGAZINE
MONTHLY JOURNAL OF FOREIGN MEDICINE – v. 1-3. Jan 1828-Jun 1829 – 1 – us UMI [610]
MONTHLY JOURNAL OF MEDICINE – v. 1-6. Jan 1823-Dec 1825 – 1 – us UMI [616]
MONTHLY JURIST – (Cont by: The Weekly Jurist 1879-81. Not yet offered by LLMC) – Bloomington, IN. v1-2. 1877-79 (all publ) – 18mf – 9 – $27.00 – LLMC 82-947 – us L.L.M.C. [073]
MONTHLY LABOR REVIEW / U.S. Department of Labor – (Updates planned) – Bureau of Labor Statistics. v1-117 no 10. 1915-Oct 1994 – 2042mf – 9 – $3,063.00 – LLMC 81-216 – us L.L.M.C. [331]
MONTHLY LABOR REVIEW – v. 1-96. 1915-1973 – 1 – us Princeton Micro [331]
MONTHLY LABOR REVIEW – (v. 92- 1969- 5,6. v. 93- 1970- 9) – v. 1- 1915- – 1 – us UMI [331]
THE MONTHLY LAW DIGEST AND REPORTER – Montreal: A Periard, [1892?-1893] – 9 – cn C.I.H.M. [340]
THE MONTHLY LAW MAGAZINE – London. v1-10. 1838-41 (all publ) – 9 – LLMC 84-618 – us L.L.M.C. [073]
MONTHLY LAW REPORTER – v. 1-27. 10 Mar 1838-May 1866 – 1 – us UMI [340]
THE MONTHLY LAW REPORTER – Boston. v1-27. 1838-66 (all publ) – 9 – LLMC 82-946 – us L.L.M.C. [073]
MONTHLY LEAFLET OF THE CANADA CONGREGATIONAL WOMAN'S BOARD OF MISSIONS – (Merged with: Missionary Messenger. Merged with: Missionary Outlook. Merged with: Monthly Letter. Merged with: The Message. Merged to become: Missionary Monthly) – Montreal: [Canada Congregational Woman's Board of Missions, 1895-1925?] – 9 – cn C.I.H.M. [240]
MONTHLY LEAFLET OF THE CANADA CONGRETATIONAL WOMAN'S BOARD OF MISSIONS *see* MONTHLY LETTER
MONTHLY LETTER – (Cont: Missionary Leaflet. Merged with: Missionary Messenger, Missionary Outlook, Monthly Leaflet of the Canada Congretational Woman's Board of Missions, The Message. Merged to become: Missionary Monthly) – Toronto: Woman's Missionary Society of the Methodist Church, Canada, [1893-1925] – 9 – cn C.I.H.M. [240]
MONTHLY LETTER : MENNONITE WOMEN'S MISSIONARY SOCIETY – nos11-18 v4-9. 1921-28 (complete) – 1r – 1 – ATLA 1994-S039 – us A.T.L.A. [073]
MONTHLY LETTER *see*
– MISSIONARY LEAFLET
– MONTHLY LEAFLET OF THE CANADA CONGREGATIONAL WOMAN'S BOARD OF MISSIONS
MONTHLY LETTER LEAFLET / Presbyterian Church in Canada. Woman's Foreign Missionary Society. Western Division – (Cont: Presbyterian Church in Canada, Woman's Foreign Missionary Society. Western Division, Woman's Foreign Missionary Society. Cont by: Presbyterian Church in Canada, Woman's Foreign Missionary Society, Western Division, Foreign missionary tidings) – Toronto: Printed for the Society by the Mall Job Dep. [1886-1897] – 9 – cn C.I.H.M. [240]
MONTHLY LETTER LEAFLET *see* LETTER LEAFLET OF THE WOMAN'S AUXILIARY TO THE BOARD OF DOMESTIC AND FOREIGN MISSIONS OF THE CHURCH OF ENGLAND IN CANADA
MONTHLY MAGAZINE – v. 1-2. 1808-09 – 1 – us UMI [073]
MONTHLY MAGAZINE – v. 1-3s, v.9. Feb 1796-Jun 1843 – 1 – us UMI [073]
THE MONTHLY MAGAZINE – (New York). 1897 – 1 – us A.J.P.C. [073]
MONTHLY MAGAZINE AND AMERICAN REVIEW – v. 1. Apr 1799-Dec 1800 – 1 – us UMI [073]
MONTHLY MAGAZINE AND LITERARY JOURNAL – v. 1-2. May 1812-Apr 1813 – 1 – us UMI [073]
MONTHLY MAXIMUM OF FAMILY EXPENDITURE FOR TRIPOLI CITY / Libya – Aug 1964. BNE-614 1 – 9 – ne IDC [339]
MONTHLY MILITARY REPOSITORY – v. 1-2. 1796-97 – 1 – us UMI [355]
MONTHLY MISCELLANY OF RELIGION AND LETTERS – v. 1-9. Apr 1839-Dec 1843 – 1 – us UMI [240]

MONTHLY MISCELLANY; OR MEMOIRS FOR THE CURIOUS – v. 1-3. Jan 1707-Oct 1709 – 1 – us UMI [073]

MONTHLY MISCELLANY; OR VERMONT MAGAZINE – v. 1. Apr-Sep 1794 – 1 – us UMI [073]

MONTHLY MUSICAL RECORD – v. 1-88. 1871-1958 – 1 – 261.00 – us L of C Photodup [780]

MONTHLY NOTES – [Toronto: s.n, 189?-19–] – 9 – cn C.I.H.M. [240]

MONTHLY NOTES, FARM MANAGEMENT AND FARM ECONOMICS *see* AGRICULTURAL SITUATION

MONTHLY NOTICES OF THE PRIMITIVE METHODIST MISSIONARY SOCIETY – (Cont as: Records of Missionary of the Primitive Methodist Missionary Society. London 1870-1892; Cont as: The Record. Organ of the Primitive Home, Colonial and Foreign Missionary Society. London 1893-1904. Cont as: The Herald of the Primitive Methodist Missionary Society. London 1905-1922. Cont as: Advance. Missionary Organ of the Primitve Methodist Church. London 1923-1932. Missing: 1848-1850(1-81); 1871(13); 1875(40); 1899-1902) – London, 1848-1869 – 131mf – 9 – ne IDC [240]

MONTHLY PAPER – [Victoria, BC?: s.n, 1892-189- or 19–] – 9 – cn C.I.H.M. [240]

MONTHLY RADIO BROADCASTS / Alabama. Polytechnic Institute. Extension Service. Negro Division – 1940-41 – 1,5,6 – us Spaulding [630]

THE MONTHLY RECORD OF THE CHURCH OF SCOTLAND IN NOVA SCOTIA – Halifax [NS]: Printed for the Proprietor by J Bowes, [1855?-18– or 19–] – 9 – cn C.I.H.M. [240]

MONTHLY RECORD OF THE FREE CHURCH OF SCOTLAND – 1886-1900, 1959-79 – 1 – us A.T.L.A. [240]

MONTHLY RECORDER, A MAGAZINE – 1. Apr-Aug 1813 – 1 – us UMI [073]

MONTHLY REGISTER MAGAZINE AND REVIEW OF THE UNITED STATES – v. 1-4. Jan 1805-Dec 1807 – 1 – us UMI [073]

MONTHLY REPOSITORY – 1-ns1. Jan 1806-Apr 1838 – 1 – us UMI [073]

MONTHLY REPOSITORY AND REVIEW OF THEOLOGY AND GENERAL LITERATURE *see* MONTHLY REPOSITORY

MONTHLY REPOSITORY OF THEOLOGY AND GENERAL LITERATURE *see* MONTHLY REPOSITORY

MONTHLY RETAIL PRICES IN TRIPOLI TOWN / Libya. Ministry of Planning. Census and Statistical Department – Jan-Dec 1972, Jan-Mar 1973. Tripoli. 1972. BNE-629 1 – 9 – ne IDC [338]

MONTHLY RETURNS OF IMPORTS AND EXPORTS AT THE PORT OF TORONTO FOR... / Board of Trade of the City of Toronto – Toronto: [s.n, 18–?-18– or 19–] – 9 – cn C.I.H.M. [380]

MONTHLY REVIEW – 1-5 (all publ). 1934-35 – 2mf – 9 – $35.00 – us UPA [335]

MONTHLY REVIEW / Bank of Nova Scotia – 1980-82 – 9 – cn Micromedia [330]

MONTHLY REVIEW / Bank of Nova Scotia – v1-5. Jan 1927-Mar 1960. (not pub. 1944-Feb. 1945) – 1 – cn Precision [332]

MONTHLY REVIEW / Federal Reserve Bank of New York – v1-58 1919-76 1; v53-58 1971-76 5,6; v57-58 9 – us UMI [336]

MONTHLY REVIEW : AN INDEPENDENT SOCIALIST MAGAZINE – New York. 1-12. 1949-60 – 74mf – 9 – $305.00 – us UPA [335]

MONTHLY REVIEW – London. v1-27. 1900-07 – 14r – 1 – us Ross [073]

MONTHLY REVIEW – May 1749-1844 – 1 – us UMI [073]

MONTHLY REVIEW – (v.31-. 1979- 5,6,9) – v.1-. 1949$ – 1 – us UMI [073]

THE MONTHLY REVIEW – (Other geographic edition: Monthly review (London, England: 1900)) – Toronto: G N Morang, [1900-1907] – 9 – cn C.I.H.M. [971]

THE MONTHLY REVIEW – Toronto: Print and pub. by H Scobie, [1840?-1841] – 9 – cn C.I.H.M. [971]

A MONTHLY REVIEW DEVOTED TO CANADIAN EMANCIPATION AND COMMERCIAL UNION WITH THE UNITED STATES = EMANCIPATION COLONIALE ET L'UNION DOUANIERE AVEC LES ETATS-UNIS – Montreal: J X Perrault, [1880] – 9 – cn C.I.H.M. [380]

MONTHLY REVIEW (LONDON, ENGLAND: 1900) *see* THE MONTHLY REVIEW

MONTHLY REVIEW OF THE IMMIGRATION AND NATURALIZATION SERVICE / U.S. Immigration and Naturalization Service – (No issues publ Mar-Jun 1948. Cont by: The I. and N. Reporter)) – Jul 1943-Jun 1952 (all publ) – 26mf – 9 – $39.00 – LLMC 81-504 – us L.L.M.C. [324]

MONTHLY REVIEW OF THE REPUBLIK PERSATAAN INDONESIA – N.p., 1960-1961 – 5mf – 9 – ne IDC [950]

THE MONTHLY REVIEW OF THE TORONTO YOUNG MEN'S CHRISTIAN ASSOCIATION – Toronto: Young Men's Christian Association, [1887?-18– or 19–] – 9 – cn C.I.H.M. [360]

MONTHLY REVIEW (SOVIET UNION. TORGOVOE PREDSTAVITELSTVO V VELIKOBRITANII) – (Includes c.1: v.11:no.1 1938:Jan.-v.11:no.12 (1938:Dec.)) – [London]: U.S.S.R. Trade Delegation in the United Kingdom, 19uu – 1 – CSUXAKY5453-S – us Hoover Inst Photo [947]

THE MONTHLY ROSE – (Cont: The Rose of Sharon Monthly. Cont by: The Protestant Review) – Bridgewater, NS: D F Hutchinson, 1868-[1869?] – 9 – cn C.I.H.M. [240]

THE MONTHLY ROSE *see*
- THE PROTESTANT REVIEW
- THE ROSE OF SHARON MONTHLY

MONTHLY SCIENTIFIC JOURNAL – Containing disquisitions in natural philosophy, chemistry, and the arts. v. 1. Feb-Jul 1818 – 1 – us UMI [500]

MONTHLY STATISTICS OF PRODUCTION AND EMPLOYMENT IN SELECTED LARGE MANUFACTURING ESTABLISHMENTS / Libya. Technical Planning Body. Census and Statistical Department – Jan Mar 1970-Sep 1972. BNE-537 1 – 9 – ne IDC [310]

MONTHLY SURVEY : STATE BANK OF THE U.S.S.R. – (Includes c.1: 1926:July-Aug.,Nov.-1927:July) – Moscow: The Bank, 1926-1927. 2v – 1 – CSUXAKZ1295-S – us Hoover Inst Photo [332]

MONTHLY VISITANT – 1$6. Jul-Dec 1816 – 1 – us UMI [073]

THE MONTHLY VISITOR – (Cont: The Saturday Evening Visitor) – Halifax [NS]: R Nugent, [1842-18– or 19–] – 9 – cn C.I.H.M. [240]

THE MONTHLY VISITOR *see* THE SATURDAY EVENING VISITOR

MONTHLY VISITOR OF THE MONTREAL TEMPERANCE SOCIETY – [Montreal?: Montreal Temperance Society, 1847?-184-?] – 9 – cn C.I.H.M. [360]

MONTHLY WEATHER REVIEW – v1-101 1872-1973 1; v99-101 1971-71 5,6 – us UMI [550]

MONTHLY WEATHER REVIEW – v1-100 1872-1972 – 1,5,6 – us Princeton Micro [550]

THE MONTHLY WESTERN JURIST – v1-3. 1874-77 (all publ) – 25mf – 9 – $37.50 – LLMC 84-619 – us L.L.M.C. [073]

Monti, G L *see* INDICES BOTANICI ET MATERIAE MEDICAE, QUIBUS PLANTARUM GENERA

MONTICELLO BAPTIST CHURCH. JASPER COUNTY. GEORGIA : CHURCH RECORDS – 1865-1906 – 1 – 6.84 – us Baptist [240]

Montignot *see* DICTIONNAIRE DIPLOMATIQUE, OU ETYMOLOGIES DES TERMES DES BAS SIECLES

Montijo. Ayuntamiento *see*
- NOTA DE LOS FUNDAMENTOS AL RECURSO...EN PLEITO AL...MERIDA
- PROGRAMA OFICIAL DE FERIAS Y FIESTAS EN HONOR DE LA STMA. VIRGEN DE BARBANOS. SEPTIEMBRE 1966

Montilus, G *see*
- MYTHES, ECOLOGIE, ACCULTURATION EN HAITI
- LES REPAS SACRIFICIELS DU VODOU HAITIEN

MONTJOIE – Organe de l'imperialisme artistique francais. Dir. Canudo. I, no. 1-12; II, no. 1-6. Paris. fevr 1913-avr juin 1914 – 1 – fr A.C.R.P.P. [073]

MONT-JOLI NOUVELLES – Mont-Joli, Canada. v4 n4. 16 avr 1958; v4 n6. 19 jun 1958; v18 n17. 29 avr 1971 – 1r – 1 – Can$25.00 – cn Can Microfilming [072]

MONT-LAURIER JOURNAL – Mont-Laurier, Canada. 19 avr 1956-v1 n3. 3 mai 1956 – 1r – 1 – Can$25.00 – cn Can Microfilming [072]

MONTLEY SURVEY (MOSCOW, R.S.F.S.R.) *see* MONTHLY SURVEY

Montmignon, J B *see* SYSTEME DE PRONONCIATION FIGUREE

MONTMORENCI BAPTIST CHURCH. AIKEN COUNTY. SOUTH CAROLINA : CHURCH RECORDS – 1934-70; 1974-89. Deacon's Minutes: 1952-59 – 1 – $73.54 – us Baptist [240]

MONTMORENCY / Carrion-Nisas – (French Theatre Series). Paris. Impr. Duval, an XI. 1803 – 9 – fr Hachette [820]

Montmort, Pierre-R de *see* ESSAI D'ANALYSE SUR LES JEUX DE HASARD

Montolin, Manuel de *see* VIDA DE PIZARRO

EL MONTONERO – (c.1: v.1:no.3 1959: Aug) – 1 – CSUXAJA7605-S – us Hoover Inst Photo [073]

MONTONEROS : LA SOBERBIA ARMADA / Giussani, Pablo – Buenos Aires: Sudamericana/Planeta, 5th ed c1984 – 1 – CSUXAHZ7342-B – us Hoover Inst Photo [355]

MONTONI OU LE CHATEAU D'UDOLPHE / Duval, Alexandre – (French Theatre Series). Paris. Migneret et Vente, an VI. 1797 – 9 – fr Hachette [820]

Montoto de Sedas Castor *see* BLANCAS Y NEGRAS (CRONICAS)

Montoto de Sedas, Castor *see* MUNOZ PABON, PREDICADOR

Montoto, Jose Maria *see* DE LOS MALEFICIOS Y LOS DEMONIOS

Montoto, Santiago *see*
- COLECCION DE DOCUMENTOS INEDITOS PARA LA HISTORIA DE IBEROAMERICA
- NOBILIARIO DE REINOS, CIUDADES Y VILLAS DE LA AMERICA ESPANOLA...TOMO 3

MONTOUR AMERICAN – Danville, PA. -w 1900-1910 – 13 – $25.00r – us I.M.R. [071]

MONTPARNASSE – Revue fondee en 1914 par Paul Husson. no. 1-2; n.s., no. 1-58. Paris. juin-juil 1914, juil 1921-janv 1930 – 1 – fr A.C.R.P.P. [073]

MONTPELIER ENTERPRISE – Montpelier, Ohio, 1880-1924 – 16r – 1 – $32.50r – us Archival [978]

Montpelier. Ohio. Saint Paul's United Methodist Church *see* RECORDS

Montpensier, de *see* MEMOIRS

MONTRAL WEEKLY TRANSCRIPT – Montreal. v1 n51. 25 mai 1842-v1 n27. (N.S.) 4 jul 1872 – 1r – 1 – Can$50.00 – cn Can Microfilming [072]

LE MONTREAL : LITTERATURE, THEATRE, SPORT – Montreal, Canada. 8,15 oct 1899 – 1r – 1 – Can$25.00 – cn Can Microfilming [073]

Montreal. Archives Judiciaires *see*
- GREFFES DES NOTAIRES (1648-1663) (BASSET, GASTINEAU, CLOSSE, ST-PERE)
- REPERTOIRES ET/OU INDEX DES NOTAIRES (NON-PUBLIES) (1673-1799)

Montreal. Archives judiciaires *see* RECENSEMENT, COMPAGNIE DES INDES (1741)

MONTREAL BIBLE REPORTER – Montreal: Montreal Auxiliary Bible Society, [1889?-189- or 19–] – 9 – cn C.I.H.M. [210]

THE MONTREAL BUILDER : OFFICIAL ORGAN OF THE MASTER PLUMBERS ASSOCIATION / Master Plumbers Association. Canada – Montreal, 1894-? SEM35P26 – 1r – 1 – Can$15.00 – cn Bibl Nat [690]

MONTREAL CHURCH REGISTER – (Cont by: Montreal Church Register and Parish Visitor) – [Montreal?]: H W Nye, [1876] – 9 – cn C.I.H.M. [240]

MONTREAL CHURCH REGISTER *see* MONTREAL CHURCH REGISTER AND PARISH VISITOR

MONTREAL CHURCH REGISTER AND PARISH VISITOR – (Cont: Montreal Church Register) – [Montreal?]: H W Nye, [1876-18– or 19–] – 9 – cn C.I.H.M. [240]

MONTREAL CHURCH REGISTER AND PARISH VISITOR *see* MONTREAL CHURCH REGISTER

THE MONTREAL CHURCHMAN : ANGLICAN CHURCH – (Montreal jan 1959-dec 1968 1r Can$50.00) – St-Jean, nov 1912-dec 1946 – 4r – 1 – Can$50.00 – cn Can Microfilming [072]

MONTREAL CONDENSED REPORTS / Canada. Quebec – 1v. 1853-54 (all publ) – 2mf – 9 – $3.00 – LLMC 81-076 – us L.L.M.C. [340]

MONTREAL CONFIDENTIEL – Montreal. v2 n15. 13 oct 1954-v18 n5. jul 1970 – 1r – 1 – Can$30.00 – cn Can Microfilming [072]

MONTREAL COURRIER AND COMMERCIAL ADVERTISER – Montreal. v3 n75. 18 may-16 aug 1862 – 1r – 1 – Can$25.00 – cn Can Microfilming [072]

THE MONTREAL DAILY MAIL – Montreal, Canada. 8 oct 1913-v5 n209. 31 aut 1917 – 10r – 1 – Can$65.00r – cn Can Microfilming [072]

MONTREAL DAILY NEWS – Montreal. v1 n1. 15 mar 1988-v1 n65. 31 may 1988 – 1r – 1 – cn Can Microfilming [072]

THE MONTREAL DAILY NEWS – Montreal, Canada. 3-26 oct 1887 (26 consecutive issues) – 1r – 1 – Can$30.00 – cn Can Microfilming [072]

MONTREAL DAILY STAR – (Cont: Montreal Daily Star 1869) – Montreal, 26 jun 1884 (Special numer – St-Jean-Baptiste Parade) – 1r – 1 – Can$25.00 – cn Can Microfilming [072]

MONTREAL DAILY STAR *see* MONTREAL DAILY STAR

MONTREAL DAILY WITNESS – Montreal, Canada. 12 aut 1860-11 jul 1913 – 37r – 1 – Can$60.00r – cn Can Microfilming [072]

THE MONTREAL DIOCESAN THEOLOGICAL COLLEGE MAGAZINE – Montreal: [s.n, 1892-189- or 19–] (Montreal: S C Kyte) – 9 – cn C.I.H.M. [240]

MONTREAL ET SES MONUMENTS – [S.l.]: [s.n.], [entre 1909 et 1919]. SEM105P1467 – 3mf – 9 – Can$6.75 – cn Bibl Nat [910]

MONTREAL EVENING – Montreal, 24 dec 1918 + Holiday Issue – 1r – 1 – Can$25.00 – cn Can Microfilming [072]

THE MONTREAL EVENING JOURNAL / ed by Wilson, L M – Montreal, 24 dec 1928 – 1r – 1 – Can$25.00 – cn Can Microfilming [072]

MONTREAL EXTRA – Montreal. v1 n2. 2 jul 1975 – 1r – 1 – Can$25.00 – cn Can Microfilming [072]

MONTREAL FIN-DE-SIECLE : HISTOIRE DE LA METROPOLE DU CANADA AU DIX-NEUVIEME SIECLE – Montreal: The Gazette Printing Company, 1899. SEM105P1796 – 3mf – 9 – Can$6.75 – cn Bibl Nat [910]

MONTREAL GAZETTE = GAZETE DE MONTREAL / ed by Mesplet, Fleury – Montreal, Canada. 25 aut 1785-13 fev 1794 – 2r – 1 – Can$35.00r – cn Can Microfilming [072]

MONTREAL GAZETTE = GAZETTE DE MONTREAL / ed by Edwards, Edward – Montreal, Canada. 3 aut 1795-v11 n123. 4 dec 1797 – 1r – 1 – Can$35.00 – cn Can Microfilming [072]

MONTREAL GAZETTE = GAZETTE DE MONTREAL / ed by Roy, Louis – Montreal, Canada. v1 n2. 24 aut 1795-v3 n15. 20 nov 1797(?) – 1r – 1 – Can$35.00 – cn Can Microfilming [072]

MONTREAL GAZETTE – Montreal, Canada. 1785-1877 – 79r – 1 – $5,135.00 – cn Library Assoc [971]

Montreal Gazette *see* CALENDAR

THE MONTREAL GAZETTE = GAZETTE DE MONTREAL / ed by Edwards, Edward – Montreal. n233. 6 jan 1800-28 dec 1801 – 1r – 1 – Can$35.00 – cn Can Microfilming [072]

MONTREAL HERALD – Montreal. Annual review 1922; national Number 1929; special Issue 1941 – 1r – 1 – Can$60.00 – cn Can Microfilming [072]

MONTREAL HERALD – Montreal, Canada. 1811-26; 1863-73 – 25r – 1 – $1,625.00 – cn Library Assoc [971]

THE MONTREAL HERALD – Montreal, Canada. v1 n6. 23 nov 1811-27 dec 1823 – 6r – 1 – Can$50.00r – cn Can Microfilming [072]

MONTREAL HERALD AND DAILY COMMERCIAL GAZETTE – Montreal. v27 n172. 17 nov 1835-18 jun 1886 + 22 jul 1886-12 apr 1933 – 4r – 1 – Can$50.00 – cn Can Microfilming [072]

MONTREAL HERALD FOR THE COUNTRY – Montreal, Canada. v20 n96. 2 nov 1837-v39 n21. 26 mai 1847 – 1r – 1 – Can$40.00 – cn Can Microfilming [072]

MONTREAL HERALD SATURDAY EDITION – Montreal, Ju1905-1910Ma – 1r – 1 – cn Preston [971]

MONTREAL ILLUSTRATED, 1869-1870 : CHRISTMAS AND NEW YEAR'S PICTORIAL ALBUM – Montreal: T.F.S. Kirkpatrick, [1869 ?]. SEM105P1435 – 3mf – 9 – Can$6.75 – cn Bibl Nat [910]

MONTREAL ILLUSTRATED, OR, THE STRANGER'S GUIDE TO MONTREAL: A COMPLETE HAND-BOOK, DIRECTING VISITORS..., CONTAINING A FINE MAP OF THE CITY.. – Montreal: C.R. Chisolm & Bros., 1875. 02981. (Pre-1900 Canadiana) – 9 – cn C.I.H.M. [971]

MONTREAL IN HALFTONE : PICTORIAL ALBUM... – Grand Rapids, MI: James Bayne Co, ?(1927 ?]. SEM105P1419 – 2mf – 9 – Can$4.50 – cn Bibl Nat [910]

MONTREAL LA NUIT ET LE JOUR : INDISCRET, FANTAISISTE, NOCTAMBULEUX – Montreal, v1 n5. 23 nov 1918-v3 n17. 19 fev 1921 – 1r – 1 – Can$35.00 – cn Can Microfilming [073]

MONTREAL – LA VRAIE VILLE – (numero unique de 32 pages publie a l'ocassion d'un emission televisee: "Montreal, ville ouverte") – Montreal. v1 n1. 31 jan 1992 – 1r – 1 – Can$25.00 – cn Can Microfilming [072]

MONTREAL LAW REPORTS : QUEEN'S BENCH / Canada. Quebec – v1-7. 1885-91 (all publ) – 42mf – 9 – $63.00 – LLMC 81-077 – us L.L.M.C. [340]

MONTREAL LAW REPORTS : SUPERIOR COURT / Canada. Quebec – v1-7. 1885-91 (all publ) – 42mf – 9 – $63.00 – LLMC 81-078 – us L.L.M.C. [340]

Montreal. Laws, Statutes, etc *see*
- REGLES ET REGLEMENS DE POLICE POUR LA CITE ET LES FAUBOURGS DE MONTREAL
- REGLES ET REGLEMENTS DE POLICE, ADDITIONNELS, POUR LA CITE ET LES FAUBOURGS DE MONTREAL
- REGLES ET REGLEMENTS DE POLICE POUR LES FAUXBOURGS ET LA CITE DE MONTREAL

MONTREAL LIFE – (Absorbed: Metropolitan (Montreal, Quebec)) – Montreal: Metropolitan Co, [1891-190?] – 9 – cn C.I.H.M. [910]

THE MONTREAL LITERARY MAGAZINE – [Montreal?: s.n, 1856-18–?] – 9 – cn C.I.H.M. [400]

MONTREAL MEDICAL GAZETTE – Montreal, Canada. 22 jan 1845 (Petition Bill) – 1r – 1 – Can$25.00 – cn Can Microfilming [610]

MONTREAL MESSENGER AND BRITISH CANADIAN LITERARY GAZETTE – Montreal, Canada. v4 n38. 31 mar 1843 – 1r – 1 – Can$25.00 – cn Can Microfilming [072]

MONTREAL MIRROR – Montreal, 14 oct 1969 – 1r – 1 – Can$25.00 – cn Can Microfilming [072]

THE MONTREAL MONTHLY MAGAZINE – Montreal, Canada. mar 1831 – 1r – 1 – Can$25.00 – cn Can Microfilming [073]

MONTREAL MUSEUM = MUSEE DE MONTREAL / ed by Gosselin, L – Montreal, Canada. dec 1832-nov 1833 – 1r – 1 – Can$35.00 – cn Can Microfilming [060]

THE MONTREAL NORTH GUIDE DE MONTREAL-NORD *see*
- LE GUIDE DE MONTREAL-NORD
- LE MONTREAL-NORD

THE MONTREAL ORACLE – Montreal. v2 n21. 17 aut 1977 – 1r – 1 – Can$20.00 – cn Can Microfilming [072]

MONTREAL PHARMACEUTICAL JOURNAL – Montreal: J D Paterson, [1890-1932] – 9 – cn C.I.H.M. [615]

MONTREAL PHILATELIST – Montreal, Canada. v3 n1. mar 1878 – 1r – 1 – Can$25.00 – cn Can Microfilming [760]

THE MONTREAL PHILATELIST – Montreal: Montreal Philatelic Pub. Co, [1898-1902] – 9 – cn C.I.H.M. [760]

THE MONTREAL POCKET ALMANACK AND GENERAL REGISTER FOR.. – Montreal: Jas Starke & Co, 1842-57. SEM16P352 – 1r – 5 – Can$15.00 – cn Bibl Nat [910]

MONTREAL POST – Montreal, 4 jun 1956-25 mar 1957 – 1r – 1 – Can$45.00 – cn Can Microfilming [072]

MONTREAL QUI CHANTE : REVUE MUSICALE – Montreal. v1 n5. nov 1908-v15 n9. sep 1923 – 1r – 1 – Can$65.00 – cn Can Microfilming [072]

MONTREAL RECORD – Montreal. 13 sep 1978-v1 n13. 29 sep 1978 – 1r – 1 – Can$30.00 – cn Can Microfilming [072]

THE MONTREAL REGISTER – Montreal, Canada. v1 n25. 22 jun 1848; v1 n33. 17 aut 1848 – 1r – 1 – Can$25.00 – cn Can Microfilming [072]

MONTREAL SATURDAY NIGHT – Montreal: Saturday Night Pub. Co, [1895-189- or 19–] – 9 – cn C.I.H.M. [910]

MONTREAL SOUVENIR / Catholic Order of Foresters. De Breboeuf Court. Montreal – Montreal, 1892. 00515. (Pre-1900 Canadiana) – 9 – cn C.I.H.M. [971]

MONTREAL SPECIAL LIBRARIES ASSOCIATION BULLETIN – 1935-57 – 1r – 1 – $68.00 – cn Library Assoc [020]

MONTREAL STANDARD – Montreal, Se1905-1951De – 410r – 1 – cn Preston [971]

MONTREAL STAR – Montreal, Quebec, CN. Nov 1869-Dec 1979 – 1 – cn Commonwealth Micro [072]

MONTREAL STOCK EXCHANGE DAILY RECORD – (1977-1985/86 1) – Montreal, 1977-88 – 1,5 – Can$200.00y – cn Micromedia [332]

THE MONTREAL SUN – Montreal, Canada. v1 n1. 10 nov 1958 – 1r – 1 – Can$25.00 – cn Can Microfilming [072]

THE MONTREAL TATTLER : CARICATURES – Montreal, Canada. v1 n4. 5 sep 1844; v1 n6. 12 sep 1844 – 1r – 1 – Can$25.00 – cn Can Microfilming [073]

THE MONTREAL TATTLER – [Montreal?]: J Jameson, [1844-18–] – 9 – cn C.I.H.M. [072]

MONTREAL TRANSCRIPT – Montreal, Canada. 1836-65 – 33r – 1 – $2,145.00 – cn Library Assoc [971]

THE MONTREAL TRANSCRIPT – Montreal, Canada. v1 n1. 4 oct 1836-v29 n53. 30 jun 1865 – 30r – 1 – Can$50.00r – cn Can Microfilming [072]

MONTREAL TRIBUNE – Montreal, Canada. 4 aut 1910-v4 n11. 20 mar 1913 – 1r – 1 – Can$45.00 – cn Can Microfilming [072]

MONTREAL VILLE OUVERTE : COLLECTION L'EXPRESS, LA PATRIE – Montreal. numero unique. fin jan 1992 – 1r – 1 – Can$25.00 – cn Can Microfilming [072]

MONTREAL WEEKLY HERALD – Canada. -w. Feb 1893-Nov 1896. 2 1 2 reels – 1 – uk British Libr Newspaper [072]

MONTREAL WEEKLY HERALD – Montreal, Canada. v43 n92. 18 oct 1851-v47 n39. 29 sep 1855 – 1r – 1 – Can$45.00 – cn Can Microfilming [072]

THE MONTREAL WEEKLY HERALD AND TOWN AND COUNTRY FAMILY NEWSPAPER – Montreal. v77 n35. 9 sep 1886 – 1r – 1 – Can$25.00 – cn Can Microfilming [072]

MONTREAL WEEKLY PILOT / ed by Hincks, Francis – Montreal, Canada. v4 n198. 25 dec 1847-v6 n6. 5 jun 1852 – 1r – 1 – Can$25.00 – cn Can Microfilming [072]

MONTREAL WEEKLY WITNESS *see* THE MONTREAL WITNESS

"MONTREAL WITNESS" : HISTORICAL SOUVENIR AND REVIEW... – Montreal: presented with the compliments of John Dougall and Son [1919?]. SEM105P1498 – 1mf – 9 – Can$2.25 – cn Bibl Nat [971]

MONTREAL WITNESS – Montreal, Canada. 1846-62 – 7r – 1 – $455.00 – cn Library Assoc [971]

THE MONTREAL WITNESS – Montreal: printed by J C Beckett, 1846-1938. SEM35P6 – 61r – 1 – Can$2,782.00 – cn Bibl Nat [072]

LE MONTREALAIS CATHOLIQUE – Montreal. v1 n3. mai 1934 – 1r – 1 – Can$25.00 – cn Can Microfilming [072]

THE MONTREALER – Montreal. v7 n17. 14 oct 1933-v- n-. 15 jun 1936 – 1r – 1 – Can$35.00 – cn Can Microfilming [072]

MONTREALER ICOR BULLETIN – Montreal, CN, 1930 – 1r – 1 – Can$25.00 – cn Can Microfilming [072]

MONTREALER NACHRICHTEN – Montreal: [s.n]. v1-22. 1955-75. SEM35P96 – 10r – 1 – Can$593.00 – cn Bibl Nat [072]

MONTREALER ZEITUNG : THE GERMAN NEWSPAPER WITH THE CANADIAN SPIRIT – (Cont by: Kanada-Kurier, Winnipeg) – Pickering, Ont., Canada. 1972-77; 1979-5 Sep 1980 – 1 – gw Mikrofilm [072]

MONTREAL-MATIN – (Cont: L'Illustration-Nouvelle) – Montreal, Canada. 13 aut 1941-31 dec 1976 – 238r – 1 – cn Can Microfilming [072]

MONTREAL-MATIN *see* L'ILLUSTRATION-NOUVELLE

MONTREAL-METROPOLITAIN / ed by Hart, Normand – Montreal, Canada. v1 n1. aut 1960 – 1r – 1 – Can$25.00 – cn Can Microfilming [072]

MONTREAL-MODE : REVUE – (Filmed with: La Broderie Gorcy 1 mar 1924-1 sep 1927. Filmed with: La Revue de Musique et de Broderie Vennat v5 1 oct 1931- v11 n5/6 mar/avr 1936) – Montreal, Canada. v1 n2. 15 mar 1904-v1 n35. 1 aut 1905 – 1r – 1 – Can$50.00 – cn Can Microfilming [073]

LE MONTREAL-NORD – (Cont by: Le Guide de Montreal-Nord/The Montreal North Guide. Cont by: The Montreal North Guide de Montreal-Nord) – Montreal-Nord, Canada. v3 n9. dec 1950-v9 n13. 15 dec 1956 – 1r – 1 – Can$60.00 – cn Can Microfilming [072]

LE MONTREAL-NORD *see* LE GUIDE DE MONTREAL-NORD

MONTREAL-PARIS-LONDRES : REVUE MENSUELLE MODERNE – Montreal. v1 n7. jun 1934 – 1r – 1 – Can$25.00 – cn Can Microfilming [072]

Montreuil, Denise *see* LE ROMAN CANADIEN-FRANCAIS, DES DEBUTS A NOS JOURS

Montreuil, Fr *see* RITES MORTUAIRES ET REPRESENTATION COLLECTIVE DE LA MORT A LA MARTINIQUE

Montreuil, Madeleine *see* BIOBIBLIOGRAPHIE DU LIEUTENANT ERNEST PAICHARI [SIC], SOLDAT DE FRANCE

MONTROSE AND BRECHIN CHRONICLE *see* MONTROSE CHRONICLE

MONTROSE ARBROATH AND BRECKIN REVIEW ETC – (Montrose Review etc. 1920-64. Missing: 1848. 1886. 1890) – Scotland, UK. 18 Apr 1818; 18 Oct 1839; 1844-75; 1884-1964 – 105r – 1 – uk British Libr Newspaper [072]

MONTROSE CHRONICLE – (Montrose and Brechin Chronicle. 1897-98) – Scotland, UK. 7 Aug 1895-20 Jul 1898. -w – 2r – 1 – uk British Libr Newspaper [072]

MONTROSE DEMOCRAT – Montrose, PA. -w 1889-1900; 1900-1923 – 13 – $25.00r – us I.M.R. [071]

MONTROSE INDEPENDENT – Montrose, PA., 1889-1981 – 13 – $25.00r – us I.M.R. [071]

MONTROSE MIRROR – Flint. Mich. 1940-1941 – 1 – us UMI [071]

MONTROSE REVIEW – 1 – £42.00r – uk Scot News [072]

MONTROSE REVIEW ETC *see* MONTROSE ARBROATH AND BRECKIN REVIEW ETC

MONTROSE STANDARD – Scotland, UK. 1844-70. -w. 110 reels – 1 – uk British Libr Newspaper [072]

MONTROSE TIMES – Flint. Mich. 1960-1963 – 1 – us UMI [071]

Montseny, Frederica *see*
- EL ANARQUISMO MILITANTE Y LA REALIDAD ESPANOLA
- LA INCORPORACION DE LAS MASAS POPULARES A LA HISTORIA
- INTERNATIONAL ANTIFASCIST SOLIDARITY: AN APPEAL TO THE WOMEN OF AMERICA

MONTSERRAT : STATISTICAL DIGEST 1973-1976 / Montserrat. Statistics Office – (1973 not available. Coll title: Latin American and Caribbean Official Statistical Serials, 1821-1982) – 6mf – 9 – £50.00 – uk Chadwyck [946]

Montserrat *see* DEVELOPMENT PLAN, 1966-70

Montserrat. Statistics Office *see* MONTSERRAT

MONTSSCHRIFT FUER RHEINISCH-WESTFAELISCHE GESCHICHTSFORSCHUNG UND ALTERTHUMSKUNDE – Bonn. Jahrg. 1-3; 1875-77. "Hrsg. von Richard Pick." Continued by Monatsschrift fuer die Geschichte Westdeutschlands. Film Mas C 720 – 1 – us H.U. Library [073]

Montucci, A *see* DE STUDIIS SINICIS...

Montuses, Ernest *see* LE DEPUTE EN BLOUSE

Montville. Connecticut. Baptist Church *see* CHURCH RECORDS, MS 1204

Monty, Jeanne R *see* ETUDE SUR LE STYLE POLEMIQUE DE VOLTAIRE

Montzheimer *see* PAST AND PRESENT OF O'BRIEN AND OSCEOLA COUNTIES

LE MONUMENT : ORGANE OFFICIEL DE LA KERMESSE / La Kermesse. Canada – Sherbrooke. 1v. 6 fev 1906-12 fev 1906. SEM35P27 – 1r – 1 – Can$15.00 – cn Bibl Nat [073]

MONUMENT FACTS AND HIGHER CRITICAL FANCIES / Sayce, Archibald Henry – (Includes index) – New York: Fleming H Revell, [190-?] – 1mf – 9 – 0-8370-9418-6 – 1986-3418 – us A.T.L.A. [220]

MONUMENT IN CANTOS AND ESSAYS – Columbia, MO. v1-2. 1968-70 – 5mf – 9 – $5.00f – us Ross [073]

MONUMENT MAISONNEUVE: SOUVENIR DE LA CEREMONIE D'INAUGURATION, LE LER JUILLET 1895 / Comite du Monument de Maisonneuve. Montreal, Quebec – Montreal?: Comite, 1895?, 00722. (Pre-1900 Canadiana) – 9 – cn C.I.H.M. [971]

MONUMENT ORDER RECORDS / Eckhardt Monument Company. Tiffin, Ohio – 1903-1963 – 3r – 1 – $32.50r – us Archival [978]

MONUMENTA CARTOGRAPHICA AFRICAE ET AEGYPTI / Kamal, Youssouf – [Le Caire], 1926-51 – us Res Libr [520]

MONUMENTA ERPHESFURTENSIA SAEC. 12, 13, 14 (MGH 7: 42.BD) – 1899 – Dfl56.00 – ne Slangenburg [240]

MONUMENTA FRANCISCANA (RS4) / ed by Brewer, J S & Howlett, R – (v1 1858 Dfl49.00. v2 1882 Dfl28.00) – ne Slangenburg [240]

MONUMENTA GERMANIAE HISTORICA : ITS INHERITANCE IN SOURCE-VALUATION AND CRITICISM / Miller Gamble, WT – Washington, 1927 – 4mf – 9 – Dfl1,162.00 – ne Slangenburg [943]

MONUMENTA GERMANIAE HISTORICA : SCRIPTORES IN FOLIO – v1-32 – 717mf – 9 – ne IDC [943]

MONUMENTA GERMANIAE HISTORICA 3 (MGH 3: 1 BD) : SCRIPTORES RERUM LANGOBARDICARUM ET ITALICARUM SAEC. 6-9 / ed by Waitz, G et al – 1878 – Dfl60.00 – ne Slangenburg [240]

MONUMENTA GERMANIAE HISTORICA 9 : LIBELLI DE LITE IMPERATORUM ET PONTIFICUM SAECULIS 11. ET 12. CONSCRIPTI – (1. Bd: 1891 Dfl63.00. 2. Bd: 1892 Dfl67.00. 3. Bd: 1897 Dfl67.00) – ne Slangenburg [240]

MONUMENTA GERMANIAE HISTORICA ANTIQUITATES. 1. POETAE LATINI MEDIIAEVI *see*
- NACHTRAEGE ZU DEN POETAE AEVI CAROLINI (MGH ANTIQUITATES 1: 6.BD. 1.TEIL)
- DIE OTTONENZEIT (MGH ANTIQUITATES 1: 5.BD. 1.TEIL 1 UND 2 HEFT))
- POETA LATINI AEVI CAROLINI (MGH ANTIQUITATES 1: 2.BD)
- POETAE LATINI AEVI CAROLINI (MGH ANTIQUITATES 1: 1.BD)
- POETAE LATINI AEVI CAROLINI (MGH ANTIQUITATES 1: 3.BD)
- POETAE LATINI AEVI CAROLINI (MGH ANTIQUITATES 1: 4.BD. 1.TEIL)
- POETAE LATINI AEVI CAROLINI (MGH ANTIQUITATES 1: 4.BD. 2.UND 3.TEIL)

MONUMENTA GERMANIAE HISTORICA ANTIQUITATES. 2. NECROLOGIA GERMANIAE *see*
- DIOECESES BRIXINENSIS, FRISINGENSIS, RATISBONENSIS (MGH ANTIQUITATES 2: 3.BD)
- DIOECESIS AUGUSTENSIS, CONSTANTIENSIS, CURIENSIS (MGH ANTIQUITATES 2: 1.BD)
- DIOECESIS PATAVIENSIS (MGH ANTIQUITATES 2: 4.BD)
- DIOECESIS PATAVIENSIS (MGH ANTIQUITATES 2: 5.BD)
- DIOECESIS SALISBURGENSIS (MGH ANTIQUITATES 2: 2.BD)
- LIBRI CONFRATERNITATUM SANCTI GALLI, AUGIENSIS, FABARIENSIS (MGH ANTIQUITATES 2: 6.BD)

MONUMENTA GERMANIAE HISTORICA ANTIQUITATES. 3. LIBRI MEMORIALES *see* LIBER MEMORIALIS VON REMIREMONT (MGH ANTIQUITATES 3: 1.BD)

MONUMENTA GERMANIAE HISTORICA. DEUTSCHES MTTELALTER. KRITISCHE STUDIENTEXTE *see*
- DIE BRIEFE HEINRICHS 4 (MGH DEUTSCHES..: 1.BD)
- BRUNOS BUCH VOM SACHSENKRIEG (MGH DEUTSCHES..: 2.BD)
- DAS LEBEN DER LIUTBIRG (MGH DEUTSCHES..: 3.BD)
- DIE SCHRIFTEN DES ALEXANDER VON ROES (MGH DEUTSCHES..: 4.BD)

MONUMENTA GERMANIAE HISTORICA, DIPLOMATA : DIPLOMATA IN FOLIO – v1 – 7mf – 9 – ne IDC [943]

MONUMENTA GERMANIAE HISTORICA DIPLOMATA. 1. DIPLOMATA IN FOLIO *see* DIPLOMATA REGUM FRANCORUM E STIRPE MEROVINGICA (MGH DIPLOMATA 1: 1.BD)

MONUMENTA GERMANIAE HISTORICA DIPLOMATA. 2. DIPLOMATA KAROLINORUM *see*
- DIE URKUNDEN LOTHARS 1. UND LOTHARS 2. (MGH DIPLOMATA 2: 3.BD)

MOORE'S PRIVY COUNCIL CASES : REPORTS OF CASES HEARD AND DETERMINED BY THE JUDICIAL COMMITTEE OF HIS MAJESTY'S MOST HONOURABLE PRIVY COUNCIL / Moore, Edmund F – (This series also had an "Indian Cases" component. Not yet available) – os: v1-15. 1836-62; ns: v1-9. 1862-73. London: W T Clarke/ Stevens & Sons, n.d. (all publ) – 142mf – 9 – $213.00 – LLMC 95-291 – us L.L.M.C. [324]
MOORE'S RURAL NEW YORKER – Rochester. N.Y. 1855; 1859; 1862 – 1 – us UMI [071]
Moorhouse, James *see* DANGERS OF THE APOSTOLIC AGE
THE MOORISH CIVILIZATION IN SPAIN / McCabe, Joseph – Girard, KS. 1927 – 1r – 1 – us Ross [946]
THE MOORLAND COTTAGE / Gaskell, Elizabeth Cleghorn – London: Chapman & Hall, 1850 – 1 roll – 1 – 1-55879-526-X – uk Libr Preservation [830]
MOORLAND IDYLLS / Allen, Grant – London: Chatto & Windus. 1896. 05054. (Pre-1900 Canadiana) – 9 – cn C.I.H.M. [830]
Moormann, F R *see* REPORT TO THE GOVERNMENT OF JORDAN ON THE SOILS OF EAST JORDAN
MOORSHEDABAD NEWS – Berhampore, India. -w. 22 Sept 1838-13 July 1839. 1 reel – 1 – uk British Libr Newspaper [072]
MOORUVALLABOK, AM 132 FOL : 1: INDEX AND CONCORDANCE 2: TEXT – 1987 – 34mf – 9 – ne Brill [400]
Moos, Eugen *see* HEINE UND DUESSELDORF
Moosdijk, P van der *see* EENVOUDIGE JAPANSCHE SPRAAKKUN EERSTE DEEL. EERSTE DRUK
MOOSE JAW TIMES-HERALD – (1971-1992.- 210r) – Moose Jaw, 1993 – 10r – 1 – cn Preston [971]
MOOSE JAW TIMES-HERALD – Moose Jaw, Canada. 1890-99 – 5r – 1 – $325.00 – cn Library Assoc [971]
Moose, Karen S *see* ATHLETIC DIRECTORS' PERCEIVED PREVALENCE OF NORTH CAROLINA HIGH SCHOOL ATHLETES' DRUG AND SUBSTANCE USE
MOOSFLORA DES HARZES / Loeske, L – Leipzig. 1903. B-947 2 – 8 – ne IDC [580]
MOOSSTUDIEN / Lorentz, P G – Leipzig, 1864. 172 pp., 5 pls. B07387 1 – 9 – ne IDC [580]
MOOTED QUESTIONS OF HISTORY / Desmond, Humphrey J – Boston: Marlier, 1902, c1900 – 1mf – us A.T.L.A. [900]
Mooyaart, A *see* MEMOIR BY ANTHONY MOOYART, COMMANDER OF JAFFNAPATAM, FOR THE INFORMATION AND GUIDANCE OF HIS SUCCESSOR, NOEL ANTHONY LEBECK, 1766
THE MOP SONG FOR VOICE AND PIANO : CONTAINS ALSO: C.J. ROBINSON "WHEN I'M WITH YOU"; A. BENNET "CONSTANCY" OLD ENGLISH: "WHEN LOVE IS KIND"; M.L. MORROW "MY WISH" / Nairns, N – 1 – us Sibley [780]
MOPAC NEWS – 1923- 1; 1974- 5,6 – us UMI [073]
Moquet, A *see* ETUDE MONOGRAPHIQUE DE LA COMMUNE DE DRY (LOIRET)
Moquin-Tandon, C H B A *see*
– CHENOPODEARUM MONOGRAPHICA ENUMERATIO
– MONOGRAPHIE DE LA FAMILLE DES HIRUDINEES
Mora, Angel *see* A.S.M. DEL REY DON ALFONSO 13, RECUERDO DE SUMPASO REGIO POR EXTREMADURA...SERENATA DEL PRIMER CUARTETO
Mora, D *see* PARERE...SOPRA L'ORDINE DI GUERREGGIARE LA POTENZA DEL TURCO, & QUELLO, CHE IN CIO EGLI GIUDICA NECESSARIO DI FARE PER SUPERARLO
MORA TIDNING – Borlange, Sweden. 1979- – 1 – sw Kungliga [072]
MORA TIDNING – Filipstad, Hedemora, Borlange, Sweden. 1892-1920, 1975-78 – 35r – 1 – sw Kungliga [072]
Mora y Araujo, Manuel *see* EL VOTO PERONISTA
Morachevskii, N Ia. *see* OBZOR BIBLIOGRAFICHESKIKH IZDANII GOS. PUBLICHNOI BIBLIOTEKI ZA 1917-1957 GG
Moraes Sequeira, V M *see* LA POTERIE DE CARNARU, NORD-EST DU BRESIL
Morainville *see* DIALOGUE ENTRE VICTOR ET LE PERE ANDRE SUR LA RELIGION SAINT-SIMONIENNE
Morais Filho, Melo *see* FESTAS E TRADICOES POPULARES DO BRASIL
Morais, Henry Samuel *see* THE JEWS OF PHILADELPHIA
MORAL / Jarrin, Francisco – 1895 – 9 – 1.50f – sp Bibl Santa Ana [830]
MORAL ADVOCATE – A monthly publication on war, duelling, capital punishment, and prison discipline. v. 1-3. Mar 1821-Oct 1824 – 1 – us UMI [360]
MORAL AND MILITARY ASPECTS OF THE WAR IN SOUTHEAST ASIA: HEARINGS... MAY 7 AND 12, 1970 / U.S. Congress. Senate. Committee on Foreign Relations – Washington, Govt. Print. Off., 1970. 108 p. LL-2359 – 1 – us L of C Photodup [340]
MORAL AND RELIGIOUS CABINET – Containing short accounts of Christian experience. vtogether vwith: Instructive and useful extracts, intended to promote the happiness of pious minds. v. 1-26. 2 Jan-25 Jun 1808 – 1 – us UMI [240]
THE MORAL ARGUMENT AGAINST COMPULSORY VACCINATION / Hutton, A W – 1895. 1 fiche (29x) – 9 – 1.00f – at Libertarian Micro [320]
THE MORAL BASIS OF CAPITALISM / Burke, T Patrick – 12p – 9 – 1.00f – at Libertarian Micro [335]
MORAL BRIEFS : A CONCISE, REASONED AND POPULAR EXPOSITION OF CATHOLIC MORALS / Stapleton, John Henry – New York: Benziger, 1904 – 1mf – 9 – 0-8370-6394-9 – 1986-0394 – us A.T.L.A. [230]
THE MORAL CHARACTER OF CHRIST, OR, THE PERFECTION OF CHRIST'S HUMANITY, A PROOF OF HIS DIVINITY : A THEOLOGICAL TRACT FOR THE PEOPLE / Schaff, Philip – Chambersburg, Pa.: M. Kieffer, 1861 – 1mf – us A.T.L.A. [240]
DIE MORAL DER EVANGELIEN UND DES TALMUD : EIN VERGLEICHENDE STUDIE IM GEISTE UNSERER ZEIT / Duschak, Moritz – Bruenn: Gernhard Epstein, 1877 – 1mf – 9 – 0-8370-5983-6 – 1985-3983 – us A.T.L.A. [270]
MORAL DEVELOPMENT LEVELS OF ATHLETES IN SPORT SPECIFIC AND GENERAL SOCIAL SITUATIONS / Hall, Elizabeth R – 1981 – 2mf – 9 – $8.00 – us Microform Publ [790]
MORAL DIFFICULTIES CONNECTED WITH THE BIBLE / Hessey, James Augustus – London: S.P.C.K., 1871. 1 fiche – 9 – us A.T.L.A. [240]
MORAL DISCIPLINE IN THE CHRISTIAN CHURCH : BEING LECTURES DELIVERED DURING LENT 1904 IN WESTMINSTER ABBEY / Henson, H Hensley – London, New York: Longmans, Green, 1905 – 1mf – us A.T.L.A. [240]
THE MORAL ECONOMY / Perry, Ralph Barton – (Includes bibliographical references & index) – New York: Charles Scribner, 1909 – 1mf – 9 – 0-8370-6301-9 – 1985-0301 – us A.T.L.A. [170]
MORAL EDUCATION : ITS LAWS AND METHODS / Buchanan, Joseph Rodes – 2nd ed. New York: Printed for the author by S W Green, c1882 – 1mf – 9 – 0-8370-7531-9 – 1986-1531 – us A.T.L.A. [370]
THE MORAL IDEAL : A HISTORIC STUDY / Wedgwood, Julia – (Includes bibliographical references and index) – London: Truebner, 1888 – 1mf – 9 – 0-8370-6449-X – 1986-0449 – us A.T.L.A. [170]
THE MORAL INFLUENCE OF MANUFACTURING TOWNS : A DISCOURSE / Dexter, Henry M – Andover: Printed by W.H. Wardwell, 1848 – 1mf – us A.T.L.A. [240]
MORAL INSTRUCTION IN SCHOOLS AND COLLEGES – Albany, NY: Moral Education Board, [ca 1906] – 1mf – 9 – 0-8370-7570-X – 1986-1570 – us A.T.L.A. [370]
LA MORAL ISLAMICA Y TIRSO GONZALEZ DE SANTALLA / Santos Neila, Francisco – Badajoz: (Imprenta de la Diputacion Provincial), 1975. Sep. Rev. Est Extremenos – 1 – sp Bibl Santa Ana [260]
MORAL JUDGMENT AND THE PERCEIVED LEGITIMACY OF INJURIOUS ACTS AMONG COLLEGIATE ATHLETES / Hacker, Colleen M & Youngen, Lois J – 1992 – 2mf – 9 – $8.00 – us Microform Publ [150]
MORAL LAW AND CIVIL LAW : PARTS OF THE SAME THING / Ritter, Eli Foster – Rev ed. Westerville, OH: American Issue Publ, 1910 – 1mf – 9 – 0-8370-6350-7 – 1986-0350 – us A.T.L.A. [170]
THE MORAL OBLIGATION OF PARENTS TO EDUCATE THEIR CHILDREN FOR MARRIAGE : THE CATHOLIC UNIVERSITY OF AMERICA STUDIES IN SACRED THEOLOGY / O'Sullivan, J J – 1955 – 2mf – 8 – ne Slangenburg [240]
THE MORAL ORDER OF THE WORLD : IN ANCIENT AND MODERN THOUGHT / Bruce, Alexander Balmain – (Includes index) – New York: Scribner's, 1899 – 1mf – 9 – 0-8370-2444-7 – 1985-0444 – us A.T.L.A. [170]
Moral OSB Tomas *see* RAMON MENDEZ PIDAL, FILOLOGO E HISTORIADOR DE LA LITERATURA ESPANOLA MEDIEVAL
MORAL PHILOSOPHY : ANALYTICAL, SYNTHETICAL, AND PRACTICAL / Winslow, Hubbard – 6th ed. New York: D Appleton, 1890, c1861 – 2mf – 9 – 0-8370-6466-X – 1986-0466 – us A.T.L.A. [170]
MORAL PHILOSOPHY : OR, ETHICS AND NATURAL LAW / Rickaby, Joseph – (Includes bibliographical references and index) – London: Longmans, Green, 1888 – 1mf – 9 – 0-8370-6346-9 – 1986-0346 – us A.T.L.A. [170]
MORAL PRINCIPLES AND MEDICAL PRACTICE : THE BASIS OF MEDICAL JURISPRUDENCE / Coppens, Charles – 4th rev ed. New York: Benziger, 1905, c1897 – 1mf – 9 – 0-8370-7375-8 – 1986-1375 – us A.T.L.A. [170]
MORAL PRINCIPLES IN EDUCATION / Dewey, John – Boston: Houghton, Mifflin, c1909 – 1mf – 9 – 0-8370-8500-4 – 1986-2500 – us A.T.L.A. [230]
LA MORAL PROFESIONAL DEL EMPLEADO DE LA CAJA DE AHORROS / Leal Ramos, Leon – Madrid: Graficas Iberica, s.a. – 1 – sp Bibl Santa Ana [946]
MORAL SCIENCE : A COMPENDIUM OF ETHICS / Bain, Alexander – New York: D Appleton, 1886, c1869 – 1mf – 9 – 0-8370-6003-6 – 1985-0003 – us A.T.L.A. [170]
THE MORAL UNITY OF THE HUMAN RACE : A SERMON PREACHED AT THE ORDINATION OF LUTHER HALSEY GULICK, M.D., AS A MISSIONARY TO THE MICRONESIAN ISLANDS / Thompson, Joseph Parrish – New York: M.W. Dodd, 1851 – 1mf – us A.T.L.A. [240]
MORAL USES OF DARK THINGS / Bushnell, Horace – London: Richard D Dickinson, 1880 – 1mf – 9 – 0-8370-6091-5 – 1986-0091 – us A.T.L.A. [210]
MORAL VIEWS OF COMMERCE, SOCIETY AND POLITICS / Dewey, Orville – 1838 – 9 – us A.T.L.A. [240]
MORAL WELFARE *see* CHURCH AND SOCIETY
MORAL WORLD – London. 1845 – 1 – uk Microform Academic [073]
LA MORALE DE CALVIN D'APRES L'INSTITUTION DE LA RELIGION CHRETIENNE / Nazelle, L – Lausanne: G. Bridel, 1882 – 1mf – us A.T.L.A. [170]
LA MORALE LAIQUE ET SES ADVERSAIRES / Bayet, Albert – 4th ed. Paris: F. Rieder et cie., 1935.222p – 1 – us U.W. Library [240]
LA MORALE UNIVERSELLE OU LES DEVOIRS DE L'HOMME FONDES SUR SA NATURE / Holbach, Paul-Thiry d' – (D'Holbach series). 1776 – 9 – fr Hachette [170]
Moraleja. Ayuntamiento *see*
– FIESTAS DE SU SANTO PATRON SAN BUENAVENTURA DURANTE...JULIO 1958
– FIESTAS DE SU SANTO PATRON. SAN BUENAVENTURA. DURANTE...JULIO 1962
Morales, Adolfo de *see*
– PARENTESCO ENTRE LOS CONQUISTADORES ESPANOLES...
– VIDA DE HERNANDO CORTES HECHA PEDAZOS..
Morales, Alan D *see* EFFECT OF THE ACHILLES TENDON ADHESIVE TAPING AND PRO M-P ACHILLES STRAP ON ECCENTRIC PLANTAR FLEXION PEAK TORQUE
Morales, Ambrosio *see*
– LAS ANTIGUEDADES DE LAS CIUDADES DE ESPANA. TOMO 9
– DE LOS CAMINOS O VIAS MILITARES FABRICADAS POR LOS ROMANOS EN ESPANA
Morales, Antonio y otros *see*
– LAS ANTIGUEDADES DE...CIUDADES DE ESPANA
– UNA RAZA DE LOBOS
Morales, Ascencio *see* CRISIS HISTORICA DE LA CIUDAD DE BADAJOZ
Morales, C *see* HISPANIAE SCHOLA MUSICA SACRA/OPERA VARIA [SAECAL 15, 16, 17 ET 18]...
Morales, C de *see* CHRISTOPHORI MORALIS HYSPANIENSIS MISSARUM LIBER PRIMUS (-SECUNDUS)
Morales, Cristobal *see* OPERA OMNIA
Morales Fernandez, Francisco *see* COMPENDIO DE ELEMENTOS DE MATEMATICAS
Morales Grinazu, Fernando *see* LOS CORREGIDORES Y SUBDELEGADOS DEL C.
Morales Guinazu, Fernando *see* GENEALOGIA DE LOS CONQUISTADORES DE CUYO
Morales, Julio *see* JOURNAL OF HIV/ AIDS PREVENTION AND EDUCATION FOR ADOLESCENTS AND CHILDREN
Morales Marquez, Angeles *see* NOMBRES CLAROS DE EXTREMADURA
Morales Oliver, Luis *see* AVANCE PARA LA BIBLIOGRAFIA DE OBRAS IMPRESAS DEL D. BENITO ARIAS MONTANO
MORALIA / Gregory the Great – 14th century. Ms 112. Emmanuel College – 14 – uk Microform Academic [240]
MORALIA HORATIANA : DAS IST DIE HORATZISCHE SITTEN-LEHRE, AUS DER ERNST-SITTIGEN GESELSCHAFT DER ALTEN WEISE-MEISTER GEZOGEN... / Zesen, Phillip von – Amsterdam, 1656 – 3mf – 9 – ne IDC [700]
MORALIA IN JOB (SIECLE 10) / Gregorio, San – Barcelona – 1r – 5,6 – sp Cultura [220]
LE MORALISTE / ed by Alepin, Sam – Montreal, Canada. 19 sep 1942-v4 n24. 2 mar 1946 – 1r – 1 – Can$60.00 – cn Can Microfilming [072]
THE MORALITY OF PROHIBITORY LIQUOR LAWS : AN ESSAY / Weeden, William Babcock – Boston: Roberts, 1875 – 1mf – us A.T.L.A. [170]
THE MORALITY OF THE OLD TESTAMENT / Smyth, Newman – London, NY: Cassell, 1886 – 1mf – 9 – 0-8370-53161 – 1985-3316 – us A.T.L.A. [170]
THE MORALITY OF TRACTARIANISM : A LETTER FROM ONE OF THE PEOPLE TO ONE OF THE CLERGY / Drane, Augusta Theodosia – London: William Pickering, 1850 – 1mf – us A.T.L.A. [240]
MORALS AND MISSILES – Catholic essays on the problems of war today. 1 fiche (29x) – 9 – 1.00f – at Libertarian Micro [320]
MORALS IN EVOLUTIONS : A STUDY IN COMPARATIVE ETHICS / Hobhouse, LT – New York: Henry Holt & Co, 1915 – 7mf – 9 – $10.50 – LLMC 92-137 – us L.L.M.C. [170]
MORALS, NOT ART OR LITERATURE / New York Society for the Suppression of Vice – (Ibid.New York: Trow, 1914. 68p. LL-711) – New York? 1895. 53p. LL-1674 – 1 – us L of C Photodup [340]
THE MORAN COMMITTEE REPORT *see* CRIMINAL JUSTICE / ABA STANDARDS / MILITARY PRACTICE
Moran, Neil K *see* THE ORDINARY CHANTS OF THE BYZANTINE MASS
Moran, Patrick Francis *see* IRISH SAINTS IN GREAT BRITAIN
Moran Triana, Eduardo *see* MANUAL ETIMOLOGICO GRECOLATINO
Morandini d'Eccatage, F *see* GRAND DICTIONNAIRE DES RIMES FRANCAISES
Morato Roma, F *see* LUZ DE MEDICINA...
Moratuwa, Ceylon. Holy Emmanuel Church *see* JUBILEE MEMORIALS, 1860-1910
Moratuwa. Ceylon. Holy Emmanuel Church *see* SEVENTY-FIFTH JUBILEE MEMORIALS, 1860-1935
Moravcsik, J *see* UNGARISCHE BIBLIOGRAPHIE DER TURKOLOGIE UND DER ORIENTALISCH-UNGARISCHEN BEZIEHUNGEN 1914-1925
MORAVEC – 1925-27 – 1 – us I.U. Libraries [073]
Moravia. Landesausschuss *see* RECHENSCHAFTS-BERICHT UEBER DIE AMTSWIRKSAMKEIT DES MAEHRISCHEN LANDESAUSSCHUSSES
Moravian Archives. Bristol *see* CATALOGUE
Moravian Archives. London *see* INDEX AND CATALOGUE
Moravian Archives. Manchester *see* CATALOGUE
Moravian Church *see* RECORDS OF THE MORAVIAN MISSION AMONG THE INDIANS OF NORTH AMERICA

Moravian Church. Bristol *see* ARCHIVES. 1756-1806
Moravian Church. General Synod, Herrnhut, 1869 *see* RESULTS OF THE SYNOD OF THE PROTESTANT CHURCH OF THE UNITED BRETHREN, OR UNITAS FRATRUM: HELD AT HERRNHUT IN THE YEAR 1869
Moravian Church. Yorkshire *see* REGISTERS
MORAVIAN HERESY, WHEREIN THE PRINCIPAL ERRORS OF THAT DOCTRINE, AS TAUGHT THROUGHOUT SEVERAL PARTS OF EUROPE AND AMERICA BY COUNT ZINZENDORF, MR. CENNICK AND OTHER MORAVIAN TEACHERS,... / Roche, J – Dublin, 1751 – 4mf – 9 – MP-343/1 – ne IDC [240]
MORAVIAN MESSENGER – 1962-90 (complete) – 7r – 1 – ATLA S0681 – us A.T.L.A. [073]
THE MORAVIAN MISSIONARY – 1929-58. (American Indian Periodicals in the Princeton University Library). 49 fiches – 9 – $200.00 – us UPA [240]
MORAVIAN MISSIONS : TWELVE LECTURES / Thompson, Augustus Charles – New York: Scribner, 1882 – 1mf – us A.T.L.A. [240]
MORAVIAN SHIPPING LIST, 14 OCTOBER 1735 – Ms. 2pp. xerox prints – 16 – uk Microform Academic [947]
THE MORAVIANS IN GEORGIA, 1735-1740 / Fries, Adelaide L – 1967. Orig. publ. 1905.Indexed. 5 fiches. F-0857 – 9 – us A.G.L.L. [240]
THE MORAVIANS IN GEORGIA, 1735-1740 / Fries, Adelaide L – Raleigh, N.C.: Printed for the author by Edwards & Broughton, c1905 – 1mf – us A.T.L.A. [240]
MORAVSKE NOVINY – Brno, Czechoslovakia. 1943-Jan 1944 (scattered issues) – 1r – 1 – us L of C Photodup [072]
MORAY AND NAIRN EXPRESS. (NORTHERN SCOT) – Elgin, Scotland. 29 Oct 1880. -w. 1mqn reels – 1 – uk British Libr Newspaper [072]
MORAY WEEKLY NEWS – Elgin, Scotland. -w. 10 Feb 1877-23 Oct 1880. 1 1 2 reels – 1 – uk British Libr Newspaper [072]
MORAYSHIRE ADVERTISER – Elgin, Scotland. -w. 8 July 1858-31 Jan 1877. 16 reels – 1 – uk British Libr Newspaper [072]
Moraze, Charles et al *see*
- ETUDES DE SOCIOLOGIE ELECTORALE
- SCIENCE AND THE FACTORS OF INEQUALITY

THE MORBID ANATOMY OF SOME OF THE MOST IMPORTANT PARTS OF THE HUMAN BODY / Baillie, M – 1v. text; 1 v. atlas. 2nd ed. M-36. 1793-1812 – 9 – ne IDC [611]
MORBIDITY AND MORTALITY – v1-25. 1952-Mar 1976 – 1 – us UMI [073]
Morbihan. France (Department) *see* DESCRIPTION ABREGEE DU DEPARTEMENT DU MORBIHAN
MORCEAUX CHOISIS DE LITTERATURE ARAMEENNE / Manna, J E – (Premiere partie. Mossoul 1901 7mf; deuxieme partie. Mossoul 1901 8mf) – 8 – ne Slangenburg [240]
MORCEAUX CHOISIS DE LITTERATURE FRANCAISE ET POESIE / Lebaigue, Charles – Paris: E. Belin, 1890. 4eme ed.viii,592p. 7 fiches. (Literature Collection) – 9 – 17.00 – fr Bibl Nationale [800]
Morcos, Selim A *see* RED SEA, GULD OF ADEN AND SUEZ CANAL
DER MORD AM POLIZEIAGENTEN BLAU / Trautner, Eduard – Berlin: Verlag Die Schmiede, c1924 – 1r – 1 – us U.W. Library [360]
Mordecai, Samuel Fox *see*
- MECHANICS' LIENS IN NORTH CAROLINA
- THE NEGOTIABLE INSTRUMENTS LAW IN NORTH CAROLINA

Mordike, B L *see* LASERS IN ENGINEERING
MORDOVIIA V GODY PERVOI RUSSKOI REVOLIUTSII / Firstov, I I – Saransk, 1955 – 1 – 35.00r – us Hoover Inst Photo [335]
MORDRED AND HILDEBRAND: A BOOK OF TRAGEDIES / Campbell, Wilfred – Ottawa: J. Durie, 1895. 00411. (Pre-1900 Canadiana) – 9 – cn C.I.H.M. [830]
Mordret, Ambroise Eusebe *see* ETUDE SUR LA DEMOGRAPHIE ET LA DEPOPULATION DE LA SARTHE
MORE – v1-8 1971-78 1; v7-8 5,6,9 – us UMI [073]
MORE ABOUT ABRAHAM BAR HIYYA'S PHILOSOPHICAL TERMINOLOGY / Efros, II – (Jewish Quaterly Review, ns no 20). Philadelphia. 1929-30. BJ-33-3 1 – 9 – ne IDC [180]
MORE CONSTITUTIONS FOR PALAU / Shuster, Donald R – 1 Sept 1981 – 1mf – 9 – $24.00 – LLMC 82-100G Title ? – us L.L.M.C. [324]
MORE "COPY" : A SECOND SERIES OF ESSAYS FROM AN EDITOR'S DRAWER ON RELIGION, LITERATURE AND LIFE / Thompson, Hugh Miller – New York: Thomas Whittaker, 1897 – 1mf – 9 – 0-8370-5594-6 – 1985-3594 – us A.T.L.A. [240]
More de Chedeville *see* SAUL
MORE DOCTORS FOR INDONESIA; A PICTURE STORY OF THE AFFILIATION BETWEEN THE SCHOOLS OF MEDICINE OF THE UNIVERSITY OF INDONESIA IN DJAKARTA AND THE UNIVERSITY OF CALIFORNIA IN SAN FRANCISCO / Jakarta. Universitas Indonesia. Fakultas Kedokteran – SE-2816 1. 1960? – 9 – ne IDC [610]
A MORE EFFECTIVE ROLE FOR SOCIAL WELFARE IN ECONOMIC AND SOCIAL DEVELOPMENT IN JORDAN / United Nations – M. Iskander. (Program of technical assistance). 1966. BNE-9797 1 – 9 – ne IDC [360]
MORE GLIMPSES OF THE WORLD UNSEEN / ed by Lee, Frederick George – London: Chatto & Windus, 1878 – 1mf – us A.T.L.A. [240]
More, Hannah *see* SACRED DRAMAS
More, Rene la *see* D'ALGER A TOMBOUCTOU
MORE THAN ENOUGH : AN OPTIMISTIC ASSESSMENT OF WORLD ENERGY / ed by Clarke, Robin – 1982 – 183p – 9 – 92-3-101986-4 – fr UNESCO [333]
More, Thomas *see* IDEE D'UNE REPUBLIQUE HEUREUSE, OU L'UTOPIE DE THOMAS MORUS. CONTENANT LE PLAN D'UNE REPUBLIQUE DONT LES LOIS, LES USAGES ET LES COUTUMES TENDENT UNIQUEMENT A RENDRE HEUREUSES LES SOCIETES QUI LES SUIVRONT
More, Thomas, Sir *see*
- VOM KREIGE; OF WARFARE
- VOYAGE A L'ILE D'UTOPIE

MORE WORK FOR MR. JOHN WESLEY : OR, A VINDICATION OF THE DECREES AND PROVIDENCE OF GOD FROM THE DEFAMATIONS OF A LATE PRINTED PAPER ENTITLED 'THE CONSEQUENCE PROVED' / Toplady, Augustus Montague – London, 1772 – 2mf – 9 – MP-476/1 – ne IDC [240]
Moreas, Jean *see* LES STANCES.
Moreau *see* STATISTIQUE COMMERCIALE DU DEPARTEMENT D'INDRE ET LOIRE ET DES CINQ DEPARTEMENTS LIMITROPHES, MAINE ET LOIRE, SARTHE, LOIR ET CHER, INDRE ET VIENNE, TOURS
Moreau de Jonnes, Alexandre *see*
- RECHERCHES STATISTIQUES SUR L'ESCLAVAGE COLONIAL ET SUR LES MOYENS DE LE SUPPRIMER
- STATISTIQUE DE L'INDUSTRIE DE LA FRANCE

Moreau de Saint Mery, ML E *see* CONSIDERATIONS PRESENTEES AUX VRAIS AMIS DU REPOS ET DU BONHEUR DE LA FRANCE, A L'OCCASION DES NOUVEAUX MOUVEMENTS DE QUELQUES SOI-DISANT AMIS DES NOIRS
Moreau de Saint-Mery, Mederic Louis Elie *see* DESCRIPTION TOPOGRAPHIQUE, PHYSIQUE, CIVILE, POLITIQUE ET HISTORIQUE DE LA PARTIE FRANCAISE DE L'ISLE SAINT-DOMINGUE
Moreau de Saint-Mery, Mederic Louis Elie (1750-1819) *see* LOIX ET CONSTITUTIONS DES COLONIES FRANCOISES DE L'AMERIQUE SOUS LE VENT
Moreau, Jacob N *see*
- MEMOIRE

Moreau, Marcel *see* VIE DE LA VENEREE ANNE-ELISABETH GOTTRAU, ABBESE DES BERNARDINES DE LA MAIGRAUGE
Moreau, Paul Joseph *see* LES INDIGENES D'A O F
Moreau-Christophe, L M *see* DU PROBLEME DE LA MISERE ET DE SA SOLUTION CHEZ LES PEUPLES ANCIENS ET MODERNES. TOME 3: PEUPLES MODERNES
Morecraft, Robert Jet al *see* THE CORTICAL AND SUBCORTICAL EFFERENT AND AFFERENT CONNECTIONS OF A PROPOSED CINGULATE MOTOR CORTEX AND ITS TOPOGRAPHICAL RELATIONSHIP TO THE PRIMARY AND SUPPLEMENTARY MOTOR CORTICES OF THE RHESUS MONKEY
MOREHEAD CITY FIRST BAPTIST CHURCH. MOREHEAD CITY, NORTH CAROLINA : CHURCH RECORDS – Sept 1873-1926 – 1 – 9.54 – us Baptist [240]
Morehouse, Ward *see* MISCELLANEOUS SCIENCE POLICY DOCUMENTS
Moreira, Dario *see* CULTURAL POLICY IN ECUADOR
Moreira de Azevedo, Manuel Duarte *see* CURIOSIDADES: NOTICIAS E VARIEDADES HISTORICAS BRAZILEIRAS
Moreira, Nicolau Joaquim *see* ...BRAZILIAN COFFEE
Morel, Benedict A *see* TRAITE DES DEGENERESCENCES PHYSIQUES, INTELLECTUELLES ET MORALES DE L'ESPECE HUMAINE ET DES CAUSES QUI PRODUISENT CES VARIETES MALADIVES
Morel de la Durantaye, A *see* EXPATRIATION ACADIENNE, NOTES FOURNIES...LE 24 MAI, 1885. BANISHMENT AND REMOVAL OF THE ACADIANS
Morel, J FN *see* CATALOGUE DES PLANTES DU JARDIN BOTANIQUE ETABLI A BESANCON...
Morel, Jean Marie *see* THEORIE DES JARDINS
Moreland, W H *see* FROM AKBAR TO AUSINGZEB
Morelet, P M A *see* SERIES CONCHYLIOLOGIQUES
Morell, Charles, Sir *see* THE TALES OF THE GENII, OR, THE DELIGHTFUL LESSONS OF HORAM THE SON OF ASMAR
Morell de Santa Cruz, Pedro Agustin *see* HISTORIA DE LA ISLA Y CATEDRAL DE CUBA
Morellet, Andre *see* LE MANUEL DES INQUISITEURS A 'USAGE DES INQUISITIONS D'ESPAGNE ET DU PORTUGAL. OU ABREGE DE L'OUVRAGE INTITULE: DIRECTORIUM INQUISITORUM
Morelly *see* NAUFRAGE DES ISLES FLOTTANTES OU BASILIADE DU CELEBRE PILPAI, POEME HEROIQUE TRADUIT DE L'INDIEN.
Morelos. Mexico (State) *see* PERIODICO OFICIAL
Morenas, Joseph-Elzear *see*
- PRECIS HISTORIQUE DE LA TRAITE DES NOIRS ET DE L'ESCLAVAGE COLONIAL, CONTENANT L'ORIGINE DE LA TRAITE, SES PROGRES, SON ETAT ACTUEL ET UN EXPOSE DES HORREURS PRODUITES PAR LE DESPOTISME DES COLONS
- PRECIS HISTORIQUE DE LA TRAITE DES NOIRS ET DE L'ESCLAVAGE COLONIAL, CONTENANT L'ORIGINE DE LA TRAITE, SES PROGRES, SON ETAT ACTUEL, ET UN EXPOSE DES HORREURS PRODUITES PAR LE DESPOTISME DES COLONS

Moreni, D *see* DELLE TRE SONTUOSE CAPELLE MEDICEE SITUATE NELL' IMP. BASILICA DI S. LORENZO DESCRIZIONE ISTORICO-CRITICA
Morenne, Daniel *see* LE PROBLEME DU LOGEMENT OUVRIER EN FRANCE
Moreno de Arteaga, Antonio *see*
- 1ST CONGRESO SINDICAL AGRARIO DE EXTREMADURA. PONENCIA 7. SITUACION DE LA, PRODUCCION GANADERA
- EXPLOTACION RACIONAL DEL SERDO

Moreno de Robles, Francisco *see* EN NOTAS DE BIBLIOGRAFIA FRANCISCANA
Moreno de Vargas, Bernabe *see*
- DISCURSO...NOBLEZA...ESPANA
- DISCURSOS DE LA NOBLEZA DE ESPANA
- DISCURSOS...NOBLEZA
- HISTORIA...MERIDA

Moreno, Enrique *see*
- CATHOLICISME ET LOYALISME
- CATHOLICS AND THE SPANISH STATE

Moreno, Francisco *see* CARTILLA HISTORICO-POLITICA
Moreno Izquierdo, Juan *see*
- LA FILOSOFIA EN LA CIENCIA. ENSAYO SOBRE EL CONCEPTO Y CONDICIONES DE AMBAS...
- IN OTHER WORDS

Moreno, Joaquin *see* UN LINAJE EXTREMENOS, LOS MORENO DE DON BENITO
Moreno, Juan Carlos *see* NUESTRAS MALVINAS, UN VIAJE DE ESTUDIOS Y OBSERVACION...
Moreno Lazaro, J *see* BREVE GUIA DE TRUJILLO, CUNA DE CONQUISTADORES
Moreno Maldonado, Jose *see* GRANDEZAS DE LA CIUDAD DE DIOS
Moreno Marquez, Victor *see*
- APUNTES BILOGICOS SOBRE EL POJO DE LAS HABAS
- CONTRIBUCION AL ESTUDIO DE LOS PASTOS EXTREMENOS
- EXPERIENCIAS SOBRE EL PODER ATRAYENTE, PARA LA MOSCA DEL OLIVO, DEL FOSFATO AMONICO A DIVERSAS CONCENTRACIONES
- IDEAS ACTUALES SOBRE LAS PLAGAS DE LANGOSTA
- LA LANGOSTA Y LAS ROTUACIONES
- UNAS PRUEBAS DE LABORES EN TERRENOS INFESTADOS CONCANUTOS DE LANGOSTA
- SEIS FORMULAS DE CEBO CONTRA LA LANGOSTA
- LAS TROCHAS

Moreno Nieto, Jose *see*
- DISCURSO PRONUNCIADO POR...EL 30 DE NOVIEMBRE DE 1881 EN EL ATENEO CIENTIFICO Y LITERARIO DE MADRID CON MOTIVO DE LA APERTURA DE SUS CATEDRAS
- DISCURSO PRONUNCIADO POR...EL DIA 8 DE NOVIEMBRE DE 1877 EN EL ATENEO CIENTIFICO LITERARIO DE MADRID, CON MOTIVO DE LA APERTURA DE SUS CATEDRAS
- DISCURSO PRONUNCIADO POR...EL DIA 10 DE NOVIEMBRE DE 1880 EN EL ATENEO CIENTIFICO Y LITERARIO DE MADRID CON MOTIVO DE LA APERTURA DE SUS CATEDRAS
- DISCURSO PRONUNCIADO POR...EL DIA 31 DE OCTUBRE DE 1878 EN EL ATENEO CIENTIFICO Y LITERARIO DE MADRID CON MOTIVO DE LA APERTURA DE SUS CATEDRAS
- DISCURSO...CATEDRAS
- DISCURSOS..
- DISCURSOS ACADEMICOS DEL..
- GRAMATICA DE LA LENGUA ARABIGA
- ORACION INAUGURAL...LICEO DE GRANADA
- UNDECIMA CONFERENCIA: INFLUENCIA DE LA MUJER EN LA SOCIEDAD
- VELADA EN HONOR

Moreno Torrado, Luis *see*
- EL AVARO
- CONSEJOS AUN JOVEN
- EXHALACIONES DEL ALMA
- EXPLOSIONES DEL SENTIMIENTO
- HUMORISMOS Y SATIRAS
- IDILIOS Y ELEGIAS
- LIRISMOS
- MOSTAZA Y ORTIGAS
- NUEVAS ELEGIAS
- PALPITACIONES DE UN CORAZON
- POEMAS Y EPISODIOS
- POESIAS SERIAS
- POSESIAS SERIAS
- SIN HIJOS Y CON BIENES
- TEORIA DEL TRABAJO
- VIBRACIONES DE UNA LIRA

Moreno Villa, Jose *see* LOCOS, ENANOS, NEGROS Y NINOS PALACIEGOS..
Morenz, S *see* DIE GESCHICHTE VON JOSEPH DEM ZIMMERMANN (T.U.U. 5-56)
Morera, J M *see* HIPPOCRATICAS THESES EX LIBRIS APHOR, PROGNOSTIC. Y VICT....
Moreri, Louis *see*
- GRAN DICCIONARIO HISTORICO. TOMO 1
- GRAN DICCIONARIO HISTORICO. TOMO 2
- GRAN DICCIONARIO HISTORICO. TOMO 3, 1ST PARTE
- GRAN DICCIONARIO HISTORICO. TOMO 3, 2ND PARTE
- GRAN DICCIONARIO HISTORICO. TOMO 4
- GRAN DICCIONARIO HISTORICO. TOMO 5
- GRAN DICCIONARIO HISTORICO. TOMO 6
- GRAN DICCIONARIO HISTORICO. TOMO 7
- GRAN DICCIONARIO HISTORICO. TOMO 8, 1ST PARTE
- GRAN DICCIONARIO HISTORICO. TOMO 8, 2ND PARTE
- LE GRAND DICTIONNAIRE HISTORIQUE OU LE MELANGE CURIEUX DE L'HISTOIRE SACREE ET PROFANE
- SUPPLEMENT AU GRAND DICTIONNAIRE HISTORIQUE, GENEALOGIQUE, GEOGRAPHIQUE, ETC..

Moresby, John *see* TWO ADMIRALS: ADMIRAL OF THE FLEET SIR FAIRFAX MORESBY, G.C.B. (1786-1877), AND HIS SON, JOHN MORESBY
Moresco, Larry L *see* INTERNATIONAL JOURNAL OF MICROELECTRONICS PACKAGING MATERIALS AND TECHNOLOGIES
Moreton de Chabrillan, Elizabeth Celeste Venard de *see* UNE MECHANTE FEMME
Moretti, G *see* PRODROMI DI UNA MONOGRAFIA DELLE SPECIE DEL GENERE MORUS

Moretti, Pietro *see* RITUS DANDI PRESBYTERIUM PAPAE, CARDINALIBUS ET CLERICIS NONNULLARUM ECCLESIARUM URBIS
Morev, I *see* "KAMEN VERY" STEFANA IAVORSKAGO
Morewood, Caroline C et al *see* ENGLISH EPISCOPAL PALACES
Morgagni, G B *see* DE SEDIBUS, ET CAUSIS MORBORUM PER ANATOMEN INDAGATIS
Morgan, Anne Eugenia *see* SCRIPTURE STUDIES ON THE ORIGIN AND DESTINY OF MAN
Morgan, B F *see* DIRECTORY OF PREBLE COUNTY 1875
Morgan, Bayard Quincy *see* DER LEX VON GUTENHAG
MORGAN COUNTY. ALABAMA : CHURCH RECORDS – Austinville First Baptist Church, 1949-50; Belview Baptist Church, 1935-60; Bethel Baptist Church, 1884-1933; Belthlehem Baptist Church, 1922-60; Brookhaven Baptist Church, 1957-60; Calvary Baptist Church, 1954-60 – 1 – 53.55 – us Baptist [240]
MORGAN COUNTY. ALABAMA : CHURCH RECORDS – Danville Baptist Church, 1884-1958; Decatur First Baptist Church, 1911-60; Eastside Decatur Baptist Church, 1952-60 – 1 – 43.20 – us Baptist [240]
MORGAN COUNTY. ALABAMA : CHURCH RECORDS – Falkville, 1887-1955; Decatur, Fifth Avenue Baptist Church, 1956-60; Gum Springs Baptist Church, 1871-1959; Hartselle, First Baptist Church, 1883-1960 – 1 – 50.40 – us Baptist [240]
MORGAN COUNTY. ALABAMA : CHURCH RECORDS – Hopewell Baptist Church, 1895-1959; Lacy's Springs, Bethlehem Baptist Church, 1943-57; Lebanon Baptist Church, 1850-96; Mt. Carmel Baptist Church, 1930-60; Mt. Nebo Baptist Church, 1887-1904 – 1 – 43.20 – us Baptist [240]
MORGAN COUNTY. ALABAMA : CHURCH RECORDS – Mt. View Baptist Church, 1952-59; Mt. Zion Baptist Church, 1853-1954; Decatur, Northside, 1947-58; Pleasant Hill Baptist Church, 1913-59; Rock Creek Baptist Church, 1957-60 – 1 – 53.55 – us Baptist [240]
MORGAN COUNTY. ALABAMA : CHURCH RECORDS – Shady Grove Baptist Church, 1889-1960; Shiloh Baptist Church, 1947-59; Shoals Creek Baptist Church, 1900-59; Summitt Baptist Church, 1948-60; Trinity Baptist Church, 1947-60 – 1 – 43.88 – us Baptist [240]
MORGAN COUNTY. ALABAMA : CHURCH RECORDS – Walden's Chapel Baptist Church, 1942-60; West Harselle Baptist Church, 1953-60; Westside Decatur Baptist Church, Membership Roll – 1 – 35.10 – us Baptist [240]
Morgan, Dale L *see* COLLECTION
Morgan, Dick Thompson *see* MORGAN'S DIGEST OF OKLAHOMA STATUTES AND SUPREME COURT DECISIONS
MORGAN, GARRETT A., PAPERS, MS 3534 – (Personal papers of Garrett A. Morgan of Cleveland, Ohio, a prominent African-American businessman and inventor, famed for his invention of a traffic control light, and a gas mask) – 1894-1970 – 1r – 1 – us Western Res [920]
Morgan, George Campbell *see*
- DISCIPLESHIP
- FIRST CENTURY MESSAGE TO 20TH CENTURY CHRISTIANS
- STUDIES IN THE PROPHECY OF JEREMIAH

Morgan, Henry J *see* THE CANADIAN MEN AND WOMEN OF THE TIME: A HANDBOOK OF CANADIAN BIOGRAPHY OF LIVING CHARACTERS
Morgan, Herschel Darrell *see* A PROGRAM FOR ESTABLISHING THE PRIMARY OPERATIVE ROLES OF THE PASTOR AT THE FIRST BAPTIST CHURCH OF BENTON, KENTUCKY
MORGAN HILL SUN – Morgan Hill, CA. 1894-1901 – 2r – 1 – $100.00 – B02488 – us Library Micro [071]
MORGAN HILL TIMES – Morgan Hill, CA. 1909-28; 1930-66; 1991-97; 1967- – 68+ r – 1 – $3,400.00 ($160.00y) – B02491 – us Library Micro [071]
Morgan, James *see* THE IMPORTANCE OF TERTULLIAN IN THE DEVELOPMENT OF CHRISTIAN DOGMA
Morgan, John *see* THE GIFT OF THE HOLY GHOST ACCORDING TO THE TEACHING OF THE SCRIPTURE
Morgan, Kenneth William *see* ISLAM THE STRAIGHT PATH
THE MORGAN MERCURY – Berkeley Springs. West Virginia. 1882-1893 – 1 – us UMI [071]
MORGAN MESSENGER – Berkeley Springs. West Virginia. 1894-1925; 1928-1968 – 1 – us UMI [071]
Morgan, PW *see* HISTORY OF WYANDOTTE COUNTY
Morgan, Rod *see* POLICING AND SOCIETY
Morgan, Sydney O *see* THE MISSIONARY, AN INDIAN TALE
Morgan, W B et al *see* RESOURCE MANAGEMENT AND OPTIMIZATION
Morgan, Wallace *see* HISTORY OF KERN COUNTY
Morgand, Leon Francois Theophile *see* LA LOI MUNICIPALE.
MORGANFIELD FIRST BAPTIST CHURCH. MORGANFIELD, KENTUCKY : CHURCH RECORDS – 1888-1963 – 1 – 50.31 – us Baptist [240]
Morgans *see* HISTORY OF SULLIVAN COUNTY
MORGAN'S DIGEST OF OKLAHOMA STATUTES AND SUPREME COURT DECISIONS / Morgan, Dick Thompson – Kansas City, Mo.: Hudson-Kimberley. 1897. 307p. LL-884 – 1 – us L of C Photodup [340]
DER MORGEN – (Also available: Ausgabe Berlin und Randgebiete, jul 1 1965-jun 29 1979; Republik-Ausgabe, aug 1 1945-jun 11 1991) – Berlin, aug 3 1945-jun 11 1991 – 1 – Inquire at Mikrofilmarchiv for details – gw Misc Inst [072]
DER MORGEN – Berlin, 2 Jan-11 Jun 1991 – 3r – DM225.00 – gw Mikro Press [072]
DER MORGEN – Berlin, 3 Aug 1945-52 – 10r – 1 – DM700.00 – gw Mikro Press [072]
DER MORGEN – Berlin, feb 1-jun 15 1901 – 2r – 1 – Inquire at Mikrofilmarchiv for details – gw Misc Inst [943]
DER MORGEN – Berlin, Germany. 1962-74 – 36r – 1 – us L of C Photodup [072]
DER MORGEN – Berlin. Germany. Aug. 1945-Dec. 1949 (gaps) – 1 – 35.00r – us Hoover Inst Photo [072]
DER MORGEN – East Berlin, Germany. Ausg. Berlin: 3 Aug 1945-1990. Republik-Ausg: Jul 1965-Jun 1979 – 87r; 28r – 1 – gw Mikrofilm [072]
DER MORGEN – (Title changes: Der Mannheimer Morgen, 8 Oct 1946; Mannheimer Morgen, 2 Oct 1947) – Mannheim, West Germany. 1953- – ca 10r per yr – 1 – gw Mikrofilm [072]
DER MORGEN – Zagreb, Yugoslavia. Jul 1925-May 1926 – 2r – 1 – us L of C Photodup [949]
DIE MORGEN STUNDEN EINES KOENIGES AN SEINEN BRUDER SOHN 1766 : GLAUBENSBEKAENNTNISS SEINER KOENIGLICHEN MAJESTAET VON PREUSSEN / Friedrich 2nd; ed by Massenbach, Eugen Freiherr von – Muenchen, 1924 – 70p – 9 – DM48.00 – 3-89349-077-9 – gw Hänsel [943]
DER MORGEN ZHURNAL = THE JEWISH MORNING JOURNAL – (In Yiddish) – New York City, NY. v17 no4834 7 Aug 1917-v27 no7923 30 Oct 1927 – 1r – 1 – $30.00 – cn Can Microfilming [071]
MORGENBLATT – Zagreb, Yugoslavia. May 1926-Apr 1929; Sept 1938; Jan-Jul 1939; Aug-Nov 1940 (incomplete) – 9r – 1 – us L of C Photodup [949]
MORGENBLATT DER BONNER ZEITUNG – Bonn, apr 1 1884-90 – 1 – Inquire at Mikrofilmarchiv for details – gw Misc Inst [943]
MORGENBLATT FUER GEBILDETE LESER *see* MORGENBLATT FUER GEBILDETE STAENDE
MORGENBLATT FUER GEBILDETE STAENDE – Stuttgart, 1807-1865 – 44r – 1 – DM3,300.00 – gw Mikro Press [072]
MORGENBLATT FUER GEBILDETE STAENDE – (Title change: Morgenblatt fuer gebildete Leser, 1837) – Tuebingen-Stuttgart, Germany. 1807-1865 – 44r – 1 – gw Mikrofilm [072]
DAS MORGENLAENDISCHE MOENCHTUM / Schiwietz, St – (Erster Band: Das Ascetentum der drei ersten christl. Jahrhunderte und das egyptische Moenchtum...Mainz, 1904. 6mf. Dfl25.00; Zweiter Band: Das Moenchtum auf Sinai und in Palaestina im vierten Jahrhundert. Mainz, 1913. 4mf. Dfl19.00; Dritter Band: Das Moenchtum in Syrien und Mesopotamien und das Aszetentum in Persien. Moedling bei Wien, 1938. 8mf. Dfl30.00) – 3v – 8 – ne Slangenburg [240]
MORGENLAND UND ABENDLAND / Lindau, Rudolf – Hamburg-Grossborstel: Verlag der Deutschen-Gedaechtnis-Stiftung, 1917 – 1 – us U.W. Library [830]
MORGENPOST *see* BREMER MORGENPOST
MORGENROETE – v52-72. 1970-90 (complete) – 1r – 1 – ATLA S0351 – us A.T.L.A. [073]
DER MORGENSHTERN = THE MORNING STAR – (In Yiddish. Monthly) – Leeds, GB. v1 no1 15 Jul 1897-v1 no2 15 Sep 1897 – 1r – 1 – $25.00 – cn Can Microfilming [072]
DER MORGENSTERN – New York. v1. 1890 – 1r – 1 – us Ross [071]
Morgenstern, Christian *see*
- EPIGRAMME UND SPRUECHE
- MELANCHOLIE
- UEBER DIE GALGENLIEDER

Morgenstern, Lina *see* ALLGEMEINER FRAUENKALENDER, 1.1885-2.1886 DIE FRAUENBESTREBUNGEN UNSERER ZEIT, 3.1887 (HQ, 17)
Morgenstern, Lina (Bauer) et al *see* DIE STELLUNG DER FRAU IM LEBEN
MORGEN-STERNE – Newark. N.J. 1921; 1922; 1932 – 1 – us A.J.P.C. [071]
THE MORGENTHAU DIARIES, 1933-1945 : DEPRESSION AND NEW DEAL, 1933-1939 – (With printed guide. Series: Research Collections in American Politics) – 63r – 1 – $7,095.00 – 1-55655-563-6 – us UPA [977]
THE MORGENTHAU DIARIES, 1933-1945 – (Individual titles listed separately. Series: Research Collection in American Politics) – 3pts 250r – 1 – $25,325.00 coll – us UPA [977]
THE MORGENTHAU DIARIES, 1933-1945 : PRELUDE TO WAR AND WAR, 1940-1942 – (With printed guide. Series: Research Collections in American Politics) – 1996 – 114r – 1 – $12,830.00 – 1-55655-564-4 – us UPA [977]
THE MORGENTHAU DIARIES, 1933-1945 : WORLD WAR 2 AND POSTWAR PLANNING, 1943-1945 – (With printed guide. Series: Research Collections in American Politics) – 1997 – 73r – 1 – $8,215.00 – 1-55655-565-2 – us UPA [977]
Morgenthau, Henry Jr. *see* PRESIDENTIAL DIARIES OF HENRY MORGENTHAU JR. (1938-45)
MORGEN-ZEITUNG – (Also suppl available: Wochen-Chronik, jul 16-30 1854, 1r) – Bremen, may 5-aug 5 1854 (incomplete) – 1 – Inquire at Mikrofilmarchiv for details – gw Misc Inst [072]
MORGENZEITUNG – Maehrisch-Ostrau, (Ostrava), Czechoslovakia. 23 Feb 1923-15 Mai 1933 – 15r – 1 – gw Mikrofilm [072]
MORGENZEITUNG *see*
- BRESLAUER ANZEIGER
- BRESLAUER MORGENZEITUNG
- DER HAMBURGER BEOBACHTER UND DAS ARCHIV WISSENSCHAFT UND KUENSTE

DER MORGN = THE MORNING – (In Yiddish) – Munich, DE. v1 no2 4 Mar 1949-v1 no35 4 Nov 1949 – 1r – 1 – $25.00 – cn Can Microfilming [072]
MORGNSTAYTUNG = MORNING JOURNAL – Buenos Aires, AG. v3 no735. 19 Sep 1937 – 1r – 1 – $25.00 – cn Can Microfilming [072]
MORGONBLADET *see* SVENSKA MORGONBLADET
MORGONBRIS – Stockholm, Sweden. 1904-23, 1928 – 3r – 1 – sw Kungliga [073]
MORGONPOSTEN – Motala, 1987-94 – 1 – sw Kungliga [072]
MORGONTIDNINGEN – Stockholm, 1942-58. Socialdemokraten, 1885-1942 – 487r – 1 – sw Kungliga [072]
MORGON-TIDNINGEN SOCIAL-DEMOKRATEN – Stockholm, oct 1942-43 (14r); 1944-jun 1950 (78r) – 92r – 1 – us Res Libr [072]
Morgues, Mathieu de *see* DIVERSES PIECES POUR LA DEFENSE DE LA ROYNE, MERE DU ROY LOUIS 13TH...
MORGUNBLADID – Reykjavik: [s.n.] 1956-69 (107r); [1970-apr 1979] (112r); [may 1979-may 15 1985] (81r); [may 16 1985-dec 31 1990] (135r); [jan 1991-jan 14 1996] (120r); jan 16 1996- – 1 – us Res Libr [072]
Morhofen, D G *see* UNTERRICHT VON DER TEUTSCHEN SPRACHE UND POESIE, DEREN URSPRUNG, FORTGANG UND LEHR-SAETZEN...
Mori, Kyozo *see* (KYOKUTO KOKUSAI GUNJI SAIBAN KIROKU MOKUROKU OYOBI SAKUIN)
MORIAH – Antwerpen. v1-2. 1935-1936 – 4mf – 9 – ne IDC [949]
Moriarty, David *see* ALLOCUTIONS TO THE CLERGY AND PASTORALS OF THE LATE RIGHT REV. DR. MORIARTY, BISHOP OF KERRY
Moriarty, James Joseph *see* THE KEYS OF THE KINGDOM
Moricand, M E *see* PLANTES NOUVELLES D'AMEA1RIQUE
Moricca, U *see* STORIA DELLA LITTERATURA LATINA CHRIST
Morice, Adrien G *see*
- DICTIONNAIRE HISTORIQUE DES CANADIENS ET DES METIS FRANCAIS DE L'OUEST
- THE GREAT DENE RACE

Morienval, Henri *see* LA GUERRE DU DAHOMEY
MORILLO, SANTIAGO. LAS IGLESIAS CRISTIANAS DE ORIENTE. TEXTO DE TEOLOGIA ORIENTAL. GRANADA, 1946 / Aldama, J A – Madrid: Razon y Fe, 1947 – 1 – sp Bibl Santa Ana [240]
Morillo Trivino, Santiago *see*
- ALCANCE MISIONAL DE LA LITURGIA DEL CANACULO O EL PROBLEMA DE LA ADAPTACION
- CURSO DE LENGUA GRIEGA
- CURSO DE LENGUA GRIEGA. MORFOLOGIA. FASCICULO 1
- CURSO DE LENGUA GRIEGA. MORFOLOGIA. FASCICULO 2. EJERCICIO Y ANTOLOGIA
- CURSO DE LENGUA GRIEGA. MORFOLOGIA. FASCICULO 2. EJERCICIOS Y ANTOLOGIA
- LAS IGLESIAS CRISTIANAS DE ORIENTE
- MISA DE SAN JUAN CRISOSTOMO
- EL PADRE PABLO DE GRAYMOOR...

Morillo-Velarde, D *see* RIMAS DE JUVENTUD. POESIAS
MORIM BULLETIN OF THE J.T.A. – (continues: J.T.A. bulletin. Continued by: Morim newsletter of the J.T.A.) – (New York, New York) v41, no. 1 (Oct.1967) – us A.J.P.C. [071]
MORIM NEWSLETTER OF THE J.T.A. – (Continues: Morim bulletin of the J.T.A.) – (New York, N.Y.) Feb. 1969-Feb. 1989 – us A.J.P.C. [270]
Morin, Augustin-Norbert *see* LA MINERVE
Morin, C *see* LIBER COMICUS MAREDSOLI
Morin, D G *see* MISCELLANEA AGOSTINIANA TESTI E STUDI, VOL 1
Morin, G *see*
- ANECDOTA MAREDSOLANA
- REGULAE S. BENEDICTI TRADITIO

Morin, J *see* COMMENTARIUS DE SACRIS ECCLESIAE ORDINATIONIBUS
Morin, Jacques *see* BIBLIOGRAPHIE DE L'OEUVRE DE MONSIEUR ROLLAND DUMAIS, CONSEILLER PEDAGOGIQUE EN SCIENCES NATURELLES A LA COMMISSION DES ECOLES CATHOLIQUES DE QUEBEC, DIRECTEUR-FONDATEUR DU CAMP MARIE-VICTORIN
Morin, Leopol *see* LE NIGOG
Morin, Louis *see* LES COMMUNAUTES DES CORDONNIERS, BASANIERS ET SAVETIERS DE TROYES
Morin, Maurice *see* BIO-BIBLIOGRAPHIE ANALYTIQUE DES DISCOURS ET CONFERENCES DE L'HONORABLE TELESPHORE-DAMIEN BOUCHARD
Morin, Pierre *see* HEBDO DE L'EST
Morin, Romuald *see* BIBLIOGRAPHIE ANALYTIQUE DE L'OEUVRE DE M. L'ABBE LOUIS O'NEILL, AUMONIER A L'ACADEMIE DE QUEBEC, PROFESSEUR DE MORALE SOCIALE
Morin, Victor *see*
- 1 LA CHANSON FRANCAISE A TRAVERS LES SIECLES
- THE AMERICAN PORTION OF THE HISTORICAL LIBRARY OF VICTOR MORIN
- CHALET DES BRISES
- LA CHANSON CANADIENNE
- CROQUIS MONTREALAIS
- DINER EN MUSIQUE
- DINER EN MUSIQUE: FANTAISIE GASTRONOMICO-MUSICALE EN DEUX ACTES..
- DINER EN MUSIQUE: FANTAISIE GASTRONOMICO-MUSICALE EN DEUX ACTES:... 28 NOVEMBRE 1935
- DINER – OPERETTE EN DEUX ACTES
- L'EMPLACEMENT DU FORT DE DOLLARD DES ORMEAUX: ETUDE REPRODUITE DE LA REVUE D'HISTOIRE DE L'AMERIQUE FRANCAISE
- LES FASTES HISTORIQUES DU VIEUX MONTREAL

- FLEURY MESPLETS, PIONNIER DE L'IMPRIMERIE A MONTREAL
- LE GOUVERNEUR ET MADAME DE RAMEZAY RECOIVENT: CHRONIQUE DES FETES DU 250E ANNIVERSAIRE DU CHATEAU DE RAMEZAY
- IN CHORDIS ET ORGANO (FASTES D'ORGANIERS)
- LA LEGENDE DOREE DE MONTREAL
- LES MEDAILLES DECERNEES AUX INDIENS
- LES MEMOIRES DE CAILLETTE ET AUTRES RECITS
- OLD MONTREAL WITH PEN AND PENCIL
- LES ORDRES DE CHEVALERIE RELIGIEUSE AU CANADA
- LES RAMEZAY ET LEUR CHATEAU
- LA ROSSE-QUI-DETELLE
- LA SCIENCE DU BLASON
- SEIGNEURS ET CENSITAIRES, CASTES DISPARUES
- TROIS DOCTEURS
- L'UTILE ET LE FUTILE
- LE VIEUX MONTREAL
- LA VILLE AUX CLOCHERS DANS LA VERDURE
- VILLE MYSTIQUE
- VINGT ANS APRES, 1884-1904: RECIT VERIDIQUE, HISTORIQUE, ANECDOTIQUE, EPIQUE ET TYPIQUE D'UN CONVENTUM D'ANCIENS COLLEGIENS

Morio, Simone *see* TWO STUDIES ON UNEMPLOYMENT AMONG EDUCATED YOUNG PEOPLE

Moriones, Ildefonso *see* ANA DE JESUS Y LA HERENCIA TERESIANA...ROMA, 1968

Moris, G G *see*
- ENUMERATIC SEMINUM REGII HORTI BOTANICI TAURINENSIS
- FLORA SARDOA

LOS MORISCOS DE HORNACHOS, CORSARIOS DE SALE / Sanchez Perez, Andres – Badajoz: (Imprenta de la Diputacion Provincial), 1964. Rev. Estudios Extremenos – 1 – sp Bibl Santa Ana [946]

THE MORISCOS OF SPAIN : THEIR CONVERSION AND EXPULSION / Lea, Henry Charles – Philadelphia: Lea Bros., 1901 – 2mf – us A.T.L.A. [305]

Morison *see* ST. BASIL AND HIS RULE

Morison, James C *see*
- A CRITICAL EXPOSITION OF THE THIRD CHAPTER OF ST PAUL'S EPISTLE TO THE ROMANS
- EXPOSITION OF THE NINTH CHAPTER OF THE EPISTLE TO THE ROMANS
- THE LIFE AND TIMES OF SAINT BERNARD, ABBOT OF CLAIRVAUX, A.D. 1091-1153
- ST. PAUL'S TEACHING ON SANCTIFICATION: A PRACTICAL EXPOSITION OF ROMANS 6

Morison, James Cotter *see*
- GIBBON
- THE SERVICE OF MAN

Morison, James Henderson Stuart *see* THE RULES OF PLEADING AS ADAPTED TO COURTS OF LAW IN TENNESSEE.

Morisse, Anne-Marie *see* DIE EPISCHE KUNST UND KUNSTTECHNIK ERNST VON WILDENBRUCHS

Morisse, Avocat *see* ESSAI SUR LA NATURE ET L'EXERCICE DE L'AUTORITE DU PEUPLE DANS UN ETAT

Morisset-Andersen, C *see* EVOLUTION D'UNE EXPLOITATION AGRICOLE DANOISE DE 1924 A 1972

Morissette, J-F *see*
- LE FEU-FOLLET
- LE FIGARO
- LE MUSEE CANADIEN

Morissette, Lucy *see* BIO-BIBLIOGRAPHIE DE S.E. LE CARDINAL NICOLAS WISEMAN

Morissette, Rachel *see* BIBLIOGRAPHIE ANALYTIQUE DE MADAME YOLANDE CHENE

MORITATEN / Kremer, Hannes – 3. Aufl. Muenchen: F Eher, 1943 – 1r – 1 – us U.W. Library [830]

MORITZ AUGUST VON THUEMMELS ROMAN "REISE IN DIE MITTAEGLICHEN PROVINZEN VON FRANKREICH" / Kyrieleis, Richard – (Includes bibliographical references) – Marburg a.L.: N G Elwert, 1908 – 1r – 1 – us U.W. Library [430]

MORITZ VON SACHSEN : TRAUERSPIEL IN FUENF AKTEN / Prutz, Robert Eduard – Zürich: Verlag des literarischen Comptoirs, 1845 – 1r – 1 – us U.W. Library [820]

Moritzi, A *see* SYSTEMATISCHES VERZEICHNISS DER VON H. ZOLLINGER IN 1842-1844 AUF JAVA GESAMMELTEN PFLANZEN, NEBST KURZER BESCHREIBUNG DER NEUEN GATTUNGEN UND ARTEN

Morla Vicuna, Carlos *see* ESTUDIO HISTORICO SOBRE EL DESCUBRIMIENTO Y CONQUISTA DE LA PATAGONIA Y DE LA TIERRA DE FUEGO

Morley, Henry *see* SKETCHES OF LONGER WORKS IN ENGLISH VERSE AND PROSE

Morley, John *see*
- CRITICAL MISCELLANIES
- THE LIFE OF RICHARD COBDEN
- RECOLLECTIONS
- STUDIES IN LITERATURE

Morley, Thomas *see*
- A PLAINE AND EASIE INTRODUCTION TO PRACTICALL MUSICKE..
- A PLAINE AND EASIE INTRODUCTION TO PRACTICALL MUSICKE

Morlighem, H *see* LES COMMUNICATIONS DES INDIGENES DU KASAI AVEC LES AMES DES MORTS

MORMOLYCE, NOVUM COLEOPTERORUM GENUS / Hagenbach, J J – Norimbergae, 1825. Z/1325/2 – 8 – ne IDC [590]

THE MORMON – New York. v1-2. 1855-56 – 1r – 1 – us Ross [240]

THE MORMON – Weekly. New York. v. 1-2, no. 25. Feb 17 1855-Aug 9 1856. Incomplete – 1 – us NY Public [240]

THE MORMON CULTURE REGION: STRATEGIES AND PATTERNS IN THE GEOGRAPHY OF THE AMERICAN WEST – 1847-1964. By D.W. Meinig 1965. Item B. Taken from: Annals of Association of American Geographers. v55, no.2, Jun 1965. p191-220. SW16-0087 – 5 – us A.G.L.L. [978]

MORMON NEWSPAPERS OF THE 19TH CENTURY – Nauvoo, IL. 1842-91 – 1r – 1 – us Ross [071]

MORMONISM EXPOSED / Danielson, Vernon J – 1933 – 1 – 5.00 – us Baptist [240]

THE MORMONS AND THE SILVER MINES / Bonwick, James – London: Hodder and Stoughton, 1872 – 1mf – us A.T.L.A. [240]

Mornet, Daniel *see* HISTOIRE DE LA CLARTE FRANCAISE, SES ORIGINES, SON EVOLUTION, SA VALEUR

MORNING ADVERTISER – London. -d. 1818-99. (268mqn reels) – 1 – uk British Libr Newspaper [072]

MORNING ADVERTISER – New York. June 8 1891-Apr 1 1897. Not collated – 1 – us NY Public [071]

MORNING ADVERTISER – Portland OR. June 5 1891 – 1 – us U.O. Library [071]

MORNING AGE – Clinton. Iowa. 1894-1904 – 1 – us UMI [071]

MORNING ALBERTAN – Calgary, Canada. -d. Jan 1907; April-May 1910; July-Sept 1912; April-June 1913; Oct-Dec 1917; June-Sept 1918; April-June 1919. Imperfect. 9 1 2 reels – 1 – uk British Libr Newspaper [072]

MORNING AMERICAN – Portland OR. June 5 1891 – 1 – us U.O. Library [071]

A MORNING AND EVENING CHURCH SERVICE IN F / Wesley, S – London: Author, Balls, 181- – 1 – us Sibley [780]

MORNING APPEAL *see*
- CARSON DAILY APPEAL
- NEVADA APPEAL

MORNING BULLETIN – Edmonton, Canada. Dec 1915-June 1922 – 49r – 1 – uk British Libr Newspaper [971]

MORNING BULLETIN – Portland OR. Sep 21 1870-May 11 1875 – 1 – us U.O. Library [071]

MORNING CALL – Allentown. Pa. and Sunday Call Chronicle. 1895- – 1 – us UMI [071]

MORNING CALL – San Francisco. Calif. 1867-1875; 1877; 1878-1914 – 1 – us UMI [071]

THE MORNING CALL – Harrisburg, PA. -d 1885-1897 – 13 – $25.00r – us I.M.R. [071]

MORNING CALM – Korea. 1890-1939 – 1 – us UMI [072]

MORNING CHRONICLE – Halifax, Canada. 1862-79 – 34r – 1 – $2,210.00 – cn Library Assoc [971]

MORNING CHRONICLE – Halifax, Canada. -d. Dec 1852-June 1922. 102 1 2 reels – 1 – uk British Libr Newspaper [072]

MORNING CHRONICLE – London. -d. 1801-65. (275 reels) – 1 – uk British Libr Newspaper [072]

MORNING CHRONICLE – London, England. 1791-1794 – 1 – us Res Libr [072]

MORNING CHRONICLE – New York. N.Y. 1802-07 – 3 – us Readex [071]

MORNING CHRONICLE – Quebec, 1853-1919 – 22r – 1 – cn Preston [971]

MORNING CHRONICLE – Quebec, Canada. 1847-73 – 48r – 1 – $3,120.00 – cn Library Assoc [971]

MORNING CHRONICLE – St. John's, Canada. The Chronicle. -d. 25 Nov 1870-7 May 1881. 17 1 2 reels – 1 – uk British Libr Newspaper [072]

MORNING CHRONICLE – St. John's, Newfoundland, Canada. 1862-73 – 13r – 1 – $845.00 – cn Library Assoc [971]

MORNING CHRONICLE *see*
- CARSON-CHRONICLE
- THE CHRISTMAS BELLS AND NEW YEAR'S CALL
- MORNING CHRONICLE AND COMMERCIAL AND SHIPPING GAZETTE

THE MORNING CHRONICLE – Quebec, Canada. 18 mai 1847-v2 n412. 29 dec 1848 – 1r – 1 – Can$40.00 – cn Can Microfilming [072]

MORNING CHRONICLE (1847) – Quebec: R Middleton & C St-Michel. v1-4. 1847-50. SEM35P233 – 4r – 1 – Can$172.00 – cn Bibl Nat [072]

MORNING CHRONICLE (1888) – (Cont: Morning Chronicle and Commercial and Shipping Gazette. Cont by: Quebec Morning Chronicle) – Quebec: J J Foote. v42 no 14 906-14 981 1888. SEM35P235 – 1r – 1 – Can$28.00 – cn Bibl Nat [072]

THE MORNING CHRONICLE (1888) *see* MORNING CHRONICLE AND COMMERCIAL AND SHIPPING GAZETTE

MORNING CHRONICLE AND BALTIMORE ADVERTISER – Baltimore, Maryland. Apr 8-Oct 7 1819; Feb 10 1821; Apr 26 1825-Dec 11 1828 – 2r – 1 – us L of C Photodup [071]

MORNING CHRONICLE AND COMMERCIAL AND SHIPPING GAZETTE : EDITION QUOTIDIENNE – (Cont: Morning Chronicle. Absorbs: The Quebec Gazette. Cont by: The Morning Chronicle (1888)) – Quebec: Charles St. Michel. v4-42. 1850-88. SEM35P234 – 65r – 1 – Can$3,313.00 – cn Bibl Nat [380]

MORNING CHRONICLE AND COMMERCIAL AND SHIPPING GAZETTE *see* MORNING CHRONICLE (1888)

MORNING COURIER – Corvallis, OR. -d. 6 Feb 1923-22 Apr 1923. 1 roll – 1 – us U.O. Library [071]

MORNING COURIER – Visalia, CA. 1905-07 – 4r – 1 – $200.00 – B03076 – us Library Micro [071]

MORNING COURIER – Visalia. Calif. 1905-07 – 1 – us UMI [071]

THE MORNING COURIER – (Filmed together with: The Commercial Advertiser) – Montreal, Canada. v1 n5. 3 mar 1835-18 mar 1850 – 3r – 1 – Can$45.00r – cn Can Microfilming [072]

THE MORNING COURIER *see* THE COMMERCIAL ADVERTISER

MORNING COURIER AND DUBLIN JOURNAL – Dublin. Ireland. -d. 29 Jul-23 Nov 1825. (1 reel) – 1 – uk British Libr Newspaper [072]

MORNING COURIER AND NEW YORK ENQUIRER – New York. v1-59. 1827-61 – 90r – 1 – us Ross [071]

MORNING COURIER AND NEW YORK ENQUIRER FOR THE COUNTRY – New York. (Semi-Weekly). June 16 1829-Dec 27 1856. Incomplete – 1 – us NY Public [071]

MORNING CRITIC – Beatrice, NE. -d. Mar. 1899-Oct. 1899 – 1 – us NE Hist [071]

MORNING DAILY HERALD – Albany, OR. 5,6,9,10,11 Aug 1898; 17 Feb, 12 Oct 1905 – 1 – us U.O. Library [071]

MORNING DAILY UNION AND HERALD *see* THE UNION

MORNING DEMOCRAT – Baker, OR. -d. 15 Feb 1890-31 Jan 1929. 44 rolls – 1 – us U.O. Library [071]

MORNING DEMOCRAT – Davenport. Iowa. 1887-1897; 1940-1964 – 1 – us UMI [071]

MORNING EAGLE – Wichita. Kan. 1884-1964 – 1 – us UMI [071]

MORNING ECHO – Olympia. Wash. 1875-1877 – 1 – us UMI [071]

MORNING ENQUIRER – Battle Creek. Mich. 1903-1918 – 1 – us UMI [071]

MORNING ENQUIRER AND OAKLAND TIMES – Oakland, CA. 1913-1914; 1916-1919 – 10r – 1 – $500.00 – C03366 – us Library Micro [071]

MORNING FREE PRESS – Easton. Pa. 1938-43 – 1 – us UMI [071]

MORNING FREE PRESS – Grand Island, NE. -d. Aug 1914-Feb 1915 – 1 – us NE Hist [071]

MORNING FREEMAN – Saint John, Canada. 1851-84 – 24r – 1 – $1,560.00 – cn Library Assoc [971]

MORNING FREEMAN – St. John's, Canada. -d. Oct 1866-Nov 1878. 6 reels – 1 – uk British Libr Newspaper [072]

MORNING GLOBE – Tacoma. Wash. 1888-1892 – 1 – us UMI [071]

MORNING HERALD : DAILY EDITION – Halifax, 1877-1880 – 4r – 1 – cn Preston [971]

MORNING HERALD – Decatur. Ill. 1880-90 – 1 – us UMI [071]

MORNING HERALD – Gloversville. New York.1937-55 – 1 – us UMI [071]

MORNING HERALD – Greenville. Tex. (State Edition). 1922-50 – 1 – us UMI [071]

MORNING HERALD – Hagerstown. Md. 1896- – 1 – us UMI [071]

MORNING HERALD – London. -d. 1801-02; 1830-33; 1858-61. (23mqn reels) – 1 – uk British Libr Newspaper [072]

MORNING HERALD – Modesto, CA. 1908-25 – 61r – 1 BR02470 – $3,050.00 – us Library Micro [071]

MORNING HERALD – New York. N.Y. 1835-1919 – 1 – us UMI [071]

MORNING HERALD – Newport News. Va. 1900-01 – 1 – us UMI [071]

MORNING HERALD – Perth, Australia. -d. Nov 1881-Jan 1909. Lacking July 1886-June 1901; Dec 1902-Feb 1903. 51 reels – 1 – uk British Libr Newspaper [072]

MORNING HERALD – Providence. RI.1867-68 – 1 – us UMI [071]

MORNING HERALD – Saginaw. Mich. 1879-1884; 1889 – 1 – us UMI [071]

MORNING HERALD : TRI-WEEKLY EDITION – Halifax, 1875-1877 – 3r – 1 – cn Preston [971]

MORNING HERALD – Uniontown. Pa. 1907-1917; 1920- – 1 – us UMI [071]

MORNING HERALD – Utica. N.Y. 1847-1900 – 1 – us UMI [071]

MORNING HERALD – Vallejo, CA. Jan-Apr 1922 – 1r – 1 – $50.00 – B03064 – us Library Micro [071]

MORNING HERALD – Yakima. Wash. 1889-1967 – 1 – us UMI [071]

MORNING HERALD *see* INDEPENDENT HERALD

THE MORNING HERALD AND COMMERCIAL ADVERTISER – Quebec, Canada. 25 avr 1837-v1 n95. 29 nov 1837 – 1r – 1 – Can$40.00 – cn Can Microfilming [072]

MORNING HERALD AND ECONOMICAL ADVERTISER – Dublin. Ireland. -d. 10 Mar-29 May 1838. (1 reel) – 1 – uk British Libr Newspaper [072]

MORNING HERALD DISPATCH – Decatur. Ill. 1890-1931 – 1 – us UMI [071]

THE MORNING HOUR OF THE AMERICAN BAPTIST MISSIONS / Vail, Albert L – 1907 – 1 – 16.87 – us Baptist [240]

MORNING HOURS IN PATMOS : THE OPENING VISION OF THE APOCALYPSE AND CHRIST'S EPISTLES TO THE SEVEN CHURCHES OF ASIA / Thompson, Augustus Charles – Boston: Gould and Lincoln, 1860 – 1mf – 9 – 0-8370-9426-7 – 1986-3426 – us A.T.L.A. [220]

MORNING JOURNAL – Daytona Beach. Fl. 1915-27; 1936- – 1 – us UMI [071]

MORNING JOURNAL – Glasgow. Scotland. -d. 1861-65. (30 reels) – 1 – uk British Libr Newspaper [072]

MORNING JOURNAL – Hanford. Calif. -w. 1944-55 – 1 – us UMI [071]

MORNING JOURNAL *see*
- HANFORD JOURNAL
- UNIONIST AND HALIFAX JOURNAL

MORNING LEADER – London. -d. Jan 1900-May 1912. (50 reels) – 1 – uk British Libr Newspaper [072]

MORNING MIRROR – Providence. R.I. 1849-1850; 1899-1901 – 1 – us UMI [071]

MORNING NEWS – (Also known as: Carson City News) – Carson City, NV. 1891-1930; Jan-Apr 1961 – 41r – 1 – $2,050.00 – U04459 – us Library Micro [071]

MORNING NEWS – Bridgeport. Conn. 1885-1886; 1887-1891 – 1 – us UMI [071]

MORNING NEWS – Clinton. Iowa. 1883-1890 – 1 – us UMI [071]

MORNING NEWS – Dallas. Tex. 1885- – 1 – us UMI [071]

MORNING NEWS – Enid. Okl. 1912-48; 1964 – 1 – us UMI [071]

MORNING NEWS – Florence. S.C. 1924- – 1 – us UMI [071]
MORNING NEWS – Hagerstown, Maryland. 1874-94 – 1 – us MD Archives [071]
MORNING NEWS – St. John's, Canada. Daily Morning News St. John Daily News. -d. 10 March 1858, 2 Sept-11 Nov 1864; 22 Oct-5 Nov 1866; Feb 1871-Jan 1879. 21 1 2 reels – 1 – uk British Libr Newspaper [072]
THE MORNING NEWS – Khartoum: Beshir Mohamed Said, [1960-sep 15 1963; feb 18 1964-apr 4 1969] – 18r – 1 – us Res Libr [072]
THE MORNING NEWS ADVERTISER – San Leandro, CA. 1971-72 – 1r – 1 – $50.00 – B05064 – us Library Micro [071]
MORNING NEWS; NEWS DEMOCRAT – Canton. Ohio. 1906-1913 – 1 – us UMI [071]
MORNING NEWS-EVENING NEWS – Williamsport, PA. -d 1894-1895 – 13 – $25.00r – us I.M.R. [071]
THE MORNING NEWS-EVENING NEWS – Danville, PA. -d 1898-1955 – 13 – $25.00r – us I.M.R. [071]
MORNING NEWS-TRIBUNE – Lawrence. Kan. -d. 1883-84 – 1 – us UMI [071]
MORNING OREGONIAN – Portland OR. Mar 26 1900-June 30 1905 + – 1 – us U.O. Library [071]
MORNING POST – Apapa, Nigeria: 1961-69 – 31r – 1 – us Ross [072]
MORNING POST – Belfast, Ireland. Jan-10 Apr 1858. -w.1/2 reel – 1 – uk British Libr Newspaper [072]
MORNING POST – Camden. N.J. 1947-49 – 1 – us UMI [071]
MORNING POST – London. -d. 1809; Jan 1818-Dec 1920. 439mqn reels – 1 – uk British Libr Newspaper [072]
MORNING PRESS – Asbury Park. N.J. 1905-1917 – 1 – us UMI [071]
MORNING PRESS – Bloomsburg. Pa. 1902-08; 1914- – 1 – us UMI [071]
MORNING PRESS – Oroville, CA. 1928-29 – 3r – 1 – $150.00 – B02573 – us Library Micro [071]
MORNING PRESS *see* SANTA BARBARA NEWS PRESS
THE MORNING PRESS – East Stroudsburg, PA. -d 1913-1929 – 13 – $25.00r – us I.M.R. [071]
MORNING REGISTER – Dublin, Ireland. 29 Oct 1824-7 Jan 1843 – 37r – 1 – uk British Libr Newspaper [072]
MORNING REGISTER – Fort Worth. TX.1897-1902 – 1 – us UMI [071]
(MORNING) REPORTER – Sumpter, OR. -d. 5 Dec 1900-20 Aug 1901. 1 roll – 1 – us U.O. Library [071]
MORNING REPUBLICAN – (Also known as: Daily Republican) – Fresno, CA. 1887-99; 1892-95; Jul-Dec 1896; Jan-Jun 1897 (scats); 1897-1932 – 298r – 1 – $14,900.00 – B02258 – us Library Micro [071]
MORNING REPUBLICAN – Findlay, Ohio. 1888-1932 – 25r – 1 – $32.50r – us Archival [071]
MORNING REVIEW – Greensburg. Pa. 1908-35; 1952-55 – 1 – us UMI [071]
MORNING SENTINEL – Orlando. Fl. 1913-May 1951 – 1 – us P.K. Yonge [071]
MORNING SENTINEL – Red Bluff, CA. 1920-21 – 1r – 1 – $50.00 – C02659 – us Library Micro [071]
MORNING SENTINEL – South Haven. Mich. 1901-1903 – 1 – us UMI [071]
MORNING SPOTLIGHT – Hastings, NE. -w. (-d 1935-42). Apr 1883; May 1886; Aug 1889; Jul 1892; Aug 1895-Mar 1942 – 1 – us NE Hist [071]
MORNING STANDARD – Portland. Or. 1881-1884 – 1 – us UMI [071]
MORNING STANDARD – Portland, OR. -d. 17 June, 18,19 Oct 1884 – 1 – us U.O. Library [071]
MORNING STANDARD – Portland, OR. -d. 1881-84 – 1 – 168.00 – us Oregon Hist [071]
MORNING STAR – Casper. Wyoming. 1954- – 1 – us UMI [071]
MORNING STAR – Greenwood. Miss. 1946-1954 – 1 – us UMI [071]
MORNING STAR – Huntington. Ind. 1906-1908 – 1 – us UMI [071]
MORNING STAR – Jaffna, Sri Lanka. 1841-1980 – 19r – 1 – us L of C Photodup [072]
MORNING STAR – London, 17 Mar 1856-13 Oct 1869 – 50r – 1 – uk British Libr Newspaper [072]
MORNING STAR – London, 1966-93. Continued annually. Continues: The Daily Worker – 1 – uk World [072]
MORNING STAR – Providence. R.I. 1870-1886 – 1 – us UMI [071]
MORNING STAR *see* MORNING STAR AND FREE BAPTIST
THE MORNING STAR – (Filmed with: The Evening Star v3 n109 22 mai 1869-v9 n78. 3 avr 1877 and Carnaval issue 1885) – Montreal, Canada. n107. 20 mai 1869 – 1r – 1 – Can$35.00 – cn Can Microfilming [072]
THE MORNING STAR – London, England. n2854. 27 apr 1865 (Assassination of A Lincoln) – 1r – 1 – Can$25.00 – cn Can Microfilming [072]
MORNING STAR AND FREE BAPTIST – (Title varies: Morning Star, 1826-1904. Some pgs and issues lacking) – v1-86. 11 May 1826-28 Dec 1911 – 26r – 1 – ATLA S0289 – us A.T.L.A. [073]
MORNING STAR AND REPUBLICAN GAZETTE – Lima, Ohio. 1896-1933 – 26r – 1 – us Archival [071]
THE MORNING STAR AND TORONTO TRANSCRIPT – 1841-42 – 1 – 130.00 – cn McLaren [072]
MORNING STAR OR PHILANSTENIAN GAZETTE – London, UK. 1833-34 – 1ft – 1 – uk British Libr Newspaper [072]
MORNING STAR & REPUBLICAN GAZETTE – Lima, Ohio. 1930-33 – 26r – 1 – $32.50r – us Archival [071]
MORNING STATE JOURNAL – The Dalles OR. May 2 1863 + – 1 – us U.O. Library [071]
MORNING SUN – Baltimore. Md. 1837-1842; 1845-1877; 1879-1892; 1895- – 1 – us UMI [071]
MORNING SUN – Watsonville. Calif. 1937-1942 – 1 – us UMI [071]
MORNING SUN – Yuma. Ariz. 1916-1935 – 1 – us UMI [071]
MORNING SUN *see* SUN
THE MORNING SUN – Stroudsburg, PA. -d 1926-1938. (Missing 1927) – 13 – $25.00r – us I.M.R. [071]
MORNING TELEGRAM – Bridgeport. Conn. 1901-1903; 1907-1917 – 1 – us UMI [071]
MORNING TELEGRAM – Utica. N.Y. 1920-22 – 1 – us UMI [071]
MORNING TELEGRAM – Winnipeg, Canada. Mar 1905-Sep 1920 (imperfect) – 148 1/2r – 1 – uk British Libr Newspaper [072]
MORNING TELEGRAM UNION – Bridgeport. Conn. 1904-1907 – 1 – us UMI [071]
MORNING TELEGRAPH – Brownsville. PA. 1927-28 – 1 – us UMI [071]
MORNING TELEGRAPH – New York. v3-54. 1841-92 – 5r – 1 – us Ross [071]
MORNING THOUGHTS FOR BUSY DAYS / Bruce, George – Saint John, N. B.: L. McMillan, 1890. 00289. (Pre-1900 Canadiana) – 9 – cn C.I.H.M. [810]
MORNING TIMES – Huntington. Ind. 1907-1911 – 1 – us UMI [071]
MORNING TIMES – Kokomo. Ind. 1964-1968 – 1 – us UMI [071]
MORNING TIMES – Mobile. Ala. 1881-1895 – 1 – us UMI [071]
MORNING TIMES – New York. N.Y. 1895-1907 – 1 – us UMI [071]
MORNING TIMES – Tulsa. Okl. 1916-19 – 1 – us UMI [071]
MORNING TIMES AND RED BLUFF SENTINEL – Red Bluff, CA. 1927-31 – 8r – 1 – $400.00 – B02660 – us Library Micro [071]
MORNING TRIBUNE – Lewiston. Id. 1896- – 1 – us UMI [071]
MORNING TRIBUNE – Providence. R.I. 1906-08 – 1 – us UMI [071]
MORNING TRIBUNE – San Luis Obispo, CA. 1906; 1907; 1910-1911; 1914-1915 – 6r – 1 – $300.00 – B03680 – us Library Micro [071]
MORNING TRIBUNE *see* TRIBUNE
MORNING UNION – Bridgeport. Conn. 1895-1900 – 1 – us UMI [071]
MORNING UNION – Springfield. Mass. 1911- – 1 – us UMI [071]
MORNING UNION – Tacoma. Wash. 1893-1897 – 1 – us UMI [071]
MORNING UNION *see* THE UNION
MORNING WATCH – v. 1-9. 1842-1845 – 1 – us UMI [240]
MORNINGS IN FLORENCE : BEING SIMPLE STUDIES OF CHRISTIAN ART, FOR ENGLISH TRAVELLERS / Ruskin, John – Orpington, Kent: G. Allen, 1875-1877 – 1 roll – 1 – 1-55879-493-X – uk Libr Preservation [700]
MORO BULLETIN – Moro, OR. -w. 5 Jun 1902-13Nov 1902. 1 roll – 1 – us U.O. Library [071]
Moro Cardenas, Ezequiel *see* EL EJERCITO EN LA SOCIODAD CONTEMPORANEA...CONFERENCIA PRONUNCIADA EN EL ISTITUTO BARBARA DE BRAGANZA DE BADAJOZ EL 11 DE ABRIL DE 1969
MORO LEADER – Moro, OR. -w. 2 Mar 1898-21 Feb 1900. 1 roll – 1 – us U.O. Library [071]
MORO OBSERVER – Moro OR. July 16 1896-Aug 25 1897 – 1 – us U.O. Library [071]
EL MORO VIZCAINO (JOSE MARIA DE MURGA). MADRID, 1944 / Ibarra y Berge, Javier de – Madrid: Razon y Fe, 1947 – 1 – sp Bibl Santa Ana [946]
MOROCCO : ANNUAIRE STATISTIQUE DU MAROC 1925-1976 / Morocco. al'Maslahah al-Markaziyah lil-Ihsa'iyat – (1930, 1931 not available. Coll title: African Official Statistical Serials, 1867-1982) – 103mf – 9 – £650.00 – uk Chadwyck [960]
MOROCCO : AN ECONOMIC STUDY / First National City Bank of New York. Morocco – 1967. BNE-3206 1 – 9 – ne IDC [330]
Morocco *see*
- AL-JARIDAH AL-RASMIYAH
- BOLETIN OFICIAL DE LA ZONA NORTE DE MARRUECOS
- BULLETIN OFFICIAL
- BULLETIN OFFICIEL
- L'ECONOMIE MAROCAINE EN 1968
- LOIS DE FINANCES. (RABAT IMPR. OFFICEILLE)
- RAPPORT ECONOMIQUE AU GROUPE CONSULTATIF

Morocco. Administration des Douanes et Impots Indirects *see*
- REGLEMENTATION DES DOUANES ET IMPOTS INDIRECTS
- TARIF DES DROITS DE DOUANE: DROITS D'IMPORTATION

Morocco. African Training and Research Centre in Administration for Development *see* PLANIFICATION ET DEVELOPPEMENT RURAL AU MAROC
Morocco. al'Maslahah al-Markaziyah lil-Ihsa'iyat *see* MOROCCO
Morocco. Banque Commerciale du Maroc *see* RAPPORTS ET BILAN
Morocco. Banque d'Etat du Maroc *see* ASSEMBLEE GENERALE ORDINAIRE
Morocco. Banque du Maroc *see* RAPPORT JUI-DEC 1959-1977
Morocco. Banque Marocaine du Commerce Exterieur *see*
- LE CONTROLE DES CHANGES DANS LES OPERATIONS DU COMMERCE EXTERIEUR
- HOW TO INVEST IN MOROCCO: STATEMENT OF THE GENERAL REGULATIONS REGARDING THE INVESTMENTS OF CAPITAL; ENCOURAGEMENT MEASURES DESTINED TO PROMOTE THESE INVESTMENTS
- RAPPORT

Morocco. Banque Marocaine du Commerce exterieur *see* BANQUE MAROCAINE DU COMMERCE EXTERIEUR, 1959/1969; DIX ANNEES DE DEVELOPPEMENT ECONOMIQUE
Morocco. Banque Nationale pour le Developpement Economique *see*
- RAPPORT ANNUEL
- STATUS

Morocco. Bureau de Recherches et de Participations Minieres *see* ORGANISATION ET ROLE DU B.R.P.M. DANS L'ECONOMIE MAROCAINE
Morocco. Caisse de Depot et de Gestion *see* RAPPORT
Morocco. Caisse de Prets Immobiliers du Maroc *see* ASSEMBLEE GENERALE ORDINAIRE DES ACTIONNAIRES
Morocco. Caisse Marocaine des Marches *see* ASSEMBLEE GENERALE ORDINAIRE
Morocco. Caisse Nationale de Credit Agricole *see*
- LE CREDIT AGRICOLE AU MAROC
- RAPPORT

Morocco. Centre National de Documentation. Secretariat d'Etat charge du Plan *see* INDEX SPECIAL: PROJET SEBOU
Morocco. Compagnie Marocaine de Credit et de Banque *see* EXERCISE
Morocco. Conseil Superieur du Plan *see*
- AVANT PROJECT DU PLAN QUINQUENNAL 1960-1964
- PLAN QUINQUENNAL 1960-1964

Morocco. Conseil superieur du Plan *see* PLAN TRIENNAL 1965-1967: TRAVAUX
Morocco. Council for Middle East Trade *see* REPORT OF THE BRITISH TRADE MISSION TO MOROCCO
Morocco. Delegation Generale a la Promotion Nationale et au Plan *see* THREE YEAR PLAN, 1965-1967
Morocco. Delegation Generale a la Promotion. Nationale et au Plan *see* LA PROMOTION AU MAROC
Morocco. Direction de l'Industrie *see*
- ETUDES D'ENTREPRISES INDUSTRIELLES RECOMMANDEES AUX CAPITAUX NATIONAUX
- L'INDUSTRIE SUCRIERE AU MAROC
- SITUATION ACTUELLE ET PREVISIONS D'EVOLUTION POUR 1970 DES INDUSTRIES DE TRANSFORMATION

Morocco. Direction des Mines et de la Geologie *see*
- ACTIVITE DU SECTEUR MINIER
- ETAT DES STATISTIQUES MINIERES
- NOTE SUR L'ACTIVITE MINIERE AU COURS DE L'ANNEE

Morocco. Direction des Statistiques *see* POPULATION LEGALE DU MAROC D'APRES LE RECENSEMENT GENERAL DE LA POPULATION ET DE L'HABITAT
Morocco. Division de la Coordination Economique et du Plan *see*
- LE DEVELOPPEMENT ECONOMIQUE ET SOCIAL DE LA PROVINCE DE FES
- PLAN BIENNAL D'EQUIPEMENT 1958-1959 RAPPORT GENERAL
- PLAN QUINQUENNAL, 1960-1964
- PLAN QUINQUENNEL 1960-1964: LE DEVELOPPEMENT INDUSTRIEL
- PLAN QUINQUENNEL: 1960-1964: MEMENTO DES OBJECTIFS DE L'INDUSTRIE, 1961
- PLAN QUINQUENNEL; INDUSTRIALISATION ET CROISSANCE ECONOMIQUE GLOBAL
- PLAN TRIENNAL, 1965-1967

Morocco. Division de l'Energie *see* NOTE SUR L'ACTIVITE DU SECTEUR PETROLIER DURANT L'ANNEE 1970
Morocco. Division du Commerce et de la Marine Marchande *see*
- MAROC CINQ ANS DE REALISATION DU PROGRAMME D'EQUIPEMENT, 1949-1953
- PROGRAMME D'EQUIPEMENT A LONG TERME, 1949-1952
- PROGRAMME D'EQUIPEMENT A LONG TERME RESULTATS DU 1ER
- TROIS ANS DE REALISATION DU PROGRAMME D'EQUIPEMENT, 1949-1952

Morocco. Division du commerce et de la Marine Marchande *see* PROGRAMME D'EQUIPEMENT A LONG TERME RESULTAT DU 2EME
Morocco. Division du Plan et des Etudes Economiques *see*
- L'INDUSTRIE, L'ENERGIE ET LES MINES: COMPTES D'EXPLOITATION, EMPLOI, INVESTISSEMENTS
- PLAN QUINGUENNAL, 1968-1972: RAPPORT SUR L'EXECUTION DU PLAN. ET PROGRAMME D'ACTION

Morocco. Division du Plan et des Statistiques *see*
- COMPTE DE LA NATION
- ETUDE SUR LE COMMERCE INTERIEUR
- PROJET DU PLAN QUINQUENNAL 1968-1972
- VIANDE

Morocco. Empire Cherifien Protectorat Francais *see* BUDGET
Morocco. European Economic Community *see* AGREEMENT ESTABLISHING AN ASSOCIATION BETWEEN THE EUROPEAN ECONOMIC COMMUNITY AND THE KINGDOM OF MAROCCO
Morocco. Haut Commissariat au Plan et a la Promotion Nationale. Division du Plan et des Statistiques *see* ETUDE SUR LE COMMERCE INTERIEUR
Morocco. ILO *see*
- RAPPORT AU GOUVERNEMENT DU ROYAUME DU MAROC SUR LA CREATION D'UN CENTRE DE PERFECTIONNEMENT DE CADRES DIRIGEANTS
- LE REVENU DES TRAVAILLEURS AGRICOLES AU MAROC

Morocco. ILO. Institute National de Formation des Cadres Techniques *see* PROGRAMME DES NATIONS UNIES POUR LE DEVELOPPEMENT. RAPPORT DE MISSION D'EVALUATION

Morocco. Institut International d'Administration Publique. Encyclopedie administrative *see* L'ADMINISTRATION MAROCAINE

Morocco. Ministere de Finances *see* PROJETS PROPOSES POUR UN FINANCEMENT EXTERIEUR AU GROUPE CONSULTATIF

Morocco. Ministere de la Sante Publique *see*
- ENQUETE D'OPINION SUR LA PLANIFICATION FAMILIALE: MILIEU RURAL
- ENQUETE D'OPINION SUR LA PLANIFICATION FAMILIALE: MILIEU URBAIN

Morocco. Ministere de l'Agriculture *see*
- ACTUALISATION DES STATISTIQUES AGRICOLES MAROCAINES 1959/1960 A 1966/1967
- ANALYSE DE LA GESTION DES COOPERATIVES MAROCAINES AGRICOLES ET SOCIETES COOPERATIVES AGRICOLES MAROCAINES
- ETUDE STATISTIQUE PAR PRODUIT 1959-1967
- ETUDE STATISTIQUE PAR PRODUIT, 1967-1968
- LA FORET MAROCAINE
- MEMENTO PRATIQUE DE L'ECONOMIE AGRICOLE MAROCAINE
- LE RIF AGRICOLE
- LES SOCIETES DE CREDIT AGRICOLE ET DE PREVOYANCE (SO.C.A.R.)

Morocco. Ministere de l'Economie Nationale *see*
- CE QU'IL FAUT SAVOIR SUR L'ECONOMIE MAROCAINE
- FINANCES PUBLIQUES DU MAROC
- LA PLANIFICATION ECONOMIQUE ET SOCIALE AU MAROC

Morocco. Ministere de l'Economie Nationale et des Finances *see* PLAN QUINQUENNAL 1960-1964 LE DEVELOPPEMENT INDUSTRIEL

Morocco. Ministere de l'Education Nationale *see* LA BANQUE MONDIALE ET L'EDUCATION AU MAROC

Morocco. Ministere de l'Enseignement *see* L'ENSEIGNEMENT: SITUATION, PROBLEMES PERSPECTIVES

Morocco. Ministere des Affaires Economiques *see* FIVE YEAR PLAN, 1968-1972

Morocco. Ministere du Commerce *see* GUIDE DE L'INDUSTRIEL DESIRANT S'ETABLIR AU MAROC

Morocco. Ministere du Developpement *see* PREPARATION DU PLAN DE DEVELOPPEMENT, 1968-1972; NOTE D'ORIENTATION POUR LA COMMISSION DE LA POLITIQUE FINANCIERE

Morocco. Ministere du Tourisme *see*
- RAPPORT SUR LE SECTEUR TOURISTIQUE PRESENTE AU GROUPE CONSULTATIF MAROC-BIRD
- STATISTIQUES TOURISTIQUES

Morocco. Ministere du Travail et des Affaires Sociales *see* LE MAROC AU TRAVAIL

Morocco. Ministry of Economic Affairs, Planning and Training Div *see* FIVE YEAR PLAN 1968-1972

Morocco. Office des Changes *see*
- BALANCES DES PAIEMENTS DU MAROC
- STATISTIQUES DU COMMERCE EXTERIEUR DU MAROC
- STATISTIQUES DU COMMERCE EXTERIEUR DU MAROC, ANNEES 1966-1970

Morocco. Office National de la Modernisation Rurale *see* RAPPORT PRELIMINAIRE SUR LA ZONE D'ATTAQUE SAHELA-SRA

Morocco. Organisation des Nations Unies. Centre National de Documentation. Secretariat d'Etat au Plan du Developpement Regional et a la Formation des Cadres *see* INDEX ONU-MAROC

Morocco. Secretariat d'Etat au Plan *see*
- LA CONSOMMATION ET LES DEPENSES DES MENAGES AU MAROC
- POPULATION LEGALE DU MAROC D'APRES LE RECENSEMENT GENERAL DE LA
- RECENSEMENT GENERAL DE LA POPULATION ET DE L'HABITAT, 1971

Morocco. Secretariat d'Etat au Plan, au Developpement regional et a la Formation des Cadres *see* PLAN DE DEVELOPPEMENT ECONOMIQUE ET SOCIAL, 1973-1977

Morocco. Secretariat d'Etat charge du Plan *see*
- ANNUAIRE STATISTIQUE DU MAROC
- LA SITUATION DE L'INDUSTRIE. ET PERSPECTIVES. 1962-1971

Morocco. Service Central des Statistiques *see*
- LA CONSOMMATION ET LES DEPENSES DES MENAGES MAROCAINS MUSULMANS: RESULTATS DE L'ENQUETE 1959-1960
- PROGRAMME QUINQUENNAL DE DEVELOPPEMENT DES TRAVAUX STATISTIQUES ET ETUDES ECONOMETRIQUES ET DEMOGRAPHIQUES AU MAROC
- RAPPORT SUR LES STATISTIQUES DU COMMERCE EXTERIEUR AU MAROC
- RECENSEMENT DEMOGRAPHIQUE, JUIN 1960: POPULATION LEGALE DU MAROC
- RECENSEMENT DEMOGRAPHIQUE, JUIN 1960: POPULATION RURALE DU MAROC
- RESULTATS DE L'ENQUETE A OBJECTIFS MULTIPLES, 1961-1963
- RESULTATS DU RECENSEMENT DE 1960
- RESULTATS PAR CULTURE DE LA CAMPAGNE AGRICOLE 1968-1969

Morocco. Societe Cherifienne des Petroles *see* RAPPORT ANNUEL

Morocco. Societe Generale pour favoriser le Developpement du Commerce et de l'Industrie en France *see* LES RELATIONS COMMERCIALES ENTRE LE MAROC ET LES ETATS-UNIS

Morocco. (Spanish Zone) *see* BOLETIN OFICIAL DE LA ZONA DE PROTECTORADO ESPANOL EN MORROCCO

MOROCCO: THE MARKET FOR SELECTED MANUFACTURED PRODUCTS FROM DEVELOPING COUNTRIES / International Trade Centre UNCTAD GATT – 1970. BNE-3060 1 – 9 – ne IDC [380]

MOROCCO, TRIAL IN RABAT ARISING OUT OF DISTURBANCES ON 20 AND 21 JUNE 1981 – sz I.C.J. [340]

Morodovtsev, D *see* POLITICHESKIE DVIZHENIIA RUSSKOGO NARODA

Morogues, Bigot de *see*
- DE LA MISERE DES OUVRIERS ET DE LA MARCHE A SUIVRE POUR Y REMEDIER
- DU PAUPERISME, DE LA MENDICITE ET DES MOYENS D'EN PREVENIR LES FUNESTES EFFETS
- RECHERCHES DES CAUSES DE LA RICHESSE ET DE LA MISERE DES PEUPLES CIVILISES

Morojele, C M H *see* 1960 AGRICULTURAL CENSUS, BASUTOLAND

Moros Planelles, Alfonso *see* INTERPRETACIONES ACTUALES SOBRE LA AGRESION

LA MOROSOPHIE DE GUILLAUME DE LA PERRIERE TOLOSAIN / Perriere, Guillaume de la – O-663 1. 1553 – 9 – ne IDC [999]

Morotius, C *see* CISTERCII REFLORESCENTIS

Moroy, Elie *see* LA LITTERATURE FEMININE DEFINIE PAR LES FEMMES ECRIVAINS

Morozov, P O *see*
- FEOFAN PROKOPOVICH KAK PISATEL'
- ISTORIIA RUSSKOGO TEATRA DO POLOVINY XVIII STOLETIIA

MORPETH AND EAST MAITLAND WANT – Jan 6 1899-Dec 30 1904 – 9 – at Pascoe [072]

MORPETH HERALD ETC – England, 1856-59; 1877; 1889; 1901-85; 1993- – 102+ r – 1 – uk British Libr Newspaper [072]

MORPETH TIMES – Feb 18 1884-Dec 7 1885 – 9 – at Pascoe [072]

A MORPHOLOGICAL STUDY OF CERTAIN ASCLEPIADEA / Frye, T C – (Botanical Gazette). v. 34. 1902. B-628 2 – 8 – ne IDC [580]

MORPHOLOGIE COMPAREE, PHYLOGENIE ET CLASSIFICATION DES GASTEROPODES PULMONES STYLOMMATOPHORES (MOLLUSCA) / Tillier, S – 9 – F100.00 – fr Ethnologie [590]

MORPHOLOGIE DE LA KAHANI CHEZ PREMCAND / Thomas, Catherine – 1975 – 9 – fr Orientalistes [490]

MORPHOLOGIE DES ATLANTISCHEN OZEANS *see* WISSENSCHAFTLICHE ERGEBNISSE DER DEUTSCHEN ATLANTISCHEN EXPEDITION AUF DEM FORSCHUNGS-UND VERMESSUNGSSCHIFF "METEOR", 1925-1927

DAS MORPHOLOGISCHE SYSTEM DER RUSSISCHEN SPRACHE / Trubeckoj, N S – 776 2. 1934 – 8 – ne IDC [460]

MORPHOLOGISCHE UNTERSUCHUNGEN AN SCHMELZKRISTALLISIERTEM PLOYAETHYLEN UND POLYAMID / Maier, Georg – Berlin, 1974 – 2mf – DM62.00 – 3-89349-887-7 – gw Hänsel [660]

DIE MORPHOLOGISCHEN VERAENDERUNGEN DURCH RADIUM AN LEBER UND MILZ / Radloff, Carl Adolf – 1995 – 1mf – 9 – DM60.00 – 3-8267-2231-0 – gw Hänsel [540]

MORPHOLOGISCHER IDEALISMUS UND NEUE LYRIKDEUTUNG / Hellwig, Elsa – (Includes bibliographical references) – Bonn a. Rh.: L Roehrschied, 1934 – 1r – 1 – us U.W. Library [400]

MORPHOLOGISCHES JAHRBUCH : EINE ZEITSCHRIFT FUER ANATOMIE UND ENTWICKLUNGSGESCHICHTE / ed by Gegenbaur, C von – Leipzig. v1-86. 1876-1941 – 1104mf – 9 – ne IDC [574]

Morphy, Michel *see* UNE NUIT DE NOCES, ROMAN INEDIT

Morpurgo, R *see* UGAV RACHEL

Morre, Karl *see* 'S NULLERL

Morrell, L A *see* THE AMERICAN SHEPHERD

Morrell, Z N *see* FLOWERS AND FRUITS IN THE WILDERNESS

Morren, C *see* BELGIQUE HORTICOLE

MORRILL COUNTY SUN – Bridgeport, NE. -w. Jan 1936-May 1942 – 1 – us NE Hist [071]

Morrill, Justin S *see* PAPERS

MORRILL MAIL – Morrill, NE. -w. Jun 1907-Dec 1923; Jan 1924-Sep 1970 – 1 – us NE Hist [071]

THE MORRIN COLLEGE – [Quebec?]: The College, [1882?-1884?] – 9 – cn C.I.H.M. [370]

MORRIN DISTRICT NEWS – Alberta, CN. 1920-21 – 1r – 1 – cn Commonwealth Micro [072]

Morris and Orange. Presbytery (Pres. Ch. in the U.S.A.) *see* MINUTES, 1870-1902

MORRIS ARBORETUM NEWSLETTER – (v.8-Jan 1979- 5,6,9) – v.6- Sep 1977- – 1 – us UMI [580]

Morris, Ben *see* SOME ASPECTS OF PROFESSIONAL FREEDOM OF TEACHERS

Morris, BF *see* CHRISTIAN LIFE AND CHARACTER OF THE CIVIL INSTITUTIONS OF THE UNITED STATES

Morris, Charles Harwood *see* KENTUCKY LAWS MADE PLAIN.

MORRIS COUNTY ENTERPRISE – Parkerville. Kan. 1878-1884 – 1 – us UMI [071]

MORRIS COUNTY REPUBLICAN-DEMOCRAT – Council Grove. Kan. 1874-1879 – 1 – us UMI [071]

Morris, D M *see* THE EFFECT OF BICYCLE CRANK ARM LENGTH ON OXYGEN CONSUMPTION AT A CONSTANT WORKLOAD AND CADENCE

Morris, Daniel *see* THE COLONY OF BRITISH HONDURAS, ITS RESOURCES AND PROSPECTS.

Morris, Ebenezer Joseph *see* PRAYER-MEETING THEOLOGY

Morris, Edward D *see*
- A CALM REVIEW OF THE INAUGURAL ADDRESS OF PROF. CHARLES A. BRIGGS
- A FRIENDLY TALK ABOUT REVISION

Morris, Edward Dafydd *see* OUTLINES OF LECTURES ON THE CHRISTIAN DOCTRINE

Morris, Edward Ellis *see* TRACTATE OF EDUCATION

Morris, F O *see*
- A HISTORY OF BRITISH BIRDS
- A NATURAL HISTORY OF THE NESTS AND EGGS OF BRITISH BIRDS

Morris, George Sylvester *see*
- HEGEL'S PHILOSOPHY OF THE STATE AND OF HISTORY
- PHILOSOPHY AND CHRISTIANITY

Morris, Gouverneur *see* PAPERS

Morris, H *see* A DESCRIPTIVE AND HISTORICAL ACCOUNT OF THE GODAVIRY DISTRICT

Morris, Harold H *see* PHYSICAL AGGRESSION AS A FUNCTION OF ANGER IN MEN AND WOMEN

Morris, Henry *see*
- THE FOUNDERS AND FIRST THREE PRESIDENTS OF THE BIBLE SOCIETY
- THE LIFE OF JOHN MURDOCH, LL.D.

Morris, Henry Francis *see* HISTORY OF ANKOLE

MORRIS HILLQUIT PAPERS / Hillquist, Morris – (With printed guide £44.00) – 1886-1944 – 10r – 1 – £575.00 – uk Chadwyck [920]

Morris, J W *see* LETTERS TO AN UNIVERSALIST

Morris, John Brande *see* JESUS THE SON OF MARY, OR, THE DOCTRINE OF THE CATHOLIC CHURCH UPON THE INCARNATION OF GOD THE SON

Morris, John G *see*
- BIBLIOTHECA LUTHERANA
- THE LIFE OF JOHN ARNDT
- QUAINT SAYINGS AND DOINGS CONCERNING LUTHER

MORRIS KETCHUM JESUP : A CHARACTER SKETCH / Brown, William Adams – New York: Scribner, 1910 – 1mf – us A.T.L.A. [240]

Morris, Leslie R *see* JOURNAL OF INTERLIBRARY LOAN, DOCUMENT DELIVERY AND INFORMATION SUPPLY

Morris, Lewis *see* SONGS OF TWO WORLDS. BY THE AUTHOR OF THE EPIC OF HADES

Morris, M F *see* AN INTRODUCTION TO THE HISTORY OF THE DEVELOPMENT OF LAW

Morris, Martin *see* A BRIEF HISTORY OF NYASALAND

Morris, Max *see* HEINRICH VON KLEISTS REISE NACH WUERZBURG

MORRIS REPORT / Minnesota. Agricultural Experiment Station. St. Paul. West Central Experiment Station – 1915-26 – 1,5,6 – us Spaulding [630]

MORRIS' REPORTS – (A Pre-NRS title) – Iowa. 1v. 1839-46 (all publ) – 6mf – 9 – $9.00 – LLMC 94-005 – us L.L.M.C. [340]

Morris, Robert *see*
- JOURNAL OF AGING AND SOCIAL POLICY
- PAPERS
- QUIZ ON CRIMINAL LAW, 1896-1897
- STUDIES IN MATHEMATICS EDUCATION

Morris, Samuel Leslie *see* AT OUR OWN DOOR: A STUDY OF HOME MISSIONS

MORRIS' STATE CASES / Mississippi. Supreme Court – (Not a Pre-NRS title) – v1-2. 1818-1872 (all publ) – 24mf – 9 – $31.50 – LLMC 95-101 – us L.L.M.C. [340]

Morris, Thelma *see* L'ABBE DESFONTAINES ET SON ROLE DANS LA LITTERATURE DE SON TEMPS

Morris, William *see*
- THE COLLECTED WORKS OF WILLIAM MORRIS. WITH INTRODUCTIONS BY HIS DAUGHTER MAY MORRIS
- A DREAM OF JOHN BALL; AND, A KING'S LESSON
- HOPES AND FEARS FOR ART
- NEWS FROM NOWHERE
- OLD FRENCH ROMANCES DONE INTO ENGLISH. WITH AN INTRODUCTION BY JOSEPH JACOBS
- POEMS BY THE WAY
- THE STORY OF SIGURD THE VOLSUNG AND THE FALL OF THE NIBLUNGS
- A TALE OF THE HOUSE OF THE WOLFINGS
- THE WATER OF THE WONDROUS ISLES
- THE WELL AT THE WORLD'S END

"THE MORRISES AS PIONEERS" / Davidson, Donna Morris – ca1949 – 1 – us KS Hist [978]

MORRISET SUN – Jul 15 1915; Feb 25 1930 – 9 – at Pascoe [072]

Morrisey, Richard Alburtus *see* BIBLE HISTORY OF THE NEGRO

Morrison, Charles Robert *see*
- JUSTICE AND SHERIFF AND ATTORNEY'S ASSISTANT.
- NEW HAMPSHIRE PROBATE LAW AND DIRECTORY, CONTAINING THE GENERAL LAWS OF 1878.
- PROOFS OF CHRIST'S RESURRECTION: FROM A LAWYER'S STANDPOINT

Morrison, R *see* VOCABULARY OF THE CANTON DIALECT

Morrison. R *see* A DICTIONARY OF THE CHINESE LANGUAGE IN THREE PARTS...

Morrison, Robert *see* A PARTING MEMORIAL

Morrison, Robert Stewart *see*
- ABSTRACT OF THE COLLECTION AND BUSINESS LAWS OF COLORADO TERRITORY
- DIGEST OF THE LAW OF MINES AND MINERALS AND OF ALL CONTROVERSIES INCIDENT TO THE SUBJECT-MATTER OF MINING
- MINING RIGHTS IN THE WESTERN STATES AND TERRITORIES
- MINING RIGHTS ON THE PUBLIC DOMAIN
- MORRISON'S DIGEST OF THE LAW OF MINES AND MINERALS
- MORRISON'S MINING REPORTS

Morrison, Sophia *see* MANX FAIRY TALES

Morrison, W D *see* THE FUNDAMENTAL TRUTHS OF THE CHRISTIAN RELIGION

Morrison Walker, Guy *see* THE THINGS THAT ARE CAESARS, A DEFENCE OF WEALTH

Morrison, William Douglas *see* PAULUS

MORRISON'S DIGEST OF THE LAW OF MINES AND MINERALS : ENGLISH AND AMERICAN, FROM THE YEARBOOKS TO 1878 / Morrison, Robert Stewart – San Francisco: A L Bancroft & Co. 1v. 1878 (all publ) – 9 – LLMC 95-133 – us L.L.M.C. [340]

MORRISON'S MINING REPORTS / Morrison, Robert Stewart – (v1-15 comprise a retrospective survey of American and English mining cases arranged in subject order. v16 starts reporting of current cases, starting with 1889 and contains an index for v1-16. v17-22 contain current cases arranged chronologically from 1872-1903. Emilio DeSoto became co-reporter with v17) – Chicago: Callagan. v1-22. 1749-1906 (all publ) – 181mf – 9 – $271.00 – LLMC 84-706 – us L.L.M.C. [340]

MORRISON'S TRANSCRIPT OF THE DECISIONS OF THE SUPREME COURT / U.S. Supreme Court – Washington. 5v. 1880-83 – 9 – LLMC 81-422 – us L.L.M.C. [340]

Morrissette, J-F *see* LE COMBAT

MORRISTOWN FIRST BAPTIST CHURCH. MORRISTOWN, TENNESSEE : CHURCH RECORDS – 1803-1964. Minutes. 1912-28. Bulletins. 1954-71 – 1 – 183.42 – us Baptist [240]

MORRISTOWN MANUSCRIPT COLLECTION – (60,000p of MS in American history, genealogy, Revolutionary War history) – 69r – 1 – $4350.00 – us UMI [975]

Morrow, Arthur A *see* MY THIRTY-TWO YEARS IN AMERICAN SAMOA

MORROW COUNTY RECORD – Heppner OR. Mar 12 19 1891 + – 1 – us U.O. Library [071]

Morrow, Don *see* JOYRIDE

Morrow, Ellen R *see* LATITUDE OF SPORTSMANSHIP BEHAVIOR DEEMED ACCEPTABLE BY SPECTATORS OF BASKETBALL GAMES

Morrow, Felix *see* THE CIVIL WAR IN SPAIN

MORSE AND THE TELEGRAPH – 1 – us Ross [380]

Morse, Annie E *see* SUNNY SLOPE

Morse, Benjamin *see* BENJAMIN MORSE PAPERS, MS V.F. M

Morse, Frederic Clarke *see* THE LAW OF INSURANCE IN TEXAS.

Morse, John T, Jr. *see* THOMAS JEFFERSON

Morse, John Torrey *see* A TREATISE ON THE LAW OF BANKS AND BANKING

Morse, Perley *see* THE ABC OF THE GOVERNMENT OF THE UNITED STATES

Morse, Samuel *see* MANUSCRIPT COLLECTION OF MARCHES, DANCES, ETC

Morse, Samuel FB *see* PAPERS

Morse, Samuel Finley Breese *see* FOREIGN CONSPIRACY AGAINST THE LIBERTIES OF THE UNITED STATES

MORSKO I FLOT – (Library has: Feb./Mar.-Nov./Dec. 1945) – Moskva: Ministerstvo morskogo flota SSSR, 1941 – 1 – CSUX89-S872 – us Hoover Inst Photo [947]

MORSKO I FLOT : ORGAN MINISTERSTVA MORSKOGO FLOTA I T SK PROFSOI UZA RABOCHIKH MORSKOGO TRANSPORTA – (Includes c.1: v.7:no.35=no.524 1949:May 4-; v.8:no.3=no.596 1950:Jan.11) – Moskva: [s.n.], 19uu – 1 – CSUXADP4338-S – us Hoover Inst Photo [947]

MORSKO I FLOT (MOSKOW, R.S.F.S.R.: 1949) *see* MORSKO I FLOT

MORSKO I FLOT (MOSKOW, R.S.F.S.R.: 1955) – (Includes Jan. 1956-Dec. 1971; Jan. 1979-) – Moskva: Morsko i transport, 1955 – 1 – CSUX90-S561 – us Hoover Inst Photo [380]

MORSKO I TRANSPORT V...GODU : NARODNY I KOMISSARIAT VODNOGO TRANSPORTA – (Includes c.1: 1935) – Moskva: Izd. Narkomroda, 19uu – 1 – CSUXAK72535-S – us Hoover Inst Photo [947]

MORSKOE PRAVO / Keilin, A D & Vinogradov, P P – Moscow, 1939. 248p. Prewar text on maritime law, both public and private. BR-9801/1 – 9 – ne IDC [340]

MORSKOE PRAVO SSSR / Avsov, I et al – Moscow, 1932. 142p. BR-9133 1 – 9 – ne IDC [340]

MORSKOE SVECHENIE / Bal'mont, K D – Spb. 1910. BR-526 2 – 8 – ne IDC [460]

MORSKOI SLOVAR' NA ANGLIISKOM, FRANTSUSKOM I ROSSIISKOM IAZYKAKH / Shishkov, A – Spb., 1795 – 7mf – 9 – 1469/2 – ne IDC [380]

MORSKOIE FLOT – Moscow, USSR. 2 Mar 1948-11 Jan 1950 – 1r – 1 – uk British Libr Newspaper [947]

MORT A CREDIT; ROMAN / Celine, Louis-Ferdinand – Paris: Les Editions Denoel et Steele, 1936. 697p – 1 – us U.W. Library [830]

LA MORT D'ABEL / Gessner, Salomon – Lyon et Paris: Perisse et Freres, 1847. 320p. 4 fiches. (Literature Collection) – 9 – 10.00 – fr Bibl Nationale [810]

LA MORT D'ABEL / Legouve – (French Theatre Series). Paris. J. G. Merigot. 1793 – 9 – fr Hachette [820]

LA MORT D'ABEL: POEME / DuBoccage, Anne Marie – Reprod. d'un edition s.l., s.n., s.d. 74p. 1 fiche. (Literature Collection) – 9 – 6.00 – fr Bibl Nationale [810]

LA MORT D'AZAIL OU LE RAPT EN DINA / Dugat, PD – Paris: Raphel et Liely, 1798. iv,516p. 6 fiches. (Literature Collection) – 9 – 15.00 – fr Bibl Nationale [810]

LA MORT DE CESAR / Gohier, Louis – Tragedie en trois actes de Voltaire, avec les changements fait par le Citoyen, Gohier, Ministre de la Justice; Represente au theatre de la Republique, a Paris. commune Affranchie, Cutty, l'an second de la Republique. (Dans l'exemplaire que nous reproduisons est ajoute un texte manuscrit sur 13 feuillets) – 9 – fr Hachette [820]

LA MORT DE GERMANICUS DE POUSSIN / Reunion des Musees Nationaux. Paris – 1973 – 9 – fr Réunion [750]

LA MORT DE L'OPERA COMIQUE...PIECE ELEGI-SATYRI-COMI-TRAGIQUE.. / Nougaret, Pierre-Jean-Baptiste – 1797 – 9 – us Sibley [780]

MORT DE TALABOT – Paris, Everat, s.d., 24 p. Les Saint-Simoniens, 1825-1834. 6976 – 9 – fr Hachette [335]

LA MORT DE VINCENT MALIGNON, AGENT NATIONAL DE LA COMMUNE DE CLAYS(...)EN UN ACTE ET EN VERS(...) / Gosse, Etienne – Nantes: Herault, [1794] – fr Armell [320]

LA MORT DE VOLTAIRE / Palissot de Montenoy, Charles – Ode. Suivie de l'eloge de ce grand homme. Au Temple de la Gloire. 1780 – 9 – fr Hachette [810]

LA MORT DE VOLTAIRE, ODE, SUIVIE DE L'ELOGE DE CE GRAND HOMME / Palissot de Montenoy, Charles – Reprod. de l'ed. Au Temple de la Gloire, 1780. 146p. 2 fiches. (Literature Collection) – 9 – 6.00 – fr Bibl Nationale [810]

LA MORT D'HENRI 4, ROI DE FRANCE / Legouve – (French Theatre Series). Paris. A.A. Renouard. 1806 – 9 – fr Hachette [820]

LA MORT DU DIABLE JESUITIQUE – Proces des apotres de Saint-Simon. Paris, impr. de Chassaignon, 1832, in-folio plano (canard, bois grave). Les Saint-Simoniens, 1825-1834. 6995 – 9 – fr Hachette [335]

MORT, VIOLENCE ET SACRE DANS LA SOCIETE MODERNE / Baudry, P – 10mf – 9 – F150.00 – fr Ethnologie [360]

LA MORTALIDAD INFANTIL EN BUENOS AIRES. ESTUDIO COMPARATIVO... / Instituto Geografico – Buenos Aires, 1879 – 2mf – 9 – sp Cultura [304]

MORTALITY IN BENGAL IN 1943 / India. Famine Inquiry Commission – Chicago: Uni of Chicago, Photodup Dept, [19–] – us Res Libr [304]

MORTALITY SCHEDULES, 1850 / Illinois. Census – T1133-0058 – 1 – us A.G.L.L. [310]

MORTALITY SCHEDULES, 1850 / Kentucky. Census – Pendleton-Woodford Co. Includes index. T655-0013 – 1 – us A.G.L.L. [920]

MORTALITY SCHEDULES, 1860 / Illinois. Census – Alphabetical by county. T1133-0058/T1133-0059 – 1 – us A.G.L.L. [310]

MORTALITY SCHEDULES, 1860 / Kansas.Census – (Mortality Schedules, 1870. T1130-0005) – T1130-0001 – 1 – us A.G.L.L. [310]

MORTALITY SCHEDULES, 1860 / Kentucky. Census – Includes index. T655-0014 – 1 – us A.G.L.L. [920]

MORTALITY SCHEDULES, 1870 / Arizona – (Mortality Schedules, 1880. T655-0002) – Mojave-Yuma Co. Includes index.T655-0001 – 1 – us A.G.L.L. [310]

MORTALITY SCHEDULES, 1870 / Illinois. Census – Alphabetical by county, A-K is missing. T1133-0059/0060 – 1 – us A.G.L.L. [310]

MORTALITY SCHEDULES, 1870 / Kentucky. Census – Adair-Jefferson Co. Includes index. T655-0015 – 1 – us A.G.L.L. [920]

MORTALITY SCHEDULES, 1870 / Kentucky. Census – Jessamine-Woodford Co. Index included. T655-0015 – 1 – us A.G.L.L. [920]

MORTALITY SCHEDULES, 1880 / Illinois. Census – Alphabetical by county. T1133-0060/0064 – 1 – us A.G.L.L. [310]

MORTALITY SCHEDULES, 1880 / Kansas.Census – Allen-Ellsworth Co. T1130-0042 – 1 – us A.G.L.L. [310]

MORTALITY SCHEDULES, 1880 / Kansas.Census – Foote-Morris Co.T1130-0043 – 1 – us A.G.L.L. [310]

MORTALITY SCHEDULES, 1880 / Kansas.Census – Nemaha-Wyandotte Co. T1130-0044 – 1 – us A.G.L.L. [310]

MORTALITY SCHEDULES, 1880 / Kentucky. Census – Adair-Jackson Co. T655-0018 – 1 – us A.G.L.L. [920]

MORTALITY SCHEDULES, 1880 / Kentucky. Census – Jefferson-Mason Co. T655-0019 – 1 – us A.G.L.L. [920]

MORTALITY SCHEDULES, 1880 / Kentucky. Census – Meade-Woodford Co. T655-0020 – 1 – us A.G.L.L. [920]

Mortara, M *see*
- CATALOGO DEI MANOSCRITTI EBRAICI DELLA BIBLIOTHECA DELLA COMUNITA ISRAELITICA DI MANTOVA
- INDICE ALFABETICO DEI RABBINI E SCRITTORI ISRAELITTI... IN ITALIA

A MORTE DE CAMOES = TOD DES DICHTERS / Tieck, Ludwig – Lisboa: Editorial Aviz, 1944 – 1 – us U.W. Library [430]

Mortell, Rosemarie *see* THE EFFECT OF A 12-WEEK RESISTIVE TRAINING PROGRAM IN THE HOME USING THE BODY BAR ON DYNAMIC AND ABSOLUTE STRENGTH IN MIDDLE-AGE WOMEN

Mortellari, M *see*
- [ARMIDE] CALMA LA PENA AMARA
- [ARMIDE] RESTA INGRATA
- [DIDONE ABBANDONATA] AH NON LASCIARM

Mortelli, M *see* THE FAVORITE BALLET OF LA FILLE SAUVAGE, OU LE POUVOIR DE LA MUSIQUE, PERFORMED AT THE KING'S THEATRE HAYMARKET

Mortensen, T *see* STUDIES OF INDO-PACIFIC EURYALIDS

Mortensen, Theodor *see* A MONOGRAPH OF THE ECHINOIDEA

MORTGAGE BANKER – v1- 1939- 1; 1972-5,6; 1976- 4 x 6 in. 9 – us UMI [073]

THE MORTGAGE LAW FOR CUBA, PUERTO RICO, AND THE PHILIPPINES, 1893 : THE ORIGINAL LAW OF AUGUST 1 1880 AS AMENDED AND REPROMULGATED ON MAY 26 1893 – Washington: GPO, 1899 – 1mf – 9 – $1.50 – LLMC 92-312 – us L.L.M.C. [340]

MORTGAGE RECORDS / Henry County. Ohio. Recorder – 1847-1891 – 10r – 1 – $32.50r – us Archival [324]

MORTGAGE RECORDS / Wyandot County. Ohio. Recorder – 1846-1889 – 12r – 1 – $32.50r – us Archival [324]

MORTGAGES / Brown, Maurice Henry – Philadelphia, Brown & Levin, 1941. 67 p. LL-9 – 1 – us L of C Photodup [340]

Mortier, D A OP *see* HISTOIRE DES MAITRES GENERAUX DE L'ORDRE DES FRERES PRECHEURS

Mortier, Roland *see* LES ANNEES DE FORMATION DE F. H. JACOBI, D'APRES SES LETTRES INEDITES A M. M. REY (1763-1771) AVEC "LE NOBLE" DE MME. DE CHARRIERE

Mortillet, Adrien de *see* LA PREHISTOIRE

Mortillet, Gabriel de *see* LA PREHISTOIRE

Mortimer, T *see* DIE AND BE DAMNED

MORTLAKE DISPATCH – 1921-1993 – 28r – 1 – at Corangamite [072]

MORTLAKE MERCURY – 1903. MOM1 – 1r – 1 – at Corangamite [072]

MORTLAKE SHIRE COUNCIL MINUTES – 1866-1991 – 6r – 5 – at Corangamite [350]

Mortlock, Edmund *see* CHRISTIANITY AGREEABLE TO REASON IN ITS EVIDENCE,...ATONEMENT, AND... SACRAMENT

Morton, A C *see* REPORT ON THE ST LAWRENCE AND ATLANTIC RAIL-ROAD, ITS INFLUENCE ON THE TRADE OF ST LAWRENCE..

MORTON BAY COURIER *see* COURIER MAIL

Morton George A *see* LAW AND LAUGHTER

Morton, George A *see* LAW AND LAUGHTER

Morton, J Sterling *see* PAPERS

Morton, Joseph *see* NEW HARMONY OF THE FOUR GOSPEL NARRATIVES OF THE CLOSING EARTHLY LABORS OF JESUS

MORTON, MISSISSIPPI. SPRINGFIELD BAPTIST CHURCH – Church Records, 1872-June 1981. 1,170p – 1 – $52.65 – us Baptist [240]

Morton, Nathaniel *see* NEW ENGLANDS MEMORIALL

Morton, Oren F *see*
- CENTENNIAL HISTORY OF ALLEGANY COUNTY
- HISTORY OF MONROE COUNTY
- HISTORY OF PRESTON COUNTY
- HISTORY OF ROCKBRIDGE COUNTY

Morton, R *see*
- PHTHISIOLOGIA
- PHTHISIOLOGIA, SEU EXERCITATIONES DE PHTHISI

MORTUARY MANAGEMENT – v1- 1914- 1; v60- 5,6; v63- 9 – us UMI [073]

MORWELL ADVERTISER – 1921-1965. MOA1-34 – 34r – 1 – at Corangamite [072]

MOSAIC – (Some issues lacking) – v1-12 no 1. 1960-Spring 1971 – 1r – 1 – ATLA S0436 – us A.T.L.A. [073]

THE MOSAIC ACCOUNT OF CREATION...THE ONENESS OF GENESIS AND SCIENCE / Warring, Charles Bartlett – New York: J.W. Schermerhorn, 1875. 1 fiche – 9 – us A.T.L.A. [240]

THE MOSAIC ORIGIN OF THE PENTATEUCHAL CODES / Vos, Geerhardus – New York: A C Armstrong, 1886 – 1mf – 9 – 0-8370-6443-0 – 1986-0443 – us A.T.L.A. [220]

THE MOSAIC RECORD AND MODERN SCIENCE / Townsend, Luther Tracy – Boston: Howard Gannett, 1881. 1 fiche – 9 – us A.T.L.A. [240]

MOSAIC RECORD OF THE CREATION EXPLAINED / Jennings, Abraham G – New York: Fleming H. Revell, 1893. 1 fiche – 9 – us A.T.L.A. [220]

O MOSAICO : PERIODICO CHISTOSO, ANECDOTICO, CRITICO E NOTICIOSO – Estancia-SE, Brazil. 3 Nov 1872 – 1 – bl Biblioteca [072]

MOSAICO EMERITENSE / Melida, Jose Ramon – Madrid: Tip. Fortanet, 1908. B.R.A.H. 52, pp. 49-50 – sp Bibl Santa Ana [946]

MOSAICOS ROMANOS DE MERIDA. INVESTIGACION Y CIENCIA / Blanco, Antonio – 1979 – 1 – sp Bibl Santa Ana [700]

MOSAICS FROM INDIA : TALKS ABOUT INDIA, ITS PEOPLES, RELIGIONS AND CUSTOMS / Denning, Margaret Beahm – (Includes index) – Chicago: Fleming H Revell, 1906, c1902 – 1mf – 9 – 0-8370-6107-5 – 1986-0107 – us A.T.L.A. [950]

DAS MOSAISCHE STRAFRECHT IN SEINER GESCHICHTLICHEN ENTWICKELUNG / Foerster, Gerhard – (Includes index) – Leipzig: Veit, 1900 – 1mf – 9 – 0-8370-3159-1 – 1985-1159 – us A.T.L.A. [306]

DIE MOSAISCHE STUFTSHUETTE / Riggenbach, Christoph Johannes – 1867 – 1 – us A.T.L.A. [240]

MOSAISCHES RECHT : STAAT, KIRCHE UND EIGENTUM IN ISRAEL / Schall, Eduard – Leipzig: A Deichert (Georg Boehme), 1896 – 1mf – 9 – 0-8370-5074-X – 1985-3074 – us A.T.L.A. [270]

DAS MOSAISCH-TALMUDISCHE POLIZEIRECHT / Bloch, Moses – Budapest: Univ.-Buchdruckerei, 1879. 1 fiche – 9 – us A.T.L.A. [270]

Mosalud, Marques de *see* LAPIDAS INEDITAS

Moscato, Michael *see* POLLUTION

Moscheles, Ignaz *see* VARIATIONS BRILLANTES SUR LA MARCHE BOHEMIENNE...POUR LE PIANOFORTE A QUATRE MAINS..

Moscheles, J *see* GEOGRAFIA DE LAS ISLAS BRITANICAS. BARCELONA, 1929

MOSCHEROSCHS GESICHTE PHILANDERS VON SITTEWALT : VERHAELTNIS DER AUSGABEN ZU EINANDER UND ZUR QUELLE; NEBST EINEM BIOGRAPHISCHEN ANHANG / Wirth, Johann – (Includes bibliographical references) – Erlangen: E T Jacob, 1887 – 1r – 1 – us U.W. Library [430]

MOSCHKO VON PARMA / Franzos, Karl Emil – 5e. Auf. Stuttgart und Berlin. 1912 – 1 – us Res Libr [890]

Moschner, Alfred *see* HOLTEI ALS DRAMATIKER

Moschulsky, V de *see* ETUDES ENTOMOLOGIQUES

Moscoso y Montemayor, Cristobal *see* REPRESENTACIONES...AL REY

Moscov, June G, Lacourse, Michael G *see* STATIC RANGE OF MOTION, LEG POWER, AND LEG STRENGTH AS PREDICTORS OF DYNAMIC RANGE OF MOTION IN FEMALE BALLET DANCERS

MOSCOW : HISTORY, ARCHITECTURE, MONUMENTS. RARE WORKS FROM 1767-1935 – 135mf – 9 – $990.00 – us Ross [947]

Moscow *see*
- OPIS' DEL KHRANIASHCHIKHSIA V ARKHIVE MOSKOVSKOI KUPECHESKOI UPRAVY
- OPISI DEL MOSKOVSKOGO OTDELENIIA OBSHCHEGO ARKHIVA GLANOGO SHTABA

Moscow. Archaeological Institute *see* ZAPISKI MOSKOVSKAGO ARKHEOLOGICHESKAGO INSTITUTA

Moscow. Arkhivnoe delo Moskovskoi oblasti *see* SBORNIK MATERIALOV

Moscow. Biblioteka Moskovskoi Sinodal'noi tipografii *see* RUKOPISI

MOSCOW DAILY NEWS – Moscow. May 1932-Oct 1934 – 1 – 35.00r – us Hoover Inst Photo [947]

MOSCOW DAILY NEWS – Moscow. v1-3. 1932-34 – 5r – 1 – us Ross [072]

Moscow. Duchovnoi Akademii. Library *see* SISTEMATICHESKII KATALOG KNIG BIBLIOTEKI MOSKOVSKOI DUCHOVNOI AKADEMII

MOSCOW ECONOMIC CONFERENCE REPORT / Moscow Soviet of Workers, Peasants and Red Army Deputies – Moscow, USSR, 1921. In Russian – 1 – £35.00r – uk Altair [947]

Moscow. Gorodskaia Uprava. Statisticheskii Otdiel *see* EZHEMIESIACHNYI BIULLETEN POVGODU MOSKVIE

Moscow. Gorodskaya Duma *see* OBSHESTVENNOE KHOZYAAISTVO GORODA MOSKVY

Moscow. Gosudarstvennaia Biblioteka SSSR im V.I. Lenina. (V.I. Lenin state library of the U.S.S.R.) *see* BIBLIOGRAPHY OF DISSERTATIONS

Moscow. I Moskovskii i Rumiantsovskii Musei *see* OTCHET

Moscow. Koniunkturnyi institut *see* EKONOMISCHESKII BIULLETEN'

Moscow. Law Society. St. Petersburg. Law Society *see* IURIDICHESKII VESTNIK

Moscow. Literaturnogo Muzeia *see* VYSTAVKA LERMONTOVSKIKH FONDOV MOSKOVSKIKH MUZEEV

Moscow, Maine. Bakerston/Moscow Baptist Church *see* RECORDS

MOSCOW NEWS – Moscow. U.S.S.R. (In English). 1961- – 1 – us UMI [072]

MOSCOW NEWS = MOSKOVSKIE NOVOSTI – (Backfile from 1980- $85r. Moscow News (in English) 1996- 2r per y $170 standing order. Backfile from 1930- $85r) – Russia, 1996- – 2r per y – 1 – $160.00 standing order – us Ross [072]

Moscow. Patriarchate *see* ZHURNAL

MOSCOW PROVINCIAL COMMITTEE, ECONOMIC COUNCIL AND CONFERENCE REPORTS – Moscow, USSR, 1922-23. In Russian – 1 – £35.00r – uk Altair [947]

Moscow. Societe des Naturalistes *see* NOUVEAUX MEMOIRES

MOSCOW SOVIET EXECUTIVE COMMITTEE REPORTS – Moscow, USSR. 1920-23. In Russian – 1 – £35.00r – uk Altair [947]

Moscow Soviet of Workers and Red Army Delegates *see* LOCAL ADMINISTRATION BULLETIN IN SOVIET RUSSIA

Moscow Soviet of Workers, Peasants and Red Army Deputies *see* MOSCOW ECONOMIC CONFERENCE REPORT

Moscow. Universitet *see* VESTNIK

MOSCOW UNIVERSITET IZVESTIIA – 1865-72 – 1 – 115.00 – us L of C Photodup [370]

Moscow. University *see*
- OBSHCHESTVO LIUBITELEI ROSSIISKOI SLOVESNOSTI PRI MOSKOVSKOM UNIVERSITETE
- OPYT RABOTY NAUCHNOI BIBLIOTEKI MGU
- OPYT TRUDOV VOL'NAGO ROSSIISKAGO SOBRANIIA PR
- ZAPISKI I TRUDY OBSHCHESTVA ISTORII I DREVNOSTEI ROSSIISKIKH, UCHREZHDENNAGO PRI IMPERATORSKOM MOSKOVSKOM UNIVERSITETE

Moscow. University. Imperial Library *see*
- SPISOK POVREMENNYKH IZDANII POLUCHAVSHIKHSIA. 1906-1911 GG
- SPISOK POVREMENNYKH IZDANII POLUCHAVSKIKHSIA. 1906-1911 GG

Moscrip *see* PAST AND PRESENT OF MARSHALL COUNTY

MOSE : EIN BEITRAG ZUR UNTERSUCHUNG UEBER DIE URSPRUENGE DER ISRAELITISCHEN RELIGION / Volz, Paul – (Includes index) – Tuebingen: J C B Mohr (Paul Siebeck), 1907 – 1mf – 9 – 0-8370-9277-9 – 1986-3277 – us A.T.L.A. [220]

MOSELEY AND BALSALL HEATH NEWS ETC – (Birmingham, Moseley & Balsall Heath News, etc 1885. Birmingham News (South ed) 1892. South Birmingham, Moseley & Balsall Heath News etc 1886-88) – England, 26 May-29 Dec 1883; 1884-92 – 10r – 1 – uk British Libr Newspaper [072]

MOSELLAENDISCHE NOVELLEN *see* GAESTE IM PARADIES

Mosenthal, Salomon Hermann *see* CAECILIA VON ALBANO

Mosenthal, Salomon Hermann von *see*
- GESAMMELTE WERKE
- DER SONNWENDHOF

Mosenthal, Teese M *see* CORRELATION OF LABORATORY TESTS TO DISTANCE RUNNING PERFORMANCE DURING A CROSS-COUNTRY TRACK SEASON

Moser, C Daniel *see* METABOLIC RESPONSE TO ACUTE COLD AIR EXPOSURE AND TWO LEVELS OF BETA BLOCKADE IN MALES AND FEMALES

Moser, G H *see* PLOTINI ENNEADES CUM MARSILII FICINI INTERPRETATIONE CASTIG

Moser, Hans *see* DEUTSCHES VOLKSTUM IN VOLKSSCHAUSPIEL UND VOLKSTANZ

Moser, Harold D et al *see* THE PAPERS OF ANDREW JACKSON, 1770-1845

Moser, Heinrich *see* WANDLUNGEN DER GEDICHTE CONRAD FERDINAND MEYERS

Moser, J B *see* DER POLITISCHE SCHNEIDERUND DER PHLEGMATISCHE SCHUELER

Moser, S *see* GRUNDBEGRIFFE DER NATURPHILOSOPHIE BEI WILHELM VON OCKHAM

MOSES / Pearse, Mark Guy – 1894 – 9 – us A.T.L.A. [240]

Moses *see* THE WHITE CITY

Moses, Adolph *see*
- THE RELIGION OF MOSES
- YAHVISM AND OTHER DISCOURSES

MOSES ALSBACHER DOCUMENT *see* ALSBACHER, MOSES, DOCUMENT, MSS V.F. A

MOSES AND EGYPT: THE DOCUMENTATION TO THE MOTION PICTURE "THE TEN COMMANDMENTS" / Noerdlinger, H S – USC Press, 1956 – 9 – $10.00 – us I.R.C. [790]

MOSES AND THE PENTATEUCH : A POPULAR STATEMENT OF THE SO-CALLED HIGHER CRITICISM, TOGETHER WITH SOME OF THE REASONS FOR NOT ACCEPTING THEM / Johnston, Howard Agnew – Cincinnati: Elm Street, 1893 – 1mf – 9 – 0-8370-3791-3 – 1985-1791 – us A.T.L.A. [220]

MOSES AND THE PROPHETS: THE OLD TESTAMENT IN THE JEWISH CHURCH... REVIEWED / Green, William Henry – New York: Hurst, 1891. 1 fiche – 9 – us A.T.L.A. [220]

MOSES AND THE PROPHETS:...SOME OF THE POSITIONS OF MODERN BIBLICAL CRITICISM / Terry, Milton Spenser – New York: Eaton & Mains, 1901. 1 fiche – 9 – us A.T.L.A. [240]

MOSES BEN ESRA AUS GRANADA / Dukes, L – Altona. 1839. BJ-421-47 1 – 9 – ne IDC [920]

MOSES BEN MAIMON, SEIN LEBEN, SEINE WERKE UND SEIN EINFLUSS / Guttmann, J – 2v. Frankfurt am Main. Leipzig. 1908-14. BJ-33-46 1 – 9 – ne IDC [270]

Moses, Halsey H *see* THE LAW OF MANDAMUS AND THE PRACTICE CONNECTED WITH IT, WITH AN APPENDIX OF FORMS

MOSES; HIS LIFE AND TIMES / Rawlinson, George – London: James Nisbet & Co., pref. 1887. viii,205p – 1 – us U.W. Library [240]

Moses, John *see* ILLINOIS: HISTORICAL AND STATISTICAL

MOSES MENDELSSOHN : LICHTSTRAHLEN AUS SEINEN PHILOSOPHISCHEN SCHRIFTEN UND BRIEFEN: NEBST BIOGRAPHIE UND CHARAKTERISTIK MENDELSSOHN'S / Brasch, Moritz – Leipzig: F A Brockhaus, 1875 – us U.W. Library [920]

Moses, Raphel Jacob *see*
- BANK CASES. 1878
- STATE INSOLVENT LAWS

MOSES RIGHT, AND BISHOP COLENSO WRONG / Cumming, John – New York: John Bradburn, 1863. 1 fiche – 9 – us A.T.L.A. [240]

MOSES THE LAW-GIVER / Taylor, William Mackergo – (Includes bibliographical references and index) – New York: Harper, c1879 – 2mf – 9 – 0-8370-9749-5 – 1986-3749 – us A.T.L.A. [220]

Moses, W H *see* COLORED BAPTISTS FAMILY TREE: A COMPENDIUM OF ORGANIZED NEGRO BAPTISTS CHURCH HISTORY

Moses, Webster W *see* PAPERS OF WEBSTER W. MOSES

MOSHCH' KOOPERATSII : O POTREBITEL'NYKH OBSHCHESTVAKH / Totomiants, V F – Ed 3. Spb., 1907 – 1mf – 9 – COR-119/1 – ne IDC [334]

MOSIER BULLETIN – Mosier, OR. -w. 12 Mar 1909-27 Jul 1917. 2 rolls – 1 – us U.O. Library [071]

Mosina, IG *see* FORMIROVANIE BURZHUAZII V POLITICHESKUIU SILU V SIBIRI

MOSKAU NEWS – Koeln, may 1988-jun 1993 – 1r – 1 – gw Mikrofilm [947]

MOSKAUER RUNDSCHAU : INFORMATIONSWOCHENSCHRIFT FUER DAS AUSLAND – Moskau (Moskva), U.S.S.R. 1930-1933 (incomplete) – 1r – 1 – gw Mikrofilm [947]

MOSKITO – Cleveland, OH. 1902 – 1mf or 1r – 9,1 – us I.H.R.C. [972]

Moskovskago Oblastnago Byuro R K P (bol'shevikov) *see* KOMMUNIST

Moskovskai a oblastnai a planovai a komissii a *see* SPRAVOCHNIK PO STROITELSTVU MOSKOVSKOI OBLASTI NA...GOD

MOSKOVSKAIA GUB – Obzor khotinskago uezda v sel'sko-khoziaistvennom otnoshenii za 1887 g. (Sostavil K. Ermolinskii). 1888 – 8 – BRZ-211 2 – ne IDC [947]

MOSKOVSKAIA KOOPERATSIIA – M., 1927-29 n17 – 32mf – 9 – COR-652/1 – ne IDC [334]

MOSKOVSKAIA RABOCHE-KREST'IANSKAIA INSPEKTSIIA (OBZOR FONDOV RKI ZA 1918-1934 GG.) – Moscow, 1966. 166p. BR-10,939/1 – 9 – ne IDC [020]

MOSKOVSKAYA PRAVDA *see* MOSKOVSKY BOLSHEVIK

Moskovski i gorodsko i prodovolstvenny i komitet *see* SMI ETA NA PERIOD...

Moskovski i gorodsko i prodovolstvenny i komitet S.R.D., Redaktsionnoizdatelski i otdi el *see* SBORNIK POSTANOVLENI I I RASPORI AZHENI I OBSHCHIKH I MI ESTNYKH, REGULIRUI USHCHIKH PRODOVOLSTVENNOE DI ELO V MOSKVI E

MOSKOVSKI I PROPAGANDIST: ZHURNAL MK I MGK VKP(B) – (Includes c.1: 1945:no.6-no.7; 1947:no.1/2, no.4-no.5, no.11-no.12) – Moskva: Tip. izd-va "Moskovski i bolshevik", 1945 – 1 – CSUXAKZ3985-S – us Hoover Inst Photo [947]

Moskovski i sovet rabochikh, kresti anskikh i krasnoarme iskikh deputatov *see* STENOGRAFICHESKIE OTCHETY MOSKOVSKOGO SOVETA RABOCHIKH I KRASNOARME ISKIKH DEPUTATOV

MOSKOVSKI I SOVET V DVUKH REVOLIUTSII AKH / Angarskii, Nikolai Semenovich – Moskva: Moskvoski i rabochi i, 1928 – 1 – CSUX88-B5893 – us Hoover Inst Photo [947]

MOSKOVSKI YEZHENEDEL'NIK – Moscow. 1907-1909; Jan-Aug 1910 – 1 – us NY Public [073]

MOSKOVSKIE MASTERA – Zhurnal iskusstv. M. 1916. BR-1877 2 – 8 – ne IDC [073]

MOSKOVSKIE NOVOSTI – Moscow, USSR. May 8, July 3 1988-Dec 17 1989; 1990-1992 – 4r – 1 – us L of C Photodup [072]

MOSKOVSKIE NOVOSTI/MOSCOW NEWS – 1930- – 1 – sz Infoprint [947]

MOSKOVSKIE PROIZVODITEL'NO-TRUDOVYE ARTELI : PO DANNYM OBSLEDOVANIIA 1913 G / Brianskii, N G – Pg., 1915 – 2mf – 9 – COR-12/1 – ne IDC [334]

MOSKOVSKIE TSERKOVNYI VESTNIK AND OFITSIAL'NAIA KHRONIKA – 1 – sz Infoprint [947]

MOSKOVSKIE VEDOMOSTI – (Missing: Many numbers. See also: Sobranie Peredovykh Statei "Moskovskikh Vedomostei") – 1813, 1827-1917 – 270r – 1 – RF-2/3 – ne IDC [072]

MOSKOVSKIE VEDOMOSTI *see* SOBRANIE PEREDOVYKH STATEI "MOSKOVSKIKH VEDOMOSTEI" 1863-1887

MOSKOVSKII BOL'SHEVIK *see* RABOCHAIA MOSKVA

MOSKOVSKII KOMSOMOLETS – Moscow: Moskovskii komsomolets, 1919- – 2mf – 9 – $199.95y – us East View [320]

MOSKOVSKII KOOPERATOR – (Missing: 1916 n5; 1917 n4; 1918 n1-2) – M., 1916-19 n8 – 22mf – 9 – COR-653/1 – ne IDC [334]

MOSKOVSKII MITROPOLIT PLATON LEVSHIN KAK PROTIVORASKOL'NICHII DEIATEL / Lysogorskii, N V – Roston na Donu: Elektro-pechatnia A I Ter-Abramian, 1905 – us Res Libr [947]

MOSKOVSKII SBORNIK : T.1: SOCHINEIIA / Aksakova, K S et al – Moskva: V Tip Aleksandra Semena, 1852 – us Res Libr [947]

MOSKOVSKII TSERKOVNYI VESTNIK – (Inquire) – 1 – us Ross [072]

MOSKOVSKOE EZHEMESIACHNOE IZDANIE – v. 1-3. M. 1781. B-1451 2 – 8 – ne IDC [073]

Moskovskoe kommunalnoe khoziaistvo, Upravlenie vodoprovodom *see* TRUDY KOMISSII PO IZYSKANIIU NOVYKH ISTOCHNIKOV VODOSNABZHENIIA G. MOSKVY

MOSKOVSKY BOLSHEVIK – Moscow, USSR. Jan 1946-Dec 1958 – 28r – 1 – uk British Libr Newspaper [947]

MOSKVA / Belyi, A – Roman. Tom I-chast' pervaia: Moskovskii chudak. Tom I-chast'vtoraia: Moskva pod udarom. Tom II. Maski. 1926-32. BR-4835 2 – 8 – ne IDC [460]

MOSKVA / ed by Kovalyov, L – Moscow: Rabochaia Moskva Publishers, 1935 – 8mf – 9 – $80.00 – us Ross [947]

MOSKVA – Moscow. U.S.S.R – 1 – us UMI [073]

MOSKVA : PODROBNOE ISTORICHESKOE I ARKHEOLOGICHESKOE OPISANIE GORODA / Snegirev, I – Moscow, 1875 – 7mf – 9 – us Ross [947]

MOSKVA : PUTEVODITEL' / ed by Zviagintsev & Kovalenskii – Moscow: I Kushneryov & Co Publ, 1915 – 8mf – 9 – us Ross [947]

MOSKVA POD UDAROM / Belyi, A – Vtoraia chast' romana "Moskva." 1927. BR-1242 2 – 8 – ne IDC [460]

MOSKVA V EE PROSHLOM I NASTOIASHCHEM – Moscow: Obrazovaniye Book Pub. Association, 1910-11 – 23mf – 9 – $240.00 – us Ross [947]

Moskvoshve i no.5 im. Profinterna (Factory) *see* NASH KONVE IER

THE MOSLEM DOCTRINE OF GOD : AN ESSAY ON THE CHARACTER AND ATTRIBUTES OF ALLAH ACCORDING TO THE KORAN AND ORTHODOX TRADITION / Zwemer, Samuel Marinus – Edinburgh-London, 1905 – 3mf – 8 – ne Slangenburg [260]

MOSLEM WORLD – v1-37. 1911-47 – 1 – us UMI [260]

THE MOSLEM WORLD – Ulster Park, NY -m. May 1893-. Nov 1893, Jan 1895. Feb 1896. 1 reel – 1 – us Western Res [071]

MOSLEM-CHRISTIAN CASE AGAINST ZIONIST AGGRESSION – Official Statement by the Palestine Arab Delegation. London. 1922. BJ-28-126 1 – 9 – ne IDC [956]

Mosler, Hans *see* URKUNDENBUCH DES ABTEI ALTENBERG

MOSMAN DAILY – Aug 6 1920-Jun 22 1967 – 9 – at Pascoe [072]

Mosquera Gomez, Luis *see* ELOGIO DE EUGENIO HERMOSO

Mosquero Martin, Manuel *see* PAULITA CENTENO MORUNO

O MOSQUETEIRO : ORGAM RECREATIVO E NOTICIOSO – Curitiba, 16 Jun-4 Oct 1887 – 1,5,6 – bl Biblioteca [072]

O MOSQUITO – Pilar, Alagoas. 1 Jan 1886 – 1,5,6 – bl Biblioteca [072]

THE MOSQUITO – [Durban: Central News Agency]. v1-3 n18. 13 jul 1905-8 nov 1907 – 3r – 1 – us Res Libr [072]

THE MOSQUITO – New Westminster, BC: Mosquito Pub. Co, [1885-18– or 19–] – 9 – cn C.I.H.M. [072]

THE MOSQUITO – Quebec, Canada. 20 jul 1882; v1 n2. 27 jul 1882 – 1r – 1 – Can$25.00 – cn Can Microfilming [072]

MOSQUITO NEWS – v1-17. 1941-57 – 1,5,6 – 2277.00 – us Princeton Micro [073]

Moss, Lemuel *see*
- ANNALS OF THE UNITED STATES CHRISTIAN COMMISSION
- THE BAPTISTS AND THE NATIONAL CENTENARY

Moss, R I *see* A BIOMECHANICAL ANALYSIS OF PATELLOFEMORAL STRESS SYNDROME

Moss, Richard Waddy *see*
- FROM MALACHI TO MATTHEW
- THE RANGE OF CHRISTIAN EXPERIENCE

Moss, Roger W *see* BIOGRAPHICAL DICTIONARY OF PHILADELPHIA ARCHITECTS: 1700-1930

MOSS VALE POST – Jan 3 1958-Dec 29 1959 – 9 – at Pascoe [072]

Mossay, J *see*
- THESAURUS SANCTI GREGORII NAZIANZENI

THE MOSSEL BAY ADVERTISER – South Africa. 4 Jan 1871-25 Dec 1926. 36 reels – 1, 16 diazo available at reduced price – sa SA Libr [072]

Mosso, Angelo *see*
- FATIGUE
- FEAR

THE MOST DELECTABLE NIGHTS OF STRAPAROLA OF CARAVAGGIO / Straparola, Giovanni Francesco – 1906 – 1 – us I.U. Libraries [390]

A MOST EXCELLENT AND LEARNED WOORKE OF CHIRURGERIE / Lanfranc – M 374. 1565 – 9 – ne IDC [617]

A MOST EXCELLENT METHOD OF CURING WOUNDES / Arcaeus, F – M-288. 1588 – 9 – ne IDC [615]

THE MOST EXCELLENT WORCKES OF CHIRURGERY / Vigo, J de – M 417. 1550 – 9 – ne IDC [617]

THE MOST EXCELLENT WORKES OF CHIRURGERY / Vigo, J de – M 418. 1571 – 9 – ne IDC [617]

THE MOST EXCELLENT WORKES OF CHIRURGERY... / Vigo, J de – London, 1550 – 16mf – ne IDC [617]

THE MOST EXCELLENT WORKES OF CHIRURGERY... / Vigo, J de – London, 1571 – 16mf – ne IDC [617]

MOST FASHIONABLE STREET, WEBSTER – Ballarat – 10mf – 9 – at Corangamite [072]

Most, Georg Friedrich *see* AUSFUEHRLICHE ENCYKLOPAEDIE DER GESAMMTEN STAATSARZNEIKUNDE (AEL, ABT 3;23)

MOST PLAIN DIRECTIONS FOR TRUE WRITING / Hodges, Richard – 1653. 101p. (English Linguistics Series 1500-1800) – 9 – us UMI [420]

THE MOST VITAL MISSION PROBLEM OF THE DAY / Schwager, Frederick – Techny, Ill.: Mission Press, 1915 – 1mf – us A.T.L.A. [240]

Mostaert, Antoine *see* TEXTES ORAUX ORDOS, RECUEILLIS ET PUBLIES AVEC INTRODUCTION, NOTES MORPHOLOGIQUES, COMMENTAIRES ET GLOSSAIRE

Mostaert, R P A *see* DICTIONNAIRE ORDOS

MOSTAZA Y ORTIGAS / Moreno Torrado, Luis – 1886 – 9 – 1.50f – sp Bibl Santa Ana [810]

Mostras, C *see* DICTIONNAIRE GEOGRAPHIQUE DE L'EMPIRE OTTOMAN

MOSTY – Lodz, Poland. Aug-Nov 1947; 31 Jan 1948 – 1r – 1 – us L of C Photodup [943]

MOSTY-NASZE SLOWO – Lodz, Poland. Jan-Apr, Sept-Dec 1949 – 1r – 1 – us L of C Photodup [943]

Moszkowski, M *see*
- 3 PIECES FOR PIANO, OP. 54
- HUIT MORCEAUX CHARACTERISTIQUES, OP. 36. CAHIER 1-3
- MAZURKA, OP. 46, NO. 2
- QUATRE MORCEAUX, OP. 38
- VALSE, OP. 46, NO. 1

Moszynski, K *see* KULTURA LUDOWA SLOWIAN

MOT – (Missing: v1(1-11) 1933) – Amsterdam. v1-3. 1933-1935 – 3mf – 9 – ne IDC [949]

LE MOT D'ESPRIT ET SES RAPPORTS AVEC L'INCONSCIENT / Freud, Sigmund – 6e ed. [Paris]: Gallimard, 1930 – 4mf – 9 – Can$9.00 – cn Bibl Nat [150]

LE MOT D'ORDRE – Paris. no.1-87.9 juil-3 oct 1877, 10 nov 1879-1 mars 1922, 1897-99, 1916-17, 1919-21 – 1 – fr A.C.R.P.P. [073]

MOT SO CHE DO CHINH SACH... – 1968 – 1mf – 9 SEL-122/1 – ne IDC [340]

MOT SO CHE DO, CHINH SACH CUA NHA NUOC TRONG TINH HINH MOI = SOME POLICIES OF THE STATE IN THE NEW CONJUNCTURE / Ministry of Agricultural Development Projects – 1967 – 2mf – 9 SEL-110/1 – ne IDC [340]

MOT SO LUAT LE CUA NHA NUOC = SOME LAWS AND REGULATIONS OF THE STATE / People's Court of Quang Ninh Province – 1974 – 2mf – 9 SEL-109/1 – ne IDC [340]

Mota Arevalo, Horacio *see*
- ETAPA EXTREMENA EN LA BIOGRAFIA DEL MINISTRO FERNANDEZ NEGRETE
- LA ORDEN DE SANTIAGO EN TIERRAS DE EXTREMADURA
- LAS ORDENES MILITARES EN EXTREMADURA
- POLITICA SOCIAL DEL EMPERADOR CARLOS 5 A TRAVES DE DOCUMENTOS DEL ARCHIVO DE MONTEMOLIN
- PRIVILEGIOS CONCEDIDOS A MONTEMOLIN POR LOS MAESTROS DE LA ORDEN DE CABALLERIA DE SANTIAGO

Mota Padillo, Francisco *see* MUERTE DE PEDRO DE ALVARADO. CARTAS DE RELACION DE ALVARADO A HERNAN CORTES. CARTAS ANTIGUAS A LA CIUDAD DE GOATHEMALA

MOTALA TIDNING – Halmstad, Skaenninge, Motala. 1868-1909 – 9 – sw Kungliga [072]

MOTALA TIDNING – Motala, Sweden. 1979- – 1 – sw Kungliga [072]

Motay Escobar, Alonso *see* DESCRIPCION GEOGRAFICA DE LOS REINOS DE LA NUEVA GALICIA...

Mote, Frederick W *see* JAPANESE SPONSORED GOVERNMENTS IN CHINA

Motelay, L *see* MONOGRAPHIE DES ISOETEAE

MOTETS A 1, 2, ET 3 VOIX AVEC BASSE CONTINUE. LIVRE PREMIER-TROISIEME / Campra, A – Paris: Ballard, 1700-1703 – 1 – us Sibley [780]

MOTETS POUR LES PRINCIPALES FESTES DE L'ANNEE / Lebegue, Nicolas – A Paris: par Christophe Ballard, seul Imprimeur du Roy pour la musique, 1687. SEM105P2018 – 2mf – 9 – Can$4.50 – cn Bibl Nat [780]

MOTEZUMA / Masara – 1807 – 9 – 1.50f – sp Bibl Santa Ana [946]

MOTH AND RUST / Cholmondeley, Mary – British Fiction Archive: Unit 3 – 9 – uk Bell [830]

MOTHER AFRICA HITS BACK : THE NATIVE PROBLEM AND ITS SOLUTION / Chadwick, William Sydney – Stellenbosch, [1950?] – us Res Libr [305]

MOTHER BUNCH'S CLOSET – 1885 – 1 – us I.U. Libraries [390]

MOTHER COBB, OR, SIXTY YEARS' WALK WITH GOD / Chapman, Mary Weems – c1896 – 9 – us A.T.L.A. [240]

MOTHER EARTH BULLETIN – (Series 1: v1-12. no. 6. 1906-17. Series 2: no. 1-17 (all publ). 1917-18) – 66mf – 9 – $265.00 – us UPA [360]

MOTHER EARTH NEWS – v1- 1970- 1; v13- 5,6,9 – us UMI [574]

MOTHER JONES – v. 1-. 1976- – 1,5,6,9 – us UMI [410]

MOTHER LODE MAGNET – Jamestown, CA. 1898-1938 – 12r – 1 – $600.00 – C03606 – us Library Micro [071]

THE MOTHERS / Hirschfeld, Georg – Garden City, New York: Doubleday, Page, 1916 – 1r – 1 – us U.W. Library [820]

MOTHER'S MAGAZINE AND FAMILY CIRCLE – v1-56. 1833-88 – 8r – 1 – us Ross [640]

MOTHER'S PENSION CASE FILES / Allen County. Ohio. Common Pleas. Juvenile Div – 1915-1930 – 1r – 1 – $32.50r – us Archival [324]

MOTHERS' PENSION DISBURSEMENTS / Defiance County. Ohio. Auditor – 1919-1927 – 1r – 1 – $32.50r – us Archival [324]

MOTHERS' PENSION DOCKETS / Defiance County. Ohio. Auditor – 1914-1932 – 1r – 1 – $32.50r – us Archival [324]

MOTHERS' PENSION DOCKETS / Fulton County. Ohio. Common Pleas. Juvenile Division – 1914-1936 – 1r – 1 – $32.50r – us Archival [324]

MOTHER'S PENSION DOCKETS/RECS / Allen County. Ohio. Common Pleas. Juvenile Div – 1919-1934 – 1r – 1 – $32.50r – us Archival [324]

MOTHER'S PENSION JOURNALS / Allen County. Ohio. Common Pleas. Juvenile Div – 1914-1936 – 2r – 1 – $32.50r – us Archival [324]

MOTHERS' PENSION RECORDS / Ottawa County. Ohio. Common Pleas. Juvenile Division – 1914-1936 – 1r – 1 – $32.50r – us Archival [324]

MOTHERS' PENSION RECORDS / Putnam County. Ohio. Common Pleas. Juvenile Div – 1924-1936 – 1r – 1 – $32.50r – us Archival [324]

MOTHERS' PENSION RECORDS / Van Wert County. Ohio. Common Pleas. Juvenile Court – 1916-1936 – 1r – 1 – $32.50r – us Archival [324]

MOTHERS WHO MUST EARN / Anthony, Katharine Susan – New York: Survey Associates, 1914. viii,223p. plates, diagr. (West Side Studies. v2,pt.2). At head of title: Russell Sage Foundation – 1 – us U.W. Library [305]

MOTHERWELL SPEAKER ETC – Scotland, UK. 1905-15 Mar 1906.-w. 28 feet – 1 – uk British Libr Newspaper [072]

MOTHERWELL TIMES – 1 – £42.00r – uk Scot News [072]

MOTHERWELL TIMES – Wales, UK. 1983. -w. 2 reels – 1 – uk British Libr Newspaper [072]

MOTHERWELL TIMES ETC – England.1947-82. -w. 52 reels – 1 – uk British Libr Newspaper [072]

Mothopeng, Zephania *see* THE BETHAL TRIAL: STATE VS. Z. MOTHOPENG AND 17 OTHERS, IN THE SUPREME COURT OF SOUTH AFRICA, SOUTHEASTERN LOCAL DIVISION

MOTHS / Ouida – British Fiction Archive: Unit 3 – 9 – uk Bell [830]

MOTHS AND BUTTERFLIES OF THE UNITED STATES / Denton, S F – 2148 2. 2 v. 1900 – 8 – ne IDC [590]

Motinggo, Busje *see*
- BUANG TONDJAM
- DOSA KITA SEMUA; SEBUAH ROMAN
- PEREMPUAN ITU BERNAMA BARABAH; SEBUAH NOVEL

MOTION – (v1-6 1972-1976/77 Can$28.00. v7 1977/78 Can$20.00y. Ceased v7 no 2 1977/78) – Toronto. v1-7. 1972-77/78 – 9 – cn Micromedia [073]

MOTION PICTURE CATALOGS BY AMERICAN PRODUCERS AND DISTRIBUTORS, 1894-1908 – (With printed guide) – 6r – 1 – $580.00 – us UPA [790]

MOTION PICTURE CLASSIC – v. 1-33. Sep 1915-Aug 1931. 10 scattered issues wanting – 1 – 249.00 – us L of C Photodup [770]

MOTION PICTURE HERALD – v. 178-197. 1950-54 – 1 – us UMI [790]

MOTION PICTURE LAW REVIEW – (Lacking: v9 p7-8,13-14. no 12) – Los Angeles. v1-21. 1938-59 (all publ) – 21mf – 9 – $94.00 – LLMC 84-620 – us L.L.M.C. [073]

MOTION PICTURE MAGAZINE – v1-61. 1911-41 – 17r – 1 – us Ross [790]

MOTION PICTURE NEWS – New York. v4-42. 1911-30 – 47r – 1 – us Ross [790]

MOTION PICTURE STUDIO DIRECTORY – 4th ed. [New York]: [Motion Picture News], 1918-. SEM16P237 – 1r – 5 – Can$12.00 – cn Bibl Nat [790]

MOTION TIME ANALYSIS BULLETIN – 1940-68 1; 1969-73 5,6 – us UMI [650]

DAS MOTIV DER ORGANISATION UND WIRKUNG VON MACHT IN PETER WEISS' EPISCHEN STUECKEN "MARAT / SADE" UND "HOELDERLIN" / Boehner, Claus-Peter – 1992 – 83p – 9 – DM75.00 – 3-89349-492-8 – gw Hänsel [430]

MOTIVATION AND EMOTION – v1-18. 1977-94 – 1,5 – $80.00 – us UMI [150]

MOTIVATION OF AQUATIC PROFESSIONALS : AN ANALYSIS OF FOUR DIFFERENT TYPES OF AQUATIC DIRECTORS AND SWIMMING COACHES / Smith, Jonathan B – 1994 – 3mf – $12.00 – us Microform Publ [150]

MOTIVE : MAGAZINE OF THE METHODIST STUDENT MOVEMENT – v1-32. Feb 1941-Apr 1972 (complete) – 10r – 1 – ATLA S0226 – us A.T.L.A. [073]

MOTIVE – v. 1-32. 1941-72 – 1 – us UMI [073]

DIE MOTIVE DER STURM- UND DRANG-DRAMATIKER : EINE UNTERSUCHUNG IHRER HERKUNFT UND ENTWICKLUNG / Zorn, Joseph – Bonn 1909 – 1 – DM30.00 – gw Mikro Press [430]

MOTIVE POWER INTERNATIONAL – 1973-1,5,6; 1975- 9 – us UMI [073]

MOTIVE UND WIRKUNGEN DES KOMMUNALWAHLSYSTEMS IN BADEN-WUERTTEMBERG / Hamberger, Wolfgang – Heidelberg, 1966 – 2mf – 9 – DM62.00 – 3-89349-370-0 – gw Hänsel [320]

MOTIVES FOR A SUBSCRIPTION TOWARDS THE RELIEF OF THE SUFFERERS AT MONTREAL IN CANADA, BY A FIRE ON THE 18TH MAY 1765 – 2nd ed. Montreal, 1765. SEM35P75 – 1 – Can$15.00 – cn Bibl Nat [360]

DIE MOTIVIERUNG DER ASKESE IN DER ALTEN KIRCHE UND DER URSPRUNG DES MOENCHTUMS (T.U.U. 5.95) / Nagel, P – Berlin, 1966 – 3mf – 9 – ne Slangenburg [240]

MOTIVOS DE BELLEZA / Botto, Antonio – Lisbon, 1923 – 1 – us Res Libr [810]

MOTIVOS EXTREMENO / Martin Gil, Thomas – Madrid: Escuelas Profesionales del Sagrado Corazon de Jesus, 1968 – 1 – sp Bibl Santa Ana [946]

MOTLEY: VERSES GRAVE AND GAY / Bengough, John Wilson – Montreal: W. Coates, 1895. 00130. (Pre-1900 Canadiana) – 9 – cn C.I.H.M. [810]

MOTO CLUB EMERITENSE. 4 TROFEO PRUEBA DE REGULARIDAD – (V Trofeo Prueba de regularidad.-1962, 1963, 1965) – 1964 – 1 – sp Bibl Santa Ana [946]

MOTOGRAPHY EXPLOITING MOTION PICTURES – Chicago. v1-20. 1909-18 – 10r – 1 – us Ross [790]

MOTOLINIA'S HISTORY OF THE INDIANS OF NEM SPAIN / Bayle, Constantino – Madrid: Missionalia Hispanica, 1952 – 1 – sp Bibl Santa Ana [946]

MOTOMBI MYTHES ET ENIGMES INITIATIQUES DES MITSOGHO DU GABON CENTRAL / Sillans, R – Route de la vie – 9 – F100.00 – fr Ethnologie [306]

MOTOR – London. v58-113. 1931-58 – 1,5,6 – us Princeton Micro [073]

MOTOR – New York. v61-102. 1934-54 – 1,5,6 – us Princeton Micro [073]

MOTOR – The Automotive Business Magazine – v1- 1903- 1; 1976- 5,6,9 – us UMI [073]

MOTOR ABILITY TESTING OF SPEECH HANDICAPPED PRESCHOOL CHILDREN : A VALIDATION STUDY / Reeves, Lynda P & Gench, Barbara E – 1991 – 3mf – 9 – $12.00 – us Microform Publ [150]

MOTOR AGE – v1- 1899- 1; v90- 5,6; v95- 9 – us UMI [629]

MOTOR BOAT AND YACHTING – 1904- 1; 1973-5,6; 1975- 4 x 6 in. 9 – apply; x 6 in9 – us UMI [073]

MOTOR BOATING AND SAILING – 1909- 1; 1964- 5,6; 1977- 4 x 6 in. 9 – us UMI [073]

MOTOR BUS LAWS AND REGULATIONS / Meighan, John M – Washington, D.C.: National Association of Motor Bus Operators 1932. 819p. LL-351 – 1 – us L of C Photodup [340]

MOTOR CARRIER CASES / U.S. Interstate Commerce Commission – v1-133. Jun 1936-86 (all publ?) – 1350mf – 9 – $2,025.00 – LLMC 78-224A – us L.L.M.C. [324]

MOTOR CYCLE – 1903- – 1 – us UMI [790]

THE MOTOR DEVELOPMENT OF INFANTS AND CHILDREN EXPOSED TO COCAINE WHILE IN UTERO / Reid, Michael E & Ridenour, Marcella – 1991 – 2mf – 9 – $8.00 – us Microform Publ [150]

MOTOR FINANCE – London, UK. Dec 1906. -irr. 9 feet – 1 – uk British Libr Newspaper [072]

MOTOR PERFORMANCE OF YOUNG EXCEPTIONAL CHILDREN / Nestroy, Jerry A – 1981 – 2mf – 9 – $8.00 – us Microform Publ [790]

MOTOR PROFICIENCY OF MALES WITH ATTENTION DEFICIT HYPERACTIVE DISORDER AND MALES WITH LEARNING DISABILITIES / Beyer, Roberta – Texas Woman's University, 1993 – 2mf – 9 – $8.00 – PSY 1881 – us Microform Publ [150]

MOTOR SHIP – v1- 1920- 1; v56- 5,6,9 – us UMI [623]

MOTOR TRAFFIC ADVOCATE – Portland OR. Oct 7 Nov 1 Dec 6 26 1933 – 1 – us U.O. Library [071]

MOTOR TREND MAGAZINE – v1- 1947- 1; 1971- 5,6,9 – us UMI [073]

MOTOR TREND YEARBOOK – 1966-72 1; v23-5,6 – us UMI [629]

MOTOR VARIANCE OF BASKETBALLS RELATED TO KINESTHETIC SENSE IN FREE THROW SHOOTING / Pangman, John R – 1982 – 2mf – 9 – $8.00 – us Microform Publ [790]
MOTOR VEHICLE SAFETY ACT, REGULATIONS & TEST METHODS / Canada. Laws, Statutes, etc – (Amendment Service. YX76-M10EM) – Basic set. YX76-M10-1-EM – 9 – Can$24.00 – cn Communication [380]
MOTOR VEHICLE TIRE SAFETY ACT, REGULATIONS & TEST METHODS / Canada. Laws, Statutes, etc – (Amendment service. YX76-M11EM. Standing order) – Basic set. YX76-M11-1-EM – 9 – Can$7.50 – cn Communication [380]
MOTORNAI A VSPASHKA, KAK SREDSTVO V BORBI E S GOLODOM V ROSSII = MOTOR PLOUGHING, AS A REMEDY AGAINST THE FAMINE IN RUSSIA / Benzin, Vasilii M – Praga: Sklad izd. Rudolf R. Tes arek, 1922 (Praga: Tip. "Politika") – 1 – CSUX89-B3363 – us Hoover Inst Photo [630]
DES MOTS A LA MODE / Callieres, F de – 2e ed. 1693 – 9 – fr I.C.S. [440]
LES MOTS FRANCOIS SELON L'ORDRE DES LETTRES / Estienne, Robert – 1576 – 9 – fr I.C.S. [440]
Mott, Frederick Blount *see* A SHORT HISTORY OF THE UNITARIANISM SINCE THE REFORMATION
Mott, George Scudder *see* THE PRODIGAL SON
Mott, J R *see* THE SUMMONS TO A LARGER EVANGELISM (CCC255)
Mott, John Raleigh *see*
- THE DECISIVE HOUR OF CHRISTIAN MISSIONS
- THE EVANGELIZATION OF THE WORLD IN THIS GENERATION
- THE FUTURE LEADERSHIP OF THE CHURCH
- THE PASTOR AND MODERN MISSIONS
- THE PRESENT WORLD SITUATION
- STRATEGIC POINTS IN THE WORLD'S CONQUEST

MOTT NORTH STAR – Dunsmuir, CA. 1887-90 – 1r – 1 – $50.00 – B02186 – us Library Micro [071]
Motta, J F et al *see* LES OEUVRES RUPESTRES DU SITE D'ALTAMIRA, JOSE DE MELLO, MINAS GERAIS, BRESIL
MOTTETI A DUE, TRE, E QUATTRO VOCI CO'L, TE DEUM, LE LETANIE DELLA B. VERGINE CONCERTTATI, ET IL PASIJ DELLA DOMENICA DELLE PALME, ET DEL VENERDI SANCTO CO'L, TAMTUM ERGO SACRAMENTUM; VENI CREATOR... : OPERA SECONDA / Beria, G B – (3 parts) – Milano: C Compagno, [1647] – 1 – us Sibley [780]
Mottoulle, Leopold *see* CONTRIBUTIONS A L'ETUDE DU DETERMINISME FONCTIONNEL DE L'INDUSTRIE DANS L'EDUCATION DE L'INDIGENE CONGOLAIS
MOTVS MONASTERIENSIS LIBRI 10 / Bolandus, J F – Coloniae, M. Gymnicus. 1546. BME165 1 – 9 – ne IDC [240]
MOTZE AND JESUS (CCC332) = ME TIH YU YEH SU / Wu, Lei-ch'uan – (In Chinese) – Shanghai: Association Press of China, 1940 – 1r – 1 – 1984-6671 – us A.T.L.A. [230]
LA MOUCHE LITTERAIRE [PUIS] MOUCHE (LA) DE SAONE-ET-LOIRE ET DE L'AIN – Macon, August 1843 – July 1848 – 1r – fr Armell [440]
Mouchet, Carlos *see* DERECHO HISPANICO Y "COMMON LAW" EN PUERTO RICO
MOUDJAHID *see* EL-MOUDJAHID
Moulds, J *see* STERN'S MARIA, A PATHETIC SONG...
Moule, Arthur Evans *see* HALF A CENTURY IN CHINA
Moule, G H *see* THE SPIRIT OF JAPAN
Moule, Handley Carr Glynn *see*
- COLOSSIAN STUDIES: LESSONS IN FAITH AND HOLINESS
- EPHESIAN STUDIES: EXPOSITORY READINGS ON THE EPISTLE
- EPISTLE OF ST PAUL TO THE ROMANS

Moule, Handly Carr Glynn *see* THE EPISTLES TO THE COLOSSIANS AND TO PHILEMON
LES MOULES A FROMAGE EN ROUMANIE / Gateau, M – 9 – F50.00 – fr Ethnologie [949]
Moulieras, Auguste *see* LE MAROC INCONNU...
Moulinet, Jean *see* LA DENTELLE A L'AIGUILLE EN BASSE-NORMANDIE
Moulton, George Ernest *see* THE IDENTIFICATION OF THE 144,000 OF REVELATION 7
Moulton, H *see* L'HEURE ESPAGNOL. TRIO SUR L'OPERA...
Moulton, James Hope *see*
- A FIRST READER IN NEW TESTAMENT GREEK
- AN INTRODUCTION TO THE STUDY OF NEW TESTAMENT GREEK

Moulton, Richard Green *see*
- THE LITERARY STUDY OF THE BIBLE
- A SHORT INTRODUCTION TO THE LITERATURE OF THE BIBLE

Moulton, Richard Green et al *see* THE BIBLE AS LITERATURE
Moulton, Warren J *see* UEBER DIE UEBERLIEFERUNG UND DEN TEXTKRITISCHEN WERT DES DRITTEN ESRABUCHS
Moulton, William Fiddian *see* THE HISTORY OF THE ENGLISH BIBLE
A MOUND OF MANY CITIES (TELL EL HESY EXCAVATED) / Bliss, F J – PEF, 1898 – 9 – $10.00 – us I.R.C. [930]
THE MOUND OF THE JEW AND THE CITY OF ONIAS (MEES VOL 7) / Naville, E – (Also: F.L. Griffith: The Antiquities of Tell el Yahudiyeh) – London, 1890 – 6mf – 8 – Dfl25.00 – ne Slangenburg [930]
Mouneimne, N *see* POISSONS DES COTES DU LIBAN (MEDITERRANEE ORIENTALE): BIOLOGIE ET PECHE
Mounfield, A *see* A SHORT HISTORY OF INDEPENDENT METHODISM
Mounier, Jean-Joseph *see* PLAN D'EDUCATION NATIONALE, ADRESSE AUX ETATS GENERAUX PAR UN PERE DE FAMILLE DAUPHINOIS
MOUNT ALEXANDER MAIL – 1864-1867. MAMA-H – 8r – 1 – at Corangamite [072]
MOUNT ALEXANDER MAIL – 1901-1917. MAM1-34 – 34r – 1 – at Corangamite [072]
MOUNT ALEXANDER MAIL – Castlemaine, Australia. Sep 1892-May 1900.-w. 3mqn reels – 1 – uk British Libr Newspaper [072]
THE MOUNT ALLISON ACADEMIC GAZETTE / Mount Allison Wesleyan Academy – (Cont by: Mount Allison Wesleyan Academy, The Mount Allison gazette) – Sackville, NB: Mount Allison Wesleyan Academy, [1853?-1862?] – 9 – cn C.I.H.M. [370]
THE MOUNT ALLISON ACADEMIC GAZETTE *see* THE MOUNT ALLISON GAZETTE
THE MOUNT ALLISON GAZETTE / Mount Allison Wesleyan Academy – (Cont: Mount Allison Wesleyan Academy, The Mount Allison Academic Gazette) – Sackville, N.B.: Mount Allison Wesleyan Academy, [1863] – 9 – cn C.I.H.M. [370]
THE MOUNT ALLISON GAZETTE *see* THE MOUNT ALLISON ACADEMIC GAZETTE
MOUNT ALLISON WESLEYAN ACADEMY *see*
- THE MOUNT ALLISON ACADEMIC GAZETTE
- THE MOUNT ALLISON GAZETTE

Mount Allison Wesleyan Academy *see*
- THE ACADEMY GOSSIP
- THE MOUNT ALLISON ACADEMIC GAZETTE
- THE MOUNT ALLISON GAZETTE

MOUNT ANGEL NEWS – Mount Angel, OR. -w. 12 May 1921-31 Dec 1970; 15 July 1976 – 13r – 1 – us U.O. Library [071]
MOUNT ARARAT BAPTIST CHURCH. CHEROKEE COUNTY. SOUTH CAROLINA : CHURCH RECORDS – 1844-82 – 1 – 11.16 – us Baptist [240]
MOUNT CALVARY BAPTIST CHURCH. BARNWELL COUNTY. SOUTH CAROLINA : CHURCH RECORDS – 1856-1972 – 1 – 29.25 – us Baptist [240]
MOUNT CARMEL BAPTIST CHURCH. NEW YORK : CHURCH RECORDS – 1790-1959 (7 vols). (Peekskill, Philipstown, Carmel). 2258p – 1 – 101.61 – us Baptist [240]
MOUNT CARMEL ITEM – Mount Carmel, PA. -d 1902-1924; 1909-1912; 1937-1946 – 13 – $25.00r – us I.M.R. [071]
MOUNT CARMEL LEDGER – Mount Carmel, PA., 1892-1895 – 13 – $25.00r – us I.M.R. [071]
MOUNT CARMEL NEWS – Mount Carmel, PA., 1925-1930 – 13 – $25.00r – us I.M.R. [071]
Mount Clemens, Michigan *see* MISCELLANEOUS EARLY NEWSPAPERS
MOUNT DESERT HERALD – Bar Harbor, ME: Mount desert Pub Co, jul 1881-jun 24 1891 – us Res Libr [071]
MOUNT FREEDOM BAPTIST CHURCH. WILMORE, KENTUCKY : CHURCH RECORDS – Wilmore, Kentucky. Mount Freedom Baptist Church, June 1832-1961. 1,480p – 1 – $66.60 – us Baptist [240]
MOUNT GILEAD BAPTIST CHURCH. MONTGOMERY ASSOCIATION. NORTH CAROLINA : CHURCH RECORDS – 1883-94 – 1 – 5.00 – us Baptist [240]
MOUNT HARMONY BAPTIST CHURCH. ROUGEMONT, NORTH CAROLINA : CHURCH RECORDS – Nov 1855-Jun 1951. (Incomplete) – 1 – 5.85 – us Baptist [240]
MOUNT JULIET FIRST BAPTIST CHURCH. MOUNT JULIET, TENNESSEE : CHURCH RECORDS – Apr 1972-Dec 1978. 178p – 1 – 8.01 – us Baptist [240]
Mount Juliet. Tennessee. Rutland Baptist Church *see* DWIGHT L. MOODY MATERIALS CONCERNING RUTLAND BAPTIST CHURCH
MOUNT MORRIS TIMES – Flint. Mich. 1928-1940 – 1 – us UMI [071]
Mount Nebo Sunday School, Mount Nebo, KS *see* SECRETARY'S BOOK
MOUNT OLIVE BAPTIST CHURCH. LOWES, LENTUCKY : CHURCH RECORDS – Aug 1836-1958 – 1 – 44.37 – us Baptist [240]
MOUNT OLIVE TRIBUNE – Mount Olive. Miss. 1943-1950 – 1 – us UMI [071]
MOUNT PARAN BAPTIST CHURCH. BROAD RIVER ASSOCIATION. CHEROKEE COUNTY. GROVER, SOUTH CAROLINA : CHURCH RECORDS – 1853-1959; 1965-76 – 1 – 30.60 – us Baptist [240]
MOUNT PISGAH BAPTIST CHURCH. BOWLING GREEN, MISSOURI : CHURCH RECORDS – 1916-46. 284p – 1 – 12.78 – us Baptist [240]
MOUNT PLEASANT BAPTIST CHURCH. CUMBERLAND COUNTY. KENTUCKY : CHURCH RECORDS – Sep 1850-Nov 1876 – 1 – 5.00 – us Baptist [240]
MOUNT PLEASANT BAPTIST CHURCH. NICHOLAS COUNTY. WEST VIRGINIA : CHURCH RECORDS – 1851-1907. 590p – 1 – 26.55 – us Baptist [240]
MOUNT PLEASANT BAPTIST CHURCH. PIKE COUNTY. MISSOURI (EXTINCT) : CHURCH RECORDS – 1833-1911. 460p – 1 – 20.70 – us Baptist [240]
MOUNT ROYAL / Braddon, Mary Elizabeth – British Fiction Archive: Unit 5 – 9 – uk Bell [830]
MOUNT ROYAL / Evans, Walter Norton – Montreal: J. Robinson, 1886. 02929. (Pre-1900 Canadiana) – 9 – cn C.I.H.M. [971]
MOUNT ROYAL ASSSURANCE COMPANY *see* PLANS D'ASSURANCES DE VILLES DU QUEBEC
MOUNT ROYAL STAMP NEWS *see* THE MOUNT ROYAL STAMP NEWS
THE MOUNT ROYAL STAMP NEWS – (Merged with: The Jubilee Philatelist. Merged to become: The Jubilee Philatelist and Mount Royal Stamp News) – Montreal: Holmes Stamp and Pub. Co, [1900] – 9 – cn C.I.H.M. [760]
THE MOUNT ROYAL STAMP NEWS *see* THE JUBILEE PHILATELIST
MOUNT SALEM BAPTIST CHURCH. NEWARK, MISSOURI : CHURCH RECORDS – 1877-1946 – 1 – 17.37 – us Baptist [240]
MT. SCOTT HERALD – Lents OR. Feb 19 1914-Aug 22 1918 – 1 – us U.O. Library [071]
MOUNT SCOTT HERALD – Portland OR. Aug 29 1918-Apr 29 1923 – 1 – us U.O. Library [071]
MOUNT SCOTT NEWS – Portland, OR. -w. 30 Nov 1911-19 Dec 1913. – 1 – us U.O. Library [071]
MOUNT SHASTA HERALD – Mt Shasta, CA. 1887-92; 1922-82; 1983- – 41+ r – 1 – $2,050.00 ($90.00y) – B02495 – us Library Micro [071]
MOUNT SINAI JOURNAL OF MEDICINE – (v.46-. 1979- 5,6,9) – v.37-. 1970- – 1 – us UMI [073]
MOUNT ST HELENS NEWSPAPER MICROFILM AND INDEX – ($35.00; 1) – Compilation of diverse newspaper coverage of the 1980 volcanic eruptions and resultant impacts on surrounding regions. Articles from over 80 newspapers (local, national, and international) dated Mar 1980-Jan 1981. Newspaper microfilm on 12 reels; index on 32 fiches – 9 – $240.00 – us U.W. Libraries [550]
MOUNT ST HELENS NEWSPAPER MICROFILM AND INDEX – (Provides access to a part of the U.W. Libraries' extensive collection. An extensive index to the microfilm set is available on microfiche. A reel guide and description of the indexing project is included with the index) – 1,9 – 12r $240.00 1; 32mf $35.00 9 – us U.W. Libraries [071]
MOUNT UNION BAPTIST CHURCH. RIVERSIDE BAPTIST ASSOCIATION. CLARKRANGE, TENNESSEE : CHURCH RECORDS – 1870-1941 – 1 – 7.38 – us Baptist [240]
MOUNT UNION TIMES – Mount Union, PA. -w 1889-1967 – 13 – $25.00r – us I.M.R. [071]
MOUNT VERNON BAPTIST CHURCH. BUTTS COUNTY. GEORGIA : CHURCH RECORDS 1878-1916 – 1 – 23.22 – us Baptist [240]
MOUNT VERNON BAPTIST CHURCH. RALEIGH ASSOCIATION. WAKE COUNTY. NORTH CAROLINA : CHURCH RECORDS – 1840-59 – 1 – 6.75 – us Baptist [240]
MOUNT VERNON GAZETTE – Mount Vernon. Ohio. -w. 1831-35. Incomplete – 1 – us Western Res [071]
Mount Vernon, Maine. Particular Baptist Church *see* RECORDS
MOUNT WASHINGTON 1745-1903 – (mf ed 1988) – 28mf – 9 – 0-87623-079-6 – us Holbrook [920]
MOUNT WILSON SOLAR OBSERVATORY / Carnegie Institution. Washington – v. 1-21. 1905-1935 – 1,5,6 – us Princeton Micro [520]
MOUNT ZION BAPTIST CHURCH. COLUMBUS, GEORGIA : CHURCH RECORDS – 1868-1961 – 1 – 41.20 – us Baptist [240]
MOUNT ZION BAPTIST CHURCH. FAIRFIELD COUNTY. SOUTH CAROLINA : CHURCH RECORDS – October 1964-1983 – 1 – $31.95 – us Baptist [240]
MOUNT ZION BAPTIST CHURCH. HARTFORD, TENNESSEE : CHURCH RECORDS – 1889-1936 – 1 – 10.53 – us Baptist [240]
MOUNT ZION BAPTIST CHURCH. SNELLVILLE, GEORGIA : CHURCH RECORDS – Jul 1853-Feb 1932; 1974-77 – 1 – 59.72 – us Baptist [240]
MT. ZION UNITED METHODIST CHURCH – Arlington, Ohio. 1886-1915 – 1 reel – 1 – us Archival [240]
Mt. Zion United Methodist Church (Arlington, Ohio) *see* RECORDS
A MOUNTAIN BOY'S LIFE STORY *see* MISCELLANEOUS BOOKS AND PAMPHLETS
MOUNTAIN BREEZE – Frazier Park. Calif. 1950-1954 – 1 – us UMI [071]
MOUNTAIN BROOK BAPTIST CHURCH. BIRMINGHAM, ALABAMA : CHURCH RECORDS – 1944-63 – 1 – 32.49 – us Baptist [240]
MOUNTAIN CHAMPION – Belmont, NV. 1868-69 – 1r – 1 – $50.00 – U04416 – us Library Micro [071]
MOUNTAIN COURIER – Crestline, CA. 1980-90 – 11r – 1 – $550.00 – R02152 – us Library Micro [071]
MOUNTAIN CREEK BAPTIST CHURCH. ANDERSON COUNTY. SOUTH CAROLINA : CHURCH RECORDS – 1798-1981; Building Committee Book 1869-1870 – 1 – $30.33 – us Baptist [240]
MOUNTAIN CREEK BAPTIST CHURCH. EDGEFIELD COUNTY. SOUTH CAROLINA : CHURCH RECORDS – (162p) – 1971-1989 – 1 reel – 1 – $7.29 – us Baptist [240]
MOUNTAIN CREEK BAPTIST CHURCH. GREENVILLE COUNTY. GREENVILLE, SOUTH CAROLINA : CHURCH RECORDS – 1831-37, 1837-1952, 1952-74. (32 reels) – 1 – 262.49 – us Baptist [240]
MOUNTAIN CREEK BAPTIST CHURCH. GREENWOOD COUNTY. SOUTH CAROLINA : CHURCH RECORDS – 1910-58.217p – 1 – 9.77 – us Baptist [240]
MOUNTAIN DAILY (KATOOMBA) – Jul 26 1919-Feb 7 1920 – 9 – at Pascoe [072]
MOUNTAIN DEMOCRAT – Auburn. Calif. 1910-1941 – 1 – us UMI [071]
MOUNTAIN DEMOCRAT – LaGrande OR. July 9 1870 + – 1 – us U.O. Library [071]
MOUNTAIN DEMOCRAT – Placerville. Calif. -w., sw. 1854-70, 1872-84, 1886-1900, 1909-13, 1915-32, 1936-1940- – 1 – us UMI [071]
THE MOUNTAIN DEMOCRAT – Placerville, CA. 1871-72; 1900-05; 1942- – 142+ r – 1 – $7,100.00 ($250.00y) – C02630 – us Library Micro [071]
MOUNTAIN ECHO – Keyser. West Virginia. 1963-1965 – 1 – us UMI [071]

THE MOUNTAIN ECHO – Mount Holly Springs, PA. -w 1889-1904. 4 rolls – 13 – $25.00r – us I.M.R. [071]
THE MOUNTAIN ECHO NEWSPAPER – Yellville, AR. 5 Mar 1886-3 Nov 1927. V10-0001 to V10-0006 – 1 – us A.G.L.L. [071]
MOUNTAIN HERALD – Yreka, CA. 1853-54 (scats) – 1r – 1 – $50.00 – B03580 – us Library Micro [071]
THE MOUNTAIN HOTELMAN – Ellenville. N.Y. 1930-33 – 1 – us A.J.P.C. [071]
MOUNTAIN ILLNESS SYMPTOMOLOGY ON MOUNT MCKINLEY, ALASKA : EFFECT OF RATE OF ASCENT AND MAXIMUM ALTITUDE / Moe, Frank R – University of North Carolina at Chapel Hill, 1995 – 1mf – 9 – $4.00 – PH1470 – us Microform Publ [612]
MOUNTAIN LIFE AND WORK – 1925- 1; 1971- 5,6; 1977- 4 x 6 in. 9 – us UMI [073]
MOUNTAIN MAGIC – Reno, NV. 1947-1948 – 1r – 1 – $50.00 – U04882 – us Library Micro [071]
MOUNTAIN MESSENGER – Downieville, CA. 1865-66; 1872-1977 – 39r – 1 BC02179 – $1,950.00 – us Library Micro [071]
MOUNTAIN MESSENGER – Downieville. Calif. -w. 1953-67 – 1 – us UMI [071]
MOUNTAIN MESSENGER : NEVADA COUNTY EDITION – Nevada City, CA. May 1979-Aug 1980; Apr 1981-1986 – 8r – 1 – $400.00 – B02517 – us Library Micro [071]
MOUNTAIN MIRROR – Bluefield. West Virginia. 1951-1953 – 1 – us UMI [071]
MOUNTAIN NEWS AND MOUNTAINEER – Lake Arrowhead, CA. 1987 – 5+ r – 1 – $300.00 ($50.00y) – R04042 – us Library Micro [071]
MOUNTAIN NEWS AND VIEWS / Kentucky Baptist Convention – Oct 1957-79. Publ. by Kentucky Baptist Mountain Missions – 1 – 20.68 – us Baptist [240]
MOUNTAIN PRESS – Bass Lake, CA. 5 Jan 1977-1978 – 2r – 1 – $100.00 – B02050 – us Library Micro [071]
MOUNTAIN PRESS – Prather, CA. Jan 1977-85 – 9r – 1 – $450.00 – B02649 – us Library Micro [071]
MOUNTAIN RESEARCH IN EUROPE : AN OVERVIEW OF MAB RESEARCH FROM THE PYRENEES TO SIBERIA – 1995 – 230p – 9 – 92-3-103050-7 – Co-publ with Parthenon/UNESCO Publishing – fr UNESCO [550]
MOUNTAIN SENTINEL – La Grande and Union, OR. 1872-77, 1881, 1883, 1886. Incomplete – 1 – 17.00 – us Oregon Hist [071]
MOUNTAIN SENTINEL – LaGrande. Or. 1872-1886 – 1 – us UMI [071]
MOUNTAIN SENTINEL – LaGrande OR. Nov 22 1873-Jan 1 1876, June 8 Dec 14 1872 – 1 – us U.O. Library [071]
MOUNTAIN SENTINEL – Union OR. Jan 3 July 10 Oct 23 1880, Dec 14 1886 + – 1 – us U.O. Library [071]
MOUNTAIN SENTINEL – Union, OR. -w. 2 May 1868-11 Dec 1886; 19 Feb, 12 Aug-30 Dec 1876; 7 July 1877-29 Dec 1877; 5 Jan-29 June 1878 – 1r – us U.O. Library [071]
MOUNTAIN SPRINGS BAPTIST CHURCH. PIEDMONT, SOUTH CAROLINA : CHURCH RECORDS – 1860-Jul 1923 – 1 – 37.80 – us Baptist [240]
MOUNTAIN STATES BANKER – v. 36-40. 1951-55 – 1 – us UMI [336]
MOUNTAIN TRIBUNE – Bieber, CA. 1881-1892 – 3r – 1 – $150.00 – C03584 – us Library Micro [071]
THE MOUNTAIN VIEW – Mountain View, CA. Jan-Dec 1961 – 1r – 1 – $50.00 – B02500 – us Library Micro [071]
MOUNTAIN VIEW BAPTIST CHURCH. PICKENS COUNTY. PICKENS, SOUTH CAROLINA : CHURCH RECORDS – 1941-77 – 1 – 31.32 – us Baptist [240]
MOUNTAIN VIEW HERALD – Mountain View, CA. 1964-65 – 3r – 1 – $150.00 – B02499 – us Library Micro [071]
MOUNTAIN VIEW NEWS HERALD – Mountain View, CA. 1969-70 – 2r – 1 – $100.00 – B02501 – us Library Micro [071]
MOUNTAINEER – Alsea, OR. -sm. 7 Nov 1914-3 Jun 1915. 1 roll – 1 – us U.O. Library [071]
MOUNTAINEER – Big Bear, CA. Apr 1933-Nov 1938 – 1r – 1 – $50.00 – R02063 – us Library Micro [071]
MOUNTAINEER – Choteau. Mont. 1892-1901; 1904-1905; 1913-1924 – 1 – us UMI [071]
MOUNTAINEER – The Dalles OR. Feb 29 1860 – 1 – us U.O. Library [071]
THE MOUNTAINEER – Big Sandy. Mont. -w. 1966 – 1 – us UMI [071]
MOUNTAINEER HERALD – Ebensburg. Pa. -w. 1959- – 1 – us UMI [071]
THE MOUNTAINEER HERALD – Ebensburg, PA. -w 1972-81; 1977-1981. 9 rolls – 13 – $25.00r – us I.M.R. [071]
MOUNTAINEER TRADER – Parsons. West Virginia. 1964-1966 – 1 – us UMI [071]
Mountain-Plains Library Association *see*
– MPLA NEWSLETTER
– QUARTERLY
MOUNTAIN-PLAINS LIBRARY QUARTERLY – (See now: Mountain-Plains Library Association Quarterly) – v1-17 1956-73 1; v15-17 5,6 – us UMI [020]
Mountford, William *see* EUTHANASY, OR, HAPPY TALK TOWARDS THE END OF LIFE
Mountmorres, William Geoffrey Bouchard de Montmorency *see* THE CONGO INDEPENDENT STATE
MOUNTVILLE BAPTIST CHURCH. LAURENS COUNTY. SOUTH CAROLINA : CHURCH RECORDS – (Also, WMU Records, 1916-1932. 698p) – 1892-1988 – 1 reel – 1 – $31.41 – us Baptist [240]
Mouravieff, AN *see* A HISTORY OF THE CHURCH OF RUSSIA
Mourbhunj, Sri Ram Chandra Bhanja Deo *see* THEISM
Mourgue, Jacques Antoine *see* ESSAI DE STATISTIQUE
Mourgues, Le P Michel *see* TRAITE DE LA POESIE FRANCAISE
Mouric, Rene *see* LE CODE DU TRAVAIL MALGACHE
MOURNE OBSERVER – Newcastle, Co. Down, Ireland. 8 Oct 1949-Dec 1977. -w. 26 reels – 1 – uk British Libr Newspaper [072]
THE MOURNING BRIDE : A TRAGEDY / Congreve, W – London, [1720] – 1mf – 9 – ne IDC [820]
MOUSAION – v. 1-100. 1955-72 – 1 – us UMI [020]
Mousinho, Manuel de Abreu *see* BREVE DISCURSO EM QUE SE CONTA A CONQUISTA DO REINO DO PEGU
Mousnier, Roland *see* URBAN LIFE UNDER THE OLD REGIME
LE MOUSQUETAIRE – Journal de M. Alexandre Dumas. Paris. nov 1853-fevr 1857 – 1 – fr A.C.R.P.P. [073]
LE MOUSQUETAIRE ET L'ECHO DE LAVAL : JOURNAL OFFICIEL DES ETUDIANTS DE LAVAL – Quebec. v1 n6. 24 nov 1917-v2 n10. 30 dec 1918 – 1r – 1 – Can$45.00 – cn Can Microfilming [072]
MOUSSA ET GI-GLA : HISTOIRE DE DEUX PETITS NOIRS / Sonolet, L – Paris: A Colin, 1946 – us Res Libr [960]
Moussa, P *see* LES CHANCES ECONOMIQUES DE LA COMMUNAUTE FRANCO-AFRICAINE
MOUSSES / Renauld, F & Cardot, J – From: Grandidier, A. Historie physique. v. 39. 1915. B-5936R 2 – 8 – ne IDC [580]
Mousset, Louis Marie *see* DICTIONNAIRE TAMOUL-FRANCAIS
Mousson, J R A *see*
– DIE LAND- UND SUESSWASSER-MOLLUSKEN VON JAVA
– REVISION DE LA FAUNE MALACOLOGIQUE DES CANARIES
Moustier, M *see* EXPEDITION C. A. VERMINCK
MOUTAKID *see* EL-MOUTAKID
Moutie, A *see* CARTULAIRE DE L'ABBAYE DE NOTRE DAME DES VAUX DE GERNAY
Mouton, Eugenio *see* EL LIBRO JAPONES
LE MOUTON: TRAITE PRATIQUE SUR L'ELEVAGE DES MOUTONS EN CANADA / Casgrain, Eugene – Ste. Anne de la Pocatiere, Quebec: Gazette des campagnes, 1879. 00514. (Pre-1900 Canadiana) – 9 – cn C.I.H.M. [636]
Moutonnet de Clairfons, Julien-Jacques *see*
– LES ILES FORTUNEES, OU LES AVENTURES DE BATHYLLE ET DE CLEOBULE, PAR M.M.D.C.A.S
– LE VERITABLE PHILANTHROPE, OU L'ISLE DE LA PHILANTHROPIE, SUIVIE DE LA BONNE MERE, DE LA PROMENADE SOLITAIRE, DU SOMMEIL ET DE LA TOILETTE DE VENUS. PRECEDE D'ANECDOTES ET DE DETAILS PEU CONNUS SUR J. J. ROUSSEAU
LE MOUVEMENT – Revue mensuelle, artistique et sociale. Dir. Maurice Magre. no. 1-9. Paris. mars 1906-janv 1907 – 1 – fr A.C.R.P.P. [073]
MOUVEMENT : REVUE DE LA FEDERATION D'EDUCATION PHYSIQUE ET DE RECREATION DU QUEBEC – Quebec: Association des professionnels de l'activite physique. v1-11. 1966-1976. SEM35P143 – 1r – 1 – Can$70.00 – cn Bibl Nat [790]
MOUVEMENT BURKINABE DES DROITS DE L'HOMME ET DES PEUPLES = BURKINA MOVEMENT OF HUMAN AND PEOPLES' RIGHTS – Ouagadougou. 8 docs. 1990-1991 – 2mf – 9 – ne IDC [320]
LE MOUVEMENT CATHOLIQUE – Trois-Rivieres [Quebec]: P V Ayotte, [1898-1900] – 9 – cn C.I.H.M. [240]
Mouvement Croix de Feu *see* LE FLAMBEAU DES ANCIENS COMBATTANTS DE L'AVANT
MOUVEMENT DE LA POPULATION / Bulgaria – 1881-1945 46. (1940-41 wanting) – 1 – 240.00 – us L of C Photodup [949]
LE MOUVEMENT DE LA POPULATION ET SES CONDITIONS ECONOMIQUES / Denis, Hector – Bruxelles: Hayez, 1897. 1 fiche. (Statistics Series: Demography). (Economics Collection) – 9 – 6.00 – fr Bibl Nationale [310]
LE MOUVEMENT DOCTRINALE DU 19E AU 14E SIECLE (13) – Paris, 1951 – Dfl46.00 – ne Slangenburg [240]
Mouvement Frontiste *see* FRONT COMMUN
LE MOUVEMENT GEOGRAPHIQUE – Brussels, Belgium. -w. 6 April 1884-16 Aug 1914; 5 Jan 1919-31 Dec 1922. 14 reels – 1 – uk British Libr Newspaper [949]
LE MOUVEMENT GEOGRAPHIQUE – Bruxelles: Institut national de geographie. v1-3 1884-1886 (lacks v3 n13); [v5-14, 16-18,31] 1888-1897, 1899-1901, 1914 – us Res Libr [900]
LE MOUVEMENT GEOGRAPHIQUE : A POPULAR JOURNAL OF GEOGRAPHICAL SCIENCES – Brussels, Belgium. 1884-1922. With printed Introduction and Finding List – 10r – 1 – £400.00 – uk Altair [960]
LE MOUVEMENT MACEDONIEN – Red. en chef Simon Radeff. no. 1-24. Paris. 20 avr 1902-5 mai 1903 – 1 – fr A.C.R.P.P. [073]
LE MOUVEMENT OUVRIER – Sherbrooke, Canada. avr 1939-v6 n1. oct 1944 – 1r – 1 – Can$60.00 – cn Can Microfilming [072]
MOUVEMENT OUVRIER INTERNATIONAL / Conseil International Provisoire des Syndicats Ouvriers – Bulletin. no. 1. Moscou. janv nov 1921 – 1 – fr A.C.R.P.P. [073]
Mouvement pour le Triomphe des Libertes Democratiques *see* LA NATION ALGERIENNE
Mouvement Republicain Populaire *see*
– L'EVEIL DU PEUPLE
– FORCES NOUVELLES
LE MOUVEMENT SOCIALISTE – Revue Bi-mensuelle Internationale. Paris. v. 1-35. Jan 1899-June 1914 – 1 – us NY Public [335]
LE MOUVEMENT SOCIALISTE – Revue bimensuelle internationale puis Revue de critique sociale, litteraire et artistique. no. 1-264. Paris. 1899-juin 1914 – 1 – fr A.C.R.P.P. [335]
MOUVEMENT SOCIALISTE – Paris. v1-35. 1899-1914 – 301mf – 9 – ne IDC [335]
MOUVEMENT SOCIALISTE : REVUE DE CRITIQUE SOCIALE, LITTERAIRE ET ARTISTIQUE – Paris. v1-35. 1899-1914 – 6r – 1 – us Ross [073]
Mouvement Socialiste International *see* LA NOUVELLE REVUE SOCIALISTE
MOUVEMENTS DE POPULATIONS ET PROJETS DE DEVELOPPEMENT DES ECONOMIES RURALES DE LA HAUTE-GAMBIE / Toure, O – Etude de la region du Wuuli – 6mf – 9 – F90.00 – fr Ethnologie [306]
MOUVEMENTS MIGRATOIRES ET DEVELOPPEMENT ECONOMIQUE DANS LA ZONE DENSE A L'OUEST DE BOUAKE / Michotte, J – (Africa series). 1968 – 9 – fr Hachette [338]
Movchanovskii, BF *see* TRUDOVYE ARTELI
MOVEMENT : ANTI-PERSECUTION GAZETTE AND REGISTER OF PROGRESS – 1-2 (all publ). 1843-1845 – 6mf – 9 – $65.00 – us UPA [360]
MOVEMENT – (Cont: Bilbo) – v3-61. 1973-86 (complete) – 2r – 1 – ATLA S0820 – us A.T.L.A. [073]
MOVEMENT – London. 1843-45 – 1 – uk Microform Academic [073]
THE MOVEMENT FOR REFORM IN THE TEACHING OF RELIGION IN THE PUBLIC SCHOOLS OF SAXONY / Show, Arley Barthlow – (Includes index) – Washington: Government Printing Office, 1910 – 1mf – 9 – 0-8370-7588-2 – 1986-1588 – us A.T.L.A. [370]
THE MOVEMENT TOWARDS CATHOLIC REFORM IN THE EARLY XVI CENTURY / Jourdan, George V – London: J. Murray, 1914 – 1mf – us A.T.L.A. [240]
MOVEMENTS OF RELIGIOUS THOUGHT IN BRITAIN DURING THE NINETEENTH CENTURY / Tulloch, John – (St. Giles' lectures 5th ser.). 1885 – 1 – us A.T.L.A. [240]
MOVIE – 1962- 1; 1972- 5,6; 1975- 4 x 6 in. 9 – apply; x 6 in9 – us UMI [073]
MOVIE MAKER *see* AMATEUR CINE WORLD
MOVIE WEEKLY – v. 1-5, no. 34. 12 Feb 1921-26 Sep 1925 – 1 – 119.00 – us L of C Photodup [770]
MOVIE/TV MARKETING – 1953- 1; 1974- 5,6; 1975- 4 x 6 in. 9 – us UMI [073]
IL MOVIMENTO – Chicago, IL, 1914 – 3r – 1 – us I.H.R.C. [978]
MOVIMENTO – Camaragibe, Alagoas. 3 Jul 1889 – 1,5,6 – bl Biblioteca [072]
MOVIMENTO – Rio de Janeiro, Oct-Dec 1928 – 1,5,6 – bl Biblioteca [072]
MOVIMENTO – San Pablo, MX. 1975-1977 – 1r – $50.00 – R63575 – us Library Micro [072]
MOVIMENTO – Sao Paulo, 7 Jul 1975-31 Dec 1978 – 1,5,6 – bl Biblioteca [072]
MOVIMENTO – Sao Paulo, BL. 1975-1977 – 1r – $50.00 – R04185 – us Library Micro [072]
O MOVIMENTO : ORGAM DA ACCAO SOCIAL CATHOLICA – Cidade de Uba, 10 Aug 1910 – 1,5,6 – bl Biblioteca [072]
O MOVIMENTO – Ouro Preto, 23 Jan 1889-5 May 1892 – 1,5,6 – bl Biblioteca [072]
O MOVIMENTO – Villa de Contagem, 12 Oct 1915-19 Jan 1919 – 1,5,6 – bl Biblioteca [072]
MOVIMENTO BRASILEIRO – Rio de Janeiro, Jan-Sep, Nov-Dec 1929; Jan-May 1930 – 1,5,6 – bl Biblioteca [072]
MOVIMENTO DELLA POPOLAZIONE E CAUSE DI MORTE / Italy. Istituto Centrale di Statistica – v. 1-80. 1862-1941 – 1 – 246.00 – us L of C Photodup [945]
MOVIMENTO DOS TRABALHADORES RURAIS SEM TERRA = MOVEMENT OF RURAL LANDLESS WORKERS – Sao Paulo. 21 docs. 1990-1991 – 7mf – 9 – ne IDC [320]
IL MOVIMENTO INTERNAZIONALE PER L'UNIFICAZIONE DEL DIRITTO COMMERCIALE / Giannini, A – Milano, 1931 – 2mf – 1 – ILM-2954/1 – ne IDC [327]
MOVIMIENTO DE LA POBLACION DE ESPANA. ANOS 1861-1870 / Instituto Geografico – Madrid, 1877 – 9mf – 9 – sp Cultura [304]
MOVIMIENTO DE POBLACION DE BUENOS AIRES...HASTA LA FECHA – Buenos Aires, 1879 – 2mf – 9 – sp Cultura [304]
MOVIMIENTO DE POBLACION DE LA PLATA / Instituto Geografico – Buenos Aires, 1884-1890 – 3mf – 9 – sp Cultura [304]
MOVIMIENTO DE POBLACION DE LA REPUBLICA DE GUATEMALA DURANTE EL ANO DE 1881 – Guatemala, 1882 – 2mf – 9 – sp Cultura [304]
MOVIMIENTO DE POBLACIONES DE BUENOS AIRES...DE 1879 – Buenos Aires, 1880 – 3mf – 9 – sp Cultura [304]
EL MOVIMIENTO DE UNION LATINA EN EXTREMADURA / Becerro de Bengoa, Ricardo – Caceres: Imp. Vda. de Garcia Floriano, 1955 – sp Bibl Santa Ana [320]
EL MOVIMIENTO ESPANOL Y EL CRITERIO CATOLICO / Franceschi, Gustavo Juan – 3rd ed. Buenos Aires, 1937. Fiche W 890. (Blodgett Collection of Spanish Civil War Pamphlets) – 9 – us H.U. College Libr [946]
MOVING PICTURE STORIES – v. 1-35, no. 1-834. 3 Jan 1913-29 Oct 1929. Scattered nos. wanting – 1 – 220.00 – us L of C Photodup [770]
MOVING PICTURE WORLD – 1-89. 1907-27 – 1 – 1,553.00 – us L of C Photodup [770]
MOVING TO A FREE-TRADE ZONE OR A TRADE-FREE ZONE / Cuthbertson, Sandy – 1987. 1p – 9 – 1.00f – at Libertarian Micro [380]
Mowat, Oliver *see* CHRISTIANITY, AND SOME OF ITS EVIDENCES: AN ADDRESS
Mowatt *see* SIXTEEN OLD MAPS OF OXFORDSHIRE
Mowlana, Hamid *see* COMMUNICATION TECHNOLOGY AND DEVELOPMENT
Mowrey, Rebecca J *see* INCENTIVE MOTIVATION DIFFERENCES IN UNITED STATES MASTERS SWIMMERS

MOWY SWIAT – New York, N.Y., Jan-June, Sept 1920-1926, 1928-1952, Mar, Aug-Oct 1962, April 1963-Oct 1969, Jan-June 1970 – 1 – us Res Libr [071]
Moxom, Phillip Stafford *see* JESUS' VIEW OF HIMSELF IN MARK'S GOSPEL: AN INDUCTIVE STUDY
Moya, Francisco J *see* ESTUDIOS SOCIALES
MOYEN DE RENDRE LES PEUPLES LIBRES ET HEUREUX, OU, IDEES SUR LEUR EDUCATION / Simonne, Jean-Claude – Paris: Gregoire, 1791. 6787 – 9 – fr Hachette [320]
MOYENS D'APPRENDRE A COMPTER SUREMENT ET AVEC FACILITE / Condorcet, Marie Jean Antoine Nicolas de – Paris: Moutardier, 1798.ii,132p. 2 fiches. (Science Collection) – 9 – 6.00 – fr Bibl Nationale [510]
MOYENS DE RENDRE LA FRANCHE-MACONNERIE PLUS UTILE A L'HUMANITE... / Wurtz, Georges-Chr. – Paris: Onfroi, 1790 – 1 – F50.00 – fr Armell [360]
MOYENS PROPOSES A L'ASSEMBLEE NATIONALE POUR RETABLIR LA PAIX ET L'ORDRE DANS LES COLONIES / Kersaint, Armand G S – Paris. Imp. du Cercle Social. 1792 – 9 – fr Hachette [321]
MOYER SITE : A PRE-HISTORIC VILLAGE IN WATERLOO COUNTY / Wagner, Norman E et al – 1973 – vi/110p – $12.00 – 0-88920-047-5 – cn W.L.U. Press [930]
Moyer, Steve W *see* THE EFFECTS OF A "PRESCRIPTIVE INDIVIDUALIZED PROGRAM" AND A "NONPRESCRIPTIVE GROUP TASK PROGRAM" ON FUNDAMENTAL MOTOR PATTERN AND ABILILTY ACQUISITION, SELF-CONCEPT, AND SOCIALIZATION SKILLS OF KINDERGARTEN CHILDREN
Moyes, James *see* THE EXISTENCE OF GOD
Moyle, Alice *see* COMPUTERISED INDEX OF AUSTRALIAN ABORIGINAL SONGS, CAPE YORK AREA
Moyne, Pierre 1e *see* DE L'ART DES DEVISES. AVEC DIVERS RECUEILS DE DEVISES DU MESME AUTHEUR
MOYSA – Montijo, 1934 – 5 – sp Bibl Santa Ana [073]
DE MOZAISCHE OORSPRONG VAN DE WETTEN IN DE BOEKEN EXODUS, LEVITICUS EN NUMERI / Hoedemaker, Philippus J – Leiden: D.H. Daamen, 1895. 1 fiche – 9 – us A.T.L.A. [220]
MOZAISCHE OORSPRONG VAN DE WETTEN IN DE BOEKEN EXODUS, LEVITICUS EN NUMERI = DER MOSAISCHE URSPRUNG DER GESETZE: IN DEN BUECHERN EXODUS, LEVITICUS UND NUMERI / Hoedemaker, Philippus Jacobus – (In German. Includes bibliographical references) – 1mf – 9 – 0-8370-4876-1 – 1985-2876 – us A.T.L.A. [220]
MOZAMBIQUE = STATISTICAL YEARBOOK 1926-1973 : ANUARIO ESTATISTICO 1926-1973 / Mozambique. Reparticao Tecnica de Estatistica – (Coll title: African Official Statistical Serials, 1867-1982) – 290mf – 9 – £1,520.00 – uk Chadwyck [960]
Mozambique *see*
- BOLETIM OFICIAL
- PLANO DE FOMENTO (LEI NO. 2058) REVISAO DE 1955 (LEI NO. 2077)

MOZAMBIQUE (MOCAMBIQUE) – BIBLIOGRAPHY *see* BIBLIOGRAFIA GERAL DE MOCAMBIQUE
Mozambique. (Portugal). Ministerios da Economia e do Ultramar *see* PLANO DE FOMENTO (1953-1958)
Mozambique. (Portugal). Presidencia do Conselho *see* 3 PLANO DE FOMENTO PARA 1968-1973
Mozambique. Presidencia do Conselho *see* PLANO INTERCALAR DE FOMENTO PARA 1965-1967
Mozambique. Reparticao Tecnica de Estatistica *see* MOZAMBIQUE
MOZAMBIQUE REVOLUTION – [Dar-es-Salaam: Mozambique Liberation Front]. n28-57. may 1967-73 – us Res Libr [072]
THE MOZARABIC PSALTER / Gilson, J P – 1905 – 7mf – 8 – ne Slangenburg [200]
MOZART AUF DER REISE NACH PRAG : NOVELLE / Moerike, Eduard Friedrich – 9. Aufl. Leipzig: G J Goeschen, 1905 – 1r – 1 – us U.W. Library [830]
MOZART AUF DER REISE NACH PRAG : EINE NOVELLE / Moerike, Eduard Friedrich – Regensburg: G Bosse [1940] – 1r – 1 – us U.W. Library [830]
Mozart, L *see* GRONDIG ONDERWYS IN HET BEHANDELEN DER VIOOL
Mozart, Leopold *see*
- VERSUCH EINER GRUENDLICHEN VIOLINSCHULE
- VERSUCH EINER GRUENDLICHEN VIOLINSCHULE, ENTWORFEN UND MIT 4 KUPFERTAFELN SAMMT EINER TABELLE VERSEHEN VON LEOPOLD MOZART

Mozart, Wolfgang Amadeus *see*
- 10 VARIATIONEN FUER KLAVIER UEBER EIN ALLEGRETTO AUS SARTIS OPER "I FINTO EREDI"
- ANLEITUNG SO VIEL ENGL. CONTRE-DAENZE, MIT ZWEI WUERFELN ZU COMPONIEREN, SO VIEL MAN WILL
- DUET FOR TWO PERFORMERS ON ONE GRAND PIANOFORTE, [K.521]
- DUET, MOZART'S FIRST, FOR VIOLIN AND TENOR [KOECH. VERZ.423]
- FIVE PIECES SELECTED FROM THE OPERA [LA CLEMENZA DI TITO]...ADAPTED FOR THE PIANOFORTE WITH AN ACCOMPAGNEME FOR THE FLUTE BY F. FIORILLO
- GRAND CONCERT [K.414] POUR LE CLAVECIN OU FORTE PIANO, AVEC L'ACCOMPAGNEMENT DES PLUSIERS INSTRUMENTS
- KONZERT RONDO K. 386, A MAJOR
- MARCHES POUR PIANOFORTE... NOS 1-5
- MUSKALISCHE WURFELSPIELE, WALZER
- QUATUOR POUR LE CLAVECIN OU PIANOFORTE, VIOLA ET VIOLONCELLE. OEUVRE 25
- RONDO PER CLAVICEMBALO O FORTE-PIANO
- RONDO POUR LE VIOLON AVEC ACCOMPAGNEMENT DE GRAND ORCHESTRA COMPOSE PAR MOZART. OUEVRE 85ME. [K. 373]
- TROIS QUATUORS POUR FLUTE, VIOLON, ALTO ET VIOLONCELLE...OEUVRE 78

MOZART-JAHRBUCH – Muenchen. v1-3. 1923-1929 – 9mf – 9 – ne IDC [780]
MOZART-JAHRBUCH – Muenchen. v1-3. 1923-1929 – 9mf – ne IDC [780]
Mozin, Abbe *see* DICTIONNAIRE COMPLET DES LANGUES FRANCAISE ET ALLEMANDE
Mozley, Francis Woodgate *see* THE PSALTER OF THE CHURCH
Mozley, James Bowling *see*
- EIGHT LECTURES ON MIRACLES
- ESSAYS HISTORICAL AND THEOLOGICAL
- LECTURES AND OTHER THEOLOGICAL PAPERS
- THE PRIMITIVE DOCTRINE OF BAPTISMAL REGENERATION
- RULING IDEAS IN EARLY AGES AND THEIR RELATION TO OLD TESTAMENT FAITH
- A TREATISE ON THE AUGUSTINIAN DOCTRINE OF PREDESTINATION

MOZNAYIM / Hebrew Writer's Association – v. 1-41. Tel Aviv. 1933-48, 1955-76. Lacking: 1955, v. 1 (1-4); 1956, v. 2 (3-4). BJ-91-66 1 – 9 – ne IDC [470]
MOZNAYIM – v. 1-41. Tel Aviv. 1933-48, 1955-76. BJ-91-66 1 – 9 – ne IDC [470]
Mozoomdar, Protap Chunder *see* THE ORIENTAL CHRIST
MPLA *see* BOLETIM DO MILITANTE
MPLA NEWSLETTER / Mountain-Plains Library Association – v20- 1975- 1,5,6; v22- 1977- 9 – us UMI [020]
MR. AND MS – Manila. 1983-.(Series for Justice and Reconciliation). ill. -w – 1 – us U.W. Library [073]
MR. BAILLAIRGE'S ADDRESS OF WELCOME TO THE MONTREAL SECTION OF CANADIAN ARCHITECTS:...OCT 2, 1895 / Baillairge, Charles – 1895?. 05405. (Pre-1900 Canadiana) – 9 – cn C.I.H.M. [720]
MR BALDWIN'S VISIT : THE HOUSE DINNER / Gray's Inn. London. Library – 1930 – 1mf – 9 – $1.50 – LLMC 84-289 – us L.L.M.C. [340]
MR. BEMISTER'S REPORT OF THE FLOOD AT BERTHIER IN THE MONTHS OF APRIL AND MAY, 1876 / Bemister, George – Montreal, 1876. 03568. (Pre-1900 Canadiana) – 9 – cn C.I.H.M. [971]
MR. BROCKWAY'S APOLOGY TO THE REV. NATHAN S.A. BEMAN.. / Brockway, Josephus – 1827 – 1 – $50.00 – us Presbyterian [240]
MR. CAVERLEY'S SLOW MINUET : A NEW DANCE FOR A GIRL / Firbank, Mr. – London: Pemberton, 173- – 1 – us Sibley [780]
MR. CENNICKS LAID OPEN AND THE DESIGN OF THE MORAVIAN METHODISTS IN PART DISCOVER'D, IN A LETTER TO A FRIEND / McConnell, James – Dublin, 1746 – 1mf – 9 – MP-329/1 – ne IDC [240]
MR. CHESSON ON MANITOBA / Chesson, Frederick William – London: European Mail, 1872? 02990. (Pre-1900 Canadiana) – 9 – cn C.I.H.M. [971]
MR. GLADSTONE / Lathbury, D C – London: Mowbray; New York: T. Whittaker, [1905?] (Leaders of the church, 1800-1900) – 1mf – us A.T.L.A. [240]
MR. GLADSTONE : WITH APPENDIX, CONTAINING THE ACCUMULATED EVIDENCE OF FIFTY-FIVE YEARS : A RETROSPECT AND PROSPECT, WITH SUMMARY AND NOTES / Denison, George Anthony – London: William Ridgway, 1886 – 1mf – us A.T.L.A. [240]
MR GRAEME'S GLOSSARY OF WORDS AND PHRASES RELATING TO THE LAND TENURES AND LAND ASSESSMENTS OF MALABAR : WITH NOTES AND ETYMOLOGICAL HEADINGS – Madras, 1882 – us Res Libr [333]
MR. HUGHES' ATTITUDE TOWARD THE NEGRO / Hughes, Charles Evans – Camden? N.J., 1916?. 7p. LL-1211 – 1 – us L of C Photodup [340]
MR. JUSTICE BRANDEIS AND THE PROBLEMS OF LABOR / Luney, Kenneth Dean – Urbana, Ill., 1932. 5, 1 p. LL-614 – 1 – us L of C Photodup [340]
MR. PERKINS OF NOVA SCOTIA, OR, THE EUROPEAN ADVENTURES OF A WOULD-BE ARISTOCRAT / Harris, Carrie Jenkins – Windsor: J. Anslow, 1891. 05376. (Pre-1900 Canadiana) – 9 – cn C.I.H.M. [830]
MR. PISISTRATUS BROWN, M.P. IN THE HIGHLANDS / Black, William – British Fiction Archive: Unit 4 – 9 – uk Bell [830]
MR. REMI BENOIT TO THE ELECTORS OF RICHMOND, NOVA SCOTIA – 1892?. 02316. (Pre-1900 Canadiana) – 9 – cn C.I.H.M. [971]
MR. SANDDEMAN REFUTED BY AN OLD WOMAN : OR, THOUGHTS ON HIS LETTERS TO THE AUTHOR OF 'THERON AND ASPASIO'... – London, 1761 – 1mf – 9 – MP-410/1 – ne IDC [240]
MR. SPOONER'S ISLAND COMMUNITY / Stanwood, Edward – In Radical Review, p.578-581. 3 fiches (29x) – 9 – 1.00f – at Libertarian Micro [320]
MR. SWIFT, VICE-PRES. OF THE AMERICAN RED CROSS, GIVES HIS IMPRESSIONS OF REPUBLICAN SPAIN / Swift, Ernest John – n.p., n.d. Fiche W1220. (Blodgett Collection of Spanish Civil War Pamphlets) – 9 – us H.U. College Libr [946]
MR. THOMAS ATKINS / Hardy, Edward John – Toronto: W. Briggs, 1900. 05361. (Pre-1900 Canadiana) – 9 – cn C.I.H.M. [971]
MR. WESLEY'S PRINCIPLES DETECTED : OR, A DEFENSE OF THE PREFACE TO THE EDINBURGH EDITION OF 'ASPASIO VINDICATED', IN ANSWER TO MR. KERSHAW'S 'EARNEST APPEAL'... / Erskine, J – Edinburgh, 1765 – 1mf – 9 – MP-431/1 – ne IDC [240]
MR. WHITFIELD'S DOCTRINES CONSIDERED AND CONFUTED, AND SOME CONSEQUENCES DEDUCED FROM THEM WHICH TEND TO DESTROY THE ESSENTIALS OF THE CHRISTIAN RELIGION;... – Ipswich, 1741 – 1mf – 9 – MP-288/1 – ne IDC [240]
Mrochek-Drozdovskii, P N *see* MATERIALY DLIA SLOVARIA PRAVOVYKH I BYTOVYKH DREVNOSTEI PO RUSSKOI PRAVDE
Mros, M *see* A DESCRIPTION OF THE CAUSAL ATTRIBUTIONS MADE TO PERCEIVED TEACHING BEHAVIOR ACROSS THREE ELEMENTARY PHYSICAL EDUCATION CONTEXTS
Mrozinski, J *see*
- ODPOWIEDZ NA UMIESZCZONA W GAZECIE LITERACKIEJ RECENZYE DZIELA POD TYTULEM: PIERWSZE ZASADY GRAMMATYKI JEZYKA POLSKIEGO
- PIERWSZE ZASADY GRAMMATYKI JEZYKA POLSKIEGO

MRS. BLIGH: A NOVEL / Broughton, Rhoda – British Fiction Archive: Unit 4 – 9 – uk Bell [830]
MRS. DYMOND / Thackeray, Anne – British Fiction Archive: Unit 3 – 9 – uk Bell [830]
MRS. HALLIBURTON'S TROUBLES / Wood, Ellen – British Fiction Archive: Unit 1 – 9 – uk Bell [830]
MRS. HILL'S NEW COOK BOOK / Hill, A P – By the widow of Hon. Edward Y. Hill. Book used by Miss Lottie Moon – 1 – $15.75 – us Baptist [640]
MRS. OVERTHEWAYS REMEMBRANCES / Ewing, Juliana Horatia – British Fiction Archive: Unit 1 – 9 – uk Bell [830]
MRS. VAN COTT'S PRAISE BOOK / Van Cott, Maggie Newton – c1877 – 9 – us A.T.L.A. [240]
MS – v1- 1972- 1,5,6; 1975- 9 – us UMI [360]
MS 16. K16 / York Minster Library – Fifteenth century – 1 – uk Microform Academic [025]
MS. 38 / Bath. Archives (Marquess). Longleat – 1 – uk Microform Academic [025]
MS. RECORDS / Tar River Association. North Carolina – 1831-90 – 1 – 42.08 – us Baptist [240]
Mseriants, Z M *see*
- ZAKONY O PECHATI

MSL LAW REVIEW – Massachusetts School of Law: v1-3. 1993-1996 – 9 – $31.00 set – us Hein [340]
MSS. 29, 30 AND 32 / Bath. Archives (Marquess). Longleat – 1 – uk Microform Academic [025]
MSS CODICES HEBRAICI BIBLIOTH... ACCEDIT APPENDIX QUA CONTINENTUR MSS CODICES RELIQUI AL. LINGUARUM / Rossi, J B de – Parmae. 3v. 1803 – 8mf – ne IDC [470]
MSS COLLECTION IN THE A.R. WENTZ LIBRARY. (MIMEO) / Lutheran Theological Seminary – Gettysburg, PA. 1977 – 1mf – 9 – ne IDC [240]
MSS. LETTERS, 1912-50 / Wijewardene, D R – 1 – us Res Libr [950]
MSS (MANUFACTURERS STANDARDIZATION SOCIETY OF THE VALVE AND FITTINGS INDUSTRY) – Standards. Printed index. Updated every 60 days – 6,9 – us Info Handling [680]
Mstislavskii, S *see* OKTIABR'SKIE DNI
MSU BUSINESS TOPICS / Michigan State University – v1- 1953- 1; 1971- 5,6; 1975- 4 x 6 in. 9 – us UMI [380]
MT. ANGEL MAGAZINE – v1-28. 1900-27 (gaps) – 16r – 1 – ATLA S0908 – us A.T.L.A. [073]
MT. ARARAT BAPTIST CHURCH. HENDERSON COUNTY. DARDEN, TENNESSEE : CHURCH RECORDS – 1867-1965 – 1 – 18.27 – us Baptist [240]
Mt. Auburn Cemetery, Topeka, KS *see* LEDGER, MINUTES, AND BURIAL RECORDS
MT. BETHEL BAPTIST CHURCH (ALSO CALLED "BRUSHY TOP" AND "STRAWPEN"). ANDERSON COUNTY. SOUTH CAROLINA : CHURCH RECORDS – 1863-1975 – 1 – $57.29 – us Baptist [240]
MT. CARMEL BAPTIST CHURCH. CINCINNATI, OHIO : CHURCH RECORDS – 1835-1905. Incomplete. 222p – 1 – 9.99 – us Baptist [240]
MT. CARMEL BAPTIST CHURCH. PICKENS COUNTY. SOUTH CAROLINA : CHURCH RECORDS – (889p) – 1836-1979 – 1 reel – 1 – $40.00 – us Baptist [240]
MT. ELON BAPTIST CHURCH. RICHLAND COUNTY. SOUTH CAROLINA : CHURCH RECORDS – 1949-53, 1956-72. Deacons' Minutes. 1954-61 – 1 – 13.73 – us Baptist [240]
MT. HOREB BAPTIST CHURCH. WASHINGTON COUNTY. GEORGIA : CHURCH RECORDS – (108p) – Treasurer's Book. 1939-1953 – 1 reel – 1 – $5.00 – us Baptist [240]
MT. JOY BAPTIST CHURCH. UNION COUNTY. SOUTH CAROLINA : CHURCH RECORDS – 1943-Jan 1973 – 1 – 18.99 – us Baptist [240]
MT. LEBANON BAPTIST CHURCH. GIBSLAND, LOUISIANA : CHURCH RECORDS – 1835-1939 – 1 – 29.12 – us Baptist [240]
MT. MORIAH BAPTIST CHURCH. GREENWOOD COUNTY. SOUTH CAROLINA : CHURCH RECORDS – 1855-Jul 1900 – 1 – 11.34 – us Baptist [240]
MT. NEBO BAPTIST CHURCH. PILOT GROVE, MISSOURI : CHURCH RECORDS – 1829-1970 – 1 – 59.22 – us Baptist [240]
MT. NEBO BAPTIST CHURCH. TANGIPAHOA PARISH. LOUISIANA : CHURCH RECORDS – 1813-1903 – 1 – 17.19 – us Baptist [240]
MT. OLIVE BAPTIST CHURCH. COWPENS, SOUTH CAROLINA : CHURCH RECORDS – 1898-1978. Mountain View Baptist Church, 1898-1900 – 1 – 36.99 – us Baptist [240]
MT. OLIVET BAPTIST CHURCH. DARLINGTON COUNTY. SOUTH CAROLINA : CHURCH RECORDS – (462p) – 1895-1919, 1922-1930, 1958-1980 – 1 reel – 1 – $20.79 – us Baptist [240]

MT. OLIVET BAPTIST CHURCH. FLORENCE COUNTY. SOUTH CAROLINA : CHURCH RECORDS – (409p) – 1852-1879, 1883-1918, 1928-1939, 1943-1952 – 1 reel – 1 – $18.41 – us Baptist [240]

MT. OLIVET BAPTIST CHURCH. SCOTT COUNTY. MISSISSIPPI : CHURCH RECORDS – 1902-26. 88p – 1 – 5.00 – us Baptist [240]

MT. PARON PRIMITIVE BAPTIST CHURCH. CLAIBOURN PARISH. LOUISIANA : CHURCH RECORDS – 1853-81 – 1 – 8.91 – us Baptist [240]

MT. PISGAH BAPTIST CHURCH. ANDERSON COUNTY. SOUTH CAROLINA : CHURCH RECORDS – 1824-79 – 1 – 18.09 – us Baptist [240]

MT. PISGAH BAPTIST CHURCH. JEFFERSON, SOUTH CAROLINA : CHURCH RECORDS – 1837-1970 – 1 – 55.62 – us Baptist [240]

MT. PLEASANT BAPTIST CHURCH. HARTSBURG, MISSOURI : CHURCH RECORDS – 1858-1958 – 1 – 59.22 – us Baptist [240]

MT. PLEASANT BAPTIST CHURCH. LAURENS COUNTY. SOUTH CAROLINA : CHURCH RECORDS – 1860-1943 – 1 – 16.65 – us Baptist [240]

MT. PLEASANT BAPTIST CHURCH. SPARTANBURG, SOUTH CAROLINA : CHURCH RECORDS – 1919-Aug 1964 – 1 – 12.74 – us Baptist [240]

Mt. Pleasant. South Carolina. Christ (Episcopal) Church *see* RECORDS

Mt. Pleasant. South Carolina. St. Andrew's (Episcopal) Church *see* RECORDS

MT. SINAI BAPTIST CHURCH. SHELBY, NORTH CAROLINA : CHURCH RECORDS – 1848-1963 – 1 – 5.00 – us Baptist [240]

MT. SINAI BAPTIST CHURCH. STEWART COUNTY. ERIN, TENNESSEE : CHURCH RECORDS – 1946-67 – 1 – 6.39 – us Baptist [240]

MT. TABOR BAPTIST CHURCH. OCONEE COUNTY. WESTMINSTER, SOUTH CAROLINA : CHURCH RECORDS – 1884-90, 1908-12, 1951-72 – 1 – 11.34 – us Baptist [240]

MT. TABOR BAPTIST CHURCH. ORANGEBURG COUNTY. SOUTH CAROLINA : CHURCH RECORDS – 1912-38, 1955-Jan 1973 – 1 – 8.37 – us Baptist [240]

MT. ZION BAPTIST CHURCH. COLUMBUS, MISSISSIPPI : CHURCH RECORDS – 1843-1965 – 1 – 98.16 – us Baptist [240]

MT. ZION BAPTIST CHURCH. ELIZABETHTOWN, KENTUCKY : CHURCH RECORDS – 1838-1968 – 1 – 62.19 – us Baptist [240]

MT. ZION BAPTIST CHURCH (FORMERLY: AN ARM OF BETHLEHEM BAPTIST CHURCH). SPARTANBURG COUNTY. SOUTH CAROLINA : CHURCH RECORDS – 1815-1955 – 1 – 31.14 – us Baptist [240]

MT. ZION BAPTIST CHURCH (FORMERLY: WEAVER STORE). FORT CAMPBELL MILITARY BASE, TENNESSEE : CHURCH RECORDS – 1922-42 – 1 – $5.00 – us Baptist [240]

MT. ZION BAPTIST CHURCH. TRENTON, KENTUCKY : CHURCH RECORDS – 1857-98 – 1 – 11.88 – us Baptist [240]

MTS *see* MASHINNO-TRAKTORNAI A STANT SII A

MUA VA BAN – Achats et ventes. no. 1-54. Saigon. 15 juin 1927-20 sept 1929 – 1 – fr A.C.R.P.P. [073]

MU'AHEDAT MECMU'ASI – (2nd series: 1927-1931. – 27mf. $375.00) – Istanbul, 1294-1298 [1877-1881] – 5v 27mf – 9 – $375.00 – us MEDOC [949]

MUALLIM – (Mueduer-i Mes'ul: Hueseyin Ragib, Nafi Atuf[Kansu]. Nos. 1, 7, 10-21 (15 Temmuz 1332-10 Nisan 1334[1916-1918])) – Istanbul: Kader Matbaasi, Evkaf-i Islamiye Matbaasi, 1916-1918 – 9mf – 9 – $145.00 – us MEDOC [949]

MUALLIM ALMANAGI 1928-1929 – 3mf – 9 – $40.00 – us MEDOC [949]

MUALLIMLER BIRLIGI – Erzurum, 1924-19? – 9 – $10.00 – us MEDOC [956]

O MUATA CAZEMBE / Gamitto, A C P – 2v. Lisbonne, 1937. BA-161-2 – 8 – ne IDC [960]

MUBASSIR *see* AL-MUBASSIR

Mubi, S *see* FUTURE OF LIVESTOCK INDUSTRIES IN EAST AND SOUTHERN AFRICA

LES MUCEDINEES SIMPLES / Costantin, J – Histoire classification, culture et role des champignons inferieurs dans les maladies des vegetaux et des animaux. Paris. 1888 – 8 – ne IDC [590]

MUCH ADO ABOUT NOTHING : OR, ARMINIAN METHODISM TURNED OUT RANK POPERY AT LAST:... / Candid Calvinists – London, 1773 – 1mf – 9 – MP-488/1 – ne IDC [240]

MUCHACHAS EN FLOR. MADRID, 1946 / Guerrero, E & Gallardo y Gomez, Manuela – Madrid: Razon y Fe, 1947 – 1 – sp Bibl Santa Ana [946]

LOS MUCHACHOS PERONISTAS : HISTORIAS PARA CONTAR A LOS PIBES / Arbelos, Carlos & Roca, Alfredo M – Madrid: Emiliano Escolar, 1981 – 1 – CSUXADH4035-B – us Hoover Inst Photo [946]

Muckle, J T *see* ALGAZEL'S METAPHYSICS

MUCORINEAE / Zycha, H – 1935 – 7 – uk Microform Academic [580]

O MUCUM : ORGAO REPUBLICANO DANNADO – Manaos, Amazonas. 30 Maio 1895; Maio 1898 – 1,5,6 – bl Biblioteca [072]

O MUCURY – Theophilo Ottoni, 17 Nov 1901; Nov 1907; Sep 1908; Sep 1923; Dec 1926; Jan-Mar, May, Nov-Dec 1927; Dec 1929-5 Oct 1930 – 1,5,6 – bl Biblioteca [072]

Muczkowski, J *see*
- GRAMATYKA JEZYKA POLSKIEGO
- GRAMMATYKA JEZYKA POLSKIEGO

Mudd, W *see* A MANUAL OF BRITISH LICHENS

Mudge, Isadore Gilbert *see* A THACKERAY DICTIONARY

MUDGEE GUARDIAN – Jan 6 1899-Dec 30 1909 – 9 – at Pascoe [072]

MUECAHEDE-I MILLIYE – Sivas. No. 36 (20 Tesrinisani 1338 [1922]), 40 (15 Mart 1339 [1923]), 40 (19 Nisan 1339 [1923]), 41 (6 Mayis 1339 [1923]) – 9 – $20.00 – us MEDOC [956]

Muecke, Albert *see*
- DIE DOGMATIK DES NEUNZEHNTEN JAHRHUNDERTS
- GESCHICHTE DER DEUTSCHEN EVANGELISCHEN SYNODE VON NORD-AMERIKA

Muegge, Theodor *see* DIE FREIEN BAUERN

Muehlau, Ferdinand *see*
- BESITZEN WIR DEN URSPRUENGLICHEN TEXT DER HEILIGEN SCHRIFT?
- DE PROVERBIORUM QUAE DICUNTUR AGURI ET LEMUELIS ORIGINE ATQUE INDOLE HENRICUS FERDINANDUS MUEHLAU

Muehlbach, Luise *see* PRINZ, ODER, SCHLOSSERGESELLE

Muehlbauer, Manfred *see* RECHTLICHE UND POLITISCHE ASPEKTE DES GRUNDWASSERSCHUTZES IN DER BUNDESREPUBLIK DEUTSCHLAND

Muehleisen, Wilhelm *see* UNTERSUCHUNGEN UBER DIE VERWANDTSCHAFT DER UBERLIEFERUNGEN VON BARBOUR'S BRUCE

Muehlen, Hermynia zur *see*
- ENDE UND ANFANG
- DAS RIESENRAD

MUEHLENBERGIA : A JOURNAL OF BOTANY... / ed by Heller, A A – Los Gatos. v1-9. 1900/1906-1915 – 32mf – 9 – ne IDC [580]

Muehlher, Robert *see* KLEISTS UND ADAM MUELLERS FREUNSCHAFTSKRISE

Muehlpfordt, Herbert Meinhard *see* KOENIGSBERGER SKULPTUREN UND IHRE MEISTER 1255-1945

MUEKALEME-I MAZBATASI ICMAL-I SEBEB-I ZUHUR SEFER-I MOSKO VE NEMCE – Istanbul: Matbaa-i Takvimhane-i Amire, 1273 [1857] – $200.00 – us MEDOC [956]

MUEKEMMEL VE MUFASSAL TUERKIYE CUMHURIYETI ATLASI / Ruesdi, Mehmed & Abduelkadir, Mehmed – Istanbul: 1928 – $65.00 – us MEDOC [956]

Muela Ezquerra, Julian *see* LA FARSA MEDIEVAL EN FRANCIA

Muela, Jose de la *see* DISCURSO...CURSO

Muelberger, Arthur *see* P.J. PROUDHON, LEBEN UND WERKE

MUELHAUSER ARBEITERFREUND – Colmar, France. 1890-1914 – 1 – fr A.C.R.P.P. [072]

MUELHAUSER TAGBLATT – (Ausgabe Altkirch) – Altkirch, mar 11 1942-nov 15 1944 – 1 – Dist. gw Mikrofilm – fr A.C.R.P.P. [944]

MUELHAUSER TAGBLATT – Mulhouse, France. 1884-1944 – 1 – fr A.C.R.P.P. [072]

MUELHAUSER VOLKSZEITUNG – Mulhouse, France. 1904-18 – 1 – fr A.C.R.P.P. [072]

MUELHEIMER ZEITUNG *see* WESTDEUTSCHE ALLGEMEINE ZEITUNG (WAZ)

MUELKIYE – (Nesreden: Muelkiye Mektebi Mezumlari Ittihad ve Teavvuen Cemiyeti, Mueduerue: Ali Resad. Nos. 5 (1 Haziran 1325[1909], 17 (1 Haziran 1326[1910])) – Istanbul: Matbaa-i Ahmed Ihsan ve Suerekasi, Matbaa-i Kader, 1908-1911 – 2mf – 9 – $30.00 – us MEDOC [949]

Mueller, Adam *see* VON DER NOTHWENDIGKEIT EINER THEOLOGISCHEN GRUNDLAGE DER GESAMMTEN STAATSWISSENSCHAFTEN UND DER STAATSWIRTHSCHAFT INSBESONDRE

Mueller, Adolf *see*
- ENTWICKELUNGSGEDANKE UND GOTTESERFAHRUNG
- JOHANN JAKOB VON WILLEMER

Mueller, Andreas *see* ONTOGENESE DES STOFFWECHSELS UND DER TEMPERATURREGULATION BEI DER NORDAFRIKANISCHEN DICKSCHWANZMAUS PACHYUROMIS DUPRASI

Mueller, Curt *see* GRILLPARZERS "AHNFRAU" UND DIE WIENER VOLKSDRAMATIK

Mueller, David Heinrich *see*
- DIE ALTSEMITISCHEN INSCHRIFTEN VON SENDSCHIRLI IN DEN KOENIGLICHEN MUSEEN ZU BERLIN
- EZECHIEL-STUDIEN

Mueller, Eberhard Johannes *see* AUGUSTINS LEHRE VON DER EINHEIT UND DREIEINHEIT IN IHRER BEDEUTUNG FUER SEIN UND ERKENNEN

Mueller, Ernst *see*
- DER BAUERN-SPIEGEL
- DER BAUERN-SPIEGEL, ODER, LEBENSGESCHICHTE DES JEREMIAS GOTTHELF
- DER HERZOG UND DAS GENIE
- SCHILLERS MUTTER

Mueller, Ernst Friedrich Karl *see*
- SYMBOLIK
- ZUR CHRISTLICHEN ERKENNTNIS

Mueller, Eugen *see*
- GEDICHTE DER GEBRUEDER WOLF
- STRASSBURGER THEOLOGISCHE STUDIEN

Mueller, F A *see* BRIEFE UEBER DIE CHRISTLICHE RELIGION

Mueller, Ferdinand Jakob Heinrich von *see*
- ANALYTICAL DRAWINGS OF AUSTRALIAN MOSSES
- CENSUS OF THE GENERA OF PLANTS HITHERTO KNOWN AS INDIGENOUS TO AUSTRALIA
- CONTRIBUTIONS TO THE PHYTOGRAPHY OF AUSTRALIA
- DEFINITIONS OF RARE OR HITHERTO UNDESCRIBED AUSTRALIAN PLANTS
- DESCRIPTION AND ILLUSTRATIONS OF THE MYOPORINOUS PLANTS OF AUSTRALIA. 2. LITHOGRAMS
- DESCRIPTION OF AN UNRECORDED ARDISIA OF NEW GUINEA
- DESCRIPTIVE NOTES ON PAPUAN PLANTS
- ESSAY ON THE PLANTS COLLECTED BY MR. EUGENE FITZALAN
- EUCALYPTOGRAPHIA. A DESCRIPTIVE ATLAS OF THE EUCALYPTS OF AUSTRALIA AND THE AJOINING ISALNDS. DECAS I-X
- FIRST GENERAL REPORT OF THE GOVERNMENT BOTANIST ON THE VEGETATION OF THE BOTANY OF VICTORIA
- FRAGMENTA PHYTOGRAPHIAE AUSTRALIAE
- GEOLOGICAL SURVEY OF VICTORIA. OBSERVATIONS ON NEW VEGETABLE FOSSILS OF THE AURIFEROUS DRIFTS
- DAS GROSSE ILLUSTRIERTE KRAEUTERBUCH
- ICONOGRAPHY OF AUSTRALIAN SALSOLACEOUS PLANTS
- ICONOGRAPHY OF AUSTRALIAN SPECIES OF ACACIA AND COGNATE GENERA
- ICONOGRAPHY OF CANDOLLEACEOUS PLANTS
- ILLUSTRATED DESCRIPTION OF THISTLES
- INDEX PERFECTUS AD CAROLI LINNAEI SPECIES PLANTARUM...
- INDUSTRIAL PLANTS DESERVING CULTURE IN THE COLONY OF VICTORIA
- KEY TO THE SYSTEM OF VICTORIAN PLANTS
- LECTURE ON THE FLORA OF AUSTRALIA
- THE NATIVE PLANTS OF VICTORIA SUCCINCTLY DEFINED
- THE NATURAL CAPABILITIES OF THE COLONY OF VICTORIA, CONSIDERED IN REFERENCE TO INDIGENOUS OR INTRODUCED VEGETATION
- NOTES SUR LA VEGETATION INDIGENE ET INTRODUITE DE L'AUSTRALIE
- ON THE ADVANCEMENT OF THE NATURAL SCIENCES THROUGH MINISTERS OF THE CHRISTIAN CHURCH
- ON THE APPLICATION OF PHYTOLOGY TO THE INDUSTRIAL PURPOSES OF LIFE
- ON THE SYSTEMATIC POSITION OF THE NARDOO PLANT AND THE PHYSIOLOGICAL CHARACTERISATION OF ITS FRUIT
- OTTELIA PRAETERITA
- THE PLANTS INDIGENOUS AROUND SHARKS BAY AND ITS VICINITY
- REPORT FOR THE YEAR ENDING 30TH
- REPORT ON THE PLANTS, COLLECTED DURING MR. BABBAGES' EXPEDITION INTO THE N.W. INTERIOR
- SELECT PLANTS READILY ELIGIBLE FOR INDUSTRIAL CULTURE OR NATURALISATION IN VICTORIA, WITH INDICATIONS OF THEIR NATIVE COUNTRIES AND SOME OF THEIR USES

Mueller, Franz Karl Friedrich *see* DER RING DES NIBELUNGEN

Mueller, Frederick O *see* THE ECONOMIC IMPACT OF DEAN E. SMITH ACTIVITIES CENTER EVENTS ON CHAPEL HILL, NORTH CAROLINA

Mueller, Friedrich Max *see*
- THE BHAGAVADGITA, WITH THE SANATSUGATIYA AND THE ANUGITA
- BUDDHIST SUTTAS
- BUDDIST MAHAYANA TEXTS
- DEUTSCHE LIEBE
- THE DHAMMAPADA
- THE FO-SHO-HING-TSAN-KING
- GAINA-SUTRAS
- THE GAINA-SUTRAS
- THE GRIHYA-SUTRAS, RULES OF VEDIC DOMESTIC CEREMONIES
- HYMNS OF THE ATHARVA-VEDA
- THE INSTITUTES OF VISHNU
- THE MAHAPARINIBBANA SUTTANTA
- MANU
- THE MINOR-LAW-BOOKS
- ON MISSIONS: A LECTURE
- PAHLAVI TEXTS
- PHLAVI TEXTS
- THE QUESTIONS OF KING MILINDA
- THE QUR'AN
- THE SACRED BOOKS OF CHINA
- THE SACRED BOOKS OF CHINA. THE TEXTS OF CONFUCIANISM
- THE SACRED BOOKS OF CHINA. THE TEXTS OF TAOISM
- THE SACRED BOOKS OF THE EAST
- THE SACRED LAWS OF THE ARYAS, AS TAUGHT IN THE SCHOOLS OF APASTAMBA, GAUTAMA, VASISHTHA AND BAUDHYANA
- THE SACRED LAWS OF THE ARYAS, AS THAUGHT IN THE SCHOOLS OF APASTAMBA, GAUTAMA, VASISHTA AND BAUDHAYANA
- THE SADDHARMA-PUNDARIKA; OR THE LOTUS OF THE TRUE LAW
- THE SATAPATHA-BRAHMANA
- THE SATAPATHA-BRAHMANA, ACCORDING TO THE TEXT OF THE MADHYANDINA SCHOOL
- THEOSOPHY, OR, PSYCHOLOGICAL RELIGION
- THE UPANISHADS
- THE VEDANTA-SUTRAS
- THE VEDANTA-SUTRAS, WITH RAMANUGA'S SRIBHASHYA
- THE VEDANTA-SUTRAS, WITH THE COMMENTARY BY SANKARAKARYA
- VEDIC HYMNS
- VINAYA TEXTS
- THE ZEND-AVESTA

Mueller, Friedrich von *see*
- DEUTSCHE DICHTUNG
- GOETHES PERSOENLICHKEIT

Mueller, Fritz *see* KRAMER UND FRIEMANN

Mueller, Georg *see* NIETZSCHE UND DIE DEUTSCHE KATASTROPHE

Mueller, George *see* A NARRATIVE OF SOME OF THE LORD'S DEALINGS WITH GEORGE MUELLER

Mueller, Gisela D *see* STUDIEN ZUR VORGOTISCHEN MOEBELFORM

Mueller, Gottfried Ephraim *see* GOTTFRIED EPHRAIM MUELLERS A.M. HISTORISCH-PHILOLOGISCHES SENDSCHREIBEN AN EINEN HOHEN GOENNER, VON ORGELN, IHREM URSPRUNGE UND GEBRAUCHE IN DER ALTEN UND NEUEN KIRCHE GOTTES

Mueller, Gustav Adolf *see*
- AUS LAVATERS BRIEFTASCHE
- UNGEDRUCKTES AUS DEM GEOTHE-KREISE

Mueller, Hannelore *see*
- DAS GEDOPPELTE TUN
- DER MANN UND DAS WEIB. DIE HERRSCHAFT DER DIFFERENZ. ZUR BEWUSSTSEINSGESCHICHTE VON NATUR UND GESCHLECHT

Mueller, Hans von *see*
- HEINRICH LOEST UEBER E.T.A. HOFFMANN
- DER SCHOEPFER

Mueller, Herman A *see* HISTORY OF MADISON COUNTY AND ITS PEOPLE

Mueller, Hermann *see* SCHILLERS JOURNALISTISCHE TAETIGKEIT AN DEN "NACHRICHTEN ZUM NUZEN UND VERGNUEGEN" IM JAHRE 1781

Mueller, J *see*
- MAFTEAH LI-TESHUVOT HA-GE'ONIM
- DIE RESPONSEN DER SPANISCHER LEHRER DES 10. JAHRHUNDERTS
- SYSTEM DER ASTERIDEN

Mueller, J A *see*
- DIAGNOSES LICHENUM SOCOTRENSIUM NOVORUM A PARTICIBUS EXPEDITIONUM BAYLEY BALFOUR ET SCHWEINFURTH LECTORUM
- GRAPHIDEAE FEEANAE
- LICHENES KNIGHTIANI IN NOVA ZELANDIA LECTI ADDITIS NONNULLIS ALIIS EJUSDEM REGIONES, QUOS EXPONIT
- LICHENOLOGISCHE BEITRAEGE
- LICHENS PARAGUAYENSES
- PYRENOCARPAE CUBENSES
- PYRENOCARPEAE FEEANAE
- REVISION DES GRAPHIDEES EXOTIQUES
- THEOLOTREMEAE ET GRAPHIDEAE NOVAE QUAS PRAESERTIM EX HB. REG. KEWENSIS

Mueller, Jakob *see* RECOLLECTIONS OF A 48'ER

Mueller, Joachim *see*
- GESTALTUNG, UMGESTALTUNG
- GRILLPARZERS MENSCHENAUFFASSUNG

Mueller, Joerg *see* REGULAERE UND CHAOTISCHE BEWEGUNG EINES ELEKTRONS IM WAKEPOTENTIAL EINES SCHNELLEN IONS IM FESTKOERPER

Mueller, Johann Tobias *see* DIE SYMBOLISCHEN BUECHER DER EVANGELISCH-LUTHERISCHEN KIRCHE

Mueller, Josef *see* DER REFORMKATHOLIZISMUS

Mueller, Joseph *see* DIE BISCHOEFLICHEN DIOEZESANBEHOERDEN, INSBESONDERE DAS BISCHOEFLICHE ORDINARIAT

Mueller, K A F W *see*
- DEUTSCHLANDS MOOSE
- SYNOPSIS MUSCORUM FRONDOSORUM OMNIUM HUCUSQUE COGNITORUM

Mueller, K (Kurt) *see* VERWEGENES SPIEL

Mueller, Karl *see* NEUTESTAMENTLICHE THEOLOGIE: GRUNDRISS FUER VORLESUNGEN

Mueller, Karl Friedrich *see* DIE LITERARISCHE KRITIK IN DER MITTELHOCHDEUTSCHEN DICHTUNG UND IHR WESEN

Mueller, Max *see* A HISTORY OF GERMAN LITERATURE

Mueller, Max Ludwig *see* FUER DAS VOELKERRECHT

Mueller, Nikolaus *see* GEORG SCHWARTZERDT, DER BRUDER MELANCHTHONS UND SCHULTHEISS ZU BRETTEN

Mueller, Otfried *see* DER KRIEG UND DIE INFEKTIONSKRANKHEITEN

Mueller, Otto *see* AUSGEWAEHLTE SCHRIFTEN

Mueller, Otto Frederik *see*
- ANIMALCULA INFUSORIA FLUVIATILIA ET MARINA
- ENTOMOSTRACA SEU INSECTA TESTACEA..
- FLORA FRIDRICHSDALINA

Mueller, Paula et al *see* MITTEILUNGEN DES DEUTSCH-EVANGELISCHEN FRAUENBUNDES, 1. 1900/01 - 4. 1903/04; EVANGELISCHE FRAUENZEITUNG, 5. 1904/05 - 42. 1940/41 (HQ 25)

Mueller, Peter *see* BEITRAEGE ZUR WUERDIGUNG VON KARL GUTZKOW ALS LUSTSPIELDICHTER

Mueller, Renate *see* DIE VARIANZ PHRASEOLOGISCHER WENDUNGEN UNTER BESONDERER BERUECKSICHTIGUNG DER LEXIKALISCHQUANTITAVEN VARIANTEN VON PHRASEOLOGISMEN IM RUSSISCHEN

Mueller, Thea *see* THEODOR STORMS ERZAEHLUNG "AQUIS SUBMERSUS"

Mueller, Theodor *see* DAS KONKLAVE PIUS' 4

Mueller, Ulrich *see* FORM UND GESCHICHTE

Mueller, Ulrich et al *see* NELLY SACHS BRIEFREGISTER

Mueller, Wilhelm *see* STUDIEN UEBER DIE RASSISCHEN GRUNDLAGEN DES "STURM UND DRANG"

Mueller, Wolfgang *see* DER FALL

Mueller, Wulf Dieter *see* ERNST JUENGER

Mueller-Burbach, Heinrich *see* DER LANDSTRASSE VERSCHWOREN

Mueller-Ems, Richard *see* OTTO LUDWIGS ERZAEHLUNGSKUNST

Mueller-Gangllaff, Erich *see* VORLAEUFER DES ANTICHRIST

Mueller-Guttenbrunn, Adam *see* KLEIST'S HERMANNSSCHLACHT

Mueller-Hamburg, K H *see* DER SUEZKANAL

Muelleri, C *see* FRAGMENTA HISTORICORUM GRAECORUM

Mueller-Jabusch, Maximilian *see* THERSITES

Mueller-Jahnke, Clara *see* WINTERSAAT

Mueller-Krueger, Th *see* SEDJARAH GEREDJA DI INDONESIA

Mueller-Langenthal *see* DIE GESCHICHTE UNSERES VOLKS. BILDER AUS DER VERGANGENHEIT UND GEGENWART DER DEUTSCHEN IN RUMANIEN

Muena, Zelmira Urra *see*
- ARAB-ISLAMIC BIOGRAPHICAL ARCHIVE (AIBA)
- CESKY BIOGRAFICKY ARCHIV A SLOVENSKY BIOGRAFICKY ARCHIV

Muench, Ernst *see* VOLLSTAENDIGE SAMMLUNG ALLER AELTEREN UND NEUEREN KONKORDATE NEBST EINER GESCHICHTE IHRES ENTSTEHENS UND IHRER SCHICKSALE VON ERNST MUENCH

Muench, Roger *see* JOHANN FRIEDRICH FREIHERR COTTA VON COTTENDORF (1764-1832)

MUENCHEN-AUGSBURGER ABENDZEITUNG *see* AUGSBURGER ABENDZEITUNG

MUENCHENER ALLEGEMEINE *see* BAYERISCHE LANDESZEITUNG

MUENCHENER BEOBACHTER : AUSGABE MUENCHEN – (Cont by: Voelkischer Beobachter, jan 3 1920) – Muenchen, 1932-apr 20 1945 – 51r – 1 – gw Mikrofilm [943]

MUENCHENER BEOBACHTER – Muenchen, DE. 1915-18 – 1r – 1 – DM100.00 – gw Mikro Press [072]

MUENCHENER BEOBACHTER : SUEDDEUTSCHE AUSGABE – (Cont by: Voelkischer Beobachter, jan 3 1920) – Muenchen, 1933-44 – 47r – 1 – gw Mikrofilm [943]

MUENCHENER BEOBACHTER – (Title changes to: Voelkischer Beobachter from 3 Jan 1920) – Muenchen, DE. 1915-45 – 1 – gw Mikrofilm [072]

MUENCHENER ILLUSTRIERTE – Muenchen, DE. 1952-Jun 1954 – 1 – gw Mikrofilm [072]

MUENCHENER KOLEOPTEROLOGISCHE ZEITSCHRIFT – Muenchen. v1-3. 1902-1908 – 23mf – 9 – ne IDC [590]

MUENCHENER MEDIZINISCHE WOCHENSCHRIFT – v. 92-116. 1950-74 – 1,5,6 – us Princeton Micro [610]

MUENCHENER MUSIK *see* DUR UND MOLL

MUENCHENER POST – Munich, DE. 5 June 1917-7 Aug 1919 (incomplete) – 4r – 1 – uk British Libr Newspaper [072]

MUENCHENER POST UND AUGSBURGER VOLKSZEITUNG *see* SCHWAEBISCHE VOLKSZEITUNG

MUENCHENER THEOLOGISCHE ZEITSCHRIFT – 1(1950)-6(1955) – 41mf – 9 – Dfl144.00 – ne Slangenburg [073]

MUENCHENER THEOLOGISCHE ZEITSCHRIFT – Muenchen. v1-6. 1950-1955 – 41mf – 9 – ne IDC [240]

MUENCHHAUSEN : EINE GESCHICHTE IN ARABESKEN / Immermann, Karl Leberecht – Leipzig: P Reclam jun., [18–] – 1r – 1 – us U.W. Library [830]

Muenchhausen, Boerries, Freiherr von *see* DIE BALLADEN UND RITTERLICHEN LIEDER DES FREIHERRN BOERRIES VON MUENCHHAUSEN

MUENCHHAUSENS BERICHTE UEBER SEINE MISSION NACH BERLIN IN JUNI 1740 / Frensdorf, F – Berlin, 1904 – 3mf – 8 – Dfl13.00 – ne Slangenburg [240]

Muenchmeyer, AF O *see* DAS DOGMA VON DER SICHTBAREN UND UNSICHTBAREN KIRCHE

MUENCHNER ILLUSTRIERTE PRESSE – Muenchen, dec 5 1923-jun 1928, 1929-30, 1932-feb 8 1945, feb 4 1950-60 – 46r – 1 – gw Mikrofilm [072]

MUENCHNER ILLUSTRIERTE PRESSE – Munich, DE. Apr 1933-Aug 1944; Sep 1940-Aug 1944 – 19r – 1 – uk British Libr Newspaper [072]

MUENCHNER JAHRBUCH DER BILDENDEN KUNST – Muenchen. v1-13 1906-1923; N.S. v1-13 1924-1939 – 170mf – 9 – ne IDC [700]

MUENCHNER MERKUR – Muenchen, DE. 1948- – 1 – gw Mikrofilm [072]

MUENCHNER MORGENBLATT – Muenchen, DE. 1 Jan-21 Jun 1848 – 1r – 1 – gw Mikrofilm [072]

MUENCHNER NEUESTE NACHRICHTEN – (1934-45 49r DM3,675.00) – Muenchen, 1886-1933 – 273r – 1 – DM20,475.00 – gw Mikro Press [072]

MUENCHNER NEUESTE NACHRICHTEN – (Cont by: Sueddeutsche Zeitung, Muenchen) – Muenchen, DE. Apr 1848-1849 – 4r – 1 – gw Mikrofilm [072]

MUENCHNER NEUESTE NACHRICHTEN – (Cont by: Sueddeutsche Zeitung, Muenchen) – Munich, DE. 12 May-7 Jul 1935; Jan-Dec 1936; 1, 10 Jan, 6, 17 Jun 1937-23 Jul 1939 – 2 1/2r – 1 – uk British Libr Newspaper [072]

MUENCHNER NEUSTE NACHRICHTEN – Munich. Germany. Aug. 1914-Aug. 1919 – 1 – 35.00r – us Hoover Inst Photo [072]

MUENCHNER POLITISCHE ZEITUNG – (Previously publ under various titles. Title change 1 Jul 1848: Neue Muenchner Zeitung. 14 Apr 1862: Bayerische Zeitung. 1 Jan 1869: Bayerische Landeszeitung) – Muenchen, DE. 1769-1819 – 80r – 1 – gw Mikrofilm [072]

Muenscher, Joseph *see* THE BOOK OF PROVERBS

MUENSE'AT-I 'AKIF – Bulak, 1262 – 3mf – 9 – $18.00 – us MEDOC [949]

MUENSE'AT-I 'AKIF – Istanbul, 1259 – 4mf – 9 – $24.00 – us MEDOC [949]

MUENSE'AT-I 'IZZET BEG – Istanbul, 1263 – 1mf – 9 – $6.00 – us MEDOC [949]

MUENSE'AT-I NU'MAN MAHIR BEG – Istanbul, 1261 – 2mf – 9 – $12.00 – us MEDOC [949]

MUENSE'AT-I RIF'AT EFENDI – Bulak, 1254 – 4mf – 9 – $24.00 – us MEDOC [949]

Muenster, G von *see* BEITRAEGE ZUR PETREFACTEN-KUNDE

Muenster, S *see*
- ARUK. DICTIONARIVM CHALDAICUM,...
- ARUK HAS-SORASOT. DICTIONARIVM HEBRAICVM,...
- DICTIONARIVM TRILINGVE, IN QVO SCILICET LATINIS VOCABVLIS...RESPONDENT GRAECA ET HEBRAICA
- SILLUS LESONOT. DICTIONARIVM TRILINGVE,...

MUENSTERLAENDISCHE HEIMAT *see* MUENSTERSCHE ZEITUNG

MUENSTERLAENDISCHE TAGESZEITUNG – Cloppenburg, West Germany. 1978- – ca 8r per yr – 1 – gw Mikrofilm [072]

MUENSTERLAENDISCHE VOLKSZEITUNG *see*
- VOLKS-ZEITUNG FUER RHEINE UND UMGEBUNG

MUENSTERSCHE BEITRAEGE ZUR GESCHICHTSFORSCHUNG – Paderborn. v. 1-12, 1882-88; n.s., v. 1-39, 1903-27; ser III, v. 1-24, 1933-39. Film Mas C 724 – 1 – us H.U. Library [073]

MUENSTERSCHE ZEITUNG : RHEINER ZEITUNG – (Bereichsausgabe der Muensterschen Zeitung. Partly Kreisausgaben. Filmed with suppl Muensterlaendische Heimat.) – Rheine, 1927-33 (incomplete), jul 1 1934-sep 30 1943 (incomplete), aug 5 1914-feb 28 1959 (isolated issues) – 40r – 1 – gw Mikrofilm [943]

MUENSTERSCHES TAGEBLATT – (Title change: Muensterscher Morgen-Anzeiger, 1 Jul 1878; Muenstersche Zeitung, 1 Dec 1897) – Muenster-Westf., West Germany. 1992- – 9r per yr – 1 – gw Mikrofilm [072]

MUENTAHABAT-I DIVAN-I FEVZI – np., n.d. – 1mf – 9 – $6.00 – us MEDOC [949]

MUENTAHABAT-I ES'AR-I SINASI – Istanbul, 1289 – 1mf – 9 – $6.00 – us MEDOC [949]

Muente, Ava Sinikka *see* ELEKTROPHYSIOLOGISCHE UNTERSUCHUNGEN ZUR VERARBEITUNG GRAMMATISCHER INFORMATION IN DER FINNISCHEN SPRACHE

Muentzer, T *see*
- BEKANTNUS
- PROTESTATION ODDER EMPIETUNG

Muenz, Bernhard *see* FRIEDRICH HEBBEL ALS DENKER

Muenzer, Jeronimo *see* VIAJE POR ESPANA Y PORTUGAL EN LOS ANOS 1494 Y 1495...

MUERTE DE D. FRANCISCO BARRADO Y FONT / Castaneda, Vicente – Madrid: Ed. Reus, 1922. B.R.A.H. 80. pp. 189-190 – 1 – sp Bibl Santa Ana [946]

LA MUERTE DE LUIS 16 / Cagigal, Jose – 1825 – 9 – 1.50f – sp Bibl Santa Ana [944]

MUERTE DE PEDRO DE ALVARADO. CARTAS DE RELACION DE ALVARADO A HERNAN CORTES. CARTAS ANTIGUAS A LA CIUDAD DE GOATHEMALA / Mota Padillo, Francisco – (Guatemala): Editorial Jose de Pineda Ibarra. v4. 67 – sp Bibl Santa Ana [350]

LA MUERTE, TRANSITO PASCUAL / Sanchez Aliseda, Casimiro – Madrid: PPC, 1966 – 1 – sp Bibl Santa Ana [946]

EL MUERTO RESUCITADO – 1888. No.4 – 9 – 1.50f – sp Bibl Santa Ana [072]

MUERUEVVET : FIRST SERIES – Istanbul: Mahmud Bey Matbaasi; Mueruevvet Matbasi, 1886-87. Cikaran: Ma'rufuzade Mehmed Ziyaeddin. Nos. 1-52 (28 Rebiuelahir 1304-3 Cemaziyelevvel 1305 [1886-87]) – $30.00 – us MEDOC [073]

MUERUEVVET : SECOND SERIES – Istanbul: Mahmud Bey Matbaasi; Mueruevvet Matbasi, 1888-89. Cikaran: Ma'rufuzade Mehmed Ziyaeddin. Nos. 1-406 (5 Mart 1304-2 Eyluel 1305 [1888-89]) – $75.00 – us MEDOC [073]

MUESAVAT – Izmir, 1918-1919 – 9 – $10.00 – us MEDOC [956]

Muesebeck, Ernst *see* ERNST MORITZ ARNDT

Muestak, Efendi *see* DIVAN

MUETTER : ROMAN / Waggerl, Karl Heinrich – Leipzig: Insel-Verlag, 1938 – 1r – 1 – us U.W. Library [830]

LAS MUGERES VINDICADAS DE LAS CALUMNIAS DE LOS HOMBRES / Cubie, Juan Bautista – Madrid, 1768. 138p. Libros en Microficha no 3 – 1mf – 9 – Pta1,000.00 – 84-85422-29-5 – sp Pentalfa [305]

MUGHAL EMPIRE – 1995 – 36p – 9 – 92-3-102681-X – fr UNESCO [950]

MUHADARAT – (Sahibleri: Fuad Arifi, Vessaf. Nos. 1 (1 Rebiyuelevvel 1300[1884]), 9-12) – Istanbul, 1884-1885 – 2mf – 9 – $30.00 – us MEDOC [949]

Muhammad Ghazali bin Shafie *see* CONFRONTATION; A MANIFESTATION OF THE INDONESIAN PROBLEM

Muhammad ibn Muhammad, al-Idrisi *see* DE GEOGRAPHIA VNIUERSALI

Muhammad ibn Muhammad, al-Sinhaji, called Ibn Ajurrum *see* KITAB AL-AJURRUMIYA FI L-NAHW TA'LIF AL-SHAIK AL-IMAM AL-ALLAMAH MUHAMMAD IBN DAUDAL-SINHAJI AL-SHAHIR BI AJURRUM

Muhammad Kazim *see* ALAMGIR-NAMAH

Muhammad Saqi *see* MAASIR I' ALAMGIRI

MUHAMMAD SPEAKS – Chicago, IL. 1971-75 – 7r – 1 – $350.00 – R04302 – us Library Micro [071]

MUHAMMAD SPEAKS – Chicago, IL. v1-10. 1960-71 – 8r – 1 – us Ross [071]

MUHAMMAD SPEAKS – Chicago. Ill. 1955- – 1 – us UMI [071]

MUHAMMAD, THE APOSTLE OF GOD AND HIS ASCENSION / Widengren, C – Uppsala, 1955 – 6mf – 8 – ne Slangenburg [260]

MUHARRERAT-I RESMIYYE VE GAYRI RESMIYYE / Mihri – Istanbul: Matbaasi, 1303 1887. 248p. LL-12018 – 1 – us L of C Photodup [340]

MUHARRIR – Izmir. Mueduer ve Nasiri: M. Sefik. Sermuharriri: A. Selahaddin. No. 2 (19 Mayis 1909) – 9 – $20.00 – us MEDOC [956]

Muhibbi *see* DIVAN

MUHIT-I MESAI – Selanik: Yeni Asir Matbaasi. Mueduer-i Mes'ul: Abdullah Feyzi, 1910-1911 – 9 – $25.00 – us MEDOC [956]

Muhle, H *see* DE ORIGINE LINGUARUM VARIARUM...

Muhlenberg, G H E *see* CATALOGUS PLANTARUM AMERICAE SEPTENTRIONALIS

MUHLENBERGIA – Reno, University of Nevada: v1 1900-v9 1915 – 2r – 1 – $100.00 – B06077 – us Library Micro [370]

MUHSU KORI UN DSEESMAS: LATWIJAS BAPTISTU DRAUDSCHU KORU WEHSTURES MATERIALU KRAHJUMS / Kronlins, Janis – Riga: Union of Latvian Baptist Churches, 1925. Publ. No. 6299 b. One of five items on a reel – 1 – us Baptist [240]

Muhtar, Ahmed *see* REHBER-I MUZAFFERAT-I BAHRIYE

Muir, John *see*
- JOHN MUIR PAPERS, 1858-1957
- ORIGINAL SANSKRIT TEXTS ON THE ORIGIN AND HISTORY OF THE PEOPLE OF INDIA, THEIR RELIGION AND INSTITUTIONS

Muir, William *see*
- ANNALS OF THE EARLY CALIPHATE, FROM THE ORIGINAL SOURCES
- THE CALL OF THE NEW ERA

Muirhead, J *see* A REVIEW OF THE PRINCIPLES OF SUCH METHODISTS AS ARE UNDER THE DIRECTION OF THE REV. MR. JOHN WESLEY
Muirhead, John Henry *see*
- THE ELEMENTS OF ETHICS
- PHILOSOPHY AND LIFE
Muirhead, Lewis A *see* THE ESCHATOLOGY OF JESUS, OR, THE KINGDOM COME AND COMING
Muirhead, Lewis Andrew *see* THE TIMES OF CHRIST
Muis, A *see* DOKUMEN DARI 'MALAYSIA.' SE-10,766/1. 1964
MUJAHID – (Sal-i 1: shumarah-'i 1-215 (1 Murdad 1358-18 Murdad 1363[23 Jul 1979-9 Aug 1984]). Missing issues: 112-114, 123, 133, 137-138, 146, 156) – [S.l.]: Sazman-i Mujahidin-i Khalq-i Iran, 1979- – 2r – 1 – $250.00 – us MEDOC [950]
MUJAHID – (Shumarah-'i 212-289 (28 Tir 1363-22 Urdibisht 1365[19 Jul 1984-12 May 1986]). Missing issues: Shumarah-'i 213-215, 266-67, 279, 281) – London: Sazman-i Mujahidin-i Khalq-i Iran – 2r – 1 – $50.00 – us MEDOC [950]
LA MUJER : ESCLAVA DE LA HISTORIA O HISTORIA DE ESCLAVA? / Hollander, Nancy – Buenos Aires: La Pleyade, 1974 – 1 – CSUXADH5743-B – us Hoover Inst Photo [305]
UNA MUJER / Barreda, Ernesto Maria – Buenos Aires. 1924 – 1 – us Res Libr [830]
UNA MUJER ARGENTINA : DONA MARIA EVA DUARTE DE PERON / Diez Gomez, Adolfo – Buenos Aires: Biblioteca Infantil "General Peron", 1948 – 1 – CSUXADH8402-B – us Hoover Inst Photo [320]
LA MUJER ARGENTINA ANTES Y DESPUES DE EVA PERON / Abejon, Carlos & Lafauci, Jorge Santos – Buenos Aires: Editorial Cuarto Mundo, c1975 – 1 – CSUXADH4008-B – us Hoover Inst Photo [972]
LA MUJER: ESCLAVA DE LA HISTORIA O HISTORIA DE ESCLAVA? *see* WOMEN, SLAVES OF HISTORY OR HISTORY OF SLAVES
LA MUJER FUERTE : ORACION FUNEBRE...EN CONVENTO...DE SANTA CLARA DE...GUADALCANAL...A...SOR ANA DE SAN PEDRO...15 FEBRERO 1740 / Francisco de la Encarnacion – Sevilla: Florencio Joseph de Blas y Quesada, s.a. – 1 – sp Bibl Santa Ana [240]
MUJER...!COQUETA! / Sanchez-Arjona, Vicente – Sevilla: Imp. Zambrano, 1957 – 1 – sp Bibl Santa Ana [810]
Mukarto, Notowidigdo *see* SPEECH TO THE CONFERENCE ON AMERICAN LIBRARY RESOURCES ON SOUTHERN ASIA IN WASHINGTON, D.C. ON NOV. 21, 1957
Mukasa-Mugerwa, E *see*
- THE CAMEL (CAMELUS DROMEDARIUS)
- A REVIEW OF REPRODUCTIVE PERFORMANCE OF FEMALE BOS INDICUS (ZEBU) CATTLE
Mukerjee, Radhakamal *see* THE SYMBOLIC LIFE OF MAN
Mukhtiar, Kaur *see* PORTUGUESE EURASIANS IN MALAYSIA
MUKLUKS HEMCUNGA – Klamath Falls OR. Apr 1973-Apr 1983 – 1 – us U.O. Library [071]
Mukundan, V *see* AN ASSESSMENT OF SELECTED RISK MANAGEMENT PRACTICES IN LOCAL INDIANA PARK AND RECREATION DEPARTMENTS
O MULATO, OU O HOMEM DE COR – (Cont: O Homem de Cor) – Rio de Janeiro, 16 Oct-4 Nov 1833 – 1,5,6 – bl Biblioteca [072]
O MULATO, OU O HOMEM DE COR *see* O HOMEM DE COR
MULBERRY BAPTIST CHURCH (FORMERLY: BALL FORK BAPTIST CHURCH). FAYETTEVILLE, TENNESSEE : CHURCH RECORDS – 1818-69.Ball Fork records – 1 – 11.25 – us Baptist [240]
MULBERRY CULTIVATION – 1988 – 134p – it F.A.O. [634]
Mulcaster, Richard *see* THE FIRST PART OF THE ELEMENTARIE
Mulchahey, James *see* THE INSPIRATION OF HISTORY
Mulert, H *see* ANTI-MODERNISTENEID, FREIE FORSCHUNG UND THEOLOGISCHE FAKULTAETEN
Mulford, Elisha *see* THE REPUBLIC OF GOD
A MULHER DO SIMPLICIO, OU A FLUMINENSE EXALTADA – Rio de Janeiro, 10-24 Mar, Sep 1832; Dec 1835; Jun 1836; Mar 1837; Dec 1838; Dec 1839-Dec 1840; May, Jul-Dec 1841; Oct-Dec 1842; Dec 1843; Apr-Jun 1844; 30 Apr 1846 – 1,5,6 – bl Biblioteca [072]
Mulia, Todung gelar Sutan Gunung *see* ENGLISH TEXTS FOR THE USE OF STUDENTS AND PUPILS PREPARING FOR THE FINAL EXAMINATION OF HIGH SCHOOLS
Mulia, Wanda *see* THE MECHANIZATION OF SMALL-SCALE INDUSTRIES
MULIAKANLAH ASMA TUHAN / Indonesia. Departemen Agama – SE-4765 1. 1963 – 9 – ne IDC [324]
Muliono, Anton Mudardo *see* ON GRAMMATICAL CATEGORIES IN INDONESIAN
Muljono, Djojopranoto *see* BEBERAPA SEGI PATOLOGI TUMOR GANAS NASOPHARYNX DI DJAWA-TIMUR
Muljono, Sri *see* AKADEMI AURI
Mulkins, Hannibal *see* REPORT TO THE CANADA TEMPERANCE SOCIETY ON THE WORKING AND EFFECTS OF PROHIBITORY LEGISLATION TO SUPPRESS INTEMPERANCE IN THE NEW ENGLAND STATES
M.U.L.L. MODERN USES OF LOGIC IN LAW *see* JURIMETRICS JOURNAL (ABA)
MULL (MODERN USES OF LOGIC IN LAW) *see* JURIMETRICS
MULLA NASR AL-DIN – (Missing nos. 16, 19-20. Vol 9, nos. 1-25 (18 Sefer 1331-Zilhicce 1332[13 Jan 1913-18 Oct 1914])) – Tiflis. v8, nos. 1-28 – 15mf – 9 – $100.00 – us MEDOC [949]
Mullach, Friedrich Wilhelm August *see* GRAMMATIK DER GRIECHISCHEN VULGARSPRACHE IN HISTORISCHER ENTWICKLUNG
MULLEN ENQUIRER – Mullen, NE. -w. Dec 1892; Aug 1895-Mar 1896 – 1 – us NE Hist [071]
Mullendore, William C *see* HISTORY OF THE UNITED STATES FOOD ADMINISTRATION
Mullens, W H *see* A BIBLIOGRAPHY OF BRITISH ORNITHOLOGY...
Muller, Eugene *see* SOUVENIRS D'UN JEUNE FRANC-TIREUR
Muller, F *see* REHOBOTH BASTARDS, 1916
Muller, George F *see* A DIPLOMATIC HISTORY OF THE CONGO FREE STATE
Muller, P J *see* DE GODSLEER DER MIDDELEEUWSCHE JODEN
Muller, William Henry *see* EARLY HISTORY OF THE FEDERAL SUPREME COURT
Mullik, B N *see* CIVIL DISTURBANCES
Mullinger, J Bass *see* THE NEW REFORMATION
Mullinger, James Bass *see*
- CAMBRIDGE CHARACTERISTICS IN THE SEVENTEENTH CENTURY, OR, THE STUDIES OF THE UNIVERSITY AND THEIR INFLUENCE ON THE CHARACTER AND WRITINGS OF THE MOST DISTINGUISHED GRADUATES DURING THAT PERIOD
- THE SCHOOLS OF CHARLES THE GREAT AND THE RESTORATION OF EDUCATION IN THE NINTH CENTURY
Mullins, E Y *see* BAPTISM AND THE REMISSION OF SINS
Mullins, Edgar Young *see* THE AXIOMS OF RELIGION
MULLINS FIRST BAPTIST CHURCH. MULLINS, SOUTH CAROLINA : CHURCH RECORDS – 1880-1920, 1924-34, 1957-72 – 1 – 19.71 – us Baptist [240]
MULL'S MEMORIAL BAPTIST CHURCH. SHELBY, NORTH CAROLINA : CHURCH RECORDS – 1939-1963 – 1 – 23.36 – us Baptist [240]
MULLUMBIMBY STAR – Feb 3 1906-Dec 21 1938; Jan 2 1940 -Dec 12 1941; Jan 14 1943-Dec 22 1945 – 9 – at Pascoe [072]
Mulot, R *see* JOHN KNOX, 1505-1572
Mulson *see* VOCABULAIRE LANGROIS
A MULTI-CASE STUDY OF BEGINNING PHYSICAL EDUCATION TEACHERS AT THE ELEMENTARY SCHOOL LEVEL / Cruz, L M – 1991 – 4mf – 9 – $16.00 – us Microform Publ [370]
A MULTI-CASE STUDY OF FIRST YEAR ATHLETIC TRAINERS AT THE HIGH SCHOOL LEVEL / Curtis, Neil & Anderson, William G – 1993 – 3mf – 9 – $12.00 – us Microform Publ [617]
MULTICHANNEL NEWS – New York, 1980- – 1 – $175.00y – us Fairchild Micro [073]
A MULTI-CHASE STUDY OF PHYSICAL EDUCATION RESOURCE TEACHERS / Balke, Martina – Columbia University, 1995 – 4mf – 9 – $16.00 – PE 3628 – us Microform Publ [370]
MULTICULTURAL EDUCATION ABSTRACTS – 1982- 12v – 9 – £197.00 – 0260-9770 – uk Carfax [370]
MULTICULTURAL EDUCATION JOURNAL – Edmonton. v1-12. 1983-94 – 9 – Can$20.00y – cn Micromedia [370]
MULTI-CULTURAL SCHOOL – 1973- 1; 1976- 5,6,9 – us UMI [370]
MULTIFARM USE OF AGRICULTURAL MACHINERY / Loennemark, H – 1985 – 63p – it F.A.O. [630]
MULTILATERAL EXCHANGE OF EDUCATIONAL AUDIO-VISUAL MATERIALS : EXISTING MECHANISMS AND SUGGESTIONS FOR THE FUTURE – 1980 – 128p – 9 – 92-3-101694-6 – fr UNESCO [370]
MULTILITH BULLETIN / Montana. Agricultural Extension Service – nos.1000-1069. 1949-69 – 1,5,6 – us Spaulding [630]
MULTILITH CIRCULAR / Montana. Agricultural Extension Service – nos.1000-1101. 1949-69 – 1,5,6 – us Spaulding [630]
MULTINATIONAL BUSINESS – 1971-92. Continued annually – 1 – uk World [338]
MULTINATIONAL CORPORATIONS, OPEC, CARTELS, FOREIGN INVESTMENTS, AND TECHNOLOGY TRANSFER, 1971-88 : SPECIAL STUDIES SERIES / ed by Kesaris, Paul – (1971-81: ISBN 0-89093-507-6. $1,105.00; 1982-85: 5r. ISBN 0-89093-552-1. $550.00; 1985-88: ISBN 1-55655-147-9. $1,105.00) – 1 – us UPA [338]
MULTINATIONAL ENTERPRISES PROGRAMME / International Labour Organisation – 45v. 1980-1986 – 17 – Sfr500.00 – 92-2-106094-2 – sz I.L.O. [330]
MULTINATIONAL MONITER – v.1-. 1980- – 1,5,6,9 – us UMI [073]
MULTIPLE LINEAR REGRESSION VIEWPOINTS – v1- 1970- 1; v8- 5,6,9 – us UMI [510]
MULTIVARIATE BEHAVIORAL RESEARCH – v1- 1966- 1; v11- 5,6,9 – us UMI [073]
MULTNOMAH CITIZEN – Multnomah, OR. -w. 19 Jul 1929-6 Feb 1931. 1 roll – 1 – us U.O. Library [071]
MULTNOMAH COMMUNITY LEDGER – Multnomah OR. Apr 9 1925 – 1 – us U.O. Library [071]
MULTNOMAH PRESS – Multnomah, OR. -w. 7 Jan 1927-29 Dec 1933. 2 rolls – 1 – us U.O. Library [071]
MUMBAI SAMACARA *see* BOMBAY SAMACHAR
Mumford, New York. First Baptist Church *see* RECORDS
Mummenhoff, Wilhelm *see* DIE DARSTELLUNGSWEISE LESSINGS IN SEINEN PROSAISCHEN SCHRIFTEN
Mumps Users' Group Meeting *see* PROCEEDINGS
Munarriz, Urtasun *see* MICHETO, EL PIRATA
Munby, G *see* FLORE DE L'ALGEA1RIE
MUNCA – Bucharest, Romania. Mar 1953-1975 – 35r – 1 – us L of C Photodup [949]
MUNCA – (Cont as: Romania Muncitoare ab 1989. Realitatea Romanesca ab 1990) – Rumaenien, 1976-1992ff – 17r – 1 – DM1,275.00 – gw Mikro Press [949]
MUNCHEN-AUGSBURGER ABENDZEITUNG – Munich, Germany. Sept-Dec 1912; Jul 1914-Jul 1934 – 19r – 1 – us L of C Photodup [072]
MUNCHNER NEUESTE NACHRICHTEN – Munich, Germany. Jul-Aug 1914; Oct 1919-Apr 1945 – 63r – 1 – us L of C Photodup [072]
Muncie, Indiana *see* MISCELLANEOUS EARLY NEWSPAPERS
MUNCITORUL FORESTIER – Bucharest, Romania. -w. 1969-70. 1 reel – 1 – uk British Libr Newspaper [949]
Muncker, Franz *see*
- JOHANN KASPAR LAVATER
- ODEN
- WIELANDS "PERVONTE"
Muncy, Pennsylvania. Muncy Baptist Church *see* RECORDS
DIE MUNDARTEN IM HOCHDEUTSCHEN DRAMA BIS GEGEN DAS ENDE DES ACHTZEHNTEN JAHRHUNDERTS : EIN BEITRAG ZUR GESCHICHTE DES DEUTSCHEN DRAMAS UND DER DEUTSCHEN DIALEKTDICHTUNG / Lowack, Alfred – (Includes bibliographical references) – Leipzig: M Hesse, 1905 – 1r – 1 – us U.W. Library [430]
MUNDARTLICH HEITERES / Adler, Carl – New York, NY: E Steiger, 1886 – 1r – 1 – us U.W. Library [430]
THE MUNDAS AND THEIR COUNTRY / Roy, Sarat Chandra – [Calcutta: Kuntaline Press], 1912 – us Res Libr [950]
Munden, Cecil L *see* BILATERAL STAFF CONVERSATIONS WITH LATIN AMERICAN REPUBLICS
EL MUNDO – Buenos Aires, Argentina. -d. Oct 1960-Dec 1967. 96 reels – 1 – uk British Libr Newspaper [072]
EL MUNDO – Habana: J M Govin, [1901-69]. [jan-sep 19 1933; sep 1935-apr 1936; jan-feb, may-jun, sep-dec 1937; 1938-43; 1946-47] (119r); [1956-apr 5 1969] (136r) – 1 – us Res Libr [072]
EL MUNDO – Madrid, Spain. -d. 1 Sept 1914-30 March 1915; 3 May 1916-10 Aug 1919. Imperfect. 11 reels – 1 – uk British Libr Newspaper [072]
EL MUNDO – Oakland, CA. 1971-77; 1979; 1981; 1984; 1986- – 6+ r – 1 RB02545 – $300.00 ($50.00y) – us Library Micro [071]
EL MUNDO – Panama City, Panama. 29 Sept 1965-31 Dec 1967 – 11r – 1 – us L of C Photodup [072]
EL MUNDO – San Juan. Puerto Rico. 1951-61, 1975 – 1 – us UMI [071]
MUNDO – Madrid. Spain. -w. 7 Jul-29 Dec 1940, 4 Jan 1942-30 Dec 1945. (Imperfect). (9 reels) – 1 – uk British Libr Newspaper [072]
EL MUNDO CATOLICO Y LA CARTA COLECTIVA DEL EPISCOPADO ESPANOL / Bayle, Constantino – Burgos: Razon y Fe, 1938 – 1 – sp Bibl Santa Ana [240]
MUNDO PERONISTA – Buenos Aires, AG. 1951-1955 – 4r – $200.00 – R04160 – us Library Micro [072]
MUNDO PERONISTA – Buenos Aires. Jul 1951-1 Sep 1955 – 1 – 35.00r – us Hoover Inst Photo [073]
Mundt, Theodor *see* ALLGEMEINE LITERATURGESCHICHTE
MUNDUS ATRIUM – v1- 1967- 1; v4- 5,6; v10- 9 – us UMI [073]
Muneles, O *see* BIBLIOGRAPHICAL SURVEY OF JEWISH PRAGUE
Munez de Castro, J *see* TRATADO UNIVERSAL...(SOBRE) LA PESTE...
Mungen. Ohio. Church of Christ *see* CHURCH RECORDS
Munger, Angele *see* BIBLIOGRAPHIE ANALYTIQUE DE LA VIE PERSONNELLE DE L'INFIRMIERE D'APRES LA DOCUMENTATION DES REVUES D'INFIRMIERES...
Munger, C *see* THE CHRONOLOGY OF BIBLE HISTORY, AND HOW TO REMEMBER IT
Munger, Theodore Thornton *see*
- ESSAYS FOR THE DAY
- THE FREEDOM OF FAITH
- ON THE THRESHHOLD
MUNGINDI NEWS – Apr 2 1898-Dec 19 1907 – 9 – at Pascoe [072]
Munhall, L W *see* ANTI-HIGHER CRITICISM
Munhall, Leander Whitcomb *see* THE HIGHEST CRITICS VS THE HIGHER CRITICS
MUNICIPAL ACT OF LOWER CANADA, 10 AND 11 VICT. 1847. / Canada. Laws, Statutes, etc – Montreal: Printed by Stewart Derbishire & George Desbarats, 1847. SEM105P171 – 1mf – 9 – Can$2.25 – cn Bibl Nat [324]
MUNICIPAL AFFAIRS – (Lacking: v4 p646-648. v6 p329-330) – New York. v1-6. 1897-1902 (all publ) – 19mf – 9 – $85.00 – LLMC 84-621 – us L.L.M.C. [073]
Municipal Archives Rotterdam *see* DUTCH THEATRE POSTERS, 1853-1926
MUNICIPAL ATTORNEY – (Lacking: v8 no 7. v18 p97-98,127-128) – National Institute of Municipal Law Officers. v1-25. 1959-84 – 29mf – 9 – $130.00 – LLMC 84-622 – us L.L.M.C. [073]
MUNICIPAL BULLETIN / Massachusetts. Dept. of Corporations and Taxation. Bureau of Accounts – 1910-78. 55 fiches. (Harvard Law School Library Collection.) – 9 – 1.50f – us H.U. Law [324]
MUNICIPAL CORPORATION CASES, ANNOTATED – Charlottesville: Michie Co. v1-11. 1894-1903 (all publ) – 109mf – 9 – $163.00 – LLMC 84-707 – us L.L.M.C. [340]
THE MUNICIPAL COURT PRACTICE ACT, ANNOTATED. / Collins, Cornelius Francis – New York, Banks, 1902. 381 p. LL-686 – 1 – us L of C Photodup [340]
MUNICIPAL COURT RECORD – Chicago. Ill. 1955- – 1 – us UMI [071]

MUNICIPAL COURT REVIEW – New York: Lawyer's Co-op. v1 no 1 Jan 1904 (all publ) – 1mf – 9 – $1.50 – LLMC 84-623 – us L.L.M.C. [073]

THE MUNICIPAL COURT REVIEW – North American Judges Association for Judges of First Jurisdiction. v1-9. 1961-69 (all publ) – 14mf – 9 – $21.00 – LLMC 84-624 – us L.L.M.C. [073]

THE MUNICIPAL EMPLOYEE – San Francisco, CA. v1-12. 1927-1937 – 2r – 1 – $100.00 – B02843a – us Library Micro [071]

MUNICIPAL FINANCE JOURNAL – v1-13. 1980-92 – 9 – $325.00set – us Hein [340]

MUNICIPAL GAZETTE / Calcutta. India – May 1944-Aug. 9, 1969- Silver Jubliee Number. 1924-1949 – 1 – us NY Public [324]

MUNICIPAL HISTORY OF ESSEX COUNTY IN MASSACHUSETTS / ed by Arrington, Benjamin F – Historical and biographical. New York, Lewis Historical Publ. Co., 1922. Vols. 1-2, Massachusetts Reel 4; Vols. 3-4, Massachusetts Reel 5. (The Cox Library Collection) – 5 – us Americana [978]

MUNICIPAL LAW COURT DECISIONS : A MONTHLY DIGEST.... – (Lacking: v14 p86-end. v24,41,42) – v1-43. 1942-84 – 62mf – 9 – $93.00 – LLMC 84-625 – us L.L.M.C. [073]

MUNICIPAL LAW JOURNAL – (Supplemented by: Municipal Law Survey) – v1-38. 1936-73 (all publ) – 51mf – 9 – $76.00 – LLMC 84-84-626 – us L.L.M.C. [073]

MUNICIPAL LAW JOURNAL *see* MUNICIPAL LAW SURVEY

MUNICIPAL LAW SURVEY – (Supplements: Municipal Law Journal) – nos 1-6 Mar-Oct 1942 (all publ) – 4mf – 9 – $6.00 – LLMC 84-627 – us L.L.M.C. [073]

MUNICIPAL LAW SURVEY *see* MUNICIPAL LAW JOURNAL

MUNICIPAL LEGISLATIVE BULLETIN – (Title changes to: Municipal Ordinance Review with v6. Lacking: v16,18,32,33,36) – v1-37. 1948-84 – 32mf – 9 – $48.00 – LLMC 84-628 – us L.L.M.C. [073]

MUNICIPAL ORDINANCE REVIEW *see* MUNICIPAL LEGISLATIVE BULLETIN

MUNICIPAL OWNERSHIP – Portland OR. Nov 1929 – 1 – us U.O. Library [071]

MUNICIPAL REVIEW : OFFICIAL ORGAN OF THE ASSOCIATION OF MUNICIPAL CORPORATIONS / Association of Municipal Corporations. London – London. v1-44. 1930-73 (all publ) – 246mf – 9 – $369.00 – LLMC 84-629 – us L.L.M.C. [336]

THE MUNICIPAL SITUATION / Baillairge, Charles – 1878. 00063. (Pre-1900 Canadiana) – 9 – cn C.I.H.M. [624]

MUNICIPAL WORLD – 1891-1994. Tracing the legislation of local government in Canada. Printed or machine-readable author subject index available separately. Periodic updates. Complete or partial sets available – 457mf – 9 – $1,500.00 – cn Municipal [340]

LAS MUNICIPALIDADES HISPANO-PORTUGUESAS SU ORIGEN Y DESARROLLO HASTA EL SIGLO 15 / Lumbreras Valiente, Pedro – Badajoz, 1958 – 1 – sp Bibl Santa Ana [946]

LAS MUNICIPALIDADES HISPANO-PORTUGUESAS. SU ORIGEN Y DESARROLLO HASTA EL SIGLO 15 / Alvarez, Arturo – Badajoz: Dip. Provincial, 1958 – sp Bibl Santa Ana [946]

THE MUNICIPALIST : INTERNAL RELATIONS OF THE CITIES, TOWNS, VILLAGES, COUNTIES AND THE STATES OF THE UNION – (A collection of materials on both the US and NY constitutions) – 2nd ed. New York: Ross & Tousey, Dexter & Brother, & Wm. Raddle, 1859 – 4mf – 9 – $6.00 – LLMC 95-076 – us L.L.M.C. [323]

THE MUNICIPALIST : INTERNAL RELATIONS OF THE CITIES, TOWNS, VILLAGES, COUNTIES, AND THE STATES OF THE UNION; A HIGHLY USEFUL BOOK FOR VOTERS, TAX-PAYERS, STATESMEN, POLITICIANS AND FAMILIES – 2nd ed. New York: Ross & Tousey et al, 1859 – 4mf – 9 – $6.00 – LLMC 95-076 – us L.L.M.C. [340]

MUNICIPALITES ET PAROISSES DANS LA PROVINCE DE QUEBEC / Deschamps, Clement E – Quebec: Impr. Leger Brousseau, 1896-97. SEM105P52 – 15mf – 9 – Can$33.75 – cn Bibl Nat [350]

MUNICIPALITES ET PAROISSES DANS LA PROVINCE DE QUEBEC = MUNICIPALITIES AND PARISHES IN THE PROVINCE OF QUEBEC / Deschamps, Clement E – 1896 (i.e.) 1897. SEM35P170 – 1r – 1 – Can$42.00 – cn Bibl Nat [350]

MUNICIPALITES, PAROISSES, CANTONS, ETC. DE LA PROVINCE DE QUEBEC DE 1896 A 1924 / Piche, Odessa – Quebec: Ministere de la colonisation des mines et des pecheries, 1924. SEM105P385 – 7mf – 9 – Can$15.75 – cn Bibl Nat [350]

MUNICIPIO : ORGAO DOS INTERESSES LOCAES – Itacoatiara, Amazonas. 11 Jun, Out 1893; Dez 1894; Jan-10 Fev 1895 – 1,5,6 – bl Biblioteca [072]

O MUNICIPIO – Bicas, 1 Jul 1956 – 1,5,6 – bl Biblioteca [072]

O MUNICIPIO – Manacapuru, Amazonas. 17 Set 1912-23 Mar 1913 – 1,5,6 – bl Biblioteca [072]

O MUNICIPIO : ORGAM INDEPENDENTE, POLITICO E NOTICIOSO – Lavras, 15 Feb 1914; 12 Dec 1926 – 1,5,6 – bl Biblioteca [072]

O MUNICIPIO : ORGAO DA LAVOURA, COMMERCIO E INDUSTRIA – S. Luiz Do Quitunde, Alagoas. 29 Jan, 18 Nov 1880 – 1,5,6 – bl Biblioteca [072]

O MUNICIPIO : ORGAO DOS INTERESSES DO MUNICIPIO DE CAMARAGIPE – Camaragibe, Alagoas. 1 Set, 3 Nov 1892 – 1,5,6 – bl Biblioteca [072]

O MUNICIPIO : ORGAO DOS INTERESSES LOCAES – Itacoatiara, Amazonas. 25 Set 1921 – 1,5,6 – bl Biblioteca [072]

O MUNICIPIO : ORGAO IMPARCIAL – S. Joao Nepomuceno, 17 Mar, Aug 1895; Jul-2 Dec 1897 – 1,5,6 – bl Biblioteca [072]

O MUNICIPIO : ORGAO INDEPENDENTE E DEDICADO AOS INTERESSES GERAES DO MUNICIPIO – Cidade do Rio Preto, 27 Jan 1916; Aug 1919; Mar 1924; Jan, Mar-31 Dec 1979 – 1,5,6 – bl Biblioteca [072]

O MUNICIPIO : ORGAO OFFICIAL DO GOVERNO MUNICIPAL – Diamantina, 25 Feb-Mar, May-Dec 1896; Jan-Mar, Apr-Jun, Dec 1897; Jan, Apr-Jun 1898; Feb-Apr, Jun-Jul, Sep-Dec 1899; Mar, May-Dec 1900; Jan-Aug, Nov 1901; Feb, 4 Jul 1903 – 1,5,6 – bl Biblioteca [072]

O MUNICIPIO – S. Jose d'Alem Parahyba, 18 Mar 1888 – 1,5,6 – bl Biblioteca [072]

O MUNICIPIO – Sao Paulo, 15 Aug, 17 Oct 1895 – 1,5,6 – bl Biblioteca [072]

O MUNICIPIO – Villa Seabra, Acre. 28 Set 1910-Set 1916; Jan-Mar 1917; Maio-Jun, Ago 1918; Jan 1930-Fev 1933; Maio, Jul-Ago, Out-26 Dez 1937 – 1,5,6 – bl Biblioteca [072]

MUNICIPIO DE ELECCION ENMIENDAS A LA CARTA DE MANILA / Papa, Ramon R – Presentadas a la legislatura...3 octubre 1914. (Manila): Esfuerzo Obrero, 1914. 10p – 1 – us U.W. Library [950]

MUNICIPIO DE PITANGUI : ORGAO OFICIAL DOS PODERES MUNICIPAIS – Pitangui, 5 May-Sep 1957; Jun 1963; Dec 1977; Jan-30 Dec 1979 – 1,5,6 – bl Biblioteca [072]

MUNICIPIO DO CURVELLO : ORGAO DO PARTIDO REPUBLICANO – Curvello, 1-21 Aug 1895; Jan, Mar, Jul, Nov 1896; Mar-Sep, 18 Dec 1897 – 1,5,6 – bl Biblioteca [072]

O MUNICIPIO DO PARA : ORGAM DOS INTERESSES DO MUNICIPIO – Cidade do Para, 22 Sep 1895 – 1,5,6 – bl Biblioteca [072]

EL MUNICIPIO EN AMERICA DURANTE LA ASISTENCIA DE ESPANA, 1930 / Navarro, Jose Gabriel – Madrid: Razon y Fe, 1931 – 1 – sp Bibl Santa Ana [970]

LOS MUNICIPIOS Y LOS INDIOS / Bayle, Constantino – Madrid: Missionalia Hispanica, 1950 – 1 – sp Bibl Santa Ana [240]

Munier, F *see* DICTIONNAIRE DES LOCUTIONS VICIEUSES

Munier, Pierre Marie *see* L'ASSABA; ESSAI MONOGRAPHIQUE

Munif *see* DIVAN

MUNIMENTA ACADEMICA : DOCUMENTS ILLUSTR. OF ACADEMICAL LIFE AND STUDIES AT OXFORD (RS50) / Oxford University; ed by Anstey, H – v1,2 1868 – Dfl32.00v – ne Slangenburg [370]

MUNIMENTA GILDHALLAE LONDONIENSIS (RS12) / LONDON CORPORATION; ed by Riley, H Th – (v1: Liber Albus 1859 Dfl56.00. v2: Liber Custumarum 1860 Dfl67.00. v3: Translation Of The Anglo-Norman Passages In Liber Albus, Glossaries, ASO Liber Horn, 1311 1862 Dfl35.00) – ne Slangenburg [941]

UN MUNITIONNAIRE DU ROI A LA NOUVELLE FRANCE, JOSEPH CADET (1756-1781) / Barbier, Alfred – Poitiers: Blais et Roy, 1900. 02974. Canadiana) – 9 – cn C.I.H.M. [971]

Muniz, A E *see* BIOMECHANICAL ANALYSIS OF FORCES AND TORQUES AT THE SUPPORT LOWER EXTREMITY DURING TWO RUNNING-IN-PLACE EXERCISES AT THREE PACES

Munk, S *see* MANUSCRITS HEBREUX DE L'ORATOIRE A LA BIBLIOTHEQUE NATIONALE DE PARIS

MUNKASOK UJSAGA – Budapest: Tancsics Mihal, apr 2-sep 24 1848 – 1r – 1 – us Res Libr [072]

Munkasy, B A *see* THE EFFECTS OF A DIFFERENT ARM SWING ON VERTICAL JUMP AND TOE-TOUCH JUMP PERFORMANCE

Munn, Lewis C *see* THE AMERICAN ORATOR

Munn Memorial Commission. Kansas *see* RECORDS

EL MUNO HISPANICO Y SU REITEGRACION HISTORICA BAJO EL SIGNO DE GUADALUPE / Becerro de Bengoa, Ricardo – Santander: Imp. El Escritorio, 1960 – 1 – sp Bibl Santa Ana [972]

Munoz, A *see* INSTRUCCION DE LOS BARBEROS FLEBOTONIANOS...

Munoz, A Lopez *see* APOSTOL BAUTISTA EN LA PERLA ANTILLANA

Munoz Arconada, Felipe *see* LA JUVENTUD QUE DEFIENDE MADRID; CONFERENCIA NACIONAL DE JUVENTUDES

Munoz Carrero, Pedro *see* HEROES EXTREMENOS

Munoz Casillas, Joaquin *see* CONTESTACIONES AL DERECHO HIPOTECARIO

Munoz Casillas, Juan *see*
- CONTESTACIONES AL DERECHO HIPOTECARIO
- LA EVOLUCION ECONOMICA 2
- LA EVOLUCION ECONOMICA 3
- LA EVOLUCION ECONOMICA 4
- MONOPOLIOS O CUASI MONOPOLIOS
- LA RENTA NACIONAL Y EL PRESUPUESTO

Munoz de Dieste, Carmen *see* TRABAJOS Y FIESTAS DE UN PUEBLO ESPANOL

Munoz de la Pena, Arsenio *see*
- LOS GRANDES SABIOS
- LOS JUDIOS EN EXTREMADURA
- EL MISTERIOSO CORONEL POLACO (HISTORIA NOVELADA)

Munoz de Rivera, Antonio *see*
- GEOGRAFIA DE...BADAJOZ
- MONOGRAFIA HISTORICO-...HORNACHOS

Munoz de Rivera, Juan *see* COMPENDIO DE ARITMETICA

Munoz de San Pedro, Miguel *see*
- ACTUACION POLICIAL DE UNNEXTREMENO EN EL SIGLO 17
- LA ANTIHISTORIA EXTREMENA
- EL ARCHIVO DE LOS CONDES DE CANILLEROS
- AVENTURAS Y DESVENTURAS DEL TERCER DIEGO GARCIA DE PAREDES
- EL BACULO DE SAN PEDRO DE ALCANTARA
- BIBLIOGRAFIA DE LAS PUBLICACIONES
- LOS CABALLEROS DE NUESTRA SENORA DE SALOR
- EL CAPITAN DIEGO DE CACERES OVANDO PALADIN EXTREMENO DE LOS REYES CATOLICOS
- CAROLINA CORONADO
- LA COFRADIA CACERENA DE NUESTRA SENORA DE LA PAZ
- CORIA Y EL MANTEL DELA SAGRADA CENA (LA CIUDAD, SU CATEDRAL, SU RELICARIO Y SU GRAN RELIQUIA)
- DESCUBRIMIENTO DE LOS RESTOS DE FREY NICOLAS DE OVANDO, PRIMER GOVERNADOR DE LAS INDIAS
- DIEGO GARCIA DE PAREDES. HERCULES Y SANSON DE ESPANA
- DIEGO GARCIA DE PAREDES, HERCULES Y SANTON DE ESPANA. MADRID, 1946
- DOCUMENTOS PARA LA HISTORIA DE LA GUERRA DE SUCESION EN EXTREMADURA
- LA ESPOSA DE DONOSO CORTES
- LA EXTREMADURA DEL S.15 EN TRES DE SUS PALADINES
- EXTREMADURA EN 1829 (DATOS DE SUS PARTIDOS Y LOCALIDADES)
- UN EXTREMENO EN LA CORTE DE LOS AUSTRIAS
- UN FRAILE EXTREMENO EN FILIPINAS
- FRANCISCO DE HINOJOSA. EL PERSONAJE INEDITO DE UN DRAMA HISTORICO
- FRANCISCO DE LIZAUR (1477-1535)
- FRANCISCO DE LIZAUR. HIDALGO INDIANO DE PRINCIPIOS DE SIGLO 16
- FRANCISCO PIZARRO DEBIO LLAMARSE DIAZ O HINOJOSA
- HERNANDO DE SOTO, PALADIN DE FLORIDA Y DESCUBRIDOR DEL MISSISIPI
- INFORMACION SOBRE EL LINAJE DE HERNANDO PIZARRO
- INFORME SOBRE EL LUGAR DE NACIMIENTO DE HERNANDO DE SOTO
- INFORME SOBREEL NACIMIENTO DE FRANCISCO PIZARRO
- JUAN VAZQUEZ DE LA PARRA, EL EXTREMENO AL QUE AMO COMO A UN HIJO SAN MARTIN DE PORRES
- LISES, VERSOS
- LISES (VERSOS Y PROSAS)
- EL MANUSCRITO DELAS REVELACIONES SOBRE LA FUNDACION DEL CONVENTO DE SERRADILLA
- EL MAYORAZGO DE BLASCO MUNOZ. FUNDACION VINCULAR DE PRINCIPIOS DEL S. 16
- UN MEMORIAL DEL I. MARQUES DE LA CONQUISTA
- MENSAJE DE EXTREMADURA
- PUNTUALIZACIONES HISTORICAS SOBRE EL LINAJE DE MONROY
- RECUERDOS. VEINTICINCO ANOS DE AMISTAD INSUSTITUIBLE
- REFLEJOS DE SIETE SIGLOS DE VIDA EXTREMENA EN CIEN DOCUMENTOS NOTARIALES
- LA RELACION DE LAS INDIAS DE FRAY ANTONIO
- EL SENORIO DE CASTELLANOS
- LA SOMBRA DE DONA ISABEL DE MERCADO
- SOR MARIANA DE LA PRESENTACION EJEMPLAR CLARISA CACERENA
- LOS TITULOS NOBILIARIOS DE LOS GODOY EN LA DOCUMENTACION DEL ARCHIVO HISTORICO NACIONAL
- LAS ULTIMAS DISPOSICIONES DEL ULTIMO PIZARRO DE LA CONQUISTA
- VIEJA BIOGRAFIA DE D. PEDRO DE ALVARADO. LUGARTENIENTE DE HERNAN CORTES Y CONQUISTADOR DE GUATEMALA

Munoz del Castillo, Jose *see* EL VANADIO EN ESPANA

Munoz Gallardo, Juan Antonio *see*
- APUNTES HISTORICOS DE LA QUE FUE SEDE ARZOBISPAL DE MERIDA DEL 507 AL 910 (403 ANOS)
- CACERES PRIMERA CUNA DE LA ORDEN MILITAR DE SANTIAGO
- HIDALGUIA EXTREMENA
- LA HISTORIA, VERDADERA ENSENANZA EN LOS CAMINOS DE LA RURA DE ESPANA
- LA PAZ DEL CAMPO PERSONALIDAD E INMORTALIDAD DE GABRIEL Y GALAN
- LA PAZ DEL CAMPO. PERSONALIDAD E INMORTALIDAD DE GABRIEL Y GALAN

Munoz Garcia, Juan *see* LAS LUCHAS DEL SIGLO 6

Munoz, J *see* LIBRO DEL NUEVO COMETA...

Munoz, Jimenez, Francisco *see* EL MILICIANO REMIGIO

Munoz, Jose *see* HISTORIA DE LA "CUERDA GRANADINA", CONTADA POR ALGUNOS DE SUS...MADRID, 1926

Munoz, Juan Antonio *see* BIOGRAFIA Y CRITICA DE D. JOSE ESPRONCEDA ISAGOGE

Munoz, Juan Bautista *see* JUICIO DEL TRATADO DE EDUCACION DE POZZI

Munoz, Luis *see* VIDA...DONA LUISA DE CARVAJAL

Munoz Olave, Reinaldo *see*
- LECTURAS DE HISTORIA NACIONAL RELACIONADAS CON EL SANTISIMO SACRAMENTO. SANTIAGO DE CHILE, 1928
- LA VIRGEN MARIA EN LA DIOCESIS DE LA CONCEPCION DURANTE LA DOMINACION ESPANOLA (1550-1810)

MUNOZ PABON, PREDICADOR / Montoto de Sedas, Castor – Sevilla, 1930; Madrid: Razon y Fe, 1931 – 1 – sp Bibl Santa Ana [240]

Munoz, Pedro de san *see* DON ALVARO DE SANDE CRONISTA DEL DESASTRE DELOS GELVES

Munoz Pizarro, C *see* INDICE DE K. REICHE: ESTUDIOS CRITICOS DE LA FLORE CHILENA

Munoz San Pedro, Miguel *see* DOCUMENTACION HISTORICA DE DIEGO GARCIA DE PAREDES

MUNOZ TORRERO / Fernandez de los Rios, Angel – 1864 – 9 – 1.50f – sp Bibl Santa Ana [830]
MUNOZ TORRERO, APUNTES HISTORICOS-BIOGRAFICOS / Romero Rizo, Jose Maria – Cadiz: Imp. de M. Alvarez Rodriguez, 1910 – 1 – sp Bibl Santa Ana [946]
MUNOZ TORRERO Y SU EPOCA / Perez Jimenez, Nicolas – 1888 – 9 – 1.50f – sp Bibl Santa Ana [920]
Munoz y Peralta, M *see* ESCRUTINIO PHISICO MEDICO DE UN PEREGRINO ESPECIFICO DE LAS CALENTURAS INTERMITENTES
Munoz-Epelde, Melchor *see* MEMORIAS DE UN AMNISTIADO
Munro, James *see* ACTS OF THE PRIVY COUNCIL OF ENGLAND
Munro, R *see* ANABOLIC STEROIDS
Munro, Robert *see* PALEOLITHIC MAN AND TERRAMARA SETTLEMENTS IN EUROPE, BEING THE MUNRO LECTURES IN ANTHROPOLOGY AND PREHISTORIC ARCHAEOLOGY...UNIVERSITY OF EDINBURGH...FEBRUARY AND MARCH 1912
Munro, W *see* A MONOGRAPH OF THE BAMBUSACEAE
Munro-Butler-Johnstone, Henry Alexander *see* A TRIP UP THE VOLGA TO THE FAIR OF NIJNI-NOVGOROD
Munroe, Richard A *see* OREGON CABLE-TENSION STRENGTH TEST BATTERIES FOR BOYS AND GIRLS FROM FOURTH GRADE THROUGH COLLEGE
Munro-Fraser, J P *see*
– HISTORY OF MARIN COUNTY
– HISTORY OF SOLANO COUNTY
Munsell Publishing Co *see*
– HISTORICAL ENCYCLOPEDIA OF ILLINOIS AND HISTORY OF KENDALL COUNTY
– HISTORICAL ENCYCLOPEDIA OF ILLINOIS AND HISTORY OF SANGAMON COUNTY
– HISTORICAL ENCYCLOPEDIA OF ILLINOIS AND HISTORY OF ST CLAIR COUNTY
– HISTORICAL ENCYCLOPEDIA OF ILLINOIS AND KNOX COUNTY
– HISTORY OF MCHENRY COUNTY
MUNSEY'S MAGAZINE *see* ALL-STORY COMBINED WITH MUNSEY'S
Munson, Carlton *see* THE CLINICAL SUPERVISOR
THE MUNSON MAIL – Alberta, CN. 1916-18 – 1r – 1 – cn Commonwealth Micro [072]
MUNSTER ADVERTISER – Cork. Ireland. -w. 20 Apr 1839-8 May 1841. (1 reel) – 1 – uk British Libr Newspaper [072]
MUNSTER CITIZEN – Carrick on Suir and Dunga, Ireland. 28 Feb-11 Sept 1852. -w. 1/4 reel – 1 – uk British Libr Newspaper [072]
MUNSTER EXPRESS – 1908-1980 – ca 100r – 1 – ie Microforms [941]
MUNSTER EXPRESS – Waterford, Ireland. -d.1908-86. 124 reels – 1 – PS27.50r – ie European Micro [072]
MUNSTER EXPRESS – Waterford, Ireland. Jul 1860-66; 1870-88; 1890; 1892-96. -w. 27 reels – 1 – uk British Libr Newspaper [072]
MUNSTER JOURNAL AND LIMERICK COMMERCIAL REPORTER – Limerick. Ireland. -w. 14 Dec 1832-9 Jan 1833. (6 ft) – 1 – uk British Libr Newspaper [072]
MUNSTER LIFE – Tralee, Ireland. -w. 6 March-5 June 1897. 15 ft – 1 – uk British Libr Newspaper [072]
MUNSTER NEWS – Limerick, Ireland. -sw. 7 June 1851-7 Jan 1871; June 1873-Dec 1927. 50 1 2 reels – 1 – uk British Libr Newspaper [072]
Muntada y Andrade, Jose *see* MEMORIA... INSTITUTO DE BADAJOZ
Muntadas, V *see* SOBRE LAS MUERTES CAUSADAS EN LA POBLACION CIVIL POR LA REVOLUCION COMUNISTA ESPANOLA
MUNTAHAB *see* AL-MUNTAHAB
MUNTAKHAB AL-LUBAB / Khafi Khan – (Bibliotheca Indica: Oriental Works). 3 v. Calcutta. 1869-1925. BI-783 2 – 8 – ne IDC [490]
MUNTAKHAB AL-TAWARIKH / Abd Al-Qadir Bin-i-Maluk – Bibliotheca Indica: Oriental Works. 3 v. Calcutta. 1864-69. BI-780 – 8 – ne IDC [890]
LES MU'O'NG : GEOGRAPHIE HUMAINE ET SOCIOLOGIE / Cuisinier, Jeanne – Paris: Institut d'ethnologie, 1946 – fr Armell [301]
MUQUYENSE : ORGAO REPUBLICANO – Villa de S. Joao do Muquy, Mar 1915; Jan 1917; 12 May 1918 – 1,5,6 – bl Biblioteca [072]
LE MUR D'AUVERGNE – Organe hebdomadaire regional de la Resistance. no. 11-79. Clermont-Ferrand. 9 sept 1944-45. mq no. 21, 26-27, 59 – 1 – fr A.C.R.P.P. [073]
MURACOLI – Madras, India. Jul-Sept 1966; Mar 1968-Jun 1970 – 6r – 1 – us L of C Photodup [072]
MURACU – Tirunelveli, India. Jul 1966-Aug 1984; Jan-1985-Nov 1994 – 84r – 1 – us L of C Photodup [072]
Murad, Emri *see* DIVAN
Murakami, Joan R *see* EFFECT OF TRAINING ON LACTATE UTILIZATION BY RAT MUSCLE MITOCHONDRIA
MURAL ART : SUBJECT COLLECTIONS – (Individual titles not listed separately) – 6 catalogues on 10mf – 9 – £85.00 – uk Chadwyck [700]
LA MURALLA – Trujillo, 1934-1936 – 5 – sp Bibl Santa Ana [073]
LAS MURALLAS ROMANAS DE ZARAGOZA / Monsalud, Marques de – Madrid: Fortanet, 1910. B.R.A.H. 57, 1910. p513 – sp Bibl Santa Ana [946]
Murari *see* (ANARGHARAGHAVA....)
Muratori, Lodovico A *see*
– ANECDOTA AMBROSIANA
– ANNALI D'ITALIA DAL PRINCIPIO DELL'ERA VOLGARE SINO ALL'ANNO 1749
– ANTIQUITATES ITALICAE MEDII AEVI
– LITURGIA ROMANA VETUS
– RERUM ITALICORUM SCRIPTORES
MURAVEINIK – (Missing: 1913 n1-11, 13-28, 33, 39-40, 42, 44-45, 51; 1914 n14-22, 25-34, 36-41; 1914 n43-1915 n38; 1915 n40-1916 n5; 1916 n9-11, 13-34, 36-40; 1916 n42-1917 n2; 1917 n4) – Kiev, 1913-17 n7 – 19mf – 9 – COR-654/1 – ne IDC [334]
Murav'ev, M N *see* SOCHINENIIA
Murayi, T et al *see* LA PRODUCTIVITE DES PETITS RUMINANTS DANS LES STATIONS DE RECHERCHE DE L'INSTITUT DES SCIENCES AGRONOMIQUES DU RWANDA
MURCHISON MINER (W.A.) – 1893-1894 – 1r – 1 – at Corangamite [980]
Murchison, R I de *see* THE GEOLOGY OF RUSSIA IN EUROPE AND THE URAL MOUNTAINS
Murcia, P J de *see* DISCURSO POLITICO SOBRE LA IMPORTANCIA DE LOS HOSPICIOS, CASAS DE EXPOSITOS CON Y HOSPITALES
THE MURDER OF DELICIA / Corelli, Marie – British Fiction Archive: Unit 1 – 9 – uk Bell [830]
MURDERED MILLIONS / Dowkontt, George D – New York: Medical Missionary Record, [1897?, c1894] – 1mf – 9 – 0-8370-7216-6 – 1986-1216 – us A.T.L.A. [240]
Murdoch, John *see*
– CLASSIFIED CATALOGUE OF PRINTED TRACTS AND BOOKS IN SINHALESE
– CLASSIFIED CATALOGUE OF TAMIL PRINTED BOOKS, WITH INTRODUCTORY NOTICES
– ETHNOLOGICAL RESULTS OF THE POINT BARROW EXPEDITION
– INDIAN MISSIONARY MANUAL
– ON THE SIBERIAN ORIGIN OF SOME CUSTOMS OF THE WESTERN ESKIMOS
– SKETCHES OF INDIAN CHRISTIANS
– A STUDY OF THE ESKIMO BOWS IN THE U.S. NATIONAL MUSEUM
THE MURDOCHVILLE MINER – Murdochville, Canada. v3 n1. 23 aut 1954; v4 n3. 30 mar 1955 – 1r – 1 – Can$25.00 – cn Can Microfilming [072]
MURDOCK TRIBUNE – Murdock, NE. -w. Mar-Dec 1915 – 1 – us NE Hist [071]
Murdowo, Raden *see*
– BALINESE ARTS AND CULTURE
– REFLECTIONS ON INDONESIAN ARTS AND CULTURE
Muret, Jean-Louis *see* MEMOIRE SUR L'ETAT DE LA POPULATION DANS LE PAYS DE VAUD.
Muretov, SD *see* OPISANIE RUKOPISEI BIBLIOTEKI VIFANSKOI DUKHOVNOI SEMINARII
Murfree, William Law *see*
– LAW OF FOREIGN CORPORATIONS
– A TREASTISE ON THE LAW OF OFFICIAL BONDS AND OTHER PENAL BONDS
– A TREATISE ON THE LAW OF SHERIFFS AND OTHER MINISTERIAL OFFICERS
MURFREESBORO FIRST BAPTIST CHURCH. MURFREESBORO, TENNESSEE : CHURCH RECORDS – (10,902p) – 1915-1917, 1953-1988 – 6r – 1 – $436.08 – us Baptist [240]
MURFREESBORO FIRST BAPTIST CHURCH. MURFREESBORO, TENNESSEE : CHURCH RECORDS – 1843-1976. Lacking: Apr 1862-Jun 1868, 1917-36 – 1 – 175.77 – us Baptist [240]
Murfreesboro. North Carolina. Chowan College *see* CATALOGS AND COLLEGE RECORDS
MURFREESBORO THIRD BAPTIST CHURCH. MURFREESBORO, TENNESSEE : CHURCH RECORDS – 1947-70 – 1 – 34.29 – us Baptist [240]
O MURIAHE – Muriae, Brazil. Jan 1923 – 1 – bl Biblioteca [072]
Muriel Jimenez, Vicente et al *see* 1ST CONGRESO SINDICAL AGRARIO DE EXTREMADURA. PONENCIA 6. MECANIZACION E INDUSTRIALIZACION DEL CAMPO
Murillo, A *see* PLANTES MEDICINALES DU CHILI
Murillo y Velarde Jurado, T *see*
– NUEVA Y VARIA DECISION SI SE PUEDE POR LOS CADAVERES CONOCER SI HA MUERTO...DE VENENOS...
– RESOLUCION PHILOSOPHICA Y MEDICA...DEL VERDADERO TEMPERAMENTO FRIO Y HUMEDO DE LA NIEVE
– TRATADO DE RARAS Y PEREGRINAS YERVAS
Muris, J de *see* EPYTOMA JOHANNIS DE MURIS. IN MUSICAM BOECII. IN QUO OMNES COCLUSIONES MUSICE
Murlin, J *see* SERMONS
Murmellius, J *see* PROTREPTICUS STUDIOSORUM POETICES
MURMURE DU LAC SAINT-JEAN : PREMIER JOURNAL AU LAC ST-JEAN – Pointe-Bleue, Canada. prospectus 1879; 15 nov 1879 – 1r – 1 – Can$25.00 – cn Can Microfilming [072]
MURO INVENCIBLE...CONTRA LOS.. / San Pedro de Alcantara, Domingo de – 1747 – 9 – 1.50f – sp Bibl Santa Ana [240]
Muro Orejon, Antonio *see* HERNANDO CORTES, EXEQUIAS, ALMONEDA E INVENTARIO DE SUS BIENES
MURO'S OLD CAP COLLIER LIBRARY – 1883-99. 461 issues – 1 – $128.00 – us L of C Photodup [830]
Murphey, Edward *see* MANUSCRIPT COLLECTION OF TUNES FOR TREBLE INSTRUMENT
Murphy, Aron J *see* TESTING STRENGTH AND POWER
Murphy, Arthur *see* THE GRAY'S INN JOURNAL
Murphy, Debra *see* APPLICATION OF THE TRANSTHEORETICAL MODEL TO EXERCISE ADHERENCE
Murphy, Edgar G *see* PAPERS
Murphy, G *see* THE ATTITUDE OF PHYSICAL EDUCATION TEACHERS IN IRELAND TOWARD THE ASSESSMENT IN SECOND LEVEL TEACHING PROGRAM
Murphy, Gardner *see* AN HISTORICAL INTRODUCTION TO MODERN PSYCHOLOGY
Murphy General Store. Tecumseh, Kansas *see* RECORDS
Murphy, Henry *see* THE CONQUEST OF QUEBEC
Murphy, James Gracey *see*
– THE BOOK OF DANIEL
– BOOK OF REVELATION, OR, THE LAST VOLUME OF PROPHECY
– A CRITICAL AND EXEGETICAL COMMENTARY ON THE BOOK OF EXODUS
– A CRITICAL AND EXEGETICAL COMMENTARY ON THE BOOK OF LEVITICUS
– SACRIFICE AS SET FORTH IN SCRIPTURE
Murphy, James J *see* RENAISSANCE RHETORIC, 1479-1602
Murphy, Walter *see* CORPORATIONS IN PENNSYLVANIA
Murray *see*
– THE HISTORY OF ADAMS COUNTY, ILLINOIS
– MURRAY STANLEY GREAT WAR DIARY
Murray, A W *see* MISSIONS IN WESTERN POLYNESIA..
Murray, Alexander *see*
– ACCOUNT OF THE LIFE AND WRITINGS OF JAMES BRUCE
– MEMOIR OF THE NAVAL LIFE AND SERVICES OF ADMIRAL SIR P.C.H.C. DURHAM
Murray, Andrew *see* THE INNER CHAMBER AND THE INNER LIFE
MURRAY BANNER – Murray, NE. -w. Jul 1891-Oct 1892, scattered issues missing; Dec 1892-Mar 1893 – 1 – us NE Hist [071]
MURRAY BAY ATLAS AND MAPS OF ITS ENVIRONS / DuBerger, C C – Murray Bay Quebec: A. Cimon, 1895. 04301. (Pre-1900 Canadiana) – 9 – cn C.I.H.M. [910]
THE MURRAY BAY HABITANT – Pointe-au-Pic. jul 1907-v2 n14. 15 aut 1922 – 1r – 1 – Can$30.00 – cn Can Microfilming [072]
Murray, Chalmers S *see* BOOK DRAFTS
Murray, Daniel *see* PAPERS OF DANIEL MURRAY, 1881-1955
Murray, David *see* THE BLACK BOOK OF PAISLEY, AND OTHER MANUSCRIPTS OF THE SCOTICHRONICON: WITH A NOTE UPON JOHN DE BURDEUS...AND THE PESTILENCE
Murray, F H M *see* THE HORIZON: A JOURNAL OF THE COLOR LINE
Murray, Geoffrey *see* VOLTAIRE'S 'CANDIDE': THE PROTEAN GARDENER, 1755-1762
Murray, Henry Anthony *see* LANDS OF THE SLAVE AND THE FREE
Murray, Hugh *see* HISTOIRE COMPLETE DES VOYAGES ET DECOUVERTES EN AFRIQUE. ACCOMPAGNEE D'UN PRECIS GEOGRAPHIQUE SUR CE CONTINENT
Murray, J *see*
– THE FINISHING STROKE TO MR. WESLEY'S 'CALM ADDRESS' TO THE PEOPLE OF ENGLAND
– SERMONS TO ASSES
Murray, J Lovell *see* A SELECTED BIBLIOGRAPHY OF MISSIONARY LITERATURE
Murray, James *see* A COMPLEAT ANSWER TO MR. WESLEY'S OBSERVATIONS UPON DR. PRICE'S ESSAY ON CIVIL LIBERTY, WHEREIN THE FATALISM AND INFIDELITY OR MR. WESLEY'S PRINCIPLES ARE CONFUTED,...
Murray, John *see*
– A HANDBOOK FOR TRAVELLERS ON THE CONTINENT: BEING A GUIDE..
– THE LIFE OF REV. JOHN MURRAY, PREACHER OF UNIVERSAL SALVATION
Murray, John Clark *see* AN INTRODUCTION TO ETHICS
Murray, Lindley *see* ENGLISH GRAMMAR
Murray, M A *see* LAHUN 2
Murray, Margaret *see* THE SPLENDOUR THAT WAS EGYPT
Murray, Mimi *see*
– GENDER CLASSIFICATIONS OF FEMALE ATHLETES AND NONATHLETES AT WOMEN'S AND COEDUCATIONAL COLLEGES
– INFLUENCE OF MENTAL IMAGERY ON TENNIS SERVICE ACCURACY OF INTERMEDIATE LEVEL TENNIS PLAYERS
– MOOD STATES AND INJURY IN INTERCOLLEGIATE FIELD HOCKEY PLAYERS
– PERCEIVED AND PREFERRED COACH LEADER BEHAVIORS OF HIGH SCHOOL AND COLLEGE FOOTBALL PLAYERS
– PERCEIVED COMPETENCE AND INTRINSIC MOTIVATION AMONG JUNIOR TENNIS PLAYERS
– THE PORTRAYAL OF WOMEN IN SPORT ADVERTISING IN TWO WOMEN'S FITNESS MAGAZINES
– THE RELATIONSHIP BETWEEN PRECOMPETITIVE ANXIETY AND TEAM COHESION
– THE RELATIONSHIP OF PHYSICAL SELF-PERCEPTION TO INJURY POTENTIAL OF COLLEGE FOOTBALL ATHLETES
– SELF-EFFICACY OF MALE AND FEMALE GOLFERS AT DIFFERING ABILITY LEVELS
– SPORT ACHIEVEMENT ORIENTATION OF MALE AND FEMALE INTERCOLLEGIATE ATHLETES, INTRAMURAL ATHLETES, AND NONATHLETES
MURRAY MIRROR – Murray, NE. -w. Mar 1895-Feb 1896 – 1 – us NE Hist [071]
MURRAY STANLEY GREAT WAR DIARY / Murray & Stanley – 1914-1918 – 2r – 1 – at Corangamite [980]
Murray, Teena *see* EVALUATION OF METABOTRIM(TM) SUPPLEMENTATION OF BODY COMPOSITION, STRENGTH AND VO2MAX IN TRAINING FEMALE ATHLETES
Murray, Thomas Chalmers *see* LECTURES ON THE ORIGIN AND GROWTH OF THE PSALMS
MURRAY'S HANDBOOKS FOR TRAVELLERS – (Pt 1, Abroad: $6,570.00; Pt 2, United Kingdom: $1,990.00) – 1836-1916. Late 19th and early 20th century British travel guides on many countries world-wide – 9 – $8,125.00 set – us UPA [910]
MURRAY'S WEEKLY VOLUNTEER : WEEKLY DEMOCRATIC NEWSPAPER – Hamilton, OH. 20 Aug 1822-26 July 1824 – 1r – 1 – us Western Res [071]
MURRE *see* NYASTE FORPOSTEN

MURRELET – v. 30-35. 1949-54 – 1 – us UMI [590]
Murri, R *see* LETTERE DI UN PRETE MODERNISTA
MURRIETA WEEK – Murrieta, CA. 1989 – 2+ r – 1 – $100.00 ($50.00y) – R04071 – us Library Micro [071]
Murrow, Edward R *see* EDWARD R. MURROW PAPERS, 1927-1965
Murry, John Middleton *see* KEATS
Murs, M A P O 'des *see* TRAITE GENERAL D'OOLOGIE ORNITHOLOGIQUE
Murschhauser, F X. *see* ACADEMIA MUSICO-POETICO BIPARTITA. ODER: HOHE SCHUEL DER MUSICALISCHEN COMPOSITION IN ZWEY THEIL EINGETHEILT
MURTOA OBSERVER AND DUNMUNKLE GAZETTE – 1895-1896 – 1r – 1 – at Corangamite [980]
Murua, Martin, Fray *see*
– HISTORIA GENERAL DEL PERU
Mus, Paul *see* BARABUDUR
MUSA CLIFFORTIANA FLORENS HARTECAMPI / Linnaeus, Carl – Lugduni Batavorum. 1736. B-171 2 – 8 – ne IDC [580]
LA MUSA DEL PECADO / Cordero, Juan Luis – Badajoz: Imp. del Hospicio Provincial, 1932 – 1 – sp Bibl Santa Ana [946]
MUSA ENTRE HIERROS (POESIAS VARIAS) / Ruiz Gonzalez Valero, Manuel – Badajoz: Tip. Vda. de Antonio Arqueros, 1945 – 1 – sp Bibl Santa Ana [440]
MUSA IBN EBI'L GAZAN YAHUT HEMIYYET – Istanbul: Matbaa-i Ebuezziya, 1299 [1882] – $10.00 – us MEDOC [470]
LA MUSA INGENUA...LA MUSA DEL CONSUELO...LA MUSA CIVICA / Cordero, Juan Luis – Badajoz: Imprenta del Hospicio Provincial, 1931 – 1 – sp Bibl Santa Ana [946]
MUSAEUM / Grew, N – M 363. 1681 – 9 – ne IDC [580]
MUSAEUM ZEYLANICUM, SIVE CATALOGUS PLANTARUM, IN ZEYLANA SPONTE NASCENTIUM / Hermannus, P – Lugduni Batavorum. 1726. B-114 2 – 8 – ne IDC [580]
MUSAHABAH RUHANIYA BAIN AL-ALIMAIN / Sinan, Shaikh – (A dialogue between two Muslims, Shaikh Sinan and Ahmad al-'Alim on their return from pilgrimage to Mecca) – Rome, 1570 – 2mf – 9 – H-8432/1 – ne IDC [956]
Musart, C *see* ADOLESCENS ACADEMICUS SUB INSTITUTIONE SALOMONIS
MUSAVVER MUHIT – v1-2 (1324-1325) – 21mf – 9 – $52.50 – us MEDOC [949]
MUSAVVER NEVSAL-I MESAHIR – 1314 [1896] – 2mf – 9 – $23.50 – us MEDOC [949]
MUSAVVER NEVSAL-I OSMANI – (1325[1909]. – 4mf. $36.75; 1326[1910]. – 5mf. $39.00; 1327M[1911]. – 5mf. $36.75; 1328M[1928]. – 5mf. $200.00) – 9 – us MEDOC [949]
MUSAVVER NEVSAL-I SERVET-I FUENUN – (1310[1894]. – 2mf. $40.00; 1312[1895]. – 2mf. $40.00; 1326[1910]. – 5mf. $39.00; 1327[1911]. – 6mf. $50.00; 1328[1912]. – 8mf. $42.00; 1329[1913]. – 2mf. $23.50) – 9 – us MEDOC [949]
MUSAVVER SEYF VE KALEM – (Mueessisi: Ebue'l Fuad Refik. No. 1 (1 Tesrinievvel 1324[1908])) – Istanbul: Mekteb-i Harbiye Matbaasi, 1908-1909 – 2mf – 9 – $30.00 – us MEDOC [949]
Muscat, Eduardo y *see* LA JOVEN Y EL ZAPATERO
DAS MUSCHELHORN : SCHICKSAL UND VOLLENDUNG DER ABDENAS: ROMAN / Leip, Hans – Stuttgart: J G Cotta, c1940 – 1r – 1 – us U.W. Library [830]
Muschg, Walter *see* JEREMIAS GOTTHELF
Muschler, Reinhold Conrad *see* DIE UNBEKANNTE H
MUSCI ALLEGHANIENSES SIVE ENUMERATIO / Sullivant, W S – Columbus, 1846. 87 pp. B-5755 1 – 9 – ne IDC [580]
MUSCI APPALACHIANI / Austin, C F – Tickets of Specimens of Mosses collected mostly in the eastern parts of North America. New Jersey. 1870. B-5453 2 – 8 – ne IDC [580]
MUSCI AUSTRO-AMERICANI / Mitten, W – Journ. Linn. Soc., London, 1869. v. 12, 659 pp. B-439 2 – 8 – ne IDC [580]
MUSCI BORNMULLERIANA; BRYOPHTEN AUS IRAN / Schiffner, V & Froelich, J – (And other articles by I. Therlot and M. Bizot. French text) – 7 – uk Microform Academic [580]
DIE MUSCI DER FLORA VON BUITENZORG... / Fleischer, M – Leiden, 1902-1922. 4vols. Flore de Buitenzorg, pt 5 – 9 – ne IDC [580]
MUSCI ELEISTOCARPI. UEBERSICHT UEBER DIE ELEISTOCARPISCHEN MOOSE / Jaeger, H – (Verhandlungen der St. Gallischen naturwissenschaftlichen Gesellschaft). St. Gallen. 1869. B-6183 2 – 8 – ne IDC [580]
MUSCI EUROPAEI NOVI, VEL BYROLOGIAE EUROPAEAE SUPPLEMENTUM / Schimper, W P – 2v. Stuttgartiae. 1864-66. B-5713 2 – 8 – ne IDC [580]
MUSCI EXOTICI, CONTAINING FIGURES AND DESCRIPTIONS OF NEW OR LITTLE KNOWN FOREIGN MOSSES / Hooker, W J – 2v. London. 1818-20. B-227 2 – 8 – ne IDC [580]
MUSCI FRONDOSI INEDITI ARCHIPELAGI INDICI... / Dozy, F & Molkenboer, J H – Lugduni Batavorum, 1845-1854 – 10mf – 9 – ne IDC [590]
MUSCI INDIAE ORIENTALIS / Mitten, W – London. 1859. B-999 2 – 8 – ne IDC [580]
MUSCI NEPALENSES / Hooker, W J – Description of several new Mosses from Nepal. (Transact. Linn. Soc.). v. 9. London. 1808. B-411 2 – 8 – ne IDC [580]
MUSCI YUNNANENSES / Bescherelle, E – (Ann. Sc. Nat. Bot. S. 7, v. 15). Paris. 1892. B-744 2 – 8 – ne IDC [580]
MUSCINEES ANNAMITES RECOLTEES PAR M. POILANE / Potier de la Varde, R – (Bull. Mus. Hist. Nat.). v. 29. Paris. 1923. B-6192 2 – 8 – ne IDC [580]
MUSCINEES DE LA FRANCE / Boulay, A – Paris, 1884 – 624p – 9 – ne IDC [580]
MUSCLE AND NERVE – (v.3-. 1980- 5,6,9) – v.1-. 1978- – 1 – us UMI [073]
MUSCLE REHABILITATION OF PATIENTS WITH OSTEOARTHRITIS OF THE KNEES / Fisher, N M – 1991 – 3mf – 9 – $12.00 – us Microform Publ [612]
MUSCOLIJUAN – New Concord. Ohio. 1907-1908; 1910-1968 – 1 – us UMI [071]
MUSCOLOGIA BRITANNICA / Hooker, W J & Taylor, T – London. 1818. B-5002 2 – 8 – ne IDC [580]
MUSCOLOGIA GALLICA / Husnot, T – Cahan, Paris. 1884-94. B-6500 2 – 8 – ne IDC [580]
MUSCOLOGIA GERMANICA / Huebener, J W P – Leipzig. 1833. B-5067 2 – 8 – ne IDC [580]
MUSCOLOGIA ITALICAE SPICILEGIUM / Notaris, G de – Mediolani. 1837. B-5318 2 – 8 – ne IDC [580]
MUSCOLOGIA ITINERIS ASSAMICI / Griffith, W – (Calcutta Journ. Nat. Hist.). v. 2. 1842; v. 3. 1845. B-420 2 – 8 – ne IDC [580]
MUSCOLOGIA RECENTIORUM SEU ANALYSIS / Bridel, S E de – v. 1. Gotha. 1797; v. 2, pt. 1. Gotha. 1798; v. 2, pt. 2. Gotha. 1801; v. 2, pt. 3. Gotha. 1803; Suppl., pt. 1. Gotha. 1807; Suppl., pt. 2. Gotha. 1812; Suppl., pt. 4. Gotha. 1819. (Methodus nova muscorum.). B-5329 1 – 9 – ne IDC [580]
MUSCOLOGIAE HIBERNICAE SPICILEGIUM / Turner, D – 5006. 1804 – 9 – ne IDC [580]
MUSCOLOGIE, OU TRAITE SUR LES MOUSSES / Palisot de Beauvois, A M F J – (Mem. Soc. Linneenne de Paris, v. 1). Paris. 1822. B-5064 2 – 8 – ne IDC [580]
MUSCORUM FRONDOSORUM NOVAE SPECIES EX ARCHIPELAGO INDICO ET JAPONICA / Dozy, F & Molkenboer, J H – Lugduni Batavorum, 1844 – 1mf – 9 – ne IDC [590]
Muscovius, Johannes *see* GEBRAUCH UND MISSBRAUCH DES LATEINISCHEN SINGENS UND BETENS..
MUSCULAR ENDURANCE IN WOMEN THROUGH ADULTHOOD : A PREDICTOR OF MUSCULAR STRENGTH / Kuramoto, Anna K – 1994 – 2mf – $8.00 – us Microform Publ [612]
"MUSCULAR STRENGTH AND ENDURANCE IN MAN" 1966 / Clarke, Henry Harrison – 1966 – 3mf – 9 – $12.00 – us Microform Publ [790]
Musculus, W *see* EEN CLAERE ENDE SCHRIFTELICKE ONDERRICHTINGHE VANDEN EEDT. WAER TOEGHEDAEN IS EEN CLEIN ANHANCKSEL DEN SELUEN HANDEL ANGAENDE
MUSE – Ottawa. v1-11. 1983/84-1993/94 – 9 – Can$20.00y – cn Micromedia [420]
DIE MUSE DES ARETIN : DRAMA IN VIER AUFZUEGEN / Widmann, Joseph Viktor – Frauenfeld: J Huber, 1902 – 1r – 1 – us U.W. Library [820]
LA MUSE FRANCAISE – Paris. juil 1823-juin 1824 (I-II) – 1 – fr A.C.R.P.P. [073]
LA MUSE FRANCAISE / Societe des textes francais modernes – Paris. 2v. 1823-1824 – 14mf – 9 – ne IDC [440]
LA MUSE LYRIQUE DEDIEE A [...]. RECUEIL D'AIR AVEC ACCOMPAGNEMENT DE GUITARRE; PAR MR. PATUOART FILS – (Also contains works by Gretey. For one or two voices and guitar. Volume 10 only.) – Imprints and dedications vary – 1 – us Sibley [780]
MUSE WHANGS: POEMS, AMOROUS, BACCHANALIAN, POLITICAL, MEMORIAL, HUMOROUS AND MISCELLANEOUS / Davidson, Judson France – s.l.: s.n., 1887 (s.l.: Will-o-the-Wisp). 03170. (Pre-1900 Canadiana) – 9 – cn C.I.H.M. [810]
MUSEE BOTANIQUE DE B. DELESSERT / Lasegue, A – Paris. 1845. B-434 2 – 8 – ne IDC [580]
LE MUSEE CANADIEN : ILLUSTRE / ed by Morissette, J-F – Quebec, 8 sep 1880 – 1r – 1 – Can$25.00 – cn Can Microfilming [060]
LE MUSEE CANADIEN – Quebec, Canada. prospectus 15 jul 1875; v1. 1 aut 1875 – 1r – 1 – Can$30.00 – cn Can Microfilming [060]
Musee Central des Arts. Paris *see* LA DIRECTION GENERALE...19 NOVEMBRE 1802
Musee de l'Homme (Paris). Phototheque *see* ENREGISTREMENT DES PROJECTIONS, ENREGISTREMENT DES NEGATIFS
Musee de Peinture et de Sculpture. Bagneres-de-Bigorre *see* CATALOGUE DE MUSEE...DONNE PAR M. ACHILLE JUBINAL...A LA VILLE DE BAGNERES-DE-BIGORRE: 1852-1857
MUSEE DES ARTS DECORATIFS CATALOGUE – (Individual titles not listed separately) – Paris, 1904-1976 – 118 catalogues on 194mf – 9 – £1,220.00 – uk Chadwyck [700]
Musee des Beaux Arts. Reims, France *see* LES LE NAIN
MUSEE DU BARDO A TUNIS ET LES FOUILLES DE M. GAUCKLER A CARTHAGE / Perrot, Georges – Paris: Librairie de l'Art Ancien et Moderne, 1900 – 1mf – 9 – $6.00 – fr Bibl Nationale [700]
Musee du Congo Belge. Brussels *see* BIBLIOGRAPHIE ETHNOGRAPHIQUE DU CONGO BELGE ET DES REGIONS AVOISINANTES
Musee du Louvre. Paris *see* DESSINS D'ARCHITECTURE DU 15 AU 19 SIECLE
LE MUSEE FRANCAIS : ECOLES FRANCAISE, ALLEMANDE, ITALIENNE – Paris, France. 1v. 1815 – 1r – 1 – Can$45.00 – cn Can Microfilming [700]
LE MUSEE FRANCAIS : TABLEAUX, STATUES ET BAS-RELIEFS DU LOUVRE – Paris, France. 1v. 1815 – 1r – 1 – Can$45.00 – cn Can Microfilming [700]
Musee Gustave Moreau. Paris *see* DESSINS DE GUSTAVE MOREAU
Musee. Lille *see* CATALOGUE DES TABLEAUX... PRECEDE D'UNE NOTICE HISTORIQUE PAR JULES LENGLART.
LE MUSEE ROYALE : RECUEIL DE GRAVURES – Paris, France. 1v. 1816 – 1r – 1 – Can$45.00 – cn Can Microfilming [760]
LE MUSEE ROYALE : TABLEAUX, STATUES ET BAS-RELIEFS – Paris, France. 1v. 1816 – 1r – 1 – Can$45.00 – cn Can Microfilming [700]
MUSEI DI ZOOLOGIA ED ANATOMIA / Comparata delle R. Universita di Torino – Torino. v8-9. 1893-1894 – 12mf – 9 – ne IDC [590]
Musei di Zoologia ed Anatomia *see* COMPARATA DELLE R. UNIVERSITA DI TORINO
MUSEO ARQUEOLOGICO DE BADAJOZ. ADQUISICIONES DE 1958-61 – Madrid: ALDUS, 1963 – 1 – sp Bibl Santa Ana [930]
MUSEO ARQUEOLOGICO DE MERIDA. ADQUISICIONES DE 1958-61 – Madrid: ALDUS, 1963 – 1 – sp Bibl Santa Ana [930]
MUSEO ARQUEOLOGICO NACIONAL. ADQUISICIONES EN 1920. NOTAS DESCRIPTIVAS / Melida, Jose Ramon – Madrid, 1923 – 1 – sp Bibl Santa Ana [060]
MUSEO ARQUEOLOGICO NACIONAL. HOMENAJE A D. JOSE MELIDA. NOTAS BIOGRAFICAS Y BIBLIOGRAFICAS – Madrid, 1939 – 1 – sp Bibl Santa Ana [930]
IL MUSEO CAPITOLINO... / Bottari, MN & Foggini, N – Milano. 3v. 1819-1821 – 16mf – ne IDC [720]
MUSEO COMICO...CHISTES / Palacio, Manuel, y otro – (v2. 1861) – 1863 – 9 – 1.50f – sp Bibl Santa Ana [820]
MUSEO DE AMERICA. SUS PRECURSORES EN EL SIGLO 16 / Bayle, Constantino – Madrid: Razon y Fe, 1941 – sp Bibl Santa Ana [970]
MUSEO DI PIANTE RARE DELLA SICILIA, MALTA, CORSICA / Boccone, P – Viennae. 1697. B-804 2 – 8 – ne IDC [580]
MUSEO EXTREMENO – Badajoz.1866, no.24 – 9 – 1.50f – sp Bibl Santa Ana [073]
MUSEO INTELECTUAL. VANGUARDIA. MEXICO, 1928 / Elguero, Francisco; ed by Bayle, Constantino – Madrid Razon y Fe, 1928 – 9 – sp Bibl Santa Ana [190]
MUSEO MILITAR HISTORIA. INDUMENTARI.. / Barado, Francisco – 1886. 3 tomos – 9 – 1.50f – sp Bibl Santa Ana [946]
MUSEO NACIONAL DE ARQUEOLOGIA : HISTORIA Y ETNOLOGIA / ed by Bayle, Constantino – Madrid: Razon y Fe, 1927 – 1 – sp Bibl Santa Ana [930]
MUSEO ORGANICO ESPANOL / Eslava, DH – Madrid – 7mf – 9 – us Sibley [780]
Museo Pitre *see* ANNALI
MUSEO POPULAR – Tomo Primero. Madrid. 1887 – 1 – us Res Libr [073]
Museo provincial de Bellas artes *see* CATALOGO
MUSEO TAURINO DE MAHIZFLOR. CATALOGO GUIA 1950 / Aceuchal – Badajoz: Tip. Vda. de A. Argueros, 1950 – 1 – sp Bibl Santa Ana [060]
MUSEOGRAPHIA ODER ANLEITUNG ZUM RECHTEN BEGRIFF UND NUETZLICHER ANLEGUNG DER MUSEORUM ODER RARITAETEN-KAMMERN / Neickelio, CF – Leipzig, Breslau. 1727. BO-379 1 – 9 – ne IDC [060]
LE MUSEON : REVUE D'ETUDES ORIENTALES – 1(1882)-52(1939) – 22mf – 9 – Dfl1,477.00 – ne Slangenburg [073]
MUSEON – 1(1882)-52(1939) – 422mf – 8 – ne Slangenburg [060]
LES MUSES DE LA MODE – Paris. aout-dec 1851 – 1 – fr A.C.R.P.P. [073]
LES MUSES DE LA NOUVELLE FRANCE / Lescarbot, Marc – Paris: Chez Jean Millot, 1609. SEM105P288 – 1mf – 9 – Can$2.25 – cn Bibl Nat [440]
Muset, Colin *see* LES CHANSONS DE COLIN MUSET
MUSEUM – 1948- 1; 1974- 5,6; 1977- 4 x 6 in. 9 – us UMI [073]
MUSEUM ART EDUCATION LIBRARY : 50 CURRICULUM GUIDES WITH INDEX – 1990 – 9 – inquire – National Art Education Association – us Ross [020]
MUSEUM BOTANICUM LUGDUNO-BATAVUM... / Blume, C L – Leiden. 2v. 1849-1851[-1857] – 14mf – ne IDC [580]
MUSEUM FUER KUENSTLER UND FUER KUNSTLIEBHABER / ed by Meusel, Johann G – 1787-92.3v – 2 – us Sibley [700]
MUSEUM HELVETICUM – Basel. v1-40. 1944-83 – 5,9 – Dfl3,200.00; Dfl80.00v – ne Swets [949]
MUSEUM JOURNAL / University of Pennsylvania – v3 no.2; v12 no.1; v14 no.4; v15 no.4; v18 no.4; v19 no.2; v20 no.1. 1913-29 – 9 – $30.00 – us I.R.C. [930]
MUSEUM LUDOVICAE ULRICAE REGINAE / Linnaeus, Carl – B-2399 2. 1764 – 8 – ne IDC [574]
Museum National d'Histoire Naturelle, Paris *see* PHYTOPLANKTON MANUAL
Museum National d'Histoire Naturelle. Paris *see*
– ANNALES
– MEMOIRES
MUSEUM NEWS – 1924-1946 – 1,5,6 us Princeton Micro [060]
MUSEUM OF CONTEMPORARY ART CATALOGUE – (Individual titles not listed separately) – Chicago, 1967-1976 – 54 catalogues on 54mf – 9 – £400.00 – uk Chadwyck [700]
Museum of Early Southern Decorative Arts *see*
– BRITISH REGIONAL CHURCH CARVING (1000-1040) AND FURNITURE (1600-1800)
– GUIDE TO THE INDEX OF EARLY SOUTHERN ARTISTS AND ARTISANS

MUSEUM OF FOREIGN LITERATURE, SCIENCE AND ART – v. 1-45. Jul 1822-Dec 1842 – 1 – us UMI [073]

THE MUSEUM OF FOREIGN LITERATURE, SCIENCE AND ART *see* AMERICAN ECLECTIC

Museum of Mankind (British Museum, Dept. of Ethnography). London *see*
- LIBRARY CATALOGUE OF THE MUSEUM OF MANKIND
- NIGERIAN BRONZES
- NORTHWEST COAST COLLECTION OF AMERICAN INDIAN ART

Museum of Modern Art *see* BULLETIN

Museum of Modern Art. New York *see*
- CATALOG
- CATALOG OF THE LIBRARY OF THE MUSEUM OF MODERN ART
- THE FILM CATALOG: A LIST OF FILM HOLDINGS

Museum Pasat *see* BULETIN MUSEUM

MUSEUM QUARTERLY – (v13-15 1984-87 Can$50.00v. v16-18 1987/88-1989/90 Can$20.00 9. Cont: Ontari Museum Association Quarterly at v13 1984/85. Ceased v18 1990) – Toronto. v13-18. 1984/85-1989/90 – 5,9 – Price varies – cn Micromedia [060]

MUSEUM QUARTERLY *see* ONTARIO MUSEUM ASSOCIATION QUARTERLY

MUSEUM S. R. M. ADOLPHI FREDERICI REGIS SUECORUM / Linnaeus, Carl – 1754 – 8 – B-2588/2 – ne IDC [574]

MUSEUM SENCKENBERGIANUM – Frankfurt am Main. v1-3. 1833/1834-1839/1845 – 24mf – 9 – ne IDC [500]

MUSEUM 'SONO BUDOJO' (SIC) / Indonesia. Jogjakarta – In: Jogjakarta: a Brief Guide. SE-11,667 1 – 9 – ne IDC [060]

MUSEUMJOURNAAL – Amsterdam, 1955-74 – 4r – 1 – £230.00 – uk Chadwyck [700]

MUSEUMS : THEIR USE AND PLACE IN LEARNING AND IN THE TRANSMISSION OF CULTURE / Pearce, James Edwin – Austin, TX: Univ. of Texas, 1921. 20p. (Univ. of Texas Bulletin, no. 2133, 10 Jun 1921) – 1 – us U.W. Library [060]

MUSEUMS AND CHILDREN / Olofsson, Ulla Keding; ed by Teichert, Gerard – 1979 – 9 – 92-3-101692-X – fr UNESCO [060]

MUSEUMS, IMAGINATION AND EDUCATION / Lewis, Sulwyn – 2nd ed 1977 – 9 – 92-3-101036-0 – fr UNESCO [060]

Musgrave, George Clarke *see* TO KUMASI WITH SCOTT

MUSIC – Chicago. v1-22. 1891-1902 – 11r – 1 – £545.00 – uk Chadwyck [780]

MUSIC : LEISURE OR WORK? AMATEUR AND PROFESSIONAL MUSICIANS' PERCEPTIONS OF REHEARSAL AND PERFORMANCE / Juniu, Susana & Tedrick, Raymond E Ted – 1993 – 2mf – $8.00 – us Microform Publ [150]

MUSIC : A REVIEW – New York City. v1-7. 1882-83 – 2r – 1 – £115.00 – uk Chadwyck [780]

MUSIC 1930-1972 (PVB 1895-1977, PT 4) – (With printed bibliography & subject index) – 84mf – 9 – £350.00 – uk Chadwyck [780]

MUSIC. A MONTHLY MAGAZINE DEVOTED TO THE ART, SCIENCE, TECHNIC AND LITERATURE OF MUSIC – v. 1-22. 1891-1902 – 1 – us UMI [780]

MUSIC AMERICA MAGAZINE – (See also: Musician, Player, and Listener) – v1. 1976-1977 – 1,5,6,9 – us UMI [780]

MUSIC ANALYSIS – v1-. 1982- – 1,5,6,9 – us UMI [073]

MUSIC AND DANCE IN SURINAM / Jaap Kunst Centre for Ethnomusicology; ed by Gieben, Claartje & Ijzermans, Jan – (This collection includes finding aids and a plastic binder) – 116mf – 9 – P-958/1 – ne IDC [780]

MUSIC AND EDUCATION : A COMPOSER WRITES ABOUT MUSICAL EDUCATION / Kabalevsky, D B – 1988 – 9 – 92-3-102449-3 – Co-published with Jessica Kingsley Publishers, London – fr UNESCO [780]

MUSIC AND LETTERS – v1- 1920- 1; v57- 5,6,9 – us UMI [780]

MUSIC AND LITURGY – (1985-. 5,6,9) – v1-. 1974- – 1 – us UMI [240]

MUSIC AND RHYTHM – v1-3, no. 8 (all publ). Nov 1940-Aug 1942. (Jazz Periodicals) – 1 reel – 1 – $110.00 – us UPA [780]

MUSIC BOOK MADE BY WILLIAM WALKER FOR MISS ELIZABETH R. ADAMS / Walker, William – ca 1832-1833 – 1r – 1 – $5.00 – us Baptist [780]

MUSIC BOOK OF THE EPHRATA CLOISTER / Ephrata Community – Manuscript with colored ornamentation, written by one of the sisters, with printed index, 1772. This book contains the music to which were sung the hymns in the "Neu vermehrte Turtel Taube." MUSIC 1154, Reel 2 – 1 – us L of C Photodup [780]

THE MUSIC CATALOG / U.S. Library of Congress – (Replaces "Music, Books on Music, and Sound Recordings." Subscription Service available quarterly. Cataloging records for music, scores, sound recordings, books and serials. Also available: Registers and cumulated indexes from 1981-94) – 9 – $130.00 – us L of C Cataloging [780]

MUSIC CITY NEWS – Nashville. 1967-76. 3 reels – 1 – 54.00 – us L of C Photodup [780]

MUSIC CLUBS MAGAZINE – v1- 1922- 1; v50-5,6; v56- 9 – us UMI [780]

MUSIC COLLECTION / Bibliotheque Nationale – 5titles in French & Italian 10 fiches by Ademollo, Fabre d'Olivet, Gautier, Noufflard and Wagner. Titles available separately – 9 – 25.00 – fr Bibl Nationale [080]

MUSIC COLLECTION: 15TH-19TH CENTURIES / Lincoln Cathedral. Library – Parts 1 and 2. With printed index – 1 – £2,400.00 – uk World [025]

MUSIC EDUCATORS JOURNAL – v1- 1914- 1; v55- 5,6; v62- 9 – us UMI [370]

MUSIC EFFECTS ON THE ACQUISITION OF A MOTOR SKILL / Holoway, Ron – University of North Carolina at Chapel Hill, 1995 – 2mf – 9 – $8.00 – PSY1846 – us Microform Publ [611]

MUSIC FOR FORTEPIANO FOUR HANDS : 1770-1820 – 101mf – 9 – MS-k – ne IDC [780]

MUSIC FOR INSTRUMENTAL ENSEMBLE, 1600-1820 – 1997 – 900mf – 9 – ne MMF Publ [780]

MUSIC FOR SOLO INSTRUMENT – 1997 – 550mf – 9 – ne MMF Publ [780]

MUSIC FOR SOLO INSTRUMENT AND ENSEMBLE / ed by Hul, Dick van den – (Music for Solo Instrument (with and without accompaniment) 742mf. Ensemble music 1: Duets and Trios 812mf. Ensemble Music 2: Quartets and Larger Ensembles 868mf. Includes printed guide) – 2422mf – 9 – MS-2000-4917/1 – ne IDC [780]

MUSIC FOR THE HYMNS IN TURTEL-TAUBE / Ephrata Community – Manuscript, ca.1747. This book was called the Mittel-Buch. MUSIC 1154, Reel 1 – 1 – us L of C Photodup [780]

MUSIC FOR THE ZIONITISCHER WEYRAUCHS HUEGEL / Ephrata Community – Manuscript containing the music to which the hymns of the Weyrauchs Huegel were sung, with printed index, ca.1745. MUSIC 1154, Reel 2 – 1 – us L of C Photodup [780]

MUSIC FROM DUTCH LIBRARIES *see* EARLY MUSIC FROM LOW COUNTRIES LIBRARIES

MUSIC HALLS' GAZETTE – London. -w. Apr-Dec 1868. (1 reel) – 1 – uk British Libr Newspaper [073]

MUSIC IN CHRISTIAN HYMNODY / Routley, Erik – 1951 – 1 – 54.95 – us Baptist [240]

MUSIC IN THE RELIGIOUS EDUCATION OF PRIMARY CHILDREN / Ball, Louis, Jr – Aug 1961 – 1 – 8.64 – us Baptist [240]

MUSIC JOURNAL – 1943- 1; 1970 5,6; 1975- 9 – us UMI [780]

MUSIC JOURNALS *see*
- MUZYKA
- MYZUKAL'NAIA SAMODEIATEL'NOST

MUSIC JOURNALS FROM THE RUSSIAN NATIONAL LIBRARY, ST PETERSBURG ON MICROFICHE *see*
- GITARIST
- GRAMMOFON I FONOGRAF
- GRAMMOFON I FOTOGRAFIIA
- GRAMMOFONNAIA ZHIZN'
- GRAMMOFONNYI MIR
- GUSEL'KI-IAROVCHATY
- MUZYKA I ZHYZN
- MUZYKAL'NAIA SAMODEIATEL'NOST
- MUZYKAL'NOE EKHO
- MUZYKAL'NOE OBOZRENIE
- MUZYKAL'NOE SAMOOBRAZOVANIE
- MUZYKAL'NO-TEATRAL'NYI SOVREMENNIK
- MUZYKAL'NYI LISTOK
- MUZYKAL'NYI MIR
- MUZYKAL'NYI TRUZHENNIK
- MUZYKAL'NYI VESTNIK
- MUZYKAL'NYIA UVESELENIIA
- NOVOSTI GRAMMOFONA
- OFITSIAL'NYE IZVESTIIA AKTSIONERNOGO OBSHCHESTVA GRAMMOFON
- PISHUSHCHII AMUR
- PISHUSHCHII AMUR I GRAMMOFONNYE NOVOSTI

MUSIC JOURNALS FROM THE RUSSIAN NATIONAL LIBRARY, ST PETERSBURG ON MICROFICHE – (Individual titles also listed) – 57 titles 817mf complete coll – 9 – $4,450.00 coll – us Ross [780]

MUSIC JOURNALS FROM THE RUSSIAN NATIONAL LIBRARY, ST PETERSBURG ON MICROFICHE *see*
- AKKORD
- ANTRAKT
- ARTISTE RUSSE
- ARTIST-MUZYKANT
- BAIAN
- BIRIUCH PETROGRADSKIKH GOSUDARSTVENNYKH TEATROV
- BIULLETEN' "DOMA PESNI"
- BIULLETEN' TEATRA I MUZYKA
- DETSKII MUZYKAL'NYI MIROK
- EZHENEDEL'NIK PETROGRADSKIKH GOSUDARSTVENNYKH AKADEMICHESKIKH TEATROV
- IUZHNYI MUZYKAL'NYI VESTNIK
- IZVESTIIA S-PETERBURGSKOGO OBSHCHESTVA MUZYKAL'NYKH SOBRANII
- KHOROVOE I REGENTSKOE DELO
- MEZHDUNARODNAIA MUZYKA
- MUZYKA
- MUZYKA DLIA VSEKH
- MUZYKA I BYT
- MUZYKA I TEATR
- NIZHEGORODSKIE MUZYKAL'NYE NOVOSTI
- ORKESTR
- PERSIMFANS
- PROLETARSKII MUZYKANT
- RUSSKII MUZYKAL'NYI VESTNIK
- SOVETSKAIA FILARMONIA
- SOVREMENNYI TEATR I MUZYKA
- STSENA I MUZYKA
- SVET I ZVUK
- SVIREL' PANA
- TEATR I MUZYKA
- TEATRAL'NAIA ROSSIA – MUZYKAL'NYI MIR
- VOSKRESNYI LISTOK MUZYKI I OB'IAVLENII
- ZA PROLETARSKUIU MUZYKU

MUSIC LADY – (1979- 5,6,9) – 1949- – 1 – us UMI [073]

THE MUSIC LIBRARY.. / Watson, Henry – 1730-1810 – 1 – uk Microform Academic [780]

MUSIC MADE EASY TO EVERY CAPACITY, IN A SERIES OF DIALOGUES / Bemetzrieder, A – 1785 – 9 – us Sibley [780]

MUSIC MAGAZINE AND MUSICAL COURIER – v1-164. 1880-1962 – 1 – us UMI [780]

MUSIC MAKER – 1950-71 – 5r – 1 – us Ross [780]

MUSIC MANUSCRIPTS / Wise, Michael et al – From York Minster Library – 1 – uk Microform Academic [240]

MUSIC MANUSCRIPTS / York Minster – Mss. M14, 26, 173, 20, 3 1-4 – 1 – uk Microform Academic [240]

MUSIC MANUSCRIPTS FROM THE GREAT ENGLISH COLLECTIONS, SERIES 1 – (Part 2: The Court Odes of William Boyce. Part 3: The Music Manuscripts of William Boyce and Maurice Greene. Part 4: Section A. Unpublished English Music Mss. before c1850. Part 5: Section B. Unpublished English Music Mss. before c1850. Part 6: Unpublished Continental Music Mss. of the 16th, 17th, and 18th Centuries) – The Oxford Music School Collection at the Bodleian Library, Oxford. Part 1. Unpublished music manuscripts of the 16th and 17th cents – 1 – us Primary [025]

MUSIC MANUSCRIPTS FROM THE GREAT ENGLISH COLLECTIONS, SERIES 2 – (Part 2: Unpublished English Music Mss. 1650-1800. Part 3: Unpublished Continental Music Mss. of the 17th, 18th, and 19th Centuries. Part 4: Section B. Unpublished Continental Music Mss. of the 17th, 18th and 19th Centuries. Part 5: Unpublished English Music Mss. of the 19th Century) – The Music Collection of St. Michael's College, Tenbury, at the Bodleian Library, Oxford. Part 1. Unpublished music manuscripts of the 16th and 17th cents – 1 – us Primary [025]

MUSIC MANUSCRIPTS FROM THE GREAT ENGLISH COLLECTIONS, SERIES 3 – (Part 2: Unpublished Music Mss. of the 16th and 17th Centuries. Part 3: Unpublished Continental Music Mss. of the 16th and 17th Centuries) – The Music Collection of Christ Church, Oxford. Part 1. Unpublished English music manuscripts of the 16th and 17th cents – 1 – us Primary [025]

MUSIC MANUSCRIPTS FROM THE GREAT ENGLISH COLLECTIONS, SERIES 4 – (Part 2: Section B. Polyphonic Music Mss. before c1640. Part 3: Section A. English Music Mss. c1640-1714. Part 4: Section B. English Music Mss. c1640-1714. Part 5: The Chapel Royal Part Books c1670-c1850. Part 6: Section A. Handel Mss: Operas, Serenades and Odes. Part 7: Section B. Handel Mss: Oratorios and Church Music. Part 8: Section C. Handel Mss: Instrumental Music, Cantatas and Other Music. Part 9: Section A. English Music Mss. c1714-c1810. Part 10: Section B. English Music Mss. c1714-c1810) – The Music Manuscript Collection of the British Library, London. Part 1. Section A. Polyphonic music manuscripts before about 1640 – 1 – us Primary [025]

MUSIC MANUSCRIPTS FROM THE GREAT ENGLISH COLLECTIONS, SERIES 5 – (Part 2. Section B. English Music Mss. before c1800. Part 3: Section A. Continental Music Mss. before c1850. Part 4: Section B. Continental Music MSs. before c1850. Part 5: Section C. Continental Music Mss. before c1850. Part 6: Section D. Continental Music Mss. before c1850. Part 7: Section A. English Music Mss. c1800-c1870. Part 8: Section B. English Music Mss. c1800-c1870. Part 9: English Music Mss. c1870-c1930) – The Music Collection of the Royal College of Music, London. Part 1. Section A. English music manuscripts before c1800 – 1 – us Primary [025]

MUSIC MANUSCRIPTS FROM THE GREAT ENGLISH COLLECTIONS, SERIES 6 – (Part 1: Music mss. before 1850 from Cambridge Univ. Library and Ely Cathedral. Part 2: Music mss. from the Rowe Music Library, King's College, Cambridge. Part 3: Handel mss. from the Fitzwilliam Museum. Part 4: English Music mss. from the Fitzwilliam Museum. Part 5: Continental Music mss. from the Fitzwilliam Museum, Section A. Part 6: Continental Music mss. from the Fitzwilliam Museum, Section B) – Music Collections of the Cambridge Libraries – 1 – us Primary [025]

MUSIC MANUSCRIPTS FROM THE GREAT ENGLISH COLLECTIONS, SERIES 7 – (Part 1: British and Continental Music Manuscripts, Section A. Part 2: British and Continental Music Manuscripts, Section B. Part 3: Previously Uncatalogued Music Manuscripts) – Music Manuscripts from the Royal Academy of Music, London – 1 – us Primary [025]

MUSIC MANUSCRIPTS FROM THE GREAT ENGLISH COLLECTIONS, SERIES 8 – (Part 1: Gerald Coke Handel Collection: Mss. of individual works. Part 2: Gerald Coke Handel Collection: Composite vols. and additional printed and manuscript items. Part 3: Geral Coke Handel Collection: The Shaftesbury Manuscripts) – Music Manuscripts from Private Collections – 1 – us Primary [025]

MUSIC MANUSCRIPTS FROM THE GREAT ENGLISH COLLECTIONS, SERIES 9 – (Part 1: The Music Collection of St. George's Chapel, Windsor) – Music Manuscripts from Chapel and Cathedral Libraries – 1 – us Primary [025]

MUSIC MANUSCRIPTS OF THE CLASSICAL AND ROMANTIC ERAS : SERIES ONE: AUTOGRAPH MUSIC MANUSCRIPTS, LETTERS AND DOCUMENTS FROM THE BRITISH LIBRARY, LONDON – (Pt 1: Manuscripts from the Royal, Stowe, Printed Books and Additional Collections 20r $2,400.00. Pt 2: Sources from Additional Manuscripts 21r $2,500.00. Pt 3: Sources from Additional Manuscripts 21r $2,500.00. Pt 4: Sources from Additional Manuscripts 21r $2,500.00. Pt 5: Manuscripts from the Additional, Egerton & Zweig Collections 21r $2,500.00) – Marlborough: Adam Matthew Publications, 1996 – 1 – uk Matthew [780]

THE MUSIC OF NATURE. / Gardiner, William – 1857 – 9 – us Sibley [780]

MUSIC PART BOOKS / Byrd, William & Dering, Richard – York Minster mss. P2 5-5s – 1 – uk Microform Academic [240]

MUSIC PART BOOKS / Dunnington & Jefferson – York Minster Ms 295 – 1 – uk Microform Academic [240]

MUSIC PART-BOOKS / Gostling, William – York Minster ms. music – 1 – uk Microform Academic [780]

MUSIC PERCEPTION – (1985/86- . 5,6,9) – v1- . 1983- – 1 – us UMI [073]

MUSIC REFERENCE SERVICES QUARTERLY / ed by Studwell, William – v5 n1. 1996- – 1,9 – $75.00 in US $105.00 outside hardcopy subsc – us Haworth [780]

MUSIC REVIEW – v1- 1940- 1; 1972- 5,6; 1976- 4 x 6 in. 9 – us UMI [780]

MUSIC REVIEW – Boston. v1-2. 1898-1900 – 1r – 1 – £60.00 – uk Chadwyck [780]

THE MUSIC REVIEW – Chicago, 1891-94 – 1 – £60.00 – uk Chadwyck [780]

MUSIC SCENE – (Incorporated in: Probe Magazine following no 371 1990) – nos 237-371. 1967-1990 – 9 – Can$20.00y – cn Micromedia [780]

MUSIC SCENE *see* SCENE MUSICALE

THE MUSIC STUDENT – v. 1-4. 1915-17 – 1 – 19.00 – us L of C Photodup [780]

MUSIC SUBJECT HEADINGS. SECOND EDITION ENLARGED / New York Public Library. Reference Department – 1966.-12,800 cards 1 reel.-ISBN: 0-8161-1358-0 – 1 – $80.00 – uk Hall [780]

MUSIC TRADE JOURNAL – v1-90. Aug 1879-Aug 1892 – 1 – 2100.00 – us Opus [073]

THE MUSIC TRADE REVIEW – New York City. v1-11. 1875-80 – 3r – 1 – £165.00 – uk Chadwyck [780]

MUSIC TRADES – 1890- 1; v33- 5,6; v37- 9 – us UMI [073]

MUSIC TRADES REVIEW – London. n1-305. 1877-1902 – 5r – 1 – us Ross [780]

MUSIC WEEK – 1959- 1; 1974- 5,6; 1975- 4 x 6 in. 9 – us UMI [780]

MUSIC WORKS – (1978-88 Can$115.00. nos 43-45 1989-90 Can$60.00y. Nos 46-60 1990-94 Can$20.) – Toronto, 1978-94 – 1,9 – Price varies – cn Micromedia [780]

MUSICA – v1- 1947- 1; v29- 5,6,9 – us UMI [780]

MUSICA – 1855, 1857-59, Repertoire International de la Presse Musicale Collection – 1 reel – 1 – us UMI [780]

MUSICA – 1876-78, 1883-85, Repertoire International de la Presse Musicale Collection – 1 reel – 1 – us UMI [780]

MUSICA AUTOSCHEDIASIKOU, QUAE PER ALIQUOT ACCESSIONES IN GRATIAM PHILOMUSORUM / Burmeister, J – P 188. n1601 – 9 – ne IDC [780]

MUSICA CHORALIS DEUDSCH / Agricola, Martin – 1533 – 9 – us Sibley [780]

MUSICA DIVINA – v. 1-10, 16-26. 1913-1938 – 1 – us Schnase [780]

MUSICA D'OGGI – v. 1-24. 1919-1942 – 1 – us Schnase [780]

MUSICA ECCLESIASTICA DA CAPELLA, A QUATTRO VOCI DIVISA IN MESSE, MOTETTI / Grancini, M – Alto, tenor, bass, and organ parts only. 1645 – 9 – us Sibley [780]

MUSICA FIGURALIS DEUDSCH / Agricola, Martin – 1532 – 9 – us Sibley [780]

MUSICA FIGURALIS ODER NEUE KLAERICHE RICHTIGE UND VERSTAENDLICHE UNTERWEISUNG DER SINGE KUNST MIT GEWISSEN REGULEN KLAREN UND VERSTAENDLICHEN EXEMPELN NEBEN VOLLKOMMENER ERKLAERUNG DER MODORUM MUSICORUM / Frederici, Daniel – Rostock: J Richeln, 1649 – 1 – us Sibley [780]

MUSICA INCANTANS, SIVE POEMA EXPRIMENS MUSICAE VIRES / South, R – Oxonii. 1667. BP-474 1 – 9 – ne IDC [780]

MUSICA INSTRUMENTALIS DEUDSCH / Agricola, Martin – P-112. 1529 – 9 – ne IDC [780]

MUSICA INSTRUMENTALIS DEUDSCH.. / Agricola, Martin – 1532 – 9 – us Sibley [780]

MUSICA LIBRIS QUATOR DEMONSTRATA / Faber, J – P 263. 1551 – 9 – ne IDC [780]

MUSICA MECHANICA ORGANOEDI.. / Adlung, Jacob – 2v. 1768 – 2 – us Sibley [780]

MUSICA MODERNA PRATTICA / Herbst, Johannes A – ed. 3. Frankfurt. 1658. BP-315 1 – 9 – ne IDC [780]

MUSICA NICOLAI LISTENII, AB AUTHORE DENUO RECOGNITA, MULTISQUE NOVIS REGULIS ET EXEMPLIS ADAUCTA / Listenius, Nicolaus – 1548 – 9 – us Sibley [780]

MUSICA NICOLAUS LISTENII, AB AUTHORE DENUO RECOGNITA, MULTISQ NOUIS REGULIS ET EXEMPLIS ADAUCTA / Listenius, Nicolaus – Francofordiae a O J Eichord, [1550] – 1 – us Sibley [780]

MUSICA NOVA QUA TAM FACILIS OSTEN DITUR CANECDI SCIENTIA,...(ETC) / Orgosinus, H – (Latin and German text) – Leipzig: Grosse/Lantzenberger, 1603 – 1 – us Sibley [780]

MUSICA POETICA, SIVE COMPENDIUM MELOPOETICUM / Herbst, Johannes A – 1643 – 9 – us Sibley [780]

MUSICA POETICA, SIVE COMPENDIUM MELOPOETICUM, DAS IST: EINE KURZE ANLEITUNG. HARMONIAM. COMPONIREN UND MACHEN SOLL / Herbst, Johannes A – P 314. 1643 – 9 – ne IDC [780]

MUSICA POPOLARE – Giornale ebdomandario illustrato di testo, musica e desegni. v.1-4. 1882-85 – 9 – us Sibley [780]

MUSICA PRACTICA SIVE INSTRUCTIO PRO SYMPHONIACIS / Herbst, Johannes A – 1642 – 9 – us Sibley [780]

MUSICA SACRA – (Caecilienvereinsorgan). v. 1-68. 1866-1937 – 1 – us Schnase [780]

MUSICA SACRA – "Sancta Sancte". Soc. de St. Gregoire. Ghent. Bruges. v1-47, no1. 1881-1940 – 1 – us Schnase [780]

MUSICA SACRA: BEITRAEGE ZUR REFORM UND FOERDERUNG DER KATHOLISCHEN KIRCHENMUSIK – (Includes Supplements) – Regensburg. 1868-1937. v1-67. – 250mf – 9 – ne IDC [240]

MUSICA SACRA; RIVISTA LITURGICA MUSICALE – Milano. Anno. 58-67. 1932-1940 – 1 – us NY Public [780]

MUSICA SACRE / Hastings, Thomas & Warriner, Solomon – 1822 with APPENDIX, 1834 – 1 – 12.67 – us Baptist [240]

MUSICA THEORICA / Fogliano, L – 1529 – 9 – us Sibley [780]

MUSICA UNIVERSALE ARMONICO PRATICA DETTATA DALL'ISTINTO. E PER I SUONATORI DI GRAVE CEMBALO, ED ORGANO ESPOSTA IN VENTIQUATTRO ESERCIZI / Basili, A – 1775? – 9 – us Sibley [780]

MUSICACHE – (Original Eulenburg editions published by Breithoff and Hartel. 95,000p of music scores covering 300 years of classical music, 1600-1900.) – 1002mf – 9 – $2360.00 – us UMI [780]

MUSICAE ACTIVAE MICROLOGUS ANDREAE ORNITOPARCHI OSTROFRANCI MEYNINGENSIS, ARTIUM MAGISTRI, LIBRO QUATUOR DIGESTUS... / Ornithoparcus, Andrea – Leipzig: Valentin Schumann, 1517 – 1 – us Sibley [780]

MUSICAE ARTIS PRAECEPTA NOVA ET FACILIMA, PER SEPTEM VOCES MUSICALES / Calvisius, S – Jena. 1612. BP-199 1 – 9 – ne IDC [780]

MUSICAE EPITOME SIVE COMPENDIUM EX GLAREANI DODECACHORDO / Glarean, Heinrich – 1557 – 2 – us Sibley [780]

MUSICAE EROTEMATUM LIBRI DUO...CUM PRAEFATIONE D. JOANNIS FREIGII / Beurhusius, Friedrich – 1580 – 9 – us Sibley [780]

MUSICAE INSTITUTIONES OTHAMARI NACHTGALL ARGENTINI A NEMINE UN QUA PRIUS PARI FACILITATE TENTATE STUDIOSO, QUI AMOUSOI ESSE NOLINT NO MEDIPCRITER CONDUCIBILES / Luscinius, Ottmar – Ioannes Knoblouch notis areis excepit Argentoraci, [1515] – 1 – us Sibley [780]

MUSICAE MATHEMATICAE / Werckmeister, A – 1686 – 9 – us Sibley [780]

MUSICAE MATHEMATICAE HODEGUS CURIOSUS, ODER RICHTIGER MUSICALISCHER WEG-WEISER / Werckmeister, A – P 514 1. 1687 – 9 – ne IDC [780]

MUSICAE PRACTICAE SIVE ARTIS CANENDI RATIO, QUAMVIS SUCCINCTA / Burmeister, J – P 189. 1601 – 9 – ne IDC [780]

MUSICAE RUDIMENTA / Faber, Nicolaus – 1516 – 2 – us Sibley [780]

MUSICAL AMERICA – New York City, 1898-99; 1910-40 – 1 – £2,150.00 – uk Chadwyck [780]

MUSICAL AMERICA – v.3-84. 1905-64 – 1 – us UMI [780]

MUSICAL AND DRAMATIC WORLD – Liverpool. England. -w. Oct 1881-7 Jul 1883. (1 reel) – 1 – uk British Libr Newspaper [780]

MUSICAL AND SEWING MACHINE GAZETTE (MUSICAL COURIER) – New York City. v8-32. 1884-96 – r4-9 – 1 – £4,410.00 – uk Chadwyck [780]

Musical Art Club. Charleston, South Carolina *see* MINUTES

MUSICAL BULLETIN : A JOURNAL – Chicago. v1-4. 1879-83 – 1r – 1 – £60.00 – uk Chadwyck [780]

THE MUSICAL BULLETIN – New York, 1867-73 – 1 – £60.00 – uk Chadwyck [780]

THE MUSICAL CABINET – v. 1, PT. 1-12. Jul 1841-Jun 1842 – 9 – us Sibley [780]

MUSICAL CLIPPER – Philadelphia, 1895 – 1 – £60.00 – uk Chadwyck [780]

MUSICAL COURIER *see* MUSIC MAGAZINE AND MUSICAL COURIER

A MUSICAL DICTIONARY : BEING A COLLECTION OF TERMS AND CHARACTER... / Grassineau, J – London, 1740 – 5mf – ne IDC [780]

MUSICAL EDUCATION AND MUSICAL ART / Eastman, E – Boston: Damrell and Upham, 1893 – 1 – us Sibley [780]

THE MUSICAL GALAXY – Toronto: [s.n, 1875?-18–] – 9 – cn C.I.H.M. [790]

MUSICAL GAZETTE – New York. v1. 1854-55 – 1r – 1 – us Ross [780]

THE MUSICAL GAZETTE – New York, 1854-55 – 1 – £60.00 – uk Chadwyck [780]

THE MUSICAL GAZETTE – New York. v. 1, no. 1-17, 19, 22-26. Nov 11 1854-May 25 1855 – 1 – us NY Public [780]

THE MUSICAL HERALD – Boston, Chicago. v1-14. 1880-93 – 6r – 1 – £330.00 – uk Chadwyck [780]

THE MUSICAL INDEPENDENT – Chicago. v1-3. 1868-71 – 1r – 1 – £60.00 – uk Chadwyck [780]

THE MUSICAL JOURNAL – Toronto: Timms, Moor, [1886?-18– or 19–] – 9 – cn C.I.H.M. [780]

THE MUSICAL JOURNAL FOR THE PIANO-FORTE IN TWO SECTIONS, ONE OF VOCAL AND ONE OF INSTRUMENTAL MUSIC – Selected and arranged by Benjamin Carr. Baltimore: J. Carr 1800-1804. MUSIC 1135 – 1 – us L of C Photodup [780]

MUSICAL LEADER AND CONCERTGOER – Chicago, 1895- – 1 – £220.00 – uk Chadwyck [780]

MUSICAL MAGAZINE – v1. 1792 – 1 – us UMI [780]

THE MUSICAL NEWS – San Francisco. 1944-76. 5 reels – 1 – 99.00 – us L of C Photodup [780]

MUSICAL NEWS AND HERALD – 1891-1920 – 1 – uk Manchester Libr [780]

MUSICAL NEWSLETTER – 1971- 1,5,6; 1976- 9 – us UMI [073]

MUSICAL OPINION – 1877- 1; 1976- 5,6,9 – us UMI [780]

THE MUSICAL OPINION – 1877-1992. Continued annually – 1 – £3,895.00 – uk World [073]

MUSICAL OPINION AND MUSIC TRADE REVIEW – London. v16-65. 1893-1942 – 16r – 1 – us Ross [780]

MUSICAL ORNAMENTS, SIMPLY EXPLAINED WITH NUMEROUS EXAMPLES FROM THE WORKS OF J.S. BACH, HANDEL, CLEMENTI, CZERNY ET AL / Harding, H – 2nd rev ed. London: Weekes & Co; Chicago: C F Summy Co, [190?] – 1 – us Sibley [780]

MUSICAL QUARTERLY – (v. 55- 1969- 5,6. v. 57- 1971- 9) – v. 1- 1915- – 1 – us UMI [780]

MUSICAL QUARTERLY – v1-41. 1915-55 – 1,5,6 – us Princeton Micro [780]

MUSICAL RECORD – Boston. 1-502. 1878-1903 – 15r – 1 – £820.00 – uk Chadwyck [780]

THE MUSICAL RED BOOK OF MONTREAL / ed by Sandwell, Bernard K – Montreal: F A Veitch, 1907. SEM105P1491 – 3mf – 9 – Can$6.75 – cn Bibl Nat [780]

MUSICAL REVIEW – New York City. v1-3. 1879-81 – 1r – 1 – £60.00 – uk Chadwyck [780]

MUSICAL TIMES – New York. v1-5. 1849-52 – 1r – 1 – us Ross [780]

MUSICAL TIMES – v. 1-71. 1844-1930 – 1 – us UMI [780]

THE MUSICAL TIMES – London, 1844-1992. Continued annually – 1 – £3,695.00 – uk World [073]

THE MUSICAL TOUR OF MR. DIBDIN, IN WHICH PREVIOUS TO HIS EMBARKATION FOR INDIAN HE FINISHED HIS CAREER AS A PUBLIC CHARACTER.. / Dibdin, Charles – Sheffield: Printed for the author by J. Gales, 1788 – 1 – us U.W. Library [780]

MUSICAL TRAVELS THROUGH ENGLAND / Collier, J – P 223. 1774 – 9 – ne IDC [780]

MUSICAL VISITOR – v. 1-26. 1871-97 – 1 – us UMI [780]

MUSICAL VISITOR – v.1-26. Oct 1871-Dec 1897 – 1 – 69.00 – us L of C Photodup [780]

MUSICAL WORLD – Boston. Feb 1901-Jan 1904 – 1 – us Schnase [073]

MUSICAL WORLD – Boston. v1-4. 1901-04 – 1r – 1 – us Ross [780]

MUSICAL WORLD – v. 1-71. 1836-91 – 1 – us UMI [780]

THE MUSICAL WORLD – Boston. v. 1, no. 1-v. 4, no. 1. Feb 1901-Jan 1904 – 1 – us NY Public [780]

MUSICALIA – Havana. no. 1-17. May 1928-Dec 1932; Second Series, no. 1-6. Nov 1940-Apr 1942 – 1 – us NY Public [780]

MUSICALISCHE BIBLIOTHEK, HERAUSGEGEBEN VON H. A. FR. V. ESCHSTRUTH / Eschstruth, H AF von – 2v. 1784-85 – 9 – us Sibley [780]

MUSICALISCHE DISCURZE DURCH DIE PRINCIPIA DEDUCIRT, UND IN GEWISSE CAPITEL EINGETHEILT / Beer, J B – Deren Innhalt nach der Vorrede zu finden. Nuernberg. 1719. BP-638 1 – 9 – ne IDC [780]

MUSICALISCHE HANDLEITUNG ODER GRUENDLICHER UNTERRICHT / Niedt, Friedrich E – Erster Theil. 1710 – 9 – us Sibley [780]

MUSICALISCHE PARODOXALDISCOURSE, ODER UNGEMEINE VORSTELLUNGEN / Werckmeister, A – Qvedlinburg. 1707. BP-775 1 – 9 – ne IDC [780]

DER MUSICALISCHE PATRIOT, WELCHER SEINE GRUENDLICHE BETRACHTUNGEN UEBER GEIST- UND WELTL. HARMONIEN / Mattheson, J – 1728 – 9 – us Sibley [780]

DER MUSICALISCHE PATRIOT WELCHER SEINE GRUENDLICHE BETRACHTUNGEN, UEBER GEIST-UND WELTL. HARMONIEN / Mattheson, J – P 723. 1728 – 9 – ne IDC [780]

MUSICALISCHER HANDLEITUNG DRITTER UND LETZTER THEIL / Niedt, Friedrich E – 1717 – 9 – us Sibley [780]

MUSICALISCHER-TRICHTER, DADURCH EIN... / Fuhrmann, MH – Frankfurt an der Spree: in Verlegung des Autoris, [1706] – 3mf – 9 – us Sibley [780]

MUSICALISCHES GESPRAECHE UBER DIE EUANGELIA, MIT 4, 5, 6 UND 7 STIMMEN NEBENST DA BASSO CONTINUO / Hammerschmidt, Andreas – Dresden: Verlegts Christian Bergen und in Wolfgang Seyfferts Druckerey, 1655-56 – 1 – us Sibley [780]

MUSICALISCHES HALLELUJA, ODER SCHONE UND GEISTREICHE GESANGE / Bachofen, J C – Zurich: Burklischer Druckery, 1786 – 1 – us Sibley [780]

MUSICALISCHES LEXICON / Walther, J G – 1732 – 9 – us Sibley [780]

MUSICALISCHES LEXICON ODER MUSICALISCHE BIBLIOTHEC... / Walther, J G – Leipzig, 1732 – 8mf – ne IDC [780]

MUSICALS – (Lists 122 productions) – 157mf – 9 – £700.00 – uk Chadwyck [790]

MUSICBUECHLEIN FUER DIE JUGEND IN DEUTSCHEN UND LATEINISCHEN SCHULEN ZU GEBRAUCHEN / Quitschreiber, G – Jehna. 1607. BP-441 1 – 9 – ne IDC [780]

MUSIC-CLASS JOURNAL AND ORGANIST'S COMPANION – Dubuque. v1-2 n2. 1865-66 – 1r – 1 – £60.00 – uk Chadwyck [780]

MUSICE ACTIVE MICROLOGUS / Ornithoparchus, Andrea – Apr 1519 – 9 – us Sibley [780]

MUSICI OPERIS, HARMONIARUM QUATUOR, QUINQUE, SEX, OCTO, ET PLURIUM VOCUM / Handl, Jacob – v. 1-4. 1586-1590 – 9 – us Sibley [780]

MUSICIAN – v42-. 1982- – 1,5,6,9 – us UMI [073]

MUSICIAN *see* THE CANADIAN MUSICIAN

THE MUSICIAN – Boston, 1928-39 – 1 – £165.00 – uk Chadwyck [780]

MUSICIAN AND ARTIST – (Boston Periodical). v.1, n.1-5. 1876 – 9 – us Sibley [073]

MUSICIAN, PLAYER, AND LISTENER – (See also: Music America Magazine) – v1- 1977- – 1,5,6,9 – us UMI [780]

LE MUSICIEN PRATIQUE / Azopardi, F – Tome 1-2. 1786 – 9 – us Sibley [780]

LES MUSICIENS NORMANDS, ESQUISSE BIOGRAPHIQUES; COMPRENANT LES NORMS DES ARTISTES MUSICIENS LES PLUS CELEBRES NEE EN NORMANDIE DU 11E AU 19E SIECLE : SUPPLEMENT OU 2E SERIE / Fallouard, P – Honfleur: C de Baudre, 1860 – 1 – us Sibley [780]
MUSICK BOOK / Adams, William O – London, 4 Sept 1795. Manuscript collection of British and American tunes for treble instrument. Includes: Columbia, a New Country Dance with Figures; Drink to Me Only; Yankee Doodle. Music 1970 – 1 – us L of C Photodup [780]
Musick, Thomas Hubbard *see* THE GENESIS OF LIFE AND THOUGHT
A MUSICK-LECTOR.. / Eccles, Salomon – 1667 – 2 – us Sibley [780]
MUSICK'S MONUMENT / Mace, Thomas – 1676 – 2 – us Sibley [780]
MUSICK'S MONUMENT; OR A REMEMBRANCER OF THE BEST PRACTICAL MUSICK / Mace, Thomas – P-707. 1676 – 9 – ne IDC [780]
MUSICO PRATTICO CHE BREVEMENTE DIMOSTRA IL MODO DI GIUNGERE / Bononcini, G M – Opera Ottava. 1673 – 9 – us Sibley [780]
MUSICO PRATTICO CHE BREVEMENTE DIMOSTRA IL MODO DI GIUNGERE / Bononcini, G M – Opera Ottava. 1688 – 9 – us Sibley [780]
IL MUSICO TESTORE DEL P. BAC ZACCARIA TEVO / Tevo, Z – 1706 – 9 – us Sibley [780]
MUSICOLOGY GENERAL CATALOGUE / ed by Davidsson, Ake – (Serials 16,269mf. Monographs 2,090mf. Individual titles available) – 9 – ne IDC [780]
MUSICUS AUTODIDACTOS. DER SICH SELBST INFORMIRENDE MUSICUS / Eisel, J P – 1762 – 9 – us Sibley [780]
MUSICUS AUTODIDAKTOS / Eisel, J P – P 674. 1738 – 9 – ne IDC [780]
DIE MUSIK – Berlin etc. v. 1-35. Oct 1901-Jan 1943. Incomplete – 1 – us NY Public [780]
MUSIK – Berlin. v1-35. 1901-43 – 21r – 1 – us Ross [780]
MUSIK *see* MUSIK IM KRIEGE
DER MUSIK DOCTORS TAGEBUCH SEINER MUSIKALISCHEN REISEN / Burney, Charles – Dritter Band. Durch Boehmen, Sachsen, Brandenburg, Hamburg und Holland. Hamburg. 1773. BP-657 1 – 9 – ne IDC [943]
DER MUSIK DOCTORS TAGEBUCH SEINER MUSIKALISCHEN REISEN / Burney, Charles – Zweyter bd. Durch Flandern, die Niederlande und am Rhein bis Wien. Hamburg. 1773. BP-656 1 – 9 – ne IDC [910]
MUSIK IM KRIEGE – War-merger of "Musik", "Neue Zeitschrift fuer Musik" and "Neues" – 1 – us Schnase [780]
MUSIK OCH MUSIKINSTRUMENT – 1934 – 1 – us I.U. Libraries [390]
MUSIK UND BEWEGUNGSSCHULUNG BEI SCHUELERN DER SEKUNDARSTUFE 1 / Lietz, Uwe – 1991 – 2mf – 9 – DM98.00 – 3-89349-418-9 – gw Hänsel [780]
MUSIK UND GESELLSCHAFT – 1966-1983 – 440mf – 1 – DM2,508.00 – gw Mikro Press [780]
MUSIK UND GOTTESDIENST – v27- 1973-1,5,6; v29- 9 – us UMI [073]
MUSIK UND KIRCHE – v. 1-16. 1929-1944 – 1 – us Schnase [780]
MUSIK VON CARL FRIEDRICH CRAMER. ERSTES VIERTELJAHR / Cramer, Carl F – 1789 – 9 – us Sibley [780]
MUSIKALISCHE BIBLIOTHEK ODER GRUENDLICHE NACHRICHT NEBST UNPARTHEYISCHEM URTHEIL VON ALTEN UND / Mizler, L C – P 726. 1743 – 9 – ne IDC [780]
MUSIKALISCHE BIBLIOTHEK, ODER GRUENDLICHE NACHRICHT NEBST UNPARTHEYISCHEM URTHEIL VON ALTEN UND / Mizler, L C – Leipzig. 1752. BP-727 1 – 9 – ne IDC [780]
DER MUSIKALISCHE DILLETTANT / Daube, J F – 1773. 2bd – 9 – us Sibley [780]
MUSIKALISCHE DYNAMIK UND AGOGIK / Riemann, H – Hamburg: Rahten etc., 1884 – 1 – us Sibley [780]
MUSIKALISCHE KORRESPONDENZ DER TEUTSCHEN FILARMONISCHEN GESELLESCHAFT FUER DAS JAHR JUL 1790-DEZ 1791 / Bossler, H P K – 9 – us Sibley [780]
MUSIKALISCHE SYNTAXIS / Riemann, H – Leipzig: Breitkopf & Haertel, 1877 – 1 – us Sibley [780]
MUSIKALISCHER ALMANACH AUF DAS JAHR 1782. MUSIKALISCHES HANDBUCH AUF DAS JAHR 1782 – 1782. Often attributed to J. F. Reichardt or C. L. Junker – 9 – us Sibley [780]
MUSIKALISCHER ALMANACH AUF DAS JAHR 1784. MUSIKALISCHES TASCHENBUCH AUF DAS JAHR 1784 – (Often attributed to C. L. Junker) – 9 – us Sibley [780]
MUSIKALISCHER ALMANACH FUER DEUTSCHLAND AUF DAS JAHR, 1782-1784 / Porkel, J N – P 273. 2 v – 9 – ne IDC [780]
MUSIKALISCHER ALMANACH FUER DEUTSCHLAND AUF DAS JAHR 1782-1784, 1789 / Forkel, J N – Leipzig: Schwickert, 1782-1789 – 13mf – 9 – us Sibley [780]
MUSIKALISCHER ANDACT / Hammerschmidt, A – 5 pts. [c1646-c1652] – 1 – us Sibley [780]
MUSIKALISCHER STAARSTECHER / Mizler, L C – 1739-40 – 9 – us Sibley [780]
MUSIKALISCHER UND KUENSTLER-ALMANACH AUF DAS JAHR 1783 – 9 – us Sibley [780]
MUSIKALISCHES CENTRALBLATT – Leipzig. 1881-4. 1 reel – 1 – 21.00 – us L of C Photodup [780]
MUSIKALISCHES CONVERSATIONS-LEXIKON UND ERGAN ZUNGSBAND / Mendel, Herman – Berlin. 1870-79. 11v. in 6 – 1 – 69.00 – us L of C Photodup [780]
MUSIKALISCHES KUNSTMAGAZIN.. / Reichardt, Johann F – 1-2 bd. 1-8 stueck. 1782-91 – 2,9 – us Sibley [780]
MUSIKALISCHES MAGAZIN – Langensalza. no. 1-74. 1901-1929. Incomplete – 1 – us NY Public [780]
MUSIKALISCHES MAGAZIN – v1-74. 1901-29 – 1r – 1 – us Ross [780]
MUSIKALISCHES OPFER SR. KOENIGLICHEN MAJESTAET IN PREUSSEN UND C. ALLERUNTERTHAENIGST GEWIDMET... / Bach, Johann Sebastian – (1st ed. Imperfect copy: lacks title page, trio sonata and all but 3 of the canons) – Zella: J G Schuebler, 1747 – 1 – us Sibley [780]
MUSIKALISCHES WOCHENBLATT – Leipzig. v. 1-41. Jan 1 1870-Dec 22 1910. Incomplete – 1 – us NY Public [780]
MUSIKALISCHES WOCHENBLATT – Leipzig. v1-41. 1870-1910 – 12r – 1 – us Ross [780]
MUSIKALISCHES WOCHENBLATT *see* – NEUE ZEITSCHRIFT FUER MUSIK
MUSIKALISCHES WOCHENBLATT. ORGAN FUER TONKUENSTLER UND MUSIKFREUNDE – Leipzig. 1870-1910. v1-41. – 536mf – 9 – ne IDC [073]
MUSIKALISCH-KRITISCHE BIBLIOTHEK / Forkel, J N – 3v. 1778-79 – 9 – us Sibley [780]
MUSIKALISCH-KRITISCHE BIBLIOTHEK / Forkel, J N – Gotha. 2v. 1778-1779 – 13mf – ne IDC [780]
Musikbibliothek Peters *see* JAHRBUCH DER MUSIKBIBLIOTHEK PETERS
MUSIKBLAETTER DER SUDETENDEUTSCHEN – Bruenn. v. 1-2. 1936-1938 – 1 – us Schnase [780]
MUSIKDIDAKTISCHE AUFGABEN IM KINDERCHOR (1984) / Bechtel, Christine – 1993 – 2mf – 9 – DM80.00 – 3-89349-838-9 – gw Hänsel [780]
DIE MUSIKHANDSCHRIFTEN DER STAATS- UND STADTBIBLIOTHEK AUGSBURG – (mf ed 1997) – 600mf – 9 – DM9,500.00 – 3-89131-240-7 – gw Fischer [090]
MUSIKHANDSCHRIFTEN DER STAATSBIBLIOTHEK ZU BERLIN – PREUSSISCHER KULTURBESITZ = MUSIC MANUSCRIPTS OF THE STAATSBIBLIOTHEK ZU BERLIN – PREUSSICHER KULTURBESITZ : TEIL 1: DIE BACH-SAMMLUNG – (mf ed 1997-) – ca 1500mf (1:24) in 5 installments – 9 – DM9,980.00 – 3-598-34420-1 – gw Saur [780]
DIE MUSIKHANDSCHRIFTEN DER UNIVERSITAETSBIBLIOTHEK MUENCHEN – (Gesamtedition: Die Handschriften der Universitaetsbibliothek Muenchen) – 1995 – 263mf – 9 – DM5,500.00 – 3-89131-203-2 – gw Fischer [780]
MUSIKLAISCHES VIERLERLEY HRSG. VON HERRN CARL PHILIP EMANUEL BACH : CONTAINS INTRUMENTAL AND VOCAL CHAMBER MUSIC BY VARIOUS GERMAN COMPOSERS INCLUDING C.P.E.BACH, GRAUN, FASCH, CRAMER, J.C.F. BACH, AND J.E. BACH / Bach, C P E – Hamburg: Gedruckt und verlegt von M C Bock, 1770 – 5 – us Sibley [780]
MUSIK-MAPPE; EINE ZEITSCHRIFT MIT NOTEN-BEILAGEN – Berlin. bd. 1 5. 1904-1911 – 1 – us NY Public [780]
MUSIKPAEDAGOGISCHE ZIELVORSTELLUNGEN VON EMILE JAQUES-DALCROZE / Lietz, Uwe – 1991 – 157p – 9 – DM98.00 – 3-89349-448-0 – gw Hänsel [780]
MUSIKPFLEGE – v. 1-15. 1930-1944 – 1 – us Schnase [780]
MUSIK-WELT – Berlin, 1880-82 – 1 – Inquire at Mikrofilmarchiv for details – gw Misc Inst [780]
"MUSIK-WELT." MUSIKALISCHE WOCHENSCHRIFT FUER DIE FAMILIE UND DEN MUSIKER – v. 1-2, no. 1-13. 1880-82 – 1 – 19.00 – us L of C Photodup [780]
Musil, Robert *see* DREI FRAUEN
MUSIM BERAHI / Rifai, Ali – SE 5426 1961 – 9 – ne IDC [950]
MUSINGS OVER THE "CHRISTIAN YEAR" AND "LYRA INNOCENTIUM" / Yonge, Charlotte Mary – Oxford: Printed by J. Parker for Messrs. Pott and Amery, [1871?] – 2mf – us A.T.L.A. [240]
LA MUSIQUE / Fabre d'Olivet, Antoine – Paris, 1896. 93p. 1 fiche. (Music Collection) – 9 – 6.00 – fr Bibl Nationale [780]
LA MUSIQUE / Gautier, Theophile – Paris: E. Fasquelle, 1911. 310p. 4 fiches. (Music Collection) – 9 – 10.00 – fr Bibl Nationale [780]
MUSIQUE DES CHANSONS DE BERANGER / Beranger, Pierre Jean de – Paris: Garnier freres, 1868. SEM105P935 – 6mf – 9 – Can$13.50 – cn Bibl Nat [780]
LA MUSIQUE DES FAMILLES – Paris. v. 1-4. Oct 20 1881-Oct 8 1885 – 1 – us NY Public [780]
LA MUSIQUE DES FAMILLES – Paris. v1-4. 1881-85 – 1r – 1 – us Ross [780]
MUSIQUE ET LITURGIE – v1-22. 1916/17-1938/39 – 1 – us Schnase [780]
MUSIQUE: REVUE D'HISTOIRE DE CRITIQUE – Paris. v. 1-3. no. 6. 1927-30 – 1 – us Schnase [780]
MUSIQUE SACREE – v. 1-40 46. 1902-42. (v. 37, 39 missing) – 1 – us Schnase [780]
MUSKALISCHE WURFELSPIELE, WALZER : INSTRUCTION TO COMPOSE, WITHOUT KNOWLEDGE OF MUSIC, GERMAN WALTZES BY THROWING TWO DICE / Mozart, Wolfgang Amadeus – (In 4 languages.[Authentically doubtful]) – Bonn: Simrock, 1798 – 1 – us Sibley [780]
Muskalla, Konstantin *see* DIE ROMANE VON JOHANN TIMOTHEUS HERMES
MUSKINGAM MESSENGER – Zanesville. Ohio. 1816-1829 – 1 – us UMI [071]
Muskingham. Ohio. Presbytery *see* CHURCH RECORDS, MS 384
MUSKINGUM MESSENGER – New Concord. Ohio. 1814-1815 – 1 – us UMI [071]
MUSKOGEE AND NORTHEASTERN OKLAHOMA / Benedict, John D – Including the counties of Muskogee, McIntosh, Wagoner, Cherokee, Sequoyah, Adair, Delaware, Mayes, Rogers, Washington, Nowata, Craig and Ottawa. Chicago: S.J. Clarke Publ. Co., 1922.v1-2, Oklahoma Reel 2.v3, Oklahoma Reel 3. (The Cox Library Collection) – 5 – us Americana [978]
MUSKOKA ILLUSTRATED: WITH DESCRIPTIVE NARRATIVE OF THIS PICTURESQUE REGION / Adam, Graeme Mercer – Toronto: Wm. Bryce, c1888. 02389. (Pre-1900 Canadiana) – 9 – cn C.I.H.M. [971]
MUSK-OX – (No issues publ in 1984, 1985, 1990 or 1993. Ceased no 40 1994) – Saskatoon. nos 1-40. 1967-94 – 9 – Can$20.00y – cn Micromedia [073]
THE MUSK-OX – 1967-78. (American Indian Periodicals in the Princeton University Library). 19 fiches – 9 – $75.00 – us UPA [305]
MUSLIM CHRONICLE – Calcutta, India. 1895-1905 – 1 – uk Microform Academic [072]
MUSLIM COURIER – Djakarta, 1965 – 1mf – 9 – ne IDC [260]
MUSLIM REVIEW – Calcutta. 1926-30. v1-4. – 32mf – 8 – ne IDC [260]
THE MUSLIM REVIEW – v12-38. Jan 1933; Jan 1949-Jun 1951 (complete) – 1r – 1 – ATLA S0536 – us A.T.L.A. [260]
THE MUSLIM WORLD : IN THE VICTORIA AND ALBERT MUSEUM / Victoria and Albert Museum. National Art Library. London – (Part 1: Paintings and Drawings in the Searight Collection. Part 2: Prints in the Searight Collection. Part 3: Color Prints in the Searight Collection. Part 4: Paintings, Drawings and Prints in the Design, Prints and Drawings Department. Part 5: Prints in the Design, Prints and Drawings Department) – 1990 – 9 – $2,800.00 – 0-8161-1756-X – uk Hall [700]
THE MUSLIM WORLD / Victoria and Albert Museum. London – (With printed index) – 62 colour 101 b/w 6 Com mf – 15,9,17 – $2,302.00 – 1-869934-15-6 – uk Emmett [260]
THE MUSLIM WORLD.. : ISLAMIC STUDY AND...CHRISTIAN INTERPRETATION AMONG MUSLIMS – v1-38. 1911-48 (complete) – 10r – 1 – ATLA S0056 – us A.T.L.A. [260]
MUSLIN WORLD – (1985-. 5,6,9) – v38-. 1948- – 1 – us UMI [073]
MUSOMACHIA: ID EST BELLUM MUSICALE / Lauremberg, P – Rostochii. 1642. BP-357 1 – 9 – ne IDC [780]
MUSSELBURGH NEWS – 1 – £42.00r – uk Scot News [072]
Mussolini, Benito *see* JOHN HUSS
MUSSOLINI EN ESPANA: SANTANDER, PRESA DEL FASCISMO – Madrid, 1937. Fiche W1067. (Blodgett Collection of Spanish Civil War Pamphlets) – 9 – us H.U. College Libr [946]
Mussulman, Laura M *see* PREDICTION OF FAT FREE MASS IN AFRICAN AMERICAN WOMEN
MUST FULL EMPLOYMENT COST MONEY? / Beckerath, Ulrich von – 2fiches (24x) – 9 – 1.00f – at Libertarian Micro [320]
MUST THE BIBLE GO? : A REVIEW OF THE DECISION OF THE SUPREME COURT OF WISCONSIN IN THE EDGERTON BIBLE CASE / McAtee, William A – Madison, WI: Tracy, Gibbs, 1890 – 1mf – 9 – 0-8370-8594-2 – 1986-2594 – us A.T.L.A. [370]
MUST THE OLD TESTAMENT GO? : OR, THE RELATION OF THE OLD TESTAMENT TO THE CHRISTIAN LIFE OF TODAY / Crafts, Wilbur Fisk – Boston: James H Earle, 1883 – 1mf – 9 – 0-8370-2767-5 – 1985-0767 – us A.T.L.A. [220]
MUST WE DEPEND UPON POLITICAL PROTECTION? / Lefevre, Robert – With E. A. Opitz. 1962. Also: Justice. 1 fiche (24x) – 9 – 1.00f – at Libertarian Micro [320]
Mustafa, Husain *see* POSTAL TECHNOLOGY AND MANAGEMENT
Mustafa Nyzuli, Al-Kulavi *see* DIVAN
Mustajab Khan *see* THE LIFE OF HAFIZ OOL-MOOLK, HAFIZ REHMUT KHAN
THE MUSTANG – (Also known as: The Polygram; The Polytechnic Californian) – San Luis Obispo, CA. Polytechnic State University: 1916-1987 – 2r – 1 – $1,200.00 – B02903 – us Library Micro [370]
MUSTAQBAL *see* AL-MUSTAQBAL
Muste, A J *see* THE PAPERS OF A.J. MUSTE, 1920-1967
MUSTER ROLLS / U.S. Marine Corps (Navy) – 1798-1892. Selected records. 16 rolls. T1118 – 1 – us Nat'l Archives [355]
MUSTER ROLLS AND PAYROLLS OF MILITIA AND REGULAR ARMY ORGANIZATIONS IN THE BATTLE OF TIPPECANOE, NOV. 1811 / U.S. War Department. Adjutant General's Office – 1roll. T1085 – 1 – us Nat'l Archives [324]
Musters, George Chaworth *see* AT HOME WITH THE PATAGONIANS; A YEAR'S WANDERINGS OVER UNTRODDEN GROUND FROM THE STRAITS OF MAGELLAN TO THE RIO NEGRO
MUSUL'MANSKAIA PECHAT' ROSSII V 1910 GODU – Spb. 1911. BR-4405 2 – 8 – ne IDC [260]
MUSURGIA SEU PRAXIS MUSICAE / Luscinius, Ottmar – 1536 – 9 – us Sibley [780]
MUSURGIA SEU PRAXIS MUSICAE ILLIUS PRIMO QUAE INSTRUMENTIS AGITUR CERTA RATIO / Luscinius, Ottmar – P 706. 1536 – 9 – ne IDC [780]
MUSURGIA UNIVERSALIS SIVE ARS MAGNA CONSONI ET DISSONI IN 10 LIBROS DIGESTA / Kircher, Athanasius – 1650. 2v – 9 – us Sibley [780]

MUSWELLBROOK CHRONICLE – Jan 1 1898-Dec 31 1910 – 9 – at Pascoe [072]
THE MUTABLE MANY: A NOVEL / Barr, Robert – New York, London: F. Stokes Co., c1896. 03350. (Pre-1900 Canadiana) – 9 – cn C.I.H.M. [830]
MUTATION RESEARCH – v1-141. 1964-84 – 1,5,6,13 – sz Elsevier [575]
Mutch, William James *see* HISTORY OF THE BIBLE: ARRANGED FOR USE AS A TEXT-BOOK
Mutchmore, Samuel Alexander *see* A VISIT OF JAPHETH TO SHEM AND HAM
MUTESA OF BUFANDA / Gray, J M – Uganda Journal. 1934 – 1 – us Res Libr [960]
Muth, Julius Bernhard *see* UEBER DAS VERHAELTNIS VON MARTIN OPITZ ZU DANIEL HEINSIUS
Muth, Karl *see* DIE WIEDERGEBURT DER DICHTUNG AUS DEM RELIGIOESEN ERLEBNIS
Muthmann, Fritz *see* UNTERSUCHUNGEN ZUR "EINKLEIDUNG" EINIGER PLATONISCHER DIALOGE
Mutiara, Dali *see* PEDOMAN PROPAGANDA
THE MUTINY ON BOARD H.M.S. BOUNTY, AND THE SUBSEQUENT VOYAGE OF A PART OF THE CREW.. / Bligh, William – London: Bankside Press, (1900?).140p. ill – 1 – us U.W. Library [910]
Mutschler, Harry *see* VERGLEICHENDE STUDIE ZWEIER UNTERSCHIEDLICHER LAKTATMESSMETHODEN
MUTTER : GEDICHTE / Johst, Hanns – Muenchen: A Langen/G Mueller, c1930 – 1r – 1 – us U.W. Library [810]
MUTTER : ROMAN / Tovote, Heinz – Berlin: Ullstein, [1912?] – 1r – 1 – us U.W. Library [830]
MUTTER MARIE : ROMAN / Mann, Heinrich – Berlin: P Zsolnay, 1927 – 1r – 1 – us U.W. Library [830]
MUTTER OHNE TOD – DIE BEGEGNUNG : ZWEI ERZAEHLUNGEN / Johst, Hanns – Muenchen: A Langen/G Mueller, 1933 – 1r – 1 – us U.W. Library [830]
MUTTERS SCHLEIER : HUMORIGE VERSE / Pleyer, Wilhelm – Karlsbad; Leipzig: A Kraft, 1944 – 1r – 1 – us U.W. Library [810]
MUTTERSCHUTZ (HQ 5) / ed by Stoecker, Helene – Frankfurt/M., 1(1905) -3(1907) (mf ed 1992) – 17mf – 9 – DM179.00 – 3-89131-059-5 – gw Fischer [640]
Mutua Aseguradora de Transportistas *see*
– ESTADO DE LAS CUENTAS DE PARTICIPACION EN LOS FONDOS SOCIALES DE LOS SENORES MUTUALISTAS CON POLIZAS EN VIGOR EN 31 DE DICIEMBRE DE 1962
– MEMORIA. EJERCICIO 1962
– MEMORIA. EJERCICIO 1968
– MEMORIA. EJERCICIO 1969
– MEMORIA-EJERCICIO 1961
Mutua Cerealista de Caceres *see*
– MEMORIA. 1970
– MEMORIA 1973
– MEMORIA 1976
– MEMORIA. EJERCICIO 1958
MUTUA CEREALISTA DE CACERES. MEMORIA EJERCICIO DE 1961 – Caceres: Tip. La Minerva, 1962 – 1 – sp Bibl Santa Ana [946]
Mutua Extremana de Vehiculos *see* MEMORIA. EJERCICIO 1970
Mutua Extremena de Seguros. Caceres *see*
– MEMORIA. EJERCICIO 1975
– MEMORIA EJERCICIO 1977
– MEMORIA EJERCICIO 1979
Mutua Extremena de Vehiculos *see*
– ESTATUTOS Y REGLAMENTOS DE LA...
– MEMORIA EJERCICIO 1972
MUTUAL AID / Kropotkin, Peter – 1902. 396p. 1 fiche (29x) – 9 – 1.00f – at Libertarian Micro [320]
MUTUAL BANKING / Greene, William B – 1fiche (24x) – 9 – 1.00f – at Libertarian Micro [320]
MUTUAL REVIEW – v.1-45. 1934-76. Continued as yProfessional Agent – 1 – us UMI [073]
MUTUAL RIGHTS AND CHRISTIAN INTELLIGENCER – (Title varies) – v1-2. 1828-30 (complete) – 1r – 1 – ATLA S0168A – us A.T.L.A. [073]
MUTUAL RIGHTS AND METHODIST PROTESTANT – (Cont by: Methodist Protestant) – v1-4 no 22. 7 Jan 1831-30 May 1834 (complete) – 1r – 1 – ATLA S0169 – us A.T.L.A. [240]
MUTUAL RIGHTS AND METHODIST PROTESTANT – v1. 1824-25 – 1 – us UMI [073]
MUTUAL RIGHTS AND METHODIST PROTESTANT *see* METHODIST PROTESTANT
MUTUAL RIGHTS OF THE MINISTERS AND MEMBERS OF THE METHODIST EPISCOPAL CHURCH – v1-4. Aug 1824-Jul 1828; v1-2. 1828-30 (complete) – 1r – 1 – ATLA S0168B – us A.T.L.A. [240]
LAS MUTUALIDADES LABORALES DE TRABAJADORES AUTONOMOS DE SERVICIOS, DE LA INDUSTRIA Y DE LAS ACTIVIDADES DIRECTAS PARA EL CONSUMO. COMPENDIO... / Lancho Moreno, Juan Jose – Caceres: Tip. El Noticiero, 1962 – 1 – sp Bibl Santa Ana [946]
A MUTUCA : ORGAM HUMORISTICO E NOTICIOSO – Manaos, Amazonas. 19 Nov 1893 – 1,5,6 – bl Biblioteca [072]
A MUTUCA : SEMANARIO CRITICO E NOTICIOSO – Senna Madureira, Acre. 2 Mar 1930 – 1,5,6 – bl Biblioteca [072]
Muurling, Willem *see* RESULTATEN VAN ONDERZOEK EN ERVARING OP GODSDIENSTIG GEBIED
MUVAFFAKIYET-I MILLIYE – Ordu, 1923-19? – 9 – $10.00 – us MEDOC [956]
MUVAZENE-I 'UMUMIYYE KANUN VE ESBAB-I MUCIBE LAYIHALARI – (1330[1913].-9mf. $75.00; 1333[1915].-12mf. $75.00; 1332[1914].-11mf. $75.00) – us MEDOC [650]
EL MUY MAGNIFICO SENOR DON GONZALO PIZARRO / Pino y Caza, Gabriel – Guayaquil: Imprenta de la Universidad, 1950 – sp Bibl Santa Ana [920]
MUY NOBLE, MUY LEAL Y MUY BENEFICA / Guia. Plasencia – Plasencia: Excelent. Ayuntamiento, 1961 – 1 – sp Bibl Santa Ana [946]
O MUYRAKYTA E OS IDOLOS SYMBOLICOS... / Barbosa Rodrigues, Joao – 2nd ed. Rio de Janeiro: Imp. nacional, 1899 – 1 – F301.72 – fr Armell [972]
Muyser, J *see* MARIA'S HEERLIJKHEID IN EGYPTE
MUZA – Ezhemesiachnoe izdanie. v. 1-4. Spb. 1796. B-1452 2 – 8 – ne IDC [073]
MUZAKIRAT-I MAJLIS-I SHURA-YI MILLI-'I IRAN – (Dawrah-'i 21, jalsah-'i 1-dawrah-'i 24, jalsah-'i 209 (14 Mihr 1342-17 Bahman 1357[6 Oct 1963-9 Feb 1979])) – Tehran: Majlis-i Shura-yi Milli-i Iran – 15r – 1 – $1,200.00 – us MEDOC [950]
MUZAKIRAT-I MAJLIS-I SHURA-YI MILLI-'I IRAN – (Dawrah-'i 3, jalsah-'i l-dawrah-'i 18, jalsah-'i 231 (17 Muharram 1333-23 Farvardin 1335[Nov 1914-12 Apr 1956]. Session 10 $150.00. Session 19 3r $150.00. Session 20 $150.00) – Tehran: Majlis-i Shura-yi Milli-i Iran – ca 22r – 1 – $1,200.00 – us MEDOC [950]
MUZAKIRAT-I MAJLIS-I SHURA-YI MILLI-I IRAN – (24 Sessions. Available individually) – 1324-1357 [1906-1979] – 9 – $150.00 ea – us MEDOC [320]
MUZAKIRAT-I MAJLIS-I SINA – (Dawrah-'i 1: jalsah-'i 38-126 (15 Mihr 1329-13 Mihr 1330[7 Oct 1951-5 Oct 1951]); dawrah-'i 2: jalsah-'i 1-116 (27 Isfand 1332-4 Azar 1334[18 Mar 1954-25 Nov 1955])) – Tehran: Majlis-i Sina-yi Iran – 3r – 1 – $125.00 – us MEDOC [950]
MUZE I REVOLIUTSII – Petrograd: Muze i revoliutsii, 1923. 1v – 1 – CSUX89-S735 – us Hoover Inst Photo [947]
MUZEI PAMIATI F.M. DOSTOEVSKAGO V IMP. ROSSIISKOM ISTORICHESKOM MUZEE IM. IMPERATORA ALEKSANDRA 3 V MOSKVE, 1846-1903 GG / Dostoevskaia, A – Spb. 1906. BR-5889 2 – 8 – ne IDC [060]
Muzhev, I F *see*
– KAZACHESTVO DONA, KUBANI I TEREKA V REVOLIUTSII 1905-1907 GG
– OCHERKI ISTORII REVOLIUTSIONNOGO DVIZHENIIA NA SEVERNOM KAVKAZE V 1905-1907 GG
– SOVETY RABOCHIKH DEPUTATOV V 1905 GODU NA DONU I SEVERNOM KAVKAZE
MUZIJAKAL KUNST-WOORDENBOEK / Verschuere Reynvaan, J – Amsterdam, 1795 – 14mf – ne IDC [780]
MUZIJKAAL KUNST-WOORDENBOEK / Verschuere Reynvaan, J – Amsterdam. 1795. BP-496 1 – 9 – ne IDC [780]
MUZYKA – 1956- 1; 1974- 5,6; 1975- 9 – us UMI [073]
MUZYKA – Moscow, 1910-16 – 100mf – 9 – $575.00 – us Ross [780]
MUZYKA – Moscow, 1937 (weekly) – 6mf – 9 – us Ross [780]
MUZYKA – Moscow. n1-255. 1910-16 (weekly) – 100mf – 9 – $575.00 – us Ross [780]
MUZYKA DLIA VSEKH – (Suppl to the journal: 30 dnei) – Moscow, 1928 (monthly) – 2mf – 9 – us Ross [780]
MUZYKA I BYT – Leningrad, 1927 (monthly 12 issues publ) – 1mf – 9 – us Ross [780]
MUZYKA I REVOLIUTSIIA – Moscow. v1-4. 1926-29 – 1r – 1 – us Ross [073]
MUZYKA I REVOLYUTZIYA – Moscow. 1926-1929 – 1 – us NY Public [780]
MUZYKA I TEATR – Moscow, 1922-24 (weekly) – 9mf – 9 – us Ross [780]
MUZYKA I TEATR – St Petersburg, 1867-68 (bimonthly 17 issues publ) – 5mf – 9 – us Ross [780]
MUZYKA I ZHYZN – Moscow. n1-11 1908; n1-12 1909; n1-12 19010; n1-12 1911; n1-6 1912 (monthly) – 28mf – 9 – $160.00 – us Ross [780]
MUZYKALE SPRAAKKONST / Lustig, Johann Wilhelm – P 380. 1754 – 9 – ne IDC [780]
MUZYKAL'NAIA SAMODEIATEL'NOST – Moscow. n1-12 1933; n1-12 1934; n1-12 1935; n1-2 1936 (monthly) – 27mf – 9 – $160.00 – us Ross [780]
MUZYKAL'NAYA KULTURA – Moscow. no. 1-3. 1924 – 1 – us NY Public [780]
MUZYKAL'NAYA LETOPIS' – Leningrad. v. 1-3. 1922-1926 – 1 – us NY Public [780]
MUZYKAL'NAYA NOV' – Moscow. v. 1-2, no. 1-12. Oct 20 1923-1924 – 1 – us NY Public [780]
MUZYKAL'NOE EKHO – Vil'na, Lithuania. n1-5. 1914 (monthly) – 3mf – 9 – $25.00 – us Ross [780]
MUZYKAL'NOE NASLEDIE CHAIKOVSKOGO / Tchaikovsky, Peter Ilyich – Iz istorii ego proizvedenii. Moscow, 1958. 542p. BR-10,656/1 – 9 – ne IDC [780]
MUZYKAL'NOE OBOZRENIE : A MONTHLY SUPPL WITH MUSIC – St Peterburg, 1885-88 (weekly 105 issues publ) – 31mf – 9 – us Ross [780]
MUZYKAL'NOE OBRAZOVANIE = MUSIKALISCHE BILDUNG : ZEITSCHRIFT FUER MUSIKPADAGOGIK, MUSIKWISSEN-SCHAFTLICHE FORSCHUNG UND SOZIALE FRAGEN DES MUSIKLEBENS – Moscow. v1-5. 1926-30 – 1r – 1 – us Ross [780]
MUZYKAL'NOE SAMOOBRAZOVANIE – Odessa, 1906-07 (biweekly) – 4mf – 9 – us Ross [780]
MUZYKAL'NO-TEATRAL'NYI SOVREMENNIK – St Peterburg, 1900-01 (weekly 48 issues publ) – 15mf – 9 – us Ross [780]
MUZYKAL'NOYE OBRAZOVANIYE – Moscow. v. 1-5. 1926-1930 – 1 – us NY Public [780]
MUZYKAL'NYI I TEATRAL'NYI VESTNIK – v. 1-5. Spb. 1856-60. BR-4136 2 – 8 – ne IDC [780]
MUZYKAL'NYI LENINGRAD, 1917-1957 / ed by Golubovskii, I V – Leningrad, 1958. 527p. BR-10,745/1 – 9 – ne IDC [780]
MUZYKAL'NYI LISTOK – St Petersburg, 1972/73-1876/77 – 35mf – 9 – us Ross [780]
MUZYKAL'NYI MIR – St Petersburg, 1882-83 (weekly) – 7mf – 9 – us Ross [780]
MUZYKAL'NYI TRUZHENNIK – Moscow, 1906-10 (biweekly) – 27mf – 9 – us Ross [780]
MUZYKAL'NYI VESTNIK – (Includes: Literaturmoe pribavlenie k Muzykal'nomu vestniku [n1-12 1870; n1-12 1871]) – Moscow. n1-12 1870; n1-12 1871 (monthly) – 23mf – 9 – $135.00 – us Ross [780]
MUZYKAL'NYIA UVESELENIIA – Moscow, 1774 – 1mf – 9 – $25.00 – us Ross [780]
MUZYKOZNANIYE – Leningrad. v. 1-4. 1925-1928 – 1 – us NY Public [780]
Muzzey, David Saville *see* THE RISE OF THE NEW TESTAMENT
MVHAMEDIS ALFRAGANI ARABIS CHRONOLIGCA ET ASTRONOMICA ELEMENTA, ... / Ahmad ibn Muhammad ibn Kathir, Al Farghani – Francofvrdi, 1590 – 7mf – 9 – H-8423/1 – ne IDC [956]
MVP: MODERN VETERINARY PRACTICE – v.46-53. 1965-72. Continued by Modern Veterinary Practice – 1 – us UMI [073]
MVSICA GETUTSCHT VND AUSSGEZOGE DURCH SEBASTIANU VIRDUG PRIESTERS VO AMBERG VN ALLES GESANG AUS DEN NOTE IN DIE / Virdung, S – Basel. 1511. BP-768 1 – 9 – ne IDC [780]
MVSVRGIA VNIVERSALIS SIVE ARS MAGNA CONSONI ET DISSONI IN X LIBROS DIGESTA. ROMAE / Kircher, Athanasius – v. 1-(2). 1650. BP-341 1 – 9 – ne IDC [780]
M.W. Wood, Publisher *see* HISTORY OF ALAMEDA COUNTY
MWANGAZA – Zanzibar, Tanzania. -w. 7 Jan 1959-5 Oct 1960. Lacking Jan-May 1960. 1 reel – 1 – uk British Libr Newspaper [072]
MWONGOZI – Zanzibar, Tanzania. -w. 2 Jan 1959-15 June 1962. 1 reel – 1 – uk British Libr Newspaper [072]
MY BONDAGE AND MY FREEDOM / Douglass, Frederick – New York: Miller, Orton, & Mulligan, 1855 – 1 reel – 1 – us Western Res [920]
MY BOY LIFE, PRESENTED IN A SUCCESSION OF TRUE STORIES: A BOOK FOR OLD OR YOUNG / Carroll, John – Toronto: W. Briggs, 1882. 00485. (Pre-1900 Canadiana) – 9 – cn C.I.H.M. [920]
MY CAMPAIGN IN IRELAND : CATHOLIC UNIVERSITY REPORTS AND OTHER PAPERS / Newman, John Henry – Aberdeen: Printed for private circulation only by A. King, 1896 – 2mf – us A.T.L.A. [240]
MY CLERICAL FRIENDS AND THEIR RELATIONS TO MODERN THOUGHT / Marshall, T W – London: Burns, Oates, 1873 – 1mf – us A.T.L.A. [240]
MY DIOCESE DURING THE WAR : EXTRACTS FROM THE DIARY OF ARTHUR HAMILTON BAYNES / Baynes, Arthur Hamilton – London: G. Bell, 1900 – 1mf – us A.T.L.A. [240]
MY EXPERIENCE IN PRISON (CCC73) = HSI YU CHI / Chao, Tzu-ch'en – (In Chinese) – Shanghai: Association Press of China, 1948 – 1r – 1 – 1984-B500 – us A.T.L.A. [920]
MY EXPERIENCE IN RURAL WORK (CCC190) = NUNG-TS'UN KUNG-TSO CHING-YEN-T'AN / Hsu, Pi-chang – Shanghai: Association Press of China, 1936 – 1r – 1 – 1984-B500 – us A.T.L.A. [240]
MY EXPERIENCES IN MANIPUR AND THE NAGA HILLS / Johnstone, James – London: S. Low, Marston, 1896. xxvii,286p – 1 – us U.W. Library [950]
MY FOUR RELIGIOUS TEACHERS : CHARLES G. FINNEY, DAVID HAWLEY, ALIAS R. BEADLE, HORACE BUSHNELL / Trumbull, Henry Clay – Philadelphia: Sunday School Times Co., 1903 – 1mf – us A.T.L.A. [240]
MY GRANDMOTHER: A MUSICAL ENTERTAINMENT / Storace, Stephen – (Vocal score). 1796 – 9 – us Sibley [780]
"MY HOME ON THE SMOKY" / Bamberg, Elma L – 1 – us KS Hist [920]
MY IMPRESSIONS OF SPAIN / Atholl, Katharine Marjory – Essex. 1937. Fiche W 734. (Blodgett Collection of Spanish Civil War Pamphlets) – 9 – us H.U. College Libr [946]
MY LADY NICOTINE / Barrie, James Matthew – London: Hodder and Stoughton, 1890 – 1 roll – 1 – 1-55879-598-7 – uk Libr Preservation [830]
MY LADY OF THE CHINESE COURTYARD / Cooper, Elizabeth – New York: Frederick A. Stokes, 1914. xvi,262p. plates – 1 – us U.W. Library [950]
MY LAI MASSACRE, MEDINA COURT-MARTIAL : AFTER ACTION REPORT – PUBLIC AFFAIRS ACTIVITIES PERTAINING TO THE COURT-MARTIAL OF CAPTAIN L. MEDINA AND RELATED ACTIVITIES, JANUARY 1970 TO OCTOBER 1971 – Fort McPherson, GA: HQ 3rd Army, n.d – 3mf – 9 – $4.50 – LLMC 97-008 – us L.L.M.C. [340]
MY LAND / Johnson, James B – (An unpaginated, bilingual booklet explaining the essentials of the land registration system in the TTPI) – TTPI Publ Off, jul 1971 – 1mf – 9 – $1.50 – LLMC 82-100F, Title 78 – us L.L.M.C. [980]
MY LIFE / Duncan, Isadora – New York: Boni and Liveright, 1927. 359p. plates, ports – 1 – us U.W. Library [920]
MY LIFE AMONG THE BLUEJACKETS / Weston, Agnes Elizabeth – 1909 – 9 – uk Libr Preservation [920]
MY LIFE AND TIMES / Hamlin, Cyrus – Boston: Congregational Sunday School Publ Society, c1893 – 2mf – 9 – 0-8370-6190-3 – 1986-0190 – us A.T.L.A. [920]

MY LIFE AS AN AUTHOR / Tupper, Martin Farquhar – London: S. Low, Marston, Searle, & Rivington, 1886 – 1 roll – 1 – 1-55879-496-4 – uk Libr Preservation [420]
MY LIFE DECISIONS (CCC269) / Pu, Hua-jen – (In Chinese) – 2nd ed. Shanghai: Association Press of China, 1921 – 1r – 1 – 1984-6608 – us A.T.L.A. [920]
MY LIFE WITH THE ESKIMO / Stefansson, Vilhjalmur – BN 403 2. 1913 – 8 – ne IDC [306]
MY LITERARY LIFE : WITH A PREFATORY NOTE BY MISS BEATRICE HARRADEN / Linton, Elizabeth Lynn – London: Hodder and Stoughton, 1899 – 1 roll – 1 – 1-55879-757-2 – uk Libr Preservation [420]
MY LORD DANBY: HIS BOOK : TRANSCRIPTIONS FOR LUTE OF EARLY 18TH-CT MUSIC – (French manuscript in lute tablature. Composers include Corelli, Handel and a few unknown and illegible names) – Manuscript, [between 1756 and 1770] – 1 – us Sibley [780]
MY MEMORIES OF EIGHTY YEARS / Depew, Chauncy M – NY: Charles Scribner's Sons, 1922 – 5mf – 9 – $7.50 – LLMC 96-040 – us L.L.M.C. [920]
MY MOTHER: IN MEMORIAM / Albyn – Halifax: J. Bowes, 1868. 06131. (Pre-1900 Canadiana) – 9 – cn C.I.H.M. [920]
MY NAVAL CAREER AND TRAVELS / Seymour, Edward Hobart – 1911 – 9 – uk Libr Preservation [910]
MY NOTEBOOK : FRAGMENTARY STUDIES IN THEOLOGY AND SUBJECTS ADJACENT THERETO / Phelps, Austin – London: T Fisher Unwin, 1891, c1890 – 1mf – 9 – 0-8370-5204-1 – 1985-3204 – us A.T.L.A. [240]
MY PATH TO ATHEISM / Besant, Anne Wood – London: Freethought Publishing Company, 1877 – viii/256p – 1 – us U.W. Library [210]
MY PHILOSOPHY OF RELIGION (CCC347) = WO TI TSUNG CHIAO KUAN / Yin, Tzu-heng – (In Chinese) – [S.l.]: Printed privately by the author, 1932 – 1r – 1 – 1984-6686 – us A.T.L.A. [200]
MY POLICY FOR THE CONSTRUCTION OF THE CANADA PACIFIC RAILWAY: AS A GOVERNMENT WORK, WITH IRREFUTABLE ARGUMENTS IN FAVOR OF THIS POLICY / Crouter, John Wesley – s.l. s.n., 18??. 04192. (Pre-1900 Canadiana) – 9 – cn C.I.H.M. [971]
MY PORTFOLIO : A COLLECTION OF ESSAYS / Phelps, Austin – New York: Charles Scribner, 1882 – 1mf – 9 – 0-8370-5194-0 – 1985-3194 – us A.T.L.A. [240]
MY RAMBLES IN THE NEW WORLD / Biart, Lucien – London: S. Low, Marston, Searle & Rivington: 1877. 00107. (Pre-1900 Canadiana) – 9 – cn C.I.H.M. [910]
MY SCRAP BOOK OR ROUGH NOTES ON INDIAN OOLOGY AND ORNITHOLOGY / Hume, A O – Calcutta. 1870. BZ-271 2 – 8 – ne IDC [590]
MY SERVANTS THE PROPHETS / Young, E J – Erdmans, 1952 – 9 – $10.00 – us I.R.C. [220]
MY SPIRITUAL AUTOBIOGRAPHY, OR, HOW I DISCOVERED THE UNSELFISHNESS OF GOD / Smith, Hannah Whitall – c1903 – 9 – us A.T.L.A. [240]
MY STORY / Caine, Hall – New York: D. Appleton and Company, 1909, [c1908] – 1 roll – 1 – 1-55879-783-1 – uk Libr Preservation [920]
MY STUDY : AND OTHER ESSAYS / Phelps, Austin – New York: Charles Scribner, 1886, c1885 – 1mf – 9 – 0-8370-5451-6 – 1985-3451 – us A.T.L.A. [240]
MY THIRTY-TWO YEARS IN AMERICAN SAMOA / Morrow, Arthur A – jan 25 1974 – 1mf – 9 – $1.50 – LLMC 82-100C Title 44 – us L.L.M.C. [920]
MY TRIP TO SAMOA / Tripp, Bartlett – Cedar Rapids, IA: The Torch Press, 1911 – 3mf – 9 – $4.50 – LLMC 82-100C Title 23 – us L.L.M.C. [910]
MY TRIP TO THE ORIENT / White, Alma – Bound Brook, N.J.: Pentecostal Union (Pillar of Fire), 1911 – 1mf – us A.T.L.A. [910]
MY WEEKLY READER EYE 5 – (v54. 5,6,9. See also: My Weekly Reader-5) – v52-54. 1973-76 – 1 – us UMI [370]
MY WEEKLY READER-1 – (See now: Buddy's Weekly Reader) – 1930-1976 – 1 – us UMI [073]
MY WEEKLY READER-2 – (See now: Weekly Reader News Hunt) – 1934-1976 – 1 – us UMI [073]
MY WEEKLY READER-3 – (See now: Weekly Reader Whiz) – 1929-1976 – 1 – us UMI [073]
MY WEEKLY READER-5 – (See now: My Weekly Reader Eye 5) – 1930-1973 – 1 – us UMI [073]
MY WEEKLY READER-SUPRISE – 1959- 1; 1974- 5,6,9 – us UMI [073]
MY WITNESSES / Hogben, Thomas – London: "One by One" Band, 1909 – 1mf – 9 – 0-8370-6265-9 – 1986-0265 – us A.T.L.A. [240]
Mya, U. *see* EPIGRAPHIA BIRMANICA: BEING LITHIC AND OTHER INSCRIPTIONS OF BURMA
MYCENAE: AN ARCHAEOLOGICAL HISTORY AND GUIDE / Wace, Alan – Princeton. 1949 – 9 – $12.00 – us I.R.C. [930]
THE MYCENAEAN AGE : A STUDY OF THE MONUMENTS AND CULTURE OF PRE-HOMERIC GREECE / Tsountas, Chrestos – Introd. by Dr. Doerpfeld. Boston, New York: Houghton, Mifflin, 1897. xxxi,417p. illus., map, plans – 1 – us U.W. Library [930]
MYCENAEAN POTTERY FROM THE LEVANT / Stubbings, Frank H – Cambridge. 1951 – 9 – $10.00 – us I.R.C. [930]
MYCOGRAPHIA, SEU LCONES FUNGORUM / Cooke, M C – Figures of fungi from all parts of the world. London. 1875-79 – 8 – ne IDC [580]
MYCOGRAPHIE SUISSE, OU DESCRIPTION DES CHAMPIGNONS QUI CROISSENT EN SUISSE / Secretan, G A S J L – 3v. Geneve. 1833. B-6314 1 – 9 – ne IDC [580]
MYCOLOGIA – v1- 1949- 1; v62- 5,6; 1976- 9 – us UMI [580]
MYCOLOGIA – v. 1-52. 1909-1960 – 1,5,6 – us Princeton Micro [580]
MYCOLOGIA *see* JOURNAL OF MYCOLOGY
MYCOLOGIA EUROPAEA / Gonnermann, WE & Rabenhorst, G L – Dresden. 1869-70. B-883 2 – 8 – ne IDC [580]
MYCOLOGIA EUROPAEA / Persoon, C H – 3v. Erlangae. 1822-28. B-6299 2 – 8 – ne IDC [580]
MYCOLOGIA SCOTICA / Stevenson, J – Fungi of Scotland and their geographical distribution. 6318. 1879 – 9 – ne IDC [580]
MYCOLOGICA FENNICA / Karsten, B A – 1871-79 – 1 – uk Microform Academic [580]
MYCOLOGICAL NOTES / ed by Lloyd, C G 1500 Cincinnati (Ohio). v1-7. 1898-1923 – (Index included) – 26mf – 9 – ne IDC [580]
MYCOLOGISCHES CENTRALBLATT – Jena. v1-5. 1912-1914/1915 – 21mf – 9 – ne IDC [580]
MYCOTAXON – v1- 1974- 1; v5- 5,6,9 – us UMI [580]
MYCOTOXIN SURVEILLANCE : A GUIDELINE – 1982 – 72p – it F.A.O. [640]
MYCOTOXINS : REPORT ON THE JOINT F.A.O./WHO/UNEP CONFERENCE. NAIROBI, 1977 – 1977 – 115p – it F.A.O. [640]
Mydorge, Claude *see* PRODROMI CATOPTRICORVM ET DIOPTRICORVM: SIVE, CONICORVM OPERIS AD ABDITA RADII REFLEXI ET REFRACTI MYSTERIA PRAEUIJ ET FACEM PRAEFERENTIS: LIBRI PRIMVS ET SECVNDVS
Myer, Albert James *see* REPORT OF THE OPERATIONS AND DUTIES OF THE SIGNAL DEPARTMENT OF THE ARMY
Myer, William G *see* FEDERAL DECISIONS
Myers, A C *see* WALTER WHARTON'S LAND SURVEY REGISTER 1675-1679
Myers, Betty *see* JOB SATISFACTION AMONG SECONDARY LEVEL TEACHERS
Myers, Bettye *see* THE ATHLETIC ORGANIZATIONAL STRUCTURE AND ADMINISTRATIVE VIEWS OF UNIVERSITY AND ATHLETIC GOVERNING PERSONNEL IN THE SOUTHWEST CONFERENCE
Myers, Cortland *see* WOULD CHRIST BELONG TO A LABOR UNION?, OR, HENRY FIELDING'S DREAM
Myers, DP *see* MANUAL OF COLLECTIONS OF TREATIES...
Myers, Emmanuel Moses *see* THE JEWS: THEIR CUSTOMS AND CEREMONIES
Myers, Frederic *see* CATHOLIC THOUGHTS ON THE BIBLE AND THEOLOGY
Myers, George A *see*
– THE GEORGE A. MYERS PAPERS
– PAPERS
Myers, John Brown *see*
– THE CONGO FOR CHRIST
– WILLIAM CAREY
Myers, Kurtz *see* INDEX TO RECORD REVIEWS, 1978-1983, FIRST SUPPLEMENT
MYER'S MERCANTILE ADVERTISER – England. Liverpool Mercantile Gazette. -w. 1825, 1828, 1833, 1838, 1843, 1848, 1853, 1858, 1863, 1868, 1873. 5 1 2 reels – 1 – uk British Libr Newspaper [072]
Myers, OL *see*
– THE BUCHEUM (MEES VOL 41, 2)
– THE BUCHEUM (MEES VOL 41, 3)
– THE BUCHEUM (MEES VOL 41,1)
Myers, Philip Van Ness *see* ANCIENT HISTORY FOR COLLEGES AND HIGH SCHOOLS
Myers, Robin *see* RECORDS OF THE STATIONERS' COMPANY, 1554-1920
Myers, Sarah Ann *see* SELF-SACRIFICE, OR, THE PIONEERS OF FUEGIA
Myers, T A *see* ACCOUNTS
Myles, W *see*
– A CHRONOLOGICAL HISTORY OF THE PEOPLE CALLED METHODISTS, CONTAINING AN ACCOUNT OF THEIR RISE AND PROGRESS, FROM THE YEAR 1729 TO THE YEAR 1799;...
– A CHRONOLOGICAL HISTORY OF THE PEOPLE CALLED METHODISTS, OF THE CONNEXION OF THE LATE REV. JOHN WESLEY
– A LIST OF ALL THE METHODIST PREACHERS WHO HAVE LABOURED IN CONNEXION WITH THE LATE REV. JOHN WESLEY...
Mylius-Erichsen, L *see* GROANLAND, ILL, SKILDRING AF DEN DANSKE LITERAERE GROANL. EXP
Myl'nikov, A S *see*
– RUKOPISNYE FONDY LENINGRADSKIKH KHRANILISHCH
– RUKOPISNYE FONDY PUBLICHNOI BIBLIOTEKI. PECHATNYE KATALOGI I OBZORY
MYNCHIN BUCKLAND PRIORY CHARTULARY – 15th century – 1 – uk Microform Academic [930]
Mynsicht, Adrian von *see* THESAURUS ET ARMAMENTARIUM MEDIOCHYMICUM.
MYOCARDIAL STRUCTURE AND FUNCTION DIFFERENCES BETWEEN STEROID USING AND NON-STEROID USING ELITE POWERLIFTERS AND ENDURANCE ATHLETES / Climstein, M – 1990 – 2mf – 9 – $8.00 – us Microform Publ [612]
MYOTOMIA REFORMATA / Cowper, William – M 330. 1694 – 9 – ne IDC [610]
Myrand, Ernest *see* NOELS ANCIENS DE LA NOUVELLE-FRANCE
MYRA'S JOURNAL OF PRESS AND FASHION – London, UK. 1875-1912. -m. 19 reels – 1 – uk British Libr Newspaper [073]
Myrberg, Otto Ferdinand *see* DIE BIBLISCHE THEOLOGIE UND IHRE GEGNER
Myrer, William *see* A SINGLE STAGE SUBMAXIMAL TREADMILL JOG TEST TO ESTIMATE VO2 MAX IN SUBJECTS AGES 30 TO 39 YEARS
MYRICK'S PROBATE DECISIONS / California – 1v. 1872-1879 – 4mf – 9 – $6.00 – LLMC 91-025 – us L.L.M.C. [340]
Myrinaei, Agathiae *see* HISTORIARUM LIBRI 5 (CSHB 1)
DIE MYRIOPODEN DER OESTERREICHISCH-UNGARISCHEN MONARCHIE / Latzel, R – 2463 2. 1880-1884 – 8 – ne IDC [943]
MYRON T. HERRICK PAPERS *see* HERRICK, MYRON T. PAPERS, MS 2925
MYRTACEEN STUDIEN / Burret, M – (Notizblatt Bot. Garten und Mus. Berlin-Dahlem). v. 15. 1941. B-1568 2 – 8 – ne IDC [580]
MYRTLE CREEK MAIL – Myrtle Creek, OR. -w. 1916-42, 1945-52 – 1 – 233.00 – us Oregon Hist [071]
MYRTLE POINT ENTERPRISE – Myrtle Point OR. Nov 16 1895-June 5 1908 + – 1 – us U.O. Library [071]
MYRTLE POINT ENTERPRISE – Myrtle Point, OR. -w. 1907-17 – 1 – 96.00 – us Oregon Hist [071]
MYRTLE POINT HERALD – Myrtle Point, OR. -w. 29 Mar 1928-. – 1 – us U.O. Library [071]
MYRTLEFORD MAIL – 1911-1936. MM1-11 – 11r – 1 – at Corangamite [072]
MYRTLEFORD TIMES – 1930-1963. MYT1-3 – 10r – 1 – at Corangamite [072]
MYRTO E ACACIA : ORGAM DO INSTITUTO NEO-PYTHAGORICO – '(s.l.')-Curitiba, Brazil. Jan 1916-Dec 1920 – 1,5,6 – bl Biblioteca [072]
Mysh, M I *see* OB INOSTRATSAKH V ROSSII; SBORNIK UZAKONENII, TRAKTATOV I KONVENTSII, S
MYSHKINA DUKOCHKA / Remizov, A – Izd. Opleshnik: Paris, 1953. 200, (7)p. BR-827 2 – 8 – ne IDC [460]
MYSL PANSTWOWA – London, UK. Oct 1954-Mar 1955 – 1 – uk British Libr Newspaper [072]
MYSL POLSKA – London, UK. 1 Dec 1942-1/15 Jan 1943; 15 Aug 1943-25 Jul 1945 – 1 – uk British Libr Newspaper [072]
MYSLI O RUSSKOM FUTURIZME / Markov, V – Novyi Zhurnal. v. 38. 1954. BR-3573 2 – 8 – ne IDC [700]
MYSLI OB USTROISTVIE BUDUSHCHEI ROSSIISKO I VOORUZHENNOI SILY / Golovin, Nikolai Nikolaevich – Bielgrad: Russkai a tip., 1925 – 1 – CSUX89-B2538 – us Hoover Inst Photo [947]
MYSORE CENSUS – Bangalore: Supt Govt Press. pt 5 1901 (administrative report); pt c 1901 (Talukwar tables); pt 3 1911 (administrative report); pt 5 1911 (village population table); pt 3 1941 (administrative) – us Res Libr [310]
MYSORE ECONOMIC JOURNAL – Bangalore. 1915-43. v1-29. Lacking: 1915-26, v. 1-12; 1929, v. 15 (9); 1932, v. 18 (10-11); 1933, v. 19 (1-2, 4, 6); 1935, v. 21 (1); 1936, v. 22 (1-2); 1937, v. 23 (7); 1939, v. 25 (12); 1940, v. 26 (4-6, 11-12); 1941, v. 27, (1-2, 6, 9); 1942, v. 28 (5-8, 11-12); 1943, v. 29 (7-12). – 167mf – 8 – ne IDC [330]
MYSORE GAZETTE / Mysore. India – Bangalore. 1963-1966 – 1 – us NY Public [324]
Mysore. India *see*
– MYSORE GAZETTE
– SECOND FIVE-YEAR PLAN PROGRAMME FOR 1959-60
THE MYSORE TRIBES AND CASTES / Iyer, LAK & Nanjundayya, H V – 4v. Bangalore. 1928-35. BI-594 2 – 8 – ne IDC [306]
THE MYSORE TRIBES AND CASTES. / Anantha Krishna Iyer, L K – (Appendix to the four volumes. Mysore, 1936. 70p. 1) – Mysore, under the auspices of Mysore Univ., 1928-35. 4v. fronts., plates, ports., maps, fold. geneal. tab – 1 – us U.W. Library [306]
LES MYSTERES DE MONTREAL : ROMAN DE MOEURS / Berthelot, Hector – 4e ed. [Montreal: Imprimerie A.P. Pigeon, limitee, entre 1906 et 1920]. SEM105P1654 – 2mf – 9 – Can$4.50 – cn Bibl Nat [880]
LES MYSTERES DE MONTREAL: ROMANS DE MOEURS / Berthelot, Hector – Montreal: A.P. Pigeon, 1898. 07160. (Pre-1900 Canadiana) – 9 – cn C.I.H.M. [830]
THE MYSTERIE OF RHETORIQUE UNVAIL'D / Smith, John – 1657. 309p. (English Linguistics Series 1500-1800) – 9 – us UMI [400]
MYSTERIENGLAUBE UND GNOSIS IN CORPUS HERMETICUM 13 (T.U.U. 5-110) / Troeger, K W – Berlin, 1971 – 4mf – 9 – ne Slangenburg [240]
MYSTERIES OF CHRISTIANITY / Crawford, Thomas J – Edinburgh: William Blackwood, 1874. 1 fiche – 9 – us A.T.L.A. [240]
THE MYSTERIES OF CHRISTIANITY : BEING THE BAIRD LECTURE FOR 1874 / Crawford, Thomas Jackson – Edinburgh:William Blackwood, 1874 – 1mf – 9 – 0-8370-2773-X – 1985-0773 – us A.T.L.A. [240]
THE MYSTERIES OF LOVE AND ELOQUENCE / Phillips, Edward – 1658. 411p. (English Linguistics Series 1500-1800) – 9 – us UMI [400]
THE MYSTERIES OF MITHRA / Cumont, Franz – Chicago: Open Court; London: Kegan Paul, Trench, Truebner, 1903 – 1mf – us A.T.L.A. [250]
THE MYSTERIES, PAGAN AND CHRISTIAN : BEING THE HULSEAN LECTURES FOR 1896-97 / Cheetham, S – London; New York: Macmillan, 1897 – 1mf – us A.T.L.A. [230]
LE MYSTERIEUX MONSIEUR DE L'AIGLE / Lacerte, E A Bourgeois – Montreal: E Garand, ca 1928. SEM105P67 – 2mf – 9 – Can$4.50 – cn Bibl Nat [830]
MYSTERIOUS EAST – v. 1-18. 1969-71 – 1 – us UMI [073]
THE MYSTERY OF GOD : A CONSIDERATION OF SOME INTELLECTUAL HINDRANCES TO FAITH / Tymms, Thomas Vincent – (Includes bibliographical references) – 2nd ed. New York: Anson D F Randolph, 1887 – 1mf – 9 – 0-8370-5664-0 – 1985-3664 – us A.T.L.A. [230]

THE MYSTERY OF LIFE / Knox, George William – Tokyo, Japan:[s.n.], 1890 – 1mf – 9 – 0-8370-4443-X – 1985-2443 – us A.T.L.A. [240]
THE MYSTERY OF LIFE : A STUDY OF REVELATION IN THE LIGHT OF SCIENCE / Richards, Harry Edward – New York:Dodd, Mead, 1898 – 1mf – 9 – 0-8370-4893-1 – 1985-2893 – us A.T.L.A. [210]
THE MYSTERY OF MARTHA WARNE : A TALE OF MONTREAL / Cambell, Arthur – Montreal: J Theo Robinson, 1888. SEM16P22 – 1r – 5 – Can$9.00 – cn Bibl Nat [830]
THE MYSTERY OF MARTHA WARNE: A TALE OF MONTREAL / Campbell, Alfred – Montreal: J. Robinson, 1888. 04022. (Pre-1900 Canadiana) – 9 – cn C.I.H.M. [830]
THE MYSTERY OF MIRACLES / Reynolds, Joseph William – London:C Kegan Paul, 1879 – 1mf – 9 – 0-8370-4885-0 – 1985-2885 – us A.T.L.A. [210]
THE MYSTERY OF NEWMAN / Bremond, Henri – London: Williams and Norgate, 1907 – 1mf – us A.T.L.A. [240]
THE MYSTERY OF SUFFERING / Pressense, Edmond Dehault de – 1879 – 9 – us A.T.L.A. [240]
THE MYSTERY OF THE ISLAND / Kingsley, Henry – British Fiction Archive: Unit 2 – 9 – uk Bell [830]
THE MYSTERY OF THE TEMPTATION : A COURSE OF LECTURES / Hutchings, William Henry – 2nd rev enl ed. London: J Masters, 1889 – 1mf – 9 – 0-8370-3701-8 – 1985-1701 – us A.T.L.A. [240]
A MYSTERY PLAY : IN HONOUR OF THE NATIVITY OF OUR LORD / Benson, Robert Hugh – (Includes bibliographical references) – London; New York: Longmans, Green, 1908 – 1mf – 9 – 0-8370-7043-0 – 1986-1043 – us A.T.L.A. [820]
MYSTIC (FIRST SERIES) – Issue Nos. 1-5 March 1940-March 1941 – 5mf – 15 – $31,95 – us Comics [760]
MYSTIC (FIRST SERIES) – Issue Nos. 6-10 Oct 1941-Aug 1942 – 5mf – 15 – $31,95 – us Comics [760]
MYSTIC LONDON, OR, PHASES OF OCCULT LIFE IN THE METROPOLIS / Davies, Charles Maurice – London: Tinsley, 1875 – 1mf – us A.T.L.A. [941]
Mystic Seaport Museum. Library *see* CARD CATALOG
THE MYSTIC TREASURES OF THE HOLY MASS / Coppens, Charles – Freiburg i.B.; St Louis, MO: B Herder, c1905 – 1mf – 9 – 0-8370-6973-4 – 1986-0973 – us A.T.L.A. [230]
MYSTIC TREATISES BY ISAAC OF NINEVEH : TRANSL. FROM THE BEDJAN'S SYRIAC TEXT WITH INTR. AND REG. / Wensinck, A J – Amsterdam, 1923 – 15mf – 9 – ne Slangenburg [240]
MYSTICA THEOLOGIA / Guadelupe, Andres – 1665 – 9 – 1.50f – sp Bibl Santa Ana [240]
MYSTICISM AND THE CREED / Cobb, William Frederick – London, New York: Macmillan, 1914 – 2mf – us A.T.L.A. [240]
MYSTICISM IN CHRISTIANITY / Fleming, W K – New York: F.H. Revell, [1913?] (Library of historic theology) – 1mf – us A.T.L.A. [240]
THE MYSTICISM OF JOHANN JOSEPH VON GOERRES AS A REACTION AGAINST RATIONALISM / Gonzaga, Mary – (Includes bibliographical references) – Washington, DC: [s.n.] 1920 – 1r – 1 – us U.W. Library [210]
THE MYSTICISM OF ST PAUL / Schweitzer, Albert – 1931 – 9 – $15.00 – us I.R.C. [240]
MYSTICKE THEOLOGIE-SERAPHINSCHE PRACTYCKE-OPRRECHTE DEVOTIE-BRANT DER LIEFDE / Maes, Bonifacius – Ghendt, 1673 – 8mf – 8 – ne Slangenburg [240]
MYSTICUS AQUILO, SIVE DECLARATION VATICINII JEREMIE PROPHETAE / Graminaeus, Diederich – Cologne, 1576 – 1 – us U.W. Library [240]
DIE MYSTIK LUTHERS : IM ZUSAMMENHANGE SEINER THEOLOGIE UND IN IHREM VERHAELTNIS ZUR AELTEREN MYSTIK / Hering, Hermann – Leipzig: J.C. Hinrichs, 1879 – 1mf – us A.T.L.A. [240]
MYSTIK UND LYRIK BEI NOVALIS : TEILDRUCK / Herzog, Werner – (Includes bibliographical references) – [S.l.: s.n.], 1926 (Jena: Druck von B Vopelius) – 1r – 1 – us U.W. Library [430]
LA MYSTIQUE DE RUYSBROECK L'ADMIRABLE. UN ECHO DU NEOPLATONISME AU 14TH SIECLE / D'Asbeck, M – Paris, 1930 – 6mf – 8 – ne Slangenburg [180]
LES MYSTIQUES EXTATIQUES ET LES STIGMATISES / Maury, Louis Ferdinand Alfred – Paris, L. Mattinet, s.d., 52 p. 1 fiche. (Statistics Series: Medical Studies) – 9 – 6.00 – fr Bibl Nationale [310]
MYTER OG SAGN FRA GRONLAND KJOBENHAVN, ETC / Rasmussen, Knud – BH 494 2. v. 1-3. 1921-1925 – 8 – ne IDC [910]
MYTH AND RITUAL / Hooke, SH – 1933 – 9 – $10.00 – us I.R.C. [240]
MYTH AND SCIENCE : AN ESSAY / Vignoli, Tito – (Includes index) – New York: D Appleton, 1882 – 1mf – 9 – 0-8370-5822-8 – 1985-3822 – us A.T.L.A. [230]
MYTH, MAGIC AND MORALS: A STUDY OF CHRISTIAN ORIGINS / Conybeare, Frederick C – London: Watts, 1910. 1 fiche – 9 – us A.T.L.A. [240]
MYTHEN, SAGEN UND MARCHEN AUS DEM DEUTSCHEN HEIDENTHUME. 1855 – 1 – us I.U. Libraries [390]
MYTHES, ECOLOGIE, ACCULTURATION EN HAITI / Montilus, G – Essai sur la reinterpretation des mythes du Golfe de Guinee dans le vaudou haitien sous l'influence des Fon du Bas-Dahomey – 9 – F70.00 – fr Ethnologie [306]
MYTHOGRAPHI VATICANI 1 ET 2 – 1987 – 6mf – 9 – Bf975.00 – 2-503-60912-0 – be Brepols [240]
MYTHOLOGIE DER CHRISTLICHEN KUNST / Piper, F – O 1257 1. 2 v. 1847 – 9 – ne IDC [240]
MYTHOLOGIE DES BUDDHISMUS IN TIBET UND DER MONGOLEI / Gruenwedel, A – Fuehrer durch die lamaistische Sammlung des Fuersten E. Uchtomskij. Leipzig. 1900. Illus. BU-800 2 – 8 – ne IDC [280]
MYTHOLOGIE DES INDOUS / Polier, Marie Elisabeth – 1809 – 1 – us I.U. Libraries [390]
LA MYTHOLOGIE SLAVE / Leger, Louis – Paris: E. Leroux, 1901 – 1mf – us A.T.L.A. [240]
MYTHOLOGISCHE PARALLELEN / Hahn, Johann Georg von – 1859 – 1 – us I.U. Libraries [390]
MYTHOLOGY AND FOLK-TALES OF THE NORTH AMERICAN INDIANS / Boas, Franz – BN 144 2. 1914 – 8 – ne IDC [390]
THE MYTHOLOGY OF GREECE AND ROME: WITH SPECIAL REFERENCE TO ITS USE IN ART / Seemann, Otto – From the German.Ed. by G.H. Bianchi. New York, 1881. 311p. ill – 1 – us U.W. Library [250]
THE MYTHOLOGY OF KODIAK ISLAND, ALASKA / Lantis, Margaret – BN 292 2. 1938 – 8 – ne IDC [390]
THE MYTHOLOGY OF THE BELLA COOLA INDIANS / Boas, Franz – 1898? 02420. (Pre-1900 Canadiana) – 9 – cn C.I.H.M. [390]
MYTHOS PAPERS – (1986-. 1,5,6) – 1982- – 9 – us UMI [073]
MYTHS AND FOLK-LORE OF IRELAND / Curtin, Jeremiah – Boston: Little, Brown, 1890. vi,345p – 1 – us U.W. Library [390]
MYTHS AND MYTH-MAKERS : OLD TALES AND SUPERSTITIONS INTERPRETED BY COMPARATIVE MYTHOLOGY / Fiske, John – Boston: J.R. Osgoodt, 1873, c1872 – 1mf – us A.T.L.A. [390]
THE MYTHS AND TRADITIONS FROM NORTHERN ALASKA, THE MACKENZIE DELTA, AND CORONATION GULF / Jenness, D – Rep. Canad. Arct. Exp. 1913-18; v. 13: Eskimo Folklore. BN 271 2. 1924 – 8 – ne IDC [290]
MYTHS OF GREECE EXPLAINED AND DATED / St Clair, George – An embalmed history from Uranus to Persus: Including the Fleusinian mysteries and the Olympic Games. London: Williams and Norgate, 1901. 2v – 1 – us U.W. Library [250]
MYTHS OF ISRAEL: THE ANCIENT BOOK OF GENESIS / Fiske, Amos Kidder – New York: Macmillan, 1897. 1 fiche – 9 – us A.T.L.A. [220]
THE MYTHS OF THE NEW WORLD: A TREATISE ON THE SYMBOLISM AND MYTHOLOGY OF THE RED RACE OF AMERICA / Brinton, Daniel Garrison – New York: Leypoldt & Holt, 1868. 02056. (Pre-1900 Canadiana) – 9 – cn C.I.H.M. [290]
DIE MYXOMYCETEN DER FLORA VON BUITENZORG... / Penzig, A J O – Leiden, 1898 – 1mf – 9 – 12,053/1 – ne IDC [580]
LES MYXOPHYCEES DE L'AFRIQUE EQUATORIALE FRANCAISE / Fremy, P – (Arch. Bot.). v. 3. Caen. 1929. B-1026 2 – 8 – ne IDC [580]
MYZUKAL'NAIA SAMODEIATEL'NOST – Moscow, 1933-1936 – 27mf – 9 – $160.00 – us Ross [780]
N. A. S. S. P. (National Association of Secondary School Principals) *see* BULLETIN
N. CHIPMAN'S REPORTS / Chipman, N – (A Pre-NRS title) – 1v. 1789-1791 (all publ) – 2mf – 9 – $3.00 – LLMC 90-307 – us L.L.M.C. [340]
N. J. E. A. (New Jersey Education Association) *see* REVIEW
N, N *see* PRESBYTERS AND DEACONS NOT COMMISSIONED TO PREACH WITHOUT THE BISHOP'S ALLOWANCE
NA AGRARNOM FRONTE – Moscow. Jan. 1926-Apr. 1935 – 1 – 35.00r – us Hoover Inst Photo [943]
NA ANTENIE – London, UK. 7 Apr 1963-22/29 Dec 1968; Apr/May 1969-1972 – 1 – uk British Libr Newspaper [072]
NA BEREGAKH NEVY / Odoevsteva, I – Novyi Zhurnal. nr. 71, nr. 72. New York. 1963. BR-3689 2 – 8 – ne IDC [380]
NA BOEVOM POSTU – (1994-98 2r per y) – Russia, 1999- – 2r per y standing order – 1 – us Ross [072]
NA CHUZHBINE (OB EMIGRANTSKOI LITERATURE) / Liubumov, L – NR. 2, 4. Novyi mir. 1957. BR-3273 2 – 8 – ne IDC [305]
NA GRANITSIE – (Includes c.1: no.101 1937:Mar.7-no.250 (1940:Feb.11)) – Progranichnai a: Izd-vo "Na granitsie", 193u – 1 – CSUXAKB0771-S – us Hoover Inst Photo [947]
NA IUG! NA IUG! / Baratov, Boris – Moskva: Gos. izd-vo, 1919 – 1 – CSUX88-B8464 – us Hoover Inst Photo [947]
NA KATORGE : VOSPOMINANIIA REVOLIUTSIONERA / Brilon, Izrail – Moskva: Moskovski i rabochi i, 1927 – 1 – CSUX89-B7299 – us Hoover Inst Photo [947]
NA KRESTNOM PUTI : ROMAN V TREKH CHASTI AKH / Elets, I Ulii Lukianovich – Sofiia, Berlin: Izd-vo "Zarnitsy", 1924 – 1 – CSUX89-B2075 – us Hoover Inst Photo [947]
NA LITERATURNOM POSTU – Moscow. v. 2-7. 1927-May 1932 – 1 – us NY Public [460]
NA LITERATURNOM POSTU – Moscow. v2-7. 1927-32 – 4r – 1 – us Ross [460]
NA MOSKVU / Davatts, Vladimir Khristianovich – Paris: Tip. Akt s. o-va I. Rirakhovski i, 1921 – 1 – CSUX89-B3123 – us Hoover Inst Photo [947]
NA NOVYI GOD – Almanakh v podarok chitateliam Moskvitianina. M. 1850. B-2343 2 – 8 – ne IDC [947]
NA OBSHCHESTVENNYIA TEMY / Minskii, N – Ed. 2. Spb. 1909. BR-808 2 – 8 – ne IDC [460]
NA OBSHCHESTVENNYIA TEMY / Minskii, N – Spb. 1909. BR-807 2 – 8 – ne IDC [460]
NA OKHOTE / Narbut, V – Razskazy. M. 1912. BR-1207 2 – 8 – ne IDC [460]
NA PARNASE SEREBRIANOGO VEKA / Makovskii, S K – Izd. ZOPE. Munich. 1962. BR-1404 2 – 8 – ne IDC [460]
NA PEREVALE – Iaroslav. Jan.-Dec. 1923; Jubilee No. "k 25 letiiu R.K. (b)", 1923 – 1 – 35.00r – us Hoover Inst Photo [073]
NA PIRU BOGOV : PRO I CONTRA: SOVREMENNYE DIALOGI / Bulgakov, Sergei Nikolaevich – Sofiia: Rossi isko-Bolgarskoe kn-vo, 1921 – 1 – CSUX88-B1890 – us Hoover Inst Photo [947]
NA PODSTUPAKH K OKTIABRIU : STATI I RECHI, MAI-DEKABR 1917 G / Bukharin, Nikolai Ivanovich – Moskva: Gos. izd-vo, 1926 – 1 – CSUX88-B1316 – us Hoover Inst Photo [947]
NA POROGIE NOVYKH MYSLEI / Golitsyn-Muravlin – [Paris]: Tip. Rossii a, 1925 – 1 – CSUX88-B9815 – us Hoover Inst Photo [947]
NA PROSHCHANIE *see* ALMANAKH NA PROSHCHANIE
NA PUTI AKH KOLLEKTIVIZATSII : VSESOI UZNY I SOVET KOLKHOZOV – (Includes c.1: v.21929-v.3(1929)) – Moskva: Knigosoi uz, 1929 – 1 – CSUXAKZ4049-S – us Hoover Inst Photo [947]
NA PUTI K EDINOMU INTERNATSIONALU PROFSOIUZOV / Galperin, S – Moskva: Izd-vo MGSPD "Trud i kniga", 1925 – 1 – CSUX88-B7198 – us Hoover Inst Photo [947]
NA PUTI K OBOBSHCHESTVLENIIU SEL'SKOGO KHOZIAISTVA : PROIZVODSTENNO-SBYTOVYE SISTEMY SEL'SKOKHOZIAISTVENNOI KOOPERATSII – M., L., 1925 – 3mf – 9 – COR-494/1 – ne IDC [334]
NA RASPUT'I / Krivenko, S N – Kul'turnye skity i kul'turnye odinochki. Ed. 2. M. 1901. BR-10.594 2 – 8 – ne IDC [460]
NA RASSVETE (SAN FRANCISCO, CALIF.) – (Library has: no. 8-10, 12-14, 16-17 (1937-1938)) – San Francisco: Izd-vo Mladorossko i partii, 1937- – 1 – CSUX89-S18 – us Hoover Inst Photo [947]
NA RODINU IZ STANA BELYKH / Bulatsel, A – Moskva: Gos. izd-vo, [1924?] – 1 – CSUX88-B1843 – us Hoover Inst Photo [947]
NA RUBEZHE DVUKH EPOKH / Zelinskii, K – Literaturnye vstrechi. 1917-1920 gg. Izd. "Sov. pisatel". 1959. BR-2231 2 – 8 – ne IDC [460]
NA RUBEZHE DVUKH STOLETII / Belyi, A – Ed. 2. M. 1931. BR-576 2 – 8 – ne IDC [460]
NA RUBEZHE DVUKH STOLETII / Belyi, A – M., L. 1930. BR-575 2 – 8 – ne IDC [460]
NA STRAZHE : ORGAN T SENTRALNOGO I MOSKOVSKOGO SOVETOV OSOAVIAKHIMA – (Includes c.1: 1934:Mar.28) – [Moskva]: T SS Osoaviakhima SSSR, 1934 – 1 – CSUXAKG5807-S – us Hoover Inst Photo [947]
NA STRAZHI E RODINY : ODNODNEVNAI A GAZETA KHARBINSKAGO OTDI ELENII A R.O.V.S. – (Includes c.1: no.1 1932:June, no.3 (1934:Apr.8)) – [Kharbin: Otdi elenie], 1932- – 1 – CSUXAKG1777-S – us Hoover Inst Photo [947]
NA TEMY DNIA : DVIERIECHI, PROIZNESENNYIA V ZASIEDANII KHARKOVSKAGO IURIDICHESKAGO OBSHCHESTVA 19-GO MARTA 1905 GODA / Gredeskul, Nikolai Andreevich – Kharkov: Tip. i litografiia N.V. Petrova, 1905 – 1 – CSUX89-B4316 – us Hoover Inst Photo [340]
NA TURUPATU NA LOTU KATOLIKA / Catholic Mission, Solomon Islands – (Mainly in the Gari language of Guadalcanal) – n1, 3-143, 145-186, 188-198, 1911-1958, and n1, 3-5, 1970-1971 – reels 1-3 – 1 – PMB Doc423 – at Pacific Mss [240]
NA ZAPADE / Adamovich, G – Paris. 1939. BR-1108 2 – 8 – ne IDC [460]
NA ZEMLE / Gorodetskii, S – Razskazy. Spb. 1914. BR-1127 2 – 8 – ne IDC [460]
NAACOG'S CLINICAL ISSUES IN PERINATAL AND WOMEN'S HEALTH NURSING *see* AWHONN'S CLINICAL ISSUES IN PERINATAL AND WOMEN'S HEALTH NURSING
NAAM-BOEK DER HOGE INDISCHE REGEERING TE BATAVIA... – Amsterdam, 1805 – 2mf – 9 – ne IDC [950]
NAAM-BOEK VAN DE WEL EDELE HEEREN DER HOGE INDISCHE REGEERING,... – Batavia, 1762-1808 – 22mf – 9 – ne IDC [950]
NAAMBOEKJE VAN DE WEL-ED. HEEREN DER HOGE INDISCHE REGERINGE,... – Amsterdam. 1748-1794. – 70mf – 9 – ne IDC [950]
NAAMLIJST DER EUROPESCHE INWONERS...IN NEDERLANDSCH-INDIE... – Batavia, 1864-1902 – 155mf – 9 – ne IDC [950]
NAAMREGISTER VAN DE E: MOG: HEEREN GECOMMITEERDE RADEN... : VAN DE OOST -EN WESTINDISCHE COMPAGNIE – Amsterdam. 1736-89. – 31mf – 9 – ne IDC [950]
NAAPI ACCOUNT *see*
– API ACCOUNT
– API NEWSLETTER
NAATSIILID – 1966-73. (American Indian Periodicals in the Princeton University Library). 8 fiches – 9 – $45.00 – us UPA [305]
NAAUWKEURIGE BESCHRYVINGE VAN MALABAR EN CHOROMANDEL, DERZELVER AANGRENZENDE KONINCKRIJCKEN. NEVENS DE AFGODERIJE DER OOST-INDISCHE HEYDENEN / Baldaeus, P – Amsterdam. 1672. BI-1068 1 – 9 – ne IDC [950]

NABARD-I BALUCH – [S.l.]: Sazman-i Paykar dar rah-i Azadi-i Tabaqah-'i Kargar, Tashkilat-i Baluchistan. Shumarah-'i 39 (16 Shahrivar 1359 [7 Sep 1980]) – 1 reel – 1 – $25.00 – us MEDOC [950]

NABARD-I KHALQ – [S.l.]: Sazman-i Chirik'ha-yi Fada'i-i Khalq-i Iran. Shumarah-'i 2-8 (Farvardin 1353-Khurdad 1355 [Mar 1974-May 1976]) – 1 reel – 1 – $60.00 – us MEDOC [950]

NABARD-I MILLAT – (Sal-i 28-31: shumarah-'i musalsal-i 126-231 (=dawrah-'i Inqilab[Series]: shumarah-'i 1-105) Day 1357-Shahrivar 1360[Jan 1979-Sep 1981]). Missing issues: 71, 73, 75, 77-79, 81-83, 85-86, 88-90, 98, 101) – Tehran – 1 reel – 1 – $55.00 – us MEDOC [950]

NABAT : EZHEDNEVNAI A GAZETA SERPUKHOVSKOGO UEZDKOMA R.K.P.(B), UISPOLKOMA I SERPUKHOVSKOGO OTDEL. VSEROS. PROFESS. SOI UZA TEKSTILSHCHIKOV – (Includes c.1: 1922: Mar.12; 1929:June 14, 21) – Serpukhov: Otd-nie, 191u – 1 – CSUXANR9741-S – us Hoover Inst Photo [947]

NABAT : GAZETA PODLINNO-RUSSKAI A, PERIODICHESKAI A, ORGAN 150-MILLIONNAGO RUSSKAGO KRESTI ANSTVA – (Library has: no. 1, 3-4, 6-9, 11-13 (May 1930-Feb. 1933)) – Paris: Nabat, 1930- – 1 – CSUX89-S9 – us Hoover Inst Photo [947]

NABAT (MUNICH, GERMANY) – (Includes c.1: v.1:no.1 1950:July 20-v.2:no.20 (1951:July 8); v.2:no.23 1951:Aug.19-v.2:no.24 (1951:Sept.2); v.2:no.26 1951:Oct.14; v.2:no.29 1951:Dec.23-v.3:n)) – Munchen: Bratstvo Sv. Georgii a, 1950- – 1 – CSUXADQ2120-S – us Hoover Inst Photo [947]

NABAT (ODESSA, UKRAINE) – (Library has: no. 15 (20 i anv. 1919) – Odessa: Odesski i soi uz russkikh li ude i v lit si e N.N. Rodzevicha, 19uu – 1 – CSUX88-S463 – us Hoover Inst Photo [947]

NABAT (PARIS, FRANCE: 1930) *see* NABAT

NABAT REVOLIUTSII – (Library has: no. 1 (Dec. 6, 1917)) – Petrograd: Nabat revoliutsii, 1917- – 1 – CSUX89-S4 – us Hoover Inst Photo [947]

NABAT (SERPUKHOV, RUSSIA) *see* NABAT

NABAT (SOFIA, BULGARIA) – (Library has: no. 4 (July 20, 1921)) – Sofiia: Nabat, 19uu – 1 – CSUX89-S16 – us Hoover Inst Photo [947]

NABATAEISCHE INSCHRIFTEN AUS ARABIEN / Euting, Julius – (Includes bibliographical references and index) – Berlin: Georg Reimer, 1885 – 1mf – 9 – 0-8370-7292-1 – 1986-1292 – us A.T.L.A. [470]

AN NABI / Gibran, Kahlil – (Translation of THE PROPHET). SE-5228 1. 1949 – 9 – ne IDC [800]

Nabi *see*
– TARIH-I KAMANICE
– TARIH-I OSMANI

NABLYUDENIYA NAD ARANEINA / Wagner, W – Z 2210 2. 1890 – 8 – ne IDC [590]

Nabokov, V D *see* VTORAIA GOSUDARSTVENNAIA DUMA

NABORSHCHIK I PECHATNYI MIR – Vestnik pechatnago iskusstva i literatury. Spb. 1905-06, 1911-16. Lacking: 1905 (107, 109, 112-114), 1906 (119, 124-126), 1912 (145-146), 1914 (172), 1915 (187). BR-4320 2 – 8 – ne IDC [073]

NACADA JOURNAL – (National Academic Advising Association).v.1-. 1981- – 1,5,6,9 – us UMI [073]

A NACAO – S. Paulo, 2 Aug-Dec 1897; Mar 1898-7 Feb 1899 – 1,5,6 – bl Biblioteca [072]

A NACAO – Sao Luiz, 12 May 1869-Apr 1870; Jan 1871 – 1,5,6 – bl Biblioteca [072]

NACCA LAW JOURNAL – National Assoc. of Claimants' Compensation Attorneys. 1948-59 – 1 – us UMI [073]

NACCA LAW JOURNAL – National Assoc. of Claimants' Council of America. 1960-64. Continued as Journal of the American Trial Lawyers Association – 1 – us UMI [073]

NACCA NEWSLETTER / National Assoc. of Claimants' Compensation Attorneys – v. 1-3, 1957-59 – us UMI [073]

NACCA NEWSLETTER – National Assoc. of Claimants' Counsel of America. v.4-7. 1960-74. Continued as yAmerican Trial Lawyers Association Newsletter – 1 – us UMI [073]

Naccari, F L *see*
– ALGOLOGIA ADRIATICA
– FLORA VENETA

NACE (NATIONAL ASSOCIATION OF CORROSION ENGINEERS) – Printed index. Updated every 60 days – 6,9 – us Info Handling [620]

LA NACELLE DE SAINTE-URSULE – Trois-Rivieres [Quebec]: Ursulines des Trois-Rivieres, 1896-1897 – 9 – cn C.I.H.M. [240]

NACH JERUSALEM / Frankl, Ludwig August – v. 1-3. Leipzig. 1858-60. BJ-27-37 1 – 9 – ne IDC [910]

NACH WELCHEM OERTLICHEN RECHT... / Greber, J – Strassburg i. E., 1900 – 1mf – 1 – ILM-3697/1 – ne IDC [327]

NACHALA – Zhurnal istorii literatury i istorii obshchestvennosti. v. 1-2. Spb. 1921-22. BR-3327 2 – 8 – ne IDC [073]

NACHALAT Z'WI = HERITAGE... – (In German) – Frankfurt, DE. v1 no2 Dec 1930-v8 no6 Mar 1938 – 1r – 1 – $25.00 – cn Can Microfilming [072]

NACHALIEL – Amsterdam. v1-8. 1925-1934 – 10mf – 9 – ne IDC [999]

NACHALNAI A SHKOLA – (Library has: 1935-1936; 1938-1940; 1944-1947; 1951; some issues missing) – [Moskva]: "Prosveshchenie.", 1933- – 1 – CSUX90-S399 – us Hoover Inst Photo [947]

NACHALO KNIGOPECHATANIIA V MOSKVE I NA UKRAINE / Zernova, A S – M. 1947. BR-10,070 1 – 9 – ne IDC [947]

NACHALO NA BALGARSKOTO KNIGO PETCHATANE / Atanasov, P – Sofia, 1959. 240p. BR-3814 2 – 8 – ne IDC [460]

NACHALO NA BALGARSKOTO VAZRAZHDANE / Penev, B – Ed 3. Sofiia, 1946 – 8 – BR-3902 2 – ne IDC [947]

NACHALO NEVMESHATEL'STVA; RASSUZHDENIE / Kamarovskii, L A – Moscow, 1874. 307p. Earliest Tsarist treatise on the principle of non-interference. BR-9150/1 – 9 – ne IDC [340]

NACHALO VEKA. VOSPOMINANIIA / Belyi, A – Moscow: Gikhl. 1933. 503p. BR-577 2 – 8 – ne IDC [460]

NACHALOTO NA SLAVIANSKATA PISMENNOST' V BALGARIIA / Georgiev, E – Sofia, 1942. BR/10,323/1 – 9 – ne IDC [947]

DAS NACHAPOSTOLISCHE ZEITALTER : GESCHICHTE DER CHRISTLICHEN GEMEINDEN VOM BEGINN DER FLAVIERDYNASTIE BIS ZUM ENDE HADRIANS / Knopf, Rudolf – Tuebingen: J.C.B. Mohr, 1905 – 2mf – us A.T.L.A. [240]

NACHERTANIE RUSSKOI ISTORII / Pogodin, M P – M. 1835. BR-8313 2 – 8 – ne IDC [947]

Nachez, T *see* CONCERTO NO. 2 IN B MINOR FOR VIOLIN AND ORCHESTRA, OP. 36

NACHGELASSENE SCHRIFTEN / Fichte, Johann Gottlieb – Berlin, 1937. – Band 2. Schriften aus den Jahren 1790-1800 – 17mf – 8 – ne Slangenburg [190]

NACHGELASSENE SCHRIFTEN / Geiger, Abraham – Ed. by L. Geiger. 5 v. Berlin. 1875-78. BJ-100-3 1 – 9 – ne IDC [900]

NACHGELASSENE SCHRIFTEN UND DICHTUNGEN / Wagner, Richard – 2. Aufl. Leipzig: Breitkopf & Haertel, 1902 – 1r – 1 – us U.W. Library [430]

NACHLESE ZUR UEBERLIEFERUNG DER MATTHAEUSERKLAERUNG DES ORIGENES (T.U.U. 4-47/4) / Klostermann, Erich – Leipzig, 1932 – 1mf – 9 – ne Slangenburg [240]

Nachmanson, Ernst *see* LAUTE UND FORMEN DER MAGNETISCHEN INSCHRIFTEN

NACHRICHT VON DER AUFFUEHRUNG DES HAENDELSCHEN MESSIAS, IN DER DOMKIRCHE ZU BERLIN / Hiller, Johann Adam – Berlin. BP-698 1 – 9 – ne IDC [780]

...NACHRICHT VON GEORG FRIEDRICH HAENDELS LEBENSUMSTAENDEN UND DER IHM ZU LONDON.. / Burney, Charles – 1785 – 2 – us Sibley [780]

NACHRICHT VON GEORG FRIEDRICH HAENDEL'S LEBENSUMSTAENDEN UND DER IHM ZU LONDON IN MAI UND JUNI 1784 ANGESTELLTEN GEDAECHTNISFEYER; AUS DEM ENGLISCHEN UBERZETZT VOM J. J. ESCHENBURG / Burney, Charles – Berlin. 1785. BP-190 1 – 9 – ne IDC [780]

NACHRICHTEN – Portland OR. Dec 10 1908-Dec 25 1919 – 1 – us U.O. Library [071]

NACHRICHTEN AUS CHEMIE, TECHNIK UND LABORATORIUM : ZEITSCHRIFT DER GDCH – v1-28. 1953-80; v31-44. 1983-96 – 1,5,6,13 – us V.C.H. [540]

NACHRICHTEN AUS DER AERTZLICHEN MISSION – nos 11-14. 1960-63 (incomplete) – 1r – 1 – ATLA S0724B – us A.T.L.A. [073]

NACHRICHTEN AUS DER AERZTLICHEN MISSION IN TSINGTAU UND TSINGCHOW – no21-49. 1939-40 (incomplete) – 1r – 1 – ATLA S0703D – us A.T.L.A. [073]

NACHRICHTEN AUS DER HEIDENWELT FUER ALT UND JUNG – v1-3. 1885-87 (complete) – 1r – 1 – ATLA 1992-S001 – us A.T.L.A. [073]

NACHRICHTEN AUS SCHLESWIG-HOLSTEIN – Oak Park, IL: H Kaul, oct 13 1914-oct 22 1940 – 4r – 1 – us Res Libr [071]

NACHRICHTEN DER AUSLANDSPRESSE – Berlin. mar 6, 1915-18 – 14r – 1 – gw Mikrofilm [072]

NACHRICHTEN DER NSDAP – Bremen, Germany. May 1933-Dec 1934 – 1 – gw Mikrofilm [072]

NACHRICHTEN DER NSDAP *see*
– BREMISCHE POLIZEIBEAMTEN-ZEITUNG

NACHRICHTEN DES AUSLANDSBUEROS "NEU BEGINNEN" – (Der Jg. 1 (1935) wird im Original faelschlich mit 1934 angegeben) – Karlsbad (Karlovy Vary)-Prag-Troppau. Czechoslovakia. Sept 1935-Apr 1937 – 1r – 1 – gw Mikrofilm [073]

NACHRICHTEN DES BUNDES DEUTSCHER KINEMATOGRAPHEN-THEATER-VEREINIGUNGEN – Berlin. dec 21, 1911 – 1 – gw Mikrofilm [790]

DIE NACHRICHTEN DES NIKETAS CHONIATES UEBER DIE ENTSTEHUNG DES ZWEITEN BULGARISCHEN STAATES / Malingoudis, Phaedon – Frankfurt a.M., 1978 – 2mf – 9 – DM62.00 – 3-89349-779-X – gw Hänsel [327]

NACHRICHTEN DES RUHR-DEPARTMENTS – Dortmund, Germany. 1811 – 1r – 1 – gw Mikrofilm [072]

NACHRICHTEN UEBER DEN ARAL SEE UND DEN UNTEREN LAUF DES AMU-DARJA VON DEN AELTESTEN ZEITEN BIS ZU 17. JAHRHUNDERT / Barthold, W – Leipzig, 1910 – XIII, 78p – 8 – ne IDC [560]

NACHRICHTEN VON DEM ZUSTANDE DER WISSENSCHAFTEN UND KUENSTE IN DEN KOENIGLICH DAENISCHEN REICHEN UND LAENDERN – Copenhagen & Leipzig. 1754-57 – 3 – us Readex [500]

NACHRICHTEN VON DER GEORG-AUGUSTS-UNIVERSITAET UND DER KOENIGL. GESELLSCHAFT DER WISSENSCHAFTEN ZU GOETTINGEN : PHILOLOGISCH-HISTORISCHE KLASSE – Goettingen, 1846-1933 – 770mf – 9 – ne IDC [400]

NACHRICHTEN VON ISLAND, GROENLAND UND DER STRASSE DAVIS / Anderson, J – BN-106 2. 1746 – 8 – ne IDC [948]

NACHRICHTEN VON KUENSTLERN UND KUNST-SACHEN / Heinecken, KH V – Leipzig. 2v. 1768-1769 – 14mf – ne IDC [700]

NACHRICHTENBLATT : JUEDISCHE WOCHENZEITUNG – Amtliches Organ fuer die Synagogen-Gemeinden Hannover und Braunschweig. Hannover, v1-15, 1924-38. Lacking: 1924-27 and misc. issues. B446. (Leo Baeck Institute. German-Jewish Periodicals, Pt 1) – 1r – 1 – $75.00 – us UPA [270]

NACHRICHTENBLATT – Mitau, Latvija. (Jelgava, USSR.). 12 Jul 1934-1935 (incomplete); 1938-29 Sept 1939 (incomplete) – 1r – 1 – gw Mikrofilm [943]

NACHRICHTENBLATT / Vereinigung deutscher Auslandsbeamten – v3-6. 1921-24. Incomplete. Berlin. (Serial publications of German trade unions in the Memorial Library, University of Wisconsin-Madison.) – 1 – us U.W. Library [330]

NACHRICHTENBLATT FUER DIE JUEDISCHE RELIGIONSGEMEINDE – Dortmund, Germany. 1933-1937 – 1r – 1 – gw Mikrofilm [072]

NACHRICHTENBLATT FUER DIE SYNAGOGEN-GEMEINDEN UND VEREINE IN STADT UND PROVINZ HANNOVER – Hanover. v1-4? 1920-1923? Most issues lacking. B445. (Leo Baeck Institute. German-Jewish Periodicals, Pt 1) – 1r – 1 – $75.00 – us UPA [270]

NACHRICHTENDIENST – Berlin. 1922-28. Incomplete. B305. (Leo Baeck Institute. German-Jewish Periodicals, Pt 2) – 1r – 1 – $60.00 – us UPA [270]

NACHRICHTENDIENST : ZENTRALWOHLFAHRTSSTELLE DER DEUTSCHEN JUDEN – Berlin, 1922 n2-1928 – 1r – 1 – Inquire at Mikrofilmarchiv for details – gw Misc Inst [360]

NACHRICHTENDIENST DES DEUTSCHLANDSENDERS – (Cont by: Pressedienst: Deutschlandsender und Reichssender, dec 3 1933; since nov 18 1934: seperate issues: Deutschlandsender, Reichssender; reunificated issue: sep 17-23 1939) – Berlin, may 30 1933-oct 7 1939 – 41r – 1 – Inquire at Mikrofilmarchiv for details – gw Misc Inst [790]

NACHRICHTSBLATT DER DEUTSCHEN MALAKOZOOLOGISCHE GESELLSCHAFT – Frankfurt am Main. v1-51. 1869-1919 – 194mf – 9 – ne IDC [590]

DIE NACHT IM TEPPICHSAAL : ERLEBNISSE EINES WANDERERS / Kurz, Isolde – Tuebingen: R Wunderlich, c1933 – 1r – 1 – us U.W. Library [830]

NACHT UEBER MALMAISON : NOVEMBER 1914 / Klaehn, Friedrich Joachim – Muenchen: F Eher, c1940 – 1r – 1 – us U.W. Library [830]

NACHTAUSGABE *see* NACHTAUSGABE-DER TAG

NACHTAUSGABE-DER TAG – (Cont by: Nachtausgabe, apr 27 1925; Berliner Nachtausgabe, mar 2 1926; Berliner Illustrierte Nachtausgabe, sep 14 1928) – Berlin, jul 12 1922-jun 30 1944 – 74r – 1 – Inquire at Mikrofilmarchiv for details – gw Misc Inst [943]

DIE NACHTEILE IM VOELKERRECHT / Bose, H von – Berlin, 1935 – 1mf – 9 – ILM-2227/1 – ne IDC [327]

NACHT-EXPRESS – (Also known as: Der Kleine Nacht-Express) – Berlin, dec 7 1945-apr 30 1953 – 18r – 1 – Inquire at Mikrofilmarchiv for details – gw Misc Inst [072]

NACHT-EXPRESS – (Kleine Nacht-Express). Berlin. Germany. -d. 7 Dec 1945-18 Nov 1949. (12 reels) – 1 – uk British Libr Newspaper [072]

Nachtigal, Gustave *see*
– SAHARA AND SUDAN
– SAHARA ET SOUDAN

NACHTRAEGE ZU BECHSTEINS NATURGESCHICHTE DEUTSCHLANDS / Leisler, J P A – heft 1. Hanau. 1812; heft 2. Hanau. 1813. B-2049 2 – 8 – ne IDC [580]

NACHTRAEGE ZU DEN POETAE AEVI CAROLINI (MGH ANTIQUITATES 1: 6.BD. 1.TEIL) – 1951 – Dfl25.00 – ne Slangenburg [240]

NACHTRAEGE ZU DER ABHANDLUNG UEBER DIE MUENZEN DER ILEKE / Dorn, B – (Melanges Asiatiques, IX. 1888). BU-654 2 – 8 – ne IDC [730]

Naci, Muallim *see* HAZIM BEY YAHUT HEDER

LA NACION – Buenos Aires, Argentina. -d. 10 July 1917-26 March 1919. 19 1 2 reels – 1 – uk British Libr Newspaper [072]

LA NACION – Buenos Aires: [s.n.], 1870- [sep 1923-mar 1924; may 1924-jun 1939] (330r); 1951-55 (29r); 1956-77 (406r); 1978-oct 1986 (212r); nov 1986-mar 31 1992 (186r); apr 1 1992- – 1 – us Res Libr [072]

LA NACION – Dominican Republic. 1944-1963 – 1 – us UMI [072]

LA NACION – Madrid, Spain. -d. 1 April 1917-31 Dec 1918. Imperfect. 6 reels – 1 – uk British Libr Newspaper [072]

LA NACION – Santiago, Chile. 1939; Jul 1940-May 1973; Jan 1981-Dec 1990 – 409r – 1 – us L of C Photodup [072]

LA NACION – Santiago: [s.n.]. jun 29 1960-sep 9 1961 – us Res Libr [072]

LA NACION *see* THE NATION/LA NACION

UNA NACION RECOBRADA : ENFOQUES PARCIALES DE LA NUEVA ARGENTINA / Argentina. Presidencia. Subsecretaria de Informaciones – [Buenos Aires, 1952] – 1 – CSUXAJA7360-B – us Hoover Inst Photo [320]

EL NACIONAL – 1929-1990 – 1 – F4,946.00 – sz Infoprint [072]

EL NACIONAL – (1991- .12r per year.$900.00) – 1929-1990 – 375r – 1 – $25,000.00 silver $75.00r – mx El Nacional [072]

EL NACIONAL – Montevideo, UY. 1953-1968 – 6r – $300.00 – R04231 – us Library Micro [072]

O NACIONAL – Maceio, Alagoas. 14 Mar 1892 – 1,5,6 – bl Biblioteca [072]

O NACIONAL : ORGAM CRITICO, HUMORISTICO, NOTICIOSO E SPORTIVO – Manaos, Amazonas. 26 Dez 1915 – 1,5,6 – bl Biblioteca [072]

LA NACIONALIDAD A LA LUZ DE LA LEGISLACION VENEZOLANA / Grisanti, C F – Caracas, 1913 – 1mf – 1 – ILM-3632/1 – ne IDC [327]
LA NACIONALIDAD ANTE EL DERECHO INTERNACIONAL PRIVADO Y EL DERECHO SUD AMERICANO / Chamorro Garrido, G – Santiago de Chile, 1936 – 2mf – 1 – ILM-3553/1 – ne IDC [327]
LA NACIONALIDAD Y EL DOMICILIO / Bielsa, R – Rosario, 1936 – 1mf – 9 – ILM-3580/1 – ne IDC [327]
NACIONAL-INTEGRISMO / Becerro de Bengoa, Ricardo – 2ª edic. Caceres: Edit. Extremadura, 1977 – 1 – sp Bibl Santa Ana [320]
NACIONALISMO, PERONISMO Y SOCIALISMO NACIONAL / Carpani, Ricardo – [Cordoba]: Editorial Centro de Estudios Politicos, [2nd ed 1974] c1973 – 1 – CSUXADJ0133-B – us Hoover Inst Photo [320]
EL NACIONALISTA DE PUERTO RICO – Vols. 1-7, Nos. 1-290. 1923-30. (Scattered issues lacking) – 1 – 40.00 – us L of C Photodup [972]
NACIONALIZACION DEL PETROLEO / Gonzalez, Julio V – Buenos Aires: El Ateneo Editorial, 1947 – 1 – CSUXADH5705-B – us Hoover Inst Photo [338]
NACIONALSINDICALISMO / Falange Espanola Tradicionalista y de las Juntas Ofensivas Nacional-Sindicalistas – Zaragoza, 1936? Fiche W 871. (Blodgett Collection of Spanish Civil War Pamphlets) – 9 – us H.U. College Libr [946]
NACIONES DE LENGUA ESPANOLA / ed by Bayle, Constantino – Madrid: Razon y Fe, 1926 – 1 – sp Bibl Santa Ana [440]
NACIONES ELEMENTALES DE ARITMETICA / Algora y Pontes, Loreto M – Badajoz: Libreria Florencio Ger, 1910 – 1 – sp Bibl Santa Ana [510]
NACKA VAERMDOE ALLEHANDA – Nacka, 1989-91 – 9 – sw Kungliga [072]
NACKA VAERMDOE ALLEHANDA – Saltsjoeoe-Boo, Sweden. 1989- – 1 – sw Kungliga [072]
NACKA-SALTSJOBADENS TIDNING – Sodertalje, Sweden. 1979-89 – 1 – sw Kungliga [072]
NACLA NEWSLETTER / North American Congress on Latin America – v1-5. Feb 1967-Oct 1971 – 1 – us UMI [073]
NACLA REPORT ON THE AMERICAS / North American Congress on Latin America – (v18-. 1984-. 5,6,9) – v11-. Sept 1977- – 1 – us UMI [073]
NACLA'S LATIN AMERICA AND EMPIRE REPORT / North American Congress on Latin America – v5-11. Nov 1971-Aug 1977 – 1 – us UMI [073]
NACWPI BULLETIN / National Association of College Wind and Percussion Instructors – (See also: National Association of College Wind and Percussion Instructors. NACWPI Journal) – v4-18. 1955-1970 – 1 – us UMI [780]
NACWPI JOURNAL / National Association of College Wind and Percussion Instructors – (See also: National Association of College Wind and Percussion Instructors. NACWPI Bulletin) – v19- 1970- 1; v27- 5,6,9 – us UMI [780]
NADA – Chicago, IL, 1905 – 7mf or 1 reel – 9,1 – us I.H.R.C. [972]
NADA / Rhodesia. Southern. Department of Native Affairs – v.1-4, 1923-63 – 1 – us Res Libr [960]
NADA DE TODO / Sanchez-Arjona, Vicente – Sevilla: Imp. Acuna, 1951 – 1 – sp Bibl Santa Ana [810]
Nadaillac *see* LE ROYAUME DE BENIN
Nadal, Augustin *see* THEATRE
Nadeau, Marie-Marthe *see* BIBLIOGRAPHIE ANALYTIQUE DE L'OEUVRE DE L'ABBE ARTHUR MAHEUX POUR LES ANNEES 1942, 1943, 1944
Nadeau, Wilfrid *see* LE DACTYLOGRAPHE CANADIEN
Nadezhin, A *see* METROPOLIT MOSKOVSKII PLATON LEVSHIN KAK PROPOVEDNIK
Nadjafi Abrandabadi, Ali Hossein *see* LA POLITIQUE CRIMINELLE IRANIENNE A L'EPREUVE DES CHANGEMENTS POLITIQUES
Nadler, Josef *see* LITERATURGESCHICHTE DES DEUTSCHEN VOLKES
AL NADWA AL'ILMIYA LI AL TA'LIM / Saudi Arabia. Ministry of Planning – (In Arabic) – Riyadh. 2v. 1983 – 17mf – 9 – DE-315/1 – ne IDC [370]
NAEB JOURNAL / National Association of Educational Broadcasters – (See: Educational Broadcasting Review). 1-26. 1941-67 – 1 – us UMI [370]
NAECHTE : GEPANZERTE LIEDER / Beck, Karl – Leipzig: W Engelmann, 1838 – 1 – us U.W. Library [810]
Naegel, Andreas *see* JULIUS GROSSES ERZAEHLENDE DICHTUNGEN
Naegele, Eugen *see* BEITRAEGE ZU UHLAND
Naegeli, Theodor *see* DER WORTSCHATZ DES APOSTELS PAULUS
NAFC NEWS MAGAZINE – 1973-75. (American Indian Periodicals in the Princeton University Library). 3 fiches – 9 – $45.00 – us UPA [305]
Naffakh, R *see* LES BEGGARA DU ZOR
NAFIRI MAUT DARI LEMBAH QAMRAN (DEAD SEA SCROLLS) / Nahdi, Saleh A – SE-11,088 1. 1964 – 9 – ne IDC [240]
NAGA BANGKIT / Oey, Hong Lee – SE-5109 1. 1962 – 9 – ne IDC [950]
NAGAH *see* AL-NAGAH
NAGALAND GAZETTE / Nagaland. India – Kohima. Oct. 15, 1966-Mar. 31, 1967 – 1 – us NY Public [324]
Nagaland. India *see* NAGALAND GAZETTE
Nagame, A V *see* THE TRAVANCORE STATE MANUAL
Nagao, Ariga *see* LA CROIX ROUGE EN EXTREME-ORIENT
NAGARA VATTA – Phnom-Penh. 6 fevr 1937-18 juil 1942 – 1 – fr A.C.R.P.P. [073]
Nagel, E *see* ZWINGLI'S STELLUNG ZUR SCHRIFT
Nagel, P *see* DIE MOTIVIERUNG DER ASKESE IN DER ALTEN KIRCHE UND DER URSPRUNG DES MOENCHTUMS (T.U.U. 5.95)
Nagel, Siegfried Robert *see* DIE HAUPTWERKE DER DEUTSCHEN LITERATUR IN ZUSAMMENHANGE MIT IHRER GATTUNG
NAGGEN – Stockholm, Sweden. 1912-22 – 1 – sw Kungliga [073]
Nagiel, Henryk *see* "DZIENNIKARSTWO POLSKIE"
Nagler, Alois Maria *see* HEBBEL UND DIE MUSIK
Nagler, Georg K *see* DIE MONOGRAMMISTEN UND DIEJENIGEN BEKANNTEN UND UNBEKANNTEN KUENSTLER ALLER SCHULEN
NAGOLD-ENZ-BOTE : BA DER SCHWARZWAELDER POST – (Title change: Schwarzwaelder Bote/C, 30 Sep 1950) – Calw-Oberndorf, Germany. 29 Oct 1948-30 Dec 1960; 2 Jul 1973-31 Dec 1979 – 77r – 1 – gw Mikrofilm [072]
NAGOYA SHIMBUN – Japan, 1906-42 – 264r – 1 – inquire – us Ross [072]
NAGOYA SHIMBUN – Nov 1906-Aug 1942 – 264r – 1 – Y2,461,200 – ja Japan Micro [950]
NAGRA BIDRAG TILL UPSALA THEOLOGISKA FAKULTETS HISTORIA / Cornelius, C A – Upsala: Akademiska boktryckeriet, 1874-1875 – 1mf – us A.T.L.A. [240]
NAGRE TROPISKE LAFVAR / Fries, E M – (Svenska Vetenskaps Akademiens). Handlinga. 1820. B-5373 – 8 – ne IDC [580]
Naguevskii, D I *see*
– BIBLIOGRAFIIA PO ISTORII RIMSKOI LITERATURY V ROSSII S 1709 PO 1889 GOD
– OSNOVY BIBLIOGRAFII PO ISTORII RIMSKOI LITERATURY
Nagy, A *see*
– DIE PHILOS. ABHANDLUNGEN DES JA'QUB BEN ISHAG AL-KINDI
– DIE PHILOSOPHISCHEN ABHANDLUNGEN DES JA'QUB BEN ISHAG AL-KINDI
Nagy, Ivan *see* MAGYARORSZAG CSALADAI
NAHALEM VALLEY REPORTER – Wheeler, OR. -w. 14 Aug 1913-9 Apr 1915. – 1 – us U.O. Library [071]
NA-HAN – (Battle Cry). v. 1-2. 1937. BCH-971 – 8 – ne IDC [999]
NAHB BUILDER – v3-4 1980-81 – 1 – us UMI [690]
Nahdi, Saleh A *see* NAFIRI MAUT DARI LEMBAH QAMRAN (DEAD SEA SCROLLS)
NAHE-ZEITUNG : BA DER RHEIN-ZEITUNG – Birkenfeld, West Germany. 1981- – 8r per yr – 1 – gw Mikrofilm [072]
NAHE-ZEITUNG *see* RHEIN-ZEITUNG
NAHID – (Purchase with Sitarah-'i Subh) – Tehran, Shumarah-'i 24 (4 Jumadi al-sani 1304 [1925]) – 1 – us MEDOC [950]
Nahke, Heinz *see* GEORG BUECHNERS AESTHETISCHE ANSCHAUUNGEN
NAHLA *see* AL-NAHLA
NAHZAT – (Shumarah-'i 69-132 (7 Tir 1363-23 Aban 1364[28 Jun 1984-14 Nov 1985]). Missing issues: Shumarah-'i 71-73, 76) – Paris: Nahzat-i Muqavamat-i Milli-i Iran – 1 reel – 1 – $50.00 – us MEDOC [950]
NAHZAT-I ZANAN-I MUSALMAN – (Shumarah-'i 21-25, 31 (10 Murdad 1358-25 Mihr 1358[1 Aug 1979-17 Oct 1979])) – Tehran: Nahzat-i Zanan-i Musalman – 1 reel – 1 – $25.00 – us MEDOC [950]
NAI DUNIA – Indore, India. Jul-Sept 1966 – 1r – 1 – us L of C Photodup [072]
NAIA NEWS – (v.29-. 1979- 5,6,9) – (National Association of Intercollegiate Athletes).v.1-. 1950- – 1 – us UMI [073]
LA NAIADE – no. 1-20; ed. impermeable no. 3-15. Paris. juin 1852-aout 1853 – 1 – fr A.C.R.P.P. [073]
Naidenov, V F *see* SISTEMATICHESKII KATALOG BIBLIOTEKI NIKOLAEVSKOI INZHENERNOI AKADEMII I UCHILISHCHA
NAIE PRESSE – La Presse nouvelle. Paris. 1934-30 sept 1939 – 1 – fr A.C.R.P.P. [073]
Naigeon, Jacques-Andre *see* LE MILITAIRE PHILOSOPHE OU DIFFICULTES SUR LA RELIGION PROPOSEES AU R.P. MALEBRANCHE, PRETRE DE L'ORATOIRE
NAIKA : JOURNAL OF THE VANUATU NATURAL SCIENCE SOCIETY – n1-42. 1981-93 – 1r – 1 – PMB Doc428 – at Pacific Mss [500]
Nail, Marvin Powell *see* THE DEVELOPMENT OF A PROGRAM OF SUPPLEMENTAL PASTORAL CARE FOR WHITSITT CHAPEL BAPTIST CHURCH
Na'ili *see* DIVAN
Naim *see*
– DIVAN
– DIVANCE
Naim, Mochtar *see* INDONESIA'S NAHDATUL ULAMA MOVEMENT: FACTORS THAT LED TO ITS EMERGENCE AS A POLITICAL PARTY
Na'ima, Mustafa *see*
– TARIH-I NA'IMA
Naiman, Robert J *see* ECOLOGY AND MANAGEMENT OF AQUATIC-TERRESTRIAL ECOTONES
NAIMUBU. BUNKYO KYOKU. NICHI MA JITEN. KAMOES BAHASA NIPPON-INDONESIA / Java – Djakarta ? Djawa Gunseikanbu (2603) vi/950p – 75-85mf – 9 – ne IDC [950]
LES LE NAIN / Musee des Beaux Arts. Reims, France – 1953. 12 illus. 1 fiche – 9 – fr Réunion [700]
LE NAIN JAUNE – puis Journal politique, litteraire et financier. Paris. mai 1863-juil 1870, juil 1872-mars 1873, juil 1876-avr 1905, 1909-10, 1912-13 – 1 – fr A.C.R.P.P. [073]
LE NAIN JAUNE – puis Le Nain jaune refugie ou Journal des arts, des sciences et de la litterature. Paris puis Bruxelles. dec 1814-juil 1815, mars-nov 1816 – 1 – fr A.C.R.P.P. [073]
Nair, Pyarelal *see* THE EPIC FAST
Nairns, N *see* THE MOP SONG FOR VOICE AND PIANO
NAIRNSHIRE, 1837 : BRITISH ISLES CENSUS DIRECTORIES PROJECT, SCOTLAND. VOL 46 – 1mf – 9 – A$9.00 – at Vine [941]
Naismith, James *see* BASKETBALL
LA NAISSANCE DE LA GRANDE INDUSTRIE EN DAUPHINE: FIN DE XVIIE SIECLE-1869 / Leon, Pierre – Paris. 1954. (La Condition Ouvriere. Part Two.) – 9 – 30.00 – fr Bibl Nationale [360]
LES NAISSANCES ILLEGITIMES EN FRANCE ET DANS QUELQUES PAYS DE L'EUROPE / Congres International d'Hygiene et de Demographie – Par Dr. Jacques Bertillon. Reprod. d'un article extr. de Internationaler Congres fuer Hygiene und Demographie. Compte-rendu. Cahier no.29, 1887. Wien, p1-55. 1 fiche. (Statistics Series: Medical Studies) – 9 – 6.00 – fr Bibl Nationale [310]
NAJAKA LALANA / Susanta Tirtapradja – Prefaces in Indonesian. SE 4490 1. 1955 – 9 – ne IDC [950]
NAJE EDUCATOR / National Association of Jazz Educators – v1-9, no. 4. 1968-Apr/May 1977. (Title varies). (Jazz Periodicals) – 2r – 1 – $150.00 – us UPA [780]
NAJE FOLKSCAJTUNG – Warsaw, Jul 1931-Dec 1933 – 10r – 1 – uk British Libr Newspaper [947]
NAJE FOLKSCAJTUNGY – (Missing: Several numbers) – Warsaw, Odessa. v1-17. 1923-1939 – 31r – 1 – J-92-26/3 – ne IDC [072]
DOS NAJE WORT – (Missing: 1936(April-June); several numbers) – Warsaw. v1-3. 1935-1937 – 5r – 1 – J-92-30/3 – ne IDC [072]
NAJWAZNIEJSZE WYNIKI SPISU LUDNOSCI I SPISU ZWIERZAD DOMOWYCH WEDLUG STANU Z DN. 31 GRUDNIA 1910 R / Kasznica, Stanislaw – Lwow, 1911 – 1r – 1 – us I.H.R.C. [947]
Nakamura, K *see* SEDJARAH NIPPON. DITERDJEMAHKAN OLEH HABIBANA-ALWIE
NAKANUNE – Berlin, mar 26-jun 30 1922, jul 13-oct 1 1922, jan 3-apr 1 1923, mar 26-jun 30 1932 – 3r – 1 – Inquire at Mikrofilmarchiv for details – gw Misc Inst [072]
NAKANUNE – On the Eve. London. -m. (In Russian). Jan 1899-Feb 1902. (36 ft) – 1 – uk British Libr Newspaper [947]
NAKAZ EIA IMPERATORSKAGO VELICHESTVA EKATERINY VTORIIA.. / Catherine 2, Tsarina of Russia – St. Petersburg, 1893. 256p. Contains French and Russian Texts of Catherine's Nakaz with extensive bibliographical notes by I. Bezgin. BR-9097/1 – 9 – ne IDC [947]
NAKED THOUGHTS ON SOME OF THE PECULIARITIES OF THE FIELD-PREACHING CLERGY, IN A LETTER TO A FRIEND – London, [1776] – 1mf – 9 – MP-512/1 – ne IDC [240]
Nakken, O *see* MANUAL OF METHODS FOR FISHERIES RESOURCE SURVEY AND APPRAISAL, PART 2
NAKORN SARN – Bangkok, Thailand. 1948-51 – 8r – 1 – us L of C Photodup [072]
NALAO BRIEF CASE *see* NLADA BRIEFCASE
Naldini, M *see* IL CRISTIANESIMO IN EGITTO
Nalivkine *see* ESQUISSE DE L'HISTOIRE DU KHANAT DE KHOKAND
NALLD JOURNAL – (National Association of Language Laboratory Directors). v.4-9. 1969-74 – 1 – us UMI [370]
NALLD JOURNAL – (v.15-. 1980- 5,6,9) – National Association of Learning Laboratory Directors. v.9-. 1975- – 1 – us UMI [370]
NALOGOVOE OBLOZHENIE CHASTNOGO SEKTORA / Russia. (1923-U.S.S.R.). Laws, Statutes, etc – Moskva: Gos. fin. izd-vo, 1931. 280p. LL-4056 – 1 – us L of C Photodup [340]
NALOGOVYI SPRAVOCHNIK DLIA KUSTAREI I REMESLENNIKOV I IKH PERVICHNIKH OB"EDINENII / Rozhdeistvenskii, N F; ed by Grossman, V IA – M., 1929 – 2mf – 9 – COR-306/1 – ne IDC [334]
Nalty, Bernard C *see* BLACKS IN THE U.S. ARMED FROCES
NAM NADU – Madras, India. Jul-Sept 1966 – 1r – 1 – us L of C Photodup [072]
NAM NU' GIO'I CHUNG – no. 1-22. Saigon. 28 mars-31 dec 1930 – 1 – fr A.C.R.P.P. [073]
NAM PHONG – Van-hoc khoa-hoc tap-chi. Hanoi. juil 1917-34. mq sept 1921 (no. 51), mars-avr 1932, aout-dec 1933, janv-15 juil 1934, aout-sept 1934, 1er-15 oct 1934, dec 1934 – 1 – fr A.C.R.P.P. [073]
NAMAH-I FARHANG – Mashhad: Sal-i 1, shumarah-i 1-9, (Day 1330-Azar 1331 [December 1951-Novmber 1952]), sal-i 2, shumarah-i 1-6 (Day 1331-Khurdad 1332 [December 1952-May 1953]) – 1 reel – 1 – $225.00 – us MEDOC [950]
NAMAH-'I KANUN-I NIVISANDIGAN-I IRAN – Tehran: Kanun-i Nivisandagan-i Iran. Shumarah-'i 1-6 (Bahar 1358-Tabistan 1360 [Spring 1979-Summer 1981]) – 1 reel – 1 – $80.00 – us MEDOC [950]
NAMAH-'I TAJADDUD – (Sal-i, shumarah-'i 1-82 (23 Hut 1302-17 Jadi 1303[13 March 1924-7 Jan 1925])) – Tehran – 1 reel – 1 – $50.00 – us MEDOC [950]
NAMAH-I TAMADDUN – Tehran: Dawrah-i 2, shumarah-i 1-8 (Mihr 1330-Urdibihisht 1333 [September 1951-April 1954]) – 1 reel – 1 – $130.00 – us MEDOC [950]
NAMBU-HAN KARO-SEKI NISSHI = POLITICAL AND ECONOMIC CALENDAR OF THE NAMBU, FEUDAL LORD OF THE MORIOKA DOMAIN, IN THE MODERN AGE – In the public hall of Morioka City. In 1644-1840 handwriting. 189 books. 220,000p – 158r – 1 – Y1,500,000.00 – ja Yushodo [950]
DER NAME : EIN BEITRAG ZU SEINER GESCHICHTE IM ALTERTUM UND BESONDERS BEI DEN GRIECHEN / Hirzel, R – Leipzig, 1927 – 3mf – 8 – ne Slangenburg [240]

NAME AND SUBJECT INDEX TO THE GENERAL CORRESPONDENCE OF THE OFFICE OF THE SECRETARY OF THE NAVY / U.S. Navy. Office of the Secretary – 1930-42. 187 rolls. M1067 – 1 – us Nat'l Archives [324]

NAME AND SUBJECT INDEX TO THE GENERAL CORRESPONDENCE OF THE WAR PLANS DIVISION / U.S. War Department. War Plans Division – 1921-42. 18 rolls. M1080 – 1 – us Nat'l Archives [324]

NAME AND SUBJECT INDEX TO THE LETTERS RECEIVED BY THE APPOINTMENT, COMMISSION, AND PERSONAL BRANCH OF THE ADJUTANT GENERAL'S OFFICE, 1871-1894 / U.S. Army. Adjutant General's Office – RG 94. M1125. 4 rolls – 1 – us Nat'l Archives [355]

NAME AUTHORITIES CUMULATIVE MICROFORM ED / U.S. Library of Congress – ISSN: 0195-9093. Item Code: 8334500 – 48mf – 9 – $310.00 – us L of C Cataloging [020]

NAME AUTHORITY LIST / British Library. National Bibliographic Service – 1992- . Monthly updated cumulations – 17 – £199.00y + VAT, £235.00y overseas – uk British Libr [020]

NAME INDEX OF JEWS WHOSE GERMAN NATIONALITY WAS ANNULLED BY THE NAZI REGIME / Germany. Berlin Documents Center – 9r – 1 – T355 – us Nat'l Archives [324]

NAME INDEX TO EARLY ILLINOIS RECORDS – Z125-0001 to Z125-0248 – 5 – us A.G.L.L. [920]

NAME INDEX TO EARLY ILLINOIS RECORDS: CHICAGO AND COOK COUNTIES – Z127-0001 to Z127-0008 – 5 – us A.G.L.L. [978]

NAME INDEX TO EARLY ILLINOIS RECORDS: SUPPLEMENT 1 – Z126-0001 to Z126-0026 – 5 – us A.G.L.L. [920]

DIE NAMEN DER MEERE IN DEN ASSYRISCHEN INSCHRIFTEN / Schrader, Eberhard – Berlin: Buchdr der koenigl Akademie der Wissenschaften: In Commission bei F Duemmler, 1878 – 1mf – 9 – 0-8370-8618-3 – 1986-2618 – us A.T.L.A. [470]

DIE NAMENGEBUNG IN DEN DRAMEN DER VORGAENGER SHAKESPEARES / Detlefsen, Hans – Kiel, 1913 – 1mf – DM48.00 – 3-8267-3050-X – gw Hänsel [420]

NAMES IN THE NEWS – 1978- Monthly Index with cumulations – 9 – us NewsBank [071]

NAMES OF COUNTRIES AND OF THEIR CAPITAL CITIES INCLUDING ADJECTIVES OF NATIONALITY AND CURRENCY UNITS – 8th rev ed 1986 – 128p – it F.A.O. [910]

NAMES OF FISHES, INCLUDING SHELLFISH AND MARINE ANIMALS : PROVISIONAL EDITION – it F.A.O. [590]

NAMES OF GOD IN HOLY SCRIPTURES: A REVELATION OF HIS NATURE AND RELATIONSHIPS / Jukes, Andrew John – New York: Thomas Whittaker, 1888. 1 fiche – 9 – us A.T.L.A. [240]

THE NAMES ON THE GATES OF PEARL: AND OTHER STUDIES / Waller, Charles Henry – London: Sampson & Rivington, 1883. 1 fiche – 9 – us A.T.L.A. [240]

O NAMESTNIKAKH, VOEVODAKH I GUBERNATORAKH / Andreevskii, I – St. Petersburg, 1864. 156p. BR-5974 2 – 8 – ne IDC [320]

NAMIBIA : THE EFFECTS OF APARTHEID ON CULTURE AND EDUCATION / O'Callaghan, Marion – 1977 – 9 – 92-3-101476-5 – fr UNESCO [320]

Namibia Office *see* GOVERNMENT OF NAMIBIA/UNICEF COUNTRY PROGRAMME OF CO-OPERATION

THE NAMIBIAN – Windhoek, Namibia. 1987-89 – 3r – 1 – us L of C Photodup [072]

NAM-KY KINH-TE BAO – Titre francais: L'Information economique de Cochinchine. Saigon. oct 1920-fevr 1924 – 1 – fr A.C.R.P.P. [073]

NAMN OCH BYGD : TIDSKRIFT FOER NORDISK ORTNAMNSFORSKNING – Uppsala, Lund. v1-29. 1913-1941 – 120mf – 9 – ne IDC [948]

NAMOI INDEPENDENT (GUNNEDAH) – Jan 2 1899-Dec 30 1907 – 9 – at Pascoe [072]

NAMOI VALLEY INDEPENDENT – Gunnedah – at Pascoe [980]

Nampon, Adrien *see* MANUEL DU MISSIONNAIRE SECULIER OU REGULIER

NAM-VIET TE-GIA NHU'T BAO – Le Journal de la famille annamite. no. 2-48. Saigon. 21 oct 1917-22 sept 1918 – 1 – fr A.C.R.P.P. [073]

NAN YANG SHANG PAO – (Some issues missing. Cont as: Nan-Yang Hsing-Chou Lie Ho Tsao Pao) – Singapore, 1960-91 – 406r – 1 – us L of C Photodup [072]

NANAIMO DAILY FREE PRESS – (1993.-12r; 1874-1976.-231r) – Nanaimo, 1977-1992 – 192r – 1 – cn Preston [971]

NANAIMO TIMES – 1980- – 1 – cn Commonwealth Micro [072]

NA-NA-KWA, OR, DAWN ON THE NORTHWEST COAST – Kitamaat, BC: G H Raley, [1898?-1907] – 9 – cn C.I.H.M. [240]

NAN-AO CHIH – 1783, 12. BCH-621 2 – 8 – no IDC [950]

NANCE COUNTY JOURNAL – Fullerton, NE. -w. May 1887; Dec 1892; Mar 1895 to date – 1 – us NE Hist [071]

NANCE COUNTY JOURNAL – Fullerton. Neb. 1887-1898; 1956-1966 – 1 – us UMI [071]

NANCE COUNTY POPULIST – Genoa, NE. -w. Oct 1895-Jun 1897. Scattered issues missing – 1 – us NE Hist [071]

NAN-CHING WEN-HSIEN – Documents on Nanking. Jan 1947-Jun 1948. No.1-18. -m.Literary writings and information on noted persons in Nanking. 1 reel – 1 – $30.00 – us Chinese Res [800]

NAN-CH'UAN HSIEN-CHIH – 1931, 14, 1. Lacking: ch. 1, 1931. BCH-714 2 – 8 – ne IDC [950]

NAN-CH'UNG HSIEN-CHIH – 1813, 7 (2). BCH-772 2 – 8 – ne IDC [950]

NANCY, A NOVEL / Broughton, Rhoda – A new ed. London: R. Bentley, 1874. 438p. illus – 1 – us U.W. Library [830]

NANCY: A NOVEL / Broughton, Rhoda – British Fiction Archive: Unit 4 – 9 – uk Bell [830]

NANDOER KAPAS ING TANAH DJAWA / Ishikawa, T – Djakarta, Djawa Goenseikanboe (Bale Poestaka), 2603. 31p – 48mf – 9 – ne IDC [950]

NANFANG RIBAO – Southern Daily. China. In Chinese. Current subscription. Annual delivery. Backfiles supplied on request. 1979- , 1 reel/y. M D15 – 1 – $55.00r – cc Microforms [072]

NAN-HAI HSIEN-CHIH – 1741, 20. BCH-588 2 – 8 – ne IDC [950]

NAN-HAI HSIEN-CHIH – 1835, 44, 2. BCH-589 2 – 8 – ne IDC [950]

NAN-HSIUNG CHIH-LI CHOU-CHIH – 1824, 34, 1. BCH-605 2 – 8 – ne IDC [950]

NANJIANG DAXUE XUEBAO – Zhexue Shehui Kexue Ban. Journal of Nanjiang University, Philosophy and Social Science. In Chinese but Table of Contents in English in each issue. F p205 – 9 – $4.50f – cc Microforms [073]

NANJING DAXUE XUEBAO – Journal of Nanjing University, Natural Sciences Edition. In Chinese but English abstracts to the main articles. F p184 – 9 – $4.50f – cc Microforms [073]

NANJING LI CHAN GONGYE XUEYUAN XUEBAO – Journal of Nanjing Forestry Technological College. In Chinese but English abstracts to the main articles. F p197 – 9 – 4.00f – cc Microforms [073]

Nanjundayya, H V *see* THE MYSORE TRIBES AND CASTES

NANKAI SOCIAL AND ECONOMIC QUARTERLY – (Missing: 1938-1940) – Tientsin, 1935-1941 – 50mf – 9 – ne IDC [300]

NANKAI XUEBAO – Zhexue Shehui Kexue Ban. Journal of Nankai University, Philosophy and Social Science. In Chinese but Table of Contents in English in each issue. F p202 – 9 – $4.50f – cc Microforms [073]

Nanking. National Central University *see* NUNG-HSUEH TS'UNG-K'AN

NANKING SEMINARY REVIEW *see* THEOLOGICAL QUARTERLY; NANKING SEMINARY REVIEW

NANKING THEOLOGICAL SEMINARY : BULLETIN / Nanking Theological Seminary – v1-7. 1939-40 (complete) – 1r – 1 – ATLA S0703E – us A.T.L.A. [073]

Nanking Theological Seminary *see* NANKING THEOLOGICAL SEMINARY

NANKING UNIVERSITY MAGAZINE – v1 no 1. Dec 1909 (incomplete) – 1r – 1 – ATLA S0703F – us A.T.L.A. [073]

NAN-NING HSIEN-CHIH – 1852, 10. BCH-668 2 – 8 – ne IDC [950]

Nannius, P *see* DECLAMATIO, DE BELLO TURCIS INFERENDO

NANOBIOLOGY : JOURNAL OF RESEARCH ON NANOSCALE LIVING SYSTEMS – 1992- 2v – 9 – £176.00 – 0958-3165 – uk Carfax [574]

NANOSTRUCTURED MATERIALS – 1,5,69 – us UMI [620]

NANOTECHNOLOGY – v1. 1990 – 1,5,6,9 – £145.00 – uk I.O.P. [530]

Nansen, Fridtjof *see* ESKIMOLIV

NANSEN IN THE FROZEN WORLD – Arr. and ed. by S.L. Berens. Chicago: Waverly, c1897. 03745. (Pre-1900 Canadiana) – 9 – cn C.I.H.M. [910]

NANSHE – Journal of the Southern Society.Feb 1910-Dec 1923. 6 reels. M-C31 – 1 – $270.00 – cc Microforms [073]

NANSIS – it F.A.O. [630]

Nantel, Alphonse *see* LA CAMPAGNE

Nantel, Bruno *see* LA NATION

Nantel, G A *see* LE NORD

Nantel, G-A *see* LA NATION

NANTES AU XIXE SIECLE. STATISTIQUE TOPOGRAPHIQUE, INDUSTRIELLE ET MORALE: HYGIENE PHYSIQUE ET MORALE / Guepin, Ange – 1835. (Condition of 19th c. French working class Series) – 9 – fr Hachette [310]

NANTES ET LE DEPARTEMENT AU 19E SIECLE... / Maillard, Emile – Nantes: Vier, 1891 – 1 – F205.89 – fr Armell [910]

Nantes, Loire-Inferieure *see* LA VILLE DE NANTES ET LA LOIRE-INFERIEURE

NANTES REALISTE / Orceau, R – Nantes: Tainon, [s.d.] – 1 – F50.00 – fr Armell [944]

NANTON NEWS – Nanton, Alberta, CN. Jun 1903- – 1r per yr – 1 – Can$57.00r – cn Commonwealth Micro [072]

NANTONG JUNSHAN NONGMIN QIYI SHILIAO – Historical materials on the peasant uprisings at Junshan Mountain, Nantong prefecture. Comp. by Guan Jincheng. 2 fiches. F-H83 – 9 – $9.00 – cc Microforms [950]

NANTUCKET 1662-1849 – (Mf 1T-5T: Vital Records 1662-1823. Mf 6T-7T: Marriages 1822-48. Mf 7T-8T: Out-of Town Marriages 1701-97. Mf 8T: Marriages 1821-27. Mf 8T-12T: Publishments 1783-1849. Mf 13T: Vital Records 1690-1726; Publishments 1744-83. Mf 13T-14T: Deaths 1841-44. Mf 14T-16T: Births 1843-49. Mf 16T-18T: Marriages 1843-49. Mf 18T-20T: Deaths 1843-49) – (mf ed 1998) – 20mf – 9 – 0-87623-299-3 – us Holbrook [920]

NANTUCKET 1662-1900 – (Mf 1-6,8: Vital Records 1662-1839. Mf 5-7: Marriages 1821-44. Mf 7: Out-of-Town Marriages 1700-97. Mf 8-11,17: Town Records 1682-1836. Mf 11-13,16: Intentions 1748-1828. Mf 18-22: Accounts 1827-37. Mf 22-36: Intentions 1828-1917. Mf 28: Deaths 1839-44. Mf 37-134: Town Records 1807-84. Mf 135-137: Census 1800. Mf 137-140: Census 1830. Mf 141-145: Census 1840. Mf 145-148: Census 1850; Tax 1853. Mf 149-152: Census 1860. Mf 152-155: Census 1865. Mf 156-158: Census 1870. Mf 158-160: Census 1880. Mf 160-161: Census 1895. Mf 162-163: Voters 1884-92. Mf 164-216: Mortgages 1830-1908. Mf 217-219: Dog Owners 1853-85. Mf 219-225: Vitals 1834-49. Mf 226-244: Vitals 1850-89. Mf 245-248: Deaths 1889-1903. Mf 249-251: Marriages 1890-1900. Mf 252-254: Births 1890-99) – (mf ed 1994) – 254mf – 9 – 0-87623-195-4 – us Holbrook [920]

NANTWICH CHRONICLE – England. 1975-81. -w. 23 reels – 1 – uk British Libr Newspaper [072]

THE NANTY GLO JOURNAL – Nanty Glo, PA. 1951-58; 1971-76. 6 rolls – 13 – $25.00r – us I.M.R. [071]

NAN-YANG HSING-CHOU LIE HO TSAO PAO *see* NAN YANG SHANG PAO

NAN-YANG HSUEH-PAO – Journal of South Seas Society. v. 1-10 (2). Singapore. 1940-54. BCH-319 2 – 8 – ne IDC [073]

NANYANG XIONGDI YANCAO GONGSI SHILIAO (SHANGHAI ZIBEN ZHUYI DIANXING QIYE SHILIAO) – Historical materials on typical bourgeois enterprises in Shanghai: Materials on the Nanyang Brothers Tobacco Company Ltd.Comp. by the Institute of Economics, Shanghai Academy of Social Sciences. 1 reel. M-H172 – 5 – 35.00 – cc Microforms [950]

NAPA CITY DIRECTORIES INCLUDING YOUNTVILLE, CALISTOGA AND ST HELENA – Napa Co, CA. 1916; 1925-1950 – 14r – 1 – $700.00 – D063 – us Library Micro [910]

NAPA COUNTY – 1909-10; 1921-33 – 12r – 1 – $600.00 – P00067 – us Library Micro [910]

NAPA COUNTY / Gunn, Harry C – Napa Co, CA. 1926 – 1r – 1 – $50.00 – B40241 – us Library Micro [978]

NAPA COUNTY DIRECTORIES – Napa Co, CA. 1871-1874; 1889-1890; 1899-1900 – 4r – 1 – $200.00 – D062 – us Library Micro [978]

NAPA COUNTY REPORTER – Napa. Calif. 1862-1864; 1881-1890 – 1 – us UMI [071]

NAPA REGISTER : SELECTED ISSUES ON WINE, GRAPES AND WINE MAKING – Napa, CA. 1872-1874 – 1r – 1 – $50.00 – B02508 – us Library Micro [630]

NAPA REGISTER AND NAPA JOURNAL *see* THE NAPA VALLEY REGISTER

NAPA VALLEY – 1909-33; 1992- – 27+ r – 1 – $1,350.00 – P00068 – us Library Micro [910]

THE NAPA VALLEY REGISTER – (Also known as: Napa Register and Napa Journal) – Napa, CA. 1952- – 453+ r – 1 – $22,650.00 ($400.00y) – B02512 – us Library Micro [071]

NAPA/SOLANO COUNTIES – 1910-20 – 10r – 1 – $500.00 – P00069 – us Library Micro [910]

NAPER INDEPENDENT – Naper, NE. -w. Apr 1916-Feb 1917 – 1 – us NE Hist [071]

NAPER NEWS – Naper, NE. -w. Feb 1900-May 1901, scattered issues missing – 1 – us NE Hist [071]

NAPHTA – Lvov, U.S.S.R. -w. 1901-08. 4 reels – 1 – uk British Libr Newspaper [947]

Napier, A S *see* THE CRAWFORD COLLECTION OF EARLY CHARTERS AND DOCUMENTS

Napier, Charles J *see* REMARKS ON MILITARY LAW AND THE PRACTICE OF FLOGGING

Napier, Edward Hungerford Delaval Elers *see* THE LIFE AND CORRESPONDENCE OF ADMIRAL SIR CHARLES NAPIER, FROM PERSONAL RECOLLECTIONS, LETTERS, AND OFFICIAL DOCUMENTS

Napier, Henry Edward *see* FLORENTINE HISTORY, FROM THE EARLIEST AUTHENTIC RECORDS TO THE ACCESSION OF FERDINAND THE THIRD, GRAND DUKE OF TUSCANY

Napiersky, C E *see* INDEX CORPORIS HISTORICODIPLOMATICI LIVONIAE, ESTHONIAE, CURONIAE. KURZER AUSZUG AUS DERJEIGEN URKUNDEN-SAMMLUNG. FUER DIE GESCHICHTE UND DAS ALTE STAATSRECHT LIV-, EST-, UND KURLANDS

Naples. (Kingdom). Laws, Statutes, etc *see* CONSTITVTIONES REGVM REGNI VTRIVSQVE SICILIAE MANDANTE FRIDERICO 2 IMPERATORE PER PETRVM DE VINEA.

NAPLO / Hungary.Orszaggyules. Kepviselohaz – Budapest. 1861-1944 – 1 – 3818.00 – us L of C Photodup [943]

NAPLO – Veszprem, Hungary. 1962-68; 1970-79 – 29r – 1 – us L of C Photodup [072]

Napolean I., Emperor of France *see* MAXIMES DE GUERRES ET PENSEES

NAPOLEON / Merezhkovskii, Dimitrii – 2v. Beograd. 1929. BR-774 2 – 8 – ne IDC [940]

NAPOLEON BONAPARTE COLLECTION – 638mf – 9 – us UMI [944]

NAPOLEON DIMEDAN ASMARA / Suwardi, Idris – SE 5461 1. 1964 – 9 – ne IDC [920]

NAPOLEON ET LA POLOGNE, 1806-1807 / Handelsman, M – Paris. 1909. BR-5488 2 – 8 – ne IDC [944]

NAPOLEON IM SPIEGEL DER GOETHESCHEN UND DER HEINESCHEN DICHTUNG : EINE KRITISCHE STUDIE / Eek, Dirk van – (Includes bibliographical references) – Amsterdam: H J Paris, 1933 – 1r – 1 – us U.W. Library [430]

NAPOLEON IN DER DEUTSCHEN LITERATUR / Schoemann, Milian – Berlin: W de Gruyter & Co, 1930 – 2r – 1 – us U.W. Library [430]

NAPOLEON NORTHWEST NEWS : WEEKLY DEMOCRATIC NEWSPAPER – Napoleon, Oh. Feb 2 1905-Dec 24 1958 – 38r – 1 – us Western Res [071]

NAPOLEON NORTHWEST-NEWS – Napoleon. Ohio. 1905-59 – 32r – 1 – $32.50r – us Archival [071]

NAPOLEON - SA FAMILLE - SON ENTOURAGE = AUTOGRAPHS OF THE STATE HISTORICAL MUSEUM IN MOSCOW : AUTOGRAPHES DE LA COLLECTION DU MUSEE HISTORIQUE NATIONAL / Petrov, F A & Ianovskii, A D - (Includes catalog in French $100) - 20r - 1 - $2,000.00 coll - us Ross [944]
NAPOLEONOVSKAIA EPOKHA / Zambornitskii, N M - Bibliograficheskii ukazatel'. v. 1-2. Spb. 1914-15. BR-5927 2 - 8 - ne IDC [940]
NAPOLEONS ANSICHTEN VON DER GOTTHEIT JESU, SOWIE VON RELIGION, PRIESTERN UND KRICHENTHUM, PROTESTANTISMUS UND KATHOLICISMUS / Ekendahl, D G von - Weimar, 1842 - 9 - DM48.00 - 3-89349-256-9 - gw Hänsel [240]
NAPONEE HERALD - Naponee, NE. -w. Aug 1912; May 1914-Jun 1916; Aug 1916-Dec 1917 - 1 - us NE Hist [071]
Nappo, Tommaso *see*
- ARCHIVES BIOGRAPHIQUES FRANCAISES. DEUXIEME SERIE (ABF 2)
- ARCHIVIO BIOGRAFICO ITALIANO (ABI 1)
- ARCHIVIO BIOGRAFICO ITALIANO, NUOVA SERIE (ABI 2)
- ARCHIVO BIOGRAFICO ITALIANO, NUOVA SERIE (ABI 2)
NAPREDEK - Cleveland, OH, 1936-1941 - 4mf or 1 reel - 9,1 - us I.H.R.C. [975]
NAPREJ - Pittsburgh, PA, 1935, 1937-1941 - 5mf or 1 reel - 9,1 - us I.H.R.C. [975]
NAPRIJED - (Some issues missing) - Zagreb, Yugoslavia. Mar 1944-Nov 1945; Jun 1946-Jan 1954 - 4r - 1 - us L of C Photodup [949]
NAPRZOD - Krakow, Poland. 28 Dec 1918-1 Jan 1919; 19,26 Aug 1945 - 2r - 1 - us L of C Photodup [943]
Narancio, Attilio *see* LAS LEYES OBRERAS Y EL 'PARTIDO COLORADO'.
Naranjo Alonso, Clodoaldo *see* TRUJILLO Y SU TIERRA
Narasayya, Maddali Lakshmi *see* THE ANGLO-TELUGU PRIMER
Narberhaus, Jozef *see* BENEDIKT VAN ANIANE
Narbonne, J *see* LES FRANCAISES FACE A LA POLITIQUE. COMPORTEMENT POLITIQUE ET CONDITION SOCIALE
Narbut, V *see*
- ALLILUIA
- NA OKHOTE
- STIKHI
NARCISS : EIN TRAUERSPIEL / Brachvogel, Albert Emil - 4. Aufl. Jena: H Costenoble, 1874 - 1 - us U.W. Library [820]
Narciss, Georg-Adolf *see* REICHSTAEDTISCHE ERZAEHLUNGEN
THE NARCISSUS : ITS HISTORY AND CULTURE... / Burbidge, FW - London, 1875 - XVI, 95p, 48pls - 8 - ne IDC [580]
NARCOTIC DRUGS : CONFERENCES AND PROTOCOLS / United Nations. Commission on Narcotic Drugs - 1947-1955 - E/F.5 E.2 F.1 - 9 (E/NT) - us U.N. Pubs [360]
NARCOTIC DRUGS : INDEX / United Nations. Commission on Narcotic Drugs - 1949-1983 - E/F.1 E.34 F.35 S.5 - 9 - us U.N. Pubs [360]
NARCOTIC DRUGS : LAWS AND REGULATIONS / United Nations. Commission on Narcotic Drugs - 1947-1979 - E.351 F.207 S.52 - 9 (E/NL) - us U.N. Pubs [340]
NARCOTIC DRUGS : SALES CODES / United Nations. Commission on Narcotic Drugs - E/F.142 E.78 F.78 R.30 S.61 - 9 - us U.N. Pubs [615]
NARCOTIC DRUGS : SUMMARIES OF ANNUAL REPORTS OF GOVERNMENTS / United Nations. Commission on Narcotic Drugs - 1939-1982 - E/F.11 E.233 F.209 S.47 - 9 (E/NR) - us U.N. Pubs [360]
NARCOTIC DRUGS / United Nations - All publications and UN official records since 1946. 1800 fiches - 9 - 3500.00; 1.90f - uk UNIMICRO [324]
NARCOTICS CONTROL DIGEST - v1- 1971- 1; v7- 1977- 5,6,9 - us UMI [610]
NARCOTICS ENFORCEMENT & PREVENTION DIGEST *see* WASHINGTON CRIME NEWS SERVICES' NARCOTICS DEMAND REDUCTION DIGEST
NARCOTICS LAW BULLETIN - v1- 1974- 1,5,6; v3- 9 - us UMI [340]
Narducci, Guglielmo *see* STORIA DELLA COLONIZZAZIONE DELLA CIRENAICA
Nares, Robert *see* ELEMENTS OF ORTHOEPY
Narfon, Julien de *see*
- LEON 13 INTIME
- POPE LEO 13
NARI EKAKH VAVILONSKIKH : ZAMI ETKI BI EZHENT SA / Gorielov, M - [S.L.: s.n.], 1921 - 1 - CSUX88-B6912 - us Hoover Inst Photo [947]
Narjoux, Felix *see*
- ARCHITECTURE COMMUNALE
- PARIS: MONUMENTS ELEVES PAR LA VILLE, 1850-1880
Narkompros RSFSR *see* UNIVERSITETY I NAUCHNYE UCHREZHDENII A
Narkomtorga R.S.F.S.R. *see* SKOROPORTIASHCHIESIA PRODUKTY I KHOLODILNOE DELO
Narkomtorga SSSR i Tsentrosoiuza *see* VOPROSY SOVETSKOI TORGOVLI
Narkomzem SSSR i Narkomsovkhozov *see* SELSKOE KHOZIAISTVO SSSR
NAROD - London, England. v1-6, 1948-53 - 1 - us I.U. Libraries [073]
NAROD - Pittsburgh, PA, 1921 - 1mf or 1 reel - 9,1 - us I.H.R.C. [975]
NAROD - Prague, Czechoslovakia. v1-4, 1917-20 - 1 - us I.U. Libraries [073]
NAROD - Sofia, Bulgaria. Oct 1944-Aug 1948 (scattered issues) - 4r - 1 - us L of C Photodup [949]
NAROD POLSKI - Chicago, Illinois. Jan 8 1987-Dec 20 1990 - 1r - 1 - us L of C Photodup [072]
NAROD POLSKI = POLISH NATION / ed by Skaryszewski, Tomasz - Chicago, 1897-1902; 1904-sep 14 1921; 1926-28; 1930-71 - 40r - 1 - us Res Libr [071]
NAROD (SAINT PETERSBURG, RUSSIA) - (Includes c.1: 1896:Dec.16) - SPB: A.P. Malshinski i, 1896 - 1 - CSUXAKF0282-S - us Hoover Inst Photo [947]
NARODEN DRUGAR - Yambol, Bulgaria. Feb 1953-1969 - 10r - 1 - us L of C Photodup [949]
NARODEN FAR - Burgas, Bulgaria. 1945-Jan 1946 - 1r - 1 - us L of C Photodup [949]
NARODEN GLAS = NATIONAL HERALD - Granite City, IL: C Nedelkoff, [aug 25 1917-jul 30 1926; apr 1947-1949] - us Res Libr [071]
NARODEN SPORT - (Some issues missing) - Sofia, Bulgaria. Oct 1944-Oct 1945; 1951-53; 1955-63 - 8r - 1 - us L of C Photodup [949]
NARODEN VOJNIK - Skopje, Yugoslavia. Mar 14,24 1945 - 1r - 1 - us L of C Photodup [949]
NARODNA ARMIIA / ed by Bilan, V - Kiev: Ministerstvo Oborony Ukrainy, 1919- - 2mf - 9 - $199.95y - us East View [320]
NARODNA ARMIIA - Sofia, Bulgaria. 1953-Sept 1991 - 46r - 1 - us L of C Photodup [949]
NARODNA ARMIJA - Beograd, 1976-80 - 5r - 1 - DM375.00 - gw Mikro Press [949]
NARODNA BESEDA - Cleveland, OH, 1899 - 1mf or 1 reel - 9,1 - us I.H.R.C. [975]
NARODNA BORBA - Sofia, Bulgaria. Sept 1946-Oct 1949 (incomplete) - 1r - 1 - us L of C Photodup [949]
NARODNA HAZETA - (Backfile 1993-98 1r per y $85y) - Ukraine, 1999- - 1r per y - 1 - $80.00 standing order - us Ross [072]
NARODNA KULTURA - (Cont as: Kultura 1990-) - Bulgarien, 1975-1991ff - 16r - 1 - DM1,200.00 - gw Mikro Press [949]
NARODNA KULTURA - Sofia, Bulgaria. -w. Jan 1959-Dec 1970. 9 reels - 1 - uk British Libr Newspaper [949]
NARODNA KULTURA *see* KULTURA
NARODNA MLADEZ - (Cont as: Mladez 1990. Faks 1991) - Sofia, 1976-1991ff - 1 - DM1,725.00 - gw Mikro Press [949]
NARODNA MLADEZ *see* FAKS
NARODNA MLADEZH - Sofia, Bulgaria. 1948-50; 1951-76; 1981-Feb 1991 (scattered issues) - 62r - 1 - us L of C Photodup [949]
NARODNA OBRODA - 1990-1993 - 1 - Sfr240.00 - sz Infoprint [947]
NARODNA OBRODA - (1990-98 4r per y $340y) - Slovakia, 1999- - 6r per y - 1 - $480.00 standing order - us Ross [072]
NARODNA OBRODA - Bratislava, Czechoslovakia. Jun 1945-May 1948 - 4r - 1 - us L of C Photodup [072]
NARODNA TRIBUNA - Kyustendil, Bulgaria. Mar 1959-1963 - 3r - 1 - us L of C Photodup [949]
NARODNA TRIBUNA - Lom, Bulgaria. Jun 1953-1963 - 2r - 1 - us L of C Photodup [949]
NARODNA VOISKA - Sofia, Bulgaria. Sept 1944-Apr 1951 (incomplete) - 3r - 1 - us L of C Photodup [949]
NARODNA VOLIA = THE PEOPLE'S WILL - Scranton, PA: Ruthenian National Union, 1914-87 - us Res Libr [071]
NARODNAI A GAZETA (PRE SOV, CZECHOSLOVAKIA) - (Library has: no. 16-24, 35-38 (1932-1933), 1-2, 15-18, 33-36 (1934), 7-14 (1935)) - Pri ashev: "Narodnaja gazeta", 19uu - 1 - CSUX89-S10 - us Hoover Inst Photo [947]
NARODNAI A VOLI A (VLADIVOSTOK, R.S.F.S.R.) - (Library has: no. 1-5, 7-8 (July 31-Aug. 9, 1921)) - Vladivostok: Narodnai a voli a, 1921- - 1 - CSUX89-S12 - us Hoover Inst Photo [947]
NARODNAIA ARMIIA - Spk. n1-2. 1907 - 8 - BR-1600 2 - ne IDC [355]
NARODNAIA BESEDA - Spb, 1862-64 - 8 - BR-1601 2 - ne IDC [947]
NARODNAIA CHITAL'NIA - Obshchedostupnyi ezhemesiachnyi zhurnal. Spb. 1903-09. Lacking: 1903-06; 1907 (1-8); 1908 (7); 1909. BR-8147 2 - 8 - ne IDC [073]
NARODNAIA DUMA I RABOCHI I SI EZD / Akselrod, Pavel Borisovich - Zheneva: Izd. "Iskry", 1905 - 1 - CSUX89-B4294 - us Hoover Inst Photo [947]
NARODNAIA DUMA I RABOCHI I SOI EZD / Akselrod, Pavel Borisovich - 2-oe izd. S.-Peterburg: "Novy i mir", 1907 - 1 - CSUX89-B1747 - us Hoover Inst Photo [947]
NARODNAIA MYSL' - Ezhemesiachnyi zhurnal. v. 1-2. M. 1911. BR-3982 2 - 8 - ne IDC [073]
NARODNAIA MYSL' - Literaturnyi obshchestvenno-politicheskii dvukhnedel'nik. v. 1-2. Petrograd. 1915. BR-3983 2 - 8 - ne IDC [320]
NARODNAIA POEZIIA / Buslaev, Fedor Ivanovich - 1887. Folk literature - 1 - us I.U. Libraries [390]
NARODNAIA UCHEBNO-VOSPITATEL'NAIA LITERATURA - Opyt kataloga obshchei pedagogiki russkoi narodnouchebnoi literatury za poslednie 25 let. (1862-1887). M. 1888. BR-7201 2 - 8 - ne IDC [370]
NARODNAIA VEST' - v. 1-2. Spb. 1906. BR-3984 2 - 8 - ne IDC [073]
NARODNAIA ZHIZN' - Izdanie ezhenedel'noe. v. 1-5. Spb. 1906. BR-3985 2 - 8 - ne IDC [073]
NARODNE HOSPODARSTVO UKRAINY V... : T SENTRALNE STATYSTYCHNE UPRAVLINIII A USSR - (Includes c.1: 1924/1925) - Kharkiv: [Upravlinni a], 1919 - 1 - CSUXAKZ1405-S - us Hoover Inst Photo [947]
NARODNE NOVINE - Zagreb. Yugoslavia. -d. 3 Feb-27 Jun 1919, 1 Sep 1941-30 Dec 1944. (11 reels) - 1 - uk British Libr Newspaper [949]
NARODNE NOVINY - Turcianske Sv. Martin, Slovakia, 1881-1914 - 4r - 1 - us I.H.R.C. [947]
NARODNE PRIPOVIJESTI I PRESUDE / ed by Vrcevic, Vuk - 1890. Yugoslavian folk literature - 1 - us I.U. Libraries [390]
NARODNI HLASNIK - Turckianske Sv. Martin, Slovakia, 1868-1881 - 1 reel - 1 - us I.H.R.C. [947]
NARODNI LIST - New York, 1898-1920 - 28r or 2mf - 1 - us I.H.R.C. [975]
NARODNI LIST - New York. Jan 1 1908-June 1911; 1912-1918; and 1920-1921. Not collated - 1 - us NY Public [073]
NARODNI LIST - Zagreb, Yugoslavia. May 1945-Jun 1959 - 21r - 1 - us L of C Photodup [949]
NARODNI OBRODA - Brno, Czechoslovakia. Aug 1945-Oct 1946 - 2r - 1 - us L of C Photodup [072]
NARODNI OSVOBOZENI - Prague, Czechoslovakia. May 1945-1948 - 4r - 1 - us L of C Photodup [072]
NARODNI POKROK - Omaha, NE. -w. Aug 1921-Dec 1945 - 1 - us NE Hist [071]
NARODNI POLITIKA - Prague, Czechoslovakia. Mar-Jun 1941 - 1r - 1 - us L of C Photodup [072]
NARODNI VESTNIK - Duluth, MN, 1911, 1917 - 2mf or 1 reel - 9,1 - us I.H.R.C. [975]
NARODNI VESTNIK - Duluth, MN, 1912-1914 - 3r - 1 - us I.H.R.C. [975]
NARODNIE NOVINY - Turcansky Sv. Martin, Czechoslovakia. Apr 1942-Jul 1944 - 1r - 1 - us L of C Photodup [072]
NARODNO DELO - Stanke Dimitrov, Bulgaria. Jul 1953-1958 (incomplete) - 1r - 1 - us L of C Photodup [949]
NARODNO DELO - Varna, Bulgaria. Apr 1945-Jan 1946; Oct 1956-1992 - 54r - 1 - us L of C Photodup [949]
NARODNO SUBRANIE - Sofia, Bulgaria, 1879-1943 - 49r - 1 - us Ross [324]
NARODNO ZEMEDELSKO ZNAME - Sofia, Bulgaria. Sept 1945-May 1947 - 2r - 1 - us L of C Photodup [949]
NARODNOE DELO - Ezhemesiachnyi illiustrirovannyi literaturnyi, obshchestvenno-ekonomicheskii i nauchno-populiarnyi zhurnal. Spb. 1910-12. Lacking: 1910 (9-12), 1912 (1, 10). B-1799 2 - 8 - ne IDC [330]
NARODNOE DELO : ORGANE DU PSR - Paris, Berne, 1902-04 - 1 - us Hoover Inst Photo [335]
NARODNOE DELO - (Partiia sotsialistov-revoliutsionerov). v. 1-5. Paris. 1902-04. Lacking: 1902 (1). BR-2345 2 - 8 - ne IDC [073]
NARODNOE DELO - Sbornik. (Partiia sotsialistov-revoliutsionerov). v. 1-7. Paris. 1909-12(?). Lacking: v. 1-3. BR-2344 2 - 8 - ne IDC [073]
NARODNOE KHOZI A ISTVO BELORUSSII : ORGAN EKONOSOVESHCHANII A PRI SOVNARKOME S.S.R.B. - (Library has: Jan.-Sept. 1922) - Minsk: Gos. izd-vo Belorussii, 1922-1924? - 1 - CSUX89-S667 - us Hoover Inst Photo [947]
NARODNOE KHOZI A ISTVO BELORUSSII (1922) *see* NARODNOE KHOZI A ISTVO BELORUSSII
NARODNOE KHOZI A ISTVO KAZAKHSTANA - (Library has: Oct./Nov. 1931, Feb./March-Nov./Dec. 1932, Jan./Feb.-Nov./Dec. 1937) - Alma-Ata: [s.n.], 1926- - 1 - CSUX90-S3 - us Hoover Inst Photo [947]
NARODNOE KHOZI A ISTVO RSFSR : T SENTRALNOE STTISTICHESKOE UPRAVLENIE PRI SOVETE MINISTROV RSFSR - Moskva: Gos. statisticheskoe izd-vo, 1958 - 1 - CSUX90-S751 - us Hoover Inst Photo [947]
NARODNOE KHOZI A ISTVO SREDNE I AZII (1924) - (Library has: Sept./Oct. 1924-Nov./Dec. 1930; some issues missing) - Tashkent: izd. Respublik sredne i Azii, 1924-1930. 7v - 1 - CSUX89-S846 - us Hoover Inst Photo [947]
NARODNOE KHOZI A ISTVO SREDNE I AZII V... : GOSUDARSTVENNAI A PLANOVAI A KOMISSII A PRI SREDNE-AZIATSKOM EKONOMICHESKOM SOVETE, BI URO KONI UNKTURNOGO SOVETA - (Includes c.1: no.1 1926/1927) - Tashkent: [Bi uro], 1927 - 1 - CSUXAKZ2501-S - us Hoover Inst Photo [947]
NARODNOE KHOZI A ISTVO UKRAINY : EZHEMESI ACHNY I ORGAN UKRSOVNARKHOZA - (Includes c.1: v.1:no.1 1919:Mar.-v.1:no.2/3 (1919:Apr./May)) - Kharkov: [Ukrsovnarkhoz], 1919- - 1 - CSUXAKZ0475-S - us Hoover Inst Photo [947]
NARODNOE KHOZI A ISTVO ZAKAVKAZI A : DVUKHNEDELNY I POLITIKO-EKONOMICHESKI I ZHURNAL ORGAN V ES'A ZSFSR - (Library has: Jan.-May 1931) - Tiflis: Sovet, 1928-1931. 4v - 1 - CSUX89-S860 - us Hoover Inst Photo [947]
NARODNOE KHOZIAISTVO - 1918-22 - 1 - 58.00 - us L of C Photodup [943]
NARODNOE KHOZIAISTVO - M., 1918-22 n10 - 163mf - 9 - R-3718/2 - ne IDC [334]
NARODNOE KHOZIAISTVO - Nauchno-obshchestvennyi zhurnal. v. 1-6. Spb. 1900-05. BR-2248 2 - 175mf - 8 - R-2248/2 - ne IDC [073]
NARODNOE KHOZIAISTVO / Vysshii Sovet Narodnogo Khoziaistva - Russia. v1,6. 1918,1922 - 1e - 1 - us Ross [947]
NARODNOE KHOZIAISTVO I VNESHNI AIA TORGOVLIA SSSR / Frumkin, Moiseilich - Moskva: Gos. izd-vo, 1926 - 1 - CSUX89-B2926 - us Hoover Inst Photo [330]
NARODNOE KHOZIAISTVO UKRAINY - Ezhemesiachnyi zhurnal. Khar'kov. 1919. BR-2257 2 - 8 - ne IDC [073]
NARODNOE KHOZIALISTVO SSR *see* PLAN
NARODNOE PRAVO / Kachorovskii, K R - Moscow, 1905. 255p. Author postulates the emergence of a new peoples' law in Russia derived from customary law of the laboring masses. BR-9759/1 - 9 - ne IDC [340]

NARODNOE PROSVESHCHENIE – Petrograd, Moscow. 1918-1922, nos. 18-111. Missing: nos. 106, 107 – 1 – 35.00r – us Hoover Inst Photo [335]

NARODNOE PROSVESHCHENIE V SSSR : T SENTRALNOE STATISTICHESKOE UPRAVLENIE SSSR – (Includes c.1: 1926/1927//) – Moskva: Upravlenie, 1929- – 1 – CSUXAKZ6202-S – us Hoover Inst Photo [947]

Narodnogo komissariata vneshne i i vnutrenne i torgovli SSSR *see* SOVETSKAI A TORGOVLI A

NARODNO-KHOZIAISTVENNYI PLAN NA 1935 G / U.S.S.R. Gosudarstvennaia Planovaia Komissiia – M. 1935. BD-248 1 – 9 – ne IDC [330]

NARODNO-KHOZIAISTVENNYI PLAN NA 1935 GOD / U.S.S.R. Gosudarstvennaia Planovaia Komissiia – Ed. 2. M. 1935. BD-249 1 – 9 – ne IDC [330]

NARODNO-KHOZIAISTVENNYI PLAN NA 1936 G / U.S.S.R. Gosudarstvennaia Planovaia Komissiia – Ed. 2. M. 1936. BD-250 1 – 9 – ne IDC [330]

NARODNO-KHOZIAISTVENNYI PLAN SOIUZA SSSR NA 1937 G / U.S.S.R. Gosudarstvennaia Planovaia Komissiia – M. 1937. BD-251 1 – 9 – ne IDC [330]

NARODNO-SOTSIALISTICHESKAIA BIBLIOTEKA – Vyp. 1. Spb. 1907. BR-1602 2 – 8 – ne IDC [335]

NARODNO-SOTSIALISTICHESKOE OBOZRENIE – Periodicheskoe izdanie Narodno-sostsialisticheskoi partii. v. 1-2. Spb. 1906. BR-4138 2 – 8 – ne IDC [073]

NARODNOST'I GOSUDARSTVO / Kazanskii, P E – Odessa, 1912. 21p – 1mf – 9 – ne IDC [320]

Narodny i komissariat finansov et al *see* GLAVNE ISHIE SVEDENII A PO GOSUDARSTVENNOMU BI UDZHETU I DENEZHNOMU OBRASHCHENII U ZA 1923-24 BI UDZHETNY I GOD

Narodny i komissariat finansov Soiuza SSR, Upravlenie gosudarstvenymi nalogami *see* STATISTIKA GOSUDARSTVENNYKH NALOGOV I POSHLIN ZA...BIUDZHETNY I GOD

Narodny i komissariat inostrannykh del *see* SOGLASHENII A S GERMANIE I ZAKLI UCHENNYE V BERLINE 6 MAI A 1921 GODA

Narodny i komissariat po inostrannym delam *see* – TREATIES, ETC

Narodny i komissariat prosveshchenii a RSFSR *see* GOSUDARSTVENNYE UNIVERSITETY

Narodny i komissariat truda *see* STATISTIKA TRUDA

Narodny i komissariat vneshne i torgovli, Glavnoe tamozhennoe upravlenie *see* STATISTIKA VNESHNE I TORGOVLI SSSR

Narodny i komissariat vnutrennikh del, Statisticheskoe biuro *see* STATISTICHESKI I OBZOR DEI ATELNOSTI MESTNYKH ADMINISTRATIVNYKH ORGANOV NARODNOGO KOMISSARIATA VNUTRENNIKH DEL RSFSR

Narodny i komissariat zemledeliia *see* TRUDOVOE KHOZIAISTVO

NARODNY NOVINY – Pittsburgh, PA: Narodny slovensky spolok v Sp s americkych, [1910-41] – us Res Libr [071]

NARODNYE SKAZKI / ed by Erlenvein, A A – 1863. Russian tales – 1 – us I.U. Libraries [390]

Narodnyi komissariat prosveshcheniia RSFSR *see* VOPROSY METODOLOGII PLANIROVANIIA PROSVETITELNOI RABOTY

Narodnyi komissariat vneshnei torgovli, Otdel tam. statistiki *see* VNESHNIAIA TORGOVLIA SOIUZA SSR

Narodnyi komissariat zdravookhraneniia, Sektsiia borby s tuberkulezom *see* TUBERKULEZ

NARODNYI TEATR I KOOPERATSIIA : DOKL. TEATR. S"EZDU V MOSKVE / Armand, L M & Evdokimov, A A – (Kultura dlia vsekh. Nos. 7-8. 24p) – [Ed 2]. M., 1917 – 1mf – 9 – COR-6/1 – ne IDC [334]

NARODNYI TRUD – Narodno-sotsialisticheskoe obozrenie. v. 1-2. Spb. 1906. BR-4139 2 – 8 – ne IDC [335]

NARODOPISNY VESTNIK CESKOSLOVANSKYY – v. 1-14. Praha. 1906-21. Illus. BR-8359 2 – 8 – ne IDC [073]

NARODOWIEC – (Consists of scattered issues) – Cleveland, OH, 1912-1919 – 1r – 1 – us I.H.R.C. [978]

NARODOWIEC – Lens, France. -d. 29 June 1958-31 Dec 1965; 30 Dec 1966-8 July 1971. 54 reels – 1 – uk British Libr Newspaper [072]

NARODY I OBLASTI – Ezhemesiachnyi zhurnal po natsional'nomu i oblastnomu voprosam. v. 1-8. M. 1914. BR-3986 – 8 – ne IDC [073]

NAROZHDENIE NOVOI ROSSII / Dan, Fedor – S.-Peterburg: "Praktik": Sklad izd. Knizhny i magazin "Trud", 1906 – 1 – CSUX89-B685 – us Hoover Inst Photo [947]

NARRABRI HERALD – Jan 2 1899-Dec 31 1912 – 9 – at Pascoe [072]

NARRACIONES DE UN MONTERO Y PRACTICA DE CAZA MAYOR / Covarsi, Antonio – Barcelona: Tercera Edicion, Editorial Juventud, 1952 – 1 – sp Bibl Santa Ana [946]

NARRACIONES DE UN TROVADOR / Guerra Hontiveros, Marcelino – 1893 – 9 – 1.50f – sp Bibl Santa Ana [830]

NARRACIONES EXTREMENAS. LA IMPRENTA EN EXTREMADURA / Barrantes Moreno, Vicente – 1783 – 9 – 1.50f – sp Bibl Santa Ana [830]

NARRACIONES EXTREMENAS. LA SERRANA DE LA VERA.. / Barrantes Moreno, Vicente – 1783 – 9 – 1.50f – sp Bibl Santa Ana [830]

NARRAGANSETT – Westerly. R.I. -w. 1858-99 – 1 – us UMI [071]

THE NARRAGANSETT DAWN – 1935-36. (American Indian Periodicals in the Princeton University Library). 5 fiches – 9 – $45.00 – us UPA [305]

THE NARRAGANSETT FRIEND'S MEETING IN THE 18TH CENTURY : WITH A CHAPTER ON QUAKER BEGINNINGS IN RHODE ISLAND / Hazard, Caroline – Boston: Houghton, Mifflin, 1899 – 1mf – us A.T.L.A. [240]

NARRAGANSETT TIMES – Wakefield. R.I. -w. 1855- – 1 – us UMI [071]

LE NARRATEUR DU SOIR : RECUEIL D'HISTOIRES ET DE LEGENDES – Montreal: Maison de la bonne presse, 1894. SEM16P73 – 1r – 5 – Can$9.00 – cn Bibl Nat [830]

NARRATIO DE INCHOATIONE DOMUS CLERICORUM IN ZWOLLIS / Traiecti, Jacobus; ed by Schoengen, Utif M – Amsterdam, 1908 – 16mf – 8 – Dfl56.00 – ne Slangenburg [240]

A NARRATION OF RELIGIOUS EXPERIENCE: IN TWELVE LETTERS / Livermore, Harriet – 1826. 1v – 9 – us A.T.L.A. [240]

NARRATION OF THE EXPERIENCE, TRAVELS AND LABOURS OF ELDER JAMES POTTER, MINISTER OF THE GOSPEL, AND PASTOR OF THE BAPTIZED CHURCH IN BOWDOIN, COMMONWEALTH OF MASSACHUSETTS / Potter, James – 1 – 5.00 – us Baptist [240]

NARRATIONE DELLA GUERRA PRINCIPIATA CONTRA IL GRAN TURCO, ... / Vltimi Auisi di Venetia – Viterbo, 1570 – 1mf – 9 – H-8170/1 – ne IDC [956]

NARRATIVA BREVE EN EL SIGLO 13 FRANCES : DITS, DEBATES Y BATALLAS / Bermejo Larrea, Esperanza – 3mf – 9 – Pta2,000.00 – 84-85422-38-4 – sp Pentalfa [440]

NARRATIVE AND CRITICAL HISTORY OF AMERICA / ed by Winsor, Justin – 8v. 1884-89 – 3r – 1 – us Ross [975]

A NARRATIVE AND EXPOSITION OF THE LATE PROCEEDINGS OF NEW ENGLAND YEARLY MEETING / ed by Wilbur, John – New York: Piercy & Reed, 1845 – 1mf – us A.T.L.A. [240]

NARRATIVE OF A JOURNEY THROUGH THE UPPER PROVINCES OF INDIA / Heber, R – London, 1928. ed. 2. v. 1-3. BI-1138 1 – 9 – ne IDC [910]

NARRATIVE OF A JOURNEY TO THE INTERIOR OF CHINA / Abel, C – London, 1818. xvi, 420p, 16 pls., 4 maps. B-6449 2 – 8 – ne IDC [910]

NARRATIVE OF A JOURNEY TO THE SHORES OF THE POLAR SEA / Franklin, John – BN 212 3rd ed. 2 v. 1824 – 8 – ne IDC [910]

NARRATIVE OF A MISSION TO CENTRAL AFRICA / Richardson, J – 2v. London. 1853. BA-347 2 – 8 – ne IDC [910]

NARRATIVE OF A RESIDENCE IN SIAM / Neale, F A – London, 1852 – 3mf – 9 – ne IDC [950]

NARRATIVE OF A SECOND EXPEDITION TO THE SHORES OF THE POLAR SEA. INCLUDING AN ACCOUNT. BY J. RICHARDSON / Franklin, John – London. 1828. BN-213 2 – 8 – ne IDC [910]

NARRATIVE OF A SECOND VOYAGE IN SEARCH OF A NORTHWEST PASSAGE. INCL THE REP. OF J. C. ROSS, AND THE DISCOVERY OF THE NORTHERN MAGNETIC POLE / Ross, James Clark – BN 377 2. 1835 – 8 – ne IDC [910]

NARRATIVE OF A VISIT TO THE SYRIAN (JACOBITE) CHURCH OF MESOPOTAMIA : WITH STATEMENTS AND REFLECTIONS UPON THE PRESENT STATE OF CHRISTIANITY IN TURKEY, AND THE CHARACTER AND PROSPECTS OF THE EASTERN CHURCHES / Southgate, Horatio – New York: D. Appleton; Philadelphia: Geo. S. Appleton, 1844 – 1mf – us A.T.L.A. [240]

NARRATIVE OF A VOYAGE OF DISCOVERY TO AFRICA AND ARABIA : PERFORMED IN HIS MAJESTY'S SHIPS, LEVEN AND BARACOUTA FROM 1821 TO 1826, UNDER THE COMMAND OF CAPTAIN F W OWEN / Boteler, Thomas – London: R Bentley, 1835 – us Res Libr [910]

NARRATIVE OF A VOYAGE TO HUDSON BAY IN H.M.S. ROSAMOND / Chappell, E – BN-162 2. 1817 – 8 – ne IDC [910]

NARRATIVE OF A VOYAGE TO THE PACIFIC AND BERING'S STRAIT / Beechey, Frederick William – v. 1-2. BN-117 2. 1831 – 8 – ne IDC [910]

NARRATIVE OF A VOYAGE TO THE SOUTHERN ATLANTIC OCEAN IN 1828, 29, 30, PERFORMED IN H.M. SLOOP CHANTICLEER / Webster, William Henry Bayley – 2v. 1834 – 9 – uk Libr Preservation [910]

NARRATIVE OF A WHALING VOYAGE AROUND THE GLOBE FROM 1833 TO 1836 / Bennett, F D – 2v. 2609 2. 1840 – 8 – ne IDC [910]

NARRATIVE OF AN EXPEDITION INTO THE INTERIOR OF AFRICA BY THE RIVER NIGER IN 1832-1834 / Laird, M & Oldfield, R AK – 2v. London. 1837. BA-330 2 – 8 – ne IDC [910]

NARRATIVE OF AN EXPEDITION TO EXPLORE THE RIVER ZAIRE, USUALLY CALLED THE CONGO. / Tuckey, James Kingston – London. 1818 – 1 – us Res Libr [960]

NARRATIVE OF AN EXPEDITION TO EXPLORE THE RIVER ZAIRE USUALLY CALLED THE CONGO IN SOUTH AFRICA IN 1816 / Tuckey, James Kingston – A 150. 1818 – 9 – ne IDC [910]

NARRATIVE OF AN EXPEDITION TO THE EAST COAST OF GREENLAND / Graah, WA – BH-480 2. 1837 – 8 – ne IDC [910]

NARRATIVE OF AN EXPEDITION TO THE SHORES OF THE ARCTIC SEA IN 1846 AND 1847 / Rae, J – BN 3552. 1850 – 8 – ne IDC [910]

A NARRATIVE OF AN EXPLORATORY VISIT TO EACH OF THE CONSULAR CITIES OF CHINA : ON BEHALF OF THE CHURCH MISSIONARY SOCIETY 1844-1846 / Smith, G – London. 1847. BCH-831 2 – 8 – ne IDC [240]

A NARRATIVE OF EVENTS CONNECTED WITH THE PUBLICATION OF THE TRACTS FOR THE TIMES : WITH AN INTRODUCTION AND SUPPLEMENT EXTENDING TO THE PRESENT TIME / Palmer, William P – London: Rivingtons, 1883 – 1mf – us A.T.L.A. [240]

A NARRATIVE OF EVENTS CONNECTED WITH THE RISE AND PROGRESS OF THE PROTESTANT EPISCOPAL CHURCH IN MARYLAND / Hawks, Francis L – New York: John S. Taylor, 1839 – 2mf – us A.T.L.A. [240]

A NARRATIVE OF EVENTS CONNECTED WITH THE RISE AND PROGRESS OF THE PROTESTANT EPISCOPAL CHURCH IN VIRGINIA : TO WHICH IS ADDED AN APPENDIX, CONTAINING THE JOURNALS OF THE CONVENTIONS IN VIRGINIA FROM THE COMMENCEMENT TO THE PRESENT TIME / Hawks, Francis L – New York: Harper, 1836, c1835 – 2mf – us A.T.L.A. [240]

A NARRATIVE OF FOUR JOURNEYS INTO THE COUNTRY OF THE HOTTENTOTS AND CAFFRARIA IN THE YEARS 1777, 1778, AND 1779 / Paterson, William – Pretoria, State Library, 1978. London: J. Johnson, 1789. 18 plates of botanical specimens. 5mf and printed booklet – 9 – sa State Libr [910]

A NARRATIVE OF SOME OF THE LORD'S DEALINGS WITH GEORGE MUELLER / Mueller, George – 8th ed. London: J Nisbet. 6v. 1872-95 – 8mf – 9 – 0-8370-7007-4 – 1986-1007 – us A.T.L.A. [920]

NARRATIVE OF THE ATTEMPTED ESCAPES OF KING CHARLES 1ST FROM CARISBROOK CASTLE, AND OF HIS DETENTION IN THE ISLE OF WIGHT FROM NOVEMBER 1647, TO THE SEIZURE OF HIS PERSON BY THE ARMY AT NEWPORT, IN NOVEMBER 1648 / Hillier, George – Includes letters of the King to Colonel Titus. London: R. Bentley, 1852. xiv,334p – 1 – us U.W. Library [920]

A NARRATIVE OF THE CONQUEST OF A FRONTIER LAND / Scrugham, James G – Chicago: American Historical Society, 1935. v1-3. Nevada reel 1. (Cox Library Collection) 5 us Americana [078]

A NARRATIVE OF THE EXPEDITION TO ALGIERS IN THE YEAR 1816, UNDER THE COMMAND OF ADMIRAL LORD VISCOUNT EXMOUTH / Salame, Abraham – Itinerary, and continuation of the introduction.2pts. 1819 – 9 – uk Libr Preservation [910]

NARRATIVE OF THE EXPEDITION TO CHINA, FROM THE COMMENCEMENT OF THE WAR TO THE PRESENT PERIOD; WITH SKETCHES OF THE MANNERS AND CUSTOMS OF THAT COUNTRY / Bingham, John Elliot – 2nd ed. 2v. 1843 – 9 – 80.00 – uk Libr Preservation [910]

A NARRATIVE OF THE EXPEDITION TO THE RIVER NIGER IN 1841 / Allen, William & Thomson, T R H – 2v. London. 1848. BA-270 2 – 8 – ne IDC [910]

A NARRATIVE OF THE EXPEDITION TO THE RIVER NIGER IN 1841 UNDER THE COMMAND OF CAPTAIN H.D. TROTTER / Allen, William & Thomson, T R H – 2v. 1848 – 9 – 80.00 – uk Libr Preservation [910]

NARRATIVE OF THE LATE EXPEDITION TO SYRIA, UNDER THE COMMAND OF ADMIRAL THE HON. SIR ROBERT STOPFORD / Hunter, W Patison – 2v. 1842 – 9 – $20.00 – uk Libr Preservation [910]

NARRATIVE OF THE NIGER, TSADDA AND BINUE EXPLORATION / Hutchinson, T J – London. 1855. BA-316 2 – 8 – ne IDC [910]

NARRATIVE OF THE ORIGIN AND PROGRESS OF THE SOUTH AMERICAN MISSION : OR, "FIRST FRUITS" ENLARGED / Marsh, John William – [enl ed]. London: South American Missionary Society, 1883 – 1mf – 9 – 0-8370-6681-6 – 1986-0681 – us A.T.L.A. [240]

A NARRATIVE OF THE PRINCIPAL CIRCUMSTANCES RELATIVE TO THE REV. MR. WESLEY'S LATE CONFERENCE HELD IN BRISTOL, AUGUST THE 6TH, 1771,... / Shirley, W – Bath, 1771 – 1mf – 9 – MP-469/1 – ne IDC [240]

NARRATIVE OF THE SECOND ARCTIC EXPEDITION / Hall, C F – BN-235 2. 1879 – 8 – ne IDC [910]

NARRATIVE OF THE SURVEYING VOYAGE OF H.M.S. FLY; COMMANDED BY CAPT. F. P. BLACKWOOD IN TORRES STRAIT, NEW GUINEA, AND OTHER ISLANDS IN THE EASTERN ARCHIPELAGO 1842-1846.. / Jukes, Joseph Beete – 2v. 1847 – 9 – 20.00 – uk Libr Preservation [910]

A NARRATIVE OF THE VISIT TO THE AMERICAN CHURCHES BY THE DEPUTATION FROM THE CONGREGATIONAL UNION OF ENGLAND AND WALES / Reed, Andrew & Matheson, James – New York: Harper, 1835 – 2mf – us A.T.L.A. [240]

NARRATIVE OF THE VOYAGE OF H.M.S. HERALD DURING THE YEARS 1845-51, UNDER THE COMMAND OF CAPTAIN H. KELLETT...CIRCUMNAVIGATION OF THE GLOBE, AND THREE CRUISES TO THE ARCTIC REGIONS IN SEARCH OF SIR J. FRANKLIN / Seemann, Berthold Carl – 2v 1853 – 9 – uk Libr Preservation [910]

NARRATIVE OF THE VOYAGE OF H.M.S. SAMARANG, DURING THE YEARS 1843-46 / Belcher, E – London. 2v. 1846 – 13mf – 9 – ne IDC [910]

NARRATIVE OF THE VOYAGES TO EXPLORE THE SHORES OF AFRICA, ARABIA AND MADAGASCAR / Owen, William Fitzwilliam – Ed. by H.B. Robinson. 2v. 1833 – 9 – 80.00 – uk Libr Preservation [910]

A NARRATIVE OF THE WESLEYAN MISSION TO JAMAICA : WITH OCCASIONAL REMARKS ON THE STATE OF SOCIETY IN THAT COLONY / Duncan, Peter – London: Partridge and Oakey, 1849 – 1mf – us A.T.L.A. [240]

NARRATIVE OF TRAVELS AND DISCOVERIES IN NORTHERN AND CENTRAL AFRICA IN THE YEARS 1822, 1823 AND 1824 / Denham, D & Clapperton, Hugh – London. 1826. BA-302 2 – 8 – ne IDC [910]

NARRATIVE ON THE DISCOVERIES OF THE NORTH COAST OF AMERICA / Simpson, Th – BN 386 2. 1843 – 8 – ne IDC [910]

NARRATIVE SUMMARY OF RECORD / International Military Tribunal for the Far East – Tokyo. On film: 1946-48. LL-029 – 1 – us L of C Photodup [340]

NARRATIVES OF REMARKABLE CONVERSIONS AND REVIVAL INCIDENTS : INCLUDING A REVIEW OF REVIVALS FROM THE DAY OF PENTECOST TO THE GREAT AWAKENING IN THE LAST CENTURY / Conant, William C – New York: Derby & Jackson, 1858 – 2mf – 9 – 0-8370-6325-6 – 1986-0325 – us A.T.L.A. [240]

NARRATIVES OF SCOTTISH CATHOLICS UNDER QUEEN MARY STUART AND KING JAMES 6TH : NOW FIRST PRINTED FROM THE ORIGINAL MANUSCRIPTS IN THE SECRET ARCHIVES OF THE VATICAN AND OTHER COLLECTIONS / ed by Forbes-Leith, William – London: T. Baker, 1889 – 1mf – us A.T.L.A. [240]

NARRATIVES OF THE EXPULSION OF THE ENGLISH FROM NORMANDY, 1449-1450 (RS32) / ed by Stevenson, J – 1863 – Dfl35.00 – ne Slangenburg [941]

NARREN VON GESTERN – HELDEN VON HEUTE : EIN ROMAN UM DIE ERSTE DEUTSCHE KRIEGSMARINE / Zerkaulen, Heinrich – Berlin: Die Heimbuecherei, c1940 – 1r – 1 – us U.W. Library [830]

NARVSKII LISTOK *see* STARYI NARVSKII LISTOK

NAS DOM – New York, NY, 1924, 1927 – 3mf or 1 reel – 1,9 – us I.H.R.C. [978]

NAS GLAS – Montevideo, Uruguay, 1932 – 1mf or 1 reel – 9,1 – us I.H.R.C. [972]

NAS GOSPODAR – Chicago, IL, 1912, 1913 – 6mf or 1 reel – 1,9 – us I.H.R.C. [978]

NAS SPORT – (Some missing issues) – Belgrade, Yugoslavia. May 1946-Apr 1950; Jun 1951 – 2r – 1 – us L of C Photodup [949]

NASA POLJOPRIVREDA – Belgrade, Yugoslavia. Jan-Mar 1950 – 1r – 1 – us L of C Photodup [949]

Nasarski, Peter Emil *see* DEUTSCHE JUGENDBEWEGUNG UND JUGENDARBEIT IN POLEN 1919-1939

NASE DOBA – v1-55. 1894-1949 – 1 – us I.U. Libraries [073]

NASE NOVINE – (In Yugoslavian) – Canada, 1971-86 – 16r – 1 – cn Commonwealth Micro [072]

NASE NOVINE – Toronto, Canada. Nov 2 1983-Dec 20 1984; Jan 10 1985-Dec 18 1986 – 2r – 1 – us L of C Photodup [072]

NASE PRAVDA – Gottwaldov, Czechoslovakia. Jun 1954-Mar 1960 – 3r – 1 – us L of C Photodup [072]

NASE REVOLUCE – Prague. 1924; 1926-1938; selected numbers – 1 – 35.00r – us Hoover Inst Photo [335]

Nasgowitz, David *see* PTOLEMAIS CYRENAICA

Nash *see* GILES OF ROME ON BOETHIUS

NASH DAUGAVPILSK I I GOLOS – (Library has holdings (incomplete) from between Dec. 2, 1932 and Dec. 13, 1938) – Daugavpils: L. I Akubovich, 1925- – 1 – CSUX87-S193 – us Hoover Inst Photo [947]

NASH DVINSK I I GOLOS *see* NASH DAUGAVPILSK I I GOLOS

NASH GOLOS – Dvukhnedel'nyl zhurnal, posviashchennyi voprosam byta i uslovii truda torgovo-promyshlennykh sluzhashchikh. nr. 1-4. Saratov. 1908. BR-3987 2 – 8 – ne IDC [073]

Nash, Henry Sylvester *see* THE HISTORY OF THE HIGHER CRITICISM OF THE NEW TESTAMENT

Nash, John C *see* AN ANNOTATED BIBLIOGRAPHY ON METHODS FOR NON-LINEAR LEAST SQUARES COMPUTATIONS INCLUDING TEST PROBLEMS

NASH KLICH – Buenos Aires, Argentina. -w. March 1950-April 1959. 5 reels – 1 – uk British Libr Newspaper [072]

NASH KONVE IER : ORGAN I ACH. VKP(B) I FABKOM F-KI MOSKVOSHVE I NO.5 IM. PROFINTERNA / Moskvoshve i no.5 im. Profinterna (Factory) – (Includes c.1: 1932:Jan.8, Feb.4) – [Moskva]: I Ach. i fabkom, 19uu – 1 – CSUXANS0487-S – us Hoover Inst Photo [947]

NASH KRA I : IZDANIE TIKHVINSKOGO SOVETA KRESTI ANSKIKH, RABOCHIKH I KRASNOARME ISKIKH DEPUTATOV – (Includes c.1: 1919:Nov.7) – Tikhvin: Sovet, 1918 – 1 – CSUXADP4316-S – us Hoover Inst Photo [947]

NASH KRA I (TIKHVIN, R.S.F.S.R.) *see* NASH KRA I

NASH KRAI – Shtomesiachnik tsentral'naga biuro kraiaznaustva pry instytutse belaruskae kul'tury. no. 4 (19) 1927. Mensk. 1927. BR-4046 2 – 8 – ne IDC [947]

Nash, Michael *see* THE SAMUEL FRANCIS DU PONT PAPERS

NASH "OSNOVNOI ZAKON" / Russia. (1917-R.S.F.S.R.). Constitution – Moskva: Izdatel'stvo Vserossiiskago tsentral'nago ispolnitel'nago komiteta sovetov "r., s., k. i k. deputatov", 1918. 40p. LL-4057 – 1 – us L of C Photodup [340]

NASH PUT (OMSK, R.S.F.S.R.) – (Includes c.1: 1919:Oct.20) – Oms: [s.n.], 1919 – 1 – CSUXADP7371-S – us Hoover Inst Photo [947]

NASH PUT (TIENTSIN, CHINA) – (Includes c.1: 1927:July 19-24, 28-Aug.5, 9-10, 12-18, 20-21,; Aug. 30-Sept.3,6,9, 13-18, Oct.9, 12-13) – Tientsin: [s.n.], 1926 – 1 – CSUXADP4860-S – us Hoover Inst Photo [947]

NASH RIECH (BUCHAREST, ROMANIA) *see* NASHA RIECH

Nash, Simeon *see* PLEADING AND PRACTICE UNDER THE CIVIL CODE

NASH SOVREMENNIK – Moscow, 1956-72.Lacking: 1968 (1,3). BR-10,427/1 – 9 – ne IDC [947]

NASH VI EK (BERLIN, GERMANY) = UNSER ZEITALTER – (Includes c.1: 1931:Nov.29-1932:Jan.1, 17-1933:Apr.23) – Berlin: Verlag "Unser Zeitalter", 1931 – 1 – CSUXANR9707-S – us Hoover Inst Photo [947]

NASHA BORBA – (Formerly: Borba. Yrly reel count varies) – Yugoslavia, dec 1995-jan 1997 – 6r – 1 – $510.00 – us Ross [072]

NASHA GAZETA – Sofia, Bulgaria. Oct 1938-Jan 1940 – 1r – 1 – us L of C Photodup [949]

NASHA GAZETA – Sofia, Bulgaria. -w. 19 Oct 1938-18 Jan 1940. 1 reel – 1 – uk British Libr Newspaper [949]

NASHA GAZETA (HARBIN, CHINA) – (Includes c.1: 1935:Jan.1, Feb.12, 19, 26) – Kharbin: [s.n.], 1935- – 1 – CSUXADP7385-S – us Hoover Inst Photo [947]

NASHA GAZETA (RIGA, LATVIA) – (Includes c.1: v.2:no8/9 1931:May 20) – Riga: Na sa gazeta, 1930 – 1 – CSUXADP4359-S – us Hoover Inst Photo [947]

NASHA NIVA – (Backfile 1991-98 $85r) – Belarus, 1999- – 2r per y standing order – 1 – us Ross [072]

NASHA NIVA – (Nasa niwa). (In Belarussian). Vilna. USSR. -w. 20 Apr 1910-17 Jan, 21 Aug 1914. (3 reels) – 1 – uk British Libr Newspaper [947]

NASHA PRAVDA : ORGAN UISPOLKOMA I UKOMA RKP (BOLSHEVIKOV) – (Includes c.1: 1922:Mar.11) – Kozlov: Uezdnoe otd-nie Rosta, 19uu – 1 – CSUXADQ1514-S – us Hoover Inst Photo [947]

NASHA PRAVDA (KOZLOV, TAMBOSVKAI A OBLAST (R.S.F.S.R.)) *see* NASHA PRAVDA

NASHA RECH (CHICAGO, ILL.) = OUR TALK – (Includes c.1: 1941:Mar.12-Apr.12, 19-June 21) – Chicago, Ill.: Russian News Publishing House, 1941- – 1 – CSUXAKF1260-S – us Hoover Inst Photo [947]

NASHA REVOLIUTSIIA : EI A VOZHDI I VEDOMYE / Aikhenvald, Iu – Moskva: "Revoliutsiia i kultura", 1918 – 1 – CSUX88-B6987 – us Hoover Inst Photo [320]

NASHA RIECH = P AREREA NOASTR A – (Includes c.1: 1926:Nov.29-Dec.6, 8-12, 14-26, 29-31) – Bucure sti: Anri Khelfant, 1922 – 1 – CSUXANR9722-S – us Hoover Inst Photo [947]

NASHA STARINA – Literaturno-istoricheskii ezhemesiachnik. Spk. 1914-17. B-1224 2 – 8 – ne IDC [460]

NASHA STRANA (MOSCOW, R.S.F.S.R.) – (Includes c.1: 1937:Oct.-1938:Jan.; 1938:May-1938:June; 1938:Oct.; 1939:Jan.-1939:Feb) – Moskva: Zhurnalno-gazetnoe obedinenie, 1937 – 1 – CSUXAKZ1625-S – us Hoover Inst Photo [947]

NASHA VOLNOST – (Includes c.1: 1917:Nov.26) – Petrograd: [s.n.], 1917 – 1 – CSUXAKG1792-S – us Hoover Inst Photo [947]

NASHA ZARI A (OMSK, R.S.F.S.R.) – (Includes c.1: 1919:Feb.23-Aug.27; Lacks some issues) – Omsk: T-vo "Nasha zari a", 1919 – 1 – CSUXAKG2042-S – us Hoover Inst Photo [947]

NASHA ZARI A (TIENTSIN, CHINA) – (Includes c.1: 1934:Sept.14; 1941:Mar.18) – Tiantszin: Izd-vo O.V. Lembich, 192u – 1 – CSUXADQ1558-S – us Hoover Inst Photo [947]

NASHA ZARIA – Obshchestvenno-politicheskii i nauchnyi zhurnal. Spb. 1910-14 (9). BR-4141 2 – 8 – ne IDC [073]

NASHA ZHIZN – St. Petersburg, Russia. 1905 – 1 – us Res Libr [072]

NASHA ZHIZN (SHANGHAI, CHINA) = UNZER LEBN – (Includes c.1: v.5:no.14=no.209 1945:Nov.23) – Shanghai: [s.n.], 19uu – 1 – CSUXAKG5932-S – us Hoover Inst Photo [306]

NASHA ZHIZN (SOFIA, BULGARIA) – (Includes c.1: 1933:Jan.22-Sept.4) – Sofiia: K.R. Gerber, 19uu – 1 – CSUXANS0313-S – us Hoover Inst Photo [947]

Nashchokin, V A *see* ZAPISKI

NASHE DELO – Ezhemesiachnyi zhurnal. v. 1-6. Petrograd. 1915. BR-2332 2 – 8 – ne IDC [073]

NASHE DELO – v. 1-10. M. 1906. Available: 1906 (1, 5-6). BR-2353 2 – 8 – ne IDC [073]

NASHE DELO – Zhurnal posviashchaetsia preimushchestvenno voprosam sel'skoi i rabochei kooperatsii. Kiev. 1909-13 (7). Lacking: 1909 (9-24); 1911 (23-24); 1912 (12-14, 17-24). BR-2354 2 – 8 – ne IDC [073]

NASHE DI ELO (IRKUTSK, R.S.F.S.R.) – (Includes c.1: 1919:Aug.21, Oct.19) – Irkutsk: [s.n.], 19uu – 1 – CSUXADQ1570-S – us Hoover Inst Photo [947]

NASHE DI ELO (PARIS, FRANCE) = NOTRE CAUSE – (Includes c.1: no.1 1939:Nov.25-no.8 (1940:Jan.6); no.11 1940:Feb.3, no.13 (1940:Feb.17); no.17 1940:Mar.16) – Paris: [s.n.], 1939- – 1 – CSUXADQ1587-S – us Hoover Inst Photo [944]

NASHE KHOZI A ISTVO : IZDANIE SEMIPALATINSKOGO GUBPLANA, PRI BLIZHA ISHEM UCHASTII GUBSTATBI URO I TOVARNO I BIRZHI – (Includes c.1: no.3 1926:Mar) – Semipalatinsk: Gubizdat, 1925 – 1 – CSUXAKY6564-S – us Hoover Inst Photo [947]

NASHE KHOZI A ISTVO (SEMIPALATINSK, KAZAKH S.S.R.) *see* NASHE KHOZI A ISTVO

NASHE KHOZIAISTVO – Elets, 1911-17 n1 – 44mf – 9 – COR-655/1 – ne IDC [334]

NASHE KHOZIAISTVO – Sel'sko-khoziaistvennyi zhurnal. Spb. 1897-1902. Available: 1897. BR-2249 2 – 8 – ne IDC [073]

NASHE SLOVO – London. nos. 1-36. Mar 1952-Jan Mar 1955 – 1 – us NY Public [073]

NASHE SLOVO = OUR WORD – (Russian Weekly) – Vilnius, LT. no1 22. Jun 1906 – 1r – 1 – $25.00 – cn Can Microfilming [072]

NASHE SLOVO – Warsaw, Poland. Oct 1956-1963. 1977-Jul 1986 – 8r – 1 – us L of C Photodup [943]

NASHE VREMI A – (Includes c.1: 1948:May 2, June 20, July 13-31; 1948:Feb., Dec.25; 1950:May 21) – [Munchen]: Serge i Novgorodt sev, 1946 – 1 – CSUXACC3454-S – us Hoover Inst Photo [947]

NASHI DNI – Ezhenedel'nyi obshestvenno-politicheskii, literaturno-khudozhestvennyi i ekonomicheskii zhurnal. v. 1-4. Petrograd. 1915. BR-3988 2 – 8 – ne IDC [320]

NASHI FINANSY ZA VREMIA GRAZHDANSKOI VOINY I NEPA / Alskii, M – Moskva: Finansovoe izd-vo NKF SSSR, 1925 – 1 – CSUX88-B8751 – us Hoover Inst Photo [947]

NASHI GOSUDARSTVENNYE I OBSHCHESTVENNYE DEIATELI / Skal'kovskii, K A – Spb, 1890 – 9 – BR-10 620 1 – ne IDC [947]

NASHI NAPRAVLENIIA / Vorontsov, V P – Spb. 1893. BR-10,647 1 – 9 – ne IDC [460]

NASHI POLITICHECKIIA ZADACHI / Trotskii, L – Geneva, 1904 – 1 – 35.00r – us Hoover Inst Photo [335]

NASHIM OBVINITELI AM : S PRILOZHENIEM "OTKRYTAGO PISMA BYVSH. TOV. LEVENSONU" / Chernov, Viktor Mikhailovich & Gardenin, U – [S.l.]: Partii a sotsialistov-revoliut sionerov, 1905 – 1 – CSUX89-B7313 – us Hoover Inst Photo [320]

NASHRIYAH-'I ANJUMAN-I DANISHJUYAN-I MUSALMAN-.DAR URUPA VA AMRIKA – (Shumarah-'i 3-64 (3 Mihr 1360-5 Azar 1361[25 Sep 1981-26 Nov 1982])) – 1 – us MEDOC [950]

NASHRIYAH-'I ANJUMAN-I DANISHJUYAN-I MUSALMAN-I FARANSAH – (Continued by Nashriyah-'i Anjuman-i Danishjuyan-i Musalman dar Urupa va Amrika. Shumarah-'i 3-5 (28 Aug 1981-18 Sep 1981)) – [S.l.]: Anjuman-i Danishjuyan-i, Musalman-i Faransah – 2r – 1 – $250.00 – us MEDOC [950]

NASHRIYAH-'I ANJUMAN-I DANISHJUYAN-I MUSALMAN-I FARANSAH *see* NASHRIYAH-'I ANJUMAN-I DANISHJUYAN-I MUSALMAN-.DAR URUPA VA AMRIKA

NASHRIYAH-'I ITTIHADIYAH ANJUMAN'HA-YI DANISHJUYAN-I MUSALMAN-I KHARIJ-I KISHVAR – (Shumarah-'i 68-107 (2 Aban 1365-20 Shahrivar 1366[24 Oct 1986-11 Sep 1987]). Missing issues: Shumarah-'i 69-76, 94-99, 101-106) – London: Ittihadiyah-'i Anjuman'ha-yi Danishjuyan-i Musliman-i Kharij-i Kishvar – 1 reel – 1 – $50.00 – us MEDOC [950]

NASHRIYAH-'I VIZHAH-'I BAHS-I DURUN-I DU SAZMAN-I MUJAHIDIN-I KHALQ-I IRAN VA CHIRIK'HA-YI FADA'I-I KHALQ-I IRAN – (Shumarah-'i 1-zamimah-'i shumarah-'i 2 (Farvardin 1355-Urdibihisht 1356[Mar 1976-Apr/May 1977])) – [S.l.]: Sazman-i Chiarik'ha-yi Fada'i-i khalq-i Iran, 1976- – 1 reel – 1 – $25.00 – us MEDOC [950]

Nashua, New Hampshire. Crown Hill Baptist Church *see* RECORDS

Nashua, New Hampshire. First Baptist Church *see* COLLECTION ON THE EXCLUSION OF DR. CALVIN AND CAROLINE CUTTER

NASHVILLE – 1973- 1,5,6; 1975- 9 – us UMI [073]

NASHVILLE BANNER – Nashville, Tenn. 1949- – 1 – us UMI [071]

NASHVILLE FIRST BAPTIST CHURCH. NASHVILLE, GEORGIA : CHURCH RECORDS – 1909-20 – 1 – 10.40 – us Baptist [240]

NASHVILLE FIRST BAPTIST CHURCH. NASHVILLE, ILLINOIS : CHURCH RECORDS – Aug 1873-Sept 1989. Lacking: Nov 1900-Mar 1903; Jan-Nov 1909 – 1 – 190.62 – us Baptist [240]

NASHVILLE FIRST BAPTIST CHURCH. NASHVILLE, TENNESSEE : CHURCH RECORDS – 1820-1966, 1985-1989 – 1 – $549.10 – us Baptist [240]

NASHVILLE MAGAZINE – 1968-70 – 1 – us UMI [073]

NASHVILLE TENNESSEAN – Nashville, Tenn. 1957- – 1 – us UMI [071]

Nashville. Tennessee. Church Archives *see* INVENTORY OF THE CHURCH ARCHIVES OF TENNESSEE

Nashville. Tennessee. Grace Baptist Church *see* CONTENTS OF 1913 CORNERSTONE

NASIB, PUTOS HARA AN / Rih, Sjeh – SE 5259 1. 1959? – 9 – ne IDC [950]

NASIH *see*
– AN-NASIH

Nasilov, V M *see* UIGURSKORUSSKII SLOVAR'

NASIONAL – Jogjakarta. Indonesia. 1957-1965 – 1 – us UMI [072]

NASIONALISME ASIA / Ruslan, Abdulgani – SE 4585 1. 1964 – 9 – ne IDC [320]

NASIONALISME, ISLAMISME DAN MARXISME / Sukarno, Pres. Indonesia – SE 4064 1. 1963 – 9 – ne IDC [324]

Nasmyth, James *see* PAPERS

Naso, Eckart von *see*
– DER RITTMEISTER
– ROSSBACH UND ZORNDORF

Nason, Elias *see* LIVES AND LABORS OF EMINENT DIVINES

NASON, P. OVIDIO. LIBROS 4, 5 Y 6 / Suarez de Figueroa, Diego – Madrid: Herederos de Francisco del Hierro, 1738 – 1 – sp Bibl Santa Ana [946]

NASPA JOURNAL / National Association of Student Personnel Administration – v1-1963- 1; v10- 5,6; v15- 9 – us UMI [073]

NASSAGAWEYA WEEK – Moffat, Ontario, CN. 1983-84 – 1r – 1 – cn Commonwealth Micro [072]

Nassarre, P *see* FRAGMENTOS MUSICOS, REPARTIDOS EN QUATRO TRATADOS

NASSAU DAILY TRIBUNE – Bahamas. The Tribune. -d. Jan 1941-Dec 1952; 11 Sept 1957-Dec 1969; July 1971-Dec 1975. 120 reels – 1 – uk British Libr Newspaper [072]

NASSAU DAILY TRIBUNE – Nassau. Bahamas. 1911-1958 and contu. thru 1968 – 1 – us UMI [072]

NASSAU GUARDIAN – Bahamas. -d. Jan 1941-May 1972. 112 reels – 1 – uk British Libr Newspaper [072]

NASSAU LAWYER – v1-43. 1953-95 – 9 – $690.00 set – us Hein [340]

Nassau. Presbytery (Pres. Ch. in the U.S.A.) *see* MINUTES, 1855-1918

Nassau, Robert Hamill *see*
- AUTOBIOGRAPHY AND CORRESPONDENCE
- CROWNED IN PALM-LAND. A STORY OF AFRICAN MISSION LIFE
- DIARIES
- HISTORY OF THE WEST AFRICA MISSION
- MAWEDO, THE PALM-LAND MAIDEN
- SELECTED DOCUMENTS
- SELECTED PUBLICATIONS

NASSAU TIMES – Nassau. Bahamas. 1874-94 – 1 – us UMI [072]

NASSAUISCHE LANDESZEITUNG : BA DER FRANKFURTER NEUEN PRESSE – (Title change: Nassauische Neue Presse) – Limburg-Lahn, West Germany. 1977- – ca 7r per yr – 1 – gw Mikrofilm [072]

NASSAUISCHE NEUE PRESSE *see* NASSAUISCHE LANDESZEITUNG

Nassen, J *see* NEUE HEINE-FUNDE

Nassouhi, E *see* TEXTES DIVERS RELATIFS A L'HISTOIRE DE L'ASSYRIE

Nassourou, S *see* UNE CRISE PAYSANNE DANS LE NORD-CAMEROUN

NASSOVIA ZEITSCHRIFT FUER NASSAUISCHE GESCHICHTE UND HEIMATKUNDE – Weisbaden etc. Jahrg. 1-18, 26-34, Nr. 6; 1900-June 1934. Ceased with Jahrg. 34, Nr. 6. Hrsg. von Christian Spielmann. Film Mas C 382 – 1 – us H.U. Library [073]

Nast, Albert Andre *see* LA LOI ET L'AVORTEMENT

Nast, Thomas *see* CARTOONIST AND ILLUSTRATOR

Nasta, M *see* THESAURUS PSEUDO-DIONYSII AREOPAGITAE

NASTOIASHCHEE I BUDUSHCHEE RUSSKOGO OBSHCHESTVENNOGO KHOZIAISTVA / Isaev, A A – Spb., 1896 – 3mf – 9 – COR-36/1 – ne IDC [334]

O NASTOIASHCHEM I BUDUSHCHEM SUDA 21 PRISIAZHNYKH / Zakrevskh, I – Sbornik statei. Spb, 1897 – 9 – BR-9781 1 – ne IDC [947]

NASTOL'NYI ENTSIKLOPEDICHESKII SLOVAR' = ENCYCLOPEDIC DICTIONARY : SIXTH SUPPLEMENTARY EDITION / ed by Abramov, A V et al – Moscow: Tovarishchestvo br. A.i I Granat' i K Publishers. 9v. 1903 – 126mf – 9 – $800.00 – us Ross [030]

Nasution, A Diapari *see* SIMPLIFIED ENGLISH GRAMMAR FOR INDONESIAN STUDENTS

Nasution, Abdul Haris *see*
- ADDRESS BY H. E. THE MINISTER OF SECURITY AND DEFENCE, ON JAN. 5, 1960,AT THE PRESS CLUB
- MENGAMANKAN PANDJI-PANDJI REVOLUSI
- TENTARA NASIONAL INDONESIA
- TO SAFEGUARD THE BANNER OF THE REVOLUTION
- TOWARDS A PEOPLE'S ARMY

Nasution, Amir Taat *see*
- KAMUS POLITIK
- MANIPOL-USDEK DAN ISLAM
- PENDIDIKAN DI RUMAH TANGGA

Nasution, Basarudin *see* PENGANTAR ILMU POLITIK

Nasution, Jahja Udin *see*
- PUDJANGGA SANUSI PANE
- SITOR SITUMORANG SEBAGAI PENJAIR DAN PENGARANG TJERITA PENDEK

Nasution, M Yunan *see* ILMU BERGAUL

Nasution, Muchtar *see* ICHTISAR AKAR-AKAR MARXISME DAN FASCISME

NASW NEWS / National Association of Social Workers – v. 1-. 1955- – 1 – us UMI [360]

NASZ GLOS – London, UK. Published by the Polish Ex-Combatants Association in Great Britain. 1957-Nov 1958 – 1 – uk British Libr Newspaper [072]

NASZ KRAJ – Cesky Tesin, Czechoslovakia. Jan-May 1932 – 1r – 1 – us L of C Photodup [072]

NASZ PRZEGLAD = OUR REVIEW – (In Polish) – Warsaw, PL. v17 no190 9 Jul 1939-no232 20 Aug 1939 – 1r – 1 – $25.00 – cn Can Microfilming [072]

NASZ PRZEGLAD – Warsaw. July 1 1937-Aug 29 1939 – 1 – us NY Public [072]

NASZA TRIBUNA – New York. N.Y. Our tribune. 1940-51 – 1 – us A.J.P.C. [071]

NASZA TRYBUNA = OUR TRIBUNE – (In Yiddish and Polish) – New York City, NY. v2 no16(20) 20 Sep 1941-v2 no9(61) 22 Sep 1944 – 1r – 1 – $35.00 – cn Can Microfilming [071]

NASZE SLOWO = OUR WORD – (In Yiddish) – Warsaw, PL. no12 31 Dec 1946; no? 19 Apr 1947 – 1r – 1 – $25.00 – cn Can Microfilming [072]

NASZE SLOWO = OUR WORD : UNZER VORT – (In Yiddish) – v5 no7(16) 31 Aug 1947-v- no8(no27) – 1r – 1 – $25.00 – cn Can Microfilming [072]

Natal *see* GOVERNMENT GAZETTE

O NATAL – Manaos, Amazonas. Sem Data – 1,5,6 – bl Biblioteca [072]

NATAL ADVERTISER – Durban, South Africa. Jul 1918 – 1 – sa State Libr [072]

NATAL ADVERTISER AND MERCANTILE GAZETTE – Durban, South Africa. 1854-55 – 1 – sa State Libr [072]

NATAL AND THE BOERS : THE BIRTH OF A COLONY / Rowell, T – (Filmed with: Souvenir of the Union of South Africa) – London: J M Dent, 1900 – us Res Libr [960]

DE NATAL BODE – Pietermaritzburg, South Africa. 1862 – 1 – sa State Libr [072]

DE NATAL BOEREN FRIEND – Pietermaritzburg, South Africa. 1885-86 – 1 – sa State Libr [072]

NATAL BULLETIN – Durban, South Africa. 1899 – 1 – sa State Libr [072]

NATAL CHRONICLE – Pietermaritzburg, South Africa. 1855-56 – 1 – sa State Libr [072]

NATAL COLONIST AND HERALD – Durban, South Africa. 1871-80 – 1 – sa State Libr [072]

Natal Colony *see* GOVERNMENT PUBLICATIONS

Natal Colony. Native Affairs Commission *see* EVIDENCE

NATAL COMMERCIAL ADVERTISER AND AGRICULTURAL REPORTER – Durban, South Africa, March 1860-July 1860 – 1 reel – 1 – sa State Libr [630]

NATAL COURIER AND PIETERMARITZBURG ADVERTISER – Pietermaritzburg, South Africa. 1859-65 – 1 – sa State Libr [072]

NATAL DAILY NEWS – Durban, South Africa. 1879-1973 – 1 – sa Microfile [960]

NATAL ECHO – Durban, South Africa. 1893-94 – 1 – sa State Libr [072]

NATAL, GENERAL REPORT OF THE PROVINCIAL AUDITOR. PIETERMARITZBURG, 1910-50 – 4r – 9 – sa SA Libr [324]

NATAL GUARDIAN – Pietermaritzburg, South Africa. 1856 – 1 – sa State Libr [072]

NATAL HERALD – Durban, South Africa. 1866-67 – 1 – sa State Libr [072]

NATAL INDEPENDENT AND GENERAL ADVERTISER – Pietermaritzburg, South Africa. 1853-54 – 1 – sa State Libr [072]

Natal Indian Association *see* FINAL STATEMENT TO THE INDIAN PENETRATION COMMISSION APPOINTED BY THE UNION GOVERNMENT OF SOUTH AFRICA, 1940-1941

Natal Indian Congress *see* AGENDA BOOK OF THE...PROVINCIAL CONFERENCE

Natal. Indian Immigrants Commission *see* REPORT OF THE INDIAN IMMIGRANTS COMMISSION, 1885-87

Natal. Laws, Statutes, etc *see* THE LAWS OF NATAL

NATAL MERCANTILE ADVERTISER – Durban, South Africa. 1864 – 1 – sa State Libr [072]

NATAL MERCURY – Durban, South Africa. 1 Jan 1852- – 814r – 1 – sa Microfile [960]

NATAL MERCURY – Pietermaritzburg, South Africa. 1865 – 1 – sa State Libr [072]

NATAL PATRIOT – Pietermaritzburg, South Africa. 1846-48 – 1 – sa State Libr [072]

NATAL RECORD – Mariannhill, South Africa. 1888-89 – 1 – sa State Libr [072]

NATAL SEARCHLIGHT – Durban, South Africa. 1893-94 – 1 – sa State Libr [072]

NATAL (SOUTH AFRICA) DIOCESAN RECORDS / United Society for the Propagation of the Gospel. Archives – 19th Century – 1 – uk Microform Academic [025]

NATAL SPORTING TIMES – Pietermaritzburg, South Africa. 1885-86 – 1 – sa State Libr [072]

NATAL STANDARD AND FARMERS' COURANT – Pietermaritzburg, South Africa. 1852 – 1 – sa State Libr [072]

NATAL STAR – Durban, SA. 1855-63 – 1 – sa State Libr [072]

NATAL TIMES AND DURBAN MERCANTILE SHIPPING GAZETTE – Durban, SA. 1853 – 1 – sa State Libr [072]

NATAL WHO'S WHO – [Durban: s.n, 1906?] – us Res Libr [920]

NATAL WITNESS – Pietermaritzburg, SA. 1846- – 1 – sa State Libr [072]

NATAL WITNESS – Pietermaritzburg, South Africa. 1905-08.-d. 16 reels – 1 – uk British Libr Newspaper [072]

NATALIA : A CONDENSED HISTORY OF THE EXPLORATION AND COLONISATION OF NATAL AND ZULULAND FROM THE EARLIEST TIMES TO THE PRESENT DAY / Ingram, J Forsyth – London: H Marshall, [1897] – us Res Libr [960]

DE NATALIER AND PIETERMARITZBURG TRUE RECORDER – Pietermaritzburg, South Africa. 1844-46 – 1 – sa State Libr [072]

LA NATALITE A SAINT-PIERRE-DE-CLAIRAC (LOT-ET-GARONNE): ESSAI DE SOCIOLOGIE CONCRETE / Dumont, Arsene – Reprod. d'un extrait de la Revue internationale de Sociologie, 1901. 16p. 1 fiche.(Statistics Series: Medical Studies) – 9 – 6.00 – fr Bibl Nationale [310]

DE NATALSE AFRIKANER – Pietermaritzburg, South Africa. 1886-1931 – 1 – sa State Libr [072]

Natansson, Hans *see* RIMUR AF SIGURDI SNARFARA OG AETTMONNUM HANS: KVEDNAR ARIN 1879-81

Nataprawira, P *see* BASA SUNDA

NATAYIJ-I BAR'RASI-I BUDJAH-'I KHANVAR'HA-YI SHAHRI-I IRAN DAR SAL-I 2533 – Tehran: Bank-i Markazi-i Iran. Sal-i 2533 (1974/1975) – 1 reel – 1 – $25.00 – us MEDOC [950]

Natchez, Mississippi *see* MISCELLANEOUS EARLY NEWSPAPERS

Natesan, Ganapati Agraharam *see* CORRESPONDENCE WITH HY. S.L. POLAK, 1917-1929?, CHARLES ROBERTS, 1917-1919, AND WILLIAM WEDDERBURN, 1904?-1918

Nathan ben Jehiel, of Rome *see* SEFER HE-'ARUKH

NATHAN DER WEISE / Lessing, Gotthold Ephraim – (German text with introd & notes in English) – New York: The Macmillan Company, 1899 – 1 – us U.W. Library [820]

NATHAN LE SQUATTER, OU, LE PREMIER AMERICAIN AU TEXAS = NATHAN; DER SQUATTER-REGULATOR : ROMAN / Sealsfield, Charles – Geneve: Jules Sandoz, 1880 – 1r – 1 – us U.W. Library [830]

"THE NATHAN REPORT" : ECONOMIC DEVELOPMENT PLAN FOR MICRONESIA. A PROPOSED LONG-RANGE PLAN FOR DEVELOPING THE TTPI – Washington: Nathan Associates, dec 1966 – 10mf – 9 – $1.50 – LLMC 82-100F – us L.L.M.C. [324]

NATHANAEL – Berlin, 1885-1905 – 1 – Inquire at Mikrofilmarchiv for details – gw Misc Inst [072]

NATHANAEL : ZEITSCHRIFT FUER DIE ARBEIT DER EVANGELISCHEN KIRCHE AN ISRAEL – (Lacking: 13(1897)-23(1907). Beilage: DER MESSIASBOTE. 3(1908)-9(1914)) – 19mf – 9 – Dfl238.00 – ne Slangenburg [073]

NATHANAEL – Zeitschrift fuer die Arbeit der evangelischen Kirche an Israel. Berlin, Karlsruhe, Leipzig. v1-34. 1885-1918. Lacking: v18-20, 1902-1904. B483. (Leo Baeck Institute. German-Jewish Periodicals, Pt 1) – 3r – 1 – $205.00 – us UPA [270]

NATHANAEL GREENE PAPERS / Greene, Nathanael – 1775-85 – 1 – $45.00 – us L of C Photodup [920]

NATHANAEL: VORTRAEGE UEBER DAS CHRISTENTHUM, DEN GEBILDETEN IN DER GEMEINDE / Dalton, Hermann – St. Petersburg: H. Schmitzdorff, 1864. 1 fiche – 9 – us A.T.L.A. [240]

NATHANIEL MASSIE PAPERS, MS 3282 / Massie, Nathaniel – 1782-1852. Correspondence, legal briefs, court dockets, land warrants, fiscal material. 4 reels – 1 – us Western Res [920]

Nathhorst, T E *see* FLORA MONSPELIENSIS

NATICK 1718-1849 – (Mf 1T: Vital Records 1729-1845. Mf 2T: Vital Records 1736-77. Mf 3T: Vital Records 1767-99. Mf 4T: Vital Records 1768-1816. Mf 5T: Vital Records 1796-1832. Mf 6T-7T: Vital Records 1735-1857. Mf 7T-8T: Births 1843-49. Mf 8T: Marriages 1841-50; Out-of-Town Marriages 1718-99; Deaths 1843-49; Births & Deaths 1845-49. Mf 9T: Marriage Intentions 1844-49) – (mf ed 1997) – 9mf – 9 – 0-87623-300-0 – us Holbrook [920]

THE NATION : ENGLISH-LANGUAGE DIALY NEWSPAPER – (Jul 1985-Dec 1985 $150.00v; Jan 1986-Dec 1986 $300.00v; Jan 1987-Dec 1988 $350.00v; Jan 1989-Dec 1990 $500.00v; Jan 1991-Dec 1991 $600.00v) – Bangkok, Thailand. Formerly: The Nation Review and Voice of the Nation – 1 – us Asia Libr [072]

LA NATION / ed by Bouchard, Paul & Hamel, Marcel – Quebec, Canada. 15 fev 1936-1 aut 1939 – 1r – 1 – Can$50.00 – cn Can Microfilming [072]

LA NATION / La Federation Republicaine de France – Bulletin puis Organe Fond. Georges Ducrocq. Paris. juil 1925-mai 1940 – 1 – fr A.C.R.P.P. [073]

LA NATION – Manchester, MA. v1 n17. 29 avr 1908-v1 n24. 17 jun 1908 – 1r – 1 – Can$30.00 – cn Can Microfilming [071]

LA NATION – Montreal, Canada. 13 sep 1911 – 1r – 1 – Can$25.00 – cn Can Microfilming [072]

LA NATION / ed by Nantel, G-A & Nantel, Bruno – St-Jerome, Canada. 18 jul 1901-26 dec 1908 – 2r – 1 – Can$40.00r – cn Can Microfilming [072]

LA NATION – no. 1-3035. Paris. 5 mars 1962-28 29 juin 1974. mq. no. 1226-1227, 1713 – 1 – fr A.C.R.P.P. [073]

LA NATION – Plantagenet, Ontario. v1 n4. 10 Oct 1885-v1 n37. 2 jul 1886 – 1r – 1 – Can$35.00 – cn Can Microfilming [072]

LA NATION : RALLIEMENT NATIONAL – Quebec, v1 n2. jan 1965-v2 n10. fev 1967 – 1r – 1 – Can$40.00 – cn Can Microfilming [072]

LA NATION – St-Hyacinthe, Canada. v1 n2. 21 sep 1871-v1 n110. 22 jun 1872 – 1r – 1 – Can$35.00 – cn Can Microfilming [072]

NATION – (1966- 5,6. 1970- 9) – 1865- – 1 – us UMI [073]

NATION – Red Cloud. Neb. 1892-1908 – 1 – us UMI [071]

NATION – Toronto, Canada. 1874-76 – 1 reel – 1 – $68.00 – cn Library Assoc [971]

NATION – v. 1-150. 1865-1940 – 1 – us Princeton Micro [073]

THE NATION – 1988(Sept 2)-1989(Apr 3) – 4r – 1,5,6 – ne IDC [073]

THE NATION – Bridgetown, November 1973-1977 – 9r – $445.50 – us African Imprint [072]

THE NATION – Ireland.12 Aug-14 Nov 1922 – 1 – ie Microforms [072]

THE NATION – Ireland.16 Oct 1924-23 Apr 1925 – 1 – ie Microforms [072]

THE NATION – Ireland.1842-91, 1896/7. 43 reels – 1 – PS27.50r – ie European Micro [072]

THE NATION – Ireland.1927-31 – 1 – Ir£75.00 – ie Microforms [072]

THE NATION – London. -w. Jan 1907-Feb 1931. (48 reels) – 1 – uk British Libr Newspaper [073]

THE NATION – New York. N.Y. 1901-08 – 1 – us A.J.P.C. [071]

THE NATION – Port of Spain. Trinidad and Tobago. -w. 20 Dec 1958-24 Aug 1962. (2 reels) – 1 – uk British Libr Newspaper [072]

THE NATION – Rangoon. Burma. 1962-1964 – 1 – us UMI [072]

THE NATION – Rangoon, Burma. Aug 1948-Aug 1950; Jan-Dec 1960 – 8r – 1 – us L of C Photodup [072]

THE NATION – Rangoon, Burma. -d. 4 Aug 1950-16 Jan 1964. 37 reels – 1 – uk British Libr Newspaper [072]

THE NATION – Rangoon: U Law Yone, aug-oct 1960 – 1r – 1 – us Res Libr [072]

THE NATION – (Weekly Nation). Dublin. Ireland. -d and w. 15 Oct 1842-22 Jul 1848, 1 Sep 1849-11 Jul 1891, 13 Jun 1896-1 Sep 1900. (133 reels) – 1 – uk British Libr Newspaper [072]

THE NATION (1842-52) – 1 – ie Microforms [420]

LA NATION ALGERIENNE / Mouvement pour le Triomphe des Libertes Democratiques – Organe central. Dir. Hocine Lahouel. Alger. sept-oct 1954 – 1 – fr A.C.R.P.P. [073]
THE NATION AND ATHENAEUM – v. 1-48. 1907-31 – 1 – 344.00 – us L of C Photodup [320]
LA NATION ARABE / La Delegation Syro-Palestinienne. aupres de la Societe des Nations – Revue mensuelle, politique, litteraire, economique et sociale. juin 1930-38 – 1 – fr A.C.R.P.P. [073]
LA NATION ARMEE, ORGANIZATION MILITAIRE ET GRANDE TACTIQUE MODERNE / Goltz, Colmar von der – Paris: Hinrichsen, 1884. viii/472p. Strategy of War Series – 9 – fr Hachette [355]
LA NATION CANADIENNE: ETUDE HISTORIQUE SUR LES POPULATIONS FRAN CAISES DU NORD DE L'AMERIQUE / Gailly de Taurines, Charles – Paris: E. Plon, 1894. 03281. (Pre-1900 Canadiana) – 9 – cn C.I.H.M. [971]
Nation, Carry Amelia Moore *see* THE USE AND NEED OF THE LIFE OF CARRY A. NATION
LA NATION ET LE DROIT DES GENS / Henrion, C – Malzeville, Nancy, 1911 – 2mf – 1 – ILM-2487/1 – ne IDC [327]
LA NATION FRANCAISE – Paris. 1955-60 – 1 – fr A.C.R.P.P. [073]
NATION REVIEW : ENGLISH-LANGUAGE DAILY NEWSPAPER – (Oct 1976-Dec 1976 $50.00v; Jan 1977-Dec 1977 $200.00v; Jan 1978-Dec 1978 $250.00v; Jan 1979-Dec 1984 $300.00v; Jan 1985-Jun 1985 $150.00v Continued as The Nation) – Bangkok, Thailand. Formerly: Voice of the Nation – 1 – us Asia Libr [072]
THE NATION REVIEW – Bangkok, Thailand. 1978-79; Jul 1982-Sept 1993 – 193r – 1 – us L of C Photodup [072]
LA NATION ROUMAINE – Paris, France. -m. Aug 1948-Dec 1970. 2 reels – 1 – uk British Libr Newspaper [072]
LA NATION SOUVERAINE – Red. en chef Alexandre Rey. Paris. 15 avr-20 aout 1871 – 1 – fr A.C.R.P.P. [073]
NATION SPANNED, 1860-1906 – 1 – us Ross [977]
NATION SUNDERED, 1815-1865 – 1 – us Ross [977]
NATION UND STAAT / Seipel, I – Wien. Leipzig. 1916. BR-4946 2 – 8 – ne IDC [320]
NATIONAAL ONTWIKKELINGSPLAN SURINAME RAAMWERK VOOR HET TWEEDE VIJFJARENPLAN 1972-1976 / Surinam. (Netherlands). Stichting Planbureau Suriname – (Surinam National Development Plan: Framework for the Second Five-Year Plan 1972-1976). BD-1744 1 – 9 – ne IDC [338]
LE NATIONAL / ed by Desaulniers, G – Quebec, Canada. 14 dec 1889-7 mar 1896 – 2r – 1 – Can$45.00r – cn Can Microfilming [072]
LE NATIONAL : LITTERAIRE ET SPORTIF – Montreal, Canada. 28 aut 1914 – 1r – 1 – Can$25.00 – cn Can Microfilming [073]
LE NATIONAL – Lowell, MA. v8 n13. 29 jul 1890-v2 n168. 30 dec 1893 – 2r – 1 – Can$50.00r – cn Can Microfilming [071]
LE NATIONAL – Manchester, NH. 3 aut 1891-7 aut 1891 – 1r – 1 – Can$25.00 – cn Can Microfilming [071]
LE NATIONAL – Montreal, Canada. 24 avr 1872-22 fev 1879 – 7r – 1 – Can$40.00r – cn Can Microfilming [072]
LE NATIONAL – Montreal, Canada. v1 n1. 20 nov 1855-14 jun 1859 – 2r – 1 – Can$45.00r – cn Can Microfilming [072]
LE NATIONAL – no. 48. Paris. 27 nov 1927; no. 10, 14, 38, 45, 49, 52. 1928; no. 47-52. 1931; 1938-25 mai 1940. mq no. 8, 29, 31, 36, 38 – 1 – fr A.C.R.P.P. [073]
LE NATIONAL – Paris. Dir., I. Rousset. 1869-1 aout 1914, 17,19 juil 1923, 6 dec 1924 – 1 – fr A.C.R.P.P. [073]
LE NATIONAL – Plattsburg, NY. 7 jun 1883-v5 n40. 16 fev 1888 – 1r – 1 – Can$25.00 – cn Can Microfilming [071]
LE NATIONAL – St-Jerome, Canada. v1 n21. 26 aut 1886; v1 n37. 5 nov 1886 – 1r – 1 – Can$25.00 – cn Can Microfilming [072]
NATIONAL : A LIBRARY FOR THE PEOPLE – London, 1839 – 1r – 1 – us Ross [073]
NATIONAL : A LIBRARY FOR THE PEOPLE – v1-26 (all publ). 1839 – 5mf – 9 – $55.00 – us UPA [335]
NATIONAL – Lima, Ohio. 1860-1861 – 1r – 1 – $32.50r – us Archival [071]
National academy of science *see* PROCEEDINGS
National Academy of Sciences of the United States of America *see*
- PROCEEDINGS
- PROCEEDINGS: PHYSICAL SCIENCES

National Academy of Sciences. Washington *see* PROCEEDINGS
THE NATIONAL ACCOUNTS / Jordan. Department of Statistics – 11 v. 1959-72; 1952-1976. BNE-9774 1 – 9 – ne IDC [339]
NATIONAL ACCOUNTS OF THE LIBYAN ARAB REPUBLIC, 1962-1969 / Libya. National Accounts Section – Directorate General of Economic and Social Planning. 1971. BNE-630 1 – 9 – ne IDC [339]
NATIONAL ACCOUNTS STATISTICS / United Nations – (ST/ESA/STAT/Ser.X/11 is not yet available in microfiche) – 1982-1986 – E.163 – 9 (ST/ESA/STAT/Ser.X/1-10; 12) – us U.N. Pubs [650]
NATIONAL ADULT EDUCATION PROGRAMME : MONITORING, EVALUATION AND RESEARCH; EXTRACTS FROM THE REPORT OF THE WORKING GROUP ON ADULT EDUCATION FOR MEDIUM TERM PLAN 1978-1983 / India. Directorate of Adult Education – New Delhi, 1978 – 1mf – 9 – DE-545/1 – ne IDC [370]
NATIONAL ADVERTISER – Dublin, Ireland.May 1850-Jun 1855. -w. 2 reels – 1 – uk British Libr Newspaper [072]
NATIONAL ADVISORY COMMISSION ON CIVIL DISORDERS : "KERNER COMMISSION" REPORT – (App by President Lyndon B. Johnson) – Washington: GPO. 1v. 1 Mar 1968 (all publ) – 5mf – 9 – $7.50 – LLMC 95-032 – us L.L.M.C. [360]
National Advisory Committee on Aeronautics *see*
- ANNUAL REPORTS
- BIBLIOGRAPHY

NATIONAL ADVOCATE – New York, NY. 1812-20 – 1,3 – us Readex [071]
NATIONAL AEGIS – Worcester. Mass. 1801-1820 – 1,3 – us Readex [071]
NATIONAL AGRICULTURAL LIBRARY PRE-1870 AMERICAN SEED TRADE CATALOGS – (Includes index £57.00) – 577mf – 9 – £3,500.00 – uk Chadwyck [631]
NATIONAL AGRICULTURAL RESEARCH : REPORT OF AN EVALUATION STUDY IN SELECTED COUNTRIES. UNDP/FAO – 1984 – 109p – it F.A.O. [630]
National American Woman Suffrage Association *see* HANDBOOK AND PROCEEDINGS OF THE ANNUAL CONVENTION
THE NATIONAL AMERICAN WOMAN SUFFRAGE ASSOCIATION RECORDS – 73r – 1 – $2,555.00 – Dist. us Scholarly Res – us L of C Photodup [320]
NATIONAL AND ENGLISH REVIEW – v. 1-154. 1883-1960 – 1 – us UMI [073]
NATIONAL ANTI-SLAVERY STANDARD – 1-30 (all publ). 1840-1870 – 6r – 1 – $720.00 – us UPA [976]
NATIONAL ANTI-SLAVERY STANDARD – 1840-72 – 1 – 112.00 – us L of C Photodup [976]
NATIONAL ANTI-SLAVERY STANDARD – New York. v. 1-30. June 11 1840-Apr 16 1870; n.s. 3, v. 1-2. July 30 1870-Dec 23 1871. Incomplete – 1 – us NY Public [305]
National Arbitration Peace Congresses *see* PROCEEDINGS
THE NATIONAL ARCHAEOLOGICAL MUSEUM, NAPLES : PICTORIAL CATALOGUE / The Archaeological Museum. Naples – (Over 20,000 reproductions with descriptive notes. Roman and Graeco-Roman antiquities. Binders) – 398mf – 9 – $2,250.00 – 0-907006-59-0 – uk Mindata [930]
NATIONAL ARCHIVES / Great Britain. Public Record Office – 11th to 20th centuries – 1 – uk G.B.P.R.O. [941]
National Archives and Records Administration, Office of the Federal Register *see* FEDERAL REGISTER
National Archives of Canada *see*
- BIRD'S EYE VIEWS
- THE CANADIAN ROCKY MOUNTAINS IN TOPOGRAPHIC MAPS (1888-1892)
- CLOSE-UP ON THE LAND

National Archives of India *see* POLITICAL RECORDS FILMED SPRING 1969
NATIONAL ARCHIVES PROCEDURE: A GENERAL SERVICES ADMINISTRATION HANDBOOK (1960) / U.S. National Archives and Records Service – 1roll. M604 – 1 – us Nat'l Archives [025]
National Archives Trust Fund Board. Washington, D.C *see*
- DATA SHEETS TO MICROFILMED CAPTURED GERMAN RECORDS
- GUIDES TO GERMAN RECORDS FILMED AT ALEXANDRIA, VA

National Art Library *see* ART PERIODICALS COLLECTION AT VICTORIA AND ALBERT MUSEUM
National Art Library. Art Periodicals Collection at the V&A Museum *see*
- PART FIVE: CHRISTIAN ART 2
- PART FOUR: CHRISTIAN ART 1
- PART THREE: ART AND DECORATION

National Art Library. Art Periodicals Collection at V&A Museum *see* PART TWO: THE ARTIST, 1880-1902, L'ART AND COURRIER DE L'ART, 1875-1907 AND OTHER PERIODICALS
NATIONAL ART LIBRARY CATALOGUE, VICTORIA AND ALBERT MUSEUM. AUTHOR CATALOGUE / Victoria and Albert Museum. National Art Library. London – 1972. 326,000 cards on 19 reels – 1 – $1,165.00 export $1,410.00 – 0-8161-1265-7 – uk Hall [700]
National Assoc. of Claimants' Compensation Attorneys *see* NACCA NEWSLETTER
National Association for Promotion of Technical Education. Great Britain *see* ANNUAL REPORTS
National Association for the Advancement of Colored People *see*
- CRISIS!
- CRISIS

NATIONAL ASSOCIATION FOR THE PROMOTION OF SOCIAL SCIENCE TRANSACTIONS – 1862-84 annual meetings (all publ?) – 9 – LLMC 84-632 – us L.L.M.C. [073]
National Association for Women Deans, Administrators, and Counselors *see* JOURNAL
National Association for Women Deans and Counselors *see* JOURNAL
NATIONAL ASSOCIATION OF ATTORNEYS GENERAL PROCEEDINGS – (Lacking: 1st-6th. 10th-26th meetings) – 1st to 67th annual meetings – 99mf – 9 – $148.00 – LLMC 84-630 – us L.L.M.C. [073]
National Association of College Wind and Percussion Instructors *see*
- NACWPI BULLETIN
- NACWPI JOURNAL

National Association of Colored Graduate Nurses *see* A SELECTION OF ITEMS BY AND ABOUT THE NACGN
NATIONAL ASSOCIATION OF COLORED GRADUATE NURSES RECORDS, 1908-1951 : FROM THE HOLDINGS OF THE SCHOMBURG CENTER FOR RESEARCH IN BLACK CULTURE, MANUSCRIPTS, ARCHIVES AND RARE BOOKS DIVISION: THE NEW YORK PUBLIC LIBRARY, ASTOR, LENOX AND TILDEN FOUNDATIONS – (Guide which covers all coll under "African-American Organizations" sold separately for $20.00 D3305.G1) – 1995 – 2r – 1 – $170.00 – D330503 – Dist. us Scholarly Res – us L of C Photodup [610]
The National Association of Colored Women *see* NATIONAL NOTES
NATIONAL ASSOCIATION OF CONGREGATIONAL CHRISTIAN CHURCHES (U.S.) : HANDBOOK – 1962-1971-1972 (complete) – Inquire – 1 – ATLA S0914 – us A.T.L.A. [240]
NATIONAL ASSOCIATION OF CONGREGATIONAL CHRISTIAN CHURCHES (U.S.) : YEARBOOK – 1972-73 (complete) – Inquire – 1 – ATLA S0915 – us A.T.L.A. [240]
National Association of Die Casting Workers, CIO *see* CIO NEWS
National Association of Educational Broadcasters *see* NAEB JOURNAL
NATIONAL ASSOCIATION OF INDIAN AFFAIRS BULLETIN – 1924-37. (American Indian Periodicals in the Princeton University Library). 5 fiches – 9 – $45.00 – us UPA [305]
NATIONAL ASSOCIATION OF INSURANCE COMMISSIONERS PROCEEDINGS – (Lacking: Pre-1913, 1914-17, 1921-24, 1926, 1931-33, 1938-39, 1942, 1948) – 1913-69 – 225mf – 9 – $337.00 – LLMC 84-631 – us L.L.M.C. [073]
NATIONAL ASSOCIATION OF INTERNAL REVENUE EMPLOYEES BULLETINS – v1-25. 1941-66 (all publ) – 9 – LLMC 84-370 – us L.L.M.C. [073]
National Association of Jazz Educators *see* NAJE EDUCATOR
National Association of Negroes in American Industries *see* BROWN AMERICAN
National Association of Purchasing Management *see* PRINCIPLES AND STANDARDS OF PURCHASING PRACTICE
NATIONAL ASSOCIATION OF RAILWAY AND UTILITY COMMISSIONERS PROCEEDINGS – (Updates planned) – 1st to 21st annual meetings. 1889-1908 – 9 – LLMC 84-633 – us L.L.M.C. [073]
National Association of Social Workers *see* NASW NEWS
National Association of Student Personnel Administration *see* NASPA JOURNAL
National Association of Teachers of Singing *see* NATS BULLETIN
NATIONAL AUDOBON SOCIETY FIELD NOTES *see* AMERICAN BIRDS
NATIONAL AUTHORITIES EMPOWERED TO ISSUE CERTIFICATES AND AUTHORIZATIONS FOR THE IMPORT AND EXPORT OF NARCOTIC DRUGS AND PSYCHOTROPIC SUBSTANCES / United Nations. Commission on Narcotic Drugs – 1947-1982 – E/F.21 – 9 (E/NA) – us U.N. Pubs [350]
THE NATIONAL BANK ACT. / Homans, Isaac Smith – New York: Bankers', 1870. 100, 20, 63p. LL-416 – 1 – us L of C Photodup [340]
NATIONAL BANK CASES – (...decisions of both the Federal and State Courts relating to national banks. v1 by Israel G. Thompson, covers 1864-78 and is also known as Thompson's National Bank Cases. v2-3, by Irving Browne, cover 1878-89, and also known as Browne's National Bank Cases) – Albany, Parson. v1-3. 1864-89 (all publ) – 27mf – 9 – $40.50 – LLMC 84-708 – us L.L.M.C. [336]
NATIONAL BANK DECISIONS DIGEST / Office of the Comptroller of the Currency – Washington: GPO. v1-5. 1864-1936 (all publ) – 28mf – 9 – $42.00 – LLMC 84-394 – us L.L.M.C. [340]
NATIONAL BANKING REVIEW – v. 1-4. 1963-67 – 1 – us UMI [336]
NATIONAL BANKRUPTCY NEWS AND REPORTS – (Cont by: American Bankruptcy Reports) – Detroit: Collector Publ Co; Sprague Publ Co. v1-4. 1898-1901 (all publ) – 89mf – 9 – $133.00 – LLMC 89-200 – us L.L.M.C. [332]
NATIONAL BANKRUPTCY NEWS AND REPORTS *see* AMERICAN BANKRUPTCY REPORTS, ANNOTATED
NATIONAL BANKRUPTCY REGISTER – (v1-3 have the title "The Bankrupt Register") – NY: US Law Association. v1-4. 1867-1871 (all publ) – LLMC 82-406 – us L.L.M.C. [073]
NATIONAL BANKRUPTCY REGISTER REPORTS – New York: McDivitt & Campbell. v1-19 + digest for v1-10. 1868-82 (all publ) – 145mf – 9 – $217.00 – LLMC 82-407 – us L.L.M.C. [332]
NATIONAL BANKRUPTCY REGISTER REPORTS *see* THE BANKRUPT REGISTER
NATIONAL BAPTIST – Philadelphia. 1865-Mar 1873. (Complete) – 1 – 95.23 – us Baptist [240]
THE NATIONAL BAPTIST – Philadelphia. v1-30 no 19. 1865-10 May 1894 (complete) – 18r – 1 – ATLA R0104 – us A.T.L.A. [073]
National Baptist Convention *see* ANNUALS
National Baptist Convention of America, Unincorporated *see* ANNUALS
National Baptist Convention. U.S.A., Inc *see* ANNUALS
NATIONAL BAPTIST CONVENTIONS, VARIOUS : ANNUAL REPORTS OF GENERAL ASSOCIATIONS AND STATE CONVENTIONS. TENNESSEE – 1865-1929 – 1r – 1 – $127.92 – us Baptist [240]
NATIONAL BAPTIST MAGAZINE – Washington, DC: American National Baptist Convention. v1-8. 1894-1901 – $20.00r – us A.B.H.S. [073]
National Baptist Publication Board *see* MATERIALS
NATIONAL BAPTIST UNION-REVIEW – 1914-19, 1901-10, 1926-62 – 1 – 764.12 – us Baptist [240]
NATIONAL BAR ASSOCIATION MAGAZINE – v1-8. 1983-94 – 9 – $59.00 set – us Hein [340]
NATIONAL BASIC INTELLIGENCE FACTBOOK/ WORLD FACTBOOK / U.S. Central Intelligence Agency – 1979-85.28 fiches – 9 – 80.00 – us Updata [324]

National Biographical Publishing Co *see* BIOGRAPHICAL CYCLOPEDIA OF MARYLAND AND DISTRICT OF COLUMBIA

NATIONAL BLACK LAW JOURNAL – UCLA. v1-13. 1971-94 – 9 – $215.00 set – us Hein [305]

NATIONAL BROAD-ARC – Estherville. Iowa. 1882-1884 – 1 – us UMI [071]

NATIONAL BULLETIN ON LITURGY – (1985-. 5,6,9) – Nos.5-.1965- – 1 – us UMI [240]

NATIONAL BUSINESS EDUCATION QUARTERLY – 1932-70 – 1 – us UMI [380]

NATIONAL BUSINESS EDUCATION YEARBOOK – 1963- 1; 1971- 5,6; 1977- 4 x 6 in. 9 – us UMI [380]

NATIONAL BUSINESS REGISTER OF INDONESIA – Djakarta, 1954-1963 – 54mf – 9 – ne IDC [650]

National Cancer Institute *see*
– JOURNAL

National Canners Association *see* INFORMATION LETTER

NATIONAL CASE STUDIES ON THE DEVELOPMENT OF OUT-OF SCHOOL POPULATION EDUCATION PROGRAMMES / Thailand. Ministry of Education – 1977 – 2mf – 9 – DE-295/1 – ne IDC [370]

National Catholic Congress. 1st *see* OFFICIAL REPORT

National Catholic Education Association *see*
– BULLETIN
– CATHOLIC HIGH SCHOOL QUARTERLY

National Catholic Educational Association *see* BULLETIN

NATIONAL CATHOLIC REPORTER – v. 1-. 1964- – 1 – us UMI [240]

National Catholic Theatre Conference *see* PRODUCTION CALENDAR

NATIONAL CENTER FOR STATE COURTS : ARCHIVE PUBLICATIONS – (Includes Library Card Catalog) – Williamsburg: National Ctr for State Courts, 1971-1996 no 1 update – 9 – $5,565.00 set – 0-89941-537-7 – us Hein [340]

National Child Labor Committee *see* AMERICAN CHILD

NATIONAL CHILD LABOR COMMITTEE COLLECTION / U.S. Library of Congress. Prints and Photographs Division – (Lewis Hine's captions for the photographs. 2r. P&P15) – 5000 photographs by Lewis Hine. P&P7475-7483 – 3r – 1 – 23.00r – us L of C Photodup [331]

NATIONAL CHRISTIAN COUNCIL : BULLETIN – 1929-37 (complete) – 1r – 1 – ATLA S0725C – us A.T.L.A. [073]

NATIONAL CHRISTIAN COUNCIL : BULLETIN – nos 139-208. 1935-41; nos 1-155. 1950-63 (complete) – 1r – 1 – ATLA S0717C – us A.T.L.A. [073]

NATIONAL CHRISTIAN COUNCIL : REVIEW – (Some pgs missing) – 1971-87 – 7r – 1 – ATLA S0673 – us A.T.L.A. [073]

NATIONAL CHRISTIAN COUNCIL OF CHINA : BULLETIN – v1-61. Nov 1922-Mar 1937 (complete) – 1r – 1 – ATLA S0084 – us A.T.L.A. [073]

National Christian Council of China *see* CHI TU HUA CHING CHI KUAN HSI CH'UAN KUO TA HUI PAO KAO (CCC253)

National Christian Council of India, Burma and Ceylon *see* NATIONAL CHRISTIAN COUNCIL REVIEW

NATIONAL CHRISTIAN COUNCIL REVIEW / National Christian Council of India, Burma and Ceylon – Cont. of "The Harvest Field," organ of the N.C.C. of India, Burma and Ceylon. v. 46-70. 1926-50. Zug. 1977. BH-2008 1 – 9 – ne IDC [073]

NATIONAL CHRISTIAN NEWS – 1963- – 1 – us UMI [240]

A NATIONAL CHURCH / Huntington, William Reed – New York: Scribner, 1898, c1897. (The Bedell lectures for 1897) – 1mf – us A.T.L.A. [240]

THE NATIONAL CHURCH : ESSAYS ON ITS HISTORY AND CONSTITUTION AND CRITICISMS OF ITS PRESENT ADMINISTRATION / Henson, H Hensley – London, New York: Macmillan, 1908 – 2mf – us A.T.L.A. [240]

THE NATIONAL CHURCH OF SWEDEN / Wordsworth, John – London: A.R. Mowbray; Milwaukee: Young Churchman, 1911 – 2mf – us A.T.L.A. [240]

NATIONAL CITIZEN AND BALLOT BOX – v1-6. no. 6 (monthly: all publ). 1876-1881 – 1 reel – 1 – $65.00 – us UPA [360]

NATIONAL CIVIC REVIEW – v44- 1955- 1; v59- 5,6; v65- 9 – us UMI [323]

NATIONAL CIVIC REVIEW – (v1-73 1912-84 on reel $780.00. v74-95 1985-95 on mf $219.00. Title varies: v1-47 1912-58 as National Municipal Review) – v1-84. 1912-95 – 5,6,9 – $999.00 – us Hein [340]

NATIONAL CIVIC REVIEW *see* NATIONAL MUNICIPAL REVIEW

THE NATIONAL CIVIC REVIEW – 1v. 1888 (all publ) – 6mf – $9.00 – LLMC 82-948 – us L.L.M.C. [073]

NATIONAL COAL BOARD REPORTS AND ACCOUNTS 1945-1964/65 – (Coll title: British Government Publications...1801-1977, Minerals) – 3r – 1 (£1,890.00 minerals set of 36r) – uk Chadwyck [333]

NATIONAL COALITION FOR HAITIAN REFUGEES – New York. 58 docs. 1986-1991 – 6mf – 9 – ne IDC [320]

NATIONAL CODE OF THE REPUBLIC OF PALAU, 1985 / Palau. (The Republic of Belau) – (With 1986 supplementation) – Koror: Palau National Code Commission. 2v. 1985-86 – 23mf – 9 – $34-50 – LLMC 82-100G Title 2 – us L.L.M.C. [324]

National Collection of Fine Arts. Smithsonian Institution *see* AMERICAN ART IN THE BARBIZON MOOD

THE NATIONAL COLLECTION OF WATERCOLOURS / Victoria and Albert Museum. London – (Over 6,500 works by 1,600 artists, from 1580-1980. Index on fiche) – 1982 – 80 colour 2 bw mf – 15,9 – $2,890.00 – 0-907716-00-8 – uk Mindata [750]

National College of Education. Evanston, IL *see* PLAY MATERIALS FOR PRE-SCHOOL CHILDREN

NATIONAL COMMERCIAL NEWS – San Francisco, CA. 1983-84 – 2r – 1 – $100.00 – B03486 – us Library Micro [071]

NATIONAL COMMISSION ON LAW OBSERVANCE AND ENFORCEMENT : "WICKERSHAM COMMISSION" OFFICIAL RECORDS – Washington: GPO. v1-5. 1931 – 36mf – 9 – $54.00 – LLMC 90-355 – us L.L.M.C. [340]

NATIONAL COMMISSION ON LAW OBSERVANCE AND ENFORCEMENT : "WICKERSHAM COMMISSION" REPORTS / U.S. National Commission on Law Observance and Enforcement – Washington: GPO. v1-6. 1930-31 – 50mf – 9 – $75.00 – LLMC 81-231 – us L.L.M.C. [324]

NATIONAL COMMITTEE FOR MONETARY REFORM, SUBSCRIPTION APPEAL / Blanchard, Jim – 1mf – 9 – $1.00f – at Libertarian Micro [335]

NATIONAL COMMUNICATION POLICY COUNCILS : PRINCIPLES AND EXPERIENCES / Dias, Marco Antonio Rodriguez et al – 1979 – 44p – 9 – 92-3-101661-X – fr UNESCO [350]

NATIONAL COMMUNICATION SYSTEMS : SOME POLICY ISSUES AND OPTIONS / Sommerlad, Lloyd E – 1975 – 9 – 92-3-101248-7 – fr UNESCO [380]

NATIONAL CONFERENCE OF CHARITIES AND CORRECTIONS PROCEEDINGS – (Lacking: 1-15th, 21st, 24-29th sessions) – 1st to 41st annual sessions. 1873?-1914 – 9 – LLMC 84-266 – us L.L.M.C. [073]

NATIONAL CONFERENCE OF COMMISSIONERS ON UNIFORM STATE LAWS : ARCHIVE PUBLICATIONS – 1930-95 (complete) – 9 – $4,995.00 set ca $175.00y – 0-89941-418-4 – us Hein [340]

NATIONAL CONFERENCE OF COMMISSIONERS ON UNIFORM STATE LAWS : HANDBOOK... PROCEEDINGS – 1st-98th. 1891-1989 – 9 – $1,068.00 set – 0-89941-419-2 – us Hein [340]

National Conference of Commissioners on Uniform State Laws *see*
– AMERICAN UNIFORM MARRIAGE AND MARRIAGE LICENSE ACT
– UNIFORM PUBLIC UTILITIES ACT

National Conference of Social Welfare *see* CONFERENCE BULLETINS

National Conference of the Social Workers of Methodism *see* THE SOCIALIZED CHURCH

NATIONAL CONFERENCE ON LABOR (NEW YORK UNIVERSITY) : PROCEEDINGS – v1-42. 1948-89 – 1,5,6 – $450.00 – us Hein [331]

National Conference on Law and Poverty. Washington, DC. 1965 *see* CONFERENCE PROCEEDINGS

NATIONAL CONFERENCE ON SOCIAL WELFARE : OFFICIAL PROCEEDINGS / Social Welfare Forum – 1-96. 1874-1969 – 565mf – 9 – $1,965.00 – us UPA [360]

National Conference on Social Welfare *see* PROCEEDINGS AND BULLETIN

NATIONAL CONFERENCE ON SOVIET JEWRY – New York. 506 docs. 1980-1991 – 54mf – 9 – ne IDC [320]

The National Congress of American Indians *see* THE SENTINEL

NATIONAL CONGRESS OF MOTHERS MAGAZINE *see* PTA MAGAZINE

NATIONAL CONGRESS ON SURVEYING AND MAPPING *see* BULLETIN

NATIONAL CONSERVATION COMMISSION : "PINCHOT COMMISSION" REPORT – Washington: GPO. v1-3. 1909 – 22mf – 9 – $33.00 – LLMC 90-372 – us L.L.M.C. [340]

National Consumer's League *see* RECORDS

NATIONAL CORPORATION REPORTER – Chicago, Ill. 1968- – 1 – us UMI [071]

NATIONAL CORPORATION REPORTER – Chicago. On film: v1-19, 21-60, 62-155; Sept 1890-Feb 1900, Aug 1900-Jul 1920, Feb 1921-Nov 1967. Lacking: v1, no10; v2, no7; v20; v73, no9. LL-0129 – 1 – us L of C Photodup [340]

National Council for Children and Television (U.S.) *see* NCCT FORUM

NATIONAL COUNCIL FOR CIVIL LIBERTIES – London. 45 docs. 1984-1991 – 5mf – 9 – ne IDC [320]

National Council for Civil Liberties. London *see* A MODEL BILL TO PREVENT DISCRIMINATION ON GROUNDS OF SEX.

National Council for the Social Studies *see* YEARBOOK

NATIONAL COUNCIL OF CHURCHES IN THE PHILIPPINES – Quezon City. 48 docs. 1985-1991 – 43mf – 9 – ne IDC [240]

NATIONAL COUNCIL OF CHURCHES OF CHRIST IN THE U.S.A : NCCC CHRONICLES – v1-86. 1975-86 (complete) – 1r – 1 – ATLA S0442 – us A.T.L.A. [240]

NATIONAL COUNCIL OF CHURCHES OF CHRIST IN THE U.S.A : TRIENNIAL REPORTS – (Lacking: 1961-62) – 1952-84 – 2R – 1 – ATLA S0667 – us A.T.L.A. [240]

NATIONAL COUNCIL OF CHURCHES OF CHRIST IN THE U.S.A. COMMISSION ON HIGHER EDUCATION : NEWS NOTES – 1960-88 (complete) – Inquire – 1 – ATLA S0410 – us A.T.L.A. [240]

NATIONAL COUNCIL OF CHURCHES OF CHRIST IN U.S.A – memo from the Washington Office. v.6-25. 1960-79 – 1 – us A.T.L.A. [240]

NATIONAL COUNCIL OF CHURCHES REVIEW – 1987-92 (complete) – 1r – 1 – ATLA S0925 – us A.T.L.A. [073]

THE NATIONAL COUNCIL OF CONGREGATIONAL CHURCHES OF THE UNITED STATES / Hood, E Lyman – Boston: Pilgrim Press, [1901?] – 1mf – us A.T.L.A. [240]

National Council of La Raza *see* AGENDA

National Council of Teachers of Mathematics *see* YEARBOOK

National Council of the Churches of Christ in the United States of America *see* NCCC CHRONICLES

National Council of the Jewish Community. Palestine. (Va'ad Le'umi) *see*
– REGULATIONS APPROVED BY THE HIGH COMMISSIONER
– REPORTS, 1921-1934

NATIONAL COUNCIL OF THE Y.M.C.A : BULLETIN – (Cont: Home Work Bulletin) – v6-37. 1932-63 (incomplete) – 1r – 1 – ATLA S0719A – us A.T.L.A. [073]

National Council of the Y.M.C.A *see* HOME WORK BULLETIN

NATIONAL COUNCIL OF THE Y.M.C.A. BULLETIN *see* HOME WORK BULLETIN

National Council of Women of Canada *see* YEARBOOK

THE NATIONAL COUNCIL OF WOMEN OF CANADA : WHAT IT MEANS AND WHAT IT DOES / Aberdeen and Temair, Ishbel Gordon – s.l., s.n. 1900. (Pre-1900 Canadiana) – 9 – cn C.I.H.M. [971]

National Council of Women of the United States *see*
– ARCHIVES
– TRANSACTIONS

NATIONAL COUNTY AGENT AND EXTENSION REVIEW *see* FARM TECHNOLOGY AND AGRI-FIELDMAN

NATIONAL COUNTY AGENT AND VO-AG TEACHER *see* FARM TECHNOLOGY AND AGRI-FIELDMAN

National Credit Union Administration *see*
– NCUA BULLETIN
– NCUA QUARTERLY

NATIONAL CULTURE AND THE DEVELOPMENT OF THE INDIVIDUAL (CCC232) = NGO SHENG SHIH SHIH : A SERIES OF ADDRESSES DELIVERED TO STUDENTS IN SHANGHAI, MAY 1926 / Lu, Szu-wei – (In Chinese) – Shanghai: Association Press of China, 1926 – 1r – 1 – 1984-6571 – us A.T.L.A. [950]

NATIONAL DAILY – Jun 1915-30 Dec 1916. Related Guide Book may be purchased separately from publisher – 2 rolls 35mm set – 1 – us Ohio Hist [360]

NATIONAL DEBT : RETURN 1888-1967/68 – (Coll title: British Government Publications... 1801-1977, Finance) – 3r – 1 (£2,260.00 finance set of 93mf + 30r) – uk Chadwyck [339]

NATIONAL DEFENSE – (v60- ; 9. See also: Ordnance) – v58- 1973- – 1,5,6 – us UMI [355]

NATIONAL DEFENSE TRANSPORTATION JOURNAL – v1-17. Feb 1945-Dec 1961 – 1 – $176.00 – us L of C Photodup [380]

NATIONAL DEMOCRAT – Ireland.1907 – 1 – ie Microforms [072]

THE NATIONAL DEVELOPMENT OF CANADA / Bourinot, John George – London: Unwin Bros., 1880. 00203. (Pre-1900 Canadiana) – 9 – cn C.I.H.M. [971]

NATIONAL DEVELOPMENT PLAN / Botswana – D-877 1. 1968-1973 – 9 – ne IDC [338]

NATIONAL DEVELOPMENT PLAN / Botswana – D-959 1. 1970-1975 – 9 – ne IDC [338]

NATIONAL DEVELOPMENT PLAN, 1965 (1965-68) – D 1199 1. 1965 – 9 – ne IDC [338]

NATIONAL DEVELOPMENT PLAN, 1962-66 / Brunei – Kuala Belait. 1962. BD-338 1 – 9 – ne IDC [338]

NATIONAL DEVELOPMENT PLAN, 1962-68 / Nigeria. Ministry of Economic Development – Lagos. 1962 – 9 – ne IDC [338]

NATIONAL DEVELOPMENT PLAN, 1967-1970 / Liberia – BD-1116 1 – 9 – ne IDC [338]

NATIONAL DEVELOPMENT PLAN, 1970-1974 / Iraq. Planning Board and Ministry of Planning – Apr 1970. Baghdad. 1971. BD-2029 1 – 9 – ne IDC [338]

NATIONAL DEVELOPMENT PLAN. 1973-1978 / Botswana. Ministry of Finance and Development Planning – Pt. 1. Policies and objectives. Gaborone. 1973. BD-1815 1 – 9 – ne IDC [960]

NATIONAL DEVELOPMENT PLAN. 1973-1978 / Botswana. Ministry of Finance and Development Planning – Pt. 2. September, 1973. Gaborone. 1973. BD-1797 1 – 9 – ne IDC [960]

NATIONAL DEVELOPMENT PLAN FOR 1970-1974 : LAW NO. 70 OF 1970 / Iraq – D-1339 1. 1970 – 9 – ne IDC [340]

NATIONAL DEVELOPMENT PLAN PROGRESS REPORT, 1964 / Nigeria. Ministry of Economic Development – Lagos. 1965 – 9 – ne IDC [338]

NATIONAL DEVELOPMENT PLANS / Europe – (Social and Economic Development Plans on microfische from more than 200 countries. This collection is updated annually. Catalogues by region free on request.) – 281 titles. – 9 – ne IDC [338]

NATIONAL EAGLE – Portland, OR. 1962-66 – 1 – 24.00 – us Oregon Hist [071]

THE NATIONAL ECHO – Penang: Straits Echo Press, Sdn Bhd, nov 15 1976-1981 – 62r – 1 – us Res Libr [072]

NATIONAL ECONOMIC DEVELOPMENT PLAN 1961-1966 SECOND PHASE, 1964-1966 / Thailand. National Economic Development Board – Bangkok. 1964. BD-352 1 – 9 – ne IDC [338]

NATIONAL ECONOMIC DEVELOPMENT PLAN 1961-1966(REV.). D 1215/1 / Thailand. National Economic Development Board – 9 – ne IDC [338]

NATIONAL ECONOMIC DEVELOPMENT PLAN 1971-1975 / Israel. Economic Planning Authority – D-1532 1. 1971 – 9 – ne IDC [338]

THE NATIONAL ECONOMIC DEVELOPMENT PROGRAMME, B.E. 2504 2506 (1961-1966) / Thailand – Bangkok. 1961. BD-633 1 – 9 – ne IDC [338]

NATIONAL ECONOMIC PLAN, 1974-1978 / Israel. Ministry of Finance – Jerusalem. 1973. BD-1670 1 – 9 – ne IDC [336]

NATIONAL ECONOMIC PLAN 1974-1983 / Israel. Economic Planning Authority – Jerusalem. 1973. Text in Hebrew. BD-1672 1 – 9 – ne IDC [338]
NATIONAL ECONOMIC TRENDS / Federal Reserve Bank of St. Louis – (1986-. 1,5,6) – 1976- – 9 – us UMI [073]
NATIONAL ECONOMIST / National Farmers Alliance and Industrial Union – Washington, D.C. v. 1-8, no. 26. Mar 14 1889-Mar 11 1893 – 1 – us NY Public [330]
NATIONAL ECONOMIST – Washington. v1-8. 1889-93 – 3r – 1 – us Ross [330]
THE NATIONAL ECONOMY UNDER PRESIDENT JOHNSON: ADMINISTRATIVE HISTORIES / Johnson, Lyndon B – 1983. (Presidential Documents Series) – 1 – $860.00 – 0-89093-488-6 – us UPA [330]
NATIONAL EDITION – (Back Files are available for $85.00r Vesicular $99.00r Negative or Positive Silver) – 1 – $990.00 Vesicular $1,175.00 Negative or Positive Silver – cn Globe Info [971]
NATIONAL EDUCATION ASSOCIATION *see* TODAY'S EDUCATION
NATIONAL EDUCATION POLICY (SALIENT FEATURES) / Pakistan. Ministry of Education – Islamabad, 1978 – 1mf – 9 – DE-573/1 – ne IDC [370]
NATIONAL EDUCATION SCHEME 1977 / Thailand. Ministry of Education – Bangkok, 1977 – 1mf – 9 – DE-279/1 – ne IDC [370]
NATIONAL EDUCATIONAL SECRETARY – v1-1936- 1; v40- 5,6; v42- 9 – us UMI [073]
National Eight-Hour Delegation *see* THE EIGHT-HOUR LAW.
NATIONAL ELEMENTARY PRINCIPAL – v1-1921- 1; v48- 5,6; v55- 1975- 9 – us UMI [370]
THE NATIONAL ENDOWMENT FOR THE ARTS DANCE PROGRAM, 1965-1971 : A SOCIAL AND CULTURAL HISTORY / Graham, Angela H – Temple University, 1996 – 5mf – 9 – $20.00 – PE 3647 – us Microform Publ [790]
NATIONAL ENQUIRER – 1926 1; 1977- 5,6,9 – us UMI [073]
NATIONAL ERA – 1-14 (all publ). 1847-1860 – 4r – 1 – $440.00 – us UPA [305]
NATIONAL ERA – Washington. v1-13. 1847-59 – 5r – 1 – us Ross [073]
NATIONAL EXAMINATIONS : DESIGN, PROCEDURES AND REPORTING / Keeves, John P – 1994 – 112p – 9 – 92-803-1154-9 – fr UNESCO [370]
National Extension Homemakers Council *see* HOMEMAKER
NATIONAL FARM HOLIDAY NEWS – Minneapolis. v. 1-2, no. 9. Aug 28 1936-Dec 31 1937 – 1 – us NY Public [630]
National Farmers Alliance and Industrial Union *see* NATIONAL ECONOMIST
National Federation of Women Workers *see* THE WOMAN WORKER
NATIONAL FISHERMAN – 1968-70 – 4r – 1 – us Ross [790]
NATIONAL FISHERMAN *see* PACIFIC FISHERMAN
NATIONAL FOOD REVIEW – v1- 1978- – 1,5,6,9 – us UMI [640]
NATIONAL FORUM – (See also: Phi Kappa Phi Journal) – v58- 1978- – 1,5,6,9 – us UMI [370]
NATIONAL FORUM, THE PHI KAPPA PHI JOURNAL – 1985- – 1 – us UMI [073]
National Free Will Baptist Bodies of the United States *see* MINUTES
NATIONAL FREEDMAN / National Freedmen's Relief Association – v1-2, no. 9 (all publ). 1865-66 – 1 reel – 1 – $55.00 – us UPA [976]
National Freedmen's Relief Association *see*
- FREEDMAN'S ADVOCATE
- NATIONAL FREEDMAN

National Gallery of Canada *see* EXHIBITION CATALOGUES
THE NATIONAL GAZETTE – Philadelphia, PA. 1791-93. Also: The Level of Europe, 1794-96, and Philadelphia Minerva, 1795-98.Sold as one unit – 1,3 – us Readex [071]
THE NATIONAL GAZETTE AND LITERARY REGISTER – Philadelphia, PA. -d 1820-1842. 13 rolls – 13 – $25.00r – us I.M.R. [071]
THE NATIONAL GAZETTE AND LITERARY REGISTER – Philadelphia: William Fry, 1820-41. may 1837-may 1838 (1r) – 1 – us Res Libr [410]
NATIONAL GAZETTE AND LITERARY REGISTER (DAILY) – Philadelphia, PA., 1820-1841 – 13 – $25.00r – us I.M.R. [071]
National Genealogical Society *see* QUARTERLY
NATIONAL GEOGRAPHIC – Black and white edition. v. 153-. 1978- – 1,5,6,9 – us UMI [910]
NATIONAL GEOGRAPHIC – v.1- 1888- – 1 – us UMI [910]
NATIONAL GEOGRAPHIC MAGAZINE – v. 1-10. 1888-1899 – 1 – us Princeton Micro [073]
NATIONAL GEOGRAPHIC RESEARCH – v1-. 1985- – 1,5,6,9 – us UMI [910]
NATIONAL GEOGRAPHIC TRAVELLER – v1-. 1984- – 1,5,6,9 – us UMI [910]
NATIONAL GEOGRAPHIC WORLD – 1975- – 1,5,6,9 – us UMI [910]
NATIONAL GOVERNOR'S CONFERENCE PROCEEDINGS – (Lacking: 1909-1923. 1943) – 1908-1976 – 162mf – $243.00 – LLMC 84-475 – us L.L.M.C. [073]
NATIONAL GRAIN POLICIES, 1975 – 1976 – 271p – it F.A.O. [340]
NATIONAL GREENBACK – (Greenback party newspaper) – Salem, OH. Jan 13 1880 – 1r – 1 – us Western Res [071]
NATIONAL HERALD – Lucknow, India. 1962-Mar 1986; May 1987-Jul 1994 – 122r – 1 – us L of C Photodup [072]
National Historical Co *see*
- HISTORY OF AUDRAIN COUNTY
- HISTORY OF CALDWELL AND LIVINGSTON COUNTIES
- HISTORY OF CALLAWAY COUNTY
- HISTORY OF CASS AND BATES COUNTIES
- HISTORY OF CLAY AND PLATTE COUNTIES
- HISTORY OF CLINTON COUNTY
- HISTORY OF GENTRY AND WORTH COUNTIES
- HISTORY OF HENRY AND ST CLAIR COUNTIES
- HISTORY OF HOLT AND ATCHISON COUNTIES
- HISTORY OF HOWARD AND COOPER COUNTIES
- HISTORY OF MONROE COUNTY AND SHELBY COUNTY
- HISTORY OF RANDOLPH AND MACON COUNTIES

NATIONAL HOG FARMER – (1986-. 1,5,6) – 1982- – 9 – us UMI [636]
NATIONAL HOME MONTHLY – Winnipeg, 1904-50 – 29r – 1 – $1,885.00 – cn Library Assoc [640]
NATIONAL HOME READING JOURNAL ARTIZANS SECTION – London, UK. 1889-90. -irr. 4 feet – 1 – uk British Libr Newspaper [073]
NATIONAL HORTICULTURAL MAGAZINE *see* AMERICAN HORTICULTURAL MAGAZINE
National Housing and Town Planning Council. London, England *see*
- BRITISH HOUSING AND PLANNING REVIEW
- HOUSING AND PLANNING NEWS BULLETIN
- MINUTES AND REPORTS OF THE NATIONAL HOUSING AND TOWN PLANNING COUNCIL

THE NATIONAL HOUSING MANUAL / Aldridge, Henry R – London, 1923 – 1 – £35.00r – uk Altair [340]
NATIONAL HUMANE REVIEW – (v. 59-61. 1971-76. 5,6. v. 64. 1976. 9) – v. 1-64. 1913-76. Supreseded by yAmerican Humane Magazine – 1 – us UMI [360]
NATIONAL HUMANE REVIEW *see* AMERICAN HUMANE MAGAZINE
NATIONAL IMMIGRATION PROJECT OF THE NATIONAL LAWYERS GUILD – Boston. 76 docs. 1980-1991 – 26mf – 9 – ne IDC [320]
NATIONAL INCOME AND EXPENDITURE 1938/45-1967/77 – (Coll title: British Government Publications...1801-1977, Finance) – 48mf – 9 (£2,260.00 finance set of 93mf + 30r) – uk Chadwyck [339]
NATIONAL INCOME ESTIMATES / Libya. Central Statistics Office. Ministry of National Economy – 1958. BNE-717 1 – 9 – ne IDC [310]
NATIONAL INCOME ESTIMATES OF SYRIA / Syria. Dept. of Statistics – 1952-58. BNE-9694 1 – 9 – ne IDC [310]
NATIONAL INCOME OF EGYPT FOR 1953; OFFICIAL ESTIMATE, DEC 1954 / Egypt – 1955. BNE-4664 1 – 9 – ne IDC [339]
THE NATIONAL INCOME OF INDONESIA, 1951-1952: A CRITICAL COMMENTARY OF THE NEUMARK ESTIMATES / Hollinger, William C – SE-2196 1 – 9 – ne IDC [339]
NATIONAL INCOME OF SUDAN / Sudan. Dept. of Statistics – 3v. in 1. 1955 56-1959 60-1962. BNE-7618 1 – 9 – ne IDC [310]
THE NATIONAL INCOME OF THE NETHERLANDS INDIES, 1921-1939. SE-11,679/1 / Polak, Jacques Jacobus – 9 – ne IDC [339]
National Indian Association *see* REPORT OF MISSIONS
NATIONAL INSTITUTE ECONOMIC REVIEW – 1959-to date – 9 – uk Microform Academic [330]
NATIONAL INSTITUTE ECONOMIC REVIEW – (1983-. 1,5,6,9) – 1959- – 1 – us UMI [330]
National Institute. London *see* ECONOMIC REVIEW
National Institute of Animal Health. Tokyo *see* QUARTERLY
National Institute of Compilation and Translation of North China *see* KUO-LI HUA-PEI PIEN-I-KUAN KUAN-K'AN
National Institute of Culture *see* CULTURAL POLICY IN THE REPUBLIC OF PANAMA
National Institute of Oceanography *see* DISCOVERY REPORTS
NATIONAL INTELLIGENCER – Washington, DC. 1800-01, 1812 – 2r – 1 – us Ross [071]
NATIONAL INTELLIGENCER – Washington. D.C. 1800-1812. yDaily National Intelligencer. 1813-1820 – 3 – us Readex [071]
NATIONAL INTELLIGENCER – Washington, DC. 1820-56 – 5r – 1 – us Ross [071]
NATIONAL INTELLIGENCER – Washington, DC. 31 Oct 1800-8 Jan 1870 – 117r – 1 – us L of C Photodup [071]
NATIONAL INTELLIGENCER – Washington, DC. -w. Jan-Dec 1820. 1 reel – 1 – uk British Libr Newspaper [071]
NATIONAL INVENTORY OF DOCUMENTARY SOURCES IN THE UNITED KINGDOM AND IRELAND – (Finding aids to thousands of archive & manuscript colls in more than 120 libraries & record offices, museums & private colls throughout the UK & Ireland) – 8 units per yr + accompanied by COM index – more than 14,000 unpubl finding aids – 9 – enquire for price plans – uk Chadwyck [010]
NATIONAL INVENTORY OF DOCUMENTARY SOURCES IN THE UNITED STATES – (Pt 1: Federal Records: The National Archives, the Smithsonian Institution Archives, the Presidential Libraries 2054mf £7,045. Pt 2: Manuscript Division, Library of Congress 924mf £3,530 Pts 1 and 2 each include 1988 suppl + index. Pt 3: State Archives, State Libraries, State Historical Societies, Academic Libraries and other Repositories – publ in 10 units per yr + accompanied by cumulative COM indexes) – 3pts – 9 (enquire for price plans) – uk Chadwyck [010]
NATIONAL ISSUES : A SURVEY OF POLITICS AND LEGISLATION / Communist Party. U.S.A. National Committee – 1-9 (all publ). 1939 – 3mf – 9 – $35.00 – us UPA [335]
THE NATIONAL JEWISH DAILY – Van Nuys, CA. 21 Nov 1986-3 Apr 1987. Continued by: Israel Today – 1 – us A.J.P.C. [071]
NATIONAL JEWISH MONTHLY – v1- 1886- 1; v91- 5,6,9 – us UMI [073]
THE NATIONAL JEWISH NEWS – (Missing Dec. 1989) – Los Angeles, California. July 1988-Dec. 1989 – us A.J.P.C. [270]
National Joint Committee for Spanish Relief *see* REPORT
NATIONAL JOURNAL – (1982-. 5,6) – 1969 – 1,9 – us UMI [073]
NATIONAL JOURNAL OF CRIMINAL DEFENSE – University of Houston. v1-7. 1975-81 (all publ) – 9 – $70.00 set – us Hein [340]
THE NATIONAL JOURNAL OF LEGAL EDUCATION – (This curious publication was issued by the American Association of Law Schools. None of the three issues are dated or given volume or issue numbers, but from internal evidence it appears that the three issues came out between 1937 & 1939) – Issues 1-3 (all publ) – 2mf – $3.00 – LLMC 95-113 – us L.L.M.C. [073]
National Junior College Athletic Association *see*
- JUCO REVIEW
- NJCAA MINUTES OF MEETINGS

National Junior College Athletic Association. Executive Committee *see* OFFICIAL HANDBOOK AND CASEBOOK..
NATIONAL KINDERGARTEN MANUAL / Pollock, Louise – Containing practical model lessons. Boston: De Wolfe, Fiske and Co., 1889. iv,177p – 1 – us U.W. Library [370]
NATIONAL LABOR BOARD DECISIONS / U.S. National Labor Relations Board – Washington: GPO. 2v. Aug 1933-Jul 1934 (all publ) – 4mf – 9 – $6.00 – LLMC 81-234 – us L.L.M.C. [324]
NATIONAL LABOR RELATIONS ACT (NLRA) : WAGNER ACT – 2v in 4bks. 1935 – 9 – $95.00 set – 0-89941-194-0 – us Hein [331]
NATIONAL LABOR RELATIONS ACT (WAGNER ACT), 1935 : LEGISLATIVE HISTORY / U. S. National Labor Relations Board – Washington: GPO. 2bks. 1949 – 37mf – 9 – $55.00 – LLMC 80-037 – us L.L.M.C. [323]
NATIONAL LABOR RELATIONS BOARD : DECISIONS AND ORDERS / U.S. National Labor Relations Board – Washington: US GPO, v1-317. 1935-95 – 9 – $6,941.00 set – us Hein [331]
NATIONAL LABOR RELATIONS BOARD DECISIONS / U.S. National Labor Relations Board – (Add vols planned) – v1-313. 1935-94 – 9 – $7,706.00 – LLMC 78-208 – us L.L.M.C. [340]
NATIONAL LABOR RELATIONS BOARD DECISIONS *see*
- ANNUAL REPORTS OF THE NATIONAL LABOR RELATIONS BOARD
- CLASSIFICATION OUTLINE WITH TOPICAL INDEX FOR DECISIONS OF THE N.L.R.B. AND RELATED COURT DECISIONS
- CLASSIFIED INDEX, REGIONAL DIRECTORS' DECISIONS IN REPRESENTATION PROCEEDINGS
- INDEX OF DECISIONS OF THE NLRB – CLASSIFIED INDEX OF THE NLRB DECISIONS AND RELATED COURT CASES

NATIONAL LABOR TRIBUNE / Amalgamated Association of Iron, Steel, and Tin Workers of America – Pitts. 1873-1909 – 1 – us UMI [331]
NATIONAL LABOR TRIBUNE / Amalgamated Association of Iron, Steel, and Tin Workers of America – Pittsburgh. v3 n17-v84 n8. 1875-1958 – 28r – 1 – us Ross [331]
NATIONAL LABOR TRIBUNE – Pittsburgh. 1875-Nov 1958. Incomplete – 1 – us NY Public [331]
NATIONAL LAMPOON – (1985- . 5,6,9) – 1970- – 1 – us UMI [073]
NATIONAL LAMPOON – London, UK. 1972-1974 – 3r – $150.00 – R63562 – us Library Micro [073]
NATIONAL LAMPOON – v1. 1970-71 – 28mf – 9 – $5.00f – us Ross [073]
NATIONAL LAND COMMITTE – Johannesburg. 18 docs. 1985-1991 – 5mf – 9 – ne IDC [320]
NATIONAL LANGUAGE WORKBOOK FOR GRADE 6 / Soriano, Josefina P – Rev. ed. Manila, 1971, c1951. 108p – 1 – us U.W. Library [370]
NATIONAL LANGUAGES AND TEACHER TRAINING IN AFRICA : A METHODOLOGICAL GUIDE FOR THE USE OF TEACHER TRAINING INSTITUTES / Poth, Joseph – 9 – fr UNESCO [370]
NATIONAL LAUNDRY RECORD, ETC – London, England. Laundry Record. -w. March 1891-1914. 21 reels – 1 – uk British Libr Newspaper [072]
NATIONAL LAW JOURNAL – Aug 1978- . -w – 1,9 – us New York Law [073]
THE NATIONAL LAW REVIEW – 1v. 1888 – 6mf – 9 – $9.00 – LLMC 82-948 – us L.L.M.C. [073]
NATIONAL LAWYERS GUILD QUARTERLY *see* GUILD PRACTITIONER
National League and American Association of Professional Baseball Clubs *see*
- CONSTITUTION AND PLAYING RULES

National League for Nursing *see*
- NLN NEWS
- NURSING AND HEALTH CARE

THE NATIONAL LEAGUE JOURNAL : WORKING MEN'S NATIONAL LEAGUE FOR THE REPEAL OF THE CONTAGIOUS DISEASES ACTS – (Missing: 1876(6-10); 1877(18, 27-28)) – Liverpool, 1875-1884 – 27mf – 9 – ne IDC [331]
National Liberal Federation. (Great Britain) *see* ANNUAL REPORTS
NATIONAL LIBRARY CATALOGUE ON MICROFICHE, 1994 / National Library of New Zealand – (3 issues/y. Register + indexes NZ$252.00. Indexes only NZ$198.00) – nz Nat'l Libr [010]
National Library of Anthropology and History. Mexico City *see*
- CATALOG

- CATALOGO DE LA BIBLIOTECA NACIONAL DE ANTROPOLOGIA E HISTORIA

National Library of Australia *see*
- FILM AND VIDEO LENDING COLLECTION 1/2 INCH VHS CATALOGUE
- FILM AND VIDEO LENDING COLLECTION CATALOGUE
- GUIDE TO COLLECTIONS OF MANUSCRIPTS RELATING TO AUSTRALIA
- NUCOM 4
- NUCOM 5

National Library of Canada *see*
- CANADIAN THESES
- CANADIAN UNION CATALOGUE OF LIBRARY MATERIALS FOR THE PRINT-HANDICAPPED (CANUC:H)
- CANADIANA
- CANADIANA 1867-1900: MONOGRAPHS/ MONOGRAPHIES
- CANADIANA 1973-1980
- CANADIANA AUTHORITIES/CANADIANA VEDETTES D'AUTORITE
- CANADIANA MULTI-YEAR CUMULATIONS
- CONSER MICROFICHE
- PEEL BIBLIOGRAPHY
- UNION LIST OF CANADIAN NEWSPAPERS
- UNION LIST OF SERIALS IN THE SOCIAL SCIENCES AND HUMANITIES (CANUC:S)

National Library of New Zealand *see* NATIONAL LIBRARY CATALOGUE ON MICROFICHE, 1994

NATIONAL LIBRARY OF PEIPING RARE BOOKS – (Three finding aids for this collection are available: 1: The Catalog of microfilm reproductions lists all the titles in this collection $30.00 1r. 2: The Notices contains annotations on all of the titles $90.00 3r. 3: The Shelflist lists the titles according to their call numbers $30.00 1r. The set is in Chinese) – 1074r – 1 – $37,590.00 in US $40.00 outside – L9300066 – Dist. us Scholarly Res – us L of C Photodup [090]

National Lubricating Grease Institute *see* NLGI SPOKESMAN

NATIONAL MAGAZINE – A political, historical, bibliographical and literary repository. v. 1-2. 1 Jun 1799-1800 – 1 – us UMI [073]

NATIONAL MAGAZINE – Devoted to Literature, Art and Religion. v. 1-13. Jul 1852-Dec 1858 – 1 – us UMI [073]

NATIONAL MAGAZINE – v. 1-15. Nov 1856-May 1864 – 1 – us UMI [073]

NATIONAL MAGAZINE – v. 1-61. 1894-1933 – 1 – us UMI [073]

NATIONAL MAGAZINE AND GENERAL REVIEW – v. 1. 1826-May 1827 – 1 – us UMI [073]

NATIONAL MAGAZINE OR CABINET OF THE UNITED STATES – v. 1-8. 22 Oct 1801-02 – 1 – us UMI [073]

National Maritime Museum. London *see* DOCUMENTS RELATING TO THE AMERICAN REVOLUTION

NATIONAL MEDIATION BOARD ANNUAL REPORTS / U.S. National Mediation Board – 1st-48th. 1935-82 – 74mf – 9 – $111.00 – LLMC 80-626 – us L.L.M.C. [324]

NATIONAL MESSENGER – Georgetown. D.C. 1817-1820 – 1,3 – us Readex [071]

NATIONAL METHODS OF AGRICULTURAL PRICE DATA COLLECTION – 1986 – 150p – it F.A.O. [300]

NATIONAL MILITARY ACADEMY / Indonesia – SE-2065 1. 1958 – 9 – ne IDC [355]

National Model Railroad Association *see* BULLETIN

NATIONAL MONETARY COMMISSION PUBLICATIONS : LEGAL STUDIES ON MONETARY LEGISLATION IN THE U.S. AND ABROAD / U.S. National Monetary Commission – (Studies issued by the Commission, which was created on 30 May 1908) – Washington: GPO. v1-20. 1911-12 (all publ) – 9 – LLMC 84-121 – us L.L.M.C. [336]

NATIONAL MUNICIPAL LEAGUE PROCEEDINGS – (Also covers meetings of the National Conferences for Good City Government) – 1894- – LLMC 84-634 – us L.L.M.C. [073]

NATIONAL MUNICIPAL REVIEW – (Post 1956 vols not supplied for copyright reasons. Title changes to: National Civic Review from v48 onwards) – v1-45. 1912-56 – 371mf – 9 – $556.00 – LLMC 81-410 – us L.L.M.C. [073]

NATIONAL MUNICIPAL REVIEW *see*
- NATIONAL CIVIC REVIEW

NATIONAL MUSEUM AND WEEKLY GAZETTE – v. 1. 13 Nov 1813-12 Mar 1814 – 1 – us UMI [073]

NATIONAL MUSEUM OF CIVILIZATION : MERCURY SERIES ANTHROPOLOGY PAPERS – 1961-1974 – 9 – cn Micromedia [900]

National Museum of Ethnology, Leiden *see* VON SIEBOLD COLLECTION

National Museum of Man *see*
- MERCURY SERIES: ARCHAEOLOGICAL SURVEY
- MERCURY SERIES: CANADIAN CENTRE FOR FOLK CULTURE STUDIES
- MERCURY SERIES: CANADIAN WAR MUSEUM PAPERS
- MERCURY SERIES: COMMUNICATIONS DIVISION
- MERCURY SERIES: ETHNOLOGY DIVISION
- MERCURY SERIES: HISTORY DIVISION

NATIONAL MUSEUM OF MANITOBA : BULLETIN SERIES – (See: Government Documents Catalogue) – Ottawa, Backfile 1913-1970 – 9 – cn Micromedia [060]

National Museum of Natural History, Smithsonian Institution *see* THE RICHMOND INDEX TO THE GENERA AND SPECIES OF BIRDS

National Museums of Canada *see* BULLETIN SERIES: ANNUAL REPORT SERIES

NATIONAL MUSEUMS OF FRANCE CATALOGUES – (Individual titles not listed separately) – Paris, 1885-1974 – 211 catalogues on 395mf – 9 – £2,975.00 – uk Chadwyck [700]

NATIONAL NEGRO HEALTH NEWS / U.S. Public Health Service – v1-18 2+2 (all publ). 1933-1950 – 26mf – 9 – $115.00 – us UPA [610]

NATIONAL NEGRO VOICE – Nos. 1-11 (all publ). 1941 – 1mf – 9 – $55.00 – us UPA [975]

NATIONAL NEW DEMOCRATIC COALITION NEWSLETTER – 1970- 1; 1975- 5,6,9 – us UMI [073]

NATIONAL NEWS – New York. N.Y. 18 Feb 1932-3 Jun 1932. No. 77-5 One reel – 1 – 15.00 – us Partington [071]

NATIONAL NEWSPAPER INDEX – Monthly cumulative index of the Wall Street Journal, The New York Times, Christian Science Monitor, Los Angeles Times and Washington Post – 5,17 – us I.A.C. [071]

National Nonpartisan League *see*
- MEMBERSHIP, SPEECH AND NEWSPAPER FILES
- PAPERS
- PRINTED MATERIALS

NATIONAL NOTES / The National Association of Colored Women – (Organ of the National Association of Colored Women) Kansas City, Missouri. v. 26, no. 10-v. 35, no. 5. Jun Sep 1924-Mar 1933 – 1 – us NY Public [073]

NATIONAL NOW TIMES – (1986- 1,5,6) – v9-1976- – 9 – us UMI [360]

NATIONAL OBJECTIVES FOR TEACHERS COLLEGE COURSES / Papua New Guinea. Department of Education – (Missing: Pt 1) – 5mf – 9 – DE-224/1 – ne IDC [370]

NATIONAL OBSERVER – Albany, NY. Aug 1827-1828. -w. Anti-Masonic – 1 – us Western Res [071]

THE NATIONAL OBSERVER – 1962-77 – 1 – us UMI [071]

NATIONAL OBSERVER AND ANTI-MASONIC PIONEER – Albany, NY. 1829-Jul 1830. -d – 1 – us Western Res [071]

NATIONAL OBSERVER AND BRITISH REVIEW OF POLITICS, ECONOMICS, LITERATURE, SCIENCE AND ART – v. 1-18. 24 Nov 1888-7 Aug 1897 – 1 – us UMI [073]

NATIONAL OPINION POLLS POLITICAL BULLETIN – 1959-78 and other surveys – 1 – us Primary [320]

NATIONAL OVERALL DEVELOPMENT PLAN, 1961-1969; LIST OF PROJECTS / Indonesia. Dewan Perantjang Nasional – SE-5362 1. 1961 – 9 – ne IDC [338]

National Paint, Varnish and Lacquer Association. Scientific Section *see* PROCEEDINGS

NATIONAL PARENT TEACHER *see* PTA MAGAZINE

NATIONAL PARENT-TEACHER *see* PTA MAGAZINE

NATIONAL PARENT-TEACHER MAGAZINE *see* PTA MAGAZINE

NATIONAL PARK LIFE, BANFF – Banff. Alberta. Canada. 7 Je 1888 – 1 – cn Commonwealth Micro [073]

National Park Service *see* NEW ECHOTA, BIRTHPLACE OF THE AMERICAN INDIAN PRESS

National Park Service et al *see* HISTORIC AMERICAN ENGINEERING RECORD (HAER)

NATIONAL PARKS AND CONSERVATION MAGAZINE – v1- 1919- 1,5,6; v46- 1972- 9 – us UMI [333]

NATIONAL PARKS PLANNING : A MANUAL WITH ANNOTATED EXAMPLES – 1988 – 111p – it F.A.O. [333]

NATIONAL PATENT PLANNING COMMISSION : "KETTERING COMMISSION: 1ST THRU 3RD REPORTS – Washington: GPO, 1943-45 (all publ) – 3mf – 9 – $4.50 – LLMC 82-502 – us L.L.M.C. [324]

NATIONAL PEACE JUBILEE AND MUSICAL FESTIVAL, NATIONAL PEACE JUBILEE AND MUSICAL REPORTER – Boston, 1869 – 1r – 1 – £60.00 – uk Chadwyck [780]

National Peiping University. Normal College for Women *see* NU-SHIH TA HSUEH-SHU CHI-K'AN

National Peking University. Chinese Agricultural Economics Research Institute *see*
- SANTOA4 NO ICHI SHUA4SHICHIN NO SHAKAITEKI KOA4ZOA4
- SANTOA4-SHOA4 KEIMIN-KEN NOA4SON CHOA4SA HOA4KOKU

NATIONAL PERILS AND HOPES : A STUDY BASED ON CURRENT STATISTICS AND THE OBSERVATIONS OF A CHEERFUL REFORMER / Crafts, Wilbur F – Cleveland, Ohio: F.M. Barton, 1910 – 1mf – us A.T.L.A. [240]

NATIONAL PETROLEUM NEWS – v1- 1909- 1; v58- 5,6; v68- 9 – us UMI [660]

NATIONAL PETROLEUM NEWS – v16-48 1924-56 – 1,5,6 – us Princeton Micro [660]

THE NATIONAL PHOTOGRAPHIC RECORD AND SURVEY / British Museum. London – (Records important buildings and monuments in Britain and Ireland between 1897-1904) – 1991 – 79mf – 9 – $470.00 – 0-907006-44-2 – uk Mindata [770]

THE NATIONAL PLAN / Great Britain. Department of Economic Affairs – London. 1965. BD-192 1 – 9 – ne IDC [339]

A NATIONAL PLAN FOR JAMAICA, 1957-1967 / Jamaica – Kingston. 1957 – 9 – ne IDC [338]

National Planning Commission *see* FOURTH PLAN 1970-1975

National Planning Office *see* WESTERN SAMOA

National Portrait Gallery. London *see* THE HILL-ADAMSON ALBUMS

NATIONAL PREACHER AND VILLAGE PULPIT – 1-NS v. 9. Jun 1826-66 – 1 – us UMI [240]

NATIONAL PRINCIPIA – 1-5 2+27 (all publ). 1858-1866 – 2r – 1 – $185.00 – us UPA [975]

NATIONAL PRINCIPIA – v. 1-5. 19 Nov 1858-14 Jun 1866 – 1 – us UMI [073]

NATIONAL PROBATION AND PAROLE ASSOCIATION YEARBOOK – (Title between 1928-49: National Probation Association. Lacking: 1st, 7th) – 1st to 45th. 1908-1952 – 129mf – 9 – $193.00 – LLMC 84-268 – us L.L.M.C. [340]

NATIONAL PRODUCTIVITY REVIEW – v1-. Winter 1981- – 1,5,6,9 – us UMI [338]

NATIONAL PROHIBITIONIST PERIODICAL / Union Signal – undated – 1 – us KS Hist [978]

NATIONAL PUBLIC ACCOUNTANT – v1- 1956- 5,6; v17- 1; v20- 9 – us UMI [650]

NATIONAL PUBLIC ACCOUNTANT – v. 1-6. 1949-56 – 5 – us UMI [650]

National Publishing Co *see* HISTORY OF HARRISON COUNTY

NATIONAL QUARTERLY REVIEW – v. 1-41. 1860-1880 – 1 – us Princeton Micro [073]

NATIONAL QUARTERLY REVIEW – v. 1-41. Jun 1860-Oct 1880 – 1 – us UMI [073]

NATIONAL RACQUETBALL – (1986-. 1,5,6) – 1982- – 9 – us UMI [790]

NATIONAL RAILROAD ADJUSTMENT BOARD, 1ST DIVISION AWARDS / U.S. National Railroad Adjustment Board – nos 1-21965. v1-168. 1934-72 (all publ) – 1665mf – 9 – $2,497.00 – LLMC 84-117 – us L.L.M.C. [324]

NATIONAL RAILROAD ADJUSTMENT BOARD, 2ND DIVISION AWARDS / U.S. National Railroad Adjustment Board – nos 1-6327. v1-67. 1935-72 (all publ) – 653mf – 9 – $979.00 – LLMC 84-118 – us L.L.M.C. [324]

NATIONAL RAILROAD ADJUSTMENT BOARD, 3RD DIVISION AWARDS / U.S. National Railroad Adjustment Board – nos 1-19195. v1-191. 1934-72 – 1958mf – 9 – $2,937.00 – LLMC 84-119 – us L.L.M.C. [324]

NATIONAL RAILROAD ADJUSTMENT BOARD, 4TH DIVISION AWARDS / U.S. National Railroad Adjustment Board – nos 1-2320. v1-21. 1935-72 (all publ) – 221mf – 9 – $331.00 – LLMC 84-120 – us L.L.M.C. [324]

NATIONAL REAL ESTATE AND BUILDING JOURNAL – v. 50-57. 1949-56 – 1 – us UMI [650]

NATIONAL RECORD (WASHINGTON, D.C.: 1943) – (Library has: v.1,no.1-v.3,no.4/5; Mar. 1943-July/Aug. 1945 (v.1,no.7 (Aug. 1943) issue missing) – Washington, D.C.: The Continental Publishing Co., 1943- – 1 – CSUX86-S182 – us Hoover Inst Photo [978]

THE NATIONAL REFORMER – 1860-93 – 5 – £595.00 – uk World [073]

NATIONAL REFORMER AND MANX WEEKLY REVIEW OF HOME AND FOREIGN AFFAIRS – 1-35 (all publ). 1846-1847 – 6mf – 9 – $65.00 – us UPA [335]

THE NATIONAL REGISTER OF HISTORIC PLACES – (Nearly 50,000 properties are included with over 200,000 photographs. Pts are listed separately. Also available by state) – 2pts – ca 11,500mf – 9 – £23,645.00 coll – uk Chadwyck [720]

THE NATIONAL REGISTER OF HISTORIC PLACES, PT 1 : PROPERTIES REGISTERED THROUGH DECEMBER 1982 – (Contains 15,000 photographs and text describing 27,000 properties) – (mf ed 1989) – 6497mf – 9 – £12,625.00 – uk Chadwyck [720]

THE NATIONAL REGISTER OF HISTORIC PLACES, PT 2 : PROPERTIES REGISTERED 1983-1988 – (Contains 57,000 photographs & text describing 19,000 properties) – (mf ed 1992) – ca 5000mf – 9 – £18,190.00 – uk Chadwyck [720]

NATIONAL REGISTER OF MICROFORM MASTERS / U.S. Library of Congress – 1965-75 – 9 – 125.00 – us Opus [010]

NATIONAL RENAISSANCE BULLETIN – 1950- 1; 1970- 5,6; 1975- 9 – us UMI [073]

NATIONAL REPORTER – v9-. Winter 1985- – 1,5,6,9 – us UMI [073]

NATIONAL REPORTER ON LEGAL ETHICS AND PROFESSIONAL RESPONSIBILITY – (Indiv. years avail. $80.00y) – 1995. 4 vols, 10 install./y – 9 – $730.00 – us UPA [340]

NATIONAL REPORTER SYSTEM 1879 THRU 1919 – (Add vols to be filmed as they fall out of copyright. Individual titles also listed separately) – 10 units – 17,512mf – 9 – $26,268.00 set – LLMC 79-404 – us L.L.M.C. [340]

NATIONAL REPORTER SYSTEM, 1879 THRU 1919 *see*
- ATLANTIC REPORTER
- THE FEDERAL REPORTER
- FEDERAL SUPPLEMENT
- NEW YORK SUPPLEMENT
- NORTHEASTERN REPORTER
- PACIFIC REPORTER
- SOUTHEASTERN REPORTER
- SOUTHERN REPORTER
- SOUTHWESTERN REPORTER
- THE SUPREME COURT REPORTER

NATIONAL REPORTS AND SELECTED PAPERS PRESENTED AT THE 1ST SESSION OF THE WORKING PARTY ON FISHERIES ECONOMICS AND PLANNING : ST. GEORGE'S GRENADA, 1989 / W.E.C.A.F.C. – 1990 – 134p – it F.A.O. [338]

NATIONAL REPORTS AND SELECTED PAPERS PRESENTED AT THE 5TH SESSION OF THE WORKING PARTY ON ASSESSMENT OF MARINE FISHERY RESOURCE. SAINT GEORGE, BERMUDA, NOV 1986 / W.E.C.A.F.C. – 1988 – 115p – it F.A.O. [639]

NATIONAL REPORTS AND SELECTED PAPERS PRESENTED AT THE 6TH SESSION OF THE WORKING PARTY ON ASSESSMENT OF MARINE FISHERY RESOURCES; SUPPLEMENT : ST. GEORGE'S, GRENADA, 1989 / W.E.C.A.F.C. – 1991 – 249p – it F.A.O. [639]

NATIONAL REPORTS OF EIFAC MEMBER COUNTRIES FOR THE PERIOD JANUARY 1984-DEC 1985 – 1986 – 138p – it F.A.O. [630]

NATIONAL REPOSITORY, DEVOTED TO GENERAL AND RELIGIOUS LITERATURE, CRITICISM AND ART – v. 1-8. Jan 1877-Dec 1880 – 1 – us UMI [240]
NATIONAL REPUBLIC – v. 41-47. 1953-60 – 1 – us UMI [975]
National Research Council *see* BULLETIN
NATIONAL RESEARCH COUNCIL, CANADA-COLLECTION / Canada. National Aeronautics Establishment and Division of Mechanical Engineering – 1951-89 Aero Reports – 500 fiches – 9 – 800.00 – us Updata [629]
National Research Council of Canada *see* CANADIAN JOURNAL OF RESEARCH
NATIONAL RESOURCES PLANNING BOARD (NRPB) : REPORTS AND RECORDS – (1934-1943. Cataloging available) – 18r + 470mf – 1 – $2625.00 – us UMI [977]
NATIONAL REVIEW – (1969- 5,6. 1970- 9) – 1955- – 1 – us UMI [073]
NATIONAL REVIEW – Manila, Philippines. -w. 1985?- – 1 – us U.W. Library [073]
NATIONAL REVIEW – Shanghai. China. -w. 5 Apr 1913-22 Jul 1916. (6 reels) – 1 – uk British Libr Newspaper [072]
NATIONAL REVIEW – v. 1-19. July 1855-Nov. 1864 – 1 – us UMI [073]
NATIONAL RIP-SAW – St. Louis etc. v. 9, no. 6-v. 15, no. 3; n.s. 4-46. Aug 1912-May 1918; Feb 1921-Sept 1924. Incomplete – 1 – us NY Public [073]
NATIONAL ROLLING PLAN 1991-1993 / Nigeria. Planning Office – [Lagos]. 2v. 1991 – 16mf – 9 – ne IDC [338]
NATIONAL SAFETY CONGRESS TRANSACTIONS / National Safety Council – 1912- 1; 1975- 5,6,9 – us UMI [610]
National Safety Council *see* NATIONAL SAFETY CONGRESS TRANSACTIONS
NATIONAL SAFETY NEWS – 1919- 1; 1975-5,6,9 – us UMI [360]
NATIONAL SCHEME OF EDUCATION B.E. 2503 (1960 A.D.) / Thailand. Ministry of Education. Division of Eductional Information – Bangkok, 1960 – 1mf – 9 – DE-278/1 – ne IDC [370]
NATIONAL SCIENCE AND TECHNOLOGY POLICIES IN EUROPE AND NORTH AMERICA 1978 : PRESENT SITUATION AND FUTURE PROSPECTS – (Text in English and French) – 1979 – 458p – 9 – 92-3-001584-9 – fr UNESCO [500]
NATIONAL SCIENCE COUNCIL MONTHLY – Taiwan. v1,no.1-v11,no.12. 1973-84. 223 fiches – 9 – 195.00 – ch Transmission [500]
NATIONAL SCIENCE COUNCIL REVIEW – Taiwan. 1965-82. 34 fiches – 9 – 40.00 – ch Transmission [500]
National Science Council. Taiwan *see*
- ANNUAL REPORT
- PROCEEDINGS
- SPECIAL SUBJECT STUDIES REPORTS

National Security Agency *see* TOP SECRET STUDIES ON U.S. COMMUNICATIONS INTELLIGENCE DURING WORLD WAR 2
NATIONAL SECURITY ARCHIVE, WASHINGTON D.C. THE MAKING OF U.S. POLICY *see*
- AFGHANISTAN
- THE BERLIN CRISIS, 1958-1962
- THE CUBAN MISSILE CRISIS, 1962
- EL SALVADOR
- IRAN
- THE IRAN-CONTRA AFFAIR
- NICARAGUA
- THE PHILIPPINES
- SOUTH AFRICA
- THE U.S. INTELLIGENCE COMMUNITY
- U.S. MILITARY USES OF SPACE, 1945-1991
- U.S. NUCLEAR HISTORY
- U.S. NUCLEAR NON-PROLIFERATION, 1945-1991

NATIONAL SECURITY ARCHIVE, WASHINGTON D.C. THE SPECIAL COLLECTIONS *see*
- EL SALVADOR 2
- IRAQGATE
- PRESIDENTIAL DIRECTIVES ON NATIONAL SECURITY FROM TRUMAN TO CLINTON
- THE SOVIET ESTIMATE
- U.S. ESPIONAGE AND INTELLIGENCE, 1947-1995

NATIONAL SECURITY FILES *see*
- THE JOHN F. KENNEDY NATIONAL SECURITY FILES, 1961-63
- THE LYNDON B. JOHNSON NATIONAL SECURITY FILES, 1963-69

NATIONAL SECURITY FILES, 1961-69 – (See listings under John F. Kennedy and Lyndon B. Johnson) – 1 – $22,575.00 coll – us UPA [324]
NATIONAL SEMINAR ON CURRICULUM DEVELOPMENT IN TEACHER EDUCATION PENANG 1970 : SEMINAR REPORT / Malaysia. Ministry of Education – Kuala Lumpur, [1971] – 2mf – 9 – DE-215/1 – ne IDC [370]
National Shorthand Reporters' Association *see* DIGEST OF STATUTES AND LEGAL DECISIONS RELATING TO OFFICIAL STENOGRAPHERS
NATIONAL SOCIALIST – Cincinnati. v1. 1878 – 1r – 1 – us Ross [335]
National Socialist German Labor Party *see* RECORDS
National Society for Performance and Instruction *see*
- NSPI JOURNAL
- NSPI NEWSLETTER

National Society for the Prevention of Blindness *see* GLAUCOMA DISCUSSION MEETINGS & REPORTS
National Society. Great Britain *see* ANNUAL REPORTS
National Speech Arts Association *see* PROCEEDINGS
NATIONAL SPEED SPORT NEWS – July 20, 1933- – 1 – us L of C Photodup [790]
NATIONAL SPIRITUALIST : SUMMIT OF SPIRITUAL UNDERSTANDING – v20. 1938; v48-68. 1966-91 (complete) – 9r – 1 – ATLA S0802 – us A.T.L.A. [073]
NATIONAL SPOTLIGHT – v.1-2. 1975-76. Continued as ySpotlight – 1 – us UMI [073]
NATIONAL STANDARD : A TEMPERANCE AND LITERARY JOURNAL – New York. v1-30; ns: 3 v1-2. 1840-71 – 10r – 1 – us Ross [073]
NATIONAL STAR – Feb 1974-Nov 1975 – 1 – us UMI [073]
NATIONAL STATISTICAL REPORTS – (This collection is updated annually; Catalogues by region free on request) – 9 – ne IDC [304]
National Student Forum of the Paris Pact *see* NEW STUDENT
National Student League *see* STUDENT REVIEW
NATIONAL SUMMARY ISRAEL / Israel. Prime Minister's Office – Report submitted to UNESCO for the Minespol II Conference. Jerusalem, Aug 1977. 45 p. Diagr – 9 – 2.00 – is I.T.T.I. [324]
NATIONAL TAX ASSOCIATION. BULLETIN *see* NATIONAL TAX JOURNAL
NATIONAL TAX JOURNAL – v1- 1948- 1; v22-5,6; v28- 9 – us UMI [336]
NATIONAL TAX JOURNAL – (Supersedes National Tax Association. Bulletin) – v1-48. 1948-95 – 9 – $741.00 set – us Hein [340]
National Teacher's Research Association *see* NEGRO EDUCATIONAL REVIEW
NATIONAL TELEGRAPH – Clarksburg. West Virginia. 1862; 1864-1868 – 1 – us UMI [071]
NATIONAL TELEPHONE JOURNAL – London. v.1-6. 1906-1912 – 1,5,6 – 2229.00 – us Princeton Micro [073]
NATIONAL TIMES – Jan 1981- – 9 – at Pascoe [073]
NATIONAL TIMES : TIMES ON SUNDAY – 1971-88 – 58r – 1 – at Pascoe [072]
NATIONAL TRANSPORTATION SAFETY BOARD DECISIONS / U.S. National Transportation Safety Board – v1-2. Apr 1967-Dec 1976 – 55mf – 9 – $82.00 – LLMC 81-235 – us L.L.M.C. [380]
National Transportation Safety Board's *see* AVIATION AND MARINE ENFORCEMENT DECISIONS
National Trust. London *see* PICTURES IN NATIONAL TRUST PROPERTIES
NATIONAL TUBERCULOSIS AND RESPIRATORY DISEASE ASSOCIATION BULLETIN *see* AMERICAN LUNG ASSOCIATION BULLETIN
National Tuberculosis Association *see* BULLETIN
NATIONAL UNDERWRITER: LIFE AND HEALTH – (v. 83- 1979- 5,6,9) – v. 24-1920- – 1 – us UMI [336]
NATIONAL UNDERWRITER: PROPERTY AND CASUALTY – (v. 83- 1979- 5,6,9) – v. 1-1897- – 1 – us UMI [336]
NATIONAL UNION CATALOG : BOOKS, 1983-1996 / U.S. Library of Congress – (1997 current subscription includes registers and indexes) – Cumulative indexes, 1983-87, 1988-1992. Registers 1983-1996 – 9 – us Advanced Libr [010]
NATIONAL UNION CATALOG / U.S. Library of Congress – Quinquennia: 1953-57; 1958-62; 1963-67; 1968-72; 1973-77. Annuals: 1978-82 – 9 – us Advanced Libr [010]
NATIONAL UNION CATALOG. AUDIOVISUAL MATERIALS: INDEXES AND REGISTERS / U.S. Library of Congress – Includes motion pictures, videorecordings, filmstrips, transparency sets and slide sets released in U.S. or Canada. -q. ISSN: 0734-7669. Item Code: 8337500 – 9 – $130.00 – us L of C Cataloging [010]
NATIONAL UNION CATALOG: BOOKS. INDEXES AND REGISTERS / U.S. Library of Congress – Replaces the NUC, Subject Catalog, Chinese Cooperative Catalog and Monographic Series, National Register of Microform Masters. -m. ISSN: 0734-7650. Item Code: 8337100 – 9 – $790.00 – us L of C Cataloging [010]
NATIONAL UNION CATALOG: CARTOGRAPHIC MATERIALS. INDEXES AND REGISTER / U.S. Library of Congress – Entire Library of Congress maps database plus entries for currently cataloged maps. -q. ISSN: 0734-7634. Item Code: 8337700 – 9 – $235.00 – us L of C Cataloging [910]
NATIONAL UNION CATALOG: PRE-1956 IMPRINTS / U.S. Library of Congress – National and international from 15th cent. through 1955 – 9 – us Advanced Libr [010]
NATIONAL UNION CATALOG: REGISTER OF ADDITIONAL LOCATIONS / U.S. Library of Congress – Cumulative Microform ed. Issued quarterly. ISSN: 0361-5251. Item Code: 8333100 – 9 – $235.00 – us L of C Cataloging [010]
National Union of Ships' Stewards, Cooks, Butchers and Bakers *see* UNION MAGAZINE
NATIONAL UNIONIST – 15 Apr 1864-22 Aug 1865 – 1 – $60.00 – us OmniSys [071]
NATIONAL VOCATIONAL TRAINING ACT 1970 / Ghana. Vocational Training Institute – 1972 – 1mf – 9 – DE-433/1 – ne IDC [370]
NATIONAL VOICE OF CONSERVATIVE BAPTISTS – 1953-55 – 1 – 32.83 – us Baptist [240]
THE NATIONAL VOLUNTEER – Dublin, Ireland.17 Oct 1914-22 Apr 1916 – 1 – ie Microforms [072]
NATIONAL WAGE STABILIZATION BOARD : A DOCUMENTARY HISTORY...: 1 JAN 1946-24 FEB 1947 – Washington: GPO, 1948 – 7mf – 9 – $10.50 – LLMC 94-010 – us L.L.M.C. [340]
NATIONAL WAR LABOR BOARD – TERMINATION REPORT : INDUSTRIAL DISPUTES AND WAGE STABILIZATION IN WARTIME, 12 JAN 1942-31 DEC 1945 – Washington: GPO. 3v. 1947 – 38mf – 9 – $57.00 – LLMC 95-008 – us L.L.M.C. [340]
National Westminster Bank *see* QUARTERLY REVIEW
NATIONAL WHOLESALERS GUIDE – 1959- 1; 1975- 5,6,9 – us UMI [073]
NATIONAL WILDLIFE – (v. 7- 1968- 5,6. v. 9- 1970- 9) – v. 1- 1962- – 1 – us UMI [574]
NATIONAL WINE MERCHANT AND BREWER GAZETTE – Providence. R.I. 1894-1899 – 1 – us UMI [640]
National Woman's Party *see*
- PAPERS

NATIONAL WOMAN'S PARTY PAPERS : COMPLETE COLLECTION – 9 – $19,535.00 – us UPA [305]
NATIONAL WOMAN'S PARTY PAPERS, PART 1 : 1913-1974 – (Guide to Part 1 $210.00) – 9 – $13,620.00 – 0-667-00538-2 – us UPA [305]
NATIONAL WOMAN'S PARTY PAPERS, PART 2 : THE SUFFRAGE YEARS, 1913-1920 – (Includes printed guide) – 9 – $8,670.00 – 0-667-00627-3 – us UPA [305]
NATIONAL WOMAN'S PARTY PAPERS. SERIES 1 : CORRESPONDENCE – (Section A: 1877-1933 $4,820.00; Section B: 1933-1945 $3,460.00; Section C: $2,690.00) – 9 – us UPA [305]
NATIONAL WOMAN'S PARTY PAPERS. SERIES 1 : CORRESPONDENCE, 1891-1940 – (Section A: 1891-1915 $2,425.00; Section B: 1916-1917 $3,520.00; Section C: 1917-1940 $3.520.00) – 9 – us UPA [305]
NATIONAL WOMAN'S PARTY PAPERS. SERIES 2 : ADMINISTRATIVE FILES, PRINTED MATTER AND PHOTOGRAPHS, 1889-1936 – (Guide to Part 2 $135.00) – 9 – $1,210.00 – us UPA [305]
NATIONAL WOMAN'S PARTY PAPERS. SERIES 2 : MINUTES; LEGAL PAPERS AND FINANCIAL RECORDS, 1912-1972 – 9 – $1,250.00 – us UPA [305]
NATIONAL WOMAN'S PARTY PAPERS. SERIES 3 : PRINTED MATERIALS, 1850-1972 – 9 – $4,425.00 – us UPA [305]
NATIONAL WOMAN'S PARTY PAPERS. SERIES 4 : WORLD WOMAN'S PARTY PAPERS, 1938-1958 – 9 – $580.00 – us UPA [305]
NATIONAL WOOL GROWER – v1- 1911- 1; v61- 5,6; v66- 9 – us UMI [636]
National Workers' Committee Movement *see* SOLIDARITY
NATIONAL WORKMAN – New York. v1-2. 1866-67 – 1r – 1 – us Ross [331]
THE NATIONAL WORKMAN – New York. v. 1, no. 2-v. 2, no. 9. Oct 20 1866-Mar 2 1867. Incomplete – 1 – us NY Public [330]
NATIONAL WORKSHOP ON POPULATION EDUCATION, 4-16 OCTOBER 1971 KUALA LUMPUR : LAPORAN (REPORT) / Malaysia. Ministry of Education – Kuala Lumpur, 1971 – 8mf – 9 – DE-216/1 – ne IDC [370]
NATIONAL WORKSHOPS / Strachey, Loe – 1mf (29x) – 9 – $1.00f – at Libertarian Micro [320]
NATIONAL ZEITUNG – Basel, Switzerland. -d. 28 Aug 1939-31 Dec 1946. Imperfect. 81 reels – 1 – uk British Libr Newspaper [949]
NATIONAL ZEITUNG – Berlin, Germany. 1963-71 – 28r – 1 – us L of C Photodup [072]
NATIONAL ZIP CODE AND POST OFFICE DIRECTORY – U.S. territories and possessions included. Alphabetical by community under state headings – 9 – us UMI [380]
National-Demokratische Partei Deutschlands (German Democratic Republic) *see* PARTEITAG. STENOGRAPHISCHE NIEDERSCHRIFT
DER NATIONALDEUTSCHE JUDE – Mitteilungsblatt des Verbandes nationaldeutscher Juden. Berlin. 1922-1934. Lacking 1924, no. 2. B307 (Leo Baeck Institute. German-Jewish Periodicals, Pt 1) – 1r – 1 – $75.00 – us UPA [270]
DER NATIONALDEUTSCHE JUDE *see* MITTEILUNGSBLATT DES VERBANDES NATIONALDEUTSCHER JUDEN
NATIONALDEUTSCHE JUDE – Berlin, 1924-33 – 1r – 1 – us Ross [270]
DIE NATIONALE AUTONOMIE... MINDERHEITSENRECHTS / Mintz, M – Riga, 1927 – 2mf – 9 – ILM-1564/1 – ne IDC [320]
DER NATIONALE GEDANKE BEI HEINRICH VON KLEIST / Iwanowa, Gora – (Includes bibliographical references) – Sofia: [s.n.], 1942 – 1r – 1 – us U.W. Library [430]
NATIONALE MERKEN – (Missing: 1954(3); 1957(6); 1959(6); 1961(7); 1962(1-2)) – Hollandia, 1953-1962(10) – 27mf – 9 – ne IDC [949]
NATIONALE PFLICHTEN ZUR LOESUNG DER JUDENFRAGE / Max, Robert – Kiel: Lipsius und Tischer, 1893 – 1r – 1 – us U.W. Library [170]
NATIONALE RESOURCES PLANNING BOARD : REPORTS AND RECORDS – 18r, 470mf – 1,9 – us UMI [350]
NATIONALE RUNDSCHAU *see* BREMER ZEITUNG
DER NATIONALE SOZIALIST – Berlin, apr 4 1926-feb 23 1930 – 1 – Inquire at Mikrofilmarchiv for details – gw Misc Inst [320]
NATIONALE UND HUMANISTISCHE ERZIEHUNG / Kalckstein, Carl von et al – Kiel: Lipsius und Tischer, 1891 – 1r – 1 – us U.W. Library [943]
Nationale Vergadering representeerende het Volk van Nederland *see* DAGVERHAAL DER HANDELINGEN
DIE NATIONALE WIEDERGEBURT DES JUEDISCHEN VOLKES IN SEINEM LANDE ALS MITTEL ZUR LOESUNG DER JUDENFRAGE / Birnbaum, N – Wien. 1893. BJ-28-54 – 9 – ne IDC [956]
Nationalen Arbeiter Union *see* ARBEITER UNION
NATIONALISM, REVOLUTION AND EVOLUTION IN SOUTH-EAST ASIA / ed by Leifer, M – SE-255 1. 1970 – 9 – ne IDC [320]
LE NATIONALISME AFRICAIN : APERCU SUR LA NAISSANCE ET SON DEVELOPPEMENT / Donnafe, P – F50.00 – fr Ethnologie [320]
LES NATIONALISMES MAGHREBINS / Duclos, L Jet al – F50.00 – fr Ethnologie [320]

NATIONALIST – 1-3 (all publ). 1889-1891 – 14mf – 9 – $85.00 – us UPA [335]
NATIONALIST – Manhattan. Kan. 1871-1926 – 1 – us UMI [071]
THE NATIONALIST – Clonmel, Ireland. -w. 1890-92. 2 reels – 1 – uk British Libr Newspaper [072]
THE NATIONALIST – Dar es Salaam, [Tanganyika]: Mwananchi Pub Co Ltd, mar 15 1965-oct 14 1968 – 8r – 1 – us Res Libr [072]
THE NATIONALIST – Ireland.21 Sept 1905-29 Mar 1906 – 1 – ie Microforms [072]
NATIONALIST AND LEINSTER TIMES – 1883-1980 – ca 156r – 1 – ie Microforms [941]
NATIONALIST AND LEINSTER TIMES – Carlow, Ireland.-d. 1883-1986. 200 reels – 1 – PS27.50r – ie European Micro [072]
NATIONALIST AND MUNSTER ADVERTISER – 1890-1980 – ca 152r – 1 – ie Microforms [941]
NATIONALIST AND MUNSTER ADVERTISER – Clonmel, Ireland. -d. 1890-1986. 200 reels – 1 – PS27.50r – ie European Micro [072]
NATIONALIST AND TIPPERARY ADVERTISER – Clonmel, Ireland. 1901.-w. 1 reel – 1 – uk British Libr Newspaper [072]
LE NATIONALISTE / ed by Asselin, Olivar – (Becomes: Le Nationaliste et Le Devoir) – Montreal, Canada. 6 mar 1904-24 sep 1922 – 5r – 1 – Can$65.00r – cn Can Microfilming [072]
LE NATIONALISTE ET LE DEVOIR – Montreal, 28 sep 1922-28 dec 1939f – 8r – 1 – Can$75.00 – cn Can Microfilming [072]
LE NATIONALISTE ET LE DEVOIR *see* LE NATIONALISTE
DIE NATIONALITAET DER HANDELSGESELLSCHAFTEN WAEHREND DES KRIEGES. / Belin, W – Borna, Leipzig, 1935 – 1mf – 9 – ILM-3230/1 – ne IDC [327]
DIE NATIONALITAETENFRAGE UND DIE SOZIALDEMOKRATIE / Bauer, O – (Marx-Studien, Bd. 2). Wien. 1907. BR-5141 2 – 8 – ne IDC [335]
LA NATIONALITE DES SOCIETES / Cuq, M E – Paris, 1921 – 3mf – 1 – ILM-3505/1 – ne IDC [327]
LA NATIONALITE DES SOCIETES AVANT ET DEPUIS LA GUERRE 1914-18 / Gain, R – Paris, 1924 – 3mf – 1 – ILM-3444/1 – ne IDC [327]
LA NATIONALITE DES SOCIETES EN TUNISIE / Bismut, V – Dijon, 1927 – 3mf – 9 – ILM-3503/1 – ne IDC [327]
LA NATIONALITE DU SLESVIG / Beauvois, E – Paris, 1864 – 1mf – 9 – ILM-3216/1 – ne IDC [327]
LA NATIONALITE ET SON INFLUENCE... / Devot, J – Paris, 1893 – 2mf – 1 – ILM-3429/1 – ne IDC [327]
DENATIONALITEIT VAN DE VEREENIGING ... / Bloette, J A A – Leiden, 1921 – 3mf – 9 – ILM-3210/1 – ne IDC [327]
NATIONALITIES PAPERS – (Increases to 4 issues in 1995) – 1995, Vol 23 – £135.00 – uk Carfax [301]
NATIONALITY – Dublin, Ireland.19 Jun 1915-20 Sept 1919 – 1 – ie Microforms [072]
NATIONALITY – Ireland.Aug 1931-Aug 1932 – 1 – ie Microforms [072]
NATIONALITY WITHIN THE BRITISH COMMONWEALTH... / Gey van Pittius, E F W – London, 1930 – 3mf – 1 – ILM-900/1 – ne IDC [327]
DIE NATIONALKIRCHLICHE IDEE I.H.V. WESSENBERGS IM URTEIL DER FLUGSCHRIFTENLITERATUR 1803-1821 : EIN BEITRAG ZUR GEISTESGESCHICHTE DER AUFKLAERUNG UND RESTAURATION / Radlspeck, Carl – Kallmuenz, 1930 – xvii/142p – 9 – DM48.00 – 3-89349-061-2 – gw Hänsel [200]
NATIONALKURIREN – Goeteborg, OErebro. 1893-1922 – 9 – sw Kungliga [072]
NATIONALLIBERALE CORRESPONDENZ – Berlin, jan 5 1932-mar 31 1933 – 1 – Inquire at Mikrofilmarchiv for details – gw Misc Inst [320]
NATIONAL-MAGAZIN – Leipzig, Germany. 1834 – 1 – gw Mikrofilm [072]
Nationalmuseum, Stockholm *see* DRAWINGS OF JOHAN TOBIAS SERGEL
NATIONALOKONOMISK TIDSSKRIFT – 1873-1; 1971- 5,6; 1975- 4 x 6 in. 9 – us UMI [073]
LE NATIONAL-POPULAIRE – Dir. Marcel Deat. Paris. juin 1942-aout 1944 – 1 – fr A.C.R.P.P. [073]
DER NATIONALSOZIALIST *see* DER DEUTSCHE AAR
NATIONALSOZIALISTISCHE BIBLIOTHEK – Muenchen. Heft 1-54; 1928-35. Some vols. are later editions. Film Mas C 693 – 1 – us H.U. Library [943]
NATIONALSOZIALISTISCHE BRIEFE – Berlin, 1925-30 – 2r – 1 – Inquire at Mikrofilmarchiv for details – gw Misc Inst [320]
NATIONALSOZIALISTISCHE BRIEFE – Berlin, Germany. 1925-1930 – 2r – 1 – gw Mikrofilm [072]
Nationalsozialistische Deutsche Arbeiter-Partei *see* REICHSORGANIZATIONSAMT
NATIONALSOZIALISTISCHE LANDPOST – Berlin/ Muenchen. jan 3, 1932-dec 8, 1944 – 11r – 1 – gw Mikrofilm [072]
NATIONALSOZIALISTISCHE MONATSHEFTE – Berlin, DE. 1930-1944 (incomplete) – 1 – gw Mikrofilm [073]
NATIONALSOZIALISTISCHE MONATSHEFTE – Berlin, Muenchen. apr 1930-31, feb 1932-44 – 7r – 1 – Inquire at Mikrofilmarchiv for details – gw Misc Inst [320]
NATIONALSOZIALISTISCHE MONATSHEFTE : WISSENSCHAFTLICHE ZEITSCHRIFT DER NSDAP – Berlin, 1930-1944 – 7r – 1 – DM770.00 – gw Mikro Press [072]
NATIONALSOZIALISTISCHE POLITIK IN SUEDOSTEUROPA : ZUM PROBLEM DER DEUTSCH-GRIECHISCHEN BEZIEHUNGEN / Khauer, Frank – 1993 – 2mf – 9 – DM80.00 – 3-89349-790-0 – gw Hänsel [327]
NATIONALSOZIALISTISCHE RUNDFUNKKORRESPONDENZ : RK – Berlin, feb 1937-mar 1941 – 11r – 1 – Inquire at Mikrofilmarchiv for details – gw Misc Inst [790]
NATIONAL-ZEITUNG – (Also suppl 1970-77 available) – Berlin, apr 12 1948-jun 30 1990 – 97r – 1 – Inquire at Mikrofilmarchiv for details – gw Misc Inst [072]
NATIONAL-ZEITUNG – (Also suppl available: Allgemeine litterarische Rundschau, jan-mar 1869, may-jun 1871, jan-feb 1874, mar-apr, nov-dec 1891, sep-oct 1892, mar-apr 1894, jan-feb, nov-dec 1904) – Berlin, jul 1 1910-sep 30 1938 (incomplete) – 1 – Inquire at Mikrofilmarchiv for details – gw Misc Inst [943]
NATIONAL-ZEITUNG – Basel, apr 1950-jan 1977 – 1 – Dist. gw Mikrofilm – gw Misc Inst [949]
NATIONAL-ZEITUNG – Berlin. avr-juin 1871 – 1 – fr A.C.R.P.P. [073]
NATIONAL-ZEITUNG – Berlin, Germany. -d. Jan 1911-Dec 1917. 16 reels – 1 – uk British Libr Newspaper [072]
NATIONAL-ZEITUNG – (Cont by: Essener Nachrichten, mar 14, 1945) – Essen. dec 15, 1930-apr 7, 1945 – 44r – 1 – gw Mikrofilm [072]
NATIONAL-ZEITUNG – East Berlin, Germany. 12 Apr 1948-30 Jun 1990 – 97r – 1 – gw Mikrofilm [072]
NATIONAL-ZEITUNG – (Title change: Acht-Uhr-Abendblatt, 1 Jul 1910) – Berlin, Germany. Apr 1848-1910 – 246r – 1 – gw Mikrofilm [072]
THE NATION/LA NACION – Panama City, Panama. 17 Aug 1946-1955; Jan-Jun 1956; Jan-Jun 1956-Sp (La Nacion) – 40r – 1 – us L of C Photodup [072]
NATION'S BUSINESS – (v. 57- 1969- 5,6. v. 58- 1970- 9) – v. 1- 1912- – 1 – us UMI [073]
NATION'S CITIES – v1-16 1963-78 1; v9-16 5,6; v13-16 9 – us UMI [600]
NATION'S CITIES WEEKLY – (v2- 1979- 5,6,9. See also: City Weekly) – v1-. 1978- – 1 – us UMI [073]
NATIONS NOUVELLES – N.S. N.p. v1-22. Oct 1964-Dec 1969 – 34mf – 9 – ne IDC [320]
NATION'S RESTAURANT NEWS – v. 1- 1967- – 1 – us UMI [073]
LES NATIONS RIVALES DANS L'ART. / Chesneau, Ernest – Paris: Didier, 1868. 476p. 5 fiches. (Art Collection) – 9 – 12.00 – fr Bibl Nationale [700]
NATION'S SCHOOLS – (v83-92 1969-74. 5,6. v85-94 1970-74. 9. See also: Nation's Schools and Colleges) – v1-94. 1928-74 – 1 – us UMI [370]
NATION'S SCHOOLS AND COLLEGES – v. 1-2. 1974-75 – 1,5,6,9 – us UMI [370]
NATION'S SCHOOLS REPORT – (v. 2- 1976-5,6,9) – v. 1- 1975- – 1 – us UMI [370]
THE NATIVE AMERICAN – 1900-31. (American Indian Periodicals in the Princeton University Library). 147 fiches – 9 – $610.00 – us UPA [305]
THE NATIVE AMERICAN – Devoted to Indian education. v. 1-31. 13 Jan 1900-6 Jun 1931. Scattered issues wanting – 1 – 208.00 – us L of C Photodup [360]
NATIVE AMERICAN ARTS – n1-2. 1968-69 – 9 – $5.00f – us Ross [740]
NATIVE AMERICAN COLLECTION – (This bibliography describes an historical collection of laws, treaties, and law-related materials pertaining to Native Americans. Individual titles, with some exceptions, are too numerous to list but a free catalogue is available on request from LLMC. Full catalogiung as a major mi microform collection available from OCLC) – 6669mf 1659 titles – 9 – $9,000.00 coll – us L.L.M.C. [340]
NATIVE AMERICAN COLLECTION *see*
- BOARD OF INDIAN APPEALS DECISIONS AND ORDERS
- BOARD OF INDIAN COMMISSIONERS' ANNUAL REPORTS
- COMMISSIONER OF INDIAN AFFAIRS ANNUAL REPORTS
- KAPPLER'S INDIAN AFFAIRS

Native American Rights Fund *see* ANNOUNCEMENTS
NATIVE AMERICANS AND THE NEW DEAL : THE OFFICE FILES OF JOHN COLLIER, 1933-1945 – (With printed guide) – 18r – 1 – $2,245.00 – 1-55655-491-5 – us UPA [324]
NATIVE AMERICANS OF THE PACIFIC NORTHWEST : A PHOTOGRAPHIC RECORD – (Over 4000 images and a 17,000-entry catalog with access through subject headings and tribal, place, and personal names) – 112mf – 9 – $115.00 set – us U.W. Libraries [306]
THE NATIVE AMERICANS REFERENCE COLLECTION, PART 1 : 1840-1900 / Office of Indian Affairs – (With printed guide) – 29r – 1 – $3,350.00 – 1-55655-408-7 – us UPA [975]
THE NATIVE AMERICANS REFERENCE COLLECTION, PART 2 : 1901-1948 – (With printed guide) – 47r – 1 – $5,060.00 – 1-55655-409-5 – us UPA [975]
THE NATIVE COUNCIL SYSTEM WITH SPECIAL REFERENCE TO THE TRANSVAAL LOCAL COUNCILS. / Lille, Abraham J van – Pretoria: J H de Bussy, 1938 – us Res Libr [350]
NATIVE ECONOMIC COMMISSION – 6r – 1 – sa Microfile [960]
THE NATIVE FLOWERS AND FERNS OF THE UNITED STATES / Meehan, T – Boston, 1878-1880. B-7226 1 – 9 – ne IDC [580]
THE NATIVE IN SOUTH AFRICA / Marquard, Leopold; ed by Lewin, Julius – 2nd rev ed. Johannesburg: Witwatersrand UP, 1944 – us Res Libr [305]
NATIVE LIFE IN SOUTH AFRICA, BEFORE AND SINCE THE EUROPEAN WAR AND THE BOER REBELLION / Plaatje, Solomon Tshekisho – 5th ed. London: P.S. King & Son, (1915?). 382p. map,port – 1 – us U.W. Library [960]
NATIVE LIFE IN TRAVANCORE / Mateer, Samuel – London: W.H. Allen, 1883. xvi,434p. illus – 1 – us U.W. Library [950]
THE NATIVE MAGAZINE – Sacramento, CA. 1993 – 2+ r – 1 – $100.00 ($50.00y) – B06053 – us Library Micro [071]
THE NATIVE NETWORK NEWS – Edmonton, Alberta, CN. 1988- – 1r per yr – 1 – $57.00r – cn Commonwealth Micro [072]
NATIVE NEVADAN – Reno, NV. 1975-1985 – 6r – 1 – $300.00 – U04680 – us Library Micro [071]
THE NATIVE NEVADAN – 1965-76. (American Indian Periodicals in the Princeton University Library). 19 fiches – 9 – $85.00 – us UPA [978]
NATIVE PEOPLE – 1969- – 1 – us UMI [073]
NATIVE PEOPLE – Edmonton, CN. 1968-78 – 1 – cn Commonwealth Micro [072]
NATIVE PERSPECTIVE – (Due to poor quality originals, some images are illegible) – Ottawa. v1-2. 1975-78 – 9 – Can$37.00 – cn Micromedia [305]
THE NATIVE PLANTS OF VICTORIA SUCCINCTLY DEFINED / Mueller, Ferdinand Jakob Heinrich von – Melbourne, 1879. pt. 1, 190 pp., 44 figs. B-6466 1 – 9 – ne IDC [580]
NATIVE POLICIES IN AFRICA / Mair, L P – London. 1936. Index. Bibliography. BA-409 2 – 8 – ne IDC [960]
THE NATIVE POLITY OF PONAPE / Riesenberg, Saul H – 1968 – 3mf – 9 – $5.00f – us Ross [970]
NATIVE PRESS – (v1-4 1971-74 Can$115.00. Cont by: Press Independent at v20 no 32 1990) – Yellowknife. v1-19. 1971-89 – 1 – Can$60.00y – cn Micromedia [305]
NATIVE PRESS *see* PRESS INDEPENDENT
THE NATIVE PROBLEM IN AFRICA / Buell, R L – 2v. New York. 1928. BA-285 2 – 8 – ne IDC [960]
NATIVE RELIGIONS AND CHRISTIANITY (CCC204) / Jones, A G – (In Chinese) – [s.l: s.n, 1896] – 1r – 1 – 1984-B500 – us A.T.L.A. [240]
THE NATIVE SON – Winnipeg, Canada. v3 n9. mar 1944-v16 n3. oct 1960 – 1r – 1 – Can$30.00 – cn Can Microfilming [072]
Native Sons and Daughters of Kansas *see* ESSAYS SUBMITTED IN WRITING CONTEST
THE NATIVE STATES OF THE GOLD COAST : HISTORY AND CONSTITUTION / Welman, C W – London, 1925-30 – us Res Libr [960]
NATIVE TRIBES OF SOUTH EAST AUSTRALIA / Howitt, A W – London: Macmillan & Co., 1904 – 14mf – 9 – A$36.00 – at State Libr Vic [306]
THE NATIVE TRIBES OF THE TRANSVAAL / Massie, R H – London: HMSO, 1905 – us Res Libr [305]
NATIVE URBAN EMPLOYMENT : A STUDY OF JOHANNESBURG EMPLOYMENT RECORDS, 1936-1944 / Johannesburg. University of Witwatersrand. Dept of Commerce – Johannesburg: Industrial Research Section, 1948 – us Res Libr [331]
NATIVE VOICE – (v1-12 1946-58, 13-22 1959-68 Can$115.00. v 1-6 1970-76 Can$85.00. v 7-49 197 8-96 Can$60.00y. Missing 1966 and 1977. Also, 1964 and 1978 are incomplete. Vol numbering changed by publ in 1994: v48 follows v21) – Vancouver. v1-49. 1946/47-1995/96 – 1 – Price varies – cn Micromedia [305]
Nativelle, Pierre *see* NOUVEAU TRAITE D'ARCHITECTURE.
THE NATIVES OF THE NORTHERN TERRITORIES OF THE GOLD COAST : THEIR CUSTOMS, RELIGION AND FOLKLORE / Cardinall, Allan Wolsey – London: Routledge, New York: Dutton, [1920] – us Res Libr [305]
THE NATIVES OF THE NORTHERN TERRITORIES OF THE GOLD COAST: THEIR CUSTOMS, RELIGION AND FOLKLORE / Cardinell, A W – London. 1925. BA-358 2 – 8 – ne IDC [306]
NATO IN QUEST OF COHESION / ed by Cerny, Karl H & Briefs, Henry W – Praeger Hoover, 1965. 488 pp – 1 – $35.00r – us Hoover Inst Photo [327]
NATO LETTER / North Atlantic Treaty Organization – (See also: North Atlantic Treaty Organization. NATO Review) – v1-19 no 4 1953-1971 – 1 – us UMI [327]
NATO REVIEW / North Atlantic Treaty Organization – (See also: North Atlantic Treaty Organization. NATO Letter) – v19-1971- 1; v26- 5,6,9 – us UMI [327]
Natow, Annette B *see* JOURNAL OF NUTRITION FOR THE ELDERLY
NATRONA COUNTY TRIBUNE – Casper. Wyoming. 1897-1919 – 1 – us UMI [071]
NATS BULLETIN / National Association of Teachers of Singing – 1944- 1; 1969- 5,6; 1977- 9 – us UMI [780]
Natschke, Birgit *see* ASPEKTE DES PERSONALMANAGEMENTS BEI DER EINFUEHRUNG UND DURCHSETZUNG VON GANZHEITLICH ORIENTIERTEN QUALITAETSSICHERUNGSSYSTEMEN NACH DIN ISO 9000FF
Natsentov, D I *see* IZUCHENIE RAIONA I POSTROENIE GODOVOGO OPERATIVNO-KHOZIAISTVENNOGO PLANA SEL'SKOKHOZIAISTVENNOGO KREDITNOGO TOVARISHCHESTVA
NATSIONAL NYI KAPITAL 5 EKONOMIKE INDONEZII / Pakhomova, Liudmila Fedorovna – SE-11,563 1. 1966 – 9 – ne IDC [338]
NATSIONALISTY V 3-EI GOSUDARSTVENNOI DUME – Spb., 1912. 327p – 3mf – 9 – ne IDC [320]
NATSIONALIZATSIIA BANKOV V SSSR / Atlas, M S – Moscow, 1948. 216p. BR-9029 1 – 9 – ne IDC [336]
NATSIONAL'NA TRIBUNA – (In Ukrainian. Backfile, through 1998 1r per y $85y) – USA, 1999- – 1r per y – 1 – $80.00 standing order – us Ross [071]

NATSIONAL'NI MENSHOSTI RADIANS'KOI UKRAINI, ZBIRNIK NATSMENOZNAVSTVA – Kiev, 1931 – 1r – 1 – us Ross [306]

NATSIONALNYE VOPROSY NA INORODCHESKIKH OKRAINAKH ROSSII : SKHEMA POLITICHESKO I PROGRAMMY / Evreinov, Grigorii Aleksandrovich – S.-Peterburg: Tip. A. Benke, 1908 – 1 – CSUX89-B3775 – us Hoover Inst Photo [320]

NATSIONALNYI VOPROSI AVTONOMIIA / Hrushevskyi, Mykhailo – S.-Peterburg: Tip. t-va "Obshchestvennaia polza", 1907 – 1 – CSUX89-B1085 – us Hoover Inst Photo [320]

NATSIONALNYIA PROBLEMY – Dvukhnedel'nyi zhurnal. nr. 1-4. M. 1915. BR-4137 2 – 8 – ne IDC [073]

NATSIONAL-REVOLIUTSIONER = LE NATIONAL-REVOLUTIONNAIRE – (Includes c.1: 1927:Jan.1-Feb.15, Apr.15) – Paris: Izd T Sentr. kom-ta Natsional-Revoliutsionnago soi uza, 1927- – 1 – CSUXANS0527-S – us Hoover Inst Photo [947]

NATSYIANAL'NAIA EKANAMICHNAIA GAZETA – (Backfile through 1998 $85r) – Belarus, 1999- – 2r per y standing order – 1 – us Ross [072]

DIE NATUERLICHEN PFLANZENFAMILIEN / ed by Engler, H G A & Prantl, K – Leipzig, 1887-1915 – 174mf – 9 – ne IDC [580]

NATUN ASAMIYA – (Assamese language) – Gauhati, India. Jul-Sept 1966 – 1r – 1 – us L of C Photodup [072]

DIE NATUR UND DER DETERMINISUMUS DES WILLENS BEI LEIBNIZ : EIN BEITRAG ZUR GESCHICHTE DER LOESUNG DES PROBLEMS DER WILLENSFREIHEIT / Bugarski, Georg M – Leipzig, 1897 – 1mf – DM48.00 – 3-8267-3077-1 – gw Hänsel [120]

NATUR UND GEIST ALS DIE WURZELN DES LEBENS UND DER KUNST / Huch, Ricarda – Muenchen: E Reinhardt, [1914?] – 1r – 1 – us U.W. Library [100]

NATUR UND GEIST IN GOETHES FAUST / Hertz, Gottfried Wilhelm – (Includes bibliographical references. "Das Buch bietet eine abgerundete Zusammenfassung meiner in den Jahren 1908-1930 erschienenen Aufsaetze) – Frankfurt am Main: M Diesterweg, 1931 – 1 – us U.W. Library [430]

NATUR UND GEIST: NACH DER AUFFASSUNG DES ALTEN TESTAMENTS / Koeberle, Justus – Muenchen: C.H. Beck, 1901. 1 fiche – 9 – us A.T.L.A. [240]

NATUR UND UEBERNATUR : DAS DOGMA VON DER GNADE UND DIE THEOLOGISCHE FRAGE DER GEGENWART: EINE KRITIK DER KUHN'SCHEN THEOLOGIE / Schaezler, Constantin, Freiherr von – (Includes bibliographical references) – Mainz: Franz Kirchheim, 1865 – 2mf – 9 – 0-8370-7018-X – 1986-1018 – us A.T.L.A. [210]

NATURA OGGI – 1991-1995 – 1r per y – 5,6 – Sfr401.00 – sz Infoprint [945]

NATURAE NOVITATES : BIBLIOGRAPHIE NEUER ERSCHEINUNGEN ALLER LAENDER AUF DEM GEBIETE DER NATURGESCHICHTE UND DER EXAKTEN WISSENSCHAFTEN – Berlin. v1-65. 1879-1943 – 318mf – 9 – ne IDC [015]

NATURAL AND SOCIAL MORALS / Read, Carveth – (Includes index) – London: Adam and Charles Black; New York: Macmillan [distributor], 1909 – 1mf – 9 – 0-8370-6341-8 – 1986-0341 – us A.T.L.A. [170]

NATURAL ARRANGEMENT OF BRITISH PLANTS ACCORDING TO THEIR RELATIONS TO EACH OTHER, AS POINTED OUT BY JUSSIEU, DE CANDOLLE, BROWN / Gray, S F A – London. 1821. B-96 2 – 8 – ne IDC [580]

NATURAL BANK CURRENCY AND NATIONAL BANK CURRENCY / Dean, William B – 1901 – 9 – 1.00f – at Libertarian Micro [335]

THE NATURAL CAPABILITIES OF THE COLONY OF VICTORIA, CONSIDERED IN REFERENCE TO INDIGENOUS OR INTRODUCED VEGETATION / Mueller, Ferdinand Jakob Heinrich von – Melbourne. 1875. B-8066 1 – 9 – ne IDC [580]

(NATURAL DE FUENTE DE CANTOS) EN NOTAS DE BIBLIOGRAFIA FRANCISCANA / Lopez, Atanasio & Guerro, Alonso – Archivo Ibero Americano, 1932 – 1 – sp Bibl Santa Ana [240]

NATURAL ELEMENTS OF REVEALED THEOLOGY / Matheson, George – London: James Nisbet, 1881. 1 fiche – 9 – us A.T.L.A. [240]

NATURAL GAS – 1977 – 1,5,6,9 – us UMI [660]

NATURAL GAS – v1- Aug 1984- – 1,5,6,9 – us UMI [660]

NATURAL HISTORY – (v. 78- 1969- 5,6. v. 79- 1970- 9) – v. 1- 1900- – 1 – us UMI [574]

NATURAL HISTORY. MOLLUSCA / Gosse, P H – Z-541 2. 1854 – 8 – ne IDC [590]

NATURAL HISTORY OF ATHEISM / Blackie, John Stuart – New York: Scribner, Armstrong, 1878. 1 fiche – 9 – us A.T.L.A. [240]

THE NATURAL HISTORY OF BARBADOS / Hughes, Griffith – London, 1750 – 1r – 1 – us Ross [500]

THE NATURAL HISTORY OF BRITISH BIRDS / Donovan, E – 10 v. 1794 -1819). Z-2076 2. Lacking v. 5-10. 1798-1819 – 8 – ne IDC [590]

THE NATURAL HISTORY OF BRITISH FISHES, INCLUDING SCIENTIFIC AND GENERAL DESCRIPTIONS OF THE MOST INTERESTING SPECIES, AND AN EXTENSIVE SELECTION OF ACCURATELY FINISHED COLOURED PLATES / Donovan, E – 2125 2. 5 v. 1802-1808 – 8 – ne IDC [590]

THE NATURAL HISTORY OF BRITISH INSECTS / Donovan, E – London,(1804) 1793-1813.v1-16.Z-1191/2 – 8 – ne IDC [590]

NATURAL HISTORY OF CAROLINA, FLORIDA AND THE BAHAMA ISLANDS / Catesby, M – 2v. London. 1730-31-1743-47. B-6454 2 – 8 – ne IDC [574]

THE NATURAL HISTORY OF MAN; COMPRISING INQUIRIES INTO THE MODIFYING INFLUENCE OF PHYSICAL AND MORAL AGENCIES ON THE DIFFERENT TRIBES OF THE HUMAN FAMILY / Prichard, James Cowles – With 36 coloured and 4 plain illustrations engraved on steel, and 90 engravings on wood. London, 1843 – 1 – us U.W. Library [573]

THE NATURAL HISTORY OF MANY CURIOUS AND UNCOMMON ZOOPHYTES / Ellis, J & Solander, D – London. 1786. BZ-2244 1 – 9 – ne IDC [590]

A NATURAL HISTORY OF NEW AND RARE FERNS / Lowe, E J – London, 1862. 192 pp., 72 pls. B-7215 1 – 9 – ne IDC [580]

THE NATURAL HISTORY OF PRINCE EDWARD ISLAND / Bain, Francis – Charlottetown: G. Haszard, 1890.02220.(Pre-1900 Canadiana) – 9 – cn C.I.H.M. [574]

THE NATURAL HISTORY OF RELIGIOUS FEELING : A QUESTION OF MIRACLES IN THE SOUL : AN INDUCTIVE STUDY / Cornelison, Isaac A – New York: G.P. Putnam, 1911 – 1mf – us A.T.L.A. [210]

THE NATURAL HISTORY OF THE BIBLE / Tristram, Henry Baker – 10th ed London, 1911 – 9mf – 8 – ne Slangenburg [220]

THE NATURAL HISTORY OF THE BRITISH ENTOMOSTRACA / Baird, W – Ray Society. 1850 – 1 £35.00 7 £35.00 – uk Microform Academic [590]

A NATURAL HISTORY OF THE CRINOIDEA / Miller, J S – Z-239 2. 1821 – 8 – ne IDC [580]

THE NATURAL HISTORY OF THE FISHES OF GUIANA / Schomburgk, R H – 2626 2. 1841-1843 – 8 – ne IDC [590]

THE NATURAL HISTORY OF THE HUMAN TEETH / Hunter, J – M-61. 1771 – 9 – ne IDC [611]

NATURAL HISTORY OF THE MAMMALIA OF INDIA AND CEYLON / Sterndale, R A – Z 290 2. 1884 – 8 – ne IDC [590]

THE NATURAL HISTORY OF THE MARKETABLE MARINE FISHES OF THE BRITISH ISLANDS / Cunningham, J T – Z-2096 2. 1896 – 8 – ne IDC [590]

A NATURAL HISTORY OF THE NESTS AND EGGS OF BRITISH BIRDS / Morris, F O – Z 1985. 3 v. Ed. 4. 1896 – 9 – ne IDC [590]

NATURAL HISTORY OF VICTORIA, PRODROMUS OF THE ZOOLOGY OF VICTORIA / Maccoy, F – Melbourne, 1885-1890. Decas. 1-20. B-2658 2 – 8 – ne IDC [590]

THE NATURAL HISTORY REVIEW: A QUARTERLY JOURNAL OF BIOLOGICAL SCIENCE – Dublin and London, 1854-65 – 3 – us Readex [574]

Natural History Society of Glasgow *see* TRANSACTIONS AND PROCEEDINGS

Natural History Society of Northumberland, Durham, and Newcastle-upon-Tyne *see* TRANSACTIONS

NATURAL IMMUNITY – v1-. 1981- – 1,5,9 – us UMI [616]

NATURAL KNOWLEDGE IN SOCIAL CONTEXT: THE JOURNALS OF THOMAS ARCHER HIRST / Hirst, Thomas Archer – By W.H. Brock and R.M. MacLeod. Diaries of the mathematician. 30 fiches. Printed booklet with biographical essay and bibliography – 9 – £205.00 – uk Mansell Publ [920]

NATURAL LANGUAGE & LINGUISTIC THEORY – v1-. 1983- – 1,5,6,9 – us UMI [400]

NATURAL LANGUAGE TERM LIST – v78-81; 86-89. 1973. Includes manual – 6,9 – $40.00 – us Chemical [540]

NATURAL LAW AND LEGAL PRACTICE : LECTURES DELIVERED AT THE LAW SCHOOL OF GEORGETOWN UNIVERSITY / Holaind, Rene I – N.Y.: Benziger Bros, 1899 – 4mf – 9 – $6.00 – LLMC 95-201 – us L.L.M.C. [340]

NATURAL LAW FORUM *see* – AMERICAN JOURNAL OF JURISPRUDENCE

NATURAL LAW IN THE SPIRITUAL WORLD / Drummond, Henry – New York: Lovell, Coryell & Co., 1884? – xxiv/414p – 1 – us U.W. Library [190]

THE NATURAL LAW OF MONEY: THE SUCCESSIVE STEPS IN THE GROWTH OF MONEY TRACED FROM THE DAYS OF BARTER TO THE INTRODUCTION OF THE MODERN CLEARING-HOUSE, AND MONETARY PRINCIPLES EXAMINED IN THEIR RELATION TO PAST AND PRESENT LEGISLATION / Brough, William – New York, London: G. Putnam's Sons, 1894. 03726. (Pre-1900 Canadiana) – 9 – cn C.I.H.M. [336]

THE NATURAL ORDER OF CISTUS / Sweet, R – 6473. 1825-1830 – 9 – ne IDC [580]

NATURAL PRODUCT LETTERS / Atta-ur-Rahman – 1,5,9 – us Gordon [540]

NATURAL RELIGION BY THE AUTHOR OF "ECCE HOMO" / Seeley, John Robert – 3rd ed. Boston:Roberts, 1886 – 1mf – 9 – 0-8370-5212-2 – 1985-3212 – us A.T.L.A. [210]

NATURAL RELIGION IN SERMONS / Blake, James Vila – Chicago: Charles H Kerr, 1892 – 1mf – 9 – 0-8370-2364-5 – 1985-0364 – us A.T.L.A. [210]

NATURAL RESOURCE AND ENVIRONMENT ABA) *see* NATURAL RESOURCES LAWYER (ABA)

NATURAL RESOURCES AND DEVELOPMENT POTENTIAL IN THE SOUTHERN PROVINCES OF THE SUDAN; A PRELIMINARY REPORT, 1954 / Sudan. Southern Development Investigation Team – 2v. 1955. BNE-7685 1 – 9 – ne IDC [333]

NATURAL RESOURCES AND ENVIRONMENT (ABA) – (Supersedes Natural Resources Lawyer (ABA)) – v1-10. 1985-96 – 9 – $171.00 set – us Hein [340]

NATURAL RESOURCES AND THE HUMAN ENVIRONMENT FOR FOOD AND AGRICULTURE – 1980 – 70p – it F.A.O. [333]

NATURAL RESOURCES AND THE HUMAN ENVIRONMENT FOR FOOD AND AGRICULTURE IN AFRICA – 1986 – 89p – it F.A.O. [333]

NATURAL RESOURCES JOURNAL – (v1-24 1961-84 on reel $335.00. v25-33 1985-95 on mf $257.00) – University of New Mexico. v1-35. 1961-95 – 5,6,9 – $592.00 set – us Hein [333]

NATURAL RESOURCES LAWYER (ABA) – (Includes index v1-15 1968-83 (all publ). Superseded by Natural Resource and Environment (ABA)) – v1-17. 1968-85 – 9 – $250.00 set – us Hein [340]

NATURAL RESOURCES LAWYER (ABA) *see* NATURAL RESOURCES AND ENVIRONMENT (ABA)

NATURAL RESOURCES OF ALASKA – 1967 – 9 – $5.00f – us Ross [333]

NATURAL RESOURCES OF ARIZONA – 1963 – 9 – $5.00f – us Ross [333]

NATURAL RESOURCES OF CALIFORNIA – 1967 – 9 – $5.00f – us Ross [333]

NATURAL RESOURCES OF COLORADO – 1963 – 9 – $5.00f – us Ross [333]

NATURAL RESOURCES OF IDAHO – 1965 – 9 – $5.00f – us Ross [333]

NATURAL RESOURCES OF INDIANA – 1967 – 9 – $5.00f – us Ross [333]

NATURAL RESOURCES OF MARYLAND – 1967 – 9 – $5.00f – us Ross [333]

NATURAL RESOURCES OF MINNESOTA – 1969 – 9 – $5.00f – us Ross [333]

NATURAL RESOURCES OF MONTANA – 1964 – 9 – $5.00f – us Ross [333]

NATURAL RESOURCES OF NEVADA – 1964 – 9 – $5.00f – us Ross [333]

NATURAL RESOURCES OF NEW MEXICO – 1964 – 9 – $5.00f – us Ross [333]

NATURAL RESOURCES OF NORTH DAKOTA – 1968 – 9 – $5.00f – us Ross [333]

NATURAL RESOURCES OF OHIO – 1964 – 9 – $5.00f – us Ross [333]

NATURAL RESOURCES OF OKLAHOMA – 1969 – 9 – $5.00f – us Ross [333]

NATURAL RESOURCES OF OREGON – 1964 – 9 – $5.00f – us Ross [333]

NATURAL RESOURCES OF PENNSYLVANIA – 1968 – 9 – $5.00f – us Ross [333]

NATURAL RESOURCES OF SOUTH DAKOTA – 1967 – 9 – $5.00f – us Ross [333]

NATURAL RESOURCES OF UTAH – 1965 – 9 – $5.00f – us Ross [333]

NATURAL RESOURCES OF WASHINGTON – 1970 – 9 – $5.00f – us Ross [333]

NATURAL RESOURCES OF WYOMING – 1966 – 9 – $5.00f – us Ross [333]

NATURAL SCIENCE – A Monthly Review of Scientific Progress. v. 1-15. Mar 1892-Dec 1899 – 1 – us UMI [500]

NATURAL SCIENCE IN SCHOOLS – 1963- 1; 1975- 5,6,9 – us UMI [073]

NATURAL SCIENCE IN SCHOOLS – v20, no.3-. Autumn 1982- – 1,5,6,9 – us UMI [073]

A NATURAL SYSTEM OF BOTANY / Lindley, J – ed. 2. London. 1836. B-6025 2 – 8 – ne IDC [580]

NATURAL THEOLOGY / Bascom, John – New York: G.P. Putnam, c1880 – 1mf – us A.T.L.A. [210]

NATURAL THEOLOGY / Bascom, John – New York: G.P. Putnam's Sons, 1880 – xiii/306p – 1 – us U.W. Library [240]

NATURAL THEOLOGY / Lee, Luther – 1866 – 9 – us A.T.L.A. [240]

NATURAL THEOLOGY : OR, EVIDENCES OF THE EXISTENCE AND ATTRIBUTES OF THE DEITY, COLLECTED FROM THE APPEARANCES OF NATURE / Paley, William – London: Printed for R. Faulder, 1802 – 1 roll – 1 – 1-55879-668-1 – uk Libr Preservation [290]

NATURAL THEOLOGY : OR, RATIONAL THEISM / Valentine, Milton – (Includes index) – Chicago: S C Griggs, 1885 – 1mf – 9 – 0-8370-5613-6 – 1985-3613 – us A.T.L.A. [210]

NATURAL THEOLOGY / Stokes, George Gabriel – London: Adam & Charles Black, 1893. 1 fiche – 9 – us A.T.L.A. [240]

NATURAL THEOLOGY AND MODERN THOUGHT / Kennedy, James Houghton – London: Hodder & Stoughton, 1891 – 1mf – 9 – us A.T.L.A. [240]

THE NATURAL THEOLOGY OF NATURAL BEAUTY / Tyrwhitt, Richard St John – (Includes bibliographical references) – London: SPCK, [1882] – 1mf – 9 – 0-8370-5595-4 – 1985-3595 – us A.T.L.A. [210]

THE NATURAL WAY IN MORAL TRAINING : FOUR MODES OF NURTURE / Bois, Patterson du – (Includes index) – 3rd ed. New York: Fleming H Revell, c1903 – 1mf – 9 – 0-8370-8568-3 – 1986-2568 – us A.T.L.A. [370]

NATURAL WEALTH OF CALIFORNIA / Cronise, Titus Fey – CA, 1868 – 1r – 1 – $50.00 – B40140 – us Library Micro [978]

NATURALEZA / Sociedad Mexicana de Historia Naturale – Mexico. S.1 v1-7; S.2 v1-3; S.3 v1-4 1869-1912. – 122mf – 9 – ne IDC [500]

NATURALEZA DE LA AGUA TERMAL AZIDA DE PUERTOLLANO / Vinzani del Aguila, F – Madrid, 1685 – 1mf – 9 – sp Cultura [615]

NATURALEZA DEL PERONISMO / Fayt, Carlos S – Buenos Aires: Viracocha, c1967 – 1 – CSUXADJ3438-B – us Hoover Inst Photo [320]

NATURALEZA TRIUNFANTE Y CRISOL DE MESENTERICAS... / Cerdan, F – Valencia, 1745 – 2mf – 9 – sp Cultura [600]

LA NATURALISATION / Bickart, E – Paris, 1890 – 2mf – 9 – ILM-3153/1 – ne IDC [327]

LA NATURALISATION A ATHENES / Caillemer, E – Paris, Caen, 1880 – 1mf – 1 – ILM-3331/1 – ne IDC [327]

NATURALISM AND SPIRITUALISM : SIX DISCOURSES ON THOSE FORMS OF THEISTICAL INFIDELITY / Byrne, James – Dublin: Hodges, Smith, 1856 – 1mf – us A.T.L.A. [140]
NATURALISM OR IDEALISM? : THE NOBEL LECTURE / Eucken, Rudolf – Cambridge: W. Heffer, 1912 – 1mf – us A.T.L.A. [140]
DER NATURALISMUS UND SEINE STELLUNG IN DER KUNSTENTWICKLUNG / Valentin, Veit – Kiel: Lipsius und Tischer, 1891 – 1r – 1 – us U.W. Library [700]
A NATURALIST IN THE MAGDALEN ISLANDS: GIVING A DESCRIPTION OF THE ISLANDS AND LIST OF THE BIRDS TAKEN THERE: WITH OTHER ORNITHOLOGICAL NOTES / Cory, C B – Boston: Mudge, 1878. 00253. (Pre-1900 Canadiana) – 9 – cn C.I.H.M. [971]
O NATURALISTA NO RIO AMAZONAS, VOL. 1 / Bates, Henry Walter – Sao Paulo, 1944 – 7mf – 8 – ne Slangenburg [580]
LE NATURALISTE CANADIEN : BULLETIN DE RECHERCHES, OBSERVATIONS ET DECOUVERTES SE RAPPORTANT A L'HISTOIRE NATURELLE DU CANADA – Quebec: imprime par C Darveau, 1868-. SEM16P314 – 14r – 5 – Can$552.00 – cn Bibl Nat [574]
NATURALISTE CANADIEN – 1868- 1; 1976- 5,6,9 – us UMI [500]
LE NATURALISTE. JOURNAL DES ECHANGES ET DES NOUVELLES *see* PETITES NOUVELLES ENTOMOLOGIQUES
NATURALISTES BELGES – 1920- 1; 1972- 5,6; 1975- 9 – us UMI [073]
NATURALISTISCHE UND RELIGIOESE WELTANSICHT / Otto, Rudolf – (Includes bibliographical references & index) – Tuebingen: J C B Mohr, 1909 – 1mf – 9 – 0-8370-4649-1 – 1985-2649 – us A.T.L.A. [210]
THE NATURALIST'S MISCELLANY, OR COLORED FIGURES OF NATURAL OBJECTS, DRAWN AND DESCRIBED FROM NATURE / ed by Shaw, G & Nodder, F P – (Index in Latin and English) – London. 1789, 1790-1813. 24v. – 124mf – 8 – ne IDC [760]
THE NATURALIST'S NOTE BOOK...A MONTHLY RECORD OF ANECDOTES, THEORIES, AND FACTS RELATING TO NATURAL SCIENCE. – 1868-69. v. 1-3; 1870; Series 2, v. 1 – 3 – us Readex [574]
LA NATURALIZACON EN LOS ESTADOS UNIDOS / Flores, A – Nueva York, 1881 – 1mf – 1 – ILM-3155/1 – ne IDC [327]
NATURALIZATION / Daly, C P – New York, 1860 – 1mf – 1 – ILM-3388/1 – ne IDC [327]
NATURALIZATION – ALIENS/MINORS / Ottawa County. Ohio. Probate Court – 1904-1906 – 1r – 1 – $32.50r – us Archival [324]
NATURALIZATION AND ALLEGIANCE / Abott – 5mf – 9 – ILM-3807/1 – ne IDC [340]
NATURALIZATION CERTIFICATES / Ottawa County. Ohio. Probate Court – 1910-1927 – 1r – 1 – $32.50r – us Archival [324]
NATURALIZATION FILES / Van Wert County. Ohio. Common Pleas. Civil Division – 1844-1895 – 1r – 1 – $32.50r – us Archival [324]
NATURALIZATION – MINORS / Lucas County. Ohio. Probate Court – 1885-1906 – 5r – 1 – $32.50r – us Archival [324]
NATURALIZATION OF FOREIGN PROTESTANTS IN AMERICA & WEST INDIAN COLONIES – Ed. by M.S. Giuseppi, 1921. Item O. 195p. Indexed. SW16-0076 – 5 – us A.G.L.L. [920]
NATURALIZATION RECORDS / Allen County. Ohio. Common Pleas. Civil Division – 1921-41 – 1r – 1 – $32.50r – us Archival [978]
NATURALIZATION RECORDS / Crawford County. Ohio. Clerk of Courts – 1907-1929 – 1r – 1 – $32.50r – us Archival [324]
NATURALIZATION RECORDS / Defiance County. Ohio. Common Pleas. Civil Division – 1872-1906 – 2r – 1 – $32.50r – us Archival [324]
NATURALIZATION RECORDS / Defiance County, Ohio. Probate Court – 1845-1929 – 1r – 1 – $32.50r – us Archival [324]
NATURALIZATION RECORDS / Fulton County. Ohio. Common Pleas. Civil Division – 1880-1903 – 2r – 1 – $32.50r – us Archival [324]
NATURALIZATION RECORDS / Hancock County. Ohio. Common Pleas. Civil Division – 1885-1895 – 2r – 1 – $32.50r – us Archival [324]
NATURALIZATION RECORDS / Henry County. Ohio. Common Pleas. Civil Division – 1907-1929 – 1r – 1 – $32.50r – us Archival [324]
NATURALIZATION RECORDS / Lucas County. Ohio. Common Pleas. Civil Division – 1906-1929 – 23r – 1 – $32.50r – us Archival [324]
NATURALIZATION RECORDS / Ottawa County. Ohio. Common Pleas. Civil Division – 1860-1903 – 3r – 1 – $32.50r – us Archival [324]
NATURALIZATION RECORDS / Ottawa County. Ohio. Probate Court – 1910-1940s – 1r – 1 – $32.50r – us Archival [324]
NATURALIZATION RECORDS / Paulding County. Ohio. Probate Court – 1853-1930 – 2r – 1 – $32.50r – us Archival [324]
NATURALIZATION RECORDS / Putnam County. Ohio. Common Pleas. Civil Division – 1861-1944 – 3r – 1 – $32.50r – us Archival [920]
NATURALIZATION RECORDS / Van Wert County. Ohio. Common Pleas. Civil Division – 1860-1902 – 2r – 1 – $32.50r – us Archival [324]
NATURALIZATION RECORDS / Wood County. Ohio. Probate Court – 1856-1960 – 3r – 1 – $32.50r – us Archival [324]
NATURALIZATION RECORDS CREATED BY THE U.S. DISTRICT COURTS IN COLORADO, 1877-1952 – 79r – 1 – M1192 – us Nat'l Archives [340]
NATURALIZATION RECORDS – LOOSE / Lucas County. Ohio. Probate Court – 1844-1906 – 27r – 1 – $32.50r – us Archival [324]
NATURALIZATION RECORDS OF THE U.S. DISTRICT COURTS FOR THE STATE OF ALASKA, 1900-1924 – 5r – 1 – M1539 – us Nat'l Archives [340]
NATURALIZATION RECORDS OF THE U.S. DISTRICT COURTS FOR THE STATE OF MONTANA, 1891-1929 – 3r – 1 – M1538 – us Nat'l Archives [340]
NATURALIZATION RECORDS OF U.S. DISTRICT COURTS IN THE SOUTHEAST, 1790-1958 – 107r – 1 – M1547 – us Nat'l Archives [340]
NATURALIZATION RECORDS/DECLARATION / Lucas County. Ohio. Common Pleas. Civil Division – 1906-1952 – 15r – 1 – $32.50r – us Archival [324]
NATURALIZATIONS : DECLARATIONS – 1879-1929 – 3r – 1 – $32.50r – us Archival [978]
NATURALIZATIONS : PETITION / Allen County. Ohio. Common Pleas. Civil Division – 1956-74 – 1r – 1 – $32.50r – us Archival [978]
NATURALIZATIONS, ALIENS / Hancock County. Ohio. Common Pleas. Civil Division – 1859-1881 – 1r – 1 – $32.50r – us Archival [324]
NATURALIZATIONS, DECLARATIONS / Crawford County. Ohio. Clerk of Courts – 1906-1929 – 2r – 1 – $32.50r – us Archival [324]
NATURALIZATIONS, DECLARATIONS / Defiance County. Ohio. Common Pleas. Civil Division – 1885-1903 – 2r – 1 – $32.50r – us Archival [324]
NATURALIZATIONS, DECLARATIONS / Fulton County. Ohio. Common Pleas. Civil Division – 1879-1906 – 2r – 1 – $32.50r – us Archival [324]
NATURALIZATIONS, DECLARATIONS / Hancock County. Ohio. Common Pleas. Civil Division – 1863-1905 – 2r – 1 – $32.50r – us Archival [324]
NATURALIZATIONS, DECLARATIONS / Henry County. Ohio. Common Pleas. Civil Division – 1906-1929 – 1r – 1 – $32.50r – us Archival [324]
NATURALIZATIONS, DECLARATIONS / Ottawa County. Ohio. Common Pleas. Civil Division – 1864-1903 – 2r – 1 – $32.50r – us Archival [324]
NATURALIZATIONS, DECLARATIONS / Van Wert County. Ohio. Common Pleas. Civil Division – 1852-1904 – 2r – 1 – $32.50r – us Archival [324]
NATURALIZATIONS, DECLARATIONS / Wood County. Ohio. Probate Court – 1859-1960 – 3r – 1 – $32.50r – us Archival [324]
NATURALIZATIONS. DECLARATIONS / Sandusky County. Ohio. Probate Court – (Some issues missing) – 1830-1872 – 3r – 1 – $32.50r – us Archival [324]
NATURALIZATIONS, MINORS / Hancock County. Ohio. Common Pleas. Civil Division – 1860-1903 – 2r – 1 – $32.50r – us Archival [324]
NATURALIZATIONS, SOLDIERS / Hancock County. Ohio. Common Pleas. Civil Division – 1896-1906 – 1r – 1 – $32.50r – us Archival [324]
NATURALIZATIONS, STUB BOOKS / Crawford County. Ohio. Clerk of Courts – 1907-1928 – 1r – 1 – $32.50r – us Archival [324]
NATURANSCHAUUNG UND MALERISCHES EMPFINDEN BEI WILHELM HEINSE / Sprengel, Hans Rolf – (Includes bibliographical references) – Frankfurt am Main: M Diesterweg, 1930 – 1r – 1 – us U.W. Library [700]
NATURE (1068 6,6. 1974- 9) – England. 1869- – 1 – us UMI [500]
NATURE / Emerson, Ralph Waldo – 1836 – 9 – 10.00 – us Scholars' Facs [840]
NATURE – France. 1952-55 – 1 – us UMI [500]
NATURE : THE UTILITY OF RELIGION, AND THEISM / Mill, John Stuart – London: Longmans, Green, Reader, and Dyer, 1874 – 1 roll – 1 – 1-55879-569-3 – uk Libr Preservation [100]
NATURE – v. 1-204. 1869-1964 – 1,5,6 – us Princeton Micro [574]
NATURE – v157-160. A weekly journal of Science. London: McMillan, 1946-47. 253/2 – 8 – ne IDC [574]
NATURE AND CHRIST : A REVELATION OF THE UNSEEN / Beet, Joseph Agar – New York: Eaton & Mains, 1896 – 1mf – 9 – 0-8370-2249-5 – 1985-0249 – us A.T.L.A. [210]
NATURE AND DEITY : A STUDY OF RELIGION AS A QUEST OF THE IDEAL / Meakin, Frederick – Chicago: Charles H Kerr, 1895 – 1mf – 9 – 0-8370-4371-9 – 1985-2371 – us A.T.L.A. [210]
THE NATURE AND EXTENT OF DIVINE INSPIRATION...DEDUCED FROM...THE N.T / Row, Charles Adolphus – London: Longmans, Green, 1864. 2 fiches – 9 – us A.T.L.A. [240]
THE NATURE AND FITNESS OF THINGS : OR, THE PERFECTIONS OF GOD A STANDING RULE TO TRY ALL DOCTRINES AND EXPERIENCE BY,... / Gurney, T – London, 2nd ed 1752 – 1mf – 9 – MP-298/1 – ne IDC [240]
NATURE AND MANAGEMENT OF TROPICAL PEAT SOILS – 1988 – 175p – it F.A.O. [631]
NATURE AND METHOD OF REVELATION / Fisher, George Park – New York: Scribner, 1890. 1 fiche – 9 – us A.T.L.A. [240]
NATURE AND PROPERTIES OF WOOL / Luccock – 1805 – 7 – uk Microform Academic [680]
THE NATURE AND REALITY OF RELIGION: A CONTROVERSY BETWEEN...HARRISON AND...SPENCER / Harrison, Frederic – New York: D. Appleton, 1885. 1 fiche – 9 – us A.T.L.A. [240]
THE NATURE AND STATUS OF HEALTH-PROMOTION PROGRAMS IN NOVA SCOTIAN GOODS-PRODUCING INDUSTRIES / Matthews, Margaret & Belzer, Edwin G – 1988 – 3mf – 9 – $12.00 – us Microform Publ [613]
NATURE AND THE BIBLE : A COURSE OF LECTURES DELIVERED IN NEW YORK IN DEC 1874 / Dawson, John William – (Includes appendixes) – New York:Robert Carter, 1875 – 1mf – 9 – 0-8370-2853-1 – 1985-0853 – us A.T.L.A. [210]
NATURE AND THE SUPERNATURAL, AS TOGETHER CONSTITUTING THE ONE SYSTEM OF GOD / Bushnell, Horace – 2d ed. 1858 – 1 – us A.T.L.A. [140]
THE NATURE AND VALUE OF JURISPRUDENCE / Chan-toon – 2nd ed. London: Reeves & Turner, 1889 – 3mf – 9 – $4.50 – LLMC 95-193 – us L.L.M.C. [340]
NATURE AND WORTH OF THE SCIENCE OF CHURCH HISTORY : AN INAUGURAL ADDRESS / Smith, Henry Boyton – Andover: W.F. Draper, 1851 – 1mf – us A.T.L.A. [240]
LA NATURE ET DIVERSITE DES POISSONS / Belon, P – 2668 2. 1555 – 8 – ne IDC [590]
THE NATURE, FOLLY, SIN AND DANGER OF BEING RIGHTEOUS OVER-MUCH, WITH A PARTICULAR VIEW TO THE DOCTRINES AND PRACTICES OF CERTAIN MODERN ENTHUSIASTS;... / Trapp, J – London, 1739 – 1mf – 9 – MP-251/1 – ne IDC [240]
NATURE GUARD / Rhode Island. Agricultural Extension Service – v. 1-107. 1900-14 – 1,5,6 – us Spaulding [630]
NATURE IN SCRIPTURE : A STUDY IN BIBLE VERIFICATION IN THE RANGE OF COMMON EXPERIENCE / Cummings, Ephraim Chamberlain – (Includes index) – [2nd ed]. Boston: Cupples & Hurd, 1887 – 1mf – 9 – 0-8370-2789-6 – 1985-0789 – us A.T.L.A. [210]
LA NATURE, LA RACE, LA SANTE: DANS LEURS RAPPORTS AVEC LA PRODUCTIVITE DU TRAVAIL:.. / Baillairge, Frederic Alexandre – 1890. 00083. (Pre-1900 Canadiana) – 9 – cn C.I.H.M. [306]
NATURE MAGAZINE – v. 42-52. 1949-59 – 1 – us UMI [574]
LA NATURE MORTE DE L'ANTIQUITE A NOS JOURS / Reunion des musees nationaux. Paris – 1952. 48 illus. 3 fiches – 9 – fr Réunion [700]
THE NATURE OF GOTHIC : A CHAPTER OF THE STONES OF VENICE / Ruskin, John – Hammersmith: Printed by William Morris at the Kelmscott Press; London, Orpington, Kent: G. Allen, 1892 – 1 roll – 1 – 1-55879-918-4 – uk Libr Preservation [720]
THE NATURE OF MAN AND HIS GOVERNMENT / Lefevre, Robert – 1970. 1 fiche (24x) – 9 – 1.00f – at Libertarian Micro [320]
THE NATURE OF POSITIVE LAW / Lightwood, John M – London: Maxmillan & Co, 1883 – 5mf – 9 – $7.50 – LLMC 95-195 – us L.L.M.C. [340]
THE NATURE OF THE CORPORATION AS A LEGAL ENTITY, WITH ESPECIAL REFERENCE TO THE LAW OF MARYLAND / Carter, James Treat – Baltimore: Curlander, 1919. 239p. LL-507 – 1 – us L of C Photodup [340]
THE NATURE OF THE LIABILITY OF SHAREHOLDERS OF A CORPORATION, UNDER STATUTE IMPOSING A LIABILITY ADDITIONAL TO THAT FOR STOCK SUBSCRIBED. / Israeli, Samuel Michael – Philadelphia, Avil Printing Co., 1901. 40 p. LL-472 – 1 – us L of C Photodup [340]
NATURE STUDIES / Royal Library. Windsor Castle – (57 drawings, 80 details, 10 infra-red images. Fully indexed) – 1983 – 4 colour mf – 15 – $125.00 – 0-907716-01-6 – uk Mindata [740]
NATURE STUDY – v1- 1947- 1; v30- 5,6,9 – us UMI [073]
NATURE, THE UTILITY OF RELIGION, AND THEISM / Mill, John Stuart – London: Watts & Co., 1914 – 108p – 1 – us U.W. Library [190]
THE NATURE, USEFULNESS AND REGULATION OF RELIGIOUS ZEAL : A SERMON PREACHED AT ST. MARY'S, OXON,... / Trapp, J – London, [1739] – 1mf – 9 – MP-267/1 – ne IDC [240]
NATURENS VERDEN – 1985- – 1 – us UMI [574]
Naturforschende Gesellschaft. Bamberg *see* BERICHT
Naturforschende Gesellschaft. Danzig *see* VERSUCHE UND ABHANDLUNGEN.
Naturforschende Gesellschaft in Basel *see* BERICHT UEBER DIE VERHANDLUNGEN.
Naturforschende Gesellschaft zu Halle *see* ABHANDLUNGEN
Naturforschende Gesselschaft. Dessau *see* ABHANDLUNGEN
Naturforschenden Gesellschaft in Zurich *see* ABHANDLUNGEN
DER NATURFORSCHER – Halle, 1774-1804 – 3 – us Readex [500]
DAS NATURGEFUEHL BEI F.L. ZACHARIAS WERNER / Schubert, Paul – (Includes bibliographical references) – Muenster: F Baer's Buchdruckerei, 1914 – 1r – 1 – us U.W. Library [790]
DAS NATURGEFUEHL IN GOETHES LYRIK : STRASSBURG-FRANKFURTER LIEDER / Kutscher, Artur – [S.l.: s.n.], 1904 (Hannover: Druck von A Eberlein) – 1 – us U.W. Library [430]
DAS NATURGEFUEHL IN GOETHES LYRIK BIS ZUR AUSGABE DER SCHRIFTEN 1789 / Kutscher, Artur – (Includes bibliographical references) – Leipzig: M Hesse, 1906 – 1 – us U.W. Library [430]
NATURGESCHICHTE ALLER DEUTSCHEN ZIMMER-, HAUS- UND JAGDVOEGEL, NEBST EINEM ANHANGE UEBER DIE AUSLAENDISCHEN VOEGEL, WELCHE IN DEUTSCHLAND IM HANDEL VORKOMMEN / Friderich, C G – 2083 2. 1849 – 8 – ne IDC [590]

NATURGESCHICHTE DER DEUTSCHEN SUMPE- UND STRANDVOGEL / Floericke, C E – Z 1755. 1897 – 9 – ne IDC [590]
NATURGESCHICHTE DER EUROPAASISCHEN LEBERMOOSE / Nees von Esenbeck, C G D – Berlin, Breslau, 1833-1838. 4 vols. B-7119 1 – 9 – ne IDC [580]
NATURGESCHICHTE DER FLECHTEN / Wallroth, C F W – 2v. Frankfurt a.M. 1825-27. B-590 2 – 8 – ne IDC [580]
NATURGESCHICHTE DER INSECTEN DEUTSCHLANDS / Erichson, W F – Continuation of: H. Schaum, G. Kraatz und H. von Kiesenwetter. Berlin, 1860-82/93. 6v. Z/1218/2 – 8 – ne IDC [590]
NATURGESCHICHTE DER INSEKTEN, BESONDERS IN HINSICHT IHRER ERSTEN ZUSTAENDE ALS LARVEN UND PUPPEN / Bouche, P F – Berlin, 1834. v1. v,216p. 10 pls. Z-1088/2 – 8 – ne IDC [590]
NATURGESCHICHTE DER LAUB- UND LEBERMOOSE LIV-, ESTH- UND KURLANDS / Girgensohn, G K – Dorpat. 1860. B-5063 2 – 8 – ne IDC [580]
NATURGESCHICHTE DER VOEGEL EUROPAS / Fritsch, A J – Prag, 1858/1870-71. 2v.Index, 61 plts. Z/1758/2 – 8 – ne IDC [590]
NATURGESCHICHTE DEUTSCHER LAND- UND SUESSWASSERMOLLUSKEN / Pfeiffer, C – Z-708 2. 1821-1828 – 8 – ne IDC [590]
NATURGESCHICHTE.KLASSIFICATION UND NOMENCLATUR DER INSEKTEN VOM BIENEN / Christ, J L – Frankfurt am Main, 1791.535p. 60 pls.Z-1137/2 – 8 – ne IDC [590]
NATURGETREUE ABBILDUNGEN UND BESCHREIBUNGEN DES ESSBAREN SCHWAEMME / Krombholz, J V von – 10 Hefte. Prag. 1831-47. B-5425 2 – 8 – ne IDC [580]
NATURHISTORISCHE BRIEFE UEBER OESTREICH, SALZBURG, PASSAU UND BERCHTESGADEN / Schrank, F von & Paula, A von & Moll, KE von – 2v. Salzburg. 1785. B-948 2 – 8 – ne IDC [574]
NATURISMO Y AFINES / Bayle, Constantino – Madrid: Razon y Fe, 1929 – 1 – sp Bibl Santa Ana [946]
DIE NATURLICHEN PFLANZENFAMILLIEN / Engler, H G A & Prantl, K – 1897-1907 – 7 – uk Microform Academic [580]
NATURSCHUTZ DURCH NATURSCHUTZVERWALTUNGEN? : UNTERSUCHUNGEN ZUR PRAXIS DER AUSWEISUNG UND BESTANDSSICHERUNG VON SCHUTZGEBIETEN ANGESICHTS KONKURRIERENDER ADMINISTRATIVER UND GESELLSCHAFTLICHER INTERESSEN / Osberghaus, Michael – 1995 – 2mf – 9 – DM80.00 – 3-8267-2092-X – gw Hänsel [630]
NATURSTUDIUM UND CHRISTENTUM / Bettex, Frederic – 8. durchges. Aufl. Bielefeld: Velhagen & Klasing, 1900 – 1mf – 9 – 0-8370-2318-1 – 1985-0318 – us A.T.L.A. [210]
NATURSTUDIUM UND CHRISTENTUM / Bettex, Frederic – (In English) – Cincinnati: Jennings & Pye, c1901 – 1mf – 9 – 0-8370-2320-3 – 1985-0320 – us A.T.L.A. [210]
NATURSYSTEM UNGEFLUEGELTEN INSEKTEN / Herbst, J FW – Berlin, 1797-1800. 4pts. BZ/1342/2 – 8 – ne IDC [590]
NATURWISSENSCHAFT UND BIBEL : BEITRAEGE ZUR WEITERBILDUNG DER RELIGION: AUSBLICKE AUF EINE NEUE STAATSKUNST: EINE NATURWISSENSCHAFTLICHE ANTWORT AUF DAS GLAUBENSBEKENNTNIS KAISER WILHELM 2 / Lehmann-Hohenberg, Johannes – Jena: Hermann Costenoble, 1904, c1901 – 1mf – 9 – 0-8370-4084-1 – 1985-2084 – us A.T.L.A. [210]
DIE NATURWISSENSCHAFTEN – v. 33-67. 1946-80 – 1,5,9 – 2651.00 – us UMI [500]
NATURWISSENSCHAFTEN – v1-42. 1913-55 – 1,5,6 – us Princeton Micro [500]
NATURWISSENSCHAFTLICHE ABHANDLUNGEN – Vienna, 1847-51. v. 1-4 – 3 – us Readex [500]
Naturwissenschaftlicher Verein. Regensburg *see* ABHANDLUNGEN DES ZOOLOGISCH-MINERALOGISCHEN VEREINES IN REGENSBURG
Naturwissenschaftlicher Verein zu Bremen *see* ABHANDLUNGEN
NATUURKUNDIG TIJDSCHRIFT VOOR NEDERLANDSCH INDIE,... : INDONESIAN JOURNAL OF NATURAL SCIENCES – (Continues as: Natuurwetenschappelijk Tijdschrift voor Nederlandsch Indie Batavia, 1941-1942. V.101-102: Continues as: Chronica Naturae. Batavia, 1947-1950. V.103-106: Continues as: Madjalah Ilmu Alam untik Indonesia. Index v1-90) – Batavia, 1850-1940. v1-100. – 589mf – 9 – ne IDC [500]
NATUURKUNDIGE UITSPANNINGEN... / Baster, J – Haarlem, 1759-1765. 2v – 6mf – 9 – ne IDC [615]
NATUURKUNDIGE VERHANDELINGEN VAN DE HOLLANDSCHE MAATSCHAPPIJ DER WETENSCHAPPEN TE HAARLEM / Hollandsche maatschappij der wetenschappen, Haarlem – 1799-1922 – 3 – us Readex [500]
NATUURKUNDIGE VERLUSTIGINGEN. / Slabber, Martinus – Haarlem: J. Bosch, 1778.viii,166p. 3 fiches. (Science Collection) – 9 – 8.00 – fr Bibl Nationale [590]
NATUURLIJKE HISTORIE OF UITVOERIGE BESCHRIJVING DER DIEREN, PLANTEN EN MINERAALEN,... / ed by Houttuyn, M – Amsterdam. 14pts. 1773-1783 – 108mf – 9 – ne IDC [500]
NAU CABLE – (The Cable). The weekly journal of the National Agricultural Union. London. -w. Mar 1893-Dec 1900. (9 reels) – 1 – uk British Libr Newspaper [630]
NAUCHNAI A LITERATURA SSSR. OBSHCHESTVENNYE NAUKI : KOMITET PO ZAVEDYVANII U UCHENYMI I UCHEBNYMI UCHREZHDENII AMI PRI T SIK SSSR, KOMISSII A PO SOSTAVENII U I IZDANII U INDEKSOV NAUCHNO I LITERATURY – (Includes c.1: 1928) – Moskva: Sovetskai a ent siklopedii a: OGIZ RSFSR, 1932- – 1 – CSUXAKZ2879-S – us Hoover Inst Photo [947]
NAUCHNAIA MYSL' – Riga. v1. 1908 – 4mf – 9 – ne IDC [947]
NAUCHNOE OBOZRENIE – Ezhenedel'nyi nauchnyi zhurnal. Spb. 1894-1903 (5). Lacking: 1895 (1-12); 1896 (1-12). B-1800 2 – 8 – ne IDC [073]
Nauchno-Issle Dovatel'skaia Assotsiatsiia Poizucheniiu Natsional'nykh i Kolonial'nykh Problem *see* REVOLIUTSIONNYI VOSTOK
NAUCHNO-ISSLEDOVATELSKI I KONI UNKTURNY I INSTITUT *see* BIULLETEN INOSTRANNO I KOMMERCHESKO I INFORMAT SII. PRILOZHENIE
Nauchno-issledo-vatel'skoi assotsiatsii po izucheniiu natsional'nykh i kolonial'nykh problem *see* REVOLIUTSIONNYI VOSTOK
NAUCHNO-TEKHNICHESKI I VESTNIK : R.S.F.S.R. NAUCHNO-TEKHNICHESKI I OTDEL V.S.N.KH. – (Library has: nos.1-2, 1920 and no. 3, 1921) – Moskva: Nauchno-tekhnicheski i otdel V.S.N.Kh., 1920-1921 – 1 – CSUX89-S620 – us Hoover Inst Photo [947]
NAUCHNYI ISTORICHESKII ZHURNAL – Spb. 1913-14. B-1433 2 – 8 – ne IDC [947]
Nauchnyi sovet po istorii mirovoi kultury Akademii nauk SSSR, Gosudarstvennaia ordena Lenina biblioteka SSSR imeni V I Lenina [redaktsionnaia 111=Markushevich, A I et al *see* CHITATEL I KNIGA
NAUCHNYIE DOKLADY VYSSHEI SHKOLY – Istoricheskie nauki. Moscow, 1958-61. BR-10,429/1 – 9 – ne IDC [947]
Naud, Denise *see* BIBLIOGRAPHIE (1915 A 1940) DU DR GEORGES MAHEUX, ENTOMOLOGISTE, MEMBRE DE LA SOCIETE ROYALE DU CANADA
Naudet, Paul Antoine *see* POUR LA FEMME: ETUDES FEMINISTES
NAUFRAGE DE LA FREGATE "LA MEDUSE" / Correard, A.Savigny, H. – Paris, Correard. 1821 – 9 – $15.00 – fr Orientalistes [910]
NAUFRAGE DES ISLES FLOTTANTES OU BASILIADE DU CELEBRE PILPAI, POEME HEROIQUE TRADUIT DE L'INDIEN. / Morelly – (Utopias in the Enlightenment series). 1753 – 9 – fr Hachette [830]
NAUFRAGE DU BRICK FRANCAIS "LA SOPHIE" PERDU LE 30 MAI 1819, SUR LA COTE OCCIDENTALE D'AFRIQUE / Cochelet, Charles – Paris. 1821 – 9 – 22.50 – fr Orientalistes [910]
NAUFRAGE DU BRIGANTINE AMERICAIN "LE COMMERCE" / Riley, James – Traduction de l'anglais. Paris. 1818 – 9 – 30.00 – fr Orientalistes [910]
LES NAUFRAGES DU JONATHAN / Verne, Jules – Paris: J. Hetzel, c1909.2v. 7 fiches.(Literature Collection) – 9 – 17.00 – fr Bibl Nationale [830]
NAUKA – Uzhhorod, July 1897-Nov. 20, 1921 – 2r – 1 – us I.H.R.C. [073]
NAUKA I RELIGIIA – (Backfile through 1998 $85r) – 1999- – 1r per y – 1 – $80.00 standing order – us Ross [072]
NAUKA I SHKOLA – Nauchno-pedagogicheskii zhurnal-sbornik. nr. 17. Khar'kov. 1915-16. BR-3990 2 – 8 – ne IDC [073]
NAUKA I SSSR / Bukharin, Nikolai Ivanovich – Leningrad: Rabotnik prosveshchenii a, 1928 – 1 – CSUX89-B5289 – us Hoover Inst Photo [500]
NAUKA I ZHIZN – Moscow. U.S.S.R. 1966- – 1 – us UMI [360]
NAUKA I ZHIZN' – Ezhemesiachnyi nauchno-populiarnyi, khudozhestvennyi i literaturnyi zhurnal. Spb. 1904-06. Lacking: 1905 (10-12), 1906 (1, 4-12). B-1801 2 – 8 – ne IDC [073]
NAUKEURIGE BESCHRIJVINGE DER AFRIKAENSCHE GEWESTEN; VAN EGYPTEN, BARBARYEN, LIBYEN, BILEDULGERID, NEGROSLANT, GUINEA, ETHIOPIEN, ABYSSINIE / Dapper, O – Amsterdam: J. van Meurs, 1668 – 1 – us U.W. Library [910]
Naukove Tovaristvo Imeni Shevchenka *see*
– KHRONIKA
– ZAPYSKY
Naukove Tovaristvo Imeni Shevchenka. Fil'ol'ogichna Sektsiia *see*
– ZBIRNYK
NAUKOVI PRATSI / Akademiia Nauk. URSR. Kiev. Instytut Budivel'noi Mekhaniky – Kiev. v1-16, 18-43. 1934-41 – 1r – 1 – us Ross [621]
NAUKOVY ZAPYSKY / Akademiia Nauk. URSR. Kiev. Instytut Movy i Literatury – Kiev. v2-3. 1946 – 1r – 1 – us Ross [460]
NAUKRATIS (MEES VOL 3) : PART 1, 1884-5 / Flinders Petrie, W M – London, 1886 – 9mf – 8 – Dfl32.00 – ne Slangenburg [930]
NAUKRATIS (MEES VOL 6) : PART 2 / Gardner, E A – London, 1888 – 7mf – 8 – Dfl28.00 – ne Slangenburg [930]
Naumann, O *see*
– DAS ERSTE BUCH DER BIBEL: NACH SEINER INNEREN EINHEIT UND ECHTHEIT
– WELLHAUSEN'S METHODE
NAUMANNIA – (Cont as: Journal fuer Ornithologie. Cassel etc. v1-90 1853-1942; Missing: v85 1937) – Stuttgart etc. v1-8. 1849-1858 – 1109mf – 9 – ne IDC [590]
Naumov, E *see*
– MAIAKOVSKII V PERVYE GODY SOVETSKOI VLASTI
– RUSSKAIA SOVETSKAIA LITERATURA
– SERGEI ESENIN
Naunyn, B *see* ARCHIV FUER EXPERIMENTELLE PATHOLOGIE UND PHARMAKOLOGIE
NAUNYN SCHMIEDEBERG'S ARCHIV FUER EXPERIMENTELLE PATHOLOGY UND PHARMAKOLOGIE – v63-227.1910-55 – 1,5,6 – us Princeton Micro [610]
NAUNYN-SCHMIEDEBERG'S ARCHIVES OF PHARMACOLOGY – v. 204-315. 1947-80 – 1,5,9 – 16,716.00 – us UMI [073]
Naurath, Hans Joachim *see* DIABETES MELLITUS IM ALTER
NAUTICAL ECONOMY : OR, FORECASTLE RECOLLECTIONS OF EVENTS DURING THE LAST WAR, BY A SAILOR, POLITELY CALLED JACK NASTY-FACE / Robinson, William – 1836 – 9 – $20.00 – uk Libr Preservation [941]
NAUTICAL GAZETTE – New York, 1871-1939 – 29r – 1 – us Ross [380]
THE NAUTICAL GAZETTE – New York. v1-148 no 1. July 1 1871-Jan 1954 – 1 – us NY Public [623]
NAUTICAL STANDARD AND STEAM NAVIGATION GAZETTE – London. 10 Jan 1846-11 Feb 1854. w – 8r – 1 – uk British Libr Newspaper [623]
NAUTILUS – Philadelphia. v1-20. 1886-1907 – 67mf – 9 – ne IDC [590]
NAUVOO EXPOSITOR – Nauvoo, Ill. v. 1, no. 1. June 7 1844 – 1 – us NY Public [071]
NAUVOO NEIGHBOR – Nauvoo, Ill. Weekly. v. 1, no. 35-v. 3, no. 22. Dec 27 1843-Oct 1 1845. Incomplete – 1 – us NY Public [071]
NAUVOO NEW CITIZEN – Nauvoo, Ill. v. 1, no. 3. Dec 23 1846 – 1 – us NY Public [071]
NAUWKEURIGE BESCHRYVING VAN DE GUINESE GOUD-, TAND-, EN SLAVE-KUST... / Bosman, Willem – Amsterdam: J Verheide, 1737 – us Res Libr [960]
NAV JIWAN – Lucknow, India. 25 Apr-31 Dec 1950; 23 Jul 1951-1953 – 6r – 1 – us L of C Photodup [072]
NAVA BHARATA TAIMSA – New Delhi, India. 10 Apr 1947-Dec 1989 – 145r – 1 – us L of C Photodup [072]
NAVA GUJARAT – Baroda, India. Apr 1944-49 – 3r – 1 – us L of C Photodup [072]
NAVABHARATH – Mangalore, India. Jul-Sept 1966 – 1r – 1 – us L of C Photodup [072]
NAVAJEEVAN – (Oriya language) – Calicut, India. Jul-Sept 1966 – 1r – 1 – us L of C Photodup [072]
Navajo Community College *see* NEWSLETTER
NAVAJO TIMES – Window Rock, AZ. 1976-87 – 23r – 1 – $1,150.00 – R01504 – us Library Micro [071]
NAVAL ACTIONS OF THE WAR OF 1812 / Barnes, James – New York: Harper, 1896. 03313. (Pre-1900 Canadiana) – 9 – cn C.I.H.M. [971]
NAVAL ADMINISTRATION : THE CONSTITION, CHARACTER AND FUNCTIONS OF THE BOARD OF ADMIRALTY, AND OF THE CIVIL DEPARTMENT IT DIRECTS / Hamilton, Richard Vesey – 1896 – 9 – uk Libr Preservation [355]
NAVAL ADMINISTRATIVE HISTORIES OF WORLD WAR 2 / U.S. Navy – (1989 Sections Available: Office of the Secretary of the Navy 176mf $880.00. Commander in Chief, United States Fleet 9mf $45.00. Office of the Deputy Chief of Naval Operations (Air) 125mf $625.50. Office of the Commandant, United States Marine Corps 10mf $50.00. Bureau of Aeronautics 105mf $525.50. Bureau of Medicine and Surgery 25mf $125.00. Bureau of Ordnance 91mf $455.00. Bureau of Naval Personnel 239mf $1,195.00. Bureau of Ships 16mf $80.00. Bureau of Supplies and Accounts 113mf $565.50. Bureau of Yards and Docks 12mf $60.00. Naval Districts 441mf $2,200.00. Chief of Naval Operations Shore Activities 32mf $160.00. Bureau of Ordnance Shore Activities 102mf $510.00. Bureau of Supplies and Accounts Activities 24mf $120.00. Atlantic 142mf $710.00. Pacific 215mf $1,075.00. Sea Frontiers and Operating Bases 135mf $675.00. Topical Histories 33mf $165.00. Printed guide available $45.00 S3220.G) – 2,130mf – 9 – $10,650.00 set – S3220 – us Scholarly Res [355]
NAVAL ARCHITECTURAL DRAWINGS / American Ship Building Company. Cleveland, Ohio – 1867-1920 – 33r – 1 – $32.50r – us Archival [623]
NAVAL AVIATION NEWS – 1919-68 – 1 – $575.00 – us L of C Photodup [355]
NAVAL CHRONICLE – v. 1-40. 1799-1818 – 1,5,6 – us Princeton Micro [073]
NAVAL CHRONOLOGY: OR, AN HISTORICAL SUMMARY OF NAVAL AND MARITIME EVENTS, FROM THE TIME OF THE ROMANS TO THE TREATY OF PEACE, 1802 / Schomberg, Isaac – With an appendix. 5v. 1802 – 9 – uk Libr Preservation [355]
NAVAL DEVELOPMENT IN THE 19TH CENTURY / Barnaby, Nathaniel – 1902 – 9 – $20.00 – uk Libr Preservation [355]
NAVAL ESSAYS; OR, ESSAYS ON THE MANAGEMENT OF PUBLIC CONCERNS AS EXEMPLIFIED IN THE NAVAL DEPARTMENT, CONSIDERED AS A BRANCH OF THE BUSINESS OF WARFARE. ESSAY 1: EFFICIENCY OF THE MATERIEL. PART 1 / Bentham, Samuel – 1828 – 9 – $20.00 – uk Libr Preservation [355]
Naval, Francisco *see* NUEVAS ARAS FUNERARIAS EN JEREZ DE LOS CABALLEROS
THE NAVAL GAZETTEER, BIOGRAPHER, AND CHRONOLOGIST : CONTAINING A HISTORY OF THE LATE WARS, FROM THEIR COMMENCEMENT IN 1793, TO THEIR CONCLUSION IN 1801...AND TO THEIR FINAL CONCLUSION IN 1815 / Norie, John William – New ed. 1827 – 9 – $20.00 – uk Libr Preservation [941]
THE NAVAL HISTORY OF GREAT BRITAIN, FROM THE DECLARATION OF WAR BY FRANCE, 1793, TO THE ACCESSION OF GEORGE 4, 1820 / James, William – New ed., with additions and notes, bringing the work down to 1827. 6v. 1886 – 9 – $220.00 – uk Libr Preservation [941]

NAVAL MAGAZINE – v1-2. Jan 1836-Nov 1837 – 1 – us UMI [355]
NAVAL & MILITARY GAZETTE – London, UK. 9 Feb 1833-17 Feb 1886. -w. 57 reels – 1 – uk British Libr Newspaper [073]
NAVAL & MILITARY RECORD – Plymouth, England. 1908-12. -w. 5 reels – 1 – uk British Libr Newspaper [072]
Naval Observatory. Washington, D.C. *see* CATALOG OF THE NAVAL OBSERVATORY LIBRARY
THE NAVAL OFFICER : OR, SCENES AND ADVENTURES IN THE LIFE OF FRANK MILDMAY / Marryat, Frederick – London: Henry Colburn, 1829 – 1 roll – 1 – 1-55879-160-4 – uk Libr Preservation [355]
THE NAVAL OPERATIONS OF THE WAR BETWEEN GREAT BRITAIN AND THE UNITED STATES, 1812-1815 / Roosevelt, Theodore – 1910 – 9 – $20.00 – uk Libr Preservation [975]
NAVAL RESEARCH LOGISTICS QUARTERLY – v1- 1954- 1; v18- 5,6; v22- 9 – us UMI [355]
NAVAL RESEARCH LOGISTICS QUARTERLY – v1-31. 1954-84 – 1,5,6 – us Princeton Micro [355]
NAVAL RESEARCH REVIEWS – v1-31 1954-78 1; v23-31 5,6; v28-31 9 – us UMI [355]
THE NAVAL SERVICE : OR OFFICERS' MANUAL, FOR EVERY GRADE IN HIS MAJESTY'S SHIPS / Glascock, William Nugent – 2v. 1836 – 9 – $20.00 – uk Libr Preservation [355]
THE NAVAL SIDE OF THE SPANISH WAR / Emanuel, W V – London, n.d. Fiche W 857. (Blodgett Collection of Spanish Civil War Pamphlets) – 9 – us H.U. College Libr [946]
NAVAL SUMMARY COURTS-MARTIAL / Lemly, Samuel Conrad – Washington, D.C., Army and Navy Register Publishing Co., 1891. 28p. LL-184 – 1 – us L of C Photodup [340]
NAVAL TACTICS, AND TRIALS OF SAILING; ALSO THE ESTABLISHED PLAN OF LIGHTS FOR STEAM-VESSELS, AND REGULATIONS TO AVOID COLLISION / Biddlecombe, George – 1850 – 9 – $20.00 – uk Libr Preservation [355]
NAVAL WAR COLLEGE, BATTLE ANALYSIS SERIES / U.S. Navy – (With printed guide) – 1990 – 3r – 1 – $255.00 – S3176 – us Scholarly Res [355]
NAVAL WARFARE : ITS RULING PRINCIPLES AND PRACTICE, HISTORICALLY TREATED / Colomb, Philip Howard – 2nd ed. 1895 – 9 – $20.00 – uk Libr Preservation [355]
NAVAL YARNS : LETTERS AND ANECDOTES COMPRISING ACCOUNTS OF SEA FIGHTS AND WRECKS FROM 1616 TO 1831 / ed by Long, William Henry & Long, A H – 1899 – 9 – $60.00 – uk Libr Preservation [355]
Navalmoral de La Mata. Ayuntamiento *see* FERIAS Y FIESTAS DURANTE LOS DIAS 28, 29 Y 30...1960
Navalmoral de la Mata. (Spain).Ayuntamiento *see* ORDENANZAS MUNICIPALES
NAVAMANI – Madras, India. Jul-Sept 1966 – 1r – 1 – us L of C Photodup [072]
NAVARAHTRA – Patna, India. 1953 – 1r – 1 – us L of C Photodup [072]
Navaro Reverter, J *see* MEMORIA...CONFERENCIAS DE PARIS..COMPARACION...TARIFAS ARANCELARIAS DE ESPANA Y FRANCIA
Navarre, Jean *see* DISCOURS QUI A REMPORTE LE PRIX, PAR LE JUGEMENT DE L'ACADEMIE DES JEUX FLORAUX EN L'ANNEE 1763, SUR CES PAROLES, QUE SEROIT EN FRANCE LE PLAN D'ETUDE LE PLUS AVANTAGEUX?
Navarrete y Sabogal, P *see* RESPONDESE AL...DOCTOR CUSPRILLI
Navarro Castellanos, Gonzalo *see* DISCURSOS POLITICOS Y MORALES EN CARTAS APOLOGETICAS CONTRA LOS QUE DEFIENDEN EL VSO DE LA COMEDIAS MODERNAS QUE SE REPRESENTAN EN ESPANA, EN COMPARACION DEL TEATRO ANTIGUO...
Navarro del Castilio, Vicente *see* SANTA EULALIA DE MERIDA, SU VIDA, MARTIRIO Y CULTO A TRAVES DE LA MODERNA CRITICA HISTORICA Y DE LOS RECIENTES DESCUBRIMIENTOS ARQUEOLOGICOS
Navarro, Jose Gabriel *see*
- LA ESCULTURA EN EL ECUADOR, 1929
- EL MUNICIPIO EN AMERICA DURANTE LA ASISTENCIA DE ESPANA, 1930

Navarro, Marysa *see* EVA PERON
Navarro Muzquiz, Fernando *see* MEMORIA
Navarro, Nicolas *see* DON RODRIGO DE BASTIDAS
Navarro, Nicolas E *see*
- ANALES ECLESIASTICOS VENEZOLANOS. CARACAS, 1929
- LA CATEDRAL DE CARACAS Y SUS FUNCIONES DE CULTO
- LA IGLESIA Y LA MASONERIA EN VENEZUELA...

Navarro Tomas, Tomas *see* AN OPEN LETTER
Navas del Madrono. Ayuntamiento *see*
- FERIAS Y FIESTAS 1974
- FERIAS Y FIESTAS...MAYO 1959...FERIA DE GANADOS DE TODAS CLASES

LAS NAVAS DEL MARQUES / Melida, Jose Ramon & Ramon, Vives – Madrid: Tip. Fortanet, 1894 – 1 – sp Bibl Santa Ana [946]
NAVASAKTI – Madras, India. Jul-Sept 1966 – 1r – 1 – us L of C Photodup [072]
Navasfrias (Salamanca) *see* COMUNIDAD DE REGANTES. ORDENANZAS
NAVASHAKTI – Bombay, India. Mar 1948-94 – 110r – 1 – us L of C Photodup [072]
LA NAVE IN ALTO MARE;... / Da Vella, O – Florence, 1892 – 1mf – 1 – ILM-468/1 – ne IDC [327]
NAVEGAMTES Y DESCUBRIDORES ESPANOLES DEL MAR PACIFICO. VASCO NUNEZ DE BALBOA / Garcia, Telesforo – Mexico: Imp. y Fotocopia de la Secretaria de Fomento, 1913 – sp Bibl Santa Ana [910]
LAS NAVES DE CORTES DESTRUIDAS / Fernandez de Moratin, Nicolas – Madrid: Rivadeneyra, 1854 – 1 – sp Bibl Santa Ana [946]
Navet, E *see* RECHERCHES SUR LA VIE D'UNE COMMUNE DU COTENTIN-BIVILLE (HAGUE)
NAVHIND TIMES – Panjim, India. Jul 1966-Apr 1970; Jul 1970-Jul 1994 – 83r – 1 – us L of C Photodup [072]
NAVIDAD 74 / Caceres. Obra Sindical de Educacion y Descanso – Caceres: Edit. Extremadura, 1974 – 1 – sp Bibl Santa Ana [370]
THE NAVIES OF THE WORLD : THEIR PRESENT STATE AND FUTURE CAPABILITIES / Busk, Hans – 1859 – 9 – uk Libr Preservation [355]
NAVIGABLE WATERS PROTECTION ACT AND REGULATIONS / Canada. Laws, Statutes, etc – (Amendment service. YX76-N22EM. Standing order) – Basic set. YX76-N22-1-EM – 9 – Can$5.00 – cn Communication [340]
LA NAVIGATION AERIENNE... / Grovalet, C – Nantes, 1909 – 2mf – 1 – ILM-1781/1 – ne IDC [327]
THE NAVIGATION LAWS AS THEY AFFECT THE MANNING OF THE NAVY : WITH SUGGESTIONS FOR IMPROVING ITS DISCIPLINE, AND THE CONDITION OF ITS SEAMEN / Hamilton, William – 1848 – 9 – $20.00 – uk Libr Preservation [340]
LA NAVIGATION: POEME / Esmenard, Joseph Alphonse – Paris: Giguet et Michaud, 1805. 2v. 9 fiches. (Literature Collection) – 9 – 22.00 – fr Bibl Nationale [810]
LE NAVIGATIONI ET VIAGGI NELLA TVRCHIA / Nicolay, N de – Anversa, 1576 – 5mf – 9 – H-8349/1 – ne IDC [910]
LES NAVIGATIONS PEREGRINATIONS ET VOYAGES, FAICTS EN LA TURQUIE AVEC SOIXANTE FIGURES AU NATUREL TANT D'HOMMES QUE DE FEMMES SELON LA DIVERSITE DES NATIONS / Nicolay, Nicolas de – Anvers, G. Silvius, 1557, xxii-305-25 p. French Voyagers in the Mediterranean 16th to 18th Centuries. 5958 – 9 – fr Hachette [944]
LES NAVIGATIONS, PEREGRINATIONS ET VOYAGES, FAICTS EN LA TVRQVIE / Nicolay, N de – Anvers, 1577 – 5mf – 9 – H-8348/1 – ne IDC [910]
NAVIGATOR – v1- 1953- 1; v19- 5,6; v23- 9 – us UMI [073]
LA NAVIGAZIONE FLUVIALE... / Catellani, E L – Torino, 1883 – 2mf – 1 – ILM-2350/1 – ne IDC [327]
Naville, E *see*
- THE 11TH DYNASTY TEMPLE AT DEIR EL-BAHARI (MEES VOL 28)
- THE 11TH DYNASTY TEMPLE AT DEIR EL-BAHARI (MEES VOL 30)
- THE 11TH DYNASTY TEMPLE AT DEIR EL-BAHARI (MEES VOL 32)
- AHNAS EL MEDINEH (MEES VOL 11)
- BUBASTIS (MEES VOL 8)
- THE FESTIVAL-HALLOF CSORKON 2 IN THE GREAT TEMPLE OF BUBASTIS (MEES VOL 10)
- GOSHEN AND THE SHRINE OF SAFT EL HENNEH (MEES VOL 4)
- INSCRIPTION HISTORIQUE DE PINODJEM 3
- THE MOUND OF THE JEW AND THE CITY OF ONIAS (MEES VOL 7)
- THE STORY-CITY OF PITHOM AND THE ROUTE OF THE EXODUS (MEES NO 1)
- THE TEMPLE OF DEIR EL BAHARI (MEES VOL 12)

Naville, E et al *see* THE CEMETERIES OF ABYDOS (MEES VOL 33)
Naville, Ernest *see*
- HEAVENLY FATHER: LECTURES ON MODERN ATHEISM
- LA VIE ETERNELLE

Naville, Jules Ernest *see* LE LIBRE ARBITRE ETUDE PHILOSOPHIQUE
Naville, P *see* LA VIE DE TRAVAIL ET SES PROBLEMES
O NAVIO : ORGAM SCIENTIFICO E LITTERARIO – Manaus, Amazonas. 28 Feb-15 Mar 1913 – 1,5,6 – bl Biblioteca [072]
O NAVIO PESSOA DE DIREITO INTERNACIONAL PUBLICO / Diniz, A – Rio de Janeiro, 1927 – 1mf – 1 – ILM-1785/1 – ne IDC [327]
LE NAVIRE D'ARGENT – Dir. Adrienne Monnier. no. 1-12. Paris. 1er juin 1925-1er mai 1926 – 1 – fr A.C.R.P.P. [073]
Navoigille, H *see* SIX QUARTETTOS IN THE COMIC STILE, OP. 2
NAVVY'S GUIDE – (Navvy's and Labourer's Guide). Eccles. England. -m. Jan-Jun 1891. (6 ft) – 1 – uk British Libr Newspaper [331]
NAVY – v1-14 1958-71 – 1 – us UMI [355]
THE NAVY AND PRIZE / Anderson, M H – London – 1mf – 9 – ILM-796/1 – ne IDC [340]
THE NAVY AND THE NATION; OR, NAVAL WARFARE AND IMPERIAL DEFENCE / Clarke, George Sydenham & Thursfield, James R – 1897 – 9 – $20.00 – uk Libr Preservation [941]
THE NAVY AS I HAVE KNOWN IT, 1849-1899 / Fremantle, Edmund Robert – 1904 – 9 – $20.00 – uk Libr Preservation [355]
NAVY CHAPLAIN'S BULLETIN – 1980-90 (complete) – 3r – 1 – ATLA S0878 – us A.T.L.A. [073]
NAVY DEPARTMENT GENERAL ORDERS AND CIRCULARS / U.S. Navy – 1798-1862. RG 45, 71, 80. M977 – 2r – 1 – us Nat'l Archives [355]
NAVY TIMES – (v28- 1978- 5,6,9) – v1- 1952- – 1 – us UMI [355]
NAW RUZ – (Sal-i 1, shumarah-i 1-48 (2 Su'l Hijjah 1320-2 Muharram 1321[2 March 1903-20 March 1904])) – Tehran – 1 reel – 1 – $75.00 – us MEDOC [950]
Nawa, Y *see* ICONES JAPONICORUM INSECTORUM
Nawab, Samsamu-D-Daula *see* MA-AASAMIRU-L-UMARA
Nawab Samsamud$Dowla, Shah Hawaz Khan *see* MAAA1SIR UL-UMARA
NAWKI I RELIGIA – Moscow. U.S.S.R. -m. 1968- – 1 – us UMI [240]
Nawroth, Peter Paul *see* DIE REGULATION DER GERINNUNG DURCH DAS ENDOTHEL
NAY LEBN [VIDA NUEVA] = NEW LIFE – (In Yiddish and Spanish) – Buenos Aires, AG. v3 no30/31 Aug/Sept 1946-v3 no32 Oct 1946 – 1r – 1 – $25.00 – cn Can Microfilming [072]
NAYA SAVERA – Lucknow, India. 1950-51 (scattered issues) – 1r – 1 – us L of C Photodup [072]
NAYA ZAMANA – Jullundur, India. Jun 1953-1954 – 4r – 1 – us L of C Photodup [072]
Nayarit. Mexico (State) *see* PERIODICO OFICIAL-GOBIERNO DEL ESTADO DE NAYARIT
NAYE FOLKSTSAYTUNG = NEW PEOPLE'S JOURNAL – (In Yiddish) – Warsaw, PL. v4 no4 5 Jan 1931-v14 no122 29 Apr 1939 – 1r – 1 – $25.00 – cn Can Microfilming [072]
DOS NAYE LAND = THE NEW LAND – (In Yiddish) – New York City, NY. v1 no1 15 Sep 1911-v2 no26 8 Mar 1912 – 1r – 1 – $30.00 – cn Can Microfilming [071]
DOS NAYE LEBEN – New York. N.Y. 1908-14 – 1 – us A.J.P.C. [071]
DOS NAYE LEBEN – New York. N.Y. v. 1. 1923 – 1 – us A.J.P.C. [071]
DOS NAYE LEBN = NEW LIFE – (In Yiddish) – Bialystok, PL. v10 no200 27 Aug 1928; v11 no110 13 May 1929 – 1r – 1 – $25.00 – cn Can Microfilming [072]
DOS NAYE LEBN = NEW LIFE – (In Yiddish) – Lodz, PL. v? no1 10 Mar 1945-no122(no546) 25 Oct 1950 – 4r – 1 – $60.00 – cn Can Microfilming [072]
NAYE POLESER SZTYME = NEW TIMES... – (In Yiddish) – Brzesc, PL. no1 1 Jan-no7 17 Feb 1926 – 1r – 1 – $30.00 – cn Can Microfilming [072]
NAYE PRESSE = NEW PRESS – (In Yiddish) – Paris, FR. Dec 1948-Jan 1949 – 1r – 1 – $25.00 – cn Can Microfilming [072]
NAYE PRESSE = PRESSE NOUVELLE – (In Yiddish) – Paris, FR. (-) 12 Fev 1939; Special 1934-1946; Dec 1948-Jan 1949 – 1r – 1 – $35.00 – cn Can Microfilming [072]
NAYE SHTAMEN = NEW STEMS – (In Yiddish) – Tel Aviv, IS. (-) May 1938 – 1r – 1 – $25.00 – cn Can Microfilming [072]
DI NAYE TSAYT – New York, N.Y. 1898-99 – 1 – us A.J.P.C. [071]
NAYE TSAYT *see* DI NAYE TSAYT
DI NAYE VAHRHEIT – New York. v. 1 no. 1-249. Mar 14-Nov 19 1925 – 1 – us NY Public [305]
NAYE VELT – New York, NY. 1909-10 – 1 – us A.J.P.C. [071]
DI NAYE WELT = THE NEW WAY – (In Yiddish) – New York City, NY. v6 no38 28 Sep 1917-v6 no40 17 Oct 1919 – 1r – 1 – $35.00 – cn Can Microfilming [071]
NAYE YIDISHE TSAYTUNG = JEWISH JOURNAL – (In Yiddish) – Munich, DE. no84 18 Jul 1952-no263 26 Mar 1956 – 1r – 1 – $25.00 – cn Can Microfilming [072]
DER NAYER VEG = THE NEW PATH – (In Yiddish – Zionist) – New York City, NY. v1 no1. Jan 1935 – 1r – 1 – $25.00 – cn Can Microfilming [071]
NAYER WOLIN = WOLIN NEWS – (In Yiddish) – New Wolin, PL. v1 no1 27 Jan 1928 – 1r – 1 – $25.00 – cn Can Microfilming [072]
DER NAYER ZHURNAL = THE NEW JOURNAL – (In Yiddish) – Paris, FR. v2 no1 2 Jan 1911-v4 no6 28 Nov 1913 – 1r – 1 – $25.00 – cn Can Microfilming [072]
NAYES LEMBERGER TOGBLAT – (In Yiddish) – Lwow, PL. no79. 20 Sep 1906 – 1r – 1 – $25.00 – cn Can Microfilming [072]
NAYLAND = NEWLAND – Montreal, CN, 1926 – 1r – 1 – Can$25.00 – cn Can Microfilming [072]
Naylor, Wilson Samuel *see* DAYBREAK IN THE DARK CONTINENT
Nayrac, Jean Paul *see* GRANDEUR ET MISERE DE LA FEMME
Nay-Reine, Lucien *see*
- FO-YAL
- SOUS LE FOULARD CREOLE

NAYS (NAUJIENOS) = NEWS – (In Yiddish) – Kaunas, LT. v1 no32 26 Dec 1921-v2 no92(128) 6 Feb 1922 – 1r – 1 – $25.00 – cn Can Microfilming [072]
DI NAY-TSAYT = THE NEW TIMES – (In Yiddish) – Warsaw, PL. v1 no1. 1907 – 1r – 1 – $25.00 – cn Can Microfilming [072]
Naz, R *see* L'AVOUERIE DE L'ABBAYE DE SAINT-ARMAND EN PEVELE
LE NAZAREEN OU LE CHRISTIANISME DES JUIFS, DES GENTILS ET DES MAHOMETANS / Toland, John – (D'Holbach series). 1777 – 9 – fr Hachette [240]
THE NAZARENE MESSENGER – Listowel, Ont: W L Kells, [1888-188-?] – 9 – cn C.I.H.M. [240]
THE NAZARENE MESSENGER – (Some original pgs damaged) – v2-14. 1898-Jan 1910 – 5r – 1 – ATLA S0419 – us A.T.L.A. [240]
NAZARENUS OR, JEWISH, GENTILE, AND MAHOMETAN CHRISTIANITY / Toland, John – London, 2nd rev ed 1718 – 4mf – 8 – ne Slangenburg [240]
NAZARETH AND THE BEGINNINGS OF CHRISTIANITY : A NEW VIEW BASED UPON PHILOLOGICAL EVIDENCE... / Burrage, Champlin – Oxford: University Press; London: H. Milford, 1914 – 1mf – us A.T.L.A. [240]
Nazarevskii, V *see* IZ ISTORII GORODA MOSKVY

NAZAR-I SERIATTE KUVVET-I BERIYE VE BAHRIYE'NIN EHEMMIYET VE VUECUBU / Atif, Mehmet – Istanbul: Matbaa-i Bahriye, 1326 [1910] – $13.00 – us MEDOC [956]
Nazelle, L *see* LA MORALE DE CALVIN D'APRES L'INSTITUTION DE LA RELIGION CHRETIENNE
Nazelle, L J *see* ETUDE SUR ALEXANDRE VINET
NAZI CONSPIRACY AND AGGRESSION : OPINION AND JUDGMENT / U.S. Chief of Counsel for Prosecution of Axis Criminality – The Nuremberg Trials – 188mf – 9 – $435.00 – us UPA [340]
NAZI CONSPIRACY AND AGRESSION / ed by Office of United States Chief of Counsel for Prosecution of Axis Criminality – Muenchen. 9v. 1979 – 130mf – 9 – subsc: DM780.00 diazo DM900.00 silver – gw Olms [320]
NAZI INTERVENTION IN SPAIN – Washington, DC, 193? Fiche W1182. (Blodgett Collection of Spanish Civil War Pamphlets) – 9 – us H.U. College Libr [946]
NAZIM HIKMET / ed by Oktay, M Fahri – Nos. 1-10 (1950) – 1mf – 9 – $10.50 – us MEDOC [949]
Nazim, Nabizade *see* HEVES ETTIM
LA NAZIONALITA / Albicini, C – Bologna, 1871 – 1mf – 9 – ILM-2385/1 – ne IDC [340]
LA NAZIONALITA DELLE PERSONE GIURIDICHE / Fadda, C – Napoli, 1902 – 1mf – 1 – ILM-3766/1 – ne IDC [327]
LA NAZIONE – Florence, Italy. -d. 19 July 1859-8 Aug 1919. Lacking 1866. 129 reels – 1 – uk British Libr Newspaper [072]
NAZIONE – 1987-1995 – 4r per y – 5,6 – Sfr1,123.00 – sz Infoprint [320]
Nazir, Datuk Pamontjak *see* INDONESIA IN PERSPECTIVE
Nazirzadah *see* IRAN-I IMRUZ
NAZWISKA POLSKIE / Bystron, J S – Lwow, 1927 – 8 – B-1237 2 – ne IDC [943]
NBFAA SIGNAL – (National Burglar and Fire Alarm Association). 1951- – 1951- 1; 1976- 5,6,9 – us UMI [360]
NC SHOPOWNER – (Numerical Control).v1-. 1980- – 1,5,6,9 – us UMI [073]
NCC (NATIONAL CHRISTIAN COUNCIL) NEWS SERVICE – (Some original pgs damaged) – 1975-87 – 2r – 1 – ATLA S0800 – us A.T.L.A. [073]
NCCC CHRONICLES / National Council of the Churches of Christ in the United States of America – v1-86,no.1. 1975-86. Ceased publication – 1 – us UMI [073]
NCCT FORUM / National Council for Children and Television (U.S.) – v1-3. 1978-80 – 1 – us UMI [073]
NCIO NEWS – 1970-72. (American Indian Periodicals in the Princeton University Library). 2 fiches – 9 – $45.00 – us UPA [305]
NCJRS MICROFICHE COLLECTION / U.S. National Institute of Justice NCJRS – (1980 14,714 documents, indexed $5500.00; 1981 suppl. 2500 docs, indexed $990.00; 1982 suppl. 2477 docs, indexed $990.00; 1983-84 suppl. 2540 docs, indexed $1010.00; 1985 suppl. 1077 docs, indexed $550.00; 1986 suppl. 1209 docs, indexed $740.00; 1987 suppl. 1738 docs, indexed $810.00; 1988 suppl. 2205 docs, indexed $940.00; 1989 suppl. 1315 docs, indexed $915.00; 1990 suppl. 1496 docs, $728.00; 1991 suppl. 1183 docs, $934.00) – More than 30,000 full-text documents, indexed – 9 – us N.C.J.R.S. [360]
NCJW JOURNAL – New York, NY. Jan/Feb 1982-May/Jun 1985. Missing some issues. Ceased publication – 1 – us A.J.P.C. [071]
NCR INDEPENDENT USER MONTHLY – 1984- – 1,5,6,9 – us UMI [510]
NCUA BULLETIN / National Credit Union Administration – 1970-72 – 1 – us UMI [073]
NCUA QUARTERLY / National Credit Union Administration – v. 1-5. 1973-77 – 1 – us UMI [336]
NDAA: JOURNAL OF THE NATIONAL DISTRICT ATTORNEYS ASSOCIATION – v1-3. 1965-67 – 1 – us UMI [340]
NDEMBU DIVINATION, ITS SYMBOLISM AND TECHNIQUES / Turner, V W – 7 – uk Microform Academic [960]
THE N.D.G. JOURNAL DE N.D.G. – Montreal, Canada. v1 n3. 17 dec 1954 – 1r – 1 – Can$25.00 – cn Can Microfilming [072]
Ndiaye, Moussa *see* GALAAY
Ndoye, Mbengue nee Mariama *see* INTRODUCTION A LA LITTERATURE ORALE LEBOUE
N'Dua, Edouard *see* L'INSTALLATION DES TUTSHOKWE DANS L'EMPIRE LUNDA 1850-1903
NE GOEPPS VULL : GESCHICHTEN IN MOENSTERLAENNSK PLATT / Wagenfeld, Karl – Muenster in Westf.: Aschendorff, 1909 – 1r – 1 – us U.W. Library [430]
NE MIR, NO MECH / Merezhkovskii, Dimitrii – Spb. 1908. BR-775 2 – 8 – ne IDC [460]
NE MOGU MOLCHAT / Akimov, A & Menshchikova, L – Ni u-lork: L. Menshchikov, 1912 – 1 – CSUX89-B7266 – us Hoover Inst Photo [999]
NE VOENNYI DNEVNIK / Merezhkovskii, Dimitrii – 1914-16. Ot voiny do revoliutsii. Petrograd. 1917. BR-776 2 – 8 – ne IDC [460]
NEA HELLAS – Athens, Greece. -d. 2 Oct 1915-13 Sept 1916; 1 Dec 1917-26 Jan 1919. Imperfect. 4 reels – 1 – uk British Libr Newspaper [949]
NEA HELLAS – Athens, Greece. -d. 2 Oct 1939-4 April 1941. Imperfect. 6 reels – 1 – uk British Libr Newspaper [949]
NEA HEMERA – Athens, Greece. -d. 15 Nov 1915-17 Nov 1916; 15 March 1917-31 July 1918. Imperfect. 5 reels – 1 – uk British Libr Newspaper [949]
N.E.A. JOURNAL *see* TODAY'S EDUCATION
NEA REPORTER – (v. 15- 1976- 5,6,9) – (National Education Association). v. 1- 1962- – 1 – us UMI [370]
NEA TODAY: A NEWSPAPER FOR MEMBERS OF THE NATIONAL EDUCATION ASSOCIATION – v1-. 1982- – 1,5,6,9 – us UMI [073]
Neal, Bart C *see* A STUDY OF ACCOUNTABILITY IN SECULAR EDUCATION IN THE UNITED STATES TO DETERMINE POSSIBLE PRINCIPLES FOR THEOLOGICAL EDUCATION AMONG SOUTHERN BAPTISTS
Neal, John *see*
- RACHEL DYER
- WANDERING RECOLLECTIONS OF A SOMEWHAT BUSY LIFE

Neale, F A *see* NARRATIVE OF A RESIDENCE IN SIAM
Neale, John Mason *see*
- CATECHETICAL NOTES AND CLASS QUESTIONS, LITERAL AND MYSTICAL
- ECCLESIOLOGICAL NOTES ON THE ISLE OF MAN, ROSS, SUTHERLAND AND THE ORKNEYS, OR, A SUMMER PILGRIMAGE TO S. MAUGHOLD AND S. MAGNUS
- A HISTORY OF THE SO-CALLED JANSENIST CHURCH OF HOLLAND
- LECTURES ON CHURCH DIFFICULTIES
- NOTES, ECCLESIOLOGICAL AND PICTURESQUE, ON DALMATIA, CROATIA, ISTRIA, STYRIA
- NOTES ON THE DIVINE OFFICE, HISTORICAL AND MYSTICAL
- THE PATRIARCHATE OF ANTIOCH
- SEATONIAN POEMS
- SERMONS ON THE SONG OF SONGS: PREACHED IN...S. MARGARET'S, EAST GRINSTED
- THE UNSEEN WORLD

NEAL'S CREEK BAPTIST CHURCH. ANDERSON COUNTY. SOUTH CAROLINA : CHURCH RECORDS – 1901-82.661p – 1 – 29.75 – us Baptist [240]
Neander, August *see*
- GENETISCHE ENTWICKLUNG DER VORNEHMSTEN GNOSTISCHEN SYSTEME
- GESCHICHTE DER PFLANZUNG UND LEITUNG DER CHRISTLICHEN KIRCHE DURCH DIE APOSTEL
- MEMORIALS OF CHRISTIAN LIFE IN THE EARLY AND MIDDLE AGES
- THEOBALD THAMER

Neander, Augustus *see*
- THE EMPEROR JULIAN AND HIS GENERATION: AN HISTORICAL PICTURE
- THE LIFE AND TIMES OF ST. BERNARD

NEAR EAST READINGS ON AGRICULTURAL INVESTMENT PROJECTS : SELECTED PAPERS PRESENTED AT THE NEAR EAST WORKSHOP ON AGRICULTURAL INVESTMENT PROJECTS, ROME, 1978 – 1979 – 299p – it F.A.O. [338]
NEAREST THE POLE / Peary, Robert E – BN 337 2. 1907 – 8 – ne IDC [910]
NEARING HOME : COMFORTS AND COUNSELS FOR THE AGED / Schenck, William Edward – Philadelphia: Presbyterian Board of Publication, c1868 – 2mf – 9 – 0-8370-6318-3 – 1986-0318 – us A.T.L.A. [240]
Neatby, William Blair *see* A HISTORY OF THE PLYMOUTH BRETHREN
Neath Burgage *see* PRESENTMENTS OF THE COURT LEET
Neath. England *see*
- COURT MINUTE BOOKS OF THE BOROUGH
- DEEDS OF THE BOROUGH
- RECORDS AND VESTRY BOOKS OF THE BOROUGH
- VESTRY BOOKS, 1830-1912/NEATH, MINUTE BOOK

NEATKARIGA CINA = INDEPENDENT STRUGGLE – (1991-93 2r per y $170y. 1994 3r $255. 1995-96 6r $510. Cont as: Neatkariga Rita Avize in 1995, 1997-98 4r per y $340y) – Latvia, 1999- – 4r per y – 1 – $320.00 standing order – us Ross [072]
NEATKARIGA RITA AVIZE *see* NEATKARIGA CINA
NEATKARIGD CINA – 1991-1995 – 1 – Sfr240.00 – sz Infoprint [947]
NEBB (NATIONAL ENVIRONMENTAL BALANCING BUREAU) – Printed index. Updated every 60 days – 6,9 – us Info Handling [621]
Nebel, Abraham Lincoln *see* CLEVELAND JEWISH MISCELLANY, MS 3669
Nebel, Gerhard *see* ERNST JUENGER UND DAS SCHICKSAL DES MENSCHEN
NEBESHEH AND DEFENNEH / Petrie, William Matthew Flinders – 1888 – 9 – $10.00 – us I.R.C. [930]
NEBESNAJA CARICA = QUEEN OF HEAVEN – McKeesport, PA: [United Societies of Greek Catholic Religion of USA. v1-29 n8. 1927-aug 1955] – us Res Libr [240]
NEBESNYE VERBLIUZHATA / Guro, E – ("Zhuravl'"). Spb. 1914. BR-931 2 – 8 – ne IDC [460]
NEBESNYIA SLOVA I DRUGIE RAZSKAZY / Gippius, Z N – Paris. 1921. BR-717 2 – 8 – ne IDC [460]
Nebie, M A *see* ETUDE ETHNOLINGUISTIQUE D'UN CORPUS DE CONTES DIOULA (HAUTE VOLTA)
NEBO GOLUBOE / Sologub, F – Stikhi. Izd. "Bibliofil". Revel. 1921. BR-868 2 – 8 – ne IDC [460]
NEBRASKA : REVISED STATUTES OF NEBRASKA / Lincoln, Nebraska Unicameral Legislature – 1943-Apr 1996 update – 9 – $3,228.75 – us Hein [340]
NEBRASKA : SESSION LAWS OF AMERICAN STATES AND TERRITORIES – 1855-1995 – 9 – $1,369.00 set – us Hein [340]
Nebraska *see*
- REPORTS AND OPINIONS (A-G)
- REPORTS, POST-NRS
- REPORTS, PRE-NRS
- SESSION LAWS, 1855-

NEBRASKA ADVERTISER – Brownville, NE. -d. Sep. 1870-Dec. 1870 – 1 – us NE Hist [071]
NEBRASKA ADVERTISER – Brownville. Neb. 1856-1908 – 1 – us UMI [071]
NEBRASKA ADVERTISER – Nemaha, NE. -w. Jun 1858-Sept 1863; Jan 1864-Nov 1865; Mar 1866-Nov 1882; Jun 1892; Oct 1895-Feb 1896; Apr 1896-May 1898; Oct 1898-Jan 1901; Apr 1901-Dec 1902; Feb 1903-Dec 1908 – 1 – us NE Hist [071]
Nebraska. Agricultural Experiment Station. Lincoln *see*
- ANNUAL REPORTS 1880-1969
- BULLETIN
- CIRCULAR
- MISCELLANEOUS PUBLICATIONS
- OUTSTATE TESTING PROGRAM CIRCULAR
- PRESS BULLETIN
- QUARTERLY
- RESEARCH BULLETIN
- SPECIAL REPORT

DER NEBRASKA ANSIEDLER – Lincoln, NE. -m. June 1878; May 1880. Continued as: Mennonitische Rundschau. In German – 1 – us NE Hist [071]
NEBRASKA ATTORNEY GENERAL REPORTS AND OPINIONS – (6 1877-1978 $210.00. 9 1977-1984 $82.50) – 1877-1984 – 6,9 – $292.50set – us Hein [340]
NEBRASKA BANNER – Omaha, NE. -w. 1 Jun 1892-8 Jun 1892. In German – 1 – us NE Hist [071]
NEBRASKA BEACON – Lincoln, NE. -irr. Jun 1899-Jan 1901, scattered issues missing; Apr 1901-Mar 1911; May-Jul 1911; Jan 1914-Dec 1921; Mar 1922-Jan 1929; Oct 1929-Oct 1968; Jan-Dec 1969 – 1 – us NE Hist [071]
NEBRASKA BEACON – Lincoln.Nebraska. And pred. 1899-1954 – 1 – us UMI [071]
NEBRASKA BEEF CATTLE REPORT / Nebraska. College of Agriculture. Dept. of Animal Science – 1952-69 – 1, 5 – us Spaulding [636]
NEBRASKA BIENE – Columbus, NE. -w. Jan. 1897-Dec. 1900; Oct. 1901-Jun. 1918 – 1 – us NE Hist [071]
NEBRASKA BLIZZARD – Lincoln, NE. -w. Nov 1894-Oct 1898, scattered issues missing; Dec 1898-Oct 1904 – 1 – us NE Hist [071]
NEBRASKA BLUE BOOK AND HISTORICAL REGISTER 1918 / ed by Sheldon, Addison E – Lincoln: Nebraska Legislative Reference Bureau, 1918. Nebraska Reel 4. (The Cox Library Collection) – 5 – us Americana [978]
NEBRASKA CHRISTIAN NEWS – Bethany, NE. -w. Dec. 1894; Oct. 1895-Jan. 1907 – 1 – us NE Hist [071]
NEBRASKA CITY DAILY CHRONICLE – Nebraska City, NE. Aug 1868-Feb 1869; Sep 1870-Feb 1871; May 1871-May 1872; Jan-Jun 1873; Dec 1873-Apr 1874 – 1 – us NE Hist [071]
NEBRASKA CITY DAILY NEWS – Nebraska City, NE. (-tw 1867-69). Dec 1864-Apr 1865; July 1865; Jan 1867-Jun 1870; Aug 1872; Jan 1877-Dec 1881; Oct 1895-Dec 1896, scattered issues missing; Jan 1897-May 1898; Jan 1899-Dec 1912; May 1914; July 1916-Oct 1917; Dec 1922; Aug 1923; Aug 1925 – 1 – us NE Hist [071]
NEBRASKA CITY NEWS-PRESS – Nebraska City, NE. -w. (-d 1867-93, 1894-95, 1918 to date; -sw 1893, 1896-1918). Jan-Apr 1857; Aug-Sept 1857; Nov 1857-Sept 1861; Jan-Nov 1862; Jan-Oct 1865; Feb 1866-Nov 1868; Jan-Dec 1869; May 1870; Jan 1871 to date – 1 – us NE Hist [071]
NEBRASKA CITY STAATS-ZEITUNG – Nebraska City, NE. -w. Jul 1892; Jun 1907-Jan 1912 – 1 – us NE Hist [071]
NEBRASKA CITY WEEKLY – Nebraska City, NE. -sw. Jun-Sept 1902; Aug 1904 – 1 – us NE Hist [071]
Nebraska. College of Agriculture *see*
- AGGIE TATLER
- AGRICULTURAL NOTEBOOK: ENGINEERING NEWS
- AGRICULTURAL NOTEBOOK: INSECT LETTER
- AGRICULTURAL NOTEBOOK: PLANT PATHOLOGY
- AGRICULTURE
- CORNHUSKER COUNTRYMAN
- FOREST CLUB ANNUAL
- HORTICULTURE PROGRESS REPORT

Nebraska. College of Agriculture. Dept. of Agricultural Economics *see*
- DEPARTMENT REPORT
- REPORT
- STAFF PAPER

Nebraska. College of Agriculture. Dept. of Agricultural Education *see*
- NEBRASKA TRACTOR TEST DATA
- PROGRESS REPORT

Nebraska. College of Agriculture. Dept. of Agronomy *see*
- AGRONOMY VIEWS
- NEBRASKA SEED AND SOIL
- PESTICIDE POINTERS

Nebraska. College of Agriculture. Dept. of Animal Science *see*
- NEBRASKA BEEF CATTLE REPORT
- NEBRASKA SWINE REPORT

Nebraska. College of Agriculture. Extension Service *see*
- THE AGRICULTURAL ENGINEER: FARM BUILDING
- THE AGRICULTURAL ENGINEER: IRRIGATION
- THE AGRICULTURAL ENGINEER: RURAL ELECTRIFICATION
- ANNUAL REPORT OF NEBRASKA IRRIGATION: DEVELOPMENT FARMS
- CAMPAIGN CIRCULAR
- EXTENSION BULLETIN
- EXTENSION CIRCULAR
- NEBRASKA FARM AND RANCH ECONOMICS

NEBRASKA COMMONWEALTH – Lincoln. Neb. 1867-1869 – 1 – us UMI [071]
Nebraska. Conservation and Survey Division *see*
- BULLETIN
- NEBRASKA CONSERVATION BULLETIN
- NEBRASKA GEOLOGICAL SURVEY BULLETIN
- NEBRASKA GEOLOGICAL SURVEY PAPER
- NEBRASKA GEOLOGICAL SURVEY RESOURCE REPORT
- NEBRASKA WATER SURVEY PAPER

NEBRASKA CONSERVATION BULLETIN / Nebraska. Conservation and Survey Division – n.1-36. 1928-64 – 1, 5 – us Spaulding [639]

NEBRASKA DAILY DEMOCRAT – Omaha, South, NE. -w. (-d 1901-1915). May-Sept 1902; Jan 1903-Mar 1904; May 1904-Apr 1921 – 1 – us NE Hist [071]

NEBRASKA DAILY PRESS – Nebraska City, NE. (-sw 1862-63; -d 1863-1925). Nov 1859-Nov 1860; May 1862-Apr 1863; Sept 1863-Mar 1865; Jun 1885-Jun 1887; Apr 1892; Jun-Jul 1892; Sept 1893-Feb 1895; Oct 1895-Nov 1925 – 1 – us NE Hist [071]

Nebraska. Dept. of Labor *see* STATE LABOR REPORTS

NEBRASKA DIGEST – Lincoln, NE. -w. Aug 1935-May 1939, scattered issues missing – 1 – us NE Hist [071]

NEBRASKA DISPATCH – Lincoln, NE. -bw. Apr 1974-Feb 1976 – 1 – us NE Hist [071]

NEBRASKA ENQUIRER – DeSoto, NE. -w. Aug. 1859-Sep. 1861. Incomplete – 1 – us NE Hist [071]

NEBRASKA FARM AND RANCH ECONOMICS / Nebraska. College of Agriculture. Extension Service – n.96-198. 1956-65 – 1, 5 – us Spaulding [630]

NEBRASKA FARMER – Brownville. Neb. 1860-1862 – 1 – us UMI [071]

NEBRASKA FARMER – Omaha. Neb. 1877-1959 – 1 – us UMI [071]

NEBRASKA FARMERS' ALLIANCE PAPERS / ed by Bakken, Douglas A – 1887-1901. 7 reels. Printed guide ($0.25) – 1 – us UMI [630]

NEBRASKA FRIEND – Plainview, NE. -m. Jun 1908-Nov 1909; Jan 1910-Feb 1911, scattered issues missing; Apr 1911-May 1915 – 1 – us NE Hist [071]

NEBRASKA GEOLOGICAL SURVEY BULLETIN / Nebraska. Conservation and Survey Division – n.1-20. 1927-63 – 1, 5 – us Spaulding [550]

NEBRASKA GEOLOGICAL SURVEY PAPER / Nebraska. Conservation and Survey Division – n.1-18. 1933-69 – 1, 5 – us Spaulding [550]

NEBRASKA GEOLOGICAL SURVEY RESOURCE REPORT / Nebraska. Conservation and Survey Division – n.1, 2. 1968-69 – 1, 5 – us Spaulding [550]

NEBRASKA HERALD – Nemaha, NE. -w. Nov 1859-Nov 1860; Jan-Mar 1861 – 1 – us NE Hist [071]

NEBRASKA HERALD – Plattsmouth. Neb. 1865-1882 – 1 – us UMI [071]

NEBRASKA JOURNAL-LEADER – Ponca, NE. -w. Jan-Nov 1884; Apr 1885-Jun 1888; Aug 1888-Nov 1891; Jan 1892-Dec 1908; Feb 1909 to date – 1 – us NE Hist [071]

NEBRASKA LAW BULLETIN *see* NEBRASKA LAW REVIEW

NEBRASKA LAW REVIEW – (Title varies: v1-19 1922-1940 as Nebraska Law Bulletin) – v1-75. 1922-95 – 9 – $1,018.00 set – us Hein [340]

NEBRASKA MEDICAL JOURNAL – (v.64-. 1979- 5,6,9) – v.56-. 1971- – 1 – us UMI [073]

NEBRASKA NEWS – Elsmere, NE. -w. Oct. 1912-Mar. 1917 – 1 – us NE Hist [071]

NEBRASKA NUGGET – Holdrege, NE. -w. Feb 1883; Jun-Oct 1883; Jan 1884-Jun 1885; Jan 1886-Jun 1887 – 1 – us NE Hist [071]

NEBRASKA PALLADIUM – Bellevue, NE. -w. Jul. 1854-Apr. 1855 – 1 – us NE Hist [071]

DIE NEBRASKA POST – Beatrice, NE. -w. Sep. 1895-May 1897 – 1 – us NE Hist [071]

Nebraska Press Association *see* WHO'S WHO IN NEBRASKA

NEBRASKA REPUBLICAN – Auburn, NE. -w. Dec. 1884-Jun. 1886. Incomplete – 1 – us NE Hist [071]

NEBRASKA SEED AND SOIL / Nebraska. College of Agriculture. Dept. of Agronomy – n.1-5. 1953-57 – 1, 5 – us Spaulding [631]

NEBRASKA SIGNAL – Fairmont, NE. -w. Oct. 1881-Apr. 1896 – 1 – us NE Hist [071]

NEBRASKA SIGNAL – Fairmont. Neb. 1881-1896 – 1 – us UMI [071]

NEBRASKA SIGNAL – Geneva, NE. -w. Nov 1882-Mar 1885; Oct 1889-Oct 1891; June 1892; Oct 1892-Dec 1922; Jan 1925 to date – 1 – us NE Hist [071]

NEBRASKA STAATS-ANZEIGER – Grand Island, NE. -w. Sept 1891-Sept 1906; Nov 1906-Jun 1918 – 1 – us NE Hist [071]

NEBRASKA STAATS-ANZEIGER – Lincoln, NE. -w. Nov 1883; Aug 1885; Sept 1891-Mar 1901 – 1 – us NE Hist [071]

NEBRASKA STAATS-ANZEIGER UND HEROLD – Grand Island, NE. 18 Sept 1891-27 June 1918. In German. Continued as: Grand Island Herald – 1 – us NE Hist [071]

NEBRASKA STAATS-JOURNAL – Omaha, NE. -w. 19 Sept 1868. In German – 1 – us NE Hist [073]

NEBRASKA STAATS-ZEITUNG – Nebraska City, NE. -w. 15 Jul 1892-31 Jan 1912 – 1 – us NE Hist [071]

DIE NEBRASKA STAATS-ZEITUNG-TRIBUNE – Grand Island, NE. -w. 6 Dec 1879 – 1 – us NE Hist [071]

Nebraska. State Bar Association *see* PROCEEDINGS

NEBRASKA STATE BAR ASSOCIATION PROCEEDINGS – v1-37. 1900-46 (all publ) – 38mf – 9 – $171.00 – LLMC 84-635 – us L.L.M.C. [073]

NEBRASKA STATE BAR JOURNAL – (Superseded by: NSBA News) – v1-20. 1952-71 (all publ) – 9 – $95.00 set – us Hein [340]

NEBRASKA STATE BAR JOURNAL *see* NSBA NEWS

NEBRASKA STATE CAPITAL – Lincoln, NE. -w. Jul-Aug 1892; Sept 1895-Dec 1899; Dec 1900-Sept 1902, scattered issues missing; Jul 1908-Nov 1912; Sept 1914 – 1 – us NE Hist [071]

NEBRASKA STATE DEMOCRAT – Lincoln, NE. -w. Jan 1893-Mar 1899; May-Sept 1899; Mar 1908-Apr 1921 – 1 – us NE Hist [071]

Nebraska State Historical Society *see* PUBLICATIONS

NEBRASKA STATE JOURNAL – Lincoln, NE. -d. Jul 1870-Sept 1871; Nov 1871-Jul 1873; Oct 1873; Jan 1874-Jan 1951 – 1 – us NE Hist [071]

NEBRASKA STATE JOURNAL – Lincoln. Neb. 1869-1951 – 1 – us UMI [071]

NEBRASKA STATE MEDICAL JOURNAL – v.1-56. 1916-71. Continued as Nebraska Medical Journal – 1 – us UMI [073]

NEBRASKA STATESMAN – Lincoln, NE. -irr. Apr-Oct 1866; Jul 1868-Jan 1871; Jun 1871 – 1 – us NE Hist [071]

Nebraska. Supreme Court *see*
- NEBRASKA SUPREME COURT REPORTS
- NEBRASKA UNOFFICIAL REPORTS
- POUND'S CASES ON PRACTICE

NEBRASKA SUPREME COURT REPORTS / Nebraska. Supreme Court – (Pre-NRS: v1-8 1860-79 53mf $79.00. Updates planned) – v1-103. 1855-1919 – 987mf – $1,481.00 – LLMC 82-984 – us L.L.M.C. [340]

NEBRASKA SUPREME COURT REPORTS *see*
- NEBRASKA UNOFFICIAL REPORTS
- POUND'S CASES ON PRACTICE

NEBRASKA SWINE REPORT / Nebraska. College of Agriculture. Dept. of Animal Science – 1953-69 – 1, 5 – us Spaulding [636]

NEBRASKA: THE LAND AND THE PEOPLE / Sheldon, Addison E – Chicago: Lewis Publ. Co., 1931. v1-2, Nebraska Reel 2. v3, Nebraska Reel 3. (The Cox Library Collection) – 5 – us Americana [978]

NEBRASKA TRACTOR TEST DATA / Nebraska. College of Agriculture. Dept. of Agricultural Education – 1920-69 – 1, 5 – us Spaulding [631]

NEBRASKA TRANSCRIPT – Stella, NE. -w. Jun 1888-Jun 1892 – 1 – us NE Hist [071]

NEBRASKA UNOFFICIAL REPORTS / Nebraska. Supreme Court – (A Pre-NRS title) – v1-5. 1901-1904 (all publ) – 54mf – 9 – $81.00 – LLMC 90-006 – us L.L.M.C. [340]

NEBRASKA VOLKSBLATT – West Point, NE. -w. Sep 1879; Jan 1885-Dec 1887; Jan 1889-Dec 1916 – 1 – us NE Hist [071]

NEBRASKA VOLKSFREUND – Hastings, NE. -w. Nov 1895-Aug 1896; Jan-Mar 1899 – 1 – us NE Hist [071]

NEBRASKA VOLKSFREUND – Hastings. Neb. 1895-1899 – 1 – us UMI [071]

NEBRASKA VORWAERTS – Omaha, NE. -d,w. 27 Sept 1894-9 Sept 1897. Title varies – 1 – us NE Hist [071]

NEBRASKA WATER SURVEY PAPER / Nebraska. Conservation and Survey Division – Nos 1-24 1944-69 – 1, 5 – us Spaulding [630]

NEBRASKANS 1854-1904 / Bee Publishing Co – Omaha, 1904. Nebraska Reel 4. (The Cox Library Collection) – 5 – us Americana [978]

Nebridius a Muendelheim *see* PHILOSOPHIEAE MAGNI PATRIS ET ECCLESIAE DOCTORIS AUGUSTINI...PARS ALTERA

NEBULO NEBULONUM HOC EST : IOCO-SERIA VERNACULAE NEQUITIAE CENSURA... / Flitner, J – Leeuwarden, 1634 – 3mf – 9 – ne IDC [700]

THE NECESSARY FOUNDATIONS OF INDIVIDUAL AND NATIONAL WELL-BEING, AND OF CIVILIZATION / Baird, Henry Carey – 20p – 9 – 1.00f – at Libertarian Micro [335]

NECESSITE D'UN NOUVEAU PARTI POLITIQUE / Freslon, A – Angers, impr. E. Le Sourd, 1832, 4 p. Lettre adressee a M. Hawke ibid., 4 P. L'attente (par Enfantin), ibid., 6 P. Les Saint-Simoniens, 1825-1834. 6914 – 9 – fr Hachette [335]

THE NECESSITY, NATURE, AND FRUITS, OF SANCTIFICATION / Bangs, Nathan – 1881 – 9 – us A.T.L.A. [240]

THE NECESSITY OF PERSONAL COMMUNION WITH CHRIST : A SERMON / Fowles, J H – Philadelphia: C. Sherman, 1853 – 1mf – us A.T.L.A. [240]

A NECESSITY OF SEPARATION FROM THE CHURCH OF ENGLAND *see* PUBLICATIONS

A NECESSITY OF SEPARATION FROM THE CHURCH OF ENGLAND PROVED BY THE NONCONFORMIST PRINCIPLES....1849 / Canne, John – 1 – us A.T.L.A. [240]

Nechaev, A I *see* SOIUZY POTREBITEL'SKIKH OBSHCHESTVO

Nechaeva, V S *see* OPISANIE RUKOPISEI F.M. DOSTOEVSKOGO

NECHEB UND NECHBET : UNTERSUCHUNGEN ZUR GESCHICHTE DES KULTORTES ELKAB / Hartmann, Hartwig – 1993 – 5mf – 9 – DM118.00 – 3-89349-822-2 – gw Hänsel [930]

Nechkina, M V *see* DVIZHENIE DEKABRISTOV

DER NECKAR-BOTE – (Also known as: Der Neckarbote) – Heidelberg, Germany. 1845-4 May 1850 – 2r – 1 – gw Mikrofilm [072]

DER NECKARBOTE *see* DER NECKAR-BOTE

NECKAR-CHRONIK : BA DER SUEDWEST-PRESSE – Horb, Germany. 2 Jan 1980- – 70r (1980-1990) – 1 – gw Mikrofilm [072]

NECKAR-ENZ-BOTE – Besigheim, 1960-dec 7 1979 – 1 – Inquire at Mikrofilmarchiv for details – gw Misc Inst [072]

NECKAR-ENZ-BOTE – Besigheim, Germany. Jan 1960-7 Dec 1979 – 30r – 1 – gw Mikrofilm [072]

NECKAR-ZEITUNG – Heilbronn, Germany. 1896-31 Dec 1934 – 1 – gw Mikrofilm [072]

Necker de Saussure, Louis Albert *see* VOYAGE EN ECOSSE ET AUX ILES HEBRIDES

Necker, N J de *see*
- COROLLARIUM AD PHILOSOPHIAM BOTANICAM
- DELICIAE GALLO-BELGICAE SILVESTRES
- ELEMENTA BOTANICA
- METHODUS MUSCORUM
- PHYTOZOOLOGIE PHILOSOPHIQUE

Neckham, A *see* DE NATURIS RERUM

Necmi *see* DIVAN

NECM-I ATI – Trabzon, 1928-19? – 9 – $10.00 – us MEDOC [956]

NECROLOGIA DEL MARQUES DE MONSALUD / Fita, Fidel & Rodriguez Villa, Antonio – Madrid: Fortanet, 1910. B.R.A.H. 56, 1910, p. 234 – sp Bibl Santa Ana [920]

NECROLOGICA / Barrado Manzano, Arcangel; ed by Pazos, Manuel R – Madrid: Graf. Calleja, 1971 – 1 – sp Bibl Santa Ana [946]

NECROLOGIE, KRONIEK EN CARTULARIUM C.A. VAN HET FRATERHUIS TE DOESBURG (1432-1559) / Weiler, A G – Leiden, 1974 – 6mf – 8 – Dfl25.00 – ne Slangenburg [240]

NECROLOGIO DE LA PROVINCIA SERAFICA DE CARTAGENA DESDE SU RESTAURACION EN 1878. MURCIA, 1967 / Garcia, Antonio – Madrid: Graf. Calleja, 1967 – 1 – sp Bibl Santa Ana [946]

HET NECROLOGIUM DIOECESIS HARLEMENSIS / Buccaeus, I – Dfl9.00 – ne Slangenburg [240]

Nectario Maria, H *see*
- CATALOGO DE LOS DOCUMENTOS REFERENTES A LA ANTIGUA PROVINCIA DE MARACAIBO, EXISTENTES EN EL ARCHIVO GENERAL DE INDIAS DE SEVILLA
- INDICE DE LOS DOCUMENTOS REFERENTES A LOS OBISPOS DE VENEZUELA (1532-1816) EXISTENTES EN EL ARCHIVO GENERAL DE INDIAS DE SEVILLA

Nectoux, G *see* LA SITUATION ECONOMIQUE DE L'ALGERIE

NED FORTESCUE, OR, ROUGHING IT THROUGH LIFE: A STORY FOUNDED ON FACT / Forrest, Edmund William – Ottawa; Toronto: Hunter, Rose, 1869. 03153. (Pre-1900 Canadiana) – 9 – cn C.I.H.M. [830]

NEDELYA – Moscow. U.S.S.R. 1961- – 1 – us UMI [072]

NEDERDUYTSCHE POEMATA / Heinsius, D – Amsterdam, 1618 – 1mf – 9 – O-3225/1 – ne IDC [430]

NEDERDUYTSCHE POEMATA / Heinsius, D – Amsterdam, 1618 [after 1620] – 2mf – 9 – O-3078/1 – ne IDC [430]

NEDERDUYTSCHE POEMATA / Heinsius, D – O 630. 1616 – 9 – ne IDC [430]

NEDERDUYTSCHE POEMATA / Hoffer, A – O 295. 1635 – 9 – ne IDC [430]

NEDERLAND EN INDONESIE IN DE 20STE / Damste, Onno – Eeuw. 1947. SE-11,784 1 – 9 – ne IDC [960]

NEDERLAND EN INDONESIE IN DE 20STE / Damste, Onno – Eeuw. 1948. 2DE DRUK. SE-11,785 1 – 9 – ne IDC [950]

NEDERLANDS JURISTEN COMITE VOOR DE MENSENRECHTEN = INTERNATIONAL COMMISSION OF JURISTS, DUTCH SECTION – Leiden. 84 docs. 1980-1991 – 97mf – 9 – ne IDC [320]

NEDERLANDS KUNSTHISTORISCH JAARBOEK – 's-Gravenhage. v1-20. 1947-1969 – 101mf – 9 – ne IDC [700]

NEDERLANDS TIJDSCHRIFT VOOR GENEESKUNDE – v.101-23. 1957-79 – 1,5,6 – us Princeton Micro [610]

NEDERLANDSCH ARCHIEF VAN KERKELIJKE GESCHIEDENIS – (1829-1840: Archief van Kerkelijke Geschiedenis; 1852-1854: Nieuw Arch. van Kerkelijke Geschiedenis. 50mf) – 1(1841)-9(1849) – 9 – Dfl175.00 – ne Slangenburg [073]

NEDERLANDSCH ARCHIEF VOOR KERKGESCHIEDENIS – 1(1902)-31(1940) – 147mf – 9 – Dfl515:00 – ne Slangenburg [073]

NEDERLANDSCH KRUIDKUNDIG ARCHIEF / ed by De Vriese, Dozy & Molkenboer – Leyden, 1846-1860; S.1 v1-5 1868-1895; S.2 v1-6 1899-1903; S.3 v1-2 1904-1932 – 173mf – 9 – ne IDC [949]

NEDERLANDSCH OF BELGISCH? / Beekman, A A – 's-Gravenhage, 1919 – 9 – 1mf – ILM-1883/1 – ne IDC [327]

NEDERLANDSCH TIJSCHRIFT VOOR VOLKSKUNDE – v39-42. 1934-38 – 1 – us I.U. Libraries [390]

NEDERLANDSCHE BIBLIOGRAPHIE VAN KERKGESCHIEDENIS / Knuttel, Willem Pieter Cornelius – Amsterdam: F. Muller, 1889 (Bijdragen tot eene Nederlandsche bibliographie; 3. deel) – 1mf – us A.T.L.A. [240]

NEDERLANDSCHE COMMISSARISSEN AAN DE KAAP, 1657-1700 / Boeseken, A J – The Hague: M Nijhoff, 1938 – us Res Libr [960]

NEDERLANDSCHE EMBLEMATA : GESCHIEDENIS EN BIBLIOGRAPHIE TOT DE 18E EEUW / Vries, A G C de – Amsterdam, 1899 – 4mf – ne IDC [700]

DE NEDERLANDSCHE ISRAELIET – s'Gravenhage. v1. 1843 – 1mf – 9 – ne IDC [305]

NEDERLANDSCHE RECHTSPRAAK, OF VERZAMELING VAN ARRESTEN EN GEWIJSDEN VAN DEN HOOGEN RAAD DER NEDERLANDEN – v. 1-222. 1839-1913 – 1 – 767.00 – us L of C Photodup [340]

NEDERLANDSCHE VOGELEN; VOLGENS HUNNE HUISHOUDING, AERT EN EIGENSCHAPPEN BESCHREEVEN / Nozeman, C & Sepp, C & Houttuyn, M – 2107 5 v. 1770-1829 – 8 – ne IDC [590]

NEDERLANDSCHE ZIONISTENBOND, 1899-1924 – Ed. by F. Bernstein, K. J. Edersheim, M. J. Simons. Amsterdam. 1925. BJ-262-41 1 – 9 – ne IDC [270]

NEDERLANDSCH-INDIE, OUD EN NIEUW – Amsterdam, 1916/1917-1935 – 94mf – 9 – ne IDC [950]

NEDERLANDSCH-ISRAELIETISCH NIEUWS-EN ADVERTENTIEBLAD – Amsterdam. v1-2. 1849-1850 – 5mf – 9 – ne IDC [949]

DE NEDERLANDSE ECONOMIE IN 1970. EEN VOORWAARDELIJKE PROGNOSE VAN DE ONTWIKKELINGSMOGELIJKHEDEN VOOR DE NEDERLANDSE ECONOMIE OP MIDDELLANGE TERMIJN(1966-1970). (THE NETHERLANDS' ECONOMY IN 1970. A PRELIMINARY PROGNOSIS) / Netherlands. Centraal Planbureau – 's-Gravenhage. 1966. BD-1701/1 – 9 – ne IDC [338]
DE NEDERLANDSE ECONOMIE IN 1973. EEN VOORWAARDELIJKE PROGNOSE VAN DE ONTWIKKELINGSMOGELIJKHEDEN VOOR DE NEDERLANDSE ECONOMIE OP MIDDELLANGE TERMIJN 1968-1973 / Netherlands. Centraal Planbureau – (The Netherlands' Economy in 1973. A preliminary prognosis of medium term development possibilities for the Dutch Economy). 's-Gravenhage. 1970. BD-1705 1 – 9 – ne IDC [338]
NEDERLANDSE HERVORMDE KERK : WEEKBULLETIN VAN HET PERSBUREAU – 1953; 1968-93 (complete) – 16r – 1 – ATLA S0482 – us A.T.L.A. [073]
Nederlandse Hervormde Kerk *see*
– WEEKBULLETIN
– WEEKBULLETIN VAN HET PERSBUREAU
NEDERLANDSE STAATSCOURANT / Netherlands – 's-Gravenhage. -d. 1814- . Texts of ministerial decisions, other official and judicial announcements. Yearly subscriptions available – 9 – ne Sdu MICRO [324]
Nedim *see* DIVAN
Nedobrovo, N V *see* ANNA AKHMATOVA
Nedoncelle, M et al *see* ARCHEOLOGIE PALEOCHRETIENNE ET CULTE CHRETIEN
THE NEED FOR AND FINANCING OF AN IDEAL MARKET FOR FREEDOM IDEAS AND FOR OTHER IDEALS AS WELL / Zube, John & Zube, David – 2fiches. (24X) – 9 – 1.00f – at Libertarian Micro [320]
A NEEDFUL ATTEMPT TO MAKE LANGUAGE AND DIVINITY PLAIN AND EASIE – Anon. 1711. 29p. (English Linguistics Series 1500-1800) – 9 – us UMI [400]
NEEDHAM 1711-1858 – (Mf 1-2: Births 1711-63. Mf 3-4: Birth Transcript 1711-63. Mf 5-7: Births 1762-1844. Mf 8-10: Birth Transcript 1762-1844. Mf 11-12: Births 1844-58. Mf 13: Marriages 1720-1801. Mf 14: Marriage Transcript 1720-1801. Mf 15-16: Marriages: 1801-45. Mf 17: Marriage Transcript 1802-45. Mf 18-20: Intentions 1802-63. Mf 21-22: Intent Transcript 1802-63. Mf 23: Marriages: 1844-58. Mf 24: Deaths 1711-1800. Mf 25: Death Transcript 1711-1800. Mf 26: Deaths 1800-44. Mf 27: Death Transcript 1776-1847. Mf 28: Deaths 1844-54) – (mf ed 1983) – 28mf – 9 – 0-931248-14-0 – us Holbrook [920]
Needham, Elizabeth A *see* WOMAN'S MINISTRY: A SPIRITUAL EXPOSITION OF WOMAN'S PLACE IN THE CHURCH OF GOD
Needham, J *see* THE DEVELOPMENT OF IRON AND STEEL TECHNOLOGY IN CHINA
NEEDHAM LAW SCHOOL, 1821-1842, CUMBERLAND COUNTY, VIRGINIA / Brock, Robert Kincaid – Farmville, Va., The Farmville Herald, 1935 24 p. LL-370 – 1 – us L of C Photodup [340]
Needham, M *see* MEDELA MEDICINAE
Needham, Philip Dennis *see* REDEMPTION AND SOCIAL REFORMATION
THE NEEDLE – Ireland.Dec 1932 – 1 – ie Microforms [072]
THE NEEDLE – v. -, no. 1 (all publ). Jun 1944-Jan 1945. (Jazz Periodicals) – 1 reel – 1 – $60.00 – us UPA [780]
Neefe, CG *see* DER DUMME GARTNER, ODER DIE BEYDEN ANTON, EIN COMISCHES SINGSPIEL IN ZWEY AUFZUGEN FURS CLAVIER GESETZT
Neel, Wallace B *see* A FIELD SYSTEMS ANALYSIS OF DUAL LEARNING ENVIRONMENTS
NEERIM NEWS – 1891-1894. NN1-2 – 2r – 1 – at Corangamite [072]
NEERLAND'S JODENDOM – Amsterdam. v1-4. 1934-1937 – 23mf – 9 – ne IDC [270]
Nees von Esenbeck, C G D *see*
– AGROSTOGRAPHIA CAPENSIS
– FLORAE AFRICAE AUSTRALIORIS
– GENERA ET SPECIES ASTEREARUM
– GENERA PLANTARUM FLORAE GERMANICAE
– HORAE PHYSICAE BEROLINENSIS
– NATURGESCHICHTE DER EUROPAASISCHEN LEBERMOOSE
– DAS SYSTEM DER PILZE UND SCHWAEMME
Nees von Esenbeck, CG D *see*
– BEITRAG ZUR FLORA BRASILIENS
– BRYOLOGIA GERMANICA
LA NEF – Revue de lettres independante. no. 1-9. Paris. sept 1913-mai 1914 – 1 – fr A.C.R.P.P. [073]
Nef, J U *see* LA ROUTE DE LA GUERRE TOTALE
Nefertiti, pseud *see* BETWEEN YOU AND ME
Nef'i *see* DIVAN
NEFTI ANOE I SLANT SEVOE KHOZI A ISTVO = PETROLEUM AND OIL-SHALE INDUSTRIES : ORGAN GLAVNYKH KOMITETOV V.S.N.KH.–NEFTI ANOGO I SLANT SEVOGO – (Includes c.1: 1921:Jan./Apr.-May/Aug; 1924:July-1925:June) – [Moskva, Petrograd: V.S.N.Kh., 1920-1925]. 6v – 1 – CSUXAKY6216-S – us Hoover Inst Photo [947]
NEFTI ANOE KHOZI A ISTVO = PETROLEUM INDUSTRY : ORGAN SOVETA NEFTI ANO I PROMYSHLENNOSTI – (Includes c.1: 1925:July-1932:May. Many issues missing) – Moskva, Leningrad: Sovet, [1925-1940] – 1 – CSUXAKZ0099-S – us Hoover Inst Photo [947]
NEFTI ANOE KHOZI A ISTVO (1945) – (Includes c.1: 1948:Apr.-May, Aug.-Dec.) – Moskva: Izd-vo "Nedra", 1945 – 1 – CSUXAKY6178-S – us Hoover Inst Photo [947]
NEFTIANOE DELO – 1899-1918 – 391mf – 9 – $1,990.00 – us Ross [330]
NEFTIANOE KHOZIAISTVO – Moscow. U.S.S.R. 1934-39. Petroleum Industry – 1 – us UMI [660]
NEGARA SOEMATERA TIMOER. SOME ANNOTATIONS REGARDING – SE-10,535 1. 1948? – 9 – ne IDC [950]
NEGARIT GAZETA – Ethiopia, 1942-64 – 2r – 1 – us Ross [324]
THE NEGATIVE CRITICISM AND THE OLD TESTAMENT : AN ALL AROUND SURVEY... / Schmauk, Theodore Emanuel – (Includes bibliographical references) – Lebanon, PA: Aldus, 1894 – 1mf – 9 – 0-8370-5103-7 – 1985-3103 – us A.T.L.A. [220]
NEGERENGELSCH-HOLLANDSCH WOORDENBOEK : MET BIJVERMELDING VAN ALLE VREEMDE WOORDEN DIE ZICH DE NEGERS HEBBEN TAAL EIGEN GEMAAKT / Halfhide, J J – Coronie. 7v. 1889-1904 – 24mf – ne IDC [430]
NEGINOT / Landau, J L – Cracow. 1895. BJ-422-40 – 9 – ne IDC [830]
NEGLIGENCE AND COMPENSATION CASES, ANNOTATED – (Cont: American Negligence Reports) – Chicago: Callaghan. v1-17. 1911-18 – 226mf – 9 – $339.00 – LLMC 90-420 – us L.L.M.C. [340]
NEGLIGENCE COMPENSATION CASES, ANNOTATED *see* AMERICAN NEGLIGENCE REPORTS, CURRENT SERIES
NEGLIGENCE; RULES–DECISIONS–OPINIONS. 2D ED / Thomas, Edward Beers – Albany, N.Y., Banks, 1904. 2 v. LL-1157 – 1 – us L of C Photodup [340]
LAS NEGOCIACIONES DIPLOMATICAS DEL CANAL DE PANAMA / Concha, J V – Bogota, 1904 – 2mf – 1 – ILM-2330/1 – ne IDC [327]
LE NEGOCIANT CANADIEN – Montreal, Canada. 12 oct 1871-2 avr 1874 – 1r – 1 – Can$40.00 – cn Can Microfilming [072]
NEGOCIATIONS DIPLOMATIQUES ENTRE LA FRANCE ET L'AUTRICHE DURANT LES TRENTE PREMIERES ANNEES DU 16 SIECLE / Glay, [A JG] Le – Paris. 2v. 1845 – 18mf – 9 – ne IDC [944]
NEGOTIA A SUPERIORIBUS FRANCISCALIBUS... / Simeone, Laurentius – Madrid: Arch. Ibero Americano, 1964 – 1 – sp Bibl Santa Ana [946]
NEGOTIABLE INSTRUMENTS / Williston, Samuel – New York, American Institute of Banking 1915 296 p. LL-1242 – 1 – us L of C Photodup [340]
NEGOTIABLE INSTRUMENTS AND PRINCIPAL AND SURETY. / Chadman, Charles Erehart – Chicago: Henneberry, 1901. 260p. LL-223 – 1 – us L of C Photodup [340]
NEGOTIABLE INSTRUMENTS IN PENNSYLVANIA / Remak, Gustavus – Philadelphia: Welsh, 1887. 237p. LL-1341 – 1 – us L of C Photodup [340]
NEGOTIABLE INSTRUMENTS LAW / Mills, Jared Warner – Denver: Mills, 1897. 147p. LL-598 – 1 – us L of C Photodup [340]
THE NEGOTIABLE INSTRUMENTS LAW IN NORTH CAROLINA / Mordecai, Samuel Fox – Raleigh: Capital, 1899. 95p. LL-619 – 1 – us L of C Photodup [340]
NEGOTIATED RULEMAKING SOURCEBOOK / Pritzker, David M & Dalton, Deborah S – Washington: GPO, 1990 (all publ) – 10mf – 9 – $15.00 – LLMC 94-338 – us L.L.M.C. [340]
NEGOTIATION JOURNAL – v1-10. 1985-94 – 1,5 – $65.00v – us UMI [340]
NEGOTIATION RESEARCH DIGEST – v1-8 1963-75 1; v7-8 5,6 – us UMI [073]
LA NEGRESSE OU LE POUVOIR DE LA RECONNAISSANCE, COMEDIE EN UN ACTE. MELEE DE DIVERTISSEMENTS / Radet et Barre – (African Library series). 1787 – 9 – fr Hachette [820]
Negri, Cesare *see* NOUVE INVENTIONI DI BALLI, OPERA VAGHISSIMA DI CESARE NEGRI MILANESE DETTO IL TROMBONE...
Negrin, Juan *see*
– CHRISTIANITY AND SPAIN
– DISCURSO DEL PRESIDENTE DEL CONSEJO Y MINISTRO DE DEFENSA, PRONUNCIADO EN MADRID, EL 18 DE JUNIO DE 1938
– PREMIER NEGRIN'S ADDRESS TO THE LEAGUE OF NATIONS ASSEMBLY ON SEPT. 18, 1937
NEGRIN Y PRIETO CULPABLES DE ALTA TRAICION; INFORME SOBRE LAS COMISIONES DE COMPRAS, LA SUBSECRETARIA DE ARMAMENTO Y EL DESPILFARRO ESCANDALOSO DE LAS FINANZAS DE LA REPUBLICA – Buenos Aires, 1939. Fiche W1073. (Blodgett Collection of Spanish Civil War Pamphlets) – 9 – us H.U. College Libr [946]
NEGRO AMERICAN LITERATURE FORUM – v1-10 1967-76 1; v5-10 1971-76 5,6 – us UMI [305]
NEGRO ANTHOLOGY 1931-1933 / Cunard, Nancy – London, 1934 – 1r – 1 – us Ross [305]
NEGRO APPRENTICESHIP IN THE BRITISH COLONIES / London Anti-Slavery Society. Committee – London, 1838. 32 p. LL-3 – 1 – us L of C Photodup [340]
NEGRO BAPTIST HISTORY / Jordan, Lewis G – 502p – 1 – 17.57 – us Baptist [240]
THE NEGRO CHURCH / Smith, Allen Hart – 1961 – 1 – us A.T.L.A. [240]
THE NEGRO CHURCHES OF MANHATTAN – New York: Greater New York Federation of Churches, 1930 – 1r – 1 – us Ross [240]
NEGRO COLLEGE QUARTERLY – Wilberforce, OH. v1-5. 1943-47 – 1r – 1 – us Ross [370]
NEGRO EDUCATION : A STUDY OF THE PRIVATE AND HIGHER SCHOOLS FOR COLORED PEOPLE IN THE UNITED STATES – 2v. 1917 – us Ross [370]
NEGRO EDUCATION IN KENTUCKY / Taylor, Lewis N – Frankfort, 1943 – 1r – 1 – us Ross [370]
NEGRO EDUCATIONAL REVIEW / National Teacher's Research Association – v1-16. 1950-65 – 2r – 1 – $150.00 – us UPA [370]
NEGRO FARMER AND MESSENGER – v1-5, no. 1 (all publ). 1914-18 – 1 reel – 1 – $65.00 – us UPA [976]
NEGRO FOLK-SONGS – 1918-19 – 1 – us I.U. Libraries [390]
NEGRO HERITAGE – Chicago. v1-6. 1961-67 – 1r – 1 – us Ross [305]
NEGRO HERITAGE – (See also: Black Heritage) – v1-16 1961-1977 1; v15-16 5,6; v16- 9 – us UMI [305]
NEGRO HISTORY BULLETIN – (v. 32- 1969- 5,6. v. 33- 1970- 9) – v. 1- 1937- – 1 – us UMI [976]
THE NEGRO IN AMERICAN HISTORY : MEN AND WOMEN EMINENT IN THE EVOLUTION OF THE AMERICAN OF AFRICAN DESCENT / Cromwell, John W – Washington: American Negro Academy, 1914 – 1mf – us A.T.L.A. [305]
THE NEGRO IN PENNSYLVANIA : SLAVERY-SERVITUDE-FREEDOM, 1639-1861 / Turner, Edward Raymond – Washington, 1911 – 1r – 1 – us Ross [976]
THE NEGRO IN THE CHRISTIAN PULPIT, OR, THE TWO CHARACTERS AND TWO DISTINIES / Haygood, Atticus Greene – Raleigh: Edwards, Broughton, 1884 – 1mf – us A.T.L.A. [240]
THE NEGRO IN THE MILITARY SERVICE OF THE UNITED STATES / U.S. Army – 1639-1886. 5 rolls. M858 – 1 – us Nat'l Archives [355]
NEGRO LABOR COMMITTEE RECORD GROUP, 1925-1969 : FROM THE HOLDINGS OF THE SCHOMBURG CENTER FOR RESEARCH IN BLACK CULTURE, MANUSCRIPTS, ARCHIVES AND RARE BOOKS DIVISION: THE NEW YORK PUBLIC LIBRARY, ASTOR, LENOX AND TILDEN FOUNDATIONS – (Guide which covers all coll under "African-American Organizations" sold separately for $20.00 D3305.G1) – 1995 – 17r – 1 – $1,445.00 – D3305P02 – Dist. us Scholarly Res – us L of C Photodup [331]
NEGRO LIBERATOR – New York, 1929-35 – 1 – us Ross [071]
NEGRO MUSIC JOURNAL – A Monthly, devoted to the Educational Interest of the Negro in Music. v1-2 (i.e. nos. 1-15; all publ). 1902-1903 – 5mf – 9 – $55.00 – us UPA [780]
O NEGRO NA BAHAI / Viana, Luiz – Rio de Janeiro. 1946 – 1 – us Res Libr [972]
Negro Needs Society *see* EDUCATION
NEGRO NEIGHBORS, BOND AND FREE : LESSONS IN HISTORY AND HUMANITY / Whipple, Phila M – Boston, Mass.: Woman's American Baptist Home Mission Society, 1907 – 1mf – us A.T.L.A. [976]
NEGRO QUARTERLY! : A REVIEW OF NEGRO LIFE AND CULTURE – 1-4 (all publ). 1942-1943 – 5mf – 9 – $55.00 – us UPA [975]
THE NEGRO SOLDIER – 9bks. 1852-99 – 1r – 1 – us Ross [355]
NEGRO STAR – 1936-53 (complete) – 5r – 1 – ATLA R0141 – us A.T.L.A. [240]
NEGRO STORY – A Magazine for All Americans. v1-2 2+3 (all publ). 1944-1946 – 8mf – 9 – $55.00 – us UPA [975]
NEGRO TRAVELER AND CONVENTIONEER – v1- 1944- 1; v26- 5,6,9 – us UMI [073]
NEGRO WORKER / Red International of Labour Unions & International Trade Union Committee of Negro Workers – ns: v1-7. 1931-37 – 1r – 1 – us Ross [331]
THE NEGRO WORKER – Paris etc. v. 1-7, no. 7 8. Jan 1931-Sept Oct 1937. Incomplete – 1 – us NY Public [331]
NEGRO WORLD – New York. July 3 1926-June 3 1933. Incomplete – 1 – us NY Public [073]
NEGRO WORLD – New York. v14-32. 1923-33 – 5r – 1 – us Ross [071]
NEGRO WORLD DIGEST : FROM THE HOLDINGS OF THE SCHOMBURG CENTER FOR RESEARCH IN BLACK CULTURE, MANUSCRIPTS, ARCHIVES AND RARE BOOKS DIVISION: THE NEW YORK PUBLIC LIBRARY, ASTOR, LENOX AND TILDEN FOUNDATIONS – (Guide which covers all colls under "Black Periodicals" sold separately for $20.00 D3305G4) – 1995 – 1r – 1 – $85.00 – D3305P13 – us Scholarly Res [073]
NEGRO YEAR BOOK – An Annual Encyclopedia of the Negro. Tuskegee, Alabama. 1918-1919 – 1 – us NY Public [073]
NEGROES OF NEW YORK – 1936-41 – 5r – 1 – us Ross [975]
THE NEGRO'S CHURCH / Mays, Benjamin Elijah & Nicholson, Joseph William – New York, 1933 – 1r – 1 – us Ross [240]
NEHALEM ENTERPRISE – Nehalem OR. June 24 1910-June 20 1913 – 1 – us U.O. Library [071]
NEHAWKA ENTERPRISE – Nehawka, NE. -w. Jul 1931-Jun 1952 – 1 – us NE Hist [071]
NEHAWKA REGISTER – Nehawka, NE. -w. Aug 1892; Mar 1893; Oct 1895-Oct 1898; Dec 1898; Jan-Mar 1899; Oct 1901; Jan 1902-Apr 1904; Jul 1904; Mar 1906- Aug 1909 – 1 – us NE Hist [071]
NEHIRO-IRINIUI AIAMIHE MASSINAHIGAN, SHATSHEGUTSH, MITINEKAPITSH, ISKUAMISKUTSH, NETSHEKATSH, MISHT', ASSINITSH, SHEKUTIMITSH, EKUANATSH, ASHUABMUSHUANITSH, PIAKUAGAMITSH... / LaBrosse, Jean Baptiste de – Massinahitsetuau: Broun gaie Girmor, 1767. SEM35P68 – 1r – 1 – Can$15.00 – cn Bibl Nat [240]
Nehrkorn, A *see* KATALOG DER EIERSAMMLUNG
Nehrkorn, Hans *see* WILHELM HEINSE UND SEIN EINFLUSS AUF DIE ROMANTIK
NEI MONGGUO RIBAO = INNER MONGOLIA DAILY – China. 1983-. M-D80 – 1 – $55.00r – cc Microforms [072]
Neickelio, CF *see* MUSEOGRAPHIA ODER ANLEITUNG ZUM RECHTEN BEGRIFF UND NUETZLICHER ANLEGUNG DER MUSEORUM ODER RARITAETEN-KAMMERN

NEID : EINE ERZAEHLUNG / Wildenbruch, Ernst von – Berlin: G Grote, 1903 – 1r – 1 – us U.W. Library [830]
DI NEIE ZEIT = NEW YIMES – (In Yiddish) – Buenos Aires, AG. v2 no59 9 Dec 1949-16 Dec 1949 – 1r – 1 – $25.00 – cn Can Microfilming [072]
Neiges, Marie-des *see* ANALYSE BIBLIOGRAPHIQUE DE REVERENDE MERE SAINTE-LOUISE-DE-MARILLAC...
NEIGHBORHOOD ASSOCIATION NEWSLETTERS – Eugene OR. ca 1970's Rolls 1-6. 1980-1983 – 1 – us U.O. Library [071]
NEIGHBORHOOD NEWS – Cleveland, Ohio. 6 Jan 1966-26 Dec 1990. 17 reels – 1 – us Western Res [071]
Neill, Edward D *see*
- HISTORY OF DAKOTA COUNTY AND THE CITY OF HASTINGS
- HISTORY OF FILMORE COUNTY
- HISTORY OF FREEBORN COUNTY
- HISTORY OF HENNEPIN COUNTY AND THE CITY OF MINNEAPOLIS
- HISTORY OF RICE COUNTY
- HISTORY OF THE CITY OF ST PAUL AND RAMSEY COUNTY
- HISTORY OF THE MINNESOTA VALLEY
- HISTORY OF THE UPPER MISSISSIPPI VALLEY
- HISTORY OF WASHINGTON COUNTY AND THE CROIX VALLEY

NEI-MENG-KU JIH-PAO – Huhehot, Inner Mongolia, China. Inner Mongolian Daily. 1952-65. 24 reels – 1 – 615.00 – us Chinese Res [072]
NEIN / Benedix, Roderich – Boston: D C Heath, c1900 – 1 – us U.W. Library [890]
NEIRANJI GONGCHENG – Internal Combustion Engineering. In Chinese but English abstracts to the main articles. F p111 – 9 – $4.50f – cc Microforms [073]
NEIZDANNYE PIS'MA INOSTRANNYKH PISATELEI XVIII-XIX VEKOV IZ LENINGRADSKIKH RUKOPISNYKH SOBRANII – Moscow, Leningrad, 1960. 380p. BR-10,781/1 – 9 – ne IDC [460]
NEIZDANNYE SOCHINENIIA I PEREPISKA / Karamzin, Nikolai M – pt. 1. Spb. 1862. BR-6046 2 – 8 – ne IDC [460]
NEK MITTEILUNGEN – 1980-90 (complete) – Inquire – 1 – ATLA S0783 – us A.T.L.A. [073]
NEKOTORYE FAKTY I ITOGI CHETYREKH LET GRAZHDANSKOI VOINY 1917-1921 / Ignatev, VI – Moskva: Gos. izdvo, 1922- – 1 – CSUX88-B5890 – us Hoover Inst Photo [947]
NEKOTORYE VOPROSY EKONOMICHESKO I POLITIKI : SBORNIK STATE I / Bukharin, Nikolai Ivanovich – Moskva: T Sentr. upr. pechati VSNKh SSSR, 1925 – 1 – CSUX89-B4608 – us Hoover Inst Photo [330]
NEKOTORYE VOPROSY IZUCHENIIA ISTORICHESKIKH DOKUMENTOV 19-NACHALA 20 V. SBORNIK STATEI – Leningrad, 1967. 264p. BR-10,723/1 – 9 – ne IDC [025]
O NEKOTORYKH VOPROSAKH UCHASTII OBSHCHESTVENNOSTI. / Avrakh, Ia. S – Kazan, 1964. 64p. BR-8428 1 – 9 – ne IDC [340]
Nekrasov, G A *see* RUSSKO-SHVEDSKIE OTNOSHENIIA I POLITIKA VELIKIKH DERZHAV V 1721-1726 GG
Nekrasov, Nikolai Alekseevich *see* OPIS' DOKUMENTAL'NYKH MATERIALOV LICHNOGO FONDA NO. 338
NEKROLOG / ed by Schlichtegroll, Friedrich – Gotha. 28v. 1790-1806 – 125mf – 9 – subsc: DM950.00 diazo DM1100.00 silver – gw Olms [430]
NEKROPOL' / Khodasevich, V – Vospominaniia. (Blok, Belyi, Gumilev i dr.). Brussels. 1939. BR-697 2 – 8 – ne IDC [920]
NEL SUD DELL'IMPERO / Vecchi, Bernardo Valentino – Milano: Fratelli Bocca, 1937 – us Res Libr [960]
Neledinskii-Meletskii, Iu. A *see* STIKHOTVORENIIA
NELIGH ADVOCATE – Neligh, NE. -w. Aug 1881-Oct 1885; Jan 1886-Nov 1894; Jan 1896-Nov 1901 – 1 – us NE Hist [071]
NELIGH JOURNAL – Neligh, NE. -w. (-bw 1873-74). Sept 1873-Nov 1877, scattered issues missing – 1 – us NE Hist [071]
NELIGH LEADER – Neligh, NE. -w. Jun 1885-May 1963 – 1 – us NE Hist [071]
NELIGH NEWS AND LEADER – Neligh, NE. -w. (-sw 1915-16). Sept 1923 to date – 1 – us NE Hist [071]
NELIGH REGISTER – Neligh, NE. -w. Feb 1905-Dec 1924 – 1 – us NE Hist [071]
Nelken, Margarita *see*
- CONDICION SOCIAL DE LA MUJER EN ESPANA, LA. SU ESTADO ACTUAL
- LAS ESCRITORAS ESPANOLAS
- HISTORIA DEL HOMBRE QUE TUVO EL MUNDO EN LA MANO
- POR QUE HICIMOS LA REVOLUCION

Nell, William C *see* THE COLORED PATRIOTS OF THE AMERICAN REVOLUTION
NELLA ROTTA DELL' ARMATA DE SVLTAN SELIN, VLTIMO RE DE TVRCHI / Blessi, M – N.p., [1572] – 1mf – 9 – H-8336/1 – ne IDC [956]
Nellis, Andrew J *see* STREET RAILROAD ACCIDENT LAW.
NELLIS CENTURY – Las Vegas, NV. 1969-1973 – 3r – 1 – $150.00 – N04605 – us Library Micro [071]
Nellist, George F *see* MEN OF HAWAII
NELLY SACHS BRIEFREGISTER : 3454 BRIEFE AUF MIKROFICHES / ed by Mueller, Ulrich et al – 1989 – 17mf – 9 – DM168.00 – 3-88099-192-8 – gw Heinz [430]
Nelme, LD *see* AN ESSAY TOWARDS AN INVESTIGATION OF THE ORIGIN AND ELEMENTS OF LANGUAGE AND LETTERS
NELSON AND HIS CAPTAINS: SKETCHES OF FAMOUS SEAMEN / Fitchett, William Henry – 1902 – 9 – $20.00 – uk Libr Preservation [920]
NELSON DAILY NEWS – British Columbia, CN. 1970- – 4r per yr – 1 – Can$55.00r – cn Commonwealth Micro [072]
Nelson, Dave Paul *see* VALIDITY CONCERNS IN PREVIOUS STUDIES EXAMINING THE FREQUENCY OF ANOREXIA NERVOSA IN FEMALE BALLET DANCERS
Nelson, David *see* CORRESPONDENCE AND PAPERS OF DAVID NELSON
Nelson, E W *see* THE ESKIMO ABOUT BERING STRAIT
Nelson, Erik *see* YEARS ON THE AMAZON, 1891-1938
Nelson, Erik Alfred *see* COLLECTION
Nelson, G *see* THE USE OF HUMAN REASON IN RELIGION, IN ANSWER TO THE METHODISTS; THE DOCTRINE OF FREE-GRACE BEING EXPLAINED IN THE MEDIUM, ACCORDING TO THE CHURCH OF ENGLAND
NELSON GAZETTE – Nelson, NE. -w. Oct 1895-Feb 1896; Apr 1896-May 1898; Feb -Nov 1899; Jan 1900-Sept 1902; Aug 1908-Sept 1919; Jan 1920 to date – 1 – us NE Hist [071]
Nelson, Horatio *see* THE DISPATCHES AND LETTERS OF VICE ADMIRAL LORD VISCOUNT NELSON, WITH NOTES BY SIR N.H. NICOLAS
Nelson, J H *see* MADURA COUNTRY
Nelson, James M *see* THE THEOLOGICAL SIGNIFICANCE OF CITY EVANGELISM
NELSON LEADER – London, UK. 1928. -w. 2 reels – 1 – uk British Libr Newspaper [072]
Nelson, Lisa H *see* DIET COMPOSITION AND BODY FAT
Nelson, New Hampshire. Nelson Baptist Church *see* RECORDS
Nelson, OM *see* THE SWEDISH ELEMENT IN OMAHA
Nelson, S B *see* HISTORY OF BALTIMORE, MARYLAND FROM ITS FOUNDING AS A TOWN TO THE CURRENT YEAR–1729-1898
Nelson, William *see* THE OFFICE AND AUTHORITY OF A JUSTICE OF PEACE.
Nelson, William E *see* CITY OF DECATUR AND MACON COUNTY
Nelson, Wolfred *see*
- RAPPORT DE DRS. NELSON ET MACDONNELL, ET ZEPHIRIN PERRAULT, ECR., AVOCAT, SUR L'HOPITAL DE MARINE ET DES EMIGRES DE QUEBEC ET CORRESPONDANCE RELATIVE AUX SERVICES DU DR. ROBITAILLE DANS LE DIT HOPITAL
- RAPPORT DU DR. WOLFRED NELSON...SUR LA CONDITION, LA DISCIPLINE, L'ADMINISTRATION ET L'ENTRETIEN DES PRISONS DE DISTRICT ET AUTRE PRISONS, DU BAS-CANADA
- RAPPORT...SUR L'HOPITAL DE MARINE ET DES EMIGRES DE QUEBEC, ET CORRESPONDANCE RELATIVE AUX SERVICES DU DR. ROBITAILLE DANS LE DIT HOPITAL
- REPORT OF DR. WOLFRED NELSON,... ON THE PRESENT STATE DISCIPLINE, MANAGEMENT AND EXPENDITURE OF THE DISTRICT AND OTHER PRISONS IN CANADA EAST
- REPORT...ON THE PRESENT STATE OF DISCIPLINE, MANAGEMENT AND EXPENDITURE OF THE DISTRICT AND OTHER PRISONS IN CANADA EAST

NEMA (NATIONAL ELECTRICAL MANUFACTURERS ASSOCIATION) – Standards. Printed index. Updated every 60 days – 6,9 – us Info Handling [621]
NEMAHA COUNTY HERALD – Auburn, NE. -w. Jan. 1889-Mar. 1893. Incomplete; Oct. 1895-Nov. 1898; Feb. 1899-Jan. 1901; Apr. 1901- – 1 – us NE Hist [071]
NEMAHA COUNTY HERALD – Auburn. Neb. 1889-1892; 1896-1959 – 1 – us UMI [071]
NEMAHA COUNTY JOURNAL – Auburn, NE. -w. Oct. 1882-Apr. 1883 – 1 – us NE Hist [071]
NEMAHA COUNTY JOURNAL – Auburn. Neb. 1882-1893 – 1 – us UMI [071]
NEMAHA COUNTY REPUBLICAN – Auburn, NE. -w. Aug. 1883-May 1885. Incomplete; Jan. 1887-Dec. 1892. Incomplete; Mar. 1894-Dec. 1914; Jan. 1916-Aug. 1916; Feb. 1917-Dec. 1922; Jan. 1925-Nov. 1929 – 1 – us NE Hist [071]
NEMAHA COUNTY REPUBLICAN – Auburn. Neb. and pred. 1883-85, 1894-1914, 1917-22, 1925-29 – 1 – us UMI [071]
NEMAHA COUNTY REPUBLICAN – Sabetha. Kansas. 1876-1893 – 1 – us UMI [071]
NEMAHA VALLEY – Falls City. Neb. 1869-1909; 1910- – 1 – us UMI [071]
NEMATOLOGICA – Leiden. v1-36. 1956-90 – 5,9 – Dfl6,480.00; Dfl180.00v – ne Swets [590]
Nemerovskaia, O *see* SUD'BA BLOKA
NEMESII EPISCOPI, PREMNON PHYSICON...A N. ALFANO...IN LATINUM TRANSLATUS. RECOGN. C. BURKHARD – Lipsiae, 1917 – 3mf – 8 – ne Slangenburg [999]
NEMESIOS VON EMESA : QUELLENFORSCHUNGEN ZUM NEUPLATONISMUS UND SEINEN ANFAENGEN BEI POSEIDONIOS / Jaeger, Werner Wilhelm – Berlin: Weidmann, 1914 – 1mf – us A.T.L.A. [180]
THE NEMESIS OF FAITH / Froude, James Anthony – London: J. Chapman, 2nd ed 1849 – 1 roll – 1 – 1-55879-566-9 – uk Libr Preservation [240]
Nemoshkalenko, V V *see* PHYSICS OF METALS
LE NEMROD – Haute-Rive, Canada. dec 1960; v9 n4. dec 1969 – 1r – 1 – Can$45.00 – cn Can Microfilming [072]
NENAGH GAZETTE – Ireland. -w. 1 Jan 1841-25 Jun 1842. (40 ft) – 1 – uk British Libr Newspaper [072]
NENAGH GUARDIAN – Ireland. 1878-99; 1885-99. -w. 17 reels – 1 – uk British Libr Newspaper [072]
NENG YUAN – Journal of Energy. 1984. F/P 265 – 9 – $3.50f – cc Microforms [073]
Nennius, Abbott of Bangor *see* HISTORIA BRITONUM
NEO – Dir. B. Montagnon. Saint-Ouen. dec 1934-mars 1936 – 1 – fr A.C.R.P.P. [073]
NEOBKHODIMOST OTKRYTIIA PORTO-FRANKO V USTIAKH RI EK OBI I ENISEI A : DOKLAD, CHITANNY I 30 APRIELIA 1907 GODA V CHREZVYCHAINOM OBSHCHEM SOBRANII TOBOLSKOI GORODSKOI DUMY / Dunin-Gorkavich, Aleksandr Aleksandrovich – Tobolsk: Gub. tip., 1907 – 1 – CSUX89-B3491 – us Hoover Inst Photo [947]
LE NEO-CLASSICISME FRANCAIS / Reunion des musees nationaux. Paris – 1974. 167 illus. 2 fiches – 9 – fr Réunion [700]
NEO-COLONIALISM, A THREAT TO WORLD-PEACE – SE-10,949 1. 1964 – 9 – ne IDC [320]
NEO-COLONIALISM IN INDONESIA : HOW A NEW COLONIALISM HAS BEEN ESTABLISHED UNDER COVER OF THE CRY OF 'ANTI-COLONIALISM.' ADDRESS TO 16TH GENERAL ASSEMBLY OF THE UN / Tiro, Hasan Muhammad – 6049/1. 1961 – 9 – ne IDC [950]
Neodesha House. Neodesha, Kansas *see* HOTEL REGISTER
NEODESHA SCRAPBOOK / Allen, Joe W – 1861-1929 – 1 – us KS Hist [978]
NEO-FUTURIZM – Sbornik. Kazan'. 1913. BR-1884 2 – 8 – ne IDC [300]
NEOGENYTON / Rafinesque-Schmaltz, Constantine S – or Indication of 66 new genera of plants of North America. Lexington. 1825. B-5652 1 – 9 – ne IDC [580]
NEO-GEORGISM: A PANEL DISCUSSION / Andelson, Robert V – 1982. Led by Prof. Andelson – 9 – 1.00f – at Libertarian Micro [320]
NEOLIT I BRONZOVYI VEK PRIBAIKAL'IA / Okladnikov, A P – Istoriko-arkheologicheskoe issledovanie. 3 v. M., L. 1950, 1955. BU-574 2 – 8 – ne IDC [930]
THE NEOLITH – London, 1907-08 – 1r – 1 – £60.00 – uk Chadwyck [760]
LA NEOLOGIE OU VOCABULAIRE DES MOTS NOUVEAUX A RENOUVELER, AN 9 / Mercier, LS – 1801 – 9 – fr I.C.S. [440]
NEOLOGOS – Istanbul, Turkey. In Greek. -w. 27 Feb 1871-16 April 1892. 40 reels – 1 – uk British Libr Newspaper [949]
NEOPHYTON NO. 3 : ON A NEW MEDICAL PLANT, PRENANTHUS OPICRINA, AND A NEW KIND OF OPIUM, OPICRINE / Rafinesque-Schmaltz, Constantine S – Cincinnati Literary Gazette, 1824 – 1mf – 9 – ne IDC [615]
NEOPLATONISM / Bigg, Charles – London: S.P.C.K.; New York: E.& J.B. Young, 1895. (Chief ancient philosophies) – 1mf – us A.T.L.A. [180]
NEOPLATONISM IN RELATION TO CHRISTIANITY : AN ESSAY / Elsee, Charles – Cambridge: University Press; New York: Putnam, 1908 – 1mf – us A.T.L.A. [180]
NEOSHO COUNTY JOURNAL – Osage Mission. Kan. 1872-1895 – 1 – us UMI [071]
NEOSHO COUNTY JOURNAL – St. Paul. KS. 1895-1901 – 1 – us UMI [071]
NEOSHO VALLEY REGISTER – Iola. Kan. 1868-1874 – 1 – us UMI [071]
NEOTESTAMENTICA – v1-16. 1967-82 – 1 – us UMI [073]
Nepal *see*
- DRAFT FIVE YEAR PLAN, A SYNOPSIS
- NEPALA RAJAPATRA

Nepal. Economic plans *see* FOURTH PLAN 1970-75
NEPAL, ETUDE HISTORIQUE D'UN ROYAUME HINDOU / Levi, S – 3v. Paris. 1905-08. BI-591 2 – 8 – ne IDC [950]
NEPAL. HISTORICAL DOCUMENTS AND MANUSCRIPTS *see* HISTORICAL DOCUMENTS AND MANUSCRIPTS
Nepal. Ministry of Education and Culture. Planning Division *see* EDUCATIONAL STATISTICS OF NEPAL AT A GLANCE 1976-1981
Nepal. Ministry of Education. Planning Division *see* EDUCATIONAL PROGRAMMES IN THE FIFTH PLAN 1975-1980
Nepal. Ministry of Education. Planning, Statistics and Research Division *see*
- DEVELOPMENT OF PRIMARY EDUCATION IN NEPAL
- DEVELOPMENT OF SECONDARY EDUCATION IN NEPAL

Nepal. National Planning Council *see*
- AN OUTLINE OF THE SECOND PLAN
- THE THIRD PLAN, 1965-70
- THE THREE YEAR PLAN (1962-1965)

NEPAL PRESS REPORT, NO. 1/67 – Kathmandu: Regmi Research Project, 1967- . Includes trans. from the Nepal press reports, Nepal gazette, and of articles from newspapers and periodicals – 1 – us U.W. Library [950]
Nepal. Social Service National Co-ordination Council. Women Service Co-ordination Committee *see* STATISTICS ON WOMEN IN NEPAL
Nepal. Tribhuvan University. Research Centre for Educational Innovation and Development *see* EDUCATION AND DEVELOPMENT 1980-1983
NEPALA RAJAPATRA / Nepal – April 1967- – 1 – 25.00y – us L of C Photodup [950]
NEPHRON – v. 3-13. 1966-74 – 1,5,6 – us UMI [073]
NEPHRON – v14-. 1975- – 1,5,9 – us UMI [610]
Nepluyeff, Nicolas de *see* LA CONFRERERIE ET SES ECOLES
NEPOBEDIMOE ORUZHIE / Maiakovskii, Vladimir – Oboronnye stikhi. M. 1938. BR-984 2 – 8 – ne IDC [460]
Nepotis, Ducae Michaelis *see* HISTORIA BYZANTINA (CBH 15)
Nepotis, Michaelis Ducae *see* HISTORIA BYZANTINA (CSHB 21)

NEPSPORT – Budapest, Hungary. 1962-67; 1969-70 – 15r – 1 – us L of C Photodup [072]
NEPSZABADSAG – (Backfile through 1998 $85r) – Hungary, 1999- – 12r per y – 1 – $960.00 standing order – us Ross [072]
NEPSZABADSAG – Budapest, Hungary. Dec 1956-1976 – 60r – 1 – us L of C Photodup [072]
NEPSZABADSAG – Ungarn, 1976-1992ff – 73r – 1 – DM5,475.00 – gw Mikro Press [072]
NEPSZAVA – 1976- – 4r per y – 1 – us Ross [072]
NEPSZAVA – 1976-1995 – 12 times per yr – 1 – F1,039.00 – sz Infoprint [072]
NEPSZAVA – Budapest, 1917-1919, 1940-44 – 125r – 1 – uk British Llbr Newspaper [072]
NEPSZAVA – Budapest, 1976-1992ff – 59r – 1 – DM4,425.00 – gw Mikro Press [072]
NEPSZAVA – Budapest, Hungary. 1962-76 – 39r – 1 – us L of C Photodup [072]
NEPSZAVA / Magyar Szocial-Demokrata Part – 1906, 1914-15, 1918, 1919-21 1939-44, 1946-49, 1962-67 (all incompl), 1968- – 1 – us Hoover Inst Photo [335]
NEPSZAVABADSAG – 1976-1995 – 12 times per yr – 1 – F1,039.00 – sz Infoprint [072]
LE NEPTUNE FRANCOIS OU ATLAS NOUVEAU DES CARTES MARINES / Sauveur, Joseph – Paris: Chez Hubert Jaillot aux deux globes, 1700. SEM35P174 – 1r – 1 – Can$23.00 – cn Bibl Nat [910]
NEPUJSAG – Eger, Hungary. Sept 1962-1964 – 2r – 1 – us L of C Photodup [072]
NER HA'MAARABI – New York. 1895-97. The Western Light – 1 – us A.J.P.C. [071]
Nerchakhy, Mohammed *see* DESCRIPTION TOPOGRAPHIQUE ET HISTORIQUE DE BOUKHARA
Neree Quepat *see* DICTIONNAIRE DE L'ANCIEN DEPARTEMENT DE LA MOSELLE
NEREIS BRITANNICA / Stackhouse, J – 1795 – 1 £35.00 7 £52.50 – uk Microform Academic [590]
Nergararian, Garabed *see* A BRIEF HISTORY OF THE BEGINNING OF THE MISSION WORK IN NICOMEDIA BY THE AMERICAN BOARD OF FOREIGN MISSIONS
Neria Serranos, Vicente *see* ROSAS Y LIRIOS
NERIKES ALLEHANDA – (Allehanda Karlskoga-Degerfors, 1979-83; Karlskoga-Degerfors Allehanda, 1984-87) – Orebro, Sweden. 1979- – 1 – sw Kungliga [072]
NERIKES ALLEHANDA – Orebro, Sweden. 1843-1978 – 647r – 1 – sw Kungliga [072]
DIE NERONISCHE CHRISTENVERFOLGUNG : EINE KRITISCHE UNTERSUCHUNG ZUR GESCHICHTE DER AELTESTEN KIRCHE / Arnold, Carl Franklin – Leipzig: Fr. Richter, 1888 – 1mf – us A.T.L.A. [900]
Nerrincq, F *see* VOOR-BEELDT DER WAERE DEUGHT, NAMENTLIJCK VAN DE MAEGHDELIJCKE REYNIGHEYDT...
NERTOBRIGA BETURICA / Fita, Fidel – Madrid: Fortanet, 1893. B.R.A.H. 22, pp. 379-383 – sp Bibl Santa Ana [946]
NERVA OR A COLLECTION OF PAPERS PUBLISHED IN THE "MONTREAL HERALD" / Gale, Samuel – Montreal: William Gray, 1814. SEM16P44 – 1r – 5 – Can$9.00 – cn Bibl Nat [080]
DER NERVENARZT – v. 18-51. 1947-80 – 1,5,9 – 3621.00 – us UMI [616]
Neser, J *see* HYMNI SACRI IN USUM LUDI ILLUSTRIS AD FONTES SALUTARES MELODIIS & NUMERIS COMPOSTI & COLLECTTI A JOHANNE NESERO, MUSICAE IN EODEM LUDO MODERATORE
Nes'et, Efendi *see* DIVAN
NESHKIN, SAMUEL, SCRAPBOOKS, MS 3804 – 1917-1977 – 1 reel – 1 – us Western Res [338]
NESHOBA DEMOCRAT – Philadelphia. Miss. 1943-1953 – 1 – us UMI [071]
NESIKA / Union of British Columbia Indian Chiefs – 1972-77. (American Indian Periodicals in the Princeton University Library). 10 fiches – 9 – $50.00 – us UPA [305]
NESKOL'KO SLOV O MANDEL'SHTAME / Adamovich, G – Vozdushnye Puti, II. New York, 1961. p.87-101. BR-3636 2 – 8 – ne IDC [460]
NESKOLKO SLOV OB AGITATSII : PISMO-LEKTSIIA / Balabanoff, Angelica – Moskva: Gos. izd-vo, 1920 – 1 – CSUX89-B6288 – us Hoover Inst Photo [947]
NESPAPER CLIPPINGS / Republic Airlines Predecessor Companies – 1941-1979 – 35r – 1 – $1,050.00 $30.00r – us M.H.S. [380]
Nesri *see* KITAB-I CIHAN-NUEMA [NESRI TARIHI]
NESS, ELIOT, PAPERS, MS 3699 – 1928-1960 – 3r – 1 – us Western Res [360]
Nesselrode, A de *see* LETTRES ET PAPIERS DU CHANCELIER COMTE DE NESSELRODE 1760-1850
Nestle, E *see* DIE KIRCHENGESCHICHTE DES EUSEBIUS (T.U.U. 2-21/2)
Nestle, Eberhard *see*
- BREVIS LINGUAE SYRIACAE GRAMMATICA, LITTERATURA, CHRESTOMATHIA CUM GLOSSARIO
- INTRODUCTION TO THE TEXTUAL CRITICISM OF THE GREEK NEW TESTAMENT
- NOVI TESTAMENTI GRAECI: SUPPLEMENTUM EDITIONIBUS DE GEBHARDT TISCHENDORFIANIS
- PHILOLOGICA SACRA...URGESTALT DER EVANGELIEN UND APOSTELGESCHICHTE
- VETERIS TESTAMENTI GRAECI
- ZUR GESCHICHTE DER SYRISCHEN PUNCTUATION

Nestler, C G *see* MONOGRAPHIA DE POTENTILLA
NESTLES COMPANY PHOTOGRAPHS – 1911-1987 – 1r – 1 – at Corangamite [338]
Nestmann, Ralf *see* TEXTKONSTITUIERENDE GRAMMATISCHE KATEGORIEN IN ENGLISCHEN FACHTEXTEN DER HUMANMEDIZIN
NESTOR : RUSSICHE ANNALEN / ed by Schloezer, A L von – Goettingen. 1802-09. 5v. – 18mf – 8 – ne IDC [947]
NESTORIAN QUESTIONS ON THE ADMINISTRATION OF THE EUCHARIST, BY ISHO'YABH 4 / Unnik, W C van – Haarlem, 1937 – 7mf – 8 – Dfl30.00 – ne Slangenburg [240]
NESTORIANA : DIE FRAGMENTE DES NESTORIUS / Nestorius, Patriarch of Constantinople; ed by Loofs, Friedrich – Halle a.S.: Niemeyer, 1905 – 1mf – us A.T.L.A. [240]
LE NESTORIANISME ET L'INSCRIPTION DE KARA-BALGASSOUN / Chavannes, E – Ser 9 v9. JA. 1897. BU-600 2 – 8 – ne IDC [240]
THE NESTORIANS AND THEIR RITUALS / Badger, George Percy – London. v1-2. 1852 – v1 9mf; v2 8mf – 8 – Dfl60.00 – ne Slangenburg [280]
THE NESTORIANS AND THEIR RITUALS : WITH THE NARRATIVE OF A MISSION TO MESOPOTAMIA AND COORDISTAN IN 1842-1844, AND OF A LATE VISIT TO THOSE COUNTRIES IN 1850... / Badger, George Percy – London: Joseph Masters, 1852 – 3mf – us A.T.L.A. [305]
THE NESTORIANS, OR, THE LOST TRIBES : CONTAINING EVIDENCE OF THEIR IDENTITY, AN ACCOUNT OF THEIR MANNERS, CUSTOMS, AND CEREMONIES, TOGETHER WITH SKETCHES OF TRAVEL IN ANCIENT ASSYRIA, ARMENIA, MEDIA, AND MESOPOTAMIA, AND ILLUSTRATIONS OF SCRIPTURE PROPHECY / Grant, Asahel – New York: Harper, 1841 – 1mf – us A.T.L.A. [305]
NESTORIOUS: A PHANTASY / Fletcher, Edward Taylor – Ottawa?: s.n., 1892 (Ottawa: A. Bureau). 03167. (Pre-1900 Canadiana) – 9 – cn C.I.H.M. [971]
Nestorius *see* LE LIVRE D'HERACLIDE DE DAMAS
NESTORIUS AND HIS PLACE IN THE HISTORY OF CHRISTIAN DOCTRINE / Loofs, Friedrich – Cambridge: University Press; New York: Putnam [distributor], 1914 – 1mf – us A.T.L.A. [240]
NESTORIUS AND HIS TEACHING : A FRESH EXAMINATION OF THE EVIDENCE / Bethune-Baker, James Franklin – Cambridge: University Press, 1908 – 1mf – us A.T.L.A. [240]
NESTORIUS ET LA CONTROVERSE NESTORIENNE / Jugie, Martin – Paris: G. Beauchesne, 1912 – 1mf – us A.T.L.A. [240]
Nestorius, Patriarch of Constantinople *see*
- LE LIVRE D'HERACLIDE DE DAMAS
- NESTORIANA

Nestroev, G *see* BIBLIOTEKA SOTSIALISTA
NESTROY ALS BEARBEITER : STUDIEN ZU "DIE VERHAENGNISVOLLE FASCHINGSNACHT", "DER UNBEDEUTENDE" UND "JUDITH UND HOLOFERNES" / Boege, Guenther – Frankfurt a.M., 1968 – 4mf – 9 – DM90.00 – 3-89349-364-6 – gw Hänsel [430]
Nestroy, Jerry A *see* MOTOR PERFORMANCE OF YOUNG EXCEPTIONAL CHILDREN
Nestroy, Johann *see*
- EULENSPIEGEL, ODER, SCHABERNACK UEBER SCHABERNACK
- DIE VERHAENGNISVOLLE FASCHINGSNACHT

NESTS AND EGGS OF AUSTRALIAN BIRDS / Campbell, A J – Z-1970. 2 v. 1901 – 9 – ne IDC [590]
THE NESTS AND EGGS OF INDIAN BIRDS / Hume, A O – Ed. 2 by E. W. Oates. 3 v. Calcutta. 1889-90. BZ-273 2 – 8 – ne IDC [590]
NETA'IC UEL-VUKU'AT / Pasa, Mustafa Nuri – Istanbul: Matba'a-i Amire, 1294-1327 – 4v 9mf – 9 – $150.00 – us MEDOC [949]
Neteler, Bernhard *see*
- DAS BUCH GENESIS DER VULGATA UND DES HEBRAEISCHEN TEXTES
- DIE BUECHER DER CHRONIK DER VULGATA UND DES HEBRAEISCHEN TEXTES

NETHERLANDS = STATISTICAL YEARBOOK OF THE NETHERLANDS 1850/51-1965/66 : JAACIJFERS VOOR NEDERLAND 1850/51-1965/66 / Netherlands. Centraal Bureau voor de Statistiek – ("Kolonien" section is continued as a separate publ not included here. Coll title: European Official Statistical Serials, 1841-1984) – 379mf – 9 – £4.00f (set £2,450.00 466mf) – uk Chadwyck [949]
NETHERLANDS : STATISTISCH JAARBOEK 1985-1881 / Netherlands. Centraal Bureau voor de Statistiek – (Coll title: European Official Statistical Serials, 1841-1984) – 87mf – 9 – £6.00f (set £2,450.00 466mf) – uk Chadwyck [949]
Netherlands *see*
- NEDERLANDSE STAATSCOURANT
- TELEPHONE BOOK (DUTCH)
- VERHANDELINGEN VAN HET KONINKLIJK INSTITUUT VOOR TAAL-, LAND- EN VOLKENKUNDE

NETHERLANDS ANTILLES : STATISTISCH JAARBOEK 1956-1971 / Netherlands Antilles. Bureau voor de Statistiek – (1962, 1964 not publ. Coll title: Latin American and Caribbean Official Statistical Serials, 1821-1982) – 9mf – 9 – £175.00 – uk Chadwyck [972]
Netherlands Antilles *see* TIENJARENPLAN CURACAO
Netherlands Antilles. Bureau voor de Statistiek *see* NETHERLANDS ANTILLES
Netherlands. Cabinet and Parliament *see* KAMERSTUKKEN
Netherlands. Centraal Bureau voor de Statistiek *see*
- NETHERLANDS

Netherlands. Centraal Planbureau *see*
- CENTRAAL ECONOMISCH PLAN, 1947. VOL. 1, EERSTE NOTA, GLOBAAL PLAN. (CENTRAL ECONOMIC PLAN, 1947. VOL. 1, FIRST MEMORANDUM, GLOBAL PLAN). 'S-GRAVENHAGE. 1946. BD-1699/1
- CENTRAAL ECONOMISCH PLAN, 1949
- CENTRAAL ECONOMISCH PLAN, 1950
- CENTRAAL ECONOMISCH PLAN, 1951
- CENTRAAL ECONOMISCH PLAN, 1952
- CENTRAAL ECONOMISCH PLAN, 1953
- CENTRAAL ECONOMISCH PLAN, 1954
- CENTRAAL ECONOMISCH PLAN, 1955
- CENTRAAL ECONOMISCH PLAN, 1956
- CENTRAAL ECONOMISCH PLAN, 1957
- CENTRAAL ECONOMISCH PLAN, 1958
- CENTRAAL ECONOMISCH PLAN, 1959
- CENTRAAL ECONOMISCH PLAN, 1960
- CENTRAAL ECONOMISCH PLAN, 1961
- CENTRAAL ECONOMISCH PLAN, 1962
- CENTRAAL ECONOMISCH PLAN, 1963
- CENTRAAL ECONOMISCH PLAN, 1964
- CENTRAAL ECONOMISCH PLAN, 1965
- CENTRAAL ECONOMISCH PLAN, 1966
- CENTRAAL ECONOMISCH PLAN, 1967
- CENTRAAL ECONOMISCH PLAN 1973
- CENTRAAL ECONOMISCH PLAN, 1974
- CENTRAAL ECONOMISCH PLAN, 1975
- CENTRAL ECONOMIC PLAN, 1952
- CENTRAL ECONOMIC PLAN, 1954
- CENTRAL ECONOMIC PLAN, 1955
- CENTRAL ECONOMIC PLAN, 1961
- CENTRAL ECONOMIC PLAN, 1964 SUMMARY
- CENTRAL ECONOMIC PLAN FOR 1970. SUMMARY
- EERSTE NOTA OVER HET NATIONAAL WELVAARTSPLAN 1946
- FIRST MEMORANDUM ON THE CENTRAL ECONOMIC PLAN, 1946
- DE NEDERLANDSE ECONOMIE IN 1970. EEN VOORWAARDELIJKE PROGNOSE VAN DE ONTWIKKELINGSMOGELIJKHEDEN VOOR DE NEDERLANDSE ECONOMIE OP MIDDELLANGE TERMIJN(1966-1970). (THE NETHERLANDS' ECONOMY IN 1970. A PRELIMINARY PROGNOSIS)
- DE NEDERLANDSE ECONOMIE IN 1973. EEN VOORWAARDELIJKE PROGNOSE VAN DE ONTWIKKELINGSMOGELIJKHEDEN VOOR DE NEDERLANDSE ECONOMIE OP MIDDELLANGE TERMIJN 1968-1973
- SUMMARY OF THE NETHERLANDS CENTRAL ECONOMIC PLAN, 1967
- SUMMARY OF THE NETHERLANDS CENTRAL ECONOMIC PLAN, 1968
- SUMMARY OF THE NETHERLANDS CENTRAL ECONOMIC PLAN, 1969
- SUMMARY OF THE NETHERLANDS CENTRAL ECONOMIC PLAN, 1973

THE NETHERLANDS EAST INDIES AND JAPAN / Zyll de Jong, E van – New York City, 1942. SE 812/1. Booklets of the Neth. Inform. Bur. No. 3 – 1mf – 9 – ne IDC [950]
Netherlands East Indies. (Netherlands). O.E.E.C *see*
- MEMORANDUM ON THE LONG TERM ECONOMIC PROGRAMME OF THE NETHERLANDS DEPENDENT OVERSEAS TERRITORIES (INDONESIA)
- REPORT TO THE ECONOMIC COOPERATION ADMINISTRATION OF THE 1949/50 PROGRAMME

Netherlands. Economic plans *see* CENTRAAL PLANBUREAU
Netherlands. General State Archives *see*
- HET ARCHIEF VAN PROF. DR. W.H. DE VRIESE BETREFFENDE ZIJN ONDERZOEK NAAR DE KULTURES IN NEDERLANDS INDIE, 1857-1862
- DOCUMENTATIE OVER KOLONISCHE ONDERWERPEN: INDONESIE (OOST-INDIE), 1819-1933; EN WEST INDIE, 1815-1929
- INDEX OVER INDISCHE ONDERWERPEN IN NEDERLANDSE COURANTEN, 1843-1947
- INDEX VAN HET OPENBAAR ARCHIEF VAN HET MINISTERIE VAN KOLONIEN VAN NEDERLAND, 1850-1921
- INDICES OP DE GEWONE RESOLUTIES VAN DE STATEN VAN HOLLAND, 1524-1795
- INDICES OP DE RESOLUTIES VAN DE GECOMMITTEERDE RADEN IN HET ZUIDERKWARTIER, 1621-1795
- INDICES OP DE SECRETE RESOLUTIES VAN DE STATEN VAN HOLLAND, 1653-1795
- KOHIEREN VAN DE TIENDE PENNING 1543
- REGISTER OVER DE INDISCHE COURANTEN, 1810-1923
- RESOLUTIES VAN DE HEREN ZEVENTIEN DER VERENIGDE OOSTINDISCHE COMPAGNIE, 1602-1796

NETHERLANDS INTERNATIONAL LAW REVIEW – v1-41. 1953-1994 – 9 – $1,495.00set – us Hein [340]
NETHERLANDS JOURNAL OF AGRICULTURAL SCIENCE – 1953- 1; 1974- 5,6; 1975- 9 – us UMI [073]
NETHERLANDS JOURNAL OF PLANT PATHOLOGY – Wageningen. v1-31. 1895-1925 – 5,9 – Dfl2,480.00; Dfl80.00v – ne Swets [580]
Netherlands. (Kingdom, 1815-). Department van Binnenlandsche Zaken *see* VIJFJARIG OVERZICHT VAN DE STERFTE NAAR DEN LEEFTIJD EN DE OORZAKEN VAN DEN DOOD IN ELKE GEMEENTE VAN NEDERLAND
Netherlands. Laws, Statutes, etc *see* STAATSBLAD VAN HET KONINKRIJK DER NEDERLANDEN
NETHERLANDS MILK AND DAIRY JOURNAL – 1947- 1; 1974- 5,6; 1975- 9 – us UMI [073]
The Netherlands. Ministry of Foreign Affairs. The Hague. *see* INVENTORIES AND GUIDES TO DIPLOMATIC ARCHIVES
Netherlands Office for Fine Arts *see* THEO VAN DOESBURG ARCHIVE
Netherlands. Parliament *see*
- HANDELINGEN
- KAMERVRAGEN

NETHERLANDS REFORMED CHURCH ARCHIVES C. 1560-1810 – (Includes the printed inventory by H.Q. Janssen, 1878 and the printed inventory by A. Fris, 1991) – 3,143mf – 9 – ne IDC [240]

Netherlands. Royal Library. The Hague. Newspaper Department *see*
- ALGEMEEN DAGBLAD VAN NEDERLANDSCH INDIE, 1873-1886
- BATAVIASCH KOLONIALE COURANT, 1810-11
- JAVASCHE COURANT, 1828-1939
- SOERABAIASCH HANDELSBLAD, 1866-1917
- SUMATRA POST, 1898-1940

Netherlands. Royal Library. The Hague. Newspaper Department *see* BATAVIAASCH NIEUWSBLAD, 1885-1926

Netherlands. Treaties, etc., 1948- *see* FINANCIAL AND ECONOMIC AGREEMENT (BETWEEN KINGDOM OF THE NETHERLANDS AND THE GOVERNMENT OF THE REPUBLIK INDONESIA SERIKAT)

Netherlands West Indies. Curacao *see* DE CURACAOSCHE COURANT

NETHERLANDS YEARBOOK OF INTERNATIONAL LAW – v1-24. 1970-1994 – 9 – $495.00set – us Hein [340]

Nethery, V M *see* PASSIVE SENSORY MEDIATION OF RATINGS OF PERCEIVED EXERTION IN TRAINED AND UNTRAINED MALES AT LIGHT AND MODERATE WORKLOADS

NETIVOT – Providence, RI. 1973-82 – 1 – us A.J.P.C. [071]

O NETO DO DIARIO : FOLHA DA TARDE – Aracaju, 2-13 Apr 1886 – 1,5,6 – bl Biblioteca [072]

O NETO DO DIARIO : PERIODICO NOTICIOSO, LITTERARIO E JOCO-SERIO – Maceio, Alagoas. 2 Jun, 28 Ago 1889 – 1,5,6 – bl Biblioteca [072]

NETSAH YISRAEL = ETERNAL ISRAEL – (In Yiddish) – Munich, DE. no1 May-no4 Sep 1948 – 1r – 1 – $25.00 – cn Can Microfilming [072]

Netscher, P M *see* OS HOLANDESES NO BRASIL

THE NETSILIK ESKIMOS / Rasmussen, Knud – 1931 – 8 – BN 365 2 – ne IDC [305]

NETSTUCCA VALLEY NEWS – Cloverdale, OR. -w. 4 Aug 1938-18 Sept 1941. 1 roll – 1 – us U.O. Library [071]

NETSUKE : JAPANESE MINIATURE CARVINGS / Victoria and Albert Museum. London – (Over 500 of the traditional Japanese miniature carvings are reproduced. Includes printed index) – 1983 – 7 colour mf – 15 – $196.00 – 0-907696-09-0 – uk Emmett [730]

Netter, Thomas *see* FASCICULI ZIZANIORUM MAGISTRI WYCLIF CUM TRITICO (RS5)

Netterville, J J *see* CENTENNIAL HISTORY OF MADISON COUNTY

Nettlau, Max *see*
- MICHAEL BAKUNIN, EINE BIOGRAPHIE, 1814-1876
- LA RESPONSABILITE ET LA SOLIDARITE DANS LA LUTTE OUVRIERE

THE NETTLE CREEK CHURCH CASE OR WHO ARE THE REGULAR BAPTISTS / Bradley, James – 1891 – 1 – 11.90 – us Baptist [240]

Nettleton, Lucy *see* LETTERS

NETWORK – 1970- – 1 – us UMI [073]

NETWORK : COMPUTATION IN NEURAL SYSTEMS – v1. 1990 – 1,5,6,9 – £169.00 – uk I.O.P. [530]

NETWORK – New York, NY. May 1969-1 Jun 1971. Lacking v2,no.4. Continued by: North American Jewish Students' Network – 1 – us A.J.P.C. [071]

NETWORK WORLD – v3-. 1986- – 1,5,6,9 – us UMI [380]

NETWORKING AND INTEGRATING (SYSTEMS AND SOCIETY) – Proceedings of the Annual Canadian Conference of Information Science, 12th. 14-16 May 1984, Toronto. ED 243-460 – 9 – us EDRS [020]

THE NETWORKING GAME / Wagner, Pat & Smith, Leif – Pamphlet. 1 fiche (29x) – 9 – 1.00f – at Libertarian Micro [320]

NETWORKING IN BRUCELLOSIS RESEARCH : REPORT OF THE UNITED NATIONS UNIVERSITY, BRUCELLOSIS RESEARCH NETWORK / ed by Frank, Julius F – 9 – $14.00 – 92-808-0756-0 – ja U.N. Univ [616]

NETWORKS – v. 1-. 1971- – 1,5,6,9 – us UMI [510]

NETWORKS OF CONTACT : THE PORTUGUESE AND TORONTO / Anderson, Grace M – 1974 – xvi/195p – Can$18.00 – 0-88920-046-7 – cn W.L.U. Press [302]

Netz, Peter *see* PSYCHISCH KRANKE ALTE MENSCHEN UND SOZIALE UNTERSTUETZUNG

Netzer, Ofra *see* EFFECTS OF AGE AND GENDER ON FUNCTIONAL ROTATION AND LATERAL FLEXION OF THE BACK AND THE NECK

NETZWERKANALYSE ZUR GENERIERUNG DER ZUSTANDSGLEICHUNGEN / Badstuebner, Frank – 1995 – 1mf – 9 – DM60.00 – 3-8267-2176-4 – gw Hänsel [621]

NEU AUFGEFUNDENE ABBILDUNG DES DRONTE UND EINES ZWEITEN KURZFLUEGELIGEN VOGELS / Frauenfels, G Ritter von – Wien, 1868. vi,16p,4pls. Account of the dodo, describing the discovery in Vienna of a painting of that extinct bird. Z/1757/2 – 8 – ne IDC [590]

NEU ERFUNDENE UND GRUENDLICHE ANWEISUNG / Heinichen, Johann David – 1711 – 9 – us Sibley [780]

NEU ERFUNDENE UND GRUENDLICHE ANWEISUNG WIE EIN MUSIKLIEBENDER AUSS GEWISSE VORTHEILHAFFTIGE ART KOENNE BIS ZU VOLKOMMENER ERLERNUNG / Heinichen, J D – Hamburg. 1711. BP-694 1 – 9 – ne IDC [780]

NEU EROEFFNETE MUSIKALISCHE BIBLIOTHEK ODER GRUENDLICHE NACHRICHT NEBST UNPARTHEYISCHEM URTHEIL VON MUSIKALISCHEN SCHRIFTEN UND BUECHERN / Mizler, L C – Leipzig. 1739. BP-729 1 – 9 – ne IDC [780]

NEU EROEFFNETE MUSIKALISCHE BIBLIOTHEK ODER GRUENDLICHE NACHRICHT NEBST UNPARTHEYISCHEM URTHEIL VON MUSIKALISCHEN SCHRIFTEN UND BUECHERN / Mizler, L C – 1739-54.4v – 9 – us Sibley [780]

NEU EROEFFNETES IN HUNDERT SPRACHEN BESTEHENDES A.B.C. BUCH,... / Fritz, J F – Leipzig, 1743 – 2mf – ne IDC [400]

Neu, Lois *see* AN INVESTIGATION OF ATHLETE SATISFACTION WITH THE SPORT TEAM SELECTION PROCESS

NEU METHOD – MESSIGE VIOL D'AMOUR STUECKE AUS ALLEN THOENEN, OHNE VERSYUEMUNG, THEILS MIT BASSE, THEILS ALLEINE, AUCH MIT AUSGESUCHTEN ARIETTEN VERMUESCHT AM ENDE DES BUCHS... / Huberty, A – Wien: [1780] – 1 – us Sibley [780]

NEUAUFGEFUNDENE HEBRAEISCHE BIBELHANDSCHRIFTEN / Harkavy, A – St. Petersbourg: Eggers, 1884. 1 fiche – 9 – us A.T.L.A. [220]

NEUBABYLONISCHE BRIEFE AUS UKRUK. / Ebeling, Erich – Berlin. 1930-34 – 1 – us Res Libr [930]

NEUBABYLONISCHE RECHTS- UND VERWALTUNGSURKUNDEN. / ed by San Nicolo, Mariano – Leipzig. 1935 – 1 – us Res Libr [930]

DIE NEUBABYLONISCHEN KOENIGSINSCHRIFTEN / Langdon, S – (Vorderasiatische Bibl). Leipzig, 1912. BNE-20,031 1 – 9 – ne IDC [410]

DER NEUBAU DES DEUTSCHEN KREDITSYSTEMS / Rittershausen, Heinrich – 1932; Das Andere System. Ein Wirtschafts- und Finanz- vorschlag in vier Gesetzentwuerfen. 1932. 332p. 2 fiches (24x) – 9 – 1.00f – at Libertarian Micro [320]

Neubauer, A *see*
- CATALOGUE OF THE HEBREW MSS IN THE BODLEIAN LIBRARY
- LES ECRIVAINS JUIFS FRANCAIS DU 14 SIECLE
- MEDIEVAL JEWISH CHRONICLES, VOL 2
- MELEKHET HA-SHIR
- OHEV NASHIM

Neubauer, Ernst *see* GOETHES RELIGIOESES ERLEBEN IM ZUSAMMENHANG SEINER INTUITIV-ORGANISCHEN WELTANSCHAUUNG

Neubert, W *see* DEUTSCHES MAGAZIN FUER GARTEN- UND BLUMENKUNDE

NEUBESTELLTES ABENTEUERLICHES TIERHAUS; EIN ZOOLOGIE DES ABERGLAUBENS, DER MYSTIK UND MYTHOLOGIE VOM MITTELALTER BIS AUF UNSERE ZEIT, VON WATER MEHRING / Mehring, Walter – Potsdam: Gustav Kiepenheuer, 1925 – 1 – us U.W. Library [390]

Neuburger, Max *see* SCHILLERS BEZIEHUNGEN ZUR MEDIZIN

Neucourt, F *see* DU MOUVEMENT DE LA POPULATION DANS LA VILLE DE VERDUN, D'APRES LES REGISTRES DE L'ETAT CIVIL

DIE NEUE – (Null-Nummern: sep 22 and 27 1978. Since feb 3 1979: issued twice a week. Since may 3 1979: issued daily. Since jan 1 1982: issued weekly) – Berlin, sep 22 1978-oct 29 1982 – 1 – Inquire at Mikrofilmarchiv for details – gw Misc Inst [072]

DIE NEUE – (Tageszeitung bis Ende 1981, dann Wochenzeitung) – West Berlin, Germany. 22 Sept 1978-12 Dec 1981 – 6r – 1 – gw Mikrofilm [072]

DIE NEUE AERZTLICHE : ALLEGEMEINE ZEITUNG FUER KLINIK UND PRAXIS – (Alles Erschienene) – Frankfurt, 16 Sept 1985-31 Mar 1991 – 16r – 1 – DM1,200.00 – gw Mikro Press [073]

NEUE ALLGEMEINE DEUTSCHE GARTEN- UND BLUMENZEITUNG – (Cont as: Hamburger Garten- und Blumenzeitung. Hamburg v8-37 1852-1881) – Hamburg. v1-7. 1844-1851 – 407mf – 9 – ne IDC [630]

NEUE ARBEITER-ZEITUNG – (Cont: Braunschweiger Arbeiter-Zeitung. Organ der Dritten Internationale, -jan 1921; Niedersaechsische Arbeiterzeitung/Organ der Vereinigten Kommunistischen Partei Deutschlands, -oct 1926) – Braunschweig, nov 13 1920-feb 26 1933 – 20r – 1 – Inquire at Mikrofilmarchiv for details – gw Misc Inst [335]

NEUE ARBEITERZEITUNG *see* BRAUNSCHWEIGER ARBEITER-ZEITUNG

NEUE ATHENER ZEITUNG – Athen, oct 14 1934-dec 16 1939 – 1 – Dist. gw Mikrofilm – gw Misc Inst [949]

NEUE BACS-BODROGER ZEITUNG – Apatin, jan 1-dec 22 1929 – 1r – 1 – Dist. gw Mikrofilm – gw Misc Inst [949]

NEUE BACS-BODROGER ZEITUNG – Apatin, Yugoslavia. May 1925-28 – 1r – 1 – us L of C Photodup [072]

DAS NEUE BADEN : ORGAN DER DEMOKRATISCHEN PARTEI SUED- UND MITTELBADENS – Lahr-Schwarzw., West Germany. 1947-1949 – 1 – gw Mikrofilm [072]

NEUE BADISCHE LANDES-ZEITUNG – Mannheim, Germany. Jul 1914-Jul 1919 – 17r – 1 – us L of C Photodup [072]

NEUE BAHNEN : DER UNTERRICHT IN DER CHRISTLICHEN RELIGION IM GEIST DER MODERNEN THEOLOGIE / Baumgarten, Otto – 2. erw Aufl. Tuebingen: J C B Mohr (Paul Siebeck), 1909 – 1mf – 9 – 0-8370-7607-2 – 1986-1607 – us A.T.L.A. [240]

NEUE BALLADEN UND LIEDER / Strauss und Torney, Lulu von – 6. und 7. Aufl. Stuttgart: Deutsche Verlags-Anstalt, 1923 – 1 – us U.W. Library [780]

NEUE BANATER ZEITUNG / ed by Kreiskomitee Temesch der RKP – Temeschburg (Timisoara), Rumaenien. 1976- – 1 – gw Mikrofilm [949]

NEUE BANATER ZEITUNG – Temeswar, 1976-1991 – 25r – 1 – DM1,875.00 – gw Mikro Press [072]

NEUE BAUSTEINE ZU EINER LEBENSGESCHICHTE WOLFRAMS VON ESCHENBACH / Schreiber, Albert – (Includes bibliographical references) – Frankfurt am Main: M Diesterweg, 1922 – 1 – us U.W. Library [430]

NEUE BAYREUTHER ZEITUNG *see* BAYREUTHER ZEITUNG

NEUE BEITRAEGE ZU KLOPSTOCKS MESSIAS : APOSTROPH, HIATURS, ALLITERATION / Pawel, Jaro – (Includes bibliographical references) – Wien: Verlag der Oberrealschule in der Josefstadt, 1881 – 1r – 1 – us U.W. Library [430]

NEUE BEITRAEGE ZUR DIPTERENFAUNA DER BALKAN-HALBINSEL / ed by Strobl, G – Wissensch. Mitthl. Bosnien und Hercegovina. v9. Wien, 1904. v9. 63p – 8 – ne IDC [590]

NEUE BEITRAEGE ZUR KENNTNISS DER EMBRYOBILDUNG DER PHANEROGAMEN / Hofmeister, W F B – (Abhandlungen der Saechsischen Gesellschaft der Wissenschaften. v. 6, v. 7.). 2 pts. Leipzig. 1859-61. B-7102 2 – 8 – ne IDC [580]

NEUE BEITRAEGE ZUR SEMITISCHEN SAGENKUNDE / Gruenbaum, Max – Leiden: E J Brill, 1893 – 1mf – 9 – 0-8370-3414-0 – 1985-1414 – us A.T.L.A. [390]

NEUE BEITRAEGE ZUR SEMITISCHEN SPRACHWISSENSCHAFT / Noeldeke, T – Strassburg. 1910. BNE-481 1 – 9 – ne IDC [470]

NEUE BEITRAEGE ZUR SEMITISCHEN SPRACHWISSENSCHAFT / Noeldeke, Theodor – (Includes bibliographical references) – Strassburg: Karl J Truebner, 1910 – 1mf – 9 – 0-8370-8604-3 – 1986-2604 – us A.T.L.A. [470]

NEUE BERLINER MUSIKZEITUNG – Berlin. v1-50. 1847-1896 – 412mf – 9 – ne IDC [780]

NEUE BERLINER MUSIKZEITUNG / ed by Boch, Gustav – Berlin, 1847-56. Hildesheim, 1990 – 49mf – 9 – DM350.00 diazo DM400.00 silver – gw Olms [780]

NEUE BERLINER MUSIKZEITUNG – v. 1-43. 1847-89 – 1 – 227.00 – us L of C Photodup [780]

NEUE BERLINER ZEITUNG – (Cont by: Das 12-Uhr-Blatt, jan 27 1931) – Berlin, 1919-44 (incomplete) – 82r – 1 – Inquire at Mikrofilmarchiv for details – gw Misc Inst [943]

NEUE BERLINER ZEITUNG – (Title changes in Jan 1931 to: Das 12 Uhr Blatt) – Berlin, 1919-44 (incomplete) – 82r – 1 – gw Mikrofilm [072]

NEUE BEYTRAEGE ZUR BOTANIK / Roth, A W – pt. 1. Frankfurt am Mayn. 1802. B-5692 2 – 8 – ne IDC [580]

NEUE BIBELSTUDIEN : SPRACHGESCHICHTLICHE BEITRAEGE, ZUMEIST AUS DEN PAPYRI UND INSCHRIFTEN, ZUR ERKLAERUNG DES NEUEN TESTAMENTS / Deissmann, Gustav Adolf – (Includes bibliographical references and index) – Marburg: N G Elwert, 1897 – 1mf – 9 – 0-8370-9459-3 – 1986-3459 – us A.T.L.A. [220]

DAS NEUE BILD – Berlin, Germany.Jul-Aug, Nov 1930; 1931 – 1 – gw Mikrofilm [072]

DAS NEUE BILD – Berlin, jul, aug, nov 1930, 1931 – 1 – Inquire at Mikrofilmarchiv for details – gw Misc Inst [072]

NEUE BILDUNGSWEGE = FREEDOM IN EDUCATION / Bartmann, Bernard & Zube, John – 1987. 250p – 9 – 1.00f – at Libertarian Micro [335]

NEUE BILDZEITUNG – Berlin, may 1957-71 – 6r – 1 – Inquire at Mikrofilmarchiv for details – gw Misc Inst [072]

NEUE BILDZEITUNG – East Berlin, Germany. May 1957-71 – 6r – 1 – gw Mikrofilm [072]

NEUE BLAETTER FUER DEN SOZIALISMUS – v1-4 no 6. 1930-Jun 1933 (complete) – 2r – 1 – ATLA B0068 – us A.T.L.A. [073]

NEUE BLAETTER FUER STADT UND LAND – Oldenburg i.O., Germany. 1843-1851 – 2r – 1 – gw Mikrofilm [072]

DAS NEUE BLATT – Leipzig, Germany. 1870; 1875-1877 – 3r – 1 – gw Mikrofilm [072]

NEUE BONNER ZEITUNG *see*
- BONNER ZEITUNG

NEUE BREMER ZEITUNG – Bremen, Germany. 7 Okt 1813-30 Sept 1815; 2 Jun 1849-8 Sept 1851 – 7r – 1 – gw Mikrofilm [072]

NEUE BREMER ZEITUNG – Bremen, jun 2 1849-jun 1852 – 1 – Inquire at Mikrofilmarchiv for details – gw Misc Inst [943]

NEUE BREMER ZEITUNG – Bremen, oct 7 1813-sep 30 1815 – 1 – Inquire at Mikrofilmarchiv for details – gw Misc Inst [943]

NEUE BREMER ZEITUNG *see* BREMER ZEITUNG

NEUE BRESLAUER ZEITUNG – (Title change: Breslauer Zeitung, 1 Jan 1828) – Breslau (Wroclaw), Poland. 1820-1827 – 12r – 1 – gw Mikrofilm [943]

NEUE BRESLAUER ZEITUNG *see* BRESLAUER ZEITUNG

NEUE BRIEFE CHR. MART. WIELANDS : VORNEHMLICH AN SOPHIE VON LA ROCHE / Wieland, Christoph Martin; ed by Hassencamp, Robert – (Includes bibliographical references and index) – Stuttgart: J G Cotta, 1894 – 1r – 1 – us U.W. Library [430]

NEUE BRUCHSALER ZEITUNG – Bruchsal, sep 4 1942-43 – 1 – Inquire at Mikrofilmarchiv for details – gw Misc Inst [943]

NEUE BUKARESTER ZEITUNG – Bukarest, jan 4-mar 31 1929 – 1r – 1 – Inquire at Mikrofilmarchiv for details – gw Misc Inst [949]

NEUE BUKARESTER ZEITUNG – Bukarest, Rumaenien. 4 Jan-31 Mar 1929 – 1r – 1 – gw Mikrofilm [949]

NEUE DEISTER-ZEITUNG – Springe, West Germany. 1981- – 6r – 1 – gw Mikrofilm [072]

NEUE DEUTSCHE BAUERNZEITUNG – (Also known as: Der freie Bauer; Der Genossenschaftsbauer) – East Berlin, Germany. 4 Nov 1960-1 Nov 1991 – 1 – gw Mikrofilm [072]

NEUE DEUTSCHE BAUERNZEITUNG *see*
– DER FREIE BAUER
– DER GENOSSENSCHAFTSBAUER

NEUE DEUTSCHE BLAETTER : MONATSCHRIFT FUER LITERATUR UND KRITIK – Prag (Praha), Czechoslovakia. Sept 1933-Aug 1935 – 1r – 1 – gw Mikrofilm [430]

NEUE DEUTSCHE DORFZEITUNG – Coburg, Germany. 15 Jan 1849-29 Jun 1851 – 2r – 1 – gw Mikrofilm [072]

NEUE DEUTSCHE FORSCHUNGEN / Abteilung neuere deutsche Literaturgeschichte – Berlin: Junker und Duennhaupt, 1935- – 2r – 1 – us U.W. Library [430]

NEUE DEUTSCHE LITERATUR – 1969-1989 – 983mf – 1 – DM5,603.10 – gw Mikro Press [430]

NEUE DEUTSCHE PRESSE – 1947-1989 – 583mf – 1 – DM3,323.10 – gw Mikro Press [070]

NEUE DEUTSCHE ZEITUNG – Darmstadt (till 1849) u. Frankfurt-Main, Germany. 1 Nov 1849-30 Jun 1850 – 4r – 1 – gw Mikrofilm [072]

NEUE DEUTSCHE ZEITUNG *see*
– FRANKFURTER GESCHAEFTSBERICHT

NEUE DICHTUNGEN / Wagner, Christian – Heilbronn: Schroeder, 1897 – 1r – 1 – us U.W. Library [810]

NEUE DORFZEITUNG *see* OSTERODER DORFZEITUNG

NEUE ENCYCLOPAEDIE DER WISSENSCHAFTEN UND KUENSTE (AEL, ABT 1;24) : FUER DIE DEUTSCHE NATION GESCHRIEBEN VON ARNETH, BENSEN, BERNOULLI U.A. / Arneth & Bensen – 2. Aufl. Stuttgart. 8 bde. 1858 (mf ed 1994) – 89mf – 9 – DM820.00 – 3-89131-174-5 – gw Fischer [030]

NEUE ENTDECKUNGEN IM GANZEN UMFANG DER PFLANZENKUNDE / Sprengel, K P J – 5751. 3 V. 1820-1822 – 9 – ne IDC [590]

NEUE ENTWICKLUNGEN IM MINDERHEITENSCHUTZ IN EUROPA / Menhart, Ursula – 1995 – 2mf – 9 – DM80.00 – 3-8267-2084-9 – gw Hänsel [320]

NEUE EPPINGER ZEITUNG – (Title change: Eppinger Zeitung, BA der Heilbronner Stimme, 3 Jan 1972) – Eppingen, Germany. 1974- – 9r per yr – 1 – gw Mikrofilm [072]

NEUE EUROPAEISCHE ZEITUNG *see* EUROPAEISCHE ZEITUNG

NEUE EVANGELISCHE KIRCHENZEITUNG – 1(1859)-28(1886) – 390mf – 9 – Dfl1,365.00 – ne Slangenburg [073]

NEUE EVANGELISCHE KIRCHENZEITUNG – Berlin, Leipzig. v1-28. 1859-1886 – 390mf – 9 – ne IDC [240]

NEUE FRAENKISCHE ZEITUNG – Wuerzburg, Germany. 23 Dec 1848-May 1850 – 2r – 1 – gw Mikrofilm [072]

NEUE FRAGMENTE DES PAPIAS, HEGESIPPUS UND PIERIUS (T.U.U. 1-5/2B) / Boor, C de – Leipzig, 1888 – 1mf – 9 – ne Slangenburg [240]

NEUE FRAGMENTE UND UNTERSUCHUNGEN ZU DEN JUDENCHRISTLICHEN EVANGELIEN (T.U.U. 3-37/1) / Schmidtke, Alfred – Leipzig, 1911 – 5mf – 9 – ne Slangenburg [240]

NEUE FRANKFURTER ZEITUNG *see*
– FRANKFURTER GESCHAEFTSBERICHT

NEUE FREIBURGER ZEITUNG *see* FREIBURGER ZEITUNG

NEUE FREIE PRESSE – (Filmed with: Neues Wiener Tagblatt, Neue Freie Presse, jan 23-31 1939) – Wien [Vienna]: Adolf Werther et al, [1890-99] (61r); [jul 1938-jan 22 1939] (7r) – 1 – us Res Libr [072]

NEUE FREIE PRESSE – Vienna, Austria. aug. 1914-Dec. 1917 (gaps) – 1 – 35.00r – us Hoover Inst Photo [072]

NEUE FREIE PRESSE – Vienna, Austria. -d. 1 Jan 1885-20 Jan 1939. 530 reels – 1 – uk British Libr Newspaper [072]

NEUE FREIE PRESSE *see* VOLKSSTIMME

NEUE FREIE PRESSE (VIENNA, AUSTRIA: 1864) – (This microfilmed segment covers period for: Sept. 1864-Sept. 1866 (reels 1-24); Oct. 1866 (reel 26); Nov. 1866 (reel 28); Dec. 1866 (reel 25); Jan. 1867-Nov. 18) – Wien: Neue freie Presse, 1864-1939 – 1 – CSUX86-S457 – us Hoover Inst Photo [943]

NEUE FREUNDSCHAFT – Berlin, 1928 n1-27 – 1r – 1 – Inquire at Mikrofilmarchiv for details – gw Misc Inst [072]

NEUE FRIEDBERGER ZEITUNG : BEILAGE: SONNTAGSBLATT – Friedberg. 1902 – 1r – 1 – gw Mikrofilm [072]

NEUE FRIEDBERGER ZEITUNG – Friedberg. mar 1, 1896-1920 – 14r – 1 – gw Mikrofilm [072]

DIE NEUE FRONT : DEUTSCHE GEWERKSCHAFTSZEITUNG – Essen, West Germany. 1956-1971 – 1 – gw Mikrofilm [072]

DIE NEUE FRONT : ORGAN DER SOZIALISTISCHEN ARBEITER-PARTEI DEUTSCHLANDS – Paris. Jul 1933-Aug 1939 – 1r – 1 – gw Mikrofilm [072]

NEUE FUNKSTUNDE *see*
– OSTDEUTSCHE ILLUSTRIERTE FUNKSTUNDE

DIE NEUE FUSSBALL-WOCHE : (FUWO) – Berlin, jan 3 1956-90 – 32r – 1 – Inquire at Mikrofilmarchiv for details – gw Misc Inst [790]

DIE NEUE FUSSBALL-WOCHE (FUWO) – East Berlin, Germany. 3 Jan 1956-1990 – 32r – 1 – gw Mikrofilm [072]

DIE NEUE GARTENLAUBE *see* DIE GARTENLAUBE

NEUE GEDICHTE / Hauptmann, Gerhart – Berlin: Aufbau-Verlag, 1946 – 1r – 1 – us U.W. Library [810]

NEUE GEDICHTE / Hesse, Hermann – (Includes indexes) – Berlin: S Fischer, 1937 – 1r – 1 – us U.W. Library [810]

NEUE GEDICHTE / Knortz, Karl – 2. verb. Aufl. Glarus: J Vogel, 1893 – 1r – 1 – us U.W. Library [810]

NEUE GEDICHTE / Pfungst, Arthur – 3., verm. Aufl. Berlin: F Duemmler, 1903 – 1r – 1 – us U.W. Library [810]

NEUE GEDICHTE / Wilbrandt, Adolf von – Stuttgart: J G Cotta, 1889 – 1r – 1 – us U.W. Library [810]

DIE NEUE GEIGE : ERZAEHLUNG / Thiel, Georg – Karlsbad: A Kraft, 1944 – 1r – 1 – us U.W. Library [430]

DIE NEUE GENERATION (HQ 6) / ed by Stoecker, Helene – 4(1908)-28(1932) (mf ed 1992) – 131mf – 9 – DM980.00 – 3-89131-060-9 – gw Fischer [305]

DER NEUE GOETTINGISCHE ABER VIEL SCHLECHTER / Mattheson, J – 1727 – 9 – us Sibley [780]

NEUE HALL- UND THONKUNST, ODER MECHANISCHE GEHEIM-VERBINDUNG DER KUNST UND NATUR / Kircher, Athanasius – trans. A. Carione. Noerdlingen, 1684. BP-702 1 – 9 – ne IDC [780]

NEUE HAMBURGER PRESSE – Hamburg. Germany. -w. 9 Jun 1945-30 Mar 1946. (53 ft) – 1 – uk British Libr Newspaper [072]

NEUE HAMBURGER PRESSE – Hamburg, Jun 1945-Mar 1946 – 1r – 1 – DM75.00 – gw Mikro Press [072]

NEUE HAMBURGER PRESSE – Hamburg, West Germany. 9 Jun 1945-30 Mar 1946 – 1r – 1 – gw Mikrofilm [072]

NEUE HAMBURGISCHE BOERSEN-HALLE *see* PRIVILIGIRTE LISTE DER BOERSENHALLE

DAS NEUE HANDWERK – Berlin, 1959-86 (incomplete) – 5r – 1 – Inquire at Mikrofilmarchiv for details – gw Misc Inst [072]

DAS NEUE HANDWERK – East Berlin, Germany. 1959-1986 – 5r – 1 – gw Mikrofilm [072]

NEUE HANNOVERSCHE PRESSE – Hanover, Germany. 1974-Aug 1977 – 37r – 1 – us L of C Photodup [072]

NEUE HANNOVERSCHE PRESSE *see*
– HANNOVERSCHE PRESSE

NEUE HANNOVERSCHE ZEITUNG *see*
– HANNOVERSCHE ZEITUNG

NEUE HEIDELBERGER JAHRBUECHER – Heidelberg. v1-21 1891-1919; N.S. 1924-1938 – 163mf – 9 – ne IDC [943]

NEUE HEINE-FUNDE / Heine, Heinrich; ed by Nassen, J – Leipzig: H Barsdorf, 1898 – 1r – 1 – us U.W. Library [800]

NEUE HESSISCHE ZEITUNG – Kassel, Germany. 15 Mar-24 Jun, 1 Oct-31 Dec 1848 – 1r – 1 – gw Mikrofilm [072]

NEUE HOMILIEN DES MAKARIUS/SYMEON : 1 AUS TYPUS 3 (T.U.U. 5-72) / ed by Klostermann-Berthold – Berlin, 1961 – 4mf – 9 – ne Slangenburg [240]

NEUE ILLUSTRIERTE ZEITUNG – (Cont: Hackebeils Illustrierte Zeitung, since 1931 n41) – Berlin, 1935-36, 1940-41 (incomplete) – 1 – Dist. gw Mikrofilm – gw Misc Inst [072]

NEUE ILLUSTRIERTE ZEITUNG *see* HACKEBEILS ILLUSTRIERTE ZEITUNG

NEUE ILLUSTRIRTE ZEITUNG – Leipzig, Germany. 1888 – 1 – gw Mikrofilm [072]

NEUE INTERNATIONALE RUNDSCHAU DER ARBEIT – Berlin, 1942-44 n3 – 1 – Inquire at Mikrofilmarchiv for details – gw Misc Inst [331]

NEUE INTERNATIONALE RUNDSCHAU DER ARBEIT – Berlin, Germany. 1942-Heft 3, 1944 – 1r – 1 – gw Mikrofilm [331]

NEUE INTERNATIONALE RUNDSCHAU DER ARBEIT – Berlin. v. 1, no. 1-v. 4, no. 3. 1941-1944 – 1 – us NY Public [331]

NEUE JAHRBUECHER FUER DAS KLASSICHE ALTERTUM, GESCHICHTE UND DEUTSCHE LITERATUR UND FUER PAEDAGOGIK / ed by Ilberg, J – Leipzig. v1-54. 1898-1924 – 587mf – 9 – H-220/2 – ne IDC [430]

NEUE JAHRBUECHER FUER PHILOLOGIE UND PAEDAGOGIK – v. 156. 1831-97 – 1 – 712.00 – us L of C Photodup [370]

NEUE JENAISCHE ALLGEMEINE LITERATUR-ZEITUNG *see* JENAISCHE ALLGEMEINE LITERATUR-ZEITUNG

NEUE JUEDISCHE MONATSHEFTE – Berlin, 1916-20 – 1r – 1 – Inquire at Mikrofilmarchiv for details – gw Misc Inst [073]

NEUE JUEDISCHE MONATSHEFTE : ZEITSCHRIFT FUER POLITIK, WIRTSCHAFT UND LITERATUR IN OST UND WEST – Berlin. v1-4. 1916-20. Complete. B309 (Leo Baeck Institute. German-Jewish Periodicals, Pt 2) – 1r – 1 – $75.00 – us UPA [270]

NEUE JUGEND – Berlin, 1931-35 – 1 – Inquire at Mikrofilmarchiv for details – gw Misc Inst [072]

NEUE JURISTISCHE WOCHENSCHRIFT – Germany, 1947/48-1970 – 9 – inquire – us Ross [340]

NEUE JURISTISCHE WOCHENSCHRIFT : NJW – 115mf – 9 – ca DM898.00 – 3-406-30563-6 – gw Beck [340]

NEUE JUSTIZ – 1947-1983 – 783mf – 1 – DM4,463.10 – gw Mikro Press [340]

NEUE JUSTIZ – v1-6. 1947-Sept 1952. -m. Oct 1952-Dec 1955, -sm. Berlin, Deutscher Zentralverlag – 1 – us U.W. Library [073]

NEUE KIRCHE – Bielefeld-Bethel, 1958-jan 25 1959, apr 1 1959-66 – 1 – Inquire at Mikrofilmarchiv for details – gw Misc Inst [240]

NEUE KIRCHLICHE ZEITSCHRIFT – 10(1899) – 18mf – 9 – Dfl63.00 – ne Slangenburg [073]

NEUE KOELNISCHE ZEITUNG FUER BUERGER, BAUERN UND SOLDATEN – Koeln, Germany. Jan-14 Jun 1849 – 2r – 1 – gw Mikrofilm [072]

NEUE KRIEGSGEDICHTE : DER TAG DES DEUTSCHEN ZWEITER TEIL / Presber, Rudolf – Stuttgart: Deutsche Verlags-Anstalt, c1915 – 1r – 1 – us U.W. Library [810]

NEUE KUNDE ZU HEINRICH VON KLEIST / Steig, Reinhold – (Includes bibliographical references) – Berlin: G Reimer, 1902 – 1r – 1 – us U.W. Library [430]

DER NEUE KURS; ERINNEERUNGEN VON OTTO HAMMANN / Hammann, Otto – Berlin: R. Hobbing, 1918. vii,240p – 1 – us U.W. Library [943]

DAS NEUE LEBEN – Eupen, Belgium. 4 Jan 1930-1935; 2 Jan 1937-1939 – 1 – gw Mikrofilm [949]

NEUE LIEDER ZUM SINGEN BEYM CLAVIER / Marpurg, Friedrich Wilhelm – Berlin: G A Lange, 1756 – 1 – us Sibley [780]

NEUE LITERATUR *see* LITERARISCHES ZENTRALBLATT FUER DEUTSCHLAND 1850-1945

NEUE LODZER ZEITUNG – Lodz, Poland. Jan 1920-29 Jun 1922; Apr-Jun 1923; Jan 1924-Apr 1925; Jul-Sept 1925; Jan-26 Nov 1926; Dec 1927-28 Jun 1931; May 1935-Aug 1939 – 29r – 1 – gw Mikrofilm [943]

NEUE LONDONER ZEITUNG – London, England. -w. 30 April 1932-7 Oct 1933. 1 reel – 1 – uk British Libr Newspaper [072]

DAS NEUE MAGAZIN *see* DAS MAGAZIN

NEUE MANNHEIMER ZEITUNG *see* WOECHENTLICHES FRAG- UND KUNDSCHAFFTS-BLATH

NEUE MANNIGFALTIGKEITEN – Aurich, 1795 – 1 – Dist. gw Mikrofilm – gw Misc Inst [072]

NEUE MARKSTEINE : ERZAEHLENDE DICHTUNGEN / Pichler, Adolf – Leipzig: A G Liebeskind, 1890 – 1 – us U.W. Library [810]

DER NEUE MERKUR – Berlin [etc]: G Müller. v1-3 n7. apr 1914-19 – us Res Libr [072]

NEUE METHODE, ALLERLEY ARTEN VON TEMPERATUREN DEM CLAVIERE AUFS BEQUEMSTE MITZUTHEILEN / Marpurg, Friedrich Wilhelm – 1790 – 9 – us Sibley [780]

DAS NEUE MONTAGSBLATT : BERLINER SOZIALISTISCHE MONTAGSSCHAU – Berlin, Germany. 2 May-21 Nov 1904 – 1r – 1 – gw Mikrofilm [072]

DAS NEUE MONTAGSBLATT : BERLINER SOZIALISTISCHE MONTAGSSCHAU – Berlin, may 2-nov 21 1904 – 1 – Inquire at Mikrofilmarchiv for details – gw Misc Inst [335]

NEUE MONTAGS-ZEITUNG – Berlin, jan-jun 1932 – 1r – 1 – Inquire at Mikrofilmarchiv for details – gw Misc Inst [943]

NEUE MUENCHNER ZEITUNG *see* MUENCHNER POLITISCHE ZEITUNG

NEUE MUSIK-ZEITUNG – Cologne, Stuttgart, Leipzig. 1880-1928. 17 reels – 1 – 367.00 – us L of C Photodup [780]

NEUE MUSIK-ZEITUNG – Stuttgart Leipzig. no. 1-49. 1880-Sept 1928. Incomplete – 1 – us NY Public [780]

NEUE MUSIK-ZEITUNG – v. 1-49. no. 24. 1880-1928 – 1 – us Schnase [780]

NEUE MUSIK-ZEITUNG – v1-49. 1880-1928 – 10r – 1 – us Ross [780]

NEUE MUTHMASUNGEN UEBER DIE SONNENFLECKEN.. / Wiedeburg, Johann Ernst Basilius – Gotha: C.W. Ettinger, 1776. 48p. 1 reel. 1226 – 1 – us U.W. Library [000]

NEUE NACHRICHTEN VON KUENSTLERN UND KUNSTSACHEN / Heinecken, KH V – Leipzig. 3pts. 1786 – 6mf – ne IDC [700]

NEUE NATIONAL ZEITUNG : JUEDISCHPOLITISCHE WOCHENSCHRIFT – Vienna. v1-17?, 1899-1915? Lacking: v1-8, 1899-1906 and misc. issues. B310 (Leo Baeck Institute.German-Jewish Periodicals, Pt 1) – 2r – 1 – $135.00 – us UPA [270]

NEUE NIEDERSAECHSISCHE VOLKSSTIMME *see* DIE WAHRHEIT

EINE NEUE NOTVERORDNUNG ZUR BEHEBUNG DER KRISE = ONE NEW EMERGENCY LAW TO REMOVE THE EMERGENCY / Beckerath, Ulrich von – 1931 – 9 – 1.00f – at Libertarian Micro [335]

NEUE NOVELLEN / Franzos, Karl Emil – 2e. Auf. Stuttgart und Berlin. 1905 – 1 – us Res Libr [430]

NEUE ODER-ZEITUNG *see*
– ALLGEMEINE ODER-ZEITUNG

NEUE OESTERREICHISCHE BIOGRAPHIE 1815-1918 – (Available: v1(1-8) Biographies: v2(1) Bibliographies) – Wien. 2v. 1923-1925 – 25mf – 9 – ne IDC [920]

DAS NEUE OKONOMISCHE SYSTEM DER PLANUNG UND LEITUNG DER VOLKSWIRTSCHAFT IN DER PRAXIS: DISKUSSION ZUM REFERAT UND ZU DEN VORGELEGTEN ENTWURFEN DER DOKUMENTS.. / Ulbricht, Walter – Berlin: Dietz, 1965 – 1 – us U.W. Library [943]

NEUE ORDNUNG – Basel, oct 2-dec 31 1920 – 1 – Dist. gw Mikrofilm – gw Misc Inst [072]

NEUE ORDNUNG – Zagreb. Yugoslavia. -w. 19 Apr 1942-23 Jul 1944, 7, 14 Jan 1945. (Imperfect). (3 reels) – 1 – uk British Libr Newspaper [949]

DER NEUE ORIENT – Berlin. Zeitschrift fua5r das politische, wirtschaftliche, und geistige Leben im gesamten Osten. Apr. 1917-July 1927; Jan.-Feb. 1940. Suspended Oct. 1929-1935 – 1 – 35.00r – us Hoover Inst Photo [073]

NEUE OZ/OSNABRUECKER ZEITUNG – Osnabrueck, West Germany. 1 Jul 1969- – ca 9r per yr – 1 – gw Mikrofilm [072]

NEUE PASSAUER ZEITUNG *see* PASSAUER ZEITUNG

NEUE PHILOSOPHISCHE ABHANDLUNGEN / Akademie der Wissenschaften. Munich – Munich, 1778-97 – 3 – us Readex [100]

NEUE POLITISCHE BRIEFE *see* RHEINHART-BRIEFE

NEUE PREDIGTEN : NACH DEN HANDSCHRIFTEN DER WIENER NATIONALBIBLIOTHEK / Sancta Clara, Abraham a; ed by Bertsche, Karl – (Includes bibliographical references) – Leipzig: K W Hiersemann, 1932 – 1 – us U.W. Library [850]

DIE NEUE PRESSE – Titre français: La Presse nouvelle. no. 1-11. Paris. janv-avr 1939. mq no. 8 – 1 – fr A.C.R.P.P. [073]

NEUE PRESSE – Coburg, West Germany. 1952-1953; 1976-1991 – ca 7r per yr – 1 – gw Mikrofilm [072]
NEUE PRESSE – (Cont by: Neue Rhein-Zeitung, 1954) – Duesseldorf. 1983-96 – 126r – 1 – gw Mikrofilm [072]
NEUE PRESSE – Libau, Latvija. (Liepaja, U.S.S.R.). Oct 1932-3 May 1933 (incomplete) – 1r – 1 – gw Mikrofilm [943]
NEUE PRESSE *see* HANNOVERSCHE PRESSE
NEUE PREUSSISCHE KREUZ-ZEITUNG *see* – NEUE PREUSSISCHE ZEITUNG
NEUE PREUSSISCHE ZEITUNG – (Cont by: Neue Preussische Kreuz-Zeitung, mar 1 1929; Kreuz-Zeitung, jun 29 1932. Spec suppl available: Deutsche Wacht, apr-dec 1924) – Berlin, jun 30 1848-jan 31 1939 – 1 – Inquire at Mikrofilmarchiv for details – gw Misc Inst [943]
NEUE PREUSSISCHE ZEITUNG : KREUZZEITUNG BERLIN, 1848-1939 – 1984 – 201r – 1 – diazo DM16,800.00 – 3-598-30673-3 – gw Saur [943]
NEUE PREUSSISCHE ZEITUNG – (Kreuzzeitung). Berlin. Aug. 1914-Sept. 1919. Missing: 15 scattered issues – 1 – 35.00r – us Hoover Inst Photo [073]
NEUE PREUSSISCHE ZEITUNG – (Title change 1 Mar 1929: Neue Preussische Kreuz-Zeitung. 29 Jun 1932: Kreuz-Zeitung) – Berlin, DE. 30 Jun 1848-31 Jan 1939 – 461r – 1 – uk British Libr Newspaper [072]
NEUE PREUSSISCHE ZEITUNG – (Title changes: Neue Preussische Kreuz-Zeitung, 1 Mar 1929; Kreuz-Zeitung, 29 Jun 1932) – Berlin, Germany. 30 Jun 1848-31 Jan 1939 – 461r – 1 – gw Mikrofilm [072]
NEUE RHEINISCHE ZEITUNG / ed by Britischen Militaerbehoerde – Duesseldorf, West Germany. 8 May 1945-23 Feb 1946 – 1r – 1 – gw Mikrofilm [072]
NEUE RHEINISCHE ZEITUNG – Koeln, 1848-1849 – 2r – 1 – DM150.00 – gw Mikro Press [072]
NEUE RHEINISCHE ZEITUNG – Koeln, Germany. Jun 1848-19 May 1849 – 1r – 1 – gw Mikrofilm [072]
NEUE RHEIN-ZEITUNG – Duesseldorf, 2 Jan 1954-30 Dec 1956 – 11r – DM825.00 – gw Mikro Press [072]
NEUE RHEIN-ZEITUNG (NRZ) : BA DER NEUEN RUHR-ZEITUNG – Koeln, West Germany. 1950-1975 – 1 – gw Mikrofilm [072]
NEUE RUHR-ZEITUNG – Essen, Germany. 1962-71 – 80r – 1 – us L of C Photodup [072]
NEUE RUHR-ZEITUNG (NRZ) – Essen, 1946-49 – 3r – 1 – DM225.00 – gw Mikro Press [072]
NEUE RUHR-ZEITUNG (NRZ) – (Grundausgabe) – Essen. feb 27, 1978-aug 17, 1979 – 15r – 1 – gw Mikrofilm [072]
NEUE RUHR-ZEITUNG (NRZ) – Wesel-Essen, West Germany. 1992- – 10r per yr – 1 – gw Mikrofilm [072]
DER NEUE RUNDFUNK – Berlin, Germany. 1926-1927 (No. 44) – 1 – gw Mikrofilm [072]
DER NEUE RUNDFUNK – (Cont by: Arbeiterfunk, 1927 n45; Volksfunk, 1932 n10) – Berlin, 1926-33 – 1 – Inquire at Mikrofilmarchiv for details – gw Misc Inst [790]
DIE NEUE RUNDSCHAU – (Freie Buehne fuer modernes Leben 1890-91. Freie Buehne fuer den Entwicklungskampf der Zeit) – Berlin, 1890-1949 – 37r – 1 – DM3,700.00 – gw Mikro Press [072]
DIE NEUE RUNDSCHAU – (Title changes: Freie Buehne fuer modernes Leben, 1890-1891; Freie Buehne fuer den Entwicklungskampf der Zeit, 1892-1893) – Berlin. 1890-1949 – 38r – 1 – gw Mikrofilm [072]
NEUE SCHWEIZER RUNDSCHAU – 18-22. 1950-55 – 1 – us UMI [073]
NEUE SPEYERER ZEITUNG – Speyer, Germany. 13 Jan 1848-30 Dec 1849 – 1r – 1 – gw Mikrofilm [072]
NEUE STUDIEN UEBER HEINRICH VON KLEIST / Schulze, Berthold – (Includes bibliographical references) – Heidelberg: K Winter, 1904 – 1 – us U.W. Library [430]
NEUE STUDIEN ZU MARCION (T.U.U. 3-44/4) / Harnack, Adolf von – Leipzig, 1923 – 1mf – 9 – ne Slangenburg [240]
NEUE SYSTEMATISCHE ERDBESCHREIBUNG VON AFRIKA / Bruns, Paul Jakob – Nuernberg: Schneider & Weigel, 1799 – us Res Libr [960]
NEUE TAEGLICHE RUNDSCHAU *see* – TAEGLICHE RUNDSCHAU
DER NEUE TAG – Bonn, feb 2 1934-may 31 1940, sep 1 1940-sep 29 1942 – 1 – Inquire at Mikrofilmarchiv for details – gw Misc Inst [943]
DER NEUE TAG – Prague, Czechoslovakia. Oct 1940-Oct 1941; 1944-Apr 1945 – 3r – 1 – us L of C Photodup [072]
DER NEUE TAG – Weiden, West Germany. 1976- – ca 10r per yr – 1 – gw Mikrofilm [072]
DAS NEUE TAGE-BUCH – Paris-Amsterdam. Jul 1933-11 May 1940 – 4r – 1 – gw Mikrofilm [072]
DAS NEUE TAGEBUCH – Paris, Amsterdam. v1-8. 1933-40. Complete. B616 (Leo Baeck Institute. German-Jewish Periodicals, Pt 2) – 5r – 1 – $335.00 – us UPA [270]
DAS NEUE TAGEBUCH *see* DAS TAGEBUCH
NEUE TAGESZEITUNG (NTZ) : BEILAGE: ILLUSTRIERTE KRIEGSCHRONIK – Friedberg. 1914-17 – 1 – gw Mikrofilm [940]
NEUE TAGESZEITUNG (NTZ) – (With suppl) – Friedberg. 1908-mar 17, 1934 – 45r – 1 – gw Mikrofilm [073]
DAS NEUE TESTAMENT UM DAS JAHR 200 : THEODOR ZAHN'S GESCHICHTE DES NEUTESTAMENTLICHEN KANONS / Harnack, Adolf von – (Includes bibliographical references) – Freiburg i.B: J C B Mohr, 1889 – 1mf – 9 – 0-8370-3479-5 – 1985-1479 – us A.T.L.A. [220]
NEUE THALIA / ed by Schiller, Friedrich von – Leipzig, 1792-93. Hildesheim, 1977 – 24mf – 9 – DM200.00 diazo DM240.00 silver – gw Olms [430]
NEUE THALIA *see* THALIA
NEUE THEOLOGISCHE ZEITSCHRIFT – (Zehnten Jahrganges, erster und zweiter Band) – Wien, 10(1837) – 16mf – 9 – Dfl56.00 – ne Slangenburg [073]
NEUE TISCHLER-ZEITUNG – Hamburg, Germany. 1 Jan-25 Jun 1893 – 1 – gw Mikrofilm [072]
NEUE UND SELTENE PFLANZEN, NEBST EINIGEN ANDERN BOTANISCHEN BEOBACHTUNGEN / Schmidt, F W – Praha. 1793. B-6486 1 – 9 – ne IDC [580]
NEUE UNTERSUCHUNGEN DER LEHRGEGENSAETZE ZWISCHEN DEN KATHOLIKEN UND PROTESTANTEN / Moehler, Johann Adam – Eine Verheidigung meiner Symbolik gegen die Kritik des Herrn Professors Dr. Baur in Tuebingen.... 1835 – 1 – us A.T.L.A. [240]
NEUE UNTERSUCHUNGEN ZUR APOSTELGESCHICHTE UND ZUR ABFASSUNGSZEIT DER SYNOPTISCHEN EVANGELIEN / Harnack, Adolf von – Leipzig, 1911 – 2mf – 8 – ne Slangenburg [220]
DAS NEUE VATERLAND – Stuttgart, West Germany. 10 May 1946-25 Mar 1955 – 2r – 1 – gw Mikrofilm [072]
NEUE VOLKSBLAETTER – Osnabrueck, Germany. 3 Jan-31 Mar 1944 – 2r – 1 – gw Mikrofilm [072]
NEUE VOLKSSTIMME – Budapest, 1895-96 – 1r – 1 – Inquire at Mikrofilmarchiv for details – gw Misc Inst [943]
NEUE VOLKSSTIMME – Budapest, Hungary. 1895-1896 – 1r – 1 – gw Mikrofilm [072]
NEUE VOLKS-ZEITUNG : DEN INTERESSEN DES ARBEITENDEN VOLKES GEWIDMET – New York. 17 Dec 1932-6 Aug 1949. 7r – 1 – gw Mikrofilm [071]
NEUE VOLKS-ZEITUNG – New York. v. 1-18, no. 32. Dec 17 1932-Aug 6 1949. Incomplete – 1 – us NY Public [071]
NEUE WAGNER-FORSCHUNGEN – v. 1. 1943 – 1 – us Schnase [780]
NEUE WALDGESCHICHTEN / Rosegger, Peter – 13. Aufl. Leipzig: L Staackmann, 1905 – 1r – 1 – us U.W. Library [830]
DER NEUE WEG – Halle/Saale, East Germany. Jul 1954-31 Jan 1992 – 56r – 1 – gw Mikrofilm [072]
NEUE WEG – Vienna. 1946-1949 – 1 – us NY Public [305]
NEUE WEGE IN DER RUSSISCHEN LITERATUR ENDE DES 18./ANFANG DES 19. JAHRHUNDERTS : DIE DICHTERGRUPPE G.R. DERZAVIN, V.V. KAPNIST, N.A. L'VOV, I.I. CHEMNICER / Peter, Simone – 1993 – 3mf – 9 – DM98.00 – 3-89349-744-7 – gw Hänsel [460]
DIE NEUE WELT – (Beilage zum Vorwaerts) – Leipzig, Stuttgart, Hamburg, 1876-77; 1881-84; 1892-1913; 1914; 1916; 1918 – 11r – 1 – DM825.00 – gw Mikro Press [072]
DIE NEUE WELT – Breslau, 1876, 1877 (incomplete), 1878-82, 1883-87 (incomplete), 1892-93 – 1 – Inquire at Mikrofilmarchiv for details – gw Misc Inst [943]
DIE NEUE WELT – Breslau (Wroclaw), Poland. 1876-1880; 1881-1887 (incomplete); 1892-93 – 1 – gw Mikrofilm [943]
DIE NEUE WELT – Le Monde nouveau. devenu: L' Humanite de Strasbourg. Strasbourg. 1923-28 – 1 – fr A.C.R.P.P. [073]
DIE NEUE WELT – (Missing: 1909 v1; 1910 (Dec)) – Warsaw, Odessa. v1-2. 1909-1910 – 1r – 1 – J-92-23/3 – ne IDC [072]
DIE NEUE WELT – Revue. Vienna. Nos. 1-734. 1927-1938. Lacking misc. issues. B312 (Leo Baeck Institute. German-Jewish Periodicals, Pt 1) – 3r – 1 – $205.00 – us UPA [270]
DER NEUE WELT BOTT : MIT ALLERHAND NACHRICHTEN DEREN MISSIONARIEN SOC. IESU / ed by Stoecklein, J et al – (Missing: Pts 37-38) – Augsburg, Graz. 6v. Pts 1-38. 1726-1758 – 88mf – 9 – H-20/1 – ne IDC [240]
DIE NEUE WELT: REISESKIZZEN AUS DEM NORDEN UND SUEDEN DER VEREINIGTEN STAATEN SOWIE AUS KANADA UND MEXICO / Deckert, Emil – Berlin: Paetel, 1892. 02694. (Pre-1900 Canadiana) – 9 – cn C.I.H.M. [910]
DIE NEUE WELTBUEHNE : WOCHENSCHRIFT FUER POLITIK, KUNST, WIRTSCHAFT – Prag-Bruessel-Paris. Apr 1933-Aug 1939 – 5r – 1 – gw Mikrofilm [072]
NEUE WERSCHETZER ZEITUNG – Vrsac, Yugoslavia. Aug 1893-Aug 1904 (scattered issues) – 2r – 1 – us L of C Photodup [949]
NEUE WESTFAELISCHE *see* – FREIE PRESSE – WESTFAELISCHE ZEITUNG
NEUE WESTFAELISCHE GEDICHTE / Wette, Hermann – Leipzig: F W Grunow, 1909 – 1r – 1 – us U.W. Library [810]
NEUE WESTFAELISCHE VOLKSZEITUNG – Bielefeld, mar 31 1877-1921 – 1 – Inquire at Mikrofilmarchiv for details – gw Misc Inst [943]
NEUE WESTFAELISCHE ZEITUNG : MUENSTERLAENDISCHE AUSGABE – jun 1 1945-jul 30 1946 – 1 – Inquire at Mikrofilmarchiv for details – gw Misc Inst [943]
NEUE WESTFAELISCHE ZEITUNG : NACHRICHTENBLATT DER ALLIIERTEN MILITAERBEHOERDE – Oelde/Westf., West Germany. 1 Jun 1945-28 Jun 1946 – 2r – 1 – gw Mikrofilm [072]
NEUE WESTFAELISCHE ZEITUNG : NACHTRICHTENBLATT DER ALLIIERTEN MILITAERBEHOERDE – Oelde, Westf. 1945-1946 – 2r – 1 – DM150.00 – gw Mikro Press [072]
NEUE WIRTSCHAFT – Bremen, aug 15, aug 31, sep 16, oct 3, oct 18 1926 – 1 – Inquire at Mikrofilmarchiv for details – gw Misc Inst [330]
DAS NEUE WISSEN UND DER NEUE GLAUBE : MIT BESONDERER BERUECKSICHTIGUNG VON D.F. STRAUSS' NEUESTER SCHRIFT, "DER ALTE UND DER NEUE GLAUBE" / Frohschammer, J – Leipzig: F.A. Brockhaus, 1873 – 1mf – us A.T.L.A. [240]
NEUE WOECHTLICHE ROSTOCK'SCHE NACHRICHTEN UND ANZEIGEN – Rostock, Germany. 1841 – 1r – 1 – gw Mikrofilm [072]
NEUE WUERZBURGER ZEITUNG – Wuerzburg, Germany. 1848-1849 – 2r – 1 – gw Mikrofilm [072]
DIE NEUE ZEIT – Berlin. Germany. July 1945-Dec. 1949 (gaps) – 1 – 35.00r – us Hoover Inst Photo [072]
DIE NEUE ZEIT – New York, NY. -w. 25 Sept 1869-9 Sept 1871. 2 reels – 1 – uk British Libr Newspaper [071]
DIE NEUE ZEIT – Ravensburg, oct 1-dec 31 1848; may 18, jun 22 1849 – 1 – gw Mikrofilm [943]
DIE NEUE ZEIT – Reval (Tallinn, U.S.S.R.). 1935-Feb 1936 – 1r – 1 – gw Mikrofilm [072]
DIE NEUE ZEIT : WOCHENSCHRIFT DER DEUTSCHEN SOZIALDEMOKRATIE – Stuttgart, Germany. 1883-22 Sept 1922 – 24r – 1 – gw Mikrofilm [072]
DIE NEUE ZEIT : WOCHENSCHRIFT DER DEUTSCHEN SOZIALDEMOKRATIE – Stuttgart, v1-40. 1883-1922 – 24r – 1 – DM2,400.00 – gw Mikro Press [072]
DIE NEUE ZEIT – Wochenscrift der deutschen Sozialdemokratie. Stuttgart. v. 1-41 bd. 2, no. 10. 1883-Aug 1923. Incomplete – 1 – us NY Public [943]
DIE NEUE ZEIT – Worms, Germany. 15 Mar 1848-30 Dec 1849 – 2r – 1 – gw Mikrofilm [072]
NEUE ZEIT – (1957-58 4r DM300.00) – Berlin, 1945-49 – 5r – 1 – DM375.00 – gw Mikro Press [072]
NEUE ZEIT – Berlin, Germany. 22-31 Jul 1945; 1962-70 – 19r – 1 – us L of C Photodup [072]
NEUE ZEIT – Berlin-Charlottenburg, jan-jun 1905, jan-jun 1923 – 3r – 1 – Inquire at Mikrofilmarchiv for details – gw Misc Inst [072]
NEUE ZEIT – East Berlin, Germany. 1992-5 Jul 1994 – 7r per yr – 1 – gw Mikrofilm [072]
NEUE ZEIT – Kattowitz (Katowice), Poland. 27 Apr 1935-17 Dec 1937 – ORGAN DES DEUTSCHEN VOLKSBLOCKS – 1 – gw Mikrofilm [943]
NEUE ZEIT – Novi Sad, Yugoslavia. Nov-Dec 1930 – 1r – 1 – us L of C Photodup [949]
NEUE ZEIT – Opava, Czechoslovakia. Nov 1907-May 1909; Jun 1913-Aug 1914; Jul 1918-1930 (incomplete) – 7r – 1 – us L of C Photodup [072]
NEUE ZEIT : WOCHENSCHRIFT DER DEUTSCHEN SOZIAL-DEMOKRATIE – v1-41. 1883-1923 + index 1883-1912 – 20r – 1 – us Ross [320]
NEUE ZEIT : ZEITUNG DER CDU/DDR – Berlin, jul 22 1945-jul 5 1994 – 1 – Inquire at Mikrofilmarchiv for details – gw Misc Inst [072]
NEUE ZEIT – Zrenjanin, Yugoslavia. Aug 1920-Nov 1930 – 6r – 1 – us L of C Photodup [949]
NEUE ZEIT (MOSKAU) – 1946-1989 – 2,396mf – 1 – DM13,657.20 – gw Mikro Press [320]
DIE NEUE ZEIT. ORGAN DER DEMOKRATIE – London, England. -w. 3 July 1858-16 April 1859. 27 ft – 1 – uk British Libr Newspaper [072]
DIE NEUE ZEIT UND DER ALTE GLAUBE : EINE CULTURGESCHICHTLICHE STUDIE / Schell, Herman – 2. Aufl. Wuerzburg: Andreas Goebel, 1898 – 1mf – 9 – 0-8370-8942-5 – 1986-2942 – us A.T.L.A. [230]
NEUE ZEITSCHRIFT FUER MISSIONSWISSENSCHAFT – 1(1945)-10(1954) – 40mf – 9 – Dfl140.00 – ne Slangenburg [073]
NEUE ZEITSCHRIFT FUER MISSIONSWISSENSCHAFT – Beckenreid. v1-10. 1945-1954 – 40mf – 9 – ne IDC [240]
NEUE ZEITSCHRIFT FUER MUSIK – (Cont as: Musikalisches Wochenblatt 1906) – Leipzig, 1864-1912 – 13r – 1 – DM1,300.00 – gw Mikro Press [780]
NEUE ZEITSCHRIFT FUER MUSIK – (Missing: v84(p25-32) 1917; v100(p.309-End) 1933; v101 1934) – Leipzig. v1-108. 1834-1941 – 1335mf – 9 – ne IDC [780]
NEUE ZEITSCHRIFT FUER MUSIK – (Title change: Musikalisches Wochenblatt, 1906) – Leipzig. 1864-1912 – 13r – 1 – gw Mikrofilm [073]
NEUE ZEITSCHRIFT FUER MUSIK – v31-91. 1864-1924 – 14r – 1 – us Ross [780]
NEUE ZEITSCHRIFT FUER MUSIK *see* MUSIK IM KRIEGE
NEUE ZEITSCHRIFT FUER SPECULATIVE PHYSIK – Tubingen, 1802 – 3 – us Readex [530]
NEUE ZEITSCHRIFT FUER SYSTEMATISCHE THEOLOGIE – v1-33. 1959-91 (complete) – 9r – 1 – ATLA S0558 – us A.T.L.A. [073]
DIE NEUE ZEITUNG : EINE AMERIKANISCHE ZEITUNG FUER DIE DEUTSCHE BEVOELKERUNG – Frankfurt M., Berlin, Muenchen, 1945-1955 – 17r – 1 – DM1,700.00 – gw Mikro Press [072]
DIE NEUE ZEITUNG : AUSGABE BERLIN – Berlin, jan 6-dec 30 1947, sep 13 1953-jan 30 1955 – 1 – Inquire at Mikrofilmarchiv for details – gw Misc Inst [072]
DIE NEUE ZEITUNG – Berlin. Germany. oct. 1945-July 1949 (gaps) – 1 – 35.00r – us Hoover Inst Photo [072]
DIE NEUE ZEITUNG – Hermannstadt (Sibiu), Rumaenien. 1930-1941 – 8r – 1 – gw Mikrofilm [949]

DIE NEUE ZEITUNG – Muenchen: Publ Operations Section, Information Control Div, USFET, US Army, -1955. Berliner Ausg. 1949-jan 1955 – 38r – 1 – us Res Libr [072]
DIE NEUE ZEITUNG – Muenchen-Frankfurt a.M.-Berlin. 18 Oct 1945-30 Jan 1955 – 17r – 1 – gw Mikrofilm [072]
DIE NEUE ZEITUNG – Munich, Berlin, Germany. Mar 1947-48 – 2r – 1 – us L of C Photodup [072]
DIE NEUE ZEITUNG – Munich, Frankfurt, Berlin. DE. 18 Oct 1945-6 Mar 1951, 2 Jan 1952-30 Dec 1954 – 39r – 1 – uk British Libr Newspaper [072]
NEUE ZEITUNG – Budapest, 1976-81 – 6r – 1 – DM450.00 – gw Mikro Press [949]
NEUE ZEITUNG *see* KAYSERLICH-PRIVILEGIRTE HAMBURGISCHE NEUE ZEITUNG
NEUE ZEITUNG FUR STADT UND LAND – (Cont as: Rigaer Tagesblatt, Riga, 1882-96) – 1876-82 – 35r – 1 – inquire – us Ross [072]
NEUE ZUERCHER ZEITUNG – (1780-1994 also available on 35mm) – Switzerland. 1988-1994 – 8r per y – 6 – Sfr1,230.00 – sz Infoprint [949]
NEUE ZUERICHER ZEITUNG – 1 – sz Infoprint [072]
NEUE ZUERICHER ZEITUNG ED. COMPLETE – 1780-1877 – 2 times per yr – 1 – Sfr195.00 – sz Infoprint [072]
NEUE ZUERICHER ZEITUNG ED. COMPLETE – 1878-1909 – 3 times per yr – 1 – Sfr521.00 – sz Infoprint [072]
NEUE ZUERICHER ZEITUNG ED. COMPLETE – 1910-1919 – 4 times per yr – 1 – Sfr852.00 – sz Infoprint [072]
NEUE ZUERICHER ZEITUNG ED. COMPLETE – 1920-1944 – 7 times per yr – 1 – Sfr1,243.00 – sz Infoprint [072]
NEUE ZUERICHER ZEITUNG ED. COMPLETE – 1946-1949 – 8 times per yr – 1 – Sfr1,243.00 – sz Infoprint [072]
NEUE ZUERICHER ZEITUNG ED. COMPLETE – 1950-1952 – 9 times per yr – 1 – Sfr1,243.00 – sz Infoprint [072]
NEUE ZUERICHER ZEITUNG ED. COMPLETE – 1953-1954 – 11 times per yr – 1 – Sfr1,243.00 – sz Infoprint [072]
NEUE ZUERICHER ZEITUNG ED. COMPLETE – 1955- – 12 times per yr – 1 – Sfr1,633.00 – sz Infoprint [072]
NEUE ZUERICHER ZEITUNG ED. COMPLETE – 1956- – 13 times per yr – 1 – Sfr1,633.00 – sz Infoprint [072]
NEUE ZUERICHER ZEITUNG ED. COMPLETE – 1957- – 12 times per yr – 1 – Sfr1,633.00 – sz Infoprint [072]
NEUE ZUERICHER ZEITUNG ED. COMPLETE – 1958- – 14 times per yr – 1 – Sfr1,633.00 – sz Infoprint [072]
NEUE ZUERICHER ZEITUNG ED. COMPLETE – 1959- – 12 times per yr – 1 – Sfr1,633.00 – sz Infoprint [072]
NEUE ZUERICHER ZEITUNG ED. COMPLETE – 1960- – 17 times per yr – 1 – Sfr1,633.00 – sz Infoprint [072]
NEUE ZUERICHER ZEITUNG ED. COMPLETE – 1961- – 21 times per yr – 1 – Sfr1,633.00 – sz Infoprint [072]
NEUE ZUERICHER ZEITUNG ED. COMPLETE – 1962-1963 – 20 times per yr – 1 – Sfr1,633.00 – sz Infoprint [072]
NEUE ZUERICHER ZEITUNG ED. COMPLETE – 1964- – 22 times per yr – 1 – Sfr1,633.00 – sz Infoprint [072]
NEUE ZUERICHER ZEITUNG ED. COMPLETE – 1965- – 21 times per yr – 1 – Sfr1,633.00 – sz Infoprint [072]
NEUE ZUERICHER ZEITUNG ED. COMPLETE – 1966-1995 – 22 times per yr – 1 – Sfr2,083.00 – sz Infoprint [072]
NEUE ZURCHER ZEITUNG – 22r per y – 1 – inquire – us Ross [072]
NEUE ZURCHER ZEITUNG – Switzerland, 1982- – 1 – us Primary [949]
NEUE ZURCHER ZEITUNG – Zurich, Switzerland. 1938-55 – 1 – us Res Libr [949]
DIE NEUEN ARGONAUTEN : KOMISCHER ROMAN / Dingelstedt, Franz, Freiherr von; ed by Heidelbach, Paul – (Includes bibliographical references) – Kassel: Baerenreiter, 1931 – 1 – us U.W. Library [830]
DER NEUENTDECKTE CODEX SYRUS SINAITICUS / Holzhey, Carl – Muenchen: J.J. Lentner, 1896. 1 fiche – 9 – us A.T.L.A. [240]
DIE NEUENTDECKTE URCHRISTLICHE SCHRIFT : "LEHRE DER ZWOELF APOSTEL AN DIE VOELKER" / Volkmar, Gustav – Leipzig, 1885 – Dfl6.00 – ne Slangenburg [220]
NEUER ANZEIGER FUER BIBLIOGRAPHIE UND BIBLIOTHEKWISSENSCHAFT *see* ANZEIGER FUER LITERATUR DER BIBLIOTHEKWISSENSCHAFT
NEUER ARBEITER – Vienna. Jan 1, 1961-Feb 1972 – 1 – 46.00 – us L of C Photodup [073]
NEUER BUECHER-SAAL DER GELEHRTEN WELT ODER AUSFUEHRLICHE NACHRICHTEN VON ALLERHAND NEUEN BUECHERN UND ANDERN ZUR HEUTIGEN HISTORIE DER GELEHRSAMKEIT GEHOERIGEN SACHEN / ed by Krause, J G & Walch, J G – Leipzig, 1710-1717. Oeffnung 1-60 (mf ed 1993) – 20mf – 9 – DM540.00 – 3-89131-089-7 – gw Fischer [073]
NEUER BUECHERSAAL DER SCHOENEN WISSENSCHAFTEN UND FREYEN KUENSTE / ed by Gottsched, Johann Christoph – Leipzig, 1745-50. Hildesheim, 1977 – 63mf – 9 – DM530.00 diazo DM600.00 silver – gw Olms [430]
NEUER CLAVIER UBUNG, ANDRER THEIL.. / Kuhnau, J – 1695 – 9 – us Sibley [780]
NEUER CLAVIER UBUNG, ERSTER THEIL.. / Kuhnau, J – 1695 – 9 – us Sibley [780]
NEUER GLAUBE / Wagner, Christian – Stuttgart: Deutsche Verlags-Anstalt, [1894?] – 1r – 1 – us U.W. Library [430]
NEUER HANNOVERSCHER KURIER – Hannover, May 1945-Jul 1946 – 1r – 1 – DM75.00 – gw Mikro Press [072]
NEUER HANNOVERSCHER KURIER – Hannover, West Germany. 29 May 1945-16 Jul 1946 – 1r – 1 – gw Mikrofilm [072]
NEUER NEKROLOG DER DEUTSCHEN / ed by Schmidt, F A – Weimar. 30 sets. 1824-56 – 430mf – 9 – subsc: DM2,900.00 – gw Olms [430]
NEUER SCHLUESSEL ZU RUMPH'S HERBARIUM AMBOINENSE... / Hasskarl, J K – Halle, 1866 – 3mf – 9 – ne IDC [580]
NEUER SCHWEIZERISCHER PAPIERHANDEL – Bern, Switzerland. -f. Jan 1884-Jan 1889. 40 ft – 1 – uk British Libr Newspaper [949]
NEUER SOCIAL-DEMOKRAT – Berlin, Jul 1871-Sep 1876 – 10r – 1 – gw Mikrofilm [335]
NEUER SOCIAL-DEMOKRAT – Berlin, Jul 1871-Sept 1876 – 10r – 1 – DM700.00 – gw Mikro Press [335]
NEUER SOCIAL-DEMOKRAT – Berlin, jul 2 1871-sep 29 1876 – 4r – 1 – Inquire at Mikrofilmarchiv for details – gw Misc Inst [943]
NEUER SUEDFUNK – Stuttgart, jan 30-dec 25 1949 – 1r – 1 – gw Mikrofilm [790]
NEUER TAG – (Cont by: Maerkische Oderzeitung, mar 17 1990. Also Bereichsausgaben available (nur Kreisseiten): ANGERMUENDE, apr 1 1958-oct 31 1961, jan 5 1967-aug 30 1969 (incomplete); BEESKOW, apr 2 1958-oct 27 1961, jan 6 1976-sep 21 1977; BERNAU, apr 1 1958-oct 31 1961, jul 3 1984-sep 26 1990; EBERSWALDE, apr 1 1958-oct 31 1961, nov 25-dec 19 1963; EISENHUETTENSTADT, apr 1 1958-oct 31 1961; BAD FREIENWALDE, apr 1 1958-oct 31 1961, jan 25-sep 2 1967; FUERSTENBERG, apr 1 1958-nov 25 1961; FUERSTENWALDE, apr 1 1958-oct 31 1961, sep 14-nov 4 1963, jul 3 1984-oct 26 1990; SCHWEDT, jul 20 1983-sep 26 1990 (incomplete); SEELOW, apr 1 1958-oct 31 1961, mar 1-25 1963, jan 26-dec 19 1965, jun 21-sep 7 1966; STRAUSBERG, apr 1 1958-oct 31 1961, jan 7 1967-nov 8 1968 (incomplete), jul 3 1984-sep 25 1990) – Frankfurt/Oder, aug 1954- – 1 – Inquire at Mikrofilmarchiv for details – gw Misc Inst [072]
NEUER TAG – (Title change: Maerkische Oderzeitung, 17 Mar 1990) – Frankfurt/Oder, East Germany. 1992- – 6r per yr – 1 – gw Mikrofilm [072]
NEUER VORWAERTS – (Cont by: Vorwaerts, Berlin (1891-1933)) – Karlsbad (Karlovy Vary)-Paris-London. 18 June 1933-12 Mai 1940 – 3r – 1 – gw Mikrofilm [072]
NEUER VORWAERTS – Karlovy Vary, Czechoslovakia. 25 Feb-14 Mar 1934; 16 Aug 1936; 3 Jan-31 Dec 1937 – 1r – 1 – us L of C Photodup [072]
NEUER VORWAERTS – Karlsbad, Paris, London. 1933-1940 – 3r – 1 – DM400.00 – gw Mikro Press [072]
NEUER VORWAERTS – Karlsbad/Paris, 1933-40 (incompl) – 1 – us Hoover Inst Photo [072]
NEUER VORWAERTS *see* – VORWAERTS
NEUER WEG – 1946-1989 – 1,192mf – 1 – DM6,794.40 – gw Mikro Press [320]
NEUER WEG – Berlin. 1-25; 1946-7O. Organ des Zentralkomitees der Sozialistischen Einheitspartei Deutschlands fuer Fragen des Parteiaufbaus und des Parteilebens. Film Mas C 740 – 1 – us H.U. Library [073]
NEUER WEG – Bucharest, Romania. May 1950-1976 – 52r – 1 – us L of C Photodup [949]
NEUER WEG – (Cont by: Allgemeine deutsche Zeitung fuer Rumaenien, 1993) – Bukarest, 1972- – 1 – Inquire at Mikrofilmarchiv for details – gw Misc Inst [949]
NEUER WEG / ed by Front der Sozialistischen Demokratie und Einheit – (Title change: Allgemeine deutsche Zeitung fuer Rumaenien, 1993) – Bukarest, Romania. 1972- – 1 – gw Mikrofilm [072]
NEUER WEG : REVUE MENSUELLE – Paris. Mar 1937-Jan 1939 – 1r – 1 – gw Mikrofilm [073]
NEUER WESTFAELISCHER KURIER – (Bereichsausgabe des Neuen Westfaelischen Kuriers, Werl) – Hamm. sep 6, 1946-sep 2, 1947 – 1r – 1 – gw Mikrofilm [943]
NEUER WESTFAELISCHER KURIER : KREISAUSGABE STEINFURT/AUSGABE F/AUSGABE F-G/AUSGABE F-L – (Different Bereichsausgaben of the Neuer Westfaelischer Kurier, Werl. Various subtitles) – Rheine, sep 6 1946-49 (incomplete) – 2r – 1 – gw Mikrofilm [072]
NEUER WESTFAELISCHER KURIER *see* SAUERLAENDISCHES VOLKSBLATT
NEUERE BEITRAEGE ZUR SCHMETTERLINGSKUNDE / Freyer, CF – Augsburg, 1833-58. 7v. Z/1261/2 – 8 – ne IDC [590]
NEUERE DEUTSCHE DICHTUNG UND DIE SCHULE / Walzel, Oskar Franz – Bonn a. Rh.: L Roehrscheid, 1929 – 1r – 1 – us U.W. Library [430]
DIE NEUERE PHILOSOPHIE UND DER CHRISTLICHE GLAUBE IN IHREM VERHAELTNISSE / Ehrenhauss, M – Wittenberg: P. Wunsehmann, 1881.1 fiche – 9 – us A.T.L.A. [240]
NEUERE TRISTANDICHTUNGEN (TANTRIS DER NARR) / Schuster, Ludwig – (Includes bibliographical references) – Darmstadt: K F Bender, 1912 – 1r – 1 – us U.W. Library [430]
DIE NEUEREN ENTDECKUNGEN UND DIE BIBEL. ERSTER BAND, VON DER SCHOEPFUNG BIS ZU ABRAHAM = MODERN DISCOVERIES AND THE BIBLE / Urquhart, John – (Includes bibliographical references) – 3. Aufl. Stuttgart: Max Kielmann, 1903 – 1mf – 9 – 0-8370-9752-5 – 1986-3752 – us A.T.L.A. [220]
DIE NEUEREN KATHOLISCHEN ORDEN UND CONGREGATIONEN BESONDERS IN DEUTSCHLAND / Schulte, Johann Friedrich von – Berlin: C.G. Luederitz, 1872 – 1mf – us A.T.L.A. [240]
NEU-EROEFFNETER ANMUTHIGER BILDERSCHATZ / Hiltebrandt, G A – O 292. 1674 – 9 – ne IDC [700]
NEU-EROEFFNETER THEORETISCH- UND PRACKTISCHER MUSIC-SAAL / Majer, J F B C – 1741. Zweyte und viel-Vermehrte Auflage – 9 – us Sibley [780]
NEU-EROEFFNETER THEORETISCH-UND PRACKTISCHER MUSIC-SAAL / Majer, J F B C – Nuernberg. 1741. BP-708 1 – 9 – ne IDC [780]
NEUES *see* MUSIK IM KRIEGE
NEUES ALLGEMEINES JOURNAL DER CHEMIE – Berlin. 1803-06 – 3 – us Readex [540]
NEUES ALLGEMEINES REPERTORIUM DER NEUESTEN IN- UND AUSLAENDISCHEN LITERATUR – Leipzig. 4v. 1833 – 24mf – 9 – ne IDC [400]
NEUES ARCHIV / Gesellschaft fuer aeltere Deutsche Geschichtskunde – Hannover, etc. Bd. 1-40; 1876-1916. Film Mas C 278 – 1 – us H.U. Library [073]
NEUES ARCHIV DER GESELLSCHAFT FUER AELTERE DEUTSCHE GESCHICHTSKUNDE – 1(1876)-50(1935) – 654mf – 9 – Dfl2,289.00 – ne Slangenburg [943]
NEUES ARCHIV DER GESELLSCHAFT FUER AELTERE DEUTSCHE GESCHICHTSKUNDE – Hannover. v1-50. 1876-1935 – 654mf – 9 – ne IDC [240]
NEUES ARCHIV FUER SAECHSISCHE GESCHICHTE UND ALTERTUMSKUNDE – Dresden. Bd. 1-63; 1880-1943. Film Mas C 273 – 1 – us H.U. Library [073]
NEUES BERLINER TAGEBLATT *see* BERLINER FLIEGENDE BLAETTER
NEUES DEUTSCHES MUSEUM – Leipzig, 1789-91 – 3 – us Readex [943]
NEUES DEUTSCHES MUSEUM *see* DEUTSCHES MUSEUM
NEUES DEUTSCHLAND – (1980-84 15r DM1,125.00. 1985-94 32r DM2,400.00. Subsc 1995 4r DM240.00) – Berlin, 1946-1979 – 79r – 1 – DM5,925.00 – gw Mikro Press [072]
NEUES DEUTSCHLAND – Berlin, 1946- – ca 4r per y – 1 – inquire – us Ross [072]
NEUES DEUTSCHLAND – Berlin. 1966-79 – 1 – gw Mikrofilm [072]
NEUES DEUTSCHLAND – Berlin, apr 23 1946- – 1 – Inquire at Mikrofilmarchiv for details – gw Misc Inst [072]
NEUES DEUTSCHLAND – Berlin, Germany. 1962-89 – 94r – 1 – us L of C Photodup [072]
NEUES DEUTSCHLAND – East Berlin. Germany. apr. 1946-Dec. 1950. Missing Mar. 13, 1949 – 1 – 35.00r – us Hoover Inst Photo [072]
NEUES DEUTSCHLAND : ORGAN DES ZENTRALKOMITEES DER SOZIALISTISCHEN EINHEITSPARTEI DEUTSCHLANDS – Berlin: Neues Deutschland, A-Ausg. jul 1955-1980 (79r); jan-may 1981 (1r) – 1 – us Res Libr [072]
NEUES DEUTSCHLAND *see* VORWAERTS
NEUES DEUTSCHLAND (BERLIN) – 1946-1995 – 3 times per yr – 1 – DM230.00 – sz Infoprint [072]
NEUES DEUTSCHLAND IM NEUEN EUROPA / ed by Union deutscher Sozialisten und Gewerkschafter in der Schweiz – Zuerich, Apr 1945-Mar, Apr 1946 – 1r – 1 – gw Mikrofilm [949]
NEUES FORUM – Vienna, AU. 1973-1980 – 8r – $400.00 – R63561 – us Library Micro [072]
NEUES HAMBURGISCHES MAGAZIN, ODER FORTSETZUNG GESAMMLETER SCHRIFTEN, AUS DER NATURFORSCHUNG, DER ALLGEMEINEN STADT- UND LAND-OEKONOMIE, UND DEN ANGENEHMEN WISSENSCHAFTEN UBERHAUPT – Hamburg und Leipzig, 1767-81 – 3 – us Readex [500]
NEUES HOEFER INTELLIGENZ-BLATT – (Cont by: Hoefer Intelligenz-Blatt, jan 7 1802. Hoefer Intelligenz-Zeitung, 1809. Intelligenz-Blatt der Stadt Hof, jan 3 1824. Wochen-Blatt der Stadt Hof, jan 3 1829. Hoefer Wochen-Blatt, jan 1 1852. Anzeiger fuer Hof und Umgegend, jan 1 1854. Hofer Tag-Blatt, jun 30 1860. Anzeiger fuer Hof und Umgegend, oct 2 1860. Hofer Anzeiger, oct 1 1867. Hofer Anzeiger. Frankenpost, jan 2, 1968) – Hof, 1968-apr 30 1984 – 1 – gw Mikrofilm [072]
NEUES JOURNAL DER PHYSIK / Annalen der Physik – Leipzig, 1795-1797 – 3 – us Readex [530]
NEUES LEBEN – 1926- – 1 – sz Infoprint [947]
NEUES LEBEN – 1966-1983 – 432mf – 1 – DM2,462.40 – gw Mikro Press [320]
NEUES LEBEN = NOVAIA ZHIZN' – (Backfile through 1998 $85r) – Russia, 1999- – 1r per y – 1 – $80.00 standing order – us Ross [072]
NEUES LEBEN : WOCHENSCHRIFT DER SOWJETDEUTSCHEN BEVOELKERUNG – Moskau (Moskva), U.S.S.R. 1986- – 1 – gw Mikrofilm [943]
NEUES LEBEN = NOVAIA ZHIZN' – (Backfile through 1998 $85r. In German and Russian) – Russia, 1999- – 1r per y standing order – 1 – us Ross [072]
NEUES LEBEN AUS KLOPSTOCK / Zimmermann, Felix – Dresden: Im Sibyllen-Verlag, 1922 – 1r – 1 – us U.W. Library [430]
NEUES MAGAZIN [...] *see* MAGAZIN ALLER NEUEN ERFINDUNGEN
NEUES MAGAZIN FUER DIE LIEBHABER DER ENTOMOLOGIE *see* MAGAZIN FUER DIE LIEBHABER DER ENTOMOLOGIE
NEUES MUSIKBLATT – Berlin. nos. 1-85. 1934-1943 – 1 – us Schnase [780]

NEUES OESTERREICH – Vienna. Austria. -d. 28 Apr 1945-30 Jun 1950. (13 reels) – 1 – uk British Libr Newspaper [072]
NEUES PESTER JOURNAL – Hungary. -d. 1 Jan 1892-31 Dec 1893; 1 Jan 1917-13 May 1919. Imperfect. 22 reels – 1 – uk British Libr Newspaper [072]
NEUES POLITISCHES VOLKSBLATT – Budapest, Hungary. 20 Sep 1921-26 Oct 1940 – 11r – 1 – gw Mikrofilm [072]
NEUES POLITISCHES VOLKSBLATT – Budapest, sep 20-dec 1921, 1923-oct 26 1940 – 11r – 1 – Inquire at Mikrofilmarchiv for details – gw Misc Inst [943]
NEUES SCHWEIZERISCHES MUSEUM; ZEITSCHRIFT FUER DIE HUMANISTISCHEN STUDIEN UND DAS GYMNASIALWESEN IN DER SCHWEIZ – Bern, etc. Jahrg. 1-6; 1861-66. No more published. Film Mas 8615 – 1 – us H.U. Library [073]
NEUES SONNTAGSBLATT – Budapest, Hungary. 7 Jan 1934-15 Sept 1940 – 3r – 1 – gw Mikrofilm [073]
NEUES SONNTAGSBLATT – Budapest, jan 7 1934-sep 15 1940 – 3r – 1 – Inquire at Mikrofilmarchiv for details – gw Misc Inst [072]
NEUES TAGEBLATT : RIGAER MORGENZEITUNG – Riga, Latvija. 5 Apr-Dec 1925 – 1r – 1 – gw Mikrofilm [943]
NEUES VOLK – Berlin, 1933 (incomplete), 1934-38, 1939-40 (incomplete) – 1 – Inquire at Mikrofilmarchiv for details – gw Misc Inst [943]
NEUES WIENER TAGBLATT – (This microfilmed segment covers period for: Jul. 23, 1914 (v. 48, no. 201)-Dec. 31, 1919 (v. 126, no. 356); only few issues missing) – Wien: Neues Wiener Tagblatt, 186?-1944 – 1 – CSUX89-S581 – us Hoover Inst Photo [943]
NEUES WIENER TAGBLATT – Wien [Vienna]: Ostmarkische Zeitungsverlagsgesellschaft mBH, nov 1939-mar 20 1940 (5r); apr 1940-jun 10 1941 (10r); 1943-44 (7r) – 1 – us Res Libr [072]
NEUES WOCHENBLATT FUER DIE AMTSBEZIRKE ACHIM UND THEDINGHAUSEN *see* ACHIMER KREISBLATT
DIE NEUESTE BEURTEILUNG DES ERASMUS : VORTRAG / Walter, Johannes von – Breslau: Grass, Barth, 1911 – 1mf – us A.T.L.A. [190]
NEUESTE DOGMENGESCHICHTE : VON SEMLER BIS AUF DIE GEGENWART: VORLESUNGEN / Landerer, Maximilian Albert; ed by Zeller, Paul – (Includes bibliographical references and index) – Heilbronn: Gebr Henninger, 1881 – 1mf – 9 – 0-8370-8689-2 – 1986-2689 – us A.T.L.A. [240]
DIE NEUESTE LEHRE GEYSERS UEBER DAS KAUSALITAETSPRINZIP / Franzelin, Bernhard – Innsbruck, 1924 – 1mf – 9 – DM48.00 – 3-89349-297-6 – gw Hänsel [120]
NEUESTE NACHRICHTEN – Budapest, 1978-85 – 1 – Inquire at Mikrofilmarchiv for details – gw Misc Inst [072]
NEUESTE NACHRICHTEN – Budapest, Hungary. 1970-1990 – 40 – 1 – us L of C Photodup [072]
NEUESTE NACHRICHTEN – Budapest, Hungary. 1978-1985 – 1 – gw Mikrofilm [072]
NEUESTE NACHRICHTEN – Oberhausen, oct 2 1929-32 – 11r – 1 – gw Mikrofilm [943]
NEUESTE PRINZIPIEN DER ALTTESTAMENTLICHEN KRITIK / Koenig, Eduard – (Includes bibliographical references and index of biblical passages cited) – Gr. Lichterfelde-Berlin: Edwin Runge, 1902 – 1mf – 9 – 0-8370-3969-X – 1985-1969 – us A.T.L.A. [220]
NEUESTE SAMMLUNG JENER SCHRIFTEN, DIE VON EINIGEN JAHREN HER UEBER VERSCHIEDENE WICHTIGSTE GEGENSTAENDE ZUR STEUER DER WAHRHEIT IM DRUCK ERSCHIENEN SIND / ed by Merz, A – Augsburg. 40v. 1783-88 – 204mf – 9 – CA-54/1 – ne IDC [240]
NEUESTE TRAUMGESCHICHTE DES ANTISEMITISCHEN PROPHETEN : SENDSCHREIBEN AN PROF. ZOECKLER IN GREIFSWALD / Delitzsch, Franz – Erlangen: Deichert, 1883 – 1mf – us A.T.L.A. [240]
DIE NEUESTE UNTERSUCHUNG DER SINGSPIELE / Mattheson, J – 1744 – 9 – us Sibley [780]
DIE NEUESTEN ENTDECKUNGEN IN DER CHEMIE – Leipzig, 1781-1786 – 3 – us Readex [540]
DIE NEUESTEN ERFINDUNGEN, ETC – Vienna, Austria. -w. Jan 1868-Dec 1872. 2 reels – 1 – uk British Libr Newspaper [072]
DIE NEUESTEN RELIGIONSBEGEBENHEITEN MIT UNPARTHEYISCHEN ANMERKUNGEN – Giessen. v1-20. 1778-1797 – 205mf – 9 – ne IDC [200]
NEUESTES KOMISCHES THEATER / Angely, Louis – Hamburg: Magazin fuer Buchhandel, Musik und Kunst. 3v. 1836-41 – 1 – us U.W. Library [820]
AIN NEUEW MANDAT JESU CHRISTI / Herman, N – Augspurg, V. Othmar. 1546. BME-43 1 – 9 – ne IDC [240]
NEUF CANTATES / Clerambault, Louis Nicolas et al – (Quatre Cantates, dont celle de Didon, de Campra, L'Amant trompe et l'amant vainqueur, de Bernier, et Didon, de Mouret) – 18th c. – fr Armell [780]
Neufchateau, Francois de *see* PAMELA OU LA VERTU RECOMPENSEE
Neufville, Gilbert de *see* EN CHALAND SOUS LES TROPIQUES
Neufville, J J *see* SEX MELEA, S. ARIAE CUM VARIATIONIBUS
Neugebauer, S *see* SELECTORUM SYMBOLORUM HEROICORUM CENTURIA GEMINA ENOTATA ATQUE ENODATA
NEUHEBRAEISCHES UND CHALDAEISCHES WOERTERBUCH UEBER DIE TALMUDIM UND MIDRASCHIM / Levy, J – v. 1-4, with INDEX OF ALL PASSAGES QUOTED. Ed. 2. Berlin. Wien. 1924. (Ed. 1. 1876-89). BJ-412-15 1 – 9 – ne IDC [470]
DER NEUIGKEITSBOTE – Berlin, jan-aug 19 1837 – 1r – 1 – Inquire at Mikrofilmarchiv for details – gw Misc Inst [072]
DER NEUIGKEITSKRAEMER – Bremen, aug 13-dec 1853, 1854 (incomplete), jan-dec 29 1855 – 1r – 1 – Inquire at Mikrofilmarchiv for details – gw Misc Inst [072]
NEUKOELLNER ILLUSTRIERTE WOCHE – Berlin, 1919-20, 1921-22 (incomplete) – 1 – Inquire at Mikrofilmarchiv for details – gw Misc Inst [072]
NEULAND : MONATSSCHRIFT FUER POLITIK, WISSENSCHAFT, LITTERATUR UND KUNST – Berlin, Paris. 3v. 1896-98 – 15mf – 9 – subsc: DM110.00 diazo DM130.00 silver – gw Olms [320]
Neulat, L *see* LES DROITS DE LA FEMME DEVANT LA LOI FRANCAISE
Neumann *see* MIKHTAV MI-YERUSHALAYIM
Neumann, Alfred *see* AUS FRIEDRICH HEBBELS WERDEZEIT
Neumann, Arno *see* JESUS
Neumann, B *see* DIE HEILIGE STADT
Neumann, C F *see*
- GESCHICHTE DES ENGLISCH-CHINESISCHEN KRIEGES
- GESCHICHTE DES ENGLISCHEN REICHES IN ASIEN
- OSTASIATISCHE GESCHICHTE VOM ERSTEN CHINESISCHEN KRIEG BIS ZU DEN VERTRAEGEN IN PEKING, 1840-1860

Neumann, Carl Wilhelm *see* LUDWIG ANZENGRUBER
Neumann, Karl Johannes *see*
- HIPPOLYTUS VON ROM IN SEINER STELLUNG ZU STAAT UND WELT
- DER ROEMISCHE STAAT UND DIE ALLGEMEINE KIRCHE BIS AUF DIOCLETIAN

Neumann, L *see* RECUEIL DES TRAITES ET CONVENTIONS CONCLUS PAR L'AUTRICHE AVEC LES PUISSANCES ETRANGERS, DEPUIS 1763 JUSQU'A NOS JOURS
Neumann, Robert *see* DIE PEST VON LIANORA
Neumann, Wilhelm *see* DIE STIFTSHUETTE IN BILD UND WORT
NEUMARKTER TAGBLATT : BA DER MITTELBAYERISCHEN ZEITUNG – Neumarkt-Oberpfalz, West Germany. Jul 1952-Jul 1973; 1978- – ca 11r per yr – 1 – gw Mikrofilm [072]
Neumayer, Robert J *see* HOW LEISURE BELIEFS RELATE TO ATTITUDES TOWARD THE NORMALIZATION PRINCIPLE AS PERCEIVED BY SERVICE PROVIDERS FOR PEOPLE WITH MENTAL RETARDATION
Neumeyer, Fredrik *see* THE LAW OF EMPLOYED INVENTORS IN EUROPE
NEUMOLCHNOE SLOVO : ORGAN T SENTRALNOGO KOMITETA TRUDOVO I NARODNO-SOT SIALISTICHESKO I PARTII – (Includes c.1: no.1 1917:Dec.12-no.2 (1917:Dec.13)) – Petrograd: Partii a, 1917- – 1 – CSUXAKB0324-S – us Hoover Inst Photo [947]
NEUN FASTEN: U. PASSIONS PREDIGTEN:... / Cramer, D – Hamburg, 1611 – 3mf – 9 – ne IDC [240]
NEUN GESCHICHTEN / Utermann, Wilhelm – 2. Aufl. Muenchen: F Eher, 1944 – 1 – us U.W. Library [830]
NEUN NOVELLEN : AUSWAHL / Kroeger, Timm – Hamburg: A Janssen, 1909 – 1r – 1 – us U.W. Library [830]
DER NEUNUNDZWANZIGSTER – New York, NY. 1898. The Twenty-Ninth – 1 – us A.J.P.C. [071]
NEUNZEHN BRIEFE UEBER JUDENTHUM = THE NINETEEN LETTERS OF BEN UZIEL : BEING A SPIRITUAL PRESENTATION OF THE PRINCIPLES OF JUDAISM / Hirsch, Samson Raphael – (In English) – New York, London: Funk & Wagnalls, 1899 – 1mf – 9 – 0-8370-3590-2 – 1985-1590 – us A.T.L.A. [270]
DAS NEUNZEHNTE JAHRHUNDERT IN DER KARIKATUR / Wendel, Friedrich – Berlin, 1925 – 2mf – DM62.00 – 3-8267-3081-X – gw Hänsel [900]
NEUPHILOLOGISCHE MITTEILUNGEN – Helsinki. v1-33. 1899-1932 – 132mf – 9 – ne IDC [400]
NEUPHILOLOGISCHE MITTEILUNGEN – Helsinki. v1-76. 1899-1975 – 5,9 – Dfl4,940.00; Dfl65.00v – ne Swets [400]
NEURAL NETWORKS – 1,5,69 – us UMI [616]
NEURAL VERSUS MUSCULAR RESPONSES TO ISOMETRIC STRENGTH TRAINING OF THE TRICEPS BRACHII / Barr, John O & Nielsen, David H – 1989 – 3mf – 9 – $12.00 – us Microform Publ [612]
Neurath, Otto *see* FAUST
NEUREN SPRACHEN – v66- 1967- 1; v76- 5,6,9 – us UMI [400]
NEUROBEHAVIORAL TOXICOLOGY – v.1-2. 1979-80. Continued by Neurobehavioral Toxicology and Teratology – 1 – us UMI [073]
NEUROBEHAVIORAL TOXICOLOGY AND TERATOLOGY – 1981- – 1,5,6,9 – us UMI [073]
NEUROBIOLOGY OF AGING – v1- 1980- – 1,5,6,9 – us UMI [610]
NEUROCHEMICAL RESEARCH – (v5-19 1980-94 $110.00v) – v1-4. 1976-79 – 1,5 – $65.00 – us UMI [073]
NEUROCHEMISTRY INTERNATIONAL – v1- 1980- – 5,6,9 – us UMI [610]
NEUROCHIRURGIA – 1958- 1; 1973- 5,6; 1975- 9 – us UMI [073]
NEUROELECTRIC NEWS – 1970- 1; 1971- 5,6; 1975- 9 – us UMI [073]
NEUROENDOCRINOLOGY – v17-. 1975- – 1,5,9 – us UMI [616]
NEUROENDROCRINOLOGY – v1-16 1965-74 1; v2-16 5,6; v6-16 9 – us UMI [616]
NEUROEPIDEMIOLOGY – v1-. 1982- – 1,5,9 – us UMI [616]
NEUROLOGIC CLINICS – 1983- – 1,5,6,9 – us UMI [616]
NEUROLOGICAL RESEARCH – v. 1-. 1979- – 1,5,6,9 – us UMI [616]
NEUROLOGIE, PSYCHIATRIE, PSYCHOLOGIE *see* ACTA NEUROLOGICA BELGICA
NEUROLOGY – (v.31-. 1981-. 5,6,9) – v.1-. 1951- – 1 – us UMI [610]
NEUROLOGY – v34-. Dec 1984- – 1,5,6,9 – us UMI [073]
NEUROMUSCULAR AND KINESTHETIC ADAPTATIONS FOLLOWING STRENGTH TRAINING OF VISUALLY IMPAIRED AND NON-VISUALLY IMPAIRED CHILDREN / Ozmun, J C – 1991 – 2mf – 9 – $8.00 – us Microform Publ [150]
NEUROMUSCULAR DISORDERS – 1,5,69 – us UMI [616]
NEUROPEPTIDES – (1982-. 1,5,6,9) – v1-. 1980- – 1 – us UMI [073]
NEUROPHARMACOLOGY – (Formerly: International Journal of Neuro-Pharmacology) – v1- 1962- – 5,6,9 – us UMI [615]
NEUROPHYSIOLOGY – v1-25. 1969-93 – 1,5 – $80.00v – us UMI [612]
NEUROPSIHIJATRIJA – v18- 1970- 1; v20- 5,6; v23- 9 – us UMI [073]
NEUROPSYCHOBIOLOGY – v1-. 1975- – 1,5,9 – us UMI [616]
NEUROPSYCHOLOGIA – v1- 1963- – 5,6,9 – us UMI [150]
NEUROPSYCHOLOGY REVIEW – v1-4. 1990-94 – 1,5 – $65.00v – us UMI [150]
NEURORADIOLOGY – v. 1-20. 1970-80 – 1,5,9 – 1410.00 – us UMI [616]
NEUROSCIENCE – v1- 1976- – 5,6,9 – us UMI [610]
NEUROSCIENCE AND BEHAVIORAL PHYSIOLOGY – v1-24. 1967-94 – 1,5 – $80.00v – us UMI [612]
NEUROSCIENCE AND BIOBEHAVIORAL REVIEWS – (See also: Biobehavioral Reviews) – v2- 1978- – 1,5,6,9 – us UMI [616]
NEUROSCIENCE LETTERS – v1-51. 1975-84 – 1,5,6,13 – sz Elsevier [073]
NEUROSCIENCE TRANSLATIONS – v. 1-16. 1967-1971 – 1,5,6 – us Princeton Micro [610]
NEUROSCIENCES RESEARCH PROGRAM BULLETIN – v2-14. 1964-76 – 1,5,6 – us Princeton Micro [073]
THE NEUROSCIENTIST : A REVIEW JOURNAL BRIDGING NEUROBIOLOGY, NEUROLOGY AND PSYCHIATRY – v1-2. 1995-1996 – 1 – $80.00r – us Williams [616]
NEUROSURGERY – v1-39. 1977-96 – 1,5,6,9 – $110.00r – us Williams [617]
NEUROTOXICOLOGY AND TERATOLOGY – 1,5,69 – us UMI [616]
Neusel, Manfred *see* ZUR EPOCHENGESCHICHTE DES NATURKUNDLICHEN UNTERRICHTS IN HESSEN-DARMSTADT
NEUSPRACHLICHE MITTEILUNGEN AUS WISSENSCHAFT UND PRAXIS – (v. 32- 1979- 5,6,9) – v. 18-. 1965- – 1 – us UMI [370]
NEUSTRIA PIA SEU DE OMNIBUS ET SINGULIS ABBATIIS ET PRIORATIBUS TOTIUS NORMANDIAE / Monstier, A du OF M – Rothomagi, 1663 – Dfl140.00 – ne Slangenburg [240]
Neustroev, A N *see*
- BIBLIOTEKA UCHENAIA, EKONOMICHESKAIA I PROCH., IZDAVAVSHAIASIA P.P. SUMAROKOVYM V 1793-1794 GG. V TOBOL'SKE
- EKONOMICHESKII MAGAZIN, (SEL'SKO-KHOZIAISTVENNYI ZHURNAL IZDAVAVSHIISIA V 1780-1789 GG
- UKAZATEL'K RUSSKIM POVREMENNYM IZDANIIAM I SBORNIKAM ZA 1703-1802 GG. I K ISTORICHESKOMU ROZYSKANIIU O NIKH

EINE NEU-TESTAMENTLICHE ENTDECKUNG UND DEREN BESTREITUNG, ODER DIE GESCHICHTS-VISION DES BUCHES HENOCH IM ZUSAMMENHANG / Volkmar, Gustav – Zuerich, 1862 – 1mf – 8 – ne Slangenburg [220]
DIE NEUTESTAMENTLICHE FORMEL ST "IN CHRISTO JESU" / Deissmann, Gustav Adolf – Marburg:N G Elwert, 1892 – 1mf – 9 – 0-8370-2861-2 – 1985-0861 – us A.T.L.A. [220]
NEUTESTAMENTLICHE THEOLOGIE: GRUNDRISS FUER VORLESUNGEN / Mueller, Karl – Erlangen: Rudolf Merkel, 1907. 1 fiche – 9 – us A.T.L.A. [240]
NEUTESTAMENTLICHE ZEITGESCHICHTE / Holtzmann, Oskar – Tuebingen: J.C.B. Mohr, 1906. 1 fiche – 9 – us A.T.L.A. [240]
NEUTESTAMENTLICHE, ZEITGESCHICHTE / Hausrath, Adolf – Heidelberg 3 Teile 1868-74 – 32mf – 8 – ne Slangenburg [220]
NEUTESTAMENTLICHES WOERTERBUCH : EIN KURZGEFASSTES NACHSCHLAGEBUCH / Kuhne, Berthold – Gotha: Friedrich Andreas Perthes, 1892 – 1mf – 9 – 0-8370-9290-6 – 1986-3290 – us A.T.L.A. [052]
NEU-TITSCHEINER ZEITUNG *see* DEUTSCHE VOLKSZEITUNG FUER DAS KUHLAENDCHEN
NEUTRAL RIGHTS... / Campbell, R G – Baltimore, 1908 – 2mf – 9 – ILM-358/1 – ne IDC [327]
LA NEUTRALITE SUR L'ESCAUT / Beer Poortugael, J C C den – La Haye, 1911 – 9 – 1mf – ILM-1889/1 – ne IDC [327]
THE NEUTRALITY OF... / Callahan, J M – Baltimore, 1898 – 3mf – 9 – ILM-351/1 – ne IDC [327]
LA NEUTRALIZZAZIONE DEL CANALE DI SUEZ... / Contuzzi, F P – Firenze, 1888 – 1mf – 1 – ILM-2296/1 – ne IDC [327]
NEUTRON NEWS / ed by Lander, Gerry – 9,5,1 – us Gordon [530]
NEU-ULMER ZEITUNG : BA DER AUGSBURGER ALLGEMEINEN – Neu-Ulm, Germany. 1 Jun 1983- – 9r per yr – 1 – gw Mikrofilm [072]
NEUVAINE A L'HONNEUR DE ST-FRANCOIS (SIC) XAVIER – Montreal: J Brown, 1811. SEM16P31 – 1r – 5 – Can$9.00 – cn Bibl Nat [240]
NEUVAINE EN L'HONNEUR DE ST-FRANCOIS XAVIER – Nouv. ed. Quebec: J Neilson, 1818. SEM16P32 – 1r – 5 – Can$9.00 – cn Bibl Nat [240]

NEU-VERMEHRTES HISTORISCH UND GEOGRAPHISCHES ALLGEMEINES LEXICON (AEL, ABT.1;9) / Iselin, Jacob Christoph – 3. Aufl. Basel. 1742-44 (mf ed 1992) – 70mf – 9 – DM590.00 – 3-89131-078-1 – gw Fischer [943]
NEUVIEME CONCERTO DE FLUTE PRINCIPALE, DEUX VIOLONS, ALTO, BASSE, CORS ET HAUTBOIS / Devienne, Francois – 179-? – 9 – us Sibley [780]
NEUVOSTO-KARJALA *see* SOVETSKAIA KARELIIA
Neuwinger, Rudolf *see* VERNUNFT UND SCHOENHEIT
DIE NEUZEIT – Wochenschrift fuer politische, religioese und Cultur-Interessen. Vienna. v1-43. 1861-1903. Lacking misc. issues. B314 (Leo Baeck Institute. German-Jewish Periodicals, Pt 1) – 8r – 1 – $545.00 – us UPA [270]
NEVA – 1955-58, 1973-85 – 1 – us I.U. Libraries [073]
NEVA – Moscow, 1955-72.Lacking: 1955 (1-3,8-9); 1957 (7-9). BR-10,430/1. Suspended: Jul 1941-Jun 1945 – 9 – ne IDC [947]
NEVA – Moscow. U.S.S.R. 1961- – 1 – us UMI [073]
NEVADA : SESSION LAWS OF AMERICAN STATES AND TERRITORIES – 1861-1995 – 9 – $1,075.50 set – us Hein [340]
Nevada *see*
- REPORTS AND OPINIONS (A-G)
- REPORTS, POST-NRS
- REPORTS, PRE-NRS
- SESSION LAWS, 1861-

NEVADA AMERICAN – Stewart, NV. 1914 – 1r – 1 – $50.00 – U04757 – us Library Micro [071]
NEVADA APPEAL – Carson City. Nev. 1947- – 1 – us UMI [071]
NEVADA APPEAL – (Cont by: Carson Daily Appeal; Morning Appeal) – Carson City, NV. Mar-Apr 1877; 1947-71 – 81r – 1 UN04460 – $4,050.00 – us Library Micro [071]
NEVADA APPEAL *see* CARSON DAILY APPEAL
NEVADA ATTORNEY GENERAL REPORTS AND OPINIONS – (6 1865-1978 $175.00. 9 1978-1994 $120.00) – 1865-1994 – 6,9 – $295.00set – us Hein [340]
THE NEVADA BAPTIST – Reno, NV. 1986-1991. 204p – 1 – $25.60 – us Baptist [071]
NEVADA BAR ASSOCIATION PROCEEDINGS – (Lacking: 1918-20) – 1912-18 (all publ) – 17mf – 9 – $25.50 – LLMC 84-636 – us L.L.M.C. [073]
NEVADA BELL : AUSTIN, CARSON CITY, FERNLEY, LOVELOCK, RENO, SPARKS, ETC. – 1992- – 6+ r – 1 – $300.00 – P00144 – us Library Micro [910]
NEVADA BUGLE – Reno, NV. Jun-Aug 1912 – 1r – 1 – $50.00 – U04681 – us Library Micro [071]
NEVADA BULLETIN – Winnemucca. Nev. 1964- – 1 – us UMI [071]
NEVADA CAPITOL NEWS – Carson City, NV. 1950 – 1r – 1 – $50.00 – U04461 – us Library Micro [071]
NEVADA CHURCHMAN – Reno, NV. 1908-12 – 1r – 1 – $50.00 – U04682 – us Library Micro [071]
NEVADA CITIZEN – Las Vegas, NV. 1954-56 – 1r – 1 – $50.00 – U04606 – us Library Micro [071]
NEVADA CITIZEN – Reno, NV. Jun 1897 – 1r – 1 – $50.00 – U04683 – us Library Micro [071]
NEVADA CITY NEWS – Nevada City, CA. 1991 – 1r – 1 – $50.00 – B06041 – us Library Micro [071]
NEVADA CITY NUGGET – Nevada City, CA. 1928-1950 – 13r – 1 – $650.00 – B03351 – us Library Micro [071]
NEVADA COUNTY, 1867; 1871-1872; 1895 – 3r – 1 – $150.00 – D064 – us Library Micro [978]
NEVADA COUNTY CITIZEN – Nevada City, CA. 1959-60 – 1r – 1 – $50.00 – C02522 – us Library Micro [071]
NEVADA COUNTY MORNING MINER – Nevada City, CA. Apr 1903-Jul 1904 – 3r – 1 – $150.00 – B02518 – us Library Micro [071]
NEVADA COUNTY NUGGET – Nevada City, CA. 1959-84 – 24r – 1 – $1,200.00 – C02521 – us Library Micro [071]
NEVADA COUNTY NUGGET – Nevada City. Calif. -w. 1959-67 – 1 – us UMI [071]
NEVADA DAILY BULLETIN – Winnemucca. Nev. 1964- – 1 – us UMI [071]
NEVADA DAILY GAZETTE – Nevada City, CA. 1869-1870 – 1r – 1 – $50.00 – C03352 – us Library Micro [071]
NEVADA DAILY TRANSCRIPT – Nevada City, CA. 1860-1904 – 76r – 1 – $3,800.00 – B02519 – us Library Micro [071]
NEVADA DEMOCRAT – Carlin, NV. Feb, Apr 1917; Oct-Nov 1914 – 1r – 1 – $50.00 – U04436 – us Library Micro [071]
NEVADA DEMOCRAT – Reno, NV. Oct-Nov 1914; 1914-15 – 1r – 1 – $50.00 – U04684 – us Library Micro [071]
THE NEVADA DEMOCRAT – Nevada City, CA. 1856-62 – 2r – 1 – $100.00 – B02520 – us Library Micro [071]
NEVADA DEMOCRATIC RECORD – Tonopah. Nev. 1963-1970 – 1 – us UMI [071]
NEVADA DEMOCRATIC RECORD – Tonopah, NV. 1962-70 (broken series) – 2r – 1 – $100.00 – U04769 – us Library Micro [071]
NEVADA ENTERPRISE – Nevada, Ohio. 1872-73 – 1r – 1 – $32.50r – us Archival [071]
NEVADA FEDERATIONIST – Reno, NV. 1915-19 (scats) – 1r – 1 – $50.00 – U04685 – us Library Micro [071]
NEVADA FIRST BAPTIST CHURCH. NEVADA, MISSOURI : CHURCH RECORDS – 1835-1983 – 1 – 140.45 – us Baptist [240]
NEVADA FORUM – (Also known as: Daily Forum; The Forum) – Sparks, NV. 1905-10 (scats) – 6r – 1 – $300.00 – us Library Micro [071]
NEVADA GAY TIMES – Las Vegas, NV. 1983-1985 – 1r – 1 – $50.00 – U04861 – us Library Micro [305]
NEVADA HISTORICAL SOCIETY QUARTERLY – 1957- 1; 1973- 5,6; 1977- 4 x 6 in. 9 – us UMI [073]
NEVADA HORSE LIFE – Reno, NV. 1977-1980 – 1r – 1 – $50.00 – U04885 – us Library Micro [071]
NEVADA INDEPENDENT (AND RENO REPORTER) – Reno, NV. Aug-Oct 1938; Apr-May 1950; 1956-58 – 1r – 1 – $50.00 – U04686 – us Library Micro [071]
NEVADA INDEX-UNION – Carson City, NV. 1887-88 – 2r – 1 – $100.00 – U04462 – us Library Micro [071]
NEVADA LABOR RECORD – Reno, NV. 1932-33 – 1r – 1 – $50.00 – U04687 – us Library Micro [071]
NEVADA LAWYER – (Supersedes Inter Alia) – v1-2. 1993-94 – 9 – $45.00 set – us Hein [340]
NEVADA LAWYER *see* INTER ALIA
NEVADA LEGIONNAIRE – Lovelock, NV. 1934-1958 – 1r – 1 – $50.00 – U04621 – us Library Micro [071]
NEVADA LEGIONNAIRE – Sparks, NV. 1934-35; 1939-49 (scats); 1941-58 – 4r – 1 – $200.00 – U04749 – us Library Micro [071]
NEVADA LIBERAL – (Also known as: Intermountain Liberal) – Reno, NV. 1924-26 (scats) – 1r – 1 – $50.00 – U04688 – us Library Micro [071]
NEVADA LUTHERAN – Gardnerville, NV. 10 Jun 1918 (only known issue) – 1r – 1 – $50.00 – U04533 – us Library Micro [240]
NEVADA MAGAZINE – Gardnerville, NV. 1889-1900; 1945-1949 – 4r – 1 – $200.00 – U04843 – us Library Micro [071]
THE NEVADA MAGAZINE – Reno, NV. 1889-1900; 1945-1949 – 5r – 1 – $250.00 – U04886 – us Library Micro [071]
NEVADA MAPS 1 : CITIES AND TOWNS – 1885-1906. 193 maps. 21 communities. Sanborn Company Fire Insurance Maps – 1 – $40.00r – us Shkurkin [910]
NEVADA MAPS 2 : CITIES AND TOWNS – 1906-43. 195 maps. 21 communities – 1 – $40.00r – us Shkurkin [910]
NEVADA MAPS 3 : CITIES AND TOWNS – 1907-50. 222 maps. 16 towns – 1 – $43.00r – us Shkurkin [910]
NEVADA MINER – Golconda, NV. Feb-Sep 1902 – 2r – 1 – $100.00 – U04542 – us Library Micro [071]
NEVADA MINES AND FARMS – Reno, NV. 1911-12 – 1r – 1 – $50.00 – U04689 – us Library Micro [071]
NEVADA MINING BULLETIN – Goldfield, NV. Dec 1906 – 1r – 1 – $50.00 – U04554 – us Library Micro [071]
NEVADA MINING FINANCIAL NEWS – Reno, NV. 1907-09 – 1r – 1 – $50.00 – U04690 – us Library Micro [071]
NEVADA MINING INVESTOR – Reno, NV. 1906-07 – 1r – 1 – $50.00 – U04691 – us Library Micro [071]
NEVADA MINING NEWS – Goldfield, NV. Jun 1906 – 1r – 1 – $50.00 – U04555 – us Library Micro [071]
NEVADA MINING PRESS – Reno, NV. 1921-31; 1939-46 – 11r – 1 – $550.00 – U04678 – us Library Micro [071]
NEVADA MINING PRESS – Reno, NV. 1927 – 1r – 1 – $50.00 – U03712 – us Library Micro [622]
NEVADA MINING RECORD – Winnemucca, NV. Jan-Mar 1901; Feb-Mar 1966 – 1r – 1 – $50.00 – U04817 – us Library Micro [071]
THE NEVADA MONTHLY – Virginia City, NV. 1880 – 1r – 1 – $50.00 – U04901 – us Library Micro [071]
NEVADA NATION – (Also known as: Nevada National, Grass Valley National, Daily National) – Grass Valley, CA. 1859-1860; 1861-1862; 1863-1865 – 5r – 1 – $250.00 – C03602 – us Library Micro [071]
NEVADA NATIONAL *see* NEVADA NATION
NEVADA NEW ERA – Kennedy, NV. 1894 – 1r – 1 – $50.00 – U04592 – us Library Micro [071]
NEVADA NEW ERA – Lovelock, NV. v2 (no date) – 1r – 1 – $50.00 – U04622 – us Library Micro [071]
NEVADA NEWS – Winnemucca, NV. 3 Jan 1901 – 1r – 1 – $50.00 – U04818 – us Library Micro [071]
NEVADA NEWSLETTER AND ADVERTISER – Reno, NV. 1914-1927 – 9r – 1 – $450.00 – U04887 – us Library Micro [071]
NEVADA OBSERVER – Reno, NV. 1904-07; 1916-18 (broken series) – 1r – 1 – $50.00 – U04692 – us Library Micro [071]
NEVADA PATRIOT – Carson City, NV. Jul-Aug 1876 (scattered issues) – 1r – 1 – $50.00 – U04463 – us Library Micro [071]
THE NEVADA PEACE OFFICER – Las Vegas, NV. 1938-1959 – 2r – 1 – $100.00 – U04857 – us Library Micro [071]
NEVADA PROGRESSIVE – Austin, NV. 1924-26 – 1r – 1 – $50.00 – U04403 – us Library Micro [071]
THE NEVADA PROHIBITIONIST – Genoa, NV. 1 Apr 1889 (only known issue) – 1r – 1 – $50.00 – U04538 – us Library Micro [071]
THE NEVADA PROSPECTOR – Mina, NV. 1978-1990 – 1r – 1 – $50.00 – U04870 – us Library Micro [622]
NEVADA RANCHER – Sparks, NV. 1971 – 8+ r – 1 – $400.00 ($90.00y) – N04750 – us Library Micro [071]
NEVADA REGISTER – Reno. Nev. 1953-56; 1960- – 1 – us UMI [071]
NEVADA REVIEW MONTHLY – Reno, NV. 1928 – 1r – 1 – $50.00 – U04888 – us Library Micro [071]
NEVADA REVISED STATUTES – Carson City, Nevada Legislative Counsel Bureau – 9 – Inquire – us Hein [340]
NEVADA REVISED STATUTES ANNOTATED – Charlottesville, Michie Company. Superseded vols – 9 – Inquire – us Hein [340]
NEVADA ROCKROLLER – Reno, NV. Jun-Sep 1914 – 1r – 1 – $50.00 – U04693 – us Library Micro [071]
NEVADA SEARCHLIGHT – Reno, NV. 1922 – 1r – 1 – $50.00 – U04694 – us Library Micro [071]
NEVADA SILVER TIDINGS – Elko, NV. 1897; Jan-Jul 1899 – 2r – 1 – $100.00 – U04498 – us Library Micro [071]
NEVADA SOCIALIST – Reno, NV. 1914-16 – 1r – 1 – $50.00 – U04695 – us Library Micro [071]
NEVADA SPORTSMAN – Sparks, NV. 1956-57 – 1r – 1 – $50.00 – U04752 – us Library Micro [071]
NEVADA STATE ANNUAL AND LABOR REVIEW – Reno, NV. 1912-1915 – 1r – 1 – $50.00 – U04889 – us Library Micro [331]
Nevada. State Bar Association *see* PROCEEDINGS
NEVADA STATE BAR JOURNAL – (Missing: v1 no 3) – v1-37. 1936-73 – 37mf – 9 – $55.00 – LLMC 84-638 – us L.L.M.C. [073]
NEVADA STATE BAR JOURNAL *see* INTER ALIA
NEVADA STATE BAR REPORTS – v1-8. 1928-35 (all publ) – 9mf – 9 – $13.50 – LLMC 84-637 – us L.L.M.C. [073]
NEVADA STATE BUILDER – Reno, NV. May 1927, 1931-32 – 1r – 1 – $50.00 – U04696 – us Library Micro [071]
Nevada. State Dept *see* BIENNIAL REPORT OF THE SECRETARY OF STATE
NEVADA STATE GAZETTEER AND BUSINESS DIRECTORY, 1914-1915 / R.L. Polk and Co – Feb 1914. Nevada Reel 2. The Cox Library Collection – 5 – us Americana [978]
NEVADA STATE HERALD – Wells, NV. 1897-1932; 1900-29 (scats) – 36r – 1 – $1,800.00 – U04808 – us Library Micro [071]
NEVADA STATE JOURNAL – Carson City, NV. May 1886 – 1r – 1 – $50.00 – U04464 – us Library Micro [073]
NEVADA STATE JOURNAL – (Cont by: Reno Gazette Journal) – Reno, NV. 1874-1983 – 872r – 1 RB04698 – $43,600.00 – us Library Micro [073]
NEVADA STATE JOURNAL – Reno, NV. 1851-1863; 1870-1896; 1912 – 16r – 1 – $800.00 – UB04697 – us Library Micro [073]
NEVADA STATE JOURNAL *see* RENO GAZETTE JOURNAL
NEVADA STATE LABOR NEWS – Reno, NV. 1942-51 (broken series) – 5r – 1 – $250.00 – U04700 – us Library Micro [071]
NEVADA STATE LABOR NEWS – Reno-Las Vegas. Nev. 1949-51 – 1 – us UMI [331]
NEVADA STATE NEWS – Reno. Nev. 1952-57 – 1 – us UMI [071]
NEVADA STATE NEWS – Reno, NV. 1952-1957 – 2r – 1 – $100.00 – U04701 – us Library Micro [071]
NEVADA STATE OBSERVER – Sparks, NV. 1904-07; Dec 1964 – 1r – 1 – $50.00 – U04753 – us Library Micro [071]
NEVADA STATE RECORDER – Carson City, NV. 1984-1986 – 3r – 1 – $150.00 – N03703 – us Library Micro [071]
NEVADA STATE REGISTER – Reno, NV. 1953-1973 – 14r – 1 – $700.00 – U04702 – us Library Micro [071]
THE NEVADA STATE VETERAN – Carson City, NV. 17, 30 Apr 1946; Mar-Dec 1949 – 1r – 1 – $50.00 – U04465 – us Library Micro [071]
THE NEVADA STATESMAN – Carson City, NV. 1960-66 – 1r – 1 – $50.00 – U04466 – us Library Micro [071]
Nevada. Supreme Court *see* NEVADA SUPREME COURT REPORTS
NEVADA SUPREME COURT REPORTS / Nevada. Supreme Court – (Pre-NRS: v1-16 1865-82 95mf $142.00. Vols after v53 still in copyright. Updates not poss before year 2006) – v1-53. 1865-1931 – 327mf – $490.00 – LLMC 82-985 – us L.L.M.C. [340]
NEVADA TIMES – Laughlin, NV. 1990 – 10+ r – 1 – $500.00 ($90.00y) – U04867 – us Library Micro [071]
NEVADA TRIBUNE – Carson City, NV. 1875-96 – 22r – 1 – $1,100.00 – U04467 – us Library Micro [071]
NEVADA TRI-WEEKLY HERALD – Nevada City, CA. 1878-1881 – 4r – 1 – $200.00 – B03353 – us Library Micro [071]
NEVADA UNION – Carson City, NV. 1886-87 – 1r – 1 – $50.00 – U04468 – us Library Micro [071]
Nevada United Methodist Church (Nevada, Ohio) *see* RECORDS
NEVADA VETERAN – Las Vegas, NV. 17, 30 Apr 1946 – 1r – 1 – $50.00 – U04607 – us Library Micro [071]
NEVADA VETERAN JOURNAL – Reno, NV. 1963-1970 – 1r – 1 – $50.00 – U04703 – us Library Micro [073]
NEVADA VETERAN JOURNAL – Tonopah. Nev. 1963-1970 – 1 – us UMI [071]
NEVADA VOICE – Reno, NV. 1926-72 – 1r – 1 – $50.00 – U04704 – us Library Micro [071]
NEVADA WOMEN – Reno, NV. 1987-1990 – 1r – 1 – $50.00 – U04890 – us Library Micro [305]
NEVADA WORKMAN – Goldfield, NV. 7 Sep 1907 – 1r – 1 – $50.00 – U04566 – us Library Micro [071]
NEVADAN – Reno, NV. Oct 1916 – 1r – 1 – $50.00 – U04706 – us Library Micro [071]
NEVADAN – Tonopah, NV. Oct-Dec 1912 – 1r – 1 – $50.00 – U04770 – us Library Micro [071]
NEVADA'S GOLDEN STARS / Sullivan, Maurice J – A Memorial Volume of Those Who Died in the World War I. Reno: A. Carlisle and Co. Nevada reel 2. (Cox Library Collection) – 5 – us Americana [978]
THE NEVADIAN – Reno, NV. 1979-1981 – 1r – 1 – $50.00 – N03711 – us Library Micro [071]

NEVADIAN TIMES – Carson City, NV. Mar-Jul 1935 – 1r – 1 – $50.00 – U04469 – us Library Micro [071]
Neve, J L *see* A BRIEF HISTORY OF THE LUTHERAN CHURCH IN AMERICA
Nevenberger, Nadia *see* ISRAEL MEDICAL BIBLIOGRAPHY: 1948-1959
NEVER LEAVE HISTORY / Sukarno, Pres. Indonesia – SE 11,690 1. Address on 17 August, 1966 – 9 – ne IDC [324]
Nevers, Edmond de *see* L'AVENIR DU PEUPLE CANADIEN-FRANCAIS
Neveux *see* DIALOGUES D'UN SAINT-SIMONIEN SUR LA RELIGION SAINT-SIMONIENNE
NEVHAT UEL-'USSAK / Receb, M ibn-i – Istanbul, 1261 – 2mf – 9 – $12.00 – us MEDOC [949]
NEVILE AND MANNING'S REPORTS : REPORTS OF CASES ARGUED AND DETERMINED IN THE COURT OF KING'S BENCH... / Nevile, Sanford & Manning, William M Manning – v1-6. 1832-36. London: S Sweet, 1834-39 (all publ) – 58mf – 9 – $87.00 – LLMC 84-780 – us L.L.M.C. [324]
NEVILE AND PERRY'S REPORTS : REPORTS OF CASES ARGUED AND DETERMINED IN THE COURT OF KING'S BENCH AND UPON WRITS OF ERROR...TO THE EXCHEQUER CHAMBER.... / Nevile, Sanford & Perry, Thomas E Perry – (This series became "Queen's Bench Reports" with the accession of Victoria in 1838) – v1-3. 1836-38. London: Sweet, Maxwell & Stevens, 1837-38 (all publ) – 25mf – 9 – $37.50 – LLMC 84-781 – us L.L.M.C. [324]
Nevile, Sanford *see*
– NEVILE AND MANNING'S REPORTS
– NEVILE AND PERRY'S REPORTS
Neville, R C *see* SAXON OBSEQUIES
Neville, Robert G *see* THE YORKSHIRE MINERS, 1881-1926
NEVILS CREEK BAPTIST CHURCH. STEWART COUNTY. MODEL, TENNESSEE : CHURCH RECORDS – 1887-Feb 1963 – 1 – 30.83 – us Baptist [240]
Nevin, AF *see* POIA
Nevin, Alfred *see* POPULAR EXPOSITOR OF THE GOSPELS AND ACTS
Nevin, John W *see* THE ANXIOUS BENCH
Nevin, Robert Peebles *see* BLACK-ROBES
Nevinson, Henry Woodd *see* A SKETCH OF HERDER AND HIS TIMES
NEVIS: 1841-1882 – September 1991, M.A.P. West Yorkshire – 7r – 1 – uk Microform Academic [972]
Nevius, Helen Sanford Coan *see* THE LIFE OF JOHN LIVINGSTON NEVIUS
Nevius, John L *see*
– CHINA AND THE CHINESE
Nevius, John Livingston *see* METHODS OF MISSION WORK
Nevole, George J, Jr. *see* VISUAL CUE UTILIZATION IN SKILLED SOFTBALL PLAYERS
Nevostruev, K I *see*
– OPISANIE SLAVIANSKIKH RUKOPISEI MOSKOVSKOI SINODAL'NOI (PATRIARSHEI) BIBLIOTEKI
– OPISANIE VELIKIKH CHETIKH-MINEI MAKARIIA MITROPOLITA VSEROSSIISKAGO
Nevres *see* DIVAN
NEVROSES : HOFFMANN, QUINCEY, EDGAR POE, G. DE NERVAL / Barine, Arvede – (Includes bibliographical references) – Paris: Hatchette, 1898 – 1 – us U.W. Library [410]
NEVSAL-I AFIYET (SALNAME-I-TIBBI) – (1315[1899]. – 5mf. $150.00; 1316[1900]. – (7mf). $150.00; 1320[1904]. – (9mf). $175.00; 1322[1906]. – (10mf). $175.00) – 9 – us MEDOC [949]
NEVSAL-I ASKERI – (1316[1898]. – 2mf. $10.00; 1321[1903]. – 3mf. $40.00) – 9 – us MEDOC [949]
NEVSAL-I MARIFET – 1309-1310 [1891-92], 11. Sene – 9 – $47.00 – us MEDOC [324]
NEVSAL-I SERVET-I FUENUN – (1314M[1898], 5. sene. $150.00) – 1313M [1897], 4. sene – 9 – $150.00 – us MEDOC [324]
NEVSKOE VREMIA – (Backfile through 1998 $85r) – 1999- – 4r per y – 1 – $320.00 standing order – us Ross [072]
NEVZAD-I VATAN – Istanbul. Sahib-i Imtiyaz ve Sermuharriri: Mehmed Suad. No. 1 (26 Agustos 1908) – 1mf – 9 – $12.00 – us MEDOC [949]
THE NEW ADVANCE – Charlotte, NC. v1-4 no 9. 1938-Jan 1947 – Inquire – 1 – ATLA S0685B – us A.T.L.A. [073]
NEW AFRICAN – (See also: New African Development and African Development) – 1978- – 1,5,6,9 – us UMI [305]
NEW AFRICAN DEVELOPMENT – 1977-1978 – 1,5,6,9 – us UMI [305]
NEW AFRICAN DEVELOPMENT *see* AFRICAN DEVELOPMENT
NEW AGE – Cape Town. Jun 1952-Oct 1954 gaps – 1 – 35.00r – us Hoover Inst Photo [072]
NEW AGE – Portland, OR. -w. 25 Nov 1899-4 May 1907. 2 rolls – 1 – us U.O. Library [071]
NEW AGE *see* GUARDIAN
THE NEW AGE – London. -w. Oct 1894-Apr 1938. (34 reels) – 1 – uk British Libr Newspaper [072]
NEW AGE, 1955-62 – Cape Town, South Africa – 1, 16 diazo available at reduced price – sa SA Libr [072]
NEW AGE DISPATCH – Los Angeles. Calif. Jan. 1, 8, 1937 – 1 – us NY Public [071]
NEW AGE JOURNAL – (1985-. 1,5,6) – 1974- – 9 – us UMI [073]
THE NEW AID TO MEMORY: PT. 4, ADAPTED TO THE NEW TESTAMENT / Knott, R R – O-870. 1846 – 9 – ne IDC [240]
A NEW ALICE IN THE OLD WONDERLAND / Richards, Anna Matlock – With 67 illus. by Anna M. Richards, jr.Philadelphia: J. Lippincott, c1895.309p. 1 reel.1243 – 1 – us U.W. Library [830]
NEW AMERICA – (1979- 5,6,9) – 1960- – 1 – us UMI [073]
NEW AMERICA – New York, 1963-65, 1974-76, 1978, 1981 (all incompl), 1979-80 – 1 – us Hoover Inst Photo [071]
NEW AMERICA – New York, NY. 1966-83 – 3r – 1 – $150.00 – R04914 – us Library Micro [071]
NEW AMERICAN – v1-. 1985- – 1,5,6,9 – us UMI [073]
THE NEW AMERICAN CHURCH MONTHLY – v43-45. 1938-39 (complete) – Inquire – 1 – ATLA 1994-S541 – us A.T.L.A. [073]
NEW AMERICAN MAGAZINE – no. 1-27. Jan 1758-Mar 1760 – 1 – us UMI [073]
NEW AMERICAN REVIEW *see* AR
NEW AMERICAN WOMAN – Los Angeles, CA. 1916-1918 – 1r – 1 – $50.00 – C03313 – us Library Micro [071]
A NEW AND CHOICE COLLECTION OF FLUTE MELODIES; CONSISTING OF DUETS, WALTZES, COTILLIONS, AIRS, MARCHES, &C. TO WHICH ARE PREFIXED THE INSTRUCTIONS FOR THE GERMAN FLUTE, AND PATENT FLAGELET – Utica, N.Y.: William Williams, 1817. Includes: "Comin' thro' the Rye." MUSIC 1990 – 1 – us L of C Photodup [780]
A NEW AND CHOICE SELECTION OF HYMNS AND SPIRITUAL SONGS / Thomas, E D – 1877. 4th ed – 1 – $19.60 – us Baptist [240]
A NEW AND COMPLETE DICTIONARY OF TERMS OF ART / Buys, Egbert – (konstwoordenboek). O-185. 2 v. 1768-1769 – 9 – ne IDC [700]
A NEW AND COMPLETE DICTIONARY OF TERMS OF ART... KONSTWOORDENBOEK / Buys, Egbert – Amsterdam. 2v. 1768-1769 – 24mf – ne IDC [700]
A NEW AND COMPLETE LAW DICTIONARY, OR, GENERAL ABRIDGMENT OF THE LAW:... / Cunningham, Thomas – London. 2v. 1764-1765 – 25mf – ne IDC [340]
A NEW AND COMPLETE PRECEPTOR FOR THE GERMAN FLUTE – 1819 – 5,15 – us Sibley [780]
A NEW AND EASIE FRENCH GRAMMAR / Festeau, Paul – 1667. 297p. (English Linguistics Series 1500-1800) – 9 – us UMI [440]
A NEW AND EASIE METHOD TO LEARN TO SING BY BOOK.. – 1686 – 2 – us Sibley [780]
NEW AND FORTHCOMING BOOKS – Published weekly – 17 – £85.00 (£99.00 Europe £105.00 Out Europe) – uk Whitaker [070]
A NEW AND GENERAL SYSTEM OF MUSIC OR THE ART OF MUSIC / Borghese, A D R – 1790 – 9 – us Sibley [780]
THE NEW AND HERE TO FORE UNFIGURED SPECIES OF THE BIRDS OF NORTH AMERICA / Elliot, Daniel Giraud – New York, (1866)-1869 – 2 vols – 8 – ne IDC [590]
NEW AND RARE LICHENS / Stirton, J – (Various articles in the "Scottish Naturalist.") 517. v. 4-5. 1877-1880 – 9 – ne IDC [580]
NEW ANNUAL REGISTER – 1780-1825 – 1 – us UMI [073]
THE NEW APOLOGETIC:...METHODS OF MEETING...ATTACKS UPON THE CHRISTIAN RELIGION / Terry, Milton Spenser – New York: Eaton & Mains, 1897. 1 fiche – 9 – us A.T.L.A. [240]
NEW APPROACH TO ENERGY PLANNING FOR SUSTAINABLE RURAL DEVELOPMENT – 1990 – 47p – it F.A.O. [333]
THE NEW APPROACH TO FREEDOM / Riegel, E C – New and original ed. with: Essays on the Separation of Money and the State.2 fiches. (24x) – 9 – 1.00f – at Libertarian Micro [320]
NEW APPROACHES TO RURAL YOUTH AND DEVELOPMENT IN LATIN AMERICA AND THE CARIBBEAN – 1981 – 104p – 9 – 92-3-101910-4 – fr UNESCO [307]
NEW ARABIAN NIGHTS / Stevenson, Robert Louis – London: Chatto & Windus, 1882 – 1 roll – 1 – 1-55879-963-X – uk Libr Preservation [830]
THE NEW ARCHAEOLOGICAL DISCOVERIES / Cobern, Camden M – 1921 – 9 – $24.00 – us I.R.C. [930]
NEW ARMUCHEE BAPTIST CHURCH. ARMUCHEE, GEORGIA : CHURCH RECORDS – 1900-78. 1896p – 1 – 85.32 – us Baptist [240]
A NEW ARRANGEMENT OF THE PROVERBS OF SOLOMON : CLASSIFIED ACCORDING TO THE SUBJECT OF EACH: TOGETHER WITH CRITICAL AND EXPLANATORY REMARKS, VARIOUS READINGS, ETC FOR THE USE OF BIBLE CLASSES AND SUNDAY-SCHOOL TEACHERS / Brooks, J W – London: Seeley, Jackson, and Halliday, 1860 – 1mf – 9 – 0-8370-9206-X – 1986-3206 – us A.T.L.A. [220]
NEW ASHANTI TIMES – Kumasi, Ghana, 1966-67 – 1r – 1 – us Ross [072]
NEW ASHFORD 1755-1859 – (Mf 1T: Marriage Intentions 1785-1842; Marriages 1834-38; Births & Deaths 1755-1859. Mf 2T: Marriages & Intentions 1805-15; Births 1838-49; Marriages 1837-52; Deaths 1843-49) – (mf ed 1998) – 9 – 0-87623-301-9 – us Holbrook [920]
NEW ASHFORD 1844-1920 – (Mf 1: Births 1844-1920, Marriages 1837-1921. Mf 2: Deaths 1846-1921) – (mf ed 1988) – 2mf – 9 – 0-87623-071-0 – us Holbrook [920]
NEW ATLAS – Vale, OR. -w. 5 Sept 1889-25 Oct 1890. 1 roll – 1 – us U.O. Library [071]
THE NEW AURORA *see*
– L'AURORA
– IL CHRISTIANO
NEW BAPTIST PRAISE BOOK – Ed. by Benjamin Shepard and William M. Lawrence. 1923 – 1 – 19.11 – us Baptist [240]
NEW BEDFORD 1650-1849 – (Mf 1T-6T: Marriage Intentions 1787-1815. Mf 4T-5T: Marriages 1787-1814. Mf 6T-8T: Births & Deaths 1754-1819. Mf 8T: Marriages 1812-22; Deaths 1785-1833. Mf 8T-22T: Marriage Intentions 1823-47. Mf 10T-11T: Marriages 1822-36. Mf 16T,22T-23T: Marriages 1830-43. Mf 24T-25T: Births & Deaths 1650-1844; Quaker Vitals 1764-1861. Mf 25T-26T: Marriage Intents 1815-23. Mf 27T: Births 1779-1835. Mf 28T-33T: Births 1843-46. Mf33T-35T: Marriages 1839-46. Mf 35T-36T: Births 1846-48. Mf 35T,38T: Deaths 1844-48. Mf 37T-38T: Marriages 1844-48. Mf 38T-41T: Marriage Intents 1847-49. Mf 41T-43T: Births 1848-49. Mf 43T-44T: Marriages 1848-49. Mf 44T-45T: Deaths 1848-49. Mf 45T: Depositions 1811-47) – (mf ed 1998) – 45mf – 9 – 0-87623-302-7 – us Holbrook [920]
NEW BETHEL BAPTIST CHURCH. EDDYVILLE, KENTUCKY : CHURCH RECORDS – 1812-38 – 1 – 57.87 – us Baptist [240]
NEW BETHEL BAPTIST CHURCH. KINGS MOUNTAIN ASSOCIATION. LAWNDALE, NORTH CAROLINA : CHURCH RECORDS – 1850-1963 – 1 – 60.12 – us Baptist [240]
NEW BIOTECH – (Ceased v4 1990) – Ottawa. v4. 1990 – 9 – Can$20.00y – cn Micromedia [660]
THE NEW BIRTH : OR, THE WORK OF THE HOLY SPIRIT / Phelps, Austin – (British ed publ as: Man's renewal, or, The work of the Holy Spirit) – Boston: Gould and Lincoln, 1867, c1866 – 1mf – 9 – 0-8370-5452-4 – 1985-3452 – us A.T.L.A. [240]
NEW BLACKFRIARS – v1- 1920- 1; v52- 5,6; v57- 9 – us UMI [073]
A NEW BOOKE OF DESTILLATYON / Gesner, C – Trans. from Latin by P. Morwyng. M 355 – 9 – ne IDC [540]
New Boston, New Hampshire. New Boston Baptist Church and Society *see* RECORDS
NEW BOSTON REVIEW – Boston, MA. 1975-1985 – 3r – 1 – $150.00 – R04377 – us Library Micro [071]
NEW BOSTON REVIEW – v. 1-6. 1975-81 – 1 – us UMI [410]
NEW BRAINTREE 1729-1849 – (Mf 1T,3T: deaths 1772-99. Mf 1T-3T: Marriage Intentions 1787-1836. Mf 1T-5T: Marriages 1755-1843. Mf 1T-2T: Births & Deaths 1729-99. Mf 4T-5T: Births 1752-1843. Mf 5T: Deaths 1793-1841; Marriage Intentions 1836-49. Mf 6T: Vital Records 1843-49) – (mf ed 1998) – 6mf – 9 – 0-87623-303-5 – us Holbrook [920]
NEW BRAINTREE 1751-1913 – (Mf 1-7: Town & Vital Records 1751-99. Mf 8: Intentions 1800-35; Marriages 1796-1826. Mf 8-9: Births & Deaths 1732-1843. Mf 10: Marriages 1833-42; Intentions 1836-1912. Mf 11: Biths & Marriages 1843-63. Mf 12: Deaths 1843-63. Mf 13: Births 1864-1897. Mf 14: Births 1898-1913; Marriages 1864-83. Mf 15: Marriages 1883-1913. Mf 16: Deaths 1864-93. Mf 17: Deaths 1894-1913) – (mf ed 1988) – 17mf – 9 – 0-87623-086-9 – us Holbrook [920]
THE NEW BREED – Regina, Saskatchewan. 1970-79. (American Indian Periodicals in the Princeton University Library). 20 fiches – 9 – $85.00 – us UPA [305]
NEW BREED NEWS – 1970-75. (American Indian Periodicals in the Princeton University Library). 5 fiches – 9 – $45.00 – us UPA [305]
NEW BRITAIN – Quarterly organ of the 11th Hour Group. London. Oct 1932-Autumn 1934, 29 Jan-25 Mar 1935. (2 reels) – 1 – uk British Libr Newspaper [073]
NEW BRITAIN PATROL REPORTS, 1926-1931 / Mack, Ian McCallum – 1r – 1 – at Pacific Mss [350]
NEW BRITISH LADY'S MAGAZINE – v. 1-NS v. 3. 1815-19 – 1 – us UMI [073]
New Brunswick *see* ROYAL GAZETTE
New Brunswick. Canada *see*
– NEW BRUNSWICK EQUITY REPORTS
– NEW BRUNSWICK REPORTS
– NEW BRUNSWICK STATUTES, SESSION LAWS AND REVISIONS
– ROYAL GAZETTE
– STOCKTON'S VICE-ADMIRALTY CASES
– TRUEMAN'S NEW BRUNSWICK EQUITY CASES
New Brunswick. Canada. Court of Chancery *see* RULES AND STATUTES REGULATING THE PRACTICE OF THE COURT OF CHANCERY IN THIS PROVINCE
New Brunswick. Canada. Supreme Court *see* GENERAL RULES AND ORDERS.
NEW BRUNSWICK COURIER – (Also known as: Courier) – Saint John, Canada. 1811-65 – 14r – 1 – $910.00 – cn Library Assoc [971]
NEW BRUNSWICK EDUCATIONAL ADMINISTRATOR – Fredericton. nos 6-32. 1987-94 – 9 – Can$20.00y – cn Micromedia [370]
NEW BRUNSWICK EQUITY REPORTS / New Brunswick. Canada – (v1-3 are by Trueman. v4 by Forbes) – v1-4. 1894-1911 (all publ) – 27mf – 9 – $40.50 – LLMC 81-027 – us L.L.M.C. [340]
THE NEW BRUNSWICK JOURNAL OF EDUCATION – Saint John, NB: Barnes, [1886-1887] – 9 – cn C.I.H.M. [370]
NEW BRUNSWICK MAGAZINE – Saint John. v1-5. 1898-1905 – 5 – Can$100.00 – cn Micromedia [073]
New Brunswick & Nova Scotia. Presbytery (Ref. Pres. Ch. of N.A.) *see* MINUTES, 1832-1919
New Brunswick. Presbytery (Pres. Ch. in the U.S.A.) *see* MINUTES, 1738-1798
NEW BRUNSWICK REPORTER – Fredericton, Canada. 1844-1902 – 26r – 1 – $1,690.00 – cn Library Assoc [971]
NEW BRUNSWICK REPORTS / New Brunswick. Canada – (Cont by 2nd series not offered by LLMC) – 1st series: v1-54. 1825-29 (all publ) – 391mf – 9 – $586.00 – LLMC 81-026 – us L.L.M.C. [340]
NEW BRUNSWICK ROYAL GAZETTE – (v127-140 1969-82 Can$105.00y 5. v141- 1983-9) – v115- 1957- – 1,5,9 – Price varies – cn Micromedia [971]

NEW BRUNSWICK STATUTES, SESSION LAWS AND REVISIONS / New Brunswick. Canada – (Updates planned) – 1871-47th Legislative 3rd sess. 1871-1973 – 639mf – 9 – $958.00 – LLMC 90-140 – us L.L.M.C. [324]
NEW BULBOUS AND TUBEROUS ROOTED PLANTS / Tubergen, C G van – 737. 1947 – 9 – ne IDC [580]
NEW BULLETIN *see* ACCOUNTING EDUCATION
New Caledonia *see* JOURNAL OFFICIEL DE LA NOUVELLE-CALEDONIE
NEW CAMP CREEK BAPTIST CHURCH. KINGS MOUNTAIN, NORTH CAROLINA : CHURCH RECORDS – 1957-63 – 1 – 5.00 – us Baptist [240]
THE NEW CAMPAIGN *see* AGE OF FREEDOM
NEW CANADA; ANTI-IMPERIALIST NEWSPAPER – v. 1-7. 1970-76 – 1 – 130.00 – cn McLaren [072]
NEW CANADIAN – (In Japanese) – Canada, 1939- – 1 – cn Commonwealth Micro [072]
NEW CANADIAN REVIEW – (Ceased v3 no 1 1991) – Pointe-Claire Dorval. v1-3. 1987/88/89-1991 – 9 – Can$20.00y – cn Micromedia [420]
NEW CARAVAN – New York. v1-5. 1927-36 – 1r – 1 – us Ross [073]
NEW CASTLE COURANT – New Castle, PA. -w 1870-1896 – 13 – $25.00r – us I.M.R. [071]
NEW CASTLE DEMOCRAT – New Castle, PA. -w 1886-1921 – 13 – $25.00r – us I.M.R. [071]
NEW CASTLE HERALD, THE HERALD – New Castle, PA. -w, -d 1906-1924 – 13 – $25.00r – us I.M.R. [071]
New Castle. Presbytery (Pres. Ch. in the U.S.A.) *see*
– MINUTES
– RECORDS
NEW CATALOGUS CATALOGORUM : AN ALPHABETICAL REGISTER OF SANSKRIT AND ALLIED WORKS AND AUTHORS / ed by Raghavan, V – Madras. v1-8. 1966-1974 – 40mf – 9 – ne IDC [490]
NEW CATHOLIC WORLD – (v. 208- 1968- 5,6. v. 210- 1969- 9) – v. 1- 1865- – 1 – us UMI [240]
NEW CENTURY REVIEW – A Monthly International Review of Literature, Politics, Religion and Sociology. London. v. 1-8. 1897-1900 – 1 – us NY Public [320]
NEW CENTURY REVIEW – London. v1-8. 1897-1900 – 2r – 1 – us Ross [073]
NEW CHALLENGE – Boston. v1-2. 1934-37 – 1r – 1 – us Ross [073]
NEW CHALLENGE – v1-2 2+2 (all publ). 1934-1937 – 4mf – 9 – $55.00 – us UPA [335]
A NEW CHAMELEON FROM MT. RUWENZORI / Parker, H W – Z-139 2. 1929 – 8 – ne IDC [590]
A NEW CHAPTER ADDED TO POLITICAL ECONOMY: POINTING OUT A 100 MILLION DOLLARS CAPITAL THAT MAY BE MADE AVAILABLE TO CANADIAN INDUSTRIES BY THE ESTABLISHMENT OF A MORTGAGE BANK OF ISSUE / Galbraith, Thomas – Toronto: Hunter, Rose, 1882. 03284. (Pre-1900 Canadiana) – 9 – cn C.I.H.M. [336]
New, Charles *see* LIFE, WANDERINGS AND LABOURS IN EASTERN AFRICA..
NEW CHINA – v1- 1975- 1; v4- 5,6,9 – us UMI [950]
THE NEW CHINA WEEKLY – v1, no.1-3. 17-31 May 1946. Published by Communist Party of China. Shanghai. Banned by the Kuomintang government after 3 issues.F-E9 – 9 – $20.00f – cc Microforms [073]
THE NEW CHRISTIANITY – v1-16. 1935-50 (complete) – Inquire – 1 – ATLA 1994-S537 – us A.T.L.A. [073]
THE NEW CHRONICLE – Roseau, Dominica. Jan 22 1983; Nov 15 1985; Apr 11 1986-Nov 27 1987 – 1r – 1 – us L of C Photodup [072]
NEW CHURCH REVIEW – Boston. 1894-1906 – 1 – us UMI [240]
NEW CHURCH REVIEW – Chicago. v. 1-2. Apr 1882-Jan 1884 – 1 – us UMI [240]
NEW CHURCH TIDINGS – Toronto: [s.n, 1888?-18– or 19–] – 9 – cn C.I.H.M. [240]
NEW CITY SONGSTER – 9 – $55.00 – us UPA [780]
THE NEW CLERK'S ASSISTANT, OR BOOK OF PRACTICAL FORMS; CONTAINING NUMEROUS PRECEDENTS AND FORMS FOR ORDINARY BUSINESS TRANSACTIONS. / Jenkins, John Stilwell – Albany, N.Y., Little, 1869. 620 p. LL-376 – 1 – us L of C Photodup [340]
A NEW CODE OF INTERNATIONAL LAW / Internoscia, Jerome – In English, French and Italian. Very good on minority rights. 11 fiches (24x) – 9 – 1.00f – at Libertarian Micro [340]
A NEW COLLECTION OF INSTRUMENTAL MUSIC, IN THREE PARTS, ARRANGED FOR THE VIOLIN, CLARIONETT, BASS-VIOL, ETC / Floyd, Thomas – Boston: Musical Gazette Press–Kldeer & Wright, Printers, 1839. MUSIC 1996 – 1 – us L of C Photodup [780]
NEW COMMENTARY ON GENESIS / Delitzsch, Franz – 1889 – 9 – $30.00 – us I.R.C. [220]
A NEW COMMENTARY ON THE GOSPEL ACCORDING TO MATTHEW / Nicholson, Edward Byron – London: C. Kegan Paul, 1881. 1 fiche – 9 – us A.T.L.A. [240]
NEW COMMUNICATION TECHNOLOGIES : A CHALLENGE FOR PRESS FREEDOM / ed by Sparks, Colin – 1994 – 119p – 9 – 92-3-102791-3 – fr UNESCO [303]
NEW COMMUNICATION TECHNOLOGIES : RESEARCH TRENDS – 1991 – 9 – 92-3-102678-X – fr UNESCO [303]
THE NEW COMPREHENSIVE NATIONAL DEVELOPMENT PLAN (SUMMARY) AND ITS IMPLEMENTATION / Japan. Office for Research on R and D Economic Planning Agency – Dec. 1972. BD-1810 1 – 9 – ne IDC [338]
NEW CONCEPT OF DEVELOPMENT : BASIC TENETS / Perroux, Francois – 1983 – 224p – 9 – 92-3-102057-9 – fr UNESCO [338]
A NEW CONCORDANCE TO THE HOLY SCRIPTURES : BEING THE MOST COMPREHENSIVE AND CONCISE OF ANY BEFORE PUBLISHED / Butterworth, John – Boston: Crocker and Brewster; New York: Jonathan Leavitt, 1843 – 2mf – 9 – 0-8370-9369-4 – 1986-3369 – us A.T.L.A. [220]
A NEW CONSTITUTION FOR A NEW AMERICA / MacDonald, William – New York: B W Huebsch, 1921 – 3mf – 9 – $4.50 – LLMC 95-085 – us L.L.M.C. [323]
NEW CONVERSATIONS – v1-13. 1975-91 (complete) – Inquire – 1 – ATLA S0808 – us A.T.L.A. [073]
A NEW COURSE OF ENGLISH FOR SCHOOLS IN INDONESIA / Rottier, Ch. J M – SE-4893 1. v. 1-2 only. v. 2. 3rd ed 1948-1949 – 9 – ne IDC [370]
A NEW COVENANT / Smith, L Neil – 1p – 9 – 1.00f – at Libertarian Micro [335]
NEW COVENANT – (1985-. 5,6,9) – v1-. 1971- – 1 – us UMI [240]
NEW CRITERION – (1986- . 5,6,9) – v1- . 1982- – 1 – us UMI [410]
NEW CRUSADER – Chicago. Ill. 1940- – 1 – us UMI [071]
NEW CUBAHATCHIE BAPTIST CHURCH. SHORTER, ALABAMA : CHURCH RECORDS – 1850-64 – 1 – 8.91 – us Baptist [240]
NEW DAILY CHRONICLE – Georgetown, Guyana. -d. 1 Jan 1930-19 May 1936. 39 reels – 1 – uk British Libr Newspaper [072]
NEW DAILY CHRONICLE – Guiana. 1927-1935 – 1 – us UMI [072]
NEW DAY – National and International. Featuring the Works of Father Divine. New York, Philadelphia etc. v. 1-33. May 28 1936-1969. Incomplete – 1 – us NY Public [240]
NEW DAY – Philadelphia. v1-38. 1936-74 – 52r – 1 – us Ross [071]
NEW DAY! : THE NATIONAL SOCIALIST WEEKLY – 1-4 2+29 (all publ). 1920-22 – 1r – 1 – $115.00 – us UPA [335]
NEW DEAL AGENCIES AND BLACK AMERICA / ed by Kriby, John B – 25 reels with printed guide – 1 – $2,750.00 – 0-89093-656-0 – us UPA [360]
NEW DEAL ECONOMIC POLICIES : FDR AND THE CONGRESS, 1933-1938 – (Guide only $215.00) – 9 – $2,015.00 – 1-55655-283-1 – us UPA [330]
A NEW DEAL FOR PAPUA / Cranswick, G H – Melbourne: F.W. Cheshire, (1949). xiii,159p. Plates, ports., map – 1 – us U.W. Library [240]
A NEW DICTIONARY FRENCH AND ENGLISH / Miege, Guy – 1677 – 9 – fr I.C.S. [440]
NEW DIGEST / Dominican Province of Saint Joseph – v1-23, Nov 1958-82. 1 reel – 1 – uc A.T.L.A. [073]
NEW DIMENSIONS *see* ONTARIO EDUCATION DIMENSIONS
NEW DIRECTIONS – (Incorporated in: Pacific Current v1 no 1 1994) – Vancouver. v1-8. 1985/86-1993/94 – 9 – Can$20.00y – cn Micromedia [100]
NEW DIRECTIONS *see* PACIFIC CURRENT
NEW DIRECTIONS FOR CHILD DEVELOPMENT – 1978- – 1,5,6,9 – us UMI [073]
NEW DIRECTIONS FOR COMMUNITY COLLEGES – v1- 1973- 1; v3- 5,6,9 us UMI [370]
NEW DIRECTIONS FOR CONTINUING EDUCATION – 1979- – 1,5,6,9 – us UMI [073]
NEW DIRECTIONS FOR EDUCATION AND WORK – v.1-5. 1978-79. Continued by New Directions for Education, Work and Careers – 1 – us UMI [073]
NEW DIRECTIONS FOR EDUCATION, WORK, AND CAREERS – v.6-8. 1979 – 1 – us UMI [073]
NEW DIRECTIONS FOR EXCEPTIONAL CHILDREN – v.1-. 1980- – 1,5,6,9 – us UMI [073]
NEW DIRECTIONS FOR EXPERIMENTAL LEARNING – no.20-.1983- – 1,5,6,9 – us UMI [073]
NEW DIRECTIONS FOR EXPERIMENTAL LEARNING – v.1-. 1978- – 1,5,6,9 – us UMI [073]
NEW DIRECTIONS FOR HIGHER EDUCATION – v1- 1973- 1; v9- 5,6,9 – us UMI [370]
NEW DIRECTIONS FOR INSTITUTIONAL ADVANCEMENT – v.1-. 1978- – 1,5,6,9 – us UMI [073]
NEW DIRECTIONS FOR INSTITUTIONAL RESEARCH – Spring 1974- 1,5,6; 1976- 9 – us UMI [370]
NEW DIRECTIONS FOR MENTAL HEALTH SERVICES – v.1-. 1979- – 1,5,6,9 – us UMI [073]
NEW DIRECTIONS FOR METHODOLOGY OF BEHAVIORAL SCIENCE – v.1-2. 1979. Continued by New Directions for Methodology of Social and Behavioral Science – 1,5,6,9 – us UMI [073]
NEW DIRECTIONS FOR METHODOLOGY OF SOCIAL AND BEHAVIORAL SCIENCE – v.3-. 1980- – 1,5,6,9 – us UMI [073]
NEW DIRECTIONS FOR PROGRAM EVALUATION – v.1-. 1978- – 1,5,6,9 – us UMI [073]
NEW DIRECTIONS FOR STUDENT SERVICES – v.1-. 1978- – 1,5,6,9 – us UMI [073]
NEW DIRECTIONS FOR TEACHING AND LEARNING – v.1-. 1980- – 1,5,6,9 – us UMI [073]
NEW DIRECTIONS FOR TESTING AND MEASUREMENT – v1- 1979- – 1,5,6,9 – us UMI [670]
NEW DIRECTIONS IN AV VIDEO *see*
– AV VIDEO
NEW DIRECTIONS OF COLLEGE LEARNING ASSISTANCE – 1980- – 1,5,6,9 – us UMI [073]
A NEW DISCOVERY OF THE OLD ART OF TEACHING SCHOOLE / Hoole, Charles – 1660. 341p. (English Linguistics Series 1500-1800) – 9 – us UMI [400]
THE NEW DISCUSSION OF THE TRINITY – 1867 – 9 – us A.T.L.A. [240]
THE NEW DOMINION – Morgantown. West Virginia. 1877-1917 – 1 – us UMI [071]
THE NEW DOMINION – Ormstown, Canada. v2 n14. 9 avr 1874-v10 n1. 5 jan 1882 – 1r – 1 – Can$40.00 – cn Can Microfilming [072]
NEW DOMINION AND TRUE HUMORIST – Saint John, Canada. 1864-78 – 4r – 1 – $260.00 – cn Library Assoc [971]
NEW DOMINION MONTHLY – v1-4. Oct 1867-Jan 1879. Missing 1872-73 – 1 – cn Precision [971]
NEW DRIVER – 1984- – 1,5,6,9 – us UMI [380]
NEW EARTH CATALOG – 1973- 1; 1974- 5,6; 1975- 4 x 6 in. 9 – us UMI [073]
THE NEW EAST – v3-27. 1908-33 (incomplete) – 1r – 1 – ATLA S0703G – us A.T.L.A. [073]
NEW ECHOTA, BIRTHPLACE OF THE AMERICAN INDIAN PRESS / National Park Service – 1941. (American Indian Periodicals in the Princeton University Library). 1 fiche – 9 – $45.00 – us UPA [305]
NEW ECONOMIC AND SOCIAL DEVELOPMENT PLAN, 1970-1975 / Japan. Economic Planning Agency – May. 1970. BD-1799 1 – 9 – ne IDC [338]
A NEW EDITION OF SIX CONCERTOS, FOR THE HARPSICHORD OR ORGAN / Handel, George Frederic – London: H Wright, [ca. 1785] – 1 – us Sibley [780]
NEW EDUCATION POLICY AND NEW SYSTEM OF SCHOOL FEES / Nigeria. North-Central State. Ministry of Information – 1971 – 1mf – 9 – DE-105/1 – ne IDC [370]
NEW EDUCATION SYSTEM (PRIMARY LEVEL) : IMPLEMENTATION GUIDELINES / Singapore. Ministry of Education – Singapore, 1979 – 1mf – 9 – DE-257/1 – ne IDC [370]
NEW EDUCATION SYSTEM (SECONDARY LEVEL) : IMPLEMENTATION GUIDELINES / Singapore. Ministry of Education – Singapore, 1980 – 1mf – 9 – DE-258/1 – ne IDC [370]
NEW ELLER BYNES (OG BUVIK) EN BYGDEBESKRIVELSE / Hoyem, OJ – 2nd ed. Trondhjem, 1894. 310p – 1 – us U.W. Library [948]
THE NEW ENCYCLOPAEDIA BRITANNICA ON THEOLOGY / Charteris, Archibald Hamilton – (The Edinburgh courant, April 15, 1876) – 9 – us A.T.L.A. [240]
THE NEW ENCYCLOPAEDIA OF SOCIAL REFORM / ed by Bliss, W D P – 1909. 1416p – 9 – 1.00f – at Libertarian Micro [335]
NEW ENGINEER – v1-8 1971-79 1; v5-8 5,6,9 – us UMI [620]
NEW ENGLAND ADVERTISING WEEK – (1985-. 5,6,9) – v1-v23,no.5. 1964-Jan 1986 – 1 – us UMI [073]
NEW ENGLAND ADVERTISING WEEK *see* ADWEEK
THE NEW ENGLAND BAPTIST – Northboro, MA. 1986-91. 583p – 1 – $30.44 – us Baptist [071]
NEW ENGLAND BASE BALLI NATIONAL CHRONICLE – Boston, MA. 1868, 1869 – 1r – 1 – $40.00r – us U.N.D. Archives [790]
NEW ENGLAND BUSINESS REVIEW – (See: New England Economic Review). 1919-68 – 1 – us UMI [380]
New England Cooperative Extension *see* PUBLICATION NEC
NEW ENGLAND ECONOMIC INDICATORS – 1969- 1; 1970 5,6; 1976- 4 x 6 in. 9 – us UMI [339]
NEW ENGLAND ECONOMIC REVIEW – 1969- 1; 1970- 5,6; 1976- 4 x 6 in. 9 – us UMI [330]
New England Emigrant Aid Co. Trustees *see* MINUTES OF MEETINGS
New England Emigrant Aid Company *see* PAPERS
NEW ENGLAND FARMER – v. 1-n.s. v. 5. 9 Dec 1848-Dec 1871 – 1 – us UMI [630]
NEW ENGLAND FARMER AND HORTICULTURAL JOURNAL, 1822-1846 – 213mf – 9 – £790.00 – uk Chadwyck [630]
NEW ENGLAND FARMER AND HORTICULTURAL REGISTER – 1822-46.24v – 9 – 410.00 – us Opus [630]
NEW ENGLAND FARMER AND HORTICULTURAL REGISTER – v. 1-4. Aug 1822-90 – 1 – us UMI [630]
NEW ENGLAND GALAXY – Boston. Mass. 1817-20 – 3 – us Readex [071]
THE NEW ENGLAND GAZETTEER: CONTAINING DESCRIPTIONS OF ALL THE STATES, COUNTIES, & TOWNS IN NEW ENGLAND – By John Hayward, 1839. Alphabetially arranged. 8 fiches. F-0625 – 9 – us A.G.L.L. [920]
New England Historic Genealogical Society *see* THE GREENLAW INDEX..
NEW ENGLAND HISTORICAL AND GENEALOGICAL RECORD, 1865-1911 – (Missing: 1866, 1868, 1876, 1879, 1886, 1893, 1896, 1898, 1899) – 269mf – 9,5 – $200.00 – B50012 – us Library Micro [920]
NEW ENGLAND HISTORICAL AND GENEALOGICAL REGISTER – Jan 1847-1905 – 1 – us UMI [920]
THE NEW ENGLAND HISTORICAL AND GENEALOGICAL REGISTER ON MICROFILM – (Reel 1: Index to v1-50. Reel 2: v1-8 1847-1854. Reel 3: v9-16 1855-1862. Reel 4: v17-24 1863-1870. Reel 5: v25-31 1871-1877. Reel 6: v32-39 1878-1885. Reel 7: v40-45 1886-1891. Reel 8: v46-50 1892-1896. Reel 9: v51-55 1896-1901. Reel 10: v56-59 1902-1905. Reel 11: v60-64 1906-1910. Reel 12: v65-69 1911-1915. Reel

13: v70-75 1916-1921. Reel 14: v76-80 1922-1926. Reel 15: v81-84 1927-1930. Reel 16: v85-89 1931-1935. Reel 17: v90-94 1936-1940. Reel 18: v95-99 1941-1945. Reel 19: v100-105 1946-1951. Reel 20: v106-111 1952-1957. Reel 21: v112-116 1958-1962. Reel 22: v117-121 1963-1967. Reel 23: v122-126 1968-1972. Reel 24: v127-131 1973-1977. Reel 25: v132-136 1978-1982. Reel 26: v137-141 1983-1987) – v1-141. 1847-1987 – 26r – 1 – $780.00 $30.00r – us New England [920]

THE NEW ENGLAND HISTORICAL AND GENEALOGICAL REGISTERS – v1-88, 105, 108, 119. 1847-1934, 1951, 1954, 1965. Z100-0001 to Z100-0019, SW16-0140, SW16-0123, SW16-0050 – 5 – us A.G.L.L. [978]

New England Historical & Genealogical Register *see* INDEXES

NEW ENGLAND JOURNAL OF DENTISTRY AND ALLIED SCIENCE – v. 1-3, no. 12. Jan 1882-Dec 1884 – 1 – us UMI [617]

NEW ENGLAND JOURNAL OF HUMAN SERVICES – v.1-. 1981- – 1,5,6,9 – us UMI [073]

NEW ENGLAND JOURNAL OF MEDICINE – (v. 272- 1965- 5,6. v. 282- 1970- 9) – v. 1-1828- – 1 – us UMI [610]

NEW ENGLAND JOURNAL OF MEDICINE – v1-309. 1828-1983. Continues: Boston Medical and Surgical Journal – 1,5,6,9 – us Princeton Micro [610]

NEW ENGLAND JOURNAL OF MEDICINE AND SURGERY, AND COLLATERAL BRANCHES OF SCIENCE – Jan 1812-Oct 1826 – 1 – us UMI [616]

NEW ENGLAND JOURNAL ON CRIMINAL AND CIVIL CONFINEMENT – (Cont: New England Journal on Prison Law) – v1-20. 1974-94 – 1,5,6 – $225.00 – us Hein [073]

NEW ENGLAND JOURNAL ON PRISON LAW *see* NEW ENGLAND JOURNAL ON CRIMINAL AND CIVIL CONFINEMENT

THE NEW ENGLAND KITCHEN : A MONTHLY JOURNAL OF DOMESTIC SCIENCE – Boston, MA: The New England Kitchen Publ Co. v1 n1-2 apr-may 1894 – us Res Libr [640]

NEW ENGLAND LAW REVIEW – (v1-20 1965-85 on reel $245.00. v21-30 1986-96 on mf $186.00. Title varies: v1-4 1965-68 as Portia Law Journal) – v1-30. 1965-96 – 5,6,9 – $431.00 set – us Hein [340]

NEW ENGLAND LITERARY HERALD – no. 1-2. Sep 1809-Jan 1810 – 1 – us UMI [410]

NEW ENGLAND MAGAZINE – An Illustrated Monthly. 1-n.s. 56, no. 6. Jan 1884-Mar 1917 – 1 – us UMI [073]

NEW ENGLAND MAGAZINE – v. 1-9. Jul 1831-Dec 1835 – 1 – us UMI [073]

NEW ENGLAND MAGAZINE OF KNOWLEDGE AND PLEASURE – v. 1-3. Aug1758- Mar 1759 – 1 – us UMI [073]

NEW ENGLAND MARRIAGES PRIOR TO 1700 / Torrey, Clarence Almon – (Contains the bibliographical references not in the published volume) – 7r – 1 – $200.00 – us New England [920]

NEW ENGLAND MISSIONARY INTELLIGENCER AND GENERAL REPOSITORY – v. 1. Jan-Oct 1819 – 1 – us UMI [240]

NEW ENGLAND MISSIONARY MAGAZINE – For Promoting Useful Knowledge and Evangelical Doctrine. no. 1-4. 1815 – 1 – us UMI [240]

NEW ENGLAND MONTHLY – 1984- – 1,5,6,9 – us UMI [073]

THE NEW ENGLAND PSALM-SINGER: OR, AMERICAN CHORISTER / Billings, William – Boston: Edos and Gill 1770?. MUSIC 1099 – 1 – us L of C Photodup [780]

NEW ENGLAND QUARTERLY – v. 1-18. 1928-1945 – 1 – us Princeton Micro [073]

NEW ENGLAND QUARTERLY – (v. 43- 1970- 5,6. v. 48- 1975- 9) – v. 23- 1950- – 1 – us UMI [978]

NEW ENGLAND QUARTERLY MAGAZINE – no. 1-3. Apr Jun-Oct Dec 1802 – 1 – us UMI [073]

New England Railroad Club *see* OFFICIAL PROCEEDINGS

THE NEW ENGLAND REPORTER – (Covers ME, NH, VT, MA, RI and CT) – Rochester: Lawyers' Co-op. v1-6. 1885-88 (all publ) – 9 – LLMC 95-117 – us L.L.M.C. [340]

NEW ENGLAND REVIEW AND BREAD LOAF QUARTERLY: NER/BLQ – v5-. 1982- – 1,5,6,9 – us UMI [800]

NEW ENGLAND SOCIAL STUDIES BULLETIN – v1- 1944- 1; v28- 5,6; v34- 9 – us UMI [300]

New England. Synod *see* MINUTES, 1776-1782

New England. Synod (Pres. Ch. in the U.S.A.) *see* MINUTES, 1912-1958

THE NEW ENGLAND THEOCRACY : A HISTORY OF THE CONGREGATIONALISTS IN NEW ENGLAND TO THE REVIVALS OF 1740 / Uhden, H F – Boston: Gould and Lincoln, 1859, c1858 – 1mf – us A.T.L.A. [240]

NEW ENGLAND TOWNSMAN – Hallowell, ME: Maine Municipal Association. v1-9. 1939-47 – 1r – 1 – us Res Libr [073]

New England Water Works Association *see* – JOURNAL

NEW ENGLAND WINE MERCHANT – Hartford. Conn. And Brewers Gazette 1894-99 – 1 – us UMI [640]

NEW ENGLAND WOMEN AND THEIR FAMILIES IN THE 18TH AND 19TH CENTURIES: PERSONAL PAPERS, LETTERS, AND DIARIES : SERIES A, MANUSCRIPT COLLECTIONS FROM THE AMERICAN ANTIQUARIAN SOCIETY. PART 1: SELECTED NEW ENGLAND COLLECTIONS / ed by Rothman, Ellen K – (With printed guide) – 1997 – ca 35r – 1 – ca $4,595.00 – 1-55655-644-6 – us UPA [305]

NEW ENGLANDER AND YALE REVIEW – v. 1-56. 1843-92 – 1 – us UMI [073]

NEW ENGLANDERS IN NOVA SCOTIA / Crowell, Fred E – 1979 – 1r – 1 – $30.00 – us New England [920]

NEW ENGLANDS MEMORIALL / Morton, Nathaniel – 1669 – 9 – 15.00 – us Scholars' Facs [978]

NEW ENGLAND'S STRUGGLES FOR RELIGIOUS LIBERTY / Ford, David B – 1896 – 1 – 10.01 – us Baptist [240]

A NEW ENGLISH DICTIONARY / Kersey, John – 1702. 293p. (English Linguistics Series 1500-1800) – 9 – us UMI [420]

A NEW ENGLISH GRAMMAR / Duncan, Daniel – 1731. 92p. (English Linguistics Series 1500-1800) – 9 – us UMI [420]

A NEW ENGLISH GRAMMAR / Kirkby, John – 1746. 209p. (English Linguistics Series 1500-1800) – 9 – us UMI [420]

NEW ENGLISH WEEKLY – London. -w. Apr 1932-Sep 1949. (12 reels) – 1 – uk British Libr Newspaper [072]

NEW EQUIPMENT DIGEST – v. 1- 1936- – 1 – us UMI [621]

NEW ERA – A Monthly Periodical, Devoted to the Interests of Religion and Humanity and to the Diffusion of Knowledge on Judaism and Jewish Literature. v. 1-6. Oct 1870-76 – 1 – us UMI [290]

NEW ERA – Alturas, CA. Feb 1901-Aug 1925 – 10r – 1 – $500.00 – B02009 – us Library Micro [071]

NEW ERA – Auburn. Ind. 1860-1864 – 1 – us UMI [071]

NEW ERA – Corning, CA. 1906-20 – 2r – 1 – $100.00 – B02140 – us Library Micro [071]

NEW ERA – Grasshopper Falls. Kan. 1866-1877 – 1 – us UMI [071]

NEW ERA – Lancaster. Pa. 1923-1940; 1945- – 1 – us UMI [071]

NEW ERA / ed by McGee, T D'Arcy – Montreal, Canada. 27 May 1857-1 May 1858 – 1r – 1 – Can$50.00 – cn Can Microfilming [072]

NEW ERA – Monterey, CA. 1890-1909; 1904-10 (scats) – 5r – 1 – $250.00 – B02483 – us Library Micro [071]

NEW ERA – Montreal, Canada. 1857-58 – 1 reel – 1 – $68.00 – cn Library Assoc [971]

NEW ERA – Omaha, NE. -w. Jul 1922-Aug 1926 – 1 – us NE Hist [071]

NEW ERA – Perris. Calif. 1894-1896 – 1 – us UMI [071]

NEW ERA – Sargent, NE. -w. Apr 1899-Oct 1902 – 1 – us NE Hist [071]

NEW ERA – Sweet Home, OR. -w. 3 Jan 1930-. – 1 – us U.O. Library [071]

NEW ERA – Tupelo. Miss. -w. 1919-20 – 1 – us UMI [071]

NEW ERA – Valley Falls. Kan. 1878-1916 – 1 – us UMI [071]

NEW ERA – Wahoo. Neb. 1890-1899 – 1 – us UMI [071]

THE NEW ERA – (New York). 1870-76 – 1 – us A.J.P.C. [071]

THE NEW ERA – Trois-Rivieres, Canada. 11 avr 1885 – 1r – 1 – Can$25.00 – cn Can Microfilming [072]

NEW ERA BAPTIST CHURCH. SEVIERVILLE, TENNESSEE : CHURCH RECORDS – 1928-58. 320p – 1 – 14.40 – us Baptist [240]

A NEW ERA IN OLD MEXICO / Winton, George B – Nashville, Tenn.: M.E. Church, South: Smith & Lamar [agents], 1905 – 1mf – us A.T.L.A. [240]

THE NEW ERA IN SOUTH AFRICA : WITH AN EXAMINATION OF THE CHINESE LABOUR QUESTION / Markham, Violet Rosa – (Filmed with: South Africa. Parliament. Joint Sitting, 1956) – London: Smith, Elder, 1904 – us Res Libr [331]

NEW ERA JOURNAL – Huntingdon, PA. -sw 1904-1912 – 13 – $25.00r – us I.M.R. [071]

THE NEW ERA, OR, CANADIAN CHRONICLE – Brockville [Ont: s.n, 1841?-18– or 19–] – 9 – cn C.I.H.M. [072]

THE NEW ERA, OR, THE COMING KINGDOM / Strong, Josiah – New York: Baker & Taylor, c1893 – 1mf – us A.T.L.A. [240]

A NEW ESKIMO CULTURE IN HUDSON BAY / Jenness, D – BN 273 2. 1925 – 8 – ne IDC [306]

NEW ESSAYS / United Workers Party – 1-6 2+4 (all publ). 1934-43 – 24mf – 9 – $135.00 – us UPA [335]

NEW EVENING POST – Dublin. Ireland. -d. 17 Oct-7 Dec 1782. (Imperfect). (10 ft) – 1 – uk British Libr Newspaper [072]

NEW FACTS CONCERNING JOHN ROBINSON : PASTOR OF THE PILGRIM FATHERS / Burrage, Champlin – Oxford: Printed by H. Hart at the University Press; London: Henry Frowde, 1910 – 1mf – us A.T.L.A. [240]

THE NEW FAR WEST AND THE OLD FAR EAST: BEING NOTES OF A TOUR IN NORTH AMERICA, JAPAN, CEYLON ETC / Barneby, William Henry – London: E. Stanford, 1889. 03374. (Pre-1900 Canadiana) – 9 – cn C.I.H.M. [910]

NEW FARM – v1- 1979- – 1,5,6,9 – us UMI [630]

NEW FEDERATION – Ottawa. v1-4. 1988/89-1993/94 – 9 – Can$20.00y – cn Micromedia [073]

NEW FEED RESOURCES : PROCEEDINGS OF A TECHNICAL CONSULTATION – 1977 – 304p – it F.A.O. [636]

THE NEW FEMINIST – 1969-73 – 1 – $65.00 – cn McLaren [305]

THE NEW FICTION : AND OTHER ESSAYS ON LITERARY SUBJECTS / Traill, Henry Duff – London: Hurst and Blackett, 1897 – 1 roll – 1 – 1-55879-575-8 – uk Libr Preservation [840]

NEW FLORA AND BOTANY OF NORTH AMERICA / Rafinesque-Schmaltz, Constantine S – Philadelphia. 1836. B-5220 1 – 9 – ne IDC [580]

NEW FOUNDATIONS – 1-7 2+2 (all publ). 1947-54 – 12mf – 9 – $75.00 – us UPA [335]

A NEW FRANCE IN NEW ENGLAND / Bender, Prosper – 1885? 03571. (Pre-1900 Canadiana) – 9 – cn C.I.H.M. [971]

NEW FREEDOM – Portland OR. Sep 26 1914 – 1 – us U.O. Library [071]

NEW FREEWOMAN – (The Egoist). London. -w. Jun 1913-Dec 1919. (1 reel) – 1 – uk British Libr Newspaper [305]

NEW FRESH WATER SHELLS OF THE UNITED STATES / Conrad, T A – Z-477 2. 1834 – 8 – ne IDC [590]

NEW FRIENDSHIP BAPTIST CHURCH. AUBURN, KENTUCKY : CHURCH RECORDS – 1834-Sep 1974 – 1 – 31.68 – us Baptist [240]

NEW FRIENDSHIP BAPTIST CHURCH. PARAGOULD, ARKANSAS : CHURCH RECORDS – Aug 1913 – Sept 1979 – 1 – 12.42 – us Baptist [240]

NEW FRONTIER – 1936-37 – 9 – 75.00 – cn McLaren [335]

NEW FRONTIERS – 1952-56 – 9 – 70.00 – cn McLaren [335]

NEW FRONTIERS IN EDUCATION – 1971- 1; 1975- 5,6,9 – us UMI [073]

NEW FRUITS FROM AN OLD FIELD / Whitaker, Epher – (Includes bibliographical references) – NY: Anson D F Randolph, 1865 – 1mf – 9 – 0-8370-5754-X – 1985-3754 – us A.T.L.A. [240]

NEW GAZETTE – Minden, NE. -w. Nov 1878; Dec 1879-Oct 1902; Dec 1902-Feb 1904, scattered issues missing – 1 – us NE Hist [071]

NEW GAZETTE – Minden. Neb. and pred. 1878-1904 – 1 – us UMI [071]

A NEW GENERAL COLLECTION OF VOYAGES AND TRAVELS / ed by Astley, T – London. 1745-47. 4v. – 115mf – 8 – ne IDC [910]

NEW GENERATION – v1- 1919- 1; v53- 5,6; v59- 9 – us UMI [305]

NEW GERMAN CRITIQUE – (v.16-. 1979- 5,6,9) – v.1-. 1973- – 1 – us UMI [073]

THE NEW GERMANIA. / Burditt, B A – Boston: Oliver Ditson & Co., 1885. MUSIC 1991, Item 2 – 1 – us L of C Photodup [780]

NEW GLASS: A WORLDWIDE SURVEY – 1979. 287p. 5 fiches. Fiche No. 6661 – 9 – $8.75 – us Corning Mus [730]

NEW GLASS REVIEW 1 – 1980. 16p., 10 color illus. Objects made in 1979. 1 fiche. Fiche no. 6669 – 9 – $2.50 – us Corning Mus [730]

NEW GLASS REVIEW 2 – 1981. 16p., 100 color illus. Objects made in 1980. 1 fiche Fiche no. 6670 – 9 – $2.50 – us Corning Mus [730]

NEW GLASS REVIEW 3 – 1982. 32p., 100 color illus. Objects made in 1981. Check list of book and articles on glass. 1 fiche. Fiche no. 6671 – 9 – $2.50 – us Corning Mus [730]

NEW GLASS REVIEW 4 – 1983. 48p. 100 color illus. Objects made in 1982. Check list of books and articles on glass, directory of contemporary galleries. 1 fiche. Fiche No.7375 – 9 – $2.50 – us Corning Mus [730]

NEW GLASS REVIEW 5 – 1984. 48p. 100 color illus. Objects made in 1983. Check list of books and articles on glass, directory of contemporary galleries. 1 fiche. Fiche No. 8409 – 9 – $2.50 – us Corning Mus [730]

NEW GLASS REVIEW 6 – 1985. 64p. 2 fiches. Fiche No. 9186 – 9 – $5.00 – us Corning Mus [730]

NEW GLASS REVIEW 7 – 1986. 54p. 2 fiches. Fiche No. 9187 – 9 – $2.50 – us Corning Mus [730]

NEW GLASS REVIEW 8 – 1987. 68p, 102 color illus. Objects made in 1986. 2 fiches. Fiche No. 9980 – 9 – $5.00 – us Corning Mus [730]

NEW GLASS REVIEW 9 / Corning Museum of Glass – Corning, NY. 1988. 54p. 2 fiches. Fiche No. 11,726 – 2mf – 9 – $5.00 plus $0.55 postage and handling plus N.Y. State tax as applicable – 0-87290-117-3 – us Corning Mus [740]

NEW GLASS REVIEW 10 / Corning Museum of Glass – Corning, NY. 1989. 54p. Fiche No. 11,763 – 2mf – 9 – $5.00 plus $0.55 postage and handling plus N.Y. State tax as applicable – 0-87290-119-X – us Corning Mus [740]

NEW GLASS REVIEW 11 / Corning Museum of Glass – Corning, NY. 1990. 55p. 2 fiche. Fiche no. 11,764 – 9 – $5.00 plus $0.55 postage and handling plus N.Y. State tax as applicable – 0-87290-122-X – us Corning Mus [740]

NEW GLASS REVIEW 12 / Corning Museum of Glass – 1991. 56p. col., ill. 2 fiche. Fiche no. 12,752 – 9 – $6.00 – us Corning Mus [740]

NEW GLASS REVIEW 13 / Corning Museum of Glass – 1992. 56p. col., ill. Fiche no. 12,753 – 2mf – 9 – $6.00 – us Corning Mus [740]

NEW GLASS REVIEW 14 / Corning Museum of Glass – 1993. 60p. col., ill. Fiche no. 13,889 – 2mf – 9 – $5.00 – us Corning Mus [740]

THE NEW GOVERNMENT'S ECONOMIC POLICY / Mexico. Banco Nacional de Comercio Exterior – Mexico City. 1971. BD-1695 1 – 9 – ne IDC [330]

A NEW GRAMMAR / Fisher, Ann – 1750. 173p. (English Linguistics Series 1500-1800) – 9 – us UMI [420]

A NEW GRAMMAR OF THE ENGLISH LANGUAGE / Fenning, Daniel – 1771. 220p. (English Linguistics Series 1500-1800) – 9 – us UMI [420]

NEW GRAND QUARTETS, TWO / Pleyel, Ignaz J – (Parts) – London: C Wheatstone, 180- – 1 – us Sibley [780]

THE NEW GREAT IRON WHEEL / Graves, J R – Published in Memphis, Tenn. 1884 – 1 – 21.00 – us Baptist [240]

NEW GROSS DISTILLIER-BUCH.. / Ryff, Walther Hermann – Frankfurt, 1556 – 1 – us U.W. Library [025]

A NEW GUIDE TO ELOQUENCE / Girard, Gabriel – 1762. 67p. (English Linguistics Series 1500-1800) – 9 – us UMI [400]

A NEW GUIDE TO THE ENGLISH TONGUE / Dilworth, Thomas – 1751. 175p. (English Linguistics Series 1500-1800) – 9 – us UMI [420]

New Guinea Compagnie, Landesverwaltung in Herbertshohe (New Guinea Company, Territorial Administration at Herbertshohe) *see* EINGANGSJOURNAL DAILY REGISTER OF LETTERS RECEIVED, 1895-1914

New Guinea, Dutch. Laws, statutes, etc *see* REGLEMENT OP DE BURGERLIJKE RECHTSVORDERING

NEW GUINEA'S IMPROVEMENT PLAN FOR 1973-1974(AND) / Papua New Guinea. Central Planning Office – Districts Supplement. Port Moresby. 1973. BD-1729 1 – 9 – ne IDC [338]

NEW HAMPSHIRE : REVISED STATUTES ANNOTATED – Oxford: Equity Pub Co, 1955 Apr 1996 update – 9 – $915.00 set – us Hein [340]

NEW HAMPSHIRE : SESSION LAWS OF AMERICAN STATES AND TERRITORIES – 1783-1995 – 9 – $862.00 set – us Hein [340]

New Hampshire *see*
- CATALOGUE OF PASTORS OF BAPTIST CHURCHES OF NEW HAMPSHIRE
- REPORTS AND OPINIONS (A-G)
- REPORTS, POST-NRS
- REPORTS, PRE-NRS
- SESSION LAWS, 1783-
- STATE LABOR REPORTS

NEW HAMPSHIRE 1776 CENSUS – (Census tells what over 9,000 New Hampshire residents thought in 1776 about the War for Independence. This completely-indexed census represents the most inclusive list of New Hampshire names available for the Revolutionary War period) – (mf ed 1976) – 1mf – 9 – 0-931248-02-7 – us Holbrook [978]

New Hampshire. Agricultural Experiment Station *see*
- ANNUAL REPORT AND BULLETIN
- PROGRESS REPORT
- RESOURCE ECONOMICS RESEARCH MIMEOGRAPH
- SCIENTIFIC CONTRIBUTIONS
- STATE SERVICE REPORT
- STATION CIRCULAR
- TECHNICAL BULLETIN

NEW HAMPSHIRE ATTORNEY GENERAL REPORTS AND OPINIONS – (1969 not availbale) – 1896-1966 – 6 – $35.00set – us Hein [340]

New Hampshire Baptist Historical Society *see* RECORDS

NEW HAMPSHIRE BAPTIST NEWS – Manchester, NH. United Baptist Convention of NH. 1924-64. Single reels available – 1 – 102.20 – us A.B.H.S. [073]

NEW HAMPSHIRE BAPTIST REGISTER – 1834-44 (complete) – 2r – 1 – ATLA R0109 – us A.T.L.A. [240]

NEW HAMPSHIRE BAR ASSOCIATION REPORTS OF PROCEEDINGS – (Lacking: 1956-1961/62) – 1900-63 (all publ) – 26mf – 9 – $117.00 – LLMC 84-639 – us L.L.M.C. [073]

NEW HAMPSHIRE BAR JOURNAL – v1-35. 1959-94 – 9 – $356.00 set – us Hein [340]

NEW HAMPSHIRE BAR NEWS (NS) – v1-6. 1960-96 – 9 – $97.00set – us Hein [340]

New Hampshire Charitable Society *see* RECORDS

New Hampshire. College of Agriculture (or N.H. College of Agriculture & Mechanical Arts) *see*
- NEWSLETTER
- REPORT

New Hampshire. Conference of Baptist Ministers *see* RECORDS

New Hampshire. Cooperative Extension Service *see*
- 4-H CIRCULAR/JUNIOR CIRCULAR
- CHIPS
- EXTENSION BULLETIN
- EXTENSION CIRCULAR
- EXTENSION FOLDER
- INFORMATION GUIDE
- NEW HAMPSHIRE FARM MANAGEMENT LETTER

New Hampshire. Department of Forest Resources (also called Department of Forestry) *see*
- FORESTRY MIMEOGRAPH
- FORESTRY TECHNICAL NOTE

NEW HAMPSHIRE FARM MANAGEMENT LETTER / New Hampshire. Cooperative Extension Service – v. 1-45. 1955-62 – 1,5,6 – us Spaulding [630]

NEW HAMPSHIRE GAZETTE – Portsmouth. N.H. 1756-1820. yFreeman's Journal. 1776-1778. Sold as one unit – 3 – us Readex [071]

NEW HAMPSHIRE JOURNAL OF MUSIC – 1872-82 – 1 – £165.00 – uk Chadwyck [780]

NEW HAMPSHIRE LAW REPORTER – New Hampshire Supreme Court. 1v. 1897-98 (all publ) – 4mf – 9 – $6.00 – LLMC 84-640 – us L.L.M.C. [073]

NEW HAMPSHIRE MAGAZINE – v. 1. Jun-Nov 1793 – 1 – us UMI [073]

NEW HAMPSHIRE NEW JERUSALEM MAGAZINE AND PRIMITIVE RELIGIOUS INTELLIGENCER – v. 1. 5 Feb 1805 – 1 – us UMI [240]

NEW HAMPSHIRE PROBATE LAW AND DIRECTORY, CONTAINING THE GENERAL LAWS OF 1878. / Morrison, Charles Robert – Concord, N.H.: Sanborn, 1884. 321p. LL-94 – 1 – us L of C Photodup [340]

NEW HAMPSHIRE PROFILES – 1951- 1; 1973-5,6; 1975- 9 – us UMI [073]

NEW HAMPSHIRE REGISTER AND BUSINESS DIRECTORY 1921/22 / Eastman Company – Concord. New Hampshire Reel 8. (The Cox Library Collection) – 5 – us Americana [978]

NEW HAMPSHIRE SPY – Portsmouth. N.H. 1786-93 – 1,3 – us Readex [071]

New Hampshire. State Bar Association *see* PROCEEDINGS

NEW HAMPSHIRE STATE DIRECTORY AND GAZETTEER – 1917. New Hampshire Reel 1. (The Cox Library Collection) – 5 – us Americana [978]

New Hampshire. Superior and Supreme Courts *see* SMITH'S REPORTS

New Hampshire. Supreme Court *see* NEW HAMPSHIRE SUPREME COURT REPORTS

NEW HAMPSHIRE SUPREME COURT REPORTS / New Hampshire. Supreme Court – (Pre-NRS: v1-63 1816-85 439mf $658.00. Updates planned) – v1-78. 1816-1919 – 538mf – $807.00 – LLMC 82-986 – us L.L.M.C. [340]

NEW HAMPSHIRE SUPREME COURT REPORTS *see* SMITH'S REPORTS

NEW HAMPSHIRE TOWN AND VITAL RECORDS *see* BROOKLINE 1748-1928

New Hampshire Yearly Meeting of Free Will Baptists *see* RECORDS

NEW HARBINGER: A JOURNAL OF THE COOPERATIVE MOVEMENT – v2-5. 1973-79. Superseded by Co-op: the Harbinger of Economic Democracy – 1,5,6,9 – us UMI [334]

NEW HARMONY OF THE FOUR GOSPEL NARRATIVES OF THE CLOSING EARTHLY LABORS OF JESUS / Morton, Joseph – Chicago: J.W. Morton, 1888. 1 fiche – 9 – us A.T.L.A. [240]

New Hartford, New York. New Hartford Baptist Church and Society *see* RECORDS

NEW HAVEN CHRONICLE – New Haven. Conn. 1786-1787. New Haven Gazette. 1784-1786. New Haven Gazette and Connecticut Magazine. 1786-1789 – 1,3 – us Readex [071]

NEW HAVEN GAZETTE AND THE CONNECTICUT MAGAZINE – v. 1-3. 16 Feb 1786-4 Dec 1788 – 1 – us UMI [073]

NEW HAVEN GENEALOGICAL MAGAZINE *see* AMERICAN GENEALOGIST

NEW HAVEN STAR – New Baltimore. Mich. 1926-41 – 1 – us UMI [071]

A NEW HEBREW GRAMMAR : COMPOSED PRINCIPALLY WITHOUT POINTS, BUT CONTAINING A BRIEF EXPLANATION OF THE MASORETIC SYSTEM, AND EXHIBITING THE RESPECTIVE POWERS OF THE PUNCTUARY VOWELS AND ACCENTS / Duncan, William Wallace – London: William Tegg, 1866 – 1mf – 9 – 0-8370-9140-3 – 1986-3140 – us A.T.L.A. [470]

New Hebrides. British Service *see* ANNUAL REPORT ON EDUCATION 1974-1979

New Hebrides British Service. Southern District Administration *see* FILES ON THE JOHN FRUM MOVEMENT

New Hebrides Chamber of Commerce *see* BULLETIN OF THE NEW HEBRIDES CHAMBER OF COMMERCE, INDUSTRY AND AGRICULTURE / BULLETIN OF THE VANUATU CHAMBER OF COMMERCE

NEW HEBRIDES FRENCH RESIDENCY : MONTHLY REPORTS – dec 1966-dec 1978 – 3r – 1 – PMB 1135 – at Pacific Mss [980]

NEW HEIGHTS BAPTIST CHURCH. BROAD RIVER ASSOCIATION. CHEROKEE COUNTY. GAFFNEY, SOUTH CAROLINA : CHURCH RECORDS – Dec 1977-Nov 1978 – 1 – 5.00 – us Baptist [240]

NEW HERALD – Kilgore. Tex. 1972- – 1 – us UMI [071]

A NEW HERBAL / Dodoens, R – M344. 1619 – 9 – ne IDC [580]

A NEW HISTORICAL RELATION OF THE KINGDOM OF SIAM / Loubere, S de La – London. 2v. 1693 – 4mf – 9 – ne IDC [950]

THE NEW HISTORY : ESSAYS ILLUSTRATING THE MODERN HISTORICAL OUTLOOK / Robinson, James Harvey – New York: Macmillan, 1912 – 1mf – us A.T.L.A. [240]

A NEW HISTORY OF METHODISM / ed by Townsend, W J et al – London, 1909. 2v: xx/598p; xvi/676p – 16mf – 9 – ne IDC [240]

A NEW HISTORY OF SOCIALISM (CCC277) = SHE-HUI-CHU-I-SHIN-SHIH / Shen, J Wesley – (In Chinese) – 1st ed. Shanghai: Association Press of China, 1934 – 1r – 1 – 1984-6616 – us A.T.L.A. [335]

A NEW HISTORY OF THE BOOK OF COMMON PRAYER : WITH A RATIONALE OF ITS OFFICES: ON THE BASIS OF THE FORMER WORK BY FRANCIS PROCTER / Frere, Walter H – London, New York: Macmillan, 1902 – 2mf – us A.T.L.A. [240]

A NEW HISTORY OF THE EMPIRE OF CHINA,... / [Magalhaes, G de] – London, 1689 – 4mf – 9 – ne IDC [950]

THE NEW HOME MISSIONS : AN ACCOUNT OF THEIR SOCIAL REDIRECTION / Douglass, Harlan Paul – New York: Missionary Education Movement of the United States and Canada, 1914 – 1mf – us A.T.L.A. [240]

NEW HOPE BAPTIST CHURCH. BON AQUA, TENNESSEE : CHURCH RECORDS – 1872-July 1978 – 1 – 32.76 – us Baptist [240]

NEW HOPE BAPTIST CHURCH. DECATUR COUNTY. DECATURVILLE, TENNESSEE : CHURCH RECORDS – 1842-Mar 1928 – 1 – 7.47 – us Baptist [240]

NEW HOPE BAPTIST CHURCH. KINGS MOUNTAIN ASSOCIATION. EARL, NORTH CAROLINA : CHURCH RECORDS – 1911-63 – 1 – $45.00 – us Baptist [240]

NEW HOPE BAPTIST CHURCH. LANCASTER COUNTY. SOUTH CAROLINA : CHURCH RECORDS – Aug 1950-1983. 625p – 1 – 28.13 – us Baptist [240]

NEW HOPE BAPTIST CHURCH. LAWRENCE COUNTY. ARKANSAS : CHURCH RECORDS – 1844-1976 – 1 – 57.51 – us Baptist [240]

NEW HOPE BAPTIST CHURCH. MCFALL, MISSOURI : CHURCH RECORDS – 1855-Apr 1963 – 1 – 27.23 – us Baptist [240]

NEW HOPE BAPTIST CHURCH. NASHVILLE ASSOCIATION. TENNESSEE : CHURCH RECORDS – 1846-April 1990 – 1 – $67.23 – us Baptist [240]

NEW HOPE BAPTIST CHURCH. OCONEE COUNTY. SOUTH CAROLINA : CHURCH RECORDS – 1835-1953 – 1 – 52.11 – us Baptist [240]

NEW HOPE BAPTIST CHURCH. SPARTAN ASSOCIATION. CROSS ANCHOR, SOUTH CAROLINA : CHURCH RECORDS – 1834-95. (lacking 1804-1833) – 1 – 18.36 – us Baptist [240]

NEW HOPE BAPTIST CHURCH. SPARTANBURG COUNTY. SOUTH CAROLINA : CHURCH RECORDS – 1834-95, 1910-52 – 1 – 28.17 – us Baptist [240]

NEW HOPE BAPTIST CHURCH. WAUCHULA, FLORIDA : CHURCH RECORDS – December 1879-1990 – 2r – 1 – $91.53 – us Baptist [240]

NEW HOPE BAPTIST CHURCH. WHITEVILLE, NORTH CAROLINA : CHURCH RECORDS – 1874-1974 – 1 – 5.49 – us Baptist [240]

New Hope. Ohio. Second Creek New Hope Baptist Church *see* CHURCH RECORDS, MS 1509

NEW HOPE PRIMITIVE BAPTIST CHURCH. DOUGLAS COUNTY. GEORGIA : CHURCH RECORDS – Dec 1828-Apr 1988 – 1 – 47.52 – us Baptist [240]

NEW HORIZONS – Chicago. v. 1-3, no. 3. Nov 1938-Mar Apr 1941 – 1 – us NY Public [073]

NEW HORIZONS : THE SCIENCE AND PRACTICE OF ACUTE MEDICINE – v1-4. 1993-1996 – 4r – 1,5,6,9 – $80.00r – us Williams [615]

NEW HORIZONS OF HUMAN KNOWLEDGE : A SERIES OF PUBLIC TALKS GIVEN AT UNESCO / Kinnon, Colette M – 1981 – 98p – 9 – 92-3-101903-1 – fr UNESCO [500]

THE NEW HOROSCOPE OF MISSIONS / Dennis, James Shepard – New York: Fleming H. Revell, 1908. 248p. 1 fiche – 9 – us A.T.L.A. [240]

NEW HUMAN SERVICES REVIEW – v1-5 1974-79 1,5,6; v2-5 9 – us UMI [650]

A NEW HYDROSTATIC METHOD : THE NATANT DISKS / Jorgensen, Arlo G – 1994 – 1mf – $4.00 – us Microform Publ [612]

NEW IBERIA FIRST BAPTIST CHURCH. NEW IBERIA, LOUISIANA : CHURCH RECORDS – Jul 1926-Dec 1980. 2038p. Lacks Oct 1961-Jun 1965, Feb 1968-Sep 1969 – 1 – 91.71 – us Baptist [240]

NEW IDEAS IN PSYCHOLOGY – v1- 1983- – 5,6,9 – us UMI [150]

NEW ILLUSTRATED SELF-INSTRUCTOR IN PHRENOLOGY AND PHYSIOLOGY / Fowler, OS & Fowler, LN – New York: Samuel R Wells, 1871 – 2mf – 9 – $3.00 – LLMC 92-113 – us L.L.M.C. [340]

THE NEW IMMIGRATION : A STUDY OF THE INDUSTRIAL AND SOCIAL LIFE OF SOUTHEASTERN EUROPEANS IN AMERICA / Roberts, Peter – New York: Macmillan, 1913, c 1912 – 1mf – us A.T.L.A. [305]

THE NEW IMPORT REGULATIONS AND LISTS OF COMMODITIES, 1960 / Indonesia. Commercial Advisory Foundation – SE-6201 1 – 9 – ne IDC [380]

NEW IMPRESSIONS ON NEW NEIGHBOR PEOPLE / Indonesia – SE-11,911 1. 1946 – 9 – ne IDC [950]

NEW INDIAN – Carson City, NV. Sep 1899; 1903-04 – 1r – 1 – $50.00 – U04470 – us Library Micro [071]

NEW INDIAN ANTIQUARY / ed by Katre, S M & Gode, P K – Bombay. 1938-47. 9v. – 88mf – 8 – ne IDC [930]

NEW INDIVIDUALIST REVIEW – 1961-68 – 1 – us UMI [073]

NEW INDIVIDUALIST REVIEW – Chicago. v1-5. 1961-68 – 17mf – 9 – $5.00f – us Ross [073]

NEW INTERNATIONAL / Socialist Workers Party – 1-24 2+3 (all publ). 1934-58 – 3r – 1 – $345.00 – us UPA [335]

NEW INTERNATIONAL – v. 1-24. 1934-1958 – 1 – us UMI [073]

NEW INTERNATIONAL ECONOMIC ORDER : LINKS BETWEEN ECONOMICS AND COMMUNICATION / Pavlic, Breda & Hamelink, Cees J – 1985 – 65p – 9 – 92-3-102311-X – fr UNESCO [330]

NEW INTERNATIONAL ORDER – (Documentation Service on microfiche. A cooperative RIO/IDC Project. 233 documents from the period between 1975 and 1979. Including catalogue cards.) – 1975-1979 – 346mf – 9 – RIO-1975 – 1979/1 – ne IDC [330]

NEW INTERNATIONALIST – (nos 1-34 1973-75 Can$55.00. nos 35-226 1976-91 Can$20.00y) – Toronto. nos 1-274. 1973-95 – 9 – Can$28.00y – cn Micromedia [073]

NEW IRELAND – Ireland.1903-04 – 1 – ie Microforms [072]

NEW IRELAND / Sullivan, Alexander Martin – Philadelphia: J.B. Lippincott, 1878. 532p – 1 – us U.W. Library [941]

NEW IRELAND/OLD IRELAND – Dublin, Ireland.15 May 1915-1922 – 1 – ie Microforms [072]

NEW IRISH JURIST AND LOCAL GOVERNMENT REVIEW *see* IRISH JURIST AND LOCAL GOVERNMENT REVIEW

A NEW ITALIAN GRAMMAR: OR, A GUIDE TO THE ITALIAN TONGUE / Barton, John – 1719. 164p. (English Linguistics Series 1500-1800) – 9 – us UMI [440]

NEW JERSEY : SESSION LAWS OF AMERICAN STATES AND TERRITORIES – 1776-1994 – 9 – $2,750.00 set – us Hein [340]

NEW JERSEY : STATUTES ANNOTATED – St Paul: West Pub Co, 1939-Apr 1996 update – 9 – $2,223.00 set – us Hein [340]

New Jersey *see*
- NEW JERSEY LAW REPORTS
- REPORTS AND OPINIONS (A-G)
- REPORTS, POST-NRS
- REPORTS, PRE-NRS
- SESSION LAWS, 1776-
- STATE LABOR REPORTS

New Jersey Academy of Science *see* BULLETIN

NEW JERSEY AND PENNSYLVANIA AGRICULTURAL MONTHLY INTELLIGENCER AND FARMER'S MAGAZINE – v. 1. 1825-26 – 1 – us UMI [630]

NEW JERSEY ATTORNEY GENERAL REPORTS AND OPINIONS – (6 1878-1978 $140.00. 9 1978-1991 $20.00) – 1878-1991 – 6,9 – $160.00set – us Hein [340]

NEW JERSEY BAPTIST BULLETIN/BULLETIN – Newark/Somerville/Plainfield/East Orange, NJ. NJ Baptist State Convention/NJ Bap. Conv./American Bap. Ch. of NJ. 1891-1980. Single reels available – 1 – 342.70 – us A.B.H.S. [073]

New Jersey. Board of Equalization of Taxes *see* REPORTS

New Jersey. Board of Public Utility Commissioners *see* REPORTS

New Jersey. Board of Railroad Commissioners *see* REPORTS

New Jersey. (Colony). Court of General Quarter Sessions of the Peace. (Cape May County) *see* REPRODUCTION OF THE SECOND MINUTE BOOK OF THE COURT OF QUARTER SESSIONS AND COMMON PLEAS...,1715

New Jersey. Commissioner of Insurance *see* REPORTS BY THE NEW JERSEY SECRETARY OF STATE AS COMMISSIONER OF INSURANCE

New Jersey Corporation Guarantee and Trust Company. Camden, NJ *see* THE CORPORATION LAWS OF NEW JERSEY

New Jersey. Courts *see* RULES OF THE NEW JERSEY COURTS.

New Jersey. Dept. of Banking *see* REPORTS OF THE COMMISSIONER OF BANKING

New Jersey. Dept. of Insurance *see* REPORT OF THE COMMISSIONER OF INSURANCE OF NEW JERSEY

New Jersey. Dept. of Labor and Industry. Division of Planning and Research *see* COVERED EMPLOYMENT TRENDS IN NEW JERSEY BY GEOGRAPHICAL AREAS OF THE STATE

New Jersey. Division of Employment Security *see* REPORTS

New Jersey. Division of Savings and Loan Associations *see* REPORTS

New Jersey. Division of Taxation *see* REPORT...IN THE DEPARTMENT OF THE TREASURY

New Jersey. Division of Workmen's Compensation *see* INDUSTRIAL ACCIDENT REPORTS

New Jersey. Employment Security Council *see* REPORTS

NEW JERSEY EQUITY REPORTS – (Pre-NRS: v1-40 1830-85 302mf $453.00. Cont by: N.J. Superior Court Reports. Not offered by LLMC) – v1-142. 1830-1948 (all publ) – 1145mf – 9 – $1,717.00 – LLMC 80-813 – us L.L.M.C. [340]

NEW JERSEY FAMILY LAWYER – v1-14. 1981-94 – 9 – $135.00 set – us Hein [340]

NEW JERSEY FORESTER *see* AMERICAN FORESTS

NEW JERSEY HISTORY – (v.97$ 1979$ 5,6,9) – v.85-. 1967- – 1 – us UMI [073]

NEW JERSEY JOURNAL – Chatham. N.J. 1779-1783 – 1 – us UMI [071]

NEW JERSEY JOURNAL OF PHARMACY – v. 24-27. 1951-54 – 1 – us UMI [615]

NEW JERSEY LAW JOURNAL – (1982-. 5,6,9) – 1878- – 1 – us UMI [073]

NEW JERSEY LAW JOURNAL – v1-58. 1878-1935 (all publ) – 9 – LLMC 82-949 – us L.L.M.C. [073]

NEW JERSEY LAW REPORTS / New Jersey – (Pre-NRS: v1-47 1790-1886 318mf $477.00. Cont by: New Jersey Reports. Not offered by LLMC) – v1-137. 1790-1948 (all publ) – 1056mf – 9 – $1,584.00 – LLMC 80-812 – us L.L.M.C. [340]

NEW JERSEY LAW REVIEW *see* RUTGERS LAW REVIEW

New Jersey. Laws, Statutes, etc *see* THE GENERAL CORPORATION ACT OF NEW JERSEY.

NEW JERSEY LAWYER : THE JOURNAL OF THE NEW JERSEY LAW SCHOOL – v1-2. 1935-36 (all publ) – 3mf – 9 – $4.50 – LLMC 84-641 – us L.L.M.C. [340]

NEW JERSEY LAWYER – (v1-17 + no 58-113 1957-85 on reel or mf $180.00. no 114-159 1985-94 on mf $126.50. Title varies: v1-15 no 58-87 1957-85 as New Jersey State Bar Journal) – v1-17 + no 58-159. 1957-94 – 5,6,9 – $306.50 set – us Hein [340]

NEW JERSEY MAGAZINE – Dec 1786-Feb 1787 – 1 – us UMI [073]

NEW JERSEY MIRROR – Wrightstown. N.J. -w. 1958- – 1 – us UMI [071]

NEW JERSEY MONTHLY MAGAZINE – v. 1. Apr 1825 – 1 – us UMI [073]

THE NEW JERSEY OFFICE OF CONSUMER PROTECTION: A PROMISE UNFULFILLED / Powell, Robert S – Princeton, N.J.: Center for Analysis of Public Issues 1970. LL-2365 – 1 – us L of C Photodup [340]

NEW JERSEY PATRIOT : DEVOTED TO THE INTERESTS OF THE PATRIOTIC SONS OF AMERICA AND KINDRED ORGANIZATIONS – Phillipsburg, NJ: Patriotic Order of Sons of America, 1895-97 – 1r – 1 – us Ross [975]

NEW JERSEY REALTY TITLE NEWS – v1 nos 1-8. 1944-48 (all publ) – 2mf – 9 – $3.00 – LLMC 84-642 – us L.L.M.C. [073]

NEW JERSEY REPORTS *see* NEW JERSEY LAW REPORTS

New Jersey. State Bar Association *see* PROCEEDINGS

NEW JERSEY STATE BAR ASSOCIATION QUARTERLY – v1-4. 1934-1937 (all publ) – 9 – $32.00 set – us Hein [340]

NEW JERSEY STATE BAR ASSOCIATION QUATERLY – v1-4. 1934-37 (all publ) – 17mf – 9 – $25.50 – LLMC 84-643 – us L.L.M.C. [073]

NEW JERSEY STATE BAR ASSOCIATION YEARBOOK – 1902-51 – 47mf – 9 – $211.00 – LLMC 84-644 – us L.L.M.C. [340]

NEW JERSEY STATE BAR JOURNAL *see* NEW JERSEY LAWYER

New Jersey. State Board of Mediation *see* REPORTS

New Jersey. State Board of Taxation *see* REPORTS

New Jersey. State Board of Taxes and Assessment *see* REPORTS

New Jersey. State Investment Council *see* REPORTS

New Jersey. State Tax Dept *see* REPORTS

New Jersey. Statistics and records bureau *see* REPORT

NEW JERSEY SUPERIOR COURT REPORTS *see* NEW JERSEY EQUITY REPORTS

New Jersey. Synod (Pres. Ch. in the U.S.A.) *see*
- MINUTES
- MINUTES, 1823-1889

THE NEW JERUSALEM AND THE OLD JERUSALEM : THE PLACE AND SERVICE OF THE JEWISH CHURCH AMONG THE AEONS OF REVELATION:WITH OTHER ESSAYS / Wilkinson, James John Garth – London:James Speirs, 1894 – 1mf – 9 – 0-8370-5850-3 – 1985-3850 – us A.T.L.A. [270]

NEW JERUSALEM CHURCH REPOSITORY – v. 1. Jan 1817-Oct 1818 – 1 – us UMI [240]

NEW JERUSALEM MISSIONARY AND INTELLECTUAL REPOSITORY – v. 1. May 1823-Apr 1824 – 1 – us UMI [240]

NEW JERUSALEM RECORD – v. 1. Jul 1820 – 1 – us UMI [240]

NEW JEWISH TIMES – New York, NY. 1980-81 – 1 – us A.J.P.C. [071]

THE NEW JOINT STOCK ACT OF CONNECTICUT, PASSED JANUARY SESSION, 1880. / Connecticut – 4th ed. New Haven: Peck, 1880. 145p. LL-1046 – 1 – us L of C Photodup [340]

NEW JUSTICE : A RADICAL MAGAZINE – 1-17 (all publ). 1919-20 – 4mf – 9 – $35.00 – us UPA [335]

EIN NEW KUNSTLICH MODELBUCH / Quentel, P – O 1133 1. 1541 – 9 – ne IDC [760]

NEW LABOR REVIEW – 1978- – 1,5,6,9 – us UMI [331]

A NEW LAW DICTIONARY / Burn, Richard – v1-2. 1709-85. London: T Cadell, 1792 – 10mf – 9 – $15.00 – LLMC 95-408 – us L.L.M.C. [340]

A NEW LAW DICTIONARY : CONTAINING EXPLANATIONS OF SUCH TECHNICAL TERMS AND PHRASES AS OCCUR IN THE WORKS OF THE VARIOUS LAW-WRITERS OF GREAT BRITAIN, TO WHICH IS ADDED AN OUTLINE OF AN ACTION OF LAW, AND OF A SUIT IN EQUITY, DESIGNED EXPRESSLY FOR THE USE OF STUDENTS / Holthouse, Henry James – London: W Crafts. 1v. 1839 – 5mf – 9 – $7.50 – LLMC 95-441 – us L.L.M.C. [340]

NEW LAW DICTIONARY / Burrill, Alexander – New York: Voorhies. pts 1 + 2 in 2 bks. 1850-51 – 12mf – 9 – $18.00 – LLMC 84-713 – us L.L.M.C. [340]

A NEW LAW-DICTIONARY: CONTAINING, THE INTERPRETATION AND DEFINITION OF WORDS AND TERMS... / Jacob, G – London, 1732 – 10mf – ne IDC [340]

NEW LEADER – (Combined with: The American Appeal) – New York: New Leader Pub Association. v15 n26-v17 n26. jul 1933-jun 1934 – us Res Libr [071]

NEW LEADER – New York. v1-33. 1924-50 – 15r – 1 – us Ross [071]

NEW LEADER – (v.54- 1971- 5,6. v.58- 1975-9) – 1924- – 1 – us UMI [073]

THE NEW LEADER – New York, 1924-50 – 1 – us NY Public [071]

THE NEW LEADER – New York, 1925, 1927-50 (all incompl) – 1 – us Hoover Inst Photo [071]

THE NEW LEADER – New York. v. 1-33, no. 17. Jan 19 1924-Apr 29 1950 – 1 – us NY Public [071]

New Leon. Mexico *see* PERIODICO OFICIAL

NEW LIBRARY SCENE – (1985-. 5,6,9) – v1-. 1982- – 1 – us UMI [020]

NEW LIBRARY WORLD – v1- 1898- 1; 1974-5,6; 1976- 4 x 6 in. 9 – us UMI [073]

THE NEW LIBYA. A GEOGRAPHICAL, SOCIAL, ECONOMIC AND POLITICAL STUDY / Libya. Ministry of Information and Culture – Tripoli. 1967. Hajjaji, S. A. BNE-523 1 – 9 – ne IDC [956]

NEW LICHENS, PRINCIPALLY FROM THE HERBARIUM OF W. J. HOOKER / Taylor, T – 324. 1847 – 9 – ne IDC [580]

A NEW LIFE IN EDUCATION / Durell, Fletcher – 2nd ed. Philadelphia: American Sunday-School Union, 1894 – 1mf – 9 – 0-8370-8665-5 – 1986-2665 – us A.T.L.A. [370]

NEW LIGHT FROM ARMAGEDDON / Guy, PLO – 1931 – 9 – $10.00 – us I.R.C. [930]

A NEW LIGHT ON ANNEXATION: A POLITICAL BROCHURE / Clarke, Samuel Robinson – (Toronto: J. Murray), 1891. 03054. (Pre-1900 Canadiana) – 9 – cn C.I.H.M. [971]

NEW LIGHT ON THE LIFE OF CHRIST / Briggs, Charles Augustus – New York: Scribner's, 1904. 1 fiche – 9 – us A.T.L.A. [240]

NEW LIGHT ON THE NEW TESTAMENT / Flournoy, Parke P – Philadelphia: Westminster Press, 1903. 1 fiche – 9 – us A.T.L.A. [240]

NEW LIGHT ON THE OLD PRAYER / Campbell, John – Toronto: W. Briggs; Montreal: C. Coates; Halifax: S. Huestis, 1895. 00381. (Pre-1900 Canadiana) – 9 – cn C.I.H.M. [240]

NEW LIGHT ON THE TEN COMMANDMENTS / Shipley, Maynard – Girard, KS: Haldeman-Julius Pub., 1929. 32p. (Little Blue Book, no 1499) – 1 – us U.W. Library [240]

NEW LISBON GAZETTE – New Lisbon, OH. Jan 8 1824 – 1r – 1 – us Western Res [071]

NEW LISBON JOURNAL – (Weekly independent newspaper) – New Lisbon, OH. Apr 11 1870-Mar 12 1888 – 5r – 1 – us Western Res [071]

NEW LISBON, OHIO, RECORDS, MS 1255 – (Delinquent list vol and misc enclosures) – 1844-51 – 1r – 1 – us Western Res [978]

A NEW LIST OF THE FLOWERING PLANTS AND FERNS GROWING WILD IN THE COUNTRY OF DEVON / Ravenshaw, T F T – London. 1860. B-7249 1 – 9 – ne IDC [580]

NEW LITERARY HISTORY – v1- 1969- 1; v6-5,6; v7- 9 – us UMI [410]

New London County. Connecticut *see*
- FIRST CONGREGATIONAL CHURCH, STONINGTON, CONNECTICUT HISTORY
- THE HOMES OF OUR ANCESTORS IN STONINGTON, CONNECTICUT
- STONINGTON, COUNTY OF NEW LONDON, CONNECTICUT

THE NEW LONDON GAZETTE – New London. Conn. 1763-73. Sold with the Connecticut Gazette, 1774-1820 – 3 – us Readex [071]

NEW LONG-RANGE ECONOMIC PLAN OF JAPAN, 1961-70 / Japan. Keizai Kikakucho – Tokyo, 1961. 127p. BD-313/1 – 9 – ne IDC [338]

NEW LONG-RANGE ECONOMIC PLAN OF JAPAN (FY1958-FY1962 / Japan. Keizai Kikakucho – Tokyo, Economic Planning Agency, 1957. 196p. BD-144- – 9 – ne IDC [338]

THE NEW MAN AND THE ETERNAL LIFE : NOTES ON THE REITERATED AMENS OF THE SON OF GOD / Jukes, Andrew John – NY: Thomas Whittaker, 1882 – 1mf – 9 – 0-8370-3820-0 – 1985-1820 – us A.T.L.A. [240]

EIN NEW MANDAT JESU CHRISTI / Herman, N – 1546. BME-42 1 – 9 – ne IDC [240]

EIN NEW MANDAT JESU CHRISTI / Herman, N – Strasszburg, H. Grymmen. 1547. BME-44 1 – 9 – ne IDC [240]

EIN NEW MANDAT JHESU CHRISTI / Herman, N – Gegeben inn diesem 56. Jar. Schleusingen, H. Hamsing. 1556. BME-45 1 – 9 – ne IDC [240]

NEW MANUAL OF THE COSTS, FORMS AND RULES, IN THE COMMON LAW COURTS OF UPPER CANADA / McMillan, Alexander Guy – Toronto, Rollo & Adam, 1865. 142 p. LL-2316 – 1 – us L of C Photodup [340]

NEW MARITIMES – (v1-6 1982/83-1987/88 Can$60.00y 1) – Halifax. v1-12. 1982/83-1993/94 – 1,9 – Can$20.00y – cn Micromedia [073]

NEW MARLBORO 1734-1890 – (Mf 1-3: Birth Index 1734-1858. Mf 3-4: Marriage Index 1734-1858. Mf 4-5: Death Index 1734-1858. Mf 6-7: Birth Index 1852-1950. Mf 8-9: Marriage Index 1852-1950. Mf 9-11: Death Index 1852-1950. Mf 12-14: Births 1734-1858. Mf 15,16: Births 1734-1858. Mf 17: Births 1844-55. Mf 18: Births 1855-58; Marriages 1766-95. Mf 19: Marriages 1795-1824. Mf 20: Marriages 1824-53. Mf 21: Marriages 1766-1850. Mf 21-22: Deaths 1750-1852. Mf 23: Deaths 1843-53. Mf 24-25: Births 1854-90. Mf 25-27: Marriages 1852-91. Mf 27-29: Deaths 1853-91) – (mf ed 1983) – 29mf – 9 – 0-931248-45-0 – us Holbrook [920]

NEW MASSES – New York, NY. -w. Jan 1934-Sept 1935. 3 reels – 1 – uk British Libr Newspaper [071]

NEW MASSES – v.1-66. 1926-48 – 1 – 22316.00 – us Princeton Micro [320]

NEW MCCLURE'S MAGAZINE – v. 1-62. 1893-1929 – 1 – us UMI [073]

NEW MEANING FOR EDUCATION : LOOKING AT THE EUROPE REGION / Aitken, Douglas J – 1990 – 51p – 9 – 92-3-102702-6 – fr UNESCO [370]

NEW MEMOIRS OF LITERATURE – Containing an account of new books printed both at home and abroad, with dissertations upon several subjects, miscellaneous observations, etc. v. 1-6. January 1725-December 1727 – 1 – us UMI [410]

DER NEW MENSCH / Crauthwaldt, S von – Augspurg, Ph. Ulhart. 1543. BME-76 1 – 9 – ne IDC [240]

NEW MENTOR – Portland OR. Feb 13 21 1932 – 1 – us U.O. Library [071]

A NEW METHOD OF LEARNING WITH GREATER FACILITY THE GREEK TONGUE / Lancelot, Claude – 1746. 2v. (English Linguistics Series 1500-1800) – 9 – us UMI [450]

NEW MEXICO : SESSION LAWS OF AMERICAN STATES AND TERRITORIES – 1846-1994 (all publ) – 9 – $1,212.00 set – us Hein [340]

New Mexico *see*
- REPORTS AND OPINIONS (A-G)
- REPORTS, PRE-NRS

THE NEW MEXICO – Santa Fe. N.M. 1868- – 1 – us UMI [978]

NEW MEXICO AGRICULTURAL STATISTICS / New Mexico State University – No.7-10.1972-81. 1 reel – 1,5 – us Spaulding [630]

New Mexico Association of Indian Affairs *see* INDIAN ART SERIES

NEW MEXICO ATTORNEY GENERAL REPORTS AND OPINIONS – (6 1909-1977 $210.00. 9 1978-1993 $140.00) – 1909-1993 – 6,9 – $350.00set – us Hein [340]

New Mexico Baptist Convention *see* ANNUALS

NEW MEXICO BAR JOURNAL – v1. 1995 – 9 – $10.00set – us Hein [340]

NEW MEXICO BUSINESS CURRENT ECONOMIC REPORT – (1984-. 5,6,9) – v1-. 1980- – 1 – us UMI [330]

New Mexico Conservation Needs Committee *see* NEW MEXICO SOIL AND WATER CONSERVATION NEEDS INVENTORY

New Mexico Crop Improvement Association *see* NEW MEXICO SEED CERTIFICATION HANDBOOK

New Mexico. Department of Agriculture *see*
- MISCELLANEOUS PUBLICATIONS
- REGISTERED PESTICIDES AND LICENSED PESTICIDE APPLICATORS, DEALERS AND CONSULTANTS

New Mexico. (District) *see*
- LETTERS RECEIVED BY HEADQUARTERS, DISTRICT OF NEW MEXICO
- LETTERS SENT BY THE NINTH MILITARY DEPARTMENT, DEPARTMENT OF NEW MEXICO, AND DISTRICT OF NEW MEXICO

New Mexico. Engineering Department *see* STATE WATER RESOURCES REPORTS

New Mexico. Fort Cummings *see* HEADQUARTERS RECORDS

NEW MEXICO HISTORICAL REVIEW – v1-1926- 1; v46- 5,6; v51- 9 – us UMI [978]

New Mexico Inter-Agency Range Committee *see* REPORT

NEW MEXICO JEWISH COMMUNITY LINK – (v11 no 2 (Feb 1982)-v11 no 6 (June 1982). v13 no 2 (Feb 1984)-v13 no 4 (Mar 1984). Missing: v11 no 7-v13 no 1 (June 1982-Jan 1984). Ceased 1984) – Albuquerque, New Mexico – 1 – us A.J.P.C. [305]

NEW MEXICO LAW REVIEW – (v1-14 1971-84 on reel $145.00. v15-24 1985-94 on mf $239.00) – v1-25. 1970-95 – 5,6,9 – $384.00 set – us Hein [340]

NEW MEXICO MAPS : CITIES AND TOWNS – 1883-1908. 390 maps. 30 towns. Sanborn Company Fire Insurance Maps – 1 – $56.00r – us Shkurkin [910]

NEW MEXICO QUARTERLY – v. 1-39. 1931-69 – 1 – us UMI [073]

NEW MEXICO SEED CERTIFICATION HANDBOOK / New Mexico Crop Improvement Association – 1980. 1 reel – 1,5 – us Spaulding [631]

NEW MEXICO SOIL AND WATER CONSERVATION NEEDS INVENTORY / New Mexico Conservation Needs Committee – Jan 1970. 1 reel – 1,5 – us Spaulding [639]

New Mexico. State Bar Association *see* PROCEEDINGS

NEW MEXICO STATE BUSINESS DIRECTORY / The Gazetteer Publishing and Printing Co – Denver, 1938. New Mexico reel 3. (Cox Library Collection) – 5 – us Americana [978]

New Mexico State College *see* NEW MEXICO TREES

New Mexico State Library *see* PUBLICATIONS FILED BY NEW MEXICO STATE AGENCIES WITH THE NEW MEXICO STATE LIBRARY

New Mexico. State Records Center and Archives *see*
- CURRENT RULE LISTINGS OF NEW MEXICO STATE AGENCIES
- LAND RECORDS OF NEW MEXICO
- MEXICAN ARCHIVES
- SPANISH ARCHIVES OF NEW MEXICO SERIES 2
- TERRITORIAL ARCHIVES OF NEW MEXICO

New Mexico State University *see*
- AN ACTION PLAN OF ASSISTANCE FOR THE SMALL FARMERS OF NEW MEXICO
- NEW MEXICO AGRICULTURAL STATISTICS
- PROCEEDINGS

New Mexico State University. Agricultural Experiment Station *see*
- BULLETIN
- MISCELLANEOUS PUBLICATIONS
- RESEARCH REPORT
- SPECIAL REPORT

New Mexico State University. Agricultural Extension Service *see* ECONOMIC SURVEY-REFERENCE MATERIAL AND REPORTS-MIDDLE RIO GRANDE CONSERVANCY DISTRICT

New Mexico State University. College of Architecture and Home Economics *see* IMPORTANCE OF THE FORT STANTON EXPERIMENTAL RANCH AND ITS IMPACT ON RANGE LIVESTOCK INDUSTRY OF NEW MEXICO

New Mexico State University. Cooperative Extension Service *see*
- 4-H SERVICE BULLETIN, SERIES 100
- BULL SESSION
- MISCELLANEOUS PUBLICATIONS
- SPECIALIST SERVICE BULLETIN

New Mexico State University. Department of Agronomy *see* THE AGRONOMIST

New Mexico State University. Department of Animal and Range Sciences *see* DAIRY TEACHING, RESEARCH AND EXTENSION AT NEW MEXICO STATE UNIVERSITY

New Mexico State University. Range Improvement Task Force *see* MISCELLANEOUS PUBLICATIONS

NEW MEXICO STATUTES ANNOTATED – Charlottesville, Michie Company. Superseded vols – 9 – Inquire – us Hein [340]

NEW MEXICO SUPREME COURT REPORTS – (Pre-NRS: v1-2 1852-83 5mf $22.50. Vols after v29 remain in copyright. Updates poss only after 1999) – v1-29. 1852-1924 – 84mf – 9 – $378.00 – LLMC 84-165 – us L.L.M.C. [340]

New Mexico Territory *see* SESSION LAWS

NEW MEXICO TREES / New Mexico State College – 1939. 1 reel – 1,5 – us Spaulding [580]

NEW MEXICO WILDLIFE – 1961- 1; 1973- 5,6; 1975- 9 – us UMI [073]

NEW MEXICO'S NEWS AND VIEWS *see* BAR BULLETIN

NEW MILITANT / Workers Party. U.S.A – 1-2 2+22 (all publ). 1934-36 – 1 reel – 1 – $115.00 – us UPA [335]

NEW MILTON DISTRICT ADVERTISER – England.Jun 1828-1830; Jul-Dec 1831. -w. 1 reel – 1 – uk British Libr Newspaper [072]

NEW MIRROR – v. 1-3. 8 Apr 1843-28 Sep 1844 – 1 – us UMI [073]

NEW MISCELLANEOUS MUSICAL WORK / Jackson, G K – For the voice and piano forte. Consisting of songs, serenades, cantatas, canzonetts, canons, glees &c. &c.n.p., n.d. music 3082, item 7 – 1 – us L of C Photodup [780]

THE NEW MITRE *see* THE MITRE

DIE NEW MODEL ARMY UND DIE LEVELLERS (1647/48) / Ludwig, Roland – 1992 – 9 – DM98.00 – 3-89349-498-7 – gw Hänsel [941]

NEW MODELBUCH. MUEMPELGARTEN / Foillet, J – O-1134 1. 1598 – 9 – ne IDC [999]

NEW MONTHLY MAGAZINE – Feb 1814-Jan 1884 – 1 – us UMI [073]

NEW MONTHLY MAGAZINE AND HUMORIST *see* NEW MONTHLY MAGAZINE

NEW MONTHLY MAGAZINE AND LITERARY JOURNAL – v. 1-nsv.3 Jan 1821-Jun 1834 – 1 – us UMI [073]

NEW MONTHLY MAGAZINE AND UNIVERSAL REGISTER *see* NEW MONTHLY MAGAZINE

THE NEW MONTREAL GAZETTE / ed by Ferguson, Archibald – Montreal, Canada. v1 n4. 6 aut 1827-v2 n9. 15 sep 1828 – 1r – 1 – Can$30.00 – cn Can Microfilming [072]

NEW MORAL WORLD – London. 1834-45 – 1 – uk Microform Academic [073]

NEW MORAL WORLD – Robert Owen. 1-13 (all publ). 1834-1845 – 69mf – 9 – $210.00 – us UPA [335]

THE NEW MORAL WORLD – Gazette of the Rational Society.v1-13, 1835-45 – 1 – 65.00 – us L of C Photodup [335]

THE NEW MORAL WORLD 1834-1845; MORAL WORLD, 1945 – September 1990 – 5r – 1 – uk Microform Academic [900]

NEW MUSIC – A quarterly of modern compositions. v. 1-8. 1927-1935 – 1 – us Schnase [780]

NEW MUSIC REVIEW AND CHURCH MUSIC REVIEW – New York. v1-34. 1901-35 – 8r – 1 – us Ross [780]

NEW MUSICAL EXPRESS – London, UK. 4 Oct 1946-1971. -w. 18 reels – 1 – uk British Libr Newspaper [073]

NEW MUSICAL EXPRESS AND PREDECESSORS, 1946-71 – 1 – us Primary [780]

NEW NATION – 1-4 2+5 (all publ). 1891-1894 – 24mf – 9 – $135.00 – us UPA [335]

NEW NATION – British Guyana. 1962- – 1 – us UMI [072]

NEW NATION – Johannesburg, South Africa. 1 Jan 1986- – 15r – 1 – sa Microfile [072]

NEW NATION – Johannesburg, South Africa. Jan 12/18-Dec 15/19 1989 – 1r – 1 – us L of C Photodup [072]

NEW NATIONAL ERA AND CITIZEN – 1870-74 – 1 – us UMI [073]

NEW NEBRASKAN – Omaha, NE. -w. Jan 1914; Apr 1914; Dec 1914-Sept 1920 – 1 – us NE Hist [071]

THE NEW NEGRO WORLD – Cleveland. v. 3, no. 8-11; 4, no. 1, 4; 5, no. 2. Jun 1943-Feb 1945 – 1 – us NY Public [073]

THE NEW NIETZSCHE – Contemporary styles of interpretation. Ed. and introd. by David B. Allison. New York: Dell Publishing Co., 1977.xxviii,274p – 1 – us U.W. Library [190]

NEW NIGERIAN – Kaduna, Nigeria, 1966-69 – 10r – 1 – us Ross [072]

NEW NIGERIAN – Kaduna, Nigeria. -d. Jan 1968-Dec 1970. 9 reels – 1 – uk British Libr Newspaper [072]

THE NEW NORTH – Rhinelander. Wis. 1891-1947 – 1 – us UMI [071]

NEW NORTHWEST – Portland, OR. -w. 1871-87 – 1 – 113.00 – us Oregon Hist [071]

NEW OR CRITICAL NORWEGIAN ALGAE / Foslie, M – (K. Norske Vidensk. Selsk. Skrifter). Trondhjem. 1894. B-6364 2 – 8 – ne IDC [580]

NEW ORDER IN VALENCIA – An article from "The Times", London, 1937. Fiche W1074. (Blodgett Collection of Spanish Civil War Pamphlets) – 9 – us H.U. College Libr [946]

NEW ORLEANS AS IT WAS, EPISODES OF LOUISIANA LIFE / Castellanos, H C – New Orleans: L. Graham and Son, Ltd., Printers, 1895. Louisiana Reel 1. (The Cox Library Collection) – 5 – us Americana [978]

New Orleans Baptist Seminary *see* MAGNET

New Orleans Baptist Theological Seminary *see*
- ADDRESSES AND LECTURES..
- INAUGURAL ADDRESSES OF PRESIDENTS

New Orleans Baptist Theological Seminary. (Formerly: Baptist Bible Institute). New Orleans, Louisiana *see* CATALOGS AND COLLEGE RECORDS

New Orleans Jazz Club *see* THE SECOND LINE

NEW ORLEANS MISCELLANY – 1847-1848 – 1 – us UMI [073]

THE NEW ORLEANS SENTINEL – New Orleans. La. june 15, Oct. 26, 1940 – 1 – us NY Public [071]

THE NEW ORLEANS TIMES PICAYUNE INDEX – 1 – us UMI [071]

NEW OUTLOOK – (The Independent was merged with Outlook and Independent in 1928). v58-164. 1898-1934 – 1,5,6 – us Princeton Micro [073]

NEW OUTLOOK – v1-165 n6. 1870-Jun 1935 – 1 – us UMI [073]

NEW OUTLOOK FOR THE BLIND – (See also: Journal of Visual Impairment and Blindness) – v1-70. 1907-76 – 1 – us UMI [370]

THE NEW PACIFIC COAST LAW JOURNAL – v1-3. 1924-1926 (all publ) – 11mf – $16.50 – LLMC 84-645 – us L.L.M.C. [073]

THE NEW PACIFIC CONSTITUTIONAL LAW JOURNAL – v1-3. 1924-26 (all publ) – 11mf – 9 – $16.50 – LLMC 84-645 – us L.L.M.C. [073]

NEW PAGE / Mayor, Federico – 1995 – 98p – 9 – 92-3-102949-5 – Co-publ with Dartmouth/UNESCO Publishing – fr UNESCO [320]

NEW PALESTINE (AMERICAN ZIONIST) – New York, NY. 14 Jan 1921-Oct/Nov 1985.English. Ceased publication – 1 – us A.J.P.C. [071]

THE NEW PANAMA CANAL TREATY : LEGISLATIVE HISTORY AND TEXTS, 1975-1979 / Panama Canal Zone – (Comprises roughly 12,000p of legislative hearings and reports, transcripts of debates, speeches, treaty drafts etc.) – New Orleans: Staff of the Library of the US 5th Circuit Court for Appeals, 1975-79 – 144mf – 9 – $216.00 – LLMC 82-100D Title 16 – us L.L.M.C. [340]

NEW PARENTS (CCC227) / ed by Liu, Yu-chen & Sun, Hui-lan – (In Chinese) – Hong Kong: Bible Book and Tract Depot, 1953 – 1r – 1984-B500 – us A.T.L.A. [640]

NEW PARTNERSHIP : INDIGENOUS PEOPLES AND THE UNITED NATIONS SYSTEM / Zinsser, Judith P – 1995 – 120p – 9 – 92-3-103046-9 – fr UNESCO [320]

'NEW PARTY' BULLETIN – Toronto: New Party, [1889-188- or 189-] – 9 – cn C.I.H.M. [324]

NEW PATH – 1863-65 – 5mf – 9 – £32.00 – uk Chadwyck [700]

NEW PERSPECTIVES : A CIVIL RIGHTS QUARTERLY – (v1-11 were titled "Civil Rights digest". Add vols planned) – v1-18 no2. 1968-86 – 56mf – 9 – $84.00 – LLMC 81-206 – us L.L.M.C. [340]

NEW PERSPECTIVES: CIVIL RIGHTS QUARTERLY *see* CIVIL RIGHTS DIGEST

NEW PHYSICIAN – (v.28-. 1979- 5,6,9) – v.6-. 1957- – 1 – us UMI [073]

NEW PHYTOLOGIST – Cambridge. v1-40. 1902-1941 – 270mf – 9 – ne IDC [580]

NEW PIONEER – London, England. -m. Dec 1938-Jan 1940. 32 ft – 1 – uk British Libr Newspaper [072]

NEW PLEASANT BAPTIST CHURCH. BROAD RIVER ASSOCIATION. CHEROKEE COUNTY. GAFFNEY, SOUTH CAROLINA : CHURCH RECORDS – 1909-22; 1930-71 – 1 – 34.65 – us Baptist [240]

NEW POEMS / Arnold, Matthew – London: Macmillan, 1867 – 1 roll – 1 – 1-55879-188-4 – uk Libr Preservation [810]

NEW POEMS BY CHRISTINA ROSSETTI : HITHERTO UNPUBLISHED OR UNCOLLECTED / Rossetti, Christina; ed by Rossetti, William Michael – New York, London: Macmillan and Co., 1896 – 1 roll – 1 – 1-55879-172-8 – uk Libr Preservation [810]

THE NEW POINT OF VIEW (CCC99) : A COMPILATION OF ARTICLES ON RELIGION AND CHRISTIANITY BY VARIOUS AUTHORS / ed by Chien, Timothy Yu-wan – (In Chinese) – 2nd ed. Shanghai: Publication Dept., National Committee, YMCAs of China, 1923 – 1r – 1 – 1984-B500 – us A.T.L.A. [240]

NEW POLITICS – v1-12 1961-78 1; v9-12 5,6; v12- 9 – us UMI [073]

A NEW PRACTICAL HEBREW GRAMMAR : WITH HEBREW-ENGLISH AND ENGLISH-HEBREW EXERCISES AND A HEBREW CHRESTOMATHY / Deutsch, Solomon – New York: Leypoldt & Holt, 1868 – 1mf – 9 – 0-8370-9136-5 – 1986-3136 – us A.T.L.A. [470]

THE NEW PRACTICAL NAVIGATOR / Moore, John Hamilton – 19th ed. 1814 – 9 – $20.00 – uk Libr Preservation [623]

THE NEW PRACTICE AND PROCEDURE IN THE MUNICIPAL COURT OF THE CITY OF NEW YORK UNDER THE MUNICIPAL COURT CODE (LAWS OF 1915, CHAP. 279). / Lauer, Edgar Jacob – (A supplement. New York, 1919. 432 p. L.C. copy imperfect: suppl. wanting) – New York, Baker, Voorhis, 1916. 1069 p. LL-264 – 1 – us L of C Photodup [340]

THE NEW PRINCE FORTUNATUS / Black, William – British Fiction Archive: Unit 4 – 9 – uk Bell [830]

A NEW PROGRAMME OF MISSIONS : A MOVEMENT TO MAKE THE COLLEGES IN ALL LANDS CENTERS OF EVANGELIZATION / Wishard, Luther Deloraine – New York: Fleming H Revell, 1895 – 1mf – 9 – 0-8370-7355-3 – 1986-1355 – us A.T.L.A. [240]

THE NEW PROPELLOR / The Aircraft Shop Stewards National Council – Journal of the Aircraft Shop Stewards, National Council.1935-46 – 1 – uk World [380]

NEW PROTECTIONISM AND ATTEMPTS AT LIBERALIZATION IN AGRICULTURAL TRADE – it F.A.O. [338]

NEW PROVIDENCE BAPTIST CHURCH. WARREN COUNTY. GEORGIA : CHURCH RECORDS – 1835-Feb 1930. 916p – 1 – 41.22 – us Baptist [240]

THE NEW PUBLIC SCHOOLS / Erickson, Donald A – CIE, 1977, 11p with publications list of CIE (Center for Independent Education) – 9 – 1.00f – at Libertarian Micro [335]

NEW QUARTERLY MAGAZINE – 1-n.s. 3. 1873-80 – 1 – us UMI [073]

NEW QUARTERLY MUSICAL REVIEW – v. 1-3. May 1893-Feb 1896 – 1 – us UMI [780]

NEW QUARTERLY REVIEW – 1-10. 1852-61 – 1 – us UMI [073]

NEW QUARTERLY REVIEW – 1-9. 1843-47 – 1 – us UMI [073]

THE NEW RAT TRACK / Darby, Douglas – 1971, 16p. Anti-Communist pamphlet – 9 – 1.00f – at Libertarian Micro [080]

NEW READINGS OF OLD PARABLES / Anderson, Charles – New York: T Whittaker, 1876 – 1mf – 9 – 0-8370-2091-3 – 1985-0091 – us A.T.L.A. [220]

THE NEW REFORMATION : A NARRATIVE OF THE OLD CATHOLIC MOVEMENT FROM 1870 TO THE PRESENT TIME / Mullinger, J Bass – London: Longmans, Green, 1875 – 1mf – us A.T.L.A. [240]

THE NEW REFORMATION : RECENT EVANGELICAL MOVEMENTS IN THE ROMAN CATHOLIC CHURCH / Bain, John A – (Includes bibliographical references and index) – Edinburgh: T & T Clark, 1906 – 1mf – 9 – 0-8370-8401-6 – 1986-2401 – us A.T.L.A. [240]

NEW REGULATION ON STATE OF EMERGENCY. PRESIDENT'S DECISION NO. 315/1959 / Indonesia. President. (Sukarno) – SE-2190 1. 1959 – 9 – ne IDC [950]
NEW RELIGIOUS MOVEMENTS AND RAPID SOCIAL CHANGE / ed by Beckford, James A – 1986 – xv/247p – 9 – 92-3-102402-7 – Co-published with Sage Publications, Ltd, London – fr UNESCO [306]
NEW RELIGIOUS MOVEMENTS UPDATE – 1977-81 – 1 – us UMI [200]
NEW REMEDIES *see* AMERICAN DRUGGIST
NEW REPUBLIC – (1967- 5,6. 1970- 9) – 1914- – 1 – us UMI [073]
NEW REPUBLIC – 3 Jan 1913-29 Dec 1916. Related Guide Book may be purchased separately from publisher – 1 roll 35mm set – 1 – us Ohio Hist [360]
NEW REPUBLIC – v. 1-112. 1914-1945 – 1 – us Princeton Micro [073]
NEW REPUBLIC – Vancouver, British Columbia, CN. Sept 1957-Dec 1970 – 27r – 1 – cn Commonwealth Micro [072]
NEW RESEARCHES INTO THE COMPOSITION AND EXEGESIS OF THE QORAN / Hirschfeld, H – 1902 – 1 – uk Microform Academic [260]
NEW RESERVOIRS IN AFRICA, 1980-2000 – 1984 – 28p – it F.A.O. [639]
NEW REVIEW – 1-4 2+6 (all publ). 1913-16 – 28mf – 9 – $160.00 – us UPA [335]
NEW REVIEW : AN INTERNATIONAL NOTEBOOK FOR THE ARTS, PUBLISHED FROM PARIS – Paris. v1-2. 1931-32 – 1r – 1 – us Ross [700]
NEW REVIEW – Milwaukie OR. Nov 22 1978-June 23 1983 – 1 – us U.O. Library [071]
NEW REVIEW – v. 1-17. June 1889-Dec 1897 – 1 – us UMI [073]
NEW REVIEW – v. 31-32. 1950 – 1 – us UMI [073]
THE NEW REVIEW – Alberta, CN. 1935-36 – 1r – 1 – cn Commonwealth Micro [072]
THE NEW REVIEW – Paris. v. 1, no. 1-v. 2, no. 5. Jan 1931-Apr 1932 – 1 – us NY Public [073]
NEW REVIEW OF BOOKS AND RELIGION – v.1-4. 1976-80 – 1 – us UMI [410]
NEW REVIEW OR MONTHLY ANALYSIS OF GENERAL LITERATURE – v1-2. 1813 – 1 – us UMI [073]
THE NEW REVOLUTIONARY LANDMARK BAPTIST FACTION / Ray, D B – 1 – 5.00 – us Baptist [240]
NEW RIVER BAPTIST CHURCH. BOOKER, FLORIDA : CHURCH RECORDS – 1899-May 1974. History. 1833-1912 – 1 – 35.82 – us Baptist [240]
NEW ROCHELLE-HER PART IN THE GREAT WAR / Pallen, Conde B – Historical and biographical sketches. Walter-Castell Tindall, 1920. New York Reel 38. (The Cox Library Collection) – 5 – us Americana [978]
NEW ROSS STANDARD – Ross, Ireland. -d. 1898-1903, 1986. 8 reels – 1 – PS27.50r – ie European Micro [072]
NEW ROTTERDAMSCHE COURANT, 1845-1970 – 1845-1970 – 10,898mf – 9 – Dfl55,708.00 silver Dfl50,887.00 diazo – ne MMF Publ [320]
NEW SALEM 1742-1894 – (Mf 1: Baptisms & Marriages 1742-82. Mf 2: Baptisms 1807-43; Marriages 1748-82, 1808-68. Mf 3: Church Business 1809-58. Mf 4-8: Parish Records 1788-1848. Mf 9-11: Parish Records 1864-1962. Mf 12-13: Church Trustees Records 1820-1909. Mf 14-15: Church Treasurers Records 1823-1963. Mf 16: Ladies Society Treasurers Records 1856-66. Mf 17: Birth Index 1857-94. Mf 18: Marriage Index 1748-99, 1857-94. Mf 19: Death Index 1857-94. Mf 20-21: Births 1769-1893. Mf 21-22: Marriages 1748-99, 1857-93. Mf 22-23: Deaths 1857-93) – (mf ed 1993) – 23mf – 9 – us Holbrook [920]
NEW SALEM BAPTIST CHURCH. COXS CREEK, KENTUCKY : CHURCH RECORDS – 1801-Nov 1960 – 1 – 83.61 – us Baptist [240]
NEW SALEM BAPTIST CHURCH. JONESBORO, TENNESSEE : CHURCH RECORDS – (528p) – 1845-1908 – 1 reel – 1 – $23.76 – us Baptist [240]
NEW SCHOLASTICISM – v1- 1927- 1; v45- 5,6; v50- 9 – us UMI [140]
NEW SCHOLASTICISM *see* AMERICAN CATHOLIC PHILOSOPHICAL QUARTERLY
New Schools Exchange *see* NEWSLETTER
NEW SCIENCE REVIEW – A Miscellany of Modern Thought and Discovery. v. 1-2. Jul 1894-Jan 1896 – 1 – us UMI [500]
NEW SCIENTIST – London – 9 – 23.00 – uk I.P.C. [500]
New Sharon, Maine. New Sharon Baptist Church *see* RECORDS
NEW SIDE-LIGHTS ON PREPARATION OF MILITARY REBELLION: AN INTERESTING DOCUMENT – Valencia, 193? Fiche W1075. (Blodgett Collection of Spanish Civil War Pamphlets) – 9 – us H.U. College Libr [946]
THE NEW SOCIETY BLUE BOOK / Pinchard, Marguerite M – San Francisco, 1928. Calif. reel 38. (Cox Library Collection) – 5 – us Americana [978]
NEW SOLIDARITY (NEW YORK, N.Y.) – (Includes c.1: v.9:no.9 1978:Mar.31-v.14:no.61 (1983:Dec.19), LACKS many issues) – New York: Campaigner Publications Ltd., 19uu – 1 – CSUX86-S417 – us Hoover Inst Photo [978]
NEW SOUTH – 1946-73 1; 1971-73 5,6 – us UMI [360]
NEW SOUTH – Birmingham. v. 1, no. 1-6. May 1937-Oct 1938. Incomplete – 1 – us NY Public [073]
NEW SOUTH – Communist Party. v1. 1937-38 – 1r – 1 – us Ross [335]
NEW SOUTH – Port Royal, SC. v1-2. 1862-64 – 1r – 1 – us Ross [071]
NEW SOUTH (BEAUFORT, SOUTH CAROLINA), MARCH 7, 1895 / ed by Bampfield, S J – (Also contains: Palmetto Herald 1864; Camp Kettle 1861-62; Hospital Transcript 1865) – 1991 – 1r – 1 – $75.00 – D3275.P11 – Co-publ with the South Caroliniana Library, University of South Carolina – us Scholarly Res [975]
New South Wales *see* MITCHELL LIBRARY TOWN AND COUNTRY INDEX
New South Wales. Australia. Parliament *see*
– LEGISLATIVE ASSEMBLY
– LEGISLATIVE COUNCIL
– PARLIAMENTARY DEBATES
New South Wales. Australia. Supreme Court *see* NEW SOUTH WALES REPORTS
NEW SOUTH WALES: HER COMMERCE AND RESOURCES / Griffin, Gilderoy Wells – Sydney: C. Potter, 1888. 293p. 1 folded leaf of plates. Col. map. With: veld trails, C.S. Stokes – 1 – us U.W. Library [380]
NEW SOUTH WALES JOURNAL OF OPTOMETRY – 1934- 1; 1972- 5,6; 1975- 9 – us UMI [073]
NEW SOUTH WALES PROVINCIAL NEWSPAPERS – (Apply to publ for details) – at Pascoe [072]
NEW SOUTH WALES REPORTS / New South Wales. Australia. Supreme Court – 10 yr. index. 21v. 1960-70 – 5,9 – $275.00 – at Butterworths [340]
NEW SPAIN; ITS PEOPLE, ITS RULER / Godden, Gertrude M – N.Y., 1939. Fiche W920. (Blodgett Collection of Spanish Civil War Pamphlets) – 9 – us H.U. College Libr [946]
THE NEW SPANISH INQUISITION / United American Spanish Aid Committee – N.Y., 1940. Fiche W1076. (Blodgett Collection of Spanish Civil War Pamphlets) – 9 – us H.U. College Libr [946]
A NEW SPELLING BOOK / Lye, Thomas – 1677. 151p. (English Linguistics Series 1500-1800) – 9 – us UMI [420]
NEW STAR – 2Feb 1796 – 1 – us UMI [073]
NEW STAR – ns 1-26. 11 Apr-3 Oct 1797 – 1 – us UMI [073]
NEW STARTS IN LIFE AND OTHER SERMONS / Brooks, Phillips – New York: E.P. Dutton, 1896 – 1mf – us A.T.L.A. [240]
NEW STATESMAN – 1931-1994 – 1 – sz Infoprint [073]
NEW STATESMAN – (1971- 5,6. 1976- 9) – 1931- – 1 – us UMI [320]
NEW STATESMAN – os v1-36 1913-31; ns v1-56 1931-58 – 1 – us Princeton Micro [073]
THE NEW STRUCTURE AND CONTENT OF EDUCATION FOR GHANA / Ghana. Ministry of Education – Accra, 1974 – 1mf – 9 – DE-434/1 – ne IDC [370]
NEW STUDENT / National Student Forum of the Paris Pact – 1-8 2+9 (all publ). 1922-29 – 2r – 1 – $230.00 – us UPA [370]
NEW STUDIES IN LITERATURE / Dowden, Edward – London: Kegan Paul, Trench, Trbner, 1895 – 1 roll – 1 – 1-55879-823-4 – uk Libr Preservation [410]
NEW SUN – Sheridan, OR. -w. 1 Jul 1904-2 Feb 1908. 1 roll – 1 – us U.O. Library [071]
NEW SUNDAY TRANSCRIPT *see* SUNDAY TRANSCRIPT
NEW SYLLABUS FOR PRIMARY SCHOOLS IN THE SOUTH-EASTERN STATE OF NIGERIA : OFFICIAL DOCUMENTS 1973(9) / Nigeria. South Eastern State – Calabar, 1973 – 2mf – 9 – DE-125/1 – ne IDC [370]
NEW SYSTEM OF WOODEN RAIL / Foster, John – Montreal?: s.n. 1869?. 05595. (Pre-1900 Canadiana) – 9 – cn C.I.H.M. [971]
NEW TECHNOLOGIES AND DEVELOPMENT / ed by Johnston, Ann & Sasson, Albert – 1986 – 9 – 92-3-102454-X – fr UNESCO [338]
NEW TELLER – York, NE. -w. Aug 1897-Mar 1949 – 1 – us NE Hist [071]
THE NEW TESTAMENT – Translated by William Tyndale, 1534...Cambridge Eng.: The University Press, 1938 – 1 – us U.W. Library [240]
NEW TESTAMENT ABSTRACTS – 1(1956)-15(1971) – 110mf – 9 – Dfl385.00 – ne Slangenburg [073]
THE NEW TESTAMENT AGAINST ITS ENVIRONMENT / Filson, FV – S.C.M. Press, 1950 – 9 – $10.00 – us I.R.C. [240]
THE NEW TESTAMENT AND ITS WRITERS / M'Clymont, James Alexander – New York: A.D.F. Randolph, 1893.1 fiche – 9 – us A.T.L.A. [240]
THE NEW TESTAMENT (CCC312) = HSIN YUEH CH'UAN SHU – (In Chinese) – [S.l: s.n, 1933] – 1r – 1 – 1984-6651 – us A.T.L.A. [220]
NEW TESTAMENT CHARACTERS (CCC181) / Hsieh, Sung-kao – (In Chinese) – Hong Kong: Bible Book and Tract Depot, 1952 – 1r – 1 – 1984-B500 – us A.T.L.A. [220]
THE NEW TESTAMENT CHURCH / Marsh, W H H – Philadelphia: American Baptist Publication Society, 1898 – 2mf – us A.T.L.A. [240]
NEW TESTAMENT CRITICISM : ITS HISTORY AND RESULTS / M'Clymont, James Alexander – London; New York: Hodder and Stoughton, 1913 printing – 1mf – 9 – 0-8370-9716-9 – 1986-3716 – us A.T.L.A. [220]
NEW TESTAMENT CRITICISM : LECTURES BY DR C W HODGE BEFORE THE JUNIOR CLASS, PRINCETON THEOLOGICAL SEMINARY / Hodge, Caspar Wistar – Princeton: [Sn.], 1890 – 1mf – 9 – 0-8370-3606-2 – 1985-1606 – us A.T.L.A. [220]
NEW TESTAMENT CRITICISM: LECTURES / Hodge, Caspar Wistar – Princeton, 1890.1 fiche – 9 – us A.T.L.A. [240]
NEW TESTAMENT DIFFICULTIES. FIRST SERIES:...FOR WORKING MEN / Winnington Ingram, Arthur F – London: S.P.C.K., 1901. 1 fiche – 9 – us A.T.L.A. [240]
"THE NEW TESTAMENT ELDER" / Witherow, Thomas – Toronto: J. Bain, 1873 – 1r – 1 – $50.00 – us Presbyterian [240]
NEW TESTAMENT GREEK : A COURSE FOR BEGINNERS / Rodwell, George – (In Greek. Includes index) – London: Methuen, 1899 – 1mf – 9 – 0-8370-9303-1 – 1986-3303 – us A.T.L.A. [450]
THE NEW TESTAMENT IN CHINESE (CCC130) : TRANSLATED FROM THE GREEK FOR THE AMERICAN AND FOREIGN BIBLE SOCIETY BY J. GODDARD – (In Chinese) – 1st ed. Ningpo: American and Foreign Bible Society, 1853 – 1r – 1 – 1984-B500 – us A.T.L.A. [220]
THE NEW TESTAMENT IN THE CHRISTIAN CHURCH: EIGHT LECTURES / Moore, Edward Caldwell – New York: Macmillan, 1904. 1 fiche – 9 – us A.T.L.A. [240]
NEW TESTAMENT: ITS AUTHORSHIP, DATE AND WORTH / Beet, Joseph Agar – London: Robert Culley, (1908). 1 fiche – 9 – us A.T.L.A. [240]
NEW TESTAMENT OF OUR LORD AND SAVIOUR JESUS CHRIST ACCORDING TO THE AUTHORIZED VERSION / How, William W – London: S.P.C.K., 1890. 2 fiches – 9 – us A.T.L.A. [240]
NEW TESTAMENT SCRIPTURES: THEIR CLAIMS, HISTORY, AND AUTHORITY / Charteris, Archibald Hamilton – London: James Nisbet, 1882. 1 fiche – 9 – us A.T.L.A. [240]
NEW TESTAMENT STUDIES – v1- 1954- 1; v23- 1976- 5,6,9 – us UMI [240]
NEW TESTAMENT STUDIES – 1(1955)-13(1967) – 93mf – 9 – Dfl326.00 – ne Slangenburg [073]
NEW TESTAMENT STUDIES. 1: LUKE THE PHYSICIAN / Harnack, Adolf von – London: Williams & Norgate, 1909. 1 fiche – 9 – us A.T.L.A. [240]
NEW TESTAMENT TESTIMONIES – Published by the Conservative Baptist. Mar 1969-Nov 1972 – 1 – 5.00 – us Baptist [240]
NEW TESTAMENT THEOLOGY, PT I : PRINTED FOR CLASSROOM USE / Evans, Milton G – Chester, PA: John Spencer, 1900 – 1mf – 9 – 0-8370-3081-1 – 1985-1081 – us A.T.L.A. [220]
THE NEW TESTAMENT VIEW OF THE OLD : A CONTRIBUTION TO BIBLICAL INTRODUCTION AND EXEGESIS / Turpie, David McCalman – (Includes bibliographical references and indexes) – London: Hodder & Stoughton, 1872 – 1mf – 9 – 0-8370-5588-1 – 1985-3588 – us A.T.L.A. [220]
THE NEW TESTAMENT VIEW OF THE OLD TESTAMENT : AN ESSAY / Donehoo, James Ramsey – (Includes appendixes) – Philadelphia, PA: Westminster Press, 1900 – 1mf – 9 – 0-8370-2949-X – 1985-0949 – us A.T.L.A. [220]
NEW THEATRE – New York. Sept. Oct. 1933-April 1937 – 1 – us NY Public [790]
NEW THEMES FOR THE PROTESTANT CLERGY : CREEDS WITHOUT CHARITY, THEOLOGY WITHOUT HUMANITY, AND PROTESTANTISM WITHOUT CHRISTIANITY : WITH NOTES BY THE EDITOR ON THE LITERATURE OF CHARITY, POPULATION, PAUPERISM, POLITICAL ECONOMY, AND PROTESTANTISM / Colwell, Stephen – Philadelphia: Lippincott, Grambo, 1851 – 1mf – us A.T.L.A. [240]
THE NEW THEOLOGY / Bascom, John – New York: Putnam, 1891. 1 fiche – 9 – us A.T.L.A. [240]
THE NEW THEOLOGY / Campbell, Reginald John – New York:Macmillan, 1907 – 1mf – 9 – 0-8370-3149-4 – 1985-1149 – us A.T.L.A. [240]
THE NEW THEOLOGY : OR, ADVANCED TRUTHS ON SPIRITUAL SUBJECTS / ed by Browning, Henry B – (Includes index) – Philadelphia: J B Lippincott, 1873 – 1mf – 9 – 0-8370-2873-6 – 1985-0873 – us A.T.L.A. [240]
THE NEW THEOLOGY AND THE OLD RELIGION / Gore, Charles – London: John Murray, 1908. 1 fiche – 9 – us A.T.L.A. [240]
NEW THEOLOGY SERMONS / Campbell, R J – London: Williams and Norgate, 1907 – 1mf – us A.T.L.A. [240]
NEW THEORY OF THE FORMATION OF VEINS; WITH ITS APPLICATION TO THE ART OF WORKING MINES / Werner, A G – G 143 2. Edinburgh Review, v18. 1811 – 8 – ne IDC [550]
NEW THOUGHT, ITS HISTORY AND PRINCIPLES, OR, THE MESSAGE OF THE NEW THOUGHT : A CONDENSED HISTORY OF ITS REAL ORIGIN WITH STATEMENT OF ITS BASIC PRINCIPLES AND TRUE AIMS / Atkinson, William Walker – Holyoke, Mass.: Elizabeth Towne; London: L.N. Fowler, c1915 – 1mf – us A.T.L.A. [200]
THE NEW TIDE – Hollywood. v. 1, no. 1. Oct Nov 1934 – 1 – us NY Public [073]
THE NEW TIDE – Hollywood. v1. 1934 – 1r – 1 – us Ross [073]
NEW TIMES – 1973-79 1,5,6; 1975- 79 9 – us UMI [073]
NEW TIMES – 1975-77 – 9 – us UMI [073]
NEW TIMES – 2-7. 1970-76. Superseded by N.T – 1 – us UMI [073]
NEW TIMES – (Cont: Marxism Today. Yrly reel count varies) – 1957- – 1 – us Ross [072]
NEW TIMES – Die neue Zeit. London. (In Yiddish). -w. 4 Mar 1904-22 Sep 1905, 6 Apr, 1, 18 May 1906. (1 reel) – 1 – uk British Libr Newspaper [072]
NEW TIMES – (Morning Journal). London. -d. Jan 1818-May 1830. (27 reels) – 1 – uk British Libr Newspaper [072]
NEW TIMES – Moscow, 1945-71 – 27r – 1 – us Ross [072]
NEW TIMES – (Published by Trud). Moscow. 1945-July 3 1963 – 1 – us NY Public [073]
NEW TIMES – (1989-92 4r per y. 1993 3r. 1994-95 1r per y. 1996-98 2r per y. In English) – Russia, 1999- – 2r per y standing order – 1 – us Ross [072]
NEW TIMES AND ETHIOPIA NEWS – London. May 9, 1936-May 5, 1956 – 1 – us NY Public [072]

NEW TIMES OF BURMA – Rangoon: "Burmese Review" Press, [1946-60]. 1954-55 (4r); 1956-jul 1960 (10r) – 1 – us Res Libr [072]

NEW TIP TOP WEEKLY – New York. no. 2-120. Aug 10 1912-Nov 14 1914. Incomplete – 1 – us NY Public [071]

A NEW TRANSLATION OF THE PROVERBS, ECCLESIASTES, AND THE CANTICLES : WITH INTRODUCTIONS, AND NOTES, CHIEFLY EXPLANATORY / Noyes, George Rapall – (Includes bibliographical references) – Boston: James Munroe; London: Chapman, 1846 – 1mf – 9 – 0-8370-9407-0 – 1986-3407 – us A.T.L.A. [220]

NEW TRAVELS INTO THE INTERIOR PARTS OF AFRICA, BY THE WAY OF THE CAPE OF GOOD HOPE, IN THE YEARS 1783, 1784 AND 1785 / Le Vaillant, Francois – London. 3v. 1796 – 1r – 1 – us Ross [910]

A NEW TREATISE ON THE LAW RELATING TO THE POWERS AND DUTIES OF JUSTICES OF THE PEACE AND CONSTABLES IN THE STATE OF KANSAS...REVISED TO CONFORM TO THE STATUTES IN FORCE 1872 / Swan, Joseph Rockwell – Cincinnati, Clarke, 1872. 683 p. LL-1292 – 1 – us L of C Photodup [340]

NEW TRENDS – v1, no. 1-7 (all publ). 1945-1946 – 2mf – 9 – $35.00 – us UPA [073]

NEW TRENDS AND NEW RESPONSIBILITIES FOR UNIVERSITIES IN LATIN AMERICA – 1980 – 96p – 9 – 92-3-101830-2 – fr UNESCO [370]

NEW TRENDS IN BIOLOGY TEACHING / ed by Heller, R – 9 – fr UNESCO [370]

NEW TRENDS IN CHEMISTRY TEACHING / ed by Cartmell, E – 9 – fr UNESCO [370]

NEW TRENDS IN HOME ECONOMICS EDUCATION – 9 – fr UNESCO [370]

NEW TRENDS IN INTEGRATED SCIENCE TEACHING – 9 – fr UNESCO [370]

NEW TRENDS IN MATHEMATICS TEACHING – 9 – fr UNESCO [370]

NEW TRENDS IN PHYSICS TEACHING – 9 – fr UNESCO [370]

NEW TRENDS IN THE UTILIZATION OF EDUCATIONAL TECHNOLOGY FOR SCIENCE EDUCATION – 1974 – 247p – 9 – 92-3-101143-X – fr UNESCO [370]

THE NEW TRISMAGISTER, OR THE NEW TEACHER OF THREE LANGUAGES / Colsoni, Francesco – 1688. 328p. (English Linguistics Series 1500-1800) – 9 – us UMI [400]

NEW UNESCO SOURCE BOOK FOR GEOGRAPHY TEACHING / ed by Graves, Norman J – 1982 – 394p – 9 – 92-3-101935-X – fr UNESCO [370]

NEW UNESCO SOURCEBOOK FOR SCIENCE TEACHING – 3rd ed 1979 – 270p – 9 – 92-3-101058-1 – fr UNESCO [370]

NEW UNION BAPTIST CHURCH. DAYTON, TENNESSEE : CHURCH RECORDS – April 1898-April 1989. 689p – 1 – $31.01 – us Baptist [240]

NEW UNITY – 1- 1971- – 1 – us UMI [073]

NEW UNIVERSAL HISTORY OF THE RELIGIOUS RIGHTS, CEREMONIES AND CUSTOMS OF THE WHOLE WORLD / Hurd – 1780 – 1 – uk Microform Academic [200]

NEW UNIVERSITY – (Cont: The Anthill) – Irvine, CA: UC Irvine, 1968-90 – 18r – 1 – $900.00 – R02310 – us Library Micro [370]

NEW UNIVERSITY – Riverside, CA. UC Riverside: 1968-1990 – 18r – 1 – $900.00 – R03413 – us Library Micro [370]

NEW UNIVERSITY THOUGHT – (See: Journal of University Studies) – 1960-73 1; 1969-73 5,6 – us UMI [900]

THE NEW VISION – Kampala, Uganda. April 30 1986-1991 – 14r – 1 – us L of C Photodup [072]

NEW VOICE – 1-23 V. Sep 1884-Dec 1906 – 1 – 202.00 – us L of C Photodup [360]

NEW VOICE – London. (National Citizen). The journal of the Middle Classes Union. Apr 1920-May Jun 1939.-m. 4 reels – 1 – uk British Libr Newspaper [072]

NEW VOICE – Toronto, CN. v2 no 7. 1946-1948 – 1r – 1 – Can$30.00 – cn Can Microfilming [072]

THE NEW VOICE IN RACE ADJUSTMENTS : ADDRESSES AND REPORTS PRESENTED AT THE NEGRO CHRISTIAN STUDENT CONFERENCE, ATLANTA, GEORGIA, MAY 14-18, 1914 / ed by Trawick, A M – New York City: Student Volunteer Movement, [1914?] – 1mf – us A.T.L.A. [305]

THE NEW WARHEIT – New York. N.Y. 1925 – 1 – us A.J.P.C. [071]

NEW WASHINGTON HERALD – New Washington, Ohio. 1975-88 – 7r – 1 – $32.50r – us Archival [071]

New Washington. Ohio. St. John's Lutheran Church *see* RECORDS

NEW WAVE – 1971- – 1 – us UMI [073]

THE NEW WAY – Ireland.Oct 1917 – 1 – ie Microforms [072]

NEW WEST – (v.4-. 1979- 5,6,9) – v.1-. 1976- – 1 – us UMI [073]

THE NEW WEST – Reno, NV. 1912 – 1r – 1 – $50.00 – B06066 – us Library Micro [071]

THE NEW WEST EDUCATION COMMISSION, 1880-93 / Hood, Edmund Lyman – Jacksonville, FL: H & W B Drew, 1905 – 1mf – 9 – 0-8370-8521-7 – 1986-2521 – us A.T.L.A. [240]

NEW WINE SKINS : PRESENT-DAY PROBLEMS: LECTURES – Boston, MA: Morning Star Publ House, 1901 – 1mf – 9 – 0-8370-3933-9 – 1985-1933 – us A.T.L.A. [240]

NEW WOMEN'S FEMINIST REVIEW – Rochester, NY. no23-30. 1983 – 1r – 1 – $50.00 – R04932 – us Library Micro [305]

NEW WOMEN'S TIMES – Rochester, NY. 1979-1984 – 3r – 1 – $150.00 – R04933 – us Library Micro [305]

NEW WORLD – (In Japanese) – San Francisco, CA. 1912-1932 – 75r – 1 – $3,750.00 – C03487 – us Library Micro [071]

NEW WORLD – London. -m. Dec 1908-Apr 1909. (4 ft) – 1 – uk British Libr Newspaper [072]

THE NEW WORLD – v1-9. 1892-1900 (complete) – 5r – 1 – ATLA 1993-S510 – us A.T.L.A. [073]

THE NEW WORLD – Vancouver: [Vancouver Typographical Union, 1892-189- or 19–] – 9 – cn C.I.H.M. [331]

THE NEW WORLD AND THE NEW THOUGHT / Bixby, James Thompson – New York: Thomas Whittaker, 1902 – 1mf – 9 – 0-8370-2710-1 – 1985-0710 – us A.T.L.A. [210]

NEW WORLD DAILY NEWS – (In Japanese) – San Francisco, CA. 1932-1935 – 9r – 1 – $450.00 – C03488 – us Library Micro [071]

THE NEW WORLD OF CENTRAL AFRICA : WITH A HISTORY OF THE FIRST CHRISTIAN MISSION ON THE CONGO / Guinnes, H Grattan – London: Hodder and Stoughton, 1890 – 2mf – us A.T.L.A. [240]

THE NEW WORLD OF ENGLISH WORDS / Phillips, Edward – 1658. 284p. (English Linguistics Series 1500-1800) – 9 – us UMI [420]

THE NEW WORLD, OR, RECENT VISIT TO AMERICA: TOGETHER WITH INTRODUCTORY OBSERVATIONS FOR TOURISTS, AND FOUR APPENDIXES CONTAINING ALL SUITABLE INFORMATION FOR EMIGRANTS, ETC / Campbell, W Graham – London: E. Stock, 1871. 00403. (Pre-1900 Canadiana) – 9 – cn C.I.H.M. [910]

NEW WORLD REVIEW – v1- 1932- 1; v39-5,6; v44- 9 – us UMI [073]

NEW WORLD REVIEW – 1-28. 1932-60 – 157mf – 9 – $640.00 – us UPA [073]

NEW WORLD SCREWWORM ERADICATION PROGRAMME : NORTH AFRICA 1988-1992 – 1992 – 192p – it F.A.O. [660]

NEW WORLD SUN – (In Japanese and English) – San Francisco, CA. 1935-1941 – 20r – 1 – $1,000.00 – C03489 – us Library Micro [071]

THE NEW WORLD-LIFE / Strong, Josiah – Garden City: Doubleday, Page, 1913 – 1mf – us A.T.L.A. [240]

THE NEW WORLD-RELIGION / Strong, Josiah – Garden City: Doubleday, Page, 1915 – 2mf – us A.T.L.A. [240]

NEW YEAR'S GIFT – 1829-34 – 14mf – 9 – £118.00 – uk Chadwyck [800]

NEW YEAR'S SERMON, LORD, WHAT WILT THOU HAVE ME TO DO?: ...CHURCH OF ST ALBAN, THE MARTYR, OTTAWA, SUNDAY, JANUARY 2, 1881 / Bedford-Jones, T – Ottawa: Citizen, 1881. 03305. (Pre-1900 Canadiana) – 9 – cn C.I.H.M. [240]

NEW YORK – v1- 1968- 1; v3- 5,6,9 – us UMI [073]

NEW YORK – 2r – 1 – $160.00 – us Scholarly Res [370]

NEW YORK : COUNTY AND REGIONAL HISTORIES AND ATLASES – 1 – us Primary [920]

NEW YORK : MCKINNEY'S CONSOLIDATED LAWS OF NEW YORK ANNOTATED – St Paul: West Pub Co, 1916-Jun 1996 update – 9 – $6,582.00 set – us Heln [340]

NEW YORK : MCKINNEY'S CONSOLIDATED LAWS OF NEW YORK ANNOTATED. SUPPLEMENT – St Paul: West Pub Co. Superseded Pocket Parts 1919-95 – 9 – $17,250.00 set – us Hein [340]

NEW YORK : SESSION LAWS OF AMERICAN STATES AND TERRITORIES – 1777-1994 – 9 – $6,112.00 set – us Hein [340]

New York *see*
- REPORTS AND OPINIONS (A-G)
- REPORTS, PRE-NRS
- SESSION LAWS
- STATE LABOR REPORTS
- STATE WATER RESOURCES REPORTS

New York Academy of Medicine *see*
- AUTHOR CATALOG OF THE LIBRARY OF THE NEW YORK ACADEMY OF MEDICINE
- BULLETIN
- CATALOG OF BIOGRAPHIES IN THE LIBRARY OF THE NEW YORK ACADEMY OF MEDICINE
- ILLUSTRATION CATALOG OF THE LIBRARY OF THE NEW YORK AKADEMY OF MEDICINE
- ILLUSTRATION CATALOG OF THE LIBRARY. THIRD EDITION REV. AND ENL
- SUBJECT CATALOG OF THE LIBRARY OF THE NEW YORK ACADEMY OF MEDICINE

New York Academy of Medicine. Library *see*
- AUTHOR CATALOG
- PORTRAIT CATALOG
- SUBJECT CATALOG

New York. Advisory Council on Employment and Unemployment Insurance *see* REPORTS

New York. Advisory Council on the Labor and Management Improper Practices Act *see* REPORTS

New York. African Academy of Arts and Research *see* AFRICA, TODAY AND TOMORROW

NEW YORK AGE – New York. 1905-60 – 31r – 1 – us Ross [071]

NEW YORK AGE – New York. Jan 5 1905-Feb 27 1960 – 1 – us NY Public [071]

NEW YORK AMSTERDAM NEWS – New York. Nov 29 1922-Dec 25 1965. Incomplete – 1 – us NY Public [071]

NEW YORK AND ADMIRAL SIR PETER WARREN AT THE CAPTURE OF LOUISBOURG, 1745: AN ADDRESS AT THE INAUGURATION OF THE MONUMENT AT LOUISBOURG, ON THE ONE HUNDRED AND FIFTIETH ANNIVERSARY OF ITS CAPTURE BY THE SOCIETY OF COLONIAL WARS, 1895 / De Lancey, Edward Floyd – s.l.: s.n., 1895. 03792. (Pre-1900 Canadiana) – 9 – cn C.I.H.M. [971]

NEW YORK AND HOLLYWOOD FASHION AND COSTUME DESIGN FROM THE BROOKLYN MUSEUM COLLECTION – 9 – $1,060.00 – us UPA [740]

New York and New Jersey. Synod (Pres. Ch. in the U.S.A.) *see*
- MINUTES, 1788-1822
- MINUTES, 1840-1869

New York and Vermont. Synod (Welsh Cal. Meth.Pres. Ch. in the U.S.A.) *see* MINUTES, 1879-1936

NEW YORK ANNOTATED CASES / New York. (State) – (Includes suppl) – v1-20. 1894-1912 (all publ) – 127mf – 9 – $190.00 – LLMC 79-514 – us L.L.M.C. [340]

NEW YORK APPELLATE DIVISION RECORDS AND BRIEFS – 2d. 39-99 – 5,6 – Inquire – us Hein [340]

NEW YORK APPELLATE DIVISION REPORTS / New York. (State). Intermediate Court of Appeals – (No Pre-NRS vols. 2nd series in copyright. No updates planned) – 1st series: v1-286. 1896-1955 (all publ) – 2943mf – 9 – $4,414.00 – LLMC 78/79-098 – us L.L.M.C. [340]

NEW YORK APPELLATE DIVISION REPORTS, 1ST SERIES – 1-286. 1896-1955 – 9 – $4,414.00 set – us Hein [340]

NEW YORK ARTS JOURNAL – v. 1-. 1976- – 1 – us UMI [700]

NEW YORK ATTORNEY GENERAL REPORTS AND OPINIONS – (6 1777-1978 $665.00. 9 1979-1994 $180.00) – 1777-1994 – 6,9 – $845.00set – us Hein [340]

New York. Banking Dept *see*
- REPORT OF THE SUPERINTENDENT OF BANKS RELATIVE TO SAVINGS AND LOAN ASSOCIATIONS, SAVINGS AND LOAN BANK OF THE STATE OF NEW YORK AND CREDIT UNIONS
- REPORT OF THE SUPERINTENDENT OF BANKS RELATIVE TO SAVINGS BANKS, INVESTMENT COMPANIES, SAFE DEPOSIT COMPANIES AND LICENSED LENDERS

New York. Banking Dept. Superintendent of Banks *see* REPORTS

THE NEW YORK BAPTIST – Syracuse, NY. 1986-1991. 594p – 1 – $29.12 – us Baptist [071]

New York Baptist Convention. Executive Board *see* MINUTES

New York. Bar of the City of New York *see*
- MEMOIR OF NICHOLAS HILL, A MEMBER OF THE BAR OF NEW YORK, WHO DIED IN THE CITY OF ALBANY, ON THE 1ST OF MAY, 1859
- TESTIMONIAL OF RESPECT OF THE BAR OF NEW YORK, TO THE MEMORY OF ALEXANDER W. BRADFORD, ESQ

New York. Board of Railroad Commissioners *see* REPORTS

New York Botanical Garden. Library *see* BIOGRAPHICAL NOTES UPON BOTANISTS

NEW YORK BOTANICAL GARDEN VASCULAR PLANT TYPE COLLECTION – (Families can be purchased separately. Index £240.00) – 1,241mf – 9 – £5,900.00 – uk Chadwyck [580]

NEW YORK CALL : A NEWSPAPER FOR THE WORKERS – New York, 1908-23 – 1 – us Hoover Inst Photo [331]

New York. Chamber of Commerce of the State of New York *see* POWERS OF THE ARBITRATION COMMITTEE...AND THE FORMS OF SUBMISSION, AWARDS, ETC

NEW YORK CHANCERY REPORTS, ANNOTATED LAWYER'S EDITION / New York. (State) – (Title replicates and adds annotations to Barbour's, Clarke's, Edward's, Hoffman's and Hopkins' Reports. Comes with a digest. Not a Pre-NRS title) – v1-7. 1814-47 (all publ) – 113mf – 9 – $169.00 – LLMC 80-013 – us L.L.M.C. [340]

NEW YORK CHRONICLE – v1-16. 1850-65 (complete) – 4r – 1 – ATLA R0119 – us A.T.L.A. [240]

NEW YORK CHRONICLE, 1769-70; CONSTITUTIONAL GAZETTE, 1775-76; WEEKLY VISITOR, 1817-20 – Sold as one unit – 1,3 – us Readex [071]

NEW YORK CIRCUS – New York. 48 docs. 1980-1991 – 29mf – 9 – ne IDC [975]

NEW YORK CITY : SMALL AREA CENSUS DATA 1910-60 – 1 – us Primary [310]

New York. (City) *see*
- A GUIDE TO THE CHURCHES AND MISSIONS IN THE CITY OF NEW YORK
- NEW YORK CITY HALL RECORDER

New York (City). Board of Alderman, 1902-37. Special Committee to Investigate the Police Dept *see* REPORT

New York. (City) Board of Estimate and Apportionment *see* JOURNAL OF PROCEEDINGS

New York. (City). Court of Common Pleas *see* BARRATRY. ITS ORIGIN, HISTORY AND MEANING IN THE MARITIME LAWS

NEW YORK CITY COURT REPORTS / New York. (City). Marine Court – v1-2. 1874-89 (all publ) – 12mf – 9 – $18.00 – LLMC 79-508 – us L.L.M.C. [340]

NEW YORK CITY HALL RECORDER / New York. (City) – v1-6. 1816-22 (all publ) – 18mf – 9 – $27.00 – LLMC 80-028 – us L.L.M.C. [340]

New York. (City). Marine Court *see* NEW YORK CITY COURT REPORTS

New York. (City). Mayor's Court *see* MAYOR'S COURT, NEW YORK CITY

New York. (City). State Bar Association *see* PROCEEDINGS

THE NEW YORK CIVIL AND CRIMINAL JUSTICE. / McCall, Henry Strong – 7th ed. Albany, Gould, 1885. 912 p. LL-187 – 1 – us L of C Photodup [340]

NEW YORK CIVIL PROCEDURE REPORTS / New York. (State) – ns: v1-4. 1908-1913 (all publ) – 15mf – 9 – $22.50 – LLMC 80-052 – us L.L.M.C. [340]

NEW YORK CIVIL PROCEDURE REPORTS / New York. (State) – v1-40. 1881-1909 (all publ) – 229mf – 9 – $343.00 – LLMC 78-110 – us L.L.M.C. [340]

NEW YORK CLIPPER – (Some years and issues missing) – 1857-1883 – 7r – 1 – $40.00r – us U.N.D. Archives [790]
NEW YORK CODE REPORTER / New York. (State) – 1st series: v1-3. 1848-51. ns: 1v. 1850-52 – 12mf – 9 – $18.00 – LLMC 79-510 – us L.L.M.C. [340]
NEW YORK COLONIZATION JOURNAL – New York. Dec 1850-Dec 1863. Incomplete – 1 – us NY Public [073]
NEW YORK COLONIZATION JOURNAL – v.l, Dec. 1850; ceased with v.13, Dec. 1863. New York: Colonization Society of the State of New York – 1 – us U.W. Library [073]
NEW YORK COMMERCIAL – New York. 1898-Sept 1917; 1918-1926 – 1 – us NY Public [071]
NEW YORK COMMERCIAL – New York. v1-80. 1815-1926 – 48r – 1 – us Ross [071]
NEW YORK COMMERCIAL BULLETIN – New York, 1879-81 – 2r – 1 – us Ross [071]
NEW YORK COMMERCIAL BULLETIN – (Semi-Weekly). New York. Nov 1 1879-Dec 31 1881. Not collated – 1 – us NY Public [073]
NEW YORK COMMON LAW REPORTS : ANNOTATED LAWYER'S EDITION, 1791-1847 / New York. (State) – (Not a Pre-NRS title. Replicates all titles in New York Common Law Reports, adding annotations) – New York: Lawyers' Coop. v1-18. 1883-99 (all publ) – 218mf – 9 – $327.00 – LLMC 79-114 – us L.L.M.C. [340]
NEW YORK COMMON LAW REPORTS / New York. (State) – (A Pre-NRS title) – v1-81. 1791-1847 (all publ) – 496mf – 9 – $744.00 – LLMC 78-512 – us L.L.M.C. [340]
NEW YORK COMMON LAW REPORTS *see* LALOR'S SUPPLEMENT TO HILL AND DENIO'S REPORTS
NEW YORK COMMON PLEAS REPORTS / New York. (State) – (Includes: Daley's v1-14 1859-91. Hilton's v1-2 1855-60. E D Smith's v1-4 1850-58) – v1-20. 1849-88 (all publ) – 149mf – 9 – $223.00 – LLMC 79-502 – us L.L.M.C. [340]
NEW YORK COMMUNIST / Socialist Party. U.S.A – 1-10 (all publ). 1919 – 1 reel – 1 – $65.00 – us UPA [335]
NEW YORK COUNTY LAWYER'S ASSOCIATION BAR BULLETIN – v1-27. 1943-70 – 9 – $156.00 set – us Hein [340]
NEW YORK COUNTY LAWYERS' ASSOCIATION BAR BULLETIN – v1-22. 1943-65 (all publ) – 22mf – 9 – $99.00 – LLMC 84-646 – us L.L.M.C. [073]
NEW YORK COURIER – New York. N.Y. 1815-17 – 3 – us Readex [071]
New York. Court of Admiralty *see* CASE PAPERS
NEW YORK COURT OF APPEALS 2D RECORDS AND BRIEFS – NY 2d. v1-89; NY 265-309 – 5 – Inquire – us Hein [340]
NEW YORK COURT OF APPEALS REPORTS / New York. (State). Court of Appeals – (No Pre-NRS vols. 2nd series in copyright. No updates planned. 1st 14v of this title are more properly cited by the name of their reporters) – 1st series: v1-309. 1847-1956 (all publ) – 2641mf – 9 – $3,961.00 – LLMC 78/79-118 – us L.L.M.C. [340]
THE NEW YORK CRIMINAL JUSTICE / Headley, Russel – New York: Banks, 1890. 640p. LL-627 – 1 – us L of C Photodup [340]
NEW YORK CRIMINAL REPORTS / New York. (State) – (Includes: Connoly & Vilas' Cases v1-6 1881-89. Cowen's Criminal Cases v1-2 1867-78. Parker's Criminal Cases v1-6 1823-68. Wheeler's Criminal Cases v1-3 1791-1825. All published) – New York. v1-17. 1878-1910 (all publ) – 127mf – 9 – $190.00 – LLMC 79-504 – us L.L.M.C. [340]
NEW YORK DAILY ADVERTISER – New York, 1801-35 – 12r – 1 – us Ross [071]
THE NEW YORK DAILY COMMERCIAL BULLETIN AND AUCTION RECORD – New York. June 4 1867-June 10 1893. Not collated – 1 – us NY Public [073]
NEW YORK DAILY EVENING MIRROR – New York, 1844-47 – 4r – 1 – us Ross [071]
New York. Dept. of Labor. Division of Research and Statistics *see* COLLECTIVE BARGAINING SETTLEMENTS IN NEW YORK STATE
New York. Dept. of Taxation and Finance *see* REPORTS
THE NEW YORK DETECTIVE LIBRARY – 1883-97. 652 issues – 1 – $216.00 – us L of C Photodup [830]
New York. Division of the Treasury *see* REPORTS
New York. Division of Water Power and Control *see* REPORTS
New York. Division of Water Resources *see* REPORTS
NEW YORK DRAMA – Library ed. New York. v1-5. 1873-80 – 1r – 1 – us Ross [790]
NEW YORK DRAMA – Library Edition. New York. v. 1-5. 1873-1880. Incomplete – 1 – us NY Public [790]
NEW YORK DRAMATIC MIRROR – New York. v. 1-85, no. 2249. Jan 1879-Apr 1922 – 1 – us NY Public [071]
NEW YORK EVENING EXPRESS – New York, 1843-81 – 47r – 1 – us Ross [071]
NEW YORK EVENING POST – New York. Nov 16 1801-June 30 1939 – 1 – us NY Public [071]
NEW YORK EVENING POST – New York. N.Y. 1801-1820 – 3 – us Readex [071]
NEW YORK EVENING POST LITERARY REVIEW – New York. N.Y. v. 1-7. 11 Sep 1920-28, May 1927 – 1 – 102.00 – us L of C Photodup [410]
NEW YORK EXAMINER – New York, 1843 – 1 reel – 1 – $68.00 – cn Library Assoc [971]
NEW YORK FARMER – v. 1-10. January 1828-December 1837 – 1 – us UMI [630]
NEW YORK FIRESIDE COMPANION – Apr 1896-Sep 1897 – 1 – us Res Libr [073]
NEW YORK FOLKLORE – v. 1- 1975- – 1,5,6,9 – us UMI [390]
NEW YORK FOLKLORE QUARTERLY – v1-30 1945-74 1; v27-30 5,6 – us UMI [390]
NEW YORK GAZETTE / ed by Bradford, William – New York, 1726-44 – 2r – 1 – us Ross [071]
NEW YORK GAZETTE AND GENERAL ADVERTISER – New York, 1811-16 – 4r – 1 – us Ross [071]
NEW YORK GAZETTE AND GENERAL ADVERTISER – New York. Nov 5 1801; Feb 11 1802; 1806; Jan-June 1811; Feb 11 1812-Dec 1815; July-Dec 1816; May 26 1817; July 31 1817; Nov 22 1820; Aug 18 1824; Nov 10 1825; June 27 1829; Nov 1833-July 24 1839. Not collated – 1 – us NY Public [071]
NEW YORK GAZETTE AND GENERAL ADVERTISER – New York, N.Y. 1880 – 1 – us Res Libr [071]
NEW YORK GAZETTE AND WEEKLY MERCURY – New York, 1752-83 – 9r – 1 – us Ross [071]
NEW YORK GUILD LAWYER – (Lacking: v17 nos 7-9. v18 nos 2,4,5. v19 nos 1-2,9-10. v7. v21 after no 2) – v1-21. 1943-63 (all publ) – 23mf – 9 – $34.50 – LLMC 84-648 – us L.L.M.C. [073]
NEW YORK HERALD – New York. (Munsey period). Jan 1920-Mar 18 1924. (For period of Feb-Sept 1920 title was: The Sun & New York Herald.) – 1 – us NY Public [071]
NEW YORK HERALD – New York. New York. 1794-1797 – 3 – us Readex [071]
NEW YORK HERALD – New York. New York. 1802-1817 – 1,3 – us Readex [071]
NEW YORK HERALD TRIBUNE – European ed. Paris.1887-1940 – 156r – 1 – us Ross [072]
NEW YORK HEROLD MORGENBLATT – New York. Oct 18-Nov 23 1860; Jan 19 1863; Apr 17 1865; Mar 7 1916-Nov 30 1919 – 1 – us NY Public [071]
NEW YORK HISTORY – v31- 1950- 1; v52-5,6; v56- 9 – us UMI [978]
NEW YORK ILLUSTRATED MAGAZINE – v. 1-3. September 20, 1845-March 20, 1847 – 1 – us UMI [073]
New York. Insurance Dept *see*
– FEES AND TAXES CHARGED INSURANCE COMPANIES UNDER THE LAWS OF NEW YORK TOGETHER WITH ABSTRACTS OF FEES, TAXES AND OTHER REQUIREMENTS OF OTHER STATES
– REPORTS OF THE SUPERINTENDENT OF INSURANCE
THE NEW YORK JEWISH VOLKSZEITUNG – New York. N.Y. 1886-89 – 1 – us A.J.P.C. [071]
THE NEW YORK JOURNAL, AND GENERAL ADVERTISER – New York. July 7 1777-Jan 6 1782. Incomplete – 1 – us NY Public [071]
NEW YORK JOURNAL AND THE GENERAL ADVERTISER – Kingston and Poughkeepsie, NY. v1-6. 1777-82 – 1r – 1 – us Ross [071]
NEW YORK JOURNAL OF COMMERCE – New York. Jan. 1828-June 30, 1948 – 1 – us NY Public [071]
NEW YORK JOURNAL OF DENTISTRY – (v.49-. 1979- 5,6,9) – v.1-. 1931- – 1 – us UMI [073]
NEW YORK JOURNAL OF MEDICINE – 1-3s6-8. July 1843-May 1860 – 1 – us UMI [610]
NEW YORK JOURNAL (OR GENERAL ADVERTISER) – New York. N.Y. 1766-76 – 3 – us Readex [071]
THE NEW YORK JOURNAL OR GENERAL ADVERTISER, 1766-1776 / New York, NY – 1972 – 5r – 1 – $425.00 – S1713 – us Scholarly Res [978]
NEW YORK JUDICIAL REPOSITORY / New York. (State) – (Also known as: Bacon's Judicial Repository) – 1v. 1818-19 – 4mf – 9 – $6.00 – LLMC 80-015 – us L.L.M.C. [340]
NEW YORK LAW FORUM – (See also: New York Law School. Law Review) – v1-21. 1955-1976 – 1 – us UMI [340]
NEW YORK LAW FORUM *see* NEW YORK LAW SCHOOL LAW REVIEW
NEW YORK LAW JOURNAL – New York, NY. 26 Mar 1888- – 1,9 – us New York Law [073]
NEW YORK LAW REVIEW – Cornell Pub House. v1 nos 1-7. 1895 (all publ) – 4mf – 9 – $6.00 – LLMC 84-649 – us L.L.M.C. [073]
NEW YORK LAW REVIEW – v1-7. 1923-29 – 1,5,6 – us Princeton Micro [073]
New York Law School *see* LAW REVIEW
NEW YORK LAW SCHOOL LAW REVIEW – (v1-29 1955-85 on reel/mf $549.00. v30-39 1985-94 on mf $254.00. Title varies: v1-21 1955-76 as New York Law Forum. Supersedes Student Law Review, New York Law School) – v1-39. 1955-94 – 9 – $803.00 set – us Hein [340]
NEW YORK LEADER – New York. May 30 1908-Nov 12 1923 – 1 – us NY Public [071]
NEW YORK LEADER – New York. v1-16. 1908-23 – 69r – 1 – us Ross [071]
NEW YORK LEADER – New York. v1-17. 1855-71 – 7r – 1 – us Ross [071]
THE NEW YORK LEADER – New York. v. 1, no. 1-v. 17, no. 52. May 27 1855-Dec 1871. Incomplete – 1 – us NY Public [071]
NEW YORK LEGAL OBSERVER – v1-12. 1842-54 (all publ) – 9 – LLMC 84-650 – us L.L.M.C. [073]
NEW YORK LIQUOR TAX LAW REPORTS / Schenck, William E – Albany: Brandon. v1-3. 1905 – 20mf – 9 – $30.00 – LLMC 80-027 – us L.L.M.C. [340]
NEW YORK LITERARY GAZETTE – v. 1-24. February 2-July 13, 1839 – 1 – us UMI [073]
NEW YORK LITERARY GAZETTE AND AMERICAN ANTHENAEUM – v. 1-3. September 10, 1825-March 3, 1827 – 1 – us UMI [073]
NEW YORK LITERARY GAZETTE AND JOURNAL OF BELLES LETTRES, ARTS, SCIENCES AND ETC – v. 6-15. Sept. 1, 1834-Mar. 14, 1835 – 1 – us UMI [073]
NEW YORK LITERARY JOURNAL, AND BELLES-LETTRES REPOSITORY – v. 1-4. May 1819-April 1821 – 1 – us UMI [410]
NEW YORK LOCAL LAWS : SESSION LAWS OF AMERICAN STATES AND TERRITORIES – 1924-1973 (all publ) – 9 – $765.00 set – us Hein [340]
NEW YORK MAGAZINE AND GENERAL REPOSITORY OF USEFUL KNOWLEDGE – v. 1. May-July 1814 – 1 – us UMI [073]
NEW YORK MAGAZINE; OR LITERARY REPOSITORY – v. 1-2. January 1790-December 1797 – 1 – us UMI [073]
NEW YORK MASONIC CODE... : CONSTITUTIONS AND GENERAL REGULATIONS / Woodruff, R W & Woodruff, William T – Rev ed. New York: Masonic Publishing and Manufacturing Co, 1870 – 2mf – 9 – $3.00 – LLMC 91-509 – us L.L.M.C. [340]
NEW YORK MEDICAL AND PHILOSOPHICAL JOURNAL AND REVIEW – v. 1-3. 1809-1811 – 1 – us UMI [610]
NEW YORK MEDICAL AND PHYSICAL JOURNAL – v. 1-9. January 1822-1830 – 1 – us UMI [610]
NEW YORK MEDICAL MAGAZINE – v. 1. January 1814-January 1815 – 1 – us UMI [610]
NEW YORK MERCURY – New York. (Hugh Gaine). 1752-1783 – 1 – us NY Public [071]
NEW YORK MERCURY – New York. N.Y. 1752-1768 – 1,3 – us Readex [071]
NEW YORK MESSENGER – New York. v. 1, no. 2-v. 2, no. 20. May 25 1844-Dec 15 1845 – 1 – us NY Public [071]
NEW YORK MIRROR – A Journal of Literature, News and the Fine Arts. New York. v. 1-6. Oct 12 1844-Oct 2 1847 – 1 – us NY Public [800]
NEW YORK MIRROR; A WEEKLY GAZETTE OF LITERATURE AND THE FINE ARTS – 1-20. August 2, 1823-December 3, 1842 – 1 – us UMI [073]
NEW YORK MIRROR AND LADIES LITERARY GAZETTE : BEING A REPOSITORY OF MISCELLANEOUS PRODUCTIONS IN PROSE AND VERSE – New York. v3-7. 1825-30 – 1r – 1 – us Ross [073]
NEW YORK MIRROR AND LADIES LITERARY GAZETTE – New York. v. 3-7. July 30 1825-July 3 1830 – 1 – us NY Public [800]
NEW YORK MISCELLANEOUS REPORTS / New York. (State) Lower Courts – (No Pre-NRS vols. 2nd series in copyright. No updates planned) – 1st series: v1-208. 1893-1955 (all publ) – 2066mf – 9 – $3,099.00 – LLMC 78/79-106 – us L.L.M.C. [340]
NEW YORK MISCELLANEOUS REPORTS, 1ST SERIES – 1-208. 1893-1955 – 9 – $3,099.00 set – us Hein [340]
NEW YORK MISSIONARY MAGAZINE, AND REPOSITORY OF RELIGIOUS INTELLIGENCE – v. 1-4. January 1800-December 1803 – 1 – us UMI [240]
NEW YORK MONTHLY CHRONICLE OF MEDICINE AND SURGERY – v. 1. July 1824-June 1825 – 1 – us UMI [610]
NEW YORK MONTHLY LAW BULLETIN – v1-5. 1879-83 (all publ) – 9 – LLMC 84-652 – us L.L.M.C. [073]
NEW YORK MONTHLY MAGAZINE – v. 1. Januar-March 1824 – 1 – us UMI [073]
NEW YORK MORNING EXPRESS – New York, 1836-61 – 29r – 1 – us Ross [071]
NEW YORK MORNING POST – New York. N.Y. 1810-12 – 3 – us Readex [071]
NEW YORK MUNICIPAL GAZETTE – v1-2. 1841-55 (all publ) – 9 – LLMC 84-651 – us L.L.M.C. [073]
New York. Museum of Modern Art *see*
– ARTIST FILES
– ARTISTS SCRAPBOOKS
THE NEW YORK MUSICAL ECHO – New York, 1891-99 – 1 – £60.00 – uk Chadwyck [780]
THE NEW YORK MUSICAL PIONEER AND CHORISTER'S BUDGET – New York City. v1-16. 1855-71 – 2r – 1 – £115.00 – uk Chadwyck [780]
THE NEW YORK NEWS – New York. N.Y. Feb. 24, 1921; Mar. 12, 1927 – 1 – us NY Public [071]
New York, NY *see* THE NEW YORK JOURNAL OR GENERAL ADVERTISER, 1766-1776
NEW YORK OBSERVER – (Lacks some pgs) – v1-40. 17 Aug 1823-1862 – 23r – 1 – ATLA S0126 – us A.T.L.A. [073]
NEW YORK PEDIATRICIAN – (1985-. 1,5,6) – 1983- – 9 – us UMI [618]
NEW YORK PO GENERAL NEWS INDEX – New York. 1873; 1875-1877; 1880-1884; 1886-1903; 1905-1921. Incomplete. Price includes New York Post. Editorial index. 1902-1903; 1906-1923 – 1 – us NY Public [071]
NEW YORK POST : GENERAL NEWS INDEX AND EDITORIAL INDEX – New York, 1873-1923 – 11r – 1 – us Ross [071]
NEW YORK POST – New York, 1801-1939 – 418r – 1 – us Ross [071]
NEW YORK POST – New York. N.Y. 1939- – 1 – us UMI [071]
New York. Presbytery (Pres. Ch. in the U.S.A.) *see* MINUTES, 1810-1840
NEW YORK PRESS – New York, 1887-1916 – 123r – 1 – us Ross [071]
NEW YORK PRESS – New York. Dec 1887-July 2 1916 – 1 – us NY Public [071]
NEW YORK PRICE CURRENT – New York. v. 60, 63-66, 69-70, 72-74. 1874, 1877-1880, 1883-1884, 1886-1888 – 1 – us NY Public [073]
NEW YORK PRICE-CURRENT – New York, NY. 1796-1817 – 3 – us Readex [071]
New York Produce Exchange *see* ANNUAL STATISTICAL REPORT

New York. (Province). Vice Admiralty Court *see* RECORDS

New York Public Library *see*
- NORMAN THOMAS PAPERS
- SCHOMBURG CLIPPING FILE

New York. Public Library *see*
- ARTISTS FILES
- THE NEW YORK PUBLIC LIBRARY

THE NEW YORK PUBLIC LIBRARY : THE PRINT FILE / New York. Public Library – (With index) – 4456mf – 9 – £11,355.00 coll – uk Chadwyck [760]

New York Public Library. Library and Museum of the Performing Arts *see* NEW YORK THEATER 1919-1961

New York Public Library. Lincoln Center Music Collection *see* AMERICAN POPULAR SONGS

New York Public Library. Reference Department *see*
- DICTIONARY CATALOG OF THE JEWISH COLLECTION
- DICTIONARY CATALOG OF THE MUSIC COLLECTION
- MUSIC SUBJECT HEADINGS. SECOND EDITION ENLARGED

NEW YORK PUBLIC LIBRARY REGISTER OF MICROFORM MASTERS: MONOGRAPHS – 200,000 cards representing monographs and pamphlets – 9 – us NY Public [010]

New York Public Library. Research Libraries *see*
- CATALOG OF GOVERNMENT PUBLICATIONS IN THE RESEARCH LIBRARIES
- CATALOG OF THE THEATRE AND DRAMA COLLECTIONS. 1967
- DICTIONARY CATALOG AND SHELF LIST OF THE SPENCER COLLECTION OF ILLUSTRATED BOOKS AND MANUSCRIPTS AND FINE BINDINGS
- DICTIONARY CATALOG OF THE HENRY W. AND ALBERT A. BERG COLLECTION OF ENGLISH AND AMERICAN LITERATURE
- DICTIONARY CATALOG OF THE LOCAL HISTORY AND GENEALOGY DIVISION
- DICTIONARY CATALOG OF THE MANUSCRIPT DIVISION
- DICTIONARY CATALOG OF THE ORIENTAL COLLECTION
- DICTIONARY CATALOG OF THE RESEARCH LIBRARIES
- DICTIONARY CATALOG OF THE SLAVONIC COLLECTION, SECOND EDITION REVISED AND ENLARGED
- GUIDE TO FESTSCHRIFTEN
- THE HEBREW-CHARACTER TITLE CATALOG OF THE JEWISH DIVISION
- PHOTOGRAPHICA: A SUBJECT CATALOG OF BOOKS ON PHOTOGRAPHY
- SECOND EDITION OF THE DICTIONARY CATALOG OF THE MUSIC COLLECTION
- SUBJECT CATALOG OF THE WORLD WAR 1 COLLECTION
- U.S. LOCAL HISTORY CATALOG

New York Public Library. Research Libraries. Astor, Lenox & Tilden Foundations *see* DICTIONARY CATALOG OF THE RARE BOOK DIVISION

New York Public Library. Research Libraries. Local History and Genealogy Division *see* U.S. LOCAL HISTORY CATALOG

New York Public Library. Research Libraries. Music Collection *see* SECOND EDITION OF THE DICTIONARY CATALOG

New York Public Library. Research Libraries. Theatre and Drama Collections *see* CATALOG OF THE THEATRE AND DRAMA COLLECTIONS

New York Public Library. Schomburg Collection *see* DICTIONARY CATALOG OF THE SCHOMBURG COLLECTION OF NEGRO LITERATURE AND HISTORY

New York Public Library.Schomburg Collection *see* DICTIONARY CATALOG

New York Public Library.Schomburg Collection of Negro Literature and History *see* CALENDAR OF MANUSCRIPTS

New York Public Library.Theatre Collection *see* SUBJECT HEADINGS

New York. Public Service Commission *see* REPORTS

New York. Public Service Commission. First District *see*
- PROCEEDINGS
- REPORTS
- REPORTS OF DECISIONS

New York. Public Service Commission. Second District *see*
- REPORTS
- REPORTS OF DECISIONS

THE NEW YORK PULPIT IN THE REVIVAL OF 1858 : A MEMORIAL VOLUME OF SERMONS / Alexander, James W – New York: Sheldon, Blakeman, 1858 – 1mf – us A.T.L.A. [240]

NEW YORK QUARTERLY – Devoted to science philosophy and literature. v. 1-4. 1852-1855 – 1 – us UMI [073]

NEW YORK RECORDER – New York. July 1 1891-Oct 11 1896. Not collated – 1 – us NY Public [071]

NEW YORK RECORDER – v1-11. 1845-55 (complete) – 3r – 1 – ATLA R0107 – us A.T.L.A. [240]

NEW YORK RECORDER AND REGISTER – Jan-Jun 1855 – 1 – 15.90 – us A.B.H.S. [071]

NEW YORK RELIGIOUS CHRONICLE – v. 2-4. 28 Feb 1824-31 Dec 1825 – 1 – us UMI [240]

NEW YORK REPORTS, 1ST SERIES – 1-309. 1847-1956 – 9 – $3,961.00 set – us Hein [340]

THE NEW YORK REVIEW : A JOURNAL OF ANCIENT AND MODERN THOUGHT – v1-3 no 6. Jun 1905-Jun 1908 (complete) – 1r – 1 – ATLA S0187 – us A.T.L.A. [073]

NEW YORK REVIEW AND ATHENEUM MAGAZINE – v. 1-2. Jun 1825-May 1826 – 1 – us UMI [073]

NEW YORK REVIEW OF BOOKS – New York, NY. 1964-77 – 15r – 1 – $750.00 – R04915 – us Library Micro [071]

NEW YORK REVIEW OF BOOKS – v. 1-. 1963- – 1,5,6,9 – us UMI [410]

NEW YORK REVIEW OF THE TELEGRAPH AND TELEPHONE *see* FACTORY

THE NEW YORK SATURDAY PRESS, 1860-1866 – 1972 – 1r – 1 – $85.00 – S1714 – us Scholarly Res [978]

NEW YORK SEMI-WEEKLY TRIBUNE – New York, 1850-95 – 17r – 1 – us Ross [071]

NEW YORK SOCIALIST – New York. v11-18. 1901-08 – 2r – 1 – us Ross [071]

New York Society for the Suppression of Vice *see* MORALS, NOT ART OR LITERATURE

NEW YORK SPECTATOR – New York, 1801-64 – 12r – 1 – us Ross [071]

NEW YORK SPECTATOR AND SEMI-WEEKLY COMMERCIAL ADVERTISER – New York. Jan 1867-Dec 1869. Not collated – 1 – us NY Public [071]

NEW YORK SPORTS – (1985-. 5,6,9) – v1-. 1983- – 1 – us UMI [790]

NEW YORK STAR – New York. June 23 1948-Jan 28 1949. (v. 1, no. 1-186) – 1 – us NY Public [071]

New York. (State) *see*
- ABBOTT'S APPEALS DECISIONS
- ABBOTT'S NEW CASES
- ABBOTT'S PRACTICE REPORTS
- ARMSTRONG'S CONTESTED ELECTION CASES
- BAXTER'S CONTESTED ELECTION CASES
- BRADBURY'S PLEADING AND PRACTICE REPORTS
- BROWNE'S INDEX/DIGEST TO THE NEW YORK COURT OF APPEALS REPORTS
- CLARKE'S CHANCERY APPEALS REPORTS
- COLONIAL HISTORY OF THE STATE OF NEW YORK
- CRARY'S NEW YORK PRACTICE
- EDMOND'S SELECT CASES
- EDWARD'S CHANCERY APPEALS REPORTS
- HOFFMAN'S CHANCERY APPEALS REPORTS
- HOPKIN'S CHANCERY APPEALS REPORTS
- HOUGH'S VICE ADMIRALTY REPORTS
- HOWARD'S PRACTICE REPORTS
- JOHNSON'S CHANCERY APPEALS REPORTS
- KEYES' APPEALS REPORTS
- LALOR'S SUPPLEMENT TO HILL AND DENIO'S REPORTS
- LIVINGSTON'S JUDICIAL OPINIONS
- MCCARTY'S CIVIL PROCEDURE REPORTS
- NEW YORK ANNOTATED CASES
- NEW YORK CHANCERY REPORTS, ANNOTATED LAWYER'S EDITION
- NEW YORK CIVIL PROCEDURE REPORTS
- NEW YORK CODE REPORTER
- NEW YORK COMMON LAW REPORTS
- NEW YORK COMMON PLEAS REPORTS
- NEW YORK CRIMINAL REPORTS
- NEW YORK JUDICIAL REPOSITORY
- NEW YORK STATE REPORTER
- NEW YORK WEEKLY DIGEST
- NOBLE'S CURRENT COURT DECISIONS
- OFFICIAL PUBLICATIONS
- PAIGE'S CHANCERY APPEALS CASES
- PRIZE CASES IN NEW YORK
- REPORTS, POST-NRS
- RULES OF ALL THE COURTS OF RECORD OF NEW YORK
- SANDFORD'S CHANCERY APPEALS REPORTS
- SELDEN'S NOTES OF CASES

NEW YORK STATE ASSEMBLY DOCUMENTS AND NEW YORK STATE SENATE DOCUMENTS – (Superseded by New York State Legislative Documents) – 1830-1918 – 1 – $19,250.00 set – us Hein [324]

New York State Bar Association *see* JUDICIAL CENTENNIAL BANQUET GIVEN AT THE LENOX LYCEUM, NEW YORK, FEBRUARY 4TH, 1890

NEW YORK STATE BAR ASSOCIATION BULLETIN *see* NEW YORK STATE BAR JOURNAL

NEW YORK STATE BAR ASSOCIATION REPORTS – v1-141. 1876-1968 – 9 – LLMC 84-653 – us L.L.M.C. [073]

NEW YORK STATE BAR BULLETIN *see* NEW YORK STATE BAR JOURNAL

NEW YORK STATE BAR JOURNAL – (Title varies: v1-22 1928-50 as New York State Bar Association Bulletin. v23-32 1951-60 as New York State Bar Bulletin) – v1-67. 1928-95 – 9 – $851.00 set – us Hein [340]

New York. State Board of Tax Commissioners *see* REPORTS

New York. (State). Commissioners of the Code *see* BOOK OF FORMS, ADAPTED TO THE CODE OF PROCEDURE

New York. (State). Commissioners to Report a Code of Evidence *see* THE CODE OF EVIDENCE...

New York. (State). Court of Appeals *see*
- NEW YORK COURT OF APPEALS REPORTS
- SILVERNAIL'S APPEALS CASES
- TIFFANY'S TRANSCRIPT APPEALS

New York. (State). Courts *see* WAIT'S TABLE OF NEW YORK CASES

NEW YORK STATE CURRICULUM DOCUMENTS – 710mf – 9 – $5.00f – us Ross [978]

NEW YORK STATE DENTAL JOURNAL – v1-1933- 1; v37- 5,6; v42- 9 – us UMI [617]

New York. State Engineer and Surveyor *see* REPORTS ON THE RAILROADS

New York State. Executive Branch *see*
- DEPARTMENT REPORTS OF THE STATE OF NEW YORK
- NEW YORK STATE LABOR RELATIONS BOARD DECISIONS AND ORDERS

New York. (State). Intermediate Court of Appeals *see* NEW YORK APPELLATE DIVISION REPORTS

NEW YORK STATE JOURNAL OF MEDICINE – (v.79-. 1979- 5,6,9) – v.1-. 1901- – 1 – us UMI [073]

New York. State Labor Relations Board *see* ANALYSIS OF DECISIONS

NEW YORK STATE LABOR RELATIONS BOARD DECISIONS AND ORDERS / New York State. Executive Branch – Albany: NYLRB. v1-37. 1937/38-1974 – 291mf – 9 – $437.00 – LLMC 94-109 – us L.L.M.C. [340]

NEW YORK STATE LAW DIGEST – (l.229-. 1979- 5,6,9) – 1965- – 1 – us UMI [073]

New York. (State). Laws, Statutes, etc *see*
- THE ACT AUTHORIZING THE FORMATION OF CORPORATIONS FOR MANUFACTURING, MINING, MECHANICAL, CHEMICAL.
- PROPOSED AMENDMENTS TO THE CODE OF PROCEDURE

NEW YORK STATE LEGISLATIVE DOCUMENTS – (Supersedes N.Y. Assembly Documents and N.Y. Senate Documents) – 1919-1976 – 9 – $10,250.00 set – us Hein [324]

NEW YORK STATE LEGISLATIVE DOCUMENTS *see* NEW YORK STATE ASSEMBLY DOCUMENTS AND NEW YORK STATE SENATE DOCUMENTS

NEW YORK STATE LIBRARY YEARBOOK OF LEGISLATION – (Updates planned) – v1-10 + Legislative bulletins nos 1-39 – 9 – LLMC 84-654 – us L.L.M.C. [340]

New York. (State) Lower Courts *see* NEW YORK MISCELLANEOUS REPORTS

NEW YORK STATE MECHANIC, A JOURNAL OF THE ARTS, TRADES AND MANUFACTUERS – v. 1-2. 20 Nov 1841-17 Jun 1843 – 1 – us UMI [621]

New York. (State). Moreland Act Commission on Nursing Homes and Residential Facilities *see* [MISCELLANEOUS PUBLICATIONS]

New York State Nurses Association *see* JOURNAL

New York. (State). Public Service Commission *see* PUBLIC UTILITIES REPORTS ANNOTATED, CONTAINING DECISIONS OF THE PUBLIC SERVICE COMMISSIONS AND OF STATE AND FEDERAL COURTS

NEW YORK STATE REGISTER – (Updated as released) – v1-16. 1979-94 – 9 – $3,250.00 set (1995 subsc $260.00v) – us Hein [324]

NEW YORK STATE REPORTER / New York. (State) – v1-75. 1886-97 (all publ) – 847mf – 9 – $1,270.00 – LLMC 78-122 – us L.L.M.C. [340]

New York State Society of Certified Public Accountants. Committee on Federal Taxation *see* RECOMMENDATIONS FOR MODIFICATIONS OF THE INTERNAL REVENUE CODE

New York. (State). State Bar Association *see* PROCEEDINGS

New York. (State). Superior Court *see* NEW YORK SUPERIOR COURT REPORTS

New York. (State). Supreme Court *see*
- BARBOUR'S SUPREME COURT CASES
- HUN'S SUPREME COURT REPORTS
- LANSING'S SUPREME COURT REPORTS
- SILVERNAIL'S SUPREME COURT REPORTS
- THOMPSON AND COOK'S SUPREME COURT REPORTS

New York. (State). Surrogate Court *see*
- BRIDGEN'S SURROGATE'S REPORTS
- NEW YORK SURROGATE COURT REPORTS

New York. State Tax Commission *see* REPORTS

THE NEW YORK STOCK EXCHANGE : A DISCUSSION OF THE BUSINESS DONE, ITS RELATION TO OTHER BUSINESSES, TO INVESTMENT, SPECULATION AND GAMBLING, THE SAFEGUARDS PROVIDED BY THE EXCHANGE, AND THE MEANS TAKEN TO IMPROVE THE CHARACTER OF SPECULATION / Martin, H S – NY: n.p., 1919 – 3mf – 9 – $4.50 – LLMC 96-056 – us L.L.M.C. [332]

NEW YORK (SUNDAY) DISPATCH – New York. Aug 22, Nov 21 1847; Nov 1855-Nov 13 1858; Apr 23 1859-Sept 1894; and 1897. Not collated – 1 – us NY Public [071]

NEW YORK SUPERIOR COURT REPORTS / New York. (State). Superior Court – (Reprint of nominative reports cited by name of their reporters) – v1-61. 1828-92 – 476mf – 9 – $714.00 – LLMC 79-500 – us L.L.M.C. [340]

NEW YORK SUPPLEMENT – (Add vols planned) – v1-177. 1888-1919 – 2302mf – 9 – $3,453.00 – LLMC 79-404J – us L.L.M.C. [340]

NEW YORK SURROGATE COURT REPORTS / New York. (State). Surrogate Court – (Reprint of nominative reports cited by name of their reporters) – v1-21. 1849-98 (all publ) – 147mf – 9 – $220.00 – LLMC 79-506 – us L.L.M.C. [340]

New York. Synod *see* MINUTES, 1745-58

New York. Synod (Assoc. Ref. Ch.) *see* MINUTES, 1803-1901

NEW YORK THEATER 1919-1961 / New York Public Library. Library and Museum of the Performing Arts – (26,000 photos fr the Vandamm Coll. Also available: Handlist of Stage Productions in the Vandamm Collection £17 16p ISBN:0-85964-126-0. A card catalogue is available separately £280 on 37mf. Individual subject groups of coll also listed separately) – 1919-61 – 877mf – 9 – £2,935.00 coll – uk Chadwyck [790]

NEW YORK THEATERS – 1858-1941 – 45r – 1 – us Ross [790]

New York. Third Presbytery (Pres. Ch. in the U.S.A.) *see* MINUTES, 1831-1870

NEW YORK TIME-PIECE – New York. N.Y. 1797-98 – 3 – us Readex [071]

NEW YORK TIMES – 1851-1994 – 1 – sz Infoprint [071]

NEW YORK TIMES – Current Events Edition – 9 1979-1980 – current subscription; 165.00 – us UMI [970]

NEW YORK TIMES INDEX – 1851-1994 – 1 – sz Infoprint [071]

NEW YORK TIMES MAGAZINE – 1896-1994 – 6,1 – sz Infoprint [071]

New York Times. Paris Bureau *see*
- PHOTOGRAPHS

THE NEW YORK TIMES REFERENCE LIBRARY – Minimum order – 20 titles – 9 – 3.00t – us UMI [020]

NEW YORK TIMES WEEKLY REVIEW – Stockholm, Sweden. 1980-82 – 1 – sw Kungliga [072]

NEW YORK TIMES WEEKLY REVIEW *see* TEMPUS

NEW YORK TRACT MAGAZINE – v. 1. Nov 1824 – 1 – us UMI [240]

New York. Transit Commission *see* REPORTS

NEW YORK TRIBUNE – New York, 1841-96 – 12r – 1 – us Ross [071]

NEW YORK TRIBUNE – New York, 1903-07 – 1 – us Ross [071]

New York. Unemployment Insurance Appeal Board *see* REPORTS

New York University. Annual National Conference on Labor *see* PROCEEDINGS

NEW YORK UNIVERSITY EDUCATIONAL QUARTERLY – Fall 1969- 1; 1977- 5,6,9 – us UMI [073]

New York University. Institute of Fine Arts *see* LIBRARY CATALOG OF THE CONSERVATION CENTER

NEW YORK UNIVERSITY JOURNAL OF INTERNATIONAL LAW AND POLITICS – v1-26. 1968-94 – 1,5,6 – $540.00 – us Hein [073]

NEW YORK UNIVERSITY LAW REVIEW – v1-71. 1924-96 – 1,5,6,9 – $2,430.00 – us Hein [073]

New York University. Tamiment Institute Library *see* CATALOG OF THE TAMIMENT INSTITUTE LIBRARY

New York. Water Power Commission *see* REPORTS

NEW YORK WEEKLY DIGEST / New York. (State) – v1-28. 1883-88 – 195mf – 9 – $292.00 – LLMC 79-516 – us L.L.M.C. [340]

NEW YORK WEEKLY NEWS – New York, 1844-46 – 1r – 1 – us Ross [071]

NEW YORK WEEKLY POST – New York. ns: v11-12. 1898-99 – 1 – us Ross [071]

NEW YORK WEEKLY REVIEW – v1-24. 1850-73.11 reels – 1 – 500.00 – us Opus [073]

NEW YORK WEEKLY REVIEW OF MUSIC, LITERATURE, FINE ARTS AND SOCIETY – New York. v1-17. 1850-66 – 4r – 1 – us Ross [073]

NEW YORK WEEKLY SUN *see* THE EXTRA SUN

NEW YORK WEEKLY TRIBUNE – New York City, NY. 4 nov 1846; v6 n9. 7 nov 1846 (whole n260); 29 mar 1847 – 1r – 1 – Can$25.00 – cn Can Microfilming [071]

NEW YORK WEEKLY WITNESS – New York, 1877-89 – 3r – 1 – us Ross [071]

NEW YORK WEEKLY WITNESS – New York. Sept 6 1877-Oct 1879; 1882-1884; 1886-1889; June 15, Sept 30 1896 and June 14 1899. Not collated – 1 – us NY Public [071]

NEW YORK WOMAN – v1- . 1986- – 1,5,6,9 – us UMI [305]

NEW YORK WORLD – New York, 1860-1924 – 46r – 1 – us Ross [071]

NEW YORK WORLD – New York. Semi-weekly. Aug 21 1860-1878; 1880-Sept 30 1895. Not collated – 1 – us NY Public [071]

NEW YORK WORLD – New York. Thrice a week. Oct 2 1895-Feb 25 1924. Incomplete. Not collated – 1 – us NY Public [071]

NEW YORK WORLD – New York. Weekly Edition. July 7 1860-Sept 5 1894. Incomplete. Monthly: Oct 1893-Sept 1894. Incomplete. Not collated – 1 – us NY Public [071]

NEW YORK-CANADA – New York City, NY. v1 n36. 9 jul 1892-v1 n39. 30 jul 1892 – 1r – 1 – Can$25.00 – cn Can Microfilming [071]

NEW YORKER – 1925-1994 – 1 – sz Infoprint [073]

NEW YORKER – v. 1-11. 26 Mar 1836-11 Sep 1841 – 1 – us UMI [073]

NEW YORKER – (v. 45- 1969- 5,6. v. 46- 1970- 9) – v. 1- 1925- – 1 – us UMI [073]

NEW YORKER DEMOKRAT – New York, feb 18, sep 1 1860; feb 9-may 4, may 18 1861 – 1r – 1 – gw Mikrofilm [978]

NEW YORKER REVUE – New York. Jan 14 1880-Jan 12 1881; Oct 1882-June 28 1914. Not collated – 1 – us NY Public [071]

NEW YORKER STAATS-ZEITUNG – (Library has: v. 81, no. 261-v. 83, no. 130; Nov. 1, 1915-May 31, 1917; few issues are missing) – New York, [N.Y.]: C. Braker, 1834-1934. 100v – 1 – CSUX87-S110 – us Hoover Inst Photo [978]

NEW YORKER STAATS-ZEITUNG – New York. v12-20. 1846-54 – 2r – 1 – us Ross [071]

NEW YORKER STAATS-ZEITUNG UND HEROLD : AN AMERICAN NEWSPAPER PUBLISHED IN THE GERMAN LANGUAGE – Long Island City, NY. 3 Jul 1972- – 1 – gw Mikrofilm [071]

NEW YORKER STAATS-ZEITUNG WOCHENBLATT – New York. Weekly Edition of the New Yorker Staats-Zeitung). Dec 21 1836-1914. Incomplete – 1 – us NY Public [071]

NEW YORKER VOLKSZEITUNG – New York, 1894-1932 – 107r – 1 – us Ross [071]

NEW YORKER VOLKSZEITUNG – New York, 1894-June 1932; Sept-Oct 15 1932. Not collated – 1 – us NY Public [071]

NEW YORKER WOCHENBLAT – New York, NY. 1935-60 – 1 – us A.J.P.C. [071]

NEW YORKER YIDDISCHE VOLKZEITUNG – New York. v1-4. 1886-89 – 1r – 1 – us Ross [071]

NEW YORKER YUDISCHE FOLKSAITUNG – New York. v. 1-4. June 25 1886-Dec 20 1889 – 1 – us NY Public [071]

NEW YORKIN UUTISET – Brooklyn, Jan. 4, 1912-Dec. 24, 1915; July 25, 1917-Dec. 31, 1918 – 6r – 1 – us I.H.R.C. [975]

NEW YORK-STATESMAN – Albany, NY. 1820. Also: Plough Boy. 1819-20. Sold as one unit – 3 – us Readex [071]

NEW ZEALAND ANNUAL REPORT FILE : THE TOP 70 PUBLIC COMPANIES – (1980-88. 630 reports A$965.00; 1989-91. 210 reports A$720.00; 1992. 70 reports A$265.00; 1993. 70 reports A$290.00; 1994. 70 reports A$290.00) – Sydney, Australia: Australian Graduate School of Management, University of New South Wales, 1980- – 9 – at A.G.S.M. [650]

NEW ZEALAND BAPTIST – Wellington, New Zealand.1935-1980. Single reels available – 1 – 384.50 – us A.B.H.S. [073]

New Zealand. Census and Statistics Office *see*
- STATISTICAL REPORT ON THE FACTORY AND BUILDING PRODUCTION..
- STATISTICAL REPORT ON THE FACTORY PRODUCTION..
- STATISTICAL REPORT ON THE INDUSTRIAL MANUFACTURES..
- STATISTICAL REPORT ON TRADE AND SHIPPING..

NEW ZEALAND COMMERCIAL DIRECTORY *see* WISE'S NZ DIRECTORY 1872-1873

NEW ZEALAND DIRECTORY 1866-67 – Stevens & Bartholomew – 4mf – 9 – NZ$16.00 – 0-908797-45-1 – nz BAB [980]

NEW ZEALAND EXAMINER – London, England. -m. 16 Jan 1860-21 Sept 1877. 4 reels – 1 – uk British Libr Newspaper [072]

NEW ZEALAND EXPEDITIONARY FORCE 1914-1918 WAR – (The items included are: NZEF Embarkation Rolls 1914-18 (NZNB610-613), Australian Infantry Force 1918 (NZNB509 N510 not found), Roll of Honour 1924 (N620), Second NZEF Reserve List 1917 (N860) and Medal Roll List) – 51mf – 9 – NZ$130.00 – 0-908797-01-X – nz BAB [355]

NEW ZEALAND EXPEDITIONARY FORCE NOMINAL ROLLS 1939-1948 – (Entries contain full name, regimental number, occupation, address and name, address and relationship of next-of-kin of enlisted person) – 16v. 1940-48 – 29mf – 9 – NZ$75.00 – 0-908797-09-5 – NZNB N737-752n – nz BAB [355]

NEW ZEALAND FORESTRY – v1- 1925- – 9 – NZ$400.00 – nz Forest [634]

NEW ZEALAND HERALD – Auckland, 1992- – 36r per y – 1 – us Ross [072]

NEW ZEALAND INDEX 1908 : WISE'S EVERY PLACE IN NEW ZEALAND – (Place names listed alphabetically, with description of each) – Wellington: H Wise & Co, 1908 – 4mf – 9 – NZ$16.00 – 0-908797-11-7 – NZNB N2364 – nz BAB [980]

NEW ZEALAND INDEX ANNUAL 1899 – (Pt 1: Information about commerce, crops, manufacturing, farming etc. Pt 2: Cities, towns, localities, alphabetically listed and described) – Dunedin: NZ Index Co, 1899 – 4mf – 9 – NZ$13.00 – 0-908797-10-9 – NZNB N2359 – nz BAB [980]

NEW ZEALAND JOURNAL – London, England. -w. 8 Feb 1840-20 Dec 1845. 2 reels – 1 – uk British Libr Newspaper [072]

NEW ZEALAND JOURNAL OF AGRICULTURE – v1- 1910- 1; v128- 5,6; v130- 9 – us UMI [073]

NEW ZEALAND JOURNAL OF HEALTH, PHYSICAL EDUCATION AND RECREATION – 1953- 1; 1972- 5,6; 1974- 9 – us UMI [073]

NEW ZEALAND JURIST : REPORTS OF CASES ARGUED AND DETERMINED IN THE SUPREME COURT OF NEW ZEALAND IN ITS RESPECTIVE DISTRICTS, AND ON APPEAL TO THE COURT OF APPEAL – (V1 contains an "Appendix of important cases decided in previous years" by Gerald D Branson. v2 is reported by Frederick R. Chapman) – v1-2. 1873-75. Dunedin: Mackay, Fenwick & Co, 1874-76 (all publ) – 7mf – 9 – $10.50 – LLMC 97-015 – us L.L.M.C. [340]

NEW ZEALAND LABOUR PARTY JOURNAL – Wellington, 1965-70 (incompl) – 1 – us Hoover Inst Photo [335]

THE NEW ZEALAND LAW JOURNAL – 1965-77 – 9 – 428.00 – at Butterworths [340]

NEW ZEALAND LIBRARIES – v2- 1937- 1; v34- 5,6; v40- 9 – us UMI [020]

NEW ZEALAND LUTHERAN – (Some original pgs damaged) – 1956-90 – 3r – 1 – ATLA S0781 – us A.T.L.A. [073]

NEW ZEALAND MEDICAL JOURNAL – v1- 1887- 1; v85- 5,6,9 – us UMI [610]

New Zealand. Methodist Church. Methodist Overseas Mission. Solomon Islands Mission *see* CHAIRMAN'S CORRESPONDENCE (INDEXED)

New Zealand. Methodist Church. Overseas Mission *see* FOREIGN MISSION EXECUTIVE MINUTE BOOKS

New Zealand. Methodist Church. Overseas Mission Board *see* MINUTES

NEW ZEALAND MONTHLY REVIEW – v1- 1960- 1; v15- 5,6; v16- 9 – us UMI [073]

NEW ZEALAND NATIONAL BIBLIOGRAPHY – (Annual cumulation only 1993, 1994. NZ$180.00; Back issues NZ$160.00ea; Cumulated ed. 1983-93. NZ$330.00) – Publ. 11 times a year with annual cumulation – NZ$270.00y – nz Nat'l Libr [010]

NEW ZEALAND NATIONAL BIBLIOGRPHY *see* NEW ZEALAND SERIALS

NEW ZEALAND REGISTERED SHIPS 1840-1950 / Watt, Morris W – (Compiled from the NZ section of the Register of all British ships. Ships, owners, builders amd masters are each listed alphabetically. Details of size and weight of vessel, builder, owner(s), registration and eventual fate, where known. Addenda and corrigenda included) – Wellington: Ship and Marine Society, 1962 – 7mf – 9 – NZ$28.00 – nz BAB [380]

NEW ZEALAND SERIALS / Baker, Alyson et al – (All serials in New Zealand National Bibliography from 1982 – Feb 1992) – Wellington, New Zealand, 1992 – 9 – NZ$170.00 – nz Nat'l Libr [073]

New Zealand. Special Law Reform Committee on Admiralty Jurisdiction *see* ADMIRALTY JURISDICTION: REPORT

NEW ZEALAND SPEECH THERAPISTS JOURNAL – v1- 1946- 1; v27- 5,6; v30- 9 – us UMI [073]

NEW ZEALAND THEOLOGICAL REVIEW *see* COLLOQUIUM

NEWARK ADVERTISER – England. -w. 1859-1968. (114 reels) – 1 – uk British Libr Newspaper [072]

NEWARK ADVERTISER – Nottinghamshire. 1866 to date – 1 – uk Microform Academic [072]

NEWARK HERALD – England. -w. Jan 1873-Sep 1960. (80 reels) – 1 – uk British Libr Newspaper [072]

NEWARK HERALD – Newark, NE. -w. Jun 1881-Mar 1882 – 1 – us NE Hist [071]

NEWAYGO COUNTY SUN – Big Rapids. Mich. -w. 1973- – 1 – us UMI [071]

NEWBERG ENTERPRISE – Newberg, OR. -w. 29 Dec 1910-4 Jul 1918. 3 rolls – 1 – us U.O. Library [071]

NEWBERG GRAPHIC – Newberg, OR. -w. 1899-1900, 1903-43 – 1 – 408.00 – us Oregon Hist [071]

NEWBERG GRAPHIC – Newberg, OR. -w. 22 Dec 1888-22 Aug 1902; 6 Jan 1944-.; 7-14 June 1901 – 2r – 1 – us U.O. Library [071]

NEWBERG SCRIBE – (Set incl. Newberg Scribe and Carlton Sentinel) – Newberg, OR. -w. 17 Mar 1932-28 Mar 1940. – 3r – 1 – us U.O. Library [071]

NEWBERG SCRIBE AND CARLTON SENTINEL – Newberg OR. Dec 3 1931-Mar 10 1932 – 1 – us U.O. Library [071]

NEWBERN BAPTIST CHURCH. GREEN COUNTY, ALABAMA : CHURCH RECORDS – 1848-1959 – 1 – 9.00 – us Baptist [240]

NEWBERRY FIRST BAPTIST CHURCH. NEWBERRY, SOUTH CAROLINA : CHURCH RECORDS – 1831-1972. WMU Minutes. 1885-1901 – 1 – 61.34 – us Baptist [240]

THE NEWBERRY GOSPELS / Goodspeed, Edgar Johnson – (Includes bibliographical references) – Chicago: University of Chicago, 1902 – 1mf – 9 – 0-8370-9235-3 – 1986-3235 – us A.T.L.A. [220]

Newberry, J S *see* NEWBERRY REPORTS OF ADMIRALTY CASES IN THE DISTRICT COURTS OF THE U.S., 1842-1957

Newberry Library. Chicago *see*
- CATALOGUE OF THE GREENLEE COLLECTION
- DICTIONARY CATALOG OF THE EDWARD E. AYER COLLECTION OF AMERICANA AND AMERICAN INDIANS
- DICTIONARY CATALOGUE OF THE HISTORY OF PRINTING FROM THE JOHN M. WING FOUNDATION
- THE GENEALOGICAL INDEX
- THE GENEALOGICAL INDEX OF THE NEWBERRY LIBRARY

NEWBERRY LIBRARY COLLECTIONS – (Micheud, Biographie Universelle 1843-65 21 reels $1550; Covent Garden Prompt Books 3 reels $220; Early English Courtesy Books 1571-1773 19 reels $1405; French Political Pamphlets 1560-1653 28 reels $2075; Nouvelle Biographie Generale 1853-1866 9 reels $665; Siebmacher Armorial Collection 18 reels $1330) – 98r – 1 – $7245.00 – us UMI [090]

Newberry, Percy *see* RESCUED ESSAYS OF THOMAS CARLYLE

Newberry, Percy E *see*
- BENI HASAN: PART 2
- EL BERESH I: THE TOMB OF TEHUTI-HETEP
- EL BERESH, PART 2

NEWBERRY REPORTS OF ADMIRALTY CASES IN THE DISTRICT COURTS OF THE U.S., 1842-1957 / Newberry, J S – New York: Banks/Gould. 1v. 1857 (all publ) – 7mf – 9 – $10.50 – LLMC 81-463 – us L.L.M.C. [324]

Newbold, D *see* ROCK PICTURES AND ARCHEAEOLOGY IN THE LIBYAN DESERT

Newborn, William *see* THE BAPTIST HYMN BOOK

THE NEW-BRUNSWICK AGRICULTURIST – Saint John [NB Agricultural and Horticultural Society of the County of Saint John, 1841] – 9 – cn C.I.H.M. [630]

THE NEW-BRUNSWICK RELIGIOUS AND LITERARY JOURNAL – Saint John, NB: A M'Leod, [1829-1830] – 9 – cn C.I.H.M. [240]

NEWBURY 1635-1849 – (Mf 1T: Vital Records 1645-1705. Mf 1T-4T: Births 1636-1705. Mf 4T: Deaths & Marriages 1649-99. Mf 5T: Marriages/Intentions 1695-1701. Mf 5T-10T: Births 1635-1730. Mf 10T-12T: Deaths 1635-1735; Marriages/Intents 1703-17. Mf 12T-24T: Births 1730-1832. Mf25T-28T: Marriages 1724-1819. Mf 28T-29T: Marriages/Intents 1716-30. Mf 30T-40T: Intentions 1730-1849. Mf 40T-41T: Marriages 1819-44. Mf 41T-44T: Deaths 1691-1844. Mf 44T-45T: Births 1831-49. Mf 46T-47T: Births 1844-49. Mf 47T: Marriages 1844-49. Mf 48T: Deaths 1844-49. Mf 49T: Out-of-Town Marriages 1662-1799) – (mf ed 1998) – 49mf – 9 – 0-87623-304-3 – us Holbrook [920]

NEWBURY EXPRESS – England.1891-98. 8 reels – 1 – uk British Libr Newspaper [072]

NEWBURY WEEKLY NEWS ETC – Feb 7-Dec 27 1867; 1868; Jul 15 1869-1906; 1908-Jun 1997 – 233 1/4r – 1 – uk British Libr Newspaper [072]

NEWBURYPORT 1740-1849 – (Mf 1T-13T: Births 1740-1844. Mf 13T-17T: Marriages 1764-1844. Mf 17T-22T: Births 1740-1805. Mf 22T-26T: Deaths 1745-1832. Mf 27T-28T: Deaths 1833-44. Mf 28T-32T: Births 1844-49. Mf 32T-34T: Marriages 1844-49. Mf 34T-36T: Deaths 1844-49. Mf 36T-48T: Intentions 1764-1849) – (mf ed 1998) – 48mf – 9 – 0-87623-305-1 – us Holbrook [920]

NEWCASTLE CHRONICLE – Newcastle-upon-Tyne. England. -w. Sept 1770-Dec 1781; 15 Jan-22 Mar 1897 (Wanting 1777). (6 reels) – 1 – uk British Libr Newspaper [072]

NEWCASTLE COURANT – Newcastle-upon-Tyne. England. -w. 1778-84. (2 reels) – 1 – uk British Libr Newspaper [072]

NEWCASTLE DAILY CHRONICLE – Newcastle-upon-Tyne, England. -d. 1868; 1871-74; 1899-1904. Lacking 1903. 30 reels – 1 – uk British Libr Newspaper [072]

NEWCASTLE DAILY JOURNAL – Newcastle-upon-Tyne, England. -d. 1871-74. 8 1 2 reels – 1 – uk British Libr Newspaper [072]
NEWCASTLE DISEASE VACCINES : THEIR PRODUCTION AND USE / Allan, W H et al – 1978 – 163p – it F.A.O. [616]
NEWCASTLE ECHO – Newcastle, SA. 1881-84 – 1 – sa State Libr [072]
NEWCASTLE FARMER – Cobourg [Ont]: Chatterton and Ruttan, [1846-1849?] – 9 – cn C.I.H.M. [630]
NEWCASTLE GENERAL MAGAZINE – 1-14. 1746-60 – 1 – us UMI [073]
NEWCASTLE GUARDIAN – Newcastle-under-Lyme. England. -w. 1881-95, 1897-1906, 1908-09. (26 reels) – 1 – uk British Libr Newspaper [072]
NEWCASTLE HERALD – 1 – F1,830.00 – sz Infoprint [072]
NEWCASTLE HERALD – Newcastle, SA. 1885-93 – 1 – sa State Libr [072]
NEWCASTLE JOURNAL – (Newcastle and North Staffordshire Pioneer Staffordshire Times and Newcastle Pioneer Staffordshire Times Staffordshire Weekly Times). Newcastle-under-Lyme. England. -w. 1855-82. (21 reels) – 1 – uk British Libr Newspaper [072]
NEWCASTLE MORNING HERALD – Newcastle, New South Wales, Australia. -d. 1 Jan 1941-29 April, 1 Aug-30 Nov 1942; 1 Jan 1943-31 Oct 1952; 1 Aug 1957-31 Aug 1961. 88 reels – 1 – uk British Libr Newspaper [072]
NEWCASTLE MORNING HERALD AND MINERS ADVOCATE – (Current issues avail on subscription) – Sydney, 1873- – 500r – 1 – at Pascoe [072]
NEWCASTLE NEWS – Newcastle, CA. 1887-1923 – 8r – 1 – $400.00 – C03354 – us Library Micro [071]
NEWCASTLE TIMES – Newcastle, NE. -w. Oct 1895-Jun 1898; Jan- Feb 1900; Oct 1902-Dec 1903; May 1937-Jun 1944 – 1 – us NE Hist [071]
NEWCASTLE TIMES – Newcastle-under-Lyme, England. 4 Mar 1938-23 Mar 1951 – 11r – 1 – uk British Libr Newspaper [072]
NEWCASTLE UPON TYNE RECORDS COMMITTEE – (Coll title: Publications of the English Record Societies, 1835-1972...) – v1-12. 1920-33 – 39mf – 9 – £330.00 – uk Chadwyck [941]
NEWCASTLE WEEKLY CHRONICLE – Newcastle-upon-Tyne, England. 1865; 1871-74; 1898; Jan-Nov 1912 – 6r – 1 – uk British Libr Newspaper [072]
NEWCASTLE-UNDER-LYME TIMES – England, Apr 1951-May 1973 – 31r – 1 – uk British Libr Newspaper [072]
THE NEW-CENTURY BIBLE *see* CHRONICLES
Newcomb, Harry Turner *see* THE FEDERAL COURTS AND THE ORDERS OF THE INTERSTATE COMMERCE COMMISSION
Newcomb, Harvey *see*
- A CYCLOPEDIA OF MISSIONS
- A PRACTICAL DIRECTORY FOR YOUNG CHRISTIAN FEMALES

Newcomen Society *see* TRANSACTIONS
THE NEWCOMES : MEMOIRS OF A MOST RESPECTABLE FAMILY / Thackeray, William Makepeace; ed by Pendennis, Arthur – London: Smith, Elder, 1869 – 1 roll – 1 – 1-55879-735-1 – uk Libr Preservation [830]
A NEWE BOKE OF PHISICKE / Bullein, W – M 318. 1559 – 9 – ne IDC [610]
NEWE GEOMETRISCHE UND PERSPECTIUISCHE INUENTIONES ETLICHER SONDERBAHRER INSTRUMENT / Faulhaber, Johann – Franckfurt am Mayn: Wolffgang Richter, 1610 – 1 – us U.W. Library [510]
Newell, Martin L *see*
- THE LAW OF DEFAMATION, LIBEL AND SLANDER IN CIVIL AND CRIMINAL CASES AS ADMINISTERED IN THE COURTS OF THE UNITED STATES OF AMERICA
- THE LAW OF SLANDER AND LIBEL IN CIVIL AND CRIMINAL CASES

Newell, William Wells *see* KING ARTHUR AND THE TABLE ROUND: TALES CHIEFLY AFTER THE OLD FRENCH OF CRESTIEN OF TROYES, WITH AN ACCOUNT OF ARTHURIAN ROMANCE.
Newell, William Whiting *see* REVIVALS
THE NEW-ENGLAND COURANT – Boston, MA. 1721-27. Also: The Weekly Rehearsal. 1731-35. Sold as one unit – 1,3 – us Readex [071]
THE NEW-ENGLAND WEEKLY JOURNAL – Boston. Mass. 1727-1741 – 1,3 – us Readex [071]
THE NEWER CRITICISM AND THE ANALOGY OF THE FAITH: A REPLY TO...W. ROBERTSON SMITH / Watts, Robert – Edinburgh: T.& T. Clark, 1881. 1 fiche – 9 – us A.T.L.A. [240]
THE NEWER DISTRICTS OF ONTARIO: INFORMATION FOR PROSPECTIVE SETTLERS: RAINY RIVER VALLEY, WABIGOON COUNTRY, TEMISCAMINGUE, ALGOMA/ REPORT OF INPECTION. / Anderson, Duncan – Toronto, Warwick & Rutter. 1898. 00877. (Pre-1900 Canadiana) – 9 – cn C.I.H.M. [971]
THE NEWER RELIGIOUS THINKING / Beach, David Nelson – Boston: Little, Brown, 1893 – 1mf – 9 – 0-8370-4672-6 – 1985-2672 – us A.T.L.A. [240]
NEWFOUNDLAND / Fane, Cecil – London?: s.n., 1893?. 05485. (Pre-1900 Canadiana) – 9 – cn C.I.H.M. [971]
Newfoundland *see*
- JOURNAL OF LEGISLATIVE ASSEMBLY
- ROYAL GAZETTE AND NEWFOUNDLAND ADVERTISER

Newfoundland. Canada *see*
- NEWFOUNDLAND GAZETTE
- NEWFOUNDLAND STATUTES, SESSION LAWS AND REVISIONS
- TUCKER'S SELECT NEWFOUNDLAND CASES

Newfoundland. Canada. Supreme Court *see* NEWFOUNDLAND SUPREME COURT REPORTS
NEWFOUNDLAND EXPRESS – St. John's, Canada. 1851-72 – 17r – 1 – $1,105.00 – cn Library Assoc [971]
NEWFOUNDLAND GAZETTE / Newfoundland. Canada – v. 30-43. 1955-1968 – 1 – us UMI [324]
NEWFOUNDLAND GAZETTE – (v44-57 1969-82 5. v58- 1983- 9) – Saint John's. v28- 1955- – 1,5,9 – Price varies – cn Micromedia [971]
NEWFOUNDLAND IN 1897: BEING QUEEN VICTORIA'S DIAMOND JUBILEE YEAR AND THE FOUR HUNDREDTH ANNIVERSARY OF THE DISCOVERY OF THE ISLAND BY JOHN CABOT / Harvey, Moses – London: Low, Marston & Co., 1897. 05210. (Pre-1900 Canadiana) – 9 – cn C.I.H.M. [971]
NEWFOUNDLAND IN 1900: A TREATISE OF THE GEOGRAPHY, NATURAL RESOURCES AND HISTORY OF THE ISLAND...FINELY ILLUSTRATED WITH MAPS AND HALF-TONE ENGRAVINGS / Harvey, Moses – St. John's, Newfoundland: S. Garland, 1900. 05209. (Pre-1900 Canadiana) – 9 – cn C.I.H.M. [910]
NEWFOUNDLAND: ITS CLIMATE, GEOGRAPHICAL POSITION, RESOURCES, ETC.: AND BENARES, THE SACRED CITY OF THE HINDUS: TWO LECTURES DELIVERED BEFORE THE Y.M.C.A / Budden, Heber – Quebec: Morning Chronicle, 1880. 00330. (Pre-1900 Canadiana) – 9 – cn C.I.H.M. [910]
Newfoundland. Laws, Statutes, etc *see* REGULATIONS MADE UNDER DEFENCE ACT, 1939 AND EMERGENCY POWERS (DEFENCE) ACT, 1940, SEPT. 1ST, 1939, TO FEB. 28TH, 1943
THE NEWFOUNDLAND MAGAZINE – (Cont by: Newfoundland Quarterly) – [S.l.]: Newfoundland Pub. Co, [1900] – 9 – cn C.I.H.M. [910]
NEWFOUNDLAND MONTHLY MESSENGER – St. John's, Nfld: [s.n, 18--1878] – 9 – cn C.I.H.M. [240]
NEWFOUNDLAND QUARTERLY *see* THE NEWFOUNDLAND MAGAZINE
NEWFOUNDLAND STATUTES, SESSION LAWS AND REVISIONS / Newfoundland. Canada – (Updates planned) – 1900-1989 – 580mf – 9 – $870.00 – LLMC 90-150 – us L.L.M.C. [324]
NEWFOUNDLAND SUPREME COURT REPORTS / Newfoundland. Canada. Supreme Court – v1-15. 1817-1946 – 97mf – 9 – $145.00 – LLMC 81-030 – us L.L.M.C. [340]
NEWFOUNDLAND, THE OLDEST BRITISH COLONY: ITS HISTORY, ITS PRESENT CONDITION, AND ITS PROSPECTS IN THE FUTURE / Hatton, Joseph – London: Chapman and Hall, 1883. 05514. (Pre-1900 Canadiana) – 9 – cn C.I.H.M. [971]
NEWFOUNDLANDER – St. John's, Canada. 1827-82 – 26r – 1 – $1,690.00 – cn Library Assoc [971]
Newhall, Guy *see* THE DISTRIBUTION OF ESTATES OF DECEASED PERSONS IN MASSACHUSETTS
NEWHALL SIGNAL – (Also known as: Valencia Valley News, Saugus Enterprise) – Newhall, CA. 1919-1923; 1925-1981; 1984-1985 – 79r – 1 – $3,950.00 – H03355 – us Library Micro [071]
NEWHAM RECORDER – 1986-Jun 1997 – 54r – 1 – uk British Libr Newspaper [072]
THE NEW-HAMPSHIRE JOURNAL – Walpole, NH, 1793-97. Also: The Farmer's Weekly Museum, 1797-1810; The New Hampshire Mercury.Portsmouth, 1784-88. Sold as one unit – 1,3 – us Readex [071]
Newill-Planson Company (Delta, Ohio) *see* FUNERAL REGISTERS
THE NEW-JERSEY GAZETTE – Burlington and Trenton. N.J. 1777-86 – 1,3 – us Readex [071]
Newland, John *see* A TREATISE ON CONTRACTS, WITHIN THE JURISDICTION OF COURTS OF EQUITY
NEWLIGHT BAPTIST CHURCH. RALEIGH ASSOCIATION. NORTH CAROLINA : CHURCH RECORDS – 1850-1920. (Membership book) – 1 – 19.80 – us Baptist [240]
THE NEW-LONDON SUMMARY – New London. Conn. 1758-1763 – 1,3 – us Readex [071]
NEWLY FILMED MATERIAL ONLY – 1503-1550 (26 Farvardin 1374-26 Isfand 1374 [14 April 1995-15 March 1996]) – $150.00 – us MEDOC [470]
NEWMAN / Barry, William Francis – London: Hodder and Stoughton, 1904 – 1mf – us A.T.L.A. [240]
NEWMAN : SA VIE ET SES OEUVRES / Goyau, Lucie Felix-Faure – Paris: Perrin, 1901 – 1mf – us A.T.L.A. [240]
Newman, Albert Henry *see*
- A HISTORY OF ANTI-PEDOBAPTISM
- HISTORY OF ANTI-PEDOBAPTISM
- A HISTORY OF THE BAPTIST CHURCHES IN THE UNITED STATES
- MATERIALS

NEWMAN AS A MAN OF LETTERS / Reilly, Joseph John – New York: Macmillan Co., 1925. ix,329p – 1 – us U.W. Library [920]
NEWMAN CATHOLIQUE : D'APRES DES DOCUMENTS NOUVEAUX / Thureau-Dangin, Paul – Paris: Plon-Nourrit, 1912 – 1mf – us A.T.L.A. [240]
Newman, E *see*
- ENTOMOLOGICAL MAGAZINE
- A HISTORY OF BRITISH FERNS AND ALLIED PLANTS

Newman, Francis *see* A HISTORY OF THE HEBREW MONARCHY: FROM THE ADMINISTRATION OF SAMUEL TO THE BABYLONIAN CAPTIVITY
Newman, Francis William *see*
- CONTRIBUTIONS CHIEFLY TO THE EARLY HISTORY OF THE LATE CARDINAL NEWMAN
- IS ROMANISM REAL CHRISTIANITY?
- PHASES OF FAITH
- THE SOUL, HER SORROWS AND HER ASPIRATIONS

NEWMAN GROVE ADVERTISER – Newman Grove, NE. -w. Oct 1895-Dec 1896 – 1 – us NE Hist [071]
NEWMAN GROVE REPORTER – Newman Grove, NE. -w. Mar 1886-Jul 1888; Jan 1892-May 1899; Apr 1907; Apr-May 1908 – 1 – us NE Hist [071]
NEWMAN GROVE WEEKLY GAZETTE – Newman Grove, NE. Oct 1895-Feb 1896; Dec 1896 – 1 – us NE Hist [071]
Newman, J S *see* HISTORY OF PRIMITIVE BAPTISTS IN TEXAS, OKLAHOMA AND INDIAN TERRITORY
Newman, John Henry *see*
- THE ARIANS OF THE FOURTH CENTURY
- DISCUSSIONS AND ARGUMENTS ON VARIOUS SUBJECTS
- AN ESSAY IN AID OF A GRAMMAR OF ASSENT
- AN ESSAY ON THE DEVELOPMENT OF CHRISTIAN DOCTRINE
- FIFTEEN SERMONS PREACHED BEFORE THE UNIVERSITY OF OXFORD BETWEEN A.D. 1826 AND 1843
- HISTORY OF MY RELIGIOUS OPINIONS
- HYMNI ECCLESIAE; PARS 1: E BREVIARIO PARISIENSI, PARS 2: E BREVIARIIS ROMANO, SARISBURIENSI, ABORACENSI, ET ALIUNDE
- LECTURES ON CERTAIN DIFFICULTIES FELT BY ANGLICANS IN SUBMITTING TO THE CATHOLIC CHURCH
- LECTURES ON THE PRESENT POSITION OF CATHOLICS IN ENGLAND
- LETTERS AND CORRESPONDENCE OF JOHN HENRY NEWMAN DURING HIS LIFE IN THE ENGLISH CHURCH, WITH A BRIEF AUTOBIOGRAPHY
- LOSS AND GAIN
- MY CAMPAIGN IN IRELAND
- PAROCHIAL SERMONS
- SERMONS BEARING ON SUBJECTS OF THE DAY
- SERMONS PREACHED ON VARIOUS OCCASIONS
- TWO ESSAYS ON BIBLICAL AND ON ECCLESIASTICAL MIRACLES
- VERSES ON VARIOUS OCCASIONS
- THE VIA MEDIA OF THE ANGLICAN CHURCH, ILLUSTRATED IN LECTURES, LETTERS AND TRACTS WRITTEN BETWEEN 1830 AND 1841, WITH PREFACE AND NOTES
- WORKS

Newman, John Henry Cardinal *see* THE VIA MEDIA OF THE ANGLICAN CHURCH
NEWMAN, SUSAN A., DIARY – (Daily account of this upper class Jewish woman, noting the effects of the Great Depression, and Newman's husband's involvement in Anti-Prohibition activities) – Cleveland, Cuyahoga, OH. 1 Jan 1931-31 Dec 1935 – 1r – 1 – us Western Res [920]
NEWMARKET ERA – Newmarket, Canada. 1862-73 – 4r – 1 – $260.00 – cn Library Assoc [971]
NEWMARKET ERA – Newmarket, Ontario, CN. 1978- – 2r per yr – 1 – Can$57.00r – cn Commonwealth Micro [072]
NEWMARKET JOURNAL – England, Dec 1882- – 131+ r – 1 – uk British Libr Newspaper [072]
Newmarket, New Hampshire. Newmarket Free Will Baptist Church *see* RECORDS
NEWMILNS, GALSTON AND DARVEL GAZETTE – Scotland, Nov 1900-Aug 1901 – 28ft – 1 – uk British Libr Newspaper [072]
NEWNAN FIRST BAPTIST CHURCH. NEWNAN, GEORGIA : CHURCH RECORDS – 1828-Oct 1941 – 1 – 56.66 – us Baptist [240]
Newnham, William Orde *see* ALRESFORD
NEWPORT BALBOA TIMES *see* BALBOA TIMES, COSTA MESA HERALD, NEWPORT BALBOA TIMES, NEWPORT NEWS
NEWPORT COUNTY SENTINEL – Tiverton. R.I. 1925-1950 – 1 – us UMI [071]
NEWPORT EAGLE – Newport, NE. -w. Aug 1895-Dec 1897; Jun 1898-Aug 1903 – 1 – us NE Hist [071]
NEWPORT ENSIGN – Newport Beach, CA. 1983 – 11+ r – 1 – $550.00 ($50.00y) – H04079 – us Library Micro [071]
NEWPORT FIRST (UNITED BAPTIST CHURCH). RHODE ISLAND : CHURCH RECORDS – Alphabetical, 1644-1946; Chronological, 1644-1946; Typescript, 1644-63, c1720-92. 298p – 1 – us Baptist [240]
NEWPORT GAZETTE – Newport, PA., 1858-1860 – 13 – $25.00r – us I.M.R. [071]
NEWPORT GRAPHIC-REVIEW – Newport, OR. -w. 5 Dec 1963 – 3 Nov 1966. 2 rolls – 1 – us U.O. Library [071]
NEWPORT HARBOR CITY DIRECTORY – Orange Co, CA. 1942 – 2r – 1 – $100.00 – D072 – us Library Micro [910]
NEWPORT HARBOR DAILY PILOT – Newport Beach, CA. 1968 – 1r – 1 – $50.00 – H04032 – us Library Micro [071]
NEWPORT HISTORY – v1- 1912- 1; v46- 5,6; v48- 9 – us UMI [073]
THE NEWPORT INDEPENDENT – Newport, VT. v2 n9. 13 apr 1899 – 1r – 1 – Can$25.00 – cn Can Microfilming [071]
NEWPORT JOURNAL – Newport, OR. -w. 4 Mar 1925-26 Nov 1947. 5 rolls – 1 – us U.O. Library [071]
NEWPORT LEDGER – Newport, PA. -w 1878-1908. 7 rolls – 13 – $25.00r – us I.M.R. [071]
NEWPORT MERCURY – Newport, RI. 1758-1820 – 3 – us Readex [071]
NEWPORT MERCURY – Newport, RI. n27. 27 dec 1758 – 1r – 1 – Can$25.00 – cn Can Microfilming [071]
Newport, New Hampshire. Newport Baptist Church *see* RECORDS
NEWPORT NEWS – Newport OR. Jan 1 1948-Oct 28 1965 – 1 – us U.O. Library [071]
NEWPORT NEWS *see* BALBOA TIMES, COSTA MESA HERALD, NEWPORT BALBOA TIMES, NEWPORT NEWS
THE NEWPORT NEWS – Newport, PA. 1842-1918; 1887-1928 – 13 – $25.00r – us I.M.R. [071]
NEWPORT NEWS AND LINCOLN COUNTY TIMES – Newport OR. Nov 4 1965-June 3 1976 – 1 – us U.O. Library [071]
NEWPORT NEWSCASTER – Newport, OR. -w. 8 Jun 1961-7 Dec 1961. 1 roll – 1 – us U.O. Library [071]

NEWPORT REPUBLICAN – Newport, NE. - w. Jul-Oct 1894; Jul 1896-Jun 1906; Oct 1906-Dec 1912 – 1 – us NE Hist [071]
NEWPORT SECOND BAPTIST CHURCH. RHODE ISLAND : CHURCH RECORDS – Misc. unbound mss, 1720-94 and n.d.; Typescript, 1716-31, 1759. 250p – 1 – us Baptist [240]
NEWPORT SENTINEL – Newport, VT. v1 n8. 27 apr 1888-v3 n4. 29 mar 1889 – 1r – 1 – Can$35.00 – cn Can Microfilming [071]
NEWPORT SIGNAL – Newport, OR. -w. 10 Oct 1910-22 Jun 1911. 1 roll – 1 – us U.O. Library [071]
NEWPORTER NEWS – Newport Beach, CA. 1959-1972 – 8r – 1 – $400.00 – R03357 – us Library Micro [071]
NEWPORTER-MESA NEWS – Newport Beach, CA. 1973-1975 – 1r – 1 – $50.00 – R03356 – us Library Micro [071]
NEWQUAY EXPRESS *see* NEWQUAY GUARDIAN AND CORNISH COUNTY CHRONICLE
NEWQUAY EXPRESS AND CORNWALL COUNTY CHRONICLE – Newquay, England. Aug 1905-Dec 1955 – 58 1/2r – 1 – uk British Libr Newspaper [072]
NEWQUAY GUARDIAN AND CORNISH COUNTY CHRONICLE – (See: Newquay Express) – England, 1945-55 – 1 – uk British Libr Newspaper [072]
NEWQUAY GUARDIAN AND CORNISH COUNTY CHRONICLE *see* NEWQUAY EXPRESS AND CORNWALL COUNTY CHRONICLE
NEWRY COMMERCIAL TELEGRAPH – Ireland, 1828-67 – 39r – 1 – uk British Libr Newspaper [072]
NEWRY EXAMINER – Ireland, 1836-38 – 3r – 1 – uk British Libr Newspaper [072]
NEWRY HERALD – Ireland, 1858-63 – 6r – 1 – uk British Libr Newspaper [072]
NEWRY REPORTER – (1871, 1892 imperfect) – Ireland, 16 Nov 1867-Dec 1910; 28 Mar 1911-1974; Jul 1975-Dec 1977; 1986- – 200+ r – 1 – uk British Libr Newspaper [072]
NEWS – Albany, CA. 1986-1988 – 1r – 1 – $50.00 – B06008 – us Library Micro [071]
NEWS – Chafey, NV. 1908-09 – 1r – 1 – $50.00 – U04477 – us Library Micro [071]
NEWS – Churchill, NV. 31 Mar 1888 – 1r – 1 – $50.00 – U04479 – us Library Micro [071]
NEWS / Coalition for Alternatives in Jewish Education – 30 May 1984-4 Sept 1987.Continued by: News from the Coalition for the Advancement of Jewish Education – 1 – us A.J.P.C. [071]
NEWS – Dutch Creek, NV. 1 Feb, Mar, May 1907 – 1r – 1 – $50.00 – U044991 – us Library Micro [071]
NEWS – Fairview, NV. 1906-08 – 1r – 1 – $50.00 – U04519 – us Library Micro [071]
NEWS – Fostoria, Ohio. 1860-61 – 1r – 1 – $32.50r – us Archival [071]
NEWS – Gold Center, NV. 29 Sep 1906; 12 Jan 1907 – 1r – 1 – $50.00 – U04544 – us Library Micro [071]
NEWS – Gold Circle, NV. 26 Sep 1908 – 1r – 1 – $50.00 – U04546 – us Library Micro [071]
NEWS – Gold Creek, NV. 1896-97 – 1r – 1 – $50.00 – U04548 – us Library Micro [071]
NEWS – Hawthorne, NV. Jan-Apr 1931; 1934-35 – 2r – 1 – $100.00 – U04582 – us Library Micro [071]
NEWS = HSIA HSI – (In Chinese) – 1930-50 (complete) – 1r – 1 – us A.T.L.A. [073]
NEWS – Jasper. Fl. -w. 1948- – 1 – us P.K. Yonge [071]
NEWS – Kimberly, NV. Feb-Dec 1910 – 1r – 1 – $50.00 – U04593 – us Library Micro [071]
NEWS – Lake Tahoe, NV. 6 Jul, 31 Dec 1916 – 1r – 1 – $50.00 – U04594 – us Library Micro [071]
NEWS – Las Vegas, NV. 1941 – 1r – 1 – $50.00 – U04608 – us Library Micro [071]
NEWS – Le Grande, CA. 1946-1948 – 1r – 1 – $50.00 – B06034 – us Library Micro [071]
NEWS – Livermore, CA. 1951-62 – 6r – 1 – $300.00 – B02352 – us Library Micro [071]
NEWS – Los Gatos, CA. 1881-1904; 1906-15 – 7r – 1 – $350.00 – B02407 – us Library Micro [071]
NEWS – Manhattan, NV. 1906-07 – 2r – 1 – $100.00 – U04631 – us Library Micro [071]
NEWS – Molokai, HA, 1984-1993 – 3r – 1 – $150.00 – B05069 – us Library Micro [071]
NEWS – Monticello. Fl. -w. 1926-1941, 1945- – 1 – us P.K. Yonge [071]
NEWS – Okeechobee. Fl. -w. 1926-30, 1934-35, 1946- – 1 – us P.K. Yonge [071]
NEWS – Orland, CA. Apr-Dec 1887; 1889-90 – 1r – 1 – $50.00 – B02560 – us Library Micro [071]
NEWS – Rawhide, NV. 7 Mar, 1 Aug 1908 – 1r – 1 – $50.00 – U04654 – us Library Micro [071]
NEWS – Red Bluff, CA. 1893; 1897-1915; Jan-Oct 1928 – 19r – 1 – $950.00 – B02662 – us Library Micro [071]
NEWS – Reno, NV. 27 Jul 1930; Jul-Sep 1959 – 1r – 1 – $50.00 – U04707 – us Library Micro [071]
NEWS – Richmond, CA. 1918-19 – 1r – 1 – $50.00 – B02694 – us Library Micro [071]
NEWS – San Francisco, CA. 1930-59 – 265r – 1 – $13,250.00 – C02843 – us Library Micro [071]
NEWS – Santa Clara, CA. 1901-56; 1966 – 21r – 1 BC02947 – $1,050.00 – us Library Micro [071]
NEWS – Sebring. Fl. -w. 1948- – 1 – us P.K. Yonge [071]
NEWS – Srinagar, India. 1969-6 Jan 1970 – 1r – 1 – us L of C Photodup [072]
NEWS – Stuart. Fl. -w. 1946- – 1 – us P.K. Yonge [071]
NEWS – Virginia City, NV. 1936-51 – 7r – 1 – $350.00 – UN04794 – us Library Micro [071]
NEWS – Waverly, NE. -w. Jun 1972 to date – 1 – us NE Hist [071]
NEWS *see* TRI-VALLEY NEWS
THE NEWS – Anaheim, CA. 1962 – 2r – 1 – $100.00 – R04003 – us Library Micro [071]
THE NEWS : EASTERN ONTARIO AND OTTAWA VALLEY ADVOCATE – L'Orignal, Ontario. v1 n34. 7 nov 1876 – 1r – 1 – Can$25.00 – cn Can Microfilming [072]
THE NEWS – (Fifeshire News, 17 May-15 Nov 1862) – Cupar, Scotland, UK. 1858-59; 1860-15 Nov 1862 – 2r – 1 – uk British Libr Newspaper [072]
THE NEWS – (Formerly: Tri-Valley News) – Dublin, CA. 1981-82 – 38r – 1 – $1,900.00 – B02181 – us Library Micro [071]
THE NEWS – Fort Erie. Toronto. 1941-46 – 1 – 185.00 – cn McLaren [072]
THE NEWS – Garden Grove. Calif. 1954-1963- – 1 – us UMI [071]
THE NEWS – Golconda, NV. Jul-Dec 1899 – 1r – 1 – $50.00 – U04543 – us Library Micro [071]
THE NEWS – Kidron. Ohio. 1935- – 1 – us UMI [071]
THE NEWS – Kingston, Ontario. v4 n13. 14 dec 1843 – 1r – 1 – Can$25.00 – cn Can Microfilming [072]
THE NEWS – London. 19 May-29 Dec 1805; Jan-Dec 1807; Jan 1819-Dec 1832.-w. 16 reels – 1 – uk British Libr Newspaper [072]
THE NEWS – Pennsboro. West Virginia. -w. 1959- – 1 – us UMI [071]
THE NEWS – San Antonio, TX. 1818 - – 1 – us UMI [071]
THE NEWS – Shelbyville. Ind. 1948- – 1 – us UMI [071]
THE NEWS – Tenaga, Canada. 11 oct 1973; v1 n10. 13 dec 1973 – 1r – 1 – Can$25.00 – cn Can Microfilming [072]
THE NEWS – Toronto, Canada. v24 n227. 15 oct 1904; v25 n67. 6 apr 1905; n68. 7 apr 1905; n74. 14 apr 1905 – 1r – 1 – Can$35.00 – cn Can Microfilming [072]
THE NEWS / University of Tennessee.Institute of Agriculture – 1981-82.1 reel – 1,5 – us Spaulding [630]
THE NEWS – Worthington. Ohio. 1925- – 1 – us UMI [071]
THE NEWS *see*
– THE SAINT-LAURENT NEWS
– TRI-VALLEY NEWS
NEWS ADVERTISER – (1955-1992.-100r) – Ajax, 1993 – 8r – 1 – cn Preston [971]
NEWS ADVERTISER – Creston. Iowa. 1928- – 1 – us UMI [071]
NEWS ADVERTISER – Flint. Mich. -w. 1933-1944; 1950-1957 – 1 – us UMI [071]
NEWS ADVERTISER – Harlan. Iowa. -w. 1951- – 1 – us UMI [071]
NEWS ADVERTISER – Whitby, 1974-1983 – 30r – 1 – cn Preston [971]
NEWS AND ARKANSAS NEWS – West Memphis. Ark. 1946-48 – 1 – us UMI [071]
NEWS AND BEATTY BULLETIN – Goldfield, NV. 1947-56 – 4r – 1 – $250.00 – U04557 – us Library Micro [071]
NEWS AND CHRONICLE *see* THE LAKESHORE NEWS
THE NEWS AND EASTERN TOWNSHIPS ADVOCATE – St-Jean. v100 n10. 29 jan 1948 Centennial Edition-v125 n22. 13 sep 1972f – 14r – 1 – Can$80.00 – cn Can Microfilming [072]
THE NEWS AND FRONTIER ADVOCATE – St-Jean, Canada. v2 n18. 8 jun 1849-7 mai 1931 – 1r – 1 – Can$80.00 – cn Can Microfilming [072]
NEWS AND GRAPHIC – Greenwich. Conn. 1915-1937 – 1 – us UMI [071]
NEWS AND LETTERS – Detroit, MI. 1976-1983 – 3r – 1 – $150.00 – R04390 – us Library Micro [071]
NEWS AND LETTERS – (v. 24- 1979- 5,6,9) – v.1- 1955- – 1 – us UMI [073]
NEWS AND NEVADA NEWS – Winnemucca, NV. 1900-01 – 1r – 1 – $50.00 – U04819 – us Library Micro [071]
NEWS AND NEWS TRIBUNE – Providence. R.I. 1891-1906; 1918-1937 – 1 – us UMI [071]
NEWS AND NOTES – series 13-28. 1925-40 (complete) – 1r – 1 – ATLA S0528 – us A.T.L.A. [240]
NEWS AND OBSERVER – Raleigh. N.C. 1877-1880; 1910- – 1 – us UMI [071]
NEWS AND PRESS – Darlington. S.C. 1911-1939 – 1 – us UMI [071]
NEWS AND REVIEW – Garden City. Mich. 1940-1959 – 1 – us UMI [071]
NEWS AND SMYTHE COUNTY NEWS – Marion. Va. 1925-1941 – 1 – us UMI [071]
NEWS AND STAR *see* CUMBERLAND NEWS (EVENING ED)
NEWS AND TRUTHS / ed by Taylor, H Boyce – Murray. KY. 1907-32 – 1 – $612.64 – us Baptist [240]
NEWS AND VALLEY TIMES – North Las Vegas, NV. 1951-1958; 1959-1970 – 21r – 1 – $1,050.00 – N04634 – us Library Micro [071]
NEWS AND VIEWS – 1957- 1; v34- 5,6; v39- 9 – us UMI [073]
NEWS AND VIEWS / The Conservative Baptist Foreign Mission Society – News and Views. May 1944-46; Conservative Baptist. 1947-Aug 1965; Impact. Sep 1965-71 – 1 – $91.35 – us Baptist [240]
NEWS AND VIEWS : PERMANENT MISSION OF THE REPUBLIK OF INDONESIA TO THE UNITED NATIONS – (Missing: v1(26-28), 30-31) 1963; v2(89) 1963; 1965) – New York, 1963-1965 – 62mf – 9 – ne IDC [950]
NEWS AND VIEWS FROM USSR : BULLETIN OF THE PRESS BUREAU OF THE EMBASSY OF THE USSR IN CHINA – (Includes c.1: no.1457 1946:Mar.20-; no. 2243 1948:Nov.13) – Chungking: The Bureau, 19uu – 1 – CSUXAKZ3756-S – us Hoover Inst Photo [947]
NEWS AND VIEWS INDONESIA – (Missing: v1(1,11,20) 1955; v2(2-5,7) 1956/57) – Canberra, 1955-1957 – 9mf – 9 – ne IDC [950]
NEWS AND WEEKLY TRIBUNE – Goldfield, NV. 1914-46 – 7r – 1 – $350.00 – U04558 – us Library Micro [071]
NEWS ARGUS – Goldsboro. N.C. 1890-1897; 1929- – 1 – us UMI [071]
NEWS BEE – Toledo. Ohio. 1903-38 – 1 – us UMI [071]
NEWS BULLETIN – Bakersfield. Calif. 1962-1967 – 1 – us UMI [071]
NEWS BULLETIN / Council of Action for Peace and Reconstruction – London. 19 Jan 1938 – 26 Jul 1939. (30 ft) – 1 – uk British Libr Newspaper [320]
NEWS BULLETIN – Harvard. Ill. -w. 1958-59 – 1 – us UMI [071]
NEWS BULLETIN / Our American Heritage Committee – 1963- 1; v8- 5,6; v13- 9 – us UMI [970]
NEWS BULLETIN *see* ARGUS
NEWS BULLETIN IOWA STATE BAR ASSOCIATION *see* IOWA LAWYER
NEWS CHRONICLE – (Issues for oct-nov 19 1955 filmed with: News Chronicle and Daily Dispatch nov 21 1955-dec 1955) – London, [England]: Daily News, jul 1938-nov 19 1955 – 89r – 1 – us Res Libr [072]
NEWS CHRONICLE – Thunder Bay, 1929-1972 – 323r – 1 – cn Preston [971]
NEWS CHRONICLE – Vallejo. Calif. 1945- – 1 – us UMI [071]
THE NEWS CHRONICLE – Shippensburg, PA., 1882-1990 – 13 – $25.00r – us I.M.R. [071]
NEWS COMET – East Berlin. Pa. 1928-1952 – 1 – us UMI [071]
NEWS COMMERCIAL – Collins. Miss. 1950-1957 – 1 – us UMI [071]
NEWS COURIER – Athens. Ala. 1944; 1969- – 1 – us UMI [071]
NEWS DEMOCRAT – Belleville. Ill. 1901-03; 1905- – 1 – us UMI [071]
NEWS DEMOCRAT – Columbus. Mont. 1918-1919 – 1 – us UMI [071]
NEWS DEMOCRAT – Huntington. Ind. 1897-1911 – 1 – us UMI [071]
NEWS DEMOCRAT – New Philadelphia. Ohio. 1901-1902 – 1 – us UMI [071]
NEWS DEMOCRAT – Uhrichsville. Ohio. 1901-1902 – 1 – us UMI [071]
NEWS DIGEST – Portland OR. Oct 1 1933 – 1 – us U.O. Library [071]
NEWS DISPATCH – Jeannette. Pa. 1890- – 1 – us UMI [071]
NEWS DISPATCH – Shamokin. Pa. 1923- – 1 – us UMI [071]
NEWS ENTERPRISE – Wasco OR. Aug 16 1923-Aug 12 1927 – 1 – us U.O. Library [071]
NEWS EXAMINER – Centralia. Wash. -w. 1901-16 – 1 – us UMI [071]
NEWS EXAMINER – Portland OR. Mar 30-May 4 1932 – 1 – us U.O. Library [071]
NEWS FARM JOURNAL – Kalispell. Mont. 1958-1959; 1966- – 1 – us UMI [071]
NEWS FROM ABROAD – Manchester. England. -w. 17 Nov, 22, 29 Dec 1722. (4 ft) – 1 – uk British Libr Newspaper [072]
NEWS FROM INDONESIA – (Missing: v1(1-13) 1948) – New York, 1948-1949 – 4mf – 9 – ne IDC [950]
NEWS FROM NOWHERE : OR, AN EPOCH OF REST, BEING SOME CHAPTERS FROM A UTOPIAN ROMANCE / Morris, William – Hammersmith [Eng.]: Kelmscott Press; London: Sold by Reeves & Turner, 1892 – 1 roll – 1 – 1-55879-198-1 – uk Libr Preservation [830]
NEWS FROM THE BASE – Stead, NV. 1945 (scattered issues) – 1r – 1 – $50.00 – U04756 – us Library Micro [071]
NEWS FROM THE COMMITTEE – New York, NY. Sept 1968-1987. English.Incomplete – 1 – us A.J.P.C. [071]
NEWS FROM UKRAINE – (Backfile through 1998 1r per y $85r) – 1999- – 1r per y – 1 – $80.00 standing order – us Ross [072]
NEWS FROM UKRAINE – Kiev – 1mf – 9 – $99.95y – us East View [947]
NEWS FROM WOMEN IN GERMAN – no.2, Feb. 1975-no.5, Dec. 1975. Madison, Wis.: Women in German, German Dept. University of Wisconsin, 1975. Wisconsin, 1975 – 1 – us U.W. Library [305]
NEWS FROM WOMEN IN GERMANISTIK – no.1, Dec. 1974. s.l.: s.n., 1974. Continued by: News from women in German – 1 – us U.W. Library [305]
NEWS GAZETTE – Champaign. Ill. 1953- – 1 – us UMI [071]
NEWS HERALD – Franklin, PA., 1920-1972 – 13 – $25.00r – us I.M.R. [071]
NEWS HERALD – Franklin. Pa. -d. 1959- – 1 – us UMI [071]
NEWS HERALD – Joplin. Mo. 1942- – 1 – us UMI [071]
NEWS HERALD – Modesto, CA. 1925-33 – 42r – 1 RB02471 – $2,100.00 – us Library Micro [071]
NEWS HERALD – Olneyville. R.I. 1928-1931 – 1 – us UMI [071]
NEWS HERALD – Panama City. Fl. 1940-57 – 1 – us P.K. Yonge [071]
NEWS HERALD – Perry. Fl. -w. 1959- – 1 – us P.K. Yonge [071]
NEWS HERALD – Plattsmouth. Neb. 1865-1912 – 1 – us UMI [071]
NEWS HERALD – Suffolk. Va. 1935- – 1 – us UMI [071]
THE NEWS HERALD – Santa Rosa, CA. 1961-1988 – 27r – $1,350.00 – B05065 – us Library Micro [071]
NEWS ITEM – Mobile. Ala. 1917-31 – 1 – us UMI [071]
THE NEWS ITEM – Shamokin, PA., 1972-1987 – 13 – $25.00r – us I.M.R. [071]
THE NEWS ITEM – Shamokin, PA. -d 1968-1970 – 13 – $25.00r – us I.M.R. [071]
NEWS JOURNAL – Chesterfield. Va. -w. 1957- – 1 – us UMI [071]

NEWS JOURNAL – Euclid. Ohio. 1938-1970 – 1 – us UMI [071]
NEWS JOURNAL – Mansfield. Ohio. and predecessors. 1891- – 1 – us UMI [071]
NEWS JOURNAL – Radford. Va. 1974- – 1 – us UMI [071]
NEWS JOURNAL – Wilmington. Ohio. 1920- – 1 – us UMI [071]
NEWS LEADER – Alexandria. La. 1968- – 1 – us UMI [071]
NEWS LEADER – Baton Rouge. La. 1968- – 1 – us UMI [071]
NEWS LEADER – Homestead. Fl. 1967- – 1 – us UMI [071]
NEWS LEADER – Homestead. Pa. 1970- – 1 – us UMI [071]
NEWS LEADER – Lake Charles. La. 1968- – 1 – us UMI [071]
NEWS LEADER – Monroe. La. 1968- – 1 – us UMI [071]
NEWS LEADER – Richwood. West Virginia. -w. 1951- – 1 – us UMI [071]
NEWS LEADER – Rockwood. West Virginia. 1948-1949 – 1 – us UMI [071]
NEWS LEADER – San Mateo, CA. 1916-24 – 14r – 1 – $700.00 – B02919 – us Library Micro [071]
NEWS LEDGER – Sacramento/West Sacramento, CA. 1964-1988 – 13r – 1 – $650.00 – C03647 – us Library Micro [071]
THE NEWS LEDGER – West Sacramento, CA. 1964 – 19+ r – 1 – $950.00 ($50.00y) – B03693 – us Library Micro [071]
THE NEWS / LES NOUVELLES *see* THE SAINT-LAURENT NEWS
NEWS LETTER / Mississippi. State College. Cooperative Extension Work in Agriculture and Home Economics – v. 1-687. 1924-35 – 1,5,6 – us Spaulding [630]
THE NEWS, LIVERMORE *see* TRI-VALLEY NEWS
NEWS MEDIA AND THE LAW – (v.3-. 1979- 5,6,9) – v.1-. Oct. 1977- – 1 – us UMI [380]
THE NEWS MESSENGER – Lincoln, CA. 1913-50 – 20r – 1 – $1,000.00 – C02342 – us Library Micro [071]
THE NEWS MESSENGER – Lincoln. Calif. -w. 1944-50 – 1 – us UMI [071]
NEWS MINER – Republic. Wash. -w. 1907-09, 1911-26, 1928-53 – 1 – us UMI [071]
NEWS MIRROR – Williamsport, PA. -w 1933 – 13 – $25.00r – us I.M.R. [071]
NEWS MIRROR – Yucaipa, CA. 1912- – 121+ r – 1 – $6,050.00 ($180.00y) – R03130 – us Library Micro [071]
THE NEWS (MONTREAL, QUEBEC) = LES NOUVELLES – Montreal: Miller Pub Co. v15-26. 1965-1978. SEM35P131 – 13r – 1 – Can$625.00 – cn Bibl Nat [072]
NEWS NOTES: BULLETIN OF THE TEXAS LIBRARY ASSOCIATION – 1 – us UMI [073]
NEWS OBSERVER – Herndon. Va. 1925-1943 – 1 – us UMI [071]
NEWS OF DELAWARE COUNTY – Upper Darby. Pa. 1939- – 1 – us UMI [071]
NEWS OF MALAYA AND SINGAPORE MARKET – Singapore. -m. Oct, Nov 1931, Mar, Apr 1932. (15 ft) – 1 – uk British Libr Newspaper [072]
NEWS OF ORANGE COVE – Dinuba, CA. 1983-1984 – 1r – 1 – $50.00 – B06022 – us Library Micro [071]
NEWS OF PORT ORFORD – Gold Beach OR. July 23-30 1953 – 1 – us U.O. Library [071]
NEWS OF THE NORTH – Yellowknife, CN. Oct 1945-1979 – 1 – cn Commonwealth Micro [072]
NEWS OF THE SWEDISH TRADE UNION CONFEDERATION / Landsorganisationen i Sverige – Stockholm, 1986- – 1 – us U.W. Library [331]
NEWS OF THE WEEK – Geelong, Australia. 22 Mar 1906-25 Dec 1918; 13 Nov 1919-29 Jun 1922 – 27r – 1 – uk British Libr Newspaper [072]
NEWS OF THE WORLD – London, Oct 1843- – 256+ r – 1 – uk British Libr Newspaper [072]
NEWS OF THE WORLD *see*
- POPULAR NEWSPAPERS DURING WORLD WAR 1
- POPULAR NEWSPAPERS DURING WORLD WAR 2
NEWS PALLADIUM – Benton Harbor. Mich. 1004 1 uo UMI [071]
NEWS PALLADIUM – Benton Harbor. Mich. -w. 1868-1901 – 1 – us UMI [071]
NEWS POST LEADER (BLYTH EDITION) – Mar 28 1974-82; 1986; Jan 8 1987-Mar, Jul 1989-96 – 69r – 1 – uk British Libr Newspaper [072]
NEWS POST LEADER (WANSBECK ED) – 1987-Mar 1988; Jan 1990-Jun, Jul 4-Aug 22, Sep-Oct, Nov 7-Dec 23 1991; Jan 9 1992-96 – 43 1/2r – 1 – uk British Libr Newspaper [072]
NEWS PRESS – Fort Myers. Fl. 1931- – 1 – us UMI [071]
NEWS PRESS – St. Joseph. MO.1904- – 1 – us UMI [071]
NEWS PRESS AND PRED – Santa Barbara. Calif. 1869- – 1 – us UMI [071]
NEWS PULSE – Claremont, CA. Apr 1973-Feb 1975 – 1r – 1 – $50.00 – R02113 – us Library Micro [071]
NEWS RECORD – DuBois. Neb. 1900-1906 – 1 – us UMI [071]
NEWS RECORD – Enterprise, OR. -w. 31 Aug 1907-7 Jun 1911. 1 roll – 1 – us U.O. Library [071]
NEWS REGISTER – Wheeling. West Virginia. 1863- – 1 – us UMI [071]
NEWS RELEASE FROM THE OFFICE OF JEWISH INFORMATION – New York, NY. 18 Dec 1967-13 Nov 1981. English. Ceased publication – 1 – us A.J.P.C. [071]
NEWS REPORTER – Dayton, NV. Mar-Dec 1886 – 1r – 1 – $50.00 – U04485 – us Library Micro [071]
NEWS REPORTER – Hubbard. Ohio. 1961- – 1 – us UMI [071]
NEWS REPORTER – McMinnville OR. Aug 5 1904-Feb 5 1953 – 1 – us U.O. Library [071]
NEWS REPORTER – McMinnville, OR. -w. 5 Feb 1953-. – 1 – us U.O. Library [071]
NEWS REPORTER – Pasco. Wash. -w. 1898-1901 – 1 – us UMI [071]
NEWS REPORTER – Three Rivers. Mich. -w. 1881-1905 – 1 – us UMI [071]
NEWS REVIEW – Albany, CA. 1964-1965 – 1r – 1 – $50.00 – B06009 – us Library Micro [071]
THE NEWS REVIEW – Petoskey. Mich. 1969- – 1 – us UMI [071]
NEWS SEARCHLIGHT – Bremerton. Wash. 1922-1945 – 1 – us UMI [071]
NEWS SENTINEL – Knoxville. Tenn. 1926- – 1 – us UMI [071]
NEWS SERVICE / American Indian Press Association – 229 issues. n.d. (American Indian Periodicals in the Princeton University Library). 7 fiches – 9 – 25.00 – us UPA [073]
NEWS SHEET, 1955-1965 / British Solomon Islands Protectorate – reels 1-2 – 1 – PMB Doc422 – at Pacific Mss [980]
NEWS SIGNAL – Middletown. Ohio. and pred. 1905-20 – 1 – us UMI [071]
NEWS STANDARD – Uniontown. Pa. 1894-1941 – 1 – us UMI [071]
NEWS SUN – Kendallville. Ind. 1909-1945; 1949- – 1 – us UMI [071]
NEWS SUN – Newport, PA., 1946-1990 – 13 – $25.00r – us I.M.R. [071]
NEWS SUN – Waukegan. Ill. 1930- – 1 – us UMI [071]
NEWS TELEGRAM – Portland. Or. 1907-1939 – 1 – us UMI [071]
NEWS TELEGRAPH – Portland OR. Oct 18-Dec 31 1940 – 1 – us U.O. Library [071]
NEWS TELEGRAPH – Sharon. Pa. 1928-1935 – 1 – us UMI [071]
NEWS TIMES – Goshen. Ind. and Democrat. 1934-54 – 1 – us UMI [071]
NEWS TRIBUNE – Beaver Falls. Pa. 1949- – 1 – us UMI [071]
NEWS TRIBUNE – Fort Pierce. Fl. 1952- – 1 – us UMI [071]
NEWS TRIBUNE – LaSalle. Ill. 1948- – 1 – us UMI [071]
NEWS TRIBUNE – Madera. Calif. 1945-1959 – 1 – us UMI [071]
NEWS TRIBUNE – Marion. Ind. 1901-1912 – 1 – us UMI [071]
NEWS TRIBUNE – Rome. Ga. 1922-23; 1956- – 1 – us UMI [071]
NEWS VALUES AND PRINCIPLES OF CROSS-CULTURAL COMMUNICATION / Costa, Alcino Louis da et al – 1980 – 9 – 92-3-101697-0 – fr UNESCO [302]
NEWS VIRGINIAN – Waynesboro. Va. 1930- – 1 – us UMI [071]
NEWS WEEKLY – Victoria, 1955-1983 – 13r – 0 at Paoooo [71]
NEWS WEEKLY – Westville. Miss. 1874-1900 – 1 – us UMI [071]
NEWS-ADVOCATE – Manistee. Mich. 1914- – 1 – us UMI [071]
NEWS-ADVOCATE – Yutan, NE. -w. Feb 1917-Sept 1918 – 1 – us NE Hist [071]
The NewsBank Library *see* ALL CATEGORIES
The NewsBank Review of the Arts *see*
- ALL CATEGORIES
- FILM AND TELEVISION CATEGORY
- FINE ARTS AND ARCHITECTURE CATEGORY
- LITERATURE CATEGORY
- PERFORMING ARTS CATEGORY
NEWS-BANNER – Bluffton. Ind. and pred. 1893- – 1 – us UMI [071]
NEWS-BEACON – Zelienople. Pa. 1932-1942 – 1 – us UMI [071]
NEWS-BLADE – Bridgeport. Neb. 1901-1963 – 1 – us UMI [071]
NEWS-BULLETIN – Brookfield. Mo. 1957- – 1 – us UMI [071]
NEWS-BULLETIN *see* HERALD ENTERPRISE
NEWS-CALL BULLETIN – San Francisco, Calif. 1959-65 – 1 – us UMI [071]
NEWS-CHRONICLE – Thousand Oaks, 1965 – 348+ r – 1 – $17,400.00 ($600.00y) – H04073 – us Library Micro [071]
NEWS-CHRONICLE – Wisner. Neb. and pred. 1892-1963 – 1 – us UMI [071]
NEWSCIENTIST – 1985-. -w – 1 – us UMI [500]
NEWS-CITIZEN – Vandergrift. Pa. 1904-1921; 1969- – 1 – us UMI [071]
NEWS-COURIER – Saginaw.Mich. 1918-27 – 1 – us UMI [071]
NEWSDAY – Long Island. N.Y. 1940- – 1 – us UMI [071]
NEWS-DEMOCRAT – Providence. R.I. 1906-09 – 1 – us UMI [071]
NEWS-DISPATCH – Michigan City. Ind. 1882-1901; 1938- – 1 – us UMI [071]
NEWS-FREE PRESS – Chattanooga. Tenn. 1933- – 1 – us UMI [071]
NEWS-GAZETTE – Lexington. Va. 1941-1945; 1948- – 1 – us UMI [071]
NEWS-GAZETTE – Martinez. Calif. 1945- – 1 – us UMI [071]
NEWS-GUARD – Lincoln City, OR. -w. 11 Mar 1965-. – 1 – us U.O. Library [071]
NEWS-HERALD – Litchfield. Ill. 1961- – 1 – us UMI [071]
NEWS-HERALD – Los Molinos, CA. 1932-42 – 3r – 1 – $150.00 – B02411 – us Library Micro [071]
NEWS-HERALD – Marshfield. Wis. 1927- – 1 – us UMI [071]
NEWS-HERALD – Willoughby. Ohio. 1961- – 1 – us UMI [071]
NEWS-HERALD – Wyandotte. Mich. 1944- – 1 – us UMI [071]
THE NEWS-HERALD – Franklin, PA., 1937-1970 – 13 – $25.00r – us I.M.R. [071]
NEWS-JOURNAL – Chester. Pa. 1957-1959 – 1 – us UMI [071]
NEWS-JOURNAL – Fullerton. Neb. 1898-1930 – 1 – us UMI [071]
NEWS-LEADER – Fernandina Beach. Fl. -w. 1949- – 1 – us P.K. Yonge [071]
NEWS-LEDGER – Nehawka, NE. -w. Oct 1911-Aug 1919 – 1 – us NE Hist [071]
NEWS-LETTER / American Antiquarian Society – v. 1-. 1968- – 1. – apply; v.15-1975- 5,6,9 – us UMI [930]
NEWSLETTER / American Council on Consumer Interests. (ACCI) – v. 1- 1954- – 1,5,6,9 – us UMI [380]
NEWSLETTER / American Historical Association – (1972- . 5,6. 1976- . 9) – v. 1- 1962- – 1 – us UMI [970]
NEWSLETTER – American Library Assoc., Exhibits Round Table. v.17-19. 1971-74. Superseded by Exhibits – 1 – us UMI [020]
NEWSLETTER / Association for the Sociological Study of Jewry – v. 1. 1973-74 – 1 – us UMI [290]
NEWSLETTER / Boston Theological Institute – 1968-88 – 1 – us A.T.L.A. [073]
NEWSLETTER / Canadian Education Association – (v380- 1986/87- 9) – v1-1946- – 5,9 – cn Micromedia [370]
NEWSLETTER / Cape Town. South Africa. Civil Rights League – Cape Town, jun-jul, oct 1954; feb, jun, aug-sep, nov-dec 1955; jan, apr-jun, aug 1956 – us Res Libr [320]
NEWSLETTER – (Cincinnati Reform Jewish High School) July 26, 1987-Dec. 1989 – us A.J.P.C. [270]
NEWSLETTER – Freedom from Religion Foundation. -1903. Continued by: Freethought Today – 1 – us U.W. Library [290]
NEWSLETTER – Group for the use of Psychology in History. v.1-4. 1972-76. Continued by Psychohistory Review – 1 – us UMI [900]
NEWSLETTER – International Assoc. of College and University Security Directors. v.1-2. 1971-72. Continued by Campus Law Enforcement Journal – 1 – us UMI [360]
NEWSLETTER / Israel. Ministry of Agriculture – Jerusalem, 1968 69-. Quarterly – 9 – 30.00; 3.00y – is I.T.T.I. [630]
NEWSLETTER / Mervyn Peake Society – (See also: Mervyn Peake Review) – v1-2. 1975-76 – 1 – us UMI [000]
NEWSLETTER – Miami, FL. South Florida Conference on Soviet Jewry. 18 Aug 1976-Oct 1981. Continued by: Lifeline (Miami, FL). Ceased publication – 1 – us A.J.P.C. [071]
NEWSLETTER / Midwest Inter-Library Center. Chicago – v1-25 1949-51 – 1 – us Res Libr [020]
NEWSLETTER / Navajo Community College – 1969-73. (American Indian Periodicals in the Princeton University Library). 4 fiches – 9 – $45.00 – us UPA [370]
NEWSLETTER / New Hampshire. College of Agriculture (or N.H. College of Agriculture & Mechanical Arts) – v1-8. 1962-69 – 1,5,6 – us Spaulding [630]
NEWSLETTER / New Schools Exchange – 1969-1978 1; 1973-78 5,6 – us UMI [073]
NEWSLETTER / Ontario Museum Association – v1-7. 1972-78 – 5 – cn Micromedia [060]
NEWSLETTER / PEN. American Center of PEN International – Oct 1978- – 1 – us U.W. Library [410]
NEWSLETTER / St. Christopher's Mission to the Navajo – 1964-77. (American Indian Periodicals in the Princeton University Library). 5 fiches – 9 – $45.00 – us UPA [240]
NEWSLETTER : SAN QUENTIN STATE PRISON / American Indian Cultural Group – 1968-72. (American Indian Periodicals in the Princeton University Library) – 4mf – 9 – $45.00 – us UPA [305]
NEWSLETTER / Special Libraries Association. Business and Finance Division – (v42-. 1976-. 5,6,9) – v. 1-. 1962- – 1 – us UMI [020]
NEWSLETTER / ed by Union of German Socialist Organizations in Great Britain – London. May-Aug 1941 (2 nos) – 1 – gw Mikrofilm [073]
NEWSLETTER – Washington, DC. Jewish Institute for National Security Affairs. Jun 1977-Oct 1984. Continued by: Security Affairs – 1 – us A.J.P.C. [071]
NEWSLETTER / Wisconsin. Land Tenure Center – Oct 1962-Jan 1970. n.1-30 – 1,5 – us Spaulding [630]
NEWSLETTER / American Council on Consumer Interests – (Cont by: Consumer new and reviews. Former titles: Council on Consumer Information (oct 1953-may 1969)) – Columbia. v1-43 oct 1953-dec 1995 1*; v23-43 jan 1975-dec 1995 5*; v23-43 jan1975-dec 1995 9* – 1,5,9 – D9141 – us UMI [338]
NEWSLETTER / American Library Association. Resources and Technical Services Division – (Ceased publ. Cont by: ALCTS Newsletter) – Chicago. v1-14 jan 1976-1989 1*; 4-14 jan 1979-1989 5*,9 – 1,5,9 – D12524 – us UMI [020]
NEWSLETTER, ALLERGY INFORMATION ASSOCIATION / Allergy Information Association – (All that is currently available. Former title: Allergy Information (1964-1970)) – Weston. Spr 1973-Win 1974 – 1 – D8711 – us UMI [616]
NEWSLETTER. AMERICAN INTRA-OCULAR IMPLANT SOCIETY – v.1-2. 1975-76. Continued as American Intra-Ocular Implant Society, Journal – 1 – us UMI [073]
NEWSLETTER – FUSION ENERGY FOUNDATION – 1975-77 – 1 – us UMI [621]
NEWSLETTER. LIBRARY ADMINISTRATION AND MANAGEMENT ASSOCIATION *see* LAD NEWSLETTER
NEWS-LETTER OF THE AMERICAN ANTIQUARIAN SOCIETY / American Antiquarian Society – Worcester. v1-. 1968-* – 1 – D10337 – us UMI [000]
NEWSLETTER OF THE DEMOCRATIC LEFT – New York, 1973-79 (incompl) – 1 – us Hoover Inst Photo [335]

NEWSLETTER OF THE DEVELOPMENT BANK OF INDONESIA – (Monthly. In English and Indonesian. Missing: v2 1969/1970; v3(4) 1970) – Djakarta, 1968-1972 – 5mf – 9 – SE-1338/1 – ne IDC [332]
NEWSLETTER OF THE INTERNATIONAL ASSOCIATION OF ORIENTALIST LIBRARIANS : NO 1-9. 1971-1975 – (Cont as: Bulletin of the International Association of Orientalist Librarians. v1-20 1976-1982) – 15mf – 9 – ne IDC [020]
NEWSLETTER OF THE PROGRAM ON PUBLIC CONCEPTIONS OF SCIENCE – v.1-16. 1972-76. Continued by Newsletter on Science, Technology and Human Values – 1 – us UMI [500]
NEWSLETTER ON COMPARATIVE STUDIES OF COMMUNISM – v. 1-6. 1968-1973 – 1 – us UMI [073]
NEWSLETTER ON INTELLECTUAL FREEDOM – v1- 1952- 1; v20- 5,6; v24- 9 – us UMI [070]
NEWSLETTER ON SCIENCE, TECHNOLOGY AND HUMAN VALUES – v.17-24. 1976-78. Continued by Science, Technology and Human Values – 1 – us UMI [500]
NEWSLETTER ON SCIENCE, TECHNOLOGY AND HUMAN VALUES *see* HARVARD UNIVERSITY – PROGRAM ON PUBLIC CONCEPTIONS OF SCIENCE
NEWSLETTER (VBA) *see* VERMONT BAR JOURNAL AND LAW DIGEST
NEWSLETTER-ORGANIZATION OF AMERICAN HISTORIANS – v1-9. 1973-81 – 1 – us UMI [073]
NEWSLIFE – Houston. Tex. 1967-1968 – 1 – us UMI [071]
NEWS-MESSENGER – Fremont. Ohio. 1941- – 1 – us UMI [071]
NEWS-MIRROR – Moorpark, CA. 1978 – 16+ r – 1 – $800.00 ($50.00y) – H04052 – us Library Micro [071]
NEWS/NORTH : YELLOWKNIFE – 1980-95 – 1 – cn Commonwealth Micro [072]
Newson. Spencer County.Kentucky *see* ATLAS
Newson, T M *see* PEN PICTURES OF ST PAUL AND BIOGRAPHICAL SKETCHES OF OLD SETTLERS FROM THE EARLIEST SETTLEMENT OF THE CITY TILL 1857
NEWSPAPER / Granite City. Illinois. First Baptist Church – 1934-1940. (This reel includes a history of the beginning of Northwest Baptist Church, Austin, Texas) – 1 – 14.76 – us Baptist [240]
NEWSPAPER – Portland OR. Sep 3 1970 – 1 – us U.O. Library [071]
THE NEWSPAPER – Pomona, CA. 1973-75 – 3r – 1 – $150.00 – R04090 – us Library Micro [071]
NEWSPAPER AND NEWSLETTER COLLECTION "AKWESASNE NEWS THRU TREATY COUNSEL NEWS" / American Indian Studies Dept. CSU San Francisco – 6r – 1 – $300.00 – B63013 – us Library Micro [071]
NEWSPAPER BULLETIN / Kentucky. Agricultural Experiment Station – v. 1-119. 1911-15 – 1,5,6 – us Spaulding [630]
NEWSPAPER CLIPPINGS / Minnesota Citizens Concerned for Life – 1962, 1966-1985 – 19r – 1 – $570.00 $30.00r – us M.H.S. [360]
NEWSPAPER CLIPPINGS / Republic Airlines – 1979-1984 – 15r – 1 – $450.00 $30.00r – us M.H.S. [380]
[NEWSPAPER CLIPPINGS] : [RACE RELATIONS SERIES 1922-1961] / South African Institute of Race Relations – Johannesburg: Microfile, [19–?] – us Res Libr [070]
NEWSPAPER CLIPPINGS, COLLECTION OF THE C.E.P. AT THE I.R.E.S / Congo – Kinshasa. Arr. after provinces, and each province after subject and chronologically. BA-566/2 – 8 – ne IDC [960]
NEWSPAPER COVERAGE OF SESSIONS / Southern Baptist Convention – May 6-10, 1953. Houston, Texas – 1 – 5.00 – us Baptist [240]
NEWSPAPER CUTTINGS BOOKS / Society for Psychical Research – 7 – uk Microform Academic [150]
NEWSPAPER CUTTINGS FILES / Great Britain. Council of Foreign Bondholders – 1870 onwards. From the Guildhall Library, London – 1 – uk Microform Academic [330]
NEWSPAPER CUTTINGS FILES OF THE COUNCIL OF FOREIGN BONDHOLDERS, 2ND SERIES : FROM THE GUILDHALL LIBRARY, LONDON – 18r – 1 – uk Microform Academic [337]
NEWSPAPER INDEX / Toledo Blade (Toledo, Ohio) – 1925-1935 – 7r – 1 – $32.50r – us Archival [978]
NEWSPAPER LIBEL, A HANDBOOK FOR THE PRESS / Merrill, Samuel – Boston: Ticknor, 1888. 304p. LL-243 – 1 – us L of C Photodup [340]
NEWSPAPER MISCELLANY : SCATTERED ISSUES FROM 63 OAKLAND NEWSPAPERS – Oakland, CA. 13 May 1854-31 Oct 1961 – 1r – 1 – $50.00 – B03367 – us Library Micro [071]
NEWSPAPER PRODUCTION – v1- 1972- 1,5,6; v4- 9 – us UMI [073]
NEWSPAPER RESEARCH JOURNAL – v.1-. 1979- – 1,5,6,9 – us UMI [073]
NEWSPAPER TRANSCRIPTS INDEX / ed by Babcock, Willoughby Maynard 2 – 1849-1863, 1896-1897 – 4r – 5 – $120.00 $30.00r – us M.H.S. [978]
NEWSPAPERS – 194 titles – 9 – ne IDC [071]
NEWSPAPERS / Niagara Peninsula. Canada – 1799-1898. Part I: Niagara-on-the-Lake Papers (complete set) includes Canada Constellation, Echo of Niagara, Mercantile Sheet Almanack, Niagara Argus, Niagara Chronicle, Niagara Fountain, Niagara Gleaner, Niagara Herald, Niagara Mail, Niagara News, Niagara Reporter, Niagara Spectator, Niagara Telegraph, Spirit of the Times, The Times, Upper Canada Guardian – 11r – 1 – $715.00 – cn Library Assoc [971]
NEWSPAPERS / Niagara Peninsula. Canada – 1827-74. Part II: St. Catharines Papers, including Port Robinson (complete set) includes British American Journal, British Colonial Argus, Constitutional, Farmers' Journal, Journal, Merchants Herald, Weekly News, Weekly Times, Welland Advocate & Review – 11r – 1 – $715.00 – cn Library Assoc [971]
NEWSPAPERS AND PERIODICALS OF THE GERMAN OCCUPATION OF BELARUS : FROM THE NATIONAL ARCHIVES OF BELARUS IN MINSK – (In German, Russian, Polish, Ukrainian and Belarusian. Pts also listed separately) – 3pts 68 titles 713mf – 9 – $4,300.00 coll – us Ross [947]
NEWSPAPERS AND PERIODICALS OF THE GERMAN OCCUPATION OF BELARUS, PT 1 : FROM THE NATIONAL ARCHIVES OF BELARUS IN MINSK – (Collaborationist publ in the Belarusian language publ during WW2) – 23 titles 210mf – 9 – $1,470.00 coll – us Ross [947]
NEWSPAPERS AND PERIODICALS OF THE GERMAN OCCUPATION OF BELARUS, PT 1 : FROM THE NATIONAL ARCHIVES OF BELARUS IN MINSK – (Collaborationist publ in the Belarusian language publ during WW2. In German, Russian, Polish, Ukrainian and Belarusian) – 23 titles 210mf – 9 – $1,470.00 coll – us Ross [947]
NEWSPAPERS AND PERIODICALS OF THE GERMAN OCCUPATION OF BELARUS, PT 2 : FROM THE NATIONAL ARCHIVES OF BELARUS IN MINSK – (Collaborationist publ in Russian, Polish & Ukrainian languages publ during WW2) – 34 titles 241mf – 9 – $1,685.00 coll – us Ross [947]
NEWSPAPERS AND PERIODICALS OF THE GERMAN OCCUPATION OF BELARUS, PT 3 : FROM THE NATIONAL ARCHIVES OF BELARUS IN MINSK – (Periodicals in German from WW1 and 2 publ on Belarusian territory) – 11 titles 262mf – 9 – $1,835.00 coll – us Ross [947]
NEWSPAPERS FROM THE RUSSIAN REVOLUTIONARY ERA – (Based on the holdings of Columbia University Libraries, New York Public Library, and the British Library) – 1 – us Primary [947]
NEWSPAPERS OF THE AMERICAN COMMUNIST PARTY, 1919-1991 : RETROSPECTIVE SET – 9 – $20,860.00 – us UPA [320]
NEWSPAPERS OF THE PARIS COMMUNE / Paris – 1870-72 – 1 – us Res Libr [072]
NEWSPAPERS OF THE TAIWANESE CHURCH = TAI-OAN KAU-HOE KONG-PO – (In Chinese) – 1923-67 (complete) – 3r – 1 – ATLA S0313 – us A.T.L.A. [073]
NEWSPAPERS PUBLISHED IN INTERNMENT CAMPS – (Includes: Heart Mountain Sentinel, Wyoming 1942-44. Pomona (CA) News Jun-Aug 1942. Santa Anita (CA) Pacemaker 1942-43.) – 3r – 1 – $150.00 – B63004 – us Library Micro [977]
NEWSPEACE – 1971-87 (complete) – 3r – 1 – ATLA S0341 – us A.T.L.A. [240]
NEWS-PILOT – San Pedro, CA. 1906 – 2100+ r – 1 – $105,000.00 ($1,200.00y) – H03510 – us Library Micro [071]
NEWS-PRESS – Arvin. Calif. 1962-1967 – 1 – us UMI [071]
NEWS-PRESS – Nebraska City. Neb. 1857-1882; 1949- – 1 – us UMI [071]
NEWS-PRESS – Stillwater. Okl. 1953- – 1 – us UMI [071]
NEWS-REGISTER – Aurora. Neb. 1942-1960 – 1 – us UMI [071]
NEWS-REGISTER – Fremont, CA. 1955-72 – 65r – 1 – $3,250.00 – B02250 – us Library Micro [071]
NEWS-REGISTER – McMinnville, OR -d. 1953 – 1 – 41.00 – us Oregon Hist [071]
NEWS-REGISTER – McMinnville, OR. -sw. 12 Feb 1953-. – 1 – us U.O. Library [071]
NEWS-REPORTER – Alma, NE. -w. Jul. 1892-Sep. 1897. Incomplete; Oct. 1897-Jun. 1899 – 1 – us NE Hist [071]
NEWS-REPORTER – Gretna, NE. -w. Sept 1891-Jan 1893, scattered issues missing; Nov 1895-May 1898; Jan-Feb 1899; Apr 1899-Jun 1900 – 1 – us NE Hist [071]
THE NEWS-REPORTER – Cozad, NE. -w. 10 Oct 1891-25 Jun 1892. Discolored and mutilated – 1 – us NE Hist [071]
NEWS-REPUBLICAN – Kenton, Ohio. 1946-53 – 18r – 1 – $32.50r – us Archival [071]
NEWS-REVIEW – Roseburg, OR. -d. 1 Apr 1920-. – 1 – us U.O. Library [071]
NEWS-REVIEW – Roseburg, OR. -w. 8 Apr 1920 – 19 May 1927. 2 rolls – 1 – us U.O. Library [071]
NEWS-SENTINEL – Fort Wayne. IN.1918- – 1 – us UMI [071]
Newstead, R *see* MONOGRAPH OF THE COCCIDAE OF THE BRITISH ISLES
NEWS-TIMES – Goshen. Ind. 1902-33 – 1 – us UMI [071]
NEWS-TIMES – Newport, OR. -w. 9 Jun 1976-. – 1 – us U.O. Library [071]
NEWS-TIMES – York. Neb. 1949- – 1 – us UMI [071]
NEWS-TRIBUNE – Britt. Iowa. -w. 1951-55 – 1 – us UMI [071]
NEWS-TRIBUNE – Fort Pierce. Fl. 1920-1926, 1928-1930, 1932-1933, 1935, 1939, 1941, 1943, 1947-Jan 1952 – 1 – us P.K. Yonge [071]
NEWS-TRIBUNE – Keyser. West Virginia. 1943-44; 1951; 1953; 1955- – 1 – us UMI [071]
NEWS-TRIBUNE – Tacoma. Wash. 1906-1918; 1920- – 1 – us UMI [071]
NEWS-TRIBUNE – Woodbridge. N.J. 1925- – 1 – us UMI [071]
NEWSWEEK – 1933-1994 – 1 – sz Infoprint [073]
NEWSWEEK – 1939-71 – 73r – 1 – us Ross [073]
NEWSWEEK – (New York ed.). 81- 1973- – 9 – apply; 1,5,6; v,85- – us UMI [073]
NEWSWEEK – (v. 73- 1969- 5,6. v. 75- 1970-9) – v. 1- 1933- – 1 – us UMI [073]
NEWSWEEK INDEX – 1933-69 – 5,6 – us UMI [073]
Newth, Samuel *see* LECTURES ON BIBLE REVISION
Newton *see*
– HISTORY OF BARRON COUNTY
– THE OLNEY HYMNS AND A BAPTIST HYMN BOOK
NEWTON 1621-1849 – (Mf 1T-4T: Births 1674-1801. Mf 4T-5T: Deaths 1687-1813. Mf 5T-6T: Marriages 1689-1799. Mf 6T-7T: Births 1733-1845. Mf 7T-9T: Marriages 1792-1843. Mf 9T: Deaths 1811-44. Mf 9T-10T: Out-of-Town Marriages 1695-1800. Mf 10T-11T: Births 1621-1850. Mf 11T: Marriages 1649-1838; Deaths 1643-1849. Mf 11T-15T: Publishments 1735-1849. Mf 15T-17T: Births 1784-1849. Mf 17T: Marriages 1844-49. Mf 18T: Deaths 1826-49) – (mf ed 1998) – 18mf – 9 – 0-87623-306-X – us Holbrook [920]
Newton, A *see* A DICTIONARY OF BIRDS
Newton, Adelaide Leaper *see* THE SONG OF SOLOMON: COMPARED WITH OTHER PARTS OF SCRIPTURE
NEWTON FALLS ECHO : WEEKLY REPUBLICAN NEWSPAPER – Newton Falls, Trumbull, OH. 12 Jul 1884 – 1r – 1 – us Western Res [071]
Newton, George *see* AN EXPOSITION WITH NOTES
NEWTON, ILLINOIS. BOGOTA BAPTIST CHURCH – Church Records, 1880-November 1950. Catalog Update: Bogota BC. 1880-November 1950. Formerly Independence BC of Christ, 1880-1910. 664p – 1 – $29.88 – us Baptist [240]
Newton, Isaac *see* OPTIQUE DE NEWTON
Newton, J T *see* NEWTON'S DIGEST OF THE PATENT OFFICE TRADEMARK DECISIONS
Newton, John *see* A CONCORDANCE TO THE OLNEY HYMNS OF JOHN NEWTON AND WILLIAM COWPER
Newton, Louis Devotie *see*
– COLLECTION
– PAPERS AS PRESIDENT OF SBC, 1946-48
Newton, Massachusetts. First Baptist Church and Society *see* RECORDS
Newton. Presbytery (Pres. Ch. in the U.S.A.) *see* MINUTES, 1817-1900
Newton, Richard *see*
– COVENANT NAMES AND PRIVILEGES
– THE JEWISH TABERNACLE AND ITS FURNITURE, IN THEIR TYPICAL TEACHINGS
Newton, Richard Heber *see*
– THE BOOK OF THE BEGINNINGS
– THE BOOK OF THE BEGINNINGS; A STUDY OF GENESIS WITH AN INTRODUCTION TO THE PENTATEUCH
– CHURCH AND CREED
– THE RIGHT AND WRONG USES OF THE BIBLE
Newton, William M *see* HISTORY OF BARNARD
NEWTONIANISME DE VOLTAIRE / Serane, Philippe – Amsterdam. Paris. B. Morin. 1779. IV – 9 – fr Hachette [520]
NEWTON'S DIGEST OF THE PATENT OFFICE TRADEMARK DECISIONS / Newton, J T – Chicago: Callaghan. 1v. 1896 (all publ) – 3mf – 9 – $4.50 – LLMC 84-340 – us L.L.M.C. [340]
NEWTON'S LONDON JOURNAL OF ARTS AND SCIENCES; BEING A RECORD OF THE PROGRESS OF INVENTION AS APPLIED TO THE ARTS – 1820-66 – 3 – us Readex [700]
NEWTOWN BAPTIST CHURCH. WILKES COUNTY. GEORGIA : CHURCH RECORDS – (398p) – November 1886-February 1924 – 1 reel – 1 – $17.91 – us Baptist [240]
NEWTOWN CHRONICLE – Jan 7 1899-Dec 28 1907 – 9 – at Pascoe [072]
NEWTOWNARDS CHRONICLE ETC – 1874-1986; Jan 8 1987-Jun 1997 – 199 1/4r – 1 – uk British Libr Newspaper [072]
NEW-YORK AMERICAN – New York: [s.n.], 1821- [daily ed]. jan 2 1827-dec 1828 (3r) – 1 – us Res Libr [071]
NEW-YORK GAZETTE – New York, NY. Also: Weekly Mercury. 1768-83 – 1,3 – us Readex [071]
NEW-YORK GAZETTE – New York. William Bradford. 1726-1741; 1744 – 1 – us NY Public [071]
NEW-YORK GAZETTE (WEYMAN'S) – New York. N.Y. 1759-1767 – 1,3 – us Readex [071]
NEW-YORK LITERARY GAZETTE, AND AMERICAN ATHENAEUM *see* AMERICAN ATHENAEUM, A REPOSITORY OF BELLES LETTRES, SCIENCE AND THE ARTS
NEW-YORK WEEKLY JOURNAL – New York. N.Y. 1733-1751 – 1,3 – us Readex [071]
NEXT – v.1-. 1980- – 1,5,6,9 – us UMI [073]
THE NEXT GREAT AWAKENING / Strong, Josiah – 1902 – 9 – us A.T.L.A. [240]
THE NEXT STAGE IN PALESTINE / Kaznelson, B – London, 1938. 17p. BJ-28-10/1 – 9 – ne IDC [956]
THE NEXT STEP IN EVOLUTION : THE PRESENT STEP / Funk, Isaac Kaufman – 5th ed. New York: Funk & Wagnalls, c1902 – 1mf – 9 – 0-8370-3217-2 – 1985-1217 – us A.T.L.A. [210]
NEXT STEPS TO WIN THE WAR IN SPAIN / Browder, Earl – New York, 1938. Fiche W 765. (Blodgett Collection of Spanish Civil War Pamphlets) – 9 – us H.U. College Libr [946]
THE NEXT WORLD WAR AND CHINA (CCC14) = TI ERH TZU TA CHAN YU CHUNG-KUO / Chang, Nae-Ch'i – (In Chinese) – Hong Kong: Association Press of China, 1936 – 1r – 1 – 0-8370-1714-9 – 1984-6098 – us A.T.L.A. [900]
NEXT YEAR COUNTRY – Regina. v1-11. 1972/74-1983/84 – 9 – Can$20.00y – cn Micromedia [073]
Ney, Julius *see*
– PFALZGRAF WOLFGANG
– DIE REFORMATION IN TRIER 1559 UND IHRE UNTERDRUECKUNG
Ney, Napoleon *see* CONFERENCE ET LETTRES DE P. SAVORGNAN DE BRAZZA SUR SES TROIS EXPLORATIONS DANS L'OUEST AFRICAIN DE 1875 A 1886
Neyre, Juan Carlos et al *see* JAURETCHE

NEYYIR-I HAKIKAT – Manastir: Osmanli Ittihad ve Terakki Cemiyeti, Neyyir-i Hakikat Matbaasi. Mueduer-i Mes'ul: Mustafa Asim; Umur-i Tahririyye: Ahmed Eyueb; Sermuharriri: Mehmed Hasib, 1908-1911 – 9 – $25.00 – us MEDOC [956]
THE NEZ PERCE INDIANS / Spinden, H J – Inc. bibliography. BN 398 2. 1908.m – 8 – ne IDC [970]
THE NEZ PERCES SINCE LEWIS AND CLARK / McBeth, Kate C – (Includes appendix) – New York: Fleming H Revell, c1908 – 1mf – 9 – 0-8370-6683-2 – 1986-0683 – us A.T.L.A. [305]
NEZAVISIMAIA GAZETA / ed by Tret'iakov, Vitalii – Moscow: Moskovskii gorodskoi sovet narodnykh deputatov, 1990- – 2mf per year – 9 – $199.95y – us East View [320]
NEZAVISIMY I GORET S – (Includes c.1: 1921:Jan.24-Feb.14) – Tiflis: Osman Seid-Nur, 1921- – 1 – CSUXANS1926-S – us Hoover Inst Photo [947]
NEZDESHNIE VECHERA / Kuzmin, M – Stikhi. 1914-20; Spb. 1921. BR-1193 2 – 8 – ne IDC [460]
NEZHNAIA TAINA / Ivanov, V – Lepta. Izd. "Ory". Spb. 1912. BR-737 2 – 8 – ne IDC [460]
NFPA (NATIONAL FIRE PROTECTION ASSOCIATION) – Standards. Printed index. Updated every 60 days – 6,9 – us Info Handling [628]
NFP(A) (NATIONAL FLUID POWER ASSOCIATION) – Standards. Printed index. Updated every 60 days – 6,9 – us Info Handling [621]
N.G. CHERNYSHEVSKII KAK PERVYI TEORETIK KOOPERATSII V ROSSII / Pazhitnov, K A – Ed 2. M., 1916 – 1mf – 9 – COR-92/1 – ne IDC [334]
NGAMILAND DISTRICT DEVOLOPMENT PLAN 1989-1995 / Botswana. Ngamiland District – Gaborone – 4mf – 9 – ne IDC [338]
NGANDO = LE CROCODILE / Lomami-Tshioamba, Paul – Brussels; G A Deny, [1949] – us Res Libr [960]
Ngatu, Ishmael *see* DIARIES
NGAY NAY – Hanoi. 7 fevr 1937, juil 1938, nov 1938-7 sept 1940, 5 mai-18 aout 1945 – 1 – fr A.C.R.P.P. [073]
NGO-BAO – Le plus grand quotidien d'information illustre en langue annamite. no. 1019-2196. Hanoi. 1931-34. mq no. 1540, 1676 – 1 – fr A.C.R.P.P. [073]
N'Goura, C *see*
- L'EDUCATION TRADITIONNELLE CHEZ LES VUTE, CAMEROUN CENTRAL
- INTRODUCTION A L'ETUDE DE LA LITTERATURE ORALE DES VOUTE, CAMEROUN CENTRAL

NGUOI VIET – Wilmington, US. 1986- – 23+ r – $1,150.00 ($145.00y) – R04235 – us Library Micro [072]
Nguyen Hung Tru'o'ng *see* BO LUAT DAN-SU' VA THU'O'NG-SU' TO-TUNG
DEN NHA NAM – (Transformation de la revue Nu-gioichung du Courrier saigonnais). no. 2-5. Saigon. 11 dec 1918-8 janv 1919 – 1 – fr A.C.R.P.P. [073]
NHA NUOC VA PHAP LUAT = THE STATE AND THE LAW / Vietnamese Lawyer's association – 4v. 1971 – 8mf – 9 SEL-119/1 – ne IDC [340]
NHAN DAN : CO QUAN TRUNG UONG CUA DANG LAO DONG VIET-NAM – Hanoi: Nhan Dan, 1963; dec 1964-1979 (32r); 1980-84 (10r); 1985-86 (4r) – 1 – us Res Libr [072]
NI DIEU, NI MAITRE – Red. en chef A. Blanqui. no. 1-71; n.s., no. 1. Paris. 20 nov 1880-6 nov 1881, 1er mai 1899 – 1 – fr A.C.R.P.P. [073]
NI EL TIO NI EL SOBRINO / Espronceda, Jose de – Madrid: Imprenta Repulles, 1834 – 1 – sp Bibl Santa Ana [946]
NI INCREDULO NI INTOLERANTE / Romero de Castilla, Tomas – 1882 – 9 – 1.50f – sp Bibl Santa Ana [830]
NI ODIO NI MIEDO : RECONSTRUIR EL PAIS / Frondizi, Arturo – Buenos Aires: Servicio Editorial y Periodistico Argentino, 1956 – 1 – CSUXADQ0035-B – us Hoover Inst Photo [320]
NIAGARA COUNTY-A CONCISE RECORD OF HER PROGRESS AND PEOPLE 1821-1921 / Williams, Edward T – Chicago, J. H. Beers and Co., 1921. New York Reel 23. (The Cox Library Collection) – 5 – us Americana [978]
Niagara Falls. New York. La Salle Baptist Church *see* SPECIAL BULLETINS, SPECIAL PROGRAMS, MISC. MEETINGS
THE NIAGARA FALLS PHILATELIST – (Absorbed: Canadian Philatelic Journal) – Niagara Falls, Ont: Niagara Falls Pub. Co, [1887-1889] – 9 – cn C.I.H.M. [760]
THE NIAGARA FALLS PHILATELIST *see* THE CANADIAN PHILATELIC JOURNAL
NIAGARA FALLS REVIEW – (1914-1992.-693r) – Niagara Falls, 1993 – 24r – 1 – cn Preston [971]
NIAGARA ONE HUNDRED YEARS AGO: THE ANCIENT CAPITAL AND ITS VICINITY / Carnochan, Janet – Welland, Publ. by direction of the Lundy's Lane Historical Society, 1892? 00463. (Pre-1900 Canadiana) – 9 – cn C.I.H.M. [971]
Niagara Peninsula. Canada *see*
- NEWSPAPERS

NIANJUN SHILIAO CONGKAN, 1-3 – Series of materials on the Nian Army, v1-3. Comp. by Wang Shirong. 1 reel. M-H99 – 5 – $34.00 – cc Microforms [950]
NIANJUN ZILIAO BIEJI – Special collection of materials on the Nian Army. Comp. by Nei Chongqi. 4 fiches. F-H100 – 9 – $31.50 – cc Microforms [950]
NIBBLE – (1982-. 1,5,6,9) – v1-. 1980- – 1 – us UMI [073]
NIBBLE MAC – v1-. 1985- – 1,5,6,9 – us UMI [510]
DAS NIBELUNGENLIED – 6. Aufl. Stuttgart: J G Cotta, 1848 – 1r – 1 – us U.W. Library [810]
DIE NIBELUNGENSAGE : VORTRAG / Hertz, Wilhelm – Berlin: C Habel, 1877 – 1r – 1 – us U.W. Library [390]
Niblack, A P *see* THE COAST INDIANS OF SOUTHERN ALASKA AND NORTHERN BRITISH COLUMBIA
Niblack, William Caldwell *see* THE LAW OF VOLUNTARY SOCIETIES, MUTUAL BENEFIT INSURANCE AND ACCIDENT INSURANCE
DAS NICAENISCH-KONSTANTINOPOLITANISCHE SYMBOL / Kunze, Johannes – Leipzig: A. Deichert, 1898 – 1mf – us A.T.L.A. [240]
NICARAGUA : ANUARIO ESTADISTICO 1938-1947 / Nicaragua. Direccion General de Estadistica – (1938, 1946 not available. Coll title: Latin American and Caribbean Official Statistical Serials, 1821-1982) – 17mf – 9 – £7.00f (set £200.00 24mf) – uk Chadwyck [972]
NICARAGUA : ANUARIO ESTADISTICO 1968-1969 / Nicaragua. Ministerio de Economia, Industria y Commercio and Banco Central de Nicaragua – (Coll title: Latin American and Caribbean Official Statistical Serials, 1821-1982) – 4mf – 9 – £7.00f (set £200.00 24mf) – uk Chadwyck [972]
NICARAGUA : THE MAKING OF U.S. POLICY, 1978-1990 – (With 2-vol printed guide & index £630.00) – 579mf – 9 – £2,940.00 – uk Chadwyck [327]
NICARAGUA : RESUMEN ESTADISTICA 1950-1960 / Nicaragua. Direccion General de Estadistica – (Coll title: Latin American and Caribbean Official Statistical Serials, 1821-1982) – 3mf – 9 – £7.00f (set £200.00 24mf) – uk Chadwyck [972]
Nicaragua *see*
- EVALUATION OF THE NATIONAL ECONOMIC AND SOCIAL DEVELOPMENT PLAN OF NICARAGUA, 1965-1969
- FIVE YEAR DEVELOPMENT PROGRAM (1952-1957)
- LA GACETA DIARIO OFICIAL

NICARAGUA, 1930-45 / U.S. Department of State – (See also series listing) – 38 reels with printed guide. Series: Confidential U.S. Diplomatic Post Records: Central America and the Caribbean – 1 – $4,185.00 – us UPA [972]
Nicaragua. Cons. Nac. de Econ. Oficina de Plan *see* PLAN NACIONAL DE DESARROLLO ECONOMICO Y SOCIAL, 1965-1969
Nicaragua. Direccion General de Estadistica *see*
- NICARAGUA

Nicaragua. Inter-American Economic and Social Council *see* EVALUACION DEL PLAN NACIONAL. DE NICARAGUA, 1965-1969
Nicaragua. Ministerio de Economia, Industria y Commercio and Banco Central de Nicaragua *see* NICARAGUA
Niccolls, Samuel J *see* WOMEN'S POSITION AND WORK IN THE CHURCH
Niccols, Richard *see*
- THE BEGGERS APE
- SIR THOMAS OVERBURY'S VISION (1616) BY RICHARD NICCOLS AND OTHER ENGLISH SOURCES OF NATHANIEL HAWTHORNE'S 'THE SCARLET LETTER'

NICE-MATIN – Nice. Toutes eds. 1960-mar 1987 – 1 – fr A.C.R.P.P. [073]
Nicephori, S, Patriarchae Constantinopolitani *see* BREVIARIUM HISTORICUM (CBH 2,2)
Nicephorus Cp *see* CORPUS SCRIPTORUM HISTORIAE BYZANTINAE (CSHB 12, 13)
Niceron, Jean Francois *see* LA PRESPECTIVE CVRIEVSE: OU, MAGIE ARTIFICIELLE DES EFFETS MERVEILLEVX
NICETA OF REMESIANA : HIS LIFE AND WORKS / ed by Burn, A E – Cambridge: University Press, 1905 – 1mf – us A.T.L.A. [240]
Nicetas, A C *see*
- DELLA HISTORIA...DELLE COSE DELL' IMPERIO DI CONSTANTINOPOLI LIBRI 7
- HISTORIA DEGLI IMPERATORI GRECI

Niceville, L de *see* THE BUTTERFLIES OF INDIA, BURMAH AND CEYLON
Nichelmann, C *see* DIE MELODIE NACH IHREM WESEN SOWOHL. ALS NACH IHREN EIGENSCHAFTEN, VON CHRISTOPH NICHELMANN
Nichelson, William *see* A TREATISE ON PRACTICAL NAVIGATION AND SEAMANSHIP
NICHI-DJO NIPPONGO RADJIO KOZA / Sato, T – (Microfiche Nos 159-160) – N.p., Barisan Propaganda, 2603?. 2pts in 1v – 2mf – 9 – SE-2002/1 – ne IDC [950]
NICHOLAS CHRONICLE – Summerville. West Virginia. 1881-1967 – 1 – us UMI [071]
NICHOLAS NICKLEBY: A FARCE IN TWO ACTS, TAKEN FROM THE POPULAR WORK OF THAT NAME BY "BOZ" / Stirling, Edward – New York: S. French, (19??). 82p. (French's minor drama, no. 264) – 1 – us U.W. Library [820]
NICHOLAS REPUBLICAN – Richwood. West Virginia. -w. 1932-38, 1959-63 – 1 – us UMI [071]
Nicholas, Samuel Smith *see*
- HABEAS CORPUS, THE LAW OF WAR, AND CONFISCATION
- MARTIAL LAW

Nicholls, G F *see* A GRAMMAR OF THE SAMARITAN LANGUAGE
Nichols, Clarina Irene (Howard) Carpenter *see* PAPERS OF CLARINA IRENE (HOWARD) CARPENTER NICHOLS
Nichols, Clark Asahel *see* A TREATISE ON PLEADING AND PRACTICE IN THE COURTS OF RECORD OF NEW YORK.
Nichols, David L *see* THE EFFECTS OF ATHLETIC TRAINING ON BONE MINERAL DENSITY IN FEMALE COLLEGIATE GYMNASTS
Nichols, Effingham H *see* A LETTER ON THE VALIDITY AND CONSTITUTIONALITY OF THE LEGAL TENDER ACT
Nichols, Egbert Ray *see* SELECTED ARTICLES ON MINIMUM WAGES AND MAXIMUM HOURS
Nichols, Harry Peirce *see* THE TEMPORARY AND THE PERMANENT IN NEW TESTAMENT REVELATION
Nichols, J G *see* THE BOOK OF NOBLESSE: ADDRESSED TO KING EDWARD THE FOURTH ON HIS INVASION OF FRANCE IN 1475
Nichols, John *see* HISTORY AND ANTIQUITIES OF THE COUNTY OF LEICESTER
Nichols, Philip *see* THE LAW OF EMINENT DOMAIN.
Nichols, Thomas Low *see* FORTY YEARS OF AMERICAN LIFE
Nicholson, E *see* INDIAN SNAKES
Nicholson, Edward Byron *see*
- A NEW COMMENTARY ON THE GOSPEL ACCORDING TO MATTHEW
- OUR NEW NEW TESTAMENT

Nicholson, Edward Williams Byron *see* KELTIC RESEARCHES; STUDIES IN THE HISTORY AND DISTRIBUTION OF THE ANCIENT GOIDELIC LANGUAGE AND PEOPLES
Nicholson, F A *see* THE COIMBATORE DISTRICT MANUAL
Nicholson, J *see* CLASSIFIED CATALOGUE OF PRINTED TRACTS AND BOOKS IN SINHALESE
Nicholson, J J *see* NICHOLSON J.J. WAR DIARY
NICHOLSON J.J. WAR DIARY / Nicholson, J J – 1914-1918 – 1r – 1 – at Corangamite [980]
Nicholson, John *see* JOHN NICHOLSON PAPERS
Nicholson, John Charles *see* PAPERS OF JOHN CHARLES NICHOLSON
Nicholson, Joseph William *see* THE NEGRO'S CHURCH
Nicholson, M J *see* A GUIDE TO CONDITION SCORING OF ZEBU CATTLE
Nicholson, Vincint De Witt *see* A TREATISE ON THE LAW RELATING TO REAL ESTATE IN PENNSYLVANIA
NICHTANDALUSISCHE POESIE ANDALUSISCHER DICHTER AUS DEM XI, XII UND XIII JAHRHUNDERT / Kaempf, Saul Isaac – 2v. Prag. 1858. BJ-421-19 1 – 9 – ne IDC [440]
NICHTKANONISCHE KORANLESARTEN IM MUHTASAB DES IBN GINNI / Bergstraesser, G – Muenchen, 1933 – 1mf – 9 – DM48.00 – 3-89349-311-5 – gw Hänsel [260]
DIE NICHTKIRCHLICHEN UND DIE FREIE THEOLOGIE : MEINE VORTRAEGE IN SOLINGEN, IHRE GEGNER UND IHRE FREUNDE / Weinel, Heinrich – Tuebingen: J C B Mohr (Paul Siebeck), 1903 – 1mf – 9 – 0-8370-6450-3 – 1986-0450 – us A.T.L.A. [240]
NICHTLIMITIERTE KOMPONENTEN IM ABGAS VON OTTOMOTOREN : EINFLUSS VON KRAFTSTOFFZUSAMMENSETZUNG UND ABGASNACHBEHANDLUNG / Huettenberger, Peter – 1993 – 2mf – 9 – DM80.00 – 3-89349-836-2 – gw Hänsel [621]
NICKEL BULLETIN – v24-41 1951-68 – 1 – us UMI [660]
THE NICKEL ORES OF SUDBURY (CANADA) / Frossard, John D – London: G. Philip, 1893. 03263. (Pre-1900 Canadiana) – 9 – cn C.I.H.M. [622]
Nickl, Georg *see* DER ANTEIL DES VOLKES AN DER MESSLITURGIE IM FRANKENREICHE
Nicodemus Colony *see* PAPERS..
Nicol, Jacob *see* LA TRIBUNE
Nicol, Thomas *see* THE FOUR GOSPELS IN THE EARLIEST CHURCH HISTORY
Nicoladoni, Alexander *see* JOHANNES BUENDERLIN VON LINZ UND DIE OBEROESTERREICHISCHEN TAEUFERGEMEINDEN IN DEN JAHREN 1525-31
Nicolaevsky, Boris I *see* POWER AND THE SOVIET ELITE
NICOLAI CUSANI DE CONCILII UNIVERSALIS POTESTATE SENTENTIA EXPLICATUR / Brockhaus, Clemens Friedrich – Leipzig, 1867 – 2mf – 9 – DM62.00 – 3-89349-330-1 – gw Hänsel [943]
Nicolai, Friedrich *see*
- ALLGEMEINE DEUTSCHE BIBLIOTHEK 1765-1796/NEUE ALLGEMEINE DEUTSCHE BIBLIOTHEK 1793-1806
- ALLGEMEINE DEUTSCHE BIBLIOTHEK; NEUE DEUTSCHE BIBLIOTHEK

NICOLAIS FEYNER KLEYNER ALMANACH : EIN BEITRAG ZUR GESCHICHTE DER WUERDIGUNG DES VOLKSLIEDES / Cleve, Karl – (Includes bibliographical references) – Schwedt a.O.: F Freyhoff, 1895 – 1r – 1 – us U.W. Library [780]
Nicolardot, Firmin *see*
- LA COMPOSITION DU LIVRE D'HABACUC
- LES PROCEDES DE REDACTION DES TROIS PREMIERS EVANGELISTES

Nicolas *see* PROCEEDINGS AND ORDINANCES OF THE PRIVY COUNCIL OF ENGLAND, 1385-1422
Nicolas, Augustin *see* SI LA TORTURE EST UN MOYEN SEUR A VERIFIER LES CRIMES SECRETS
NICOLAS DE BONNEVILLE AND THE CERCLE SOCIAL: 1787-1800 – Ed. by Francois Furet. Complete collection, 47 titles on 201 fiches – 9 – fr Hachette [321]
NICOLAS DIAZ PEREZ / Blanco Garcia, Francisco – Madrid: Saenz de Jubera, 1909 – sp Bibl Santa Ana [440]
NICOLAS FRERET, ACADEMICIEN, 1688-1749 / Simon, Renee – (Studies on Voltaire and the eighteenth century, v17) – Oxford. 1961 – 9 – $27.00 – 0-7294-0071-9 – uk Voltaire [920]
NICOLAS GOGOL / Leger, L – Paris, 1914 – 5mf – 9 – ne IDC [460]
Nicolas, H *see* HISTORY OF THE ORDERS OF KNIGHTHOOD
Nicolas, Louis *see* LE CHAT BOTTE
Nicolas, P *see* CONTRIBUTION A L'ETUDE PHYTOGEOGRAPHIQUE DE LA FORET DU GABON
NICOLAS POUSSIN ET SON TEMPS. LE CLASSICISME FRANCAIS ET ITALIEN CONTEMPORAIN DE POUSSIN / Réunion des musees nationaux. Paris – 1961. 48 illus. 2 fiches – 9 – fr Réunion [700]

Nicolas, Victor *see* L'EXPEDITION DU DAHOMEY

Nicolau y Vergara, Luis *see* RESPUESTA DEL DR. LUIS NICOLAU Y VERGARA...A LA MANIFESTACION DEL DR. ANDRES PIQUER

Nicolay, N de *see*
- LE NAVIGATIONI ET VIAGGI NELLA TVRCHIA
- LES NAVIGATIONS, PEREGRINATIONS ET VOYAGES, FAICTS EN LA TVRQVIE

Nicolay, Nicolas de *see* LES NAVIGATIONS PEREGRINATIONS ET VOYAGES, FAICTS EN LA TURQUIE AVEC SOIXANTE FIGURES AU NATUREL TANT D'HOMMES QUE DE FEMMES SELON LA DIVERSITE DES NATIONS

Nicole, P *see*
- PREJUGEZ LEGITIMES CONTRE LES CALVINISTES
- LES PRETENDUS REFORMEZ CONVAINCUS DE SCHISME...

Nicole, Pierre *see* NOUVELLE METHODE POUR APPRENDRE FACILEMENT ET EN PEU DE TEMPS LA LANGUE LATINE.

LE NICOLETAIN / ed by Duguay, M & Duguay, Camille – (Cont by: La Boussole 9 jan 1959-28 oct 1966) – Victoriaville, Canada. 6 dec 1933-26 dec 1958 – 6r – 1 – Can$65.00r – cn Can Microfilming [072]

LE NICOLETAIN – Nicolet, Canada. v1 n28. 29 oct 1886-v5 n68. 16 jun 1891 – 1r – 1 – Can$30.00 – cn Can Microfilming [072]

Nicoll, Maurice *see* DREAM PSYCHOLOGY

Nicoll, W Robertson *see* LITERARY ANECDOTES OF THE NINETEENTH CENTURY

Nicoll, William Robertson *see*
- THE CHURCH'S ONE FOUNDATION
- THE LAMB OF GOD
- LAMB OF GOD: EXPOSITIONS IN THE WRITINGS OF ST JOHN
- LITERARY ANECDOTES OF THE NINETEENTH CENTURY

Nicolliere Teijeiro, Stephane Praude de la *see* LA MARINE BRETONNE AUX 15E ET 16E SIECLES

Nicolson, Harold *see* VITA SACKVILLE WEST AND HAROLD NICOLSON

Nicolson, W Millar *see* CLASSICAL REVISION OF THE GREEK NEW TESTAMENT

Nicolson, William *see* DIARIES, 1701-1714

Nicolson, William (Bishop) *see* CORRESPONDENCE, 1697-1725

Nicot, J *see* THRESOR DE LA LANGUE FRANCOYSE

NIDA – Nigde. Sahibi ve Sermuharriri: Ali Riza, Mesul Mueduerue: Riza Ratib. No. 11 (23 Subat 1924) – 9 – $20.00 – us MEDOC [956]

Nida, E *see*
- BIBLE TRANSLATING
- GOD'S WORD IN MAN'S LANGUAGE
- MESSAGE AND MISSION

NIDA-YI IRAN-I NUVIN – (Missing issues: 1558-1635) – Tehran: Hizb-i Iran-i Nuvin. Sal-i 1, shumarah-'i 1-1791 (7 Tir 1343-19 Isfand 1350 [28 Jun 1964-10 Mar 1971]) – 9r – 1 – $650.00 – us MEDOC [950]

NIDA-YI VATAN – (Sal-i 1, shumarah-'i–sal-i 2, shumarah-'i 211 (Zu'l-qa'dah 1324-22 Safar 1326[27 Dec 1906-25 Mar 1907])) – Tehran – 2r – 1 – $80.00 – us MEDOC [950]

NIE STIRBT DAS LAND : GEDICHTE / Oberkofler, Joseph Georg – Jena: E Diederichs, 1942 – 1r – 1 – us U.W. Library [810]

Niebergall, Ernst Elias *see* DES BURSCHEN HEIMKEHR

Niebuhr, Barthold Georg *see* BRIEFE UND SCHRIFTEN

Niebuhr, Carl *see*
- DIE CHRONOLOGIE DER GESCHICHTE ISRAELS, AEGYPTENS, BABYLONIENS UND ASSYRIENS VON 2000-700 V. CHR.
- VERSUCH EINER RECONSTELLATION DES DEBORALIEDES

Niebuhrii, B G *see* HISTORIARUM QUAE SUPERSUNT (CSHB 14)

NIEDER MIT DEN SOZIALDEMOKRATEN / Brake, Wilhelm – Braunschweig, 1876 – 1 – DM30.00 – gw Mikro Press [335]

NIEDERDEUTSCHE ZEITUNG – Hamburg, Germany. 10 Feb 1947-25 Jan 1950 – 4r – 1 – uk British Libr Newspaper [072]

NIEDERGANG UND AUFSTIEG DER DEUTSCHEN FAMILIE / Buch, Walter – Muenchen: F. Eber, 1932. 52p – 1 – us U.W. Library [305]

NIEDERHEINISCHE MUSIKZEITUNG FUER KUNSTFREUNDE UND KUENSTLER – Koeln. 15v. 1853-67 – 70mf – 9 – subsc: DM420.00 diazo DM500.00 silver – gw Olms [780]

Niederle, L *see* OBOZRENIE SOVREMENNAGO SLAVIANSTVA

Niederpruem, Michael G *see* DIETARY FAT AND CARBOHYDRATE IN RELATION TO BODY FATNESS IN LEAN AND OBESE MEN AND WOMEN

NIEDERRHEINISCHE MUSIK-ZEITUNG FUER KUNSTFREUNDE UND KUNSTLER – Cologne. 1853-67. 4 reels – 1 – 92.00 – us L of C Photodup [780]

NIEDERRHEINISCHE NACHRICHTEN – Duisburg, Germany. 1914 (Nrn.211-361); 1915-19; 1922 (Nr.134); 1925; 1929 (Nr.1-298) – 1 – gw Mikrofilm [072]

NIEDERRHEINISCHE VOLKS-ZEITUNG *see* DUESSELDORFER KREISBLATT UND TAEGLICHER ANZEIGER

NIEDERRHEINISCHE ZEITUNG – Emmerich, Germany. 1889-1915 – 1 – gw Mikrofilm [072]

NIEDERRHEINISCHER KURIER – Titre francais: Courrier du departement du Bas-Rhin puis Courrier du Bas-Rhin. Strasbourg. 1817, 1828-32, 1846-47 – 1 – fr A.C.R.P.P. [073]

NIEDERRHEINISHE MUSIK-ZEITUNG FUER KUNSTFREUNDE UND KUENSTLER – Koeln. v1-15. 1853-1867 – 129mf – 9 – ne IDC [780]

NIEDERSACHSEN: HALBMONATSSCHRIFT FUER GESCHICHTE, LANDS- UND VOLKSKUNDE, SPRACHE UND LITERATUR NIEDERSACHSENS – Bremen. Jahrg. 1-26; 1895-1921. Film Mas C 491 – 1 – us H.U. Library [073]

NIEDERSACHSEN-STUERMER – (Publ in (Hannover-) Buchholz until jul 1932, in (Hamburg-) Harburg until mar 31 1937, in Lueneburg since apr 1 1937) – Lueneburg, may 9 1930-may 14 1932, jan 3 1934-dec 25 1943 – 7r – 1 – gw Mikrofilm [943]

NIEDERSAECHISISCHE ARBEITERZEITUNG ORGAN DER VKPD *see* BRAUNSCHWEIGER ARBEITER-ZEITUNG

NIEDERSAECHSISCHE ARBEITERZEITUNG/ ORGAN DER VEREINIGTEN KOMMUNISTISCHEN PARTEI DEUTSCHLANDS *see* NEUE ARBEITER-ZEITUNG

NIEDERSAECHSISCHE BEOBACHTER – (Title changes: Niedersaechsische Tageszeitung, 1 Feb 1931; Hannoversche Zeitung, 1 Mar 1943) – Hannover, Germany. Feb-Sep 1931 – 24r – 1 – gw Mikrofilm [072]

NIEDERSAECHSISCHE TAGESZEITUNG – (Change of title: Braunschweiger Tageszeitung 1931-45) – Hannover, Feb-Sep 1931 – 42r – 1 – DM3,150.00 – gw Mikro Press [072]

NIEDERSAECHSISCHE TAGESZEITUNG – (Cont by: Hannoversche Zeitung, mar 1, 1943) – Hannover. jul 5, 1943-apr 6, 1945 – 2r – 1 – gw Mikrofilm [072]

NIEDERSAECHSISCHE TAGESZEITUNG – (Cont by: Hannoversche Zeitung, mar 1 1943. Also Bereichsausgabe available: Braunschweiger Tageszeitung, oct 1 1931-39) – Hannover, feb 1 1931-apr 6 1945 – 1 – Inquire at Mikrofilmarchiv for details – gw Misc Inst [943]

NIEDERSAECHSISCHE TAGESZEITUNG *see*
- NIEDERSAECHSISCHE BEOBACHTER
- NIEDERSAECHSISCHER BEOBACHTER

NIEDERSAECHSISCHE VOLKSSTIMME *see* HANNOVERSCHE VOLKSSTIMME

NIEDERSAECHSISCHER BEOBACHTER – (Title changes: Niedersaechsische Tageszeitung, 1 Feb 1931; Hannoversche Zeitung, 1 Mar 1943) – Hannover, Germany. 2 May 1944-6 Apr 1945 (incomplete) – 2r – 1 – gw Mikrofilm [072]

NIEDERSCHLESISCHE TAGESZEITUNG – Legnica, Poland. Oct 1935-Apr 1936; 2-9 Jan 1937 – 2r – 1 – us L of C Photodup [943]

NIEDERSCHLESISCHER ANZEIGER – Glogau (Glogow), Germany. 1811 (incomplete); 1849 – 4r – 1 – gw Mikrofilm [072]

NIEDERSCHRIFT DER KONSTITUIERENDEN SITZUNG...: ABGEHALTEN...12 DEC 1919. / Zentralarbeitsgemeinschaft der Industriellen und Gewerblichen Arbeitgeber und Arbeitnehmer Deutschlands. Zentralausschuss – Berlin: s.n., 1919?. (Serial publications of German trade unions in the Memorial Library, University of Wisconsin-Madison.) – 1 – us U.W. Library [331]

NIEDERSCHRIFT DER VERHANDLUNGEN / Kongress der Christlichen Gewerkschaften Deutschlands – Berlin. v3-4, 8, 10, 12-13. 1901-32. Title varies. Some vols. have distinctive title. (Serial publications of German trade unions in the Memorial Library, University of Wisconsin-Madison.) – 1 – us U.W. Library [330]

NIEDERSCHRIFT DER VERHANDLUNGEN AM 15 UND 16 MAI 1921. 104P. (SERIAL PUBLICATIONS OF GERMAN TRADE UNIONS IN THE MEMORIAL LIBRARY, UNIVERSITY OF WISCONSIN-MADISON.) / Reichskonferenz der Forstarbeiter – Jena. 1921 – 1 – us U.W. Library [331]

NIEDERSCHRIFT DER VERHANDLUNGEN DER ERSTEN REICHSKONFERENZ.. / Verband der Maler, Lackierer, Anstreicher, Tuencher und Weissbinder Deutschlands – v1. 1930. Hamburg. 1v. (Serial publications of German trade unions in the Memorial Library, University of Wisconsin-Madison.) – 1 – us U.W. Library [330]

NIEDERSCHRIFT VOM GEWERKSCHAFT-SKONGRESS / Allgemeiner Freier Angestelltenbund – 1st, 1921-. Berlin, Freier Volksverlag GmbH. v2. 1925. (Serial publications of German trade unions in the Memorial Library, University of Wisconsin-Madison) – 1 – us U.W. Library [331]

NIEDERSCHRIFTEN UEBER DIE VERHANDLUNGEN.. / Deutscher Baugewerksbund – v1-2. 1924-27. Hamburg. (Serial publications of German trade unions in the Memorial Library, University of Wisconsin-Madison.) – 1 – us U.W. Library [330]

Niedt, Friedrich E *see*
- HANDLEITUNG ZUR VARIATION
- MUSICALISCHE HANDLEITUNG ODER GRUENDLICHER UNTERRICHT
- MUSICALISCHER HANDLEITUNG DRITTER UND LETZTER THEIL

DER NIEGEKUESSTE MUND : DREI ERZAEHLUNGEN / Wassermann, Jakob – Berlin: S Fischer [190-?] – 1r – 1 – us U.W. Library [830]

Nieh, E C *see* OLD TESTAMENT CHARACTERS (CCC256)

Nielen, J M *see* GEBET UND GOTTESDIENST IM NEUEN TESTAMENT

Nielle, Henri *see* MON ROMAN AU NIGER

Nielsen, Anton *see* FRA FORST TIL SIDST: GAMLE OG NY FORTAELLINGER

Nielsen, David H *see* NEURAL VERSUS MUSCULAR RESPONSES TO ISOMETRIC STRENGTH TRAINING OF THE TRICEPS BRACHII

Nielsen, FE *see* A COMPETENCY ANALYSIS OF NCAA ATHLETIC ADMINISTRATORS

Nielsen, Fredrik *see* STATSKIRKE OG FRIKIRKE

Nielson, Jens Christian *see*
- HISTORY

Nielson, L C *see* TWELVE EASY DUETS FOR TWO FLUTES

NIEMAN REPORTS – v1- 1947- 1; v29- 5,6; v30- 9 – us UMI [073]

Nieman-Beckman Funeral Home (Pemberville, Ohio) *see* FUNERAL REGISTERS

NIEMANDS LAND : ERZAEHLUNG / Wiessalla, Josef – Leipzig: P Reclam, 1942 – 1r – 1 – us U.W. Library [830]

Niemann, August *see* CREDIT

Niemann, Frank-Michael *see*
- AUFBEREITUNG UND INTERPRETATION VON ERGEBNISSEN EXTERNER QUALITAETSSICHERUNGSMASSNAHMEN ALS EINSTIEG IN DIE INTERVENTIONEN VON QUALITAETSPROBLEMEN
- STATISTISCHE METHODEN ZUR UNTERSUCHUNG VON ASSOZIATIONEN ZWISCHEN ANTIGENEN UND KRANKHEITEN

Niemeyer, August Hermann *see* CHARAKTERISTIK DER BIBEL

Niemeyer, Eduard *see* LESSINGS NATHAN DER WEISE

Niemeyer, N *see* ENGLISH EPISCOPAL PALACES

NIEMEYER'S ZEITSCHRIFT *see* ZEITSCHRIFT FUER INTERNATIONALES PRIVAT- UND STRAFRECHT (T. NIEMEYER)

Niemeyerus, H A *see* DE ISIDORI PELUSIOTAE VITA, SCRIPTIS ET DOCTRINA COMMENTATIO, HISTORICA THEOLOGICA

Niemoeller, Heinrich *see* REFORMATIONSGESCHICHTE VON LIPPSTADT

Niemojowski, Ludwik *see* SIBERIAN PICTURES

Niemtschek, FX. *see* LEBENSBESCHREIBUNG DES KK. KAPELLMEISTERS W.A. MOZART, AUS ORIGINALQUELLEN

Niendorf, Emma *see* LENAU IN SCHWABEN

NIEPODLEGLOSC – Warsaw. Index: 1929-1937, Vols. I-XVI – 1 – 35.00r – us Hoover Inst Photo [335]

Nierengarten, Mark E *see* EFFECTS OF IMITATIVE LEARNING ON THE ACQUISITION OF ROTARY PURSUIT SKILL BY EDUCABLE MENTALLY RETARDED BOYS

Nieritz, Gustav *see*
- DES KOENIGS LEIBWACHE
- DER REICHE ARME MANN
- DIE WUNDERPFEIFE, ODER, DIE KINDER VON HAMELN

Nierop, D R van *see* WIS-KONSTIGE MUSYKA VERTOONENDE DE OORSAECKE VAN 'T GELUYT, DE REDENS DER ZANGH TOONEN TELKONSTIGH UYTGEREECKENT ENDE HET MAKEN EN STELLEN DER SPEELTUYGEN, ALSMEDE VAN DER OUDEN MUSIJCK

Nierszesovicz, Deodatus (Astuatsatur) *see* DICTIONARIUM LATINO-ARMENUM SUPER SACRAM SCRIPTURAM

Niese, Benedictus *see* FLAVII IOSEPHI ANTIQUITATUM IUDAICARUM EPITOME

Niess, J *see* DE ORTU ET OCCASU LINGUAE LATINAE

LA NIETA DEL ZAPATERO / Hurtado, Antonio – 1869 – 9 – 1.50f – sp Bibl Santa Ana [830]

Nieten, Otto *see*
- LESSINGS RELIGIONSPHILOSOPHISCHE ANSICHTEN BIS ZUM JAHRE 1770 IN IHREM HISTORISCHEN ZUSAMMENHANG UND IN IHREN HISTORISCHEN BEZIEHUNGEN
- UEBER CHR. D. GRABBES TRAGOEDIE "DON JUAN UND FAUST"

Niethammer, F J *see* PHILOSOPHISCHES JOURNAL EINER GESELLSCHAFT TEUTSCHER GELEHRTEN

Nieto de Pina, C *see*
- HISTORIA DE LA EPIDEMIA DE CALENTURAS BENIGNAS...EN SEVILLA
- MEMORIAS DE LAS ENFERMEDADES EXPERIMENTADAS EN SEVILLA EN 1785
- MEMORIAS DE LAS ENFERMEDADES EXPERIMENTADAS EN SEVILLA EN 1786

Nieto, Manuel *see* UN LINAJE EXTREMENOS, LOS MORENO DE DON BENITO

Nieto y Serrano, M *see*
- CONSIDERACIONES SOBRE DIVERSAS CATEGORIAS DE FUERZAS...
- DISCURSO...DE LAS SESIONES DEL ANO 1853 EN LA REAL ACADEMIA DE MEDICINA...
- DISCURSOS...DE LA REAL ACADEMIA DE MEDICINA Y CIRUGIA DE MADRID EN EL ANO. 1861
- ENSAYO DE MEDICINA GENERAL O SEA DE FILOSOFIA MEDICA...
- FILOSOFIA DE LA NATURALEZA
- FILOSOFIA Y FISIOLOGIA COMPARADAS EN SU HISTORIA CON EL CRITERIO DE LA CIENCIA VIVIENTE... 3 VOL
- HISTORIA CRITICA DE LOS SISTEMAS FILOSOFICOS...
- LA LIBERTAD MORAL...
- MEMORIA ACERCA DE LA NECESIDAD Y UTILIDAD DE UNA ASOCIACION GENERAL DE PROFESORES DE CIENCIAS MEDICAS
- PROGRAMA DE ENCICLOPEDIA FILOSOFICA
- LA REFORMA MEDICA...
- VEJECES, (RECUERDOS AUTOBIOGRAFICOS)

NIETZSCHE : EINE CHRISTLICHE BESINNUNG / Steinbuechel, Theodor – Stuttgart: Deutsche Verlags-Anstalt, c1946 – 1r – 1 – us U.W. Library [190]

NIETZSCHE / Juenger, Friedrich Georg – Frankfurt am Main: V Klostermann, 1949 – 1r – 1 – us U.W. Library [190]

NIETZSCHE ALS GESCHICHTSPHILOSOPH : EINE QUELLENSTUDIE / Lory, Carl – (Includes bibliographical references) – Berlin: A Kohler, 1904 – 1r – 1 – us U.W. Library [190]

NIETZSCHE ALS PHILOSOPH / Vaihinger, Hans – Berlin: Reuther & Reichard, 1902 – 1r – 1 – us U.W. Library [190]

NIETZSCHE ALS RICHTER UNSRER ZEIT / Gundolf, Ernst – Breslau: F Hirt, 1923 – 1r – 1 – us U.W. Library [190]

NIETZSCHE AND OTHER EXPONENTS OF INDIVIDUALISM / Carus, Paul – Chicago: Open Court, 1914 – 1mf – us A.T.L.A. [190]

NIETZSCHE DER FALSCHE PROPHET / Ernst, Otto – Leipzig: L Staackmann, 1914 – 1r – 1 – us U.W. Library [190]

Nietzsche, Friedrich Wilhelm *see* VON NEUEN FREIHEITEN DES GEISTES

NIETZSCHE UND DAS CHRISTENTUM / Jaspers, Karl – Hameln: F Seifert, [1946] – 1r – 1 – us U.W. Library [190]

NIETZSCHE UND DIE DEUTSCHE KATASTROPHE / Mueller, Georg – Guetersloh: C Bertelsmann, 1946 – 1r – 1 – us U.W. Library [190]

NIETZSCHE UND TOLSTOI / Grot, Nikolaus – Berlin: H Steinitz, 1898 – 1r – 1 – us U.W. Library [920]

NIETZSCHES STELLUNG ZUR CHRISTLICHEN DEMUT / Hauff, Reinhard von – (Includes bibliographical references) – Tuebingen: C Gulde, 1939 – 1r – 1 – us U.W. Library [190]

NIETZSCHES WELT- UND LEBENSANSCHAUUNG IN IHRER ENTSTEHUNG UND ENTWICKLUNG / Ritschl, Otto – Freiburg i. B.: J.C.B. Mohr, 1899 – 1mf – us A.T.L.A. [190]

EEN NIEU GHEESTELIJCK LIEDT-BOECXKEN. WT DEN O. ENDE N.T. GHEMAECT / Soetken Gerijts v. Rotterdamme – 1592. BME-350 1 – 9 – ne IDC [240]

NIEUW ARCHIEF VAN KERKELIJKE GESCHIEDENIS – (1829-1840...Arch. van Kerkelijke Geschiedenis; 1841-1849...Nederl. archief v. Kerkel. Geschiedenis. 12mf) – 1(1852)-2(1854) – 9 – Dfl42.00 – ne Slangenburg [240]

NIEUW CHRISTENDOM – Door Saint-Simon, Gravenhage, Bij M. de Lyon, 6 Junij 1835, iv-84 p. Les Saint-Simoniens, 1825-1834. 6903 – 9 – fr Hachette [335]

EEN NIEUW GELUID OVER DEN VOLKENBOND / Cleymaet, G – Gent, 1935 – 3mf – 1 – ILM-4010/1 – ne IDC [327]

NIEUW ISRAELIETISCH WEEKBLAD – (Missing: 1887(July 7)-1892; 1911(22); 1922) – Amsterdam, 1865-1940 – 763mf – 9 – ne IDC [956]

NIEUW JOODSCH LEVEN – Amsterdam. v1. 1932-1933 – 5mf – 9 – ne IDC [949]

NIEUW THEOLOGISCH TIJDSCHRIFT – v1-33. 1912-46 (complete) – Inquire – 1 – ATLA 1994-S503 – us A.T.L.A. [073]

DE NIEUWE 2-JARIGE KWEEKSCHOOL / Dutch East Indies. Dept. van Onderwijs en Eredienst – SE-3994 1. 1947 – 9 – ne IDC [324]

NIEUWE AFBELDINGHE VAN DE VIER UYTERSTEN BESCHREVEN IN HET LATYN DOOR DEN EERWEERDIGHEN PATER GUILLIELMUS STANIHURSTUS PRIESTER DER SOCIETEYT IESU : VERTAELT, ENDE VERCIERT MET PRINTEN EN POESIE DOOR EENEN PRIESTER DER SELVE SOCIETEYT / Poirters, Adrianus – Antwerpen, 1662 – 4mf – 9 – O-3155/1 – ne IDC [760]

DE NIEUWE AMSTERDAMMER – Amsterdam, Netherlands. -w. 2 Jan 1915-13 July 1918. Very imperfect. 1 reel – 1 – uk British Libr Newspaper [949]

NIEUWE LITERATUUR OVER OORLOG EN VREDE / Polemologisch Instituut Rijksunivers. Groningen – 1964 – 9 – BH-1821 1 – ne IDC [940]

NIEUWE NAAMLIJST VAN NEDERLANDSCHE SCHILDVLEUGELIGE INSECTEN (INSECTA COLEOPTERA) / Everts, E J G – Haarlem, 1887. iii,237p. Z/1222/2 – 8 – ne IDC [590]

NIEUWE ROTTERDAMSCHE COURANT – Rotterdam, Netherlands. Mar 1910-Dec 1922 – 154r – 1 – uk British Libr Newspaper [949]

NIEUWE ROTTERDAMSE COURANT – [Rotterdam: s.n.], jul 1938-may 4 1945 – 46r – 1 – us Res Libr [072]

DE NIEUWE SCHOUBOURGH DER NEDERLANTSCHE KUNSTSCHILDERS EN SCHILDERESSEN... / Gool, J van – 's-Gravenhage. 2v. 1750-1751 – 20mf – ne IDC [700]

DE NIEUWE SCHOUBURGH DER NEDERLANTSCHE KUNSTSCHILDERS EN SCHILDERESSEN / Gool, J van – 2v. 's-Gravenhage. 1750-51. BO-275 1 – 9 – ne IDC [700]

NIEUWE VERHANDELINGEN / Bataafsch Genootschap der Proefondervindelijke Wijsbegeerte, Rotterdam – 1800-6 – 3 – us Readex [190]

NIEUWE VERHANDELINGEN / Zeeuwsch Genootschap der Wetenschappen. Middelburg – Middelburg, 1807-35. v. 1-5 – 3 – us Readex [500]

NIEUWE WEEKBLAD VOOR NAMAQUA EN DAMARALAND – Windhoek, South West Africa. 1914-15 – 1 – sa State Libr [072]

NIEUWE WERKEN VAN HET ZEEUWSCH GENOOTSCHAP DER WETENSCHAPPEN / Zeeuwsch Genootschap der Wetenschappen. Middelburg – Middelburg. 1839-45 – 3 – us Readex [500]

Nieuwenhuijze, Christoffel Anthonie Olivier Van *see* WHAT THE JAPANESE DID TO ISLAM IN JAVA

Nieuwenhuis, G J *see* BRONNENBOEK VOOR HET NIEUWE TAALONDERWIJS IN INDIE

HET NIEUWS VAN DEN DAG – Amsterdam. Oct 1906-Dec 1915 – 1 – us NY Public [072]

NIEUWSBLAD VOOR ISRAELIETEN – Amsterdam. v1-3. 1884-1887 – 22mf – 9 – ne IDC [956]

NIEUW-SEMARANG "DE HEUVELSTAD" : AANGEBODEN DOOR DE "NILLMIJ" – Weltevreden, 1917. 17p – 1mf – 9 – ne IDC [950]

NIF-10S MODEL DATA BASE ON MICROFICHE – 9 – at Statistics [304]

Niftrik, Gerrit Cornelis van *see* DOGMATIKA MASAKINI

NIGER : ANNUAIRE STATISTIQUE 1962, 1967 / Niger. Direction de la Statistique – (Coll title: African Official Statistical Serials, 1867-1982) – 5mf – 9 – £42.00 – uk Chadwyck [960]

Niger *see*
- JOURNAL OFFICIEL DE LA REPUBLIQUE DU NIGER
- JOURNAL OFFICIEL DU TERRITOIRE DU NIGER
- PLAN DE DEVELOPPEMENT ECONOMIQUE ET SOCIAL, 1961-1963 (PLAN INTERIMAIRE)
- PLAN QUADRIENNAL, 1965-1968
- SUMMARY TRANSLATION OF THE NIGER REPUBLIC'S ECONOMIC AND SOCIAL DEVELOPMENT PLAN: INTERIM PLAN, 1961-1963

NIGER AND YORUBA NOTES – London: E Stock. v1-10 n120. jul 1894-jun 1904 – us Res Libr [960]

Niger. Commissariat General au Developpement *see* PROGRAMMATION 1971-1974

Niger. Commissariat General au Plan *see*
- PERSPECTIVES DECENNALES DE DEVELOPPEMENT, 1965-1974
- PLAN INTERIMAIRE, 1964

Niger. Direction de la Statistique *see* NIGER

NIGER: PAPERS RELATIVE TO THE EXPEDITION TO THE RIVER – 1843 – 1 – uk Microform Academic [910]

NIGERIA : ANNUAL ABSTRACT OF STATISTICS 1960-1973 / Nigeria. Federal Office of Statistics – (1962 not publ. Coll title: African Official Statistical Serials, 1867-1982) – 38mf – 9 – £7.00f (set £660.00 90mf) – uk Chadwyck [960]

NIGERIA : ANNUAL STATISTICAL DIGEST 1963-1965 / Nigeria. Eastern Region. Statistics Division – (Coll title: African Official Statistical Serials, 1867-1982) – 9 – £7.00f (set £660.00 90mf) – uk Chadwyck [960]

NIGERIA – Lagos, n9-56. 1937-58 – us Res Libr [960]

NIGERIA : STATISTICAL ABSTRACT 1959-1972 / Nigeria. Western State. Statistics Division – (Coll title: African Official Statistical Serials, 1867-1982) – 39mf – 9 – £7.00f (set £660.00 90mf) – uk Chadwyck [960]

NIGERIA : STATISTICAL YEARBOOK 1964-1966 / Nigeria. Northern Region. Ministry of Economic Planning – (Coll title: African Official Statistical Serials, 1867-1982) – 9mf – 9 – £7.00 (set £660.00 90mf) – uk Chadwyck [960]

Nigeria *see*
- ANNUAL REPORT ON THE GENERAL PROGRESS OF DEVELOPMENT AND WELFARE SCHEMES, 1945-46
- DEVELOPMENT FINANCE, 1955-56 (INTERIM DEVELOPMENT PLAN)
- DEVELOPMENT PLANS
- FIRST PROGRESS REPORT ON THE ECONOMIC PROGRAMME, 1955-60
- GOVERNMENT PUBLICATIONS
- SECOND PROGRESS REPORT ON THE ECONOMIC PROGRAMME, 1955-60
- SOUTHERN NIGERIA CIVIL SERVICE LIST, WITH HANDBOOK
- TEN-YEAR PLAN OF DEVELOPMENT AND WELFARE FOR NIGERIA
- THIRD PROGRESS REPORT ON THE ECONOMIC PROGRAMME, 1055 60

Nigeria and British Cameroons *see* ANNUAL DEPARTMENTAL REPORTS

Nigeria. Bendel State. Ministry of Finance and Economic Planning. Statistics Office *see* DIRECTORY OF EDUCATIONAL INSTITUTIONS 1983/84-1984/85

Nigeria. Bendel State. Statistics Office *see* DIGEST OF EDUCATION STATISTICS ... 1977/78-1984/85

Nigeria. Benue State. Ministry of Education *see* STATISTICAL DATA 1976/77-1984/85

Nigeria. Central Planning Office *see* THIRD NATIONAL DEVELOPMENT PLAN, 1975-1980

Nigeria. Central Planning Office. Ministry of Economic Development and Reconstruction *see* GUIDELINES FOR THE THIRD NATIONAL DEVELOPMENT PLAN 1975-1980

Nigeria. Central-West State *see* GAZETTE

Nigeria. Cross River State *see*
- CONCLUSIONS OF THE GOVERNMENT ... ON THE REPORT AND RECOMMENDATIONS OF THE TECHNICAL COMMITTEE FOR THE ASSESSMENT OF THE VIABILITY OF THE EXISTING PRIMARY SCHOOLS ...
- CONCLUSIONS OF THE GOVERNMENT ... ON THE REPORT OF THE ADMINISTRATIVE INQUIRY INTO ALLEGATIONS OF MISMANAGEMENT IN THE SCHOOL OF BASIC STUDIES, AKAMKPA

Nigeria. Cross River State. Adult Education Division *see* THE ADULT EDUCATION ANNUAL REPORT 1982

Nigeria. Cross River State. Ministry of Local Government *see* ANNUAL REPORT ON UNIVERSAL PRIMARY EDUCATION 1984

Nigeria. Department of Statistics *see* POPULATION CENSUS OF THE NORTHERN REGION OF NIGERIA, 1952

Nigeria. East Central State *see* PUBLIC EDUCATION EDICT 1970

Nigeria. East Central State. Ministry of Education *see*
- DIRECTORY OF POST-PRIMARY INSTITUTIONS IN THE EAST CENTRAL STATE OF NIGERIA
- DIRECTORY OF POST-PRIMARY INSTITUTIONS IN THE EAST CENTRAL STATE OF NIGERIA 1973
- POLICY OF PUBLIC EDUCATION

Nigeria. East Central State of Nigeria, Ministry of Economic Development and Reconstruction *see* FIRST DEVELOPMENT PLAN 1970-74

Nigeria. Eastern *see*
- EASTERN NIGERIA DEVELOPMENT PLAN, 1962-68
- REVISED DEVELOPMENT PROGRAMME, 1958-62 (REVISED APR 1960)

Nigeria. Eastern. Ministry of Economic Planning *see* EASTERN NIGERIA DEVELOPMENT PLAN, 1962-68 FIRST PROGRESS REPORT

Nigeria. Eastern Region. House of Assembly *see* DEBATES

Nigeria. Eastern Region. Statistics Division *see* NIGERIA

Nigeria. Federal Ministry of Economic Development *see* FEDERAL GOVERNMENT DEVELOPMENT PROGRAMME, 1962-68 FIRST PROGRESS REPORT

Nigeria. Federal Office of Statistics *see* NIGERIA

Nigeria. General Agreement on Tariffs and Trade *see* THE FIRST SIX-YEAR PLAN OF NIGERIA

Nigeria. House of Representatives *see* DEBATES

Nigeria. Imo State. Imo State Manpower Committee *see* UNEMPLOYMENT PROBLEM IN IMO STATE

Nigeria. Kaduna State. Ministry of Economic Development. Statistics Division *see* TRACER STUDY OF KADUNA STATE PRIMARY / POST SCHOOL-LEAVERS 1977-1978 EDUCATIONAL YEAR

Nigeria. Kaduna State. Ministry of Economic Planning and Rural Development *see* STATISTICAL YEARBOOK 1975

Nigeria. Kaduna State. Ministry of Information *see* ADULT EDUCATION MEMORANDA

Nigeria. Kwara State, Ministry of Finance, Economic Planning Division *see* FIRST DEVELOPMENT PLAN, 1970-1974

Nigeria. Lagos State. Ministry of Education and Community Development. School Service Board *see* THE TECHAER'S HANDBOOK

Nigeria. Land and Survey Department *see* NOTES ON LAND TENURE IN THE BENIN, KUKURUKU, ISHAN AND ASABA DIVISIONS OF BENIN PROVINCE

NIGERIA LAWYERS QUARTERLY – v1- 1964-1; v7- 5,6,9 – us UMI [073]

Nigeria. Legislative Council *see* DEBATES

Nigeria. Mid-Western. Ministry of Internal Affairs *see* MID-WESTERN NIGERIA DEVELOPMENT PLAN, 1964-68

Nigeria. Mid-Western State *see* MIDWEST TEACHERS SERVICE REGULATIONS 1971

Nigeria. Mid-Western State. Department of Internal Affairs and Information *see* THE EDUCATION WE WANT, MILITARY GOVERNOR, MID-WESTERN NIGERIA

Nigeria. Mid-Western State. Ministry of Education. Planning Division *see* POST-PRIMARY SCHOOL DIRECTORY OF MIDWESTERN STATE OF NIGERIA 1971 (SECONDARY LEVEL)

Nigeria. Mid-Western State of Nigeria, Ministry of Economic Development and Reconstruction *see* DEVELOPMENT PLAN 1970-74

Nigeria. Ministry of Economic Development *see*
- NATIONAL DEVELOPMENT PLAN, 1962-68
- NATIONAL DEVELOPMENT PLAN PROGRESS REPORT, 1964

NIGERIA NEWSLETTER – 1978- – 1,5,6,9 – us UMI [073]

Nigeria. North Central State of Nigeria, Economic Planning Division *see* FIRST DEVELOPMENT PLAN 1970-74

Nigeria. North Eastern State of Nigeria, Ministry of Economic Planning *see* FIRST DEVELOPMENT PLAN 1970-1974

Nigeria. North Western State of Nigeria *see* FOUR YEAR DEVELOPMENT PLAN 1970-1974 (IN BRIEF)

Nigeria. North-Central State. Ministry of Information *see* NEW EDUCATION POLICY AND NEW SYSTEM OF SCHOOL FEES

Nigeria. North-Central State. Ministry of Information. Adult Education Division *see* ADULT EDUCATION MEMORANDA

Nigeria. North-Central States Legislature. House of Assembly *see* DEBATES: OFFICIAL REPORT

Nigeria. North-Eastern State *see* GAZETTE

Nigeria. Northern. Ministry of Economic Planning *see* DEVELOPMENT PLAN, 1962-68

Nigeria. Northern Region *see*
- THE CONSTITUTION OF NORTHERN NIGERIA LAW, 1953
- EDUCATION LAW OF NORTHERN NIGERIA 1964

Nigeria. Northern Region. Ministry of Economic Planning *see* NIGERIA

Nigeria. North-Western State *see* GAZETTE

Nigeria. Ogun State. Ministry of Economic Planning. Statistics Division *see*
- REPORT OF A SAMPLE SURVEY OF UNEMPLOYMENT AMONG SCHOOL-LEAVERS 1977
- REPORT OF A SURVEY OF THE UNIVERSAL PRIMARY EDUCATION SCHEME 1978

Nigeria. Ogun State. Ministry of Finance and Economic Development *see* REPORT OF A SAMPLE SURVEY OF UNEMPLOYMENT AMONG SCHOOL-LEAVERS 1975

Nigeria. Ondo State. Ministry of Finance and Economic Development *see* A SUMMARY OF CURRENT EDUCATION

Nigeria. Oyo State. Ministry of Economic Planning. Statistics Division *see*
- ANNUAL DIGEST OF EDUCATION STATISTICS...
- A SUMMARY OF CURRENT EDUCATION STATISTICS 1976/77-1987

Nigeria. Oyo State. Ministry of Finance and Economic Planning. Statistics Division *see* A SUMMARY OF CURRENT EDUCATION STATISTICS 1976-1977

Nigeria. Oyo State. Statistics Division *see* UNIVERSAL PRIMARY EDUCATION

Nigeria. Planning Office *see* NATIONAL ROLLING PLAN 1991-1993

Nigeria. Planning Office 1500 Lagos, 1990 *see* GUIDELINES FOR THE NATIONAL ROLLING PLAN (1990-1992)

Nigeria. Sokoto State. Ministry of Education. Statistics Section *see*
- EDUCATIONAL STATISTICS 1975/76-1977/78
- POST-PRIMARY STATISTICS 1980-1981

Nigeria. South Eastern State *see* NEW SYLLABUS FOR PRIMARY SCHOOLS IN THE SOUTH-EASTERN STATE OF NIGERIA

Nigeria. South-Eastern State of Nigeria, Ministry of Economic Development and Reconstruction *see* FIRST STATE DEVELOPMENT PLAN 1970-74

Nigeria. Western *see*
- AN APPRAISAL OF THE DEVELOPMENT OF WESTERN NIGERIA, 1959-60
- DEVELOPMENT OF THE WESTERN REGION OF NIGERIA, 1955-1960
- PROGRESS REPORT ON THE DEVELOPMENT OF THE WESTERN REGION OF NIGERIA, 1955-60
- WESTERN NIGERIA DEVELOPMENT PLAN, 1962-68
- WESTERN REGION DEVELOPMENT PLAN, 1960-65

Nigeria. Western. Ministry of Planning and Community Development *see* WESTERN NIGERIA DEVELOPMENT PLAN, 1962-68, FIRST PROGRESS REPORT

Nigeria. Western Provinces. House of Assembly *see* DEBATES

Nigeria. Western Region *see*
- GAZETTE
- WHITE PAPER ON THE ESTABLISHMENT OF A UNIVERSITY IN WESTERN NIGERIA

Nigeria. Western Region. Commission Appointed to Review the Educational System of Western Nigeria *see* REPORT OF THE COMMISSION

Nigeria. Western Region. House of Assembly *see*
- DEBATES
- OFFICIAL REPORT

Nigeria. Western Region. House of Chiefs *see*
- DEBATES
- OFFICIAL REPORT

Nigeria. Western Region. Ministry of Economic Planning and Social Development *see* INTERIM REPORT ON EDUCATION IN A RURAL AREA ...

Nigeria. Western State of Nigeria, Ministry of Economic Planning and Reconstruction *see* DEVELOPMENT PLAN 1970-74

Nigeria. Western State. Statistics Division *see* NIGERIA

[NIGERIA/BIAFRA INFORMATION COLLECTION] – (Inquire for list of contents) – Chicago: Uni of Chicago, Photodup Dept, 1973 – us Res Libr [960]

NIGERIAN BAPTIST – 1923-61 – 1 – us Res Libr [073]

NIGERIAN BAPTIST – 1923-78 – 1 – 447.79 – us Baptist [240]

NIGERIAN BRONZES / Museum of Mankind (British Museum, Dept. of Ethnography). London – (Over 530 colour images of bronzes from 14th-19th C. Fully indexed) – 1985 – 9 colour mf – 15 – $360.00 – 0-907716-03-2 – uk Mindata [730]

NIGERIAN BUSINESS DIGEST – 1971- 1; 19974- 5,6; 1976- 4 x 6 in. 9 – us UMI [073]

NIGERIAN CHRISTIAN – v1-11, Apr 1967-77. 2 reels – 1 – us A.T.L.A. [073]

NIGERIAN CHRONICLE – Lagos. Nigeria. -w. Nov 1908-Mar 1915. (4 reels) – 1 – uk British Libr Newspaper [072]

NIGERIAN CITIZEN – Zaria, Nigeria. -w. 5 July 1951-26 June 1952; 7 Jan 1954-30 Oct 1965. Imperfect. 11 reels – 1 – uk British Libr Newspaper [072]

NIGERIAN DAILY SKETCH – Ibadan, Nigeria. 1965-69 – 11r – 1 – us Ross [072]

NIGERIAN DAILY TIMES – Lagos, Nigeria. Daily Times. -d. 1941-55. 39 reels – 1 – uk British Libr Newspaper [072]

NIGERIAN GEOGRAPHICAL JOURNAL – v1-9. 1957-1966 – 28mf – 9 – ne IDC [960]

Nigerian Institute of Social and Economic Research *see* CONFERENCE PROCEEDINGS

NIGERIAN LABOUR STUDIES / ed by Waterman, P – (Chief O.A. Fagbenro Beyioku Personal Archive 62mf Dfl558.00. Labour in the Nigerian Press 1976-1977 30mf Dfl270.00. Lagos Port Labour Archive 219mf Dfl1,971.00. Nigerian Trade Union Tribunal of 1976 73mf Dfl657.00. Includes a printed guide. Wage Labour Relations in Africa 16mf Dfl144.00.) – 9 – ne IDC [331]

NIGERIAN LANGUAGES – BIBLIOGRAPHY *see* A VERNACULAR BIBLIOGRAPHY FOR THE LANGUAGES OF NIGERIA

NIGERIAN MORNING POST – Lagos, Nigeria. Morning Post. -d. Jan 1963-Dec 1965. Imperfect. 13 reels – 1 – uk British Libr Newspaper [072]

NIGERIAN OFFICIAL PUBLICATIONS, 1869-1959 / U.S. Library of Congress. General Reference and Bibliography Division – Washington. 1959 – 1 – us Res Libr [324]

NIGERIAN OUTLOOK – Enugu, Nigeria, 1965-66 – 3r – 1 – us Ross [072]

NIGERIAN PAMPHLETS FILMED FROM THE COLLECTIONS OF THE IBADAN UNIVERSITY LIBRARY – (Inventory available in Its Africana pamphlets) – [Ibadan, Nigeria, 19–?] – us Res Libr [960]

NIGERIAN PAMPHLETS FROM THE UNIVERSITY OF NIGERIA LIBRARY FILMED AT IBADAN UNIVERSITY LIBRARY – (Inventory available) – [v.p.], 1844-1949 – us Res Libr [960]

NIGERIAN PIONEER – Lagos. Nigeria. -w. Feb 1914-Jul 1934. (18 reels) – 1 – uk British Libr Newspaper [072]

NIGERIAN TIMES – (Times of Nigeria). Lagos. Nigeria. -w. Apr 1910-Oct 1911, Jan 1914-Jun 1915, Nov 1915-Nov 1920. (2 reels) – 1 – uk British Libr Newspaper [072]

NIGERIAN TRIBUNE – Ibadan, Nigeria. -d. 11 Jan-6 Dec 1950; 8 Aug 1951-25 March 1953; 2 Jan 1958-29 Sept 1960; 8 Oct 1964-31 July 1965. Imperfect. 13 reels – 1 – uk British Libr Newspaper [072]

NIGERIEN, AM NIL DER SCHWARZEN / Haenel, Karl – Leipzig: W. Goldmann, (c1943). 145p. map – 1 – us U.W. Library [950]

Nigg, W *see* DIE KIRCHENGESCHICHTSS-CHREIBUNG

THE NIGGER OF THE "NARCISSUS" / Conrad, Joseph; ed by Bayle, Constantino – Leipzig, Madrid: Razon y Fe, 1928 – 9 – sp Bibl Santa Ana [830]

THE NIGGER OF THE "NARCISSUS" : A TALE OF THE SEA / Conrad, Joseph – London: William Heinemann, 1898 – 1 roll – 1 – 1-55879-510-3 – uk Libr Preservation [830]

NIGHTINGALE – 10 May-30 Jul 1796 – 1 – us UMI [073]

Nightingale, Florence *see*
- LETTERS AND PAPERS
- NOTES ON HOSPITALS
- NOTES ON NURSING

Nightingale, J *see* A PORTRAITURE OF METHODISM

THE NIGHT-SIDE OF NATURE; OR, GHOSTS AND GHOST SEERS / Crowe, Catherine – New ed., intro. by Thomson Jay Hudson. Philadelphia: H.T. Coates & Co., 1901. xiv,(7)-451p – 1 – us U.W. Library [830]

LE NIGOG / ed by Roquebrune, Robert de & Morin, Leopol – Montreal, Canada. jan-dec 1918 – 1r – 1 – Can$30.00 – cn Can Microfilming [072]

LA NIGRIZIA – Rome [etc]: Missionari comboniani [etc]. [v36-61] (1918-43); v66-70 (1947-51); 1952-59 – us Res Libr [073]

Nihan, Charles W *see* ADMINISTERING THE FEDERAL JUDICIAL CIRCUITS

NIHILISM AS IT IS, BEING STEPNIAK'S PSEUD. PAMPHLETS .. / Stepniak, S – Trans. by E.L. Voynich, and Felix Volkhovsky's Claims of the Russian Liberals, with an introd. by Dr. R. Spence Watson. London: T.F. Unwin, 1894?. xi,122p – 1 – us U.W. Library [335]

NIHON BIJUTSU : 1898-1916 – (Nos 196, 197 not published) – Nihon Bijutsu-in: nos 1-79. Nihon Bijutsu-sha: nos 80-198- – 18r – 1 – Y240,000 – ja Yushodo [700]

NIHON KEIZAI SHIMBUN – (1945-85 713r) – Tokyo, 1876-1944 – 317r – 1 – inquire – us Ross [072]

NIHON KEIZAI SHIMBUN : TOKYO EDITION – (Jan 1945-Dec 1988 1028r Y9,108,000) – 1876-Dec 1944 – 317r – 1 – Y3,384,000 – ja Japan Micro [950]

NIHON KENCHIKU-SHI ZUROKU – Historical Album of Japanese Architecture. By Amanuma Shun'ichi. 6 v. Kyoto, Hoshino Shoten. 1933-38. BCH-540 2 – 8 – ne IDC [720]

NIHON KINSEI KAYO SHIRYO-SHU = COLLECTION OF SONGS AND BALLADS IN THE PRE-MODERN JAPAN – 44r – 1 – Y572,000 – ja Yushodo [390]

NIHON MEITO-SEN – Plates of masterpieces of Japanese ceramics. Ed. by Nihon Meito sen Kankokai. 10 v. Tokyo. 1932-35. BCH-545 2 – 8 – ne IDC [740]

NIHON RINSEISHI CHOSA SHIRYO = HISTORICAL SOURCES OF THE LAND AND FOREST SYSTEM IN JAPAN, FROM THE 16TH TO THE 19TH CENTURIES / Japan. Ministry of Agriculture and Forestry; ed by Tokugawa Institute of Forestry, Tokyo – Ed. by the Ministry in 1924-34. 800,000p. 1400v Maps. Printed guide (200p) – 706r – 1 – Y4,968,000.00 – ja Yushodo [630]

NIHONSI KANKEI SHIRYO / Harvard University. Law School Library; ed by Fujii, Joji – 130p with English introd. 309 items – 88r – 1 – Y1,130,000.00 – ja Yushodo [340]

Nii Kwabena Bonne 3 *see* MILESTONES IN THE HISTORY OF THE GOLD COAST

NIIGATA NIPPO – (Includes: Yukan Niigata) – Japan, 1942-80 – 422r – 1 – inquire – us Ross [072]

NIIGATA NIPPO – (Includes Yukan Niigata) – November 1942-December 1994 – 778r – 1 – Y7,026,400 – ja Japan Micro [950]

NIJAT-I IRAN – (Shumarah-'i 6-38 (7 Khurdad 1364-8 Bahman 1364[28 May 1985-28 Jan 1986]). Missing issue: 29) – Paris: Jibhah-'i Nijat-i Iran – 1 reel – 1 – $50.00 – us MEDOC [950]

Nijhoff, I A *see* GEDENKWAARDIGHEDEN UIT DE GESCHIEDENIS VAN GELDERLAND

A NIKA-ENGLISH DICTIONARY. / Krapf, Ludwig & Rebmann, Johannes; ed by Sparshott, T H – London: Society for Promoting Christian Knowledge, 1887. vii,391p – 1 – us U.W. Library [490]

Nikishov, P P *see* IZ ISTORII KRAKHA LEVYKH ESEROV V TURKESTANE

Nikitin, S N *see* UKAZATEL' LITERATURY PO BUROVYM NA VODU SKVAZHINAM V ROSSII

Nikitina, E *see*
- POETICHESKOE ISKUSSTVO BLOKA
- RUSSKAIA LITERATURA OT SIMVOLIZMA DO NASHIKH DNEI

Nikitopoulos, Ingeborg *see* ASPEKTE DER SELBSTBESTIMMUNGSPROBLEMATIK IN DEN VEREINTEN NATIONEN

NIKKAN MINSHU = THE DAILY PEOPLE – Vancouver, BC. May-Dec 1941 – 1r – 1 – Can$125.00 – cn U.B.C. Preserve [072]

NIKKAN SPORT – Mar 1946-Dec 1994 – 471r – 1 – Y4,710,000 – ja Japan Micro [072]

THE NIKKEI WEEKLY : MICROFILM – (Significant news stories pertaining to business in Japan) – 1963-. annual – 1 – Y48,000y – ja Nihon Keizai [650]

NIKKEI WEEKLY (JAPAN ECONOMIC JOURNAL) – (This is the English version of Nikkei) – January 1963-December 1994 – 40r – 1 – Y704,000 – ja Japan Micro [950]

Nikolaev, A A *see*
- KOOPERATSIIA
- KOOPERATSIIA I SOTSIALIZM
- OBSHCHESTVENNYE OGORODY I UCHASTIE V IKH USTROISTVE KOOPERATIVNYKH ORGANIZATSII
- SPRAVOCHNIK DLIA USTROITELEI I RUKOVODITELEI TRUDOVYKH ZEMLEDEL'CHESKIKH ARTELEI
- TEORIA I PRAKTIKA KOOPERATIVNOGO DVIZHENIIA

Nikolaev, IN *see* UKAZATEL' CHERTEZHEI MOSKOVSKIM TSERKVAM I SOSTOIAVSHIM V IKH PRIKHODAKH DVORAM I LAVKAM ZA 1775-1782 GG

Nikolaeva, V V *see* BORBA ZA USTANOVLENIE I UPROCHENIE SOVETSKOI VLASTI V IAKUTII

NIKOLAI MIKHAILOVICH KARAMZIN, PO EGO SOCHINENIIAN, PIS'MAM I OTZYVAM SOVREMENNIKOV / Pogodin, M P – 2pts. M. 1866. BR-7777 2 – 8 – ne IDC [947]

Nikolai Mikhailovich, Vel. Kn *see* GRAF P. A. STROGANOV, 1774-1817

NIKOLAI NOVIKOV I RUSSKOE PROSVESHCHENIE 18 VEKA / Makogonenko, G P – M., L. 1951. BR-7677 2 – 8 – ne IDC [460]

NIKOLAI SEPANOVICH GUMILEV / Gumileva, A – Novyi zhurnal. New York. 1956. BR-3661 2 – 8 – ne IDC [073]

NIKOLAIER ANZEIGER UND PLESSER STADTBLATT *see* ANZEIGER FUER DEN KREIS PLESS

NIKOLAUS LENAU : ZUR JAHRHUNDERTFEIER SEINER GEBURT / Castle, Eduard – (Includes bibliographical references) – Leipzig: M Hesse, 1902 – 1r – 1 – us U.W. Library [920]

NIKOLAUS LENAU UND DAS JUNGE DEUTSCHLAND / Hessen, Jozef van – 's-Gravenhage: G Vormer, 1925 – 1r – 1 – us U.W. Library [430]

NIKOLAUS LENAUS BRIEFE AN EMILIE VON REINBECK UND DEREN GATTEN GEORG VON REINBECK / ed by Schlossar, Anton – Stuttgart: A Bonz, 1896 – 1r – 1 – us U.W. Library [430]

NIKOLAUS LENAU'S DICHTERISCHER NACHLASS / ed by Gruen, Anastasius – Stuttgart: Tuebingen: J G Cotta, 1851 – 1r – 1 – us U.W. Library [430]

NIKOLAUS LENAUS LYRIK : IHRE GESCHICHTE, CHRONOLOGIE UND TEXTKRITIK / Bischoff, Heinrich – (Includes bibliographical references) – Berlin: Weidmann, 1921 – 1r – 1 – us U.W. Library [430]

NIKOLAUS LENAUS SAEMTLICHE WERKE IN ZWEI BAENDEN = WORKS / Lenau, Nikolaus; ed by Castle, Eduard – Leipzig: Max Hesse, [1900?] – 1 – us U.W. Library [800]

NIKOLAUS ZURKINDEN VON BERN, 1506-1588 : EIN VERTRETER DER TOLERANZ IM JAHRHUNDERT DER REFORMATION / Baehler, Eduard – Zuerich: Beer, 1912 – 1mf – us A.T.L.A. [240]

NIKOLAUSKULT UND NIKOLAUSBRAUCH IM ABENDLANDE (FVK HFT 9-12) / Meisen, A – Duesseldorf, 1931 – Dfl67.00 – ne Slangenburg [240]

Nikol'skii, A A *see* POLNYI SPRAVOCHNYI UKAZATEL' KNIG, BROSHIUR, GAZET ZHURNALOV, AREST NA KOTORYE UTVERZHDEN SUBDEBNYMI USTANOVLENIIAMI PO 1-E IANVARIA 1912 GODA

Nikol'skii, D P *see* BIBLIOGRAFICHESKII UKAZATEL' LITERATURY O BASHKIRAKH

Nikolskii, N K *see* RUKOPISNAIA KNIZHNOST' DREVNERUSSKIKH BIBLIOTEK (XI-XVII) MATERIALY DLIA SLOVARIA VLADELTSEV RUKOPISEI PISTSOV, PEREVODCHIKOV.

Nikonov, S P *see* GRAZHDANSKOE PRAVO. UKAZATEL' LITERATURY

Nikov, P *see* VUZRAZHDANIE NA BALGARSKIIA NAROD TSARKOVNO-NATSIONALNI BORNI I POSTIZHENIIA

NIKU-DAN KOERBAN MANOESIA : BOEKOE TJATATAN SEORANG OPSIR NIPPON WAKTOE MENGEPOENG DAN MENJERANG PORT-ARTHUR / Sakurai, T – (Microfiche Nos 148-150) – Djakarta: Djawa Goenseikanboe (Balai Poestaka), 2604 – 3mf – 9 – SE-2002/1 – ne IDC [950]

Nikuradse, Alexander *see* KAUKASIEN, NORDKAUKASIEN, ASERBEIDSCHAN, ARMENIEN, GEORGIEN, GESCHICHTLICHER UMRISS

Nilakanta Sastri, K A *see* HISTORY OF SRI VIJAYA

THE NILE TRIBUTARIES OF ABYSSINIA / Baker, Samuel White – new ed. London. 1874. BA-167 2 – 8 – ne IDC [910]

NILES DAILY NEWS : DAILY GENERAL NEWSPAPER – Niles, OH. 22 Feb 1895 – 1r – 1 – us Western Res [071]

NILES' NATIONAL REGISTER – v. 1-77. 1811-49 – 1 – us UMI [073]

NILES' NATIONAL REGISTER – v1-76. 1811-49 – 1 – us Princeton Micro [323]

NILES TOWNSHIP REGISTER – Fremont, CA. Apr 1927-1954 – 14r – 1 – $700.00 – B02251 – us Library Micro [071]

NILES TOWNSHIP REGISTER – Niles, CA. Apr 1927-54 – 14r – 1 – $800.00 – B02526 – us Library Micro [071]

NILGIN NEWS *see* SOUTH OF INDIA OBSERVER

Nilsson, N A *see* OSIP MANDEL'SHTAM AND HIS POETRY

Nilsson, S *see*
- ANALECTA ORNITHOLOGICA
- HISTORIA MOLLUSCORUM SVECIAE TERRESTRIUM ET FLUVIATILIUM BREVITER DELINEATA
- ORNITHOLOGIA SVECICA

NILUEFER – Bursa: Feraizcizade Matbaasi, 1889-1893 – 9 – $10.00 – us MEDOC [956]

NILUEFER – Seydibesir. Sahib-i Imtiyaz ve Mueduer-i Mes'ul: Edib; Sermuharriri: Idris Subhi; Karikatueristi: Kerameddin Hilmi, 1920-19? – 9 – $25.00 – us MEDOC [956]

Nimal, H *see* VIE DE QUELQUES-UNES DE NOS GRANDES SAINTES AU PAYS DE LIEGE

Nimat Allah *see* HISTORY OF THE AFGHANS

THE NIMBORAN LANGUAGE: PHONOLOGY AND MORPHOLOGY / Anceaux, Johannes Cornelis – SE-4781 1. 1965 – 9 – ne IDC [490]

Nimchuk, V V *see* STARO-UKRAINS'KA LEKSYKOHRAFIIA V II ZV'IAZKAKH Z ROSIIS'KOIU TA BILORUS'KOIU

NIMM MICH MIT UND BERLINER WOCHE – Berlin, 1906/07 – 1 – Inquire at Mikrofilmarchiv for details – gw Misc Inst [072]

NIMM MICH MIT UND BERLINER WOCHE – Berlin, Germany.1906-07 – 1 – gw Mikrofilm [073]

Nin Frias, Alberto *see* ESTUDIOS SOBRE JESUS Y SU INFLUENCIA

[NINA] AIR DE NINA / Dalayrac, N – Paris: Louis, 179- – 1 – us Sibley [780]

[NINA] OVERTURE : ROMANCE ET CHOER, ARR. PIANO OR HARPSICHORD WITH AD LIB VIOLIN / Dalayrac, N – Paris: Louis, 179- – 1 – us Sibley [780]

NINE HONEST MEN / Lawrence, David – New York, Appleton-Century, 1936. 164 p. LL-640 – 1 – us L of C Photodup [340]

NINE LEAFLETS / Association of Libertarian Feminists – 1fiche (29x) – 9 – 1.00f – at Libertarian Micro [320]

NINE LECTURES ON THE EARLIER CONSTITUTIONAL HISTORY OF CANADA DELIVERED BEFORE THE UNIVERSITY OF TORONTO IN EASTER TERM, 1899 / Ashley, William James – Toronto: Rowsell & Hutchinson, Printers to the University, 1899. 00050. (Pre-1900 Canadiana) – 9 – cn C.I.H.M. [971]

NINE O'CLOCK NEWS, 1939-1945 / BBC (British Broadcasting Corporation) Home Service – 745mf – 9 – £2,865.00 – uk Chadwyck [900]

NINE YEARS AT THE GOLD COAST / Kemp, Dennis – London, New York: Macmillan, 1898 – us Res Libr [920]

NINETEEN CENTURIES OF MISSIONS : A HANDBOOK PRIMARILY PREPARED FOR YOUNG PEOPLE / Scudder, William W (Mrs) – (Includes index) – New York: Fleming H Revell, c1899 – 1mf – 9 – 0-8370-6699-9 – 1986-0699 – us A.T.L.A. [240]

NINETEENTH AND TWENTIETH CENTURY ENGLISH AND AMERICAN DRAMA – 13,538mf – 9 – $48,138.00 $1,282.50y – us OmniSys [820]

NINETEENTH AND TWENTIETH CENTURY MARITIME AND TRADING RECORDS / Merseyside Maritime Museum (National Museums and Galleries on Merseyside). Liverpool – (Waterloo Dock Registers, 1827-50. ca 35 reels. £1300.00; 1. Minutes and Reports of the Liverpool Steamship Owners' Assoc., 1859-1964. ca 60 reels. £2,500.00; ALT; 1) – Customs Registers of Shipping, 1786-1823 – ca 20r – 1 – £750.00 – uk Altair [380]

NINETEENTH CENTURY – v1- 1975- 1; v4- 5,6,9 – us UMI [700]

THE NINETEENTH CENTURY *see*
- NINETEENTH CENTURY BOOKS ON ART AND ARCHITECTURE
- VISUAL ARTS AND ARCHITECTURE SPECIALIST COLLECTION

NINETEENTH CENTURY AMERICAN MUSIC PERIODICALS – (Based on: A Checklist of American Music Periodicals, 1850-1900 by William J Weichlein. Full list available) – (mf ed 1986-) – 1 – uk Chadwyck [780]

NINETEENTH CENTURY AMERICAN MUSIC PERIODICALS *see*
- THE AEOLIAN QUARTERLY
- THE BATON
- THE BOSTON MUSICAL GAZETTE
- THE BOSTON MUSICAL TIMES
- THE BOSTON MUSICAL YEARBOOK
- BRAINARD'S MUSICAL
- THE CABINET
- CAECILIA
- CHICAGO MUSICAL TIMES
- THE CHOIR JOURNAL
- THE CHORAL ADVOCATE AND SINGING CLASS JOURNAL
- CHURCH'S MUSICAL VISITOR
- THE CONCORDIA
- THE COURIER
- DEXTER SMITH'S MUSICAL, LITERARY, DRAMATIC AND ART PAPER
- THE ETUDE
- THE FOLIO
- FREUND'S DAILY MUSIC AND DRAMA
- J C FREUND'S WEEKLY
- H E FREUND'S WEEKLY / MUSICAL AGE
- GITTIT
- THE GLOBE
- GOLDBECK'S MUSICAL INSTRUCTOR
- HENRY DE MARSAN'S NEW COMIC AND SENTIMENTAL SINGERS JOURNAL
- THE INDICATOR
- JUBILEE DAYS
- THE KEYNOTE
- KUNKEL'S MUSICAL REVIEW
- LOOMIS' MUSICAL JOURNAL
- MASSACHUSETTS MUSICAL JOURNAL
- MELLOR'S MUSICAL MIRROR
- THE MESSAGE BIRD
- METRONOME
- MOORE'S MUSICAL RECORD
- MUSIC
- MUSIC REVIEW
- THE MUSIC REVIEW
- THE MUSIC TRADE REVIEW
- MUSICAL AMERICA
- MUSICAL AND SEWING MACHINE GAZETTE (MUSICAL COURIER)
- THE MUSICAL BULLETIN
- MUSICAL BULLETIN
- MUSICAL CLIPPER
- THE MUSICAL GAZETTE
- THE MUSICAL HERALD
- THE MUSICAL INDEPENDENT
- MUSICAL LEADER AND CONCERTGOER
- MUSICAL RECORD
- MUSICAL REVIEW
- MUSIC-CLASS JOURNAL AND ORGANIST'S COMPANION
- NATIONAL PEACE JUBILEE AND MUSICAL FESTIVAL, NATIONAL PEACE JUBILEE AND MUSICAL REPORTER
- NEW HAMPSHIRE JOURNAL OF MUSIC
- THE NEW YORK MUSICAL ECHO
- THE NEW YORK MUSICAL PIONEER AND CHORISTER'S BUDGET
- NORTH'S PHILADELPHIA MUSICAL JOURNAL
- OPERA GLASS
- THE ORGAN
- ORGANIST'S QUARTERLY JOURNAL AND REVIEW
- ORPHEUS
- PIANIST
- ROCHESTER MUSICAL TIMES
- SARONI'S MUSICAL TIMES
- THE SCORE
- THE SONG JOURNAL
- SOUTHERN JOURNAL OF MUSIC
- SOUTHERN MUSICAL ADVOCATE
- TRIFET'S MONTHLY GALAXY OF MUSIC
- THE VIOLIN WORLD
- THE VOICE
- THE VOX HUMANA
- WATSON'S WEEKLY ART JOURNAL
- WESTERN MUSICAL WORLD
- WILLARD'S MUSICAL VISITOR
- WORCH'S MUSICAL MONTHLY

NINETEENTH CENTURY AMERICAN MUSIC PERIODICALSIC PERIODICALS *see* THE MUSICIAN

NINETEENTH CENTURY AND AFTER *see* TWENTIETH CENTURY

NINETEENTH CENTURY ART : MAJOR SUBJECT COLLECTIONS – (Individual titles not listed separately) – 345 catalogues on 475mf – 9 – £2,495.00 – uk Chadwyck [700]

NINETEENTH CENTURY BOOKS ON ART AND ARCHITECTURE / ed by Fawcett, Trevor – (Includes a free CD-ROM index wh provides full bibliographic details of all items publ. Free to purchasers of coll) – 2440 Eng-lang titles publ between 1801-1900 (mf ed 1997) – ca 10,000mf – 9 – £29,500.00 – uk Chadwyck [700]

NINETEENTH CENTURY BOOKS ON CHINA / British Library – (Each unit consists of ca 500mf and a printed short title list. Cumulated lists will be publ end of 1996 and 1997) – Units 1,2,3 available; Units 4,5 1997 – ca 2,500mf – 9 – £9,200 – uk Chadwyck [950]

NINETEENTH CENTURY FICTION – v1- 1945- 1; v23- 5,6; v30- 9 – us UMI [420]

NINETEENTH CENTURY FRENCH STUDIES – v1- 1972- 1,5,6; v6- 9 – us UMI [073]

THE NINETEENTH CENTURY GENERAL COLLECTION : SOCIETY AND CULTURE / British Library – 7 units per yr – ca 500mf per unit – 9 – £1,565.00 standing order (£1,845.00 per unit) – uk Chadwyck [941]

NINETEENTH CENTURY LEGAL TREATISES – (Subject breakouts available) – 9 – us Primary [340]

NINETEENTH CENTURY LITERARY MANUSCRIPTS – (Pt: 1 The Browning, Eliot, Thackeray and Trollope Manuscripts from the British Library, London 20r $2,400.00. Pt 2: The Correspondence and Records of Smith, Elder & Co. from the National Library of Scotland 7r $840.00. Includes guide) – Marlborough: Adam Matthew Publications, 1996 – 1 – uk Matthew [420]

THE NINETEENTH CENTURY LITERATURE SPECIALIST COLLECTION : PART 1: WOMEN WRITERS / ed by Alston, R C & Sutherland, J A – 3 units per yr – ca 500mf per unit – 9 – £1,030.00 standing order (£2,145.00 per unit) – uk Chadwyck [800]

THE NINETEENTH CENTURY LITERATURE SPECIALIST COLLECTION : PART 2: CHILDREN'S LITERATURE / British Library – 1 unit per yr – ca 500mf per unit – 9 – £1,830.00 standing order (£2,145.00 per unit) – uk Chadwyck [800]

NINETEENTH CENTURY MUSIC – v. 1-. 1977- – 1,5,6,9 – us UMI [780]

NINETEENTH CENTURY POLITICAL LEADERS : SERIES A: HOLDINGS OF THE VIRGINIA HISTORICAL SOCIETY / ed by Barney, William L – 1996 – ca 50r – 1 – ca $6,250.00 – 1-55655-633-0 – us UPA [975]

NINETEENTH CENTURY QUESTIONS / Clarke, James Freeman – Boston: Houghton, Mifflin, 1897 – 1mf – us A.T.L.A. [240]

NINETEENTH CENTURY RUSSIAN PUBLICISTS / ed by O'Flaherty, Dennis M – 88 titles – 9 – ne IDC [070]

NINETEENTH CENTURY THEATRE PERIODICALS – (Pt 1: From the British Library, Bloomsbury. Pt 2: From the British Library, Colindale. Pt 3: From the Theatre Museum, London and the Bodleian Library, Oxford) – 1 – us Primary [790]

NINETEENTH CENTURY THEATRE RESEARCH – v. 1-4. 1973-76 – 1,5,6,9 – us UMI [790]

NINETEENTH CENTZRY AMERICAN MUSIC PERIODICALS *see* LEADER

NINETEENTH-CENTURY AMERICAN LITERATURE AND HISTORY – (Pt 1: The Ohio Valley and the South; Pt 2: The Trans-Mississippi West) – Includes selected titles from Dr. J. Christian Bay's bibliog., Three Handfuls of Western Books, and other material with an emphasis on late 19th century imprints – 9 – us Primary [800]

NINETEENTH-CENTURY CONTEXTS / ed by Kucich, Greg & Hanley, Keith – 9,5,1 – us Gordon [400]

NINETEENTH-CENTURY DIPLOMATIC RECORDS RELATING TO CHINA – (Diplomatic Instructions, 1843-1906. 7 rolls. $161.00; Diplomatic Despatches, 1843-1906. 131 rolls. $3,013.00; Notes to the Chinese Legation, 1868-1906. 2 rolls. $46.00; Notes from the Chinese Legation, 1868-1906. 6 rolls. $138.00; Consular Despatches: Amoy, 1844-1906. 15 rolls. $345.00; Antung, Manchuria, 1904-1906. 1 roll. $23.00; Canton, 1790-1906. 20 rolls. $460.00; Chefoo, 1863-1906. 9 rolls. $207.00; Chinkiang, 1864-1902. 7 rolls. $161.00; Chungking, 1896-1906. 1 roll. $23.00; Foochow, 1849-1906. 10 rolls. $230.00; Hangchow, 1904-1906. 1 roll. $23.00; Hankow, 1861-1906. 8 rolls. $184.00; Macao, 1849-1869. 2 rolls. $46.00; Mukden, Manchuria, 1904-1906. 1 roll. $23.00; Nanking, 1902-1906. 1 roll. $23.00; Newchwang, Manchuria, 1865-1906. 7 rolls. $161.00; Ningpo, 1853-96. 7 rolls. $161.00; Shanghai, 1847-1906. 53 rolls. $1,219.00; Swatow, 1860-1881. 4 rolls. $92.00; Tientsin, 1863-1906. 8 rolls. $184.00) – 9 – Dist. us Scholarly Res – us L of C Photodup [324]

NINETEENTH-CENTURY DIPLOMATIC RECORDS RELATING TO KOREA – (Diplomatic Instructions, 1883-1905. 1 roll. $23.00; Diplomatic Despatches, 1883-1905. 22 rolls. $506.00; Notes to the Korean Legation, 1888-1906. 1 roll. $23.00; Notes from the Korean Legation, 1883-1906. 1 roll. $23.00; Consular Despatches: Seaoul, 1886-1906. 2 rolls. $46.00) – 27 rolls – 9 – Dist. us Scholarly Res – us L of C Photodup [324]

NINETEENTH-CENTURY DIRECTORIES FOR THE DUTCH BOOK TRADE = ADRESBOEKEN VOOR DEN NEDERLANDSCHEN BOEKHANDEL, [1828] 1848-1896 : DUTCH DIRECTORIES – 1992 – 198mf – 9 – Dfl2,725.00 – ne MMF Publ [380]

NINETEENTH-CENTURY DIRECTORIES FOR THE GERMAN BOOK TRADE = ADRESSBUCH FUER DEN DEUTSCHEN BUCHHANDEL UND VERWANDTE GESCHAEFTSZWEIGE, 1839-1900 : GERMAN DIRECTORIES – 1839-1900 – 257mf – 9 – Dfl4,775.00 – ne MMF Publ [380]

NINETY SECOND CYCLE ERGOMETER TESTS FOR ASSESSING ANAEROBIC GLYCOLYTIC POWER / Pearman, SN – 1990 – 2mf – 9 – $8.00 – us Microform Publ [613]

NINETY SIX FIRST BAPTIST CHURCH. NINETY SIX, SOUTH CAROLINA : CHURCH RECORDS – 1875-1926 – 1 – 12.78 – us Baptist [240]

NINETY YEARS' HISTORY OF THE PRESBYTERIAN CHURCH IN NORTH FORMOSA (CCC188) / Hsu, C H – (In Chinese) – Taipei: [s.n.], 1962 – 1r – 1 – 1984-B500 – us A.T.L.A. [240]

NINETY-NINE YEAR LEASES AND FORTUNES MADE THEREIN. / Pryor, Charles Foster – Cincinnati: Anderson, 1928. 191p. LL-1236 – 1 – us L of C Photodup [340]

NINGBO RIBAO = NINGBO DAILY – China. 1985-. M-D87 – 1 – $55.00r – cc Microforms [072]

NINGEN-KOGAKU = HUMAN ENGINEERING – (Japan). v1-20 – 113mf – 9 – inquire – us Ross [300]

NINGXIA RIBAO = NINGXIA DAILY – China. 1983-. M-D52 – 1 reel/y – 1 – $52.00r – cc Microforms [072]

NINIAN UND SEIN EINFLUSS AUF DIE AUSBREITUNG DES CHRISTENTHUMS IN NORD-BRITANNIEN / Mackinnon, James – Heidelberg: J. Hoerning, 1891 – 1mf – us A.T.L.A. [941]

NINON CHEZ MME. DE SEVIQNE. OPERA EN UN ACT ET EN VERS / Berton, H – Paris: Duhan et Co, 1808? – 1 – us Sibley [780]

LOS NINOS CON LA REPUBLICA Y CON LA REACCION / Spain. Ministerio de Propaganda – Children with Republic and with reaction. n.p., 1936. Fiche W1077. (Blodgett Collection of Spanish Civil War Pamphlets) – 9 – us H.U. College Libr [946]

LOS NINOS INDIGENAS EN LA CRISTIANIZACION DE AMERICA UNA PAGINA CONMOVEDORA EN LA HISTORIA / Bayle, Constantino – Madrid: Razon y Fe, 1944 – 1 – sp Bibl Santa Ana [240]

LOS NINOS (UN LIBRO PARA LOS GRANDES) CONSIDERACIONES SOBRE LA PRIMERA EDUCACION Y LA PRIMERA INSTRUCCION / Alcaraz Segura, Lorenzo – Caceres: Imp. Moderna, 1923 – 1 – sp Bibl Santa Ana [370]

NINTH ALABAMA NATIONAL EGG LAYING DEMONSTRATION / Alabama. Polytechnic Institute. Extension Service – 1932-33 – 1,5,6 – us Spaulding [636]

NINTH CENSUS OF THE UNITED STATES / U.S. Bureau of the Census – 1870. 1748 rolls. M593 – 1 – us Nat'l Archives [324]

NINTH CENSUS OF THE U.S. – Arkansas, 1870 – 1r – 1 – $50.00 – B50002 – us Library Micro [975]

NINTH CENSUS OF THE U.S. : EL DORADO AND LOS ANGELES COUNTIES ONLY – California, 1870 – 1 – $50.00 – C50008 – us Library Micro [975]

NINTH MEETING OF THE EAST AND SOUTHERN AFRICAN SUB-COMMITTEE FOR SOIL CORRELATION AND LAND EVALUATION : LILONGWE, 1991 – 1992 – 123p – it F.A.O. [631]

NINTH REPORT ON THE DEMAND FOR AND SUPPLY OF TEACHERS / Great Britain. Ministry of Education – 1963-1986 – 9 – uk Microform Academic [324]

NINUS 2 / Brifaut, Charles – (French Theatre Series). Paris. F. Didot. 1815 – 9 – fr Hachette [820]

NIOBRARA PIONEER – Niobrara, NE. -w. May 1877-Jan 1880; Sept 1880-Jul 1882, scattered issues missing; Aug-Sept 1887; Jul 1888-Apr 1901; Mar 1902-Jul 1904 – 1 – us NE Hist [071]

NIOBRARA TRIBUNE – Niobrara, NE. -w. Oct 1885 to date – 1 – us NE Hist [071]

Nipho, Francisco Mariano *see*
- CORREO GENERAL DE ESPANA
- DISCURSOS ELOCUENTES Y POLITICOS
- DISCURSOS ERUDITOS DE INGENIOS ESPANOLES
- VOCES LLENAS DE AMOR A FERNANDO 6

NIPOMA'S ADOBE PRESS – Arroyo Grande, CA. 1983 – 13+ r – 1 – $650.00 ($50.00y) – R03145 – us Library Micro [071]

NIPON O DAI ITSI RAN, OU ANNALES DES EMPEREURS DU JAPON – Traducteur by Isaac Titsingh. Traduction du japonais. 1834 – 9 – 15.00 – fr Orientalistes [950]

Nippold, Friedrich *see*
- DIE ALTKATHOLISCHE KIRCHE DES ERZBISTHUMS UTRECHT
- EIN BISCHOFSBRIEF VOM CONCIL UND EINE DEUTSCHE ANTWORT
- DAVID JORIS VON DELFT. SEIN LEBEN, SEINE LEHRE UND SEINE SECTE
- KATHOLISCH ODER JESUITISCH?
- MEINE GUTACHTEN VOR GERICHT IN SACHEN DER LIGUORISCHEN MORAL
- URSPRUNG, UMFANG, HEMMNISSE, UND AUSSICHTEN DER ALTKATHOLISCHEN BEWEGUNG

NIPPON BOEKI NENPYO = ANNUAL RETURN OF THE FOREIGN TRADE OF THE EMPIRE OF JAPAN / Japan – 1866-1964 – 123r – 1 – Y1,100,000 – ja Yushodo [380]

NIPPON DI MASA PERANG ! KESAN RINGKAS JANG DIDAPAT SELAMA TOEROET DALAM SEKAWAN OETOESAN DJAWA MELAWAT KE NIPPON, 2603 / Harahap, P – Djakarta (Djawa Shimbun Sha) 2604. 130p – 37-38mf – 9 – ne IDC [950]

NIPPON KAGAKU KAISHI – (1975- 5,6,9) – 1973- – 1 – us UMI [073]

NIPPONGO : MOEDAH DAN GAMPANG OENTOEK DAPAT BERBAHASA NIPPON, PENERBITAN JANG BAROE / Kurono Maisaichi – Djakarta Gunhodobu, Pentjetak Kung Yung Pao, 2605. 408p – 93-97mf – 9 – ne IDC [950]

NIRRANDA CEMETERY REGISTER – 1888-1993 – 2mf – 9 – at Corangamite [920]

Nirschl, Joseph *see* DIE THEOLOGIE DES HEILIGEN IGNATIUS

NIRU – [S.l.]: Jami'ah-'i Susyalist'ha-yi Irani dar Urupa. Shumarah-'i 2, 4-11 (Isfand 1339-Isfand 1341 [Feb/Mar 1961-Feb/Mar 1963]) – 1 reel – 1 – $25.00 – us MEDOC [950]

NIRWANA : DREI BUECHER AUS DER GESCHICHTE FRANKREICHS. ROMAN / Jensen, Wilhelm – Breslau: S Schottlaender, 1877 – 1r – 1 – us U.W. Library [830]

Nisancizade, Mehmed b. Ahmed *see* MIR'AT UEL-KA'INAT

Nisard, Ch *see* ETUDE SUR LE LANGAGE POPULAIRE

Nisbet, Charles *see* ADDRESS...DICKINSON COLLEGE

Nisbet, J *see* BURMA UNDER BRITISH RULE – AND BEFORE

NISEI AFFAIRS – Japanese Canadian Committee for Democracy. 1945-47 – 1 – 75.00 – cn McLaren [971]

NISHI-NIHON (FUKUOKA NICHINICHI SHIMBUN) – Mar 1877-Dec 1988 – 767r – 1 – Y6,136,000 – ja Japan Micro [950]

NISHI-NIHON SHIMBUN FUKUOKA NICHINICHI SHIMBUN – Japan, 1877-1984 – 767r – 1 – inquire – us Ross [072]

THE NISHNAWBE NEWS / Organization of North American Indian Students – 1971-82. (American Indian Periodicals in the Princeton University Library). 1 reel – 1 – $75.00 – us UPA [305]

NISQUALLY VALLEY NEWS – Yelm, WA. Feb-Dec 1922; 1924-79; 1983- – 30+ r – 1 – $1,500.00 ($50.00y) – B05405 – us Library Micro [071]

O NISSEI : ORGAO DE IMPRENSA E PUBLICIDADE DA A.N.N.B.A. – Manaus, Amazonas. Jul 1962 – 1,5,6 – bl Biblioteca [072]

Nissel, Carl *see* ULRICH VON HUTTEN

NITHARDI HISTORIARUM LIBRI 3 (MGH 7: 44.BD) : ACCEDIT ANGELBERTI RHYTHMUS DE PUGNA FONTANETICA – Ed 3a. 1907 – Dfl9.00 – ne Slangenburg [240]

NITRO JOURNAL – Nitro, Canada. 8 aut 1941-21 jul 1942 – 1r – 1 – Can$25.00 – cn Can Microfilming [072]

NITROGEN – 1959- 1; v87- 5,6; v93- 9 – us UMI [073]

Nitsche, Richard *see* GESCHICHTE DER WIEDERTAEUFER IN DER SCHWEIZ ZUR REFORMATIONSZEIT

Nitschke, Otfried *see* GOETHES PAEDAGOGISCHE PROVINZ

NITSOTS = THE SPARK – (Title in Yiddish. In Hebrew) – Munich, DE. v13 no80. 11 Jul 1947 – 1r – 1 – $25.00 – cn Can Microfilming [072]

NITTETI: DEH VIEN MECO AMATO / Anfossi, P – London: John Preston – 1 – us Sibley [780]

Nitti, Francesco S *see* CATHOLIC SOCIALISM

Nitzsch, Carl Immanuel *see*
- URKUNDENBUCH DER EVANGELISCHEN UNION
- ZWEI VORTRAEGE

Nitzsch, Friedrich *see*
- GRUNDRISS DER CHRISTLICHEN DOGMENGESCHICHTE
- LUTHER UND ARISTOTELE

NIULI ZAMZAM... LES OISEAUX S'EBATTENT / Kabore, O – Essai d'etude ethnolinguistique des chansons enfantines moose de Koupela, Burkina Faso (ex Haute Volta) – 9 – F120.00 – fr Ethnologie [306]

NIVA – Bialystok, Poland. May 1959-61 – 1r – 1 – us L of C Photodup [943]

NIVA – Ezhemesiachnyia literaturnyia i populiarnonauchnyia prilozheniia k zhurnalu "Niva". Spb. 1894-1916. B-1401 2 – 8 – ne IDC [320]

NIVA – Illiustrirovannyi zhurnal literatury, politiki i sovremennoi zhizni. v. 1-48. Spb. 1870-1917. B-1400 2 – 8 – ne IDC [320]

Nive *see* BIO-BIBLIOGRAPHIE ANALYTIQUE DE L'OEUVRE DE MARCEL TRUDEL, DOCTEUR ES LETTRES

Nivers, G G de *see*
- TRAITE DE LA COMPOSITION DE MUSIQUE

Nivers, Guillaume-G *see* LAMENTATIONES JEREMIAE PROPHETAE(...)

THE NIXON ADMINISTRATION : A COMPREHENSIVE MICROFICHE LIBRARY WITH ANALYTICAL INDEXES / ed by Weinstein, Stephen – 1008mf + index – 9 – $5.00f – us Ross [975]

Nixon, Robert *see* FREE ENTERPRISE MARKETING

NIXUS PLANTARUM / Lindley, J – Londini. 1833. B-6026 2 – 8 – ne IDC [580]

NIXUS PLANTARUM / Lindley, J – Translated into German by C. T. Beilschmied. Nuernberg. 1834. B-7104 2 – 8 – ne IDC [580]

Niyazi, Mehmet *see* SARK ORDUSIDA AZIZ PASA FIRKASI

Niza' Muddin Ahmad *see*
- TABAQAA8T-I-AKBARIA8
- TABAQAT-I-AKBARI

NIZAM – UEmmet-i Islamiye ve Millet-i Osmaniyeye hizmet eden kalemlere mahsus fikir ve ictihad sahifeleri. Sahib-i Imtiyaz: Ebu'l-Cihad Ali Riza. No. 5 (15 Kanunievvel 1918) – 9 – $20.00 – us MEDOC [956]

Nizami *see* LAILI AND MAJNUM: WOMEN OF PERSIA

Nizami, 'Aruzi' *see* THE CHAHAR MAQALA

NIZHEGORODSKAI A KOMMUNA : ORGAN NIZHEGORODSKOGO GUBERNSKOGO KOMITETA ROSSI ISKO I KOMMUNISTICHESKO I PARTII, GUBERNSKOGO I GORODSKOGO SOVETOV RABOCHIKH, KRASNOARME ISKIKH I KRESTI ANSKIKH DEPUTATOV – (Includes c.1: 1921:Nov.6) – N-Novgorod: Nizhegorodski i gubispolkom, 19uu – 1 – CSUXANS0352-S – us Hoover Inst Photo [947]

NIZHEGORODSKAIA GUB – Sel'sko-khoziaistvennyi obzor Nizhegorodskoi gubernii za 1896 god; za 1903 god (Vypusk vtoroi). Nizhii-Novgorod. 1897; 1905. BRZ-213 2 – 8 – ne IDC [947]

NIZHEGORODSKIE MUZYKAL'NYE NOVOSTI – Nizhnii Novgorod, 1901-12 (weekly) – 5mf – 9 – us Ross [780]

NIZHEGORODSKII SBORNIK, IZDAVAEMYI NIZHEGORODSKIM GUBERNSKIM STATISTICHESKIM KOMITETOM / ed by Gatsiskii, A S – Nizhnii Novgorod. 10v. 1867-1890 – 61mf – 9 – ne IDC [947]

NIZHEGORODSKIIA GUBERNSKIIA VIEDOMOSTI / Russia – 1894-96 – 1 – $52.00 – us L of C Photodup [947]

NIZHGORODSKII KOOPERATOR *see* BIULLETEN' NIZHEGORODSKOGO GUBERNSKOGO KOOPERATIVNOGO SOVETA

NIZHNEE PRIOB'E V I TYSIACHELETII NASHEI ERY / Chernetsov, V N – In. MIA. v.58. p.136-245. Moscow. 1957. Ills. BU-571 2 – 8 – ne IDC [335]

Nizigiyimana, D *see* LES CONTES D'OGRES (IBISIZIMWE)

NJANJIAN KANAK-KANAK, DENGAN ARANSEMEN PIANO / Kau Besin, AF – Djakarta, Balai Pustaka, 1961. xvi,68p.illus.Vocal music. SEM-10089-10090/1 – 9 – ne IDC [780]

NJCAA MINUTES OF MEETINGS / National Junior College Athletic Association – 1976 – 9 – us UMI [073]

NJIOER MELAMBAI. (SEPATAH KATA PENJONGSONG, OLEH SOEKARNO) / Yuji, Isobe – (Microfiche Nos 186-187) – Djakarta, Kakumin Toshokyoku, 2605 – 2mf – 9 – SE-2002/1 – ne IDC [950]

NJIVA – Buenos Aires, Argentina, 1937 – 2mf or 1 reel – 1,9 – us I.H.R.C. [972]

Njoto *see* STRIVE FOR THE VICTORY OF THE INDONESIAN REVOLUTION WITH THE WEAPON OF DIALECTICAL AND HISTORICAL MATERIALISM

N.K.F. *see* TRUDY SEKTSII PROMYSHLENNOSTI I TOVAROOBMENA

N.K.F., Institut ekonomicheskikh issledovanii *see* TRUDY SELSKO-KHOZIAISTVENNOI SEKTSII

Nkhonjera, LP *see* EVALUATION OF THE PRODUCTIVITY OF CROSSBRED DAIRY CATTLE ON SMALLHOLDER AND GOVERNMENT FARMS IN THE REPUBLIC OF MALAWI

NKT–RSFSR, Glavnoe upravlenie sotsialnogo strakovaii a *see* STATISTICHESKIE DANNYE PO SOTSIALNOMU STRAKHOVANII U V RSFSR ZA...POLUGODIE...

N.K.V.T., Glavnoe tamozhennoe upravlenie S.S.S.R. *see* VNESHNIAIA TORGOVLIA PO EVROPEISKO I GRANITSE

Nkwenti-Azeh, Blaise *see* TERMINOLOGICAL PROBLEMS INVOLVED IN THE PROCESS OF EXCHANGE OF NEW TECHNOLOGY BETWEEN DEVELOPING AND DEVELOPED COUNTRIES

N.K.Z. Upravlenie po opytnomu delu Sredne-chernozemnoi oblasti *see* VESTNIK OPYTNOGO DELA

NLADA BRIEFCASE – (Title varies: v1-7 no 10 1962-49 as NALAO Brief Case. v7 no 11-v8 no 6 1949-50 as Brief Case. v9-29 1950-71 as Legal Aid Brief Case) – v1-39. 1942-82 – 9 – $242.50 set – us Hein [340]

NLGI SPOKESMAN / National Lubricating Grease Institute – v1- 1937- 1; v34- 5,6; v40- 9 – us UMI [621]

NLN NEWS / National League for Nursing – v1- 1952- 1; v20- 5,6; v23- 9 – us UMI [073]

NLP-ANKER-KOLLABIEREN ALS KURZZEITTHERAPIE VON STUDIERENDEN MIT PRUEFUNGSANST : EINE THERAPIEVERGLEICHSSTUDIE MIT MENTALEM TRAINING / Reckert, Horst-Walter – 1993 – 2mf – 9 – DM80.00 – 3-89349-798-6 – gw Hänsel [150]

NMR-SPEKTROSKOPISCHE METHODEN ZUR DETEKTION VON METABOLITEN IM PHYSIOLOGISCHEN MEDIUM / Stryjewski, Detlef – 1992 – 98p – DM98.00 – 3-89349-494-4 – gw Hänsel [540]

NMU PILOT – New York. N.Y. 1958- – 1 – us UMI [071]

NO "BEGINNING", OR, THE FUNDAMENTAL FALLACY: A COMMON-SENSE DEMONSTRATION OF THE NON-EXISTENCE OF A "FIRST CAUSE", THEREBY IDENTIFYING GOD WITH NATURE / Maple, William H – 3rd ed. Chicago: Ingersoll Beacon Co., 1906, c1899 – 1 – us U.W. Library [240]

NO BEGINNING, OR, THE FUNDAMENTAL FALLACY:...IDENTIFYING GOD WITH NATURE / Maple, William H – Chicago: W.H. Maple, 1899. 1 fiche – 9 – us A.T.L.A. [240]

NO COMPROMISE, NO POLITICAL TRADING / Liebknecht, Wilhelm – Trans. by A.M. Simons and Marcus Hitch. Chicago: C.H. Kerr, 1900. 64p – 1 – us U.W. Library [335]

NO DEMOCRATIC GOVERNMENT IN SPAIN. RUSSIA'S PART IN SPAIN'S CIVIL WAR. MURDER AND ANTIRELIGION IN SPAIN / Carney, William P – New York. 1937. Fiche W 774. (Blodgett Collection of Spanish Civil War Pamphlets) – 9 – us H.U. College Libr [946]

NO DISTANT MILLENNIUM : THE INTERNATIONAL LAW OF HUMAN RIGHTS / Humphrey, John – 1989 – 204p – 9 – 92-3-102615-1 – fr UNESCO [340]

NO FUE TEA, FUE BARRENO / Jimenez de la Espada, Marcos – Madrid: Fortanet, 1887. B.R.A.H. XI, pp. 235-238 – sp Bibl Santa Ana [946]

NO HAY JUSTICIA SIN LIBERTAD : PODER JUDICIAL Y "PODER PERJUDICIAL" / Gonzalez Calderon, Juan Antonio – Buenos Aires: V.P. de Zavalia, [1956] – 1 – CSUXADJ1815-B – us Hoover Inst Photo [360]

NO HAY MAS POSIBILIDAD DE GOBERNAR NI DE VICTORIA QUE A TRAVES DEL FRENTE POPULAR / Ibarruri, Dolores – Barcelona, 1938? Fiche W1758. (Blodgett Collection of Spanish Civil War Pamphlets) – 9 – us H.U. College Libr [946]

NO IMPORTA – Villafranca de los Barros, 1913 – 5 – sp Bibl Santa Ana [073]

NO MAN HATH SEEN GOD (CCC338) = MEI YU JEN KAN CHIEN KUO SHANG TI / Wu, Yao-tsung – (In Chinese) – [s.l: s.n, 1943] – 1r – 1 – 1984-6677 – us A.T.L.A. [210]

THE NO MO CO – Havre. Mont. 1935-1967 – 1 – us UMI [071]

NO MORE LEGAL POWER OF THE NETHERLANDS IN INDONESIA / Maramis, A A – SE-11,998 1. 1946 – 9 – ne IDC [950]

NO REFUGE BUT IN TRUTH / Smith, Goldwin – New York: G.P. Putnam, 1909. 1 fiche – 9 – us A.T.L.A. [240]

NO SONG, NO SUPPER: A COMIC OPERA IN TWO ACTS. / Storace, Stephen – (Vocal score). 1790 – 9 – us Sibley [780]

NO TAXES – Stockton, CA. Nov 1935-40 – 1r – 1 – $50.00 – C03014 – us Library Micro [071]

NO TAXES – Stockton. Calif. 1935-40 – 1 – us UMI [071]

NO UNITED FRONT WITH COMMUNISM / Trades Union Congress – Speeches at the Trades Union Congress, Plymouth, 1936. London, 1936. Fiche W1078. (Blodgett Collection of Spanish Civil War Pamphlets) – 9 – us H.U. College Libr [946]

NOAA / U.S. National Oceanic and Atmospheric Administration – (v7- . 1977- . 9) – v. 3-. 1973- – 1,5,6 – us UMI [073]

Noack, Ingolf *see* RECHTE UND PFLICHTEN DER JUGENDLICHEN IM ARBEITSPROZESS

Noack, Ludwig *see*
- DIE BIBLISCHE THEOLOGIE
- THARRAQAH UND SUNAMITH

NO-ACTION AND INTERPRETATIVE LETTERS / U.S. Securities and Exchange Commission – Current year – 9 – $985.00 – us Washington [336]

NO-ACTION AND INTERPRETATIVE LETTERS / U.S. Securities and Exchange Commission – v1-3. 1971-87 – 9 – $1915.00 – us Washington [324]

Noailles, Anna Elizabeth de Brancovan *see* LES INNOCENTES, OU LA SAGESSE DES FEMMES

NOB HILL NEWS – Portland OR. Sep 16 1954 – 1 – us U.O. Library [071]

Nobel, Alphons *see* FRAU VON STEIN

Nobele, Edouard de *see* LE CONGRES INTERNATIONAL DE DROIT COMMERCIAL A ANVERS. L'UNIFICATION DE LA LEGISLATION EN MATIERE DE LETTRES DE CHANGE

Noberasco, Felipe *see* EL ESPIRITU Y EL APOSTOLADO DE SOR MARIA JOSEFA ROSELLO...

NOBILARIO DEL CONDE DON PEDRO, HIJO DEL REY DON DIONIS DE PORTUGAL / Pedro, Conde de Barcellos – Traduzido castigado y con nuevas ilustraciones de varias notas por Manuel de Faria i Sousa, cavallero dela Orden de Christo i de la Casa Real. Madrid: A. de Paredes, 1646 – 1 – us U.W. Library [946]

NOBILIAIRE D'AUVERGNE / Bouillet, Jean B – Clermont-Ferrand, 1846-1853. 7v – 9mf – 9 – F270.00 – fr F.F.G. [920]

NOBILIAIRE DE GUYENNE ET DE GASCOGNE / O'gilvy – Paris, 1858-83. 4v – 7mf – 9 – F210.00 – fr F.F.G. [920]

NOBILIAIRE DE TOURAINE / Touraine – (T. 1: documents genealogiques; T. 2: chevaliers bannerets) – 19th cent – 1 – F330.18 – fr Armell [920]

NOBILIAIRE DU PONTHIEU DE DU VIMEU / Belleval – Paris, 2nd ed., 1876. 1v – 2mf – 9 – F60.00 – fr F.F.G. [920]

NOBILIARIO DE CONQUISTADORES DE INDIAS – 1892 – 9 – 1.50f – sp Bibl Santa Ana [946]

NOBILIARIO DE REINOS, CIUDADES Y VILLAS DE LA AMERICA ESPANOLA...TOMO 3 / Montoto, Santiago – Madrid: Razon y Fe, 1929 – 1 – sp Bibl Santa Ana [946]

LA NOBILISSIMA, ANZI ASINISSIMA COMPAGNIA DELLI BRIGANTI DELLA BASTINA... COMPOSITIONE DI CAMILLO SCAGLIERI DALLA FRATTA / Banchieri, A – (pseud.) 1597 – 9 – us Sibley [780]

NOBILITY OF ENGLAND WITH THEIR DESCENT / Douai Abbey – Ms. 100ff – 1 – uk Microform Academic [920]

THE NOBLE AND GENTLE MEN OF ENGLAND; OR, NOTES TOUCHING THE ARMS AND DESCENTS OF THE ANCIENT KNIGHTLY AND GENTLE HOUSES OF ENGLAND / Shirley, Evelyn Philip – Arranged in their respective counties. Westminster: J. Bowyer Nichols and Sons, 1859. vii,(1),315,(1)p – 1 – us U.W. Library [920]

Noble, CF *see* A VOYAGE TO THE EAST INDIES IN 1747 AND 1748

NOBLE DEPOSITARIO DE UNA HERENCIA DE AMOR / Argentina. Presidencia. Subsecretaria de Informaciones – [Buenos Aires, 1952?] – 1 – CSUXADP9148-B – us Hoover Inst Photo [972]

Noble, Earl G *see* ALTERATIONS IN 72 KILODALTON STRESS PROTEIN LEVELS FOLLOWING ECCENTRICALLY BIASED EXERCISE

Noble, Eustache Le *see* L'ECOLE DU MONDE OU INSTRUCTION D'UN PERE A SON FILS

Noble, Frederick Alphonso *see*
- DISCOURSES ON PHILIPPIANS
- OUR REDEMPTION: ITS NEED, METHOD AND RESULT

Noble, John *see* DESCRIPTIVE HANDBOOK OF THE CAPE COLONY: ITS CONDITION AND RESOURCES

A NOBLE QUEEN: A ROMANCE OF INDIAN HISTORY / Taylor, Philip Meadows – British Fiction Archive: Unit 5 – 9 – uk Bell [830]

NOBLE'S CURRENT COURT DECISIONS / New York. (State) – v1-2. 1908-10 (all publ) – 9 – $12.00 – LLMC 80-043 – us L.L.M.C. [340]

NOBLEZA DE CATALUNA / Corral, Juan del – Madrid: Hidalguia, s.a. – 1 – sp Bibl Santa Ana [946]

Nobre de Guzman, Armando *see* LIVROS IMPRESSOS NO SECULO 16 EXISTENTES... EVORA

Nocca, D *see*
- FLORA FARMACEUTICA...
- INSTITUZIONI DI BOTANICA PRACTICA

NOCES D'OR DE LA SAINT-JEAN-BAPTISTE: COMPTE-RENDU OFFICIEL DES FETES DE 1884 A MONTREAL / Charette, Pierre Ph – Montreal: Le Monde, 1884. 00579. (Pre-1900 Canadiana) – 9 – cn C.I.H.M. [971]

NOCES D'OR DE PIE IX: DISCOURS PRONONCE A CETTE OCCASION A LA SEANCE LITTERAIRE ET MUSICALE DONNEE A L'UNIVERSITE LAVAL, EN L'HONNEUR DU CINQUANTIEME ANNIVERSAIRE DU SACERDOCE DE SA SAINTETE, LE 10 AVRIL 1869 / Chauveau, Pierre J O – Quebec?: A. Cote. 1869. 02982. (Pre-1900 Canadiana) – 9 – cn C.I.H.M. [240]

NOCH EIN TSCHERNOBYL, WENN DAS VOLK ES WHYL-EINE ANARCHISTISCHE KRITIK AN DER GRUENEN FORDERUNG NACH VOLKSENTSCHEID / Blankertz, Stefan – 6p – 9 – 1.00f – at Libertarian Micro [335]

Noche, Diego de *see* PLACEME DE...AL EXCMO.SR.SECRETARIO DE ESTADO Y DEL DESPACHO D. JOSE M^A CALATRAVA...

NOCHE-BUENA EN FAMILIA / Gomez Bravo, Vicente – 1899 – 9 – $1.50f – sp Bibl Santa Ana [240]

NOCHE-BUENA EN FAMILIA : POESIAS Y DIALOGOS / Gomez Bravo, Vicente – 2nd ed. Madrid: Imp. de San Francisco de Sales, 1901 – 9 – sp Bibl Santa Ana [800]

NOCICONES Y TABLAS DE ARITMETICA / Sanchez Rodrigo, A – Plasencia Editorial Sanchez Rodrigo, SA, 1977 – 1 – sp Bibl Santa Ana [510]

NOCIONES DE AGRIMENSURA / Romero Morera, Joaquin – 1896 – 9 – $1.50f – sp Bibl Santa Ana [630]

NOCIONES DE ANATOMIA Y FISIOLOGIA HUMANA PARA USO DE LOS ALUMNOS DE PRIMERA ENSENANZA POR... / Pesado Blanco, Sergio – Trujillo: Tip. Benito Pena Pena, 1901 – 1 – sp Bibl Santa Ana [612]

NOCIONES DE ARITMETICA Y GEOMETRIA / Luna Gomez, Sergio – 2nd ed. Sevilla: Est. Tip. de Angel Saavedra, 1910 – 1 – sp Bibl Santa Ana [510]

NOCIONES DE ARITMETICA Y SU METRICO DECIMAL...ELEMENTALES DE NINOS... SEXOS / Cerro y Contreras, Felix – 1895 – 9 – 1.50f – sp Bibl Santa Ana [510]

NOCIONES DE DERECHO INTERNACIONAL MARITIMO,... / ed by Fernandez, C – Habana, 1863 – 2mf – 1 – ILM-1784/1 – ne IDC [327]

NOCIONES DE GEOGRAFIA DESCRIPTIVO-FISICO-POLITICA DE ESPANA / Rodriguez y Rivero, Cecilio – Valladolid: Im y Li. Nacional y Extranjera Andres Martin, 1903 – 1 – sp Bibl Santa Ana [320]

NOCIONES DE INDUSTRIA Y COMERCIO / Martinez Escobar, Jose – 1893 – 9 – 1.50f – sp Bibl Santa Ana [380]

NOCIONES ELEMENTALES DE ARITMETICA / Crespo, Nicasio – Badajoz: Tip. La Economica, 1905 – sp Bibl Santa Ana [510]

NOCIONES ELEMENTALES...QUIMICA / Martin y Castro, Florencio – 1847 – 9 – 1.50f – sp Bibl Santa Ana [540]

NOCIONES GENERALES SOBRE LAS OBLIGACIONES CONVENCIONALES... / Diez, J – Caracas, 1934 – 1mf – 1 – ILM-3026/1 – ne IDC [327]

NOCIONES Y TABLAS DE ARITMETICA... / Rodrigo, A S – Plasencia: Editorial Sanchez Rodrigo s.a. Imp. E.S.R., 1978 – sp Bibl Santa Ana [510]

NOCTES MUSICAE, STUDIO ET INDUSTRA MATTAEI REYMANI TORONENSIS BORUSSI CONCINNATAE / Reymann, Mathaeus – [Leipzig]. Editio est Voegeliana, 1598 – 1 – us Sibley [780]

NOCTURNES, TROIS, EN DUO POUR PIANO ET VIOLONCELLE (OU VIOLON)...1ER LIVRE / Duport, J L – (Score and parts) – Paris: Pacini, [182-?] – 1 – us Sibley [780]

Nodder, F P *see* THE NATURALIST'S MISCELLANY, OR COLORED FIGURES OF NATURAL OBJECTS, DRAWN AND DESCRIBED FROM NATURE

Node, P Le *see* DECLAMATION CONTRE L'ERREUR EXECRABLE DES MALEFICIERS, SORCIERS, ENCHANTEURS, MAGICIENS

DI NODEL = THE NEEDLE – (In Yiddish) – Vilnius, LT. 1913 – 1r – 1 – $25.00 – cn Can Microfilming [072]

Nodier, Charles *see* EXAMEN CRITIQUE DES DICTIONNAIRES DE LA LANGUE FRANCOISE

NODL ARBETER – New York, NY. 1924, 1932 – 1 – us A.J.P.C. [071]

NODULAR GRANITE FROM PINE LAKE, ONTARIO / Adams, Frank Dawson – Montreal: 1898. 02281. (Pre-1900 Canadiana) – 9 – cn C.I.H.M. [550]

Noe, B *see* VIAGGIO DA VENETIA AL SANTO SEPOLCRO, ET AL MONTE SINAI

Noel, Conrad *see* SOCIALISM IN CHURCH HISTORY

Noel de la Moriniere, Simon B J *see* PREMIER ESSAI (SUIVI DE SECOND ESSAI) SUR LE DEPARTEMENT DE LA SEINE-INFERIEURE

Noel et Chapsal *see* NOUVELLE GRAMMAIRE FRANCAISE

Noel, Martin *see* ESTUDIOS PARA LA HISTORIA DEL ARTE COLONIAL. VOL 1. ARQUITECTURA VIRREINAL SEGUIDA DE UNA ADICION DOCUMENTAL POR JOSE TORRE...BUENOS AIRES, 1934

Noel, Martin S *see* ESPANA VISTA OTRA VEZ

Noel, P *see* PETIT MANUEL FRANCAIS-KANOURI

Noel, Roden Berkeley Wriothesley *see*
- ESSAYS ON POETRY AND POETS
- LIFE OF LORD BYRON

Noeldechen, Ernst *see*
- DIE ABFASSUNGSZEIT DER SCHRIFTEN TERTULLIANS (T.U.U. 1-5/2A)
- TERTULLIAN'S GEGEN DIE JUDEN AUF EINHEIT, ECHTHEIT, ENTSTEHUNG
- TERTULLIAN'S GEGEN DIE JUDEN (T.U.U. 1-12/2A)

Noeldeke, T *see*
- BEITRAEGE ZUR SEMITISCHEN SPRACHWISSENSCHAFT
- NEUE BEITRAEGE ZUR SEMITISCHEN SPRACHWISSENSCHAFT

Noeldeke, Theodor *see*
- BEITRAEGE ZUR SEMITISCHEN SPRACHWISSENSCHAFT
- COMPENDIOUS SYRIAC GRAMMAR
- GESCHICHTE DER PERSER UND ARABER ZUR ZEIT DER SASANIDEN
- DIE INSCHRIFT DES KOENIGS MESA VON MOAB
- KURZGEFASSTE SYRISCHE GRAMMATIK
- NEUE BEITRAEGE ZUR SEMITISCHEN SPRACHWISSENSCHAFT
- DIE SEMITISCHEN SPRACHEN
- UNTERSUCHUNGEN ZUR KRITIK DES ALTEN TESTAMENTS

Noelle, Fritz *see* SICKINGENS RING

NOELS ANCIENS DE LA NOUVELLE-FRANCE / Myrand, Ernest – 4e ed. Montreal: Librairie Beauchemin, limitee, 1926 (imprime en Belgique). SEM105P1626 – 4mf – 9 – Can$9.00 – cn Bibl Nat [780]

Noer, Graf Friedrich Christian Karl August von *see* THE EMPEROR AKBAR, A CONTRIBUTION TOWARDS THE HISTORY OF INDIA IN THE 16TH CENTURY

Noerdlinger, H S *see* MOSES AND EGYPT: THE DOCUMENTATION TO THE MOTION PICTURE "THE TEN COMMANDMENTS"

NOESANTARA – (Lacking: 1946, V.1(2, 3, p. 32-96)) – Djakarta, 1946 – 3mf – 9 – ne IDC [073]

Noesgen, Karl Friedrich *see* DAS EIGENARTIGE DES CHRISTENTUMS ALS RELIGION

Noetscher, F *see* ELLIL IN SUMER UND AKKAD

Noeyes, H E *see* CHURCH REFORM IN SPAIN AND PORTUGAL

NOGALES INTERNATIONAL – Nogales, AZ. 1925- – 55r – 1 – $2,750.00 ($170.00y) – R01502 – us Library Micro [071]

Nogales, Rafael de *see* CUATRO ANOS BAJO LA MEDIA LUNA...

NOGLE UGRAESPLANTERS INDVANDRING I NORGE / Holmboe, J – (Nyt Magazin for naturvidenskaberne. v. 38. 1900). B-5295 2 – 8 – ne IDC [580]

Nohl, Ludwig *see* LIFE OF LISZT

NOI SAN NHIEN CUU LICH SU DANG = THE INTERNALLY-CIRCULATED JOURNAL STUDYING THE HISTORY OF THE PARTY / The Central Study Committee on the History of the Party – 1971 – 1mf – 9 SEL-126/1 – ne IDC [340]

Noie, Dennis R *see* USE OF VARIABLE BODY WEIGHT RESISTANCE IN DEVELOPING UPPER BODY STRENGTH

Noilhan, Henri *see* HISTOIRE DE L'AGRICULTURE A L'ERE INDUSTRIELLE

LE NOIR DE BONDOUKOU : KOULANGOS, DYOULAS, ABRONS(...) / Tauxier, Louis – Paris: Leroux, 1921 – fr Armell [944]

Noir, Louis Salmon *see* VOYAGES, EXPLORATIONS, AVENTURES

NOIR OR : LE BASUTOLAND, MISSION NOIRE, MOISSON D'OR / Bonhomme, Joseph – Montreal: Les Missionaires Oblats de M I, [1934] – us Res Libr [960]

Noirot, Ernest *see* A TRAVERS LE FOUTA-DIALLON ET LE BAMBOUC (SOUDAN OCCIDENTAL)

Noirot, Ernst *see* A TRAVERS LE FOUTA-DIALLON ET LE BAMBOUC (SOUDAN OCCIDENTAL)

Noirot, Louis *see*
- ETUDES STATISTIQUES SUR LA MORTALITE ET LA DUREE DE LA VIE DANS LA VILLE ET L'ARRONDISSEMENT DE DIJON DEPUIS LE 17EME SIECLE JUSQU'A NOS JOURS
- ETUDES SUR LE RECENSEMENT DE LA POPULATION DE DIJON EN 1872

Noiset, L *see* ROBESPIERRE ET LES FEMMES

A NOITE : FOLHA INDENPENDENTE – Manaos, Amazonas. 5, 13 Dez 1928 – 1,5,6 – bl Biblioteca [072]

A NOITE – Manaos, Amazonas. Jun 1914 – 1,5,6 – bl Biblioteca [072]

Noja Ruiz, Higinio *see* EL ARTE EN LA REVOLUCION; CONFERENCIA PRONUNCIADA EN EL CINE COLISEUM DE BARCELONA, EL DIA 21 DE MARZO DE 1937

NOKA KEIZAI CHOSA HOKOKU / South Manchurian Railway. North China Research Bureau – 5issues, 1937, 1938 and 1939. Agriculture and rural conditions of selected areas of North China. 1937-1939. (J 612.221 Mi37n). 1939. (J 612.221 Mi37na). 1940. (J 612.221 Mi37nb) – 1 – 35.00r – us Hoover Inst Photo [380]

Nolan, Edmond *see* THE GREEK GRAMMAR OF ROGER BACON AND A FRAGMENT OF HIS HEBREW GRAMMAR

Nolasco de Llano, Pedro *see*
- COMPENDIO DE LOS COMENTARIOS EXTENDIDOS POR EL MAESTRO ANTONIO GOMEZ A LAS OCHENTA Y TRES LEYES DE TORO...
- COMPENDIO DE LOS COMENTARIOS... ANTONIO GOMEZ...TORO

Nolcken, J H W von *see* LEPIDOPTEROLOGISCHE FAUNA VON ESTLAND, LIVLAND UND KURLAND

Nold, Guenter *see* MIMESIS DER WIRKLICHKEIT IM ROMANWERK C.P. SNOWS

Nolde, Clara *see* DIE SCHLUESSELGEWALT DER EHEFRAU INSBESONDERE BEI GETRENNT LEBENDEN EHEGATTEN

Noldeke, T *see* BEITRAEGE ZUR SEMITISCHEN SPRACHWISSENSCHAFT

Noldius, C *see* CONCORDANTIAE PARTICULORUM EBRAEOCHALDAICARUM VETERIS TESTAMENTI

Nolen, Desire *see* LA CRITIQUE DE KANT ET LA METAPHYSIQUE DE LEIBNIZ: HISTOIRE ET THEORIE DE LEURS RAPPORTS

NOLYNN BAPTIST CHURCH. HODGENVILLE, KENTUCKY : CHURCH RECORDS – 1857-1966 – 1 – 63.90 – us Baptist [240]

NOMADES ET NOMADISME EN ENNEDI / Massip, J M – 9 – F60.00 – fr Ethnologie [306]

NOMADISCHE STREIFEREIEN UNTER DEN KALMUEKEN / Bergmann, B – Riga, 1804-1805 – v1-4, 351, 352, 302, 355p – 8 – ne IDC [947]

NOMASTICON CISTERCIENSE / Paris, D Julian – New ed. Parisiis, 1670 – 34mf – 8 – Dfl119.00 – ne Slangenburg [240]

LE NOMBRE DES CHEVALLIERS QVI SONST MORTS AU SIEGE DE MALTE, L'AN MIL CINQ CENS SOIXANTE CINQ, TANT AU BOURG SAINCT ELME, QUE SAINCT MICHEL – Lyon, 1566 – 1mf – 9 – H-8167/1 – ne IDC [956]

EL NOMBRE NUESTRO DE CADA DIA. (MECANOGRAFIADO) / Belloso Rodriguez, Pedro – 1975? – 1 – sp Bibl Santa Ana [810]

NOMBRES CLAROS DE EXTREMADURA / Morales Marquez, Angeles – Badajoz: Tip.Vicente Rodriguez, 1914 – 1 – sp Bibl Santa Ana [946]

NOMBRES CLAROS DE EXTREMADURA, POR ANGELES MORAN MARQUEZ / T'Serclaes, Duque de – Madrid: Fortanet, 1915. B.R.A.H. 67, pp. 33-35 – sp Bibl Santa Ana [946]

NOMBRES DE ARTISTAS EN LA ESPANA ROMANA / Garcia y Bellido, Antonio – Madrid, 1955 – 1 – sp Bibl Santa Ana [700]

NOMENCLATOR AVIUM MUSEI ZOOLOGICI BEROLINENSIS / Lichtenstein, MH C – Berlin. 1854. Text in Latin and German. Z-1839 2 – 8 – ne IDC [590]

NOMENCLATOR AVIUM NEOTROPICALIUM / Sclater, P L & Salvin, O – Z 312 2. 1873 – 8 – ne IDC [590]

NOMENCLATOR BOTANICUS / Oeder, G C – Havniae. 1769. B-891 2 – 8 – ne IDC [580]

NOMENCLATOR BOTANICUS / Raeuschel, E A – Ed. 3. Lipsiae. 1797. B-6434 2 – 8 – ne IDC [580]

NOMENCLATOR BOTANICUS / Steudel, E G – 2nd ed, Stuttgardiae, Tubingae, 1840-1841. 2 vols. B-424 2 – 8 – ne IDC [580]

NOMENCLATOR BOTANICUS ENUMERATIO ALPHABETICA OMNIUM HUCUSQUE COGNITORUM VEGETABILIUM ADJECTIS PRAECIPUIS SYNONYMIS / Dennstedt, A W – 2v. Eisenbergae. 1810. B-630 2 – 8 – ne IDC [580]

NOMENCLATOR BOTANICUS HORTENSIS / Heynhold, G – 2v. Dresden, Leipzig. 1840-46. B-796 2 – 8 – ne IDC [580]

NOMENCLATOR DE ESPANA DE 1888, TOMO 1-5 / Instituto Geografico – Madrid, 1893-1894 – 55mf – 9 – sp Cultura [946]

NOMENCLATOR DE LAS CIUDADES, VILLAS, LUGARES, ALDEAS Y DEMAS ENTIDADES DE POBLACION DE ESPANA... / Instituto Nacional de Estadistica – Madrid: Scres. de Rivadeneyra, S.A., 1950 – 1 – sp Bibl Santa Ana [946]

NOMENCLATOR DE LAS CIUDADES, VILLAS, LUGARES, ALDEAS Y DEMAS ENTIDADES DE POBLACION DE ESPANA...CON REFERENCIA AL 31-12-1940. PROVINCIA DE BADAJOZ / Direccion General de Estadistica – Madrid: Barranco – 1 – sp Bibl Santa Ana [946]

NOMENCLATOR DE LAS CIUDADES, VILLAS, LUGARES...PROVINCIA DE BADAJOZ – Madrid, Tomo 4-6. 1973 – 1 – sp Bibl Santa Ana [946]

NOMENCLATOR DE LOS PUEBLOS DE ESPANA / Comision de Estadistica – Madrid, 1958 – 17mf – 9 – sp Cultura [946]

NOMENCLATOR ENTOMOLOGICUS / Herrich-Schaeffer, G A W – Regensburg, 1835-40. 2pts. Z/1344/2 – 8 – ne IDC [590]

NOMENCLATOR INSIGNIUM SCRIPTORUM,... / Gessner, C & Constantin, R – Parisiis: Apud A Wechelum, 1555 – 2mf – 9 – H-2545/1 – ne IDC [010]

NOMENCLATOR LITERARIUS RECENTIORIS THEOLOGIAE CATHOLICAE / ed by Hurter, H – Oeniponte. 4v. 1892-1899 – 67mf – 9 – ne IDC [240]

NOMENCLATOR LITERARIUS RECENTIORIS THEOLOGIAE CATHOLICAE, 1109-1899. / ed by Hurter, H – Oeniponte. 5v. 1903-1913 – 83mf – 9 – ne IDC [240]

NOMENCLATOR LITRARIUS THEOLOGIAE CATHOLICAE : TOME 1-4 / Hurter, H – Oeniponti, 1903-1911 – 96mf – 8 – ne Slangenburg [290]

NOMENCLATOR ZOOLOGICUS / Scudder, S H – (Alphabetical list of all generic names to close of the year 1879). 1. Supplemental list. 2. Universal index. 2053 2. 1882-1884 – 8 – ne IDC [590]

NOMENCLATORIS ZOOLOGICI INDEX UNIVERSALIS / Agassiz, J L R – Soloduri, 1848 – 17mf – ne IDC [590]

NOMENCLATURA DE LAS CIUDADES, VILLAS, LUGARES, ALDEAS Y DEMAS ENTIDADES DE POBLACION DE ESPANA...CON REFERENCIA AL 31-12-1940. PROVINCIA DE CACERES / Direccion General de Estadistica – Madrid: Barranco – 1 – sp Bibl Santa Ana [946]

THE NOMENCLATURE OF BRITISH INSECTS... / Stephens, J F – London, 1829 – [II], 68p – 8 – ne IDC [590]

NOMER PERINGATAN SETAHOEN PEMBANGOENAN DJAWA BAROE / Sinar, Baroe – (Microfiche Nos 165-167) – Semarang, 2603 – 3mf – 9 – SE-2002/1 – ne IDC [950]

NOMER SETAHOEN PERINGATAN / Sinar, Baroe – (Microfiche Nos 162-164) – Semarang, 2603.-1v – 3mf – 9 – SE-2002/1 – ne IDC [950]

NOMINAL INDEX FOR PRE-1904 SOUTH AUSTRALIAN NATURALIZATIONS, 1848-1903 – 12mf – 9 – CRS A7419 – at Archives [920]

NOMINAL INDEX FOR PRE-1904 VICTORIAN NATURALIZATIONS, 1847-1903 – 29mf – 9 – CRS A7796 – at Archives [920]

NOMINAL ROLL OF BETHUNE'S MOUNTED INFANTRY FOR SERVICE IN THE BOER WAR, 1899-1901 / Department of Defence, Victoria – 12r – 1 – CRS B5203 – at Archives [920]

NOMINAL ROLLS AND LISTS OF MEDALS AND CLASPS FOR NEW SOUTH WALES MILITARY FORCES WHO SERVED IN THE BOER WAR, 1899-1907 – 3r – 1 – CRS B5204 – at Archives [920]

NOMINAL ROLLS OF BATTALIONS FOR SERVICE IN SOUTH AFRICA, 1902-1902 / Department of Defence 1 – 15r – 1 – CRS B5207 – at Archives [920]

NOMINAL ROLLS OF THE 3RD MOUNTED RIFLES AND 3RD NSW IMPERIAL BUSHMEN, 1901-1902 – 6r – 1 – CRS B5198 – at Archives [920]

NOMINAL ROLLS OF THE QUEENSLAND DEFENCE FORCE FOR SERVICE IN SOUTH AFRICA, 1900-1903 / Chief Secretary's Office, Queensland – 4r – 1 – CRS B5172 – at Archives [920]

NOMINAL ROLLS OF VICTORIAN CONTINGENTS FOR SOUTH AFRICA, 1900-1900 / Department of Defence, Victoria – 5r – 1 – CRS B5179 – at Archives [920]

DIE NOMINALSUFFIXE IM RUSSISCHEN / Le Juge, Vasil von – Leipzig: R. Gerhard, 1906 – 1 – us U.W. Library [460]

NOMINATION PAPERS / Royal Institute of British Architects – 1834-1914 – uk World [720]

NOMMO – Los Angeles, CA. 1977-82 – 2r – 1 – $100.00 – R02395 – us Library Micro [071]

NOMS DE NAISSANCE: CONCEPTION DU MONDE ET SYSTEME DE VALEURS CHEZ LES GUN AU SUD BENIN / Saulnier, P – 9 – F70.00 – fr Ethnologie [306]

NOMS FEODAUX OU NOMS DE CEUX QUI ONT TENU FIEFS EN FRANCE DEPUIS LE XIIE JUSQU'AU MILIEU DU XVIIIE / Betencourt – Paris, 1826 – 3mf – 9 – F90.00 – fr F.F.G. [920]

NOMS GEOGRAPHIQUES DE LA PROVINCE DE QUEBEC ET DES PROVINCES MARITIMES EMPRUNTES AUX LANGUES SAUVAGES / Rouillard, Eugene – Quebec: Ed. Marcotte, 1906. SEM105P89 – 2mf – 9 – Can$4.50 – cn Bibl Nat [910]

LES NOMS PROPRES ASSYRIENS : RECHERCHES SUR LA FORMATION DES EXPRESSIONS IDEOGRAPHIQUES / Menant, Joachim – Paris: Benjamin Duprat, 1861 – 1mf – 9 – 0-8370-8598-5 – 1986-2598 – us A.T.L.A. [470]

LES NOMS REVOLUTIONNAIRES DES COMMUNES DE FRANCE, PAR DEPARTEMENT ET ORDRE ALPHABETIQUE... L'HISTOIRE DE LA REVOLUTION FRANCAISE / Figueres – Paris, 1901 – 1mf – 9 – F30.00 – fr F.F.G. [944]

NOMZANO WINNIE MANDELA, APPELLANT VERSUS THE STATE, RESPONDENT, IN THE SUPREME COURT OF SOUTH AFRICA (APPELLATE DIVISION) : RECORD OF APPEAL [CASE NO R5023/70.A.290/71] – Pretoria, 1971 – us Res Libr [340]

THE NONCONFORMI (THE INDEPENDENT AND NONCONFORMI-THE INDEPENDENT) – London. 14 Apr 1841-25 Mar 1900.-w. 66 reels – 1 – uk British Libr Newspaper [072]

NONCONFORMIST – 1841-80 – 1 – uk World [240]

THE NONCONFORMIST – London. -w. Apr 1841-Dec 1880. (40 reels) – 1 – uk British Libr Newspaper [072]

NON-CONFORMITY : ITS ORIGIN AND PROGRESS / Selbie, W B – London: Williams and Norgate; New York: Henry Holt, [1912?] – 1mf – us A.T.L.A. [302]

NONCONFORMITY IN THE 19TH CENTURY / Horne, C Silvester – London: National Council of Evangelical Free Churches, 1905. (Eras of nonconformity; 11) – 1mf – us A.T.L.A. [240]

NONCONFORMITY IN WALES / Lewis, Howell Elvet – London: National Council of Evangelical Free Churches, 1904 (Eras of nonconformity; 4) – 1mf – us A.T.L.A. [240]

NON-DECENNIAL CENSUS PUBLICATIONS IN MICROFORM, 1820-1945 : PART 1 / U.S. Bureau of the Census – (Individual sections may be purchased separately) – 16 sections. 1950 – 5934mf – 9 – $9,720.00 – us CIS [310]

NON-DECENNIAL CENSUS PUBLICATIONS IN MICROFORM, 1946-1967 : PART 2 / U.S. Bureau of the Census – (1 section on film. Individual sections may be purchased separately) – 14 sections. 1974 – 4226mf 181r – 9,1 – $13,080.00 – us CIS [310]

NONDESTRUCTIVE TESTING AND EVALUATION / ed by Palmer, S B – 1,5,9 – us Gordon [621]

NONDESTRUCTIVE TESTING INFORMATION ANALYSIS CENTER (NTIAC) – (Updated Every 60 Days) – Information Handling Services – 5 – us Info Handling [621]

Nonell, Iacobus *see* ARS IGNATIANA ANIMORUM AD DEUM PER CHRISTUM ADDUCENDORUM

NON-EXTINCTION OF CHRISTIANITY / Kennedy, R J Sinclair – London: Arthur H. Stockwell, 1901. 1 fiche – 9 – us A.T.L.A. [240]

NON-FICTIONAL WORKS OF H.G. WELLS / Wells, H G – 53mf – 9 – us UMI [880]

NON-FORMAL EDUCATION AND EDUCATION POLICY IN GHANA AND SENEGAL / Sine, Barbara – 1979 – 35p – 9 – 92-3-101659-8 – fr UNESCO [370]

NON-FORMAL EDUCATION FOR NATIONAL HARMONY AND DEVELOPMENT : A PROJECT FOR THE DEVELOPMENT OF LOCALLY RELEVANT ADULT EDUCATION PROGRAMS / Thailand. Ministry of Education – Bangkok, 1974 – 5mf – 9 – DE-290/1 – ne IDC [370]

NONFORMAL EDUCATION IN BANGLADESH : A STRATEGY FOR DEVELOPMENT / Bangladesh. Committee on Nonformal Education – Dacca, 1975 – 4mf – 9 – DE-531/1 – ne IDC [370]

NONG-CO MIN-DAM – Moi tuan le in ngay thu ba puis Causeries sur l'agriculture et le commerce. Saigon. mars 1910-12, 1915-nov 1924 – 1 – fr A.C.R.P.P. [073]

NONG-CONG-THU'O'NG – Journal d'agriculture, d'industrie et de commerce. Saigon. 1938-39 – 1 – fr A.C.R.P.P. [073]

NONGMIN RIBAO = CHINESE PEASANTS DAILY – In Chinese. Current subscription. Annual delivery. M D7. Apr 1980- . 1r per yr. As Zhongguo Nongmin Bao (Chinese Peasants Gazette) until 1985 – 1 – $55.00r – cc Microforms [072]

NON-GOVERNMENTAL SOCIETY / Carpenter, Edward – 1911, 14p. Extract only from his 1911 book: Prisons, Police and Punishment – 9 – 1.00f – at Libertarian Micro [335]

NONGYE JINGJI WENTI – Problems of Agricultural Economics. In Chinese but Table of Contents in English in each issue. F p6 – 9 – $4.50f – cc Microforms [630]

NONGYE JIXIE XUEBAO – Transactions of the Chinese Society of Agricultural Machinery. 1983. F/P 292 – 9 – $4.50f – cc Microforms [630]

NONLINEAR ANALYSIS – v1- 1977- – 5,6,9 – us UMI [510]

NONLINEAR OPTICS / ed by Kobayashi, Takayoshi – 9,5,1 – us Gordon [530]

NONLINEARITY – v1-. 1988- – 1,5,6,9 – £315.00 – uk I.O.P. [530]

NON-MILITARY ASPECTS OF INTERNATIONAL SECURITY – 1995 – 264p – 9 – 92-3-103073-6 – fr UNESCO [320]

NON-MULBERRY SILKS – 1979 repr 1981 – 195p – it F.A.O. [670]

NONNENSPIEGEL UND MOENCHSSPIEGEL DES EUAGRIOS PONTIKOS (T.U.U. 3-39/4B) / Gressmann, H – Leipzig, 1913 – 1mf – 9 – ne Slangenburg [240]

NONPAREIL – Burlington. Kansas. 1886-1893 – 1 – us UMI [071]

NONPAREIL – Central City. Neb. 1882-1953 – 1 – us UMI [071]

THE NONPAREIL – Toronto: Toronto Typographical Union, no 91, [1898-189- or 19–] – 9 – cn C.I.H.M. [331]

NONPOPULATION CENSUS SCHEDULES / Minnesota – 1860-80 – 17r – 1 – $30.00r – us M.H.S. [324]

NONPOPULATION CENSUS SCHEDULES / U.S. Bureau of the Census – 1850-80. Kansas. 48 rolls. A1130 – 1 – us Nat'l Archives [324]

NONPOPULATION CENSUS SCHEDULES / U.S. Bureau of the Census – 1860-80. Washington. 8 rolls. A1154 – 1 – us Nat'l Archives [324]

NONPOPULATION CENSUS SCHEDULES, 1850-60 / U.S. Bureau of the Census – Michigan. In the custody of the Michigan State Archives, Division of Michigan History, Department of State. 77 rolls. T1164 – 1 – us Nat'l Archives [310]

NONPOPULATION CENSUS SCHEDULES, 1850-60 / U.S. Bureau of the Census – Michigan, Mortality. In the custody of the State Library of Ohio. 1 roll. T1163 – 1 – us Nat'l Archives [310]

NONPOPULATION CENSUS SCHEDULES, 1850-60 / U.S. Bureau of the Census – Ohio. In the custody of the State Library of Ohio. 104 rolls. T1159 – 1 – us Nat'l Archives [310]

NONPOPULATION CENSUS SCHEDULES, 1850-60 / U.S. Bureau of the Census – Pennsylvania, Manufacturers. 9 rolls. T1157 – 1 – us Nat'l Archives [310]

NONPOPULATION CENSUS SCHEDULES, 1850-80 / U.S. Bureau of the Census – Massachusetts. 40 rolls. T1204 – 1 – us Nat'l Archives [310]

NONPOPULATION CENSUS SCHEDULES, 1850-80 / U.S. Bureau of the Census – (Virginia. 34 rolls. T1132.. Illinois. 64 rolls. T1133. Texas. 59 rolls. T1134. Tennessee. 39 rolls. T1135. Louisiana. 15 rolls. T1136. Georgia. 27 rolls. T1137. Iowa. 62 rolls. T1156) – 1 – us Nat'l Archives [310]

NONPROTEIN NITROGEN IN THE NUTRITION OF RUMINANTS / Loosli, J K & McDonald, IW – 2nd printing 1975 – 94p – it F.A.O. [636]

NON-SECTARIAN AND UNIVERSAL EDUCATION : IN RESPONSE TO THE SENTIMENT, OUR COMMON SCHOOLS, THE GLORY OF OUR REPUBLIC, UNDEFILED BY SECTARIANISM; OUR HOPE AND BOAST / Ullmann, Daniel – New York: Baker & Godwin, 1876 – 1mf – 9 – 0-8370-7596-3 – 1986-1596 – us A.T.L.A. [370]

THE NON-SLAVEHOLDER – (Series 1: v1-5 (all publ). 1846-1850. Series 2: v1-2 (all and last publ). 1853-54) – 20mf – 9 – $75.00 – us UPA [976]

THE NONSUCH PROFESSOR IN HIS MERIDIAN SPLENDOR / Secker, William – 1848. 262p – 1 – 9.17 – us Baptist [240]

NON-TIMBER USES OF SELECTED ARID ZONE TREES AND SHRUBS IN AFRICA – 1988 – 183p – it F.A.O. [634]

NONVERBAL BEHAVIOR OF NATIONAL FIGURE SKATING COACHES : EFFECTS UPON FEMALE ATHLETES DIFFERING IN AGE AND ATHLETIC MATURITY LEVELS / Miller-Tait, Jennifer & Bleuler, Sharon A – 1993 – 2mf – 9 – $8.00 – us Microform Publ [150]

NONVIOLENT DIRECT ACTION GROUP – Chavakachcheri. 79 docs. 1979-1991 – 23mf – 9 – ne IDC [320]

NON-VOTING DELEGATES, GUAM AND THE VIRGIN ISLANDS : HEARING BEFORE THE SUBCOMMITTEE ON TERRITORIAL AND INSULAR AFFAIRS... / Guam. US Congress – 91st Congress 2nd sess. 18-19 May 1970. Washington: GPO, 1970 – 2mf – 9 – $3.00 – LLMC 95-039 – us L.L.M.C. [327]

NON-VOTING DELEGATES, GUAM AND THE VIRGIN ISLANDS : HEARING BEFORE THE SUBCOMMITTEE ON TERRITORIAL AND INSULAR AFFAIRS... / Guam. US Congress – 92nd Congress 1st sess. 22 Apr 1971. Washington: GPO, 1971 – 1mf – 9 – $1.50 – LLMC 95-040 – us L.L.M.C. [327]

Nonweiler, T R F *see* LISTED ORDINATES OF THE "GUNACA" AEROFOILS A REVISION OF THE NACA 6 SERIES OF LOW-DRAG SECTIONS

NON-WOOD FOREST PRODUCTS : THE WAY AHEAD – 1991 – 45p – it F.A.O. [634]

DE NOODZAKELIJKHEID VAN DE INSTELLING EENER INDISCHE VOLKSVERTEGENWOORDIGING MET WETGEVENDE MACHT / Dwidjo Sewojo, MN G – 1mf – 9 – ne IDC [950]

NOOKS AND CORNERS OF THE NEW ENGLAND COAST / Drake, Samuel Adams – New York: Harper, 1875. 03761. (Pre-1900 Canadiana) – 9 – cn C.I.H.M. [910]

THE NOON PRAYER MEETING OF THE NORTH DUTCH CHURCH : FULTON STREET, NEW YORK : ITS ORIGIN, CHARACTER AND PROGRESS, WITH SOME OF ITS RESULTS / Chambers, Talbot Wilson – New York: Board of Publication of the Reformed Protestant Dutch Church, 1858 – 1mf – us A.T.L.A. [240]

NOONMARK – Exeter, NH. 1967-74 – 11mf – 9 – $5.00f – us Ross [830]

Noot, Jan van der *see* A THEATRE FOR VOLUPTUOUS WORLDLINGS

EEN NOOTWENDICH VERMANEN VNDE BEDACHTE REDEN, ALLEN GHOETWILLIGHEN IN EEN OPSIEN TER BETERINGE VOORGESCHREUEN / Joris, David – BME-375 1 – 9 – ne IDC [240]

NOOTWENDIGE VERANTWOORDINGE DER VERDRUCTER WAERHEYT / Iacob Iansen Kist en Hans De Ries – Nu Anno. 1591. Door Pieter Cornelisz predicant binnen Alckmaer... bestreden... BME-221 1 – 9 – ne IDC [240]

NOOTWENDIGE VERANTWOORDINGHE ENDE CLAER BEWIJS WT DE HEYLIGE SCHRIFTUERE / Outerman, J – 1599. BME-228 1 – 9 – ne IDC [240]

Nor. Evang. Luth. Kirke in Amerika *see* LUTHERANEN OG BIBEL-BUDET

NOR KYANK – Bucharest, Romania. Mar 1959-1961; 1972-83 – 7r – 1 – us L of C Photodup [949]

NORA MCCARTY / Webb, G J – Ms, Boston, 186- – 1 – us Sibley [780]

NORA STADS OCH BERGSLAGS TIDNING – Nora, Sweden. 1866-1964 – 1 – sw Kungliga [072]

DIE NORAG – Hamburg. may 16, 1924-nov 12, 1933 – 13r – 1 – gw Mikrofilm [072]

LA NORAMBEGUE: DECOUVERTE D'UNE QUATRIEME COLONIE PRECOLOMBIENNE DANS LE NOUVEAU MONDE, AVEC DES PREUVES DE SON ORIGINE SCANDINAVE FOURNIES PAR LA LANGUE, LES INSTITUTIONS ET LES CROYANCES DES INDIGENES DE L'ACADIE / Beauvois, Eugene – Bruxelles: F. Hayez, 1880. 04068. (Pre-1900 Canadiana) – 9 – cn C.I.H.M. [971]

NORBA – Caceres, 1928 – 5 – sp Bibl Santa Ana [073]

NORBA – Revista del Archivo Municipal de Caceres. Ano I, no 1, Octubre-Diciembre, 1928 – sp Bibl Santa Ana [020]

Norberg, D *see* LA POESIE LATINE RYTHMIQUE DU HAUT MOYEN-AGE

NORBORNE FIRST BAPTIST CHURCH. NORBORNE, MISSOURI : CHURCH RECORDS – 1868-1901 – 1 – 36.99 – us Baptist [240]

LE NORD – Brussels, Belgium. -w. 1 July 1855-30 June 1870; 17 March 1871-30 Jan 1892; 6 Jan 1894-17 Oct 1907. 75 reels – 1 – uk British Libr Newspaper [949]

LE NORD / ed by Hervieux, J-A & Nantel, G A – St-Jerome, Canada. v1 n2. 21 nov 1878-v23 n49. 21 mar 1901 – 4r – 1 – Can$60.00r – cn Can Microfilming [072]

LE NORD – Montreal, Canada. v1 n16. 29 jul 1915-v20 n28. 10 jan 1935 – 1r – 1 – Can$30.00 – cn Can Microfilming [072]

LE NORD – Ste-Scholastique, Canada. 12 mai 1864-4 mai 1866 – 1r – 1 – Can$40.00 – cn Can Microfilming [072]

NORD CONTRE SUD / Verne, Jules – Paris: J. Hetzel, 1887. 2v. 8 fiches. (Literature Collection) – 9 – 20.00 – fr Bibl Nationale [830]

NORD DEUTSCHE ALLGEMEINE ZEITUNG – Berlin. Jan. 1910-Dec. 1914 – 1 – 35.00r – us Hoover Inst Photo [072]

Nord, F R *see* DIE DROHENDE SICHEL

NORD HEBDO – Mont-Laurier, Canada. 1 sep 1972-v1 n10. 13-20 dec 1972 – 1r – 1 – Can$30.00 – cn Can Microfilming [072]

LE NORD MAURICIEN : REGARD SUR LE NORD MAURICIEN: SUPPLEMENT DU NOUVELLISTE – La Tuque. v1 n1. 22 jan 1980-16 dec 1980 – 1r – 1 – Can$35.00 – cn Can Microfilming [072]

LE NORD SOCIAL – Organe de l'Union regionale des syndicats libres du Nord de la France puis Organe des syndicats professionnels du Nord (C.F.T.C.). no. 18-415. Lille. aout 1921-35. mq no. 115, 298, 300, 303, 384 – 1 – fr A.C.R.P.P. [073]
DAS NORD- UND OSTLICHE THEIL VON EUROPA, UND ASIA / IN SO WEIT SOLCHES DAS GANTZE RUSSISCHE REICH MIT SIBERIEN UN DER GROSSEN TATAREN IN SICH BEGREIFFET... / Strahlenberg, P J von – Stockholm, 1730 – 11mf – 9 – ne IDC [947]
NORD UND SUD – July 1914-Dec. 1919. Missing: Dec. 1915; Apr. 1919 – 1 – 35.00r – us Hoover Inst Photo [072]
NORD UND SUED – (Publ since 1921 in Breslau) – Berlin. apr-jun, oct-dec 1877. 1879-95. jul-sep 1897. jan-apr 1908. jul 1908-09. 1912-20, 1927-28 – 26r – 1 – gw Mikrofilm [943]
NOR-DAR – (Missing: 1902(7,160-161,178,189)) – Tiflis, 1889-1903 – 3r – 1 – AR-2413/3 – ne IDC [072]
Nordau, Max Simon *see*
– ENTARTUNG
– THE RIGHT TO LOVE
NORDBAYERISCHER KURIER – Bayreuth, 1969- – ca 11r per yr – 1 – Dist. gw Mikrofilm – gw Misc Inst [072]
DER NORD-BERLINER – Berlin, 1951-82 (almost complete) – 1 – Inquire at Mikrofilmarchiv for details – gw Misc Inst [072]
Nordboehmischer Verein fuer Heimatforschung und Wanderpflege *see* MITTEILUNGEN
DIE NORDDEUTSCHE – Bremen-Vegesack, Germany. 29 Sept 1971- – 1 – gw Mikrofilm [072]
DIE NORDDEUTSCHE *see* NORDDEUTSCHE VOLKSZEITUNG
NORDDEUTSCHE ALLGEMEINE ZEITUNG – Berlin: Buchdruckerei der Nordd Allg Zeitung, jan 25 1882 (eve)-dec 29 1891 (morn) (20r); sunday suppls onyl for: 1888-mar 1893 (1r) – 1 – us Res Libr [072]
NORDDEUTSCHE ALLGEMEINE ZEITUNG – (Cont by: Die Internationale, nov 10 1918; Deutsche Allgemeine Zeitung, nov 12 1918. Also available: AUSGABE GROSS-BERLIN, 1919-apr 22 1945; REICHSAUSGABE, sep 2 1922-apr 29 1923, jul 4-dec 31 1925, jan 1-mar 31 1937) – Berlin, 1866-apr 24 1945 – 1 – Inquire at Mikrofilmarchiv for details – gw Misc Inst [943]
NORDDEUTSCHE ALLGEMEINE ZEITUNG – (Since nov 12, 1918: Deutsche Allgemeine Zeitung.) – Berlin. apr 22-dec 31, 1925. jul 1, 1936-aug 31, 1937 – 1 – gw Mikrofilm [072]
NORDDEUTSCHE FREIE PRESSE – Hamburg-Altona, Germany. Apr 1849-Jun 1850 – 2r – 1 – gw Mikrofilm [072]
NORDDEUTSCHE HANSA – Bremen, 1859-64 – 2r – 1 – Inquire at Mikrofilmarchiv for details – gw Misc Inst [072]
NORDDEUTSCHE NEUESTE NACHRICHTEN – Rostock, Germany. 1992- – 5r per yr – 1 – gw Mikrofilm [072]
NORDDEUTSCHE RUNDSCHAU *see*
– BREMER ZEITUNG
– ITZEHOER WOCHENBLATT
NORDDEUTSCHE VOLKSSTIMME – Bremerhaven, 1895, 1898-99, 1905 (single issues only), 1914-jun 1916, aug 1916-24, sep 1926-nov 1927, 1928-aug 31 1932, oct 14 1932, feb 1933 – 1 – Inquire at Mikrofilmarchiv for details – gw Misc Inst [943]
NORDDEUTSCHE VOLKSZEITUNG – (Cont: Vegesacker Wochenblatt, may 25 1846-sep 1860; Wochenschrift fuer Vegesack und Umgegend, -dec 1872; Vegesacker Wochenschrift, -jul 1881; Kreisblatt fuer den Kreis Osterholz, jul 9 1881; Vegesacker Wochenschrift, -mar 1885. Cont by: Nord-Kurier, jan 21 1971; Die Norddeutsche, mar 31 1979. Suppl available: 75 Jahre Norddeutsche Volkszeitung, may 10 1923; 80 Jahre Norddeutsche Volkszeitung, may 25 1928; Deutsche Heimat, apr 7 1929-sep 27 1931; Fuer die Jugend, 1929-31; Fuer die Landwirtschaft, oct 1932-37; Hitlers aussenpolitische Rede, may 18 1933; Illustriertes Sonntagsblatt, 1931; Die Jugend voran, 1936-37; Kreistierschau, sep 18-20 1927; Landmanns Sonntagsblatt, 1927; Die Niederweser, 1922-39; Partei-Sonderausgabe, jun 2, jun 30 1934; Ratgeber fuer Garten, Feld und Haus, 1922 (many issues missing); Unterhaltungsbeilage, 1931-apr 1934; Das Wochenende, 1934 (single issue only); Zum Zeitvertreib, jul 1934-35) – Bremen, may 25 1849-may 31 1941, sep 29 1971- – 1 – Inquire at Mikrofilmarchiv for details – gw Misc Inst [943]
NORDDEUTSCHE ZEITUNG – (Bereichsausgabe der Norddeutschen Zeitung, Hannover) – Goettingen. aug 3, 1948-oct 26, 1949 – 2r – 1 – gw Mikrofilm [072]
NORDDEUTSCHE ZEITUNG – Hanover. Germany. -d. 20 May 1948-30 Nov 1952. (Imperfect). (19 reels) – 1 – uk British Libr Newspaper [072]
NORDDEUTSCHE ZEITUNG – Schwerin, 1947 – 1r – 1 – DM75.00 – gw Mikro Press [072]
NORDDEUTSCHE ZEITUNG – Schwerin, East Germany. 1947; Jul 1954-1990 – 68r – 1 – gw Mikrofilm [072]
NORDDEUTSCHES VOLKSBLATT – Wilhelmshaven, Germany. 1887-1895 – 1 – gw Mikrofilm [072]
NORDDEUTSCHES WOCHENBLATT – Bremen, 1882, 1883 (single issues only), 1884-86, – 1 – Inquire at Mikrofilmarchiv for details – gw Misc Inst [072]
NORDDEUTSCHES WOCHENBLATT – Bremen. 1882-1886 (incomplete) – 2r – 1 – gw Mikrofilm [072]
NORDDEUTSCHES WOCHENBLATT – Germany, 1882-86 – 2r – 1 – DM150.00 – gw Mikro Press [072]
NORD-ECLAIR – Ed. de Roubaix puis Lille. Lille. sept 1944-45 – 1 – fr A.C.R.P.P. [073]
Nordeen, Lisa M *see* BELIEF IN MENTAL IMAGERY IN FREE THROW PERFORMANCE
NORDELBISCHE EVANGELISCH-LUTHERISCHE KIRCHE : GESETZ-UNE VERORDNUNGSBLATT – 1977-84 (complete) – 3r – 1 – ATLA S0590 – us A.T.L.A. [240]
NORDELBISCHE EVANGELISCH-LUTHERISCHE KIRCHE. SYNODE : BERICHT UEBER DIE VERHANDLUNGEN (1980) – 1980-91 (complete) – 5r – 1 – ATLA S0650 – us A.T.L.A. [240]
NORDELBISCHE EVANGELISCH-LUTHERISCHE KIRCHE. SYNODE : BERICHT UEBER DIE VERHANDLUNGEN DER SYNODE (1976) – 1976-79 (complete) – 4r – 1 – ATLA S0390 – us A.T.L.A. [240]
NORDELBISCHE STIMMEN – 1977-92 (complete) – Inquire – 1 – ATLA S0776 – us A.T.L.A. [073]
NORDEN *see* NORRBOTTENSKURIREN
Norden *see* SURVEY OF THE SOMERSET PROPERTIES OF THE DUCHY OF CORNWALL, 1611
Norden, Charles van *see* JESUS
Norden, E *see* AGNOSTOT THEOS
Norden, Hermann *see* FRESH TRACKS IN THE BELGIAN CONGO FROM THE UGANDA BORDER TO THE MOUTH OF THE CONGO
NORDEN INDUSTRITIDNING – Stockholm, Sweden. Industritidning Norden. -m. 1895-1905. 7 reels – 1 – uk British Libr Newspaper [073]
Nordenskiold, A E *see* VEGAS FAERD KRING ASIEN OCH EUROPA
Nordenskjoeld, O *see* WISSENSCHAFTLICHE ERGEBNISSE DES SCHWEDISCHEN SUEDPOLAR-EXPEDITION 1901-1903
Norder-Pietrzak, Michelle M *see* PERCEIVED BODY IMAGE
LE NORD-EST – Sept-Iles, 1 nov 1978-29 dec 1991 – 24r – 1 – Can$70.00 – cn Can Microfilming [072]
LE NORDEST – Sept-Iles. 14 jun 1961-v2 n46. 15 mai 1963 – 1r – 1 – Can$60.00 – cn Can Microfilming [072]
NORDFRIESLAND TAGEBLATT : BA DES FLENSBURGER TAGEBLATTS – Niebuell, West Germany. 1978- – ca 6r per yr – 1 – gw Mikrofilm [072]
NORDFRIESLAND TAGEBLATT – Flensburg, Germany. 1978- – 6r per yr – 1 – gw Mikrofilm [072]
NORDHALLAND – Kungsbacka, Sweden. 1883-1907 – 9r – 1 – sw Kungliga [072]
NORDHALLAND *see* NORRA HALLAND
NORD-HEBDO – Mont Laurier: Assoc cooperative d'information....v1-2. 1972-73. SEM35P28 – 1r – 1 – Can$20.00 – cn Bibl Nat [072]
Nordhoff, Charles *see*
– THE COMMUNISTIC SOCIETIES OF THE UNITED STATES
– GOD AND THE FUTURE LIFE
LE NORDIC – (Filmed with: Promo-Services/ Le Nordic 22 oct 1983-20 mar 1991. Le Plein-Jour sur la Manicouagan 27 mar 1991-25 dec 1991) – Baie Comeau, Haute-Rive, Canada. v4 n40. 20 sep 1967-14 oct 1983 – 34r – 1 – Can$75.00r – cn Can Microfilming [072]
NORDIC JOURNAL OF LINGUISTICS – (1981-. 1,5,6,9) – v1-. 1978- – 1 – us UMI [400]
DER NORDISCHE MERKUR : EIN JOURNAL HISTORISCHEN, POLITISCHEN UND LITERARISCHEN INHALTS. FUER DIE PREUSSISCHEN STAATEN UND DIE UEBRIGEN LAENDER DES NOERDLICHEN DEUTSCHLANDS / ed by Lange, Karl Julius – Leipzig. 3v. 1805 – 15mf – 9 – subsc: DM110.00 diazo DM130.00 silver – gw Olms [430]
NORDISCHE ZEITUNG *see* DER JUNG-DEUTSCHE ORDEN
NORDISK EKUMENISK ARSBOK – 1972-90 (complete) – Inquire – 1 – ATLA S0463 – us A.T.L.A. [240]
NORDISK LANTBRUKSEKONOMISK TIDSKRIFT – Stockholm, Sweden. 1950-74 – 4r – 1 – sw Kungliga [330]
NORDISK MISSIONSTIDSSKRIFT – v1-102. 1891-1991 (complete) – 18r – 1 – ATLA S0507 – us A.T.L.A. [240]
NORDISK ORNITHOLOGIE / Walter, J E C – 2117 2. 1828 – 8 – ne IDC [590]
NORDISK TIDSSKRIFT FOR TALE OG STEMME – Kobenhavn. 1936-64. v1-24. – 75mf – 8 – ne IDC [430]
NORDISK VETERINAERMEDICIN – v1- 1949- 1; v26- 5,6; v27- 9 – us UMI [621]
DEN NORDISKE KIRKES : GRUNDLAEGGELSE OG FORSTE UDVIKLING / Jorgensen, A D – Kobenhavn: Selskabet for Danmarks kirkehistorie, 1874-1878 – 2mf – us A.T.L.A. [240]
NORDISKE OLDSKRIFTER – v1-15, 17, 19-33. 1847-52, 1854-85 – 1 – us I.U. Libraries [390]
NORDISKT MEDICINSKT ARKIV *see* ACTA CHIRURGICA SCANDINAVICA
LE NORDISTE – Senneterre, Canada. 1 nov 1973; v1 n23. 11 avr 1974 – 1r – 1 – Can$25.00 – cn Can Microfilming [072]
NORD-KURIER *see* NORDDEUTSCHE VOLKSZEITUNG
NORDMAEHRISCHE RUNDSCHAU – Maehrisch-Neustadt (Unicov), Czechoslovakia. 7 Jan 1923-1938 – 6r – 1 – gw Mikrofilm [072]
NORDPOLEN – Pitea, Sweden. 1846 – 1 reel – 1 – sw Kungliga [072]
DER NORDSCHLESWIGER – Apenrade, 1972- – 1 – Dist. gw Mikrofilm – gw Misc Inst [072]
DER NORDSCHLESWIGER – Apenrade, jan 3 1948-91 – 1 – Dist. gw Mikrofilm – gw Misc Inst [072]
NORDSEE-ZEITUNG – Bremerhaven, jan 30, jun 22, oct 9, nov 3 1866, 1873, jul 7, dec 30 1874, aug 20 1875-jun 29 1884, 1885-jun 22 1886, 1887-89, jul 1-dec 31 1891, sep 1-dec 29 1894, jan 1-jun 30 1897, jan 1-jun 30 1898, 1899-jun 30 1901 – 1 – Inquire at Mikrofilmarchiv for details – gw Misc Inst [943]
NORDSEE-ZEITUNG – Bremerhaven, West Germany. 1968- – ca 8r per yr – 1 – gw Mikrofilm [072]
NORDSEE-ZEITUNG – (Filmed with Nordwestdeutsche Zeitung, Bremerhaven) – Bremerhaven, sep 20 1947-mar 16 1962, 1963- – 1 – Inquire at Mikrofilmarchiv for details – gw Misc Inst [072]
Nordstedt, C F O *see* INDEX DESMIDIACEARUM LOCUPLETISSIMUS
NORDSTERN : ORGAN FUER DAS DEUTSCHE VOLK – Hamburg, Germany. 4 Okt 1862-10 Feb 1866 (Incomplete) – 1 – gw Mikrofilm [072]
NORDSTJERNAN – New York, NY. 1872-1966 – 98r – 1 – sw Kungliga [071]
NORD-SUD – Revue litteraire. Paris. Dir., Pierre Reverdy.no.1-16. mars 1917-oct 1918 – 1 – fr A.C.R.P.P. [073]
NORDSVENSKA DAGBLADET *see* UMEBLADET
NORDSVENSKA POSTEN – OEstersund, Sundsvall. 1903-05 – 9 – sw Kungliga [072]
DEN NORDSVENSKE KOPMANNEN – Lulea, Sweden. 1913-56 – 5r – 1 – sw Kungliga [073]
NORDSVERIGE – Solleftea, Sweden. 1919-64 – 116r – 1 – sw Kungliga [072]
NORDSVERIGE – Solleftea, Sweden. 1965- – 1 – sw Kungliga [072]
DAS NORD-UND OSTLICHE THEIL VON EUROPA, UND ASIA : IN SO WEIT SOLCHES DAS GANTZE RUSSISCHE REICH MIT SIBERIEN UN DER GROSSEN TATAREN IN SICH BEGREIFFET / Strahlenberg, P J von – Stockholm, 1730 – 438p Index. Tabs – 8 – ne IDC [940]
NORDVARMLAND *see* FRYKSDALSBYGDEN
NORDVASTRA SKANES TIDNINGAR ENGELHOLMS OCH KLIPPANS TIDNING HOGANAS TIDNING ORESUNDSPOSTEN – Angelholm, Sweden. 1987- – 1 – sw Kungliga [072]
NORDVASTRA SKANES TIDNINGAR ENGELHOLMS TIDNING – (Eslovs Tidning, 1979-81; Hoganas Tidning, 1979-82; Hoganas Tidning Oresundsposten, 1982-84; Klippans Tidning; Landskronaposten; Oresundsposten, 1979-82) – Angelholm, Sweden 1979-84 – 1 – sw Kungliga [072]
NORDVASTRA SKANES TIDNINGAR ENGELHOLMS TIDNING OCH KLIPPANS TIDNING – (Hoganas Tidning Oresundsposten; Landskronaposten) – Angelholm, Sweden. 1984-87 – 1 – sw Kungliga [072]
NORDVESTPASSAGEN / Amundsen, R – BN-105 2. 1908 – 8 – ne IDC [910]
DIE NORD-WACHT – Wilhelmshaven, Germany. 1888-1890 – 1 – gw Mikrofilm [072]
NORDWEST – Bremen, 1878-94 – 9r – 1 – Inquire at Mikrofilmarchiv for details – gw Misc Inst [072]
NORDWEST – Bremen, Germany. 1878-1894 – 9r – 1 – gw Mikrofilm [072]
NORDWESTDEUTSCHE GASTWIRTE-ZEITUNG – Bremen, apr 1 1931-dec 20 1944 – 3r – 1 – Inquire at Mikrofilmarchiv for details – gw Misc Inst [072]
NORDWESTDEUTSCHE GASTWIRTE-ZEITUNG – Bremen, Germany. 1 Apr 1931-20 Dec 1944 – 3r – 1 – gw Mikrofilm [072]
NORDWESTDEUTSCHE HANDWERKS-ZEITUNG – (Title change: Deutsche Allgemeine Handwerks-Zeitung, 7 Oct 1932) – Hannover, Germany. 1917-1934 – 1 – gw Mikrofilm [072]
NORDWESTDEUTSCHE LANDES-ZEITUNG *see* BLUMENTHALER ZEITUNG
NORDWESTDEUTSCHE ZEITUNG – (Filmed with Nordsee-Zeitung, Bremerhaven) – Bremerhaven, aug 11 1895-mar 1906, jul 1906-may 11 1914, jul 1914-jun 1938 (incomplete), aug 11 1938-may 7 1945 – 149r – 1 – Inquire at Mikrofilmarchiv for details – gw Misc Inst [943]
NORDWESTDEUTSCHER LANDBOTE – Bremen, oct 1907 – 1 – Inquire at Mikrofilmarchiv for details – gw Misc Inst [072]
NORDWESTDEUTSCHES ECHO *see*
– DER KOMMUNIST
DER NORDWESTEN CANADAS : EINE ANREDE ZU WINNIPEG GEHALTEN / Argyll, John Douglas Sutherland Campbell, Duke of – Ottawa, 1881. 00822. (Pre-1900 Canadiana) – 9 – cn C.I.H.M. [971]
NORDWESTERN HAROLD – Wisconsin and Duluth, MN. 1901-06 – 3r – 1 – sw Kungliga [071]
NORDWEST-ZEITUNG – Oldenburg i.O., West Germany. 1969- – ca 13r per yr – 1 – gw Mikrofilm [072]
Nores, G de *see* ORATIONE...AL SERENISS. PRINCIPE DI VENETIA SEBASTIAN VENIERO, ...
Noret, J *see* THESAURUS LEONTII PRESBYTERI CONSTANTINOPOLITANI
NORFOLK – Norfolk. Va. and Portsmouth Herald. Title varies. 1802-59 – 1 – us UMI [071]
NORFOLK, 1822 : BRITISH ISLES CENSUS DIRECTORIES PROJECT, ENGLAND – (In prep) – at Vine [941]
NORFOLK, 1830 : BRITISH ISLES CENSUS DIRECTORIES PROJECT, ENGLAND – at Vine [941]
NORFOLK, 1836 : BRITISH ISLES CENSUS DIRECTORIES PROJECT, ENGLAND – (In prep) – at Vine [941]
NORFOLK, 1839 : BRITISH ISLES CENSUS DIRECTORIES PROJECT, ENGLAND. VOL 13 – 2mf – 9 – A$15.00 – at Vine [941]
NORFOLK, 1845 : BRITISH ISLES CENSUS DIRECTORIES PROJECT, ENGLAND. VOL 137 – 5mf – 9 – A$33.00 – at Vine [941]
NORFOLK, 1846 : BRITISH ISLES CENSUS DIRECTORIES PROJECT, ENGLAND – at Vine [941]
NORFOLK, 1850 : BRITISH ISLES CENSUS DIRECTORIES PROJECT, ENGLAND. VOL 85 – 2mf – 9 – A$15.00 – at Vine [941]

NORFOLK, 1858 : BRITISH ISLES CENSUS DIRECTORIES PROJECT, ENGLAND – at Vine [941]
NORFOLK, 1869 : BRITISH ISLES CENSUS DIRECTORIES PROJECT, ENGLAND. VOL 28 – 7mf – 9 – A$45.00 – at Vine [941]
NORFOLK, 1875 : BRITISH ISLES CENSUS DIRECTORIES PROJECT, ENGLAND – (In prep) – at Vine [941]
NORFOLK, 1879 : BRITISH ISLES CENSUS DIRECTORIES PROJECT, ENGLAND – (In prep) – at Vine [941]
NORFOLK, 1883 : BRITISH ISLES CENSUS DIRECTORIES PROJECT, ENGLAND. VOL 138 – 13mf – 9 – A$81.00 – at Vine [941]
NORFOLK, 1896 : BRITISH ISLES CENSUS DIRECTORIES PROJECT, ENGLAND – at Vine [941]
NORFOLK, 1912 : BRITISH ISLES CENSUS DIRECTORIES PROJECT, ENGLAND – at Vine [941]
NORFOLK, 1916 : BRITISH ISLES CENSUS DIRECTORIES PROJECT, ENGLAND – at Vine [941]
NORFOLK DAILY NEWS – Norfolk, NE. Jan 1888-Jun 1898; Oct 1898 to date – 1 – us NE Hist [071]
NORFOLK DAILY TIMES-TRIBUNE – Norfolk, NE. Oct 1898-Jun 1900, scattered issues missing – 1 – us NE Hist [071]
NORFOLK FAMILIES / Rye, Walter – 1913 – 1 – uk Microform Academic [920]
NORFOLK ISLAND / Maconochie, Alexander – London. 1848 – 1 – us Res Libr [980]
NORFOLK JOURNAL – Norfolk, NE. -w. (-sw 1897-1900). Nov 1877-Jul 1879, scattered issues missing; Jan 1880; Apr 1880-Mar 1889; May 1889; Oct 1889; Jan 1891-Jun 1894; Aug 1894-Feb 1895; Aug 1895; Oct 1895-Nov 1900 – 1 – us NE Hist [071]
NORFOLK (LYNN REGIS, NORWICH AND GREAT YARMOUTH), 1805 : BRITISH ISLES CENSUS DIRECTORIES PROJECT, ENGLAND. VOL 188 – 1mf – 9 – A$9.00 – at Vine [941]
NORFOLK NEWS – Norwich, England. -w. 1845-1918. Lacking 1898, 1912. 85 reels – 1 – uk British Libr Newspaper [072]
NORFOLK PRESS – Norfolk, NE. -w. Sept 1904-Jan 1908, scattered issues missing; Mar 1908-Oct 1938 – 1 – us NE Hist [071]
NORFOLK RECORD SOCIETY – (Coll title: Publications of the English Record Societies, 1835-1972...) – v1-39. 1931-70 – 99mf – 9 – £730.00 – uk Chadwyck [941]
NORFOLK TIMES – Norfolk, NE. -irr. Sept 1880-Sept 1881, scattered issues missing – 1 – us NE Hist [071]
NORFOLK TIMES TRIBUNE – Norfolk, NE. -w. Feb-Jul 1896; Jan 1897-Feb 1904; Apr 1904-Jan 1909 – 1 – us NE Hist [071]
Norfolk, Virginia *see* MISCELLANEOUS EARLY NEWSPAPERS
NORFOLK VIRGINIAN *see* VIRGINIAN-PILOT
NORFOLK WEEKLY NEWS-JOURNAL – Norfolk, NE. Sept 1884; Jan-Dec 1886; Sept 1887; Apr-Jun 1888; Dec 1888-Dec 1890; Apr 1892-Oct 1917 – 1 – us NE Hist [071]
NORGES HANDEL OG SJOFARTS TIDENDE = NORWEGIAN JOURNAL OF COMMERCE AND SHIPPING – Oslo, mar 1952-55 (24r); 1956-mar 1978 (83r); apr 1978-1981 (18r) – 1 – us Res Libr [380]
Norie, John William *see* THE NAVAL GAZETTEER, BIOGRAPHER, AND CHRONOLOGIST
Norlie, Olaf Morgan *see* THE UNITED CHURCH HOME MISSIONS
Norlind, Tobias *see* STUDIER I SVENSK FOLKLORE
Norlund, Poul *see* VIKING SETTLERS IN GREENLAND AND THEIR DESCENDANTS DURING FIVE HUNDRED YEARS
NORMAL ADDRESSES ON BIBLE-DIFFUSION FOR THE USE OF YOUNGER CLERGY, AND LAY-SPEAKERS IN GENERAL MEETINGS, TRAINING COLLEGES, AND SCHOOLS / Cust, Robert Needham – London:Elliot Stock, 1892 – 1mf – 9 – 0-8370-2799-3 – 1985-0799 – us A.T.L.A. [220]
THE NORMAL CLASS – v1-3. 1875-77 (complete) – 1r – 1 – ATLA S0711 – us A.T.L.A. [073]
NORMAL EVANGELISM / Green, Oscar Olin – New York: Fleming H Revell, c1910 – 1mf – 9 – 0-8370-6122-9 – 1986-0122 – us A.T.L.A. [240]
NORMAL SCHOOL APPLICATIONS / Fulton County. Ohio. Board of Education – 1914 – 1r – 1 – $32.50r – us Archival [324]
NORMAL TIMES *see* THE SPARTAN DAILY
O NORMALISTA – Rio Branco, Acre. 26 Jun-4 Ago 1969 – 1,5,6 – bl Biblioteca [072]
Norman College. Norman Park, Georgia *see* CATALOGS AND COLLEGE RECORDS
NORMAN FIRST BAPTIST CHURCH. NORMAN, OKLAHOMA : CHURCH RECORDS – 1889-September 1987. 2,686p – 2r – 1 – $120.87 – us Baptist [240]
Norman, J *see* LABOUR AND POLITICS IN LIBYA AND ARAB AFRICA
Norman Penney *see* RECORD OF THE SUFFERINGS OF QUAKERS IN CORNWALL, 1655-86
NORMAN PEOPLE AND THEIR EXISTING DESCENDANTS IN THE BRITISH DOMINIONS AND THE U.S.A – 1874 – 1 – uk Microform Academic [920]
Norman, S *see* AUTHENTIC ANECDOTES OF GEOGE LUKINS, THE YATTON DOEMONIAC, WITH A VIEW OF THE CONTROVERSY AND A FULL REFUTATION OF THE IMPOSTURE
NORMAN THOMAS PAPERS / New York Public Library – (With printed guide £26.00) – 85r – 1 – £4,800.00 – uk Chadwyck [920]
Normand, Jacques *see* LE CANARD
Normand, Rita *see* BIO-BIBLIOGRAPHIE DE GERARD MARTIN DE LA SOCIETE DES ECRIVAINS CANADIENS
Normand, Victor *see* LA CONFESSION
LA NORMANDIE ARTISTIQUE ET LITTERAIRE – Revue mensuelle. no. 1-33. Paris. sept 1896-mai 1899 – 1 – fr A.C.R.P.P. [073]
LES NORMANDS DANS LES DEUX MONDES / Lagreze, Gustave Bascle de – Paris: Firmin Didot, 1890. 03334. (Pre-1900 Canadiana) – 9 – cn C.I.H.M. [971]
THE NORMANS IN EUROPE / Johnson, Arthur Henry – 1883 – 1 – us A.T.L.A. [940]
NORMANSKII PERIOD RUSSKOI ISTORII / Pogodin, M P – M. 1859. BR-8317 2 – 8 – ne IDC [947]
NORMAS DE CONSTITUCION Y FUNCIONAMIENTO DE LOS CONSEJOS ECONOMICOS SINDICALES COMARCALES E INTERCOMARCALES O DE ZONA / Consejo Economico Sindical – Badajoz: Imp. Inca, 1967 – sp Bibl Santa Ana [330]
NORMAS DE CULTIVO PARA OBTENER BENEFICIO CON LOS MAICES... / Giralt Thovar, Arturo – Badajoz: Tip. Clasica, 1965 – 1 – sp Bibl Santa Ana [946]
NORMAS DE FUNCIONAMIENTO EN LOS CENTROS DE ALIMENTACION INFANTIL / Auxilio Social – Caceres: Tip. Garcia Floriano, s.a., 1941 – 1 – sp Bibl Santa Ana [946]
NORMAS DE HONORARIOS MINIMOS / Colegio Provincial de Abogados de Caceres – Caceres: El Noticiero, 1956 – sp Bibl Santa Ana [946]
NORMAS DE PROCEDIMIENTO EN CASO DE ACCIDENTE DEPORTIVO / Caceres. Mutualidad General Deportiva – Caceres, 1970 – 1 – sp Bibl Santa Ana [350]
NORMAS DE TRABAJO VIGENTES EN LAS INDUSTRIAS DE LA CONSTRUCCION YUNOBRAS PUBLICAS Y TABLAS DE LIQUIDACION DE SALARIOS / Rincon Martin, Jose Maria & Fermoso Palmeco, Aristides – Caceres: Tip. Jomarin, 1954 – sp Bibl Santa Ana [304]
NORMAS QUE HA DE TENER EN CUENTA EL QUE MANDA / Delegacion Provincial del Frente de Juventudes – Caceres: Tip. Floriano, s.a., 1943 – 1 – sp Bibl Santa Ana [946]
NORMAS Y CUESTIONARIOS PARA LAS CLASES ESPECIA LES DE ADULTOS / Inspeccion Provincial de Ensenanza Prima Ria – Badajoz: Grafica Jimenez, 1966 – sp Bibl Santa Ana [946]
NORMAS Y ORIENTACIONES PARA LA ENSENANZA PRIMARIA / Delegacion Provincial de Juventudes – Badajoz: Jefatura Provincial de Ensenanza, 1959 – sp Bibl Santa Ana [946]
NORMAS Y PRECEPTOS DEL JUEGO DE DOMINO. LEXICOGRAFIA, ETIMOLOGIA / Ubeda Sanchez, Jose – Badajoz: Imp. Argueros, 1961 – sp Bibl Santa Ana [946]
NOROESTE – Rio Branco, Acre. 15 Abr-Maio, 22 Jul 1917 – 1,5,6 – bl Biblioteca [072]
Norona, Andres *see* ESTATUTOS...CATEDRAL DE PLASENCIO
NORRA BOHUSLAEN – Grebbestad, Stroemstad. 1894-1933 – 9 – sw Kungliga [072]
NORRA HALLAND – Kungsbacka, Sweden. 1979- – 1 – sw Kungliga [072]
NORRA HALLAND – (Norra Hallands Veckoblad 1921-66; Norra Halland 1967-78) – Kungsbacka, Sweden – 72r – 1 – sw Kungliga [072]
NORRA HALLANDS TIDNING – Varberg, Sweden. 1864-76 – 1 – sw Kungliga [072]
NORRA HALLANDS TIDNING VESTKUSTEN – Varberg, Falkenberg, Halmstad, Sweden. 1876-1950 – 1 – sw Kungliga [072]
NORRA HALLANDS TIDNING VESTKUSTEN – Varberg, Sweden. Semiweekly ed. 1904 – 1 – sw Kungliga [072]
NORRA HALLANDS VECKOLBLAD *see* NORRA HALLAND
NORRA SKANE – AEngelholm, 1880-97 – 9 – sw Kungliga [072]
NORRA SKANE – Hassleholm, Sweden. 1899- – 1 – sw Kungliga [072]
NORRA SMALANDS TIDNING – Skaenninge, Motala. 1880-82 – 9 – sw Kungliga [072]
NORRA VASTERBOTTEN – Skelleftea, Sweden. 1910-78 – 353r – 1 – sw Kungliga [072]
NORRA VASTERBOTTEN – Skelleftea, Sweden. 1979- – 1 – sw Kungliga [072]
NORRBOTTENS ALLEHANDA – Pitea, 1891-1951 – 9 – sw Kungliga [072]
NORRBOTTENS ALLEHANDA – Pitea, Sweden. 1891-96 – 5r – 1 – sw Kungliga [072]
NORRBOTTENSKURIREN – Lulea, Sweden. 1979- – 1 – sw Kungliga [072]
NORRBOTTENSKURIREN – (Norden, 1861) – Lulea, Sweden. 1861-1978 – 463r – 1 – sw Kungliga [072]
NORRBOTTENSPOSTEN – Pitea, Sweden. 1847-1912, 1914-16 – 28r – 1 – sw Kungliga [072]
NORRBOTTNINGEN – Lulea, Sweden. 1979- – 1 – sw Kungliga [072]
Norris, J Frank *see*
– COLLECTION, 1925-52
– INFIDELITY AMONG SOUTHERN BAPTISTS ENDORSED BY HIGHEST OFFICIALS
– INSIDE HISTORY OF FIRST BAPTIST CHURCH, FORT WORTH AND TEMPLE BAPTIST CHURCH, DETROIT: LIFE STORY OF J. F. NORRIS
– INSIDE THE CUP OR MY 21 YEARS IN FORT WORTH
Norris, John Pilkington *see*
– A KEY TO THE NARRATIVE OF THE ACTS OF THE APOSTLES
– LECTURES ON BUTLER'S ANALOGY
– RUDIMENTS OF THEOLOGY: A FIRST BOOK FOR STUDENTS
Norris, Robert *see*
– MEMOIRES DU REGNE DE BOSSA-AHADEE, ROI DE DAHOME
– MEMOIRES DU REGNE DE BOSSA-AHADEE ROI DU DAHOME, ETAT, SITUE DANS L'INTERIEUR DE LA GUINEE; ET VOYAGE DE L'AUTEUR A ABOME, QUI EN EST LA CAPITALE. OBSERVATIONS SUR LA TRAITE DES NEGRES ET DESCRIPTION DE QUELQUES ENDROITS DE LA COTE DE GUINEE
Norris-Newman, Charles L *see* IN ZULULAND WITH THE BRITISH THROUGHOUT THE WAR OF 1879
NORRISTOWN REGISTER AND MONTGOMERY COUNTY DEMOCRAT – Norristown, PA. -w 1889-1912 – 13 – $25.00r – us I.M.R. [071]
NORRISTOWN WEEKLY HERALD – Norristown, PA. -w 1889-1912 – 13 – $25.00r – us I.M.R. [071]
NORRKOPINGS TIDNINGAR – Norrkoping, Sweden. 1787-1978 – 648r – 1 – sw Kungliga [072]
NORRKOPINGS TIDNINGAR – Norrkoping, Sweden. 1979- – 1 – sw Kungliga [072]
NORRKOPINGS WECKOTIDNINGAR – Norrkoping, Sweden. 1758-86 – 4r – 1 – sw Kungliga [072]
NORRKOPINGSOSTGOTEN *see* OSTGOTEN
NORRLAENDSKA ANNONSBLADET – OErnskoeldsvik, 1906-09 – 9 – sw Kungliga [072]
NORRLAENDSKA FAMILJEBLADET – Harnoesand, Sollefté. 1909-11 – 9 – sw Kungliga [072]
NORRLAENNINGEN – Sundsvall, 1887-94, 1900-02 – 9 – sw Kungliga [072]
NORRLANDSKA KORRESPONDENTEN *see* SUNDSVALLS TIDNING
NORRLANDSKA SOCIALDEMOKRATEN – Boden, Lulea, Sweden. 1918-78 – 380r – 1 – sw Kungliga [072]
NORRLANDSPOSTEN – Gavle, Sweden. 1837-67; 1901-56 – 1 – sw Kungliga [072]
NORRLANDSPOSTEN – Gavle, Sweden. 1868-1900 – 38r – 1 – sw Kungliga [072]
NORRLANDSPOSTEN – Gavle, Sweden. 1983-85 – 1 – sw Kungliga [072]
NORRON SYNTAX / Nygaard, M – Kristiania. 1905. BH-365 2 – 8 – ne IDC [400]
NORRORT – (Danderyds Tidning, 1979-82; Sigtuna Marsta Posten, 1979-82; Vaxholms Tidning, 1979-82; Vasbynytt, 1979-84) – Stockholm, Sweden. 1979-84 – 1 – sw Kungliga [072]
NORRORT – Stockholm, Sweden. 1957-78 – 34r – 1 – sw Kungliga [072]
NORRORT MED DANDERYDS TIDNING – Stockholm, Sweden. 1984-87 – 1 – sw Kungliga [072]
NORRORT MED VASBYNYTT – Stockholm, Sweden. 1984-87 – 1 – sw Kungliga [072]
NORRSKENSFLAMMAN – Lulea, Sweden. 1906-78 – 247r – 1 – sw Kungliga [072]
NORRSKENSFLAMMAN – Lulea, Sweden. 1979- – 1 – sw Kungliga [072]
NORRTELJE TIDNING – Norrtalje, Sweden. 1880-1978 – 183r – 1 – sw Kungliga [072]
NORRTELJE TIDNING – Norrtalje, Sweden. 1979- – 1 – sw Kungliga [072]
NORRTELJE WECKOBLAD – Norrtalje, Sweden. 1859-60 – 1 reel – 1 – sw Kungliga [072]
NORRTELJEBLADET – Norrtalje, Sweden. 1860-79. 3 reels; 1891-93. 2 reels – 1 – sw Kungliga [072]
NORRVIKENS TIDNING – Stromstad, Sweden. 1918-19 – 1 – sw Kungliga [072]
THE NORSEMAN – Saratoga, CA: West Valley College, Sept 1965-82 – 3r – 1 – $150.00 – B02983 – us Library Micro [370]
NORSK FLORA / Hoffstad, Olaf Alfred – Kristiania: Haschebhoug, 1893. 252p. ill – 1 – us U.W. Library [580]
NORSK GEOGRAFISK TIDSSKRIFT = NORWEGIAN JOURNAL OF GEOGRAPHY – 1959-1. 1981-. 1,5,6,9 – us UMI [910]
NORSK GEOLOGISK TIDSSKRIFT – (1981-. 1,5,6,9) – 1968- – 1 – us UMI [550]
Norsk Luthersk Kirche in Amerika *see* THEOLOGISK TIDSSKRAFT
NORSK LUTHERSK KIRKE IN AMERIKA : TEOLOGISK TIDSSKRIFT – v1-12 no 1. Oct 1917-Oct 1928 (complete) – 2r – 1 – ATLA S0243 – us A.T.L.A. [073]
NORSK TEOLOGISK TIDSSKRIFT – (Lacking: 1925) – v1-54. 1900-1952 – 8r – 1 – ATLA S0081 – us A.T.L.A. [073]
NORSK TIDSSKRIFT FOR SPROGVIDENSKAP = NORWEGIAN JOURNAL OF LIGUISTICS – v26-31. 1972-77 – 1 – us UMI [400]
NORSKE INTELLIGENSSEDLER – Oslo, Norway. -d. 1 July 1916-8 Aug 1919. 17 reels – 1 – uk British Libr Newspaper [072]
NORSKE KIRKE, TUNSBERG : BISPEDOEMME – 1951-83 (complete) – 1r – 1 – ATLA S0610 – us A.T.L.A. [073]
DEN NORSKE KIRKES GEISTLIGHED 1 REFORMATIONS-AARHUNDREDET (1536-1600) : BIOGRAFISKE, KULTURHISTORISKE OG KIRKEHISTORISKE OPLYSNINGER / Bang, A C – [S.l.]: A. Cammermeyer, [1897] (Kristiania: Centraltrykkeriet) – 1mf – us A.T.L.A. [240]
DEN NORSK-ISLANDSKE SKJALDEDIGTNING / ed by Jonssen, F – BH-361 2. 1912-1915 – 8 – ne IDC [430]
EL NORTE – Mexico, MX. 1982-1989 – 19r – $950.00 – R04217 – us Library Micro [072]
NORTE : REVISTA IBERO-AMERICANA – Paris, Jul no 1 1937 – 1 – us Hoover Inst Photo [073]
O NORTE : FOLHA DA MANHAN – Maceio, Alagoas. 20 Set 1888 – 1,5,6 – bl Biblioteca [072]
O NORTE : ORGAM DO PARTIDO CIVILISTA DAS ALAGOAS – Maceio, Alagoas. 8 Abr-Maio, Set-15 Nov 1910 – 1,5,6 – bl Biblioteca [072]
O NORTE : ORGAO DOS INTERESSES GERAES DO NORTE – Diamantina, 31 May, Aug 1906; Dec 1908; 23 Jan 1909 – 1,5,6 – bl Biblioteca [072]
NORTE DE ALAGOAS : ORGAO DO GENUINO PARTIDO DEMOCRATA NOS MUNICIPIOS DEMARAGOGY, PORTO CALVO, PORTO DE PEDRAS, SAO LUIZ E CAMARAGIBE – Passo de Camaragibe, Alagoas. 10 Jan, 5 Abr 1895 – 1,5,6 – bl Biblioteca [072]
NORTE DE GOYAZ – Porto Nacional-TO, Brazil. 15 Jul 1906; Abr 1908-31 Dez 1912 – 1 – bl Biblioteca [072]
O NORTE DE MINAS – Teofilo Otoni, 25 May, 23 Jul 1960 – 1,5,6 – bl Biblioteca [072]
O NORTE DO BRASIL – Manaos, Amazonas. 27 Jun, 15 Ago 1888 – 1,5,6 – bl Biblioteca [072]

NORTE MINEIRO : ORGAM DO PARTIDO REPUBLICANO MINEIRO DO MUNICIPIO – Pecanha, 19 Sept-11 Nov 1921 – 1,5,6 – bl Biblioteca [072]
NORTE Y GUIA PARA EL CAMINO DEL CIELO / Guerrero, Alonso – 1671 – 9 – 1.50f – sp Bibl Santa Ana [240]
NORTE Y MEDIODIA ...EXTREMADURA BAJA / Soler Arques, Carlos – 1894 – 9 – 1.50f – sp Bibl Santa Ana [946]
NORTEAMERICA Y LA GUERRA DE ESPANA: DOS DISCURSOS EN TORNO A LA ENTREGA DE UNA BANDERA DE LOS SOCIALISTAS NORTEAMERICANOS / Spain. Subcomisariado de Propaganda – n.p., 19?? Fiche W1080. (Blodgett Collection of Spanish Civil War Pamphlets) – 9 – us H.U. College Libr [946]
NORTH – (Cont by: North/Nord at v19 1972) – Ottawa. v6-18. 1959-71 – 5 – Can$100.00 – cn Micromedia [073]
NORTH = NORD – Canada: Dept of Indian Affairs and Northern Development, Jun 1959-Jan 1985 – 1 – cn Commonwealth Micro [072]
NORTH *see* NORTH/NORD
THE NORTH AFRICAN CHURCH / Lloyd, Julius – (Includes bibliographical references and index) – London: S P C K, 1880 – 1mf – 9 – 0-8370-7644-7 – 1986-1644 – us A.T.L.A. [240]
NORTH ALABAMIAN AND TIMES – Tuscumbia. Ala. 1870-72 – 1 – us UMI [071]
NORTH AMERICA / Hayden, Ferdinand Vandeveer – Ed. and enl. London: Stanford, 1883. 05648. (Pre-1900 Canadiana) – 9 – cn C.I.H.M. [970]
NORTH AMERICA – Toronto, Canada. -sw. 1850-54 – 2r – 1 – $136.00 – cn Library Assoc [971]
NORTH AMERICA / Trollope, Anthony – London: Chapman & Hall, 1862 – 2 rolls – 1 – 1-55879-980-X – uk Libr Preservation [975]
North America. Museums and Galleries *see* 196 ART EXHIBITION CATALOGS ON MICROFICHE
NORTH AMERICAN – (Biweekly newspaper publ in Mexico by Americans during the Mexican War) – oct 22, 1847-jan 1, 1848 – 1 – us Western Res [071]
NORTH AMERICAN – Swanton, VT. v1 n3. 6 apr 1839-v2 n11. 1 jul 1840. 26 jan 1841 – 1r – 1 – Can$50.00 – cn Can Microfilming [071]
NORTH AMERICAN – Toronto, Canada. -w. 1850-55 – 2r – 1 – $136.00 – cn Library Assoc [971]
THE NORTH AMERICAN – Philadelphia, PA. 1909-11 – 1 – us A.J.P.C. [071]
THE NORTH AMERICAN – Toronto. v1 n10. 15 nov 1850 – 1r – 1 – Can$25.00 – cn Can Microfilming [072]
North American Baptist General Convention *see* ANNUAL REPORTS
NORTH AMERICAN BIRD BANDER – v. 1-. 1976- – 1,5,6,9 – us UMI [590]
NORTH AMERICAN BOTANY / Eaton, A – Ed. 8. New York. 1840. B-5069 2 – 8 – ne IDC [580]
NORTH AMERICAN BOUNDARY : CORRESPONDENCE RELATING TO THE BOUNDARY BETWEEN THE BRITISH POSSESSIONS IN NORTH AMERICA AND THE UNITED STATES OF AMERICA UNDER THE TREATY OF 1783 – London: Printed by T R Harrison, 1840. SEM105P113 – 4mf – 9 – Can$9.00 – cn Bibl Nat [976]
NORTH AMERICAN COALITION FOR HUMAN RIGHTS IN KOREA (NACHRK) – Washington DC. 218 docs. 1980-1990 – 50mf – 9 – ne IDC [320]
North American Committee to Aid Spanish Democracy *see*
- FACTS ABOUT SPAIN TO BE USED BY SPEAKERS
- WHAT LIES BEHIND THE "PATRIOTISM" OF THE FASCIST EX-GENERALS: GERMANY AND ITALY AID THE REBELS IN ORDER TO TAKE POSSESSION OF SPAIN

North American Congress on Latin America *see*
- NACLA NEWSLETTER
- NACLA REPORT ON THE AMERICAS
- NACLA'S LATIN AMERICA AND EMPIRE REPORT

NORTH AMERICAN CONGRESS ON LATIN AMERICA (NACLA) – New York. 67 docs. 1980-1991 – 42mf – 9 – ne IDC [320]
THE NORTH AMERICAN CRINOIDEA CAMERATA / Wachsmuth, C & Springer, F – 1v. text, 1v. atlas. Z 2000. 1897 – 9 – ne IDC [580]
NORTH AMERICAN ENTOMOLOGIST / ed by Grote, A R – Buffalo. v1. 1879-1880 – 3mf – 9 – ne IDC [590]
NORTH AMERICAN HERPETOLOGY / Holbrook, J E – 2131 2. 5 v. 1842 – 9 – ne IDC [590]
North American Indian Association *see*
- BOW AND ARROW NEWS
- BUCKEYE SMOKE SIGNALS

NORTH AMERICAN INDIANS : FROM THE NATIONAL ANTHROPOLOGICAL ARCHIVES / Smithsonian Institution – 96mf – 9 – $105.00f – 0-226-76617-9 – us Chicago [930]
NORTH AMERICAN JEWISH STUDENTS NETWORK – New York, NY. 1 Oct 1971-18 Jan 1974. Continues: Network (New York, NY, 1970). Continued by: Network (New York, NY, 1974) – 1 – us A.J.P.C. [071]
NORTH AMERICAN LEPIDOPTERA / Grote, Augustus Radcliffe – Bremen, 1886. 63p. Z/1316/2 – 8 – ne IDC [590]
North American Metalworking Research Conference *see* PROCEEDINGS
NORTH AMERICAN MISCELLANY AND DOLLAR MAGAZINE – v. 1-4. Feb 1851-Aug 1852 – 1 – us UMI [073]
NORTH AMERICAN MORAVIAN – 1970-83 – 1 – us A.T.L.A. [073]
NORTH AMERICAN NOTES AND QUERIES – Quebec: R Renault, [1900-1901] (Quebec: Dussault & Proulx) – 9 – cn C.I.H.M. [970]
NORTH AMERICAN OOLOGY / Brewer, T M – Pt. 1: Raptores and Fissirostres. Z-1969. 1856 – 9 – ne IDC [590]
NORTH AMERICAN OR WEEKLY JOURNAL OF POLITICS, SCIENCE AND LITERATURE – v. 1. 19 May-24 Nov 1827 – 1 – us UMI [073]
THE NORTH AMERICAN PYRENOMYCETES; A CONTRIBUTION TO MYCOLOGIC BOTANY / Ellis, J B & Everhart, BM – Newfield. 1892. B-6522 2 – 8 – ne IDC [580]
NORTH AMERICAN QUARTERLY MAGAZINE – 1-9. Nov 1832-Jun 1838 – 1 – us UMI [073]
NORTH AMERICAN REVIEW – 1815- 1; v8-5,6; v260- 9 – us UMI [073]
NORTH AMERICAN REVIEW – v. 1-248. 1815-1940 – 1 – us Princeton Micro [073]
NORTH AMERICAN SHORE BIRDS... / Elliot, Daniel Giraud – New York, 1895 – xvi/268p, 72pls – 8 – ne IDC [590]
THE NORTH AMERICAN SLIME-MOULDS / Macbride, T H – 7579 2. 1899 – 8 – ne IDC [580]
NORTH AMERICAN STUDY CENTER FOR POLISH AFFAIRS – Ann Arbor. 41 docs. 1980-1990 – 22mf – 9 – ne IDC [320]
THE NORTH AMERICAN SYLVA, OR A DESCRIPTION OF THE FOREST TREES OF THE UNITED STATES / Michaux, Francois Andre – Paris, 1819. 2 vols. B-6067 2 – 8 – ne IDC [580]
NORTH AMERICAN VETERINARIAN – v.1-39. 1920-58. Continued by Modern Veterinary Practice – 1 – us UMI [073]
NORTH ANDOVER 1854-1905 – (Mf 1-2: Births 1854-87. Mf 3-4: Births 1887-1905. Mf 5-6: Marriages 1855-89. Mf 7-8: Marriages 1889-1908. Mf 9-10: Deaths 1855-90. Mf 11-13: Deaths 1890-1915. Mf 14-17: Birth Index 1843-1915. Mf 17-18: Marriage Index 1843-1915. Mf 19-21: Death Index 1844-1915) – (mf ed 1998) – 21mf – 9 – 0-87623-394-9 – us Holbrook [920]
NORTH ANTRIM STANDARD – Ballymoney. Ireland. -w. 7 Aug 1890-12 Oct 1922. (Wanting Jan-Mar 1921). (11 reels) – 1 – uk British Libr Newspaper [072]
North Atlantic Treaty Organization *see*
- NATO LETTER
- NATO REVIEW

NORTH BALTIMORE NEWS – North Baltimore, Ohio. 1975-87 – 5r – 1 – $32.50r – us Archival [071]
North Baltimore. Ohio. Church of the Good Shepherd-United Brethren *see* RECORDS
North Baptist Church *see* OUR CALENDAR
NORTH BAY NUGGET – Ontario, CN. 1908- – 12r per yr – 1 – $53.00r – cn Commonwealth Micro [072]
NORTH BEND ARGUS – North Bend, NE. -w. Apr 1890-Aug 1896, scattered issues missing; Oct 1896-Oct 1897 – 1 – us NE Hist [071]
NORTH BEND EAGLE – North Bend, NE. -w. Nov 1897 to date – 1 – us NE Hist [071]
NORTH BEND NEWS – (Set incl. Sun and North Bend News (North Bend); Sun-News (North Bend); 7 May 1970-27 Aug 1986) – North Bend, OR. -w. 4 Jan 1951-30 Dec 1976. – 18r – 1 – us U.O. Library [071]
NORTH BEND REPUBLICAN – North Bend, NE. -w. Sept 1895-Oct 1897, scattered issues missing – 1 – us NE Hist [071]
NORTH BERWICK FIRST BAPTIST CHURCH. NORTH BERWICK, MAINE : CHURCH RECORDS – 1768-1914 (Histories, 1868-1968) – 1 – 27.36 – us Baptist [240]
North Berwick, Maine. North Berwick Baptist Church *see* RECORDS
North Borneo. (United Kingdom) *see* TRADE MARKS SUPPLEMENT TO THE GOVERNMENT GAZETTE. JESSELTON. 1954-AUG. 1, 1963
North Borneo. (United Kingdom). Development Committee *see*
- DEVELOPMENT PLAN
- RECONSTRUCTION AND DEVELOPMENT PLAN

NORTH BRITISH AGRICULTURIST – Edinburgh, Scotland. v33 n32. 10 aug 1881-v34. 15 nov 1882 – 1r – 1 – Can$25.00 – cn Can Microfilming [630]
NORTH BRITISH REVIEW – v. 1-53. 1844-71 – 1 – us UMI [073]
NORTH BRITON – v. 1-46. 5 Jun 1762-12 Nov 1763 – 1 – us UMI [073]
NORTH BROOKFIELD 1841-1890 – (Mf 1-5: Births 1842-90. Mf 6-9: Marriages 1842-1890. Mf 10-13: Deaths 1841-90. Mf 14-15: Birth Index 1844-98. Mf 16-17: Marriage Index 1842-98. Mf 18-19: Death Index 1841-98. Mf 20: Births 1861, 1891-98. Mf 21: Marriages 1891-98. Mf 22: Deaths 1888-98) – (mf ed 1984) – 22mf – 9 – 0-931248-70-1 – us Holbrook [920]
NORTH BUCKS TIMES ETC *see* FENNY STRATFORD WEEKLY TIMES
North, C R *see*
- THE OLD TESTAMENT INTERPRETATION OF HISTORY
- THE SUFFERING SERVANT IN DEUTERO-ISAIAH

NORTH CALIFORNIAN – Oroville, CA. 1855-57 – 2r – 1 CB02576 – $100.00 – us Library Micro [071]
NORTH CAROLINA – 16r – 1 – $1,280.00 – us Scholarly Res [370]
NORTH CAROLINA : SESSION LAWS OF AMERICAN STATES AND TERRITORIES – 1777-1993 – 9 – $2,082.00 set – us Hein [340]
North Carolina *see*
- REPORTS AND OPINIONS (A-G)
- REPORTS, POST-NRS
- REPORTS, PRE-NRS
- SESSION LAWS, 1777-

North Carolina. Agricultural Experiment Station. Raleigh *see*
- AGRONOMY INFORMATION CIRCULAR
- ANNUAL REPORT
- BULLETIN
- CIRCULAR
- PROGRESS REPORT
- RESEARCH AND FARMING
- TECHNICAL BULLETIN
- TOBACCO ABSTRACTS

NORTH CAROLINA ATTORNEY GENERAL REPORTS AND OPINIONS – (6 1867-1979 $245.00. 9 1979-1992 $95.00) – 1867-1992 – 6,9 – $340.00 set – us Hein [340]
NORTH CAROLINA BAPTIST HISTORICAL PAPERS – With suppl. v1-3. 1896-1907 – 1 – $19.60 – us Baptist [240]
NORTH CAROLINA BAPTIST INTERPRETER – 1833-34 – 1 – 20.30 – us Baptist [240]
NORTH CAROLINA BAR – v.1-24. 1954-77. Continued by North Carolina State Bar Quarterly – 1 – us UMI [073]
NORTH CAROLINA BAR ASSOCIATION REPORTS – (With Constitution and Bylaws, 1885. Lacking: 38th meeting 1936) – 1st-50th annual meetings. 1899-1948 (all publ) – 55mf – 9 – $247.00 – LLMC 84-655 – us L.L.M.C. [340]
NORTH CAROLINA CENTRAL LAW JOURNAL – (v1-15 1969-85 on reel $170.00. v16-20 1986-92 on mf $61.00. Title varies: v1 1969 as North Carolina College Law Journal) – v1-20. 1969-92 – 5,6,9 – $231.00 – us Hein [340]
NORTH CAROLINA COLLEGE LAW JOURNAL *see* NORTH CAROLINA CENTRAL LAW JOURNAL
North Carolina. Dept. of Labor and Printing *see* STATE LABOR REPORTS
North Carolina Division of Archives and History *see*
- INDEX OF REVOLUTIONARY ARMY ACCOUNTS
- INDEX TO NORTH CAROLINA MARRIAGE BONDS, 1741-1868
- NORTH CAROLINA SUPREME COURT CASE INDEX, 1909-1929

NORTH CAROLINA EXTENSION EVALUATION STUDIES / North Carolina. State University. Raleigh. Agricultural Extension Service – v.1-5. 1957-64 – 1,5 – us Spaulding [630]
NORTH CAROLINA. GENERAL STATUTES OF NORTH CAROLINA – 1944-May 1996 update – 9 – $2,882.00 set – us Hein [340]
NORTH CAROLINA JOURNAL OF INTERNATIONAL LAW AND COMMERCIAL REGULATION – v1-18. 1976-1993 – 9 – $200.00set – us Hein [340]
NORTH CAROLINA JOURNAL OF INTERNATIONAL LAW AND COMMERCIAL REGULATION – v1-8. 1976-93 – $225.00 – us Hein [073]
NORTH CAROLINA JOURNAL OF LAW – Chapel Hill, NC. v1-2. 1904-05 (all publ) – 14mf – 9 – $21.00 – LLMC 82-950 – us L.L.M.C. [073]
NORTH CAROLINA LAW JOURNAL – v1-2. 1900-02 (all publ) – 12mf – 9 – $18.00 – LLMC 84-951 – us L.L.M.C. [073]
NORTH CAROLINA LAW REVIEW – (v1-62 1922-84 on reel $1,030.00. v63-73 1984-95 on mf $284.00) – v1-73. 1922-95 – 9 – $1,314.00 set – us Hein [340]
NORTH CAROLINA LIBRARIES – v1- 1942- 1; v28- 5,6; v35- 9 – us UMI [020]
NORTH CAROLINA MAGAZINE; OR, UNIVERSAL INTELLIGENCER – v. 1-2. Jun 1764-Jan 1765 – 1 – us UMI [073]
NORTH CAROLINA MAGAZINE: POLITICAL, HISTORICAL AND MISCELLANEOUS – v. 1. Aug 1813 – 1 – us UMI [073]
THE NORTH CAROLINA MANUAL OF LAW AND FORMS FOR JUSTICES OF THE PEACE, COUNTY OFFICERS, LAWYERS, AND BUSINESS MEN. / Jones, WN – Raleigh, Denmark, 1884. 387 p. LL-977 – 1 – us L of C Photodup [340]
NORTH CAROLINA MEDICAL JOURNAL – v1-1940- 1; v32- 5,6; v37- 9 – us UMI [610]
North Carolina Negro Associations *see* ANNUALS
NORTH CAROLINA SPECTATOR AND WESTERN ADVERTISER – Rutherfordton, NC: Roswell Elmer, Jr, mar 26 1830-feb 28 1835 – 1r – 1 – us Res Libr [071]
North Carolina. State Bar Association *see* PROCEEDINGS
NORTH CAROLINA STATE BAR ASSOCIATION PROCEEDINGS – 1st to 10th annual meetings, 1934-43 (all publ) – 12mf – 9 – $18.00 – LLMC 84-656 – us L.L.M.C. [340]
NORTH CAROLINA STATE BAR NEWSLETTER – v1-19. 1975-94 – 9 – $85.00 set – us Hein [340]
NORTH CAROLINA STATE BAR QUARTERLY – v1-42. 1954-95 – 9 – $380.00 set – us Hein [340]
NORTH CAROLINA STATE BAR QUARTERLY – v.25-. 1978- – 1,5,6,9 – us UMI [073]
North Carolina State University. Agricultural Experiment Station *see* PROGRESS REPORT SOC
North Carolina State University. Agricultural Extension Service *see* HOME ECONOMICS SERIES
North Carolina. State University. Raleigh. Agricultural Extension Service *see*
- ANNUAL REPORT
- CLUB SERIES
- EXTENSION CIRCULAR
- EXTENSION NEWS
- HOME ECONOMICS SERIES
- MISCELLANEOUS EXTENSION PUBLICATIONS
- MISCELLANEOUS PAMPHLETS
- NORTH CAROLINA EXTENSION EVALUATION STUDIES
- TAR HEEL ECONOMIST

North Carolina. State University. Raleigh. Agricultural Policy Institute *see*
- AGRICULTURAL POLICY REVIEW
- API SERIES
- UNNUMBERED PUBLICATIONS

North Carolina. State University. Raleigh. Dept. of Agronomy *see* RESEARCH REPORT
North Carolina. State University. Raleigh. Dept. of Crop Science *see* RESEARCH REPORT

North Carolina. State University. Raleigh. Dept. of Economics see
- AE INFORMATION SERIES
- ECONOMICS INFORMATION REPORT

North Carolina. State University. Raleigh. Dept. of Field Crops see RESEARCH REPORT

North Carolina. State University. Raleigh. School of Agriculture and Life Science see ANNUAL REPORT

North Carolina State University.Agricultural Experiment Station see
- BULLETIN
- RESEARCH AND FARMING
- TECHNICAL BULLETIN

North Carolina State University.Agricultural Experiment Station and Agricultural Research Service see TOBACCO ABSTRACTS

North Carolina State University.Agricultural Extension Service see
- AG
- EXTENSION CIRCULAR
- EXTENSION NEWS
- MISCELLANEOUS EXTENSION PUBLICATIONS
- TAR HEEL ECONOMIST

North Carolina State University.Agricultural Policy Institute see API SERIES

North Carolina State University.Agricultural Research Service see
- BULLETIN
- RESEARCH PERSPECTIVES

North Carolina State University.Department of Crop Science see RESEARCH REPORT

North Carolina State University.Department of Economics see
- ECONOMICS INFORMATION REPORT
- ECONOMICS RESEARCH REPORT

North Carolina State University.Department of Sociology and Anthropology see PROGRESS REPORT

North Carolina State University.Department of Soil Science. Agronomic-Economic Research on Soils of the Tropics see
- ANNUAL REPORTS 1972-75
- REPORT

North Carolina State University.Department of Soil Science. International Soil Fertility Evaluation and Improvement Program see ANNUAL REPORT TO THE AGENCY FOR INTERNATIONAL DEVELOPMENT

North Carolina State University.Department of Soil science. International Soil Fertility Evaluation and Improvement Program see TECHNICAL BULLETIN

North Carolina State University.School of Agriculture and Life Sciences see ANNUAL REPORT

North Carolina. Supreme Court see NORTH CAROLINA SUPREME COURT REPORTS

NORTH CAROLINA SUPREME COURT CASE INDEX, 1909-1929 / ed by North Carolina Division of Archives and History – Raleigh, N.C.: Division of Archives and History, 1988 – 9mf – 9 – $50.00 set – us NC Archives [340]

NORTH CAROLINA SUPREME COURT REPORTS / North Carolina. Supreme Court – (Pre-NRS: v1-95 1778-1886 614mf $921.00. Updates planned) – v1-326: 1778-1990 – 2914mf – $4,371.00 – LLMC 82-987 – us L.L.M.C. [340]

NORTH CAROLINA SUPREME COURT REPORTS see CAROLINA LAW REPOSITORY

NORTH CAROLINA'S CONTRIBUTION TO THE LAW. / Patterson, Lindsay – Charlotte, N.C.: Observer, 1906. 26p. LL-1390 – 1 – us L of C Photodup [340]

NORTH CENTRAL ASSOCIATION QUARTERLY – v1- 1926- 1; v51- 5,6,9 – us UMI [073]

North Central Weed Control Conference see PROCEEDINGS

NORTH CHESHIRE REFORMER – (Stockport Chronicle Macclesfield, Stockport, and Congleton Chronicle). 8 Jul 1836-26 Dec 1848. -w. (5 reels) – 1 – uk British Libr Newspaper [072]

NORTH CHESIRE HERALD – Hyde, England. 1860-88, 1974-77.-w. 27 reels – 1 – uk British Libr Newspaper [072]

NORTH CHINA DAILY NEWS – Shanghai. China. 1866-1951 – 1 – 8344.00 – us Chinese Res [072]

NORTH CHINA DAILY NEWS – Shanghai. China. -d. Jan-Dec 1869, Jan-Dec 1871, Jul 1872-Dec 1874, Jul 1875-Jun 1877, Jan 1878-Jun 1879, Jan 1889-Jun 1893. (25 reels) – 1 – uk British Libr Newspaper [072]

NORTH CHINA HERALD – China. 1850-1941 – 1 – us UMI [072]

NORTH CHINA HERALD AND SUPREME COURT AND CONSULAR GAZETTE – 1852-1907 – 1 – $35.00r – us Hoover Inst Photo [950]

NORTH CHINA HERALD, AND SUPREME COURT AND CONSULAR GAZETTE – (Some missing vols) – Shanghai, 1868-1886 – 385mf – 9 – ne IDC [950]

NORTH CHINA STANDARD = HUA-PEI CHENG PAO – Peking: Standard Press, jan 5-dec 1927 – 4r – 1 – us Res Libr [072]

NORTH CHINA STAR – Peking, 1919-21 – 3r – 1 – us Ross [072]

NORTH CHINA STAR – Peking Tientsin, China. Jan 19 1919-Mar 31 1921. Incomplete – 1 – us NY Public [072]

NORTH CLACKAMAS NEWS – Milwaukie OR. Jan 5 1966-Feb 22 1967 – 1 – us U.O. Library [071]

NORTH COAST RIPSAW; RANK AND FILE REPORTER; HUMBOLDT INDEPENDENT NEWS – Eureka, CA. 1969-70; 1970-80; 1973-74 – 1 – $50.00 – B03215 – us Library Micro [071]

NORTH COAST TIMES EAGLE – Wheeler, OR. -w. 13 May 1971-12 Mar 1976. – 2r – 1 – us U.O. Library [071]

NORTH COAST VIEW see NORTH COUNTY CONSTITUTION; NORTH COAST VIEW

NORTH COTSWOLD STANDARD – (Also known as: Cotswold Standard) – Jan-Dec 1986; 1987-Jun 1996 – 17r – 1 – uk British Libr Newspaper [072]

THE NORTH COUNTRY, A HISTORY OF JEFFERSON, ST LAWRENCE, OSWEGO, LEWIS AND FRANKLIN COUNTIES / Landon, Harry F – Indianapolis, Historical Publ. Co., 1932. Vols. 1-3. New York Reel 2. (The Cox Library Collection) – 5 – us Americana [978]

NORTH COUNTRY CATHOLIC – Ogdensburg. N.Y. -w. 1946- – 1 – us UMI [071]

NORTH COUNTY CONSTITUTION; NORTH COAST VIEW – Eureka, CA. 1975-76; 1982-89 – 4r – 1 – $200.00 – B03216 – us Library Micro [071]

NORTH COUNTY LIBRARIES – v.1-14. 1957-71 – 1 – us UMI [020]

NORTH COUNTY NEWS – (Also known as: Times Journal-Castroville Times) – Salinas, CA. 1978-81 – 4r – 1 – $200.00 – B02755 – us Library Micro [071]

NORTH COUNTY NEWS, SALINAS see CASTROVILLE TIMES/NORTH COUNTY NEWS

NORTH DAKOTA : CENTURY CODE ANNOTATED – Charlottesville: Michie Co, 1959-May 1996 update – 9 – $1,197.00 set – us Hein [340]

NORTH DAKOTA : SESSION LAWS OF AMERICAN STATES AND TERRITORIES – 1889-1995 – 9 – $782.00 set – us Hein [340]

North Dakota see
- REPORTS AND OPINIONS (A-G)
- SESSION LAWS

North Dakota. Agricultural Experiment Station. Dickinson see
- ANNUAL REPORT.NOS.1-6. 1909-13
- LIVESTOCK RESEARCH ROUNDUP

North Dakota. Agricultural Experiment Station. Edgely see ANNUAL REPORT

North Dakota. Agricultural Experiment Station. Fargo see
- AGRICULTURAL COLLEGE SPECIAL BULLETIN: FOOD DEPT
- AGRICULTURAL ECONOMIC REPORT
- AGRONOMY MIMEOGRAPH CIRCULAR
- ANNUAL REPORT
- BULLETIN
- CIRCULAR
- NORTH DAKOTA FARM RESEARCH BIMONTHLY BULLETIN
- NORTH DAKOTA FARMERS' INSTITUTE ANNUAL
- PAINT BULLETIN
- PRESS BULLETINS
- RESEARCH REPORT
- SPECIAL SEED BULLETIN
- STATE DEMONSTRATION FARMS ANNUAL REPORT

North Dakota. Agricultural Experiment Station. Fargo. Dept. of Agricultural Economics see
- AGRICULTURAL ECONOMICS MISCELLANY REPORT
- AGRICULTURAL ECONOMICS STATISTICAL SERIES
- AGRICULTURAL STATISTICS
- NORTH DAKOTA CROP AND LIVESTOCK STATISTICS

North Dakota. Agricultural Experiment Station. Langdon see ANNUAL REPORT

North Dakota. Agricultural Experiment Station. Williston see ANNUAL REPORT

NORTH DAKOTA ATTORNEY GENERAL REPORTS AND OPINIONS – (6 1889-1979 $140.00. 9 1979-1994 $160.00) – 1889-1994 – 6,9 – $300.00set – us Hein [340]

NORTH DAKOTA BAPTIST BULLETIN/NORTH DAKOTA BAPTIST NEWSLETTER – Lisbon/ Grand Forks/Fargo, ND; Sioux Falls, SD. ND Baptist State Convention. 1916-82. Single reels available – 1 – 125.50 – us A.B.H.S. [073]

NORTH DAKOTA BAPTIST HALF CENTURY BOOK – By Fred E. Stockton. Unpublished mss, 1934 – 1 – us A.B.H.S. [240]

NORTH DAKOTA BAR ASSOCIATION REPORTS – 1899-1928 (all publ) – 22mf – $99.00 – LLMC 84-657 – us L.L.M.C. [073]

NORTH DAKOTA BAR BRIEFS see NORTH DAKOTA LAW REVIEW

NORTH DAKOTA CROP AND LIVESTOCK STATISTICS / North Dakota. Agricultural Experiment Station. Fargo. Dept. of Agricultural Economics – 1956-57 – 1,5,6 – us Spaulding [630]

North Dakota. Dept. of Agriculture and Labor see STATE LABOR REPORTS

NORTH DAKOTA FARM RESEARCH BIMONTHLY BULLETIN / North Dakota. Agricultural Experiment Station. Fargo – v.1-33. 1938-75 – 1,5,6 – us Spaulding [630]

NORTH DAKOTA FARMERS' INSTITUTE ANNUAL / North Dakota. Agricultural Experiment Station. Fargo – nos.1-13. 1900-16 – 1,5,6 – us Spaulding [630]

NORTH DAKOTA HISTORY – v1- 1926- 1; v38- 5,6; v43- 9 – us UMI [978]

NORTH DAKOTA HISTORY AND PEOPLE / Lounsberry, Clement A – Chicago: S.J. Clarke Publ. Co., 1917. 3v. North Dakota Reel 1.(The Cox Library Collection) – 5 – us Americana [978]

THE NORTH DAKOTA JUDICIAL EDUCATION PLAN / Gladden, Ted – Bismarck 1975. LL-2366 – 1 – us L of C Photodup [340]

NORTH DAKOTA LAW REVIEW – (v1-60 1924-84 on reel $510.00. v61-71 1985-95 on mf $207.00. Title varies: v1-24 no 1 Dec 1924-Jan 1948 as Bar Briefs. v24 no 2-26 Apr 1948- Oct 1959 as North Dakota Bar Briefs) – 5,6,9 – $719.00 set – us Hein [340]

North Dakota. State Bar Association see PROCEEDINGS

NORTH DAKOTA STATE BAR NEWSLETTER – (Filming in process) – 9 – Inquire – us Hein [340]

North Dakota. Supreme Court see NORTH DAKOTA SUPREME COURT REPORTS

NORTH DAKOTA SUPREME COURT REPORTS / North Dakota. Supreme Court – (Pre-NRS vols listed under Dakota Reports. Updates planned) – v1-40. 1890-1918 – 65mf – 9 – $473.00 – LLMC 84-166 – us L.L.M.C. [340]

North Dakota. University. Agricultural Experiment Station see
- SEED CALENDAR BULLETIN
- SEED CIRCULAR
- WESTERN DAKOTA SHEEP DAY

NORTH DEVON JOURNAL – Barnstaple. England. -w. Jan 1827-Dec 1853. (Wanting 1850-52). (9 reels) – 1 – uk British Libr Newspaper [072]

NORTH DOUGLAS HERALD – Drain, OR. -w. 3 July 1914-2 Jun 1916. – 1 – us U.O. Library [071]

NORTH EAST BAPTIST CHURCH. MILLERTOWN, NEW YORK : CHURCH RECORDS – 1751, 1761-1815. (Book 1), 1815-41 and Historical Sketches, 1753-1815 (Book 2). 618p – 1 – 27.81 – us Baptist [240]

NORTH EAST BAY INDEPENDENT AND GAZETTE – (Cont: Richmond Independent. Cont by: Contra Costa Independent) – Richmond, CA. May 1978-Feb 1982 – 85r – 1 – $4,250.00 – B02695 – us Library Micro [071]

NORTH EAST BAY INDEPENDENT AND GAZETTE see
- BERKELEY DAILY GAZETTE
- CONTRA COSTA INDEPENDENT
- THE INDEPENDENT

NORTH EAST DISTRICT DEVELOPMENT PLAN 1989-1995 / Botswana. North East District – Gaborone, 1990 – 3mf – 9 – ne IDC [338]

NORTH EAST KENT NEWS see FAVERSHAM NEWS AND EAST KENT JOURNAL

NORTH & EAST LONDON STAR – London, England. North London Press & Star – North London Press. -w. 30 March 1889-25 Jan 1980. 2 reels – 1 – uk British Libr Newspaper [072]

NORTH EASTERN DAILY GAZETTE – Middlesbrough, England. -d. Jan 1889-Dec 1919. Lacking Jan-Feb 1906; Jan-Dec 1911. 73 reels – 1 – uk British Libr Newspaper [072]

North Egremont, Massachusetts. North Egremont Baptist Church see RECORDS

North, Eric McCoy see EARLY METHODIST PHILANTHROPY

North, F A see HISTORY OF PETTIS COUNTY

NORTH FAIRFIELD GAZETTE – North Fairfield, Ohio. 1856-1860 – 2r – 1 – $32.50r – us Archival [071]

NORTH FORK BAPTIST CHURCH. VIRGILINA, VIRGINIA : CHURCH RECORDS – 1884-1976 – 1 – 59.40 – us Baptist [240]

North Frodingham. Yorkshire see PARISH REGISTERS

North, George see THE DESCRIPTION OF SWEDLAND, GOTLAND, AND FINLAND

NORTH HOLLYWOOD – 1977; 1979-86 – 18r – 1 – $900.00 – P00035 – us Library Micro [910]

NORTH HOLLYWOOD (SAN FERNANDO) VALLEY TIMES – North Hollywood, CA. 1938-58; Feb-Mar 1970 – 149r – 1 – $7,450.00 – C02530 – us Library Micro [071]

NORTH INDIA / Andrews, CF – London: A.R. Mowbray, 1908 – 1mf – us A.T.L.A. [240]

NORTH INDIA CHURCHMAN – (Many issues misnumbered) – 1971-1988 (complete) – 4r – 1 – ATLA S0622 – us A.T.L.A. [073]

NORTH IOWA TIMES – McGregor. Iowa. -w. 1856-57 – 1 – us UMI [071]

NORTH ISLAND GAZETTE – (1965-1992) – Port Hardy, 1993 – 1 – cn Preston [971]

NORTH ITALIAN SERVICES OF THE 11TH CENTURY / Lambot, C – 1931 – 3mf – 8 – ne Slangenburg [240]

North, Joseph see MEN IN THE RANKS; THE STORY OF 12 AMERICANS IN SPAIN

NORTH KINGSTON BAPTIST CHURCH. RHODE ISLAND : CHURCH RECORDS – 1782-1950; Groton Baptist Association, Minutes, RI and CT, 1786-98. 1600p – 1 – us Baptist [240]

NORTH LAKE TAHOE BONANZA – Incline Village, NV. 1981 – 50+ r – 1 – $2,500.00 ($240.00y) – N04802 – us Library Micro [071]

North Laos Mission. (Pres. Ch. in the U.S.A.) see MINUTES, 1872-1902

NORTH LIGHT – (1986-. 1,5,6) – 1983- – 9 – us UMI [073]

NORTH LINCOLN COAST GUARD – Nelscott OR. Feb 25 1932-July 1 1937, Dec 21 28 1933, Mar 15 1934, Feb 18 1937 – 1 – us U.O. Library [071]

NORTH LINCOLN COUNTY NEWS – Oceanlake, OR. -tw. 20 Apr 1944-29 Mar 1951. 3 rolls – 1 – us U.O. Library [071]

NORTH LONDON ECHO – London, England. -w. 1892. 55 ft – 1 – uk British Libr Newspaper [072]

NORTH LONDON GUARDIAN – London, England. -w. 6 Oct 1888-31 March 1916. 25 1 2 reels – 1 – uk British Libr Newspaper [072]

NORTH LONDON OBSERVER – (Stoke Newington and Hackney Observer). London. -w. 1939-71. (27 reels) – 1 – uk British Libr Newspaper [072]

NORTH LONDON PRESS see HOLLOWAY PRESS

NORTH LOUP LOYALIST – North Loup, NE. -w. Oct 1888-Nov 1895; Apr 1898-Mar 1943 – 1 – us NE Hist [071]

North, Mary see CIVIL WAR ARMY NURSES' SCRAPBOOK

NORTH METROPOLITAN AND HOLLOWAY PRESS see HOLLOWAY PRESS

NORTH MISSISSIPPI HERALD – Water Valley. Miss. 1902-1908; 1915-1924; 1927-1929; 1937-1952 – 1 – us UMI [071]

NORTH NEBRASKAN – Dakota City, NE. -w. Aug. 1859-May 1860; Mar. 1861-Apr. 1861 – 1 – us NE Hist [071]

NORTH OMAHA SUN – Omaha, NE. -w. Jan 1951 to date – 1 – us NE Hist [071]

NORTH ORANGE COUNTY INDEPENDENT – Orange Co, CA. 1962 – 1r – 1 – $50.00 – R04081 – us Library Micro [071]

NORTH OXFORDSHIRE MONTHLY TIMES – Deddington, England. -m. Jan 1850-Aug 1854. 1 2 reel – 1 – uk British Libr Newspaper [072]

North Pacific History Co *see* HISTORY OF THE PACIFIC NORTHWEST: WASHINGTON AND OREGON

NORTH PLATTE DAILY BULLETIN – North Platte, NE. Apr 1932-Jun 1946 – 1 – us NE Hist [071]

NORTH PLATTE DAILY RECORD – North Platte, NE. Dec 1895-Aug 1896, scattered issues missing; Jul 1897 – 1 – us NE Hist [071]

NORTH PLATTE HERALD – North Platte, NE. -w. Oct 1924-Apr 1925 – 1 – us NE Hist [071]

NORTH PLATTE NEBRASKIAN – North Platte, NE. -w. (-sw 1875). Aug 1874-Jan 1877; Mar 1877-Oct 1887, scattered issues missing – 1 – us NE Hist [071]

NORTH PLATTE REPUBLICAN – North Platte, NE. -w. (-sw 1872). Feb 1870-Sept 1873, scattered issues missing; Nov 1873-Jan 1877; Mar 1877-Oct 1881, scattered issues missing – 1 – us NE Hist [071]

NORTH PLATTE TELEGRAPH – North Platte, NE. -w. (-sw 1897-1909; -d 1918 to date). Apr 1881-Sept 1887, scattered issues missing; May 1889-May 1907, scattered issues missing; May 1908-Aug 1918; Jul 1941 to date – 1 – us NE Hist [071]

NORTH PLATTE TELEGRAPH – North Platte, NE. -w. (-sw 1899-1945). May 1899-Dec 1901, scattered issues missing; Jan 1925-Dec 1927; Jan-Mar 1939; Feb 1942-Oct 1945, scattered issues missing – 1 – us NE Hist [071]

THE NORTH POLE / Peary, Robert E – BN338 2. 1910 – 8 – ne IDC [910]

NORTH POWDER NEWS – North Powder, OR. -w. 3 Feb 1917-25 Nov 1938. 4 rolls – 1 – us U.O. Library [071]

NORTH QUEENSLAND TELEGRAPH – Townsville, Australia. 1 Sep-12 Dec 1887; 8 May-31 Dec 1888.-w. 2 reels – 1 – uk British Libr Newspaper [072]

NORTH RENFREW TIMES – (1945-1992.-31r) – Deep River, 1993 – 1r – 1 – cn Preston [971]

NORTH RIDING RECORD SOCIETY – (NS: v1-4 1894-97 £112.00 16mf. Coll title: Publications of the English Record Societies, 1835-1972...) – OS: v1-9. 1884-92 – 38mf – 9 – £320.00 – uk Chadwyck [941]

NORTH ROYALTON SCHOOL DISTRICT RECORDS – (Minutes of the Board of Education, Royalton Twp and North Royalton, Ohio 1883-1938. Personal bonds 1922-1936. Revenue accounts 1865-1887 and 1903-1915) – 1865-1960 – 6r – 1 – us Western Res [370]

NORTH SACRAMENTO JOURNAL – North Sacramento, CA. 1926; 1929-30; 1932-33; 1938; 1945-58; 1961-63 – 20r – 1 – $1,000.00 – B02532 – us Library Micro [073]

NORTH SACRAMENTO JOURNAL – Sacramento, CA. 1924-1958; 1961-1963 – 20r – 1 – $1,000.00 – BC03429 – us Library Micro [071]

North, Safford E *see* OUR COUNTY AND ITS PEOPLE (GENESEE)

NORTH SALEM BAPTIST CHURCH. SAVANNAH, GEORGIA : CHURCH RECORDS – 1823-1952 – 1 – 20.52 – us Baptist [240]

NORTH SALEM LUTHERAN CHURCH RECORDS – Wyandot County. Ohio. 1868-1989 – 1 reel – 1 – us Archival [240]

North Salem Lutheran Church (Wyandot County, Ohio) *see* RECORDS

North Sanbornton, New Hampshire.Third Baptist Church *see* RECORDS

THE NORTH SEA / Heine, Heinrich – (Original German text and the English translation on opposite pages) – Chicago: The Open Court Publishing Company, 1916 – 1 – us U.W. Library [810]

NORTH SHORE EXPRESS – Vancouver, British Columbia, CN. 1908-12 – 4r – 1 – cn Commonwealth Micro [072]

THE NORTH SHORE GAZETTE – Rosemere, Canada. 16 jul 1975 – 1r – 1 – Can$25.00 – cn Can Microfilming [072]

NORTH SHORE NEWS – North Shore, CA. 1967 – 5+ r – 1 – $250.00 ($50.00y) – R04073 – us Library Micro [071]

NORTH SHORE NEWS – Pierrefonds, Canada. 27 jul 1962-4 sep 1980 – 12r – 1 – Can$60.00r – cn Can Microfilming [072]

NORTH SHORE PRESS – North Vancouver, Canada. -w. May 1914-Dec 1921 7 1 2 reels – 1 – uk British Libr Newspaper [072]

NORTH SHORE PRESS – Vancouver, British Columbia, CN. 1913-57 – 1 – cn Commonwealth Micro [072]

North Shore Railway Company *see* REPORTS OF CHIEF ENGINEER ON THE SURVEY OF THE NORTH SHORE RAILWAY, AND OF DIRECTORS ON THE PROPER RESOURCES OF THE SAME

NORTH SHORE REVIEW – Vancouver, British Columbia, CN. Jan 1952-Jul 1957 – 2r – 1 – cn Commonwealth Micro [072]

NORTH SHORE TIMES – Vancouver, British Columbia, CN. Apr-Dec 1929 – 1r – 1 – cn Commonwealth Micro [072]

NORTH SHORE TIMES (SYDNEY) – Sydney, 1960-1994 – 500r – 1 – at Pascoe [072]

NORTH & SOUTH SHIELDS GAZETTE AND DAILY TELEGRAPH – South Shields, England. -w. Jan 1871-Dec 1875. 10 1 2 reels – 1 – uk British Libr Newspaper [072]

NORTH STAR – Mott, CA. 1887-90 – 1r – 1 – $50.00 – B02494 – us Library Micro [071]

NORTH STAR – Oklahoma City. Okl. 1952-59 – 1 – us UMI [071]

NORTH SUMMIT TIMES – Hudson. Ohio. 1958- – 1 – us UMI [071]

North Texas Baptists Convention. 1880-85. East Baptist Convention, 1877-84 *see* PAPERS

NORTH TILLAMOOK COUNTY NEWS – Garibaldi OR. Apr 3 1936-July 17 1947 – 1 – us U.O. Library [071]

NORTH TOPEKA TIMES – Topeka. Kan. 1871-83 – 1 – us UMI [071]

NORTH TRENHOLM BAPTIST CHURCH. FAIRFIELD ASSOCIATION. RICHLAND COUNTY. COLUMBIA, SOUTH CAROLINA : CHURCH RECORDS – 1911-60. Formerly Tabernacle Baptist Church. Name changed May 1955 – 1 – 91.52 – us Baptist [240]

NORTH VANCOUVER NEWS – Vancouver, British Columbia, CN. 1954-Jul 1957 – 2r – 1 – cn Commonwealth Micro [072]

NORTH VIETNAM NEWS SERVICE – Hanoi. North Vietnam. 1965- – 1 – us UMI [072]

NORTH WALES, 1822 : BRITISH ISLES CENSUS DIRECTORIES PROJECT, WALES – (In prep) – at Vine [941]

NORTH WALES, 1835 : BRITISH ISLES CENSUS DIRECTORIES PROJECT, WALES. VOL 3 – 1mf – 9 – A$9.00 – at Vine [941]

NORTH WALES, 1844 : BRITISH ISLES CENSUS DIRECTORIES PROJECT, WALES – at Vine [941]

NORTH WALES, 1858 : BRITISH ISLES CENSUS DIRECTORIES PROJECT, WALES. VOL 1 – 2mf – 9 – A$15.00 – at Vine [941]

NORTH WALES GUARDIAN *see* WREXHAM GUARDIAN

NORTH WALES TIMES – Denbigh, Wales. 27 Apr 1895-Dec 1921 – 23r – 1 – uk British Libr Newspaper [072]

NORTH WALES WEEKLY – Conway, Llandudno, Wales, UK. 1971-75 – 13r – 1 – uk British Libr Newspaper [072]

NORTH WEST EXPRESS – 1957-1990. NWE1-12 – 12r – 1 – at Corangamite [072]

North West Frontier Province. India *see* LEGISLATIVE COUNCIL DEBATES

North West Frontier Province. India. Legislative Assembly *see* DEBATES, 1937-1946

NORTH WEST FRONTIER PROVINCE LEGISLATIVE ASSEMBLY DEBATES – (Missing: v1; v11(p 345-394)) – v1-11. 1937-1946 – 138mf – 9 – ne IDC [950]

NORTH WEST FRONTIER PROVINCE LEGISLATIVE COUNCIL DEBATES – Peshavar. v1-11. 1932-1936 – 104mf – 9 – ne IDC [950]

NORTH WEST NEWS – Portland. Or. 1883-1884 – 1 – us UMI [071]

North Western Museum of Science and Industry *see* EARLY RARE PHOTOGRAPHIC BOOKS COLLECTIONS

NORTH WILTS GAZETTE AND HERALD – Deuizes, England. 1913; 1950-Jun 1992, 1995- – 136+ r – 1 – uk British Libr Newspaper [072]

NORTH WILTS HERALD – (Lacking: 1896) – Swindon, England. 1861-1955 – 99r – 1 – uk British Libr Newspaper [072]

NORTH YAMHILL RECORD – Yamhill OR. Oct 19 1899-Feb 27 1908 – 1 – us U.O. Library [071]

North Yarmouth, Maine. Baptist Religious Society in North Yarmouth and Freeport *see* RECORDS

NORTH YORK CONSUMER – Toronto, 1977-1981 – 9r – 1 – cn Preston [971]

NORTH-AMERICAN TREES / Britton, N L & Shafer, J A – 7515 2. 1908 – 8 – ne IDC [580]

NORTHAMPTON 1650-1893 – (Mf 1-6: Proprietors 1653-83. Mf 7-14: Proprietors 1650-1839. Mf 15-27: Town Records 1653-1754. Mf 28-32: Town Records 1741-72. Mf 33-42: Town Records 1772-1801. Mf 43-50: Intentions 1789-1862. Mf 51-52: Vitals 1654-1801, 16mm. Mf 53-62: Vitals 1654-1801, 35mm. Mf 63-67: Vitals 1654-1801, Typed. Mf 68-72: Vitals 1654-1844, Trans. Mf 73: Births 1783-1852. Mf 74-76: Births 1843-53. Mf 76-78: Deaths 1844-53. Mf 76-77: Marriages 1850-53. Mf 79-83: Births 1853-72. Mf 84-88: Marriages 1834-72. Mf 89-91: Deaths 1853-72. Mf 92-95: Births 1873-83. Mf 96-99: Marriages 1873-83. Mf 100-104: Deaths 1873-83. Mf 105-112: Birth Index 1654-1883. Mf 113-119: Marr Index 1654-1883. Mf 120-124: Death Index 1654-1883. Mf 125-129: Births 1884-93. Mf 130-133: Marriages 1884-93. Mf 134-138: Deaths 1884-93) – (mf ed 1994) – 138mf – 9 – us Holbrook [920]

NORTHAMPTON CHRONICLE AND ECHO *see* CHRONICLE AND ECHO

NORTHAMPTON CORRESPONDENT – Easton. Pa. 1814-48; 1876-1903 – 1 – us UMI [071]

NORTHAMPTON COUNTY NEWS – Jackson. N.C. 1955-1957 – 1 – us UMI [071]

NORTHAMPTON COUNTY TIMES NEWS – Jackson. N.C. 1964- – 1 – us UMI [071]

NORTHAMPTON MERCURY – Northampton, England. 1720-1977 – 1 – uk Microform Academic [072]

NORTHAMPTON MISCELLANY – v. 1. Jan-Jun 1721 – 1 – us UMI [800]

NORTHAMPTONSHIRE, 1823 : BRITISH ISLES CENSUS DIRECTORIES PROJECT, ENGLAND. VOL 215 – 1mf – 9 – A$9.00 – at Vine [941]

NORTHAMPTONSHIRE, 1830 : BRITISH ISLES CENSUS DIRECTORIES PROJECT, ENGLAND. VOL 73 – 1mf – 9 – A$9.00 – at Vine [941]

NORTHAMPTONSHIRE, 1841 : BRITISH ISLES CENSUS DIRECTORIES PROJECT, ENGLAND. VOL 236 – 1mf – 9 – A$9.00 – at Vine [941]

NORTHAMPTONSHIRE, 1848 : BRITISH ISLES CENSUS DIRECTORIES PROJECT, ENGLAND – at Vine [941]

NORTHAMPTONSHIRE, 1850 : BRITISH ISLES CENSUS DIRECTORIES PROJECT, ENGLAND. VOL 81 – 2mf – 9 – A$15.00 – at Vine [941]

NORTHAMPTONSHIRE, 1864 : BRITISH ISLES CENSUS DIRECTORIES PROJECT, ENGLAND. VOL 120 – 4mf – 9 – A$27.00 – at Vine [941]

NORTHAMPTONSHIRE, 1874 : BRITISH ISLES CENSUS DIRECTORIES PROJECT, ENGLAND. VOL 57 – 10mf – 9 – A$63.00 – at Vine [941]

NORTHAMPTONSHIRE, 1877 : BRITISH ISLES CENSUS DIRECTORIES PROJECT, ENGLAND – at Vine [941]

NORTHAMPTONSHIRE, 1898 : BRITISH ISLES CENSUS DIRECTORIES PROJECT, ENGLAND. VOL 72 – 6mf – 9 – A$39.00 – at Vine [941]

NORTHAMPTONSHIRE, 1910 : BRITISH ISLES CENSUS DIRECTORIES PROJECT, ENGLAND – (In prep) – at Vine [941]

Northamptonshire Baptist Association, England *see*
- 321 MANUSCRIPTS AND LETTERS FROM 21 CHURCHES, 1775-1819
- CIRCULAR LETTERS OF MINISTERS AND MESSENGERS

NORTHAMPTONSHIRE EVENING TELEGRAPH *see* EVENING TELEGRAPH

NORTHBOROUGH 1716-1892 – (Mf 1-5: Births & Deaths 1735-1847. Mf 5-7: Marriages & Intents 1771-1847. Mf 7,16: Out-of-Town Marriages 1766-99. Mf 8: Birth, Death Index 1735-1847. Mf 9-11: Births 1716-1847- Mf 11-12: Deaths 1743-1877. Mf 13-14: Intentions 1766-1847. Mf 15: Marriage Index 1768-1844. Mf 15-16: Marriages 1766-1844. Mf 17-25: Town Records 1744-94. Mf 26-33: Town Records 1795-1819. Mf 34-43: Town Records 1819-43. Mf 44-54: Town Records 1843-66. Mf 55: Voter Registers 1884-92. Mf 56-60: Burials 1798-1904. Mf 61-62: Intent Index 1771-1899. Mf 63-65: Intentions 1887-1909. Mf 66-70: Birth Index 1844-1991. Mf 71-75: Marriage Index 1766-1980. Mf 76-79: Death Index 1844-1991. Mf 80-81: Births 1843-58. Mf 81: Marriages 1844-51. Mf 82: Deaths 1844-54. Mf 83-86: Births 1859-92. Mf 87-89: Marriages 1852-92. Mf 89-92: Deaths 1855-92) – (mf ed 1993) – 92mf – 9 – 0-87623-165-2 – us Holbrook [920]

NORTHBOROUGH HISTORY, NORTHBOROUGH, MASS / Kent, Josiah C – 1921 – 1 – 22.05 – us Baptist [240]

Northborough, Massachusetts. Evangelical Congregational Church *see* RECORDS

Northborough, Massachusetts. Northborough Baptist Church *see* RECORDS

Northborough, Massachusetts. Trinity Church *see* RECORDS

NORTHBRIDGE 1748-1849 – (Mf 1T-4T: Births & Deaths 1748-1849. Mf 4T: Out-of-Town Marriages 1772-99; Publishments & Marriages 1772-81; Births & Deaths 1748-89. Mf 5T: Publishments & Marriages 1780-1804; Births & Deaths 1769-1800. Mf 6T: Marriages & Intentions 1797-1829. Mf 7T: Marriages & Intentions 1811-24, 1829-41. Mf 8T: Births 1844-49. Mf 9T: Marriages & Deaths 1844-49. Mf 10T: Marriages & Intentions 1840-49) – (mf ed 1998) – 10mf – 9 – 0-87623-307-8 – us Holbrook [920]

NORTHBRIDGE 1748-1900 – (Mf 1-3: Births 1748-1848. Mf 3: Deaths 1771-1849. Mf 4-6: Intents, Marriages 1772-1841. Mf 6-8: Town Records 1774-1842. Mf 8-11: Indexes 1748-1849. Mf 12-13: Vital & Town 1748-1826. Mf 14-15: Marriages & Town 1824-41. Mf 16-18: Births, Deaths 1765-1845; Out-Town-Marriages 1772-99. Mf 19-22: Church Records 1782-1834. Mf 23-24: Vital Records 1844-50. Mf 25-26: Birth Index 1848-91. Mf 26-27: Death Index 1848-91. Mf 28-29: Marriage Index 1848-91. Mf 30-34: Births 1851-91. Mf 35-38: Marriages 1851-91. Mf 39-41: Deaths 1851-91. Mf 42-44: Birth Index 1892-1913. Mf 44-46: Marr Index 1892-1917. Mf 47-48: Death Index 1892-1909. Mf 49-54: Deaths 1892-1909. Mf 55-56: Marriages 1892-1900. Mf 57-58: Births 1892-1900. Mf 59-78: Town Meetings 1772-1868. Mf 79-89: Town Meetings 1869-1903. Mf 90-110: Town Meeting 1904-38) – (mf ed 1994) – 110mf – 9 – 0-87623-184-9 – us Holbrook [920]

NORTHBROOK BAPTIST CHURCH. SPARTANBURG, SOUTH CAROLINA : CHURCH RECORDS – 1959-1990 – 1r – 1 – $22.64 – us Baptist [240]

THE NORTH-CHINA DAILY NEWS – (Lacks: jun 20,22,24 1946) – Shanghai: North-China Herald, -1951 – 3r – 1 – us Res Libr [072]

NORTHCOAST OUTDOORS – Eureka, CA. 1966-69 – 2r – 1 – $100.00 – B02223 – us Library Micro [071]

NORTHCOAST SPORTING NEWS – Eureka, CA. 1973-1976 – 2r – 1 – $100.00 – B05031 – us Library Micro [071]

Northcote, J Spencer *see* ROMA SOTTERRANEA, OR, SOME ACCOUNT OF THE ROMAN CATACOMBS, ESPECIALLY OF THE CEMETERY OF SAN CALLISTO

Northcote, James Spencer *see* EPITAPHS OF THE CATACOMBS, OR, CHRISTIAN INSCRIPTIONS IN ROME DURING THE FIRST FOUR CENTURIES

NORTHCOTE LEADER – 1982-1994 – 22r – 1 – at Corangamite [072]

Northcutt, Jesse J *see* THE OLD TESTAMENT BACKGROUND FOR PAUL'S DOCTRINE OF THE RIGHTEOUSNESS OF GOD

NORTHEAST – 1962- 1; 1973- 5,6; 1975- 9 – us UMI [073]

THE NORTHEAST ASIA JOURNAL OF THEOLOGY – (Includes index 1968-72) – v1-13. Mar 1968-Sep 1974 (complete) – 1r – 1 – ATLA S0284 – us A.T.L.A. [073]

NORTHEAST BAPTIST CHURCH. MIAMI, FLORIDA : CHURCH RECORDS – 1949-67, 1969-73 – 1 – 196.56 – us Baptist [240]

THE NORTHEAST DEVELOPMENT PLAN, 1962-1966 / Thailand. National Economic Development Board – Bangkok. 1962 – 9 – ne IDC [338]

NORTHEAST LINCOLN SUN – Lincoln, NE. -w. Nov 1961 to date – 1 – us NE Hist [071]

NORTHEAST OIL REPORTER – 1984-85 – 1,5,6,9 – us UMI [660]

NORTHEAST OIL WORLD – 1985- – 1,5,6,9 – us UMI [660]

NORTHEAST PORTLAND NEWS – Portland OR. Sep 3 1937, May 13 1949 – 1 – us U.O. Library [071]

NORTH-EASTERN BOUNDARY : CORRESPONDENCE RESPECTING THE OPERATIONS OF THE COMMISSION FOR RUNNING AND TRACING THE BOUNDARY LINE BETWEEN HER MAJESTY'S POSSESSION IN NORTH AMERICA AND THE UNITED STATES.. – London: T R Harrison, 1845. SEM105P440 – 1mf – 9 – Can$2.25 – cn Bibl Nat [971]
NORTHEASTERN CHRISTIAN – (Some original pgs damaged) – 1958-81 – 1r – 1 – ATLA S0584 – us A.T.L.A. [073]
NORTHEASTERN NEVADA HISTORICAL SOCIETY QUARTERLY – Elko, NV. 1970 – 3+ r – 1 – $150.00 ($50.00y) – U04838 – us Library Micro [073]
NORTHEASTERN PART OF LABRADOR AND NEW QUEBEC / Coleman, Arthur Philemon – BN 173 2. 1921 – 8 – ne IDC [971]
NORTHEASTERN REPORTER – (Add vols planned) – 1st series: v1-123. 1885-1919 – 1463mf – 9 – $2,194.00 – LLMC 79-404D – us L.L.M.C. [340]
Northen, W F *see* MEN OF MARK IN GEORGIA
THE NORTHERN / Ohio Northern University – 1910-1995. Yearbooks – 14r – 1 – $32.50r – us Archival [370]
NORTHERN ADVANCE – Barrie, 1917-1940Fe – 11r – 1 – cn Preston [971]
NORTHERN ADVANCE – Barrie, Canada. 1854-71 – 6r – 1 – $390.00 – cn Library Assoc [971]
NORTHERN ADVERTISER – Belfast, Ireland. 16 Oct 1841-30 Jul 1842 – 1/4r – 1 – uk British Libr Newspaper [072]
NORTHERN ALABAMA – History and biography of all counties except Houston. Birmingham: Donohue and Henneberry, 1888. Alabama Reel 2. (The Cox Library Collection) – 5 – us Americana [978]
NORTHERN AQUACULTURE – (v1 1995 Can$80.00y 1. Cont: Canadian Aquaculture at v7 1991) – Victoria. v7-10. 1991-94 – 9,1 – Can$20.00y – cn Micromedia [639]
NORTHERN AQUACULTURE *see* CANADIAN AQUACULTURE
NORTHERN BANTU. AN ACCOUNT OF SOME CENTRAL AFRICAN TRIBES OF THE UGANDA PROTECTORATE / Roscoe, J – Cambridge. 1915. BA-369 2 – 8 – ne IDC [960]
Northern Baptist Convention/American Baptist Convention/American Baptist Churches in the U.S.A *see* YEARBOOKS AND DIRECTORIES
THE NORTHERN BEACON – THE BEACON/ LE PHARE – LE PHARE DU NORD – Rosemere, Canada. 3 fev 1955-27 avr 1972 – 6r – 1 – Can$60.00r – cn Can Microfilming [072]
NORTHERN BRITISH COLUMBIA INDEX AND GUIDE : GENERAL INFORMATION OF THE DISTRICT, DETAILED DESCRIPTION OF SETTLEMENTS AND INDUSTRIALS; RESIDENTS OF THE PRINCE RUPERT AND OUTLYING SETTLEMENTS – Prince Rupert, B.C.: F.S. Wright, 1916 – 1r – 1 – cn U.B.C. Preserve [971]
NORTHERN CALIFORNIA AND BUSINESS : SAN LUIS OBISPO AND NORTH – 1989- – 6+ r – 1 – $300.00 – P00143 – us Library Micro [910]
NORTHERN CALIFORNIA JEWISH BULLETIN – San Francisco, CA. 1982-86 – 1 – us A.J.P.C. [071]
THE NORTHERN CALIFORNIAN – Marysville, CA. 1866-67 – 1r – 1 – $50.00 – B02433 – us Library Micro [071]
NORTHERN CHINESE FARMERS UNION NEWSLETTER = HUA-PEI NUNG LIEN T'UNG-HSUN – (In Chinese) – nos 1-7. 1950 (complete) – 1r – 1 – ATLA S0296L – us A.T.L.A. [073]
NORTHERN CHRONICLE AND GENERAL ADVERTISER FOR THE NORTH OF SCOTLAND – Scotland, UK. 1953-26 Mar 1969 – 12r – 1 – uk British Libr Newspaper [072]
NORTHERN CHRONICLE ETC – Inverness, Scotland, UK.1881-1952. -w. 65 reels – 1 – uk British Libr Newspaper [072]
Northern Congregational Church (Toronto, Ont.). Young Men's Association *see* THE PORTFOLIO
NORTHERN CONSTITUTION *see* COLERAINE CONSTITUTION
NORTHERN COURIER (FERNMOUNT) – Sep 7 1897-Dec 25 1907 – 9 – at Pascoe [072]
NORTHERN DAILY MAIL *see* NORTHERN EVENING MAIL
NORTHERN DAILY NEWS – (1993.-6r; 1923-1974.-163r) – Kirkland Lake, 1975-1992 – 106r – 1 – cn Preston [971]
NORTHERN DEMOCRAT – Gateshead, England. -w. Sep 1927-Oct 1928. 14 feet – 1 – uk British Libr Newspaper [072]
NORTHERN DEMOCRAT – Newcastle-upon-Tyne, England. Aug 1906-Jun 1912.-m – 1 – uk British Libr Newspaper [072]
NORTHERN DISTRICTS STANDARD – 1921-1926. NDS1-2 – 2r – 1 – at Corangamite [072]
NORTHERN ENSIGN – Wick, Scotland. -w. 1854. 31 ft – 1 – uk British Libr Newspaper [072]
NORTHERN EVENING MAIL – (Also known as: Northern Daily Mail; Mail (Hartlepool)) – Feb 18 1878-95; Jan 7-Jun 30 1896; Jan 8 1897-Jun 1898; Jan-Jun 1899; 1900-09; Jul 1910-41; 1943-Aug 24 1959; Sep 1959-Feb, Apr 1996-Jun 1997 – 571 3/4r – 1 – uk British Libr Newspaper [072]
NORTHERN EVENING MAIL – (Northern Daily Mail). West Hartlepool. England. -d. Feb 1878-Dec 1981. Wanting: Jul-Dec 1896; Jul-Dec 1899; Jan-Jun 1910. (380 reels) – 1 – uk British Libr Newspaper [072]
NORTHERN HERALD – (Ballymoney Northern Herald). Ireland. -w. 11 Oct 1860-8 Jan 1863. (2 reels) – 1 – uk British Libr Newspaper [072]
NORTHERN HERALD – Belfast, Ireland. -w. 28 Sept 1833-16 Jan 1836. 1 reel – 1 – uk British Libr Newspaper [072]
NORTHERN ILLINOIS UNIVERSITY LAW REVIEW – v1-15. 1980-95 – 9 – $218.00 set – us Hein [340]
NORTHERN INDEPENDENT – (Some issues lacking) – v3-7. 1858-62 – 2r – 1 – ATLA S0137 – us A.T.L.A. [240]
NORTHERN INDIA PATRIKA – Allahabad, India. Jul-Sept 1966; Nov 1968-May 1991; Aug-Dec 1993 – 103r – 1 – us L of C Photodup [072]
NORTHERN INDIANIAN – Gary. Ind. -w. 1906-09 – 1 – us UMI [071]
NORTHERN INDIANIAN – Warsaw. Ind. 1856-1858; 1862-1865; 1867-1884; 1894-1919; 1927-1946 – 1 – us UMI [071]
Northern Ireland *see*
– THE BELFAST GAZETTE
– BELFAST GAZETTE
NORTHERN IRELAND FAMILY EXPENDITURE SURVEY 1971-1977 – (Coll title: British Government Publications...1801-1977, Health and Public Welfare) – 7mf – 9 (£1,080.00 health and public welfare set of 171mf) – uk Chadwyck [339]
Northern Ireland. Ministry of Education *see* PRIMARY EDUCATION TEACHERS' GUIDE
Northern Ireland. Parliament *see* NORTHERN IRELAND PARLIAMENTARY PUBLICATIONS
NORTHERN IRELAND PARLIAMENTARY PUBLICATIONS / Northern Ireland. Parliament – 95 reels – 1 – $3,500.00 – us Trans-Media [323]
NORTHERN IRELAND POLITICAL LITERATURE : PHASE 1 (1968-1972) PHASE 2 (1973-1975) – Ir£85.00 Phase 1 Ir£175.00 Phase 2 – ie Microforms [320]
NORTHERN IRELAND POLITICAL LITERATURE – (Phases Two and Three: Pamphlets and the very ephemeral. Indexed. 9) – 1966-85.Phase One: Periodicals. 1956 fiches. Indexed – 9 – PS5000.00 – ie European Micro [073]
NORTHERN JOURNAL – Elgin, Scotland. -w. 18 Nov 1865-16 Nov 1867. 1 reel – 1 – uk British Libr Newspaper [072]
THE NORTHERN JOURNAL – Montreal, Canada. v1 n37. 15 jun-v1 n40. 6 jul 1872 – 1r – 1 – Can$25.00 – cn Can Microfilming [072]
NORTHERN JOURNAL OF APPLIED FORESTRY – v1-. 1984- – 1,5,6,9 – us UMI [073]
NORTHERN JOURNEY – Ottawa. v1-8. 1971-76 – 9 – Can$20.00y – cn Micromedia [073]
THE NORTHERN LAKES OF CANADA: THE NIAGARA RIVER AND TORONTO, THE LAKES SIMCOE AND COUCHICHING, THE LAKES OF MUSKOKA, THE GEORGIAN BAY,.. – Toronto: Hunter, Rose, c1886. 02234. (Pre-1900 Canadiana) – 9 – cn C.I.H.M. [910]
NORTHERN LIBERATOR – Newcastle-upon-Tyne. England. -w. Oct 1837-Dec 1840. (3 reels) – 1 – uk British Libr Newspaper [072]
NORTHERN LIGHT – (1976-1992.-63r) – Bathhurst, 1993 – 3r – 1 – cn Preston [971]
NORTHERN LIGHT – Ada, Ohio. 1913-14 – 1r – 1 – $32.50r – us Archival [071]
NORTHERN LIGHT – (Cont: Far Point 1974. No issues publ in 1977, 1979, or 1982. nos 9-13 1983-85 Can$46.00) – Antigonish. nos 1-13. 1974-85 – 9 – Can$20.00y – cn Micromedia [073]
NORTHERN LIGHT – Devoted to free Discussion, and to the Diffusion of Useful Knowledge, miscellaneous literature, and general intelligence. v. 1-4. Apr 1841-44 – 1 – us UMI [073]
NORTHERN LIGHT *see* FAR POINT
THE NORTHERN LIGHT – Eastport, ME: A H Quincy, nov 1828-apr 1832 – 1r – 1 – us Res Libr [071]
NORTHERN LIGHTS ON THE BIBLE: DRAWN FROM A BISHOP'S EXPERIENCE DURING TWENTY-FIVE YEARS IN THE GREAT NORTH-WEST / Bompas, William Carpenter – London: J. Nisbet, 18??. 00171. (Pre-1900 Canadiana) – 9 – cn C.I.H.M. [240]
Northern Mariana Islands (Commonwealth) *see* WELCOMING AMERICA'S NEWEST COMMONWEALTH
NORTHERN MESSENGER – Montreal: J Dougall, 1876-[19–] – 9 – cn C.I.H.M. [072]
NORTHERN MESSENGER – Montreal, New York. v11 n17. 1 sep 1876-v44 n12. 19 mar 1909 – 4r – 1 – Can$50.00r – cn Can Microfilming [072]
NORTHERN MINER – Charters Towers, Australia. 9 May 1888-20 Feb 1889; 1 Jul 1889-23 Jun 1891. (Imperfect). -sw – 8r – 1 – uk British Libr Newspaper [622]
THE NORTHERN MINER : CANADA'S MINING NEWSPAPER – Toronto, Ontario, CN. 1915- – 2r per yr – 1 – $55.00r – cn Commonwealth Micro [072]
NORTHERN MINING REGISTER. (NORTH QUEENSLAND REGISTER) – Charters Towers, Australia. 29 Aug 1891-1 Apr 1939. -d – 176r – 1 – uk British Libr Newspaper [622]
NORTHERN MORNING NEWS AND ACCRINGTON ADVERTISER *see* ACCRINGTON WEEKLY ADVERTISER
NORTHERN MYTHOLOGY, COMPRISING THE PRINCIPAL POPULAR TRADITIONS AND SUPERSTITIONS OF SCANDINAVIA, NORTH GERMANY, AND THE NETHERLANDS / Thorpe, Benjamin – Comp. from original and other sources. London: E. Lumley, 1851-52. 3v. illus – 1 – us U.W. Library [390]
NORTHERN NECK NEWS – Warsaw. Va. 1879-1945; 1950- – 1 – us UMI [071]
NORTHERN NEIGHBORS – v1- 1956- 1; v17-5,6; v20- 9 – us UMI [073]
NORTHERN ONTARIO BUSINESS – Sudbury. v1-15. 1980/81-1994/95 – 1 – Price varies – cn Micromedia [380]
Northern Pacific Railway Company *see*
– ANNUAL REPORTS
– CLIPPINGS SCRAPBOOKS
– PAPERS OF THE NORTHERN PACIFIC RAILWAY COMPANY, PART 1
– VILLARD EXCURSION FILE
Northern Pacific Railway Company. Land Department *see* RECORDS
Northern Pacific Railway Company. Personnel Dep't *see* INDEX TO PERSONNEL FILES
Northern Pacific Railway Company. Secretary's Department *see* UNREGISTERED LETTERS RECEIVED AND RELATED RECORDS
THE NORTHERN PATRIOT – Ireland.15 Oct 1895-15 Nov 1897 – 1 – ie Microforms [072]
NORTHERN PEN – (1990-1992.-6r) – St. Anthony, 1993 – 2r – 1 – cn Preston [971]
NORTHERN PIONEER – Huddersfield, England. 22 Oct 1881-14 Jul 1883.-w. 2 reels – 1 – uk British Libr Newspaper [072]
NORTHERN PLAINS BAPTIST – Rapid City, SD. 1986-87. 198p – 1 – 5.00 – us Baptist [071]
NORTHERN POST – Aliwal North, South Africa. 2 May 1874-30 Dec 1902 – 17r – 1, 16 diazo available at reduced price – sa SA Libr [072]
NORTHERN PRESS – Liverpool. England. -w. 9 Jun 1860-10 Sep 1870. (4 reels) – 1 – uk British Libr Newspaper [072]
NORTHERN RECORD – Orleans, CA. 1870-1872 – 1r – 1 – $50.00 – C03627 – us Library Micro [071]
NORTHERN REVIEW – Ada, Ohio. 1915-83. 8 rolls – 1 – us Archival [071]
NORTHERN REVIEW – Middlesbrough, England. -w. 2 Oct 1886-31 Dec 1892. 6 reels – 1 – uk British Libr Newspaper [072]
NORTHERN REVIEW – v. 1-7. 1945-56 – 1 – 140.00 – cn McLaren [700]
NORTHERN REVIEW – Whitehorse. nos 1-11. 1988-93 – 9 – Can$20.00y – cn Micromedia [073]
NORTHERN RHODESIA GOVERNMENT GAZETTE – v1-54. 1911-64 – 29r – 1 – us Ross [324]
NORTHERN RHODESIA HANDBOOK – [Lusaka: Govt Printer, 1953] – 1 – us Res Libr [960]
NORTHERN RHODESIA JOURNAL – Livingstone: Northern Rhodesia Society. v1 n2-v6 n3. dec 1950-1965; index v1-6 – us Res Libr [073]
THE NORTHERN RHODESIAN JOURNAL – (Cont as: The Zambia[Northern Rhodesia] Journal. Zambia, 1965) – Fort Jameson, 1909-1962/1964 – 81mf – 9 – ne IDC [960]
NORTHERN SCOT – 1 – £42.00r – uk Scot News [072]
NORTHERN STANDARD – Monaghan, Ireland. -d. 1885-1986. 200 reels – 1 – PS27.50r – ie European Micro [072]
NORTHERN STAR – Belfast. Ireland. -sw. Jan 1792-Dec 1794. (3 reels) – 1 – uk British Libr Newspaper [072]
NORTHERN STAR – (Cont: Press Independent at v23 no 17 1993) – v23- 1993- – 1 – Can$115.00y – cn Micromedia [070]
NORTHERN STAR – Fort Chimo, Canada. v2 n18. 30 mar 1963-v4 n3. 30 jan 1965 – 1r – 1 – Can$30.00 – cn Can Microfilming [072]
NORTHERN STAR – Leeds, England. 1838-52 – 1 – uk Microform Academic [072]
NORTHERN STAR – Snohomish. Wash. -w. 1876-79 – 1 – us UMI [071]
NORTHERN STAR *see* PRESS INDEPENDENT
THE NORTHERN STAR – Belfast, Ireland. 1792-96. 3 reels – 1 – ie Microforms [072]
THE NORTHERN STAR – Quebec, Canada. 20 nov 1875 – 1r – 1 – Can$25.00 – cn Can Microfilming [072]
THE NORTHERN STAR – (The Star and National Trades Journal The Star of Freedom). Leeds and London. -w. Jan 1838-May 1852, Aug-Nov 1852. (30 reels) – 1 – uk British Libr Newspaper [331]
NORTHERN STAR (LISMORE) – Jan 1 1909-Dec 31 1913 – 9 – at Pascoe [072]
NORTHERN STAR OR THE YORKSHIRE MAGAZINE – England. v. 1-3. 1817-18 – 1 – uk Microform Academic [072]
NORTHERN TERRITORY ADELAIDE REGISTER FOR LAND ORDERS MAY 1871-NOVEMBER 1873 – (Adelaide Register Allotment Selected May 1871-November 1873) – 1988 – 1mf – 9 – A$5.00 – 0-949124-48-6 – item 18 – at G.S.N.T. [920]
NORTHERN TERRITORY GOLD MINING/MINERAL LANDS/PASTORAL LEASES/PEARLING – (Pastoral Leases, 21.9.1886-12.9.1903. ISBN: 0-949124-24-9; Applications for Mineral Lands. ISBN: 0-949124-23-0; Goldmining Leases for the Northern Territory. ISBN: 0-949124-22-2; Pearling Luggers Port Darwin, 1903-1919. ISBN: 0-949124-45-1) – 1988 – 1mf – 9 – A$5.00 – item 15 – at G.S.N.T. [920]
NORTHERN TERRITORY LAND APPLICATIONS-VARIOUS – (Various Northern Territory Colonial Register Vol 1 and 2, 1864. ISBN: 0-949124-31-X; English Applications to Pay Deposit, 1864. ISBN: 0-949124-34-6; Colonial Application for Land – 160 Acres. ISBN: 0-949124-30-3; Colonial Application for Extended Land Area Vol 2, 1869. ISBN: 0-949124-27-3) – 1988 – 1mf – 9 – A$5.00 – item 12 – at G.S.N.T. [920]
NORTHERN TERRITORY LAND ORDERS/ ADELAIDE AND LONDON REGISTERS 1870 BALLOT – (1870 Ballot for Priority of Choices in Selection of Country Sections. ISBN: 0-949124-31-1; List of Applications of Preliminary Land Orders. ISBN: 0-949124-28-1; Adelaide List – List of the Numbers and Names of the Holders of Preliminary Land Orders in the Northern Territory. ISBN: 0-949124-41-9; Northern Territory Land Orders – Adelaide Register. ISBN: 0-949124-29-X; Northern Territory Land Orders – London Register. ISBN: 0-949124-46-X; Northern Territory Lease on Purchase – on Credit 1882. ISBN: 0-949124-33-8) – 1988 hr – 9 – A$5.00 – item 17 – at G.S.N.T. [920]

NORTHERN TERRITORY NEWS – 1 – F1,805.00 – sz Infoprint [072]

NORTHERN TERRITORY PASTORAL LEASE APPLICATIONS 1875-1899 – 1988 – 1mf – 9 – A$5.00 – 0-949124-35-4 – item 14 – at G.S.N.T. [920]

NORTHERN TERRITORY PASTORAL PERMITS 17.11.1902-14.04.1924 – 1988 – 1mf – 9 – A$5.00 – 0-949124-25-7 – item 11 – at G.S.N.T. [920]

NORTHERN TERRITORY SCHEDULE OF LAND TRANSACTIONS 1895-1909 – 2mf – 9 – A$10.00 – 0-949124-26-5 – item 13 – at G.S.N.T. [920]

NORTHERN TERRITORY SHIPPING 1901-1921 – 11mf – 9 – A$50.00 set – 0-949124-49-4 – item 19 – at G.S.N.T. [380]

NORTHERN TERRITORY TIMES AND GAZETTE NAME INDEX 1875 – 1988 – 9 – A$5.00 – 0-949124-38-9 – item 7 – at G.S.N.T. [072]

NORTHERN TERRITORY TIMES AND GAZETTE NAME INDEX 1877 – 1988 – 9 – A$5.00 – 0-949124-39-7 – item 9 – at G.S.N.T. [072]

NORTHERN TERRITORY TIMES AND GAZETTE NAME INDEX 1882 – 1988 – 9 – A$5.00 – 0-949124-36-2 – item 10 – at G.S.N.T. [072]

NORTHERN TERRITORY TIMES & GAZETTE – Darwin, Australia. Jan 1885-Jun 1932.-d. 20men reels – 1 – uk British Libr Newspaper [072]

NORTHERN TERRITORY'S PALMERSTON CEMETERY AND SOME OF ITS OCCUPANTS – 9 – A$10.00 – 0-949124-51-6 – item 20 – at G.S.N.T. [920]

NORTHERN TIMES – 1 – £42.00r – uk Scot News [072]

NORTHERN TIMES : WHITEHORSE – July 1978-Aug 1979 – 1 – cn Commonwealth Micro [072]

NORTHERN TIMES (KERANG) – 1973, 1978, 1980. NT3,11 – 5r – 1 – at Corangamite [072]

NORTHERN TOURS – Montreal: Desbarats, [1898-189- or 19–] – 9 – cn C.I.H.M. [910]

NORTHERN TRIBUNE – A periodical for the people. 1-2 2+9 (all publ). 1854-1855 – 6mf – 9 – $65.00 – us UPA [335]

NORTHERN TRIBUNE – Gouverneur. N.Y. 1887-1929 – 1 – us UMI [071]

NORTHERN VINDICATOR – Estherville. Iowa. 1868-1874; 1884-1899 – 1 – us UMI [071]

NORTHERN VIRGINIA DAILY – Strasburg. Va. 1934- – 1 – us UMI [071]

NORTHERN VIRGINIA SUN – Arlington. Va. 1971- – 1 – us UMI [071]

NORTHERN WARDER – Dundee, Scotland, UK. 1846. -w. 1 reel – 1 – uk British Libr Newspaper [072]

NORTHERN WEEKLY AND TEDDY ASHTON'S JOURNAL *see* TEDDY ASHTON'S JOURNAL

NORTHERN WEEKLY INDEPENDENT – Eureka, CA. 1870-1872 – 1r – 1 – $50.00 – B03593 – us Library Micro [071]

NORTHERN WHEELER – Bolton, England. The Wheeler. -w. 27 April 1892-15 Feb 1893; 18 Oct 1893-17 May 1899. 12 reels – 1 – uk British Libr Newspaper [072]

NORTHERN WHIG – Belfast. Ireland. -tw. 1840-44. (5 reels) – 1 – uk British Libr Newspaper [072]

THE NORTHERNMOST INHABITANTS OF THE EARTH / Bessels, Emil – (Ethnographic sketch). BN 123 1884 – 8 – ne IDC [305]

NORTHFIELD 1717-1902 – (Mf 1-8: Vital Records Index 1717-1922. Mf 9: Births, Marriages, Deaths 1717-71. Mf 10-13: Vital Records 1727-1838. Mf 14-15: Church Records 1752-94. Mf 16-17: Marriage Intentions 1842-50. Mf 17-19: Marriages 1717-99, 1817-62. Mf 20: Births 1843-55. Mf 20-21: Marriages 1843-55. Mf 21: Deaths 1843-54. Mf 22-24: Births 1855-1902. Mf 24-26: Marriages 1855-1902. Mf 26-28 Deaths 1855-1902) – (mf ed 1987) – 28mf – 9 – 0-87623-056-7 – us Holbrook [920]

NORTHFIELD ECHOES *see* THE RECORD OF CHRISTIAN WORK

NORTHFIELD (MINNESOTA) BANK ROBBERY OF 1876: SELECTED MANUSCRIPTS COLLECTIONS AND GOVERNMENT RECORDS – 1876-1979. 2 rolls including filmed inventory – 1 – $90.00; $45.00r – us M.H.S. [360]

NORTHGATE BAPTIST CHURCH. FLORENCE, SOUTH CAROLINA : CHURCH RECORDS 1960-72. (Mission of FBC, 1960-63) – 1 – 6.89 – us Baptist [240]

NORTHIAN – (v1-9 1964-73, 10-12 1974-76 Can$100.00. v13 1978 Can$50.00.) – Saskatoon. v1-13. 1964-78 – 5 – Price varies – cn Micromedia [073]

THE NORTHLAND POST – Sept-Iles, Canada. v1 n5. 6 mar 1965 – 1r – 1 – Can$25.00 – cn Can Microfilming [072]

THE NORTHMEN / Maclear, George Frederick – London: S.P.C.K.; New York: Pott, Young, [1878?] (Conversion of the West) – 1mf – us A.T.L.A. [240]

NORTH/NORD – (v19-30 1972-83 Can$100.00v. v 31 1985 Can$50.00. Cont: North at v19 1972. C) – Ottawa. v19-31. 1972-85 – 5 – Price varieS – cn Micromedia [073]

NORTH/NORD *see* NORTH

Northport, Maine. Northport Baptist Church *see* RECORDS

Northrup, Gordon *see* RESIDENTIAL TREATMENT FOR CHILDREN AND YOUTH

Northrup, W M *see* ALHAMBRA COMMUNITY BOOK

NORTH'S PHILADELPHIA MUSICAL JOURNAL – Philadelphia. v1-6 n12. 1886-91 – 1r – 1 – £60.00 – uk Chadwyck [780]

NORTHSIDE BAPTIST CHURCH. ORANGEBURG COUNTY. SOUTH CAROLINA : CHURCH RECORDS – 1962-72 – 1 – 5.27 – us Baptist [240]

NORTHSIDE MEMORIAL BAPTIST CHURCH. SUMTER COUNTY. SOUTH CAROLINA : CHURCH RECORDS – 1949-64 – 1 – 25.83 – us Baptist [240]

NORTHSIDE REPORTER – Jackson. Miss. 1954-1964; 1966-1967 – 1 – us UMI [071]

NORTHSIDE (WOODRUFF MILLS) BAPTIST CHURCH. SPARTANBURG COUNTY. SOUTH CAROLINA : CHURCH RECORDS – 1904-22, 1926-48, 1952-55, 1959-72. Deacons' Minutes. 1952-55. 1959-72 – 1 – 17.55 – us Baptist [240]

NORTH-SOUTH TECHNOLOGY TRANSFER: FINANCING AND INSTITUTION BUILDING / Baranson, Jack – 1981. 160p. – 9 – $12.75 – 0-912338-28-8 – us Lomond [600]

NORTHUMBERLAND, 1828 : BRITISH ISLES CENSUS DIRECTORIES PROJECT, ENGLAND – at Vine [941]

NORTHUMBERLAND, 1834 : BRITISH ISLES CENSUS DIRECTORIES PROJECT, ENGLAND – at Vine [941]

NORTHUMBERLAND, 1848 : BRITISH ISLES CENSUS DIRECTORIES PROJECT, ENGLAND – at Vine [941]

NORTHUMBERLAND, 1855 : BRITISH ISLES CENSUS DIRECTORIES PROJECT, ENGLAND – at Vine [941]

NORTHUMBERLAND, 1872 : BRITISH ISLES CENSUS DIRECTORIES PROJECT, ENGLAND – at Vine [941]

NORTHUMBERLAND, 1879 : BRITISH ISLES CENSUS DIRECTORIES PROJECT, ENGLAND. VOL 245 – 7mf – 9 – A$45.00 – at Vine [941]

NORTHUMBERLAND ADVERTISER ETC – North Shields, England. 1 Aug 1831-5 Mar 1834 – 1r – 1 – uk British Libr Newspaper [072]

NORTHUMBERLAND COUNTY DEMOCRAT – Northumberland, PA., 1861-1912 – 13 – $25.00r – us I.M.R. [071]

NORTHUMBERLAND (EAST), 1887 : BRITISH ISLES CENSUS DIRECTORIES PROJECT, ENGLAND. VOL 50 – 6mf – 9 – A$39.00 – at Vine [941]

NORTHUMBERLAND ECHO – Heathsville. Va. 1968- – 1 – us UMI [071]

NORTHUMBERLAND GAZETTE *see* ALNWICK AND COUNTY GAZETTE

NORTHUMBERLAND (NEWCASTLE), 1805 : BRITISH ISLES CENSUS DIRECTORIES PROJECT, ENGLAND. VOL 187 – 1mf – 9 – A$9.00 – at Vine [941]

NORTHUMBERLAND (NEWCASTLE AND GATESHEAD), 1837 : BRITISH ISLES CENSUS DIRECTORIES PROJECT, ENGLAND. VOL 200 – 1mf – 9 – A$9.00 – at Vine [941]

NORTHUMBERLAND (NEWCASTLE ETC), 1928 : BRITISH ISLES CENSUS DIRECTORIES PROJECT, ENGLAND – at Vine [941]

NORTHUMBERLAND REPUBLICANER – Sunbury, PA. 1812-18. Also: Nordwestliche Post. 1818-22. Sold as one unit – 1,3 – us Readex [071]

NORTHWARD JOURNAL – (Cont: Boreal, 1979) – Toronto. v13- 1979- – 9 – Can$20.00y – cn Micromedia [073]

NORTHWARD JOURNAL *see* BOREAL

NORTHWARD OVER THE "GREAT ICE."BN 336/2. 2 V. 1898 / Peary, Robert E – 8 – ne IDC [910]

NORTHWEST – Port Townsend. Wash. -w. 1860-62 – 1 – us UMI [071]

NORTHWEST – (Weekly Democratic newspaper) – Napoleon, OH. sept 8, 1852-dec 28, 1865 – 3r – 1 – us Western Res [071]

THE NORTHWEST – Freeport. Ill. 1865-67 – 1 – us UMI [071]

NORTHWEST ARKANSAS TIMES – Fayetteville. AR. And pred. 1892- – 1 – us UMI [071]

NORTHWEST BAPTIST CHURCH. OKLAHOMA CITY, OKLAHOMA : CHURCH RECORDS – 1930-34 – 1 – 8.46 – us Baptist [240]

NORTHWEST BAPTIST WITNESS – (Pacific Coast Baptist. 1931-74) – 1931-1991 – 1 – $347.80 – us Baptist [240]

NORTHWEST CLARION – Portland OR. Dec 7 1956-May 30 1957 – 1 – us U.O. Library [071]

NORTHWEST COAST COLLECTION OF AMERICAN INDIAN ART / Museum of Mankind (British Museum, Dept. of Ethnography). London – (Complete pictorial catalogue of NW Coast artefacts acquired before 1875. Printed index) – 1987 – 35mf – 15 – $1,600.00 – 0-907716-44-X – uk Mindata [760]

Northwest Colony and Russell Townsite Company *see* LEDGER

NORTHWEST DEFENDER – Portland OR. Jan 25 1962-Sep 22 1965 – 1 – us U.O. Library [071]

NORTHWEST ENTERPRISE – Anacortes. Wash. -w. 1882-86 – 1 – us UMI [071]

NORTHWEST HERALD – Portland OR. June 10 1899 – 1 – us U.O. Library [071]

THE NORTHWEST HERALD – Seattle. Wash. feb. 27, May 22, 29, June 26, 1945 – 1 – us NY Public [071]

NORTHWEST ITALIEN NEWS – Seattle, WA. Sept 1961-Dec 1987 – 2r – 1 – us I.H.R.C. [071]

NORTHWEST JOURNAL – Chicago. Ill. 1960-1965 – 1 – us UMI [071]

NORTHWEST JOURNAL OF OPTOMETRY *see* AMERICAN JOURNAL OF OPTOMETRY AND ARCHIVES OF AMERICAN ACADEMY OF OPTOMETRY

NORTHWEST LIBERAL – Portland OR. Oct 20 22 1934 – 1 – us U.O. Library [071]

NORTHWEST LINCOLN SUN – Lincoln, NE. -w. Jan 1973 to date – 1 – us NE Hist [071]

NORTHWEST MOTOR – v. 45-47. 1950-55 – 1 – us UMI [629]

NORTHWEST NEBRASKA NEWS – Crawford, NE. -w. May 1914-Oct. 1914; Nov. 1929-Dec. 1942 – 1 – us NE Hist [071]

NORTHWEST NEWS – Paisley OR. May 1912 – 1 – us U.O. Library [071]

NORTHWEST NEWS – Portland, OR. -d. 1883-84 – 1 – 48.00 – us Oregon Hist [071]

NORTHWEST PACIFIC FARMER – Portland, OR. -w. 9 Feb 1893-1 Aug 1918. 9 rolls – 1 – us U.O. Library [071]

NORTHWEST POULTRY JOURNAL – Salem, OR. -m. Feb 1911-Jul 1919. 1 roll – 1 – us U.O. Library [071]

Northwest Provinces and Oudh. India *see* INDIAN ARCHITECTURAL DRAWINGS. P. I

NORTHWEST REFORM JOURNAL – Portland OR. Feb 19 26 1892 – 1 – us U.O. Library [071]

NORTHWEST REVIEW – v1- 1957- 1; v15- 5,6; v16- 9 – us UMI [073]

NORTHWEST SIGNAL – Napoleon, Ohio. 1961- – 75r – 1 – $32.50r – us Archival [071]

NORTHWEST SIGNAL – Napoleon. Ohio. 1961- – 1 – us UMI [071]

NORTHWEST SIGNAL AND COURIER Napoleon. Ohio. 1974- – 1 – us UMI [071]

NORTHWEST SUNDIAL – Portland, OR. 2 Jan 1954-8 Mar 1957. 1 roll – 1 – us U.O. Library [071]

Northwest Territories. Canada *see* TERRITORIES LAW REPORTS

Northwest Territories. Canada. Supreme Court *see* NORTHWEST TERRITORIES SUPREME COURT REPORTS

NORTHWEST TERRITORIES GAZETTE – Regina, Canada, 1887-1905 – 2r – 1 – us Ross [324]

NORTHWEST TERRITORIES GAZETTE – (v4-1983- 9) – Yellowknife, 1887- – 1,9 – Price varies – cn Micromedia [971]

NORTHWEST TERRITORIES SUPREME COURT REPORTS / Northwest Territories. Canada. Supreme Court – v1-2. 1887-90 (all publ) – 11mf – 9 – $16.50 – LLMC 81-032 – us L.L.M.C. [340]

NORTHWEST TERRITORY : REPORTS OF PROGRESS, TOGETHER WITH A PRELIMINARY AND GENERAL REPORT ON THE ASSINIBOINE AND SASKATCHEWAN EXPLORING EXPEDITION.. / Hind, Henry Youle – Toronto: John Lovell, 1859. SEM105P284 – 4mf – 9 – Can$9.00 – cn Bibl Nat [910]

NORTHWEST TERRITORY : SESSION LAWS OF AMERICAN STATES AND TERRITORIES – 1788-1801 (all publ) – 9 – $17.50 set – us Hein [340]

Northwest Territory *see* SESSION LAWS, 1788-1801

NORTHWEST TRIBUNE – Spokane. Wash. Index. 1887-1895 – 1 – us UMI [071]

NORTHWEST TRIBUNE – Stevensville. Mont. 1951-1954; 1956-1958; 1967- – 1 – us UMI [071]

Northwest Vigilante Committee, Franklin County, KS *see* RECORDS

NORTHWEST WEST VIRGINIA PANHANDLE / Boyd, Peter – Indianapolis, Historical Publishing Co., 1927. Vols. 1-2. West Virginia Reel 4. (The Cox Library Collection) – 5 – us Americana [978]

NORTHWESTERN – Klamath Falls, OR. -w. 13 Mar 1912-26 Dec 1915. 3 rolls – 1 – us U.O. Library [071]

NORTHWESTERN AREA : BEVERLY HILLS, BURBANK, CANOGA PARK, ENCINO, GLENDALE, MALIBU, SAN FERNANDO, ETC, – 1992-94 – 3r – 1 – $150.00 – P00070 – us Library Micro [910]

NORTHWESTERN DEMOCRAT – Perrysburg, Ohio. 1852-58 – 1r – 1 – $32.50r – us Archival [071]

Northwestern Historical Association *see* MEMOIRS OF ALLEGHENY COUNTY

NORTHWESTERN INDIANA 1800-1900 / Ball, T H – Crown Point, Valparaiso, LaPorte, Knox, Winamac, Monticello, Rensselaer, Kentland. 1900. Indiana Reel 3. (The Cox Library Collection) – 5 – us Americana [978]

NORTHWESTERN IOWA: ITS HISTORY AND TRADITIONS 1804-1926 / Allen, Arthur F – (Chicago: S. J. Clarke Publ. Co., 1927). Vol. 1-3. Iowa Reel 5. (The Cox Library Collection) – 5 – us Americana [978]

NORTHWESTERN JOURNAL OF INTERNATIONAL LAW AND BUSINESS – v1-15. 1979-95 – 1,5,6 – $270.00 – us Hein [073]

NORTHWESTERN LAW REVIEW – (Add vols as copyright expires) – v1-14. 1906/7-1919/20 – 96mf – $144.00 – LLMC 95-140 – us L.L.M.C. [073]

NORTHWESTERN LAW REVIEW – (Lacking: v2 nos 3,5,6) – v1-4. 1893-96 (all publ) – 15mf – 9 – $22.50 – LLMC 82-952 – us L.L.M.C. [073]

NORTHWESTERN LUTHERAN – (Lacks some pgs. Some original pgs damaged) – v11-73. 1924-86 – 19r – 1 – ATLA S0816 – us A.T.L.A. [073]

NORTHWESTERN MILLER – v7-280 1879-1973 1; 1971-73 5,6 – us UMI [660]

NORTHWESTERN MILLER *see* AMERICAN BAKER

NORTHWESTERN PRESS – Harrison, NE. -w. Apr 1896-Jun 1899, scattered issues missing – 1 – us NE Hist [071]

Northwestern Provinces and Oudh. India *see*
– DISTRICT CENSUS STATISTICS

NORTHWESTERN REPORTER – (Add vols planned) – 1st series: v1-173. 1879-1919 – 2079mf – 9 – $3,445.00 – LLMC 79-404F – us L.L.M.C. [340]

NORTHWESTERN REPUBLICAN – Wauseon, Ohio. 1868-94 – 10r – 1 – $32.50r – us Archival [071]

Northwestern University *see* CATALOG OF THE MELVILLE J. HERSKOVITS LIBRARY OF AFRICAN STUDIES, NORTHWESTERN UNIVERSITY LIBRARY, AND AFRICANA IN SELECTED LIBRARIES

NORTHWESTERN UNIVERSITY LAW REVIEW – v1-90. 1906-96 – 1,5,6,9 – $1,890.00 – us Hein [073]

Northwestern University. Library *see* UMAR-FALKE COLLECTION OF HAUSA MANUSCRIPTS IN ARABIC SCRIPT

Northwestern University. School of Law *see* BY-PRODUCTS OF THE STUDY OF LAW

Northwestern University.Melville J. Herskovits Library of African Studies *see* AFRICANA CONFERENCE PAPER INDEX

NORTHWICH AND KNUTSFORD GUARDIAN *see* NORTHWICH GUARDIAN AND WINSFORD, MIDDLEWICH AND WEAVERHAM ADVERTISER

NORTHWICH AND WINSFORD CHRONICLE ETC – Apr 6-Dec 28 1889; 1892; Mar 13-Dec 25 1897; Jan 7-Dec 19 1911; Jan 9 1986-Jun 1995; 1996 – 40 1/2r – 1 – uk British Libr Newspaper [072]

NORTHWICH AND WINSFORD GUARDIAN ETC *see* NORTHWICH GUARDIAN AND WINSFORD, MIDDLEWICH AND WEAVERHAM ADVERTISER

NORTHWICH GUARDIAN AND WINSFORD, MIDDLEWICH AND WEAVERHAM ADVERTISER – (Northwich & Knutsford Guardian, 1876-91. Northwich & Winsford Guardian etc, 1864-75. Missing: 1911) – England, 1 Jun 1861-1946; 1985- – 156+ r – 1 – uk British Libr Newspaper [072]

Northwood, New Hampshire. Northwood Baptist Church *see* RECORDS

NORTON 1688-1849 – (Mf 1T-4T: Vital Records 1688-1833. Mf 5T-10T: Vital Records 1747-1854. Mf 10T: Out-of-Town Marriages 1720-99; Births 1843-49. Mf 11T: Marriages 1843-49; Deaths 1843-49. Mf 11T-12T: Marriage Intentions 1721-71. Mf 13T-16T: Marriage Intentions 1773-1849) – (mf ed 1998) – 16mf – 9 – 0-87623-308-6 – us Holbrook [920]

NORTON 1688-1900 – (Mf 1-3: Vital Records 1688-1833. Mf 4: Vitals Index 1688-1833. Mf 4-7: Vital Records 1688-1833. Mf 8-12: Vitals (copy) 1735-1855. Mf 12,20: Out-of-Town Marriages 1712-99. Mf 13-14: Vitals Index 1735-1855. Mf 15-20: Vital Record 1735-1855. Mf 21-25: Town Records 1715-69. Mf 26-33: Town Records 1769-1808. Mf 34-43: Town Records 1808-62. Mf 44-46: Militia 1857-1902. Mf 47-48: Intentions 1711-71. Mf 49-52: Intentions 1773-1881. Mf 53-54: Intentions 1882-1905. Mf 55-56: Vital Records 1843-57. Mf 57-59: Birth Index 1858-1969. Mf 59-61: Intentions Index 1858-1915. Mf 62-64: Death Index 1858-1968. Mf 65-68: Marriage Index 1858-1968. Mf 69-71: Births 1858-1900. Mf 71-73: Marriages 1858-1900. Mf 73-75: Deaths 1858-1900) – (mf ed 1991) – 75mf – 9 – 0-87623-129-6 – us Holbrook [920]

Norton, A Banning *see* A HISTORY OF KNOX COUNTY, OHIO 1779-1862

Norton, Andrews *see*
- A DEFENCE OF LIBERAL CHRISTIANITY
- THE EVIDENCES OF THE GENUINENESS OF THE GOSPELS
- INAUGURAL DISCOURSE DELIVERED BEFORE THE UNIVERSITY IN CAMBRIDGE, 10 AUG 1819
- INTERNAL EVIDENCES OF THE GENUINENESS OF THE GOSPELS

Norton, Arthur O *see* READINGS IN THE HISTORY OF EDUCATION

Norton, Charles Basil *see* PERSONAL JOURNAL OF EVENTS ABOARD HMS CHALLENGER 1909-1910

Norton, Charles Eliot *see* TWO NOTEBOOKS OF THOMAS CARLYLE FROM 23D MARCH, 1822, TO 16TH MAY, 1832

Norton Family *see* DIARIES

Norton, Francis Collins *see* A POPULAR HANDBOOK OF USEFUL AND INTERESTING INFORMATION FOR BEGINNERS IN THE ELEMENTARY STUDY OF ASSYRIOLOGY

Norton, Frederick Owen *see* A LEXICOGRAPHICAL AND HISTORICAL STUDY OF DIATHEKE

Norton, George *see* COMMENTARIES ON THE HISTORY, CONSTITUTION, AND CHARTERED FRANCHISES OF THE CITY OF LONDON

Norton, Margaret Cross *see*
- ILLINOIS CENSUS RETURNS, 1810 & 1818
- ILLINOIS CENSUS RETURNS, 1820

Norton, Raquel *see* THE RELATIONSHIP BETWEEN CAFFEINE CONSUMPTION AND SYMPTOMS OF PREMENSTRUAL SYNDROME IN COLLEGE AGE FEMALES

Norton, Robert *see* THE RESTORATION OF APOSTLES AND PROPHETS IN THE CATHOLIC APOSTOLIC CHURCH

NORTON: THE COLLECTED WRITINGS OF CAROLINE NORTON (1808-1877) – Marlborough: Adam Matthew Publications, 1995 – 8r – 1 – $970.00 – uk Matthew [305]

Norton, William *see* REVISED ENGLISH VERSION OF THE OLD-COVENANT SCRIPTURES: COMPARED

NORTON'S LITERARY LETTER, COMPRISING AMERICAN PAPERS OF INTEREST AND A CATALOGUE OF RARE AND VALUABLE BOOKS RELATIVE TO AMERICA – 1-252. 1857-60 – 1 – us UMI [073]

NORU : NORDDEUTSCHE RUNDSCHAU FUER FUNK UND FILM – Hamburg, Berlin. may-jun 1926 – 1r – 1 – gw Mikrofilm [790]

Norval, Leigh *see* WOMEN OF THE BIBLE

NORVEG – v1-13. 1951-68 – 1 – us I.U. Libraries [390]

NORWALK AFTER TWO HUNDRED AND FIFTY YEARS / Fairfield County. Connecticut – By the Norwalk Historical & Memorial Library Assn., 1902. Biog. and hist. sketches. 7 fiches. F-0082 – 9 – us A.G.L.L. [920]

Norwalk. Ohio. First Presbyterian Church *see* RECORDS

Norwalk.Ohio. St. Paul's Episcopal Church *see* RECORDS

NORWAY : HISTORISK STATISTISK 1968 / Norway. Statistiske Sentralbyra – (Coll title: European Official Statistical Serials, 1841-1984) – 7mf – 9 – £7.00f (set £1,510.00 288mf) – uk Chadwyck [948]

NORWAY : STATISTISK ARBOK FOR NORGE 1879-1965 / Norway. Statistisk Sentralbyra – (Coll title: European Official Statistical Serials, 1841-1984) – 281mf – 9 – £4.00f (set £1,510.00 288mf) – uk Chadwyck [948]

Norway *see*
- OM ET LANGTIDSPROGRAM FOR 1954-1957
- UTBYGGINGSPROGRAMMET FOR NORD-NORGE, 1952-1960

NORWAY BAPTIST CHURCH. ORANGEBURG COUNTY, SOUTH CAROLINA : CHURCH RECORDS – 1893-Aug. 1991 (incomplete). WMU 1906-1922 – 1r – 1 – $29.21 – us Baptist [240]

NORWAY, CHANGING AND CHANGELESS / Rothery, Agnes Edwards – New York: The Viking Press, 1939. 294p.plates – 1 – us U.W. Library [948]

Norway. Finans- og Toll departementet *see*
- LANGTIDSPROGRAMMET, 1962-1965
- LANGTIDSPROGRAMMET 1966-1969
- NORWEGIAN LONG TERM PROGRAMME, 1962-1965
- REVISJON AV LANGTIDSPROGRAMMET 1966-1969

Norway. Royal Norwegian Ministry of Finance *see* NORWEGIAN LONG TERM PROGRAMME 1974-1977

Norway. Statistisk Sentralbyra *see* NORWAY

Norway. Statistiske Sentralbyra *see* NORWAY

NORWEGIAN ARCHAEOLOGICAL REVIEW – (1981-. 1,5,6,9) – v1-. 1968- – 1 – us UMI [073]

NORWEGIAN BAPTIST YEARBOOKS AND BANNERET YEARBOOKS – 1877-1962; Bannaret 1880-1962 – 1 – $996.45 – us Baptist [240]

THE NORWEGIAN FORMS OF CERAMIUM / Foslie, M – (K. Norske Vidensk. Selsk. Skrifter). Trondhjem. 1893. B-6362 2 – 8 – ne IDC [580]

THE NORWEGIAN FORMS OF LITHOTHAMNION / Foslie, M – (K. Norske Vidensk. Selsk. Skrifter). Trondhjem. 1895. B-6363 2 – 8 – ne IDC [580]

NORWEGIAN LONG TERM PROGRAMME, 1962-1965 / Norway. Finans- og Toll departementet – Oslo. 1961 – 9 – ne IDC [336]

NORWEGIAN LONG TERM PROGRAMME 1974-1977 / Norway. Royal Norwegian Ministry of Finance – Extracts from Parliamentary Report nr. 71, 1972-1973. BD-2011 1 – 9 – ne IDC [948]

NORWELL 1633-1900 – (Mf 1-5: Scituate Vital Records 1636-1799. Mf 6-9: Scituate Town & Vital Records 1659-1795. Mf 10-17: Scituate Town & Vital Records 1736-1845. Mf 18-24: Scituate Land Records 1633-1707. Mf 25: South Scituate Rebellion Records 1861-65. Mf 26-30: South Scituate Vital Records 1849-65. Mf 31-32: South Scituate Births 1849-91. Mf 32-33: South Scituate Marriages 1866-92. Mf 34: South Scituate Deaths 1866-92. Mf 35-36: Index of Norwell Births 1888-1940. Mf 37-38: Index of Norwell Marriages 1889-1940; FICHES 39-40: Index of Norwell Deaths 1892-1940. Mf 40: Norwell Deaths 1892-1914. Mf 41: Norwell Births 1888-1900. Mf 42: Norwell Marriages 1889-1912) – (mf ed 1991) – 42mf – 9 – 0-87623-123-7 – us Holbrook [920]

NOR'WEST FARMER – Winnipeg, CN. 1886-1936 – 46r – 1 – cn Commonwealth Micro [073]

NOR-WEST FARMER – Winnipeg, Canada. Mar 1905-Jun 1922; 1935-36 – 1 – uk British Libr Newspaper [072]

NOR'WESTER – Red River Settlement, Winnipeg, Canada. 1859-69 – 2r – 1 – $136.00 – cn Library Assoc [971]

NOR'WESTER JOURNAL – Guelph. v1-2. 1970-73 – 9 – Can$20.00 – cn Micromedia [073]

Norwich. (Diocese) *see*
- BISHOPS REGISTERS
- TANNER'S INDEX TO THE BISHOPS' REGISTERS

NORWICH GAZETTE – England, 7 Jan 1744-19 Dec 1747 (imperfect) – 1r – 1 – uk British Libr Newspaper [072]

NORWICH PACKET – Norwich. Connecticut. 1773-1802 – 1,3 – us Readex [071]

NORWICH THEATRICAL OBSERVER AND RANELAGH SPECTATOR – 1-42. 1827 – 1 – us UMI [790]

NORWOOD NEWS – (Norwood News & Tuesday Edition 1923-25) – London, UK. 29 Feb 1868-26 Nov 1965 – 112r – 1 – uk British Libr Newspaper [072]

NORWOOD NEWS AND TUESDAY EDITION *see* NORWOOD NEWS

Norwood, Richard *see* THE JOURNAL OF RICHARD NORWOOD 1639-1640, SURVEYOR OF BERMUDA

NO.S / Maiakovskii, Vladimir – (Novye stikhi). M. 1928. BR-985 2 – 8 – ne IDC [460]

NOS AFRICAINS... / Percher, Jules Hippolyte – Paris, 1894 – us Res Libr [960]

NOS AMIS LES QUEBECQUOIS : ALBUM DE CARICATURES / Huard, Charles – Montreal: Jules Fournier, editeur, [1913?]. SEM105P1505 – 1mf – 9 – Can$2.25 – cn Bibl Nat [740]

NOS ARCHIVES: LES STATISTIQUES / Bedard, Theophile Pierre – Quebec: A. Cote, 1880. 03307. (Pre-1900 Canadiana) – 9 – cn C.I.H.M. [310]

NOS DOCTRINES. / Daly, Cesar – Paris, 1863, 16p.; DES DROITS ET DES DEVOIRS DE L'ARCHITECTE. Paris, 1870, 22p.; INGENIEURS ET ARCHITECTES. Paris, 1877, 12 p.; DES HAUTES ETUDES D'ARCHITECTURE. Paris. 1888, 44p., ill. (Architecture Series) – 9 – fr Hachette [720]

NOS DROITS – Cap-de-la-Madeleine, Canada. 25 jun 1948-26 mar 1969 – 7r – 1 – Can$55.00r – cn Can Microfilming [072]

NOS GRAND'MERES: DISCOURS PRONONCE DEVANT LA SOCIETE DES DAMES DE CHARITE DE MONTREAL / Bourassa, Napoleon – Montreal: Cadieux & Derome, 1887. 00206. (Pre-1900 Canadiana) – 9 – cn C.I.H.M. [971]

NOS IMAGES – Leopoldville, Belgian Congo. French and Lingala Edition. Dec. 15, 1949 – 1 – us NY Public [960]

NOS IMAGES – Leopoldville, Belgian Congo. Swahili Edition. 1948 49-1950 – 1 – us NY Public [072]

NOS IMAGES – Leopoldville, Belgian Congo. Tshiluba language.15 Mar 1949; 15 Jan- 15 Sept 1950 – 1 – us NY Public [072]

NOS JEUNES DETENUS. ETUDE SUR L'ENFANCE COUPABLE AVANT, PENDANT ET APRES SON SEJOUR AU QUARTIER CORRECTIONNEL / Raux – (French Precursors of Psychiatry Series). Lyon. A. Storck. 1890 – 9 – fr Hachette [305]

NOS LIVRES / Quebec. (Province). Office des Communications Sociales – Montreal: Office des communications sociales. v8-19. 1970-1988. SEM16P240 – 2r – 5 – Can$106.00 – cn Bibl Nat [010]

NOS PAYSANNES / L'Estoille, Antoine de – Paris. 1885. (La Condition Ouvriere. Part Two.) – 9 – 5.00 – fr Bibl Nationale [360]

NOS SAINTS PATRONS : SAINT THOMAS D'AQUIN, PATRON DES ECOLES, SAINTE CECILE, PATRONNE DES MUSICIENS, SAINT JEAN-BAPTISTE, PATRON DES CANADIENS FRANCAIS / Allaire, J-B-A – Saint-Hyacinthe: [s.n.], 1921. SEM105P692 – 1mf – 9 – Can$2.25 – cn Bibl Nat [240]

NOSCE TE IPSUM / Davis, John – 16th century. Holkham Ms 758 – 1 – uk Microform Academic [810]

Nosgen, CF *see* COMMENTAR UEBER DIE APOSTELGESCHICHTE DES LUKAS

Noske, S *see* ASPECTS OF THE BEHAVIOUR AND ECOLOGY OF THE WHITE COCKATOO AND GALAH IN CROPLANDS IN NORTH-EASTERN NEW SOUTH WALES

NOSOGRAPHIE PHILOSOPHIQUE. OU LA METHODE DE L'ANALYSE APPLIQUEE A LA MEDECINE / Pinel, Philippe – (French Precursors of Psychiatry Series). Paris. Maradan, an VI – 9 – fr Hachette [120]

NOSOTROS; REVISTA MENSUEL DE LETRAS, ARTE HISTORIA Y FILOSOFIA – Buenos Aires. v. 1, no. 2-v. 81, no. 299 300. Sep 1907-Dec 1934 – 1 – us NY Public [073]

NOSOTROS...LIBRO DE PRECES DE LA MILITANTE DEACCION CATOLICA / Aradillas Agudo, Antonio – Madrid: Maribel A.G., 1964 – 1 – sp Bibl Santa Ana [946]

Nosovich, II *see* SLOVAR' BELORUSSKOGO NARECHIIA

Noss, James *see* MANUSCRIPTS RELATING TO PAPUA NEW GUINEA, (1943)

A NOSSA FOLHA : ORGAO POLITICO, PROGRESSISTA, DEDICADO A REORGANISACAO DO MUNICIPIO – Guanhaes, 5 Mar-16 May 1937 – 1,5,6 – bl Biblioteca [072]

NOSTALGIA DE DIOS EN AGUSTIN Y EN PASCAL / Caba, Pedro – Madrid. pp. 305-314 – sp Bibl Santa Ana [240]

LA NOSTALGIA DE LOS DOS / Reyes Huertas, Antonio – Badajoz: Tipgrafia el Noticiero extremeno, 1910 – 1 – sp Bibl Santa Ana [946]

NOSTALGIAS / Reyes Huertas, Antonio & Monterrey, Manuel – Badajoz: Arqueros, 1910 – 1 – sp Bibl Santa Ana [946]

LA NOSTRA LOTTA – Koper, Yugoslavia. Oct 1949-1952 – 2r – 1 – us L of C Photodup [949]

NOT INTERVENTION...CONQUEST / Ehrenburg, Ilia Grigorevich – n.p. 1937? Fiche W 854. (Blodgett Collection of Spanish Civil War Pamphlets) – 9 – us H.U. College Libr [946]

NOT OF MAN BUT OF GOD / Manning, Jacob Merrill – Boston: D. Lothrop, 1883. 1 fiche – 9 – us A.T.L.A. [240]

NOT "THEIR" JESUS (CCC345) / Yeh, Tu – (In Chinese) – Shanghai: Christian Literature Society, 1923 – 1r – 1 – 1984-6684 – us A.T.L.A. [240]

NOT WISELY, BUT TOO WELL: A NOVEL / Broughton, Rhoda – British Fiction Archive: Unit 4 – 9 – uk Bell [830]

NOT WITHSTANDING / Cholmondeley, Mary – British Fiction Archive: Unit 3 – 9 – uk Bell [830]

NOT YOURS TO GIVE / Crockett, David – 1884, 8p – 9 – 1.00f – at Libertarian Micro [335]

A NOTA – Manaos, Amazonas. 26 Ago-18 Nov 1917 – 1,5,6 – bl Biblioteca [072]

NOTA DE LOS FUNDAMENTOS AL RECURSO...EN PLEITO AL...MERIDA / Montijo. Ayuntamiento – 1897 – 9 – 1.50f – sp Bibl Santa Ana [946]

NOTA DEL DIA / Garcia Jimeno, Fernando – Badajoz: Tip. y Lit. El Progreso, 1902 – 1 – sp Bibl Santa Ana [946]

NOTA EXPLICATIVA DE LOS PRODUCTOS QUE EXHIBE... / Velasco y Rodriguez, Antonio – Almendralejo: Tip. de los Caballeros, s.a. – 1 – sp Bibl Santa Ana [946]

NOTA OVER DE CONVERSIE VAN COMMUNAAL IN ERFELIJK INDIVIDUEEL GRONDBEZIT OP JAVA EN MADOERA – Batavia, 1902 – 3mf – 9 – ne IDC [333]

NOTA OVER DE VERVANGING VAN HET ERFELIJK INDIVIDUEEL GRONDBEZIT DOOR EIGENDOM OP JAVA EN MADOERA – Batavia, 1902 – 3mf – 9 – ne IDC [333]

NOTA OVER VOLKSBEWEGINGEN IN DE PREANGER 1925 – KITLV,H 795,8. BSD-102/1 mf. 85-86 – 9 – ne IDC [950]

NOTA SOBRE DOCUMENTOS INEDITOS DE PIZARRO, DE CUNEO VIDAL / Perez de Guzman, Juan – Madrid: Fortanet, 1920. B.R.A.H. 77 p. 478 – 1 – sp Bibl Santa Ana [946]

NOTA SOBRE LA IMPROCEDENCIA DEL RECURSO...POR PLASENZUELA...EN PLEITO CON EL AYUNTAMIENTO DE TRUJILLO... – Madrid: Sucesores de Rivadeneyra s.a., 1897? – 1 – sp Bibl Santa Ana [946]

Notabene, Nicolaus *see* FORORD

NOTABILITIES OF TORONTO IN 1877 / Edwards, David – Toronto: P. Gross, 1877. 02886. (Pre-1900 Canadiana) – 9 – cn C.I.H.M. [971]

A NOTABLE HISTORIE OF THE SARACENS. BRIEFLY AND FAITHFULLY DESCRYBING THE ORIGINALL BEGINNING CONTINUAUNCE AND SUCCESSE ASWELL OF THE SARACENS, AS ALSO OF TURKES, SOULDANS, MAMALUKES, ASSASSINES, TARTARIANS AND SOPHIANS / Curio, C A – London, 1575 – 4mf – 9 – H-8346/1 – ne IDC [956]

NOTABLE MEN OF WISCONSIN / Williams Publishing Co – Milwaukee: ca. 1902. Wisconsin Reel 3. (The Cox Library Collection) – 5 – us Americana [978]

UN NOTABLE MOSAICO EN SANTA MARTA (BADAJOZ). EL ARTE ANTIGUO EN LOS CAMPOS / Viniegra de Vera, Virgilio – Madrid: Tip. Rev. Arch. Bibl. y Mus, 1925. B.R.A.H. 87, pp 294-298, 2 lam – sp Bibl Santa Ana [750]
NOTABLE TRIALS SERIES – (Notable British Trials. $1,466.25. Notable War Crimes Trials. $184.00) – Original publ., Hodge and Co. Ltd. 93 titles in two series: Notable British Trials and War Crimes Trials. Includes index. Individual series available – 9 – $1,650.25 – us UMI [340]
NOTAE SEU ELUCIDATIONES BREVES IN PETRI DORLANDI CHRONICI CARTUSIENSIS LIBROS / Petraeus, Theodorus – Col. Agrippinae, 1608 – 2mf – 8 – Dfl9.00 – ne Slangenburg [240]
THE NOTARIAL LAWS OF CUBA AND PUERTO RICO, 1893 : ORIGINAL DECREE OF THE SPANISH REPUBLIC IN 18973 AS AMENDED BY SUBSEQUENT ROYAL DECRESS THRU 1893 – Washington: GPO, 1899 – 1mf – 9 – $1.50 – LLMC 92-310 – us L.L.M.C. [340]
THE NOTARIES' AND COMMISSIONERS' MANUAL, CONTAINING FULL INSTRUCTIONS AS TO THEIR APPOINTMENT, POWERS, RIGHTS, AND DUTIES, UNDER FEDERAL AND NEW YORK LAWS. / Snyder, William Lamartine – New York, Baker, Voorhis, 1898. 184 p. LL-1288 – 1 – us L of C Photodup [340]
NOTARIES' COMMISSIONS RECORDS / Huron County. Ohio. Clerk of Courts – 1858-1876 – 1r – 1 – $32.50r – us Archival [324]
NOTARIES JOURNAL – New York. On film: v1-6; 1877-83. LL-0154 – 1 – us L of C Photodup [340]
THE NOTARIES' MANUAL. / Rex, Benjamin F – (3d ed. St. Louis: Gilbert, 1889. 285p. LL-1172) – St. Louis: Gilbert, 1882. 283p. LL-1169 – 1 – us L of C Photodup [340]
UN NOTARIO ESPANOL EN RUSIA / Hidalgo, Diego – 3rd ed. Madrid: Edit. Cenit S.A., 1930 – 1 – sp Bibl Santa Ana [340]
Notaris, G de *see*
- CRONACA DELLA BRIOLOGIA ITALIANA
- EPILOGO DELLA BRIOLOGIA ITALIANA
- JUNGERMANNIARUM AMERICANARUM PUGILLUS
- MANTISSA MUSCORUM AD FLORAM PEDEMONTANAM
- MUSCOLOGIA ITALICAE SPICILEGIUM
- SYLLABUS MUSCORUM IN ITALIA ET IN INSULIS CIRCUMSTANTIBUS HUCUSQUE COGNITORUM

NOTARISIA – Venezia. v1-11. 1886-1896 – 42mf – 9 – ne IDC [945]
NOTARUM SPONGIA QUIBUS ALEXIPHARMACUM CIVIBUS SYLVAE-DUCENSIBUS, ASPERSIT GISBERTUS VOETIUS MINISTER SYLVAE-DUCENSIS / Jansenius, Corn. – Lovanii, 1631 – 10mf – 8 – ne Slangenburg [240]
THE NOTARY'S MANUAL: SHOWING THE RIGHTS, DUTIES, AND LIABILITIES OF NOTARIES, ACCORDING TO THE COMMON LAW THROUGHOUT THE UNION – Detroit: Richmond, Backus, 1881. 67 29p. LL-744 – 1 – us L of C Photodup [340]
NOTARY'S NOTE-BOOK AND NOTE-HOLDER'S MANUAL. – Little Rock, Ark.: Arkansas Democrat, 1892. 44p. LL-954 – 1 – us L of C Photodup [340]
NOTAS A LAS ANTIGUEDADES DE EXTREMADURA / Guerra, Felipe Leon – (1854 ed.1.50f; 9. 1872 ed.1.50f; BSA; 9. 1883 ed.1.50f; BSA; 9) – 1865 – 9 – 1.50f – sp Bibl Santa Ana [930]
NOTAS A LAS ANTIGUEDADES E EXTREMADURA DE JOSE VIU / Guerra, Felipe Leon – Caceres: Imp. de la Vda. de Burgos e hijos, 1854 – 1 – sp Bibl Santa Ana [946]
LAS "NOTAS A LAS LEYES DE INDIAS" DE MANUEL JOSE DE AYALA. MADRID, 1935 / Manzano Manzano, Juan – Madrid: Razon y Fe, 1936 – 1 – sp Bibl Santa Ana [946]
NOTAS ACERCA DEL TEATRO RELIGIOSO EN LA AMERICA COLONIAL / Bayle, Constantino – Madrid: Razon y Fe, 1947 – 1 – sp Bibl Santa Ana [240]
NOTAS ARQUEOLOGICAS / Roso de Luna, Mario – Caceres: Tip. Enc. y Lib. Jimenez, 1906 – 1 – sp Bibl Santa Ana [930]
NOTAS BIOGRAFICAS DE ANTONIO RODRIGUEZ MONINO / Segura Otano, Enrique – Badajoz: Imprenta Diputacion Provincial, 1971 – sp Bibl Santa Ana [920]
NOTAS DOCUMENTALES SOBRE ARTISTAS Y ARTESANOS DE EXTREMADURA / Martinez Quesada, Juan – (Badajoz): Imprenta de la Diputacion Provincial, 1960 – sp Bibl Santa Ana [700]
NOTAS EPIGRAFICAS / Roso de Luna, Mario – Caceres: Tip. Enc. y Lib. de N.M. Jimenez, 1900 – 1 – sp Bibl Santa Ana [946]
NOTAS EPIGRAFICAS. CACERES / Berjano, Daniel Escobar – 1899 – 1 – sp Bibl Santa Ana [946]
NOTAS LITERARIAS DE EXTREMADURA / Lopez Prudencio, Jose – Badajoz: Artes Graficas, 1932 – 1 – sp Bibl Santa Ana [440]
NOTAS PARA LA HISTORIA DE LA CIUDAD DE BADAJOZ A FINES DEL SIGLO 18 / Agundez Fernandez, Antonio – Badajoz: Diputacion Provincial de Badajoz, 1959 – 1 – sp Bibl Santa Ana [946]
NOTAS PARA SUS BIOGRAFIAS Y PARA LA HISTORIA DOCUMENTAL DE LA SANTA IGLESIA CATEDRAL Y CIUDAD DE PLASENCIA / Benabides Checa, Jose – Plasencia, 1907 – sp Bibl Santa Ana [240]
NOTAS PARA UN CATALOGO ARTISTICO DE LLERENA / Lepe de la Camara, Jose Maria – Badajoz: Dip. Provincial, 1966. Sep. REE – sp Bibl Santa Ana [700]
NOTAS PARA UNA BIBLIOGRAFIA GUADALUPANA / Montejano & Aguinaga, R – Mexico, Bay, (Bajo el signo de "Abside"), 1940 – 2mf – 9 – ne IDC [972]
NOTAS Y DOCUMENTOS ACERCA DE LA DESCENDENCIA DE MOCTEZUMA 3RD / Lopez de Meneses, Amada – mayo-junio, 1955 – 1 – sp Bibl Santa Ana [920]
NOTAS Y TEXTOS. INFORME SOBRE LOS NATURALES DE LA DIOCESIS DE CEBU / Bayle, Constantino – Madrid: Missionalia Hispanica, 1949 – 1 – sp Bibl Santa Ana [240]
NOTAS Y TEXTOS. PLANES ANTIGUOS DE SEMINARIOS DE MISIONES Y DE RECLUTAR CLERO SECULAR PARA LA EVANGELIZACION DE AMERICA / Bayle, Constantino – Madrid: Missionalia Hispanica, 1949 – 1 – sp Bibl Santa Ana [240]
NOTATIONES IN TOTAM SCRIPTURAM SACRAM / Sa, E – Antverpiae, 1598 – 6mf – 9 – CA-62/1 – ne IDC [240]
NOTATIONES IN TOTAM SRIPTURAM SACRAM / Sa, E – Antverpiae, 1598 – 12mf – 8 – ne Slangenburg [220]
NOTE ON 2 PRESCRIPTIONS : MEMOIRES CONCERNANT L'HISTOIRE, LES SCIENCES... DES CHINOIS... / Remedes – Paris, 1776-1783 – 1mf – 9 – ne IDC [615]
NOTE ON EDUCATION IN PALESTINE, 1920-1929 / Palestine. Department of Education – Jerusalem. 1929. BJ-28-112 1 – 9 – ne IDC [956]
A NOTE ON EDUCATIONAL DEVELOPMENT AND RELATED SCHEMES IN RAJASTHAN / India. Rajasthan. Directorate of Primary and Secondary Education – Bikaner, 1970 – 2mf – 9 – DE-554/1 – ne IDC [370]
A NOTE ON ORGANIZATION AND EXECUTION OF THE RECLAMATION CONTRACT BY NASA / United Nations. Food and Agriculture Organization. The Development of the Tribal Lands and Settlement Project. Libya Mission – Benghazi. Aug 1966. Singh, H. (Farm Management Expert). BNE-1011 1 – 9 – ne IDC [333]
NOTE ON THE KHAKSAR MOVEMENT / Orde, P L et al – [s.l: s.n.], 1940 (Lahore: SGPP) – us Res Libr [950]
NOTE RELATIVE AUX TRAVAUX PREPARATOIRES DU IVE PLAN 1973-76 / Tunisia. Ministere du Plan – (Preparatory Framework for the Fourth Plan 1973-76). Tunis. Jul 1972. BD-1763 1 – 9 – ne IDC [330]
NOTE SUR LA FAUNE DES LEPIDOPTERES DE LOJA (EQUATEUR) ET DESCRIPTIONS D'ESPECES NOUVELLES / Dognin, P – Paris, 1887-91. v1-4. (Extrait du Naturaliste). Z-1190/2 – 8 – ne IDC [590]
NOTE SUR LA MORTALITE PARMI LES FORCATS DU BAGNE DE ROCHEFORT, SUR LA FREQUENCE DE LEURS MALADIES / Villerme, Louis Rene – Reprod. d'un extrait des Annales d'Hygiene publique et de Medecine legale. v6, 1831. p113-127. 1 fiche. (Statistics Series: Medical Studies) – 9 – 6.00 – fr Bibl Nationale [310]
NOTE SUR L'ACTIVITE DU SECTEUR PETROLIER DURANT L'ANNEE 1970 / Morocco. Division de l'Energie – BNE-3043 1 – 9 – ne IDC [660]
NOTE SUR L'ACTIVITE MINIERE AU COURS DE L'ANNEE / Morocco. Direction des Mines et de la Geologie – 1968-70. BNE-3038 1 – 9 – ne IDC [622]
NOTE SUR LE MOUVEMENT DE LA POPULATION ET LA QUESTION DE LA NATALITE DANS LE CANTON DE CRIQUETCH-L'ESNEVAL / Lechevalier, A – Reprod. d'un extrait du Recueil des Publications de la Societe havraise d'Etudes diverses. 1817. p39-63. 1 fiche. (Statistics Series; Demography) – 9 – 6.00 – fr Bibl Nationale [310]
NOTE SUR LES RAVAGES DU CHOLERA-MORBUS EN MAISONS GARNIES DE PARIS DEPUIS LE 19 MARS JUSQU'AU LE 1ER AOUT 1832 / Villerme, Louis Rene – Reprod. d'un extrait des Annales d'Hygiene publique et de Medecine legale. v11, 1834. p385-409.1 fiche. (Statistics Series: Medical Studies) – 9 – 6.00 – fr Bibl Nationale [310]
NOTE SUR LES TABLEAUX STATISTIQUES / France. Ministere de l'Interieur – P., imp. de la Republique, an IX – 9 – fr Hachette [944]
NOTE SUR LES TOU-YU-HOUEN ET LES SOU-P'I / Pelliot, P – T'ount Pao, v. 20. Leide. 1921. BU-588 2 – 8 – ne IDC [950]
NOTE SUR LES TUYUYUN / Hambis, L – v. 236. 1948. BU-589 2 – 8 – ne IDC [999]
NOTE SUR UNE ANCIENNE TRADUCTION FRANCAISE MANUSCRITE DE L'ITINERAIRE DE BENJAMIN DE TUDELE / Weil, Julien – Madrid: Est. Tip. Fortanet, 1907. B.R.A.H. Tomo 50, 1907, pp. 150-153 – 1 – sp Bibl Santa Ana [946]
NOTEBOOK / Whilden, R Furman – 1 – 8.96 – us Baptist [240]
NOTEBOOKS / Anderson, Alexander – Records of Anderson's experiments in puffing cereal grains and other starch-containing materials conducted between 1900 and 1931 – 9r, including filmed inventory – 1 – $270.00; $30.00r – us M.H.S. [660]
NOTEBOOKS / Irving, Washington – v1-15. 1807-35 – 1r – 1 – us Ross [880]
NOTEBOOKS / Scharf, George – 1820-95. National Portrait Gallery. With printed index – 1 – PS1350.00 – uk World [025]
NOTEBOOKS, 1836-1838 / Clowes, W – (Coll title: The People Called Methodists, Phase 3: Primary Sources, 1801-1850) – 4mf – 9 – MP-685/1 – ne IDC [240]
NOTEBOOKS CONTAINING QUERIES, EXTRACTS FROM PRINTED SOURCES, ETC. RELATING TO ASTORIA / Irving, Washington – 1835. Ms notebooks 1-15 – 1 – us NY Public [830]
NOTEBOOKS OF JOHN WINDELE / Royal Irish Academy – 1801-1865 – 31r with printed guide – £1,300.00 – uk World [880]
NOTED LIVING ALBANIANS AND STATE OFFICIALS / Harsha, David A – Biographical sketches. Albany: Weed, Parsons and Co., 1891. New York Reel 7. (The Cox Library Collection) – 5 – us Americana [978]
NOTE-LINE IN THE HEBREW SCRIPTURES / Kennedy, James – Edinburgh: T. & T. Clark, 1903. 1 fiche – 9 – us A.T.L.A. [220]
DAS NOTENBLATT : MONTHLY, LATER WEEKLY, GERMAN LANGUAGE, FRATERNAL NEWSPAPER – Cleveland, OH. Mar 1906-Oct 1909 (incomplete) – 1 – us Western Res [071]
NOTES / Montana. Forest and Conservation Experiment Station. Missoula – nos.1-8. 1964-69 – 1,5,6 – us Spaulding [630]
NOTES / Taft, Robert – undated, Related to Frederic Remington and biography of Remington – 1 – us KS Hist [920]
NOTES ADDITIONNELLES SUR LES TON-KINE (TURCS) OCCIDENTAUX / Chavannes, E – (T'oung Pao, S. 2, v. 5.). BU-590 2 – 8 – ne IDC [956]
NOTES ADDITIONNELLES A L'HISTOIRE DE LA FAMILLE GILL / Gill, Charles – Montreal: E. Senecal, 1889. 03062. (Pre-1900 Canadiana) – 9 – cn C.I.H.M. [920]
NOTES ALGOLOGIQUES / Bornet, J BE & Thuret, G – 1876 and 1880 – 1 – uk Microform Academic [580]
NOTES ALGOLOGIQUES / Bornet, J BE & Thuret, G – Paris. 1876-80. B-39 2 – 8 – ne IDC [580]
NOTES AND MEMORANDA, 1784-1868 / Everett, J – (Coll title: The People Called Methodists, Phase 3: Primary Sources, 1801-1850) – 60mf – 9 – MP-675/1 – ne IDC [240]
NOTES AND QUERIES – Series 1-13. 1849-1953 – 1,5,6 – us Princeton Micro [010]
NOTES AND QUERIES FOR READERS AND WRITERS, COLLECTORS AND LIBRARIANS – v1- 1849- 1; v18- 5,6; v23- 9 – us UMI [010]
NOTES AND REMINISCENCES OF A JOURNEY TO ENGLAND / Godden, John – Montreal: J. Lovell, 1873. 03455. (Pre-1900 Canadiana) – 9 – cn C.I.H.M. [910]
NOTES AND STUDIES IN THE PHILOSOPHY OF ANIMAL MAGNETISM AND SPIRITUALISM / Ashburner, John – New York: H. Bailliere, etc., 1867. xxiv,444p – 1 – us U.W. Library [150]
NOTES ARCHEOLOGIQUES: LE FORT DE CHAMBLY, 1709 A 1760 / Dion, J O – s.l.: s.n., 1875. 02180. (Pre-1900 Canadiana) – 9 – cn C.I.H.M. [971]
NOTES BIO-BIBLIOGRAPHIE DU REVEREND FRERE PATRICE, S.C. / Ulderic, Frere – 1961. SEM105P4 – 1mf – 9 – Can$2.25 – cn Bibl Nat [240]
NOTES BIO-BIBLIOGRAPHIQUES SUR "TANTE CHANTAL", MADAME CECILE LACHAINE-BROSSEAU / Saint-Gilbert-de-la-Croix, Soeur – 1963. SEM105P4 – 1mf – 9 – Can$2.25 – cn Bibl Nat [920]
NOTES, CORRESPONDENCE AND CLIPPINGS RELATING TO JOSEPH KINCHEN GRIFFIS / Jaderboeg, Elizabeth – 1 – us KS Hist [978]
NOTES CRITICAL AND EXPLANATORY ON PAUL'S EPISTLE TO THE GALATIANS GREEK TEXT OF TISCHENDORF / Boise, James Robinson – Cambridge: University Press, c1881 – 1mf – 9 – 0-8370-5989-5 – 1985-3989 – us A.T.L.A. [220]
NOTES, CRITICAL AND EXPLANATORY, ON THE ACTS OF THE APOSTLES / Jacobus, Melancthon Williams – New York: Robert Carter, 1864. 1 fiche – 9 – us A.T.L.A. [240]
NOTES, CRITICAL AND EXPLANATORY, ON THE BOOK OF EXODUS / Jacobus, Melancthon Williams – New York: Robert Carter, 1874. 1 fiche – 9 – us A.T.L.A. [220]
NOTES, CRITICAL AND EXPLANATORY, ON THE BOOK OF GENESIS : FROM THE COVENANT TO THE CLOSE / Jacobus, Melancthon Williams – (Includes appendix on various events and people in Genesis) – New York: Robert Carter, 1866 – 1mf – 9 – 0-8370-3749-2 – 1985-1749 – us A.T.L.A. [220]
NOTES, CRITICAL AND PRACTICAL, ON THE BOOK OF GENESIS : DESIGNED AS A GENERAL HELP TO BIBLICAL READING AND INSTRUCTION / Bush, George – (V2 includes index of subjects and phrases) – 26th ed. New York: Ivison, Phinney, 1860, c1838 – 2mf – 9 – 0-8370-4871-0 – 1985-2871 – us A.T.L.A. [220]
NOTES DE LEXICOGRAPHIE HEBRAIQUE / Jouan, P – (Extrait des Melanges de la Fac. Orientale de l'Universite St. Joseph a Beyrouth). 1908. BNE-467 1 – 9 – ne IDC [470]
NOTES DE SYNTHESE SUR L'ECONOMIE DE LA VILLE DE BOUAKE / Castella, P & Baillon, D – Africa series. 1970 – 9 – fr Hachette [338]
NOTES DE TERRAIN, DOGON, OGOTEMMELI / Griaule, M – 9 – F160.00 – fr Ethnologie [960]
NOTES DE VOYAGE / Fabre, Paul – Couverture de George Auriol. Paris: Capitaine, 1895. 02938. (Pre-1900 Canadiana) – 9 – cn C.I.H.M. [910]
NOTES DE VOYAGE: LE GOLFE ET LES PROVINCES MARITIMES / Genand, J A – Montreal: Senecal, 1872.03323.(Pre-1900 Canadiana) – 9 – cn C.I.H.M. [910]
NOTES D'ETHNO-BOTANIQUE SUR L'ILE DES PINS, NOUVELLE-CALEDONIE / Dubois, M J – 9 – F20.00 – fr Ethnologie [580]
NOTES D'ETHNOLOGIE NEO-CALEDONIENNE / Leenhardt, Maurice – 9 – F100.00 – fr Ethnologie [306]
NOTES D'UN VOYAGE DANS L'OUEST DE LA FRANCE / Merimee, Prosper – Paris: Fournier, 1836 – fr Armell [910]

NOTES, ECCLESIOLOGICAL AND PICTURESQUE, ON DALMATIA, CROATIA, ISTRIA, STYRIA : WITH A VISIT TO MONTENEGRO / Neale, John Mason – London: J.T. Hayes, 1861 – 1mf – us A.T.L.A. [240]

NOTES ET DOCUMENTS / Congo. Institut de Recherches Economiques et Sociales – Leopoldville. 1960-61. – 22mf – 9 – ne IDC [960]

NOTES ET DOCUMENTS SUR LA FAMILLE DU BELLAY – 1579-19th c. – fr Armell [920]

NOTES ET ETUDES DOCUMENTAIRES – 1992-1995 – 33 times per yr – 9 – F5,280.00 – sz Infoprint [072]

NOTES ET ETUDES DOCUMENTAIRES / Libya. Secretariat General du Gouvernement – 27 Nov 1970. Nrs. 3740-3741. La Rep. Arabe Libyenne. La documentation francaise. Paris. BNE-519 1 – 9 – ne IDC [324]

NOTES ET REMARQUES SUR LA BRESSE LOUHANNAISE: ESQUISSE D'UNE TOPOGRAPHIE PHYSIOLOGIQUE ET MEDICALE DE L'ARRONDISSEMENT DE LOUHANS / Guillemaut, Lucien – Louhans: A. Romand, 1879. 529p.6 fiches. (Statistics Series: Topography). (Statistics Series: Medical Studies) – 9 – 15.00 – fr Bibl Nationale [944]

NOTES, EXPLANATORY AND PRACTICAL ON THE ACTS OF THE APOSTLES : DESIGNED FOR SUNDAY-SCHOOL TEACHERS AND BIBLE-CLASSES / Barnes, Albert – rev ed. New York: Harper & Bros, c1870 – 1mf – 9 – 0-8370-2179-0 – 1985-0179 – us A.T.L.A. [220]

NOTES, EXPLANATORY AND PRACTICAL, ON THE FIRST EPISTLE OF PAUL TO THE CORINTHIANS / Barnes, Albert – New York: Harper, 1867, c1837 – 1mf – 9 – 0-8370-6322-1 – 1986-0322 – us A.T.L.A. [220]

NOTES FOR BIBLE STUDY – Toronto: S R Briggs, [1881?-18– or 19–] – 9 – cn C.I.H.M. [210]

NOTES FOR READINGS ON THE LIFE OF JESUS / Moore, Edward Caldwell – Cambridge: Riverside Press, 1907. 1 fiche. 8370-4477-4 – 9 – us A.T.L.A. [240]

NOTES FROM CENTRAL AMERICAN LEGATIONS IN THE U.S. TO THE DEPT. OF STATE, 1823-1906 / U.S. Department of State – 10r – 1 – T34 – us Nat'l Archives [972]

NOTES FROM FEE / Read, Leonard E – Jan 1982. With comments. 1 fiche (29x) – 9 – 1.00f – at Libertarian Micro [320]

NOTES FROM FOREIGN CONSULS IN THE U.S. TO THE DEPT. OF STATE, 1789-1906 / U.S. Department of State – 11r – 1 – M664 – us Nat'l Archives [975]

NOTES FROM IRELAND – Ireland.1901-Aug 1918 – 1 – ie Microforms [072]

NOTES FROM MISCELLANEOUS FOREIGN STATES TO THE DEPT. OF STATE, 1817-1906 / U.S. Department of State – 4r – 1 – T953 – us Nat'l Archives [975]

NOTES FROM THE ARGENTINE LEGATION IN THE U.S. TO THE DEPT. OF STATE, 1811-1906 / U.S. Department of State – 15r – 1 – M47 – us Nat'l Archives [972]

NOTES FROM THE AUSTRIAN LEGATION IN THE U.S. TO THE DEPARTMENT OF STATE, 1820-1906 / U.S. Department of State – 15r – 1 – $510.00 – M48 – us Scholarly Res [327]

NOTES FROM THE BELGIAN LEGATION IN THE U.S. TO THE DEPT. OF STATE, 1832-1906 / U.S. Department of State – 12r – 1 – M194 – us Nat'l Archives [949]

NOTES FROM THE BOLIVIAN LEGATION IN THE U.S. TO THE DEPT. OF STATE, 1837-1906 / U.S. Department of State – 1r – 1 – T795 – us Nat'l Archives [972]

NOTES FROM THE BRAZILIAN LEGATION IN THE U.S. TO THE DEPT. OF STATE, 1824-1906 / U.S. Department of State – 8r – 1 – M49. Printed guide – us Nat'l Archives [972]

NOTES FROM THE BRITISH LEGATION IN THE U.S. TO THE DEPT. OF STATE, 1791-1906 / U.S. Department of State – 145r – 1 – M50 – us Nat'l Archives [941]

NOTES FROM THE CHILEAN LEGATION IN THE U.S. TO THE DEPT. OF STATE, 1811-1906 / U.S. Department of State – 6r – 1 – M73 – us Nat'l Archives [972]

NOTES FROM THE CHINESE LEGATION IN THE U.S. TO THE DEPT. OF STATE, 1868-1906 / U.S. Department of State – 6r – 1 – M98. Printed guide – us Nat'l Archives [950]

NOTES FROM THE COLOMBIAN LEGATION IN THE U.S. TO THE DEPT. OF STATE, 1810-1906 / U.S. Department of State – 11r – 1 – M51 – us Nat'l Archives [972]

NOTES FROM THE COSTA RICAN LEGATION IN THE U.S. TO THE DEPT. OF STATE, 1878-1906 / U.S. Department of State – 2r – 1 – T799 – us Nat'l Archives [972]

NOTES FROM THE CUBAN LEGATION IN THE U.S. TO THE DEPT. OF STATE, 1844-1906 / U.S. Department of State – 2r – 1 – T800 – us Nat'l Archives [972]

NOTES FROM THE DANISH LEGATION IN THE U.S. TO THE DEPT. OF STATE, 1801-1906 / U.S. Department of State – 9r – 1 – M52 – us Nat'l Archives [948]

NOTES FROM THE DEPT. OF STATE TO FOREIGN MINISTERS AND CONSULS IN THE U.S., 1793-1834 / U.S. Department of State – 5r – 1 – M38 – us Nat'l Archives [975]

NOTES FROM THE ECUADOREAN LEGATION IN THE UNITED STATES TO THE DEPARTMENT OF STATE / U.S. Department of State – 1839-1906. 2 rolls. T810 – 1 – us Nat'l Archives [972]

NOTES FROM THE ECUADOREAN LEGATION IN THE U.S. TO THE DEPT. OF STATE, 1839-1906 / U.S. Department of State – 2r – 1 – T810 – us Nat'l Archives [972]

NOTES FROM THE FRENCH LEGATION IN THE U.S. TO THE DEPT. OF STATE, 1789-1906 / U.S. Department of State – 32r – 1 – M53 – us Nat'l Archives [944]

NOTES FROM THE GREEK LEGATION IN THE U.S. TO THE DEPT. OF STATE, 1823-1892 / U.S. Department of State – 1r – 1 – T808 – us Nat'l Archives [949]

NOTES FROM THE HAITIAN LEGATION IN THE U.S. TO THE DEPT. OF STATE, 1861-1906 / U.S. Department of State – 6r – 1 – T803 – us Nat'l Archives [972]

NOTES FROM THE HAWAIIAN LEGATION IN THE U.S. TO THE DEPT. OF STATE, 1841-1899 / U.S. Department of State – 4r – 1 – T160 – us Nat'l Archives [978]

NOTES FROM THE HONDURAN LEGATION IN THE U.S. TO THE DEPT. OF STATE, 1878-1906 / U.S. Department of State – 1r – 1 – T796 – us Nat'l Archives [972]

NOTES FROM THE ITALIAN LEGATION IN THE U.S. TO THE DEPT. OF STATE, 1861-1906 / U.S. Department of State – 18r – 1 – M202. Printed guide – us Nat'l Archives [945]

NOTES FROM THE JAPANESE LEGATION IN THE U.S. TO THE DEPT. OF STATE. 1858-1906 / U.S. Department of State – 9r – 1 – M163. Printed guide – us Nat'l Archives [950]

NOTES FROM THE KOREAN LEGATION IN THE U.S. TO THE DEPT. OF STATE, 1883-1906 / U.S. Department of State – 1r – 1 – M166 – us Nat'l Archives [950]

NOTES FROM THE LEGATION OF EL SALVADOR IN THE U.S. TO THE DEPT. OF STATE, 1879-1906 / U.S. Department of State – 2r – 1 – T798 – us Nat'l Archives [972]

NOTES FROM THE LEGATION OF THE DOMINICAN REPUBLIC IN THE U.S. TO THE DEPT. OF STATE, 1844-1906 / U.S. Department of State – 3r – 1 – T801 – us Nat'l Archives [972]

NOTES FROM THE LEGATION OF THE KINGDOM OF THE TWO SICILIES TO THE DEPT. OF STATE, 1826-1860 / U.S. Department of State – 2r – 1 – M55 – us Nat'l Archives [945]

NOTES FROM THE LEGATIONS OF THE GERMAN STATES AND GERMANY IN THE U.S. TO THE DEPT. OF STATE, 1817-1906 / U.S. Department of State – 35r – 1 – $805.00 – M58 – us Nat'l Archives [327]

NOTES FROM THE LIBERIAN LEGATION IN THE U.S. TO THE DEPARTMENT OF STATE, 1862-1898 / U.S. Department of State – 1r – 1 – T807 – us Nat'l Archives [960]

NOTES FROM THE LUXEMBOURG LEGATION IN THE U.S. TO THE DEPT. OF STATE, 1876-1903 / U.S. Department of State – 1r – 1 – T814 – us Nat'l Archives [949]

NOTES FROM THE MADAGASCAN LEGATION IN THE U.S. TO THE DEPT. OF STATE, 1883-1894 / U.S. Department of State – 1r – 1 – T806 – us Nat'l Archives [960]

NOTES FROM THE MEXICAN LEGATION IN THE U.S. TO THE DEPT. OF STATE, 1821-1906 / U.S. Department of State – 39r – 1 – M54. Printed guide – us Nat'l Archives [972]

NOTES FROM THE MONTENEGRAN LEGATION IN THE U.S. TO THE DEPT. OF STATE, 1896-1905 / U.S. Department of State – T614 – 1r – 1 – us Nat'l Archives [949]

NOTES FROM THE NETHERLANDS LEGATION IN THE U.S. TO THE DEPT. OF STATE, 1784-1906 / U.S. Department of State – 13r – 1 – M56 – us Nat'l Archives [949]

NOTES FROM THE NICARAGUAN LEGATION IN THE U.S. TO THE DEPT. OF STATE, 1862-1906 / U.S. Department of State – 4r – 1 – T797 – us Nat'l Archives [972]

NOTES FROM THE NORWEGIAN LEGATION IN THE U.S. TO THE DEPT. OF STATE, 1905-6 / U.S. Department of State – 1r – 1 – T811 – us Nat'l Archives [948]

NOTES FROM THE PANAMANIAN LEGATION IN THE U.S. TO THE DEPT. OF STATE, 1903-6 / U.S. Department of State – 1r – 1 – T812 – us Nat'l Archives [972]

NOTES FROM THE PARAGUAYAN LEGATION IN THE U.S. TO THE DEPT. OF STATE, 1853-1906 / U.S. Department of State – 1r – 1 – M350 – us Nat'l Archives [972]

NOTES FROM THE PERSIAN LEGATION IN THE UNITED STATES TO THE DEPARTMENT OF STATE, 1887-1906 / U.S. Department of State – 1r – 1 – M511 – us Nat'l Archives [956]

NOTES FROM THE PERUVIAN LEGATION IN THE U.S. TO THE DEPT. OF STATE, 1827-1906 / U.S. Department of State – 6r – 1 – T802 – us Nat'l Archives [972]

NOTES FROM THE PORTUGUESE LEGATION IN THE U.S. TO THE DEPT. OF STATE, 1796-1906 / U.S. Department of State – 8r – 1 – M57 – us Nat'l Archives [946]

NOTES FROM THE ROYAL BOTANIC GARDEN EDINBURGH – (Index included) – Glasgow-Edinburgh. v1-14. 1908-1924 – 76mf – 9 – ne IDC [580]

NOTES FROM THE RUSSIAN LEGATION IN THE U.S. TO THE DEPT. OF STATE, 1809-1906 / U.S. Department of State – 12r – 1 – M39. Printed guide – us Nat'l Archives [947]

NOTES FROM THE SAMOAN LEGATION IN THE U.S. TO THE DEPT. OF STATE, 1856-1894 / U.S. Department of State – 1r – 1 – T805 – us Nat'l Archives [980]

NOTES FROM THE SARDINIAN LEGATION IN THE U.S. TO THE DEPT. OF STATE, 1838-61 / U.S. Department of State – 1r – 1 – M201 – us Nat'l Archives [945]

NOTES FROM THE SIAMESE LEGATION IN THE UNITED STATES TO THE DEPARTMENT OF STATE, 1876-1906 / U.S. Department of State – 1r – 1 – M512 – us Nat'l Archives [950]

NOTES FROM THE SPANISH LEGATION IN THE U.S. TO THE DEPT. OF STATE, 1790-1906 / U.S. Department of State – 31r – 1 – M59 – us Nat'l Archives [946]

NOTES FROM THE SWEDISH LEGATION IN THE U.S. TO THE DEPT. OF STATE, 1813-1906 / U.S. Department of State – 9r – 1 – M60 – us Nat'l Archives [948]

NOTES FROM THE SWISS LEGATION IN THE U.S. TO THE DEPT. OF STATE, 1882-1906 / U.S. Department of State – 6r – 1 – T813 – us Nat'l Archives [949]

NOTES FROM THE TEXAN LEGATION IN THE U.S. TO THE DEPT. OF STATE, 1836-1845 / U.S. Department of State – 1r – 1 – T809 – us Nat'l Archives [978]

NOTES FROM THE TUNISIAN LEGATION IN THE U.S. TO THE DEPT. OF STATE, 1805-6 / U.S. Department of State – 1r – 1 – M67 – us Nat'l Archives [960]

NOTES FROM THE TURKISH LEGATION IN THE U.S. TO THE DEPT. OF STATE, 1867-1906 / U.S. Department of State – 8r – 1 – T815 – us Nat'l Archives [956]

NOTES FROM THE URUGUAYAN LEGATION IN THE U.S. TO THE DEPT. OF STATE, 1834-1906 / U.S. Department of State – 1r – 1 – T804 – us Nat'l Archives [972]

NOTES FROM THE VENEZUELAN LEGATION IN THE U.S. TO THE DEPT. OF STATE, 1835-1906 / U.S. Department of State – 8r – 1 – T93 – us Nat'l Archives [972]

NOTES FROM WORKSHOP CENTER FOR OPEN EDUCATION – v. 4-. 1975- – 1,5,6,9 – us UMI [073]

NOTES HISTORIQUES : LIVRE DEDIE AUX VENERABLES JUBILAIRES DE L'INSTITUT DES FILLES DE LA CHARITE SERVANTES DES PAUVRES DITES SOEURS DE LA PROVIDENCE / Marie-Antoinette, Mere FCS P – Montreal: Providence (maison mere), 1922. SEM105P1546 – 2mf – 9 – Can$4.50 – cn Bibl Nat [240]

NOTES HISTORIQUES SUR LA PAROISSE DE SAINT-GUILLAUME D'UPTON AVEC LA GENEALOGIE DES FAMILLES DE SERRE, VANASSE... / Desaulniers, Francois Lesieur – Montreal: A.-P. Pigeon, imprimeur, 1905. SEM105P1348 – 2mf – 9 – Can$4.50 – cn Bibl Nat [971]

NOTES HISTORIQUES SUR L'ORIGINE DE LA FAMILLE GILL DE SAINT FRANCOIS DU LAC ET SAINT THOMAS DE PIERREVILLE: ET HISTOIRE DE MA PROPRE FAMILLE / Gill, Charles – Montreal: E. Senecal, 1887. 03220. (Pre-1900 Canadiana) – 9 – cn C.I.H.M. [971]

NOTES OF A COURSE OF LECTURES ON SMITH'S MERCANTILE LAW / Gilmore, James Houston – Charlottesville? VA, 1891. 400p LL-341 – 1 – us L of C Photodup [340]

NOTES OF A TOUR FROM BANGALORE TO CALCUTTA: THENCE TO DELHI, AND SUBSEQUENTLY, TO BRITISH SIKKIM DURING THE EARLY PART OF 1867 / Bulger, George Ernest – Secunderabad, India: Regimental Press, 1869. 00855. (Pre-1900 Canadiana) – 9 – cn C.I.H.M. [950]

NOTES OF AN OVERLAND JOURNEY THROUGH FRANCE AND EGYPT TO BOMBAY...: WITH A MEMOIR / Roberts, E – London: Allen, 1841. KHT-124-1 – 9 – ne IDC [910]

NOTES OF DEBATES IN THE FEDERAL CONVENTION OF 1787 / Madison, James – Athens: Ohio UP, n.d. – 6mf – 9 – $9.00 – LLMC 90-022 – us L.L.M.C. [323]

NOTES OF EVIDENCE : TAKEN BY THE COMMISSION OF INQUIRY APPOINTED TO INQUIRE INTO THE DISTURBANCE IN THE CALABAR AND OWERRI PROVINCES, DECEMBER 1929 / ABA Commission of Inquiry – London: Waterlow, 1930 – us Res Libr [960]

NOTES OF LECTURES ON THE EPISTLE TO THE HEBREWS / Lincoln, William – Kilmarnock, Scotland: John Ritchie, [18–?] – 1mf – 9 – 0-8370-7236-0 – 1986-1236 – us A.T.L.A. [220]

NOTES OF MATERIALS : FOR THE HISTORY OF PUBLIC DEPARTMENTS – London, 1846 – Dfl35.00 – ne Slangenburg [240]

NOTES OF MY LIFE, 1805-1878 / Denison, George Anthony – Oxford: J. Parker,1879 – 1mf – us A.T.L.A. [240]

NOTES OF MY MINISTRY / Henson, H Hensley – London: H. Rees, 1913 – 1mf – us A.T.L.A. [240]

NOTES OF SELECTED DECISIONS OF HER MAJESTY'S HIGH COURT IN UGANDA, ON CASES ORIGINATING FROM THE BUGANDA COURTS, 1940-1958 / Haydon, Edwin Scott – Nairobi: Boyd's 1958. 96p. LL-12046 – 1 – us L of C Photodup [340]

NOTES ON A NEW KIND OF A PITHECANTHROPUS MANDIBLE / Sartono, S – SE 6235 1. 1961 – 9 – ne IDC [590]

NOTES ON AFRICA : PARTICULARLY THOSE PARTS WHICH ARE SITUATED BETWEEN CAPE VERDE AND THE RIVER CONGO... / Robertson, G A – London: Sherwood, Neely, & Jones, 1819 – us Res Libr [960]

NOTES ON ALGAE / Collins, G N – v. 3. Rhodora. 1901. B-518 2 – 8 – ne IDC [580]

NOTES ON AN ETHNOGRAPHICAL COLLECTION FROM THE WEST COAST OF NORTH AMERICA FORMED DURING THE VOYAGE OF CAPT. VANCOUVER, 1790 / Dalton, O M – BN-189 2. 1897 – 8 – ne IDC [910]

NOTES ON, AND THE PRECISE GEOLOGICAL HORIZON OF SIPHONOTRETA SCOTICA, DAVIDSON / Ami, Henry Marc – 1887? 02412. (Pre-1900 Canadiana) – 9 – cn C.I.H.M. [550]

NOTES ON COMMON FORMS: A BOOK OF MASSACHUSETTS LAW / Crocker, Uriel Haskell – Boston, Little, Brown, 1867. 235 p. LL-719 – 1 – us L of C Photodup [340]

NOTES ON DIFFICULT PASSAGES OF THE NEW TESTAMENT / Riggs, Elias – Boston:Congregational Sunday-School and Pub. Society, c1889 – 1mf – 9 – 0-8370-4907-5 – 1985-2907 – us A.T.L.A. [220]

NOTES ON ENGLAND... / Taine, Hippolyte – London: Strahan & Co., 1872 – 1 roll – 1 – 1-55879-534-0 – uk Libr Preservation [941]

NOTES ON GENESIS / Robertson, Frederick William – London:Kegan Paul, Trench, Truebner, 1903 – 1mf – 9 – 0-8370-4922-9 – 1985-2922 – us A.T.L.A. [220]

NOTES ON HOSPITALS / Nightingale, Florence – M 257. 1859 – 9 – ne IDC [360]

NOTES ON INDONESIAN VILLAGERS' PARTICIPATION IN PROGRAMS TO MODERNIZE RURAL LIFE / Textor, Robert B – SE 1152 1 – 9 – ne IDC [360]

NOTES ON INGERSOLL / Lambert, Louis Aloisius – Buffalo: Buffalo Catholic, 1883.1 fiche – 9 – us A.T.L.A. [240]

NOTES ON LAND TENURE IN THE BENIN, KUKURUKU, ISHAN AND ASABA DIVISIONS OF BENIN PROVINCE / Nigeria. Land and Survey Department – Lagos: Govt Printer, 1948 – us Res Libr [333]

NOTES ON MEDIAEVAL SERVICES IN ENGLAND : WITH AN INDEX OF LINCOLN CEREMONIES / Wordsworth, Charles – London: T. Baker, 1898 – 1mf – us A.T.L.A. [240]

NOTES ON MILITARY LAW : PROCEEDINGS OF COURTS-MARTIAL... / Griffiths, Frederick A – Woolwich, England: E Jones, 1841 – 3mf – 9 – $4.50 – LLMC 90-025 – us L.L.M.C. [340]

NOTES ON MISSIONARY SUBJKECTS / Cust, Robert Needham – London: Elliot Stock, 1889 – 2mf – us A.T.L.A. [240]

NOTES ON MUSIC IN OLD BOSTON / Fisher, William A – 1918 – 1 – 5.00 – us Baptist [240]

NOTES ON NEW TESTAMENT GRAMMAR / Burton, Ernest De Witt – rev ed. Chicago: University of Chicago Press, 1904 – 1mf – 9 – 0-8370-9131-4 – 1986-3131 – us A.T.L.A. [450]

NOTES ON NEW TESTAMENT LITERATURE & ECCLESIASTICAL HISTORY / Alexander, Joseph Addison – New York: Scribner, 1867. 1 fiche – 9 – us A.T.L.A. [240]

NOTES ON NORTH-WESTERN AMERICA / Anderson, Alexander – Montreal? s.n. 1876. 12401. (Pre-1900 Canadiana) – 9 – cn C.I.H.M. [971]

NOTES ON NURSING / Nightingale, Florence – M-136. 1859 – 9 – ne IDC [610]

NOTES ON PARASITES OF FRESHWATER FISHES IN INDONESIA / Sachlan, M – Bogor, Balai Penjelidikan Perikanan Darat, 1952. 59p, illus. 25 cm. (Pemberitaan, no.2) Indonesian abstract – 9 – ne IDC [639]

NOTES ON PERSPECTIVE OF DEVELOPMENT, INDIA 1960-61 TO 1975-76 / India. Planning Commission – New Delhi. 1964. BD-449 1 – 9 – ne IDC [338]

NOTES ON POPULAR RATIONALISM / Henson, H Hensley – London: Isbister, 1904 – 1mf – us A.T.L.A. [140]

NOTES ON PREHISTORIC MAN EGYPT AND THE LEBANON: BEING A PAPER READ BEFORE A MEETING OF THE VICTORIA INSTITUTE, HELD AT THE HOUSE OF THE SOCIETY OF ARTS, MAY 6, 1884 / Dawson, John William – s.l.: s.n., 1884?. 02627. (Pre-1900 Canadiana) – 9 – cn C.I.H.M. [560]

NOTES ON PRIMITIVE MAN IN ONTARIO: BEING AN APPENDIX TO THE REPORT OF THE MINISTER OF EDUCATION FOR ONTARIO / Boyle, David – Toronto: Printed by order of the Legislative Assembly by Warwick & Rutter, 1895. 02175. (Pre-1900 Canadiana) – 9 – cn C.I.H.M. [971]

NOTES ON PROCEDURES / Hong Kong. University and Polytechnic Grants Committee – Hong Kong, 1980 – 3mf – 9 – DE-184/1 – ne IDC [370]

NOTES ON SCRIVENER'S PLAIN INTRODUCTION TO THE CRITICISM OF THE NEW TESTAMENT / Abbot, Ezra – Boston: Houghton, Mifflin, 1885.1 fiche – 9 – us A.T.L.A. [240]

NOTES ON SUITS BETWEEN STATES; INTERSTATE WATERS IRRIGATION / Randolph, Carman Fitz – New York? 1902 53 p. LL-1210 – 1 – us L of C Photodup [340]

NOTES ON THE AMERICAN DECISIONS AND REPORTS – (Coll title: American State Reports) – SF/NY: Bancroft-Whitney/Lawyers' Co-op. 20v. 1909-12 (all publ) – 272mf – 9 – $408.00 – LLMC 84-694 – us L.L.M.C. [340]

NOTES ON THE BOOK OF GENESIS / McIntosh, Charles H – Boston: Believers' Book Rooms, 1861?. 1 fiche – 9 – us A.T.L.A. [240]

NOTES ON THE BOOK OF LEVITICUS / Mackintosh, Charles Henry – New York: Fleming H Revell, [18–?] – 1mf – 9 – 0-8370-6755-3 – 1986-0755 – us A.T.L.A. [220]

NOTES ON THE BOOK OF REVELATIONS TO ASSIST INQUIRERS IN SEARCHING INTO THAT BOOK / Darby, John N – 1839 – 1 – us A.T.L.A. [240]

NOTES ON THE CHALCOLITHIC AND EARLY BRONZE AGE POTTERY AT MEGIDDO / Engberg, Robert M – 1934 – 9 – $10.00 – us I.R.C. [930]

NOTES ON THE CHRONOLOGICAL LIST OF MISSIONARIES TO CHINA AND THE CHINESE / Boynton, Charles Luther – 1807-1942 – 1 – us A.T.L.A. [240]

NOTES ON THE CHURCHES IN THE COUNTIES OF KENT, SUSSEX AND SURREY, MENTIONED IN DOMESDAY BOOK, AND THOSE OF MORE RECENT DATE / Hussey, Arthur – London: J.R. Smith, 1852. 388p. 1 illus. 20pl – 1 – us U.W. Library [720]

NOTES ON THE COLES AND LIGNITES OF THE CANADIAN NORTH-WEST: CHIEFLY DERIVED FROM THE REPORTS OF THE GEOLOGICAL SURVEY OF CANADA / Dawson, George M – Montreal: Herald, 1884. 02355. (Pre-1900 Canadiana) – 9 – cn C.I.H.M. [550]

NOTES ON THE DIVINE OFFICE, HISTORICAL AND MYSTICAL : FROM ANCIENT AND MODERN SOURCES / Neale, John Mason – London: J.T. Hayes, [1877?] – 1mf – us A.T.L.A. [240]

NOTES ON THE EARLY HISTORY OF BABYLONIA / Rawlinson, Henry Creswicke – (Includes bibliographical references) – [S.l.: s.n., 1854?] – 1mf – 9 – 0-8370-8608-6 – 1986-2608 – us A.T.L.A. [930]

NOTES ON THE EARLY HISTORY OF THE VULGATE GOSPELS / Chapman, John – Oxford: Clarendon Press, 1908. 1 fiche – 9 – us A.T.L.A. [240]

NOTES ON THE EASTERN CREE AND NORTHERN SAULTEAUX / Skinner, A – BN 388 2. 1911 – 8 – ne IDC [305]

NOTES ON THE EPISTLE TO THE HEBREWS / Huntington, Ezra Abel – Auburn: Wm J Moses, 1866 – 1mf – 9 – 0-8370-3697-6 – 1985-1697 – us A.T.L.A. [220]

NOTES ON THE FEASTS OF THE LORD PRESCRIBED TO THE JEWS – London: Thomas Bosworth, 1884. 1 fiche – 9 – us A.T.L.A. [240]

NOTES ON THE "FEASTS OF THE LORD", PRESCRIBED TO THE JEWS, AND THEIR BEARING UPON THE FAITH AND HOPE OF THE CHRISTIAN CHURCH – London: Thomas Bosworth, 1884 – 1mf – 9 – 0-8370-2566-4 – 1985-0566 – us A.T.L.A. [270]

NOTES ON THE FERNS OF HONG KONG AND THE ADJACENT MAINLAND / Matthew, C G – Edinburgh, 1908. 35 pp. B-7225 1 – 9 – ne IDC [580]

NOTES ON THE FOLK-LORE OF THE NORTHERN COUNTIES OF ENGLAND AND THE BORDERS / Henderson, William – London: Satchell, Peyton and Co., 1879. xvii,391p – 1 – us U.W. Library [390]

NOTES ON THE GEOLOGY AND BOTANY OF DIGBY NECK / Bailey, Loring Woart – 1895?. 05974. (Pre-1900 Canadiana) – 9 – cn C.I.H.M. [550]

NOTES ON THE HAGUE RULES, 1921 / Berlingieri, F – Genova, 1922 – 1mf – 9 – ILM-3221/1 – ne IDC [327]

NOTES ON THE HEBREW TEXT OF SAMUEL / Driver, Samuel Rolles – 1913 – 9 – $18.00 – us I.R.C. [220]

NOTES ON THE HEBREW TEXT OF THE BOOK OF GENESIS : WITH TWO APPENDICES / Spurrell, George James – Oxford:Clarendon Press, 1887 – 1mf – 9 – 0-8370-5351-X – 1985-3351 – us A.T.L.A. [220]

NOTES ON THE HISTORY AND THE MATERIAL CULTURE OF THE TONKAWA INDIANS / Jones, William K – 1969 – 1mf – 9 – $5.00f – us Ross [970]

NOTES ON THE KENTUCKY AGRICULTURAL SITUATION / Kentucky. Agricultural Extension Service – 1929-56 – 1,5,6 – us Spaulding [630]

NOTES ON THE LATE REVISION OF THE NEW TESTAMENT VERSION / Goodwin, Daniel Raynes – New York. Thomas Whittaker, 1883 – 1mf – 9 – 0-8370-3340-3 – 1985-1340 – us A.T.L.A. [220]

NOTES ON THE LAW OF RULE DAYS IN VIRGINIA AND WEST VIRGINIA / Kittle, Warren Brance – Charleston, W. Va., Union Publishing Co. 1912. 61 p. LL-278 – 1 – us L of C Photodup [340]

NOTES ON THE LIFE OF DR. JOSEPH WORKMAN / Boyle, David – Toronto: Arbuthnot Bros., 1894. 00230. (Pre-1900 Canadiana) – 9 – cn C.I.H.M. [920]

NOTES ON THE LOCUST INVASION OF 1874, IN MANITOBA AND THE NORTH-WEST TERRITORIES / Dawson, George M – Montreal: s.n., 1876 (Montreal: Mitchell & Wilson). 02357. (Pre-1900 Canadiana) – 9 – cn C.I.H.M. [971]

NOTES ON THE MEGGIDO POTTERY / Shipton, Geoffrey M – 1939 – 9 – $10.00 – us I.R.C. [930]

NOTES ON THE NAGA TRIBES, IN COMMUNICATION WITH ASSAM / Owen, J – I-1004 2. 1844 – 8 – ne IDC [950]

NOTES ON THE NESTORIAN INSCRIPTION OF SI-AN (CCC129) / Fung, Ch'eng-chun – (In Chinese) – 1st ed. Shanghai: Y.W. Wong, 1931 – 1r – 1 – 1984-B500 – us A.T.L.A. [240]

NOTES ON THE NEW TESTAMENT / Sherwood, Adiel – v. 1-2 – 1 – 28.07 – us Baptist [240]

NOTES ON THE NEW YORK LAW OF LIFE INSURANCE / Alexander, Charles Beatty – New York, Baker, Voorhis, 1887. 156 p. LL-263 – 1 – us L of C Photodup [340]

NOTES ON THE OCCURENCE OF MAMMOTH-REMAINS IN THE YUKON DISTRICT OF CANADA AND IN ALASKA / Dawson, George M – s.l.: s.n., 1894?. 02358. (Pre-1900 Canadiana) – 9 – cn C.I.H.M. [560]

NOTES ON THE ORNITHOLOGY OF THE SEASONS: AS ILLUSTRATED BY THE ARRIVAL AND DEPARTURE OF SOME OF OUR MIGRATORY BIRDS / Allan, George William – Toronto: Copp, Clark, 1885?. 05678. (Pre-1900 Canadiana) – 9 – cn C.I.H.M. [590]

NOTES ON THE PALESTINE PROBLEM / Great Britain. G.H.Q. Middle East – Jerusalem. 1945. BJ-28-105 1 – 9 – ne IDC [956]

NOTES ON THE PHOSPHATES OF THE LAURENTIAN AND CAMBRIAN ROCKS OF CANADA / Dawson, John William – s.l.: s.n., 1876?. 02628. (Pre-1900 Canadiana) – 9 – cn C.I.H.M. [560]

NOTES ON THE PHYSIOLOGICAL ACTION OF THE CALABAR POISON BEAN / Fraser, T T – (Physostigma venenosum, Balfour). Transact. Bot. Soc., Edinburgh. v. 7. 1862, 1863. B-6118 2 – 8 – ne IDC [580]

NOTES ON THE PLAINS CREE / Skinner, A – BN 389 2. 1914 – 8 – ne IDC [305]

NOTES ON THE POST-PLIOCENE GEOLOGY OF CANADA: WITH ESPECIAL REFERENCE TO THE CONDITIONS OF ACCUMULATION OF THE DEPOSITS AND THE MARINE LIFE OF THE PERIOD / Dawson, John William – Montreal: s.n., 1872 (Montreal: Mitchell & Wilson). 02277. (Pre-1900 Canadiana) – 9 – cn C.I.H.M. [560]

NOTES ON THE PUBLIC STATUTES OF MASSACHUSETTS / Crocker, Uriel Haskell – (2nd ed., Boston, Little, Brown, 1891. 859 p. LL-70) – Boston, Houghton, Mifflin, 1882. 691 p. LL-1664 – 1 – us L of C Photodup [340]

NOTES ON THE REVISED STATUTES OF THE U.S. : AND SUBSEQUENT LEGISLATION OF CONGRESS TO JULY 1, 1889 / Gould, John M & Tucker, George F – Boston: Little, Brown & Co, 1889 – 27mf – 9 – $40.50 – LLMC 94-111 – us L.L.M.C. [340]

NOTES ON THE RUINS OF MUQEYER / Taylor, J E – [S.l.: s.n., 1854?] – 1mf – 9 – 0-8370-8624-8 – 1986-2624 – us A.T.L.A. [930]

NOTES ON THE SECOND PLENARY COUNCIL OF BALTIMORE / Smith, Sebastian – New York: P O'Shea, 1874 – 2mf – 9 – 0-8370-7340-5 – 1986-1340 – us A.T.L.A. [240]

NOTES ON THE SMELTING PROCESSES AT FREIBERG / Brown, Walter H & Philipps, W B – Freiberg, Saxony: Gerlach's Printing House, 1886 – us Res Libr [670]

NOTES ON THE TINNEH OF CHEPEWYAN INDIANS OF BRITISH AND RUSSIAN AMERICA / Gibbs, G – BN 219 2. 1866 – 8 – ne IDC [306]

NOTES ON TITLES. / Miller, Edgar George, Jr – Baltimore: Title Guarantee & Trust Co., 1903. 462p. LL-515 – 1 – us L of C Photodup [340]

NOTES ON TREES ON THE GROUNDS OF MCGILL UNIVERSITY / Dawson, John William – Montreal?: s.n., 1891?. 02629. (Pre-1900 Canadiana) – 9 – cn C.I.H.M. [971]

NOTES ON VANCOUVER ISLAND / Begg, Alexander – 1895? 02431. (Pre-1900 Canadiana) – 9 – cn C.I.H.M. [910]

NOTES ON VIRGINIA CORPORATION LAWS / Staples, Abram Penn – Charlottesville, Va., Michie, 1909. 52 p. LL-1398 – 1 – us L of C Photodup [340]

NOTES POUR SERVIR A L'HISTOIRE DE LA MEDECINE DANS LE BAS-CANADA... / Ahern, M J – Quebec: [s.n.], 1923 [Quebec: Imprimerie Laflamme]. SEM105P1554 – 6mf – 9 – Can$13.50 – cn Bibl Nat [610]

NOTES POUR SERVIR A L'HISTOIRE DE L'EMPEREUR MAXIMILIEN: D'APRES SES OEUVRES, LES RECITS DU CAPITAINE D'ARTILLERIE ALBERT HANS, DU MEDECIN PARTICULIER DE S. M. LE DOCTEUR BASCH ET DES TEMOINS OCULAIRES DE L'EXECUTION / Faucher de Saint-Maurice, Narcisse – Quebec: A. Cote, 1889. 03068. (Pre 1900 Canadiana) – 9 – cn C.I.H.M. [971]

NOTES POUR SERVIR A L'HISTOIRE DES OFFICIERS DE LA MARINE ET DE L'ARMEE FRANCAISE QUI ONT FAIT LA QUERRE DE L'INDEPENDANCE AMERICAINE / Faucher de Saint-Maurice, Narcisse – Quebec: L. Demers, 1896. 03067. (Pre-1900 Canadiana) – 9 – cn C.I.H.M. [971]

NOTES RELATIVES AUX INSCRIPTIONS DU MONUMENT DE CHAMPLAIN / Casgrain, Henri-Raymond – Quebec: Dussault & Proulx, 1898. 00524. (Pre-1900 Canadiana) – 9 – cn C.I.H.M. [971]

NOTES SUR DE VIEUX MANUSCRITS ABENAKIS / Gill, Charles – s.l., s.n., 1886 (Montreal: E. Senecal). 03136. (Pre-1900 Canadiana) – 9 – cn C.I.H.M. [971]

NOTES SUR LA COUTUME DE PARIS INDIQUANT LES ARTICLES ENCORE EN FORCE, AVEC TOUT LE TEXTE DE LA COUTUME.. / Ramsay, Thomas Kennedy – Montreal: C.O. Beauchemin and Valois..., 1864. SEM105P452 – 2mf – 9 – Can$4.50 – cn Bibl Nat [944]

NOTES SUR LA FORMATION DU FRANCO-NORMAND ET DE L'ANGLO-SAXON / Faucher de Saint-Maurice, Narcisse – s.l.: s.n., 1892 (Montreal: E. Senecal). 03071. (Pre-1900 Canadiana) – 9 – cn C.I.H.M. [971]

NOTES SUR LA LITTERATURE DES JUIFS HISPANO-PORTUGAIS / Kayserling, M – N.p., n.d. – 1mf – ne IDC [470]

NOTES SUR LA PAROISSE DE ST FRANCOIS DE LA BEAUCE / Demers, Benjamin – Quebec: s.n., 1891 (Quebec: C. Darveau). 03765. (Pre-1900 Canadiana) – 9 – cn C.I.H.M. [971]

NOTES SUR LA RUSSIE, 1835-1840 / Barante, Guillaume-Prosper de – (Russia – 19th C. series). 1875 – 9 – fr Hachette [947]

NOTES SUR LA VEGETATION INDIGENE ET INTRODUITE DE L'AUSTRALIE / Mueller, Ferdinand Jakob Heinrich von – Transl. by E. Lissignol. Melbourne. 1866. B-8067 1 – 9 – ne IDC [580]

NOTES SUR LE JAPON / Chassiron, Ch. de – Paris, E. Dentu. 1861 – 9 – 12.50 – fr Orientalistes [950]

NOTES SUR LE "TURKESTAN" BARTHOLD, DE M.W. / Pelliot, P – (T'oung Pao, v. 27. 1930). BU-804 2 – 8 – ne IDC [950]

NOTES SUR LES COUTUMES DES PEULS AU FOUTA DJALLON / Viellard, Gilbert Pierre – Paris: Larose, 1939 – us Res Libr [960]

NOTES SUR LES ESQUIMAUX DE BAIE HUDSON / Turquetil, A – BN 428 2. 1926 – 8 – ne IDC [971]

NOTES SUR LES JUGES ET LES ASSESSEURS DU PROCES DE CONDEMNATION DE JEANNE D'ARC / Beaurepaire, Charles de Robillard de – Rouen: E. Cagniard, 1890. 135p.2 fiches. (Law Collection) – 9 – 6.00 – fr Bibl Nationale [900]

NOTES SUR LES LIVRES LITURGIQUES DES DIOCESES D'AUTUN, CHALON ET MACON / Pellechet, M – Paris, 1883 – 14mf – 8 – Dfl49.00 – ne Slangenburg [240]

NOTES SUR LES SAUVAGES TAHL-TAN / Callbreath, J C – BN 155 2. 1889 – 8 – ne IDC [306]

NOTES SUR LES ZONES DE DEVELOPPEMENT DE BROBO ET DE BIABO / Anooy, G – (Africa series). 1969 – 9 – fr Hachette [338]

NOTES SUR L'IRLANDE / Dumont, Georges A – s.l.: s.n., 1883?. 02796. (Pre-1900 Canadiana) – 9 – cn C.I.H.M. [971]
NOTES SUR QUELQUES CATEGORIES RELIGIEUSES DES INDIENS WAURA DU HAUT-XINGU, BRESIL / Chiara, V – 9 – F20.00 – fr Ethnologie [290]
NOTES SUR QUELQUES PLANTES CRITIQUES, RARES OU NOUVELLES, ET ADDITIONS A LA FLORE DES ENVIRONS DE PARIS / Cosson, E S C – Paris. 1848-52 – 8 – ne IDC [580]
NOTES TO FOREIGN CONSULS IN THE U.S. FROM THE DEPT. OF STATE, 1853-1906 / U.S. Department of State – 4r – 1 – M663 – us Nat'l Archives [975]
NOTES TO THE AUSTRIAN LEGATION, 1853-1906 – M99 – 3r – 1 – $69.00 – us Scholarly Res [327]
NOTES TO THE LEGATIONS OF THE GERMAN STATES, 1834-1906 / U.S. Department of State – 9r – 1 – $102.00 – M99 – us Scholarly Res [327]
NOTES TO V. 1 MINOR'S INSTITUTES / Lile, William Minor – 4th ed. Charlottesville, Michie, 1899. 299 p. LL-528 – 1 – us L of C Photodup [340]
NOTES UPON RUSSIA AND KINGDOMS LYING THAT WAY / ed by Major, R H – Hakluyt Society. 1517-26 – 7 – uk Microform Academic [910]
NOTES WRITTEN IN 1749 BY THE SISTERS OF THE SISTERHOOD IN THE SISTERHOUSE OF THE SEVEN DAY BAPTISTS, AT EPHRATA IN LANCASTER COUNTY, PENNSYLVANIA / Ephrata Community – Manuscript with printed index, 1749. MUSIC 1154, Reel 1 – 1 – us L of C Photodup [780]
Notestein, Wallace *see* A HISTORY OF WITCHCRAFT IN ENGLAND FROM 1558 TO 1718
Nothardt, Fritz *see* GOERRES UND SEIN "ROTHES BLATT"
NOTHERN TERRITORY CENSUS 1881 AND 1891 – 2mf – A$10.00 – 0-949124-16-8 – item 1 – at G.S.N.T. [920]
NOTHING BUT NAMES: AN INQUIRY INTO THE ORIGIN OF THE NAMES OF THE COUNTIES AND TOWNSHIPS OF ONTARIO / Gardnier, Herbert Fairbairn – Toronto: G. Morang, 1899. 03289. (Pre-1900 Canadiana) – 9 – cn C.I.H.M. [971]
NOTHSTAENDE DER PROTESTANTISCHEN KIRCHE UND DIE INNERE MISSION : ZUGLEICH ALS ZWEITE NACHRICHT UEBER DIE BRUEDER DES RAUHEN HAUSES ALS SEMINAR FUER INNERE MISSION / Wichern, Johann Hinrich – Hamburg: Agentur des Rauhen Hauses, 1844 – 1mf – us A.T.L.A. [240]
DIE NOTHWENDIGKEIT UND GESTALT EINER KIRCHLICHEN REFORM : DER KIRCHE DER REFORMATION GEWIDMET / Kreyenbuehl, Johannes – (Includes bibliographical references) – Freiburg i. B: J C B Mohr (Paul Siebeck), 1896 – 1mf – 9 – 0-83704-000-0 – 1985-2000 – us A.T.L.A. [240]
DIE NOTHWENDIGSTEN ANMERCKUNGEN UND REGELN WIE DER BASSUS CONTINUUS ODER GENERAL-BASS WOL KOENNE TRACTIRET WERDEN / Werckmeister, A – Aschersleben. 1698. BP-515 1 – 9 – ne IDC [780]
NOTICE BIOGRAPHIQUE MGR C.-E. LEGARE, PROTONOTAIRE APOSTOLIQUE A. J. P., VICAIRE GENERAL DE S. E. LE CARDINAL TASCHEREAU, ARCHEVEQUE DE QUEBEC / Cote, Georges-Pierre – Quebec: A. Cote, 1892. 00462. (Pre-1900 Canadiana) – 9 – cn C.I.H.M. [971]
NOTICE BIOGRAPHIQUE SUR LE PERE FERDINAND VERBIEST, MISSIONAIRE A LA CHINE / Carton, C L – Bruges, 1839 – 1mf – 9 – ne IDC [240]
NOTICE BIOGRAPHIQUE SUR LE REVEREND J. AUCLAIR: CURE DE NOTRE DAME DE QUEBEC: DECEDE LE 29 NOVEMBRE, 1887 / Cote, Georges-Pierre – Quebec: A. Cote, 1888. 00410. (Pre-1900 Canadiana) – 9 – cn C.I.H.M. [971]
NOTICE BIOGRAPHIQUE SUR LE REVEREND J. AUCLAIR, CURE DE NOTRE-DAME DE QUEBEC, DECEDE LE 29 NOVEMBRE 1887 / Cote, Georges-Pierre – Quebec: Imp. Gen A Cote, 1888. SEM105P46 – 1mf – 9 – Can$2.25 – cn Bibl Nat [240]
NOTICE BIOGRAPHIQUE SUR LE R.P. NEWMAN DE L'ORATOIRE DE SAINT-PHILIPPE DE NERI / Gondon, Jules – Paris: Sagnier et Bray, 1853 – 1mf – us A.T.L.A. [240]
NOTICE DE L'OUVRAGE DE GREGOIRE INTITULE: DE LA LITTERATURE DES NEGRES / Lanjuinais, J D – Paris, Maradam. 1808 – 9 – $5.00 – fr Orientalistes [490]
NOTICE DU CONG-FOU DES BONZES TAO-SEE = NOTE ON THE MEDICAL VALUE OF TAOIST EXERCISES : MEMOIRES CONCERNANT L'HISTOIRE, LES SCIENCES...DES CHINOIS... / Cibot, P M – Paris, 1776-1783 – 1mf – 9 – ne IDC [615]
NOTICE DU MUSEE HISTORIQUE DE VERSAILLES / Clement de Ris, Louis Torterat – Paris: Mourgues, 1881. 132p. (Art Collection) – 2mf – 9 – $6.00 – fr Bibl Nationale [944]
NOTICE OF GRIESBACH'S EDITION OF THE NEW TESTAMENT / Buckminster, Joseph Stevens – (The Monthly Anthology and Boston Review, v. 5, Jan. 1808, p. 18-21) – 9 – us A.T.L.A. [240]
NOTICE ON THE MEDICAL PROPERTIES OF SOME NORTH-AMERICAN PLANTS / Rafinesque-Schmaltz, Constantine S – Medical Repository, 1808 – 1mf – 9 – ne IDC [615]
NOTICE REGISTER / Ottawa County. Ohio. Carroll Township. Board of Trustees – 1r – 1 – $32.50r – us Archival [324]
NOTICE SUR ABOU-IOUSOUF HASDAI' IBN-SCHAPROUT / Luzzatto, P – Paris. 1852. BJ-421-26 1 – 9 – ne IDC [470]
NOTICE SUR EUGEN BONAMY : DOCUMENTS INEDITS SUR LE MAGNOLIA DE LA MAILLARDIERE / Rostaing de Rivas, Eugene P de – Nantes: Mellinet, 1862 – fr Armell [580]
NOTICE SUR HUET DE COETLISAN / Gueraud, Armand – Rennes: Marteville et Lefas, 1851 – 1 – F50.00 – fr Armell [920]
NOTICE SUR JEAN VAUQUELAIN DE DIEPPE: LIEUTENANT DE VAISSEAU (1727-1764): D'APRES M. FAUCHER DE SAINT-MAURICE / Faucher de Saint-Maurice, Narcisse – par Gabriel Gravier. s.l.: s.n., 1885 (Rouen France: E. Cagniard). 03070. (Pre-1900 Canadiana) – 9 – cn C.I.H.M. [971]
NOTICE SUR LA COLONIE DU SENEGAL ET SUR LES PAYS QUI SONT EN RELATIONS AVEC ELLE / Faidherbe, Louis Leon Cesar – Paris: A Bertrand, 1859 – us Res Libr [960]
NOTICE SUR LA DESTRUCTION DES ARCHIVES ET BIBLIOTHEQUES DES DEUX CHAMBRES LEGISLATIVES DU CANADA, LORS DE L'EMEUTE QUI A EU LIEU A MONTREAL LE 25 AVRIL 1849 / Faribault, Georges Bartelemy – Quebec: Imp. du Canadien, s.d. SEM105P219 – 1mf – 9 – Can$2.25 – cn Bibl Nat [971]
NOTICE SUR LA FAMILLE GUY: ET SUR QUELQUES AUTRES FAMILLES / Daniel, Francois – Montreal E. Senecal, 1867. 02155. (Pre-1900 Canadiana) – 9 – cn C.I.H.M. [971]
NOTICE SUR LA VIE ET LES ECRITS DE M. MERLE D'AUBIGNE / Bonnet, Jules – Paris: Grassart; Geneve: Emile Beroud, 1874 – 1mf – us A.T.L.A. [240]
NOTICE SUR LA VIE ET LES OUVRAGES DE NICOLAS PICCINNI / Ginguene, P L – P 297- 1800 01 – 9 – ne IDC [920]
NOTICE SUR LE DICTIONNAIRE INTITULE : MIROIR DES LANGUES MANDCHOUE ET MONGOLE / Abel-Remusat – (Notices et Extraits des Manuscrits de la Bibliotheque du Roi) – Paris. v13(p1-125). 1838 – 5mf – 8 – U-485/2 – ne IDC [040]
NOTICE SUR LE PAYS ET LE PEUPLE DES YEBOUS EN AFRIQUE / Avezac-Macaya, Armand d' – (African Library). Paris. Libraire orientale Dondey-Dupre. 1845 – 9 – fr Hachette [960]
NOTICE SUR LE PAYS ET LE PEUPLE DES YEBOUS EN AFRIQUE / Avezac-Macaya, Armand d' – [Paris: Dondey-Dupre, 1845] – us Res Libr [960]
NOTICE SUR LE PEUPLE DU BENIN : LUE A LA SEANCE PUBLIQUE DE L'INSTITUT DU 15 NIVOSE AN 9 / Palisot-Beauvois, C – [Paris?, 179?] – us Res Libr [300]
NOTICE SUR LES ECOLES RELEVANT DU BUREAU...DE LA CITE DE MONTREAL / Bureau des commissaires d'ecoles catholiques romains de Montreal – Montreal, Le Bureau, 1893. 00335. (Pre-1900 Canadiana) – 9 – cn C.I.H.M. [370]
NOTICE SUR LES PLANTES A AJOUTER A LA FLORE DE FRANCE / Loiseleur-Deslongchamps, J L A – Flora Gallica. Paris. 1810. B-6039 1 – 9 – ne IDC [580]
NOTICE SUR L'IMPOSSIBLITE D'ETABLIR UNE RELIGION NOUVELLE EN REPONSE A LA FOI NOUVELLE DES SIMONIENS SANS MISSION LEGITIME NI AUTHENTIQUE – Lyon, impr. A. Idt, 1831, 24 p. Les Saint-Simoniens, 1825-1834. 6991 – 9 – fr Hachette [335]
NOTICE SUR M. JOS. O. LEPROHON: ARCHIPRETRE, DIRECTEUR DU COLLEGE DE NICOLET, ETC. ETC / Bois, Louis Edouard – Quebec: A. Cote, 1870. 00086. (Pre-1900 Canadiana) – 9 – cn C.I.H.M. [920]
NOTICE SUR MISSILLAC ET SUR LA BARONNIE DE LA ROCHE-BERNARD / Prevel – 19th c. – fr Armell [920]
NOTICE SUR QUELQUES RELATIONS DIPLOMATIQUES DES MONGOLS DE LA CHINE AVEC LES PAPES D'AVIGNON / Jacquet, E – JA. 1831. BU-708 2 – 8 – ne IDC [950]
NOTICE SUR SON BUT ET SON ORGANISATION / Compagnie de colonisation et de credit des cantons de l'est – Sherbrooke: "Pionnier", 1881. 05249. (Pre-1900 Canadiana) – 9 – cn C.I.H.M. [971]
NOTICES / American Mathematical Society – (1975- . 5,6. 1977- . 9) – 1- 1954- – 1 – us UMI [510]
NOTICES / American Mathematical Society – Providence. v1-44 feb 1954- 1; 22-44 jan 1975- 5,9 – 1,5,9 – D1679 – us UMI [510]
NOTICES BIOGRAPHIQUES / Chalmel, J L – 19th cent – 1 – F247.00 – fr Armell [920]
NOTICES BIOGRAPHIQUES ET BIBLIOGRAPHIQUES SUR LES JESUITES DE L'ANCIENNE MISSION DE CHINE 1552-1773 / Pfister, L – Chang-Hai. 2v. 1932-1934 – 23mf – 9 – ne IDC [240]
NOTICES DE MANUSCRITS ARMENIENS VUS DANS QUELQUES BIBLIOTHEQUES DE L'EUROPE CENTRALE / Macler, F – Paris, 1913 – 2mf – 9 – ne IDC [460]
NOTICES DES TABLEAUX EXPOSES DANS LES GALERIES DU MUSEE NATIONAL DE LOUVRE : TROISIEME PARTIE: ECOLE FRANCAIS / Villot, Marie Joseph Frederic – Paris: de Mourgues Freres, 1881 – 6mf – 9 – $15.00 – fr Bibl Nationale [700]
NOTICES ET PORTRAITS / France. Chambre des Deputes – 1916, 1928, 1932, 1936, 1940, 1951 – 1 – fr A.C.R.P.P. [323]
NOTICES ET PORTRAITS / France. Senat – 1910, 1921, 1933, 1936, 1939 – 1 – fr A.C.R.P.P. [323]
NOTICES GENERALES DES GRAVEURS / Huber, M – O-993 1. 1787 – 9 – ne IDC [760]
NOTICES HISTORIQUES SUR LES GENERAUX ET MARINS DU 18E SIECLE / Dussieux, Louis – Paris: V. Lecoffre, 1889. 02810. (Pre-1900 Canadiana) – 9 – cn C.I.H.M. [971]
NOTICES OF BRITISH FUNGI / Berkeley, M J & Broome, C E – 1837-85 – 7 – uk Microform Academic [580]
NOTICES OF BRITISH FUNGI / Berkeley, M J & Broome, C E – London, 1837-83. B-5013/2 – 8 – ne IDC [580]
NOTICES OF MATERIA MEDICA / Rafinesque-Schmaltz, Constantine S – Western Minerva, 1821 – 1mf – 9 – ne IDC [615]
NOTICES OF THE ENGLISH COLLEGES AND CONVENTS ESTABLISHED ON THE CONTINENT AFTER THE DISSOLUTION OF RELIGIOUS HOUSES IN ENGLAND / Petre, Edward; ed by Husenbeth, F C – Norwich: Bacon and Kinnebrook, 1849 – 1mf – us A.T.L.A. [370]
NOTICES OF THE JEWS BY THE CLASSIC WRITERS OF ANTIQUITY; BEING A COLLECTION OF FACTS AND OPINIONS FROM THE WORKS OF ANCIENT HEATHEN AUTHORS PREVIOUS TO A.D. 500 / Gill, John – 1870 – 1 – us A.T.L.A. [270]
NOTICES SUR LES 70 SERVITEURS DE DIEU : MIS A MORT POUR LA FOI EN CHINE, AU TONG-KING ET EN COCHINCHINE: DECLARES VENERABLES PAR N.S.P. LE PAPE GREGOIRE 16 / Rousseau, Abbe – Paris: Gaspard P Alexandre, 1855 – 1mf – 9 – 0-8370-7099-6 – 1986-1099 – us A.T.L.A. [240]
NOTICES SUR LES COLONIES ANGLAISES / Avalle, Ernest – Paris: Berger-Levrault, 1883. 00898. (Pre-1900 Canadiana) – 9 – cn C.I.H.M. [971]
NOTICES SUR LES OEUVRES DE THEATRE / Argenson, Marquis; ed by Lagrave, H – (Studies on Voltaire and the eighteenth century, v42-43) – Oxford. 1966 – 9 – $87.00 – 0-7294-0130-8 – uk Voltaire [820]
NOTICES SUR LES PLANTES RARES CULTIVEES DANS LE JARDIN BOTANIQUE DE GENEVE / Candolle, A P de – Geneve, Paris. 1823-47 – 8 – ne IDC [580]
NOTICES SUR L'HISTOIRE ANCIENNE DE L'ARMENIE ET LES INSCRIPTIONS CUNEIFORMES DU BASSIN DE VAN / Hyvernat, Henri – (Includes bibliographical references) – Strasbourg: Imprimerie Alsacienne, 1892 – 1mf – 9 – 0-8370-8581-0 – 1986-2581 – us A.T.L.A. [930]
NOTICES SUR QUELQUES MANUSCRITS ARABES / Dozy, R – Leyde, 1847-1851 – Dfl22.00 – ne Slangenburg [470]
A NOTICIA – Palmyra, 26 Sep 1925 – 1,5,6 – bl Biblioteca [072]
A NOTICIA – Rio Branco, Acre. 10 Mar 1918-11 Maio 1919 – 1,5,6 – bl Biblioteca [072]
A NOTICIA – Sao Paulo, Brazil. Dec 1906; Jan-Oct 1907; May-Nov 1908 – 1 – bl Biblioteca [072]
NOTICIA DE UN LIBRO VIEJO Y DE UNA GLORIA OLVIDADA / Bayle, Constantino – Madrid: Razon y Fe, 1920 – 1 – sp Bibl Santa Ana [946]
NOTICIA DEL VIAJE DE ESPANA / Velazquez de Velasco, Luis J – 1765 – 1mf – 9 – Pta1,000.00 – 84-7848-274-1 – sp Pentalfa [910]
NOTICIA GENERAL PARA LA ESTIMACION DE LAS ARTES... / Gutierrez de Los Rios, G – Madrid, 1600 – 7mf – 9 – sp Cultura [700]
NOTICIA HISTORICA DE LA RIQUEZA MINERA DE MEXICO... / Ramirez, Santiago – Mexico: Secretaria de Fomento, 1884 – 1 – F391.85 – fr Armell [972]
NOTICIA HISTORICA DE...BADAJOZ / Diaz Perez, Nicolas – 1899 – 9 – 1.50f – sp Bibl Santa Ana [946]
NOTICIA INEDITA / Sanguino y Michel, Juan – Caceres: Tip. Enc. y Lib. Jimenez, 1904 – 1 – sp Bibl Santa Ana [946]
LA NOTICIA MUNDIAL – Chicago: Noticia Mundial Newspaper Co, aug 7 1927-feb 12 1928 – 1r – 1 – us Res Libr [071]
NOTICIA NECROLOGICA DE DON FELIPE-LEON GUERRA / Barrantes Moreno, Vicente – Madrid: Fortanet, 1890. B.R.A.H. 17, pp. 429-430 – sp Bibl Santa Ana [946]
NOTICIA SOBRE LA SEPULTURA DE PIZARRO, DE CUNEO VIDAL / Perez de Guzman, Juan – Madrid: Tip. Fortunat, 1920. B.R.A.H 77, p. 478 – sp Bibl Santa Ana [946]
NOTICIA SOBRE REVISTA DE EXTREMADURA Y LAPIDAS / Fita, Fidel – Madrid: Tip. Fortanet, 1899 – 1 – sp Bibl Santa Ana [946]
NOTICIA SOBRE SAN GERMAN Y SAN SERVAN / Melida, Jose Ramon – Madrid: Fortanet, 1920. B.R.A.H. 76. pp. 287-288 – 1 – sp Bibl Santa Ana [946]
NOTICIA VERDADEIRA DA GUERRA DA AMERICA ENTRE OS FRANCEZES, E INGLEZES, COM A TOMADA DO FORTE DE SAM JORZE GANHADO PELOS FRANCEZES E C – Lisbon: Domingos Gonsalves, 1757. SEM105P883 – 1mf – 9 – Can$2.25 – cn Bibl Nat [971]
O NOTICIADOR – Penedo, Alagoas. 26 Out, Dez 1890; Jan-Fev 1891; 27 Fev 1892 – 1,5,6 – bl Biblioteca [072]
O NOTICIADOR : PERIODICO NOTICIOSO, COMMERCIAL, AGRICOLA E IMPARCIAL – Penedo, Alagoas. 30 Mar, 13, 27 Maio 1877 – 1,5,6 – bl Biblioteca [072]
NOTICIADOR CUIABANO – Cuiaba, 28 Jun, Nov-Dec 1857; Mar-3 Apr 1859 – 1,5,6 – bl Biblioteca [072]
NOTICIADOR DE MINAS – Ouro Preto, 19 Aug 1868-Nov 1869; Aug-Oct 1870; Feb 1871-27 Jan 1873 – 1,5,6 – bl Biblioteca [072]
NOTICIADOR SERGIPENSE – Aracaju, 9, 27 Oct 1835; Jan-Apr, Sep 1836; 1837 – 1,5,6 – bl Biblioteca [072]
NOTICIARIO / Interamerican Children's Institute. Montevideo – Nos 1-167 1942-63. 9 scattered nos. missing – 1 – $25.00 – us L of C Photodup [305]
NOTICIARIO OBRERO INTERAMERICANO – Mexico City. March 1951-65 – 1 – 40.00 – us L of C Photodup [330]
LAS NOTICIAS – Barcelona, 6 May-25 Oct 1916; 1 Jan 1917-30 June 1919 (imperfect) – 12r – 1 – uk British Libr Newspaper [072]

NOTICIAS / Fita, Fidel & Fernandez D, Cesareo – Madrid: Fortanet, 1899, p.288. B.R.A.H. 35, 1899 – 1 – sp Bibl Santa Ana [946]

NOTICIAS – Lourenco Marques: [s.n., 1956-] – us Res Libr [072]

NOTICIAS ALEMANAS : DEUTSCHE NACHRICHTEN – Asuncion, oct 1 1943-45 n41 (incomplete) – 1 – Dist. gw Mikrofilm – gw Misc Inst [972]

NOTICIAS ALIADAS = LATINAMERICA PRESS – Lima. 577 docs. 1980-1991 – 68mf – 9 – ne IDC [972]

NOTICIAS AMERICANAS / Ulloa, Antonio de – 1772 – 2mf – 9 – Pta1,500.00 – 84-7848-336-5 – sp Pentalfa [970]

NOTICIAS BIBLIOGRAFICAS : COLECCION SAULO.-VIDA DEL VENERABLE JUAN BAUTISTA BERTRAN / ed by Bayle, Constantino – Madrid: Razon y Fe, 1925 – 1 – sp Bibl Santa Ana [010]

NOTICIAS BIBLIOGRAFICAS : EARLY JESUIT...BY C. WESSELS / ed by Bayle, Constantino – Madrid: Razon y Fe, 1925 – 1 – sp Bibl Santa Ana [240]

NOTICIAS BIBLIOGRAFICAS : ROSAS DE MARTIRIO.-LUIS CARPIO MORAGAS.-LES SAINTS.-BIBLIOGRAFIA HISPANO-AMERICANA... / ed by Bayle, Constantino – Madrid: Razon y Fe, 1925 – 1 – sp Bibl Santa Ana [240]

NOTICIAS BIBLIOGRAFICAS : UNITED STATES CATHOLIC, TOMO 1-13 / ed by Bayle, Constantino – Madrid: Razon y Fe, 1925 – 1 – sp Bibl Santa Ana [240]

NOTICIAS BIBLIOGRAFICAS DE TEXTOS Y DISPOSIONES LEGALES DE LOS REINOS DE CASTILLA... / Gil Ayuso, F – Madrid, 1935 – 8mf – 9 – sp Cultura [340]

NOTICIAS DE... / Fita, Fidel & Rodriguez Villa, Antonio – Madrid: Fortanet, 1899, p.93. B.R.A.H. 34, 1899 – 1 – sp Bibl Santa Ana [946]

NOTICIAS DE EL CAPHE... / Tariol, J – SL, SA: s. XVIII? – 2mf – 9 – sp Cultura [946]

NOTICIAS DE LA HISTORIA GENERAL DE CANARIAS. TOMO 1 / Viera Clavijo, Jose – 1772 – 2mf – 9 – Pta1,500.00 – 84-7848-339-X – sp Pentalfa [946]

NOTICIAS DE LA HISTORIA GENERAL DE CANARIAS. TOMO 2 / Viera Clavijo, Jose – 1773 – 2mf – 9 – Pta1,500.00 – 84-7848-340-3 – sp Pentalfa [946]

NOTICIAS DE LA HISTORIA GENERAL DE CANARIAS. TOMO 3 / Viera Clavijo, Jose – 1776 – 2mf – 9 – Pta1,500.00 – 84-7848-341-1 – sp Pentalfa [946]

NOTICIAS DE LA HISTORIA GENERAL DE CANARIAS. TOMO 4 / Viera Clavijo, Jose – 1783 – 2mf – 9 – Pta1,500.00 – 84-7848-342-X – sp Pentalfa [946]

NOTICIAS DE LA PENINSULA AMERICANA DE CALIFORNIA. INTRODUCION Y NOTAS POR PAUL KIRCHHOFF... / Baegetr, Juan Jacobo – Madrid: Razon y Fe, 1944 – 1 – sp Bibl Santa Ana [972]

NOTICIAS DE LA VILLA DE SEGURA DE LEON / Casquete Hernando, Antonio – Sevilla: Graficas Tirvia, 1951 – 1 – sp Bibl Santa Ana [946]

NOTICIAS ESTADISTICAS DE LA ISLA DE CUBA EN 1862 – La Habana, 1864 – 4mf – 9 – sp Cultura [304]

NOTICIAS GENERALES / Bayle, Constantino – Madrid: Razon y Fe, 1920 – 1 – sp Bibl Santa Ana [946]

NOTICIAS GENERALES / Bayle, Constantino – Madrid: Razon y Fe, 1921 – 1 – sp Bibl Santa Ana [946]

NOTICIAS GENERALES / Bayle, Constantino – Madrid: Razon y Fe, 1922 – 1 – sp Bibl Santa Ana [946]

NOTICIAS GENERALES / Bayle, Constantino – Madrid: Razon y Fe, 1924 – 1 – sp Bibl Santa Ana [946]

NOTICIAS GENERALES / Bayle, Constantino – Madrid: Razon y Fe, 1925 – 1 – sp Bibl Santa Ana [946]

NOTICIAS GENERALES / ed by Bayle, Constantino – Madrid: Razon y Fe, 1926 – 1 – sp Bibl Santa Ana [946]

NOTICIAS GENERALES – Madrid: Razon y Fe, 1926 – 1 – sp Bibl Santa Ana [946]

NOTICIAS GENERALES Y UN DATO INEDITO PARA LA BIOGRAFIA DE VASCO DIAZ TANCO, DE FREGENAL, EN RELACION CON CANARIAS / Santiago Rodriguez, Miguel – Badajoz: Imp. Diput. Prov., 1982 – sp Bibl Santa Ana [920]

NOTICIAS (HALLAZGOS POR EL MARQUES DE CASTROFUERTE EN CACERES / Castrofuerte, Marques de – Madrid: Fortanet, 1886. B.R.A.H. IX, pp. 393-394 – sp Bibl Santa Ana [946]

NOTICIAS. PIEDRA OSCILANTE DE MONTANCHEZ / Paredes Guillen, Vicente – Madrid: Fortanet, 1887. B.R.A.H. XI, pp. 279-280, 1 lam – sp Bibl Santa Ana [946]

NOTICIAS REFERENTES...TEATRO EN SEVILLA / Sanchez Arjona y Sanchez Arjona, Jose – 1898 – 9 – 1.50f – sp Bibl Santa Ana [790]

NOTICIAS SOBRE EL ESTADO DE LA BASILICA DE SANTA EULALIA Y NUEVOS HALLAZGOS EN MERIDA / Fita, Fidel – Madrid: Fortanet, 1893. B.R.A.H. 23, pp. 361-362 – sp Bibl Santa Ana [946]

NOTICIAS SOBRE LAS PROVINCIAS FRANCISCANAS DE CANARIAS. TENERIFE, 1966 / Inchambre, Diego de – Madrid: Graf. Calleja, 1967 – 1 – sp Bibl Santa Ana [946]

NOTICIAS SOBRE SU OBRA. "EL TEATRO TAGALO" / Barrantes Moreno, Vicente – Madrid: Fortanet, 1890. B.R.A.H. 16, pp. 472 – sp Bibl Santa Ana [946]

EL NOTICIERO – Caceres, 1903-1908, 1910-1912 y 1914-1931 – 5 – sp Bibl Santa Ana [073]

EL NOTICIERO – Plasencia. 1887. No.12 – 9 – 1.50f – sp Bibl Santa Ana [072]

EL NOTICIERO – Plasencia, 1887-1888 – 5 – sp Bibl Santa Ana [073]

EL NOTICIERO EMERITENSE – Merida, 1900. 2 numeros – 5 – sp Bibl Santa Ana [073]

NOTICIERO EXTREMENO – Badajoz, 1905, 1909-1911, 1914 y 1917-1926 – 5 – sp Bibl Santa Ana [073]

NOTICIERO EXTREMENO – Badajoz, 1908 y 1913. 2 numeros – 5 – sp Bibl Santa Ana [073]

LA NOTION D'ADAPTATION EN TRADUCTION : ETUDE DE L'ADAPTATION PONCTUELLE ET GLOBALE DE LA VERSION ESPAGNOLE DE L'ANALYSE DU DISCOURS COMME METHODE DE TRADUCTION, DE J. DELISLE / Bastin, Georges – 3mf – 9 – 10371 – fr Atelier National [440]

LA NOTION DE CONGREGATION, SA PORTEE EN DROIT CIVIL FRANCAIS. / Buzy, Odette – Paris: Librairie generale de droit & de jurisprudence, 1940. 219p. LL-4090 – 1 – us L of C Photodup [340]

LA NOTION JOHANNIQUE DE L'ESPRIT ET SES ANTECEDENTS HISTORIQUES / Goguel, Maurice – Paris: Fischbacher, 1902 – 9 – us A.T.L.A. [240]

LES NOTIONS D'ACTIVITIES ET D'ACTIFS A L'INTERIEUR D'UNE EXPLOITATION AGRICOLE / Ancey, G – (Black Africa series). 1968 – 9 – fr Hachette [630]

NOTIONS DE DROIT MARITIME INTERNATIONAL / Antraygues, E – Paris, 1923 – 2mf – 9 – ILM-1614/1 – ne IDC [340]

NOTIONS DE DROIT MARITIME INTERNATIONAL / Charnet, J – Paris, Nancy, 1907 – 2mf – 1 – ILM-1610/1 – ne IDC [327]

NOTIONS ELEMENTAIRES D'HARMONIE MODERNE... / Loquin, A – Bordeaux: G Gounouilhou, 1862 – 1 – us Sibley [780]

THE NOTIONS OF THE METHODISTS FARTHER DISPROV'D, IN ANSWER TO THEIR 'EARNEST APPEAL',... / Smith, G – (Reprinted in London in 1744) – Newcastle, 1743 – 1mf – 9 – MP-306/1 – ne IDC [240]

THE NOTIONS OF THE METHODISTS FULLY DISPROV'D, BY SETTING THE DOCTRINE OF THE CHURCH OF ENGLAND CONCERNING JUSTIFICATION AND REGENERATION IN A TRUE LIGHT;... / Smith, G – (Reprinted in London for Jacob Robinson in 1744 under the combined title of The notions of the Methodists fully disprov'd) – Newcastle, 1743 – 1mf – 9 – MP-305/1 – ne IDC [240]

NOTIONS PRATIQUES DE DROIT MARITIME INTERNATIONAL ET COMMERCIAL / Doneaud, A – Paris, 1866 – 3mf – 1 – ILM-1502/1 – ne IDC [327]

NOTITIA CONSTANTINOPOLITANAE *see* NOTITIA DIGNITATUM, ACCEDUNT NOTITIA CONSTANTINOPOLITANAE ET LATERCULI PROVINCIARUM

NOTITIA DIGNITATUM : ACCEDUNT NOTITIA CONSTANTINOPOLITANAE ET LATERCULI PROVINCIARUM / ed by Seeck, O – Berolini, 1876 – Dfl28.00 – ne Slangenburg [240]

NOTITIA DIGNITATUM, ACCEDUNT NOTITIA CONSTANTINOPOLITANAE ET LATERCULI PROVINCIARUM / ed by Seeck, O – Berolini, 1876 – 7mf – 8 – Dfl28.00 – ne Slangenburg [240]

NOTITIA DIGNITATUM IMPERII ROMANI (CBH 27) / ed by Labbe, Ph – Parisiis, 1651 – Dfl22.00 – ne Slangenburg [930]

NOTITIA EPISCOPATUUM ORBIS CHRISTIANI SIVE CODEX PROVINCIALIS ROMANUS / Miraeus, A – Parisiis, 1610 – Dfl9.00 – ne Slangenburg [240]

NOTITIA SCRIPTORUM SS. PATRUM ALIORUMQUE VETERIS ECCLESIAE MONUMENTORUM : QUAE IN COLLECTIONIBUS ANECDOROTUM POST ANNUM CHRISTI MDCC. IN LUCEM EDITIS CONTINENTUR / Dowling, Joannis Goulter – Oxonii: Typographeo Academico, 1839 – 1mf – us A.T.L.A. [240]

NOTITIA VTRAQVE CVM ORIENTIS TVM OCCIDENTIS VLTRA ARCADII HONORIIQVE CAESARVM TEMPORA, ILLUSTRE UETUSTATIS MONUMENTUM, IMO THESAURUS PRORSUM INCOMPARABILIS – Basileae, 1552 – 4mf – 9 – H-8154/1 – ne IDC [956]

NOTIZBLATT DES KOENIGL. BOTANISCHEN GARTENS UND MUSEUMS ZU BERLIN – Berlin. v1-15. 1895-1941 – 181mf – 9 – ne IDC [580]

NOTIZIE DE' PROFESSORI DEL DISEGNO DA CIMABUE IN QUA, PER LE QUALI SI DIMOSTRA COME, E PER CHI LE BELL' ARTI DI PITTURA, SCULTURE, E ARCHITETTURA LASCIATA LA ROZZEZZA DELLE MANIERE GRECA, E GOTTICA... / Baldinucci, Filippo – 6v. Firenze. 1681-1728. BO-135 1 – 9 – ne IDC [700]

NOTIZIE ISTORICHE DELLE CHIESE FIORENTINE DIVISE NE' SUOI QUARTIERI / Richa, G – Firenze, 1754-1762 – 10 vols – 9 – ne IDC [720]

NOTKERI BALBULI GESTA KAROLI MAGNI IMP. (MGH 6: 12.BD) / ed by Haefele, H F – 1959 – Dfl19.00 – ne Slangenburg [240]

Notkerus *see* TROPI CARMINUM : LIBER HYMNORUM

Notman, John *see* THE LAW AND PRACTICE CONCERNING CONTROBERTED [I.E. CONTROVERTED] PARLIAMENTARY ELECTIONS IN THE PROVINCE OF CANADA

NOTNYI KATALOG TSENTRAL'NOI BIBLIOTEKI / Russia. Central Library – M. 1895. BR-4774 2 – 8 – ne IDC [020]

THE NOTORIOUS MRS. EBBSMITH : A DRAMA IN FOUR ACTS / Pinero, Arthur Wing – London: W. Heinemann, 1895 – 1 roll – 1 – 1-55879-467-0 – uk Libr Preservation [820]

NOTOSOETARSO : HET DRAMA VAN INDIE – 's-Gravenhage, 1945 – 1mf – 9 – ne IDC [950]

Notosutardjo, Achmad *see*
- BUNG KARNO DIHADAPAN PENGADILAN KOLONIAL
- BUNG KARNO MENDJAWAB

LE NOTRE : DANS LES INTERETS DES OUVRIERS – Montreal, Canada. 10 aut 1895 – 1r – 1 – Can$25.00 – cn Can Microfilming [072]

NOTRE BEAU NIGER / Dubois, Felix – Paris: E Flammarion, 1911 – us Res Libr [910]

NOTRE COLONIE – Brussels. Belgium. Oct. 1919-June 1929 – 1 – 35.00r – us Hoover Inst Photo [949]

NOTRE COLONIE DE LA COTE D'IVOIRE / Villamur, Roger & Richaud, Leon – Paris: A Challamel, 1903 – us Res Libr [960]

NOTRE COURRIER – [Quebec]: Manufacturers Life Assurance Co, [1896-1908?] – 9 – cn C.I.H.M. [360]

NOTRE DAME ENGLISH JOURNAL – v1-nsv15. 1961-83 – 1 – us UMI [420]

NOTRE DAME JOURNAL OF EDUCATION – v1-7 1970-76 1; v3-7 5,6; v6-7 9 – us UMI [073]

NOTRE DAME JOURNAL OF LAW, ETHICS AND PUBLIC POLICY – v1-9. 1984-1995 – 9 – $163.00 set – us Hein [340]

NOTRE DAME JOURNAL OF LEGISLATION – (See also: Journal of Legislation) – v1-2 1974-1975 1,5,6; v2 1975 9 – us UMI [340]

NOTRE DAME LAW REVIEW – (Title varies: v1-57 1928-82 as Notre Dame Lawyer. Available on reel or mf) – v1-71. 1925-96 – 9 – $1,047.00 set – us Hein [340]

NOTRE DAME LAW REVIEW – v1-70. 1925-95 – 1,5,6,9 – $1,305.00 – us Hein [073]

NOTRE DAME LAW REVIEW – (v60-. 1984-. 5,6,9) – v58-. Oct 1982- – 1 – us UMI [073]

NOTRE DAME LAWYER – v1-57. Nov 1925-Jun 1982 – 1 – us UMI [073]

NOTRE DAME LAWYER *see* NOTRE DAME LAW REVIEW

NOTRE FRONTIERE / Comtat, Paulin – Paris: [s.n.]; Montreal: Le Devoir, [1914?] (Paris: Impr. P Feron-Vrau). SEM105P1548 – 2mf – 9 – Can$4.50 – cn Bibl Nat [440]

NOTRE REPUBLIQUE – no. 1-110. Paris. juil 1959-63 – 1 – fr A.C.R.P.P. [073]

NOTRE TEMPS – Paris. juin 1927-juin 1940 – 1 – fr A.C.R.P.P. [073]

NOTRE VOIE – (In French) – Geneva, SZ. v2 no9-10. Jan-Feb 1947 – 1r – 1 – $25.00 – cn Can Microfilming [072]

NOTRE VOIX – Hebdomadaire politique paraissant le dimanche. no. 1-32. Hanoi. 1er janv-25 aout 1939 – 1 – fr A.C.R.P.P. [073]

NOTRE-DAME DU LAUS ET LA VENERABLE SOEUR BENOITE : D'APRES LES MANUSCRITS AUTHENTIQUES: CONSERVES AU PIEUX SANCTUAIRE – Laus: en vent chez Peres Missionnaires; Gap: En vente chez J-C Richard, 1895 – 2mf – 9 – 0-8370-7502-5 – 1986-1502 – us A.T.L.A. [920]

NOTRE-DAME-DES-CANADIENS ET LES CANADIENS AUX ETATS-UNIS / Chandonnet, Thomas Aime – Montreal: G. Desbarats, 1872. 00555. (Pre-1900 Canadiana) – 9 – cn C.I.H.M. [971]

NOTRE-TEMPS / ed by Richer, Leopold & Richer, Julia – Montreal, Canada. 18 oct 1945-25 aut 1962 – 8r – 1 – Can$55.00r – cn Can Microfilming [072]

NOTT AND M'CORD'S LAW REPORTS / South Carolina. Supreme Court – (A Pre-NRS title) – v1-2. 1817-1820 (all publ) – 14mf – 9 – $21.00 – LLMC 94-013 – us L.L.M.C. [340]

Nott, Eliphalet *see* RESURRECTION OF CHRIST: A SERIES OF DISCOURSES

Nott, Josiah Clark *see* TWO LECTURES ON THE CONNECTION BETWEEN THE BIBLICAL AND PHYSICAL HISTORY OF MAN

LA NOTTE – 1991-1995 – 3r per y – 5,6 – Sfr936.00 – sz Infoprint [945]

NOTTE – 1991-1995 – 3 times per yr – 6 – F3,500.00 – sz Infoprint [072]

Notter, Friedrich *see* LUDWIG UHLAND

NOTTING HILL & BAYSWATER TIMES – London. 29 Dec 1860-24 Sep 1870.-w. 9mqn reels – 1 – uk British Libr Newspaper [072]

NOTTINGHAM AND NEWARK MERCURY – (Nottingham Mercury). England. -w. 24 Jan 1827-17 Sep 1852. (22 reels) – 1 – uk British Libr Newspaper [072]

NOTTINGHAM CHRONICLE – England.May-Nov 1903. -d. 1/2 reel – 1 – uk British Libr Newspaper [072]

NOTTINGHAM CITIZEN – (Weekly newspaper, publ in a Cleveland suburb later annexed to the city; issues are intermixed on the film with those of The Citizen and Collinwood Citizen) – Nottingham, OH. feb 2, 1900-dec 4, 1903 – 1r – 1 – us Western Res [071]

NOTTINGHAM JOURNAL – England. -w, -d. 1832-33; 1847; 1851-70; 1874-77; 1881-87. 79 reels – 1 – uk British Libr Newspaper [072]

NOTTINGHAM JOURNAL – England. -w. Jan-Dec 1866. 1 reel – 1 – uk British Libr Newspaper [072]

NOTTINGHAM MEDIAEVAL STUDIES – Cambridge. H 790. v. 1-11. 1957-1967 – 9 – ne IDC [073]

Nottingham, New Hampshire. Nottingham Baptist Church *see* RECORDS

NOTTINGHAM REVIEW – Nottingham. England. -w. Jan 1827-Dec 1852. (18 reels) – 1 – uk British Libr Newspaper [072]

NOTTINGHAMSHIRE, 1822 : BRITISH ISLES CENSUS DIRECTORIES PROJECT, ENGLAND – (In prep) – at Vine [941]

NOTTINGHAMSHIRE, 1828 : BRITISH ISLES CENSUS DIRECTORIES PROJECT, ENGLAND. VOL 100 – 1mf – 9 – A$15.00 – at Vine [941]

NOTTINGHAMSHIRE, 1841 : BRITISH ISLES CENSUS DIRECTORIES PROJECT, ENGLAND. VOL 237 – 1mf – 9 – A$9.00 – at Vine [941]

NOTTINGHAMSHIRE, 1848 : BRITISH ISLES CENSUS DIRECTORIES PROJECT, ENGLAND – at Vine [941]

NOTTINGHAMSHIRE, 1850 : BRITISH ISLES CENSUS DIRECTORIES PROJECT, ENGLAND – at Vine [941]

NOTTINGHAMSHIRE, 1853 : BRITISH ISLES CENSUS DIRECTORIES PROJECT, ENGLAND – at Vine [941]

NOTTINGHAMSHIRE, 1864 : BRITISH ISLES CENSUS DIRECTORIES PROJECT, ENGLAND. VOL 103 – 5mf – 9 – A$33.00 – at Vine [941]

NOTTINGHAMSHIRE, 1888 : BRITISH ISLES CENSUS DIRECTORIES PROJECT, ENGLAND – at Vine [941]

NOTTINGHAMSHIRE, 1916 : BRITISH ISLES CENSUS DIRECTORIES PROJECT, ENGLAND – at Vine [941]

NOTTINGHAMSHIRE (NEWARK AND NOTINGHAM), 1805 : BRITISH ISLES CENSUS DIRECTORIES PROJECT, ENGLAND. VOL 189 – 1mf – 9 – A$9.00 – at Vine [941]

NOTTINGHAMSHIRE (NORTH), 1868 : BRITISH ISLES CENSUS DIRECTORIES PROJECT, ENGLAND. VOL 25 – 1mf – 9 – A$9.00 – at Vine [941]

NOTTINGHAMSHIRE (NORTH WEST), 1852 : BRITISH ISLES CENSUS DIRECTORIES PROJECT, ENGLAND. VOL 256 – 2mf – 9 – A$15.00 – at Vine [941]

NOTTOWAY RECORD – Crewe. Va. 1922-1930 – 1 – us UMI [071]

NOTTURNO, NO 7, POUR LE PIANOFORTE AVEC ACCOMP. D'UN VIOLON ET VIOLONCELLE / Gyrowetz, Adalbert – (Pts) – Augsburg: Gombert, 180- – 1 – us Sibley [780]

NOTTURNO POUR DEUX ALTOS ET VIOLONCELLE / Brandl, J – Offenbach s/M: J Andre, ca 1800 – 1 – us Sibley [780]

NOTULAE AD PLANTAS ASIATICAS / Griffith, W – 4v. Calcutta. 1847-54. B-5269 2 – 8 – ne IDC [580]

NOTULAE ENTOMOLOGICAE – Helsingfors. 1921-1942. v1-22. – 66mf – 8 – ne IDC [590]

NOTULAE SYSTEMATICAE EX HERBARIO HORTI BOTANICI PETROPOLITANI – Petrograd. v1-5. 1919-1924 – 13mf – 9 – ne IDC [580]

NOTULAE SYSTEMATICAE EX INSTITUTO CRYPTOGAMICO HORTI BOTANICI PETROPOLITANI – Petrograd, Petropolis. v1-3. 1922-1924 – 9mf – 9 – ne IDC [580]

NOTWENDIGE ENDECKUNG WIE D. LUCAS OSIANDER IN SEINER PREDIGT VON DER GNADEN-WAHL DIE VERZWEYFFELTE CALUINISCHE LERE VERSTECKT MIT FUERSATZ DIESELBIGE IN DIE REINE CHRISTLICHE KIRCHEN IN WUERTEMBERG... / Huber, S – N.p., 1596 – 1mf – ne IDC [240]

DIE NOTWENDIGKEIT DES RELIGIONSUNTERRICHTS IN DER STAATSSCHULE : EIN VORTRAG / Dickmann, Fritz – Berlin: Georg Nauck (Fritz Ruehe), 1906 – 1mf – 9 – 0-8370-7692-7 – 1986-1692 – us A.T.L.A. [370]

DIE NOTWENDIGKEIT UND VERBINDLICHKEIT DES KIRCHLICHEN BEKENNTNISSES : EINE FESTSCHRIFT ZUM 300JAEHRIGEN JUBILAEUM DES LUTHERISCHEN KONKORDIENBUCHES (25. JUNI 1880) / Philippi, Ferdinand – Guetersloh: C. Bertelsmann, 1880 – 1mf – us A.T.L.A. [240]

Noufflard, Georges *see* BERLIOZ ET LE MOUVEMENT DE L'ART CONTEMPORAIN

Nougaret, Pierre-Jean-Baptiste *see* LA MORT DE L'OPERA COMIQUE...PIECE ELEGI-SATYRI-COMI-TRAGIQUE..

Nougayrol, J *see*
- LE PALAIS ROYAL D'UGARIT 1
- LE PALAIS ROYAL D'UGARIT 4

Nougues Secall, Mariano *see* RESENA HISTORICA...BOTOA

Noulens *see* MAISONS HISTORIQUES DE GASCOGNE ET DE GUYENNE

Noulet, J B *see* ESSAI SUR L'HISTOIRE LITTERAIRE DES PATOIS DU MIDI DE LA FRANCE AUX XVIEET XVIIESIECLES

O NOUMAS – Athens, Greece. -w. 2 Jan 1903-28 Dec 1913. 5 reels – 1 – uk British Libr Newspaper [949]

THE NOURISHMENT OF THE CHRISTIAN SOUL = NOURRITURE DE L'AME CHRETIENNE : OR, MENTAL PRAYER RENDERED EASY BY MEDITATION ON THE PASSION OF OUR LORD JESUS CHRIST WITH EXERCISES AND PRAYERS / Pinart, Desire – (In English) – London: Joseph Masters, 1852 – 1mf – 9 – 0-8370-7254-9 – 1986-1254 – us A.T.L.A. [240]

Nourse, Robert *see* WHY I AM NOT AN INFIDEL: A LECTURE

NOUVELLES DE LA CITE DE AFRICQUE EN BARBARIE PRINSE PAR LES CAPITEINES DE LARMEE DE LEMPEREUR – Louayn au Lupart, 1550 – 1mf – 9 – H-8153/1 – ne IDC [956]

NOUVE INVENTIONI DI BALLI, OPERA VAGHISSIMA DI CESARE NEGRI MILANESE DETTO IL TROMBONE... / Negri, Cesare – Milano: G Bordone, 1604 – 1 – us Sibley [780]

NOUVEAU BULLETIN DES SCIENCES, PAR LA SOCIETE PHILOMATIQUE DE PARIS – Paris. v4-8. 1814-1820 – 31mf – 9 – ne IDC [500]

LE NOUVEAU CAMPUS ESTRIEN *see* LE JOURNAL DES ETUDIANTS DE L'UNIVERSITE DE SHERBROOKE

NOUVEAU CHRISTIANISME / Saint Simon, Claude Henri de – Dialogue entre un conservateur et un novateur. Paris, Bossange. 1825. 91 p. Les Saint-Simoniens, 1825-1834. 6840 – 9 – fr Hachette [240]

LE NOUVEAU CLAIRON *see* LE CLAIRON

NOUVEAU CLASSEMENT DES MONNAIES ARSACIDES D'APRES LE CATALOGUE DU BRITISH MUSEUM / Allotte de la Fuye – Paris, 1904 – 1mf – ne IDC [900]

LE NOUVEAU CODE CIVIL DU TONKIN. / Darras, Maxime – Paris, Domat-Montchrestien, 1934. 171 p. LL-10001 – 1 – us L of C Photodup [340]

LE NOUVEAU CODE CONJUGAL, ETABLI SUR LES BASES DE LA CONSTITUTION / Bonneville, Nicolas de – Paris. Chez les Directeurs de l'Imp. du Cercle Social. 1792 – 9 – fr Hachette [321]

UN NOUVEAU COLONIALISME; DOCUMENT HISTORIQUE PUBLIE PAR LE GOUVERNEMENT DE LA REPUBLIQUE DES MOLUQUES DU SUD / South Moluccas. (Republic). Dept. of Public Information – SE 2655 1. 1958? – 9 – ne IDC [324]

LE NOUVEAU CONTRAT SOCIAL / Casaubon, E A – ou Place a la femme. Paris, Delaunay, 1834, 77 p. Les Saint-Simoniens, 1825-1834. 6912 – 9 – fr Hachette [305]

NOUVEAU COURRIER DE LA COTE SUD *see* LE COURRIER DE MONTMAGNY

LE NOUVEAU COURRIER RIVIERA *see* LE RIVIERA

NOUVEAU DICTIONNAIRE DE LA LANGUE ALLEMANDE ET FRANCOISE, FRANCOISE ET ALLEMANDE (AEL, ABT 2;13) / Schwan, Christian Friedrich – Mannheim, 1782-1793, 1798 (mf ed 1995) – 56mf – 9 – DM890.00 – 3-89131-196-6 – gw Fischer [040]

NOUVEAU DICTIONNAIRE DE LA LANGUE FRANCAISE / Dochez, L – 1859-1860 – 9 – fr I.C.S. [440]

NOUVEAU DICTIONNAIRE DE LA LANGUE FRANCAISE / Laveaux, J -Ch. Thibault de – 1820 – 9 – fr I.C.S. [440]

NOUVEAU DICTIONNAIRE DE LA LANGUE FRANCAISE / Laveaux, J -Ch. Thibault de – 2e ed. 1828 – 9 – fr I.C.S. [440]

NOUVEAU DICTIONNAIRE DES COMMUNES, HAMEAUX...DU ROYAUME DE BELGIQUE – Bruxelles vers, 1892 – 2mf – 9 – F60.00 – fr F.F.G. [949]

NOUVEAU DICTIONNAIRE D'HISTOIRE NATURELLE – Ed 2. Paris. v1-36. 1816-1819 – 342mf – 9 – ne IDC [500]

NOUVEAU DICTIONNAIRE PORTATIF DE LA LANGUE FRANCAISE / Gattel, C M – 1797 – 9 – fr I.C.S. [440]

NOUVEAU DICTIONNAIRE POUR SERVIR DE SUPPLEMENT AUX DICTIONNAIRES DES SCIENCES, DES ARTS ET DES METIERS / Diderot, Denis – 1776-1777 – 9 – fr I.C.S. [500]

NOUVEAU DICTIONNAIRE UNIVERSEL / La Chatre, M – 1865-70 – 9 – fr I.C.S. [400]

NOUVEAU DICTIONNAIRE UNIVERSEL DE LA LANGUE FRANCAISE / Poitevin, P – 1856-60 – 9 – fr I.C.S. [440]

UN NOUVEAU DIT DES FEMMES PUBLIE POUR LA PREMIERE FOIS / ed by Raynaud, Gaston – Paris: Imp. Jouast et Sigaux, 1886. 12p. (Les Femmes Collection) – 1mf – 9 – $6.00 – fr Bibl Nationale [305]

LE NOUVEAU DROIT INTERNATIONAL ET SA NOUVELLE METHODE D'ETUDE / Alvarez, Arturo – Paris, 1934 – 3mf – 9 – ILM-1690/1 – ne IDC [340]

LE NOUVEAU DROIT INTERNATIONAL PUBLIC... / Alvarez, Arturo – Paris, 1934 – 1mf – 9 – ILM1716/1 – ne IDC [340]

NOUVEAU GLOSSAIRE GENEVOIS / Humbert, J – 1852 – 9 – fr I.C.S. [440]

LE NOUVEAU GULLIVER, OU VOYAGE DE JEAN GULLIVER, FILS DU CAPITAINE GULLIVER, TRADUIT D'UN MANUSCRIT ANGLOIS / Desfontaines, Pierre-Francois Guyot – (Utopias in the Enlightment). 1730 – 9 – fr Hachette [440]

LE NOUVEAU JOURNAL / ed by Gagnon, Jean-Louis – Montreal, Canada. 5 sep 1961-21 jun 1962 – 6r – 1 – Can$60.00r – cn Can Microfilming [072]

LE NOUVEAU JOURNAL – puis Litterature, sciences et arts. Red. en chef Amedee Rolland. no. 1-23; II, no. 1-20. Paris. nov 1850-avr 1851, fevr-juin 1852 – 1 – fr A.C.R.P.P. [073]

LE NOUVEAU JOURNAL *see* LE JOURNAL DE MAGOG

LE NOUVEAU JOURNAL D'ALEXANDRIA – Rigaud, Canada. 7 nov 1962; v1 n9. 2 jan 1963 – 1r – 1 – Can$25.00 – cn Can Microfilming [072]

LE NOUVEAU JOURNAL DE LAVAL – Ville de Laval. v1 n2. 21 dec 1964 – 1r – 1 – Can$25.00 – cn Can Microfilming [072]

NOUVEAU JOURNAL DES SCAVANS, DRESSE A BERLIN / ed by Chauvin, Etienne – Berlin. Annee 1-3. 1696-1698 (mf ed 1993) – 9mf – 9 – DM220.00 – gw Fischer [073]

LE NOUVEAU LEVIS – Levis, Canada. 23 mar 1907-v1 n2. 30 mar 1907 – 1r – 1 – Can$25.00 – cn Can Microfilming [072]

NOUVEAU MANUEL COMPLET DU MARQUETEUR DU TABLETIER ET DE L'IVOIRIER / Maigne, W – Paris: Librairie Encyclopedique de Roret, 1889. SEM16P284 – 1r – 5 – Can$9.00 – cn Bibl Nat [740]

NOUVEAU MANUEL COMPLETE DE L'ORGANISTE – Paris: Roret, 1855-1863 – 1 – us Sibley [780]

NOUVEAU MANUEL DE LA PURETE DU LANGAGE / Biscarrat, F – 1835 – 9 – fr I.C.S. [440]

LE NOUVEAU MONDE – (Becomes: Le Monde 3 jan 1882-31 dec 1886. Becomes: Le Monde Canadien 5 aut 1897) – Montreal, Canada. 17 aut 1867-30 sep 1868 – 4r – 1 – Can$65.00r – cn Can Microfilming [072]

LE NOUVEAU MONDE / ed by Blumhart, W F – (Becomes: La Presse 20 oct 1884) – Montreal, Canada. 15-18 oct 1884 – 1r – 1 – Can$25.00 – cn Can Microfilming [072]

LE NOUVEAU MONDE – Montreal, Canada. 1867-1900 – 56r – 1 – $3,640.00 – cn Library Assoc [971]

LE NOUVEAU MONDE – Theorie de Charles Fourier. Paris. juin 1839-41, fevr-nov 1843, janv-fevr 1844 (I-IV) – 1 – fr A.C.R.P.P. [073]

LE NOUVEAU MONDE: DRAME EN 5 ACTES, EN PROSE / Villiers de L'Isle Adam, Auguste de – Couronne au concours institue en l'honneur du centenaire de la proclamation de l'independance des Etats-Unis. Paris: Richard, 1880. xiv,190p. 3 fiches. (Literature Collection) – 9 – 8.00 – fr Bibl Nationale [820]

LE NOUVEAU MONDE: POEME / Lesuire, Robert Martin – Paris: Quillau, Vve. Duchesne, Vve. Tilliard, 1781. 2v in 1. 5 fiches. (Literature Collection) – 9 – 12.00 – fr Bibl Nationale [810]

NOUVEAU PLAN D'EDUCATION ET D'INSTRUCTION PUBLIQUE DEDIE A L'ASSEMBLEE NATIONALE / Villier, Joseph – Angers. Impr. Mame. 1789 – 9 – fr Hachette [370]

NOUVEAU PLAN D'EDUCATION POUR FORMER DES HOMMES INSTRUITS ET DES CITOYENS UTILES / Carpentier – Paris. 1775. 6740 – 9 – fr Hachette [320]

NOUVEAU PLAN D'EDUCATION POUR LES CLASSES DE CITOYENS / Verlac, Bertrand – Vannes, Bizette et Paris: Maisonneuve, 1789. 150p. 2 fiches. (Education Collection) – 9 – 6.00 – fr Bibl Nationale [370]

NOUVEAU PLAN D'ETUDES: ESSAI SUR LA MANIERE DE REMPLIR LES PLACES DANS LES COLLEGES QUE LES JESUITES OCCUPOIENT CI-DEVANT / Chaumeix, Abraham J de – Cologne. 1762 – 9 – fr Hachette [370]

LE NOUVEAU QUEBEC – (Becomes: Le Bastion 14 avr 1965) – Sept-Iles, Canada. 16 avr 1959-13 mar 1962 – 1r – 1 – Can$65.00 – cn Can Microfilming [072]

LE NOUVEAU QUOTIDIEN – 1991-1995 – 3r per y – 5,6 – Sfr1,123.00 – sz Infoprint [949]

NOUVEAU RECUEIL DE DIVERTISSEMENS COMIQUES / Oudin, Cesar Francois – Paris, 1670 – 1 – us U.W. Library [830]

NOUVEAU RECUEIL DE LEGISLATION CANTONALE ET COMMUNALE ANNAMITE DE COCHINCHINE / Outrey, Ernest – Saigon: Menard et Rey, 1905. 254p. LL-10013 – 1 – us L of C Photodup [340]

NOUVEAU RECUEIL DE PLANCHES COLORIEES D'OISEAUX / Temminick, C J & Laugier, M – Paris. 1838, 1820-39. Z-1948 2 – 8 – ne IDC [590]

NOUVEAU RECUEIL DE TRAITEZ,... / Dumont, J – Amsterdam, 1710 – 5mf – 1 – ILM-161/1 – ne IDC [327]

NOUVEAU RECUEIL DES FACTUMS DU PROCEZ / Furetiere, Antoine – 1694 – 9 – fr I.C.S. [400]

LE NOUVEAU REGIONAL – Chicoutini. v3 n16. 3 mar 1937 – 1r – 1 – Can$25.00 – cn Can Microfilming [072]

LE NOUVEAU SAMEDI – Montreal, 1963?-81. SEM35P104 – 36r – 1 – Can$1,550.00 – cn Bibl Nat [072]

LE NOUVEAU SIECLE – Journal de la fraternite nationale pour la politique de la victoire. Dir. G. Valois. Paris. 26 fevr 1925-1er avr 1928 – 1 – fr A.C.R.P.P. [073]

LE NOUVEAU SPECTATEUR – Dir. Roger Allard. no. 1-20. Paris. 10 mai 1919-20 fevr 1921 – 1 – fr A.C.R.P.P. [073]

NOUVEAU SUPPLEMENT DU DICTIONNAIRE D'ARGOT / Larchey, L – 1889 – 9 – fr I.C.S. [440]

NOUVEAU SYSTEME DE MINERALOGIE / Berzelius, Jons Jakob – G-131 2. 1819 – 8 – ne IDC [550]

NOUVEAU SYSTEME DE MUSIQUE THEORIQUE / Rameau, Jean-Philippe – 1726 – 9 – us Sibley [780]

LE NOUVEAU TESTAMENT DE NOTRE SEIGNEUR. – Avec notes explicatives et des introductions a chaque livre par L Bonnet et Ch. Baup. Geneve, Paris: Emile Beroud, 1846-52. 2v – 1 – us U.W. Library [240]

NOUVEAU THEATRE ITALIEN / Dominique, Joseph Biancolelli – 1 – us U.W. Library [790]

NOUVEAU TRAITE... / Brocher, C A – Paris, 1876 – 5mf – 1 – ILM-442/1 – ne IDC [327]

NOUVEAU TRAITE ABREGE DE LA SPHERE, D'APRES LE SYSTEME DE COPERNIC – Nouv ed. Trois-Rivieres: L Duvernay, 1824. SEM16P190 – 1r – 5 – Can$9.00 – cn Bibl Nat [520]

NOUVEAU TRAITE D'ARCHITECTURE. / Nativelle, Pierre – Paris, J. Dupuis, 1729. 2v., 125 pl. (Architecture Series) – 9 – fr Hachette [720]

NOUVEAU TRAITE DE DIPLOMATIQUE : PAR DEUX RELIGIEUX BENEDICTINS DE LA CONGREGATION DE S. MAUR / Toustain, Ch & Tassin, R – Paris. Tom. 1-6. 1750-1765 – Dfl828.00 – ne Slangenburg [240]

NOUVEAU TRAITE DE DIPLOMATIQUE / Toustain, Ch & Tassin, R – Paris. Tome 1-6. 1750-1765 – Dfl828.00 – ne Slangenburg [240]

NOUVEAU TRAITE DE TOUTE L'ARCHITECTURE. / Cordemoy, J L de – Paris, Coignard, 1706. In-12, 14, 230p., ill. (Architecture Series) – 9 – fr Hachette [720]

LE NOUVEAU TROIS-RIVIERES – Trois-Rivieres, Canada. 17 jul 1908-v9 n37. 27 avr 1917 – 3r – 1 – Can$40.00r – cn Can Microfilming [072]

NOUVEAU VOYAGE DANS LA PARTIE MERIDIONALE DE L'AFRIQUE / Barrow, John – Traduction de l'anglais. Paris, Dentu. 1806 – 9 – 20.00 – fr Orientalistes [910]

NOUVEAU VOYAGE DANS LE PAYS DES NEGRES : SUIVI D'ETUDES SUR LA COLONIE DU SENEGAL / Raffenel, Anne – Paris: Impr et Librairie Centrales des Chemins de Fer, 1856 – us Res Libr [910]

NOUVEAU VOYAGE DANS LE PAYS DES NEGRES SUIVI D'ETUDES SUR LA COLONIE DU SENEGAL / Raffenel, Jean-Baptiste A – Paris, Imprimerie et Librairie Centrale des chemins de fer de Napoleon, Chaix et Cie. 1856 – 9 – 27.00 – fr Orientalistes [910]

NOUVEAU VOYAGE DE GUINEE, DESCRIPTION DES COUTUMES, MANIERES, TERRAIN, CLIMAT, ETC. HABILLEMENTS, BATIMENTS, EDUCATION, ARTS MANUELS, AGRICULTURE, COMMERCE, EMPLOIS, LANGAGES, RANGS DE DISTINCTION, HABITATIONS, DIVERTISSEMENTS / Smith, Guillaume – (African Library series). 1751 – 9 – fr Hachette [960]

NOUVEAU VOYAGE EN GUINEE / Smith, William – Traduction de l'anglais. Paris, Durand, Pissot. 1751 – 9 – 17.50 – fr Orientalistes [910]

NOUVEAUX CAHIERS – Paris. mars 1937-avr 1940 – 1 – fr A.C.R.P.P. [073]

NOUVEAUX DOCUMENTS POUR LA FLORE BRYOLOGIQUE DU JAPON / Bescherelle, E – (Ann. Sc. Nat. Bot., S. 7, v. 17, 1893). B-988 2 – 8 – ne IDC [580]

NOUVEAUX ENTRETIENS POLITIQUES – Par M. Le Noble. no. 1-87. Paris. juil 1702-juil 1709. mq no. 70, 78-79 – 1 – fr A.C.R.P.P. [073]

NOUVEAUX GASCONISMES CORRIGES, AN 10 / Villa, E de – 1802 – 9 – fr I.C.S. [440]

LES NOUVEAUX HORIZONS DE LA RENAISSANCE FRANCAISE / Atkinson, G – Paris, 1935 – 9mf – 8 – ne Slangenburg [100]

NOUVEAUX MATERIAUX POUR LA FLORE ATLANTIQUE / Pomel, A – (Bull. Soc. Sc. Physiques Naturelles et Climatologiques de l'Algerie, Ann. XI-XIII). Paris. Alger. 1874. B-5306 2 – 8 – ne IDC [580]

NOUVEAUX MELANGES ORIENTAUX – Publies par les professeurs de l'Ecole des langues orientales vivantes. Congres de Vienne en 1886 – 9 – fr Orientalistes [480]

NOUVEAUX MEMOIRES : ACADEMIE DE SCIENCE A BERLIN – Berlin, 1783, 1786/87 – 1 – Inquire at Mikrofilmarchiv for details – gw Misc Inst [072]

NOUVEAUX MEMOIRES / Akademie der Wissenschaften. Berlin – 17v 1770-1786 – 1 – us Schnase [500]

NOUVEAUX MEMOIRES / Moscow. Societe des Naturalistes – 1837-39 – 1 – uk Microform Academic [580]

NOUVEAUX MEMOIRES DE L'ACADEMIE ROYALE DES SCIENCES ET BELLES-LETTRES / Akademie der Wissenschaften. Berlin – 1772-88 – 3 – us Readex [500]

NOUVEAUX MEMOIRES DE L'ACADEMIE ROYALE DES SCIENCES ET BELLES-LETTRES : ANNEE 1770-1786. AVEC L'HISTOIRE POUR LA MEME ANNEE – Berlin, 1770-1786 – 345mf – 9 – ne IDC [500]

NOUVEAUX MEMOIRES DES MISSIONS DE LA COMPAGNIE DE JESUS DANS LE LEVANT / ed by Fleuriau d'Armenonville, T – Paris. 8v. 1717-1745 – 36mf – 9 – ne IDC [240]

NOUVEAUX MEMOIRES SUR L'ETAT PRESENT DE LA CHINE / Le Comte, LD – Ed 3. Paris. 2v. 1697 – 11mf – 9 – HT-537/1 – ne IDC [920]

NOUVEAUX POURTRAITZ ET FIGURES DE TERMES POUR USER EN L'ARCHITECTURE... / Boillot, Joseph – Langres: Jehan des Prey, [1592] – 1 – F67.36 – fr Armell [720]

LES NOUVEAUX TEMPS – Dir. Jean Luchaire. Paris. 1er nov 1940-17 aout 1944 – 1 – fr A.C.R.P.P. [073]

LES NOUVEAUX TRAVAUX SUR LA RIVIERE OTTAWA POUR FACILITER LA DESCENTE DES BILLOTS – 1872? SEM105P638 – 1mf – 9 – Can$2.25 – cn Bibl Nat [627]

NOUVEAUX VOYAGES DE MR LE BARON DE LAHONTAN DANS L'AMERIQUE SEPTENTRIONALE / Lahontan, Louis A de L d'A – La Haye: les Freres l'Honore. 2v. 1703. SEM16P53 – 1r – 5 – Can$9.00 – cn Bibl Nat [971]

LE NOUVEL AGE – Paris. mai 1934-juin 1940, 1 aout 1945-oct 1948. Suite de: Chantiers cooperatifs, voir a ce titre – 1 – fr A.C.R.P.P. [073]

NOUVEL AGE – (Maison Coopea1rative du Livre). Paris. no 1-764. June 1 1934-June 8 10 1940; n.s. 1-26 Aug 1945-Dec 1947. Incomplete – 1 – us NY Public [073]

LE NOUVEL AN – Montreal, Canada. 1 jan 1887 – 1r – 1 – Can$25.00 – cn Can Microfilming [073]

NOUVEL ATLAS DE LA CHINE / Anville, J B B d' – La Haye, 1737 – 5mf – 9 – ne IDC [950]

NOUVEL AVIS AUX MERES QUI VEULENT NOURRIR / Gaultier de Claubry, Charles Daniel – Paris, 1783, 273 p. 3 fiches. (Statistics Series: Medical Studies) – 9 – 8.00 – fr Bibl Nationale [310]

LE NOUVEL ECONOMISTE – (Also available on CD-ROM) – France. 1988-1995 – 2r per y – 5,6 – Sfr695.00 – sz Infoprint [330]

NOUVEL HERBIER DE L'AMATEUR / Loiseleur-Deslongchamps, J L A – Paris. 1838. B-6041 1 – 9 – ne IDC [580]

LE NOUVEL HOMME / Saint Martin, Louis Claude de – Paris. Chez les Directeurs du Cercle Social. 1792 – 9 – fr Hachette [321]

LE NOUVEL LIB : PUBLIE DURANT LA GREVE DU NOUVELLISTE – Trois Rivieres, Canada. 17 mar 1976-28 avr 1976 – 1r – 1 – Can$40.00 – cn Can Microfilming [072]

LE NOUVEL OBSERVATEUR – (Also available on CD-ROM) – 1988-1995 – 3r per y – 5,6 – Sfr642.00 – sz Infoprint [072]

LE NOUVEL OBSERVATEUR – France. 1957-1987 – 6 times per yr – 6 – F2,300.00 – sz Infoprint [944]

LE NOUVEL OBSERVATEUR – (Yrly reel count varies) – 1950- – 1 – inquire – us Ross [072]

NOUVEL OBSERVATEUR – 1957-1995 – 1 – sz Infoprint [072]

NOUVEL OBSERVATEUR – (1979- 5,6,9) – 1964- – 1 – us UMI [073]

NOUVELLE METHODE POUR APPRENDRE FACILEMENT LES PRINCIPES DE LA LANGUE / Irson, Cl – 1656 – 9 – fr I.C.S. [400]

LA NOUVELLE – East-Angus, Canada. v2 n18. 23 dec 1975 – 1r – 1 – Can$25.00 – cn Can Microfilming [072]

LA NOUVELLE – Ottawa: Eleves du College d'Ottawa, [1887-18– ou 19–] – 9 – cn C.I.H.M. [370]

LA NOUVELLE – Victoriaville, Canada. 25 fev 1956 – 1r – 1 – Can$25.00 – cn Can Microfilming [072]

NOUVELLE ARMEE DE FEMMES SAINT-SIMONIENNES – Organisation en corps mobile. Paris, Garson, 1832, in-folio plano, canard, bois grave. Les Saint-Simoniens, 1825-1834. 6996 – 9 – fr Hachette [335]

LA NOUVELLE ATLANTIDE / Bacon, Francis – The New Atlantis. Paris: J. Musier, 1702. In French. xix, 253p. 3 fiches. (Literature Collection) – 9 – 8.00 – fr Bibl Nationale [190]

NOUVELLE BIBLIOTHEQUE – ou Histoire litteraire des principaux ecrits qui se publient. La Haye. oct dec 1738-avr juin 1744 (I-XIX) – 1 – fr A.C.R.P.P. [073]

NOUVELLE BIBLIOTHEQUE GERMANIQUE – ou Histoire litteraire de l'Allemagne, de la Suisse et des pays du Nord. Amsterdam. 1746-60 (I-XXVI) – 1 – fr A.C.R.P.P. [073]

NOUVELLE BIBLIOTHEQUE POPULAIRE – Paris: Henri Gautier, 1887-1900.209 fiches. (Literature Collection) – 9 – 517.00 – fr Bibl Nationale [800]

NOUVELLE BIOGRAPHIE GENERALE – 46v 1853-66. Newberry Library Collections – 9r – 1 – $665.00 – us UMI [920]

NOUVELLE BIOGRAPHIE GENERALE DEPUIS LE TEMPS LES PLUS RECULES JUSQU'A NOS JOURS / ed by Hoefer, F de – Paris. 46v. 1855-66 – 273mf – 9 – 8840/1 – ne IDC [920]

NOUVELLE CHRONIQUE DE JERSEY – Saint Helier. 1859; 4 Jan 1865-29 Dec 1866; 1873-29 Dec 1875; 3 Jan 1889-31 Mar 1917 – 1 – uk British Libr Newspaper [072]

NOUVELLE CHYMIE RAISONNEE / Ettmueller, Michael – Lyon, 1693 – 1 – us U.W. Library [540]

LA NOUVELLE CONVENTION DE GENEVE (6 JUILLET 1906)... / Delpech, J – Paris, 1907 – 2mf – 1 – ILM-922/1 – ne IDC [327]

LA NOUVELLE CRITIQUE – Paris. dec 1948-jan fev 1980 – 1 – fr A.C.R.P.P. [073]

NOUVELLE DECOUVERTE DU PRINCIPE DE L'HARMONIE / Esteve, P – 1752 – 9 – us Sibley [780]

NOUVELLE DOGMATIQUE: LETTRE À M. LE PROFESSEUR GRETILLAT *see* COLLECTED WORKS

NOUVELLE EPARGNE *see* EPARGNE

NOUVELLE ET PARFAITE GRAMMAIRE ROYALE FRANCOISE ET ALLEMANDE / Des Pepliers, J R – 1719 – 9 – fr I.C.S. [440]

NOUVELLE FLORE DES LICHENS / Boistel, A – 2v. Paris. 1896-1902. B-1001 2 – 8 – ne IDC [580]

NOUVELLE FLORE DU PELOPONNESE ET DES CYCLADES / Bory de Saint-Vincent, J B C M & Chaubard, LA – Paris. 1838. B-6507 1 – 9 – ne IDC [580]

LA NOUVELLE FRANCE : HEBDO – Montreal, Canada. 18,25 avr 1896 – 1r – 1 – Can$25.00 – cn Can Microfilming [072]

LA NOUVELLE FRANCE – Montreal, Canada. 21 aut 1875; v1 n3. 11 sep 1875 – 1r – 1 – Can$25.00 – cn Can Microfilming [072]

LA NOUVELLE FRANCE, LE CANADA: APPEL AUX CLASSES NECESSITEUSES DE FRANCE / Bossange, Gustave – Paris: G. Bossange, 1871? 00192. (Pre-1900 Canadiana) – 9 – cn C.I.H.M. [971]

NOUVELLE GRAMMAIRE FRANCAISE / Noel et Chapsal – 1845 – 9 – fr I.C.S. [440]

NOUVELLE HISTOIRE D'ABISSINIE OU D'ETHIOPIE, TIREE DE L'HISTOIRE LATINE DE M. LUDOLF / Ludolf, Hiob – (African Library series). 1684 – 9 – fr Hachette [960]

NOUVELLE HISTOIRE DE L'AFRIQUE FRANCAISE ENRICHIE DE CARTES ET D'OBSERVATIONS ASTRONOMIQUES ET GEOGRAPHIQUES, DE REMARQUES SUR LES USAGES LOCAUX, LES MOEURS, LA RELIGION ET LA NATURE DU COMMERCE DE CE PAYS / Demanet – (African library series). 1767 – 9 – fr Hachette [960]

NOUVELLE HISTOIRE DE L'AFRIQUE FRANCOISE / Demanet – Paris, Duchesne. 1767 – 9 – 17.50 – fr Orientalistes [960]

NOUVELLE HISTOIRE DES VOYAGES ET DES GRANDES DECOUVERTES GEOGRAPHIQUES DANS TOUS LES TEMPS ET DANS TOUS LES PAYS. TOME PREMIER / Cortambert, Richard – Paris: E. Junod, 1883?. 04306. (Pre-1900 Canadiana) – 9 – cn C.I.H.M. [910]

NOUVELLE ICONOLOGIE HISTORIQUE, OU ATTRIBUTS HIEROGLYPHIQUES = NIEUWE HISTORISCHE BEELDSPRAK OF HIEROGLYPHISCHE MERKBEELDEN / Fosse, J C de la – Amsterdam, 1781. BO-257 1 – 9 – ne IDC [700]

NOUVELLE INSTITUTION NATIONALE PAR L'AUTEUR DES VUES D'UN SOLITAIRE PATRIOTE / Feroux, Christophe-Leon – Paris. impr. Clousier. 1788. 6756 – 9 – fr Hachette [944]

LA NOUVELLE MAISON RUSTIQUE : OU ECONOMIE GENERALE DE TOUS LES BIENS DE CAMPAGNE, LA MANIERE DE LES ENTRETENIR & DE LES MULTIPLIER / Liger, Sieur – 8e ed. Augmentee...et Mise en Meilleur Ordre,...Paris: Durand, 1762. SEM35P351 – 1r – 1 – Can$49.00 – cn Bibl Nat [600]

NOUVELLE MANIERE DE FORTIFIER LES PLACES / Blondel, Jacques Francois – Paris, Langlois, 1683. 4v. 5, 68p., ill. (Architecture Series) – 9 – fr Hachette [720]

NOUVELLE MANIERE D'ECRIRE COMME ON PARLE EN FRANCE / Vaudelin, le P G – 1713 – 9 – fr I.C.S. [440]

NOUVELLE METHODE.. / Poisson, Leonard – 1745 – 2 – us Sibley [780]

NOUVELLE METHODE FACILE ET CURIEUSE POUR APPRENDRE. / Marquet, Francois-Nicolas – 2nd. ed. 1769 – 9 – us Sibley [780]

NOUVELLE METHODE POUR APPRENDRE FACILEMENT ET EN PEU DE TEMPS LA LANGUE LATINE. / Lancelot, Claude & Arnauld, Antoine & Nicole, Pierre – (Paris: A. Vitre, 1650. 6 fiches. (Language Collection). 15.00; 9. Paris: P. LePetit, 1662. 10 fiches. (Language Collection). 25.00; BN; 9) – Paris: A. Vitre, 1644. 4 fiches. (Language Collection) – 9 – 10.00 – fr Bibl Nationale [450]

NOUVELLE METHODE POUR APPRENDRE L'ANGLOIS / Miege, Guy – 1685. 281p. (English Linguistics Series 1500-1800) – 9 – us UMI [420]

LA NOUVELLE METHODE RAISONNEE DU BLASON / Menestrier, Claude-Francois – Lyons: Bruyset, 1750. SEM105P948 – 5mf – 9 – $11.25 – cn Bibl Nat [720]

NOUVELLE METODE POUR APPRENDRE LES PRINCIPES ET L'USAGE DES LANGUES FRANCOISE ET HOLLANDOISE / Marin, P – 1712 – 9 – fr I.C.S. [440]

LA NOUVELLE NEMESIS – no. 1-9. Paris. aout-oct 1868 – 1 – fr A.C.R.P.P. [073]

NOUVELLE PHASE DE LA LITTERATURE RUSSE / Herzen, Aleksandr I – (Russia – 19th C. series). 1864 – 9 – fr Hachette [460]

LA NOUVELLE PRESSE MEDICALE – v1-12. 1972-83 – 1,5,6 – us Princeton Micro [610]

NOUVELLE RELATION DE L'AFRIQUE OCCIDENTALE / Labat, Jean-Baptiste – 5v. Paris. 1728. BA-328 2 – 8 – ne IDC [960]

NOUVELLE RELATION DE L'AFRIQUE OCCIDENTALE / Labat, Jean-Baptiste – Paris, Guillaume Cavelier. 1728 – 9 – 60.00 – fr Orientalistes [960]

NOUVELLE RELATION DE L'INTERIEUR DU SERRAIL DU GRAND SEIGNEUR CONTENANT PLUSIEURS SINGULARITEZ QUI JUSQU'ICI N'ONT POINT ESTE MISES EN LUMIERE / Tavernier, Jean-Baptiste – Paris, O. de Varennes, 1675, xiv-277 p. French Voyagers in the Mediterranean 16th to 18th Centuries. 5966 – 9 – fr Hachette [956]

LA NOUVELLE REVUE – Paris. s. 1, v. 20-s. 4, v. 167, no. 2. Jan 1883-May 1940 – 1 – 1,765.00 – us L of C Photodup [800]

LA NOUVELLE REVUE *see* LA REVUE DE GRANBY

LA NOUVELLE REVUE DE GATINEAU – Gatineau: s.n, (196-?)-1966. SEM35P284 – 1r – 1 – Can$28.00 – cn Bibl Nat [073]

NOUVELLE REVUE DE PARIS – Lettres, histoire, philosophie. janv-oct nov 1864. devenu: Revue de Paris. Litterature, histoire, philosophie. nov dec 1864-fevr mars 1865. Paris – 1 – fr A.C.R.P.P. [073]

NOUVELLE REVUE DES DEUX MONDES – (1971- 5,6; 1975- 9) – v. 1- 1831- – 1 – us UMI [800]

LA NOUVELLE REVUE FRANCAISE – Revue mensuelle de litterature et de critique. Paris. 15 nov 1908, 1er fevr 1909-1er juin 1943. N'a pas paru de sept. 1914 a mai 1919 – 1 – fr A.C.R.P.P. [073]

NOUVELLE REVUE FRANCAISE D'HEMATOLOGIE – v.20-23, 1978-81. v.1-19 details upon request. ISSN: 0029-4810 – 1,5,6,9,13 – 115.00v – us UMI [073]

LA NOUVELLE REVUE MARXISTE – no. 1, 3. Paris. juin 1961, fevr avr 1962 – 1 – fr A.C.R.P.P. [073]

LA NOUVELLE REVUE SOCIALISTE / Mouvement Socialiste International – Revue mensuelle. Dir. L.-O. Frossard, Jean Longuet. no. 1-35. Paris. 5 dec 1925-janv fevr 1931 – 1 – fr A.C.R.P.P. [335]

NOUVELLE REVUE THEOLOGIQUE – 1(1869)-66(1939) – 762mf – 9 – Dfl2,667.00 – ne Slangenburg [073]

NOUVELLE REVUE THEOLOGIQUE – Paris. v1-66. 1869-1939 – 762mf – 9 – ne IDC [240]

NOUVELLE RIVE GAUCHE – Politique et litteraire. no. 1-61. nov 1882-mars avr 1883. devenu: Lutece. Journal litteraire, politique. no. 61 bis-259. mars avr 1883-nov 1886; n.s., no. 1-8. avr-nov 1897. Paris – 1 – fr A.C.R.P.P. [073]

LA NOUVELLE VOIE MARITIME LE CANAL DE PANAMA / Bellet, D – Paris, n.d. – 4mf – 9 – ILM-1807/1 – ne IDC [327]

LA NOUVELLE-FRANCE – Quebec: [s.n.], 1881-[1882] – 9 – cn C.I.H.M. [440]

LA NOUVELLE-FRANCE *see* LE CANADA-FRANCAIS

NOUVELLE-FRANCE – v1-17, no. 6. 1902-June 1918 – 1 – cn Precision [073]

Nouvelle-France. Lois, etc. *see* EDITS, ORDONNANCES ROYAUX

LES NOUVELLES : JOURNAL DU DIMANCHE / ed by Lafontaine, V – Montreal, Canada. 1 sep 1895-6 fev 1898 – 1r – 1 – Can$40.00 – cn Can Microfilming [072]

LES NOUVELLES – Montreal. v26-31. 1978-83. SEM35P271 – 12r – 1 – Can$492.00 – cn Bibl Nat [072]

LES NOUVELLES – Paris. 28 dec 1908-1910, juil 1911-14/15 juin 1912, 27-28 aout-5/6 nov 1912, 1913-1 aout 1914 – 1 – fr A.C.R.P.P. [073]

LES NOUVELLES – Ville St-Laurent, 7 jan 1960 – 1 – cn Can Microfilming [072]

NOUVELLES ANNALES DU MUSEUM D'HISTOIRE NATURELLE : OU, RECUEIL DE MEMOIRES / Paris. Museum national d'histoire naturelle – Paris, 1832-35 – 3 – us Readex [580]

NOUVELLES ANNALES DU MUSEUM D'HISTOIRE NATURELLE – Paris, 1832-1835. 4v – 71mf – 9 – ne IDC [500]

NOUVELLES ARCHIVES DU MUSEUM D'HISTOIRE NATURELLE – Paris. 1865-1874; S.1, v1-10. 1878-1889; S.2, v1-10. 1889-1898; S. 3, v1-10. 1899-1908; S.4, v1-10. 1909-1914/19; S.5, v1-6 – 589mf – 9 – ne IDC [500]
NOUVELLES ASTED – Montreal: Asted. no 84/85 1974-no 130 1981; v1(1982)-. SEM35P208 – 2r – 1 – Can$80.00 – cn Bibl Nat [073]
NOUVELLES DE FRANCE ET DU MONDE *see* JOURNAL DU CAMP
NOUVELLES DE LA REPUBLIQUE DES LETTRES ET DES ARTS – Paris. nov ? 1777, fevr 1779-87 (I-VIII) – 1 – fr A.C.R.P.P. [073]
NOUVELLES DE L'ACBLF – Montreal: l'Acblf. no 1-83. 1965-73. SEM16P346 – 1r – 51 – Can$27.00 – cn Bibl Nat [500]
LES NOUVELLES DE L'ECOLE DES H.E.C – (Becomes: Le Caducee mai 1952-nov/dec 1991) – Montreal, Canada. fev 1927-jun 1936 – 2r – 1 – Can$55.00r – cn Can Microfilming [073]
NOUVELLES DE L'EST – Montreal. v3 n22. 21 mar 1952-v24 n43. 7 nov 1962 – 1r – 1 – Can$25.00 – cn Can Microfilming [072]
NOUVELLES DE STE-GENEVIEVE – Pierrefonds, Canada. v2 n1. 25 jun 1958; v2 n10. 24 sep 1958 – 1r – 1 – Can$25.00 – cn Can Microfilming [072]
NOUVELLES DE VERSAILLES – Paris. 25 juin, 28-29 juil 1789 – 1 – fr A.C.R.P.P. [073]
NOUVELLES DECOUVERTES SUR LA GUERRE DANS UNE DISSERTATION SUR POLYBE / Folard, Jean Charles de – Paris. Josse. 1726. Reproduction de l'Epitre de la Preface. xlvii p. HISTOIRE DE POLYBE...Amsterdam. 1729. Reproduction de la Preface, de la vie de Polybe et du traite de la colonne. (Strategy of War Series) – 9 – fr Hachette [355]
NOUVELLES DONNEES HISTORIQUES DANS L'EPIGRAPHIE MAYA / Davoust, M – 9 – F120.00 – fr Ethnologie [306]
NOUVELLES DU CONGO / Congo – Leopoldville. 1960-61. 2v. – 27mf – 9 – ne IDC [960]
NOUVELLES DU CONGO – DE L'AFRIQUE – DU MONDE : AGENCE CONGOLAISE DE PRESSE – Leopoldville. 81v. 1961(Apr 18)-1967 – 981mf – 9 – ne IDC [960]
NOUVELLES DU ZAMBEZE – Geneva. Jan. 1898-Sept. 1934. Missing: Sept. 1932 – 1 – 35.00r – us Hoover Inst Photo [072]
NOUVELLES ECCLESIASTIQUES – ou Memoires pour servir a l'histoire ecclesiastique puis a l'histoire de la Constitution Unigenitus. Utrecht. 1713 1728, fevr 1728-24 mai 1803 – 1 – fr A.C.R.P.P. [073]
NOUVELLES ECCLESIASTIQUES: SUPPLEMENT – 1734-48 – 1 – fr A.C.R.P.P. [073]
NOUVELLES ETUDES MORALES SUR LE TEMPS PRESENT / Caro, Elme – (Includes bibliographical references) – Paris: L Hachette, 1869 – 1mf – 9 – 0-8370-7206-9 – 1986-1206 – us A.T.L.A. [170]
NOUVELLES ETUDES SUR LES GROUPES DE PRESSION EN FRANCE / Meynaud, J – 8mf – 9 – F120.00 – fr Ethnologie [360]
LES NOUVELLES GUEPES – Montreal, Canada. 23 mar-v1 n4. 14 avr 1872 – 1r – 1 – Can$25.00 – cn Can Microfilming [072]
NOUVELLES ILLUSTREES – Montreal: Alpha inc. v4-34. 1958-1985. SEM35P29 – 60r – 1 – Can$2,899.00 – cn Bibl Nat [072]
NOUVELLES INVENTIONS POUR BIEN BASTIR ET A PETIT FRAIS. / Delorme, Philibert – Paris. F. Morel. 1561. 6, 617 f. (Architecture Series) – 9 – fr Hachette [720]
NOUVELLES LECONS DE CLAVECIN OU INSTRUCTIONS GENERALES SUR LA MUSIQUE VOCALE ET INSTRUMENTALE, SUR LA MELODIE ET L'HARMONIE / Bemetzrieder, A – Seconde ed. augmentee d'une introduction. 1783 – 9 – us Sibley [780]
LES NOUVELLES LITTERAIRES, ARTISTIQUES ET SCIENTIFIQUES – Paris. 21 oct 1922-juin 1940, avr 1945-86 – 1 – fr A.C.R.P.P. [073]
NOUVELLES LITTERAIRES CONTENANT CE QUI SE PASSE DE PLUS CONSIDERABLE DANS LA REPUBLIQUE DES LETTRES – La Haye puis Amsterdam. 1715-juin 1720 (I-XI) – 1 – fr A.C.R.P.P. [073]
NOUVELLES LITTERAIRES DE FRANCE – Puis et D'Angleterre. Par Clement. Paris, Londres. fevr 1751-janv 1753 – 1 – fr A.C.R.P.P. [073]
LES NOUVELLES LITTERATURES, ARTISTIQUES ET SCIENTIFIQUES – Paris. no. 1-1060. 1922-47. (LC lacks nos. 47, 116, 904-05.) – 1 – 180.00 – us L of C Photodup [800]
NOUVELLES MOSCOU – 1990-1991 – 2 times per yr – 5,6 – Sfr588.00 – sz Infoprint [073]
NOUVELLES NOTES SUR L'HISTOIRE DE LA FAMILLE GILL / Gill, Charles – Montreal?: s.n., 1892.02492.(Pre-1900 Canadiana) – 9 – cn C.I.H.M. [971]
NOUVELLES OBSERVATIONS OU GUERRE CIVILE DES FRANCOIS SUR LA LANGUE / Alemand, L A – 1688 – 9 – fr I.C.S. [440]
NOUVELLES OBSERVATIONS SUR LA LANGUE FRANCOISE / Buffet, M – 1668 – 9 – fr I.C.S. [440]
NOUVELLES RECHERCHES SUR LA POPULATION DE LA FRANCE: AVEC DES REMARQUES IMPORTANTES SUR DIVERS OBJETS D'ADMINISTRATION / Messance, receveur des tailles – Lyons: Perisse Freres, 1788. viii,131p.2 fiches. (Statistics Series: Demography) – 9 – 6.00 – fr Bibl Nationale [310]
NOUVELLES RECHERCHES SUR LE STATUS DES FORGERONS D'AFRIQUE NOIRE / Boyer, Pascal – Nanterre. 1978 – 2mf – 9 – F30.00 – fr Ethnologie [305]
NOUVELLES REFLEXIONS DE M. RAMEAU SUR SA DEMONSTRATION DU PRINCIPE DE L'HARMONIE / Rameau, Jean-Philippe – 1752 – 9 – us Sibley [780]
NOUVELLES REFLEXIONS SUR L'ART POETIQUE / Lamy, B – 1668 – 9 – fr I.C.S. [410]
NOUVELLES REMARQUES SUR LA LANGUE FRANCAISE / Favre de Vaugelas, Cl – (Linguistic series) – 9 – fr Hachette [440]
NOUVELLES REMARQUES SUR LA LANGUE FRANCOISE / Leven de Templery, J – 1698 – 9 – fr I.C.S. [440]
NOUVELLES REMARQUES SUR LA LANGUE FRANCOISE / Vaugelas, Cl. Favre de – 1690 – 9 – fr I.C.S. [440]
LES NOUVELLES SAINT LAURENT – Saint Laurent. v31- 1983-. SEM35P248 – 20r – 1 – Can$1,021.00 – cn Bibl Nat [072]
NOUVELLES SOIREES CANADIENNES *see* LES SOIREES CANADIENNES
NOUVELLES SOUREES CANADIENNES – (Fait suite a: Les Soirees canadiennes) – Quebec: L H Tache, 1882-1888 – 9 – cn C.I.H.M. [440]
LES NOUVELLES SOVIETIQUES / La Societe pour les Ralations Culturelles entre l'U.R.S.S. et l'etranger – Organe mensuel. Moscou. juil 1931-mai 1934 – 1 – fr A.C.R.P.P. [947]
LES NOUVELLES / ST-LAURENT NEWS *see* THE SAINT-LAURENT NEWS
NOUVELLES-EXPRESS – Montreal, Canada. 26 fev 1956; v1 n7. 8 avr 1956 – 1r – 1 – Can$25.00 – cn Can Microfilming [072]
NOUVELLES-SOIREES CANADIENNES – v1-7. 1882-Aug. 1888 – 1 – cn Precision [073]
LE NOUVELLISTE / ed by Fortier, J H et al – Trois-Rivieres, Canada. 30 oct 1920-31 dec 1992 – 433r – 1 – Can$75.00r – cn Can Microfilming [072]
LE NOUVELLISTE – Journal du soir. Marseille. 1848-51 – 1 – fr A.C.R.P.P. [073]
LE NOUVELLISTE – Port-au-Prince, 1956-70; 1976-dec 16 1979 – us Res Libr [072]
LE NOUVELLISTE – Port-au-Prince. Haiti. 1899-1913, 1925-1950 – 1 – us UMI [072]
LE NOUVELLISTE : QUOTIDIEN – Quebec, Canada. 27 nov 1876-23 oct 1886 – 7r – 1 – Can$40.00r – cn Can Microfilming [072]
NOUVELLISTE *see* L'AMI DES CAMPAGNES
LE NOUVELLISTE DE BRETAGNE – Rennes. Parait sous des titres divers. 1918-29 – 1 – fr A.C.R.P.P. [073]
LE NOUVELLISTE DE LA GUADELOUPE – French West Indies. 1909-1927; 1929; 1930; 1945-1962 – 1 – us UMI [072]
LE NOUVELLISTE DE PARIS – Ancienne Assemblee nationale. Red. en chef Xavier Eyma. Paris. 22 avr-juin 1874 – 1 – fr A.C.R.P.P. [073]
LE NOUVELLISTE DE RIMOUSKI – Rimouski, Canada. 23 dec 1876-2 dec 1880 – 1r – 1 – Can$35.00 – cn Can Microfilming [072]
NOV'. DVUCHNEDEL'NYI ZHURNAL – v. 1-8. M. 1910. Lacking: 1910 (1, 3). B-1808 2 – 8 – ne IDC [073]
NOV ZHIVOT – Kurdzhall, Bulgaria. Aug 1958-1987 – 28r – 1 – us L of C Photodup [949]
NOVA ACTA ACADEMIAE SCIENTIARUM IMPERIALIS PETROPOLITANAE – Petropoli, 1783-1802. S.4. V.1-15 – 219mf – 9 – ne IDC [500]
NOVA ACTA PHYSICO-MEDICA ACADEMIAE CAESAREAE LEOPOLDINI-CAROLINAE NATURAE CURIOSORUM EXHIBENTIA EPHEMERIDES... – Norimbergiae, etc., 1757-1783. V.1-7 – 130mf – 9 – ne IDC [610]
NOVA ACTA REGIAE SOCIETATIS SCIENTIARUM UPSALIENSIS. UPSALIAE, 1773-1850 / Vetenskaps-Societeten i Upsala – Series 2 – 3 – us Readex [500]
NOVA APPENDIX : OPERA GEORGII PISIDAE, THEODOSII DIACONI ET CORIPPI AFRICANI GRAMMATICI (CBH 35) / ed by Fogginius, P – Romae, 1777 – Dfl88.00 – ne Slangenburg [240]
NOVA BORBA – Prague, Czechoslovakia. May-Aug 1953 – 1r – 1 – us L of C Photodup [072]
NOVA CANZONE PER LA GLORIOSISSIMA VITTORIA DELL' ARMATA CHRISTIANA CONTRA LA TURCHESCA – Venetia, 1572 – 1mf – 9 – H-8193/1 – ne IDC [956]
A NOVA CRENCA – Maceio, Alagoas. 27 Jan, 27 Abr 1884 – 1,5,6 – bl Biblioteca [072]
NOVA DOBA – Cleveland, OH, 1938, 1940, 1945 – 4mf or 1 reel – 9,1 – us I.H.R.C. [975]
NOVA DOBA – Omaha, NE. -sw. Oct 1911-Oct 1914, scattered issues missing; May-Dec 1918 – 1 – us NE Hist [071]
NOVA DOBA – Organ of the Ukranian Communist Party in Exile. Vienna. 1920-21 – 1 – 75.00 – cn McLaren [335]
NOVA DOBA – Pittsburgh, PA, 1914 – 1mf or 1 reel – 1,9 – us I.H.R.C. [975]
NOVA DOBA – Schuyler, NE. (New Era). 5 Jan 1892-7 Jun 1892 – 1 – us NE Hist [071]
NOVA DOMOVINA – Cleveland, OH, 1901, 1902, 1906 – 5mf or 1 reel – 9,1 – us I.H.R.C. [975]
A NOVA EPOCHA : FOLHA POLITICA E INDUSTRIAL – '(s.l.')-Sao Luiz, Brazil. 12 Jul 1856-20 Nov 1858 – 1,5,6 – bl Biblioteca [072]
NOVA ET AMPLISSIMA COLLECTIO CONCILIORUM / Mansi, J D – v1-53. Venetiis, 1759 – Arnhem, 1937 – Dfl4,025.00 – ne Slangenburg [240]
NOVA FRANCIA / Societe d'histoire du Canada – Paris: la Societe. v1 no 1-1925-. SEM16P341 – 1r – 5 – Can$36.00 – cn Bibl Nat [971]
NOVA GENERA AC SPECIES PLANTARUM QUAS IN REGNO CHILENSI PERUVIANO / Poeppig, E F & Endlicher, S L – 3v. Lipsiae. 1835-45. B-2264 2 – 8 – ne IDC [580]
NOVA GENERA ET SPECIES PLANTARUM / Martius, Karl Friedrich Philipp von – Monachii, 1824-1832. 3 vols. B-5257 2 – 8 – ne IDC [580]
NOVA GENERA ET SPECIES PLANTARUM SEU PRODROMUS DESCRIPTIONUM VEGETABILIUM / Swartz, O P – Holmiae, Upsaliae, 1788. 152 pp. B-5756 2 – 8 – ne IDC [580]
NOVA GENERA PLANTARUM / Micheli, P A – 1729 – 7 – uk Microform Academic [580]
NOVA GENERA PLANTARUM / Schrader, H A – pars. 1. Lipsiae. 1797. B-5723 2 – 8 – ne IDC [580]
NOVA GENERA PLANTARUM / Thunberg, C P – Upsaliae. 1781-1801. B-341 2 – 8 – ne IDC [580]
NOVA HROMADA – Literaturno-naukovyi misiachnyk. nr. 1-2. Kiev. 1906. BR-4146 2 – 8 – ne IDC [073]
NOVA HRVATSKA – Zagreb, Yugoslavia. -a. 23 Dec 1941-11 Aug 1944; 16 Jan-25 Feb, 20-22 March 1945. Lacking Sept 1942. 23 reels – 1 – uk British Libr Newspaper [949]
NOVA INSTRUCCAO MUSICAL, OU THEORICA PRATICA DA MUSICA RYTHMICA / Solano, F I – Lisboa. 1764. BP-473 1 – 9 – ne IDC [780]
NOVA KAMBANA – Sofia, Bulgaria. Oct-Dec 1944 – 1r – 1 – us L of C Photodup [949]
NOVA LAW JOURNAL *see* NOVA LAW REVIEW
NOVA LAW REVIEW – (v1-9 1977-85 on reel $120.00. v10-20 1985-96 on mf $217.00. Title varies: v1-10 1977-86 as Nova Law Journal) – v1-20. 1977-96 – 5,6,9 – $337.00 set – us Hein [340]
NOVA LITERARIA CIRCULI FRANCONICI ODER FRAENCKISCHE GELEHRTEN-HISTORIE, 1725 FRAENCKISCHE ACTA ERUDITA ET CURIOSA, 1726-1732 NUETZLICHE UND AUSERLESENE ARBEITEN DER GELEHRTEN IM REICH, 1733-1736 – Nuernberg, 1725-1736 (mf ed 1995) – 17mf – 9 – DM490.00 – 3-89131-211-3 – gw Fischer [430]
NOVA LITERARIA GERMANIAE COLLECTA HAMBURGI, 1703-1706; NOVA LITERARIA GERMANIAE ALLIORUMQUE EUROPAE REGNORUM COLLECTA HAMBURGI, 1707-1709 / ed by Lehmann, Peter Ambros – Leipzig, Frankfurt, 1703-09 (mf ed 1993) – 20mf – 9 – DM490.00 – 3-89131-092-7 – gw Fischer [430]
NOVA LUZ BRASILEIRA – Rio de Janeiro, 9 Dec 1829-13 Oct 1831 – 1,5,6 – bl Biblioteca [072]
NOVA MAKEDONIJA – Jugoslawien, 1976-1993ff – 104r – 1 – DM7,800.00 – gw Mikro Press [949]
NOVA MAKEDONIJA – Skopje, Yugoslavia. 30 Nov 1944-1974 – 99r – 1 – us L of C Photodup [949]
NOVA MAKEDONIJA – (Yrly reel count varies) – 1976- – 1 – us Ross [072]
NOVA MISAO – v1. 1953 – 1 – us I.U. Libraries [073]
NOVA MYSL – (Coll title: Czech/Slovakian Periodicals. Missing: 1947-1950 (p1-768); 1951 (p1-96, 623-728); 1953 (p641-End); 1954 (p649-952). In Czech) – 1947-1989 – 710mf – 9 – R-15381/1 – ne IDC [320]
NOVA PATRUM BIBLIOTHECA / ed by Mai, Angelo & Cozza-Luzi, J – Romae. Tom 1-10. 1844-1905 – 200mf – 9 – Dfl700.00 – ne Slangenburg [240]
A NOVA PHASE – Mar de Hespanha, 28 Dec 1902 – 1,5,6 – bl Biblioteca [072]
NOVA PHASE – Leopoldina, 14 Feb 1932 – 1,5,6 – bl Biblioteca [072]
NOVA PLANTARUM AMERICANARUM GENERA / Plumier, C – Parisiis. 1703. B-1116 2 – 8 – ne IDC [580]
NOVA PLANTARUM GENERA JUXTA TOURNEFORTII METHODUM DISPOSITA / Micheli, P A – Florentiae, 1729. 234 pp., 108 pls. B-6068 prSF 41,00 IDC 9 – ne IDC [580]
NOVA POLJOPRIVREDA – Zagreb, Yugoslavia. Nov 1949-Mar 1951 – 1r – 1 – us L of C Photodup [949]
NOVA QUATUOR VOCIBUS COMPONENDI METHODUS / Bontempi, G A A – Dresdae. 1660. BP-179 1 – 9 – ne IDC [780]
NOVA SCOTIA – 3rd ed 1993 – 9 – cn Communication [971]
Nova Scotia *see*
- HALIFAX GAZETTE
- ROYAL GAZETTE

THE NOVA SCOTIA AND NEW BRUNSWICK WESLEYAN METHODIST MAGAZINE – [Halifax, N.S.?: s.n., 1832] – 9 – cn C.I.H.M. [240]
Nova Scotia. Canada *see*
- NOVA SCOTIA REPORTS
- NOVA SCOTIA SESSION LAWS AND REVISIONS
- RITCHIE'S EQUITY REPORTS
- RUSSELL'S ELECTION CASES
- STEWART'S NOVA SCOTIA ADMIRALTY REPORTS
- YOUNG'S VICE-ADMIRALTY DECISIONS

NOVA SCOTIA CHURCH CHRONICLE – Windsor [N.S.: King's College), 1865-1868] – 9 – cn C.I.H.M. [240]
NOVA SCOTIA. (COLONIAL) AND NEW BRUNSWICK : BAPTIST AND (NEW LIGHT) CHURCH RECORDS – 1778-1868. 910p – 1 – us Baptist [240]
NOVA SCOTIA GAZETTE – Halifax, Canada. -w. 13 Aug 1767-27 July 1769. 33 ft – 1 – uk British Libr Newspaper [072]
NOVA SCOTIA HISTORICAL QUARTERLY – (1979- 5,6,9) – 1971- – 1 – us UMI [073]
NOVA SCOTIA HISTORICAL REVIEW – Halifax. v1-14. 1981-94 – 9 – Can$20.00y – cn Micromedia [971]
NOVA SCOTIA ILLUSTRATED – Halifax, N.S.: G.H. Bradford, v1 no 1 (Apr 1895)- – 9 – cn C.I.H.M. [971]
NOVA SCOTIA IN ITS HISTORICAL, MERCANTILE AND INDUSTRIAL RELATIONS / Campbell, Duncan – Montreal: J. Lovell, 1873. 02016. (Pre-1900 Canadiana) – 9 – cn C.I.H.M. [971]

NOVA SCOTIA, ITS CLIMATE, RESOURCES AND ADVANTAGES: BEING A GENERAL DESCRIPTION OF THE PROVINCE FOR THE INFORMATION OF INTENDING EMIGRANTS / Crosskill, Herbert – Halifax n.s.: Province of Nova Scotia, 1872 (Halifax n.s.: C. Annuad). (Pre-1900 Canadiana) – 9 – cn C.I.H.M. [971]

THE NOVA SCOTIA JOURNAL OF AGRICULTURE *see* JOURNAL OF AGRICULTURE

Nova Scotia. Laws, Statutes, etc *see* INDEX TO THE LOCAL AND PRIVATE ACTS OF NOVA SCOTIA PASSED BY THE LEGISLATURE DURING THE YEARS 1924 TO 1934 BOTH INCLUSIVE

THE NOVA SCOTIA MAGAZINE – Halifax, N.S.: [s.n., 1894] – 9 – cn C.I.H.M. [971]

THE NOVA SCOTIA NEW MONTHLY MAGAZINE – [Halifax, N.S.: J. Kirk, 1842] – 9 – cn C.I.H.M. [971]

THE NOVA SCOTIA NORMAL – Truro, N.S.: Provincial Normal School Institute, [1894?-19–] – 9 – cn C.I.H.M. [370]

NOVA SCOTIA REPORTS / Nova Scotia. Canada – (Cont by 2nd series not offered by LLMC) – 1st series: v1-60. 1834-1929 (all publ) – 428mf – 9 – $642.00 – LLMC 81-034 – us L.L.M.C. [340]

NOVA SCOTIA ROYAL GAZETTE – 1801-1824 – 6r – 1 – cn Library Assoc [971]

NOVA SCOTIA. ROYAL GAZETTE – (v178-191 1969-1982 Can$105.00 5. v192- 1983- 9) – Halifax. v157- 1949- – 1,5,9 – Price varies – cn Micromedia [073]

NOVA SCOTIA SESSION LAWS AND REVISIONS / Nova Scotia. Canada – (Updates planned) – 1864-1945 – 519mf – 9 – $778.00 – LLMC 90-160 – us L.L.M.C. [324]

NOVA SCOTIA, THE LAND OF EVANGELINE AND THE TOURIST'S PARADISE:.. / Anderson, Thomas F – Boston: Yarmouth Steamship Co., 1892. 06146. (Pre-1900 Canadiana) – 9 – cn C.I.H.M. [910]

NOVA SCOTIAN CHURCH MONTHLY – Springhill, N.S.: J.A. Stansfield, [1894?-189- or 19–] – 9 – cn C.I.H.M. [240]

Nova Scotian Institute of Science *see* PROCEEDINGS

THE NOVA SCOTIAN JOURNAL OF AGRICULTURE – Halifax, N.S.: A. & W. MacKinlay, [1866-1885] – 9 – cn C.I.H.M. [630]

THE NOVA SCOTIAN PHILATELIST – Amherst, N.S.: Nova Scotian Philatelic Pub Co, [1893-1894?] – 9 – cn C.I.H.M. [760]

NOVA SENTINELA DA LIBERDADE : NA GUARITA DO FORTE DE S. PEDRO NA BAHIA DE TODOS OS SANTOS – '(s.l.')- Bahia, Brazil. 29 May-23 Oct 1831 – 1,5,6 – bl Biblioteca [072]

NOVA SVOBODA – Ostrava, Czechoslovakia. Jul 1953-Jun 1966 – 18r – 1 – us L of C Photodup [072]

NOVA UKRAINA – Prague. 1922-1928. Gaps – 1 – 35.00r – us Hoover Inst Photo [335]

NOVA VECHER – Sofia, Bulgaria. May 1941-Mar 1944 – 5r – 1 – us L of C Photodup [949]

NOVA ZAPOVID : ROMAN / Vynnychenko, Volodymyr – [s.l.]: Ukraina, 1950 – us Res Libr [830]

NOVAE AC INFESTAE DESTILLATIONIS... QUAE CIVITATI BARCINONESIS ANNI 1562 ACCIDIT BREVIS ENARATIO / Bruguera, O – Barcelona, 1563 – 2mf – 9 – sp Cultura [610]

NOVAE BIBLIOTHECAE MANUSCRIPT LIBRORUM THOMUS PRIMUS : HISTORIAS, CHRONICA, SANCTORUM, SANCTARUMQUE VITAS...REPRAESENTANS / Labbe – Parisiis, 1657 – 36mf – 8 – ne Slangenburg [240]

NOVAE BIBLIOTHECAE MANUSCRIPT LIBRORUM TOMUS SECUNDUS : RERUM AQUITANICARUM PRAESERTIM BITURICENSIUM UBERRIMA COLLECTIO / Labbe – Parisiis, 1657 – 37mf – 8 – ne Slangenburg [240]

NOVAE FUNGORUM SPECIES IN BELGIO SEPTENTRIONALI / Dozy, F & Molkenboer, J H – Lugduni Batavorum. 1846. B-5092 2 – 8 – ne IDC [580]

NOVAE HOLLANDIAE PLANTARUM SPECIMEN / Billiardiere – 1904-06 – 5 – uk Microform Academic [580]

NOVAE HOLLANDIAE PLANTARUM SPECIMEN / Labillardiere, J J H de – 2v. Parisiis. 1804-1806-07. B-5998 2 – 8 – ne IDC [580]

NOVAE PLANTARUM SPECIES / Kerner von Marilaun, A – Decas 1-3. Innsbruck. 1870-71. B-859 2 – 8 – ne IDC [580]

NOVAE PLANTARUM SPECIES PRAESERTIM INDIAE ORIENTALIS, EX COLLECTIONE HEYNII / Roth, A W – Halberstadii. 1821. B-400 2 – 8 – ne IDC [580]

NOVA-FRANCIA : GRUNDLICHE HISTORIE VON ERFUNDUNG DER GROSSEN LANDSCHAFT NOVA FRANCIA, ODER NEU FRANKREICH GENANNT. / Lescarbot, Marc – Augspurg: Chrysostomo Dabertzhofer, 1613. SEM105P882 – 2mf – 9 – Can$4.50 – cn Bibl Nat [971]

NOVAI A DEREVNI A : EZHEDNEVNAI A GAZETA GOMELSKOGO GUBERNSKOGOKOMITETA ROSSI ISKO I KOMMUNISTICHESKO I PARTII (BOLSHEVIKOV) – (Includes c.1: 1922:Mar.12) – Gomel: 1-i a gos. tip., 19uu – 1 – CSUXANR9792-S – us Hoover Inst Photo [947]

NOVAI A DEREVNI A (HOMEL, BELARUS) *see* NOVAI A DEREVNI A

NOVAI A DEREVNI A (SEMIPALATINSK, KAZAKHSTAN) – (Includes c.1: 1928:Mar.9, Apr.20, May 1, 11-18, June 1-8; SUPPLEMENTS: 1928:May 18:suppl) Semipalatinsk: Gubizdat, 1925 – 1 – CSUXANR9817-S – us Hoover Inst Photo [947]

NOVAI A GAZETA (PETROGRAD, R.S.F.S.R.) – (Includes c.1: 1918:May 29) – Petrograd: V. Timkovski i, 1918- – 1 – CSUXAKF0446-S – us Hoover Inst Photo [947]

NOVAI A MYSL (MYKOLA IV, UKRAINE) – (Includes c.1: 1944:Feb.20) – Nikolaev: [s.n.], 1943 – 1 – CSUXANS0387-S – us Hoover Inst Photo [947]

NOVAI A RUSSKAI A ZHIZN – (Includes c.1: 1919:Dec.19; 1920:Jan.20-21, July 31, Sept.21, 28, Oct.1-12, 14-31; 1920:Nov.1-3, 5-12, 14, 17, 23, 25-26, 28, Dec.2, 4-7, 10-14, 18-19, 22) – Helsingfors: G.A. Grigorkov, 1919 – 1 – CSUXANR0030-S – us Hoover Inst Photo [947]

NOVAI A ZHIZN (SHANGHAI, CHINA) = THE NEW IFE – (Includes c.1: 1945:Nov.17-1946:May 13; Lacks many issues) – Shankhai: M.N. Kulesh, 19uu – 1 – CSUXALC2075-S – us Hoover Inst Photo [947]

NOVAIA EKONOMICHESKAIA POLITIKA I KRIZIS PARTI I POSLE SMERTI LENINA / Valentinov, N – (The New Economic Policy and the Party Crisis after the Death of Lenin). 1971. 256p – 1 – 35.00r – us Hoover Inst Photo [947]

NOVAIA EZHEDNEVNAIA GAZETA – Moscow: Novaia ezhednevnaia gazeta, 1993- – 2mf – 9 – $199.95y – us East View [947]

NOVAIA IUDEIA – v. 1-4. Odessa. 1908. BR-3991 2 – 8 – ne IDC [073]

NOVAIA KNIGA – Kritiko-bibliograficheskii ezhenedel'nik. Spb. 1907 (1-14). BR-4322 2 – 8 – ne IDC [460]

NOVAIA KOOPERATSIIA V SEL'SKOM KHOZIAISTVE I KARTOFELEKRAKHMAL'NOE PROIZVODSTVO / Makarov, N P – Ed.2. M., 1913 – 2mf – 9 – COR-66/1 – ne IDC [334]

NOVAIA LITERATURA – Kritiko-bibliograficheskii zhurnal. Spb. 1907. BR-4323 2 – 8 – ne IDC [460]

NOVAIA MUZYKA – Leningrad. v. 1-2, no. 2. 1927-1928 – 1 – us NY Public [780]

NOVAIA RUSSKAIA BIBLIOTEKA, ZAKLIUCHAIUSHCHAIA V SEBE DO 15000 NAZVANII KNIG, VYSHEDSHIKH S 1850 PO 1 OKT. 1877 G. ENTSIKLOPEDICHESKII (PREDMETNYI) UKAZATEL' / Ivkin, A – Spb. 1878. BR-4342 2 – 8 – ne IDC [010]

NOVAIA STUDIIA – Zhurnal literatury, iskusstva i stseny. v. 1-13, 1. M. 1912. BR-3992 2 – 8 – ne IDC [073]

NOVAIA ZHIZN' – Bespartiinyi zhurnal literatury, nauki, iskusstva i obshchestvennoi zhizni. M. 1910-18. Lacking: 1913 (3-11), 1914 (3), 1916 (6-12), 1917 (2-12), 1918 (1-12). B-1809 2 – 8 – ne IDC [073]

NOVAIA ZHIZN' – Literaturno-obshchestvennyi al'mamakh. v. 1-5. M. 1916. Lacking: v. 2-3. BR-1885 2 – 8 – ne IDC [460]

NOVAIA ZHIZN' – (Missing: 1917 n1, 16-19) – Orsha, 1917-18 n3 – 5mf – 9 – COR-658/1 – ne IDC [334]

NOVAIA ZHIZN' – Murom, 1919 n1-2 – 1mf – 9 – COR-657/1 – ne IDC [334]

NOVAIA ZHIZN' – Petrograd. Apr. 18, 1917-July 16, 1918 – 1 – 35.00r – us Hoover Inst Photo [335]

Novakovic, S *see* SRPSKA BIBLIOGRAFIJA ZA NOVIJU KNIZEVNOST, 1741-1867

NOVALIS / Pastor, Willy – Berlin: Schuster & Loeffler, [1904] – 1r – 1 – us U.W. Library [430]

Novalis *see*
– DER HUETER DER SCHWELLE
– WORKS. 1805

NOVALIS ALS NATURPHILOSOPH / Pixberg, Hermann – (Includes bibliographical references) – Guetersloh: C Bertelsmann, 1928 – 1r – 1 – us U.W. Library [430]

NOVALIS ALS PHILOSOPH / Fridell, Egon – Muenchen: F Bruckmann, 1904 – 1r – 1 – us U.W. Library [430]

NOVALIS DEVANT LA CRITIQUE / Spenle, E – (Includes index) – Paris: Hachette, 1903 – 1r – 1 – us U.W. Library [430]

NOVALIS "HEINRICH VON OFTERDINGEN" UND DER "GUIDO" DES GRAFEN VON LOEBEN / Kollmann, Fritz – (Includes bibliographical references) – Budweis: Selbstverlag der deutschen k. k. Staatsrealschule, [19–?] – 1r – 1 – us U.W. Library [430]

NOVALIS' HYMNEN AN DIE NACHT UND GEISTLICHE LIEDER / Woerner, Roman – Muenchen: K. Hof- und Universitaets-Buchdruckerei von C Wolf, 1885 – 1r – 1 – us U.W. Library [780]

NOVALIS' LYRIK / Busse, Carl – (Includes bibliographical references) – Oppeln: G Maske, 1898 – 1r – 1 – us U.W. Library [430]

NOVALIS UND DER PIETISMUS / Thierstein, Johann R – [1910?] – 1mf – us A.T.L.A. [240]

NOVALIS UND DIE WELT DES OSTENS : VOM WERDEN UND VON DEN GESCHICHTLICHEN BILDEKRAEFTEN ROMANTISCHER WELTANSCHAUUNG UND RELIGIOSITAET / Goldammer, Kurt – Stuttgart: Kreuz-Verlag, [1948] – 1r – 1 – us U.W. Library [430]

NOVALIS UND SOPHIE VON KUEHN : EINE PSYCHOPHYSIOLOGISCHE STUDIE / Schlaf, Johannes – Muenchen, Schwabing: E W Bonsels, 1906 – 1r – 1 – us U.W. Library [430]

NOVARUM AUT RAIORUM PLANTARUM HORTI REG. BOTAN. MATRITENSIS DESCRIPTIONUM / Ortega, C G (de) – Matriti. 1797-1800. B-5531 2 – 8 – ne IDC [580]

NOVARUM ET MINUS COGNITARUM STIRPIUM PUGILLUS 1-10 / Lehmann, J G C – Hamburgi. 1828-57. B-5511 2 – 8 – ne IDC [580]

NOVARUM OBSERVATIONUM PHYSICO-MATHEMATICARUM F. MARINI MERSENNI MINIMI TOMUS 3, QUIBUS ACCESSIT ARISTARCHUS SAMIUS DE MUNDI SYSTEMATE / Mersenne, Marin – Avec une introduction de A. Beaulieu, Paris, A. Bertier, 1647, pieces liminaires et 245 p. Histoire des Sciences 17e-19e Siecles. 7966 – 9 – fr Hachette [510]

NOVARUM STIRPIUM BRASILIENSIUM DECADES (1-10) / Casaretto, G – Genoa. 1842-45. B-5116 2 – 8 – ne IDC [580]

NOVARUM STIRPIUM DECADES / Endlicher, S L – Vindobonae. 1839. B-5923 2 – 8 – ne IDC [580]

THE NOVA-SCOTIA AND NEW-BRUNSWICK MAGAZINE, OR, THE HISTORICAL, LITERARY, THEOLOGICAL, AND MISCELLANEOUS REPOSITORY – [Halifax, N.S.?: s.n., 1806?] – 9 – cn C.I.H.M. [971]

NOVASCOTIAN – Halifax, Canada. 1824-70 – 28r – 1 – $1,820.00 – cn Library Assoc [971]

THE NOVASCOTIAN AND WEEKLY CHRONICLE – Halifax, Canada. Weekly Chronicle & Nova Scotian Nova Scotian. -w. Nov 1899-Dec 1921. 25 reels – 1 – uk British Libr Newspaper [072]

NOVATO ADVANCE – Novato, CA. 1922- – 81+ r – 1 – $4,050.00 ($100.00y) – B02534 – us Library Micro [071]

NOVATORE – New York, NY, 1910-1911 – 1r – 1 – us I.H.R.C. [978]

NOVAYA I NOVEISHAYA ISTORIA – (Modern and Recent History). Moscow. U.S.S.R. 1961- – 1 – us UMI [947]

NOVAYA ZHIZN – (Svobodnaya zhizn). Leningrad. USSR. -d. 20 Apr 1917-4 May, 6 Jul 1918. (Imperfect). (2 reels) – 1 – uk British Libr Newspaper [947]

NOVE ATHENEUM – v1-2, 1920-21 – 1 – us I.U. Libraries [073]

NOVE CECHY – v3-17, 19. 1920-34, 1937 – 1 – us I.U. Libraries [073]

NOVE KNIHY – (Backfile through 1998 2r per y $170y) – Czech Republic, 1999- – 2r per y – 1 – $160.00 standing order – us Ross [072]

LAS NOVEDADES – New York, 2 Jan 1889-31 Mar 1898 – 20r – 1 – uk British Libr Newspaper [071]

NOVEDADES – Mexicali, MX. 1982 – 7r – $350.00 – R04216 – us Library Micro [072]

NOVEDADES – Mexico: R C Garza, oct 1970-jan 1978 (173r); feb 1978-aug 1980 (62r); sep 1980-1981 (32r) – 1 – us Res Libr [072]

NOVEISHAIA EVOLIUTSIIA ADMINISTRATIVNOGO PRAVA / Karadzhe-Iskrov, N P – Irkutsk, 1927. 40p. Precis of recent innovations in Soviet administrative law. BR-9434/1 – 9 – ne IDC [340]

NOVEISHAIA NATSIONAL'NAIA ISTORIOGRAFIIA GERMANII, ANGLII I FRANTSII / Petrov, M – Sravnitel'nyi istoriko-bibliograficheskii obzor. Khar'kov. 1861. BR-7210 2 – 8 – ne IDC [900]

NOVEISHAIA RUSSKAIA POEZIIA / Iakobson, R – Nabrosok pervyi. Prague. 1921. BR-1319 2 – 8 – ne IDC [460]

O NOVEISHEI LITERATURE MORSKAGO I VOENNAGO PRAVA / Kamarovskii, L A – Moscow, 1885. 115p. Appraisal of Western international legal literature on the law of warfare land and sea, with critical commentary. BR-7114/2 – 8 – ne IDC [340]

O NOVEISHIKH TEORETICHESKIKH ISKANIIAKH V OBLASTI KHUDOZHESTVENNOGO SLOVA / Ivanov, V – Nauchnye izvestiia. M. v. 2. 1922. BR-740 2 – 8 – ne IDC [460]

NOVEL REVIEW – 1- 45. 1867-92 – 1 – us UMI [830]

NOVELAS. JARILLA / Coronado, Carolina – 1873 – 9 – 1.50f – sp Bibl Santa Ana [830]

NOVELETTE, OP. 18 / Liapunov, S – [19–] – us Sibley [780]

NOVELLA 2000 – 1988-1995 – 1r per y – 5,6 – Sfr401.00 – sz Infoprint [945]

NOVELLEN / Arnim, Ludwig Achim, Freiherr von – Berlin: Veit, 1839 – 1r – 1 – us U.W. Library [830]

NOVELLEN : AUS DEM NACHLASSE DES DICHTERS / Kuernberger, Ferdinand; ed by Lauser, Wilhelm – Stuttgart: Deutsche Verlags-Anstalt, 1893 – 1 – us U.W. Library [830]

NOVELLEN / Heyse, Paul – Stuttgart und Berlin, J. C. Cotta, 1904-1910. 24 v. Film Mas C 544 – 1 – us H.U. Library [830]

NOVELLEN / Keller, Gottfried – Leipzig: P Reclam jun, [1941] – 1 – us U.W. Library [830]

NOVELLEN / Kroeger, Timm – (v.1 Eine stille Welt. v.2 Aus alter Truhe. v.3 Leute eigener Art. v.4 Wege nach dem Glueck. v.5 Des Lebens Wegzoelle. v.6 Dem unbekannten Gott) – Gesamtausgabe. 4.-13. Tausend. Hamburg, etc., G. Westermann, 1918. 6 v. Film Mas 8191 – 1 – us H.U. Library [830]

NOVELLEN / Storm, Theodor – Leipzig: Philipp Reclam jun., [1936] – 1r – 1 – us U.W. Library [830]

NOVELLEN AUS DER HEIMAT / Wilbrandt, Adolf von – Stuttgart: J G Cotta, [1880?] – 1r – 1 – us U.W. Library [830]

NOVELLEN DER LIEBE / Storm, Theodor – 3. Aufl. Berlin: Verlag der Nation, 1960 – 1r – 1 – us U.W. Library [830]

DIE NOVELLEN UM CLAUDIA : ROMAN / Zweig, Arnold – Berlin: G Kiepenheuer, 1931, c1930 – 1r – 1 – us U.W. Library [830]

NOVELLENSCHATZ DES AUSLANDES / ed by Heyse, Paul & Kurz, Hermann – Muenchen, 187-?. 14 v. Vol. ix-xiv herausgegeben von Paul Heyse. Film Mas C 650 – 1 – us H.U. Library [800]

DU NOVELLINE TOSCANE – 1890 – 1 – us I.U. Libraries [390]

THE NOVELS OF CHARLES DICKENS : A BIBLIOGRAPHY AND SKETCH / Kitton, Frederic George – London: Elliot Stock, 1897 – 1 roll – 1 – 1-55879-646-0 – uk Libr Preservation [420]

THE NOVELS, POEMS, AND MEMORIES OF CHARLES KINGSLEY / Kingsley, Charles – New York: Taylor, 1899 – 7 rolls – 1 – 1-55879-227-9 – uk Libr Preservation [420]

THE NOVELTIES OF ROMANISM : IN THREE PARTS, 1. DEVELOPMENT OF DOCTRINES, 2. CHRONOLOGICAL ARRANGEMENT, 3. OLD AND NEW CREEDS CONTRASTED / Collette, Charles Hastings – (In English and Latin. Includes bibliographical references) – 2nd rev enl ed. London: Religious Tract Society, [186-?] – 1mf – 9 – 0-8370-8412-1 – 1986-2412 – us A.T.L.A. [240]

NOVENA A JESUS NAZARENO EN SU.. / Burguillos, Pedro – 1824 – 9 – 1.50f – sp Bibl Santa Ana [240]

NOVENA A LA SACRATISIMA VIRGEN DEL CARMEN, MADRE DE DIOS Y SENORA NUESTRA – Almendralejo: Tip. L.C. Becerro, 1904 – 1 – sp Bibl Santa Ana [240]

NOVENA A LA SANTISIMA VIRGEN DE LA MONTANA PATRONA DE CACERES – Caceres: Tip. Floriano, 1940 – 1 – sp Bibl Santa Ana [240]

NOVENA A LA VIRGEN DE LA VICTORIA DE TRUJILLO – Caceres – 1 – sp Bibl Santa Ana [240]

NOVENA A MARIA SANTISIMA...LLERENA – 1883 – 9 – 1.50f – sp Bibl Santa Ana [240]

NOVENA A NUESTRA SENORA DE CONSOLACION QUE SE VENERA...EN MONTANCHEZ – Caceres: Tip. Garcia Floriano Cumbreno, 1941 – 1 – sp Bibl Santa Ana [240]

NOVENA A NUESTRA SENORA DE SANTA MARIA DE GUADALUPE – Sevilla: Imp. San Antonio, 1912 – 1 – sp Bibl Santa Ana [240]

NOVENA A SANTA RITA DE CASIA / Pastor, Juan Jose – Zorita: Imp. Montes, 1970 – 1 – sp Bibl Santa Ana [240]

NOVENA A...BOTOA – 1864 – 9 – 1.50f – sp Bibl Santa Ana [240]

NOVENA A...CHRISTO DE LA BUENA MUERTE / Nunez, Pedro C – 1819 – 9 – 1.50f – sp Bibl Santa Ana [240]

NOVENA A...DE LA GRANADA / Llerena – 1793 – 9 – 1.50f – sp Bibl Santa Ana [240]

NOVENA AL GLORIOSSIMO SAN ROQUE – 1885 – 9 – 1.50f – sp Bibl Santa Ana [240]

NOVENA AL SANTISIMO CRISTO DE LA SALUD. BROZAS / Carrasco Montero, Gregorio – Caceres: Im. M. Sergio, 1974 – 1 – sp Bibl Santa Ana [240]

NOVENA CONSAGRADA EN HONOR DE MARIA SANTISIMA QUE CON EL TITULO DE MARIA SANTISIMA VIRGEN DE LA CORONADA SE VENERA EN VILLAFRANCA DE LOS BARROS (EXTREMADURA BAJA) – Jaen Est. Tip. de los Sres. Rubio y Alcazar, 1878 – 1 – sp Bibl Santa Ana [240]

NOVENA DE CONFIANZA Y AGRADECIMIENTO AL CORAZON DOLORIDO E INMACULADO DE MARIA – Caceres: Imp. La Minerva, 1958 – 1 – sp Bibl Santa Ana [240]

NOVENA DE LA MILAGROSA SANTA RITA DE CASIA CON LA BENDICION DE SUS ROSAS – Caceres: Edit. Extremadura, 1975 – 1 – sp Bibl Santa Ana [240]

NOVENA DE MARIA SANTISIMA DE CORONADA QUE SE VENERA EN LA VILLA DE VILLAFRANCA DE LOS BARROS EN LA ESTREMADURA BAJA – Sevilla: Imprenta de Hidalgo y Compania, 1930 – 1 – sp Bibl Santa Ana [240]

NOVENA DE MARIA SANTISIMA DE LA SALUD CUYA...EN LA PUERTA QUE LLAMAN DE TRUJILLO – Plasencia: Imp. y Lib. Montero, 1962 – sp Bibl Santa Ana [240]

NOVENA DE NUESTRA SENORA DE BELEN – (Incompleta) – 1 – sp Bibl Santa Ana [946]

NOVENA DE NUESTRA SENORA DE SOPETRAN ORDENADA DE NUEVE PRECIOSAS PIEDRAS DE QUE SE COMPONE EL NOMBRE SOPETRANA... / Gomez Acedo, Francisco – Plasencia: Graf. Sandoval, 1959 – 1 – sp Bibl Santa Ana [240]

NOVENA DE SAN GREGORIO OBISPO DE OSTIA PATRONO POPULAR DE LA VILLA DE RUANES POR... / Arias Regodon, Publio – Caceres: El Noticiero – 1 – sp Bibl Santa Ana [250]

NOVENA DE SANTA LUCIA VIRGEN Y MARTIR ABOGADA DE LA VISTA – Caceres: Imprenta Moderna, 1939 – 1 – sp Bibl Santa Ana [240]

NOVENA DEPRECATORIA...MERCED – 1859 – 9 – 1.50f – sp Bibl Santa Ana [946]

NOVENA DIARIA DEL GLORIOSO SAN ANTONIO DE PADUA – Caceres: Edit. Extremadura, 1972 – 1 – sp Bibl Santa Ana [240]

NOVENA DIARIA DEL GLORIOSO SAN ANTONIO DE PADUA REVELADA POR EL MISMO... – Caceres: Imp. Nicolas M. Jimenez, 1871 – 1 – sp Bibl Santa Ana [240]

NOVENA EN HONOR DEL GLORIOSO PENITENTE SAN PEDRO DE ALCANTARA... / Lopez Cruz, Lorenzo – Caceres: Tip. Luciano Jimenez Merino, 1919 – sp Bibl Santa Ana [240]

NOVENA EN HONOR DEL GLORIOSO SAN BLAS OBISPO DE SEBASTE MARTIN – Caceres: Imp. Garcia Floriano Cumbreno, 1944 – 1 – sp Bibl Santa Ana [240]

NOVENA EN HONOR DEL SANTISIMO CRISTO DE LA VICTORIA QUE SE VENERA EN EL CONVENTO...DE SERRADILLA (CACERES) – Plasencia: Imp. Sanchez Rodrigo, 1963 – 1 – sp Bibl Santa Ana [240]

NOVENA Y DUODENARIO DE NUESTRA... MARIA – 1788 – 9 – 1.50f – sp Bibl Santa Ana [240]

NOVENA Y EJERCICIO DE LOS SABADOS A LA SANTISIMA VIRGEN DE LA MONTANA. PATRONA DE CACERES – Caceres: Imp. Floriano, 1947 – 1 – sp Bibl Santa Ana [240]

NOVENA...CONSOLACION...MONTANCHEZ – 1866 – 9 – 1.50f – sp Bibl Santa Ana [240]

NOVENA...DE LA PIEDAD – 1851 – 9 – 1.50f – sp Bibl Santa Ana [240]

NOVENA-MARIA SANTISIMA MADRE DE DIOS Y SENORA NUESTRA QUE CON EL TITULO DEL PUERTO VENERA Y TIENE POR PATRONA LA CIUDAD DE PLASENCIA... / Varela, Cipriano – Plasencia: Imp. Montero, 1962 – 1 – sp Bibl Santa Ana [240]

NOVENA...NTRA. SRA. PUERTO.. / Varela, Cipriano – 1845 – 9 – 1.50f – sp Bibl Santa Ana [240]

NOVENA...PATRIARCA SAN JOSE – 1867 – 9 – 1.50f – sp Bibl Santa Ana [240]

NOVENA...PIEDRAESCRITA...CAMPANARIO / San Jose, Francisco de – 1866 – 9 – 1.50f – sp Bibl Santa Ana [972]

NOVENARIO DEL GLORIOSO APOSTOL Y MARTIR SAN BARTOLOME... / Presbitero Secular – Caceres: Tip. El Noticiero, s.a. – 1 – sp Bibl Santa Ana [240]

NOVENARIO DOLOROSO...NTRA. SRA. DE LA SOLEDAD – 1805 – 9 – 1.50f – sp Bibl Santa Ana [240]

NOVENE ZU UNSERER LIEBEN FRAU VON LOURDES / Meschler, Moritz – (Includes bibliographical references) – 4. Aufl. Freiburg i.B.; St Louis, MO: Herder, 1880 – 1mf – 9 – 0-8370-8459-8 – 1986-2459 – us A.T.L.A. [240]

NOVGORODSKAIA LETOPIS' PO SINODAL'NOMU KHARATEINOMU SPISKU – Spb. 1888. BR-10,310 1 – 9 – ne IDC [950]

NOVGORODSKIE GRAMOTY NA BERESTE (IZ RASKOPOK 1952 G.) / Artsikhovskii, A V – Moscow, 1954. 92p. 19 plates. BR-10,112 1 – 9 – ne IDC [340]

NOVGORODSKIE GRAMOTY NA BERESTE (IZ RASKOPOK 1953-54 GG.) / Artsikhovskii, A V & Borkovskii, V I – Moscow, 1958. 160p Plates. BR-10,110 1 – 9 – ne IDC [340]

NOVGORODSKIE GRAMOTY NA BERESTE (IZ RASKOPOK 1956-57 GG.) / Artsikhovskii, A V & Borkovskii, V I – Moscow, 1963. 328p Br-11,197 1 – 9 – ne IDC [340]

NOVGORODSKIE GRAMOTY NA BERESTE (IZ RASKOPOK 1958-1961 GG.) / Artsikhovskii, A V – Moscow. 1963. 118p. plates. BR-11,200 1 – 9 – ne IDC [947]

NOVGORODSKIE GRAMOTY NA BERESTE (IZ RASPOKOK 1955 G.) / Artsikhovskii, A V & Borkovskii, V I – Moscow, 1958. 152p Plates.BR-10,111 1 – 9 – ne IDC [340]

NOVGORODSKII SBORNIK : IZDANIE NOVGORODSKOGO STATISTICHESKOGO KOMITETA / ed by Bogoslovskii, N – Novgorod. 5v. 1865-1866 – 25mf – 9 – RET-9/1 – ne IDC [947]

NOVI COMMENTARII ACADEMIAE SCIENTIARUM IMPERIALES PETROPOLITANAE – Petropoli. v1-20. 1750-1776 – 304mf – 9 – ne IDC [500]

NOVI COMMENTARII SOCIETATIS REGIAE SCIENTIARUM GOETTINGENSIS / Akademie der Wissenschaften. Goettingen – Gottingae et Gothae, 1771-78 – 3 – us Readex [500]

NOVI FRUCTUS SACRORUM LAUDUM GUIBUS INSUNT DUAE MISSAE, SACRAE CANTIONES. / Gambalo – 1619 – 9 – us Sibley [780]

NOVI LIST – Buenos Aires, Argentina, 1933 – 1mf or 1 reel – 9,1 – us I.H.R.C. [972]

NOVI LIST – Rijeka, Yugoslavia. Aug 1954; Aug 1956-1970 (incomplete) – 41r – 1 – us L of C Photodup [949]

NOVI PROVENTUS HORTI MEDICI... / Heucher, J H von – Vitembergae, 1711 – 2mf – 9 – ne IDC [615]

NOVI PROVENTUS HORTORUM HALENSIS ET BEROLENSIS / Sprengel, K P J – Halae, 1819. 48 pp. B-7301 1 – 9 – ne IDC [580]

NOVI SREDNJOSKOLAC – Belgrade, Yugoslavia. Oct-Dec 1950 – 1r – 1 – us L of C Photodup [949]

NOVI TESTAMENTI..., ANNOTATIONIBUS ERUDITIS AND PIJS IAM PRIMUM EXPLICATI AND ILLUSTRATI,...LVCAS AND IOANNES / Lossius, L – Franc., [1554]. V.2 – 5mf – ne IDC [240]

NOVI TESTAMENTI GRAECI JESU CHRISTI TAMEION / Schmid, Erasmus – 2v. 1819 – 1 – us A.T.L.A. [240]

NOVI TESTAMENTI GRAECI: SUPPLEMENTUM EDITIONIBUS DE GEBHARDT TISCHENDORFIANIS / Nestle, Eberhard – Leipzig: Bernhard Tauchnitz, 1896. 1 fiche – 9 – us A.T.L.A. [240]

NOVI VJESNIK – (Cont: Vjesnik. Yrly reel count varies) – 1976- – 1 – us Ross [072]

NOVI VJESNIK *see* VJESNIK

Novichenko, Leonid *see* TARAS SHEVCHENKO

NOVIDADE – Maceio, Alagoas. 11 Abr-26 Set 1931 – 1,5,6 – bl Biblioteca [072]

NOVIDADES – Rio de Janeiro, 25 Jan-Dec 1887; Jan-Mar, Jul-Dec 1888; Jan-31 Dec 1889 – 1,5,6 – bl Biblioteca [072]

NOVIEMBRE 1975. SESIONES CINEMATOGRAFICAS DE ARTE Y ENSAYO / Casa de la Cultura. Cine Club de la O.S. de E. y D. – Caceres: Imp. D. Rodriguez, 1975 – 1 – sp Bibl Santa Ana [790]

NOVIEMBRE DE MADRID / Espinar, Jaime – Barcelona. 1938. Fiche W 863. (Blodgett Collection of Spanish Civil War Pamphlets) – 9 – us H.U. College Libr [946]

Novigenti, Guibertus *see* QUO ORDINE SERMO FIERI DEBEAT. DE BUCELLA IUDAE DATA ET DE VERITATE DOMINI CORPORIS. DE SANCTIS ET EORUM PIGNERIBUS

Novikov, I I *see* DISSIPATIVNYE SVOISTVA METALLOV I METALLICHESKIKH SPLAVOV

NOVIKOV I MOSKOVSKIE MARTINISTY / Longinov, M N – 1867. BR-7661 2 – 8 – ne IDC [460]

Novikov, N I *see*
- IZBRANNYE SOCHINENIIA
- RODOSLOVNAIA KNIGA KNIAZEI I DVORIAN ROSSIISKIKH
- SATIRICHESKIE ZHURNALY
- TRUTEN'
- ZHIVOPISETS

Novikov, S P *see* MATHEMATICAL PHYSICS REVIEWS

Novikov, V *see* V.V. MAIAKOVSKII

NOVINI – Sofia, Bulgaria. Feb 1945-Sept 1947 (scattered issues) – 1r – 1 – us L of C Photodup [949]

LOS NOVIOS / Manzoni, Alejandro – Trans., Gabino Tejado. Tomo I-III. 1859 – 9 – 1.50f – sp Bibl Santa Ana [830]

LA NOVISSIMA GRAMMATICA DELLE TRE LINGUA ITALIANA, FRANZESE E SPAGNUOLA / Lonchamps, A – 1664 – 9 – fr I.C.S. [440]

NOVITATES CONCHOLOGICAE – (Cont as: Conchologische Mittheilungen. Cassel v1-3 1881-1894) – Cassel. S.1 v1-5; 1854-1879; S.2 v1-15 1858-1865 – 59mf – 9 – ne IDC [590]

NOVITATES ZOOLOGICAE – London. v1-34. 1894-1928 – 361mf – 9 – ne IDC [590]

Novitskii, I P *see* UKAZATEL'K IZDANIIAM VREMENNOI KOMMISSII DLIA RAZBORA DREVNIKH AKTOV. 1-2

O NOVO BAHIANO : JORNAL POLITICO E COMMERCIAL – '(s.l.')-Bahia, Brazil. 31 Jul 1833 – 1,5,6 – bl Biblioteca [072]

NOVO DIA – Manaos, Amazonas. 27 Jul-21 Set 1890 – 1,5,6 – bl Biblioteca [072]

NOVO DIARIO DA BAHIA : JORNAL POLITICO E COMMERCIAL – Bahia, Brazil. 30 Nov-Dez 1837; 6-16 Jan 1838 – 1 – bl Biblioteca [072]

NOVO MONDO – (In Portuguese) – Canada, 1907-73 – 4r – 1 – cn Commonwealth Micro [072]

NOVO SECULO – S. Manoel, 14 Jul 1901; 16 Jan 1902 – 1,5,6 – bl Biblioteca [072]

O NOVO SETE DE NOVEMBRO : PERIODICO MORAL, POLITICO E COMMERCIAL – '(s.l.')-Bahia, Brazil. 18-30 Dec 1837-16 Jan 1838 – 1,5,6 – bl Biblioteca [072]

NOVO VREME – Belgrade, Yugoslavia. May 1941-Apr 1944 – 7r – 1 – us L of C Photodup [949]

Novo y Colson, Pedro de *see* INFORME DE LA OBRA TITULADA "ESTUDIO BIOGRAFICO DE ESPRONCEDA" POR JOSE CASCALES Y MUNOZ

NOVOE DELO – Ezhemesiachnyi literaturnyi zhurnal. v. 1-12. Spb. 1902. B-1810 2 – 8 – ne IDC [073]

NOVOE OTKROVENIE O SOVETSKO I EKONOMIKE II KAK MOZHNO POGUBIT RABOCHE-KRESTI ANSKI I BLOK : K VOPROSU OB EKONOMICHESKOM OBOSNOVANII TROT SKIZMA / Bukharin, Nikolai Ivanovich – Moskva: Gos. izd-vo, 1925 – 1 – CSUX89-B4182 – us Hoover Inst Photo [320]

NOVOE RUSSKOE SLOVO – (Library has: Vol. 35, no. 11,119[i.e. 12,119]-12,299 July 1-Dec.31, 1945;[missing Aug. 4; some issues slightly mutilated]) – New York: Novoye Russkoye Slovo Pub. Co., 1920 – 1 – CSUX86-S346 – us Hoover Inst Photo [947]

NOVOE SLOVO – Ezhemesiachnyi obshchestvenno-literaturnyi illustrirovannyi zhurnal. M. 1905 06-1907. Lacking: 1906 (45). B-1225 2 – 8 – ne IDC [073]

NOVOE SLOVO – Ezhemesiachnyi zhurnal. Spb. 1908-14. B-1226 2 – 8 – ne IDC [073]

NOVOE SLOVO – DAS NEUE WORT : NATIONALE ZEITUNG IN RUSSISCHER UND DEUTSCHER SPRACHE – Berlin, 1933-45 n95 – 6r – 1 – Inquire at Mikrofilmarchiv for details – gw Misc Inst [072]

NOVOE VREMIA – Belgrade, Yugoslavia. 5 Feb 1924; 1927-Oct 1930 – 7r – 1 – us L of C Photodup [949]

NOVOE VREMIA – Dvukhnedel'nyi zhurnal. M. 1945-66. BR-4147 2 – 8 – ne IDC [073]

NOVOE VREMIA – Leningrad, U.S.S.R. -w. Jan 1888-Nov 1889; Jan 1891-Oct 1917. Imperfect. 151 reels – 1 – uk British Libr Newspaper [947]

NOVOE VREMIA – Moscow. Jun 1943-Dec 1966. Incomplete – 1 – $35.00r – us Hoover Inst Photo [947]

NOVOE VREMIA – St. Petersburg. 1876-1882 (scattered issues missing). 1893-1916 (many gaps; complete holdings available on request). Dec. 19, 1916-Oct. 26, 1917 complete – 1 – 35.00r – us Hoover Inst Photo [335]

NOVOE VREMIA – St Petersburg. Jan 1900-June 1901; Jan 1902-June 1916; Oct 1916-June 1917. Incomplete – 1 – us NY Public [073]

NOVOE VREMJA – En russe. Titre francais: Nouveau temps. Saint-Petersbourg. janv-juin 1881, juil 1882-juin 1885, 1886, juil-dec 1887, 1899 – 1 – fr A.C.R.P.P. [073]

NOVOGORODSKIE GRAMOTY NA BERESTE (IZ RASKOPOK 1951 G.) / Artsikhovskii, A V & Tikhomirov, M N – Moscow, 1953. 65p. 25 plates. BR-10,113 1 – 9 – ne IDC [340]

O NOVOI SILIE V REVOLIUTSIONNYKH KADRAKH : OCHERK / Diachkov-Tarasov, V – Parizh: Izd. gazety "Parizhskii vi estnik", 1911 – 1 – CSUX88-B6925 – us Hoover Inst Photo [947]

Novorossiiskago. University *see* ZAPISKI IMPERATORSKAGO NOVOROSSIISKAGO UNIVERSITETA

Novorossiiskago. University. Faculty of Historical Philology *see* ZAPISKI NOVOROSSIISKAGO UNIVERSITETA

NOVORUM VEGETABILIUM DESCRIPTIONES / Llave, P de la & Lexarza, J de – Mexico. 1824-25. B-6001 2 – 8 – ne IDC [580]

NOVOS RUMOS – Rio de Janeiro, 28 Feb 1959-23 Mar 1964 – 1,5,6 – bl Biblioteca [072]

NOVOS TEMPOS – Rio de Janeiro, BL. 1957-1958 – 1r – $50.00 – R04177 – us Library Micro [073]

NOVOSADSKI DNEVNIK – Novi Sad, Yugoslavia. Oct 1954-Apr 1956 – 1r – 1 – us L of C Photodup [949]

NOVOSTI – Belgrade, Yugoslavia. 9,13,18 Nov 1945 – 1r – 1 – us L of C Photodup [949]

NOVOSTI – (In Croatian) – Canada, 1944-48 – 1r – 1 – cn Commonwealth Micro [072]

NOVOSTI – Zagreb, Yugoslavia. Nov 1944-Jan 1945 – 1r – 1 – us L of C Photodup [949]

NOVOSTI DESTKOI LITERATURY – Kritiko – bibliograficheskii ezhemesiachnyi zhurnal. M. 1912-16. Lacking: v. 1 (1-5, 7-9), 1912; v. 2 (7, 9), 1913; v. 3 (8), 1914; v. 4 (11-12), 1915; v. 5 (11-12), 1916. BR-4325 2 – 8 – ne IDC [460]

NOVOSTI GRAMMOFONA – St Petersburg. n1-9 1907; n1-3 1908 (monthly) – 6mf – 9 – $40.00 – us Ross [780]
NOVOSTI I BIRZHEVAIA GAZETA – (Missing: Many numbers) – 1889-1906 – 39r – 1 – RF-4/3 – ne IDC [072]
NOVOSTI I BIRZHEVOIA GAZETA – 1889-1906. BRF-4 3 – 1 – ne IDC [947]
NOVOSTI KOMMERCHESKOI LITERATURY – Ezhemesiachnyi bibliograficheskii zhurnal. Spb. 1913 (1-4). Lacking: 1913 (3). BR-4333 2 – 8 – ne IDC [460]
NOVOSTI LITERATURY – v. 1-18. Spb. 1822-25. B-1417 2 – 8 – ne IDC [073]
NOVOSTI PECHATI – Ezhemesiachnyi zhurnal literatury, kritiki, bibliografii, pechatnago i izdatel'skogo dela. M. 1895-96. Lacking: 1895 (12). BR-4326 2 – 8 – ne IDC [460]
NOVOSTI RUSSKOI LITERATURY – v. 1-14. M. 1802-05. Lacking: v. 2-3, 5-8, 10-14. B-1418 2 – 8 – ne IDC [073]
NOVOYE RUSSKOYE SLOVO – New York. NY. 1961- – 1 – us UMI [071]
NOVUM – (Lacking: v1-3,5 1974) – 1973-81 – 9r – 1 – ATLA S0748 – us A.T.L.A. [073]
NOVUM TESTAMENTUM – Leiden. v1-32. 1956-90 – 5,9 – Dfl2,880.00; Dfl90.00v – ne Swets [240]
NOVUM TESTAMENTUM GRAECE / ed by Tischendorf, Constantin – 2v. 1869-72 – 45mf – 9 – $150.00 – us OmniSys [240]
NOVUS THESAURUS PHILOLOGICO-CRITICUS SIVE LEXICON IN 70 ET RELIQUOS INTERPRETES GRAECOS AC SCRIPTORES APOCRYPHOS VETERIS TESTAMENTI / Schleusner, J F – Lipsiae. Pars 1-5. 1820-1821 – 9 – Dfl189.00 – ne Slangenburg [450]
NOVVELLES DES VICTOIRES SIGNALEES OBTENVES PAR L'ARMEE IMPERIALE CONTRE LES TURCS ET TARTARES – Arras, 1596 – 1mf – 9 – H-8215/1 – ne IDC [956]
NOVVM INSTRUMENTUM OMNE – Basileae, 1516 – 1 – us A.T.L.A. [240]
NOVVM TESTAMENTVM...ANNOTATIONIBUS ERUDITIS AND PIJS IAM PRIMUM EXPLICATUM AND ILLUSTRATUM,...MATTHAEUVS AND MARCVS / Lossius, L – Franc., [1553] V.1 – 6mf – ne IDC [240]
NOVVS ORBIS REGIONVM AC INSVLARVM VETERIBVS INCOGNITARVM, UNA CUM TABULA COSMOGRAPHICA, ET ALIQUOT ALIJS CONSIMILIS ARGUMENTI LIBELLIS, QUORUM OMNIUM CATALOGUS SEQUENTI PATEBIT PAGINA / ed by Grynaeus, S – (Collection of travel accounts of the newly discovered regions of the world, with a copious index. It includes Marco Polo, Marci Pauli Veneti De Regionibus orientalibus. Het'owm Patmich, Haithoni Armeni...De Tartaris liber) – Basileae, 1532. [48], 585, [586, wrongly numbered 584] p – 12mf – 9 – H-8143/1 – ne IDC [910]
NOVY DEN – Plzen, Czechoslovakia. Jun-Nov 1945 – 1r – 1 – us L of C Photodup [072]
NOVY DOMOV – Toronto, Canada. -w. 10 May 1958-Dec 1970. 5 reels – 1 – uk British Libr Newspaper [072]
NOVY I PUT : ORGAN SOVI ETA NARODNAGO KHOZI A ISTVA SI EVERNAGO RA IONA – (Library has: June 1918-Sep. 1919, Mar./Apr. 1920-Dec. 1921) – Petrograd: Sovet, 1917-1922. 6v – 1 – CSUX89-S969 – us Hoover Inst Photo [947]
NOVY I PUT (1917: PETROGRAD, R.S.F.S.R. *see* NOVY I PUT
NOVY I ZHURNAL = THE NEW REVIEW – (Includes c.1: v.1 1942-v.162 (1986)) – Ni u-lork: [s.n.], 1942- – 1 – CSUX89-S42 – us Hoover Inst Photo [947]
NOVY MIR – (New World). Moscow. U.S.S.R. 1961- – 1 – us UMI [460]
NOVY MIR – New York, 1911-38 – 16r – 1 – us Ross [071]
NOVY SHLYAKH – Saskatoon, Canada. New Pathway. -w. 7 Jan 1936-28 Dec 1939. 4 reels – 1 – uk British Libr Newspaper [072]
NOVY SVET : DAILY, LATER WEEKLY CZECH LANGUAGE NEWSPAPER – Cleveland, OH. Sept 16 1950-Jan 30 1976. – 37r – 1 – us Western Hes [071]
NOVY ZIVOT – (Some issues missing) – Presov, Czechoslovakia. Jan-Nov 1956 – 1r – 1 – us L of C Photodup [072]
NOVYE IDEI V KOOPERATSII : SBORNIK STATEI – M., 1919 – 1mf – 9 – COR-338/1 – ne IDC [334]
NOVYE LIUDI / Gippius, Z N – Razskazy. Spb. 1896. BR-718 2 – 8 – ne IDC [460]
NOVYE MATERIALY DLIA ISTORII RUSSKOI DUKHOVNOI LITERATURY / lazykov, D D – Spb. 1885. BR-5908 2 – 8 – ne IDC [460]
NOVYE POSTROENIIA V IDEOLOGII I TEORII KOOPERATIZMA-ARTEL'NOSTI / Slobozhanin, M – Pg., 1919 – 1mf – 9 – COR-221/1 – ne IDC [334]
NOVYE POSTUPLENIIA V OTDELE RUKOPISEI GPB (1952-1966) – Kratkii otchet. Moscow, 1968. 200p. BR-10,846/1 – 9 – ne IDC [025]
NOVYE PUTI KOOPERATSII : PT. 1 KOMMUNIZM I KOOPERATSIIA – M., 1922 – 1mf – 9 – COR-176/1 – ne IDC [334]
NOVYE TRUDY PO ISTOCHNIKOVEDENIIU DREVNE-RUSSKOI LITERATURY / Peretts, V N – Kritikobibliograficheskii obzor. Vtoraia seriia. v. 1-15. Kiev. 1905; v. 31-46. 1907-08; v. 1-55. 1909-14. BR-7315 2 – 8 – ne IDC [460]
NOVYE ZAKONY O KOOPERATSII : SISTEMATICHESKII SBORNIK ZAKONOV, POSTANOVLENII, INSTRUKTSII, PRIMERNYKH USTAVOV I PR. / Dolmatovskii, A M – M., 1925 – 6mf – 9 – COR-729/1 – ne IDC [334]
NOVYE ZHYTTIA – Presov, Czechoslovakia. 1967-1991 – 9r – 1 – us L of C Photodup [072]
NOVYI BIBLIOGRAFICHESKII UKAZATEL' – Polnaia entsiklopediia. Zakliuchaiushchaia v sebe do 15000 nazvanii knig, vyshedshikh za posledniia 30 let, po vsem otrasliam znaniia. Sost. A.J. n. (A. Ivkin?). Spb. 1880. BR-4363 2 – 8 – ne IDC [010]
NOVYI EKONOMIST : EZHENEDEL'NYI, NAUCHNYI I POLITICHESKII ZHURNAL POSVIASHCHENNYI EKONOMICHESKOI I FINANSOVOI ZHIZNI RUSSKOI I ZAGRANICHNOI / ed by Migulin, P P – (Missing: 1917 n8-end) – Spb. v1-5. 1913-17 – 121mf – 9 – R-2320/2 – ne IDC [334]
NOVYI ENTSIKLOPEDICHESKII SLOVAR' BROKGAUZA-EFRONA – (V.30-48 have not been published; Missing: V.8/p. 329-344); V.13(p. 157-160); V.15(p. 201-204); V.18(p. 197-200)) – Spb., Pg., 1911-1916. v1-29. A-Otto – 195mf – 9 – R-18350/1 – ne IDC [947]
NOVYI I POLNYI GEOGRAFICHESKII SLOVAR' ROSSIISKOGO GOSUDARSTVA / Maksimovich, L – M., 1788-1789. v1-6 – 46mf – 9 – R-8395/2 – ne IDC [947]
NOVYI KORABL' – Literaturnyi zhurnal. v. 1-4. Paris. 1927-28. BR-4149 2 – 8 – ne IDC [073]
NOVYI KORABL' – Paris. no. 1-4. 1927-1928 – 1 – us NY Public [073]
NOVYI LEF – Moscow, 1927-28 – 1r – 1 – us Ross [335]
NOVYI LEF – Moscow. no. 1-10. 1927 – 1 – us NY Public [073]
NOVYI LEF – Zhurnal levogo fronta iskusstv. M. 1927-28. BR-3606 2 – 8 – ne IDC [073]
NOVYI MIR – Moscow, USSR. 1938-1979 – 58r – $2,900.00 – R63623 – us Library Micro [072]
NOVYI MIR – Russkaya Rabochaya Gazeta. New York etc. Apr 1911-Sept 1938. Incomplete – 1 – us NY Public [073]
NOVYI PUT' – Leningrad. v1-2. 1903-04 – 3r – 1 – us Ross [073]
NOVYI PUT' – Obshchestvenno-politicheskii, literaturnyi ezhemesiachnyi zhurnal. nr. 1-24. Spb. 1903-04. B-1109 2 – 8 – ne IDC [320]
NOVYI PUT' – St Petersburg. year 1-2. 1903-1904 – 1 – us NY Public [073]
NOVYI RUSSKII BAZAR – St Petersburg, 1865, 1867, 1869-98 – 463mf – 9 – $2,490.00 coll – us Ross [073]
NOVYI SATIRIKON – St Petersburg. 1913-1914; 1915-1917; 1918. no. 1-5, 8 – 1 – us NY Public [460]
NOVYI STROI I PRAVA SVOBODNYKH GRAZHDAN / Gerasimov, P V – Petrograd: "Osvobozhdennai a Rossii a", 1917 – 1 – CSUX89-B3499 – us Hoover Inst Photo [947]
NOVYI VEK – Ezhemesiachnyi illiustrirovannyi politicheskii, nauchnyi i literaturnyi zhurnal. Spb. 1900-03. Lacking: 1900 (6), 1905 (5-12), 1903 (4-12). B-1814 2 – 8 – ne IDC [320]
NOVYI VIK – Bucharest, Romania. 1972-83 – 4r – 1 – us L of C Photodup [949]
NOVYI VOSKHOD – Ezhenedel'nik posviashchennyi evreiskim interesam. v. 1-6. Spb. 1910-15. BR-4150 2 – 8 – ne IDC [073]
NOVYI VOSTOK – Moscow. 1922-1930, nos. 1-29 – 1 – 35.00r – us Hoover Inst Photo [335]
NOVYI VOSTOK – Moscow. v. 1-29. 1922-1930 – 1 – us NY Public [073]
NOVYI VOSTOK – Moscow. v1-29. 1922-30 – 4r – 1 – us Ross [335]
NOVYI VOSTOK – Zhurnal Vserossiiskoi nauchnoi assotsiatsii vostokovedeniia pri Narodnom Komissariate po delam natsional'nostei. V. 1-29. M. 1922-30. BR-4151 2 – 8 – ne IDC [073]
NOVYI ZAKON O PROMYSLOVOI KOOPERATSII 11 MAIA 1927 G. S POSTATEINYMI RAZ"IASNENIIAMI / Genkin, D M & Filatov, VB – M., 1927 – 2mf – 9 – COR-292/1 – ne IDC [334]
NOVYI ZHURNAL – (Backfile available. Inquire) – Russia, 1999- – 12mf per y standing order – 9 – us Ross [072]
NOVYI ZHURNAL = THE NEW REVIEW – (Complete backfile available 1942-97 500mf $4,000) – 1998- – 12mf per y – 9 – $100.00 standing order – us Ross [460]
NOVYI ZHURNAL DLYA VSEKH – St Petersburg. Nov 1908-Sept Oct 1916. Incomplete – 1 – us NY Public [073]
NOVYI ZHURNAL INOSTRANNOI LITERATURY, ISKUSSTVA I NAUKI – Illiustrirovannoe ezhemesiachnoe izdanie. v. 4. Spb. 1897-1909. Lacking: 1901, v. 1-2, v. 3: 1-2; 1907, v. 1, v. 2: 3; 1908, v. 2: 2-4, v. 3-4; 1909, v. 1: 2-3, v. 2-4. B-1816 2 – 8 – ne IDC [073]
NOVYI ZHURNAL VSEKH – Obshchedostupnyi literaturno-kriticheskii, obshchestvenno-politicheskii, illiustrirovannyi ezhemesiachnyi zhurnal. Spb. 1908-16. Lacking: 1909 (5); 1913 (3); not published, 1914 (7-10); 1916 (11-12). B-1815 2 – 8 – ne IDC [410]
NOVYIA EZHEMESIACHNYIA SOCHINENIIA – v. 1-120. Spb. 1786-96. B-1453 2 – 8 – ne IDC [073]
NOVYIA MYSLI – Zhurnal. Spb. 1907-08. BR-3993 2 – 8 – ne IDC [073]
NOVYIA STIKHOTVORENIIA / Merezhkovskii, Dimitrii – (1891-95). Spb. 1896. BR-777 2 – 8 – ne IDC [460]
NOW – Los Angeles. July, 1943-July 1946 – 1 – us NY Public [073]
NOW / Montana. Agricultural Extension Service – 1965-1978. v.1-14 – 1,5,6 – us Spaulding [630]
NOW – v.1-. 1979- – 1,5,6,9 – us UMI [073]
NOWA DOBA – Bautzen, Germany. Dec 1952-1953; 1956-Jun 1979; Jan-May 1982; Jan-May 1983 – 27r – 1 – us L of C Photodup [072]
NOWA KULTURA – Warsaw. Poland. -w. 3 Apr 1950-9 Jun 1963. (14 reels) – 1 – uk British Libr Newspaper [947]
NOWE DROGI – 1941-43 – 1r – 1 – inquire – us Ross [072]
NOWE DROGI – Warsaw. v. 1-20. 1947-1966. Incomplete – 1 – us NY Public [073]
NOWE SYGNALY – Wroclaw. Poland. -w. Dec 1956-Nov 1957. (1 reel) – 1 – uk British Libr Newspaper [947]
NOWE WIDNOKREGI – Moscow, 1942-46 – 1r – 1 – us Ross [072]
NOWE WIDNOKREGI – Moscow. June 1942-Sept 1946. Not collated – 1 – us NY Public [073]
NOWINY PODKARPACKIE – Krosno, Poland. Feb-Nov 1953 – 1r – 1 – us L of C Photodup [943]
NOWINY POLSKIE – (In Polish and English) – Milwaukee, WI. 1939-43 – 12r – 1 – $1,020.00 – D3381 – us Scholarly Res [071]
NOWINY PRZEMYSKIE – Przemysl, Poland. Feb-Nov 1953 – 1r – 1 – us L of C Photodup [943]
NOWINY RZESZOWSKIE – Rzeszow, Poland. Jul 1952-May 1979 – 53r – 1 – us L of C Photodup [943]
Nowland, John H B *see* EARLY REMINISCENCES OF INDIANAPOLIS
Nowlis, Helen *see* DRUGS DEMYSTIFIED
NOWY CASNIK – Cottbus, Germany. 1956-Jun 1979 – 3r – 1 – us L of C Photodup [072]
NOWY DZIENNIK – (In Polish. Backfile through 1998 $85r) – USA, 1999- – 6r per y – 1 – $480.00 standing order – us Ross [071]
NOWY KURIER WARSZAWSKI – (Scattered issues missing) – Warszawa, [oct 11 1939-jul 22/23 1944] – 16r – 1 – us Res Libr [943]
NOWY KURJER POLSKI – Warsaw, Poland. Feb-Apr 1926 – 1r – 1 – us L of C Photodup [943]
NOWY SWIAT – (Film includes scattered issues of other eds; not collated) – New York: Polish Daily Nowy Swiat, [1920-jun 1970] [New York ed] – us Res Libr [071]
Noyes, George Rapall *see*
- CAUSES OF THE DECLINE OF INTEREST IN CRITICAL THEOLOGY
- A NEW TRANSLATION OF THE PROVERBS, ECCLESIASTES, AND THE CANTICLES
- REVIEW OF CHRISTOLOGIE DES ALTEN TESTAMENTES, VON E. W. HENGSTENBERG
- STUART ON THE OLD TESTAMENT

Noyes, H E *see* SEVENTEEN YEARS IN PARIS
Noyes, John Humphrey *see* HOME-TALKS
Noyon, CN *see* STATISTIQUE DU DEPARTEMENT DU VAR
NOYYI GRAD – NR. 1-14. Paris. 1931-39. BR-4148 2 – 8 – ne IDC [073]
Nozeman, C *see* NEDERLANDSCHE VOGELEN; VOLGENS HUNNE HUISHOUDING, AERT EN EIGENSCHAPPEN BESCHREEVEN
NOZHET-ELHADI – Texte arabe et traduction par O. Houdas. 1888, 1889 – 9 – fr Orientalistes [800]
NOZIONI ELEMENTARI DI DIRITTO PENALE INTERNAZIONALE E DELLE PROCEDURE AD ESSO ATTINENTI / Bellegotti, L – Pontremoli, 1889 – 2mf – 9 – ILM-2263/1 – ne IDC [327]
[LE NOZZE DI DORINA]. IO NON ERA / Storace, S – [London]: J Dale, [1793] – 1 – us Sibley [780]
NPPA JOURNAL *see* CRIME AND DELINQUENCY
THE N.R.A. REPORTER – v1-2. 1933-34 (all publ) – 7mf – 9 – $10.50 – LLMC 84-658 – us L.L.M.C. [073]
NRA'S "BLUE EAGLE," A WEEKLY NEWSPAPER, JUNE 11, 1934-MAY 17, 1935 / U.S. National Recovery Administration – 1roll. T692 – 1 – us Nat'l Archives [324]
NRAVY RUSSKOGO OBSHCHESTVA V EKATERINSKUIU EPOKHU / Pavlenko, I – Arkhangel'sk. 1912. BR-7748 2 – 8 – ne IDC [947]
NRC HANDELSBLAD – 1970- – us Ross [072]
NRPB *see* NATIONAL RESOURCES PLANNING BOARD (NRPB)
NS FUNK – v. 1-7. 1933-39 – 1 – 224.00 – us L of C Photodup [621]
NS VOLKSBLATT FUER WESTFALEN – Bielefeld, dec 13 1933-aug 14 1935 – 1 – Inquire at Mikrofilmarchiv for details – gw Misc Inst [320]
LES N'SAKKARAS, LEUR PAYS, LEURS MOEURS. AVEC UN GLOSSAIRE N'SAKKARA – Bar le Duc: Imprimerie Comte-Jacquet. 1895 – 9 – 5.00 – fr Orientalistes [960]
NSBA NEWS – (Supersedes Nebraska State Bar Journal) – 1970-94 – 9 – $144.00 set – us Hein [340]
NSBA NEWS *see* NEBRASKA STATE BAR JOURNAL
NSDAP – Germany – 1 – 35.00r – us Hoover Inst Photo [943]
NSF (NATIONAL SANITATION FOUNDATION) – Printed index. Updated every 60 days – 6,9 – us Info Handling [628]
NSPI JOURNAL / National Society for Performance and Instruction – (See also: NSPI Newsletter) – v15- 1976- – 1,5,6,9 – us UMI [073]
NSPI NEWSLETTER / National Society for Performance and Instruction – v1-14 1962-75 1; v10-14 5,6 – us UMI [073]
NSPI NEWSLETTER *see* NSPI JOURNAL
NS-TAGEBLATT FUER DEN KREIS ROTENBURG A F UND NACHBARGEBIETE *see* BEBRAER TAGESZEITUNG
NS-TAGEBLATT FUER OSTKURHESSEN UND NACHBARGEBIETE *see* BEBRAER TAGESZEITUNG
NS-TAGESZEITUNG FUER BAUTZEN *see* BAUTZENER NACHRICHTEN
NSW PARLIAMENTARY PAPERS : 1ST SESSION, 49TH PARLIAMENT – 1988 – ca 140mf – 9 – $146.00 – at Parliament [324]

NSW PARLIAMENTARY PAPERS : 2ND SESSION, 48TH PARLIAMENT – 1984-86 – ca 600mf – 9 – $577.00 – at Parliament [324]

NSW PARLIAMENTARY PAPERS : 3RD SESSION, 48TH PARLIAMENT – 1986-88 – ca 900mf – 9 – $910.00 – at Parliament [324]

NSW PARLIAMENTARY PAPERS : 49TH PARLIAMENT, 2 SESSIONS – 1989-90 – 9 – A$1,369.00 – at Parliament [324]

NSZ RHEINFRONT – Saarbruecken, Germany. -d. Jan 1937-Jan, Oct 1939. 11 reels – 1 – uk British Libr Newspaper [072]

NT – (See also: New Times) – v8-. 1976- – 1 – us UMI [073]

NT – v.8-. 1976- – 1 – us UMI [073]

NT TIMES – (1969-1974: 28r. 1981-1996: 128r. Current issues avail on subscription.) – Northern Territory, 1952-1968 – 30r – 1 – at Pascoe [072]

NT TIMES – 1981-84 – 20r – 1 – at Pascoe [072]

NTIS REFERENCE FILES – Years: 1943-1972 – 1,5,6 – us Princeton Micro [010]

THE NTU GOD-NAMES / Wanger, W – (Filmed with: Bibliotheca africana) – Innsbruck: F Rauch, 1927 – us Res Libr [960]

O NU : HEBDOMADARIO CRITICO, HUMURISTICO E NOTICIOSO – Manaos, Amazonas. 23 Abr 1903 – 1,5,6 – bl Biblioteca [072]

NUBIE / Cherubini, S – Paris, Firmin Didot Freres. 1847 – 9 – 5.00 – fr Orientalistes [960]

NUCKOLLS COUNTY HERALD – Nelson, NE. -w. Dec 1892; Dec 1893-Dec 1921; Jan 1924-Oct 1948 – 1 – us NE Hist [071]

NUCKOLLS COUNTY SUN – Nelson, NE. -w. Mar-Jul 1900 – 1 – us NE Hist [071]

NUCLEAR AND CHEMICAL WASTE MANAGEMENT – v. 1-. 1980- – 5,6,9 – us UMI [360]

NUCLEAR AND RELATIVISTIC ASTROPHYSICS AND NUCLIDIC COSMOCHEMISTRY / Kuchowicz, B – 1963-67 – 1,5,9 – 35.00 – us Gordon [530]

NUCLEAR DATA AND LOW ENERGY: NUCLEAR RESEARCH IN ISRAEL / Israel. Prime Minister's Office – By Shimon Yiftah. Apr 1977. 58 p – 9 – 2.00 – is I.T.T.I. [324]

NUCLEAR ENERGY : BASIC DOCUMENTS ON TECHNOLOGICAL, ECONOMIC, ENVIRONMENTAL AND LEGAL ISSUES, 1945-1979 / U.S. Nuclear Regulatory Commission, et al – 1982 – 1 – $2,310.00 – 0-89093-300-6 – us UPA [338]

NUCLEAR ENGINEERING – 1956-60 – 1 – uk Microform Academic [600]

NUCLEAR ENGINEERING AND DESIGN – v1-86 1965-84 – 1,5,6,13 – sz Elsevier [621]

NUCLEAR FUSION – v1-7 1960-67 – 1 – us UMI [621]

NUCLEAR GEOPHYSICS – 1,5,69 – us UMI [550]

NUCLEAR INSTRUMENTS AND METHODS IN PHYSICS RESEARCH – v1-233. 1957-84 – 1,5,6,13 – sz Elsevier [073]

NUCLEAR LAW BULLETIN / Nuclear Regulatory Commission – v1- 1968- – 9 – LLMC 81-902 – us L.L.M.C. [340]

NUCLEAR MEDICINE AND BIOLOGY – v1- 1973- – 5,6,9 – us UMI [616]

NUCLEAR MEDICINE COMMUNICATIONS – (v4-. 1983-. 5,6,9) – v1-. Mar 1980- – 1 – us UMI [073]

NUCLEAR PHYSICS – (Section A: Nuclear Physics Proper. v90-429. 1956-84. Section B: High Energy Physics. v1-247.1967-84) – 1,5,6,13 – sz Elsevier [073]

NUCLEAR PHYSICS – v1-89. 1956-66 – 1,5,6,13 – sz Elsevier [073]

NUCLEAR PHYSICS NEWS / ed by Koerner, Gabriele-Elisabeth – 1,5,9 – us Gordon [530]

NUCLEAR POWER – 1956-59 – 1 – uk Microform Academic [073]

NUCLEAR POWER – v1-8. May 1956-Apr 1963. Continued as: Nuclear Engineering International – 1 – us UMI [621]

Nuclear Regulatory Commission *see* NUCLEAR LAW BULLETIN

NUCLEAR REGULATORY COMMISSION ANNUAL REPORTS – (Lacking: 1975-78. 1984 and vols after 1985) – 1979-82; 1985 – 14mf – 9 – $21.00 – LLMC 95-021 – us L.L.M.C. [340]

NUCLEAR REGULATORY COMMISSION OPINIONS AND DECISIONS / U.S. Nuclear Regulatory Commission – (Includes issuances Jul 1987-June 1994 (v39). With cumulative index/digest for 1980-90. Lacking: v23-25 + index for v32) – v1-22. 1975-85 – 472mf – 9 – $708.00 – LLMC 80-512 – us L.L.M.C. [340]

NUCLEAR REGULATORY COMMISSION OPINIONS AND DECISIONS *see* NUCLEAR REGULATORY COMMISSION ANNUAL REPORTS

NUCLEAR SAFETY – v1- 1959- 1; v12- 5,6; v16- 9 – us UMI [621]

NUCLEAR SCIENCE ABSTRACTS – v1-33 1948-76 1; v15-33 1961-76 5,6 – us UMI [530]

NUCLEAR SCIENCE ABSTRACTS – (Indexes only). v. 1-33. 1948-76 – 1,5,6 – us Princeton Micro [530]

NUCLEAR SCIENCE ABSTRACTS – v. 1-33. 1947-1976 – 1,5,6 – us Princeton Micro [530]

NUCLEAR SCIENCE ABSTRACTS *see* ABSTRACTS OF DECLASSIFIED DOCUMENTS

NUCLEAR SCIENCE APPLICATIONS: SECTIONS A AND B – 1983- – 1,5,9 – us Harwood [530]

NUCLEAR TECHNIQUES FOR INCREASED FOOD PRODUCTION – 1969 – 76p – it F.A.O. [338]

NUCLEAR TRACKS AND RADIATION MEASUREMENTS – v1- 1977- – 5,6,9 – us UMI [530]

NUCLEAR TRACKS: METHODS, INSTRUMENTS AND APPLICATIONS – v.1- 1977- – 5,6,9 – us UMI [073]

NUCLEAR WEAPONS, ARMS CONTROL, AND THE THREAT OF THERMONUCLEAR WAR : SPECIAL STUDIES / ed by Kesaris, Paul – (Basic Set 1969-81 17r $1,965.00 ISBN 0-89093-494-0. 1st suppl 1981-82 9r $1,040.00 ISBN 0-89093-568-8. 2nd suppl 1983-84 12r $1,385.00 ISBN 0-89093-570-X. 3rd suppl 1985-86 7r $810.00 ISBN 0-89093-992-6. 4th suppl 1987-88 10r $1,160.00 ISBN 1-55655-109-6. 5th suppl 1989-90 12r $1,500.00 ISBN 1-55655-385-4. 6th suppl 1991-92 12r $1,500.00 ISBN 1-55655-466-4. 7th suppl 1993-95 12r $1,500.00 ISBN 1-55655-539-3. All pts with printed guides) – 1982 – 1 – us UPA [327]

O NUCLEO : ORGAO DO NUCLEO AMAZONENSE DE TRETAS – Manaos, Amazonas. 12 Fev 1907 – 1,5,6 – bl Biblioteca [072]

UN NUCLEO DE NETERRAMIENTOS ROMANOS EN LA CAMPINA DE MERIDA / Alvarez y Saenz de Buruaga, Jose – Zaragoza, 1951 – 1 – sp Bibl Santa Ana [946]

NUCLEONICS – v1-25 1947-67 1; v25- 5,6 – us UMI [530]

NUCLEOSIDES & NUCLEOTIDES – (1984-. 5,6,9) – v1-. 1982- – 1 – us UMI [073]

NUCLEUS EMBLEMATUM SELECTISSIMORUM / Rollenhagen, G – O 414. 1611-1613 – 9 – ne IDC [760]

NUCLEUS TOTIUS MEDICINAE QUINQUE PARTITUS (AEL, ABT 3;11) / Ernsting, Arthur Conrad – Helmstaedt, 1741 (mf ed 1994) – 24mf – 9 – DM560.00 – 3-89131-179-6 – gw Fischer [610]

NUCOM 4 / National Library of Australia – 1980-89 – 9 – A$100.00 – at Nat'l Libr [020]

NUCOM 5 / National Library of Australia – Cumulative annual with suppl – 9 – A$100.00y – at Nat'l Libr [020]

NUCOM 6 : NATIONAL UNION CATALOGUE OF MONOGRAPHS ON NATIONAL BIBLIOGRAPHIC DATABASE – (Semi-annual; March 1994-) – Canberra: National Library of Australia, 1994 – 2 sets – 9 – A$140.00y – at Nat'l Libr [020]

NUE ERFUMDESE UND GRUNDLICHE ANWEISUNG... / Heinichen, J D – Hamburg: Benjamin Schiller, 1711 – 5mf – 9 – us Sibley [780]

NUE VUE *see* THE MITRE

NUERNBERG TRIALS RECORDS : REGISTER CARDS TO THE NG DOCUMENT SERIES, 1946-1949 – M1278 – 3r – $69.00 – us Nat'l Archives [340]

NUERNBERG TRIALS RECORDS : REGISTER CARDS TO THE NI DOCUMENT SERIES, 1946-1949 – M1397 – 8r – $184.00 – us Nat'l Archives [340]

NUERNBERG TRIALS RECORDS : REGISTER CARDS TO THE NOKW DOCUMENT SERIES, 1946-1949 – M1291 – 2r – $46.00 – us Nat'l Archives [340]

DER "NUERNBERGER AERZTEPROZESS" 1946/47 : WORTPROTOKOLLE, ANKLAGE- UND VERTEIDIGUNGSDOKUMENTE / Linne, Karsten; ed by Hamburger Stiftung fuer Sozialgeschichte des 20. Jahrhunderts – 1997/98 – ca 307mf (1:24) + guide – 9 – diazo ca DM3,980.00 (silver ca DM4,600.00 ISBN: 3-598-32031-3) – 3-598-32020-5 – gw Saur [943]

NUERNBERGER ANZEIGER – Nuernberg, feb 4 1971-jan 7 1997 – 50r – 1 – gw Mikrofilm [072]

NUERNBERGER KURIER – Nuernberg, Germany. Jan-Jun 1848; Jan-9 Oct 1849 – 2r – 1 – gw Mikrofilm [072]

NUERNBERGER NACHRICHTEN : AUSGABE A – Nuernberg, oct 1-31 1966; 1971-87 – 1 – gw Mikrofilm [072]

NUERNBERGER NACHRICHTEN : AUSGABE B – Nuernberg, apr 1 1971-96 – 1 – gw Mikrofilm [072]

NUERNBERGER NACHRICHTEN – Nuernberg, West Germany. 11 Oct 1945-1947; 1950-1960; 1968- – ca 11r per yr – 1 – gw Mikrofilm [072]

NUERNBERGER NACHRICHTEN *see* FUERTHER NACHRICHTEN

NUERNBERGER PROZESSE : TRIALS OF WAR CRIMINALS BEFORE THE NUERNBERG MILITARY TRIBUNAL UNDER CONTROL COUNCIL LAW NO. 10 – Washington D.C. 15v. 1950-53 – 215mf – 9 – subsc: DM1,500.00 diazo DM1,750.00 silver – gw Olms [340]

NUERNBERGER RATSVERLAESSE UEBER KUNST UND KUENSTLER IM ZEITALTER DER SPAETGOTIK UND RENAISSANCE (1449)1474-1618 (1633) / Hampe, Th – O-517z – 9 – ne IDC [700]

DIE NUERNBERGER REISE / Hesse, Hermann – Berlin: S Fischer, 1928, c1927 – 1r – 1 – us U.W. Library [920]

NUERNBERGER TAGBLATT – Nuernberg, Germany. Jul-Dec 1848 – 1r – 1 – gw Mikrofilm [072]

NUERNBERGER ZEITUNG – Nuernberg, West Germany. 1976- – ca 12r per yr – 1 – gw Mikrofilm [072]

NUERNBERGISCHES GELEHRTEN-LEXICON / Will, Georg Andreas – Nuernberg und Altdorf, 1755-1808. Hildesheim, 1983 – 52mf – 9 – DM350.00 diazo DM410.00 silver – gw Olms [430]

NUERTINGER KREISNACHRICHTEN – Nuertingen, Germany. 4 Mar 1950-1960 – 22r – 1 – gw Mikrofilm [072]

NUERTINGER ZEITUNG – Nuertingen, West Germany. 1978- – ca 7r per yr – 1 – gw Mikrofilm [072]

NUESTRA CONTRIBUCION A LA PAZ DE LA PATRIA : DECLARACION EPISCOPAL DENUNCIANDO LA PERSECUCION RELIGIOSA EN LA ARGENTINA – [Buenos Aires, 1955] – 1 – CSUXAHZ3531-B – us Hoover Inst Photo [240]

NUESTRA CUESTION DE LIMITES CON LAS REPUBLICAS DEL ECUADOR Y COLOMBIA / Angulo y Puente-Arnao, J – Lima, 1908 – 2mf – 9 – ILM-2537/1 – ne IDC [340]

NUESTRA INDUSTRIA-REVISTA ECONOMICA – Havana. Jun 1963-Aug 1967 – 1 – 35.00r – us Hoover Inst Photo [072]

NUESTRA OPCION POR EL PERONISMO / Concatti, Rolando – [Buenos Aires]: Sacerdotes para el Tercer Mundo–Mendoza, 2nd ed [1972] – 1 – CSUXADL6991-B – us Hoover Inst Photo [320]

NUESTRA ORGANIZACION Y NUESTROS CUADROS: J. S. U. DE ESPANA / Alvarez, Segis – Valencia, 1937? Fiche W 712. (Blodgett Collection of Spanish Civil War Pamphlets) – 9 – us H.U. College Libr [946]

NUESTRA SENORA DE FATIMA / Gallardo de Alvarez, Isabel – Madrid: Sociedad de Educacion. Atenas S.A., 1948 – 1 – sp Bibl Santa Ana [946]

NUESTRA SENORA DE LA ESTRELLA / Manzano Garias, A – Los Santos de Maimona: Imp. Los Santos, 1946 – 1 – sp Bibl Santa Ana [946]

NUESTRA SENORA DE LAS CRUCES. TRADICION – 1852 – 9 – 1.50f – sp Bibl Santa Ana [946]

NUESTRA SENORA DE LOURDES / Lasserre, Enrique; ed by Bayle, Constantino – Madrid: Razon y Fe, 1928 – 9 – sp Bibl Santa Ana [240]

NUESTRAS MALVINAS, UN VIAJE DE ESTUDIOS Y OBSERVACION... / Moreno, Juan Carlos – Madrid: Razon y Fe, 1940 – 1 – sp Bibl Santa Ana [946]

NUESTRO CONCEPTO DE LA RAZON...SANTO TOMAS DE AQUINO / Romero de Castilla, Tomas – 1881 – 9 – $1.50f – sp Bibl Santa Ana [240]

NUESTRO CONCEPTO DE LA RAZON...SANTO TOMAS DE AQUINO / Romero de Castilla, Tomas – 1883 – 9 – $1.50f – sp Bibl Santa Ana [180]

NUESTRO DOMINIO FLUVIAL... / Carbajal, C – Montevideo, 1937 – 2mf – 1 – ILM-2113/1 – ne IDC [327]

NUESTRO PROGRAMA DE RECONSTRUCCION POR GASTON LEVAL (PSEUD.); CONFERENCIA PRONUNCIADA EN EL CINE COLISEUM DE BARCELONA, EL DIA 10 DE ENERO DE 1937 / Piller, Pedro R – Barcelona, 1937. Fiche W1108. (Blodgett Collection of Spanish Civil War Pamphlets) – 9 – us H.U. College Libr [946]

NUESTROS CORSARIOS 1. BROWN Y BOUCHARD EN EL PACIFICO, 1815-1816 / Cailler-Bois, Ricardo – Buenos Aires, 1930 – 1 – sp Bibl Santa Ana [910]

NUESTROS HERMANOS, LOS CAMPESINOS / Uribe, Vicente – Valencia? 1937? Fiche W1241. (Blodgett Collection of Spanish Civil War Pamphlets) – 9 – us H.U. College Libr [946]

NUESTROS LIMITES CON LA REPUBLICA DEL ECUADOR / Angulo y Puente-Arnao, J – Lima, 1905 – 2mf – 9 – ILM-2538/1 – ne IDC [340]

NUESTROS NINOS – 1924. 212p – 1 – 7.42 – us Baptist [240]

NUETZLICHES UNTERHALTUNGS- UND WOCHENBLATT FUER VERSCHIEDENE LESER *see* ANZEIGER VOM OBERLAND

LA NUEVA – Tijuana, MX. 1986 – 1r – $50.00 – R04226 – us Library Micro [072]

NUEVA ARGENTINA – (Includes c.1: v.9:no.85 1944:Dec.- v.10:no.98/100 (1946:Jan./Mar.)) – 1 – CSUXAJA8066-S – us Hoover Inst Photo [972]

UNA NUEVA ARGENTINA / Bunge, Alejandro Ernesto – Buenos Aires: G. Kraft ltda., 1940 – 1 – CSUXADP8835-B – us Hoover Inst Photo [947]

LA NUEVA CONQUISTA DE LA AMERICA ESPANOLA / Bayle, Constantino – Madrid: Razon y Fe, 1925 – 1 – sp Bibl Santa Ana [972]

NUEVA DISPOSICION Y REGIMEN QUE SU EXCELENCIA HA DADO PARA LOS COLEGIOS DE NINAS POBRES. HUERFANAS DE SU VILLA Y TIERRA DE BEJAR EN ESTE ANO DEL SENOR DE MIL SETECIENTOS Y VEINTICINCO / Bejar, Duque de – s.l., s.i., s.a. – 1 – sp Bibl Santa Ana [946]

NUEVA ECONOMIA NACIONAL – Madrid. Spain. -w. 30 Oct 1941-18 Oct 1945. (7 reels) – 1 – uk British Libr Newspaper [330]

LA NUEVA ESPANA AGRARIA – Bilbao, 1937. Fiche W1084. (Blodgett Collection of Spanish Civil War Pamphlets) – 9 – us H.U. College Libr [946]

NUEVA FASE DE LA COMPANA / Bayle, Constantino – Madrid: Razon y Fe, 1931 – 1 – sp Bibl Santa Ana [946]

NUEVA FASE DE UNA CAMPANA : LA EDUCACION POPULAR EN AMERICA / Bayle, Constantino – Madrid: Razon y Fe, 1932 – 1 – sp Bibl Santa Ana [370]

NUEVA FIGURACION DEL RAYO LUMINOSO PARA MEJOR EXPLICAR LA POLIZACION ROTATORIA POR... / Sanchez Rodrigo, Angel – Serradilla: Tip. El Cronista, s.a. (1921?) – 1 – sp Bibl Santa Ana [946]

NUEVA FILOSOFIA DE LA NATURALEZA DEL HOMBRE / Sabuco, M – Madrid, 1587 – 13mf – 9 – sp Cultura [610]

NUEVA GEOGRAFICA DE COLOMBIA / Vergara y Velasco, Francisco J – Bogota: Vapor, 1901 – 1 – F577.82 – fr Armell [910]

NUEVA GRAMATICA TAGALOG.TEORICO-PRACTICA / Coria, Joaquin de – 1872 – 9 – 1.50f – sp Bibl Santa Ana [490]

NUEVA IDEA PHYSICA NATURAL DEMOSTRATIVA, ORIGEN DE LAS MATERIAS QUE MUEVEN LAS COSAS / Juanini, J – Zaragoza, 1685 – 7mf – 9 – sp Cultura [530]

NUEVA IMAGEN DE SAN PEDRO DE ALCANTARA EN CACERES – Madrid: Graf. Calleja, 1967 – 1 – sp Bibl Santa Ana [240]

NUEVA INSCRIPCION ROMANA DE SANTA AMALIA / Fita, Fidel – Madrid: Fortanet, 1912. B.R.A.H. LX, pp. 233-247 – sp Bibl Santa Ana [946]

NUEVA INSCRIPCION ROMANA DE VILLAMESIAS... / Roso de Luna, Mario – Madrid: Fortanet, 1913. B.R.A.H. 63, p. 570 – sp Bibl Santa Ana [946]

NUEVA INSCRIPCION ROMANA DEL ESCURIAL (TRUJILLO) / Roso de Luna, Mario – Madrid: Est. Tip. Fortanet, 1914. B.R.A.H. Tomo 64, 1914, pp. 246 – 1 – sp Bibl Santa Ana [946]

LA NUEVA LAPIDA ROMANA DE IBAHERNANDO / Sanguino y Michel, Juan – Madrid: Fortanet, 1904. B.R.A.H. 44, 1904, p. 524 – sp Bibl Santa Ana [920]

NUEVA LAPIDA ROMANA DE IBAHERNANDO / Sanguino y Michel, Juan – Madrid: Fortanet, 1904. B.R.A.H. 44, 1904, p. 424 00100103 – sp Bibl Santa Ana [946]

NUEVA LAPIDA ROMANA DE MERIDA / Monsalud, Marques de – Madrid: Fortanet, 1896. pp. 429-430. Boletin de la Real Academia de la Historia, 28, 1896 – 1 – sp Bibl Santa Ana [946]

NUEVA LAPIDA ROMANA DE MONTANCHEZ, CAPITAL DE PARTIDO EN LA PROVINCIA DE CACERES / Codera, Francisco – Madrid: Fortanet, 1915. B.R.A.H. lxvi/pp. 577-582 – 1 – sp Bibl Santa Ana [946]

NUEVA LAPIDA ROMANA DEL ESCURIAL (TRUJILLO) / Fita, Fidel – Madrid: Fortanet, 1912. B.R.A.H. 60, pp. 158-161 – sp Bibl Santa Ana [946]

NUEVA LAPIDA ROMANA EN SERRADILLA (CACERES) / Fita, Fidel – Madrid: Fortanet, 1916. B.R.A.H. lxviii/pp. 282-284 – 1 – sp Bibl Santa Ana [946]

NUEVA PRESENCIA – Buenos Aires, Argentina. Nov 10 1978-Dec 20 1980; Jan 1-Dec 11 1981; May 21 1982-1990 – 14r – 1 – us L of C Photodup [072]

NUEVA RECONQUISTA DE ESPANA. VALLADOLID, 1938 / Rodriguez, Teodoro – Burgos: Razon y Fe, 1938 – 1 – sp Bibl Santa Ana [946]

NUEVA REVISTA CUBANA – Havana. v1-2. 1959-62 – 1r – 1 – us Ross [073]

NUEVA SELECCION DE LECTURAS FRANCESAS / Guzman y Martinez, Jesus – Madrid: Talleres Poligraficos, 1922 – 1 – sp Bibl Santa Ana [440]

LA NUEVA UNION – Plasencia, 1907-1912 – 5 – sp Bibl Santa Ana [073]

NUEVA Y VARIA DECISION SI SE PUEDE POR LOS CADAVERES CONOCER SI HA MUERTO...DE VENENOS... / Murillo y Velarde Jurado, T – SL, SA: 1675 – 3mf – 9 – sp Cultura [614]

NUEVAS ACTAS CAPITULARES DE LA PROVINCIA DES CALZA DE SAN GABRIEL (1621-1644) / Barrado Manzano, Arcangel – Madrid: Archivo Ibero-Americano, 1961 – 1 – sp Bibl Santa Ana [946]

NUEVAS APORTACIONES AL ESTUDIO DE LA NECROPOLIS ORIENTAL DE MERIDA / Alvarez Saenz de Buruaga, Jose & Garcia de Soto, Jesus – Madrid, 1946 – 1 – sp Bibl Santa Ana [946]

NUEVAS ARAS FUNERARIAS EN JEREZ DE LOS CABALLEROS / Naval, Francisco – Madrid: Tip. Arch., Bibl. y Mus, 1930. B.R.A.H. 97, pp. 836-845, 2 lam – sp Bibl Santa Ana [946]

NUEVAS BASES Y PRINCIPIOS PARA LA REORGANIZACION POLITICA DE LA REPUBLICA ARGENTINA, MADRID, NUEVA YORK, 1951-1953 / Arce, Jose – Buenos Aires: Editoriales Reunidas, 1956 – 1 – CSUXAGP9560-B – us Hoover Inst Photo [320]

NUEVAS CASTELLANAS / Gabriel y Galan, Jose Maria – Salamanca: Imp. y Lib. Francisco Nunez, vol 3. 1905 – 1 – sp Bibl Santa Ana [946]

NUEVAS CONSIDERACIONES SOBRE LA LIBERTAD ABSOLUTA DE COMERCIO Y PUERTOS FRANCOS... / Gutierrez, M – Madrid, 1839 – 17mf – 9 – sp Cultura [380]

NUEVAS ELEGIAS / Moreno Torrado, Luis – 1894 – 9 – 1.50f – sp Bibl Santa Ana [810]

NUEVAS ESCULTURAS ZOOMORFAS PREHISTORICAS EN EXTREMADURA / Ramon y Fernandez, Jose – Barcelona, 1950 – 1 – sp Bibl Santa Ana [946]

NUEVAS INSCRIPCIONES CRISTIANAS DE EXTREMADURA Y ANDALUCIA (MERIDA, LA PUEBLA DEL PRIOR Y SEVILLA) / Monsalud, Marques de – Madrid: Fortanet, 1900. B.R.A.H. 36, 1900, pp. 518-520 – sp Bibl Santa Ana [946]

NUEVAS INSCRIPCIONES DE EXTREMADURA (MERIDA Y TORREMEJIA) / Monsalud, Marques de – Madrid: Fortanet, 1900. B.R.A.H. 37, 1900, pp. 488-491 – sp Bibl Santa Ana [946]

NUEVAS INSCRIPCIONES DE EXTREMADURA Y ANDALUCIA : ALBURQUERQUE, BADAJOZ, BURGUILLOS, MEDINA DE LAS TORRES, REINA, CASAS DE REINA, ALANJE, ECIJA / Monsalud, Marques de – Madrid: Est. Tip. Fortanet, 1898. B.R.A.H. 33, 1898, pp. 150-160 – 1 – sp Bibl Santa Ana [946]

NUEVAS INSCRIPCIONES DE IBAHERNANDO / Monsalud, Marques de – Caceres: Tip. Enc. Lib. Jimenez, 1902 – 1 – sp Bibl Santa Ana [946]

NUEVAS INSCRIPCIONES DE IBAHERNANDO, CUMBRE Y SANTA ANA / Roso de Luna, Mario – Caceres: Tip. Enc. y Lib. de Jimenez, 1903 – 1 – sp Bibl Santa Ana [946]

NUEVAS INSCRIPCIONES DE IBAHERNANDO, CUMBRE Y SANTA ANA / Roso de Luna, Mario – Madrid: Fortanet, 1903. B.R.A.H. 42, 1903, pp. 232-235 – sp Bibl Santa Ana [946]

NUEVAS INSCRIPCIONES DE MERIDA Y SEVILLA / Fita, Fidel – Madrid: Tip. Fortanet, 1914. B.R.A.H. LIV, pp. 236-242 – sp Bibl Santa Ana [946]

NUEVAS INSCRIPCIONES EXTREMENAS / Paredes Guillen, Vicente – Caceres: Tip. Enc. y Lib. de Jimenez, 1902 – 1 – sp Bibl Santa Ana [946]

NUEVAS INSCRIPCIONES ROMANAS : JEREZ DE LOS CABALLEROS, LA MORERA, ALMENDRALEJO / Monsalud, Marques de – Madrid: Establec. Tip. Fortanet, 1897. B.R.A.H. 30, 1897, pp. 415-422 – 1 – sp Bibl Santa Ana [946]

NUEVAS INSCRIPCIONES ROMANAS : VALVERDE DE BURGUILLOS, MERIDA / Monsalud, Marques de – Madrid: Est. Tip. Fortanet, 1898. B.R.A.H. 32, 1898, pp. 364-366 – 1 – sp Bibl Santa Ana [946]

NUEVAS INSCRIPCIONES ROMANAS (CORIA, GIJON) / Fita, Fidel – Madrid: Fortanet, 1905. B.R.A.H. XLVI, pp. 76-81 – sp Bibl Santa Ana [946]

NUEVAS INSCRIPCIONES ROMANAS DE EXTREMADURA : BADAJOZ, MERIDA, RIBERA DEL FRESNO, VILLAFRANCA DE LOS BARROS, CASTUERA / Monsalud, Marques de – Madrid: Est. Tip. Fortanet, 1898. B.R.A.H. 32, 1898, pp. 149-153 – 1 – sp Bibl Santa Ana [946]

NUEVAS INSCRIPCIONES ROMANAS DE EXTREMADURA. MALPARTIDA DE LA SERENA, ESPARRAGOSA DE LA SERENA, MERIDA / Monsalud, Marques de – Madrid: Est. Tip. Fortanet, 1899. B.R.A.H. 34, 1899, pp. 133-138 – sp Bibl Santa Ana [946]

NUEVAS INSCRIPCIONES ROMANAS DE EXTREMADURA. (MERIDA E IBAHERNANDO) / Monsalud, Marques de – Madrid: Fortanet, 1900. B.R.A.H. 36, 1900, pp. 5-13 – sp Bibl Santa Ana [946]

NUEVAS INSCRIPCIONES ROMANAS DE EXTREMADURA (VILLAMIEL, MERIDA Y HORNACHOS) / Monsalud, Marques de – Madrid: Fortanet, 1900. B.R.A.H. 37, 1900, pp. 322-325 – sp Bibl Santa Ana [946]

NUEVAS INSCRIPCIONES ROMANAS DE EXTREMADURA Y ANDALUCIA (MEDELLIN, VILLAFRANCA DE LOS BARROS E ITALICA) / Monsalud, Marques de – Madrid: Fortanet, 1899, pp. 415-422. B.R.A.H. 34, 1899 – 1 – sp Bibl Santa Ana [946]

NUEVAS INSCRIPCIONES ROMANAS DE IBAHERNANDO / Fita, Fidel – Madrid: Tip. de Fortanet, 1900 – sp Bibl Santa Ana [946]

NUEVAS INSCRIPCIONES ROMANAS DE LA REGION NORBENSE / Roso de Luna, Mario – Madrid: Est. Tip. Fortanet, 1905. B.R.A.H. Tomo 47, 1905, pp. 60-71 – 1 – sp Bibl Santa Ana [946]

NUEVAS INSCRIPCIONES ROMANAS DE LA REGION NORBENSE / Roso de Luna, Mario – Madrid: Fortanet,1904. B.R.A.H. 44, 1904, pp. 113-137 – sp Bibl Santa Ana [946]

NUEVAS INSCRIPCIONES ROMANAS DE MERIDA / Fita, Fidel – Madrid: Fortanet, 1909. B.R.A.H. 55, pp. 363-365 – sp Bibl Santa Ana [946]

NUEVAS INSCRIPCIONES ROMANAS DE MERIDA / Monsalud, Marques de – Madrid: Fortanet, 1899. pp. 518-523. B.R.A.H. 34, 1899 – 1 – sp Bibl Santa Ana [946]

NUEVAS INSCRIPCIONES ROMANAS EN EXTREMADURA. (MERIDA Y ALANGE) / Monsalud, Marques de – Madrid: Est. Tip., 1907. B.R.A.H. Tomo 50, 1907, 357-358 – 1 – sp Bibl Santa Ana [946]

NUEVAS INSCRIPCIONES ROMANAS Y VISIGOTICAS / Fita, Fidel – Madrid: Tip. de Fortanet, 1897 – sp Bibl Santa Ana [946]

NUEVAS INSCRIPCIONES ROMANAS Y VISIGOTICAS DE EXTREMADURA : MERIDA, ALMENDRAL, ACEUCHAL / Monsalud, Marques de – Madrid: Est. Tip. Fortanet, 1901. B.R.A.H. 38, 1901, p. 474-477 – sp Bibl Santa Ana [946]

NUEVAS INSCRIPCIONES ROMANAS Y VISIGOTICAS DE EXTREMADURA (MERIDA, FERIA, Y SALVATIERRA DE LOS BARROS) / Monsalud, Marques de – Madrid: Fortanet, 1903. B.R.A.H. 43, 1903, pp. 240-250 – sp Bibl Santa Ana [946]

NUEVAS INSCRIPCIONES ROMANAS Y VISIGOTICAS DE EXTREMADURA (MERIDA, SOLANA DE LOS BARROS, Y LA ALCONERA) / Monsalud, Marques de – Madrid: Est. Tip. Fortanet, 1906. B.R.A.H. tomo 48, 1906, pp. 485-491 – 1 – sp Bibl Santa Ana [946]

NUEVAS INSCRIPCIONES ROMANAS Y VISIGOTICAS DE TALAVAN Y MERIDA / Fita, Fidel – Madrid: Tip. Fortanet, 1914. B.R.A.H. LIV, pp. 304-313 – sp Bibl Santa Ana [946]

NUEVAS INSCRIPCIONES ROMANAS Y VISIGOTICAS. MERIDA / Monsalud, Marques de – Madrid: Est. Tip. Fortanet, 1897. B.R.A.H. 31, 1897, pp. 391-404 – sp Bibl Santa Ana [946]

NUEVAS INSCRIPCIONES VISIGOTICAS DE EXTREMADURA (MERIDA Y ALANJE-SIC) / Monsalud, Marques de – Madrid: Fortanet, 1899, pp. 222-225. B.R.A.H. 35, 1899 – 1 – sp Bibl Santa Ana [946]

NUEVAS INSCRIPTIONES ROMANAS DE EXTREMADURA : MERIDA, IBAHERNANDO / Monsalud, Marques de – Madrid: Tip. Fortanet, 1902. B.R.A.H. 40, 1902, pp.541-546 – sp Bibl Santa Ana [946]

NUEVAS LAPIDAS ROMANAS DE EXTREMADURA : FERIA, MERIDA, SANTA AMALIA, MALPARTIDA DE LA SERENA / Monsalud, Marques de – Madrid: Est. Tip. Fortanet, 1897. B.R.A.H. 31, 1897, pp. 436-442 – sp Bibl Santa Ana [946]

NUEVAS LAPIDAS ROMANAS DE EXTREMADURA (IBAHERNANDO, ARROYO DEL PUERCO Y ALISEDA) / Monsalud, Marques de – Madrid: Fortanet, 1903. B.R.A.H. 43, 1903, pp. 528-535 – sp Bibl Santa Ana [946]

NUEVAS LAPIDAS ROMANAS DE NOYA, CANDO, CEREZO Y JUMILLA / Fita, Fidel – Madrid: Fortanet, 1911. B.R.A.H. LIX, pp. 398-417 – sp Bibl Santa Ana [946]

NUEVAS LAPIDAS ROMANAS DE SANTISTEBAN DEL PUERTO, BERLANGA (BADAJOZ), AVILA Y RETORTILLO (SALAMANCA) / Fita, Fidel – Madrid: Fortanet, 1913. B.R.A.H. 62. pp. 529-545 – 1 – sp Bibl Santa Ana [946]

NUEVAS LAPIDAS ROMANAS DE TARRAGONA, PALENCIA, SALVARIERRA DE LOS BARROS BAEZA Y NAVA DE MENA / Fita, Fidel – Madrid: Tip. de Fortanet, 1895 – 1 – sp Bibl Santa Ana [946]

NUEVAS LAPIDAS VISIGOTICAS : MERIDA, LA PUEBLA DE SANCHO PEREZ / Monsalud, Marques de – Madrid: Est. Tip. Fortanet, 1898. B.R.A.H. 32, 1898, pp. 433-435 – 1 – sp Bibl Santa Ana [946]

NUEVAS NOTAS SOBRE EL CONDADO DE LA GOMERA / Siete Iglesias, Antonio de & Montero de Espinosa, Marques de – Madrid, s.i., 1956 – 1 – sp Bibl Santa Ana [920]

NUEVAS POESIAS SERIAS / Salas, Francisco Gregorio de – 1775 – 9 – 1.50f – sp Bibl Santa Ana [810]

NUEVAS UTILIDADES DE LA QUINA / Alsinet, J – Madrid, 1774 – 4mf – 9 – sp Cultura [615]

NUEVAS Y RARAS OBSERVACIONES PARA DIAGNOSTICAR CRISIS POR EL PULSO... / Roche, J – Puerto de Santa Maria, 1761 – 8mf – 9 – sp Cultura [616]

LAS NUEVE LAMENTACIONES...SEMANA SANTA / Salas, Francisco Gregorio de – 1773 – 9 – $1.50f – sp Bibl Santa Ana [810]

LOS NUEVE LIBROS DE LOS EXEMPLOS MORALES DE VALERIO MAXIMO TRADUCIDOS POR DIEGO LOPEZ / Lopez, Diego – Madrid: Imp. Real, 1654 – 1 – sp Bibl Santa Ana [170]

NUEVE MESES DE ACTUACION DE LA CORPORACION MUNICIPAL DE ALJUCEN / Prieto Gonzalvez, Pedro – Badajoz: Edicion Patrocinada pro Org. Oficiales. Emp. Ex, 1955 – 1 – sp Bibl Santa Ana [350]

NUEVO CANTORAL DE LOS FIELES / Parroquia de San Jose – Caceres: Ed. Extremadura, 1975 – 1 – sp Bibl Santa Ana [240]

EL NUEVO DERECHO SOCIAL ARGENTINO : [DISCURSOS PRONUNCIADOS POR S.E. EL SENOR INTERVENTOR DE LA PROVINCIA DE BUENOS AIRES, DOCTOR JUAN ATILIO BRAMUGLIA: LA PLATA, ABRIL DE 1945 / Bramuglia, Juan Atilio – [La Plata, Argentina: s.n., 1945?] – 1 – CSUXADJ0057-B – us Hoover Inst Photo [340]

NUEVO DESCUBRIMIENTO DEL GRAN RIO DE LAS AMAZONAS / Acuna, Cristobal de – 9 – 1.50f – sp Bibl Santa Ana [972]

NUEVO DIA – Caceres, 1926-1932 – 5 – sp Bibl Santa Ana [073]

NUEVO DIARIO DE BADAJOZ – Badajoz, 1893-1906, 1908-1913 y 1917-1923 – 5 – sp Bibl Santa Ana [072]

EL NUEVO DON JUAN / Lopez de Ayala, Adelardo – 1863 – 9 – $1.50f – sp Bibl Santa Ana [820]

EL NUEVO HUMANISMO / Frutos Cortes, Eugenio – Badajoz: Dip. Provincial, 1970 – sp Bibl Santa Ana [946]

Nuevo Leon. Mexico (State) *see* PERIODICO OFICIAL-GOBIERNO CONSTITUCIONAL DEL ESTADO LIBRE Y SOBERANO DE NUEVO LEON

NUEVO LIBRO DE YERBAS DE CACERES O SEA DESCRIPCION DE TODAS LAS DEHESAS SOTOS... : PROLOGO DE D. DANIEL BERJANO / Villegas, Alfredo – Caceres: Est. Tip. Lib y Enc. de El Noticiero, 1909 – 1 – sp Bibl Santa Ana [946]

NUEVO METODO PARA CURAR FLATOS, HIPOCONDRIAS, VAPORES Y ATAQUES HYSTERICOS... / Alsinet, J – Madrid, 1776 – 7mf – 9 – sp Cultura [610]

NUEVO MUNDO ISRAELITA – (Some nos missing) – Caracas, 1973-1976 – 65mf – 9 – ne IDC [956]

NUEVO NOMENCLATOR DE LAS CIUDADES / Instituto Geografico – Madrid, 1876 – 18mf – 9 – sp Cultura [946]

NUEVO REPERTORIO EPIGRAFICO DE LA PROVINCIA DE CACERES / Callejo Serrano, Carlos – Madrid: Diana Graf, 1972 – 1 – sp Bibl Santa Ana [930]

NUEVO SALTERIO LATINO-ESPANOL / Sanchez Ruiz, Valentin M – Madrid: Apostolado de la Prensa, 1946 – 1 – sp Bibl Santa Ana [240]

NUEVO SALTERIO LATINO-ESPANOL. 2ND EDICION / Sanchez Ruiz, Valentin M – Madrid: Apostolado de la Prensa, 1948 – 1 – sp Bibl Santa Ana [240]

NUEVO SALTERIO LATINO-ESPANOL. VERSION LATINA PROMULGADA POR S.S. PIO 12... / Errandonea, Ignacio & Sanchez Ruiz, Valentin – Madrid: Razon y Fe, 1946 – 1 – sp Bibl Santa Ana [946]

LOS NUEVOS BEATOS MARTIRES DEL PARAGUAY, SIMIENTE DE LAS REDENCIONES / Bayle, Constantino – Madrid: Razon y Fe, 1934 – 1 – sp Bibl Santa Ana [240]

NUEVOS COLABORADORES. DON JUAN FERNANDEZ Y FERNANDEZ / Revista Espanola de Estudios Biblicos – Malaga: R.E.E.B., 1928 – 1 – sp Bibl Santa Ana [946]

NUEVOS CUENTOS POPULARES / Trueba, Antonio de – 1880 – 1 – us I.U. Libraries [390]

NUEVOS DIALOGOS DE LOS MUERTOS... / Pan Duro, Luciano – Madrid, 1932; Madrid: Razon y Fe, 1933 – 1 – sp Bibl Santa Ana [390]

NUEVOS DOCUMENTOS RELATIVOS A LOS BIENES DE HERNANDO CORTES (1547-1947) – Mexico: Imp. Universitaria, 1946 – sp Bibl Santa Ana [920]

NUEVOS ELEMENTOS DE GEOGRAFIA GENERAL ASTRONOMICA / Garcia, Juan Justo – 1818. 2v – 9 – 1.50f – sp Bibl Santa Ana [520]

NUEVOS HALLAZGOS EN TURMULES / Sanguino y Michel, Juan – Caceres: Tip. Enc. y Lib. Jimenez, 1906 – 1 – sp Bibl Santa Ana [946]
NUEVOS JENEROS I ESPECIES DE PLANTAS PARA LA FLORANEO-GRANADINA / Triana, J J – Bogota. 1854. B-5779 1 – 9 – ne IDC [580]
LOS NUEVOS SANTOS INGLESES / Bayle, Constantino – Madrid: Razon y Fe, 1935 – 1 – sp Bibl Santa Ana [240]
NUGGET – Chehalis. Wash. -w. 1897-98 – 1 – us UMI [071]
NUGGET – Round Mountain, NV. 1 Jun 1906; 1908-10 – 1r – 1 – $50.00 – U04734 – us Library Micro [071]
NU'-GIO'I-CHUNG – Femina annamite. no. 1-22. Saigon. 1er fevr-19 juil 1918 – 1 – fr A.C.R.P.P. [073]
Nugroho, Notosusanto *see*
– ADDRESSES
– THE COUP ATTEMPT OF THE "SEPTEMBER 30 MOVEMENT" IN INDONESIA
Nuh, Muhammad *see*
– KSATRYA DICTIONARY : KAMUS INGGERIS-INDONESIA
– KSATRYA VOCABULARY. KAMUS INGGERIS-INDONESIA, INDONESIA-INGGERIS
NUHBET UEL-TEVARIH VE'L AHBAR / Mehmed, Mehmed ibn – Istanbul: Matba'a-i Amire, 1276 [1859/60] – 6mf – 9 – $98.00 – us MEDOC [949]
NUHUN GEMISI / ed by Uestemir, Nahit – Istanbul: Mizah Gazetesi, Sene 1, sayi 1-31 (1949-1950) – 3mf – 9 – $65.00 – us MEDOC [949]
UNE NUIT DE NOCES, ROMAN INEDIT / Morphy, Michel – Paris: Nouvelle Librairie, A. Soirat, 1886. 126p. (Les Femmes Collection) – 2mf – 9 – $6.00 – fr Bibl Nationale [830]
Nuix, Juan *see* REFLEXIONES SOBRE LA HUMANIDAD DE LOS ESPANOLES EN LAS INDIAS
Nulli, Siro Attilio *see* SHAKESPEARE IN ITALIA
NUMA YA DUA – Yerington, NV. v3 1975-1976. v1 1979-1980 – 2r – 1 – $100.00 – U04906 – us Library Micro [071]
Numa, Yamu *see* THE PRIDE OF URHOBO NATION
NUMANTIA, EINE TOPOGRAPHISCH-HISTORISCHE UNTERSUCHUNG / Schulten, Aolf – Berlin, 1905 – 4mf – 8 – Dfl19.00 – ne Slangenburg [240]
THE NUMBER OF MAN : THE CLIMAX OF CIVILIZATION / Mauro, Philip – New York: Fleming H Revell, 1909 – 1mf – 9 – 0-8370-2397-1 – 1985-0397 – us A.T.L.A. [210]
NUMBER SEVENTEEN / Kingsley, Henry – British Fiction Archive: Unit 2 – 9 – uk Bell [830]
NUMBERED DOCUMENT FILE OF THE ADVISORY COMMISSION TO THE COUNCIL OF NATIONAL DEFENSE, 1940-41 / U.S. War Production Board – 2 rolls. M187. Printed guide – 1 – us Nat'l Archives [324]
NUMBERED DOCUMENT FILE OF THE COUNCIL OF THE OFFICE OF PRODUCTION MANAGEMENT, 1940-42 / U.S. War Production Board – 1roll. M195. Printed guide – 1 – us Nat'l Archives [324]
NUMBERED DOCUMENT FILE OF THE SUPPLY PRIORITIES AND ALLOCATIONS BOARD, SEPT. 2, 1941-JAN. 15, 1942 / U.S. War Production Board – 1roll. M196. Printed guide – 1 – us Nat'l Archives [324]
NUMBERED DOCUMENTS. / U.S. President. Commission on the Assassination of President Kennedy – RG 272. M1124. 42 rolls – 1 – us Nat'l Archives [977]
NUMBERED DOCUMENTS OF THE PRESIDENT'S COMMISSION ON THE ASSASSINATION OF PRESIDENT KENNEDY – 42r – 1 – M1124 – us Nat'l Archives [324]
NUMBERED RECORD BOOKS CONCERNING MILITARY OPERATIONS AND SERVICE, PAY AND SETTLEMENT OF ACCOUNTS, AND SUPPLIES IN THE WAR DEPARTMENT COLLECTION OF REVOLUTIONARY WAR RECORDS / U.S. War Department. Collection of Revolutionary War Records – 41 rolls. M853 – 1 – us Nat'l Archives [324]
NUMBERS IN HISTORY: HOW THE GREEKS DEFEATED THE PERSIANS, THE ROMANS CONQUERED THE WORLD, THE TEUTONS OVERTHREW THE ROMAN EMPIRE, AND WILLIAM THE NORMAN TOOK POSSESSION OF ENGLAND / Delbrueck, Hans – Two lectures delivered before University of London, 6 and 7 October, 1913. London: Holder & Stoughton, 1913. 77p – 1 – us U.W. Library [900]
NUMEN – Leiden. v1-37. 1954-90 – 5,9 – Dfl2,960.00; Dfl80.00v – ne Swets [073]
NUMERI / Holzinger, Heinrich – (Includes subject index) – Tuebingen: J C B Mohr (Paul Siebeck), 1903 – 1mf – 9 – 0-8370-3648-8 – 1985-1648 – us A.T.L.A. [220]
NUMERICAL AND MINOR FILES OF THE DEPARTMENT OF STATE / U.S. Department of State – 1906-10. 1241 rolls. M862 – 1 – us Nat'l Archives [975]
NUMERICAL FUNCTIONAL ANALYSIS AND OPTIMIZATION – (1985-. 5,6,9) – v1-. 1979- – 1 – us UMI [073]
A NUMERICAL LIST OF DRIED SPECIMENS OF PLANTS IN THE EAST INDIA COMPANY'S MUSEUM / Wallich, N – London. 1828-49. B-1049 2 – 8 – ne IDC [580]
NUMERICAL LIST OF PRESIDENTIAL PROCLAMATIONS, 1-2317, 1789-1938 / U.S. Congress – 1r – 1 – M1331 – us Nat'l Archives [324]
NUMERICAL METHODS FOR PARTIAL DIFFERENTIAL EQUATIONS – 1985- – 1,5,6,9 – us UMI [510]
NUMERISCHE MATHEMATIK – v. 1-36. 1959-80 – 1,5,9 – 3456.00 – us UMI [073]
NUMERISCHE SIMULATION DER PARTIKELBEWEGUNG IN EINEM INSTATIONAEREN STROEMUNGSFELD / Maleki-Ardebili, Mansour – 1994 – 2mf – DM80.00 – 3-8267-2058-X – gw Hänsel [620]
NUMEROUS CASES OF SURGICAL OPERATIONS WITHOUT PAIN IN THE MESMERIC STATE / Elliotson, J – M-99. 1843 – 9 – ne IDC [150]
NUMERUS FIGURATUS: SIVE, ARITHMETICA ANALYTICA, NOUA, IN AUDITA, & MIRABILI ARTE CONSTANS – s.l.: s.n., 1614?. Filmed with Faulhaber, Johann. Arithmetischer Tausendkunstler. Ulm, 1762 and Newe geometrische und perspectiuische Inventiones...Frankfurt am Mayn, 1610 – 1 – us U.W. Library [510]
DIE NUMINOSE BALLADE : VERSUCH EINER TYPOLOGIE DER BALLADE / Kaempchen, Paul Ludwig – (Includes bibliographical references) – Bonn: L Roehrscheid, 1930 – 1r – 1 – us U.W. Library [780]
NUMISMATIC CHRONICLE AND JOURNAL / The Royal Numismatic Society – v1- 1838-. Superseded by: Numismatic Chronicle – 1,5,6,9 – us UMI [760]
NUMISMATIC FINE ARTS, INC – v1- 1977- – 1,5,6,9 – us UMI [730]
NUMISMATIC NEWS – v1-31 1952-83 – 1 – us Princeton Micro [730]
NUMISMATIC SCRAPBOOK – v1-42 1935-76 1; v37-42 5,6 – us UMI [730]
NUMISMATIQUE JAPONAISE / Villaret, E de – 1892 – 9 – $10.00 – fr Orientalistes [730]
NUMIZMATICHERSKII SBORNIK – Moscow, 1911-15, v1-3. B/1491/2 – 8 – ne IDC [730]
NUMURKAH GUARD AND WUNGHNU OBSERVER – 1884-1885. NGWO1 – 1r – 1 – at Corangamite [072]
NUMURKAH LEADER – 1895-1994 – 62r – 1 – at Corangamite [072]
NUMURKAH SHIRE COMMITTEE MINUTES – 1929-1974. NSCCM1 – 1r – 1 – at Corangamite [910]
NUMURKAH SHIRE COUNCIL MINUTES – 1879-1993 – 16r – 1,5 – at Corangamite [910]
NUMURKAH SHIRE NOTICES OF MOTION – 1957-1979. NSCN1 – 1r – 1 – at Corangamite [910]
NUMURKAH SHIRE SEWERAGE AUTHORITY – 1969-1983. NSCSA1 – 1r – 1 – at Corangamite [910]
Nunciatura Apostolica *see* AUTO Y SENTENCIA EN FAVOR DEL R. PADRE FR. SEBASTIAN DE MORATILLA VICARIO PATERNO DEL MONATERIO DE GUADALUPE...
NUNEATON AND DISTRICT RECORD – England. The Record. -w. 5 March 1907-27 Oct 1908. 1 reel – 1 – uk British Libr Newspaper [072]
NUNEATON CHRONICLE – England. -w. 1868-1956. (72 reels) – 1 – uk British Libr Newspaper [072]
NUNEATON EVENING NEWS *see* MIDLAND DAILY TRIBUNE
NUNEATON EVENING TRIBUNE *see* MIDLAND DAILY TRIBUNE
NUNEATON OBSERVER AND DISTRICT ADVERTISER – England. The Observer & District Advertiser Nuneaton Observer. -w. 9 Nov 1877-Dec 1978. Lacking 1897; July 1959. 116 1 2 reels – 1 – uk British Libr Newspaper [072]
Nunez, A *see*
– PARECER DEL DOCTOR...SOBRE EL GARROTILLO...
– TRATADO REPARTIDO EN CINCO PARTES... (SOBRE)...PESTE...
Nunez Coronado, J *see*
– GRAMATICA FRANCESA
Nunez de Acosta, D *see* TRATADO PRACTICO DE LAS SANGRIAS
NUNEZ DE BALBOA / Gaffarel, Paul – 1882 – 9 – 1.50f – sp Bibl Santa Ana [946]
Nunez de Balboa *see* REAL DECRETO DECLARANDO OFICIAL EL CUARTO CENTENARIO DEL DESCUBRIMIENTO DEL OCEANO PACIFICO Y NOTICIA
NUNEZ DE BALBOA. CONGRESO DE HISTORIA Y GEOGRAFIA HISPANOAMERICANA, CELEBRADO EN SEVILLA / Fita, Fidel & Perez Guzman J – Madrid: Fortanet, 1914. B.R.A.H. 64, p. 556 – sp Bibl Santa Ana [910]
NUNEZ DE BALBOA. EL TESORO DEL DABAIBE / Mendez Pereira, Octavio – Madrid: Ediciones Nuestra Raza, s.a. – 1 – sp Bibl Santa Ana [920]
Nunez de Balboa, Vasco *see*
– CONGRESO DE HISTORIA Y GEOGRAFIA HISPANO-AMERICANAS EN COMMEMORACION DEL DESCUBRIMIENTO DEL MAR PACIFICO POR VASCO NUNEZ DE BALBOA
– REAL DECRETO DE 26 DE MARZO DE 1913 DECLARANDO OFICIAL EL CUARTO CENTENARIO DEL OCEANO PACIFICO
– VASCO NUNEZ DE BALBOA
Nunez de Coria, F *see* AVISO DE SANIDAD QUE TRATA DE TODOS LOS GENEROS DE ALIMENTOS Y DEL REGIMIENTO...
Nunez de Esquivel, G *see* RESPUESTA...AL PAPEL DEL DOCTOR LORENCO DE SAN MILLAN
Nunez de Torres, Juan *see* INSTITUCION... IGLESIA
Nunez Gonzalez, Salvador *see* ETICA ELEMENTAL
Nunez, Pedro C *see* NOVENA A...CHRISTO DE LA BUENA MUERTE
NUNG TSUN CHING CHI CHIN JUNG FA KUEI HUIPIEN / China. Laws, Statutes, etc – A compendium of laws and regulations on agricultural economy and Financing. Chungking, 1942. 1 reel – 1 – 12.10 – us Chinese Res [340]
NUNG TS'UN FU HSING WEI YUAN HUI HUI PAO / China. Commission on Rural Reconstruction of the Executive Yuan – Official bulletin. Nanking. 1933-35. Lacking: v. 2 (1, 5) 1934; v. 2 (10-12) 1935. BCH-1077 1 – 9 – ne IDC [950]
NUNG-HSUEH PAO – (Agriculture Bulletin). v. 1-315. Shanghai. 1897-1905. BCH-803 2 – 8 – ne IDC [630]
NUNG-HSUEH TS'UNG-K'AN / Nanking. National Central University – (Lacking: v3-4 1936-37) – Nanking. 4v. 1933-37. – 9 – BCH-321 1 – ne IDC [630]
NUNGUSIUTTUQ INUUSIQ (THE ETERNAL LIFE) / Antoine, J – A composite translation of the synoptic gospels in dialect of Tarramiut Eskimos. N-464. 1964 – 9 – ne IDC [240]
NUNO BELTRAN DE GUZMAN Y SU OBRA EN LA NUEVA ESPANA / Santana, Jose Epigmeno – Mexico, 1930; Madrid: Razon y Fe, 1932 – 1 – sp Bibl Santa Ana [440]
NUN'S ISLAND TRIBUNE DE L'ILE DES SOEURS : MENSUEL / ed by Dubee, Bernard – Verdun, Canada. n7. avr 1972-n9. jun1972 – 1r – 1 – Can$25.00 – cn Can Microfilming [072]
THE NUNS OF PORT ROYAL : AS SEEN IN THEIR OWN NARRATIVES / Lowndes, Mary E – (Includes bibliographical references and index) – London; New York: Oxford University Press, 1909 – 1mf – 9 – 0-8370-8445-8 – 1986-2445 – us A.T.L.A. [920]
NUOVA DESCRIZIONE DEL VATICANO O SIA DELLA SACROSANTA BASILICA DI S. PIETRO / Chattard, G P – 3v. Roma. 1762-67. BO-957 1 – 9 – ne IDC [700]
NUOVA DOMOVINA – Buenos Aires, Argentina, 1952 – 1mf or 1 reel – 9,1 – us I.H.R.C. [972]
LA NUOVA FRANCIA: ANTICA COLONIA FRANCESE: APPELLO ALLE CLASSI OPERAIE / Bossange, Gustave – Parigi: G. Bossange, 1873. 02838. (Pre-1900 Canadiana) – 9 – cn C.I.H.M. [971]
LE NUOVE LEGGI SUL MATRIMONIO ... / Bosco, G – Roma, 1930 – 1mf – 9 – ILM-3016/1 – ne IDC [327]
NUOVI E NUOVE SPECIE DI PIANTE MONOCOTILEDONI / Parlatore, F – Firenze. 1854. B-6145 2 – 8 – ne IDC [580]
NUOVI STUDI SULLA QUESTIONE DI PAPA LIBERIO / Savio, Fedele – (Includes bibliographical references) – Roma: Federico Pustet, 1909 – 1mf – 9 – 0-8370-8546-2 – 1986-2546 – us A.T.L.A. [240]
NUOVI TEMPI – (Cont by: Confronti) – 1967-89 (complete) – 12r – 1 – ATLA S0635 – us A.T.L.A. [073]
NUOVI TEMPI – Paterson, NJ, 1918 – 1mf or 1r – 1,9 – us I.H.R.C. [978]
NUOVI TEMPI *see* CONFRONTI
IL NUOVO AVANTI – Paris, 1928-40 – 1 – us Hoover Inst Photo [072]
NUOVO BULLETTINO DI ARCHEOLOGIA CHRISTIANA – 1(1895)-28(1922) – 196mf – 8 – ne Slangenburg [240]
NUOVO BULLETTINO DI ARCHEOLOGIA CHRISTIANA – 1(1895)-28(1922) – 192mf – 9 – Dfl672.00 – ne Slangenburg [073]
IL NUOVO CIMENTO – Lettere Al. Series 1. v. 1-4. 1969-70. Series 2. v. 1-5. 1970-72 – 1,5,6 – us Princeton Micro [540]
IL NUOVO CIMENTO – Revista Del Series 1, v. 1-2. 1969-1970 – 1,5,6 – us Princeton Micro [540]
IL NUOVO CIMENTO – Revista Del Series 2. v. 1-4. 1971-74 – 1,5,6 – us Princeton Micro [540]
IL NUOVO CIMENTO – Series 10, Part A and B. 1965-1970 – 1,5,6 – us Princeton Micro [540]
IL NUOVO CIMENTO – Series 11, Part A and B. 1971-74 – 1,5,6 – us Princeton Micro [540]
IL NUOVO CIMENTO – Series 9, v1-12.1949-54. Series 10, v1-35. 1955-65 – 1,5,6 – us Princeton Micro [540]
IL NUOVO CIMENTO – Supplement Series 1, v. 1-6. 1963-68 – 1,5,6 – us Princeton Micro [540]
IL NUOVO CIMENTO – Supplement Series 10, v. 1-26. 1955-1962 – 1,5,6 – us Princeton Micro [540]
IL NUOVO DIRITTO INTERNAZIONALE... / Gabba, C F – Roma, 1910 – 1mf – 1 – ILM-2490/1 – ne IDC [327]
NUOVO DRITTO INTERNAZIONALE... / Fiore, P – Milan, 1865 – 8mf – 1 – ILM-105/1 – ne IDC [327]
IL NUOVO FAN FULLA *see* JOURNAUX DIVERS
IL NUOVO PROLETARIO – Chicago, IL. Nov 30, 1918, Dec 27 1919 – 1r – 1 – us I.H.R.C. [978]
NUOVO SAGGIO DI CRITICA BIBLICA / Scerbo, Francesco – Firenze: Editrice Fiorentina, 1903. 1 fiche – 9 – us A.T.L.A. [240]
NUOVO STUDIO DI PITTURA, SCOLTURA, ED ARCHITETTURA NELLE CHIESE DI ROMA / Titi, F – O 1053 1. 1721 – 9 – ne IDC [945]
NUR *see* AN-NUR
NUR AL-ISLAM – (Missing: 1935, V.6(1)) – Cairo, 1930-1936. V.1-7 – 102mf – 9 – NE-20331/1 – ne IDC [073]
Nur, Riza *see* HUERRIYET VE ITILAF NASIL DOGDU, NASIL OLDU?
Nureddin, Tevfik *see* SULTAN AZIN'IN HAL'I VE INTIHARI
NUREMBERG CHRONICLE : A PICTORIAL WORLD HISTORY FROM THE CREATION TO 1493, WITH A LEAF FROM THE PIRATED AUGSBURG LATIN EDITION OF 1497 / Shaffer, Ellen K – (Original from Cleveland Public Library) – Los Angeles: Platinum Press, 1950 – 1r – 1 – us Western Res [943]
Nuri, Celal *see*
– ISTIRAK ETMEDIGIMIZ HAREKAT
– ITTIHAD-I ISLAM VE ALMANYA
NUR-I 'ILM / ed by Yazdi, Muhammad – (Missing Issues: 7 and 10; Dawrah-'i sivvum: Shumarah-'i 1-7, Missing Issue: 5. (Day 1362-Tir 1368[January 1984-July 1989])) – Nashriyah-'i Jami'ah-'i Hawzah'i Ilmiyah i Qum. Qum: Majallah-'i Nur-i 'Ilm. Dawrah-'i avval: Shumarah-'i 2-12; Dawrah-'i duvvum: Shumarah-'i 1-12. – $250.00 – us MEDOC [956]

NURNBERGER NACHRICHTEN – (Some issues missing) – Nurnberg, Germany. Oct 1945-54; Jul 1967-Aug 1978; 1980-1990 – 187r – 1 – us L of C Photodup [072]

NURSE EDUCATION TODAY – v1-. 1981- – 1,5,6,9 – us UMI [073]

NURSE EDUCATOR – v. 1- 1976- – 1,5,6,9 – us UMI [370]

NURSE PRACTITIONER – v1- 1975- 1,9; v2- 5,6 – us UMI [610]

NURSERY-BEGINNER LEADER – 1950-60 – 1 – 60.27 – us Baptist [240]

NURSERYMEN'S NOTEBOOKS: DISEASES OF ORNAMENTALS / Virginia. Polytechnic Institute. Extension Division – 1fiche – 9 – us Spaulding [580]

NURSES FAR AND NEAR – v112-193. 1934-54 (incomplete) – 1r – 1 – ATLA S0706B – us A.T.L.A. [073]

NURSE'S JOURNAL OF THE PACIFIC COAST – v1-8. 1904-12 – 1 – us UMI [073]

NURSES' JOURNAL OF THE PACIFIC COAST *see* PACIFIC COAST JOURNAL OF NURSING

NURSES RECORD / Putnam County. Ohio. Probate Court – 1916-1957 – 1r – 1 – $32.50r – us Archival [324]

NURSING ADMINISTRATION QUARTERLY – (v.4-. 1979-. 5,6,9) – v.1-. 1976- – 1 – us UMI [073]

NURSING AND HEALTH CARE / National League for Nursing – (v5- 1984- 5,6,9) – v1- Jul 1980- – 1 – us UMI [610]

NURSING CAREERS AMONG THE AMERICAN INDIANS – 1970 – 9 – $5.00f – us Ross [610]

NURSING CLINICS OF NORTH AMERICA – v1- 1966- 1; v6- 5,6; v10- 9 – us UMI [610]

NURSING FORUM – v1- 1961- 1; v12- 5,6,9 – us UMI [610]

NURSING HOME ADMINISTRATOR *see* MODERN NURSING HOME

NURSING JOURNAL OF INDIA – 1912- 1; v65- 5,6; v66- 9 – us UMI [610]

NURSING LEADERSHIP – v.1-. 1978- – 1,5,6,9 – us UMI [073]

NURSING MANAGEMENT – v12-. 1981- – 1,5,6,9 – us UMI [073]

NURSING MIRROR – (See also: Nursing Mirror and Midwives Journal) – v144- 1977- – 1,5,6,9 – us UMI [610]

NURSING MIRROR AND MIDWIVES JOURNAL – v1-143 1886-1977 1; v144- 5,6,9 – us UMI [610]

NURSING NEWS – v1- 1929- 1; v45- 5,6; v53- 1979- 9 – us UMI [610]

NURSING OUTLOOK – (v. 16- 1968- 5,6. v. 18- 1970- 9) – v. 1- 1953- – 1 – us UMI [610]

NURSING RESEARCH – (v. 14- 1965- 5,6. v. 22- 1973- 9) – v. 1- 1952- – 1 – us UMI [610]

NURSING SCAN IN ADMINISTRATION *see* AONE'S LEADERSHIP PROSPECTIVES

NURSING SUCCESS TODAY – v1-. 1984- – 1,5,6,9 – us UMI [610]

NURSING TIMES – v1- 1905- 1; v67- 5,6,9 – us UMI [610]

NURSING WORLD – v. 122-134. 1949-1960 – 1 – us UMI [610]

NURSINGLIFE – v.1-. 1981- – 1,5,6,9 – us UMI [610]

NUSA TENGGARA SURVEY REPORT. SE 4792/1. 1960 / United Nations. Food and Agriculture Organization – (Report to the government of Indonesia on aspects of forestry in relation to the rayon plant project in South Sumatra, by F. Lootoh. SE 11,480; 1. 1960. SF 9.00; 9. Report to the government of Indonesia on cotton production, by A. C. Dennison. SE 10,467; 1. 1962. SF 9.00; IDC; 9. Report to the government of Indonesia on development of soil microbial research and educational programs, by R. E. Carlyle. SE 3785; 1. 1961. SF 9.00; IDC; 9. Report to the government of Indonesia on grassland and fodder development, by Pierre Bonnemaison. SE 10,312; 1. 1961. SF 9.00; IDC; 9) – ne IDC [333]

NUSA TENGGARA TIMUR *see* INFORMATION ABOUT NUSA TENGGARA TIMUR

NUSANTARA – Djakarta, Indonesia. Oct 1 1967-Jan 16 1974 – 10r – 1 – us L of C Photodup [072]

NUSANTARA; ATLAS INDONESIA UNTUK SEKOLAH DAN UMUM – SE-4454 1 – 9 – ne IDC [910]

NU-SHIH TA HSUEH-SHU CHI-K'AN / National Peiping University. Normal College for Women – "Quarterly Magazine of Research Studies". v. 1-2 (2). Peiping. 1930-31. BCH-323 1 – 9 – ne IDC [073]

NUSIMATA AEREA IMPERATORUM, AUGUSTARUM ET CAESARUM, IN COLONIIS, MUNICIPIIS, ET URBIBUS JURE LATIO DONATUS, EX OMNI MODULO PERCUSSA / Foy-Vaillant, Jo. – Parisiis, 1695 – Dfl84.00 – ne Slangenburg [240]

Nusret, Mehmed *see* TARIHCE-I ERZURUM YAHUT HEMSERILERE ARMAGAN

Nussberger, Max *see*
- CONRAD FERDINAND MEYER
- SCHILLER ALS POLITISCHER DICHTER. SHAKESPEARE UND DAS DEUTSCHE DRAMA

Nussen, F *see* SIX SONATAS FOR A VIOLIN, TENOR AND VIOLONCELLE

Nuszbaum, O *see* KLOSTER, PRIESTERMOENCH UND PRIVATMESSE

EEN NUT ENDE PROFITELIJCK BOECXKEN. AENGAENDE DE VERCLARINGHE DER MENSCHWERDINGE ONS HEEREN JESU CHRISTI / Tricht, J – 1578. BME-218 1 – 9 – ne IDC [240]

NUTCRACKER – Calgary, Alberta, CN. Nov 1916-1917 – 1r – 1 – cn Commonwealth Micro [072]

Nute, Grace Lee *see*
- THE CARE AND CATALOGUING OF MANUSCRIPTS: AS PRACTICED BY THE MINNESOTA HISTORICAL SOCIETY
- INDEX TO NORTHWEST MISSIONS MANUSCRIPTS

NUTRITION ABSTRACTS AND REVIEWS – v1-46 1931-76 – 1,5,6 – us Princeton Micro [612]

NUTRITION CHEZ UN INVERTEBRE MARIN DETRITIVORE: LEPTOSYNAPTA GALLIENNEI (HOLOTHURIOIDEA: ECHINODERMATA) / Feral, J P – 9 – F100.00 – fr Ethnologie [590]

NUTRITION IN MALAYSIA : AN INTERDISCIPLINARY GUIDE / Salleh, Salmah – 1985 – A$10.00 – 0-86758-183-2 – at BISA [613]

NUTRITION NEWS – v1- 1937- 1; v37- 5,6,9 – us UMI [610]

NUTRITION REPORTS INTERNATIONAL – v1- 1970- 1; v5- 5,6; v13- 9 – us UMI [610]

NUTRITION RESEARCH – v1- 1981- – 5,6,9 – us UMI [612]

NUTRITION REVIEW – (v23- 1965- 5,6 v28- 1970- 9) – v1- 1942- – 1 – us UMI [612]

Nutrition Society. London *see* PROCEEDINGS

NUTRITION SOCIETY. PROCEEDINGS – (v1-5 12-35 Dfl60.00v. v36-46 Dfl120.00v. v6-11 as part of British Journal of Nutrition) – London. v1-5, 12-46. 1941-87 – 5,9 – Dfl3,060.00 – ne Swets [612]

NUTRITION TODAY – v1- 1966- 1; v8- 5,6; v11- 9 – us UMI [073]

NUTRITION TODAY – v18-31. 1983-96 – 1,5,6,9 – $65.00r – us Williams [613]

NUTRITIONAL FISH PATHOLOGY : MORPHOLOGICAL SIGNS OF NUTRIENT DEFICIENCY AND TOXICITY IN FARMED FISH – 1992 – 80p – it F.A.O. [639]

NUTRITIONAL IMPLICATIONS OF FOOD AID : AN ANNOTATED BIBLIOGRAPHY – 1985 – 119p – it F.A.O. [640]

NUTRITIONAL KNOWLEDGE, ATTITUDES, AND PRACTICES AND THE ACTUAL DIETARY INTAKES OF FEMALE COLLEGE ATHLETES / Lundell, Lynda & Smith, Joe F – 1991 – 2mf – 9 – $8.00 – us Microform Publ [613]

THE NUT-SHELL – Barrie, Ont.: W.B. Baikie, [1889?-189-?] – 9 – cn C.I.H.M. [073]

THE NUT-SHELL – Brockville, Ont.: Lewis and Patterson [1890?-189- or 19–] – 9 – cn C.I.H.M. [073]

THE NUT-SHELL – Cobourg, Ont.: A. Hewson, [1889?-189-?] – 9 – cn C.I.H.M. [073]

THE NUT-SHELL – Galt, Ont: J.K. Cranston, [1889?-189-?] – 9 – cn C.I.H.M. [073]

THE NUT-SHELL – Montreal: J Row, [1889?-1890?] – 9 – cn C.I.H.M. [073]

THE NUT-SHELL – Newmarket, Ont: Brunton Bros, [1890?-189- or 19–] – 9 – cn C.I.H.M. [971]

THE NUT-SHELL – Ottawa: Bryson, Graham, [1889-189-] – 9 – cn C.I.H.M. [073]

THE NUT-SHELL – Peterborough, Ont: Sailsbury Bros, [1889?-189-] – 9 – cn C.I.H.M. [073]

THE NUT-SHELL – Strathroy, Ont: M Springer, [1889?-189-?] – 9 – cn C.I.H.M. [073]

THE NUT-SHELL – Toronto: E and C Gurney Co, [1889?-189-?] – 9 – cn C.I.H.M. [073]

Nuttall, T *see* THE GENERA OF NORTH AMERICAN PLANTS

Nuttall, Thomas *see* A JOURNAL OF TRAVELS INTO THE ARKANSA TERRITORY, DURING THE YEAR 1819...

NUTTELIJK MENGELMOES / Abraham a Sancta Clara – O-532. 1718 – 9 – ne IDC [999]

NUTZBARES, GALANTES UND CURIOESES FRAUENZIMMER-LEXIKON...(HQ 14) / Corvinus, Gottlieb S – Leipzig, 1715 (mf ed 1993) – 13mf – 9 – DM160.00 – 3-89131-126-5 – gw Fischer [305]

NUUANU BAPTIST CHURCH. HONOLULU, HAWAII : CHURCH RECORDS – Apr 1943-Jul 1948; Oct 1980-Sept 1985. Histories, 1943-62 – 1 – 32.36 – us Baptist [240]

NUVID – [S.l.]: Hizb-i Tudah-'i Iran. Sal 1, shumarah 1-sal 4, shumrah 73 (Day 1354-26 Isfand 1357 [1975-1979]) – 1 reel – 1 – $60.00 – us MEDOC [950]

NUZDAH-I BAHMAN-I TI'URIK – (Missing issues: shumarah-'i 7) – Shumarah-'i 1-8 (Shahrivar 1353-Azar 1355 [Aug 1974-Nov 1976]) – 1 reel – 1 – $35.00 – us MEDOC [950]

Nuzum, George *see* BIOGRAPHY OF IOWA INDIANS OF KANSAS AND NEBRASKA FROM 1880-96

N.V. GOGOL / Ovsianiko-Kulikovskii, D N – R-210 2. Ed. 2 enlarged. 1907 – 8 – ne IDC [920]

NVOVA CANZONE NELLA FELICISSIMA VITTORIA CONTRA INFEDELI / Malombra, B – Venetia, 1571 – 1mf – 9 – H-8315/1 – ne IDC [956]

NWZ GOEPPINGER KREISNACHRICHTEN – Goeppingen, Germany. 1978- – ca 8r per yr – 1 – gw Mikrofilm [072]

N.Y. ASSEMBLY SOCUMENTS AND N.Y. SENATE DOCUMENTS *see* NEW YORK STATE LEGISLATIVE DOCUMENTS

NY DAG – Stockholm, Sweden. 1930-74 – 166r – 1 – sw Kungliga [072]

NY DAG – Stockholm, Sweden. 1983-90 – 1 – sw Kungliga [072]

NY DIKISIONARY MALAGASY : MIZARA ROA ENGLISH SY MALAGASY, ARY MALAGASY SY ENGLISH / Johns, David – Tananarive: Tamy Ny Press..., 1835 – us Res Libr [040]

NY FANDROSOAM-BAOVAO / Tananarive – Gazety mivoaka isan' alakamisy. 1er juil 1926-1er dec 1927, 27 fevr 1931-19 dec 1939. du 1er juil 1926 au 1er sept 1927 a paru sous le titre de: Ny Fandrosoana – 1 – fr A.C.R.P.P. [073]

NY GAZETY MALAGASY – Tananarive. n1-14. mai 1875-juin 1876 – 1 – fr A.C.R.P.P. [490]

NY LAKOLOSY VOLAMENA – n1-228. Tananarive. 1er avr 1910-7 aout 1914. mq no. 33, 96, 167, 197-209 – 1 – fr A.C.R.P.P. [073]

NY LOHARANO – Tananarive. n1-19. 17 juin-16 dec 1915 – 1 – fr A.C.R.P.P. [073]

NY MASOANDRO : GAZETY MOMBA NY SCIENCES, NY HEVITRA LAIQUE, NY LITTERATURE MALAGASY – Tananarive. n1-164. 14 oct 1910-19 dec 1913 – 1 – fr A.C.R.P.P. [073]

NY MAZAVA – Tananarive. n1-24. 15 juil-23 dec 1915 – 1 – fr A.C.R.P.P. [073]

NY TANAMASOANDRO – no. 1-524. Tananarive. 30 juin 1922-27. mq no. 182, 227-228, 231, 241, 445, 472 – 1 – fr A.C.R.P.P. [073]

NY TID – Goteborg, Sweden. 1892-1966 – 497r – 1 – sw Kungliga [072]

NYA ALGER FRAN MEXICO / Agardh, J G – (Oefversigt af Kongl. Vetenskaps-Akademiens Foerhandlingar 4 Arg 1847) B-5513 2 – 8 – ne IDC [580]

NYA ARBOGABLADET *see* ARBOGABLADET

NYA CIMBRISHAMNSBLADET – Simrishamn, Sweden. 1882-83 – 1 – sw Kungliga [072]

NYA DAGLIGT ALLEHANDA – Stockholm, Sweden. 1859-1944 – 391r – 1 – sw Kungliga [072]

NYA FOLKVILJAN *see* FOLKVILJAN

NYA KLARAN – Molkom, Sweden. 1905-06 – 1 – sw Kungliga [072]

NYA KRISTINEHAMNSPOSTEN – Kristinehamn, Sweden. 1979- – 1 – sw Kungliga [072]

NYA KRISTINEHAMNSPOSTEN – Orebro, Kristinehamn, Sweden. 1884-1978 – 152r – 1 – sw Kungliga [072]

NYA KUNGALVSPOSTEN – Molndal, Sweden. 1979-81 – 1 – sw Kungliga [072]

NYA LANSTIDNINGEN NYA LIDKOPINGSTIDNINGEN – Lidkoping, Sweden. 1979- – 1 – sw Kungliga [072]

NYA LANSTIDNINGEN NYA LIDKOPINGSTIDNINGEN – (Nya Lidkopingstidningen, 1903-61; Nya Lanstidningen Nya Lidkopingstidningen, 1961-78) – Lidkoping, Sweden – 210r – 1 – sw Kungliga [072]

NYA LERUMS TIDNING *see* ALINGSAS TIDNING

NYA LIDKOPINGSTIDNINGEN *see* NYA LANSTIDNINGEN NYA LIDKOPINGSTIDNINGEN

NYA LUDVIKA TIDNING – Ludvika, 1993- – 9 – sw Kungliga [072]

NYA LUND – Lund, Sweden. 1892-93 – 2r – 1 – sw Kungliga [072]

NYA LYSEKILSKURIREN *see* LYSEKILSKURIREN

NYA MARSTRANDSPOSTEN – Marstrand, 1868-73 – 9 – sw Kungliga [072]

NYA NORRLAENNINGEN – Sundsvall, 1894-98 – 9 – sw Kungliga [072]

NYA NORRLAND – Harnosand, Sweden. 1907, 1910, 1911, 1913-78 – 330r – 1 – sw Kungliga [072]

NYA NORRLAND – Harnosand, Sweden. 1979- – 1 – sw Kungliga [072]

NYA PERSPEKTIV – Stockholm, Sweden. 1967-74 – 2r – 1 – sw Kungliga [410]

NYA PRESSEN – Stockholm, 1881-82 – 9 – sw Kungliga [072]

NYA SAMHALLET *see* DAGBLADET NYA SAMHALLET

NYA SIGTUNA TIDNING – Sigtuna, Sweden. 1887-88 – 1 – sw Kungliga [072]

NYA SKANDINAVISKA LAFARTER / Fries, T M – (Bot. Not. 1865). 1866, 1867. B-5310 2 – 8 – ne IDC [580]

NYA ST TIDNINGEN – Stenungsund, Sweden. 1988- – 1 – sw Kungliga [072]

NYA WECKOBLADET I ABROGA *see* ARBOGA WECKOBLAD

NYA WERMLANDSPOSTEN – Karlstad, 1855-60, 1862-71 – 9 – sw Kungliga [072]

NYA WERMLANDSTIDNINGEN – Karlstad, Sweden. 1979- – 1 – sw Kungliga [072]

NYA WERMLANDSTIDNINGEN – (Wermlands Tidning, 1836-42; Wermlandstidningen, 1842-50; Nya Wermlandstidningen, 1851-1978) – Karlstad, Sweden – 603r – 1 – sw Kungliga [072]

NYA WEXJOBLADET – Vaxjo, Sweden. 1847-95 – 28r – 1 – sw Kungliga [072]

NYAH AND PIANGIL TIMES – 1921-1942 – 5mf – 9 – at Corangamite [980]

NYAISHES OR ZOROASTRIAN LITANIES / ed by Dhalla, Maneckji Nusservanji – (Avestan text with the Pahlavi, Sanskrit, Persian and Gujarati versions) – New York, 1908 – 3mf – NE-20155/1 – ne IDC [180]

NYANJA-ENGLISH VOCABULARY / Barnes, Herbert – (New enl rev ed by M W Bully) – London: Sheldon, [1929] – us Res Libr [040]

Nyanteng, V K *see* ECONOMIC ORGANISATION OF YAM MARKETING IN GHANA

NYARE SKENINGE TIDNING – Motala, Skaenninge. 1868-85 – 9 – sw Kungliga [072]

NYARE UMEATIDNINGEN – Umea, Sweden. 1856-57 – 1 reel – 1 – sw Kungliga [072]

Nyasaland *see*
- ANNUAL DEPARTMENTAL REPORTS
- CAPITAL DEVELOPMENT PLAN, 1957/61
- DEVELOPMENT PROGRAMME
- GOVERNMENT GAZETTE
- GOVERNMENT PUBLICATIONS
- REVISED REPORT OF THE POST-WAR DEVELOPMENT COMMITTEE (1946-1955)

Nyasaland. Development Committee *see* REPORT OF THE POST-WAR DEVELOPMENT COMMITTEE (1946-1955)

NYASALAND JOURNAL – (Cont as: Society of Malawi Journal. Blantyre v18(2)-v19 1964-1966) – Blantyre. v1-18(1). 1948-1965 – 60mf – 9 – ne IDC [960]

Nyasaland. Native Administration *see* ANNUAL REPORT OF THE PROVINCIAL COMMISSIONERS

NYASALAND TIMES – (The Times). Blantyre. Malawi. -w and sw. 5 Jan 1911-Dec 1932. (16 reels) – 1 – uk British Libr Newspaper [072]

NYASTE FORPOSTEN – (Suppl: Murre, 1888-91) – Goteborg, Sweden. 1875-91 – 16r – 1 – sw Kungliga [072]

NYASTE RIKSGRANSEN – Haparanda, Sweden. 1873-82 – 1 – sw Kungliga [072]

NYBRO TIDNING – Nybro, Kalmar, Sweden. 1931-78 – 1 – sw Kungliga [072]

NYBRO TIDNING *see* KALMAR LANS TIDNING

DET NYE AAR – (Some yrs on 16mm film) – 1951-89 – 4r – 1,5 – ATLA S0609 – us A.T.L.A. [073]

NYE COUNTY NEWS – Ione, NV. 1865-66 – 1r – 1 – $50.00 – U04590 – us Library Micro [071]

NYE FREMSKRIDT INDEN FOR ESKIMOFORSKNINGEN / Birket-Smith, K – BN 139 1950 – 8 – ne IDC [970]

NYE MENNESKER / Rasmussen, Knud – BN 358 2.1905 – 8 – ne IDC [910]

Nye. Nevada *see* ASSESSORS RECORDERS

NYE SAMLING AF DET KONGELIGE DANSKE VIDENSKABERNES SELSKABS SKRIFTER / Danske Videnskabernes selskab. Copenhagen – Kiobenhavn, 1781-99 – 3 – us Readex [500]

NYELETI YA MISO – Cleveland, South Africa. 1 Jan 1921-30 Jun 1949 – 2r – 1, 16 diazo available – sa SA Libr [960]

Nygaard, M *see* NORRON SYNTAX

Nyhart, J Daniel *see* THE ROLE OF LAW AND ECONOMIC DEVELOPMENT

NYHETERNA – Kalmar, Sweden. 1985- – 1 – sw Kungliga [072]

NYHETERNA – Malmo, Sweden. 1983 – 1 – sw Kungliga [072]

NYHETERNA *see* SKANSKA SOCIALDEMOKRATEN

NYHETSBLADET – Stockholm, Sweden. 1867-68 – 1 – sw Kungliga [072]

NYKTERHETSBASUNEN – Holdrege, NE. -w. 18 Jun 1890-3 Sept 1890. In Swedish – 1 – us NE Hist [071]

NYLA BULLETIN – New York Library Association – v1- 1953- 1; v23- 1975- 5,6,9 – apply; v.23-. 1975- 5,6,9 – us UMI [020]

Nylander, Gustavus Reinhold *see* GRAMMAR AND VOCABULARY OF THE BULLOM LANGUAGE

Nylander, W *see*
- CONSPECTUS SYNOPTICUS STICTEORUM
- ENUMERATIO LICHENUM FRETI BEHRINGII
- ENUMERATION GENERALE DES LICHENS, AVEC L'INDICATION SOMMAIRE DE LEUR DISTRIBUTION GEOGRAPHIQUE
- LICHENES FUEGIAE ET PATAGONIAE
- LICHENES IN REGIONIBUS EXOTICIS QUIBUSDAM VIGENTES
- LICHENES. IN: TRIANA, J. E. PLANCHON. PRODROMUS FLORAE NOVO-GRANATENSIS
- LICHENES INSULARUM GUINEENSIUM
- LICHENES JAPONIAE. ACCEDUNT OBSERVATIONIBUS LICHENES INSULAE LABUAN
- LICHENES LAPPONIAE ORIENTALIS
- LICHENES NOVAE-ZELANDIAE
- LICHENES PYRENAEORUM ORIENTALIUM OBSERVATIS NOVIS
- LICHENES SCANDINAVIAE
- RECOGNITIO MONOGRAPHICA RAMALINARUM
- SERTUM LICHENAEAE TROPICAE E LABUAN ET SINGAPORE ACCEDENT OBSERV
- SYNOPSIS DU GENRE ARTHONIA
- SYNOPSIS METHODICA LICHENUM

Nyman, CF *see*
- ANALECTA BOTANICA
- CONSPECTUS FLORAE EUROPAEAE
- SYLLOGE FLORAE EUROPAEAE, SEU PLANTARUM VASCULARIUM EUROPAE INDIGENARUM ENUMERATIO

NYNAES NYHETER – Nynaeshamn, 1923-25 – 9 – sw Kungliga [072]

NYNASHAMNSPOSTEN – Nynashamn, Sweden. 1979- – 1 – sw Kungliga [072]

Nynauld, I de *see* DE LA LYCANTHROPIE, TRANSFORMATION, EXTASE DES SORCIERS

NYNGAN OBSERVER – Apr 21 1894-Dec 14 1895; Jan 1898- Dec 1909; Jan 1916-Dec 1925; Feb 12 1926-Oct 6 1939; Jun 25 1942-Dec 15 1945; Jan 13 1955-Dec 18 1968 – 9 – at Pascoe [072]

Nyrop, Kristoffer *see* DEN OLDFRANSKE HELTEDIGTNING

NYSSA GATE CITY JOURNAL – Nyssa, OR. -w. 14 Apr 1910-. – 1 – us U.O. Library [071]

Nyssens, A et al *see* SOURCES BIBLIOGRAPHIQUES... CONGRES INTERNATIONAL DE DROIT COMMERCIAL D'ANVERS 1885

NYT FRA BIBELSELSKABET *see* DET DANSKE BIBELSELSKABS ARBOG

NYTHEROY – Rio de Janeiro, Brazil. 1836 – 1 – bl Biblioteca [072]

NYTT ALLVAR OCH SKAMT *see* SUNDSVALLS TIDNING

NYTT OCH GAMMALT *see* LUNDS WECKOBLAD NYTT OCH GAMMALT

NYU FORUM – (Continued by: Forum (New York, N.Y.)) – (New York, N.Y.) v1, no. 1 (week of Mar. 25, 1980) – us A.J.P.C. [073]

NYUANSN = NUANCES – Montreal, CN, 1921 – 1r – 1 – Can$25.00 – cn Can Microfilming [072]

NZ ELECTORAL ROLLS 1880 AND 1881 – 32mf – 9 – NZ$140.00 – 0-908797-57-5 – nz BAB [324]

NZ ELECTORAL ROLLS 1887 – 23mf – 9 – NZ$102.00 – 0-908797-60-5 – nz BAB [980]

NZ ELECTORAL ROLLS 1890 – (Missing: East Coast and supplements for Marsden and Palmerston) – 24mf – 9 – NZ$106.00 – 0-908797-61-3 – nz BAB [980]

NZ ELECTORAL ROLLS 1893 – (The first election where women were entitled to vote) – 43mf – 9 – NZ$190.00 – 0-908797-26-5 – nz BAB [980]

NZ ELECTORAL ROLLS 1894 – 39mf – NZ$173.00 – 0-908797-27-3 – nz BAB [980]

NZ ELECTORAL ROLLS 1896 – (Missing: supplement for Otaki) – 47mf – 9 – NZ$206.00 – 0-908797-62-1 – nz BAB [980]

NZ ELECTORAL ROLLS 1897 – 37mf – 9 – NZ$163.00 – 0-908797-63-X – nz BAB [980]

NZ ELECTORAL ROLLS 1899 – 53mf – 9 – NZ$230.00 – 0-908797-64-8 – nz BAB [980]

NZ ELECTORAL ROLLS 1900 – 43mf – 9 – NZ$190.00 – 0-908797-81-8 – nz BAB [920]

NZ ELECTORAL ROLLS 1902 – 56mf – 9 – NZ$242.00 – 0-908797-82-6 – nz BAB [920]

NZ ELECTORAL ROLLS 1903 – 44mf – 9 – NZ$194.00 – 0-908797-83-4 – nz BAB [920]

NZ ELECTORAL ROLLS 1908 – 90mf – 9 – NZ$326.00 – 0-908797-85-0 – nz BAB [920]

NZ ELECTORAL ROLLS 1911 – 93mf – 9 – NZ$340.00 – 0-908797-86-9 – nz BAB [920]

NZ ELECTORAL ROLLS 1914 – 94mf – 9 – NZ$344.00 – 0-908797-87-7 – nz BAB [920]

NZ ELECTORAL ROLLS 1919 – 114mf – 9 – NZ$384.00 – 0-908797-88-5 – nz BAB [920]

NZ ELECTORAL ROLLS 1922 – 108mf – 9 – NZ$366.00 – 0-908797-89-3 – nz BAB [920]

NZ ELECTORAL ROLLS 1925 – 114mf – 9 – NZ$384.00 – 0-908989-13-X – nz BAB [920]

NZ ELECTORAL ROLLS 1928 – 136mf – 9 – NZ$428.00 – 0-908989-14-8 – nz BAB [920]

NZ ELECTORAL ROLLS 1931 – 136mf – 9 – NZ$428.00 – 0-908989-30-X – nz BAB [320]

NZ ELECTORAL ROLLS 1935 – 139mf – 9 – NZ$447.00 – 0-908989-31-8 – nz BAB [320]

NZ ELECTORAL ROLLS 1938 – 153mf – 9 – NZ$460.00 – 0-908989-32-6 – nz BAB [320]

NZ ELECTORAL ROLLS 1941 – 127mf – 9 – NZ$400.00 – 0-908989-33-4 – nz BAB [320]

NZ ELECTORAL ROLLS 1943 – 153mf – 9 – NZ$460.00 – 0-908989-15-6 – nz BAB [320]

NZ ELECTORAL ROLLS 1946 – 160mf – 9 – NZ$481.00 – 0-908989-34-2 – nz BAB [320]

NZ ELECTORAL ROLLS 1949 AND 1951 SUPPLEMENTARY ROLLS – (1949 and 1951 Maori Rolls included) – 203mf – 9 – NZ$610.00 – 0-908989-35-0 – nz BAB [320]

NZ ELECTORAL ROLLS 1954 – (Maori Rolls included) – 176mf – 9 – NZ$529.00 – 0-908989-36-9 – nz BAB [320]

NZ ELECTORAL ROLLS 1905-6 – 66mf – 9 – NZ$282.00 – 0-908797-84-2 – nz BAB [920]

NZ ELECTORAL ROLLS 1865-1866 – (Missing: Grey & Bell, Omata, New Plymouth & Westland) – 6mf – 9 – NZ$29.00 – 0-908797-30-3 – nz BAB [324]

NZ ELECTORAL ROLLS 1866-1867 – 9mf – 9 – NZ$42.00 – 0-908797-31-1 – nz BAB [324]

NZ ELECTORAL ROLLS 1867-1868 – 8mf – 9 – NZ$38.00 – 0-908797-39-7 – nz BAB [324]

NZ ELECTORAL ROLLS 1868-69 – 7mf – 9 – NZ$34.00 – 0-908797-32-X – nz BAB [324]

NZ ELECTORAL ROLLS 1869-70 – 9mf – 9 – NZ$42.00 – 0-908797-18-4 – nz BAB [324]

NZ ELECTORAL ROLLS 1870-71 – 15mf – 9 – NZ$65.00 – 0-908797-19-2 – nz BAB [324]

NZ ELECTORAL ROLLS 1871-72 – 9mf – 9 – NZ$42.00 – 0-908797-20-6 – nz BAB [324]

NZ ELECTORAL ROLLS 1872-73 – 11mf – 9 – NZ$50.00 – 0-908797-21-4 – nz BAB [324]

NZ ELECTORAL ROLLS 1873-74 – 10mf – 9 – NZ$46.00 – 0-908797-22-2 – nz BAB [324]

NZ ELECTORAL ROLLS 1874-75 – 11mf – 9 – NZ$50.00 – 0-908797-23-0 – nz BAB [324]

NZ ELECTORAL ROLLS 1875-76 – 13mf – 9 – NZ$58.00 – 0-908797-24-9 – nz BAB [324]

NZ ELECTORAL ROLLS 1876-77 – 11mf – 9 – NZ$50.00 – 0-908797-25-7 – nz BAB [324]

NZ ELECTORAL ROLLS 1877-78 – (Missing: Wellington City & Wellington Country) – 12mf – 9 – NZ$54.00 – 0-908797-54-0 – nz BAB [324]

NZ ELECTORAL ROLLS 1878-79 – (Missing: Auckland City East, East Coast, Lyttelton, Mataura, Port Chalmers, Riverton & Waitaki) – 12mf – 9 – NZ$54.00 – 0-908797-55-9 – nz BAB [324]

NZ ELECTORAL ROLLS 1879-80 – (Missing: Christchurch, Wakatipu & Wallace) – 12mf – 9 – NZ$54.00 – 0-908797-56-7 – nz BAB [324]

NZ ELECTORAL ROLLS 1882-84 – (Missing: Parnell, Taieri, Wakanaui & suppl 1 for Marsden) – 21mf – 9 – NZ$93.00 – 0-908797-58-3 – nz BAB [324]

NZ ELECTORAL ROLLS 1885-86 – (Incomplete set, many supplementary rolls) – 10mf – 9 – NZ$50.00 – 0-908797-59-1 – nz BAB [324]

NZ MAORI ELECTORAL ROLL 1919 : NORTHERN, EASTERN, WESTERN AND SOUTHERN MAORI – 3mf – 9 – NZ$15.00 – 0-908989-16-4 – nz BAB [920]

NZ MAORI VOTERS' ROLL 1908 : NORTHERN, EASTERN AND WESTERN MAORI – (A Southern Maori roll has not been found. Contains: full name, address, tribe and hapu for each voter) – 3mf – 9 – NZ$15.00 – 0-908797-90-7 – nz BAB [920]

NZ – NEUE ZEITUNG – Budapest, 1972- – 6r – 1 – Inquire at Mikrofilmarchiv for details – gw Misc Inst [072]

NZ – NEUE ZEITUNG *see* DIE WAHRHEIT

Nzabakomada, R *see* LA GUERRE DE KONGO-WARA 1928-1931. UN CHAPITRE DE LA RESISTANCE ANTI-COLONIALE EN AFRIQUE EQUATORIALE

NZ-NEUE ZEITUNG – Budapest, Hungary. 1990- – 1 – gw Mikrofilm [072]

O A H NEWSLETTER – (1982-. 1,5,6,9) – v9-. 1981- – 1 – us UMI [073]

O AND M – (Organization and Methods) – 1962- 1; 1972- 5,6; 1975- 9 – us UMI [073]

O CARMO DO RIO CLARO – Carmo do Rio Claro, Brazil. Nov 1925; Feb 1927 – 1 – bl Biblioteca [072]

O CENSOR : PERIODICO MENSAL, POLITICO, HISTORICO E LITTERARIO – '(s.l.')-BA, Brazil. 6 set-nov 1837 – 1,5,6 – bl Biblioteca [072]

O CENSOR – '(s.l.')-Sao Luis, Brazil. 24 Jan-Mar, Dec 1825. Feb-Mar, May, July 1826. Mar 1827. Oct 1828. Apr, May, Nov 1829. May 1830 – 1,5,6 – bl Biblioteca [072]

O CENSOR BRASILEIRO – Rio de Janeiro, 4 Apr-27 Jun 1828 – 1,5,6 – bl Biblioteca [072]

O Estlund, KE M *see* COLLECTION OF DRAWINGS WITH NOTES OF ORCHIDACEAE OF MEXICO

O FUTURO – Curitiba, 4 Sep-27 Nov 1892 – 1,5,6 – bl Biblioteca [072]

O FUTURO : ORGAO DOS INTERESSES REGIONAIS – Rio Branco, Acre. 7 Dez 1919-26 Jun 1921 – 1,5,6 – bl Biblioteca [072]

O GAFANHOTO – Rio Branco, Acre. Ago, Out, Dez 1984; Jul, Set-Out 1985 – 1,5,6 – bl Biblioteca [072]

O GAROTO : ORGAM CRITICO, HUMORISTICO, ENOFENSIVO, FRANCO-POPULAR – Manaos, Amazonas. 22 Jun-20 Jul 1919 – 1,5,6 – bl Biblioteca [072]

O GENIO : PERIODICO LITTERARIO DE EDUCACAO E RECREIO – Maceio, Alagoas. 25 Ago-18 Set 1889 – 1,5,6 – bl Biblioteca [072]

OA : OFFICE MANAGEMENT AND AUTOMATION – (Publ ceases under this title at v6 no 9 1990. Incorporated within Office Systems and Technology at v36, No.8, 1990) – Willowdale. v1-6. 1985-1990 – 9 – Can$28.00y – cn Micromedia [650]

OA *see* OFFICE SYSTEMS AND TECHNOLOGY

THE O.A.C. REVIEW – Guelph, Ont.: Literary Society of the Ontario Agricultural College, v1 no 1 (Nov 1889)- – 9 – cn C.I.H.M. [630]

OAG AIR CARGO GUIDE – (All that is currently offered. Cont the guide section of: Air Cargo) – Oak Brook. v21-24. jan 1977-dec 1980 1,5*,9 – 1,5,9 – us UMI [380]

OAG AIR CARGO GUIDE *see* AIR CARGO

OAK FOREST STAR – Chicago Heights. Ill. 1972- – 1 – us UMI [071]

OAK GROVE BAPTIST CHURCH. CRAWFORD COUNTY. GEORGIA : CHURCH RECORDS – 1838-1908. Formerly: Lebanon Baptist Church. 326p – 1 – 14.67 – us Baptist [240]

OAK GROVE BAPTIST CHURCH. MODEL, TENNESSEE : CHURCH RECORDS – 1932-May 1965 – 1 – 27.27 – us Baptist [240]

OAK GROVE BAPTIST CHURCH. SPARTANBURG COUNTY. SOUTH CAROLINA : CHURCH RECORDS – 1850-67, 1936-40, 1951-72 – 1 – 20.61 – us Baptist [240]

OAK GROVE MISSIONARY BAPTIST CHURCH. CEDARTOWN, GEORGIA : CHURCH RECORDS – 1898-1930 – 1 – 5.04 – us Baptist [240]

Oak Harbor. Ohio. St. Joseph's Catholic Church *see* RECORDS

Oak Harbor. Ohio. St. Paul's United Church of Christ *see* RECORDS

OAK HILL BAPTIST CHURCH. APPLE CREEK ASSOCIATION. ST CLAIR COUNTY. ILLINOIS : CHURCH RECORDS – 1851-63 – 1 – 10.62 – us Baptist [240]

OAK HILL BAPTIST CHURCH. APPLE CREEK ASSOCIATION. ST CLAIR COUNTY. ILLINOIS : CHURCH RECORDS – 1851-63 – 1 – 10.62 – us Baptist [240]

OAK LEAF – Oak, NE. -w. Apr-Jun 1914; Feb 1915-Jun 1920 – 1 – us NE Hist [071]

OAK LEAVES – Oak Park. Ill. 1963- – 1 – us UMI [071]

OAK NEWS – Oak, NE. -w. Sept-Dec 1897; Jul 1899-Sept 1906; Nov 1906; Feb-May 1907; Aug 1907-Aug 1911 – 1 – us NE Hist [071]

OAK PARK LEDGER – (Also known as: Sacramento County Ledger) – Oak Park, CA. 1901-1917 – 5r – 1 – $250.00 – C03624 – us Library Micro [071]

OAK PRESS SENTINEL – Ojai, CA. 1961-1962 – 1r – 1 – $50.00 – B03626 – us Library Micro [071]

OAK REPORT – v.1-. 1980- – 1,5,6,9 – us UMI [073]

OAK RIDGE BAPTIST CHURCH. LINCOLN COUNTY. MISSOURI : CHURCH RECORDS – 1896-1926. 230p – 1 – 10.35 – us Baptist [240]

Oak Ridge Institute of Nuclear Studies *see* OAK RIDGE TENNESSEE NEWS LETTER

OAK RIDGE TENNESSEE NEWS LETTER / Oak Ridge Institute of Nuclear Studies – v. 1, no. 1-18, no. 6. Jul 1948-Dec 1965 – 1 – us NY Public [500]

OAK RIDGER – Oak Ridge. Tenn. 1949-1963 – 1 – us UMI [071]

Oak Shade Methodist Church (Fulton County, Ohio) *see* RECORDS

OAK VIEW BAPTIST CHURCH. KINGS MOUNTAIN, NORTH CAROLINA : CHURCH RECORDS – 1938-63 – 1 – 5.00 – us Baptist [240]

OAKDALE GRAPHIC – Oakdale, CA. 1884-88; Jan-Jun 1890 – 3r – 1 – $150.00 – B02535 – us Library Micro [071]

OAKDALE JOURNAL – Oakdale, NE. -w. Jun 1959-Apr 1961 – 1 – us NE Hist [071]

OAKDALE JOURNAL – Oakdale, NE. -w. May 1877; Sept 1877-May 1886; Jul 1887-Apr 1891 – 1 – us NE Hist [071]

OAKDALE LEADER – Oakdale, CA. 1885-90; 1904-10; 1925-26; 1944-60; 1972- – 65+ r – 1 BC02536 – $3,250.00 ($135.00y) – us Library Micro [071]

OAKDALE SENTINEL – Oakdale, NE. -w. Jun 1887-Nov 1929; Jan 1930; Mar 1930-Apr 1958 – 1 – us NE Hist [071]

OAKDALE TIMES – Oakdale, PA. -w 1899-1907 – 13 – $25.00r – us I.M.R. [071]

Oakdale United Methodist Church (Deshler, Ohio) *see* RECORDS
OAKDALE UNITED METHODIST CHURCH, RECORDS – Deshler, Ohio. 1854-1989 – 1 reel – 1 – us Archival [240]
Oakeley, Frederick *see* HISTORICAL NOTES ON THE TRACTARIAN MOVEMENT, A.D. 1833-1845
Oakes, R A *see* GENEALOGICAL AND FAMILY HISTORY OF JEFFERSON COUNTY
Oakey, C C *see* GREATER TERRE HAUTE AND VIGO COUNTY
OAKFIR LOOKOUT – Oakridge, OR. -w. 4 Aug 1939-2 Oct 1942. 1 roll – 1 – us U.O. Library [071]
OAK-GRINER BAPTIST CHURCH. OCALA, FLORIDA : CHURCH RECORDS – 1915-78 – 1 – 85.19 – us Baptist [240]
OAKHAM 1739-1849 – (Mf 1T: Births & Deaths 1739-1821; Publishments 1766-1813. Mf 2T: Births & Deaths 1777-1843; Intentions & Marriages 1809-36. Mf 3T: Publishments 1827-38. Mf 3T-4T: Marriages 1819-45. Mf 4T: Out-of-Town Marriages 1771-99; Deaths 1837-45. Mf 4T-5T: Vital Records 1844-49. Mf 6T: Cemetry Inscriptions 1761-1849; Church Deaths/Marriages 1806-32) – (mf ed 1998) – 6mf – 9 – 0-87623-309-4 – us Holbrook [920]
OAKHAM 1750-1895 – (Mf 1-6: Town Records 1750-83. Mf 6,15: Vital Records 1744-1822. Mf 7-15: Town Records 1783-1803. Mf 16-19: Town Records 1803-12. Mf 19-22: Vital Records 1773-1843. Mf 23-24: Births 1786-1844. Mf 25: Marriages 1771-99, 1836-45. Mf 26: Deaths 1837-45. Mf 27-28: Marriages Intentions 1837-1905. Mf 29-31: Births, Marriages, Deaths 1844-59. Mf 32-33: Births 1860-95. Mf 34-35: Marriages 1856-95. Mf 35-37: Deaths 1860-95) – (mf ed 1987) – 37mf – 9 – 0-87623-033-8 – us Holbrook [920]
OAKHURST BAPTIST CHURCH. DECATUR, GEORGIA : CHURCH RECORDS – 1913-1946 – 1 – 30.16 – us Baptist [240]
OAKHURST BAPTIST CHURCH. DECATUR, GEORGIA : CHURCH RECORDS – 1913-85. 3951p – 1 – $177.80 – us Baptist [240]
OAKLAND – 1906-23; 1979-87; 1989-92 – 83r – 1 – $4,150.00 – P00071 – us Library Micro [910]
OAKLAND ADVANCE – Oakland OR. Apr 22 1910-Aug 14 1914 – 1 – us U.O. Library [071]
OAKLAND ALAMEDA COUNTY GAZETTE – Oakland, CA. 1856-75 – 2r – 1 – $100.00 – C02538 – us Library Micro [071]
OAKLAND ENQUIRER *see* INDEPENDENT ENQUIRER
OAKLAND HISTORY BOOKS – (Includes 10 titles. Apply for list) – Oakland, CA. 1885-1935 – 3r – 1 – $150.00 – B40326 – us Library Micro [978]
OAKLAND INDEPENDENT AND REPUBLICAN – Oakland, NE. -w. Nov 1881; Oct 1895-Feb 1897; Apr 1897 to date – 1 – us NE Hist [071]
OAKLAND MAIL – Oakland, NE. -w. May 1908-Feb 1912 – 1 – us NE Hist [071]
OAKLAND OBSERVER – Oakland OR. Apr 10 1891 – 1 – us U.O. Library [071]
OAKLAND OWL – Oakland OR. Nov 14 1902-Apr 15 1910 – 1 – us U.O. Library [071]
THE OAKLAND POST – Oakland, CA. 1976-77; 1978- – 23+ r – 1 BR02549 – $1,150.00 ($90.00y) – us Library Micro [071]
OAKLAND POST ENQUIRER – (Also known as: Enquirer) – Oakland, CA. 1891-1950 – 561r – 1 – $28,050.00 – C02550 – us Library Micro [071]
THE OAKLAND POST ENQUIRER – Oakland, CA: Post-Enquirer Publ Co, [1924-1928] – 61r – 1 – us Res Libr [071]
OAKLAND REPUBLICAN – Oakland, NE. -w. Oct 1895-Feb 1896; Apr 1896-Apr 1907 – 1 – us NE Hist [071]
OAKLAND TIMES – Oakland, CA. 1925-1927 – 5r – 1 – $250.00 – C03369 – us Library Micro [071]
OAKLAND TRIBUNE – (Also known as: The Tribune) – Oakland, CA. 1874- – 2137+ r – 1 – $106,850.00 ($880.00y) – B02552 – us Library Micro [071]
OAKLAND TRIBUNE – Oakland OR. Jan 5 1928-July 31 1942 – 1 – us U.O. Library [071]
OAKLAND TRIBUNE YEARBOOK – Oakland, CA. 1914-1949 – 3r – 1 – $150.00 – B03370 – us Library Micro [071]
OAKLAND/ALAMEDA – 1993- – 4+ r – 1 – $200.00 – P00072 – us Library Micro [910]
OAKLANDER – Pittsburgh. Pa. 1911-1928 – 1 – us UMI [071]
Oakley, Edward Ellsworth *see* DIARIES AND ACCOUNT BOOKS
OAKLEY JOHNSON PAPERS : FROM THE HOLDINGS OF THE SCHOMBURG CENTER FOR RESEARCH IN BLACK CULTURE, MANUSCRIPTS, ARCHIVES AND RARE BOOKS DIVISION: THE NEW YORK PUBLIC LIBRARY, ASTOR, LENOX AND TILDEN FOUNDATIONS – (Guide which covers all coll under "Civil Rights Advocates" sold separately for $20.00 D3305.G3) – 1995 5r – 1 – $425.00 – D3305P09 – Dist. us Scholarly Res – us L of C Photodup [320]
Oakley, P *see* GUIDE TO EXTENSION TRAINING
OAKRIDGE REVIEW – Oakridge, OR. -w. 26 Sep 1924-25 Mar 1926. – 1r – 1 – us U.O. Library [071]
OAKRIDGE TELEGRAM – Oakridge, OR. -sw. 23 Oct 1952-22 Jun 1974. – 10r – 1 – us U.O. Library [071]
THE OAKS OF THE UNITED STATES / Engelmann, G – 7536 2. 1876-1877 – 8 – ne IDC [580]
OAKSHOTT CASTLE, BY GRANBY DIXON / Kingsley, Henry – British Fiction Archive: Unit 2 – 9 – uk Bell [830]
OAKVILLE BEAVER – Oakville. Ontario. Canada. Ap 1975- – 1 – cn Commonwealth Micro [072]
OAKVILLE JOURNAL-RECORD – Oakville, Ontario, Canada. Nov 1947-Aug 1962; Apr 1975-78. Title varies – 1 – cn Commonwealth Micro [072]
OAKWOOD CEMETERY RECORDS / Baldwin City Cemetery Company – 1879-1970 – 1 – us KS Hist [025]
OAKWOOD NEWS – Oakwood, Ohio. 1908-82 – 21r – 1 – $32.50r – us Archival [071]
OAMARU TIMES AND WAITAKI REPORTER – New Zealand. -sw. 2 Nov 1866-27 Oct 1868. (1 reel) – 1 – uk British Libr Newspaper [072]
OAR RESEARCH REVIEW *see* AIR FORCE RESEARCH REVIEW
OAS ANNALS / Organization of American States – v1-10. 1949-58 (all publ) – 9 – LLMC 81-900 – us L.L.M.C. [340]
OAS CHRONICLE / Organization of American States – v1-12. 1965-77 (all publ) – 9 – LLMC 81-901 – us L.L.M.C. [340]
OASIS – Hawthorne, NV. 8 Sep 1881 – 1r – 1 – $50.00 – U04583 – us Library Micro [071]
OASIS : PERIODICO IMPARCIAL – Corumba, 3 May-Jun 1888; Aug 1889; May 1890; Jun 1891; Oct, Dec 1892; Jan-Feb, Jun 1893; Jan, Feb, Apr 1894; 31 Mar 1896 – 1,5,6 – bl Biblioteca [072]
THE OASIS : S. NEVADA HISTORICAL SOCIETY NEWLETTER – 1r – 1 – $50.00 – U04909 – us Library Micro [071]
Oates, James F *see* CHARACTER STUDIES
Oaxaca. Mexico (State) *see* PERIODICO OFICIAL
OB A. BLOKE / Mirskii, D S – 'Zvezda' no 8 1936. BR-3280 2 – 8 – ne IDC [460]
OB ALEKSANDRE BLOKE – Stat'i. Izd. "Kartonnyi domik". Spb. 1921. BR-1467 2 – 8 – ne IDC [920]
OB ESTETIKAKH I VZGLIADAKH MAIAKOVSKOGO / Vladimirov, S – L. 1959. BR-2200 2 – 8 – ne IDC [460]
OB IASNITEL'NYI MORSKOI SLOVAR' / Vakhtin, V V – Ed.2. Enlarged. Spb., 1893 – 8mf – 9 – 1383/2 – ne IDC [380]
OB INOSTRATSAKH V ROSSII; SBORNIK UZAKONENII, TRAKTATOV I KONVENTSII, S / ed by Mysh, M I – Spb, 1911 – 8 – BR 4277 2 – ne IDC [947]
OB ITOGAKH VYPOLNENIIA GOS. PLANA RAZVITIIA NARODNOGO KHOZIAISTVA SSSR NA 1960 G. ZA PERVOE POLUGODIE / U.S.S.R. Tsentralnoe Statisticheskoe Upravlenie – M. 1960. BD-788 1 – 9 – ne IDC [310]
OB ITOGAKH VYPOLNENIIA GOSUDARSTVENNOGO PLANA RAZVITIIA NARODNOGO KHOZIAISTVA SSSR V 1955 G / U.S.S.R. Tsentralnoe Statisticheskoe Upravlenie – M.1956. BD-783 1 – 9 – ne IDC [310]
OB ITOGAKH VYPOLNENIIA GOSUDARSTVENNOGO PLANA RAZVITIIA NARODNOGO KHOZIAISTVA SSSR V 1956 G / U.S.S.R. Tsentralnoe Statisticheskoe Upravlenie – M.1957. BD-784 1 – 9 – ne IDC [310]
OB ITOGAKH VYPOLNENIIA GOSUDARSTVENNOGO PLANA RAZVITIIA NARODNOGO KHOZIAISTVA SSSR V 1957 G / U.S.S.R. Tsentralnoe Statisticheskoe Upravlenie – M.1958. BD-785 1 – 9 – ne IDC [310]
OB ITOGAKH VYPOLNENIIA GOSUDARSTVENNOGO PLANA RAZVITIIA NARODNOGO KHOZIAISTVA SSSR V 1958 G / U.S.S.R. Tsentralnoe Statisticheskoe Upravlenie – M.1959. BD-786 1 – 9 – ne IDC [310]
OB ITOGAKH VYPOLNENIIA GOSUDARSTVENNOGO PLANA RAZVITIIA NARODNOGO KHOZIASISTVA SSSR V 1959 G / U.S.S.R. Tsentralnoe Statisticheskoe Upravlenie – M.1960. BD-787 1 – 9 – ne IDC [310]
OB ITOGAKH VYPOLNENIIA PIATOGO PIATILETNEGO PLANA RAZVITIIA SSSR I SOIUZNYKH RESPUBLIK NA 1951-1955 GG / U.S.S.R. Tsentralnoe Statisticheskoe Upravlenie – M.1956. BD-243 1 – 9 – ne IDC [310]
OB IZDANIIAKH ZAKONOV ROSSIISKOI IMPERII 1830-1917 / Korevo, N N – 4pts. Spb. 1900-17. Available: pts. 1-3. BR-11,238 1 – 9 – ne IDC [340]
OB IZUCHENII KOOPERATSII / Fortunatov, AF – Ed 2. M., 1914 – 1mf – 9 – COR-129/1 – ne IDC [334]
OB ORGANAKH SUDEBNOI VLASTI V ROSSII OT OSNOVANIIA GOSUDARSTVA DO VSTUPLENIIA NO PRESTOL' ALEKSEIA MIKHAILOVICHA / Cheglokov, P N – Kazan, 1855. 104p. BR-9547/1 – 9 – ne IDC [340]
OB ORGANIZATSII NASHEGO SEL'SKOGO BYTA : TEORIIA I PRAKTIKA: K VOPR. O VYSSH. PREPODAVANII / Stolypin, D A – M., 1892 – 2mf – 9 – COR-110/1 – ne IDC [334]
OB (OSSEWABRANDWAG) – 12 Nov 1941 – 17 Dec 1952 – 1 – us Res Libr [960]
OB OZHIDOVLENII BYVSHE I GOSUDARSTV. DUMY : ZAIMSTVOVANO IZ "NOVAGO VREMENI" / D.L.I. – S-Peterburg: Nevskai a tip., 1907 – 1 – CSUX89-B5903 – us Hoover Inst Photo [947]
OB USLOVIIAKH RAZVITIIA KREST'IANSKOGO KHOZIAISTVA V ROSSII : OCHERKI PO EKONOMIKI SEL'SKOGO KHOZIAISTVA / Kablukov, N A – M., 1899 – 4mf – 9 – COR-40/1 – ne IDC [334]
OB USTROISTVE ARENDNYKH KHUTOROV NA VLADEL'CHESKIKH ZEMLIAKH I KREST'IANSKOM KHOZIAISTVE VOOBSHCHE : IZ SEL'SKO-KHOZIASTVENNOI PRAKTIKI / Stolypin, D A – M., 1892 – 1mf – 9 – COR-111/1 – ne IDC [334]
OBADIAH RICH COLLECTION / ed by Brownrigg, Edwin Blake – Based on Colonial Latin American Manuscripts and Transcripts in the Obadiah Rich Collection. An inventory and index (New York Public Library, 1978) – 1 – us Primary [972]
Oban. Scotland. Old Parish Church *see* REGISTER OF BURIALS
OBAN TIMES – 1 – £42.00r – uk Scot News [072]
Obando, Luis de *see* CORRECCION DEL LENGUAJE...
O'Bannon, Jane P *see* VALIDATION OF FITNESSGRAM ONE-MILE RUN/WALK CRITERION-REFERENCED STANDARDS IN MEN AND WOMEN 18 TO 25 YEARS OF AGE
OBAT-OBAT JANG HARUS DIKETAHUI / Goei, Bian Sioe (The) – SE-4602 1. 1961 – 9 – ne IDC [950]
OBAT-OBATAN DAN PEMBUATANNJA / Kwik, Hok Tiang – 1959 – 9 – SE-4279 1 – ne IDC [615]
OBEDIENCIA Y AMOR : CARTA PASTORAL DEL...ADOLFO P.MUNOZ. OBISPO DE BADAJOZ / Perez Munoz, Adolfo – Badajoz: Tip.Uceda Hnos, 1916 – 1 – sp Bibl Santa Ana [240]
OB'EDINENIE : IZDANIE MOSKOVSKOGO SOIUZA POTREBITEL'SKIKH OBSHCHESTV – (Cont as: Izdanie Vserossiiskogo Tsentral'nogo Soiuza Potrebitel'skikh Obshchestv M., 1917 n13-1919 n4) – M., 1911-17 n12 – 40mf – 9 – COR-660/1 – ne IDC [334]
O'Beirne, H F *see* LEADERS AND LEADING MEN OF THE INDIAN TERRITORY
OBELISK – Carrara, NV. 1914-16 – 1r – 1 – $50.00 – U04439 – us Library Micro [071]
OBERAMMERGAU PASSION-PLAY = DAS PASSIONS-SCHAUSPIEL IN OBERAMMERGAU : MIT DEM VOLLSTAENDIGEN TEXTE DER CHORGESAENGE – Augsburg: B Schmid (A Manz), 1870 – 1 – us U.W. Library [820]
OBERAMMERGAU UND SEIN PASSIONSSPIEL / Trautmann, Karl – (Includes bibliographical references) – 6. Aufl. Bamberg: Buchner, 1890 – 1r – 1 – us U.W. Library [430]
OBERBADISCHES VOLKSBLATT – Loerrach, West Germany. 1977- – ca 9r per yr – 1 – gw Mikrofilm [072]
OBERBAYERISCHES VOLKSBLATT – Rosenheim, West Germany. 1969- – ca 10r per yr – 1 – gw Mikrofilm [072]
OBERBERGISCHE VOLKS-ZEITUNG / ed by Ausgabe O (Gummersbach) der Koelnischen Rundschau – Gummersbach, West Germany. 1992- – 7r per yr – 1 – gw Mikrofilm [072]
Oberbreyer, Max *see* JUS POTANDI
OBERDEUTSCHE ALLGEMEINE LITERATURZEITUNG UND NEUE OBERDEUTSCHE ALLGEMEINE LITERATURZEITUNG – Salzburg, spaeter Muenchen, 1788-1811 (mf ed 1987) – 340mf – DM2,850.00 – 3-89131-031-5 – gw Fischer [430]
OBERDEUTSCHE ZEITSCHRIFT FUER LAND- UND HAUSWIRTHE, KAUFLEUTE, FABRIKANTEN UND MANUFAKTURISTEN – Augsburg, jul 2-dec 31 1803, jan 7-dec 29 1804, jul 6-dec 28 1805, jul 5-dec 27 1806 – 1 – Dist. gw Mikrofilm – gw Misc Inst [072]
OBERELSAESSISCHE LANDESZEITUNG – Mulhouse, France. 1897-1918 – 1 – fr A.C.R.P.P. [072]
OBERFRAENKISCHE VOLKSZEITUNG – Hof B., Feb 1946-Mar 1971 – 60r – 1 – DM4,500.00 – gw Mikro Press [072]
OBERFRAENKISCHE VOLKSZEITUNG – Hof, West Germany. 22 Feb 1946-Mar 1971 – 1 – gw Mikrofilm [072]
Oberge, Eilhart von *see* TRISTRANT UND ISALDE
OBERHESSISCHE PRESSE *see* OBERHESSISCHER ANZEIGER
OBERHESSISCHE TAGESZEITUNG – (Bereichsausgabe der Oberhessischen Tageszeitung, Giessen) – Friedberg. jan 3, 1936-jun 30, 1938. 1940. 1942 (incomplete) – 14r – 1 – gw Mikrofilm [072]
OBERHESSISCHE ZEITUNG – Alsfeld, 1977- – ca 5r per yr – 1 – Dist. gw Mikrofilm – gw Misc Inst [072]
OBERHESSISCHE ZEITUNG *see* OBERHESSISCHER ANZEIGER
OBERHESSISCHER ANZEIGER – (Title changes: Oberhessische Zeitung, 1 Apr 1867; Marburger Presse, 14 Sep 1945; Oberhessische Presse, 1 Jun 1951) – Marburg Lahn, West Germany. 1976- – ca 7r per yr – 1 – gw Mikrofilm [072]
OBERHESSISCHER ANZEIGER *see* INTELLIGENZBLATT FUER DIE PROVINZ OBERHESSEN
DER OBERHOF : ERZAEHLUNG / Immermann, Karl Leberecht – Leipzig: P Reclam, [1940?] – 1r – 1 – us U.W. Library [830]
Oberholtzer, Ernest C *see* PAPERS
Oberholtzer Family *see* GENEALOGICAL MATERIAL, MS 2500
OBERKASSELER ZEITUNG – Bonn-Oberkassel, 1914-40, jan 16 1948-73 – 12r – 1 – Inquire at Mikrofilmarchiv for details – gw Misc Inst [943]
Oberkofler, Joseph Georg *see* NIE STIRBT DAS LAND
OBERKOMMANDO DES HEERES / Germany. Heer. Oberkommando – Heeres-Druck Vorschrift. Berlin, 1930-1944. no. 1A-488 5 – 1 – us NY Public [943]
OBERLIN : THE COLONY AND THE COLLEGE, 1833-1883 / Fairchild, James H – Oberlin, [Ohio]: E.J. Goodrich, 1883 – 1mf – us A.T.L.A. [370]
OBERLINS DREI STUFEN : UND, STURREGANZ / Wassermann, Jakob – Berlin: S Fischer, 1922 – 1r – 1 – us U.W. Library [810]
OBERMAIN-TAGBLATT – Lichtenfels, West Germany. 1 Sept 1978- – ca 7r per yr – 1 – gw Mikrofilm [072]
Obermann, H A *see* ARCHBISHOP THOMAS BRADWARDINE
OBERNDORFER NACHRICHTEN *see* SCHWARZWAELDER BOTE

OBERON : EIN GEDICHT IN ZWOELF GESAENGEN / Wieland, Christoph Martin; ed by Sallwuerk, Edmund von – Bielefeld: Velhagen & Klasing, 1926 – 1r – 1 – us U.W. Library [810]
OBERON : EIN GEDICHT IN ZWOELF GESAENGEN / Wieland, Christoph Martin – Stuttgart: J G Cotta'sche Buchhandlung Nachfolger, [1887?] – 1r – 1 – us U.W. Library [810]
OBERON : A POEM / Wieland, Christoph Martin – London: Printed for Cadel and Davies [etc.], 1798 – 1r – 1 – us U.W. Library [810]
OBERON : EIN ROMANTISCHES HELDENGEDICHT IN ZWOELF GESAENGEN / Wieland, Christoph Martin – Leipzig: A Schumann, 1898 – 1r – 1 – us U.W. Library [810]
OBERPFAELZISCHES ZEITBLATT – Amberg, 1848-49 – 1r – 1 – Dist. gw Mikrofilm – gw Misc Inst [943]
OBERRHEINISCHE ZEITUNG – Freiburg, Br., Germany. 12 Jul 1842-31 Dec 1846; 1 Jan-12 Jul 1849 – 7r – 1 – gw Mikrofilm [072]
Oberschlep, Reinhard *see* GESAMTVERZEICHNIS DES DEUTSCHSPRACHIGEN SCHRIFTTUMS, 1911-1965
DER OBERSCHLESIER – Oppeln (Opole), Poland. 1926-1940 – 1r – 1 – gw Mikrofilm [943]
DER OBERSCHLESISCHE KURIER – Koenigshuette (Chorzow), Poland. Jul 1925-1938; 1 Jan-15 Aug 1939; 1 Oct 1939-Mar 1943 – 48r – 1 – gw Mikrofilm [072]
OBERSCHLESISCHE ZEITUNG – Beuthen, 1908, feb 16 1930 – 1 – Inquire at Mikrofilmarchiv for details – gw Misc Inst [943]
OBERSCHLESISCHE ZEITUNG – Beuthen, Germany. 1908 – 3r – 1 – gw Mikrofilm [943]
OBERSCHLESISCHE ZEITUNG – Katowice. Poland. -w. 21 Mar 1943-17 Jan 1945. (Imperfect). (5 reels) – 1 – uk British Libr Newspaper [943]
OBERSCHLESISCHE ZEITUNG *see* KATTOWITZER ZEITUNG
Oberthur, C *see* ETUDES DE LEPIDOPTEROLOGIE COMPAREE
OBESITY AND METABOLISM – v.1-. 1981- – 1,5,6,9 – us UMI [073]
Obi-Okoye, A *see* ENFORCEMENT OF JUDGMENTS AND ORDERS
EL OBISPO DE BADAJOZ...A LOS CATOLICOS / Ramirez Vazquez, Fernando – 1873 – 9 – 1.50f – sp Bibl Santa Ana [240]
EL OBISPO DE BADAJOZ...CATOLICOS / Rodriguez Obregon, Francisco Xavier – 1848 – 9 – 1.50f – sp Bibl Santa Ana [240]
EL OBISPO DE ORENSE EN LA REGENCIA DEL ANO 1810 / Lopez Aydillo, Eugenio – Madrid: Imprenta Fortanet, 1918 – 1 – sp Bibl Santa Ana [240]
EL OBISPO DE QUITO DON ALONSO DE LA PENA MONTENEGRO / Baudin Hesmo, Manuel – Madrid: Missionalia Hispanica, 1952 – 1 – sp Bibl Santa Ana [240]
LOS OBISPOS DE LA ORDEN DE LA MERCED EN AMERICA (1601-1926). SANTIAGO DE CHILE, 1927 / Perez, Pedro – Madrid: Razon y Fe, 1929 – 1 – sp Bibl Santa Ana [240]
OBITER DICTA / Birell, Augustine – London: E. Stock, 1884 – 1 roll – 1 – 1-55879-764-5 – uk Libr Preservation [890]
OBITUAIRE DU MONASTERE DE GROENENDAEL DANS LA FORET DE SOIGNES / Dykmans, M – Bruxelles, 1942 – 12mf – 8 – Dfl25.00 – ne Slangenburg [240]
OBITUARY CARD FILES BRO-CLY / Jefferson County, KS – 1 – us KS Hist [920]
OBITUARY CARD FILES GOB-SCH / Jefferson County, KS – 1 – us KS Hist [920]
OBITUARY CARD FILES SCH-ZWY / Jefferson County, KS – Includes the Oskaloosa Church Records 1862-1925 – 1 – us KS Hist [920]
OBJECTIONS TO ANARCHISM / Barrett, George Slayter – Freedom Press pamphlet, 1921 – 9 – 1.00f – at Libertarian Micro [335]
OBJECTIONS TO THE CONTINUANCE OF THE WAR... / Bowles, J – Ed 2. London, 1794 – 1mf – 1 – ILM-2561/1 – ne IDC [327]
OBJECTIVE JUSTICE – v1- 1969- 1; v8- 5,6,9 – us UMI [321]
OBJECTIVES OF THE SECOND FIVE YEAR PLAN (1960-65) / Pakistan. Planning Commission – Karachi. 1959. BD-502 1 – 9 – ne IDC [338]
OBJECTIVIST – v1-10 1962-71 1; v10- 5,6 – us UMI [100]
OBJETOS INGRESADOS EN EL MUSEO PROVINCIAL (DE CACERES) / Sanguino y Michel, Juan – Madrid: Fortanet, 1913. B.R.A.H. 62, pp. 65-69 – sp Bibl Santa Ana [060]
OBJETS DES PHILIPPINES (MINDORO, PALAWAN) / MacDonald, Ch – Notes techniques et ethnographiques – 9 – F90.00 – fr Ethnologie [980]
OBJETS DU HAUT-SEPIK, NOUVELLE-GUINEE / Juillerat, B – (Amanab et Kwomtari) – 9 – F130.00 – fr Ethnologie [980]
OBJETS ETHNOGRAPHIQUES D'AMAZONIE / Caron, R – (Caraja, Cayapo, Tapirape, Timbira) – 9 – F60.00 – fr Ethnologie [305]
OBLASTNYE UCHREZHDENIIA ROSSII V 17 V / Chicherin, Boris N – Moscow, 1856. 600p. Local governmental administration in pre-Petrine Russia; based primarily on Polnoe Sobranie and publs. of the Archeographical Commissions. BR-9770/1 – 9 – ne IDC [947]
OBLICZE TYGODNIA *see* ODGLOSY
Obligado, Pastor S *see* TRADICIONES DE BUENOS AIRES
L'OBLIGATION – Montreal, Canada. n5. 24 oct 1918; n5. 10 oct 1919 – 1r – 1 – Can$30.00 – cn Can Microfilming [072]
THE OBLIGATIONS AND DUTIES OF THE FEMALE SEX TO CHRISTIANITY / Rogers, Ebenezer Platt – 1849 – 9 – us A.T.L.A. [240]
OBLIGATORY EXERCISE AND PATHOGENIC WEIGHT CONTROL IN COLLEGE STUDENTS / Stodel, Emma J – Springfield College, 1995 – 2mf – 9 – $8.00 – PSY1866 – us Microform Publ [150]
LE OBLIGAZIONI... / Cereti, C – Torino, 1925 – 3mf – 1 – ILM-3052/1 – ne IDC [327]
OBNOVA – Belgrade, Yugoslavia. Jun-Aug 1942 – 1r – 1 – us L of C Photodup [949]
Obol'ianinov, N *see* KATALOG RUSSKIKH ILLIUSTRIROVANNYKH IZDANII 1725-1860 GG
OBORONNYE STIKHI / Maiakovskii, Vladimir – M. 1936. BR-987 2 – 8 – ne IDC [460]
OBOZRENIE ARKHIVNYKH MATERIALOV / Arkhiv Akademii nauk SSSR – Moscow, Leningrad, 1933-71. 6v. General guide and description of holdings for Archive of Academy of Sciences of the USSR. BR-10,949/1 – 9 – ne IDC [500]
OBOZRENIE KOLLEKTSII SOBRANIIA FOTOARKHIVA INSTITUTA ISTORII MATERIAL'NOI KUL'TURY IM. N. IA. MARRA AN SSSR / Devel', T M – (Sovetskaia Arkheologiia, nr. 12, 1950). BR-10,994 1 – 9 – ne IDC [930]
OBOZRENIE KORMCHEI KNIGI V ISTORICHESKOM VIDE / Rozenkampf, G A – St. Petersburg, 1839. Ed.2. BR-11,138/1 – 9 – ne IDC [240]
OBOZRENIE LITERATURY PO TEATRU I MUZYKE 1889-1891 GG / Lisovskii, N M – Bibliograficheskii ocherk. Spb. 1893. BR-7135 2 – 8 – ne IDC [780]
OBOZRENIE PREDMETOV MEZHDUNARODNOGO PRAVA / Kapustin, MN – Moscow, 1856-59.360p. Based on author's lectures on international law at Moscow University. BR-9496/1 – 9 – ne IDC [340]
OBOZRENIE PREPODAVANIIA PREDMETOV V IMPERATORSKOM VARSHAVSKOM UNIVERSITETE V 1897/98. AKADEMICHESKOM GODU – Warsaw. n.d. BR-5746 2 – 8 – ne IDC [370]
OBOZRENIE RUKOPISEI I STAROPECHATNYKH KNIG V KNIGOKHRANILISHCHAKH MONASTYREI GORODSKIKH I SEL'SKIKH TSERKVEI KALUZHSKOI EPARKHII / Leonid, Arkhimandrit – Moscow, 1865. 115p. BR/7294/2 – 8 – ne IDC [240]
OBOZRENIE RUKOPISEI LOMONOSOVA I MATERIALOV O NEM, KHRANIASHCHIKHSIA V MOSKOVSKIKH I LENINGRADSKIKH ARKHIVAKH, MUZEIAKH I BIBLIOTEKAKH – Moscow, Leningrad, 1951.BR-10,658/1 – 9 – ne IDC [025]
OBOZRENIE RUSSKOI LITERATURY PO GRECHESKOI FILOLIGII ZA 1882-1883 GODY / Mishchenko, F – Kiev. 1884. BR-7172 2 – 8 – ne IDC [450]
OBOZRENIE RUSSKOI UCHEBNOI LITERATURY I KNIG DLIA CHTENIIA PO GEOGRAFII – (I.V. Ianchin, Red.). M. 1877. BR-7196 2 – 8 – ne IDC [910]
OBOZRENIE SLAVIANO-RUSSKOI BIBLIOGRAFII – 1: 2. Spb. 1849. BR-7197 2 – 8 – ne IDC [010]
OBOZRENIE SOSTAVA I USTROISTVA REGULIARNOI RUSSKOI KAVALERII OT PETRA VELIKOGO I DO NASHIKH DNEI / Ivanov, P A – Spb. 1864. BR-6188 2 – 8 – ne IDC [947]
OBOZRENIE SOVREMENNAGO SLAVIANSTVA / Niederle, L – (Entsiklopediia slavianskoi fiologii. nr. 2). Spb. 1909. BR-4969 2 – 8 – ne IDC [400]
OBOZRENIE TRUDOV PO SLAVIANOVEDENIIU – 1913 gg. v. 1-3. Petrograd. 1915-18. BR-5650 2 – 8 – ne IDC [460]
OBRA DE AGRICULTURA COMPILADA DE DIVERSOS AUTORES / Herrera, G – Alcala de Henares, 1513 – 6mf – 9 – sp Cultura [630]
Obra de Ayuda Nacional-Sindicalista *see* ESTAUTOS DE LA...
LA OBRA DE DON ANDRES MANJON / Marquez, Gabino – Madrid: Razon y Fe, 1923 y 1924 – 1 – sp Bibl Santa Ana [946]
OBRA DE LA PROPAGACION DE LA FE : MEMORIA / Badajoz. Junta Diocesana – (1929, 1931, 1932, 1933, 1937, 1938, 1939, 1940, 1941, 1942, 1943, 1944, 1945, 1947, 1948, 1949, 1950, 1951, 1951-52, 1952-53, 1953-54, 1954-55, 1955-56, 1956-57, 1957-58, 1958-59, 1959-60, 1960-61, 1961-62, 1962-63, 1963-64, 1964-65, 1965-66, 1966-67, 1967-68, 1968-69, 1969-70, 1970-71, 1971-72, 1972-73, 1973-74) – Badajoz: Tip. Espanola, s.a. – 1 – sp Bibl Santa Ana [946]
OBRA DE LA PROPAGACION DE LA FE : MEMORIA, 1928 / Badajoz. Junta Diocesana – Badajoz: Tip. Espanola, 1928 – 1 – sp Bibl Santa Ana [946]
LA OBRA DE LA REPUBLICA ESPANOLA / Peydro, Miguel – Casablanca, 1945. Fiche W1106. (Blodgett Collection of Spanish Civil War Pamphlets) – 9 – us H.U. College Libr [946]
LA OBRA DE LOS TRABAJADORES UNIDOS / Confederacion Nacional de Trabajo. Spain – Valparaiso, 1937. Fiche W 817. (Blodgett Collection of Spanish Civil War Pamphlets) – 9 – us H.U. College Libr [946]
LA OBRA DE PERON / Peron, Juan – Buenos Aires: [s.n.], 1954 – 1 – CSUXADH9482-B – us Hoover Inst Photo [320]
OBRA PONTIFICIA DE LA PROPAGACION DE LA FE...SECRETARIADO DE MEMORIA ANUAL DE – 1971 – Badajoz: Tipografia Clasica, 1971 – 1 – sp Bibl Santa Ana [946]
OBRA PONTIFICIA DE LA SANTA INFANCIA : MEMORIA / Badajoz. Santa Infancia – (1949-50, 1950-51, 1951-52, 1952-53, 1953-54, 1955-56, 1956-57, 1958-59, 1959-60, 1961-62, 1962-63, 1963-64, 1964-65, 1965-66, 1966-67, 1967-68, 1968-69, 1969-70, 1970-71, 1971-72, 1972-73) – Badajoz – 1 – sp Bibl Santa Ana [240]
OBRA REVOLUCIONARIA – Havana, CU. 1960-1961 – 2r – $100.00 – R04203 – us Library Micro [320]
OBRA REVOLUCIONARIA – Havana. May 1960-June July 1965 – 1 – 35.00r – us Hoover Inst Photo [073]
Obra Sindical *see* PREVENCION DE ACCIDENTES Y SOCORRISMO EN EL TRABAJO
OBRA SINDICAL DE COLONIZACION. GRANJA ESCUELA SINDICAL AGRARIA. NUESTRA SENORA DE BOTOA / Delegacion Provincial e Sindicatos – Badajoz: Granja Escuela Sindical Agraria, 1968 – sp Bibl Santa Ana [630]
Obra Sindical de Educacion y Descanso *see*
– 2ND JORNADAS DE PROMOCION DEL DEPORTE LABORAL 1976
– BASES DE LA 1ST EXPOSICION DE FOTOGRAFIAS...
– I JORNADAS DE PROMOCION DEL DEPORTE LABORAL
OBRA SINDICAL DE EDUCACION Y DESCANSO. ACTOS ORGANIZADOS PARA EL DIA 1 DE MAYO CON MOTIVO DE LA FESTIVIDAD DE SAN JOSE ARTESANO / Organizacion Sindical – Badajoz: Imp. Inca, 1970 – sp Bibl Santa Ana [946]
Obra Sindical de Formacion Profesional *see* REGLAMENTO DEL PATRONATO DEL CENTRO SINDICAL MINERO 9 DE FORMACION PROFESIONAL ACELERADA DE BADAJOZ
Obra Sindical de Formacion Profesional. Organizacion Sindicazl *see* TALLER ESCUELA-SINDICAL "VIRGEN DEL PUERTO"
Obra Sindical Educacion y Descanso. Caceres *see* EXPOSICION PROVINCIAL DE ARTE
OBRA Y ACCI ON DEL PERONISMO – (Includes c.1: v.2:no.3/4 1948:Feb) – Buenos Aires: Orientaci on Peronista, 194?- – 1 – CSUXADP1494-S – us Hoover Inst Photo [972]
OBRA...DE LA GRANDE Y TERRIBLE MORTANDAD / Bovea, A – Valencia, 1582 – 1mf – 9 – sp Cultura [616]
OBRANA L'UDU – Bratislava, Czechoslovakia. 1947-1992 – 49r – 1 – us L of C Photodup [072]
OBRANA L'UDU – Prague, Czechoslovakia. Jun 1948-Sept 1951 – 2r – 1 – us L of C Photodup [072]
OBRAS / Cabello de Balboa, Miguel – Madrid: Missionalia Hispanica, 1948.-v1 – 1 – sp Bibl Santa Ana [440]
OBRAS / Donoso Cortes, Juan Francisco – 1854. 5v – 9 – 1.50f – sp Bibl Santa Ana [946]
OBRAS / Donoso Cortes, Juan Francisco – 1891-94.4v – 9 – 1.50f – sp Bibl Santa Ana [946]
OBRAS / Donoso Cortes, Juan Francisco – (Tambien Vol 2; 3; 4) – Madrid: Edit. San Francisco de Sales, 1903.-v1 – 1 – sp Bibl Santa Ana [946]
OBRAS / Forner Segarra, Juan Pablo – v1. 1843 – 9 – 1.50f – sp Bibl Santa Ana [840]
OBRAS / Lasso de la Vega, Garcia – 1604 – 9 – 1.50f – sp Bibl Santa Ana [900]
OBRAS / Lopez de Ayala, Adelardo – Madrid, 1881-85.7v. (Coleccion de escritores castellanos). 1 reel. 1248 – 1 – us U.W. Library [890]
OBRAS / Lopez de Ayala, Adelardo – (Teatro III. 1882. 1.50f; 9. Teatro III. 1883. 1.50f; BSA; 9. Teatro IV. 1884. 1.50f; BSA; 9. Teatro V. 1884.1.50f; BSA; 9) – Teatro II. 1882 – 9 – 1.50f – sp Bibl Santa Ana [820]
OBRAS / Mena, Juan de – (1582. 1.50f; 9) – 1804 – 9 – 1.50f – sp Bibl Santa Ana [240]
OBRAS / Orozco, Alfonso de – v1-2. 1882 – 9 – 1.50f – sp Bibl Santa Ana [240]
OBRAS / Sarmiento, Domingo F – Paris. 1889-1909. 53 v – 1 – 162.00 – us L of C Photodup [972]
OBRAS COMPLETAS / Acuna de Figueroa, Francisco Esteban – 12v. 1890 – 1 – 69.00 – us L of C Photodup [890]
OBRAS COMPLETAS / Arenal de Garcia Carrasco, Concepcion – 13v. 1894-96. Lacks v.5-11 – 1 – 23.00 – us L of C Photodup [360]
OBRAS COMPLETAS / Bolivar, Simon – Comp. y notas de Vicente Lecuna, con Esther Barret de Nazaris. 2nd ed. 1950. 3v – 1 – us U.W. Library [920]
OBRAS COMPLETAS / Chamizo, Luis – 1892 – 9 – 1.50f – sp Bibl Santa Ana [890]
OBRAS COMPLETAS / Gabriel y Galan, Jose Maria – Castellanas: Nuevas Castellanas: Extremenas. Quinta Edicion. Madrid. Rivadeneyra, 1921.-v1 – 1 – sp Bibl Santa Ana [946]
OBRAS COMPLETAS / Gabriel y Galan, Jose Maria – Zamora: Tip. Jacinto Gonzalez, s.a. vol 1 – 1 – sp Bibl Santa Ana [946]
OBRAS COMPLETAS / Lopez de Ayala, Adelardo – 1881 – 9 – 1.50f – sp Bibl Santa Ana [820]
OBRAS COMPLETAS = WORKS / Peron, Juan Domingo – (Includes c.1: v.2-v.4:no.2, v.5-v.7:no.3, v.14, v.17, v.21-25:no.2; v.26-27) – Buenos Aires, Argentina: Proyecto Hernandarias, 1984- – 1 – CSUXAJA7202-B – us Hoover Inst Photo [320]
OBRAS COMPLETAS... / Gonzolo Picon, Febres – Madrid: Razon y Fe, 1940 – sp Bibl Santa Ana [780]
OBRAS COMPLETAS 1. MERCEDARIOS ILUSTRES INTRODUCCION Y NOTAS DE RICARDO SANLES MARTINEZ. MADRID, 1966 / Vasquez Nunez, Guillermo – Madrid: Graf. Calleja, 1967 – 1 – sp Bibl Santa Ana [946]

OBRAS COMPLETAS DE DON JOSE CLEMENTE FABRES, RECOPILADAS Y PUBLICADAS POR LA UNIVERSIDAD CATOLICA DE SANTIAGO DE CHILE / Fabres y Fernandez, Jose Clement – Santiago de Chile, Cervantes, 1908-1914. 16 v – 1 – $46.00 – us L of C Photodup [440]

OBRAS COMPLETAS, ORDENADAS Y PROLOGADAS POR ALBERTO GHIRALDO / Marti, Jose Julian – Madrid. v1-6. 1925 – 1r – 1 – us Ross [440]

OBRAS COMPLETAS Y CORRESPONDENCIA CIENTIFICA / Ameghino, F; ed by Forelli, A J – La Plata. v1-24. 1913-1936 – 340mf – 9 – ne IDC [500]

OBRAS DE ALBEYTERIA / Arredondo, Martin – 1669 – 9 – 1.50f – sp Bibl Santa Ana [946]

OBRAS DE ALBEYTERIA / Arredondo, Martin – 1728 – 9 – 1.50f – sp Bibl Santa Ana [946]

OBRAS DE ANTONIO RAFAEL MENGS / Azara, Jose Nicolas – 1780 – 2mf – 9 – Pta1,500.00 – 84-7848-163-X – sp Pentalfa [440]

OBRAS DE D....TEATRO 6. CASTIGO Y PERDON. EL NUEVO DON JUAN / Lopez do Ayala, Adelardo – Madrid: Imp. Perez Dubrull, 1885 – 1 – sp Bibl Santa Ana [440]

OBRAS DE JENOFONTE. TOMO 1 / Florez Canseco, Casimiro – 1781 – 2mf – 9 – Pta1,500.00 – 84-7848-142-7 – sp Pentalfa [440]

OBRAS DE JENOFONTE. TOMO 2 / Florez Canseco, Casimiro – 1781 – 2mf – 9 – Pta1,500.00 – 84-7848-143-5 – sp Pentalfa [440]

LAS OBRAS DE PUBLIO V. MARON / Lopez, Diego – 1614; 1641; 1679; 1721 – 9 – $1.50f – sp Bibl Santa Ana [450]

LAS OBRAS DE PUBLIO VIRGILIO MORAN. TRADUCIDO EN PROSA CASTELLANA POR...NATURAL... / Lopez, Diego – Madrid: Juan de la Cuesta, 1614 – sp Bibl Santa Ana [946]

LAS OBRAS DE VIRGILIO MARON, TRADUCIDO EN PROSA CASTELLANA... / Lopez, Diego – Madrid: Angel Pascual Rubio, 1721 – 1 – sp Bibl Santa Ana [946]

LAS OBRAS DEL FAMOSO POETA JUAN DE MENA / Sanchez, Francisco – Salamanca, 1582 – 1 – sp Bibl Santa Ana [810]

LAS OBRAS DEL...JUAN DE MENA / Sanchez de las Brozas, Francisco – 1582 – 9 – $1.50f – sp Bibl Santa Ana [240]

OBRAS. EL TEJADO DE VIDRIO / Lopez de Ayala, Adelardo – Tomo II.1882 – 9 – 1.50f – sp Bibl Santa Ana [820]

OBRAS. EN SU LENGUA ORIGINAL CON LA TRADUCCION LATINA Y ALGUNAS ANOTACIONES POR PEDRO ARMENGOL VALENZUELA / Pedro Pascual, Saint, Bp. of Jaen – Roma: Tip. della Pace di F. Cuggiani, 1905-08 – 1 – us U.W. Library [240]

OBRAS ESCOGIDAS / Donoso Cortes, Juan Francisco – Buenos Aires: Editorial Difusion, 1944 – sp Bibl Santa Ana [946]

OBRAS INEDITAS, ORDENADAS Y PROLONGADAS POR ALBERTO GHIRALDO / Perez Galdos, Benito – Madrid: Renacimiento, 1923- – 1 – us U.W. Library [820]

OBRAS MISTICAS DEL ANOTADAS Y PRECEDIDAS DE UNA INTRODUCCION...POR EL P. FR. JAIME SALA. PARTE 1... / Juan de los Angeles – Madrid: Bailly Bailliere, 1912 – 1 – sp Bibl Santa Ana [946]

OBRAS MISTICAS...OBRA PREPARADA POR EL P. FR. JAIME SALA Y REVISADA POR EL P. FR. GREGORIO FUENTES... / Juan de los Angeles – Madrid: Bailly-Bailliere, 1917 – 1 – sp Bibl Santa Ana [140]

OBRAS MUSICALES DE RODRIGUEZ ORDONEZ Y GUERRERO RIBERA (SIECLE 16-17) – Avila – 1r – 5,6 – sp Cultura [780]

OBRAS. POESIAS / Lopez de Ayala, Adelardo – 1885 – 9 – 1.50f – sp Bibl Santa Ana [810]

OBRAS POETICAS / Espronceda, Jose de – (1871 ed.1.50f; 9. 1875 ed.1.50f; BSA; 9. 1883 ed.1.50f; BSA; 9. 1884 ed.1.50f; BSA; 9. 1891 ed.1.50f; BSA; 9) – 1869 – 9 – 1.50f – sp Bibl Santa Ana [810]

OBRAS POETICAS COMPLETAS / Espronceda, Jose de – (Con un estudio preliminar y notas) – Madrid: Aguilar. S.A., 1951 – sp Bibl Santa Ana [810]

OBRAS POETICAS DE / Espronceda, Jose de – Barcelona: Casa Editorial Maucci, 1906 – 9 – sp Bibl Santa Ana [440]

OBRAS POETICAS DE / Espronceda, Jose de – Paris: Baudry Libreria Europea, 1865 – 9 – sp Bibl Santa Ana [440]

OBRAS POETICAS DE D..., ORDENADAS Y ANOTADAS POR J.E. HARTZENBUSCH A SABER : EL PELAYO, ENSAYO EPICO... / Espronceda, Jose de – Paris: Bandry, 1870 – sp Bibl Santa Ana [810]

OBRAS POETICAS DE.... PRECEDIDAS DE LA BIOGRAFIA DEL AUTOR / Espronceda, Jose de – Valladolid: Jorge Montoro, 1907 – 1 – sp Bibl Santa Ana [440]

OBRAS POETICAS Y ESCRITOS EN PROSA / Espronceda, Jose de – (1865 ed.1.50f; 9. 1870 ed.1.50f; BSA; 9. 1876 ed.1.50f; BSA; 9. 1890 ed.1.50f; BSA; 9) – 1884 – 9 – 1.50f – sp Bibl Santa Ana [810]

OBRAS POETICAS Y ESCRITOS EN PROSA. COLECCION COMPLETA...ORDENADA POR DON PATRICIO DE LA ESNOSURA / Espronceda, Jose de – Madrid: Eduardo Mengibar, Editor. 1884 – 9 – sp Bibl Santa Ana [440]

OBRAS POETICASIDE PINDARO.. / Berguizas, Francisco P – 1798 – 9 – 1.50f – sp Bibl Santa Ana [450]

OBRAS QUE DEDICA A LA REINA. TOMO 1 / Vaca de Guzman, Jose Maria – 1789 – 1mf – 9 – Pta1,000.00 – 84-7848-276-8 – sp Pentalfa [946]

OBRAS QUE DEDICA A LA REINA. TOMO 2 / Vaca de Guzman, Jose Maria – 1792 – 1mf – 9 – Pta1,000.00 – 84-7848-277-6 – sp Pentalfa [946]

OBRAS QUE DEDICA A LA REINA. TOMO 3 / Vaca de Guzman, Jose Maria – 1792 – 1mf – 9 – Pta1,000.00 – 84-7848-278-4 – sp Pentalfa [946]

OBRAS SUELTAS. TOMO 1 / Iriarte, Juan de – 1774 – 2mf – 9 – Pta1,500.00 – 84-7848-183-4 – sp Pentalfa [440]

OBRAS SUELTAS. TOMO 2 / Iriarte, Juan de – 1774 – 2mf – 9 – Pta1,500.00 – 84-7848-184-2 – sp Pentalfa [440]

OBRAS. TOMO 1 / Castellanos, Juan de – Caracas, 1930; Madrid: Razon y Fe, 1931 – 1 – sp Bibl Santa Ana [440]

OBRAS Y HECHOS DEL PERONISMO – (Includes c.1: v.1:no.1 1947:Aug) – Buenos Aires: Orientaci on Peronista, 1947- – 1 – CSUXADP1485-S – us Hoover Inst Photo [972]

OBRAS Y SERVICIOS DE LAS CORPORACIONES LOCALES, SANIDAD Y ASSISTENCIA ANEXO AL PLAN. 1964/67 / Spain. Comisaria del Plan de Desarrollo Economico y Social – Madrid. 1964. BD-857 1 – 9 – ne IDC [338]

OBRAS...POETA / Silvestre, Gregorio – 1592 – 9 – 1.50f – sp Bibl Santa Ana [810]

OBRAZ NIKOLAIA CHUDOTVORSTA. ALATYR'-KAMEN' RUSSKOI VERY / Remizov, A – Paris, 1931. 90p. BR-829 2 – 8 – ne IDC [460]

OBRAZTSY PIS'MA DREVNEISHEGO PERIODA ISTORII RUSSKOI KNIGI / Karinskii, N M – Leningrad, 1925.BR-10,332/1 – 9 – ne IDC [947]

OBRAZTSY SLAVIANSKOGO, KIRILLOVSKOGO PIS'MA S X DO XVIII VEK / Karskii, E F – Warsaw, 1912/13.BR-10,336/1 – 9 – ne IDC [460]

Obrecht, Jacob *see* WERKEN

Obregon, B *see* CONSTITUCIONES Y REGLA DE LA MINIMA CONGREGACION DE LOS HERMANOS ENFERMEROS

EL OBRERO / Gonzalez y Grez, Juan J – 1898 – 9 – 1.50f – sp Bibl Santa Ana [305]

EL OBRERO DEL CAMPO / Merino, Alberto – Badajoz: Imp. de Vicente Rodriguez, 1912 – 1 – sp Bibl Santa Ana [946]

EL OBRERO DEL CAMPO (ESTUDIO SOCIAL) / Merino de Torres, Alberto – 2nd ed. corregida y aumentada. Badajoz: Imp. V. Rodriguez, 1920 – sp Bibl Santa Ana [300]

EL OBRERO LUSTRADOR DE CALZADO (PERIODICAL) AHORRE : EL AHORRO ES LA BASE FUNDAMENTAL DEL BIENESTAR DE LOS PUEBLOS; APOYE EL 20. PLAN QUINQUENAL – [Buenos Aires]: Sindicato Obrero de Lustradores de Calzado de la Rep. Argentina, [1953] – 1 – CSUXADH6497-B – us Hoover Inst Photo [073]

O'Brian, Jeanne M *see* ISOKINETIC EVALUATION OF THE POSTERIOR ROTATOR CUFF MUSCULATURE FOLLOWING A STRENGTHENING PROGRAM UTILIZING RUBBER TUBING

O'Brien, Archbishop *see*
- PASTORAL LETTER ADDRESSED TO THE CLERGY AND LAITY OF THE ARCHDIOCESE OF HALIFAX
- TO THE CLERGY AND LAITY OF THE DIOCESE, HEALTH AND BENEDICTION IN THE LORD
- TO THE CLERGY AND LAITY OF THE DIOCESE OF HALIFAX, HEALTH AND BENEDICTION IN THE LORD
- TO THE CLERGY, RELIGIOUS ORDERS AND LAITY OF THE DIOCESE, HEALTH AND BENEDICTION IN THE LORD

O'Brien, Cornelius *see* MATER ADMIRABILIS

O'Brien, Mary *see* THE PIOUS INCENDIARIES

O'Brien, Richard Barry *see* FIFTY YEARS OF CONCESSIONS TO IRELAND, 1831-1881

Obrman, Jan *see*
- CZECH/SLOVAKIAN PERIODICALS
- PRAGUE SPRING 1968

O'Bryan, W *see* DIARY, 1825-1827, 1831-1834, 1836-1838, 1840, 1842, 1845, 1848, 1855, 1857-1864

OBSCENITY AND PORNOGRAPHY COMMISSION : "LOCKHART COMMISSION" TECHNICAL REPORTS – Washington: GPO. v1-8 + Final Report. 1970 (all publ) – 35mf – 9 – $52.00 – LLMC 81-232 – us L.L.M.C. [324]

OBSCHCHESTVA ISTORII I DREVNOSTEI ROSSIIKIKH / Russia – Cheteniia. Moscow. 1846-1918 – 1 – us UMI [947]

OBSCHEE DELO – Titre francais: La Cause commune. Quotidien russe. Red. en chef Victor Bourzeff. Paris. sept 1918-21 – 1 – fr A.C.R.P.P. [073]

OBSCURE CHARACTERS AND MINOR LIGHTS OF SCRIPTURE / Hastings, Frederick – New York: Funk & Wagnalls, 1885 – 1mf – 9 – 0-8370-3520-1 – 1985-1520 – us A.T.L.A. [220]

OBSEQUIES, REV. G.W. LYON / Lyon, George A – 1871 – 9 – $50.00 – us Presbyterian [920]

OBSERVACION SOBRE EL VOMITO PERIODICO... / Vidal, Fabian – Madrid, 1742 – 1mf – 9 – sp Cultura [616]

OBSERVACION Y SUMARIA RELACION DE LAS VIRUELAS / Sola, F – SL, SA: 1622? – 1mf – 9 – sp Cultura [616]

OBSERVACIONES AL LIBRO DE AUBSEY F.C. BELL SOBRE FRAY LUIS DE LEON. EL ESCORIAL, 1931 / Velez, Pedro M – Madrid: Razon y Fe, 1932 – 1 – sp Bibl Santa Ana [420]

OBSERVACIONES DEL ECLIPSE...OFICIAL – 1900 – 9 – 1.50f – sp Bibl Santa Ana [520]

OBSERVACIONES DIRIGIDAS A DEMOSTRAR LA JUSTICIA DEL RECURSO DE SUPLICA / Tans de Monsalve, Agustin – Caceres, 1849 – 1 – sp Bibl Santa Ana [340]

OBSERVACIONES PRACTICAS SOBRE LOS RECURSOS DE FUERZA.... 1794 / Canada, Conde de la – 9 – 1.50f – sp Bibl Santa Ana [340]

OBSERVACIONES...CONTRA LA SENTENCIA... DUQUE DE MEDINACELI / Santos Cuenda, Juan y Consortes – 1879 – 9 – 1.50f – sp Bibl Santa Ana [946]

OBSERVACIONES...INTERPUESTO POR DON AGUSTIN TOUS DE MONSALVEZ – 1849 – 9 – $1.50f – sp Bibl Santa Ana [946]

EL OBSERVADOR – Ano 1810 (6-VII/7-IX) – 6mf – 9 – sp Cultura [946]

O OBSERVADOR : ORGAO DOS INTERESSES GERAES DO MUNICIPIO – S. Luiz Do Quitunde, Alagoas. 11 Mar 1882 – 1,5,6 – bl Biblioteca [072]

O OBSERVADOR – Sao Luis, 29 Jul 1847-Dec 1849. Jan, Mar-Dec 1850. Jan 1851-11 Feb 1861 – 1,5,6 – bl Biblioteca [072]

O OBSERVADOR DAS GALLERIAS DA ASSEMBLEA GERAL EM 1830 – Rio de Janeiro, 11 May-9 Sep 1930 – 1,5,6 – bl Biblioteca [072]

L'OBSERVATEUR – (Cont: Echo Laval) – Laval, Canada. v4 n1. 8 jan 1969-26 sep 1973 – 4r – 1 – Can$60.00r – cn Can Microfilming [072]

L'OBSERVATEUR – (Cont: La Bibliotheque Canadienne) – Montreal, Canada. 10 jul 1830-2 jul 1831 – 1r – 1 – Can$30.00 – cn Can Microfilming [073]

L'OBSERVATEUR / ed by Darveau, L M – Quebec, Canada. 9 mar 1858-21 mar 1860 – 1r – 1 – Can$30.00 – cn Can Microfilming [072]

L'OBSERVATEUR / ed by Guilbault, George – Joliette, Canada. v1 n14. 6 oct 1882-v3 n80. 5 mai 1885 – 1r – 1 – Can$30.00 – cn Can Microfilming [072]

L'OBSERVATEUR – Montreal, Canada. 6 mai 1899 – 1r – 1 – Can$25.00 – cn Can Microfilming [072]

L'OBSERVATEUR – Par M. Feydel. I, no. 1-91; II, no. 1-40. Paris. aout 1789-oct 1790 – 1 – fr A.C.R.P.P. [073]

L'OBSERVATEUR *see*
- BIBLIOTHEQUE CANADIENNE
- ECHO LAVAL
- L'OMBUDSMAN

L'OBSERVATEUR CANADIEN – Montreal, Canada. 3 mar; v1 n5. 20 mar 1838 – 1r – 1 – Can$25.00 – cn Can Microfilming [072]

L'OBSERVATEUR CATHOLIQUE – Montreal, Canada. 26 jun 1854-v1 n3. 10 jul 1854 – 1r – 1 – Can$30.00 – cn Can Microfilming [240]

OBSERVATEUR ECONOMIQUE CANADIEN *see* REVUE STATISTIQUE DU CANADA

L'OBSERVATEUR FEMININ – Par Madame de Verte-Allure. devenu: L' Etoile du matin ou Les Petits mots de Madame de Verte-Allure, ex-religieuse. no. 1-6. Paris. mars 1790 – 1 – fr A.C.R.P.P. [073]

L'OBSERVATEUR FRANCAIS – Journal politique quotidien. Dir. Denis Gilbert. Paris. juil-dec 1891 – 1 – fr A.C.R.P.P. [073]

OBSERVATEUR FRANCAIS – London, UK. 17 May 1845-5 Aug 1848 – 1 – uk British Libr Newspaper [072]

L'OBSERVATEUR LITTERAIRE – Par M. l'abbe de La Porte. Amsterdam. 1758-61 (I-XVII) – 1 – fr A.C.R.P.P. [073]

L'OBSERVATEUR MUNICIPAL – Montreal, Canada. 21 jul 1894 – 1r – 1 – Can$25.00 – cn Can Microfilming [072]

L'OBSERVATEUR NATURALISTE – Quebec, Canada. jan, fev 1904; jan 1907 – 1r – 1 – Can$25.00 – cn Can Microfilming [072]

OBSERVATION AND STUDY : CRITIQUE AND RECOMMENDATIONS ON FEDERAL PROCEDURES / Farmer, Larry C – Washington: FJC, Dec 1977 – 1mf – 9 – $1.50 – LLMC 95-811 – us L.L.M.C. [340]

OBSERVATION AND STUDY IN THE FEDERAL DISTRICT COURTS / Horney, Julie – Washington: FJC, 1985 – 1mf – 9 – $1.50 – LLMC 95-360 – us L.L.M.C. [340]

OBSERVATION CAR / Cleveland, Akron and Columbus Railway – 1892. 1 reel – 1 – us Ohio Hist [380]

OBSERVATION ON THE AUTHENTICITY OF BRUCE'S TRAVELS IN ABYSSINIA : IN REPLY TO SOME PASSAGES IN BROWN'S TRAVELS THROUGH EGYPT, AFRICA, AND SYRIA / Wharton, Richard – Newcastle upon Tyne, 1800 – 1 – us Res Libr [910]

OBSERVATION POST : VETERAN'S HOME OF CALIFORNIA – Yountville, CA. Jul 1944-Nov 1978 – 5r – 1 – $250.00 – B03115 – us Library Micro [071]

OBSERVATIONAL LEARNING AND ACQUISITION OF COMPLEX MOTOR PATTERNS BY CHILDREN : A PERCEPTION/ACTION APPROACH / Romack, Jennifer L – Indiana University, 1995 – 2mf – 9 – $8.00 – PSY1860 – us Microform Publ [611]

OBSERVATIONES ACADEMICAE, QUIBUS VIA MUNITUR AD ORIGINES GRAECAS INVESTIGANDAS, LEXICORUMQUE DEFECTUS RESARCIENDOS / Valckenaer, L C – (Linguistic series). 1805 – 9 – fr Hachette [450]

OBSERVATIONES ANATOMICAE... / Stensen, N – Lugduni Batavorum, 1662 – 3mf – 9 – ne IDC [611]

OBSERVATIONES BOTANICAE / Dahl, A – Havniae. 1787. B-5885 2 – 8 – ne IDC [580]

OBSERVATIONES BOTANICAE / Medikus, F K – (Historia et Commentationes Academie. v. 3. Theodoro-Palatinae. 1775). B-8128 1 – 9 – ne IDC [580]

OBSERVATIONES BOTANICAE / Mohr, D M H – Kiliae, 1803. 45, 2 pp. B-6077 2 – 8 – ne IDC [580]

OBSERVATIONES BOTANICAE / Retzius, A J – Lipsiae. 1779-91. B-2231 2 – 8 – ne IDC [580]

OBSERVATIONES BOTANICAE / Swartz, O P – 5757. 1791 – 9 – ne IDC [580]

OBSERVATIONES BOTANICAE IN LINNEI SPECIES PLANTARUM EX EDITIONE C.L. WILLDENOW / Schultes, J A – Oeniponti. 1809. B-5730 2 – 8 – ne IDC [580]
OBSERVATIONES BOTANICAS / Meyen, F J F – (Nova Acta Academiae Leopoldino-Carolinae Naturae Curiosorum, 1842, v. 19, suppl. 1, 512 pp., 13 pls.). B-5227 prSF 48,00 IDC 8 – ne IDC [580]
OBSERVATIONES BOTANICO-MEDICAE / Lachenal, W de – Basel, [1776] – 1mf – 9 – ne IDC [615]
OBSERVATIONES ENTOMOLOLGICAE / Heer, Oswald – Turici, 1836. Z/1135/2 – 8 – ne IDC [590]
OBSERVATIONES EPIGRAPHICAE DE PRAEPOSITIONUM GRAECARUM : FORMA ET USU / Geyer, Mauritius – (Includes bibliographies) – Altenburgi: O Bondi, 1880 – 1mf – 9 – 0-8370-9146-2 – 1986-3146 – us A.T.L.A. [450]
OBSERVATIONES ET EMENDATIONES AD FRANCISCI GEORGII VENETI PROBLEMATA / Mersenne, Marin – Lutetiae Parisiorum, 1623 – 10mf – 8 – ne Slangenburg [220]
OBSERVATIONES IN MATERIAM MEDICAM / Linnaeus, Carl – Upsaliae, 1772 – 1mf – 9 – ne IDC [610]
OBSERVATIONES MEDICAE CIRCA MORBORUM AUCTORUM HISTORIAM ET CURATIONEM / Sydenham, T – Londini, 1676 – 10mf – 9 – ne IDC [615]
OBSERVATIONES MYCOLOGICAE / Fries, E M – v. 1. Havnaie. 1815; v. 2. Havniae. 1818. B-5235 2 – 8 – ne IDC [580]
OBSERVATIONES MYCOLOGICAE / Persoon, C H – 1796 – 1 – uk Microform Academic [580]
OBSERVATIONES MYCOLOGICAE / Persoon, C H – v. 1. Lipsiae. 1796; v. 2. Lipsiae. 1799. B-5095 2 – 8 – ne IDC [580]
OBSERVATIONES QUAEDAM BOTANICAE ET ANATOMICAE / Zinn, J G – Goettingae. 1753. B-5822 2 – 8 – ne IDC [580]
OBSERVATIONES...DE PACTIS / Colenbrander, G J – Lugduni-Batavorum, 1810 – 2mf – 1 – ILM-1125/1 – ne IDC [327]
OBSERVATIONIS DE SACRIS AMPHIARAI THEBANIS ET OROPIIS / Dittenberger, Wilhelm – 1889. 8p – 1 – us U.W. Library [250]
OBSERVATIONS AND REMARKS ON MR. SEAGRAVE'S CONDUCT AND WRITINGS, IN WHICH HIS ANSWER TO THE REV. DR TRAPP'S FOUR SERMONS IS MORE PARTICULARLY CONSIDERED – London, 1739 – 1mf – 9 – MP-254/1 – ne IDC [240]
OBSERVATIONS CONCERNING THE NATURE AND DUE METHOD OF TREATING THE GOUT / Cheyne, G – M-89 2. 1720 – 8 – ne IDC [610]
OBSERVATIONS CONCERNING THE NATURE AND ORIGIN OF THE MEETINGS OF THE TWELVE JUDGES FOR THE CONSIDERATION OF CASES RESERVED FROM THE CIRCUITS / Alcock, John Congreve – Dublin, Milliken, 1838. 39 p. LL-101 – 1 – us L of C Photodup [340]
OBSERVATIONS DE L'ACADEMIE FRANCOISE SUR LES REMARQUES DE M. DE VAUGELAS / Vaugelas, Cl. Favre de – 1704 – 9 – fr I.C.S. [440]
LES OBSERVATIONS DE PLUSIEURS SINGULARITEZ ET CHOSES MEMORABLES, TROUVEES EN GRECE, ASIE, IUDEE, EGYPTE, ARABIE, ET AUTRES PAYS ESTRANGES / Belon, Pierre – Paris, G. Corrozet, 1553, xxii p. -210 ff. French Voyagers in the Mediterranean 16th to 18th Centuries. 5955 – 9 – fr Hachette [949]
LES OBSERVATIONS DE PLVSIEVRS SINGVLARITEZ ET CHOSES MEMORABLES, TROUUEES EN GRECE, ASIE, IUDEE, EGYPTE, ARABIE, ET AUTRES PAYS ESTRANGES, ... / Belon, P – Paris, 1555 – 5mf – 9 – H-8288/1 – ne IDC [956]
OBSERVATIONS DE POULKOVA, PUBLIEES PAR OTTO STRUVE, DIRECTEUR DE L'OBSERVATOIRE CENTRAL NICOLAS – v1-14. St. Petersburg. Impr. de l'Academie imperiale des Sciences. Suppl. no.1-3 (1881-91). Some vols. publ. out of order. Continued by: Publications de l'Observatoire central Nicolas – 1 – us U.W. Library [520]
OBSERVATIONS ET MEMOIRES SUR LA PHYSIQUE, SUR L'HISTOIRE NATURELLE ET SUR LES ARTS... – (Cont as: Journal de Physique, de Chimie et d'Histoire naturelle... Paris v44-46 1794-1823) – Paris. v1-43. 1772-1793 – 1088mf – 9 – ne IDC [500]
OBSERVATIONS GRAMMATICALES / Deplace, G M – 1810 – 9 – fr I.C.S. [440]
OBSERVATIONS IURIS NATURALIS,... / Darjes, J G – Jena, 1751-54 – 8mf – 1 – ILM-463/1 – ne IDC [327]
OBSERVATIONS MADE AT THE MAGNETICAL AND METEOROLOGICAL OBSERVATORY AT TRINITY COLLEGE, DUBLIN / Dublin. University. Magnetical and Meteorological Observatory – Dublin, 1865-69 – 3 – us Readex [530]
OBSERVATIONS NONNULLAE IN COLEOPTERA INDIAE ORIENTALIS / Perty, M – Monachii. 1831. BZ-1541 2 – 8 – ne IDC [590]
OBSERVATIONS ON A LETTER FROM JAMES STEWART...RELATING TO ANIMADVERSIONS AND IMPUTATIONS ON HIS CONDUCT AND CHARACTER IN CERTAIN PROCEEDINGS OF THE ASSEMBLY OF LOWER CANADA – s.l., s.n, 1832. SEM105P399 – 3mf – 9 – Can$6.75 – cn Bibl Nat [971]
OBSERVATIONS ON A LETTER FROM JAMES STUART,...TO THE RIGHT HONORABLE LORD VISCOUNT GODERICH RELATING TO ANIMADVERSIONS AND IMPUTATIONS ON HIS CONDUCT AND CHARACTER IN CERTAIN PROCEEDINGS OF THE ASSEMBLY OF LOWER CANADA / Viger, Denis Benjamin – [s.l.]: [s.n.], 1832. SEM105P399 – 3mf – 9 – Can$6.75 – cn Bibl Nat [971]
OBSERVATIONS ON CERTAIN PROPHECIES IN THE BOOK OF DANIEL AND THE REVELATION OF ST JOHN WHICH RELATE TO THE SECOND APPEARING OF OUR LORD,... / Moody, Robert – [London], 1787 – 1mf – 9 – MP-552/1 – ne IDC [240]
OBSERVATIONS ON MAN / Hartley, David – 2v in 1. 1749 – 9 – $55.00 – us Scholars' Facs [190]
OBSERVATIONS ON MILITARY LAW, AND THE CONSTITUTION AND PRACTICE OF COURTS MARTIAL. / de Hart, William Chetwood – New York, Wiley and Putnam, 1846. 433 p. LL-1264 – 1 – us L of C Photodup [340]
OBSERVATIONS ON MR. STUART'S LETTER, AND C – [s.l.]: [s.n.], [183-?] – 1mf – 9 – Can$2.25 – cn Bibl Nat [971]
OBSERVATIONS ON PALESTINE PLANTS/ KNOWLEDGE OF THE FLORA OF PALESTINE / Eig, A – 7 – uk Microform Academic [580]
OBSERVATIONS ON PROFESSOR W. R. SMITH'S ARTICLE "BIBLE." / Kennedy, James – 1877 – 9 – us A.T.L.A. [240]
OBSERVATIONS ON SHEEP, WOOL, PLOUGHS AND OXEN / Somerville, J – 1809 – 7 – uk Microform Academic [636]
OBSERVATIONS ON SOME OF THE MOST FREQUENT AND IMPORTANT DISEASES OF THE HEART / Burns, A – M-44. 1809 – 9 – ne IDC [616]
OBSERVATIONS ON SOME POINTS OF SEAMANSHIP, WITH PRATICAL HINTS ON NAVAL ECONOMY / Griffiths, Anselm John – 2nd ed. 1828 – 9 – $20.00 – uk Libr Preservation [355]
OBSERVATIONS ON THE ATTEMPTED APPLICATION OF PANTHEISTIC PRINCIPLES... TO GOSPEL / Mill, William Hodge – Cambridge: Deighton, Bell, 1861.1 fiche – 9 – us A.T.L.A. [240]
OBSERVATIONS ON THE AUTHENTICITY OF THE GOSPELS / Chandler, Peleg W – Chicago: Myers & Chandler, 1867 – 9 – us A.T.L.A. [240]
OBSERVATIONS ON THE CHANGES OF THE AIR AND THE CONCOMITANT EPIDEMICAL DISEASES IN THE ISLAND OF BARBADOS / Hillary, W – London, 1759 – 7mf – 9 – ne IDC [614]
OBSERVATIONS ON THE CONSTITUTION, CUSTOMS, AND USAGE OF MIDDLE TEMPLE / Downing, William – London: Society of the Middle Temple, 1896 – 3mf – 9 – $4.50 – LLMC 84-280 – us L.L.M.C. [323]
OBSERVATIONS ON THE COURT OF CLAIMS / Phillips, Philip – Washington, D.C.: Polkinhorn, 1859. 31,1p. LL-1220 – 1 – us L of C Photodup [340]
OBSERVATIONS ON THE DERANGED MANIFESTATIONS OF THE MIND AND INSANITY / ed by Spurzheim, Johann Gaspar – Boston: Marsh, Capen & Lyon, 1833 – 3mf – 9 – $4.50 – LLMC 92-197 – us L.L.M.C. [340]
OBSERVATIONS ON THE DISEASES OF THE ARMY / Pringle, J – M 233. 1752 – 9 – ne IDC [610]
OBSERVATIONS ON THE DROPSY IN THE BRAIN / Whytt, R – M 134. 1768 – 9 – ne IDC [616]
OBSERVATIONS ON THE EMBRYOLOGY OF INSECTS AND ARACHNIDS / Bruce, A T – Baltimore, 1887.xiv,31p. 6 pls. Z-1101/2 – 8 – ne IDC [590]
OBSERVATIONS ON THE GOAT / French, MH – 1970 – 204p – it F.A.O. [636]
OBSERVATIONS ON THE INTELLECTUAL CULTURE OF THE CARIBOU ESKIMOS / Rasmussen, Knud – 1930 – 8 – BN 363 2 – ne IDC [306]
OBSERVATIONS ON THE MEANS OF EXCITING A SPIRIT OF NATIONAL INDUSTRY... / Anderson, J – Edinburgh, 1777 – 7mf – 9 – ne IDC [338]
OBSERVATIONS ON THE MUSLIM SETTLEMENTS OF MINAHASA / Bhatta, Jitandra Nath – In Indonesian and English. SE-4090 1. 1958? – 9 – ne IDC [305]
OBSERVATIONS ON THE NATURAL GROUP OF PLANTS CALLED POMACEAE / Lindley, J – Trans. Linn. Soc. v. 13. London. 1822. B-6023 2 – 8 – ne IDC [580]
OBSERVATIONS ON THE NATURE AND CONSEQUENCES OF WOUNDS AND CONTUSIONS OF THE HEAD,... / Pott, P – London, 1760 – 4mf – 9 – ne IDC [617]
OBSERVATIONS ON THE NATURE OF CIVIL LIBERTY,... / Price, R – London, 1776 – 1mf – 9 – ne IDC [320]
OBSERVATIONS ON THE ORGANS AND MODE OF FECUNDATION IN ORCHIDEAE AND ASCLEPIADEAE / Brown, R – Transactions of the Linnean Society of London, 1883. V.16 – 3mf – 9 – ne IDC [615]
OBSERVATIONS ON THE PENSIONING OF SOLDIERS – London: Printed by S & R Bentley, s.d. SEM105P100 – 1mf – 9 – Can$2.25 – cn Bibl Nat [355]
OBSERVATIONS ON THE PRACTICE AND FORMS OF DISTRICT, REGIMENTAL AND DETACHMENT COURTS-MARTIAL : WITH REFERENCES TO THE MUTINY ACT OF 1839 AND EXISTING REGULATIONS... / D'Aguilar, George C D – Dublin/London: W Frazer/W Clowes, 1839 – 3mf – 9 – $4.50 – LLMC 89-033 – us L.L.M.C. [340]
OBSERVATIONS ON THE REAL RIGHTS OF WOMEN: WITH THEIR APPROPRIATE DUTIES, AGREEABLE TO SCRIPTURE, REASON AND COMMON SENSE / Crocker, Hannah Mather – 1818 – 9 – us A.T.L.A. [240]
OBSERVATIONS ON THE REVEREND MR. WHITEFIELD'S ANSWER TO THE BISHOP OF LONDON'S LAST PASTORAL LETTER – London, [1739] – 1mf – 9 – MP-264/1 – ne IDC [240]
OBSERVATIONS ON THE STRUCTURE OF FOSSIL PLANTS FOUND IN THE CARBONIFEROUS STRATA / Binney, E W – G-174 1. 1868-1875 – 9 – ne IDC [560]
OBSERVATIONS ON THE SUPPLEMENTARY MEMORANDUM BY THE GOVERNMENT OF PALESTINE / Jewish Agency for Palestine. Jerusalem – Including notes on evidence given to the U.N.S.C.O.P. up to the 2 Jul 1947. Submitted to U.N.S.C.O.P. 1947. BJ-28-156 1 – 9 – ne IDC [956]
OBSERVATIONS ON THE SUPREME APPELLATE JURISDICTION OF GREAT BRITAIN. / Burge, William – London, Saunders, and Benning, 1841. 63 p. LL-106 – 1 – us L of C Photodup [340]
OBSERVATIONS ON THE WESTERN ESQUIMAUX / Simpson, J – BN 387 2. 1875 – 8 – ne IDC [305]
OBSERVATIONS PHYTOLOGIQUES / Lestiboudois, T G – Lille. 1826. B-6017 2 – 8 – ne IDC [580]
OBSERVATIONS SUR DIFFERENS POINTS D'HARMONIE / Roussier, Pierre-Joseph – 1755 – 9 – us Sibley [780]
OBSERVATIONS SUR LA LANGUE FRANCAISE / Menage, G – 1675-76 – 9 – fr I.C.S. [440]
OBSERVATIONS SUR LA LITTERATURE MODERNE – La Haye puis Amsterdam, Londres et Paris. 1749-52 – 1 – fr A.C.R.P.P. [073]
OBSERVATIONS SUR LA SITUATION DU DEPARTEMENT DE LA DROME / Colin – an IX – 9 – fr Hachette [944]
OBSERVATIONS SUR LA STATISTIQUE DU DEPARTEMENT DES BASSES-PYRENEES QUI PARUT EN L'ANNEE 1802, ET PROJETS D'AMELIORATION / Lacoste, D – 1815 – 9 – fr Hachette [944]
OBSERVATIONS SUR L'ARCHITECTURE / Laugier, M A – La Haye, Paris, Desaint, 1765. xvi, 326p. (Architecture Series) – 9 – fr Hachette [720]
OBSERVATIONS SUR LE CONTRAT SOCIAL DE J.-J. ROUSSEAU / Berthier, Guillaume F – Paris, Merigot. 1789 – 9 – fr Hachette [190]
OBSERVATIONS SUR LE PRINCIPE QUI A PRODUIT LES REVOLUTIONS DE FRANCE, DE GENEVE ET D'AMERIQUE, DANS LE DIX-HUITIEME SIECLE / Isnard, Achille N – Evreux: Imp. Vve. Malassis, 1789 – 9 – fr Hachette [900]
OBSERVATIONS SUR LE TRAITE HISTORIQUE ET CRITIQUE DE MONSIEUR FOURNIER LE JEUNE / Gando, Pere et Fils – Berne et Paris. 1766. BP-682 1 – 9 – ne IDC [780]
OBSERVATIONS SUR L'EDUCATION PUBLIQUE POUR SERVIR DE REPONSE AUX QUESTIONS POSEES PAR MM. LES AGENTS GENERAUX DU CLERGE DE FRANCE / Eyrard, Francois – Paris. Berton et Morin. 1786. 6753 – 9 – fr Hachette [944]
OBSERVATIONS SUR LES CORDES A INSTRUMENTS DE MUSIQUE TANT DE BOYAU QUE SOIE; SUIVIES D'UNE LETTRE DU C. GOSSEC AU C. BAUD; ET DE L'EXTRAIT PROCES, VERBAL DE L'INSTITUT NATIONAL, RELATIF A CE RAPPORT / Baud, C – Versailles: Ph D Pierres, 1803 – 1 – us Sibley [780]
OBSERVATIONS SUR LES ECRITS DE M. DE VOLTAIRE / Gibert, E G – Principalement sur la religion. Londres. Spilsburg. 1788. XXIV – 9 – fr Hachette [240]
OBSERVATIONS SUR LES ECRITS MODERNES – Par Desfontaines. Paris. mars 1735-aout 1743 (I-XXXIV) – 1 – fr A.C.R.P.P. [073]
OBSERVATIONS SUR LES ETATS DE SITUATION DU DEPARTEMENT DE L'AUBE / Barante, Claude I B de – an IX – 9 – fr Hachette [944]
OBSERVATIONS SUR LES LOIS DE NATURALISATION DES ETRANGERS EN ALGERIE / Fabre de Parrel, R – Alger, 1901 – 2mf – 1 – ILM-3767/1 – ne IDC [327]
OBSERVATIONS SUR LES PRINCIPES DE L'HARMONIE OCCASIONNEES PAR QUELQUES ECRITS MODERNES SUR CE SUJET / Serre, J A – Geneve. 1763. BP-758 1 – 9 – ne IDC [780]
OBSERVATIONS SUR L'ETAT DES CLASSES OUVRIERES / Fix, Theodore – (Condition of 19th C. French working class series). 1846 – 9 – fr Hachette [360]
OBSERVATIONS SUR L'ETUDE ARCHEOLOGIQUE DU DR. DIONNE / Cazes, Paul de – (Montreal: L'Etendard), 1891. 00649. (Pre-1900 Canadiana) – 9 – cn C.I.H.M. [930]
OBSERVATIONS SUR L'HISTOIRE NATURELLE, SUR LA PHYSIQUE ET SUR LA PEINTURE, AVEC DES PLANCHES IMPRIMEES EN COULEUR. – Paris, 1752-57 – 3 – us Readex [530]
OBSERVATIONS SUR L'ORGINE DE LA LANGUE FRANCAISE VULGAIRE LEBER, [J.M.]C. COLLECTION DES MEILLEURES DISSERTATIONS, NOTICES ET TRAITES PARTICULIERS RELATIFS A L'HISTOIRE DE FRANCE / Liron, D – Paris. v14(p64-79). 1838 – 1mf – 9 – ne IDC [440]
OBSERVATIONS SUR L'ORTHOGRAPHE / Firmin-Didot, A – 2e ed. 1868 – 9 – fr I.C.S. [070]
OBSERVATIONS SUR NOTRE INSTINCT POUR LA MUSIQUE / Rameau, Jean-Philippe – 1754 – 9 – us Sibley [780]
OBSERVATIONS SUR PLUSIEURS PLANTES NOUVELLES, RARES, OU CRITIQUES DE LA FRANCE / Jordan, A. – Paris. 1846-49. B-730 2 – 8 – ne IDC [580]
OBSERVATIONS UPON THE CONDUCT AND BEHAVIOUR OF A CERTAIN SECT USUALLY DISTINGUISHED BY THE NAME OF METHODISTS / Gibson, E – [London, 1744] – 1mf – 9 – MP-309/1 – ne IDC [240]
OBSERVATIONS UPON THE PELOPONNESUS AND GREEK ISLANDS / Anderson, Rufus – Boston: Crocker and Brewster; New York: J. Leavitt, 1830 – 1mf – us A.T.L.A. [949]
OBSERVATIONS UPON THE WINDWARD COAST OF AFRICA / Corry, J – London. 1807. BA-294 2 – 8 – ne IDC [960]
OBSERVATIONUM BOTANICARUM / Jacquin, N J von – 4v. Vindobonae. 1764-71. B-5254 2 – 8 – ne IDC [580]

OBSERVATIONUM BOTANICARUM FASCICULUS PRIMUS / Hedwig, R A – Lipsiae. 1802. B-5951 2 – 8 – ne IDC [580]

OBSERVATIONUM BOTANICARUM PUGILLUS / Retzius, A J – Lundae. 1810. B-5483 2 – 8 – ne IDC [580]

OBSERVATIONUM LIBRI DUO / Albaspinaeus, Gabr. – Parisiis, 1631 – 15mf – 8 – ne Slangenburg [240]

OBSERVATONS ON THE LAW OF EVIDENCE / Thayer, Ezra Ripley – Ann Arbor, Mich., Ann Arbor Press, 1915 13 p. LL-1228 – 1 – us L of C Photodup [340]

OBSERVATOR – v. 1-11. Apr 1702-Jul 1712 – 1 – us UMI [073]

OBSERVATOR – v. 1-3. 13 Apr 1681-9 Mar 1687 – 1 – us UMI [073]

OBSERVATORIO RUSTICO / Salas, Francisco Gregorio de – (1816. 1.50f; 9. 1772. 1.50f; BSA; 9) – 1802 – 9 – 1.50f – sp Bibl Santa Ana [810]

OBSERVATORIO RUSTICO: SEGUNDA PARTE / Salas, Francisco Gregorio de – 1774 – 9 – 1.50f – sp Bibl Santa Ana [810]

OBSERVER – 1791-1995 – 9 – F3,166.00 – sz Infoprint [072]

OBSERVER – (1977-1992.-202r) – Sarnia, 1993 – 18r – 1 – cn Preston [971]

OBSERVER – (Also known as: Times-Observer, Los Gatos Times) – Saratoga, CA. 1960 – 74+ r – 1 – $3,700.00 ($120.00y) – B02984 – us Library Micro [071]

OBSERVER – Alton. Ill. 1836-38 – 1 – us UMI [071]

OBSERVER – Conrad. Mont. 1905-1923 – 1 – us UMI [071]

OBSERVER – Euclid. Ohio. 1937-1939 – 1 – us UMI [071]

OBSERVER – Grand Rapids. Mich. -w. 1908-26 – 1 – us UMI [071]

OBSERVER – Greenwich. Conn. 1877-1882 – 1 – us UMI [071]

OBSERVER – Henty – at Pascoe [980]

OBSERVER – Hudson. Ohio. and Telegraph. 1830-33 – 1 – us UMI [071]

OBSERVER – Lanark, 1850-1853 – 1r – 1 – cn Preston [971]

OBSERVER – London. 1791-to date – 1 – uk Microform Academic [072]

OBSERVER – Massena. N.Y. 1891-1900 – 1 – us UMI [071]

OBSERVER – Moultrie. Ga. 1905- – 1 – us UMI [071]

OBSERVER – Moultrie. Ga. -w. 1894- – 1 – us UMI [071]

OBSERVER – Ontario. Calif. 1888-1897 – 1 – us UMI [071]

OBSERVER – Portland. Or. 1939-1946 – 1 – us UMI [071]

OBSERVER – Portland OR. Mar 19 1945-Oct 1948, July 1950, July 1-Dec 30 1976 – 1 – us U.O. Library [071]

OBSERVER – Princeton. West Virginia. 1928-1956 – 1 – us UMI [071]

OBSERVER – Rochester. N.Y. 1827-32 – 1 – us UMI [071]

OBSERVER – Sacramento. Calif. 1963-1965 – 1 – us UMI [071]

OBSERVER – v. 1-2. 29 Nov 1806-26 Dec 1807 – 1 – us UMI [073]

OBSERVER – v. 1-25. 19 Feb-6 Aug 1809 – 1 – us UMI [073]

OBSERVER – v. 1-28. 14 Oct 1810-21 Apr 1811 – 1 – us UMI [073]

OBSERVER – Washington. Pa. 1872-1966 – 1 – us UMI [071]

OBSERVER – Westover. West Virginia. 1952-1959 – 1 – us UMI [071]

THE OBSERVER – Bangor. Maine. 1959-1965 – 1 – us UMI [071]

THE OBSERVER – Cowansville, Canada. 2 sep 1870-22 oct 1908 – 1r – 1 – Can$60.00 – cn Can Microfilming [072]

THE OBSERVER – Flushing. Mich. 1935-1969 – 1 – us UMI [071]

THE OBSERVER – Greenville. R.I. 1956- – 1 – us UMI [071]

THE OBSERVER – (Includes The Observer Magazine beginning with 1991. Index also available) – 1791- – 12r per y – 1 – inquire – us Ross [072]

THE OBSERVER – London. -w. 1791-93, 1795-1812, 1815-1927. (158 reels) – 1 – uk British Libr Newspaper [072]

THE OBSERVER – Monrovia. Liberia. -f. 26 Sep, 24 Oct, 12 Dec 1878, 11 Sep 1879-22 Dec 1881, 12 Jan-11 May, 15 Sep, 12 Oct 1882, 12 Apr 1883. (1 reel) – 1 – uk British Libr Newspaper [072]

THE OBSERVER – (New York) v14, no. 5 (Dec. 9, 1971)-v45, no. 4 (Jan. 11, 1984) – us A.J.P.C. [071]

THE OBSERVER – Plymouth. Montserrat. -w. 1957-59. (1 reel) – 1 – uk British Libr Newspaper [072]

THE OBSERVER – Portland, OR. 1943-50. and pred. Portland Observer. 1938-39 – 1 – 24.00 – us Oregon Hist [071]

THE OBSERVER – Toronto: [s.n., 1891-1892] – 9 – cn C.I.H.M. [072]

THE OBSERVER / U.S. Military Assistance Command. Vietnam – Tokyo. May 1964-Jan 27, 1973. v. 3, n. 1-v. 11, n. 25. 2 reels – 1 – 55.00 – us L of C Photodup [977]

OBSERVER AND OTTAWA VALLEY ADVOCATE – Pembroke, 1906-1926 – 10r – 1 – cn Preston [971]

OBSERVER AND UPPER OTTAWA ADVERTISER – Pembroke, 1900-1902 – 1r – 1 – cn Preston [971]

OBSERVER COLOUR SUPPLEMENT – London, UK. 6 Sept 1964-1967. -w. 7 reels – 1 – uk British Libr Newspaper [072]

OBSERVER DISPATCH – Utica. N.Y. 1922- – 1 – us UMI [071]

THE OBSERVER MAGAZINE – 1964-1990 – ca 4r per y – 1 – inquire – us Ross [072]

OBSERVER PROGRAM OPERATIONS MANUAL – 1986 – 218p – it F.A.O. [630]

OBSERVER REPORTER – Washington. Pa. Final Ed. 1967- – 1 – us UMI [071]

OBSERVER REPORTER – Washington. Pa. Home Ed. 1967 – 1 – us UMI [071]

OBSERVER, SARATOGA *see* TIMES-OBSERVER

OBSERVER & TELEGRAPH – (Weekly Presbyterian newspaper, succeeded by the Ohio Observer) – Hudson, OH. mar 5, 1830-sept 21, 1833 – 1r – 1 – us Western Res [071]

OBSERVER WEEKLY COLOUR MAGAZINE – London. 1964-to date – 1 – uk Microform Academic [072]

OBSERVER-STAR – La Grande, OR. -w. 1922-30 – 1 – 96.00 – us Oregon Hist [071]

OBSHCHEE DELO : IZD MOSKOVSKOGO SOIUZA-POTREBITEL'NYKH OBSHCHESTV – (Missing: 1919 n9...; 1920 n3) – M., 1916-20 n5 – 23mf – 9 – COR-659/1 – ne IDC [334]

OBSHCHEE DI ELO *see* V BORBIE S BOLSHEVIKAMI I NIEMTSAMI

OBSHCHEE UCHENIE O KOOPERATSII / Balabanov, MS – M., L., 1928 – 4mf – 9 – COR-243/1 – ne IDC [334]

OBSHCHESTRIO ISTORII I DREVNOSTEI ROSSIISKIKH PRI MOSKOVSKOM UNIVERSITETE: VREMENNIKH / Russia – Moscow. 1849-1857 – 1 – us UMI [947]

OBSHCHESTVA, TOVARISHCHESTVA, TRESTY, ARTELI, KOOPERATIVY I DRUGIE OB"EDINENIIA / Braginskii, M et al – Moscow, 1924 – 2mf – 9 – COR-713/1 – ne IDC [334]

OBSHCHESTVENNOE DVIZHENIE V ROSSI NACHALE 20 VV – St Petersburg. v. 1-4. 1909-1911 – 1 – us NY Public [073]

OBSHCHESTVENNO-KOOPERATIVNAIA SHKOLA / Kil'chevskii, V A – Iaroslavl', 1919 – 2mf – 9 – COR-251/1 – ne IDC [334]

OBSHCHESTVENNYE I UMSTVENNYE TECHENIIA V ROSSII, 1870-1905 / Martov, L – M., L., 1924. 202p – 3mf – 9 – ne IDC [320]

OBSHCHESTVENNYE OGORODY I UCHASTIE V IKH USTROISTVE KOOPERATIVNYKH ORGANIZATSII / Nikolaev, A A – Iaroslavl', 1921 – 2mf – 9 – COR-496/1 – ne IDC [334]

OBSHCHESTVO I GOSUDARSTVO V DO-MONGOL'SKII PERIOD RUSSKOI ISTORII / Khlebnikov, N I – Saint Petersburg, 1872. 540p. State, law and social fabric of pre-Mongol Russia from earliest days to 1237. BR-9762/1 – 9 – ne IDC [320]

OBSHCHESTVO ISTORII I DREVNOSTEI ROSSIISKIKH: CHTENIIA – (Society of Russian History). 264 v. Moscow. 1846-1918 – 3 – us Readex [947]

OBSHCHESTVO LIUBITELEI ESTESTVOZNANIIA ANTROPOLOGII I ETNOGRAFII – Moscow: Fiziologicheskoe Otdelenie. Memuary. n1. 1925 – 1r – 1 – us Ross [305]

OBSHCHESTVO LIUBITELEI ROSSIISKOI SLOVESNOSTI PRI MOSKOVSKOM UNIVERSITETE / Moscow. University – Istoricheskaia zapiska i materialy za sto let, 1811-1911. M. 1911. B-1566 2 – 8 – ne IDC [370]

OBSHCHESTVO LIUBITELEI RUSSKOI SLOVESNOSTI – Moscow: Sochineniia v Prozie i Stikhakh, 1822-28 – 1r – 1 – us Ross [460]

OBSHCHEZANIMATEL'NYI VESTNIK – Zhurnal literatury, nauk, iskusstv, promyshlennosti, torgovli i obshchezhitiia. Spb. 1857-58. BR-4152 2 – 8 – ne IDC [073]

"OBSHCHIE PRINTSIPY PRAVA" V MEZHDUNARODNOM PRAVE / Koretskii, V M – Kiev. 1957. BR-8641 2 – 8 – ne IDC [460]

OBSHCHII KURS SCHETOVODSTVA POTREBITEL'SKIKH OBSHCHESTV / Shalov, I S; ed by Kompaneiskii, B N – (Missing: V7) – v1-13 – 9mf – 9 – COR-285/1 – ne IDC [334]

OBSHCHII TSERKOVNO-SLAVIANOROSSIISKII SLOVAR' / Sokolov, P – Spb., 1834. v1-2 – 31mf – 9 – R-8404/2 – ne IDC [290]

OBSHCHIMI SILAMI K OBSHCHEMU BLAGU : KNIGA DLIA CHTENIIA PO KOOPERATSII / Kholmogorskii, FD – M., 1925 – 4mf – 9 – COR-284/1 – ne IDC [334]

OBSHCHINA I KOOPERATSIIA : OCHERKI PO ISTORII KREST'IANSKOGO KHOZIAISTVA V ZAPADNOI EVROPE I ROSSII / Krainskii, V V – Spb., 1907 – 2mf – 9 – COR-53/1 – ne IDC [334]

OBSHCHINNOE PRAVO : OPYT SOTSIAL'NO-IURIDICHESKOGO ANALIZA OBSHCHINNOGO ZEMLEVLADENIIA, KAK INSTITUTA GRAZHDANSKOGO PRAVA / Izgoev, A S – Spb., 1906 – 2mf – 9 – COR-34/1 – ne IDC [334]

OBSHCHINNOE VLADENIE V ROSSII / Karelin, A A – Spb., 1893 – 4mf – 9 – COR-44/1 – ne IDC [334]

OBSHESTVENNOE KHOZYAAISTVO GORODA MOSKVY / Moscow. Gorodskaya Duma – v. 1863-1887. Godakh. Moscow. v. 1-4. 1888-1895 – 1 – us NY Public [323]

OBSTACLES TO DISARMAMENT AND WAYS OF OVERCOMING THEM / ed by Rana, Swadesh – 1981 – 233p – 9 – 92-3-101879-5 – fr UNESCO [320]

OBSTETRICAL AND GYNECOLOGICAL SURVEY – v1-51. 1946-96 – 1,5,6,9 – $110.00r – us Williams [618]

OBSTETRICS AND GYNECOLOGY – v1- 1952-1; v41- 5,6; v45- 9 – us UMI [073]

OBSTOIATEL'NOE OPISANIE SLAVIANO-ROSSIISKIKH RUKOPISEI, KHRANIASHCHIKHSIA...V BIBLIOTEKE...F.A. TOLSTOGO / Kalaidovich, K F & Stroev, P M – Moscow, 1825. lxvii,817p. Describes Slavic MS collection from the library of F.A. Tolstoi, most of which is now in Saltykov-Shchedrin Library. BR-7113/2 – 8 – ne IDC [010]

OBSTOIATEL'NOE OPISANIE STAROPECHATNYKH KNIG SLAVIANSKIKH I ROSSIISKIKHM KHRANIASHCHIKHSIA V BIBLIOTEKE...GRAFA F.A. TOLSTOVA / Stroev, P M – Moscow, 1829. 592p. BR-5615/2 – 8 – ne IDC [947]

OBUKHOVSKOE DELO. S PRILOZHENIEM SUDEBNAGO PRIGOVORA / Riazanov, N (pseud.) – 2nd ed. St. Petersburg, 1906 – 1 – $35.00r – us Hoover Inst Photo [947]

OBYCHNOE PRAVO : MATERIALY DLIA BIBLIOGRAFII OBYCHNOGO PRAVA / Iakushkin, E I – (Missing: v4) – Iaroslavl'. 4v. 1875-1910 – 25mf – 9 – ne IDC [340]

OBZOR – Skalica, Slovakia, 1863-1905 – 13r – 1 – us I.H.R.C. [071]

OBZOR – Zagreb, Yugoslavia. -d. 13 Feb-25 July 1919; 23 June 1920-11 July 1940. Imperfect. 37 reels – 1 – uk British Libr Newspaper [949]

OBZOR BIBLIOGRAFICHESKIKH IZDANII GOS. PUBLICHNOI BIBLIOTEKI ZA 1917-1957 GG / Morachevskii, N Ia. & Ivkov, Iu. P – BR-10,840/1 – 9 – ne IDC [010]

OBZOR DEI ATELNOSTI GROZNENSKOGO OKRUZHNOGO OTDELA ZDRAVOOKHRANENII A ZA...BI UDZHETNY I GOD / Groznenski i okrug (R.S.F.S.R.). Otdel zdravookhranenii a – (Includes c.1: 1924/1925) – [Grozny i: s.n.], 19uu – 1 – CSUXAKZ2467-S – us Hoover Inst Photo [947]

OBZOR DETSKOI LITERATURY – 1. Knigi izdannyia v 1883 godu. Spb. 1885; 2. Knigi izdannyia v 1884 godu. Spb. 1886; 3. Obzor detskoi literatury za 1885-1888 gg. Spb. 1889. BR-7198 2 – 8 – ne IDC [460]

OBZOR DOKUMENTAL'NYKH MATERIALOV PO ISTORII G. MOSKVY S DREVNEISHIKH VREMEN DO 19 V – Moscow, 1949. 187p. BR-10,707/1 – 9 – ne IDC [947]

OBZOR DOKUMENTAL'NYKH MATERIALOV TSENTRAL'NOGO GOSUDARSTVENNOGO ISTORICHESKOGO ARKHIVA SSSR PO ISTORICHI OBRABATYVAIUSHCHEI PROMYSHLENNOSTI ROSSII V PERVOI POLOVINE 19 VEKA – 2 pts. BR-10,734/1 – 9 – ne IDC [025]

OBZOR DOKUMENTOV OTNOSIASHCHIKHSIA K ISTORII BALTIISKOGO KRAIA I KHRANIASHCHIKHSIA V MOSKOVSKIKH ARKHIVAKH MINISTERSTV.. / Kharuzin, N – 1894. v2, p30 54. Brief survey of materials relating to the Baltic area (17th and 18th centuries). BR-11,317/1 – 9 – ne IDC [947]

OBZOR FONDA TSENTRAL'NOGO KOMITETA TSENZURY INOSTRANNOI / Polianskaia, L – (Arkhivnoe delo. v. 45, nr. 1, 1938). BR-10,731 1 – 9 – ne IDC [335]

OBZOR "GRAMOT KOLLEGII EKONOMII" / Shumakov, S A – 4v. M. 1899-1917. (Originally published in Chteniia v obshchestve istorii i drevnostei rossiiskikh). PKG-B-84.5 Surveys early Russian charters (1300-1795) from the Economic Kollegiia collection now in TsGADA. BR-11,158 1 – 9 – ne IDC [321]

OBZOR IURIDICHESKOI LITERATURY ZA 1884-94 GG / Kirkhengeim, A von – Moscow, 1895. 62p. Vol. 1 of survey of German legal literature for the period 1884-94 in the fields of legal philosophy, history of German law, comparative jurisprudence . Trans. by P.N. Apostol'. BR-5633/2 – 8 – ne IDC [340]

OBZOR IUZHNO-RUSSKIKH I ZAPADNO-RUSSKIKH PAMIATNIKOV PISMENNOSTI OT 11 DO 17 ST / Vladimirov, P V – Kiev, 1890. 42p. BR-7044/2 – 8 – ne IDC [025]

OBZOR LITERATURY PO PSIKHOLOGII DETSTVA / Rumiantsev, N E – Ed. 2 Spb. 1912. BR-7241 2 – 8 – ne IDC [150]

OBZOR MIROVO I NEFTEPROMYSHLENNOSTI ZA...G. I NEFTEPROMYSHLENNOSTI SSSR ZA...G. : SOVET NEFTI ANO I PROMYSHLENNOSTI – (Library has: 1927) – Moskva, Leningrad: Nefti anoe izd-vo NTU VSNKh SSSR, 1926 – 1 – CSUX90-S945 – us Hoover Inst Photo [947]

OBZOR RUKOPISNYKH MATERIALOV UCHENOGO ARKHIVA VSESOIUZNOGO GEOGRAFICHESKOGO OBSHCHESTVA O NARODAKH PRIBALTIKI (LATYSHI, LITOVTSY, ESTY) / Zelenin, D K – (Sovetskaia etnografiia, 1947, nrs. 6-7). BR-10,993 1 – 9 – ne IDC [947]

OBZOR RUKOPISNYKH MATERIALOV UCHENOGO ARKHIVA VSESOIUZNOGO GEOGRAFICHESKOGO OBSHCHESTVA O NARODAKH SSSR. I. BASHKIRY, BESERMIANE, BOLGARY, VENSY, EVREI, KALMYKI, KARELY, KOMI, KOMI-PERMIAKI / Zelenin, DK – (Sovetskaia etnografiia, v4. 1941). PKG-C-81 BR-10,992 1 – 9 – ne IDC [947]

OBZOR RUKOPISNYKH PAMIATNIKOV PO ISTORII SLOBODSKOI UKRAINY, KHRANIASHCHIKHSIA V VOENNO-UCHENOM ARKHIVE V S-PETERBURGE / Kataev, I – Kharkov, 1902. 60p. Catalog of materials now in TsGVIA. BR-11,118/1 – 9 – ne IDC [460]

OBZOR RUSSKOGO I INOSTRANNOGO ZAKONODATEL'STVA O KOOPERATIVNYKH TOVARISHCHESTVAKH / Kulisher, IM – Spb., 1906 – 4mf – 9 – COR-54/1 – ne IDC [334]

OBZOR SOVREMENNOI LITERATURY PO MEZDUNARODNOMU PRAVU / Kamarovskii, L A – Moscow, 1887. 400p. Critical appraisal of mid-19th century international legal literature intended for Russian law students. BR-9482/1 – 9 – ne IDC [340]

OBZOR VNESHNIKH SNOCHENII ROSSII (PO 1800 GOD.) / Bantysh-Kamenskii, N – Moscow, 1894-1902. 4v. 303p; 271p; 319p; 463p. BR-5982/2 – 8 – ne IDC [947]

OBZOR ZAPISOK, DNEVNIKOV, VOSPOMINANII, PISEM, PUTESHESTVII OTNOSIASHCHIKSIA K ISTORII ROSSII I NAPECHATNNYKH NA RUSSKOM IAZYKE / Mintslov, S R – v. 1-5. Novgorod. 1911-12. BR-7171 2 – 8 – ne IDC [947]

OBZOR ZHIZNI I TRUDOV RUSSKIKH PISATELEI I PISATEL'NITS / Iazykov, D D – 1-2 (2-oe izd.), 2-10. M. 1885-1915. BR-5909 2 – 8 – ne IDC [460]

OC ANA D IEGO DE-A L V A REZ, A RTURO *see* UN VIAJE FASCINANTE POR LA AMERICA HISPANA DEL SIGLO 16. MADRID, 1969

OCAK – Konya: Babalik Matbassi, 1917-19? – 9 – $10.00 – us MEDOC [956]

O'Callaghan, E B *see* DOCUMENTS RELATING TO THE COLONIAL HISTORY OF THE STATE OF NEW YORK

O'Callaghan, Marion *see* NAMIBIA

Ocampo, Florian de *see* CRONICA GENERAL DE ESPANA. BOOK 1-4

Ocana, H *see* RESPUESTA CRITICA DE...AL OPUSCULO DE...CURAR LOS MORBOS

Ocaranza, Fernando *see*
- LA BEATIFICACION DEL VENERABLE SEBASTIAN DE APARICIO. MEXICO, 1934
- HISTORIA DE LA MEDICINA EN MEXICO. MEXICO, 1934
- EL IMPERIAL COLEGIO DE INDIOS DE LA SANTA CRUZ DE TLALTELOCO. MEXICO, 1934

O'Caroll, J *see* MONASTIC RULES IN MEROVINGIAN GAUL

Occam, Guillelmus de *see*
- DIALOGUS DE IMPERIO ET PONTIFICA POTESTATE
- QUOTLIBETA SEPTEM
- SUPER 4 LIBROS SENTENTIARUM 1-2-3-4 + TABULAE 1-4 ET CENTILOGIUM THEOLOGICUM

OCCASIO ARREPTA, NEGLECTA, HUIUS COMMODA; ILLIUS INCOMMODA / David, I – O 219. 1605 – 9 – ne IDC [450]

THE OCCASIONAL – Virginia City, NV. 1886 – 1r – 1 – $50.00 – U04795 – us Library Micro [071]

OCCASIONAL BULLETIN OF MISSIONARY RESEARCH – v.1-4. 1977-80 – 1 – us UMI [240]

THE OCCASIONAL MAGAZINE – Halifax, N.S.: Smith & Williams, [1895] – 9 – cn C.I.H.M. [073]

OCCASIONAL PAPER OF THE QU'APPELLE ASSOCIATION – nos 156-88. 1934-50 (complete) – 1r – 1 – ATLA S0548 – us A.T.L.A. [073]

OCCASIONAL PAPERS / American Negro Academy. Washington, D.C – no. 1-22. 1897-1924 – 1 – 18.00 – us L of C Photodup [305]

OCCASIONAL PAPERS / Papua New Guinea Church Partnership. Formerly, the New Guinea Mission – 1905-1980 – 1 – uk Microform Academic [240]

OCCASIONAL PAPERS / Qu'appelle Association – ns.156-88. 1934-50 – 1 – us A.T.L.A. [240]

OCCASIONAL PAPERS / Rhodes-Livingstone Museum – 1934-51. BA-469 2 – 8 – ne IDC [960]

OCCASIONAL PAPERS : SELECTED FROM THE GUARDIAN, THE TIMES, AND THE SATURDAY REVIEW, 1846-1890 / Church, R W – London; New York: Macmillan, 1897 – 3mf – us A.T.L.A. [240]

OCCASIONAL PAPERS AND REVIEWS / Keble, John – Oxford, Eng.: J. Parker, 1877 – 1r – 1-55879-852-8 – uk Libr Preservation [999]

OCCASIONAL PAPERS FROM ST AUGUSTINE'S COLLEGE, CANTERBURY, 1853-1935 / Trustees of St. Augustine's College – 5r – 1 – £270.00 – 1-897955-34-0 – uk Academic [240]

OCCASIONAL PAPERS IN OLD COLONY STUDIES – 1973- 1,5,6; 1975- 9 – us UMI [073]

OCCASIONAL PAPERS SERIES – 1965- – 1,5,6 – us UMI [073]

OCCASIONAL REVERBERATOR – v. 1-4. 7 Sep-5 Oct 1753 – 1 – us UMI [073]

OCCASIONAL THOUGHTS OF AN ASTRONOMER ON NATURE AND REVELATION / Pritchard, Charles – London: John Murray, 1889. 1 fiche. 8370-4802-8 – 9 – us A.T.L.A. [240]

L'OCCHIO – Italy, 1979-81 – 27r – 1 – inquire – us Ross [072]

THE OCCIDENT – Chicago. 17 Apr 1885-6 Sep 1895 (imperfect).-w. 11 reels – 1 – uk British Libr Newspaper [071]

THE OCCIDENT – (Chicago). 1878-95 – 1 – us A.J.P.C. [071]

THE OCCIDENT – San Francisco, CA. 1885-91 (broken series) – 1r – 1 – $50.00 – C02844 – us Library Micro [071]

OCCIDENT AND AMERICAN JEWISH ADVOCATE – (Philadelphia). 1843-69 – 1 – us A.J.P.C. [270]

OCCIDENT AND ORIENT IN HONOUR OF M. GASTER'S 80TH / Gaster, M – birthday. London. 1936. BJ-100-21 1 – 9 – ne IDC [920]

OCCIDENT ET ORIENT. ETUDES POLITIQUES, MORALES ET RELIGIEUSES PENDANT 1833-1834 DE L'ERE CHRETIENNE, 1249-1250 DE L'HEGYRE / Barrault, Emile – Paris, Desessart, 1835, 498 p. Les Saint-Simoniens, 1825-1834. 6968 – 9 – fr Hachette [335]

OCCIDENT, WITH PRELUDES ON CURRENT EVENTS / Cook, Joseph – Boston: Houghton, Mifflin, 1884 – 1mf – us A.T.L.A. [240]

Occidental Publishing Co *see* ILLUSTRATED ALBUM OF BIOGRAPHY OF SOUTHWESTERN MINNESOTA

Occola. Ohio. United Brethren Church *see* RECORDS

L'OCCONOMIE DES TROIS FAMILLES DV MONDE SVBLVNAIRE, A SCAVOIR ANIMALE, VEGETALE, ET MINERALE : ET PARTICVLIEREMENT DE LA NATVRE DE L'HOMME / Pages, Jean – Paris, 1625 – 1 – us U.W. Library [190]

OCCULT – (See also: Psychic World and Psychic World and the Occult) – v1-7. 1969-1976 – 1. v5-7 5,6 – us UMI [130]

OCCULT JAPAN; OR, THE WAY OF THE GODS; AN ESOTERIC STUDY OF JAPANESE PERSONALITY AND POSSESSION / Lowell, Percival – Boston, New York: Houghton, Mifflin and Company, 1895. 3p,1 leaf,379p. front., 3 pl – 1 – us U.W. Library [130]

L'OCCUPATION DE TOMBOUCTOU / Bonnier, Gaetan – Paris: Editions du Monde Moderne, [1926] – us Res Libr [960]

L'OCCUPATION DU SOL ET LE PEUPLEMENT FRANCAIS DES TERRES ATLANTIQUES DU CANADA AUX 17E ET 19E SIECLES A PARTIR DES CARTES NAUTIQUES MANUSCRITES FRANCAISES / Azard, M M – F160.00 – fr Ethnologie [380]

THE OCCUPATION OF JAPAN, 1942-45 – (Pt 1: U.S. Planning Documents. $2,535.00 ISBN 0-88692-107-4, guide only $315.00; Pt 2: U.S. and Allied Policy. $3,195.00 ISBN 1-55655-213-0, guide only $405.00; Pt 3: Reform, Recovery and Peace. $4,510.00 ISBN 0-88692-200-3, guide only $515.00) – us UPA [950]

THE OCCUPATION OF JAPAN, 1945-52 : ECONOMIC REFORM – (Pt 1: Deconcentration and Modernization of Economic Power. 651mf $4,815.00 ISBN 1-55655-515-6, guide only $395.00; Pt 2: Land Reform and Japan's Place in the Postwar World Economy. ca 55mf ca $4,100.00 ISBN 1-55655-516-4, guide only $375.00) – 1995 – $7,235.00 set – us UPA [950]

OCCUPATIONAL AND GEOGRAPHICAL MOBILITY IN AND OUT OF THAI FISHERIES – 1986 – it F.A.O. [338]

OCCUPATIONAL HAZARDS – v1- 1938- 1; v33- 5,6; v38- 9 – us UMI [360]

OCCUPATIONAL HEALTH – (See also: Journal for Industrial Nurses) – v15- 1963- 1; v30- 5,6,9 – us UMI [610]

OCCUPATIONAL HEALTH NURSING *see*
- AAOHN JOURNAL
- AMERICAN ASSOCIATION OF INDUSTRIAL NURSES JOURNAL

OCCUPATIONAL HEALTH REVIEW – v. 1-22. 1949-71 – 1 – us UMI [614]

OCCUPATIONAL HYGIENE / ed by Guillemin, Michel P – 9,5,1 – us Gordon [360]

OCCUPATIONAL OUTLOOK QUARTERLY – v1- 1957- 1; v15- 5,6; v19- 9 – us UMI [650]

OCCUPATIONAL REGULATION AND THE PUBLIC INTEREST, COMPETITION OR MONOPOLY / ed by Albon, Robert & Lindsay, Greg – 1984. 215p. Indexed, CIS – 9 – 1.00f – at Libertarian Micro [320]

OCCUPATIONAL SAFETY AND HEALTH ADMINISTRATION REPORTS / U.S. Department of Labor – (1952-72 are entitled: "Safety Standards". 1972-78 are entitled: "Job Safety and Health". Lacking: 1952-68. v1 nos 7-8, v2 nos 11-12 of "Job Safety and Health") – v1-21. 1952-72 (all publ) – 9 – LLMC 80-624 – us L.L.M.C. [324]

OCCUPATIONAL SAFETY AND HEALTH REVIEW COMMISSION DECISIONS AND REPORTS / U.S. Occupational Safety and Health Review Commission – (Includes indexes) – v1-20. 1971-75 – 248mf – 9 – $372.00 – LLMC 79-414 – us L.L.M.C. [360]

OCCUPATIONAL SKILLS OF REFUGEES / International Refugee Organization – Geneva. Jan. 1948-Jan. 1951 – 1 – us NY Public [331]

OCCUPATIONAL STRESS AND JOB SATISFACTION RELATED TO MANAGEMENT STYLES OF AMERICAN- AND JAPANESE-OWNED COMPANIES IN AMERICA / Garrison, DR – 1991 – 2mf – 9 – $8.00 – us Microform Publ [150]

OCCUPATIONAL STRESS, EXERCISE, AND HEALTH / Leonard, Anne C – 1994 – 1mf – $4.00 – us Microform Publ [150]

OCCUPATIONAL THERAPY IN HEALTH CARE : A JOURNAL OF CONTEMPORARY PRACTICE / ed by Kaplan, Susan – v1- 1984- – 1, 9 ($125.00 in US $175.00 outside hardcopy subsc) – us Haworth [615]

OCCUPATIONAL THERAPY IN MENTAL HEALTH : A JOURNAL OF PSYCHOSOCIAL PRACTICE AND RESEARCH / ed by Blount, Marie-Louise & Donohue, Mary – v1- 1980- – 1, 9 ($125.00 in US $175.00 outside hardcopy subsc) – us Haworth [615]

OCCUPATIONS FOR WOMEN / Willard, Frances Elizabeth – c1897 – 9 – us A.T.L.A. [240]

OCCUPATIONS NEUTRALITE MILITAIRE ET ANNEXION DE LA SAVOIE / Ducis, C A – Paris, 1877 – 2mf – 1 – ILM-873/1 – ne IDC [327]

L'OCCUPAZIONE DEI MARI COSTIERI / Cansacchi, G – Torino, 1936 – 3mf – 1 – ILM-1500/1 – ne IDC [327]

D'OCEAN A OCEAN: IMPRESSIONS D'AMERIQUE / Bonnaud, Dominique – Preface d'Armand Silvestre. Paris: Bibliotheque de la Vie Moderne, 18??. 02814. (Pre-1900 Canadiana) – 9 – cn C.I.H.M. [910]

OCEAN AND COASTAL LAW – v1. 1994-95 – 9 – $20.00 – us Hein [340]

OCEAN AND COASTAL LAW *see* TERRITORIAL SEA JOURNAL

OCEAN COUNTY TIMES – Lakewood. N.J. 1966- – 1 – us UMI [071]

OCEAN DEVELOPMENT AND INTERNATIONAL LAW – v1- 1973- 1; v5- 5,6,9 – us UMI [340]

OCEAN DEVELOPMENT AND INTERNATIONAL LAW – v1-26. 1993-95 – 9 – $1,040.00 set – us Hein [340]

OCEAN ENGINEERING – v1- 1968- – 5,6,9 – us UMI [550]

OCEAN INDUSTRY – v1- 1966- 1; v5- 5,6; v11- 9 – us UMI [550]

OCEAN MANAGEMENT – v1-9. 1973-84 – 1,5,6,13 – sz Elsevier [550]

OCEAN OBSERVING SYSTEM DEVELOPMENT PROGRAMME : A WORLD CLIMATE RESEARCH PROGRAMME ACTION PLAN – 1984 – 9 – 92-3-102289-X – fr UNESCO [550]

OCEAN ROUTE TO AUSTRALASIA THROUGH ATLANTIC AND PACIFIC / Clarke, Andrew – 1894? 00915. (Pre-1900 Canadiana) – 9 – cn C.I.H.M. [910]

OCEAN ROUTES AND MODERN TRANSPORTATION: CANADA'S SPLENDID OPPORTUNITY / Dobson, George H – s.l.: s.n., 1898 (Halifax, N.S.: Herald Print). 02728. (Pre-1900 Canadiana) – 9 – cn C.I.H.M. [910]

OCEAN SCIENCE AND ENGINEERING – (1984-. 5,6,9) – v6-. 1981- – 1 – us UMI [550]

OCEAN SCIENCE FOR THE YEAR 2000 – 1984 – 9 – 92-3-102198-2 – fr UNESCO [550]

OCEAN VIEW BAPTIST CHURCH. HORRY COUNTY. SOUTH CAROLINA : CHURCH RECORDS – 1964-72 – 1 – 15.53 – us Baptist [240]

OCEAN WAVE – Woods OR. Aug 16 1900 – 1 – us U.O. Library [071]

OCEAN YEARBOOK – 1978- – 1,5,6,9 – us UMI [550]

OCEANA, OR, ENGLAND AND HER COLONIES / Froude, James Anthony – London: Longmans, Green, 2nd ed 1886 – 1r – 1 – 1-55879-958-3 – uk Libr Preservation [941]

OCEANA, OR, ENGLAND AND HER COLONIES / Froude, James Anthony – New York: Scribner, 1886 – 1mf – us A.T.L.A. [941]

THE OCEANIC HYDROZOS: A DESCRIPTION OF THE CALYCOPHORIDAE AND PHYSOPHORIDAE / Huxley, Thomas – Ray Society. 1859 – 1 – uk Microform Academic [580]

OCEANIC ICHTHYOLOGY / Goode, C B & Bean, T H – Z-2108 2. 2 v. 1895 – 8 – ne IDC [590]

OCEANIC ICHTHYOLOGY / Goode, G B & Bean, T H – F180.00 – fr Ethnologie [590]

OCEANIS (SYDNEY-GREEK LANGUAGE) – Sept 3-Dec 3 1915 – 9 – at Pascoe [072]

OCEANOGRAPHIC ABSTRACTS AND OCEANOGRAPHIC BIBLIOGRAPHY *see* DEEP SEA RESEARCH AND OCEANOGRAPHIC LITERATURE REVIEW

OCEANOGRAPHIC COMPONENTS OF THE GLOBAL ATMOSPHERIC RESEARCH PROGRAMME – 1978 – 9 – 92-3-101535-4 – fr UNESCO [550]

OCEANOGRAPHIC INDEX / Sears, Mary – (Subject Cumulation 1946-1971, 1972. 95,500 entries 8 reels. $380.00 export $460.00. – ISBN 0-8161-1263-0; Cumulation 1946-1973: Marine Organisms, Chiefly Planktonic, 1974. 48,400 entries 6 reels. $220.00 export $265.00. – ISBN 0-8161-1324-6) – 1 – uk Hall [550]

OCEANOGRAPHIC INDEX / Woods Hole Oceanographic Institution – (Subject Cumulation 1946-71, 1972.-95,500 entries. 8 reels. $420.00 ISBN: 0-8161-1263-0; Cumulation 1946-73: Marine Organisms, chiefly Planktonic, 1974.- 48,400 entries 6 reels. $240.00 ISBN: 0-8161-1324-6) – Dr. Mary Sears, comp. 1971 – 1 – 380.00 – uk Hall [574]

OCEANOGRAPHIC LITERATURE REVIEW – v1- 1953- – 5,6,9 – us UMI [550]

OCEANOLOGY – v1-7 1966-72 1; v6-7 5,6 – us UMI [550]

OCEANS – v1- 1969- 1; v4- 5,6; v8- 9 – us UMI [550]

OCEANSIDE BLADE TRIBUNE – Oceanside, CA. Jul 1934-Dec 1934. 1 roll – 1 – 20.00 – uk Libr Preservation [071]

OCEANSIDE BLADE TRIBUNE INDEX – Oceanside, CA. 1975-84.25 fiches. Individual fiches available – 9 – 50.00 – uk Libr Preservation [071]

OCEANSIDE HERALD; THE OLIVE LEAF – Oceanside, CA. 1892-1897. Olive Leaf, 1896-97.1 roll – 1 – 25.00 – uk Libr Preservation [071]

OCEANSIDE NEWS – Oceanside, CA. 1926-34; 1936-49; 1953-54; 1956-57. 11 rolls. Individual rolls available – 1 – 275.00 – uk Libr Preservation [071]

OCEANSIDE RECORD – Oceanside, CA. 1913-14.1 roll – 1 – 25.00 – uk Libr Preservation [071]

OCEANSIDE REGISTER – Oceanside, CA. 1915-16.1 roll – 1 – 25.00 – uk Libr Preservation [071]

OCEANUS – v1- 1952- 1; v18- 5,6; v19- 9 – us UMI [073]

OCERK ISTORII RUSSKOJ KUL'TURY / Pokrovskij, M N – R 8096. 4-oe izd. (v. 2 has not been published). 1925 – 9 – ne IDC [947]

OCHEREDNAIA ZADACHA POTREBITEL'SKOI KOOPERATSII V GORODAKH ROSSII / Pazhitnov, K A – Pg., 1916 – 1mf – 9 – COR-90/1 – ne IDC [334]

OCHEREDNYE ZADACHI KHOZIAISTVENNOGO STROITEL'STVA : SBORNIK STATEI / Vladimirov, M K – M., L., 1925 – 1mf – 9 – COR-149/1 – ne IDC [334]

OCHEREDNYE ZADACHI MAKSIMALIZMA / Berdnikov, Aleksandr Ivanovich & Svetlov, F – Moskva: "Soi uz maksimalistov", 1919 – 1 – CSUX89-B3848 – us Hoover Inst Photo [330]

OCHEREDNYE ZADACHI PO RABOTE SREDI ZHENSHCHIN : DOKLAD NA VSEROSSIISKOM SOVESHCHANII ORGANIZATOROV OTDELOV PO RABOTE SREDI ZHENSHCHIN 28 MARTA 1920 G. V MOSKVE / Blonina, El – Moskva: Gos. izd-vo, 1920 – 1 – CSUX89-B3421 – us Hoover Inst Photo [947]

OCHEREDNYE ZADACHI PROMYSHLENNO I POLITIKI : SBORNIK STATE / Dzerzhinskii, Felix Edmundovich – Moskva: T Sentr. upr. pechati VSNKh SSSR, 1925 – 1 – CSUX88-B7001 – us Hoover Inst Photo [320]

OCHERK EKONOMICHSKO I BORBY RABOCHIKH V ROSSII : IZ ISTORII VOLNENI I I ZABASTOVOK / Gordon, Maks – 2-e izd. perer. Leningrad: Izd. Leningradskogo gub. soveta professionalnykh soi uzov, 1924 – 1 – CSUX89-B7331 – us Hoover Inst Photo [330]

OCHERK ISTORII BIBLIOTECHNOGO DELA V ROSSII 11-18 VV / Vasil'chenko, V E – Moscow, 1948. 157p. BR-10,788/1 – 9 – ne IDC [020]

OCHERK ISTORII NOVE ISHE I RUSSKO I LITERATURY : ETI UDY I KHARAKTERISTIKI / Evgenev-Maksimov, Vladislav Evgenevich – Leningrad: Gos. izd-vo, 1925 – 1 – CSUX89-B1533 – us Hoover Inst Photo [460]

OCHERK ISTORII ZEMELNYKH OTNOSHENII V ODESSKOI GUBERNII / Chernenkov, N N – Odessa: [Odesskoe gubernskoe statisticheskoe bi uro], 1925 – 1 – CSUX91-B3151 – us Hoover Inst Photo [947]

OCHERK IZUCHENIIA MAN'CHZHURSKAGO IAZYKA V KITAE / Grebenshchikov, A V – (Izvestiia Vostochnago instituta, v. 32). 1913. BR-501 2 – 8 – ne IDC [460]

OCHERK KOOPERATIVNOGO SBYTA ZERNA / Makarov, N P – M., 1914 – 2mf – 9 – COR-67/1 – ne IDC [334]

OCHERK LITERATURNOI ISTORII STARINNYKH POVESTEI I SKAZOK RUSSKIKH / Pypin, AN – Spb. 1857. BR-4083 2 – 8 – ne IDC [460]

OCHERK SRAVNITEL'NOI GRAMMATIKI SLAVIANSKIKH IAZYKOV / Bernshtein, S B – M. 1961. BR-11,242 1 – 9 – ne IDC [400]

OCHERK USLOVI I RAZVITII A OTECHESTVENNAGO TORGOVAGO MOREPLAVANIIA / Filipov, I Urii Dmitrievich – Petrograd: Tip. Red. period. izd. Ministerstva finansov, 1916 – 1 – CSUX89-B2703 – us Hoover Inst Photo [947]

OCHERKI DEREVENSKOI KOOPERATSII / Vil'do, Iu et al – Moscow, Leningrad, 1925 – 1mf – 9 – COR-468/1 – ne IDC [334]

OCHERKI DEREVNI SSSR, 1917-1927 / Bol'shakov, A M – (Pedagogicheskie Kursy na domu. Nos. 19-25) – M., 1928 – 3mf – 9 – COR-463/1 – ne IDC [334]

OCHERKI FEDERAL'NOGO UPRAVLENIIA SSSR / Ananov, I N – Leningrad, 1925. 211p. BR-9426 1 – 9 – ne IDC [335]

OCHERKI I FANTAZII / Skal'kovskii, K A – Spb. 1903. BR-10,624 2 – 8 – ne IDC [460]

OCHERKI I RAZSKAZY IZ RUSSKOI ISTORIIA XVIII VEKA. TSARITSA PRASKOV'IA 1664-1723 / Semevskii, M I – ed. 2. Spb. 1883. BR-10,531 1 – 9 – ne IDC [947]

OCHERKI I RECHI / Kliuchevskii, V O – Vtoroi sbornik statei, 1915 – 8 – BR-6055 2 – ne IDC [947]

OCHERKI ISTORII GRAZHDANKSOI VOINY 1917-1920 / Anishev, A – Leningrad: Gos. izd-vo, 1925 – 1 – CSUX88-B3937 – us Hoover Inst Photo [947]

OCHERKI ISTORII ISPANO-RUSSKIH LITERATURNYKH OTNOSHENII. XVI-XIX VV / Alekseev, M P – Leningrad, 1964. 216p. BR-6073 2 – 8 – ne IDC [460]

OCHERKI ISTORII REVOLIUTSIONNOGO DVIZHENIIA NA SEVERNOM KAVKAZE V 1905-1907 GG / Muzhev, I F – Nal'chik, 1957 – 1 – 35.00r – us Hoover Inst Photo [947]

OCHERKI ISTORII RUSSKOI TSENZURY (1700-1863) / Skabichevskii, A M – Spb. 1892. BR-7870 2 – 8 – ne IDC [947]

OCHERKI ISTORII S. PETERBURGSKOI SINODAL'NOI TIPOGRAFII / Gavrilov, A V – Vyp. 1. 1711-1839. Spb. 1911. Suppl. Index. BR-4564 2 – 8 – ne IDC [070]

OCHERKI IZ ISTORII RUSSKOI LITERATURY 17 I 18 STOLETII / Maikov, L N – Spb. 1889. BR-7672 2 – 8 – ne IDC [460]

OCHERKI KHOZIAISTVENNOGO PRAVA SSSR / Asknazii, S I – Leningrad, 1926. 200p. BR-9401 1 – 9 – ne IDC [330]

OCHERKI KRASNOI ARMII / Gorodnev, A – Izd. 2-e. Moskva: Gos. voen. izd-vo, 1926 – 1 – CSUX88-B1903 – us Hoover Inst Photo [947]

OCHERKI KRASNOI ARMII / Gorodnev, A – Moskva: Gos. voen. izd-vo, 1924 – 1 – CSUX88-B4720 – us Hoover Inst Photo [947]

OCHERKI KREDITNOI KOOPERATSII V SSSR / Lur'e, ML – L., 1926 – 2mf – 9 – COR-391/1 – ne IDC [334]

OCHERKI LITERATURNOGO DVIZHENIIA REVOLIUTSIONNOI EPOKHI, 1917-1927 / Polonskii, V – Ed. 2. M., L. 1929. BR-2078 2 – 8 – ne IDC [335]

OCHERKI OSVOBODITELNAGO DVIZHENIIA "SHETSTIDESIATYKH GODOV" / Lemke, M K – Po neizdannym dokymentam s portretami. Spb, 1908 – 9 – BR-10 088 1 – ne IDC [947]

OCHERKI PO BALGARSKIIA FOLKLOR / Arnaudov, M P – Sofiia. 1934. BR-3948 2 – 8 – ne IDC [390]

OCHERKI PO ISTORII ARKHIVNOGO DELA V SSSR / Maiakovskii, IL – Ed. 2. Moscow, 1960. 338p. BR-10,767/1 – 9 – ne IDC [025]

OCHERKI PO ISTORII EKONOMICHESKIKH NAUK V ROSSII 18 VEKA / Karataev, N K – M. 1960. BR-6202 2 – 8 – ne IDC [947]

OCHERKI PO ISTORII KRASNOI GVARDII / Georgievskii, G – Moskva: "Fakel", 1919 – 1 – CSUX88-B6998 – us Hoover Inst Photo [355]

OCHERKI PO ISTORII NOVEISHEI RUSSKOI LITERATURY / Kogan, P – M. 1910-11. BR-1341 2 – 8 – ne IDC [460]

OCHERKI PO ISTORII OBSHCHESTVENNAGO DVIZHENIIA I KREST'IANSKAGO DELA V ROSSII / Kornilov, A A – Spb. 1905. B-1562 2 – 8 – ne IDC [947]

OCHERKI PO ISTORII PROFESSIONALNOGO DVIZHENIIA RABOTNIKOV SVIAZI 1905-1906 / Bazilevich, K V – Moskva: T S.K. Soi uza svi azi, 1925 – 1 – CSUX88-B582 – us Hoover Inst Photo [947]

OCHERKI PO ISTORII RUSSKIKH FINANSOV V TSARSTVORANIE EKATERINY 2 / Chechulin, N D – Spb. 1906. BR-4111 2 – 8 – ne IDC [947]

OCHERKI PO ISTORII RUSSKOI KOOPERATSII / Korotkov, M A – L., 1925 – 2mf – 9 – COR-205/1 – ne IDC [334]

OCHERKI PO ISTORII RUSSKOI LITERATURY OT EPOKHI PETRA VELIKOGO DO PUSHKINA / Lipovskii, A L – Spb. 1912. BR-7653 2 – 8 – ne IDC [460]

OCHERKI PO ISTORII RUSSKOI POEMY 18 I PERVOI POLOVINY 19 VEKA / Sokolov, A N – M. 1955. BR-7889 2 – 8 – ne IDC [460]

OCHERKI PO ISTORII RUSSKOI SOVETSKOI POEZII / Selivanovskii, A – M. 1936. BR-2117 2 – 8 – ne IDC [460]

OCHERKI PO ISTORII RUSSKOI ZHURNALISTIKI I KRITIKI – v.1. L. 1950. BR-7737 2 – 8 – ne IDC [070]

OCHERKI PO ISTORII SOVETOV RABOCHIKH DEPUTATOV V 1905 G / Gorin, Pavel Osipovich – Moskva: Izd. Kommunisticheskogo un-ta im. I A.M. Sverdlova, 1925 – 1 – CSUX88-B756 – us Hoover Inst Photo [947]

OCHERKI PO KOOPERATSII : LEKTSII I STAT'I / Antsyferov, A N – Ed 2. M., 1915 – 4mf – 9 – COR-3/1 – ne IDC [334]

OCHERKI PO SEL'SKO-KHOZIASTVENNOI I KREDITNOI KOOPERATSIIA : (STAT'I DOKLADY ZAMETKI), 1900-1918 GG / Kulyzhnyi, A E – Pg., 1918 – 1mf – 9 – COR-58/1 – ne IDC [334]

OCHERKI PO TEORII KOOPERATSII / Ilimskii, D I (D I Golenishchev-Kutuzov) – M., 1925 – 2mf – 9 – COR-197/1 – ne IDC [334]

OCHERKI PO TEORII TRUDOVOGO KHOZIAISTVA / Chaianov, A V – ([Pt 1] 1912. Pt 2: Osnovy slozheniia potrebitel' skogo biudzheta 1913) – M., 1912-1913 – 2mf – 9 – COR-139/1 – ne IDC [334]

OCHERKI PRAVA RODOVOGO, NASLEDSTVENNOGO I OBYCHNOGO / Bashmakov, A A – Spb. 445p. 1911 – 7mf – 9 – R-9743/1 – ne IDC [947]

OCHERKI REVOLIUTSIONNOGO DVIZHENIIA V AZERBAIDZHANE / Guseinov, Ragim – Baku: Kooperativnoe izdvo pri BK AKP (b) "Bakinski i rabochi i", 1926- – 1 – CSUX88-B1331 – us Hoover Inst Photo [947]

OCHERKI RUSSKO I REVOLIUTSII = THROUGH THE RUSSIAN REVOLUTION : PEREVOD S ANGI ISKOGO / Williams, Albert Rhys – Moskva: Gos. izdvo, 1924 – 1 – CSUX88-B5817 – us Hoover Inst Photo [320]

OCHERKI RUSSKOI LITERATURY KONTSA 19NACHALA 20 VEKOV / Volkov, A – Gozlitizdat. M. 1952. BR-2208 2 – 8 – ne IDC [460]

OCHERKI RUSSKOI NARODNOI SLOVESNOSTI / Miller, V F – M. 3v. 1897-1924 – 24mf – 9 – R-2299/2 – ne IDC [947]

OCHERKI RUSSKOI SMUTY / Denikin, Anton Ivanovich – Paris: J Povolozky, [1921-1926]. 5v – 1 – CSUX88-B9772 – us Hoover Inst Photo [947]

OCHERKI TEORII I ISTORII KOOPERATSII : POSOBIE DLIA SOVPARTSHKOL I KOMVUZOV / Kantor, M – M., 1931 – 3mf – 9 – COR-250/1 – ne IDC [334]

OCHERKI TRUDOVOGO PRAVA / Dogadov, Vasilii Mikhailovich – L. 1927. BR-9416 1 – 9 – ne IDC [947]

OCHERKI TRUDOVOGO PRAVA / Kaminskaia, PD – Moscow, 1927. 136p. Labor law, concentrating on collective contract and labor contract; Soviet institutions contrasted with those of capitalist countries. BR-9418/1 – 9 – ne IDC [340]

OCHERKII PO ISTORII RUSSKOI PROMYSHLENNOSTI 17, 18 I NACHALA 19 VEKA / Liubomirov, P G – M. 1947. BR-7657 2 – 8 – ne IDC [947]

OCHO SEMANAS EN LOS CALABOZOS PERONISTAS : PRECEDIDO DE UNA CARTA POLITICA DEL PRESIDENTE PERON AL DR. LUIS A. DE HERRERA / Azarola Saint, Jose Luis – Montevideo: Imp. San Luis, 1954 – 1 – CSUXADQ6529-B – us Hoover Inst Photo [320]

OCHOCO REVIEW – Prineville, OR. 5 Sep 1885-2 June 1894 – 1 – us U.O. Library [071]

Ochotorena, Manuel D *see* CODIGO PENAL PARA LAS ISLAS DE CUBA Y PUERTO RICO

Ochs Funeral Home (Ottawa, Ohio) *see* FUNERAL RECORDS

Ochse, J J *see*
– INDISCHE VRUCHTEN
– TROPISCHE GROENTEN GETEELD EN IN HET 'T WILD GROEIENDE GEWASSEN, DIE DOOR DE INDISCHE BEVOLKING WORDEN GEGETEN

OCHT SGEALTA O CHOILLTE MAGHACH / Ui Chathasaigh, Thomais – 1936. Irish tales – 1 – us I.U. Libraries [390]

O OCIO – Manaos, Amazonas. 22 Out, 5 Nov 1906 – 1,5,6 – bl Biblioteca [072]

OCIOS DE MI JUVENTUD / Cadalso Vazquez, Jose – 1781 – 1mf – 9 – Pta1,000.00 – 84-7848-137-0 – sp Pentalfa [440]

OCIOS Y VERSOS / Cacharron, Francisco de Paula – Badajoz: Tipografia el Progreso, de Antonio Arqueros, 1901 – 1 – sp Bibl Santa Ana [780]

LA OCIOSIDAD EN SONETOS / Sanchez-Arjona, Vicente – Sevilla: Imp. Alvarez, Tomo 4-6. 1957 – 1 – sp Bibl Santa Ana [810]

LA OCIOSIDAD EN SONETOS / Sanchez-Arjona, Vicente – Sevilla: Imp. Cuadrado, Tomo 1-3. 1957 – 1 – sp Bibl Santa Ana [810]

LA OCIOSIDAD EN SONETOS / Sanchez-Arjona, Vicente – Sevilla: Imp. Zambrano, Tomo 7-9. 1958 – 1 – sp Bibl Santa Ana [810]

LA OCIOSIDAD EN...¡SONETOS! / Sanchez-Arjona, Vicente – Sevilla: Imp. Alvarez, Tomo 10-12. 1958 – 1 – sp Bibl Santa Ana [810]

Ockley, Simon *see* AN ACCOUNT OF SOUTH-WEST BARBARY: CONTAINING WHAT IS MOST REMARKABLE IN THE TERRITORIES OF THE KING OF FEZ AND MOROCCO

OCMULGEE BAPTIST CHURCH. PERRY COUNTY. OCMULGEE, ALABAMA : CHURCH RECORDS – 4May 1820-2 May 1948 – 1 – 19.71 – us Baptist [240]

OCMULGEE NATIONAL MONUMENT, GEORGIA / Pope, G D – 1956 – 2mf – 9 – $5.00f – us Ross [720]

Ocoee. Presbytery (Cumberland Presbyterian Church) *see* MINUTES, 1887-1889

O'Connell, Cornelius Joseph *see* CHRISTIAN EDUCATION

O'Connell, Daniel *see* CORRESPONDENCE OF DANIEL O'CONNELL, THE LIBERATOR; ED. WITH NOTICES OF HIS LIFE AND TIMES.

O'Conner, V C Scott *see* MANDALAY AND OTHER CITIES OF THE PAST IN BURMA

O'Connor, C *see* PRODUCTION AND PROCESSING OF MILK FROM CATTLE IN SUB-SAHARAN AFRICA

O'Connor, C B *see*
INTRODUCTION A L'ETUDE DU LAIT
– AN INTRODUCTION TO MILK
– MILK PROCESSING TECHNIQUES
– TECHNIQUES DE TRANSFORMATION DU LAIT FERMENTE
– TRADITIONAL CHEESEMAKING MANUAL

O'Connor, John *see* FOOD, COOKERY, AND CATERING MICROFICHE LIBRARY

O'Connor, Johnson *see* CHARACTERISTICS COMMON TO LAWYERS

O'Connor, Kimberly A *see* LIFE STRESS AND ITS EFFECTS ON INJURY AND PERFORMANCE AMONG COLLEGIATE SOCCER PLAYERS

O'Connor, MaryLou *see* CAFFEINE, CARBOHYDRATE LOADING, AND PHYSICAL PERFORMANCE

OCONTO REGISTER – Oconto, NE. -w. Jan 1908-Jun 1920 – 1 – us NE Hist [071]

OCP, ON CONTINUING PRACTICE / Ontario College of Pharmacy – v1- 1973- 1; v3-5,6,9 – us UMI [971]

OCTAGON – v. 1-15. 1929-43 – 1 – us UMI [073]

OCTAGON *see* AIA JOURNAL

OCTAVA SAGRADAMENTE CULTA...UNICO MILAGRO DE SAN LORENZO DEL ESCORIAL / Luis de Santa Maria, Fray – Madrid, 1664 – 8mf – 9 – sp Cultura [240]

OCTOBER – (1979- 5,6,9) – 1976- – 1 – us UMI [073]

OCTOBER – [Egypt], 1976 – 52mf per y – 9 – $300.00y – us Ross [072]

OCTOPUS *see* CANADIAN FREE PRESS

O'Curry, Eugene *see* ON THE MANNERS AND CUSTOMS OF THE ANCIENT IRISH; A SERIES OF LECTURES DELIVERED BY THE LATE EUGENE O'CURRY

OD KLADSKEHO POMEZI – v3-9, 1925-32 – 1 – us I.U. Libraries [073]

ODA SAFICA A...WELLINGTON DE CIUDAD RODRIGO – 1812 – 9 – 1.50f – sp Bibl Santa Ana [810]

ODAL – Berlin, 1933/34 n4, 1934/35-1941 (incomplete) – 1 – Inquire at Mikrofilmarchiv for details – gw Misc Inst [072]

O'Daniel *see* DOMINICANS IN EARLY FLORIDA

Odarial Publicidad *see* FERIAS Y FIESTAS. CACERES, MAYO 1958

ODAS A LA MUSICA / Olloqui, Emilio – 1848 – 9 – 1.50f – sp Bibl Santa Ana [780]

THE ODD FELLOW – London, Ontario. v1 n20. 30 may 1853 – 1r – 1 – Can$25.00 – cn Can Microfilming [072]

ODD FELLOW'S MAGAZINE – v. 1. 1825-26 – 1 – us UMI [073]

THE ODD FELLOW'S RECORD : A MONTHLY MAGAZINE DEVOTED TO THE INTERESTS OF THE INDEPENDENT ORDER OF ODD FELLOWS – v1-2. 1846-47. SEM105P496 – 6mf – 9 – Can$13.50 – cn Bibl Nat [360]

THE ODDFELLOWS' GAZETTE – Montreal: J.T. Courtenay, [1894-189- or 19–] – 9 – cn C.I.H.M. [360]

ODDITIES OF THE LAW / Heard, Franklin Fiske – San Francisco: Sumner Whitney and Co, 1885 – 3mf – 9 – $4.50 – LLMC 95-165 – us L.L.M.C. [340]

ODE QVAM SVPER DIVINA AC FOELICISSIMA VICTORIA EX CELEBERRIMA PUGNA AD SCOPULOS ECHINEOS NONIS OCTOB. MDLXXI / Zannius, F – Venetijs, 1571 – 1mf – 9 – H-8319/1 – ne IDC [956]

ODE SUR LA VIE HUMAINE / Haren, Willem van – (D'Holbach series). 1768 – 9 – fr Hachette [810]

ODELL ORACLE – Odell, NE. -w. Dec 1919-Nov 1958 – 1 – us NE Hist [071]

ODEN / Klopstock, Friedrich Gottlieb; ed by Muncker, Franz & Pawel, Jaro – Stuttgart: Goeschen, 1889 – 1r – 1 – us U.W. Library [810]

ODENWAELDER HEIMAT ZEITUNG *see* GRAEFLICH ERBACHISCHES WOCHEN-BLATT FUER DEN LANDKREIS ERBACH

Odenwald, Theodor *see* DAS RELIGIONSPROBLEM BEI FRIEDRICH NIETZSCHE

ODER-BLATT – Kostryzn, Poland. Oct-Dec 1942 – 1r – 1 – us L of C Photodup [943]

ODES AND ADDRESSES TO GREAT PEOPLE / Hood, Thomas – London: Printed for Baldwin, Craddock & Joy, 1825 – 1r – 1 – 1-55879-620-7 – uk Libr Preservation [810]

THE ODES OF SOLOMAN / ed by Bernard, J H – 1912 – 3mf – 9 – ne Slangenburg [240]

ODESSEY OF THE SPIRIT – v1-2. 1978-80 (complete) – 1r – 1 – ATLA S0652 – us A.T.L.A. [073]

ODESSKII VESTNIK SEL'SKOKHOZIAISTVENNOI KOOPERATSII – Odessa, 1922 n1 – 1mf – 9 – COR-661/1 – ne IDC [334]

ODESSKOYE OBSHCHESTVO ISTORII I DREVNOSTEI – Zapiski. Odessa. v. 1-33. 1844-1919 – 1 – us NY Public [947]

Odgers, Len *see* DIARY AND TRANSCRIPT, 1942-1943

Odgers, William B *see* SIX LECTURES ON THE INNS OF COURT AND CHANCERY

ODGLOSY – (Oblicze Tygodnia: 4 Oct 1958 27 Aug 1966) – London, UK. 28 Jun 1957-13 Sept 1958 – 1 – uk British Libr Newspaper [072]

ODINOCHESTVO I SVOBODA. IZD. IMENI CHEKHOVA / Adamovich, G – New York, 1955. BR-1110 2 – 8 – ne IDC [460]

ODISEA Y GESTA DE OVEIDO; EPOPEYA DE UNA CIUDAD MARTIR Y HEROICA, 18 JULIO 1936-21 OCTUBRE 1937 / Rivero Sanchez, Manuel – Las Palmas, 1938. Fiche W1143. (Blodgett Collection of Spanish Civil War Pamphlets) – 9 – us H.U. College Libr [946]

ODNA LIUBOV / Sologub, F – Stikhi. Petrograd. 1921. BR-870 2 – 8 – ne IDC [460]

ODNODNEVNYE GAZETY SSSR 1917-1983 : THE ONE-DAY NEWSPAPER COLLECTION OF THE SALTYKOV-SHCHEDRIN STATE PUBLIC LIBRARY / ed by Grigor'iants, T S & Snigireva, I A – (Printed guide 3v $290) – 1993 – 46r – 1 – $3,600.00 – us Ross [072]

Odoevsteva, I *see*
- ANGEL SMERTI
- DVOR CHUDES
- IZOL'DA
- KONTRAPUNKT
- NA BEREGAKH NEVY
- OSTAV' NADEZHDU NAVSEGDA
- ZERKALO

O'Donnell, James H *see* LITURGY FOR THE LAITY, OR, AN EXPLANATION OF SACRED OBJECTS CONNECTED WITH DIVINE WORSHIP

O'Donnell, Roger *see* PROCEDURE AND FORMS COMMON LAW PLEADING, COVERING ALL COMMON LAW ACTIONS

ODONTOGRAPHY, OR A TREATISE ON THE COMPARATIVE ANATOMY, OF THE TEETH / Owen, R – London, 1840-1845 – 35mf – 9 – ne IDC [611]

ODONTOLOGIA SANITARIA POR... / Dominguez Villagra, David – Plasencia: Imp. Hontineros, 1933 – 1 – sp Bibl Santa Ana [617]

ODPOWIEDZ NA UMIESZCZONA W GAZECIE LITERACKIEJ RECENZYE DZIELA POD TYTULEM: PIERWSZE ZASADY GRAMMATYKI JEZYKA POLSKIEGO / Mrozinski, J – Warszawa. 1824. BR-4845 2 – 8 – ne IDC [460]

ODRA – Wroclaw, Poland. -w. Feb 1958-Jan 1961. 3 reels – 1 – uk British Libr Newspaper [947]

Odriozola, Manuel de *see* COLECCION DE... DEL PERU

ODRODZENIE – Cracow and Warsaw. Poland. -w. Jun 1946-Mar 1950. (4 reels) – 1 – uk British Libr Newspaper [947]

ODRUN : TRAGOEDIE / Hartz, Erich von – Berlin: A Langen/G Mueller, 1939 – 1r – 1 – us U.W. Library [820]

Odyniec, Antoni Edward *see* LISTY Z PODROZY: WYBOR

ODYSSEUS AUF ITHAKA : DRAMATISCHE DICHTUNG IN DREI AUFZUEGEN / Lienhard, Friedrich – 2. bearb. Aufl. Stuttgart: Greiner & Pfeiffer, 1914 – 1r – 1 – us U.W. Library [820]

ODYSSEY – v.1-. 1979- – 1,5,6,9 – us UMI [073]

THE ODYSSEY OF THE PHILIPPINE COMMISSION / Williams, Daniel Roderick – Chicago: A.C. McClurg, 1913. 264p – 1 – us U.W. Library [950]

OE AND M : OFFICE EQUIPMENT AND METHODS – (Cont by: Office Systems and Technology at v36 no 8 1990) – Toronto. v17-35. 1970-1989 – 9 – Can$28.00y – cn Micromedia [650]

OE AND M *see* OFFICE SYSTEMS AND TECHNOLOGY

O.E. MANDEL'SHTAM / Mochul'skii, K – Vstrecha, 2. 1945. BR-3683 – 8 – ne IDC [460]

OEA FOCUS / Oklahoma Education Association – v1-. 1982- – 1,5,6,9 – us UMI [073]

OEBAR KAMPOENG. TJITAKAN 1 / Prawirangara, R I – (Microfiche No 131) – Djakarta: Gunseikanbu Kokumin Tosyokyoku (Bale Poestaka), 2604 – 1mf – 9 – SE-2002/1 – ne IDC [950]

Oecolampad, J *see*
- AIN GESPRECH ETLICHER PREDICANTEN ZU BASEL
- DER PROPHET MALEACHI, MIT AUSZLEGUNG. VERDEUETSCHT D. L. HAETZER
- UNDERRICHTUNG VON DEM WIDERTAUFF
- VOM SACRAMENT DER DANCKSAGUNG. VERTEUETSCHT D. L. HAETZER

OECOLOGIA – v. 1-47. 1968-80 – 1,5,9 – 7332.00 – us UMI [073]

OECONOMISCHE PFLANZENHISTORIE / Ehrhart, B – ed. 2. 4 v. Ulm, Memmingen. 1756-62. B-824 2 – 8 – ne IDC [580]

OECONOMISCHE PFLANZENHISTORIE / Ehrhart, B – v. 1-4. Ulm, Memmingen. 1753-54. Lacking: v. 5-12. B-7126 – 9 – ne IDC [580]

THE OECUMENICAL COUNCIL AND THE INFALLIBILITY OF THE ROMAN PONTIFF : A PASTORAL LETTER TO THE CLERGY ETC / Manning, Henry Edward – (Includes bibliographical references) – 2nd ed. London: Longmans, Green, 1869 – 1mf – 9 – 0-8370-8448-2 – 1986-2448 – us A.T.L.A. [240]

OECUMENISME – (1985-. 5,6,9) – Eng. ed.1974- – 1 – us UMI [240]

Oeder, G C *see*
- FLORA DANICAE
- FLORAE DANICAE. ICONES PLANTARUM SPONTE NASCENTIUM IN REGNIS DANICAE ET NORVEGIAE
- NOMENCLATOR BOTANICUS

OEDIPUS JUDAICUS / Drummond, William – London: Reeves & Turner, 1866. 1 fiche – 9 – us A.T.L.A. [240]

OEDIPUS ON THE SPHINX OF THE NINETEENTH CENTURY; OR, POLITICO-POLEMICAL RIDDLES INTERPRETED / Brade, William – London: G. Manwaring, 1862. 363p. illus – 1 – us U.W. Library [320]

OEDIPUS TYRANNUS OF SOPHOCLES / Paine, John Knowles – Boston: Arthur P. Schmidt, 1881. Piano-vocal score. music 295 – 1 – us L of C Photodup [780]

OEEC. GENERAL MEMORANDUM ON THE 1950/51 AND 1951/52 PROGRAMME / Greece – D-1310 1. 1950 – 9 – ne IDC [330]

OEEC. REPORT TO ECONOMIC COOPERATION ADMINISTRATION ON THE 1949/50 PROGRAMME, V. 2 – GREECE / Greece – D-1309 1. 1949 – 9 – ne IDC [330]

OEFFENTLICHE ANZEIGEN *see* BRAUNSCHWEIGISCHE ANZEIGEN

OEFFENTLICHE ANZEIGEN DER GRAFSCHAFT RAVENSBERG *see* WESTFAELISCHE ZEITUNG

OEFFENTLICHE ANZEIGEN DES DISTRICTES [...] *see* WESTFAELISCHE ZEITUNG

OEFFENTLICHE ANZEIGEN DES WESERDEPARTEMENTS *see* JOURNAL DER DISTRIKTE MINDEN, BIELEFELD UND RINTELN

DER OEFFENTLICHE BEDIENSTETE – Wien, Austria. 1953-72 – 1 – gw Mikrofilm [072]

DIE OEFFENTLICHE MEINUNG IN DER STAATSPHILOSOPHIE VON THOMAS HOBBES / Flieger, Heinrich – Frankfurt a.M., 1975 – 2mf – 9 – DM62.00 – 3-89349-378-6 – gw Hänsel [190]

OEFFENTLICHE RECHENSCHAFT UEBER MEINE ZWOELFJAEHRIGE DIENSTFUEHRUNG ALS ZWEITER ARZT DES KOENIGL. CHARITE-KRANKENHAUSES ZU BERLIN NEBST ERFAHRUNGEN UEBER KRANKENHAEUSER UND IRRENANSTALTEN / Horn, Ernst – Berlin, 1818 – 9 – DM48.00 – 3-89349-022-1 – gw Hänsel [610]

OEFFENTLICHER ANZEIGER *see*
- DER DEUTSCHE REDNER FUER RECHT UND FREIHEIT
- OEFFENTLICHER ANZEIGER FUER BAD KREUZNACH UND UMGEBUNG

OEFFENTLICHER ANZEIGER FUER BAD KREUZNACH UND UMGEBUNG : BA DER RHEIN-ZEITUNG – (Title change: Oeffentlicher Anzeiger, 23 Aug 1978) – Bad Kreuznach, West Germany. 1977- – ca 9r per yr – 1 – gw Mikrofilm [072]

OEFFENTLICHER ANZEIGER FUER DAS VEREINIGTE WIRTSCHAFTSGEBIET *see* BUNDES-ANZEIGER

OEFFENTLICHER ANZEIGER FUER DEN KREIS BOCHUM *see* DER DEUTSCHE REDNER FUER RECHT UND FREIHEIT

OEFFENTLICHER ANZEIGER FUER DIE GRAFSCHAFT LIMBURG – (Title changes: Iserlohner Kreisanzeiger, 18 Mar 1875; Iserlohner Kreisanzeiger und Zeitung, 24 Nov 1949) – Iserlohn, West Germany. 1992- – 11r per yr – 1 – gw Mikrofilm [072]

OEGUET – Konya, Ankara, 1918-19? – 9 – $20.00 – us MEDOC [956]

Oehler, Dolf *see* DIE ANTIBOURGEOISE AESTHETIK DES JUNGEN BAUDELAIRE

Oehler, G F *see* THEOLOGY OF THE OLD TESTAMENT

Oehler, Hugo *see* SIXTH ANNIVERSARY OF THE SPANISH REPUBLIC IN BARCELONA; EYEWITNESS ACCOUNT BY EDWARD H. OLIVER

Oehler, Rolf *see* DIE TARIFLICHEN LOHNGARANTIEN DES AKKORDWEBERS IN DER DEUTSCHEN TEXTIL-INDUSTRIE

L'OEIL – Journal de Cayenne absolument independant. Dir. S.-H. Melesse, E. Gregoire, E. Menopole. Cayenne. fevr-mars 1902, juin-aout 1904, juin 1907, sept 1911 – 1 – fr A.C.R.P.P. [073]

L'OEIL – Quebec, Canada. v1 n31. 1 fev 1924-v4 n8. 3 dec 1926 – 1r – 1 – Can$25.00 – cn Can Microfilming [072]

L'OEIL : REVUE MENSUELLE / ed by Ayotte, Alfred – Montreal, Canada. 1 oct 1940-jul 1951 – 3r – 1 – Can$55.00r – cn Can Microfilming [073]

L'OEIL ILLUSTRE – Montreal. v3 n32. 9 oct 1954 – 1r – 1 – Can$25.00 – cn Can Microfilming [072]

L'OEIL REGIONAL – Beloeil. v1- 1970-. SEM35P211 – 1 – cn Bibl Nat [073]

Oei-Tan Soey Nio *see* DIE ENTWICKLUNG DER HOHEREN SCHULBILDUNG IN INDONESIEN VON 1600-1941

OEKONOMISCHE ANALYSE DES RECHTS AM BEISPIEL DES GEWAESSERSCHUTZES / Pennekamp, Markus – 1995 – 3mf – 9 – DM98.00 – 3-8267-2254-X – gw Hänsel [340]

OEKONOMISCH-TECHNISCHE ENZYKLOPAEDIE.. / Kruenitz, Johann Georg – Berlin, 1773-1858. Hildesheim, 1982 – 2028mf – 9 – DM11,000.00 diazo DM13,000.00 silver – gw Olms [330]

Oelgeklaus, Rainer *see* IMPEDANZSPEKTRONISCHE UNTERSUCHUNGEN ZUR ADSORPTIONSGESCHWINDIGKEIT AN POLY- UND MONOKRISTALLINEN PLATIN-ELEKTRODEN

Oelmann, Klaus Henning *see*
- EDVARD GRIEGS BRIEFWECHSEL, BAND 1
- DIE GRATULANTEN KOMMEN

Oelrichs, J C C *see* HISTORISCHE NACHRICHT VON DEM AKADEMISCHEN WUERDEN IN DER MUSIK UND OEFFENTLICHEN MUSIKALISCHEN AKADEMIEN UND GESELLSCHAFTEN

Oels, Friedrich *see* LUETZOWS LAGER

Oelsner, L *see* JAHRBUECHER DES FRAENKISCHEN REICHES UNTER KOENIG PIPPIN

Oelsner, Werner *see* DER BEGRIFF KLASSISCH BEI HERDER

OENDANG-OENDANG SEKOLAH, JAITOE PADA MENJATAKAN PERATOERAN HAL PENGADJARAN – Weltevreden, 1919 – 3mf – 9 – ne IDC [370]

'Oerfi ve 'Avnuellah, Al-Kazimi *see* DIVAN

OERNSKOELDSVIKS ALLEHANDA – OErnskoeldsvik, 1901-48 – 9 – sw Kungliga [072]

OERNSKOELDSVIKS ALLEHANDA WEEKLY EDITION – OErnskoeldsvik, 1901-02 – 9 – sw Kungliga [072]

OERNSKOELDSVIKS NYHETER – OErnskoeldsvik, 1894-1900 – 9 – sw Kungliga [072]

OERNSKOELDSVIKS TIDNING – Haernoesand, 1890-91 – 9 – sw Kungliga [072]

OERNSKOELDSVIKSPOSTEN – OErnskoeldsvik, OEstersund. 1890-1951 – 9 – sw Kungliga [072]

OERNSKOELDSVIKSPOSTEN VECKOUPPLAGA – OErnskoeldsvik, Sweden. 1907 – 1 – sw Kungliga [072]

Oersted, A S *see*
- DE REGIONIBUS MARINIS
- GESNERACEAE CENTRO-AMERICANAE. CENTRALAMERICAS GESNERACEER, ET SYSTEMATISK, PLANTEGEOGRAPHISK BIDRAG TIL CENTRALAMERICAS FLORA

Oersted, Hans *see* RECHERCHES SUR L'IDENTITE DES FORCES CHIMIQUES ET ELECTRIQUES

Oertel, J R *see* PAULUS IN DER APOSTELGESCHICHTE: DER HISTORISCHE CHARAKTER DIESER SCHRIFT

Oertmann, Paul Ernst Wilhelm *see* DIE RECHTSBEDINGUNG (CONDICIO IURIS) UNTERSUCHEUNGEN ZUM BURGERLICHEN RECHT UND ZUR ALLGEMEINEN RECHTSLEHRE

Oertzen-Strehlow, Heinrich Ulrich von *see* TIERZUCHT IM POMMERN

Oeser, Willy *see* MALER MUELLER

OESTE : QUINZENAL SOB OS AUSPICIOS DA PREFEITURA MUNICIPAL – Xapuri, Acre. 25 Jun 1949; 20 Out 1957 – 1,5,6 – bl Biblioteca [072]

OESTE-JORNAL : ORGAM DOS INTERESSES DO MUNICIPIO – Dores do Indaya, 2-7 Dec 1919; Mar 1920; Sep 1924; Dec 1926-3 Apr 1927 – 1,5,6 – bl Biblioteca [072]

OESTERGOETLANDS NYHETER – Motala, 1891-93 – 9 – sw Kungliga [072]

Oesterley, William Oscar Emil *see*
- EVOLUTION OF THE MESSIANIC IDEA: A STUDY IN COMPARATIVE RELIGION
- AN INTRODUCTION TO THE BOOKS OF THE APOCRYPHA
- THE PSALMS IN THE JEWISH CHURCH
- THE RELIGION AND WORSHIP OF THE SYNAGOGUE: AN INTRODUCTION TO THE STUDY OF JUDAISM FROM THE NEW TESTAMENT PERIOD
- THE WISDOM OF JESUS THE SON OF SIRACH

Oesterly, William Oscar Emil *see* AN INTRODUCTION TO THE BOOKS OF THE OLD TESTAMENT

OESTERREICH IM DICHTEN UND DENKEN GRILLPARZERS / Kosch, Wilhelm – (Includes index) – Nymwegen: Waechter-Verlag, 1946 – 1r – 1 – us U.W. Library [430]

OESTERREICH UND PREUSSEN IM BEFREIUNGSKRIEGE / Oncken, Wilhelm – Berlin. 2v. 1876-1879 – 13mf – 9 – ne IDC [943]

DER OESTERREICHISCHE ARBEITER UND ANGESTELLTE – (Solidaritaet). Vienna. Austria. -w. 8 Jun 1945-1 Sep 1958. (4 reels) – 1 – uk British Libr Newspaper [331]

OESTERREICHISCHE BOTANISCHE ZEITSCHRIFT *see* OESTERREICHISCHES BOTANISCHES WOCHENBLATT

OESTERREICHISCHE FESTDICHTUNGEN / Saar, Ferdinand von – (Includes bibliographical references) – Wien: Theodor Daberkow, [1903] – 1r – 1 – us U.W. Library [810]

OESTERREICHISCHE MONATSSCHRIFT FUER DEN ORIENT – Wien etc. Jahrg. 1-44, Heft 9; 15 Jan. 1875-Okt. 1918. 1875-1916 issued by Oesterreichisches Handels-Museum, Vienna, 1917-18 issued by Oesterreichische Orient- und Uebersee-Gesellschaft. Set lacks Jahrg. 25. Film Mas C 576 – 1 – us H.U. Library [950]

Oesterreichische Nationalbibliothek Wien. Musiksammlung *see*
- DIE BACH-DRUCKE DER HOBOKEN-SAMMLUNG MUSIKALISCHER ERST- UND FRUEHDRUECKE
- DIE DRUCKE DER BACHSOEHNE DER HOBOKEN-SAMMLUNG MUSIKALISCHER ERST- UND FRUEHDRUCKE
- DIE HAYDN-DRUCKE DER HOBOKEN-SAMMLUNG MUSIKALISCHER ERST- UND FRUEHDRUCKE

OESTERREICHISCHE NATIONAL-ENZYKLOPAEDIE ODER ALPHABETISCHE DARLEGUNG DER WISSENSWUERDIGSTEN EIGENTHUEMLICHKEITEN DES OESTERREICHISCHEN KAISERTUMS (AEL, ABT.1;10) / Graeffer, Franz & Czikann, Johann – Wien, 1835-1838 (mf ed 1992) – 45mf – 9 – DM370.00 – 3-89131-076-5 – gw Fischer [943]

OESTERREICHISCHE REVUE 1. 1863-5.1867. OESTERREICHISCH-UNGARISCHE REVUE 1.1886-37.1910 – Wien, 1863-1910 (mf ed 1994) – 227mf – 9 – DM2,250.00 – 3-89131-166-4 – gw Fischer [430]

DER OESTERREICHISCHE VOLKSWIRT – Vienna, Austria. -w. 7 Oct 1916-26 July 1919. 4 reels – 1 – uk British Libr Newspaper [072]

OESTERREICHISCHE WASSERWIRTSCHAFT – v.1-3, 1949-51; v.5-20, 1953-68; v.22-23, 1970-71; v.25-33, 1973-81. ISSN: 0029-9588 – 1,5,6,9,13 – 80.00v – us UMI [333]

OESTERREICHISCHE WOCHENSCHRIFT = AUSTRIAN WEEKLY – (In German) – Vienna, AU. v16 no5 Feb 1899-v16 no43 27 Oct 1899 – 1r – 1 – $25.00 – cn Can Microfilming [072]

OESTERREICHISCHE WOCHENSCHRIFT – Vienna. v. 1-37. no. 7. Oct 15 1884-Feb 20 1920 – 1 – us NY Public [305]

OESTERREICHISCHE ZEITSCHRIFT FUR OFFENTLICHES RECHT UND VOLKERRECHT – v.1-32, 1946-81. ISSN: 0378-3073 – 1,5,6,9,13 – 133.00v – us UMI [073]

OESTERREICHISCHE ZEITUNG – (Zeitung der Sowjetarmee fuer die Bevoelkerung Oesterreichs). Vienna. Austria. -d. 15 Jul 1945-15 Feb 1948. (9 reels) – 1 – uk British Libr Newspaper [072]

EIN OESTERREICHISCHER GESCHICHTSSCHREIBER, THEOLOGE UND DIPLOMAT DES 15. JAHRHUNDERTS 1957 (MGH SCHRIFTEN..: 15.BD) / Lhotsky, A & Ebendorfer, Thomas – Dfl19.00 – ne Slangenburg [240]
OESTERREICHISCHER NEUE TAGESZEITUNG – Vienna, Austria. 1956-May 1964 – 1 – us Res Libr [072]
OESTERREICHISCHER REICHSRAT – (Stenographische Protokolle des Herrenhauses 1861-1918 698mf DM4,600.00 diazo DM5,400.00 silver. Stenographische Protokolle des Abgeordnetenhauses 1861-1918 5229mf DM23,800.00 diazo DM28,800.00 silver. Stenographische Protokolle ueber die Sitzungen der Provisorischen Nationalversammlung fuer Deutschoesterreich 1918 und 1919, Der Konstituierenden Nationalversammlung der Republik OEsterriech 1919 und 1920, des Nationalrates der Republik OEsterreich 1920-1934 und des Bundesrates 1916-1934 812mf DM5,200.00 diazo DM5,900.00 silver) – 9 – gw Olms [943]
OESTERREICHISCHES BOTANISCHES WOCHENBLATT – (Cont as: Oesterreichische Botanische Zeitschrift. Wien v8-90 1858-1941) – Wien. v1-7. 1851-1857 – 716mf – 9 – ne IDC [580]
OESTERREICHISCHES CENTRAL-ORGAN FUER GLAUBENSFREIHEIT – Ed. by I. Busch and M. Letteris. Vienna. 1848. BJ-23-60 1 – 9 – ne IDC [360]
OESTERREICHISCHES GEFALLS-STRAFRECHT VON HEINRICH VETTER / Vetter, Heinrich – Wien, Selbstverlag, Brezezowsky, 1890. 51 p. LL-4026 – 1 – us L of C Photodup [340]
Oesterreichisches Handelsmuseum *see* DAS HANDELSMUSEUM
OESTERREICHISCHES INGENIEUR-ARCHIV – v1-16 1946-62 – 1 – us Princeton Micro [620]
OESTERREICHISCHES WIRTSCHAFTSPOLITISCHES ARCHIV – v. 1-9. 1901-09 – 1 – 142.00 – us L of C Photodup [330]
OESTERREICHISCH-UNGARISCHE MONTAN-UND METALLINDUSTRIE-ZEITUNG – Vienna, Austria. -w. Oct 1886-Dec 1910. 10 reels – 1 – uk British Libr Newspaper [072]
OESTERREICHISCH-UNGARISCHE MUELLER-ZEITUNG – Vienna, Austria. -w. Oct 1886-Dec 1890; 1897-1908. 6 reels – 1 – uk British Libr Newspaper [072]
OESTERREICHS DICHTERFUERSTIN MARIE VON EBNER-ESCHENBACH / Siegl, Dora – Prag [i.e., Prague]: A Haase, [1917?] – 1r – 1 – us U.W. Library [430]
OESTERREICHS THEILNAHME AN DEN BEFREIUNGSKRIEGEN / ed by Metternich-Winneburg, R – Wien, 1887 – 10mf – 9 – ne IDC [943]
OESTERREICH-UNGARNS AUSSENPOLITIK / Austro-Hungarian Monarchy. Ministerium des K. und K. Hauses und des aussern – Wein. v. 1-9. 1908-14 – 1 – $85.00 – us L of C Photodup [943]
OESTERREICH-UNGARNS AUSSENPOLITIK VON DER BOSNISCHEN KRISE 1908 BIS ZUM KRIEGSAUSBRUCH 1914 – Vienna. 1930. v1-9. – 147mf – 8 – ne IDC [943]
OESTERREICH-UNGARUS AUSSENPOLITIK VON DER BOSNISCHEN KRISE 1908 BIS ZUM KRIEGSAUSBRUCH 1914 – 1908-14 – 9 – us UMI [943]
OESTRA SOERMLAND – Nykoeping, 1991 – 9 – sw Kungliga [072]
OESTRA VESTMANLAND – Sala, Vaesterås. 1887-1906 – 9 – sw Kungliga [072]
OESTREICHS FLORA / Schultes, J A – 5309. 2 V. 1794 – 9 – ne IDC [580]
Oestrop, E *see* DANSKE DIATOMEER
Oettingen, A J *see* HARMONIESYSTEM IN DUALEN ENTWICKLUNG
Oettingen, W von *see* ANTONIO AVERLINO FILARETE'S TRACTAT UEBER DIE BAUKUNST NEBST SEINEN BUECHERN VON DER ZEICHENKUNST UND DEN BAUTEN DER MEDICI
OETTINGEN-WALLERSTEIN'SCHE MUSIKSAMMLUNG – (Catalogue available) – 1985 – 3819mf (1:24) – 9 – diazo DM9,980.00 – 3-598-30730-6 – gw Saur [780]
OETTINGER UND BURGHAUSER ANZEIGER – (Cont: Koeniglich-Baierisches Salzach-Kreis-Blatt; Wochenblatt der Koeniglich baierischen Stadt Burghausen, -1835; Wochenblatt der Stadt Burghausen, -1838; Burghauser-Wochen-Blatt, -mar 1839; Burghauser-Muehldorfer Wochenblatt, -1843; Wochenblatt fuer die Bezirke der koeniglichen Landgerichte Burghausen, Altoetting und Muehldorf -1851; Wochenblatt fuer die Bezirke der koeniglichen Landgerichte Burghausen, Altoetting, Muehldorf, Neumarkt und Tittmoning, -1862; Der Amtsbote am Inn, an der Rott und Salzach, -1873; Amtsblatt des Koeniglichen Bezirksamtes Altoetting und der Koeniglichen Landgerichte Altoetting und Burghausen, -1935) – Burghausen, 1809, jul 1 1832-74, nov 2 1935-apr 30 1945, sep 2-dec 31 1949 – 1 – Inquire at Mikrofilmarchiv for details – gw Misc Inst [943]
Oettlie, Sam *see* GREIFSWALDER STUDIEN: THEOLOGISCHE ABHANDLUNGEN HERMANN CREMER
L'OEUVRE – Dir. G. Tery. Paris. mai 1904-14, sept 1915-17 aout 1944 – 1 – fr A.C.R.P.P. [073]
L'OEUVRE – Port Louis, Mauritius. May 1942-Dec 1950 (imperfect) – 9r – 1 – uk British Libr Newspaper [072]
L'OEUVRE – Publication mensuelle puis Revue internationale des arts et du theatre. Dir. Lugne-Poe. Paris. fevr 1909-juil 1914, juil-nov 1919, 1920-mars 1930 – 1 – fr A.C.R.P.P. [073]
OEUVRE / Atget, Eugene – Six albums, 60 plates each, comp. by Atget, depict Paris during La Belle Epoque. 1 reel.(Collections of the Department of Prints and Photographs) – 1 – $50.00 – fr Bibl Nationale [760]
OEUVRE / Laliberte, Alfred – Montreal: Bibliotheque nationale du Quebec, 1977. SEM35P149 – 1r – 1 – Can$18.00 – cn Bibl Nat [730]
OEUVRE / Le Secq, Henri – Sepia calotypes including Amiens, Strasbourg, Reims and Chartres cathedrals; still-lifes; landscapes. 1 reel. (Collections of the Department of Prints and Photographs) – 1 – $50.00 – fr Bibl Nationale [760]
OEUVRE / Lyman, John – Montreal: Bibliotheque Nationale du Quebec, 1975. SEM35P124 – 3r – 1 – Can$168.00 – cn Bibl Nat [760]
OEUVRE / May, Leon Pamphile Le – Montreal: Bibliotheque nationale du Quebec, 1978. SEM35P158 – 4r – 1 – Can$219.00 – cn Bibl Nat [920]
OEUVRE / Pellan, Alfred – Montreal: Bibliotheque nationale du Quebec, 1973. SEM35P1 – 4r – 1 – Can$195.00 – cn Bibl Nat [760]
L'OEUVRE DE LA MISSION MARISTE EN NOUVELLE-CALEDONIE – Noumea. 1901. 100p. (Religion Series) – 9 – 6.00 – fr Bibl Nationale [240]
OEUVRE DES ECOLES D'ORIENT – devenu: Oeuvre d'Orient. no. 1-553. Paris. nov 1857-avr 1940, avr 1945-66 – 1 – fr A.C.R.P.P. [073]
L'OEUVRE DES MISSIONS PROTESTANTES A MADAGASCAR / Bianquis, Jean – Paris: Maison des missions evangeliques, 1907 – us Res Libr [240]
L'OEUVRE DU PAIN DES PAUVRES: DISCOURS POUR LA BENEDICTION D'UNE STATUE DE SAINT ANTOINE DE PADOUC:.. / Gohiet, Francois – 15 mars 1896, Basilique d'Ottawa. Quebec: Faveur, 1896. 02087. (Pre-1900 Canadiana) – 9 – cn C.I.H.M. [240]
L'OEUVRE DU QUATRIEME JOUR DE LA CREATION / Lefebvre, J – (Includes bibliographical references) – Rouen: Esperance Cagniard, 1882 – 1mf – 9 – 0-8370-4082-5 – 1985-2082 – us A.T.L.A. [220]
L'OEUVRE DU SAINT-ESPRIT DANS L'HOMME : DISCOURS / Tophel, Gustave – 2e ed. Lausanne: Georges Bridel, 1875 – 1mf – 9 – 0-8370-5659-4 – 1985-3659 – us A.T.L.A. [210]
L'OEUVRE DU SAINT-ESPRIT DANS L'HOMME = THE WORK OF THE HOLY SPIRIT IN MAN : DISCOURSES DELIVERED AT GENEVA / Tophel, Gustave – (In English) – 2nd rev ed. Chicago, IL: Chicago Foundlings' Home, 1883, c1880 – 1mf – 9 – 0-8370-5384-6 – 1985-3384 – us A.T.L.A. [240]
OEUVRE GRAVEE D'APRES TIZIANO VECELLI, DIT LE TITIEN, 1485-1576 – Copies of many of Titian's engravings by prominent 16th and 17th cent. artists. 728 images by or after Titian. 1 reel. (Collections of the Department of Prints and Photographs) – 1 – 50.00 – fr Bibl Nationale [700]
L'OEUVRE ISOPODOLOGIQUE D'ALBERT VANDEL / Dalens, H & Saporte, C – F50.00 – fr Ethnologie [590]
L'OEUVRE LITTERAIRE DE NAN, AUTEUR CAMBODGIEN DE LA FIN DU XVIIIE SIECLE ET DU DEBUT DU XIXE / Khing, H D – 9 – F130.00 – fr Ethnologie [306]
L'OEUVRE MILITAIRE DE LA GALISSONIERE AU CANADA / Girerd, Sylvain – St. Etienne: Societe de l'Imp. Theolier: J. Thomas et cie., 1902. SEM105P470 – 1mf – 9 – Can$2.25 – cn Bibl Nat [355]
OEUVRES / Barth, Auguste – v. 1-4. Paris. 1914-18. B-520 2 – 8 – ne IDC [240]
OEUVRES / Champlain, Samuel de – (This edition has never been published) – Epreuves de l'edition de Quebec: Impr. de G E Desbarats, 1869. SEM16P123 – 1r – 5 – Can$35.00 – cn Bibl Nat [971]
OEUVRES / La Mothe Le Vayer, F de – 1756-59 – 9 – fr I.C.S. [890]
OEUVRES / Lavoisier, Antoine-Laurent – Paris, 1864-93, 6 v. Histoire des Sciences XVIIe-XIXe Siecles. 7955 a 7960 – 9 – fr Hachette [540]
OEUVRES / Pons, Jean Francois de – Paris: Prault fils, 1738. 354p.4 fiches. (Literature Collection) – 9 – 10.00 – fr Bibl Nationale [890]
OEUVRES CHIRURGICALES / Desault, P J – M 148. 3 v. 1801-1803 – 9 – ne IDC [617]
OEUVRES CHOISIES / Prevost, AF – Paris, Leblanc (I-X, XIII). 1810-16 – 1 – fr A.C.R.P.P. [440]
OEUVRES CHOISIES, PUBLIEES POUR LA PREMIERE FOIS PAR GAGARIN / Tchadaie, Pierre – (Russia – 19th C. series). 1862 – 9 – fr Hachette [460]
OEUVRES COMPLETES : 63 OPUSCULES TRAITANT SURTOUT DE POESIE OU DES GUERRES DE VENDEE / Rousse, Joseph – 2r – 1 – F1,314.09 – fr Armell [440]
OEUVRES COMPLETES / Bastiat, Frederic – 6v, from the 2nd and 4th ed., 1854, 1860, 1862. 6 fiches – 9 – 1.00f – at Libertarian Micro [335]
OEUVRES COMPLETES = COMPLETE WORKS: 48 HISTORICAL, LITERARY, DRAMATIC AND POETIC WORKS MICROFILMED TOGETHER : 48 OEUVRES HISTORIQUES, LITTERAIRES, THEATRALES ET POETIQUES (1882-1931), MICROFILMEES ENSEMBLE / Gourcuff, Olivier de – 2r – fr Armell [400]
OEUVRES COMPLETES / Laforgue, Jules – Paris: Mercure de France, 1902. 272p. 3 fiches. (Literature Collection) – 9 – 8.00 – fr Bibl Nationale [810]
OEUVRES COMPLETES DE FRERET...MISES DANS UN NOUVEL ORDRE, AUGMENTEES... PAR M. CHAMPOLLION-FIGEAC... / Freret, Nicolas – Paris: Didot, 1825 – 1 – F315.95 – fr Armell [944]
OEUVRES COMPLETES DE JULES LAFORGUE / Laforgue, Jules – Paris: Societe du Mercure de France, 1902-03. 3v – 1 – us U.W. Library [810]
OEUVRES COMPLETES DE OCTAVE CREMAZIE / Cremazie, Octave – Montreal: Librairie Beauchemin limitee, [entre 1900 et 1924]. SEM105P1429 – 6mf – 9 – Can$13.50 – cn Bibl Nat [890]
OEUVRES COMPLETES DE RACAN : T. 1. – NOUV. ED. REV. ET ANNOTEE PAR M. TENANT DE LATOUR, AVEC UNE NOTICE BIOGR. DE M. ANTOINE DE LATOUR / Racan, Honorat de Bueil, Mis de – Paris: Jannet, 1857 – 1 – F86.34 – fr Armell [944]
OEUVRES COMPLETES DE THOMAS...PRECEDEES D'UNE NOTICE SUR LA VIE ET LES OUVRAGES DE L'AUTEUR PAR M. CARET / Thomas, Antoine Leonard – Paris: Verdiere, 1822-25. 6v in 7. 33 fiches. (Literature Collection) – 9 – 82.00 – fr Bibl Nationale [890]
OEUVRES COMPLETES DU TROUVERE ADAM DE LA HALLE / Halle, Adam de la – Paris: A Durand & Pedone-Lauriel, 1872 – 1 – us Sibley [780]
LES OEUVRES D'ARCHITECTURE / Le Pautre, Antoine – Paris, Jombert, 1652. 38p., ill. (Architecture Series) – 9 – fr Hachette [720]
OEUVRES D'ARCHITECTURE / Peyre, Marie Joseph – Nouvelle ed. Paris, 1795. 32p, 25 pl. (Architecture Series) – 9 – fr Hachette [720]
OEUVRES DE AUGUSTE BARTH / Barth, Auguste – Paris. 5v. 1914-1927 – 37mf – 9 – ne IDC [240]
OEUVRES DE CORELLY EN TRIO [TRIO SONATAS OP. 1 – 4] / Corelli, Arcangelo – (Manuscript in unknown hand) – [Early 18th-cent.] – 1 – us Sibley [780]
LES OEUVRES DE HUGUES DE SAINT-VICTOR / Haureau, B – Paris, 1886 – 5mf – 8 – ne Slangenburg [240]
OEUVRES DE MADAME ET DE MADEMOISELLE DESHOULIERES / Deshoulieres, Antoinette du L de la G – Nouvelle ed. Paris. 2v. 1764. SEM16P232 – 1r – 5 – Can$9.00 – cn Bibl Nat [890]
OEUVRES DE MR. DUPLESSIS, ANCIEN AVOCAT DU PARLEMENT / Duplessis, Claude – Paris: chez Nicolas Gosselin, 1726-28. SEM35P325 – 1r – 1 – $66.00 – cn Bibl Nat [944]
OEUVRES DIVERSES / Dulard, Paul Alexandre – Amsterdam: Arkstee et Merkus, 1758. 2v.8 fiches. (Literature Collection) – 9 – 20.00 – fr Bibl Nationale [890]
LES OEUVRES DU DIVIN ST DENYS AREOPAGITE – Trans. J. de S. Francois. 1608 – 8 – ne IDC [180]
LES OEUVRES ET LA DOCTRINE DE SIGER DE BRABANT / Steenbergen, F van – Bruxelles, 1938 – 4mf – 8 – ne Slangenburg [140]
LES OEUVRES ET LA DOCTRINE DE SIGER DE BRABANT / Steenbergen, F van – Bruxelles, 1938 – 4mf – 8 – ne Slangenburg [180]
OEUVRES MELEES CONTENANT 6 SONATES POUR LE CLAVESSIN DE TANT DE PLUS CELEBRES COMPOSITEURS, RANGES EN ORDRE ALPHABETIQUE – Nuremberg. 12v – 1 – $23.00 – us L of C Photodup [780]
OEUVRES MILITAIRES / Bugeaud de la Piconnerie, T R – Paris. L. Baudoin. 1883. vii, 394p. tables. (Strategy of War Series) – 9 – fr Hachette [355]
OEUVRES (REMARQUES SUR LES SONS DE LA LANGUE) / Boindin, N – 1753 – 9 – fr I.C.S. [410]
LES OEUVRES RUPESTRES DE L'ABRI DE MALHADOR (MUNICIPIO DE JANUARIA, MINAS GERAIS, BRESIL) / Borges, M et al – F350.00 – fr Ethnologie [760]
LES OEUVRES RUPESTRES DU MASSIF DE CAETANO, REGION DE LAGOA SANTA, MINAS GERAIS, BRESIL / Anthonioz-Russel, S et al – 9 – F70.00 – fr Ethnologie [306]
LES OEUVRES RUPESTRES DU MASSIF DE CERCA GRANDE, REGION DE LAGOA SANTA, MINAS GERAIS, BRESIL / Anthonioz-Russel S et al – 9 – F200.00 – fr Ethnologie [972]
LES OEUVRES RUPESTRES DU MASSIF DE SUMIDOURO, REGION DE LAGOA SANTA, MINAS GERAIS, BRESIL / Clement, G – Paris. 1979 – 9 – F100.00 – fr Ethnologie [930]
LES OEUVRES RUPESTRES DU SITE D'ALTAMIRA, JOSE DE MELLO, MINAS GERAIS, BRESIL / Motta, J F et al – 9 – F90.00 – fr Ethnologie [306]
OEUVRES SPIRITUELLES / Pedro de Alcantara, Saint – 1862 – 9 – 1.50f – sp Bibl Santa Ana [240]
OEUVRES TRADUITES EN FRANCAIS, AVEC UNE INTRODUCTION DE P. DUGAC / Cantor, Georg – ACTA MATHEMATICA, t. 2 1883 et t. 4 1884, MEMOIRES DE LA SOCIETE PHYSIQUE ET NATURELLE DE BORDEAUX, t. 3 1889, 220 pp. Histoire des Sciences XVIIe-XIXe Siecles. 7997 – 9 – fr Hachette [510]
Oey, Hong Lee *see*
– INDONESIAN GOVERNMENT AND PRESS DURING GUIDED DEMOCRACY
– NAGA BANGKIT
– POWER STRUGGLE IN SOUTHEAST ASIA
OEZ DILEK – Erzurum, Trabzon: Vilayet Matbaasi (Erzurum), 1923-1928 – 9 – $10.00 – us MEDOC [956]
OF CONSUMING INTEREST – v. 1- 1967- – 1. ; 5,6. ; 9 – apply; v.6-; v.10- – us UMI [073]
OF EDUCATION ESPECIALLY OF YOUNG GENTLEMEN / Walker, Obadiah – 1673. 302p. (English Linguistics Series 1500-1800) – 9 – us UMI [400]
OF JUSTIFICATION BY FAITH AND WORKS : A DIALOGUE BETWEEN A METHODIST AND A CHURCHMAN / Law, W – (This was an octavo issue. There was also a duodecimo issue with identical imprint but different pagination) – London, 1760 – 1mf – 9 – MP-396/1 – ne IDC [240]
OF SEA AND SHORE – v1- 1970- 1; v3- 5,6; v6- 9 – us UMI [073]

OF SIX MEDIAEVAL WOMEN; TO WHICH IS ADDED A NOTE ON MEDIAEVAL GARDENS / Welch, Alice Kemp – London: MacMillan, 1913.xxix,188p. plates – 1 – us U.W. Library [305]

OF THE ADVANCEMENT OF LEARNING / Bacon, Francis – M-291 2. 1640 – 8 – ne IDC [500]

OF THE CONDUCT OF THE UNDERSTANDING / Locke, John – Biography, critical opinions, and explanatory notes by A. Louise M. Gilbert. New York: Maynard, Merrill & Co., 1901. 132p. Bibliography. (Maynard's English Classic Series, no 228-9) – 1 – us U.W. Library [190]

OF THE DOCTRINE OF MORALITY IN ITS RELATION TO THE GRACE OF REDEMPTION / Fairbairn, Robert B – New York: T. Whittaker, 1887 – 1mf – us A.T.L.A. [240]

OF THE ORIGIN AND PROGRESS OF LANGUAGE / Burnet, James Lord Monboddo – 1773. 6v. (English Linguistics Series 1500-1800) – 9 – us UMI [400]

OF THE RECONCILEABLENESS OF SPECIFICK MEDICINES TO THE CORPUSCULAR PHILOSOPHY / Boyle, R – London, 1685 – 5mf – 9 – ne IDC [610]

OF THE SYMPATHETICK POWDER / Digby, K – M 343. 1669 – 9 – ne IDC [615]

OF TORONTO THE GOOD; A SOCIAL STUDY : THE QUEEN CITY OF CANADA AS IT IS / Clark, Christopher Saint George – Montreal: Toronto Pub., 1898. 00659. (Pre-1900 Canadiana) – 9 – cn C.I.H.M. [910]

O'Ferrall, Arturo *see* BOSQUEJO PARA UN CURSO DE GIMNASIA PARA EL USO DE ORGANIZACIONES JUVENILES DE F.E.T. Y DE LAS JONS DE LA PROVINCIA DE CACERES POR...

Off of Micronesian Status Negotiations *see*
- OFFICIAL RECORDS OF THE 4TH ROUND OF MICRONESIAN FUTURE POLITICAL STATUS TALKS
- PROCEEDINGS OF THE 6TH ROUND OF FUTURE POLITICAL STATUS NEGOTIATIONS
- RECORDS OF THE 5TH ROUND OF MICRONESIAN FUTURE POLITICAL STATUS NEGOTIATIONS
- SUMMARY RECORD OF THE U.S.-MICRONESIA ROUNDTABLE CONFERENCE ON THE FUTURE POLITICAL STATUS OF THE TRUST TERRITORY OF THE PACIFIC

OFF OUR BACKS – Washington, DC. 1971-84 – 2r – 1 – $100.00 – R05502 – us Library Micro [071]

OFF SEASON RESIDENT CAMP UTILIZATION IN THE CONTIGNOUS UNITED STATES / Cloninger, Karl W – 1980 – 2mf – 9 – $8.00 – us Microform Publ [790]

OFFALY INDEPENDENT – Athlone, Ireland. 4 Feb 1922-2 Jun 1923. -w. 1 1/4 reels – 1 – uk British Libr Newspaper [072]

OFF-BROADWAY PLAYS – Harmondsworth, Middlesex, England: Penguin Books, 1971- . -irr.v1. 1971- – 1 – us U.W. Library [820]

Offenbach, J *see*
- LA BELLE HELENE
- LA GRAND DUCHESSE DE GEROLSTEIN
- [OPERAS (SKETCHES)]. HOLOGRAPH

OFFENBACH-POST – Offenbach, West Germany. 1969- – ca 10r per yr – 1 – gw Mikrofilm [072]

DIE OFFENBARUNG DES HL. JOHANNES : IM LICHTE DES EVANGELIUMS NACH JOHANNES: EINE SKIZZE DER KOENIGLICHEN HERRSCHAFT VON JESU CHRISTI / Krementz, Ph – Freiburg i.B.: Herder, 1883 – 1mf – 9 – 0-8370-6745-6 – 1986-0745 – us A.T.L.A. [220]

DIE OFFENBARUNG JOHANNIS : NEU UNTERSUCHT UND ERLAEUTERT / Voelter, Daniel – (Includes bibliographical references) – Strassburg: J H Ed Heitz, 1904 – 1mf – 9 – 0-8370-9434-8 – 1986-3434 – us A.T.L.A. [220]

DIE OFFENBARUNG JOHANNIS INS LICHT GESTELLT / Wepf, Louis – Cincinnati: Cranston & Stowe, 1885. 1 fiche. 8370-5789-2 – 9 – us A.T.L.A. [240]

DIE OFFENBARUNG JOHANNIS (T.U.U. 1-2/3) / Vischer, Eberhard – Leipzig, 1886 – 2mf – 9 – ne Slangenburg [240]

OFFENBARUNG UND INSPIRATION = REVELATION AND INSPIRATION / Seeberg, Reinhold – (In English) – London; New York:Harper, 1909 – 1mf – 9 – 0-8370-5210-6 – 1985-3210 – us A.T.L.A. [220]

OFFENBARUNGEN DES WACHOLDERBAUMS : ROMAN EINES ALLSEHERS / Wille, Bruno – 2. Aufl. Leipzig: Eugen Diederich, 1903 – 1r – 1 – us U.W. Library [830]

DER OFFENBARUNGSBEGRIFF DES ALTEN TESTAMENTES / Koenig, Eduard – (Includes bibliographical references and index) – Leipzig: J C Hinrichs. 2v. 1882 – 2mf – 9 – 0-8370-9483-6 – 1986-3483 – us A.T.L.A. [220]

Offenburg, Benno *see* DAS ERWACHEN DES DEUTSCHEN NATIONALBEWUSSTSEINS IN DER PREUSSISCHEN JUDENHEIT (VON MOSES MENDELSSOHN BIS ZUM BEGINN DER REAKTION

OFFENBURGER TAGEBLATT – Offenburg, West Germany. 1976- – ca 9r per yr – 1 – gw Mikrofilm [072]

OFFENE KIRCHE – (Cont: Fuer eine offene Kirche) – 1970-89 (complete) – 3r – 1 – ATLA S0789 – us A.T.L.A. [073]

OFFENER BRIEF AN DEN VERFASSER DER SCHRIFT "ERNSTE GEDANKEN" / Rietschel, Georg – Leipzig:H.G. Wallmann, 1890 – 1mf – 9 – 0-8370-4902-4 – 1985-2902 – us A.T.L.A. [920]

OFFENER BRIEF AN HERRN PROFESSOR SCHIRREN UEBER DESSEN BUCH "LIVLAENDISCHE ANTWORT VON PROF. POGODIN" / Pogodin, M P – Berlin, 1870 – 2mf – 9 – ne IDC [460]

OFFENES SENDSCHREIBEN AN HERRN. STRECKFUSS / Jost, I M – Berlin. 1833. BJ-23-114 1 – 9 – ne IDC [360]

A OFFENSIVA – Rio de Janeiro, 17 May 1934-19 Mar 1938 – 1,5,6 – bl Biblioteca [072]

OFFENTLICHE GESUNDHEITSWESEN – 1920-1; 1975- 5,6,9 – us UMI [073]

Offermann, Volker *see* RATIONALE INVESTITIONSPLANUNG

OFFICAL REGISTER / U.S. Civil Service Commission – 1817-1959 – 1,5,6 – 22978.00 – us Princeton Micro [324]

OFFICE – v1- 1935- 1; v69- 5,6; v81- 9 – us UMI [650]

OFFICE ADMINISTRATION AND AUTOMATION – v44-. 1983- – 1,5,6,9 – us UMI [650]

OFFICE ADMINISTRATION AND AUTOMATION *see*
- ADMINISTRATIVE MANAGEMENT

THE OFFICE AND AUTHORITY OF A JUSTICE OF PEACE. / Nelson, William – London: Gosling, Mears, 1736. 2v. LL-140 – 1 – us L of C Photodup [340]

THE OFFICE AND HOME – Ottawa: B. Sawyer, G. Blatch, v1 no 1 (July 1890)- – 9 – cn C.I.H.M. [650]

OFFICE AUTOMATION REPORT – v28-. 1985- – 1,5,6,9 – us UMI [380]

L'OFFICE CANADIEN : JOURNAL EN LANGUE ARABE, ANGLAISE ET FRANCAISE – Montreal, Canada. v1 n4. 1910 – 1r – 1 – Can$25.00 – cn Can Microfilming [072]

Office de la Recherche Scientifique et Technique Outre Mer (ORSTROM) *see* DIRECTION DES ETUDES DU DEVELOPPEMENT

L'OFFICE DE L'EGLISE – Quebec: John Neilson, 1820. SEM16P33 – 1r – 5 – Can$9.00 – cn Bibl Nat [240]

OFFICE EQUIPMENT AND METHODS – v1-1955- 1; v21- 5,6,9 – us UMI [650]

OFFICE EQUIPMENT DIGEST *see* ADMINISTRATIVE MANAGEMENT

OFFICE EQUIPMENT INDEX – (See also: Index to Office Equipment and Supplies) – 1974-1; 1975- 5,6,9 – us UMI [680]

OFFICE EQUIPMENT NEWS – 1984-. -m – 1 – us UMI [680]

OFFICE EQUIPMENT SALESMAN *see* AMERICAN BUSINESS

Office for Micronesian Status Negotiations *see*
- MICRONESIAN STATUS NEGOTIATIONS, 7TH ROUND
- MICRONESIAN STATUS NEGOTIATIONS, 8TH ROUND

OFFICE LAO DE TRADUCTIONS : FRENCH-LANGUAGE DAILY NEWS SUMMARY – Vientiane, Laos. Jul 1975-Dec 1976. Mimeograph format – 1 – $75.00v – us Asia Libr [072]

L'OFFICE LIEGEOIS DE LA FETE-DIEU, SA VALEUR ET SON DESTIN / Cottiaux, J – Leuven, 1963 – 3mf – 8 – ne Slangenburg [240]

OFFICE MANAGEMENT – v. 1-26. 1947-72 – 1 – us UMI [650]

OFFICE MANAGEMENT *see*
- ADMINISTRATIVE MANAGEMENT
- AMERICAN BUSINESS

OFFICE MANAGEMENT AND AMERICAN BUSINESS *see*
- ADMINISTRATIVE MANAGEMENT
- AMERICAN BUSINESS

OFFICE MANAGEMENT AND EQUIPMENT *see* ADMINISTRATIVE MANAGEMENT

Office of Indian Affairs *see* THE NATIVE AMERICANS REFERENCE COLLECTION, PART 1

OFFICE OF LEGAL COUNSEL OPINIONS / U.S. Department of Justice – (Updates planned) – v1-16. 1977-92 – 70mf – 9 – $105.00 – LLMC 82-206 – us L.L.M.C. [340]

OFFICE OF LEGAL POLICY, REPORTS TO THE ATTORNEY GENERAL *see*
- THE CONSTITUTION IN THE YEAR 2000
- FEDERAL HABEAS CORPUS REVIEW OF STATE JUDGEMENTS, 27 MAY 1988
- JUSTICE WITHOUT LAW
- THE LAW OF PRE-TRIAL INTERROGATION, 12 FEB 1986
- ORIGINAL MEANING JURISPRUDENCE
- REDEFINING DISCRIMINATION
- RELIGIOUS LIBERTY UNDER THE FREE EXERCISE CLAUSE, 13 AUG 1986
- THE SEARCH AND SEIZURE EXCLUSIONARY RULE, 26 FEB 1986
- USING AND MISUSING LEGISLATIVE HISTORY

Office of the Comptroller of the Currency *see* NATIONAL BANK DECISIONS DIGEST

Office of United States Chief of Counsel for Prosecution of Axis Criminality *see* NAZI CONSPIRACY AND AGRESSION

OFFICE PRODUCTIVITY – (Cont: Office Systems and Technology at v39 1993. Ceased: v39 no 9 1993) – v39- 1993- – 9 – Can$28.00y – cn Micromedia [650]

OFFICE PRODUCTIVITY *see* OFFICE SYSTEMS AND TECHNOLOGY

OFFICE PRODUCTS – Superseded by Office Products Dealer – 1904-79 1; 1969-79 5,6; 1976-79 9 – us UMI [680]

OFFICE PRODUCTS DEALER – v.107-. 1979- – 1,5,6,9 – us UMI [380]

OFFICE SYSTEMS – v1-. Jul 1984- – 1,5,6,9 – us UMI [073]

OFFICE SYSTEMS AND TECHNOLOGY – (Cont and incorporates: OA and OE and M at v36 no 8 1990. Cont by: Office Productivity at v39 1993) – Toronto. v36-38. 1990-92 – 9 – Can$28.00y – cn Micromedia [650]

OFFICE SYSTEMS AND TECHNOLOGY *see*
- OA
- OE AND M
- OFFICE PRODUCTIVITY

Officer, M *see* DIARY, 1848-1852

Officer, R R *see* AUSTRALIAN TAKEOVERS: THE EVIDENCE

OFFICES OF MOST CHARGES APPERTAINING UNTO A CAMP / Holkham Hall. Norfolk. England – Holkham MS 708 – 1 – uk Microform Academic [025]

OFFICIA SANCTORUM ARCHIEPISCOPATUS ULTRAJECTENSIS ET EPISCOPATUM SUFFRAGENORUM HARLEMENSIS...ET ADDENDA – Coloniae, 1640 – 4mf – 8 – Dfl19.00 – ne Slangenburg [240]

THE OFFICIAL AND CONFIDENTIAL FILES OF FBI DIRECTOR JOHN EDGAR HOOVER / U.S. Federal Bureau of Investigation – (With printed guide) – 1988 – 6r – 1 – $510.00 – S3156 – us Scholarly Res [360]

THE OFFICIAL AND PRIVATE PAPERS OF LT. COL. GIDEON GORREQUER / Gorrequer, Gideon, Lt. Col – 1 – uk World [025]

OFFICIAL ARCHITECTURE AND PLANNING – (Continued as: Built Environment) – v1-35 no 3. 1937-72 – 1 – us UMI [720]

THE OFFICIAL BARONAGE OF ENGLAND, SHOWING THE SUCCESSION, DIGNITIES, AND OFFICES OF EVERY PEER FROM 1066 TO 1885 / Doyle, James William Edmund – With 1600 illus.London: Longmans, Green and Co., 1886.3v. illus. Includes ports., coats of arms, facsims – 1 – us U.W. Library [920]

OFFICIAL BASEBALL RECORD – New York, NY. 1885 Jul 15-1886 Oct 9 – 1r – 1 – $40.00r – us U.N.D. Archives [790]

OFFICIAL BATTLE LISTS OF THE CIVIL WAR / U.S. War Department. Adjutant General's Office – 1861-65. 2 rolls. M823 – 1 – us Nat'l Archives [324]

OFFICIAL BOARD MARKETS – v46. 1970 – 9mf – 9 – $5.00f – us Ross [600]

OFFICIAL BULLETIN / International Labour Organisation – 1920-92. Continued annually – 9 – uk World [323]

OFFICIAL BULLETIN / International Labour Organisation – v1-76. 1920-1993 – 9 – Sfr4,000.00 – 92-2-109736-6 – sz I.L.O. [330]

OFFICIAL BULLETIN *see* AMERICAN JOURNAL OF HOSPITAL PHARMACY

OFFICIAL BULLETIN OF THE NATIONAL DENTAL ASSOCIATION *see* JOURNAL OF THE AMERICAN DENTAL ASSOCIATION

THE OFFICIAL CATHOLIC DIRECTORY AND CLERGY LIST FOR THE YEAR OF OUR LORD... – Milwaukee: M H Wiltzius and Co, 1906-1911 – 8r – 1 – $40.00r – us U.N.D. Archives [240]

THE OFFICIAL CATHOLIC DIRECTORY FOR THE YEAR OF OUR LORD... – New York: P J Kennedy and Sons, 1912-1970 – 59r – 1 – $40.00r – us U.N.D. Archives [240]

OFFICIAL CONVERSATIONS AND MEETINGS OF DEAN ACHESON, 1949-53 / Acheson, Dean – 1980. (Presidential Documents Series) – 1 – $480.00 – 0-89093-354-5 – us UPA [977]

OFFICIAL DIRECTORY. CATHOLIC DIRECTORY, ALMANAC AND CLERGY LIST FOR THE YEAR OF OUR LORD... – Milwaukee: M H Wiltzius and Co, 1903-1905 – 3r – 1 – $40.00r – us U.N.D. Archives [240]

OFFICIAL DIRECTORY. CATHOLIC DIRECTORY, ALMANAC AND CLERGY LIST – QUARTERLY, FOR THE YEAR OF OUR LORD... – (Includes suppls) – Milwaukee: M H Wiltzius and Co., 1900-1902 – 3r – 1 – $40.00r – us U.N.D. Archives [240]

OFFICIAL GAZETTE = AMTSBLATT – Berlin, 1950-65 – 1r – 1 – us Ross [324]

OFFICIAL GAZETTE – Bridgetown, Barbados, 1966-68 – 5r – 1 – us Ross [324]

OFFICIAL GAZETTE / British Guiana – 1845-1903 – 1 – us UMI [324]

OFFICIAL GAZETTE – Capetown, South Africa, 1957-70 – 14r – 1 – us Ross [324]

OFFICIAL GAZETTE / Dominica. British West Indies – 1865-1956 – 1 – us UMI [324]

OFFICIAL GAZETTE / East Africa High Commission – Nairobi. Supplements. 1957-Nov. 1961 – 1 – us NY Public [960]

OFFICIAL GAZETTE – Entebbe, Uganda. v51-63. 1958-70 – 16r – 1 – us Ross [324]

OFFICIAL GAZETTE / Great Britain. High commissioner for Basutoland, the Bechuanaland Protectorate, and Swaziland – Bechuanaland protectorate edition. Mafeking. Jan.-Oct. 1963 – 1 – us NY Public [960]

OFFICIAL GAZETTE / Great Britain. High Commissioner for Basutoland, the Bechuanaland Protectorate, and Swaziland – v194-228. 1951-63 – 4r – 1 – us Ross [324]

OFFICIAL GAZETTE – (Includes annual suppls) – Georgetown, Guyana, 1957-68 – 13r – 1 – us Ross [324]

OFFICIAL GAZETTE – (Includes suppls) – Nairobi. v23-72. 1921-70 – 66r – 1 – us Ross [324]

OFFICIAL GAZETTE – (Includes suppls) – Nassau, Bahamas, 1968-70 – 2r – 1 – us Ross [324]

OFFICIAL GAZETTE – Manila, Philippines. v1-66. 1902-70 – 131r – 1 – us Ross [324]

OFFICIAL GAZETTE – Nairobi. v10-14. 1957-61 – 1r – 1 – us Ross [324]

OFFICIAL GAZETTE – Nairobi. v1-4. 1967-70 – 1r – 1 – us Ross [324]

OFFICIAL GAZETTE – Nairobi. v1-6. 1962-67 – 2r – 1 – us Ross [324]

OFFICIAL GAZETTE / Philippines – 1970- – 1 – $255.00y – us L of C Photodup [950]

OFFICIAL GAZETTE – Pietermaritzburg, South Africa, 1958-70 – 12r – 1 – us Ross [324]

OFFICIAL GAZETTE – Pretoria, South Africa. v132-211. 1950-69 – 28r – 1 – us Ross [324]

OFFICIAL GAZETTE / Quebec – pt 2. 1979-81 – 9 – cn Micromedia [971]

OFFICIAL GAZETTE / South Africa – Pretoria, South Africa. 1980- – 9 – sa State Libr [324]

OFFICIAL GAZETTE / South Africa. High Commissioner – Johannesburg. South Africa. 1901-42 – 1 – sa State Libr [960]

OFFICIAL GAZETTE – St John's, Antigua. v3-4. 1969-70 – 1r – 1 – us Ross [324]

OFFICIAL GAZETTE – Tokyo, 1946-52 – 19r – 1 – us Ross [324]

OFFICIAL GAZETTE – Tripoli, Libya. v1-8. 1951-58 – 1r – 1 – us Ross [324]

OFFICIAL GAZETTE / U.S. Patent Office – 1872-1971 – 5,6 – us UMI [324]

OFFICIAL GAZETTE / U.S. Patent Office – 1958-81 – 3 – us Readex [340]

OFFICIAL GAZETTE / U.S. Patent Office – Patents. v. 883- 1971$ – 1,5,6 – us UMI [324]

OFFICIAL GAZETTE / U.S. Patent Office – v1-1073.1872-1986 – 1,5,6. ; 1,5,6 – apply; Annual subscription. 138.00y – us Princeton Micro [340]

OFFICIAL GAZETTE / Yemen – (1978-. ca $20.00y) – 1971-77 – 2r – 1 – $45.00; outside North America add $1.25r – us L of C Photodup [324]

THE OFFICIAL GAZETTE / Zanzibar – 1957-1966 – 1 – us NY Public [960]

OFFICIAL GAZETTE OF THE ALLIED KOMMANDATURA : AMTSBLATT DER ALLIIERTEN KOMMANDATURA BERLIN – Berlin, feb 28 1950-aug 31 1965 – 1 – Inquire at Mikrofilmarchiv for details – gw Misc Inst [350]

OFFICIAL GAZETTE OF THE GOVERNMENT OF PALESTINE / Palestine – Jerusalem. 1921-30 – 1 – us Res Libr [956]

THE OFFICIAL GAZETTE OF THE UGANDA PROTECTORATE / Uganda – v1-50. 1908-1957 – 1 – $907.00 – us L of C Photodup [960]

OFFICIAL GAZETTE: TRADEMARKS / U.S. Patent Office – v894-1061. 1972-85 – 1,5,6. 51.00; 1,5,6 – apply; y – us Princeton Micro [340]

OFFICIAL GAZETTES OF SOUTH WEST AFRICA, 1915-1978 – February 1991, M.A.P. West Yorkshire – 29r – 1 – uk Microform Academic [320]

OFFICIAL GAZETTE-STAATSKOERANT VAN DIE UNIE VAN SUID-AFRIKA / South Africa – Pretoria. South Africa. 1910-79 – 1 – sa State Libr [960]

OFFICIAL GAZETTE-TRADEMARKS / U.S. Patent Office – v. 883- 1971- – 1,5,6 – us UMI [324]

OFFICIAL HANDBOOK AND CASEBOOK.. / National Junior College Athletic Association. Executive Committee – 1976-77 – 9 – us UMI [073]

THE OFFICIAL HANDBOOK OF NEW ZEALAND / ed by Vogel, Julius – London: Wyman, 1875. 272p. illus. maps. Includes index – 1 – us U.W. Library [910]

OFFICIAL HISTORICAL ATLAS MAPS OF FRESNO COUNTY / Thompson, T H – Fresno Co. CA, 1891 – 1r – 1 – $50.00 – B40220 – us Library Micro [310]

OFFICIAL HISTORY. / Whitfield County. Georgia – 1936. Indexed. 4 fiches. F-0736 – 9 – us A.G.L.L. [324]

OFFICIAL HISTORY OF THE FIRST WORLD WAR – With printed index – 5,9 – £1,200.00 Fiche: £1,695.00 – uk World [940]

OFFICIAL INSPECTIONS / Maine. Agricultural Experiment Station – v. 1-293. 1958-69 – 1,5,6 – us Spaulding [630]

OFFICIAL JOURNAL / Amalgamated Meat Cutters and Butcher Workmen of North America – Syracuse. v1-9. 1899-1908 – 2r – 1 – us Ross [331]

OFFICIAL JOURNAL / League of Nations – 27r – 1 – $950.00 – us Trans-Media [900]

OFFICIAL JOURNAL *see*
- CARRIAGE AND WAGON WORKERS JOURNAL, 1899-1908 : OFFICIAL JOURNAL, 1912-1915 : MESA EDUCATOR, 1944-1951
- MACHINISTS AND BLACKSMITHS' MONTHLY JOURNAL, 1870-1875 : THE BRASS WORKER, 1895-1896 : OFFICIAL JOURNAL, 1902-1904

OFFICIAL JOURNAL OF THE AMALGAMATED MEATCUTTERS AND BUTCHER WORKMEN : 1800 1900 / Amalgamated Meat Cutters and Butcher Workmen of North America – (Coll title: Labor Union Periodicals, Pt 3) – 1996 – 3r – 1 – $405.00 – 1-55655-627-6 – us UPA [331]

OFFICIAL JOURNAL OF THE AMERICAN MEDICAL TECHNOLOGISTS *see* JOURNAL OF THE AMERICAN MEDICAL TECHNOLOGISTS

OFFICIAL JOURNAL OF THE EUROPEAN COMMUNITIES, SERIES C : INFORMATION AND NOTICES – (Available in 11 languages. Subsc comprises series L and C, directory of current Community legal instruments, alphabetical index and methodological table) – 6,9 – ECU595.00 subsc – FX-AC-96-000-EN-A – lu EEC [340]

OFFICIAL JOURNAL OF THE EUROPEAN COMMUNITIES, SERIES L : LEGISLATION – (Available in 11 languages. Subsc comprises series L and C, and directory of current Community legal instruments, alphabetical index and methodological table) – 9,6 – ECU595.00 subsc – FX-AL-96-000-EN-A – lu EEC [340]

OFFICIAL PAPERS OF FLEET ADMIRAL ERNEST J. KING / King, Ernest J – (With printed guide) – 1991 – 10r – 1 – $306.00 – S3213 – us Scholarly Res [355]

OFFICIAL PAPERS OF SIR JEFFERY AMHERST / Amherst, Jeffery – 1740-83. With printed index – 1 – £6,995.00 – uk World [920]

OFFICIAL PREMIUM LIST / Louisiana State University. Agricultural Extension Service. Dixie Jubilee Horse Show Division – 1971-76.1 reel – 1,5 – us Spaulding [630]

OFFICIAL PROCEEDINGS / Central Railway and Engineering Club of Canada – Toronto: The Club, [1907-1915] – 9 – cn C.I.H.M. [380]

OFFICIAL PROCEEDINGS / Chicago Medical Society – May 1888, Dec. 1888, Feb. 1889-Feb. 1891 – 1 – us Res Libr [610]

OFFICIAL PROCEEDINGS / International Irrigation Congress – v. 1-16. 1891-1914 – 1 – 48.00 – us L of C Photodup [330]

OFFICIAL PROCEEDINGS / New England Railroad Club – 1894- 1; 1970- 5,6; 1975- 4 x 6 in. 9 – us UMI [625]

OFFICIAL PUBLICATION OF THE AMERICAN SOCIETY OF CLINICAL LABORATORY TECHNICIANS *see* AMERICAN JOURNAL OF MEDICAL TECHNOLOGY

OFFICIAL PUBLICATION OF THE LITHOGRAPHER'S INTERNATIONAL PROTECTIVE AND BENEFICIAL ASSOCIATION *see* LITHOGRAPHER'S BULLETIN, 1901-1904 : OFFICIAL PUBLICATION OF THE LITHOGRAPHER'S INTERNATIONAL PROTECTIVE AND BENEFICIAL ASSOCIATION, 1910-1913 : THE LITHOGRAPHER'S JOURNAL, 1918-1955

OFFICIAL PUBLICATIONS / New York. (State) – 1974-82 – 5,6,9 – us Primary [324]

OFFICIAL PUBLICATIONS OF SOUTH AFRICAN STATES – (First supplement) – State Library Pretoria, 1983-87 – 9 – sa State Libr [324]

OFFICIAL PUBLICATIONS OF SOUTH AFRICAN STATES – (First supplement) – State Library Pretoria. Up to 1982 – 9 – sa State Libr [324]

OFFICIAL PUBLICATIONS OF SOUTH AFRICAN STATES – State Library Pretoria, 1988-1994 – 9 – sa State Libr [324]

THE OFFICIAL RECOGNITION OF WOMAN IN THE CHURCH: AN HISTORICAL STUDY / Rishell, Charles Wesley – c1892 – 9 – us A.T.L.A. [240]

OFFICIAL RECORDS OF THE 4TH ROUND OF MICRONESIAN FUTURE POLITICAL STATUS TALKS : HELD AT KOROR, PALAU (BELAU), APR 1972 / Off of Micronesian Status Negotiations – Washington: Off of Micronesian Status Negotiations, 1972 – 1mf – 9 – $1.50 – LLMC 82-100F, Title 83 – us L.L.M.C. [323]

OFFICIAL RECORDS OF THE UNION AND CONFEDERATE ARMIES, 1861-65 / U.S. Army – 128r – 5 – M262 – us Nat'l Archives [324]

OFFICIAL RECORDS OF THE UNION AND CONFEDERATE NAVIES, 1861-65 / U.S. Navy – 31r – 5 – M275 – us Nat'l Archives [355]

OFFICIAL REGISTER / Iowa – 1899. Iowa Reel 44. (The Cox Library Collection) – 5 – us Americana [978]

THE OFFICIAL REGISTER OF IOWA 1911-12 / Iowa. Secretary of State – W.C. Hayward, Secretary of State. Des Moines: Emory H. English, State Printer, 1911.Iowa Reel 44. (The Cox Library Collection) – 5 – us Americana [978]

OFFICIAL REPORT / Kenya. National Assembly. House of Representatives – 1907-1971 – 1,5,6 – us Princeton Micro [324]

OFFICIAL REPORT / National Catholic Congress. 1st – London: Sands; St Louis, MO: B Herder, 1910 – 2mf – 9 – 0-8370-7412-6 – 1986-1412 – us A.T.L.A. [240]

OFFICIAL REPORT / Nigeria. Western Region. House of Assembly – 1952-65 – 1 – $88.00 – us L of C Photodup [960]

OFFICIAL REPORT / Nigeria. Western Region. House of Chiefs – 7 Jan 1952-9 Dec 1965 – 1 – $25.00 – us L of C Photodup [960]

OFFICIAL REPORT OF THE PROCEEDINGS / Democratic Party. National Convention – 1832-1932 – 1 – 167.00 – us L of C Photodup [324]

OFFICIAL REPORT OF THE PROCEEDINGS / Republican Party. National Convention – 1856-1968 – 1 – 119.00 – us L of C Photodup [324]

OFFICIAL REPORT OF THE SPEECH ON THE IRISH QUESTION / Blake, Edward – Delivered by Hon. Edward Blake, Ottawa, 1882. 02169. (Pre-1900 Canadiana) – 9 – cn C.I.H.M. [971]

OFFICIAL REPORTS / Lesotho. National Assembly – Feb 3, 1967-Oct 15, 1969 – 1 – us Res Libr [323]

OFFICIAL ROSTER OF OFFICERS AND EMPLOYEES.. / Philippines. Bureau of Civil Service – 1904- .Manila: Bureau of Printing – 1 – us U.W. Library [324]

OFFICIAL ROSTER OF OFFICERS AND EMPLOYEES IN THE CIVIL SERVICE OF THE PHILIPPINE ISLANDS – The Government of the Philippine Islands, Bureau of Civil Service. Manila: Bureau of Printing, 1904- – 1 – us U.W. Library [323]

OFFICIAL SCHOOL DISTRICT TREASURER'S RECORD BOOK / Shawnee County. Kansas. School District 35 – 1895-1907 – 1 – us KS Hist [978]

OFFICIAL SUMMARY OF STOCK TRANSACTIONS AND HOLDINGS / U.S. Securities and Exchange Commission – v1-58. 1935-92 – 1191mf – 9 – $1,786.00 – LLMC 84-357 – us L.L.M.C. [332]

OFFICIAL TRANSCRIPT OF THE WATERGATE TRIAL, 1974-75 – 97mf; 3r – 1,9 – $280.00 – us UMI [977]

OFFICIAL U.S. BULLETIN / U.S. Committee on Public Information – Published daily under order of the President of the United States by Committee on Public Information. v1-3. 10 May 1917-31 Mar 1919 – 1 – $140.00 – us L of C Photodup [977]

OFFICIALS' BONDS / Hancock County. Ohio. Biglick Township. Township Clerk – 1867-1962 – 1r – 1 – $32.50r – us Archival [324]

OFFICIALS' BONDS / Ottawa County. Ohio. Carroll Township. Board of Trustees – 1880-1964 – 1r – 1 – $32.50r – us Archival [324]

OFFICIEEL NIEUWSBLAD VAN NEDERLANDS-NIEUW-GUINEA – (Missing: 1951(3-13); 1962(1-2); Suppl: 1950; 1952(5-7); 1955(3); 1959(5-8); 1961(3)-1962(7)) – Hollandia. Suppl 1950-1962 – 47mf – 9 – ne IDC [980]

OFFICIEEL ORGAAN VAN DE JOODSCHE INVALIDE – Amsterdam. v1-12. 1927-1938 – 53mf – 9 – ne IDC [270]

OFFICINA BIBLICA / Walther, Michael – 1703 – 1 – us A.T.L.A. [240]

OFFICIUM ECCLESIASTICUM ABBATUM SECUNDUM USUM EVESHAMENSIS MONASTERII / Wilson, H Austin – 1893 – 3mf – 8 – Dfl13.00 – ne Slangenburg [240]

OFFICIUM IN HONOREM DOMINI NOSTRI J. C., SUMMI SACERDOTIS ET OMNIUM SANCTORUM SACERDOTUM AC LEVITARUM – Montreal: apud Fleurium Mesplet, 1777. SEM16P74 – 1r – 5 – Can$9.00 – cn Bibl Nat [240]

OFFISIELE KOERANT – Bloemfontein, South Africa, 1958-67 – 10r – 1 – us Ross [324]

OFF-LEAD – v. 1-3. 1972-74 – 1,5,6 – us UMI [073]

Offord, Daniel B *see* ORIGINAL SHAKER MUSIC

OFFRANDE AUX SAINT-SIMONIENS. LE NAIN MYSTERIEUX, PROVERBE DRAMATIQUE / Montherot, F de – Lyon, impr. Ayme, 1832, 32 p. Les Saint-Simoniens, 1825-1834. 6997 – 9 – fr Hachette [335]

OFFSHORE – 1954- 1; 1971- 5,6; 1977- 4 x 6 in. 9 – us UMI [073]

OFF-TASTES IN RAW RECONSTITUTED MILK – 1984 – it F.A.O. [636]

OFICINA DE FARMACIA DEL LICENCIADO ANTONIO GONZALEZ – Jerez de los Caballeros – 1 – sp Bibl Santa Ana [946]

OFICINA PROVINCIAL DE INVERSIONES INFORME ANUAL. DICIEMBRE DE 1978 / Diputacion Provincial – Badajoz: Imp. Provincial, 1978 – sp Bibl Santa Ana [946]

OFICIO A NTR. SRA....MARIA – 1763 – 9 – 1.50f – sp Bibl Santa Ana [240]

OFIT SIALNY I SBORNIK NARKOMZDRAVA RSFSR – (Includes c.1: 1935:no.16/17-19, 21-22; 1936:no.1-4, 6-9) – Moskva: Biomedgiz, 1935 – 1 – CSUXAKY6058-S – us Hoover Inst Photo [947]

OFITSERY, OCHERKI / Denikin, Anton Ivanovich – Parizh: [Rodnik], 1928 – 1 – CSUX88-B6131 – us Hoover Inst Photo [355]

OFITSIAL'NAIA KHRONIKA MOSKOVSKOGO PATRIARKHATA – 1993-94 – 1r – 1 – $85.00r – us Ross [072]

OFITSIAL'NYE IZVESTIIA AKTSIONERNOGO OBSHCHESTVA GRAMMOFON – (In 1910 title changed to: Pishushchii amur i Grammofonnye novosti) – Moscow. n1-7,9-13 1908-09; n14-21 1910 (monthly) – 7mf – 9 – $45.00 – us Ross [780]

O'Flaherty, Dennis M *see*
- CENSORSHIP IN TSARIST RUSSIA
- NINETEENTH CENTURY RUSSIAN PUBLICISTS
- PERSONAL SOURCES FOR THE HISTORY OF RUSSIA IN THE 19TH CENTURY

OFRECIMIENTO AL...CORAZON DE JESUS – 1869 – 9 – 1.50f – sp Bibl Santa Ana [240]

Ofterdinger, Ludwig Felix *see* CHRISTOPH MARTIN WIELAND'S LEBEN UND WIRKEN IN SCHWABEN UND IN DER SCHWEIZ

Ogallah. Kansas. Swedish Evangelical Lutheran Church *see* CHURCH REGISTER

OGALLALA TRIBUNE – Ogallala, NE. -w. Jul 1916-Dec 1918 – 1 – us NE Hist [071]

THE OGAM INSCRIBED MONUMENTS OF THE GAEDHIL IN THE BRITISH ISLAND; WITH A DISSERTATION ON THE OGAM CHARACTER, ETC / Brash, Richard Rolt; ed by Atkinson, George M – Illus. with 50 photolithographic plates. London: G. Bell and Sons, 1879. xvi,425p. pl., fold. map – 1 – us U.W. Library [410]

Oganovskii, N P *see*
- AGRARNYI VOPROS I KOOPERATSIIA
- INDIVIDUALIZATSIIA ZEMLEVLADENIIA V ROSSII I EE POSLEDSTVIIA OTTISK IZ "VESTNIK SEL. KHOZ" 1914 G
- PERSPEKTIVY RAZVITIIA SEL'SKOGO KHOZIAISTVA SSSR
- VOINA I ZEMEL'NAIA KOOPERATSIIA

Ogarev, N P *see* ESSAI SUR LA SITUATION RUSSE

Ogarev, Nikolai Platonovich *see* OPIS' DOKUMENTAL'NYKH MATERIALOV KICHNOGO FONDA NO. 359

Ogbemudia, SO *see* THE EDUCATION WE WANT, MILITARY GOVERNOR, MID-WESTERN NIGERIA

Ogden, Ellen Seton *see* THE ORIGIN OF THE GUNU-SIGNS IN BABYLONIAN

Ogden, John *see* THE SCIENCE OF EDUCATION AND ART OF TEACHING

Ogden, John Cosens (1751-1800) *see* A TOUR THROUGH UPPER AND LOWER CANADA

Ogden, Rollo *see* WILLIAM HICKLING PRESCOTT

Ogden, Uzal *see* ANTIDOTE TO DEISM..

Ogel-Ros, L *see*
- L'ABRI CHAPADA DOS CRUZES, SITE DE LA VARIETE SERRA DA CAPIVARA ET DE STYLE SERRA DO TAPUIO, SUD-EST DU PIAUI, BRESIL
- UN ABRI LIMITROPHE DE L'AIRE DE SAO RAIMUNDO NONATO: LA TOCA DA PEDRA SOLTA DO BOM JESUS, BRESIL
- UN ABRI PEINT LIMITROPHE DE L'AIRE DE SAO RAIMUNDO NONATO, LA TOCA DAS LETRAS, SUD DU PIAUI, BRESIL
- ABRI TOCA DO PINGA DO BOI, SITE TYPIQUE DE LA VARIETE SERRA BRANCA, STYLE VARZEA GRANDE, BRESIL
- L'ABRI TOCA DO SALITRE, SITE TYPIQUE DE LA SOUS-TRADITION SALITRE
- LES ABRIS TOCAS DO BAIXAO DO PERNA 1 ET 2, SITES DU STYLE VARZEA GRANDE, SUD-EST DU PIAUI, BRESIL

OGEMAW COUNTY HERALD AND HERALD TIMES – West Branch. Mich. -w. 1923- – 1 – us UMI [071]

Ogg, David *see* EUROPE IN THE SEVENTEENTH CENTURY

OGGI – 1987-1995 – 2r per y – 5,6 – Sfr615.00 – sz Infoprint [072]

Ogilby, John *see* THE ENTERTAINMENT OF HIS MOST EXCELLENT MAJESTIE CHARLES 2

Ogilvie, James Nicoll *see* THE PRESBYTERIAN CHURCHES

Ogilvie-Forbes of Boyndlie. Archives *see* PAPERS RELATING TO AMERICA

O'gilvy *see* NOBILIAIRE DE GUYENNE ET DE GASCOGNE

Ogilvy, J *see* COLLECTION OF AFRICAN TRAVELS

Ogilvy, Maud *see* GOLD AND SILVER: THE BEST TWENTY POEMS AND THOUGHTS EXTANT, SELECTED WITH SOME APPROACH TO ANALYTICAL CERTAINTY

OGLACH *see* AN T-OGLACH

Ogle, George A *see* COMPENDIUM OF HISTORY AND BIOGRAPHY OF NORTH DAKOTA

Ogle, Marbury Bladen *see* ENGLISH AND LATIN: A MANUAL OF PROSE COMPOSITION

Oglesby, Carole *see* ATTENTION IN YOUNG SOCCER PLAYERS

Ogletree, R J *see* SELECTED FACTORS REALTED TO HELP-SEEKING BEHAVIOR IN COLLEGE WOMEN VICTIMS OF SEXUAL COERCION

OGNENNAIA ROSSIIA / Remizov, A – Revel', (1923). 89p. BR-830 2 – 8 – ne IDC [460]

OGNENNYI STOLP / Gumilev, Nikolai Sepanovich – Ed. 2. Spb., Berlin. 1922. BR-1147 2 – 8 – ne IDC [460]

OGNISKO – New York: [s.n.], jul 7 1887-jun 22 1889 – 1r – 1 – us Res Libr [073]

OGNISKO DOMOWE – Detroit, MI: Trybuna Codzienna Pub Co, [apr 19-jul 1918; oct 1918-jan 14 1921; sep 10 1920; 1929-30] – us Res Libr [071]

OGNIWO PRZJAZNI – Glasgow, UK. 11 Jan 1941-28 Mar 1942 – 1 – uk British Libr Newspaper [072]

OGONEK – Ezhenedel'nyi khudozhestvenno-literaturnyi zhurnal. Spb. 1908-17. Lacking: 1900-07; 1908 (15, 51); 1909 (1, 3-5, 11, 14, 52); 1915 (22, 43); 1916 (3); 1917 (25, 27-29, 39-40, 42, 52). B-1818 2 – 8 – ne IDC [073]

OGONEK – Illiustrirovannyi zhurnal literatury, nauk i iskusstv. Spb. 1879-1883. Lacking: 1879; 1880 (34); 1881-83. B-1819 2 – 8 – ne IDC [760]

OGONEK – M. 1934-35. Available: 1934 (19, 20, 21, 23, 24); 1935 (1-21). BR-5747 2 – 8 – ne IDC [073]

OGONYOK – (Flame). Moscow. U.S.S.R. 1961- – 1 – us UMI [460]

O'Gorman, Thomas *see* A HISTORY OF THE ROMAN CATHOLIC CHURCH IN THE UNITED STATES

O'Grady, Standish *see* THE STORY OF IRELAND

Oguchi-Chen, Fumiko *see* CHARACTERISTICS OF THOUGHT PROCESSES AND KNOWLEDGE STRUCTURES OF NOVICE TENNIS PLAYERS

Oguz, Remzi *see* ADANA TICARET REHBERI

OH HE YOH NOH – 1970-76. (American Indian Periodicals in the Princeton University Library). 26 fiches – 9 – $100.00 – us UPA [305]

OH YEAH? / Angly, Edward – Compiled from newspapers and public records. New York: Viking Press, 1931. 64p. illus. diagrs – 1 – us U.W. Library [330]

O'Hagan, A P *see* MATERIAL RE-CREATION IN THE APOSTOLIC FATHERS (T.U.U. 5-100)

O'Hare, Kate Richards *see*
- CASE FILE 35-30
- IN PRISON

O'Hart, John *see* IRISH PEDIGREES: OR, THE ORIGIN AND STEM OF THE IRISH NATION

OHEL YA'AKOV: AL HAMISHAH HUMSHE TORAH. / Kranz, Jacob ben Wolf – 1874. 5v in 1 – 1 – us U.W. Library [270]

OHEV NASHIM / Jedaiah Ha-Penini (Jedaiah ben Abraham Bedersi); ed by Neubauer, A – In Jubelschrift. L. Zunz. Berlin. 1884. BJ-421-78 1 – 9 – ne IDC [470]

O'Heyne, John *see* EPILOGUS CHRONOLOGICUS EXPONENS SUCCINTE CONVENTUS ET FUNDATIONES SACRI ORDINIS PRAEDICATORUM IN REGNO HYBERNIAE

OHIO – (1985-. 1,5,6) – Apr 1978- – 9 – us UMI [073]

OHIO : ATTORNEY GENERAL OPINIONS – (1846-1972 on reel $1,190.00. 1973-94 on mf $688.00) – 1846-1994 – 9,6 – $1,878.00 set – us Hein [340]

OHIO : PAGE'S OHIO REVISED CODE ANNOTATED – Cincinnati: Anderson Pub Co, 1953-May 1996 update – 9 – $1,623.50 set – us Hein [340]

OHIO : SESSION LAWS OF AMERICAN STATES AND TERRITORIES – 1803-1994 – 9 – $2,328.00 set – us Hein [340]

Ohio *see*
- LAND GRANT RECORDS
- OHIO DECISIONS REPRINT
- OHIO LAW REPORTER
- REPORTS AND OPINIONS (A-G)
- REPORTS, POST-NRS
- REPORTS, PRE-NRS
- SESSION LAWS
- STATE LABOR REPORTS
- WEEKLY LAW BULLETIN

OHIO AGRICULTURAL REPORT – 12-25. 1857-1870 – 1,5,6 – us Princeton Micro [338]

Ohio Anti-Slavery Society *see* REPORT OF ANNIVERSARY

OHIO APPELLATE DECISIONS ON FICHE / Ohio. District Courts of Appeals – (No NRS cases) – 1981-92 (all publ) – 5358mf – 9 – $4,000.00 – LLMC 82-889 – us L.L.M.C. [340]

OHIO APPELLATE DECISIONS ON FICHE *see*
- CINCINNATI SUPERIOR COURT DECISIONS
- GOEBEL'S PROBATE REPORTS
- GOTTSCHALL'S REPORTS
- IDDINGS' TERM REPORTS
- OHIO CIRCUIT COURT REPORTS
- OHIO CIRCUIT COURT REPORTS, NEW SERIES
- OHIO CIRCUIT DECISIONS
- OHIO COURTS OF APPEALS REPORTS
- OHIO DECISIONS
- OHIO DECISIONS REPRINT
- OHIO FEDERAL DECISIONS
- OHIO LAW REPORTER
- OHIO NISI PRIUS REPORTS, NEW SERIES
- OHIO NISI PRIUS REPORTS, OLD SERIES
- TAPPAN'S COMMON PLEAS REPORTS
- WEEKLY LAW BULLETIN

OHIO APPELLATE REPORTS : CASES IN COURTS OF APPEALS / Ohio. Court of Appeals – (Pre-NRS: v1-19. Updates planned) – v1-10. 1913-1918/19 – 69mf – 9 – $103.00 – LLMC 90-304 – us L.L.M.C. [340]

OHIO ARGUS – Lebanon. Ohio. 1831-34 – 1 – us UMI [071]

Ohio Association of School Librarians *see* BULLETIN

OHIO ATLASES – (Athens County. 1905. Fayette Co. 1875. Knox Co. 1896. Jackson Co. 1875. Washington Co. 1875. Champaign Co. 1874. Licking Co. 1875. Miami Co. 1875. Holmes Co. 1875. Union Co. 1877. Greene Co. 1874. Sandusky Co. 1874. Mercer Co. 1900. Madison Co. 1875. Lucas Co. 1875. Fairfield Co. 1875. Morgan Co. 1875. Ashland Co. 1874) – 1874-1905. 3 rolls – 1 – us Ohio Hist [910]

OHIO BAPTIST – Granville, OH. Ohio Baptist Convention.1920-63. Single reels available – 1 – 132.00 – us A.B.H.S. [073]

OHIO BAPTIST MESSENGER – Columbus, Ohio. State Convention of Baptists of Ohio, Nov 1952-1991 – 1 – $488.08 – us Baptist [240]

Ohio Bar Association *see* REPORTS

OHIO BAR ASSOCIATION REPORTS – v1-55. 1928-90 – 9 – LLMC 84-660 – us L.L.M.C. [073]

Ohio. Bureau of Unemployment Compensation *see* THE COMPENSATOR

Ohio. Bureau of Unemployment Compensation. State Advisory Council *see* REPORTS

OHIO C P A – (v.38-. 1979- 5,6,9) – v.18-. 1959- – 1 – us UMI [073]

OHIO CENTENNIAL ANNIVERSARY CELEBRATION AT CHILLICOTHE, 20-21 MAY 1903 / ed by Randall, E O – Columbus: Ohio State Archaeological and Historical Society, 1903. Ohio Reel 10. (The Cox Library Collection) – 5 – us Americana [978]

OHIO CERTIFIED PUBLIC ACCOUNTANT – v.1-17. 1942-58. Continued by Ohio C P A – 1 – us UMI [073]

Ohio. Chenot, George. *see* PASTOR'S REGISTER

Ohio. Circuit Court *see*
- OHIO CIRCUIT COURT REPORTS
- OHIO CIRCUIT COURT REPORTS, NEW SERIES
- OHIO CIRCUIT DECISIONS

OHIO CIRCUIT COURT REPORTS / Ohio. Circuit Court – (Merges with: Ohio Circuit Decisions at v13) – Jahn Publ Co. v1-22. 1885-1901 (all publ) – 180mf – 9 – $270.00 – LLMC 80-815 – us L.L.M.C. [340]

OHIO CIRCUIT COURT REPORTS *see* OHIO CIRCUIT DECISIONS

OHIO CIRCUIT COURT REPORTS, NEW SERIES / Ohio. Circuit Court – Ohio Law Book Co. v1-26. 1903-17 – 194mf – 9 – $291.00 – LLMC 82-888 – us L.L.M.C. [340]

OHIO CIRCUIT COURT REPORTS, NEW SERIES *see* OHIO COURTS OF APPEALS REPORTS

OHIO CIRCUIT DECISIONS / Ohio. Circuit Court – (Merged with: Ohio Circuit Court Reports) – Laning Publ Co. v1-29. 1885-1918 – 69mf – 9 – $382.00 – LLMC 80-816 – us L.L.M.C. [340]

OHIO CIRCUIT DECISIONS *see* OHIO CIRCUIT COURT REPORTS

OHIO CITY ARGUS : WEEKLY NATIONAL REPUBLICAN (WHIG) NEWSPAPER – Cleveland, OH. May 26, 1836-June 7, 1838 – 1r – 1 – us Western Res [071]

Ohio City. Ohio. Methodist Episcopal Church *see* RECORDS

Ohio. Cleveland Baptist Association/Rocky River Association *see* PRINTED MINUTES

OHIO COMMON SCHOOL DIRECTOR – v. 1. Mar-Nov 1838 – 1 – us UMI [370]

OHIO CORRESPONDENT : WEEKLY CLEVELAND WEST SIDE NEWSPAPER – Cleveland, Oh. 30 Apr 1910-13 Aug 1910 – 1r – 1 – us Western Res [071]

OHIO: COUNTY AND REGIONAL HISTORIES AND ATLASES – 1 – us Primary [978]

Ohio. Court of Appeals *see*
- OHIO APPELLATE REPORTS
- OHIO COURTS OF APPEALS REPORTS
- OHIO DECISIONS

OHIO COURTS OF APPEALS REPORTS / Ohio. Court of Appeals – (Cont: Ohio Circuit Court Reports, New Series. Complete set is v27-32 1917-22. Updates planned) – Ohio Law Reporter Co. v27-30. 1917-20 – 28mf – 9 – $42.00 – LLMC 88-882B – us L.L.M.C. [340]

OHIO CPA JOURNAL – v39-. 1980- – 1,5,6,9 – us UMI [073]

OHIO CRIMINAL LAW AND PRACTICE; A PRACTICAL TREATISE, WITH DIRECTIONS AND FORMS / Laning, Jay Ford – Norwalk, OH, Laning Printing Co., 1901. 1088 p. LL-287 – 1 – us L of C Photodup [340]

OHIO CULTIVATOR – v. 1-22. Jan 1845-66 – 1 – us UMI [071]

Ohio. Dayton *see* IDDINGS' TERM REPORTS

OHIO DECISIONS / Ohio. Court of Appeals – (Cont: Ohio Nisi Reports, Old Series starting with v12) – Laning: American Publ Co/Ohio Law Book Co. v1-31. 1894-1920 (all publ) – 262mf – 9 – $393.00 – LLMC 94-206 – us L.L.M.C. [340]

OHIO DECISIONS REPRINT / Ohio – (Reprints of foll titles: Western Law Journal. Western Law Monthly. Weekly Law Gazette. Law and Bank Bulletin. American Law Register. American Law Record. Weekly Law Bulletin. Handy's Cincinnati Reports. Disney's Cincinnati Reports. Cincinnati Superior Court Reporter) – v1-13 (all publ) – 111mf – 9 – $166.00 – LLMC 94-206 – us L.L.M.C. [340]

OHIO DEMOCRAT – New Philadelphia. Ohio. 1866-1897 – 1 – us UMI [071]

OHIO DEMOCRAT – New Philadelphia. Ohio. and Times. 1900-25 – 1 – us UMI [071]

Ohio. Dept. of Commerce. Division of Banks *see* REPORTS

Ohio. Dept. of Commerce. Division of Building and Loan Associations *see* REPORTS

Ohio. Dept. of Commerce. Division of Insurance *see* REPORTS OF THE DIRECTOR OF INSURANCE

Ohio. Dept. of Industrial Relations *see* REPORTS

Ohio. Dept. of Taxation *see* REPORTS

Ohio. District Courts of Appeals *see* OHIO APPELLATE DECISIONS ON FICHE

OHIO FARMER – Cleveland. Ohio. 1895-1942 – 1 – us UMI [071]

OHIO FARMER & MECHANIC'S ASSISTANT – (Weekly agricultural newspaper, which William Dean Howells edited) – Cleveland, OH. jan 1, 1852-dec 30, 1854 – 1r – 1 – us Western Res [071]

OHIO FEDERAL DECISIONS / U.S. District Court of Ohio – v1-16. 1809-1911 (all publ) – 132mf – 9 – $198.00 – LLMC 84-174 – us L.L.M.C. [324]

OHIO FIERY CROSS : NEWSPAPER OF THE OHIO KU KLUX KLAN – Dayton, OH. 1924 – 1r – 1 – us Western Res [071]

OHIO FOLKLIFE – v6-. 1979- – 1,5,6,9 – us UMI [073]

Ohio Genealogical Society *see* FIRST FAMILIES OF OHIO

Ohio Genealogical Society. Crawford County Chapter *see* PIONEER FAMILIES OF CRAWFORD COUNTY

Ohio Genealogical Society. Ottawa County Chapter *see* FIRST FAMILIES OF OTTAWA COUNTY, OHIO

Ohio Genealogical Society. Wood County Chapter *see* FIRST FAMILIES OF WOOD COUNTY, OHIO

Ohio. Grand Army of the Republic. Army & Navy Post No.187 *see* RECORDS

OHIO HISTORICAL QUARTERLY *see* OHIO HISTORY

Ohio Historical Society *see*
- CENTENNIAL HOMESTEADS, 1977 APPLICATIONS
- EARLY OHIO POLITICAL LEADERS
- TEMPERANCE AND PROHIBITION COLLECTION

OHIO HISTORY – v1- 1887- 1; 1968- 5,6; 1975- 9 – us UMI [978]

OHIO HISTORY – (Formerly: Ohio Historical Quarterly). v.1-80. 1886-1971 – 1 – 415.00 – us Princeton Micro [978]

OHIO INDEPENDENT PRESS – Rossville. Ohio. 1830-1832 – 1 – us UMI [071]

Ohio. Industrial Commission *see* REPORTS

OHIO JOURNAL OF SCIENCE – v. 1-75. 1900-1975 – 1 – us Princeton Micro [500]

THE OHIO JUSTICES' CODE / Whittaker, William Henry – Cincinnati, Anderson, 1898. 593 p. LL-1548 – 1 – us L of C Photodup [340]

THE OHIO LAW JOURNAL – (Lacking: v1) – v1-6. 1880-84 (all publ) – 16mf – 9 – $72.00 – LLMC 82-953 – us L.L.M.C. [073]

THE OHIO LAW OF APPELLATE PROCEDURE AND THE PRACTICE INCIDENT TO APPEALS IN ALL OHIO COURTS. / Laning, Jay Ford – Norwalk, OH, The Ohio Law Book Co., 1899. 334 p. LL-831 – 1 – us L of C Photodup [340]

THE OHIO LAW OF OPINION EVIDENCE, EXPERT AND NON-EXPERT / James, Francis Bacon – Cincinnati, Anderson, 1889. 85 p. LL-893 – 1 – us L of C Photodup [340]

OHIO LAW REPORTER / Ohio – v1-16. 1903-19 (all publ) – 123mf – 9 – $184.00 – LLMC 84-171 – us L.L.M.C. [340]

OHIO LAWYER – v1-9. 1987-95 – 9 – $118.00 set – us Hein [340]

OHIO LIBERAL – Mansfield. Ohio. 1873-1875; 1880-1883 – 1 – us UMI [071]

OHIO LUMINARY : WEEKLY ANTI-MASONIC NEWSPAPER – Jefferson, OH, Dec 10 1828-June 12 1830 – 1r – 1 – us Western Res [071]

OHIO LUMINARY AND ASHTABULA PIONEER : WEEKLY ANTI-MASONIC NEWSPAPER – Jefferson, OH, Aug 14-Dec 11 1830 – 1r – 1 – us Western Res [071]

OHIO MEDICAL AND SURGICAL JOURNAL – v. 1-ns 14. Sep 1848-Jul 1878 – 1 – us UMI [616]

OHIO MEDICAL REPOSITORY OF ORIGINAL AND SELECTED INTELLIGENCE – v. 1. Apr 1826-18 Apr 1827 – 1 – us UMI [616]

OHIO MINING JOURNAL – Columbus. Ohio. 1883-93 – 1 – us UMI [622]

OHIO MISCELLANEOUS MUSEUM – v1 Jan-May 1822 – 1 – us UMI [978]

Ohio. Montgomery County. Dayton *see* GOTTSCHALL'S REPORTS

OHIO NISI PRIUS REPORTS, NEW SERIES – Cincinnati, OH: Ohio Law Reporter Co. v1-32. 1902-34 (all publ) – 231mf – 9 – $346.00 – LLMC 84-178 – us L.L.M.C. [340]

OHIO NISI PRIUS REPORTS, OLD SERIES – Jahn Publ Co. v1-8. 1893-1901 (all publ) – 47mf – 9 – $70.00 – LLMC 84-177 – us L.L.M.C. [340]

OHIO NISI REPORTS, OLD SERIES *see* OHIO DECISIONS

OHIO NORTHERN INTRAMURAL *see* OHIO NORTHERN UNIVERSITY LAW REVIEW

Ohio Northern University *see* THE NORTHERN

OHIO NORTHERN UNIVERSITY LAW REVIEW – (v1-11 1973-84 incl Ohio Northern Intramurel 1-3 1970-73 on reel $202.00. v12-21 1985-95 on mf $206.00) – v1-21. 1973-95 – 5,6,9 – $383.00 set – us Hein [340]

OHIO OBSERVER – Hudson. Ohio. 1833-1855 – 1 – us UMI [071]

OHIO OBSERVER – (Weekly Presbyterian newspaper, succeeded by the Cleveland Observer) – Hudson, OH. sept 28, 1833-sept 21, 1837 – 1r – 1 – us Western Res [071]

OHIO OBSERVER – (Weekly Presbyterian newspaper, successor to the Cleveland Observer) – Hudson, OH. apr 16, 1840-june 20, 1855 – 5r – 1 – us Western Res [071]

OHIO PATRIOT – New Philadelphia. Ohio. 1878-1880 – 1 – us UMI [071]

OHIO PATRIOT – (Weekly Democratic newspaper) – New Lisbon, OH. Feb 21 1840-Dec 30 1880 – 10r – 1 – us Western Res [071]

OHIO PATRIOT – (Weekly Democratic newspaper) – New Lisbon, OH. Nov 26 1831-May 25 1833 – 1r – 1 – us Western Res [071]

OHIO PATRIOT – (Weekly newspaper) – New Lisbon, OH. Jun 16 1810-Jan 24 1824 – 1r – 1 – us Western Res [071]

OHIO PATRIOT, AND FARMERS' AND MECHANICS' SHIELD – (Weekly Democratic newspaper) – New Lisbon, OH. Nov 22 1833-Aug 23 1839 – 2r – 1 – us Western Res [071]

OHIO PATRIOT AND NEW LISBON GAZETTE – (Weekly Democratic newspaper) – New Lisbon, OH. Mar 8 1828-Nov 19 1831 – 1r – 1 – us Western Res [071]

OHIO PATRIOT AND NEW LISBON WEEKLY ADVERTISER – (Weekly Democratic newspaper) – New Lisbon, OH. Feb 10 1824-Mar 1 1828 – 1 – us Western Res [071]

Ohio. Presbytery (Assoc. ChurchUnited Pres. Ch. of No. Am.) *see* MINUTES, 1808-1867

Ohio. Public Service Commission *see* REPORT

Ohio. Public Utilities Commission *see* REPORTS

Ohio. Railroad Commission *see* REPORTS

OHIO READING TEACHER – (v.14-. 1979- 5,6,9) – v.1-. 1967- – 1 – us UMI [073]

OHIO REPUBLICAN – Youngstown. Ohio. 1847-52 – 1 – us UMI [071]

OHIO REPUBLICAN – Zanesville. Ohio. 1823-1845 – 1 – us UMI [071]

OHIO SCHOOLS – v. 1-. 1923- – 1. – apply; v.53- 1975- 5,6,9 – us UMI [370]

THE OHIO SOCIALIST, 1919 : THE TOILER, 1919-1922 : THE WORKER, 1922 – 9 – $100.00 – us UPA [320]

OHIO SOLDIER : BI-WEEKLY NEWSPAPER SERVING UNION CIVIL WAR VETERANS – Chillicothe, OH. 20 Aug 1887-28 Feb 1891 – 3r – 1 – us Western Res [071]

OHIO SOLDIER AND NATIONAL PICKET GUARD : BI-WEEKLY NWESPAPER SERVING UNION CIVIL WAR VETERANS – Chillicoth, OH. 14 Mar 1891-1 Oct 1902 – 5r – 1 – us Western Res [071]

OHIO STAATS-ZEITUNG – Toledo, Ohio. 1854-56 – 1r – 1 – $32.50r – us Archival [071]

OHIO STAR – Ravenna. Ohio. 1830-1835; 1838-1840 – 1 – us UMI [071]

OHIO STAR : WEEKLY ANTI-MASONIC NEWSPAPER – Ravenna, OH. 6 Jan 1830-31 Dec 1835 – 3r – 1 – us Western Res [071]

OHIO STATE BAR ASSOCIATION *see* OHIO STATE BAR ASSOCIATION REPORT

Ohio. State Bar Association *see* PROCEEDINGS

OHIO STATE BAR ASSOCIATION REPORT – (Title varies: v1-50 1928-77 as Ohio State Bar Association) – v1-68. 1928-95 – 5,6 – $2,430.00 set – us Hein [340]

OHIO STATE BAR ASSOCIATION REPORTS – (Missing: 1899 pp7-9. 1900 pp16-17) – v1-48. 1880-1927 (all publ) – 48mf – 9 – $216.00 – LLMC 84-659 – us L.L.M.C. [340]

OHIO STATE DEMOCRAT – Urbana. Ohio. 1855-1858 – 1 – us UMI [071]

OHIO STATE JOURNAL – Columbus. Ohio. -d. 1842-56; 1857-1939 – 1 – us UMI [370]

OHIO STATE JOURNAL – Columbus. Ohio. -w. 1821-22; 1825-53; 1856-96; 1898-1914 – 1 – us UMI [370]

OHIO STATE JOURNAL ON DISPUTE RESOLUTION – v1-10. 1985-95 – 9 – $137.00 set – us Hein [340]

OHIO STATE LAW JOURNAL – (v1-45 1935-84 on reel/mf $700.00. v46-56 1985-95 on mf $301.00) – v1-56. 1935-95 – 5,6,9 – $1,001.00 set – us Hein [340]

THE OHIO STATE NEWS – Columbus. Feb. 14, 21, 1942 – 1 – us NY Public [073]

Ohio. State University. School of Home Economics *see* CATALOG OF THE LIBRARY

OHIO STATESMEN AND HUNDRED YEAR BOOK 1788-1892 / Taylor, William A – Columbus: Westbote Co., State Printers, 1892. Ohio Reel 10. (The Cox Library Collection) – 5 – us Americana [978]

OHIO SUN : WEEKLY DEMOCRATIC NEWSPAPER – Batavia, OH. 22 Apr 1829 – 1r – 1 – us Western Res [071]

OHIO SUN : WEEKLY DEMOCRATIC NEWSPAPER – Batavia, OH. 7 Dec 1840-24 May 1844 – 1r – 1 – us Western Res [071]

Ohio. Superior Court *see*
- CINCINNATI SUPERIOR COURT DECISIONS

Ohio. Supreme Court *see*
- GOEBEL'S PROBATE REPORTS
- OHIO SUPREME COURT REPORTS
- OHIO UNREPORTED CASES
- WRIGHT'S REPORTS

OHIO SUPREME COURT PRACTICE; CONTAINING THE LAW, DECISIONS AND FORMS, WITH FULL DIRECTIONS FOR PROCEEDING IN MANDAMUS, QUO-WARRANTO, HABEAS CORPUS. / Green, Arnold – Cleveland: Ingham, Clarke, 1877. 465p. LL-610 – 1 – us L of C Photodup [340]

OHIO SUPREME COURT REPORTS : OHIO REPORTS – OHIO STATE REPORTS / Ohio. Supreme Court – (Ohio Reports: v1-20 1821 (all publ). Ohio State Reports: v1-100 1852-1919 894mf $1,341.00. Pre-NRS: Ohio Reports: v1-20 and Ohio State Reports v1-42 1821-85 457mf $685.00. Updates planned) – 2 titles – 9 – LLMC 80-814 – us L.L.M.C. [340]

OHIO SUPREME COURT REPORTS *see*
- OHIO UNREPORTED CASES
- WRIGHT'S REPORTS

THE OHIO SUPREME COURT REPORTS REDUCED TO QUESTIONS AND ANSWERS. / Hoffman, Frederick Lewis – Cincinnati: Anderson Co., 1908. 350p. LL-914 – 1 – us L of C Photodup [340]

Ohio. Tax Commission *see* REPORTS

Ohio. Turnpike Commission *see* OHIO TURNPIKE COMMISSION SCRAPBOOKS

OHIO TURNPIKE COMMISSION SCRAPBOOKS / Ohio. Turnpike Commission – 1947-75 – 1 – us Ohio Hist [978]

OHIO UNREPORTED CASES / Ohio. Supreme Court – (A Pre-NRS title) – Laning, Norwalk. 1v. 1889-99 (all publ) – 10mf – 9 – $15.00 – LLMC 84-172 – us L.L.M.C. [340]

THE OHIO VALLEY IN COLONIAL DAYS / Fernow, Bertold – Albany, N.Y.: J. Munsell, 1890. 05476. (Pre-1900 Canadiana) – 9 – cn C.I.H.M. [971]

Ohio. Volunteer Infantry. 105th Regiment *see* RECORDS, MS 2400

OHIO WATCHMAN : MONTHLY LIBERAL FREE-THINKER NEWSPAPER – Ravenna, Portage, OH. 1 Jan 1835-18 Jan 1837 – 1r – 1 – us Western Res [071]

OHIO WATCHMAN AND LIBERAL ENQUIRER : SEMI-WEEKLY LIBERAL FREE-THINKER NEWSPAPER – Ravenna & Mantua, Portage, OH. 13 May 1837-8 Jul 1837 – 1r – 1 – us Western Res [071]

OHIO WHIG – Perrysburg, Ohio. 1838-40 – 1r – 1 – $32.50r – us Archival [071]

OHIOWA ADVERTISER – Ohiowa, NE. -w. Feb 1925-Jan 1930 – 1 – us NE Hist [071]

OHIOWA OPINION – Ohiowa, NE. -w. Mar 1930-Jan 1934 – 1 – us NE Hist [071]

OHIOWA SPOTLIGHT – Ohiowa, NE. -w. Oct 1895-Jan 1896; May 1896-May 1898; Dec 1898-Dec 1900; Apr 1901-Mar 1907; Jan 1908-Dec 1912; May 1914-Sept 1917 – 1 – us NE Hist [071]

Ohl, J F *see* THE INNER MISSION

Ohlenburg, Salomon *see* DIE BIBLISCHEN ASYLE IN TALMUDISCHEM GEWANDE

OHLONE COLLEGE MONITOR – Fremont, CA: Ohlone College, 1970-71; 1973-80 – 6r – 1 – $300.00 – B02252 – us Library Micro [370]

Ohly, Karl *see* ROTHE LIEDER UND ZWANGLOSE REIME

DIE OHNE : HALBMONATS-ZEITSCHRIFT FUER JUNGGESELLINNEN – Berlin, 1925 n1-2 – 1r – 1 – Inquire at Mikrofilmarchiv for details – gw Misc Inst [072]

OHNE BEFEHL : EINE ERZAEHLUNG AUS DEN BEFREIUNGSKRIEGEN / Pergel, Walter – Stuttgart: Deutsche Verlags-Expedition, c1939 – 1r – 1 – us U.W. Library [830]

DIE OHNEHOSEN : ROMAN / Schulte vom Bruehl, Walther – Leipzig: Verlag der Wiking-Buecher, H Wille, [18-?] – 1 – us U.W. Library [830]

Ohorn, Anton *see* DIE BRUEDER VON ST BERNHARD

OHRAI-MONO BUNRUI SHUSEI / Tokyo University. General Library; ed by Ishikawa, Matsutaro – Collection of Textbooks of Modern Japanese Education for the Common People in the Tokyo University Library – 66r – 1 – Y660,000.00 – ja Yushodo [370]

OHRAI-MONO BUNRUISHUSEI JOSHIYO OHRAI-HEN / Kensei-Bunko; ed by Ishikawa, Matsutaro – (Collection of textbooks of modern Japanese education for women) – 32r – 1 – Y432,000 – ja Yushodo [305]

Ohsson, M C d' *see*
- DES PEUPLES DU CAUCASE ET DES PAYS AU NORD DE LA MER NOIRE ET DE LA MER CASPIENNE DANS LE 10E
- TABLEAU GENERALE DE L'EMPIRE OTHOMAN, DIVISE EN DEUX PARTIES

Ohtani, S *see* SHIMOFUSA SAKURA-HAN HOTTA-KE MONJO

OI TREIS HIERARCHAI – Athens, Greece. -f. 1 July 1921-16 31 May 1926. 1 reel – 1 – uk British Libr Newspaper [949]

OIEBLIKKET / Kierkegaard, Soren – Kjobenhavn: C.A. Reitzels, 1855 – 1mf – us A.T.L.A. [190]

OIF KATOVES – (Chicago). 1920 – 1 – us A.J.P.C. [073]

OIL : THE FEDERAL INVESTIGATIONS – (1970-74: ISBN 0-89093-010-4. $860.00; The Energy Crisis, Supplements. 1974-76: ISBN 0-89093-124-0. $580.00; 1976-78: 6r ISBN 0-89093-184-4. $580.00; 1978-80: 6r ISBN 0-89093-185-2. $580.00; 1980-85: 12r ISBN 0-89093-695-1. $1,150.00. All with printed guides) – 1 – $3,565.00 set – us UPA [337]

OIL AND FAT INDUSTRIES *see* JOURNAL OF THE AMERICAN OIL CHEMISTS' SOCIETY

OIL AND GAS JOURNAL – Tulsa, OK. v17-53. 1918-55. Continues: Oil Investors' Journal – 1,5,6 – us Princeton Micro [660]

OIL AND GAS JOURNAL – (v63- 1965- 5,6; v68- 1970- 9) – 1- 1902- – 1 – us UMI [660]

OIL AND GAS TAX QUARTERLY – v1- 1951- 1; v26- 1977- 5,6,9 – us UMI [336]

OIL AND GAS TAX QUARTERLY – v1-42. 1951-94 – 1,5,6 – $495.00 – us Hein [073]

OIL AND SOAP *see* JOURNAL OF THE AMERICAN OIL CHEMISTS' SOCIETY

OIL AND WINE / Tyrrell, George – London; New York: Longmans, Green, 1907 – 1mf – 9 – 0-8370-8557-8 – 1986-2557 – us A.T.L.A. [240]

Oil, Chemical and Atomic Workers International Union *see* UNION NEWS

OIL DAILY – v1- 1951- – 1,5,6,9 – us UMI [338]

OIL FACTS – 22- ns. 11 1957-69 – 1 – us UMI [660]

OIL FOR INDONESIA'S FUTURE; AN OUTLINE OF TASKS AHEAD FOR THE OIL INDUSTRY / Shell Oil Company. Marketing Organization in Indonesia – SE 3463 1. 1958 – 9 – ne IDC [660]

OIL ON ICE : THE ALASKAN WILDERNESS AT THE CROSSROADS / Brown, Tom – 1r – 5,9 – $50.00 – B70006 – us Library Micro [333]

OIL, PAINT AND DRUG REPORTER – Los Angeles, CA. v183-192 – 1r – 1 – $50.00 – R03315 – us Library Micro [071]

OIL, PAINT AND DRUG REPORTER – v133-164. 1938-53 – 1,5,6 – us Princeton Micro [540]

OILSEEDS AND OILS : NATIONAL POLICIES OF SELECTED COUNTRIES – 1984 – 77p – it F.A.O. [350]

OILSPILL WESLEY MARX – 1r – 5,9 – $50.00 – B70010 – us Library Micro [360]

OILWEEK – (v38-46 1987/88-1995 Can$37.00y 9. Nos 3-5 in v6 not available for filming) – Toronto. v5-46. 1954/55-1995 – 5,9 – Price varies – cn Micromedia [660]

Olschinger, Johann Nepomuk Paul *see* DIE EINHEITSLEHRE DER GOETTLICHEN TRINITAET NACH DER KIRCHLICHEN TRADITION BEWIESEN UND GEGEN DIE IRRLEHREN

Oise. France. (Department) *see* BUDGET DES RECETTES ET DES DEPENSES DEPARTEMENTALES

L'OISEAU-MOUCHE : REVUE LITTERAIRE ET HISTORIQUE – Chicoutimi, Canada. 1 jan 1893-27 dec 1902 – 1r – 1 – Can$50.00 – cn Can Microfilming [073]

LES OISEAUX DE LA CHINE / David, A & Oustalet, E – 2077 2. v. 1 text. v. 2 atlas. 1877 – 8 – ne IDC [590]

OISEAUX DE L'ILE DE LA TRINIDAD (ANTILLES) / Leotaud, A – Z 1829. 1866 – 9 – ne IDC [590]

OITO DE JULHO : ORGAO DOS ALUNOS DO GRUPO ESCOLAR PAULA ROCHA – DIRETOR-X – Sabara, 21 Oct 1932 – 1,5,6 – bl Biblioteca [072]

OITO DE MAIO – Manaos, Amazonas. 8 Maio 1912 – 1,5,6 – bl Biblioteca [072]

OIZ : OESTERREICHISCHE INGENIEUR-ZEITSCHRIFT – v1-11 1958-68; v13-15 1970-72; v17-24 1974-81. ISSN: 0029-9219 – 1,5,6,9,13 – $88.00v – us UMI [620]

THE OJAI – Calif. 1958- – 1 – us UMI [071]

OJAI VALLEY NEWS – Ojai, CA. 1947- – 94+ r – 1 – $4,700.00 ($150.00y) – C02555 – us Library Micro [071]

OJE *see* VALE QUIEN SIRVE

Ojea, Julio Oscar *see* LA INTERVENCION FEDERAL EN LA PROVINCIA DE BUENOS AIRES, 5 DE ENERO A 5 DE MAYO DE 1944

OJF DER WACH (NA STRAZY) = ON GUARD – (In Yiddish. Only one issue publ) – Warsaw, PL. v1 no1. Apr 1948 – 1r – 1 – $25.00 – cn Can Microfilming [072]

OJFGANG = FORWARD – (In Yiddish) – Linz, DE. no39 28 Nov 1947-no40 12 Dec 1947 – 1r – 1 – $25.00 – cn Can Microfilming [072]

THE OJIBWA WOMAN / Landes, R – BN 290 2. 1938 – 8 – ne IDC [306]

O'JORNAL BATISTA – (Some issues lacking) – 1921-44 – 11r – 1 – ATLA S0728 – us A.T.L.A. [073]

Ojuka, Edward O *see* COCAINE AND EXERCISE

Ok Park, Hye *see* ALICAT. THE ONLINE CATALOG

OKALOOSA NEWS JOURNAL – Crestview. Fla. Aug 1937-41, 1953- – 1 – us P.K. Yonge [071]

OKAMURA : PERDJOEANGAN SINGAMANGARADJA JANG KE-12 – N.p. Balatentera Pertahanan Soematera Oetara (2605). 15p – 116mf – 9 – ne IDC [950]

OKANAGAN SUNDAY – (1990-1992.-6r) – Kelowna, 1993 – 2r – 1 – cn Preston [971]

OKANOGAN RECORD – Conconully. Wash. -w. 1903-15 – 1 – us UMI [071]

OKAZ – (Yrly reel count varies) – Saudi Arabia,1965- – 1 – inquire – us Ross [072]

O'Kelly, James *see*
- AUTHOR'S APOLOGY FOR PROTESTING AGAINST THE METHODIST EPISCOPAL GOVERNMENT
- A VINDICATION OF THE AUTHOR'S APOLOGY, WITH REFLECTIONS ON THE REPLY..

Oken, L *see* ELEMENTS OF PHYSIOPHILOSOPHY

Okey, Thomas *see* THE STORY OF PARIS

OKHA = O.J.A. – (In Yiddish) – Virginia, Sante Fe, AG. no4(46). Aug 1946 – 1r – 1 – $25.00 – cn Can Microfilming [072]

OKHOTNIK I PUSHNIK SIBIRI – Novosibirsk, 1925-28 n12 – 54mf – 9 – COR-663/1 – ne IDC [334]

OKHOTNIK I RYBAK SIBIRI – (Missing: 1931 n11-12) – Novosibirsk, 1929-33 n6 – 52mf – 9 – COR-664/1 – ne IDC [334]

OKHOTNIK I RYBOLOV – Viatka, 1926-27 n4 – 7mf – 9 – COR-665/1 – ne IDC [334]

OKHRANA I REVOLIUTSIIA : K ISTORII TAINYKH POLIT / Men'shchikov, L – M., 1925-1932. 3v: v1. 1885-1898. M., 1925. 431p; v2, pt1. M., 1898-1903. M., 1928. 187p; v3. M., 1932. 280p – 5mf – 9 – ne IDC [320]

OKINAWA TIMES – (1991- 12r per year Y120,000) – June 1948-December 1988 – 418r – 1 – Y4,180,000 – ja Japan Micro [950]

OKINAWA TIMES – (Yrly reel count varies) – Japan, 1948- – 1 – inquire – us Ross [072]

Okladnikov, A P *see* NEOLIT I BRONZOVYI VEK PRIBAIKAL'IA

OKLAHOMA – 1r – 1 – $80.00 – us Scholarly Res [370]

OKLAHOMA : SESSION LAWS OF AMERICAN STATES AND TERRITORIES – 1890-1995 – 9 – $1,056.00 set – us Hein [340]

OKLAHOMA : STATUTES ANNOTATED – St Paul: West Pub Co, 1936-May 1996 update – 9 – $2,577.00 set – us Hein [340]

Oklahoma *see*
– REPORTS AND OPINIONS (A-G)
– REPORTS, PRE-NES
– STATE REPORTS, PRE-NRS

OKLAHOMA AND INDIAN TERRITORY BAR ASSOCIATION REPORTS – 1st to 3rd annual meetings. 1904-07 (all publ) – 8mf – 9 – $12.00 – LLMC 84-661 – us L.L.M.C. [073]

OKLAHOMA ATTORNEY GENERAL REPORTS AND OPINIONS – (6 1897-1979 $70.00. 9 1979-1994 $190.00) – 1897-1994 – 6,9 – $260.00set – us Hein [340]

Oklahoma Baptist Associations *see* ANNUALS

Oklahoma Baptist State B.Y.P.U. Conventions *see* PROCEEDINGS

Oklahoma Baptist State Convention *see* MATERIALS

OKLAHOMA BAR ASSOCIATION JOURNAL *see* OKLAHOMA BAR JOURNAL

OKLAHOMA BAR ASSOCIATION JOURNAL QUARTERLY SUPPLEMENT – 1972-77 (all publ?) – 9 – LLMC 84-664 – us L.L.M.C. [073]

OKLAHOMA BAR JOURNAL – (Title varies: v1-10 1931-40 as Oklahoma State Bar Journal. v11 1941 as Oklahoma Bar Association Journal. v12-49 1942-79 as Journal of the Oklahoma Bar Association) – v1-66. 1931-95 – 9 – $2,688.00 set – us Hein [340]

Oklahoma, Choctaw-Chickasaw Sunday School Convention *see* MINUTES

Oklahoma City, Oklahoma *see* MISCELLANEOUS EARLY NEWSPAPERS

OKLAHOMA CITY STAR. HUDSON AVENUE BAPTI TRUMPET ED – Oklahoma City, OK. 1934-35 – 1 – 36.70 – us A.B.H.S. [073]

OKLAHOMA CITY UNIVERSITY LAW REVIEW – (v1-9 1976-84 on reel $130.00. v10-19 1985-94 on mf $190.00. Includes index 1-5 1976-80) – v1-19. 1976-94 – 5,6,9 – $320.00 set – us Hein [340]

Oklahoma. Criminal Court of Appeal *see* OKLAHOMA CRIMINAL REPORTS

OKLAHOMA CRIMINAL REPORTS / Oklahoma. Criminal Court of Appeal – (No Pre-NRS vols. Updates planned) – v1-15. 1908-1919 – 130mf – 9 – $195.00 – LLMC 90-402 – us L.L.M.C. [340]

OKLAHOMA CURRENT FARM ECONOMICS – v1- 1927- 1; 1971- 5,6; 1977- 4 x 6 in. 9 – us UMI [330]

OKLAHOMA CURRENT FARM ECONOMICS / Oklahoma State University. Agricultural Experiment Station – No.43-55. 1970-82 – 1,5 – us Spaulding [330]

OKLAHOMA EAGLE – Tulsa. Oklahoma. oct. 11, 1941; Feb. 5, 22, 1942 – 1 – us NY Public [071]

Oklahoma Education Association *see* OEA FOCUS

OKLAHOMA HISTORY-SOUTH OF THE CANADIAN / Johnson, Roy M – Chicago: S.J. Clarke Publ. Co., 1925. 3v. Oklahoma Reel 3. (The Cox Library Collection) – 5 – us Americana [978]

OKLAHOMA INDIAN LAND LAWS. / Mills, Lawrence – St. Louis, MO: Thomas Law Book Co., 1924. 1254p. LL-194 – 1 – us L of C Photodup [340]

OKLAHOMA JEWISH REVIEW – Oklahoma City. Okl. 1912-13 – 1 – us A.J.P.C. [071]

THE OKLAHOMA LAW JOURNAL – OK: Guthrie. v1-14. 1902-1916 (all publ) – 73mf – $109.00 – LLMC 95-109 – us L.L.M.C. [073]

OKLAHOMA LAW REVIEW – (v1-37 1948-84 on reel $440.00. v38-47 1985-94 on mf $231.00) – v1-47. 1948-94 – 5,6,9 – $671.00 set – us Hein [340]

OKLAHOMA LEADERS / Harlow, Rex – Oklahoma City: Harlow Publ. Co., 1928. Oklahoma Reel 2.(The Cox Library Collection) – 5 – us Americana [978]

OKLAHOMA LIBRARIAN – v1- 1950- 1; v21-5,6; v27- 9 – us UMI [020]

OKLAHOMA OBSERVER – (v. 11- 1979-5,6,9) – v. 1- 1969- – 1 – us UMI [073]

OKLAHOMA STANDARD – Stillwater. Okl. 1889-1890 – 1 – us UMI [071]

Oklahoma. State Bar Association *see* PROCEEDINGS

OKLAHOMA STATE BAR ASSOCIATION REPORTS – v1-23. 1907-30 (all publ) – 27mf – 9 – $121.00 – LLMC 84-662 – us L.L.M.C. [340]

OKLAHOMA STATE BAR JOURNAL – v1-1931- – 9 – LLMC 84-663 – us L.L.M.C. [073]

OKLAHOMA STATE BAR JOURNAL *see* OKLAHOMA BAR JOURNAL

Oklahoma State University. Agricultural Experiment Station *see*
– ANIMAL SCIENCE RESEARCH REPORT
– ANNUAL REPORT
– BULLETIN
– MISCELLANEOUS PUBLICATIONS
– OKLAHOMA CURRENT FARM ECONOMICS
– RESEARCH REPORT
– TECHNICAL BULLETIN

Oklahoma State University. Cooperative Extension Service *see*
– AGRICULTURAL CHEMICALS CONFERENCE FOR PESTICIDE DEALERS AND APPLICATORS 1967-82
– CIRCULAR
– OSU EXTENSION FACTS

Oklahoma. Supreme Court *see* OKLAHOMA SUPREME COURT REPORTS

OKLAHOMA SUPREME COURT REPORTS / Oklahoma. Supreme Court – (No Pre-NRS vols. Updates planned) – v1-64. 1890-1919 – 581MF – 9 – $871.00 – LLMC 81-804 – us L.L.M.C. [340]

OKLAHOMA TEACHER – (1979-82. 5,6,9) – 1919-82 – 1 – us UMI [073]

Oklahoma. Territory *see* SESSION LAWS

OKLAHOMA TERRITORY AND THE NATIONAL ARCHIVES : A STUDY IN FEDERAL LANDS / Chapman, Berlin B – undated – 1 – us KS Hist [978]

Oklahoma Territory and the National Archives *see* STUDY

OKLAHOMA WAR CHIEF – Caldwell. Kan. -w. 1883-86 – 1 – us UMI [071]

OKLAHOMAN – Oklahoma City. Okl. -w. 1895, 1909 – 1 – us UMI [071]

OKMULGEE OBSERVER – Okmulgee. Okla. Feb. 12, 19, 1942 – 1 – us NY Public [071]

Oko, Adolph S *see* THE SPINOZA BIBLIOGRAPHY

OKOLAKICIYE WAKAN WOTANIN WOWAPI – 1970-74. (American Indian Periodicals in the Princeton University Library). 2 fiches – 9 – $45.00 – us UPA [305]

OKOLO PRAVOSUDIIA : STAT'I SOOBSHCHENIIA I SUDEBNYE OCHERKI / Karabchevskii, N P – 2nd ed. Spb., 1908. 540p – 6mf – 9 – ne IDC [320]

Okolowicz, Jozef *see* WYCHODZTWO I OSADNICTWO POLSKIE PRZEDWOJNA SWIATOWA

OKOTOKS REVIEW – (Some issues missing) – Alberta, CN. 1962-69 – 3r – 1 – cn Commonwealth Micro [072]

OKOTOKS TIMES AND WESTERN STAR – Alberta. Canada. Jan-Dec 1903 – 1 – cn Commonwealth Micro [072]

Oksenov, I *see* O KOMPOZITSII "DVENADTSATI"

DIE OKTATEUCHCATENE DES PROKOP VON GAZA UND DIE SEPTUAGINTAFORSCHUNG / Lindl, Ernest – Muenchen: Hermann Lukaschik, 1902. 1 fiche – 9 – us A.T.L.A. [240]

Oktay, M Fahri *see* NAZIM HIKMET

OKTIABR' – Literaturno-khudozhestvennyi i obshchestvenno-bytovoi Zhurnal. Moscow, 1924-72. Lacking: 1924 (1-2); 1925-29; 1930 (7-12); 1939 (10-12); 1941 (1-4,11-12); 1943 (6-12). BR-10,433/1. BR-10,433/1 – 9 – ne IDC [460]

OKTIABR' : LITERATURNO-KHUDOZHESTVENNYI I OBSHCHESTVENNO-POLITICHESKII ZHURNAL – Moscow, 1924-44 – 17r – 1 – us Ross [320]

OKTIABR 1917 GODA V MOSKVE I MOSKOVSKOI GUBERNII – Obzor dokumentov Gosudarstvennogo arkhiva Oktiabr'skoi revoliutsii sotsialisticheskogo stroitel'stva Moskovskoi oblasti. Moscow, 1957. 174p. BR-10,942/1 – 9 – ne IDC [947]

OKTIABR'SKAIA POEMA MAIAKOVSKOGO / Abramov, A – Voronezh. 1958. BR-1953 2 – 8 – ne IDC [460]

OKTIABR'SKAIA REVOLIUTSIIA I GRAZHDANSKAIA VOINA NA DAL'NEM VOSTOKE; 1917-1922 GG / Tsypkin, S – Moscow, 1933 – 1 – 35.00r – us Hoover Inst Photo [335]

OKTIABR'SKIE DNI / Mstislavskii, S – M., 1927. 64p – 1mf – 9 – ne IDC [320]

OKTIABRSKOE VOORUZHENNOE VOSSTANIE – Semnadtsatyi god v Petrograde. (S.N. Valk, Red.). v. 1-2. L. 1967 – 8 – BR-8239 2 – ne IDC [947]

OKTOBER HARI PERINGATAN KESAKTIAN PANTJA SILA / Indonesia. Angkatan Darat – SE-5834 1. 1966? – 9 – ne IDC [324]

OKTYABR – Moscow. 1924-1941; 1942 – 1 – us NY Public [305]

OKTYABR – Moscow. U.S.S.R. 1961- – 1 – us UMI [073]

OKUMA MONJO = OKUMA RECORDS – Documents, letters of Shigenobu Okuma (1838-1922), Japanese statesman in the Meiji-Taisho era, now in Waseda Univ. Library, Tokyo. 4800 documents, 6640 letters. Index. 186 reels. Classified catalog suppl. – 186r – 1 – Y1,896,000 – ja Yushodo [950]

OKURASHO GINKO-KYOKU NEMPYO = STATISTICAL ANNUALS OF THE BANKING BUREAU OF THE MINISTRY OF FINANCE, JAPANESE GOVERNMENT – 1st-65th reports, 1873-1940 – 41r – 1 – Y680,000 – ja Yushodo [336]

OKURASHO NENPO = ANNUAL REPORT OF THE MINISTRY OF FINANCE, JAPANESE GOVERNMENT – 1st report to 67th reports, 1875-1941 – 32r – 1 – Y221,000.00 – ja Yushodo [336]

O.L. Baskin and Co *see*
– HISTORY OF CLEAR CREEK AND BOULDER VALLEYS
– HISTORY OF DELAWARE COUNTY
– HISTORY OF GRUNDY COUNTY
– HISTORY OF MENARD AND MASON COUNTIES
– HISTORY OF MORROW COUNTY
– HISTORY OF POTTAWATTAMIE COUNTY
– HISTORY OF THE ARKANSAS VALLEY, COLORADO
– HISTORY OF THE CITY OF DENVER AND ARAPAHOE COUNTY AND COLORADO

Olabarrieta, Francisco de *see* DISCURSO..

OLAFS SAGA HELGA. SAGA OLAFS KONUNGS ENS HELGA – 1853 – 1 – us I.U. Libraries [390]

OLAFS SAGA TRYGGVASONAR – Danish. King Olaf Tryggvesons Saga. 1826-27 – 1 – us I.U. Libraries [390]

OLALLA. REVISTA DE POESIA – Merida: Imp. Cardoso, 1957. Abril a Septiembre (6 numeros, todo lo publicado) – sp Bibl Santa Ana [946]

OLAM HA-BA – Hanau. 1620. BJ-43-69 1 – 9 – ne IDC [270]

OLAMENU / ed by Glikson, M – Odessa-Moscow. 1917. BJ-422-64 1 – 9 – ne IDC [400]

OLANDSBLADET – Borgholm, Sweden. 1867-1950 – 60r – 1 – sw Kungliga [072]

OLANDSBLADET – Borgholm, Sweden. 1951- – 1 – sw Kungliga [072]

Olarra y Garmendia, Jose de et al *see* CORRESPONDENCIA ENTRE LA NUNCIATURA...

Olathe. Kansas. School for the Deaf *see* RECORDS OF PUPILS

Olavarrieta y Huarte, Eugenio *see* EL FOLKLORE DE MADRID

Olavide, I *see* INDICE DE LOS PAPELES DE LA JUNTA CENTRAL SUPREMA GUBERNATIVA DEL REINO Y...

OLBIE OU ESSAI SUR LES MOYENS DE REFORMER LES MOEURS D'UNE NATION / Say, Jean Baptiste – (Utopias in the Enlightenment series). 1800 – 9 – fr Hachette [320]

Olbrich, Carl *see* GOETHE'S SPRACHE UND DIE ANTIKE

Olcott, E R *see* OLCOTT'S REPORTS OF CASES IN THE DISTRICT COURT FOR THE SOUTHERN DISTRICT OF NEW YORK, 1843-1847

Olcott, Edward Rufus *see* THE LOUISIANA MAGISTRATE, AND PARISH OFFICERS' GUIDE.

OLCOTT'S REPORTS OF CASES IN THE DISTRICT COURT FOR THE SOUTHERN DISTRICT OF NEW YORK, 1843-1847 / Olcott, E R – New York: Halstead. 1v. 1857 (all publ) – 6mf – 9 – $9.00 – LLMC 81-464 – us L.L.M.C. [340]

OLD AGE PENSIONER – Newport Beach, CA. 1942-48 – 1r – 1 – $50.00 – C02525 – us Library Micro [071]

OLD AND NEW – v. 1-11. Jan 1870-May 1875 – 1 – us UMI [073]

OLD AND NEW CANADA, 1753-1844: HISTORIC SCENES AND SOCIAL PICTURES, OR, THE LIFE OF JOSEPH FRANCOIS PERRAULT / Bender, Prosper – Montreal: Dawson Bros., 1882. 00122. (Pre-1900 Canadiana) – 9 – cn C.I.H.M. [971]

THE OLD AND NEW MONONGAHELA / Van Voorhis, John S – Bellevernon, 1893. Pennsylvania Reel 23. (The Cox Library Collection) – 5 – us Americana [978]

OLD AND NEW TESTAMENT THEOLOGY = LEHRE DER BIBEL VON GOTT / Ewald, Heinrich – (Includes bibliographical references and indexes) – Edinburgh: T & T Clark; New York: Scribner and Welford [distributor], 1888 – 2mf – 9 – 0-8370-9466-6 – 1986-3466 – us A.T.L.A. [220]

OLD AND NEW THEOLOGY : A CONSTRUCTIVE CRITIQUE / Heard, John Bickford – Edinburgh:T & T Clark, 1885 – 1mf – 9 – 0-8370-4501-0 – 1985-2501 – us A.T.L.A. [240]

THE OLD AND THE NEW MAN, OR, SIN AND SALVATION / West, Anson – Nashville, TN: Southern Methodist Publ House, 1886, c1885 – 1mf – 9 – 0-8370-5765-5 – 1985-3765 – us A.T.L.A. [210]

OLD ANGLICANISM AND MODERN RITUALISM / Meyrick, F – London: Skeffington, 1901 – 1mf – us A.T.L.A. [240]

OLD AUTHOR'S FARM : SALE LISTS; NUMISMATS, PHILATELISTS – Morrisburg, Ontario. nos 190, 191, 193 (after 1950) – 1r – 1 – Can$25.00 – cn Can Microfilming [072]

OLD BABYLONIAN CONTRACTS FROM NIPPUR, VOL 1 : SELECTED TEXTS FROM THE UNIVERSITY MUSEUM, UNIVERSITY OF PENNSYLVANIA / Stone, Elizabeth C & Zimansky, Paul E – 1976 – 1mf – 9 – $4.50f – 0-226-77551-8 – us U.C. Orient [930]

OLD BABYLONIAN INSCRIPTIONS CHIEFLY FROM NIPPUR / Hilprecht, H V – (The Babylonian expedition of the University of Pennsylvania. Series A: Cuneiform texts). 2v. Philadelphia, 1893-96. BNE-426 1 – 9 – ne IDC [410]

OLD BALLADS, HISTORICAL AND NARRATIVE, WITH SOME OF THE MODERN DATE – 1784 – 1 – us I.U. Libraries [390]

OLD BAPTIST BANNER – Nashville. Tenn. 20 Jan 1838-Apr 1839; and The Correspondent. Murfreesboro. Tenn. May 1839-Apr 1840 – 1 – 13.09 – us Baptist [240]

THE OLD BENCHERS OF THE INNER TEMPLE / Lamb, Charles – London: Clarendon Press, 1927 – 2mf – 9 – $3.00 – LLMC 84-300 – us L.L.M.C. [340]

THE OLD BIBLE AND THE NEW SCIENCE: AN ESSAY AND FOUR LECTURES / Thomas, Jesse Burgess – New York: Daniel C. Potter, 1877. 1 fiche – 9 – us A.T.L.A. [240]

THE OLD BREWERY: AND THE NEW MISSION HOUSE AT THE FIVE POINTS – 1854 – 9 – us A.T.L.A. [240]

OLD BROTHERHOOD ARCHIVES – 1 – uk Microform Academic [240]

OLD CALABAR AND NOTES ON THE IBIBIO LANGUAGE / Jeffreys, Mervyn David Waldegrave – Calabar: HWTI Press, 1935 – us Res Libr [470]

OLD CARS – v. 1-5. 1971-76 – 1,5,6 – us Princeton Micro [629]

OLD CARS – v5-12. 1976-83 – 1 – us Princeton Micro [380]

OLD CHRIST CHURCH, PHILADELPHIA *see* ARCHIVES OF OLD CHRIST CHURCH, PHILADELPHIA, 1695-1976

OLD COLONISTS' JUBILEE, AUCKLAND, NZ 1842-1892 / Craig, J J – (Includes roll of settlers who arrived before 1843. Lists name, age, ship, port and year of arrival) – 1mf – 9 – NZ$5.00 – 0-908797-67-2 – NZNB C1693 – nz BAB [980]

THE OLD COUNTRYMAN'S EMIGRANT GUIDE TO CANADA – Quebec, Canada. v1 n2. 9 mai 1862 – 1r – 1 – Can$25.00 – cn Can Microfilming [323]

THE OLD COURT HOUSE : REMINISCENCES AND ANECDOTES OF THE COURTS AND BAR OF CINCINNATI / Carter, Alfred George Washington – Cincinnati: Thomson, 1880. 466p. LL-1545 – 1 – us L of C Photodup [340]

THE OLD DOCUMENTS AND THE NEW BIBLE / Smyth, John Paterson – New York: James Pott, 1890. 1 fiche – 9 – us A.T.L.A. [240]

OLD DOMINION SUN – Staunton. Va. 1902-1907 – 1 – us UMI [073]

THE OLD ENGLISH BIBLE : AND OTHER ESSAYS / Gasquet, Francis Aidan – (Includes bibliographical references and index) – London: John C Nimmo, 1897 – 1mf – 9 – 0-8370-9233-7 – 1986-3233 – us A.T.L.A. [220]

THE OLD ENGLISH MARTYROLOGY / Herzfeld, G – (Re-edited from mss. in libraries of British Museum and of Corpus Christi College, Cambridge.) H.P.25. 1900 – 9 – ne IDC [240]

THE OLD FAITH AND THE NEW LEARNING : READY TO-DAY TO GIVE AN ACCOUNT CONCERNING THE HOPE WHICH IS IN YOU / Bethune-Baker, James Franklin – London: S.P.C.K.; New York: E.S. Gorham, 1907 – 1mf – us A.T.L.A. [240]

THE OLD FAITH AND THE NEW WOMAN / Tyrrell, George – (The American Catholic Quarterly Review, v. 22, Sept. 1897, p. 630-645) – 9 – us A.T.L.A. [240]

OLD FAITHS AND NEW FACTS / Kinsley, William Wirt – NY: D Appleton, 1896, c1895 – 1mf – 9 – 0-8370-3901-0 – 1985-1901 – us A.T.L.A. [210]

THE OLD FINNISH LITERATURE ON MICROFICHE 1562-1827 – (Collection increases irregularly) – Helsinki – ca 12,000mf – 9 – fi H.U. Libr [490]

AN OLD FOX TARR'D AND FEATHER'D, OCCASIONED BY WHAT IS CALLED MR. JOHN WESLEY'S 'CALM ADDRESS TO OUR AMERICAN COLONIES' / Toplady, Augustus Montague – London, 2nd ed 1775 – 1mf – 9 – MP-502/1 – ne IDC [240]

OLD FRENCH ROMANCES DONE INTO ENGLISH. WITH AN INTRODUCTION BY JOSEPH JACOBS / Morris, William – London: G. Allen, 1896 – 1 roll – 1 – 1-55879-590-1 – uk Libr Preservation [830]

OLD GLORY AND THE GOSPEL IN THE PHILIPPINES : NOTES GATHERED DURING PROFESSIONAL AND MISSIONARY WORK / Condict, Alice Byram – Chicago:Fleming H. Revell, 1902, c1901 – 1mf – 9 – 0-8370-5458-3 – 1985-3458 – us A.T.L.A. [240]

OLD GUARD – v. 1-8. Jun 1863-Dec 1870 – 1 – us UMI [073]

OLD HALL MANUSCRIPT – 1 – uk Microform Academic [240]

OLD HANOVER CHURCH, PA / Robinson, Thomas H – 1878 – 1 – $50.00 – us Presbyterian [240]

OLD JEWISH NEWSPAPERS FROM LATVIA – (Titles include: Dos Idise Folk; Libauer Folksblat etc. Enquire for detailed listing) – 7r set – 1 – $550.00 set – us Ross [072]

OLD JEWISH NEWSPAPERS FROM LITHUANIA *see* OVENT KURJER

OLD JEWISH NEWSPAPERS FROM LITHUANIA – (Individual titles also listed separately) – 50r coll – 1 – $3,500.00 coll – us Ross [072]

OLD JEWISH NEWSPAPERS FROM LITHUANIA *see*
- DI CAIT
- HEINTIGE NAIS
- VILNER RADIO

OLD JUDGE PRIEST / Cobb, Irvin S – New York: George H Doran Co, 1916 – 5mf – 9 – $7.50 – LLMC 92-142 – us L.L.M.C. [870]

OLD KASKASKIA / Catherwood, Mary Hartwell – Boston: Houghton, Mifflin, 1893. 00509. (Pre-1900 Canadiana) – 9 – cn C.I.H.M. [830]

OLD KENSINGTON / Thackeray, Anne – British Fiction Archive: Unit 3 – 9 – uk Bell [830]

OLD KENTUCKY ENTRIES & DEEDS – By Willard Jillson, 1926. Item J. Complete index to all of the earliest land entries, military warrants, deeds & wills of the Commonwealth of Lincoln, Fayette & Jefferson Cos., KY. Indexed by county. 571p. SW16-0028 – 5 – us A.G.L.L. [920]

AN OLD LANDMARK / Pendleton, J M – 1899 – 1 – 5.00 – us Baptist [240]

OLD LANDMARKISM, WHAT IS IT? / Graves, J R – 1880 – 1 – 10.08 – us Baptist [240]

OLD LANDMARKISM: WHAT IS IT? / Graves, J R – 1880 – 1 – us A.T.L.A. [240]

OLD LANDMARKS OF CANTON AND STARK COUNTY / Danner, John – Logansport: B. F. Bowen and Co., 1904. Ohio Reel 59. (The Cox Library Collection) – 5 – us Americana [978]

THE OLD LATIN AND THE ITALA / Burkitt, FC – 1896 – 2mf – 9 – ne Slangenburg [240]

OLD LIBERTY BAPTIST CHURCH. BEAVERDAM ASSOCIATION. MADISON, SOUTH CAROLINA : CHURCH RECORDS – 1818-54, 1869 – 1 – 7.38 – us Baptist [240]

Old Malton. Yorkshire *see* PARISH REGISTERS

THE OLD MAN'S DARLING: A SERIES OF CHARACTER SKETCHES / Garland, Bessie – Toronto: B. Garland, 1881. 03292. (Pre-1900 Canadiana) – 9 – cn C.I.H.M. [830]

AN OLD MAN'S LOVE / Trollope, Anthony – Edinburgh: Blackwood, 1884 – 1 roll – 1 – 1-55879-968-0 – uk Libr Preservation [830]

OLD MARGARET / Kingsley, Henry – British Fiction Archive: Unit 2 – 9 – uk Bell [830]

OLD MASTER AND CONTINENTAL DRAWINGS, WATERCOLOURS AND PRINTS – (12,000 images) – 71mf – 9 – $650.00 – 0-907006-08-6 – uk Mindata [700]

OLD MASTER, CONTINENTAL AND 19TH CENTURY PICTURES – (10,000 illustrations) – 95mf – 9 – $590.00 – 0-907006-03-5 – uk Mindata [700]

OLD MASTER PAINTINGS – (Over 45,000 reproductions, 5,500 artists) – 464mf – $2,550.00 – 1-900853-75-2 – uk Mindata [750]

OLD MASTER PAINTINGS AND DRAWINGS – (Over 7,000 reproductions) – 116mf – 9 – $725.00 – 0-907006-72-8 – uk Mindata [750]

OLD MASTERS DRAWINGS AT HOLKHAM HALL / Popham, A E – (138p accompanying text) – 1986 – 5mf – 9 – $150.00f – 0-226-69273-6 – Copubl by Oxford Microform Publications – us Chicago [740]

THE OLD MASTERS OF THE BLUEGRASS – By Samuel Woodson Price, 1902. Biog. sketches of six of Kentucky's most eminent artists. 5 fiches. F-0154 – 9 – us A.G.L.L. [920]

OLD MONTREAL WITH PEN AND PENCIL / Morin, Victor – Montreal, 1929. SEM105P785 – 1mf – 9 – Can$2.25 – cn Bibl Nat [971]

OLD NORTHWEST – v1- 1975- 1; v3- 5,6,9 – us UMI [978]

OLD PANTHER CREEK BAPTIST CHURCH. BLACKFORD ASSOCIATION. OHIO COUNTY. WHITESVILLE, KENTUCKY : CHURCH RECORDS – 1959-88 – 1 – 36.81 – us Baptist [240]

OLD PLANTATION HYMNS : A COLLECTION OF HITHERTO UNPUBLISHED MELODIES OF THE SLAVE AND THE FREEDMAN, WITH HISTORICAL AND DESCRIPTIVE NOTES / Barton, William E – Boston: Lamson, Wolffe, 1899 – 1mf – us A.T.L.A. [780]

OLD PORTLAND TODAY – Portland OR. Jan 1973-May 1 1975 – 1 – us U.O. Library [071]

THE OLD RABBINIC DOCTRINE OF GOD / Marmorstein, Arthur – (1: The Names and Attributes of God. London, 1927. 4mf; 2: Essays in Anthropomorphism. London, 1937. 3mf) – 8 – ne Slangenburg [270]

OLD REDSTONE...WESTERN PRESBYTERIANISM *see* AMERICAN PRESBYTERIANA 1

OLD SALEM BAPTIST CHURCH. LIVINGSTON, KENTUCKY : CHURCH RECORDS – 1805-1902 – 1 – 19.71 – us Baptist [240]

OLD SALINE BAPTIST CHURCH. RED RIVER ASSOCIATION. SALINE, LOUISIANA : CHURCH RECORDS – 1844-1880 – 1 – 14.67 – us Baptist [240]

OLD SCHOOL PRESBYTERIAN *see* ST. LOUIS PRESBYTERIAN

OLD SCHOOL SONNETS, OR A SELECTION OF CHOICE HYMNS / Osbourn, James – 1836 – 1 – 13.58 – us Baptist [810]

THE OLD SERVICE-BOOKS OF THE ENGLISH CHURCH / Wordsworth, Charles & Littlehales, H – 2nd ed. London, 1910 – 7mf – 8 – Dfl28.00 – ne Slangenburg [240]

THE OLD SERVICE-BOOKS OF THE ENGLISH CHURCH / Wordsworth, Charles & Littlehales, H – H 1350 2. 1904 – 8 – ne IDC [240]

OLD SETTLER CHEROKEE CENSUS ROLL, 1895, AND INDEX TO PAYMENT ROLL, 1896 / U.S. Bureau of Indian Affairs – 2 rolls.T985 – 1 – us Nat'l Archives [324]

THE OLD SHOWMAN AND THE OLD LONDON FAIRS / Frost, Thomas – A new ed. London: Chatto & Windus, 1881. 388p – 1 – us U.W. Library [390]

Old Slave Mart Museum and Library. Charleston, South Carolina *see* CATALOG OF THE OLD SLAVE MART MUSEUM AND LIBRARY

OLD SOUTH LEAFLETS – Boston. v1-9. n.d. – 3r – 1,9 – inquire – us Ross [978]

'OLD SPOOKSES' PASS": 'MALCOLM'S KATIE' AND OTHER POEMS / Crawford, Isabella Valancy – s.l.: s.n., 1844. 00026. (Pre-1900 Canadiana) – 9 – cn C.I.H.M. [810]

OLD SYRIAC ELEMENT IN THE TEXT OF CODEX BEZAE / Chase, Frederic Henry – London: Macmillan, 1893 – 9 – us A.T.L.A. [240]

THE OLD SYRIAC GOSPELS OR EVANGELION DA-MEPHARRESHE / Smith Lewis, A – 11mf – 8 – ne Slangenburg [220]

OLD TABERNACLE THEOLOGY FOR NEW TESTAMENT TIMES / Moore, Robert Braden – (Includes index) – Philadelphia: Presbyterian Bd of Publ, c1894 – 1mf – 9 – 0-8370-4478-2 – 1985-2478 – us A.T.L.A. [220]

THE OLD TESTAMENT AND MODERN LIFE / Brooke, Stopford Augustus – New York: Dodd, Mead, 1896 – 1mf – 9 – 0-8370-2466-8 – 1985-0466 – us A.T.L.A. [220]

OLD TESTAMENT AND SEMITIC STUDIES IN MEMORY OF W.R. HARPER / Harper, William Rainey – Ed. by R. F. Harper, F. Brown and G. Foot Moore. 2 v. Chicago. 1908. BNE-20,037 – 9 – ne IDC [220]

THE OLD TESTAMENT AND THE CHINESE CLASSICAL BOOKS (CCC285) = CHUNG-KUO CHUAN-TUNG WEN-HUA YU TIEN-CHU KU-CHIAO / Su, Hsueh-Lin – (In Chinese) – 2nd ed. [S.l.: s.n., 1957] – 1r – 1 – 1984-6624 – us A.T.L.A. [230]

THE OLD TESTAMENT AND THE NEW CRITICISM / Blomfield, Alfred – 1895 – 9 – us A.T.L.A. [240]

THE OLD TESTAMENT AND THE NEW SCHOLARSHIP / Peters, John John Punnett – New York: Macmillan, 1902. 1 fiche – 9 – us A.T.L.A. [240]

THE OLD TESTAMENT BACKGROUND FOR PAUL'S DOCTRINE OF THE RIGHTEOUSNESS OF GOD / Northcutt, Jesse J – 1947 – 1 – 11.56 – us Baptist [240]

OLD TESTAMENT CANON AND PHILOLOGY / Green, William Henry – Princeton: Press Printing, 1878 – 9 – us A.T.L.A. [240]

OLD TESTAMENT CHARACTERS (CCC256) / ed by Nieh, E C & Chang, Shao-ching – (In Chinese) – Hong Kong: Bible Book and Tract Depot, 1952 – 1r – 1 – 1984-6595 – us A.T.L.A. [220]

OLD TESTAMENT CRITICISM AND THE RIGHTS OF THE UNLEARNED / Kennedy, John – 1897 – 9 – us A.T.L.A. [220]

OLD TESTAMENT CRITICISM IN NEW TESTAMENT LIGHT / Rouse, George Henry – London: Religious Tract Society, 1905. 1 fiche – 9 – us A.T.L.A. [240]

OLD TESTAMENT DIFFICULTIES:...PAPERS WRITTEN FOR WORKING MEN / Winnington Ingram, Arthur F – London: S.P.C.K., 1900. 1 fiche – 9 – us A.T.L.A. [240]

OLD TESTAMENT ETHICS VINDICATED : BEING AN EXPOSITION OF OLD TESTAMENT MORALS,... / Jarrel, Willis Anselm – [Greenville, TX]: W A Jarrel, 1882 – 1mf – 9 – 0-8370-3773-5 – 1985-1773 – us A.T.L.A. [220]

OLD TESTAMENT FROM THE MODERN POINT OF VIEW / Batten, Loring Woart – New York: Edwin S. Gorham, 1901.1 fiche – 9 – us A.T.L.A. [240]

OLD TESTAMENT HISTORY (CCC65) / Chao, Tsung-fu – (In Chinese) – [s.l: s.n, 1938] – 1r – 1 – 1984-6404 – us A.T.L.A. [220]

OLD TESTAMENT HISTORY OF REDEMPTION : LECTURES / Delitzsch, Franz – Edinburgh:T. & T. Clark, 1881 – 1mf – 9 – 0-8370-2874-4 – 1985-0874 – us A.T.L.A. [220]

THE OLD TESTAMENT IN GREEK / Brooke, Alan E – 1906-40. 3v – 9 – $66.00 – us I.R.C. [220]

THE OLD TESTAMENT IN THE JEWISH CHURCH / Smith, William Robertson – 2nd ed. 1895 – 9 – us A.T.L.A. [220]

OLD TESTAMENT IN THE NEW / Gibson, Edgar CS – London: Wells, Gardner, 1907. 1 fiche – 9 – us A.T.L.A. [240]

THE OLD TESTAMENT IN THE NEW : A CONTRIBUTION TO BIBLICAL CRITICISM AND INTERPRETATION / Turpie, David McCalman – (Includes indexes) – Edinburgh: Williams and Norgate, 1868 – 1mf – 9 – 0-8370-5589-X – 1985-3589 – us A.T.L.A. [220]

THE OLD TESTAMENT IN THE NEW : THE WARBURTONIAN LECTURES FOR 1903-1907 / Gibson, Edgar Charles Sumner – London: Wells Gardner, Darton, c1907 – 1mf – 9 – 0-8370-3263-6 – 1985-1263 – us A.T.L.A. [220]

THE OLD TESTAMENT INTERPRETATION OF HISTORY / North, C R – Epworth. 1953 – 9 – $10.00 – us I.R.C. [220]

THE OLD TESTAMENT ITS OWN DEFENCE: BEING A REPLY TO "THE OLD TESTAMENT VINDICATED" / Cook, Joseph Simpson – Introduction by Rev. Principal Shaw. Toronto: W. Briggs; Montreal: C. Coates; Halifax, N.S.: S. Huestis, 1898. 00315. (Pre-1900 Canadiana) – 9 – cn C.I.H.M. [971]

OLD TESTAMENT LITERATURE: LECTURES ON THE POETICAL BOOKS OF THE OLD TESTAMENT / Green, William Henry – Princeton: E. Fitzgeorge, 1884. 1 fiche – 9 – us A.T.L.A. [220]

THE OLD TESTAMENT NARRATIVE / ed by Sheffield, Alfred Dwight – (Includes index) – Boston: Houghton, Mifflin, 1910 – 2mf – 9 – 0-8370-9823-8 – 1986-3823 – us A.T.L.A. [220]

OLD TESTAMENT PROPHECY: ITS WITNESS AS A RECORD OF DIVINE FOREKNOWLEDGE / Leathes, Stanley – London: Hodder & Stoughton, 1880. 1 fiche – 9 – us A.T.L.A. [240]

THE OLD TESTAMENT PROPHECY OF THE CONSUMMATION / Orelli, Conrad von – 1885 – 9 – $15.00 – us I.R.C. [220]

OLD TESTAMENT PROPHECY...AND NEW TESTAMENT FULFILMENT / Elliott, Charles – New York: A.C. Armstrong, 1889. 1 fiche – 9 – us A.T.L.A. [240]

OLD TESTAMENT REVISION : A HANDBOOK FOR ENGLISH READERS / Roberts, Alexander – (Includes bibliographical references and indexes) – New York:Charles Scribner, 1883 – 1mf – 9 – 0-8370-4917-2 – 1985-2917 – us A.T.L.A. [220]

OLD TESTAMENT SHADOWS OF NEW TESTAMENT TRUTHS / Abbott, Lyman – New York: Harper, 1870, c1869 – 1mf – 9 – 0-8370-9681-2 – 1986-3681 – us A.T.L.A. [220]

OLD TESTAMENT STORY : A MANUAL FOR TEACHERS OF YOUNG STUDENTS / Corbett, Charles H – (Includes index) – Chicago, IL: University of Chicago Press; New York: Baker & Taylor [distributor], 1912 – 1mf – 9 – 0-8370-9371-6 – 1986-3371 – us A.T.L.A. [220]

OLD TESTAMENT STUDIES : AN OUTLINE OF OLD TESTAMENT THEOLOGY / Foster, Robert Verrell – (Includes subject index) – Chicago:Fleming H. Revell, c1890 – 1mf – 9 – 0-8370-3170-2 – 1985-1170 – us A.T.L.A. [220]

OLD TESTAMENT THEOLOGY AND MODERN IDEAS / Girdlestone, Robert Baker – (Includes index of authors) – London, New York: Longmans, Green, 1909 – 1mf – 9 – 0-8370-3299-7 – 1985-1299 – us A.T.L.A. [220]

THE OLD TESTAMENT UNDER FIRE / Behrends, Adolphus Julius Frederick – New York: Funk & Wagnalls, 1897 – 1mf – 9 – 0-8370-2254-1 – 1985-0254 – us A.T.L.A. [220]

OLD TESTAMENT WORD STUDIES : AN ATTEMPT TO MAKE CLEAR TO THE READER OF THE ENGLISH BIBLE THE EXACT MEANING OF ONE HUNDRED AND SIXTY-FIVE HEBREW WORDS, ARRANGED IN GROUPS OF SYNONYMS / Butler, C E; ed by Maggs, Joseph Thomas Lawrence – New York: Abbey Press, c1902 – 1mf – 9 – 0-8370-9210-8 – 1986-3210 – us A.T.L.A. [220]

THE OLD THEOLOGY AND THE NEW : A DISCOURSE IN ALL SOUL'S CHURCH, NEW YORK / Bellows, Henry Whitney – New York:G P Putnam, 1878 – 1mf – 9 – 0-8370-2625-3 – 1985-0625 – us A.T.L.A. [210]

OLD TIME STUDENT VOLUNTEERS : MY MEMORIES OF MISSIONARIES / Trumbull, Henry Clay – New York: F.H. Revell, 1902 – 1mf – us A.T.L.A. [240]

OLD TRUTHS IN MODERN LIGHTS: THE BOYLE LECTURES FOR 1890 WITH OTHER SERMONS / Bonney, Thomas G – New York: James Pott, 1891. 1 fiche – 9 – us A.T.L.A. [240]

THE OLD VIC ARCHIVES IN THE UNIVERSITY OF BRISTOL THEATRE COLLECTION – 1990 – 1200mf – 9 – $5,600.00 – 0-8161-1761-6 – uk Hall [790]

OLD VINCENNES / Indiana – By Joseph Henry Vanderburgh Somes. 1962. Item I. Includes index, 243p. SW16-0092 – 5 – us A.G.L.L. [978]

OLD WALLED CITY OF SAN'A' / Lewcock, Ronald – 1986 – 132p – 9 – 92-3-102362-4 – fr UNESCO [910]
OLD WANG : THE FIRST CHINESE EVANGELIST IN MANCHURIA: A SKETCH OF HIS LIFE AND WORK, WITH A CHAPTER UPON NATIVE AGENCY IN CHINESE MISSIONS / Ross, John – London: Religious Tract Society, 1889 – 1mf – us A.T.L.A. [240]
OLD WAR INDEX TO PENSION FILES, 1815-1926 / U. S. Veterans Administration – 7rolls. T316 – 5 – us Nat'l Archives [324]
THE OLD WORLD AND THE NEW / Dewey, Orville – 2v. 1836 – 9 – us A.T.L.A. [240]
THE OLD YELLOW BOOK / Hodell, Charles W – (Source of Browning's The Ring and the Book. In complete photo-reproduction with translation, essay and notes) – 2nd ed. Washington: Carnegie Institution, 1908 – 7mf – 9 – $10.50 – LLMC 91-050 – us L.L.M.C. [340]
OLD YUKON TALES, TRAILS AND TRIALS / Wickersham, James – Washington, DC: Washington Law Book Co., 1938. Alaska Reel 1. (The Cox Library Collection) – 5 – us Americana [978]
Oldcastle, John *see* MEMORIALS OF CARDINAL MANNING
OLDEN TIME – 1-2. 1846-47 – 1 – us UMI [073]
OLDEN TIMES IN COLORADO / Davis, Carlyle C – Los Angeles: Phillips Publ. Co., 1916. Colorado Reel 1.(Cox Library Collection) – 5 – us Americana [978]
OLDENBURGER ZEITUNG – Oldenburg i.O., Germany. 1848 – 1r – 1 – gw Mikrofilm [072]
DER OLDENBURGISCHE VOLKSFREUND – Oldenburg i.O., Germany. 1849-Jun 1852 – 1r – 1 – gw Mikrofilm [072]
OLDENBURGISCHE VOLKSZEITUNG – Vechta, West Germany. 1976- – ca 9r per yr – 1 – gw Mikrofilm [072]
OLDEN-TIME MUSIC : A COMPILATION FROM NEWSPAPERS AND BOOKS / Brooks, Henry M – Boston: Ticknor, 1888, c1887. (Ye Olden time series; [7]) – 1mf – us A.T.L.A. [780]
Ol'derogge, D A *see* SUAKHILI-RUSSKII SLOVAR'
THE OLDEST DRAMA IN THE WORLD: THE BOOK OF JOB: ARRANGED IN DRAMATIC FORM / Walls, Alfred – New York: Hunt & Eaton, 1891. 1 fiche – 9 – us A.T.L.A. [240]
OLD-FASHIONED FAIRY TALES / Ewing, Juliana Horatia – British Fiction Archive: Unit 1 – 9 – uk Bell [830]
Oldfield, R AK *see* NARRATIVE OF AN EXPEDITION INTO THE INTERIOR OF AFRICA BY THE RIVER NIGER IN 1832-1834
DEN OLDFRANSKE HELTEDIGTNING / Nyrop, Kristoffer – 1883 – 1 – us I.U. Libraries [390]
OLDHAM EVENING CHRONICLE *see* EVENING CHRONICLE
Oldham, Joseph Houldsworth *see* STUDIES ON THE TEACHING OF JESUS: AS RECORDED IN THE SYNOPTIC GOSPELS
Oldham, W F *see* INDIA, MALAYSIA, AND THE PHILIPPINES
OLDIN – (In Icelandic) – Canada, Sept 1881-Feb 1892 – 1r – 1 – cn Commonwealth Micro [072]
Oldmixon, John *see* REFLECTIONS ON DR. SWIFT'S LETTER TO THE EARL OF OXFORD, ABOUT THE ENGLISH TONGUE
OLDS GAZETTE – Alberta, CN. 1921-25 – 2r – 1 – cn Commonwealth Micro [072]
Olds, Irving S *see* THE PRICE OF PRICE CONTROLS
THE OLD-TIME PARSON / Ditchfield, P H – London: Methuen; New York: E.P. Dutton [distributor], [1909] – 1mf – us A.T.L.A. [240]
OLD-TIME PRIMITIVE METHODISM IN CANADA, 1829-1884 / Hopper, R P – Toronto: William Briggs, 1904 – 1mf – us A.T.L.A. [240]
OLEAGINEUX – v.24-32. 1969-77 – 1,5,6 – 22161.00 – us Princeton Micro [540]
O'Leary, Daniel F *see* MEMORIAS DEL GENERAL O'LEARY
O'Leary, Walter-P *see* L'INDEPENDANCE
Olena Presbyterian Church (Bronson Township, Huron County, Ohio) *see* RECORDS
Olentangy. Ohio. Emmanuel Lutheran Church *see* RECORDS
DIE OLEWAGEN SAGA / Grimm, Hans – Muenchen: A Langen, 1928 – 1r – 1 – us U.W. Library [390]
DIE OLEWAGEN-SAGA / Grimm, Hans – 2. Aufl. der Feldpostausg. Gueterslоh: C Bertelsmann, 1943 – 1r – 1 – us U.W. Library [390]
Olgiati, Francesco *see*
– L'IDEALISMO DI GEORGIO, BERKELEY...
– SILLABARIO...
Olguin, Eduardo Fernandez *see* LOS ARCHIVOS DE SALTA Y JUJUY
O OLHO DA RUA – Curityba, 13 Apr 1907-Nov 1909; May-22 Nov 1911 – 1,5,6 – bl Biblioteca [072]
OLIA / Remizov, A – Paris, 1927. 345, (5)p. BR-831 2 – 8 – ne IDC [460]
LA OLIGARQUIA EN LA CRISIS DE LA ECONOMIA ARGENTINA / Guillen, Abraham – Buenos Aires: Comision Nacional de Homenaje a Lisandro de la Torre, 1956 – 1 – CSUXAHZ5812-B – us Hoover Inst Photo [320]
OLIGARQUIA Y PODER EN LA ARGENTINA / Cuneo, Dardo – Buenos Aires: Libreria Piloto, [1969?] – 1 – CSUXAD02781-B – us Hoover Inst Photo [972]
Oliger, L *see* DER PAEPSTLICHE ZEREMONIEN-MEISTER JOHANNES BURCKARD VON STRASSBURG 1450-1506
Oligny, Odette *see* CHIC
[OLIMPIADE] THE FAVORITE SONGS IN THE OPERA : WORDS BY METASTASIO / Gluck, Paisiello – London: Napier, 178- – 1 – us Sibley [780]
OLIMPICAS Y PITICAS (GRIEGO) (SIECLE 15) / Pindaro – Madrid – 1r – 5,6 – sp Cultura [090]
L'OLIMPINDE (PASTICCIO). THE FAVOURITE SONGS... / Bertoni, F – London: William Napier, [178-?] – 1 – us Sibley [780]
Olin *see* CENTENNIAL HISTORY OF AKRON 1825-1925
Olin, Oscar E *see* AKRON AND ENVIRONS: HISTORICAL BIOGRAPHICAL AND GENEALOGICAL
Olin, Stephen *see*
– GREECE AND THE GOLDEN HORN
– TRAVELS IN EGYPT, ARABIA, PETRAEA, AND THE HOLY LAND
OLINDE RODIGUES AUX SAINT-SIMONIENS / Rodrigues, O – 13 fevrier 1832. Paris, Everat, 13 p. LE DISCIPLE DE SAINT-SIMON AUX SAINT-SIMONIENS ET AU PUBLIC. S.1.n.d., 28 p. RELIGION SAINT-SIMONIENNE. Olindes Rodrigues a Michel Chevalier. (12-18 mars 1832). Paris, Lachevardiere, 8 p. Les Saint-Simoniens, 1825-1834. 6953 – 9 – fr Hachette [335]
THE OLIO – [Whitby, Ont.?]: Literary Society of the Whitby Collegiate Institute, [1885?-18– or 19–] – 9 – cn C.I.H.M. [370]
OLIPHANT : THE COLLECTED WRITINGS OF MARGARET OLIPHANT (1828-1897) – (Pt 1: 20r $2,400.00. Pt 2: 20r $2,400.00. Pt 3: 20r $2,400.00) – Marlborough: Adam Matthew Publications, 1995 – 1 – uk Matthew [420]
OLIPHANT : THE CORRESPONDENCE AND LITERARY MANUSCRIPTS OF MARGARET OLIPHANT (1828-1897) FROM THE NATIONAL LIBRARY OF SCOTLAND – Marlborough: Adam Matthew Publications, 1996 – 20r – 1 – $2,400.00 – uk Matthew [420]
Oliphant, Laurence *see* PICCADILLY
Oliphant, Margaret *see*
– A BELEAGUERED CITY
– THE LIFE OF EDWARD IRVING, MINISTER OF THE SCOTCH CHURCH, LONDON
– SALEM CHAPEL
Oliva de la Frontera *see*
– FERIAS Y FIESTAS
– FIESTAS DE SAN MARCOS. DESDE EL CERRO DE LA SALVE
– OLIVA DE LA FRONTERA EN FIESTAS. 1980
– REVISTA OFICIAL, DE FERIA
OLIVA DE LA FRONTERA EN FIESTAS. 1980 / Oliva de la Frontera – Jerez de los Caballeros: Imp. Moderna, 1980 – 1 – sp Bibl Santa Ana [390]
OLIVAER ZEITUNG – Danzig (Gdansk)-Oliva, Poland. 1927 – 2r – 1 – gw Mikrofilm [943]
Olivares del Valle, Francisco Javier *see* CONTRIBUCION AL ESTUDIO DE LOS VINAGRE DE VINO DE "TIERRA DE BARROS" Y ESTUDIO DE ALGUNOS COMPONENTES VOLATILES DE LOS MISMOS
Olivares, Miguel de, y otro *see* COLECCION DE HISTORIADORES DE CHILE
Olivart, R de *see* BIBLIOGRAPHIE DU DROIT INTERNATIONAL
Olivas y Frances, Francisco *see* DIVINO... GARCIA GOLFIN DE CARVAJAL. MANIFIESTO
OLIVE BRANCH – Boston, MA. v11 n2. 18 jul 1846-v13 n19. 11 nov 1848 – 1r – 1 – Can$40.00 – cn Can Microfilming [071]
OLIVE BRANCH – Freeport, PA., 1835 – 13 – $25.00r – us I.M.R. [071]
OLIVE BRANCH – Oliveburg, PA., 1834 – 13 – $25.00r – us I.M.R. [071]
OLIVE BRANCH – Sherburne, NY. 1806-1808; Olive Branch. Norwich, NY. 1808-1809; Republican Messenger. Sherburne, NY. 1810-1811. Sold as one unit – 3 – us Readex [071]
OLIVE BRANCH – Youngstown. Ohio. and New County Advocate. 1843-45 – 1 – us UMI [071]
THE OLIVE BRANCH – Montreal: A.T. Patterson, W.E. Fudger, [18–1882?] – 9 – cn C.I.H.M. [971]
THE OLIVE BRANCH : PETITION OF THE AMERICAN CONGRESS TO GEORGE 3, 1775 LETTERS OF THE AMERICAN ENVOYS, AUGUST-SEPTEMBER 1775 / U.S. Continental Congress – 1954 – 9 – $5.00f – us Ross [975]
OLIVE BRANCH BAPTIST CHURCH. LIVINGSTON ASSOCIATION. MISSOURI : CHURCH RECORDS – 1909-69 – 1 – 14.13 – us Baptist [240]
OLIVE BY-PRODUCTS FOR ANIMAL FEED – 1985 – 49p – it F.A.O. [636]
OLIVE CHAPEL BAPTIST CHURCH. APEX, NORTH CAROLINA : CHURCH RECORDS – 1850-1942 – 1 – 30.24 – us Baptist [240]
THE OLIVE LEAFE: OR, UNIVERSALL ABCE / Top, Alexander – 1603. 34p. (English Linguistics Series 1500-1800) – 9 – us UMI [400]
OLIVE OIL TECHNOLOGY – 1983 – 173p – it F.A.O. [660]
OLIVE PESTS AND THEIR CONTROL IN THE NEAR EAST – 1992 – 187p – it F.A.O. [590]
OLIVENCA / Matos Sequeira, Rocha – Lisboa: Portugalia editora, 1924 – 1 – sp Bibl Santa Ana [920]
OLIVENCA ILLUSTRADA...MARIA DA CRUZ / Torre, Joao de – 1747 – 9 – 1.50f – sp Bibl Santa Ana [240]
Olivenza *see*
– ESCUELAS PARROQUIALES EL SAGRADO CORAZON
– FERIA Y FEISTAS DE...AGOSTO 1970
Olivenza. Ayuntamiento *see* FERIAS Y FIESTAS DE AGOSTO. 1975
Olivenza. Escuelas Parroquiales Sagrado Corazon *see* MEMORIA DE...ANO 1979
Olivenza, Teleclub no 23 *see* FIESTAS PATRONALES EN LA BARRIADA DEL SAGRADO CORAZON...
Oliver, Alexander *see*
– A COLLECTION OF THE STATUTES OF PRACTICAL UTILITY, COLONIAL AND IMPERIAL, IN FORCE IN NEW SOUTH WALES
– IN DEFENCE OF THE FAITH
Oliver, Ann *see* TEST CASE ON THE ORDINATION OF WOMEN: APPEALED FROM THE NEW ENGLAND CONFERENCE TO GENERAL CONFERENCE
Oliver, Benjamin Lynde *see* PRACTICAL CONVEYANCING
OLIVER CROMWELL : HIS LIFE, TIMES, BATTLEFIELDS, AND CONTEMPORARIES / Hood, Paxton – London: Hodder and Stoughton, 1882 – 1mf – us A.T.L.A. [941]
Oliver, D *see* THE BOTANY OF THE SPEKE AND GRANT EXPEDITION
Oliver, D et al *see* FLORA OF TROPICAL AFRICA
Oliver, David D *see* CENTENNIAL HISTORY OF ALPENA COUNTY
OLIVER FAMILY PAPERS, 1419-1946 – Massachusetts Historical Society – 28r – 1 – $2105.00 – us UMI [920]
Oliver, G *see* MONASTICON DIOCOECIS EXONIENSIS
OLIVER OPTIC'S MAGAZINE. OUR BOYS AND GIRLS – v. 1-18. Jan 1867-Dec 1875 – 1 – us UMI [617]
Oliver, Vere Langford *see* THE HISTORY OF THE ISLAND OF ANTIGUA
THE OLIVER WENDELL HOLMES, JR. PAPERS / Holmes, Oliver Wendell, Jr – (Guide only $100.00) – 72r – 1 – $7,920.00 – 0-89093-803-2 – us UPA [340]
Oliveres, Luis *see* EL COLERA
OLIVER'S MAGAZINE – 1. Oct 1841 – 1 – us UMI [073]
Olivet, A *see* L'EVANGELISATION EN PAYS DE LANGUE FRANCAISE AU 19ME SIECLE
Olivet, P J d' *see*
– REMARQUES DE GRAMMAIRE SUR RACINE
– TRAITE DE LA PROSODIE FRANCOISE
OLIVETUM : ODER, DER OELBERG – LATEINISCHES EPOS / Gryphius, Andreas – Weimar: H Boehlau, 1862 – 1r – 1 – us U.W. Library [810]
Olivier, Aime, Vicomte de Sanderval *see* DE L'ATLANTIQUE AU NIGER PAR LE FOUTAH-DJALLON
OLIVIER, BELL AND FITZGERALD'S REPORTS OF CASES DECIDED IN THE COURT OF APPEAL AND THE SUPREME COURT OF NEW ZEALAND, 1878-79-80 – (Originally issued in separate pts) – Wellington: Lyon & Blair. 1v. 1880? – 5mf – 9 – $7.50 – LLMC 9-017 – us L.L.M.C. [340]
Olivier, H *see*
– FLORE ANALYTIQUE ET DICHOTOMIQUE DES LICHENS DE L'ORNE DEPARTMENT CIRCONVOISINS
– TABLEAUX ANALYTIQUES ET DICHOTOMIQUES DE TOUS LES GENRES ET ESPECES DE LICHENS DECRITS DANS LE LICHENOGRAPHIA SCANDINAVICA DE TH. M. FRIES
THE OLLA PODRIDA – [Halifax, N.S.?: s.n., 1899?-19–] – 9 – cn C.I.H.M. [971]
Ollard, Sidney Leslie *see*
– A DICTIONARY OF ENGLISH CHURCH HISTORY
– A SHORT HISTORY OF THE OXFORD MOVEMENT
Ollelaprune, Leon *see* LA RAISON ET LE RATIONALISME
Ollenhauer, Erich *see*
– ARBEITER-JUGEND
– DAS PROGRAMM DER OPPOSITION
– WIR BRAUCHEN EINE NEUE AUSSENPOLITIK
Ollero, Meliton *see* DISCURSO...APERTURA DE CURSO...CACERES
Ollier, Marie-Louise *see* LEXIQUE ET CONCORDANCES DE CHRETIEN DE TROYES D'APRES LA COPIE GUIOT
Ollivier, Charles P *see* DICTIONNAIRE HISTORIQUE DE LA MEDECINE ANCIENNE ET MODERNE (AEL, ABT 3;17)
Ollone, Charles-A *see* LES DERNIERS BARBARES
Olloqui, Emilio *see* ODAS A LA MUSICA
Olmedo, Alfaro *see* EL CANAL DE PANAMA EN LAS GUERRAS FUTURAS
Olmstead, Dwight Hinckley *see* THE PROTESTANT FAITH, OR, SALVATION BY BELIEF
Olmsted, Frederick Law *see*
– FREDERICK L. OLMSTED PAPERS
– SELECTED WORKS
OLNEY / Baptist Associations. Illinois – 1860-1987 – 1 – us Baptist [240]
THE OLNEY HYMNS AND A BAPTIST HYMN BOOK / Newton & Cowper – 1 – $36.89 – us Baptist [780]
Olnhausen, Gerd von *see* LAL BANGLA
Olofsson, Ulla Keding *see* MUSEUMS AND CHILDREN
OLOFSTROMS NYHETER *see* KARLSHAMNS ALLEHANDA
OLOGICAL COMET OR FIRE THINKING ENGLISHMAN – London, UK. 1819. -irr. 6 feet – 1 – uk British Libr Newspaper [072]
OLONETSKI SBORNIK : IZDANIE OLONETSKOGO GUBERNSKOGO STATISTICHESKOGO KOMITETA / ed by Ivanov, A & Blagoveshchenskii – Petrozavodsk. 4pts. 1875-[1902] – 20mf – 9 – RET-10/1 – ne IDC [947]
OLONETSKII KOOPERATOR – Petrozavodsk, 1918-20 n6 – 11mf – 9 – COR-662/1 – ne IDC [334]
Olozaga, Juan de *see* MAYOREZGO DE HERNANDO CORTES
OLPER INTELLIGENZ-BLATT *see* SAUERLAENDISCHES VOLKSBLATT
OLPER KREIS-BLATT *see* SAUERLAENDISCHES VOLKSBLATT
Olpin, Michael N *see* THE RELATIONSHIP OF SUBLIMINAL RELAXATION AFFIRMATIONS AND THE DEGREE OF RELAXATION ACHIEVED
Olrich, Tracy W *see* THE RELATIONSHIP OF MALE IDENTITY, THE MESOMORPHIC IMAGE, AND ANABOLIC STEROID USE IN BODYBUILDING
Olrik, Axel *see* KILDERNE TIL SAKSES OLDHISTORIE

Olschner, Gerhard Konrad *see* DER EINFLUSS EINES NEUEN 30 MM BALLONKATHETERS AUF CORONARARTERIENDISSEKTIONEN BEI PERKUTANTER TRANSLUMINALER CORONARANGIOPLASTIE IM VERGLEICH ZUM KONVENTIONELLEN 20 MM BALLONKATHETER
Olsen, Sandra Haller *see*
- FRENCH DRAWINGS AND SKETCHBOOKS OF THE NINETEENTH CENTURY, VOL 1
- FRENCH DRAWINGS AND SKETCHBOOKS OF THE NINETEENTH CENTURY, VOL 2
- FRENCH DRAWINGS OF THE SIXTEENTH AND SEVENTEENTH CENTURIES
- ITALIAN DRAWINGS OF THE 18TH AND 19TH CENTURIES AND SPANISH DRAWINGS OF THE 17TH THROUGH 19TH CENTURIES

Olshausen, Hermann *see* BIBLICAL COMMENTARY ON ST PAUL'S EPISTLES TO THE GALATIANS, EPHESIANS, COLOSSIANS, AND THESSALONIANS
Olshausen, Waldemar von *see* LESSINGS WERKE
Ol'shevskii, I *see* BOR'BA SO SHTUNDOI
Olson *see* HISTORY OF THE SWEDES OF ILLINOIS
Olson, Ernest W *see* THE SWEDISH ELEMENT IN ILLINOIS
Olson, Gary L *see* DRUG DESIGN AND DISCOVERY
Olson, KR *see* LEG LENGTH AND DISTANCE OF APPROACH STEPS FOR THE OPTIMAL SOCCER STYLE PLACEKICK
Olson, Linda K *see* THE RELATIONSHIP OF TASK AND EGO INVOLVEMENT TO SPORTSMANSHIP AND AGGRESSION TENDENDENCIES
Olson, Susan M *see* CALENDARING PRACTICES OF THE EASTERN DISTRICT OF NORTH CAROLINA
OLSSONS TIDNING – Vaernamo, 1990- – 9 – sw Kungliga [072]
Oltrogge, Jens *see* IN-VITRO-INFEKTION VON HUMANEN ENDOTHELZELLEN MIT ZYTOMEGALIEVIRUS
Olympe, Gouges d' *see* LE COUVENT OU LES VOEUX FORCES
OLYMPIAN – Olympia. Wash. 1891- – 1 – us UMI [071]
OLYMPIA-ZEITUNG : SOMMERSPIELE 1936 – Berlin. jul 21-aug 19, 1936 – 1r – 1 – gw Mikrofilm [790]
OLYMPIA-ZEITUNG : WINTERSPIELE 1936 – Berlin, feb 5-13/17 1936 – 1r – 1 – Inquire at Mikrofilmarchiv for details – gw Misc Inst [790]
OLYMPIC EDUCATION : BREAKING GROUND FOR THE 21ST CENTURY – (Series: United States Olympic Academy, 13) – Evergreen State College, 1989 – 4mf – 9 – $16.00 – us Microform Publ [790]
THE OLYMPIC IDEAL : 776 B.C. TO THE 21ST CENTURY – (Series: United States Olympic Academy, 4) – Indiana University at Bloomington, 1980 – 11mf – 9 – $44.00 – us Microform Publ [790]
OLYMPIC TRIBUNE – Port Angeles. Wash. -w. 1918-24, 1932-44 – 1 – us UMI [071]
OLYMPIC USA : A TEAM EFFORT – (Series: United States Olympic Academy, 15) – Colorado State University, 1989 – 3mf – 9 – $12.00 – us Microform Publ [790]
THE OLYMPICS : SERVING ALL PEOPLE AND ALL NATIONS – (Series: United States Olympic Academy, 11) – Indianapolis, Indiana, 1987 – 4mf – 9 – $16.00 – us Microform Publ [790]
OLYMPISM : A COMMITMENT TO A BETTER WORLD TOMORROW THROUGH SPORT – (Series: United States Olympic Academy, 9) – State University of New York, Pittsburg, 1985 – 3mf – 9 – $12.00 – us Microform Publ [790]
OLYMPISM : A MOVEMENT OF THE PEOPLE – (Series: United States Olympic Academy, 7) – Texas Tech University, 1983 – 5mf – 9 – $20.00 – us Microform Publ [790]
OLYMPISM, THE OLYMPIC GAMES AND THE WORLDWIDE OLYMPIC MOVEMENT – (Series: United States Olympic Academy, 10) – U.S. Olympic Complex, Colorado Springs, 1986 – 5mf – 9 – $20.00 – us Microform Publ [790]
OM ALGEVEGETATIONEN VED FAEROERNES KYSTER / Boergesen, FC E – Kobenhavn, Kristiania, 1904 – [2], 122, [4]p, 12pls – 8 – ne IDC [580]
OM BEGREBET IRONI : MED STADIGT HENSYN TIL SOCRATES / Kierkegaard, Soren – Kjobenhavn: P.G. Philipsen, 1841 – 1mf – us A.T.L.A. [190]
OM BEVISEN FOER GUDS VERKLIGHET / Edfeldt, Hans – (In Swedish.) – Upsala: Almqvist & Wiksells, 1897 – 1mf – 9 – 0-8370-3026-8 – 1985-1026 – us A.T.L.A. [210]
OM BEVISEN FOR GUDS VERKLIGHET / Edfeldt, Hans – Upsala: Almqvist & Wiksells, 1897. 1 fiche – 9 – us A.T.L.A. [240]
OM CHARACEERNAS KNOPPAR OCH OEFVERINTRING / Wahlstedt, L J – Lund. 1864. B-6415 2 – 8 – ne IDC [580]
OM DE SKANDINAVISKA ARTENA AF LAFSLAGTENA SCHISMATOMMA, OPEGRAPHA OCH BACTROSPORA / Almqvist, S – Upsala. 1869. B-6501 2 – 8 – ne IDC [590]
OM DET RELIGIOSE I DETS ENHED MED DET HUMANE : ET POSITIVT SUPPLEMENT TIL "PROBLEMET OM TRO OG VIDEN" / Brochner, H – Kjobenhavn: P.G. Philipsen, 1869 – 1mf – us A.T.L.A. [240]
OM DYAEFWLSENS FRAESTILSE. JOHANNES FABRI / Gerson, J – 87 2. 1495 – 9 – ne IDC [999]
OM ESKIMOERNES HERKOM AARBOG FOR NORDISK OLDKYNDIGHED / Rink, H J – BN 373 2. 1871 – 8 – ne IDC [305]
OM ESKIMOKULTURENS OPRINDELSE / Steensby, H P – BN 399 2. 1905 – 8 – ne IDC [306]
OM ET LANGTIDSPROGRAM FOR 1954-1957 / Norway – Oslo. 1953 – 9 – ne IDC [338]
OM GILTIGHETEN AF UTOMLANDS INGANGNA AEKTENSKAP / Hellner, J – Stockholm, 1896 – 1mf – 1 – ILM-3557/1 – ne IDC [327]
OM INDIANSKA KRASSENS BLICKANDE / Linnaea, E C – With additions of Carolus Linnaeus and H. C. Wilcke. 1762. B-6141 2 – 8 – ne IDC [580]
OM KALLORNA TILL 1526 ARS OFVERSATTNING AF NYA TESTAMENTET / Stave, Erik – Upsala: Almqvist & Wiksell, 1893. 1 fiche – 9 – us A.T.L.A. [240]
OM KALLORNA TILL 1541 ARS OFVERSATTNING AF NYA TESTAMENTET / Stave, Erik – Upsala: Almqvist & Wiksell, 1896. 1 fiche – 9 – us A.T.L.A. [240]
OM NOGLE RELIGIONSFILOSOFISKE ARBEJDER FRA DEN NYESTE TID / Hoffding, Harald – Kjobenhavn: Universitetsbogtrk., 1903. 1 fiche – 9 – us A.T.L.A. [240]
OM RICHARD WAGNER OG HANS TANNHAEUSER / Forchhammer, Ejnar – Kobenhavn: Gyldendalske Boghandel, Nordisk Forlag, 1910 – 1r – 1 – us U.W. Library [790]
OM UTVECKLINGEN AF MOLLUSCA ACEPHALA / Loven, S L – Z-632 2. 1849 – 8 – ne IDC [590]
OM VERKAN AF UTLAENDSK STRAFFDOM / Ehrensvaerd, A – Lund, 1895 – 2mf – 1 – ILM-2581/1 – ne IDC [327]
OMAHA ARROW – Omaha, NE. -irr. Jul-Dec 1854 – 1 – us NE Hist [071]
OMAHA BEE-NEWS – Omaha, NE. -d. Morning ed. Dec 1872-Oct 1879, scattered issues missing; May 1880-Sept 1937 – 1 – us NE Hist [071]
OMAHA DAILY HERALD – Omaha, NE. Jan 1866; Jan-Dec 1867; Mar 1868-Jan 1869; Sept 1870; Jan-Nov 1871; Jan 1873-Jul 1889 – 1 – us NE Hist [071]
OMAHA DAILY NEBRASKIAN – Omaha, NE. Dec 1859-Jan 1860; Sep-Nov 1860; Feb-Aug 1861; Jan 1863 – 1 – us NE Hist [071]
OMAHA DAILY NEWS – Omaha, NE. May 1878-Jun 1880 – 1 – us NE Hist [071]
OMAHA DAILY NEWS – Omaha, NE. Oct 1899-Sep 1902; Nov 1902-May 1906; Jul-Dec 1906; Mar 1907-Feb 1927 – 1 – us NE Hist [071]
OMAHA DAILY NEWS-REPUBLICAN – Omaha, NE. Aug-Dec 1895; Feb-Mar 1896 – 1 – us NE Hist [071]
OMAHA DAILY UNION – Omaha, NE. Jan-Oct 1874 – 1 – us NE Hist [071]
OMAHA EVENING BEE-NEWS – Omaha, NE. -d. May 1872-Oct 1874; Jan 1875-Sep 1937 – 1 – us NE Hist [071]
OMAHA EVENING DISPATCH – Omaha, NE. -d. Jun 1883-Apr 1885 – 1 – us NE Hist [071]
OMAHA EXCELSIOR – Omaha, NE. -w. Oct 1884-Apr 1887, scattered issues missing; Sep 1891-Dec 1892; Jan 1893-Apr 1894, scattered issues missing; Sep 1895-Dec 1915; Aug 1916; Dec 1917-Dec 1921 – 1 – us NE Hist [071]
OMAHA GUIDE – Omaha, NE. -w. Jul 1932-Feb 1936; Sep 1936-Apr 1940; Jul 1940-Mar 1947; Apr 1954; May 1955-Mar 1957; Jul-Oct 1957; Mar 1958 – 1 – us NE Hist [071]
THE OMAHA GUIDE – Omaha. Neb. sept. 21, 1940; Nov. 29, 1941; Feb. 14, 1942 – 1 – us NY Public [071]
OMAHA MERCURY – Omaha, NE. -w. Feb 1873-Aug 1890, scattered issues missing; Nov 1891-Dec 1900; May 1901-Jul 1906 – 1 – us NE Hist [071]
OMAHA MONITOR – Omaha, NE. -w. Jul 1915-Jan 1929 – 1 – us NE Hist [071]
OMAHA NEBRASKIAN – Omaha, NE. -w. Nov 1855; Jan 1856-Dec 1858; Feb 1859-Dec 1860 – 1 – us NE Hist [071]
OMAHA POSTEN – Omaha, NE. -w. Sep-Dec 1890; Aug 1891-Jan 1954 – 1 – us NE Hist [071]
OMAHA PUBLIC LEDGER – Omaha, NE. -w. Feb 1954-Apr 1959; Oct 1960-Nov 1968 – 1 – us NE Hist [071]
OMAHA REPUBLICAN – Omaha, NE. -d. Jan 1864-Mar 1874, scattered issues missing; Jul 1874-Oct 1879; Dec 1879-Jun 1881; Aug-Nov 1881; Jan 1882-Jun 1886; Sep 1886-Jul 1890 – 1 – us NE Hist [071]
OMAHA STAR – Omaha, NE. -w. Jul-Sep 1938; Mar 1940; May 1940 to date – 1 – us NE Hist [071]
OMAHA SVENSKA TRIBUN – Omaha, NE. -w. 29 Nov 1889-29 Jan 1892. In Swedish – 1 – us NE Hist [071]
OMAHA: THE GATE CITY AND DOUGLAS COUNTY / Wakeley, Arthur C – Chicago: S.J. Clarke Publ. Co., 1917. 2v. Nebraska Reel 8. (The Cox Library Collection) – 5 – us Americana [978]
OMAHA TIMES – Omaha, NE. -w. Jun 1857-Mar 1859 – 1 – us NE Hist [071]
OMAHA TRI-WEEKLY NEBRASKA REPUBLICAN – Omaha, NE. Jan 1862-Jan 1864, scattered issues missing – 1 – us NE Hist [071]
OMAHA WEEKLY HERALD – Omaha, NE. Oct 1865-Dec 1888 – 1 – us NE Hist [071]
OMAHA WEEKLY REPUBLICAN – Omaha, NE. (-tw 1862-64). Nov 1859-Nov 1860; Feb-Oct 1861, scattered issues missing; Jan 1862-Jul 1863; Sep 1863; Nov 1863-Dec 1883 – 1 – us NE Hist [071]
OMAHA WEEKLY TRIBUNE – Omaha, NE. Aug 1870-Jun 1871 – 1 – us NE Hist [071]
OMAHA WEEKLY WORLD HERALD – Omaha, NE. Jul 1889-Sep 1891; Dec 1891; Mar-Aug 1892; Nov 1892-Oct 1894, scattered issues missing; Mar-Oct 1895; Jan 1896; Apr 1896-Apr 1898; Nov 1898 – 1 – us NE Hist [071]
OMAHA WORLD HERALD – Omaha, NE. -d. Morning ed. Oct-Dec 1889; Apr 1890 to date – 1 – us NE Hist [071]
OMAHA WORLD-HERALD – Omaha, NE. -d. Evening ed. Aug 1885-Aug 1888; Jan-Dec 1889; Jan 1968 to date – 1 – us NE Hist [071]
O'Mahony, Frank *see* RURAL DAIRY TECHNOLOGY
O'Malley, Lewis Sydney Steward *see* SARAN
Oman *see* AL-JARIDAH AL-RASMIYAH
Oman, R F *see* EFFICACY COGNITIONS, INTRINSIC MOTIVATION, AND EXERCISE BEHAVIOR
O'Mara, C M *see* VALIDITY OF TECHNIQUES FOR MEASURING BLOOD CHOLESTEROL WITH THE REFLOTRON
L'OMBRE DU BEFFROI. / Lacerte, E A Bourgeois – Montreal: Ed. E Garand, c.1925. SEM105P68 – 2mf – 9 – Can$4.50 – cn Bibl Nat [830]
L'OMBRE D'URBAIN GRANDIER DE LOUDUN – 1634 – 9 – fr Hachette [360]
OMBRES ET LUMIERES : EXTRAIT DU JOURNAL D'UNE INSTITUTRICE, MISSIONAIRE AU ZAMBEZE, 1913-1919 / Kuntz, Marthe – 2. ed. Paris: Spciete des missions evangeliques, 1925 – us Res Libr [360]
L'OMBUDSMAN – (Cont by: Echo Laval. Cont by: L'Observateur) – Laval, Canada. 23 nov 1966-27 jan 1967 – 1r – 1 – Can$30.00 – cn Can Microfilming [072]
L'OMBUDSMAN *see* ECHO LAVAL
THE OMBUNDSMAN : A PRIMER FOR FEDERAL AGENCIES / Anderson, David R & Hill, Larry B – Washington: GPO, 1991 (all publ) – 1mf – 9 – $1.50 – LLMC 94-341 – us L.L.M.C. [340]
O'Meara, Kathleen *see* A HEROINE OF CHARITY AND A QUEEN BY RIGHT DIVINE
OMEGA : THE INTERNATIONAL JOURNAL OF MANAGEMENT SCIENCE – v1- 1973- – 5,6,9 – us UMI [650]
OMEGA *see* HEALTH
O-MEI HSIEN-CHIH – 1813, 10, 1. BCH-757a – 8 – ne IDC [950]
OMEO STANDARD – 1921-1928. OS1-7 – 7r – 1 – at Corangamite [072]
OMER – Tel Aviv. 1951- Available: 1960-76. BJ-91-101 3 – 9 – ne IDC [956]
UNA OMISION EN LA POLEMICA FORNERIANA : RAFAEL DE FLORANES / Garcia Salinero, Fernando – Badajoz: Imp. Dip. Provincial, 1966. Sep. REE – sp Bibl Santa Ana [946]
OMKRING SPROGTEORIENS GRUNDLAEGGELSE / Hjeimslev, L – Kobenhavn. 1943. B-1113 2 – 8 – ne IDC [400]
OMLADINA – Belgrade, Yugoslavia. 4 Nov 1944; Jul 1945-1955 – 7r – 1 – us L of C Photodup [949]
Ommer, Beduja *see* WANDEL DER KLINISCHEN PAEDIATRIE, DARGESTELLT AM STATIONAERN KRANKENGUT DER LANDESKINDERKLINIK KOHLHOF IN DEN JAHREN 1963-1977
Ommerborn, Rainer *see* PROFESSIONELLES BEWUSSTSEIN VON GEWERBE- UND GYMNASIALLEHRAMTSKANDIDATEN IN DER ERSTEN AUSBILDUNGSPHASE
OMNES FERE TITULI TAM IURIS CIVILIS... / Lopez de Tovar, Gregorio – Valladolid: Diego Fernandez de Cordova, 1588 – 1 – sp Bibl Santa Ana [946]
OMNES FERE...LEGUNTUR / Lopez de Tovar, Gregorio – (1588. 1.50f; 9) – 1611 – 9 – 1.50f – sp Bibl Santa Ana [946]
OMNES UNUM – v1-15. May 1931-Dec 1945 (complete) – 2r – 1 – ATLA S0487 – us A.T.L.A. [073]
OMNIA LATINA SCRIPTA... / Flacius Illyricus d.A E, M – [Magdeburgae, 1550] – 6mf – 9 – ne IDC [240]
L'OMNIBUS – Montreal, Canada. 4 jul-31 oct 1860 – 1r – 1 – Can$30.00 – cn Can Microfilming [072]
L'OMNIBUS – Quebec, Canada. 14 aut-18 sep 1869 – 1r – 1 – Can$25.00 – cn Can Microfilming [072]
OMNIBUS – Sao Paulo, Brazil. Dec 1872-Feb 1874 – 1 – bl Biblioteca [072]
THE OMNIBUS – St. Catherines [Ont.]: T. Stumps, [1857-18–?], v1 no 1 (Dec 18 1857)- – 9 – cn C.I.H.M. [072]
OMNIBUS COPYRIGHT REVISION: LEGISLATIVE HISTORY / ed by Grossman, George S – (Includes C.O. studies, all published hearings and reports of the Senate and House, as well as drafts and reports submitted by the C.O. Micro) – v1-17. 1960-76 – 9 – $445.00 set – us Hein [324]
L'OMNIBUS DU LANGAGE / Barthelemy, P – 1839 – 9 – fr I.C.S. [400]
LES OMNIBUS DU LANGAGE / Levi-Alvares, D & Marie, C L – 1842 – 9 – fr I.C.S. [400]
THE OMNIPRESENCE OF THE DEITY : A POEM / Montgomery, Robert – London: S. Maunder, 1828 – 1 roll – 1 – 1-55879-673-8 – uk Libr Preservation [810]
OMNIUM GATHERUM – 1. Nov 1809-Oct 1810 – 1 – us UMI [073]
OMNIUM OPERUM DIUI EUSEBII HIERONYMI STRIDONENSIS / Hieronymus, Saint – 1516. 9v. in 5 – 1 – us A.T.L.A. [240]
Omont, H *see* MINIATURES DES PLUS ANCIENS MANUSCRITS GRECS... DU 6E AU 14E SIECLE...
Ompteda, DH L *see* LITTERATUR DES GESAMMTEN SOWOHL NATUERLICHEN ALS POSITIVEN VOELKERRECHTS
Ompteda, Georg, Freiherr von *see*
- AUS GROSSEN HOEHEN
- DENISE DE MONTMIDI

OMR : ORGANIC MAGNETIC RESONANCE – (1982- 5,6,9) – v1- 1969- – 1 – us UMI [621]
OMS: ORGANIC MASS SPECTROMETRY – (1982-. 1,5,6,9) – v1-. 1968- – 1 – us UMI [073]
OMS (ORIENTAL MISSIONARY STANDARD) OUTREACH – (Lacking some early issues. Title varies) – v1-74. 1902-75 – 9r – 1 – ATLA S0290 – us A.T.L.A. [073]
Omsk. Siberia. (Province). Upravlenie vnutrennikh Arkhivnyi otdel'. del' *see* REVOLIUTSIONNOE DVIZHENIE V OMSKE V GODY PERVOI RUSSKOI REVOLIUTSII 1905-1907

OMSTAENDELIG OG UDFORLIG RELATION ANGAAENDE DEN GRONLANDSKE MISSIONS BEGYNDELSE OG FORTSAETTELSE SAMT HVAD ELLERS MERE DER / Egede, P – Kjobenhavn. 1738. BH-471 2 – 8 – ne IDC [430]

ON A COLLECTION OF SIERRA LEONE LEPIDOPTERA / Schaus, W & Clements, W G – London, 1893. vi,46p. 3 pls. Z-1603/2 – 8 – ne IDC [590]

ON A FRESH REVISION OF THE ENGLISH NEW TESTAMENT / Lightfoot, Joseph Barber – (Includes bibliographical references, appendix on the Greek words epiousios and periousios and indexes of biblical passages and topical subjects) – 3rd ed. London, New York: Macmillan, 1891 – 1mf – 9 – 0-8370-4125-2 – 1985-2125 – us A.T.L.A. [220]

ON A NEW OR HITHERTO UNRECOGNIZED GEOLOGICAL HORIZON IN THE GAS AND OIL REGION OF WESTERN ONTARIO / Ami, Henry Marc – Montreal, 1899. 00797. (Pre-1900 Canadiana) – 9 – cn C.I.H.M. [550]

ON A SYRIAC MS. BELONGING TO THE COLLECTION OF ARCHBISHOP USSHER / Gwynn, John – Dublin: Royal Irish Academy, 1886. 1 fiche – 9 – us A.T.L.A. [240]

ON ACTORS AND THE ART OF ACTING / Lewes, George Henry – London: Smith, Elder, 1875 – 1 roll – 1 – 1-55879-567-7 – uk Libr Preservation [790]

ON ANABAPTISM, THE INDEPENDENTS, AND QUAKERISM / ed by Bennett, W J E – London: J.T. Hayes, [1867?] (The church's broken unity / edited by W.J.E. Bennet; v2) – 1mf – us A.T.L.A. [240]

ON ANTI-RELIGION (CCC124) = FEI TSUNG-CHIAO TA-T'UNG-MING – (In Chinese) – [s.l.: s.n, 1922] – 1r – 1 – 1984-B500 – us A.T.L.A. [210]

ON BOARD THE "ROCKET" / Adams, Robert Chamblet – Boston: D. Lothrop Co., c1879. 00871. (Pre-1900 Canadiana) – 9 – cn C.I.H.M. [971]

ON BUYING A JOB, THE REGULATION OF TAXI CABS IN CANBERRA / Swan, Peter L – 2fiches (29x) – 9 – 1.00f – at Libertarian Micro [320]

ON CAMPUS WITH WOMEN – v1- 1971- 1; v8- 5,6; 1976- 9 – us UMI [073]

ON CHLOROFORM AND OTHER ANAESTHETICS: THEIR ACTION AND ADMINISTRATION / Snow, J; ed by Richardson, B W – M 153. 1858 – 9 – ne IDC [615]

ON COLOURED BOOKS FOR CHILDREN / Welsh, Charles – Read before the Sette...Friday, May 6th, 1887. With a catalogue of the books exhibited. London: Bror. C.W.H. Wyman, 1887. 255 copies for private circulation – 1 – us U.W. Library [070]

ON COMMUNICATIONS – v1-3. 1984-86 – 1,5,6,9 – us UMI [380]

ON COMPUTING – v.1-. Sum 1979- – 1,5,6,9 – us UMI [073]

ON CRYSTAL FORMATION OF THE ELEMENTS AND THEIR ALLOTROPIC MODIFICATIONS: WITH DEDUCTION OF THE ATOMIC FORMS THEREFROM / Addison, William L T – Toronto?: s.n., 1898 (Toronto: Mail Job). 02392. (Pre-1900 Canadian) – 9 – cn C.I.H.M. [530]

ON DISEASES OF THE LIVER / Budd, G – M-43. 1845 – 9 – ne IDC [616]

ON EUROPEAN SPIDERS / Thorell, T T T – Z 2203 2. 1869-1870 – 8 – ne IDC [590]

ON FORAMINIFERA FROM THE GULF AND RIVER ST LAWRENCE / Dawson, George M – s.l.: s.n., 1870?. 02360. (Pre-1900 Canadiana) – 9 – cn C.I.H.M. [550]

ON GRAMMATICAL CATEGORIES IN INDONESIAN / Muliono, Anton Mudardo – (Thesis). SE-5000 1. 1965 – 9 – ne IDC [490]

ON GRANDFATHER'S FARM / Frechette, Annie Thomas – Philadelphia: American Baptist Publication Society, c1897. 00153. (Pre-1900 Canadiana) – 9 – cn C.I.H.M. [830]

ON HEROES, HERO WORSHIP AND THE HEROIC IN HISTORY : REPORTED, WITH EMENDATIONS AND LECTURES / Carlyle, Thomas – London: James Fraser, 1841 – 1 roll – 1 – 1-55879-443-3 – uk Libr Preservation [390]

ON HOLY SCRIPTURE AND CRITICISM: ADDRESSES AND SERMONS / Ryle, Herbert Edward – London: Macmillan, 1904.1 fiche – 9 – us A.T.L.A. [240]

ON INDIAN OOLOGY / Theobald, W – Z 296 2. 1855 – 8 – ne IDC [590]

ON JURISPRUDENCE... / Harrison, F – Oxford, 1919 – 2mf – 1 – ILM-545/1 – ne IDC [327]

On, Lan *see* FAR ABOVE RUBIES (CCC257)

ON LIBERTY / Mill, John Stuart – 1fiche (29x) – 9 – 1.00f – at Libertarian Micro [320]

ON LIBERTY / Mill, John Stuart – 3rd ed. London: Longman, Green, Longman, Roberts and Green, 1864 – 207p – 1 – us U.W. Library [190]

ON MASKS, LABRETS, AND CERTAIN ABORIGINAL CUSTOMS / Dall, W H – BN 188 2. 1884 – 8 – ne IDC [306]

ON MEGRIM, SICKHEADACHE AND SOME ALLIED DISORDERS : A CONTRIBUTION TO THE PATHOLOGIE OF NERVE-STORMS / Liveing, E – London, 1873 – 10mf – 9 – ne IDC [616]

ON METHODISM AND THE SWEDENBORGIANS / ed by Bennett, W J E – London: J.T. Hayes, [1867?] (The church's broken unity / edited by W.J.E. Bennet; v3) – 1mf – us A.T.L.A. [240]

ON MIRACLES AND MODERN SPIRITUALISM: THREE ESSAYS / Wallace, Alfred Russel – London: James Burns, 1875. 1 fiche – 9 – us A.T.L.A. [240]

ON MISSIONS: A LECTURE / Mueller, Friedrich Max – New York: Scribner, Armstrong, 1874. 77p. 1 fiche – 9 – us A.T.L.A. [240]

ON NEW HUMAN RELATIONS / Werkheiser, Don – p. 491-498. 1 fiche (29x) – 9 – 1.00f – at Libertarian Micro [320]

ON NEW LICHENS FROM AUSTRALIA AND NEW ZEALAND / Shirton, J – (Transact. New Zealand Institute. v. 30, p. 382-393, 1897; v. 32, p. 70-82, 1899). B-340 2 – 8 – ne IDC [580]

ON PAPAL INFALLIBILITY : OPPORTUNE OR INOPPORTUNE?: WHAT DO YOU THINK OF IT? / Weninger, Francis Xavier – Baltimore: Kreuzer, 1870 – 1mf – 9 – 0-8370-6862-2 – 1986-0862 – us A.T.L.A. [240]

ON POISONS IN RELATION TO MEDICAL JURISPRUDENCE AND MEDICINE / Taylor, Alfred S – 2nd Am ed. Philadelphia: Blanchard & Lea, 1859 – 8mf – 9 – $12.00 – LLMC 92-109 – us L.L.M.C. [340]

ON PRESBYTERIANISM AND IRVINGISM / ed by Bennett, W J E – London: J.T. Hayes, [1867?] (The church's broken unity / edited by W.J.E. Bennet; v1) – 1mf – us A.T.L.A. [240]

ON RELIGIOUS LIBERTY IN RUSSIA : OPEN LETTER TO THE HEAD OF THE RUSSIAN SYNOD, PRIVY COUNCILLOR CONSTANTINE POBIEDONOSIEFF / Dalton, Hermann – Leipzig: Duncker & Humblot, 1890 – 1mf – us A.T.L.A. [240]

ON ROMANISM / ed by Bennett, W J E – London: J.T. Hayes, [1867?] (The church's broken unity / edited by W.J.E. Bennett; v4-5) – 2mf – us A.T.L.A. [240]

ON SCENE – 1973- 1; 1974- 5,6; 1975- 4 x 6 in. 9 – us UMI [073]

ON SELF-CULTURE : INTELLECTUAL, PHYSICAL, AND MORAL: A VADE MECUM FOR YOUNG MEN AND STUDENTS / Blackie, John Stuart – Edinburgh: Edmonston and Douglas, 1874 – 1mf – us A.T.L.A. [240]

ON SNOW-SHOES TO THE BARREN GROUNDS / Whitney, C – BN 451 2. 1896 – 8 – ne IDC [910]

ON SOME DYKES CONTAINING HURONITE / Barlow, Alfred Ernest – Ottawa?, 1894. 03367. (Pre-1900 Canadiana) – 9 – cn C.I.H.M. [550]

ON SOME INFLUENCES OF CHRISTIANITY UPON NATIONAL CHARACTER : THREE LECTURES DELIVERED IN ST. PAUL'S CATHEDRAL FEBRUARY 4TH, 11TH, AND 18TH, 1873 / Church, R W – London: Macmillan, 1873 – 1mf – us A.T.L.A. [240]

ON SOME PECULIARITIES OF THE ESKIMO DIALECT / Dall, W H – BN 184 2. 1871 – 8 – ne IDC [490]

ON THE ADVANCEMENT OF THE NATURAL SCIENCES THROUGH MINISTERS OF THE CHRISTIAN CHURCH / Mueller, Ferdinand Jakob Heinrich von – Melbourne, etc. 1877. B-8068 1 – 9 – ne IDC [500]

ON THE ALLEGED OBSCURITY OF PROPHECY / Stuart, Moses – The Biblical Repository, v. 2, no. 6, April 1832, p. 217-245) – 9 – us A.T.L.A. [240]

ON THE ALTERNATION OF GENERATIONS / Steenstrup, J J S – Ray Society. 1845 – 1. 16.00; ; 7 – uk Microform Academic [580]

ON THE APOSTOLICAL AND INFALLIBLE AUTHORITY OF THE POPE, WHEN TEACHING THE FAITHFUL = APOSTOLISCHE VOLLMACHT DES PAPSTES IN GLAUBENS-ENTSCHEIDUNGEN : AND ON HIS RELATION TO A GENERAL COUNCIL / Weninger, Francis Xavier – (In English. Later ed issued under title: Die Unfehlbarkeit des Papstes als Lehrer der Kirche) – New York: D & J Sadlier; Cincinnati: John P Walsh, 1868 – 1mf – 9 – 0-8370-6863-0 – 1986-0863 – us A.T.L.A. [240]

ON THE APPLICATION OF PHYTOLOGY TO THE INDUSTRIAL PURPOSES OF LIFE / Mueller, Ferdinand Jakob Heinrich von – Melbourne. 1870. B-8069 1 – 9 – ne IDC [631]

ON THE ASCLEPIADEAE / Brown, Robert – (Memoirs of the Wernerian Society, v. 1, 1811). London. 1810. B-5863 2 – 8 – ne IDC [580]

ON THE AUTHORIZED VERSION OF THE NEW TESTAMENT : IN CONNEXION WITH SOME RECENT PROPOSALS FOR ITS REVISION / Trench, Richard Chenevix – (Includes indexes) – 2nd rev enl ed. London: John W Parker, 1859 – 1mf – 9 – 0-8370-9192-6 – 1986-3192 – us A.T.L.A. [220]

ON THE BOOK OF JONAH : A MONOGRAPH: A CONTRIBUTION TO THE EVIDENCE OF ITS HISTORIC TRUTH / Kennedy, John – London: Alexander and Shepheard, 1895 – 1mf – 9 – 0-8370-3884-7 – 1985-1884 – us A.T.L.A. [220]

ON THE CLASSIFICATION AND GEOGRAPHICAL DISTRIBUTION OF THE MAMMALIA / Owen, R – 2490 2. 1859 – 8 – ne IDC [590]

ON THE CLASSIFICATION OF BIRDS / Huxley, T H – Z 1808. 1868 – 9 – ne IDC [590]

ON THE COMMERCIAL IMPORTANCE OF HUDSON'S BAY: WITH REMARKS ON RECENT SURVEYS AND INVESTIGATIONS / Bell, Robert – London: W. Clowes, 1881?. 06718. (Pre-1900 Canadiana) – 9 – cn C.I.H.M. [550]

ON THE CONFLICTS... / Bartolus, de Saxoferrato – Cambridge, 1914 – 1mf – 9 – ILM-423/1 – ne IDC [340]

ON THE CONSTITUTIONAL AND LOCAL EFFECTS OF DISEASE OF THE SUPRA-RENAL CAPSULES / Addison, T – M-31. 1855 – 9 – ne IDC [616]

ON THE CULTIVATION OF THE PLANTS BELONGING TO THE NATURAL ORDER OF PROTEAE / Knight, J – London. 1809. B-350 2 – 8 – ne IDC [580]

ON THE DIATOMS OF THE BALTIC SEA / Juhlin-Dannfelt, H J B – v6(21), 52p. 1882 – 2mf – 9 – ne IDC [574]

ON THE DIFFERENCE BETWEEN PHYSICAL AND MORAL LAW : THE FERNLEY LECTURE OF 1883 / Arthur, William – London: T. Woolmer, 1883 – 1mf – us A.T.L.A. [240]

ON THE DIURNAL VARIATION OF AIR TEMPERATURE / Sutrisno, C – Djakarta, Departemen Perhubungan Udara Lembaga Meteorologi dan Geofisik, 1960. 8p, graphs, tables – 9 – ne IDC [550]

ON THE DOMICIL OF ENGLISHMEN IN FRANCE / Cole, H W – London, 1857 – 2mf – 1 – ILM-3585/1 – ne IDC [327]

ON THE EARLY HISTORY OF THE DOCTRINE OF THE HOLY SPIRIT : WITH ESPECIAL REFERENCE TO THE CONTROVERSIES OF THE FOURTH CENTURY / Swete, Henry Barclay – Cambridge: Deighton, Bell, 1873 – 1mf – us A.T.L.A. [240]

ON THE ENGLISH TRANSLATIONS OF THE "IMITATIO CHRISTI" / Copinger, WA – Manchester: [s.n.], 1900 (Bibliographiana; no. 3) – 1mf – us A.T.L.A. [220]

ON THE ESKIMO MUSIC IN GREENLAND / Thuren, Hj – 1911. BH-183 2 – 8 – ne IDC [780]

ON THE EVE = AM VORABEND : DRAMA IN THREE ACTS / Kampf, Leopold – New York: International Library Publishing, c1907 – 1r – 1 – us U.W. Library [820]

ON THE EVE OF CIVIL WAR IN SPAIN / Ramos-Oliveira, Antonio – London, 1937. Fiche W1128. (Blodgett Collection of Spanish Civil War Pamphlets) – 9 – us H.U. College Libr [946]

ON THE GEOLOGY OF NATURAL GAS AND PETROLEUM IN SOUTHWESTERN ONTARIO: NOTES ON THE OCCURENCE OF PETROLEUM IN GASPE, QUEBEC / Brumell, Henry Peareth H – Rochester, NY: Geological Society of America, 1893. 02178. (Pre-1900 Canadiana) – 9 – cn C.I.H.M. [550]

ON THE GEOLOGY OF THE OTTAWA AND PARRY SOUND RAILWAY / Ells, Robert Wheelock – Ottawa: Painter & Abbott, 1897. 05238. (Pre-1900 Canadiana) – 9 – cn C.I.H.M. [550]

ON THE GEOLOGY OF THE ST CLAIR TUNNEL / Adams, Frank Dawson – 1891?. 02537. (Pre-1900 Canadiana) – 9 – cn C.I.H.M. [550]

ON THE GERMINATION, DEVELOPMENT AND FRUCTIFICATION OF THE HIGHER CRYPTOGAMIA AND ON THE FRUCTIFICATION OF THE CONIFERAE / Hofmeister, W F B – Ray Society. 1862 – 1 – uk Microform Academic [580]

ON THE HEIGHTS : A NOVEL / Auerbach, Berthold – (Translation of: Auf der Hoehe) – Boston: Roberts, 1874 – 1r – 1 – us U.W. Library [830]

ON THE HIGHER CRYPTOGAMOUS PLANTS / Griffith, W – (Notulae ad plantas asiaticas). v. 2. 1849. B-419 2 – 8 – ne IDC [580]

ON THE HISTORY OF THE DOCTRINE OF THE PROCESSION OF THE HOLY SPIRIT : FROM THE APOSTOLIC AGE TO THE DEATH OF CHARLEMAGNE / Swete, Henry Barclay – Cambridge: Deighton, Bell; London: G. Bell, 1876 – 1mf – us A.T.L.A. [240]

ON THE INDIANS AND ESKIMOS OF THE UNGAVA DISTRICT, LABRADOR / Turner, L M – BN 426 2. 1887 – 8 – ne IDC [971]

ON THE INDIANS OF THE MACKENZIE AND YUKON RIVERS / Bompas – BN 149 2. 1893 – 8 – ne IDC [305]

ON THE INDONESIAN STRUGGLE AGAINST IMPERIALISM / Wang, Jen-shu – In Chinese. SE 10,343 1. 1947 – 9 – ne IDC [320]

ON THE INSCRIPTIONS OF ASSYRIA AND BABYLONIA / Rawlinson, Henry Creswicke – (Includes bibliographical references and index) – [S.l.: s.n., 1850?] – 1mf – 9 – 0-8370-8609-4 – 1986-2609 – us A.T.L.A. [470]

ON THE INTERPRETATION OF STATUTES / Maxwell, Peter Benson – 2d ed. London: Maxwell, 1883. 688p. LL-120 – 1 – us L of C Photodup [340]

ON THE LAWS AND PRACTICE OF HORSE RACING / Rous, H J – 1866 – 1 – uk Microform Academic [340]

ON THE MANNERS AND CUSTOMS OF THE ANCIENT IRISH; A SERIES OF LECTURES DELIVERED BY THE LATE EUGENE O'CURRY / O'Curry, Eugene – Edited with introd., appendixes, etc. by W.K. Sullivan. London and Edinburgh: Williams and Norgate, 1873.3v. ill – 1 – us U.W. Library [390]

ON THE MINERAL NUTRITION OF LOWLAND RICE / Go, Ban Hong – (Thesis). Indonesian or Dutch with summary in English. SE-10,357 1. 1957 – 9 – ne IDC [630]

ON THE MOLLUSCA OF PECONIC AND GARDINER'S BAYS, LONG ISLAND, NEW YORK / Smith, S – Z 794 2. 1862 – 8 – ne IDC [590]

ON THE NATURAL HISTORY AND CLASSIFICATION OF BIRDS / Swainson, W – (The cabinet cyclopaedia). Z 1943.m 1836-1837 – 9 – ne IDC [590]

ON THE NECESSITY OF A SCHOOL OF ARTS FOR THE DOMINION: A PAPER READ BEFORE THE CANADIAN SOCIETY OF CIVIL ENGINEERS...26TH MAY 1887 / Baillairge, Charles – 1887?. 00065. (Pre-1900 Canadiana) – 9 – cn C.I.H.M. [624]

ON THE OCCURRENCE OF MAMMOTH AND MASTODON REMAINS AROUND HUDSON'S BAY / Bell, Robert – Rochester, NY: Geological Society of America, 1898. 03559. (Pre-1900 Canadiana) – 9 – cn C.I.H.M. [550]

ON THE OCCURRENCE OF SCOLITHUS IN ROCKS OF THE CHAZY FORMATION ABOUT OTTAWA, ONTARIO / Ami, Henry Marc – 1886?. 06602. (Pre-1900 Canadiana) – 9 – cn C.I.H.M. [550]

ON THE ORIGIN AND RELATIONS OF THE GRENVILLE AND HASTINGS SERIES IN THE CANADIAN LAURENTIAN / Adams, Frank Dawson – 1897? 00775. (Pre-1900 Canadiana) – 9 – cn C.I.H.M. [550]

ON THE ORIGIN OF THE FERRAR-GROUP : A LECTURE ON THE GENEALOGICAL RELATIONS OF THE NEW TESTAMENT MSS DELIVERED..ON NOVEMBER 6TH 1893 / Harris, James Rendel – (Includes appendix on Syriac stichometry) – London: C J

Clay, 1893 – 1mf – 9 – 0-8370-3494-9 – 1985-1494 – us A.T.L.A. [220]

ON THE PAGANISM OF THE CIVILISED IROQUOIS OF ONTARIO / Boyle, David – 1900? 00921. (Pre-1900 Canadiana) – 9 – cn C.I.H.M. [290]

ON THE PATHOLOGY AND TREATMENT OF GLAUCOMA / Smith, P – M 431 2.m 1891 – 8 – ne IDC [616]

ON THE PHENOMENA OF FERTILIZATION IN FICUS ROXBURGHII WALL / Cunningham, D D – (Annals Royal Bot. Garden, Calcutta). 1888 – 8 – ne IDC [580]

ON THE PHILOSOPHY OF KANT / Adamson, Robert – Edinburgh: D. Douglas, 1879 – 1mf – us A.T.L.A. [140]

ON THE PHONETIC TRANSCRIPTION OF INDIAN LANGUAGES / Thalbitzer, W – BN 418 2. 1924 – 8 – ne IDC [490]

ON THE PLAINS IN 1867-68 / McIntyre, W E – 1 – us KS Hist [978]

ON THE POLYPHONY OF THE ASSYRIO-BABYLONIAN CUNEIFORM WRITING : A LETTER TO PROFESSOR RENOUF / Hincks, Edward – Dublin: John F Fowler, 1863 – 1mf – 9 – 0-8370-8350-8 – 1986-2350 – us A.T.L.A. [470]

ON THE POWER, WISDOM, AND GOODNESS OF GOD AS MANIFESTED IN THE ADAPTATION OF EXTERNAL NATURE TO THE MORAL AND INTELLECTUAL CONSTITUTION OF MAN / Chalmers, Thomas – London: William Pickering, 1833 – 1 roll – 1 – 1-55879-163-9 – uk Libr Preservation [210]

ON THE RELATION OF ISLAM TO THE GOSPEL / Moehler, Johann Adam – Calcutta: Ostell and Lepage, 1847 – 1mf – us A.T.L.A. [230]

ON THE REMAINS OF LATER PRE-HISTORIC MAN IN THE CATHERINE ARCHIPELAGO, ALASKA TERRITORY / Dall, W H – BN 187 2. 1878 – 8 – ne IDC [573]

ON THE REVISION OF THE CONFESSION OF FAITH *see* THEOLOGICAL MISCELLANY 1

ON THE RIGHTS OF THE INDIANS OF THE AMERICAS / ed by Vermeer, B – (Includes a printed guide and a plastic binder) – 152mf – H-2625/1 – ne IDC [340]

ON THE SIBERIAN ORIGIN OF SOME CUSTOMS OF THE WESTERN ESKIMOS / Murdoch, John – BN 322 2. 1888 – 8 – ne IDC [306]

ON THE STUDY OF CHARACTER : INCLUDING AN ESTIMATE OF PHRENOLOGY / Bain, Alexander – London: Parker, Son and Bourn, 1861 – 1mf – us A.T.L.A. [150]

ON THE SUPERFICIAL GEOLOGY OF BRITISH COLUMBIA / Dawson, George M – s.l.: s.n., 1878?. 02359. (Pre-1900 Canadiana) – 9 – cn C.I.H.M. [550]

ON THE SYSTEMATIC POSITION OF THE NARDOO PLANT AND THE PHYSIOLOGICAL CHARACTERISATION OF ITS FRUIT / Mueller, Ferdinand Jakob Heinrich von – 1862. B-8070 1 – 9 – ne IDC [580]

ON THE THRESHHOLD / Munger, Theodore Thornton – Boston: Houghton, Mifflin, 1886, c1880 – 1mf – 9 – 0-8370-6226-8 – 1986-0226 – us A.T.L.A. [240]

ON THE THRESHOLD OF CENTRAL AFRICA / Coillard, Francois – London. 1897. BA-293 2 – 8 – ne IDC [960]

ON THE THRESHOLD OF THREE CLOSED LANDS : THE GUILD OUTPOST IN THE EASTERN HIMALAYAS / Graham, J A – Edinburgh: R.& R. Clark; London: A. and C. Black, [1897?] – 1mf – us A.T.L.A. [240]

ON THE TRINITY / Edwards, Jonathan – (Unpublished). With remarks on Edwards and his theology by George P. Fisher. 1903 – 9 – us A.T.L.A. [240]

ON THE UNION OF PRESBYTERIANS IN CANADA: PRIZE ESSAY / Campbell, Robert, 1835-1921 – Montreal: F. Grafton, 1871. 00399. (Pre-1900 Canadiana) – 9 – cn C.I.H.M. [240]

ON THE WATER SUPPLY OF MONTREAL AND ITS SUBURBS / Edwards, J Baker – s.l.: s.n., 1879?. 05220. (Pre-1900 Canadiana) – 9 – cn C.I.H.M. [971]

ON THE WING – Sacramento, CA. 1986-1989 – 2r – 1 – $100.00 – B05057 – us Library Micro [071]

ON THE WING WITH THE WORD – 1922-61 – 1 – 311.08 – us Baptist [240]

ON TREK IN THE TRANSVAAL; OR, OVER BERG AND VELDT IN SOUTH AFRICA / Roche, Harriet A – London: S. Low Marston, Searle & Rivington, 1878. xv,367,(1)p. Fold. map. 1 reel. 1290 – 1 – us U.W. Library [910]

ON WAR / Clausewitz, C von – rev ed. London. 3v. 1908 – 9mf – 1 – ILM-1359/1 – ne IDC [327]

ON WINGS OF EAGLES. A HISTORY OF THE FIRST BAPTIST CHURCH OF WHITE SETTLEMENT, TEXAS / Semple, James H – 1868-1968. 1968 – 1 – 7.21 – us Baptist [240]

Onabamiro, Sanya Dojo *see* THE ECOLOGY OF CYCLOPS IN SOUTH-WEST NIGERIA AND THEIR RELATION TO THE OCCURRENCE OF DRACUNCULUS MEDINENSIS, THE GUINEA-WORM, IN THAT REGION

ONAFHANKELIJK ISRAELIETISCH ORGAAN VOOR NEDERLAND – (Missing: 1875-1877, v1-3; 1882-1886, v7-12; 1891-1900, v16-26) – Amsterdam. v1-35. 1875-1910 – 87mf – 9 – ne IDC [270]

Onahan, William James et al *see* READINGS FROM THE BIBLE

Onaindia, Alberto *see* PRIEST WHO SAW PLANE ATTACK TELLS OF GUERNICA "MASSACRE."

Onana, L *see* ESIE, RITE DE GUERISON ET DE PURIFICATION BETI (CAMEROUN)

O.N.C. JOTTINGS *see* ONTARIO NORMAL COLLEGE MONTHLY

ONCE A MONTH – Toronto: Provident Life Assurance and Investment Co, [1859?-18–] – 9 – cn C.I.H.M. [360]

ONCE THEIR HOME OR OUR LEGACY FROM THE DAHKOTAHS / Holley, Frances C – Chicago: Donohue and Hemeberry, 1892. South Dakota Reel 5. (The Cox Library Collection) – 5 – us Americana [978]

Oncken Archives. Hamburg, Germany *see* BERLIN BAPTIST CHURCH DOCUMENTS 1837-41

Oncken, Johann Gerhard *see*
– LICHT UND RECHT
– PAPERS

Oncken, Wilhelm *see*
– ALLGEMEINE GESCHICHTE IN EINZELDARSTELLUNGEN
– OESTERREICH UND PREUSSEN IM BEFREIUNGSKRIEGE

ONCOLOGY – v. 20-28. 1966-74 – 1,5,6 – us UMI [616]

ONCOLOGY – v31-. 1975- – 1,5,9 – us UMI [616]

ONCOLOGY RESEARCH – 1,5,69 – us UMI [616]

Ondaatje, Aelian *see* SAWERS' DIGEST OF THE KANDYAN LAW

L'ONDE ELECTRIQUE – Paris. v. 1-25, 28-50. 1922-45, 1948-70 – 1,5,6 – us Princeton Micro [621]

ONDER KRUGERS' HOLLANDERS GESCHIEDENIS VAN DE NEDERLANDSCHE ZUID-AFRIKAANSCHE SPOORWEG-MAATSCHAPPIJ / Winter, Peter van – 2v. Amsterdam. 1937-38. B-346 2 – 8 – ne IDC [960]

ONDER VERBETERINGE. KORTE INLEYDINGE DER FEESTEN ISRAELS, TWELCK RECHTE TIJTKAARTEN ZIJN / Robert Robertsz – 1593. BME-338 1 – 9 – ne IDC [240]

ONDER VERBETERINGHE. DE RECHTER VLUEGEL / Robert Robertsz – 1596. BME-256 1 – 9 – ne IDC [240]

ONDER VERBETERINGHE. DE SLINCKER VLUEGEL / Robert Robertsz – 1596. BME-255 1 – 9 – ne IDC [240]

ONDER VERBETERINGHE. EEN TUCHT ROEDE GHEMAECKT WT LIEFDE VAN JACOB JANSZ. KIST, OMDAT HY DIE WAERHEYT IN ZIJN GHEDRUCKTEN BRIEF AEN L.G. HEEFT GHEMIST / Robert Robertsz – 1597. BME-257 1 – 9 – ne IDC [240]

DEN ONDERGANCK DES ROOMSCHEN ARENTS / Hulsius, B – O 643. 1642 – 9 – ne IDC [920]

ONDERSTEPOORT JOURNAL OF VETERINARY RESEARCH – (See also: Onderstepoort Journal of Veterinary Science and Animal Industry) – v25- 1951- – 1 – us UMI [636]

ONDERSTEPOORT JOURNAL OF VETERINARY RESEARCH – v. 1-35. 1933-1968 – 1,5,6 – us Princeton Micro [636]

ONDERSTEPOORT JOURNAL OF VETERINARY SCIENCE AND ANIMAL INDUSTRY – (See also: Onderstepoort Journal of Veterinary Research) – v1-24. 1933-1950 – 1 – us UMI [636]

DE ONDERWERPING VAN DJAMBI, 1901-1907. BEKNOPTE GESCHIEDENIS, NAAR OFFICIEELE GEGEVENS SAMENTGESTELD / Velds, G J – Batavia, 1909 – 3mf – 9 – SE-1598/1 – ne IDC [350]

ONDERWIJSINGHE, TEGHENS DE DWALINGHE DER WEDERDOOPEREN / Taffin, I – Haerlem, G. Rooman. 1590. BME-247 1 – 9 – ne IDC [240]

ONDERWYS OM OP EENE TUIGWERKELYKE WYZE CLAVIEREN, CLAVECIMBELS EN ORGELS IN ALLE 24 TOONEN EVEN ZUIVER TE STEMMEN / Fritz, B – Amsterdam. 1756. BP-277 – 9 – ne IDC [780]

ONDERWYZINGE HOE EMEN ALLE DE TOON EN EN HALVE TOONEN, DIE MEEST GEBRUYCKELYCK ZYN, OP DE HANDTFLUYT ZAL KONNEN T'EENEMAEL ZUYVER BLAEZEN, EN HOE MEN OP YEDER, 'T GEMACKELYCKST EEN TRAMMELANT ZAL KONNEN MAKEN, HEEL DIENSTIGH VOOR DE LIEFHEBBERS / Blanckenburgh, G van – Amsterdam. P. Matthysz. 1654. BP-173 1 – 9 – ne IDC [780]

ONDERZOEK NAAR DE ECHTHEID VAN CLEMENS' EERSTEN BRIEF AAN DE CORINTHIERS / Bergh, G van den – Leiden: E.J. Brill, 1908 – 1mf – us A.T.L.A. [240]

ONDERZOEK NAAR DEN JURIDISCHEN WERELDBOUW / Asbeck, F M van – Amsterdam, 1916 – 4mf – 9 – ILM-2136/1 – ne IDC [340]

ONE BIG UNION MONTHLY / Industrial Workers of the World – Series 1: v1-3; 2+1 (all publ.). 1919-21. Series 2: v1-2 (all publ). 1927-28 – 23mf – 9 – $130.00 – us UPA [331]

ONE DAY'S COURTSHIP : THE HERALDS OF FAME / Barr, Robert & Hall, Robert – New York: F. Stokes Co., c1896. 03351. (Pre-1900 Canadiana) – 9 – cn C.I.H.M. [830]

ONE DIME *see* THE INTERNATIONAL PHILATELIST

ONE FAULT : A NOVEL / Trollope, Frances Milton – London: Richard Bentley, 1840 – 2 rolls – 1 – 1-55879-266-X – uk Libr Preservation [830]

THE ONE HUNDRED AND FIFTY CHAPTERS / Palamas, Gregory; ed by Sinkewicz, Robert E – 1988 – 1mf – 9 – Can$39.00 – 0-88844-083-9 – cn Pontif [240]

ONE HUNDRED AND TEN MIRACLES OF OUR LADY MARY, TRANSLATED FROM ETHIOPIC MANUSCRIPTS FOR THE MOST PART IN THE BRITISH MUSEUM.. / ed by Budge, Sir Ernest Alfred Thompson Wallis – London, Boston: Medici Society, 1923. lviii,359p – 1 – us U.W. Library [240]

ONE HUNDRED AND TWO (102) MONITOR – v1- 1971- 1,5,6; v6- 9 – us UMI [073]

ONE HUNDRED THIRTY-TWO PUBLICATIONS IN THE LOMA LANGUAGE *see* 132 PUBLICATIONS IN THE LOMA LANGUAGE

ONE HUNDRED YEARS IN THE PAJARO VALLEY : 1969-1868 / Watkinson, F – Santa Cruz, CA. – 1r – 1 – $50.00 – B40264 – us Library Micro [978]

ONE HUNDRED YEARS OF FABIAN PUBLISHING / Kareh, Rashid – Full cumulative indexes by author and title, 1883-1937. Printed text – 9 – £60.00 – uk World [320]

ONE HUNDRED YEARS OF MEDICINE IN DEKALB COUNTY / Weaver, J Calvin – 1822-1922. 1952. Biog. and hist. sketches. Indexed. 2 fiches. F-0681 – 9 – us A.G.L.L. [978]

ONE HUNDRED YEARS OF THE AFRICAN METHODIST EPISCOPAL ZION CHURCH, OR, THE CENTENNIAL OF AFRICAN METHODISM / Hood, J W – New York City: A.M.E. Zion Book Concern, 1895 – 2mf – us A.T.L.A. [240]

ONE HUNDREDTH ANNIVERSARY / Wilmington. Delaware. Hanover Street Presbyterian Church. Sunday School – 1914 – 9 – $50.00 – us Presbyterian [240]

ONE IN CHRIST – v1- 1965- 1; v12- 5,6,9 – us UMI [240]

ONE LIFE, ONE LAW / Reed, Mrs. Myron – New York: John W. Lovell, 1890. 1 fiche – 9 – us A.T.L.A. [240]

ONE LIFE, ONE LOVE / Braddon, Mary Elizabeth – British Fiction Archive: Unit 5 – 9 – uk Bell [830]

THE ONE MEDIATOR : OR, SACRIFICE AND SACRAMENTS / Humphrey, William – London: Burns & Oates; New York: Catholic Publ Society, [1890?] – 1mf – 9 – 0-8370-6986-6 – 1986-0986 – us A.T.L.A. [240]

THE ONE MEDIATOR: SELECTIONS AND THOUGHTS ON THE PROPITIATORY SACRIFICE AND INTERCESSION PRESENTED BY THE LORD JESUS CHRIST AS OUR GREAT HIGH PRIEST: WITH APPENDED CHAPTERS ON THE CONDITIONS OF SALVATION: ALSO APPENDED EXPOSITION OF ROMANS V. 11-21.. / Evans, John Swanton – Toronto: W. Briggs; Montreal: C. Coates; Halifax N.S.: S. Huestis, 1884. 02926. (Pre-1900 Canadiana) – 9 – cn C.I.H.M. [971]

ONE MICROFICHE PUBLISHED AUGUST 1996 – (Index to the Northern Territory's Star Newspaper 1 July 1976 to 1 August 1978) – 1996 (complete) – 1mf – A$5.00 – 0-949124-84-2 – at G.S.N.T. [072]

ONE OF CHINA'S SCHOLARS : THE CULTURE AND CONVERSION OF A CONFUCIANIST / Taylor, Howard (Mrs) – (Includes bibliographical references) – Philadelphia: China Inland Mission, 1900 – 1mf – 9 – 0-8370-6707-3 – 1986-0707 – us A.T.L.A. [920]

ONE OF THE JESUITS: ALEXIS CLERC, SAILOR AND MARTYR / Daniel, Charles – With a preface by Thomas S. Preston. New York: Montreal: D. Sadlier, 1880. 05415. (Pre-1900 Canadiana) – 9 – cn C.I.H.M. [971]

THE ONE POUND NOTE/ SCOTLAND/ ENGLAND / Graham, William – 1fiche (29x) – 9 – 1.00f – at Libertarian Micro [320]

THE ONE RELIGION: TRUTH, HOLINESS, AND PEACE DESIRED BY THE NATIONS / Wordsworth, John – New York: E.P. Dutton, 1881. 1 fiche – 9 – us A.T.L.A. [240]

ONE SMALL CANDLE: THE PILGRIMS' FIRST YEAR IN AMERICA – By Thomas J. Fleming 1963. Item G. Indexed, 220p. SW16-0092 – 5 – us A.G.L.L. [978]

ONE THING AND ANOTHER : A BOOK OF ESSAYS BY JUDGE CHARLES FORREST MOORE – (Moore was a well known NY judge) – New York: William Edwin Rudge, 1924 – 3mf – 9 – $4.50 – LLMC 92-129 – us L.L.M.C. [340]

ONE THING NEEDFUL / Braddon, Mary Elizabeth – Includes: Cut by the County. British Fiction Archive: Unit 5 – 9 – uk Bell [830]

ONE THIRD OF THE NATION'S LAND : A REPORT TO THE PRESIDENT AND THE CONGRESS – Washington: GPO, 1970 – 4mf – 9 – $6.00 – LLMC 85-302 – us L.L.M.C. [340]

ONE THIRD OF THE NATION'S LAND: A REPORT TO THE PRESIDENT AND TO THE CONGRESS / U.S. Public Land Law Review Commission – Washington Govt. Print. Off. 1970. 342p. LL-2278 – 1 – us L of C Photodup [340]

ONE THOUSAND LEGAL FACTS. / Arnold, Edward W – Girard, Kan., Derry, 1900. 180 p. LL-581 – 1 – us L of C Photodup [340]

ONE THOUSAND LEGAL QUESTIONS ANSWERED BY THE PEOPLE'S LAWYER OF THE BOSTON DAILY GLOBE / Bridgham, Percy Albert – Boston, Brooks, 1891. 236 p. LL-1606 – 1 – us L of C Photodup [340]

ONE THOUSAND MALAYALAM PROVERBS – (Filmed with: A Wreath of Malayalam Proverbs) – Mangalore: Printed by Stolz & Reuther, Basel Mission Press, 1868 – us Res Libr [390]

ONE: VSESOIUZNAIA PEREPIS' NASELENIIA 17 DEKABRIA 1926 A. GODA. PREDVARITEL'NYE ITOGI / Russia. Tsentral'noe Statisticheskoe Upravlenie – M. 1927-28. B-2207 a2 – 8 – ne IDC [324]

ONE: VSESOIUZNAIA PEREPIS' NASELENIIA. KRATKIE SVODKI, V. 4-7 / Russia. Tsentral'noe statisticheskoe upravlenie – M. 1928; Sistema razrabotki. M. 1927. B-2207 b 2 – 8 – ne IDC [310]

ONE WORLD – 1974- 1; 1977- 5,6,9 – us UMI [073]

ONE YEAR IN SPAIN; A PICTURE STORY OF AMERICAN DOCTORS AND NURSES / Medical Bureau and North American Committee to Aid Spanish Democracy – N.Y., 1937. Fiche W 1037. (Blodgett Collection of Spanish Civil War Pamphlets) – 9 – us H.U. College Libr [946]

THE ONE-ACT PLAYS.. / Pirandello, Luigi – Ed. by Arthur Livingston; trans. by Elizabeth Abbott, Arthur Livingston and Blanche Valentine Mitchell. New York: E.P. Dutton & Company, c1928. 1 reel. 1268 – 1 – us U.W. Library [820]
O'Neall *see* ANNALS OF NEWBERRY COUNTY
ONEIDA CIRCULAR – 1-n.s. 13. Nov 1851-Mar 1876 – 1 – us UMI [073]
Oneida Community *see* BOOKS, PAMPHLETS AND SERIALS
ONEIDA MORNING HERALD – Utica. N.Y. 1847-1900 – 1 – us UMI [071]
ONEIDA WEEKLY HERALD – Utica. N.Y. 1851-1897 – 1 – us UMI [071]
ONEIDA WHIG – Utica. N.Y. 1834-1846 – 1 – us UMI [071]
O'Neil, J L *see* JEROME SAVONAROLA
O'NEILL – (Lists 16 productions) – 17mf – 9 – £110.00 – uk Chadwyck [790]
O'Neill, James H *see* INDIVIDUALITY AND INTIMACY IN PASTORAL MARITAL COUNSELING
O'Neill, Simeon Wilberforce *see* A CONTRIBUTION TO THE CAUSE OF CHRISTIAN UNITY, OR, THE THOUGHTS OF AN INDIAN MISSIONARY ON THE CONTROVERSIES OF THE DAY
O'NEILL SUN – O'Neill, NE. -w. Jul 1892; Aug 1895-Sep 1897 – 1 – us NE Hist [071]
O'NEILL TRIBUNE – O'Neill, NE. -w. Jun 1887-Apr 1890, scattered issues missing – 1 – us NE Hist [071]
ONESIMUS : MEMOIRS OF A DISCIPLE OF ST PAUL / Abbott, Edwin Abbott – (Includes notes) – London: Macmillan, 1882 – 1mf – 9 – 0-8370-2016-6 – 1985-0016 – us A.T.L.A. [830]
ONE-YEAR DEVELOPMENT PLAN / Ghana – July 1970 to June 1971. D-1077 1. 1970 – 9 – ne IDC [338]
ON-FARM MAIZE DRYING AND STORAGE IN THE HUMID TROPICS – 1980 – 69p – it F.A.O. [660]
ONFEYLBARE GHEPEYSEN TER SALIGHEYDT, VOOR EEN NIEUW-IAER TOE-GHE-EYGHENT AEN ALLE VYERIGHE BE-YVERAERS DER SALIGHEYDT, VAN HAERE SIELE : ECCLES. CAP.7.V.40. ZIJT IN ALLE UWE WERCKEN UWER UYTERSTEN GHEDACHTIGH, EN INDER EEUWIGHEYDT EN SULT GHY NIET SONDIGHEN / Smidt, A de – Antwerpen, 1666 – 1mf – 9 – O-3259/1 – ne IDC [760]
DE ON-GHEMASKERDE LIEFDE DES HEMELS / Castro, I A – O 192. 1686 – 9 – ne IDC [700]
Oni-Orisan, B A *see* A BIBLIOGRAPHY OF NIGERIAN HISTORY
ONKRUIDFLORA DER JAVASCHE SUIKERRIETGRONDEN / Backer, C A – (Lacking: pl. 1-32; 129-160) – Soerabaja, [1928-1941] – 5mf – 9 – ne IDC [580]
ONLINE DATA ACCESS *see* ACCESS
THE ONLOOKER – 1920-22 – 1 – 65.00 – cn McLaren [800]
ONLY A CLOD / Braddon, Mary Elizabeth – British Fiction Archive: Unit 5 – 9 – uk Bell [830]
THE ONLY GOOD THING IN ALL THE WORLDS / Turner, Jonathan Baldwin – Chicago: Open Court, 1891 – 1mf – 9 – 0-8370-5652-7 – 1985-3652 – us A.T.L.A. [240]
THE ONLY KEY TO DANIEL'S PROPHECIES / Auchincloss, William Stuart – (Includes chronological tables & index) – New York: D van Nostrand, 1903 – 1mf – 9 – 0-8370-2129-4 – 1985-0129 – us A.T.L.A. [220]
DE ON-NOODSAKELIJKHEID EN ONDIENSTIGHEID VAN CIS EN DIS IN DE BASSEN DER KLOKKEN, VERTOONT UYT VERSCHEYDE ADVYSEN VAN ERVAREN ORGANISTEN ENDE KLOKKENSPEELDERS BIJ EEN VERSAMELT / Hemony, P – Delft. Oosterhout. 1678. BP-313 1 – 9 – ne IDC [780]
ONOMASTICA SACRA : UNTERSUCHUNGEN ZUM LIBER INTERPRETATIONIS NOMINUM HEBRAICORUM DES HEILIGEN HIERONYMUS (T.U.U. 3-41) / Wutz, F – Leipzig, 1915 – 21mf – 9 – ne Slangenburg [240]
ONOMASTIKON MEDICINAE / Brunfels, Otto – Argentorarti, 1534 – 1 – us U.W. Library [610]
ONOMASTIKON MEDICINAE (AEL, ABT 3;9) / Brunfels, Otto; ed by Stolberg, Michael – Straßburg, 1534 (mf ed 1994) – 5mf – 9 – DM150.00 – 3-89131-177-X – gw Fischer [610]
ONOMATOLOGIA BOTANICA COMPLETE / Gmelin, J F – 10 v. Frankfurt-Leipzig. 1772-78. B-832 2 – 8 – ne IDC [580]
ONOMATOLOGIA MEDICA COMPLETA ODER MEDICINISCHES LEXICON...VON EINER GESELLSCHAFT GELEHRTER AERZTE, MIT EINER VORREDE ALBRECHT VON HALLERS (AEL, ABT.3;4) – Ulm, Frankfurt, Leipzig, 1755-1756 (mf ed 1993) – 18mf – 9 – DM240.00 – 3-89131-154-0 – gw Fischer [610]
ONO-MEDEDELINGEN – (Cont as: O.S.R. News. Djakarta 1950-1951 v2-3; Cont as: Journal for Scientific Research. Djakarta 1952-1954 v1-3(2); Missing: 1949(10-12) has never been published) – Batavia. v1(1-9). 1949 – 31mf – 9 – ne IDC [500]
ONONDAGA'S CENTENNIAL / Boston History Co – Boston, 1896. Vols. 1-2. New York Reel 26. (The Cox Library Collection) – 5 – us Americana [978]
ONOWAY – Canada, Jan 1980-Dec 1982 – 1 – cn Commonwealth Micro [072]
ONS COURANT *see* ONZE COURANT
ONS GEESTELIJK ERF – 1(1927)-23(1949) – 196mf – 9 – Dfl686.00 – ne Slangenburg [073]
ONS LAND – South Africa. 14 Jan 1892-13 Jan 1894. 2 reels – 1, 16 diazo available at reduced price – sa SA Libr [072]
ONS LAND *see* DE ZUID-AFRIKAAN
ONS MOOI INDIE BATAVIA: OUD EN NIEUW / Balbian Verster, Jan Francois Leopold de – Amsterdam: J.M. Meulenhoff, 1921. 174p. illus – 1 – us U.W. Library [950]
ONS VOLKSLEVEN – v1-12. 1889-1900 – 1 – us I.U. Libraries [390]
ONS VRIEND – Windhoek, SA. 1925-26 – 1 – sa State Libr [072]
ONSCHULDT DAUIDS JORIS. GEDAEN VNDE GEPRESENTEERT AN DIE WOLGEBORENE VROUW, VROUW ANNA, GHEBORENE GRAUINNE VAN OLDENBURCH / Joris, David – Z. BME-361 1 – 9 – ne IDC [240]
ONSCHULDT DAUIDS JORISZ. GEDAEN VNDE GEPRESENTEERT AN DIE WOLGEBORENE VROUW, VROUW ANNA, GHEBORENE GRAUINNE VAN OLDENBURCH INT JAER 1540 / Joris, David – BME-360 1 – 9 – ne IDC [240]
Onstot, T G *see* LINCOLN AND SALEM
THE ONTARIAN GENEALOGIST AND FAMILY HISTORIAN – Toronto: Rolph, Smith [1898-1901] – 9 – cn C.I.H.M. [920]
Ontario *see*
– CURRENT PUBLICATIONS
– LEGISLATIVE ASSEMBLY JOURNALS
ONTARIO AND WEST VICTORIA GAZETTE – Beaverton, Ont.: J.J.Cave, [1894-189- or 19–] – 9 – cn C.I.H.M. [971]
ONTARIO APPEAL REPORTS / Ontario. Canada – v1-27. 1876-1900 (all publ) – 213mf – 9 – $319.00 – LLMC 81-048 – us L.L.M.C. [340]
ONTARIO ARGUS – Ontario OR. June 11 1909-Nov 11 1915, Feb 10 1916-June 27 1918, May 1 1919-Aug 28 1947 – 1 – us U.O. Library [071]
ONTARIO ARGUS-OBSERVER – Ontario, OR. -d. 2 sep 1947-12 nov 1970 – 1 – us U.O. Library [071]
ONTARIO ATHELETICS *see* ATHLETICS
Ontario. Canada *see*
– CLARK AND SCULLY'S ONTARIO DRAINAGE CASES
– DRAPER'S UPPER CANADA KING'S BENCH REPORTS
– GRANT'S ONTARIO ERROR AND APPEAL REPORTS
– GRANT'S UPPER CANADA CHANCERY REPORTS
– HARRISON AND HODGIN'S UPPER CANADA MUNICIPAL REPORTS
– HODGIN'S CANADA ELECTION CASES
– ONTARIO APPEAL REPORTS
– ONTARIO CHANCERY CHAMBER REPORTS
– ONTARIO ELECTION CASES
– ONTARIO LOCAL COURTS AND MUNICIPAL GAZETTE
– ONTARIO PRACTICE REPORTS
– ONTARIO WEEKLY REPORTER
– PATRICK'S ONTARIO ELECTION CASES
– TAYLOR'S UPPER CANADA KING'S BENCH REPORTS
– UPPER CANADA CHAMBERS
– UPPER CANADA COMMON PLEAS
– UPPER CANADA COURT RECORDS
– UPPER CANADA JURIST
– UPPER CANADA QUEEN'S BENCH
– UPPER CANADA QUEEN'S BENCH REPORTS
ONTARIO CHANCERY CHAMBER REPORTS / Ontario. Canada – v1-4. 1858-72 (all publ) – 20mf – 9 – $30.00 – LLMC 81-042 – us L.L.M.C. [340]
THE ONTARIO CHRISTIAN MAGAZINE AND MONTHLY JOURNAL – Sharon [Ont.]: Ontario Christian Conference, [1891?-189- or 19–] – 9 – cn C.I.H.M. [240]
ONTARIO CITY DIRECTORIES INCLUDING CHINO, ALTA AND LOMA LINDA – San Bernardino Co, CA. 1945-1949 – 2r – 1 – $100.00 – D082 – us Library Micro [978]
Ontario College of Art. Council *see* RECORDS
Ontario College of Pharmacy *see* OCP, ON CONTINUING PRACTICE
Ontario. Commission on Metropolitan Toronto *see* BRIEFS AND TRANSCRIPTS OF PUBLIC HEARINGS
ONTARIO CRAFT – (Cont: Craftsman at v6 1981) – Toronto. v6-19. 1981-94 – 9 – Can$20.00y – cn Micromedia [740]
ONTARIO CRAFT *see* CRAFTSMAN
ONTARIO DAILY REPORT – Ontario, CA. 1910-1959 – 137r – 1 – $6,850.00 – R04075 – us Library Micro [071]
ONTARIO DEMOCRAT – Ontario, OR. -w. 21 Jun 1902-4 Jul 1918. 1 roll – 1 – us U.O. Library [071]
ONTARIO DIVORCE LAW NOTEBOOK / Heaton, Sydney Lewell – Hamilton, Ont.: Lewell Publishing Co. 1941. 64p. LL-2219 – 1 – us L of C Photodup [340]
THE ONTARIO DOCKET – Toronto: Docket Pub. Co, [1894-19–?] v1 no 1(Mar 1894)- – 9 – cn C.I.H.M. [340]
ONTARIO ECONOMIC REVIEW – Toronto. v1-12. 1963-74 – 5 – Can$100.00 – cn Micromedia [330]
ONTARIO EDUCATION DIMENSIONS – (Film contains New Dimensions 1969-73 and Dimensions in Education 1967-69) – Toronto. v8-9. 1973/74-1974/75 – 5 – Can$100.00 – cn Micromedia [370]
ONTARIO ELECTION CASES / Ontario. Canada – v1-2. 1884-1900 (all publ) – 9mf – 9 – $13.50 – LLMC 81-049 – us L.L.M.C. [340]
THE ONTARIO EPISCOPAL GAZETTE – Ottawa: J Hoyland, [1862?-186-] – 9 – cn C.I.H.M. [240]
THE ONTARIO EVANGELIST – (Cont: The Christian Worker. Cont by: The Canadian Evangelist) – Guelph, Ont: T.L. Fowler, G Munro, [1886-1890] – 9 – cn C.I.H.M. [240]
THE ONTARIO FARMER – Toronto: Pub. for the proprietor by Hunter, Rose, 1869-[1871] – 9 – cn C.I.H.M. [630]
ONTARIO FEDERATION OF LABOUR BULLETIN – Don Mills, 1948-1956 – 5 – Can$100.00 – cn Micromedia [331]
L'ONTARIO FRANCAIS – Ottawa, Ontario. 2 mai 1902-v2 n32. 31 dec 1903 – 1r – 1 – Can$50.00 – cn Can Microfilming [072]
ONTARIO GAZETTE – Toronto, 1958-68 – 19r – 1 – us Ross [324]
ONTARIO GAZETTE – (v101-115 1968-82 Can$155.00y 5. v116- 1983- 9) – Toronto. v90- 1958- – 1,5,9 – Price varies – cn Micromedia [971]
ONTARIO GAZETTE PART 2 – Toronto. v112-116. 1979-1983 – 9 – Can$175.00y – cn Micromedia [971]
ONTARIO HERALD – Ontario, CA. 1922-1949 – 1r – 1 – $50.00 – R04076 – us Library Micro [071]
ONTARIO HOUSING – (Cont by: Housing Ontario) – Toronto. v1-18. 1955-74 – 5 – Can$100.00 – cn Micromedia [360]
ONTARIO HOUSING *see* HOUSING ONTARIO
ONTARIO JOURNAL OF EDUCATIONAL RESEARCH – Toronto. v1-10. 1958/59-1967/68 – 5 – Can$100.00 – cn Micromedia [370]
ONTARIO LABOUR – (1986-87 Can$20.00y 9. Cont: Labor Review, 1978. Ceased 1987) – Don Mills, 1978-87 – 5,9 – Can$50.00y – cn Micromedia [331]
ONTARIO LABOUR *see* LABOUR REVIEW
ONTARIO LAWYERS WEEKLY – (1985-. 5,6,9) – v1-. 1983- – 1 – us UMI [340]
ONTARIO LIBRARY REVIEW – 1916-71 – 9r – 1 – $585.00 – cn Library Assoc [971]
ONTARIO LIVING – (v7 1991 Can$20.00y. Incorporated into: London Magazine at v1 no 1 1991) – London. v1-7. 1985-91 – 9 – Can$28.00y – cn Micromedia [306]
ONTARIO LIVING *see* LONDON MAGAZINE
ONTARIO LOCAL COURTS AND MUNICIPAL GAZETTE / Ontario. Canada – v1-8. 1865-72 (all publ) – 24mf – 9 – $36.00 – LLMC 81-047 – us L.L.M.C. [340]
ONTARIO MEDICINE – Toronto. v9- 1990- – 1 – Price varies – cn Micromedia [610]
Ontario Museum Association *see* NEWSLETTER
ONTARIO MUSEUM ASSOCIATION NEWSLETTER *see* ONTARIO MUSEUM ASSOCIATION QUARTERLY
ONTARIO MUSEUM ASSOCIATION QUARTERLY – (Contains: Ontario Museum Association Newsletter v1-7 1972-78. Cont by: Museum Quarterly at v13 1984/85) – Toronto. v8-12. 1979-83/84 – 5 – Price varies – cn Micromedia [060]
ONTARIO MUSEUM ASSOCIATION QUARTERLY *see* MUSEUM QUARTERLY
ONTARIO NATURALIST – v1- 1963- 1; v13-5,6; v16- 9 – us UMI [574]
ONTARIO NATURALIST – (Cont by: Seasons at v20 1980) – Don Mills. v1-19. 1963-1979 – 9 – Can$28.00y – cn Micromedia [574]
ONTARIO NATURALIST *see* SEASONS
ONTARIO NEWS – Ontario, Oregon.1893-98 – 1 – 48.00 – us Oregon Hist [071]
ONTARIO NORMAL COLLEGE MONTHLY – (Cont: ONC Jottings) – Hamilton, Ont: [s.n. 1898-19–] – 9 – cn C.I.H.M. [370]
ONTARIO OBSERVER – Ontario, CA. 1888-1897 – 3r – 1 – $150.00 – R04077 – us Library Micro [071]
ONTARIO OUT OF DOORS – (v1-22 1969-90 Can$37.00y) – Toronto. v1-26. 1969-94 – 9 – Can$28.00y – cn Micromedia [790]
ONTARIO PHILATELIST *see* THE PHILATELIC AND ADVOCATE
THE ONTARIO PHILATELIST – (Is absorbed by: The Philatelic Advocate) – St. Catharines, Ont: Widdicombe and Beatty, [1896-1898] – 9 – cn C.I.H.M. [760]
ONTARIO PRACTICE REPORTS / Ontario. Canada – (v1-5: Practice Court and Chamber Reports. v6-8: and theorts of Cases Decided in Common Law Chambers, Chancery Chambers, and the Master's Office) – v1-19. 1850-1900 (all publ) – 117mf – 9 – $175.00 – LLMC 81-051 – us L.L.M.C. [340]
ONTARIO PSYCHOLOGIST – v1- 1969- 1; v5-5,6; v7- 9 – us UMI [073]
ONTARIO PSYCHOLOGIST – Toronto. v1-26. 1969-94 – 9 – Can$20.00y – cn Micromedia [150]
ONTARIO RECORD – Ontario, CA. 1882-1956 – 29r – 1 – $1,450.00 – R02556 – us Library Micro [071]
ONTARIO REFORMER – Oshawa, Canada. 1871-73 – 1 reel – 1 – $68.00 – cn Library Assoc [971]
ONTARIO REPORT – Ontario, CA. 1917-1918 – 3r – 1 – $150.00 – C03627 – us Library Micro [071]
ONTARIO REPOSITORY – Canadaigua. N.Y. and Freeman. 1803-37 – 1 – us UMI [071]
ONTARIO REVIEW – Princeton, 1974-1984/85; nos 23-40 1985/86-1993/94 – 9 – Can$20.00y – cn Micromedia [910]
Ontario. Royal Commissions *see* REPORTS
ONTARIO SECURITIES COMMISSION BULLETIN – Toronto. v1- 1981- – 9 – Price varies – cn Micromedia [332]
ONTARIO SEMI WEEKLY ARGUS – Ontario OR. Nov 16 1915-Jan 25 1916 – 1 – us U.O. Library [071]
THE ONTARIO STAMP JOURNAL – Niagara Falls South, Ont: M.H. Bigger, [1888] – 9 – cn C.I.H.M. [760]
ONTARIO STATUTES, SESSION LAWS AND REVISIONS / Ontario.Canada – (Updates planned) – 10th Legislative 1st sess-31st Legislative 3rd sess. 1903-1979 – 1156mf – 9 – $1,734.00 – LLMC 90-170 – us L.L.M.C. [324]
THE ONTARIO TEACHER – Strathroy, Ont: Ross and M'Coll, 1873-1876 – 9 – cn C.I.H.M. [370]
ONTARIO WEEKLY REPORTER / Ontario. Canada – v1-27. 1901-16 (all publ) – 298mf – 9 – $447.00 – LLMC 81-039 – us L.L.M.C. [340]
ONTARIO WORKMAN – 1872-74 – 1 – 140.00 – cn McLaren [971]
Ontario.Canada *see* ONTARIO STATUTES, SESSION LAWS AND REVISIONS
ONTDECKINGE VAN DAT PUNCT UNDE DIE REDEN ONS HEEREN CHRISTI JESU WOORDT: VAN DIE REIN VAN HERTEN SYN / Joris, David – Wtghegaen int Jaer, 1551. BME-427 1 – 9 – ne IDC [240]

ONTOGENESE DES STOFFWECHSELS UND DER TEMPERATURREGULATION BEI DER NORDAFRIKANISCHEN DICKSCHWANZMAUS PACHYUROMIS DUPRASI / Mueller, Andreas – 1992 – 108p – 9 – DM98.00 – 3-89349-466-9 – gw Hänsel [574]

THE ONTOLOGICAL AND NORMATIVE STRUCTURE IN THE SOCIAL REALITY OF A BANTU SOCIETY : A SYSTEMATIC STUDY OF GANDA ONTOLOGY AND ETHICS / Sempebwa, Joshua Wantate – Heidelberg, 1978 – 4mf – 9 – DM90.00 – 3-89349-785-4 – gw Hänsel [306]

DER ONTOLOGISCHE GOTTESBEWEIS : KRITISCHE DARSTELLUNG SEINER GESCHICHTE SEIT ANSELM BIS AUF DIE GEGENWART / Runze, Georg – (Includes bibliographical references) – Halle: C E M Pfeffer, 1882 – 1mf – 9 – 1985-2998 us A.T.L.A. [210]

ONTWIKKELINGSPLAN / Aruba. (Netherlands) – 2V. D-1534 1. 1961-1971 – 9 – ne IDC [330]

ONUC-BULLETIN MENSUEL DE STATISTIQUE / Congo. Operations civiles des Nations Unies au Congo – Leopoldville. 1963-64. 3v. – 13mf – 8 – ne IDC [960]

ONUC-CHRONOLOGIES / Congo. Press Services Office of Public Information, United Nations, NY – Leopoldville, New York. 1960-64. 2v. – 9mf – 8 – ne IDC [960]

ONUITGE GEVEN BRIEVEN VAN EENIGE PATERS DER SOCIETEIT VAN JESUS, MISSIONARISSEN IN CHINA VAN DE 17 EN 18 EEUW / Visschers, P – Arnhem, 1857 – 3mf – 9 – HTM-233/1 – ne IDC [240]

DIE ONURIS-LEGENDE / Junker, H – Wien, 1917. BNE-20,030/1 – 9 – ne IDC [390]

DE ONWAARDIGE WERELD / Luiken, J – O 352. 1710 – 9 – ne IDC [760]

THE ONWARD CRY AND OTHER SERMONS / Brooke, Stopford Augustus – London: Duckworth, 1911 – 1mf – us A.T.L.A. [240]

ONZE BOND – (Missing: 1928(1-3)) – Arnhem. v1-7. 1928-1933 – 10mf – 9 – ne IDC [331]

ONZE COURANT – (Suspended: 1901-02. 1905, 1913 not available for microfilming) – Graaff-Reinet, South Africa. 4 Jul 1892-31 Dec 1923 – 27r – 1,16 diazo available at reduced price – sa SA Libr [072]

OO MEYO ACHIMOOWIN ST MARK – The Gospel according to St. Mark trans. into cree...by James Hunter. London: Printed for the British and Foreign Bible Society, 1876. 01021. (Pre-1900 Canadiana) – 9 – cn C.I.H.M. [240]

OOLENOY BAPTIST CHURCH. PICKENS COUNTY. PICKENS, SOUTH CAROLINA : CHURCH RECORDS – 1832-1977 – 1 – 53.15 – us Baptist [240]

OORKONDENBOEK DER GRAAFSCHAPPEN GELRE EN ZUTPHEN / Sloet, L – Den Haag, 1872 – Dfl60.00 – ne Slangenburg [240]

OORSPRONG EN BETEKENIS VAN DE NEDERLANDSE BEGIJNEN : EN BEGARDENBEWEGING / M ENS, A – Antwerpen, 1947 – Dfl35.00 – ne Slangenburg [240]

Oort, Henricus *see*
- DE BERGREDE
- DE DIENST DER BAALIM IN ISRAEL: NAAR AANLEIDING VAN...R. DOZY, DE ISRAELIETEN TE MEKKA
- HET MENSCHENOFFER IN ISRAEL
- OUD-ISRAELS RECHTSWEZEN
- TEXTUS HEBRAICI EMENDATIONES QUIBUS IN VETERE TESTAMENTO NEERLANDICE VERTENDO
- WAT GELOOFDEN DE JODEN IN DEN TIJD VAN JEZUS?
- WORSHIP OF BAALIM IN ISRAEL: BASED UPON...R. DOZY, THE ISRAELITES AT MECCA

HET OOSTEN – Paterson, NJ: Lont & Overkamp Pub Co, dec 1917-jan 2 1920 – us Res Libr [071]

DIE OOSTERLIG – Port Elizabeth, SA. 1937-82 – 1 – sa State Libr [072]

OOSTERLIG – (Continued as DIE BURGER (OOSKAAP)) – Port Elizabeth, South Africa. 2 Jul 1990-30 Nov 1990 – 4r – 1, 16 diazo available – sa SA Libr [960]

Oosterzee, J J van *see* DER BRIEF DES JAKOBUS

Oosterzee, Johannes Jacobus van *see*
- THE EPISTLE OF PAUL TO PHILEMON
- THE EPISTLE OF PAUL TO TITUS
- GOETHE'S STELLUNG ZUM CHRISTENTHUM
- DIE PASTORALBRIEFE UND DER BRIEF AN PHILEMON
- PRACTICAL THEOLOGY
- THE TWO EPISTLES OF PAUL TO TIMOTHY
- VIER AKADEMISCHE VORTRAEGE UND FUENFZIG APHORISMEN

OOST-WEST – v. 1-3. Den Haag. 1962-64. BH-1807 1 – 9 – ne IDC [073]

OP. 1 / Sayers, Dorothy Leigh – Oxford, B. H. Blackwell, 1916 – 1 – us U.W. Library [830]

OPAL MINER (WHITE CLIFFS) – Mar 21 1903-Jun 4 1904 – 9 – at Pascoe [072]

EN OPBYGGELIG TALE / Kierkegaard, Soren – Kjobenhavn: C.A. Reitzel, 1850 – 1mf – us A.T.L.A. [190]

OPC – 1984- – 1,5,6,9 – us UMI [510]

OPEC REVIEW – v1- 1981- – 5,6,9 – us UMI [338]

OPEN – v1- 1969- 1; v4- 5,6; v8- 9 – us UMI [073]

OPEN COMMUNION AND THE BAPTISTS OF NORWICH : REPORT OF THE PROCEEDINGS IN ATTORNEY-GENERAL V. GOULD, BEFORE THE RIGHT HONORABLE THE MASTER OF THE ROLLS, AND HIS HONOR'S JUDGMENT THEREON / Gould, George – Norwich: J. Fletcher; London: Hamilton, Adams, 1860 – 2mf – us A.T.L.A. [240]

OPEN COURT; A QUARTERLY MAGAZINE – v. 1-19. Feb 1887-Dec 1905 – 1 – us UMI [073]

THE OPEN DOOR : A CHALLENGE TO MISSIONARY ADVANCE: ADDRESSES DELIVERED... / General Missionary Convention of the Methodist Episcopal Church. 1st; ed by Fahs, Charles Harvey et al – (Includes index) – New York: Eaton & Mains; Cincinnati: Jennings & Graham, 1903 – 1mf – 9 – 0-8370-6256-X – 1986-0256 – us A.T.L.A. [240]

THE OPEN DOOR AND... / Gerig, B – London, 1930 – 3mf – 1 – ILM-1902/1 – ne IDC [327]

OPEN FILE REPORTS COLLECTION / U.S. Bureau of Mines – 1962-86 – 5169mf – 9 – $9000.00 – us Updata [622]

THE OPEN FORUM (LOS ANGELES, CALIF.: 1924) – (Library has: v.2, no.1-v.30, no.3; Jan. 3, 1925-Mar./Apr. 1953 (many issues missing)) – Los Angeles, Calif.: The American Civil Liberties Union, Southern California Branch, 1924- – 1 – CSUX86-S203 – us Hoover Inst Photo [320]

OPEN LEARNING : SYSTEMS AND PROBLEMS IN POST-SECONDARY EDUCATION / MacKenzie, Norman & Postgate, Richmond & Scupham, John – 1975 – 498p – 9 – 92-3-101332-7 – fr UNESCO [370]

OPEN LEARNING – v1-. 1986- – 1,5,6,9 – us UMI [370]

AN OPEN LETTER / Navarro Tomas, Tomas – n.p., 193? Fiche W 1069. (Blodgett Collection of Spanish Civil War Pamphlets) – 9 – us H.U. College Libr [946]

OPEN LETTER – (Series 1 1966-69 Can$20.00y) – London. series 1-8. 1966-94 – 9 – Can$37.00y – cn Micromedia [073]

AN OPEN LETTER ON CULTURE AND DEMOCRACY IN SPAIN – N.Y., 1938. Fiche W1087. (Blodgett Collection of Spanish Civil War Pamphlets) – 9 – us H.U. College Libr [946]

AN OPEN LETTER ON THE QUESTION, DO YOU WANT ANNEXATION TO THE UNITED STATES?: WRITTEN TO AN AMERICAN FRIEND BY BASTION OLD – Toronto: J. Ferguson, 1890. 03003. (Pre-1900 Canadiana) – 9 – cn C.I.H.M. [971]

AN OPEN LETTER TO HIS EMINENCE CARDINAL GIBBONS : APROPOS OF HIS INTERVIEW ON THE SEPARATION OF CHURCH AND STATE IN FRANCE / Sabatier, Paul – Boston: Sherman, French, 1908 – 1mf – us A.T.L.A. [240]

OPEN LETTER TO PRES. EISENHOWER / Sutomo – Written at the time of the A-A Conference. SE 11,584 1. 1955 – 9 – ne IDC [950]

Open Network. Denver, CO *see* PAMPHLETS, NEWSLETTERS, ETC

THE OPEN POLAR SEA / Hayes, Isaac Israel – New ed. BN 246 2. 1867 – 8 – ne IDC [910]

THE OPEN POLAR SEA: A NARRATIVE OF A VOYAGE OF DISCOVERY TOWARDS THE NORTH POLE IN THE SCHOONER UNITED STATES / Hayes, Isaac Israel – New York: Hurd and Stoughton, 1867, c1866. 05521. (Pre-1900 Canadiana) – 9 – cn C.I.H.M. [910]

OPEN PROCESS – San Francisco, CA. SF State University: 1967-1969 – 1r – 1 – $50.00 – B03718 – us Library Micro [370]

THE OPEN SECRET, OR, THE BIBLE EXPLAINING ITSELF / Smith, Hannah Whitall – Toronto: S.R. Briggs, 1885. 1 fiche – 9 – us A.T.L.A. [240]

AN OPEN VERDICT / Braddon, Mary Elizabeth – British Fiction Archive: Unit 5 – 9 – uk Bell [830]

OPEN WINDOWS – 1937-61 – 1 – 349.37 – us Baptist [240]

OPEN YARD HOUSING FOR YOUNG CATTLE – 1981 – 133p – it F.A.O. [636]

OPENING ADDRESS AT MEETING OF MINISTERS IN PREPARATION OF THE SECOND ASIAN-AFRICAN CONFERENCE, DJAKARTA / Subandrio – SE 4690 1. 10 Apr 1964 – 9 – ne IDC [950]

OPENING CEREMONY ASIAN GAMES 4 – Djakarta, 1962 (official program). In English and Indonesian. SE-3859 1 – 9 – ne IDC [790]

OPENING SERMON BEFORE THE HUDSON RIVER ASSOCIATION SOUTH, THE / Armitage, Thomas – 1851 – 1 – 5.00 – us Baptist [240]

OPENING SPEECH OF THE STATE TEACHERS COLLEGE IN BANDUNG, INDONESIA, DELIVERED ON OCT. 20, 1954 / Yamin, Muhammad – SE 3968 1 – 9 – ne IDC [370]

OPERA – v1- 1950- 1; v22- 5,6; v27- 9 – us UMI [780]

OPERA / Abaelardus, Petrus; ed by Cousin, V – Parisiis. Tomus 1-2. 1849-1859 – 51mf – 8 – ne Slangenburg [240]

OPERA / Cano, M – Coloniae Agrippinae, 1605 – 11mf – 9 – CA-9/1 – ne IDC [100]

OPERA / Horatius – Persius Satirae.1497. Holkham ms. 318. Holkham Hall, Norfolk, England – 1,14 – uk Microform Academic [760]

OPERA / Hosius, Stanislaus; ed by Dunghen, Henry – Antwerpen, 1566 – 33mf – 8 – ne Slangenburg [240]

OPERA / Vergil – 11th, 12th cents. Holkham ms. 303. Holkham Hall, Norfolk, England – 1 – uk Microform Academic [760]

OPERA / Vergil – Flemish.1473. Holkham ms. 311. Holkham Hall, Norfolk, England – 14 – uk Microform Academic [760]

OPERA ASCETICA / Rievallensis, Aelredus – 1989 – 12mf – 9 – Bf2,450.00 – 2-503-63012-X – be Brepols [240]

OPERA BEFORE 1820 – 2001 – 1200mf – 9 – ne MMF Publ [780]

OPERA BOTANICA – A societate botanica Lundensi. 7702. v1-25. 1953-1969 – 9 – ne IDC [580]

OPERA BOTANICA / Gessner, C – Norimbergae: Impensis I.M. Seligmanni, typis I.I. Fleischmanni. 2v. 1751-1771 – 14mf – ne IDC [580]

OPERA BOTANICA PER DUO SAECULA / Gesner, C – 2v. Norimbergae. 1754-71. B-7927 1 – 9 – ne IDC [580]

OPERA BOTANICA PER DUO SAECULA / Gesner, C – 5927 1. 2 v. 1751-1771 – 9 – ne IDC [580]

OPERA CANADA – v1- 1960- 1; v13- 5,6; v18- 9 – us UMI [073]

OPERA CHIAMATA CONFVSIONE DELLA SETTA MACHVMETANA, ... / Andres, J – Seuiglia, 1537 – 2mf – 9 – H-8245/1 – ne IDC [956]

OPERA COLLECTION / ed by Hul, Dick van den – (Collection includes a printed guide) – 1603mf – 9 – OPR – ne IDC [780]

OPERA CUM EDITA TUM INEDITA / Hernandez, F – v. 1. Matriti. 1790; v. 2. 1790; v. 3. 1790. B-911 2 – 8 – ne IDC [580]

OPERA CUM OBSERVATIONIBUS ET NOTIS GABR. ALBASPINAEI / Optatus, Milevitanus – Parisiis, 1631 – 25mf – 8 – ne Slangenburg [240]

OPERA DIPLOMATICA ET HISTORICA / Miraeus, A; ed by Foppens, J F – Ed. 2a. Lovanii. Tom 1-2. 1723 – Dfl214.00 – ne Slangenburg [240]

OPERA DIPLOMATICA ET HISTORICA, TOM. 3-4 *see* DIPLOMATUM BELGICORUM NOVA COLLECTIO

OPERA DOCTORIS...IN HIS PANIAE REGIAS CONSTITUTIONES / Acevedo, Alfonso de – Madrid: J. Haxrey, 1612 – 1 – sp Bibl Santa Ana [340]

OPERA ET VITA... / Bruno Cartusiense – Paris, 1704 – 9 – sp Cultura [920]

OPERA GLASS – Boston. v1-4. 1894-98 – 1r – 1 – £60.00 – uk Chadwyck [780]

OPERA GLASS, DEVOTED TO THE FINE ARTS, LITERATURE AND THE DRAMA – Sep 1828-29 – 1 – us UMI [700]

OPERA, HACTENUS IN LUCEM NON EDITA / Goropius, J (Called Becanus) – O 620. 1580 – 9 – ne IDC [450]

OPERA HISTORICA / Trithemius, J – Franceforti, 1601 – 46mf – 8 – Dfl161.00 – ne Slangenburg [240]

OPERA LATINA 134 / Lulle, Raymond – 1985 – 9mf – 9 – Bf975.00 – 2-503-63392-7 – be Brepols [240]

OPERA LATINA 76-81 / Lulle, Raymond – 1989 – 9mf – 9 – Bf1,675.00 – 2-503-63794-9 – be Brepols [240]

OPERA LATINA 114-117 / Lulle, Raymond – 1982 – 9mf – 9 – Bf975.00 – 2-503-63362-5 – be Brepols [240]

OPERA LATINA 123-127 / Lulle, Raymond – 1984 – 9mf – 9 – Bf1,550.00 – be Brepols [240]

OPERA LATINA 135-141 / Lulle, Raymond – 1983 – 9mf – 9 – Bf975.00 – 2-503-63372-2 – be Brepols [240]

OPERA LATINA 190-200 / Lulle, Raymond – 1988 – 8mf – 9 – Bf1,550.00 – 2-503-63782-5 – be Brepols [240]

OPERA LATINA 201-207 / Lulle, Raymond – 1987 – 13mf – 9 – Bf1,850.00 – 2-503-63762-0 – be Brepols [240]

OPERA LATINA 208-212 / Lulle, Raymond – 1991 – 4mf – 9 – Bf1,250.00 – 2-503-63802-3 – be Brepols [240]

OPERA LATINA SIVE IN LINGUAM LATINAM TRANSLATA 86-91 / Lulle, Raymond – 1993 – 8mf – 9 – Bf1,700.00 – 2-503-64112-1 – be Brepols [450]

OPERA MEDICA / Galeno – Venecia, 1490 – 14mf – 9 – sp Cultura [610]

OPERA MINORA / Iunior, Arnobius – 1992 – 12mf – 9 – Bf1,050.00 – 2-503-60252-5 – be Brepols [450]

OPERA NEWS – v1- 1936- 1; v35- 5,6,9 – us UMI [780]

OPERA NOVA CHIAMATA PORTOLANO... – Vineggia, [1539/1540] – 1mf – 9 – H-8146/1 – ne IDC [956]

OPERA OMNIA / Agobardus Lugdunensis; ed by Acker, L van – 1981 – 12mf – 9 – Bf5,500.00 – 2-503-03521-3 – be Brepols [450]

OPERA OMNIA / Arnobius iunior – 1992 – 12mf – 9 – Bf2,500.00 – be Brepols [240]

OPERA OMNIA / Bochartus, Sam; ed by Villemandy, Leusdende – Leiden, 1692 – 105mf – 8 – ne Slangenburg [290]

OPERA OMNIA / Calvin, J – Amsterdam, 1667.-9v – 324mf – 8 – ne Slangenburg [290]

OPERA OMNIA / Covarrubias y Leyra, D de – Lugduni. 2v. 1661 – 22mf – 9 – CA-65/1 – ne IDC [240]

OPERA OMNIA / Dionysius, Cart. – Monstrolii-Tornaci. v42. 1896-1913 – 707mf – 8 – ne Slangenburg [240]

OPERA OMNIA / Erasmus, Desiderius; ed by Clerc, Jean le – 10v. 1703-6 – 5r – 1 – $365.00 – us OmniSys [450]

OPERA OMNIA / Erasmus, Desiderius; ed by Clerici, J – Leiden, 1703.-10v – 266mf – 8 – ne Slangenburg [290]

OPERA OMNIA / Galen – 108mf – 9 – us UMI [080]

OPERA OMNIA / Gerson, John – Antwerpen, 1706.-5v – 167mf – 8 – ne Slangenburg [290]

OPERA OMNIA / Huberinus, Caspar – Ed. by G. Franz. Together with the Seelenasznei Medicina AnimaeOF Urbanus Rhegius, and other related works. 69 titles – 9 – ne IDC [150]

OPERA OMNIA / Malpighi, M – London, 1686 – 32mf – 9 – ne IDC [610]

OPERA OMNIA / Melanchton, P – Wittemb., 1562. 4v – 91mf – 8 – ne Slangenburg [290]

OPERA OMNIA / Molinaeus, Car. – Parisiis. Tomi 1-4. 1658 – 167mf – 8 – ne Slangenburg [240]

OPERA OMNIA / Morales, Cristobal – Madrid: Arch. Ibero Americano, 1965 – 1 – sp Bibl Santa Ana [780]
OPERA OMNIA / Origenis; ed by Lommatzsch, C H E – Tomus 1-25 – 192mf – 9 – ne Slangenburg [240]
OPERA OMNIA / Sanchez de las Brozas, Francisco – Tomos I-IV. 1766 – 9 – 1.50f – sp Bibl Santa Ana [890]
OPERA OMNIA / Sepulvada, Ion. Gen. – Col. Agrippinae, 1602 – 19mf – 8 – ne Slangenburg [240]
OPERA OMNIA / Stapleton, Thomas – Lutetiae Parisiorum, 1620 – 212mf – 8 – ne Slangenburg [240]
OPERA OMNIA / Thomasio, J M; ed by Blanchini, J – Tomus Primus... Romae, 1744 – 50mf – 8 – ne Slangenburg [290]
OPERA OMNIA / Thomasius – Roma, 1747. 7v – 91mf – 8 – ne Slangenburg [290]
OPERA OMNIA BOTANICA / Plukenet, L – 4v. Londini. 1720-25. B-6154 2 – 8 – ne IDC [580]
OPERA OMNIA, GRAECE, SYRIACE ET LATINE / Ephraemi Syri – Romae 1737-1746. 6v – 164mf – 8 – ne Slangenburg [240]
OPERA OMNIA IN UNIVERSUM VETUS ET NOVUM TESTAMENTUM / Caro, Hugo de S – Coloniae Agrippinae. Tomi 8. 1621 – 188mf – 8 – ne Slangenburg [220]
OPERA OMNIA MEDICO-PRATICA ET ANATOMICA HAC SEXTA EDITIONE, POST ULTIMAN ULTRAJECTINAM AUCTA, NOVISQUE LOCUPLETATA DISSERTATIONIBUS EPISTOLIS AND PRAEFATIONE QUAE SYSTEMATIS BAGLIVIANI USUM APERIT, ADVERSARIORUMQUE DILUIT OBJECTIONES / Baglivi, Georgii – London, Paris. 1704. SEM35P89 – 1r – 1 – Can$20.00 – cn Bibl Nat [610]
OPERA OMNIA QUAE SUPERSTES ADHUC EDITIT / D'Espence, C – Lutetiae Parisiorum, 1619 – 23mf – 9 – CA-95/1 – ne IDC [240]
OPERA OMNIA QUOTQUOT IN SACRAE SCRIPTURAE EXPOSITIONUM REPERIUNTUR / Cajetan, T de V – Lugduni. 5v. 1639 – 53mf – 9 – CA-72/1 – ne IDC [240]
OPERA OMNIA (RS75) / Simeon Of Durham; ed by Arnold, T – (v1 1882 Dfl30.00. v2 1885 Dfl32.00) – ne Slangenburg [240]
OPERA OMNIA THEOLOGICA / Coccejus, J – Amsterdam, 1673.-8v – 358mf – 8 – ne Slangenburg [290]
OPERA OMNIA THEOLOGICA / Symons, Menno – Amsterdam, 1681 – 22mf – 8 – ne Slangenburg [290]
OPERA OMNIA THEOLOGICA... / Grotius, Hugo de – Amsterdam, 1679.-4v – 135mf – 8 – ne Slangenburg [290]
OPERA OMNIA...FAUSTINO AREVALO...TOMUS OCTAVUS ET ULTIMUS / Isidore de Seville, Saint – Paris: Migne, 1862 – 1 – sp Bibl Santa Ana [240]
OPERA OMNIA...FAUSTINO AREVALO...TOMUS QUARTUS... / Isidore de Seville, Saint – Paris: Migne, 1862 – 1 – sp Bibl Santa Ana [240]
OPERA OMNIA...MARSILIO FICINO INTERPRETE / Platonis – Ludg., 1590 idem, Francof, 1602 – 39mf – 8 – ne Slangenburg [180]
OPERA OMNIA...RECENSENTE / Arevalo, Faustino – v. 1-7. 1797-1803 – 9 – 1.50f – sp Bibl Santa Ana [780]
OPERA OMNIA...RECENSENTE FAUSTINO AREVALO... : TOMO 4. ETYMOLOGIARUM / Isidore de Seville, Saint – Roma, Antonii Fulgonii, 1801 – 1 – sp Bibl Santa Ana [240]
OPERA OMNIA...RECENSENTE FAUSTINO AREVALO... : TOMO 5. LIBRI DIFFERENTIARUM / Isidore de Seville, Saint – Roma: Antonii Fulgonii, 1802 – 1 – sp Bibl Santa Ana [780]
OPERA OMNIA...RECENSENTE FAUSTINO AREVALO, TOMO 6 : OPERA THEOLOGICA, LITURGICA ET MYSTICA... / Isidore de Seville, Saint – Roma: Antonium Fulgonium, 1802. Tambien Tomo 7 – 1 – sp Bibl Santa Ana [240]
OPERA OMNIA...RECENSENTE FAUSTINO AREVALO, TOMUS PRIMUS ET SECUNDUS / Isidore de Seville, Saint – Paris: Migne, 1862 – 1 – sp Bibl Santa Ana [240]
OPERA OMNIA...RECENSENTE FAUSTINO AREVALO...TOMI TERTIUS ET QUARTUS... / Isidore de Seville, Saint – Paris: Migne, 1850 – 1 – sp Bibl Santa Ana [240]
OPERA PHILOSOPHICA ET TRAGAEDIAE / Seneca – 14th Century. Holkham Ms 390 – 1 – uk Microform Academic [760]
OPERA PIA ET SPIRITUALIA... / Tritheme, Jean – Moguntiae, 1605 – 22mf – 9 – CA-91/1 – ne IDC [240]
OPERA POETICA / Campiliiensis, Christanus – 1993 – 7mf – 9 – Bf1,950.00 – 2-503-63192-4 – be Brepols [450]
OPERA POSTHUMA / Spinoza, Benedictus de – H 1404 2. 1677 – 8 – ne IDC [190]
OPERA QUAE EXSTNT OMNIA / Sadoleti, Iac. – Veronae. Tomus 1-4. 1737-1738 – 30mf – 8 – ne Slangenburg [240]
OPERA QVOTQVOT EXTANT OMNIA / Giovio, P – Basileae. 4pts. 1578 – 25mf – 9 – H-8374/1 – ne IDC [956]
OPERA THEOLOGICA / Arminius, Jacobus – Lugd. Batavorum, 1629 – 17mf – 8 – ne Slangenburg [240]
OPERA THEOLOGICA / Ursinus, Zach – (Tomus 1: Heidelberg, 1612. 21mf; Tomus 2: id. 1612. 38mf; Tomus 3: id. 1612. 20mf) – 8 – ne Slangenburg [290]
OPERA THEOLOGICA OMNIA... / Gomarus, F – Amsterdam, 1644 – 53mf – 8 – ne Slangenburg [290]
OPERA THOMAE / Campis, Thoma a – Paris, 1549 – 19mf – 8 – ne Slangenburg [290]
OPERA VARIA / Swedenborg, Emanuel von – Amsterdam, 1763-1769 – 29mf – 8 – ne Slangenburg [290]
OPERA VARIA, IN QUIBUS CONTINENTUR FUNDAMENTA BOTANICA, SPONSALIA PLANTARUM, ET SYSTEMA NATURAE / Linnaeus, Carl – Lucae. 1758. B-7297 2 – 8 – ne IDC [580]
OPERACION MASACRE : [UN PROCESO QUE NO HA SIDO CLAUSURADO] / Walsh, Rodolfo J – Buenos Aires: Ediciones Sigla, [1957] – 1 – CSUXADH5438-B – us Hoover Inst Photo [972]
OPERACION "ROSA NEGRA" / Flores, Jose – Buenos Aires: Editorial Errele, 1956 – 1 – CSUXADJ8418-B – us Hoover Inst Photo [972]
OPERA/EPITOME LIVII ETC / Caesar, Julius – Late 14th, 15th cents. Holkham mss. 342, 343, 366. Holkham Hall, Norfolk, England – 1 – uk Microform Academic [760]
L'OPERAIA – New York, NY, Aug. 30, 1913-Jan. 11, 1919 – 5r – 1 – us I.H.R.C. [978]
O OPERARIO – Manaos, Amazonas. 12-19 Dez 1892 – 1,5,6 – bl Biblioteca [072]
O OPERARIO – Montes Claros, Brazil. Sept 1932-Aug 1945. Very scattered issues – 1 – bl Biblioteca [072]
O OPERARIO : ORGAO DA UNAIO OPERARIA BENEFICENTE – DEUS, HONRA E TRABALHO – Diamantina, 12 Apr 1925 – 1,5,6 – bl Biblioteca [072]
O OPERARIO – '(s.l.')-Sao Luis, Brazil. 27 Nov 1892-24 Mar 1894 – 1,5,6 – bl Biblioteca [072]
OPERAS / Leonardo, Leo – 1 – 115.00 – us L of C Photodup [780]
OPERAS / Meyerbeer, Giacomo – Full scores – 1 – 187.00 – us L of C Photodup [780]
[OPERAS (SKETCHES)]. HOLOGRAPH : CONTAINS SKETCHES OF PORTION OF VARIOUS WORKS / Offenbach, J – 1 – us Sibley [780]
OPERATING ENGINEER – v. 3-4 1950-51 – 1 – us UMI [621]
OPERATION DIXIE : THE CIO ORGANIZING COMMITTEE PAPERS, 1946-1953 – 75r – 1 – $5775.00 – us UMI [331]
OPERATION LITTLE SWITCH / U.S. Army. Forces in the Far East – v. 1-4. 1 Aug 1953-15 Nov 1953 – 1 – 80.00 – us L of C Photodup [950]
OPERATION OF THE FEDERAL JUDICIAL COUNCILS / Flanders, Steven & McDermott, John T – Washington: FJC, 1978 – 2mf – 9 – $3.00 – LLMC 95-302 – us L.L.M.C. [340]
OPERATION REBUTTAL / Brookes, Patrick – AIR paper, c1972 – 9 – 1.00f – at Libertarian Micro [335]
OPERATIONAL EFFICIENCY OF AGRICULTURAL COOPERATIVES IN DEVELOPING COUNTRIES / Duelfer, E – 1977 – 188p – it F.A.O. [334]
OPERATIONES CHIRURGICAE NOVUM LUMEN EXHIBENTES OBSTETRICANTIBUS / Deventer, H van – Lugduni Batavorum, 1701 – 7mf – 9 – ne IDC [618]
L'OPERATION-LABOUR / Fadli, M – Rabat. 1961. BNE-3052 1 – 9 – ne IDC [331]
OPERATIONS MANUAL FOR A PROTECTED AREA SYSTEM : GUIDELINES FOR DEVELOPING COUNTRIES – 1984 – 91p – it F.A.O. [630]
LES OPERATIONS MILITAIRES EN ESPAGNE / International Committee of Coordination and Information to Aid Republican Spain – Paris, 1938. Fiche W1088. (Blodgett Collection of Spanish Civil War Pamphlets) – 9 – us H.U. College Libr [946]
OPERATIONS OF THE ALLIED INTELLIGENCE BUREAU, GHQ, SWPA / U.S. Army. Far East Command – 1948. 3v – 1 – 21.00 – us L of C Photodup [950]
OPERATIONS OF THE ALLIED TRANSLATOR AND INTERPRETER SECTION, GHQ, SWPA / U.S. Army. Far East Command – v. 1-2. 1948 – 1 – 25.00 – us L of C Photodup [950]
OPERATIONS OF THE CIVIL INTELLIGENCE SECTION, GHQ, FEC AND SCAP / U.S. Army. Far East Command – v. 1-4 – 5 – 28.00 – us L of C Photodup [950]
OPERATIONS OF THE COUNTER INTELLIGENCE CORPS IN THE SWPA / U.S. Army. Far East Command – v. 1-2. 1948 – 1 – 20.00 – us L of C Photodup [950]
THE OPERATIONS OF THE HOLY SPIRIT IMPERCEPTIBLE, AND HOW MEN MAY KNOW WHEN THEY ARE UNDER THE GUIDANCE AND INFLUENCE OF THE SPIRIT:... / Dockwray, T – Newcastle, [1743] – 1mf – 9 – MP-304/1 – ne IDC [240]
OPERATIONS OF THE MILITARY INTELLIGENCE SECTION, GHA, SWPA/FEC/SCAP / U.S. Army. Far East Command – 1951. 6v – 1 – 38.00 – us L of C Photodup [950]
OPERATIONS OF THE TECHNICAL INTELLIGENCE UNIT IN THE SWPA / U.S. Army. Far East Command – 1948 – 1 – 18.00 – us L of C Photodup [950]
OPERATIONS REPORTS / California. Employment Development Dept – Jul 1936-Jul 1978. 166 fiches. (Harvard Law School Library Collection.) – 9 – $1.50f – us H.U. Law [330]
OPERATIONS RESEARCH – (1985-. 5,6,9) – v4-. 1956- – 1 – us UMI [073]
OPERATIONS RESEARCH : MANAGEMENT APPLICATIONS – 1970 – 10mf – 9 – $15.00 – 0-87703-232-7 – us Univelt [629]
OPERATIONS RESEARCH : MATHEMATICAL AND COMPUTER METHODS AND MILITARY APPLICATIONS – 1970 – 23mf – 9 – $30.00 – 0-87703-234-3 – us Univelt [629]
OPERATIONS RESEARCH : URBAN PROBLEMS – 1970 – 13mf – 9 – $15.00 – 0-87703-233-5 – us Univelt [629]
Operations Research Society of America *see* JOURNAL
OPERATIONS RESEARCH-SPEKTRUM – v.1-3, 1980-81. ISSN: 0171-6468 – 1,5,6,9,13 – 64.00v – us UMI [000]
THE OPERATIVE – London. -w. Nov 1838-Jun 1839. (1 reel) – 1 – uk British Libr Newspaper [072]
OPERE E LETTERE = SELECTIONS / Wackenroder, Wilhelm Heinrich – (Includes bibliographical references. Italian translation from German) – Lanciano: R Carabba, 1916 – 1r – 1 – us U.W. Library [800]
OPERE POLITICHE E LETTERARIE. / Giannotti, Donati – Florence. 1850. 2 vols – 1 – us Res Libr [945]
OPERETTA-DINNER *see* 1 LA CHANSON FRANCAISE A TRAVERS LES SIECLES
DIE OPERNDICHTUNG DER DEUTSCHEN ROMANTIK / Ehrenhaus, Martin – (Includes bibliographical references) – Breslau: F Hirt, 1911 – 1 – us U.W. Library [430]
DIE OPERNDICHTUNG LORTZINGS : QUELLEN UND UMWELT: VERHAELTNIS ZUR ROMANTIK UND ZU WAGNER / Laue, Hellmuth – (Includes bibliographical references) – Bonn a. Rh.: L Roehrscheid, 1932 – 1r – 1 – us U.W. Library [780]
OPERNFUEHRER – Berlin. 1900-13. 2 reels – 1 – 39.00 – us L of C Photodup [780]
DAS OPFERLAMM : SONETTE / Park, A – Augsburg: Literarisches Institut von M Huttler, 1890 – 1r – 1 – us U.W. Library [810]
DIE OPHEFFING VAN DIE KLEURLINGBEVOLKING / Cruse, Henri Pierre – Stellenbosch: Christenstudenteveleniging van Suid-Afrika. v1. 1947- – us Res Libr [960]
OPHIS / Lemercier – (French Theatre Series). Paris. Rayolle, an VII. 1798 – 9 – fr Hachette [820]
OPHTALMOTONOMETRIE / Langenhan, F – M-9. 1925 – 9 – ne IDC [610]
OPHTHALMIC LITERATURE – 1947- 1; 1975- 5,6,9 – us UMI [617]
OPHTHALMIC RESEARCH – v7-. 1975- – 1,5,9 – us UMI [617]
OPHTHALMO-GRAPHIA / Briggs, W – M-313. 1676 – 9 – ne IDC [610]
OPHTHALMOLOGICA – (v. 159-169, 1969-74. 5,6) – v. 151-169, 1966-74 – 1 – us UMI [617]
OPHTHALMOLOGICA – v170-. 1975- – 1,5,9 – us UMI [617]
OPIE COLLECTION OF CHILDREN'S LITERATURE – (20,000 children's literature titles from Bodleian Library) – Units 1,2 and 3 available. Ca 600mf per unit – 9 – $1,950.00 per unit – us UMI [800]
OPINIA = OPINIONS – (In Polish) – Warsaw, PL. v2 no2 25 Jul 1946-v4 no52 28 Mar 1949 – 1r – 1 – $25.00 – cn Can Microfilming [072]
A OPINIAO – Estancia, Brazil. 18 Jul-22Aug 1880. Incomplete – 1 – bl Biblioteca [072]
A OPINIAO : ORGAM DE ALUMNOS DO GYMNASIO AMAZONENSE – Manaos, Amazonas. 27 Out 1910 – 1,5,6 – bl Biblioteca [072]
A OPINIAO : ORGAM DOS INTERESSES DO POVINHO – Manaus, Amazonas. 1 Jan 1910 – 1,5,6 – bl Biblioteca [072]
A OPINIAO : ORGAO DE ESTUDANTES – Curitiba, 3 Aug-8 Dec 1887 – 1,5,6 – bl Biblioteca [072]
A OPINIAO : PERIODICO LITTERARIO E NOTICIOSO – Corumba, 1 Jan-Dec 1878; Jan, May 1879; 10 Jun 1880 – 1,5,6 – bl Biblioteca [072]
A OPINIAO – S. Carlos do Pinhal, 6 Apr 1899 – 1,5,6 – bl Biblioteca [072]
A OPINIAO – Sao Joao d'el-Rei, 25 Mar 1908 – 1,5,6 – bl Biblioteca [072]
OPINIAO – Maceio, Alagoas. 17 Ago-15 Set 1885 – 1,5,6 – bl Biblioteca [072]
OPINIAO – Rio de Janeiro, 23 Oct 1972-4 Apr 1977 – 1,5,6 – bl Biblioteca [072]
OPINIAO MUNICIPAL : ORGAO POLITICO, CATHOLICO E NOTICIOSO – Marianna, 24 Jan 1913 – 1,5,6 – bl Biblioteca [072]
L'OPINION – Hull, Canada. 25 aut 1933-v1 n13. 18 nov 1933 – 1r – 1 – Can$30.00 – cn Can Microfilming [072]
L'OPINION – Journal des principes conservateurs. no. 1-36. Paris. 1er juil-5 nov 1847. mq no. 27 – 1 – fr A.C.R.P.P. [073]
L'OPINION – Montreal, Canada. 12 oct 1905-v4 n9. 21 oct 1908 – 1r – 1 – Can$25.00 – cn Can Microfilming [072]
LA OPINION – Los Angeles. Calif. 1926- – 1 – us UMI [071]
LA OPINION – Trujillo, 1909-1965 – 5 – sp Bibl Santa Ana [073]
LA OPINION – Veracruz, Mexico: [s.n. nov 11 1911-jan 9 1915] – 5r – 1 – us Res Libr [072]
OPINION – Branford, CT. -w. 1896-1912 – 1 – us UMI [071]
OPINION – Chinook. Mont. 1890-1948; 1956-1959; 1966- – 1 – us UMI [071]
OPINION – Los Angeles, Calif. 1900-1901 – 1 – us Res Libr [071]
OPINION AND BRIEF IN THE CASE OF MULLER VS OREGON / Brandeis, Louis Dembitz – (Commonly referred to as "The Brandeis Brief") – 1907 – 2mf – 9 – $3.00 – LLMC 82-000 – us L.L.M.C. [340]
OPINION AS TO THE VALIDITY OF THE TAX ON THE NON-RESIDENT STOCKHOLDERS OF THE NATIONAL BANKS / Thomas, Benjamin F – Boston, Mudge, 1868. 10 p. LL-2354 – 1 – us L of C Photodup [340]
OPINION DE M. CONDORCET SUR LE RAPPORT DES COMITES MILITAIRE, DIPLOMATIQUE ET DE L'ORDINAIRE DES FINANCES, REUNIS / Condorcet, Marie Jean Antoine Nicolas de – Lue le 28 decembre 1791.Paris: Imp. Nat., s.d.7p. 1 fiche. (Political Science Collection) – 9 – $6.00 – fr Bibl Nationale [320]
OPINION DES ANCIENS SUR LES JUIFS / Mirabaud, Jean-Baptiste de – (D'Holbach series). 1769 – 9 – fr Hachette [305]
LA OPINION DIARO POPULAR INDEPENDIENTE – Los Angeles, CA. 1926-70 – 197r – 1 – $9,850.00 – C02386 – us Library Micro [071]
L'OPINION DU PEUPLE – Quebec, Canada. 8 avr-v1 n11. 16 mai 1871 – 1r – 1 – Can$25.00 – cn Can Microfilming [072]

OPINION FORMADA EN EL ASUNTO DE LOS FERROCARRILES DE LA PROVINCIA DE CACERES / Calzado Pedrilla, Felipe - 1868 - 9 - 1.50f - sp Bibl Santa Ana [946]

L'OPINION FRANCAISE ET LA GUERRE DES BOERS / Pelletier, J G - 1899-1902 - 9 - fr Hachette [960]

L'OPINION NATIONALE - Journal politique quot. Paris. 1 sept 1859-16 oct 1876, 6 mars-22 dec 1883, 28 mars 1896, 1 juil 1902-04, 5 juil 1914 - 1 - fr A.C.R.P.P. [073]

L'OPINION NATIONALE - Quebec, Canada. 3 mai 1870-v1 n23. 3 aut 1870 - 1r - 1 - Can$25.00 - cn Can Microfilming [072]

OPINION OF HORACE BINNEY, ESQ., UPON THE RIGHT OF THE CITY COUNCILS TO SUBSCRIBE FOR STOCK IN THE PENNSYLVANIA RAIL-ROAD COMPANY / Binney, Horace - Philadelphia, Sherman, 1846. 32 p. LL-498 - 1 - us L of C Photodup [340]

L'OPINION OUVRIERE : QUARTIER ST-HENRI - Montreal. 5 dec 1967-v1 n2. jan 1968 - 1r - 1 - Can$25.00 - cn Can Microfilming [072]

L'OPINION PUBLIQUE : ILLUSTRE - Montreal, Canada. 1 jan 1870-27 dec 1883 - 6r - 1 - Can$60.00r - cn Can Microfilming [073]

L'OPINION PUBLIQUE - Organe des interets generaux a Madagascar. Tamatave. 1891-juil 1892 - 1 - fr A.C.R.P.P. [073]

L'OPINION PUBLIQUE / ed by Tache, Louis-H et al - Montreal, Canada. 16 dec 1892-16 jun 1893 - 1r - 1 - Can$40.00 - cn Can Microfilming [073]

L'OPINION PUBLIQUE - Worcester, MA. 27 jan 1893-31 dec 1901; 30 jan-30 jun 1931 - 7r - 1 - Can$60.00r - cn Can Microfilming [071]

L'OPINIONE - Florence, Rome. 1 Jan 1870-20 Dec 1900 - 58r - 1 - uk British Libr Newspaper [072]

L'OPINIONE - (In Italian) - Philadelphia, PA. 1927-35 - 39r - 1 - $3,315.00 - D3383 - us Scholarly Res [071]

L'OPINIONE PUBBLICA NELLE... / Cavaglieri, A - Firenze, 1907 - 1mf - 1 - ILM-1595-1 - ne IDC [327]

OPINIONI DE' CANTORI ANTICHI, E MODERNI O SIENO OSSERVAZIONI SOPRA IL CANTO FIGURATO / Tosi, P - 1723 - 9 - us Sibley [780]

OPINIONS : BOARD OF REVIEW, JAG BRANCH, EUROPEAN THEATER OF OPERATIONS, HOLDINGS, OPINIONS AND REVIEWS / U.S. Army. Judge Advocate General. Board of Review, ETO - (Covers: CM-ETO-839 to CM-ETO-19354. With 2 index/digest vols covering 1942-1 Jun 1945, and a suppl index vol covering Jun-Nov 1945) - v1-34. 1942-45. Washington: Office of the JAG, 1945-46 - 172mf - 9 - $258.00 - LLMC 82-221 - us L.L.M.C. [340]

OPINIONS : BOARD OF REVIEW. JAG BRANCH, NORTH AFRICAN AND MEDITERRANEAN THEATERS OF OPERATIONS; HOLDINGS, OPINIONS AND REVIEWS / U.S. Army. Judge Advocate General. Board of Review, NATO-MTO - (Covers: CM.NATO-1 to CM-NATO-3940. CM-MTO-4061 to CM-MTO-7658) - v1-7. 1943-46. Washington: Ofice of the JAG, 1946 - 32mf - 9 - $48.00 - LLMC 84-225 - us L.L.M.C. [340]

OPINIONS : BOARD OF REVIEW, JAG BRANCH, PACIFIC OCEAN AREA, HOLDINGS, OPINIONS AND REVIEWS / U.S. Army. Judge Advocate General. Board of Review, POA - (Covers: CM-POA-15 to CM-POA-379) - 1944-45. Washington: Office of the JAG, 1946 - 4mf - 9 - $6.00 - LLMC 84-223 - us L.L.M.C. [340]

OPINIONS : BOARD OF REVIEW, JAG BRANCH, SOUTHWEST PACIFIC AREA (A) AND PACIFIC (P); HOLDINGS, OPINIONS; AND REVIEWS / U.S. Army. Judge Advocate General. Board of Review, A&P - (Covers: CM-A-55 to CM-A-2320. CM-P-4 to CM-P-1368) - v1-4. 1942-46. Washington: Office of the JAG, 1946 - 20mf - 9 - $30.00 - LLMC 84-222 - us L.L.M.C. [340]

OPINIONS / Virginia. Industrial commission - Richmond. v. 1-21. 1919-1939 - 1 - us NY Public [330]

OPINIONS, 1817-32 / U. S. Attorney General - 3rolls. T412 - 1 - us Nat'l Archives [324]

OPINIONS (A-G) / Delaware - 1963-77.3 reels - 1 - $35.00r - us Trans-Media [340]

LES OPINIONS ALLEMANDES SUR LA RECONSTRUCTION DU DROIT INTERNATIONAL / Frachon, A - N.p., n.d. - 5mf - 1 - ILM-2115/1 - ne IDC [327]

OPINIONS AND DECISIONS / Wisconsin. Railroad Commission - v1-34, Jul 20, 1905-Jun 4, 1931. 368 fiches. (Harvard Law School Library Collection.) - 9 - $1.50f - us H.U. Law [336]

OPINIONS AND REPORTS OF THE ECONOMIC AND SOCIAL COMMITTEE : (IRREGULAR) - (Available in 9 languages. Interinstitutional catalogue available in paper version free of charge) - 9 - ECU590.00 subsc - EY-CO-96-Z00-EN-A - lu EEC [340]

OPINIONS DE L'ILE JESUS = THE CITIZEN OF ILE JESUS / ed by Lavoie, J-N - Ville de Laval, Canada. 1 fev 1962-20 jun 1966 - 3r - 1 - Can$60.00r - cn Can Microfilming [072]

OPINIONS LITERAIRES, PHILOSOPHIQUES ET INDUSTRIELLES / Saint-Simon, Leon H & Rodrigues, Olinde - Paris, Bossange. 1825. 392p Les Saint-Simoniens, 1825-1834 - 9 - fr Hachette [320]

OPINIONS OF THE ATTORNEY GENERAL OF THE U.S. / U.S. Department of Justice - (With index/digest) - v1-42. 1789-1974 - 347mf - 9 - $520.00 - LLMC 78-408 - us L.L.M.C. [324]

OPINIONS OF THE OFFICE OF LEGAL COUNSEL OF THE UNITED STATES DEPARTMENT OF JUSTICE / ed by Ulman, Leon - Washinton DC: Office of the Legal Counsel, 1980. v1-16. 1977-1992 - 9 - $175.00 set - us Hein [340]

OPINION-TRIBUNE - Glenwood. Iowa. -w. 1951- - 1 - us UMI [071]

OPIS' DEL KHRANIASHCHIKHSIA V ARKHIVE MOSKOVSKOI KUPECHESKOI UPRAVY / Moscow - (v1. Prilozhenie. M. 1890; Ukazateli. M. 1891. v2. 1863-1888 gg. 676 v. M. 1892; Ukazateli. M. 1893) - v.1. 1787-1863 gg. M. 1888; Ukazateli. M. 1889. BR-9892 1 - 9 - ne IDC [025]

OPIS' DELAM ARTILLERIISKOGO DEPARTAMENTA MORSKOGO MINISTERSTVA / Russia. Morskoe Ministerstvo - 1827-52.Saint Petersburg, 1857. 117p.Catalogue materials in TsGAVMF. BR-10,793/1 - 9 - ne IDC [324]

OPIS' DELAM DEPARTAMENTA KORABEL'NYKH LESOV MORSKOGO MINISTERSTVA, KHRANIASHCHIMSIA V GLAVNOM MORSKOM ARKHIVE, 1799-1853 G / Russia. Morskoe Ministerstvo - Spb. 1858. BR-10,794 1 - 9 - ne IDC [324]

OPIS' DELAM GLAVNOGO MEDITSINSKOGO UPRAVLENIIA MORSKOGO MINISTERSTVA, KHRANIASHCHIMSIA V ARKHIVE MINISTERSTVA / Russia. Morskoe Ministerstvo - pt. 1. 1827-52; Spb. 1853-56. BR-10,795 1 - 9 - ne IDC [324]

OPIS' DELAM I ZHURNALAM BUMAG VOENNO-POKHODNOI E.I.V. KANTSELIARII PO MORSKOI CHASTI I DELAM KANTSELIARII MORSKOGO MINISTERSTVA / Russia. Morskoe Ministerstvo - Pt 1: 1836-55. St. Petersburg, 1856.197p. Describes naval records now in TsGAVMF. BR-10,797/1 - 9 - ne IDC [355]

OPIS' DELAM KANTSELIARII FLOTA GENERAL-INTENDANTA KHRANIASHCHIMSIA V OBSHCHEM ARKHIVE...1827-55 / Russia. Morskoe Ministerstvo - St. Petersburg, 1859. 90p. Inventories records now in TsGAVMF. BR-10,798/1 - 9 - ne IDC [355]

OPIS' DELAM KORABLESTROITEL'NOGO DEPARTAMENTA MORSKOGO MINISTERSTVA KHRANIASHCHIMSIA V GLAVNOM MORSKOM ARKHIVE / Russia. Morskoe Ministerstvo - Pt 1: 1827-50. No. del 1-2449. 299p. Inventories records now in TsGAVMF. BR-10,799/1 - 9 - ne IDC [355]

OPIS' DELAM UPRAVLENIIA GENERAL-GIDROGRAFA I GIDROGRAFICHESKOGO DEPARTAMENTA MORSKOGO MINISTERSTVA, 1827-1852 GG / Russia. Morskoe Ministerstvo - Spb. 1857. BR-10,800 1 - 9 - ne IDC [324]

OPIS' DIKUMENTAL'NYKH MATERIALOV FONDA NO.129 / Gertsen, Aleksandr Ivanovich - Moscow, 1951. 31p. BR-10,689/1 - 9 - ne IDC [335]

OPIS' DOKUMENTAL'NYKH MATERIALOV ARKHIVNOGO FONDA NO.43 / Suvorov, Alexandr Vasil'evich - Moscow, 1952. 76p. BR-10,740/1 - 9 - ne IDC [025]

OPIS' DOKUMENTAL'NYKH MATERIALOV FONDA LICHNOGO PROISKHOZHDENIIA NO.1 / Chernyshevskii, Nikolai Gavrilovich - Moscow, 1955. 118p. BR-10,687/1 - 9 - ne IDC [460]

OPIS' DOKUMENTAL'NYKH MATERIALOV FONDA NO.332 / Makarenko, Anton Semenovich - Moscow, 1950. 28p. BR-10,693/1 - 9 - ne IDC [010]

OPIS' DOKUMENTAL'NYKH MATERIALOV KICHNOGO FONDA NO. 359 / Ogarev, Nikolai Platonovich - Moscow, 1950. 24p. BR-10,695/1 - 9 - ne IDC [010]

OPIS' DOKUMENTAL'NYKH MATERIALOV LICHNOGO FONDA NO. 56 / Briusov, Valerii I - Moscow, 1950. 16p. Briusov papers in TsGALI SSSR. BR-10,684/1 - 9 - ne IDC [947]

OPIS' DOKUMENTAL'NYKH MATERIALOV LICHNOGO FONDA NO. 338 / Nekrasov, Nikolai Alekseevich - Moscow, 1949. 34p. BR-10,694/2 - 8 - ne IDC [025]

OPIS' DOKUMENTAL'NYKH MATERIALOV LICHNOGO FONDA NO. 363 / Ostrovskii, Nikolai Alekseevich - Ed. by R. P. Ostrovskii. M. 1954. BR-10,806 1 - 9 - ne IDC [920]

OPIS DOKUMENTAL'NYKH MATERIALOV LICHNOGO FONDA NO. 457 / Serafimovich, Aleksandr Serafimovich - Moscow. 1955. 130p. Describes Serafimovich papers in TsGALI SSSR. BR-10,696/1 - 9 - ne IDC [025]

OPIS' DOKUMENTAL'NYKH MATERIALOV LICHNOGO FONDA NO. 905 / Tchaikovsky, Peter Ilyich - Moscow, 1955. 19p. BR-10,685/1 - 9 - ne IDC [780]

OPIS' DOKUMENTAL'NYKH MATERIALOV LICHNOGO FONDA NO. 917 / Shishkin, Ivan Ivanovich - Ed. by A. N. Shchekotov. M. 1949. BR-10.697 1 - 9 - ne IDC [920]

OPIS' DOKUMENTAL'NYKH MATERIALOV LICHNOGO FONDA NO. 1996 / Grekov, Mitrofan Borisovich & Kogan, E R; ed by Tikhomirov, M N - 1955. BR-10,805 1 - 9 - ne IDC [920]

OPIS' DOKUMENTAL'NYKH MATERIALOV LICHNOGO FONDA NO.139 / Gogol, Nikolai Vasilievich - Moscow, 1951. 20p. BR-10,690/1 - 9 - ne IDC [460]

OPIS DOKUMENTAL'NYKH MATERIALOV LICHNOGO FONDA NO.234 / Korolenko, Vladimir G - Moscow, 1949. 24p. BR-10,691/1 - 9 - ne IDC [460]

OPIS DOKUMENTAL'NYKH MATERIALOV LICHNOGO FONDA NO.509 / Turgenev, Ivan Sergeevich - Moscow, 1951. 27p. BR-10,698/1 - 9 - ne IDC [460]

OPIS' DOKUMENTAL'NYKH MATERIALOV LICHNOGO FONDA NO.522 / Furmanov, Dmitrii Andreevich - Moscow, 1949. 8p. BR-10,688/1 - 9 - ne IDC [460]

OPIS' DOKUMENTAL'NYKH MATERIALOV LICHNOGO FONDA.NO.716 / Vasnetsov, Viktor Mikhailovich - Moscow, 1949. 16p. BR-10,699/1 - 9 - ne IDC [025]

OPIS' DOKUMENTOV I DEL, KHRANIASHCHIKHSIA V SENATSKOM ARKHIVE - Otechestvennaia voina i kampanii 1813-1815 gg. Saint Petersburg, 1912. 339p. BR-10,728/1 - 9 - ne IDC [947]

OPIS' DOKUMENTOV I DEL, KHRANIASHCHIKHSIA V SENATSKOM ARKHIVE - St. Petersburg, Petrograd, 1909-1917. 9v in 3 series. BR-10,727/1 - 9 - ne IDC [947]

OPIS DREVNIKH RUKOPISEI / Prozorovskii, D I - Early Slavic mss. from the prerevolutionary museum of the Imp. Archeological Society now in the Saltykov-Shchedrin Library. BR-7321/2 - 8 - ne IDC [025]

OPIS' DYEL ARKHIVA / Russia. Gosudarstvennyi Sovyet - St Petersburg. 1908-1914. v. 1-12, 15-16, 19-21 - 1 - us NY Public [947]

OPIS' KAZACH'IKH DEL MOSKOVSKOGO OTDELENIIA OBSHCHEGO ARKHIVA GLAVNOGO SHTABA / Russia; ed by Dmitrenko, I I - Spb. 1899. BR-10,825 1 - 9 - ne IDC [947]

OPIS' STAROPECHATNYKH KNIG / Setsinskii, E - Muzei Podol'skago Tserkovnago Istorik-arkheologicheskago Obshchestva 1). Kqmenets-Podol'sk 1904. 107p. BR-4690/2 - 8 - ne IDC [930]

OPIS' ZHKANECHNYM ZHURNALAM S 1719 PO 1853 GOD I REESTR KLERKSKIM PROTOKOLAM I ZHURNALAM KANTSELIARII FLAGMANOV, S 1723 G. PO 1826 G - Morskoe ministerstvo. St. Petersburg, 1856. BR-10,801/1 - 9 - ne IDC [947]

OPISANIE / Rukopisi A P Chekhova - Moscow, 1938. 124p. BR-11,011/1 - 9 - ne IDC [460]

OPISANIE / Rukopisi IS Turgeneva - Leningrad, 1953.143p. BR-10,916/1 - 9 - ne IDC [460]

OPISANIE / Rukopisi M Iu. Lermontova - Leningrad, 1941.76p. BR-10,906/1 - 9 - ne IDC [460]

OPISANIE 432-KH RUKOPISEI, PRINADLEZHASHCHIKH S. PETERSBURGSKOI DUKHOVNOI AKADEMII / Rodosskii, Aleksei S - St. Petersburg, 1893. 427p. BR-7238/2 - 8 - ne IDC [240]

OPISANIE AKTOV SOBRANIIA GRAFA A.S. UVAROVA: AKTY ISTORICHESKIE / Kataev, IM & Kabanov, AK - Moscow, 1905. vii, 666p. Describes charters, legal acts, etc. in Uvarov collection in State Historical Museum. BR-11,202/1 - 9 - ne IDC [947]

OPISANIE AVTOGRAFOV I.S. TURGENEVA / Matorina, R P - BR-10,834/1 - 9 - ne IDC [460]

OPISANIE BUMAG EPISKOPA PORFIRIIA USPENSKOGO, POZHERTVOVANNYKH IM V BIBLIOTEKU IMP. AKADEMII NAUK PO ZAVESHCHANIIU / Syrku, P - St. Petersburg, 1891. xvi,440p. BR-7339/2 - 8 - ne IDC [240]

OPISANIE DEL ARKHIVA MINISTERSTVA NARODNOGO PROSVESHCHENIIA - Petrograd, 1917-1921. 2v. BR-10,820/1 - 9 - ne IDC [025]

OPISANIE DEL ARKHIVA MORSKOGO MINISTERSTVA ZA VREMIA S POLOVINY 17 DO NACHALA 19 STOLETIIA - St. Petersburg, 1877-1906. 10v. BR-10,679/1 - 9 - ne IDC [947]

OPISANIE DOKUMENTAL'NYKH MATERIALOV / Maiakovskii, Vladimir - Moscow, 1964-65.2v. 287p; 303p. BR-10,659/1 - 9 - ne IDC [010]

OPISANIE DOKUMENTOV ARKHIVA ZAPADNO-RUSSKIKH UNIATSKIKH MITROPOLITOV - St. Petersburg, 1897-1907. 2v. BR-10,729/1 - 9 - ne IDC [240]

OPISANIE DOKUMENTOV I DEL, KHRANIASHCHIKHSIA V ARKHIVE SVIATEISHEGO PRAVITEL'STVUIUSHCHEGO SINODA / Russia - 30v. in 31. Spb. 1868-1917. BR-10,817 1 - 9 - ne IDC [010]

OPISANIE GOSUDARSTVENNOGO ARKHIVA STARYKH DEL / Ivanov, PI - Moscow, 1850. 390p. BR-10,712/1 - 9 - ne IDC [947]

OPISANIE GRECHESKIKH RUKOPISEI MONASTYRIA SVIATOI EKATERINY NA SINAE. 1, 3: 1 / Beneshevich, V N - v. 1 3(1). Spb. 1911-17. BR-7068 2 - 8 - ne IDC [010]

OPISANIE IAPONSKIKH RUKOPISEI, KSILOGRAFOV, I STAROPECHATNYKH KNIG / Petrova, OP et al - Moscow, 1963-71. 6v. BR-10,979/1 - 9 - ne IDC [010]

OPISANIE IUR'EVSKAGO EVANGELIIA 1118-1128 G / Amfilokhii, Archimandrite - Moscow, 1877. 233, 39p. BR-10,107 1 - 9 - ne IDC [240]

OPISANIE KITAISKIKH RUKOPISEI DUN'KHUAUNSKOGO FONDA INSTITUTA NARODOV AZII / Vorob'eva-Desiatovskaia, M I et al - Moscow, 1963-67. 2v. BR-10,975/1 - 9 - ne IDC [025]

OPISANIE KNIG GRAZHDANSKOI PECHATI / Akademiia Dukhovnaia. Leningrad - 1899. 530p. Aleksei Stepanovich Rodosskii - 1 - us U.W. Library [460]

OPISANIE KOLLEKTSII NARODNYKH PISANOK / Kulzhinskii, SK - 1899 - 1 reel - 1 - us I.H.R.C. [947]

OPISANIE KOLLEKTSII PEDAGOGICHESKAGO MUZEIA VOENNO-UCHEBNYKH ZAVEDENII., 1. ISTORIIA / Andreianov, M A - St. Petersburg, 1891. 103p. BR-7054 2 - 8 - ne IDC [370]

OPISANIE KURDSKIKH RUKOPISEI LENINGRADSKIKH SOBRANII / Rudenko, M B - Moscow, 1961. 125p. BR-10,877/1 - 9 - ne IDC [010]

OPISANIE MAN'CHZHURSKIKH RUKOPISEI INSTITUTA NARODOV AZII AN SSSR / Volkova, M P - Moscow, 1965. 139p. BR-10,982/1 - 9 - ne IDC [010]

OPISANIE PAMIATNIKOV SLAVIANO-RUSSKOI LITERATURY KHRANIASHCHIKHSIA V PUBLICHNYKH BIBLIOTEKAKH GERMANII I FRANTSII / Stroev, S - Moscow, 1841. 193p. BR-7336/2 - 8 - ne IDC [025]

OPISANIE PERGAMENTNYKH RUKOPISEI GOSUDARSTVENNOGO ISTORICHESKOGO MUZEIA / Shchepkina, M V et al - Arkheograficheskii Ezhegodnik za 1965, p135-234; za 1965, p273-309. BR-10,379/1 - 9 - ne IDC [947]

OPISANIE PISEM V.G. KOROLENKO - Moscow, 1961. 659p. BR-11,014/1 - 9 - ne IDC [025]

OPISANIE PIS'MENNYKH PAMIATNIKOV KOREISKOI KUL'TURY / Petrova, OP - Moscow, 1956-63. 2v. BR-10,980/1 - 9 - ne IDC [025]

OPISANIE PUSHKINSKAGO MUZEIA IMP / Asnash, S M & Iakhontov, A N - Aleksandrovskago Litseia. 1899. BR-5875 2 - 8 - ne IDC [460]

OPISANIE ROSSIISKO-IMPERATORSKOGO STOLICHNOGO GORODA SANKTPETERBURGA I DOSTOPAMIATNOSTEI V OKRESTNOSTIAKHONOGO / Georgi, I G - 3pts. Spb. 1794 - 8 - BR-6164 2 - ne IDC [947]

OPISANIE RUKOPISEI A.I. GERTSENA / Russia; ed by Askariants, A V & Kemenova, E V - Ed. 2. M. 1950. BR-10.833 1 - 9 - ne IDC [335]

OPISANIE RUKOPISEI A.M. GOR'KOGO, PT. 1 - Moscow, 1948. 730p. BR-10,969/1 - 9 - ne IDC [460]

OPISANIE RUKOPISEI BIBLIOTEKI VIFANSKOI DUKHOVNOI SEMINARII / Muretov, SD - Moscow, 1897. xii,239p.BR-7305/2 - 8 - ne IDC [240]

OPISANIE RUKOPISEI F.M. DOSTOEVSKOGO / ed by Nechaeva, V S - Moscow, 1957. 587p. BR-10,657/1 - 9 - ne IDC [460]

OPISANIE RUKOPISEI I IZOBRAZITEL'NYKH MATERIALOV PUSHKINSKOGO DOMA - Moscow, Leningrad, 1962.7v. BR-10,963/1 - 9 - ne IDC [460]

OPISANIE RUKOPISEI I KNIG, SOBRANNYKH DLIA IMP. AKADEMII NAUK V OLONETSKOM KRAE / Sreznevskii, 6 - St. Petersburg, 1913. xxviii/688p BR-7334/2 - 8 - ne IDC [500]

OPISANIE RUKOPISEI ISTORICHESKAGO OBSHCHESTVA NESTORA LETOPISTSA / Maslov, S I - Kiev, 1908. 121p. BR-7302/2 - 8 - ne IDC [947]

OPISANIE RUKOPISEI KATALOG KNIG TSERKOVNOI PECHATI BIBLIOTEKI A.I. KHLUDOVA / Popov, AN - Moscow, 1872. x,664,54p. BR-7318/2 - 8 - ne IDC [460]

OPISANIE RUKOPISEI, KHRANIASHCHIKHSIA V ARKHIVE SVIATEISHEGO PRAVITEL'STVUIUSHCHEGO SINODA - St. Petersburg, 1904-10.2v in 3. BR-7311/2 - 8 - ne IDC [240]

OPISANIE RUKOPISEI KHRANIASHCHIKHSIA V BIBLIOTEKE CHERNIGOVSKOI DUKHOVNOI SEMINARII / Lileev, M I - 215p. BR/7298/2 - 8 - ne IDC [240]

OPISANIE RUKOPISEI, KHRANIASHCHIKHSIA V BIBLIOTEKE IMP. KAZANSKAGO UNIVERSITETA / Artemev, A I - Spb. 1882. BR-7058 2 - 8 - ne IDC [010]

OPISANIE RUKOPISEI KHUDOZHESTVENNYKH PROIZVEDENII L.N. TOLSTOGO - Moscow, 1955. 634p. BR-11,025/1 - 9 - ne IDC [460]

OPISANIE RUKOPISEI KNIAZIA PAVLA PETROVICHA VIAZEMSKOGO - St. Petersburg, 1902. BR-7309/2 - 8 - ne IDC [025]

OPISANIE RUKOPISEI MONASTYREI VOLOKOLAMSKOGO, NOVYI IERUSALIM, SAVVINA STOROZHEVSKOGO I PAFNUTIEVA BOROVSKOGO / Stroev, P M - St. Petersburg, 1891. xviii,343p. BR-7337/2 - 8 - ne IDC [025]

OPISANIE RUKOPISEI N.P. OGAREVA - Moscow, 1952. 206p. BR-11,016/1 - 9 - ne IDC [025]

OPISANIE RUKOPISEI OBSHCHESTVA LIUBITELEI DREVNEI PIS'MENNOSTI / Loparev, Kh.M - St. Petersburg. 3v. 1892-99. BR-7299/2 - 8 - ne IDC [460]

OPISANIE RUKOPISEI POCHAEVSKOI LAVRY / Berezin, V - Kiev, 1881. 86p. BR-7069/2 - 8 - ne IDC [947]

OPISANIE RUKOPISEI S. PETERSBURGSKOI DEKHOVNOI AKADEMII. SOFFIISKAIA BIBLIOTEKA / Abramovich, D I - St. Petersburg. 1905-10. 3 v. BR-11, 156 1 - 9 - ne IDC [010]

OPISANIE RUKOPISEI SAMARITIANSKOGO PIATIKNIZHNIIA KHRANIASHCHIKHSIA V IMPERATORSKOI PUBLICHNOI BIBLIOTEKE / Harkavy, A - 2v. St. Petersburg, 1874-75. 536p. BR-7103/2 - 8 - ne IDC [090]

OPISANIE RUKOPISEI SINODAL'NOGO SOBRANIIA (NE VOSHEDSHIKH V OPISANIE A.V. GORSKOGO I K.I. NEVOSTRUEVA) / Protas'eva, T N; ed by Shchepkina, M V - 2v. M. 1970-73; v1, no. 577-819; v2, no. 820-1051. BR-11,098 1 - 9 - ne IDC [240]

OPISANIE RUKOPISEI STATEI L.N. TOLSTOGO - Literatura, iskusstvo, nauka, pedagogika. Moscow, 1961.279p. BR-11,026/1 - 9 - ne IDC [460]

OPISANIE RUKOPISEI TVERSKAGO MUZEIA / Speranskii, M N - Moscow, 1891. v1, 337p.BR-7333/2 - 8 - ne IDC [460]

OPISANIE RUKOPISEI UCHENOGO ARKHIVA IMPERATORSKOGO RUSSKOGO GEOGRAFICHESKOGO OBSHCHESTVA / Zelenin, D K - Pg. 3v. 1914-1916 - 24mf - 9 - R-7046/2 - ne IDC [947]

OPISANIE RUKOPISEI UCHENOGO ARKHIVA IMPERATORSKOGO RUSSKOGO GEOGRAFICHESKOGO OBSHCHESTVA / Zelenin, D K - Pg. 3v. 1914-1916 - 24mf - 9 - ne IDC [947]

OPISANIE RUKOPISEI V.G. KOROLENKO - Moscow, 1950. 223p. BR-11,013/1 - 9 - ne IDC [025]

OPISANIE RUKOPISNOGO OTDELA BIBLIOTEKI AKADEMII NAUK SSSR - v. 5. Grecheskie rukopisi. Comp. by I. N. Lebedeva. 1973. BR-10,954 1 - 9 - ne IDC [450]

OPISANIE RUKOPISNOGO OTDELA BIBLIOTEKI AKADEMII NAUK SSSR - v3,pt.1-3; v4,pt.1; v5. BR-10,954/1 - 9 - ne IDC [947]

OPISANIE RUKOPISNYKH SOBRANII NAKHODIASHCHIKHSIA V GORODE KIEVE / Petrov, N I - 3v. M. 1891-1904. BR-7317 2 - 8 - ne IDC [947]

OPISANIE RUSSKIKH KNIZHNIKH ZNAKOV / Ivask, U G - v.2, 3. Moscow, 1910, 1918. 104, 56p. BR-11,225 1 - 9 - ne IDC [460]

OPISANIE SLAVIANO-RUSSKIKH KNIG NAPECHATATANNYKH KIRILLOVSKIMI BUKVAMI. 1491 PO 1652 / Karataev, I - Saint Petersburg, 1883. 560p. BR-5910/2 - 8 - ne IDC [460]

OPISANIE SLAVIANO-RUSSKIKH RUKOPISEI, NAKHODIASHCHIKHSIA V BIBLIOTEKE VOSKRESENSKOGO NOVO-IERUSALIMSKOGO MONASTYRIA / Sakharov, I P - Spb. 1842. BR-11,155 1 - 9 - ne IDC [947]

OPISANIE SLAVIANO-RUSSKIKH RUKOPISEI, NAKHODIASHCHIKHSIA V SOBRANII... A.A. TITOVA / Titov, A A - St. Petersburg, Moscow, 1893-1913. 6v in 7. BR-7340- - 8 - ne IDC [025]

OPISANIE SLAVIANORUSSKIKH STARO-PECHATNYKH KNIG VILENSKOI PUBLICHNOI BIBLIOTHEKI (1491-1800 GG.) / Milovidov, A I - Vil'na, 1908 - 3mf - 9 - ne IDC [947]

OPISANIE SLAVIANSKIKH RUKOPISEI BIBLIOTEKI SVIATO-TROITSKOI SERGIEVOI LAVRY / Ilarii, Ieromonakh & Arsenii, Ieromonakh - 3v. Moscow, 1878-79. xix,352p; 240p; 267, 44p. BR-7057/2 - 8 - ne IDC [010]

OPISANIE SLAVIANSKIKH RUKOPISEI MOSKOVSKOI SINODAL'NOI (PATRIARSHEI) BIBLIOTEKI / Gorskii, A V & Nevostruev, K I - 3v in 6pts. Moscow, 1855-1917. BR/10,324/1 - 9 - ne IDC [947]

OPISANIE SOBRANIIA RUKOPISNYKH MATERIALOV A.V. SUVOROVA - Leningrad, 1955.303p. BR-10,914/1 - 9 - ne IDC [025]

OPISANIE STARINNYKH ATLASOV, KART I PLANOV 16,17,18, I POLOVINY 19 VV., KHRANIASHCHIKHSIA - Arkhive Tsentral'nogo kartograficheskogo proizvodstva VMF. Leningrad, 1958. 270p. BR-10,804/1 - 9 - ne IDC [910]

OPISANIE STAROPECHATNYKH KNIG SLAVIANSKIKH NAKHODIASHCHIKHSIA V BIBLIOTEKE...I.N. TSARSKAGO / Stroev, P M - Moscow, 1836. 463p. BR-5617/2 - 8 - ne IDC [025]

OPISANIE STAROPECHATNYKH KNIG SLAVIANSKIKH SLUZHASHCHEE DOPELNENIEM K OPISANIIAM BIBLIOTEK GRAFA F.A. TOLSTOVA I KUPTSA I.N. TSARSKAGO / Stroev, P M - Moscow, 1841. 284p. BR-5616/2 - 8 - ne IDC [025]

OPISANIE TADZHIKSHIKH I PERSIDSKIKH RUKOPISEI INSTITUTA VOSTOKOVEDENIIA / Miklukho-Maklai, N D & Baevskii, S I - v. 1-5. 1955-68. Lacking v. 3. BR-10,985 1 - 9$3.00 - ne IDC [490]

OPISANIE TADZHIKSKIKH I PERSIDSKIKH RUKOPISEI VOSTOCHNOGO OTDELA BIBLIOTEKI LGU - v1, 514p. Leningrad, 1962. BR-10,923/1 - 9 - ne IDC [025]

OPISANIE TIURKSKIKH RUKOPISEI INSTITUTA NARODOV AZII - Moscow, 1965. 258p. BR-10,988/1 - 9 - ne IDC [025]

OPISANIE UIGURSKIKH RUKOPISEI INSTITUTA NARODOV AZII - Moscow, 1962. 207p. BR-10,989/1 - 9 - ne IDC [025]

OPISANIE VELIKIKH CHETIKH-MINEI MAKARIIA MITROPOLITA VSEROSSIISKAGO / Gorskii, A V & Nevostruev, K I - 9 - BR-10 374 1 - ne IDC [947]

OPISANIE VOSKRESENSKOI NOVOIERUSALEMSKOI BIBLIOTEKI S PRILOZHENIEM SNIMKOV SO VSEKH PERGAMENNYKH RUKOPISEI I NEKOTORYKH PISANNYKH NA BUMAGE / Amfilokhii, Archimandrite - Moscow. 1875. 226 p. 18 pls. BR-11,198 1 - 9 - ne IDC [240]

OPISI AKTOVYKH KNIG KIEVSKAGO TSENTRAL'NAGO ARKHIVA / Kiev. Central Archive - NR. 19, 33, 37, 39, 2037, 2051, 2093. Kiev. 1878-1909. BR-7314 2 - 8 - ne IDC [010]

OPISI DEL MOSKOVSKOGO OTDELENIIA OBSHCHEGO ARKHIVA GLANOGO SHTABA / Moscow - Ed. by N. P. Polikarpov. 7 v. (unnumbered). Spb. 1912-13. BR-9897 1 - 9 - ne IDC [025]

OPISI DELAM DOKUMENTAM KOMISSII DLIA SOSTAVLENIIA SMETNYKH ISCHISLENII NA POSTROENNIE KORABLEI I DRUGIKH SUDOV, 1824-1827 GG. I DELAM I ZHURNALAM KORABLESTROITEL'NOGO I UCHETNOGO KOMITETA, 1827-1852 GG / Russia. Morskoe Ministerstvo - Spb. 1857. BR-10,803 1 - 9 - ne IDC [324]

OPISI TSARSKOGO ARKHIVA XVIVEKA I ARKHIVA POSOL'SKOGO PRIKAZA 1614 GODA / ed by Shmidt, Sigurd Ottovich - 1960. BR-11.084 1 - 9 - ne IDC [025]

Opiso, Papirio *see* SPAGNA INDOMITA

Opitz, Georg *see* DIE STABREIMENDEN WORTBINDUNGEN IN DEN DICHTUNGEN WALTER SCOTT'S

THE OPIUM PROBLEM IN BRITISH MALAYA / Chen, Su Lan - Reel 4001. 1935 - 1 - ja CEACS [950]

Opiz, P M *see*
- BEITRAEGE ZUR NATURGESCHICHTE ALS FORTSETZUNG DES NATURALIENTAUSCH
- BOEHEIMS PHAENEROGRAMISCHE UND CRYPTOGAMISCHE GEWAECHSE
- SEZNAM ROSTLIN KVETENY CESKE

DE OPKOMST VAN HET PROTESTANTISME IN EENE NOORD-NEDERLANDSCHE STAD : GESCHIEDENIS VAN DE HERVORMING BINNEN LEIDEN, VAN DEN AANVANG TOT OP HET BELEG / Knappert, L - Leiden: S.C. van Doesburgh, 1908 - 1mf - us A.T.L.A. [240]

DIE OPKONS VAN'N REPUBLIEK : OF, DIE GESKIEDENIS VAN DIE ORANGEVRYSTAAT TOT DIE JAAR 1863 / Malen, J H - Bloemfontein: Gedr en uitg deur die Nasionale Pers Bepk, 1929 - us Res Libr [960]

DE OPLEIDING VAN DE BOUWKUNDIG INGENIEUR OF ARCHITECT IN INDONESIE / Dicke, F - SE-10,010 1. 1951 - 9 - ne IDC [720]

Oplt, Miroslav *see* BAHASA INDONESIA. UCEBNICE INDONESTINY. INDONESIAN LANGUAGE

DE OPMERKER - Arnhem, The Hague, Netherlands. -w. 7 April 1866-3 June 1916. 36 reels - 1 - uk British Libr Newspaper [949]

Opoichenko, Iakov *see* IZOBLICHENIE SHTUNDISTSKOI BOGOPROTIVNOI ERESI NA OSNOVANII SVYASHCHENNAGO PISANIYA, SVYASHCHENNAGO PREDANIYA I ISTORICHESKIKH" PAMYATNIKOV"

"OPOWIADANIE Z WEDROWKI PO KOLONIACH POLSKICH W AMERYCE POLONCNEJ" / Milkowski, Zygmunt - Paryz, 1902 - 1r - 1 - us I.H.R.C. [947]

Oppenheim, A Leo *see* GLASS AND GLASSMAKING IN ANCIENT MESOPOTAMIA

Oppenheim, M von *see* ARCHIV FUER ORIENTFORSCHUNG, BEIBAND 1

Oppenheim, Ph. *see* DAS MOENCHSKLEID IM CHRISTLICHEN ALTERTUM

Oppenheim, Samuel A *see* THE PRACTICAL BOLSHEVIK: A. I. RYKOV AND RUSSIAN COMMUNISM 1881-1938

Oppenheimer, Franz *see* THE STATE

Oppert, G *see* LISTS OF SANSKRIT MSS IN PRIVATE LIBRARIES OF SOUTHERN INDIA

Oppert, Jules *see* LE PEUPLE ET LA LANGUE DES MEDES

OPPIANOU ANAZARBEOS ALIEUTIKON BIBLIA - Parisiis, 1555 - 1 - us U.W. Library [336]

OPPORTUNITIES AND PROBLEMS OF A YOUNG COUNTRY: AN EXPLANATORY STUDY / Israel. Prime Minister's Office. Industry Science University in Israel - By S. Wald, Jerusalem, Dec. 1972. 63 p - 9 - 2.00 - is I.T.T.I. [330]

OPPORTUNITIES FOR INDUSTRIAL DEVELOPMENT IN EGYPT: REPORT TO U.S. GOVERNMENT FOREIGN OPERATIONS ADMINISTRATION - 1955. BNE-4641 1 - 9 - ne IDC [338]

OPPORTUNITIES IN THE PATH OF THE GREAT PHYSICIAN / Penrose, Valeria Fullerton - (Includes index) - Philadelphia: Westminster Press, 1902 - 1mf - 9 - 0-8370-7321-9 - 1986-1321 - us A.T.L.A. [610]

OPPORTUNITY - A Journal of Negro Life. v. 1-27. 1923- 1949 - 1 - us UMI [073]

OPPORTUNITY : A JOURNAL OF NEGRO LIFE - New York. v1-27. 1923-49 - 4r - 1 - us Ross [073]

OPPORTUNITY - Journal of Negro Life. New York. v. 1-27. no. 1. 1923-Winter 1949 - 1 - us NY Public [073]

OPPORTUNITY - London, 1921-1940 - 83mf - 9 - ne IDC [350]

OPPORTUNITY NEWS - Woodburn, OR. -w. 18 Jun 1965-25 Mar 1968. 1 roll - 1 - us U.O. Library [071]

OPPORTUNITY OF CONTINUATION TO LOWER SECONDARY EDUCATION / Thailand. National Education Commission - Bangkok, c. 1978 - 4mf - 9 - DE-305/1 - ne IDC [370]

"OPPOZITSIIA" / Vasil'ev, N P - Spb., 1910. 138p - 2mf - 9 - ne IDC [320]

LES OPPRIMES - Journal socialiste de la Guyane. Cayenne. aout 1925-26 - 1 - fr A.C.R.P.P. [073]

OPREDELENIIA UGOLOVNOI KASSATSIONNOI KOLLEGII VERKHSUDA R.S.F.S.R. ZA... / Russian S.F.S.R. Ugolovnaia kassatsionnaia kollegiia - (Includes c.1: 1926:no.2) - Moskva: Iuridicheskoe izdvo narkomi usta R.S.F.S.R., 1926 - 1 - CSUXAKZ2843-S - us Hoover Inst Photo [360]

OPREGTE AFRIKANER, DE - Bedford, South Africa. 13 May 1882-4 Apr 83. 1 reel - 1, 16 diazo available at reduced price - sa SA Libr [072]

DER OPTATIV-VOLUNTATIVE MODALITAETSTYP UND DIE ASPEKTVERHAELTNISSE DES PRAEDIKATIVEN INFINITIVS IM BEREICH DER AFFIRMATION UND NEGATION / Lohde, Michael - 1994 - 1mf - 9 - DM60.00 - 3-89349-875-3 - gw Hänsel [460]

Optatus, C *see* PRACTICA SAVONAROLE DE FEBRIBUS...

Optatus, Milevitanus *see* OPERA CUM OBSERVATIONIBUS ET NOTIS GABR. ALBASPINAEI

OPTIC - Larned. Kan. -w. 1878-1901 - 1 - us UMI [071]

OPTIC - Las Vegas. NM. 1880-88; 1910; 1920- - 1 - us UMI [071]

OPTIC - Las Vegas. NM. Also: Live Stock Grower. -w. 1910-20 - 1 - us UMI [071]

OPTICA ACTA - v. 6-21. 1959-74 - 1,5,6 - us Princeton Micro [530]

OPTICA ACTA - v.1-22. 1953-75. London - 9 - 24330.00; 2415.00v - uk Dawson [610]

OPTICAL AND QUANTUM ELECTRONICS - (v15-. 1983-. 5,6,9) - v7-. 1975- - 1 - us UMI [073]

OPTICAL INFORMATION SYSTEMS *see* VIDEODISC AND OPTICAL DISK

OPTICAL JOURNAL AND REVIEW OF OPTOMETRY - (See also: Review of Optometry) - v1-114 1891-1977 1; 1971-77 5,6; 1976-77 4 x 6 in. 9 - us UMI [617]

OPTICAL SCANNING NEWS - v1- 1970- 1; v4-5,6; v7- 9 - us UMI [617]

Optical Society of America *see*
- APPLIED OPTICS
- OPTICS LETTERS

Optical Society of AmericaInstitute of Electrical and Electronic Engineers *see* JOURNAL OF LIGHTWAVE TECHNOLOGY

OPTICAL SPECTRA – 1967- 1; 1970- 5,6; 1977- 4 x 6 in. 9 – us UMI [530]
OPTICS AND LASERS IN ENGINEERING – v1-5 1980-84 – 1,5,6,13 – sz Elsevier [620]
OPTICS AND PHOTONICS NEWS – Monthly – 9,6 – $99.00 in US $119.00 outside – us Optical Soc [621]
OPTICS AND SPECTROSCOPY – English translation of Optika i Spektroskopiya, microfilm edition: available for back numbers – 1800p per Year – us Optical Soc [621]
OPTICS AND SPECTROSCOPY – Monthly – 9,6 – $1,732.00 in US $1,778.00 outside – us Optical Soc [621]
OPTICS COMMUNICATIONS – v1-52. 1969-84 – 1,5,6,13 – sz Elsevier [073]
OPTICS LETTERS – Bimonthly – 9,6 – $855.00 in US $888.00 outside – us Optical Soc [621]
OPTICS LETTERS / Optical Society of America – (v1-17. 1977-92. $485.00v, $36.00 per issue. v18. 1993. $540.00, $569.00 outside North America) – v1-. 1977-. Semimonthly – 9 – us Optical Soc [073]
OPTIMAL DROP HEIGHT PREDICTION FROM LOWER BODY STRENGTH FOR PLYOMETRIC JUMP TRAINING / Moody, Melissa & Wilkerson, Jerry D – 1992 – 1mf – $4.00 – us Microform Publ [612]
OPTIMAL'NYE ZARMERY SEL'SKO-KHOZIAISTVENNYKH PREDPRIIATII / Chaianov, A V – Ed 3. M., 1928 – 1mf – 9 – COR-232/1 – ne IDC [334]
OPTIMIERUNG VON ROBOTERBAHNEN MIT KOLLISIONSVERMEIDUNG MITTELS DER POTENTIALFELDMETHODE / Lueth, Oliver Andreas – 1994 – 2mf – 9 – DM80.00 – 3-89349-877-X – gw Hänsel [629]
OPTIMISM : THE LESSON OF AGES / Blood, Benjamin – Boston: Bela Marsh, 1860 – 1mf – 9 – 0-8370-2711-X – 1985-0711 – us A.T.L.A. [100]
OPTIMISM OF BUTLER'S ANALOGY / Holland, Henry Scott – Oxford, Clarendon Press, 1908. 1 fiche – 9 – us A.T.L.A. [240]
THE OPTIMISM OF BUTLER'S 'ANALOGY' DELIVERED IN THE SHELDONIAN THEATRE, JUNE 13 1908 / Holland, Henry Scott – Oxford:Clarendon Press, 1908 – 1mf – 9 – 0-8370-3624-0 – 1985-1624 – us A.T.L.A. [230]
OPTIMISM: THE LESSON OF AGES / Blood, Benjamin – Boston: Bela Marsh, 1860. 1 fiche – 9 – us A.T.L.A. [240]
OPTIMIST – Portland OR. Oct 1 Nov 1 1930, May 5 1932 – 1 – us U.O. Library [071]
OPTIMIZATION / ed by Elster, K H – 9,5,1 – us Gordon [000]
OPTIMIZATION METHODS AND SOFTWARE / ed by Evtushenko, Yu. G – 9,5,1 – us Gordon [000]
OPTIMIZATION OF THE VALGUS INTERTROCHANTERIC OSTEOTOMY / Miller, John et al – 1990 – 3mf – 9 – $12.00 – us Microform Publ [612]
OPTIMUM FISHING EFFORT AND ECONOMIC RENT : A CASE STUDY OF CYPRUS – 1989 – 63p – it F.A.O. [639]
OPTION CANADA – Montreal. 1969-v6 n6. fev/mar 1970 – 1r – 1 – Can$30.00 – cn Can Microfilming [072]
OPTIONS FOR THE MANAGEMENT OF TUNA FISHERIES IN THE INDIAN OCEAN – 1990 – 79p – it F.A.O. [338]
OPTIQUE DE NEWTON / Newton, Isaac – Trad. nouvelle, faite par Jean-Paul Marat, Paris, 1787, 2 v., xxiv, 192, 308 p. Histoire des Sciences XVIIe-XIXe Siecles. 7988 9 – 9 – fr Hachette [530]
OPTO ELECTRONICS – v1-6. Feb 1909-74 – 1 – us UMI [073]
OPTOMETRIC MANAGEMENT – v1- 1965- 1; v7- 5,6; v12- 9 – us UMI [617]
OPTOMETRIC WORLD – 1914- 1; 1972- 5,6; 1975- 4 x 6 in. 9 – us UMI [617]
OPTOMETRY AND VISION SCIENCE – v53-73. 1976-96 – 1,5,6,9 – $90.00r – us Williams [617]
OPTOMETRY TODAY – 1970- – 1. 1974-; ; 5,6. 1975-; ; 4 – apply; x 6 in9 – us UMI [617]
OPUS – v1-. Nov 1984- – 1,5,6,9 – us UMI [073]
OPUS 39, LIEDERKREIS VON EICHENDORF. / Schumann, Robert – (Engraved with corrections in pencil made by Schumann for a later edition. Title page and pp. 1$4 missing. 1842 – 9 – us Sibley [780]
OPUS 39, NO. 12, FRUEHLINGSNACHT / Schumann, Robert – Ms. copy used as proof for publication – 9 – us Sibley [780]
OPUS AUREUM MUSICE CASTIGATISIIMU DE GREGORIANA ET FIGURATIVA / Wollick (Wolquier), Nicolaus – Koeln. 1501. BP-521 1 – 9 – ne IDC [780]
OPUS DE THEOLOGICIS DOGMATIBUS / Petavius, Dion – Antwerpen, 1700. 3v – 112mf – 8 – ne Slangenburg [290]
OPUS INTERNATIONAL – v1- 1967- 1; 1971- 5,6; 1975- 4 x 6 in. 9 – us UMI [073]
OPUS MORALE IN PRAECEPTA DECALOGI / Sanchez, Tomas Antonio – Coloniae Agrippinae. 2v. 1614 – 14mf – 9 – CA-69/1 – ne IDC [240]
OPUS NEOTERICUM MEDICUM THEORICO PRACTICUM DE LAXO ET ESTRICTO, JUSTA DIVINI. HIPPOCRATIS MENTEM / Arnau, J – Valencia, 1733 – 7mf – 9 – sp Cultura [610]
OPUS VEGETABILE, AUSS NIEDERLANDISCHEN MANUSCRIPTIS VERHOCHDEUTCHET, VON SOHN SENDIVOGII, GENANT J. F. H. S / Johannes Isaaci, Hollandus – Amsterdam, 1659 – 1 – us U.W. Library [631]
OPUSCULA : ESSAYS CHIEFLY PHILOLOGICAL AND ETHNOGRAPHICAL / Latham, Robert Gordon – London: Williams & Norgate; Leipzig: R Hartmann, 1860 – 1mf – 9 – 0-8370-8758-9 – 1986-2758 – us A.T.L.A. [400]
OPUSCULA 36/SONETTI E POESIE ITALIANE DI VARI AUTORI / Vergerii, P P et al – 15th cent. Holkham MSS. 487, 521. Holkham Hall: Norfolk, England – 1 – uk Microform Academic [810]
OPUSCULA ANATOMICA NOVA / Riolan, Jean – M 396. 1649 – 9 – ne IDC [611]
OPUSCULA AUREA THEOLOGICA...CIRCA PROCESSIONEM SPIRITUS SANCTI / Arcudius, P – 1630 – 12mf – 8 – ne Slangenburg [240]
OPUSCULA BOTANICO-PHYSICA / Jung, J – Coburgi. 1747. B-6494 2 – 8 – ne IDC [580]
OPUSCULA ENTOMOLOGICA / Thomson, C G – 1875 – 7 – uk Microform Academic [590]
OPUSCULA, ETC / Aretinus, L et al – 15th century. Holkham mss. 483, 484, 490. Holkham Hall, Norfolk, England – 1 – uk Microform Academic [025]
OPUSCULA OMNIA 1558 / Cajetanus – Romae, 1570 – 14mf – 8 – ne Slangenburg [290]
OPUSCULA SANCTI PATRIS FRANCISCI ASSISIENSIS / Francesco d'Assisi, Saint – 1904 – 1 – us A.T.L.A. [240]
OPUSCULA SUA BOTANICA PRIUS EDITA RECENSUIT, RETRACTAVIT, AUXIT / Haller, Albrecht von – Goettingae. 1749. B-6189 2 – 8 – ne IDC [580]
OPUSCULA VARIA POSTHUMA / Bacon, Francis – M-293 2. 1658 – 8 – ne IDC [500]
OPUSCULES / Casgrain, Henri-Raymond – Quebec: A. Cote, 1876. 00647. (Pre-1900 Canadiana) – 9 – cn C.I.H.M. [971]
OPUSCULES ET FRAGMENTS INEDITES / Leibniz, Gottfried Wilhelm von – Paris: F. Alcon, 1903. xiv,682p. L'ed. ancienne faite partie de la Collection historique des grands philosophes. 8 fiches. (Philosophy Collection) – 9 – 20.00 – fr Bibl Nationale [190]
OPUSCULES MATHEMATIQUES – 7 – uk Microform Academic [510]
OPUSCULES MATHEMATIQUES / Alembert, Jean Le Rond d' – Paris, 1761-80, 8 t. en 7 v. Histoire des Sciences XVIIe-XIXe Siecles. 7973 a 7980 – 9 – fr Hachette [510]
OPUSCULES PHYTOLOGIQUES / Cassini, A H G de – 3v. Paris. 1826-34 – 8 – ne IDC [580]
OPUSCULES SUR LA LANGUE FRANCOISE PAR DIVERS ACADEMICIENS – 1754 – 9 – fr I.C.S. [440]
UN OPUSCULO BIBLICO DEL TOSTADO DESCONOCIDO / Zamora, Hermenegildo – Verdad y Vida, 1973 – 1 – sp Bibl Santa Ana [020]
OPUSCULO FUNEBRE / Rianzuela, Marques de – 1861 – 9 – 1.50f – sp Bibl Santa Ana [880]
OPUSCULO...GOBIERNO...ESPANOLES / Rodero del Brio, Juan – 1868 – 9 – 1.50f – sp Bibl Santa Ana [946]
OPUSCULOS / Bravo Murillo, Juan – 1863. 6 tomos – 9 – 1.50f – sp Bibl Santa Ana [946]
OPUSCULOS DE ORO, VIRTUDES MORALES CHRISTIANAS / Calderon Altamirano de Chaves Hinojosa y Paredes, Luis Francisco – Madrid: Juan Garcia Infancon, 1707 – 1 – sp Bibl Santa Ana [240]
OPUSCULUM RECENS NATVM DE MORBIS PVERORVM CUM APPENICIBUS MAGISTRI PETRI TOLETI / Bagellardo, Paolo – Lyon, 1538 – 1 – us U.W. Library [920]
OPVSCVLVM DE EMENDATIONIBUS TERMPORUM AB ORBE CONDITIO ADVSQUE HANC AETATEM NOSTRAM / Lucidus, Joannes – Venetiis, 1537 – 1 – us U.W. Library [450]
OPVSCVLVN, IN QUO VNA ORATION, & DUAE QUESTIONES ALTERA DE CERTITUDINE, & ALTERA DE MEDIETATE MATHEMATICARUM CONTINENTUR / Barozzi, Francesco – Patavii, 1560 – 1 – us U.W. Library [510]
OPYT ANKETNOGO ISSLEDOVANIIA DENEZHNYKH ELEMENTOV KRESTIANSKOGO KHOZIAISTVA MOSKOVSKOI GUBERNII / Chaianov, A V – M., 1912 – 1mf – 9 – COR-138/1 – ne IDC [334]
OPYT BIBLIOGRAFICHESKAGO UKAZATELIA PO ISTORII I GENEALOGII ROSSIISKAGO DVORIANSTVA / Savelov, L M – M. 1893. BR-7247 2 – 8 – ne IDC [920]
OPYT BIBLIOGRAFII OBSHCHESTVENNYKH NAUK ZA REVOLIUTSIONNOE TREKHLETIE (1918-1920) / Durdenevski i, Vsevolod – Moskva: Gos. izd-vo, 1925 – 1 – CSUX88-B6337 – us Hoover Inst Photo [010]
OPYT I ISSLEDOVANIIA / Kliuchevskii, V O – Ed 2. 1914 – 8 – BR-6206 2 – ne IDC [947]
OPYT IUZHNO-RUSSKOGO SLOVARIA / Sheikovskii, K – M., 1861-1886 – 10mf – 9 – R-8402/2 – ne IDC [460]
OPYT IZSLEDOVANIIA URIANKHAISKAGO IAZYKA / Katanov, N F – Kazan'. 1903. BU-329 2 – 8 – ne IDC [460]
OPYT KATALOGA VSEM OTDEL'NYM SOCHINENIIAM PO 1872 GOD OB OTECHESTVENNOI VOINE 1812 GODA / Liprandi, I P – M. 1876. BR-7134 2 – 8 – ne IDC [460]
OPYT OBLASTNAGO VELIKORUSSKAGO SLOVARIA / Akademiia Nauk – Izd. Vtorym otdeleniem Imp. Akademii nauk. Spb. 1852. B-1039/2 – 10mf – 8 – ne IDC [073]
OPYT RABOTY NAUCHNOI BIBLIOTEKI MGU / Moscow. University – nr. 1. M. 1955. BR-10,835 1 – 9 – ne IDC [020]
OPYT RATSIONALIZATSII TORGOVOGO APPARATA : PO MATERIALAM KOMISSII PO RATSIONALIZATSII APPARATA TSENTROSOIUZA / ed by Kissin, A A – M., 1929 – 3mf – 9 – COR-339/1 – ne IDC [334]
OPYT ROSSIISKOI BIBLIOGRAFII, ILI POLNYI SLOVAR' SOCHINENII I PEREVODOV, NAPECHATANNYKH NA SLAVENSKOM I ROSSIISKOM IAZYKAKH, OT NACHALA ZAVEDENIIA TIPOGRAFII, DO 1813 GODA... / Sopikov, V S – Spb., 1813-1821. v1-5 – 44mf – 9 – R-4691/2 – ne IDC [460]
OPYT RUSSKOI ISTORIOGRAFII / Ikonnikov, V S – 2v. in 4. Kiev. 1891-1908. B-1141 2 – 8 – ne IDC [947]
OPYT RUSSKOI ISTORIOGRAFII / Ikonnikov, V S – Kiev. (A tentative Russian historiography). 2 v. 1891-1908 – 3 – us Readex [010]
OPYT SLOVARIA PSEVDONIMOV RUSSKIKH PISATELEI / Kartsov, S V & Mazaev, MN – Spb. 1891. BR-5911 2 – 8 – ne IDC [460]
OPYT SLOVARIA RUSSKIKH SINONIMOV / Kalaidovich, P – M., 1818. v1 – 2mf – 9 – R-8393/2 – ne IDC [460]
OPYT TERMINOLOGICHESKOGO SLOVARIA SEL'SKOGO KHOZIAISTVA... / Burnashev, VP – Spb., 1843-1844. 2 vols – 18mf – 9 – 1379/2 – ne IDC [580]
OPYT TRUDOV VOL'NAGO ROSSIISKAGO SOBRANIIA PR / Moscow. University – Imperatorskom Moskovskom Universitete. v. 1-5. M. 1774-80. BR-7738 2 – 8 – ne IDC [073]
OPYTY PO ISTORII RUSSKAGO PRAVA / Chicherin, Boris N – Moscow, 1858. 389p. Early history of the development of Russian law. B-2381/2 – 8 – ne IDC [947]
O'Quin, Patrick *see* DU DECROISSEMENT DE LA POPULATION DAN LE DEPARTEMENT DES BASSES-PYRENEES
OR *see* 'HA'OR'
L'OR BLANC – Thetford, Canada. 21 oct 1975; v1 n18. 9 dec 1975 – 1r – 1 – Can$25.00 – cn Can Microfilming [072]
OR DES SCYTHES / Reunion des Musees Nationaux. Paris – 1975 – 9 – fr Réunion [700]
L'OR ET L'ARGENT EN 1864 / Bordet, Henri – Paris: Guillaumin, 1864.62p. 1 fiche.(Economics Collection) – 9 – 6.00 – fr Bibl Nationale [336]
O.R. HERTWIG'S TABELLEN ZUR EINLEITUNG IN DIE...BUECHER DES ALTEN TESTAMENTS / Kleinert, Paul – Berlin: G.W.F. Mueller, 1869. 1 fiche – 9 – us A.T.L.A. [220]
ORA DI PALERMO – 1987-1995 – 4r per y – 5,6 – Sfr989.00 – sz Infoprint [072]
ORACION APOLOGERICA POR LA ESPANA Y SU MERITO LITERARIO / Forner Segarra, Juan Pablo – Badajoz: Imprenta de la Diputacion Provincial, 1945 – 1 – sp Bibl Santa Ana [440]
ORACION APOLOGETICA POR LA ESPANA Y SU MERITO LITERARIO / Forner Segarra, Juan Pablo – 1786 – 1mf – 9 – Pta1,000.00 – 84-7848-195-8 – sp Pentalfa [440]
ORACION APOLOGETICA POR LA ESPANA... LITERARIO / Forner Segarra, Juan Pablo – (1786. 1.50f; 9) – 1787 – 9 – 1.50f – sp Bibl Santa Ana [840]
ORACION DE LOS DEBILES AL COMENZAR EL ANO POR... / Diez Canedo, Enrique – Mexico: D.F., Talleres Graficos de la Compania Editora y Librera ARS, S.A., 1950 – 1 – sp Bibl Santa Ana [946]
LA ORACION DE TODAS LAS NOTICIAS / Aradillas Agudo, Antonio – Madrid: Sociedad de Educacion Atenas, S.A., 1966 – 1 – sp Bibl Santa Ana [240]
ORACION FUNEBRE / Bedoya, Juan Manuel – 1818 – 9 – 1.50f – sp Bibl Santa Ana [240]
ORACION FUNEBRE / Dolores y Santa Marta, Felix – 1786 – 9 – 1.50f – sp Bibl Santa Ana [850]
ORACION FUNEBRE QUE EN EL 4TH CENTENARIO DE LA MUERTE DELA REINA CATOLICA PRONUNCIO EN LA IGLESIA CATOLICA DE SANTA MARIA DE CACERES... / Escobar Prieto, Eugenio – Caceres: Tip. Jimenez, 1904 – 1 – sp Bibl Santa Ana [240]
ORACION FUNEBRE...5 DE JULIO DE 1736 / Alonso de Llerena – 9 – 1.50f – sp Bibl Santa Ana [946]
ORACION FUNEBRE...DON JUAN BALTASAR DE LOAYSA / Mier, Santiago – 1756 – 9 – $1.50f – sp Bibl Santa Ana [850]
ORACION FUNEBRE...EXEQUIAS / Garcia Bermejo, Antonio – 1824 – 9 – 1.50f – sp Bibl Santa Ana [850]
ORACION FUNEBRE...POR LOS FALLECIDOS... DE LA GUERRA CIVIL / Aguilar Gallegos, Manuel – 1876 – 9 – 1.50f – sp Bibl Santa Ana [946]
ORACION FUNEBRE...SAN ISIDRO / Garcia Bermejo, Antonio – 1831 – 9 – 1.50f – sp Bibl Santa Ana [850]
ORACION INAUGURAL...LICEO DE GRANADA / Moreno Nieto, Jose – 1857 – 9 – 1.50f – sp Bibl Santa Ana [850]
ORACION PANEGIRICA...IGLESIA METROPOLITANA...ENEMIGOS / Levanto y Vivaldo, Francisco – 1711 – 9 – 1.50f – sp Bibl Santa Ana [240]
ORACION...APERTURA DE LA AUDIENCIA DE CACERES / Mendoza, Pedro – 1850 – 9 – 1.50f – sp Bibl Santa Ana [850]
ORACION...EN EL INSTITUTO PROVINCIAL DE BADAJOZ.. / Botello del Castillo, Carlos – 1849 – 9 – 1.50f – sp Bibl Santa Ana [510]
ORACIONES / Asociacion de Hijas de la Purisima e Inmaculada...Viregen Maria. Spain – 1881 – 9 – 1.50f – sp Bibl Santa Ana [240]
ORACIONES / Asociacion de Hijas de la Purisima e Inmaculada...Viregen Maria. Spain – 1890 – 9 – 1.50f – sp Bibl Santa Ana [240]
LAS ORACIONES DEL SALTERIO "PER ANNUM" EN EL NUEVO LIBRO DE LA LITURGIA DE LAS HORAS / Pinell, J – Roma, 1974 – 2mf – 8 – Dfl9.00 – ne Slangenburg [240]
ORACIONES PARA LA REVOLUCION JUSTICIALISTA / Jass en, Raul – Buenos Aires: Editorial Patria Barbara, 1965? – 9 – us Hoover Inst Photo [972]
ORACION...MAGESTAD...CABILDOS DE LA CIUDAD DE BADAJOZ...INFANTES / Soler de los Rios, Antonio – 1784 – 9 – 1.50f – sp Bibl Santa Ana [946]

ORACLE – St. Mary's. West Virginia. 1882-99; 1932-69 – 1 – us UMI [071]
THE ORACLE – San Francisco, CA. 1966-69 – 1r – 1 – $50.00 – B02845 – us Library Micro [071]
THE ORACLE AND THE DAILY ADVERTISER. (DAILY ADVERTISER & ORACLE, DAILY ADVERTISER, ORACLE & TRUE BRITON) – London. 1801-04.-d. 8 reels – 1 – uk British Libr Newspaper [072]
ORACLE OF REASON – Bristol, then London. 1841-43 – 1 – uk Microform Academic [073]
ORACLE OF THE DAY – Portsmouth. N.H. 1793-1799. United States Oracle. 1800-1803. Sold as one unit – 1,3 – us Readex [071]
ORACLES – Santa Maria, CA. Allan Hancock College: 1950 – 3+ r – 1 – $150.00 – R04112 – us Library Micro [071]
THE ORACLES OF GOD: NINE LECTURES ON THE NATURE AND EXTENT OF BIBLICAL INSPIRATION / Sanday, William – London: Longmans, Green, 1891. 1 fiche – 9 – us A.T.L.A. [240]
ORAD HERMANOS. MEDITACIONES SOBRE TEMAS LITURGICOS / Aradillas Agudo, Antonio – Barcelona: Juan Flors, 1959 – 1 – sp Bibl Santa Ana [240]
EL ORADOR CRISTIANO / Mayans y Siscar, Gregorio – 1733 – 1mf – 9 – Pta1,000.00 – 84-7848-287-3 – sp Pentalfa [240]
Oraeus, Henricus *see* AEREOPLASTES THEOSOPHICUS, SIVE EICONES MYSTICAE
THE ORAGEAN VERSION / King, Charles Daly – 1st ed. Long Valley? N.J., 1951 – 1 – us U.W. Library [830]
ORAISON FUNEBRE DE (...)CHARLES-FERDINAND D'ARTOIS, PRONONCEE AU SERVICE SOLENNEL(...)LE 10 AVRIL, DANS L'EGLISE DES HERBIERS (VENDEE) / Jaunet, Jacques – Nantes: Busseuil, [ca 1820] – fr Armell [944]
ORAISON FUNEBRE DE LOUIS 16TH(...)PRONONCEE LE 30 JUIN 1814(...) / Roullier, H – Nantes: Busseuil, 1816 – fr Armell [944]
ORAISONS FUN EBRES DE BOSSUET : PRECEDEES DE L'ESSAI SUR L'ORAISON FUN EBRE / Bossuet, Jacques Benigne – Paris: Firmin Didot, 1859 – 2mf – 9 – 0-8370-7126-7 – 1986-1126 – us A.T.L.A. [230]
ORAISONS FUNEBRES DE MGR. BOURGET: PRONONCEES DANS L'EGLISE NOTRE-DAME LE 12 JUIN 1885 / Colin, Frederic Louis de Gonzague – Et a l'eveche le lendemain par Mgr. Tache. Montreal: Cadieux & Derome, 1885?. 03209. (Pre-1900 Canadiana) – 9 – cn C.I.H.M. [920]
ORAISONS FUNEBRES DE MONSEIGNEUR IGNACE BOURGET, SECOND EVEQUE DE MONTREAL, ARCHEVEQUE DE MARIANOPOLIS, PRONONCEE DANS L'EGLISE DE NOTRE-DAME DE MONTREAL, LE 12 JUIN 1885 / Colin, Frederic Louis de Gonzague – Montreal, 1885. 00708. (Pre-1900 Canadiana) – 9 – cn C.I.H.M. [920]
ORAL ARGUMENTS OF THE US SUPREME COURT ON MICROFICHE – 1953/54-1994/95 – 9 – Apply for prices – us CIS [340]
ORAL HEALTH – (v1-59 1911-69 Can$1,980.00 5) – Don Mills. v1-84. 1911-94 – 5,9 – Can$28.00y – cn Micromedia [617]
ORAL HISTORIES OF THE JOHNSON ADMINISTRATION – (Microfilm ed. 1-55655-085-5. $1,740.00) – Part 1: The White House and the Executive Departments. 347 fiches with printed guide – 9 – $1,740.00 – 0-89093-873-3 – us UPA [977]
ORAL HISTORIES OF THE JOHNSON ADMINISTRATION – (Microfilm ed. 1-55655-086-3. $2,015.00) – Part 2: The Congress, the Judiciary, Public Figures, and Private Individuals. 416 fiches with printed guide – 9 – $2,015.00 – 0-89093-874-1 – us UPA [977]
ORAL HISTORY ASSOCIATION NEWSLETTER – v1-21. 1967-87 – 21mf – 9 – $125.00 – us UPA [910]
ORAL ONCOLOGY *see* EUROPEAN JOURNAL OF CANCER
ORAL RESEARCH ABSTRACTS – v.1-13. 1966-78 – 1 – us UMI [073]
ORAL SURGERY, ORAL MEDICINE AND ORAL PATHOLOGY – v. 1- 1948- – 1. ; 5,6,9 – apply; v.31- – us UMI [617]
ORAL SURGERY, ORAL MEDICINE, ORAL PATHOLOGY *see* AMERICAN JOURNAL OF ORTHODONTICS
ORANG INDONESIA JANG TERKEMOEKA DI DJAWA : TJETAKAN PERTAMA – Djakarta ? Gunseikanbu, 2604. 552p – 117-122mf – 9 – ne IDC [950]
ORANGE 1767-1891 – (Mf 1-2: Birth Index 1844-91. Mf 2-3: Marriage Index 1844-91. Mf 4-5: Death Index 1844-91. Mf 6-8: Births & Deaths 1767-1849. Mf 9: Births 1844-51. Mf 9: Marriages 1777-99, 1844-50. Mf 10: Deaths 1844-53. Mf 11-15: Births 1851-91. Mf 15-19: Marriages 1851-90. Mf 19-23: Deaths 1854-90) – (mf ed 1983) – 23mf – 9 – 0-931248-47-7 – us Holbrook [920]
ORANGE, A POLITICAL RHAPSODY IN THREE CANTOS / Gifford, John – 9th ed. Dublin: Printed for J. Milliken, 1798 – 1 – us U.W. Library [780]
THE ORANGE AND PROTESTANT BANNER, 1851-1868/9 – 5r – 1 – uk Microform Academic [941]
THE ORANGE ASSOCIATION UNMASKED: A CRUSHING BLOW TO OATH-BOUND SECRET SOCIETIES / Blake, Edward – Mr. Blake's great speech to the House of Commons, March 17, 1884. Montreal: Post Print. and Pub. Co., 1884. 00166. (Pre-1900 Canadiana) – 9 – cn C.I.H.M. [971]
ORANGE BELT DAILY NEWS – San Bernardino, CA. 1934-1935 – 3r – 1 – $150.00 – R03455 – us Library Micro [071]
ORANGE CITY DIRECTORIES – Orange Co, CA. 1907, 1919, 1949-1950 – 3r – 1 – $150.00 – D066A – us Library Micro [910]
ORANGE CITY NEWS – Orange, CA. 1993-1994 – 6r – 1 – $300.00 – R04078 – us Library Micro [071]
ORANGE COAST DAILY PILOT – Orange Co, CA. 1967; 1974 – 71+ r – 1 – $3,550.00 ($170.00y) – H04033 – us Library Micro [071]
ORANGE COUNTY, 1899-1903; 1911-1951, 1991 – 26r – 1 – $1,300.00 – D066 – us Library Micro [978]
ORANGE COUNTY BUSINESS FIRST – Orange Co, CA. 1988-1989 – 2r – 1 – $100.00 – R04082 – us Library Micro [071]
ORANGE COUNTY BUSINESS WEEK – Orange Co, CA. 1986-1988 – 4r – 1 – $200.00 – R04083 – us Library Micro [071]
ORANGE COUNTY: BUSINESS-TO-BUSINESS – 1985; 1987; 1898-92 – 7r – 1 – $350.00 – P00074 – us Library Micro [910]
ORANGE COUNTY: CENTRAL – 1983 – 25+ r – 1 – $1,250.00 – P00080 – us Library Micro [910]
ORANGE COUNTY: CENTRAL AND NORTH – 1989 – 1r – 1 – $50.00 – P00079 – us Library Micro [910]
ORANGE COUNTY: CENTRAL AND SOUTH – 1975-86 – 33r – 1 – $1,650.00 – P00078 – us Library Micro [910]
ORANGE COUNTY: COASTAL – 1990 – 9+ r – 1 – $450.00 – P00081 – us Library Micro [910]
ORANGE COUNTY EVENING NEWS – Garden Grove, CA. 1964-70 – 1 – us UMI [071]
ORANGE COUNTY EVENING NEWS – Orange Co, CA. 1973-1974 – 1r – 1 – $50.00 – R04084 – us Library Micro [071]
ORANGE COUNTY: INLAND – 1990 – 9+ r – 1 – $450.00 – P00082 – us Library Micro [910]
ORANGE COUNTY: NORTH – 1983 – 20+ r – 1 – $1,000.00 – P00075 – us Library Micro [910]
ORANGE COUNTY: NORTHWEST – 1991 – 1r – 1 – $50.00 – P00076 – us Library Micro [910]
ORANGE COUNTY: ORANGE – 1907-31; 1933-36; 1993- – 62+ r – 1 – $3,100.00 – P00073 – us Library Micro [910]
ORANGE COUNTY PRESS – Middletown. N.Y. 1865-1905 – 1 – us UMI [071]
ORANGE COUNTY: SOUTH – 1981-86; 1988 – 18+ r – 1 – $900.00 – P00077 – us Library Micro [910]
ORANGE COUNTY: SPANISH – 1992 – 3+ r – 1 – $150.00 – P00083 – us Library Micro [910]
ORANGE COUNTY TIMES – Middletown. N.Y. 1891-1905 – 1 – us UMI [071]
ORANGE COUNTY TIMES PRESS – Middletown. N.Y. 1906-1925 – 1 – us UMI [071]
ORANGE COUNTY TRIBUNE – Orange Co, CA. 1908-1918 – 5r – 1 – $250.00 – R04085 – us Library Micro [071]
ORANGE COVE AND MOUNTAIN NEWS – Dinuba, CA. 1985 – 1r – 1 – $50.00 – B06023 – us Library Micro [071]
ORANGE COVE AND MOUNTAIN TIMES – Orange Cove, CA. 1984-1993 – 2r – 1 – $100.00 – B06043 – us Library Micro [071]
ORANGE COVE EVENTS AND NEWS – Orange Cove, CA. 1981 – 1r – 1 – $50.00 – B06044 – us Library Micro [071]
ORANGE COVE-NEWS – Orange Cove, CA. 1933-75; 1977-80 – 18r – 1 – $900.00 – B02557 – us Library Micro [071]
ORANGE FREE STATE, REPORTS OF THE PROVINCIAL AUDITOR. BLOEMFONTEIN, 1910-50 – 3r – 9 – sa SA Libr [324]
ORANGE JUDD AMERICAN AGRICULTURIST *see* AMERICAN AGRICLUTURIST AND THE RURAL NEW YORKER
ORANGE JUDD FARMER – Sep 8 1888-Dec 30 1893 – 5r – 1 – $150.00 $30.00r – us M.H.S. [630]
ORANGE LEADER – Jan 4 1899-Dec 31 1919 – 9 – at Pascoe [072]
THE ORANGE LILY – (Cont: The Orange Lily and Protestant Vindicator) – Bytown [Ottawa]: D Kerr, [between 1850 and 1854-18–?] – 9 – cn C.I.H.M. [072]
THE ORANGE LILY *see* THE ORANGE LILY AND PROTESTANT VINDICATOR
THE ORANGE LILY AND PROTESTANT VINDICATOR – (Cont by: The Orange Lily) – Bytwon [Ottawa]: Ottawa Advocate, [1849-between 1850 and 1854] – 9 – cn C.I.H.M. [072]
THE ORANGE LILY AND PROTESTANT VINDICATOR *see* THE ORANGE LILY
ORANGE OBSERVER AND ORANGE CITY NEWS – Orange Co, CA. 1992 – 1+ r – 1 – $50.00 ($50.00y) – R04086 – us Library Micro [071]
ORANGE POST – (Also known as: Semi-Weekly Post) – Orange, CA. 1913-1916; 1919-1922 – 3r – 1 – $150.00 – C03374 – us Library Micro [071]
THE ORANGE RECORD – Toronto: F Crapper, [1887?-18–?] – 9 – cn C.I.H.M. [360]
ORANGE STAR – Orange, CA. 1917-1921 – 2r – 1 – $100.00 – C03375 – us Library Micro [071]
ORANGE TELEGRAPH – Newburgh. N.Y. 1829-1830 – 1 – us UMI [071]
ORANGE-BELLIED PARROT RECOVERY PLAN / Brown, Peter B & Wilson, Roland I – 1984 – microfiche – A$15.00 – at R.A.O.U. [590]
Orangeburg. South Carolina. Church of the Redeemer (Episcopal) *see* REGISTER
ORANGEVILLE BANNER – (1931-1976.-33r; 1993.-10r) – Orangeville, 1977-1992 – 109r – 1 – cn Preston [971]
L'ORANGISME ET LE CATHOLICISME: SIR GEORGE E. CARTIER, LE GRAND CHEF DU BAS-CANADA CONTRE SIR JOHN A. MACDONALD, L'ENNEMI DES CATHOLIQUES ET DES CANADIENS-FRANCAIS / Bellerose, Joseph Hyacinthe – Discours prononce au senat le 2 mars 1886. Montreal, 1886. 03566. (Pre-1900 Canadiana) – 9 – cn C.I.H.M. [240]
ORANG-OUTANG / Tyson, E – M 414. 1699 – 9 – ne IDC [580]
ORANJEBLOESEMS / Tal, T – Amsterdam. 1898. BJ-262-61 1 – 9 – ne IDC [949]
ORAN-REPUBLICAIN – Le quotidien de la democratie. Dir. L. Deville. Oran. 1950-56, avr-juin 1959, janv-mars 1960, juil 1962 – 1 – fr A.C.R.P.P. [073]
ORATE FRATRES – Collegeville, 1(1926)-25(1951) – 315mf – 9 – Dfl1,103.00 – ne Slangenburg [073]
L'ORATEUR D'OUTREMONT = D'OUTREMONT ORATOR – Outremont, Canada. v1 n1. 27 aut 1958; v1 n14. 26 nov 1958 – 1r – 1 – Can$25.00 – cn Can Microfilming [072]
L'ORATEUR DU PEUPLE – Par Martel puis Journal libre par Martel. Par Freron. Paris. mai 1790-nov 1792, sept 1794-aout 1795 – 1 – fr A.C.R.P.P. [073]
LES ORATEURS DE LA REVOLUTION: LA LEGISLATIVE ET LA CONVENTION / Aulard, Francois Victor Alphonse – Nouv, ed. rev. et cor. avec illustrations hors texte. Paris: E. Cornely, 1906-1907 – 1 – us U.W. Library [944]
ORATIO AD PIUM QUINTUM PONT. MAX. QUA PRINCIPES AD BELLUM CONTRA SELINUM EXCITANTUR POST VICTAM CLASSEM TURCICAM / Franciscus, J – Venetijs, 1572 – 1mf – 9 – H-8326/1 – ne IDC [956]
ORATIO AD SERENISSIMVM CAROLVM V. SACRI ROMANI IMPERIJ CAESAREM INCLYTUM / Frangepan, W – Augustae Vindelicorum, 1530 – 1mf – 9 – H-8238/1 – ne IDC [956]
ORATIO DE BELLO ADVERSVS TVRCAM, AD FERDINANDUM VNGARIAE ET BOHEMIAE REGEM, ET PRINCIPES / Agricola, F et al – Lipsiae, 1594 – 3mf – 9 – H-8378/1 – ne IDC [943]
ORATIO DE HISTORICA RELIGIONIS CHRISTIANAE INDOLE : HODIE NIMIUM SPRETA, HAUD SINE GRAVISSIMO DAMNO CONTEMNENDA AC NEGLIGENDA / Haar, Bernard ter – Trajecti ad Rhenum: Kemink, 1860 – 1mf – 9 – 0-8370-4767-6 – 1985-2767 – us A.T.L.A. [240]
ORATIO DE JURIS PUBLICI UNIVERSALIS STUDIO,... / Cock, H – Leiden, 1826 – 1mf – 1 – ILM-725/1 – ne IDC [327]
ORATIO DE PACE FUTURA... / Hartmann, I Z – Kiliae, 1736 – 1mf – 1 – ILM-2598/1 – ne IDC [327]
ORATIO DE STATV ECCLESIARVM HOC TEMPORE IN GRAECIA, ASIA, AFRICA, VNGARIA, ... / Chrytraeus, D – VVittebergae, 1580 – 2mf – 9 – H-8355/1 – ne IDC [956]
ORATIO DE STATV ECCLESIARVM HOC TEMPORE IN GRAECIA, ASIA, BOHEMIA, ... / Chytraeus, D – Francofvrti, 1583 – 3mf – 9 – 8361/1 – ne IDC [949]
ORATIO HABITA AB ELOQUENTISSIMO VIRO. F. THOMA GUICHARDO RHODIO / Guichardus, T – Romae, 1523 – 1mf – 9 – H-8231/1 – ne IDC [956]
ORATIO HABITA AD SANCTISSIMU DUM NOSTRU LEONE 10 PONT. MAX. ... / Arnolphus, B – Rome, 1513 – 1mf – 9 – H-8226/1 – ne IDC [945]
ORATIO HABITA CORA CLEMETE 7 DE CONFOEDERATIONE NUPER INITA, PACEQUE UNIUERSALI, ATQUE EXPEDITIONE ADUERSUS TURCAS SUSPICIENDA / Balbi, G – Rome, 1533 – 1mf – 9 – H-8243/1 – ne IDC [956]
ORATIO QUAM PRO SOLEMNI STUDIORUM INSTAURATIONE...1925-1926 IN PONTIFICIO UNIVERSITATE VALENTINA – Madrid: Razon y Fe, 1926 – 1 – sp Bibl Santa Ana [370]
ORATIONE DELLA PACE, ET DELLA GUERRA CONTRA TURCHI, A'I PRENCIPI CHRISTIANI / Bucci, A – N.p., 1559 – 1mf – 9 – H-8294/1 – ne IDC [956]
ORATIONE PER LA GVERRA CONTRA TVRCHI A SISTO QVINTO PONT, MASSIMO, ... / Piccha, G – Roma, 1589 – 1mf – 9 – H-8375/1 – ne IDC [956]
ORATIONE...AD HENRICO 4. CHRISTIANISSIMO RE DI FRANCIA, E DI NAUARRA / Soranzo, L – Ferrara, 1598 – 1mf – 9 – H-8401/1 – ne IDC [240]
ORATIONE...AL SERENISS. PRINCIPE DI VENETIA SEBASTIAN VENIERO, ... / Nores, G de – Padova, 1578 – 1mf – 9 – H-8352/1 – ne IDC [945]
ORATIONE...FATTA IN VINEGIA, PER L'ALLEGREZZA DELLA UITTORIA OTTENUTA CONTRA TURCHI DALLA SANTISSIMA LEGA / Groto, L – Vinegia, 1571 – 1mf – 9 – H-8312/1 – ne IDC [956]
ORATIONES / Sallustius & Catilia & Aretinus, L – Holkham ms. 339. Holkham Hall, Norfolk, England – 1 – uk Microform Academic [025]
ORATIONES 2. 1. ADUERSUS LIB. VBERTI FOLIETAE DE MAGNITUDINE ET PERPETUA IN BELLIS FELICITATE IMPERII TURCICI. 2. AD EXPEDITIONEM IN TURCAS FORTITER ET CONSTANTER PERSEQUENDAM EXHORTATORIA / Estienne, Henri – Francofordii, 1594 – 3mf – 9 – H-8380/1 – ne IDC [956]
ORATIONS, OF ARSANES AGAYNST PHILIP THE TRECHEROUS KYNG OF MACEDONE – London, [1560] – 2mf – 9 – H-8157/1 – ne IDC [949]
ORATORIOS REGULARES...RELIGIOSOS / San Pedro de Alcantara, Domingo de – 1734 – 9 – 1.50f – sp Bibl Santa Ana [240]
GLI ORAZI E CURIAZI / Cimarosa, D – (Overture, arr. Fortepiano) – Paris: Sieber, 179- – 1 – us Sibley [780]
ORBA; A GUIDE TO THE NEW ORDER, GOVERNMENT POLICY / Indonesia. Departemen Penerangan – SE-8483 1. 1967? – 9 – ne IDC [324]
O ORBE – Maceio, Alagoas. 2 Mar-Dez 1879; Abr 1880; Maio 1881-Jun 1885; Mar-Maio, Ago-Dez 1886; Jan 1887-Mar 1890; Fev, Jun, Set-Dez 1896; Jan-Dez 1897; Jan-Maio, Set-Dez 1898; Jun 1899-Jun 1900 – 1,5,6 – bl Biblioteca [072]
Orbigny, Alcide d' *see*
– MOLLUSQUES
– PALEONTOLOGIE FRANCAISE

- VOYAGES DANS L'AMERIQUE MERIDIONALE... EXECUTE PENDANT LES ANNEES 1826-1833

ORBIS : A JOURNAL OF WORLD AFFAIRS – v1- 1957- 1; v12- 5,6; v19- 9 – us UMI [327]

ORBIS LATINUS ODER VERZEICHNIS DER WICHTIGSTEN LATEINISCHEN ORTS- UND LAENDERNAMEN. ED. 3 / Graesse, J GT; ed by Benedict, F – Berlin, 1922 – 13mf – 9 – 7717/2 – ne IDC [450]

THE ORBIS PICTUS OF JOHN AMOS COMENIUS = ORBIS SENSUALIUM PICTUS / Comenius, Johann Amos – (Text in English and Latin in parallel columns) – Syracuse, NY: C W Bardeen, 1887 – 1mf – 9 – 0-8370-7616-1 – 1986-1616 – us A.T.L.A. [450]

ORBIS SENSUALIUM PICTUS / Comenius, Johann Amos – Charles Hoole. 1659. 350p. (English Linguistics Series 1500-1800) – 9 – us UMI [400]

ORBITAL MECHANICS AND MISSION DESIGN – (Suppl to v69, Advances) – 1989 – 1mf – 9 – $10.00 – 0-87703-313-7 – us Univelt [629]

THE ORCADIAN – Kirkwall, Scotland. -w. 1870-1975. 93 reels – 1 – uk British Libr Newspaper [072]

Orceau, R *see* NANTES REALISTE

Orchard, George Herbert *see* AUTOBIOGRAPHICAL MEMOIRS, 1821-52

ORCHARD NEWS – Orchard, NE. -w. Aug 1903-Aug 1907, scattered issues missing; Jan 1908-Aug 1913; Oct 1913-Apr 1914; Jun 1914 to date – 1 – us NE Hist [071]

Orchard, William Edwin *see* THE EVOLUTION OF OLD TESTAMENT RELIGION

ORCHESTRA AND THE CHOIR – 1-n.s. 14. 1863-87 – 1 – us UMI [780]

ORCHESTRAL JOURNAL / Friederich, G WE – New York: Firth, Pond & Co., 1856. Collection of orchestral works, small ensemble, parts only. MUSIC 1985 – 1 – us L of C Photodup [780]

L'ORCHESTRE – Montreal, Canada. 16/21 oct 1893-v2 n9. 10 dec 1894 – 1r – 1 – Can$35.00 – cn Can Microfilming [780]

ORCHID HERBARIUM / Lindley, J – (Includes index on microfiche) – Kew – 320mf – 9 – 7395/2 – ne IDC [580]

ORCHID HERBARIUM OF OAKES AMES BOTANICAL MUSEUM / Harvard University Herbaria – (Includes index £90.00) – 307mf – 9 – £1,320.00 – uk Chadwyck [580]

ORCHID POLLEN/POLLINARIA : COLLECTION OF 3,100 SCANNING ELECTRON MICROPHOTOGRAPHS – 36mf – 9 – 13261/1 – ne IDC [580]

ORCHID REVIEW – London. v1-25. 1893-1917 – 172mf – 9 – ne IDC [580]

THE ORCHIDACEAE OF MEXICO AND GUATEMALA / Bateman, J – London, [1837-]1843 – 40pls – 8 – ne IDC [580]

ORCHIDEARUM SCELETOS / Lindley, J – Londini. 1826. B-5027 2 – 8 – ne IDC [580]

THE ORCHID-GROWER'S MANUAL / Williams, B S – 5341. 7TH ED. 1894 – 9 – ne IDC [580]

THE ORCHIDS OF BURMA / Grant, B – Rangoon. 1895. B-7315 2 – 8 – ne IDC [580]

ORCHIS – (Beilage zur "Gartenflora". v1-14; Missing: v1-2 1906-1908) – Berlin, 1906-1920 – 25mf – 9 – ne IDC [630]

Orcutt, Hiram *see* AMONG THE THEOLOGIES

ORD JOURNAL – Ord, NE. -w. (-sw 1898-99). Jun 1892; Jan 1895; Sep 1895-Feb 1898; May 1898-Dec 1928 – 1 – us NE Hist [071]

ORD OBSERVER – Ord, NE. -w. Dec 1930-Mar 1932 – 1 – us NE Hist [071]

ORD QUIZ – Ord, NE. -w. Feb-Nov 1885, scattered issues missing; Sep 1892; Sep 1895 to date – 1 – us NE Hist [071]

ORD REPORT ON THE WEST COAST OF AFRICA / Great Britain. Parliament – (£7.00; 7) – 1865 – 1 – uk Microform Academic [960]

ORDAINING WOMEN / Roberts, Benjamin Titus – 1891 – 9 – us A.T.L.A. [240]

DE ORDE DER JEZUIETEN : HARE GESCHIEDENIS, INRICHTING EN MORAAL / Maronier, J H – Leiden: E.J. Brill, 1908 – 1mf – us A.T.L.A. [240]

Orde, P L et al *see* NOTE ON THE KHAKSAR MOVEMENT

ORDEAL : A CRITICAL JOURNAL OF POLITICKS AND LITERATURE – v1. 7 Jan-Jul 1809 – 1 – us UMI [073]

A ORDEM – (Cont as: A Provincia de Minas) – Ouro Preto, 27 Nov 1899-31 Dec 1892 – 1,5,6 – bl Biblioteca [072]

A ORDEM – Maceio, Alagoas. 15 Nov 1888; Nov-7 Dez 1889 – 1,5,6 – bl Biblioteca [072]

A ORDEM – Maceio, Alagoas. 6 Nov 1880 – 1,5,6 – bl Biblioteca [072]

A ORDEM : ORGAM NOTICIOSO E SEM LIGACOES POLITICAS – Rio Novo, 10 Jul 1923 – 1,5,6 – bl Biblioteca [072]

A ORDEM : ORGAO DO COMMERCIO E NOTICIOSO – Vianna, 28 Mar-Apr, Jun, Aug, Oct-Nov 1882 – 1,5,6 – bl Biblioteca [072]

A ORDEM : PERIODICO NOTICIOSO, CRITICO E LITTERARIO – Aracaju, 19 Feb, Apr, 31 Aug 1876 – 1,5,6 – bl Biblioteca [072]

A ORDEM – Sao Paulo, 2 Jun-13 Oct 1862 – 1,5,6 – bl Biblioteca [072]

A ORDEM *see* A PROVINCIA DE MINAS

O ORDEM – Montes Claros, Brazil. Dec 1922; Jan 1923 – 1 – bl Biblioteca [072]

ORDEM E PROGRESSO : JORNAL POLITICO CONSERVADOR – '(s.l.')-Sao Luis,Brazil. 26 Dec 1860-30 Jan 1862 – 1,5,6 – bl Biblioteca [072]

DER ORDEN : MITTEILUNGEN DER GROSSLOGE FUER DEUTSCHLAND – Berlin, 1927-30 (incomplete), 1933-37 (incomplete) – 1 – Inquire at Mikrofilmarchiv for details – gw Misc Inst [290]

EL ORDEN – Badajoz, 1891-1895 – 5 – sp Bibl Santa Ana [072]

EL ORDEN – Caceres, 1887 – 5 – sp Bibl Santa Ana [073]

Der Orden Bne Briss *see* B'NAI B'RITH DEUTSCHLAND

ORDEN CIRCULAR RELATIVA.. / Spain. Laws, Statutes, etc – 1790 – 9 – 1.50f – sp Bibl Santa Ana [324]

ORDEN DE 31 DE ENERO DE 1958...LA INCOACION PARA LAS HERMANDADES SINDICALES DE LABRADORES Y GANADEROS...EXACCION POR LA VIA DE APREMIO DE LOS CUPONES IMPAGADOS / Camara Oficial Sindical Agraria. Caceres – Caceres: Ministerio de Trabajo, Servicio de Divulgacion y Publicaciones, 1958 – 1 – sp Bibl Santa Ana [630]

ORDEN DE DELEGACION NO 43. NUMERO 18 DE FOMENTO FUNCIONAL Y DIRECCION DE ENTIDADES LOCALES. FUNCIONES Y ATRIBUCIONES DE LAS JUNTAS SINDICALES AGROPECUARIAS DE LAS HERMANDADES / Sanz Catalan, Jose – Caceres: Tip. El Noticiero, 1946 – sp Bibl Santa Ana [946]

ORDEN DE DELEGACION NUM. 45, NO 19 DE FOMENTO FUNCIONAL Y DIRECCION DE ENTIDADES LOCALES. NORMAS PARA REDACCION POR LAS HERMANDADES DE SUS PRESUPUESTOS ORDINARIOS, ESPECIALES Y EXTRAORDINARIOS / Sanz Catalan, Jose – Caceres: Tip. El Noticiero, 1947 – sp Bibl Santa Ana [946]

ORDEN DE DELEGACION NUM. 50. NO 4 DE ELECCIONES SINDICALES Y VARIOS. CONCENTRACION DE MANDOS... / Sanz Catalan, Jose – Caceres: Tip. El Noticiero, 1947 – sp Bibl Santa Ana [946]

ORDEN DE DELEGACION NUM. 51 NUM. 5 DE ELECCIONES SINDICALES. REALIZACION PRACTICA DE LAS ELECCIONES SINDICALES EN LOS GREMIOS Y HERMANDADES SINDICALES LOCALES / Sanz Catalan, Jose – Caceres: Tip. El Noticiero, 1947 – sp Bibl Santa Ana [946]

ORDEN DE DELEGACION NUM. 52. NUM. 6 DE ELECCIONES SINDICALES. PLAN DE DESARROLLO DE LAS ELECCIONES SINDICALES DE 2ND GRADO O PROVINCIALES / Sanz Catalan, Jose – Caceres: Tip. El Noticiero, 1947 – sp Bibl Santa Ana [946]

ORDEN DE DELEGACION NUM. 53 NUM. 7 DE ELECCIONES SINDICALES. NORMAS PARA LA ELECCION DE JEFES EN LAS ENTIDADES MENORES / Sanz Catalan, Jose – Caceres: Tip – sp Bibl Santa Ana [946]

ORDEN DE DELEGACION NUM. 57 NUM. 22 DE FOMENTO FUNCIONAL Y DIRECCION ENTIDADES. NORMAS PARA EL TRASPASO DE LAS FUNCIONES DE LAS ANTIGUAS JUNTAS LOCALES A JUNTAS SINDICALES AGROPECUARIAS A LOS CABILDOS DE LAS HERMANDADES / Sanz Catalan, Jose – Caceres: Tip. El Noticiero, 1948 – sp Bibl Santa Ana [946]

ORDEN DE DELEGACION NUMERO 40 NUMERO 16 DE FOMENTO FUNCIONAL Y DIRECCION DE ENTIDADES LOCALES PLAN E INSTRUCCIONES PARA UNA ACTUACION EFICAZ Y DECISIVA DELAS HERMANDADES / Sanz Catalan, Jose – Caceres: Tip. El Noticiero, 1946 – sp Bibl Santa Ana [946]

ORDEN DE DELEGACION NUMERO 46. NUMERO 20 DE FOMENTO FUNCIONAL Y DIRECCION DE ENTIDADES LOCALES. CREACION DEL SERVICIO DEEXPLOTACION ECONOMICA Y SUMINISTROS AGRICOLAS EN LAS HERMANDADES SINDICALES DEL CAMPO / Sanz Catalan, Jose – Caceres: Tip. El Noticiero, 1947 – sp Bibl Santa Ana [338]

ORDEN DE SAN JERONIMO. DEFINITORIO DEL CAPITULO PRIVADO. SENTENCIA QUE DIO EL CONTRA EL REVERENTISIMO PADRE FRAY DIEGO DE CAZERES, GENERAL. 19.10.1641 – S.l., s.i., s.a. – 1 – sp Bibl Santa Ana [240]

LA ORDEN DE SANTIAGO EN TIERRAS DE EXTREMADURA / Mota Arevalo, Horacio – Badajoz: (Imp. de la Diputacion Provincial), 1962. Sep. Revi. Estudios Extremenos – 1 – sp Bibl Santa Ana [340]

LA ORDEN DE SANTO DOMINGO EN EL PERU : ESTUDIO BIBLIOGRAFICO ESCRITO POR EL R.P. FRAY / Angulo, D – Lima, Sanmarti, 1909 – 4mf – 9 – ne IDC [972]

ORDEN PARA LA CURA Y PRESERVACION DE LAS SECAS Y CARBUNCOS... / Zamudio de Alfaro, A – Madrid, 1599 – 1mf – 9 – sp Cultura [612]

ORDENACION DE LA ECONOMIA PORCINA / Masa Campos, A – Madrid: Mag, 1954 – 1 – sp Bibl Santa Ana [330]

ORDENAMIENTO ECONOMICO-SOCIAL / Argentine Republic. Consejo nacional de postguerra – Buenos Aires: G. Kraft ltda., 1945 – 1 – CSUXAHZ5965-B – us Hoover Inst Photo [330]

ORDENANZA / Falange Espanola Tradicionalista y de la Jons – Caceres: Tip. La Minerva, s.a. (antes de marzo de 1937) – 1 – sp Bibl Santa Ana [060]

ORDENANZA DE LA COMUNIDAD DE LABRADORES DE MERIDA – 1904 – 1 – sp Bibl Santa Ana [340]

ORDENANZA FISCAL, NUM. 3 PARA LA EXACCION DE DERECHOS Y TASAS POR PRESTACIONES DE SERVICIOS...SANITARIOS...1968 / Diputacion Provincial – Badajoz: Imprenta Provincial, 1969 – sp Bibl Santa Ana [946]

ORDENANZAS / Badajoz – 1767 – 9 – 1.50f – sp Bibl Santa Ana [340]

ORDENANZAS – Badajoz: Tip. Uceda Hnos, 1894 – 1 – sp Bibl Santa Ana [060]

ORDENANZAS / Llerena.(Spain). Ayuntamiento – 1709 – 9 – 1.50f – sp Bibl Santa Ana [340]

ORDENANZAS / Villafranca de los Barros. Comunidad de Labradores – Villafranca de los Barros: Imprenta de Ventura Rodriguez, 1907 – 1 – sp Bibl Santa Ana [350]

ORDENANZAS 1 AL 6. PRESUPUESTO EXTRAORDINARIO DE OBRAS, SERVICIOS Y URBANISMO, VIGENCIA INDEFINIDA DESDE 1957 / Caceres – Caceres: Tip. El Noticiero – 1 – sp Bibl Santa Ana [340]

ORDENANZAS (ANNO 1485) – Avila – 1r – 5,6 – sp Cultura [946]

ORDENANZAS DE 1892 / Badajoz. Spain – 1894 – 9 – 1.50f – sp Bibl Santa Ana [946]

ORDENANZAS DE LA (TIPO) / Hermandad Sindical – (Badajoz): Imprenta INCA, 1961 – 1 – sp Bibl Santa Ana [340]

ORDENANZAS DE REGIMEN INTERIOR / Grupo sindical de colonizacion num. 7959 – Caceres: Imp. Moderna, 1972 – 1 – sp Bibl Santa Ana [060]

ORDENANZAS FISCALES QUE AGREGANDO O RECTIFICANDO ALGUNAS DE 1939 FORMAN, CON LAS DE ESTE, LAS DEL EJERCICIO ECONOMICO DE 1940 / Caceres – Caceres: Tip. El Noticiero – 1 – sp Bibl Santa Ana [340]

ORDENANZAS FORMADAS PARA EL COBRO DE LOS IMPUESTOS Y ARBITRIOS DEL PRESUPUESTO 1915-26 / Caceres – Caceres: Tip. La Minerva, 1927, 1930, 1933 – 1 – sp Bibl Santa Ana [340]

ORDENANZAS FORMADAS PARA EL COBRO DE LOS IMPUESTOS Y ARBITRIOS DEL PRESUPUESTO DE 1959 / Caceres – Caceres: Tip. El Noticiero – 1 – sp Bibl Santa Ana [340]

ORDENANZAS MUNICIPALES – 1891 – 9 – 1.50f – sp Bibl Santa Ana [340]

ORDENANZAS MUNICIPALES / Alcantara. Spain – 1896 – 9 – 1.50f – sp Bibl Santa Ana [340]

ORDENANZAS MUNICIPALES / Aldeanueva del Camino. Ayuntamiento – Salamanca: Imp. de Calatrava, 1905 – sp Bibl Santa Ana [340]

ORDENANZAS MUNICIPALES / Azuaga. Spain – 1895 – 9 – 1.50f – sp Bibl Santa Ana [340]

ORDENANZAS MUNICIPALES / Badajoz – 1894 – 9 – 1.50f – sp Bibl Santa Ana [946]

ORDENANZAS MUNICIPALES / Barcarrota – 1897 – 9 – 1.50f – sp Bibl Santa Ana [946]

ORDENANZAS MUNICIPALES / Caceres. (Spain) – 1891 – 9 – 1.50f – sp Bibl Santa Ana [340]

ORDENANZAS MUNICIPALES / Campanario. Ayuntamiento – Badajoz: Imp. La Minerva Extremena, 1902 – sp Bibl Santa Ana [340]

ORDENANZAS MUNICIPALES / Don Benito. Spain. Ayuntamiento – 1896 – 9 – 1.50f – sp Bibl Santa Ana [324]

ORDENANZAS MUNICIPALES / Feria. Spain. Ayuntamiento – 1900 – 9 – 1.50f – sp Bibl Santa Ana [946]

ORDENANZAS MUNICIPALES / Fuente de Cantos. Ayuntamiento – Badajoz: Imp. La Minerva Extremena, 1903 – sp Bibl Santa Ana [340]

ORDENANZAS MUNICIPALES / Guarena. Ayuntamiento – Don Benito: Imp. Juan Trejo y Alvarez, 1904 – sp Bibl Santa Ana [340]

ORDENANZAS MUNICIPALES / Higuera La Real.Spain.Ayuntamiento – 1876 – 9 – 1.50f – sp Bibl Santa Ana [946]

ORDENANZAS MUNICIPALES / Hornovhos. Ayuntamiento – Badajoz: Imp. La Minerva Extremena, 1902 – sp Bibl Santa Ana [340]

ORDENANZAS MUNICIPALES / Lobon. Ayuntamiento – 1894 – 9 – 1.50f – sp Bibl Santa Ana [340]

ORDENANZAS MUNICIPALES / Los Santos de Maimona. Ayuntamiento – 1875 – 9 – 1.50f – sp Bibl Santa Ana [324]

ORDENANZAS MUNICIPALES / Madronera, Ayuntamiento – Caceres: Tip. La Minerva de Serafin Rojas, 1908 – sp Bibl Santa Ana [340]

ORDENANZAS MUNICIPALES / Malpartida de Plasencia. Ayuntamiento – 1885 – 9 – 1.50f – sp Bibl Santa Ana [946]

ORDENANZAS MUNICIPALES / Medellin. Colombia. Ayuntamiento – 1892 – 9 – 1.50f – sp Bibl Santa Ana [340]

ORDENANZAS MUNICIPALES / Medina de Las Torres. Ayuntamiento – Badajoz: Tip. La Economica, de Rodriguez y Cordero, 1908 – sp Bibl Santa Ana [340]

ORDENANZAS MUNICIPALES / Merida. Ayuntamiento – Merida: Tip. de Juan F. Rivera, 1902 – sp Bibl Santa Ana [340]

ORDENANZAS MUNICIPALES / Miajadas. Ayuntamiento – 1894 – 9 – 1.50f – sp Bibl Santa Ana [946]

ORDENANZAS MUNICIPALES / Montanchez, Ayuntamiento – Caceres: Tip. La Minerva de Serafin Rodas, 1907 – sp Bibl Santa Ana [340]

ORDENANZAS MUNICIPALES / Navalmoral de la Mata. (Spain).Ayuntamiento – 1880 – 9 – 1.50f – sp Bibl Santa Ana [946]

ORDENANZAS MUNICIPALES / Plasencia. (Spain). Ayuntamionto 1881 – 9 – 1.50f – sp Bibl Santa Ana [946]

ORDENANZAS MUNICIPALES / Tejeda. Ayuntamiento – Plasencia: Tip. de J. Hontiveros, 1906 – sp Bibl Santa Ana [340]

ORDENANZAS MUNICIPALES / Torre de Miguel Sesmero – Badajoz: Tip. de Antonio Arqueros, 1905 – sp Bibl Santa Ana [340]

ORDENANZAS MUNICIPALES / Trujillo. Ayuntamiento – 1895 – 9 – 1.50f – sp Bibl Santa Ana [946]

ORDENANZAS MUNICIPALES / Usagre. Ayuntamiento – Badajoz: Tip. La Minerva Extremena, 1905 – sp Bibl Santa Ana [340]

ORDENANZAS MUNICIPALES / Valverde de Leganes. Ayuntamiento – Badajoz: Tip. La Economica, 1904 – sp Bibl Santa Ana [340]

ORDENANZAS MUNICIPALES / Villar del Rey. Ayuntamiento – Badajoz: Tip. La Minerva Extremena, 1907 – sp Bibl Santa Ana [340]

ORDENANZAS MUNICIPALES... / Valdeobispo. Ayuntamiento – Plasencia: Imp. Gregorio Hontiveros, s.a., 1909 – sp Bibl Santa Ana [340]

ORDENANZAS MUNICIPALES DE POLICIA Y BUEN GOBIERNO – Caceres: Imp. La Minerva, 1971 – 1 – sp Bibl Santa Ana [350]

ORDENANZAS MUNICIPALES PARA EL REGIMEN Y GOBIERNO DE DON BENITO. ANO DE 1928 / Don Benito – Don Benito: Tip. de Trejo, 1929. 1 lam – sp Bibl Santa Ana [350]

ORDENANZAS MUNICIPALES...DE CACERES... APROBADAS EN 1912 / Caceres – Caceres: Tip. Luciano Jimenez Merino, 1913 – 1 – sp Bibl Santa Ana [340]

ORDENANZAS. ORDENANZAS. ORDENANZAS PARA EL GOBIERNO DE LA M.M. Y M.L. CIUDAD DE XEREZ DE LOS CABALLEROS PROBADAS POR LOS SENORES DEL REAL... / Jerez de Los Caballeros – S.L.m s.i., 1758 – 1 – sp Bibl Santa Ana [350]

ORDENANZAS PARA EL COBRO DE LOS IMPUESTOS Y ARBITRIOS DEL PRESUPUESTO / Caceres – 1938, 1939, 1946, 1950, 1953, 1954, 1956. Caceres: Tip. El Noticiero – 1 – sp Bibl Santa Ana [340]

ORDENANZAS PARA EL REGIMEN Y GOBIERNO DEL HOSPICIO... – Oviedo, 1752 – 1mf – 9 – sp Cultura [320]

ORDENANZAS PARA SU REGIMEN Y ADMINISTRACION. ESTATUTOS A ACTUALIZAR / Cofradia de Nuestra Senora De la Santisima Virgen de la Montana – Caceres: Tip. Estremadura, 1977 – 1 – sp Bibl Santa Ana [350]

ORDENANZAS Y REGLAMENTOS / Comunidad de Regantes de Badajoz. Canal Montijo – Comunidad Sindicato y riegos y Jurado de riegos. Badajoz: Tip. A. Mangas, 1964 – 1 – sp Bibl Santa Ana [340]

ORDENANZAS Y REGLAMENTOS / Comunidad de regantes de Merida – Merida: Imp. Rodriguez, 1960 – sp Bibl Santa Ana [340]

ORDENANZAS Y REGLAMENTOS / Comunidad de Regantes de Montijo – Badajoz: Imp. Barrena, 1964 – sp Bibl Santa Ana [340]

ORDENANZAS Y REGLAMENTOS DE LA... / Comunidad de regantes de la margen derecha del rio Salor – Caceres: Edit. Extremadura, 1975 – 1 – sp Bibl Santa Ana [350]

ORDENANZAS Y REGLAMENTOS PARA EL SINDICATO Y JURADO E RIEGO / Comunidad de regantes de Badajoz por el Canal de Lobon – Badajoz: Graf. Tejado, 1961 – sp Bibl Santa Ana [340]

ORDENANZAS Y TARIFAS PARA EL SERVICIO Y DISTRIBUCION DE AGUA DE LA CIUDAD DE ALMENDRALEJO. APROBADO POR EL EXCMO. AYUNTAMIENTO...4 DE AGOSTO 1933 – Madrid: Talleres Graficos Marsiega, 1934 – sp Bibl Santa Ana [340]

ORDENAZAS MUNICIPALES DE CORDOBA Y PUEBLOS...(ANNO 1374-1600) – Cordoba – 1r – 5,6 – sp Cultura [946]

LAS ORDENES MILITARES EN EXTREMADURA / Mota Arevalo, Horacio – Badajoz: (Imprenta de la Diputacion Provincial), 1969. Sep. Rev. Estudios Extremenos – 1 – sp Bibl Santa Ana [350]

LAS ORDENES MILITARES EN LA RECONQUISTA DE LA PROVINCIA DE BADAJOZ / Bullon de Mendoza, Alfonso – Merida: Tip. B. Vadillo, 1959 – sp Bibl Santa Ana [350]

LAS ORDENES RELIGIOSAS / Sanchez Aliseda, Casimiro – Barcelona: Ed. Seix Barral, S.A., 1952 – 1 – sp Bibl Santa Ana [240]

LAS ORDENES RELIGIOSAS DE ESPANA Y LA COLONIZACION DE AMERICA EN LA SEGUNDA PARTE DEL SIGLO 18 / Maas, Otto – Barcelona, 1917-1929; Madrid: Razon y Fe, 1933. 2v – 1 – sp Bibl Santa Ana [240]

ORDENES RELIGIOSAS NO MISIONERAS EN INDIAS / Bayle, Constantino – Madrid: Missionalia Hispanica, 1944 – 1 – sp Bibl Santa Ana [240]

ORDENSDEUTSCHE / Kroeger, Arved – Dresden: H B Schulze, 1943 – 1r – 1 – us U.W. Library [943]

DER ORDENTLICHE VERBANDSTAG; PROTOKOLL, ETC / Deutscher Metallarbeiterverband – Stuttgart. v7-8, 11, 15-20. 1905-32. Title varies. (Serial publications of German trade unions in the Memorial Library, University of Wisconsin-Madison.) – 1 – us U.W. Library [330]

ORDENTLICHER BUNDESTAG / Gerwerkschaftsbund der Angestellten – v5. 1930. (Serial publications of German trade unions in the Memorial Library, University of Wisconsin-Madison.) – 1 – us U.W. Library [330]

ORDENUNG (CHRISTLICHE) VND MANDAT DER ERBAREN WENDISCHEN STEDTE WIDER DIE WIDERTEUFFER VNND SACRAMENTIRER – 1555. BME-146 1 – 9 – ne IDC [240]

ORDER – v1-. 1984- – 1,5,6,9 – us UMI [073]

ORDER AND DISORDER (A STUDY OF MEDIAEVAL PRINCIPLES) / Slesser, Henry Herman – London: Hutchinson 1945. 112p. LL-2339 – 1 – us L of C Photodup [340]

ORDER BOOK / South Carolina. Militia. Third Regiment – 1778. 2 fiches – 9 – us South Carolina Historical [976]

ORDER BOOK / South Carolina. Volunteers. Fourth Regiment – 1861-62.5 fiches – 9 – us South Carolina Historical [978]

ORDER BOOK OF CAPTAIN JOHN B. VANSANT / U.S. Army. 5th Cavalry, Missouri. Company F – 1862-63 – 1 – us KS Hist [978]

ORDER BOOK OF THE COUNCIL OF STATE OF THE PROTECTOR / Great Britain. Council of State – 1658-9. Richard Cromwell; from Archives of Marquess of Bath, Longleat – 1 – uk Microform Academic [941]

ORDER N3027 : INTERIM TRANSITION TO GOVERNMENTS BASED ON LOCALLY DEVELOPED CONSTITUTIONS IN THE TTPI / U.S. Department of the Interior – Washington: U.S. Department of the Interior, 1978 – 1mf – 9 – $1.50 – LLMC 82-100F, Title 60 – us L.L.M.C. [323]

THE ORDER OF ASSASSINS / Hodgson, MGS – 's Gravenhage, 1955 – 8mf – 8 – ne Slangenburg [260]

Order of Canadian Home Circles *see* CONSTITUTION AND LAWS

THE ORDER OF THE CINCINNATI IN FRANCE – Providence, RI. 1905 – 1r – 1 – Can$50.00 – cn Can Microfilming [944]

THE ORDER OF THE COIF / Pulling, Alexander – London: Clowes & Sons, 1884 – 4mf – 9 – $6.00 – LLMC 84-311 – us L.L.M.C. [340]

THE ORDER OF THE COMMUNION 1548 / Wilson, H Austin – 1908 – 3mf – 8 – ne Slangenburg [240]

ORDER WITHOUT DESIGN / Society for Austrian Economics & David Hume Society. Sydney University, 1980 – Conference Papers. 1 fiche (29x) – 9 – 1.00f – at Libertarian Micro [320]

ORDERS / Wisconsin. Public Service Commission – v.1-58, Jun 11, 1931-1973. 517 fiches. (Harvard Law School Library Collection.) – 9 – 1.50f – us H.U. Law [336]

ORDERS AND CIRCULARS ISSUED BY THE ARMY OF THE POTOMAC AND THE ARMY AND DEPARTMENT OF NORTHERN VIRGINIA, C.S.A / U.S. War Department. Adjutant General's Office – 1861-65. 4 rolls. M921 – 1 – us Nat'l Archives [324]

ORDERS AND ENDORSEMENTS SENT BY THE SECRETARY..., 1846-70 / U.S. War Department. Office of the Secretary – 13 rolls. M444. Printed guide – 1 – us Nat'l Archives [324]

ORDERS AND SPECIAL ORDERS BY MAJOR GENERAL WILLIAM O. BUTLER AND MAJOR GENERAL W.J. WORTH TO THE ARMY IN MEXICO, 1848 / U.S. War Department. Adjutant General's Office – 1roll. T1114 – 1 – us Nat'l Archives [324]

ORDERS AND UNITY / Gore, Charles – London: J. Murray, 1909 – 1mf – us A.T.L.A. [240]

ORDERS ISSUED BY BRIGADE GENERAL STEPHEN W. KEARNEY AND BRIGADE GENERAL STERLING PRICE TO THE ARMY OF THE WEST, 1846-48 / U.S. Army. Army of the West – T1115 – 1reel – 1 – us Nat'l Archives [975]

ORDERS OF GENERAL ZACHARY TAYLOR TO THE ARMY OF OCCUPATION IN THE MEXICAN WAR, 1845-47 / U.S. War Department. Adjutant General's Office – 3rolls. M29 – 1 – us Nat'l Archives [324]

ORDERS, RETURNS, MORNING REPORTS, AND ACCOUNTS OF BRITISH TROOPS / U.S. War Department. Collection of Revolutionary War Records – 1776-81. 1 roll. M922 – 1 – us Nat'l Archives [324]

ORDERS, RETURNS, MORNING REPORTS AND ACCOUNTS OF BRITISH TROOPS, 1776-1781 – 1973. A British orderly book, 2v. M922-0001 – 1 – us A.G.L.L. [920]

ORDINAIRE DE L'ORDRE N.D. DU CARMEL PAR SIBERT DE BEKA (VERS 1312) / Zimmermann, B – Paris, 1910 – 8mf – 8 – Dfl30.00 – ne Slangenburg [240]

L'ORDINAIRE DE PREMONTRE D'APRES DES MANUSCRIPTS DU 12TH ET DU 13TH SIECLE / Lefevre, F – Louvain, 1941 – 4mf – 8 – Dfl19.00 – ne Slangenburg [240]

LES ORDINAIRES DES COLLEGIALES S. PIERRE A LOUVAIN ET S. PIERRE ET S. PAUL A ANDERLECHT D'APRES DES MANUSCRITS DU 14TH SIECLES / Lefevre, F – Louvain, 1960 – 7mf – 8 – Dfl28.00 – ne Slangenburg [240]

THE ORDINAL AND CUSTOMERY OF THE ABBEY OF SAINT MARY, YORK, BY THE ABBESS OF STANBROOK (LAURENTIA MCLACHLAN) / Tolhurst, J B L – (Vol 1.-3mf; Vol 2.-3mf; Vol 3.-2mf) – 1936, 1937 and 1951 – 8 – ne Slangenburg [240]

THE ORDINALE AND CUSTOMARY OF THE BENEDICTINE NUNS OF BARKING ABBEY / Tolhurst, J B L – (Vol 1.-3mf; Vol 2.-4mf) – 1927-1928 – 8 – ne Slangenburg [240]

ORDINALE EXON / Dalton, J N – 2v. 1909 – 11mf – 8 – ne Slangenburg [240]

ORDINALE EXON, VOL. 3 / Dalton, J N – 1926 – 7mf – 8 – ne Slangenburg [240]

ORDINALE EXON, VOL 4 / Doble, G H – 1940 – 4mf – 8 – ne Slangenburg [240]

ORDINALE SARUM SIVE DIRECCTORIUM SACERDOTUM LIBER / Wordworth, C – 1901-1902 – 13mf – 8 – Dfl46.00 – ne Slangenburg [240]

L'ORDINAMENTO LITURGICO DIE GABRIELE 5, 88E PATRIARCA COPTO / Abdallah, A – Cairo, 1962 – 9mf – 8 – Dfl32.00 – ne Slangenburg [240]

ORDINANCE AND RESOLUTION / Lucas County, Ohio. Maumee, City. City Council – 1839-1962 – 4r – 1 – $32.50r – us Archival [324]

ORDINANCE BOOK / Abilene. Kansas – 1869-74. Minute Book, 1870-76 – 1 – us KS Hist [324]

ORDINANCE BOOK / Erie County. Ohio. Milan, Village. Village Council – 1875-1932 – 1r – 1 – $32.50r – us Archival [324]

ORDINANCE BOOK / Wood County. Ohio. Bowling Green. City City Council – 1869-1914 – 1r – 1 – $32.50r – us Archival [324]

ORDINANCE NO. 13 OF 1873. SPECIAL EDITION OF "THE HONGKONG CODE OF CIVIL PROCEDURE,". / Hong Kong. Laws, Statutes, etc – Hongkong: Noronha, 1873. LL-10006 – 1 – us L of C Photodup [340]

ORDINANCE OF REGULATION CO-OPERATIVE SOCIETIES 1949 / Dutch East Indies. Laws, statutes, etc – SE-11,832-1 – 9 – ne IDC [324]

ORDINANCE RECORDS / Crawford County. Ohio. Galion – 1962-1979 – 4r – 1 – $32.50r – us Archival [324]

ORDINANCE RECORDS / Erie County. Ohio. Huron, City City Council – 1874-1945 – 1r – 1 – $32.50r – us Archival [324]

ORDINANCE RECORDS / Fulton County. Ohio. Archbold. Village. Village Council – 1876-1977 – 3r – 1 – $32.50r – us Archival [324]

ORDINANCE RECORDS / Wood County. Ohio. Weston. Village Council – 1873-1975 – 1r – 1 – $32.50r – us Archival [324]

ORDINANCES / Chetopa. Kansas – 1879-81 – 1 – us KS Hist [978]

ORDINANCES / Seneca County, Ohio. Tiffin, City. City Council – 1850-1989 – 7r – 1 – $32.50r – us Archival [324]

ORDINANCES AND RESOLUTIONS / Defiance County, Ohio. Hicksville, Village. Village Council – 1876-1929 – 1r – 1 – $32.50r – us Archival [324]

ORDINANCES AND RESOLUTIONS / Paulding County, Ohio. Cecil Village Council – 1906-1914 – 1r – 1 – $32.50r – us Archival [324]

ORDINANCES AND RESOLUTIONS / Paulding County. Ohio. Cecil Village Council – 1906-1914 – 1r – 1 – $32.50r – us Archival [324]

ORDINANCES AND RESOLUTIONS / Seneca County. Ohio. Fostoria, City. City Council – 1851-1922 – 3r – 1 – $32.50r – us Archival [324]

ORDINANCES AND RESOLUTIONS / Seneca County. Ohio. Fostoria, City. City Council – 1851-1922 – 3r – 1 – $32.50r – us Archival [324]

ORDINANCES AND RESOLUTIONS / Wood County. Ohio. Bowling Green. City City Council – 1869-1887 – 1r – 1 – $32.50r – us Archival [324]

ORDINANCES MADE AND PASSED BY THE GOVERNOR AND LEGISLATIVE COUNCIL OF THE PROVINCE OF QUEBEC / Quebec. Laws, Statutes, etc – Quebec: William Brown, 1777. SEM105P417 – 2mf – 9 – Can$4.50 – cn Bibl Nat [971]

ORDINANCES MADE AND PASSED BY THE GOVERNOR AND LEGISLATIVE COUNCIL OF THE PROVINCE OF QUEBEC / Quebec. Laws, Statutes, etc – Quebec: William Brown, 1780. SEM105P418 – 1mf – 9 – Can$2.25 – cn Bibl Nat [340]

ORDINANCES MADE AND PASSED BY THE GOVERNOR AND LEGISLATIVE COUNCIL OF THE PROVINCE OF QUEBEC / Quebec. Laws, Statutes, etc – Quebec: William Brown, 1787. SEM105P420 – 1mf – 9 – Can$2.25 – cn Bibl Nat [340]

ORDINANCES MADE AND PASSED BY THE GOVERNOR AND LEGISLATIVE COUNCIL OF THE PROVINCE OF QUEBEC / Quebec. Laws, Statutes, etc – Quebec: Willim sic Brown, 1786. SEM105P419 – 2mf – 9 – Can$4.50 – cn Bibl Nat [340]

ORDINANCES MADE FOR THE PROVINCE OF QUEBEC. / Quebec. (Province). Laws, Statutes, etc – Quebec: Brown & Gilmore, 1767. 81p. LL-2367 – 1 – us L of C Photodup [340]

ORDINANCES, MADE FOR THE PROVINCE OF QUEBEC, BY THE GOVERNER AND LEGISLATIVE COUNCIL OF THE SAID PROVINCE, SINCE THE ESTABLISHMENT OF THE CIVIL GOVERNMENT / Quebec. Laws, Statutes, etc – Quebec: Brown and Gilmore, 1767. SEM105P416 – 1mf – 9 – Can$2.25 – cn Bibl Nat [340]

THE ORDINANCES OF THE COLONY OF SIERRA LEONE, NOW IN FORCE, COMMENCING 12TH OCTOBER 1811, AND ENDING 5TH OCTOBER 1857 / Sierra Leone. Laws, Statutes, etc – London: Eyre and Spottiswoode, 1857. 320, 2p. LL-12019 – 1 – us L of C Photodup [340]

ORDINANCES OF THE SETTLEMENT OF SIERRA LEONE, PASSED IN THE YEARS 1875, 1876, 1877, 1878, 1879, TO JUNE 1880; ROYAL CHARTERS; TREATIES OF THE GOVERNMENT OF SIERRA LEONE WITH THE NATIVE CHIEFS. / Sierra Leone. Laws, Statutes, etc – London: Eyre and Spottiswoode, 1881. vol. VI. 199p. LL-12020 – 1 – us L of C Photodup [340]

ORDINANCES PASSED BY THE GOVERNOR AND SPECIAL COUNCIL OF LOWER CANADA, IN THE THIRD AND FOURTH YEAR OF THE REIGN OF HER MAJESTY QUEEN VICTORIA / Canada. Bas-Canada. Laws, Statutes, etc – London: Printed by W Clowes & Sons's, 1841. SEM105P92 – 3mf – 9 – Can$6.75 – cn Bibl Nat [324]

ORDINARIODE LA MISA, PARA FIELES / Secretariado Diocesano de Catequesis – Caceres: Imp. La Victoria, 1969 – 1 – sp Bibl Santa Ana [240]

THE ORDINARY CHANTS OF THE BYZANTINE MASS / Moran, Neil K – (Vol 1: Investigations, Hamburg 1975. 4mf. Dfl19.00; Vol 2: Critical Edition, Hamburg 1975. 5mf. Dfl22.00) – 8 – ne Slangenburg [240]

ORDINATION ADDRESSES / Stubbs, William – London, New York: Longmans, Green, 1901 – 1mf – us A.T.L.A. [240]

THE ORDINATION OF A PRIEST, JUNE 9TH, 1867...: TRANSLATED FROM THE ROMAN PONTIFICAL AND MISSAL – Montreal, 1867. 00513. (Pre-1900 Canadiana) – 9 – cn C.I.H.M. [240]

THE ORDINATION OF WOMEN TO THE PASTORATE IN BAPTIST CHURCHES / Hungate, Jesse Avery – 1899 – 9 – us A.T.L.A. [240]

ORDINE COL QUALE L'ILLUSTRISS. ET ECCELLENTISS. SIGNOR MARC' ANTONIO COLONNA, ... – Roma, 1572 – 1mf – 9 – H-8194/1 – ne IDC [956]

L'ORDINE DELLE GALERE ET LE INSEGNE LORO, CON LI FANO, NOMI, ET COGNOMI DELLI MAGNIFICI, ET GENEROSI PATRONI DI ESSE, ... / Camocio, G F – Venetia, 1571 – 1mf – 9 – H-8171/1 – ne IDC [945]

ORDINE FIGLI D'ITALIA IN AMERICA – New York, NY. Jan 1918-1918, Jan 1920-1920, May-Oct 1923, Jan 1925-Dec 1927, Jan 1928-Jul 1929 – 5r – 1 – us I.H.R.C. [073]

ORDINE FIGLI D'ITALIA IN AMERICA. BOLLETTINO UFFICIALE – New York, NY. - m. May,Jun,Sept,Oct 1923; 1925-27; 1928-Jul 1929. 3 reels, 60 feet – 1 – us I.H.R.C. [071]

ORDINE FIGLI D'ITALIA IN AMERICA. BOLLETTINO UFFICIALE – New York, NY. - w. 5 Jan-28 Dec 1918; 3 Jan-1 Oct 1920.2 reels, 35 feet – 1 – us I.H.R.C. [071]

ORDINE NUOVO – 1919-1922 – 1 – sz Infoprint [072]

ORDINE NUOVO – Italy, 1919-22 – inquire – us Ross [072]

DIE ORDINES FUER DIE WEIHE UND KROENING DES KAISERS UND DER KAISERIN (MGH LEGES 4: 9.BD) – 1960 – Dfl22.00 – ne Slangenburg [240]

ORDINES NATURALES PLANTARUM / Rueling, J P – Goettingae. 1774. B-863 2 – 8 – ne IDC [580]

ORDINES NATURALES PLANTARUM CORUMQUE CHARACTERES ET AFFINITATES ADJECTA GENERUM ENUMERATIONE / Bartling, F G – Goettingae. 1830. B-5832 2 – 8 – ne IDC [580]

ORDINES OF HAYMO OF FAVERSHAM / Wormald, F – 1961 – 4mf – 8 – ne Slangenburg [240]

LES ORDINES ROMANI DU H.M.A / Andrieu, M – Louvain. 5v. 1957-61 – 50mf – 8 – Dfl175.00 – ne Slangenburg [240]

ORDINIS PRAEMONSTRATENSIS CHRONICON / Miraeus, A – Colonia Agrippina, 1613 – 7mf – 8 – Dfl28.00 – ne Slangenburg [240]

ORDINIS S. HIERONYMI...OBSERVATIONIS... MEMORIALE ADDITIONALE / Jeronimos – (Discursus Facti.1729. 1.50f; 9. Episcoporum. 1788. 1.50f; BSA; 9) – 1729 – 9 – 1.50f – sp Bibl Santa Ana [240]

ORDINIS S. HIERONYMI...OBSERVATIONIS... SUMMARIUM / Jeronimos – 1728 – 9 – 1.50f – sp Bibl Santa Ana [240]

AN ORDNANCE GAZETTEER OF SCOTLAND / Groome, F H – 1 – uk Microform Academic [910]

THE ORDNANCE MANUAL FOR THE OFFICERS OF THE U.S. ARMY (3RD ED., PHILADELPHIA, 1862) / U.S. War Department. Adjutant General's Office – 1 roll. T1117 – 1 – us Nat'l Archives [324]

ORDNANCE SURVEY MAPS: LANDRANGER SERIES : OS GREAT BRITAIN / British Ordnance Survey – 1994 – 204mf – 15 – $1,300.00 – us Comics [941]

ORDNANCE SURVEY MEMOIRS / Royal Irish Academy – c. 1833-37. 21 reels with printed guide 1610 £925.00 – uk World [941]

ORDNANCE SURVEYORS' DRAWINGS, 1789-1840 – (Complete set. South-west subset. South-east subset. Heart of England subset. The East and Wales subset. The West and North-west subset) – Original manuscript maps of the first ordnance survey of England and Wales – 9 – us Primary [910]

DIE ORDNUNG DES PRIESTERTUMS / Assfalg, J – Le Caire, 1955 – 4mf – 8 – Dfl19.00 – ne Slangenburg [240]

ORDNUNG (DIE) DER WIDERTEUFFER ZU MUENSTER – 1535. BME-150 1 – 9 – ne IDC [240]

ORDNUNG UND ERKANTNUSS EINES ERSAMENN RADTS. BETREFFENT DEN EEBRUCH, HUREN, KUPLEREN ETC – Zuerich. 1526. BME-6 1 – 9 – ne IDC [360]

ORDNUNG UND VERZIERUNG : UNTERSUCHUNGEN ZUR DEUTSCHSPRACHIGEN ARCHITEKTURTHEORIE DES 18. JAHRHUNDERTS / Schuette, Ulrich – Heidelberg, 1979 – 6mf – DM118.00 – 3-89349-841-9 – gw Hänsel [720]

ORDO : ORGAN DES COMITE JUIF D'ETUDES POLITIQUES; HALBMONATSSCHRIFT – Paris. 1 Apr-15 Oct 1938 (Nrn. 1-11) – 1 – gw Mikrofilm [072]

ORDO DIVINI OFFICCI RECITANDI / Plasencia. Diocesis – Plasencia: Imp. y Librer, Montero, 1959 – 1 – sp Bibl Santa Ana [240]

ORDO DIVINI OFFICII RECITANDI, ET MISSAE CELEBRANDAE JUXTA BREVIARIUM ET MISSALE ROMANUM, PRO ANNO BISSEXTILI 1812, AD USUM DIAECESIS QUEBECENSIS – Marianapoli: apud Jacobum Brown, 1811. SEM16P75 – 1r – 5 – Can$9.00 – cn Bibl Nat [240]

ORDO DIVINI OFICCI...1828 / Badajoz – 1827 – 9 – 1.50f – sp Bibl Santa Ana [946]

ORDO DIVINI OFICCI...PROANNO...1943 / Badajoz. Diocesis – Pace Augusta (Sic) T. Espanola. 1942 – sp Bibl Santa Ana [240]

ORDO DIVINI OFICII...DIOCESIS COURIENSIS... PRO ANNO 1943 – Cauriare: T. Fernandez, 1943 – 1 – sp Bibl Santa Ana [240]

ORDO FOR THE YEAR OF OUR LORD *see*
- SADLIER'S CATHOLIC ALMANAC AND ORDO FOR THE YEAR OF OUR LORD...
- SADLIER'S CATHOLIC DIRECTORY, ALMANAC, AND ORDO FOR THE YEAR OF OUR LORD...

Ordonez de Adrian, Valeriano *see*
- MEMORIA ACERCA...INSTITUTO...SEGUNDA ENSENANZA DE BADAJOZ...1878 A 1879... CATEDRATICO Y DIRECTOR
- MEMORIA DEL INSTITUTO DE SEGUNDA ENSENANZA DE LA PROVINCIA DE BADAJOZ LEIDA EN LA APERTURA DEL CURSO...1867 A 1868 POR EL DOCTOR D...DIRECTOR
- MEMORIA DEL INSTITUTO...BADAJOZ

UNE ORDONNANCE CURIEUSE : STATUTS DU CARDINAL-LEGAT OTTO POUR LES MONASTERES D'ALSACE (1239). RCA, 43 / Gass, J – Dfl6.00 – ne Slangenburg [240]

ORDONNANCE DES CINQ ESPECES DE COLONNES SELON LA METHODE DES ANCIENS / Perrault, Claude – Paris, Coignard, 1683. 8, xxvii, 124p. (Architecture Series) – 9 – fr Hachette [720]

ORDONNANCE FAICTE PAR TOUS LES PRINCES ET ESTATZ DE LEMPIRE, TOUCHANT LA GUERRE PAR EULX ENTREPRISE CONTRE LE TURCQ, POUR LE RECOUUREMENT DE HONGRIE – Paris, 1542 – 1mf – 9 – H-8150/1 – ne IDC [956]

ORDONNANCE POUR POURVOIR A L'AMELIORATION DES CHEMINS DANS LE VOISINAGE DE LA CITE DE MONTREAL. / Canada. Bas-Canada. Laws, Statutes, etc – s.l., s.n., s.d. SEM105P101 – 1mf – 9 – Can$2.25 – cn Bibl Nat [324]

L'ORDRE / ed by Fabre, Hector – Montreal, Canada. 23 nov 1858-23 oct 1871 – 7r – 1 – Can$50.00r – cn Can Microfilming [072]

L'ORDRE – Montreal, Canada. 1858-71 – 14r – 1 – $910.00 – cn Library Assoc [971]

L'ORDRE – Ottawa, Ontario. 13 nov 1920 – 1r – 1 – Can$25.00 – cn Can Microfilming [072]

L'ORDRE : QUOTIDIEN DE CULTURE FRANCAISE ET DE RENAISSANCE NATIONALE – Montreal, Canada. 10 mar 1934-11 mai 1935 (incomplete) – 1r – 1 – Can$40.00 – cn Can Microfilming [072]

L'ORDRE : UNION CATHOLIQUE – Ed. bihebdomadaire. Montreal: David Senecal et Cie. v1-13. 1858-71. SEM35P311 – 1 – Can$15.00 – cn Bibl Nat [971]

L'ORDRE DE CITEAUX EN BELGIQUE DES ORIGINES (1132) AU 800 SIECLE / Canivez, J -M – Forges les-Chimay, 1926 – Dfl35.00 – ne Slangenburg [240]

L'ORDRE DE PARIS – Dir. Dugue de la Fauconnerie. Paris. 1874 75 – 1 – fr A.C.R.P.P. [073]

ORDRE INTERNATIONAL – London, UK. 27 Apr-22 Oct 1876 – 1 – uk British Libr Newspaper [072]

L'ORDRE NOUVEAU – Revue mensuelle. Red. R. Aron, D. Rops, D. de Rougemont. no. 1-44. Paris. mai 1933-juil 1938 – 1 – fr A.C.R.P.P. [073]

L'ORDRE NOUVEAU : SEMAINES SOCIALES – Montreal, Canada. 5 oct 1936-20 dec 1940 – 1r – 1 – Can$40.00 – cn Can Microfilming [072]

L'ORDRE SOCIAL – Quebec, Canada. 19 fev 1850-v1 n40. 26 dec 1850 – 1r – 1 – Can$30.00 – cn Can Microfilming [072]

LES ORDRES DE CHEVALERIE RELIGIEUSE AU CANADA / Morin, Victor – Hull, 1940. SEM105P767 – 1mf – 9 – Can$2.25 – cn Bibl Nat [971]

LES ORDRES RELIGIEUX AU POINT DE VUE SOCIAL: LECTURE...AU CERCLE VILLE-MARIE DE MONTREAL / Henriot, Constant – Montreal: E. Senecal, 1892. 05542. (Pre-1900 Canadiana) – 9 – cn C.I.H.M. [240]

ORDSTAV – 1923 – 1 – us I.U. Libraries [390]

ORE 12 – 1991-1995 – 2r per y – 5,6 – Sfr936.00 – sz Infoprint [073]

OREBRO LANS JORDBRUKARETIDNING – Vasteras, Sweden. 1928-50 – 1 – sw Kungliga [072]

OREBRO-BERGSLAGSKURIREN – Orebro, Sweden. 1986-87 – 1 – sw Kungliga [072]

OREBROKURIREN – (Karlskoga Bergslagskuriren, 1987-88; Karlskogakuriren, 1988-) – Orebro Sweden. 1987- – 1 – sw Kungliga [072]

OREBROKURIREN – Orebro, 1902-78 – 1 – sw Kungliga [072]

OREBROKURIREN – Orebro, Sweden. 1979-86. Bergslagskuriren, 1981-86; Karlskogakuriren – 1 – sw Kungliga [072]

OREGON : REVISED STATUTES – Salem: State of Oregon Legislative Counsel Committee – 9 – $3,199.00 set – us Hein [340]

OREGON : SESSION LAWS OF AMERICAN STATES AND TERRITORIES – 1841-1996 – 9 – $1,276.50 set – us Hein [340]

Oregon *see*
- MISCELLANEOUS NEWSPAPERS
- REPORTS AND OPINIONS (A-G)
- REPORTS, PRE-NRS
- SESSION LAWS

OREGON ADVANCE TIMES – Portland, OR. -w. 1 Feb 1968-7 Nov 1968. 1 roll – 1 – us U.O. Library [071]

OREGON ADVERTISER – Portland OR. Jan 19 1861, Feb 22 1862 – 1 – us U.O. Library [071]

OREGON ADVOCATE – Portland OR. Mar 14 1971 – 1 – us U.O. Library [071]

OREGON AGRICULTURIST – Portland, OR. 1896-1914 – 1 – 120.00 – us Oregon Hist [071]

OREGON AGRICULTURIST AND THE RURAL NORTHWEST – v6,no.6-v23,no.19. 1896-1913 – 1 – us UMI [630]

OREGON ALLICANCE HERALD – Pendleton OR. May 13 1891 – 1 – us U.O. Library [071]

OREGON AMERICAN AND EVANGELICAL UNIONIST – Tualatin Plains, OR. 1848-49 – 1 – 17.00 – us Oregon Hist [071]

OREGON AND WASHINGTON CHURCHMAN – Portland OR. Dec 1886 Jan Feb Oct 1887 – 1 – us U.O. Library [071]

OREGON AND WASHINGTON DONATION LAND FILES / U.S. Bureau of Land Management – 1851-1903. 108 rolls. M815 – 1 – us Nat'l Archives [324]

OREGON AND WASHINGTON GAZETTEER AND BUSINESS DIRECTORY 1909-1910 / Polk – Oregon reel 8. (Cox Library Collection) – 5 – us Americana [978]

OREGON ARBITRATOR – Salem OR. May 7 21 July 10 1896 – 1 – us U.O. Library [071]

OREGON ARENA – Salem OR. July 19 25 Aug 1 8 Sep 12 26 1864, Oct 3 17 31 Nov 14 Dec 5 1864, Jan 2-May 15 Sep 11 1865 + – 1 – us U.O. Library [071]

OREGON ARGUS – Oregon City OR. Apr 21 1855-Apr 11 1863 – 1 – us U.O. Library [071]

OREGON ARGUS – Salem and Oregon City, OR. -w. 1855-63 – 1 – 72.00 – us Oregon Hist [071]

OREGON ARGUS – Salem, OR. -w. 16 May 1863-Oct 26 1863. – 1 – us U.O. Library [071]

OREGON ATTORNEY GENERAL REPORTS AND OPINIONS – (6 1897-1978 $385.00. 9 1978-1993 $177.50) – 1897-1993 – 6,9 – $562.50set – us Hein [340]

OREGON BAR ASSOCIATION PROCEEDINGS – (No reports were publ for the 17th, 20th to 22nd & 24th meetings) – 1st-23rd Annual Meetings. 1891-1913 (all publ) – 21mf – $31.50 – LLMC 84-665 – us L.L.M.C. [073]

OREGON BAR ASSOCIATION REPORTS – (Lacking: 17th, 20th-22nd, 24th meetings) – 1st-23rd annual meetings. 1891-1913 – 21mf – 9 – $31.50 – LLMC 84-665 – us L.L.M.C. [340]

OREGON BUILDING RECORD – Portland OR. Jan 2 1914-May 29 1916 – 1 – us U.O. Library [071]

OREGON BUSINESS REVIEW – v1- 1941- 1; v36- 5,6,9 – us UMI [073]

OREGON CABLE-TENSION STRENGTH TEST BATTERIES FOR BOYS AND GIRLS FROM FOURTH GRADE THROUGH COLLEGE / Clarke, Henry Harrison & Munroe, Richard A – 1970 – 1mf – 9 – $4.00 – us Microform Publ [790]

OREGON CHURCHMAN – Portland OR. May 4 1876, Feb 22 1877 – 1 – us U.O. Library [071]

OREGON CITY COURIER – (Set incl. Oregon City Courier-Herald) – Oregon City, OR. -w. 23 Sep 1883-3 Jul 1919. – 8r – 1 – us U.O. Library [071]

OREGON CITY COURIER HERALD – Oregon City OR. Sep 23 1898-Oct 30 1902 – 1 – us U.O. Library [071]

OREGON CITY DAILY STAR – Oregon City OR. Sep 24 27 Nov 30 1906, Mar 28 May 17 18 June 3 1907 – 1 – us U.O. Library [071]

OREGON CITY ENTERPRISE – Oregon City, OR. -w. 27 Oct 1866-25 Dec 1942. 22 rolls – 1 – us U.O. Library [071]

OREGON CITY MORNING ENTERPRISE – Oregon City, OR. -d. 8 Jan 1911-28 Feb 1950. – 55r – 1 – us U.O. Library [071]

OREGON CITY PRESS – Oregon City, OR. -w. 9 Feb 1898-26 Apr 1899. 1 roll – 1 – us U.O. Library [071]

OREGON COAST BULLETIN – Oceanlake OR. Oct 1 1937 – 1 – us U.O. Library [071]

OREGON COMMUNITY NEWS – Eugene OR., Jan Feb 1932 – 1 – us U.O. Library [071]

OREGON CULTIVATOR – Albany, OR. -w. 16 Dec 1875-15 Feb 1877; 16 Dec 1875-18 Jan 1877 – 1r – 1 – us U.O. Library [071]

OREGON DAILY EMERALD – Eugene, OR. 29 Sep 1909-28 Sep 1920 – 1 – us U.O. Library [071]

OREGON DAILY TIMES – Portland, OR. 1860-63 – 1 – 24.00 – us Oregon Hist [071]

OREGON DEMOCRAT – Albany, OR. -w. 1 Nov. 1859-28 Jun 1864. 1 roll – 1 – us U.O. Library [071]

OREGON DEMOCRATIC NEWS – Oregon City OR. Oct 1 1941 – 1 – us U.O. Library [071]

OREGON DEUTSCHE ZEITUNG – Portland OR. Dec 10 1908-Sep 18 1917 – 1 – us U.O. Library [071]

OREGON DEUTSCHE ZEITUNG – Portland OR. Oct 24 1868, Feb 20 1869, Sep 5 1874, Oct 23 1875, May 12 1877, Apr 19 1879 – 1 – us U.O. Library [071]

OREGON EMERALD – Eugene, OR. 29 Sep 1909-28 Sep 1920 – 1 – us U.O. Library [071]

OREGON ENQUIRER – Oregon, Ohio. 1981 – 1r – 1 – $32.50r – us Archival [071]

OREGON FARM BUREAU NEWS – Pendleton OR. Sep 1949 – 1 – us U.O. Library [071]

OREGON FARM BUREAU NEWS – Salem OR. Apr 1 1950 – 1 – us U.O. Library [071]

OREGON FARMER – Portland, OR. 1858-63 – 1 – 24.00 – us Oregon Hist [071]

OREGON FARMER – Portland, OR. 1914-65 – 1 – 552.00 – us Oregon Hist [071]

OREGON FARMER – v23,no.20-v93. 1913-70 – 1 – us UMI [630]

OREGON FARMER STOCKMAN – Spokane WA. Oct 8-Dec 7 1859, June 5 1860, Jan 6 1966 + – 1 – us U.O. Library [071]

OREGON FARMERS UNION – Salem OR. June 1931-Dec 1979 – 1 – us U.O. Library [071]

OREGON FARMER-STOCKMAN – v94-102.1971-79 – 1 – us UMI [636]

OREGON FARMER-STOCKMAN. INLAND EDITION – (1985- . 5,6,9) – v103- . 1980- – 1 – us UMI [636]

OREGON FARMER-STOCKMAN. PACIFIC EDITION – (1985- . 5,6,9) – v103- . 1980- – 1 – us UMI [636]

OREGON FREE PRESS – Oregon City, OR. 15 Apr 1848-25 Nov 1848; 8 Apr 1848 – 1r – 1 – us U.O. Library [071]

OREGON FREE PRESS – Portland OR. Apr 8 1848 – 1 – us U.O. Library [071]

OREGON FREE PRESS – Salem, OR. -w. 24 Jun 1910-2 Dec 1910. 1 roll – 1 – us U.O. Library [071]

OREGON GAZETTEER – Salem OR. Oct 1 1900-Dec 15 1902 – 1 – us U.O. Library [071]

OREGON GOOD TEMPLAR – Albany, OR. -w. 21 Jul 1870-26 Jun 1872. 1 roll – 1 – us U.O. Library [071]

OREGON GOOD TEMPLAR – Portland OR. July 21 1870-July 26 1872 – 1 – us U.O. Library [071]

OREGON GRANGE BULLETIN – Portland, OR. -m,-sm. 5 Jul 1946-20 Dec 1947. 1 roll – 1 – us U.O. Library [071]

OREGON HERALD – Portland OR. Aug 12 1916-Jan 6 1917 – 1 – us U.O. Library [071]

OREGON HISTORICAL QUARTERLY – 1901-56 – 1 – us Princeton Micro [978]

OREGON HUB – Redmond OR. Oct 28 Nov 11 Dec 30 1909, Jan 6 27 1910, Nov 2 1911 – 1 – us U.O. Library [071]

OREGON INDEPENDENT – Salem, OR. -w. 14 Mar 1893-23 Dec 1897; 5 Sep, 12,15,22 Dec 1803 – 1r – 1 – us U.O. Library [071]

OREGON INTELLIGENCER – Jacksonville OR. June 20 1863, Jan 23-Nov 19 1864 – 1 – us U.O. Library [071]

OREGON INTELLIGENCER – Jacksonville, OR. -w. 1864 – 1 – 17.00 – us Oregon Hist [071]

OREGON IRRIGATOR – Irrigon, OR. -w. 27 Jan 1904-30 Aug 1906; 14 May 1909-15 Sept 1911. – 1r – 1 – us U.O. Library [071]

OREGON JOURNAL – Portland OR. Aug 15 1945 (Victory Issue) + – 1 – us U.O. Library [071]

OREGON JOURNAL – Portland, OR. -d. 1903-04 – 1 – 72.00 – us Oregon Hist [071]

OREGON LABOR PRESS – Portland, OR. -w. 6 Sept 1900-25 Aug 1905. 1 roll – 1 – us U.O. Library [071]

OREGON LABORER – Pendleton OR. June 3 1886 – 1 – us U.O. Library [071]

OREGON LAW REVIEW – v1-73. 1921-94 – 1,5,6 – $855.00 – us Hein [073]

OREGON LEGIONAIRE – Salem, OR. -m. Mar 1949-Jul 1955. 1 roll – 1 – us U.O. Library [071]

OREGON LIBERAL – Portland OR. May 7 Aug 14 Sep 11 1936 – 1 – us U.O. Library [071]

OREGON LITERARY VIDETTE – Portland OR. May 7 1881 – 1 – us U.O. Library [071]

OREGON LITERARY VIDETTE – Salem OR. Dec 1879 + – 1 – us U.O. Library [071]

OREGON MAPS : TOWNS OF 8 EASTERN COUNTIES – 1884-1949. 644 maps. 42 towns. Sanborn Company Fire Insurance Maps – 1 – $77.00r – us Shkurkin [910]

OREGON MIRROR – Portland OR. Mar 21-June 27 1962 – 1 – us U.O. Library [071]

OREGON MIST – St. Helens OR. Aug 7 1891-Dec 27 1912 – 1 – us U.O. Library [071]

OREGON NEWS – Oregon, Ohio. 1959-80 – 12r – 1 – $32.50r – us Archival [071]

OREGON OBSERVER – Grants Pass OR. Apr 3 May 7 Oct 29 1904, Jan 14 July 5 1905, June 24 1925, July 1 Sept 30 1925, July 21 1926 + – 1 – us U.O. Library [071]

OREGON OBSERVER – Grants Pass, OR. -w. 13 Feb 1892-28 Feb 1903; 1 Dec 1920-10 Oct 1923. 4 rolls – 1 – us U.O. Library [071]

OREGON OBSERVER – Grants Pass, OR. -w. 1901-27 – 1 – 233.00 – us Oregon Hist [071]

Oregon. Ohio. Saint Mark's Lutheran Church *see* RECORDS

OREGON ORACLE – Philomath, OR. -w. 11 Jun 1885-8 Oct 1885. 1 roll – 1 – us U.O. Library [071]

OREGON ORIANO – Vale, OR. -w. 17 Jan 1906-3 Feb 1912. 2 rolls – 1 – us U.O. Library [071]

OREGON PERISCOPE – Portland OR. Mar 2 Apr 6 1940 – 1 – us U.O. Library [071]

OREGON POPULIST – Albany, OR. -w. 4 Jan 1893-21 Feb 1894. 1 roll – 1 – us U.O. Library [071]

OREGON POSTEN – Portland, OR. 8 Sept 1920-25 Dec 1929; 1 Jan 1930-28 Dec 1939 – 1 – us U.O. Library [071]

Oregon. Presbytery. (Cum. Pres. Ch.) *see* MINUTES, 1889-1902

OREGON PROGRESSIVE – Eugene OR. Sep 21 Oct 6 19 Nov 15 1938 – 1 – us U.O. Library [071]

OREGON PROGRESSIVE – Portland OR. Oct 18 1934 – 1 – us U.O. Library [071]

OREGON REAL ESTATE BULLETIN – Salem OR. June 15 1928 – 1 – us U.O. Library [071]

OREGON REGISTER – Eugene, OR. 4 Jan 1917-2 May 1918. 1 roll – 1 – us U.O. Library [071]

OREGON REGISTER – Lafayette, OR. -w. 29 Jul 1887-28 Dec 1889 – 1r – 1 – us U.O. Library [071]

OREGON REGISTER – McMinnville OR. Jan 4-Feb 1 1889 – 1 – us U.O. Library [071]

OREGON REPORTER – Jacksonville OR. Jan 4-Dec 23 1865, Jan 6 13 20 Mar 10 1866, Apr 7 14 June 2 30 Sep 1 1866, Sep 22 Oct 20 Nov 3-Dec 29 1866 + – 1 – us U.O. Library [071]

OREGON REPORTER – Portland OR. Apr 1899 – 1 – us U.O. Library [071]

OREGON REPORTER – Portland OR. Apr 1947 – 1 – us U.O. Library [071]

OREGON REVIEW – LaGrande OR. Apr 26 1876 – 1 – us U.O. Library [071]

OREGON SCOUT – Union, OR. -w. 12 Dec 1884-21 Apr 1910; 6 Jan 1912 – 3r – 1 – us U.O. Library [071]

OREGON SEARCHLIGHT – Salem OR. July 20 1899-July 8 1904 – 1 – us U.O. Library [071]

OREGON SEMI MONTHLY ARGUS – Salem OR. Jan 12 1878 – 1 – us U.O. Library [071]

OREGON SENTINEL – Jacksonville OR. June 6-Dec 29 1885, Mar 27 1886 + – 1 – us U.O. Library [071]

OREGON SENTINEL – Jacksonville OR. May 23 1868, Apr 19 1873, May 9 1874, Aug 30 Sep 27 1884, Oct 4-18 Nov 8 15 1884, Feb 28 Mar 21 28 Apr 18 1885 + – 1 – us U.O. Library [071]

OREGON SENTINEL – (Set incl. Table Rock Sentinel (Jacksonville); 5 Nov 1859-24 Apr 1886; 7,14 Apr, 2,30 June, 1 Sep 1866; 22 Sep, 20 Oct, 3 Nov 1866-29 Dec 1866.) – Jacksonville, OR. -w,-sw. 13 Dec 1856-27 Nov 1886. – 7r – 1 – us U.O. Library [071]

OREGON SIFTINGS – Portland OR. Nov 19 26 1887, Feb 25 1888 – 1 – us U.O. Library [071]

OREGON SOCIALIST PARTY BULLETIN – Portland OR. Mar 15 May 25 July-Aug 1919 – 1 – us U.O. Library [071]

OREGON SPECTATOR – Oregon City, OR. -d. 5 Feb 1846-10 Mar 1855. – 1r – 1 – us U.O. Library [071]

OREGON STAATS-ZEITUNG – Portland, OR. -w. 1893-99 – 1 – 72.00 – us Oregon Hist [071]

OREGON STAATSZEITUNG – Portland OR. Aug 5 1893-Feb 4 1903 – 1 – us U.O. Library [071]

Oregon. State Bar Association *see* PROCEEDINGS

OREGON STATE BAR BULLETIN – v1- 1935- – 9 – LLMC 84-666 – us L.L.M.C. [073]

OREGON STATE BAR BULLETIN – v1-55. 1941-95 – 9 – $540.00 set – us Hein [340]

OREGON STATE DIRECTORY 1881 / Bynon, A A – Portland: Gill and Co. Oregon reel 7. (Cox Library Collection) – 5 – us Americana [978]

OREGON STATE JOURNAL – Eugene OR. Dec 4-18 1897 + – 1 – us U.O. Library [071]

OREGON STATE JOURNAL – Eugene, OR. -w. 1864-1909 – 1 – 353.00 – us Oregon Hist [071]

OREGON STATESMAN – Oregon City and Salem, OR. -w. 1851-54 – 1 – 65.00 – us Oregon Hist [071]

OREGON STATESMAN – Oregon City OR. Mar 28 1851-June 11 1853 – 1 – us U.O. Library [071]

OREGON STATESMAN – Salem. Or. 1869-1873; 1885- – 1 – us UMI [071]

OREGON STATESMAN – Salem OR. Feb 18-Apr 23 1870, Aug 18-Sep 18 1870, Oct 8-28 1870, June 2-29 1870 + – 1 – us U.O. Library [071]

OREGON STATESMAN – Salem. Or. -w. 1851-66, 1885-1924 – 1 – us UMI [071]

OREGON STATESMAN – Salem, OR. -w. 21 Jun 1853-7 Feb 1854 – 1 – us U.O. Library [071]

Oregon. Supreme Court *see* OREGON SUPREME COURT REPORTS

OREGON SUPREME COURT REPORTS / Oregon. Supreme Court – (Pre-NRS: v1-10. 1853-83 59mf $88.00. Updates planned) – v1-95. 1853-1920 – 739mf – $1,108.00 – LLMC 82-988 – us L.L.M.C. [340]

OREGON TIMES – Salem, OR. 29 Jan 1971-Apr 1976 – 1 – us U.O. Library [071]

THE OREGON TREATY AND THE HUDSON'S BAY COMPANY / Barnston, George – 186?. 02428. (Pre-1900 Canadiana) – 9 – cn C.I.H.M. [975]

OREGON UNION – Corvallis, OR. -sw, -w. 22 Sep, 6,11,25 Oct 1862; 8 Nov 1862-27 Dec 1862; 3 Jan 1863-7,28 Mar 1863 – 1 – us U.O. Library [071]

OREGON VIDETTE AND ANTI MONOPOLIST – Salem OR. May 19 1883, Feb 26 June 25 1885 – 1 – us U.O. Library [071]

OREGON WEEKLY – Eugene OR. Feb 12 1900-June 14 1909 – 1 – us U.O. Library [071]

OREGON WEEKLY HERALD – Portland, OR. 20 Mar 1866-17 Aug 1872. 2 rolls – 1 – us U.O. Library [071]

OREGON WEEKLY TIMES – Portland, OR. 1850-62. And pred – 1 – 48.00 – us Oregon Hist [071]

OREGONIAN – Portland, OR. 1861- – 1 – us UMI [071]

OREGON'S RESOURCES – Portland OR. June 30 1902 – 1 – us U.O. Library [071]

OREGON-WASHINGTON FARMERS UNION – Salem, OR. -m. Jun 1962-. – 1 – us U.O. Library [071]

OREHOT HAYYIM – Prague. 1626. BJ-43-71 1 – 9 – ne IDC [270]

O'Reilly, B *see* GREENLAND, THE ADJACENT SEAS, AND THE NORTH-WEST PASSAGE TO THE PACIFIC OCEAN; ILLUSTRATED ON A VOYAGE TO DAVIS'S STRAIT DURING THE SUMMER OF 1817

O'Reilly, Bernard *see* A LIFE OF PIUS 9TH

O'Reilly, John Boyle *see* THE STATUES IN THE BLOCK, AND OTHER POEMS

O'Reilly, Kenneth *see*
- FBI FILING AND RECORDS PROCEDURES
- FBI MANUALS OF INSTRUCTION, INVESTIGATIVE PROCEDURES, AND GUIDELINES, 1927-1978
- MCCARTHY ERA BLACKLISTING OF SCHOOL TEACHERS, COLLEGE PROFESSORS, AND OTHER PUBLIC EMPLOYEES

O'Reilly, P *see*
- BIBLIOGRAPHIE DE LA NOUVELLE-CALEDONIE
- BIBLIOGRAPHIE METHODIQUE, ANALYTIQUE ET CRITIQUE DES ILES WALLIS ET FUTUNA
- CALEDONIENS, REPERTOIRE BIO-BIBLIOGRAPHIQUE DE LA NOUVELLE-CALEDONIE

OREL – Zhurnal ucheno-literaturnyi illiustrirovannyi. nr. 1-4. Spb. 1859. BR-4153 2 – 8 – ne IDC [073]

O'Rell, Max *see*
- A FRENCHMAN IN AMERICA: THE ANGLO-SAXON RACE REVISITED
- JOHN BULL AND CO.: THE GREAT COLONIAL BRANCHES OF THE FIRM, CANADA, AUSTRALIA, NEW ZEALAND AND SOUTH AFRICA
- LA MAISON JOHN BULL & CIE.: LES GRANDES SUCCURSALES, LE CANADA, L'AUSTRALIE, LA NOUVELLE-ZELANDE, L'AFRIQUE DU SUD
- WOMAN AND ARTIST

Orellana la Vieja. Ayuntamiento *see* FIESTAS POPULARES. AGOSTO 1980

Orellana-Pizarro Perez-Aloe, Antonio. Vizconde de Amaya *see* FRANCISCO PIZARRO

Orelli, Conrad v *see* EIGENART DER BIBLISCHEN RELIGION

Orelli, Conrad von *see*
- THE OLD TESTAMENT PROPHECY OF THE CONSUMMATION
- THE PECULIARITY OF THE RELIGION OF THE BIBLE
- THE PROPHECIES OF ISAIAH
- THE PROPHECIES OF JEREMIAH
- THE TWELVE MINOR PROPHETS

ORESTES A. BROWNSON: A PILGRIM'S PROGRESS / Schlesinger, Arthur Meier – Boston: Little, Brown and Co., 1939. 320p – 1 – us U.W. Library [920]

ORESTES A. BROWNSON'S...LIFE / Brownson, Henry Francis – 3v. 1898-1900 – 1 – us A.T.L.A. [920]

ORESUNDSPOSTEN – (Suppl: Vara Hem, 1906-29) – Helsingborg, Sweden. 1847-1939 – 167r – 1 – sw Kungliga [072]

ORESUNDSPOSTEN *see* NORDVASTRA SKANES TIDNINGAR ENGELHOLMS TIDNING

Orfanel, Jacinto *see* HISTORIA...JAPON

Orfield, Lester Bernhardt *see* THE AMENDING OF THE FEDERAL CONSTITUTION

ORG. SINDICAL-BADAJOZ. 4 CONSEJO ECONOMICO S. PROV. C. 15^{A} (FACTORES HUMANOS Y SOCIALES PRODUCTIVIDAD / Igelmo Pinilia, Eulogio – Badajoz: Imp. Inca, 1966 – 1 – sp Bibl Santa Ana [330]

HET ORGAAN VAN DE BOND VAN NEDERLANDSE PREDIKANTEN – 1936; 1939; 1958; 1961; 1966-88 (complete) – 4r – 1 – ATLA S0618 – us A.T.L.A. [240]

THE ORGAN – 1921-92. Continued annually – 1 – £1,350.00 – uk World [073]

THE ORGAN – Boston. v1-2. 1892-94 – 1r – 1 – £60.00 – uk Chadwyck [780]

ORGAN BRATRSTVA – v41, no.2-v41, no.12 – 1 – us I.U. Libraries [073]

ORGAN BRATRSTVA C.S.P.S. – v1, no 1-v2, no 23; v6, no 1-v6, no 12; v15, no 1-v40, no 12. 1891-1893, 1897-1898, 1907-1932 – 1 – us I.U. Libraries [073]

ORGAN CESKOSLOVENSKYCH SPOLKU V AMERICE – v42, no 1-v47, no. 4. 1934-1939 – 1 – us I.U. Libraries [073]

ORGAN C.S.B.P. JEDNOTY : WEEKLY, LATER SEMI-WEEKLY CZECH LANGUAGE FRATERNITY NEWSPAPER – Cleveland, Oh. 7 Jan 1928-27 Dec 1930 – 2r – 1 – us Western Res [071]

Organ des Germanischen Museums *see* ANZEIGER FUER KUNDE DER DEUTSCHEN VORZEIT

ORGAN INSTITUTE QUARTERLY – v. 1-11. 1951-64 – 1 – us UMI [616]

ORGAN OF CONGREGATION SONS OF ISRAEL AND DAVID / Congregation Sons of Israel and David – Providence. R.I. 1895-98 – 1 – us A.J.P.C. [270]

THE ORGAN OF ISLAM IN ITS CHRISTIAN ENVIRONMENT / Bell, R – Edinburgh. 1926. BNE-497 1 – 9 – ne IDC [260]

THE ORGAN STUDY: BEING AN INTRODUCTION TO THE PRACTICE OF THE ORGAN; TOGETHER WITH A COLLECTION OF VOLUNTARIES, PRELUDES AND INTERLUDES / Loud, Thomas – Philadelphia: Loud's Piano Forte & Music Store, 1845. MUSIC 3082, Item 8 – 1 – us L of C Photodup [780]

Organe de la Confederation Nationale du Travail et des Unions et Federations des Syndicats Nationaux de France *see* L'AVENIR SYNDICAL

L'ORGANE DE LA MILICE – Quebec, Canada. v1 n3. 27 avr 1865-v1 n47. 29 mar 1866 – 1r – 1 – Can$25.00 – cn Can Microfilming [072]

Organe de l'opposition Communiste *see* CONTRE LE COURANT

Organe du Comite de la Troisieme Internationale *see* BULLETIN COMMUNISTE

Organe du Comite Executif de l'Internationale Communiste *see* L'INTERNATIONALE COMMUNISTE

THE ORGANIC ACT OF PORTO RICO 109 MARCH 2 1917 AS AMENDED TO MARCH 4 1927 – Washington: GPO, 1927 – 1mf – 9 – $3.00 – LLMC 92-406 – us L.L.M.C. [324]

ORGANIC GARDENING – (See also: Organic Gardening and Farming) – v25- 1978- – 1,5,6,9 – us UMI [630]

ORGANIC GARDENING AND FARMING – 1-25 1954-78 1; v17-25 5,6,9 – us UMI [630]

ORGANIC GARDENING AND FARMING – v18. 1971 – 24mf – 9 – $5.00f – us Ross [630]

ORGANIC GEOCHEMISTRY – v1- 1978- – 5,6,9 – us UMI [550]

ORGANIC MAGNETIC RESONANCE. SPECTRAL SUPPLEMENT – (1982- 5,6,9) – 1969- – 1 – us UMI [621]

ORGANIC MATERIALS AND SOIL PRODUCTIVITY – 1982 – 127p – it F.A.O. [631]

ORGANIC MATERIALS AND SOIL PRODUCTIVITY IN THE NEAR EAST – 1982 – 297p – it F.A.O. [631]

ORGANIC MATERIALS AS FERTILIZERS – 1978 – 400p – it F.A.O. [631]

ORGANIC RECYCLING IN AFRICA – 1980 – 308p – it F.A.O. [631]

ORGANIC SYNTHESES – (1984-. 5,6,9) – v1-. 1921- – 1 – us UMI [540]

ORGANIC SYNTHESES – v1-49. 1921-69 – 1,5,6 – us Princeton Micro [073]

ORGANIC UNION OF CANADIAN CHURCHES: WITH A COMPARISON OF AUTHORIZED STANDARDS / Carmichael, James – Montreal: Dawson Bros., 1887. 00504. (Pre-1900 Canadiana) – 9 – cn C.I.H.M. [240]

ORGANISASI DAN ADMINISTRASI; PENUNTUN UNTUK MEMPELADJARI ORANISASI DALAM DINAS ADMINISTRASI SERTA TANGGUNGDJAWAB DAN KEWADJIBAN PEMIMPIN / Wajong, J – SE 4503 1. 1961 – 9 – ne IDC [950]

Organisasi Exporteur Hasilbumi Indonesia *see* CONDITIONS FOR THE SALE OF PRODUCE AND ARBITRATION RULES

L'ORGANISATEUR – Journal des Progres de la science generale. Changements de sous-titre: Journal de la Doctrine de Saint-Simon (a partir du 18 avril 1830). Gazette des Saint-Simoniens (a partir du 26 mars 1831). Parait a Paris, chaque semaine, du 15 aout 1829 au 13 aout 1831. Les Saint-Simoniens, 1825-1834. 6853-6854 – 9 – fr Hachette [500]

L'ORGANISATEUR – Journal des progres de la science generale puis Gazette des Saints-Simoniens. Paris. aout 1829-aout 1831 – 1 – fr A.C.R.P.P. [073]

L'ORGANISATEUR – v.1-, a-b, 1829-. Paris, varies – 1 – us U.W. Library [073]

L'ORGANISATEUR BELGE – Journal de la doctrine de Saint-Simon. Parait a Bruxelles, chaque semaine du 29 mai 1831 (no. 1) au 27 nov 1831 (no. 24), pagination continue: 192 p. Les Saint-Simoniens, 1825-1834. 6855 – 9 – fr Hachette [073]

Organisatie voor Natuurwetenschappelijk Onderzoek in Indonesie *see*
- GUIDE OF SCIENTISTS IN INDONESIA
- GUIDE TO SCIENTISTS IN INDONESIA

ORGANISATION AND MANAGEMENT OF WATER SUPPLIES IN TROPICAL AFRICA = ORGANISATION ET GESTION DES RESSOURCES HYDRAULIQUES EN AFRIQUE TROPICALE / Sandford, S – 1983 – 9 – $14.00 – 92-9053-112-6 – et ILRI [333]

L'ORGANISATION DE LA FAMILLE D'APRES LE NOUVEAU CODE CIVIL ET COMMERCIAL SIAMOIS / Vinicchayakoul, Serm – Paris, Rousseau, 1939. 254 p. LL-10021 – 1 – us L of C Photodup [340]

ORGANISATION DES ECOLES NATIONALES / Auger, Athanase – Paris, impr. nationale, 1791. viii, 43 p. 1 fiche. (Bibliotheque nationale, Paris. Education ColLection) – 9 – 6.00 – fr Bibl Nationale [370]

DIE ORGANISATION DES HOEBEREN UNTERRICHTS IM KANADISCHEN BUND / Coffin, Victor – Munich: C. Deck, 1897. 03204. (Pre-1900 Canadiana) – 9 – cn C.I.H.M. [971]

ORGANISATION ET REFORME DE L'INDUSTRIE MODERNE / Association Professionnelle des Industriels. Congres Patronal (2e: 1946: Montreal, Quebec) – Montreal: Association Professionnelle des Industriels, 1945 [i.e. 1947] – 2mf – 9 – Can$4.50 – cn Bibl Nat [650]

ORGANISATION ET ROLE DU B.R.P.M. DANS L'ECONOMIE MAROCAINE / Morocco. Bureau de Recherches et de Participations Minieres – 1960. BNE-3015 1 – 9 – ne IDC [330]

ORGANISATION MORPHOGENETIQUE DU SYSTEME VISUEL DE LA TRUITE SALMO GAIRDNERI / Pinganaud, G – 9 – F65.00 – fr Ethnologie [574]

ORGANISATION OF AFRICAN UNITY, RESOLUTIONS OF THE ANNUAL SUMMITS AND OTHER DOCUMENTS SINCE 1963 : MATERIAL FROM THE PERSONAL LIBRARY OF COLIN LEGUM – 35mf – 9 – £200.00 – uk Altair [320]

THE ORGANISATION OF THE EARLY CHRISTIAN CHURCHES / Hatch, Edwin – 1881 – 9 – us A.T.L.A. [240]

L'ORGANISATION SCIENTIFIQUE DES USINES / Lefort-Lavauzelle – Paris. 1919. (La Condition Ouvriere. Part Two.) – 9 – 2.50 – fr Bibl Nationale [360]

L'ORGANISATION SOCIALE TRADITIONELLE DES ESQUIMAUX DE KANGIRSUJUAK. (NOUVEAU-QUEBEC) / Saladin d'Anglure, B – BH 135 2. 1964 – 8 – ne IDC [306]

ORGANISATION SOCIO-ECONOMIQUE DES MINYANKA DU MALI / Jonckers, D – 9 – F130.00 – fr Ethnologie [306]

ORGANISATIONS INTERNATIONALES ET POUVOIRS POLITIQUES DES ETATS / Hoffmann, S – F80.00 – fr Ethnologie [320]

ORGANISATIONSENTWICKLUNG UND BERATUNG IM NON-PROFIT-BEREICH / Zunft, Stefanie – 1992 – 191p – 9 – DM98.00 – 3-89349-612-2 – gw Hänsel [370]

ORGANISME REGIONAL DE DEVELOPPEMENT – RAPPORTS 1972-73 – 1r – 1 – $439.50 – us African Imprint [336]

DER ORGANISMUS DER INFUSIONSTHIERE / Stein, S F N von – Z 441 2. 3 v. 1859-1883 – 8 – ne IDC [590]

ORGANIST'S QUARTERLY JOURNAL AND REVIEW – Boston. v1-3. 1874-77 – 1r – 1 – £60.00 – uk Chadwyck [780]

ORGANISTS REVIEW – 1913- 1; 1974- 5,6; 1975- 4 x 6 in. 9 – us UMI [073]

Organizacion Sindical *see*
- COMPOSICION DEL 4 PLENO DEL CONSEJO ECONOMICO SINDICAL
- DEL 4 PLENO DEL CONSEJO ECONOMICO SINDICAL PROVINCIAL
- MANDOS POLITICOS Y REPRESENTATIVOS
- OBRA SINDICAL DE EDUCACION Y DESCANSO. ACTOS ORGANIZADOS PARA EL DIA 1 DE MAYO CON MOTIVO DE LA FESTIVIDAD DE SAN JOSE ARTESANO

Organizacion Sindical de Badajoz *see* 4 PLENO DEL CONSEJO ECONOMICO SINDICAL. CONCLUSIONES DEFINITIVAS

ORGANIZACION Y METODOS DE LOS SERVICIOS ECONOMICOS DE LAS CORPORACIONES LOCALES... / Mahillo Santos, Julio – Madrid: Escuela Nacional de Administracion Local, 1969 – sp Bibl Santa Ana [330]

ORGANIZACION Y PROCEDIMIENTO PEDAGOGICOS DE LAS ESOUELAS PARROQUIALES DE LOS SANTOS / Fernandez Santana, Ezequiel – Madrid: Ed. Pens S.A., 1920 – 1 – sp Bibl Santa Ana [370]

ORGANIZATION AND ADMINISTRATION OF NATIONAL COMMUNITY DEVELOPMENT PROGRAMMES,BY ATMOSUDIRDJO DRAJUDI. BANGKOK, 22 AUG.-1 SEPT. 1961. SE 11,616/1. 1961 / United Nations. Asian Seminar on Planning and Administration of National Community Development Programmes – 9 – ne IDC [338]

ORGANIZATION AND ADMINISTRATION OF SOCIAL WELFARE PROGRAMMES, A SERIES OF COUNTRY STUDIES / Jordan. U.N. Dept. of Economic and Social Affairs – 1968. BNE-9814 1 – 9 – ne IDC [360]

THE ORGANIZATION AND CELL LINEAGE OF THE ASCIDIAN EGG / Conklin, E C – 1905-08 – 1 – uk Microform Academic [590]

ORGANIZATION AND MANAGEMENT OF AGRICULTURAL DEVELOPMENT FOR SMALL FARMERS : ISSUES IN DECENTRALIZATION AND SMALL FARMERS' PARTICIPATION – 1992 – 69p – it F.A.O. [338]

THE ORGANIZATION AND MANAGEMENT OF BUSINESS CORPORATIONS / Clephane, Walter Collins – 2d ed. Kansas City, MO: Vernon, 1913. 479p. LL-446 – 1 – us L of C Photodup [650]

ORGANIZATION AND MANAGEMENT: THEORY AND PRACTICE / Seckler-Hudson, Catheryn – 1955. 324p. Principles and processes of managing large organizations – 9 – us Lomond [650]

ORGANIZATION AND METHODS OF MISSION WORK : BEING PART 3 OF A CONCISE HISTORY OF MISSIONS / Bliss, Edwin Munsell – New York: Fleming H Revell, c1897 – 1mf – 9 – 0-8370-7125-9 – 1986-1125 – us A.T.L.A. [240]

ORGANIZATION AND OPERATION OF THE INDUSTRIAL BANK OF EGYPT / Little, A.D., Inc. – 1953. BNE-4644 1 – 9 – ne IDC [332]

ORGANIZATION AND STRUCTURE OF F.A.O. INCLUDING TITLES OF STAFF – 5th rev ed 1984 – 219p – it F.A.O. [060]

ORGANIZATION FOR ECONOMIC CO-OPERATION AND DEVELOPMENT PUBLICATIONS (O.E.C.D.) – (Annual update) – 1961-1996 no 1 update – 9 – $2,925.00 set – 0-89941-422-2 – us Hoin [337]

Organization for European Economic Cooperation *see*
- GENERAL MEMORANDUM ON THE 1950/51 AND 1951/52 PROGRAMMES
- GENERAL MEMORANDUM ON THE 1950/51 AND 1951/52 PROGRAMMES. AUSTRIA
- GENERAL MEMORANDUM ON THE 1950/51 AND 1951/52 PROGRAMMES. DENMARK
- GENERAL MEMORANDUM ON THE 1950/51 AND 1951/52 PROGRAMMES. ICELAND
- GENERAL MEMORANDUM ON THE 1950/51 AND 1951/52 PROGRAMMES. SWEDEN
- INTERIM REPORT ON THE EUROPEAN RECOVERY PROGRAMME. VOL. 2. LONG-TERM PROGRAMME OF DENMARK
- INTERIM REPORT ON THE EUROPEAN RECOVERY PROGRAMME. VOL. 2. PORTUGUESE LONG-TERM PROGRAMME
- INTERIM REPORT ON THE EUROPEAN RECOVERY PROGRAMME. VOL. 2. THE AUSTRIAN LONG-TERM PROGRAMME 1952-53
- INTERIM-REPORT ON THE EUROPEAN RECOVERY PROGRAMME. VOL. 2. LONG-TERM PROGRAMME OF SWEDEN
- REPORT TO THE ECONOMIC COOPERATION ADMINISTRATION ON 1949/50 PROGRAMME. VOL. 2. SWEDEN
- REPORT TO THE ECONOMIC COOPERATION ADMINISTRATION ON THE 1949/50 PROGRAMME. VOL. 2. AUSTRIA
- REPORT TO THE ECONOMIC COOPERATION ADMINISTRATION ON THE 1949/50 PROGRAMME. VOL. 2. NETHERLANDS
- REPORT TO THE ECONOMIC COOPERATION ADMINISTRATION ON THE 1949/50 PROGRAMME. VOL. 2. PORTUGAL

Organization of American States *see*
- ANNALS
- OAS ANNALS
- OAS CHRONICLE

Organization of Coordination and Cooperation for the Fight Against Major Endemic Diseases, West Africa *see* RAPPORTS FINALS DES CONFERENCES TECHNIQUES DE L'OCCGE, 1963-1974

ORGANIZATION OF INFORMATION SYSTEMS FOR GOVERNMENT AND PUBLIC ADMINISTRATION / Grolier, Eric de – 2nd ed 1985 – 9 – 92-3-101595-8 – fr UNESCO [000]

Organization of North American Indian Students *see* THE NISHNAWBE NEWS

Organization of Petroleum Exporting Countries *see*
- ANNUAL STATISTICAL BULLETIN
- RESOLUTIONS
- REVIEW AND RECORD
- SELECTED DOCUMENTS OF THE INTERNATIONAL PETROLEUM INDUSTRY

THE ORGANIZATION OF THE ORTHODOX EASTERN CHURCHES / Dampier, Margaret G – London: Published for the Eastern Church Association by A.R. Mowbray, 1910 – 1mf – us A.T.L.A. [240]

THE ORGANIZATION OF THE SPANISH ARMY / Roure-Torent, J – Paris, 1937. Fiche W1150. (Blodgett Collection of Spanish Civil War Pamphlets) – 9 – us H.U. College Libr [946]

THE ORGANIZATION OF TRILOBITES / Burmeister, H – Ray Society. 1846 – 1. 32.00; ; 7 – uk Microform Academic [560]

ORGANIZATION, OPERATION AND MAINTENANCE OF IRRIGATION SCHEMES – 1982 2nd print 1986 – 174p – it F.A.O. [631]

ORGANIZATIONAL ACTIVITIES AND MATERIALS – (Various pagination) – Saipan, n.p, 1975 – 15mf – 9 – $22.50 – LLMC 82-100F, Title 88 – us L.L.M.C. [323]

ORGANIZATIONAL CHANGES IN THE CHINESE ARMY, 1895-1950 / U.S. Office of the Chief of Military History – 1968 – 1 – 21.00 – us L of C Photodup [950]

ORGANIZATSIIA I PRAKTIKA PROMYSLOVOI KOOPERATSII / Vasil'evskii, L G – M., 1928 – 5mf – 9 – COR-414/1 – ne IDC [334]

ORGANIZATSIIA I TEKHNIKA KREDITNYKH KOOPERATIVOV / Evzlin, Z P – L, 1925 – 4mf – 9 – COR-377/1 – ne IDC [334]

ORGANIZATSIIA IURIDICHESKOI RABOTY UCHREZHDENII / Gavrilenko, K & Golubov, S – M. 1927. BR-9606 1 – 9 – ne IDC [338]

ORGANIZATSIIA KHLEBOTORGOVLI I KOOPERATIVNYI SBYT KHLEBA V ROSSII : OCHERKI / Kulyzhnyi, A E – Ed 3. M., 1919 – 1mf – 9 – COR-57/1 – ne IDC [334]

ORGANIZATSIIA KHOZIAISTVENNOI ZHIZNI PETROGRADSKOI GUBERNII : DOKLADY NA GUBERNSKOM SOEZDE UEZDNYKH OTDELOV NARODNOGO KHOZIAISTVA 10-11 SENTI ABRIA 1920 G / Gubernskii sezd uezdnykh otdelov narodnogo khoziaistva (1920: Leningrad, R.S.F.S.R.) – Petrograd: Izdatelskii otdel Petrogradskogo soveta narodnogo khozia istva, 1920 – 1 – CSUX91-B1111 – us Hoover Inst Photo [330]

ORGANIZATSIIA KONTROLIA V KREDITNOI KOOPERATSII / Minervin, BM – M., 1929 – 2mf – 9 – COR-394/1 – ne IDC [334]

ORGANIZATSIIA KREST'IANSKOGO KHOZIAISTVA / Chaianov, A V – M., 1925 – 3mf – 9 – COR-233/1 – ne IDC [334]

ORGANIZATSIIA MESTNYKH KOOPERATIVNYKH KURSOV / Kil'chevskii, V A – Pg. v1. 1919 – 2mf – 9 – COR-252/1 – ne IDC [334]

ORGANIZATSIIA NARODNOGO KHOZIAISTVA I KOOPERATSIIA / Grechko, A M – Khar'kov, 1917 – 1mf – 9 – COR-20/1 – ne IDC [334]

ORGANIZATSIIA RABOCHEI SILY V 1920 GODU / Anikst, Abram – Moskva: Agit.-izdatelski i otdel G.K.T. i N.K.T., 1920 – 1 – CSUX91-B606 – us Hoover Inst Photo [947]

ORGANIZATSIIA RASPREDELENIIA RABOCHEI SILY : STATI I DOKLADY ZA 1918-20 GG / Anikst, Abram – Moskva: [Agit.-izd. otdel Glavkomtruda i Narkomtruda], 1920 – 1 – CSUX91-B3140 – us Hoover Inst Photo [947]

ORGANIZATSIIA RYNKA TRUDA ZA DVA GODA SOVETSKOI VLASTI : KRATKI I OCHERK / Anikst, Abram – Moskva: Nar. komissariat truda i sot s. obespechenii a, 1920 – 1 – CSUX89-B7282 – us Hoover Inst Photo [947]

ORGANIZATSIIA SEL'SKOGO KHOZIAISTVA / Makarov, N P – M., 1926 – 7mf – 9 – COR-210/1 – ne IDC [334]

ORGANIZATSIIA SEVERNOGO KREST'IANSKOGO KHOZIAISTVA / Chaianov, A V – Iaroslavl', 1918 – 2mf – 9 – COR-234/1 – ne IDC [334]

ORGANIZATSIIA SNABZHENCHESKOI RABOTY V SISTEME SEL'SKOKHOZIAISTVENNOI KOOPERATSII I VOPROSY PROIZVODSTVENNOGO KOOPERIROVANIIA / Dudin, K – M., 1928 – 2mf – 9 – COR-473/1 – ne IDC [334]

ORGANIZATSIIA UPRAVLENIIA POTREBITEL'SKIKH OBSHCHESTV I IKH SOIUZOV : SBORNIK / ed by Kheisin, M L – Pg., 1918 – 2mf – 9 – COR-340/1 – ne IDC [334]

ORGANIZED CRIME DIGEST – v.1-. 1980- – 1,5,6,9 – us UMI [073]

ORGANIZED LABOR : OFFICIAL PAPER OF THE STATE AND LOCAL BUILDING TRADES COUNCILS OF CALIFORNIA – San Francisco. v1-49. 1900-48 – 15r – 1 – us Ross [331]

ORGANIZED LABOR – San Francisco, CA. 1943-88 – 16r – 1 – $800.00 – C02846 – us Library Micro [071]

ORGANIZED LABOR – San Francisco. Calif. -w. 1944-66 – 1 – us UMI [331]

ORGANIZED LABOR – San Francisco. v. 1-49. Feb 3 1900-Apr 19 1948. Incomplete – 1 – us NY Public [331]

ORGANIZING EDUCATIONAL BROADCASTING / Hawkridge, David & Robinson, John – 1982 – 302p – 9 – 92-3-101878-7 – fr UNESCO [380]

ORGANIZU ITE DEREVNIU! : PRIMIERNAIA PAMIATKA, NASTAVLENIE DLIA OT IEZZHAI USHCHIKH V DEREVNIU TOV.-SOLDAT I KRESTIAN-KHODOKOV / Burov, I Akovlosifovich – Petrograd: Izd-vo Soldatskai a i kresti anskai a biblioteka, 1918 – 1 – CSUX89-B1638 – us Hoover Inst Photo [947]

ORGANIZU ITE DETVORU : ORGAN NARKOMPROSA RSFSR I T SK VLKSM – (Library has: Jan./Feb.-Mar./Apr. 1934) – Moskva: Gos. ucheb.-pedagog. izd-vo, 1930-1935. 6v – 1 – CSUX89-S773 – us Hoover Inst Photo [947]

ORGANO SUONARINO DEL P. D. ADRIANO BANCHIERI BOLOGNESE ABBATE BENEMERITO OLIVETANO. OPERA 33 / Banchieri, A – Quarta Impressione. 1638 – 9 – us Sibley [780]

L'ORGANO SUONARINO DI ADRIANO BANCHIERI BOLOGNESE / Banchieri, A – Entro il quale si practica quanto occorrer suole a gli Suonatori d'Organo. Venetia, appresso Ricciardo Amadino. 1605. BP-635 1 – 9 – ne IDC [780]

ORGANOMETALLIC COMPOUNDS – v1- 1961-1; v18- 5,6; v28- 9 – us UMI [540]

ORGANOMETALLICS – v1- 1982- – 1,5,6,9 – us A.C.S. [073]

THE ORGANON OF SCRIPTURE : OR, THE INDUCTIVE METHOD OF BIBLICAL INTERPRETATION / Lamar, James Sanford – Philadelphia: J B Lippincott, 1860 – 1mf – 9 – 0-8370-4039-6 – 1985-2039 – us A.T.L.A. [220]

ORGANOPOEIA, ODER UNTEWEIZUNG WIE EIN ORGEL. ZU ERBAUEN / Bendeler, J Ph – P-162. c.1690 – 9 – ne IDC [780]

ORGANUM DIALECTICUM ET RETORICORUM / Sanchez de las Brozas, Francisco – Salamanca: M.Serrano de Vargas, 1588 – 1 – sp Bibl Santa Ana [946]
ORGANUM GRUNINGENSE REDIVIVUM / Werckmeister, A – 1705 – 9 – us Sibley [780]
O ORGAO DA LEI – Gravata, 6 Jun 1832 – 1,5,6 – bl Biblioteca [072]
ORGAO DO POVO – Penedo, Alagoas. 17 Jun-8 Jul 1877 – 1,5,6 – bl Biblioteca [072]
ORGAO OFICIAL DOS PODERES DO ESTADO / Minas Gerais. Brazil – Belo Horizonte. 1942-1946 – 1 – us NY Public [972]
ORGELHISTORIE / Sponsel, J U – Nuernberg. 1771. BP-764 1 – 9 – ne IDC [780]
ORGEL-PROEF OF NAAUWKEURIGE BESCHRYVING VAN 'T GEENE DAT ER VOOR HET AANBESTEEDEN VAN NIEUWE EN TE RENOVEERENE OUDE ORGELS NODIG DIENE IN ACHT GENOMEN / Werckmeister, A – Volgens den laatsten druk by den auteur vermeerderd en nagezien. Uit het hoogduitsche vertaald. door Jacob Wilhelm Lustig. Amsteldam. 1755. BP-516 1 – 9 – ne IDC [780]
ORGELTOENE : GEDICHTE / Meissner, Heinrich – Bocholt: In Commission bei J & A Temming, 1887 – 1r – 1 – us U.W. Library [810]
Orgkomitet XII Mezhdunarodnogo seminara po issledovaniiu semi *see*
– DINAMIKA IZMENENIIA POLOZHENIIA ZHENSHCHINY I SEMIA
ORGONE ENERGY BULL – 1-2. 1949-50 – 1 – us UMI [530]
Orgosinus, H *see* MUSICA NOVA QUA TAM FACILIS OSTEN DITUR CANECDI SCIENTIA,... (ETC)
Orhon, Orhan Seyfi *see* PERI KIZILE COBAN HIKAVESI
ORI APOLLINIS NILIACI, DE SACRIS NOTIS / Horus Apollo – O-303. 1551 – 9 – ne IDC [760]
ORIENS CHRISTIANUS – 1(1901)-8(1908). NS: 1(1911)-14(1924). 3. S. 1(1927)-9(1934) – 252mf – 9 – Dfl882.00 – ne Slangenburg [073]
ORIENS CHRISTIANUS / Quien, M Le, OP – Parisiis. Tomi 1-3. 1740 – 61mf – 8 – Dfl214.00 – ne Slangenburg [240]
ORIENS CHRISTIANUS – Rome. v1-8. 1901-1908; NS v1-14. 1911-1924; S3 v1-9. 1927-1934 – 252mf – 9 – ne IDC [240]
ORIENS CHRISTIANUS PER GLI STUDI DELL'ORIENTE CHRISTIANO – Anno Primo. Roma, 1901 – Dfl39.00 – ne Slangenburg [240]
L'ORIENT – Paris & Brussels, 17 Sep 1889-Nov 1910 – 12r – 1 – uk British Libr Newspaper [072]
DER ORIENT : BERICHTE, STUDIEN UND KRITIKEN FUER DIE JUEDISCHE GESCHICHTE UND LITERATUR / ed by Fuerst, Julius – Leipzig, 1840-50. Hildesheim, 1992 – 108mf – 9 – DM766.00 diazo DM870.00 silver – gw Olms [470]
DER ORIENT : BERICHTE, STUDIEN UND KRITIKEN FUER JUEDISCHE GESCHICHTE UND LITERATUR – Leipzig. v1-12, 1840-51. Includes Literaturblatt des Orient. Incomplete. B320 (Leo Baeck Institute. German-Jewish Periodicals, Pt 2) – 5r – 1 – $335.00 – us UPA [270]
ORIENT : UNABHAENGIGE WOCHENSCHRIFT. ZEITFRAGEN, KULTUR, WIRTSCHAFT – Haifa, Israel. 10 Apr 1942-7 Apr 1943 – 1 – gw Mikrofilm [072]
ORIENT NEWS – Istanbul, Turkey. 17 Jun 1919-17 May 1922 (imperfect) – 6r – 1 – uk British Libr Newspaper [949]
ORIENTACIONES DE LA ESPANA FUTURA – N.Y., 1938? Fiche W1090. (Blodgett Collection of Spanish Civil War Pamphlets) – 9 – us H.U. College Libr [946]
ORIENTACIONES NECESARIAS CUBA Y PANAMA / Carrera Justiz, F – Habana, 1911 – 6mf – 1 – ILM-2329/1 – ne IDC [327]
ORIENTADOR REVOLUCIONARIO – Havana, CU. 1967 – 1r – $50.00 – R04204 – us Library Micro [072]
ORIENTAL AND INTER-AMERICAN MISSIONARY STANDARD *see* OMS (ORIENTAL MISSIONARY STANDARD) OUTREACH
ORIENTAL ART – (Individual titles not listed separately) – 77 catalogues on 154mf – 9 – £970.00 – uk Chadwyck [700]
ORIENTAL BAPTIST – Calcutta. 1847-54, v1-8; n.s. v1-2. 1879-80. Lacking: o.s., 1847-1854, v1-8. – 10mf – 8 – ne IDC [073]
Oriental Ceramic Society *see* TRANSACTIONS
THE ORIENTAL CHRIST / Mozoomdar, Protap Chunder – Boston: Geo. H. Ellis, 1883. 1 fiche. 8370-4519-3 – 9 – us A.T.L.A. [240]
THE ORIENTAL CHRISTIAN SPECTATOR – (Some issues lacking) – v1 nos 1-10; v2 nos 1-10; v3 nos 1-5; v4 nos 2-4. 1831-63 – 11r – 1 – ATLA S0234 – us A.T.L.A. [073]
ORIENTAL COLLEGE MAGAZINE – (Some missing vols) – Lahore. v1-50. 1925-1974 – 297mf – 9 – ne IDC [370]
ORIENTAL COMMERCE / Milburn, W – or THE East India Trader's Complete Guide. London. 1825. Index. BCH-823 2 – 8 – ne IDC [380]
ORIENTAL DIPLOMACY : WITH FULL VOCABULARY, GRAMMATICAL NOTES, ETC / Bezold, Carl – (In Akkadian and English. Includes bibliographical references) – London: Luzac, 1893 – 1mf – 9 – 0-8370-7445-2 – 1986-1445 – us A.T.L.A. [930]
ORIENTAL FORERUNNERS OF BYZANTINE PAINTING / Breasted, J H – 1924 – 9 – $8.50f – 0-226-07185-5 – us U.C. Orient [750]
ORIENTAL HAIR STYLES / Iki, Mme. – Indonesian and English. SE-11,044 1. 1958 – 9 – ne IDC [390]
ORIENTAL HERALD AND JOURNAL OF GENERAL LITERATURE – London. 1824-29. v1-23 – 264mf – 8 – ne IDC [480]
ORIENTAL HERALD AND JOURNAL OF GENERAL LITERATURE – v. 1-23. 1824-29 – 1 – us UMI [480]
ORIENTAL HISTORICAL MANUSCRIPTS IN THE TAMIL LANGUAGE / Taylor, William MacKergo – Translated with annotations. Madras C. J. Taylor 1835 – 1 – us U.W. Library [950]
ORIENTAL HISTORICAL MANUSCRIPTS, IN THE TAMIL LANGUAGE – Madras: [Printed by J C Talyor], 1835 – us Res Libr [090]
Oriental Institute. University of Chicago *see*
– THE 1905-1907 BREASTED EXPEDITIONS TO EGYPT AND THE SUDAN
– THE 1919-20 BREASTED EXPEDITION TO THE NEAR EAST
– PERSEPOLIS AND ANCIENT IRAN
– PTOLEMAIS CYRENAICA
AN ORIENTAL LAND OF THE FREE, OR, LIFE AND MISSION WORK AMONG THE LAOS / Freeman, John Haskell – Philadelphia: Westminster Press, 1910. 200p. 1 fiche – 9 – us A.T.L.A. [240]
THE ORIENTAL MISCELLANY : BEING A COLLECTION OF THE MOST FAVOURITE AIRS OF HINDOOSTAN / Bird, William Hamilton – Calcutta: J Cooper, 1789 – 1 – us Sibley [780]
ORIENTAL MISSIONARY STANDARD *see* OMS (ORIENTAL MISSIONARY STANDARD) OUTREACH
THE ORIENTAL QUESTION, 1840-1900 : FILES FROM THE ROYAL ARCHIVES, WINDSOR CASTLE / Great Britain. Royal Archives – 38 reels with printed guide – 1 – $3,660.00 – 0-89093-737-0 – us UPA [950]
THE ORIENTAL RELIGIONS IN ROMAN PAGANISM / Cumont, Franz – Chicago: Open Court; London: Kegan Paul, Trench, Truebner [distributor], 1911 – 1mf – us A.T.L.A. [230]
ORIENTAL STUDIES / Haupt, P – Ed. by C. Adler and A. Ember. Leipzig. 1926. BNE-20,043 1 – 9 – ne IDC [950]
ORIENTAL WORKS OF ART – (Over 2,500 items of Chinese porcelain. 8,000 reproductions) – 137mf – 9 – $750.00 – 0-907006-37-X – uk Mindata [700]
ORIENTALIA – Roma. S.I v1-55 1920-1930; N.S. v1-5 1932-1936 – 116mf – 9 – ne IDC [950]
ORIENTALIA CHRISTIANA PERIODICA – 1(1935) – 44(1978) – 491mf – 8 – ne Slangenburg [240]
ORIENTALISCH- UND OCCIDENTALISCHES A.B.C.-BUCH WELCHES HUNDERT ALPHABETE NEBST IHRER AUSSPRACHE SO BEY DENEN MEISTEN EUROPAEISCH-ASIATISCH-AFRICANISCH- UND AMERICANISCHEN VOELKERN UND NATIONEN GEBRAEUCHLICH SIND,... / Schulzen, B – Naumberg: Zeiss, 1769 – 3mf – ne IDC [400]
ORIENTALISCHE BIBLIOGRAPHIE... – Berlin. v1-25. 1887-1911 – 166mf – 9 – ne IDC [950]
DIE ORIENTALISCHE CHRISTENHEIT DER MITTELMEERLAENDER : REISESTUDIEN ZUR STATISTIK UND SYMBOLIK DER GRIECHISCHEN, ARMENISCHEN UND KOPTISCHEN KIRCHE / Beth, Karl – (Includes bibliographical references) – Berlin: C A Schwetschke, 1902 – 1mf – 9 – 0-8370-7444-4 – 1986-1444 – us A.T.L.A. [240]
EIN ORIENTALISCHES HANDELSUNTERNEHMEN IM 15. JAHRHUNDERT / Hinz, W – (Die Welt des Orients 1949). v. 4. BU-741 2 – 8 – ne IDC [950]
ORIENTALIST : A MONTHLY JOURNAL OF ORIENTAL LITERATURE, ARTS AND SCIENCES, FOLKLORE – Bombay. 1884-92. 4v. – 18mf – 8 – ne IDC [700]
ORIENTALISTISCHE LITERATUR-ZEITUNG – Berlin. v1-44. 1898-1941 – 484mf – 9 – ne IDC [480]
ORIENTATIE – Batavia, 1947-1954 – 40mf – 9 – ne IDC [950]
ORIENTE MODERNO : REVISTA MENSILE D'INFORMAZIONI DI STUDI PER LA DIFFUZIONE ET LA CONOSCENZY DELL' ORIENTE,... – Roma. v1-21. 1921-41 – 397mf – 9 – ne IDC [950]
ORIENTE MODERNO – Roma: Istituto per l'Oriente. v1-50. jun 15 1921-70 – us Res Libr [073]
ORIENTE, ZENITH Y OCASO / Soto y Marne, Francisco de – 1742? – 9 – 1.50f – sp Bibl Santa Ana [946]
DIE ORIENTPOLITIK DER 3. INTERNATIONALE / Hurwicz, Elias – Berlin, 1922 – 1 – DM30.00 – gw Mikro Press [335]
L'ORIFLAMME – Le Regulateur. Journal politique et litteraire. Paris. 1er juin-dec 1823 – 1 – fr A.C.R.P.P. [073]
ORIGEN DEL EXTREMADURA...POBLACIONES / Paredes, Guillen Vicente – 1886 – 9 – $1.50f – sp Bibl Santa Ana [946]
ORIGEN, NATURALEZA Y DESTINO DEL HOMBRE EN LOS AUTOS SACRAMENTALES DE CALDERON / Frutos Cortes, Eugenio – Madrid, 1946. Rev. Filosofia (Tomo 4, no 5) del Instituto Luis Vives – sp Bibl Santa Ana [440]
EL ORIGEN Y EL NOMBRE DE CACERES / Callejo Serrano, Carlos – Caceres: Caja de Ahorros y Monte de Piedad de Caceres, 1962 – 1 – sp Bibl Santa Ana [946]
ORIGEN Y PRINCIPIO...ALCANTARA / Diaz de la Carrera, Diego – 1663 – 9 – $1.50f – sp Bibl Santa Ana [946]
ORIGENE, LE THEOLOGIEN ET L'EXEGETE / Prat, Ferdinand – 1907 – 1 – us A.T.L.A. [240]
ORIGENES : EINE DARSTELLUNG SEINES LEBENS UND SEINER LEHRE / Redepenning, Ernst Rudolf – Bonn: Eduard Weber, 1841-1846 – 3mf – us A.T.L.A. [240]
Origenes *see*
– LE COMMENTAIRE D'ORIGENE SUR ROM. 3, 5-V, 7 D'APRES LES EXTRAITS DU PAPYRUS NO 88748 DU MUSEE DU CAIRE
– ENTRETIEN D'ORIGENE AVEC HERACLIDE ET LES EVEQUES SES COLLEGUES SUR LE PERE, LE FILS ET L'AME
LOS ORIGENES DE EUROPA. TRADUCCION DE FRANCISCO ELIAS DE TEJADA. MADRID, 1945 / Cereceda, F & Dawson, Christopher – Madrid: Razon y Fe, 1947 – 1 – sp Bibl Santa Ana [940]
ORIGENES DE LA POESIA CASTELLANA / Velazquez de Velasco, Luis J – 1754 – 1mf – 9 – Pta1,000.00 – 84-7848-335-7 – sp Pentalfa [440]
ORIGENES DE LA REVOLUCION ESPANOLA / Tusquets, Juan – Valencia, 2nd ed 1932; Madrid: Razon y Fe, 1932 – 1 – sp Bibl Santa Ana [946]
LOS ORIGENES DEL GOBIERNO VIRREINAL EN LAS INDIAS ESPANOLAS. DON ANTONIO DE MENDOZA, PRIMER VIRREY DE LA NUEVA ESPANA (1535-1550) / Perez Bustamante, Ciriaco – Madrid: Razon y Fe, 1929 – 1 – sp Bibl Santa Ana [946]
ORIGENES DEL NACIONALISMO ARGENTINO / Ibarguren, Federico – [Buenos Aires: Editorial Celcius, 1969] – 1 – CSUXADJ1482-B – us Hoover Inst Photo [320]
ORIGENES DEL NACIONALISMO ESPANOL / Garcia Morente, Manuel – Buenos Aires, 1938. Fiche W 907. (Blodgett Collection of Spanish Civil War Pamphlets) – 9 – us H.U. College Libr [946]
ORIGENES ECCLESIASTICAE: OR, THE ANTIQUITIES OF THE CHRISTIAN CHURCH, AND OTHER WORKS / Bingham, Joseph – London: W. Straker, 1840. 9v. maps, plans – 1 – us U.W. Library [240]
ORIGENES HISTORICOS DE LA AGRICULTURA Y DE LA GANADERIA EN CACERES / Floriano Cumbreno, Antonio C – Caceres: Garcia Floriano, 1935 – 1 – sp Bibl Santa Ana [630]
Origenes, M M *see* CARDIO-RESPIRATORY RESPONSE TO UPRIGHT AND AERO-POSTURE CYCLING
ORIGENES Y ARMAS DE LA CASA DE MARQUEZ DE PRADO / Maldonado y Cocat, Jose Ramon – Madrid, 1955 – 1 – sp Bibl Santa Ana [920]
Origenis *see* OPERA OMNIA
THE ORIGIN AND CAUSE OF THE ANTI-CHRISTIAN MOVEMENT BY CHINESE OFFICIALS AND GENTRY, 1860-1874 (CCC233) / Lu, Shih-Chiang – (In Chinese) – Nanking, Taipei, Taiwan: Institute of Modern History, Academia Sinica, 1966 – 1r – 1 – 1984-6572 – us A.T.L.A. [950]
'THE ORIGIN AND CAUSE OF THE BRITISH-AMERICAN ORDER OF GOOD TEMPLARS', REVIEWED / Crane, J Willard – Halifax, N.S.: s.n., 1867 (Halifax, N.S.: J. Bowes). 03622. (Pre-1900 Canadiana) – 9 – cn C.I.H.M. [360]
ORIGIN AND DEVELOPMENT OF INDIAN CALENDRICAL SCIENCE / Chakravarty, Apurba Kumar – Calcutta: Indian Studies, Past & Present, 1975. 62p. Bibliog. p61-62 – 1 – us U.W. Library [520]
THE ORIGIN AND DEVELOPMENT OF THE CHRISTIAN CHURCH IN GAUL DURING THE FIRST SIX CENTURIES OF THE CHRISTIAN ERA : BEING THE BIRKBECK LECTURES FOR 1907 AND 1908 IN TRINITY COLLEGE, CAMBRIDGE / Holmes, T Scott – London, New York: Macmillan, 1911 – 2mf – us A.T.L.A. [240]
ORIGIN AND DEVELOPMENTS OF ANGLICANISM : OR, A HISTORY OF THE LITURGIES, HOMILIES, ARTICLES, BIBLES, PRINCIPLES AND GOVERNMENTAL SYSTEM OF THE CHURCH OF ENGLAND / Waterworth, William – (Includes bibliographical references) – London: Burns & Lambert, 1854 – 1mf – 9 – 0-8370-7198-4 – 1986-1198 – us A.T.L.A. [240]
ORIGIN AND DEVELOPMENTS OF ANGLICANISM; OR A HISTORY OF THE LITURGIES, HOMILIES, ARTICLES, BIBLES, PRINCIPLES AND GOVERNMENTAL SYSTEM OF THE CHURCH OF ENGLAND / Waterworth, William – London: Burns and Lambert, 1854.419p – 1 – us U.W. Library [240]
THE ORIGIN AND GROWTH OF THE AMERICAN CONSTITUTION : A DOCUMENTARY HISTORY / Taylor, Hannis – Boston: Houghton-Mifflin, 1911 – 3mf – 9 – $4.50 – LLMC 84-254 – us L.L.M.C. [323]
THE ORIGIN AND GROWTH OF THE ENGLISH CONSTITUTION / Taylor, Hannis – New York: Houghton-Mifflin. v1-2. 1904 – 15mf – 9 – $22.50 – LLMC 84-803 – us L.L.M.C. [323]
THE ORIGIN AND HISTORY OF METHODISM IN WALES AND THE BORDERS / Young, D – London, 1893. xxvi/731p – 9mf – 9 – ne IDC [240]
ORIGIN AND HISTORY OF PREMILLENARIANISM / Briggs, Charles Augustus – (Article in the Lutheran Quarterly review, v. 9, 1879) – 1 – 5.67 – us Baptist [240]
ORIGIN AND HISTORY OF THE NEW TESTAMENT / Martin, James – London: Hodder & Stoughton, 1882. 1 fiche – 9 – us A.T.L.A. [240]
THE ORIGIN AND HISTORY OF THE PRIMITVE METHODIST CHURCH / Kendall, H B – London, [1906]. 2v: [4], 559p; 552p – 12mf – 9 – ne IDC [240]
ORIGIN AND HISTORY OF THE WESLEYAN REFORM UNION, WITH A BRIEF SUMMARY OF METHODIST SECESSIONS / Wesleyan Reform Union – Sheffield, 1896. [8], 116p – 2mf – 9 – ne IDC [060]
ORIGIN AND PROGRESS OF LANGUAGE / Burnet, James Lord Monboddo – (Linguistics series). 6 v. 1774-1792 – 9 – fr Hachette [400]
THE ORIGIN AND PROPAGATION OF SIN / Tennant, Frederick Robert – being the Hulsean lectures delivered before the University of Cambridge in 1901-2. 1902 – 1 – us A.T.L.A. [240]

ORIGIN AND RELIGIOUS CONTENT OF THE PSALTER / Cheyne, Thomas Kelly – New York: Thomas Whittaker, 1891. 2 fiches – 9 – us A.T.L.A. [240]

THE ORIGIN AND SERVICES OF THE PRINCE OF WALES REGIMENT: INCLUDING A BRIEF HISTORY OF THE MILITIA OF FRENCH CANADA AND OF THE CANADIAN MILITIA.. / ed by Chambers, Ernest J – Montreal: E. Ruddy, 1897. 00547. (Pre-1900 Canadiana) – 9 – cn C.I.H.M. [971]

ORIGIN AND TRADITIONAL HISTORY OF THE WYANDOTTS: AND SKETCHES OF OTHER INDIAN TRIBES OF NORTH AMERICA, TRUE TRADITIONAL STORIES OF TECUMSEH AND HIS LEAGUE, IN THE YEARS OF 1811 AND 1812 / Clarke, Peter Dooyentate – Toronto: Hunter, Rose, 1870. 00669. (Pre-1900 Canadiana) – 9 – cn C.I.H.M. [305]

THE ORIGIN AND VARIETIES OF THE SEMITIC ALPHABET : WITH SPECIMENS / Clarke, John Caldwell Calhoun – 2nd ed. Chicago: American Publication Society of Hebrew, 1884 – 1mf – 9 – 0-8370-8496-2 – 1986-2496 – us A.T.L.A. [470]

THE ORIGIN OF BENIN / Egharevba, Jacob U – Lagos: Ribway Printers, 1953 – us Res Libr [960]

THE ORIGIN OF BIRDS / Heilmann, G – 2324 2. 1926 – 8 – ne IDC [590]

THE ORIGIN OF CREATION, OR, THE SCIENCE OF MATTER AND FORCE: A NEW SYSTEM OF NATURAL PHILOSOPHY – Halifax, N.S., 1874. 02780. (Pre-1900 Canadiana) – 9 – cn C.I.H.M. [140]

THE ORIGIN OF GNEISS AND SOME OTHER PRIMITIVE ROCKS / Bell, Robert – Salem, MA: Salem Press, 1889. 03560. (Pre-1900 Canadiana) – 9 – cn C.I.H.M. [550]

THE ORIGIN OF HUMAN REASON : BEING AN EXAMINATION OF RECENT HYPOTHESES CONCERNING IT / Mivart, St George Jackson – (Includes bibliographical references and index) – London: Kegan Paul, Trench, 1889 – 1mf – 9 – 0-8370-6762-6 – 1986-0762 – us A.T.L.A. [150]

THE ORIGIN OF LANGUAGE AND NATIONS / Jones, Rowland – 1764. 353p. (English Linguistics Series 1500-1800) – 9 – us UMI [400]

THE ORIGIN OF PROPERTY IN LAND / Coulanges, F de – 1890. 201p – 9 – 1.00f – at Libertarian Micro [333]

THE ORIGIN OF PTOLEMY'S GEOGRAPHIA / Bagrow, L – Stockholm. 1945. B-2198 2 – 8 – ne IDC [910]

THE ORIGIN OF SPECIES BY MEANS OF NATURAL SELECTION, OR, THE PRESERVATION OF FAVOURED RACES IN THE STRUGGLE FOR LIFE / Darwin, Charles – London: John Murray, 6th ed 1872 – 1 roll – 1 – 1-55879-794-7 – uk Libr Preservation [590]

ORIGIN OF THE ABORIGINES OF CANADA: A PAPER READ BEFORE THE SOCIETY, 17TH DECEMBER 1880 / Campbell, John – 1881? 00923. (Pre-1900 Canadiana) – 9 – cn C.I.H.M. [305]

ORIGIN OF THE COPPER ESKIMOS AND THEIR COPPER CULTURE / Jenness, D – BN 269 2. 1923.m – 8 – ne IDC [306]

ORIGIN OF THE DISCIPLES OF CHRIST (CAMBELLITES) / Whitsitt, William H – A contribution to the Centennial Anniversary of the birth of Alexander Campbell. 1888 – 1 – 5.00 – us Baptist [240]

ORIGIN OF THE DISCIPLES OF CHRIST (CAMPBELLITIES) : A CONTRIBUTION TO THE CENTENNIAL ANNIVERSARY OF THE BIRTH OF ALEXANDER CAMPBELL / Whitsitt, William H – New York: A.C. Armstrong, 1888 – 1mf – us A.T.L.A. [240]

ORIGIN OF THE ENGLISH NATION / Chadwick, H M – H-1146 2. 1907 – 8 – ne IDC [941]

ORIGIN OF THE FOUR GOSPELS / Tischendorf, Constantin von – Boston: American Tract Society, 1867. 1 fiche – 9 – us A.T.L.A. [240]

THE ORIGIN OF THE GUNU-SIGNS IN BABYLONIAN / Ogden, Ellen Seton – (Includes bibliography) – Leipzig: W Drugulin, 1911 – 1mf – 9 – 0-8370-8368-0 – 1986-2368 – us A.T.L.A. [470]

THE ORIGIN OF THE KNOWLEDGE OF RIGHT AND WRONG / Brentano, Franz Clemens – Westminster: Archibald Constable, 1902 – 1mf – 9 – 0-8370-6088-5 – 1986-0088 – us A.T.L.A. [170]

THE ORIGIN OF THE LEICESTER CODEX OF THE NEW TESTAMENT / Harris, James Rendel – London: C J Clay, 1887 – 1mf – 9 – 0-8370-9788-6 – 1986-3788 – us A.T.L.A. [220]

THE ORIGIN OF THE NEW TESTAMENT = ENTSTEHUNG DER SCHRIFTEN DES NEUEN TESTAMENTS / Wrede, William – (In English) – London; New York: Harper, 1909 – 1mf – 9 – 0-8370-7278-6 – 1986-1278 – us A.T.L.A. [220]

THE ORIGIN OF THE PENTATEUCH IN THE LIGHT OF THE ANCIENT MONUMENTS / White, Henry Alexander – (Includes bibliographical references) – Richmond, VA: B F Johnson, 1894 – 1mf – 9 – 0-8370-9435-6 – 1986-3435 – us A.T.L.A. [220]

THE ORIGIN OF THE REFORMED CHURCH IN GERMANY / Good, James I – Reading, Pa.: Daniel Miller, 1887 – 2mf – us A.T.L.A. [240]

THE ORIGIN OF THE RIGHT OF FISHERY IN TERRITORIAL WATERS / Fenn, P T – Cambridge, 1926 – 3mf – 1 – ILM-1800/1 – ne IDC [327]

THE ORIGIN OF THE WORLD, ACCORDING TO REVELATION AND SCIENCE / Dawson, John William – Montreal: Dawson, 1877. 02605. (Pre-1900 Canadiana) – 9 – cn C.I.H.M. [971]

ORIGINAL AND SELECTED THOUGHTS ON THE LIFE AND TIMES OF REV. THOMAS MILLER, AND REV. THOMAS WARBURTON / Miller, Thomas B – 1860 – 1 – us A.T.L.A. [240]

ORIGINAL FABLES / Kidgell, J – (In English and French) – London, 1764. 2v – 4mf – 9 – ne IDC [390]

ORIGINAL HYMNS FOR PUBLIC, PRIVATE AND SOCIAL DEVOTION / Montgomery, James – London: Longman, Brown, Green and Longmans, 1853 – 1 roll – 1 – 1-55879-433-6 – uk Libr Preservation [780]

ORIGINAL LETTERS BETWEEN THE REVEREND MR. JOHN WESLEY AND MR. RICHARD TOMPSON RESPECTING THE DOCTRINE OF ASSURANCE AS HELD BY THE FORMER,... – London, 1760 – 1mf – 9 – MP-385/1 – ne IDC [240]

ORIGINAL LETTERS BY THE REV. JOHN WESLEY AND HIS FRIENDS, ILLUSTRATIVE OF HIS EARLY HISTORY,... / Priestly, J – Birmingham, 1791 – 3mf – 9 – MP-572/1 – ne IDC [240]

ORIGINAL LISTS OF AMERICAN EMIGRANTS, 1600-1700 / Hotten, J C – 1931 – 1 – uk Microform Academic [920]

ORIGINAL MANUSCRIPTS AND PAPERS / Hardy, Thomas – 1 – uk Microform Academic [830]

ORIGINAL MATTER CONTAINED IN LIEUT-COLONEL SUTHERLAND'S MEMOIR ON THE KAFFERS, HOTTENTOTS, AND BOSJEMANS OF SOUTH AFRICA, HEADS 1ST AND 2ND / Sutherland, John – (Commentaries & notes on text used in the compilation of the memoris) – Cape Town: Pike & Philip, 1847 – us Res Libr [960]

ORIGINAL MEANING JURISPRUDENCE : A SOURCEBOOK: 12 MAR 1987 – Washington: GPO, 1988 – 2mf – 9 – $3.00 – LLMC 94-363 – us L.L.M.C. [340]

ORIGINAL MEMBERS AND OTHER OFFICERS ELIGIBLE TO THE SOCIETY OF THE CINCINNATI 1783-1938 / Metcalf, Bryce – With the Institution, Rules of Admission, and Lists of the Officers of the General and State Societies. Strasburg: Shenandoah Publ. House Inc., 1938. Military Books reel 3. (Cox Library Collection) – 5 – us Americana [920]

ORIGINAL MONOGRAPH SERIES *see* DIGESTS OF INTERNATIONAL LAW SERIES

ORIGINAL MSS. AND ANNOTATED PROOFS / Dickens, Charles – From Foster Collection in Victoria and Albert Museum, London – 1 – uk Microform Academic [830]

ORIGINAL MSS. AND OTHER PAPERS / Dickens, Charles – From Dickens House, London – 1 – uk Microform Academic [830]

ORIGINAL OPINIONS OF THE JUSTICES OF THE U.S. SUPREME COURT DELIVERED AT THE JANUARY TERM 1832 / U.S. Department of Justice – Opinions and other case papers of Chief Justice Marshall, 1834-35 Terms. 1 roll – 1 – T57 – us Nat'l Archives [340]

ORIGINAL RECORDS OF BAPTISMS AND CORRESPONDENCE / Santa Cruz Mission. Calif – 1791-1814 – 1 – 20.00 – us Library Micro [920]

ORIGINAL SANSKRIT TEXTS ON THE ORIGIN AND HISTORY OF THE PEOPLE OF INDIA, THEIR RELIGION AND INSTITUTIONS / Muir, John – 2nd ed. 5v. 1872-74 – 1 – us A.T.L.A. [950]

ORIGINAL SHAKER MUSIC / Offord, Daniel B – New York: Wm. A. Pond, 1893 – 1mf – us A.T.L.A. [780]

ORIGINAL, SHORT AND PRACTICAL SERMONS FOR EVERY FEAST OF THE ECCLESIASTICAL YEAR : THREE SERMONS FOR EVERY FEAST / Weninger, Francis Xavier – (Includes index) – Cincinnati: C J H Lowen, c1882 – 2mf – 9 – 0-8370-6715-4 – 1986-0715 – us A.T.L.A. [230]

ORIGINAL, SHORT AND PRACTICAL SERMONS FOR EVERY SUNDAY OF THE ECCLESIASTICAL YEAR : THREE SERMONS FOR EVERY SUNDAY / Weninger, Francis Xavier – Cincinnati: C J H Lowen, c1881 – 2mf – 9 – 0-8370-6716-2 – 1986-0716 – us A.T.L.A. [240]

ORIGINAL STORIES FROM REAL LIFE : WITH CONVERSATIONS CALCULATED TO REGULATE THE AFFECTIONS AND FORM THE MIND TO TRUTH AND GOODNESS / Wollstonecraft, Mary – London: J. Johnson, 1791 – 1 roll – 1 – 1-55879-643-6 – uk Libr Preservation [830]

L'ORIGINALITA DELLA REGOLA FRANCISCANA / Quaglia, Armando – Madrid: Archivo Ibero Americano, 1960 – 1 – sp Bibl Santa Ana [240]

DIE ORIGINALITAET DES NEULICH ENTDECKTEN HEBRAEISCHEN SIRACHTEXTES : TEXTKRITISCH, EXEGETISCH UND SPRACHGESCHICHTLICH UNTERSUCHT / Koenig, Eduard – (Includes index and bibliography) – Freiburg i. B: J C B Mohr (Paul Siebeck), 1899 – 1mf – 9 – 0-8370-3970-3 – 1985-1970 – us A.T.L.A. [220]

DIE ORIGINALSPRACHE DES MATTHAEUSEVANGELIUMS : HISTORISCH-KRITISCHE UNTERSUCHUNG / Gla, Dietrich – (Includes bibliographical references) – Paderborn: Ferdinand Schoeningh, 1887 – 1mf – 9 – 0-8370-3302-0 – 1985-1302 – us A.T.L.A. [220]

ORIGINAUX ET DETRAQUES: DOUZE TYPES QUEBECQUOIS, ONEILLE, GRELOT, DRAPEAU / Frechette, Louis-Honore – Montreal: L. Patenaude, 1892. 03237. (Pre-1900 Canadiana) – 9 – cn C.I.H.M. [305]

L'ORIGINE DE L'EPISCOPAT / Michiels, A – 221 2. 1900 – 8 – ne IDC [240]

L'ORIGINE DES MENSES DANS LE TEMPOREL DES EGLISES ET DES MONASTERES DE FRANCE AU 19E SIECLE / Lesne, Emile – Lille: R. Giard; Paris: H. Champion, 1910 – 1mf – us A.T.L.A. [240]

L'ORIGINE DES RICHESSES AU JAPON – Fookoua Siriak, ou traite sur l'origine des richesses au Japon, ecrit en 1708. Traducteur by H. J. von Klaproth. Traduit de l'original chinois, Paris, Schubart et Heideloff. 1828 – 9 – 5.00 – fr Orientalistes [950]

L'ORIGINE DU NOM DE "CHINE" / Pelliot, P – T'oung Pao, v. 13. Leide. 1912. BU-566 2 – 8 – ne IDC [400]

ORIGINE ET ORGANISATION DE L'ASSOCIATION MEDICALE CANADIENNE: AVEC LES MINUTES DES ASSEMBLEES TENUE A QUEBEC, OCTOBRE 1867, ET A MONTREAL, SEPTEMBRE 1868 / Canadian Medical Association – Montreal: J. Lovell, 1868. 04095. (Pre-1900 Canadiana) – 9 – cn C.I.H.M. [610]

ORIGINE ET PROGRES DU DROIT ET DE LA LEGISLATION MARITIME,... / Azuni, D A – Paris, 1810 – 4mf – 9 – ILM-932/1 – ne IDC [340]

ORIGINELLE, KURZ-GEFASSTE, PRAKTISCHE FASTEN-PREDIGTEN : SECHS JAHRGAENGE IN EINEM BAND / Weninger, Francis Xavier – Cincinnati: [s.n.], 1883 – 1mf – 9 – 0-8370-6877-0 – 1986-0877 – us A.T.L.A. [240]

ORIGINELLE, KURZ-GEFASSTE, PRAKTISCHE FEST-PREDIGTEN ZU EHREN DER HL. APOSTEL, ORDENSSTIFTER, LANDES-PATRONE UND SCHUTZHEILIGEN / Weninger, Francis Xavier – Cincinnati: [s.n.], 1884 – 2mf – 9 – 0-8370-6957-2 – 1986-0957 – us A.T.L.A. [240]

ORIGINELLE, KURZ-GEFASSTE, PRAKTISCHE MARIANISCHE FEST-REDEN : ZUR FEIER DES MONAT MAI / Weninger, Francis Xavier – Cincinnati: [s.n.], 1882 – 2mf – 9 – 0-8370-6865-7 – 1986-0865 – us A.T.L.A. [240]

ORIGINELLE, KURZ-GEFASSTE, PRAKTISCHE PREDIGTEN ZU EHREN DES ALLERHEILIGSTEN SAKRAMENTES : 36 PREDIGTEN IN 12 ABTHEILUNGEN VON JE 3 PREDIGTEN: ZUR FEIER DES 40-STUENDIGEN GEBETES UND DER FROHNLEICHNAMS-OCTAVE / Weninger, Francis Xavier – (Later ed issued unter title: Original, short and practical sermons in honor of the blessed Sacrament) – Cincinnati: [s.n.], 1883 – 1mf – 9 – 0-8370-6795-2 – 1986-0795 – us A.T.L.A. [240]

ORIGINELLE, KURZ-GEFASSTE, PRAKTISCHE PREDIGTEN ZU EHREN DES ALLERHEILIGSTEN SAKRAMENTES = ORIGINAL, SHORT AND PRACTICAL SERMONS IN HONOR OF THE BLESSED SACRAMENT : 36 SERMONS, IN 12 DIVISIONS, 3 IN EACH / Weninger, Francis Xavier – (In English) – Cincinnati: [s.n.], 1884 – 1mf – 9 – 0-8370-6866-5 – 1986-0866 – us A.T.L.A. [240]

ORIGINELLE, KURZ-GEFASSTE, PRAKTISCHE SONNTAGS-PREDIGTEN FUER DAS GANZE KIRCHENJAHR : DREI PREDIGTEN FUER JEDEN SONNTAG / Weninger, Francis Xavier – Cincinnati: F X Weninger, 1879 – 2mf – 9 – 0-8370-6958-0 – 1986-0958 – us A.T.L.A. [240]

ORIGINELLE, KURZ-GEFASSTE, PRAKTISCHE STANDES-PREDIGTEN FUER EHEMAENNER, EHEFRAUEN, JUENGLINGE UND JUNG-FRAUEN : FUER JEDEN DIESER STAENDE 36 MONATLICHE CONFERENZEN, MITHIN DREI JAHRGAENGE / Weninger, Francis Xavier – 2. Aufl. Cincinnati: [s.n.], 1881 – 3mf – 9 – 0-8370-6959-9 – 1986-0959 – us A.T.L.A. [240]

ORIGINELLE, KURZ-GEFASSTE, PRAKTISCHE STANDESPREDIGTEN FUER EHEMAENNER, EHEFRAUEN, JUENGLINGE UND JUNGFRAUEN = ORIGINAL, SHORT AND PRACTICAL CONFERENCES FOR MARRIED MEN AND YOUNG MAIDENS / Weninger, Francis Xavier – (In English) – 2nd ed. New York: Benziger, c1883 – 2mf – 9 – 0-8370-6794-4 – 1986-0794 – us A.T.L.A. [240]

ORIGINELLE, KURZ-GEFASSTE, PRAKTISCHE STANDESPREDIGTEN FUER EHEMAENNER, EHEFRAUEN, JUENGLINGE UND JUNGFRAUEN = ORIGINAL, SHORT AND PRACTICAL CONFERENCES FOR MARRIED MEN AND YOUNG MEN / Weninger, Francis Xavier – (In English) – Cincinnati: [s.n.], 1883 – 2mf – 9 – 0-8370-6793-6 – 1986-0793 – us A.T.L.A. [240]

ORIGINES ANTWERPIANAE...; NOVEM LIBROS COMPLEXA... / Gorp, J van – Antverpiae, 1569 – 20mf – 9 – ne IDC [400]

ORIGINES BENEDICTINAE / Miraeus, A – Colonia Agrippina, 1614 – 7mf – 8 – Dfl28.00 – ne Slangenburg [240]

LES ORIGINES CHRETIENNES DANS LA PROVINCE ROMAINE DE DALMATIE / Zeiller, Jacques – Paris: H. Champion, 1906 – 1mf – us A.T.L.A. [240]

LES ORIGINES CISTERCIENNES / Othon Ducourneau, D J – (From the Revue Mabillon, 1932-33) – Liguge, 1933 – 5mf – 8 – Dfl22.00 – ne Slangenburg [240]

LES ORIGINES DE LA CROIX-ROUGE / Haje, C F & Simon, J M – Stuttgart, Amsterdam, 1900 – 1mf – 1 – ILM-827/1 – ne IDC [327]

LES ORIGINES DE LA FACULTE DE THEOLOGIE PROTESTANTE DE MONTAUBAN : ETUDE HISTORIQUE / Frossard, C L – Paris: Grassart, 1882 – 1mf – us A.T.L.A. [370]

LES ORIGINES DE LA LANGUE FRANCOISE / Menage, G – 1650 – 9 – fr I.C.S. [440]

LES ORIGINES DE LA PRIME / Froger, Dom J – Roma, 1946 – 3mf – 8 – Dfl13.00 – ne Slangenburg [240]

LES ORIGINES DE LA SCOLASTIQUE ET HUGUES DE SAINT-VICTOR / Mignon, A – (Paris, 1895.-v1.-1mf; Paris, 1895.-v2.-7mf) – 8 – ne Slangenburg [100]

LES ORIGINES DE LA SCOLASTIQUE ET HUGUES DE SAINT-VICTOR / Mignon, A – Paris: P. Lethielleux, [1895?] – 2mf – us A.T.L.A. [240]

LES ORIGINES DES LEGENDES MUSULMANES DANS LE CORAN ET DANS LES VIES DU PROPHETE / Sidersky, D – 1933 – 4mf – 8 – ne Slangenburg [260]
LES ORIGINES DIPLOMATIQUES DE LA GUERRE DE 1870-71. RECUEIL DE DOCUMENTS PAR LE MINISTERE DES AFFAIRES ETRANGERES / France. Ministere des Affaires Etrangeres – 29 v. 1910-32 – 1 – 227.00 – us L of C Photodup [944]
LES ORIGINES DU CULTE DES MARTYRS / Delehaye, Hippolyte – Bruxelles: Bureaux de la Societe des Bollandistes, 1912 – 2mf – us A.T.L.A. [240]
LES ORIGINES DU SCHISME ANGLICAN (1509-1571) / Tresal, Joseph – Paris: V. Lecoffre, 1908 – 2mf – us A.T.L.A. [240]
LES ORIGINES DU SERMON DE LA MONTAGNE / Rodrigues, Hippolyte – Paris: Michel Levy, 1868. 1 fiche – 9 – us A.T.L.A. [240]
ORIGINES ET DEVELOPPEMENT DE L'ART INTERNATIONAL INDEPENDANT / Reunion des musees nationaux. Paris – 1937. 1 fiche – 9 – fr Réunion [700]
ORIGINES ET FONDATION DU PLUS ANCIEN EVECHE DU NOUVEAU MONDE: LE DIOCESE DE GARDHS EN GROENLAND: 986-1126 / Beauvois, Eugene – Paris: E. Dufosse, 1878.04069.(Pre-1900 Canadiana) – 9 – cn C.I.H.M. [240]
ORIGINES ET PROGRES DE L'EDUCATION EN AMERIQUE: ETUDE HISTORIQUE ET CRITIQUE: LES ETATS PRIMITIFS / Barneaud, Charles – Paris: Savaete, 1898. 03373. (Pre-1900 Canadiana) – 9 – cn C.I.H.M. [370]
LES ORIGINES FRANCAISES DU JURY. LES ASSISES FEODALES / Prieur, Leon – Paris: Girard, 1924. 74p. LL-4004 – 1 – us L of C Photodup [340]
ORIGINES HAMBURGENSES SIVE RERUM HAMBURGENSIUS. LIBRI 2 / Lambecii, Petri – Hamburgi, 1706 – Dfl74.00 – ne Slangenburg [240]
ORIGINES JUDAICAE : AN INQUIRY INTO HEATHEN FAITHS AS AFFECTING THE BIRTH AND GROWTH OF JUDAISM / Cobb, William Frederick – London: A D Innes, 1895 – 1mf – 9 – 0-8370-2692-X – 1985-0692 – us A.T.L.A. [270]
ORIGINES JURIDICIALES : OR HISTORICAL MEMORIALS OF THE ENGLISH LAWS, COURTS OF JUSTICE, FORMS OF TRYAL, PUNISHMENT IN CASES CRIMINAL, LAW-WRITERS, LAW-BOOKS, GRANTS AND SETTLEMENTS OF ESTATES, DEGREE OF SERJEANT, INNS OF COURT AND CHANCERY / Dugdale, William – 2nd ed. London: Abel Roper, 1671 – 5mf – 9 – $7.50 – LLMC 95-244 – us L.L.M.C. [340]
ORIGINES LINGVAE ITALICAE / Ferrari, O – Patavii, 1676 – 6mf – 9 – ne IDC [440]
ORIGINES LITURGICAE OR ANTIQUITIES OF THE ENGLISH RITUAL AND A DISSERTATION ON PRIMITIVE LITURGIES / Palmer, William P – London. v1-2. 1845 – 16mf – 8 – Dfl56.00 – ne Slangenburg [200]
LES ORIGINES POLITIQUES DES GUERRES DE RELIGION (1547-1559) / Romier, L – H 381 2. 2 v. 1913-1914 – 8 – ne IDC [940]
ORIGINS AND DEVELOPMENT AT LOCAL LEVEL / Labour Party. Great Britain – Minutes, Reports, Correspondence, etc – 1 – uk Microform Academic [360]
ORIGINS AND FAITH: AN ESSAY OF RECONCILIATION / Compton-Rickett, Joseph – New York: F.H. Revell, 1909. 1 fiche – 9 – us A.T.L.A. [240]
THE ORIGINS OF CHRISIANITY / Bigg, Charles; ed by Strong, Thomas Banks – Oxford; New York: Clarendon Press, 1909 – 2mf – us A.T.L.A. [240]
ORIGINS OF LIFE – (v14-. 1984-. 5,6,9) – v5-14. 1974-84 – 1 – us UMI [577]
ORIGINS OF LIFE AND EVOLUTION OF THE BIOSPHERE – v15-. May 1984- – 1,5,6,9 – us UMI [577]
THE ORIGINS OF LOVE AND HATE / Suttie, Ian Dishart – London: K. Paul, Trench, Trubner, 1935. xvi,275p. diagrs – 1 – us U.W. Library [150]
ORIGINS OF MODERN FEMINISM – Part One: Diaries of Constance Maynard, feminist campaigner and founder of Westfield College, London – 1 – us Primary [920]
ORIGINS OF THE ELEMENTS OF FEDERAL COURT GOVERNANCE / Wheeler, Russell R – Washington: FJC, 1992 – 1mf – 9 – $1.50 – LLMC 95-364 – us L.L.M.C. [340]
ORIGINS OF THE WELFARE STATE IN BRITAIN / Great Britain. Unemployment Assistance Board – Minutes and memoranda of the Unemployment Assistance Board. PRO Class AST12, Files 1-25, 28-32, and 48-57 – 1 – us Primary [941]
ORIGINUM CISTERCIENSUM / Janauschek, PL – Vindobonae. Tomus 1. 1877 – 17mf – 8 – Dfl60.00 – ne Slangenburg [240]
ORIGINUM GALLICARUM LIBER... CUI ACCEDIT ANTIQUAE BRITTANICAE, LEXICON BRITTANNICO-LATINUM... / Boxhorn, MZ – Amstelodami, 1654 – 3mf – 9 – HL-8/1 – ne IDC [014]
L'ORIGNAL DECHAINE : UNIVERSITE LAURENTIENNE – Sudbury, Canada. sep 1987-v5 n12. 31 mar 1992 – 1r – 1 – cn Can Microfilming [072]
ORINDA : THE LITERARY MANUSCRIPTS OF KATHERINE PHILIPS (1631-1664) – (Includes Guide) – Marlborough: Adam Matthew Publications, 1995 – 4r – 1 – $490.00 – uk Matthew [420]
EL ORINOCO...ILUSTRADO / Gumilla, Jose – 1745 – 9 – 1.50f – sp Bibl Santa Ana [972]
Oriol Moncanut, Ana Maria *see* LA ENSENANZA EN BARCELONA A FINES DEL SIGLO 18
ORION : AN EPIC POEM IN THREE BOOKS / Horne, Richard H – London: J. Miller, 3rd ed 1843 – 1 roll – 1 – 1-55879-722-X – uk Libr Preservation [810]
ORION : A MONTHLY MAGAZINE OF LITERATURE AND ART – v1-4. Mar 1842-Aug 1844 – 1 – us UMI [073]
Orishin, A D *see*
– BELINSKII I RUSSKAIA LITERATURA 18 VEKA
– KHRESTOMATIIA KRITICHESKIKH MATERIALOV PO RUSSKOI LITERATURE 18 VEKA
ORISSA AND ITS EVANGELIZATION : INTERSPERSED WITH SUGGESTIONS RESPECTING THE MORE EFFICIENT CONDUCTING OF INDIAN MISSIONS / Sutton, Amos – Boston: W. Heath, 1850 – 1mf – us A.T.L.A. [240]
ORISSA GAZETTE / Orissa. India (State) – Cuttack. Index. 1936-1942, 1946-1966 – 1 – us NY Public [072]
ORISSA HISTORICAL RESEARCH JOURNAL – Bhubaneswar. v1-16. 1952-68 – 83mf – 9 – ne IDC [950]
Orissa Historical Research Society *see* JOURNAL
ORISSA HOMEOPATHIC BULLETIN – 1969- 1; 1972- 5,6; 1975- 4 x 6 in. 9 – us UMI [615]
Orissa. India (State) *see*
– ORISSA GAZETTE
– POST-WAR DEVELOPMENT IN ORISSA
Orissa. India (State). Advisory Council *see* SUMMARY OF PROCEEDINGS, 1936
Orissa. India (State). Legislative Assembly *see* DEBATES
ORKESTR – Moscow, 1910-12 (bimonthly) – 9mf – 9 – us Ross [780]
ORKNEY AND SHETLAND AMERICAN – 1887-1895 – 1. 118 – £42.00r – uk Scot News [072]
ORKNEY AND SHETLAND JOURNAL – Kirkwall, Scotland. Jan 1838-Aug 1839 – 1r – 1 – uk British Libr Newspaper [072]
ORKNEY AND ZETLAND CHRONICLE – 1824-1826 – 1. 119 – £42.00r – uk Scot News [072]
ORKNEY HERALD – Kirkwall, Scotland. 5 Jun 1860-10 Jan 1961 – 78r – 1 – uk British Libr Newspaper [072]
ORKNEY ISLES, 1837 : BRITISH ISLES CENSUS DIRECTORIES PROJECT, SCOTLAND. VOL 47 – 1mf – 9 – A$9.00 – at Vine [941]
ORKNEY ISLES, 1852 : BRITISH ISLES CENSUS DIRECTORIES PROJECT, SCOTLAND. VOL 17 – 1mf – 9 – A$9.00 – at Vine [941]
ORKNEY ISLES, 1915 : BRITISH ISLES CENSUS DIRECTORIES PROJECT, SCOTLAND. VOL 10 – 1mf – 9 – A$9.00 – at Vine [941]
ORL – v37-. 1975- – 1,5,9 – us UMI [610]
ORL (OTORHINOLARYNGOLOGY) DIGEST – 1971-77 – 1. 1975$77.: ; 5,6,9 – us UMI [073]
ORLAND PARK STAR TRIBUNE – Chicago Heights. Ill. 1972- – 1 – us UMI [071]
ORLAND PRESS – Orland, CA. Sept 1976-1977 – 2r – 1 – $100.00 – B02561 – us Library Micro [071]
ORLAND PRESS-REGISTER – Orland, CA. 1983- – 19+ r – 1 – $950.00 ($120.00y) – B02562 – us Library Micro [071]
Orlandi, Pellegrino Antonio *see* ABCEDARIO PITTORICO
ORLANDO / Woolf, Virginia – (Ms.) – 1 – uk Microform Academic [830]
ORLANDO FURIOSO DI M. LODOVICO ARIOSTO,... / Ariosto, Lodovico – Venetia: V. Valgrisi, 1580 – fr Armell [945]
ORLEANS 1637-1892 – (Mf 1-5: Orleans/ Eastham Records 1637-1853. Mf 6-8: Orleans/Eastham B,M,I,D 1743-98. Mf 9-12: Orleans/Eastham Accts & Deaths 1765-1840. Mf 13-14: Orleans/Eastham Marriages 1764-1844. Mf 15-17: Orleans/Eastham Marriage Intentions 1763-1905. Mf 18: B.M.D 1844-50. Mf 19-20: Births 1851-92. Mf 21-23: Marriages & Deaths 1851-92. Mf 24: Birth Index 1851-92. Mf 25-26: Marriage Index 1851-92. Mf 27-28: Index to Deaths 1851-92) – (mf ed 1987) – 28mf – 9 – 0-931248-99-X – us Holbrook [920]
ORLEANS CHRONICLE – Orleans, NE. -w. Jun 1982-Apr 1898, scattered issues missing; May 1901-Jul 1906; Sep 1907-Nov 1918; Apr 1920-Mar 1927; Jul 1927-Mar 1961 – 1 – us NE Hist [071]
Orleans, Duc d'... *see* HISTOIRE DE LOUIS-PHILIPPE-JOSEPH, DUC D'ORLEANS
ORLEANS ENTERPRISE – Orleans, NE. -w. Apr 1936-Sep 1939 – 1 – us NE Hist [071]
ORLEANS PROGRESS – Orleans, NE. -w. Oct 1895-Feb 1896, scattered issues missing; Apr 1896-Jul 1898 – 1 – us NE Hist [071]
Orleanskii, V L *see* AGRO-KOOPERATIVNYI KRUZHOK
Orliac, C *see* MATERIAUX POUR L'ETUDE DES HABITATIONS PROTO-HISTORIQUES A TAHITI
Orlov, Aleksandr Sergeevich *see* SOMOSTROI PO KONSHINSKOMU SPISKU I PODOBNYM
Orlov, N A *see* KOOPERATIV V RABOTE
Orlov, V N *see*
– ALEXANDER BLOK
– PUTI I SUD'BY
– RUSSKIE PROSVETITELI 1790-1800-KH GODOV
Orlov-Davydov, V *see* BIOGRAFICHESKII OCHERK V.G. ORLOVA
L'ORMA DEL LEONE / Prato, Stanislau – 1883 – 1 – us I.U. Libraries [390]
Ormanian, Malachia *see* THE CHURCH OF ARMENIA
Ormer, Abraham Brower Bunn van *see* STUDIES IN RELIGIOUS NURTURE
Ormerod, E A *see* A MANUAL OF INJURIOUS INSECTS
Ormsby, K A *see* PERCEPTIONS AND ATTITUDES OF DEAF AND HEARING STUDENTS IN INTEGRATED PHYSICAL EDUCATION CLASSES
Ormsby. Nevada *see* ASSESSORS RECORDERS
THE ORMSTOWN BULLETIN AND DISTRICT OF BEAUHARNOIS ADVERTISER – Ormstown, Canada. 19 dec 1895; 13 aut 1925; v38 n21. 26 mai 1932 – 1r – 1 – Can$25.00 – cn Can Microfilming [072]
THE ORMSTOWN COURIER – Ormstown, Canada. v10 n2. 12 jan 1882-v14 n37. 14 oct 1886 – 1r – 1 – Can$40.00 – cn Can Microfilming [072]
THE ORMSTOWN RECORD – Ormstown, Canada. 6 sep 1888-v4 n2. 17 sep 1891 – 1r – 1 – Can$45.00 – cn Can Microfilming [072]
Orne. France (Department) *see* DESCRIPTION ABREGEE DU DEPARTEMENT DE L'ORNE, REDIGEE PAR LE LYCEE D'ALENCON
ORNIS : INTERNATIONALE ZEITSCHRIFT FUER DIE GESAMMTE ORNITHOLOGIE – (Cont as: Ornis, Bulletin du Comite Ornithologique International, Paris v9-12 1898-1904. Cont as: Ornis, Journal of the International Ornithological Committee, London v13 1905-10) – Wien. v1-8. 1885-96 – 138mf – 9 – ne IDC [590]
ORNIS, BULLETIN DU COMITE ORNITHOLOGIQUE *see* ORNIS
ORNIS CAUCASICA / Radde, G FR – Z 1881. 1884 – 9 – ne IDC [590]
ORNIS, JOURNAL OF THE INTERNATIONAL ORNITHOLOGICAL COMMITTEE *see* ORNIS
ORNITHOGRAPHIA ROSSICA. ORNITHOLOGICESKAJA ROSSIJSKOJ IMPERII. DIE VOGEL-FAUNA DES RUSSISCHEN REICHS / Pleske, Th. D – Text in Russian and German. Z 1879. v. 2. (v. 1 not published). 1889-1891 – 9 – ne IDC [590]
ORNITHOLOGIA / Savi, P – Z 1902. 3 v. 1827-1831 – 9 – ne IDC [590]
ORNITHOLOGIA DELLA PAPUASIA E DELLE MOLUCCHE / Salvador, T A – 3v. Torino. 1880-82. BZ-1899 2 – 62mf – 8 – ne IDC [590]
ORNITHOLOGIA ITALIANA / Savi, P – Z 1903. 3 v. 1873-1876 77 – 9 – ne IDC [590]
ORNITHOLOGIA SICILIANA / Benoit, L – Z-345 2. 1840 – 8 – ne IDC [590]
ORNITHOLOGIA SIVE SYNOPSIS METHODICA / Brisson, M J – 6v. Z-364 2. 1760 – 8 – ne IDC [590]
ORNITHOLOGIA SVECICA / Nilsson, S – Z-1873. 2 pts. 1817-1821 – 9 – ne IDC [590]
ORNITHOLOGIAE SPECIMEN NOVUM / Barrere, P – Z 342. 1745 – 9 – ne IDC [590]
ORNITHOLOGICAL DICTIONARY / Montagu, G – 1802 – 8 – Z-1859 2 – ne IDC [590]
ORNITHOLOGICAL DICTIONARY... / Montagu, G – (Suppl. Exeter, 1813) – London, 1802 – 10mf – ne IDC [590]
ORNITHOLOGICAL MISCELLANY / Rowley, G D – Z 1896. 3 v. 1876-1878 – 9 – ne IDC [590]
ORNITHOLOGICAL SYNONYMS / Strickland, Hugh Edwin; ed by Strickland, Hugh Edwin & Jardine, W – London, 1855 – 5mf – ne IDC [590]
ORNITHOLOGIE D'ANGOLA / Barboza du Bocage, J V – Z-341 2. 1881 – 8 – ne IDC [590]
ORNITHOLOGIE DE LA SAVOIE / Bailly, J B – 4v. Z-337 2. 1853-1854 – 8 – ne IDC [590]
ORNITHOLOGIE DU PEROU / Taczanowski, W – Z 119 2. 3 v. 1884-1886 – 8 – ne IDC [590]
ORNITHOLOGIE NORDOST-AFRIKA'S / Heuglin, M Th. von – Z 1803. 4 v. 1869-1874 – 9 – ne IDC [590]
ORNITHOLOGIE. SUN-BIRDS / Jardine, W – v. 5 of The naturalist's library. Z 1812. 1843 – 9 – ne IDC [590]
ORNITHOLOGISCHE FRAGMENTE / Petenyi, S J von – Z-1878 2. 1905 – 8 – ne IDC [590]
ORNITHOLOGISCHE MONATSBERICHTE – Berlin. v1-28. 1893-1920 – 109mf – 9 – ne IDC [590]
ORNITHOLOGISCHER ATLAS... DER AUSSEREUROPAEISCHEN VOEGEL / Hahn, C W & Kuester, H C – Nuernberg. 17pts. 1834-1841 – 8mf – ne IDC [590]
ORNITHOLOGISCHER BEITRAG ZUR FAUNA GROENLANDS / Holboll, C P – Transl. by J. H. Paulsen. Leipzig. 1846. BZ-1804 2 – 8 – ne IDC [590]
ORNITHOLOGISCHES CENTRALBLATT : ORGAN FUER WISSENSCHAFT UND ... BEIBLATT ZUM 'JOURNAL FUER ORNITHOLOGIE' / ed by Cabanis, J & Reichenow, A – Leipzig, etc. v1-7. 1876-82 – 45mf – 9 – Z-2033/2 – ne IDC [590]
ORNITHOLOGISCHES JAHRBUCH : ORGAN FUER DAS PALAEARKTISCHE FAUNENGEBIET – Halle. 1890-1918 – 135mf – 8 – ne IDC [590]
ORNITHOLOGY – CATALOGUE *see* AVIUM GENERA
ORNITHOLOGY – DICTIONARY *see* ORNITHOLOGICAL DICTIONARY
ORNITHOLOGY – GENERAL *see*
– BIRDS OF THE BAHAMA ISLANDS
– THE BIRDS OF THE WEST INDIES
– CATALOGUE OF WEST INDIAN BIRDS
ORNITHOLOGY – GERMANY *see* TASCHENBUCH DER DEUTSCHEN VOEGELKUNDE
THE ORNITHOLOGY OF THE STRAITS OF GIBRALTAR / Irby, H L – Z 1809. Ed.2. 1895 – 9 – ne IDC [590]
ORNITHOLOGY – U.S. *see* AMERICAN ORNITHOLOGY
Ornithoparchus, Andrea *see* MUSICE ACTIVE MICROLOGUS
Ornithoparcus, Andrea *see*
– CONTAINING THE ART OF SINGING
– HIS MICROLOGVS
– MUSICAE ACTIVAE MICROLOGUS ANDREAE ORNITOPARCHI OSTROFRANCI MEYNINGENSIS, ARTIUM MAGISTRI, LIBRO QUATUOR DIGESTUS...
Ornitz, Lou *see* CAPTURED BY FRANCO
ORNIZHOLOGY – GENERAL *see* THE BIRDS OF EASTERN NORTH AMERICA
Ornsby, Robert *see* MEMOIRS OF JAMES ROBERT HOPE-SCOTT OF ABBOTSFORD, D.C.L., Q.C.
ORNSKOLDSVIKS ALLEHANDA – Ornskoldsvik, Sweden. 1949-78 – 204r – 1 – sw Kungliga [072]

ORNSKOLDSVIKS ALLEHANDA – Ornskoldsvik, Sweden. 1979- – 1 – sw Kungliga [072]
Oro, Buenaventura *see* FRAY LUIS BOLANOS, APOSTOL DEL PARAGUAY Y DEL RIO DE LA PLATA. CORDOBA (TUCUMAN). 1934
Orobio, Isaac *see* ISRAEL VENGE. OU EXPOSITION NATURELLE DES PROPHETIES HEBRAIQUE QUE LES CHRETIENS APPLIQUENT A JESUS, LEUR PRETENDU MISSIE
ORONOKO / Behn, Aphra – Amsterdam, 1745. 2v. (Les Femmes Collection) – 4mf – 9 – $10.00 – fr Bibl Nationale [830]
Oropesa, Manuel, y otros *see* RESPUESTA A...MONASTERIOS DE GUADALUPE...ESCORIAL
O'Rorke, Benjamin Garniss *see* AFRICAN MISSIONS
OROSI PROGRESS – Orosi, CA. May 1913-Oct 1914 (broken series) – 1r – 1 – $50.00 – B02567 – us Library Micro [071]
Orosius *see* HISTORIAE
O'Rourke, John *see* THE HISTORY OF THE GREAT IRISH FAMINE OF 1847, WITH NOTICES OF EARLIER IRISH FAMINES
OROVILLE REGISTER – Oroville, CA. 1887-96; 1898-1903 – 6r – 1 – $300.00 – B02577 – us Library Micro [071]
Orozco, Alfonso de *see*
- DECLAMATIONES IN OMNES SOLEMNITATES...
- DECLAMATIONES VINTIGINQUE IN EVANGELIA.
- DECLAMATIONES...DOMINICIS
- OBRAS
- RECOPILACION DE LAS OBRAS..

Orozco Avelianeda, Agustin J *see* PONENCIA PARA LA ASAMBLEA DE COLEGIO (DE PRACTICANTES DEL DIA 22 DE NOVIEMBRE DE 1944 PRESENTADA PRO EL PRESIDENTE...
Orozco y Arascot, Andres de *see* CODIGO PENAL DE 1879
Orozco y Berra, Manuel *see* HISTORIA DE LA DOMINACION ESPANOLA EN MEJICO
L'ORPHELINE DE MOSCOU OU LA JEUNE INSTITUTRICE / Woillez, Catherine – Tours: A. Mame, 1909. 240p. 3 fiches. (Literature Collection) – 9 – 8.00 – fr Bibl Nationale [830]
LES ORPHELINS ARABES D'ALGER: LEUR PASSE, LEUR PRESENT, LEUR AVENIR: OEUVRE DE LEUR ADOPTION / Charmetant, Felix – 1875. 02979. (Pre-1900 Canadiana) – 9 – cn C.I.H.M. [360]
ORPHEUS – New York City, Boston. v1-12. 1865-77 – 2r – 1 – £115.00 – uk Chadwyck [780]
ORPHEUS AND OTHER POEMS / Brownlow, Edward Burrough – Montreal: Pen and Pencil Club, 1896. 00287. (Pre-1900 Canadiana) – 9 – cn C.I.H.M. [810]
ORPHEUS, DER DICHTER UND DIE TOTEN : SELBSTDEUTUNG UND TOTENKULT BEI NOVALIS, HOELDERLIN, RILKE – Duesseldorf: L Schwann, 1950 – 1r – 1 – us U.W. Library [430]
ORPHEUS EUCHARISTICUS / Chesneau, Augustin – O-202. 1657 – 9 – ne IDC [290]
Orphicorum Fragmenta *see* COLLEGIT OTTO KERN
ORPINGTON AND KENTISH TIMES *see* ORPINGTON, ST MARY CRAY AND KENTISH TIMES
ORPINGTON, ST MARY CRAY AND KENTISH TIMES – (Orpington & Kentish Times, Mar 1962-) – London, UK. 1932-69; 1972-Nov 1978; 1984- – 155+ r – 1 – uk British Libr Newspaper [072]
Orpwood, Graham *see* SCIENCE AND TECHNOLOGY IN THE PRIMARY SCHOOL OF TOMORROW
ORQUESTA FILARMONICA MORAVA DE OLOMONE-SINFONICA DEL ESTADO / Caceres: Universidad Laboral Hispanoamericana – Caceres: Imp. La Minerva, 1977 – sp Bibl Santa Ana [780]
Orr, James *see*
- THE BIBLE UNDER TRIAL: IN VIEW OF PRESENT-DAY ASSAULTS ON HOLY SCRIPTURE
- THE PROBLEM OF OLD TESTAMENT CRITICISM
- THE RESURRECTION OF JESUS
- THE VIRGIN BIRTH OF CHRIST

Orrego Vicuna, Eugenio *see* EL LIBERTADO O'HIGGINS Y EL GENERAL DE LA CRUZ
Orsini, B *see*
- MEMOIRE DE' PITTORI PERUGINI DEL SEC. 28
- VITA, ELOGIO E MEMORIE DELL' EGREGIO PITTORE PIETRO PERUGINO F. DEGLI SCOLARI DI ESSO

Orsini, Mathieu *see* VIERGE
ORSTROM *see* DIRECTION DES ETUDES DU DEVELOPPEMENT
ORSZAGOS EVANGELIKUS HETILAP *see* EVANGELIKUS ELET; ORSZAGOS EVANGELIKUS HETILAP
ORSZAGOS REFORMATUS HETILAP *see* REFORMATUSOK LAPJA; ORSZAGOS REFORMATUS HETILAP
ORT YEDIES = O.R.T. NEWS – (In Yiddish) – Munich, DE. no40. 1 Dec 1948 – 1r – 1 – $25.00 – cn Can Microfilming [072]
Ortac, Yusuf Ziya *see* YANAR DAG
Ortega, Angel *see* FLORIANO, ANTONIO. LA IGLESIA DE SANTIAGO DE LOS CABALLEROS EN CACERES
Ortega, C G (de) *see* NOVARUM AUT RAIORUM PLANTARUM HORTI REG. BOTAN. MATRITENSIS DESCRIPTIONUM
Ortega, J *see*
- ELOGIO HISTORICO DEL...DOCTOR JOSEPH CERVI...
- TRATADO SUBTILISSIMO DE ARITMETICA Y GEOMETRIA...

Ortega Munilla, Jose *see* VIAJE...CACERES
Ortega Sanchez, Luis Miguel *see* EL PARQUE
Ortega y Cotes, Ignacio *see* BULLARIUM... ALCANTARA...PEREIRO
Ortello, A *see* THEATRO DE LA TIERRA UNIVERSAL
Orth, Samuel P *see* HISTORY OF CLEVELAND
ORTHODOX BAPTIST SEARCHLIGHT – Nov. 4, 1935-Mar 25, 1973. Formerly Missionary Baptist Searchlight. 6,302p – 1 – 220.57 – us Baptist [240]
ORTHODOX CHURCH IN AMERICA : YEARBOOK AND CHURCH DIRECTORY – 1971-91 (complete) – Inquire – 1 – ATLA S0655 – us A.T.L.A. [240]
THE ORTHODOX CHURCH OF THE EAST IN THE EIGHTEENTH CENTURY : BEING THE CORRESPONDENCE BETWEEN THE EASTERN PATRIARCHS AND THE NONJURING BISHOPS / Williams, George – London: Rivingtons, 1868 – 1mf – us A.T.L.A. [240]
THE ORTHODOX DOCTRINE OF THE APOSTOLIC EASTERN CHURCH OR, A COMPENDIUM OF CHRISTIAN THEOLOGY – London: Whittaker, 1857 – 1mf – us A.T.L.A. [240]
THE ORTHODOX EASTERN CHURCH / Fortescue, Adrian – London: Catholic Truth Society, 1911 – 2mf – us A.T.L.A. [240]
THE ORTHODOX LIFE – 1950-89 (complete) – 6r – 1 – ATLA S0386 – us A.T.L.A. [073]
ORTHODOX PATHS RETRACED : OR, THE OLD THEOLOGY: IN A SERIES OF ESSAYS, LETTERS, AND LECTURES / Williston, Timothy – New York: Wilford Hall, 1884 – 1mf – 9 – 0-8370-5752-3 – 1985-3752 – us A.T.L.A. [200]
THE ORTHODOX THEOLOGY OF TO-DAY / Smyth, Newman – NY: Charles Scribner, 1881 – 1mf – 9 – 0-8370-5392-7 – 1985-3392 – us A.T.L.A. [240]
ORTHODOXA DE EXORCISMO A QVIBVSDAM ECCLESIIS AVGVSTANAM CONFESSIONEM AMPLECTENTIBUS IN BAPTISMI ADMINISTRATIONE... / Hoffmann, David – N.p., 1591 – 1mf – ne IDC [240]
ORTHODOXIE UND PIETISMUS IM KAMPF UM DIE PREDIGT : EIN BEITRAG ZUR GESCHICHTE DES ENDENDEN 17. UND DES BEGINNENDEN 18. JAHRHUNDERTS / Schian, Martin – Giessen: A. Toepelmann, 1912 – 1mf – us A.T.L.A. [240]
ORTHODOXY AND HETERODOXY : A MISCELLANY / Shedd, William Greenough Thayer – (Includes bibliographical references) – New York: Charles Scribner, 1893 – 1mf – 9 – 0-8370-5382-X – 1985-3382 – us A.T.L.A. [230]
ORTHODOXY IN MASSACHUSETTS 1630-1650 / Miller, P – New York, 1970 – 7mf – 8 – ne Slangenburg [240]
ORTHODOXY IN MASSACHUSETTS, 1630-1650 / Miller, Perry – 1 – 12.88 – us Baptist [240]
ORTHODOXY, WITH PRELUDES ON CURRENT EVENTS / Cook, Joseph – Boston: Houghton, Mifflin, c1878 – 1mf – us A.T.L.A. [240]
AN ORTHOGRAPHIE, CONTEYNING THE DUE ORDER AND REASON / Hart, John – 1569. 160p. (English Linguistics Series 1500-1800) – 9 – us UMI [420]
DER ORTHOPAEDE – v. 1-9. 1972-80 – 1,5,9 – 662.00 – us UMI [617]
ORTHOPEDICS DIGEST – (See also: Journal of Continuing Education in Orthopedics) – v2-5 1974-77 1,5,6; v3-5 9 – us UMI [617]
ORTHOPIA ANGLICANA: OR, THE FIRST PRINCIPALL PART OF THE ENGLISH GRAMMAR / Daines, Simon – 1640. 122p. (English Linguistics Series 1500-1800) – 9 – us UMI [420]
ORTHOPOLITAN – Parkersburg. West Virginia. 1873-1875 – 1 – us UMI [071]
ORTHOPTERA DESCRIPTA ET DEPICTA / Charpentier, T von – Lipsiae, 1841-45. 60 pls. Z-1133/2 – 8 – ne IDC [590]
ORTHOPTERA EUROPAEA / Fischer, L H – Lipsiae, 1853. xx,454p,18pls. Z/1248/2 – 8 – ne IDC [590]
LES ORTHOPTERES DE LA FRANCE / Finot, P A P – Paris, 1883 – 199p, 1pl – 8 – ne IDC [590]
Orti Belmonte, Miguel Angel *see*
- CACERES BAJO LA REINA CATOLICA Y SU CAMARERO SANCHO PAREDES GOLFIN
- LAS CONQUISTAS DE CACERES POR FERNANDO 2 Y ALFONSO 9 DE LEON Y SU FUERO LATINO ANOTADO
- EPISCOPOLOGIO CAURIENSE
- FUNDACIONES BENFICAS DE LA PROVINCIA DE CACERES ANTERIORES A 1850
- HISTORIA DEL CULTO Y SAN TUARIO DE NUESTRA SENORA DE LA MONTANA PATRONA DE CACERES
- HISTORIA DEL CULTO Y SANTUARIO DE NUESTRA SENORA DE LA MONTANA
- LOS OVANDO Y SOLIS DE CACERES
- LA VIDA EN CACERES EN LOS SIGLOS 12 Y 16 AL 18

Ortique, Joseph Louis d' *see* DU THEATRE ITALIEN
Ortiz Cantero, Jose *see*
- DIRECTORIO CATHECHISTICO...ROIPALDA
- DIRECTORIO CATHEQUISTICO DEL CHRISTIANO ILUSTRADO EN LA FE CON LA GLOSA UNIVERSAL DE LA DOCTRINA CHRISTIANA...
- DIRECTORIO PARRAQUIAL
- DIRECTORIO PARROQUIAL, PRACTICA DE CONCURSOS Y DE CURAS...

Ortiz, Dionisio *see*
- CHAUCHAMAYO. ESTUDIO DE UNA REGION DE LA SELVA DEL PERU. DEPARTAMENTO... TOMO 1. LIMA, 1969
- OXAPAMPA, VISION HISTORICA Y DESARROLLO DE OXAPAMPA EN EL DEPARTAMENTO DE PASCO. TOMO 1. LIMA, 1967

Ortiz, Fernando *see* HAMPA AFRO-CUBANA. LOS NEGROS BRUJOS (APUNTES PARA UN ESTUDIO DE ETNOLOGIA CRIMINAL)
Ortiz, G *see* MADRID. BIBLIOTECA NACIONAL. CATALOGO DE INCUNABLES
Ortiz, M *see* DISCURSO...SOBRE LA EPIDEMIA DE PAMPLONA
Ortiz, Vickie J *see* CURRENT RULE LISTINGS OF NEW MEXICO STATE AGENCIES
Ortiz y Gutierrez, Luis Felipe *see* CARTA PASTORA
Ortner, Eugen *see* MEIER HELMBRECHT
ORTODOXIA – (Lacking: v1-2,6,10) – v3-40. 1951-88 – 19r – 1 – ATLA S0357 – us A.T.L.A. [073]
L'ORTOGRAFE FRANCAISE / Girard – 1716 – 9 – fr I.C.S. [440]
L'ORTOGRAFE FRANCOISE / Blegny, E de – 1667 – 9 – fr I.C.S. [440]
ORTOGRAFIA / Academia Espanola – 1763, 3rd ed – 1mf – 9 – Pta1,000.00 – 84-7848-126-5 – sp Pentalfa [946]
ORTOGRAFIA ESPANOLA. COLEGIO DE SAN JOSE, VILLAFRANCA (BADAJOZ) / Hernandez, Mariano – Toledo: Editorial Catolica Toledana, 1942 – 1 – sp Bibl Santa Ana [946]
ORTOGRAFIA KASTELLANA...EL MANUAL EPIKTETO / Correas, Gonzalo – 1630 – 9 – 1.50f – sp Bibl Santa Ana [440]
ORTOGRAFIA Y REGLAS DE LENGUA TAGALAG, ORDENADA POR... / Castro, Pedro Andres de – Madrid, 1930; Madrid: Razon y Fe, 1931 – 1 – sp Bibl Santa Ana [340]
Orton Dyslexia Society *see* ANNALS OF DYSLEXIA
Orton, Richard H *see* RECORDS OF CALIFORNIA MEN IN THE WAR OF THE REBELLION 1861-1867
ORTSAUFLOESENDE TEMPERATURMESSUNG IM NIEDRIGFELD- UND HOCHFELD KERNSPINTOMOGRAPHEN UND UNTERSUCHUNG DER MOEGLICHKEIT ZUR ANWENDUNG IN DER INTRA-TUMORALEN LASERTHERAPIE / Friebe, Michael Horst – 1995 – 2mf – 9 – DM80.00 – 3-8267-2187-X – gw Hänsel [616]
ORTUS VOCABULORUM – Anon. 1500. 486p. (English Linguistics Series 1500-1800) – 9 – us UMI [450]
ORVILLE COLLEGE / Wood, Ellen – British Fiction Archive: Unit 1 – 9 – uk Bell [830]
Orville, Glenn *see* THE ENGLISH CLASSIFICATION TESTS
ORWELL BAPTIST CHURCH. ORWELL, VERMONT : CHURCH RECORDS – 1787-1865 – 1 – 19.89 – us Baptist [240]
ORWIGSBURG NEWS – Orwigsburg, PA. 1889-1951. 12 rolls – 13 – $25.00r – us I.M.R. [071]
ORYCTOGRAPHIE DU GOUVERNEMENT DE MOSCOU / Fischer von Waldheim, G – G-105 2. 1830-1837 – 8 – ne IDC [335]
ORZEL POLSKI – Washington, Franklin Co, MO: [s.n., feb 23 1870-1972] – us Res Libr [071]
OS = LETTER – (In Yiddish) – Lodz, PL. no5 1937-no1 1938 – 1r – 1 – $25.00 – cn Can Microfilming [072]
OS DEFUNCTOS : PERIODICO POLITICO E SATYRICO – [s.l.]. 3 Out-Dez 1868; Jan-Abr 1869 – 1,5,6 – bl Biblioteca [072]
OSAGE COUNTY CHRONICLE – Burlingame. Kan. 1863-1919 – 1 – us UMI [071]
Osage County. Kansas. Elk Township *see* RECORDS
Osage County. Kansas. School District 16 *see* RECORDS
OSAGE MISSIONS / Society of Jesus. Missouri Province – 1832-88 – 1 – us KS Hist [978]
OSAKA MAINICHI : ENGLISH DAILY EDITION – Tokyo, Osaka, Japan. 1 Jul 1922-11 Aug 1925 – 7r – 1 – uk British Libr Newspaper [072]
OSAMU KANPO – (Lacking: 1943(1-7, 10); 1945(30)) – Djakarta, Jawa Gunseikanbu, 1943-1945(31) – 375-389mf – 9 – ne IDC [073]
OSAR LESON HAQ-QODES, HOC EST, THESAVRVS LINGVAE SANCTAE... / Pagninus, S – Lvgd.[vni]. [1529] – 24mf – ne IDC [400]
OSB SCRIPTORES QUI 1750-1880 FUERUNT IN IMPERIO AUSTRIACO-HUNGARICO – Vindobonae, 1881 – Dfl63.00 – ne Slangenburg [240]
Osbeck, P *see* DAGBOK OA5FVER EN OA5STENDISK RESA AA'REN 1750-1752
Osberghaus, Michael *see* NATURSCHUTZ DURCH NATURSCHUTZVERWALTUNGEN?
Osborn, Albert Sherman *see*
- JOHN FLETCHER HURST
- THE PROBLEM OF PROOF, ESPECIALLY AS EXEMPLIFIED IN DISPUTED DOCUMENT TRIALS.

Osborn, Charles B *see* FRENCH PHILOLOGY
Osborn, G *see*
- OUTLINES OF WESLEYAN BIBLIOGRAPHY
- OUTLINES OF WESLEYAN BIBLIOGRAPHY; OR, A RECORD OF METHODIST LITERATURE FROM THE BEGINNING, IN TWO PARTS:...

Osborn, Henry Fairfield *see* EVOLUTION AND RELIGION
Osborn, Henry Stafford *see* A CLASS-BOOK OF BIBLICAL HISTORY AND GEOGRAPHY
Osborn, Loran David *see* THE RECOVERY AND RESTATEMENT OF THE GOSPEL
Osborn, M C *see*
- AN ALPHABETICAL ARRANGEMENT OF ALL THE WESLEYAN-METHODIST MINISTERS, AND PREACHERS ON TRIAL, IN CONNECTION WITH THE BRITISH AND IRISH CONFERENCES
- AN ALPHABETICAL ARRANGEMENT OF ALL THE WESLEYAN-METHODIST MINISTERS, AND PREACHERS ON TRIAL, IN CONNECTION WITH THE BRITISH AND IRISH CONFERENCES;
- AN ALPHABETICAL ARRANGEMENT OF ALL THE WESLEYAN-METHODIST MINISTERS AND PREACHERS ON TRIAL, IN CONNECTION WITH THE BRITISH AND IRISH CONFERENCES

Osborn, Sh *see* STRAY LEAVES FROM AN ARCTIC JOURNAL
OSBORN STAR – Fairborn. Ohio. and Local. 1881-1916 – 1 – us UMI [071]
Osborn, Thomas *see* A RATIONAL WAY OF TEACHING ...OF THE ENGLISH TONGUE

Osborne City Town Company, Osborne, KS see MINUTE BOOK

Osborne County. Kansas. Superintendent of Schools see RECORDS

Osborne, John H see
- CRUCIFIXION
- FOUR BIBLE STUDIES: SHAMELESSNESS, REVENGE, PRAYER, FIDELITY

Osborne. Kansas. First Congregational Church see RECORDS

Osborne, Nigel see CONTEMPORARY MUSIC REVIEW

Osborne, Thomas Mott see
- SOCIETY AND PRISONS
- WITHIN PRISON WALLS

Osborne, William Alexander see THE REVISED VERSION OF THE NEW TESTAMENT

OSBORN-FAIRBORN HERALD – Fairborn. Ohio. -w. 1941-50 – 1 – us UMI [071]

Osbourn, James see OLD SCHOOL SONNETS, OR A SELECTION OF CHOICE HYMNS

Osbourne, Lloyd see
- THE EBB TIDE
- THE WRECKER
- THE WRONG BOX

OSCAR, FILS D'OSSIAN / Arnault – (French Theatre Series). Paris. DuPont, an IV. 1796 – 9 – fr Hachette [820]

OSCARSHAMNS TIDNING – Oskarshamn, Sweden. 1857-59 – 1 reel – 1 – sw Kungliga [072]

OSCARSHAMNSPOSTEN – Oskarshamn, Sweden. 1862-1923 – 1 – sw Kungliga [072]

OSCEOLA RECORD – Osceola, NE. -w. Aug 1873-Oct 1893, scattered issues missing; Jan 1894-Dec 1917; Mar 1919 to date – 1 – us NE Hist [071]

OSCEOLA SUN – Kissimmee. Fl. 1970- – 1 – us UMI [071]

Osenbaugh Family see OSENBAUGH FAMILY GENEALOGY NOTES

OSENBAUGH FAMILY GENEALOGY NOTES / Osenbaugh Family – 1793-1988 – 1r – 1 – $32.50r – us Archival [920]

OSENNIIA OZERA / Kuzmin, M – Vtoraia kniga stikhov. M. 1912. BR-1194 2 – 8 – ne IDC [460]

Osgood, C see THE ETHNOGRAPHY OF THE TANAINA. NEW HAVEN

Osgood, Elliott Irving see BREAKING DOWN CHINESE WALLS

Osgood, Howard see
- QUOTATIONS OF THE OLD TESTAMENT IN THE NEW TESTAMENT
- A REASONABLE HYPOTHESIS OF THE ORIGIN OF THE PENTATEUCH
- REFERENCES TO THE VERSIONS BY THE BRITISH REVISERS COMPARED WITH THE VERSIONS

Osgood, Howard et al see ANTI-HIGHER CRITICISM

Osgood, William Newton see EMPLOYERS' LIABILITY

OSGOODE HALL LAW JOURNAL – (v1-22 1958-84 on reel $280.00. v23-32 1985-94 on mf $322.00) – York University. v1-32. 1958-94 – 5,6,9 – $402.00 set – us Hein [340]

O'Shaughnessy, William Brooke see THE BENGAL DISPENSATORY: CHIEFLY COMPILED FROM THE WORKS OF ROXBURGH, WALLICH, AINSLIE, WIGHT, ARNOT, ROYLE, PEREIRA, LINDLEY, RICHARD AND FEE

OSHAWA TIMES EXTRA – (1985-1992) – Oshawa, 1993 – 1r – 1 – cn Preston [971]

OSHAWA VINDICATOR – Oshawa, Canada. 1862-71 – 4r – 1 – $260.00 – cn Library Assoc [971]

O'Sheridan, Mary Grant see GAELIC FOLK TALES

OSHKOSH HERALD – Oshkosh, NE. -w. Aug 1908-Jan 1917; Jan 1918-Feb 1919 – 1 – us NE Hist [071]

OSI (OPEN SYSTEMS INTERCONNECTION) – Printed index. Updated every 60 days – 6,9 – us Info Handling [621]

OSIA NEWS – Worcester, MA. Oct 1946-Dec 1971 – 2r – 1 – us I.H.R.C. [071]

OSIA NEWS – Worchester, MA. 1946- – us I.H.R.C. [071]

Osiander, Lucas see
- ANNOTATIONES IN NOVUM TESTAMENTUM
- EIN PREDIG VON DEM WIDERTAUFF. SAMPT ANGEHENCKTER HISTORIEN, WELCHER GESTALT SICH DIE WIDERTAEUFFER

Osinskii, N see VOSSTANOVLENIE KREST'IANSKOGO KHOZIAISTVA V ROSSII I NASHI ZADACHI

OSIP MANDEL'SHTAM / Ivanov, G – Novyi zhurnal. New York. 1955. BR-3663 2 – 8 – ne IDC [460]

OSIP MANDEL'SHTAM AND HIS POETRY / Nilsson, N A – In: Scando-Slavica. v. 9. 1963. BR-3687 2 – 8 – ne IDC [460]

OSIP MANDEL'SHTAM (LISTKI IZ DNEVNIKA). VOZDUSHNYE PUTI / Akhmatova, A – New York. 1965. BR-3634 2 – 8 – ne IDC [460]

OSIP MANDEL'SHTAM, SOBRANIE SOCHINENII / Ivask, I – (Review). Opyty (New York). 1956. BR-3665 2 – 8 – ne IDC [460]

Osip'yan, Yu.A et al see PHYSICS, CHEMISTRY AND THE MECHANICS OF SURFACES

OSKARSHAMNSBLADET – Oskarshamn, Sweden. 1902-08 – 6r – 1 – sw Kungliga [072]

OSKARSHAMNSNYHETERNA – Oskarshamn, Sweden. 1971-78 – 69r – 1 – sw Kungliga [072]

OSKARSHAMNSNYHETERNA see
- OSTRA SMALAND
- VASTERVIKSDEMOKRATEN

OSKARSHAMNSTIDNINGEN – Oskarshamn, Sweden. 1880-1967 – 257r – 1 – sw Kungliga [072]

OSKARSHAMNSTIDNINGEN see BAROMETERN

OSKOLKI – St Petersburg. 1881-1882; 1884; 1888-1894; 1897-1903 – 1 – us NY Public [073]

OSKOLKI – St Petersburg. v1-23. 1881-1903 – 6r – 1 – us Ross [073]

Osler, W see
- BIBLIOTHECA OSLERIANA
- INCUNABULA MEDICA
- LECTURES ON ANGINA PECTORIS AND ALLIED STATES

OSLINYI KHVOST I MISHEN' – M. 1913. BR-3607 2 – 8 – ne IDC [460]

OSLOBODENJE – Sarajevo, Yugoslavia. 1947-Apr 1992 – 235r – 1 – us L of C Photodup [949]

OSLOBODENJE SVIJET see SVIJET

OSLOBODJENJE : WEEKLY EUROPEAN EDITION – 1993 – 1 – sz Infoprint [947]

OSLOBODJENJE : WEEKLY EUROPEAN EDITION – jan 1994-jan 1996 – 4r – 1 – $340.00 – us Ross [072]

OSLOBODJENJE (WEEKLY EUROPEAN EDITION) – (Backfile through 1996 $85r) – Slovenia – 1 – us Ross [072]

Osman, Tosyali Rifat see EDIRNE RAHNUEMASI

OSMANLI ALIM VE SATIM SIRKETI NIZAMNAME-I DAHILESI – [Istanbul]: Matbaa-i Bahriye, 1326 [1908] – us MEDOC [380]

OSMANLI KUMANDANLARI / Residi, Halil – Kostantiniye: Matbaa-i Ebuezziya, 1329 [1913] – $20.00 – us MEDOC [956]

OSMANLI MUEELLIFLERI / Tahir, Bursali Mehmed – Istanbul: Matba'a-i Aire, 1915-1924 – 3v 15mf – 9 – $31.50 – us MEDOC [490]

OSMANLI MUELLIFERI, IATANBUL. MATBAA-I AMIRE-SUKRU MATBASSI, 1333-1342 / Mehmet Tahir, Bursali – 3v. in 1., Index. 1944. BA-411 2 – 8 – ne IDC [956]

OSMANLI PARLAMENTOSU BEYNELMILEL SULH HEYETI / Masliyah, Nesim – Kostantiniye: Matbaa-yi Ebuezziya, 1329 [1913] – $45.00 – us MEDOC [956]

OSMANLI TARIHI / Mithat, Ahmet – Istanbul, 1298 [1881] – $80.00 – us MEDOC [956]

OSMOND REPUBLICAN – Osmond, NE. -w. Dec 1892; Oct 1895-Aug 1902, scattered issues missing; Sept 1907-Feb 1908; May 1908 to date – 1 – us NE Hist [071]

Osmond, Samuel McClurg see SULAMITH

OSNABRUECKER MITTEILUNGEN – Osnabrueck. v.1-65. 1842-1952. Includes indexes for v.1-16, 17-32, 33-55, 56-65. Film Mas C 726 – 1 – us H.U. Library [073]

OSNABRUECKER RUNDSCHAU – Osnabrueck. Germany. -w. 1 Mar-13 Sep 1946. (1 reel) – 1 – uk British Libr Newspaper [072]

OSNABRUECKER TAGEBLATT – Osnabrueck, Germany. 22 Mar-Juni 1848; Sep-Dec 1849 – 1r – 1 – gw Mikrofilm [072]

OSNABRUECKER TELEGRAPH – Osnabrueck, Germany. April 1852-1853 – 1r – 1 – gw Mikrofilm [072]

OSNABRUECKER VOLKSBLATT – Osnabrueck, Germany. 29 Mar 1848-25 Dec 1852 – 1 – gw Mikrofilm [072]

OSNABRUECKISCHE OEFFENTLICHE ANZEIGEN see WOECHENTLICHE OSNABRUECKISCHE ANZEIGEN

OSNOVA – Iuzhno-russkii literaturno-uchenyi vestnik. Spb. 1861-62. Lacking: 1862, v. 11-12. B-1820 2 – 8 – ne IDC [460]

OSNOVA – Vistnyk pys'menstva, nauky i hromads'koho zhyttia. v. 1 3. Odessa. 1915. BR-3780 2 – 8 – ne IDC [460]

OSNOVNAIA LITERATURA OB AZIATSKOM MUSEE-INSTITUTE VOSTOKOVEDENIIA AKADEMII NAUK SSSR (1776-1954) / Livotova, O E – BR-10,971/1 – 9 – ne IDC [460]

OSNOVNO I ZAKON (KONSTITUTSIIA) SOVETSKO I SOTSIALISTICHESKO I RESPUBLIKI GRUZII – Tiflis: NKI U SSRG, 1926 – 1 – CSUX91-B2002 – us Hoover Inst Photo [340]

OSNOVNOI KATALOG DLIA VOISKOVYKH OFITSERKIKH BIBLIOTEK – Ed. 4. Spb. 1902. BR-4365 2 – 8 – ne IDC [020]

OSNOVNYE CHERTY ISTORII NOVEISEI RUSSKOI LITERATURY / Vengerov, S A – Spb. 1909. BR-2189 2 – 8 – ne IDC [460]

OSNOVNYE CHERTY ZHKONOPROEKTA O DOGOVORAKH / Amfiteatrov, G N – Moscow, 1934. 62p. BR-9809 1 – 9 – ne IDC [947]

OSNOVNYE IDEI I METODY RABOTY OBSHCHESTVENNOI AGRONOMIII / Chaianov, A V – M., 1924 – 2mf – 9 – COR-235/1 – ne IDC [334]

OSNOVNYE ITOGI RABOTY PRAVITELSTVA SSSR K PEREVYBORAM SOVETOV...G : T SIK I SNK SSSR – (Includes c.1: 1928/1929) – Moskva: Otdel pechati i informat sii SNK i STO, 1928- – 1 – CSUXAKZ1579-S – us Hoover Inst Photo [947]

OSNOVNYE MATERIALY DLIA CHTENIIA PO POEZII 20 VEKA / Levonevskii, D – V. Saianov. Ocherki po istorii russkoi poezii XX veka. L. 1929. BR-3674 2 – 8 – ne IDC [460]

OSNOVNYE MOMENTY V RAZVITII KOMMUNISTICHESKOI PARTII V ROSSII / Bubnov, Andrei – Moskva: Gos. izd-vo, 1921 – 1 – CSUX89-B6630 – us Hoover Inst Photo [947]

OSNOVNYE NACHALA KOOPERATIVNOGO PRAVA SSSR / Povolotskii, LI – L., 1925 – 2mf – 9 – COR-301/1 – ne IDC [334]

OSNOVNYE NACHALA TEORII KREDITA I KREDITNOI KOOPERATSII / Zak, L S – Pg., 1919 – 3mf – 9 – COR-378/1 – ne IDC [334]

OSNOVNYE USLOVIIA USPEKHA KOOPERATIVNOGO SBYTA PRODUKTOV SEL'SKOGO KHOZIAISTVA / Chaianov, A V – M., 1917 – 1mf – 9 – COR-236/1 – ne IDC [334]

OSNOVNYE UZAKONENII I RASPORIAZHENIIA PO NARODNOMU PROSVESHCHENIIU / ed by Kasatkin, V N – Moscow, 1929. 698p. Collected legislative and departmental regulations on public education. BR-9610/1 – 9 – ne IDC [340]

OSNOVNYE VOPROSY NAUKI MEZHDUNARODNAGO PRAVA / Kamarovskii, L A – Moscow, 1892. 201p. Theoretical treatment of the basic questions of international legal science. BR-9151/1 – 9 – ne IDC [340]

OSNOVNYE VOPROSY SOVETSKOI KOOPERATISII : SBORNIK STATEI / Fishgendler, Abram Markovich – Khar'kov, Kiev, 1925 – 3mf – 9 – COR-225/1 – ne IDC [334]

OSNOVNYE ZADACHI NAUKI SOVETSKOGO SOTSIALISTICHESKOGO PRAVA / Akademiia Nauk. SSSR Institut Prava – Moscow, 1938. 192p. BR-8996 1 – 9 – ne IDC [340]

OSNOVOI GOSUDARSTVENNYI ZAKON ROSSISSKOI IMPERII : PROEKT RUSSKOI KONSTITUTSII / vyrabotannyi gruppoi chlenov "Soiuza osvobozhdeniia – Paris: Societe nouvelle de librarie et dedition, 1905 – us Res Libr [947]

OSNOVY BIBLIOGRAFII PO ISTORII RIMSKOI LITERATURY / Naguevskii, D I – Posobie dlia studentov filologov. Kazan'. 1889. BR-7174 2 – 8 – ne IDC [460]

OSNOVY GRAZHDANSKOGO PRAVA V SVIAZI S CHAST'IU 3 SVODA UZAKONENII DEISTVUIUSHCHIKH V LATVII I ESTONII / Sinaiskii, V – Riga. 2v. 1924-1926 – 14mf – 9 – ne IDC [340]

OSNOVY I PRAKTIKA SOVETSKOGO PRAVA; SBORNIK STATEI / Kaul, A – Petrograd, 1923.120p. Nine essays by Petrograd jurists outlining basic principles of Soviet law with special attention to procuracy, the advocates, arbitral courts, and notariat. BR-9602/1 – 9 – ne IDC [340]

OSNOVY KOOPERATIVNOGO DVIZHENIIA / Posse, V A – Pg., 1916 – 1mf – 9 – COR-99/1 – ne IDC [334]

OSNOVY KOOPERATIVNOI POLITIKI RKP(B) / Kantor, M – M., L., 1926 – 1mf – 9 – COR-154/1 – ne IDC [334]

OSNOVY KOOPERATIZMA / Pazhitnov, K A – Pg., 1917 – 2mf – 9 – COR-89/1 – ne IDC [334]

OSNOVY KOOPERATSII V USLOVIIAKH NAKOPLENIIA KOOPERATIVNOGO KAPITALA / Maslov, P P – Ed.2. M., L., 1925 – 2mf – 9 – COR-392/1 – ne IDC [334]

OSNOVY PATENTNOGO PRAVA / Kheifets, Ila – Leningrad, 1925.418p. Early treatise on patent law during the NEP period. BR-8476/1 – 9 – ne IDC [340]

OSNOVY SEL'SKOI KREDITNOI KOOPERATSII / Lur'e, ML; ed by Shefler, M E – M., 1928 – 2mf – 9 – COR-390/1 – ne IDC [334]

OSOBYI ZHURNAL SOVETA MINISTROV / Russia – St. Petersburg. June 6, 1906-Feb. 15, 1917. Missing: Vol. 2, 1914 – 1 – 35.00r – us Hoover Inst Photo [324]

OSOBYI ZHURNAL ZASEDANIIA VREMENNAGO PRAVITEL'STVA – Petrograd. 1 volume. Apr. 21-Sept. 23, 1917, nos. 1-18 – 1 – 35.00r – us Hoover Inst Photo [072]

OSORIO : A TRAGEDY... / Coleridge, Samuel Taylor – London: John Pearson, 1873 – 1 roll – 1 – 1-55879-284-8 – uk Libr Preservation [820]

Osorio da Fonesca, J see DE REBVS; EMMANVELIS, LVSITANIAE REGIS INVICTISSIMI, VIRTVTE ET AVSPICIO, ...

OSPREY – Arcata, CA. 1973-1990 – 1r – 1 – $50.00 – B05027 – us Library Micro [071]

O.S.R. NEWS see ONO-MEDEDELINGEN

OSS STATE DEPARTMENT INTELLIGENCE AND RESEARCH REPORTS see GERMANY AND ITS OCCUPIED TERRITORIES DURING WORLD WAR 2

LES OSSEMENTS DE SPY ET L'ETHNOGRAPHIE DE LA TUNISIE / Topinard, Paul – Paris: A. Hennuyer, 1889. 20p. Extrait des Bulletins de la Societe d'Anthropologie, 13 decembre, 1888. 1 fiche. (Miscellaneous Selections) – 9 – 6.00 – fr Bibl Nationale [305]

OSSERVATIONI NELLA PITTURA / Sorte, C – O 1028 1. 1580 – 9 – ne IDC [760]

L'OSSERVATORE see JOURNAUX DIVERS

L'OSSERVATORE see LA VOCE D'ITALIA

L'OSSERVATORE DELLE BELLE ARTI IN ROMA OSSIA ESAME ANALITICO DE' MONUMENTI ANTICHI, E MODERNI / Prunetti, M A – O 1055. 2 v. 1808-1811 – 9 – ne IDC [930]

L'OSSERVATORE ROMANO : DEUTSCHSPRACHIGE WOCHEN-AUSGABE – Rome-Vatican, Italy. 7 Jan 1983- – 1 – gw Mikrofilm [072]

L'OSSERVATORE ROMANO – [Vatican City: s.n., 1861- ; 1951-72] – us Res Libr [072]

OSSERVATORE ROMANO – 1976-1978 – Cumul – 1 – L320,000 – sz Infoprint [072]

OSSERVATORE ROMANO – 1987- – 2r per y – 5 – inquire – us Ross [072]

OSSERVATORE ROMANO – 1987-1995 – 2r per y – 5,6 – Sfr936.00 – sz Infoprint [072]

OSSERVATORE ROMANO – (Italian ed.). 1849- – 1 – us UMI [072]

OSSERVAZIONI BOTANICHE CON UN SAGGIO D'APPENDICE ALLA FLORA PEDEMONTANA / Bellardi, C A L – Torino. 1788. B-5843 – 8 – ne IDC [580]

OSSERVAZIONI SULLE NORME DI DIRITTO INTERNAZIONALE PRIVATO... / Arminjon, P – Roma, 1933 – 1mf – 9 – ILM-3647/1 – ne IDC [340]

Ossian see POESIES GALLIQUES.

OSSIAN OU LES BARDES / Deschamps, Dercy & Deschamps, Lesueur – French Theatre Series. Paris. Ballard, an XII. 1804 – 9 – fr Hachette [820]

Ossian (supposed author) see POESIES GALLIQUES EN VERS FRANCAIS

Ossinger, J F O E S A see BIBLIOTHECA AUGUSTINIANA

OSSIUS OF CORDOVA : A CONTRIBUTION TO THE HISTORY OF THE CONSTANTINIAN PERIOD / Clercq, V C De – 1954 – 10mf – 9 – ne Slangenburg [240]

OSS/LONDON : SPECIAL OPERATIONS BRANCH AND SECRET INTELLIGENCE BRANCH WAR DIARIES / U.S. Office of Strategic Services – 8 reels with printed guide – 1 – $770.00 – 0-89093-724-9 – us UPA [977]

Ossoli, Margaret Fuller *see* MEMOIRS OF MARGARET FULLER OSSOLI
Ossorio, Angel *see*
- LA AGONIA DEL PRINCIPE DE LA PAZ. DISCURSO...1923-1924
- THE RELIGIOUS PROBLEM IN SPAIN
- SPAIN'S FUTURE SPEECH MADE AT THE MAISON DE CHIMIE, PARIS, FEB 22, 1937
- TEXTO INTERGRO DE LOS DISCURSOS PRONUNCIADOS ANTE LOS MICROFONOS DEL MINISTERIO DE LA GUERRA Y DEL PARTIDO COMUNISTA

Ossorio, Bernard M *see*
- APUNTES PARA UN DICCIONARIO DE ESCRITORES DEL S. XIX
- ESCRITORES ESPANOLES: CAROLINA CORONADO

OSSTF FORUM – (Cont by: Educational Forum at v14 no 3 1988/89) – Don Mills. v1-14. 1975-1988/89 – 9 – Can$20.00y – cn Micromedia [073]
OSSTF FORUM *see* EDUCATION FORUM
OSSZES MUNKAI / Vorosmartym, Mihaly – Budapest. 8v. 1884-85 – 1 – 23.00r – us L of C Photodup [460]
OST UND WEST : ILLUSTRIERTE MONATSSCHRIFT FUER MODERNES JUDENTUM / ed by Trietsch, D, Winz, L – (Fortgesetzt als: Ost und West. Illustrierte Monatsschrift fuer das gesamte Judentum. Charlottenburg 1909-1923. Ab 1912 mit dem Zusatz: Organ d. Alliance israelite universelle) – Charlottenburg, 1901-1908 – 110mf – 9 – subsc: DM770.00 diazo DM880.00 silver – gw Olms [320]
Ostal'skii, D V *see* SEGODNIA
OSTASIATISCHE GESCHICHTE VOM ERSTEN CHINESISCHEN KRIEG BIS ZU DEN VERTRAEGEN IN PEKING, 1840-1860 / Neumann, C F – Leipzig. 1861. BCH-826 2 – 8 – ne IDC [950]
DER OSTASIATISCHE LLOYD – Shanghai. 1891-1915, 1936-41. Beilage: Shanghaier Nachrichten und Handelsnachrichten. Shanghai. 1913-15. BCHF-1 3 – 1 – ne IDC [380]
OSTASIATISCHE ZEITSCHRIFT : BEITRAEGE ZUR KENNTNISS DER KULTUR UND KUNST DES FERNEN OSTENS – Berlin. v1-20. 1912-40 – 201mf – 9 – ne IDC [950]
OSTASIATISCHER LLOYD – Shanghai, China. Oct 1891-Sep 1892; Oct 1893-1915; Jan-Jun 1936; Jan-Jun 1937; Nov-Dec 1937; 1938-May 1941 – 56r – 1 – gw Mikrofilm [072]
OSTATNIE WIADOMOSCI – Mannheim, Germany. 1962-64 – 1r – 1 – us L of C Photodup [072]
OSTATNIE WIADOMOSCI – Mannheim, Germany. -w. 12 July 1947-25 Nov 1951; 1 Jan 1952-24 March 1972. 37 reels – 1 – uk British Libr Newspaper [072]
OSTAV' NADEZHDU NAVSEGDA / Odoevsteva, I – Roman. Izd. imeni Chekhova. New York. 1954. BR-1226 2 – 8 – ne IDC [460]
OSTBOEHMENS DEUTSCHER BOTE *see*
- DEUTSCHER BOTE

OST-COURIER – Berlin, 1922-24 – 1 – Inquire at Mikrofilmarchiv for details – gw Misc Inst [072]
OSTDEUTSCHE BEITRAEGE AUS DEM GOETTINGER ARBEITSKREIS – Wuerzburg: Holzner-Verlag, 1956- – 10r – 1 – us U.W. Library [943]
OSTDEUTSCHE FUNKWOCHE *see*
- OSTDEUTSCHE ILLUSTRIERTE FUNKSTUNDE

OSTDEUTSCHE ILLUSTRIERTE FUNKSTUNDE – (Cont by: Ostdeutsche Funkwoche, 1934; Neue Funkstunde, jan 1939; Hoer mit mir – Neue Funkstunde, 1939 n39.) – Breslau, Bochum, Berlin. jul 1927-may 31 1941 – 1 – Inquire at Mikrofilmarchiv for details – gw Misc Inst [790]
OSTDEUTSCHE ILLUSTRIERTE FUNKSTUNDE – (Cont by: Ostdeutsche Funkwoche, 1934. Neue Funkstunde, jan 1939. Hoer mit mir – Neue Funkstunde, 1939 n39) – Breslau. jul 1927-38 – 1 – gw Mikrofilm [073]
DER OSTDEUTSCHE LANDBAU ZWISCHEN FORTSCHRITT, KRISE UND POLITIK : EIN BEITRAG ZUR AGRAR- UND ZEITGESCHICHTE / Borcke-Stargordt, Henning Graf von – (Includes bibliographical references and index) – Wuerzburg: Holzner, 1957 – 1 – us U.W. Library [943]
OSTDEUTSCHE MORGENPOST – (1938: Sunday Issues only) – Beuthen. mar 4, 1921-30. jan 9-dec 25 1938. aug 2-sep 1, 1940 – 27r – 1 – gw Mikrofilm [943]
OSTDEUTSCHE MORGENPOST – (Cont: Beuthener Zeitung, -jun 14 1919) – Beuthen, mar 4 1921-30, jan 9-dec 25 1938 (only sunday issues), nov 1939-sep 1944 – 27r – 1 – Inquire at Mikrofilmarchiv for details – gw Misc Inst [943]
OSTDEUTSCHE PRESSE – Bromberg, jul 1-sep 30 1915 – 1r – 1 – Inquire at Mikrofilmarchiv for details – gw Misc Inst [943]
OSTDEUTSCHE RUNDSCHAU – (Cont by: Deutsche Rundschau) – Bromberg (Bydgoszcz), Poland. 1920 (incomplete) – 1 – gw Mikrofilm [943]
OSTDEUTSCHE RUNDSCHAU *see*
- DEUTSCHE RUNDSCHAU
- DEUTSCHE RUNDSCHAU IN POLEN

OSTDEUTSCHER BEOBACHTER – Posen (Poznan), Poland. Nov 1939-1943 – 12r – 1 – gw Mikrofilm [943]
OSTDEUTSCHER BEOBACHTER – Poznan. Poland. -d. Jan 1942-Jan 1945. (Imperfect). (13 reels) – 1 – uk British Libr Newspaper [943]
OSTDEUTSCHES VOLKSBLATT – Lemberg (Lwow), U.S.S.R. 6 Apr 1922-20 Aug 1939 – 9r – 1 – gw Mikrofilm [943]
OSTDEUTSCHLANDS ARBEITERBEWEGUNG : ABRISS IHRER GESCHICHTE, LEISTUNG UND OPFER / Matull, Wilhelm – (Includes bibliographical references and indexes) – Wuerzburg: Holzner Verlag, 1973 – 10r – 1 – us U.W. Library [331]
Osten, H von *see* IM REGIMENT
Osten, Hans Henning von der *see*
- RESEARCHES IN ANATOLIA
- RESEARCHES IN ANATOLIA, VOL 9

Osten-Sacken, C R von *see* RECORD OF MY LIFE-WORK IN ENTOMOLOGY
OSTEOGRAPHIA / Cheselden, W – or the anatomy of the bones. M-45 2. 1733 – 8 – ne IDC [611]
OSTEOLOGIA NOVA / Havers, C – M369. 1691 – 9 – ne IDC [611]
OSTEOLOGY OF THE WESTERN AND CENTRAL ESKIMOS / Cameron, J – BN 160 2. 1923 – 8 – ne IDC [305]
OSTERAKER *see* LOKALTIDNINGEN VAXHOLM/ OSTERAKER
OSTERGOTLANDS FOLKBLAD *see* FOLKBLADET OSTGOTEN
OSTERHOLZER KREISBLATT : BA DES BREMER WESER-KURIER – Osterholz-Scharmbeck, Germany. 1 Okt 1971- – 1 – gw Mikrofilm [072]
OSTERLAENDER VOLKSZEITUNG. FUER DIE KREISE ALTENBURG UND SCHMOELLN *see* LEIPZIGER VOLKSZEITUNG
Osterman *see* HISTORY OF DODGE AND WASHINGTON COUNTIES
OSTERN IM HIMMEL = EASTER IN HEAVEN / Weninger, Francis Xavier – (In German) – New York: Gebrueder Benziger, 1864 – 1mf – 9 – 0-8370-6867-3 – 1986-0867 – us A.T.L.A. [240]
Osternig, Louis R *see*
- AN INVESTIGATION OF ANATOMICAL STRUCTURES ASSOCIATED WITH THE SITE OF MEDIAL TIBIAL STRESS SYNDROME, OFTEN REFERRED TO AS "SHIN SPLINTS"
- RELATIONSHIPS BETWEEN LOWER EXTREMITY LOADING AND DEPTH JUMP PERFORMANCE

OSTERODER DORFZEITUNG – (Cont by: Neue Dorfzeitung, apr 7 1849) – Allenstein, mar-dec 26 1849 – 1r – 1 – Dist. gw Mikrofilm – gw Misc Inst [943]
OSTERREICH'S WOLEN- UND LEINEN INDUSTRIE – Liberec, Austria. 1900-09.-w. 19 reels – 1 – uk British Libr Newspaper [072]
OSTERSUNDSPOSTEN – Ostersund, Sweden. 1877-1978 – 449r – 1 – sw Kungliga [072]
OSTERSUNDSPOSTEN – Ostersund, Sweden. 1979- – 1 – sw Kungliga [072]
OSTEUROPAEISCHE BIBLIOGRAPHIE 1920-1923 – Breslau. 4v. 1921-1928 – 34mf – 9 – ne IDC [947]
OSTEUROPAEISCHE BIBLIOGRAPHIE 1920-1923 – Breslau. 4v. 1921-28 – 34mf – 9 – ne IDC [947]
OSTEUROPAEISCHE UND OSTASIATISCHE STREIFZUEGE / Marquart, J – Ethnologische und historisch-topographische Studien zur Geschichte des 9, und 10. Jahrhunderts (ca. 840-940). Leipzig. 1903. BU-628 2 – 8 – ne IDC [910]
OSTFRIESEN ZEITUNG – Leer, West Germany. 1977- – ca 9r per yr – 1 – gw Mikrofilm [072]
OSTFRIESISCHE NACHRICHTEN – Aurich, jun 1 1983- – 6r per yr – 1 – Dist. gw Mikrofilm – gw Misc Inst [072]
OSTFRIESISCHE NACHRICHTEN – Breda, IA. 1922-sep 20 1939 (incomplete) – 3r – 1 – Inquire at Mikrofilmarchiv for details – gw Misc Inst [072]
OSTFRIESISCHE ZEITSCHWINGEN – Aurich. may 7-dec 24, 1848 – 1 – gw Mikrofilm [072]
OSTFRIESISCHE ZEITSCHWINGEN – Aurich, may 7-dec 24 1848 – 1 – Dist. gw Mikrofilm – gw Misc Inst [943]
OSTFRIESISCHER KURIER – Norden, West Germany. 1977- – ca 7r per yr – 1 – gw Mikrofilm [072]
OSTFUNK *see* DER KOENIGSBERGER RUNDFUNK
OSTGOTA CORRESPONDENTEN – Linkoping, Sweden. 1838-1978 – 626r – 1 – sw Kungliga [072]
OSTGOTA CORRESPONDENTEN – Linkoping, Sweden. 1979- – 1 – sw Kungliga [072]
OSTGOTABLADET – Vadstena, Sweden. 1893-96, 1903-08 – 9r – 1 – sw Kungliga [072]
OSTGOTAKURIREN *see* WADSTENA LANS TIDNING
OSTGOTEN – Norrkoping, Sweden. 1981- – 1 – sw Kungliga [072]
OSTGOTEN – (Norrkopingsostgoten 1872-74; Linkopingsostgoten 1873-74; Ostgoten 1874-82) – Linkoping, Sweden – 8r – 1 – sw Kungliga [072]
OSTGRONLANDSKE STEMMER / Thalbitzer, W – (Det gronlandske Selskabs Aarsskrift, 1933-1934). Kobenhavn. 1934. BN-422 2 – 8 – ne IDC [910]
OSTHAMMARS TIDNING – Osthammar, Sweden. 1886-90 – 3r – 1 – sw Kungliga [072]
OSTHOLSTEINER ANZEIGER – Eutin, Germany. 1981- – 6r per yr – 1 – gw Mikrofilm [072]
Ostholsteiner Nachrichten *see* LUEBECKER NACHRICHTEN
Ostiguy, Flore-Ella *see* BIBLIOGRAPHIE DE MADAME ELLA CHARLAND-OSTIGUY
OSTJUEDISCHE ZEITUNG – Czernowitz (Cernauti), Rumaenien. 23 Mai 1928-28 Jan 1934 (1933, incomplete) – 3r – 1 – gw Mikrofilm [949]
OSTKIRLICHE STUDIEN – 1(1952)-21(1972) – 137mf – 9 – Dfl480.00 – ne Slangenburg [073]
OSTKUSTEN – Norrtalje, Sweden. 1904-06 – 2r – 1 – sw Kungliga [072]
OSTLAND – Berlin, jan 22 1926-jan 6 1928, 1930-mar 15 1936 – 4r – 1 – Inquire at Mikrofilmarchiv for details – gw Misc Inst [072]
Ostler, H *see* DIE PSYCHOLOGIE DES HUGO VON S. VIKTOR
Ostmann, Hans *see* BRAUNSCHWEIGISCHES FRIEDHOFS- UND BESTATTUNGSRECHT
OSTPOMMERSCHE HEIMAT *see* ZEITUNG FUER OSTPOMMERN
DAS OSTPREUSSENBLATT – Hamburg, West Germany. 5 Apr 1950-75 – 1 – gw Mikrofilm [072]
OSTPREUSSENS ARBEITERBEWEGUNG : GESCHICHTE UND LEISTUNG IM UEBERBLICK / Matull, Wilhelm – (Includes bibliographical references and index) – Wuerzburg: Holzner Verlag, 1970 – 10r – 1 – us U.W. Library [331]
EIN OSTPREUSSISCHES PFARRERLEBEN : AUS DEN AUFZEICHNUNGEN CHRISTIAN FRIEDRICH MUELLERS, 1805-1818 / Goettinger Arbeitskreis – Wuerzburg: Holzner-Verlag, 1959 – 10r – 1 – us U.W. Library [240]
OSTPREUSSISCHES VOLKSBLATT – Rastenburg, Germany. (Ketrzyn, Poland). 1891 (Nrn.1-149); 1892 (Nrn.151-306); 1901 (Nrn.150-305); 1903 (Nrn.152-306); 1904; 1905 (Nrn. 1-151) – 1 – gw Mikrofilm [943]
OSTRA SMALAND – Kalmar, Sweden. 1928-78 – 294r – 1 – sw Kungliga [072]
OSTRA SMALAND – (Oskarshamnsnyheterna, 1979-84. Vasterviksdemokraten, 1979-84) – Kalmar, Sweden. 1979- – 1 – sw Kungliga [072]
Ostrander, Dempster *see* THE LAW OF FIRE INSURANCE
OSTRECHT – (Cont as: Zeitschrift fuer Osteuropaeisches Recht, Breslau v1-3 1925-27. Cont as: Zeitschrift fuer Ostrecht, Berlin v1-8 1927-34. Cont as: Zeitschrift fuer Osteuropaeisches Recht, NS Berlin v1-11 1934-44) – Berlin. v1-3. 1925-27 – 216mf – 9 – ne IDC [943]
Ostrorog, Leon *see* CONSTITUTION DES SOCIETES ANONYMES EN FRANCE, DANS L'EMPIRE ALLEMAND ET EN GRANDE-BRETAGNE
Ostroumov, G *see* DOGMATICHESKOW ZNACHENIE SED'MAGO VSELENSKAGO SOBORA: NAUCHNO ISTORICHESKOW IZSLENOVANIE VAZHNOSTI I NEOPKHODIMOSTI..
Ostroumov, Vl *see* KONSPEKT LEKTSII PO SEL'SKOKHOZIAISTVENNOI KOOPERATSII
OSTROVA OCHAROVANII / Severianin, I – Al'manakh 2-i. Novya poezy. Petrograd. 1917. BR-1033 2 – 8 – ne IDC [460]
Ostrovskii, AN *see* A. N. OSTROVSKII, N. S. LESKOV RUKOPISI, PEREPISKA, DOKUMENTY
Ostrovskii, Nikolai Alekseevich *see* OPIS' DOKUMENTAL'NYKH MATERIALOV LICHNOGO FONDA NO. 363
Ostrovskii, V V *see* KOOPERATSIIA I GORODSKOE SAMOUPRAVLENIE
OSTROZHSKAIA TIPOGRAFIIA I EIA IZDANIIA / Seletskii, A K – Pochaev. 1885 – 8 – ne IDC [070]
OSTSCHLESISCHE POST – Bielitz-Biala, apr 21-nov 6 1923, feb 5 1924-mar 8 1934 – 1 – Inquire at Mikrofilmarchiv for details – gw Misc Inst [947]
OSTSCHLESISCHE POST – Bielitz-Biala (Bielsko-Biala), Poland. 21 Apr-6 Nov 1923; 5 Feb 1924-8 Mar 1934 – 1 – gw Mikrofilm [072]
OSTSEE ZEITUNG – Szczecin, Poland. Oct 1942-Aug 1944 – 4r – 1 – us L of C Photodup [943]
OSTSEE-TELEGRAPH – Flensburg, Germany. 26 Oct 1848-30 Dec 1849 – 1r – 1 – gw Mikrofilm [072]
OSTSEE-ZEITUNG – Rostock, East Germany. 1992- – 5r per yr – 1 – gw Mikrofilm [072]
OSTSEE-ZEITUNG – Rostock, Germany. 1964-Aug 1970 – 12r – 1 – us L of C Photodup [072]
OSTZEISKII VOPROS : PIS'MO K PROFESSORU SIRRENU / Pogodin, M P – M., 1869. (4) – 4mf – 9 – ne IDC [947]
OSU EXTENSION FACTS / Oklahoma State University. Cooperative Extension Service – No.100-9448 – 1,5 – us Spaulding [630]
Osuji, PO et al *see* FEED EVALUATION
O'Sullivan, Henry *see*
- REPORT OF PROGRESS OF EXPLORATION IN THE COUNTRY BETWEEN LAKE ST JOHN AND JAMES BAY MADE UNDER INSTRUCTIONS FROM THE DEPARTMENT OF COLONIZATION AND MINES, QUEBEC
- SECOND REPORT OF PROGRESS OF EXPLORATION IN THE COUNTRY BETWEEN LAKE ST JOHN AND JAMES BAY INCLUDING THE REGION OF LAKE MISTASSINI AND THE BASINS OF THE GREAT NOTTAWAY AND RUPERT RIVERS..

O'Sullivan, J J *see* THE MORAL OBLIGATION OF PARENTS TO EDUCATE THEIR CHILDREN FOR MARRIAGE
Osuna, Candido *see* PLAN DE MEJORAS... CACERES
Osuna Lara, Antonio J *see*
- APUNTES PARA LA HISTORIA DE ZAFRA
- HISTORIA LIBERAL DEL JUEGO DEL AXEDREZ

Osvaldo Inglese, Juan et al *see* UNIVERSIDAD Y ESTUDIANTES
OSVETA AMERICKE – Omaha, NE. -d. Jul 1898-Sep 1916 – 1 – us NE Hist [071]
OSVOBOZHDENIE – v. 1-4, NR. 1-79. Stuttgart, Paris. 1902-05. B-1487 2 – 8 – ne IDC [073]
OSVOBOZHDENIE ROSSII I UKRAINSKII VOPROS : STATI I ZAMIETKI / Hrushevskyi, Mykhailo – S.-Peterburg: Tip. t-va "Obshchestvennaia polza", 1907 – 1 – CSUX89-B1013 – us Hoover Inst Photo [320]
OSWALD CRAY / Wood, Ellen – British Fiction Archive: Unit 1 – 9 – uk Bell [830]
Oswald, H *see* DE INSTITUTIONIS THEOLOGICAE VIA AC RATIONE
Oswalt, Lynn T *see* THE ELEMENTS OF REMEMBRANCE AND CELEBRATION IN CHRISTIAN WORSHIP AND EDUCATION
OSWEGO HONK – Lake Oswego OR. Sep 29 1942, Jan 9 1944-Sep 2 1945 – 1 – us U.O. Library [071]
OSWEGO IRON WORKER – Lake Oswego OR. Dec 23 1893, June 30 July 7 1894 – 1 – us U.O. Library [071]
Oswego, New York *see* MISCELLANEOUS EARLY NEWSPAPERS

OSWEGO TIMES – Lake Oswego, OR. 30 Mar 1916-8 Mar 1918; 23 Mar 1916 – 1 – us U.O. Library [071]

OSWESTRY AND BORDER COUNTIES ADVERTIZER – England. Border Counties Advertizer. -w. 1949-63; 1972-75. 37 reels – 1 – uk British Libr Newspaper [072]

OSYOBOZHDENIE – Neu-Ulm. Germany. -m. Feb 1953-Sep 1956. (Imperfect). (38 ft) – 1 – uk British Libr Newspaper [947]

OT CHEKHOVA DO NASHIKH DNEI IZD / Chukovskii, K – M. O. Vol'fa. Ed. 3. Spb. 1908. BR-2034 2 – 8 – ne IDC [460]

OT DANTE DO TASSO. KATALOG PISEM I SOCHINENII ITAL'IANSKIKH GUMANISTOV V SOBRANII LOII SSSR / Katushkina, LG – L. 1972. BR-11,322 1 – 9 – ne IDC [440]

OT DANTE K BLOKU / Minskii, N – Berlin. 1922. BR-809 2 – 8 – ne IDC [460]

OT DIKTATURY IMPERIALIZMA K DIKTATURE PROLETARIATA : CZECH / Bukharin, Nikolai Ivanovich – VPraze: Nak. casopisu Socialni Demokrat, 1920 – 1 – CSUX88-B748 – us Hoover Inst Photo [943]

OT DIKTATURY IMPERIALIZMA K DIKTATURI E PROLETARIATA / Bukharin, Nikolai Ivanovich – Petrograd: Pribo i, 1918 – 1 – CSUX88-B2523 – us Hoover Inst Photo [947]

OT KRUSHENIIA TSARIZMA DO PADENIIA BURZHUAZII / Bukharin, Nikolai Ivanovich – Kharkov: Izd-vo "Proletari i", 1925 – 1 – CSUX89-B4614 – us Hoover Inst Photo [947]

OT KRUSHENIIA TSARIZMA DO PADENIIA BURZHUAZII / Bukharin, Nikolai Ivanovich – Kharkov: Kharkovskoe kooperativnoe izd-vo "Proletari i", 1923 – 1 – CSUX88-B7209 – us Hoover Inst Photo [947]

OT PUSHKINA DO BLOKA / Grossman, L – Etiudy i portrety. Izd. "Sovremennye problemy". M. 1926. BR-1286 2 – 8 – ne IDC [460]

OT RABSTVA K SVOBODE : OBIAZANNOSTII PRAVA KOMMUNISTOV V PERVOI TRUDOVOI RESPUBLIKE / Balabanoff, Angelica – Moskva: Gos. izd-vo, 1920 – 1 – CSUX89-B5610 – us Hoover Inst Photo [947]

OT SEZD K SEZDU : UPRAVLENIE DELAMI SNK I EKOSO RSFSR – (Includes c.1: 1930) – Moskva, Leningrad: Sov zakonodatelstvo, 1929 – 1 – CSUXAKY6440-S – us Hoover Inst Photo [947]

OT SEZDA K SEZDU : MATERIALY K OTCHETU PRAVITELSTVA NA...SEZDE SOVETOV SOI UZA SSR – (Includes c.1: 1927/1929) – Moskva: T SIK i SNK SSR, 1927 – 1 – CSUXAKZ3815-S – us Hoover Inst Photo [947]

OT SEZDA K SEZDU (RUSSIAN S.F.S.R. UPRAVLENIE DELAMI SNK I EKOSO) *see* OT SEZD K SEZDU

OT SEZDA K SEZDU (SOVIET UNION. T SENTRALNY I ISPOLNITELNY I KOMITET) *see* OT SEZDA K SEZDU

OT VOLGI DO BAIKALA / Dmitriev, N – Moskva: "Voen. vestnik", 1928 – 1 – CSUX88-B7664 – us Hoover Inst Photo [910]

OTADZBINA – v1-5, 7-32. 1875-1892 – 1 – us I.U. Libraries [073]

OTAVAN – v8-14. 1924-1934 – 1 – us I.U. Libraries [073]

Otayek, R W *see* LA POLITIQUE AFRICAINE DE LA LYBIE DU 1ER SEPTEMBRE 1969

OTCHE NASH, NABRANNAIA SHRIFTAMI TIPOGRAFII I SLOVOLITNI IMP. KAZANSKAGO UNIVERSITETA / Molitva Gospodnia – Kazan. 1890. BR-4583 2 – 8 – ne IDC [370]

OTCHET / Moscow. I Moskovskii i Rumiantsovskii Musei – Moscow. 33v. 1864-1915 – 1 – $46.00 – us L of C Photodup [060]

OTCHET AKT SIONERNOGO OBSHCHESTVA "KHLEBOPRODUKT" ZA...G. : AKT SIONERNOE OBSHCHESTVO TORGOVLI KHLEBNYMI I DRUGIMI SELSKO-KHOZI A ISTVENNYMI PRODUKTAMI "KHLEBOPRODUKT" / Khleboprodukt – (Includes c.1: 1927/1928) – Moskva: Soi uzkhleb, 1923 – 1 – CSUXAKZ2211-S – us Hoover Inst Photo [947]

OTCHET ARKHANGEL'SKOGO SOIUZA KOOPERATIVOV, ZA 1914-23 GG – (Missing: 1914-16 v1-3; 1920 v6) – Arkhangel'sk. v1-9. 1918-23 – 15mf – 9 – COR-731/1 – ne IDC [310]

OTCHET EKSPEDITSII KOMZETA 1927 GODA PO OBSLEDOVANIIU BIROBIDZHANSKOGO RAIONA DALNEVOSTOCHNOGO KRAIA (BIROBIDZHANA) / Ekspeditsii a Komzeta po obsledovanii u Birobidzhanskogo ra iona Dalnevostochnogo krai a (1927); ed by Viliamsa, V R – Moskva: Izd. Komzeta, 1930 – 1 – CSUX91-B372 – us Hoover Inst Photo [947]

OTCHET IMPERATORSKOI PUBLICHNOI BIBLIOTEKI ZA 1850 G.-...ZA 1913 G – St. Petersburg, Petrograd, 1851-1917. 62v. BR-10,847/1 – 9 – ne IDC [020]

OTCHET KHARKOVSKOGO GUBERNSKOGO EKONOMICHESKOGO SOVESHCHANII A : KHARKOVSKI I GUBERNSKI I ISPOLNITELNY I KOMITET SOVETA RABOCHIKH, KRESTI ANSK. I KRASNOARME ISK. DEPUTATOV – (Includes c.1: 1921:Jan./Oct.-1921:Oct./1922:Apr) – Kharkov: Gos. izd-vo, [1921-1922]. 2v – 1 – CSUXAKZ2661-S – us Hoover Inst Photo [947]

OTCHET KHARKOVSKOGO GUBISPOLKOMA I GUB EKONOMSOVESHCHANII A : KHARKOVSKI I GUBERNSKI I ISPOLNITELNY I KOMITET SOVETA RABOCHIKH, KRESTI ANSKIKH I ARME ISKIKH DEPUTATOV – (Includes c.1: no.2 1922:Apr./Oct) – Kharkov: Gubispolkom, 1922 – 1 – CSUXAKZ2673-S – us Hoover Inst Photo [947]

OTCHET LENINGRADSKOGO OBLASTNOGO ISPOLKOMA – (Includes c.1: 1927/1929-1929/1930) – [Leningrad]: Ispolkom, 1929- – 1 – CSUXAKZ3517-S – us Hoover Inst Photo [947]

OTCHET LENINGRADSKOGO RAIONNOGO SOIUZA POTREBITEL'SKIKH OBSHCHESTV "LENINGRADRAIPOTREBSOIUZ" ZA 1924 OPERATSIONNYI GOD – L., 1925 – 1mf – 9 – COR-343/1 – ne IDC [334]

OTCHET MOSKOVSKOGO SOIUZA PROMYSLOVOI KOOPERATSII ZA 1925/26 G – M., 1927 – 2mf – 9 – COR-438/1 – ne IDC [334]

OTCHET NARODNOGO KOMISSARIATA FINANSOV SOI UZA SSR OB ISPOLNENII EDINOGO GOSUDARSTVENNOGO BI UDZHETA SOI UZA SOT SIALISTICHESKIKH RESPUBLIK ZA...GOD : FINANSOVO-KONTROLNOE UPRAVLENIE NKF SSSR – (Includes c.1: 1923/1924-1926/1927) – Moskva: Komissariat, 1926- – 1 – CSUXAKY5712-S – us Hoover Inst Photo [947]

OTCHET NARODNOGO KOMISSARIATA IUSTITSII ZA... / Ukraine, Narodnyi komisariat iustytsii – (Includes c.1: 1921) – Kharkov: Komissariat, 19uu – 1 – CSUXAKY6338-S – us Hoover Inst Photo [340]

OTCHET NARODNOGO KOMISSARIATA ZEMLEDELIIA R.S.F.S.R....VSEROSSI ISKOMU S"EZDU SOVETOV ZA... / Russian S.F.S.R. Narodnyi komissariat zemledeliia – (Includes c.1: 1923/1924) – Moskva: Novaia derevnia, 192u – 1 – CSUXAKZ2907-S – us Hoover Inst Photo [630]

OTCHET NARODNOGO KOMISSARIATA ZEMLEDELIIA...VSEROSSIISKOMU S"EZDU SOVETOV ZA... / Russian S.F.S.R. Narodnyi komissariat zemledeliia – (Includes c.1: 1921) – Moskva: Red.-izd. komiteta N.K.Z., 1921 – 1 – CSUXAKZ2895-S – us Hoover Inst Photo [630]

OTCHET NARODNOGO KOMISSRIATA FINANSOV R.S.F.S.R. OB ISPOLNENII GOSUDARSTVENNOGO BI UDZHETA ROSSI ISKO I SOT SIALISTICHESKO I FEDERATIVNO I SOVETSKO I RESPUBLIKI ZA... : FINANSOVO-KONTROLNOE UPRAVLENIE N.K.F. R.S.R.S.R. – (Library has: 1924/25, 1924/25 suppl) – Moskva: Komissariat, 19uu – 1 – CSUX90-S947 – us Hoover Inst Photo [947]

OTCHET O DEI ATELNOSTI ZA...OPERAT SIONNY I GOD : AKT SIONERNY I BANK PO ELEKTRIFIKAT SII "ELEKTROBANK" / Elektrobank SSSR – (Includes c.1: 1924/1925) – Moskva: [Bank], 1926- – 1 – CSUXAKZ2199-S – us Hoover Inst Photo [332]

OTCHET O DEIATELNOSTI OTDELENIIA RUSSKAGO IAZYKA I SLOVESNOSTI / Akademiia Nauk – St. Petersburg, 1893-1919. BR-5651 2 – 8 – ne IDC [460]

OTCHET O DEIATEL'NOSTI PRAVLENIIA OBSHCHESTVA VSPOMOSHCHESTVOVANIIA NUZHDAIUSHCHIMSIA UCHASHCHIMSIA V UCHILISHCHE D-RA M.P. SIMONOVICH – za 1906-07, 1909-12 gg. v. 1-6. Odessa. 1906-07, 1909-12. BR-5749 2 – 8 – ne IDC [073]

OTCHET O DEIATELNOSTI TSENTRALNOGO STATISTICHESKOGO UPRAVLENIIA ZA...OPERATSIONNYI GOD / Ukraine, Tsentralne statystychne upravlinniaT Sentralnoe statistichesko upravlenie – (Includes c.1: 1923/1924) – Kharkov: Upravlenie, 19uu – 1 – CSUXAKZ2076-S – us Hoover Inst Photo [320]

OTCHET O DIEIATELNOSTI DANSKOGO PRAVITELSTVA ZA GRANITSE I PO 25 SENTIABRIA 1921 G / Donskoe pravitelstvo (1921) – Konstantinopol: Tip. Izd. t-va "Pressa", 1921 – 1 – CSUX88-B9219 – us Hoover Inst Photo [947]

OTCHET OTDELENIIU RUSSKOGO IAZYKA SLOVESNOSTI IMP. AKADEMII NAUK O POEZDKE V OLONETSKUIU, VOLOGODSKUIU PERMSKUIU GUBERNII (IIUN' 1902 G.) / Sreznevskii, 6 – Spb. 1904. PKG-C-24.66 BR-11,178 1 – 9 – ne IDC [947]

OTCHET PO GOSUDARSTVENNOI TIPOGRAFII ZA 1907 GOD – Spb. 1907. BR-4604 2 – 8 – ne IDC [070]

OTCHET PO REVIZII TURKESTANSKAGO KRAIA. / Palen, Konstantin Konstantinovich, Graf – St. Petersburg, Senatskaia tip., 1909-1910. 5v in 2 – 1 – us U.W. Library [947]

OTCHET RABOTY URALSKO I TRESTIROVANNO I PROMYSHLENNOSTI ZA...OPERAT SIONNOGO GODA PO PROTOKOLAM ZASEDANI I PREDIDIUMA *see* URALOBLSOVNARKHOZA

OTCHET SEVERO-ZAPADNOGO OBLASTNOGO EKONOMICHESKOGO SOVESHCHANII A : SEVERO-ZAPADNOE OBLASTNOE EKONOMICHESKOE SOVESHCHANIE – (Includes c.1: 1921:no.1) – Petrograd: Gos. izd-vo, 1921- – 1 – CSUXAKZ6269-S – us Hoover Inst Photo [947]

OTCHET SOVETU TRUDA I OBORONY ZA... : ODESSKOE GUB EKONOMSOVESHCHANIE – (Includes c.1: 1921:July/Sept) – Odessa: Vseukainskoe gos. izd-vo, 1921- – 1 – CSUXAKZ1372-S – us Hoover Inst Photo [947]

OTCHET TSENTRAL'NAGO KOMITETA KONSTITUTSIONNO-DEMOKRATICHESKOI PART 2 (PARTII NARODNOI SOVBODY) ZA DVA GODA – S 18 oktiabra 1905 g po oktabr' 1907 g. Spb. 1907. BR-3523 2 – 8 – ne IDC [321]

OTCHET URALSKOGO OBLASTNOGO EKONOMICHESKOGO SOVESHCHANII A SOVETU TRUDA I OBORONY ZA... – (Includes c.1: 1921/1922) – Ekaterinburg: [s.n.], 1923- – 1 – CSUXAKZ1562-S – us Hoover Inst Photo [947]

OTCHET VSEROSSIISKOGO KOOPERATIVNOGO BANKA ZA 1927-28 OPERATSIONNYI GOD – M., 1929 – 1mf – 9 – COR-398/1 – ne IDC [334]

OTCHET VSEROSSIISKOGO KOOPERATIVNOGO BANKA...1923-1926 GG – M., 1924-27 – 10mf – 9 – COR-732/1 – ne IDC [334]

OTCHET VSEROSSIISKOGO TSENTRAL'NOGO SOIUZA POTREBITEL'NYKH OBSHCHESTV ZA 1919 GOD – M., 1920 – 1mf – 9 – COR-341/1 – ne IDC [334]

OTCHET VSEROSSIISKOGO TSENTRAL'NOGO SOIUZA POTREBITEL'NYKH OBSHCHESTV ZA 1920 GOD – M., 1922 – 1mf – 9 – COR-342/1 – ne IDC [334]

OTCHET ZA...G / Vserossiiskii kooperativnyi lesnoi soiuz – (Includes c.1: 1927) – Moskva: Vsekoles, 19uu – 1 – CSUXAKZ6956-S – us Hoover Inst Photo [634]

Otdelenie mekhaniki i protsessov upravleniia Novosibirsk: VTS SO AN SSSR 1970-1986. v1 n1-5 (1970) *see* CHISLENNYE METODY MEKHANIKI SPLOSHNOI SREDY

OTDYKH – Khudozhestvenno-literaturnyi ezhemesiachnyi zhurnal. v. 1-12. Spb. 1899-1900. B-1821 2 – 8 – ne IDC [073]

OTECHESTVEN FRONT – Sofia, Bulgaria. -d. Oct 1944-Nov 1945; Feb 1947-Nov 1953; June 1959-Dec 1970. Imperfect. 41 reels – 1 – uk British Libr Newspaper [949]

OTECHESTVEN FRONT – Sofia, Bulgaria.Sept 1944-May 1990 – 69r – 1 – us L of C Photodup [949]

OTECHESTVEN GLAS – Plovdiv, Bulgaria. Oct 1944-Jan 1946; Jul 1951-1980; 1982-90; 1992 – 55r – 1 – us L of C Photodup [949]

OTECHESTVEN ZOV – (Some issues lacking) – Vratsa, Bulgaria. May 1953-1979 – 21r – 1 – us L of C Photodup [949]

OTECHESTVENNAIA VOINA V RUSSKOI ZHURNALISTIKE / Voenskii, K – Bibliograficheskii sbornik statei, otnoziashchikhsia k 1812 godu. Spb. 1906. BR-5922 2 – 8 – ne IDC [010]

OTECHESTVO – Paris. 1921-1923, nos. 1-6 – 1 – 35.00r – us Hoover Inst Photo [073]

OTEM – New York. 1923 – 1 – us A.J.P.C. [071]

Otero, Caroline *see* LES SOUVENIRS ET LA VIE INTIME DE LA BELLE OTERO

Otero D'Acosta, Enrique *see* COMENTOS CRITICOS SOBRE LA FUNDACION DE CARTAGENA DE INDIAS. BOGOTA

Otero Munoz, Gustavo *see* LA LITERATURA COLONIAL DE COLOMBIA

Oteyza, Luis de *see*
- DE ESPANA AL JAPON
- LA EDIFICANTE AVENTURA DE GARIN
- EN ELREMOTO CIGANGO. JORNADAS JAPONESAS
- FRASES HISTORICAS. VULGANIZACIONES
- PICARESCA PUNTANA

OTGOLOSKI STARINY / Liubetskii, S N – (Istoricheskaia mozaika). M. 1867. BR-7656 2 – 8 – ne IDC [460]

OTHELLO OU LE MORE DE VENISE / Ducis – (French Theatre Series). Paris. Maradan, an II. 1793 – 9 – fr Hachette [820]

"OTHER INDIVIDUALS AND ORGANIZATIONS" FILE OF THE PRESIDENT'S COMMISSION ON THE ASSASSINATION OF PRESIDENT KENNEDY, 1963-1964 – 39r – 1 – M1402 – us Nat'l Archives [324]

OTHER SCENES – 1967- – 1 – us UMI [500]

OTHER SCHOOLS AND GRAPHIC ART – (Includes European and North American Schools. Also Old Master and other prints, book plates and mss. 6,000 reproductions) – 108mf – 9 – $590.00 – 0-907006-12-4 – uk Mindata [760]

OTHER SIDE – (1985-. 5,6,9) – v1-. 1965- – 1 – us UMI [073]

OTHER SIDE / Minco, Marga – 1993 – 118p – 9 – Co-published with Peter Owen, UK – fr UNESCO [830]

THE OTHER SIDE OF EVOLUTION : AN EXAMINATION OF ITS EVIDENCES / Patterson, Alexander – (Includes index) – Chicago: Winona Publ Co, 1903 – 1mf – 9 – 0-8370-4675-0 – 1985-2675 – us A.T.L.A. [240]

OTHER STAND – Montreal. 12 fev 1969-v4 n2. 6 oct 1971f – 1r – 1 – Can$50.00 – cn Can Microfilming [072]

THE OTHER WOMAN; A REVOLUTIONARY FEMINIST NEWSPAPER – v. 1-5. 1972-77 – 1 – $95.00 – cn McLaren [305]

OTHERS – Grantwood, New Jersey. July 1915-July 1919. Incomplete – 1 – us NY Public [073]

OTHMAR / Ouida – British Fiction Archive: Unit 3 – 9 – uk Bell [830]

Othon Ducourneau, D J *see* LES ORIGINES CISTERCIENNES

OTIA HISPANICA / Webb, P B – Parisiis. 1839. B-5802 2 – 8 – ne IDC [580]

OTIS 1764-1849 – (Mf 1T: Marriages & Intentions 1777-1819. Mf 1T-2T: Births & Deaths 1764-1841. Mf 2T: Marriages & Banns 1797-1843. Mf 3T: Marriages & Intentions 1843-49. Mf 3T-4T: Births & Deaths 1765-1855. Mf 4T: Intentions & Marriages 1804-08. Mf 5T: B,M,D 1843-49) – (mf ed 1998) – 5mf – 9 – 0-87623-310-8 – us Holbrook [920]

OTIS 1764-1892 – (Mf 1: Vital Records 1764-1804. Mf 2-5: Vital Records 1767-1842. Mf 6-11: Vital Records 1777-1905. Mf 12-15: Loudon Records 1774-1803. Mf 16-19: Bethelem Records 1889-1910. Mf 20-29: Town records 1802-38. Mf 30-37: Town Records 1838-58. Mf 38-41: Misc Town Records 1861-94. Mf 42-43: Birth Index 1844-1987. Mf 44-45: Marriage Index 1844-1987. Mf 46-47: Death Index 1844-1987. Mf 48-51: Vital Records 1844-92) – (mf ed 1990) – 51mf – 9 – 0-87623-111-3 – us Holbrook [920]

Otis, Harrison G *see* HARRISON GRAY OTIS PAPERS, 1691-1870

Otis, Merrill Edward *see* A PROPOSED TRIBUNAL: IS IT CONSTITUTIONAL?

OTKRYTIE AMERIKI / Maiakovskii, Vladimir – New York. n.d. BR-988 2 – 8 – ne IDC [460]

OTKRYTIE PAMIATNIKA A. S. PUSHKINA V MOSKVE V 1880 GODU / Mezhov, VI – Sochineniia i stat'i napisannyia po povodu etogo torzhestva. Bibliograficheskii ukazatel'. Spb. 1885. BR-7161 2 – 8 – ne IDC [920]

OTKUDA NEUROZHAI I GOLODOVKI / Gorev, Mikhail – Moskva: Giz., 1922 – 1 – CSUX88-B9833 – us Hoover Inst Photo [947]
Otley. Yorkshire *see* PARISH REGISTERS
OTNOSHENIIA SENATA K MESTNYM UCHREZHDENIIAM V XIX VEKE / Blinov, I A – St. Petersburg, 1911. 288p. BR-4230 2 – 8 – ne IDC [947]
OTOE COUNTY GRIT – Dunbar, NE. -w. Nov. 1898-May 1899 – 1 – us NE Hist [071]
OTOE UNION – Unadilla, NE. -w. Dec 1896-Sept 1897; Jan 1902-Dec 1928 – 1 – us NE Hist [071]
OTOE WEEKLY TIMES – Otoe, NE. Sep 1918-Sep 1921 – 1 – us NE Hist [071]
OTOLARYNGOLOGIC CLINICS OF NORTH AMERICA – (v. 8- 1975- 5,6,9) – v. 1- 1968- – 1 – us UMI [617]
OtoLaryngological Society of Australia *see* JOURNAL
OTOLARYNGOLOGY – v. 86. 1978 – 1,5,6,9 – us UMI [617]
Oton, Alfonso y Zaldivar, Ignacio *see* EL DOLOR SUPREMO
OTONIS DE SANCTO BLASIO CHRONICA (MGH 7: 47.BD) : ACCEDUNT EX CHRONICA UNIVERSALI TURICENSI EXCERPTA – 1912 – Dfl13.00 – ne Slangenburg [240]
Ototskii, P V *see* LITERATURA PO RUSSKOMU POCHVOVEDENIIU S 1765 PO 1896 G
LA OTRA UNIVERSIDAD : SOCILOGIA DE LA ENSENANZA A DISTANCIA / Garcia de Leon, Ma Antonia – 3mf – 9 – Pta2,000.00 – 84-85422-19-8 – sp Pentalfa [301]
OTRAES BAPTISTU DRAUDSCHU SAWEENIBAS = HANDBOOK AND MINUTES – 1928, 1929/1930, 1930/1931, 1931/1932. Publ. No. 6344b. One of three items on reel. Total pages 1,412 – 1 – us Baptist [240]
OTRAVLENNAIA TUNIKA I DRUGIE NEIZDANNYE PROIZVEDENIIA POD. RED. G.P. STURVE. IZD. IMENI CHEKHOVA / Gumilev, Nikolai Sepanovich – 1952. BR-1148 2 – 8 – ne IDC [460]
OTRAZHENIIA RUSSKOI REVOLIUTSII NA ZAPADIE : PO LICHNYM NABLIUDENIIAM / Grigorev, Rafail – Petrograd: Izdvo "Sotsialist", 1917 – 1 – CSUX88-B2681 – us Hoover Inst Photo [947]
OTRESHENNYI / Dolinin, A S – (O Sologube). Zavety, 7. 1913. BR-3259 2 – 8 – ne IDC [460]
LOS OTROS, EL PAISAJE Y YO (MECANOGRAFIADO) / Belloso Rodriguez, Pedro – Puebla del Maestre, 1975 – 1 – sp Bibl Santa Ana [810]
Ots, Jose Maria *see* INSTITUCIONES SOCIALES DE LA AMERICA ESPANOLA EN EL PERIODO COLONIAL. LA PLATA, 1934
OTSEGO HERALD – Cooperstown. N.Y. 1795-1820 – 1,3 – us Readex [071]
Otsmane el-Hachaichi, Mohammed ben *see* VOYAGE AU PAYS DES SENOUSSIA A TRAVERS LA TRIPOLITAINE ET LES PAYS TOUAREG
Otsup, N *see*
- BEATRICHE V ADU
- DNEVNIK V STIKHAKH
- LITERATURNYE OCHERKI
- TRI TSARIA
- V DYMU. VTORAIA KNIGA STIKHOV
- VSTRECHA
- ZHIZN' I SMERT'

Ott, A *see* DICTIONNAIRE DES SCIENCES POLITIQUES ET SOCIALES
Ott, I *see* RUOTGERI VITA BRUNONIS ARCHIEPISCOPI COLONIENSIS (MGH 6: 10.BD)
OTTAGONO – Milan, 1966-77 – 5r – 1 – £290.00 – uk Chadwyck [720]
OTTAVAS Y CANCIONES ESPIRITUALES / Aldana, Cosme de – 1578 – 9 – 1.50f – sp Bibl Santa Ana [780]
OTTAWA ADVOCATE – Ottawa, Ontario. v3 n10. 26 mar 1844 – 1r – 1 – Can$25.00 – cn Can Microfilming [072]
THE OTTAWA ARGUS – Aylmer, Canada. v1 n14. 6 mar 1850-v4 n10. 6 oct 1853 – 1r – 1 – Can$25.00 – cn Can Microfilming [072]
OTTAWA BUSINESS LIFE – (Cont by: Ottawa Business Magazine, 1989) – Ottawa, 1984-89 – 9 – Can$20.00y – cn Micromedia [650]
OTTAWA BUSINESS LIFE *see* OTTAWA BUSINESS MAGAZINE
OTTAWA BUSINESS MAGAZINE – (Cont: Ottawa Business Life, 1989. Cont by: Ottawa Business Quarterly, 1992. Cont: Ottawa Business Quarterly, 1994) – Ottawa, 1990-94 – Can$20.00y – cn Micromedia [650]
OTTAWA BUSINESS MAGAZINE *see*
- OTTAWA BUSINESS LIFE
- OTTAWA BUSINESS QUARTERLY

OTTAWA BUSINESS QUARTERLY – (Cont: Ottawa Business Magazine, Spring 1992. Cont by: Ottawa Business Magazine, Winter 1994) – 1992-93 – 9 – Can$20.00y – cn Micromedia [650]
OTTAWA BUSINESS QUARTERLY *see*
- OTTAWA BUSINESS MAGAZINE

THE OTTAWA CHURCH OF ENGLAND MAGAZINE – [Ottawa? : s.n. 1891?-189- or 19–] – 9 – cn C.I.H.M. [240]
OTTAWA CITIZEN – Ottawa, Canada. 1846-92 – 57r – 1 – $3,705.00 – cn Library Assoc [971]
THE OTTAWA CITIZEN – Ottawa, Ontario, CN. 1846- – 36r per yr – 1 – Can$53.00r – cn Commonwealth Micro [072]
OTTAWA COUNTY HERALD – Port Clinton, Ohio. 1906-18 – 5r – 1 – $32.50r – us Archival [071]
OTTAWA COUNTY NEWS – Port Clinton, Ohio. 1865-80; 1931-56 – 17r – 1 – $32.50r – us Archival [071]
OTTAWA COUNTY NEWS-DEMOCRAT – Port Clinton, Ohio. 1894-1931 – 7r – 1 – $32.50r – us Archival [071]
Ottawa County. Ohio. Auditor *see*
- ANNUAL SCHOOL REPORTS
- ASSESSMENT LIST
- CIVIL WAR BOUNTY RECORD
- ENUMERATION OF DEAF, DUMB, ETC
- ENUMERATIONS OF SOLDIERS
- ENUMERATIONS OF YOUTH
- EXEMPTIONS FROM MILITARY SERVICE
- LAND SALES: SWAMP LAND
- MILITIA RECORDS, MISCELLANEOUS
- REAPPRAISEMENT RECORDS
- SCHOOL LAND RECORDS
- SOLDIERS' RELIEF APPLIC. LTTRS
- TAX LISTS

Ottawa County. Ohio. Board of County Commissioners *see*
- COMMISSIONERS' JOURNALS
- INDEX TO JOURNALS
- JOURNALS, COUNTY HOME

Ottawa County. Ohio. Board of Education *see* DAILY CLASS REGISTER
Ottawa County. Ohio. Board of Railroad Appraisers *see* RAILROAD APPRAISEMENT RECORDS
Ottawa County. Ohio. Carroll Township. Board of Education *see*
- MISCELLANEOUS RECORDS
- RECEIPTS AND EXPENDITURES RECORD
- TEACHERS' CONTRACTS

Ottawa County. Ohio. Carroll Township. Board of Elections *see* POLL BOOKS AND TALLY SHEETS
Ottawa County. Ohio. Carroll Township. Board of Health *see* MINUTES AND ORDINANCES
Ottawa County. Ohio. Carroll Township. Board of Trustees *see*
- ACCOUNT BOOKS
- ANNUAL BUDGETS
- CEMETERY DEED MEMORANDUM
- CEMETERY RECORDS
- DITCH JOURNALS
- DITCH PAPERS
- INSURANCE POLICIES
- MINUTES
- MINUTES OF DITCH PROCEEDINGS
- NOTICE REGISTER
- OFFICIALS' BONDS
- PERFORMANCE BONDS
- PETITIONS
- ROAD FUND RECORD
- ROAD RECORD
- ROAD SUPERINTENDENTS' RECORDS

Ottawa County. Ohio. Carroll Township. Fruit Commissioners *see* MINUTES
Ottawa County. Ohio. Carroll Township. Justice of the Peace *see*
- CIVIL DOCKETS
- CIVIL DOCKETS (INDEXED)
- CRIMINAL DOCKETS
- CRIMINAL DOCKETS (INDEXED)

Ottawa County. Ohio. Carroll Township. Township Clerk *see*
- ACCOUNT BOOK OF ORDERS ISSUED
- ACCOUNT BOOKS
- ANNUAL REPORTS
- CHATTEL MORTGAGES AND INDICES
- JOURNAL OF FUNDS
- MISCELLANEOUS RECORDS
- RECEIPTS AND EXPENDITURES RECORD
- RELIEF LISTS AND REPORTS
- SCHOOL FUND ACCOUNT BOOK
- SCHOOL FUND RECORD
- SETTLEMENT SHEETS

Ottawa County. Ohio. Carroll Township. Township Treasurer *see*
- ACCOUNT BOOK
- CASH BOOK

Ottawa County. Ohio. Common Pleas. Civil Division *see*
- NATURALIZATION RECORDS
- NATURALIZATIONS, DECLARATIONS
- QUADRENNIAL ENUMERATIONS

Ottawa County. Ohio. Common Pleas. Juvenile Division *see* MOTHERS' PENSION RECORDS
Ottawa County, Ohio. County Home *see* PAUPERISM STATISTICS
Ottawa County. Ohio. County Home *see*
- MINUTES
- REGISTERS

Ottawa County. Ohio. Erie Township. Board Of Trustees *see* CEMETERY DEED RECORD
Ottawa County. Ohio. Erie Township. Board of Trustees *see* CEMETERY RECORD
Ottawa County. Ohio. Middle Bass Island Board of Education *see* MINUTES
Ottawa County. Ohio. Probate Court *see*
- BIRTH RECORDS
- DECLARATIONS OF INTENTION
- INDEX DECLARATIONS OF INTENT
- INDEX TO NATURALIZATION RECORD
- MARRIAGE RECORDS
- NATURALIZATION – ALIENS/MINORS
- NATURALIZATION CERTIFICATES
- NATURALIZATION RECORDS

Ottawa County. Ohio. Put-in-Bay. Township Board of Education *see* ENUMERATIONS: SCHOOL, AGE, YOUTH
Ottawa County, Ohio. Put-in-Bay, Township Clerk/Treasurer *see* BURIAL PERMITS/ TRANSIT PERMITS
Ottawa County. Ohio. Put-in-Bay. Village. Village Council *see* MINUTES
Ottawa County. Ohio. Recorder *see*
- DEED RECORD
- REGISTER OF CONVEYANCES

Ottawa County. Ohio. Soldiers Relief Commission *see*
- CASE FILES
- CASE FILES – APPLICATIONS AND CORRESPONDENCE
- CASE FILES – REPORTS
- MINUTES

Ottawa County. Ohio. Treasurer *see* TAX DUPLICATE
OTTAWA COUNTY UNION – Port Clinton, Ohio. 1869-71 – 1r – 1 – $32.50r – us Archival [071]
OTTAWA DEMOCRAT – Port Clinton, Ohio. 1857-64 – 1r – 1 – $32.50r – us Archival [071]
Ottawa. Department of National Defence *see* CWAC NEWS LETTER (CANADIAN WOMEN'S ARMY CORPS)
Ottawa Field-Naturalists' Club *see*
- THE CANADIAN FIELD-NATURALIST
- THE OTTAWA NATURALIST

OTTAWA FIELD-NATURALISTS'CLUB *see* THE OTTAWA NATURALIST
OTTAWA FREE PRESS – Ottawa, Canada. 1871-1900 – 71r – 1 – $4,615.00 – cn Library Assoc [971]
OTTAWA FREE PRESS *see* CANADIAN FREE PRESS
OTTAWA JEWISH BULLETIN AND REVIEW – Ottawa, Canada. 26 Oct 1979-19 Jun 1987. English. Incomplete – 1 – us A.J.P.C. [072]
OTTAWA JOURNAL – (Backfiles: 1885-1939 240r Can$12,720. 1940-70 375r Can$19,875. 1971 15r Can$795. 1972-74 72r Can$3,816. 1975 23r Can41,219. 1976-77 26r Can$1,378. 1978-80 64r Can$3,392) – Ottawa, Ontario, CN. 1885-1980 – 1 – cn Commonwealth Micro [072]
OTTAWA LAW REVIEW – (v1-16 1966-84 on reel $220.00. v17-26 1985-94 on mf $261.00) – v1-26. 1966-94 – 5,6,9 – $481.00 set – us Hein [340]
OTTAWA MAGAZINE – Ottawa. v1-14. 1981-94 – 9 – Price varies – cn Micromedia [910]
Ottawa. Minister of National Defence *see* KHAKI: THE ARMY BULLETIN
THE OTTAWA NATURALIST / Ottawa Field-Naturalists' Club – (Cont: Ottawa Field-Naturalists' Club. Cont by: The Canadian Field-Naturalist) – Ottawa: Citizen Print and Pub. Co, 1887-[1919] – 9 – cn C.I.H.M. [500]
THE OTTAWA PARISH MAGAZINE – Ottawa: [s.n. 8–18– or 19–] – 9 – cn C.I.H.M. [240]
THE OTTAWA PHILATELIST – Ottawa: F.L. Chevrier, [1892-1893] – 9 – cn C.I.H.M. [760]
Ottawa Presbyterian Church (Ottawa, Ohio) *see* RECORDS
Ottawa Printing Co *see* PLATT BOOK OF LA SALLE COUNTY
OTTAWA SUN – (Se1988-1992.-100r) – Ottawa, 1993 – 24r – 1 – cn Preston [971]
OTTAWA TIMES – Ottawa, Canada. 1865-77 – 24r – 1 – $1,560.00 – cn Library Assoc [971]
Ottawa Town Company *see* MINUTES OF MEETINGS
OTTAWA TRIBUNE – Ottawa: Wrightson and Rathbone, [1896-1900?] – 9 – cn C.I.H.M. [072]
THE OTTAWA TRIBUNE – Ottawa, Ontario. v10. 29 jan 1864 – 1r – 1 – Can$25.00 – cn Can Microfilming [072]
OTTAWA'S GUIDE – [Ottawa? s.n. 1890?-189- or 19–] – 9 – cn C.I.H.M. [910]
Otte, Enrique *see* EDULARIOS DE LA MONARQUIA ESPANOLA DE MARGARITA, NUEVA ANDALUCIA...TOMO 1 Y 2. CARACAS, 1967
OTTELIA PRAETERITA / Mueller, Ferdinand Jakob Heinrich von – F.v.M. n.p. 1879. B-8071 1 – 9 – ne IDC [580]
Otten, Orvin G *see* A STUDY OF ATTITUDES TOWARD HIGH SCHOOL ACADEMICS REPORTED BY CURRENT FOOTBALL PLAYERS ENROLLING AT SELECTED BIG TEN CONFERENCE UNIVERSITIES FROM 1985 THROUGH 1989
OTTER BOARD DESIGN AND PERFORMANCE – 1974 – 79p – it F.A.O. [639]
Otterbein College *see* FAN-CARDINAL
Otterloo, A A V *see* JOHANNES RUYSBROEC
OTTETTO POUR VIOLON, VIOLA, VIOLONCELLE, FLUTE, CLARINETTE, BASSON ET DEUX CORS / Winter, Peter von – Leipzig: Breitkopf & Haertel, [1812?] – 1 – us Sibley [780]
OTTILIE WILDERMUTHS GESAMMELTE WERKE / ed by Lackowitz, Ida – Neue ill. Ausg. in 2 Bd. Berlin: Merkur, [19–?] – 1 – us U.W. Library [430]
OTTILIE WILDERMUTHS LEBEN : NACH IHREN EIGENEN AUFZEICHNUNGEN / Wildermuth, Ottilie; ed by Willms, Agnes & Wildermuth, Adelheid – 2. durchgesehene Aufl. Stuttgart: Gebrueder Kroener, [1889?] – 1r – 1 – us U.W. Library [920]
OTTILIE WILDERMUTH'S WERKE = WORKS. 1862 / Wildermuth, Ottilie – 1. Gesammt-Ausg. Stuttgart: Adolf Krabbe, 1862 – 1r – 1 – us U.W. Library [943]
Ottino, P *see* ARCHEOLOGIE DES ILES MARQUISES
Ottley, Robert Lawrence *see* THE HEBREW PROPHETS
Ottman, Ford Cyrinde *see* GOD'S OATH: A STUDY OF AN UNFULFILLED PROMISE OF GOD
Otto, C F *see* ABBILDUNG UND BESCHREIBUNG BLUEHENDER CAKTEEN
Otto, CF *see*
- ICONES PLANTARUM RARIORUM HORTI REGII BOTANICI BEROLINENSIS
- ICONES PLANTARUM SELECTARUM HORTI REGII BOTANICI BEROLINENSIS

OTTO DER SCHUETZ : EINE RHEINISCHE GESCHICHTE IN ZWOELF ABENTEUERN / Kinkel, Gottfried – Stuttgart: J G Cotta, 1888 – 1 – us U.W. Library [830]
OTTO ERICH HARTLEBEN / Landsberg, Hans – (Includes bibliographical references) – Berlin: Gose & Tetzlaff, 1905 – 1r – 1 – us U.W. Library [430]
Otto, Gottlieb Friedrich *see* LEXICON DER SEIT DEM 15. JAHRHUNDERT VERSTORBENEN UND JETZT LEBENDEN OBERLAUSITZISCHEN SCHRIFTSTELLER UND KUENSTLER
Otto, Heinrich *see* UEBER DIE BEGABTENAUSLESE BEIM UEBERGANG VON DER GRUNDSCHULE ZUR HOEHEREN SCHULE (AN HAND DER ACH'SCHEN SUCHMETHODE)
Otto, J C T *see* CORPUS APOLOGETARUM CHRISTIANORUM SAECULI SECUNDI
Otto, J CT *see* DE JUSTINI MARTYRIS SCRIPTIS ET DOCTRINA
Otto, Johannes Carl Theodor *see* DES PATRIARCHEN GENNADIOS VON KONSTANTINOPEL CONFESSION

Otto, Louise *see*
- DER GENIUS DER MENSCHHEIT. FRAUENWIRKEN IM DIENSTE DER HUMANITAT. EINE GABE FUR MADCHEN UND FRAUEN
- MEIN LEBENSGANG. GEDICHTE AUS FUNF JAHRZEHNTEN

OTTO LUDWIG IN SEINER STELLUNG ZUR ITALIENISCHEN RENAISSANCE / Scotti, Anita – (Includes bibliographical references) – Zuerich: E Kreutler, 1916 – 1r – 1 – us U.W. Library [430]

OTTO LUDWIGS ERZAEHLUNGSKUNST : MIT BERUECKSICHTIGUNG DER HISTORISCHEN VERHAELTNISSE NACH DEN ERZAEHLUNGEN UND THEORETISCHEN SCHRIFTEN DES DICHTERS / Mueller-Ems, Richard – (Includes bibliographical references (p.[127]-128)) – Berlin: A Kohler, 1905 – 1r – 1 – us U.W. Library [430]

OTTO LUDWIGS LEHRE VON DER TRAGISCHEN SCHULD / Feierfell, Georg – (Includes bibliographical references) – Reichenberg: Selbstverlag des k.k. Staatsgymnasiums, 1904 – 1r – 1 – us U.W. Library [430]

OTTO LUDWIGS TRAUERSPIELPLAN "DER SANDWIRT VON PASSEIER" : UND SEIN VERHAELTNIS ZU DEN "SHAKESPEARESTUDIEN" / Fischer, Bernhard – (Includes bibliographical references) – Anklam: R Poettcke, 1916 – 1r – 1 – us U.W. Library [410]

Otto, Max Carl *see* IS THERE A GOD?

Otto, Rudolf *see*
- THE IDEA OF THE HOLY
- LIFE AND MINISTRY OF JESUS: ACCORDING TO THE HISTORICAL AND CRITICAL METHOD
- NATURALISTISCHE UND RELIGIOESE WELTANSICHT

Otto, Wigand *see* WIGAND'S CONVERSATIONS-LEXIKON [UND] DIE NEUE ZEIT (ERSTER SUPPLEMENTBAND ZU WIGAND'S CONVERSATIONS-LEXIKON)(AEL, ABT 1;17)

OTTOKARS OESTERREICHISCHE REIMCHRONIK (MGH 8: 5.BD) – 1890-1893 – Dfl144.00 – ne Slangenburg [240]

L'OTTOMANNO / Soranzo, L – Ferrara, 1598 – 3mf – 9 – H-8400/1 – ne IDC [956]

DIE OTTONENZEIT (MGH ANTIQUITATES 1: 5.BD. 1.TEIL 1 UND 2 HEFT)) – 1937-1939 – Dfl56.00 – ne Slangenburg [240]

OTTONIS EPISCOPI FRISINGENSIS CHRONICA SIVE HISTORIA DE DUABUS CIVITATIBUS (MGH 7: 45.BD) – Ed 2a. 1912 – Dfl46.00 – ne Slangenburg [240]

OTTONIS ET RAHEWINI GESTA FRIDERICI 1 IMPERATORIS (MGH 7: 46.BD) – Ed 3a. 1912 – Dfl25.00 – ne Slangenburg [240]

OTTONIS MORENAE ET CONTINUATORUM HISTORIA FREDERICI 1 (MGH 6: 7.BD) / ed by Gaeterbock, F – 1930 – Dfl22.00 – ne Slangenburg [240]

Otto-Peters, Louise *see* SCHLOSS UND FABRIK

Otts, John Martin Philip *see*
- CHRIST AND THE CHERUBIM, OR, THE ARK OF THE COVENANT A TYPE OF CHRIST
- EVANGELISTS AND LAY-EXHORTERS
- THE FIFTH GOSPEL: THE LAND WHERE JESUS LIVED
- UNSETTLED QUESTIONS TOUCHING THE FOUNDATIONS OF CHRISTIANITY

OTUMBA RELACION DE LA BRILLANTE VICTORIA ALCANZADA POR HERNAN CORTES EN MEJICO POR DON... / Solis Rivadeneyra, Antonio de – Barcelona: Editorial FTD, 1926 – 1 – sp Bibl Santa Ana [972]

OTVET G.G. STRUVE I FILIPPOVU / Ivanov, G – Novyi zhurnal. New York. 1956. BR-3664 2 – 8 – ne IDC [073]

OTVET RUSSKIKH PISATELEI ANGLIISKIM SOBRAT'IAM – Birzhevy vedomosti. nr. 14753. 1915. BR-3330 2 – 8 – ne IDC [460]

OTVETY NA VOPROSY UCHREZHDENII MELKOGO KREDITA / Podol'skii, IM – Pg., 1915 – 4mf – 9 – COR-86/1 – ne IDC [334]

OTVI ETSTVENNOST TSARIA : RIECH, PROIZNESENNAIA V. BURTSEVYM NA MITINGIEV "KUPER-I UNION" V NI U-LORKI E 25-GO APRIELIA 1910 G., USTROENNOM OBSHCHESTVOM AMERIKANSKIKH DRUZEI RUSSKOI SVOBODY / Burtsev, Vladimir Lvovich – Parizh: Izd. red. zhurnala "Byloe", 1910 – 1 – CSUX89-B4290 – us Hoover Inst Photo [947]

Otway, A *see* AUTOBIOGRAPHY AND JOURNALS OF ADMIRAL LORD CLARENCE E. PAGET, G.C.B

Otway, Thomas *see* THOMAS OTWAY. WITH AN INTROD. AND NOTES BY THE HON. RODEN NOEL

OU VA L'INDUSTRIE? / Association Professionnelle des Industriels. Congres Patronal (4e: 1949: Montreal, Quebec) – Montreal: Association Professionnelle des Industriels, 1948 [i.e. 1949] – 2mf – 9 – Can$4.50 – cn Bibl Nat [338]

THE OUANANICHE : HOTEL ROBERVAL – Roberval, Canada. v1 n6. 18 aut 1906 – 1r – 1 – Can$25.00 – cn Can Microfilming [072]

THE OUANANICHE AND ITS CANADIAN ENVIRONMENT / Chambers, Edward Thomas Davies – New York: Harper, 1896. 00549. (Pre-1900 Canadiana) – 9 – cn C.I.H.M. [590]

Ouane, Ibrahim Manadou *see* FADIMATA, LA PRINCESSE DU DESERT

Ouane, Ibrahima Mamadou *see*
- LE COLLIER DE COQUILLAGES
- L'ISLAM ET LA CIVILISATION FRANCAISE

Ouane, Ibrahima Manadou *see* L'ENIGME DU MACINA

OUATOUR POUR FLUTE,...OP. 84 / Amon, J A – Offenbach: J Andre, 1825? – 1 – us Sibley [780]

Oubangui-Chari-Tchad *see* JOURNAL OFFICIEL

L'OUBLIE / Conan, Laure – 9e ed. Montreal: Librairie Beauchemin limitee, 1939. SEM105P1289 – 2mf – 9 – Can$4.50 – cn Bibl Nat [890]

L'OUBLIE / Conan, Laure – Montreal: C.O. Beauchemin et fils, 1902. SEM105P923 – 3mf – 9 – Can$6.75 – cn Bibl Nat [971]

L'OUBLIE / Conan, Laure – Montreal: Librairie Beauchemin Limitee, 1939 – 2mf – 9 – Can$4.50 – cn Bibl Nat [440]

OUD EN NIEUW OOST-INDIEN / Valentijn, F – Dordrecht, Amsterdam, 1724-1726 – 5v 94mf – 9 – SEP-74/1 – ne IDC [950]

OUD HOLLAND : NIEUWE BIJDRAGEN VOOR DE GESCHIEDENIS DER NEDERLANDSCHE KUNST, LETTERKUNDE – Amsterdam. v1-49. 1883-1932 – 287mf – 9 – ne IDC [700]

OUD SOERABAIA. DE GESCHIEDENIS VAN INDIE'S EERSTE KOOPSTAD VAN DE OUDSTE TIJDEN TOT DE INSTELLING VAN DE GEMEENTERAAD / Faber, G H von – Soerabaia, 1931 – 13mf – 9 – ne IDC [950]

Oudart, PL *see* LA GALERIE DES OISEAUX

DE OUDE EMIGRANT – Pretoria, South Africa. 1938 – 1 – sa State Libr [072]

OUDE GEGEVENS SEMARANG, VERZ. DOOR J.W. MEYER RANNEFT – 1913. Col.M.R., no.3. BSD-110/1 mf.1-2 – 9 – ne IDC [950]

HET OUDE KERSPEL WINTERSWIJK / Stegeman, B – Zutphen, 1927 – Dfl28.00 – ne Slangenburg [240]

DE OUDE TIJD – 1869-74 – 1 – us I.U. Libraries [390]

HET OUDE VOLK, VOORHEEN EN THANS – Amsterdam. v1-2. 1917-19 – 16mf – 9 – ne IDC [949]

OUDERLINGENBLAD – (Some pgs lacking) – 1970-92 – Inquire – 1 – ATLA S0744 – us A.T.L.A. [073]

OUDHEDEN EN GESTICHTEN / ed by Heussen, J van & Rijn, J van – Leiden. v1-13. 1719-1749 – 9 – Dfl427.00 – ne Slangenburg [949]

OUDHEDEN.. VAN GRONINGEN – Leiden, 1724 – Dfl35.00 – ne Slangenburg [240]

OUDHEDEN... VAN RHIJNLAND – Leiden, 1719 – Dfl39.00 – ne Slangenburg [240]

OUDHEDEN...VAN DELFT EN DELFLAND, MITSGADERS VAN 'S GRAVENHAGE – Leiden, 1720 – Dfl35.00 – ne Slangenburg [240]

OUDHEDEN...VAN HET BISDOM DEVENTER – Leiden. 2v. 1725 – Dfl77.00 – ne Slangenburg [240]

OUDHEDEN...VAN NOORD-HOLLAND – Leiden. 2v. 1721 – Dfl60.00 – ne Slangenburg [240]

OUDHEDEN..VAN 'S HERTOGENBOSCH – Leiden, 1749 – Dfl39.00 – ne Slangenburg [240]

OUDHEDEN...VAN VRIESLAND – Leiden. 2v. 1723 – Dfl63.00 – ne Slangenburg [240]

OUDHEDEN...VAN ZEELAND – Leiden. 2v. 1722 – Dfl49.00 – ne Slangenburg [240]

OUDHEDEN...VAN ZUID-HOLLAND – Leiden, 1719 – Dfl32.00 – ne Slangenburg [240]

OUDHEIDKUNDIGE INLICHTINGEN IN KERKELIJK OPZICHT / Rooy, K van – Brugge, 1899 – 7mf – 8 – Dfl28.00 – ne Slangenburg [240]

Oudin, A *see*
- CURIOSITEZ FRANCOISES
- GRAMMAIRE FRANCOISE, RAPPORTEE AU LANGAGE DU TEMPS. REVUEE ET AUGMENTEE DE BEAUCOUP EN CETTE SECONDE EDITION
- RECHERCHES ITALIENNES ET FRANCOISES

Oudin, C *see* THRESOR DES TROIS LANGUES, ESPAGNOLE, FRANCOISE ET ITALIENNE

Oudin, Cesar Francois *see* NOUVEAU RECUEIL DE DIVERTISSEMENS COMIQUES

OUD-ISRAELS RECHTSWEZEN / Oort, Henricus – Leiden: E.J. Brill, 1892. 1 fiche – 9 – us A.T.L.A. [270]

OUD-NEDERLANDSCH PROCESRECHT / Goede, Arian de – Utrecht: Dekker en Van de Vegt, 1948. 396p. LI-4101 – 1 – us L of C Photodup [340]

Oudschans Dentz, F *see* DE KOLONISATIE VAN DE PORTUGEESCH JOODSCHE NATIE IN SURINAME EN DE GESCHIEDENIS VAN DE JODEN SAVANNE

OUDTESTAMENTISCHE STUDIEN – Deel 1, 2+3 1942-1943 – 14mf – 8 – ne Slangenburg [220]

OUDTSHOORN COURANT – Oudtshoorn, South Africa. 11 Jun 1879-30 Dec 1932. 64 reels – 1, 16 diazo available at reduced price – sa SA Libr [072]

Ouekaki-Morikouni *see* YO-SAN-FI-ROK, L'ART D'ELEVER LES VERS A SOIE AU JAPON

Ouellet, Therese *see* BIBLIOGRAPHIE DU THEATRE CANADIEN-FRANCAIS AVANT 1900

L'OUEST AFRICAIN ET LES MISSIONS CATHOLIQUES : CONGO ET OUBANGHI / Renouard, G – Paris: H Oudin, [1906?] – us Res Libr [240]

L'OUEST AFRICAIN FRANCAIS : SES RESOURCES AGRICOLES, SON ORGANISATION ECONOMIQUE / Cosnier, Henri Charles – Paris: E Larose, 1921 – us Res Libr [630]

L'OUEST CANADIEN – Edmonton, Alberta. 3 fev 1898-v2 n53. 22 fev 1900 – 1r – 1 – Can$45.00 – cn Can Microfilming [072]

L'OUEST CANADIEN – Winnipeg, Canada. 14 fev 1889-v1 n26. 14 aut 1889 – 1r – 1 – Can$35.00 – cn Can Microfilming [072]

L'OUEST- ECLAIR – (Library has: April 17, 20-21, Oct. 17, 1918; Feb. 28, 1940-July 31, 1944. Approximately 60 scattered issues wanting) – Rennes, France: L'Quest- eclair, 1900 – 1 – CSUX89-S61 – us Hoover Inst Photo [944]

L'OUEST FRANCAIS – Bay City, MI. v1 n3. 29 jun 1888-6 avr 1889 – 1r – 1 – Can$30.00 – cn Can Microfilming [071]

L'OUEST-ECLAIR – Journal republicain du matin. Dir. politique Emmanuel Desgrees du Lou. Rennes. 1921, 1923, 1931 – 1 – fr A.C.R.P.P. [073]

OUEST-FRANCE – Rennes: Societe d'editions, 1970-78 (100r); 1979-jan 1 1982 (36r) – 1 – us Res Libr [072]

OUEST-KEBEC – Hull, Canada. 1 sep 1971; v2 n1. 23 mai 1973 – 1r – 1 – Can$25.00 – cn Can Microfilming [072]

OUGHT WE TO SAVE? / Paish, George – 1928. 1 fiche (29x) – 9 – 1.00f – at Libertarian Micro [320]

"OUI" AU REFERENDUM – Montreal, 30 jun 1977 – 1r – 1 – Can$30.00 – cn Can Microfilming [072]

OUI (L'AVENIR) – Paris, France. 2 May 1918-12 Aug 1919 (imperfect) – 4r – 1 – uk British Libr Newspaper [072]

Ouida *see*
- AN ALTRUIST
- ARIADNE
- BIMBI
- CECIL CASTLEMAINE'S GAGE
- CHANDOS
- CRITICAL STUDIES
- A DOG OF FLANDERS
- A DOG OF FLANDERS, AND OTHER STORIES
- DON GESUALDO
- FOLLE-FARINE
- FRESCOES
- FRIENDSHIP
- GUILDEROY
- HELD IN HOSTAGE
- HELIANTHUS
- A HOUSE PARTY
- IDALIA
- IN A WINTER CITY
- IN MAREMMA
- THE MASSARENES
- MOTHS
- OTHMAR
- PASCAREL
- PIPISTRELLO
- PRINCESS NAPRAXINE
- PUCK
- A RAINY JUNE
- RUFFINO
- SANTA BARBARA
- LE SELVE
- SIGNA
- THE SILVER CHRIST AND A LEMON TREE
- STRATHMORE
- STREET DUST
- LA STREGA
- SYRLIN
- THE TOWER OF TADDEO
- TOXIN
- TRICOTRIN
- TWO LITTLE WOODEN SHOES
- TWO OFFENDERS
- UNDER TWO FLAGS
- VIEWS AND OPINIONS
- A VILLAGE COMMUNE
- WANDA
- THE WATERS OF EDEIRA

Oulton, J *see* A VINDICATION OF THE SEVENTEENTH ARTICLE OF THE CHURCH OF ENGLAND FROM THE ASPERSIONS CAST ON IT IN A SERMON LATELY PUBLISHED BY MR. JOHN WESLEY

OUMA *see* EL-OUMA

OUR ADVERSARY / Braddon, Mary Elizabeth – British Fiction Archive: Unit 5 – 9 – uk Bell [830]

Our American Heritage Committee *see* NEWS BULLETIN

OUR ARCHITECTURAL HERITAGE : FROM CONSCIOUSNESS TO CONSERVATION / Erder, Cevat – 1986 – 236p – 9 – 92-3-102363-2 – fr UNESCO [720]

OUR ATTITUDE TOWARDS ENGLISH ROMAN CATHOLICS AND THE PAPAL COURT / Galton, Arthur – New York: E.P. Dutton; London: E. Stock, [1902?] – 1mf – us A.T.L.A. [240]

OUR BAPTIST MINISTERS AND SCHOOLS / Pegues, A W – 1892. 644p – 1 – 22.54 – us Baptist [240]

OUR BEST POLICY – Continental Union Association of Ontario, August, 1895. Toronto: Hunter, Rose, 1885. 02271. (Pre-1900 Canadiana) – 9 – cn C.I.H.M. [971]

OUR BIBLE : HOW IT HAS COME TO US / Talbot, Reginald Thomas – (Includes index) – New York:Thomas Whittaker, 1894 – 1mf – 9 – 0-8370-5479-6 – 1985-3479 – us A.T.L.A. [240]

OUR BOOTH'S BAZOO – Needles. Calif. 1889-1890 – 1 – us UMI [071]

OUR BOYS – [Toronto]: Boy's Committee of the Toronto Young Men's Christian Association, [1883?-18–?] – 9 – cn C.I.H.M. [240]

OUR BOYS MAGAZINE – Mimico [Ont]: Published by the Boys of Victoria Industrial School, [1894?-192-?] – 9 – cn C.I.H.M. [370]

OUR CALENDAR / North Baptist Church – [Halifax, N.S.?: The Church?, 1898?-19–] – 9 – cn C.I.H.M. [240]

OUR CHRISTIAN HERITAGE / Gibbons, James – (Includes bibliographical references and index) – Baltimore: John Murphy; London: R Washbourne, 1889 – 2mf – 9 – 0-8370-9781-9 – 1986-3781 – us A.T.L.A. [230]

OUR CHURCH HERITAGE, OR, THE SCOTTISH CHURCHES VIEWED IN THE LIGHT OF THEIR HISTORY / Walker, Norman Lockhart – London, New York: T. Nelson, 1893 – 1mf – us A.T.L.A. [240]

OUR CHURCH MONTHLY – [Springhill, N.S.: s.n. 1894?-189- or 19–] – 9 – cn C.I.H.M. [240]

OUR CHURCH MUSIC : A BOOK FOR PASTORS AND PEOPLE / Willis, Richard Storrs – New York: Dana, 1856, c1855 – 1mf – us A.T.L.A. [780]

OUR CHURCH PAPER : DEVOTED TO THE INTERESTS OF THE EVANGELICAL LUTHERAN CHURCH – (Lacking: v13-29 1885-1901) – v1-32 no 35. 1873-30 Aug 1904 – 4r – 1 – ATLA S0096 – us A.T.L.A. [073]

OUR CHURCH TIDINGS – Talbotville [Ont: s.n. 1896?-19–] – 9 – cn C.I.H.M. [240]

OUR CLERGYWOMEN / Holland, Frederic May – The Open Court, v. 6 no. 231, Jan. 28, 1892, p. 3121-3123) – 9 – us A.T.L.A. [240]

OUR COLONIAL EMPIRE / Acton, Richard – 2nd ed. London: Cassell, Petter, Galpin, 1881?.06068.(Pre-1900 Canadiana) – 9 – cn C.I.H.M. [321]

OUR COLONY OF NATAL / Peace, Walter – London: E Stanford, [1883] – us Res Libr [960]

OUR COMMERCE, IN WAR; AND HOW TO PROTECT IT / Danson, John Towne – 1897 – 9 – uk Libr Preservation [941]

OUR COMMUNITY – (Jan. 1979-Nov. 1981; May/June 1982; Dec. 1982; Feb. 1983-May/June 1984; Oct. 1984; Apr. 1985-May 1985; Sept. 1985-Nov. 1985) – South Bend, Indiana – 1 – us A.J.P.C. [978]

OUR CORNER / ed by Besant, Anne Wood – 1883-88 – 5 – PS90.00 – uk World [073]

OUR CORNER – v1-12 (all publ). 1883-1888 – 2r – 1 – $245.00 – us UPA [335]

OUR COUNTRY / Peck, George – 1865 – 9 – us A.T.L.A. [240]

OUR COUNTRY'S SIN : A SERMON / Perkins, Justin – New York: H.B. Knight, 1854 – 1mf – us A.T.L.A. [240]

OUR COUNTY AND ITS PEOPLE / Bates, Samuel P – Historical and memorial of Crawford County. W. A. Ferguson and Co., 1899. Pennsylvania Reel 17. (The Cox Library Collection) – 5 – us Americana [978]

OUR COUNTY AND ITS PEOPLE (GENESEE) / North, Safford E – Biographical. Boston, Boston History Co., 1899. New York Reel 16. (The Cox Library Collection) – 5 – us Americana [978]

OUR COUNTY AND ITS PEOPLE-ERIE / White, Truman C – Boston, Boston History Co., 1898. Vol. 1. New York Reel 14; Vol. 2. New York Reel 15. (The Cox Library Collection) – 5 – us Americana [978]

OUR COUNTY AND ITS PEOPLE-JEFFERSON / Emerson, Edgar C – Boston, Boston History Co., 1898. New York Reel 18. (The Cox Library Collection) – 5 – us Americana [978]

OUR COUNTY AND ITS PEOPLE-MADISON COUNTY / Smith, John E – Boston, Boston History Co., 1899. New York Reel 22. (The Cox Library Collection) – 5 – us Americana [978]

OUR COUNTY AND ITS PEOPLE-ONEIDA / Wager, Daniel E – Boston, Boston History Co., 1896. New York Reel 25. (The Cox Library Collection) – 5 – us Americana [978]

OUR DEBT TO SPAIN. LONDON, 1938 / Peers, A Allison – Burgos: Razon y Fe, 1938 – 1 – sp Bibl Santa Ana [946]

OUR DISRESPECT FOR LAW / Avery, Asahel George – Seattle? 1908 15 p. LL-670 – 1 – us L of C Photodup [340]

OUR EASTERN SISTERS AND THEIR MISSIONARY HELPERS / Ellis, Harriet W – 1883 – 9 – us A.T.L.A. [240]

OUR ENGLISH BIBLE: ITS TRANSLATIONS AND TRANSLATORS / Stoughton, John – London: Religious Tract Society, 1872.1 fiche – 9 – us A.T.L.A. [240]

OUR EXCELLENT WOMEN OF THE METHODIST CHURCH IN ENGLAND AND AMERICA – 1873 – 9 – us A.T.L.A. [240]

OUR FAULTY GAOL SYSTEM: MEMORANDUM OF AN ADDRESS DELIVERED ON BEHALF OF THE PRISONERS' AID ASSOCIATION IN THE METROPOLITAN CHURCH, TORONTO / Blake, Samuel Hume – 1896. 00178. (Pre-1900 Canadiana) – 9 – cn C.I.H.M. [360]

OUR FIGHT WITH TAMMANY / Parkhurst, Charles H – New York: Scribner, 1895 – 1mf – us A.T.L.A. [240]

OUR FISHERY RIGHTS IN THE NORTH ATLANTIC / Doran, Joseph I – Philadelphia: Allen, Lane & Scott, 1888. 02740. (Pre-1900 Canadiana) – 9 – cn C.I.H.M. [971]

OUR FOREST CHILDREN – 1889-90 – 1 – 65.00 – cn McLaren [970]

OUR FOUNDERS AND THEIR STORY : A SHORT HISTORY OF THREE CHURCHES AND THEIR UNION AS THE UNITED METHODIST CHURCH / Eayrs, G – 2nd ed. London, 1907. 63p – 1mf – 9 – ne IDC [240]

OUR FRIENDS IN HEAVEN / Killen, James Miller – 1857 – 9 – us A.T.L.A. [240]

OUR GENERATION – (v1-15 1961-83 Can$100.00. v 16-17 1983-86 Can$50.00.v18-26 1986/87-1995 Can) – Montreal. v1-26. 1961-95 – 5,9 – Price varies – cn Micromedia [073]

OUR HIGHWAYS TO THE SEA BY RAIL AND WATER: THE ENLARGEMENT OF THE CANALS AN INTERNATIONAL WORK / Fisher, James – Winnipeg?: s.n., 1891 (Winnipeg: McIntyre). 05469. (Pre-1900 Canadiana) – 9 – cn C.I.H.M. [971]

OUR HOME – (Cont by: Home and Youth) – Montreal: Wells and Richardson, [1893?-1897] – 9 – cn C.I.H.M. [640]

OUR HOME *see* HOME AND YOUTH

OUR HOME COMPANION – London, Ont: Companion Pub. Co, [1876?-18–?] – 9 – cn C.I.H.M. [971]

OUR HOMES AND NEWS-RECORD – DuBois, NE. -w. Jun. 1900-Sep. 1906 – 1 – us NE Hist [071]

OUR HOPE – (Cont by: Eternity) – July 1894 – December 1957 – 341mf – 9 – $875.00 – us Schnappsburg [240]

OUR ILLUSTRATED ROYAL NEWS – (Advertising circular for the Royal Baking Powder Co of New York, with local advertising content) – Warren, OH. oct, 1873 – 1r – 1 – us Western Res [071]

OUR IMPORT TRADE: COMMERCIAL RELATIONS WITH BRITAIN AS AFFECTED BY THE TARIFF – 1891?. 03697. (Pre-1900 Canadiana) – 9 – cn C.I.H.M. [971]

OUR INDIA MISSION : A THIRTY YEAR'S HISTORY OF THE INDIA MISSION OF THE UNITED PRESBYTERIAN CHURCH OF NORTH AMERICA: TOGETHER WITH PERSONAL REMINISCENCES / Gordon, Andrew – (Includes index) – Philadelphia: Andrew Gordon, 1886 – 2mf – 9 – 0-8370-6499-6 – 1986-0499 – us A.T.L.A. [240]

OUR INDIAN FIELD – v20-35. Apr 1934-6 Dec 1949 (complete) – 2r – 1 – ATLA S0486 – us A.T.L.A. [073]

OUR INHERITANCE IN THE GREAT PYRAMID / Smyth, Charles P – 1880 – 1 – us A.T.L.A. [956]

OUR INSTITUTIONS – New York. N.Y. 1924 – 1 – us A.J.P.C. [071]

OUR INTELLECTUAL STRENGTH AND WEAKNESS: A SHORT HISTORICAL AND CRITICAL REVIEW OF LITERATURE, ART AND EDUCATION IN CANADA / Bourinot, John George – Montreal: F. Brown, 1893. 00205. (Pre-1900 Canadiana) – 9 – cn C.I.H.M. [971]

OUR IRON-CLAD SHIPS; THEIR QUALITIES, PERFORMANCES AND CO WITH CHAPTERS ON TURRET SHIPS, IRONCLAD RAMS, ETC / Reed, Edward James – 1869 – 9 – $20.00 – uk Libr Preservation [623]

OUR JEWISH NEIGHBORS – Sep 1921-Jun 1931 (complete) – 1r – 1 – ATLA S0687 – us A.T.L.A. [270]

OUR JOURNAL – Quebec, Canada. v1 n34. 14 mai 1853 – 1r – 1 – Can$25.00 – cn Can Microfilming [073]

OUR JOURNAL – v1-20. 1884-1906 (complete) – 2r – 1 – ATLA R0121 – us A.T.L.A. [073]

OUR JOURNAL IN THE PACIFIC / Eardley-Wilmot, Sidney; ed by Lieutenant S – By the officers of H.M.S. Zealous; arranged and Eardley-Wilmot. London: Longmans – 9 – cn C.I.H.M. [910]

OUR JOURNEY AROUND THE WORLD: AN ILLUSTRATED RECORD OF A YEAR'S TRAVEL OF FORTY THOUSAND MILES THROUGH INDIA, CHINA, JAPAN, AUSTRALIA, NEW ZEALAND, EGYPT, PALESTINE, GREECE, TURKEY, ITALY, FRANCE, SPAIN, ETC / Clark, Francis Edward – Hartford, Conn.: A. D. Worthington, 1894. 05409. (Pre-1900 Canadiana) – 9 – cn C.I.H.M. [910]

OUR JOURNEY TO SPAIN – Madrid, 1938? Fiche W1093. (Blodgett Collection of Spanish Civil War Pamphlets) – 9 – us H.U. College Libr [946]

OUR LADY OF PELLEVOISIN – Outremont: Juvenate of the Clerics of St-Viateur, [1898 ?]. SEM105P528 – 1mf – 9 – Can$2.25 – cn Bibl Nat [240]

OUR LADY'S DIGEST – v1- 1946- 1; v26- 5,6; v30- 9 – us UMI [073]

OUR LAITY: AND THEIR EQUAL RIGHTS WITHOUT DISTINCTION OF SEX IN THE METHODIST EPISCOPAL CHURCH / Kynett, Alpha Jefferson – 1896 – 9 – us A.T.L.A. [240]

OUR LIBERAL MOVEMENT IN THEOLOGY, CHIEFLY AS SHOWN IN RECOLLECTIONS OF THE HISTORY OF UNITARIANISM IN NEW ENGLAND / Allen, Joseph Henry – 1882 – 1 – us A.T.L.A. [240]

OUR LOCAL PORTFOLIO – (Extracts from: The Halifax Guardian) – Yorkshire, 1856-69 – 7 – uk Microform Academic [072]

OUR LORD'S SIGNS IN ST JOHN'S GOSPEL : DISCUSSIONS CHIEFLY EXEGETICAL AND DOCTRINAL ON THE EIGHT MIRACLES IN THE FOURTH GOSPEL / Hutchison, John – (Includes bibliographical references) – Edinburgh: T & T Clark, 1892 – 1mf – 9 – 0-8370-3705-0 – 1985-1705 – us A.T.L.A. [220]

OUR LORD'S TEACHING / Robertson, James Craigie – (Includes bibliographical references) – New York:Anson D F Randolph; London:Adam and Charles Black, [1895?] – 1mf – 9 – 0-8370-4924-5 – 1985-2924 – us A.T.L.A. [240]

OUR LORD'S THREE RAISINGS FROM THE DEAD / Macmillan, Hugh – New York: E P Dutton, 1876 – 1mf – 9 – 0-8370-4247-X – 1985-2247 – us A.T.L.A. [240]

OUR MESS / ed by Lever, Charles James – Dublin: W. Curry; London: William S. Orr and Co., 1843-44 – 2 rolls – 1 – 1-55879-258-9 – uk Libr Preservation [920]

OUR MESSENGER – (Cont by: The Church Messenger for the Diocese of Qu'Appelle) – Fort Qu'Appelle [Sask]: Printed and pub. at the "Vidette" Office, [1888-188- or 189-] – 9 – cn C.I.H.M. [240]

OUR MISSION – (Cont: Our Mission Union) – Toronto: Willard Tract Depository, [1885-1886] – 9 – cn C.I.H.M. [240]

OUR MISSION *see* OUR MISSION UNION

OUR MISSION NEWS – (Cont by: Canadian Church Magazine and Mission News) – Hamilton, Ont: Domestic and Foreign Missionary Society of the Church of England in Canada [1886-1887] – 9 – cn C.I.H.M. [240]

OUR MISSION NEWS *see* THE CANADIAN CHURCH MAGAZINE AND MISSION NEWS

OUR MISSION UNION – (Cont by: Our Mission) – Toronto: S.R. Briggs, [1884-1885] – 9 – cn C.I.H.M. [240]

OUR MISSION UNION *see*
- OUR MISSION
- OUR YOUNG PEOPLE'S MISSION UNION

OUR MONTHLY – Toronto: G Moffat, v1 no 1(May 1896)- – 9 – cn C.I.H.M. [073]

OUR MONTHLY – Toronto: Manufacturers Life and Accident Insurance Companies, [1891-189- or 19–] – 9 – cn C.I.H.M. [360]

OUR NATIVE FERNS; OR A HISTORY OF THE BRITISH SPECIES AND THEIR VARIETIES / Lowe, E J – London, 1865-1867. 2 vols. B-7216 1 – 9 – ne IDC [580]

OUR NEGRO AND INDIAN MISSIONS – 1950-70. (American Indian Periodicals in the Princeton University Library). 9 fiches – 9 – $50.00 – us UPA [240]

OUR NEIGHBOR NICARAGUA / Cramer, Floyd – New York: Fred. A. Stokes, c1929 – 1 – us U.W. Library [972]

OUR NEW NEW TESTAMENT : AN EXPLANATION OF THE NEED AND A CRITICISM OF THE FULFILMENT / Nicholson, Edward Byron – (Includes appendixes) – London: Rivingtons, 1881 – 1mf – 9 – 0-8370-4585-1 – 1985-2585 – us A.T.L.A. [220]

OUR NEW TESTAMENT : HOW DID WE GET IT? / Vedder, Henry Clay – (Includes appendixes containing translated ancient documents bearing on the history of the N.T canon and index) – Philadelphia: Griffith & Rowland, c1908 – 1mf – 9 – 0-8370-5627-6 – 1985-3627 – us A.T.L.A. [220]

OUR NEW WEST / Bowles, Samuel – Records of travel. Hartford: Hartford Publ. Co., 1869. California Reel 1. The Cox Library Collection – 5 – us Americana [978]

OUR OLD PIONEERS: A MEMORIAL ADDRESS AT THE HILLHOUSE GRAVEYARD, SUNDAY JAN 31, 1925 / Armstrong, J W – Stoutland, MO. Missouri Reel 12. (The Cox Library Collection) – 5 – us Americana [978]

OUR OWN ENGLISH BIBLE : ITS TRANSLATORS AND THEIR WORK / Heaton, William James – (Includes bibliographical references) – London: Francis Griffiths, 1905 – 1mf – 9 – 0-8370-9155-1 – 1986-3155 – us A.T.L.A. [220]

OUR OWN FIRESIDE – Whitby, Ont: J.S. Robertson, [1883?-18–] – 9 – cn C.I.H.M. [073]

OUR OWN MAGAZINE – Toronto: Dominion Publishing Co, [1870?-18–?] – 9 – cn C.I.H.M. [073]

OUR PARISH; OR, PEN PAINTINGS OF VILLAGE LIFE / Hill, George Canning – Boston: L.P. Crown; Philadelphia: J.W. Bradley, 1856. 452p – 1 – us U.W. Library [750]

OUR PATRON – v2-3. 1929-32 (complete) – 2r – 1 – ATLA S0910 – us A.T.L.A. [073]

OUR PICTURESQUE NORTHERN NEIGHBOR: HISTORICAL AND DESCRIPTIVE SKETCHES OF THE SCENERY AND LIFE...TORONTO...CANADIAN SHORE OF LAKE HURON...NORTHWEST TERRITORIES...BRITISH COLUMBIA / ed by Grant, George Monro – Chicago: A. Belford, 1899. 05120. (Pre-1900 Canadiana) – 9 – cn C.I.H.M. [910]

OUR PROGRAMME / Ussishkin, M – New York. 1905. BJ-28-61 1 – 9 – ne IDC [956]

OUR PUBLIC LANDS – v1- 1951- 1; v22- 5,6; v26- 9 – us UMI [333]

OUR PUBLIC RECORDS: A BRIEF HANDBOOK TO THE NATIONAL ARCHIVES / Ewald, Alexander Charles – London: B.M. Pickering, 1873. viii,158p – 1 – us U.W. Library [025]

OUR QUARTERLY *see* THE PALM BRANCH

OUR RECENT VISIT TO TRINIDAD: AND THE OPENING OF THE PRESBYTERIAN COLLEGE IN SAN FERNANDO / Clark, Mary Alice – (Ottawa: J. Hope), 1892. 00917. (Pre-1900 Canadiana) – 9 – cn C.I.H.M. [910]

OUR RECORD – London, Ont: The Church,[1888-18– or 19–] – 9 – cn C.I.H.M. [240]

OUR REDEMPTION: ITS NEED, METHOD AND RESULT / Noble, Frederick Alphonso – New York: Fleming H. Revell, 1897. 1 fiche – 9 – us A.T.L.A. [240]

OUR RELIGION: AS IT WAS AND AS IT IS / Laidlaw, Robert J – (Includes index) – Toronto: Hunter, Rose, 1879 – 1mf – 9 – 0-8370-4398-0 – 1985-2398 – us A.T.L.A. [240]

OUR SCHOOLS/OUR SELVES – (Each vol is composed of 4 issues and 3-4 monographs) – Toronto. v1-5. 1988/89-1993/94 – 9 – Can$37.00y – cn Micromedia [370]

OUR SECOND YEAR'S HARVEST : BEING A BRIEF RECORD OF A YEAR OF DIVINE HEALING MISSIONS ON THE PACIFIC COAST OF AMERICA... / Dowie, John A – Chicago: International Divine Healing Association, 1891 – 1mf – us A.T.L.A. [240]

OUR SHAM DEMOCRACY OR THE MAJORITY VOTE RACKET / Guthrie, James – 1fiche (29x) – 9 – 1.00f – at Libertarian Micro [320]

OUR SHARE IN CHINA AND WHAT WE ARE DOING WITH IT / Bond, Goerge John – Toronto: Missionary Society of the Methodist Church, 1911 – 1mf – us A.T.L.A. [240]

OUR SOCIETY – [Halifax, N.S.?: s.n. 1890-189- or 19–] – 9 – cn C.I.H.M. [971]

OUR SOUTH AFRICAN EMPIRE / Greswell, William Henry Parr – London. 2v. 1885 – 1r – 1 – us Ross [960]

OUR "SPECIAL" – [Toronto]: Railway Committee of the Toronto Young Men's Christian Association, [1881-18–?] – 9 – cn C.I.H.M. [240]

OUR SUNDAY VISITOR – Huntington. Ind. -w. 1912- – 1 – us UMI [071]

OUR TENGGER / Indonesia. Kementerian Penerangan – SE-2259 1. 1959 – 9 – ne IDC [320]

OUR THEATRE – New York. N.Y. 1921 – 1 – us A.J.P.C. [071]

OUR THEOLOGICAL CENTURY . A CONTRIBUTION TO THE HISTORY OF THEOLOGY IN THE UNITED STATES / Hurst, John F – New York: A.D.F. Randolph, 1877 – 1mf – us A.T.L.A. [240]

OUR TIMES – Toronto. v1-14. 1982-95 – 9 – Can$20.00y – cn Micromedia [971]

OUR TIMES – v. 1-33. 1935-69 – 1 – us UMI [073]

OUR TRADE WITH CANADA: ARGUMENT OF HON SELWYN Z. BOWMAN OF MASSACHUSETTS IN THE HOUSE OF REPRESENTATIVES, TUESDAY, JUNE 9, 1880 / Bowman, Selwyn Zadock – Washington, 1880. 00423. (Pre-1900 Canadiana) – 9 – cn C.I.H.M. [971]

OUR UNION JACK / Fessenden, Clementine – s.l., s.n., 18??. 03092. (Pre-1900 Canadiana) – 9 – cn C.I.H.M. [971]

OUR VISIT TO TORONTO, THE NIAGRA FALLS AND THE UNITED STATES OF AMERICA: BEING A SHORT ACCOUNT OF A TOUR IN CONNECTION WITH THE MEETING OF THE BRITISH ASSOCIATION FOR THE ADVANCEMENT OF SCIENCE, HELD AT TORONTO, CANADA, AUGUST 18 TO 25, 1897 / Crosweller, William Thomas – s.l.: s.n., 1898. 00480. (Pre-1900 Canadiana) – 9 – cn C.I.H.M. [971]

OUR VOICE : WEEKLY SLOVENIAN FRATERNAL NEWSPAPER – Cleveland, Oh. 28 Jan 1971-23 Dec 1982 – 2r – 1 – us Western Res [071]

OUR VOICE – West Palm Beach. Fla. 1962-65 – 1 – us A.J.P.C. [071]

OUR WESTERN ARCHIPELAGO / Field, Henry Martyn – New York: C. Scribner, 1895. 03099. (Pre-1900 Canadiana) – 9 – cn C.I.H.M. [910]

OUR WORK IN SPAIN SAVING THE CHILDREN – Enfield, England, 1937. Fiche W1094. (Blodgett Collection of Spanish Civil Pamphlets) – 9 – us H.U. College Libr [946]

OUR YOUNG FOLKS : AN ILLUSTRATED MAGAZINE FOR BOYS AND GIRLS – Boston, 1867-68 – 1r – 1 – us Ross [073]

OUR YOUNG FOLKS – v1-9 1865-73 – 1 – us UMI [305]

OUR YOUNG PEOPLE – (Cont: Our Young People's Mission Union) – Toronto: Willard Tract Depository, [1885?-1886?] – 9 – cn C.I.H.M. [240]

OUR YOUNG PEOPLE *see* OUR YOUNG PEOPLE'S MISSION UNION

OUR YOUNG PEOPLE'S MISSION UNION – (Is supplement: Our Mission Union. Cont by: Our Young People) – Toronto: Williard Tract Depository, [1885] – 9 – cn C.I.H.M. [240]

OUR YOUNG PEOPLE'S MISSION UNION *see* OUR YOUNG PEOPLE

O OURO PRETO : JORNAL POLITICO, NOTICIOSO E LITTERARIO, ONSAGRADO A DEFENSO DOS INTERESSES DO MUNICPIO – Ouro Preto, 23 Aug 1922 – 1,5,6 – bl Biblioteca [072]

OURO PRETO : JORNAL DO POVO, ABSOLUTAMENTE SINCERO PRACTICO E LOCAL – Ouro Preto, 25 Dec 1918-12 Jan 1919 – 1,5,6 – bl Biblioteca [072]

OURO PRETO – Ouro Preto, 19 Mar 1911 – 1,5,6 – bl Biblioteca [072]

OURO PRETO : QUINZENARIO CRITICO LITTERARIO E NOTICIOSO – Ouro Preto, 15 Jan 1900-1 Jun 1901 – 1,5,6 – bl Biblioteca [072]

L'OURS EN PELUCHE – no. 1-4. Paris. 1927 – 1 – fr A.C.R.P.P. [073]

OURSELVES AND THE UNIVERSE: STUDIES IN LIFE AND RELIGION / Brierley, Jonathan – Boston: Pilgrim Press, 1906. 1 fiche – 9 – us A.T.L.A. [240]

OUSAMA IBN MOUNKIDH / Derenbourg, Hartwig – 1886 – 9 – fr Orientalistes [470]

Ouseley, Gore *see* BIOGRAPHICAL NOTICES OF PERSIAN POETS

Oustalet, E *see* LES OISEAUX DE LA CHINE

OUT OF EGYPT: BIBLE READINGS ON THE BOOK OF EXODUS / Pentecost, George Frederick – New York: Funk & Wagnalls, 1884.1 fiche – 9 – us A.T.L.A. [240]

OUT OF PRINT GPO SALES PUBLICATIONS REFERENCE FILE, 1994 / U.S. Government Printing Office – (Cites govt publ that went out of print during 1990-94. Includes a stock number index, an ISBN number index, a classification number index and an alphabetical index.) – 1994 – 101mf – $20.00 in US $25.00 outside – S-N 021-000-00169-7 – us Gov't Printing [010]

OUT OF THE DEPTHS (CCC292) / Teng, Shu-kun – (In Chinese) – 1st ed. Shanghai: Christian Literature Society, 1931 – 1r – 1 – 1984-6631 – us A.T.L.A. [240]

OUT OF THE PAST, A TALE OF TWO MODERN CITIES, SHREVEPORT-LITTLE ROCK / Hutchison, Eloise P – 1943 – 1 – 7.35 – us Baptist [240]

OUT WEST – Jun 1894-1916 – 1 – us UMI [073]

OUT WEST-STOP THE EXODUS: BEING A BRIEF EXPOSE OF THE FRAUDS OF THE UNITED STATES IMMIGRATION AGENTS, AND PAMPHLETS / Elliott, George Babington – Toronto: "Pure Gold", 1872. 02905. (Pre-1900 Canadiana) – 9 – cn C.I.H.M. [971]

L'OUTAOUAIS – Hull, Canada. 10 oct 1892 – 1r – 1 – Can$25.00 – cn Can Microfilming [072]

Outcalt, John *see* HISTORY OF MERCED COUNTY

AN OUTCAST OF THE ISLANDS / Conrad, Joseph – New York: D. Appleton, 1896 – 1 roll – 1 – 1-55079-909-5 – uk Libr Preservation [830]

OUTDOOR CANADA – Toronto. v1-23. 1972/73-1995 – 9 – Can$28.00y – cn Micromedia [790]

OUTDOOR LIFE – (v. 143- 1969- 5,6. v. 145-1970- 9) – v. 1- 1898- – 1 – us UMI [790]

OUTDOOR RECREATION ACTION – 1972-77 1,5,6; 1976-80 9 – us UMI [073]

OUTDOOR RECREATION PARTICIPATION OF MARYLAND RESIDENTS IN MARYLAND STATE FORESTS AND PARKS : AN ANALYSIS OF PARTICIPATION BARRIERS / Schaeffer, Kelly R & Graefe, Alan R – 1991 – 3mf – 9 – $12.00 – us Microform Publ [790]

OUTDOOR WORLD – Atlanta. v1-3. 1968-70 – 19mf – 9 – $5.00f – us Ross [790]

OUTDOOR WORLD'S GUIDE : A SUPPLEMENT TO OUTDOOR WORLD – v1-3. 1968-70 – 9 – $5.00f – us Ross [790]

OUTER HEBRIDES, 1915 : BRITISH ISLES CENSUS DIRECTORIES PROJECT, SCOTLAND. VOL 12 – 1mf – 9 – A$9.00 – at Vine [941]

OUTER SPACE : A SOURCE OF CONFLICT OR CO-OPERATION / ed by Jasani, Bhupendra – 9 – $14.00 – 92-808-0759-5 – ja U.N. Univ [600]

Outerman, J *see* NOOTWENDIGE VERANTWOORDINGHE ENDE CLAER BEWIJS WT DE HEYLIGE SCHRIFTUERE

THE OUTERMOST RIM AND BEYOND : A CONTRIBUTION TOWARD PATIENCE, REVERENCE, SILENCE AND SPIRITUALITY, IN THE STUDY OF NATURE AND OF GOD / Van Norden, Charles – New York: Anson D F Randolph, c1882 – 1mf – 9 – 0-8370-5668-3 – 1985-3668 – us A.T.L.A. [240]

OUTFLOW OF PROFESSIONALS WITH HIGHER EDUCATION : FROM AND AMONG STATES PARTIES TO THE REGIONAL CONVENTION ON THE RECOGNITION OF STUDIES, DIPLOMAS AND DEGREES IN HIGHER EDUCATION IN LATIN AMERICA AND THE CARIBBEAN – 1984 – 59p – 9 – 92-3-102054-4 – fr UNESCO [370]

L'OUTILLAGE NATIONAL – Paris. nov 1917-18 – 1 – fr A.C.R.P.P. [073]

OUTILS ET INSTRUMENTS SERVANT A L'EDIFICATION DES FORTERESSES FRANCAISES – Montreal: Bibliotheque Nationale du Quebec, 1971. SEM35P45 – 1r – 1 – Can$15.00 – cn Bibl Nat [355]

OUTING: SPORT, ADVENTURE, TRAVEL, FICTION – v. 1-82. May 1882-1923 – 1 – us UMI [073]

Outlaw, David *see* DAVID OUTLAW PAPERS

OUT-LETTERS, 1728-1787 / Wesley, Charles – (Coll title: The People Called Methodists, Phase 2: Primary Sources 1738-1800) – 8mf – 9 – MP-643/1 – ne IDC [240]

OUT-LETTERS, 1733-1787 / Wesley, Charles – (Coll title: The People Called Methodists, Phase 2: Primary Sources 1738-1800) – 3mf – 9 – MP-644/1 – ne IDC [240]

OUT-LETTERS, 1739-1766 / Wesley, Charles – (Coll title: The People Called Methodists, Phase 2: Primary Sources 1738-1800) – 8mf – 9 – MP-645/1 – ne IDC [240]

OUT-LETTERS, 1740-1783 / Wesley, Charles – (Coll title: The People Called Methodists, Phase 2: Primary Sources 1738-1800) – 1mf – 9 – MP-646/1 – ne IDC [240]

OUT-LETTERS, 1748-1787 / Wesley, Charles – (Coll title: The People Called Methodists, Phase 2: Primary Sources 1738-1800) – 9mf – 9 – MP-647/1 – ne IDC [240]

OUT-LETTERS, 1752-1784 / Fletcher, J W – (Coll title: The People Called Methodists, Phase 2: Primary Sources 1738-1800) – 9mf – 9 – MP-628-1 – ne IDC [240]

OUT-LETTERS, 1752-1785 / Fletcher, J W – (Coll title: The People Called Methodists, Phase 2: Primary Sources 1738-1800) – 7mf – 9 – MP-629/1 – ne IDC [240]

OUT-LETTERS, 1766-1820 / Benson, J – (Coll title: The People Called Methodists, Phase 2: Primary Sources 1738-1800) – 15mf – 9 – MP-617/1 – ne IDC [240]

OUT-LETTERS, 1769-1799 / Mather, A – (Coll title: The People Called Methodists, Phase 2: Primary Sources 1738-1800) – 9mf – 9 – MP-632/1 – ne IDC [240]

OUT-LETTERS, 1780-1840 / Moore, H – (Coll title: The People Called Methodists, Phase 3: Primary Sources, 1801-1850) – 10mf – 9 – MP-677/1 – ne IDC [240]

OUT-LETTERS 1785-1832 / Clarke, A – (Coll title: The People Called Methodists, Phase 3: Primary Sources, 1801-1850) – 20mf – 9 – MP-671/1 – ne IDC [240]

OUT-LETTERS, 1788-1826 / Wesley, Sally – (Coll title: The People Called Methodists, Phase 2: Primary Sources 1738-1800) – 1mf – 9 – MP-659/1 – ne IDC [240]

OUT-LETTERS, 1788-1830 / Wesley, Charles – (Coll title: The People Called Methodists, Phase 2: Primary Sources 1738-1800) – 2mf – 9 – MP-651/1 – ne IDC [240]

OUT-LETTERS, 1789-1797 / Wesley, Sarah – (Coll title: The People Called Methodists, Phase 2: Primary Sources 1738-1800) – 1mf – 9 – MP-669/1 – ne IDC [240]

OUT-LETTERS, 1795-1833 / Wesley, Charles – (Coll title: The People Called Methodists, Phase 2: Primary Sources 1738-1800) – 3mf – 9 – MP-652/1 – ne IDC [240]

OUT-LETTERS, 1802-1841 / Entwisle, J – (Coll title: The People Called Methodists, Phase 3: Primary Sources, 1801-1850) – 18mf – 9 – MP-673/1 – ne IDC [240]

OUT-LETTERS AND MISCELLANEOUS PAPERS, 1754-1816 / Wesley, Sarah – (Coll title: The People Called Methodists, Phase 2: Primary Sources 1738-1800) – 3mf – 9 – MP-668/1 – ne IDC [240]

OUT-LETTERS AND MISCELLANEOUS PAPERS, 1772-1835 / Wesley, Samuel – (Coll title: The People Called Methodists, Phase 2: Primary Sources 1738-1800) – 6mf – 9 – MP-661/1 – ne IDC [240]

OUT-LETTERS AND MISCELLANEOUS PAPERS, 1785-1835 / Wesley, Samuel – (Coll title: The People Called Methodists, Phase 2: Primary Sources 1738-1800) – 3mf – 9 – MP-662/1 – ne IDC [240]

OUT-LETTERS AND POEMS, 1775-1828 / Wesley, Sally – (Coll title: The People Called Methodists, Phase 2: Primary Sources 1738-1800) – 8mf – 9 – MP-658/1 – ne IDC [240]

OUT-LETTERS, SERMONS AND MISCELLANEOUS PAPERS, 1779-1815 / Bradburn, S – (Coll title: The People Called Methodists, Phase 2: Primary Sources 1738-1800) – 9mf – 9 – MP-624/1 – ne IDC [240]

AN OUTLINE HANDBOOK OF THE LIFE OF CHRIST : FROM THE FOUR GOSPELS / Stevens, Arnold William & Burton, Ernest De Witt – Boston: Bible Study Pub Co, 1892 – 1mf – 9 – 0-8370-9272-8 – 1986-3272 – us A.T.L.A. [240]

AN OUTLINE HISTORY OF PERSIAN LITERATURE, A.D. 822-1926 / Faridi, Abid Hasan – Agra: Ram Prasad, 1928 – 1 – us U.W. Library [490]

OUTLINE OF ANTI-ILLITERACY CAMPAIGN AND ITS FOLLOW-UP ACTIVITIES / Indonesia. Ministry of Basic Education and Culture. Dept. of Community Education – SE-6940 1. 1962? – 9 – ne IDC [370]

AN OUTLINE OF BAPTIST HISTORY, NEGRO / Pius, N H – 1911 – 1 – 6.30 – us Baptist [240]

OUTLINE OF BIBLE HISTORY / Hurst, John F – New York: Phillips & Hunt, 1883.1 fiche – 9 – us A.T.L.A. [240]

OUTLINE OF CHRISTIAN HISTORY, A.D.50-1880 / Allen, Joseph Henry – Boston, 1906, c1884. With index – 9 – us A.T.L.A. [240]

OUTLINE OF CHRISTIAN THEOLOGY / Clarke, William Newton – 2nd ed. 1898 – 9 – us A.T.L.A. [240]

OUTLINE OF CONSTITUTIONAL LAW / Rotwein, Noah – Brooklyn: American Book Exchange 1937. LL-1490 – 1 – us L of C Photodup [340]

OUTLINE OF DEVELOPMENT OF INCOME AND EMPLOYMENT IN ITALY IN THE TEN-YEAR PERIOD 1955-1964 / Italy. Ministero del Bilancio – Paris. 1955 – 9 – ne IDC [338]

OUTLINE OF DEVELOPMENT PLAN FOR MALTA. 1973-1980 / Malta. Office of the Prime Minister – Aug. 1973. BD-1814 1 – 9 – ne IDC [956]

OUTLINE OF ESKIMO PREHISTORY / Collins, H B – BN 172 2. 1940 – 8 – ne IDC [930]

OUTLINE OF FOOD LAW : STRUCTURE, PRINCIPLES, MAIN PROVISIONS – 1975 – 114p – it F.A.O. [340]

OUTLINE OF INFORMATION AVAILABLE AT THE CENTRAL OFFICE OF STATISTICS / Indonesia. Biro Pusat Statistik – English and Indonesian. SE-10,874 1. 1952? – 9 – ne IDC [310]

OUTLINE OF INTERNATIONAL LAW / Becker, T – New York, [1941] – 9 – 2mf – ILM-2489/1 – ne IDC [327]

OUTLINE OF INTERNATIONAL LAW = KUO CHI FA TA KANG / Chou, Keng-sheng – Shanghai, 1929 – 5mf – 1 – ILM-2442/1 – ne IDC [327]

OUTLINE OF LECTURES IN SYSTEMATIC THEOLOGY : DELIVERED IN CHICAGO THEOLOGICAL SEMINARY, JANUARY AND FEBRUARY, 1894 / Foster, Frank Hugh – Chicago: David Oliphant, 1894 – 1mf – us A.T.L.A. [240]

AN OUTLINE OF LUVALE SOCIAL AND POLITICAL ORGANISATION / White, C M N – 7 – uk Microform Academic [960]

AN OUTLINE OF MODERN CHINESE FAMILY LAW / Valk, M.H. van der – (Monumenta Serica Monograph Series no 2) – Peking, 1939 – 4mf – 9 – CH-933/2 – ne IDC [340]

OUTLINE OF NEW AND ECONOMIC DEVELOPMENT PLAN / Japan – D-1529 1. April 1970 – 9 – ne IDC [338]

OUTLINE OF NEW TESTAMENT CHRISTOLOGY: A STUDY OF GENETIC RELATIONSHIPS / Granbery, John Cowper – Chicago: University of Chicago, 1909. 1 fiche – 9 – us A.T.L.A. [240]

AN OUTLINE OF NEW TESTAMENT THEOLOGY / Estes, David Foster – (Includes indexes) – New York; Boston:Silver, Burdett, c1900 – 1mf – 9 – 0-8370-3073-0 – 1985-1073 – us A.T.L.A. [220]

OUTLINE OF NEW TESTAMENT THEOLOGY / Estes, David Foster – New York: Silver, Burdett, 1900.1 fiche – 9 – us A.T.L.A. [240]

OUTLINE OF NEW YORK CRIMINAL LAW / Alpert, Benjamin M – Brooklyn, American Book Exchange 1937 21 p. LL-445 – 1 – us L of C Photodup [340]

AN OUTLINE OF OUR HISTORY AND GOVERNMENT FOR AFRICAN METHODIST CHURCHMEN : MINISTERIAL AND LAY, IN CATECHETICAL FORM: TWO PARTS WITH APPENDIX / Tanner, B T – [Philadelphia?: s.n., 1884?] – 1mf – us A.T.L.A. [240]

AN OUTLINE OF THE CLEVELAND CRIME SURVEY / Moley, Raymond – Cleveland The Cleveland Foundation, c.1922. 64p. LL-891 – 1 – us L of C Photodup [340]

OUTLINE OF THE ECONOMIC AND SOCIAL CHANGES IN THE SYRIAN ARAB REPUBLIC DURING 1950-1970 / Syria. Central Bureau of Statistics – 9 – ne IDC [310]

AN OUTLINE OF THE FIVE YEAR PLAN FOR ISRAELS AGRICULTURE, 1966/7-1970/1 / Israel. Ministry of Agriculture – Tel-Aviv. 1967 – 9 – ne IDC [630]

AN OUTLINE OF THE GEOLOGY OF CANADA: BASED ON A SUBDIVISION OF THE PROVINCES INTO NATURAL AREAS / Chapman, Edward John – Toronto: Copp, Clark, 1876. 00624. (Pre-1900 Canadiana) – 9 – cn C.I.H.M. [550]

AN OUTLINE OF THE HISTORICAL EVIDENCE OF THE TRUTH OF THE CHRISTIAN RELIGION / MacKnight, Alexander – Halifax, N.S.: A. & W. Mackinlay, 1876. 1 fiche – 9 – us A.T.L.A. [240]

OUTLINE OF THE INDONESIAN QUESTION / Indonesia – SE-3542 1. 1950? – 9 – ne IDC [300]

OUTLINE OF THE JURISDICTION AND PROCEDURE OF THE FEDERAL COURTS / Long, Joseph Ragland – Charlottesville, Michie, 1910. 88 p. LL-1223 – 1 – us L of C Photodup [340]

AN OUTLINE OF THE LAW OF INSURANCE / Elliot, Charles Burke – 2d ed. St. Paul, West, 1896. 2 v. in 1. LL-333 – 1 – us L of C Photodup [340]

OUTLINE OF THE LAW OF LANDLORD AND TENANT IN MASSACHUSETTS / Delano, Charles G – Boston, Reed, 1884. 52 p. LL-549 – 1 – us L of C Photodup [340]

OUTLINE OF THE LAW OF PRIVATE CORPORATIONS. / Alpert, Benjamin M – New York, American Legal Publications 1948 121 p. LL-1423 – 1 – us L of C Photodup [340]

OUTLINE OF THE LAW OF WILLS, BASED ON NEW YORK CASES AND STATUTES / Duberstein, Murray W – New York, American Legal Publications 1948. LL-1382 – 1 – us L of C Photodup [340]

AN OUTLINE OF THE LAWS OF THE TTPI RELATING TO REAL PROPERTY / Farrell, John P – TTPI (U.S.) Div of Land Management. nov 15, 1968 – 1mf – 9 – $1.50 – LLMC 82-100F, Title 76 – us L.L.M.C. [980]

OUTLINE OF THE NEO-HEBRAIC APOCALYPTIC LITERATURE / Buttenwieser, Moses – Cincinnati: Jennings & Pye, 1901. 1 fiche. 8370-2561-3 – 9 – us A.T.L.A. [270]

AN OUTLINE OF THE SECOND PLAN / Nepal. National Planning Council – Kathmandu. 1962 – 9 – ne IDC [338]

OUTLINE OF THE THIRD FIVE-YEAR PLAN (1965-70) / Pakistan. Planning Commission – Karachi. 1964. BD-779 1 – 9 – ne IDC [338]

AN OUTLINE OF THE TRANSITIONAL DEVELOPMENT PLAN / Zambia. Central Planning Office – Lusaka. 1965. BD-190 1 – 9 – ne IDC [338]

OUTLINE OF THE TRANSMIGRATION DEPARTMENT IN INDONESIA / Indonesia. Kementerian Sosial – SE-4352 1. 1957 – 9 – ne IDC [321]

AN OUTLINE PICTURE OF THE BAPTIST DENOMINATION IN ALABAMA; AUTOBIOGRAPHY OF REV. ELDER BURDER TEAGUE, 1820-1902 / Teague, E P – 237p – 1 – 8.29 – us Baptist [240]

OUTLINE PLAN FOR THE CITY OF DJAKARTA / United Nations. Technical Assistance Administration – Indonesian and English on opposite pages. SE 4968 1. 1957 – 9 – ne IDC [310]

OUTLINE RESEARCH PROGRAMME FOR THE AFRICAN REGIONAL AQUACULTURE CENTRE, PORT HARCOURT, RIVERS STATE, NIGERIA : REPORT OF A TASK FORCE SPONSORED BY THE F.A.O./U.N.D.P./A.D.C.P., 1980 – 1980 – 21p – it F.A.O. [060]

OUTLINE RESEARCH PROGRAMMES FOR THE REGIONAL AQUACULTURE LEAD CENTRES IN ASIA, PARTS 1 AND 2 – 1980 – 47p – it F.A.O. [636]

OUTLINE RESEARCH PROGRAMMES FOR THE REGIONAL LEAD CENTRES IN ASIA, PART 3 – 1981 – 22p – it F.A.O. [060]

OUTLINE SKETCH OF THE VOYAGES, TRAVELS, WRITINGS, AND PUBLIC LABOURS OF JAMES SILK BUCKINGHAM. / Buckingham, James Silk – From authentic sources, with a portrait.London: P. Jackson, 1847. 153p – 1 – us U.W. Library [920]

OUTLINE STUDIES IN ACTS, ROMANS...CORINTHIANS, GALATIANS AND EPHESIANS / Moorehead, William Gallogly – Chicago: Fleming H. Revell, 1902. 1 fiche – 9 – us A.T.L.A. [240]

OUTLINE STUDIES IN THE NEW TESTAMENT : PHILIPPIANS TO HEBREWS / Moorehead, William Gallogly – New York: Fleming H Revell, 1905 – 1mf – 9 – 0-8370-4481-2 – 1985-2481 – us A.T.L.A. [220]

OUTLINES, DEFINITIONS, MAXIMS, QUOTATIONS, AND PROBLEMS IN ELEMENTARY LAW / Hawley, Charles Anthony – Pella, Iowa, 1904. 75p. LL-362 – 1 – us L of C Photodup [340]

OUTLINES FOR THE STUDY OF BIBLICAL HISTORY AND LITERATURE / Sanders, Frank Knight – New York: Charles Scribner, 1906. 1 fiche – 9 – us A.T.L.A. [240]

OUTLINES OF A GRAMMAR OF THE SUSU LANGUAGE. / Duport, J H – London: Society for Promoting Christian Knowledge, [186-?] – us Res Libr [470]

OUTLINES OF A HISTORY OF PROTESTANT MISSIONS = ABRISS EINER GESCHICHTE DER PROTESTANTISCHEN MISSIONEN : FROM THE REFORMATION TO THE PRESENT TIME: A CONTRIBUTION TO MODERN CHURCH HISTORY / Warneck, Gustav – (In English. Includes bibliographical references and indexes) – New York: Fleming H Revell, 1901 – 1mf – 9 – 0-8370-6629-8 – 1986-0629 – us A.T.L.A. [240]

OUTLINES OF A PHILOSOPHY OF RELIGION BASED ON PSYCHOLOGY AND HISTORY / Sabatier, Auguste – New York: James Pott, 1902. 1 fiche – 9 – us A.T.L.A. [240]

OUTLINES OF AN INTERNATIONAL CODE / Field, D D – New York, 1872 – 9mf – 1 – ILM-164/1 – ne IDC [327]

OUTLINES OF AN INTRODUCTION TO THE OLD TESTAMENT / Beardslee, John Walter – Chicago: Fleming H Revell, 1903 – 1mf – 9 – 0-8370-2222-3 – 1985-0222 – us A.T.L.A. [220]

OUTLINES OF BIBLICAL PSYCHOLOGY / Beck, Johann Tobias – Edinburgh: T. & T. Clark, 1877. 1 fiche – 9 – us A.T.L.A. [240]

OUTLINES OF BRITISH FUNGOLOGY / Berkeley, M J – London. 1860. B-6243 1 – 9 – ne IDC [580]

OUTLINES OF CHRISTIAN APOLOGETICS: FOR USE IN LECTURES / Schultz, Hermann – New York: Macmillan, 1905. 1 fiche – 9 – us A.T.L.A. [240]

OUTLINES OF CHRISTIAN THEOLOGY / Walker, Cornelius – (Includes index) – New York: Thomas Whittaker, 1894 – 1mf – 9 – 0-8370-2926-0 – 1985-0926 – us A.T.L.A. [240]

OUTLINES OF CHURCH HISTORY / Schubert, Hans von – New York: G.P. Putnam, 1907 – 1mf – us A.T.L.A. [240]

OUTLINES OF CHURCH HISTORY / Sohm, Rudolf – London, New York: Macmillan, 1895 – 1mf – us A.T.L.A. [240]

OUTLINES OF CRIMINAL LAW, FOR USE OF STUDENTS / McClain, Emlin – Iowa City, 1882. 115 p. LL-553 – 1 – us L of C Photodup [340]

OUTLINES OF DOCTRINAL THEOLOGY : WITH PRELIMINARY CHAPTERS ON THEOLOGY IN GENERAL AND THEOLOGICAL ENCYCLOPAEDIA / Drury, A W – Dayton, Ohio: Otterbein Press, 1914 – 1mf – us A.T.L.A. [240]

OUTLINES OF EVIDENCE, PREPARED FOR THE STUDENTS OF THE BROOKLYN LAW SCHOOL / Richardson, William Payson – New York: Eagle 1911. 416p. LL-1188 – 1 – us L of C Photodup [340]

OUTLINES OF GERMAN LITERATURE / Gostwick, Joseph & Harrison, Robert – (Includes index) – New York: H Holt, [1873] – 1r – 1 – us U.W. Library [430]

OUTLINES OF HEBREW ACCENTUATION, PROSE AND POETICAL / Davidson, Andrew Bruce – (Includes bibliographical references) – London: Williams and Norgate, 1861 – 1mf – 9 – 0-8370-9223-X – 1986-3223 – us A.T.L.A. [470]

OUTLINES OF HEBREW GRAMMAR = GRUNDRISS DER HEBRAEISCHEN GRAMMATIK / Bickell, Gustav – (Includes bibliographical references and index) – Leipzig: F A Brockhaus, 1877 – 1mf – 9 – 0-8370-9204-3 – 1986-3204 – us A.T.L.A. [470]

OUTLINES OF HINDU METAPHYSICS / Dutt, Manmatha Nath – 2nd ed. Calcutta: Society for the Resuscitation of Indian Literature, 1910. iii,247p – 1 – us U.W. Library [110]

OUTLINES OF HISTORICAL JURISPURDENCE / Vinogradoff, Paul – London etc: Oxford UP. 2v. 1920-22 – 9mf – 9 – $13.50 – LLMC 95-173 – us L.L.M.C. [340]

THE OUTLINES OF HUNGARIAN PREHISTORY / Sinor, D – (Chm IV; 3, 1958. p 513-540) – 8 – ne IDC [930]

OUTLINES OF INTERNATIONAL LAW... / Davis, G B – London, 1888 – 6mf – 1 – ILM-155/1 – ne IDC [327]

OUTLINES OF INTRODUCTION TO THE HEBREW BIBLE / Geden, Alfred Shenington – Edinburgh: T & T Clark, 1909 – 1mf – 9 – 0-8370-3239-3 – 1985-1239 – us A.T.L.A. [220]

OUTLINES OF LECTURES ON THE CHRISTIAN DOCTRINE : PRINTED FOR THE USE OF STUDENTS IN LANE THEOLOGICAL SEMINARY / Morris, Edward Dafydd – s.l: s.n, [1880?] – 1mf – 9 – 0-8370-4036-1 – 1985-2036 – us A.T.L.A. [240]

OUTLINES OF OLD TESTAMENT THEOLOGY / Burney, Charles Fox – London: Rivingtons, 1899. 1 fiche – 9 – us A.T.L.A. [240]

OUTLINES OF PRIMITIVE BELIEF AMONG THE INDO-EUROPEAN RACES / Keary, Charles Francis – New York: Scribner, 1882 – 2mf – us A.T.L.A. [200]

OUTLINES OF REAL PROPERTY / Tiffany, Herbert Thorndike – Chicago, Callaghan, 1929. 704 p. LL-1641 – 1 – us L of C Photodup [340]

OUTLINES OF SOCIAL THEOLOGY / Hyde, William De Witt – New York: Macmillan, 1895 – 1mf – 9 – 0-8370-4602-5 – 1985-2602 – us A.T.L.A. [240]

OUTLINES OF SPECIAL INTRODUCTION TO THE BOOKS OF THE OLD TESTAMENT / Lansing, John Gulian – New Brunswick: J. Heidingsfeld, 1897. 1 fiche – 9 – us A.T.L.A. [220]

OUTLINES OF SYSTEMATIC THEOLOGY : DESIGNED FOR THE USE OF THEOLOGICAL STUDENTS / Strong, Augustus Hopkins – Philadelphia:Griffith & Rowland, c1908 – 1mf – 9 – 0-8370-2900-7 – 1985-0900 – us A.T.L.A. [240]

OUTLINES OF TEXTUAL CRITICISM APPLIED TO THE NEW TESTAMENT / Hammond, Charles Edward – (Includes appendixes and indexes) – 5th rev ed. Oxford: Clarendon Press, 1890 – 1mf – 9 – 0-8370-3460-4 – 1985-1460 – us A.T.L.A. [220]

THE OUTLINES OF THE CHRISTIAN MINISTRY : DELINEATED AND BROUGHT TO THE TEST OF REASON, HOLY SCRIPTURE, HISTORY, AND EXPERIENCE, WITH A VIEW TO THE RECONCILIATION OF... / Wordsworth, Charles – London: Longmans, Green, 1872 – 1mf – us A.T.L.A. [240]

OUTLINES OF THE GEOGRAPHY OF PLANTS / Meyen, F J F – 1846 – 1 £35.00 7 £38.50 – uk Microform Academic [580]

OUTLINES OF THE HISTORY OF ETHICS FOR ENGLISH READERS / Sidgwick, Henry – London, New York: Macmillan, 1886. Based on article contributed to Encyclopaedia Britannica – xxiv/276p – 1 – us U.W. Library [170]

OUTLINES OF THE HISTORY OF GERMAN LITERATURE / Robertson, John George – (Includes index) – Edinburgh: W Blackwood and Sons, 1911 – 1 – us U.W. Library [430]

OUTLINES OF THE HISTORY OF PSYCHOLOGY / Dessoir, Max – Authorized trans. by Donald Fisher. New York: Macmillan Co., 1912. xxix,278p – 1 – us U.W. Library [150]

OUTLINES OF THE HISTORY OF THE ENGLISH LANGUAGE / Toller, Thomas Northcote – Cambridge: University Press, 1927 – 1 roll – 1 – 1-55879-417-4 – uk Libr Preservation [420]

OUTLINES OF THE HISTORY OF THE THEOLOGICAL LITERATURE OF THE CHURCH OF ENGLAND : FROM THE REFORMATION TO THE CLOSE OF THE EIGHTEENTH CENTURY / Dwoden, John – London: S.P.C.K.; New York: E.& J.B. Young, 1897. (The Bishop Paddock lectures; 1896-7) – 1mf – us A.T.L.A. [240]

OUTLINES OF THE LAW AGENCY / Mechem, Floyd Russell – 2nd ed. Chicago: Callaghan & Co, 1903 – 3mf – 9 – $4.50 – LLMC 96-039 – us L.L.M.C. [340]

OUTLINES OF THE LAW OF CONTRACTS, PREPARED FOR THE USE OF STUDENTS IN THE BROOKLYN LAW SCHOOL OF ST LAWRENCE UNIVERSITY / Richardson, William Payson – New York: Eagle, 1904. 8, 204p. LL-1000 – 1 – us L of C Photodup [340]

OUTLINES OF THE LIFE OF CHRIST / Sanday, William – New York: Scribner: 1905. 1 fiche – 9 – us A.T.L.A. [240]

OUTLINES OF THE NEW YORK LAW OF EVIDENCE AND PRACTICE, WITH PRACTICE TIME TABLE AND FORMS / Rothschild, Jay Leo – 3d ed. Brooklyn: Weidner, 1929. 93p. LL-1388 – 1 – us L of C Photodup [340]

OUTLINES OF THE PHILOSOPHY OF UNIVERSAL HISTORY APPLIED TO LANGUAGE AND RELIGION / Bunsen, Christian Charles Josias – London: Longman, Brown, Green, and Longmans, 1854. (Christianity and mankind. Philosophical section, v3-4) – 3mf – us A.T.L.A. [190]

OUTLINES OF THE POLITICAL HISTORY OF MICHIGAN / Campbell, James Valentine – Detroit: Schober, 1876. 00408. (Pre-1900 Canadiana) – 9 – cn C.I.H.M. [975]

OUTLINES OF THE SCIENCE OF JURISPRUDENCE : AN INTRODUCTION TO THE SYSTEMAYTIC STUDY OF LAW / Hastie, W – Edinburgh: T & T Clark, 1887 – 4mf – 9 – $6.00 – LLMC 95-206 – us L.L.M.C. [340]

OUTLINES OF TRIAL PROCEDURE / Bennett, J L – Chicago, Donohue & Henneberry 1895 55 p. LL-1369 – 1 – us L of C Photodup [340]

OUTLINES OF WESLEYAN BIBLIOGRAPHY : OR, A RECORD OF METHODIST LITERATURE FROM THE BEGINNING, IN TWO PARTS:... / Osborn, G – London, 1869 – 3mf – 9 – ne IDC [240]

OUTLINES OF WESLEYAN BIBLIOGRAPHY; OR, A RECORD OF METHODIST LITERATURE FROM THE BEGINNING, IN TWO PARTS:... / Osborn, G – London, 1869 – 3mf – 9 – ne IDC [240]

OUTLOOK – Alexander City, AL. 1865-1970 – 1 – us UMI [071]

OUTLOOK / American Crafts Council.(ACC) – v. 1-16 1960-76 – 1,5,6,9 – us UMI [740]

OUTLOOK – Center, NE. -w. Dec. 1901-Dec. 1902 – 1 – us NE Hist [071]

OUTLOOK = CHAN WANG – (In Chinese) – v1-11. 1953-67 (complete) – 3r – 1 – ATLA S0297 – us A.T.L.A. [073]

OUTLOOK – Gresham. Or. -w. 1913-63 – 1 – us UMI [071]

OUTLOOK – Karachi, PK. 1972-1974 – 3r – $150.00 – R63576 – us Library Micro [072]

OUTLOOK – Laurel. Mont. 1958-1959; 1966- – 1 – us UMI [071]

OUTLOOK – London, UK. 1905-06 – 4r – 1 – uk British Libr Newspaper [072]

OUTLOOK : MEDICAL POST – v1- 1994- – 1 – Price varies – cn Micromedia [610]

OUTLOOK – Providence. R.I. 1890- – 1 – us UMI [071]

OUTLOOK – Weekly review of politics, art, literature, and finance. v. 1-61. Feb. 5, 1898-June 30, 1928 – 1 – us UMI [073]

OUTLOOK *see* NEW OUTLOOK

THE OUTLOOK – 1870-1935 – 1 – us UMI [071]

THE OUTLOOK – Bakersfield. CA. 1957-66. Includes predecessors – 1 – us UMI [071]

THE OUTLOOK – Rathfriland, Ireland. 1959- – 52+ r – 1 – uk British Libr Newspaper [072]

THE OUTLOOK – Victoria, B.C.: F Finch-Smiles, [1900?-19–] – 9 – cn C.I.H.M. [073]

OUTLOOK ENVIRONMENTAL LAW JOURNAL *see* TEMPLE ENVIRONMENTAL LAW AND TECHNOLOGY JOURNAL

OUTLOOK FOR CHRISTIANITY / ed by Champion, L G – 1967. 194p – 1 – 6.79 – us Baptist [240]

OUTLOOK FOR PULP AND PAPER TO 1985 – 1986 – 83p – it F.A.O. [338]

OUTLOOK MAIL – Santa Monica, CA. 1977 – 33+ r – 1 – $1,650.00 ($50.00y) – R03522 – us Library Micro [071]

OUTLOOK/WATCH-TOWER – New York. 1874-75, 1878-83 – 1 – 33.65 – us A.B.H.S. [073]

OUT-OF-PRINT AAS BOOKS ON MICROFICHE / American Astronautical Society – (Vols available separately) – 9 – $440.00 set – us Univelt [629]

OUT-OF-PRINT AAS BOOKS ON MICROFICHE *see*
- AEROSPACE RESEARCH AND DEVELOPMENT
- BIOASTRONAUTICS
- DEVELOPING THE SPACE FRONTIER
- ENVIRONMENTAL CONTROL AND AGRI-TECHNOLOGY
- FROM SPACE LAB TO SPACE STATION
- FUTURE SPACE ACTIVITIES
- HANDBOOK OF SOVIET LUNAR AND PLANETARY EXPLORATION
- PHYSIOLOGICAL AND PERFORMANCE DETERMINANTS IN MANNED SPACE SYSTEMS
- POST-APOLLO EXPLORATION
- PRACTICAL SPACE APPLICATIONS
- PROCEEDINGS 1957-63
- REDUCING THE COST OF SPACE TRANSPORTATION
- THE SEARCH FOR EXTRATERRESTRIAL LIFE
- THE SKYLAB RESULTS
- SKYLAB SCIENCE EXPERIMENTS
- SOVIET SPACE PROGRAMS 1980-1985
- SPACE FLIGHT MECHANICS SPECIALISTS SYMPOSIUM
- SPACE MANUFACTURING
- SPACE RESCUE AND SAFETY 1974
- TECHNOLOGY UTILIZATION IDEAS FOR THE 70S AND BEYOND

OUT-OF-PRINT BOOKS AUTHOR GUIDE 1990-1991 – 1991 – 1262p on 14mf – 1 – us UMI [010]

OUTPOSTS OF ZION WITH LIMNINGS OF MISSION LIFE / Goode, William H – 1864 – 1 – 16.45 – us Baptist [240]

OUTPUT – v.1-2. 1980-81 – 1,5,6,9 – us UMI [073]

OUTPUT OF NATIONAL HIGH SCHOOLS / Papua New Guinea. Manpower Planning Unit – [Waigani], 1977 – 1mf – 9 – DE-235/1 – ne IDC [370]

Outram, George *see* LEGAL AND OTHER LYRICS

Outrein, J D' *see* PROEFSTUKKEN VAN HEILIGE SINNE-BEELDEN
OUTRE-MER – Revue Generale de Colonisation. Paris. 1929-1937 complete – 1 – 35.00r – us Hoover Inst Photo [073]
Outrey, Ernest *see* NOUVEAU RECUEIL DE LEGISLATION CANTONALE ET COMMUNALE ANNAMITE DE COCHINCHINE
OUTSIDE – Irvine, CA. 1983-1985 – 1r – 1 – $50.00 – R04036 – us Library Micro [071]
OUTSKIRTS OF PHYSICAL SCIENCE: ESSAYS / Dale, Thomas Nelson – Boston: Lee and Shepard, 1884. 1 fiche – 9 – us A.T.L.A. [240]
OUTSTATE TESTING PROGRAM CIRCULAR / Nebraska. Agricultural Experiment Station. Lincoln – n.1-137. 1948-69 – 1,5 – us Spaulding [630]
THE OUTWARD AND VISIBLE SIGN: A NEW AND ATTRACTIVE METHOD OF TEACHING RELIGIOUS TRUTHS, AND ESPECIALLY APPLIED TO THE TEACHING OF THE CHURCH CATECHISM. / Caswell, D J – Brantford Ont.: Caswell, 1891. 00762. (Pre-1900 Canadiana) – 9 – cn C.I.H.M. [240]
OUTWARD BOUND / Society for the Propagation of the Gospel in Foreign Parts – Westminister. v1-4. 1920-1923/24 – 40mf – 9 – ne IDC [240]
OUVERTURE DE LA CARAVANE. ARRANGEE POUR LE CLAVECIN OU LE FORTEPIANO AVEC VIOLON AD LIB PAR M. CESAR... / Gretry, A – (Parts) – Paris: Naderman, 180-? – 1 – us Sibley [780]
L'OUVERTURE DU CANAL DE PANAMA ... / Billot, F – Paris, 1913 – 2mf – 9 – ILM-1806/1 – ne IDC [327]
OUVERTURE D'UNE BIBLIOTHEQUE DE LA DOCTRINE SAINT-SIMONIENNE A PERPIGNAN / Lechevalier, J – Perpignan, impr. Alzine, 1831, 8 p. Les Saint-Simoniens, 1825-1834. 6937 – 9 – fr Hachette [335]
LES OUVRAGES D'ARCHITECTURE / Post, Pierre – O 407. 1715 – 9 – ne IDC [720]
OUVRAGES POSTHUMES DE D. JEAN MABILLON ET DE D. THIERRI RUINART / Mabillon, Jean – Paris. Tome 1-3. 1724 – v1 19mf; v2 18mf; v3 17mf – 8 – Dfl189.00 – ne Slangenburg [240]
OUVRAGES SUR VOLTAIRE, 1788-1826 / ed by Vercruysse, Jeroom – 51 titles. Available individually – 9 – fr Hachette [920]
L'OUVRE-BOITE *see* LE JOURNAL DES ETUDIANTS DE L'UNIVERSITE DE SHERBROOKE
L'OUVRIER : HEBDO / ed by Langlois, A & Rouleau, C E – Quebec, Canada. 20 oct-24 nov 1888 – 1r – 1 – Can$25.00 – cn Can Microfilming [072]
L'OUVRIER – Montreal, Canada. 19 jan 1908-v1 n5. 5 jul 1908 – 1r – 1 – Can$25.00 – cn Can Microfilming [072]
L'OUVRIER – Montreal, Canada. v1 n3. 15 dec 1883-v1 n38. 23 aut 1884 – 1r – 1 – Can$35.00 – cn Can Microfilming [072]
L'OUVRIER – Montreal: L Lepine, [1900-19–] – 9 – cn C.I.H.M. [073]
L'OUVRIER – Quebec, Canada. 8-27 nov 1877 – 1r – 1 – Can$25.00 – cn Can Microfilming [072]
L'OUVRIER – Saint Roch [Quebec]: Frs Pichet, [1851-18– ou 19–] – 9 – cn C.I.H.M. [240]
L'OUVRIER ALGERIEN – no. 1-7, 9, 13; N.S., no. 1-3. Alger puis Paris. avr 1956-janv 1957, aout-dec 1957 – 1 – fr A.C.R.P.P. [073]
L'OUVRIER CANADIEN – Montreal, Canada. 15 mai 1930-v1 n12. oct 1931 – 1r – 1 – Can$30.00 – cn Can Microfilming [072]
OUVRIER CHAPELIER. L'AVENIR DE L'OUVRIER DEDIE A LA CLASSE OUVRIERE ET PLACE SOUS SA PROTECTION / Saive, A – Paris. 1841. (La Condition Ouvriere. Part Two.) – 9 – 2.50 – fr Bibl Nationale [360]
L'OUVRIER CONSCIENT – no. 1-2, 5. Marseille. fevr-mai 1909 – 1 – fr A.C.R.P.P. [073]
L'OUVRIER DE LEVIS – Levis, Canada. 24,31 mai 1890 – 1r – 1 – Can$25.00 – cn Can Microfilming [072]
L'OUVRIER DES DEUX MONDES – Revue mensuelle d'economie sociale. fevr 1897-98. devenu: Le Monde ouvrier. janv-juil 1899. Paris – 1 – fr A.C.R.P.P. [073]
L'OUVRIER METALLURGISTE / L'Union federale des Ouvriers metallurgistes de France – Paris. 1902-09. devenu: L' Union des metaux voir a ce titre – 1 – fr A.C.R.P.P. [331]
L'OUVRIER MINEUR – Douai. oct 1883-juin 1884 – 1 – fr A.C.R.P.P. [073]
L'OUVRIER MINEUR – Paris puis Carvin. juin 1904-mars 1910 – 1 – fr A.C.R.P.P. [073]
L'OUVRIER POLONAIS EN FRANCE – Paris. 1923-24 – 1 – fr A.C.R.P.P. [073]
Ouvrier sans Travail *see* L'APPEL AU PEUPLE: DROIT AU TRAVAIL, LES CONSERVATEURS, CRISE, FAMINE, MANDAT CONTRACTUEL
L'OUVRIER TEXTILE / Federation ouvriere de l'industrie textile de France – Lille puis Paris. No.1-133. nov 1903-juil 1914. mq no.115. Paris.No.1-58. juil/sept 1919-juil 1935. mq no.7-10, 13-16, 24-27 – 1 – fr A.C.R.P.P. [073]
L'OUVRIERE – no. 1-239. Paris. 11 mars 1922-31 mars 1927; no. 1-135. 1er mai 1930-35 – 1 – fr A.C.R.P.P. [073]
LES OUVRIERES DE L'AIGUILLE A PARIS / Benoist, Charles – Paris. 1895. (La Condition Ouvriere. Part Two.) – 10.00; CPC; 9 – fr Bibl Nationale [360]
LES OUVRIERS CHRETIENS SOUS LE GOUVERNEMENT DE FRANCO / Mardones Zabalandi Koetxea, Francisco G – Paris, 1938? Fiche W 1024. (Blodgett Collection of Spanish Civil War Pamphlets) – 9 – us H.U. College Libr [946]
LES OUVRIERS D'A PRESENT ET LA NOUVELLE ECONOMIE DU TRAVAIL / Audiganne, A – (Condition of 19th C. French working class series). 1865 – 9 – fr Hachette [335]
LES OUVRIERS DE L'AIGUILLE A PARIS / Benoist, Charles – Paris: Chailley, 1895. 296p. (Les Femmes Collection) – 4mf – 9 – $10.00 – fr Bibl Nationale [360]
LES OUVRIERS DE PARIS. ALIMENTATION / Vincard, Pierre – (Condition of 19th C. French working class series). 1863 – 9 – fr Hachette [305]
LES OUVRIERS EN FAMILLE / Audiganne, A – 5eme ed. augmentee d'un manuel elementaire des Societes de Secours mutuel. (Condition of 19th C. French Working Class Series). 1858 – 9 – fr Hachette [944]
DES OUVRIERS ET DES MOYENS D'AMELIORER LEUR CONDITION DANS LES VILLES / Madre, A de – (Condition of 19th century French working class). 1863 – 9 – fr Hachette [305]
LES OUVRIERS ETRANGERS... / Auvillain, L – Paris, 1905 – 3mf – 9 – ILM-324/1 – ne IDC [340]
LES OUVRIERS EUROPEENS. ETUDES SUR LES TRAVAUX, LA VIE DOMESTIQUE ET LA CONDITION MORALE DES POPULATIONS OUVRIERES DE L'EUROPE, D'APRES LES FAITS OBSERVES DE 1829 A 1879 / Le Play, Frederic – (Condition of 19th C. French working class series). 1877-79 – 9 – fr Hachette [305]
LES OUVRIERS, HISTOIRE POPULAIRE ILLUSTREE DES TRAVAILLEURS AU XIXE SIECLE / Dupont – 1890. (Condition of the 19th c. French working class series) – 9 – fr Hachette [360]
OUVRIERS PARISIENS D'APRES-GUERRE / Valdour, Jacques – Paris. 1921. (La Condition Ouvriere. Part Two.) – 9 – $5.00 – fr Bibl Nationale [360]
Ouwerkerk, Louise *see* THE UNTOUCHABLES OF INDIA
OUYEN AND NORTH-WEST EXPRESS – 1918-1939. ONWE A-K – 11r – 1 – at Corangamite [072]
OUYEN AND NORTH-WEST EXPRESS – 1940-1957 – 6mf – 9 – at Corangamite [980]
OVA PASCHALIA SACRO EMBLEMATE INSCRIPTA DESCRIPTAQUE / Stengel Georg – O 766. 1678 – 9 – ne IDC [760]
Ovalle, Alonso de *see* COLECCION...CHILE Y DOCUMENTOS..
Ovalle, S E *see* A COMPARISON BETWEEN ANTHROPOMETRIC REGRESSION EQUATIONS AND HYDROSTATIC WEIGHING FOR PREDICTING PERCENT BODY FAT OF ADULT MALES WITH DOWN SYNDROME
LA OVANDINA, DE PEDRO MEXIA DE OVANDO / Uragon, Marques de Laurencin – Madrid: Fortanet, 1909. B.R.A.H. 55, 1909, pp. 5-34, 1 lam – sp Bibl Santa Ana [946]
Ovando, Juan de *see*
- COMENTARII..3 LIBRUM...DUNS SCOTI
- DISCURSUS...MYSTERIA FIDEI
- TRATADO PASTORAL...PROPIEDADES DEL BUEN PASTOR

Ovando Mogollon de Baredes, Francisco *see* BREVILOQUIUM...QUATOR LIBROS...SENTENTIARUM
LOS OVANDO Y SOLIS DE CACERES / Orti Belmonte, Miguel Angel – Badajoz: Tip.Artes Graficas, 1932 – 1 – sp Bibl Santa Ana [946]
OVENT KURJER – Vilniuo, 1925-39 – 10r – 1 – $750.00 – us Ross [072]
OVER AGAINST THE TREASURY : OR, COMPANIONS OF THE PRESENT CHRIST: A VISION / Fenn, Courtenay Hughes – Philadelphia: Westminster Press, 1910 – 1mf – 9 – 0-8370-6041-9 – 1986-0041 – us A.T.L.A. [240]
OVER DE AFRIKAANSE VIJGE-BOOMEN / Miquel, F A W – (Verhandl. le kl. Kon. Ned. Inst., van Wetenschappen. Amsterdam, 1849, p. 111-150, 5 pls.). B-1258 2 – 8 – ne IDC [580]
OVER DE DRUKPRS IN NEDERLANDSCH-INDIE / Schill, Jeremias J A – Leiden, 1863 – 3mf – 9 – SE-1423/1 – ne IDC [950]
OVER DE OUDSTE PORTUGESE SYNAGOGES TE AMSTERDAM / Silva Rosa, J S da – Chronicon Spinozanum, I. 1921. BJ-262-58 1 – 9 – ne IDC [270]
OVER DE VEREISCHTEN IN EENEN ORGANIST / Hess, J – Gouda. 1807. BP-317 1 – 9 – ne IDC [780]
OVER DEN BOUW DER SCHELPEN VAN BRACHIOPODEN EN CHITONEN / Bemmelen, J F van – Z-396 2. 1882 – 8 – ne IDC [590]
OVER THE BORDER / Baynes, O'Hara – 18–?. 03979. (Pre-1900 Canadiana) – 9 – cn C.I.H.M. [971]
OVER THE BORDER: ACADIA, THE HOME OF "EVANGELINE" / Chase, Eliza Brown – Illus. in heliotype from water-color sketches by the author. Boston: J. Osgood, 1884. 00584. (Pre-1900 Canadiana) – 9 – cn C.I.H.M. [971]
OVER THE SNOW, OR, THE MONTREAL CARNIVAL / Beers, William George – Montreal: W. Drysdale and J. Robinson, 1883. 03544. (Pre-1900 Canadiana) – 9 – cn C.I.H.M. [360]
THE OVERALL ECONOMIC DEVELOPMENT PROGRAM / Virgin Islands. Economic Development Board – Charlotte Amalie. 1966. BD-584 1 – 9 – ne IDC [338]
OVERALL RESOURCES BUDGET: 1969. SECOND FIVE-YEAR ECONOMIC DEVELOPMENT PLAN / Korea. South. Economic Planning Board – Sep 1968. BD-1680 1 – 9 – ne IDC [338]
OVERALL RESOURCES BUDGET FOR 1971. THE TERMINAL YEAR OF THE SECOND FIVE YEAR DEVELOPMENT PLAN / Korea. South. Economic Planning Board – Mar 1971. BD-1682 1 – 9 – ne IDC [338]
Overbeck, Franz *see*
- DIE BISCHOFSLINIEN UND DIE APOSTOLISCHE NACHFOLGE IN DER KIRCHENGESCHICHTE DES EUSEBIUS
- UEBER DEN PSEUDOJUSTINISCHEN BRIEF AN DIOGNET
- UEBER DIE CHRISTLICHKEIT UNSERER HEUTIGEN THEOLOGIE

Overbeck, J J *see*
- CATHOLIC ORTHODOXY AND ANGLO-CATHOLICISM
- RABULAE EPISCOPI EDESSENI, BALAEI ALIORUMQUE. OPERA SELECTA E CODICIBUS MSS. IN MUSEO BRITANNICO ET BIBLIOTHECA BODLEIANA ASSERVATIS
- DIE WIEDERVEREINIGUNG DER MORGEN-UND ABENDLAENDISCHEN KIRCHE

Overbeck, J Josephus *see* S. EPHRAEMI SYRI, RABULAE EPISCOPI EDESSENI, BALAEI ALIORUMQUE OPERA SELECTA
Overberg, Bernhard *see* KATECHISMUS DER CHRISTKATHOLISCHEN LEHRE ZUM GEBRAUCHE DER GROESSEREN SCHUELER, (WELCHE DEN KLEINEN KATECHISMUS GELERNT HABEN) NACH ANLEITUNG DES RELIGIONS-HANDBUCHS
THE OVERBERG COURANT – Swellendam, South Africa. 5 Oct 1859-10 May 1865 – 1r – 1, 16 diazo available – sa SA Libr [960]
OVERBERG UND FUERSTENBERG IN IHRER BEDEUTUNG FUER DIE GEISTIGE UND KULTURELLE HEBUNG DER LAENDLICHEN BEVOELKERUNG / Schroeder, August – Muenster, 1937 – iv/107p – 9 – DM48.00 – 3-89349-031-0 – gw Hänsel [943]
Overbergh, Cyr. van *see*
- LES BANGALA ST (ETAT IND. DU CONGO)
- LES BASONGE (ETAT IND. DU CONGO)
- COLLECTION DES MONOGRAPHIES ETHNOGRAPHIQUES

Overbergh, Cyrille van *see* COLLECTION DE MONOGRAPHIES ETHNOGRAPHIQUES PUBLIEES PAR CYRILLE VAN OVERBERGH
Overbrook. Kansas. Bethel Methodist Church *see* MEMBERSHIP RECORD
Overbrook Methodist Church *see* RECORDS
OVERCORRECTION AND TIMEOUT TECHNIQUES TO DECREASE TIME OFF-TASK DURING A GROSS MOTOR PERFORMANCE OF EMOTIONALLY DISTURBED MALES / Wagner, K E – 1991 – 2mf – 9 – $8.00 – us Microform Publ [150]
DE OVEREENKOMST IN HET INTERNATIONAAL PRIVAATRECHT / Eras, J F M – 's-Gravenhage, [1928] – 3mf – 1 – ILM-3049/1 – ne IDC [327]
Overend, T J *see* DETERMINANTS OF CRITICAL POWER AND ANAEROBIC WORK CAPACITY IN YOUNG AND ELDERLY MEN
Overholser, Winfred *see* THE PRACTICAL OPERATION OF THE MASSACHUSETTS LAW REQUIRING THE PSYCHIATRIC EXAMINATION OF CERTAIN PERSONS ACCUSED OF CRIME (THE "BRIGGS LAW")
OVERLAND – 1954- 1; 1972- 5,6; 1975- 4 x 6 in. 9 – us UMI [073]
THE OVERLAND CEYLON OBSERVER AND FORTNIGHTLY SUMMARY OF INTELLIGENCE – Ceylon. Feb 1873 to Dec 1875 – 1 – uk Microform Academic [072]
OVERLAND CHINA MAIL – Hong Kong: David Christian Wilson, jan 8 1931-jun 1941 – 13r – 1 – us Res Libr [072]
OVERLAND FRIEND OF CHINA – Hong Kong: William Tarrant, sep 5 1858-sep 28 1859 – 1r – 1 – us Res Libr [072]
Overland, Martha Uboe *see* A MANUAL OF STATUTORY CORPORATION LAW
THE OVERLAND MONTHLY – 1868-1935 – 1 – us UMI [071]
OVERLAND MONTHLY AND OUT WEST MAGAZINE – Jul 1868-Dec 1935 – 1 – us UMI [073]
OVERLAPPING TAXES IN THE UNITED STATES / U.S. Treasury Department. Advisory Commission on Intergovernmental Relations – Washington: GPO, 1954 – 1mf – 9 – $1.50 – LLMC 82-705 – us L.L.M.C. [336]
Overman, David Gene *see* HELPING PARENTS FACILITATE THE RELIGIOUS EDUCATION OF PRESCHOOL CHILDREN IN THE HOME
OVERSEA EDUCATION – London. 1929-1962 63. v1-34. – 140mf – 8 – ne IDC [073]
OVERSEA EDUCATION – v. 21-25. 1949-54 – 1 – us UMI [370]
OVERSEAS : THE MAGAZINE OF EDUCATIONAL EXCHANGE – 1-3. 1961-May 1964 – 1 – us UMI [073]
OVERSEAS BUSINESS REPORTS – 1972-1,5,6; 1976- 9 – us UMI [650]
OVERSEAS BUSINESS REPORTS : BASIC DATA ON THE ECONOMY OF MOROCCO 1966 / U.S. Department of Commerce – Stechschulte, R.F. BNE-3227 1 – 9 – ne IDC [360]
OVERSEAS BUSINESS REPORTS / U.S. Department of Commerce – Oct 1972. Basic data on the economy of Morocco. Jensen, L.L. and M.R. Smith. BNE-3230 1 – 9 – ne IDC [360]
OVERSEAS BUSINESS REPORTS / U.S. Department of Commerce. Bureau of International Commerce – Basic data on the basis economy in Libya. Jul 1970. BNE-517 1 – 9 – ne IDC [360]
OVERSEAS BUSINESS REPORTS / U.S. Office of International Regional Economics – Washington. (25) Jul 1970, 1-22. Basic data on the Basic Economy of Libya. BNE-529 1 – 9 – ne IDC [310]
THE OVERSEAS CHINESE / Uchida, Naosaku – 1959 – 1 – 35.00r – us Hoover Inst Photo [305]
OVERSEAS DEVELOPMENT – No.1-. Nov. 1966-. London, Information Dept., Overseas Development Administration. -bim.Suspended Oct 1978-Jun 1979 – 1 – us U.W. Library [073]
OVERSEAS HINDUSTAN TIMES – New Delhi, India. May 1950-1952; 1962-Jul 1987 – 26r – 1 – us L of C Photodup [072]
Overseas Missionary Fellowship *see* THE PRISONER LEAPS; A DIARY OF MISSIONARY LIFE IN JAVA

OVERSEAS TRADE ACCOUNTS OF THE UNITED KINGDOM 1965-1969 – (Coll title: British Government Publications...1801-1977, Foreign Trade) – 240mf – 9 (£15,875.00 foreign trade set of 220r + 824mf) – uk Chadwyck [380]

OVERSEAS TRADE STATISTICS OF THE UNITED KINGDOM 1970-1977 – (Coll title: British Government Publications...1801-1977, Foreign Trade) – 576mf – 9 (£15,875.00 foreign trade set of 220r + 824mf) – uk Chadwyck [380]

THE OVER-TAXATION OF IRELAND: SPEECH IN THE HOUSE OF COMMONS, ON 29TH MARCH, 1897: WITH INTRODUCTION, INDEX AND TABLES / Blake, Edward – Delivered by Edward Blake, M. P. (South Longford). Dublin: Sealy, Bryers and Walker, 1897? 00168. (Pre-1900 Canadiana) – 9 – cn C.I.H.M. [360]

Overton, Carl McKinely *see* DESIGNING PROCEDURES FOR THE PROVISION OF NEW FACILITIES FOR CENTRAL BAPTIST ASSOCIATION

Overton, Daniel Y *see* A TREATISE ON THE LAW OF LIENS

Overton, John H *see*
- THE ANGLICAN REVIVAL
- THE ENGLISH CHURCH FROM THE ACCESSION OF GEORGE 1 TO THE END OF THE EIGHTEENTH CENTURY (1714-1800)
- THE ENGLISH CHURCH IN THE EIGHTEENTH CENTURY
- THE ENGLISH CHURCH IN THE NINETEENTH CENTURY (1800-1833)
- THE EVANGELICAL REVIVAL IN THE EIGHTEENTH CENTURY
- JOHN WESLEY
- LIFE IN THE ENGLISH CHURCH (1660-1714)
- WILLIAM LAW, NONJUROR AND MYSTIC

OVERTON OBSERVER – Overton, NE. -w. Apr 1938-May 1940; May 1941; May 1943; May 1944-May 1946; Oct 1946-Sep 1973 – 1 – us NE Hist [071]

OVERTURE AND FAVORITE ARIEN FROM LA MOLINARA / Paisiello, G – (Piano accompaniment) – Bonn: Simrock, 1794 – 1 – us Sibley [780]

OVERTURE, ARRANGED PIANO WITH AD LIB VIOLIN FROM "NINA O LA PAZZA PER AMORE" / Paisiello, G – (Piano part only) – Paris: Boyer, 179- – 1 – us Sibley [780]

OVERTURE OF ANGELS / Beecher, Henry Ward – New York: J.B. Ford, 1870. 1 fiche – 9 – us A.T.L.A. [240]

OVERVIEW – Tucson, Arizona. v12. no 4 (Fall 1978)-v28. no 2 (Fall 1994) – 20ft – us A.J.P.C. [270]

HET OVERVLOEIJEND HERTE / Luiken, J – O 355. 1767 – 9 – ne IDC [760]

HET OVERZICHT – Michel Seuphor, Jozef Peeters. no. 1-24. Anvers. juin 1921-fevr 1925. Collection privee. Disponible en reimpression, voir p. 111 – 1 – fr A.C.R.P.P. [073]

OVERZICHT DER STAATKUNDIGE BETREKKINGEN VAN HET EUROPEES GEZAG MET DE VORSTEN OP JAVA – 1596-1830. Arch. Kol. No. 2962. BSD-113/1 mf. 1-5 – 9 – ne IDC [950]

OVERZICHT VAN DE INLANDSCHE EN MALEISCH-CHINESE PERS – (Not published 1918 (1-43)) – Batavia, 1918-1940 – 759mf – 9 – ne IDC [950]

OVERZICHT VAN DE NEDERLANDSE PERS : VOORLICHTINGS DIENST, LONDON, VOOR INTERNE CIRCULATIE – (Lacking:[1945?]-1949, V.1-5(1-7)) – London, 1945?-1949 – 1mf – 9 – ne IDC [950]

Ovesen, N Krebs *see* ADVANCES IN THE CONTINUING EDUCATION OF ENGINEERS

Oviatt Family *see* PAPERS, MS 777

Ovid *see*
- HEROIDES
- LES METAMORPHOSES D'OVIDE, AVEC DES EXPLICATIONS A LA FIN DE CHAQUE FABLE
- SELECTIONS
- SPURIOUS AND DOUBTFUL WORKS

OVID HORIZONTE – Buenos Aires, Argentina. Mar 1949-Dec 1955 – 1r – 1 – uk British Libr Newspaper [072]

Ovidio Nason, P *see* DE EL REMEDIO DE EL AMOR IMPURO

Ovidius *see* METAMORPHOSES, ETC

Oviedo, F de *see* INTEGER CURSUS PHILOSOPHICUS

Oviedo, L *see* METHODO DE LA COLLECTION Y REPOSICION DE LAS MEDICINAS SIMPLES

OVIND; A STORY OF COUNTRY LIFE IN NORWAY / Bjornson, Bjornstjerne – Trans. from Norwegian by Sivert and Elizabeth Hjerleid. London: Simpkin, 1869.202p – 1 – us U.W. Library [830]

OVNT-KURYER = EVENING COURRIER – (In Yiddish) – Vilnius, LT. v14 no159 12 Jul 1926-v14 no193 18 Aug 1937 – 1r – 1 – $25.00 – cn Can Microfilming [072]

Ovsianiko-Kulikovskii, D N *see*
- LIRIKA KAK OSOBYI VID TVORCHESTVA
- N.V. GOGOL

Ovsiannikov, VZ *see* LITERATURNAIA RECH'. TOLKOVYI SLOVAR SOVREMENNOI OBSHCHELITERATURNOI FRAZEOLOGII

OWAY – Rangoon, Burma. 1948-26 Dec 1952; Jan 1953-30 Sept 1954; Mar 1959-Mar 1960; Dec 1960-Aug 1961 – 20r – 1 – us L of C Photodup [072]

Owen, Anevrin *see* ANCIENT LAWS AND INSTITUTES OF WALES

Owen, David E *see* KIRKSTALL ABBEY

Owen, J *see* NOTES ON THE NAGA TRIBES, IN COMMUNICATION WITH ASSAM

Owen, John *see*
- EVENINGS WITH THE SKEPTICS, OR, FREE DISCUSSION ON FREE THINKERS
- THE SKEPTICS OF THE FRENCH RENAISSANCE
- THE SKEPTICS OF THE ITALIAN RENAISSANCE
- THE YOUTH'S INSTRUCTOR IN THE ENGLISH TONGUE

Owen, R *see*
- A MONOGRAPH ON THE FOSSIL REPTILIA OF THE MESOZOIC FORMATIONS
- ODONTOGRAPHY, OR A TREATISE ON THE COMPARATIVE ANATOMY, OF THE TEETH
- ON THE CLASSIFICATION AND GEOGRAPHICAL DISTRIBUTION OF THE MAMMALIA

Owen, Robert *see* CORRESPONDENCE AND PAPERS, 1825-56

OWEN ROE O'NEILL / Taylor, John Francis – London: T. Fisher Unwin; Dublin: Sealy, Bryers & Walker, 1896. vi,249p – 1 – us U.W. Library [920]

OWEN SOUND SUN TIMES – Ontario, CN. 1851- – 12r per yr – 1 – $53.00r – cn Commonwealth Micro [072]

Owen, W C *see* THE ECONOMICS OF HERBERT SPENCER

Owen, Wilber Allen *see* QUESTIONS AND ANSWERS ON TWENTY-FIVE OF THE MOST IMPORTANT LEGAL SUBJECTS

Owen, William Fitzwilliam *see* NARRATIVE OF THE VOYAGES TO EXPLORE THE SHORES OF AFRICA, ARABIA AND MADAGASCAR

OWENITE MINUTE BOOKS, 1838-1845 / International Institute of Social History. Amsterdam – Archives, British Political Sources – 1 – us Primary [335]

OWENSBORO FIRST BAPTIST CHURCH. OWENSBORO, KENTUCKY : CHURCH RECORDS – 1840-1983 – 1 – 238.32 – us Baptist [240]

Owensboro, Kentucky *see* MISCELLANEOUS EARLY NEWSPAPERS

OWL – Beaverton, OR. -w. 20 Jul 1912-16 May 1914. 1 roll – 1 – us U.O. Library [071]

OWL – Woods OR. Jan 13 1900 – 1 – us U.O. Library [071]

THE OWL – Cape Town, South Africa.10 Oct 1896-29 Nov 1907. 17 reels – 1, 16 diazo available at reduced price – sa SA Libr [072]

THE OWL – (Cont by: The University of Ottawa Review) – Ottawa: Students of the College of Ottawa, [1888-1898] – 9 – cn C.I.H.M. [370]

THE OWL – Mount Owl's Head (Bolton), Canada. 16 mar 1967 – 1r – 1 – Can$25.00 – cn Can Microfilming [072]

THE OWL – Vancouver: Owl Print and Pub. Co, [1893-189- or 19–] – 9 – cn C.I.H.M. [320]

THE OWL *see* UNIVERSITY OF OTTAWA REVIEW

Owlia, G *see* INFLUENCE OF REINFORCERS ON MOTORIZED BICYCLE ON-TASK TIME OF PROFOUNDLY MENTALLY RETARDED ADOLESCENTS

OWNER OPERATOR – v1- 1970- 1; v4- 5,6,9 – us UMI [073]

OWNERSHIP AND MANAGEMENT OF FISHERY RESEARCH VESSELS – 1983 – 55p – it F.A.O. [650]

OXALIS. MONOGRAPHIA ICONIBUS ILLUSTRATA / Jacquin, N J von – Viennae. 1794. B-5442 2 – 8 – ne IDC [580]

OXAPAMPA, VISION HISTORICA Y DESARROLLO DE OXAPAMPA EN EL DEPARTAMENTO DE PASCO. TOMO 1. LIMA, 1967 / Ortiz, Dionisio – Madrid: Graf. Calleja, 1969 – 1 – sp Bibl Santa Ana [946]

OXBERRY'S DRAMATIC BIOGRAPHY AND HISTRIONIC ANECDOTES – v. 1-7. 1 Jan 1825-12 Aug 1827 – 1 – us UMI [920]

Oxenham, H N *see* SHORT STUDIES IN ECCLESIASTICAL HISTORY AND BIOGRAPHY

Oxenstirn, Johann Turesson *see*
- DER RABBINISCHE RATIONALISMUS: EINE UNTERREDUNG
- RATIONALISME DU RABBIN

OXFORD 1690-1905 – (Mf 1-4,56: Births 1690-1841. Mf 4-7: Intentions/Marriages 1716-1839. Mf 7-9: Deaths 1717-1845. Mf 10-12: Town Meetings 1713-52. Mf 12: Vital Records 1714-40. Mf 13-16: Vital Records 1714-1800. Mf 16,20-21,25: Deaths 1721-1844. Mf 17-18: Vital Records 1751-1815. Mf 19-25: Births 1729-1874. Mf 26-31: Intentions 1839-94. Mf 31: Marriages 1839-44. Mf 32-37: Births 1821-90. Mf 33: Marriages & Deaths 1844-51. Mf 38-43: Marriages, Deaths 1851-90. Mf 44-46: Birth Index 1714-1874. Mf 47-48: Intentions Index 1742-1839. Mf 49-50: Marriage Index 1718-1851. Mf 51-52: Death Index 1717-1851. Mf 53,55: Births, Deaths 1890-97. Mf 54: Marriages 1891-1903. Mf 57,64: Out-of-Town Marriages 1718-98. Mf 58-61: Intentions/ Marriages 1799-1839. Mf 62-64: Proprietors 1712-74. Mf 64-85: Town Records 1752-1858. Mf 86-105: Taxes 1808-59. Mf 106-107: Births & Deaths 1898-1904) – (mf ed 1996) – 107mf – 9 – 0-87623-392-2 – us Holbrook [920]

OXFORD 1713-1849 – (Mf 1T: Vital Records 1713-41. Mf 1T-4T: Births 1715-1804. Mf 4T-7T: Marriages & Intentions 1735-1800. Mf 5T: deaths 1721-86. Mf 7T-8T: Vital Records 1760-1815. Mf 8T-10T: Births 1729-1841. Mf 10T-12T: Deaths 1799-1845. Mf 12T-14T: Marriage Intentions 1800-49. Mf 13T-15T: Marriages 1799-1839. Mf 14T-15T: Out-of-Town Marriages 1718-98. Mf 15T-16T: Birth 1781-1849. Mf 16T-17T: Vital Records 1844-49. Mf 18T: Vitals 1791-1856; Marriages 1833-44) – (mf ed 1998) – 18mf – 9 – 0-87623-311-6 – us Holbrook [920]

OXFORD AGRARIAN STUDIES – 1990- 21v – 9 – £132.00 – 0264-5491 – uk Carfax [630]

OXFORD AND CAMBRIDGE CONFERENCES, 1897-1899 / Rickaby, Joseph – London: Burns and Oates; New York: Benziger, 1899 – 1mf – 9 – 0-8370-7328-6 – 1986-1328 – us A.T.L.A. [240]

OXFORD AND CAMBRIDGE MAGAZINE – 1. Jan-Dec 1856 – 1 – us UMI [073]

OXFORD BULLETIN OF ECONOMICS AND STATISTICS – (1982-. 1,5,6,9) – v35-. 1973- – 1 – us UMI [330]

OXFORD CHRONICLE – Oxford, England. 1843-45; 1848-66 – 17r – 1 – uk British Libr Newspaper [072]

OXFORD CHRONICLE AND BERKS AND BUCKS GAZETTE *see* OXFORD CITY AND COUNTY CHRONICLE

OXFORD CITY AND COUNTY CHRONICLE – (Oxford Chronicle & Berks & Bucks Gazette. 1863-1900) – England. 4 Feb 1837-1845; 1848-92; 1894-95; 1901-16. -w – 71r – 1 – uk British Libr Newspaper [072]

OXFORD CITY COURIER – (Also known as: Oxford Courier; Courier Oxford) – 1986-Jun 1995; 1996 – 17 1/2r – 1 – uk British Libr Newspaper [072]

OXFORD CONSERVATIVE – England. -f. 5 July 1834-27 June 1835. 1 reel – 1 – uk British Libr Newspaper [072]

OXFORD COURIER *see* OXFORD CITY COURIER

OXFORD ECONOMIC PAPERS – v1- 1938- 1; v23- 5,6; v27- 9 – us UMI [330]

OXFORD ECONOMIC PAPERS – n.s. v. 1-20 with Henderson suppl. London. 1949-68 – 9 – 24120.00; 6.00v – uk Dawson [330]

OXFORD ECONOMIC PAPERS – orig. s. no. 1-8. London. 1938-47 – 9 – 2415.00 – uk Dawson [330]

OXFORD ENGLISH DICTIONARY – Oxford, 1884-1928 – 228mf – 9 – us UMI [420]

OXFORD FLYING POST – England. -w. 7 Jan-26 Aug 1859. 20 ft – 1 – uk British Libr Newspaper [072]

OXFORD FREE PRESS – England. -w. 2 Jan-21 Aug 1858. 21 ft – 1 – uk British Libr Newspaper [072]

OXFORD GAZETTE AND READING MERCURY – (Reading Mercury and Oxford Gazette). England. -w. 1753-57, 1767-85. (4 reels) – 1 – uk British Libr Newspaper [072]

OXFORD GERMAN STUDIES – v. 1-6. Oxford. 1966-1971 72 – 9 – 2418.00; 3.00v – uk Dawson [430]

OXFORD GUARDIAN – England. -w. Jan 1884-Dec 1887. 1 1 2 reels – 1 – uk British Libr Newspaper [072]

OXFORD HIGH ANGLICANISM AND ITS CHIEF LEADERS / Rigg, James H – London: C.H. Kelly, 1899 – 1mf – us A.T.L.A. [240]

OXFORD JOURNAL *see* JACKSONS OXFORD JOURNAL

OXFORD JOURNAL OF ARCHAEOLOGY – v1-. 1982- – 1,5,6,9 – us UMI [073]

OXFORD JOURNAL OF LEGAL STUDIES – (1983-. 1,5,6,9) – v1-. 1981- – 1 – us UMI [073]

OXFORD MAGAZINE : UNIVERSAL MUSEUM – v1-13. Jul 1768-Dec 1776 – 1 – us UMI [073]

Oxford, Maine. Baptist Auxiliary Foreign Mission Society *see* RECORDS

OXFORD MERCURY & MIDLAND COUNTY CHRONICLE – England.5 Aug 1795-26 Oct 1796. -w. 1/2 reel – 1 – uk British Libr Newspaper [072]

OXFORD MESSENGER – England. -w. 4 June-9 July 1873; 1 July 1874-16 Feb 1876. 1 reel – 1 – uk British Libr Newspaper [072]

THE OXFORD METHODISTS : MEMOIRS OF THE REV. MESSRS. CLAYTON, INGHAM, GAMBOLD, HERVEY AND BROUGHTON, WITH BIOGRAPHICAL NOTICES OF OTHERS / Tyerman, L – New York: Harper, 1873 – 1mf – us A.T.L.A. [240]

Oxford, Mississippi *see* MISCELLANEOUS EARLY NEWSPAPERS

THE OXFORD MOVEMENT : TWELVE YEARS, 1833-1845 / Church, R W – London; New York: Macmillan, 1891 – 1mf – us A.T.L.A. [240]

THE OXFORD MOVEMENT IN AMERICA, OR, GLIMPSES OF LIFE IN AN ANGLICAN SEMINARY / Walworth, Clarence A – New York: Catholic Book Exchange, c1895 – 1mf – us A.T.L.A. [240]

Oxford. Presbytery (Pres. Ch. in the U.S.A.) *see* MINUTES, 1830-1870

THE OXFORD REFORMERS JOHN COLET, ERASMUS, AND THOMAS MORE : BEING A HISTORY OF THEIR FELLOW-WORK / Seebohm, Frederic – London: Longmans, Green, 1887 – 2mf – us A.T.L.A. [240]

OXFORD REVIEW OF EDUCATION – 1975- 19v – 9 – £126.00 – 0305-4985 – uk Carfax [370]

OXFORD REVIEWS OF REPRODUCTIVE BIOLOGY – (1982-. 1,5,6,9) – v1-. 1979- – 1 – us UMI [574]

OXFORD SLAVONIC PAPERS – (1982-. 1,5,6,9) – v1-. 1950- – 1 – us UMI [460]

OXFORD SLAVONIC PAPERS – n.s. v. 1. Oxford. 1968 – 9 – $243.00 – uk Dawson [460]

OXFORD SLAVONIC PAPERS – o.s. v. 1-13. Oxford. 1950-67 – 9 – $2439.00; $3.00v – uk Dawson [460]

THE OXFORD SPELLING-BOOK / Tuite, Thomas – 1726. 153p. (English Linguistics Series 1500-1800) – 9 – us UMI [420]

OXFORD STANDARD – Oxford, NE. -w. Jun 1892; Apr 1896-Jul 1899, scattered issues missing; Aug 1902-Nov 1902, scattered issues missing; Aug 1908-Sep 1910; Jul 1914; Jan 1918-Aug 1920; May 1921 to date – 1 – us NE Hist [071]

OXFORD STAR AND WOODSTOCK ADVERTISER – 1848-49 – 1 – 65.00 – cn McLaren [072]

OXFORD TOWNSHIP, DELAWARE CO., OHIO, RECORDS – (Primary results of township elections, minutes of trustee meetings, copies of indentures and agreements....) – 1828-43 – 1r – 1 – us Western Res [978]

OXFORD TRIBUNE – Ontario Prov., Canada. Nov 1876-Oct 1879 – 1 – cn Commonwealth Micro [072]

THE OXFORD UNION MURALS / Christian, John – (80p accompanying text) – 1980 – 1 color mf – 15 – $29.00f – 0-226-68922-0 – us Chicago [760]

Oxford University *see*
- MUNIMENTA ACADEMICA
- REPORT OF THE COMMISSIONERS

OXFORD UNIVERSITY, CITY AND COUNTY HERALD. (OXFORD UNIVERSITY HERALD) – England. Jan 1845-30 Jan 1892 (missing Nov-Dec 1871).-w. 40 reels – 1 – uk British Libr Newspaper [072]

Oxford University. Colleges *see* CATALOGUE OF MANUSCRIPTS

Oxford University. Institute of Statistics *see* BULLETIN..

OXFORD WEEKLY RECORD – England. -w. 1 Dec 1882-8 June 1883. 23 ft – 1 – uk British Libr Newspaper [072]

OXFORDSHIRE, 1823 : BRITISH ISLES CENSUS DIRECTORIES PROJECT, ENGLAND. VOL 216 – 1mf – 9 – A$9.00 – at Vine [941]

OXFORDSHIRE, 1830 : BRITISH ISLES CENSUS DIRECTORIES PROJECT, ENGLAND. VOL 263 – 1mf – 9 – A$9.00 – at Vine [941]

OXFORDSHIRE, 1848 : BRITISH ISLES CENSUS DIRECTORIES PROJECT, ENGLAND – at Vine [941]

OXFORDSHIRE, 1864 : BRITISH ISLES CENSUS DIRECTORIES PROJECT, ENGLAND. VOL 117 – 4mf – 9 – A$27.00 – at Vine [941]

OXFORDSHIRE, 1877 : BRITISH ISLES CENSUS DIRECTORIES PROJECT, ENGLAND – at Vine [941]

OXFORDSHIRE, 1891 : BRITISH ISLES CENSUS DIRECTORIES PROJECT, ENGLAND. VOL 27 – 6mf – 9 – A$39.00 – at Vine [941]

OXFORDSHIRE, 1899 : BRITISH ISLES CENSUS DIRECTORIES PROJECT, ENGLAND – at Vine [941]

OXFORDSHIRE, 1915 : BRITISH ISLES CENSUS DIRECTORIES PROJECT, ENGLAND – (In prep) – at Vine [941]

OXFORDSHIRE, 1920 : BRITISH ISLES CENSUS DIRECTORIES PROJECT, ENGLAND – (In prep) – at Vine [941]

OXFORDSHIRE FREE PRESS – Abingdon, England. -w. 30 March 1906-24 March 1916. Lacking July 1910-Feb 1912. 6 reels – 1 – uk British Libr Newspaper [072]

OXFORDSHIRE MAPS – From Corpus Christi College. 17th century – 14 – uk Microform Academic [910]

OXFORDSHIRE (OXFORD), 1805 : BRITISH ISLES CENSUS DIRECTORIES PROJECT, ENGLAND. VOL 186 – 1mf – 9 – A$9.00 – at Vine [941]

OXFORDSHIRE RECORD SOCIETY : OXFORDSHIRE RECORD SERIES – (Coll title: Publications of the English Record Societies, 1835-1972) – v1-37. 1919-56 – 85mf – 9 – £625.00 – uk Chadwyck [941]

OXFORDSHIRE WEEKLY NEWS – Chipping Norton, England. -w. March 1869-Dec 1895. 26 reels – 1 – uk British Libr Newspaper [072]

OXIDATION OF METALS – v1-42. 1969-94 – 1,5 – $65.00 – us UMI [660]

Oxley *see* YOUNG'S VICE-ADMIRALTY DECISIONS

Oxoby, Jean Daramy d' *see* LE SENEGAL EN 1925

Oxomensis, Eterius *see* ADVERSUS ELIPANDUM

OXONIAN ADVERTISER – Oxford, England. Hall's Oxonian Advertiser. -m. Jan 1853-26 March 1856. 33 ft – 1 – uk British Libr Newspaper [072]

OXYGEN CONSUMPTION DURING KAYAK PADDLING / Gray, Georgina L & McKenzie, Donald C – 1992 – 1mf – 9 – $4.00 – us Microform Publ [613]

THE OXYGEN COST OF EXERCISE HYPERNEA / Aaron, Elizabeth A – 1989 – 223p 3mf – 9 – $12.00 – us Microform Publ [612]

Oyen, A A Vorsterman van *see* HUGO DE GROOTEN ZIJN GESLACHT

OYF DER FRAY = UNTO FREEDOM – (In Yiddish) – Stuttgart, DE. no1. Sep 1945 – 1r – 1 – $25.00 – cn Can Microfilming [072]

OYFBOY = BUILDER – (In Yiddish) – New York City, NY. v2 no5. Jul 1923 – 1r – 1 – $25.00 – cn Can Microfilming [071]

OYFGANG = RISE – Havana, CU. v4 no 27. 1930 – 1r – 1 – Can$25.00 – cn Can Microfilming [072]

OYFGANG = RISE – (In Yiddish) – Warsaw, PL. no4-no5. Nov,Dec 1928 – 1r – 1 – $25.00 – cn Can Microfilming [072]

OYFN TZIMBL = TAKING TO TASK – (In Yiddish) – Munich, DE. no1. 1945 – 1r – 1 – $25.00 – cn Can Microfilming [072]

OYFSNAY = RENOUVEAU – (In Yiddish) – Paris, FR. Jan 1947-v2 no6-7(13-14) Jun/Jul 1948 – 1r – 1 – $25.00 – cn Can Microfilming [072]

OZ MAGAZINE *see* THE UNDERGROUND AND ALTERNATIVE PRESS IN BRITAIN

Ozaeta, Jose Maria OS A *see* EL TRATADO INEDITO "DE FIDE QUAE REVELANDA ERAT"

OZAKI KYUYA COLLECTION = OZAKI KYUYA COLLECTION OF EDO LITERATURE, BALLADS AND SONGS / Hosa Library. Nagoya. Japan – Share-hon, Kokkei-hon, Gokan-hon and the performing arts literature including Kayo and Kabuki. Printed 140p bibliography – 120r – 1 – Y1,200,000.00 – ja Yushodo [480]

Ozanam, Antoine F *see* REFLEXIONS SUR LA DOCTRINE DE SAINT-SIMON

OZAR HA-HAYYIM, ME'ASSEF LE-TORAT YISRA'EL – Ed. by H. J. Ehrenreich. Deva. Seini (Rumania). 1925-38. BJ-100-144 1 – 9 – ne IDC [073]

OZAR HA-MESHALIM VE-HA-PITGAMIM / Tawiow, J H – Berlin. 1922. BJ-290-5 1 – 9 – ne IDC [470]

OZAR TOV – (Hebrew supplement to "Magazin fuer die Wissenschaft des Judentums"). Berlin. 1877-86. BJ-100-145 1 – 9 – ne IDC [270]

OZAR YEHUDEI SEFARAD – V. 1-12. Jerusalem. 1959-70. BJ-91-69 1 – 9 – ne IDC [270]

OZARK ACCESS CATALOG – 1973 – 1,5,6 – us UMI [073]

THE OZARK CULTURE REGION REVEALED BY TRADITIONAL MATERIALS / Miller, Joan Wilson – Item J. From Annals AAG. 26p of xeroxed material. SW16-0090 – 5 – us A.G.L.L. [978]

OZARK MOUNTAIN FOLKS / Randolph, Vance – New York: Vanguard Press, 1932. ix, 279p. Illus. 1 reel – 1 – us I.U. Libraries [390]

Ozarovskaia, O E *see* BABUSHKINY STARINY

"OZE" OESTERREICHISCHE ZEITSCHRIFT FUR ELEKTRIZITATSWIRTSCHAFT – v.1-2, 1948-49; v.4, 1951; v.8-34, 1955-81. ISSN: 0029-9618 – 1,5,6,9,13 – 80.00v – us UMI [621]

Ozeretskovskii, N E *see*
- PRAVOVAIA ORGANIZATSIIA SOVETSKOI KOOPERATSII
- SPRAVOCHNIK PO SEL'SKOKHOZIAISTVENNOI KOOPERATSII

Ozerov, I Kh. *see* CHTO TAKOE OBSHCHESTVO POTREBITELEI, KAK EGO OSNOVAT'I VESTI

Ozerov, N I *see* KOOPERATIVNYE KRUZHKI V DEREVNE

Ozmun, J C *see* NEUROMUSCULAR AND KINESTHETIC ADAPTATIONS FOLLOWING STRENGTH TRAINING OF VISUALLY IMPAIRED AND NON-VISUALLY IMPAIRED CHILDREN

Ozols, M A *see* TOKEN ECONOMY WITHIN AN ADAPTED PHYSICAL EDUCATION PROGRAM TO MODIFY UNCOOPERATIVE BEHAVIOR OF TRAINABLE MENTALLY RETARDED TEENAGERS

OZONE – v. 1-. 1979- – 5,6,9 – us UMI [540]

Ozu, S *see* WADJAH SEMANGAT

P A L LA VICINI, S *see* HISTOIRE DU CONCILE DE TRENTE

P ANCIROLUS, G *see* DE QUATTORDECIM REGIONIBUS URBIS ROMAE EARUMDEMQUE AEDIFICIIS

P. ANTONIO MARIA DE BARCELONA. O.M. MARTIRI DELLA RIVOLUTIONE MAXISTA NELLA SPANA... / Bayle, Constantino – sp Bibl Santa Ana [946]

EL P. BARTOLOME DE OLMEDO. CAPELLAN DEL EJERCITO DE CORTES / Castro Seoane, Jose – Madrid: Missionalia Hispanica, 1949 – 1 – sp Bibl Santa Ana [946]

P ELZER, A *see* ADDENDA ET EMENDANDA AD F. EHRLE HISTORIA BIBLIOTHECAE ROMANORUM PONTIFICUM TOMUS I

P. FR. TOMAS DE SAN RAFAEL, CARMELITA DESCALZO : HISTORIA DE LA CONQUISTA DE... / ed by Bayle, Constantino – Madrid: Razon y Fe, 1927 – 1 – sp Bibl Santa Ana [240]

EL P. JUAN DE MALDONADO. TEOLOGO Y ESCRITURARIO / Boner, Jose M – Madrid: Razon y Fe, 1934 – 1 – sp Bibl Santa Ana [240]

P. OVIDIO NASON. DE EL REMEDIO DEL AMOR IMPURO / Suarez de Figueroa, Diego – Madrid, Tomo tercero. 1732 – 1 – sp Bibl Santa Ana [450]

P. OVIDIO NASON. EPISTOLAS DE LAS HEROIDAS / Suarez de Figueroa, Diego – Madrid: Herederos de Francisco del Hierro, 1735 – 1 – sp Bibl Santa Ana [450]

P. OVIDIO NASON.COMENTO DEL...NASON / Suarez de Figueroa, Diego – 1733 – 9 – $1.50f – sp Bibl Santa Ana [450]

P. OVIDIO NASON.DE EL...AMOR / Suarez de Figueroa, Diego – v2-3. 1732 – 9 – $1.50f – sp Bibl Santa Ana [450]

P. OVIDIO NASON.EPISTOLAS...HERODIAS / Suarez de Figueroa, Diego – 1735 – 9 – $1.50f – sp Bibl Santa Ana [450]

P. OVIDIO NASON.FASTOS / Suarez de Figueroa, Diego – (Libros 4-6. 1738.$1.50f) – Libros 1-3. 1737 – 9 – $1.50f – sp Bibl Santa Ana [450]

P. SILVERIO DE SANTA TERESA, C.D. OBRAS DE SANTA TERESA DE JESUS / ed by Bayle, Constantino – Madrid: Razon y Fe, 1926 – 1 – sp Bibl Santa Ana [240]

P.A. DE GASPE ET FRANCIS PARKMAN / Casgrain, Henri-Raymond – Montreal: Beauchemin & Valois, 1886. 02055. (Pre-1900 Canadiana) – 9 – cn C.I.H.M. [920]

PA JOURNAL – (Cont: Physician's Associate) – Thorofare. v3-5. 1973-win 75 1; v4-5. win 1974-win 1975* 5; v4-5. win 1974-win 1975 9 – 1,5,9 – D8216.01 – us UMI [610]

Paalzow, Henriette Wach von *see* SAEMMTLICHE ROMANE

DE PAARL *see* HET DAGBLAD

PAARL DISTRICT ADVERTENTIEBLAD *see* HET DAGBLAD

PAARL POST – (Continues: Afrikaanse Patriot) – Paarl, South Africa. 8 Sept 1906-21 Dec 1950 – 73r – 1, 16 diazo available at reduced price – sa SA Libr [072]

Paas, Sigrun *see* "KUNST UND KUENSTLER" 1902-1933

Paasche, Fredrik *see* GOETHE

Paasilinna, Arto *see* YEAR OF THE HARE

Paban, C *see*
- DEFENSIONES THEOLOGIAE DIVI THOMAE AQUINATIS
- DEFENSIONES THEOLOGIAE DIVI THOMAE AQUINATIS. VOL 1-7

PABLO SARASATE CORRESPONDANCE. 30 LETTERS [1 TO 6P. EACH] WRITTES BETWEEN FEB 9 1869 AND SEPT 27 1871 / Sarasate, P – (Vault letter file) – 1 – us Sibley [780]

PABLOID – Portland OR. Aug 14 1944-Feb 17 1945 – 1 – us U.O. Library [071]

Pablos Abril, Juan *see* CONEXION DE YUSTE CON LOS PUNTOS HISTORICOS DE LA PROVINCIA DE CACERES

Pabon Guerrero, Alonso *see* RHETORICA CASTELLANA...HABLAR BIEN...ORACION

Pabst, Curt *see* LORE'S LEIDEN

Pacaud, E et al *see* LE SOLEIL

Pacault, Emile *see* LA FIN DU CHOMAGE PAR LE PARTAGE DU TRAVAIL

Paccard, E *see* LISTA DE ALGUNAS PLANTAS MEDICINALES...

Pace, Celestino *see* SAINTE ANNE / CELESTINO PACE...

PACE ENVIRONMENTAL LAW REVIEW – v1-11. 1983-94 – 9 – $151.00 set – us Hein [340]

PACE INTERNATIONAL LAW REVIEW – (Title varies: v1-4 1982-92 as Pace Yearbook of International Law) – v1-5. 1989-93 – 9 – $63.00 set – us Hein [340]

PACE LAW REVIEW – (v1-5 1980-85 on reel $70.00. v6-15 1985-95 on mf $177.00) – v1-15. 1980-95 – 5,6,9 – $247.00 set – us Hein [340]

PACE YEARBOOK OF INTERNATIONAL LAW *see* PACE INTERNATIONAL LAW REVIEW

EL PACENSE – Badajoz.1891-92; 1896.No. sueltos – 9 – 1.50f – sp Bibl Santa Ana [073]

Pacheco, Francisco *see* ARTE DE LA PINTURA, SU ANTIGUEDAD Y GRANDEZAS.

Pacheco Ortiz, Felix *see* RAYOS DE LUZ

Pachelbel, Johann *see* HEXACHORDUM APOLLINIS SEX ARIAS..

PACHOMIANA LATINA / Boon, A – 1932 – 5mf – 8 – ne Slangenburg [240]

Pachymeris, Georgii *see*
- DE MICHAEL ET ANDROICO PALAEOLOGIS LIBRI 13 (CSHB 24, 25)
- HISTORIA RERUM A MICHAELE PALAEOLOGO (CBH 28,1)
- HISTORIA RERUM AB ANDRONICO SENIORE (CBH 28,2)

PACIFIC – San Francisco CA. Sep 28 1881 – 1 – us U.O. Library [071]

THE PACIFIC – San Francisco, CA. Aug 1851-Nov 1856 (broken series) – 1r – 1 BC02847 – $50.00 – us Library Micro [071]

THE PACIFIC AERONAUTICAL INDEX 1942-1953 – 1,5,6 – us Princeton Micro [629]

PACIFIC AFFAIRS – Vancouver. v1-70. 1928-win 1998+ 1; v42-70. spr 1969-win 1998+ 5; v49-70. spr 1976-win 1998 9 – 1,5,9 – D225 – us UMI [327]

PACIFIC AFFAIRS – Vancouver. v58-66. 1985/86-1993/94 – 9 – Can$28.00y – cn Micromedia [971]

PACIFIC ARCHITECT AND BUILDER WITH CONSTRUCTION NEWS BULLETIN – Seattle. v56-59. 1949-53 – 1 – D419 – us UMI [690]

PACIFIC BUILDER – San Francisco, CA. 1945-47 – 4r – 1 – $200.00 – C02848 – us Library Micro [071]

PACIFIC BUILDER – San Francisco. CA. -w.1945-47 – 1 – us UMI [071]

PACIFIC BUILDER AND ENGINEER – Seattle. v56-63. 1950-57 – 1 – D631 – us UMI [690]

PACIFIC BUSINESS NEWS – Honolulu. v1-29 1963-mar 1992*. v30-35 mar 1992-mar 1998+ – 1 – D16683 – us UMI [650]

PACIFIC CALENDAR AND CATHOLIC BULLETIN – San Francisco, CA. 1894-1897 – 1r – 1 – $50.00 – B05068 – us Library Micro [071]

PACIFIC CHRISTIAN ADVOCATE – Portland, OR. -w. 1 Sept 1855-26 Dec 1940, 13 Jan 1904 – 48r – 1 – us U.O. Library [071]

PACIFIC CHRISTIAN ADVOCATE – Salem OR. Sep 1 1855-Dec 26 1940 – 1 – us U.O. Library [071]

PACIFIC CHRISTIAN MESSENGER – Monmouth OR. May 31 1877-Dec 23 1881 – 1 – us U.O. Library [071]

PACIFIC CITIZEN – (Also publ in Salt Lake City and San Francisco) – Los Angeles, CA. 1929- – 30+ r – 1 – $1,500.00 ($50.00y) – B02398 – us Library Micro [071]

PACIFIC CITIZEN – (In Japanese-American) – San Francisco, CA. 1940-1942 – 1r – 1 – $50.00 – B03672 – us Library Micro [071]

PACIFIC CITIZEN – Los Angeles. Calif. 1961-1965 – 1 – us UMI [071]

PACIFIC COAST DIRECTORIES – West Coast. 1867; 1871-1873; 1878; 1880-1881; 1883-1884; 1886-1889 – 12r – 1 – $650.00 – D124 – us Library Micro [978]

PACIFIC COAST DIRECTORIES INCLUDING NAPA AND SONOMA COUNTIES – Sonoma Co, CA. 1871-1874; 1883-1890; 1899-1900 – 10r – 1 – $500.00 – D063 – us Library Micro [978]

PACIFIC COAST JOURNAL OF NURSING – (Cont: Nurses' Journal of the Pacific Coast. Cont by: California State Nurses' Association, Bulletin) – San Francisco. v8-39. aug 1912-dec 1943* – 1 – D14136.01 – us UMI [640]

PACIFIC COAST LAW JOURNAL – v1-12. 1878-84 (all publ) – 102mf – 9 – $153.00 – LLMC 82-954 – us L.L.M.C. [073]

PACIFIC COAST SCANDINAVIAN – San Francisco, CA. 1937-50 – 1r – 1 – $50.00 – B02849 – us Library Micro [071]

PACIFIC COMMERCIAL ADVERTISER – Honolulu. Hawaii. 1856-1884 – 1 – us UMI [071]

PACIFIC COMMERCIAL ADVERTISER – Honolulu. Jul 1856-Jun 1868 (missing Jul 1866-Jun 1867).-w. 5 reels – 1 – uk British Libr Newspaper [071]

PACIFIC CURRENT – (Incorporates: New Directions v1 no 1 Aug/Sept 1994) – v1- 1994/95- – 9 – Can$20.00y – cn Micromedia [971]

PACIFIC CURRENT *see* NEW DIRECTIONS

PACIFIC DEMOCRAT – Portland, OR. -w. 1899 – 1 – 17.00 – us Oregon Hist [071]

PACIFIC DISCOVERY – (With cum index for v1-25 1948-72 in 1) – San Francisco. v1-50. 1948-97+ 1; v27-36 1974-83. v37-47 1984-94*. v48-50 1995-97+ 5; v28-50. 1975-97+ 9 – 1,5,9 – D6859 – us UMI [073]

PACIFIC ECHO – Napa, CA. 1862-63 – 1r – 1 – $50.00 – C02511 – us Library Micro [071]

PACIFIC ECHO – Napa. Calif. 1862-1863 – 1 – us UMI [071]

PACIFIC EXPRESS – Portland OR. May 10 1888, Jan 31 1889 + – 1 – us U.O. Library [071]

PACIFIC FISHERMAN – (Absorbed in 1967 by: National Fisherman) – Portland. v48-49 1950-51. v51-52 1953-54 – 1 – D327 – us UMI [639]

PACIFIC GROVE REVIEW – Pacific Grove, CA. 1890-1906 (broken series) – 5r – 1 – $250.00 – C02589 – us Library Micro [071]

PACIFIC HERALD – Waldport, OR. -w. 26 Nov 1925-1 Apr 1926. 1 roll – 1 – us U.O. Library [071]
PACIFIC HERALD OF HOLINESS – San Francisco, CA. Jun 1884-22 Dec 1887 – 1r – 1 – $50.00 – C02847b – us Library Micro [071]
PACIFIC HISTORIAN – (With cum index for v1-15 1957-71 in 1) – Stockton. v1-31. feb 1957-spr 1987 1; v16 1972. v19-31 spr 1975-spr 1987 5; v19-31. spr 1975-spr 1987 9 – 1,5,9 – D6717 – us UMI [978]
PACIFIC HISTORICAL REVIEW – Berkeley. v1-66. 1932-97+ 1; v38-66. 1969-97+ 5; v44-66 1975-97+ 9 – 1,5,9 – D303 – us UMI [978]
PACIFIC HOMESTEAD – Salem, OR. -w, -m. 1 Mar 1900-Aug 1930. 23 rolls – 1 – us U.O. Library [071]
PACIFIC INSECTS – Honolulu. v17-22. 1975-80 1,9; v17-19 1975-77*. v20-21 1978-mar 1980. v22 aug-dec 1980* 5 – 1,5,9 – D10398 – us UMI [590]
THE PACIFIC ISLANDERS...FAMOUS MISSIONARIES AND NATIVE CONVERTS / Pierson, Arthur Tappan – New York: Funk & Wagnalls, 1906.ix,354p. 1 fiche – 9 – us A.T.L.A. [240]
PACIFIC ISLANDS MANUSCRIPTS, DOCUMENTS AND SERIALS – (Write to publisher for information) – 1,5,9,14 – at Pacific Mss [980]
PACIFIC ISLANDS MONTHLY – Sydney, 1930-42 – 90r – 1 – at Pascoe [073]
PACIFIC JEWISH ANNUAL – San Francisco. Calif. 1897-98 – 1 – us A.J.P.C. [071]
PACIFIC JEWISH PRESS – San Francisco, CA. 4 Jan 1963 (1 issue only) – 1r – 1 – $50.00 – B02850 – us Library Micro [071]
THE PACIFIC JOURNAL OF THEOLOGY – nos 1-34. Dec 1961-1970 (complete) – 1r – 1 – ATLA S0529 – us A.T.L.A. [071]
PACIFIC LAW JOURNAL – v1-25. 1970-94 – 1,5,6 – $855.00 – us Hein [073]
PACIFIC MAIL – London. -m and f. Oct 1873-Feb 1876. (1 reel) – 1 – uk British Libr Newspaper [072]
PACIFIC MONTHLY – Portland, OR. Oct 1898-Dec 1911. 12 rolls – 1 – us U.O. Library [071]
PACIFIC NEWS SERVICE – 1970- 1; 1972- 5,6; 1975- 4 x 6 in. 9 – us UMI [073]
PACIFIC NORTHWEST – Portland, OR. June 1911-Dec 1915. 1 roll – 1 – us U.O. Library [071]
PACIFIC NORTHWEST – Seattle. v14-27 1980-93. v28 1994* 1,9; v14-20 1980-86. v21-28 1987-94* 5 – 1,5,9 – Absorbed by: Seattle, feb 1995. Cont: Pacific Search – us UMI [978]
PACIFIC NORTHWEST LIBRARY ASSOCIATION : PNLA QUARTERLY – Portland. v1-43. oct 1936-sum 1979* 1; v44-62. fal 1979-sum 1998+ 1,5,9 – 1,5,9 – D12397 – us UMI [020]
PACIFIC NORTHWEST LIBRARY ASSOCIATION QUARTERLY – 1936-54 – 2r – 1 – $136.00 – cn Library Assoc [020]
PACIFIC NORTHWEST NEWSPAPERS ON MICROFILM – (Checklist of over 1200 regional newspaper titles) – 1 – us U.W. Libraries [071]
PACIFIC NORTHWEST QUARTERLY – Formerly: Washington Historical Quarterly. v. 1-36. 1906-1945 – 1,5,6 – us Princeton Micro [978]
THE PACIFIC NORTHWEST TRIBES INDIAN LANGUAGE COLLECTION OF THE OREGON PROVINCE ARCHIVES OF THE SOCIETY OF JESUS / ed by Carriker, Robert C – (With printed guide) – 1976 – 21r – 1 – $1,785.00 – D3152 – us Scholarly Res [490]
THE PACIFIC NORTHWEST TRIBES MISSIONS COLLECTION OF THE OREGON PROVINCE ARCHIVES OF THE SOCIETY OF JESUS, 1853-1960 / ed by Carriker, Robert C – (With printed guide) – 1986 – 34r – 1 – $2,890.00 – S3038 – us Scholarly Res [240]
PACIFIC OIL AND GAS WORLD – (Merged with: Gulf Coast Oil and Gas World; Midcontinental Oil and Gas World; Southwest Oil and Gas World; to form: Hart's Oil and Gas World. Cont: Pacific Oil World) – Denver. v85-86 jun 1993-jan 1994 – 1,5,9 – D2439.01 – us UMI [550]
PACIFIC OIL AND GAS WORLD *see* HART'S OIL AND GAS WORLD
PACIFIC OIL WORLD *see* PACIFIC OIL AND GAS WORLD
PACIFIC OVERSEER – Portland OR. Mar 1 1882 – 1 – us U.O. Library [071]
PACIFIC PATRIOT – Lents OR. Oct 1916 – 1 – us U.O. Library [071]
PACIFIC PATRIOT – Portland OR. May 1914, Jan 25 Feb Mar 1915 – 1 – us U.O. Library [071]
PACIFIC RAILWAY SURVEYS, 1853-1855 : REPORTS OF EXPLORATIONS AND SURVEYS TO ASCERTAIN THE MOST PRACTICABLE AND ECONOMICAL ROUTE FOR A RAILROAD FROM THE MISSISSIPPI RIVER TO THE PACIFIC OCEAN / U.S. Congress. Senate – 7r – 1 – $595.00 – S1878 – us Scholarly Res [625]
PACIFIC RECORD HERALD – Medford, OR. -w. 3 Jan 1929-6 Apr 1933. – 2r – 1 – us U.O. Library [071]
PACIFIC REFERENCE SOURCES : A SELECT BIBLIOGRAPHY / Atjtje, Syarfuddin – Sydney: BISA, 1988 – 1mf – 9 – A$10.00 – 0-86758-279-0 – at BISA [980]
PACIFIC REPORTER – (Add vols planned) – 1st series: v1-182. 1883-1919 – 2297mf – 9 – $3,445.00 – LLMC 79-404F – us L.L.M.C. [340]
PACIFIC RIM LAW AND POLICY JOURNAL – University of Washington: v1-4. 1992-95 – 9 – $61.00 set – us Hein [340]
PACIFIC RURAL PRESS – (Cont by: California Farmer) – San Francisco, CA. 1871-1948 – 107r – 1 – $5,350.00 – B02851 – us Library Micro [071]
PACIFIC RURAL PRESS – (Cont by: California Farmer Southern Edition) – Los Angeles, CA. 1871-1948 – 107r – 1 – $5,350.00 – B02399 – us Library Micro [071]
PACIFIC RURAL PRESS *see*
– CALIFORNIA FARMER
PACIFIC SCIENCE : A QUARTERLY DEVOTED TO THE BIOLOGICAL AND PHYSICAL SCIENCES OF THE PACIFIC REGION – v1- 1947- 1; v25- 5,6; v31- 9 – us UMI [574]
Pacific Science Congress. 10th. Div of Geography *see* LAND TENURE IN THE PACIFIC
PACIFIC SEARCH *see* PACIFIC NORTHWEST
PACIFIC SENTINEL – Santa Cruz, CA. 1856-62 – 7r – 1 – $350.00 – B02959 – us Library Micro [071]
PACIFIC SKANDINADEN – Portland, OR. 16 Apr 1908-4.July 1919. – 1r – 1 – us U.O. Library [071]
PACIFIC SOUTHWEST, DAVIS' COMMERCIAL ENCYCLOPEDIA / Davis, Ellis A – California, Nevada, Utah & Arizona. Oakland: 1915. California reel 38. (Cox Library Collection) – 5 – us Americana [978]
PACIFIC STARS AND STRIPES (PWW2 COLL) : FAR EAST WEEKLY REVIEW – TOKYO – may 25 1947-dec 31 1948 – 1r (reel 122) – 1 – $100.00r – us Ross [071]
PACIFIC STARS AND STRIPES (PWW2 COLL) : TOKYO – v1 n1-v19 n364. oct 3 1945-dec 31 1963 – 75r (reels 47-121) – 1 – $100.00r – us Ross [071]
PACIFIC STATE REPORTS : EXTRA ANNOTATED – (States covered: California v1-63 bks 1-21 1906. Colorado v1-6 bks 21-23 1911. Idaho Territory v1 bk 23 1904. Kansas v1-29 bks 24-32 1912. Montana Territory v1-3 bks 32-33 1911. Nevada v1-16 bks 33-36 1911. New Mexico Territory v1-2 bks 36-37 1911. Oregon Territory and State v1-10 bks 37-39 1911. Utah Territory v1-2 bks 39-40 1911. Washington Territory v1 bk 40 1911. Wyoming Territory v1-2 bk 40 1912) – Bks 1-40. 1904-12 (all publ) – 1022mf – 9 – $1,533.00 – LLMC 94-327 – us L.L.M.C. [340]
PACIFIC STATES AND TERRITORIES – West Coast. 1878 – 1r – 1 – $50.00 – D126 – us Library Micro [978]
Pacific States Publishing Co *see* HISTORY OF NEW MEXICO
PACIFIC SUN – Mill Valley, CA. Sept 1966- – 51+ r – 1 – $2,550.00 ($90.00y) – B02459 – us Library Micro [071]
PACIFIC SUN (MILL VALLEY) – San Rafael, CA. 1966- – 48+ r – 1 – $2,400.00 ($90.00y) – B02460 – us Library Micro [071]
Pacific Theological College *see* BACHELOR OF DIVINITY AND MASTER OF THEOLOGY THESES, 1968-1993
PACIFIC TRIBUNE – Canada. v1-28. Jan. 1935-Dec. 1968. Lacking: Jan. 1943-Dec. 1944 – 1 – cn Precision [971]
PACIFIC TRIBUNE – Seattle.WA. -w. 1861-79 – 1 – us UMI [071]
PACIFIC VIEWPOINT – v1- 1960- 1; v12- 5,6; v18- 9 – us UMI [073]
PACIFIC WEEKLY CENSOR – Vancouver WA. Sep 21 1881 – 1 – us U.O. Library [071]
PACIFIC YACHTING – (Inconsistent vol numbering in 1990. Publ notes no v31) – Vancouver. v28-36. 1987-94 – 9 – Can$37.00y – cn Micromedia [790]
PACIFICA TRIBUNE – Pacifica, CA. 1959- – 55+ r – 1 – $2,750.00 ($160.00y) – B02586 – us Library Micro [071]
PACIFICA VIEWS – 1-4 2+44 (all publ). 1943-47 – 10mf – 9 – $65.00 – us UPA [320]
LA PACIFICATION DE LA COTE D'IVOIRE, 1908-1915. / Angoulvant, Gabriel Louis – Paris, 1916 – 1 – us Res Libr [960]
PACIFIC-BASIN FINANCE JOURNAL – Amsterdam. v1-5. 1993-97+ – 1,5,9 – D42716 – us UMI [330]
PACIFISM, DISARMAMENT AND INTERNATIONAL RELATIONS, SERIES 1 – (Part One: Minutes, Reports and Publications, 1921-74) – Archives of War Resisters International – 1 – us Primary [327]
PACIFISM, DISARMAMENT AND INTERNATIONAL RELATIONS, SERIES 2 – (Part One: Minute Books and Committee Papers, 1915-60) – Archives of the Fellowship of Reconciliation – 1 – us Primary [327]
PACIFISM, DISARMAMENT AND INTERNATIONAL RELATIONS, SERIES 3 – (Pt 1: Annual Reports, 1937-85, and Minute Books, 1936-72. Pt 2: The Pacifist, The PPU Journal, Pamphlets, Leaflets, and other Publications, 1936-1986) – Archives of the Peace Pledge Union – 1 – us Primary [327]
Pacioli, L *see* DIVINA PROPORTIONE
Pacios Lopez, Arsenio *see*
– LOGICA Y ETICA
– PSICOLOGIA GENERAL Y DIFERENCIAL DEL NINO
PACKAGE DEVELOPMENT AND SYSTEMS *see* PACKAGING TECHNOLOGY
PACKAGE ENGINEERING – (v25- 1980- 5,6,9) – v1- 1956- – 1 – us UMI [680]
PACKAGE ENGINEERING *see* PACKAGE ENGINEERING INCLUDING MODERN PACKAGING
PACKAGE ENGINEERING INCLUDING MODERN PACKAGING – (The micro-edition for 1981-83 incl: The Packaging Encyclopedia. Formed by the merger of: Package engineering; and: Modern Packaging. Cont by: Packaging) – Chicago. v25-28. jan 1980-aug 1983 – 1,5,9 – D12927.01 – us UMI [680]
PACKAGE ENGINEERING INCLUDING MODERN PACKAGING *see* PACKAGING
PACKAGE PRINTING – (Cont: Package Printing and Diecutting. Cont by: Package Printing and Converting) – Philadelphia. v25-34. mar 1978-jun 1987 1,9; v25-26 mar 1978-dec 1979*. v27 1980. v28-34 1978-jun 1987* 5 – 1,5,9 – D10325.02 – us UMI [680]
PACKAGE PRINTING *see*
– PACKAGE PRINTING AND CONVERTING
– PACKAGE PRINTING AND DIECUTTING
PACKAGE PRINTING AND CONVERTING – (Cont: Package Printing) – Oak Brook. v34-44. jul 1987-1997+ 1,9; v34-41 jul 1987-1994*. v42-44 1995-97+ 5 – 1,5,9 – D10325.03 – us UMI [680]
PACKAGE PRINTING AND CONVERTING *see* PACKAGE PRINTING
PACKAGE PRINTING AND DIECUTTING – (Formed by the union of: Gravure; Diemaking, Diecutting and Converting; and: Package Printing and Flexography. Cont by: Package Printing) – Philadelphia. v21-25. 1975-feb 1978 1; v22 1976*. v23-24 1977. v25 jan-feb 1978* 5; v22-25. 1976-feb 1978 – 1,5,9 – D10325.01 – us UMI [680]
PACKAGE PRINTING AND DIECUTTING *see* PACKAGE PRINTING
PACKAGE PRINTING AND FLEXOGRAPHY *see* PACKAGE PRINTING AND DIECUTTING
PACKAGING – Finchley. n1-537 1930-74*. v46-64 1975-jan 1994. v65 feb-dec 1994*. v66-68 1995-97+ 1; v46-49 1975-78. v50-53 1979-82*. v54-64 1983-jan 1994. v65 feb-dec 1994*. v66-68 1995-97+ 5; v47-64 1976-jan 1994. v65 feb-dec 1994*. v66-68 1995-97+ 9 – 1,5,9 – D10241 – us UMI [680]
PACKAGING – (The micro-edition for 1985-89 incl: The Packaging Encyclopedia and Technical Directory. Absorbed by: Packaging Digest, dec 1994. Cont: Package Engineering including Modern Packaging) – Newton. v28-39. sep 1983-nov 1994 – 1,5,9 – D12927.02 – us UMI [680]
PACKAGING *see*
– PACKAGE ENGINEERING INCLUDING MODERN PACKAGING
– PACKAGING DIGEST
PACKAGING AND MANUFACTURING ELECTRONIC DATA SERVICES – v1-. 1982- – 1,5,6,9 – us UMI [621]
PACKAGING DESIGN – (Incorporated by: Print, in 1976) – Rockville. v1-16. 1960-75 – 1 – D10256 – us UMI [760]
PACKAGING DIGEST – (Absorbed: Packaging, dec 1994) – Chicago. v1-11 dec 1963-67. v12 1975*. v13-17 1976-80. v18 1981* 1; v16 1979*. v17 1980. v18 1981* 5; v16-18 1979-81* 9; v19-28 1982-91. v29-30 1992-93*. v31-34 1994-97+ 1,5,9 – 1,5,9 – D3298 – us UMI [680]
PACKAGING DIGEST *see* PACKAGING
THE PACKAGING ENCYCLOPEDIA *see* PACKAGE ENGINEERING INCLUDING MODERN PACKAGING
THE PACKAGING ENCYCLOPEDIA AND TECHNICAL DIRECTORY *see* PACKAGING
PACKAGING REVIEW – (Absorbed by: Packaging week, may 1986) – Tonbridge. v99-100. 1979-80 1,5,9; v99 1979* 5 – 1,5,9 – D10637 – us UMI [680]
PACKAGING TECHNOLOGY – (Cont: Package Development and Systems) – Hillsdale. v10-12 may 1980-jan 1983. v13 mar-dec 1983*. v14 jul-oct 1984. v15 feb-dec 1985*. v16-17 feb 1986-aug 1987 1,9; v10-13 may 1980-dec 1983*. v14 jul-oct 1984. v15-17 feb 1985-aug 1987* 5 – 1,5,9 – D8321.02 – us UMI [680]
PACKAGING TECHNOLOGY AND SCIENCE – Chichester. v1-10. 1988-97+ 1,9; v1 1988. v2-7 1989-94*. v8-10 1995-97+ 5 – 1,5,9 – D16175 – us UMI [680]
PACKAGING WEEK *see* PACKAGING REVIEW
Packard, A S *see* THE LABRADOR COA NEW YORK, 1891. 513P., ILLUS., MAPS
Packard, Joseph *see* THE BOOK OF MALACHI
PACKER – (v69 is missing in number only) – Lincolnshire. v1-67 1893-1961*. v68 feb 1962-feb 1963. v70-104 feb 1963-97+ – 1 – D1522 – us UMI [680]
Packer, G *see* THE CENTENARY OF THE METHODIST NEW CONNEXION, 1797-1897
Packer, John *see* PAPERS
PACKET AND TIMES – (1949-1992.-357r) – Orillia, 1993 – 24r – 1 – cn Preston [971]
PACKET SWITCHING NETWORKS: AN INTRODUCTION WITH SOME ATTENTION TO SELECTED VENDORS / Sanchez, James Joseph – ED 244-641 – 9 – 0.91 – us EDRS [070]
PACKINGHOUSE WORKER : 1942-1968 / Amalgamated Meat Cutters and Butcher Workmen of North America – (Coll title: Labor Union Periodicals, Pt 3) – 1996 – 4r – 1 – $540.00 – 1-55655-621-7 – us UPA [331]
PACOLET BAPTIST CHURCH. BROAD RIVER ASSOCIATION. CHEROKEE COUNTY. SOUTH CAROLINA : CHURCH RECORDS – 20 May 1797-2 Feb 1805, 1846-73 – 1 – 20.70 – us Baptist [240]
PACOTILHA : HEBDOMADARIO CRITICO E NOTICIOSO – '(s.l.')-Sao Luiz, Brazil. 30 Oct-Dec 1880; Apr-Sept, Nov-Dec 1881; Jan 1883-Dec 1888; Jan-Mar, Jul-Dec 1889; Jan 1890-Dec 1904; Apr 1905-Dec 1928; Jan-Mar, Jun-Dec 1929; Jan-Sept 1930; Aug 1934-31 Dec 1938 – 1,5,6 – bl Biblioteca [072]
A PACOTILHA DO TIO IGNACIO DAS MERCES – Rio de Janeiro, 26 May-18 Nov 1866 – 1,5,6 – bl Biblioteca [072]
PACTE MARITIME ADRESSE AUX NATIONS NEUTRES PAR UN NEUTRE / Paine, Thomas – Paris: Imp. du Cercle social, 1800. 42p. 1 fiche. (Political Science Collection) – 9 – 6.00 – fr Bibl Nationale [976]
PACTE MARITIME ADRESSE AUX NATIONS NEUTRES PAR UN NEUTRE / Paine, Thomas – Trad. de Nicolas de Bonneville. Paris. Imprimerie-Librairie du Cercle So-Social. 1800 – 9 – fr Hachette [321]
LOS PACTOS DE BUCASELI Y EL TRATADO DE LA MESILLA... / Fernandez, Salvador Diego – Madrid: Razon y Fe, 1940 – sp Bibl Santa Ana [946]

PACTUS LEGIS SALICAE (MGH LEGES 2A: 4.BD. PARS 1A) – 1962 – Dfl35.00 – ne Slangenburg [240]

Paczolt, T M *see* SAFETY BELT KNOWLEDGE, ATTITUDES, AND BEHAVIORS AMONG MINORITY ADOLESCENTS

Paddock, BB *see*
- FORT WORTH AND THE TEXAS NORTHWEST
- HISTORY OF CENTRAL AND WESTERN TEXAS
- A TWENTIETH CENTURY HISTORY AND BIOGRAPHICAL RECORD OF NORTH AND WEST TEXAS

PADDOCK PUBLICATIONS – Arlington Heights. Ill. 1901- – 1 – us UMI [071]

Paddock, Robert Louis *see* LETTER TO THE FRIENDS OF DEMOCRACY

Paddon, Kathleen S *see* AN EVALUATION OF THE EFFECTIVENESS OF THE 1981 HEALTH WORKSHOPS FOR LANE COUNTY CETA EMPLOYEES

PADDY DRYING MANUAL – 1987 – 130p – it F.A.O. [631]

Padecopeo, Gabriel *see* SOLILOQUIOS AMOROSOS DE UN ALMA A DIOS

Padel, Wilhelm *see* DE LA LEGISLATION FONCIERE OTTOMANE

Padelford, Frank W *see* THE COMMONWEALTHS AND THE KINGDOM

THE PADEN COLLECTION OF ARABIC MATERIALS, KANO, NIGERIA / Paden, John Naber – Chicago: Uni of Chicago Photodup Dept for Cooperative Africana Microform Project, [19–?] – us Res Libr [470]

Paden, John N *see* INFLUENCE OF RELIGIOUS ELITES ON POLITICAL CULTURE AND COMMUNITY INTEGRATION IN KANO, NIGERIA

Paden, John Naber *see* THE PADEN COLLECTION OF ARABIC MATERIALS, KANO, NIGERIA

PADENIE DINASTII : TEMNYE SILY I REVOLIUTSIIA / Kadmin [Abramovich, N I] – M., 1917. 149p – 2mf – 9 – ne IDC [320]

PADENIE TSARSKOGO REZHIMA / Russia. (1917-Provisional Government). Chrezvychainaia Sledstvennaia Komissiia – Moscow, 1924-1927 – 1 – 35.00r – us Hoover Inst Photo [324]

PADENIE TSARSKOVO REZHIMA – (Fall of the Tsarist Government). 7 v. 1924-27 – 3 – us Readex [947]

Paderewski, Ignace Jan *see*
- DANS LE DESERT, OP. 15
- HUMORESQUE DE CONCERT, OP. 14, CAHIER 1, [A L'ANTIQUE]
- HUMORESQUE DE CONCERT, OP. 14, CAHIER 2, ["MODERNE"]
- MISCELLANEA: SERIES DE MORCEAUX POUR PIANO, OP. 16, NO. 1: LEGENDE
- MISCELLANEA: SERIES DE MORCEAUX POUR PIANO, OP. 16, NO. 2: MELODIE
- MISCELLANEA: SERIES DE MORCEAUX POUR PIANO, OP. 16, NO. 3: THEME VARIE
- MISCELLANEA: SERIES DE MORCEAUX POUR PIANO, OP. 16, NO. 4: NOCTURNE
- MISCELLANEA: SERIES DE MORCEAUX POUR PIANO, OP. 16, NO. 5
- MISCELLANEA: SERIES DE MORCEAUX POUR PIANO, OP. 16, NO. 7: MINUET
- MISSCELLANEA: SERIES DE MORCEAUX POUR PIANO, OP. 16, NO. 6: UN MOMENT MUSCIAL
- SONATE FOR PIANO, OP. 21

PADGETT'S CREEK BAPTIST CHURCH. UNION, SOUTH CAROLINA : CHURCH RECORDS – 1784-1955 – 1 – 85.05 – us Baptist [240]

Padirac, B de et al *see* SPINES THESAURUS

PADJADJARAN – Bandung. Lacking: 1959; v. 2(2-4). 1958-1970 – 9 – ne IDC [073]

THE PADLOCK : A COMIC OPERA IN TWO ACTS / Bickerstaff, Isaac – (Libretto without music[by Dibdin]) – New York: C Wiley, 1825 – 1 – us Sibley [780]

THE PADLOCK / Dibdin, Charles – (Vocal score) – London: J Johnston, [1768] – 1 – us Sibley [780]

EL PADRE BOSCANA, HISTORIADOR DE CALIFORNIA. PALMA DE MALLORCA, 1965 / Font Obrador, Bartolome – Madrid: Graf. Calleja, 1966 – 1 – sp Bibl Santa Ana [975]

"PADRE COBOS" PERIODICO DE POLITICA, LITERATURA Y ARTES – Madrid, 1855 – 2mf – 9 – sp Cultura [320]

EL PADRE CONSTANTINO BAYLE (1882-1953) / Mateos, Francisco – Madrid: Missionalia Hispanica, 1955 – 1 – sp Bibl Santa Ana [240]

EL PADRE CRISTOBAL, OTRO GIGANTE. VIDA DEL VENERABLE PADRE CRISTOBAL DE SANTA CATALINA / Felipe, Dionisio de – Madrid: Ed. El Perpetuo Socorro, 1967 – sp Bibl Santa Ana [240]

EL PADRE DOMINGO DE LA ANUNCIACION Y SU PERSONALIDAD MISIONERA / Salvador y Conde, Jose – Madrid: Missionalia Hispanica, 1950 – 1 – sp Bibl Santa Ana [240]

EL PADRE JOSE MHA RUIZ, MARTIR EN SIGUENZA / Riol, Eladio – San Sebastian: Editorial Coculsa, 1939 – sp Bibl Santa Ana [240]

EL PADRE JOSE QUIROGA / Furlong Cardiff, Guillermo – Buenos Aires, 1930; Madrid: Razon y Fe, 1931 – 1 – sp Bibl Santa Ana [240]

EL PADRE LA CALLE (PRIMER CENTENARIO DE SU MUERTE) / Izquierdo, Adolfo – Caceres: Tip. El Noticiero S.L., 1948 – 1 – sp Bibl Santa Ana [946]

EL PADRE PABLO DE GRAYMOOR... / Morillo Trivino, Santiago & S Granny, Tito – Madrid: Centro de Estudios Orientales, s.a. – 1 – sp Bibl Santa Ana [240]

EL PADRE TEMBLEQUE. MEXICO, 1945 / Valdes, Octavio – Madrid: Razon y Fe, 1947 – 1 – sp Bibl Santa Ana [972]

PADRES ANTE TODO / Sanchez Arjona y Sanchez Arjona, Jose – 1874 – 9 – 1.50f – sp Bibl Santa Ana [810]

PADRON GENERAL DEL ANO 1897 / Almendralejo – Badajoz: La Minerva Extremena – 1 – sp Bibl Santa Ana [946]

PADUCAH FIRST BAPTIST CHURCH. PADUCAH, KENTUCKY : CHURCH RECORDS – 1896-1961 – 1 – 235.26 – us Baptist [240]

Paducah. Kentucky. Jonathan Creek Baptist Assembly *see* TRUSTEES AND ADVISORY COMMITTEE MINUTES

PADUCHAIA STREMNINA / Severianin, I – Roman v 2-kh chastiakh. Berlin. 1922. BR-1034 2 – 8 – ne IDC [460]

PAEDAGOGICA EUROPAEA – (Cont by: European Journal of Education) – 's-Hertogenbosch. v1-13. 1965-78* – 1 – D11167 – us UMI [370]

DIE PAEDAGOGISCHE ENTWICKLUNG DES CHRISTLICHEN LEBENS / Beck, Johann Tobias; ed by Lindenmeyer, Julius – Guetersloh: Bertelsmann, 1883 – 2mf – us A.T.L.A. [240]

PAEDAGOGISCHE REFORM – Hamburg, Germany. -w. 15 May 1877-25 Dec 1901. 7 reels – 1 – uk British Libr Newspaper [072]

PAEDAGOGISCHE ZEITUNG – Berlin, 1877-87 – 1 – Inquire at Mikrofilmarchiv for details – gw Misc Inst [370]

PAEDAGOGISCHE ZEITUNG – Berlin, Germany. 1877-1887 – 1 – gw Mikrofilm [072]

DIE PAEDAGOGISCHEN ELEMENTE IN DER PHILOSOPHIE DES JAKOB BALMES / Kruse, Paul – Neuherberg, 1935 – 153p – 9 – DM48.00 – 3-89349-006-X – gw Hänsel [190]

PAEDIATRIC ANAESTHESIA – Paris. v1-4 1991-94*. v5-7 1995-97+ – 1,5,9 – D18096 – us UMI [618]

PAEDIATRIC AND PERINATAL EPIDEMIOLOGY – Oxford. v1-11. 1987-97+ 1,9; v1 1987*. v2 1988. v3-8 1989-94*. v9-11 1995-97+ 5 – 1,5,9 – D15617 – us UMI [618]

PAEDIATRICA INDONESIANA – Djakarta. SE-861 1. Lacking: 1961; v. 1 (1,3-4). 1961-1971 – 9 – 69.50 – ne IDC [618]

PAEDIATRICA INDONESIANA – (v1 was not available for filming) – Jakarta. v2-11 1962-71. v16-20 1976-80 1; v16-19 1976-79*. v20 1980 5; v16-20 1976-80 9 – 1,5,9 – D7293 – us UMI [618]

PAEDIATRICIAN – Basel. v2. 1973 – 1 – D7541 – us UMI [618]

PAEDIATRIE UND PAEDOLOGIE – v.1-16, 1965-81. ISSN: 0030-9338 – 1,5,6,9,13 – 90.00v – us UMI [370]

PAEDIATRISCHE PRAXIS – v12- 1973- 1,5,6; v16- 9 – us UMI [618]

Paenek, Joannes *see* COMMENTARIUS IN EPISTOLAM B. PAULI APOSTOLI AD HEBRAEOS

DIE PAEPSTLICHE LEGATION IN DER ERSTEN HAELFTE DES 13. JAHRHUNDERTS / Zimmermann, Heinrich – 1913 – 1 – us A.T.L.A. [240]

DIE PAEPSTLICHE UNFEHLBARKEIT UND DAS VATIKANISCHE KONCIL : VORTRAG GEHALTEN ZUM BESTEN DER DEUTSCHEN INVALIDENSTIFTUNG AM 11. FEBRUAR 1871 / Hinschius, Paul – Kiel: Universitaets-Buchh, 1871 – 1mf – 9 – 0-8370-8435-0 – 1986-2435 – us A.T.L.A. [240]

DER PAEPSTLICHE ZEREMONIEN-MEISTER JOHANNES BURCKARD VON STRASSBURG 1450-1506 / Oliger, L – Strassburg, 1934 – 1mf – 8 – Dfl6.00 – ne Slangenburg [240]

DIE PAEPSTLICHEN DECRETE VOM 18. JULI 1870 / Reinkens, Joseph Hubert – Muenster, 1871 – 3mf – 9 – DM75.00 – 3-89349-285-2 – gw Hänsel [240]

Paer, F *see*
- ACHILLE
- LA LACONDA DE VAGOBONDI

PAESE SERA – 1987-1995 – 3r per y – 5,6 – Sfr936.00 – sz Infoprint [072]

PAESI SOTTO MANDATA... / Ambrosini, G – Milano, Roma, 1932 – 2mf – 9 – ILM-2376/1 – ne IDC [340]

Paetel, F *see* MOLLUSCORUM SYSTEMA ET CATALOGUS

Paetel, Karl Otto *see* ERNST JUENGER

Paez de la Cadena, Francisco *see* MOCION FORMULADA Y EXPUESTA A LA CONSIDERACION DEL EXCMO. AYUNTAMIENTO CONSTITUCIONAL DE BADAJOZ

PAGAN : A MAGAZINE FOR EUDAEMONISTS – New York. v1-6. 1916-22 – 1r – 1 – us Ross [290]

PAGAN : A MAGAZINE FOR EUDAEMONISTS – New York. v1-6 may 1916-jan 1922* – 1 – D4676 – us UMI [130]

PAGAN AND CHRISTIAN CREEDS: THEIR ORIGIN AND MEANING / Carpenter, Edward – 2nd ed. London: G. Allen & Unwin, 1921.318p. diagrs.Includes bibliographical references and index – 1 – us U.W. Library [210]

THE PAGAN BACKGROUND OF EARLY CHRISTIANITY / Halliday, William Reginald – Liverpool: The University Press of Liverpool, 1925. xvi,334p. (The Ancient World) – 1 – us U.W. Library [240]

Pagan, Oliver Elwood *see* PRECEDENTS AND FORMS OF INDICTMENTS, INFORMATIONS, COMPLAINTS.

PAGAN POEMS / Moore, George – London: Newman, 1881 – 1 roll – 1 – 1-55879-478-6 – uk Libr Preservation [810]

Paganini, N *see* CAPRICE NO. 20, ARRANGED FOR VIOLIN AND PIANO BY KREISLER

Page, Bessie Nadine *see* LEGAL FORMS AND LAW OFFICE PRACTICE

UNE PAGE DE LA TERREUR A NANTES : LES LE LOUP DE LA BILIAIS MARTYRS DU SACRE-COEUR... / Wismes, Gaetan de – Vannes: Lafolye, 1894 – 1 – F50.00 – fr Armell [240]

Page, Elizabeth Merwin *see* IN CAMP AND TEPEE

Page, H J *see* PAGE'S INDEX OF JUDGMENTS IN THE CIRCUIT AND DISTRICT COURTS OF THE UNITED STATES FOR THE DISTRICT OF KANSAS

Page, Jean-Pierre *see* BIO-BIBLIOGRAPHIE DE HENRI [I.E. HECTOR] DE SAINT-DENYS GARNEAU (1953-1963)

Page, Jesse *see*
- BISHOP PATTESON
- DAVID BRAINERD, THE APOSTLE TO THE NORTH AMERICAN INDIANS
- HENRY MARTYN
- THE LAND OF THE PEAKS AND THE PAMPAS

Page, John *see* SIX ANTHEMS AND TEN CHANTS

Page, Kirby *see* IMPERIALISM AND NATIONALISM; A STUDY OF CONFLICT IN THE NEAR EA.

Page, N *see* L'ALLIANCE

PAGE NEWS AND COURIER – Luray. Va. 1923- – 1 – us UMI [071]

Page, O J *see* HISTORY OF MASSAC COUNTY

Page Renouf, P Le *see* WHO WERE THE LIBYANS? A 626. 1891

PAGE REPORTER – Page, NE. -w. Jan 1903-Feb 1906, scattered issues missing; Jul 1914-Jun 1942 – 1 – us NE Hist [071]

Page, Thomas Ethelbert *see* THE ACTS OF THE APOSTLES

A PAGEANT : AND OTHER POEMS / Rossetti, Christina – London: Macmillan, 1881 – 1 roll – 1 – 1-55879-171-X – uk Libr Preservation [810]

PAGEANT – London. v5-7. 1949-52 – 1 – D284 – us UMI [073]

PAGEANT *see* CHURCH AND SOCIETY

THE PAGEANT – London, 1896-97 – 1r – 1 – £60.00 – uk Chadwyck [760]

PAGEANT OF AMERICA – (Text and pictures on US history from Yale University Press material. v1 Adventurers in the Wilderness; v2 Lure of the Frontier; v3 Toilers of Land and Sea; v4 March of Commerce; v5 Epic of Industry; v6 Winning of Freedom; v7 In Defense of Liberty; v8 Builders of the Republic; v9 Makers of a New Nation; v10 American Idealism; v11 American Spirit in Letters; v12 American Spirit in Art; v13 American Spirit in Architecture; v14 American Stage; v15 Annals of American Sport) – 62mf – 9 – $160.00 – us UMI [975]

THE PAGEANTRY OF METHODIST UNION : BEING A PICTORIAL RECORD OF THE EVENTS LEADING UP TO AND CONSUMMATING IN THE HISTORIC UNITING CONFERENCE OF 1932 / Wycherley, R N – London, 1936. 411p – 5mf – 9 – ne IDC [240]

Pagel, Bjoern *see* LESSINGS "PHILOTAS" UND SEINE PRODUKTIVE REZEPTION BEI BODMER UND GLEIM

Pages, E L *see* LES INCIDENTS ET LES EXCEPTIONS DEVANT LES TRIBUNAUX MILITAIRES EN TEMPS DE PAIX ET AUX ARMEES

PAGES FROM A JOURNAL, WITH OTHER PAPERS. BY MARK RUTHERFORD / White, William Hale – London: T. Fisher Unwin, 1901 – 1 roll – 1 – 1-55879-816-1 – uk Libr Preservation [920]

Pages, G *see*
- AU RUANDA SUR LES BORDS DU LAC KIVU (CONGO BELGE)
- LE GRAND ELECTEUR ET LOUIS XIV, 1660-1688

PAGE'S INDEX OF JUDGMENTS IN THE CIRCUIT AND DISTRICT COURTS OF THE UNITED STATES FOR THE DISTRICT OF KANSAS / Page, H J – Topeka: Commonwealth, 1879. 197p. LL-1287 – 1 – us L of C Photodup [340]

Pages, Jean *see* L'OCCONOMIE DES TROIS FAMILLES DV MONDE SVBLVNAIRE, A SCAVOIR ANIMALE, VEGETALE, ET MINERALE

Pages, Leon *see*
- BIBLIOGRAPHIE JAPONAISE
- HISTOIRE DE LA RELIGION CHRETIENNE AU JAPON DEPUIS 1598 A 1651
- LE JAPON ET SES DERNIERS TRAITES AVEC LES PUISSANCES EUROPEENNES
- LA PERSECUTION DES CHRETIENS AU JAPON ET L'AMBASSADE JAPONAISE EN EUROPE

PAGES LIBRES – no. 1-457. Paris. 1901-2 oct 1909. mq no. 397, 408-413, 454 – 1 – fr A.C.R.P.P. [073]

PAGES LIBRES – Paris. No.1-457. 1901-Oct 1909. 144 fiches. (Selected Periodicals) – 9 – 356.00 – fr Bibl Nationale [073]

Pages, Pere *see* UN ROYAUME HAMITE AU CENTRE DE L'AFRIQUE

Paget, Clarence Edward *see* AUTOBIOGRAPHY AND JOURNALS OF ADMIRAL LORD CLARENCE E. PAGET, G.C.B

UNA PAGINA DE GEOGRAFIA ANEJA / Bayle, Constantino – Madrid: Razon y Fe, 1921 – 1 – sp Bibl Santa Ana [900]

PAGINAS DE EXTREMADURA. VILLANUEVA DE LA SERENA / Torres Cabrera, Marques de – Badajoz: Tip. El Progreso, 1900 – 1 – sp Bibl Santa Ana [946]

PAGINAS DE LITERATURA Y ENSAYO – Madrid: Itaca, 1982- . ill. -q – 1 – us U.W. Library [800]

PAGINAS DE SANTA MARTA / Viniegra de Vera, Virgilio – Zafra: Imp. Morera, 1925 – 1 – sp Bibl Santa Ana [946]

PAGINAS OLVIDADAS / Espronceda, Jose de – (1882 ed.1.50f; 9) – 1875 – 9 – 1.50f – sp Bibl Santa Ana [810]

PAGINAS OLVIDADAS / Espronceda, Jose de – Madrid: Casa Editorial de Medina y Navarro, s.a. – 1 – sp Bibl Santa Ana [946]

PAGINAS OLVIDADAS DE... / Espronceda, Jose de – Madrid: Libro de Los Senores Sienon y Osler, 2ª ed 1882 – 1 – sp Bibl Santa Ana [946]

PAGINAS ORTOGRAFICAS / Guzman y Martinez, Jesus – Badajoz: Tip y Enc. Uceda Hnos, 1915 – 1 – sp Bibl Santa Ana [946]

PAGINAS PARA LA HISTORIA DEL FRENTE POPULAR / Martinez Barrio, Diego – Madrid, 1937. Fiche W 1032. (Blodgett Collection of Spanish Civil War Pamphlets) – 9 – us H.U. College Libr [946]

PAGINE DI STORA DEL DIRITTO INTERNAZIONALE / Focherini, A – Carpi-Emilia, 1918 – 1mf – 1 – ILM-3561/1 – ne IDC [327]

Pagninus, S *see* OSAR LESON HAQ-QODES, HOC EST, THESAVRVS LINGVAE SANCTAE...

PAHLAVI MEDICAL JOURNAL – Shiraz. v1-4 1970-73. v6-9 1975-78 1; v3 1972. v7-9 1976-78 5; v7-9 1976-78 9 – 1,5,9 – D7404 – us UMI [610]

DER PAHLAVI TEXT : "DER KOENIG HUSRAV UND SEIN KNABE..." / ed by Huvala, J M – Wien, 1917 – 1mf – NE-20157/1 – ne IDC [490]

PAHLAVI TEXT SERIES / ed by Sanjana, D D P – Bombay, 1894-1908. 3v – 12mf – NE-20164/1 – ne IDC [490]

PAHLAVI TEXTS – (A collection of very rare titles) – 141mf – ne IDC [490]

PAHLAVI TEXTS : PART 1: THE BUNDAHIS BAHMAN YAST, AND SHAYAST LA-SHAYAST / ed by Mueller, Friedrich Max – (Translated by E.W. West) – 1880 – 9mf – 8 – ne Slangenburg [280]

PAHLAVI TEXTS : PART 2: THE DADISTAN-I DINIK AND THE EPISTLES OF MANUSKIHAR / ed by Mueller, Friedrich Max – (Translated by E.W. West) – 1882 – 9mf – 8 – ne Slangenburg [280]

PAHLAVI TEXTS : PART 3: DINA-I MAINOG-KHIRAD, GUMANIK VIGAR, AND SAD DAR / ed by Mueller, Friedrich Max – (Translated by E.W. West) – 1885 – 8mf – 8 – ne Slangenburg [280]

PAHLAVI TEXTS : PART 4: THE CONTENTS OF THE NASKS, AS STATED IN THE EIGHT AND NINTH BOOKS OF THE DINKARD / ed by Mueller, Friedrich Max – (Translated by E.W. West) – 1892 – 10mf – 8 – ne Slangenburg [280]

PAHRUMP VALLEY TIMES – Pahrump, NV. 1978 – 16+ r – 1 – $800.00 – N04636 – us Library Micro [071]

PAHRUMP VALLEY TRIBUNE – Pahrump, NV. 1979-1983 – 1r – 1 – $50.00 – N04804 – us Library Micro [071]

Paiaranus, Baptista *see* CHRONICA

Paige, Johannis, Le *see* BIBLIOTHECA PREMONSTRATENSIS ORDINIS

PAIGE'S CHANCERY APPEALS CASES / New York. (State) – (A Pre-NRS title) – v1-11. 1828-45 (all publ) – 90mf – 9 – $135.00 – LLMC 80-113 – us L.L.M.C. [340]

Paillet de Warcy, L *see* HISTOIRE DE LA VIE ET DES OUVRAGES DE VOLTAIRE

PAIMANN'S FILMLISTEN – Wien, jan 13 1916-mar 30 1943, feb 7 1946-65 – 8r – 1 – gw Mikrofilm [790]

PAIN – Amsterdam. v1-71. mar 1975-dec 1997+ 1,5; v32-71 1988-97+ 9 – 1,5,9 – D42028 – us UMI [073]

PAIN – v1-20. 1975-84 – 1,5,6,13 – sz Elsevier [073]

PAIN MEDICINE JOURNAL CLUB JOURNAL – Hagerstown. v1-3. 1995-97+ – 1,5,9 – D21916 – us UMI [615]

DU PAIN POUR GAGNER LA GUERRE – Paris, 193? Fiche W 846. (Blodgett Collection of Spanish Civil War Pamphlets) – 9 – us H.U. College Libr [946]

Paina, E S *see*
- EKONOMICHESKAIA ISTORIIA ROSSII, 1861-1917 GG
- KREST'IANSKOE DVIZHENIE V ROSSII V 19-NACHALE 20 VV

Paine, E *see* PAINE'S REPORTS OF CASES IN THE SECOND CIRCUIT, 1810-1840

Paine, John Knowles *see*
- CENTENNIAL HYMN, OP. 27
- OEDIPUS TYRANNUS OF SOPHOCLES
- ST. PETER: AN ORATORIO

Paine, Levi Leonard *see* A CRITICAL HISTORY OF THE EVOLUTION OF TRINITARIANISM AND ITS OUTCOME IN THE NEW CHRISTOLOGY

Paine, Robert T *see* PAMPHLETS, 1879-1904

Paine, Thomas *see*
- DE L'ORIGINE DE LA FRANC-MACONNERIE
- PACTE MARITIME ADRESSE AUX NATIONS NEUTRES PAR UN NEUTRE

Paine, Willis Seaver *see* PAINE'S ANALYSIS OF THE FEDERAL RESERVE ACT AND COGNATE STATUTES, INCLUDING ANALYSES OF THE FEDERAL FARM LOAN

PAINE'S ANALYSIS OF THE FEDERAL RESERVE ACT AND COGNATE STATUTES, INCLUDING ANALYSES OF THE FEDERAL FARM LOAN / Paine, Willis Seaver – (Suppl. Oct. 1, 1917. New York: Bankers, 1918. 80p. LL-1116) – New York: Bankers, 1917. 416p. LL-1116 – 1 – us L of C Photodup [340]

PAINE'S REPORTS OF CASES IN THE SECOND CIRCUIT, 1810-1840 / Paine, E – New York/Albany: Donaldson. v1-2. 1827; Banks & Bros, 1860 (all publ) – 17mf – 9 – $25.50 – LLMC 81-465 – us L.L.M.C. [340]

PAINESVILLE TELEGRAPH : WEEKLY INDEPENDENT NEWSPAPER – Painesville, OH. 16 Jul 1822-2 Jun 1829 – 3r – 1 – us Western Res [071]

PAINESVILLE TELEGRAPH – (Weekly Whig newspaper) – Painesville, OH. jan 7, 1840-nov 16, 1842 – 2r – 1 – us Western Res [071]

PAINESVILLE TELEGRAPH – (Weekly Whig newspaper) – Painesville, OH. oct 22, 1845-feb 27, 1850 – 3r – 1 – us Western Res [071]

PAINESVILLE TELEGRAPH – (Weekly Whig newspaper; scattered issues of the Painesville Republican are included in the film) – Painesville, OH. aug 9, 1831-aug 23, 1838 – 3r – 1 – us Western Res [071]

PAINESVILLE TELEGRAPH AND GEAUGA CO. WHIG – (Weekly Whig newspaper; film incl issues of the Semi-Weekly Telegraph & Whig) – Painesville, OH. sept 6, 1838-oct 22, 1839 – 1r – 1 – us Western Res [071]

PAINESVILLE TELEGRAPH AND GEAUGA FREE PRESS – (Weekly independent newspaper) – Painesville, OH. june 16, 1829-june 29, 1830 – 1r – 1 – us Western Res [071]

Paino y Hurtado, Vicente *see* SUPLICA QUE HIZO AL REY LA PROVINCIA DE EXTREMADURA SOBRE EL PLEITO CON LOS GANADORES TRASUMANTES

PAINSVILLE, OHIO, TAXES, MS V.F. O – (List of all the residents land in the District of Painsville, County of Trumbull) – 1801 – 1r – 1 – us Western Res [978]

PAINSVILLE, OHIO, TAXES, MS V.F.O. – (List of the real and personal property in the township subject to taxation for the year 1804) – 1804 – 1r – 1 – us Western Res [978]

PAINT AND COATINGS INDUSTRY – Troy. v1-9 1985-93* 1; v10 1994*. v11-13 1995-97+ 1,5,9 – 1,5,9 – D21059 – us UMI [660]

PAINT AND RESIN – (1984-. 5,6,9) – v51-. 1981- – 1 – us UMI [660]

PAINT AND VARNISH PRODUCTION – (Cont by: Modern Paint and Coatings) – Atlanta. v1-38 1910-48*. v39-63 1949-73. v65 jan-feb 1975 1, v61-65 1971-feb 1975 5; v65 jan-feb 1975 9 – 1,5,9 – D2761 – us UMI [660]

PAINT BULLETIN / North Dakota. Agricultural Experiment Station. Fargo – v.1-v.1, no.7. Feb.1910-Oct 1919 – 1,5,6 – us Spaulding [630]

PAINT INDUSTRY MAGAZINE – v.64-69. 1949-54 – 1 – us UMI [660]

PAINT MANUFACTURE – v1-49. 1962-79 – 1 – us UMI [670]

PAINT MANUFACTURE INCORPORATING RESIN NEWS – v49-51. 1979-81 – 1 – us UMI [660]

PAINT, OIL AND CHEMICAL REVIEW – Chicago. v. 89-122. 1930-59 – 1,5,6 – us Princeton Micro [540]

PAINT TECHNOLOGY – v.11-35. 1946-71 – 1,5,6 – 22207.00 – us Princeton Micro [540]

PAINT TITLES – Oxford. v17-18 1987-88. v19 1989*. v20 1990. v21 1991*. v22 1992. v23-24 1993-94*. v25-27 1995-97+ – 1,5,9 – D49547 – us UMI [073]

THE PAINTED ROCK OF CALIFORNIA : A LEGEND BY MYRON ANGEL – (Also known as: La Piedra Pintada) – Los Angeles: Grafton Publ Co, 1910 – 1r – 1 – $50.00 – B40255 – us Library Micro [978]

THE PAINTER AND THE SCULPTOR – London, 1958-63 – 1r – 1 – £60.00 – uk Chadwyck [750]

Painter, F V N *see* CHRISTIAN WORSHIP

PAINTINDIA – (v24 1974 was not available for filming) – Bombay. v1-18 1951-68*. v19-23 1969-73. v25 1975*. v26-28 1976-78. v29-44 1979-94*. v45-47 1995-97+ 1; v21-23 1971-73. v25-28 1975-78. v30 1980 5 – 1,5 – D2990 – us UMI [073]

PAINTING AND DECORATING JOURNAL – v93-1973- 1,5,6; v95- 9 – us UMI [073]

PAINTING ILLUSTRATED IN THREE DIALLOGUES / Aglionby, W – (sic) CONTAINING SOME CHOICE OBSERVATIONS UPON THE ART. together with the lives of the most eminent painters from Cimabue to the time of Raphael and Michael Angelo. O-970 1. 1685 – 9 – ne IDC [920]

PAINTING PERSONIFIED / Bicknell, A – OR, THE CARICATURE and SENTIMENTAL PICTURES, OF THE PRINCIPAL ARTISTS OF THE PRESENT TIMES, FANCIFULLY EXPLAINED. 2 V. O-990 1. 1790 – 9 – ne IDC [750]

PAINTINGS AND DRAWINGS / Rossetti, Dante Gabriel – In public and private collections in Great Britain. ed. by Virginia Surtees – 14 – uk Microform Academic [750]

PAINTINGS IN PROVINCIAL AND OTHER MUSEUMS / Caisse Nationale des Monuments Historiques et des Sites. Paris – (Over 8500 reproductions) – 143mf – 9 – $730.00 – 0-907006-60-4 – uk Mindata [750]

PAINTINGS IN THE KUNSTHISTORISCHES MUSEUM, VIENNA – (Includes printed handlist. 1,800 reproductions of Old Master paintings. The paintings are grouped according to recognised art historical Schools. The no of reproductions for each School is: Flemish 625; Italian 568; German 255; Dutch 265; French 46; Spanish 36; Austrian 18; English 15; Swiss 10) – mf ed 1984 – 24mf (23 colour 1 b/w) – 15,9 – £500.00 – 0-85964-158-9 – uk Chadwyck [750]

PAINTINGS IN THE LOUVRE / Caisse Nationale des Monuments Historiques et des Sites. Paris – (Together with public and private Modern Art Collections in Paris. Over 9000 reproductions) – 154mf – 9 – $805.00 – 0-907006-55-8 – uk Mindata [750]

PAIR TRAWLING WITH SMALL BOATS – 1980 – 78p – it F.A.O. [639]

Pairault, Claude *see* VILLAGE-SAVANE EN PAYS ADIOUKROU

EL PAIS – 6,1 – F6,548.00 – sz Infoprint [072]

EL PAIS – 1977-1985 – 6,1 – F7,378.00 – sz Infoprint [072]

EL PAIS – 1986-1988 – 6,1 – F8,775.00 – sz Infoprint [072]

EL PAIS – 1989-1994 – 6,1 – F9,517.00 – sz Infoprint [072]

EL PAIS – Cali, Colombia. Mar 1989-Dec 1991 – 54r – 1 – us L of C Photodup [072]

EL PAIS – Madrid, Spain. 1976- . Index available – 1 – us Primary [072]

EL PAIS – Madrid, Spain. -d. 12 Sept 1914-10 Aug 1919. Very imperfect. 8 reels – 1 – uk British Libr Newspaper [072]

EL PAIS – Mai 1976-Dec – 6,1 – F5,632.00 – sz Infoprint [072]

EL PAIS – Montevideo, [Uruguay]: Dr E R Larreta, 1956- – us Res Libr [072]

O PAIS – Lisbon. No.1-86. 9 Jan 1976-26 Aug 1977. Incomplete. (Portuguese Revolution of 1974. Newspapers from Portugal publ. from 21 Feb 1971 to 15 Feb 1980, collected and filmed by University of Wisconsin-Madison libraries.) – 1 – us U.W. Library [072]

EL PAIS AL SERVICIO DEL CORONEL / Aguirre Camara, Jose – [Buenos Aires?: s.n.], 1945 – 1 – CSUXAJA7090-B – us Hoover Inst Photo [972]

EL PAIS DE LA COLA DE PAJA / Benedetti, Mario – (8th ed.Montevideo: Editorial Arca, 1970, c1966). 194p. With: Army List of Her Majesty's and the Honourable Company's Forces Serving under the Bengal Presidency.... 1 reel.1257 – 1 – us U.W. Library [972]

EL PAIS INDEX – 6,1 – F2,532.00 – sz Infoprint [072]

EL PAIS INDEX – 1976-1994 – 6,1 – F2,794.00 – sz Infoprint [072]

UN PAIS SIN JUSTICIA, UN EPISODIO DE LA RESISTENCIA : ACTUACIONES PROCESALES EN JUICIOS SEGUIDOS POR LA JUSTICA DEL CRIMEN CONTRA EL DOCTOR GUILLERMO BONAPARTE, ABOGADO DEL FORO DE PARAN A, ENTRE RIOS, REPUBLICA ARGENTINA / Bonaparte, Guillermo – [Buenos Aires: Ediciones Populares Argentinas, 1956] – 1 – CSUXADQ6170-B – us Hoover Inst Photo [360]

EL PAISAJE Y EL ALMA ARGENTINA / Ibarguren, Carlos – 1938 – 1 – us I.U. Libraries [390]

Paish, George *see* OUGHT WE TO SAVE?

Paisible, J *see* THE GODOLPHIN

Paisiello *see* [IDALIDE] AH CHE NEL PETTO LO SENTO

Paisiello, G *see*
- [IL BARBIERE DI SEVIGLIA] AH CHI SA
- [IL BARBIERE FI SEVIGLIA] O CHE UMOR
- (LA DISCORDIA FORTUNATA] AH MIA CARA
- LA FRANSCATANA. OPERA BUFFA IN TRE ATTI
- [IL FRANTICO BURLATO] OVERTURE, ARRANGED PIANO WITH AD LIB VIOLIN
- [LA LOCANDA] TUTTO DA VOI DISPENDE
- [IL MARCHESE TULIPANO] OVERTURE, AIR, AND TRIO; ARRANGED PIANO WITH AD LIB VIOLIN
- IL MIO GARZONI IL PIFARO FROM "LA MOLINARA"
- OVERTURE AND FAVORITE ARIEN FROM LA MOLINARA
- OVERTURE, ARRANGED PIANO WITH AD LIB VIOLIN FROM "NINA O LA PAZZA PER AMORE"
- IL RE TEODORO IN VENEZIA. ATTO PRIMO

PAISLEY ADVERTISER – Scotland. -w. Oct 1824-Dec 1827, Jan 1842-Jul 1844. (2 reels) – 1 – uk British Libr Newspaper [072]

PAISLEY ADVOCATE – Paisley, 1871-1976 – 43r – 1 – cn Preston [971]

PAISLEY ADVOCATE AND GENERAL ADVERTISER – Paisley, 1865-1868 – 1r – 1 – cn Preston [971]

PAISLEY AND RENFREWSHIRE GAZETTE – Scotland. 29 Oct 1864-Dec 1892; 1918. -w. 28mqn reels – 1 – uk British Libr Newspaper [072]

PAISLEY AND RENFREWSHIRE STANDARD – Scotland. -w. May 1869-Feb 1871. (2 reels) – 1 – uk British Libr Newspaper [072]

PAISLEY DAILY EXPRESS – Paisley, Scotland, UK. 1886. -d. 2 reels – 1 – uk British Libr Newspaper [072]

PAISLEY HERALD AND RENFREWSHIRE ADVERTISER – Scotland. 9 Jul 1853-Dec 1877.-w. 24 reels – 1 – uk British Libr Newspaper [072]

PAISLEY NEWS – Paisley, 1899-1900 – 1r – 1 – cn Preston [971]

Paisley. Scotland. New Street Church *see* REGISTER OF BURIALS

Paiva d'Andrada, Joachim Carlos *see* MANICA

LA PAIX – Brussels, Belgium. -w. 24 Aug 1862-25 June 1887. 8 reels – 1 – uk British Libr Newspaper [949]

LA PAIX – Lac Megantic, Canada. 21 jun 1902-13 dec 1902 – 1r – 1 – Can$30.00 – cn Can Microfilming [072]

LA PAIX : LIBERAL NATIONAL / ed by Chagnon, W & Langelier, L N – Trois-Rivieres, Canada. 10 nov 1887-31 dec 1890 – 1r – 1 – Can$50.00 – cn Can Microfilming [072]

LA PAIX – Martinique. French West Indies. 1816-1961 with omissions thru 1966 – 1 – us UMI [072]

LA PAIX CONSTANTINIENNE ET LE CATHOLICISME / Batiffol, Pierre – Paris: V. Lecoffre, 1914 – 2mf – us A.T.L.A. [240]

LA PAIX D'AMIENS. LE CONCORDAT. LE CONSULAT A VIE / Reunion des musees nationaux. Paris – 1952. 20 illus. 2 fiches – 9 – fr Réunion [700]

LA PAIX DE L'AMERIQUE / Brum, B – Montevideo, 1923 – 1mf – 1 – ILM-4077/1 – ne IDC [327]

PAIX ET LIBERTE – Organe du Comite national de lutte contre la guerre et le fascisme. Fonde par Henri Barbusse. no. 1-97. Paris. dec 1935-aout 1939. mq no. 94. voir aussi: FRONT MONDIAL – 1 – fr A.C.R.P.P. [073]

PAIX ET LIBERTE – (Some issues lacking) – 1968-83 – 4r – 1 – ATLA S0519 – us A.T.L.A. [073]

LA PAIX MEDITATIONS HISTORIQUES ET RELIGIEUSES / Gratry, A – Paris, 1861 – 3mf – 1 – ILM-4022/1 – ne IDC [327]

LA PAIX PAR LE DROIT – 1891-1948 – 250mf – 9 – $1,005.00 – us UPA [320]

PAIX (TROIS-RIVIERES, QUEBEC) *see* LA SENTINELLE

O PAIZ – Manaos, Amazonas. 25 Abr, 19 Set 1886 – 1,5,6 – bl Biblioteca [072]

O PAIZ – Rio de Janeiro, 1 Oct 1884-Dec 1903; Jan-Jun, Oct-Dec 1904; Jan 1905-18 Nov 1934 – 1,5,6 – bl Biblioteca [072]
EL PAJARILLO DE LA TRADICION EXTREMENA / Gil Garcia, Bonifacio – Badajoz: Dip. Provincial, 1958 Sep. REE – sp Bibl Santa Ana [946]
THE PAJARO TIMES – Watsonville, CA. 1864-67 – 4r – 1 – $200.00 – B03085 – us Library Micro [071]
PAJARONIAN – Watsonville. Calif. -w. 1870-1914 – 1 – us UMI [071]
UN PAJE DE MARIA ANTONIETA / Palomer, Jose – Barcelona, 1932; Madrid: Razon y Fe, 1933 – 1 – sp Bibl Santa Ana [920]
PAJE, MISIONERO Y MARTIR : EL BEATO JUAN DE BRITO, DE LA COMPANIA DE JESUS. BILBAO, 1934 / Gonzalez Pintado, Gaspar – Madrid, 1936 – 1 – sp Bibl Santa Ana [240]
PAK SURA, KALIJAN PETIKAN SANES-SANESIPUN KANGGE SMA BG. A / Sastrasuwignja, S – SE 4892 1. v. 1 only. 1956- – 9 – ne IDC [950]
PAK THAI – Phuket, Thailand. Aug 1969-76 – 8r – 1 – us L of C Photodup [072]
Pakem Kedjaksaan Tinggi *see* AGNI BAWANA
PAKENHAM GAZETTE – 1917-1965 – 18r – 1 – at Corangamite [072]
Pakhomova, Liudmila Fedorovna *see* NATSIONAL NYI KAPITAL 5 EKONOMIKE INDONEZII
Pakistan *see*
– GAZETTE OF PAKISTAN
– THE SECOND FIVE YEAR PLAN (REVISED ESTIMATES)
– THE THIRD FIVE YEAR PLAN (1965-1970)
Pakistan. East *see* THE DACCA GAZETTE
PAKISTAN ECONOMICS AND COMMERCE – Lahore, Pakistan. -m. Jan 1952-Aug 1954. 2 reels – 1 – uk British Libr Newspaper [339]
PAKISTAN ECONOMIST – Karachi, PK. 1972-1979 – 14r – $700.00 – R63577 – us Library Micro [330]
Pakistan. Education Division *see* ADMINISTRATIVE SET UP OF THE EDUCATION DIVISION
PAKISTAN EDUCATION STATISTICS 1947-1979... / Pakistan. Ministry of Education. Research Wing – Islamabad, 1979 – 2mf – 9 – DE-570/1 – ne IDC [370]
PAKISTAN EDUCATION STATISTICS 1947/48 TO 1972/73 / Pakistan. Ministry of Education. Bureau of Educational Planning and Management – Islamabad, [1974] – 5mf – 9 – DE-567/1 – ne IDC [370]
PAKISTAN EDUCATION STATISTICS 1970/71 TO 1975/76 / Pakistan. Ministry of Education. Bureau of Educational Planning and Management – Islamabad, 1976 – 2mf – 9 – DE-568/1 – ne IDC [370]
Pakistan. General Agreement on Tariffs and Trade *see* STUDY OF THE SECOND FIVE-YEAR PLAN OF PAKISTAN
Pakistan Historical Society *see* JOURNAL OF THE PAKISTAN HISTORICAL SOCIETY
PAKISTAN HISTORY CONFERENCE – Karachi. 1951-56. v1-6. Lacking: 1951, v1(p1-4); 1954, v4. – 33mf – 8 – ne IDC [950]
PAKISTAN JOURNAL OF GERIATRICS/ PAKISTAN PROBIN HITAISHI – v. 9- 1963-1971 – 1 – us UMI [618]
PAKISTAN JOURNAL OF MEDICAL RESEARCH – v1- 1958- 1; v12- 5,6; v14- 9 – us UMI [073]
PAKISTAN LAW REPORTS – Dacca series: v1-12 1951-62; Lahore series: v1-8 1948-55; West Pakistan series: 1956-64 – 939mf – 9 – ne IDC [340]
Pakistan. Ministry of Economic Affairs *see* SIX YEAR DEVELOPMENT PROGRAMME JULY 1951 TO JUNE 1957. D-1408/1
Pakistan. Ministry of Economic Affairs. Village Aid Administration *see* VILLAGE AID FIVE YEAR PLAN, 1955/56-1959/60
Pakistan. Ministry of Education *see* NATIONAL EDUCATION POLICY (SALIENT FEATURES)
Pakistan. Ministry of Education. Bureau of Educational Planning and Management *see*
– BUDGET STATISTICS ON EDUCATION OF THE CENTRAL AND PROVINCIAL GOVERNMENTS 1970/71 TO 1976/77
– PAKISTAN EDUCATION STATISTICS 1947/48 TO 1972/73
– PAKISTAN EDUCATION STATISTICS 1970/71 TO 1975/76
– PRIMARY EDUCATION IN THE RURAL VILLAGES OF PAKISTAN 1976-1977
– STATISTICS ON UNIVERSITY EDUCATION 1968-1974
Pakistan. Ministry of Education. Research Wing *see* PAKISTAN EDUCATION STATISTICS 1947-1979...
Pakistan. National Planning Board *see* THE FIRST FIVE-YEAR PLAN, 1955-1960
Pakistan. National Planning Board. Education Section *see* EDUCATION AND TRAINING
PAKISTAN OBSERVER – Dacca, Bangladesh.Jan 1965-Dec 1970.-d. 58 reels – 1 – uk British Libr Newspaper [072]
Pakistan. Planning Commission *see*
– ANNUAL DEVELOPMENT PROGRAMME OF THE FEDERAL GOVERNMENT 1972-73
– ANNUAL PLAN, 1968/69
– ANNUAL PLAN, 1969-70
– ANNUAL PLAN, 1975-1976
– CENTRAL DEVELOPMENT PROGRAMME 1966-67
– CENTRAL DEVELOPMENT PROGRAMME, 1967-68
– CENTRAL DEVELOPMENT PROGRAMME 1969-70. (1 JUL 1969 TO 30 JUN 1970)
– CENTRAL DEVELOPMENT PROGRAMME 1970-71
– CENTRAL DEVELOPMENT PROGRAMME 1971-72
– DEVELOPMENT PROGRAMME (1 JUL 1960 TO 30 JUN 1961)
– DEVELOPMENT PROGRAMME. (1 JUL 1961 TO 30 JUN 1962) AS APPROVED BY THE ECONOMIC COUNCIL
– DEVELOPMENT PROGRAMME (1 JUL 1962 TO 30 JUN 1963)
– DEVELOPMENT PROGRAMME. (1 JUL 1963 TO 30 JUN 1964) 1 AS APPROVED BY THE NATIONAL ECONOMIC COUNCIL
– DEVELOPMENT PROGRAMME, 1964-65
– DEVELOPMENT PROGRAMME 1965-66 (1 JUL 1965 TO 30 JUN 1966). AS APPROVED BY THE NATIONAL ECONOMIC COUNCIL
– DEVELOPMENT PROGRAMME, 1966-76
– DEVELOPMENT PROGRAMME 1967-68
– DEVELOPMENT PROGRAMME 1969-70
– DEVELOPMENT PROGRAMME 1970-1971 (1 JUL 1970 TO 30 JUN 1971)
– MID-PLAN REVIEW EVALUATION OF PROGRESS DURING THE FIRST THREE YEARS OF THE SECOND FIVE-YEAR PLAN
– MID-PLAN REVIEW OF PROGRESS IN 1960/61-1961/62 UNDER THE SECOND FIVE-YEAR PLAN
– OBJECTIVES OF THE SECOND FIVE YEAR PLAN (1960-65)
– OUTLINE OF THE THIRD FIVE-YEAR PLAN (1965-70)
– REVISED CENTRAL DEVELOPMENT PROGRAMME, 1965-1966
– REVISED PHASING, SECTORAL PRIORITIES AND ALLOCATIONS OF THE THIRD FIVE YEAR PLAN (1965-70)
– THE SECOND FIVE YEAR PLAN (1960-65)
Pakistan. Planning Commission. *see* WORKING PAPERS FOR THE DEVELOPMENT PERSPECTIVE (1975-1980)
Pakistan. Planning Commission. Education and Training *see*
– APPROACH TO THE SECOND FIVE YEAR PLAN AND THE TENTATIVE DEVELOPMENT PROGRAMME OF VARIOUS SECTORS OF EDUCATION IN STATEMENT FORMS
– AN ASSESSMENT OF THE PERFORMANCE OF THE FIRST PLAN FOR THE FORMULATION OF THE SECOND FIVE YEAR PLAN (EDUCATION AND TRAINING)
– IMPORTANT ISSUES UNDERLYING THE SECOND FIVE YEAR PLAN OF EDUCATION AND CONCLUSIONS ARRIVED AT AS A RESULT OF THE STUDIES
– INTRODUCTION OF UNIVERSAL PRIMARY EDUCATION
PAKISTAN PRESS YEAR BOOK – Karachi: Express Publ, 1956 – us Res Libr [950]
Pakistan. Punjab. Bureau of Education *see* EDUCATION STATISTICS IN PUNJAB 1972/73-1983/84
PAKISTAN QUARTERLY – Karachi. 1949-65. v1-13 – 150mf – 8 – ne IDC [073]
PAKISTAN REVIEW – Lahore. 1953-62. v1-10. Lacking: v1 (1-4); v2 (10); v3 (1-2); v4 (1-2); v5 (4-10); v7 (4); v8 (8-9); v9 (1-2); v10 (9-12). – 203mf – 8 – ne IDC [073]
THE PAKISTAN TIMES – Lahore: Mian Iftikhar-un-Din, 1956-66 – 50r – 1 – us Res Libr [072]
Pakistan. University Grants Commission *see* STATISTICS ON HIGHER EDUCATION IN PAKISTAN 1973/74-1983/84
PAKOE BOEWANA 9 : WIRALSJWARE. SERAT WIRA ISWARA...KAWEDALAKEN...DENING KI PADMA SOESASTRA – Soerakarta, 1898 – 3mf – 9 – ne IDC [950]
Pakun, R M *see* KIDUNG SISWA: LAGU2 KRISTEN DALAM BAHASA INGGERIS, DJERMAN DAN PERANTJIS. HYMNS, WITHOUT MUSIC; ENGLISH, GERMAN AND FRENCH WORDS
LA PALABRA, EL PENSAMIENTO Y LA ACCION DE EVA PERON / Peron, Eva – n.p. n.d – 1 – us Res Libr [320]
LA PALABRA ISRAELITA – Santiago, Chile. Jan 7 1977-1991 – 9r – 1 – us L of C Photodup [072]
PALABRAS DE UN GOBERNANTE PERONISTA / Caesar, Juan Hugo – Santa Fe, Argentine Republic: [s.n.], 1951 – 1 – CSUXADQ4895-B – us Hoover Inst Photo [320]
PALABRAS LIRICAS : POESIAS / Monterrey, Manuel – Badajoz: Imp. V.Rodriguez, 1916 – 1 – sp Bibl Santa Ana [810]
THE PALACE OF PEACE – (Unpaginated, mostly photographs with captions) – Rotterdam: Nijh & Van Ditmars, n.d. – 1mf – 9 – $1.50 – LLMC 96-049 – us L.L.M.C. [770]
THE PALACE OF PROFITABLE PLEASURE / Evans, John – 1621. 152p. (English Linguistics Series 1500-1800) – 9 – us UMI [420]
PALACH PRESS – London. 34 docs. 1980-1990 – 29mf – 9 – ne IDC [360]
EL PALACIO DEL DUQUE DE LA ROCA, DE MERIDA / Alvarez Saenz de Buruaga, Jose – Merida – 1 – sp Bibl Santa Ana [946]
Palacio, Manuel, y otro *see* MUSEO COMICO...CHISTES
EL PALACIO TRISTE / Martinez Sierra, Gregorio – Madrid. 1914 – 1 – us Res Libr [830]
Palacio y de Palacio, Jose Maria *see* MISERIAS Y GRANDEZAS DE UN HABITO
Palacios, Enrique Juan *see* THE STONE OF THE SUN AND THE FIRST CHAPTER OF HISTORY IN MEXICO
Palacios, Juan Jose *see* SERMON...ALMENDRALEJO...MARIA MARTIN LLANOS
Palacky, Franz *see* DIE GESCHICHTE DES HUSSITENTHUMS UND PROF. CONSTANTIN HOEFLER
EL PALADIA – Corpus Christi, TX. Oct 1929-Jan 1939 – 1 – $100.00 – R05000 – us Library Micro [071]
PALADIN – Furman University. Greenville, SC. 1916-May 1990 – 1 – $373.96 – us Baptist [370]
O PALADINO : MENSARIO LITTERARIO, NOTICIOSO E CRITICO – Manaos, Amazonas. 23 Jan-31 Mar 1909 – 1,5,6 – bl Biblioteca [072]
O PALADINO : ORGAO LITTERARIO, RECREATIVO E NOTICIOSO – Aracaju, 14 Oct-6 Nov 1889 – 1,5,6 – bl Biblioteca [072]
O PALADINO : PERIODICO BI-MENSAL LITTERARIO E NOTICIOSO – Maceio, Alagoas. 16 Set 1903 – 1,5,6 – bl Biblioteca [072]
PALADIO : ORGAO DO CLUB RECREATIVO ITACOATIARENSE – Itacoatiara, Amazonas. 5 Set-Dez 1908; Jan-Out, Dez 1909; Jan-Set, Dez 1910; Jan-23 Jul 1911 – 1,5,6 – bl Biblioteca [072]
Paladio, A *see*
– LIBRO PRIMERO DE ARCHITECTURA
PALAEOGEOGRAPHY, PALAEOCLIMATOLOGY, PALAEOECOLOGY – v1-48. 1965-84 – 1,5,6,13 – sz Elsevier [560]
PALAEOGRAFI – 1943-54 – 1 – us I.U. Libraries [390]
PALAEOGRAFISK ATLAS : OLDNORSK-ISLANDSK AFDELING – Copenhagen: Cyldendal. n1-53. 1905 – 8mf – 9 – H-363/2 – ne IDC [560]
PALAEONTOGRAPHIA ITALICA – (Index. NS v1-10 1929/30-1940/41; 1933-42 v2 suppl 1-5) – Pisa. v1-30. [1895-]1896-1930 – 453mf – 9 – ne IDC [560]
Palaeontographical Society *see* MONOGRAPHS
PALAEONTOLOGIA INDICA – (Series and vols also available separately) – Os: 1-16; ns: v1-24. 1863-1952 – 8 – Dfl4,250.00 – ne Schierenberg [560]
PALAEONTOLOGIA SINICA – 1922-64. Old and new series in 138 numbers – 8 – Dfl3,500.00 – ne Schierenberg [560]
THE PALAEONTOLOGICAL MICROFICHE LIBRARY – (Pt A 41mf $189.75. Pt B 20mf $92.00. Pt C 37mf $172.50. Pt D 91mf $419.75. Pt E 34mf $155.25. Pt F 32mf $149.50. Pt G 58mf $264.50) – 313mf coll + guide – 9 – $1,437.50 – us UMI [560]
PALAEONTOLOGIE VON TIMOR, NEBST KLEINEREN BEITRAEGEN ZUR PALAEONTOLOGIE EINIGER ANDERN INSELN DES OSTINDISCHEN ARCHIPELS / ed by Wanner, R J – Stuttgart. 1914-1929. v1-16. – 123mf – 9 – 2546/2 – ne IDC [560]
PALAEONTOLOGISCHE ABHANDLUNGEN / ed by Dames, W & Kaiser, E – (Cont as: Geologische und Palaeontologische Abhandlungen, Jena v9-23 1901-33. Edited by J. Koken) – Berlin, Jena. v1-8. 1882-98 – 375mf – 9 – ne IDC [560]
DIE PALAESTINISCHEN MAERTYRER DES EUSEBIUS VON CAESAREA (T.U.U. 1-14/4) / Violet, B – Leipzig, 1896 – 3mf – 9 – ne Slangenburg [240]
PALAIOS – v1-. 1986- – 1,5,6,9 – us UMI [073]
Palairet, M R *see* YUGOSLAV STATISTICS, 1834-1919
PALAIS DE CRISTAL – London, UK. Journal illustre de l'Exposition de 1851. 7 May-26 Jul 1851 – 1 – uk British Libr Newspaper [900]
LE PALAIS DES CVRIEVX. AUQUEL SONT ASSEMBLEES PLUSIEURS DIURSITEZ POUR LE PLAISIR DES DOCTES / Beroalde de Verville, Francois – Paris, 1612 – 1 – us U.W. Library [370]
LE PALAIS LEGISLALIF DE QUEBEC: GOVERNMENT BUILDINGS IN QUEBEC / Gagnon, Ernest – Quebec?: s.n., 1897 (Quebec: C. Darveau). 03279. (Pre-1900 Canadiana) – 9 – cn C.I.H.M. [971]
LE PALAIS ROYAL D'UGARIT 1 / Nougayrol, J – Paris, 1955 – 14mf – 8 – Dfl49.00 – ne Slangenburg [270]
LE PALAIS ROYAL D'UGARIT 2 / Virolleaud, Ch. – Paris, 1956 – 11mf – 8 – Dfl39.00 – ne Slangenburg [270]
LE PALAIS ROYAL D'UGARIT 4 / Nougayrol, J – Paris, 1956 – 14mf – 8 – Dfl49.00 – ne Slangenburg [270]
Palamas, Gregory *see* THE ONE HUNDRED AND FIFTY CHAPTERS
PALANTE Y PALANTE – Havana, CU. 1969-1978 – 8r – $400.00 – R04205 – us Library Micro [073]
Palar, LN *see* STATEMENT TO THE UNITED NATIONS IN GENERAL DEBATE OF 18TH SESSION OF GENERAL ASSEMBLY
Palat, Barthelemy Edmond Pierre Lehautcourt *see* TEN WORKS ON MILITARY HISTORY
Palau Constitutional Convention, Koror *see* THE CONSTITUTION OF THE REPUBLIC OF PALAU, 1979
PALAU INDICATIVE DEVELOPMENT PLAN : DRAFT – Koror: Palau Political Status Commission, dec 1976 – 3mf – 9 – $4.50 – LLMC 82-100G, Title 13 – us L.L.M.C. [323]
Palau Political Status Commission *see*
– DECLARATION OF INTENT
– SITUATION REPORT
Palau. (The Republic of Belau) *see*
– THE CONSTITUTION OF THE REPUBLIC OF PALAU, 1979
– MORE CONSTITUTIONS FOR PALAU
– NATIONAL CODE OF THE REPUBLIC OF PALAU, 1985
PALAU'S CONSTITUTIONAL CONVENTION. AN INFORMAL REPORT / Freeman, Harrup A – (Typescript) – Honolulu, feb 27, 1979 – 1mf – 9 – $1.50 – LLMC 82-100G, Title 16 – us L.L.M.C. [323]
PALAU'S CONSTITUTIONAL TANGLE / Shuster, Donald R – Honolulu: Uni of Hawaii, Graduate Div, 1979 – 1mf – 9 – $1.50 – LLMC 82-100G, Title 34 – us L.L.M.C. [323]
PALAU'S EVOLVING RELATIONSHIP WITH THE U.S. : INTRODUCTION AND CHRONOLOGY OF DEVELOPMENTS / Christopher, Luella S – Washington: Library of Congress Congressional Research Service, may 28, 1988 – 1mf – 9 – $1.50 – LLMC 82-100G, Title 10 – us L.L.M.C. [327]
PALAU'S STRATEGIC POSITION PLACES DEMOCRACY AT RISK / Anglim, John – Sydney: Australian Defense Academy, apr 1988 – 1mf – 9 – $1.50 – LLMC 82-100G, Title 33 – us L.L.M.C. [355]

PALAU/UNITED STATES AGREEMENTS REGARDING THE COMPACT OF FREE ASSOCIATION ... : AND AMENDING THE MILITARY USE AND OPERATING RIGHTS AGREEMENT – (Various pagination) – Agana (Guam), jul 1983 – 1mf – 9 – $1.50 – LLMC 82-100G, Title 25 – us L.L.M.C. [327]

PALAU/U.S. AGREEMENT REGARDING MILITARY USE AND OPERATING RIGHTS OF THE U.S. GOVERNMENT IN PALAU : CONCLUDED PURSUANT TO SECTIONS 321 AND 323 OF THE COMPACT OF FREE ASSOCIATION – (Various pagination) – Initialed nov 17, 1980 – 3mf – 9 – $4.50 – LLMC 82-100G, Title 22 – us L.L.M.C. [327]

A PALAVRA : FOLHA LITTERARIA, HUMORISTICA E NOTICIOSA DA FAMILIA AMAZONENSE – Manaos, Amazonas. 21 Ago 1915-1 Jul 1916 – 1,5,6 – bl Biblioteca [072]

A PALAVRA – Maceio, Alagoas. 3 Nov-Dez 1875; Jun-24 Set 1876 – 1,5,6 – bl Biblioteca [072]

A PALAVRA – Manaoas, Amazonas. Jun 1932 – 1,5,6 – bl Biblioteca [072]

A PALAVRA : ORGAO LITTERARIO – Manaos, Amazonas. 27 Ago 1910 – 1,5,6 – bl Biblioteca [072]

A PALAVRA : REVISTA LITTERARIA DEDICADA A INSTRUCCAO E RECREIO DA MULHER – Pao d Assucar, Alagoas. 21 Jul, Out 1889; Fev-Mar, Ago-Dez 1891; Jul 1892; Jan-Nov 1893; Fev 1894-Dez 1896; Fev-Dez 1897; Jan, 10 Dez 1898 – 1,5,6 – bl Biblioteca [072]

A PALAVRA DE DEUS – S. Miguel de Campos, Alagoas. 1879 – 1,5,6 – bl Biblioteca [072]

PALAWIDJA : ROMAN-PANTJAROBA / Halim, K – Djakarta, Gunseikanbu Kokumin Tosyokyoku Balai Poestaka, 2605. 118p – 35-36mf – 9 – ne IDC [950]

PALAZZI ANTICHI DI GENOVA RACCOLTI E DESIGNATI DA PIETRO PAOLO RUBENS / Rubens, Pieter-Paul – O 419. 2 v. 1708 – 9 – ne IDC [740]

Palazzi, Giovanni Andrea *see* I DISCORSI. SOPRA L'IMPRESE

Palazzolo, Octavio *see* DIEZ ANOS DE ORGANIZACION SINDICAL

IL PALCOSCENICO – New York, NY. 1935-1936(?) – us I.H.R.C. [073]

PALEMBANG IN 1934 / Wellan, J W I – Palembang, 1934.-4 pts – 1mf – 9 – SE-1279/1 – ne IDC [950]

Palen, Konstantin Konstantinovich, Graf *see* OTCHET PO REVIZII TURKESTANSKAGO KRAIA.

PALENCIA. ARCHIVO HISTORICO PROVINCIAL INVENTARIO DE LA SECCION 1. PROTOCOLOS / Romero Cabot, R – 1mf – 9 – sp Cultura [025]

PALENCIA. ARCHIVO HISTORICO PROVINCIAL INVENTARIO DE LA SECCION 2. CONTADURIA DE HIPOTECAS / Romero Cabot, R – 5mf – 9 – sp Cultura [025]

PALENCIA. ARCHIVO HISTORICO PROVINCIAL INVENTARIO DE LA SECCION 4. DESAMORTIZACION / Romero Cabot, R – 1mf – 9 – sp Cultura [025]

PALENCIA. ARCHIVO HISTORICO PROVINCIAL INVENTARIO DE LA SECCION 7. HACIENDAS LOCALES / Romero Cabot, R – 3mf – 9 – sp Cultura [025]

PALENCIA. ARCHIVO HISTORICO PROVINCIAL INVENTARIO DE LA SECCION 9. SINDICATOS / Romero Cabot, R – 2mf – 9 – sp Cultura [025]

PALENQUE EXTREMENO – Almendralejo, 1958-1960 – 5 – sp Bibl Santa Ana [073]

PALEOBIOLOGY – v. 1- 1975- – 1,5,6,9 – us UMI [073]

PALEOCEANOGRAPHY – (v7. 1992. $180.00) – Bi-monthly. 1993 v8. 1994 v9 $215.00. 1995 v10 $270.00 – $195.00 – us A.G.U. [550]

PALEOGRAFIA ESPANOLA / Terreros Pando, Esteban – 1758 – 1mf – 9 – Pta1,000.00 – 84-7848-334-9 – sp Pentalfa [440]

PALEOGRAFICHESKII I LINGVISTICHESKII ANALIZ NOVGORODSKIKH BERESTIANYKH GRAMOT / ed by Borkovskii, V I – Sbornik, Moscow, 1955. BR-10,315/1 – 9 – ne IDC [930]

PALEOGRAFICHESKII IZBORNIK / Kamanin, IM – Kiev, 1899 1v. Materialy po istorii iuzhno-russkogo pis'ma v XV-XVIII vv. BR/10,255/1 – 9 – ne IDC [410]

PALEOGRAFICHESKOI OBOZRENIE KIRILLOVSKOGO PIS'MA / Lavrov, P A – Petrograd, 1914.BR/10,377/1 – 9 – ne IDC [947]

PALEOGRAPHIE MUSICALE – 2e Serie. Solesmes. Tome 1. 1900 – 28mf – 8 – Dfl98.00 – ne Slangenburg [240]

PALEOGRAPHIE MUSICALE : CANTORIUM DE ST.-GALL. – 2e Serie. Solesmes. Tome 2. 1924 – 8mf – 8 – Dfl30.00 – ne Slangenburg [240]

PALEOGRAPHIE MUSICALE : SOLESMES – Tournai. v1-13. 1889-1930 – 163mf – 9 – H-163/2 – ne IDC [780]

PALEOGRAPHIE MUSICALE – Solesmes. v1-16. 1899-1955 – 270mf – 8 – Dfl945.00 – ne Slangenburg [240]

THE PALEOGRAPHY COLLECTION / University of London. Library – (Available on microfilm by request) – 1968. 26,100 cards – 9 – $190.00 export $225.00 – 0-8161-0789-0 – uk Hall [090]

THE PALEOGRAPHY OF GREEK PAPYRI / Kenyon, F G – H-126 2. 1899 – 8 – ne IDC [450]

PALEOLITHIC MAN AND TERRAMARA SETTLEMENTS IN EUROPE, BEING THE MUNRO LECTURES IN ANTHROPOLOGY AND PREHISTORIC ARCHAEOLOGY...UNIVERSITY OF EDINBURGH...FEBRUARY AND MARCH 1912 / Munro, Robert – 75 plates and 174 figures in the text. Edinburgh: Oliver and Boyd, 1912. xxiii,(1),507,(1)p. illus – 1 – us U.W. Library [930]

PALEONTOLOGICAL JOURNAL – (v18-. 1984-. 5,6,9) – v1-. 1967- – 1 – us UMI [560]

PALEONTOLOGICAL MICROFICHE LIBRARY – 313mf – 9 – us UMI [560]

PALEONTOLOGIE FRANCAISE / ed by Orbigny, Alcide d' – Paris. 1840-1894. 24v. – 316mf – 8 – ne IDC [560]

Palerne, Jean *see* PEREGRINATIONS DU S. IEAN PALERNE OU EST TRAICTE DE PLUSIEURS SINGULARITES ET ANTIQUITES REMARQUEES ES PROVINCES D'EGYPTE, ARABIE DESERTE ET PIERREUSE, TERRE SAINCTE, SURIE, ANATOLIE, GRECE

PALESTINE : THE LEGAL BACKGROUND – 23 titles – 9 – ne IDC [956]

Palestine *see*
- MEMORANDA PREPARED BY THE GOVERNMENT OF PALESTINE FOR THE USE OF THE PALESTINE ROYAL COMMISSION
- OFFICIAL GAZETTE OF THE GOVERNMENT OF PALESTINE
- THE STATUS QUO IN THE HOLY PLACES
- SUPPLEMENTARY MEMORANDUM

PALESTINE AND THE BRITISH TAX-PAYER / Jewish Agency for Palestine. London – 1929. BJ-28-130 1 – 9 – ne IDC [956]

THE PALESTINE ARAB CASE: A STATEMENT / Arab Higher Committee – Apr 1947. BJ-28-151 1 – 9 – ne IDC [956]

PALESTINE BAPTIST CHURCH. CAMPBELLSVILLE, KENTUCKY : CHURCH RECORDS – 1843-1977. 886p – 1 – 39.87 – us Baptist [240]

PALESTINE BULLETIN *see* JERUSALEM POST

Palestine. Chief Secretary's Office *see* A SURVEY OF PALESTINE PREPARED IN DEC 1945 AND JAN 1946 FOR THE INFORMATION OF THE ANGLO-AMERICAN COMMITTEE OF INQUIRY

Palestine. Department of Development *see* REPORTS ON AGRICULTURAL DEVELOPMENT AND LAND SETTLEMENT IN PALESTINE

Palestine. Department of Education *see* NOTE ON EDUCATION IN PALESTINE, 1920-1929

Palestine. Department of Land Settlement and Water Commissioner *see* GEOLOGY AND WATER RESOURCES OF PALESTINE

Palestine. Department of Migration *see* ANNUAL REPORT OF THE DEPARTMENT OF MIGRATION, PALESTINE

Palestine. Department of Statistics *see* VITAL STATISTICS TABLES

PALESTINE ET SYRIE / Baedeker, K – 4e Ed. Leipzig/Paris, 1912 – 12mf – 8 – ne Slangenburg [956]

Palestine Exploration Fund *see* PHOTOGRAPHS OF THE EXPLORING PARTIES, 1865-1877

PALESTINE EXPLORATION FUND ANNUAL – 1953 – 9 – $10.00 – us I.R.C. [073]

PALESTINE EXPLORATION QUARTERLY (PEQ) – 1950-56 – 9 – $10.00 per fiche (1 fiche per year) – us I.R.C. [930]

Palestine Foundation Fund (Keren Hayesod) *see* FOUNDATIONS: A SURVEY OF 25 YEARS OF ACTIVITY OF THE PALESTINE FOUNDATION FUND-KEREN HAYESOD, FACTS AND FIGURES, 1921-1946

Palestine. Government of Palestine. Committee for Moslem religious affairs *see* REPORT

PALESTINE HUMAN RIGHTS INFORMATION CENTRE (PHRIC) – (Formerly the Database Project on Palestinian Human Rights) – Chicago, Jerusalem. 72 docs. 1986-1991 – 63mf – 9 – ne IDC [320]

PALESTINE LAND TRANSFER REGULATIONS / Great Britain. Foreign Office – Letter to the Secretary-General of the League of Nations. London. Feb 28 1940. BJ-28-92 1 – 9 – ne IDC [956]

PALESTINE MANDATE ... / Boustany, W F – Beirut, 1936 – 2mf – 9 – ILM-2159/1 – ne IDC [327]

PALESTINE NEWSPAPERS – (Also available seperately) – 537r – 1 – ne IDC [072]

PALESTINE POST *see* JERUSALEM POST

THE PALESTINE POST – Jerusalem: Palestine Telegraphic Agency, 1948-apr 21 1950 – 7r – 1 – us Res Libr [072]

PALESTINE REFERENCE FILES OF DEAN RUSK AND ROBERT MCCLINTOCK, 1947-1949 / U.S. Department of State – RG 59. M1175. 12 rolls – 1 – us Nat'l Archives [956]

Palestine Royal Commission *see* SUMMARY OF REPORT

Palestine. Secretary of State for Foreign Affairs *see* PARLIAMENTARY STATEMENT

PALESTINE TERMINATION OF THE MANDATE 15 MAY 1948 / Great Britain. Colonial Office – London. 1948. BJ-28-100 1 – 9 – ne IDC [956]

PALESTINE: THE BRITISH MANDATE – (Individual titles available) – 378mf – 9 – ne IDC [956]

PALESTINE THROUGH THE EYES OF A NATIVE / Wad-el-Ward, Gamahliel – New York:Fleming H. Revell, c1907 – 1mf – 9 – 0-8370-5679-9 – 1985-3679 – us A.T.L.A. [220]

Palestine. Treaties *see* AGREEMENT BETWEEN PALESTINE AND SYRIA AND THE LEBANON AMENDING THE AGREEMENT OF 2 FEB 1926, REGARDING FRONTIER QUESTIONS

PALESTINE WEEKLY *see* JERUSALEM POST

PALESTINE WHITE PAPER OF OCT 1930: MEMORANDUM / Jewish Agency for Palestine. London – Nov 1930. BJ-28-132 1 – 9 – ne IDC [956]

PALESTINE:THE LEGAL BACKGROUND – 1,313mf – 9 – ne IDC [340]

PALESTINIAN ARABS UNDER THE BRITISH MANDATE / Jewish Agency for Palestine. London – 1930. BJ-28-131 1 – 9 – ne IDC [956]

"THE PALESTINIAN EXPEDITION" / Rowe, Alan – University of Pennsylvania Museum Journal: Mar 1929 – 9 – $10.00 – us I.R.C. [930]

THE PALESTINIAN SYRIAC LECTIONARY OF THE GOSPELS / Lewis, A S; ed by Lewis, Agnes Smith & Gibson, Margaret Dunlop – Cambridge, 1899 – 7mf – 8 – ne Slangenburg [220]

THE PALESTINIAN VERSION OF THE HOLY SCRIPTURES – Oxford v1-pt 5 1893 – 3mf – 8 – ne Slangenburg [220]

A PALESTRA : GAZETA IMPARCIAL E HUMORISTICA – Manaos, Amazonas. 30 Abr 1882 – 1,5,6 – bl Biblioteca [072]

A PALESTRA – Maceio, Alagoas. 3-17 Ago 1902 – 1,5,6 – bl Biblioteca [072]

Palestrina, Giovanni Pierluigi *see*
- AD SANCTA SANCTORUM: OH BONE JESU MISERERE NOSTRI, SATB, LATIN TEXT
- IL PRIMO LIBRO DI MADRIGALI A QUARTO VOCI.

PALETTE AND GRAVER, 1919-1923 : INTERNATIONAL MAILER, 1946-1955 / International Photoengravers Union of North America – (Coll title: Labor Union Periodicals, Pt 2) – 1r – 1 – $135.00 – 1-55655-309-9 – us UPA [680]

Paley, William *see*
- NATURAL THEOLOGY
- A TREATISE ON THE LAW OF PRINCIPAL AND AGENT, CHIEFLY WITH REFERENCE TO MERCANTILE TRANSACTIONS

Palgen, Rudolf *see* UEBER ZACHARIAS WERNERS "SOEHNE DES TALS"

Palgrave, Francis Turner *see*
- THE GOLDEN TREASURY OF THE BEST SONGS AND LYRICAL POEMS IN THE ENGLISH LANGUAGE
- LANDSCAPE IN POETRY FROM HOMER TO TENNYSON

O PALHACO – Manaos, Amazonas. 1908 – 1,5,6 – bl Biblioteca [072]

PALI TIPITAKA – In Khmer Chrieng script and Khmer translation. 110v – 1,142 fiches – 9 – $800.00 – us I.A.S.W.R. [280]

PALI VIEW BAPTIST CHURCH. KANEOHE, HAWAII : CHURCH RECORDS – 1952-70 – 1 – 15.48 – us Baptist [240]

PALIGGENESIA – Athens, Greece. -d. 20 Oct 1862-30 Sept 1899. 38 reels – 1 – uk British Libr Newspaper [949]

PALINGENESIE PHILOSOPHIQUE, OU IDEES SUR L'ETAT PASSE ET SUR L'ETAT FUTUR DES ETRES VIVANTS, OUVRAGE DESTINE A SERVIR DE SUPPLEMENT AUX DERNIERS ECRITS DE L'AUTEUR / Bonnet, Charles – 2e ed., Geneve, 1770, 2 v., xxvi-431, ii-448 p. Histoire des Sciences XVIIe-XIXe Siecles. 7935 6 – 9 – fr Hachette [560]

Palingenius, Marcellus *see* THE ZODIAKE OF LIFE

PALINODIA / Diaz Tanco, Vasco – 1547 – 9 – 1.50f – sp Bibl Santa Ana [810]

PALINODIE CHIMIQUE: OV LES ERREVRS DE CEST ART / Fregeville, Antoine de – Paris, 1588 – 1 – us U.W. Library [540]

PALISADE PRESS – Palisade, NE. -w. Sep 1897-Jan 1898; Aug-Dec 1900; Feb-May 1901; Sep-Nov 1901 – 1 – us NE Hist [071]

PALISADE TIMES – Palisade, NE. -w. Feb 1909-Dec 1923; Jan 1925-Dec 1941; Jan 1943-Nov 1957 – 1 – us NE Hist [071]

PALISADES-MALIBU NEWS – Santa Monica, CA. 1957-1982 – 244r – 1 – $12,200.00 – R03523 – us Library Micro [071]

PALISADIAN POST – Pacific Palisades, CA. 1931 – 63+ r – 1 – $3,150.00 ($50.00y) – H04056 – us Library Micro [071]

Palisot de Beauvois, A M F J *see*
- ESSAI D'UNE NOUVELLE AGROSTOGRAPHIE
- FLORA D'OWARE SET DE BENIN EN AFRIQUE
- FLORE D'OWARE ET DE BENIN EN AFRIQUE
- MUSCOLOGIE, OU TRAITE SUR LES MOUSSES
- PRODROME DES CINQUIEME ET SIXIEME FAMILLES DE L'AETHEOGAMIE

Palisot-Beauvois, C *see* NOTICE SUR LE PEUPLE DU BENIN

Palissot de Montenoy, Charles *see*
- ELOGE DE M. DE VOLTAIRE
- LE GENIE DE VOLTAIRE
- LA MORT DE VOLTAIRE
- LA MORT DE VOLTAIRE, ODE, SUIVIE DE L'ELOGE DE CE GRAND HOMME

O PALITO : HEBDOMADARIO DE CRITICA HUMORISTICA SERIA – [s.l.] 1-8 Jun 1902; 11 Out 1903 – 1,5,6 – bl Biblioteca [072]

PALL MALL GAZETTE – London. -d. 1865-1923. (290 reels) – 1 – uk British Libr Newspaper [072]

PALL MALL MAGAZINE – v. 1-53. 1893-1914 – 1 – us UMI [073]

PALLA TOA : EIN LYRISCHES EPOS / Keilmann, Wilhelm – Heiligenstadt (Eichsfeld): F W Cordier, 1898 – 1r – 1 – us U.W. Library [810]

O PALLADIO – Curitiba, 26 May-Sep 1920 – 1,5,6 – bl Biblioteca [072]

Palladio, Andre *see* LES QUATRES LIVRES DE L'ARCHITECTURE

Palladio, Andrea *see* I QUATTRO LIBRI DELL' ARCHITETTURA

PALLADIO DRAWINGS AT THE ROYAL INSTITUTE OF BRITISH ARCHITECTS – With printed index – 14 – uk World [720]

PALLADIS TAMIA / Meres, Francis – 1598 – 9 – 35.00 – us Scholars' Facs [810]

PALLADIUM – Charlottetown, Canada. 1843-45 – 1 reel – 1 – $68.00 – cn Library Assoc [971]

PALLADIUM : A MONTHLY JOURNAL OF LITERATURE, POLITICS, SCIENCE AND ART – London. v1-2. jul 1850-mar 1851 – 1 – D4706 – us UMI [073]

PALLADIUM : ORGAM DO CENTRO ESTUDANTIL PARANAENSE – Curitiba, 15 Apr 1909-1 Nov 1910 – 1,5,6 – bl Biblioteca [072]

PALLADIUM – Oswego. N.Y. 1819-25; 1838-43 – 1 – us UMI [071]

PALLADIUM – Oswego. N.Y. and Rep. Chronicle. 1830-35 – 1 – us UMI [071]

PALLADIUM : REVISTA LITTERARIA, SCIENTIFICA E NOTICIOSA – Manaos, Amazonas. Mar 1908 – 1,5,6 – bl Biblioteca [072]

PALLADIUM – Richmond. Ind. 1878-1902; 1904-1938 – 1 – us UMI [071]

PALLADIUM – Richmond. Ind. -w. 1831-75 – 1 – us UMI [071]

PALLADIUM TIMES – Oswego. N.Y. 1959- – 1 – us UMI [071]

PALLADIUM-ITEM – Richmond. Ind. 1939- – 1 – us UMI [071]

PALLADIUS UND RUFINUS : EIN BEITRAG ZUR QUELLENKUNDE DES AELTESTEN MOENCHSTUMS / Preuschen, Erwin – Giessen, 1897 – Dfl28.00 – ne Slangenburg [240]

Pallain, G *see* TALLEYRAND'S BRIEFWECHSEL MIT KOENIG LUDWIG 18. WAEHREND DES WIENER CONGRESSES

Pallas, Peter Simon *see*
- ENUMERATIO PLANTARUM QUAE IN HORTO PROCOPII A DEMIDOF
- FLORA ROSSICA
- ICONES INSECTORUM PRAESERTIM ROSSIAE SIBIRIAEQUE PECULIARIUM
- ILLUSTRATIONES PLANTARUM IMPERFECTE VEL NONDUM COGNITARUM
- MISCELLANEA ZOOLOGICA.
- PISCES
- REISE DURCH VERSCHIEDENE PROVINZEN DES RUSSISCHEN REICHS
- SAMMLUNGEN HISTORISCHER NACHRICHTEN UEBER DIE MONGOLISCHEN VOELKERSCHAFTEN...
- SPECIES ASTRAGALORUM DESCRIPTAE ET ICONIBUS COLORATIS ILLUSTRATAE
- SPICILEGIA ZOOLOGICA.

Pallavicini *see* DEVISES ET EMBLEMES D'AMOUR ANCIENS ET MODERNES MORALISEZ ET EXPLIQUEZ EN SEPT SORTES DE LANGUES (LATIN, ITALIAN, FRENCH, SPANISH, DUTCH, ENGLISH AND GERMAN)

Pallavicini, S *see* HISTOIRE DU CONCILE DE TRENTE

Pallen, Conde B *see* NEW ROCHELLE-HER PART IN THE GREAT WAR

Palles, Jose *see* QUINCENARIO PARA HONRARA LA IMMACULADA CONCEPCION BAJO EL TITULO DE NUESTRA SENORA DE LOURDES

Pallestrini, L *see* FOUILLES DANS TROIS SITES BRESILIENS DU HAUT PARANAPANEMA: METHODE ET RESULTATS

Pallet, Jean *see* DICCIONARIO MUY COPIOSO DE LA LENGUA ESPANOLA Y FRANCESA, DICTIONNAIRE TRES AMPLE DE LA LANGUE FRANCOISE ET ESPAGNOLE (AEL, ABT 2;15)

PALLETIZER – (Cont by: Modern Materials Handling) – Boston. may-oct 1946 – 1 – D14873 – us UMI [380]

PALLIATIVE CARE : A COMPARISON OF FAMILY MEMBERS' NEEDS WITH PALLIATIVE CARE NURSES' PERCEPTIONS OF FAMILY MEMBERS' NEEDS / Thorpe, Patricia M & Belzer, Edwin G Jr. – 1992 – 2mf – 9 – $8.00 – us Microform Publ [613]

Pallme, Ignatius *see* TRAVELS IN KORDOFAN; EMBRACING A DESCRIPTION OF THAT PROVINCE OF EGYPT, AND OF SOME OF THE BORDERING COUNTRIES.

Pallone, Nathaniel J *see* JOURNAL OF OFFENDER REHABILITATION

Palm, August *see* DIE LIEDER IN DEN HISTORISCHEN BUECHERN DES ALTEN TESTAMENTES

PALM BEACH JEWISH WORLD – (Merged with Miami Jewish tribune and Broward Jewish world to form South Florida Jewish tribune) – West Palm Beach, Fla. v9 n9-n14; n18-n26; n 28-n34; n37-n38; n40-n43; v11 n4 – 95ft – us A.J.P.C. [270]

PALM BEACH JEWISH WORLD *see* BROWARD JEWISH WORLD

PALM BRANCH *see* THE PALM BRANCH

THE PALM BRANCH – (Merger of: Our Quarterly. Merger of: Palm Branch) – [St. John, N.B.: s.n. 1894?-1929?] – 9 – cn C.I.H.M. [240]

PALM DESERT COUNTRY CLUB – Palm Desert, CA. 1987 – 1+ r – 1 – $50.00 ($50.00y) – R04087 – us Library Micro [071]

PALM DESERT POST – Palm Desert, CA. 1963- – 63+ r – 1 – $3,150.00 ($160.00y) – R02593 – us Library Micro [071]

Palm, Hermann *see* MARTIN OPITZ VON BOBERFELD

Palm, Jefferson *see* COMPLETE FORMS OF PROCEEDINGS IN CIVIL AND CRIMINAL CASES BEFORE JUSTICES OF THE PEACE, IN THE STATE OF OHIO

PALM TISSUE CULTURE : STATE OF THE ART AND ITS APPLICATION TO THE COCONUT – 1981 – 76p – it F.A.O. [634]

LA PALMA NEWS – La Palma, CA. 1993-1994 – 6r – 1 – $300.00 – R04047 – us Library Micro [071]

Palma, Ricardo *see* LAS MEJORES TRADICIONES PERUANAS

Palma, S *see* CONTRIBUTION A L'ETUDE BIOLOGIQUE ET ECOLOGIQUE DE CYCLOTHONE BRAUERI JESPERSEN ET TANING, 1926 (GONOSTOMATIDAE), EN MER LIGURE

Palma y Freites, Luis de la *see* POR EL... JUAN DE LA SERENA...DEFINIDORES..

PALMA...CIUDAD DE DIOS CONTRA SATANAS / San Pedro de Alcantara, Domingo de – 1741 – 9 – 1.50f – sp Bibl Santa Ana [240]

PALMARUM FAMILIA EJUSQUE GENERA DENUO ILLUSTRATA / Martius, Karl Friedrich Philipp von – Monachii, 1824. 24 pp. B-6051 2 – 8 – ne IDC [580]

A PALMATORIA : PERIODICO CRITICO SATYRICO – Maceio, Alagoas. 12 Jun 1882 – 1,5,6 – bl Biblioteca [072]

PALMBLAETTER AUS DER MISSIONS – nos 38-43. 1934-39 (incomplete) – 1r – 1 – ATLA S0724C – us A.T.L.A. [073]

PALMDALE REPORTER *see* ANTELOPE VALLEY PRESS

PALMER 1727-1849 – (Mf 1T-3T: Births & Deaths 1727-1813. Mf 1T: Marriages 1749-92. Mf 2T-4T,6T: Marriages & Intentions 1761-1839. Mf 5T-6T: Marriage Intentions 1839-49. Mf 6T-7T: Births & Deaths 1752-1842. Mf 7T: Birth Index 1752-1842. Mf 8T: Births 1843-49. Mf 7T,9T: Marriages 1843-49. Mf 9T: Deaths 1848-49; Out-of-Town Marriages 1753-99) – (mf ed 1998) – 9mf – 9 – 0-87623-312-4 – us Holbrook [920]

PALMER 1731-1904 – (Mf 1-8: Town & Vital Records 1731-95. Mf 9-13: Proprietors of Elbows & Palmer 1732-56. Mf 14-18: Births, Marriages, Deaths 1796-1849. Mf 19-22: Birth Index 1843-1904. Mf 23-26: Marriage Index 1843-1904. Mf 27-29: Death Index 1843-1904. Mf 30-33: Births, Marriages, Deaths 1843-64. Mf 34-37: Births 1864-91. Mf 38-43: Marriages 1851-86. Mf 44-48: Deaths 1864-1904. Mf 49-53: Marriages 1886-1904. Mf 54-57: Marriage Intentions 1888-99. Mf 58: Births 1892-95) – (mf ed 1988) – 58mf – 9 – 0-87623-087-7 – us Holbrook [920]

Palmer, Albert *see* GEGEN DEN STROM

Palmer, Benjamin Morgan *see* THE THREEFOLD FELLOWSHIP AND THE THREEFOLD ASSURANCE

Palmer, Beverly Wilson *see* PAPERS OF CHARLES SUMNER

Palmer, Byron *see*
- GOD'S WHITE THRONE
- THE LIVING WAY

Palmer, Edward Henry *see*
- THE CALIPH HAROUN ALRASCHID AND SARACEN CIVILIZATION
- THE DESERT OF THE EXODUS

Palmer, Edwin O *see* HISTORY OF HOLLYWOOD

Palmer, Frederic *see*
- THE DRAMA OF THE APOCALYPSE IN RELATION TO THE LITERARY AND POLITICAL CIRCUMSTANCES OF ITS TIME
- STUDIES IN THEOLOGIC DEFINITION UNDERLYING THE APOSTLES' AND NICENE CREEDS

Palmer, F.W., State Printer *see* THE CENSUS OF IOWA

Palmer, G T *see* THE ACH INDEX OF NUTRITIONAL STATUS

Palmer, George Herbert *see*
- ETHICAL AND MORAL INSTRUCTION IN SCHOOLS
- THE FIELD OF ETHICS
- TRADES AND PROFESSIONS

Palmer, Greg *see*
- THE AMERICAN REVOLUTION IN CONTEXT
- FOREIGN OFFICE REGISTERS AND INDEXES OF CORRESPONDENCE, 1793-1919

PALMER HARTSOUGH, MICHIGAN SONG WRITER AND MINISTER, 1880-1932 / Severance, H O – 1 – 5.00 – us Baptist [240]

Palmer, J W *see* UP AND DOWN THE IRRAWADDI

Palmer, John M *see* BENCH AND BAR OF ILLINOIS

PALMER JOURNAL – Palmer, NE. -w. Jun 1914 to date – 1 – us NE Hist [071]

Palmer, Maria del Carmen Simon *see* SPANISH WOMEN WRITERS

Palmer, Patricia *see* PAPERS

Palmer, Phoebe Worrell *see*
- FAITH AND ITS EFFECTS, OR, FRAGMENTS FROM MY PORTFOLIO
- FOUR YEARS IN THE OLD WORLD: COMPRISING THE TRAVELS, INCIDENTS, AND EVANGELISTIC LABORS OF DR. AND MRS. PALMER IN ENGLAND, IRELAND, SCOTLAND AND WALES
- INCIDENTAL ILLUSTRATIONS OF THE ECONOMY OF SALVATION: ITS DOCTRINES AND DUTIES
- PRESENT TO MY CHRISTIAN FRIEND: ON ENTIRE DEVOTION TO GOD
- PROMISE OF THE FATHER, OR, A NEGLECTED SPECIALITY OF THE LAST DAYS: ADDRESSED TO THE CLERGY AND LAITY OF ALL CHRISTIAN COMMUNITIES
- THE WAY OF HOLINESS: WITH NOTES BY THE WAY, BEING A NARRATIVE OF RELIGIOUS EXPERIENCE RESULTING FROM A DETERMINATION TO BE A BIBLE CHRISTIAN

Palmer, Ray *see* HINTS ON THE FORMATION OF RELIGIOUS OPINIONS

Palmer, S B *see* NONDESTRUCTIVE TESTING AND EVALUATION

Palmer, Thomas *see* COPYBOOK

Palmer, William P *see*
- AN APPEAL TO THE SCOTTISH BISHOPS AND CLERGY AND GENERALLY TO THE CHURCH OF THEIR COMMUNION
- DISSERTATIONS ON SUBJECTS RELATING TO THE "ORTHODOX" OR "EASTERN-CATHOLIC" COMMUNION
- A NARRATIVE OF EVENTS CONNECTED WITH THE PUBLICATION OF THE TRACTS FOR THE TIMES
- ORIGINES LITURGICAE OR ANTIQUITIES OF THE ENGLISH RITUAL AND A DISSERTATION ON PRIMITIVE LITURGIES
- RUSSIA AND THE ENGLISH CHURCH DURING THE LAST FIFTY YEARS

PALMER, WILLIAM P., COLLECTION, MS 3947 : DIARY OF JOHN M. BUTLER – 1 reel – 1 – us Western Res [976]

PALMER, WILLIAM P., COLLECTION, MSS 3947 – (F.A. Flournoy Autograph Book, Dated 26 July 1862) – 1r – 1 – us Western Res [976]

PALMER, WILLIAM P., COLLECTION, MSS 3947 : JOHNSON'S ISLAND [PRISON] LISTS AND NARRATIVES... – 1 reel – 1 – us Western Res [355]

PALMER, WILLIAM P., COLLECTION, MSS 3947 – (Undated autograph book, signed by Confederate prisoners held at the Johnson's Island, Ohio, Prison, and detailing name, rank, hometown, and place of capture in the American Civil War) – 1 reel – 1 – us Western Res [355]

Palmer, William Scott *see* THE CHURCH AND MODERN MEN

PALMERS GREEN AND SOUTHGATE – Enfield, UK. 1984; Jan-Jul 1986. -w. 4 1/2 reels – 1 – uk British Libr Newspaper [072]

PALMER'S INDEX TO THE TIMES, 1790-JUNE 1941 – (Also available individually. 1790-1811 £297.00. 1812-31 £270.00. 1832-43 £162.00. 1844-53 £135.00. 1854-62 £122.00. 1863-68 £81.00. 1869-73 £67.00. 1874-78 £67.00. 1879-83 £67.00. 1884-88 £67.00. 1889-93 £67.00. 1894-99 £81.00. 1900-05 £81.00. 1906-10 £67.00. 1911-14 £54.00. 1915-19 £67.00. 1920-23 £54.00. 1924-27 £54.00. 1928-32 £67.00. 1933-37 £67.00. 1938-Jun 1941 £48.00) – London, 1790-Jun 1941 – 21r – 1 – £1,945.00 – uk Pordes [072]

PALMERSTON PAPERS AMERICAN CORRESPONDENCE, 1835-41 AND 1846-50. ADD MSS 48495, 48575. BRRAM / British Museum – 1 – uk Microform Academic [975]

PALMETTO HERALD *see* NEW SOUTH (BEAUFORT, SOUTH CAROLINA), MARCH 7, 1895

PALMETTO LEADER (COLUMBIA, SOUTH CAROLINA), 1925-1957 – 1991 – 6r – 1 – $510.00 – D3275.P01 – Co-publ with South Caroliniana Library, University of South Carolina – us Scholarly Res [071]

PALMETUM ORBIGNIANUM / Martius, Karl Friedrich Philipp von – From: A, d'Orbigny. Voyage dans l'Amerique Meridionale. Paris, 1847. 140 pp., 32 pls. B-5401B 2 – 8 – ne IDC [580]

Palmieri, A *see* THEOLOGICA DOGMATICA ORTHODOXA

THE PALM-OIL INDUSTRY ON THE EAST COAST OF SUMATRA / Hasibuan, Sayuti – SE-11,603 1. 1960 – 9 – ne IDC [380]

PALMONI, OR, THE NUMERALS OF SCRIPTURE, A PROOF OF INSPIRATION / Mahan, Milo – New York: D. Appleton, 1863. 1 fiche. 8370-4257-7 – 9 – us A.T.L.A. [240]

Palmstruch, J W *see* SVENSK BOTANIK

PALMYRA ITEMS – Palmyra, NE. -w. Sep 1887; Mar 1888; Aug 1895-Apr 1904; Jul 1907; Mar 1908; Jun 1908-May 1913; May 1937-Jun 1945 – 1 – us NE Hist [071]

PALMYRAH PALM : POTENTIAL AND PERSPECTIVES – 1983 – 82p – it F.A.O. [634]

O PALMYRENSE – Palmyra, 25 Apr, 4 Jul 1897 – 1,5,6 – bl Biblioteca [072]

THE PALO ALTAN – Palo Altan, CA. 1905-14 – 6r – 1 – $300.00 – B02598 – us Library Micro [071]

PALO ALTO CITIZEN – Palo Alto, CA. 1904-05 – 1r – 1 – $50.00 – B02597 – us Library Micro [071]

PALO ALTO LIVE OAK – Palo Alto, CA. 1896-1908 – 1r – 1 – $50.00 – B02599 – us Library Micro [071]

THE PALO ALTO NEWS – (Also known as: Mid-Peninsula News; Peninsula Mirror) – Palo Alto, CA. 1926-38 – 6r – 1 – $300.00 – C02600 – us Library Micro [071]

PALO ALTO PRESS – Palo Alto, CA. 1901-02 – 1r – 1 – $50.00 – B02601 – us Library Micro [071]

PALO ALTO SUN – Palo Alto, CA. 1933-1935 – 1 – 1 – $50.00 – C03629 – us Library Micro [071]

PALO ALTO TIMES *see* PENINSULA TIMES TRIBUNE

PALO ALTO TIMES TRIBUNE *see* TIMES TRIBUNE

THE PALO ALTO WEEKLY – Palo Alto, CA. Oct 1979- – 25+ r – 1 – $1,250.00 ($120.00y) – B02607 – us Library Micro [071]

PALO ALTO/REDWOOD CITY – 1922-38; 1978- – 46+ r – 1 – $3,000.00 – P00084 – us Library Micro [910]

PALO VERDE VALLEY HERALD – Palo Verde, CA. 1911-15 – 1r – 1 – $50.00 – R02608 – us Library Micro [071]

PALO VERDE VALLEY TIMES – Blythe, CA. 1925-89 – 71r – 1 – $3,550.00 – R02072 – us Library Micro [071]

LA PALOMBIERE / Lafargue, Fernand – Paris: E. Flammarion, 1904. 296p. 4 fiches. Roman. (Literature Collection) – 9 – 10.00 – fr Bibl Nationale [830]

Palomer, Jose *see* UN PAJE DE MARIA ANTONIETA

Palomino, A A *see*
- AN ACCOUNT OF THE LIVES AND WORKS OF THE MOST EMINENT SPANISH PAINTERS, SCULPTORS AND ARCHITECTS
- LAS VIDAS DE LOS PINTORES Y ESTATUARIOS EMINENTES ESPANOLES...
- LAS VIDAS DE LOS PINTORES Y ESTATUARIOS EMINENTES ESPANOLES

Palomino de Castro *see* TEORIA Y PRACTICA DE LA PINTURA

Palomino, Martin Alfonso *see* ATRAS HAY DIOS

Palomo Iglesias Crescensio *see* CARTA MEDITA DE LA DUQUESA DE PLASENCIA DONA LEONOR PIMENTEL. DONANDO A LOS DOMINICOS EL CONVENTO DE SAN VICENTE FERRER DE LA CIUDAD DE PLASENCIA (22 DE AGOSTO Y 10 DE OCTUBRE DE 1484)

PALOS VERDES NEWS AND ROLLING HILLS HERALD – (Also known as: Pals Verdes News, Rolling Hills Herald, Hollywood Riviera Tribune) – Palos Verdes, CA. 1938-1959; 1937-1983 – 64r – 1 – $3,200.00 – H03383 – us Library Micro [071]

PALOS VERDES PENINSULA NEWS – Palos Verdes, CA. 1961 – 33+ r – 1 – $1,650.00 ($100.00y) – H04059 – us Library Micro [071]

PALPITACIONES DE UN CORAZON / Moreno Torrado, Luis – 1886 – 9 – 1.50f – sp Bibl Santa Ana [810]

PALS VERDES NEWS *see* PALOS VERDES NEWS AND ROLLING HILLS HERALD

Palsgrave, John see
- L'ECLAIRCISSEMENT DE LA LANGUE FRANCAISE
- L'ESCLARCISSEMENT DE LA LANGUE FRANCOYSE

Palumbo, G et al see ASTROPHYSICAL LETTERS

Palz, W et al see SOLAR ENERGY

PAMATNIK CESKYCH EVANJELICKYCH CIRKVI / Siller, Vilem – 1900 – 1 – $50.00 – us Presbyterian [240]

PAMELA; OR, VIRTUE REWARDED. / Richardson, Samuel – Facs. reprod. of 1769 ed. Berwyn, PA: Private printer, 1929. 166p. illus – 1 – us U.W. Library [830]

PAMELA OU LA VERTU RECOMPENSEE / Neufchateau, Francois de – (French Theatre Series). Paris. Barba, an III. 1794 – 9 – fr Hachette [820]

PAMIATI A. BELOGO / Stepun, F A – "Sovremennye zapiski". v. 56. Paris. 1934. BR-3296 2 – 8 – ne IDC [920]

PAMIATI A.A. BLOKA – Sbornik. Poliarnaia zvezda. Spb. 1922. BR-1476 2 – 8 – ne IDC [460]

PAMIATI LET. SBORNIK STIKHOTVORENII 1912-1955 / Aseev, N – M. 1956. BR-906 2 – 8 – ne IDC [460]

PAMIATI MANDEL'SHTAMA / Margolin, I – Vozduzhnye Puti, II. New York. 1961. BR-3679 2 – 8 – ne IDC [920]

PAMIATKA L'NOVODA-KOOPERATORA / Chaianov, A V – M., 1918 – 1mf – 9 – COR-237/1 – ne IDC [334]

PAMIATKA RABOTNIKAM SEL'SKOKHOZIAISTVENNOI KOOPERATSII : SBORNIK POSTANOVLENII RUKOVODIASHCHIKH ORGANOV I TSIRKULIAROV PO OSNOVNYM VOPROSAM SEL'SKOKHOZIAISTVENNYKH...ZA 1926 GOD – M., 1926 – 2mf – 9 – COR-299/1 – ne IDC [334]

PAMIATNAIA KNIZHKA VIATSKOI GUBERNII I KALENDAR' NA 1857-1916 GOD – Viatka, 1857-1916 god – 255mf – 9 – RET-208/1 – ne IDC [947]

PAMIATNIKE SIBIRSKOI ISTORII 18 VIEKA – Ed. by A.I. Timofeev. St. Petersburg, 1882-85. 2v. In Cyrillic – 1 – us U.W. Library [947]

PAMIATNIKI DIPLOMATICHESKIKH SNOSHENII DREVNER ROSSII S DERZHAVAMI INOSTRANNYMI – Invaluable collection of early Russian diplomatic documents on relations with neighboring entities. 10 v. Spb. 1851-79 – 8 – ne IDC [947]

PAMIATNIKI DREVNERUSSKOI TSERKOVNOI-UCHITEL'NOI LITERATURY / Ponomarev, A I, red; ed by Ponomarev, A I – St. Petersburg, 1894. Pt.1. BR-10,047/2 – 8 – ne IDC [460]

PAMIATNYE VSTRECHI / Pavlovich, N – (O Bloke). Literaturnaia gazeta. nr. 141. 1955. BR-3289 2 – 8 – ne IDC [460]

PAMIETNIKI CHLOPOWISEMA DRUGA – Warszawa, 1936 – 1r – 1 – us I.H.R.C. [947]

PAMONA PRESS – Providence. R.I. 1890-1902 – 1 – us UMI [071]

LE PAMPHLET – Redige par Alfred Fabre-Luce, Pierre Dominique et Jean Prevost. no. 1-50. Paris. 3 fevr 1933-16 mars 1934 – 1 – fr A.C.R.P.P. [073]

PAMPHLET / Iowa State University. Cooperative Extension Service in Agriculture and Home Economics – No.1-978. 1945-80 – 1,5 – us Spaulding [630]

PAMPHLET / Vermont. Agricultural Experiment Station – v. 1-36. 1943-69 – 1,5,6 – us Spaulding [630]

PAMPHLET COLLECTION see SHAKESPEARE AT STRATFORD-UPON-AVON

PAMPHLETEER : DEDICATED TO BOTH HOUSES OF PARLIAMENT – (With cum index) – London. v1-29. 1813-28 – 1 – D2823 – us UMI [941]

PAMPHLETS / Communist International – Hamburg. n1-6, 8-13,14. 1921-1922 – 1 – us NY Public [080]

PAMPHLETS / Communist Party. Germany – Berlin. A collection of 24 pamphlets published by the Communist Party of Germany during its early period, 1919-1924. Authors include Karl Radek and Rosa Luxemburg – 1 – 35.00r – us Hoover Inst Photo [335]

PAMPHLETS – New York: Loyal Publ Society. v1-92. 1863-65 – 1r – 1 – us Ross [975]

PAMPHLETS / South Carolina Historical Society – 1858-1976. 14 fiches – 9 – us South Carolina Historical [975]

[PAMPHLETS] / The Indian Empire Society – [London]: The Society, n2-14. [1930?-31] – us Res Libr [950]

PAMPHLETS, 1879-1904 / Paine, Robert T – 1 – 19.00 – us L of C Photodup [920]

PAMPHLETS AND BOOKS / Labour Research Department. London – 1916-92. With printed index. Continued annually – 5. ; 9 – £895.00r £995.00mf – uk World [330]

(PAMPHLETS BY AND ABOUT RASMUS RASK) / Rask, Rasmus – 1831-1937 – 1 – us I.U. Libraries [390]

PAMPHLETS COLLECTED BY THE HOUSE COMMITTEE ON UN-AMERICAN ACTIVITIES / Library of Congress – (With free printed list of titles) – 4,189mf – 9 – £9,590.00 – uk Chadwyck [977]

PAMPHLETS IN AMERICAN HISTORY – (Individual sections and topics available. Cataloging available) – 18,589mf complete collection – 9 – $39,035 – us UMI [975]

PAMPHLETS, NEWSLETTERS, ETC / Open Network. Denver, CO – Selection. 1 fiche (29x) – 9 – 1.00f – at Libertarian Micro [320]

PAMPHLETS ON AMERICAN WRITERS – Minneapolis. n1-103. 1959-72 – 103mf – 9 – $5.00f – us Ross [420]

PAMPHLETS ON ATHEISM (AND) MISCELLANEOUS ISSUES OF PERIODICALS AND SERIALS – Madison: University of Wisconsin, Madison Libraries, 1985- – 1 – us U.W. Library [210]

PAMPHLETS ON CEYLON POLITICS, 1935-1968 – Chicago: Uni of Chicago, Photodup Dept, [1971?] – us Res Libr [320]

PAMPHLETS ON PRAYER – Twenty-four English and German titles published between 1863 and 1905 – 1 – us A.T.L.A. [080]

PAMPHLETS ON SOCIALISM, COMMUNISM, BOLSHEVISM, ETC – 164 v. 1849-1931 – 1 – 39.00 – us L of C Photodup [335]

PAMPHLETS ON THE CIVIL WAR, 1861-1865 – (Cataloging available) – 2000mf – 9 – $5490.00 – us UMI [976]

PAMPHLETS ON THE CONSTITUTION OF THE UNITED STATES : PUBLISHED DURING ITS DISCUSSION BY THE PEOPLE, 1787-1788 / ed by Ford, Paul L – Brooklyn: n.p., 1888 – 5mf – 9 – $7.50 – LLMC 95-058 – us L.L.M.C. [323]

PAMPHLETS ON THE SPANISH CIVIL WAR – 123 v. 1936-39 – 1 – 31.00 – us L of C Photodup [946]

PAMPHLETS PUBLISHED BY THE SOCIAL DEMOCRATIC PARTY OF THE FEDERAL REPUBLIC OF GERMANY FOR THE ELECTION OF 1969 – Collection of German pamphlets. With: Miscellaneous Materials Related to Politics and Elections in the Federal Republic of Germany, 1960's-1970's – 1 – us U.W. Library [080]

PAMPIERE WERELD OFTE WERELDSCHE OEFFENINGE, BEGRIJPENDE IN VIER DEELEN MEEST ALLE DE RIJMEN : EN WERKEN, VAN I.H. KRUL / Krul, J H – Amsterdam, c1650 – 9mf – 9 – O-3235/1 – ne IDC [760]

PAMPIERE WERELD OFTE WERELDSCHE OEFFENINGE, WAER IN BEGREPEN ZIJN MEEST ALLE DE RIJMEN EN WERKEN VAN I.H. KRUL : AL TE ZAMEN DOOR HEM VERBETERT, EN MET VEEL NIEUWE RIJMEN VERRIJCKT, DOOR GAENS MET SCHOONE KOPERE PLATEN VERCIERT, AFGEZONDERT IN VIER DEELEN / Krul, J H – Amsterdam, 1681 – 9mf – 9 – O-3108/1 – ne IDC [760]

PAMPLICO FIRST BAPTIST CHURCH. PAMPLICO, SOUTH CAROLINA : CHURCH RECORDS – 1921-38, 1958-72 – 1 – 10.22 – us Baptist [240]

Pamuntjak, Kasuma gelar Sutan see PERIBAHASA

PAMYATKY UKRAYINS'KO – RUS 'KOYI MOVY I LITERATURY – L'viv. v. 1-7. 1896-1912 – 1 – us NY Public [460]

PAN – Berlin, 1895-1900 – 4r (mono or colour) – 1,14 – £230.00 1 £420.00 14 – uk Chadwyck [760]

PAN – Berlin. v. 1-4. no. 2 3. Nov 1 1910-Apr 1 1915 – 1 – us NY Public [073]

PAN – Berlin. v1-4. 1910-15 – 1r – 1 – us Ross [073]

PAN – Revue artistique et litteraire. Supplement francais. no. 1-4 5. Paris. avr-dec 1895 – 1 – fr A.C.R.P.P. [073]

Pan American Union see
- BULLETIN
- PAN AMERICAN UNION BULLETIN

PAN AMERICAN UNION BULLETIN / Pan American Union – (Lacking: v1-65, v76) – v1-82. 1893-1948 (all publ) – 9 – LLMC 81-903 – us L.L.M.C. [340]

Pan Duro, Luciano see NUEVOS DIALOGOS DE LOS MUERTOS...

Panafieu, J B de see L'ALIMENTATION HIVERNALE DU MERLAN (MERLANGIUS MERLANGUS L., 1758) EN MER DU NORD

PAN-AFRICAN JOURNAL – (With cum index for v1-3 1) – New York. v1-10. 1968-77 1; v8-10. 1975-77 5; v9-10. 1976-77 9 – 1,5,9 – D6155 – us UMI [960]

PAN-AFRICAN MOVEMENT SINCE 1952, DOCUMENTS, PAPERS AND MEMORANDA ON THE GROWTH OF THE... : MATERIAL FROM THE PERSONAL LIBRARY OF COLIN LEGUM – 44mf – 9 – £250.00 – uk Altair [320]

Panaiotov, I see RUSSIA, VELIKITE SILI I BALGARSKIIAT VAPROS SLED IZBORA NA KNIAZ FERDINANDA (1888-1896

PANAMA : COMPENDIO ESTADISTICO DESCRIPTIVO DE LA REPUBLICA DE PANAMA, CON LOS DATOS SINOPTICOS DE COMERCIO INTERNACIONAL DE 1909 A 1916 / Panama. Direccion de Estadistica – (Coll title: Latin American and Caribbean Official Statistical Serials, 1821-1982) – 3mf – 9 – £7.00f (set £595.00 81mf) – uk Chadwyck [972]

PANAMA : ESTADISTICA ANUAL 1908-1911 / Panama. Direccion General de Estadistica – (1911 not available. Coll title: Latin American and Caribbean Official Statistical Serials, 1821-1982) – 5mf – 9 – £7.00f (set £595.00 81mf) – uk Chadwyck [972]

PANAMA : EXTRACTO ESTADISTICO DE LA REPUBLICA DE PANAMA 1941-1943, 1944-1946, 1951-1952 / Panama. Direccion de Estadistica y Censos – (Coll title: Latin American and Caribbean Official Statistical Serials, 1821-1982) – 40mf – 9 – £7.00f (set £595.00 81mf) – uk Chadwyck [972]

PANAMA : PANAMA EN CIFRAS 1958/62-1968/72 / Panama. Direccion de Estadistica y Censos – (Coll title: Latin American and Caribbean Official Statistical Serials, 1821-1982) – 33mf – 9 – £7.00f (set £595.00 81mf) – uk Chadwyck [972]

Panama see
- GACETA OFICIAL
- GAZETA OFICIAL

EL PANAMA AMERICA – Panama City, Panama. 3 Sept 1951-25 Apr 1955; Oct 1959-1961; 1963-Jun 1970; Sept 1976-Jan 1977 – 65r – 1 – us L of C Photodup [072]

EL PANAMA AMERICA see THE PANAMA AMERICAN/EL PANAMA AMERICA

THE PANAMA AMERICAN – Panama City, Panama. Oct 1925-28; Sept 1951-59; 1960-68; 1969-14 Jan 1977 (incomplete) – 90r – 1 – us L of C Photodup [072]

THE PANAMA AMERICAN/EL PANAMA AMERICA – Panama City, Panama. 1929-2 Sept 1951 – 136r – 1 – us L of C Photodup [072]

PANAMA, ARCHIVO NACIONAL : CATALOGO DE CEDULAS REALES, 1573-1648 – Panama: Ministerio de Educacion, 1573-1648 – 3r – 1 – $240.00 – us Ross [972]

PANAMA, ARCHIVO NACIONAL : SECCION JURIDICA: PRIMERA NOTERIA – Panama: Ministerio de Educacion, 1825-85 – 74r – 1 – $5,920.00 coll – us Ross [972]

PANAMA AREA PERSONNEL BOARD : POLICY AND REGULATIONS MANUAL / Panama Canal Zone – CZ, 1 Apr 1989 – 2mf – 9 – $3.00 – LLMC 82-100D Title 12 – us L.L.M.C. [340]

PANAMA CANAL – 1 – us Ross [977]

THE PANAMA CANAL / Arias, H – London, 1911 – 3mf – 9 – ILM-1862/1 – ne IDC [340]

THE PANAMA CANAL / Deniel, E – By permission of the Council. Montreal: Printed for the Society by J. Lovell, 1889. (Pre-1900 Canadiana) – 9 – cn C.I.H.M. [971]

PANAMA CANAL INSURANCE LAWS : EXTRACTS FROM THE CANAL ZONE CODE PERTAINING TO INSURANCE IN GENERAL, INCLUDING LAWS RELATING TO THE LICENSING OF FOREIGN CORPORATIONS UNDER WHICH INSURANCE COMPANIES ARE AUTHORIZED TO DO BUSINESS IN THE CANAL ZONE / Panama Canal Zone. National Insurance Law Service – New York: NILS, 1963; 1973 – 2mf – 9 – $3.00 – LLMC 82-100D Title 7 – us L.L.M.C. [340]

THE PANAMA CANAL PERSONNEL MANUAL, JANUARY 1 1967 : WITH REVISIONS THRU MAY 5 1975 / Panama Canal Zone – n.p; n.d. – 15mf – 9 – $22.50 – LLMC 82-100D Title 13 – us L.L.M.C. [340]

PANAMA CANAL STUDIES / U.S. Army. Caribbean Defense Command – 1946-48. 11 Titles – 1 – 269.00 – us L of C Photodup [972]

Panama Canal Zone see
- CANAL ZONE CODE, 1934
- CANAL ZONE CODE, 1962
- CANAL ZONE CODE ANNOTATED, 1962
- CANAL ZONE REPORTS, VOL 3
- CANAL ZONE RULES AND REGULATIONS, 1966
- THE CIVIL CODE OF THE REPUBLIC OF PANAMA AND AMENDATORY LAWS CONTINUED IN FORCE IN THE CANAL ZONE, ISTHMUS OF PANAMA, BY EXECUTIVE ORDER OF MAY 9 1904
- LAWS OF THE CANAL ZONE, ISTHMUS OF PANAMA
- THE NEW PANAMA CANAL TREATY
- PANAMA AREA PERSONNEL BOARD
- THE PANAMA CANAL PERSONNEL MANUAL, JANUARY 1 1967
- PRESIDENTIAL EXECUTIVE ORDERS RELATING TO THE PANAMA CANAL
- REPORTS, PRE-NRS

Panama Canal Zone. Hispanic Law Division see THE CONTROVERSY OVER A NEW CANAL TREATY BETWEEN THE U.S. AND PANAMA

Panama Canal Zone Museum. Library see SUBJECT CATALOG...THE HISTORY OF THE ISTHMUS OF PANAMA AS IT APPLIES TO INTEROCEANIC TRANSPORTATION

Panama Canal Zone. National Insurance Law Service see PANAMA CANAL INSURANCE LAWS

Panama Canal Zone. Supreme Court see CANAL ZONE SUPREME COURT REPORTS, VOLS 1-2

Panama. Direccion de Estadistica see PANAMA

Panama. Direccion de Estadistica y Censos see
- PANAMA

Panama. Direccion General de Estadistica see PANAMA

Panama. Direccion General de Planificacion y Administracion see
- PROGRAMA DE DESARROLLO ECONOMICO Y SOCIAL. 1963-1970
- PROGRAMAS Y PROYECTOS DE INVERSIONES PUBLICAS 1972-1975

Panama. Direccion General de Planificacion y Administracion, Departamento de Planificacion see ESTRATEGIA PARA EL DESARROLLO NACIONAL, 1970-80

Panama. Direccion General de Planificacion y Administracion. Departemento de Planificacion see PROGRAMAS Y PROTECTOS DE INVERSIONES PUBLICAS 1971-1975

PANAMA EN EL ARCHIVO DE INDIAS : TRES ANOS DE LABOR / Susto, Juan Antonio – Madrid: Razon y Fe, 1972 – 1 – sp Bibl Santa Ana [972]

PANAMA JOURNAL see DIARIO DE PANAMA/PANAMA JOURNAL

Panama. Laws, Statutes, etc see LEYES EXPEDIDAS POR LA CONVENCION NACIONAL CONSTITUYENTE DE LA REPUBLICA DE PANAMA EN 1904

Panama. Ministerio de Planificacion y Politica Economica see PLAN OPERATIVO DE GOBIERNO NACIONAL PARA 1974

PANAMA MORNING JOURNAL – Panama City, Panama. 3 Oct 1911-7 Nov 1918 (incomplete) – 17r – 1 – us L of C Photodup [072]

PANAMA PRESS – Panama, NE. -w. May 1922-Jan 1923 – 1 – us NE Hist [071]

PANAMA RECORD – Panama, NE. -w. Oct 1913-Mar 1915; May-Dec 1915 – 1 – us NE Hist [071]

PANAMA STAR – Panama City. Also: Herald. May 1919-Mar 1951 – 1 – us UMI [072]

PANAMA STAR AND HERALD – Panama. -d. 1 Jan 1874-21 Sep 1882. (10 reels) – 1 – uk British Libr Newspaper [072]

THE PANAMA STAR AND HERALD : 1849-1914 – (Individual reels available for $65.00ea) – 158r – 1 – $9,900.00 – us Universal [950]

THE PANAMA STAR AND HERALD – Panama, 1849-1914 – 158r – 1 – $9,900.00 – us Ross [072]

THE PANAMA TIMES – Ancon, Panama Canal Zone. 21 Mar 1925-1 Jan 1928 – 3r – 1 – us L of C Photodup [072]
THE PANAMA TRIBUNE – Panama City, Panama. 11 Nov 1928-24 Dec 1971 (incomplete) – 22r – 1 – us L of C Photodup [072]
PANAMA WEEKLY NEWS – Panama City, Panama. 11 Jul 1917-26 Oct 1918 – 1r – 1 – us L of C Photodup [072]
HET PANAMA-KANAAL / Gijselaar, N C de – Leiden, 1891 – 3mf – 1 – ILM-1808/1 – ne IDC [327]
DER PANAMAKANAL... / Beck, W C A – Stuttgart, 1911 – 9 – 1mf – ILM-1863/1 – ne IDC [327]
PAN-AMERICAN QUESTIONS / Cavalcanti, A – Rio de Janeiro, 1913 – 1mf – 1 – ILM-4085/1 – ne IDC [327]
LE PANAMERICANISME ET LA SIXIEME CONFERENCE PANAMERICAINE / Alvarez, Arturo – Paris, 1928 – 2mf – 9 – ILM-4059/1 – ne IDC [340]
EL PAN-AMERICANISMO Y EL PAN-HISPANISMO / Giberga, E – Habana, 1916 – 1mf – 1 – ILM-4099/1 – ne IDC [327]
DIE PAN-AMERIKANISCHEN KONFERENZEN / Buechi, R – Breslau, 1914 – 2mf – 1 – ILM-4078/1 – ne IDC [327]
PANAMSKI I KANAL, PADENIE KHLI EBNYKH T SI EN, VO INA I NASHI TORGOVYE DOGOVORY / Goldstein, Joseph M – Izd. 2-e, ispr. i znachitelno dop. Moskva: T-vo tip. A.I. Mamontova, 1915 – 1 – CSUX89-B3184 – us Hoover Inst Photo [320]
PANAMSKI I KANAL, PADENIE KHLI EBNYKH T SIE EN, VO INA I NASHI TORGOVYE DOGOVORY / Goldstein, Joseph M – Izd. 3-e, ispr. i znachitelno dop. Moskva: Tipo-lit. Russkago t-va pechatnago i izdatelskago di ela, 1915 – 1 – CSUX89-B2377 – us Hoover Inst Photo [320]
PANARCHIE, REVUE TRIMESTRIELLE / Puydt, P E de – Brussels. 1860. In German trans. 3 fiches (29x) – 9 – 1.00f – at Libertarian Micro [320]
PANATHENAIA – Athens, Greece. -f. Oct 1900-Feb 1915. 11 reels – 1 – uk British Libr Newspaper [949]
PANCEVOER POST – Pancevo, Yugoslavia. Mar 1932-Aug 1934 – 1r – 1 – us L of C Photodup [949]
Pancke, Florian *see* HACIA ALLA Y PARA ACA...
PANDAI MEMBUAT 80 – (i.e. Delapan Puluh) Kuwe Basah. SE-4369 1. 1963? – 9 – ne IDC [950]
Pandam, Guritno Siswoharsojo *see* SOCIAL PATHOLOGY AND CHILD HEALTH IN JOGJAKARTA
PANDANGAN KITAB SUTJI BIJBEL TENTANG PEKERDJAAN / Sudarmo, R – SE 4202 1. 1951 – 9 – ne IDC [950]
LES PANDECTES BELGES; CORPUS JURIS BELGICI; INVENTAIRE DU DROIT D'UNE NATION DE RACE EUROPEO-AMERICAINE AU 20 SIECLE – Bruxelles. On film: v1-90, 92-136; 1878-1933. Lacking: v91; 1908. LL-0230 – 1 – us L of C Photodup [340]
O PANDEGO : PERIODICO CRITICO, SATYRICO, HUMORISTICO E NOTICIOSO – Maceio, Alagoas. 24-31 Jul, Set, Nov 1882; Jan, 23 Maio 1883 – 1,5,6 – bl Biblioteca [072]
PANDITA RAMABAI : THE STORY OF HER LIFE / Dyer, Helen S – New York: Fleming H Revell, c1900 – 1mf – 9 – 0-8370-6490-2 – 1986-0490 – us A.T.L.A. [920]
PANDJI POESTAKA – (Lacking: 1925 v3(26). 1938 v16(93-94). 1939 v17(2,51-52,76,83,86). 1940 v18(14,19-?). 1941 v19) – Weltevreden. v1-23. 1922-1945 – 828mf – 9 – ne IDC [950]
PANDOE NEGARA : PEMATANG SIANTAR, PEMOEDA SOSIALIS INDONESIA – 1947. V.1(1) – 1mf – 9 – ne IDC [950]
O PANDOKEU – Rio de Janeiro, 25 Nov 1866-10 Mar 1867 – 1,5,6 – bl Biblioteca [072]
PANDORA – Seattle. v3 oct 1972-oct 1973. v6-8 nov 1975-dec 1978 1; v6 nov 1975-sep 1976. v7-8 oct 1976-dec 1978* 5; v6-8. nov 1975-dec 1978* 9 – 1,5,9 – D8131 – us UMI [073]
PANDORA TIMES – Pandora, Ohio. 1902- – 24r – 1 – $32.50r – us Archival [071]
Pandora United Methodist Chruch (Pandora, Ohio) *see* RECORDS
PANDORA'S BOX; A TRAGEDY IN THREE ACTS / Wedekind, Frank – Trans. by Samuel A. Eliot, jr., New York: Boni and Liveright, 1918. 79p. 1 reel. 1248 – 1 – us U.W. Library [820]
Pandzic, Basilio *see* ANALES MINORUM... TOMUS 32 (1671-1680). ROMA, 1964
Pane, Luigi dal *see* ANTONIO LABRIOLA: LA VITA E IL PENSIERO
PANEGIRICO AL CHOCOLATE / Castro de Torres – 1887 – 9 – 1.50f – sp Bibl Santa Ana [810]
PANEGIRICO DE SANTA BARBARA...BADAJOZ / Sanchez Juarez, Francisco – 1875 – 9 – 1.50f – sp Bibl Santa Ana [440]
PANEGIRICO POR LA POESIA / Vera Mendoza, Fernando de – Montilla: Manuel de Payna, 1627 – 1 – sp Bibl Santa Ana [810]
PANEGIRICO...SANTA OLALLA / Herrera, Bonifacio – 1878 – 9 – 1.50f – sp Bibl Santa Ana [240]
PANEGYRICO FUNERAL PREDICADO EN LAS EXEQUIAS QUE LA CIUDAD DE PLASENCIA CELEBRO EN LA MEMORIA DEL SR. DON CARLOS 2 / Xavir, Manuel – s.l.,s.i. S.A. – 1 – sp Bibl Santa Ana [240]
PANEGYRICO POR LA POESIA / Vera y Mendoza, Fernando de – Cieza: Imp.Artes Graficas Soler – 1 – sp Bibl Santa Ana [810]
PANEGYRIQUE DE L'ABBE JEAN MANDE SIGIGNE: MISSIONNAIRE FRANCAIS A LA BAIE STE. MARIE, N. ECOSSE DEPUIS 1799 JUSQU'EN 1844 / Bourgeois, Phileas Frederic – Discours prononce par Bourgeois le 19 mai 1892. Weymouth, N.E.: L'Evangeline, 1892. 00985. (Pre-1900 Canadiana) – 9 – cn C.I.H.M. [971]
Panganiban, Cirio H *see* THE FILIPINO NATIONAL LANGUAGE
Panger, M *see* THEOLOGIA SCHOLASTICA MORALI-POLEMICA...
PANGERAN; KUMPULAN TJERITA-PENDEK / Sitor Situmorang – SE 4479 1. 1963 – 9 – ne IDC [950]
Pangeri, Matthias *see* DAS BUCH DER MALERZECHE IN PRAG
Panglaykim, J *see*
- INDONESIA: STATE TRADING AND PRIVATE ENTERPRISE
- THE INDONESIAN ECONOMY: FACING A NEW ERA?
- AN INDONESIAN EXPERIENCE, ITS STATE TRADING CORPORATION
- INDONESIAN EXPORTS; PERFORMANCE AND PROSPECTS, 1950-1970
- MANAGEMENT; SUATU PENGANTAR
- REPORT ON BUSINESS MANAGEMENT TRAINING IN INDONESIA
- STATE TRADING CORPORATIONS IN INDONESIA: FIRST YEAR'S PERFORMANCE, 1961

PANGLIPUR WUJUNG – In Javanese. SE-4739 1. 1963 – 9 – ne IDC [950]
Pangman, John R *see* MOTOR VARIANCE OF BASKETBALLS RELATED TO KINESTHETIC SENSE IN FREE THROW SHOOTING
Pangputhipong, V *see* COUNTRY REPORT THAILAND; ...
PANHANDLE DIGEST – Chadron, NE. -w. Mar. 1947-Nov. 1948 – 1 – us NE Hist [071]
PANHANDLE PRESS – Big Springs, NE. -w. Mar. 1931-Sep. 1950 – 1 – us NE Hist [071]
LA PANHYPOCRISIADE OU LE SPECTACLE INFERNAL DE SEIZIEME SIECLE. SUITE DE LA PANHYPOCRISIADE OU LE SPECTACLE INFERNAL DU DIX-NEUVIEME SIECLE / Lemercier, Nepomucene – Paris: F. Didot, 1819. xii,403p. Paris: G. Doyen, 1837. xvi,119p. 7 fiches. (Literature Collection) – 9 – 17.00 – fr Bibl Nationale [810]
Panin, I *see* KREDITNAIA KOOPERATSIIA ZAURAL'IA
Panin, Ivan *see* THE STRUCTURE AND AUTHORSHIP OF THE NEW TESTAMENT
Panina, M *see* RABOCHI I KLASS I REVOLIUTSIONNOE DVIZHENIE V ROSSII
Panitia Pembina Djiwa Revolusi *see* PANTJAWARSA MANIPOL
Panitya Pasar Malam *see* SYUU HOOKOOKAI...
Panizza, Oskar *see* PARISJANA
Pankey, Robert B *see* THE EFFECTS OF ROAD SURFACE PITCH ON THE SUBTALAR JOINT WHILE RUNNING AT SELECTED VELOCITIES
Pankhurst, Estelle Sylvia *see* THE LIFE OF EMMELINE PANKHURST; THE SUFFRAGETTE STRUGGLE FOR WOMEN'S CITIZENSHIP
PANKRAZ VON FREYBERG AUF HOHENASCHAU : EIN BAIRISCHER EDELMANN AUS DER REFORMATIONSZEIT / Preger, Konrad – Halle: Verein fuer Reformationsgeschichte, 1893. ([Schriften des Vereins fuer Reformationsgeschichte; Bd. 40]) – 1mf – us A.T.L.A. [240]
PANMINERVA MEDICA – Turin. 1959-74*. v17-22 1975-80. v23-30 1981-88*. v31-32 1989-90. v33-36 1991-94*. v37-39 1995-97+ – 1 – D10019 – us UMI [610]
Pannier, J *see*
- L'EGLISE REFORMEE DE PARIS SOUS HENRI 4
- L'EGLISE REFORMEE DE PARIS SOUS LOUIS 13 (1610-1621)

Pannwitz, Rudolf *see* BALDURS TOD
Panola, Mississippi *see* MISCELLANEOUS EARLY NEWSPAPERS
LE PANORAMA : LE SEUL MAGAZINE EN LANGUE FRANCAISE CONSACRE AUX VUES ANIMEES – Montreal: Poirier & cie, 1919-. SEM35P44 – 1r – 1 – Can$48.00 – cn Bibl Nat [073]
O PANORAMA : PERIODICO LITTERARIO E NOTICIOSO – Pilar, Alagoas. 20 Maio 1901 – 1,5,6 – bl Biblioteca [072]
PANORAMA – Italy, 1980-1995 – 3r per y – 5,6 – Sfr695.00 – sz Infoprint [945]
PANORAMA – Los Angeles, CA. nos 669-681. 1980-1994 – 26r – 1 – $1,300.00 – R04063 – us Library Micro [071]
PANORAMA DE ESTUDIOS AFROAMERICANOS / Pollak-Eltz, A – (Cont as: Bibliografia afrovenezolana) – Caracas: Univ. Cat. Andres Bello, 1972 – 1mf – 9 – ne IDC [970]
PANORAMA DE LA LITTERATURE BULGARE CONTEMPORAINE / Hateau, G – Paris. 1937. BR-3962 2 – 8 – ne IDC [460]
PANORAMA RODOVIARIO : ORGAO INSTRUCTIVO E EDUCATIVO DO TRANSITO – Monte Alegre de Minas, 21 Aug-15 Dec 1979 – 1,5,6 – bl Biblioteca [072]
PANORAMA SOCIAL / Solar y Maeztu, Jose del – Badajoz: Imp. Emilio Hernandez, 1906 – 1 – sp Bibl Santa Ana [946]
PANORAMONDE : EDITE A MONTREAL POUR UNE DOUZAINE D'HEBDOS DU QUEBEC – Montreal, Canada. v1 n1. 24-29 fev 1964-v3 n45. 24-30 dec 1966 – 1r – 1 – Can$55.00 – cn Can Microfilming [072]
Pan-Pacific Trade Union Conference. Hankow. 1927 *see* BULLETIN OF PROCEEDINGS
PANS – (Cont by: Tropical Pest Management) – London. v1-25. 1955-79* – 1 – D17346 – us UMI [616]
PANSLAVIZM V PROSHLOM I NASTOIASHCHEM, 1878 / Pypin, AN – Spb. 1913. BR-4981 2 – 8 – ne IDC [305]
DER PANSLAWISMUS BIS ZUM WELTKRIEG / Fischel, A – Stuttgart, Berlin. 1919. BR-4904 2 – 8 – ne IDC [940]
Pantaleon, H *see* MILITARIS ORDINIS IOHANNITARVM RHODIORVM, AVT MELITENSIVM EQVITVM, ...
Panteleev, L *see* RESPUBLIKA BEZPRIZORNYKH (SHKID)
PANTEON INOSTRANNOSI SLOVESNOSTI – v. 1-3. M. 1818. B-1826 2 – 8 – ne IDC [073]
PANTEON LITERATURY – Ezhemesiachnyi istoriko-literaturnyi zhurnal. Spb. 1888-95. Lacking: 1892 (3); 1895 (2-4). B-1827 2 – 8 – ne IDC [073]
PANTHEISM AND CHRISTIANITY / Hunt, John – London: Wm Isbister, 1884 – 9 – 0-8370-3694-1 – 1985-1694 – us A.T.L.A. [210]
PANTHEISM: ITS STORY AND SIGNIFICANCE / Picton, James Allanson – Chicago: Open Court, 1907. 1 fiche – 9 – us A.T.L.A. [240]
PANTHEISM'S DESTRUCTION OF BOUNDARIES / Kuyper, Abraham – Bronxville: J.H. de Vries, 1893.1 fiche – 9 – us A.T.L.A. [210]
PANTHEON : MONATSSCHRIFT FUER FREUNDE UND SAMMLER DER KUNST – Muenchen. v1-30. 1928-42 – 203mf – 9 – ne IDC [700]
LE PANTHEON HAITIEN / Edouard, Emmanuel – Paris: A. Ghio, 1885. 76p. 1 fiche. (Miscellaneous Selections) – 9 – 6.00 – fr Bibl Nationale [290]
LE PANTHEON HUGUENOT DECOUVERT ET RUINE... / Richeome, L – Lyon, 1610 – 5mf – 9 – CA-106/1 – ne IDC [240]
THE PANTHER – Johnstown. Pa. 1930-1970 – 1 – us UMI [071]
PANTHER CREEK BAPTIST CHURCH. OHIO COUNTY, KENTUCKY : CHURCH RECORDS – Sep 1815-May 1959 – 1 – 68.22 – us Baptist [240]
PANTHER FORK BAPTIST CHURCH. MOUNT VERNON, ILLINOIS : CHURCH RECORDS – 1866-1950 – 1 – 19.08 – us Baptist [240]
PANTHER FORK MISSIONARY BAPTIST CHURCH. TEXICO, ILLIMOIS : CHURCH RECORDS – 1950-Oct 1964 – 1 – 8.82 – us Baptist [240]
PANTHEVM SIVE ANATOMIA ET SYMPHONIA PAPATVS,... / Himmlisch, J F – N.p., 1568-1569. 2 pts – 4mf – ne IDC [240]
PANTJA RAJA – Djakarta, Balai Poestaka, 1945-1947 – 35mf – 9 – ne IDC [073]
PANTJA SILA IDEOLOGI PEMERSATU / Ruslan, Abdulgani – SE 4462 1. 1962 – 9 – ne IDC [320]
PANTJA SILA PEMBENTUK KESATUAN BANGSA. INDONESIA / Sutoko Djojosubroto – SE 4853 1. 1961 – 9 – ne IDC [950]
PANTJA SILA, THE BASIS OF THE STATE OF THE REPUBLIC OF INDONESIA / Sukarno, Pres. Indonesia – SE 6136 1. 1964 – 9 – ne IDC [324]
PANTJASILA DOKTRIN REVOLUSI NASIONAL KITA / Ruslan, Abdulgani – SE 5434 1. 1964 – 9 – ne IDC [335]
PANTJASILA, THE PRIME MOVER OF THE INDONESIAN REVOLUTION / Ruslan, Abdulgani – SE 11,415 1. 1964? – 9 – ne IDC [335]
PANTJAWARNA – Djakarta. Incomplete. SE-942 1. 1948-1965 – 9 – ne IDC [073]
PANTJAWARSA MANIPOL / Panitia Pembina Djiwa Revolusi – SE-5317 1. 1964 – 9 – ne IDC [320]
PANTJAWARSA MANIPOL / Sukarno, Pres. Indonesia – SE 5658 1. 1964 – 9 – ne IDC [025]
Pantoja Idrovo de Castaneda, W *see* UN PROCESO, DOS JUICIOS ORALES Y UN RECURSO DE CASACION
Pantorba, Bernardino de *see*
- FRANCISCO DE ZURBARAN
- EL PINTOR EUGENIO HERMOSO

Panzer, Friedrich Wilhelm *see*
- DEUTSCHE FORSCHUNGEN
- ITALISCHE NORMANN IN DEUTSCHER HELDENSAGE

Panzer, G W F *see*
- DEUTSCHLANDS INSEKTENFAUNE ODER ENTOMOLOGISCHES TASCHENBUCH FUER DAS JAHR 1795
- FAUNAE INSECTORUM AMERICES BOREALIS PRODROMUS
- FAUNAE INSECTORUM GERMANICAE INITIA
- INDEX ENTOMOLOGICUS, SISTENS OMNES INSECTORUM SPECIES IN G.W.F. PANZERI FAUNA INSECTORUM GERMANICA DESCRIPTAS
- KRITISCHE REVISION DER INSEKTENFAUNE DEUTSCHLANDS NACH DEM SYSTEM BEARBEITET

PANZER GREIFEN AN / Kuersten, Hans – Leipzig: Hesse & Becker, [1942?] – 1r – 1 – us U.W. Library [830]
Panzer, Marianne *see* TANZ UND RECHT
O PAO : DA PADARIA ESPIRITUAL – Fortaleza, 10 Jul, 24 Dec 1892; 1895; Aug-Oct 1896 – 1,5,6 – bl Biblioteca [072]
O PAO : ORGAO LITTERARIO E CRITICO – [s.l.] 1890 – 1,5,6 – bl Biblioteca [072]
O PAO D'ASSUCAR : PERIODICO LITTERARIO E NOTICIOSO – Pao d Assucar, Alagoas. 25 Nov 1877-13 Jan 1878 – 1,5,6 – bl Biblioteca [072]
O PAO DE SANTO ANTONIO : ORGAO OFFICIAL E INDEPENDENTE DA PAROQUIA DE SANTO ANTONIO DE CURVELO – Curvelo, 13, 27 Aug 1950; Aug 1955; Aug-4 Nov 1962 – 1,5,6 – bl Biblioteca [072]
PAO DE SANTO ANTONIO : ORGAO DA "PIA UNIAO DO PAO DE SANTO ANTONIO" – Diamantina, 13 Feb 1916; Jul-Dec 1918; Jan, Apr 1919; Dec 1923; Nov 1925; Nov 1929; May 1930; Jan, Apr 1932; Jan 1933-Dec 1934; Jan-Feb, Apr-29 Dec 1935 – 1,5,6 – bl Biblioteca [072]
PAO EM PEDACINHOS – Arassuahy, 21 Sep 1918 – 1,5,6 – bl Biblioteca [072]
Pao, Kuang-lin *see* YEH SU TI YEN CHIN (CCC258)
Pao, Ssu-ching *see* KAMUS INDONESIA-TIONGHOA
Paoli, Betty *see* GRILLPARZER UND SEINE WERKE
Paoli, Deanna M *see* THE ITALIAN-AMERICAN COMMUNITY OF SAN FRANCISCO

Paoli, Francesco *see* DELLA VITA DI ANTONIO ROSMINI-SERBATI
Paolone, Albert M *see*
- EFFECT OF EXERCISE TRAINING ON THE FUNCTION OF THE RAT MYOCARDIUM DURING REPERFUSION FOLLOWING GLOBAL ISCHEMIA
- METABOLIC RESPONSE TO ACUTE COLD AIR EXPOSURE AND TWO LEVELS OF BETA BLOCKADE IN MALES AND FEMALES

Paolone, Vincent J *see*
- THE EFFECT OF WRIST WEIGHT ON THE HEMODYNAMIC RESPONSE TO EXERCISE IN CORONARY ARTERY DISEASE
- THE EFFECTS OF ALPHA-TOCOPHEROL ON METABOLIC DETERMINATIONS IN GRADED EXERCISE
- THE EFFECTS OF AMINO ACID SUPPLEMENTATION ON ENDURANCE PERFORMANCE
- RELATIONSHIP BETWEEN BIOELECTRICAL CONDUCTANCE AND LEAN BODY MASS FROM THREE ELECTRODE CONFIGURATIONS IN A COLLEGE-AGED POPULATION

Paolucci, G *see* ARTE PRATICA DI CONTRAPPUNTO
EL PAPA DE LAS BELLEZAS. LA SOMBRA. EL NAUFRAGO. A TODO HONOR / Trigo, Felipe – Madrid: Renacimiento, 1920 – sp Bibl Santa Ana [946]
IL PAPA, L'ITALIA E LA GUERRA / Quadrotta, Guglielmo – Milano: Rava, 1915 – 1mf – us A.T.L.A. [240]
Papa, Ramon R *see* MUNICIPIO DE ELECCION ENMIENDAS A LA CARTA DE MANILA
Papachatzis, Thanasis *see* A COMPARISON OF OFFENSIVE EFFICIENCY BETWEEN THREE TYPES OF BASKETBALL OFFENSE
THE PAPACY : ITS HISTORIC ORIGIN AND PRIMITIVE RELATIONS WITH THE EASTERN CHURCHES / Guettee, Abbe – New York: Carleton; London: S. Low, 1867, c1866 – 1mf – us A.T.L.A. [240]
THE PAPACY AND MODERN TIMES : A POLITICAL SKETCH, 1303-1870 / Barry, William Francis – New York: Henry Holt; London: Williams and Norgate, c1911. (Home university library of modern knowledge; no. 22) – 1mf – us A.T.L.A. [320]
THE PAPACY AND MODERN TIMES; A POLITICAL SKETCH, 1303-1870 / Barry, William Francis – London: Williams and Norgate, c1911 – 1 – us U.W. Library [240]
THE PAPACY AND SCHISM : STRICTURES ON MR. FOULKES' LETTER TO ARCHBISHOP MANNING / Bottalla, Paul – (Includes bibliographical references) – London: Burns, Oates, 1869 – 1mf – 9 – 0-8370-7529-7 – 1986-1529 – us A.T.L.A. [240]
PAPACY, SOCIALISM AND DEMOCRACY / Leroy-Beaulieu, Anatole – London: Chapman & Hall, 1892 – 1mf – us A.T.L.A. [320]
Papadopoli, N *see* TRATTATO...SOPRA IL SUCCESSO DELLA GUERRA, ...CONTRA... TURCO...
Papadopoulos, Chrysostomou *see* HISTORIKAI MELETAI
Papadopoulos-Kerameoos, A *see*
- ANALECTA HIEROSOLYMITIKES STACHYOLOGIAS
- ANALEKTA HIEROSOLYMITIKES STACHYOLOGIAS
- IEROSOLYMITIKE BIBLIOTHEKE

O PAPAGAIO : FOLHA LITTERARIA E RECREATIVA – Manaos, Amazonas. 6-20 Ago, 7-22 Out 1899 – 1,5,6 – bl Biblioteca [072]
O PAPAGAIO : ORGAO HUMORISTICO E NOTICIOSO – Manaos, Amazonas. 2-29 Jan 1915 – 1,5,6 – bl Biblioteca [072]
O PAPAGAIO : PERIODICO CRITICO E JOCO-SERIO – Maceio, Alagoas. 28 Jul, Set 1876; Jul 1877; Abr 1878; Ago 1879; Jan 1880; Mar 1882; Jan-Fev, Out 1883; Out 1884; Out 1885; 26 Mar 1887 – 1,5,6 – bl Biblioteca [072]
O PAPAGAIO – Rio de Janeiro, 4 May-8 Aug 1822 – 1,5,6 – bl Biblioteca [072]
IL PAPAGALLO – Bologna, Italy. -w. 2 Jan 1881-23 May 1915. 6 reels – 1 – uk British Libr Newspaper [072]
PAPAGAN – (Mueduer-i Mes'ul ve Sahibi: Orhan Seyfi[Orhon]. Nos. 25, 35-42, 45, 129 (8 Tesrinievvel 1924-23 Mayis 1926); v. sene, no. 17 (11 Temmuz 1928)) – Istanbul: Tanin Matbaasi, Vatan Matbaasi, Milliyet Matbaasi, 1924-28 – 2mf – 9 – $30.00 – us MEDOC [949]
PAPAL COMMISSION AND THE PENTATEUCH / Briggs, Charles Augustus – London: Longmans, Green, 1906. 1 fiche – 9 – us A.T.L.A. [240]
THE PAPAL CONCLAVES : AS THEY WERE AND AS THEY ARE / Trollope, Thomas Adolphus – London: Chapman and Hall, 1876 – 2mf – us A.T.L.A. [240]
THE PAPAL CONCLAVES / Pennington, Arthur Robert – London: S.P.C.K.; New York: E. & J.B. Young, 1897 – 1mf – us A.T.L.A. [240]
THE PAPAL CONSPIRACY EXPOSED, AND PROTESTANTISM DEFENDED, IN THE LIGHT OF REASON, HISTORY, AND SCRIPTURE / Beecher, Edward – New York: M W Dodd, 1855, c1854 – 1mf – 9 – 0-8370-8649-3 – 1986-2649 – us A.T.L.A. [240]
PAPAL CONTROVERSY INVOLVING THE ROMAN CATHOLIC CHURCH / Ray, D B – 1892 – 1 – 21.84 – us Baptist [240]
PAPAL INFALLIBILITY: "CATHOLIC'S REPLIES TO 'CIEOPHAS,' REFUTING THE VATICAN DOGMA: WITH PREFACE AND COPIOUS APPENDIX / Davenport, John M – St. John, N. B.: J. & A. McMillan, 1885. 03643. (Pre-1900 Canadiana) – 9 – cn C.I.H.M. [971]
THE PAPAL MONARCHY : FROM ST. GREGORY THE GREAT TO BONIFACE VIII (590-1303) / Barry, William Francis – New York: Putnam; London: T. Fisher Unwin, 1902. (The Story of the nations) – 2mf – us A.T.L.A. [320]
THE PAPAL SYSTEM : FROM ITS ORIGIN TO THE PRESENT TIME: A HISTORICAL SKETCH OF EVERY DOCTRINE, CLAIM AND PRACTICE OF THE CHURCH OF ROME / Cathcart, William – (Includes bibliographical references and index) – Philadelphia: Cathcart and Turner, 1872 – 2mf – 9 – 0-8370-8888-7 – 1986-2888 – us A.T.L.A. [240]
PAPALISM VERSUS CATHOLIC TRUTH AND RIGHT / Spencer, Jesse Ames – (Includes bibliographical references and index) – New York: Thomas Whittaker, 1896 – 1mf – 9 – 0-8370-8472-5 – 1986-2472 – us A.T.L.A. [240]
Papanikolaou, Zissis *see* ATTENTION IN YOUNG SOCCER PLAYERS
PAPARCHY AND NATIONALITY – (Includes bibliographical references) – [S.l.: s.n., ca 1874] – 1mf – 9 – 0-8370-8949-2 – 1986-2949 – us A.T.L.A. [240]
LES PAPAS DU NOUVEAU-MONDE RATTACHES A CEUX DES ILES BRITANNIQUES ET NORDATLANTIQUES / Beauvois, Eugene – Louvain: J. Istas, 1893.04070.(Pre-1900 Canadiana) – 9 – cn C.I.H.M. [900]
Papas, T *see* GESCHICHTE DER MESSGEWAENDER
Papayya Sastri, B *see* [ELEMENTS OF TELUGU GRAMMAR]
LE PAPE DU GHETO. PARIS / Fort, Gertrude von – Madrid: Razon y Fe, 1935 – 1 – sp Bibl Santa Ana [944]
PAPE ET CONCILE AU 19E SIECLE = ROME AND THE COUNCIL IN THE NINETEENTH CENTURY / Bungener, Felix – (In English) – Edinburgh: T & T Clark, 1870 – 1mf – 9 – 0-8370-8486-5 – 1986-2486 – us A.T.L.A. [240]
Pape, P *see* DIE PREDIGT UND DAS BRIEFFRAGMENT DES ARISTIDES (T.U.U. 1-12/2B)
EL PAPEL DE LA GENTE – Riverside, CA. 1976-77 – 2r – 1 – $100.00 – R02716 – us Library Micro [071]
EL PAPEL DE LOS SINDICATOS EN LOS MOMENTOS ACTUALES / Mije, Antonio – Valencia? 1937? Fiche W 1048. (Blodgett Collection of Spanish Civil War Pamphlets) – 9 – us H.U. College Libr [946]
EL PAPEL MONEDA / Subercaseaux, Guillermo – Santiago de Chile: Imprenta Cervantes, 1912. 406p. Incl. tables. 1 reel. 1272 – 1 – us U.W. Library [336]
PAPEL O ESCRITO...SOBRE LAS BEBIDAS HELADAS... / Eguia, F – S.L., S.A. – 1mf – 9 – sp Cultura [610]
PAPEL QUE RESPONDE A...DAMIAN DE MAYORGA Y GUZMAN, MEDICO...SOBRE...LA CALENTURA MALIGNA / Bernes, J – Madrid, 1647 – 1mf – 9 – sp Cultura [610]
PAPELES DE ECONOMIA ESPANOLA. FUNDACION FIES – No 01, (Madrid, 1979) – No 14, (Madrid, 1983) – 105mf – 9 – sp Cultura [946]
PAPELES DE SON ARMADANS – Palma. v1-35. apr 1956-dec 1964 – 1 – D9829 – us UMI [073]
PAPELES DEL ARCHIVO. PUBLICACIONES DEL ARCHIVO GENERAL DE LA NACION / Bayle, Constantino – Buenos Aires, 1942; Madrid: Razon y Fe, 1944 – 1 – sp Bibl Santa Ana [946]
PAPELES PROHIBIDOS / Aradillas Agudo, Antonio – Madrid: Sedmay, ediciones, 1977 – 1 – sp Bibl Santa Ana [240]
PAPER – (Former title: World's Paper Trade Review) – Tonbridge. v183-206. 1975-86 1,9; v183-84 1975*. v185-206 1976-86 5 – 1,5,9 – D10661 – us UMI [670]
THE PAPER – Guerneville, CA. 1979-1989 – 9r – 1 – $450.00 – B05039 – us Library Micro [071]
[PAPER, 3RD SERIES] / Black Sash (Society) – Johannesburg: Microfile, [19–?] – us Res Libr [960]
PAPER AND CONVERTING PRODUCT NEWS – (Cont by: Converting Product News) – San Francisco. v1. 1980* – 1 – D22233 – us UMI [680]
PAPER AND INK – Toronto: Buntin, Reid, [1895?-189- or 19–] – 9 – cn C.I.H.M. [680]
PAPER AND PACKAGING ANALYST – London. may 1990-93* 1; 1994*. 1995-97+ 1,5,9 – 1,5,9 – D21234 – us UMI [680]
PAPER AND PULP – London, UK. Jan 1906. -irr. 9 feet – 1 – uk British Libr Newspaper [072]
PAPER CONVERTERS AND ENVELOPE INDUSTRY – (Cont: Journal for Paper Converters. Cont by: Converter) – Chicago. oct 1934-dec 1937* – 1 – D12386.04 – us UMI [680]
PAPER, FILM AND FOIL CONVERTER – (Cont: American Paper Converter) – Chicago. sep 1953-dec 1978* 1; v53-71. 1979-97+ 1,5,9 – 1,5,9 – D12386.07 – us UMI [670]
PAPER INDUSTRY – (Cont by: Paper Industry Management Association, PIMA. Cont: American Paper Industry) – Arlington Heights. v59-60. jan 1977-jan 1978 – 1,5,9 – D6604.01 – us UMI [670]
PAPER INDUSTRY MANAGEMENT ASSOCIATION – PIMA *see* PAPER INDUSTRY
PAPER ON LA RESPONSIBILITE DES PROPRIETAIRES DE NAVIRES... / Autran, F C – London, 1910 – 1mf – 9 – ILM-3874/1 – ne IDC [340]
PAPER ON RAILWAY GAUGES / Fairlie, Robert Francis – London: C. Whiting, 1871. 05483. (Pre-1900 Canadiana) – 9 – cn C.I.H.M. [971]
A PAPER ON THE REVISED VERSION OF THE NEW TESTAMENT: AS READ BEFORE THE SUNDAY SCHOOL TEACHERS' ASSOCIATION OF THE DEANERY OF SAINT JOHN, ON OCTOBER 4TH, 1881 / Brigstocke, Frederick Hervey John – Saint John, N. B.: Daily Telegraph, 1891. 00276. (Pre-1900 Canadiana) – 9 – cn C.I.H.M. [240]
PAPER SALES – (v.41-. 1981-. 5,6,9) – v.1-. 1941- – 1 – us UMI [380]
PAPER: THE OLD BOYKIN HOME *see* MISCELLANEOUS BOOKS AND PAMPHLETS
PAPER TRADE JOURNAL – (Absorbed by: Pulp and Paper) – New York. v1-170. may 1872-nov 1986 1; v150-170. 1966-86 5; v160-170 1976-86 9 – 1,5,9 – D14 – us UMI [670]
PAPER TRADE REVIEW. (WORLD'S PAPER TRADE REVIEW) – London. Aug 1883-Dec 1913.-w. 57 reels – 1 – uk British Libr Newspaper [072]
PAPERBOARD PACKAGING – (Former titles: Fibre Containers, 1916-51. Fibre Containers and Paperboard Mills, dec 1951-jul 1959) – New York. v59-69 1974-84. v70-78 1985-93*. v79-82 1994-97+ 1; v59-69 1974-84. v78-79 1993-94*. v80-82 1995-97+ 5; v62-69 1977-84. v78 1993*. v79-82 1994-97+ 9 – 1,5,9 – D9828 – us UMI [670]
PAPERBOARD PACKAGING – v55. 1970 – 14mf – 9 – $5.00f – us Ross [680]
Papernov, Z A *see* SEL'SKOKHOZIAISTVENNAIA KOOPERATSIIA I STANDARTIZATSIIA SEL'SKOKHOZIAISTVENNOI PRODUKTSII
Papernyi, Z *see*
- O MASTERSTVE MAIAKOVSKOGO
- POETICHESKII OBRAZ U MAIAKOVSKOGO

PAPERS / Adams, Elmer E et al – Undated and 1860-1951, 1966, 1979 – 84r – 1 – $2,520.00 $30.00r – us M.H.S. [920]
PAPERS / Aldrich, Nelson W – 1777-1930 – 1 – 1520.00 – us L of C Photodup [920]
PAPERS / Allston, Robert FW – Governor of South Carolina from 1856-58, rice planter near Georgetown. Over 25,000p, including 2100-card index and calendar. 456 fiches – 9 – us South Carolina Historical [978]
PAPERS / American Agricultural Economics Association – 1978- – 1,5,6,9 – us UMI [630]
PAPERS / American Congress on Surveying and Mapping – v28-31. 1968-71. Continued by: Proceedings – 1 – us UMI [520]
PAPERS / American Home Missionary Society – 1816-94 – 1 – $7,480.00 – us Amistad [240]
PAPERS / American Issue Publishing Company – Ed. by Mary S. Higley. 1911-39, 1950 – 1 – us Ohio Hist [360]
PAPERS / Anti-Saloon League of America – Ed. by Mary S. Higley. 1880, 1894-1938 – 1 – us Ohio Hist [360]
PAPERS / Anti-Saloon League of America. District of Columbia – Ed. by Mary S. Higley. 1902-28 – 1 – us Ohio Hist [360]
PAPERS / Anti-Saloon League of America. Office of General Counsel and Legislative Superintendent – Ed. by Mary S. Higley. 1883-1933 – 1 – us Ohio Hist [360]
PAPERS / Anti-Saloon League of America. Ohio – Ed. by Mary S. Higley. 1894-95, 1902-33 – 1 – us Ohio Hist [360]
PAPERS / Anzalone, Charles – 1937-1970 – 1r – 1 – us I.H.R.C. [920]
PAPERS / Arthur, Chester A – 1843-1926 – 1 – 54.00 – us L of C Photodup [920]
PAPERS / Bacon, Anthony – Lambeth Palace Library. With printed list – 1 – £395.00 – uk World [941]
PAPERS / Baird, George W – 1874-91 – 1 – us KS Hist [920]
PAPERS / Baker, Ray Stannard – 1836-1947 – 1 – 2231.00 – us L of C Photodup [920]
PAPERS / Ball Family – 1731-1864. Rice planters of St. John's Parish, Charleston District. 3000p.Includes 58p calendar.52 fiches – 9 – us South Carolina Historical [978]
PAPERS / Baptist Association. Louisiana. – 1955, 1957-87 – 1 – $64.88 – us Baptist [240]
PAPERS / Baptist Missionary and Educational Convention. Indian Territory – 1883-1905 – 1 – $29.96 – us Baptist [240]
PAPERS / Baptist Missionary and Educational Convention. Oklahoma and Indian Territories – Jun 25-27, 1896, 1901, 1903-07 – 1 – $24.50 – us Baptist [240]
PAPERS / Baptist Missionary Association. Texas – 1901-50. 2,390p – 1 – 83.65 – us Baptist [240]
PAPERS / Baptist World Alliance, Fifth Congress, Berlin – 1934 – 1 – 10.01 – us Baptist [240]
PAPERS / Barth Family – 1877-1972 – 1 – us KS Hist [920]
PAPERS / Bayard, James A & Bayard, Richard H – 1797-1899 – 1 – 81.00 – us L of C Photodup [920]
PAPERS / Baynton, Wharton & Baynton, Morgan – 1757-87. (In Pa. State Archives). 10 reels. Guide – 1 – us Penn Hist [920]
PAPERS / Beach, Abijah Ives – 1863-69 – 1 – us KS Hist [920]
PAPERS / Bell, John – 1815-61 – 1 – 19.00 – us L of C Photodup [920]
PAPERS / Bibliographical Society of America – Chicago. v1-73. 1899-1979 – 11r – 1 – us Ross [070]
PAPERS / Biddle, Nicholas – 1681-1931 – 1 – 967.00 – us L of C Photodup [920]
PAPERS / Bingham, John A – 1840-1913. There are 5 35mm rolls in this set. Related Guide Book included in purchase of set of 5 rolls; may be purchased separately from publisher – 1 – us Ohio Hist [978]
PAPERS / Black, Jeremiah S – 1813-1904 – 1 – 747.00 – us L of C Photodup [920]
PAPERS / Blackwell family – 1848-1957 – 1 – 1356.00 – us L of C Photodup [920]
PAPERS / Blaine, James G – 1 – 378.00 – us L of C Photodup [920]
PAPERS / Blennerhassett, Harman – 1755-1866 – 1 – 52.00 – us L of C Photodup [920]
PAPERS / Bouquet, Henry – 1754-65. Printed Index – 1 – £740.00 – uk World [975]
PAPERS / Bowen, T J – 1846-76.Revised version, 1988; Nigerian Baptist – 1 – us Baptist [240]

PAPERS / Boyen, Herman von – c1787-1848. 12 rolls. M207. (World War II Collection of Seized Enemy Records) – 1 – us Nat'l Archives [920]
PAPERS / Bradlaugh, Charles – 1833-91 – uk Microform Academic [941]
PAPERS / Braunschweig-Bevern, August Wilhelm Herzog von – 1717-81. 1 roll. M954 – 1 – us Nat'l Archives [324]
PAPERS / British and Colonial Emigration Fund – London, 1870? 00864. (Pre-1900 Canadiana) – 9 – cn C.I.H.M. [971]
PAPERS / Brook Farm – 1842-61.1 reel. (Massachusetts Historical Society) – 1 – us UMI [975]
PAPERS / Brown, Ethan A – Ed. by Linda E. Kalette. 1806-45 – 1 – us Ohio Hist [978]
PAPERS / Brown, James – 1843-51. BRRAM – 1 – uk Microform Academic [970]
PAPERS / Brown, John – 1821-1961. Ed. by Kenneth W. Duckett. There are 9 35mm rolls in this set. Related Guide Book included in purchase of set of 9 rolls; may be purchased separately from publisher – 1 – us Ohio Hist [978]
PAPERS / Brown, John – 1826-1948, Correspondence and business records of John Brown and correspondence with family members and others about him. This is the complete John Brown collection at the Kansas State Historical Society; John Brown documents from other sources are on rolls MS-61 and MS-799.03 – 1 – us KS Hist [920]
PAPERS / Brown, John – 1849-60 – 1 – us KS Hist [920]
PAPERS / Buchanan, James & Johnston, Harriet L – 1825-87 – 1 – 78.00 – us L of C Photodup [920]
PAPERS / Calhoun, John C – 1 – 110.00 – us L of C Photodup [920]
PAPERS / Cambridge, George – 1838-1900. From Royal Archives, Windsor Castle – 1 – uk Microform Academic [941]
PAPERS / Cameron, Simon – 1738-CA.1919 – 1 – 463.00 – us L of C Photodup [920]
PAPERS / Carlson, Frank – Sept.-Dec. 1954 – 1 – us KS Hist [920]
PAPERS / Carter, Thomas H – 1883-1917 – 1 – 316.00 – us L of C Photodup [920]
PAPERS / Carver, George Washington – 1864-1943. 67 reels – 1 – us UMI [630]
PAPERS / Catt, Carrie Clinton Chapman – 1848-1950 – 1 – 370.00 – us L of C Photodup [920]
PAPERS / Chandler, Zachariah – 1854-99 – 1 – 93.00 – us L of C Photodup [920]
PAPERS / Chapman, Samuel M – 1866-1906. Douglas A. Bakken, ed. 10 reels. Printed guide – 1 – us UMI [920]
PAPERS / Chase, Salmon Portland – 1824-72 – 1 – 720.00 – us L of C Photodup [920]
PAPERS / Cherrington, Ernest H – 1900-50. Ed. by Laruel Bowen. 110 reels in set. Guide available – 1 – us Ohio Hist [978]
PAPERS / Cherrington, Ernest H – undated, Cherrington was a prominent prohibitionist – 1 – us KS Hist [920]
PAPERS / Chesnut, James et al – Mss. and personal papers of James Chesnut, Jr., U.S. Senator, 1858-60; Stephen D. Miller, Governor, 1828-31, U.S. Senator, 1831-33; John L. Manning, Governor, 1852-54. Cotton planters of Kershaw and Sumter Counties. Over 6000p, including 1600-card index and a calendar. 115 fiches – 9 – us South Carolina Historical [978]
PAPERS / Christian Faith Society – 17th-19th centuries. With printed index – 1 – £480.00 – uk World [240]
PAPERS / Clay, Henry – 1770-1910 – 1 – 463.00 – us L of C Photodup [920]
PAPERS / Cleveland, Grover – 1826-1945 – 1 – 3,388.00 – us L of C Photodup [920]
PAPERS / Cole Family – 1870-1981, "My Life on the Frontier," a reminiscence by Lizzie May Cole; a letter from Samuel Asa Cole; and the journals of Wallace Shively Cole – 1 – us KS Hist [920]
PAPERS / Colfax, Schuyler – 1837-82 – 1 – 26.00 – us L of C Photodup [920]
PAPERS / Comly, James M – 1856-1926. Ed. by Andrea D. Lentz. There are 3 35mm rolls in this set. Related Guide Book included in purchase of set of 3 rolls; may be purchased separately from publisher – 1 – us Ohio Hist [978]
PAPERS / Conkling, Roscoe – 1769-1895 – 1 – 26.00 – us L of C Photodup [920]
PAPERS / Connelley, William Elsey – 1906-1930, Relating to Indian folklore, the Pawnee Indians, and Manabozho – 1 – us KS Hist [305]
PAPERS / Coolidge, Calvin – 1921-29 – 1 – 4,019.00 – us L of C Photodup [920]
PAPERS : THE CORRESPONDENCE AND WRITINGS OF A CROATIAN WHO LIVED AND TRAVELLED IN U.S. CROATIAN COMMUNITIES / Lupis-Vucic, Ivo F – 1912-1957 – 18r – 1 – us I.H.R.C. [920]
PAPERS / Coxey, Jacob S, Sr – 1874-1976. Ed. by Linda E. Kalette – 1 – us Ohio Hist [025]
PAPERS / Crittenden, John Jordan – 1782-1888 – 1 – 295.00 – us L of C Photodup [920]
PAPERS / Cross Family – 1870-1982, Letters; land records; biographies; photographs; obituaries; certificates; school records, reports, and announcements; reminiscences; autographs and poetry; and genealogical information relating to the White, Cross, McKee, Franklin, Jones, Zehner, Taylor, Sage, and other families – 1 – us KS Hist [920]
PAPERS / Curry, William L – 1832-1926. Ed. by Joyce E. Harman. There are 6 35mm rolls in this set. Related Guide Book included in purchase of set of 6 rolls; may be purchased separately from publisher – 1 – us Ohio Hist [978]
PAPERS / Danish Baptist General Conference of America – 1931 – 1 – 8.89 – us Baptist [240]
PAPERS / Davis, Jefferson – 1835-1913 – 1 – 38.00 – us L of C Photodup [920]
PAPERS / Davison, Newman and Co., Ltd – 1753-1897. From Guildhall Library, London. BRRAM – 1 – uk Microform Academic [970]
PAPERS / Dekalb County Historical Society – Biog. and hist. sketches. 2 fiches. F-0680 – 9 – us A.G.L.L. [978]
PAPERS / Donelson, Andrew J – 1779-1943 – 1 – 295.00 – us L of C Photodup [920]
PAPERS / Donnelly, Ignatius – (Research Note Cards. 4 rolls including filmed inventory. $120.00; $30.00r; 1) – 1812, 1836-1943.167 reels – 1. $4950.00; 1 – $35.00r; t – us M.H.S. [920]
PAPERS / Doolittle, James R – 1858-1927 – 1 – 26.00 – us L of C Photodup [920]
PAPERS / Doster, Frank – 1922-32 – 1 – us KS Hist [920]
PAPERS / Douglass, Frederick – 1841-1964 – 1 – 672.00 – us L of C Photodup [920]
PAPERS / Dunbar, Paul Laurence – 1873-1936. Ed. by Sara S. Fuller. There are 9 35mm rolls in this set. Related Guide Book included in purchase of set of 9 rolls; may be purchased separately from publisher – 1 – us Ohio Hist [978]
PAPERS / Eddy, Elizabeth Ann (Berryman) – 1 – us KS Hist [920]
PAPERS / Eichmann, Adolph – 1 – uk Microform Academic [920]
PAPERS / Emerson, Caleb – 1795-1905. Ed. by Susan Pruul. There are 6 35mm rolls in this set. Related Guide Book separate purchase from: Western Reserve Historical Society, 10825 East Boulevard, Cleveland, Ohio 44106 – 1 – us Ohio Hist [978]
PAPERS / Ewing, Thomas, Sr – (Includes guide) – 1815-72 – 6r – 1 – $240.00 – us U.N.D. Archives [920]
PAPERS / Featherstonhaugh, George W – 1771-1856. 10 reels – 1 – $300.00; $35.00r – us M.H.S. [920]
PAPERS / Ferrua, Pietro – Nine articles on the First International Anarchist Symposium, Portland, 1980 – 9 – 1.00f – at Libertarian Micro [335]
PAPERS / Fessenden, William P – 1832-78 – 1 – 109.00 – us L of C Photodup [920]
PAPERS / Fitch, John – 1783-1854 – 1 – 58.00 – us L of C Photodup [920]
PAPERS / Francis, Edmund – 1860's – 1 – us KS Hist [920]
PAPERS / Frankfurter, Felix – 1882-1965 – 1 – 3795.00 – us L of C Photodup [920]
PAPERS / Freewill Baptist Associations. Yearly Conference. Maine. 1799-1814 – 1 – $5.00 – us Baptist [240]
PAPERS / Funston, Frederick – 1 – us KS Hist [920]
PAPERS / Furnas, Robert W – 1844-1905. Douglas A. Bakken, ed. 13 reels. Printed guide – 1 – us UMI [920]
PAPERS / Garfield, James A – 1848-81 – 1 – 3,640.00 – us L of C Photodup [920]
PAPERS / Genet, Edmond C – 1756-1895 – 1 – 858.00 – us L of C Photodup [920]
PAPERS / Germany. Reichsamt fuer Bodenforschung – 7rolls. T401. Finding Aids: GG26. (Captured German Records Filmed at Alexandria, VA.) – 1 – us Nat'l Archives [630]
PAPERS / Gibbes, Lewis R – 1793-1894 – 1 – 168.00 – us L of C Photodup [920]
PAPERS / Giddings, Joshua R – 1821-66. There are 5 35mm rolls in this set. Related Guide Book included in purchase of set of 5 rolls; may be purchased separately from publisher – 1 – us Ohio Hist [978]
PAPERS / Gladden, Washington – 1847-1921, 1970. Ed. by Gary J. Arnold. Related Guide Book included in purchase of set of 52 rolls; may be purchased separately from publisher – 1 – us Ohio Hist [978]
PAPERS / Gleason, Arthur H – 1863-1931 – 1 – 160.00 – us L of C Photodup [920]
PAPERS / Gneisenau, August von – c1785-1831. 43 rolls. M211. (World War II Collection of Seized Enemy Records) – 1 – us Nat'l Archives [920]
PAPERS / Grant, Ulysses – 1844-1908 – 1 – 660.00 – us L of C Photodup [920]
PAPERS / Great Britain. Colonial Defence Commission Under Lord Carnarvon – 1881-82 – 1 – £95.00 – uk World [941]
PAPERS / Green, John P – 1869-1910. Ed. by Olivia J. Martin. There are 6 35mm rolls in this set. Related Guide Book separate purchase from: Western Reserve Historical Society, 10825 East Boulevard, Cleveland, Ohio 44106 – 1 – us Ohio Hist [978]
PAPERS / Green, William – 1891-1952. Labor history. AFL President, 1924-52. AFL Exec. Board, 1913. Related papers and organizations – 1 – us Ohio Hist [330]
PAPERS / Griffing, James Sayre – 1841-99 – 1 – us KS Hist [920]
PAPERS / Griffing, James Sayre – 1854-81 – 1 – us KS Hist [920]
PAPERS / Grimke Family – 1761-1866. 13 fiches – 9 – us South Carolina Historical [978]
PAPERS / Groener, Wilhelm – 27 rolls. M137. (World War II Collection of Seized Enemy Records) – 1 – us Nat'l Archives [920]
PAPERS / Hadley-Allen Family – 1854-94 – 1 – us KS Hist [920]
PAPERS / Hamilton, Alexander – 1708-1903 – 1 – 961.00 – us L of C Photodup [920]
PAPERS / Hammond, James H – 1823-75 – 1 – 421.00 – us L of C Photodup [920]
PAPERS / Harding, Warren G; ed by Lentz, Andrea D – (There are 263 35mm rolls in this set. Related Guide Book included in purchase of set of 263 rolls. May be purchased separately from publisher) – 1888-1923 – 1 – us Ohio Hist [920]
PAPERS / Harrison, Benjamin – 1787-1938 – 1 – 3,158.00 – us L of C Photodup [920]
PAPERS / Harrison, William Henry – 1734-1939 – 1 – 48.00 – us L of C Photodup [920]
PAPERS / Harvey, Charles Thompson – 1858-1872 – 2r – 1 – $32.50r – us Archival [920]
PAPERS / Haupers, Clement B & Mairs, Clara Gardner – 1918-1983. 4 rolls including filmed inventory – 1 – $30.00r – us M.H.S. [920]
PAPERS / Hay, John – 1785-1914 – 1 – 478.00 – us L of C Photodup [920]
PAPERS / Hayes, Max S – 1891-1949. Ed. by Joyce E. Harman. Related Guide Book included in purchase of set of 2 rolls; may be purchased separately from publisher – 1 – us Ohio Hist [025]
PAPERS / Haynes, William Casper – 1862-1897, Letters and papers relating to his military service in Company D, 11th Kansas Cavalry – 1 – us KS Hist [350]
PAPERS / Herbert, Hilary A – 1878-1931. University of North Carolina Library. Guide – 1 – $36.00 – us U.N.C. Southern Hist [976]
PAPERS / Hertzler, Arthur Emanuel – 1898-1970 – 1 – us KS Hist [920]
PAPERS / Higginson, Thomas Wentworth – 1855-60 – 1 – us KS Hist [920]
PAPERS / Holker, John – 1777-1822 – 1 – 457.00 – us L of C Photodup [920]
PAPERS / Holliday, Cyrus Kurtz – undated – 1 – us KS Hist [920]
PAPERS / Hotchkiss, Jedediah – 1845-99 – 1 – 1160.00 – us L of C Photodup [920]
PAPERS / Huntington, Samuel; ed by Kalette, Linda E – 1776-1946 – 1 – us Ohio Hist [978]
PAPERS / Indian Rights Association – 1864-1973. 136 reels – 1 – us UMI [305]
PAPERS / Ingalls, John James and Family – (Scrapbooks. 1) – 1818-1950 – 1 – us KS Hist [920]
PAPERS / Intercollegiate Prohibition Association – Ed. by Mary S. Higley. 1885-1940, 1963 – 1 – us Ohio Hist [360]
PAPERS / International Congress of Folklore – 16-22 Aug 1954. Sao Paulo, Brazil. 1954? – 1 – us I.U. Libraries [390]
PAPERS / Ireland, John – 1825-1948. 23r – 1 – $805.00; $40.00 – us M.H.S. [920]
PAPERS / Iturbide, Agustin – 1799-1880 – 1 – 422.00 – us L of C Photodup [920]
PAPERS / Jackson, Andrew – 1775-1860 – 1 – 1,469.00 – us L of C Photodup [920]
PAPERS / Jay, John – 1776-94 – 1 – 26.00 – us L of C Photodup [920]
PAPERS / Jefferson, Thomas – 1606-1889 – 1 – 1,261.00 – us L of C Photodup [920]
PAPERS / Johnson, Andrew – 1814-1900 – 1 – 1,164.00 – us L of C Photodup [920]
PAPERS / Johnson, Martin & Johnson, Osa – 1 – us KS Hist [920]
PAPERS / Johnson, Tom L – Ed. by Raimund E. Goerler. 1901-08 – 1 – us Ohio Hist [978]
PAPERS / Johnston, Frances Benjamin – 1864-1952 – 1 – 85.00 – us L of C Photodup [920]
PAPERS / Johnston, Harriet L & Buchanan, James – 1825-87 – 1 – 78.00 – us L of C Photodup [920]
PAPERS / Jones, John Paul – 1775-88 – 1 – $65.00 – us L of C Photodup [976]
PAPERS / Jordan, David Starr; ed by Palmer, Patricia – 1861-1964. 1979. 187 reels. Includes name index (3 reels) and guide. Minimum order-50.00 – 1 – 2760.00; 18.00r – us S.U. Libraries [370]
PAPERS / Kellogg, Frank B – 1890-1942 – 54r – 1 – $1890.00; $40.00r – us M.H.S. [920]
PAPERS / Kitchin, Claude – 1879-1926, 1935-36. University of North Carolina Library. Guide – 1 – $156.00 – us U.N.C. Southern Hist [978]
PAPERS / Klein, Mary Frances Goldmann – 1942-1946. WAC overseas duty in WWII – 2r – 1 – $32.50r – us Archival [920]
PAPERS / Kovatch-McMillan-Botkin Family – 1833-1984, Family members lived in Kansas and Indiana – 1 – us KS Hist [920]
PAPERS / Lanman, Charles – 1789-1895 – 1 – 20.00 – us L of C Photodup [920]
PAPERS / Lehmann, G W – 1841-79. Material from Oncken Archives, Hamburg, Germany. 2330p – 1 – 81.55 – us Baptist [240]
PAPERS / Leicester Secular Society – 1852-1943 – 1 – uk Microform Academic [240]
PAPERS / Lincoln, Abraham – 1833-1917 – 1 – 1,900.00 – us L of C Photodup [920]
PAPERS / London Corresponding Society – 1 – uk Microform Academic [025]
PAPERS / Long, Chester I – 1890-1928. In Kansas State Historical Society. Guide – 1 – us KS Hist [978]
PAPERS / Lucas Family – 1795-1925. 142 fiches – 9 – us South Carolina Historical [978]
PAPERS / McBridge, F Scott – undated, Papers of the noted prohibitionist – 1 – us KS Hist [920]
PAPERS / McClellan, George Brinton – 1 – 1,848.00 – us L of C Photodup [920]
PAPERS / McCoy Family – 1826-95 – 1 – us KS Hist [920]
PAPERS / McKinley, William – 1847-1902 – 1 – 2,070.00 – us L of C Photodup [920]
PAPERS / McKinney, Edmund – 1847-1916, Papers of the Presbyterian mission to the Iowa, Oto, and Omaha Indians, Bellevue, Nebraska – 1 – us KS Hist [920]
PAPERS / McLean, John M – 1817-61 – 1 – 377.00 – us L of C Photodup [920]
PAPERS / Madison, James – 1723-1859 – 1 – 577.00 – us L of C Photodup [920]
PAPERS / Masters, William Gallio – undated, Correspondence, interviews, clippings, articles, research notes, and bibliographies relating to the west, trails, battles, Indians, and the Oregon Trail centennial – 1 – us KS Hist [920]
PAPERS / Maxwell, Manuel – 1853-1901. Douglas A. Bakken, ed. 8 reels. Printed guide – 1 – us UMI [920]
PAPERS / Meigs, Montgomery C. – 1849-92 – 1 – 590.00 – us L of C Photodup [920]

PAPERS / Meigs, Return J – Ed. by Linda E. Kalette. 1798-1945 – 1 – us Ohio Hist [978]
PAPERS / Memminger, Christopher G – 1821-75. University of North Carolina Library. Guide – 1 – $18.00 – us U.N.C. Southern Hist [920]
PAPERS / Methodist minister, Ohio. Caddy, Charles Chester – 1852-1897 – 1r – 1 – $32.50r – us Archival [978]
PAPERS / Middleton Place. Dorchester County. South Carolina – ca. 1781-1889. 338 fiches. (Courtesy of the Middleton Place Foundation, 1981) – 9 – us South Carolina Historical [978]
PAPERS / Minier, A M – 1823-69 – 1 – us KS Hist [920]
PAPERS / Missionary Society of Connecticut – 1759-1948. 20 reels – 1 – us UMI [240]
PAPERS / Moltke, Helmuth Carl Bernhard von – 1800-91. 6 rolls. M960 – 1 – us Nat'l Archives [324]
PAPERS / Monroe, James – 1758-1839 – 1 – 220.00 – us L of C Photodup [920]
PAPERS / Morrill, Justin S – 1825-1923 – 1 – 1,083.00 – us L of C Photodup [920]
PAPERS / Morris, Gouverneur – 1771-1816 – 1 – 127.00 – us L of C Photodup [920]
PAPERS / Morris, Robert – 1775-1829 – 1 – 253.00 – us L of C Photodup [920]
PAPERS / Morse, Samuel FB – 1791-1944 – 1 – 656.00 – us L of C Photodup [920]
PAPERS / Morton, J Sterling – 1849-1902. Douglas A. Bakken, ed. 78 reels. Printed guide (.25) – apply; 1UM; 1 – us UMI [920]
PAPERS / Murphy, Edgar G – 1891-1913. University of North Carolina Library. Guide – 1 – $18.00 – us U.N.C. Southern Hist [240]
PAPERS / Myers, George A – 1890-1929. Ed. by Thomas J. Rieder. Related Guide Book included in purchase of set of 8 rolls; may be purchased separately from publisher – 1 – us Ohio Hist [978]
PAPERS / Nasmyth, James – 1836-1922 – 1 – uk Microform Academic [920]
PAPERS / National Nonpartisan League – 1910-28 – 18r – 1 – $540.00; $35.00r – us M.H.S. [025]
PAPERS / National Woman's Party – 1913-74 – 1 – us UMI [360]
PAPERS / National Woman's Party – 1913-74 – 1 – us UMI [025]
PAPERS / New England Emigrant Aid Company – 1854-1909. In Kansas State Historical Society. Guide – 1 – us KS Hist [976]
PAPERS / North Texas Baptists Convention. 1880-85. East Baptist Convention, 1877-84 – 378p – 1 – 13.23 – us Baptist [240]
PAPERS / Oberholtzer, Ernest C – Undated and 1856-1980's – 52r – 1 – $1,820.00 $40.00r – us M.H.S. [920]
PAPERS / Oncken, Johann Gerhard – Material from Oncken Archives. Hamburg, Germany. 3200p – 1 – 112.00 – us Baptist [240]
PAPERS / Packer, John – c.1616-25 – 1 – uk Microform Academic [920]
PAPERS / Partridge, Alden – 1807-59 – 1 – 45.00 – us L of C Photodup [920]
PAPERS / Pickens, Francis W & Bonham, Milledge L – 1837-1920 – 1 – $45.00 – us L of C Photodup [920]
PAPERS / Pierce, Franklin – 1820-69 – 1 – 127.00 – us L of C Photodup [920]
PAPERS / Place, Francis – British Museum – 1 – uk Microform Academic [920]
PAPERS / Polish Association of Ohio – 1907-1930 – 1r – 1 – us I.H.R.C. [305]
PAPERS / Polk, James K – 1775-1891 – 1 – 1,518.00 – us L of C Photodup [920]
PAPERS / Poole, John E – 1900-1954. Great Lakes shipping materials – 2r – 1 – $32.50r – us Archival [920]
PAPERS / Porte, Albert – Private papers, documents and newspapers from Liberia. 10 reels – 1 – 395.50 – us African Imprint [960]
PAPERS / Prior, Matthew – From Bath. Archives (Marquess), Longleat. Index included. 1664-1721 – 1 – uk Microform Academic [920]
PAPERS / Prohibition Party – Ed. by Mary S. Higley. 1868-1933 – 1 – us Ohio Hist [360]
PAPERS / Quick, Birney McNabb – 1930-84.6 rolls including filmed inventory – 1 – $30.00r – us M.H.S. [920]
PAPERS / Quimby, Phineas P – 1859-66 – 1 – 65.00 – us L of C Photodup [920]
PAPERS / Quirnheim, Christoph Emanuel Hermann Ritter Mertz von – 1866-1947. 2 rolls. M958 – 1 – us Nat'l Archives [324]
PAPERS / Rauschenbusch, August – Material from Oncken Archives, Hamburg, Germany. 2705p – 1 – 94.67 – us Baptist [240]
PAPERS / Religious Education Association. Southern Baptist Convention – 1926-61. (Southwestern Baptist, R.E.A. Books, Southeastern, Southwestern and Western) – 1 – 125.54 – us Baptist [240]
PAPERS / Reynolds, Thomas C – 1862-66 – 1 – 26.00 – us L of C Photodup [920]
PAPERS / Rhodes-Livingstone Institute – 7 – uk Microform Academic [960]
PAPERS / Roberts, Edmund – 1 – $65.00 – us L of C Photodup [920]
PAPERS / Rochdale Equitable Pioneers – 1 – uk Microform Academic [330]
PAPERS / Roon, Albrecht, Graf von – 1803-79. 2 rolls. M956 – 1 – us Nat'l Archives [324]
PAPERS / Roosevelt, Theodore – 1759-1919 – 1 – 9,387.00 – us L of C Photodup [920]
PAPERS / Russell, Howard Hyde – 1842-1946 – 1 – us Ohio Hist [978]
PAPERS / Ruthenberg, Charles E – Ed. by Gary J. Arnold. 1906-66 – 1 – us Ohio Hist [978]
PAPERS / Sabbath School and Colportage Union – 1865-67, 1873, 1877-84, 1886-90, 1892, 1899-1900. 478p – 1 – 16.73 – us Baptist [240]
PAPERS / St Clair, Arthur – Ed. by Linda E. Kalette. 1746-1882 – 1 – us Ohio Hist [920]
PAPERS / Scharnhorst, Gerhard Johann David von – 1775-1813. 12 rolls. M959 – 1 – us Nat'l Archives [324]
PAPERS / Schellenberg, Theodore R – 1921-1970, Papers relating to activities, travels, and work as assistant archivist of the United States – 1 – us KS Hist [920]
PAPERS / Scheulh, Heinrich – 1864-1942. 1 roll. M957 – 1 – us Nat'l Archives [324]
PAPERS / Schlieffen, Alfred, Graf von – 1833-1913. 8 rolls. M961 – 1 – us Nat'l Archives [324]
PAPERS / Schmidt, Mary Emilia Schwandt – 1862-1939 – 1r – 1 – $30.00 – us M.H.S. [920]
PAPERS / Schoolcraft, Henry Rowe – 1788-1906 – 1 – 1,437.00 – us L of C Photodup [920]
PAPERS / Schurz, Carl – 1842-1932 – 1 – 2,520.00 – us L of C Photodup [920]
PAPERS / Scientific Temperance Federation – Ed. by Laurel Bowen. Temperance & Prohibition Papers. 1881-1934 – 1 – us Ohio Hist [978]
PAPERS / Shafter, William R – 1826-1938. 7 reels. Guide available separately-3.00. Minimum order: 50.00 – 1 – 140.00; 20.00r – us S.U. Libraries [920]
PAPERS / Sheridan, Philip H – General correspondence, letterbooks, dispatches, telegrams, reports, orders, scrapbooks relating to Sheridan's role in the Civil War battles and postwar campaigns against the plains Indians. 104 reels, including register – 1 – $2,704.00 $23.00r – us L of C Photodup [920]
PAPERS / Sherman, William T – 1810-96 – 1 – 1,176.00 – us L of C Photodup [920]
PAPERS / Sherman, William Tecumseh – (Includes guide) – 1808-91 – 15r – 1 – $600.00 – us U.N.D. Archives [920]
PAPERS / Short, William – 1778-1853 – 1 – 646.00 – us L of C Photodup [920]
PAPERS / Sibley, Henry H – (Research Note Cards. 2 rolls including filmed inventory. 15.00r; 1) – 1815-1930 – 32r – 1 – $960.00; $35.00r – us M.H.S. [920]
PAPERS / Sickles, Daniel E – 1859-1911 – 1 – 67.00 – us L of C Photodup [920]
PAPERS / Simerwell, Ann – 1851-1854, Papers of the daughter of Robert Simerwell while she was at boarding school – 1 – us KS Hist [920]
PAPERS / Simerwell, Robert – 1822-1867, Letters and other papers of the noted Baptist Indian missionary – 1 – us KS Hist [920]
PAPERS / Skillman, Isaac – 1864-1925 – 1r – 1 – $32.50r – us Archival [976]
PAPERS / Slight, Joseph – 1874-1957. Ed. M. Higley. 6 reels – 1 – us Ohio Hist [978]
PAPERS / Society for the Propagation of the Gospel – Early 18th century. Lambeth Palace Library. With printed index – 1 – uk World [240]
PAPERS / The South Sea Company – 1711-1856. Printed index – 1 – £1,195.00 – uk World [900]
PAPERS / Southern Historical Society – 1876-1943 – 1 – us UMI [978]
PAPERS / Southern Historical Society – v1-5, 1876-Jun 1878. F-1841/F-1845 – 9 – us A.G.L.L. [977]
PAPERS / Southern Historical Society – v1-52. 1876-1959 – 1,5,6 – us Princeton Micro [978]
PAPERS / Spencer Family (Kalida, Ohio) – 1830-1938 – 1r – 1 – $32.50r – us Archival [920]
PAPERS / Squier, Ephraim George – 1841-88 – 1 – 295.00 – us L of C Photodup [920]
PAPERS / Stanton, Elizabeth Cady – 1 – 96.00 – us L of C Photodup [920]
PAPERS / Stephens, Alexander H – 1784-1886 – 1 – 1,184.00 – us L of C Photodup [920]
PAPERS / Stewart, Ethelbert – 1877-1933. University of North Carolina Library. Guide – 1 – $36.00 – us U.N.C. Southern Hist [310]
PAPERS / Taft, William H – 1810-1930 – 1 – 14,025.00 – us L of C Photodup [920]
PAPERS / Taliaferro, Lawrence – (Research Note Cards. 1 roll including filmed inventory. $30.00; 1) – 1813-68 – 4r – 1 – $120.00; $35.00r – us M.H.S. [920]
PAPERS / Tappan, Benjamin – 1795-1900 – 1 – 214.00 – us L of C Photodup [920]
PAPERS / Tappan, Lewis – 1809-1903 – 1 – 129.00 – us L of C Photodup [920]
PAPERS / Taylor, James W – (Research Note Cards. 1 roll including filmed inventory. 15.00; 1) – 1834-92 – 10r – 1 – $300.00 $35.00r – us M.H.S. [920]
PAPERS / Taylor, Zachary – 1814-31 – 5 – 28.00 – us L of C Photodup [920]
PAPERS / Terrell, Mary Church – 1851-1962 – 1 – 598.00 – us L of C Photodup [920]
PAPERS / Terrill, Robert H – 1884-1925 – 1 – 96.00 – us L of C Photodup [920]
PAPERS / Texas. Baptist Associations – 1879-1979 – 1 – us A.B.H.S. [240]
PAPERS / Thornton, William Wheeler – 1741-1858 – 1 – 253.00 – us L of C Photodup [920]
PAPERS / Trades Council. Dublin – 1 – uk Microform Academic [941]
PAPERS / Trumbull, Lyman – 1843-94 – 1 – $463.00 – us L of C Photodup [920]
PAPERS / Tyler, John – 1691-1918 – 1 – 45.00 – us L of C Photodup [920]
PAPERS / U.S. Bureau of Indian Affairs. St. Louis Superintendency – 1807-55 – 1 – us KS Hist [324]
PAPERS / U.S. National War Labor Board – (With printed guide) – 1918-19 – 22r – 1 – $2,115.00 – 0-89093-711-7 – us UPA [330]
PAPERS / U.S. Select Commission on Immigration and Refugee Policy – (Pt 1, Meetings, Consultations, Legal Materials, Selected Subject Files and Staff Report with Appendices: 11r $1,200.00 ISBN 0-89093-580-7; Pt 2, Records of Regional Hearings: 13r $1,430.00 ISBN 0-89093-581-5) – 1 – us UPA [324]
PAPERS / Usher, John Palmer – undated, Papers of the man who became Lincoln's Secretary of the Interior – 1 – us KS Hist [920]
PAPERS / Van Buren, Martin – 1787-1868 – 1 – 765.00 – us L of C Photodup [920]
PAPERS / Van Marum, Martinus – 7 – uk Microform Academic [920]
PAPERS / Vermont Baptist Historical Society – 1786-1917 – 1 – $166.60 – us Baptist [240]
PAPERS / Wade, Benjamin Franklin – 1832-81 – 1 – 233.00 – us L of C Photodup [920]
PAPERS / Walker, Thomas – 1744-1835 – 1 – $148.00 – us L of C Photodup [920]
PAPERS / Warmoth, Henry C – 1798-1934. University of North Carolina Library. Guide – 1 – $396.00 – us U.N.C. Southern Hist [976]
PAPERS / Washburn, George P – 1879-1921, Noted Ottawa, KS, architect's papers – 1 – us KS Hist [920]
PAPERS / Washington, Booker T. – 1882-1942 – 1 – us L of C Photodup [920]
PAPERS / Washington, George – 1592-1937 – 1 – 2,586.00 – us L of C Photodup [920]
PAPERS / Waterton, Charles – 1782-1865 – 1 – uk Microform Academic [920]
PAPERS / Webster, Daniel – 1800-1855 – 1 – $168.00 – us L of C Photodup [920]
PAPERS / West, Aaron & West, Mary – 1842-1898 – 3r – 1 – $32.50r – us Archival [920]
PAPERS / Whitbread, Samuel – 1807-15. BRRAM – 1 – uk Microform Academic [240]
PAPERS / White, Wesley D – 1747-1982. 61 fiches – 9 – us South Carolina Historical [978]
PAPERS / Whitefield, Edwin & Whitefield, Wilfred J – 1854-71. 1 roll including filmed inventory – 1 – $30.00r – us M.H.S. [920]
PAPERS / Wilhelm 3, Friedrich – 1770-1840. 1 roll. M955 – 1 – us Nat'l Archives [324]
PAPERS / Wilkinson, Spenser – 1881-1935 – 1 – uk Microform Academic [920]
PAPERS / William J. Sullivan Collection/Arnold McMahan – 1863-1929 – 1r – 1 – $32.50r – us Archival [976]
PAPERS / Williams, Howard Y – 1924-46 – 20r – 1 – $700.00 $45.00r – us M.H.S. [920]
PAPERS / Williams, Micajah T – Ed. by Linda E. Kalette. 1741, 1802-1906 – 1 – us Ohio Hist [978]
PAPERS / Wilson, Woodrow – 1786-1944 – 1 – 9663.00 – us L of C Photodup [920]
PAPERS / Winterfeldt, Hans Karl von – 1707-57. 2 rolls. M953 – 1 – us Nat'l Archives [324]
PAPERS / Wisconsin. Land Tenure Center – 1965-69, n.1-68 – 1,5 – us Spaulding [630]
PAPERS / Woman's Christian Temperance Union; ed by Higley, Mary S – 1853-1939 – 1 – us Ohio Hist [360]
PAPERS / Women's Trade Union League – 1895-1921. From Congress House, London – 1 – uk Microform Academic [330]
PAPERS / Wood, Samuel Newitt – 1885-1897, Correspondence and other papers of this noted peripatetic Kansan involved in almost every major event in Kansas' early history – 1 – us KS Hist [920]
PAPERS / World League Against Alcoholism; ed by Higley, Mary S – 1900-36 – 1 – us Ohio Hist [360]
PAPERS / Worthington, Thomas; ed by Kalette, Linda E – 1731, 1779-1907 – 1 – us Ohio Hist [978]
PAPERS.. / Nicodemus Colony – 1 – us KS Hist [978]
THE PAPERS / Prankard, Graffin – 1712-57. From The Dickinson Papers. BRRAM – 1 – uk Microform Academic [920]
PAPERS, 1776-1865 / Sargent, Winthrop; ed by Kalette, Linda E – 1 – us Ohio Hist [920]
PAPERS, 1793-1794 / Wayne, Anthony – 1 – $50.00 – us Presbyterian [975]
PAPERS 1854-1910 / Cape of Good Hope. South Africa. Parliament – Cape Town: Cape Times Ltd., etc.. Includes government reports, documents, correspondence, petitions, etc., but excluding the select committee reports of both houses, which have a separate numbering system – 1 – us U.W. Library [960]
PAPERS, 1854-1916. (MIMEO.) : AN INVENTORY. COLLECTION EMORY UNIVERSITY / Wilson, A W – Atlanta, USA – 1mf – 9 – ne IDC [972]
PAPERS, 1854-1924 : AN INVENTORY. COLLECTION EMORY UNIVERSITY / Allen, Y J – n.d. – 1mf – 9 – ne IDC [950]
PAPERS, 1866-1936 / Seeckt, Hans von – 28 rolls. M132. (World War II Collection of Seized Enemy Records) – 1 – us Nat'l Archives [920]
PAPERS 1874-78 / Mississippi Valley Trading Company – BRRAM – 1 – uk Microform Academic [976]
PAPERS, 1876-1962 / Lee, E E – 11,132p – 1 – $389.62 – us Baptist [240]
PAPERS, 1887-1964 : AN INVENTORY. COLLECTION EMORY UNIVERSITY. ATLANTA, U.S.A. / Burke, W B – n.d. – 1mf – 9 – ne IDC [950]
PAPERS 1913-1923 / Roche, Josephine – 1913-1923 – 1r – 1 – us I.H.R.C. [920]
[PAPERS, 1913?-1924?] / Paranjpye, Raghunath Purushottam; ed by Ellinwood, DeWitt – New Delhi: Nehru Memorial Museum & Library, [19–?] – us Res Libr [950]
PAPERS, 1913-1969 / Eastman, George Herbert – (Excluding publ) – Suva, Fiji – 11r – 1 – PMB1073 – at Pacific Mss [240]
PAPERS, 1913-1975 / Steadman, Hilda Mary – Suva, Fiji – 1r – 1 – PMB1074 – at Pacific Mss [240]

PAPERS, 1914-1919 / Khaparde, G S; ed by Ellinwood, DeWitt – (Filmed with: Selections from the Home Political Files 1914-16, 1918 and the Army Department Filed 1914-may 1919...) – New Delhi: National Archives of India, 1969 – us Res Libr [950]
PAPERS, 1914-1920 / Indian National Congress. All-India Congress Committee; ed by Ellinwood, DeWitt – (Filmed with: Thakurdas, Purshottamdas: Papers, 1917?-1957) – New Delhi: Nehru Memorial Museum & Library, [19–?] – us Res Libr [950]
PAPERS, 1916-1925 / Jayakar, M R; ed by Ellinwood, DeWitt – (Filmed with: Selections from the Home Political Files jul 1914-16, 1918 and the Army Department Files 1914-may 1919...) – New Delhi: National Archives of India, 1969 – us Res Libr [950]
PAPERS, 1917?-1957 / Thakurda, Purshottamdas; ed by Ellinwood, DeWitt – New Delhi: Nehru Memorial Museum & Library, [19–?] – us Res Libr [950]
PAPERS, 1936-1952 / Porter, Howard N – Ed. by Mary Higley – 1 – us Ohio Hist [025]
PAPERS, 1937-1964 / Hepple, Alexander – Chicago: Uni of Chicago, Photodup Dept, [1977] Boxes 1-8 – us Res Libr [920]
PAPERS, 1946-1987 / Tuilovoni, Setareki – Suva, Fiji – 3r – 1 – PMB1072 – at Pacific Mss [240]
PAPERS, 1959-1992 / Fanua, Tupou Posesi – Tonga – 2r – 1 – PMB1058 – at Pacific Mss [980]
PAPERS AND ADDRESSES...: IMPERIAL FEDERATION AND COLONISATION, FROM 1880 TO 1894 / Brassey, Thomas & Brassey, Earl; ed by Arthur H – Arranged and Loring and R. J. Beadon. London: Longmans – 9 – cn C.I.H.M. [971]
PAPERS AND BOOKS RELATING TO 1698-1763 / Mackworth of Gnoll (Neath), Humphrey – 1 – uk Microform Academic [920]
PAPERS AND CORRESPONDENCE / Haldimand, Frederick – 1758-84. Unpublished official and private papers and correspondence. Printed Index – 1 – £4,250.00 – uk World [975]
PAPERS AND CORRESPONDENCE : SUFFRAGE-RELATED MATERIAL OWNED BY THE STOWE-DAY FOUNDATION, HARTFORD / Hooker, Isabella B; ed by Margolis, A J – (With guide index) – 145mf – 9 – $5.00f – us Ross [920]
PAPERS AND CORRESPONDENCE OF ROYAL D. SIMONS / Simons, Royal D. – 1813-32 – 1 – us KS Hist [978]
PAPERS AND DISCUSSIONS / American Academy of Medicine. Conference on Prevention of Infant Mortality. 1909, New Haven, CT – 347p. diagrs – 1 – us U.W. Library [610]
PAPERS AND DISCUSSIONS OF THE ROYAL TOWN PLANNING INSTITUTE / Town Planning Institute. London, England – 1914/15-1922/23. With printed Finding List – 1 – £35.00 – uk Altair [710]
PAPERS AND MINUTES OF MEETINGS OF PRINCIPAL WORLD WAR 2 ALLIED MILITARY CONFERENCES / U.S. Department of State – 1941-45. 4 rolls. M995 – 1 – us Nat'l Archives [324]
PAPERS AND MONOGRAPHS / American Academy in Rome – v. 16. 1955 – 1 – us NY Public [073]
PAPERS AND PROCEEDINGS / Canadian Political Science Association – v1-6 1913-34 – 1 – cn Precision [320]
PAPERS AND RECORDS / Ramsey, Alexander – (Research Note Cards. 3 rolls including filmed inventory. $90.00 $30.00r 1) – 1829-1903 – 70r – 1 – $2100.00 $35.00r – us M.H.S. [920]
PAPERS AND RECORDS / Wentworth Historical Society – v2-3. 1899-1902 – 1 – cn Precision [978]
PAPERS AND SCRAPBOOK OF LEWIS WALTER KEPLINGER / Keplinger, Lewis Walter – 1 – us KS Hist [978]
PAPERS AND SERMONS OF E.C. DARGAN / Dargan, Edwin Charles – 1893-1913. 8,560p – 1 – us Baptist [240]
PAPERS AND SERMONS OF WILLIAM HARRISON WILLIAMS, SR. / Williams, William Harrison, Sr – 1840-93. 6874p – 1 – $240.59 – us Baptist [240]
PAPERS ANDREW PICKENS / Pickens, Andrew – 1782-1804. 1 fiche – 9 – us South Carolina Historical [025]
PAPERS AS PRESIDENT OF SBC, 1946-48 / Newton, Louis Devotie – Manuscript and correspondence. Indexed on reel. 350p – 1 – us Baptist [240]
PAPERS, C. 1883-1968 / Witts Family – (Bulk: 1900-13) – 1r – 1 – PMB1075 – at Pacific Mss [920]
PAPERS CONTRIBUTED TO THE WORKSHOP ON STRATEGIES FO THE MANAGEMENT OF FISHERIES AND AQUACULTURE IN MANGROVE ECOSYSTEMS, AND COUNTRY STATUS REPORTS ON INLAND FISHERIES : PRESENTED AT THE 3RD SESSION OF THE IPFC WORKING PARTY OF EXPERTS ON INLAND FISHERIES; BANGKOK, 1986 / IPFC – 1987 – 254p – it F.A.O. [338]
PAPERS CONTRIBUTED TO THE WORKSHOP ON THE USE OF CYPRINIDS IN THE FISHERIES MANAGEMENT OF LARGER INLAND WATER BODIES OF THE INDO-PACIFIC : AND, COUNTRY REPORTS PRESENTED AT THE 4TH SESSION OF THE INDO-PACIFIC FISHERY COMMISSION WORKING PARTY OF EXPERTS ON INLAND FISHERIES; KATHMANDU, 1988 / IPFC – 1989 – 185p – it F.A.O. [338]
PAPERS: CORRESPONDENCE, CLIPPINGS, MANUSCRIPTS AND BOOK OF THE FAMILY / Warder Family – In Va., Ky., Ill. 1934. 186p – 1 – 6.51 – us Baptist [920]
PAPERS DELIVERED FROM THE ADMIRALTY RELATIVE TO THE WAR WITH AMERICA / Great Britain. Admiralty – N.p., 1815 – 4mf – 1 – ILM-2919/1 – ne IDC [327]
PAPERS: DIARIES, NOTEBOOKS AND REPORTS / Wilson, Gilbert L – 41v (1905-29) from larger collection of Wilson Papers, most of which record his anthropological studies of Hidatsa and Mandan Indians of the Fort Berthold Reservation, North Dakota. Also, studies of Dakota Indians of Standing Rock Reservation, North and South Dakota – 5r – 1 – $150.00 $30.00r – us M.H.S. [978]
PAPERS FROM THE AMERICAN INSTITUTE OF ARCHITECTS LIBRARY AND ARCHIVES / ed by American Institute of Architects – (AIA Awards Program 122r $8,125 (also available in mf). Proceedings 1867-1931 12r $520. Outgoing correspondence 20r $1,820. Papers of the Western Association of Architects 1884-89 4r $300. All 3 coll with Papers 158r $10,100) – Washington, D.C.: AIA, 1995 – 154r – 1 – $9,900.00 for 3 coll – Dist. us Ross – us A.I.A. [720]
PAPERS FROM THE ANNUAL MEETING / American Congress on Surveying and Mapping – (Papers from the 1st-27th meeting no published. Cont by: Proceedings of the American Congress on Surveying and Mapping annual meeting) – Washington. v28-31. 1972-1979* – 1 – D12486 – us UMI [520]
PAPERS FROM THE ANNUAL MEETING-AMERICAN CONGRESS ON SURVEYING AND MAPPING ANNUAL MEETING *see* PROCEEDINGS
PAPERS FROM THE BUCCLEUCH AND QUEENSBURY MUNIMENTS / Townshend, Charles – 1765-1767. BRRAM – 1 – uk Microform Academic [025]
PAPERS IN LINGUISTICS – (Cont by: Research on language and social interaction) – Edmonton. v1-19. jul 1969-86 1; v4-6 jul 1971-win 1973. v8-9 1975-76. v10-11 1977-78*. v12 1979. v13-19 1980-86* 5; v10-19. 1977-86 9 – 1,5,9 – D5417 – us UMI [400]
PAPERS IN LINGUISTICS MONOGRAPH SERIES – (Material for 1971 was not available for filming) – Edmonton. 1970-73 – 1 – D5846 – us UMI [400]
PAPERS IN THE TAMIL LANGUAGE ON MATTERS OF PUBLIC BUSINESS : WITH A GLOSSARY OF TECHNICAL TERMS IN TAMIL AND ENGLISH / Robertson, Andrew – London: W H Allen, 1890 – us Res Libr [350]
PAPERS, JOURNALS, LETTERS, SERMONS, ETC OF HEZEKIAH SMITH / Smith, Hezekiah – 609p – 1 – $21.31 – us Baptist [240]
PAPERS, MS 484 / Guilford, Linda Thayer – 1855-1906 – 1r – 1 – us Western Res [920]
PAPERS, MS 522 / Lee, Wau – 1873-75. 1 reel – 1 – us Western Res [920]
PAPERS, MS 777 / Oviatt Family – 1814-76. 1 reel – 1 – us Western Res [920]
PAPERS, MS 1085 / Wickham, Gertrude van Rensselaer – 1887-1911. 1 reel – 1 – us Western Res [920]
PAPERS, MS 1746 / Upton, Harriet Taylor – 1893-1916. 1 reel – 1 – us Western Res [920]
PAPERS, MS 2347 / Trumbull, Jonathan – 1787-1811. 1 reel – 1 – us Western Res [920]
PAPERS, MS 2729 / Elijah Wadsworth Family – (Includes a 7-pg guide) – 1792-1868 – 2r – 1 – us Western Res [920]
PAPERS, MS 3132 / Humphrey, George Magoffin – (Includes a 24-pg guide) – 1912-70 – 26r – 1 – us Western Res [300]
PAPERS, MS 3370 / Chesnutt, Charles W – (Correspondence, speeches, other writings) – 1891-1932 – 1r – 1 – us Western Res [920]
PAPERS, MS 3479 / Manry, Robert A – 1 Jun-17 Aug 1965. Log entries of 78-day crossing of the Atlantic in Tinkerbelle, a 13 1/2 foot sloop – 1 – us Western Res [920]
THE PAPERS OF A. PHILIP RANDOLPH / ed by Bracey, John H, Jr & Meier, August – (Includes a printed guide) – 35r – 1 – $3,850.00 – 1-55655-024-3 – us UPA [320]
THE PAPERS OF AARON BURR, 1756-1836 / Burr, Aaron – 27r – 1 – us UMI [920]
THE PAPERS OF A.J. MUSTE, 1920-1967 / Muste, A J – (With printed guide. From the Swarthmore College Peace Collection) – 1990 – 39r – 1 – $3,315.00 – D3251 – us Scholarly Res [331]
THE PAPERS OF ALBERT GALLATIN : INCLUDES 1985 SUPPLEMENT / Gallatin, Albert; ed by Prince, Carl E & Fineman, Helene H – (With guide 1972-85. Suppl only 5r $375.00) – 51r – 1 – $4,335.00 – S1613-14 – us Scholarly Res [920]
PAPERS OF ALBIN K. LONGREN / Longren, Albin K – 1911-47 – 1 – us KS Hist [978]
THE PAPERS OF ALEXANDER HAMILTON – 34r – 1 – $1.190.00 – Dist. us Scholarly Res – us L of C Photodup [323]
THE PAPERS OF ALEXANDER STEPHENS – 57r – 1 – $1,995.00 – Dist. us Scholarly Res – us L of C Photodup [976]
PAPERS OF ALFRED GRAF VON SCHLIEFFEN, 1833-1913 – M961 – $184.00 – 8r – us Nat'l Archives [355]
THE PAPERS OF ANDREW DONELSON – 14r – $490.00 – us L of C Photodup [976]
THE PAPERS OF ANDREW JACKSON, 1770-1845 : A MICROFILM SUPPLEMENT / ed by Moser, Harold D et al – (With printed guide and index) – 39r – 1 – $3,315.00 – S1625 – us Scholarly Res [920]
PAPERS OF ARTHUR MIDDLETON / Middleton, Arthur – 1767-83. 10 fiches – 9 – us South Carolina Historical [025]
PAPERS OF AUGUST BELMONT, JR., 1827-1965 / Belmont, August – (Engineering, opening, and operation of Cape Cod Canal) – Massachusetts Historical Society – 5r – 1 – us UMI [920]
PAPERS OF AUGUST VON GNEISENAU, CA. 1785-1831 – 43r – $989.00 – M211 – us Nat'l Archives [355]
THE PAPERS OF AUGUSTUS SAINT-GAUDENS – 55r – 1 – $865.00 set – us Dartmouth [730]
PAPERS OF AUGUSTUS SAINT-GAUDENS, 1848-1907 / Saint-Gaudens, Augustus – 55r – 1 – $4045.00 – us UMI [920]
PAPERS OF BASIL MANLY, JR. / Manly, Basil Jr. – 1840-92. 3236p – 1 – $113.26 – us Baptist [240]
PAPERS OF BASIL MANLY, JR. / Manly, Basil Jr. – (Papers, 1863-64. 116p. $5.00; 1) – 1842-1891. 440p – 1 – $15.40 – us Baptist [240]
THE PAPERS OF BENJAMIN BROWN FRENCH – 13r – 1 – $455.00 – Dist. us Scholarly Res – us L of C Photodup [976]
PAPERS OF BENJAMIN COLMAN, 1641-1763 / Colman, Benjamin – Massachusetts Historical Society – 1r – 1 – $85.00 – us UMI [920]
PAPERS OF BENJAMIN FRANKLIN / Franklin, Benjamin – 1726-1907 – 12r – 1 – $420.00 – Dist. us Scholarly Res – us L of C Photodup [975]
THE PAPERS OF BENJAMIN FRANKLIN WADE – 11r – 1 – $385.00 – Dist. us Scholarly Res – us L of C Photodup [976]
THE PAPERS OF BENJAMIN TAPPAN – 11r – 1 – $385.00 – Dist. us Scholarly Res – us L of C Photodup [976]
PAPERS OF BETTY GANNETT, 1929-1970 / Gannett, Betty – (With printed guide £22) – 17r – 1 – £1,050.00 – uk Chadwyck [920]
PAPERS OF BOSTON CORBETT / Corbett, Boston – 1854-1913 – 1 – us KS Hist [978]
PAPERS OF CAMPBELL, PRESTON AND FLOYED FAMILIES / Campbell Family – 1741-1925 – 1 – $152.00 – us L of C Photodup [920]
THE PAPERS OF CARL SCHURZ – (With guide) – 125r – 1 – $4,375.00 – Dist. us Scholarly Res – us L of C Photodup [975]
THE PAPERS OF CARLOS MONTEZUMA, M.D / Montezuma, Carlos; ed by Larner, John W Jr & Huppert, Thomas C – (With printed guide) – 1984 – 9r – 1 – $765.00 – S1618 – us Scholarly Res [920]
THE PAPERS OF CARRIE CHAPMAN CATT – 18r – 1 – $630.00 – Dist. us Scholarly Res – us L of C Photodup [320]
PAPERS OF CHARLES COTESWORTH PINCKNEY / Pinckney, Charles Cotesworth – 1775-1817. 2 fiches – 9 – us South Carolina Historical [025]
THE PAPERS OF CHARLES EVANS HUGHES – 150r – 1 – $5,250.00 – Dist. us Scholarly Res – us L of C Photodup [340]
PAPERS OF CHARLES FRANCIS ADAMS 2, 1861-1933 / Adams, Charles Francis – Massachusetts Historical Society – 55r – 1 – $4280.00 – us UMI [920]
PAPERS OF CHARLES SUMNER / Sumner, Charles; ed by Palmer, Beverly Wilson – (With printed guide and index £58) – 85r – 1 – £4,630.00 – uk Chadwyck [976]
THE PAPERS OF C.J. BLOMFIELD, BISHOP OF LONDON – 1828-1855. 250mf with printed guide – £850.00 – uk World [240]
PAPERS OF CLARINA IRENE (HOWARD) CARPENTER NICHOLS / Nichols, Clarina Irene (Howard) Carpenter – 1842-1904 – 1 – us KS Hist [978]
THE PAPERS OF CORDELL HULL – (With guide) – 118r – 1 – $4,130.00 – Dist. us Scholarly Res – us L of C Photodup [977]
PAPERS OF COUNT CIANO (LISBON PAPERS) RECEIVED FROM THE DEPARTMENT OF STATE – 4r – $69.00 – T816 – us Nat'l Archives [324]
THE PAPERS OF DANIEL C. FRENCH – 44r – 1 – $1,540.00 – Dist. us Scholarly Res – us L of C Photodup [730]
THE PAPERS OF DANIEL E. SICKLES – 5r – 1 – $175.00 – Dist. us Scholarly Res – us L of C Photodup [355]
PAPERS OF DANIEL MURRAY, 1881-1955 / Murray, Daniel – (With printed guide £17.00) – 27r – 1 – £1,545.00 – uk Chadwyck [920]
THE PAPERS OF DANIEL WEBSTER – 8r – 1 – $280.00 – Dist. us Scholarly Res – us L of C Photodup [975]
THE PAPERS OF DANIEL WEBSTER – (With Guide and Index) – 41r – 1 – $550.00 set – us Dartmouth [975]
PAPERS OF DANIEL WEBSTER, 1798-1852 / Webster, Daniel – (16,000 items in chronological order under headings General Correspondence, Business Papers, Congressional Papers, and State Department Papers) – 41r – 1 – $2780.00 – us UMI [920]
PAPERS OF DAVID AMES WELLS / Wells, David Ames – 1759-1898 – 9r – 1 – $315.00 – Dist. us Scholarly Res – us L of C Photodup [330]
PAPERS OF DAVID DUNCAN WALLACE / Wallace, David Duncan – 1822-1970. 632 fiches – 9 – us South Carolina Historical [025]
THE PAPERS OF DR. ADAM CLARKE / Lloyd, Gareth – (Coll title: The People Called Methodists, Phase 1: Reference Tools) – Manchester, 1991 – 2mf – 9 – MP-609/1 – ne IDC [240]
THE PAPERS OF EDMOND C. GENET – 41r – 1 – $1,435.00 – Dist. us Scholarly Res – us L of C Photodup [944]
PAPERS OF EDWARD VERNON AND SIR CHARLES WAGER / Vernon, Edward – 1654-1773 – 1 – $142.00 – us L of C Photodup [920]
THE PAPERS OF EDWIN DOAK MEAD AND LUCIA AMES MEAD, 1876-1936 / Mead, Edwin Doak & Mead Lucia Ames – (With printed guide. From the Swarthmore College Peace Collection) – 11r – 1 – $935.00 – D3252 – us Scholarly Res [920]
PAPERS OF EDWIN MCCANN / McCann, Edwin – 1884-1916 – 1 – us KS Hist [978]

THE PAPERS OF ELEANOR ROOSEVELT, 1933-45 / Roosevelt, Eleanor – (With printed guide) – 20r – 1 – $2,065.00 – 0-89093-925-X – us UPA [920]

PAPERS OF ELEAZAR WHEELOCK / Wheelock, Eleazar – (History of Dartmouth College, the Indian Charity School, and Hanover, NH) – Dartmouth College Library Collections – 16r – 1 – $775.00 – us UMI [920]

THE PAPERS OF ELEAZAR WHEELOCK / Wheelock, Eleazar – (Includes guide) – 16r – 1 – $160.00 set – us Dartmouth [370]

PAPERS OF ELI THAYER / Thayer, Eli – 1851-91 – 1 – us KS Hist [978]

THE PAPERS OF ELIZABETH CADY STANTON AND SUSAN B. ANTHONY / Stanton, Elizabeth Cady & Anthony, Susan B; ed by Gordon, Ann & Holand, Patricia – (Guide and Index $50.00 S3165.G) – 1991 – 45r – 1 – $3,825.00 – S3165 – us Scholarly Res [920]

THE PAPERS OF EMILY GREENE BALCH, 1875-1961 / Balch, Emily Greene; ed by Shane, Martha P – (With printed guide) – 26r – 1 – $2,210.00 – S3051 – us Scholarly Res [920]

PAPERS OF EPHRAIM BLAINE / Blaine, Ephraim – 1766-1805 – 1 – $109.00 – us L of C Photodup [920]

PAPERS OF EUGENE V. DEBS, 1834-1945 / Debs, Eugene V – 21r – 1 – $1540.00 – us UMI [920]

THE PAPERS OF FELIX FRANKFURTER – (With guide) – 165r – 1 – $5,775.00 – Dist. us Scholarly Res – us L of C Photodup [340]

PAPERS OF FRANCIS B. LOOMIS / Loomis, Francis B – 1835-1959. 9 reels. Includes guide. Minimum order: $50.00 – 1 – $180.00; $20.00r – us S.U. Libraries [025]

THE PAPERS OF FRANK O. SALISBURY (1874-1962) / Peacock, Alison – (Coll title: The People Called Methodists, Phase 1: Reference Tools) – Manchester, 1989 – 1mf – 9 – MP-610/1 – ne IDC [240]

PAPERS OF FRASER-WINTHROP / Fraser-Winthrop – ca1700-ca1905. 4 fiches – 9 – us South Carolina Historical [025]

PAPERS OF FREDRICK DOUGLASS – (With guide) – 34r – 1 – $1,190.00 – Dist. us Scholarly Res – us L of C Photodup [976]

PAPERS OF GEN. HANS DON SEECKT, 1866-1936 – 28r – $644.00 – M132 – us Nat'l Archives [355]

PAPERS OF GEN. WILHELM GROENER, 1867-1939 – 27r – $621.00 – M137 – us Nat'l Archives [355]

THE PAPERS OF GENERAL FRIEDRICH WILHELM VON STEUBEN, 1777-1794 / Steuben, Friedrich Wilhelm Baron von; ed by Zemenszky, Edith von & Schulmann, Robert J – (With guidebook) – 1984 (mf ed) – 7r – 1 – us Ross [920]

THE PAPERS OF GENERAL NATHANAEL GREENE : PART 1: DEC 23 1766-JULY 31 1780 / Greene, Nathanael; ed by McCarthy, Robert E – (With printed guide) – 4r – 1 – $340.00 – S3164 – us Scholarly Res [920]

PAPERS OF GEORGE AND MARY STEARNS / Stearns, George Luther & Stearns, Mary E – 1856-1901 – 1 – us KS Hist [978]

THE PAPERS OF GEORGE C. MARSHALL : SELECTED WORLD WAR 2 CORRESPONDENCE – (Comes with printed guide) – 40r – 1 – $4,760.00 – 1-55655-455-9 – us UPA [355]

PAPERS OF GEORGE WASHINGTON CARVER, 1864-1943 – 67 reeels – 1 – $3380.00 – us UMI [920]

PAPERS OF GERHARD JOHANN DAVID VON SCHARNHORST, 1775-1813 – 12r – $276.00 – M959 – us Nat'l Archives [355]

PAPERS OF GERMAN DIPLOMATS (NACHLASSE AND ASSERVATE), 1833-1927. (AMERICAN HISTORICAL ASSOC. PROJECT 2) – 25r – 1 – T291 – us Nat'l Archives [943]

THE PAPERS OF GIDEON WELLES – 36r – 1 – $1,260.00 – Dist. us Scholarly Res – us L of C Photodup [355]

PAPERS OF GRAF HELMUTH CARL BERNHARD VON MOLTKE, 1800-1891 – 6r – $138.00 – M960 – us Nat'l Archives [355]

PAPERS OF GREAT BRITISH STATESMEN AND POLITICIANS, SERIES 1 : THE PAPERS AND CORRESPONDENCE OF CHARLES JAMES FOX, 1749-1806 – British Library, London. Additional mss. 47559-47581. Holland House Papers additional manuscripts 51457-51475 – 1 – us Primary [920]

PAPERS OF GREAT BRITISH STATESMEN AND POLITICIANS, SERIES 2 : THE PAPERS OF SIR JAMES GRAHAM, HOME SECRETARY, STATESMAN AND REFORMER – Part 1: General Series, 1820-60. Part 2: Old Files Series, 1829-34; Irish Files, 1842-46 – 1 – us Primary [360]

PAPERS OF GRENVILLE CLARK / Clark, Grenville – 1882-1967. 15mf. Printed portfolio – 9 – $10.00 – us Dartmouth [920]

THE PAPERS OF HAMILTON FISH – 24r – 1 – $840.00 – Dist. us Scholarly Res – us L of C Photodup [975]

THE PAPERS OF HANNAH CLOTHIER HULL, 1889-1958 / Hull, Hannah Clothier – (With printed guide. From the Swarthmore College Peace Collection) – 6r – 1 – $510.00 – D3250 – us Scholarly Res [920]

THE PAPERS OF HENRY A. WALLACE AS VICE-PRESIDENT / Wallace, Henry Agard – 1941-44.54 rolls – 1 – us Roosevelt [920]

PAPERS OF HENRY DEMAREST LLOYD, 1840-1937 / Lloyd, Henry Demarest – (With printed guide £27.00) – 52r – 1 – £2,745.00 – uk Chadwyck [920]

PAPERS OF HENRY FLEMING / Fleming, Henry – 1772-1795. BRRAM – 1 – uk Microform Academic [975]

THE PAPERS OF HENRY WILLIAM ELLSWORTH, 1845-1849 / Ellsworth, Henry William – 4r – 1 – A1176 – us Nat'l Archives [324]

PAPERS OF HERMAN VON BOYEN, CA. 1787-1849 – 12r – $276.00 – M207 – us Nat'l Archives [355]

PAPERS OF HUGH DUNN FISHER / Fisher, Hugh Dunn – 1867-1911 – 1 – us KS Hist [978]

PAPERS OF I.J. VAN NESS / Van Ness, IJ – Van Ness as Edit. Secretary, 1911-17; as Exec. Secretary, 1917-35 of the Sunday School Board, SBC. 90,610p – 1 – $3,171.35 – us Baptist [240]

THE PAPERS OF JAMES A. FARLEY – 54r – 1 – $1,890.00 – Dist. us Scholarly Res – us L of C Photodup [977]

THE PAPERS OF JAMES KENT – 7r – 1 – $245.00 – Dist. us Scholarly Res – us L of C Photodup [340]

PAPERS OF JAMES WILKENSON LEGARE CLEMENT, JR. / Clement, James Wilkenson Legare, Jr. – 1895-1912. 7 fiches – 9 – us South Carolina Historical [025]

THE PAPERS OF JEDEDIAH HOTCHKISS – 61r – 1 – $2,135.00 – Dist. us Scholarly Res – us L of C Photodup [976]

PAPERS OF JOHN A. ANDREW, 1772-1895 / Andrew, John A – Massachusetts Historical Society – 43r – 1 – $3235.00 – us UMI [920]

PAPERS OF JOHN AND JAMES VERDIER / Verdier, John Mark & Verdier, James Robert – 1802-72. 2 fiches – 9 – us South Carolina Historical [025]

PAPERS OF JOHN AND LUGENIA BURNS HOPE / Hope, John & Hope, Lugenia (Burns) – 21r with printed guide – 1 – $2,310.00 – 0-89093-696-X – us UPA [360]

THE PAPERS OF JOHN C. CALHOUN – 6r – 1 – $210.00 – Dist. us Scholarly Res – us L of C Photodup [975]

PAPERS OF JOHN CHARLES NICHOLSON / Nicholson, John Charles – 1884-1916 – 1 – us KS Hist [978]

THE PAPERS OF JOHN D. ROCKEFELLER, SR. – (Pt 1: Business Correspondence, 1877-1893. 13r ISBN 1-55655-394-3. $1,430.00; Pt 2: Business Investments Correspondence, 1881-1893. 10r ISBN 1-55655-395-1. $1,105.00; Pt 3: Office Correspondence, 1879-1894. 42r ISBN 1-55655-396-X. $4,620; Pt 4: Index to the John D. Rockefeller Letterbooks at the Rockefeller Archive Center. 1r ISBN 1-55655-397-8. $110.00. With printed guides) – 66r – 1 – $6,900.00 – us UPA [650]

PAPERS OF JOHN DAVIS / Davis, John – 1775-83 – 5r – 1 – $175.00 – us L of C Photodup [355]

THE PAPERS OF JOHN ETTWEIN – 1 – us Primary [240]

THE PAPERS OF JOHN FOSTER DULLES AND OF CHRISTIAN A. HERTER, 1953-1961 : THE CHRONOLOGICAL CORRESPONDENCE SERIES – (With printed guide) – 24r – 1 – $2,310.00 – 0-89093-890-3 – us UPA [324]

THE PAPERS OF JOHN FOSTER DULLES AND OF CHRISTIAN A. HERTER, 1953-1961 : THE WHITE HOUSE CORRESPONDENCE AND MEMORANDA SERIES – (With printed guide) – 9r – 1 – $900.00 – 0-89093-891-1 – us UPA [324]

THE PAPERS OF JOHN FOSTER DULLES AND OF CHRISTIAN A. HERTER, 1953-61 : MINUTES OF TELEPHONE CONVERSATIONS / Dulles, John Foster & Christian A Herter – 1980. (Presidential Documents Series) – 1 – $1,060.00 – 0-89093-356-1 – us UPA [977]

THE PAPERS OF JOHN HOLKER – 20r – 1 – $700.00 – Dist. us Scholarly Res – us L of C Photodup [380]

PAPERS OF JOHN JOHNSON / Johnson, John – 1888-89. 11 fiches – 9 – us South Carolina Historical [025]

THE PAPERS OF JOHN JORDAN CRITTENDEN – 14r – 1 – $490.00 – Dist. us Scholarly Res – us L of C Photodup [976]

PAPERS OF JOHN L. LEWIS, 1879-1969 / Lewis, John L – (With printed guide £22.00) – 4r – 1 – £235.00 – uk Chadwyck [920]

PAPERS OF JOHN PAUL JONES / Jones, John Paul – 1776-77 – 1mf – 9 – us South Carolina Historical [975]

PAPERS OF JOHN PAUL JONES / Jones, John Paul; ed by Bradford, James C – (With printed guide £44.00) – 10r – 1 – £630.00 – uk Chadwyck [920]

THE PAPERS OF JOHN PAUL JONES – 4r – 1 – $140.00 – Dist. us Scholarly Res – us L of C Photodup [355]

THE PAPERS OF JOHN PEABODY HARRINGTON IN THE SMITHSONIAN INSTITUTION / ed by Mills, Elaine L – (Pt 1: Alaska-Northwest Coast 1982 30r $2,400. Pt 2: Northern and Central California 1985 101 $8,080. Pt 3: Southern California-Basin 1986 182r $14,560. Pt 4: Southwest 1986 58r $4,640. Pt 5: Plains 1987 17r $1,360. Pt 6: Northeast/Southeast 1987 18r $1,440. Pt 7: Mexico/Central America/South America 36r $2,880. Pt 8: Notes and Writings on Special Linguistic Studies 35r $2,800. Pt 9: Correspondence and Financial Reports $1,360) – 1907-57 – 1 – $35,520.00 coll – us Ross [306]

PAPERS OF JOHN THURLOE / Thurloe, John – London. 1742. v1-7. – 157mf – 8 – ne IDC [025]

PAPERS OF JOHN WALKER INGLESBY / Inglesby, John Walker – 1908-63. 29 fiches – 9 – us South Carolina Historical [025]

THE PAPERS OF JOSEPH BENSON / Lloyd, Gareth – (Coll title: The People Called Methodists, Phase 1: Reference Tools) – Manchester, 1991 – 2mf – 9 – MP-611/1 – ne IDC [240]

THE PAPERS OF JOSEPH HAWLEY – 29r – 1 – $1,015.00 – Dist. us Scholarly Res – us L of C Photodup [355]

PAPERS OF JOSEPH PULITZER – 1925-55 – 163r – 1 – $5,705.00 – Dist. us Scholarly Res – us L of C Photodup [070]

THE PAPERS OF JOSEPHUS DANIELS – (With guide) – 73r – 1 – $2,555.00 – Dist. us Scholarly Res – us L of C Photodup [355]

PAPERS OF JOSIAH BARTLETT / Bartlett, Josiah – Dartmouth College Library Collections – 1 reel – 1 – $75.00 – us UMI [920]

THE PAPERS OF JOSIAH BARTLETT / Bartlett, Josiah – 1r – 1 – $20.00 – us Dartmouth [610]

THE PAPERS OF J.S. BLACK – 36r – 1 – $1,260.00 – Dist. us Scholarly Res – us L of C Photodup [975]

THE PAPERS OF JUSTIN MORRILL – 52r – 1 – $1,820.00 – Dist. us Scholarly Res – us L of C Photodup [975]

PAPERS OF KATE BACHMAN / Bachman, Kate – 1862-ca.1878. 2 fiches – 9 – us South Carolina Historical [978]

THE PAPERS OF LEWIS TAPPAN – 7r – 1 – $245.00 – Dist. us Scholarly Res – us L of C Photodup [976]

PAPERS OF M. CAREY THOMAS – 1857-1935. Published in cooperation with Bryn Mawr College – 1 – us Primary [920]

PAPERS OF MANIGAULT-BURNET / Manigault-Burnet – 1752-54, 1794, 1888, 1896. 2 fiches – 9 – us South Carolina Historical [025]

THE PAPERS OF MARGARET SANGER – (With guide) – 145r – 1 – $5,075.00 – Dist. us Scholarly Res – us L of C Photodup [613]

PAPERS OF MARTIN VAN BUREN / ed by West, Lucy Fisher – (With printed guide and index £68.00) – 55r – 13 – £4,015.00 – uk Chadwyck [920]

PAPERS OF MARY CHURCH TERRELL AND ROBERT H. TERRELL – L110005 – 38r – 1 – $1,330.00 – Dist. us Scholarly Res – us L of C Photodup [320]

THE PAPERS OF MONTGOMERY C. MEIGS – 51r – 1 – $1,785.00 – Dist. us Scholarly Res – us L of C Photodup [355]

PAPERS OF NATHANIEL P. TALLMADGE / Tallmadge, Nathaniel P – (With printed guide £21.00) – 1812-62 – 3r – 1 – £195.00 – uk Chadwyck [920]

THE PAPERS OF NEIL JAMIESON – 8r – 1 – $280.00 – Dist. us Scholarly Res – us L of C Photodup [380]

THE PAPERS OF NELSON ALDRICH – (With guide) – 73r – 1 – $2,555.00 – Dist. us Scholarly Res – us L of C Photodup [332]

THE PAPERS OF NICHOLAS BIDDLE – 46r – 1 – $1,610.00 – Dist. us Scholarly Res – us L of C Photodup [332]

THE PAPERS OF PANTON, LESLIE AND CO – Over 8000 documents recording the trading company's operations; ethnographic collection for the study of American Indians of the Southeast – 1 – us Primary [975]

THE PAPERS OF PASTOR FELIX / Lockhart, Arthur John – Cincinnati: Jennings & Pye; New York: Eaton & Mains, c1903 – 1mf – 9 – 0-8370-6144-X – 1986-0144 – us A.T.L.A. [920]

PAPERS OF PAUL ZIMMERMAN / Zimmerman, Paul – 1898, 1900-65 – 1 – us KS Hist [978]

THE PAPERS OF PHILIP H. SHERIDAN – (With guide) – 104r – 1 – $3,640.00 – Dist. us Scholarly Res – us L of C Photodup [355]

THE PAPERS OF QUEEN VICTORIA ON FOREIGN AFFAIRS – (Pt 1: Russia and Eastern Europe 1846-1900 4r $460.00. ISBN 1-55655-184-3. Pt 2: Germany and Central Europe 1841-1900 33r $3,815.00 ISBN 1-55655-185-1. Pt 3: Italy 1847-1900 18r $2,080.00 ISBN 1-55655-186-X. Pt 4: Portugal and Spain 1841-1900 10r $1,160.00 ISBN 1-55655-187-8. Pt 5: France and Belgium 1848-1900 13r $1,500.00 ISBN 1-55655-188-6. Pt 6: Greece 1847-1863 3r $345.00 ISBN 1-55655-189-4) – 1 – $8,420.00 coll – us UPA [320]

THE PAPERS OF RAY STANNARD BAKER – 97r – 1 – $3,395.00 – Dist. us Scholarly Res – us L of C Photodup [320]

THE PAPERS OF R.M.T. HUNTER, 1817-1887 / Hunter, Robert Mercer Taliaferro – (With printed guide) – 13r – 1 – $1,105.00 – D3185 – us Scholarly Res [920]

PAPERS OF ROBERT M. LA FOLLETTE, 1876-1924 / La Follette, Robert M – (With printed guide £44.00) – 163r – 1 – £8,600.00 – uk Chadwyck [920]

PAPERS OF ROBERT MILLS / Mills, Robert – 1803-53. 16 fiches – 9 – us South Carolina Historical [025]

THE PAPERS OF ROBERT MILLS, 1781-1855 / Mills, Robert; ed by Scott, Pamela – (With printed guide. Sold separately $45.00 S3198.G) – 1990 – 15r – 1 – $1,275.00 – S3198 – us Scholarly Res [920]

THE PAPERS OF RUTHERFORD BIRCHARD HAYES / Hayes, Rutherford B – (With guide. Sections available: Incoming Correspondence, 1829-93 158r $13,430. Outgoing Correspondence, 1834-93 32r $2,720. White House Records, 1877-81 74r $6,290) – Fremont, Ohio. 1983 – 304r – 1 – $25,840.00 – D3196 – us Scholarly Res [920]

PAPERS OF SAMUEL CABOT, 1713-1858 / Cabot, Samuel – Massachusetts Historical Society – 4r – 1 – $305.00 – us UMI [920]

THE PAPERS OF SAMUEL PETER HEINTZELMAN – 13r – 1 – $455.00 – Dist. us Scholarly Res – us L of C Photodup [355]

PAPERS OF STEPHEN C. ROWAN, 1826-90 / U.S. Navy. Office of Naval Records and Library – 1roll. M180. Printed guide – 1 – us Nat'l Archives [324]

PAPERS OF THE 2ND MEETING : NOV 21, 1967 / Future Political Status Commission [TTPI (U.S.)] – (Typescript, various pagination) – n.p, n.d. – 10mf – 9 – $1.50 – LLMC 82-100F, Title 34 – us L.L.M.C. [323]

PAPERS OF THE ABRAHAM LINCOLN ASSOCIATION / Abraham Lincoln Association – (Cont by: Journal of the Abraham Lincoln Association) – Springfield, IL. v1-8. 1979-1986* – 1 – D16624 – us UMI [360]

PAPERS OF THE AMERICAN BOARD OF COMMISSIONERS FOR FOREIGN MISSIONS, 1812-1919 – Based on the holdings of Houghton Library, Harvard University – 1 – us Primary [240]

PAPERS OF THE ASSOCIATION AGAINST THE PROHIBITION AMENDMENT AND THE WOMEN'S ORGANIZATION FOR NATIONAL PROHIBITION REFORM – (With printed guide) – 1982 – 17r – 1 – $1,445.00 – S1844 – Co-publ with Hagley Museum and Library – us Scholarly Res [360]

PAPERS OF THE BRITISH SCHOOL AT ROME – Rome, 1902-20 – 64mf – 9 – ne IDC [370]

PAPERS OF THE CIVIL RIGHTS CONGRESS – (Part 1. Case Files. 40r. $4,410.00. ISBN 1-55655-065-0; Part 2. Files of William L. Patterson and the National Office. 42r. $4,620.00. ISBN 1-55655-066-9; Part 3. Publications. 19r. $2,090.00. ISBN 1-55655-067-7; Part 4. Communist Party USA Files. 16r. $1,760.00. ISBN 1-55655-068-5; Part 5. Citizens Emergency Defense Conference Files. 8r. $885.00. ISBN 1-55655-069-3) – 1 – $13,075.00 set – us UPA [320]

THE PAPERS OF THE CONFEDERATE STATES OF AMERICA – 70r – 1 – $2,450.00 – Dist. us Scholarly Res – us L of C Photodup [976]

PAPERS OF THE CONGRESS OF RACIAL EQUALITY, 1941-1967 – (With printed guide £58) – 49r – 1 – £3,085.00 – uk Chadwyck [977]

PAPERS OF THE CONSTITUTIONAL CONVENTION – (In English and Palauan. Various pagination) – n.p, n.d. – 7mf – 9 – $10.50 – LLMC 82-100G, Title 6 – us L.L.M.C. [323]

PAPERS OF THE CONTINENTAL CONGRESS, 1774-89 / U.S. Continental Congress – 204 rolls. printed Guide – 1 – M247 – us Nat'l Archives [324]

PAPERS OF THE FEDERAL RESERVE SYSTEM / U.S. Federal Reserve System – (See also indiv. titles: Legislation, Major Speeches and Essays and and Special Reports, 1913-60; Minutes of Meetings of the Federal Open Market Committee, 1923-75) – 1 – $4,660.00 set – us UPA [336]

PAPERS OF THE FUTURE POLITICAL STATUS NEGOTIATIONS : HELD IN HANA, MAUI, HI, OCT 1971 / [/TTPI (U.S.)/] – (Typescript, various pagination) – n.p, n.d. – 4mf – 9 – $6.00 – LLMC 82-100F, Title 39 – us L.L.M.C. [323]

PAPERS OF THE GREAT NORTHERN RAILWAY COMPANY, PART 1 / Great Northern Railway Company – (Series A: Board of Directors Minutes and Corporate Histories. 4 reels. ISBN: 0-89093-725-7. $380.00; Series B: Labor. 16 reels. ISBN: 0-89093-726-5. $1,540.00; Series C: Settlement and Development. 5 reels. ISBN: 0-89093-727-3. $480.00) – 1862-1922 – 1 – us UPA [025]

PAPERS OF THE INTERNATIONAL LABOR DEFENSE – 22r – 1 – $2,425.00 – 1-55655-037-5 – us UPA [331]

PAPERS OF THE INTERNATIONAL WORKINGMEN'S ASSOCIATION, 1868-1877 / International Working Men's Association – (With printed guide £17.00) – 2r – 1 – £125.00 – uk Chadwyck [331]

PAPERS OF THE MANLY FAMILY / Manly Family – 1742-1888 – 1 – $14.14 – us Baptist [240]

PAPERS OF THE MARYLAND STATE COLONIZATION SOCIETY, 1817-1902 / ed by Best, Randolph B – (With printed guide) – 1972 – 31r – 1 – $2,635.00 – S1859 – Co-publ with Maryland State Historical Society – us Scholarly Res [360]

PAPERS OF THE NAACP : LEGAL DEPARTMENT CASE FILES, 1956-1965 / ed by Bracey, John H, Jr & Meier, August – (Series A: The South ca 70r $8,750. Series B: The Northeast ca 10r $5,000 ISBN 1-55655-603-9. Series C: The Mid and Far West ca 30r $3,750 ISBN 1-55655-604-7. All with printed guides) – 1996 – 1 – us UPA [320]

PAPERS OF THE NAACP, PART 1 : MEETINGS OF THE BOARD OF DIRECTORS, RECORDS OF ANNUAL CONFERENCES, MAJOR SPEECHES, AND SPECIAL REPORTS, 1909-1950 / ed by Bracey, John H, Jr & Meier, August – (Supplements: 1951-55 12r ISBN 0-89093-970-5 $1,500.00. 1956-60 12r ISBN 1-55655-286-6 $1,500.00. 1961-65 9r 1-55655-542-3 $1,125.00. All with printed guides. Series: Black Studies Research Sources) – 28r – 1 – $3,500.00 – 0-89093-397-9 – us UPA [320]

PAPERS OF THE NAACP, PART 2 : PERSONAL CORRESPONDENCE OF SELECTED NAACP OFFICIALS, 1919-39 / ed by Bracey, John H, Jr & Meier, August – (With printed guide. Series: Black Studies Research Sources) – 20r – 1 – $2,510.00 – 0-89093-511-4 – us UPA [320]

PAPERS OF THE NAACP, PART 3 : THE CAMPAIGN FOR EDUCATIONAL EQUALITY, 1913-65 / ed by Bracey, John H, Jr & Meier, August – (Series A: Legal Department and Central Office Records, 1913-40 24r ISBN 0-89093-893-8 $3,005.00. Series B: Legal Department and Central Office Records, 1940-50 19r ISBN 0-89093-894-6 $2,385.00. Series C: Legal Department and Central Office Records, 1951-55 23r ISBN 1-55655-543-1 $2,875.00. Series D: General Office Files, 1956-65 13r ISBN 1-55655-553-9 $1,625.00. Series: Black Studies Research Sources) – Series A-D – 1 – us UPA [320]

PAPERS OF THE NAACP, PART 4 : THE VOTING RIGHTS CAMPAIGN, 1916-50 / ed by Bracey, John H, Jr & Meier, August – (Supplement: General Office Files, 1956-65 6r ISBN 1-55655-544-X $750.00. Includes printed guides. Series: Black Studies Research Sources) – 13r – 1 – $1,630.00 – 0-89093-897-0 – us UPA [320]

PAPERS OF THE NAACP, PART 5 : THE CAMPAIGN AGAINST RESIDENTIAL SEGREGATION, 1914-55 / ed by Bracey, John H, Jr & Meier, August – (Supplement: General Office Files 1956-65 16r ISBN 1-55655-545-8 $2,000.00. Includes printed guides. Series: Black Studies Research Sources) – 23r – 1 – $2,875.00 – 0-89093-968-3 – us UPA [320]

PAPERS OF THE NAACP, PART 6 : THE SCOTTSBORO CASE, 1931-50 / ed by Bracey, John H, Jr & Meier, August – (With printed guide. Series: Black Studies Research Sources) – 24r – 1 – $3,005.00 – 0-89093-969-1 – us UPA [320]

PAPERS OF THE NAACP, PART 7 : THE ANTI-LYNCHING CAMPAIGN, 1912-55 – (Series A: Anti-Lynching Investigative Files, 1912-53 30r ISBN 0-89093-971-3 $3,750.00. Series B: Anti-Lynching Legislative and Publicity Files, 1916-55 35r ISBN 0-89093-972-1 $4,380.00. With printed guides. Series: Black Studies Research Sources) – Series A and B – 1 – us UPA [320]

PAPERS OF THE NAACP, PART 8 : DISCRIMINATION IN THE CRIMINAL JUSTICE SYSTEM, 1910-1955 / ed by Bracey, John H, Jr & Meier, August – (Series A: Legal Department and Central Office Records, 1910-39 17r ISBN 1-55655-079-0 $2,115.00. Series B: Legal Department and Central Office Records, 1940-55 32r ISBN 1-55655-080-4 $4,000.00. With printed guides. Series: Black Studies Research Sources) – 1 – us UPA [320]

PAPERS OF THE NAACP, PART 9 : DISCRIMINATION IN THE U.S. ARMED FORCES, 1918-55 – (Series A: General Office Files on Armed Forces' Affairs, 1918-55 18r ISBN 1-55655-116-9 $2,265.00. Series B: Armed Forces' Legal Files, 1940-50 30r ISBN 1-55655-117-7. $3,880.00. Series C: The Veterans Affairs Committee, 1940-50 12r ISBN 1-55655-118-5 $1,500.00. With printed guides. Series: Black Studies Research Sources) – Series A, B and C – 1 – us UPA [320]

PAPERS OF THE NAACP, PART 10 : PEONAGE, LABOR, AND THE NEW DEAL, 1913-39 / ed by Bracey, John H, Jr & Meier, August – (With printed guide. Series: Black Studies Research Sources) – 23r – 1 – $3,235.00 – 1-55655-157-6 – us UPA [320]

PAPERS OF THE NAACP, PART 11 : SPECIAL SUBJECT FILES, 1912-39 / ed by Bracey, John H, Jr & Meier, August – (Series A: Africa through Garvey, Marcus 35r ISBN 1-55655-158-4 $4,935.00. Series B: Harding, Warren G. through YWCA 36r ISBN 1-55655-175-4 $5,065.00. Printed guide only ISBN 1-55655-176-2 $130.00. Series: Black Studies Research Sources) – Series A and B – 1 – us UPA [320]

PAPERS OF THE NAACP, PART 12 : SELECTED BRANCH FILES, 1913-39 / ed by Bracey, John H, Jr & Meier, August – (Series A: The South 20r ISBN 1-55655-287-4 $2,510.00. Series B: The Northeast 8r ISBN 1-55655-288-2 $875.00. Series C: The Midwest 27r ISBN 1-55655-289-0 $3,380.00. Series D: The West 7r ISBN 1-55655-290-4 $875.00. Series: Black Studies Research Sources) – Series A, B, C and D – 1 – us UPA [320]

PAPERS OF THE NAACP, PART 13 : THE NAACP AND LABOR, 1940-1955 / ed by Bracey, John H, Jr & Meier, August – (Series A: Subject Files on Labor Conditions and Employment Discrimination, 1940-55 21r ISBN 1-55655-420-6 $2,630.00. Series B: Cooperation with Organized Labor, 1940-55 25r ISBN 1-55655-421-4 $3,130.00. Series C: Legal Department Files on Labor, 1940-55 12r ISBN 1-55655-422-2 $1,500.00. With printed guides. Series: Black Studies Research Sources) – Series A, B and C – 1 – us UPA [320]

PAPERS OF THE NAACP, PART 14 : RACE RELATIONS IN THE INTERNATIONAL ARENA, 1940-55 / ed by Bracey, John H, Jr & Meier, August – (With printed guide. Series: Black Studies Research Sources) – 21r – 1 – $2,630.00 – 1-55655-459-1 – us UPA [320]

PAPERS OF THE NAACP, PART 15 : SEGREGATION AND DISCRIMINATION, COMPLAINTS AND RESPONSES, 1940-55 / ed by Bracey, John H, Jr & Meier, August – (Series A: Legal Department Files 19r ISBN 1-55655-460-5 $2,385.00. Series B: Administrative Files 15r ISBN 1-55655-461-3 $1,875.00. With printed guides. Series: Black Studies Research Sources) – 1993 – 1 – us UPA [320]

PAPERS OF THE NAACP, PART 16 : BOARD OF DIRECTORS CORRESPONDENCE AND COMMITTEE MATERIALS, 1919-55 – (Series A: 1919-39 8r ISBN 1-55655-477-X $1,005.00. Series B: 1940-55 24r ISBN 1-55655-478-8 $3,005.00. Supplement: 1956-65 12r $1,500.00. Includes printed guides. Series: Black Studies Research Sources) – Series A,B + suppl – 32mf – 1 – us UPA [320]

PAPERS OF THE NAACP, PART 17 : NATIONAL STAFF FILES, 1940-1955 – (Includes printed guide. Series: Black Studies Research Sources) – 29r – 1 – $3,630.00 – 1-55655-489-3 – us UPA [320]

PAPERS OF THE NAACP, PART 18 : SPECIAL SUBJECTS, 1940-1955 – (Series A: Legal Department Files 10r ISBN 1-55655-511-3 $1,250.00. Series B: General Office Files, Abolition of Government Agencies-Jews 23r ISBN 1-55655-512-1 $2,875.00. Series C: General Office Files, Justice Department-White Supremacy 33r ISBN 1-55655-517-2 $4,125.00. Series: Black Studies Research Sources) – Series A,B,C – 1 – $8,250.00 set – us UPA [320]

PAPERS OF THE NAACP, PART 19 : YOUTH FILE – (Series A: 1919-39 5r ISBN 1-55655-520-2 $625.00. Series B: 1940-55, American Jewish Congress – Motion Picture Project 25r ISBN 1-55655-521-0 $3,130.00. Series C: 1940-55 NAACP-Youth Builders 27r ISBN 1-55655-522-9 $3,375.00. All with printed guides. Series: Black Studies Research Sources) – Series A,B,C – 1 – us UPA [320]

PAPERS OF THE NAACP, PART 20 : WHITE RESISTANCE AND REPRISALS, 1956-1965 – (With printed guide. Series: Black Studies Research Sources) – 1995 – 15r – 1 – $1,875.00 – us UPA [320]

PAPERS OF THE NAACP, PART 21 : NAACP RELATIONS WITH THE MODERN CIVIL RIGHTS MOVEMENT – (With printed guide. Series: Black Studies Research Sources) – 1995 – 22r – 1 – $2,750.00 – us UPA [320]

PAPERS OF THE NAACP, PART 22 : LEGAL DEPARTMENT ADMINISTRATIVE FILES, 1956-1965 – (With a printed guide. Series: Black Studies Research Sources) – 1996 – ca 28r – 1 – ca $3,500.00 – us UPA [320]

PAPERS OF THE NAACP, PART 23 : LEGAL DEPARTMENT CASE FILES, 1955-1965 / ed by Bracey, John H, Jr & Meier, August – (Series A: South ca 70r ca $8,750. Series B: Northeast ca 40r ca $5,000. Series C: Mid and Far West ca 30r ca$3,750. With printed guides. Coll title: Black Studies Research Sources) – Series A,B,C – 1 – us UPA [320]

PAPERS OF THE NATIONAL NEGRO CONGRESS – (Part 1: Records and Correspondence, 1933-1942. 30r. $3,300.00. ISBN 1-55655-057-X; Part 2: Records and Correspondence, 1943-1947. 36r. $3,965.00. ISBN 1-55655-058-8; Part 3: Financial Records, 1940- 1947, and Publications. 19r. $2,090.00. ISBN 1-55655-059-6; Part 4: The Negro Labor Victory Committee, 1942-1945. 9r. $990.00. ISBN 1-55655-060-X) – 1 – $9,830.00 set – us UPA [320]

PAPERS OF THE NIXON WHITE HOUSE – (Includes a printed guide) – Part 8. The Nixon White House Tapes: The Complete Transcripts Prepared by the Watergate Special Prosecution Force – 73mf – 9 – $455.00 – 1-55655-399-4 – us UPA [025]

PAPERS OF THE NIXON WHITE HOUSE – Part 7. President's Personal Files, 1969-74 – 549mf – 9 – $3,335.00 – 1-55655-398-6 – us UPA [025]

PAPERS OF THE NIXON WHITE HOUSE – (Printed guide. ISBN 1-55655-032-4. $225.00) – Part 3. John Ehrlichman: Notes of Meetings with the President, 1969-73 – 77mf – 9 – $685.00 – 1-55655-031-6 – us UPA [025]

PAPERS OF THE NIXON WHITE HOUSE – (Printed guide. ISBN 1-55655-034-0. $225.00) – Part 4. The John Ehrlichman Alphabetical Subject File, 1969-73 – 175mf – 9 – $1,270.00 – 1-55655-033-2 – us UPA [025]

PAPERS OF THE NIXON WHITE HOUSE – (Printed guide. ISBN 1-55655-036-7. $225.00) – Part 5. H.R. Haldeman: Notes of White House Meetings, 1969-73 – 98mf – 9 – $810.00 – 1-55655-035-9 – us UPA [025]

PAPERS OF THE NIXON WHITE HOUSE – (Printed index. ISBN 1-55655-028-6. $125.00) – Part 1. Official Inventories and Other Historical Materials of the Nixon White House – 98mf – 9 – $710.00 – 1-55655-027-8 – us UPA [025]

PAPERS OF THE NIXON WHITE HOUSE – (Printed index. ISBN 1-55655-030-8. $225.00) – Part 2. The President's Meeting File, 1969-74 – 260mf – 9 – $1,770.00 – 1-55655-029-4 – us UPA [025]

PAPERS OF THE NIXON WHITE HOUSE – (Series B: Daily News Summaries Annotated by the President, 1969-1973. ISBN 1-55655-075-8. Printed guide. ISBN 1-55655-076-6. $215.00. Guide Series A $225.00 ISBN: 1-55655-074-X) – Part 6. The President's Office Files. Series A: Documents Annotated by the President, 1969-1974. – 370mf – 9 – $2,425.00 – 1-55655-073-1 – us UPA [025]

PAPERS OF THE NORTHERN PACIFIC RAILWAY COMPANY, PART 1 / Northern Pacific Railway Company – (Series A: Board of Directors Minutes and Corporate Histories. 10 reels. ISBN: 0-89093-728-1. $965.00; Series B: Labor. 12 reels. ISBN: 0-89093-729-X. $1,150.00; Series C: Settlement and Development. 3 reels. ISBN: 0-89093-730-3. $295.00. All with printed guides) – 1864-1922 – 1 – us UPA [025]

PAPERS OF THE OFFICE OF PRICES STABILIZATION / DiSalle, Michael V – 1951-53. Ed. by David J. Rosenblatt. There are 4 35mm rolls in this set. Related Guide Book not available – 1 – us Ohio Hist [978]

PAPERS OF THE PEERY FAMILY / Peery Family – 1846-1921 – 1 – us KS Hist [978]

PAPERS OF THE PENNSYLVANIA ABOLITIONIST SOCIETY, 1775-1916 : HISTORY BY WILLIAM J. BUCK – 5r – 1 – $425.00 – S1865 – us Scholarly Res [360]

PAPERS OF THE PINCKNEY FAMILY / Pinckney Family – 1703-1847. 74 fiches – 9 – us South Carolina Historical [025]

PAPERS OF THE PRESIDENT'S MEDIATION COMMISSION, 1917-19 / U.S. President – (With printed guide) – 3r – 1 – $295.00 – 0-89093-745-1 – us UPA [330]

PAPERS OF THE PRESIDENT'S SCIENCE ADVISORY COMMITTEE, 1957-61 – 3 reels with printed guide – 1 – $295.00 – 0-89093-979-9 – us UPA [500]

PAPERS OF THE PRIME MINISTERS OF GREAT BRITAIN, SERIES 1 / Great Britain. Prime Minister – Papers of William Pitt, the Younger (Prime Minister, 1783-1801 and 1804-1806). Part 1: PRO Class 30/8, vols. 101-135. Part 2: (PRO Class 30; 8, v136-171). Part 3: (PRO Class 30; 8, v172-94, 264-71, 325-31, 361-62. Part 4: (PRO Class 30; 8, v195-199, 228-63. Part 5: (PRO Class 30; 8, v272-315. Part 6: (PRO Class 30; 8, v317-324, 332-360 and 363 – 1 – us Primary [941]

PAPERS OF THE PRIME MINISTERS OF GREAT BRITAIN, SERIES 2 / Great Britain. Prime Minister – Papers of Sir Robert Peel (Prime Minister, 1834-35, 1841-45 and 1845-46). Part 1: British Library additional mss. 40432-40461. Part 2: British Library Add. Mss. 40462-40484. Part 3: British Library Add. Mss. 40485-40521. Part 4: British Library Add. Mss. 40522-40556. Part 5: British Library Add. Mss. 40557-40581. Part 6: British Library Add. Mss. 40582-40603 – 1 – us Primary [941]

PAPERS OF THE PRIME MINISTERS OF GREAT BRITAIN, SERIES 3 / Great Britain. Prime Minister – (Papers of Lord Liverpool (Prime Minister, 1812-1827). Pt 1: British Library add mss. 38190-38196 and 38237-38268. Pt 2: British Library add mss. 38269-38302. Pt 3: British Library add mss. 38312-38328, 38357-38372, 38377-38381, 38471-38475, 38564-38568, 38571-38577, 38580) – 1 – us Primary [941]

PAPERS OF THE PRIME MINISTERS OF GREAT BRITAIN, SERIES 4 / Great Britain. Prime Minister – (Papers of the Duke of Newcastle (Prime Minister, 1754-1756 and 1757-1762). Pt 1: British Library add mss. 32686-32701 Home Correspondence 1724-43. Pt 2: British Library add Mss. 32702-32719 Home Correspondence 1744-49. Pt 3: British Library add mss. 32720-32737 Home Correspondence 1750-54. Pt 4: British Library add mss. 32852-32869 General Correspondence 1755-56. Pt 5: British Library add mss. 32870-32886 General Correspondence 1757-58. Pt 6: British Library add mss. 32887-32907 General Correspondence 1759-Jun 1760. Pt 7: British Library Add. Mss. 32908-32932. General Correspondence Jul 1760-61. Pt 8: British Library add mss. 32933-32954 General Correspondence 1762-63. Pt 9: British Library add mss. 32955-32972 General Correspondence 1764-65. Pt 10: British Library add mss. 32973-32992 General Correspondence 1766-Nov 1768) – us Primary [941]

PAPERS OF THE PRIME MINISTERS OF GREAT BRITAIN, SERIES 5 / Great Britain. Prime Minister – (The Papers of Lord North (Prime Minister, 1770-1782)) – 1 – us Primary [941]

PAPERS OF THE PRIME MINISTERS OF GREAT BRITAIN, SERIES 6 / Great Britain. Prime Minister – (The Papers of George Grenville (Prime Minister, 1763-1782)) – 1 – us Primary [941]

PAPERS OF THE PRIME MINISTERS OF GREAT BRITAIN, SERIES 7 / Great Britain. Prime Minister – (The Papers of Spencer Perceval (Prime Minister, 1809-1812)) – 1 – us Primary [941]

PAPERS OF THE PRIME MINISTERS OF GREAT BRITAIN, SERIES 8 : THE PAPERS OF WILLIAM EWART GLADSTONE / Prime Minister, Great Britain – (Pt 1: Printed speeches and newspaper cuttings from St Deinol's Residential Library, Hawarden, and notes for speeches from the British Library. Pts 2 and 3: Special correspondence from the British Library) – 1 – us Primary [324]

PAPERS OF THE ROGER JONES FAMILY – 15r – 1 – $525.00 – Dist. us Scholarly Res – us L of C Photodup [975]

THE PAPERS OF THE SHIPPEN FAMILY – 15r – 1 – $525.00 – Dist. us Scholarly Res – us L of C Photodup [975]

PAPERS OF THE SOCIALIST LABOR PARTY OF AMERICA, 1877-1907 – (With guide £21) – 39r – 1 – £2,231.00 – uk Chadwyck [335]

PAPERS OF THE SOCIETY OF AMERICAN INDIANS, 1906-1946 / ed by Larner, John W Jr – (With printed guide) – 1986 – 10r – 1 – $850.00 – S1879 – us Scholarly Res [306]

PAPERS OF THE ST LOUIS FUR TRADE / ed by Swagerty, William R – (Pt 1: The Chouteau Collection, 1752-1925 40r $4,620.00 ISBN 1-55655-411-7. Pt 2: Fur Company Ledgers and Account Books, 1802-1871 23r $2,655.00 ISBN 1-55655-412-5. Pt 3: Robert Campbell Family Collection from the St Louis Mercantile Library Association 30r $3,755.00. ISBN 1-55655-497-4. All pts with printed guides) – 1 – $10,480.00 coll – us UPA [978]

PAPERS OF THE VAWTER FAMILY / Vawter Family – 1848-1913 – 1 – us KS Hist [978]

PAPERS OF THE WESTERN ASSOCIATION OF ARCHITECTS, 1884-1889 – 4r – 1 – $320.00 – us Ross [720]

PAPERS OF THE WORLD CONGRESS OF SOCIOLOGY – Montreal. v10. 1982* – 1,5,9 – D12761 – us UMI [301]

PAPERS OF THE WTUL AND ITS PRINCIPAL LEADERS / Women's Trade Union League – 1 – us Primary [305]

PAPERS OF THOMAS A. EDISON : A SELECTIVE MICROFILM EDITION / Edison, Thomas A – (Pt 1, 1850-78: 28r ISBN 0-89093-700-1. $2,315.00. Guide only $40.00; Pt 2, 1879-86: 69r. ISBN 0-89093-701-X. $5,710.00. Guide only $50.00; Pt 3, 1887-98: ISBN 0-89093-702-8. $5,380.00. Guide only $50.00) – 1 – $2,315.00 set – us UPA [920]

PAPERS OF THOMAS MURRAY 1593-1623 / Lambeth Palace Library – 3r – 1 – £135.00 – 1-897955-24-3 – uk Academic [090]

PAPERS OF T.J. BOWEN : MISSIONARY TO AFRICA / Bowen, T J – 1953-60. 652p – 1 – $22.82 – us Baptist [240]

PAPERS OF VINCENTE SEBASTIAN PINTADO / Pintado, Vincente Sebastian – 1781-1842 – 6r – 1 – $210.00 – Dist. us Scholarly Res – us L of C Photodup [520]

THE PAPERS OF WALT WHITMAN – L110144 – 34r – 1 – $1,190.00 – 1167-6 – us L of C Photodup [420]

PAPERS OF WASHINGTON ALLSTON / Allston, Washington – 1800-43. 2 reels. (Massachusetts Historical Society) – 1 – $130.00 – us UMI [920]

PAPERS OF W.E.B. DU BOIS / Du Bois, WE B – Speeches and radio broadcasts. Fisk University Library. No. 77-6. One reel – 1 – $15.00 – us Partington [920]

PAPERS OF W.E.B. DUBOIS, 1877-1965 / DuBois, WE Burghard – 89r – 1 – $6115.00 – us UMI [920]

PAPERS OF WEBSTER W. MOSES / Moses, Webster W – 1856-82 – 1 – us KS Hist [978]

PAPERS OF WILLIAM A. SMITH / Smith, William A – 1923-45 – 1 – us KS Hist [978]

THE PAPERS OF WILLIAM D. LEAHY – 5r – 1 – $175.00 – Dist. us Scholarly Res – us L of C Photodup [977]

PAPERS OF WILLIAM G. HINSON / Hinson, William G – 1846, ca.1861-1915. 14 fiches – 9 – us South Carolina Historical [025]

PAPERS OF WILLIAM H. SEWARD – 1 – Co-publ with the University of Rochester, Dept. of Rare Books, Manuscripts and Archives – us Primary [920]

THE PAPERS OF WILLIAM HENRY HARRISON 1800-1815 / ed by Clanin, Douglas E – (With printed guide. Reels covering 1810-15 to be publ) – Indianapolis: Indiana Historical Society, 1993 – 3r – 1 – $60.00 set $25.00r – us I.H.S. [320]

THE PAPERS OF WILLIAM HERNDON – 15r – 1 – $525.00 – Dist. us Scholarly Res – us L of C Photodup [976]

PAPERS OF WILLIAM LIVINGSTON, 1771-1790 / Livingston, William – (New Jersey's first elected Governor) – 25r – 1 – $1065.00 – us UMI [976]

THE PAPERS OF WILLIAM SHORT – 32r – 1 – $1,120.00 – Dist. us Scholarly Res – us L of C Photodup [975]

THE PAPERS OF WILLIAM TECUMSEH SHERMAN – (With guide) – 51r – 1 – $1,785.00 – Dist. us Scholarly Res – us L of C Photodup [355]

PAPERS OF WILMOT GIBBES DESAUSSURE / DeSaussure, Wilmot Gibbes – 1858-81. 4 fiches – 9 – us South Carolina Historical [025]

PAPERS OF W.J. MCGLOTHLIN, 1930-32 / McGlothlin, William Joseph – 3090p – 1 – $108.15 – us Baptist [240]

PAPERS OF WOLSELEY / Wolseley, Field Marshal Viscount – 1833-1913 – 1 – uk Microform Academic [941]

THE PAPERS OF ZACHARIAH CHANDLER – 4r – 1 – $140.00 – Dist. us Scholarly Res – us L of C Photodup [976]

THE PAPERS OF ZEBULON VANCE / ed by McKinney, Gordon & McMurry, Richard – (Includes printed guide) – 39r – 1 – $4,290.00 (Guide only: $100.00) – 0-89093-545-9 – us UPA [320]

PAPERS ON GODLINESS: BEING REPORTS OF A SERIES OF ADDRESSES DELIVERED AT JAMES'S HALL, LONDON, W., DURING 1881 / Booth, Catherine Mumford – 1890 – 9 – us A.T.L.A. [240]

PAPERS ON LANGUAGE AND LITERATURE – Edwardsville. v1-33. 1965-97+ 1; v8-33. 1972-97+ 5; v12-33. 1976-97+ 9 – 1,5,9 – D7789 – us UMI [400]

PAPERS ON PSYCHO-ANALYSIS / Jones, Ernest – London: Bailliere, Tindall and Cox, 1913. xv,432p – 1 – us U.W. Library [616]

PAPERS ON THE AALL CODE OF ETHICS / Committee on EthicsEthics Commission of the American Association of Law Libraries – (The Ethics Commission was abolished by the AALL in 1984) – Papers + correspondence (all publ) – 8mf – 9 – $12.00 – LLMC 80-430 – us L.L.M.C. [340]

PAPERS ORESTES A. BROWNSON / Brownson, Orestes A – (Includes guide) – University of Notre Dame Archives, 1823-75 – 19r – 1 – $760.00 – us U.N.D. Archives [240]

PAPERS, PART 1 / League of Women Voters – Meetings of the Board of Directors and the Executive Committees: Minutes and related documents, 1918-74. 14 reels with printed guide – 1 – $1,540.00 – 0-89093-795-8 – us UPA [360]

PAPERS, PART 1 : MEETINGS OF THE REPUBLICAN NATIONAL COMMITTEE, 1911-80 / Republican Party – (Series B: 1960-80. 18 reels with printed guide. $1,980.00. 0-89093-983-7) – Series A: 1911-60. 18 reels with printed guide – 1 – $1,980.00 – 0-89093-982-9 – us UPA [323]

PAPERS, PART 1 : NUMERICAL FILE ARCHIVE / U.S. Commission of Wartime Relocation and Internment of Civilians – 35r – 1 – $3,850.00 – 0-89093-625-0 – us UPA [324]

PAPERS, PART 1 : WESTERN REGIONAL OFFICE, 1962-65 / Congress of Racial Equality – 5 reels with printed guide – 1 – $550.00 – 0-89093-582-3 – us UPA [360]

PAPERS PART 2 : REPORTS AND MEMORANDA OF THE RESEARCH DIVISION OF THE HEADQUARTERS OF THE RNC, 1938-80 / Republican Party – 15 reels with printed guide – 1 – $1,655.00 – 0-89093-984-5 – us UPA [323]

PAPERS, PART 2 / League of Women Voters – Series A. Transcripts and records of National Conventions, 1919-44, and of General Councils, 1927-43. 20 reels with printed guide – 1 – $2,200.00 – 0-89093-796-6 – us UPA [360]

PAPERS, PART 2 / League of Women Voters – Series B. Transcripts and records of National Conventions, 1946-74, and of General Councils, 1945-73. 30 reels with printed guide – 1 – $3,300.00 – 0-89093-797-4 – us UPA [360]

PAPERS, PART 2: SOUTHERN REGIONAL OFFICE, 1959-66 / Congress of Racial Equality – 15 reels with printed guide – 1 – $1,655.00 – 0-89093-598-X – us UPA [360]

PAPERS, PART 3 / League of Women Voters – Series A. National Office Subject Files, 1920-32. 34 reels with printed guide – 1 – $3,740.00 – 0-89093-798-2 – us UPA [360]

PAPERS, PART 3: SEDFRE SERIES A, ADMINISTRATIVE FILES, 1960-76 / Congress of Racial Equality – 13 reels with printed guide – 1 – $1,430.00 – 0-89093-599-8 – us UPA [360]

PAPERS, PART 3: SEDFRE SERIES B, LEADERSHIP DEVELOPMENT FILES, 1960-76 / Congress of Racial Equality – 10 reels with printed guide – 1 – $1,105.00 – 0-89093-578-5 – us UPA [360]

PAPERS, PART 3: SEDFRE SERIES C, LEGAL DEPARTMENT FILES, 1960-76 / Congress of Racial Equality – 37 reels with printed guide – 1 – $4,070.00 – 0-89093-579-3 – us UPA [360]

PAPERS PERTAINING TO VESSELS OF OR INVOLVED WITH THE CONFEDERATE STATES OF AMERICA: "VESSEL PAPERS" / U.S. War Department – M909 – 32r – 1 – us Nat'l Archives [324]

PAPERS PRESENTED AT THE 6TH SESSION OF THE STANDING COMMITTEE ON RESOURCES RESEARCH AND DEVELOPMENT : COLOMBO, 1990 / IPFC – 1992 – 221p – it F.A.O. [333]

PAPERS PRESENTED AT THE 7TH SESSION OF THE INDO-PACIFIC FISHERY COMMISSION WORKING PARTY ON FISH TECHNOLOGY AND MARKETING : BANGKOK, 1988 / IPFC – 1990 – 314p – it F.A.O. [639]

PAPERS PRESENTED AT THE 8TH SESSION OF THE INDO-PACIFIC FISHERY COMMISSION WORKING PARTY ON FISH TECHNOLOGY AND MARKETING : YOGYAKARTA, INDONESIA, 1991 / IPFC – 1992 – 358p – it F.A.O. [639]

PAPERS PRESENTED AT THE F.A.O./UNEP MEETING ON THE EFFECTS OF POLLUTION ON MARINE ECOSYSTEMS. BLANES, SPAIN, 1985 – 1987 – 287p – it F.A.O. [574]

PAPERS PRESENTED AT THE FAO/ UNEP/WHO/IOC/IAEA MEETING ON THE BIOGEOCHEMICAL CYCLE OF MERCURY IN THE MEDITERRANEAN. SIENA, ITALY, 1984 – 1986 – 193p – it F.A.O. [574]

PAPERS PRESENTED AT THE TECHNICAL CONSULTATION ON HIGH SEAS FISHING : ROME, 1992 – 1993 – 84p – it F.A.O. [636]

PAPERS REGARDING PACIFIC LINGUISTICS, 1897-1938 / Dempwolff, Otto – (Bulk: 1913-38) – 3r – 1 – PMB1056 – at Pacific Mss [490]

PAPERS RELATING TO AMERICA / Ogilvie-Forbes of Boyndlie. Archives – BRRAM – 1 – uk Microform Academic [970]

PAPERS RELATING TO HER MAJESTY'S COLONIAL POSSESSIONS: REPORTS FOR 1879 / Great Britain. Colonial Office – Reel 4001. 1881 – 1 – ja CEACS [941]

PAPERS RELATING TO LOWER CANADA... – [London, England: s.n., 1838]. SEM105P1369 – 1mf – 9 – Can$2.25 – cn Bibl Nat [971]

PAPERS RELATING TO PAPUA NEW GUINEA, C. 1941-1945 / Ross, James Campbell – 1r – 1 – PMB1059 – at Pacific Mss [980]

PAPERS RELATING TO THE ADMISSION OF NATIVES TO THE CIVIL SERVICE OF INDIA / India – P.P., 1878-79. v. 55, paper C.2376. BI-511 2 – 8 – ne IDC [324]

PAPERS RELATING TO THE CHINESE MARITIME CUSTOMS SERVICE / Maze, Frederick – 1 – uk Microform Academic [950]

PAPERS RELATING TO THE ELECTIONS FOR THE PALESTINE LEGISLATIVE COUNCIL, 1923 / Great Britain. Colonial Office. Palestine – London. Cmd. 1889. BJ-28-68 1 – 9 – ne IDC [956]

PAPERS RELATING TO THE FOREIGN RELATIONS OF THE UNITED STATES / U.S. Department of State – 1861-1945 – 1 – us Princeton Micro [327]

PAPERS RELATING TO THE GILBERT ISLANDS, 1942-1970 / Maude, Henry Evans – 1r – 1 – PMB1077 – at Pacific Mss [980]

PAPERS RELATING TO THE PANAMA CANAL AND OUR RELATIONS WITH COLUMBIA – Senate doc no 471. 63rd Congress 2nd sess. Washington: GPO, 1914 – 1mf – 9 – $1.50 – LLMC 82-100D Title 20 – us L.L.M.C. [324]

PAPERS RELATING TO THE RED RIVER SETTLEMENT. – s.l: House of Commons, 1819. SEM105P108 – 4mf – 9 – Can$9.00 – cn Bibl Nat [971]

PAPERS RELATIVE TO THE AFFAIRS OF CANADA / Canada – London: Printed by William Clowes and Sons, 1849. SEM105P441 – 1mf – 9 – Can$2.25 – cn Bibl Nat [324]

PAPERS RELATIVE TO THE AFFAIRS OF LOWER CANADA – s.l: House of Commons, 1837. SEM105P442 – 1mf – 9 – Can$2.25 – cn Bibl Nat [971]

PAPERS RELATIVE TO THE EXPLORATION OF THE COUNTRY BETWEEN LAKE SUPERIOR AND THE RED RIVER SETTLEMENT – London: Printed by George Edward Eyre and William Spotteswoode, 1859. SEM105P286 – 2mf – 9 – Can$4.50 – cn Bibl Nat [910]

PAPERS RELATIVE TO THE SETTLEMENT OF THE DISPUTED BOUNDARIES BETWEEN THE PROVINCES OF CANADA AND NEW BRUNSWICK – London: William Clowes & Sons, 1851. SEM105P438 – 2mf – 9 – Can$2.25 – cn Bibl Nat [971]

PAPERS RESPECTING DISCUSSIONS WITH THE HOUSES OF ASSEMBLY AND LEGISLATIVE COUNCIL – [London, England: s.n., 1837]. SEM105P1365 – 1mf – 9 – Can$2.25 – cn Bibl Nat [971]

PAPERS SUBMITTED TO THE INTERNATIONAL CONGRESS OF AFRICANISTS / International Congress of Africanists. Addis Ababa – 1973. Incomplete – 3r – 1 – $148.50 – us African Imprint [960]

PAPERS: TRINIDAD / Anti-Slavery Society – 1836-42 – 1 – uk Microform Academic [972]

PAPERS UNIVERSITY SETTLEMENT SOCIETY OF NEW YORK CITY, 1886-1945 – (With printed guide £21.00) – 22r – 1 – £1,380.00 – uk Chadwyck [370]

PAPERS WHILE EXECUTIVE SECRETARY OF THE SUNDAY SCHOOL BOARD, JUNE 1935-MAY 1945 / Holcomb, T L – 33,097p – 1 – $1,158.39 – us Baptist [240]

PAPERS WHILE PRESIDENT OF SOUTHERN BAPTIST CONVENTION : BROOKS HAYS / Hays, Brooks – Index on each reel. 10,146p – 1 – $355.11 – us Baptist [240]

PAPERS...(LISBON PAPERS) RECEIVED FROM THE DEPT. OF STATE (U.S.A.) / Ciano, Galeazzo, Count – 3rolls. T816. (World War II Collection of Seized Enemy Records) – 1 – us Nat'l Archives [920]

PAPERWEIGHTS: FLOWERS WHICH CLOTHE THE MEADOWS / Hollister, Paul & Lanmon, Dwight P – 1978. 167p., 306 illus. 4 fiches. Fiche no. 4322 – 9 – $7.50 – us Corning Mus [730]

LE PAPETIER – Quebec: Service des relations publiques... v1- 1964-. SEM35P32 – 2r – 1 – Can$72.00 – cn Bibl Nat [072]

Papez, David M *see* SERVICES OFFERED BY ATHLETIC TRAINERS AT PRIVATE SPORTS MEDICINE CLINICS IN THE UNITED STATES

DAS PAPIASFRAGMENT : EXEGETISCHE UNTERSUCHUNG DES FRAGMENTES (EUSEBIUS, HIST. ECCL: 3, 39, 3-4) UND KRITIK DER GLEICHNAMIGEN SCHRIFT VON DR. WEISSENBACH / Leimbach, Carl L – Gotha: F.A. Perthes, 1875 – 1mf – us A.T.L.A. [240]

PAPIER – v1- 1947- 1; v27- 5,6; v29- 9 – us UMI [073]

DER PAPIER FABRIKANT – Berlin, Germany. 1904-09.-w. 12mqn reels – 1 – uk British Libr Newspaper [073]

DER PAPIER FABRIKANT – Berlin, Germany. 1904.-m. 1 reel – 1 – uk British Libr Newspaper [073]

PAPIERS RELATIFS A LA RECLAMATION DES ACTIONNAIRES...COMPAGNIE DU CANAL WELLAND...L'ACTE 7, VICTORIA, CHAPITRE 34 – Quebec, 1853. SEM105P811 – 1mf – 9 – Can$2.25 – cn Bibl Nat [336]

PAPIER-ZEITUNG – Berlin, Germany. -m. 1878-1926. 135 reels – 1 – uk British Libr Newspaper [072]

PAPILIO : THE ORGAN OF THE NEW YORK ENTOMOLOGICAL CLUB – New York, Philadelphia. v1-4. 1881-84 – 18mf – 9 – ne IDC [420]

PAPILLION TIMES – Papillion, NE. -w. Dec 1874-Aug 1884, scattered issues missing; Jun 1892-May 1896, scattered issues missing; Jul 1896 to date – 1 – us NE Hist [071]

LE PAPILLON : LITTERAIRE – St-Francois-du-Lac, Canada. 3 issues. aut? 1927 – 1r – 1 – Can$25.00 – cn Can Microfilming [800]

LE PAPILLON – puis Journal hebdomadaire. Paris. avr 1881-mai 1884 – 1 – fr A.C.R.P.P. [073]

Papillon, A *see* SCRIPTORES ORDINIS PRAEDICATORUM

Papillon, Alexander Frederick William *see* MEMOIRS OF THOMAS PAPILLON, OF LONDON, MERCHANT.(1623-1702)

PAPILOMA COMEO DE LA LARINGE, LARINGOTOMIA CURACION / Cisneros, Juan – Madrid: Revista clinica de los Hospitales, 1890 – 1 – sp Bibl Santa Ana [946]

PAPINEAU, 1786-1871 / DeCelles, Alfred Duclos – Montreal, 1905. SEM105P521 – 3mf – 9 – Can$6.75 – cn Bibl Nat [920]

PAPINEAU: DRAME HISTORIQUE CANADIEN EN QUATRE ACTES ET NEUF TABLEAUX / Frechette, Louis-Honore – Montreal?: s.n., 1880 (Montreal: Chapleau & Lavigne). 03238. (Pre-1900 Canadiana) – 9 – cn C.I.H.M. [820]

PAPINEAU: EXTRAITS DE SA CORRESPONDANCE INTIME / Celles, Alfred Duclos de – Montreal: Gebhardt-Berthiaume, 1891. 03783. (Pre-1900 Canadiana) – 9 – cn C.I.H.M. [971]

Papineau, Louis Joseph *see*
- AUX HONORABLES CHEVALIERS, CITOYENS ET BOURGEOIS, LES COMMUNES DU ROYAUME-UNI DE LA GRANDE-BRETAGNE ET D'IRLANDE, ASSEMBLEES EN PARLEMENT
- HISTOIRE DE L'INSURRECTION DU CANADA

Papini, Giovanni *see* IL CREPUSCOLO DEI FILOSOFI

Papon, J *see* RECUEIL D'ARRESTS NOTABLES DES COURS SOUVERAINES DE FRANCE

THE PAPOOSE – 1902-03.(American Indian Periodicals in the Princeton University Library). 4 fiches – 9 – $45.00 – us UPA [073]

Pappas, John N *see* BERTHIER'S "JOURNAL DE TREVOUX" AND THE PHILOSOPHES

Pappe, CW L *see*
- SILVA CAPENSIS
- SILVA CAPENSIS, OR A DESCRIPTION OF SOUTH AFRICAN FOREST TREES AND ARBORESCENT SHRUBS
- SYNOPSIS FILICUM AFRICAE AUSTRALIS

Pappenheim, S *see* AGGADAT ARBA KOSOT

DIE PAPPENHEIMER : EIN REITERLIED / Wolff, Julius – Philadelphia: Philadelphia Demokrat Publishing Company, [18-?] – 1r – 1 – us U.W. Library [780]

Pappritz, Richard *see* DON KARLOS IN DER GESCHICHTE UND IN DER POESIE

Pappus of Alexandria *see* MATHEMATICAE COLLECTIONES A FEDERICO COMMANDINO IN LATINVM CONVERSAE ET COMMENTARIIS ILLVSTRATAE

Paprocki, Stanislaw J *see* MINORITY AFFAIRS AND POLAND: AN INFORMATORY OUTLINE

DER PAPST, DER ABSOLUTISMUS UND DAS CONCIL – (Includes bibliographical references) – Muenchen: Theodor Ackermann, 1869 – 1mf – 9 – 0-8370-8544-6 – 1986-2544 – us A.T.L.A. [240]

PAPST LEO 13. UND DER PROTESTANTISMUS / Brecht, Theodor – Barmen: Hugo Klein, 1888 – 1mf – 9 – 0-8370-8483-0 – 1986-2483 – us A.T.L.A. [240]

PAPST PIUS 10 : EIN BILD KIRCHLICHER REFORMTAETIGKEIT / Hoch, Alexander – (Includes bibliographical references) – Leipzig: G Mueller-Mann, [ca 1907] – 1mf – 9 – 0-8370-8826-7 – 1986-2826 – us A.T.L.A. [920]

PAPST URBAN 2 (1088-1099) (MGH SCHRIFTEN..: 19.BD. 1.TEIL) : HERKUNFT UND KIRCHLICHE LAUFBAHN. DER PAPST UND DIE LATEINISCHE CHRISTENHEIT / Becker, A – 1964 – Dfl25.00 – ne Slangenburg [240]

DAS PAPSTTHUM IN SEINER SOZIAL-KULTURELLEN WIRKSAMKEIT / Hoensbroech, Paul, Graf von – 5. Aufl. Leipzig: Breitkopf und Haertel, 1905 – 4mf – 9 – 0-8370-8351-6 – 1986-2351 – us A.T.L.A. [240]

DAS PAPSTTUM. SEINE IDEE UND IHRE TRAEGER / Krueger, Gustav – 1907 – 1 – us A.T.L.A. [240]

DAS PAPSTTUM UND SEINE UNFEHLBAREN : GESCHICHTE DES ROEMISCHEN PONTIFIKATS / Rolf, A – (Includes index) – Wiesbaden: J G Birlenbach, [1895?] – 1mf – 9 – 0-8370-8373-7 – 1986-2373 – us A.T.L.A. [240]

DIE PAPSTWAHL INNOCENZ 13 / Mayer, Max, Ritter von – Wien: Wilhelm Braumueller, 1874 – 1mf – 9 – 0-8370-8769-4 – 1986-2769 – us A.T.L.A. [240]

DIE PAPSTWAHLEN UNTER DEN KAROLINGERN / Heimbucher, Max – Augsburg: M. Huttler, 1889 – 1mf – us A.T.L.A. [240]

PAPUA AND NEW GUINEA VILLAGER – (Filmed together with: Rabaul News (in Pidgin) Papua New Guinea Dept of Educ (13 jan 1951-31 jan 1959)) – Port Moresby: Papua New Guinea Dept of Education, nov-dec 1951 (in English) – 1r – 1 – PMB Doc405 – at Pacific Mss [073]

Papua New Guinea *see*
- CURRICULUM DEVELOPMENT IN PRIMARY EDUCATION, PAPUA NEW GUINEA SITUATION
- REPORT OF THE ADVISORY COMMITTEE ON EDUCATION IN PAPUA AND NEW GUINEA 1969

Papua New Guinea. Central Planning Office *see* NEW GUINEA'S IMPROVEMENT PLAN FOR 1973-1974(AND)

Papua New Guinea Church Partnership. Formerly, the New Guinea Mission *see* OCCASIONAL PAPERS

Papua New Guinea. Committee of Enquiry *see* REPORT...INTO UNIVERSITY DEVELOPMENT 1974

Papua New Guinea. Department of Education *see*
- 1975 EDUCATION PLAN
- CURRICULUM REVIEW – LATE 1973
- DEVELOPMENT AND CHANGES, PRIMARY CURRICULUM 1972
- DRAFT PROPOSAL FOR SYLLABUS DEVELOPMENT FOR GRADE 7 OF THE PROPOSED 8 YEAR COMMUNITY SCHOOL
- EDUCATION ANNUAL REPORT 1977-1981
- EDUCATION PLAN 1976-1980
- EDUCATION PORTFOLIO: MINISTER'S BRIEF 1987
- EDUCATION STAFFING AND ENROLMENT STATISTICS
- GENERAL PRIMARY CURRICULUM COMMITTEE MEETING, HOUSE OF ASSEMBLY, PORT MORESBY 1971
- NATIONAL OBJECTIVES FOR TEACHERS COLLEGE COURSES
- PRACTICE TEACHING
- PRIMARY CURRICULUM SEMINAR. HOUSE OF ASSEMBLY, PORT MORESBY 1971
- PROPOSED EDUCATION FIVE YEAR PLAN SEPTEMBER 1973
- RECENT DEVELOPMENTS IN EDUCATION
- SIX YEAR PRIMARY CURRICULUM

Papua New Guinea. Five Year Education Plan Committee *see* REPORT 1974

Papua New Guinea. Manpower Planning Unit *see*
- ANALYSIS OF SCHOOL CERTIFICATE EXAMINATION ACHIEVEMENT OF INPUTS TO SELECTED TERTIARY INSTITUTIONS 1972
- DEMAND FOR PRIMARY SCHOOL TEACHERS 1975-1985
- EDUCATION FOR NATIONAL DEVELOPMENT; SOME DIRECTIONS
- MIGRATION AND EDUCATION IN PAPUA NEW GUINEA
- OUTPUT OF NATIONAL HIGH SCHOOLS

PAPUA NEW GUINEA MEDICAL JOURNAL – Boroko. 1955-74*. v18-23 1975-80. v24-37 1981-94*. v38-40 1995-97+ – 1 – D7309 – us UMI [610]

Papua New Guinea. National Archives and Public Records Service *see* PATROL REPORTS

Papua New Guinea. National Education Board *see*
- ANNUAL REPORT FOR 1977-1978
- BIANNUAL REPORT 1979/80

Papua New Guinea National Fisheries Authority. Kanudi Research Station Library *see* PNG COLLECTION

Papua New Guinea National Fisheries Authority. Research Branch *see* MISCELLANEOUS ARCHIVES, 1948-1978

PAPUA NEW GUINEA PATROL REPORTS AND RELATED CORRESPONDENCE, 1954-1963 / Goodger, D R – 1r – 1 – PMB1060 – at Pacific Mss [980]

Papua New Guinea. Teaching Service Commission *see* ANNUAL REPORT 1980

Papua New Guinea Trades Union Congress *see* ARCHIVES

Papuan National Committee *see* VOICE OF THE NEGROIDS IN THE PACIFIC TO THE NEGROIDS THROUGHOUT THE WORLD

PAPUAN NOTES AND TROBRIAND ISLANDS LINGUISTIC MATERIAL 1940S / Baldwin, Father Bernard MSC – 1r – 1 – at Pacific Mss [490]

PAPUAN VILLAGER – v. 1-13. 1929-41 – 1 – 19.00 – us L of C Photodup [980]

Papua-New Guinea. House of Assembly. Select Committee on Constitutional Development *see* FINAL REPORT, TOGETHER WITH...MINUTES OF PROCEEDINGS

Papua-New Guinea. (Territory) *see*
- ECONOMIC DEVELOPMENT OF PAPUA AND NEW GUINEA
- GOVERNMENT GAZETTE
- PROGRAMMES AND POLICIES FOR THE ECONOMIC DEVELOPMENT OF PAPUA AND NEW GUINEA

PAPUANS OF THE TRANS-FLY / Williams, F E – Oxford. 1936. BA-188 2 – 8 – ne IDC [950]

PAPYR CYMRAEG NEWYDD *see* Y PAPYR CYMRAEG NEWYDD

PAPYRI UND TALMUD IN GEGENSEITIGER BELEUCHTUNG / Blau, L L – Leipzig. 1913. BJ-32-13 1 – 9 – ne IDC [410]

LE PAPYRUS DE NEFER RENPET / Speleers, L – Bruxelles, 1917 – 9 – ne IDC [930]

PAPYRUS DE TURIN. FACSIMILES / Rossi, F & Pleyte, W – 2v. Leiden. 1869-1876. BNE-374 1 – 9 – ne IDC [930]

DER PAPYRUS EBERS / Wreszinski, W – (Die Medizin der alten Agypter, v3) – Leipzig, 1913 – 4mf – 9 – ne IDC [930]

LES PAPYRUS EGYPTIENS DU MUSEE DE BOULAQ PUBLIES EN FAC-SIMILE SOUS LES AUSPICES DE S. A. ISMAIL-PACHAK, KHEDIVE D'EGYPTE / Mariette, A – Paris. 1871. BNE-360 1 – 9 – ne IDC [930]

PAPYRUS HIERARIQUES, NOS. 58001-58036 : CATALOGUE GENERAL DES ANTIQUITIES EGYPTIENNES DU MUSEE DU CAIRE / Golenischeff, W – Cairo. v53. 1927 – 6mf – 9 – ne IDC [930]

LES PAPYRUS HIERATIQUES NO 1115, 1116 A ET 1116 B DE L'ERMITAGE IMPERIAL A ST-PETERSBOURG / Golenischeff, W – 9 – ne IDC [930]

DER PAPYRUSFUND VON ELEPHANTINE : DOKUMENTE EINER JUEDISCHEN GEMEINDE AUS DER PERSERZEIT UND DAS AELTESTE ERHALTENE BUCH DER WELTLITERATUR / Meyer, Eduard – (Includes bibliographical references) – 2. Aufl. Leipzig: J C Hinrichs, 1912 – 1mf – 9 – 0-8370-7242-5 – 1986-1242 – us A.T.L.A. [090]

PAPYRUSFUNDE UND PAPYRUSFORSCHUNG / Preisendanz, K – Leipzig. 1933. B-978 2 – 8 – ne IDC [930]

Paquet, Alfons *see* FRAU RAT GOETHE UND IHRE WELT

Paquin, Ubald *see* LA BATAILLE

PAQUIN WORTH FASHION DRAWINGS 1865-1956 / Victoria and Albert Museum. London – (5,000 designs from the houses of Paquin and Worth, the epitome of fashion design in the late 19th and early 20th C. Includes printed index) – 60 colour mf – 15 – $1,056.00 – 0-907696-05-8 – uk Emmett [740]

PAQUITA ADORACION. NOVELAS ORIGINALES / Coronado, Carolina – 1850 – 9 – 1.50f – sp Bibl Santa Ana [830]

PARA DE MINAS : ORGAO POLITICO E NOTICIOSO – Cidade do Para, 22 Sep-Oct 1918; Apr 1919; May-Jul, Sep-Oct 1920; Sep 1922; 25 Feb 1923 – 1,5,6 – bl Biblioteca [072]

PARA E AMAZONAS; QUESTAO DE LIMITES / Verissimo de Mattos, Jose – Rio de Janeiro: Companhia typographica do Brazil, 1899. 95p. Fold. map. 1 reel. 1273 – 1 – us U.W. Library [910]

PARA EVITAR EL VACIAMIENTO DEL PERONISMO / Unamuno, Miguel – [Buenos Aires?]: Editora del Movimiento, [1984] – 1 – CSUXADJ8821-B – us Hoover Inst Photo [320]

PARA LA HISTORIA DEL MONASTERIO DE GUADALUPE : NOTICIA DE UN CODICE INTERESANTE (LIBRO DE LA HACIENDA...EN TRUJILLO, VICONDE DE AMAYA) / Blanco Sanchez, R – Madrid: Tip. R. Arch. B. y M., 1910 – 1 – sp Bibl Santa Ana [240]

PARA PIANO. (NO 4 FROM RECUERDOS DE VLAJE) / Albeniz, I – Madrid: Union Musical Espanola, [19-?] – 1 – us Sibley [780]

PARA QUE EL CAMPESINO TENGA TIERRAS, TRABAJO, LIBERTAD Y BIENESTAR / Spain. Ministerio de Agricultura – Barcelona, 19?? Fiche W1096. (Blodgett Collection of Spanish Civil War Pamphlets) – 9 – us H.U. College Libr [946]

PARA SAKSI : TJERITAPENTAS UNTUK HARI PASKAH / Rosin, B F – 1962 – 9 – SE-5429 1 – ne IDC [950]

PARA TI / Sanchez-Arjona, Vicente – Sevilla: Imp. Carlos Acuna, 1952 – 1 – sp Bibl Santa Ana [810]

PARABALOU – Farmington. v1-3. 1920-feb 1921 – 1 – D4677 – us UMI [073]

DIE PARABELN JESU, METHODISCH AUSGELEGT / Goebel, Siegfried – 1 – us A.T.L.A. [240]

THE PARABLES BY THE LAKE: THE PARABLES AND THEIR HOME / Thomson, William Hanna – New York: Harper, 1895. 1 fiche – 9 – us A.T.L.A. [240]

THE PARABLES OF OUR LORD / Dods, Marcus – London: Hodder and Stoughton, 1902?. 2v – 1 – us U.W. Library [240]

THE PARABLES OF OUR LORD : [FIRST SERIES]: THE PARABLES RECORDED BY MATTHEW / Dods, Marcus – London: Hodder & Stoughton, 1895 – 1mf – 9 – 0-8370-2939-2 – 1985-0939 – us A.T.L.A. [220]

PARABLES OF OUR LORD (SECOND SERIES): THE PARABLES RECORDED BY ST LUKE / Dods, Marcus – London: Hodder & Stoughton, 1894. 1 fiche – 9 – us A.T.L.A. [240]

THE PARABLES OF THE NEW TESTAMENT PRACTICALLY UNFOLDED / Stevens, William Bacon – Philadelphia:J.M. Stoddart, 1871 – 1mf – 9 – 0-8370-5413-3 – 1985-3413 – us A.T.L.A. [220]

PARABLES: READ IN THE LIGHT OF THE PRESENT DAY / Guthrie, Thomas – New York: E.B. Treat, (1891). 1 fiche – 9 – us A.T.L.A. [240]

PARABOLA – New York. v1-9. 1976-84* 1; v10-22. 1985-97+ 1,5,9 – 1,5,9 – D15444 – us UMI [073]

LES PARABOLES DE L'EVANGILE / Klein, Felix – Paris, Madrid: Razon y Fe, 1934 – 1 – sp Bibl Santa Ana [220]

PARABOLY / Kuzmin, M – Stikhotvoreniia. 1921-22. Berlin. 1923. BR-1195 2 – 8 – ne IDC [460]

O PARACATU : HEBDOMADARO LITTERARIO, COMMERCIAL, AGRICOLA E NOTICIOSO – Paracatu, 19 Jun-24 Jul 1897 – 1,5,6 – bl Biblioteca [072]

O PARACATUENSE : HEBDOMADARIO POLITICO, NOTICIOSO, LITTERARIO E AGRICOLA – Paracatu, 19 Dec 1909; Mar-Dec 1910; Jan, Apr-Dec 1911; Jan-11 Feb 1912 – 1,5,6 – bl Biblioteca [072]

PARACHUTE : REVUE D'ART CONTEMPORAINE – Montreal. nos 1-73. 1975-1993/94 – 9 – Can$28.00y – cn Micromedia [700]

LE PARACLET / Boulgakof, S – Paris, 1944 – 7mf – 8 – ne Slangenburg [290]

PARACLETE – Springfield. v1-18 1967-84*. v19-29 1985-95 1; v19-23 1985-89. v24-28 1990-94*. v29 1995 5; v19-29 1985-95 9 – 1,5,9 – D15284 – us UMI [073]

THE PARACLETE / Parker, Joseph – 1874 – 9 – us A.T.L.A. [240]

PARADIGMATA DE QVATOR LINGVIS ORIENTALIBVS, PRAECIPVIS ARABICA, ARMENA, SYRA, AETHIOPICA / Cayet, P V – Parisiis, 1596 – 3mf – 9 – H-8386/1 – ne IDC [956]

PARADIGMATA GRAPHICES VARIORUM ARTIFICIUM EX FORMIS NICOLAI VISSCHER / Episcopius, J – Amsterdam. n.d. vtogether vwith: Idem Signorum veterum icones. S.L. N.D. BO-246 1 – 9 – ne IDC [700]

PARADIGMENWECHSEL IN DER THEORIE DER WISSENSCHAFT / Halfmann, Jost – Frankfurt a.M., 1977 – 4mf – 9 – DM90.00 – 3-89349-371-9 – gw Hänsel [100]

PARADIGMS – (Cont by: Global Society) – Abingdon. 1987-95* – 1 – D24373 – us UMI [073]

Paradin, Claude *see*
- HEROICA M. CLAUDI PARADINI, BELLIIOCENSIS CANONICI, ET D. GABRIELIS SYMEONIS, SYMBOLAT
- PRINCELIICKE DEVIISEN VAN CLAUDE PARADIN, GABRIEL SIMEON, ENDE MEER ANDER
- QUADRINS HISTORIQUES DE LA BIBLE [SUIVIS DE] LA VIE DE MOISE, REPRESENTEE PAR FIGURES [SUIVIE DE] LES DOUZE MOIS DE L'ANNEE, REPRESENTES PAR FIGURES
- SYMBOLA HEROICA M. CLAUDII PARADINI, BELLIIOCENSIS CANONICI

Paradis, Andre *see* BIBLIOGRAPHIE DU R.P. ARCADE-M. MONETTE

LE PARADIS PERDU / Milton, John – Paradise Lost. Paris: Desaint et Saillant, 1755. 3v. 17 fiches. (Literature Collection) – 9 – 42.00 – fr Bibl Nationale [810]

LE PARADIS TERRESTRE: POEME IMITE DE MILTON / DuBoccage, Anne Marie – Londres: s.n., 1748. vi,122p. 2 fiches. (Literature Collection) – 9 – $6.00 – fr Bibl Nationale [810]

PARADISCHES WUNDER-SPIEL WELCHES SICH IN DIESEN LETZTEN ZEITEN UND TAGEN IN DENEN ABENDLAENDISCHEN WELT-THEILEN ALS EIN VORSPIEL DER NEUEN WELT HERVORGETHAN / Ephrata Community – Manuscript, 1751. Agrees in the main with the printed ed. of 1754. MUSIC 1032 – 1 – us L of C Photodup [780]

A PARADISE FOR ANGLERS AND HUNTERS: GRAND TRUNK RAILWAY AND MUSKOKA NAVIGATION COS. TO THE PICTURESQUE MUSKOKA LAKES – 1895?. 02517. (Pre-1900 Canadiana) – 9 – cn C.I.H.M. [639]

PARADISE LOST, A POEM IN TWELVE BOOKS / Milton, John – Introd. and notes on its structure and meaning by John A. Himes.New York, London: Harper & Brothers, 1898.xxxii,482p. illus – 1 – us U.W. Library [810]

THE PARADISE POST – Paradise, CA. 1946 (scats); 1947-49 (broken series); 1950- – 72+ r – 1 – $3,600.00 ($150.00y) – B02609 – us Library Micro [071]

PARADISI IN SOLE PARADISUS TERRESTRIS / Parkinson, J – or A garden of all sorts of pleasant flowers which our English ayre will permitt to be noursed up. London. 1629. B-7363 1 – 9 – ne IDC [580]

PARADISUS ANIMAE INTELLIGENTIS : DEUTSCHE TEXTE DES MITTELALTERS, BD 30 – Berlin, 1919 – 5mf – 8 – ne Slangenburg [290]

PARADISUS DELITIARUM PAULI / Trejo Placentini – 1538 – 9 – 1.50f – sp Bibl Santa Ana [240]

PARADISUS EUCHARISTICUS / Dobrowolski, Augustinus – Lublin, 1652 – 6mf – 8 – Dfl25.00 – ne Slangenburg [240]

THE PARADISUS LONDINENSIS / Salisbury, R A – 629 1. 2 v. 1805-1808 – 9 – ne IDC [580]

PARADISZ GAERTLEIN... / Arndt, Johann – Magdeburg, 1615 – 8mf – 9 – ne IDC [240]

DAS PARADOX DER METAFIKATION : SELBSTREFLEXIVITAET IN NEUEREN DEUTSCHEN ERZAEHLTEXTEN / Frank, Dirk – 1995 – 2mf – 9 – DM80.00 – 3-8267-2211-6 – gw Hänsel [430]

PARADOX REY / Baroja, P – H-558 2. 1917 – 8 – ne IDC [830]

PARADOXA / Sanchez de las Brozas, Francisco – 1582 – 9 – 1.50f – sp Bibl Santa Ana [880]

PARADOXA DVCENTA OCTOGINTA, DAS IST: ZWEYHUNDERT VNND ACHTZIG WUNDERRED / Franck von Woerd, S – Pforzheym, G. Raben. 1558. BME-81 1 – 9 – ne IDC [240]

PARADOXES / Hall, John – 1650 – 9 – 10.00 – us Scholars' Facs [840]

PARAFJA I SKOLA PARAFJALNA WSROD EMIGRACJI POLSKI W AMERYCE : STUDJUM DZIELNICY POLSKIEJ W POL. CHICAGO / Chalasinski, Jozef – Poznan, 1935 – 1r – 1 – us I.H.R.C. [947]

PARAFRASIS A VARIAS COMPOSICIONES DEL BELLISIMO LIBRO "EN VUELO HERIDO" DE LA EGREGIA POETISA EVA CERVANTES / Sanchez-Arjona, Vicente – Sevilla: Imp. Alvarez, 1957 – 1 – sp Bibl Santa Ana [810]

PARAFRASIS DE...DELORES / Salas, Francisco Gregorio de – 1774 – 9 – 1.50f – sp Bibl Santa Ana [810]

PARAFRASIS DEL MAESTRO SOBRE EL CANTAR DE LOS CANTARES EN TONO PASTORIL / Arias Montano, Benito – Madrid: Revista Espanola de Estudios Biblicos, 1928 – 1 – sp Bibl Santa Ana [780]

PARAFRASIS PEQUENAS A LA GRAN OBRA MISTICA "ESTRELLAS MINIMAS" DE LA EGREGIA POETISA EVA CERVANTES / Sanchez-Arjona, Vicente – Sevilla: Imp. Zambrano, 1958 – 1 – sp Bibl Santa Ana [810]

O PARAFUZO – Manaos, Amazonas. 7 Jan 1912 – 1,5,6 – bl Biblioteca [072]

PARAGRAPH : THE FICTION MAGAZINE – (Cont: Cross-Canada Writers' Magazine at v12 no 2 1990) – Stratford. v12-16. 1990-94 – 9 – Can$20.00y – cn Micromedia [420]

PARAGRAPH – New Rochelle. N.Y. 1891-1919 – 1 – us UMI [071]

PARAGRAPH – Oxford. v1-17 1983-94*. v18-20 1995-97+ – 1 – D18520 – us UMI [073]

PARAGRAPH *see* CROSS-CANADA WRITERS' MAGAZINE

PARAGRAPHS ON THE SUBJECT OF JUDICIAL REFORM IN MARYLAND. / Price, William – Baltimore: Toy, 1846. 73p. LL-1377 – 1 – us L of C Photodup [340]

PARAGUAY : ANUARIO ESTADISTICO 1886-1969 / Paraguay. Direccion General de Estadistica y Censos – (1886-1913, 1914-15, 1918-24, 1925-26, 1927, 1930-34 not available. Coll title: Latin American and Caribbean Official Statistical Serials, 1821-1982) – 45mf – 9 – £380.00 – uk Chadwyck [972]

Paraguay *see*
- ECONOMIC PLANS
- GACETA OFICIAL
- REGISTRO OFICIAL

Paraguay. Direccion General de Estadistica y Censos *see* PARAGUAY

THE PARAGUAYAN CHACO;... / Baez, C – New York, 1904 – 1mf – 9 – ILM-333/1 – ne IDC [340]

EL PARAGUAYO INDEPENDIENTE – 1-118. 1845-1952 – 1 – 23.00 – us L of C Photodup [972]

A PARAHYBA E SEUS PROBLEMAS / Almeida, Jose Americo de – Parahyba: Imp. Off., 1923 – 1 – us U.W. Library [972]

A PARAHYBA E SEUS PROBLEMAS / Almeida, Jose Americo de – Second ed., Porto Alegre: Livraria do Globo, 1937. – 1 – us U.W. Library [972]

O PARAISENSE : SEMANARIO DEDICADO AOS INTERESSES DO MUNICIPIO – S. Sebastiao do Paraiso, 28 Jan 1906 – 1,5,6 – bl Biblioteca [072]

A PARALEGAL TRAINER'S MANUAL FOR AFRICA / Tsanga and Ige – 1994 – sz I.C.J. [340]

PARALLEL ALGORITHMS AND APPLICATIONS / ed by Evans, David, J – 1,5,9 – us Gordon [000]

PARALLEL COMPUTING – Amsterdam. v1-23. 1984-97+ 1; v1-8 1984-oct 1988. v9-12 dec 1988-89*. v13-23 1990-97+ 5; v6-23 1988-97+ 9 – 1,5,9 – D42515 – us UMI [000]

THE PARALLEL PSALTER : BEING THE PRAYER-BOOK VERSION OF THE PSALMS AND A NEW VERSION ARRANGED ON OPPOSITE PAGES – (Includes bibliographical references) – Oxford: Clarendon Press, 1898 – 2mf – 9 – 0-8370-9464-X – 1986-3464 – us A.T.L.A. [220]

PARALLEL SOURCE PROBLEMS IN MEDIEVAL HISTORY / Krey, August C & Duncalf, Frederic – New York: Harper, 1912 – 1mf – us A.T.L.A. [900]

PARALLELE 5, REVUE MENSUELLE – French Guiana. 1950-1955 – 1 – us UMI [072]

PARALLELE DE LA PUISSANCE ANGLAISE ET RUSSE RELATIVEMENT A L'EUROPE, SUIVI D'UN APERCU SUR LA GRECE / Pradt, D G F de – (Russia – 19th C. series). 1823 – 9 – fr Hachette [940]

PARALLELE DE L'ARCHITECTURE ANTIQUE ET DE LA MODERNE. / Freart, Roland – Paris. E. Martin, 1650. 7, 109p., ill. (Architecture Series) – 9 – fr Hachette [720]

PARALLELE DE PLANS DES PLUS BELLES SALLES DE SPECTACLES D'ITALIE ET DE FRANCE AVEC DES DETAILS DE MACHINES THEATRALES / Dumont – Paris. n.d. BO-236 1 – 9 – ne IDC [790]

PARAMETERS : JOURNAL OF THE US ARMY WAR COLLEGE – Carlisle Barracks. v1-18. 1971-88* 1; v19-27. 1989-98+ 1,5,9 – 1,5,9 – D17546 – us UMI [073]

Paramos, Jose G *see* LA VERDADERA PATRIA DE CRISTOBAL COLON

O PARANA – '(s.l.')-Curitiba, Brazil. Aug-Oct 1907; Jun-Dec 1910; Feb-May, Jul-30 Nov 1911 – 1,5,6 – bl Biblioteca [072]

PARANA : ORGAO DE PROPAGANDA DO ESTADO – Curityba, Oct-Nov 1929 – 1,5,6 – bl Biblioteca [072]

Parana. Brazil *see* DIARIO OFICIAL

Parana. Brazil. Assembleia *see* DIARIO DE ASSEMBLEIA

Paranikas, M *see* ANTHOLOGIA GRAECA CARMINUM CHRISTIANORUM

Paranjpye, Raghunath Purushottam *see* [PAPERS, 1913?-1924?]

PARAPHARMEX 93 – (See also Sempex-Parapharmex-Accessoirex) – 1992. Microfiches B: Produits Dietetiques et de Parapharmacie – 9 – FF491.00 – fr S.E.M.P. [610]

PARAPHARMEX-ACCESSOIREX 93 – (See also Sempex-Parapharmex-Accessoirex) – 1992. Microfiches B: Produits Dietetiques et de Parapharmacie. Microfiches C: Accessoires et Divers Vendus en Officine – 9 – FF762.00 – fr S.E.M.P. [610]

PARAPHASIS DE LOS PSALMOS DE DAVID...Y MODO DE HABLAR DE LA LENGUA ESPANOLA / Caceres y Sotomayor, Antonio – 1616 – 9 – 1.50f – sp Bibl Santa Ana [240]

PARAPHRASE SUR LES EPISTRES CATHOLIQUES DE S. IACQUES, DE S. PIERRE, DE S. IEAN, ET DE S. IUDE – Saumur: Iean Lesnier, 1646. Publ. anonymously – 1 – us U.W. Library [240]

EEN PARAPHRASE VAN DE BRIEVEN VAN HADEWYCH DOOR HENDRIK MANDE / Mierlo, J van – Dietsche Warande: Belfort, 1909 – 1mf – 8 – ne Slangenburg [290]

PARAPLEGIA – Edinburgh. v1-19. 1963-81* 1; v20-35. 1982-97+ 1,5,9 – 1,5,9 – D13433 – us UMI [616]

PARAPSYCHOLOGY BULLETIN – (Cont by: FRNM Bulletin. Former title: Foundation for Research on the Nature of Man, FRNM Bulletin) – Durham. v1-20 sum 1965-win 1971. v21-26 1972* – 1 – D6436 – us UMI [130]

THE PARAQUAT REPORT, A HIT-AND-RUN HERBICIDE / Brennan, Paul & Sutherland, Richard – 1983, 35p – 9 – 1.00f – at Libertarian Micro [335]

PARA...!QUEMARLOS! / Sanchez-Arjona, Vicente – Sevilla: Imp. Zambrano, Tomo 1. 1956 – 1 – sp Bibl Santa Ana [810]

PARA...!QUEMARLOS! / Sanchez-Arjona, Vicente – Sevilla: Imp. Zambrano, Tomo 2,3. 1956 – 1 – sp Bibl Santa Ana [810]

PARASHAT ELLEH MASEI / Hagiz, M – Jerusalem. 1884. BJ-27 12 1 – 9 – ne IDC [956]

PARASITE IMMUNOLOGY – Oxford. v1 1979*. v2-15 1980-93. v16 1994*. v17-19 1995-97+ 1; v1-16 1979-94*. v17-19 1995-97+ 5; v1-9 1979-87*. v10-15 1988-93. v16 1994*. v17-19 1995-97+ 9 – 1,5,9 – D15542 – us UMI [615]

PARASITES, INFECTIONS AND DISEASES OF FISH IN AFRICA – 1980 – 224p – it F.A.O. [636]

PARASITICA – Belgium. v. 10. 1954; v. 16-20. 1960-64 – 1,5,6 – us Princeton Micro [631]

PARASITOLOGY – Cambridge. v1-33. 1908-41 – 329mf – 9 – ne IDC [616]

PARASITOLOGY – (With cum index for v1-10 1) – Cambridge. v1-71. 1908-75 1; v72-115. 1976-97+ 1,5,9 – 1,5,9 – D11088 – us UMI [590]

Paravicini, Werner *see* DAS UFFENBACHSCHE WAPPENBUCH

PARCHAM – Tabriz: Ahmad Kasravi. Sal 1, shumarah 1-12 (Farvardin 1322-Shahrivar 1322 [Mar 1943-Aug 1943]) – 1 reel – 1 – $170.00 – us MEDOC [950]

THE PARCHMENTS OF THE FAITH / Merrill, George Edmunds – New York: A.D.F. Randolph, 1894.1 fiche – 9 – us A.T.L.A. [240]

Pardee *see* HISTORY OF DULUTH AND ST LOUIS COUNTY PAST AND PRESENT

PARDES – v. 1-2. Odessa. 1892-96. BJ-291-14 1 – 9 – ne IDC [073]

Pardey, Ulrich *see* ZUR KONSTRUKTION EINIGER SEMANTISCHER ANTINOMIEN

Pardi *see* ALMANAK NAUTIKA

Pardi, M *see* BOEKOE PELADJARAN ILMOE PENJEBERANGAN LAOET

Pardi, N *see* KUASAILAH LAUTAN INDONESIA

Pardo, Antonio *see* PEDRO DE VALDIVIA

Pardo Bazan, Condesa Emilia de *see* LA QUIMERA

Pardo Canalis, E *see* LOS REGISTROS DE MATRICULA DE LA ACADEMIA DE SAN FERNANDO DE 1752 A 1815. MADRID, 1967

Pardo de Tavra, T H J *see* THE MEDICINAL PLANTS OF THE PHILIPPINES

Pardoko, R H *see* DUKUN AS REFERRER OF FAMILY PLANNING ACCEPTORS

PARDON PETITIONS AND RELATED PAPERS SUBMITTED IN RESPONSE TO PRESIDENT ANDREW JACKSON'S AMNESTY PROCLAMATION OF MAY 29, 1865 / U.S. Department of State – Amnesty Papers. 73 rolls. M1003 – 1 – us Nat'l Archives [324]

Pare, A *see*
- DIX LIVRES DE LA CHIRURGIE, AVEC LE MAGASIN DES INSTRUMENS NECESSAIRES A ICELLE
- WORKES

Pare, Emile E *see* LA QUEBECOISE

Pare, Richard *see* BIBLIOGRAPHIE ANALYTIQUE DES OUVRAGES EDITES PAR LES PRESSES UNIVERSITAIRES LAVAL, 1950 A 1957

Pare, Rosario *see* BIBLIOGRAPHIE DE L'OEUVRE DE MAURICE LEBEL, SECRETAIRE A LA FACULTE DES LETTRES ET PROFESSEUR DE LITTERATURE GRECQUE A L'UNIVERSITE LAVAL

PARECER ACERCA DE LA ESSENCIA Y CURA...GARROTILLO / Sola, F – SL, SA – 1mf – 9 – sp Cultura [616]

PARECER DE D. ANDRES DAVILA...QUE NO HAY MEDICINA UNIVERSAL... / Davila y Heredia, A – S.L., S.A. – 1mf – 9 – sp Cultura [610]

PARECER DEL DOCTOR...SOBRE EL GARROTILLO... / Nunez, A – Plasencia, 1605 – 1mf – 9 – sp Cultura [610]

PARECER DEL REVERENDO...DEBE SER CABEZA DE LA DICHA RELIGION / Caceres, Diego de – 1642 – 9 – 1.50f – sp Bibl Santa Ana [240]

PARECER QUE DIERON LOS DOCTORES... EN UN ACCIDENTE RECOGIDO POR... / Saavedra, J – Sevilla, 1622 – 1mf – 9 – sp Cultura [610]

PARECER QUE DIO EL R.P...ACERCA SI ERA VALIDA UNA ELECCION. VICARIO DE GUADALUPE / Virgen, Juan de la – S.l., s.i., s.a. 1639? – 1 – sp Bibl Santa Ana [946]

PARECER...ACERCA DE LOS POLVOS VENENOSOS DE MILAN / Sola, F – SL, SA – 1mf – 9 – sp Cultura [610]

PARECERES EN EL ESTADO DE SALUD DE SEVILLA / Peramato, P de – Sevilla, SA – 1mf – 9 – sp Cultura [946]

Paredes *see* TRATADO BREVE DE LA PESTE

Paredes Guillen, Ramon *see* INFORME PRESENTADO A LA JUNTA DE AGRICULTURA, INDUSTRIA Y COMERCIO DE ESTA PROVINCIA ACERCA DE LAS BASES PARA LA FORMACION DE UN PROYECTO DE ENSENANZA AGRICOLA

Paredes Guillen, Vicente *see*
- CRONICON...MUERTO RESUCITADO
- ESCULTURAS PROTOHISTORICAS DE LA PENINSULA HISPANICA
- HIDROCILO PAREDES
- HISTORIA...FRAMONTANOS CELTIVEROS
- JUNTA DE AGRICULTURA...ENSENANZA AGRICOLA
- NOTICIAS. PIEDRA OSCILANTE DE MONTANCHEZ
- NUEVAS INSCRIPCIONES EXTREMENAS
- REPOBLACION DE LA VILLA DE GARROVILLAS
- LOS ZUNIGA, SENORES DE PLASENCIA

Paredes, Guillen Vicente *see* ORIGEN DEL EXTREMADURA...POBLACIONES

Paredi, A *see* SACRAMENTARIUM BERGOMENSE

Parejo Gonzalez, Jose *see* APUNTES DE ESPARRAGALEJO

Parekh, Manilal Chhotalal *see* RAJARSHI RAM MOHAN ROY

Parennin, D *see* SECONDE LETTRE...A MESSIEURS DE L'ACADEMIE DES SCIENCES

PARENT AND SUBSIDIARY CORPORATIONS / Powell, Frederick James – Chicago: Callaghan, 1931. 172p. LL-1062 – 1 – us L of C Photodup [340]

Parent, Etienne *see* LECTURE PRONONCEE PAR E. PARENT DEVANT L'INSTITUT CANADIEN, JEUDI LE 19 NOVEMBRE 1846

Parent, J M *see* LA DOCTRINE DE LA CREATION DANS L'ECOLE DE CHARTRES

Parent, Jean-Baptiste *see* BIO-BIBLIOGRAPHIE DE MONSEIGNEUR ALEXANDRE VACHON

PARENTAL DRUG ASSOCIATION: BULLETIN – v19-28. 1965-74 – 1,5,6 – us Princeton Micro [073]

THE PARENTAL OBLIGATION TO CARE FOR THE RELIGIOUS EDUCATION OF CHILDREN / Enderbrock, D M – Washington, D.C., 1955 – 8mf – 8 – ne Slangenburg [240]

PARENTALIA : OR, MEMOIRS OF THE FAMILY OF THE WRENS / Wren, Christopher – London, 1750 – 5mf – ne IDC [700]

Parent-Duchatelet, A J B *see*
- HYGIENE PUBLIQUE OU MEMOIRES SUR LES QUESTIONS LES PLUS IMPORTANTES DE L'HYGIENE APPLIQUEE AUX PROFESSIONS ET AUX TRAVAUX D'UTILITE PUBLIQUE
- DE LA PROSTITUTION DANS LA VILLE DE PARIS, CONSIDEREE SOUS LE RAPPORT DE L'HYGIENE PUBLIQUE, DE LA MORALE ET DE L'ADMINISTRATION; OUVRAGE APPUYE DE DOCUMENTS STATISTIQUES PUISES DANS LES ARCHIVES DE LA PREFECTURE DE PARIS

Parent-Duchatelet, Alexandre Jean Baptiste *see* DE LA PROSTITUTION DANS LA VILLE DE PARIS??: CONSIDEREE SOUS LE RAPPORT DE L'HYGIENE PUBLIQUE, DE LA MORALE ET DE L'ADMINISTRATION

PARENTE RITUELLE ET SOCIETE A CHIA, PEROU / Christinat, J -L – 1979. xxxvi/748p – 9 – F210.00 – fr Ethnologie [306]

PARENTESCO ENTRE LOS CONQUISTADORES ESPANOLES... / Morales, Adolfo de – Santa Cruz de la Sierra (Bolivia): Univ. Gabriel Rene Moreno, 1958. Sep. de la Revista de la Universidad, pp. 34-41 – sp Bibl Santa Ana [946]

PARENTS – (See also: Parents' Magazine) – v53- 1978- – 5,6,9 – us UMI [640]

THE PARENT'S ASSISTANT : OR, STORIES FOR CHILDREN / Edgeworth, Maria – Paris: Baudry, Bobe e et Hingray, Galignani, 1827 – 2 rolls – 1 – 1-55879-261-9 – uk Libr Preservation [830]

PARENTS' ATTITUDES REGARDING THE LEISURE BEHAVIOR OF THEIR HANDICAPPED CHILD / Folkerth, Jean E – 1982 – 2mf – 9 – $8.00 – us Microform Publ [790]

PARENTS' MAGAZINE – v52-53 1977-1978 – 1,5,6,9 – us UMI [640]

PARENTS' MAGAZINE *see* PARENTS' MAGAZINE AND BETTER HOMEMAKING

PARENTS' MAGAZINE AND BETTER FAMILY LIVING – (v44-48. 1969-73. 5,6. v45-47. 1970-72. 9. See also: Parents' Magazine and Better Homemaking) – v1-48. 1926-73 – 1 – us UMI [370]

PARENTS' MAGAZINE AND BETTER FAMILY LIVING *see* PARENTS' MAGAZINE AND BETTER HOMEMAKING

PARENTS' MAGAZINE AND BETTER HOMEMAKING – (Cont: Parents' Magazine and Better Family Living. Cont by: Parents' Magazine) – Bergenfield. v48-52. nov 1973-jun 77 – 1,5,9 – D163.01 – us UMI [640]

PARENTS SUCCESSFULLY SEPARATING FROM ADOLESCENTS: A STUDY IN THE PHENOMENON OF SEPARATION / Grantham, David B – 1982 – 1 – 5.44 – us Baptist [240]

PARENTS, TEACHERS FIGHT OVER PLEASE-YOURSELF SCHOOL FREEDOM / Blakeney, Sally – 1972 (Currambena). 1p – 9 – 1.00f – at Libertarian Micro [335]

Parenty, Auguste *see* LES ANCIENNES CORPORATIONS D'ARTS ET METIERS DE LA VILLE D'ARRAS

PARERE...SOPRA L'ORDINE DI GUERREGGIARE LA POTENZA DEL TURCO, & QUELLO, CHE IN CIO EGLI GIUDICA NECESSARIO DI FARE PER SUPERARLO / Mora, D – Bologna, 1572 – 1mf – 9 – H-8333/1 – ne IDC [956]

PARERGA ATQUE ORNAMENTA... / Rubeis, II de – Quae extabant in ruinis domus Imperat. Titi elegantiam. Romae, s.a. – 9 – ne IDC [700]

PARERGA ATQUE ORNAMENTA. QUAE EXTABANT IN RUINIS DOMUS IMPERAT / Rubeis, II de – O 1084 – 9 – ne IDC [930]

LA PARFAICT JOALLIER, OU HISTOIRE DES PIERRERIES: OU SONT AMPLEMENT DESCRITES LEUR NAISSANCE, JUSTE PRIX, MOYEN DES LES COGNOISTRE, ET SE GARDER DES CONTREFAITES... / Boece de Boodt, Anselme – Lyon, chez Iean-Antoine Huguetan, 1644. 32p., 2 depl., 746p., 34p. (Histoire des Sciences XVIIe-XIXe Siecles) – 9 – fr Hachette [730]

LE PARFAIT CAPITAINE, AUTREMENT L'ABREGE DES GUERRES DE GAULE, DES COMMENTAIRES DE CESAR / Rohan, Henry I – Paris. J. Mouze, 1636. 390p. (Strategy of War Series) – 9 – fr Hachette [355]

LE PARFAIT MAITRE A CHANTER.. / Corrette, M – Nouvelle edition.... 1782 – 9 – us Sibley [780]

LE PARFAIT MARESCHAL, QUI ENSEIGNE A CONNOISTRE LA BEAUTE, LA BONTE ET LES DEFAUTS DES CHEVAUX / Solleysel, Jacques de – Paris: Chez Emery: Saugrain Pere: Pierre Martin, 1733. SEM105P954 – 10mf – 9 – Can$22.50 – cn Bibl Nat [590]

LE PARFAIT MISSIONNAIRE OU LA VIE DU R.P. JULIEN MAUNOIR / Boschet, A – Paris, 1697 – 6mf – 9 – CA-160/1 – ne IDC [240]

Parfusser, A *see* VERMERCKT AIN VNNDERWEYSUNG. WIDER DIE SECT DER ZWYTAUFFER

PARI; PARTAI REPOEBLIK INDONESIA / Tan Malaka – SE 2144 1. 1946 – 9 – ne IDC [320]

LE PARIA – Paris. mai 1922-avr 1926 – 1 – fr A.C.R.P.P. [073]

PARIBASAN BEBASAN SALOKA / Adi, S – SE-3970 1. 1954 – 9 – ne IDC [950]

PARIDIS CRASSI BONONIENSIS DE CAEREMONIIS CARDINALIUM – Venetiis, 1582 – 4mf – 8 – Dfl19.00 – ne Slangenburg [240]

PARINARIUM : ORGAO LITTERARIO E OPPORTUNO – Manaos, Amazonas. 26 Set 1909-24 Abr 1910 – 1,5,6 – bl Biblioteca [072]

PARINTINS : ORGAO DO PARTIDO REPUBLICANO FEDERAL – Parintins, Amazonas. 10 Jul 1907-26 Mar 1911 – 1,5,6 – bl Biblioteca [072]

PARIS – 1957- 1; 1974- 5,6; 1975- 4 x 6 in. 9 – us UMI [400]

PARIS / Allen, Grant – London: G. Richards, 1897. 05055. (Pre-1900 Canadiana) – 9 – cn C.I.H.M. [910]

PARIS – Paris. 20 oct 1852-8 dec 1853 – 1 – fr A.C.R.P.P. [073]

PARIS – Red. en chef Ch. Laurent. Paris. juil 1881-82 – 1 – fr A.C.R.P.P. [073]

Paris *see* NEWSPAPERS OF THE PARIS COMMUNE

Paris. Archives Nationales *see* LES INVENTAIRES DES ARCHIVES NATIONALES DE PARIS

Paris, Auguste Joseph *see* LA JEUNESSE DE ROBESPIERRE ET LA CONVOCATION DES ETATS GENERAUX EN ARTOIS

Paris. Biblioteka Polska *see* KATALOG REKOPISOW

Paris. Conseil Municipal *see* BULLETIN MUNICIPAL OFFICIEL

Paris, D Julian *see*
- DU PREMIER ESPRIT DE L'ORDRE DE CISTEAUX
- NOMASTICON CISTERCIENSE

PARIS – DAKAR – TOMBOUCTOU – ALGER – CASABLANCA – PARIS : QUELQUES IMPRESSIONS DE ROUTE – [Paris: Les Presses de T Brugiere, 1925] – us Res Libr [910]

Paris, E. G *see* INDEX BRYOLOGICUS

Paris. Ecole Normale Superieure *see* ANNALES SCIENTIFIQUES

Paris, Emilien *see* LIBRES-PENSEURS RELIGIEUX

PARIS EVANGELICAL MISSIONARY SOCIETY ARCHIVES 1822-1935 / Departement Evangelique Francais d'Action Apostolique (DEFAP), Paris – (Includes printed guide) – 5,984mf – 9 – ne IDC [240]

PARIS MATCH – 1948-1994 – 3r per y – 5,6 – sz Infoprint [073]

Paris, Matthew *see* CHRONICA MAIORA

PARIS MAY '68 / Bibliotheque Nationale – (This document includes a printed guide) – 391mf – 9 – ne IDC [080]

PARIS MODERNE – Revue litteraire et artistique. no. 1-32. Paris. mars 1881-mars 1883 – 1 – fr A.C.R.P.P. [073]

THE PARIS MONTHLY REVIEW OF BRITISH AND CONTINENTAL LITERATURE – No1-12. Paris. 1822-janv 1823. absorbe par: Galignani's Monthly Review and Magazine – 1 – fr A.C.R.P.P. [073]

PARIS: MONUMENTS ELEVES PAR LA VILLE, 1850-1880 / Narjoux, Felix – (v1.Edifices administratifs, judiciaires. v2.Edifices consacres a l'Instruction publique. v3.Edifices consacres aux Beaux-Arts, Edifices religieux. v4.Edifices decoratifs, etc) – Paris: Morel, 1883. 4v in fol., pl. (Architecture Series) – 9 – fr Hachette [720]

Paris. Museum national d'histoire naturelle *see* NOUVELLES ANNALES DU MUSEUM D'HISTOIRE NATURELLE

PARIS NEWS – 1916- – 1 – us UMI [072]

Paris Peace Conference *see* PUBLICATIONS

Paris, Pierre *see*
- PROMENADES ARCHEOLOGIQUES
- RESTES DU CULTE DE MITHRA EN ESPAGNE. LE MITRHEUM DE MERIDA

Paris, R. and G. Dilleman *see* COLLOQUIUM ON MEDICAL PLANTS, ORGANIZED BY THE BOTANICAL SOCIETY OF FRANCE

PARIS REVIEW – (With cum index for 1953-63. v19 is missing in number only) – Flushing. 1953-65. n36-44 win 1966-fal 1968. v12-18 1968-77. v20-39 1978-97+ 1; v13-18 sum 1970-win 1977. v20-39 1978-97+ 5; v16-18 1975-77. v20-39 1978-97+ 9 – 1,5,9 – D2132 – us UMI [073]

PARIS, SA POPULATION, SON INDUSTRIE / Cochin, Augustin – Memoire lu a l'Academie des Sciences morales et politiques les 18 et 25 juin 1864. Paris, 1864. 86p.1 fiche. (Political Science Collection) – 9 – 6.00 – fr Bibl Nationale [310]

Paris. Service de la Statistique municipale *see* RESULTATS STATISTIQUES DE DENOMBREMENT DE 1881 POUR LA VILLE DE PARIS: ET RENSEIGNEMENTS RELATIFS AUX RECENSEMENTS ANTERIEURS

PARIS STAR – Paris, 1967-1972 – 3r – 1 – cn Preston [971]

Paris. Universite. Institut Henri Poincare *see*
- ANNALES
- ANNALES. SECTION A: PHYSIQUE THEORETIQUE
- ANNALES. SECTION B: CALCUL DES PROBABILITES ET STATISTIQUES

PARIS-CANADA : ORGANE INTERNATIONAL DES INTERETS CANADIENS ET FRANCAIS – Paris, France. 11 jun 1884-15 jan 1909 – 3r – 1 – Can$70.00r – cn Can Microfilming [072]

PARIS-CAPRICE – Gazette illustree litteraire et artistique. Red. Eugene Schnert. no. 1-142. Paris. dec 1867-aout 1870 – 1 – fr A.C.R.P.P. [073]

PARIS-COMET – Paris. oct 1927-janv fevr 1930 – 1 – fr A.C.R.P.P. [073]

PARIS-DAKAR – 1933-36.-3r.$148.50; 1937-44.-13r.$643.50 – 1 – us African Imprint [072]

PARIS-DAKAR – Dir. Charles de Breteuil. Dakar. 1947-48. mq fevr 1947 – 1 – fr A.C.R.P.P. [073]

PARIS-DEMAIN / La Democratie Socialiste du XXe Arrondissement – Paris. juil 1933-mai 1936. remplace par: Le Front – 1 – fr A.C.R.P.P. [073]

PARISER KURIER – Paris. 1972-1982 – 1 – gw Mikrofilm [072]

PARISER TAGEBLATT – Paris. 12 dec 1933-18 fevr 1940 – 1 – fr A.C.R.P.P. [073]

PARISER TAGEBLATT – Paris. Dec. 12, 1933-Jan. 14, 1936. Missing: no. 193, June 23, 1934. Pariser Tagezeitung. June 12, 1936-Feb. 18, 1940 – 1 – 35.00r – us Hoover Inst Photo [072]

PARISER TAGEBLATT : QUOTIDIEN EN LANGUE ALLEMANDE – (Cont by: Pariser Tageszeitung) – Paris; FR. 1933-40 – 12r – 1 – gw Mikrofilm [072]

PARISER TAGESZEITUNG *see* PARISER TAGEBLATT

PARISER ZEITUNG – France. -w. 23 Feb 1941-24 Aug 1944. (10 reels) – 1 – uk British Libr Newspaper [072]

PARISER ZEITUNG – Paris. 1941-mars 1942 – 1 – fr A.C.R.P.P. [073]

PARIS-FLIRT – Gaite, humour et fantaisie. Paris. fevr 1957-janv 1959 – 1 – fr A.C.R.P.P. [073]

PARISH AND HOME – Toronto: Pub. for the Alumni Association of Wycliffe College by the J.E. Bryant Co, [1890-19–] – 9 – cn C.I.H.M. [240]

PARISH AND HOME/ PAUL'S CHURCH, LINDSAY – (Cont: Parish Magazine/St. Paul's Church, Lindsay) – Lindsay, Ont: Canadian Post Office, [1893 or 1892-19–] – 9 – cn C.I.H.M. [240]

PARISH AND HOME/ST. PAUL'S CHURCH, LINDSAY *see* PARISH MAGAZINE/ PAUL'S CHURCH, LINDSAY

PARISH CHOIR OR CHURCH MUSIC BOOK – v.1-3 (no. 1-63). February 1846-March 1951 – 1 – 20.00 – us L of C Photodup [780]

THE PARISH CHOIR, OR CHURCH MUSIC BOOK / Society for Promoting Church Music – London. 1846-51. 1 reel – 1 – 17.00 – us L of C Photodup [780]

THE PARISH CHURCH MAGAZINE – [S.1: s.n. 1888?-18– or 19–] – 9 – cn C.I.H.M. [240]

PARISH CHURCH RECORDS / Angus, Scotland – 1618-1941 – 1 – uk Microform Academic [920]

PARISH CHURCH REGISTER OF BURIALS / Govan, Scotland – 1710-1940 – 1 – uk Microform Academic [920]

PARISH CHURCH WORK – (Cont by: St. George's Parish Magazine) – [Toronto?: s.n. 1881)-1882] – 9 – cn C.I.H.M. [240]

PARISH CHURCH WORK *see* ST. GEORGE'S PARISH MAGAZINE

THE PARISH CLERK / Ditchfield, P H – London: Methuen, 1907 – 1mf – us A.T.L.A. [240]

PARISH COMM. MINUTES 1914-1930, FINANCIAL REPORTS, 1923-1934 / PNCC, Western Diocese, Sacred Hearth Church – Minneapolis, MN, 1914-1965 – 1r – 1 – us I.H.R.C. [240]

THE PARISH GUIDE – [Hamilton, Ont?: s.n. 1894?-189- or 19–] – 9 – cn C.I.H.M. [240]

THE PARISH GUILDS OF MEDIEVAL ENGLAND / Westlake, H F – H 1341 2. 1919 – 8 – ne IDC [360]

PARISH LIFE IN MEDIAEVAL ENGLAND / Gasquet, Abbot – London: Methuen, 1906 – 1mf – us A.T.L.A. [240]

PARISH MAGAZINE – [Toronto?: s.n. 1881?-18– or 19–] – 9 – cn C.I.H.M. [240]

PARISH MAGAZINE *see* AVON DEANERY MAGAZINE
THE PARISH MAGAZINE AND CHURCH & SUNDAY SCHOOL REGISTER – Toronto: Church Book Association [18–18– or 19–] – 9 – cn C.I.H.M. [240]
PARISH MAGAZINE/ JAMES' CHURCH, STRATFORD – Stratford, Ont: Stratford Beacon, [18—189- or 19–] – 9 – cn C.I.H.M. [240]
PARISH MAGAZINE/ PAUL'S CHURCH, LINDSAY – (Cont by: Parish and Home/ St. Paul's Church, Lindsay) – Lindsay [Ont]: Canadian Post Office, [1891-1891 or 1892] – 9 – cn C.I.H.M. [240]
THE PARISH MAGAZINE, VICTORIA – Victoria [B.C.: s.n. 1873-18–] – 9 – cn C.I.H.M. [240]
PARISH MAGAZINE/CHAPTER HOUSE – London, Ont: Southam and Brierley, [1887?-18– or 19–] – 9 – cn C.I.H.M. [240]
PARISH MAGAZINE/ST. PAUL'S CHURCH, LINDSAY *see* PARISH AND HOME/ PAUL'S CHURCH, LINDSAY
PARISH NOTES – (Cont by: St John's Church Record and Parish Notes) – St. John, N.B.: G.G. Ruel, [1891-1892] – 9 – cn C.I.H.M. [240]
PARISH NOTES *see* ST. JOHN'S CHURCH RECORD AND PARISH NOTES
PARISH OF ORLEANS REPORTS / Louisiana. Orleans Court of Appeals – v1-14. 1903-17 (all publ) – 30mf – 9 – $135.00 – LLMC 84-145 – us L.L.M.C. [340]
PARISH PAPERS / Macleod, Norman – London: Alexander Strahan, 1862 – 1mf – 9 – 0-8370-4221-6 – 1985-2221 – us A.T.L.A. [240]
PARISH PRIESTS AND THEIR PEOPLE IN THE MIDDLE AGES IN ENGLAND / Cutts, Edward L – London: S.P.C.K.; New York: E.& J.B. Young, 1898 – 2mf – us A.T.L.A. [240]
PARISH QUESTIONNAIRES AND RELATED MATERIALS / Archdiocese of St. Paul and Minneapolis – Materials (1890s-1974) documenting the history of Catholic parishes in Minnesota, North and South Dakota. 23 reels, including filmed inventory – 1 – $690.00 $30.00r – us M.H.S. [240]
PARISH RECORDS / Anthony. Kansas. Grace Episcopal Church – 1901-45 – 1 – us KS Hist [978]
PARISH RECORDS / Junction City. Kansas. Church of the Covenant – 1870-1968 – 1 – us KS Hist [978]
PARISH RECORDS / Protestant Episcopal Church in the U.S.A. Western Kansas (Diocese) – 1893-1970 – 1 – us KS Hist [978]
PARISH RECORDS / United Methodist Church – 1859-1972 – 1 – us KS Hist [978]
PARISH RECORDS OF VARIOUS TOWNS / Protestant Episcopal Church in the U.S.A. Western Kansas (Missionary District) – 1879-1968 – 1 – us KS Hist [978]
PARISH RECORDS OF VARIOUS TOWNS / Protestant Episcopal Church in the U.S.A. Western Kansas (Missionary District) – 1913-69 – 1 – us KS Hist [978]
PARISH REGISTERS / Ackworth. Yorkshire – 1558-1868 – 1 – uk Microform Academic [941]
PARISH REGISTERS / Acomb. Yorkshire – 1725-1847 – 1 – uk Microform Academic [941]
PARISH REGISTERS / Adwick-le-Street. Yorkshire – 1547-1865 – 1 – uk Microform Academic [920]
PARISH REGISTERS / Almondbury. Yorkshire. All Hallows – 1557-1812 – 1 – uk Microform Academic [941]
PARISH REGISTERS / Alverthorpe. Yorkshire. St. Paul's – 1825-92 – 1 – uk Microform Academic [941]
PARISH REGISTERS / Badsworth. Yorkshire – 1584-1879 – 1 – uk Microform Academic [941]
PARISH REGISTERS / Barnoldswick. Yorkshire – 1587-1776 – 1 – uk Microform Academic [941]
PARISH REGISTERS / Blacktoft. Yorkshire – 1813-1930 – 1 – uk Microform Academic [941]
PARISH REGISTERS / Bramham. Yorkshire – 1586-1737 – 1 – uk Microform Academic [240]
PARISH REGISTERS / Cayton. Yorkshire – 1684-1837 – 1 – uk Microform Academic [240]
PARISH REGISTERS / Crofton. Yorkshire – 1689-1886 – 1 – uk Microform Academic [920]
PARISH REGISTERS / Darrington. Yorkshire – 1754-1881 – 1 – uk Microform Academic [920]
PARISH REGISTERS / Darton. Yorkshire – 1647-1812 – 1 – uk Microform Academic [920]
PARISH REGISTERS / Dent. Yorkshire – 1611-1812 – 1 – uk Microform Academic [920]
PARISH REGISTERS / Dewsbury. Yorkshire – 1653-1699 – 1 – uk Microform Academic [941]
PARISH REGISTERS / East Ardsley. Yorkshire – 1654-1812 – 1 – uk Microform Academic [941]
PARISH REGISTERS / Edstone. Yorkshire – 1772-1812 – 1 – uk Microform Academic [941]
PARISH REGISTERS / Emley. Yorkshire. St. Michael – 1600-1812 – 1 – uk Microform Academic [941]
PARISH REGISTERS / Hanbury. Staffordshire – 1574-1812 – 1 – uk Microform Academic [920]
PARISH REGISTERS / Heptonstall. Yorkshire – 1593-1812 – 1 – uk Microform Academic [941]
PARISH REGISTERS / Howden. Yorkshire – 1770-1812 – 1 – uk Microform Academic [941]
PARISH REGISTERS / Huddersfield. Yorkshire – 1562-1812 – 1 – uk Microform Academic [941]
PARISH REGISTERS / Hutton Buscel. Yorkshire – 1572-1837 – 1 – uk Microform Academic [941]
PARISH REGISTERS / Hutton Wandsley. (Long Marston). Yorkshire – 1645-59 and 1694-1895 – 1 – uk Microform Academic [941]
PARISH REGISTERS / Keele. Staffordshire – 1540-1812 – 1 – uk Microform Academic [941]
PARISH REGISTERS / Kirkburton. Yorkshire. All Hallows – 1540-1899 – 1 – uk Microform Academic [941]
PARISH REGISTERS / Kirkheaton. Yorkshire – 1653-1873 – 1 – uk Microform Academic [941]
PARISH REGISTERS / Lawkland. Yorkshire – 1816-61 – 1 – uk Microform Academic [941]
PARISH REGISTERS / Leconfield. Yorkshire – 1551-1812 – 1 – uk Microform Academic [941]
PARISH REGISTERS / Leek. Staffordshire – 1696-1812 – 1 – uk Microform Academic [941]
PARISH REGISTERS / London. All-Hallows. (London Wall) – 1675-1812. From Guildhall Library. London – 1 – uk Microform Academic [941]
PARISH REGISTERS / London. St. Anne, Blackfriars – 1560-1837. From Guildhall Library, London – 1 – uk Microform Academic [920]
PARISH REGISTERS / London. St. Bartholomew, Exchange – 1558-1837. From Guildhall Library, London – 1 – uk Microform Academic [920]
PARISH REGISTERS / London. St. Botolph, Aldgate – 1558-1625. From Guildhall Library, London – 1 – uk Microform Academic [941]
PARISH REGISTERS / London. St. Christopher Le Stocks – 1558-1781. From Guildhall Library, London – 1 – uk Microform Academic [941]
PARISH REGISTERS / London. St. Lawrence, Pountney – 1538-1739. From Guildhall Library, London – 1 – uk Microform Academic [941]
PARISH REGISTERS / London. St. Martin's, Ironmonger Lane – 1559-1837. From Guildhall Library, London – 1 – uk Microform Academic [941]
PARISH REGISTERS / London. St. Mary Abchurch – 1558-1839. From Guildhall Library, London – 1 – uk Microform Academic [941]
PARISH REGISTERS / London. St. Mary Bothaw, Bowgate – 1536-1654. From Guildhall Library, London – 1 – uk Microform Academic [941]
PARISH REGISTERS / London. St. Mary, Colechurch – 1558-1812. From Guildhall Library, London – 1 – uk Microform Academic [941]
PARISH REGISTERS / London. St. Mildred, Poultry – 1538-1837. From Guildhall Library, London – 1 – uk Microform Academic [941]
PARISH REGISTERS / London. St. Olav, Jewry – 1558-1837. From Guildhall Library, London – 1 – uk Microform Academic [941]
PARISH REGISTERS / London. St. Stephen, Coleman Street – 1538-1837. From Guildhall Library, London – 1 – uk Microform Academic [941]
PARISH REGISTERS / London. St. Swithin, London Stone – 1615-1837. From Guildhall Library, London – 1 – uk Microform Academic [941]
PARISH REGISTERS / London. St. Andrew by the Wardrobe – 1560-1837. Also, St. Anne, Blackfriars Parish Registers, 1558-1837. From Guildhall Library, London – 1 – uk Microform Academic [941]
PARISH REGISTERS / Marston-on-Dove.Staffordshire – Also, Sudbury and Tutbury Parish Registers – 1 – uk Microform Academic [941]
PARISH REGISTERS / North Frodingham. Yorkshire – 1660-76 – 1 – uk Microform Academic [941]
PARISH REGISTERS / Old Malton. Yorkshire – 1606-1863 – 1 – uk Microform Academic [941]
PARISH REGISTERS / Otley. Yorkshire – 1745 to 1783 – 1 – uk Microform Academic [941]
PARISH REGISTERS / Penistone. Yorkshire – 1643-1844 – 1 – uk Microform Academic [920]
PARISH REGISTERS / Raskelf. Yorkshire – 1600-1746 – 1 – uk Microform Academic [941]
PARISH REGISTERS / Royston. Yorkshire. St. John the Baptist – 1 – uk Microform Academic [941]
PARISH REGISTERS / Saddleworth. Yorkshire. St. Chad's – 1613-1891 – 1 – uk Microform Academic [240]
PARISH REGISTERS / Sandal Magna. Yorkshire – 1651-1832 – 1 – uk Microform Academic [941]
PARISH REGISTERS / Scarborough. Yorkshire – 1602-82 – 1 – uk Microform Academic [941]
PARISH REGISTERS / Silkstone. Yorkshire – 1558-1830 – 1 – uk Microform Academic [941]
PARISH REGISTERS / Snaith. Yorkshire – 1656-1727 – 1 – uk Microform Academic [941]
PARISH REGISTERS / Tankersley. Yorkshire – 1595-1843 – 1 – uk Microform Academic [941]
PARISH REGISTERS / Wedmore Parish. England – Baptisms, 1561-1812. Wells: J.M. Atkins, 1890 – 1 – us U.W. Library [240]
PARISH REGISTERS / Wensley. Yorkshire – 1754-1812 – 1 – uk Microform Academic [941]
PARISH REGISTERS / Whitby. Yorkshire – 1669-1768 – 1 – uk Microform Academic [941]
PARISH REGISTERS / Woodkirk. Yorkshire – 1652-1832 – 1 – uk Microform Academic [941]
PARISH REGISTERS / Woolley. Yorkshire – 1651-1812 – 1 – uk Microform Academic [941]
PARISH REGISTERS / York. Holy Trinity – Yorkshire. 1754-1837 – 1 – uk Microform Academic [941]
PARISH REGISTERS / York. St. Martin's-cum-Gregory – Yorkshire. 1735-1837 – 1 – uk Microform Academic [941]
THE PARISH REGISTERS OF ENGLAND / Cox, John Charles – London: Methuen, 1910. (The Antiquary's books) – 1mf – us A.T.L.A. [240]
PARISH RUBRIC – Carson City, NV. Feb 1898; Mar-Apr 1901; Jun 1904 – 1r – 1 – $50.00 – U04471 – us Library Micro [071]
PARISH SCHOOL ADVOCATE AND FAMILY INSTRUCTOR *see* THE INSTRUCTOR
THE PARISH SCHOOL ADVOCATE AND FAMILY INSTRUCTOR – (Cont by: The Instructor) – [Bay Verte, N.B.?: s.n.], 1858-1859 (Halifax, N.S.: J Barnes) – 9 – cn C.I.H.M. [370]
THE PARISH SCHOOLS OF NEW YORK : A BRIEF STATEMENT GIVING REPORT OF ATTENDANCE AND EXPENSES OF PARISH SCHOOLS IN THE CITY OF NEW YORK – New York: Columbus Press, 1905 – 1mf – 9 – 0-8370-7582-3 – 1986-1582 – us A.T.L.A. [370]
THE PARISH SUNBEAM – Gorrie [Ont: s.n. 1892-189- or 19–] – 9 – cn C.I.H.M. [240]
LE PARISIEN – (Also available on CD-ROM) – France. 1988-1995 – 6r per y – 5,6 – Sfr1,176.00 – sz Infoprint [944]
LE PARISIEN – Journal politique, commercial et litteraire. Chronique des cours d'assises et des tribunaux correctionnels. Paris. 9 sept-dec 1842 – 1 – fr A.C.R.P.P. [073]
LE PARISIEN – (Yrly reel count varies) – 1988- – 5 – us Ross [072]
PARISIEN – 1944-1995 – 1 – sz Infoprint [072]
PARISIEN – 1988-1995 – 6 times per yr – 6 – F4,400.00 – sz Infoprint [072]
LE PARISIEN LIBERE – Paris. Toutes eds. 22 aout 1944-1985 – 1 – fr A.C.R.P.P. [073]
UNE PARISIENNE AU BRESIL / Toussaint-Samson, Adele – Paris, 1883. 234p. (Les Femmes Collection) – 3mf – 9 – $8.00 – fr Bibl Nationale [920]
Parisius, L *see* DEUTSCHLANDS POLITISCHE PARTEIEN UND DAS MINISTERIUM BISMARK
PARISJANA : DEUTSCHE VERSE AUS PARIS / Panizza, Oskar – Zuerich: Verlag Zuercher Diskussionen, 1899 – 1r – 1 – us U.W. Library [810]
PARIS-JOURNAL – Dir. Henry de Pene. Paris. 11 juil 1869-juin 1870, 1871-17 juil 1882, 1910-mars 1912, 1913-3 juil 1924, 21 mars 1929, 9 nov 1930, 12 fevr-12 nov 1933 – 1 – fr A.C.R.P.P. [073]
PARIS-JOURNAL – Paris. 15 mai 1891-28 dec 1910 4, janv 1911 – 1 – fr A.C.R.P.P. [073]
PARIS-LONDRES – Paris. 1837-42 – 1 – fr A.C.R.P.P. [073]
PARIS-LONDRES JOURNAL – London, UK. 2, 30 Apr-29 May 1914 – 1 – uk British Libr Newspaper [072]
PARIS-MIDI – Paris. 7 fevr 1911-10 juin 1940, 17 fevr 1941-15 aout 1944 – 1 – fr A.C.R.P.P. [073]
PARIS-MONTREAL / Bles, Numa – Montreal: [Imp. La Patrie], 1902. SEM105P1662 – 1mf – 9 – Can$2.25 – cn Bibl Nat [073]
PARIS-NORMANDIE – Rouen. 1960-66 – 1 – fr A.C.R.P.P. [073]
Parisot, Jean Patrocle *see* LA FOY DEVOILEE PAR LA RAISON, DANS LA CONNAISSANCE DE DIEU, DE SES MYSTERES, ET DE LA NATURE
Parisot, Sabastien Antoine *see* TRAITE DU CALCUL CONJECTURAL OU L'ART DE RAISONNER SUR LES CHOSES FUTURES ET INCONNUES
PARIS-PRESSE – puis Paris-presse L'Intransigeant; Paris-presse l'Intransigeant. France-soir. Paris. 14 nov 1944-13 juil 1970 – 1 – fr A.C.R.P.P. [073]
PARIS-SOIR – Paris. 22 juin 1940-17 aout 1944. Publie a Paris sous controle allemand – 1 – fr A.C.R.P.P. [073]
PARIS-SOIR – Paris. oct 1923-14 mai 1943 – 1 – fr A.C.R.P.P. [073]
PARIS-SOIR DIMANCHE – Paris. 22 dec 1935-36 – 1 – fr A.C.R.P.P. [073]
PARIS-TURF – Paris. sept 1946-86 – 1 – fr A.C.R.P.P. [073]
PARIZHSKY VESTNIK – Paris. France. -w. 14 Jun 1942-12 Aug 1944. (1 reel) – 1 – uk British Libr Newspaper [072]
Park *see* AFRICAN RESEARCHES
Park, A *see* DAS OPFERLAMM
PARK CITY DAILY NEWS – Bowling Green. Ky. 1955- – 1 – us UMI [071]
PARK COUNTY NEWS – Helena. Mont. 1950-1954 – 1 – us UMI [071]
PARK COUNTY NEWS – Livingston. Mont. 1950-1954; 1958-1959; 1966- – 1 – us UMI [071]
Park, David *see* MISSIONARY METHODS FOR MISSIONARY COMMITTEES
Park, Edwards Amasa *see*
- THE ASSOCIATE CREED OF ANDOVER THEOLOGICAL SEMINARY
- DISCOURSES ON SOME THEOLOGICAL DOCTRINES AS RELATED TO THE RELIGIOUS CHARACTER
- MEMORIAL COLLECTION OF SERMONS
- WRITINGS OF PROFESSOR B.B. EDWARDS

PARK FOREST STAR – Chicago Heights. Ill. -w. 1949- – 1 – us UMI [071]

Park, Mungo *see*
- THE JOURNAL OF A MISSION TO THE INTERIOR OF AFRICA
- MISSION TO THE INTERIOR OF AFRICA
- TRAVELS IN THE INTERIOR OF AFRICA
- VOYAGE DANS L'INTERIEUR DE L'AFRIQUE

Park, Song Yong *see* ECHANGES ECONOMIQUES ET RELATIONS SOCIALES DANS DEUX COMMUNAUTES VILLAGEOISES DE COREE

Park, Stephen *see* THE ENGLISH BOOKTRADE, 1660-1853

PARK STREET BAPTIST CHURCH (CALLED ELMWOOD PARK). COLUMBIA, SOUTH CAROLINA : CHURCH RECORDS – 1910-1913. Second Baptist. Church records. 1915-26. Park Street. Church records. 1926- – 1 – $13.40 – us Baptist [240]

PARK STREET BAPTIST CHURCH. FAIRFIELD ASSOCIATION. COLUMBIA, SOUTH CAROLINA : CHURCH RECORDS – 1923-1972 – 1 – 27.08 – us Baptist [240]

THE PARKDALE NEWS – Parkdale, Canada. v4 n13. 19 jun 1884 – 1r – 1 – Can$25.00 – cn Can Microfilming [072]

Parker, Alexander Augustine *see* THE ALLEGORICAL DRAMA OF CALDERON, AN INTRODUCTION TO THE AUTOS SACRAMENTALES

Parker, Amasa J *see* LANDMARKS OF ALBANY COUNTY

Parker, C W *see* WHO'S WHO IN WESTERN CANADA

Parker, Charles *see* REPORT...ON THE MAGNETIC NEEDLE

Parker, Daniel *see* A PUBLIC ADDRESS TO THE BAPTIST SOCIETY OF THE BAPTIST BOARD OF FOREIGN MISSIONS

PARKER FAMILY PAPERS, 1760-95 / Parker, James – 1 – uk Microform Academic [920]

Parker, H *see*
- ANCIENT CEYLON: AN ACCOUNT OF THE ABORIGINES AND OF THE EARLY CIVILISATION
- VILLAGE FOLK-TALES OF CEYLON; COLLECTED AND TRANSLATED

Parker, H W *see* A NEW CHAMELEON FROM MT. RUWENZORI

Parker, Henry Webster *see* THE AGNOSTIC GOSPEL

Parker, Irene *see* DISSENTING ACADEMIES IN ENGLAND

Parker, James *see* PARKER FAMILY PAPERS, 1760-95

PARKER, JAMES M., DAYBOOK, MS 2067 – 1840-1841 – 1 reel – 1 – us Western Res [920]

Parker, Jenny M *see* ROCHESTER-A STORY HISTORICAL

Parker, John Scott *see*
- WHERE AND HOW; A CORPORATION HAND BOOK CONTAINING THE LAWS OF DELAWARE, NEW JERSEY, NEW YORK AND PENNSYLVANIA.
- WHERE AND HOW; A HAND BOOK OF INCORPORATION. BEING A DIGEST AND COMPARISON OF THE CORPORATION LAWS OF NEW YORK, NEW JERSEY, MAINE, DELAWARE, WEST VIRGINIA, SOUTH DAKOTA, MASSACHUSETTS.

Parker, Joseph *see*
- AD CLERUM
- ECCE DEUS
- THE EPISTLE TO THE EPHESIANS
- THE PARACLETE
- THE PRIESTHOOD OF CHRIST
- PULPIT NOTES
- TYNE CHYLDE

Parker, L F *see* HISTORY OF POWESHIEK COUNTY, IOWA

Parker, Matthew *see* REGISTER

Parker, P *see*
- STATEMENTS RESPECTING HOSPITALS IN CHINA
- STATEMENTS RESPECTING HOSPITALS IN CHINA, PRECEDED BY A LETTER TO JOHN ABERCROMBRIE,...

Parker, R N *see* A FOREST FLORA OF THE PUNJAB WITH HAZARA AND DELHI

THE PARKER SOCIETY – (Basic writings of the fathers and early authors of the Church of England) – 9 – us Primary [240]

Parker, Theodore *see*
- D.F. STRAUSS' DAS LEBEN JESU
- A DISCOURSE ON THE TRANSIENT AND PERMANENT IN CHRISTIANITY
- THE RELATION OF THE BIBLE TO THE SOUL
- SPEECHES, ADDRESSES, AND OCCASIONAL SERMONS
- THEODORE PARKER PAPERS, 1826-1862
- WEST ROXBURY SERMONS

Parker, Virginia *see* BUTTE COUNTY HISTORICAL SOCIETY "DIGGIN'S"

Parker, W *see* A LETTER TO THE REV MR. JOHN WESLEY, CONCERNING HIS INCONSISTENCY WITH HIMSELF, OCCASIONED BY THE PUBLICATION OF HIS SERMON ENTITLED 'THE LORD OUR RIGHTEOUSNESS'

Parker, W K *see* A MONOGRAPH ON THE STRUCTURE AND DEVELOPMENT OF THE SHOULDER-GIRDLE AND STERNUM IN THE VERTEBRATA

Parker, William *see* THE JESUITS UNMASKED

Parkerson, Harriet *see* DIARIES

PARKES EXAMINER – Jan 4 1899-Dec 29 1906 – 9 – at Pascoe [072]

PARKES INDEPENDENT – Jan 3 1899-Nov 14 1901 – 9 – at Pascoe [072]

Parkes, Joseph *see* MEMOIRS OF SIR PHILIP FRANCIS, K.C.B., WITH CORRESPONDENCE AND JOURNALS

Parke-Taylor, G H *see* YAHWEH

PARKHASH – (Dawrah-'i piruzi: shumarah-'i 1-18 (29 Isfand 1357-18 Murdad 1358[20 Mar 1979-9 Aug 1980])) – Tehran – 1 reel – 1 – $25.00 – us MEDOC [950]

PARKHILL GAZETTE – Ontario Prov., Canada. 1893-1921 – 1 – cn Commonwealth Micro [072]

Parkhouse, Bonnie L *see*
- AQUAPRENEURSHIP
- FRESHMAN ELIGIBILITY IN INTERCOLLEGIATE ATHLETICS

Parkhurst, Charles H *see*
- A BRIEF HISTORY OF THE MADISON SQUARE PRESBYTERIAN CHURCH AND ITS ACTIVTIES
- FIRST STEPS TOWARD CHURCH UNITY
- OUR FIGHT WITH TAMMANY
- THE PULPIT AND THE PEW

Parkhurst, H E *see* TREES, SHRUBS AND VINES...

Parkhurst, J *see* A SERIOUS AND FRIENDLY ADDRESS TO THE REVEREND MR. JOHN WESLEY IN RELATION TO A PRINCIPAL DOCTRINE ADVANCED AND MAINTAINED BY HIM AND HIS ASSISTANTS

Parkhurst, John *see* A GREEK AND ENGLISH LEXICON TO THE NEW TESTAMENT.

Parkinson, J *see*
- ESSAY ON THE SHAKING PALSY
- PARADISI IN SOLE PARADISUS TERRESTRIS
- THEATRUM BOTANICUM

Parkinson, R R *see* PEN PORTRAITS

Parkinson, S *see* A JOURNAL OF A VOYAGE TO THE SOUTH SEAS IN HIS MAJESTY'S SHIP THE ENDEAVOUR

Parkinson, Thomas *see* YORKSHIRE LEGENDS AND TRADITIONS AS TOLD BY HER ANCIENT CHRONICLERS, HER POETS, AND JOURNALISTS

Parkinson, Thomas Ignatius *see* CASES AND MATERIALS ON LEGISLATION

Parkinson, William *see* REPORTS

PARKINSONISM AND RELATED DISORDERS – Kidlington. v1-3. 1995-97+ – 1,5,9 – D42780 – us UMI [616]

PARKLAND NEWS – Alberta, CN. 1979-91 – 15r – 1 – cn Commonwealth Micro [072]

Parkman, Francis *see* THE JESUITS IN NORTH AMERICA IN THE SEVENTEENTH CENTURY

PARK-RAFU SHIMPO – Monterey, CA. 1978 – 64+ r – 1 – $3,200.00 ($200.00y) – H04048 – us Library Micro [071]

PARKROSE EAST COUNTY ENTERPRISE – Parkrose OR. Oct 14 1953-May 1 1957, June 25 1958-Oct 18 1962 – 1 – us U.O. Library [071]

PARKROSE ENTERPRISE – Portland OR. Jan 30 1952 – 1 – us U.O. Library [071]

PARKS – Washington. v1-10. 1976-85 1,9; v1-6 apr 1976-mar 1982. v7-9 apr 1982-dec 1984*. v10 1985 5 – 1,5,9 – D11276 – us UMI [710]

PARKS AND RECREATION – (Formed by the union of: Parks and Recreation; Recreation; American Recreational Journal; and: Planning and Civic Comment) – Arlington. v1-32. 1966-97+ 1,5,9; v1 1966* 5 – 1,5,9 – D5678 – us UMI [710]

PARKS AND RECREATION – (Merged with: Recreation; American Recreation Journal, and: Planning and Civic Comment. To form: Parks and Recreation) – Wheeling. v1-48. 1917-65* – 1 – D11850 – us UMI [710]

PARKS AND RECREATION *see*
- PARKS AND RECREATION

PARKS AND RECREATION CANADA = PARCS ET LOISIRS CANADA – (Cont: Recreation Canada) – Gloucester. v53-55. 1996-97+ – 1,5,9 – D10554.01 – us UMI [710]

Parks, Edna D *see* ENGLISH HYMNS AND THEIR TUNES IN THE 16TH AND 17TH CENTURIES

Parks, James Giddings *see* A MANUAL OF THE LAW OF PLEADING

Parks, Stephen *see* FREEDOM OF THE PRESS

Parks, W H *see* HISTORY OF THE BAPTIST MISSIONARY ASSOCIATION OF TEXAS

PARKSVILLE BAPTIST CHURCH. MCCORMICK, SOUTH CAROLINA : CHURCH RECORDS – (446p. – Formerly Callahan's Mill Baptist Church) – 1856-1957 (scattered), 1959-1984 – 1 reel – 1 – $20.07 – us Baptist [240]

PARKWAY VILLAGE BAPTIST CHURCH. MEMPHIS, TENNESSEE : CHURCH RECORDS – 1963-75 – 1 – 18.00 – us Baptist [240]

Parlagi, I *see* DAS GEISTIGE UNGARN; BIOGRAFICHES LEXIKON

DAS PARLAMENT – (1951- $200y 9) – Hamburg/Bonn, 1951- – 2r per y – 1 – us Ross [072]

DAS PARLAMENT – (1978-94 34r DM2,550.00. 1995 subsc ca 2r DM140.00. Beilagen inklusiv) – Hamburg, Bonn. Sep 19 1951-1977 – 39r – 1 – DM3,125.00 – gw Mikro Press [943]

DAS PARLAMENT – Bonn. 1979- – 22125.00y; CPC; – gw Alpha Com [072]

DAS PARLAMENT – Bonn. v. 6-12. 1956-1962. Incomplete – 1 – us NY Public [073]

DAS PARLAMENT – Bonn-Trier, West Germany. 19 Sep 1951-. Including: Beilagen – ca 104m per yr – 1 – gw Mikrofilm [072]

DAS PARLAMENT – (Since 1970 incl suppl) – Hamburg, Bonn. 1951- – 1 – Inquire at Mikrofilmarchiv for details – gw Misc Inst [320]

DAS PARLAMENT – v1-. 19 Sept 1951-. -w. illus. Bonn: Bundeszentrale fuer politische Bildung – 1 – us U.W. Library [073]

PARLAMENT (HAMBURG/BONN) – 1951-1995 – 2 times per yr – 1 – DM140.00 – sz Infoprint [072]

EL PARLAMENTARIO – Madrid, Spain. -d. 3 May 1916-14 Aug 1919. Very imperfect. 7 reels – 1 – uk British Libr Newspaper [072]

EL PARLAMENTO ARGENTINO, 1854-1947 / Argentina. Congreso de la Nacion. Camara de Diputados de la Nacion – Buenos Aires: Impr. del Congreso de la Nacion, 1st ed 1948 – 1 – CSUXAHZ6105-B – us Hoover Inst Photo [320]

EL PARLAMENTO ARGENTINO EN EPOCAS DE CAMBIO : 1890, 1916 Y 1946 / Canton, Dario – [Buenos Aires]: Editorial del Instituto, [1st ed 1966] – 1 – CSUXADH9369-B – us Hoover Inst Photo [350]

Parlatore, F *see*
- FLORA ITALIANA
- NUOVI E NUOVE SPECIE DI PIANTE MONOCOTILEDONI
- PLANTAE NOVAE VEL MINUS NOTAE OPUSCULIS DIVERSIS

LE PARLEMENT – Journal de la republique liberale. Paris. 20 oct 1879-juin 1881, janv-juin 1882 – 1 – fr A.C.R.P.P. [073]

LE PARLEMENT – Red. en chef Gregory Ganesco. Paris. 26 oct 1869-9 sept 1870 – 1 – fr A.C.R.P.P. [073]

Parlement Indonesia *see* PENERBIT

LE PARLEMENTARISME CONTRE L'ACTION OUVRIERE / Pierrot, Marc – Paris. 1912. (La Condition Ouvriere. Part Two.) – 9 – 2.50 – fr Bibl Nationale [360]

LE PARLER ARABE DE TENES, ALGERIE / Belkaid, M – Etude phonologique, grammaticale et lexicale – 9 – F200.00 – fr Ethnologie [306]

LE PARLER POPULAIRE DES CANADIENS FRANCAIS OU LEXIQUE DES CANADIANISMES, ACADIANISMES, ANGLICISMES, AMERICANISMES, MOTS ANGLAIS LES PLUS EN USAGE AU SEIN DES FAMILLES CANADIENNES ET ACADIENNES FRANCAISES / Dionne, Narcisse Eutrope – Quebec: Laflamme & Proulx..., 1909. SEM105P505 – 8mf – 9 – Can$18.00 – cn Bibl Nat [440]

LES PARLERS DU SOUS-ENSEMBLE SONGHAY-ZARMA SEPTENTRIONAL. DOCUMENTS DE TERRAIN. DICTIONNAIRE FRANCAIS-TASAWAQ / Lacroix, PF – 9 – F150.00 – fr Ethnologie [306]

LES PARLERS DU SOUS-ENSEMBLE SONGHAY-ZARMA SEPTENTRIONAL. DOCUMENTS DE TERRAIN. DICTIONNAIRE TASAWAQ-FRANCAIS / Lacroix, PF – 9 – F150.00 – fr Ethnologie [490]

LES PARLERS DU SOUS-ENSEMBLE SONGHAY-ZARMA SEPTENTRIONAL. DOCUMENTS DE TERRAIN. LEXICOLOGIE TADAKSAHAK / Lacroix, PF – 9 – F90.00 – fr Ethnologie [490]

LES PARLERS DU SOUS-ENSEMBLE SONGHAY-ZARMA SEPTENTRIONAL. DOCUMENTS DE TERRAIN. LEXICOLOGIE TIHITIT ET TAGDALT / Lacroix, PF – 9 – F60.00 – fr Ethnologie [490]

PARLEYINGS WITH CERTAIN PEOPLE OF IMPORTANCE IN THEIR DAY / Browning, Robert – London: Smith, Elder, 1887 – 1 roll – 1 – 1-55879-587-1 – uk Libr Preservation [800]

PARLEY'S MAGAZINE – New York. v1-7 mar 1833-mar 1839. v8-12 1840-44 – 1 – D4552 – us UMI [073]

Parliament of Basutoland, Senate *see* INDEPENDENCE DEBATE

PARLIAMENT, THE CIVIL WAR, THE CONQUEST AND ADMINISTRATION OF SCOTLAND, 1640-1644 – William Clarke Manuscripts in Worcester College, Oxford – 1 – us Primary [941]

PARLIAMENTARIAN – (Former titles: Journal of the Parliaments of the Empire, 1920-48. Journal of the Parliaments of the Commonwealth, 1949-65) – London. v1-55 1920-74*. v56-78 1975-97+ 1; v57 1976*. v58-66 1977-85. v67-75 1986-94*. v76-78 1995-97+ 5; v57 1976*. v58-78 1977-97+ 9 – 1,5,9 – D2718 – us UMI [941]

PARLIAMENTARY AFFAIRS – Oxford. v1-26. win 1947-aut 1973 1; v27-50. win 1973-oct 1997+ 1,5,9 – 1,5,9 – D10978 – us UMI [321]

PARLIAMENTARY COMMITTEE MINUTES (1888-1921) AND REPORTS (1908-19) / Trades Union Congress – 1 – £375.00 – uk World [331]

PARLIAMENTARY DEBATES – New South Wales, 1879-1900 – 35r – 9 – A$1,147.00 silver A$988.00 vesicular – at Pascoe [324]

PARLIAMENTARY DEBATES / New South Wales. Australia. Parliament – New South Wales, 1879-1900 – 35r – 1 – A$1,147.00 silver A$988.00 vesicular – at Pascoe [324]

PARLIAMENTARY DEBATES / Queensland. Australia. Parliament – Queensland, 1864-1901 – 18r – 1 – A$602.00 silver A$519.00 vesicular – at Pascoe [324]

PARLIAMENTARY DEBATES – South Australia, 1857-1901 – 15r – 1 – A$482.00 silver A$415.00 vesicular – at Pascoe [324]

PARLIAMENTARY DEBATES / Victoria. Australia. Parliament – Victoria, 1856-1902 – 40r – 1 – A$1,160.00 silver A$980.00 vesicular – at Pascoe [324]

PARLIAMENTARY DEBATES ON THE SUBJECT OF THE CONFEDERATION OF THE BRITISH NORTH AMERICAN PROVINCES. / Canada. Parliament – Quebec: Hunter, Rose & Co, 1865 – 11mf – 9 – Can$24.75 – SEM105P423 – cn Bibl Nat [323]

PARLIAMENTARY GOVERNMENT IN CANADA: A CONSTITUTIONAL AND HISTORICAL STUDY / Bourinot, John George – Washington: GPO, 1892. 00207. (Pre-1900 Canadiana) – 9 – cn C.I.H.M. [971]

PARLIAMENTARY GOVERNMENT IN CANADA: A LECTURE READ BEFORE THE LAW SCHOOL OF BISHOP'S COLLEGE, SHERBROOKE / Colby, Charles Carroll – Montreal: Dawson Bros., 1886. 00699. (Pre-1900 Canadiana) – 9 – cn C.I.H.M. [971]

PARLIAMENTARY HISTORY : PART 1: MANUSCRIPT MINUTES, COMMITTEE BOOKS AND VOTING RECORDS OF THE HOUSE OF LORDS, CA 1620-1714. PART 2: THE BRAYE MANUSCRIPTS FROM THE HOUSE OF LORDS RECORD OFFICE – (Part 2: 22 reels $2,700.00) – Marlborough: Adam Matthew Publications, 1991 – 36r – 1 – $4,300.00 – uk Matthew [320]

PARLIAMENTARY HISTORY : A YEARBOOK – Gloucester. v1-8 1982-89*. v9-16 1990-97+ 1; v9-13 1990-94*. v14-16 1995-97+ 5; v9-16. 1990-97+ 9 – 1,5,9 – D18521 – us UMI [320]

PARLIAMENTARY HISTORY OF ENGLAND FROM THE NORMAN CONQUEST IN 1066 TO 1803 / Cobbett, William – (Hansard) – 3 – us Readex [941]

PARLIAMENTARY JOURNAL – Kensington. v1-38. 1960-97+ 1; v17-18 1976-77*. v19 1978. v20 1979*. v21 1980. v22-28 1981-87*. v29 1988. v30-35 1989-94*. v36-38 1995-97+ 5; v18-38. 1977-97+ 9 – 1,5,9 – D9066 – us UMI [320]

Parliamentary Labour Party. Great Britain. Archives *see* ARCHIVES OF THE PARLIAMENTARY LABOUR PARTY

PARLIAMENTARY PAPERS / Italy. Legislature. Seventh – 1976-79. Printed index – 162r – 1,5 – $10,290.00 – us UPA [945]

PARLIAMENTARY PAPERS, RELATING TO THE EAST INDIES / Great Britain. Parliament. House of Commons – Account and Papers, v. 64. London. 1909. BI-340 2 – 8 – ne IDC [324]

PARLIAMENTARY PAPERS RELATING TO THE PROPOSAL TO SEND MEMBERS OF THE QUEENSLAND DEFENCE FORCE TO THE TRANSVAAL, 1899-1899 / Queensland Legislative Assembly – 6r – 1 – CRS B5182 – at Archives [920]

PARLIAMENTARY PROCEDURE AND PRACTICE: WITH AN INTRODUCTORY ACCOUNT OF THE ORIGIN AND GROWTH OF PARLIAMENTARY INSTITUTIONS IN THE DOMINION OF CANADA / Bourinot, John George – Montreal: Dawson Bros., 1884. 00209. (Pre-1900 Canadiana) – 9 – cn C.I.H.M. [971]

PARLIAMENTARY PROCEDURES OF THE HOUSE OF REPRESENTATIVES OF THE U.S / Hinds, Asher C – 55th Congress 2nd sess. doc no 576. Washington: GPO, 1899 – 4mf – 9 – $18.00 – LLMC 84-103 – us L.L.M.C. [323]

PARLIAMENTARY PROCEEDINGS – South Australia, 1857-1901 – 41r – 9 – A$1,407.00 silver A$1,213.00 vesicular – at Pascoe [324]

PARLIAMENTARY REPORTS AND PAPERS RELATING TO EDUCATION / Great Britain. Parliament – 19th, 20th Centuries – 1, 9 – uk Microform Academic [370]

PARLIAMENTARY REPORTS AND PAPERS RELATING TO THE NAVY / Great Britain. Parliament – 1801-1900 – 1 – uk Microform Academic [941]

PARLIAMENTARY RETURNS / Great Britain. Parliament – 1213-1874 – 1 – uk Microform Academic [323]

PARLIAMENTARY REVIEW AND FAMILY MAGAZINE – London. v1-4 1833. n1-2 1834 – 1 – D5459 – us UMI [073]

PARLIAMENTARY STATEMENT / Palestine. Secretary of State for Foreign Affairs – Jerusalem. 1945. BJ-28-93 1 – 9 – ne IDC [956]

PARLIER PROGRESS – Fresno, CA. 1927-1931 – 5r – 1 – $250.00 – B06027 – us Library Micro [071]

PARLONS SPORTS – Montreal, Canada. v4 n14. 2 fev 1957-v10 n1. 15 dec 1962 – 2r – 1 – Can$55.00r – cn Can Microfilming [790]

PARLOUR COMPANION – (Supersedes: Juvenile Port-folio and Literary Miscellany) – Philadelphia. v1-3. 1817-aug 1819 – 1 – D4504 – us UMI [073]

PARLOUR REVIEW, AND JOURNAL OF MUSIC, LITERATURE, AND THE FINE ARTS – Philadelphia. v1. jan-mar 1838 – 1 – D3857 – us UMI [700]

Parma. Ohio. First Congregational Church *see* CHURCH RECORDS, MS 1468

PARMENIDES, LEUKIPPOS UND DIE GRUNDLAGE DER EPIKURISCHEN PHYSIK UND ETHIK BEI LUKREZ / Saltzer, Walter Gabriel – Frankfurt a.M., 1964 – 2mf – 9 – DM62.00 – 3-89349-735-8 – gw Hänsel [170]

PARMENIDES UND HEGEL UEBER DAS SEIN : ZUR INTERPRETATION DES ANFANGS DER HEGELSCHEN LOGIK / Constantineau, Philippe – Heidelberg, 1984 – 3mf – 9 – DM76.00 – 3-89349-703-X – gw Hänsel [110]

Parmenov, IS *see* VNESHNIAIA TORGOVLIA ROSSII I GLAVNEISHIKH EVROPEISKIKH GOSUDARSTV V DIAGRAMMAKH I TABLITSAKH

Parmly, Eleazar *see* THE BABE OF BETHLEHEM: FROM THE CRADLE TO THE CROSS

PARNASO ESPANOL. TOMO 1 / Lopez Sedano, Juan Jose – 1768 – 1mf – 9 – Pta1,000.00 – 84-7848-361-6 – sp Pentalfa [946]

PARNASO ESPANOL. TOMO 2 / Lopez Sedano, Juan Jose – 1770 – 1mf – 9 – Pta1,000.00 – 84-7848-362-4 – sp Pentalfa [946]

PARNASO ESPANOL. TOMO 3 / Lopez Sedano, Juan Jose – 1770 – 2mf – 9 – Pta1,500.00 – 84-7848-363-2 – sp Pentalfa [946]

PARNASO ESPANOL. TOMO 4 / Lopez Sedano, Juan Jose – 1770 – 2mf – 9 – Pta1,500.00 – 84-7848-364-0 – sp Pentalfa [946]

PARNASO ESPANOL. TOMO 5 / Lopez Sedano, Juan Jose – 1771 – 2mf – 9 – Pta1,500.00 – 84-7848-365-9 – sp Pentalfa [946]

PARNASO ESPANOL. TOMO 6 / Lopez Sedano, Juan Jose – 1772 – 2mf – 9 – Pta1,500.00 – 84-7848-366-7 – sp Pentalfa [946]

PARNASO ESPANOL. TOMO 7 / Lopez Sedano, Juan Jose – 1773 – 2mf – 9 – Pta1,500.00 – 84-7848-367-5 – sp Pentalfa [946]

PARNASO ESPANOL. TOMO 8 / Lopez Sedano, Juan Jose – 1774 – 2mf – 9 – Pta1,500.00 – 84-7848-368-3 – sp Pentalfa [946]

PARNASO ESPANOL. TOMO 9 / Lopez Sedano, Juan Jose – 1778 – 2mf – 9 – Pta1,500.00 – 84-7848-369-1 – sp Pentalfa [946]

LE PARNASSE – Revue des lettres et des arts. Dir. Alfred Cherie. no. 109-116. Paris. fevr-sept 1886 – 1 – fr A.C.R.P.P. [073]

LE PARNASSE CONTEMPORAIN – Recueil de vers nouveaux. Paris. 1866, 1869-71, 1876 – 1 – fr A.C.R.P.P. [073]

PARNASSUS – New York. v1-13. 1929-41 – 2r – 9 – $5.00f – us Ross [700]

PARNASSUS : POETRY IN REVIEW – New York. v1-14 1972-88*. v15-22 1989-97+ 1; v15-16 1989-90*. v17-18 1992-93. v18-19 1993-94*. v20-22 1995-97+ 5; v15-22 1989-97+ 9 – 1,5,9 – D17522 – us UMI [840]

PARNASSUS BOICUS, ODER NEU-EROEFFNETER MUSEN-BERG, 1722-1727. NEU-FORTGESETZTER PARNASSUS, ODER BAYERISCHER MUSENBERG, 1736-1737. ETWELCHE MEISTENS BAYERISCHE DENCK-UND LESSWUERDIGKEITEN, 1737-1740 – 1722-1740 (mf ed 1995) – 21mf – 9 – DM480.00 – 3-89131-210-5 – gw Fischer [943]

Parnell, Katherine Wood *see* CHARLES STEWART PARNELL; HIS LOVE STORY AND POLITICAL LIFE

PARNELL'S FAITHFUL FEW / Leamy, Margaret Hanly – New York: Macmillan, 1936. vii,235p. front., ports., facsims – 1 – us U.W. Library [920]

Parnet, Max *see* LA CULTURE PHYSIQUE DE LA FEMME

PAROCHIAL AND TOWNSHIP SUBDIVISIONS OF LOWER CANADA, IN RETURN TO THE ANNEXED ADDRESS OF THE LEGISLATIVE ASSEMBLY, 1853 / Canada. Parliament. Legislative Assembly – Quebec: Printed by E R Frechette, 1853. SEM105P134 – 2mf – 9 – Can$4.50 – cn Bibl Nat [324]

THE PAROCHIAL SCHOOL : A CURSE TO THE CHURCH, A MENACE TO THE NATION: WITH AN APPENDIX WHICH DEALS WITH THE SEPARATE OR PAROCHIAL SCHOOL IN CANADA / Crowley, Jeremiah J – 2nd ed. Chicago, IL: J J Crowley, c1905 – 2mf – 9 – 0-8370-8658-2 – 1986-2658 – us A.T.L.A. [240]

PAROCHIAL SERMONS / Newman, John Henry – London: J.G. & F. Rivington; Oxford: J.H. Parker, 1834-42 – 3 rolls – 1 – 1-55879-207-4 – uk Libr Preservation [240]

LES PARODIES THEATRALES EN FRANCE: HISTOIRE DU GENRE A TRAVERS DEUX SIECLES / Lecomte, L H – 7 fiches. (Recueils documentaires des Arts du Spectacle) – 9 – 17.00 – fr Bibl Nationale [440]

PARODY IN JEWISH LITERATURE / Davidson, I – New York. 1907. BJ-421-15 1 – 9 – ne IDC [470]

UNE PAROISSE CANADIENNE AU XVIIE SIECLE / Casgrain, Henri-Raymond – Quebec: L. Brousseau, 1880. 02543. (Pre-1900 Canadiana) – 9 – cn C.I.H.M. [240]

LA PAROISSE, OU, GEOGRAPHIE LOCALE: SAINT HUBERT (CO. DE CHAMBLY) / Baillairge, Frederic Alexandre – 1899. 04084. (Pre-1900 Canadiana) – 9 – cn C.I.H.M. [910]

PAROISSES ET FAMILLES DE TOURAINE / Touraine – 19th cent. 2v – 1 – F895.37 – fr Armell [920]

LA PAROLA DEI SOCIALISTI – Chicago, IL, 1908-1911, 1913, 1914 – 3r – 1 – us I.H.R.C. [978]

LA PAROLA DEL MEDICO – New York, NY. 2 Apr 1916-1 Jan 1919 – 1 – us I.H.R.C. [071]

LA PAROLE / ed by Duguay, Camille et al – Drummondville, Canada. 1 avr 1926-25 dec 1991 – 73r – 1 – Can$70.00r – cn Can Microfilming [072]

LA PAROLE – no. 1-65. nov 1924-aout 1935. MQ no. 7. devenu: Les Enseignements de la parole. Spiritualisme chretien. no. 66-83. sept 1935-juin juil 1937. devenu: La Parole. Enseignements. no. 84-98. aout sept 1937-mai juin 1939. Paris – 1 – fr A.C.R.P.P. [073]

LA PAROLE BULGARE – Sofia. Bulgaria. -w. 2 Mar 1936-1 Jan 1944. (Imperfect). (7 reels) – 1 – uk British Libr Newspaper [949]

LA PAROLE DANS LA VIE SOCIALE DES BAATOMBU / Schottman, W – F100.00 – fr Ethnologie [306]

LA PAROLE INTERIEURE: ESSAI DE PSYCOLOGIE DESCRIPTIVE / Egger, Victor – 2nd ed. rev. Paris: F. Alcan, 1904. 326p – 1 – us U.W. Library [150]

EL PARQUE / Ortega Sanchez, Luis Miguel – Miajadas, 1980 – 1 – sp Bibl Santa Ana [946]

Parra, Caracciolo *see* CARACAS, 1935

Parra Leon, Jose Antonio *see* CONTRIBUCION AL ESTUDIO DE LA OSTEOSINTESIS EN CARACAS

Parra Marquez, Hector *see* CARACAS POLITICA, INTELECTUAL Y MUNDANA. CARACAS, 1966

Parra Perez, C *see* 1ST BAYONA Y LA POLITICA DE NAPOLEON EN AMERICA... Y 2ND HISTORIA DE LA PRIMERA REPUBLICA DE VENEZUELA...

Parra, Victoriano C *see* ENSAYO HISTORICO DE OLIVENZA

PARRAL PAPERS = ARCHIVO DE HIDALGO DEL PARRAL – (360,000p in Spanish of offical documents of Spanish colonial era in southwestern United States and Mexico, 1631-1821. Index in Spanish or English available) – 324r – 1 – $20,350.00 – us UMI [970]

PARRAMATTA MESSENGER – Jan 16 1847-Jun 5 1847 – 9 – at Pascoe [072]

Parran, A *see* TRAITE DE LA MUSIQUE THEORIQUE ET PRATIQUE CONTENANT LES PRECEPTES DE LA COMPOSITION

Parrinder, Geoffrey *see* JESUS IN THE QUR'AN

Parrish, Edward *see* EDUCATION IN THE SOCIETY OF FRIENDS

Parrish, J *see* LA RELIGIEUSE

Parrish, Valerie D *see* THE USE OF PROXY REPORTS AS PREDICTORS OF MAXIMAL AEROBIC POWER IN CHILDREN

PARROCCHIE D'ITALIA / Elenco, Generale Delle – 1924 – 1r – 1 – us I.H.R.C. [945]

Parron Fernandez, Felipe *see* LA INDEPENDENCIA DE UN PUEBLO CON UN HIJO ILUSTRE FRAY PEDRO DE GODOY

Parroquia de Nuestra Senora de Belen *see* FIESTAS EN BELEN DE TRUJILLO 1974

Parroquia de San Jose *see* NUEVO CANTORAL DE LOS FIELES

LA PARROQUIA DE SAN MATEOS DE CACERES Y SUS AGREGADOS / Hurtado de Mendoza, Publio – Caceres: Tip. La Minerva Extremena, Cacerenas, 1918 – 1 – sp Bibl Santa Ana [946]

Parroquia del Espiritu Santo *see*
- LAS BARRIADAS DE...HONRAR AL ESPIRITU SANTO CON LOS SIGUIENTES FESTEJOS... 1976
- LAS BARRIADAS...HONRAN AL ESPIRITU SANTO CON LOS SIGUIENTES FESTEJOS. 1975

Parroquia del Salvador *see* MEMORIA 1969. PRESUPUESTOS 1970

Parrot, Andre *see*
- BABYLON AND THE OLD TESTAMENT
- GOLGOTHA AND THE CHURCH OF THE HOLY SEPULCHRE
- SAMARIA, THE CAPITAL OF THE KINGDOM OF ISRAEL
- THE TEMPLE OF JERUSALEM

PARROTS AND SUNFLOWERS IN NORTHERN NEW SOUTH WALES / Jones, D N – (M Nat Res Thesis) – 1983 – 9 – A$15.00 – at R.A.O.U. [590]

Parrott, J *see* A DIGEST OF THE HISTORY, POLITY AND DOCTRINES OF THE PRIMITIVE METHODISTS,...

Parry, C *see* INQUIRY INTO THE SYMPTOMS AND CAUSES OF THE SYNCOPE ANGINOSA

Parry, Clive *see* LAW OFFICER'S OPINIONS TO THE FOREIGN OFFICE

Parry, Edward *see* MEMOIRS OF REAR-ADMIRAL SIR W.E. PARRY

Parry, Edward A *see* VAGABONDS ALL

Parry, F J S *see* A CATALOGUE OF LUCANOID COLEOPTERA

Parry, Reginald St John *see* THE FIRST EPISTLE OF PAUL THE APOSTLE TO THE CORINTHIANS

PARRY SOUND NORTH STAR – (Some missing issues) – Parry Sound, Ontario, CN. 1879-1971 – 35r – 1 – cn Commonwealth Micro [072]

Parry, W E *see*
- JOURNAL OF A SECOND VOYAGE FOR THE DISCOVERY OF A NORTH-WEST PASSAGE FROM THE ATLANTIC TO THE PACIFIC
- JOURNAL OF A THIRD VOYAGE FOR THE DISCOVERY OF A NORTH-WEST PASSAGE FROM THE ATLANTIC TO THE PACIFIC
- JOURNAL OF A VOYAGE FOR THE DISCOVERY OF A NORTH-WEST PASSAGE FROM THE ATLANTIC TO THE PACIFIC

Parry, William *see* THE LAST DAYS OF LORD BYRON

PARS : LA REVUE LITTERAIRE PERSANE – (In Persian and French) – Istanbul: Sal-i 1, shumarah-i 1-6 (Sha'ban 1339-4 Zu'l Qadah 1339 [15 April 1921-7 July 1921]) – 1 reel – 1 – $145.00 – us MEDOC [950]

PARS 1: AULAE TURCICAE, OTHOMANNICIQ'VE IMPERII DESCRIPTIO: ...PARS 2: SOLYMANNI 12. ET SELYMI 13. TVRCAR. IMPP. CONTRA CHRISTIANOS / Geuffroy, A – Basileae, 1577 – 7mf – 9 – H-8246/1 – ne IDC [956]

Parsarew, Isadore Alvin *see* SURVEY OF LOCAL PLANNING IN MARYLAND

Parsegian, V L *see* ARMENIAN ARCHITECTURE

THE PARSI RELIGION : AS CONTAINED IN THE ZAND-AVASTA, AND PROPOUNDED AND DEFENDED BY THE ZOROASTRIANS OF INDIA AND PERSIA, UNFOLDED, REFUTED, AND CONTRASTED WITH CHRISTIANITY / Wilson, John – Bombay: American Mission Press, 1843 – 1r – 1 – us U.W. Library [230]

PARSIFAL : EIN BUEHNENWEIHFESTSPIEL / Wagner, Richard – Leipzig: Insel-Verlag, [19–?] – 1r – 1 – us U.W. Library [790]

PARSIFAL : EIN BUEHNENWEIHFESTSPIEL / Wagner, Richard – Mainz: B Schott's Soehne – 1r – 1 – us U.W. Library [790]

THE PARSIFAL OF RICHARD WAGNER = PARSIFAL DE RICHARD WAGNER : WITH ACCOUNTS OF THE PERCEVAL OF CHRETIEN DE TROIES AND THE PARZIVAL OF WOLFRAM VON ESCHENBACH / Kufferath, Maurice – New York: H Holt, 1904 – 1 – us U.W. Library [790]

THE PARSIS IN INDIA, BEING AN ENLARGED AND COPIOUSLY ANNOTATED UP TO DATE ENGLISH EDITION.. / Menant, Delphine – By M.M. Murzban.Bombay, 1917. 2v. ill – 1 – us U.W. Library [950]

Parsley, Al *see* THE MONITOR

THE PARSON'S DEVIL : LIFE OF LAWYER GEORGE M. STEARNS / Johnson, Clifton – New York: Thomas Y. Crowell, 1927 – 4mf – 9 – $6.00 – LLMC 92-198 – us L.L.M.C. [340]

Parsons, Ellen C *see*
- CHRISTUS LIBERATOR
- A LIFE FOR AFRICA

PARSONS FIRST BAPTIST CHURCH. PARSONS, TENNESSEE : CHURCH RECORDS – 1893-Feb 1981. WMU Records. 1915-48 – 1 – 121.82 – us Baptist [240]

Parsons, Geoffrey *see* THE LAND OF FAIR PLAY

Parsons, James *see*
- AN EXPOSITION OF THE PRINCIPLES OF PARTNERSHIP
- REMAINS OF JAPHET

Parsons James, J *see* THE ACARN-HOG ECONOMY OF THE OAK WOOD LANDS...

Parsons, James J *see* THE CORK OAK FORESTS AND THE EVOLUTION OF THE CORK INDUSTRY IN SOUTHERN SPAIN AND PORTUGAL

Parsons, Robert *see* THE JUDGMENT OF A CATHOLICKE ENGLISHMAN LIVING IN BANISHMENT FOR HIS RELIGION
Parsons, Samuel Holden *see* SAMUEL HOLDEN PARSONS PAPERS, MS 3204
Parsons, Theophilus *see*
- THE ELEMENTS OF MERCANTILE LAW
- THE LAW OF CONTRACTS
- LAWS OF BUSINESS FOR ALL THE STATES OF THE UNION AND THE DOMINION OF CANADA
- MEMOIR OF THEOPHILUS PARSONS, CHIEF JUSTICE OF THE SUPREME JUDICIAL COURT OF MASSACHUSETTS
- THE PERSONAL AND PROPERTY RIGHTS OF A CITIZEN OF THE UNITED STATES
- THE POLITICAL, PERSONAL AND PROPERTY RIGHTS OF A CITIZEN OF THE UNITED STATES
- A TREATISE ON THE LAW OF MARINE INSURANCE AND GENERAL AVERAGE
- A TREATISE ON THE LAW OF PARTNERSHIP

Parsons, Wilfrid *see* THE POPE AND ITALY
LA PART DU DIABLE / Auber, D F E – Annotated ms copy – 1 – us Sibley [780]
PART FIVE: CHRISTIAN ART 2 / National Art Library. Art Periodicals Collection at the V&A Museum – 1750-1920 – £1,100.00 – uk World [700]
PART FOUR: CHRISTIAN ART 1 / National Art Library. Art Periodicals Collection at the V&A Museum – 1750-1920 – £1,750.00 – uk World [700]
THE PART OF RHEIMS IN THE MAKING OF THE ENGLISH BIBLE / Carleton, James G – Oxford: Clarendon Press, 1902. 1 fiche – 9 – us A.T.L.A. [240]
PART THREE: ART AND DECORATION / National Art Library. Art Periodicals Collection at the V&A Museum – 1750-1920 – £1,425.00 – uk World [700]
PART TWO: THE ARTIST, 1880-1902, L'ART AND COURRIER DE L'ART, 1875-1907 AND OTHER PERIODICALS / National Art Library. Art Periodicals Collection at V&A Museum – (Chromolitograph, 1867-69; L'Art pour Tous, 1861-1906; L'Art Decoratif, 1900-13; The Artist, 1880-1902; L'Art, 1875-1907; Courrier de l'Art, 1881-90; Art and Decoration, 1885-86. PS2500.00; 1. Chromolitograph, 1867-69; L'Art pour Tous, 1861-1906; L'Art decoratif, 1900-13; The Artist, 1880-1902; L'Art, 1875-1907; Courrier de l'Art, 1881-90; Art and Decoration, 1885-86) – 1750-1920. 19 color reels, 37 black and white reels – 1 – PS2300.00 – uk World [073]
LE PARTAGE EN DROIT INTERNATIONAL PRIVE FRANCAIS... / Dennery, R – Paris, 1935 – 3mf – 1 – ILM-3042/1 – ne IDC [327]
LE PARTAGE EN DROIT INTERNATIONAL PRIVE FRANCAIS... / Dennery, R – Paris, 1935 – 3mf – 1 – ILM-3043/1 – ne IDC [327]
Partai Nasional Indonesia *see* MANIFESTO OF MARHAENISM
PARTANT POUR LA SYRIE. TROUBADOR ROMANCE WITH VARIATIONS, OP. 74 / Dussek, J L – London: Mitchell's Musical Library, 181- – 1 – us Sibley [780]
PARTE PRIMA (-SECONDA) SONATE A VIOLINO O CEMBALO...OP. 5 / Corelli, Arcangelo – Roma: G P Santa, (1700) – 2mf – 9 – us Sibley [780]
LA PARTE SUBJETIVA EN EL CONOCIMIENTO INTELECTUAL SEGUN SANTO TOMAS DE AQUINO / Carzo, Jose M – Zafra: Tip. Castro, 1970 – sp Bibl Santa Ana [946]
DER PARTEIARBEITER – Berlin, 1923-25 (incomplete) – 1r – 1 – Inquire at Mikrofilmarchiv for details – gw Misc Inst [320]
DER PARTEIARBEITER – Berlin, Germany. 1923-1925 (incomplete) – 1r – 1 – gw Mikrofilm [072]
PARTEIKONFERENZ / Sozialdemokratische Partei Deutschlands – Weimar, 1919 – 1 – DM80.00 – gw Mikro Press [335]
PARTEITAG. STENOGRAPHISCHE NIEDERSCHRIFT / National-Demokratische Partei Deutschlands (German Democratic Republic) – Berlin: Verlag der Nation – 1 – us U.W. Library [943]
PARTEITAGE / Sozialdemokratische Partei Deutschlands – (1946-62 DM350.00. Inkl Vorlaeufer) – 1865-1931 – 1 – DM800.00 – gw Mikro Press [335]
PARTERRE – Philadelphia. v1-2. jun 1816-jun 1817 – 1 – D3780 – us UMI [073]
LE PARTERRE DE LA RHETORIQUE FRANCOISE – 1659 – 9 – fr I.C.S. [440]
PARTES FRUCTIFICATIONIS, SEU PRINCIPIA BOTANICES ILLUSTRATA / Joerlin, E & Rumberg, E – Londini Gothorum. 1771. B-7109 1 – 9 – ne IDC [580]
Parthenay l'Archeveque, famille de *see* 23 PIECES CONCERNANT LA FAMILLE DE PARTHENAY L'ARCHEVEQUE, SEIGNEURS DE TAILLEBOURG, LE PARC, SOUBISE, MOUCHAMPS, ETC
PARTHENON : A MAGAZINE OF ART AND LITERATURE – London. v1-16. jun 1825-jan 1826 – 1 – D5461 – us UMI [700]
PARTHENON, OR LITERARY AND SCIENTIFIC MUSEUM – New York. v1. aug-dec 1827 – 1 – D5461 – us UMI [073]
Parti Agraire et Paysan Francais *see* LA VOIX DE LA TERRE
Parti autonomiste breton *see* BREIZ ATAO
Parti Communiste. Congres National, 9th, Arles, 1937 *see* LE PEUPLE DE FRANCE AUX COTES DE L'ESPAGNE REPUBLICAINE; EXTRAITS DES RAPPORTS ET INTERVENTIONS
Parti Communiste et des Soviets *see* LE COMMUNISTE
Parti communiste francais (S F IC) *see* LES CAHIERS DU MILITANT
Parti Communiste Internationaliste Bolchevik-Leniniste pour la Construction de la IVe Internationale *see* LA COMMUNE
Parti Communiste. Nancy *see* L'EST OUVRIER ET PAYSAN
Parti Communiste. Region Algerienne *see* LE PAYSAN INDIGENE
Parti Communiste (S F IC) *see* LA LORRAINE OUVRIERE ET PAYSANNE
Parti communiste S F IC *see* AL-BEIRAK-AL-AHMAR
Parti Constitutionnaliste Indochinois *see*
- LA TRIBUNE INDIGENE
- LA TRIBUNE INDOCHINOISE

Parti democratique de Guinee Congres nationale *see* 9EME CONGRES NATIONAL DU PDG (9TH: 1972 CONKARY)
Parti du Faisceau Francais *see*
- SOLIDARITE FRANCAISE
- SOLIDARITE NATIONALE

PARTI INAI A ZHIZN KAZAKHSTANA : ZHURNAL T SENTRALNOGO KOMITETA, KOMMUNISTICHESKO I PARTII KAZAKHSTANA – (Library has: Jan. 1958-Dec 1980; missing: Sept. 1969, Dec. 1971) – Alma-Ata: Izd-vo T Sk KP kazakhstana, 1958 – 1 – CSUX89-S758 – us Hoover Inst Photo [947]
PARTI INO-POLITICHESKAI A RABOTA V RKKA – (Library has: 1938, no. 10-11, 15-23/24; 1939, no. 12) – Moskva: Voenizdat, 1938-1940. 3v – 1 – CSUX90-S199 – us Hoover Inst Photo [947]
LE PARTI LIBERAL ET LE GROS BON SENS / Belgium. (before 1830) – Tournai, 18–. SEM105P564 – 2mf – 9 – Can$4.50 – cn Bibl Nat [949]
Parti National Francais *see* MONITEUR UNIVERSEL DU PARTI NATIONAL FRANCAIS
LE PARTI OUVRIER : ORGANE DES TRAVAILLEURS SOCIALISTES DE FRANCE ET D'ALGERIE – Paris, 1888-1914 – 1 – fr A.C.R.P.P. [335]
Parti Ouvrier de la Region Nord *see*
- LE REVEIL DU FORCAT
- LE TRAVAILLEUR

Parti ouvrier francais. Conseil national *see* AUX TRAVAILLEURS DE FRANCE
Parti Ouvrier Internationaliste *see* LA LUTTE OUVRIERE
Parti Ouvrier Socialiste Revolutionnaire. 9e Congres Regional de l'Union Federative du Centre. Paris du 21 aout au 11 septembre 1892 *see* COMPTE RENDU
Parti Ouvrier Socialiste Revolutionnaire. 14e Congres Regional de l'Union Federative du Centre. Paris, fevrier 1896 *see* COMPTE RENDU
Parti Ouvrier Socialiste Revolutionnaire. 15e Congres Regional, Paris, avril-mai 1899 *see* COMPTE RENDU
LE PARTI QUEBECOIS – Montreal. v1 n3. avr 1970-v2 n4. dec 1971 – 1r – 1 – Can$25.00 – cn Can Microfilming [072]
Parti Republicain Democrate et Socialiste de la Guyane *see* LE PROGRES
Parti republicain democratique et social *see* ALLIANCE REPUBLICAINE DEMOCRATIQUE
Parti republicain, democratique et social *see* LA REPUBLIQUE DEMOCRATIQUE
Parti republicain radical et radical socialiste *see* CONGRES, MAXEVILLE-NANCY, FRANCE, 1907
Parti Republicain Radical et Radical-Socialiste. Congres du Parti *see* COMPTES RENDUS
LE PARTI SOCIALISTE – Organe du Comite revolutionnaire central. Vierzon puis Paris. juin 1891-16 mars 1895 – 1 – fr A.C.R.P.P. [335]
LE PARTI SOCIALISTE ET LA CONFEDERATION DU TRAVAIL / Guesde, Jules – Paris. 1908. (La Condition Ouvriere. Part Two.) – 9 – 2.50 – fr Bibl Nationale [360]
LE PARTI SOCIALISTE ET LA TRADITION DEMOCRATIQUE EN SUISSE / Masnata, F – F60.00 – fr Ethnologie [320]
Parti Socialiste et l'Internationale *see* RAPPORT SUR LES NEGOCIATIONS CONDUITES A MOSCOU, SUIVI DES THESES PRESENTEES AU 2EME CONGRES DE L'INTERNATIONALE COMMUNISTE
Parti Socialiste Francais. Comite General. Discussion sur l'unification et l'organisation du Parti *see* COMPTE RENDU STENOGRAPHIQUE
Parti Socialiste. Section Francaise de l'Internationale Ouvriere *see* COMPTES RENDUS ET RAPPORTS DES 30-44 CONGRES
Parti socialiste. Section francaise de l'internationale ouvriere *see* CONGRES NATIONAL, 19E-38E
Parti socialiste (SFIO) *see* L'EGALITAIRE
Parti Socialiste (S.F.I.O.) et des Syndicats d'Oran *see* LA LUTTE SOCIALE
PARTIAL MANUSCRIPT CATALOG / Charleston Library Society. Charleston, South Carolina – n.d. – 2mf – 9 – us South Carolina Historical [010]
PARTIAL PAYMENT OF FILING FEES IN PRISONER IN FORMA PAUPERIS CASES IN FEDERAL COURTS : A PRELIMINARY REPORT / Willging, Thomas E – Washington: FJC, Sept 1984 – 1mf – 9 – $1.50 – LLMC 95-835 – us L.L.M.C. [340]
PARTIAL REPORT ON JOINT ICA AGRICULTURAL PROGRAMS IN INDONESIA, 1957-1959 / U.S. Operations Mission to Indonesia – SE 5471 1. 1960 – 9 – ne IDC [630]
PARTIAL TRANSCRIPT REPORT / de Brahm, William Gerard – ca.1771. 1 fiche – 9 – us South Carolina Historical [978]
PARTICIPACION POLITICA POPULAR. (GUIONES PARA UN CURSILLO MONOGRAFICO) / Hurtado Munoz de Lucas, Vicente – Caceres: Tip. Extremadura, 1976 – 1 – sp Bibl Santa Ana [320]
PARTICIPANT NEWSLETTER / U.S. Agency for International Development – Incomplete. SE 304 1. 1962-1965 – 9 – ne IDC [337]
PARTICIPANTS BENEFITS ASSESSMENT AT A CAMPUS RECREATIONAL FACILITY / Vitorino, Maria R & Theobald, William F – 1993 – 1mf – 9 – $4.00 – us Microform Publ [790]
PARTICIPATE IN DEVELOPMENT – 1986 – 371p – 9 – 92-3-102180-X – fr UNESCO [338]
Participating Shares Corporation *see* PARTICIPATING TRUST SHARES, SERIES A
PARTICIPATING TRUST SHARES, SERIES A / Participating Shares Corporation – Chicago: Gunthorp-Warren, 1933. 55p. LL-1374 – 1 – us L of C Photodup [340]
LA PARTICIPATION COLLECTIVE DES FEMMES A LA REVOLUTION FRANCAISE / Lasserre, Adrien – Paris: Alcan, 1906. 349p. (Les Femmes Collection) – 4mf – 9 – $10.00 – fr Bibl Nationale [305]
LA PARTICIPATION DES BELGES A L'OEUVRE COLONIALE DES HOLLANDAIS AUX INDES ORIENTALES / Anciaux, Leon – Brussels, 1955 – 1 – us Res Libr [950]
PARTICIPATION IN CULTURAL ACTIVITIES : THREE CASE-STUDIES – 1986 – 126p – 9 – 92-3-102420-5 – fr UNESCO [302]
PARTICIPATION IN WHITE WATER RAFTING INSTRUCTION BY ADULTS WITH DEVELOPMENTAL DISABILITIES / Gargasz, Kimberly L & Smissen, Betty van der – 1990 – 2mf – $8.00 – us Microform Publ [790]
PARTICIPATIVE ADMINISTRATION AND ENDOGENOUS DEVELOPMENT / ed by Tri, Huynh Cao – 1989 – 253p – 9 – 92-3-102408-6 – Co-published with the International Institute of Administrative Sciences, Belgium – fr UNESCO [307]
PARTICLE ACCELERATORS / ed by Keil, E et al – 1970- – 1,5,9 – us Gordon [530]
PARTICLE WORLD / ed by Levy, M – 9,5,1 – us Gordon [530]
PARTICULARS OF THE COUNTRY OF LABRADORE / Curtis, R – BN 181 2. 1774 – 8 – ne IDC [971]
PARTICULATE SCIENCE AND TECHNOLOGY – Washington. v1 1983. v2 1984*. v3-9 1985-91. v10-12 1992-94*. v13-15 1995-97+ 1,9; v1-7 1983-89*. v8 1990. v9-12 1991-94*. v13-15 1995-97+ 5 – 1,5,9 – D14335 – us UMI [073]
PARTIDA DE BAUTISMO DEL P. ANDRES DE GUADALUPE / Acemel, Isidoro – Archivo Ibero Americano, 5, 1916 – 1 – sp Bibl Santa Ana [946]
PARTIDAS 3 Y 4 / Lopez de Tovar, Gregorio – sp Bibl Santa Ana [946]
Partido Africano da Independencia da Guine e Cabo Verde *see* COMMUNIQUE
EL PARTIDO COMUNISTA ANTES, DURANTE Y DESPUES DE LA CRISIS DEL GOBIERNO LARGO CABALLERO / Hernandez, Jesus – Valencia, 1937. Fiche W942. (Blodgett Collection of Spanish Civil War Pamphlets) – 9 – us H.U. College Libr [946]
Partido Comunista de Espana. Comite Central *see*
- PROGRAMA DE ACCION COMUN PARA LA CREACION DEL PARTIDO UNICO DEL PROLETARIADO
- LA VICTORIA EXIJE EL PARTIDO UNICO DEL PROLETARIADO: CARTA DEL BURO

EL PARTIDO LIBERAL – Caceres, 1893, 1898 – 5 – sp Bibl Santa Ana [073]
PARTIDO LIBERAL – (Cont: Jornal de Maceio) – Maceio, Alagoas. 19 Jul 1872; 19 Jul 1873 – 1,5,6 – bl Biblioteca [072]
Partido nacional. Honduras *see* LIBRO DE ORO DEL PARTIDO NACIONAL HONDURENO, 1939-40
Partido Obrero de Unificacion Marxista. Spain *see* INFORMATION BULLETIN.
Partido Obrero Espanol *see* EL SOCIALISTA
EL PARTIDO OBRERO Y EL PERONISMO / ed by Prensa Obrera – [Buenos Aires?]: Prensa Obrera, [1983] – 1 – CSUXADQ6582-B – us Hoover Inst Photo [320]
Partido Sindicalista. Spain *see* COMO PIENSA EL PARTIDO SINDICALISTA EN ESTE MOMENTO HISTORICO DE LA VIDA ESPANOLA; TRES MANIFESTOS DEL COMITE NACIONAL, CON NUEVE REPRODUCCIONES DE LOS CARTELES DE PROPAGANDA ANTIFASCISTA
Partido Socialista (Argentine Republic) *see* [PUBLICACIONES]
Partido Socialista Brasileiro *see* FOLHA SOCIALISTA
Partido Socialista del Peru *see* EL SOCIALISTA
Partido Socialista Obrero Espanol *see* EL SOCIALISTA (1886-1986)
LOS PARTIDOS POLITICOS / Ferrer, Gustavo – [Buenos Aires: Centro Editor de America Latina, 1971] – 1 – CSUXADL7079-B – us Hoover Inst Photo [320]
LOS PARTIDOS POLITICOS Y EL SUFRAGIO EN UNA DEMOCRACIA ORGANICA : ANTECEDENTES PARA UNA MEJOR LEGISLACION / Christophersen, Pedro F – Buenos Aires: Guillermo Kraft ltda., soc. anon. de impresiones generales, 1945 – 1 – CSUXAGP8686-B – us Hoover Inst Photo [320]
PARTIE DE LA REPONSE A L'ADRESSE A SON EXCELLENCE LE GOUVERNEUR-GENERAL, EN DATE DU 19E MAI, 1853, AU SUJET DE LA TENURE SEIGNEURIALE DANS LE BAS-CANADA – Quebec: Imp. Bureau et Marcotte, 1853. SEM105P262 – 1mf – 9 – Can$2.25 – cn Bibl Nat [971]
PARTIE FRANCAISE DE LA REVUE MILITAIRE CANADIENNE – Quebec: Presses de L'ecole d'artillirie, [1880-1881] – 9 – cn C.I.H.M. [355]
PARTIE FRANCAISE DE LA REVUE MILITAIRE CANADIENNE *see* CANADIAN MILITARY REVIEW
LE PARTIE OPERATIONS PREVUES AU PLAN EN 1966-1967 / Togo – Chapitre IV du Plan – 9 – ne IDC [338]
PARTII A KOMMUNISTOV BOLSHEVIKOV / Bystrianskii, Vadim – Peterburg: Gos. izd-vo, 1920 – 1 – CSUX89-B6599 – us Hoover Inst Photo [320]

PARTII A V BORBE S BIUROKRATIZMOM : IZ OTCHETA T SKK VKP (B), NK RKI SSSR NA X SEZDE KP (B) U / Akovlev, Akov Arkadevich – Moskva: Gos. izdvo, 1928 – 1 – CSUX89-B7425 – us Hoover Inst Photo [320]
PARTII I KREST'IANSTVO V GOSUDARSTVENNOI DUME / L'vovich, A – Rostov n/D, n.d. 108p – 2mf – 9 – ne IDC [320]
PARTIIA BOLSHEVIKOV V 1917 GODU / Aroslavskii, Emelian – Moskva: Gos. izd vo, 1927 – 1 – CSUX88-B3700 – us Hoover Inst Photo [320]
PARTIIA NARODNOI SVOBODY – Leningrad, Viestnik, 1906-08 – 1r – 1 – us Ross [947]
PARTIIA O KOOPERATSII : POSTANOVLENIIA I REZOLIUTSII VKP(B) – M., 1928 – 5mf – 9 – COR-177/1 – ne IDC [334]
PARTIIA O KOOPERATSII : POSTANOVLENIIA PART. S"EZDOV, KONF. – M., 1928 – 5mf – 9 – COR-178/1 – ne IDC [334]
PARTIIA O KOOPERATSII : POSTANOVLENIIA PART. S"EZDOV, KONFERENTSII – M., 1929 – 5mf – 9 – COR-179/1 – ne IDC [334]
PARTIIA O KUSTARNO-PROMYSLOVOI KOOPERATSII – M., 1928 – 1mf – 9 – COR-180/1 – ne IDC [334]
PARTIIA O PROMYSLOVOI KOOPERATSII I KUSTARNOI PROMYSHLENNOSTI : SBORNIK RESHENII I POSTANOVLENII VKP (B), KOMINTERNA I TSK VLKSM / Baulin, A G & Meshkovskii, V M – M., 1931 – 3mf – 9 – COR-181/1 – ne IDC [334]
PARTIINAIA ZHIZN' – Moscow, 1946-72.Suspended: 5 Apr 1948-Mar 1954. Lacking: 1946 (1-2); 1959 (1-8); 1960 (9-16). BR-10,434/1 – 9 – ne IDC [073]
PARTIINAYA ZHIZN – Moscow. U.S.S.R. (Party Life).1947, 1954- – 1 – us UMI [335]
PARTIINOE STROITELSTVO – Moscow. 1929-41 – 1 – D16230 – us UMI [072]
Partija socialistov-revoljucionerov *see* REVOLJUCIONNAJA ROSSIJA
PARTIKELABSCHEIDUNG IN NASSENTSTAUBERN UNTER BERUECKSICHTIGUNG VON WAERME- UND STOFFAUSTAUSCHVORGAENGEN / Gemci, Tevfik – 1993 – 2mf – 9 – DM80.00 – 3-89349-842-7 – gw Hänsel [621]
PARTIKULARIST BLIEMCHEN AUS DRESDEN IN BAYREUTH / Schumann, Gustav – 11. neubearb. Aufl. Leipzig: Abel & Mueller, [between 1882 and 1900] – 1 – us U.W. Library [830]
PARTIMENTI OSSIA BASSO NUMERATO OPERA COMPLETA / Fenaroli, Fedele – 18- – 9 – us Sibley [780]
A PARTING MEMORIAL : CONSISTING OF MISCELLANEOUS DISCOURSES, WRITTEN AND PREACHED IN CHINA, AT SINGAPORE, ON BOARD SHIP AT SEA IN THE INDIAN OCEAN, AT THE CAPE OF GOOD HOPE, AND IN ENGLAND / Morrison, Robert – London: W. Simpkin and R. Marshall, 1826 – 1mf – us A.T.L.A. [240]
PARTI-PRIS : REVUE – Montreal, Canada. oct 1963-summer 1968 – 2r – 1 – Can$50.00r – cn Can Microfilming [073]
PARTIRO DEL CARO SPOSO. A FAVORITE SONG / Salieri, A – London: Longman and Broderip, [1786] – 1 – us Sibley [780]
PARTIS POLITIQUES ET CLASSES SOCIALES EN FRANCE / Duverger, Maurice – F90.00 – fr Ethnologie [320]
PARTIS POLITIQUES ET REALITES SOCIALES : CONTRIBUTION A UNE ETUDE REALISTE DES PARTIS POLITIQUES / Lavau, G – F50.00 – fr Ethnologie [320]
PARTISAN – Los Angeles, etc: John Reed Clubs of the West. v1 n1-6. 1933-34 (all publ) – 1r – 1 – us Ross [073]
PARTISAN – New York. v1-5. apr 1965-apr 1969 – 1 – D3260 – us UMI [073]
THE PARTISAN – Los Angeles etc. v. 1, no. 1-6. Dec 1933-Oct 1934 – 1 – us NY Public [073]
PARTISAN REVIEW – (Former titles: Partisan Review, feb/mar 1934-oct/nov 1935. Partisan Review and Anvil, feb-oct 1936) – Boston. v1-64. 1934-97+ 1; v36-64. 1969-97+ 5; v42-64. 1975-97+ 9 – 1,5,9 – D939 – us UMI [073]
PARTISAN REVIEW – (New York.) v. 1-11. 1934-1944 – 1,5,6 – us Princeton Micro [073]
PARTISAN REVIEW AND ANVIL *see* PARTISAN REVIEW
PARTITION RECORDS / SETTLEMENTS / Wood County. Ohio. Common Pleas. Civil Division – 1820s-1860 – 1r – 1 – $32.50r – us Archival [324]
Partito Socialisto Italiano *see* AVANTI!
Partito Socialisto Unitario dei Lavoratori Italiani *see* RINASCITA SOCIALISTA
PARTIZANSKOE DVIZHENIE V PRIMORI 1918-1920 GG / Iliukhov, Nikolai Kirillovich – Leningrad: "Pribo i", 1928 – 1 – CSUX88-B3850 – us Hoover Inst Photo [320]
PARTNERSHIP – (Cont by: Marriage Partnership) – Carol Stream. v1-4. 1984-aug 1987 – 1,5,9 – D13829 – us UMI [640]
PARTNERSHIP AND TRADERS' RECORD / Wyandot County. Ohio. Clerk of Courts – 1894-1940 – 1r – 1 – $32.50r – us Archival [324]
Partojuwono, R S Yudi *see* SERAT: WEDARAN WIRID. ISI: WEDARANWEDARAN KANTI BARESKURES ADADASAR; AKAL IAN BUDI SAHA KALAWAN BLAK-BLAKAN, MIJAK WEWADOSING GESANG KASUNJATAN
Partridge, Alden *see* PAPERS
Partridge, Anthony *see*
- THE BUDGETARY IMPACT OF POSSIBLE CHANGES IN DIVERSITY JURISDICTION
- THE CRIME CONTROL AND FINE ENFORCEMENT ACTS OF 1984
- THE QUALITY OF ADVOCACY IN THE FEDERAL COURTS
- A REEVALUATION OF THE CIVIL APPEALS MANAGEMENT PLAN
- THE SECOND CIRCUIT SENTENCING STUDY
- THE SENTENCING OPTIONS OF FEDERAL DISTRICT JUDGES
- SPEEDY TRIAL ACT OF 1974

Partridge, Anthony et al *see*
- PUNISHMENTS FOR FEDERAL CRIMES
- THE SENTENCING OPTIONS OF FEDERAL DISTRICT JUDGES

Partridge, Charles *see* CROSS RIVER NATIVES
PARTRIDGE CRICKET WEEKLY PRESS – Partridge. Kan. 1886-1887 – 1 – us UMI [071]
Partridge, Monica *see* ALEXANDER HERZEN
PARTS MANUFACTURER APPROVALS, 1992 / Transportation Dept., Federal Aviation Administration, Aviation Standards National Field Office, Engineering and Manufacturing Branch – 1992 – 35mf – 9 – $3.75 set in US $4.69 outside – 0-16-005260-2 – S-N 050-007-00963-1 – us Gov't Printing [629]
Partsch, J *see* CORIPPI AFRICANI GRAMMATICI LIBRI QUI SUPERSUNT (MGH1: 3.BD. 2.TEIL)
Parturier, Louis *see* L'ASSISTANCE A PARIS SOUS L'ANCIEN REGIME ET PENDANT LA REVOLUTION
PARTY BUILDER / Socialist Party. U.S.A – 1-88 (all publ). 1912-14 – 1 – $11500 – us UPA [335]
PARTY ORGANIZER / Communist Party. U.S.A – 1-11 2+8 (all publ). 1927-1938 – 40mf – 9 – $230.00 – us UPA [335]
THE PARTY ORGANIZER – New York. Apr. 1927-Dec. 1931. Missing: no. 2, Mar. 1931; scattered issues – 1 – 35.00r – us Hoover Inst Photo [335]
PARVARISH – (Purchase with Hikmat) – Cairo, 1900- . v.1, no.1-2 (10 Safar 1318-27 Safar 1318 [8 Jun 1900-15 Jun 1900]) – 1 – us MEDOC [950]
PARVARISH – (Shumarah-i 1-23 (10 Safar 1318-4 Sha'ban 1318[8 June 1900-22 November 1900])) – Cairo – 1 reel – 1 – $25.00 – us MEDOC [950]
Parvus *see* ROSSIIA I REVOLIUTSIIA
PARZIVAL / Eschenbach, Wolfram von; ed by Legerlotz, Gustav – 12. Aufl. Bielefeld; Leipzig: Volhagen & Klasing, 1933 – 1 – us U.W. Library [830]
PARZIVAL IN DER DEUTSCHEN LITERATUR / Golther, Wolfgang – (Includes bibliographical references) – Berlin: W de Gruyter & Co, 1929 – 2r – 1 – us U.W. Library [430]
Pas, J de *see* CARTULAIRE DE LA CHARTREUSE DU VAL DE STE-ALDEGONDE PRES SAINT-OMER
PASA A LA COMISION DE RECOMPENSAR DE LA REAL ACADEMIA DE LA HISTORIA / Fita, Fidel – Madrid: Fortanet, 1910. B.R.A.H. 56, 1910, p. 530 – sp Bibl Santa Ana [946]
Pasa, Ahmet Cevdet *see*
- ADEB-I SEDAT
- TARIH-I CEVDET

Pasa, Kamil *see* TARIH-I SIYASI DEVLET-I ALIYE-I OSMANIYE
Pasa, Luetfi *see* TEVARIH-I AL-I OSMAN
Pasa, Mahmud Mutar *see* ISTANBUL'UN KARA VE DENIZDEN HUECM VE MUEDAFAASI HAKKINDA BIR KAC SOEZ
Pasa, Mustafa Nuri *see* NETA'IC UEL-VUKU'AT
Pasa, Nisanci Mehmed *see* SIYER-I ENBIYA-I 'AZAM VE AHVAL-I HULEFA-I KIRAM
Pasa, Ragib *see* DIVANCE
Pasa, Ziya *see* EDIB-I MUHTEREM MERHUM ZIYA PASA'NIN RUHYASI
PASADENA – 1980; 1988- – 11+ r – 1 – $550.00 – P00085 – us Library Micro [910]
PASADENA CITY DIRCTORIES – Los Angeles Co, CA. 1881-1976 – 95r – 1 – $4,750.00 – D051 – us Library Micro [910]
PASADENA EVENING POST – Pasadena, CA. 1919-1921 – 1 – 1 – $50.00 – C03385 – us Library Micro [071]
THE PASADENA ORGANIZATION HANDBOOK – Los Angeles Co, 1939 – 1r – 1 – $50.00 – B06098 – us Library Micro [060]
PASADENA POST – Pasadena, CA. 1932-1945 – 67r – 1 – $3,350.00 – C03386 – us Library Micro [071]
PASADENA: THE WEEKLY *see* ALTADENA
PASAJEROS A INDIAS / Rubio Moreno, Luis – Madrid, 1931; Madrid: Razon y Fe, 1932. 2v – 1 – sp Bibl Santa Ana [830]
Pasaribu, Amir *see*
- RABANARA DANCES; PIANO SOLO
- RIWAJAT MUSIK SAN MUSISI

DEN PASAR-PONTIANAK, LAHIRNJA DOEA NEGARA / Dutch East Indies. Algemeen Regeerings-commissariaat voor Borneo en de Grote Oost – SE-4924 1. 1946? – 9 – ne IDC [324]
PASASON : LAO-LANGUAGE DAILY NEWSPAPER – (Jul 1983-Dec 1983 $50.00v; Jan 1984-Dec 1985 $100.00v; Jan 1986-Jun 1986 $50.00v; Jul 1986-Dec 1986 $100.00v; Jan 1987-Dec 1992 $200.00v) – Vientiane, Laos. Formerly: Siang Pasason – 1 – us Asia Libr [072]
PASATIEMPO DE...RESPUESTA A SU ORACION APOLOGETICA / Forner Segarra, Juan Pablo – 1787 – 9 – 1.50f – sp Bibl Santa Ana [840]
PASATIEMPO EN RESPUESTA A LAS OBJECIONES A SU ORACION / Forner Segarra, Juan Pablo – 1787 – 1mf – 9 – Pta1,000.00 – 84-7848-199-0 – sp Pentalfa [946]
PASATIEMPOS ARROYANOS / Carrasco Canales, Jose – Caceres: Imp. Linea 21, 1976 – 1 – sp Bibl Santa Ana [946]
PASCAL / Boutroux, Emile – Paris: Hachette, 1900 – 1mf – us A.T.L.A. [430]
PASCAL AND MODULA 2 – 1983 – 9 – us UMI [510]
PASCAL AND THE PORT ROYALISTS / Clark, William – Edinburgh: T. & T. Clark, 1902 – 1mf – us A.T.L.A. [240]
Pascal, Cesar *see* LA REVOCATION DE L'EDIT DE NANTES ET MME DE MAINTENON
Pascal, Joseph et al *see* LA VICTOIRE
PASCAREL / Ouida – British Fiction Archive: Unit 3 – 9 – uk Bell [830]
Paschal, George Washington *see* THE CONSTITUTION OF THE UNITED STATES DEFINED AND CAREFULLY ANNOTATED
Pascher, A *see*
- DIE SUESSWASSER-FLORA DEUTSCHLANDS, OESTERREICHS UND DER SCHWEIZ
- DIE SUESSWASSER-FLORA (VON DEUTSCHLAND, OSTERREICH UND DER SCHWEIZ)

Paschke, F *see* DIE BEIDEN GRIECHISCHEN KLEMENTINEN-EPITOMEN UND IHRE ANHAENGE (T.U.U. 5-90)
PASCO NEWS – Dade City. Fla. Sep 1973- Formerly: Pasco East and Dade City Banner – 1 – us P.K. Yonge [071]
Pascoe, F P *see* THE STUDENT'S LIST OF BRITISH COLEOPTERA, WITH SYNOPTIC TABLES OF FAMILIES AND GENERA
Pascoli, L *see*
- VITE DE' PITTORI, SCULTORI ED ARCHITETTI MODERNI...
- VITE DE' PITTORI, SCULTORI ED ARCHITETTI PERUGINI
- VITE DE'PITTORI, SCULTORI ED ARCHITETTI MODERNI
- VITE DE'PITTORI, SCULTORI ED ARCHITETTI PERUGINI

Pascual Ayago, Julian *see* EL CICERONE
Pascual, Julian *see* EL CICERONE
Pascual y Rubio, J *see* TRATADO DEL GARROTILLO MALIGNO ULCERADO O ANGINA MALIGNA GANGRENOSA...
Pashkov, V V *see* ISSLEDOVANIIA TERMODINAMICHESKIKH SVOISTV ZHIDKOGO VODORODA
Pashkov, Vasilii A *see* KRUZHESKIYA BESEDY
PASHKOVITES – (No3. Vnebogosluzhebnaya beseda o pochitanii svyatykh ikon: Otvet posledovatelyam Pashkova. St. Petersburg, 1891; No4. Sbornik statei dukhovnago soderzhaniya. Moscow, 1891) – Four titles on 1 reel – 1 – $15.00 – us Baptist [240]
PASICRISIE INTERNATIONALE : HISTOIRE DOCUMENTAIRE DES ARBITRAGES INTERNATIONAUX / Lafontaine, H – Berne, 1902 – 13mf – 9 – H-1085/2 – ne IDC [900]
Pasio, A P Francisco *see* RELATIO HISTORICA RERUM IN JAPONIAE REGNO GESTARUM ANNO DOMINI 1603
LA PASION DE UNA RELIGIOSA, BENITEZ DE CASTRO, CUARTO GALEON, IRIGARAY DE BUZO A GENERAL, TOMAS LECCION DE AMOR SIN PALABRAS Y PEREZ Y PEREZ, CABEZA DE ESTOPA / Maridos de Coral, Montemor – Madrid: Razon y Fe, 1943 – 1 – sp Bibl Santa Ana [240]
PASIONARIA; PEOPLE'S TRIBUNE OF SPAIN – N.Y., 1937? Fiche W1514. (Blodgett Collection of Spanish Civil War Pamphlets) – 9 – us H.U. College Libr [946]
Paskevicius, Juozas *see* LIETUVISKAI-VOKISKAS ZODYNAS: LITAUISCH-DEUTSCHES WOERTERBUCH
EL PASO DEL GUADIANA / Crespo, Pedro – Madrid: Sala Editorial, 1977 – 1 – sp Bibl Santa Ana [946]
PASO ROBLES DAILY PRESS – Paso Robles, CA. 1921-66; 1970-74; 1980- – 183+ r – 1 – $9,150.00 ($350.00y) – B02616 – us Library Micro [071]
PASO ROBLES RECORD – Paso Robles, CA. 1895-1917 – 8r – 1 – $400.00 – B02617 – us Library Micro [071]
PASO ROBLES SPOTLIGHT – Paso Robles, CA. Jan-Dec 1930 – 1r – 1 – $50.00 – B02618 – us Library Micro [071]
PASO ROBLES TIMES – Paso Robles, CA. 1935-37 – 1r – 1 – $50.00 – B02619 – us Library Micro [071]
Paso y Troncoso, Francisco del *see* EPISTOLARIO DE NUEVA ESPANA...
LA PASQUA DEI LAVORATORI – New York, NY, 1898 – 1mf or 1r – 1,9 – us I.H.R.C. [978]
Pasquale, G A *see* FLORA MEDICA DELLA PROVINCIA DI NAPOLI
Pasquali, N *see*
- THE ART OF FINGERING THE HARPSICHORD
- LA BASSE CONTINUE RENDUE AISEE
- SIX SONATAS (SECOND SET) FOR TWO VIOLINS WITH A TENOR AND THOROUGH BASS FOR THE HARPSICHORD OR VIOLONCELLO
- THOROUGH-BASS MADE EASY

Pasqualigus, Z *see* DISPUTATIONES META PHYSICAE...
Pasque, Ernst *see* LES CLOCHES DE PLURS
THE PASQUINO – Keyser. West Virginia. 1921-1968- – 1 – us UMI [071]
THE PASQUINO – Potomac. West Virginia. 1921-1967 – 1 – us UMI [071]
PASSAGES FROM THE LIFE AND WRITINGS OF GEORGE FOX, TAKEN FROM HIS JOURNAL / Fox, George – Philadelphia, 1881. 345p – 1 – us U.W. Library [920]
PASSAGES FROM THE PROSE WRITINGS OF MATTHEW ARNOLD / Arnold, Matthew – London: Smith, Elder, 1880 – 1 roll – 1 – 1-55879-189-2 – uk Libr Preservation [800]
PASSAGES SELECTED FROM THE WRITINGS OF THOMAS CARLYLE : WITH A BIOGRAPHICAL MEMOIR BY THOMAS BALLANTYNE / Carlyle, Thomas – London: Chapman and Hall, 1855 – 1 roll – 1 – 1-55879-364-X – uk Libr Preservation [840]
Passaic. Presbytery (Pres. Ch. in the U.S.A. Old School) *see* MINUTES, 1852-1870
LE PASSANT – no. 1-45. Paris. 1er juin 1882-16 janv 1883. contient aussi le suppl: Le Passant-Affiches. no. 1-54. 10 dec 1882-3 fevr 1883 – 1 – fr A.C.R.P.P. [073]
Passarge, Siegfried *see* ADAMAUA
PASSAUER NEUE PRESSE – Passau, West Germany. 1968- – ca 10r per yr – 1 – gw Mikrofilm [072]
PASSAUER ZEITUNG – (Title change: Neue Passauer Zeitung, 1 Oct 1848) – Passau, Germany. 1848-1849 – 2r – gw Mikrofilm [072]

PASSAVIA SACRA / Schroedel, Karl – Geschichte des Bisthums Passau bis zur Sakularisation des Fuerstenthums Passau. Passau, M. Waldbauer, 1879. 424 p. Film Mas 8116 – 1 – us H.U. Library [240]

LE PASSE, LE PRESENT, L'AVENIR / Picard – (French Theatre Series). Paris. Impr. du Postillon, Fievee, Melle sulan. s.d – 9 – fr Hachette [820]

LE PASSE, LE PRESENT, L'AVENIR: ABUS, FRAUDES, INJUSTICES – Montreal, 1875. 04065. (Pre-1900 Canadiana) – 9 – cn C.I.H.M. [971]

Passendorfer, A *see* BLEDY JEZYKOWE

PASSENGER AND ALIEN CREW LISTS OF VESSELS ARRIVING AT THE PORT OF DETROIT, MICHIGAN, 1946-1957 – 23r – 1 – M1479 – us Nat'l Archives [340]

PASSENGER AND CREW LISTS OF VESSELS ARRIVING AT NEW YORK, 1897-1919 / U.S. Immigration and Naturalization Service – 6674 rolls. T715 – 1 – us Nat'l Archives [324]

PASSENGER AND CREW LISTS OF VESSELS ARRIVING AT SAN FRANCISCO, 1954-1957 – 19r – 1 – M1411 – us Nat'l Archives [340]

PASSENGER AND CREW LISTS OF VESSELS ARRIVING AT SEATTLE, WASHINGTON, 1890-1957 – 357r – 1 – M1383 – us Nat'l Archives [340]

PASSENGER LISTS OF SHIPS COMING TO NORTH AMERICA, 1607-1825 – By A.H. Lancour 1938. Item P.26p. SW16-0020 – 5 – us A.G.L.L. [920]

PASSENGER LISTS OF THE HOLLAND-AMERICA LINE, 1900-1940 – (Indexes available separately 272mf Dfl3,750.00) – 1994 – 1,053mf – 9 – Dfl11,995.00 – ne MMF Publ [380]

PASSENGER LISTS OF VESSELS ARRIVING AT BALTIMORE, 1820-91 / U.S. Bureau of the Customs – 50 rolls. M255. Printed guide – 1 – us Nat'l Archives [324]

PASSENGER LISTS OF VESSELS ARRIVING AT BALTIMORE, 1891-1909 / U.S. Immigration and Naturalization Service – 77 rolls. T844 – 1 – us Nat'l Archives [324]

PASSENGER LISTS OF VESSELS ARRIVING AT BOSTON, 1820-91 / U.S. Bureau of the Customs – 115 rolls. M277 – 1 – us Nat'l Archives [324]

PASSENGER LISTS OF VESSELS ARRIVING AT BOSTON, 1891-1919 / U.S. Immigration and Naturalization Service – 454 rolls. T843 – 1 – us Nat'l Archives [324]

PASSENGER LISTS OF VESSELS ARRIVING AT GALVESTON, TEXAS, 1896-1951 – 36r – 1 – M1359 – us Nat'l Archives [340]

PASSENGER LISTS OF VESSELS ARRIVING AT KEY WEST, 1898-1945 / U.S. Immigration and Naturalization Service – 122 rolls. T940 – 1 – us Nat'l Archives [324]

PASSENGER LISTS OF VESSELS ARRIVING AT NEW BEDFORD, 1902 / U.S. Immigration and Naturalization Service – 8rolls. T944 – 1 – us Nat'l Archives [324]

PASSENGER LISTS OF VESSELS ARRIVING AT NEW ORLEANS, LOUISIANA / U.S. Bureau of the Customs – 1820-1902. 93 rolls. M259 – 1 – us Nat'l Archives [324]

PASSENGER LISTS OF VESSELS ARRIVING AT NEW YORK, 1820-97 / U.S. Bureau of the Customs – 675 rolls. M237. Printed guide – 1 – us Nat'l Archives [324]

PASSENGER LISTS OF VESSELS ARRIVING AT PHILADELPHIA, 1800-82 / U.S. Bureau of the Customs – 108 rolls. M425 – 1 – us Nat'l Archives [324]

PASSENGER LISTS OF VESSELS ARRIVING AT PHILADELPHIA, 1883-1919 / U.S. Immigration and Naturalization Service – 181 rolls. T840 – 1 – us Nat'l Archives [324]

PASSENGER LISTS OF VESSELS ARRIVING AT PORTLAND, MAINE / U.S. Bureau of the Customs – 29 Nov 1893-Mar 1943. 35 rolls.A1151 – 1 – us Nat'l Archives [310]

PASSENGER LISTS OF VESSELS ARRIVING AT PROVIDENCE, RHODE ISLAND / U.S. Bureau of the Customs – 1911-30. 49 rolls. M1188 – 1 – us Nat'l Archives [324]

PASSENGER LISTS OF VESSELS ARRIVING AT SAN FRANCISCO, 1893-1953 – 429r – 1 – M1410 – us Nat'l Archives [340]

PASSENGER LISTS OF VESSELS ARRIVING AT SAN FRANCISCO FROM HONOLULU, 1902-1907 – 1r – 1 – M1494 – us Nat'l Archives [340]

PASSENGER LISTS OF VESSELS ARRIVING AT SAN FRANCISCO FROM INSULAR POSSESSIONS, 1907-1911 – 2r – 1 – M1438 – us Nat'l Archives [340]

PASSENGER LISTS OF VESSELS ARRIVING AT SAVANNAH, 1906 / U.S. Immigration and Naturalization Service – 4rolls. T943 – 1 – us Nat'l Archives [324]

PASSENGER LISTS OF VESSELS ARRIVING AT SEATTLE FROM INSULAR POSSESSIONS, 1908-1917 – 1r – 1 – M1485 – us Nat'l Archives [340]

PASSENGER LISTS OF VESSELS ARRIVING AT SEATTLE, WASHINGTON, 1949-1954 – 5r – 1 – M1398 – us Nat'l Archives [340]

LE PASSE-PARTOUT : HUMORISTIQUE – Sorel, Canada. 12 mai 1888-v3 n2. 27 fev 1892 – 1r – 1 – Can$25.00 – cn Can Microfilming [072]

O PASSE-PARTOUT : ORGAO DE PROPAGANDA EXCLUSIVA DO BAZAR PASSE PARTOUT – Manaos, Amazonas. 12 Set-23 Nov 1909 – 1,5,6 – bl Biblioteca [072]

LA PASSE-TEMPS – Montreal: [s.n. 1878-188- ou 19–] – 9 – cn C.I.H.M. [971]

LE PASSE-TEMPS – Quebec, Canada. 22 jul-29 jul 1862 – 1r – 1 – Can$25.00 – cn Can Microfilming [072]

LE PASSE-TEMPS : REVUE MUSICALE ET LITTERAIRE – Montreal, Canada. 2 fev 1895-dec 1949 – 10r – 1 – Can$60.00r – cn Can Microfilming [073]

PASSE-TEMPS – Canada. v1-41. Feb. 2, 1895-Jan. 1934 – 1 – cn Precision [073]

PASSETEMPS SUR LES CHARS: RECITS ET NOUVELLES / Bourget, Joseph G – Trois Rivieres, Quebec: La Concorde, 1880. 00216. (Pre-1900 Canadiana) – 9 – cn C.I.H.M. [830]

PASSING NOTES – Hove, England. Hove Courier. -w. 5 June 1880-23 Sept 1882. 1 reel – 1 – uk British Libr Newspaper [072]

THE PASSING OF THE EMPIRES, 850 BC TO 330 BC / Maspero, Gaston – ed. by A. Sayce.Trans. by M.L. McClure. New York: Appleton, 1900. xii,824p. illus. maps – 1 – us U.W. Library [900]

PASSIO DOMINI NOSTRI JESU CHRISTI: DAS LEYDEN UND STERBEN UNSERS HERRN JESU CHRISTI..... / Mancinus, Thomas – Wolffenuttel: E Holwein, 1620 – 1 – us Sibley [780]

PASSIO S. THECLAE VIRGINIS : DIE LATEINISCHEN UEBERSETZUNGEN DER ACTA PAULI ET THECLAE (T.U.U. 2-22/2) / Gebhardt, Oscar von – Leipzig, 1902 – 5mf – 9 – ne Slangenburg [240]

DIE PASSION DES HERRN NACH DEN VIER EVANGELIEN SYNOPTISCH DARGESTELLT FUER DIE GEBILDETEN IN DER GEMEINDE / Decker, A – Kiel: Ernst Homann, 1863 – 1mf – 9 – 0-8370-2857-4 – 1985-0857 – us A.T.L.A. [240]

THE PASSION FOR MEN: A PLEA FOR ENDEAVOR IN SOUL WINNING / Hallenbeck, Edwin Forrest – New York: Fleming H. Revell, 1904. 134p. 1 fiche – 9 – us A.T.L.A. [240]

THE PASSION OF JESUS (FIRST SERIES) : SEVEN DISCOURSES FOR LENT / Baring-Gould, Sabine – (Includes bibliographical references) – London: Skeffington, 1885 – 1mf – 9 – 0-8370-4808-7 – 1985-2808 – us A.T.L.A. [240]

THE PASSION OF S. PERPETUA / ed by Robinson, J A – 1891 – 3mf – 9 – ne Slangenburg [240]

PASSIONAL BUECHLEIN... / Andreae d.A E, J – Wittenberg, 1577 – 4mf – 9 – ne IDC [240]

PASSIONES VITAEQUE SANCTORUM AEVI MEROVINGICI ET ANTIQUORUM ALIQUOT (MGH 2: 3.BD) / ed by Krusch, B – 1896 – Dfl63.00 – ne Slangenburg [240]

PASSIONES VITAEQUE SANCTORUM AEVI MEROVINGICI (MGH 2: 4.BD) / ed by Krusch, B – 1902 – Dfl74.00 – ne Slangenburg [240]

PASSIONES VITAEQUE SANCTORUM AEVI MEROVINGICI (MGH 2: 5.BD) / ed by Krusch, B & Levison, W – 1910 – Dfl81.00 – ne Slangenburg [240]

PASSIONES VITAEQUE SANCTORUM AEVI MEROVINGICI (MGH 2: 6.BD) / ed by Krusch, B & Levison, W – 1913 – Dfl63.00 – ne Slangenburg [240]

PASSIONES VITAEQUE SANCTORUM AEVI MEROVINGICI (MGH 2: 7.BD) / ed by Krusch, B & Levison, W – 1920 – Dfl84.00 – ne Slangenburg [240]

PASSIONS CANTATE, GROSZE, [DU GOTTSLICHER WARUMBIST DU SO IN DES TODES SCHMERZ VERSUNKEN?] IN MUSIK GESETZT VON KARL PHILIPP EMANUEL BACH... / Bach, C P E – Ms, [178-?] – 1 – us Sibley [780]

PASSIVE RESISTER – Johannesburg. South Africa. -w. 8 Jul 1946-8 Oct 1948. (40 ft) – 1 – uk British Libr Newspaper [072]

THE PASSIVE RESISTER : OFFICIAL ORGAN OF THE PASSIVE RESISTANCE COUNCIL OF THE TRANSVAAL INDIAN CONGRESS – Johannesburg: T N Naidoo, jul 15 1946-oct 8 1948 – 1r – 1 – us Res Libr [073]

PASSIVE SENSORY MEDIATION OF RATINGS OF PERCEIVED EXERTION IN TRAINED AND UNTRAINED MALES AT LIGHT AND MODERATE WORKLOADS / Nethery, V M – 1989 – 1mf – 9 – $4.00 – us Microform Publ [150]

Passlack, M et al *see* INFRARED SPECTRAL DATA

PASSOS DOS LUSIADAS ESTUDADOS A LUZ DA MITOLOJIA.. / Vasconcellos-Abreu, Guilherme de – Lisboa: Imprensa nacional, 1892.vii,85p. Illus. (facs.). plates. 1 reel. 1273 – 1 – us U.W. Library [390]

Passot, Luis *see* MEMORIA...MOLINO-PANADERIA...HABITANTES

PAST AND PRESENT / Carlyle, Thomas – London: Chapman and Hall, 1843 – 1 roll – 1 – 1-55879-324-0 – uk Libr Preservation [840]

PAST AND PRESENT – Oxford. v1-125. 1952-89* 1; v126-149 1990-95. v151-158 1996-97+ 1,5,9 – 1,5,9 – D18439 – us UMI [073]

PAST AND PRESENT OF ADAMS COUNTY / Barton & Lewis – Chicago: S.J. Clarke Publ. Co., 1916. 2v. Nebraska Reel 5. (The Cox Library Collection) – 5 – us Americana [978]

PAST AND PRESENT OF ALAMEDA COUNTY, CALIFORNIA / Baker, Joseph E – Chicago: S.J. Clarke Publ. Co., 1914. 2v. California Reel 10. (The Cox Library Collection) – 5 – us Americana [978]

PAST AND PRESENT OF BOONE COUNTY, ILLINOIS / H.F. Kett and Co – Chicago, 1877. Illinois Reel 12. The Cox Library Collection – 5 – us Americana [978]

PAST AND PRESENT OF BUREAU COUNTY / Pioneer Publishing Co – Chicago, 1906. Illinois Reel 13. (The Cox Library Collection) – 5 – us Americana [978]

PAST AND PRESENT OF CALHOUN COUNTY / Stonebraker, Beaumont E – (Chicago: Pioneer Publ. Co., 1915). Vols. 1-2. Iowa Reel 8. (The Cox Library Collection) – 5 – us Americana [978]

PAST AND PRESENT OF CHRISTIAN COUNTY, ILLINOIS / McBridge, J C – Chicago: S. J. Clarke Publ. Co., 1904. Illinois Reel 15. (The Cox Library Collection) – 5 – us Americana [978]

PAST AND PRESENT OF DALLAS COUNTY / Wood, R F – (Chicago: S. J. Clarke Publ. Co., 1907). Iowa Reel 12. (The Cox Library Collection) – 5 – us Americana [978]

PAST AND PRESENT OF DE KALB COUNTY, ILLINOIS / Gross, Lewis M – Chicago: The Pioneer Publ. Co., 1907. Vol. 1. Illinois Reel 21; Vol. 2. Illinois Reel 22. (The Cox Library Collection) – 5 – us Americana [978]

THE PAST AND PRESENT OF EATON COUNTY / The Michigan Historical Publishing Association – Biographical sketches. Lansing. Michigan Reel 8. (The Cox Library Collection) – 5 – us Americana [978]

PAST AND PRESENT OF FAYETTE COUNTY / B.F. Bowen and Co – Indianapolis, 1910. v1-2. Iowa Reel 16. The Cox Library Collection – 5 – us Americana [978]

PAST AND PRESENT OF FOND DU LAC COUNTY / McKenna, Maurice – Chicago: S. J. Clarke Publ. Co., 1912. Vols. 1-2. Wisconsin Reel 11. (The Cox Library Collection) – 5 – us Americana [978]

PAST AND PRESENT OF GREENE COUNTY / Fairbanks, J & Tuck, C E – Genealogical records. Indianapolis: A.W. Bowen and Co., 1915. Missouri Reel 17. (The Cox Library Collection) – 5 – us Americana [978]

PAST AND PRESENT OF GUTHRIE COUNTY – Chicago, 1907. Iowa Reel 19. The Cox Library Collection – 5 – us Americana [978]

PAST AND PRESENT OF ISABELLA COUNTY / Fancher, Issac A – Indianapolis: B. F. Bowen and Co., 1911. Michigan Reel 14. (The Cox Library Collection) – 5 – us Americana [978]

PAST AND PRESENT OF JASPER COUNTY / Weaver, James B – Indianapolis: B. F. Bowen and Co., 1912. Vol. 1, Iowa Reel 22; Vol. 2, Iowa Reel 23. (The Cox Library Collection) – 5 – us Americana [978]

PAST AND PRESENT OF KANE COUNTY / Le Baron, William Jr – Historical and biographical sketches. Chicago: 1878. Illinois Reel 30. (The Cox Library Collection) – 5 – us Americana [978]

PAST AND PRESENT OF KNOX COUNTY / Williams, Albert B – Indianapolis: B. F. Bowen and Co., 1912. Vols. 1-2. Ohio Reel 41. (The Cox Library Collection) – 5 – us Americana [978]

PAST AND PRESENT OF LA SALLE COUNTY / H.F. Kett and Co – Historical and biographical sketches. Chicago, 1877. Illinois Reel 36. The Cox Library Collection – 5 – us Americana [978]

PAST AND PRESENT OF LAKE COUNTY – Historical and biographical sketches. Chicago, 1877. Illinois Reel 35. The Cox Library Collection – 5 – us Americana [978]

PAST AND PRESENT OF MARSHALL COUNTY / Battin & Moscrip – Indianapolis: B. F. Bowen and Co., 1912. Vols. 1-2. Iowa Reel 29. (The Cox Library Collection) – 5 – us Americana [978]

PAST AND PRESENT OF O'BRIEN AND OSCEOLA COUNTIES / Peck & Montzheimer & Miller – Indianapolis: B. F. Bowen & Co., 1914. Vol. 1, Iowa Reel 31; Vol. 2, Iowa Reel 32. (The Cox Library Collection) – 5 – us Americana [978]

PAST AND PRESENT OF PIKE COUNTY / Massie, M D – Historical and biographical sketches. Chicago: S. J. Clarke Publ. Co., 1906. Illinois Reel 49. (The Cox Library Collection) – 5 – us Americana [978]

PAST AND PRESENT OF ROCK ISLAND COUNTY / H.F. Kett and Co – Historical and biographical sketches. Chicago, 1877. Illinois Reel 50. The Cox Library Collection – 5 – us Americana [978]

PAST AND PRESENT OF ROCKFORD CITY AND WINNEBAGO COUNTY / Church, Charles A – Chicago: S. J. Clarke Publ. Co., 1905. Illinois Reel 64. (The Cox Library Collection) – 5 – us Americana [978]

PAST AND PRESENT OF SAUNDERS COUNTY / Perky, Charles – Chicago: S.J. Clarke Publ. Co., 1915. 2v. Nebraska Reel 12. (The Cox Library Collection) – 5 – us Americana [978]

PAST AND PRESENT OF SHIAWASSEE COUNTY / Michigan Historical Publishing Co – Biographical sketches. Lansing. Michigan Reel 21. (The Cox Library Collection) – 5 – us Americana [978]

PAST AND PRESENT OF SIOUX CITY AND WOODBURY COUNTY / Marks, Constant R – Chicago: S.J. Clarke Publ. Co., 1904. Iowa Reel 43. (The Cox Library Collection) – 5 – us Americana [978]

PAST AND PRESENT OF SYRACUSE AND ONONDAGA COUNTY – New York, 1908. v1. New York Reel 26; v2. New York Reel 27. The Cox Library Collection – 5 – us Americana [978]

PAST AND PRESENT OF THE CITY OF DECATUR AND MACON COUNTY – Chicago, 1903. Illinois Reel 40. The Cox Library Collection – 5 – us Americana [978]

PAST AND PRESENT OF THE CITY OF LANSING AND INGHAM COUNTY / Cowles, Albert E – Lansing: Michigan Historical Publ. Asso. Michigan Reel 12. (The Cox Library Collection) – 5 – us Americana [978]

PAST AND PRESENT OF THE CITY OF QUINCY AND ADAMS COUNTY / Collins, W H & Perry, Cicero F – Chicago: S. J. Clarke Publ. Co., 1905. Illinois Reel 11. (The Cox Library Collection) – 5 – us Americana [978]

PAST AND PRESENT OF THE CITY OF SPRINGFIELD AND COUNTY OF SANGAMON / Wallace, Joseph – Chicago: S. J. Clarke Publ. Co., 1904. Vols. 1-2. Illinois Reel 53. (The Cox Library Collection) – 5 – us Americana [978]

PAST AND PRESENT OF TIPPECANOE COUNTY / DeHart, R P – Indianapolis: B.F. Bowen and Company, 1909. 2v.Indiana Reel 27. (The Cox Library Collection) – 5 – us Americana [978]

PAST AND PRESENT OF VERMILION COUNTY – Chicago, 1903. Illinois Reel 57. The Cox Library Collection – 5 – us Americana [978]

PAST AND PRESENT OF WARREN COUNTY, ILLINOIS 1877 / Kett, H.F. and Co – Chicago. (Illinois Reel 58). (The Cox Library Collection) – 5 – us Americana [978]

PAST AND PRESENT OF WASHINGTON COUNTY / Quickert, Carl – Chicago: S. J. Clarke Publ. Co., 1912. Vols. 1-2. Wisconsin Reel 21. (The Cox Library Collection) – 5 – us Americana [978]

PAST AND PRESENT OF WASHTENAW COUNTY / Beakes, Samuel W – Biographical sketches. Chicago: S. J. Clarke Publ. Co., 1906. Michigan Reel 22. (The Cox Library Collection) – 5 – us Americana [978]

PAST AND PRESENT OF WILL COUNTY / Stevens, W W – Chicago: S. J. Clarke Publ. Co., 1907. Vols. 1-2. Illinois Reel 62. (The Cox Library Collection) – 5 – us Americana [978]

PAST AND PRESENT OF WOODFORD COUNTY – Chicago, 1878. Illinois Reel 64. The Cox Library Collection – 5 – us Americana [978]

PAST AND PRESENT SUBTERRANEAN DWELLINGS OF THE TRIBES OF NORTH EASTERN ASIA AND NORTH WESTERN AMERICA / Jochelson, W – BN 276 2. 1907 – 8 – ne IDC [306]

THE PAST AND PROSPECTIVE EXTENSION OF THE GOSPEL BY MISSIONS TO THE HEATHEN : CONSIDERED IN EIGHT LECTURES / Grant, Anthony – London: Printed for J.G.F.& J. Rivington, 1844 – 2mf – us A.T.L.A. [240]

Pastalan, Leon A *see* JOURNAL OF HOUSING FOR THE ELDERLY

PASTELERIAS EN LIMA PRIMITIVA / Bayle, Constantino – Madrid: Revista de Indias, 1941 – 1 – sp Bibl Santa Ana [950]

Pastells, Pablo *see*
- CATALOGO DE LOS DOCUMENTOS RELATIVOS A LAS ISLAS FILIPINAS, EXI EN EL ARCH. D. INDIAS DE SEVILLA
- CATALOGO DE LOS DOCUMENTOS RELATIVOS A LAS ISLAS FILIPINAS EXISTENTES EN EL ARCHIVO DE INDIAS DE SEVILLA (1592-1602). BARCELONA, 1928
- HISTORIA GENERAL DE FILIPINAS. NAVAS DEL VALLE. CATALOGO DE MONUMENTOS REFERENTES A ISLAS FILIPINAS...

PASTELS, AQUARELLES ET DESSINS DE PAYSAGISTES FRANCAIS DU XIXE SIECLE / Reunion des musees nationaux. Paris – 1933. 1 fiche – 9 – fr Réunion [750]

Pasternak, B *see*
- DOKTER ZHIVAGO
- GRUZINSKIE LIRIKI
- IZBRANNYE PEREVODY
- POEZIIA
- POVERKH BAR'EROV
- SOCHINENIIA POD. RED. G.P. STRUVE
- STIKHOTVORENIIA 1 POEMY
- STIKHOTVORENIIA V ODNOM TOME
- ZEMNOI PROSTOR

PASTIME – Schenectady. v1-2. feb 1807-jun 1808 – 1 – D3626 – us UMI [790]

PASTKAIDROJUMI BAPTISTU DRAUDSCHU LOZEKLEEM SAWEENIBAS PADOMES SUHDSIBAS LEETA / Laudam, Jet al – Riga, 1926. Publ. No. 6299 e. One of five items on a reel – 1 – us Baptist [240]

Paston, William *see* A CATALOGUE OF THE LIBRARY OF THE RIGHT HONOURABLE... EARL OF YARMOUTH, LATELY DECEASED.

THE PASTOR AND MODERN MISSIONS : A PLEA FOR LEADERSHIP IN WORLD EVANGELIZATION / Mott, John Raleigh – (Includes index) – New York: Student Volunteer Movt for Foreign Missions, 1904 – 1mf – 9 – 0-8370-6285-3 – 1986-0285 – us A.T.L.A. [240]

PASTOR BONUS – (1947-: Trierer Theol. Zeitschrift) – 1(1889)-55(1944) – 510mf – 9 – Dfl1,785.00 – ne Slangenburg [073]

PASTOR BONUS – Trier. v1-55. 1889/1890-1944 – 510mf – 9 – ne IDC [240]

PASTOR C. H. SPURGEON : HIS LIFE AND WORK TO HIS FIFTIETH BIRTHDAY / Stevenson, George J – London: Passmore and Alabaster, 1885 – 1mf – us A.T.L.A. [240]

PASTOR CHINIQUY : AN EXAMINATION OF HIS "FIFTY YEARS IN THE CHURCH OF ROME" / Smith, Sydney – London: Catholic Truth Society, s.d. SEM105P379 – 1mf – 9 – Can$2.25 – cn Bibl Nat [240]

Pastor Diaz, Nicomedes *see*
- LA CUESTION ELECTORAL
- LA CUESTION SOCIAL EN DICIEMBRE DE 1839 Y ENERO DE 1840

EL PASTOR EVANGELICO – 1958. 404p – 1 – 14.14 – us Baptist [240]

PASTOR IN BUDAPEST / Meyer, Heinrich – Copy Book, 1883-1915. Material from Oncken Archives, Hamburg, Germany. 1344p – 1 – 47.04 – us Baptist [240]

PASTOR J. JEZEQUEL VISITS REPUBLICAN SPAIN / Gutierrez Marin, C – Barcelona, 1938. Fiche W936. (Blodgett Collection of Spanish Civil War Pamphlets) – 9 – us H.U. College Libr [946]

Pastor, Juan Jose *see* NOVENA A SANTA RITA DE CASIA

Pastor, Ludwig, Freiherr von *see*
- CHARAKTERBILDER KATHOLISCHER REFORMATOREN DES 16. JAHRHUNDERTS
- DIE KIRCHLICHEN REUNIONSBESTREBUNGEN WAEHREND DER REGIERUNG KARLS 5.

Pastor Serrano, Juan Jose *see*
FIESTAS COMARCALES DE SANTA CRUZ DE LA SIERRA...MAYO 1981 EN HONOR DE SANTA RITA...
- SANTA CRUZ DE LA SIERRA. FIESTAS COMARCALES A SANTA RITA. 1977

DE PASTOR VON DRIEBECK : ERZAEHLUNG IN NIEDERDEUTSCHER MUNDART / Wibbelt, Augustin – 3. Aufl. Essen (Ruhr): Fredebeul und Koenen, 1920 – 1r – 1 – us U.W. Library [390]

Pastor, Willy *see* NOVALIS

PASTORAL / Casas y Souto, Pedro – Barcelona: Imp. P. Bofarull.s.a. – sp Bibl Santa Ana [240]

PASTORAL AL...PONTIFICADO / Lopez y Zaragoza, Gregorio Mª. – 1864 – 9 – 1.50f – sp Bibl Santa Ana [240]

PASTORAL AND PERSONAL EVANGELISM / Goodell, Charles Le Roy – New York: Fleming H Revell, c1907 – 1mf – 9 – 0-8370-6121-0 – 1986-0121 – us A.T.L.A. [240]

PASTORAL CARE IN EDUCATION – 1983- – 1,5,6,9 – us UMI [073]

PASTORAL DE URGENCIA / Sanchez Aliseda, Casimiro – (Tonicos y sugerencias para el apostolado) – Madrid: Graficas Canales S.L., 1958 – 1 – sp Bibl Santa Ana [240]

PASTORAL DEL VENERABLE OBISPO DE PLASENCIA / Casas Souto, Pedro – 1885 – 9 – 1.50f – sp Bibl Santa Ana [240]

PASTORAL DISCOURSES / Brown, J C – 1847 – 1 – us A.T.L.A. [240]

PASTORAL EPISTLES / Plummer, Alfred – New York: A.C. Armstrong, (1889). 1 fiche – 9 – us A.T.L.A. [240]

THE PASTORAL EPISTLES : TIMOTHY AND TITUS: INTRODUCTION, AUTHORIZED VERSION, REVISED VERSION WITH NOTES, INDEX AND MAP / ed by Horton, Robert Forman – (Includes an index) – New York: Henry Frowde, 1901 – 1mf – 9 – 0-8370-3668-2 – 1985-1668 – us A.T.L.A. [220]

THE PASTORAL EPISTLES: A NEW TRANSLATION / Lilley, James Philip – Edinburgh: T. & T. Clark, 1901 – 1mf – 9 – us A.T.L.A. [240]

PASTORAL EPISTLES: TIMOTHY AND TITUS / Horton, Robert Forman – New York: Henry Frowde, 1901. 1 fiche – 9 – us A.T.L.A. [240]

PASTORAL LETTER ADDRESSED TO THE CLERGY AND LAITY OF THE ARCHDIOCESE OF HALIFAX / O'Brien, Archbishop – Halifax, N.S.: Morning Herald, 1883. 05105. (Pre-1900 Canadiana) – 9 – cn C.I.H.M. [240]

PASTORAL LETTER DECLARING THE DECREES OF THE FIRST COUNCIL OF ST BONIFACE / Tache, Archbishop – 1892? 03222. (Pre-1900 Canadiana) – 9 – cn C.I.H.M. [240]

PASTORAL LETTER OF THE FATHERS OF THE SIXTH COUNCIL OF QUEBEC – Quebec?, 1878?. 03218. (Pre-1900 Canadiana) – 9 – cn C.I.H.M. [240]

PASTORAL LIFE – Canfield. v1-20 1952-71*. v21-46 1972-97+ 1; v21-23 1972-74. v24-27 1975-78*. v28 1979. v29 1980*. v30 1981. v31-39 1982-90*. v40 1991. v41-43 1992-94*. v44-46 1995-97+ 5; v23 1974*. v24-46 1975-97+ 9 – 1,5,9 – D7107 – us UMI [073]

PASTORAL MUSIC – Washington. v1-3 oct 1976-oct 1979*. v4-22 oct 1979-sep 1998+ 1; v4-19 oct 1979-sep 1995*. v20-22 oct 1995-sep 1998+ 5; v4-22. oct 1979-sep 1998+ 9 – 1,5,9 – D12503 – us UMI [780]

PASTORAL PSYCHOLOGY – v1- 1950- 1; v24-5,6,9 – us UMI [150]

PASTORAL REGISTER / Graham, H Q. – 1853-1892 – 1 – $50.00 – us Presbyterian [240]

PASTORAL REVIEW AND GAZIER'S RECORD – v. 60-62. 1950-52 – 1 – us UMI [073]

PASTORAL SOBRE EL SACRAMENTO DE LA CONFIRMACION / Garcia Gil, Manuel – Badajoz, 1856 – 1 – sp Bibl Santa Ana [240]

PASTORAL SYSTEMS RESEARCH IN SUB-SAHARAN AFRICA. : PROCEEDINGS OF THE WORKSHOP HELD AT ILCA, ADDIS ABABA, ETHIOPIA, 21-24 MARCH 1983 / ILCA – 1983 – 9 – $18.00 – 92-9053-135-5 – et ILRI [630]

PASTORAL TEACHING OF PAUL: HIS MINISTERIAL IDEALS / Chadwick, William Edward – Edinburgh: T. & T. Clark, 1907. 1 fiche – 9 – us A.T.L.A. [240]

PASTORAL TIMES – Deniliquin, Australia. Jan 1885-Dec 1921.-w. 14 reels – 1 – uk British Libr Newspaper [072]

DIE PASTORALBRIEFE UND DER BRIEF AN PHILEMON / Oosterzee, Johannes Jacobus van – Bielefeld: Velhagen & Klasing, 1864. 1 fiche – 9 – us A.T.L.A. [240]

LE PASTORALE DE MALINES : SON HISTOIRE, SES SOURCES / Malherbe, G – Maline, 1940 – 1mf – 8 – Dfl6.00 – ne Slangenburg [240]

PASTORALE MECHLINIENSE – Antverpiae, 1589 – 4mf – 8 – Dfl19.00 – ne Slangenburg [240]

PASTORALE NOVELLUM / Liebegg, Rudolfus de – 1982 – 6mf – 9 – Bf750.00 – 2-503-63552-0 – be Brepols [240]

PASTORALISTS' REVIEW PASTORAL REVIEW *see* AUSTRALASIAN PASTORALISTS' REVIEW

Pastore, Annibale *see* SILLOGISMO E PROPORZIONE

PASTOR'S MONTHLY – v1-13. 1923-35 (complete) – 5r – 1 – ATLA S0264 – us A.T.L.A. [073]

PASTOR'S REGISTER / Ohio. Chenot, George. – 1897-1934. – 1r – 1 – $32.50r – us Archival [978]

LOS PASTOS. SU IMPORTANCIA A TRAVES DEL TIEMPO / Cruz Guzman, Emilio – Badajoz: Tip. A Mangas, 1970 – sp Bibl Santa Ana [946]

PASTURE AND CATTLE UNDER COCONUTS – 1988 – 330p – it F.A.O. [636]

PASTURE AND FORAGE CROPS: SHORT COURSE PROCEEDINGS / Texas A & M University. Agricultural Experiment Station and Agricultural Extension Service – 1966-74.9 fiches – 9 – us Spaulding [631]

PASUNDAN : PARLEMEN. ZAKBOEK – Bandung, 1948-1949 – 10mf – 9 – ne IDC [320]

PAT M. HOLT, SENATE SERVICE 1950-1977 : CHIEF OF STAFF, SENATE FOREIGN RELATIONS COMMITTEE – 4mf – 9 – $20.00 – us Scholarly Res [320]

PATAGONIAN FISHERY RESOURCES AND THE OFFSHORE FISHERIES IN THE SOUTH-WEST ATLANTIC – 1987 – 80p – it F.A.O. [639]

Pataky, Sophie *see* LEXIKON DEUTSCHER FRAUEN DER FEDER

Patas, Janus Robert *see* SELTENE URSACHEN DER GASTROINTESTINALEN BLUTUNG INNERHALB DER CHIRURGIE AM BEISPIEL EIGENER FAELLE UND NEUERER LITERATUR

Pate, John G *see* THE COMPARISON OF AEROBIC FITNESS LEVELS IN REPECT TO VISUAL-PERCEPTUAL PERFORMANCE AT REST AND DURING EXERCISE

PATEESIBAI JAUSWAR! = THE TRUTH WILL WIN! – Riga: Derigu Rakstu Apgande, 1927. Publ. No. 6349a. One of three items on reel. Total Pages 146 – 1 – us Baptist [240]

Pateman, Emily May *see* PATEMAN PAPERS

PATEMAN PAPERS : A COLLECTION OF GILBERTESE TRADITIONS / Pateman, Emily May – c1900 – 1r – 1 – at Pacific Mss [306]

THE PATENT ALBO-CARBON LIGHT / Albo-Carbon Light Agency – Montreal: Breton, 1894. 00780. (Pre-1900 Canadiana) – 9 – cn C.I.H.M. [621]

PATENT AND TECHNICAL INFORMATION AGREEMENTS. / U.S. Department of State. International Business Practices Division – Washington, Govt. Print. Off., 1960. 79 p. LL-2997 – 1 – us L of C Photodup [340]

PATENT AND TRADEMARK LAWS COMMISSION : PRELIMINARY AND FINAL REPORTS / Forbes, Francis et al – 1899, 1902 (all publ) – 9mf – 9 – $13.50 – LLMC 82-503 – us L.L.M.C. [324]

PATENT AND TRADEMARK OFFICE, COMMISSIONER OF PATENTS DECISIONS – 1869-1968 – 681mf – $1,021.00 – LLMC 80-700 – us L.L.M.C. [340]

PATENT AND TRADEMARK OFFICE, COMMISSIONER OF PATENTS DECISIONS *see*
- ANNUAL REPORTS OF THE ECONOMIC DEVELOPMENT ADMINISTRATION, COMMERCE DEPARTMENT
- ANNUAL REPORTS OF THE U.S. PATENT OFFICE

PATENT AND TRADEMARK REVIEW – (Add vols as copyright expires) – v1-10. 1902-12 – 40mf – 9 – $60.00 – LLMC 84-342 – us L.L.M.C. [073]

THE PATENT APPLICATION, PREPARATION AND PROSECUTION / Fishburne, Benjamin Postell – Washington, D.C.: Byree, 1933. 153p. LL-648 – 1 – us L of C Photodup [340]

PATENT CASE INDEX / Preble, William Pitt – 2d ed. Boston: Little, Brown, 1884. 707p. LL-1055 – 1 – us L of C Photodup [340]

PATENT CASES DETERMINED IN THE SUP. CT., INCLUDING COPYRIGHT AND TRADEMARK / U.S. Supreme Court – By Chas. S. Whitman, 1810-74, Washington, D.C., Morrison 1875-78, 2 vols. (cited as Whit. Pat. Cas.). 81-424 – 9 – $16.00 – us L.L.M.C. [340]

PATENT DRAWINGS, 1792-1833 / U.S. Patent Office – 2 rolls. T280 – 1 – us Nat'l Archives [324]

PATENT LAW AND PRACTICE / Schwartz, Herbert F – Washington: FJC, 1988 – 2mf – 9 – $3.00 – LLMC 95-378 – us L.L.M.C. [340]

PATENT LAW ANNUAL (SOUTHWESTERN LEGAL FOUNDATION) : PROCEEDINGS OF THE ANNUAL INSTITUTE ON PATENT LAW – v1-26. 1963-88 – 1,5,6 – $270.00 – us Hein [340]

PATENT LAW ASSOCIATION OF CHICAGO : JOURNAL OF PROCEEDINGS – 1884-1900 (all publ) – 9 – LLMC 84-343 – us L.L.M.C. [073]

PATENT LAW IN BRIEF / Kookogey, William P – New York, Baker, Voorhis, 1884. 67 p. LL-182 – 1 – us L of C Photodup [340]

PATENT LAWS AND THE PRACTICE OF OBTAINING LETTERS PATENT FOR INVENTIONS IN THE UNITED STATES AND FOREIGN COUNTRIES : INCLUDING COPYRIGHT AND TRADEMARK LAWS / Whitman, Charles S – Washington: Morrison, 1871 – 8mf – 9 – $12.00 – LLMC 84-323 – us L.L.M.C. [340]

THE PATENT LAWS OF ALL NATIONS / Abbott, Benjamin Vaughan – Brodix, Washington. 2v. 1886 – 4mf – 9 – $18.00 – LLMC 84-321 – us L.L.M.C. [340]

PATENT LAWS OF LATIN AMERICA (SOUTH AND CENTRAL AMERICA) / Geraud, Jules – Rio de Janeiro: Lamoureux, 1888. 78p. LL-8009 – 1 – us L of C Photodup [340]

PATENT LAWS OF THE REPUBLIC OF HAWAII, AND RULES OF PRACTICE IN THE PATENT OFFICE / Hawaii. Laws, Statutes, etc – 5th ed. Honolulu: Hawaiian Gazette Co., 1897. 39p. LL-394 – 1 – us L of C Photodup [340]

PATENT LAWS OF THE WORLD / ed by Carpmael, A & Carpmael, E – London: Crowes & Sons, 1885 + suppl 1889 – 4mf – 9 – $18.00 – LLMC 84-322 – us L.L.M.C. [340]

PATENT OFFICE FEES: A LEGISLATIVE HISTORY / U.S. Library of Congress. Legislative Reference Service – Washington, Govt. Print. Off., 1958. 16 p. LL-2305 – 1 – us L of C Photodup [340]

PATENT OFFICE GAZETTE *see* PREBLE'S PATENT CASE INDEX

PATENT OFFICE RECORD / Canada – v56-101.1928-73 – 1,5,6 – us Princeton Micro [073]

PATENT OFFICE RECORD – (Several indexes included) – v78-123. 1950-95 – 5 – Price varies – cn Micromedia [340]

PATENT POLICY, VARIOUS GOVERNMENTAL AND NON-GOVERNMENTAL AGENCIES, PART 1 : GENERAL STUDIES / U.S. Congress – (Covers Government Patent Policy. Government Patent Practice. National Patent Policy) – GPO. 3 issuances. 1963 – 12mf – 9 – $18.00 – LLMC 82-501A – us L.L.M.C. [340]

PATENT POLICY, VARIOUS GOVERNMENTAL AND NON-GOVERNMENTAL AGENCIES, PART 2 : AGENCY STUDIES FOR THE DEPARTMENTS OF AGRICULTURE AND COMMERCE AND FOR A NUMBER OF OTHER AGENCIES... / U. S. Congress – 9 – LLMC 82-501B – us L.L.M.C. [340]

PATENT PUBLICATIONS IN NUMERICAL ORDER, 1990 / Japan. Patent Office – 1950- . Full set as published after examination for opposition, under annually arranged serial numbers, all classes. 145 reels containing over 63,000 applications examined and published for opposition during 1990 – 5,6,9 – Y1,015,000.00 – ja Nippon Tech [340]

THE PATENT REVIEW – Ottawa: A Harvey, v1 no 1(Jan 1887)- – 9 – cn C.I.H.M. [600]

THE PATENT SYSTEM AND THE MODERN ECONOMY. / Frost, George E – Washington: GPO. 1957. 77p. LL-2298 – 1 – us L of C Photodup [340]

PATENT, TRADEMARK AND COPYRIGHT JOURNAL OF RESEARCH AND EDUCATION *see* IDEA

PATENT TRADER – Mount Kisco. N.Y. 1958- – 1 – us UMI [071]

PATENTABLE INVENTION / Renwick, Edward Sabine – Rochester, N.Y.: Lawyers' Co-operative, 1893. 155p. LL-1092 – 1 – us L of C Photodup [340]

PATENT-OFFICE MANUAL, INCLUDING THE LAW AND PRACTICE OF CASES IN THE UNITED STATES PATENT OFFICE AND THE COURTS HOLDING A REVISORY RELATION THERETO / Knight, George H – Boston, Little, Brown, 1894. 655 p. LL-181 – 1 – us L of C Photodup [340]

PATENTS AND DESIGNS JOURNAL / Israel. State Records – Jerusalem. 1953-. -m – 9 – 600.00; 24.00y – is I.T.T.I. [324]

PATENTS OF CANADA / Canada. Bureau des Brevets – Toronto: Printed by Lovell & Gibson, 1860-1865. SEM105P152 – 14mf – 9 – Can$31.50 – cn Bibl Nat [340]

Pater, Walter *see*
- ESSAYS FROM THE "GUARDIAN"
- GASTON DE LATOUR
- GREEK STUDIES
- IMAGINARY PORTRAITS
- MARIUS THE EPICUREAN
- MISCELLANEOUS STUDIES
- PLATO AND PLATONISM
- THE RENAISSANCE
- UNCOLLECTED ESSAYS

PATER WENZEL HOCKE / Doppler, Josef – Wien: G Stubenvoll, 1886 – 1 – us U.W. Library [820]

PATERNALISM AND SPECIAL OLYMPICS / Harmer, Peter A P – 1989 – 153p 2mf – 9 – $8.00 – us Microform Publ [302]

PATERNALISMO Y MUNDO NUEVO / Castro, Jorge & Bolivar, Jorge – Buenos Aires: J. Alvarez, 1969 – 1 – CSUXAJA7787-B – us Hoover Inst Photo [972]

Paterson, William *see*
- A NARRATIVE OF FOUR JOURNEYS INTO THE COUNTRY OF THE HOTTENTOTS AND CAFFRARIA IN THE YEARS 1777, 1778, AND 1779
- QUATRE VOYAGES DANS LE PAYS DES HOTTENTOTS ET LA CAFRERIE

THE PATH OF A STAR / Duncan, Sara Jeannette – By Mrs. Everard Cotes; with twelve illustrations by F. H. Townsend. Toronto: W. Gage, 1899. 05294. (Pre-1900 Canadiana) – 9 – cn C.I.H.M. [830]

PATHE FRERES – (Cont by: Pathe-Woche, apr 1, 1911?) – Berlin. sep 1909-jul 1910. apr 1-dec 2, 1911. dec 27, 1913. mar 21-jul 22, 1914 – 1 – gw Mikrofilm [790]

PATHE JORNAL : ORGAO LITTERARIO-CRITICO-HUMORISTICO – Manaos, Amazonas. 30 Jun-Out 1913; Jan-Abr, Out 1914; Maio 1915; 16 Set 1922 – 1,5,6 – bl Biblioteca [072]

PATHE-WOCHE *see* PATHE FRERES

PATH-FINDER – Glenville. West Virginia. -w. 1936-59 – 1 – us UMI [071]

PATHFINDER – v. 1. Mar-Jun 1843 – 1 – us UMI [073]

PATHOBIOLOGY – v61-. 1993- – 1,5,9 – us UMI [612]

PATHOLOGE DER PATHOLOGIE UND KLINIK – v.1-2, 1980-81. ISSN: 0172-8113 – 1,5,6,9,13 – 75.00v – us UMI [616]

PATHOLOGIA ET MICROBIOLOGIA – v29-40 1966-74 1; v35-40 5,6 – us UMI [616]

PATHOLOGIA VETERINARIA *see* VETERINARY PATHOLOGY

PATHOLOGIE DU PANCREAS ET MALNUTRITION PROTEIQUE EN ZONE INTERTROPICALE / Aholi, Paul – (Africa series). 1970 – 9 – fr Hachette [610]

PATHOLOGY INTERNATIONAL *see* ACTA PATHOLOGICA JAPONICA

PATHOMYOTOMIA / Bulwer, J – M 321. 1649 – 9 – ne IDC [610]

THE PATHWAY OF FAITH : STUDIES IN GENESIS 12-50 / Gelesnoff (Zhelieznov), Vladimir – New York: Call to Prayer, 1909 – 1mf – 9 – us A.T.L.A. [240]

PATIENT ACCOUNT RECORD / Van Wert County. Ohio. County Home – 1888-1906 – 1r – 1 – $32.50r – us Archival [324]

PATIENT AID DIGEST – Union. v1-2. sep 1970-aug 1972 1; v3-4. sep 1972-aug 1973 1,5 – 1,5 – D6640 – us UMI [615]

PATIENT CARE – Oradell. v1-31. 1967-97+ 1; v8-21 1974-87. v22 1988*. v23 1989. v24-26 1990-92*. v27-31 1993-97+ 5; v8-31. 1974-97+ 9 – 1,5,9 – D2972 – us UMI [615]

PATIENT CARE – v1-10. 1967-76.Continues: Patient Care Management Concepts – 1,5,6 – us Princeton Micro [610]

PATIENT COUNSELLING AND HEALTH EDUCATION – (Cont by: Patient Education and Counseling) – Princeton. v1-4. 1978-83* – 1 – D42564 – us UMI [615]

PATIENT COUNSELLING AND HEALTH EDUCATION *see* PATIENT EDUCATION AND COUNSELING

PATIENT EDUCATION AND COUNSELING – (Cont: Patient Counselling and Health Education) – Limerick. v5 1983*. v6-30 1984-97+ 1,5; v11-30. 1988-97+ 9 – 1,5,9 – D42564.01 – us UMI [615]

PATIENT EDUCATION AND COUNSELING *see* PATIENT COUNSELLING AND HEALTH EDUCATION

PATIENT REGISTERS / Christ's Hospital, Topeka, KS – 1884-1912 – 1 – us KS Hist [610]

PATIENTS' ACCOUNT RECORD / Wyandot County. Ohio. County Home – 1878 – 1r – 1 – $32.50r – us Archival [324]

Patil, D R *see* THE ANTIQUARIAN REMAINS IN BIHAR

PATJARA TAHBISAN IMAM – (Includes combined texts from Missal and the Pontifical in Indonesian and Latin). 1957? SE-6021 1 – 9 – ne IDC [240]

Patkanov, K P *see* BIBLIOGRAFICHESKII OCHERK ARMIANSKOI ISTORICHESKOI LITERATURY

Patke, Kathryn E *see* PHYSICAL EDUCATION OBJECTIVES AS PERCEIVED BY MIDDLE SCHOOL STUDENTS

Patmore, Coventry Kersey Dighton *see*
- AMELIA, TAMERTON CHURCH-TOWER, ETC
- POEMS
- PRINCIPLE IN ART, ETC
- THE ROD, THE ROOT, AND THE FLOWER
- THE UNKNOWN EROS AND OTHER ODES

PATNA LAW JOURNAL – Bankipur. 1916-21. v1-6 – 86mf – 8 – ne IDC [073]

PATOLOGIA – Malaga. v7. jan-oct 1974 – 1,5 – D7507 – us UMI [616]

Paton, B E *see* WELDING AND SURFACING REVIEWS

Paton, David C *see* BEHAVIOUR AND FEEDING ECOLOGY OF THE NEW HOLLAND HONEYEATER PHYLIDONYRIS NOVAEHOLLANDIAE IN VICTORIA

Paton, Frank Hume Lyall *see* LOMAI OF LENAKEL

Paton, Frank Hyme Lyall *see* JOHN G. PATON

Paton, J B *see* THE INNER MISSION

Paton, James *see* THE STORY OF JOHN G. PATON TOLD FOR YOUNG FOLKS

Paton, John Gibson *see* JOHN G. PATON

Paton, Lewis Bayles *see*
- A CRITICAL AND EXEGETICAL COMMENTARY ON THE BOOK OF ESTHER

Patouillard, N *see* DES HYMENOMYCETES

Patouillard, N T *see* CHAMPIGNONS DU TONKIN

Patranella, Kenneth W *see* ACADEMIC PERFORMANCE, ATTENDANCE, AND SCHEDULE RIGOR OF EXTRACURRICULAR PARTICIPANTS AND NONPARTICIPANTS

Patrat *see* TOBERNE OU LE PECHEUR SUEDOIS

PATRE ANTONIO LLINAS, COLLEGIORUM MISSIONARIUM IN HISPANIA ET AMERICA FUNDATORE 1635-1693 / Pozos, Emmanuel R de – Madrid: Razon y Fe, 1943 – 1 – sp Bibl Santa Ana [240]

LA PATRIA – Urussanga, Brazil. 26 May 1901-26 May 1902 – 1 – bl Biblioteca [072]

LA PATRIA *see* JOURNAUX DIVERS

PATRIA – Cluj, Romania. -d. 2 Feb-22 May 1920; 1 Sept 1921-31 Dec 1926; 26 Jan-1 Dec 1928. Imperfect. 6 reels – 1 – uk British Libr Newspaper [949]

PATRIA : FOLHA CATHOLICA E POPULAR – Pouso Alegre, 4 Jul 1897 – 1,5,6 – bl Biblioteca [072]

PATRIA – Manaos, Amazonas. 22 Abr 1906 – 1,5,6 – bl Biblioteca [072]

PATRIA : ORGAM DA COLONIA CEARENSE – [s.l.] 1 Out 1898-29 Set 1899 – 1,5,6 – bl Biblioteca [072]

PATRIA : ORGAO DO PARTIDO DEMOCRATA – Maceio, Alagoas. 6 Maio, Set-Dez 1891; Jan-Dez 1982 – 1,5,6 – bl Biblioteca [072]

PATRIA – [s.l.] 5 Out 1918 – 1,5,6 – bl Biblioteca [072]

LA PATRIA DEL ALMIRANTE... / Valero de Bernabe, Antonio et al; ed by Bayle, Constantino – Madrid: Razon y Fe, 1928 – 9 – sp Bibl Santa Ana [946]

PATRIA E LAR : ORGAM DO BRAZIL CIVICO – Curitiba, Jul 1912-Jun 1913 – 1,5,6 – bl Biblioteca [072]

A PATRIA MINEIRA : ORGAM DA IDEA REPUBLICANA – S. J. d'el-Rei, May 1889-Feb 1894 – 1,5,6 – bl Biblioteca [072]

PATRIA NOVA : FOLHA REPUBLICANA – Pilar, Alagoas. 28 Jul 1889; Fev 1890; 17 Jan 1891 – 1,5,6 – bl Biblioteca [072]

LA PATRIA POTESTAD Y LA NACIONALIZACION... / Gonzalez Revilla, L – Madrid, 1906 – 1mf – 1 – ILM-3675/1 – ne IDC [327]

PATRIA SINDICAL VERSUS PATRIA SOCIALISTA / Garcia, Roberto – Buenos Aires: Ediciones Depalma, 1980 – 1 – CSUXADH5698-B – us Hoover Inst Photo [320]

O PATRIARCA – Nepomuceno, Brazil. Jul 1897 – 1 – bl Biblioteca [072]

PATRIARCHAL DYNASTIES FROM ADAM TO ABRAHAM / Crawford, Tarleton P – Richmond: Josiah Ryland, 1877. 1 fiche – 9 – us A.T.L.A. [240]

THE PATRIARCHAL DYNASTIES FROM ADAM TO ABRAHAM : SHOWN TO COVER 10,500 YEARS, AND THE HIGHEST HUMAN LIFE ONLY 187 / Crawford, Tarleton Perry – (Includes an appendix) – Richmond, VA:Josiah Ryland, 1877 – 1mf – 9 – 0-8370-2772-1 – 1985-0772 – us A.T.L.A. [220]

PATRIARCHAL SHADOWS OF CHRIST AND HIS CHURCH...JOSEPH AND HIS BRETHREN / Winslow, Octavius – New York: Robert Carter, 1863. 1 fiche – 9 – us A.T.L.A. [240]

THE PATRIARCHATE OF ANTIOCH : TOGETHER WITH, MEMOIRS OF THE PATRIARCHS OF ANTIOCH / Neale, John Mason & Constantius; ed by Williams, George – ((A Posthumous fragment)) – London: Rivingtons, 1873 – 1mf – us A.T.L.A. [240]

DES PATRIARCHEN GENNADIOS VON KONSTANTINOPEL CONFESSION : NEBST EINEM EXCURS UEBER ARETHAS' ZEITALTER / Otto, Johannes Carl Theodor – (In Greek and German. Includes bibliographical references and index) – Wien: Wilhelm Braumueller, 1864 – 1mf – 9 – 0-8370-7494-0 – 1986-1494 – us A.T.L.A. [240]

THE PATRIARCHS AND LAWGIVERS OF THE OLD TESTAMENT / Maurice, Frederick Denison – 1855 – 1 – us A.T.L.A. [220]

THE PATRIARCHS OF CONSTANTINOPLE / Cobham, Claude Delaval – Cambridge: University Press; New York: G.P. Putnam [distributor], 1911 – 1mf – us A.T.L.A. [240]

THE PATRICIAN – Quebec, Canada. nov 1927 – 1r – 1 – Can$25.00 – cn Can Microfilming [072]

Patrick, Alfred *see* DIGEST OF "PRECEDENTS OR DECISIONS" BY SELECT COMMITTEES APPOINTED TO TRY THE MERITS OF UPPER CANADA CONTESTED ELECTIONS, FROM 1824 TO 1849

PATRICK HAMILTON, THE FIRST PREACHER AND MARTYR OF THE SCOTTISH REFORMATION : AN HISTORICAL BIOGRAPHY / Lorimer, Peter – Edinburgh: T. Constable, 1857. (Precursors of Knox, or, memoirs of Patrick Hamilton... /by Peter Lorimer; 1) – 1mf – us A.T.L.A. [240]

PATRICK HENRY / Tyler, Moses Coit – Boston & NY: Houghton, Mifflin & Co, 1899 – 5mf – 9 – $7.50 – LLMC 96-027 – us L.L.M.C. [975]

Patrick, M *see* FOUR CENTURIES OF SCOTTISH PSALMODY

Patrick, Mary Mills *see* SEXTUS EMPIRICUS AND GREEK SCEPTICISM

Patrick, Richard A *see* POLITICAL GEOGRAPHY AND THE CYPRUS CONFLICT

Patrick, William *see* JAMES, THE LORD'S BROTHER

PATRICK'S ONTARIO ELECTION CASES / Ontario. Canada – 1v. 1824-49 (all publ) – 2mf – 9 – $3.00 – LLMC 81-050 – us L.L.M.C. [340]

LA PATRIE – Dir.-red. en chef Emile Massard. Paris. juil-dec 1865, juil-dec 1914, janv-16 nov 1929 – 1 – fr A.C.R.P.P. [073]

LA PATRIE – Ed. du soir. Paris. 1848, 7 fevr-dec 1853, 9 juil-nov 1860, 31 janv-dec 1861, 1863 – 1 – fr A.C.R.P.P. [073]

LA PATRIE : EDITION QUOTIDIENNE – Montreal, Canada. 24 fev 1879-29 dec 1957 – 422r – 1 – Can$60.00r – cn Can Microfilming [072]

LA PATRIE – Petite edition du matin. Paris. janv-2 oct 1850 – 1 – fr A.C.R.P.P. [073]

LA PATRIE – Port-au-Prince. Haiti. 21-23, 25, 27, 30 Jan; 11-13 Feb; 29 Mar 1941 – 1 – us NY Public [072]

LA PATRIE : QUOTIDIEN / ed by Rambau, A-X – (Filmed with: La Patrie (hebdo) 13 jun 1857-17 jul 1858) – Montreal, Canada. 26 sep 1854-17 jul 1858 – 3r – 1 – Can$60.00r – cn Can Microfilming [072]

LA PATRIE : SUPPLEMENTS – Montreal, Canada. 1908; 1909; 1919-1930 – 1r – 1 – Can$50.00 – cn Can Microfilming [072]

LA PATRIE DU DIMANCHE – Montreal, Canada. v1 n2. 13 jan 1935-9 jan 1978 – 173r – 1 – Can$70.00r – cn Can Microfilming [072]

LA PATRIE ILLUSTREE – Montreal, Canada. 24 jun 1884 – 1r – 1 – Can$25.00 – cn Can Microfilming [072]

DIE PATRIMONIEN DER ROEMISCHEN KIRCHE BIS ZUR GRUENDUNG DES KIRCHENSTAATES / Schwarzlose, Carl – Berlin, 1887 – 1mf – 9 – DM38.00 – 3-89349-339-5 – gw Hänsel [240]

DER PATRIOT : BA DER RUHR-NACHRICHTEN – Lippstadt-Dortmund, West Germany. 1992- – 9r per yr – 1 – gw Mikrofilm [072]

DER PATRIOT – Bremen, jul-dec 1838 – 1r – 1 – Inquire at Mikrofilmarchiv for details – gw Misc Inst [072]

DER PATRIOT – Hamburg, Germany. 6 Sept 1848-8 Dec 1850 – 1r – 1 – gw Mikrofilm [072]

DER PATRIOT *see* BUERENER ZEITUNG

PATRIOT – Atchison. Kan. 1869-80 – 1 – us UMI [071]

PATRIOT – Atchison. Kan. -w. 1870-96 – 1 – us UMI [071]

PATRIOT – (Backfile through 1998 $85r) – 1999- – 1r per y – 1 – $80.00 standing order – us Ross [072]

PATRIOT – Burlington. Kan. -w. 1864-68, 1873-86 – 1 – us UMI [071]

PATRIOT – Charlottetown, Canada. 1867-90 – 26r – 1 – $1,690.00 – cn Library Assoc [971]

PATRIOT – Ezhemesiachnyi literaturno-patrioticheskii zhurnal. v. 1. Tambov. 1907. BR-3785 2 – 8 – ne IDC [947]

PATRIOT – Fort Madison. Iowa. 1838-1841 – 1 – us UMI [071]

PATRIOT – Fulton. N.Y. 1881-1906 – 1 – us UMI [071]

PATRIOT – Harrisburg. Pa. 1866-1948 – 1 – us UMI [071]

PATRIOT – Harrisburg. Pa. 1949- – 1 – us UMI [071]

PATRIOT – Jackson. Mich. 1847-1849; 1855-1857 – 1 – us UMI [071]

PATRIOT – London, UK. 1792-93. -w. 1/2 reel – 1 – uk British Libr Newspaper [072]

PATRIOT – New Delhi, India. 30 Mar 1963-1994 – 145r – 1 – us L of C Photodup [072]

PATRIOT – San Jose, CA. 1863-72; 1875-76 – 4r – 1 BC02884 – $200.00 – us Library Micro [071]

PATRIOT – Sofia, Bulgaria. Nov 1952-1964 – 4r – 1 – us L of C Photodup [949]

PATRIOT – Sofia. Bulgaria. -w. Jul 1959-Dec 1964. (3 reels) – 1 – uk British Libr Newspaper [949]

PATRIOT – Woonsocket. R.I. and Register. 1856-76 – 1 – us UMI [071]

THE PATRIOT – Delhi, India. -d. 1 July 1972-31 Dec 1974. 9 reels – 1 – uk British Libr Newspaper [072]

THE PATRIOT – Montreal, Canada. v2 n1. oct 1886; avr 1887; v6 n7. 21 fev 1891 – 1r – 1 – Can$30.00 – cn Can Microfilming [072]

THE PATRIOT – St John, N.B.: W.G. Day, [1865] – 9 – cn C.I.H.M. [971]

PATRIOT AND FARMERS' MONITOR – Kingston and Toronto, Canada. 1832-44 – 6r – 1 – $390.00 – cn Library Assoc [971]

THE PATRIOT AND FARMER'S MONITOR – Kingston, Ontario. 12 oct 1829-v1 n6. 17 dec 1829 – 1r – 1 – Can$30.00 – cn Can Microfilming [072]

THE PATRIOT (NEW YORK, N.Y.: 1970) – (Library has: v.1, no.1-2 (March 21-July 21, 1970)) – New York, N.Y.: Patriot Party, 1970- – 1 – CSUX89-S85 – us Hoover Inst Photo [947]

PATRIOT, OR SCOURGE OF ARISTOCRACY – Stoningtonport. v1. jul 1801-jul 1802 – 1 – D3627 – us UMI [073]

PATRIOT UNION – Harrisburg, PA., 1861 – 13 – $25.00r – us I.M.R. [071]

O PATRIOTA – Baependе, Jan, Mar-Jun 1938; Mar, Aug-Oct, Dec 1949; Jan, Jul, Oct-25 Nov 1950 – 1,5,6 – bl Biblioteca [072]

O PATRIOTA : JORNAL LITTERARIO POLITICO E MERCANTIL – Rio de Janeiro, Jan 1813-Dec 1814 – 1,5,6 – bl Biblioteca [072]

LE PATRIOTE : ANTI-SEMITE / ed by Arcand, Adrien – Montreal, Canada. 4 mai 1933-15 jan 1938 – 1r – 1 – Can$40.00 – cn Can Microfilming [072]

LE PATRIOTE : BI-HEBDO – Montreal, Canada. 18 sep-v1 n5. 1 oct 1886 – 1r – 1 – Can$25.00 – cn Can Microfilming [072]

LE PATRIOTE – Quebec: C.E. Rouleau, [1878-187-?] – 9 – cn C.I.H.M. [971]

LE PATRIOTE – Sorel, Canada. v1 n63. 15 jul 1887-31 dec 1891 – 1r – 1 – Can$35.00 – cn Can Microfilming [072]

LE PATRIOTE CANADIEN : JOURNAL HEBDOMADAIRE. POLITIQUE, HISTORIQUE, LITTERAIRE ET INDUSTRIEL – Burlington, VT. 7 aut 1839-5 fev 1840 – 1r – 1 – Can$45.00 – cn Can Microfilming [071]

LE PATRIOTE DE LA MAYENNE – Laval, June 1903 – June 1912 – 2r – fr Armell [320]

LE PATRIOTE DE L'OUEST – Prince Albert, Saskatchewan. 22 aut 1910-v21 n52. 2 mar 1932 – 8r – 1 – Can$60.00r – cn Can Microfilming [072]

LE PATRIOTE DU SUD-OUEST – Bordeaux. aout-dec 1944 – 1 – fr A.C.R.P.P. [073]

LE PATRIOTE FRANCAIS – Journal libre, impartial et national. Red. J.-P. Brissot de Warville puis Girey-Dupre. Paris. mai 1789-juin 1793 – 1 – fr A.C.R.P.P. [073]

LE PATRIOTE FRANCAIS – Par Lemaire. Paris. sept 1797-juin 1799 – 1 – fr A.C.R.P.P. [073]

LE PATRIOTE JURASSIEN – Journal politique et litteraire, industriel et agricole puis Journal du progres democratique. Lons-le-Saunier. 1848-13 aout 1850. mq no. 91 – 1 – fr A.C.R.P.P. [073]

PATRIOTEN – Stockholm, Sweden. 1792-94 – 1 reel – 1 – sw Kungliga [073]

LES PATRIOTES DE 1837-1838 / David, Laurent Olivier – Montreal: Senecal, 1884. 02518. (Pre-1900 Canadiana) – 9 – cn C.I.H.M. [971]

LES PATRIOTES DE 1837-38 / David, Laurent Olivier – Montreal: Eusebe Senecal et fils, 1884. SEM105P377 – 4mf – 9 – Can$9.00 – cn Bibl Nat [971]

THE PATRIOTES OF '37 : A CHRONICLE OF THE LOWER CANADIAN REBELLION / DeCelles, Alfred Duclos – Toronto, 1916. SEM105P516 – 2mf – 9 – Can$4.50 – cn Bibl Nat [971]

PATRIOTIC ADDRESS: DELIVERED AT DUNGANNON, MARCH 15, 1900 AT A CONCERT IN AID FOR THE FUND FOR THE BENEFIT OF THE WIDOWS AND ORPHANS OF THE CANADIAN SOLDIERS KILLED IN THE SOUTH AFRICAN WAR / Cameron, Malcolm Graeme – 1900? 02827. (Pre-1900 Canadiana) – 9 – cn C.I.H.M. [971]

PATRIOTIC ADDRESSES : IN AMERICA AND ENGLAND FROM 1850 TO 1885, ON SLAVERY, THE CIVIL WAR, AND THE DEVELOPMENT OF CIVIL LIBERTY IN THE UNITED STATES / Beecher, Henry Ward; ed by Howard, John R – New York: Fords, Howard & Hulbert, 1887 – 2mf – us A.T.L.A. [320]

PATRIOTIC SPEECH: IN REPLY TO THE TOAST OF PROFESSIONAL ANNEXATION BEFORE THE DENTAL SOCIETIES OF THE STATE OF NEW YORK AT SYRACUSE, NY ON OCTOBER 25, 1888 / Beers, William George – 1888. 03545. (Pre-1900 Canadiana) – 9 – cn C.I.H.M. [617]

PATRIOTISCHES ARCHIV FUER DEUTSCHLAND – Berlin, 1799, 1801 – 2r – 1 – Inquire at Mikrofilmarchiv for details – gw Misc Inst [943]

PATRIOTISCHES MAGAZIN VON UND FUER BUENDTEN [...] – Bern, 1790 – 1 – Inquire at Mikrofilmarchiv for details – gw Misc Inst [949]

PATRIOTISCHES TAGEBLATT – Bruenn, jul-dec 1803 – 1 – Inquire at Mikrofilmarchiv for details – gw Misc Inst [943]

PATRIOTISME DANS INTERNATIONALISME / Communist Party. Indonesia – By A. Anwar Sanusi et al. 1962.SE-3457-1 – 9 – ne IDC [335]

PATRIOTY BEZ OTECHESTVA / Bobrishchev-Pushkin, Aleksandr M Vladimirovich – Leningrad: Kubuch, 1925 – 1 – CSUX89-B6377 – us Hoover Inst Photo [947]

PATRIS – Athens, Greece. -d. 1 Aug-17 Nov 1916; 1 July 1917-16 July 1919. Very imperfect. 3 reels – 1 – uk British Libr Newspaper [949]

PATRISTIC STUDY / Swete, Henry Barclay – London, New York: Longmans, Green, 1902 – 1mf – us A.T.L.A. [240]

PATRISTIQUE ET MOYEN AYGE / Ghellinck, J de – (T. 1: Les recherches sur les origines...Bruxelles, 1946 5mf; T. 2: Introduction et complements Bruxelles, 1947 8mf; T. 3: Complements a l'etude...Bruxelles, 1948 9mf) – 8 – ne Slangenburg [240]

PATRISTISCHE MISCELLEN (T.U.U. 2-20/3B) / Harnack, Adolf von – Leipzig, 1900 – 2mf – 9 – ne Slangenburg [240]

Patrizi, Francesco Saverio *see* DELLA DESCRIZIONE UNIVERSALE MENTOVATA DA SAN LUCA

Patrizi, J A *see* RUTAS VENEZOLANAS...

DIE PATRIZIERIN : NOVELLE / Widmann, Joseph Viktor – 3. Aufl. Bern: A Francke, 1912 – 1r – 1 – us U.W. Library [830]

PATROCINIUM MUSICES.. / Lasso, Orlando di – v.1-5. 1574-76 – 9 – us Sibley [780]

PATROCINIUM MUSICES...CANTIONUM, QUAS MUTETAS VOCANT, OPUS NOVUM / Lasso, Orlando di – Monachij: Excudebat Adamus Berg, 1573. SEM35P232 – 1r – 1 – Can$15.00 – cn Bibl Nat [780]

PATROCINIUM MUSICES...MAGNIFICAT ALIQUOT, QUATUOR, QUINQUE, SEX ET OCTO VOCUM / Lasso, Orlando di – Monachij: Adamus Berg, 1576. SEM35P259 – 1r – 1 – Can$15.00 – cn Bibl Nat [780]

PATROCINIUM MUSICES...MISSAE ALIQUOT QUINQUE VOCUM / Lasso, Orlando di – Monachij: Adamus Berg, 1574. SEM35P257 – 1r – 1 – Can$20.00 – cn Bibl Nat [780]

PATROCINIUM MUSICES...MISSAE ALIQUOT QUINQUE VOCUM / Lasso, Orlando di – Monachij: Adamus Berg, 1589. SEM35P260 – 1r – 1 – Can$20.00 – cn Bibl Nat [780]

PATROCINIUM MUSICES...PASSIO QUINQUE VOCUM : IDEM LECTIONES JOB ET LECTIONES MATUTINAE CHRISTI; QUATUOR VOCUM / Lasso, Orlando di – Monachij: Adamus Berg, 1575. SEM35P258 – 1r – 1 – Can$15.00 – cn Bibl Nat [780]

PATROCINIVM MVSICLES – Monachij. 1573-98. 1-6 – 1 – 46.00 – us L of C Photodup [780]

PATROL AND NATIVE LOCAL GOVERNMENT SURVEY REPORTS / Symons, Craig – Western Highlands, PNG. 1960-61 – 1r – 1 – PMB1090 – at Pacific Mss [350]

PATROL REPORTS / Papua New Guinea. National Archives and Public Records Service – (Bougainville, K424.00; Chimbu, K400.00; Northern, K560.00; East New Britain, K172.00; West New Britain, K402.00; Central, K1,310.00; Gulf, K824.00; Eastern Highlands, K804.00; East Sepik, K696.00) – K4896.00 less 10% for whole set, less 5% for each complete part – 9980-909-98-6 – at Pacific Mss [980]

PATROLOGIA GRAECA, VOL 166 / Migne – 3052mf – 8 – ne Slangenburg [240]

PATROLOGIA LATINA, VOL 221 / Migne – 3951mf – 8 – ne Slangenburg [240]

PATROLOGIA ORIENTALIS – Paris. v1-22. 1907-30 – 307mf – 9 – H-2821/1 – ne IDC [480]

PATROLOGIA SYRIACA – v1-3 – 69mf – 9 – ne Slangenburg [240]

PATROLOGIA SYRIACA – v1-3. 1894-1926 – 38mf – 9 – H-2823/1 – ne IDC [470]

PATROLOGIAE : CURSUS COMPLETUS SIVE BIBLIOTHECA UNIVERSALIS ... SERIES GRAECA / ed by Migne, Jacques-Paul – (Including printed guide and index) – Paris. v1-161. 1857-68 – 1309mf – 9 – 392/2 – ne IDC [450]

PATROLOGIAE : CURSUS COMPLETUS SIVE BIBLIOTHECA UNIVERSALIS ... SERIES LATINA / ed by Migne, J P – (Including printed guide) – Paris. v1-221. 1844-64 – 1658mf – 9 – 393/1 – ne IDC [450]

PATROLOGIAE CURSUS COMPLETUS / ed by Migne, Jacques-Paul – (Series Latina Paris 1844-1885 v1-221 (in 222 vols) 1,658mf Dfl6,490.00. Series Graeco-Latina. Paris 1857-1868 v1-161 (in 168 vols) 1,309mf Dfl5,115.00; Includes printed guide) – 9 – ne IDC [240]

PATROLOGY : THE LIVES AND WORKS OF THE FATHERS OF THE CHURCH / Bardenhewer, Otto – Freiburg im Breisgau; St. Louis, Mo.: Herder, 1908 – 2mf – us A.T.L.A. [240]

LE PATRON ET L'OUVNER / Defoy, Henri – s.l.: s.n., 1892 (Quebec: L. Brousseau). 02702. (Pre-1900 Canadiana) – 9 – cn C.I.H.M. [971]

Patron, Pablo *see* LIMA ANTIGUA. ESTUDIO BIOGRAFICO DEL AUTOR POR EVARISTO SAN CRISTOVAL. LIMA, 1935

LE PATRONAGE, OEUVRE DE FORMATION POUR LA JEUNESSE : BIBLIOGRAPHIE ANALYTIQUE / Desnoyers, Paul-Henri – 1964. SEM105P4 – 2mf – 9 – cn Bibl Nat [010]

EL PATRONATO ESPANOL EN EL VIRREYNO DEL PERU DURANTE EL SIGLO 16 / Bayle, Constantino & Perez Angel, Gabriel – Tournai, 1937; Burgos: Razon y Fe, 1938 – 1 – sp Bibl Santa Ana [946]

PATRONATO LOCAL DE CANTINAS ESCOLARES (REGLAMENTO) / Caceres – Caceres: Imprenta Moderna, 1933 – 1 – sp Bibl Santa Ana [946]

Patronato Local de Formacion Profesional. Caceres *see* MEMORIA QUINQUENIO 1940-1944

Patrons of Husbandry. Dominion Grange *see* QUARTERLY REPORT OF THE DOMINION SECRETARY OF THE PATRONS OF HUSBANDRY FOR THE QUARTER ENDING...

Patrons of Husbandry. Ohio State Grange. Salem Grange No. 2259. Wood County, Ohio *see* RECORDS

Patrons of Husbandry. Pleasant Hill Grange No. 11, Reno County, KS *see* RECORDS

Patrons of Husbandry. Rose Grange No. 1384, Woodson County, KS *see* MINUTE BOOK

PATRONS OF PALOMAR COLLEGE ALBUM – San Marcos, CA. 1946-1993 – 33r – 1 – $1,650.00 – R04158 – us Library Micro [370]

DIE PATROZINIEN IM KOELNER GROSZARCHIDIAKONAT XANTEN / Stuewer, W – Bonn, 1938 – 5mf – 8 – Dfl22.00 – ne Slangenburg [240]

PATRYOTA – (In Polish) – Philadelphia, PA. 1927-54 – 11r – 1 – $935.00 – D3375 – us Scholarly Res [071]

PATRYOTA – Philadelphia, PA. -w. 15 Dec 1950-14 Jan 1955. Imperfect. 3 reels – 1 – uk British Libr Newspaper [071]

Patschovsky, A *see* DE PASSAUER ANONYMUS (MGH SCHRIFTEN..: 22.BD)

Patte, Pierre *see* MEMOIRES SUR LES OBJETS LES PLUS IMPORTANTS DE L'ARCHITECTURE

Pattee, William Sullivan *see*
- AUTHORITIES, DEDUCTIONS AND NOTES IN CONTRACTS
- AUTHORITIES, DEDUCTIONS AND NOTES IN REAL PROPERTY
- AUTHORITIES, DEDUCTIONS, AND NOTES IN THE ELEMENTS OF EQUITY
- THE ESSENTIAL NATURE OF LAW OR THE ETHICAL BASIS OF JURISPRUDENCE
- ILLUSTRATIVE CASES IN EQUITY

Patten *see* HISTORY OF THE SOMONAUK UNITED PRESBYTERIAN CHURCH

PATTERN CRIMINAL JURY INSTRUCTIONS : REPORT OF THE FJC COMMITTEE TO STUDY CRIMINAL JURY INSTUCTIONS / Marshall, Prentice H – Washington: FJC, June 1982 – 1mf – 9 – $7.50 – LLMC 95-352 – us L.L.M.C. [340]

PATTERN MAKERS JOURNAL : 1893-1955 / Pattern Makers' League of North America – (Coll title: Labor Union Periodicals, Pt 1) – 10r – 1 – $1,350.00 – 1-55655-246-7 – us UPA [331]

Pattern Makers' League of North America *see* PATTERN MAKERS JOURNAL

PATTERN RECOGNITION – Oxford. v1-30. 1968-97+ – 1,5,9 – D49154 – us UMI [150]

PATTERN RECOGNITION LETTERS – Amsterdam. v1-15 1982-94*. v16-18 1995-97+ 1,5; v7-15 1988-94*. v16-18 1995-97+ 9 – 1,5,9 – D42491 – us UMI [150]

PATTERNS OF PREJUDICE – London. v1-13. 1967-79* 1; v14-23 1980-win 1990. v24-28 sum 1990-oct 1994*. v29-31 1995-97+ 1,5,9 – 1,5,9 – D11230 – us UMI [150]

PATTERNS OF SOME GEOLOGICAL CHARACTERISTICS FROM OIL FIELDS IN THE GULF OF SUEZ / Cohen, Avigdor – Jerusalem, Aug 1977. 15p. map – 9 – $2.00 – is I.T.T.I [550]

Patterson, Alexander *see*
- THE GREATER LIFE AND WORK OF CHRIST
- THE OTHER SIDE OF EVOLUTION

Patterson, Christopher Stuart *see* THE PRINCIPLES OF THE LAW OF REAL PROPERTY

Patterson, FW *see* THE CHURCH IN THE SMALLER CITIES

Patterson, George *see* MISSIONARY LIFE AMONG THE CANNIBALES

PATTERSON GROVE BAPTIST CHURCH. KINGS MOUNTAIN ASSOCIATION. GROVER, NORTH CAROLINA : CHURCH RECORDS – 1884-1963 – 1 – 13.95 – us Baptist [240]

Patterson, H Temple *see* POETIC GENESIS: SEBASTIEN MERCIER INTO VICTOR HUGO

PATTERSON IRRIGATOR – Patterson, CA. 1911-39 – 8r – 1 – $400.00 – B02620 – us Library Micro [071]

Patterson, John Robert *see* KANURI SONGS

Patterson, Lindsay *see* NORTH CAROLINA'S CONTRIBUTION TO THE LAW.

Patterson, M L P *see*
- SOUTH ASIAN LIBRARY RESOURCES IN NORTH AMERICA

Patterson, Roberta Turner *see* CANDLE BY NIGHT: A HISTORY OF WOMAN'S MISSIONARY UNION AUXILIARY TO THE BAPTIST GENERAL CONVENTION OF TEXAS

PATTERSON SPRINGS BAPTIST CHURCH. NORTH CAROLINA : CHURCH RECORDS – 1895-Oct 1963 – 1 – 55.98 – us Baptist [240]

Patterson, T A *see* THE THEOLOGY OF J.R. GRAVES AND ITS INFLUENCE ON SOUTHERN BAPTIST LIFE

Patterson, William B *see* MODERN CHURCH BROTHERHOODS

Patti, Rino J *see* ADMINISTRATION IN SOCIAL WORK

Pattison, Everett Wilson *see*
- FORMS FOR MISSOURI PLEADING
- INSTRUCTIONS IN CRIMINAL CAUSES PASSED UPON BY THE COURTS OF MISSOURI
- MISSOURI FORM BOOK AND LEGAL MANUAL FOR LAWYERS, COUNTY OFFICERS AND BUSINESS MEN

Pattison, James *see* JAMES PATTISON PAPERS, 1777-81

Pattison, Mark *see*
- ISAAC CASAUBON, 1559-1614
- SERMONS

Pattison, Thomas Harwood *see*
- THE HISTORY OF CHRISTIAN PREACHING
- THE HISTORY OF THE ENGLISH BIBLE

Patton, Francis Landey *see* THE INSPIRATION OF THE SCRIPTURES

PATTON, JR. AND HEATH'S REPORTS / Virginia. Supreme Court. Special Court of Appeals – (A Pre-NRS title. Bound with v1 and publ simultaneously with it, but with its own title and pagination, is an additional book by the same authors entitled: "A General Index to Gratton's Reports" The "Gratton" reference is to Gratton's Reports, v1-32, which became v42-74 of the renumbered, official Virginia Reports. This "added title" is included in the LLMC fiche for P.&H) – v1-2. 1855-1857 (all publ) – 18mf – 9 – $27.00 – LLMC 90-315 – us L.L.M.C. [340]

Patton, N W *see* THE INFLUENCE OF MUSICAL PREFERENCE ON THE AFFECTIVE STATE, HEART RATE, AND PERCEIVED EXERTION RATINGS OF PARTICIPANTS IN AEROBIC DANCE/EXERCISE CLASSES

Patton, Walter Melville *see* AHMAD IBN HANBAL AND THE MIHNA

O PATUSCO : ORGAO DA RAPAZIADA – Maceio, Alagoas. 22 Jan, 19 Mar 1882 – 1,5,6 – bl Biblioteca [072]

PATZCUARO. TEXTO DE MANUEL TOUSSAINT. MEXICO, 1942 / Bayle, Constantino – Madrid: Razon y Fe, 1948 – 1 – sp Bibl Santa Ana [972]
Patze, C *see* FLORA DER PROVINZ PREUSSEN
Patzer, Georg *see* ZEN UND DER KRIMINALROMAN
O PAU – Manoas, Amazonas. 22 Set-21 Out 1912 – 1,5,6 – bl Biblioteca [072]
Pauck, Wilhelm *see*
- THE HERITAGE OF THE REFORMATION
- THE HERITAGE OF THE REFORMATION GLENCOE

Paucke, P Florian *see* HACIA ALLA Y PARA ACA
PAUL : A SERVANT OF JESUS CHRIST / Meyer, Frederick Brotherton – New York:Fleming H. Revell, c1897 – 1mf – 9 – 0-8370-4412-X – 1985-2412 – us A.T.L.A. [920]
PAUL / Wrede, William – Boston: Am. Unitarian Assoc., 1908. 1 fiche – 9 – us A.T.L.A. [240]
PAUL AND JESUS / Weiss, Johannes – London: Harper, 1909. 1 fiche – 9 – us A.T.L.A. [240]
PAUL AND THE WOMEN: AND OTHER DISCOURSES / Hawthorne, James Boardman – 1891 – 9 – us A.T.L.A. [240]
PAUL DE CHOMEDEY, SIEUR DE MAISONNEUVE, FONDATEUR DE MONTREAL: ETUDE HISTORIQUE ET BIOGRAPHIQUE / Chouinard, Honore Julien Jean Baptiste – Quebec: A. Cote, 1882. 00632. (Pre-1900 Canadiana) – 9 – cn C.I.H.M. [971]
PAUL DE LAGARDE – (Includes bibliographical references) – Kiel: Lipsius und Tischer, 1892 – 1r – 1 – us U.W. Library [943]
PAUL DE LAGARDE : REDE BEI DER GEDAECHTNISFEIER DER PHILOSOPHISCHEN FAKULTAET AM 2. NOVEMBER 1927 GEHALTEN / Schroeder, Edward – Goettingen: W F Kaestner, 1928 – 1 – us U.W. Library [100]
PAUL DE LAGARDE'S JUEDISCHE GELEHRSAMKEIT: EINE ERWIEDERUNG / Kaufmann, David – Leipzig: Otto Schulze, 1887. 1 fiche – 9 – us A.T.L.A. [270]
Paul de Rome, Soeur *see* BIBLIOGRAPHIE ANALYTIQUE DE L'OEUVRE DU DOCTEUR DE LA BROQUERIE FORTIER, M.D. F.A.A.P., PROFESSEUR TITULAIRE DE CLINIQUE PEDIATRIQUE...
Paul, Doris *see* INDIVIDUELLE UND GESELLSCHAFTLICHE REPRAESENTATIONEN VON AIDS
Paul, Eden *see* PROLETCULT (PROLETARIAN CULTURE)
PAUL FERROLL, A TALE : BY THE AUTHOR OF "IX. POEMS BY V." / Clive, Caroline – London: Saunders and Otley, 4th ed 1856 – 1 roll – 1 – 1-55879-561-8 – uk Libr Preservation [830]
PAUL GERHARDT : EIN ERINNERUNGSBLATT / Kawerau, Gustav – Halle: Verein fuer Reformationsgeschichte, 1907. (Schriften des Vereins fuer Reformationsgeschichte; 24. Jahrg., Schrift 93) – 1mf – us A.T.L.A. [240]
Paul, Gustav *see* DIE VERANLASSUNG UND DIE QUELLEN VON JOHANN ELIAS SCHLEGELS "CANUT"
PAUL HARRO-HARRING / Larsen, Asbjorn Lunge – Oslo: Cammermeyer, 1949 – 1r – 1 – us U.W. Library [920]
PAUL HEYSE : EIN DEUTSCHER LYRIKER / Petzet, Erich – Leipzig: Hesse & Becker, [1913?] – 1r – 1 – us U.W. Library [430]
PAUL HEYSE : DER DICHTER UND SEINE WERKE / Spiero, Heinrich – Stuttgart: J G Cotta, 1910 – 1r – 1 – us U.W. Library [430]
PAUL HEYSE / Farinelli, Arturo – Muenchen: Sueddeutsche Monatshefte, 1913 – 1r – 1 – us U.W. Library [920]
PAUL HEYSE / Klemperer, Victor – Berlin: Pan-Verlag, 1907 – 1r – 1 – us U.W. Library [430]
PAUL HEYSE / Ruete, Edmund – Bremen: G Winter, 1910 – 1r – 1 – us U.W. Library [430]
PAUL HEYSE ALS DRAMATIKER / Petzet, Erich – (Includes bibliographical references) – Stuttgart: J G Cotta, 1904 – 1r – 1 – us U.W. Library [430]
Paul, John *see* EVERY LANDLORD OR TENANT HIS OWN LAWYER.
THE PAUL LAURENCE DUNBAR COLLECTION / Dunbar, Paul Laurence – (Guide sold separately $10.00) – 1972 – 9r – 1 – $675.00 – D3168 – Dist. us Scholarly Res – us Ohio Hist [920]
PAUL OF TARSUS: AN INQUIRY INTO THE TIMES AND THE GOSPEL OF THE APOSTLE OF THE GENTILES – Boston: Roberts, 1872. 1 fiche – 9 – us A.T.L.A. [240]
PAUL PRY – London, UK. 28 Feb-26 Dec 1830.-w. 1/2 reel – 1 – uk British Libr Newspaper [072]
PAUL PRY – (Superseded by: Huntress) – Washington. v1-5. dec 1831-nov 1836 – 1 – D4606 – us UMI [073]
PAUL PRY – v. 1-5. 3 Dec 1831-19 Nov 1836 and successor The Huntressv. 1-16, 17, no. 1-18. 2 Dec 1836-27 May 1854; no. 1-3. 24 Jun-24 Jul 1854 – 1 – 67.00 – us L of C Photodup [975]
THE PAUL PRY – Montreal: J Huniker, [1844-18–?] – 9 – cn C.I.H.M. [971]
THE PAUL ROBESON COLLECTION – (With printed guide. Coll title: Manuscript Collections from the Schomburg Center for Research in Black Culture, the New York Public Library) – 9r – 1 – $1,040.00 – 1-55655-375-7 – us UPA [780]
Paul Sabatier *see* LEGEND. SPECULUM PERFECTIONIS. S. FRANCIS OF ASSISI: THE MIRROR OF PERFECTION
PAUL SPERATUS VON ROETLEN : EVANGLISCHER BISCHOF VON POMESANIEN IN MARIENWERDER / Tschackert, Paul – Halle: Verein fuer Reformationsgeschichte, 1891. ([Schriften des Vereins fuer Reformationsgeschichte; Bd. 33]) – 1mf – us A.T.L.A. [240]
PAUL, THE ALL-ROUND MAN / Speer, Robert Elliott – New York: Fleming H. Revell, 1909. 1 fiche – 9 – us A.T.L.A. [240]
PAUL THE APOSTLE: A POEM / Braithwaite, Joseph Bevan – London: Seele, 1885. 1 fiche – 9 – us A.T.L.A. [240]
PAUL, THE APOSTLE OF HEATHEN JUDAISM, OR, CHRISTIANITY : DISCOURSE DELIVERED BEFORE SINAI CONGREGATION, CHICAGO 1894 / Hirsch, Emil Gustav – Chicago: Bloch & Newman, [1894?] – 1mf – 9 – 0-8370-3589-9 – 1985-1589 – us A.T.L.A. [920]
PAUL THE MYSTIC : A STUDY IN APOSTOLIC EXPERIENCE / Campbell, James Mann – (Includes index) – New York:Putnam's, 1908 – 1mf – 9 – 0-8370-2575-3 – 1985-0575 – us A.T.L.A. [240]
PAUL, THE MYSTIC: A STUDY IN APOSTOLIC EXPERIENCE / Campbell, James Mann – London: A. Melrose, 1907. 285p – 1 – us U.W. Library [240]
PAUL THE POPE AND PAUL THE FRIAR : A STORY OF AN INTERDICT / Trollope, Adolphus – London: Chapman and Hall, 1861 – 1mf – us A.T.L.A. [240]
PAUL THE PREACHER; OR, A POPULAR AND PRACTICAL EXPOSITION OF HIS DISCOURSES AND SPEECHES, AS RECORDED IN THE ACTS OF THE APOSTLES / Eadie, John – 1870 – 1 – us A.T.L.A. [240]
Paul Zsolnay Verlag *see* JAHRBUCH
Paula, A von *see*
- BAIERSCHE FLORA
- NATURHISTORISCHE BRIEFE UEBER OESTREICH, SALZBURG, PASSAU UND BERCHTESGADEN
- PLANTAE RARIORES HORTI ACADEMICI MONACENSIS
- PRIMITIAE FLORAE SALISBURGENSIS

Paula, E A *see* APPRAISAL OF THE DEVELOPMENT OF KICKING BEHAVIOR OF PRESCHOOL AGE CHILDREN
Paula, Francisco de *see* DISCURSO...AUDIENCIA...CACERES. .Bl.-1838
PAULDING COUNTY GAZETTE – Paulding, Ohio. 1878-88 – 4r – 1 – $32.50r – us Archival [071]
Paulding County. Ohio. Cecil Mayor *see* COURT DOCKET
Paulding County, Ohio. Cecil Village Council *see*
- MINUTES
- ORDINANCES AND RESOLUTIONS

Paulding County. Ohio. Cecil Village Council *see*
- MINUTES
- ORDINANCES AND RESOLUTIONS

Paulding County, Ohio. Clerk of Courts *see* RECORD OF INQUESTS
Paulding County, Ohio. Crane Township. Justice of the Peace *see* CIVIL AND CRIMINAL DOCKETS
Paulding County. Ohio. Crane Township. Justice of the Peace *see* CIVIL AND CRIMINAL DOCKETS
Paulding County, Ohio. Crane Township. Township Clerk *see* SCHOOL FUND RECORD
Paulding County. Ohio. Crane Township. Township Clerk *see*
- ACCOUNT OF TOWNSHIP FUNDS
- CASH JOURNAL
- SCHOOL FUND RECORD

Paulding County. Ohio. Probate Court *see* NATURALIZATION RECORDS
Paulding County. Ohio. Soldiers Relief Commission *see* CASE FILES
PAULDING COUNTY REPUBLICAN – Paulding, Ohio. 1921-49 – 12r – 1 – $32.50r – us Archival [071]
Paulding, Mississippi *see* MISCELLANEOUS EARLY NEWSPAPERS
Paulding. Ohio. St. Joseph's Catholic Church *see* RECORDS
PAULDING PROGRESS – Paulding, Ohio. 1949- – 33r – 1 – $32.50r – us Archival [071]
Paulet, J J *see* TRAITE DES CHAMPIGNONS
PAULI HISTORIA LANGOBARDORUM (MGH 7: 48.BD) – 1878 – Dfl22.00 – ne Slangenburg [240]
PAULI HISTORIA ROMANA (MGH 7: 49.BD) – 1879 – Dfl13.00 – ne Slangenburg [240]
PAULINE AND OTHER STUDIES IN EARLY CHRISTIAN HISTORY / Ramsay, William Mitchell – (Includes bibliographical references and indexes) – New York: A C Armstrong, 1906 – 2mf – 9 – 0-8370-4836-2 – 1985-2836 – us A.T.L.A. [240]
THE PAULINE EPISTLES : A CRITICAL STUDY / Scott, Robert – (Includes indexes) – Edinburgh: T&T Clark, 1909 – 1mf – 9 – 0-8370-5192-4 – 1985-3192 – us A.T.L.A. [220]
THE PAULINE ESCHATOLOGY / Vos, Geerhardus – 1930 – 9 – $12.00 – us I.R.C. [240]
PAULINE MARIE JARICOT : FOUNDRESS OF THE ASSOCIATION FOR THE PROPAGATION OF THE FAITH AND OF THE LIVING ROSARY / Maurin, M J – New York: Benziger, 1906 – 1mf – 9 – 0-8370-6758-8 – 1986-0758 – us A.T.L.A. [920]
PAULINE METHODS OF MISSIONARY WORK / Taylor, William MacKergo – Philadelphia: National Publishing Association for the Promotion of Holiness, c1879 – 1mf – us A.T.L.A. [240]
THE PAULINE THEOLOGY...ORIGIN AND CORRELATION OF THE DOCTRINAL TEACHINGS / Stevens, George Barker – New York: Charles Scribner, 1894. 1 fiche – 9 – us A.T.L.A. [240]
PAULINE THEORY OF THE INSPIRATION OF HOLY SCRIPTURE / Atwell, William Erskine – London: Hodder & Stoughton, 1878. 1 fiche – 9 – us A.T.L.A. [240]
Pauline-Marie, Soeur *see* LES SOEURS MISSIONNAIRES DE L'IMMACULEE-CONCEPTION, PREMIER INSTITUT MISSIONNAIRE D'ORIGINE CANADIENNE, 1902-1932
DIE PAULINISCHE ANGELOLOGIE UND DAEMONOLOGIE : EIN BIBLISCHTHEOLOGISCHER VERSUCH / Everling, Otto – (Includes bibliographical references and index) – Goettingen:Vandenhoeck und Ruprecht, 1888 – 1mf – 9 – 0-8370-3084-6 – 1985-1084 – us A.T.L.A. [220]
DIE PAULINISCHE CHRISTOLOGIE : IN IHREM ZUSAMMENHANGE MIT DER HEILSLEHRE DES APOSTELS / Schmidt, Richard – (Includes bibliographical references) – Goettingen:Vandenhoeck und Ruprecht, 1870 – 1mf – 9 – 0-8370-5115-0 – 1985-3115 – us A.T.L.A. [220]
DAS PAULINISCHE EVANGELIUM / Scholten, Johannes Henricus – Elberfeld: R.L. Friderichs, 1881. 1 fiche – 9 – us A.T.L.A. [240]
DER PAULINISMUS DES IRENAEUS (T.U.U. 1-6/2) / Werner, J – Leipzig, 1889 – 4mf – 9 – ne Slangenburg [240]
DER PAULINISMUS UND DIE LOGIA JESU (T.U.U. 2-27) / Resch, A – Leipzig, 1904 – 10mf – 9 – ne Slangenburg [240]
DIE PAULINSCHE LEHRE VOM GESETZ: NACH DEN VIER HAUPTBRIEFEN / Grafe, Eduard – Freiburg i.B.: J.C.B. Mohr, 1893. 1 fiche – 9 – us A.T.L.A. [240]
O PAULISTA & LIBERAL PAULISTA – Sao Paulo, Brazil. Feb-Dec 1886; 1887; Jan-Mar 1888 – 1 – bl Biblioteca [072]
PAULITA CENTENO MORUNO / Mosquero Martin, Manuel – Badajoz: Tip.Espanola, 1942 – 1 – sp Bibl Santa Ana [946]
Paulitschke, Phillip Viktor *see* DIE AFRIKA-LITERATUR
Paullin, CO *see* GUIDE TO THE MATERIALS IN LONDON ARCHIVES FOR THE HISTORY OF THE UNITED STATES SINCE 1783
O PAULO AFFONSO : PERIODICO IMPARCIAL, NOTICIOSO, COMMERCIAL E LITTERARIO – Pao d'Assucar, Alagoas. 27 Out 1878; Fev, Jul-17 Ago 1879 – 1,5,6 – bl Biblioteca [072]
PAULO AFFONSO : REVISTA LITTERARIA ALAGOANA – Maceio, Alagoas. 6-25 Abr 1896 – 1,5,6 – bl Biblioteca [072]
Pauls, Eilhard Erich *see* DER HUETER ISRAELS
Paulsen, Friedrich *see*
- THE GERMAN UNIVERSITIES
- A SYSTEM OF ETHICS

Paulsen, Rudolf *see*
- MEIN LEBEN
- DER MENSCH AN DER WAGE

PAULUS : NACH DER APOSTELGESCHICHTE: HISTORISCHER WERTH DIESER BERICHTE / Trip, Ch. J – (Includes bibliographical references) – Leiden: D Noothoven van Goor, 1866 – 1mf – 9 – 0-8370-5574-1 – 1985-3574 – us A.T.L.A. [220]
PAULUS = ST. PAUL : THE MAN AND HIS WORK / Weinel, Heinrich; ed by Morrison, William Douglas – (In English. Includes index) – 1mf – 9 – 0-8370-5746-9 – 1985-3746 – us A.T.L.A. [920]
PAULUS = ST PAUL THE APOSTLE : A BIBLICAL PORTRAIT AND A MIRROR OF THE MANIFOLD GRACE OF GOD / Besser, Wilhelm Friedrich – (In English) – NY: Robert Carter, 1864 – 1mf – 9 – 0-8370-2311-4 – 1985-0311 – us A.T.L.A. [920]
PAULUS / Wrede, William – Tuebingen: J.C.B. Mohr, 1907. 1 fiche – 9 – us A.T.L.A. [240]
PAULUS DER APOSTEL JESUS CHRISTI... : EIN BEITRAG ZU EINER KRITISCHEN GESCHICHTE DER URCHRISTENTUMS / Bauer, FC – (2. Aufl. besorgt von E. Zeller. 2 Theile, Leipzig, 1866) – 15mf – 8 – ne Slangenburg [240]
PAULUS: DER MENSCH UND SEIN WERK: DIE ANFAENGE DES CHRISTENTUMS / Weinel, Heinrich – Tuebingen: J.C.B. Mohr, 1904. 1 fiche – 9 – us A.T.L.A. [240]
PAULUS DES APOSTELS BRIEF AN DIE ROEMER : AUS DEM GRIECHISCHEN URTEXT AUF GRUND DES SINAI-CODEX / Delitzsch, Franz – (Includes bibliographical references & glossary of Hebrew words) – Leipzig: Doerffling und Franke, 1870 – 1mf – 9 – 0-8370-2875-2 – 1985-0875 – us A.T.L.A. [220]
Paulus, Helmut *see* ELF PREUSSISCHE OFFIZIERE
PAULUS IM DRAMA / Emrich, Wilhelm – (Includes bibliographical references) – Berlin: W de Gruyter & Co, 1934 – 2r – 1 – us U.W. Library [430]
PAULUS IN DER APOSTELGESCHICHTE: DER HISTORISCHE CHARAKTER DIESER SCHRIFT / Oertel, J R – Halle a.S.: Georg Schwabe, 1868.1 fiche – 9 – us A.T.L.A. [240]
Paulus, J *see*
- HENRI DE GAND
- TRENTE ANS DE CAFE-CONCERT

Paulus, Nikolaus *see*
- DIE DEUTSCHEN DOMINIKANER IM KAMPFE GEGEN LUTHER (1518-1563)
- HEXENWAHN UND HEXENPROZESS
- JOHANN TETZEL DER ABLASSPREDIGER
- LUTHER UND DIE GEWISSENSFREIHEIT
- PROTESTANTISMUS UND TOLERANZ IM 16. JAHRHUNDERT
- DIE STRASSBURGER REFORMATOREN UND DIE GEWISSENSFREIHEIT

PAULUS' STELLUNG ZU FRAU UND EHE / Delling, G – Stuttgart, 1931 – 3mf – 8 – ne Slangenburg [220]
PAULUS UND SEINE BRIEFE : KRITISCHE UNTERSUCHUNGEN ZU EINER NEUEN GRUNDLEGUNG DER PAULINISCHEN BRIEFLITERATUR UND IHRER THEOLOGIE / Voelter, Daniel – (Includes bibliographical references) – Strassburg: J H Ed Heitz, 1905 – 1mf – 9 – 0-8370-9335-X – 1986-3335 – us A.T.L.A. [220]
PAULUS UNTER DEN JUDEN : DRAMATISCHE LEGENDE IN SECHS BILDERN / Werfel, Franz – Berlin: P Zsolnay, 1926 – 1r – 1 – us U.W. Library [820]

PAULUS VON SAMOSATA (T.U.U. 3-44/5) / Loofs, Friedrich – Leipzig, 1924 – 6mf – 9 – ne Slangenburg [240]
DIE PAULUSBRIEFE / Vischer, Eberhard – Halle a.S.: Gebauer-Schwetschke, 1904. (Religionsgeschichtliche Volksbuecher fuer deutsche christliche Gegenwart; 1. Reihe, 4. Heft) – 1mf – us A.T.L.A. [220]
Pauly, Charlotte E *see* DER TIGER UND DIE HARFE
Pauly, Ernst *see*
– 20 JAHRE CAFE DES WESTENS
Pauly, Walter *see* ALS LANDRAT IN OSTPREUSSEN
PAULYS REALENCYCLOPAEDIE DER CLASSISCHEN ALTERTUMSWISSENSCHAFT – 1991 – 589 fiches (1:24) – silver DM4,480 – 3-598-33221-1 gw Saur [450]
PAUPER REGISTERS / Van Wert County. Ohio. Pleasant Township. Township Clerk – 1876-1902 – 1r – 1 – $32.50r – us Archival [324]
PAUPERISM STATISTICS / Fulton County. Ohio. County Home – 1889-1906 – 1r – 1 – $32.50r – us Archival [324]
PAUPERISM STATISTICS / Huron County. Ohio. County Home – 1846-1900 – 1r – 1 – $32.50r – us Archival [324]
PAUPERISM STATISTICS / Ottawa County, Ohio. County Home – 1882-1904 – 1r – 1 – us Archival [350]
PAUPERISME ET ASSOCIATION / Gatti de Gamond, Zoe – (Condition of 19th C. French working class series). 1847 – 9 – fr Hachette [360]
PAUSANIAS / Trouve – Carcassone: G. Gareng, 1810. (French Theatre Series) – 9 – fr Hachette [820]
Pausewang, Ute *see* LEHRPLANGEBUNDENES UND LEHRPLANUNGSGEBUNDENES ERZAEHLEN IN KLASSE 1, UNTERSUCHT IM ZUSAMMENHANG MIT DER SOZIALEN SCHICHTUNG
Paust, Otto *see* SEINE MAJESTAET, DER REKRUT
Pautex, B *see* ERRATA DU DICTIONNAIRE DE L'ACADEMIE FRANCAISE
Pauthier, PG *see*
– CHINE OU DESCRIPTION HISTORIQUE, GEOGRAPHIQUE ET LITTERAIRE DE CE VASTE EMPIRE, D'APRES DES DOCUMENTS CHINOIS
– L'UNIVERS, OU HISTOIRE ET DESCRIPTION DE TOUS LES PEUPLES,...
PAUVRES BETES ET PAUVRES GENS / Pescow de Cherville, Gaspard Georges de – Paris: A. Parpalet, 1869. 338p.4 fiches. (Literature Collection) – 9 – 10.00 – fr Bibl Nationale [830]
PAUVRETE, SILHOUETTES PARISIENNES / Besancenet, Etienne de – Paris. 1899. (La Condition Ouvriere. Part Two.) – 9 – 7.50 – fr Bibl Nationale [360]
Pauwels, Jan Anton Frans *see*
– DE HEDENDAEGSCHE LANG-TONGE AF-GEBEELD IN TWAELF ZINNE-BEELDEN...
– PESSIMORUM PESSIMUM, ET OPTIMORUM OPTIMUM
Pauwels, Louis *see* THE DAWN OF MAGIC
...PAVANA-CAPRICHO, OP. 12. PIANO SOLO / Albeniz, I – Madrid: Union Musical Espanola, 19-? – 1 – us Sibley [780]
Pavard, C *see* FRANCE AFRICAINE, SAHARA ET SOUDAN
PAVEL / Merezhkovskii, Dimitrii – Avgustin. Berlin. 1936. BR-779 2 – 8 – ne IDC [460]
PAVEL I / Merezhkovskii, Dimitrii – Spb. 1908. BR-780 2 – 8 – ne IDC [460]
Pavet de Courteille, M *see* DICTIONNAIRE TURK-ORIENTAL
PAVILLIONS – Pattee, University Park, PA. 1982 – 63p 3mf – 9 – $0.50f – us Lawrence Pub [720]
Pavlenko, I *see* NRAVY RUSSKOGO OBSHCHESTVA V EKATERINSKUIU EPOKHU
Pavlic, Breda *see* NEW INTERNATIONAL ECONOMIC ORDER
Pavlicek, Vaclav *see* POLITICKE STRANY PO UNORU.
Pavlov, B *see* DVA KRASNYKH GODA, NOI ABR 1917 G.-NOI ABR 1919 G
PAVLOVIAN JOURNAL OF BIOLOGICAL SCIENCE – (Cont: Conditional Reflex. Cont by: Integrative Physiological and Behavioral Science) – Philadelphia. v9-25. 1974-90 1; v9 1974. v12-14 1977-79*. v15-16 1980-81. v17-25 1982-90* 5; v11-25 1976-90 9 – 1,5,9 – D6891.01 – us UMI [574]
Pavlovich, N *see* PAMIATNYE VSTRECHI
Pavluts'kii, G *see* ISTORIIA UKRAJINS'KOHO ORNAMENTU
Pavon y Jimenez, Jose Antonio *see*
– FLORA PERUVIANA ET CHILENSIS...
– FLORAE PERUVIANAE ET CHILENSIS PRODROMUS......
– SUPLEMENTO A LA QUINOLOGIA, EN EL QUAL SE AUMENTAN LAS ESPECIES DE QUINA NUEVAMENTE DESCUBIERTAS EN EL PERU...
– SYSTEMA VEGETABILIUM FLORAE PERUVIANAE ET CHILENSIS
Pavy, L-C *see* LES RECLUSERIES
PAW PAW HOLLOW BAPTIST CHURCH (FORMERLY: FORK OF FRENCH BROAD AND HOLSTON). SEVIER COUNTY. TENNESSEE : CHURCH RECORDS – 1802-80 – 1 – 10.17 – us Baptist [240]
Pawel, Jaro *see*
– BEITRAEGE ZU KLOPSTOCKS ZEITMESSUNG
– KLOPSTOCKS ODEN
– NEUE BEITRAEGE ZU KLOPSTOCKS MESSIAS
– ODEN
Pawling *see* LIVINGSTON COUNTY DIRECTORY 1873-1874
Pawlowski, Auguste *see* BIBLIOGRAPHIE RAISONEE DES OUVRAGES CONCERNANT LE DAHOMEY
PAWNBROKERS' GAZETTE – London, England. -w. April 1837-Dec 1931. Wanting Oct 1872-May 1873. 46 reels – 1 – uk British Libr Newspaper [072]
PAWNEE CHIEF – Pawnee City, NE. -w. Apr 1901-Jul 1944 – 1 – us NE Hist [071]
PAWNEE COUNTY HERALD – Larned. Kan. 1877-1878 – 1 – us UMI [071]
PAWNEE PRESS – Pawnee City, NE. -w. (-sw 1896-1903). May 1878-Jan 1879, scattered issues missing; Mar 1879-Feb 1888; Nov 1894-Jul 1908 – 1 – us NE Hist [071]
PAWNEE REPUBLICAN – Pawnee City, NE. -w. Oct 1874; Jul 1875; Sep 1878-Dec 1881, scattered issues missing; Jan 1883-Mar 1891; May-Jul 1891; Oct 1891-May 1906; Jan 1907 to date – 1 – us NE Hist [071]
Pawson, J *see* A CHRONOLOGICAL CATALOGUE OF ALL THE TRAVELLING PREACHERS NOW IN THE METHODIST CONNEXION...
PAWTUCKET VALLEY GLEANER – Phenix. R.I. 1878-1902; 1905-1906 – 1 – us UMI [071]
PAWTUXET VALLEY DAILY TIMES – West Warwick. R.I. 1892- – 1 – us UMI [071]
Paxon, FL *see* GUIDE TO THE MATERIALS IN LONDON ARCHIVES FOR THE HISTORY OF THE UNITED STATES SINCE 1783
PAXTON 1749-1890 – (Mf 1-2: Births 1749-1845. Mf 2-3: Marriages 1784-1852. Mf 3-4: Deaths 1756-1845. Mf 5-6: Births: 1843-61. Mf 6: Marriages; Deaths 1844-62. Mf 7: Births 1862-93; Marriages 1862-92. Mf 8: Deaths 1862-91) – (mf ed 1985) – 8mf – 9 – 0-931248-38-8 – us Holbrook [920]
PAXTON ADVOCATE – Paxton, NE. -w. Jan-Jul 1892 – 1 – us NE Hist [071]
Paxton, J *see* MAGAZINE OF BOTANY
PAXTON PAPERS: INDEX AND CALENDAR – 1 – uk Microform Academic [520]
Paxton, S *see* A CONCERTO FOR THE VIOLINCELLO. WITH ACCOMPANIMENT FOR 2VLNS/TENOR/BASS/2FL/2HNS
PAXTON TIMES – Paxton, NE. -w. Jun 1924-Jun 1966; Aug 1966-Apr 1967 – 1 – us NE Hist [071]
Paxton, W M *see* ANNALS OF PLATTE COUNTY
Paxton, William Miller *see* THE MISSION OF THE PRESBYTERIAN CHURCH
PAY LEDGER FOR NEW SOUTH WALES MILITARY FORCES WHO SERVED IN THE BOER WAR, 1899-1903 – 12r – 1 – CRS B5202 – at Archives [920]
PAY LEDGERS FOR NEW SOUTH WALES MILITARY FORCES INVOLVED IN THE BOER WAR, 1899-1902 – 2r – 1 – CRS B5205 – at Archives [920]
PAY LISTS FOR "H" COMPANY, 4TH CONTINGENT, QUEENSLAND DEFENCE FORCE, CHRONOLOGICAL SERIES, 1900-1901 / Chief Secretary's Office, Queensland – 3r – 1 – CRS B5164 – at Archives [920]
PAY PLANNING IDEAS – (v.20-. 1979-5,6,9) – v.1-. 1960- – 1 – us UMI [073]
PAY SHEETS OF THE 5TH AND 6TH CONTINGENTS FROM THE QUEENSLAND DEFENCE FORCE WHO SERVED IN THE BOER WAR, CHRONOLOGICAL SERIES, 1901-1902 / Chief Secretary's Office, Queensland – 5r – 1 – CRS B5180 – at Archives [920]
PAYAM-I AZADI – (Shumarah-'i 3-19 (9 Mihr 1360-Urdibihisht 1362[Oct 1981-Apr/May 1983]). Missing issues: shumarah-'i 15) – [S.l.]: Shura-yi Muttahid-i Chap bara-yi Dimukrasi va Istiqlal – 1 reel – 1 – $25.00 – us MEDOC [950]
PAYAM-I DANISHJU – Austin, Texas: Sazman-i Danishju'i-i Astin dar Iyalat-i Tigzas. Sal-i 1, shumarah-'i 1-sal-i 3, shumarah-'i 5 (Khurdad 1353-Day 1357 [Jun 1974-Dec 1978]) – 1 reel – 1 – $25.00 – us MEDOC [950]
PAYAM-I DANISHJU – Frankfort: Danishjuyan-i Pishraw dar kharih-i kishvar, havadar-i Rah-i Fada'i. Sal-i 1, shumarah-'i 1-7 (Azar 1360-Tir 1361 [Dec 1981-Jul 1982]) – 1 reel – 1 – $25.00 – us MEDOC [950]
PAYAM-I DANISHJU – (Shumarah-'i 9 (20 Tir, 1340[Jul 11, 1961]-dawrah-'i jadid, shumarah-'i 2 (16 Azar 1342[Dec 7, 1962])) – [S.l.] Kumitah-'i Danishjuyan-i Danishgah-'i Tehran – 1 reel – 1 – $25.00 – us MEDOC [950]
PAYAM-I DANISHJU – (Unnumbered: 19 issues) – [S.l.]: Sazman-i Danishjuyan-i Jibhah-'i Milli-i Iran. (3 Mihr 1342-Murdad/ Shahrivar 1344 [25 Sep 1963-Aug 1965]) – 1 reel – 1 – $25.00 – us MEDOC [950]
PAYAM-I JIBHAH-'I MILLI – (Purchase with Jabhah) – Tehran: Jabhah-'i Milli-i Iran – 1 – us MEDOC [950]
PAYAM-I KHALQ – (Sal-i 1: shumarah-'i 1-21 (1 Isfand 1357-8 Murdad 1358[20 Feb 1979-30 Jun 1979])) – Tehran: Sazman-i Mujahidin-i Khalq-i Iran, 1979- – 1 reel – 1 – $25.00 – us MEDOC [950]
Payette, Ange-Albert *see* L'HONORABLE MAURICE TELLIER
Payeur-Didelot *see* TRENTE MOIS AU CONTINENT MYSTERIEUX
PAYKAR – (Missing issues: 41-43, 55-65, 67-68, 55-68, 70-76, 78-79, 87, 89-91, 93-97, 99-119, 121-122, 124-125) – Tehran: Sazman-i Paykar dar rah-i Azadi-i Tabaqah-'i Kargar, 1979-. No. 16-126 (18 Urdibihisht 1358-18 Aban 1360 [28 Apr 1979-9 Nov 1981]) – 1 reel – 1 – $125.00 – us MEDOC [950]
Paykull, G von *see* FAUNA SVECICA: INSECTA
PAYLISTS AND PAY INSTRUCTION ROLLS FOR THE QUEENSLAND DEFENCE FORCE MEMBERS WHO SERVED IN THE BOER WAR, 1901-1902 / Chief Secretary's Office, Queensland – 1 reel – 1 – CRS B5161 – at Archives [920]
PAYMAN – (Sal 1, shumarah 1-sal 7, shumarah 9 (Azar 1312-Khurdad 1321[Oct 1933-May 1942])) – Tabriz: Ahmad Kasravi – 2r – 1 – $65.00 – us MEDOC [950]
PAYMAN – (Shumarah-'i 7, 9, 12, 14-16 (15?) (7 Mihr 1344-21 Bahman 1344[29 Sep 1965-7 Feb 1966])) – London: Kumitah-'i Difa' az Farigh al-Tahsilan-i Zindani, vabastah bih Kunfidirasyun-i Danishjuyan-i Irani – 1 reel – 1 – $25.00 – us MEDOC [950]
PAYMENT SYSTEMS STRATEGIES – (Cont by: Retail Delivery Strategies) – Washington. v1-4. sum 1994-spr 1995* – 1,5,9 – D21315 – us UMI [330]
PAYMENTS SYSTEMS REPORT – (Cont: Automated Payments Update) – Herndon. v11-12. 1996-97+ – 1,5,9 – D20203.01 – us UMI [330]
Payn, James *see* SOME LITERARY RECOLLECTIONS
Payne, Charles Henry *see* GUIDES AND GUARDS IN CHARACTER-BUILDING
Payne, Daniel A *see* WELCOME TO THE RANSOMED, OR, DUTIES OF THE COLORED INHABITANTS OF THE DISTRICT OF COLUMBIA
Payne, Daniel Alexander *see* HISTORY OF THE AFRICAN METHODIST EPISCOPAL CHURCH
Payne, J *see* CARRINGTON AND PAYNE'S REPORTS
Payne, Joseph *see* MOORE AND PAYNE'S REPORTS
Payne Smith, Robert *see*
– DANIEL
– PROPHECY
PAYNE STAR – Payne, Ohio, 1884-1885 – 1r – 1 – $32.50r – us Archival [978]
Payne, V Gregory *see*
– AGE-RELATED CHANGES IN THE RELEASE POINT, VELOCITY AND ACCELERATION IN GIRLS' OVERARM THROWING PERFORMANCE
– EFFECTS OF AGE AND GENDER ON FUNCTIONAL ROTATION AND LATERAL FLEXION OF THE BACK AND THE NECK
Payne, WO *see* HISTORY OF STORY COUNTY
Payne-Smith, Robert *see*
– THE AUTHENTICITY AND MESSIANIC INTERPRETATION OF THE PROPHECIES OF ISAIAH VINDICATED IN A COURSE OF SERMONS PREACHED BEFORE THE UNIVERSITY OF OXFORD
– SYRIAC DICTIONARY
PAYROLL RECORD / Van Wert County. Ohio. County Home – 1901-1912 – 1r – 1 – $32.50r – us Archival [324]
PAYROLL RECORDS / Atchison, Topeka and Santa Fe Railroad Company – 1893-1895 – 1 – us KS Hist [380]
LE PAYS – Journal de l'Empire. Politique, litteraire, agricole. Paris. 1858-juin 1863 – 1 – fr A.C.R.P.P. [073]
LE PAYS – Montreal, Canada. 15 jan 1910-3 dec 1921 (incomplete) – 3r – 1 – Can$45.00r – cn Can Microfilming [072]
LE PAYS – Montreal, Canada. 1862-71 – 13r – 1 – $845.00 – cn Library Assoc [971]
LE PAYS – Paris. 1er juin 1917-26 dec 1919 – 1 – fr A.C.R.P.P. [073]
LE PAYS : RADICAL – Montreal, Canada. 15 jan 1852-23 dec 1871 – 12r – 1 – Can$50.00r – cn Can Microfilming [072]
PAYS D' OUEST / Geffroy, Gustave – Paris: E. Fasquelle, 1897 – fr Armell [944]
LES PAYS D'ALBANIE ET LEUR HISTOIRE... / Gibert, Frederic – Paris: Rosier, 1914 – 1 – F166.99 – fr Armell [949]
LE PAYS DE HAMI OU KHAMIL / Imbault-Huart, C – Description, histoire, d' apres les auteurs chinois. (Bulletin du Comite des travaux historiques et scientifiques. Section de geographie). Annee. 1892; Paris. 1893. BU-617 2 – 8 – ne IDC [950]
LE PAYS DES NEGRES ET LA COTE DES ESCLAVES. / Laffitte, J – 2e ed. Tours, 1878 – 1 – us Res Libr [960]
LES PAYS D'OCCIDENT D'APRES LE HEOU CHOU / Chavannes, E – (T'oung Pao, S. 2, v. 8). Leide. 1907. BU-556 2 – 8 – ne IDC [900]
LES PAYS DU BAS-MUNGO, BAS-WOURI / Moby-Etia, P – Etude geographique de la vie rurale et des relations avec Douala – 9 – F70.00 – fr Ethnologie [910]
LE PAYS MOSSI / Marc, L – Paris. 1909. BA-340 2 – 8 – ne IDC [956]
LE PAYS SOCIALISTE – Dir. Paul Faure. no. 1-36. Paris. 18 mars-29 dec 1939. mq no. 6 – 1 – fr A.C.R.P.P. [073]
LE PAYSAGE ITALIEN DANS LES ROMANS DE LAMARTINE : BIBLIOGRAPHIE / Williamson, Jean Bisset – 1953. SEM105P4 – 1mf – 9 – cn Bibl Nat [440]
PAYSAGES CANADIENS / Chevillard, Valbert – Paris: A. Lemerre, 1891. 00604. (Pre-1900 Canadiana) – 9 – cn C.I.H.M. [910]
PAYSAGES DE FRANCOIS DESPORTES, 1661-1743 / Reunion des musees nationaux. Paris – 1961. 13 illus. 1 fiche – 9 – fr Réunion [700]
PAYSAN AU DAHRA ORIENTAL (ALGERIE) DJEBEL BISSA / Kergoat, J – Contribution a la connaissance de la condition paysanne en montagne forestiere (Essai socio-historique) – 9 – F100.00 – fr Ethnologie [960]
LE PAYSAN DE COCHINCHINE – Hebdomadaire de soutien des interets agricoles. Dir. H. Chene. Saigon. oct 1934-39 – 1 – fr A.C.R.P.P. [073]
LE PAYSAN DE FRANCE – Journal republicain agricole. Paris. 1901-11 – 1 – fr A.C.R.P.P. [073]
LE PAYSAN DE LA MAYENNE – Laval, May 1941 – May 1944 – 1r – fr Armell [630]
LE PAYSAN DU CENTRE-OUEST – Organe agraire et professionnel. Dir.-gerant H. d'Halluin-Dorgeres. Rennes. dec 1932-juin 1940 – 1 – fr A.C.R.P.P. [073]
LE PAYSAN INDIGENE / Parti Communiste. Region Algerienne – Journal. Alger. mars 1933 – 1 – fr A.C.R.P.P. [335]
PAYSANA : REVUE D'ARTISANAT / ed by Gaudet-Smet, Francoise – Montreal, mar 1938-hiver 1980f – 3r – 1 – Can$50.00 – cn Can Microfilming [073]
LES PAYSANS DE MORETTE : UN SIECLE DE VIE RURALE DANS UNE COMMUNE DU DAUPHINE / Garavel, J – F30.00 – fr Ethnologie [944]
LES PAYSANS ET LA POLITIQUE DANS LA FRANCE CONTEMPORAINE / Fauvet, J & Mendras, H – F90.00 – fr Ethnologie [320]
LES PAYSANS NOIRS / Delavignette, Hobert Louis – ed. nouv. Paris, 1947 – 1 – us Res Libr [960]

Payson, Edward *see* AN ADDRESS TO SEAMEN, DELIVERED AT PORTLAND, 28 OCT 1821; AT THE REQUEST OF THE PORTLAND MARINE BIBLE SOCIETY
Payte, J Thomas *see* JOURNAL OF MAINTENANCE IN THE ADDICTIONS
PAYVAND – (Shumarah-'i 1-5 (Tir 1362-Farvardin 1363[Jun 1983-Mar 1984])) – Miami: Jibhah-'i Hambastagi-i bayn al-millali bara-yi Difa az Huquq-i Dimukratik-i Mardum-i Iran – 1 reel – 1 – $25.00 – us MEDOC [950]
A PAZ – Labrea/Manicore, Amazonas. 19 Maio-Jun 1901; Abr-Jul 1902; Mar, Out 1903; Jan-Abr 1904; Maio, Out-Dez 1905; Fev-8 Abr 1906 – 1,5,6 – bl Biblioteca [072]
A PAZ : ORGAO OFFICIAL DA EGREIJA BETHESDA – Manoas, Amazonas. 21 Mar 1898 – 1,5,6 – bl Biblioteca [072]
LA PAZ. CANTO HEROICO / Forner Segarra, Juan Pablo – 1796 – 9 – 1.50f – sp Bibl Santa Ana [810]
LA PAZ DEL CAMPO PERSONALIDAD E INMORTALIDAD DE GABRIEL Y GALAN / Munoz Gallardo, Juan Antonio – Badajoz: Imprenta Diputacion Provincial, 1967. Sep. Rev. Est. Extrem. – 1 – sp Bibl Santa Ana [946]
LA PAZ DEL CAMPO. PERSONALIDAD E INMORTALIDAD DE GABRIEL Y GALAN / Munoz Gallardo, Juan Antonio – Badajoz: Imp. de la Diputacion Provincial, 1967 – sp Bibl Santa Ana [946]
PAZ E TERRA – Rio de Janeiro, BL. 1966-1969 – 1r – $50.00 – R04178 – us Library Micro [240]
Paz, Ireneo *see* ALBUM DE LA PAZ Y EL TRABAJO
Paz, J *see*
- CATALOGO DE TOMOS VARIOS (B.N. DEPARTAMENTO DE MANUSCRITOS)
- MADRID. BIBLIOTECA NACIONAL. CATALOGO DE LOS MANUSCRITOS DE AMERICA
- VALLADOLID. ARCHIVO GENERAL DE SEMANCAS. SECRETARIA DE ESTADO. CAPITULACIONES CON INGLATERRA ...
- VALLADOLID. ARCHIVO GENERAL DE SIMANCAS DIVERSOS DE CASTILLA. CAMARA DE CATILLA
- VALLADOLID. ARCHIVO GENERAL DE SIMANCAS. SECRETARIA DE ESTADO. CAPITULACIONES CON FRANCIA Y NEGOCICACIONES...
- VALLADOLID. ARCHIVO GENERAL DE SIMANCAS. SECRETARIA DE ESTADO. CAPITULACIONES CON LA CASA DE AUSTRIA...

Paz Sanchez, Abdon de *see* LUZ EN LA TIERRA
Pazhitnov, K A *see*
- IZ ISTORII RABOCHIKH ARTELEI NA ZAPADE I V ROSSII
- MEZHDUNARODNYI KOOPERATIVNYI SOIUZ
- N.G. CHERNYSHEVSKII KAK PERVYI TEORETIK KOOPERATSII V ROSSII
- OCHEREDNAIA ZADACHA POTREBITEL'SKOI KOOPERATSII V GORODAKH ROSSII
- OSNOVY KOOPERATIZMA
- PERVYI GOD SUSHCHESTVOVANIIA PETROGRADSKOGO KOOPERATIVNOGO INSTITUTA
- POPULIARNYE OCHERKI PO TEORII KOOPERATSII

PAZIFISCHE RUNDSCHAU / ed by Ackermann's Advertising & News Service Ltd – Vancouver, Canada. 1971-1981; 29 Jan-24 Dec 1983 – 1 – gw Mikrofilm [072]
DER PAZIFIST – Hagen, Germany. 1921-11 Mar 1933; 2 Aug-10 Dec 1947; 1948; 1951-Jun 1969 – 4r – 1 – gw Mikrofilm [072]
Pazos, Manuel R *see*
- LOMAX, DEUK V. LA ORDEN DE SANTIAGO, 1,170-1,275. MADRID, 1965
- NECROLOGICA
- EL REINO DE GALICIA, TOMO 1. VIGO 1966

Pazos, Matias *see* LAPIDAS ROMANAS. ALCOLLARIN
Pazukhin, A A *see* SBORNIK GRAMOT I DOGOVOROV O PRISOEDINENII TSARSTVE I OBLASTEI K GOSUDARSTVU ROSSIISKOMU V 17-19 VEKAKH
PC BUSINESS WORLD – London. v1-7. 1985-91* – 1 – D15410 – us UMI [650]
PC DESIGN – Alpharetta. v1-2. sep 1984-apr 1985* – 1 – Cont by: Printed Circuit Design – us UMI [073]
PC JR – 1984 – 1 – us UMI [510]
PC MIKRODATA MED PC WORLD NORGE – 1985- – 1,5,6,9 – us UMI [510]
PC MUNDO – 1986- – 1,5,6,9 – us UMI [510]
PC PRODUCTS – Boston. v1-3. jun 1984-oct 1986* – 1 – D14874 – us UMI [073]
PC RESOURCE – (Absorbed by: PC World) – Peterborough. v1-21. 1987-88* 1; v22-41. 1989-aug 1990 1,5,9 – 1,5,9 – D16873 – us UMI [073]
PC RESOURCE *see* PC WORLD
PC TECH JOURNAL – (1986-. 1,5,6) – 1984- – 9 – us UMI [629]
PC TECH JOURNAL – v1-. 1983- – 1,5,6,9 – us UMI [073]
PC: THE INDEPENDENT GUIDE TO IBM PERSONAL COMPUTERS – v1-. 1982- – 1,5,6,9 – us UMI [073]
PC USER – (Cont by: Programmable Controls) – St Clair Shores. v1-3. mar 1982-84* – 1 – D14418 – us UMI [000]
PC WEEK – 1983- – 1,5,6,9 – us UMI [073]
PC WEEK – (1986-. 1,5,6) – v1-. 1984- – 9 – us UMI [510]
PC WELT – (1985-. 5,6,9) – 1983- – 1 – us UMI [510]
PC WORLD – (Absorbed: PC Resource 1990) – San Francisco. v1-15. 1983-97+ – 1,5,9 – D13583 – us UMI [073]
PC WORLD : BENELUX-EDITION – Amsterdam. 1984-88* 1; 1989-94*. 1995-97+ 1,5,9 – 1,5,9 – D15252 – us UMI [073]
PC WORLD – Danmark.v1-. 1985- – 1,5,6,9 – us UMI [510]
PC WORLD – Espana. 1985- – 1,5,6,9 – us UMI [510]
PC WORLD : LOTUS-EDITION – (Cont: Lotus) – Boston. v10-11 dec 1992-dec 1992*. v12-13 jan 1994-jul 1995 – 1,5,9 – D20311 – us UMI [073]
PC WORLD – Swedish ed. 1984- – 1,5,6,9 – us UMI [510]
PC WORLD *see* PC RESOURCE
PDB *see* DESCRIPTION ABREGEE DE L'EMPIRE DE LA CHINE,...
PEABODY 1855-1905 – (Mf 1-3: Birth Index 1855-80. Mf 4-6: Birth Index 1880-1903. Mf 7-9: Marriage Index 1855-90. Mf 10-12: Marriage Index 1891-1912. Mf 13-14: Death Index 1855-80. Mf 15-17: Death Index 1880-1906. Mf 18-22: Births 1855-79. Mf 23-25: Births 1880-90. Mf 26-30: Marriages 1855-91. Mf 31-35: Deaths 1855-79. Mf 36-37: Deaths 1880-90. Mf 38-41: Births 1891-1902. Mf 42-47: Marriages 1891-1912. Mf 48-51: Deaths 1891-1905) – (mf ed 1984) – 37mf – 9 – 0-931248-63-9 – us Holbrook [920]
Peabody, Andrew Preston *see*
- BACCALAUREATE SERMONS
- CHRISTIAN BELIEF AND LIFE
- CHRISTIANITY AND SCIENCE: A SERIES OF LECTURES
- CHRISTIANITY, THE RELIGION OF NATURE
- LECTURES ON CHRISTIAN DOCTRINE

Peabody, Elizabeth Palmer *see*
- LECTURES IN THE TRAINING SCHOOLS FOR KINDERGARTNERS
- REMINISCENCES OF THE REV. WM. ELLERY CHANNING, D.D

PEABODY ESSEX MUSEUM COLLECTIONS – (Cont: Essex Institute Historical Collections) – Salem. v129-133. oct 1993-dec 1997+ – 1,5,9 – D3464.01 – us UMI [700]
Peabody, Francis Greenwood *see* THE RELIGION OF AN EDUCATED MAN
Peabody, Joel R *see* A WORLD OF WONDERS, OR, DIVERS DEVELOPMENTS, SHOWING THE THOROUGH TRIUMPH OF ANIMAL MAGNETISM IN NEW ENGLAND.
PEABODY MUSEUM: A VISUAL RECORD OF ARTIFACTS / Peabody Museum of Archaeology and Ethnology, Harvard University – Boston: G.K. Hall & Co., 1990 – 600 images on 8 84 frame color mf – 15 – $250.00 export $325.00 – 0-8161-1754-3 – uk Hall [301]
Peabody Museum of Archaeology and Ethnology, Harvard University *see*
- AUTHOR AND SUBJECT CATALOGS OF THE TOZZER LIBRARY, 2ND ENLARGED EDITION ON MICROFICHE
- PEABODY MUSEUM: A VISUAL RECORD OF ARTIFACTS

PEACE : A MONTHLY REVIEW OF THE PEACE MOVEMENT – Apr 1933 – Sept/Oct 1941 – 15mf – 9 – $65.00 – us UPA [320]
PEACE – New York. v1-4. jul 1963-69 1; v4. 1969 5 – 1,5 – D2283 – us UMI [073]
PEACE ACTION – 1934-49 – 15mf – 9 – $65.00 – us UPA [320]
PEACE ACTION : NEWSLETTER – (Cont: Sanefreeze News) – Washington. v32-36. spr 1993-win 1998+ 1,5,9; v32-33. spr 1993-win 1995* 5 – 1,5,9 – D6055.03 – us UMI [073]
PEACE AND CHANGE – Sonoma. v1-13 1972-88*. v14-18 1989-93. v19 1994*. v20-22 1995-97+ 1; v14-15 1989-90*. v16-18 1991-93. v19 1994*. v20-22 1995-97+5; v14-18 1989-93. v19 1994*. v20-22 1995-97+ 9 – 1,5,9 – D17058 – us UMI [073]
PEACE AND CONFLICT ISSUES AFTER THE COLD WAR – 9 – 92-3-102770-0 – fr UNESCO [320]
PEACE AND HAPPINESS / Lubbock, John – (Includes bibliographical references) – New York: Macmillan, 1909 – 1mf – 9 – 0-8370-6074-5 – 1986-0074 – us A.T.L.A. [200]
PEACE AND SECURITY = PAIX ET SECURITE – (Ceased v7 no 1 1992) – Ottawa. v1-7. 1986/87-1992 – 9 – Can$20.00y – cn Micromedia [320]
PEACE AND SECURITY OF THE DEVELOPING NATIONS / Indonesia. Permanent Mission to the United Nations – Subandrio, Deputy Prime Minister and Minister for Foreign Affairs, at General Assembly of United Nations, 11 Dec 1964. SE-6187-1 – 9 – ne IDC [950]
THE PEACE CONFERENCE... / Darby, W E – London, [1899] – 1mf – 9 – ILM-459/1 – ne IDC [327]
PEACE CORPS / Sumarga – SE 10,543 1. 1964 – 9 – ne IDC [360]
THE PEACE EGG / Ewing, Juliana Horatia – British Fiction Archive: Unit 1 – 9 – uk Bell [830]
PEACE FORUM – Mar 1912 – Jun 1915. Continuation of: Peace. Continued as: World Court Magazine – 18mf – 9 – $80.00 – us UPA [320]
PEACE MAGAZINE – Toronto. v1-10. 1985-94 – 9 – Can$20.00y – cn Micromedia [320]
THE PEACE MOVEMENT – (1914-39 have been publ in French) – Berne, 1912-39 – 65mf – 9 – ILM-4002/1 – ne IDC [327]
THE PEACE MOVEMENT – International Peace Bureau, Berne. 1912-July 1914 – 18mf – 9 – $80.00 – us UPA [320]
PEACE NEWS – 1936-78 – us Primary [073]
PEACE NEWS – London, UK. 1969-1992 – 15r – $750.00 – R63563 – us Library Micro [072]
PEACE NEWS *see* THE LEFT IN BRITAIN, PART 1
PEACE NEWSLETTER – (1985- . 5,6,9) – 1936- – 1 – us UMI [073]
THE PEACE OF AMERICA / Brum, B – Montevideo, 1923 – 1mf – 1 – ILM-4076/1 – ne IDC [327]
THE PEACE OF THE CHURCH / Huntington, William Reed – New York: Scribner, 1892, c1891. (The Bohlen lectures for 1891) – 1mf – us A.T.L.A. [240]
PEACE OFFICER – v1- 1957- 1; v15- 5,6; v18- 9 – us UMI [073]
PEACE ON EARTH (CCC220) / Lin, Han-ying – (In Chinese) – 1st ed. Hong Kong: Council on Christian Literature for Overseas Chinese, 1959 – 1r – 1 – 1984-B500 – us A.T.L.A. [240]
Peace Palace Library. The Hague *see* CARD CATALOGUE
PEACE PLANS AND LIBERTARIAN MICROFICHE PUBLISHING – Lists of plans published so far and publishing programme. 1 fiche – 9 – 1.00f – at Libertarian Micro [320]
PEACE PLEDGE UNION *see* PACIFISM, DISARMAMENT AND INTERNATIONAL RELATIONS, SERIES 3
PEACE PRINCIPLES EXEMPLIFIED IN THE EARLY HISTORY OF PENNSYLVANIA / Janney, Samuel M – Philadelphia: Friends' Book Association, 1876 – 1mf – us A.T.L.A. [978]
THE PEACE PROBLEM : THE TASK OF THE TWENTIETH CENTURY / Lynch, Frederick – New York: F.H. Revell, c1911 – 1mf – us A.T.L.A. [320]
PEACE RESEARCH – Brandon. v1-27. 1969-95 – 9 – Can$20.00y – cn Micromedia [320]
PEACE RIVER BLOCK NEWS – Peace River. B.C. Canada. May 1930-Dec 71; 1974- – 1 – cn Commonwealth Micro [072]
PEACE STUDIES CURRICULUM – 1990 – 9 – $5.00f – Educators for Social Responsibility – us Ross [370]
Peace, Walter *see* OUR COLONY OF NATAL
PEACEFUL USES OF ATOMIC ENERGY / United Nations – Proceedings of International Conferences on Peaceful Uses of Atomic Energy. Conferences 1, 1955; 2, 1958; 3, 1964; 4, 1972 – 9 – 298.00; 1.90f – uk UNIMICRO [621]
PEACEKEEPING AND INTERNATIONAL RELATIONS – (Incorporates: International Perspectives at v20 no 2 1991) – Toronto. v20-23. 1991-94 – 9 – Can$20.00y – cn Micromedia [327]
PEACEKEEPING AND INTERNATIONAL RELATIONS *see* INTERNATIONAL PERSPECTIVES
PEACEMAKER AND COURT OF ARBITRATION – 1882-1913 – 98mf – 9 – $395.00 – us UPA [320]
PEACH STREET BAPTIST CHURCH. SHELBY, NORTH CAROLINA : CHURCH RECORDS – 1954-62 – 1 – 9.36 – us Baptist [240]
Peacham, Henry *see*
- THE GARDEN OF ELOQUENCE
- MINERVA BRITANNA OR A GARDEN OF HEROICAL DEVISES

Peacock, Alison *see* THE PAPERS OF FRANK O. SALISBURY (1874-1962)
Peacock, Thomas Love *see*
- GRYLL GRANGE...
- THE MISFORTUNES OF ELPHIN...

PEAK OXYGEN DEFICIT AS A PREDICTOR OF SPRINT AND MIDDLE-DISTANCE TRACK PERFORMANCE / Weyand, Peter G & Cureton, Kirk J – 1992 – 2mf – 9 – $8.00 – us Microform Publ [612]
PEAK TORQUE RELIABILITY OF BIODEX B-2000 ISOKINETIC DYNAMOMETER DURING CONCENTRIC LOADING OF BACK FLEXORS AND EXTENSORS / Hoffert, Troy A & Kimura, Iris F – 1992 – 1mf – 9 – $4.00 – us Microform Publ [612]
Peake, Arthur S *see* CHRISTIANITY
Peake, Arthur Samuel *see*
- HEBREWS
- THE PROBLEM OF SUFFERING IN THE OLD TESTAMENT: THE HARTLEY LECTURE
- THE RELIGION OF ISRAEL

Peake, T De Witt *see* THE SYMBOLISM OF SOLOMON'S TEMPLE
PEALE, CHARLES WILLSON : COLLECTED PAPERS – (With printed guide) – Smithsonian Institution, National Portrait Gallery – 449mf – 1 – us Ross [920]
PEANUT – v1-. 1984- – 1,5,6,9 – us UMI [073]
PEANUT VARIETIES FOR ALABAMA / Alabama. Agricultural Experiment Station – 1960-64 – 1,5,6 – us Spaulding [630]
Pearce Edcumbe, E R *see* POPULAR FALLACIES REGARDING TRADE AND FOREIGN DUTIES
Pearce, H G *see* SEVEN LECTURES ON ECONOMICS
Pearce, J *see*
- BURNING AND SHINING LIGHTS
- DINNA FORGET

Pearce, James Edwin *see* MUSEUMS
PEARL (MIDDLE ENGLISH POEM) – A Modern version in the metre of the original, by Sophie Jewett.New York: T.Y. Crowell & Co., 1908. xvi,102p – 1 – us U.W. Library [810]
THE PEARL OF DAYS – v1-2. 1887-88 (complete) – 1r – 1 – ATLA T0087 – us A.T.L.A. [073]
THE PEARL OF PARABLES : NOTES ON LUKE 15, 11-32 / Hamilton, James – (Includes index) – New York: Robert Carter, 1869 – 1mf – 9 – 0-8370-3459-0 – 1985-1459 – us A.T.L.A. [220]
PEARL OF PARABLES: NOTES ON LUKE 15, 11-32 / Hamilton, James – New York: Robert Carter, 1869. 1 fiche – 9 – us A.T.L.A. [240]
PEARL OF THE ORIENT – (Some original pgs damaged) – v30-35. 1933-38 – 1r – 1 – ATLA S0725D – us A.T.L.A. [073]
PEARL RIVER BANNER – Monticello. Miss. 1838-1839 – 1 – us UMI [071]
Pearman, SN *see* NINETY SECOND CYCLE ERGOMETER TESTS FOR ASSESSING ANAEROBIC GLYCOLYTIC POWER
Pearse, Mark Guy *see*
- BRIDGETSTOW
- THE CHRISTIANITY OF JESUS CHRIST
- CHRIST'S CURE FOR CARE
- DANIEL QUORM, AND HIS RELIGIOUS NOTIONS
- DANIEL QUORM, AND HIS RELIGIOUS NOTIONS: SECOND SERIES
- GOLD AND INCENSE
- GOOD WILL
- HOMELY TALKS

- IN THE BANQUETING HOUSE
- JESUS CHRIST AND THE PEOPLE
- MISTER HORN AND HIS FRIENDS
- MOSES
- THE PRETTY WAYS O' PROVIDENCE
- THE PROPHET'S RAVEN
- THE STORY OF A ROMAN SOLDIER
- WOUNDS OF THE WORLD

Pearson, Alfred *see* CHRISTUS MAGISTER
Pearson, H *see* MEMOIRS OF THE LIFE AND WRITINGS OF THE REV. CLAUDIUS BUCHANAN
Pearson, John Batteridge *see* THE DIVINE PERSONALITY
Pearson, K B *see* EXPOSITION OF THE CREED
Pearson, Karl *see*
- THE ETHIC OF FREETHOUGHT AND OTHER ADDRESSES AND ESSAYS
- THE GRAMMAR OF SCIENCE

Pearson, Richmond Mumford *see* THE LAW LECTURES TREATING OF THE RIGHTS WHICH RELATE TO THINGS REAL AND PERSONAL.
Pearson, Thomas *see*
- INFIDELITY DISSECTED
- INFIDELITY: ITS ASPECTS, CAUSES AND AGENCIES

Peary, Robert E *see*
- NEAREST THE POLE
- THE NORTH POLE
- NORTHWARD OVER THE "GREAT ICE."BN 336/2. 2 V. 1898
- SELECTED TIDE-STAFF READINGS AND HYDROGRAPHIC SURVEY SOUNDINGS

THE PEASANT – Ireland.9 Feb 1907-26 Dec 1908 – 1 – ie Microforms [072]
PEASANT LIFE IN THE HOLY LAND / Wilson, Charles Thomas – (Includes glossary & indexes) – New York: E P Dutton, 1906 – 1mf – 9 – 0-8370-5862-7 – 1985-3862 – us A.T.L.A. [270]
PEASANTRY OF PALESTINE / Grant, Elihu – Boston: Pilgrim Press, 1907. 1 fiche – 9 – us A.T.L.A. [956]
PEASANTS AND PROPHETS / Byford, Charles T – 1912 – 1 – 6.86 – us Baptist [240]
THE PEASANTS WAR IN GERMANY, 1525-1526 / Bax, Ernest Belfort – London: Swan Sonnenschein; New York: Macmillan, 1899. (Social side of the Reformation in Germany / by E. Belfort Bax; 2) – 1mf – us A.T.L.A. [943]
Pease, Aaron Gaylord *see* PHILOSOPHY OF TRINITARIAN DOCTRINE
PEASE, SETH, PAPERS, MS 3234 – 1769-1837 – 1 reel – 1 – us Western Res [910]
PECAN QUARTERLY – v1- 1967- 1; v6- 5,6; v10- 9 – us UMI [073]
Pecevi, Ibrahim *see* TARIH-I PECEVI
Pechar, Gary S *see*
- THE EFFECTS OF BODY SEGMENT LENGTH AND HEAD POSITION UPON SIT AND REACH FLEXIBILITY PERFORMANCE
- AN EVALUATION OF THE PHYSICAL FITNESS EFFECTS OF A HIGH SCHOOL AEROBIC DANCE CURRICULUM

PECHAT' I REVOLIUTSIIA / Kommunisticheskaia Akademiia – Moscow. v1-10. 1921-30 – 5r – 1 – us Ross [320]
PECHAT I REVOLUTZIYA – Moscow. May 1921-June 1930 – 1 – us NY Public [073]
PECHAT' PERED SUDOM RECHI PO DELAM "RUSI", "NASHEI ZHIZNI" I "SYNA OTCHESTVA" / Goldshtein, ML – St. Petersburg, 1906. BR-10,101-1 – 9 – ne IDC [460]
PECHAT' Y TOBOL'SKOM NAMESTNICHESTVE V KONTSE 18 STOLETIIA / Dmitriev-Mamanov, A I – Istoriko-bibliograficheskiia izzledovaniia. Omsk. 1891. BR-4675 2 – 8 – ne IDC [947]
"DEN PECHATI" : KLICH: SBORNIK NA POMOSHCH ZHERTVAM VOINY / ed by Bunina, I A et al – Moskva: [T-vo skorpechatni A.A. Levenson], 1915 – 1 – CSUX88-B9675 – us Hoover Inst Photo [947]
PECHAT'I REVOLIUTSIIA – May 1921-June 1930 – 1 – 35.00r – us Hoover Inst Photo [335]
PECHATNIK – v. 1-4, 8. M. 1906. BR-4327 2 – 8 – ne IDC [073]
PECHATNOE DIELO – Leningrad. v1-4. 1909-12 – 1r – 1 – us Ross [072]
PECHATNOE ISKUSSTVO – Ezhemesiachnyi illiustrirovannyi sbornik. Spb. 1901-03. B-1829 2 – 8 – ne IDC [760]
PECHATNOE ISKUSSTVO / Russkoe Obshchestvo Dieiatelei Pechatnago Diela – Leningrad. v1-2. 1901-03 – 1r – 1 – us Ross [072]
PECHATNOYE DELO – St Petersburg. v. 1-4. Nov 24 1909-Mar 21 1912. Incomplete – 1 – us NY Public [072]
PECHATNOYE ISKUSSTVO – St Petersburg. v. 1-2. Oct 1901-Sept 1903 – 1 – us NY Public [700]
PECHATNYI VESTNIK – St Petersburg. v. 1, no. 1-18, v. 2, no. 1-5. May 15-Nov 27 1905; Feb 12-Mar 19 1906 – 1 – us NY Public [072]
PECHATNYI VIESTNIK – St Petersburg. v1-2. 1905-06 – 1r – 1 – us Ross [072]
PECHAT'SSSR – Moscow. 10v. 1922-38 – 1 – 23.00r – us L of C Photodup [070]
LA PECHE A SAINT JEAN DE LUZ / Louit, Ch – 9 – F60.00 – fr Ethnologie [240]
LA PECHE MARITIME... / David, R P F – Paris, 1897 – 2mf – 1 – ILM-471/1 – ne IDC [327]
PECHENEGI, TORKI I POLOVTSY DO NASHESTVIIA TARTAR / Golubovskii, P – Istoriia Iuzhno-Russkikh stepei IX-XIII vv. Izvestiia Universiteta Kiev. 1884. BU-631 2 – 8 – ne IDC [940]
Pecher, Erich *see* KOMPANIE IN POLEN
LES PECHERIES DE LA PROVINCE DE QUEBEC / Chambers, E T D – [Quebec]: Ministere de la colonisation, des mines et de pecheries de la province de Quebec, [1912]. SEM105P1950 – 3mf – 9 – Can$6.75 – cn Bibl Nat [639]
LES PECHERIES FRANCAISES SUR LES COTES D'ISLANDE / Gicquel, Francisque – Saint-Brieuc: Prud'homme, 1893 – 1 – F50.00 – fr Armell [630]
Pechey, J *see* A GENERAL TREATISE ON THE DISEASES OF INFANTS AND CHILDREN
Pechmeja, Jean de *see* TELEPHE EN 12 LIVRES
Peck *see*
- HISTORY OF CUMBERLAND COUNTY, MAINE
- HISTORY OF SUSQUEHANNA AND JUNIATA VALLEYS
- PAST AND PRESENT OF O'BRIEN AND OSCEOLA COUNTIES

Peck, C H *see*
- INDEX TO REPORTS OF SPECIES
- REPORTS OF SPECIES

Peck, Epaphroditus *see* THE PROPERTY RIGHTS OF HUSBAND AND WIFE UNDER THE LAW OF CONNECTICUT
Peck, George *see*
- AN ANSWER TO THE QUESTION, WHY ARE YOU A WESLEYAN METHODIST?
- APPEAL FROM TRADITION TO SCRIPTURE AND COMMON SENSE
- CHRISTIAN EXERTION
- THE LIFE AND TIMES OF REV. GEORGE PECK
- OUR COUNTRY
- THE SCRIPTURE DOCTRINE OF CHRISTIAN PERFECTION
- SKETCHES AND INCIDENTS, OR, A BUDGET FROM THE SADDLEBAGS OF A SUPERANNUATED ITINERANT
- SLAVERY AND THE EPISCOPACY
- SOUL PROBLEMS

Peck, George Bacheler *see* THE GATE AND THE CROSS, OR, PILGRIM'S PROGRESS IN ROMANS
Peck, George W *see* CYCLOPEDIA OF WISCONSIN
Peck, Harry Thurston *see* THE SEMITIC THEORY OF CREATION: A STUDY IN LANGUAGE
Peck, Hiram David *see* THE LAW OF MUNICIPAL CORPORATIONS IN THE STATE OF OHIO.
Peck, J M *see* DRAPER MANUSCRIPT, 24 NOV. 1842-27 OCT. 1869
Peck, Jesse Truesdell *see* THE TRUE WOMAN, OR, LIFE AND HAPPINESS AT HOME AND ABROAD
Peck, John M *see* THE TRAVELER'S DICTIONARY FOR ILLINOIS
Peck, John Mason *see*
- FATHER CLARK, OR, THE PIONEER PREACHER
- JOURNAL

Peck, Jonas Oramel *see* THE REVIVAL AND THE PASTOR
Peck, Melville *see* THE DOCTRINE OF PROXIMATE CAUSE AND LAST CLEAR CHANGE
Peck, S L *see* HISTORY OF IRA, VERMONT
Peck, Theodore S *see* REVISED ROSTER OF VERMONT VOLUNTEERS AND LISTS OF VERMONTERS WHO SERVED IN THE ARMY AND NAVY OF THE U.S. DURING THE WAR OF THE REBELLION 1861-66
Peckham, George A *see* AN INTRODUCTION TO THE STUDY OF OBADIAH
Pecock, Reginald *see* THE REPRESSOR OF OVERMUCH BLAMING OF THE CLERGY (RS19)
Pecquet, J *see* EXPERIMENTA NOVA ANATOMICA, QUIBUS
PECULIARITIES OF BEHAVIOR; WANDERING MANIA, DIPSOMANIA, CLEPTOMANIA, PYROMANIA AND ALLIED IMPULSIVE ACTS / Stekel, Wilhelm – Authorized Eng. version by James S. Van Teslaar.New York: Liveright, 1943. 2v – 1 – us U.W. Library [150]
THE PECULIARITIES OF DIVINE REVELATION IN ITS EARLIEST STAGE, OR, GENESIS FROM A MODERN POINT OF VIEW / Chapman, Charles – A lecture delivered before the Young Men's Association of Zion Church, and published at their request. Montreal: F. Grafton, 1871. 00617. (Pre-1900 Canadiana) – 9 – cn C.I.H.M. [240]
THE PECULIARITY OF THE RELIGION OF THE BIBLE / Orelli, Conrad von – New York: Eaton & Mains, 1908. 1 fiche – 9 – us A.T.L.A. [240]
PEDAGOGIA GENERAL / Malaga Garcia, Eduardo – Caceres: Tip. El Noticiero, 1946 – 1 – sp Bibl Santa Ana [370]
LA PEDAGOGIA JURIDICA NORTEAMERICANA / Chacon Zamora, Fernando – Santiago de Chile, 1948. 260p. LL-357 – 1 – us L of C Photodup [340]
PEDAGOGIA SOCIAL DEL GENERAL PERON / Bertotto, Jose Guillermo – Buenos Aires: Ediciones Hechos e Ideas, [1951] – 1 – CSUXADJ9170-B – us Hoover Inst Photo [370]
PEDAGOGIC THEORIES IN THE AGE OF ENLIGHTENMENT – Rare works. 66 titles on 163 fiches. Available individually – 9 – fr Hachette [944]
PEDAGOGICHESKAIA SISTEMA AKADEMII KHUDOZHESTV 18 VEKA / Moleva, N & Beliutin, E – M. 1956. BR-7706 2 – 8 – ne IDC [370]
PEDAGOGICHESKII LISTOK – Dlia roditelei i vospitatelei. Spb. 1871-85. Lacking: 1881, v. 2. BR-4156 2 – 8 – ne IDC [370]
PEDAGOGICHESKII LISTOK S. PETERBURGSKIKH ZHENSKIKH GIMNAZII – v. 1-3. Spb. 1873-74. BR-4155 2 – 8 – ne IDC [370]
PEDAGOGICHESKII VESTNIK MOSKOVSKAGO UCHEBNAGO OKRUGA – Sredniaia shkola. M. 1911-16. Lacking: v. 4 (2), 1912. BR-3776 2 – 8 – ne IDC [370]
PEDAGOGICHESKOE OBOZRENIE – Periodicheskoe izdanie dlia uchitelei srednei i nachal'noi shkol, roditelei i vospitatelei. v. 1-8. M. 1912-14. BR-3786 2 – 8 – ne IDC [370]
LA PEDAGOGIE FEMININE / Rousselot, Paul – Paris: Delagrave, 1881. 234p. (Les Femmes Collection) – 3mf – 9 – $8.00 – fr Bibl Nationale [370]
PEDAGOGISK FORSKNING – v1-14. 1957-70 – 1 – us UMI [073]
LES PEDAGOGUES DE PORT-ROYAL / Carre, I – 1887 – 9 – fr I.C.S. [240]
Pedamon, Michel *see* LA REFORME MONETAIRE DE 1948 EN ALLEMAGNE OCCIDENTALE ET LE DROIT DES OBLIGATIONS
PEDANG KILAT DARI GUNUNG THIAN SAN;.. / An, Todjin – Djakarta: Marga Raya, 1963. 6 pts. in 1v. 384p – 1 – us U.W. Library [950]
PEDANG PEMBUNUH ASMARA / Kwee, Oen Keng – 8v. 1963 – 9 – SE-5242 1 – ne IDC [360]
PEDAS BELUH. KITAB OGEN MAN DANAK-DANAK SI MBARU ERLADJAR NGOGE HURUP LATIN, IBAS SEKOLAH-SEKOLAH SI MAKE TJAKAP KARO / Soaloon, A Sutan – SE 5445 1. v. 1 only. 1962 – 9 – ne IDC [950]
Pedashenko, A D *see* UKAZATEL' KNIG, ZHURNAL'NYKH I GAZETNYKH STATEI PO SEL' SKOMU KHOZIAISTVU ZA 1890-1911 GG
Pedde, Dennis R *see* AN ANALYSIS OF JOHANN LYDWIG KREBS' EIGHT CHORALE PRELUDES FOR ORGAN WITH TRUMPET OR OBOE
Pede, I, N N -v *see* ROSPIS' OTDEL'NYKH KNIG PO SEL'SKOMU KHOZIAISTVU NAPECHATANNYKH S 1730 PO 1884 GOD
Pedersen, Paul B *see* THE TOBA BATAK LANGUAGE: INTRODUCTION GRAMMAR AND SENTENCE PATTERNS
Pederson, Lee *see* LINGUISTIC ATLAS OF THE GULF STATES
Pederson, Troy S *see* THE EFFECTS OF SPATTING AND ANKLE TAPING ON INVERSION BEFORE AND AFTER EXERCISE
THE PEDESTAL – Vancouver. 1969-74 – 1 – $75.00 – cn McLaren [640]
PEDIATRIA – v1- 1958- 1; v15- 5,6; v18- 9 – us UMI [618]
PEDIATRIC AND ADOLESCENT GYNECOLOGY / International Federation of Infantile and Juvenile Gynecology – v1-. 1983- – 1,5,6,9 – us UMI [073]
PEDIATRIC CARDIOLOGY – v.1, 1979 80. ISSN:0172-0643 – 1,5,6,9,13 – 64.00v – us UMI [618]
PEDIATRIC CLINICS OF INDIA – v1- 1966- 1; v7- 5,6; v10- 9 – us UMI [618]
PEDIATRIC CLINICS OF NORTH AMERICA – v1- 1954- 1; v14- 5,6; v22- 9 – us UMI [618]
PEDIATRIC EMERGENCY CARE – v1-12. 1985-96 – 12r – 1,5,6,9 – $70.00r – us Williams [618]
PEDIATRIC INFECTIOUS DISEASE JOURNAL – (Also available on CD-ROM: 1984-90 $395.00) – v1-15. 1982-96 – 15r – 1,5,6,9 – $90.00r – us Williams [610]
PEDIATRIC NEUROSURGERY – v1-. 1975- – 1,5,9 – us UMI [617]
PEDIATRIC NURSING – v1- 1975- 1; v4- 5,6,9 – us UMI [610]
PEDIATRIC PATHOLOGY – v1-. 1983- – 1,5,6,9 – us UMI [618]
PEDIATRIC PHYSICAL THERAPY : OFFICIAL PUBLICATION OF THE SECTION ON PEDIATRICS OF THE AMERICAN PHYSICAL THERAPY ASSOCIATION – v1-8. 1989-1996 – 8r – 1,5,6,9 – $65.00r – us Williams [618]
PEDIATRIC PULMONOLOGY – v1-. 1985- – 1,5,6,9 – us UMI [618]
PEDIATRIC RADIOLOGY – v. 1-10. 1973-80 – 1,5,9 – 675.00 – us UMI [618]
PEDIATRIC RESEARCH – v1-40. 1967-96 – 1,5,6,9 – $105.00r – us Williams [618]
PEDIATRIC REVIEWS AND COMMUNICATIONS / ed by Burman, David & Lanzkowsky, Philip – 9,5,1 – us Harwood [618]
PEDIATRICS – v1- 1948- 1; v49- 5,6; v55- 9 – us UMI [618]
PEDIATRICS AND RELATED TOPICS / ed by Schneeweiß, Burkhard – 1,5,9 – us Gordon [618]
PEDIATRIE – v29- 1974- 1,5,6; v30- 9 – us UMI [618]
Pedigo, Virginia G *see* HISTORY OF PATRICK AND HENRY COUNTIES
A PEDIGREE OF THE FORSTERS AND FOSTERS, OF THE NORTH OF ENGLAND, AND OF SOME OF THE FAMILIES CONNECTED WITH THEM / Foster, Joseph – Printed for private circulation, 1871. 2v. in 1. fold. geneal. tables. 2nd ed – 1 – us U.W. Library [920]
PEDIGREES OF THE COUNTY FAMILIES OF YORKSHIRE...AND AUTHENTICATED BY THE MEMBERS OF EACH FAMILY / Foster, Joseph – London: The compiler, 1874. 3v genealogical tables (part fold.), coats of arms – 1 – us U.W. Library [920]
PEDOMAN / Indonesian Socialist Party – Djakarta, 1947, 1951-57 (all incompl) – 1 – us Hoover Inst Photo [335]
PEDOMAN / Indonesian Socialist Party – Djakarta, Indonesia. Nov 29 1968-Jan 23 1974 – 11r – 1 – us L of C Photodup [072]
PEDOMAN DAN BEKAL OENTOEK GOEROE... – (Lacking: 1915(3). 1917(3,4,12)) – 1915-1917 – 16mf – 9 – ne IDC [950]
PEDOMAN GURU – (Lacking: 1949 v2(3,10). 1950 v3(2)) – Djakarta, Dep. Pendidikan, Keboedajaan dan Pengetahoean. Dec., 1947/48-1950. v1-3(3) – 16mf – 9 – ne IDC [370]
PEDOMAN KOTA BANDUNG / Indonesia. Bandung – 1951 – 9 – SE-5338 1 – ne IDC [910]
PEDOMAN PROPAGANDA / Mutiara, Dali – SE-4448 1. 1946? – 9 – ne IDC [950]
PEDOMAN PUASA / Ashshiddiqy, Muhammad Hasbi – SE-4591 1. 1963 – 9 – ne IDC [950]
PEDOMAN RAKJAT – Ujung Pandang, Indonesia. June 1965-Dec 1965; Aug 1967-Jun 1993 – 74r – 1 – us L of C Photodup [072]

PEDOMAN SEMENTARA / Jakarta. Universitas Indonesia. Fakultas Sastra – SE-2935 1 – 9 – ne IDC [950]
PEDOMAN-KERDJA PENERANGAN DALAM ALAM MANIPOL / Ruslan, Abdulgani – SE 4562 1. 1962 – 9 – ne IDC [320]
Pedot, Lino M *see* LA S.C. DE PROPAGANDA FIDE E LE MISSIONI DEL GINPPANE (1622-1838)
Pedrajas y Nunez-Moreno, Eloy *see*
- COMPENDIO HISTORIA ECLESIASTICA
- LECCIONES DE HISTORIA SAGRADA

Pedrajas y Nunez-Romero, Eloy *see* GUADALUPE, IMPRESIONES ARTISTICO-RELIGIOSAS
Pedreira, Antonio S *see* BIBLIOGRAFIA PUERTORRIQUENA (1493-1930). MADRID, 1932
PEDRERIAS DAVILA. CONTRIBUCION AL ESTUDIO DE LA FIGURA DEL "GRAN JUSTADOR", GOBERNADOR DE CASTILLA DEL ORO Y NICARAGUA. MADRID, 1934 / Alvarez Rubiano, Pablo – Madrid: Razon y Fe, 1945 – 1 – sp Bibl Santa Ana [350]
Pedrero Nieto, G *see* CATALOGO PARCIAL I DEL ARCHIVO HISTORICO DIOCESANO DE SAN CRISTOBAL DE LAS CASAS, CHIAPAS
Pedret de Falgas, Ramon *see* PRINCIPIOS BASICOS Y ESTRUCTURAS DE LA ORGANIZACION SINDICAL; NOTAS ACERCA DE "LO SINDICAL"
PEDRO 2 Y EL INFANTE ALFONSO (ANNO 1276-1285) – Barcelona – 1r – 5,6 – sp Cultura [946]
PEDRO ALVARADO, 4TH CENTENARIO DE LA MUERTE DE...1541-1941 / Herrero, Miguel – Madrid: Revista de Indias, 1941 – 1 – sp Bibl Santa Ana [920]
Pedro, Conde de Barcellos *see* NOBILARIO DEL CONDE DON PEDRO, HIJO DEL REY DON DIONIS DE PORTUGAL
Pedro de Alcantara, Saint *see*
- COMPENDIOSO...TRATADO DE LA ORACION
- ESTUDIOS SOBRE SAN PEDRO DE ALCANTARA
- OEUVRES SPIRITUELLES
- TRATADO DE LA ORACION
- TRATADO DE LA ORACION Y LA MEDITACION
- TRATADO DE LA ORACION Y MEDITACION
- TRATADO DE LA ORACION Y MEDITACION. CON BREVE INTRODUCCION Y UN TRATADO DE LOS TRES VOTOS DE LA RELIGION POR FRAY GERONYMO DE FERRERA

Pedro de Almendralejo *see* SERMON...ORDEN SERAPHICA
PEDRO DE ALVARADO, CONQUISTADOR. PRINCETON, 1932 / Kelly, John Eogan – Madrid: Razon y Fe, 1936 – 1 – sp Bibl Santa Ana [910]
PEDRO DE SAN BUENAVENTURA : VOCABULARIO DE LA LENGUA TAGALA – Madrid, SP. 1613 – 1,5 – sp Cultura [240]
PEDRO DE VALDIVIA / Errazuriz, Crescente – Santiago de Chile: Imp. Cervantes, Tomo 1. 1911...y Tomo 2 – sp Bibl Santa Ana [920]
PEDRO DE VALDIVIA / Pardo, Antonio – Madrid: Publicaciones Espanolas, 2nd ed 1959. Col. Temas espanoles, no 43 – sp Bibl Santa Ana [920]
PEDRO DE VALDIVIA / Valdivia, Pedro de – Madrid: Ed. Fe, 1945 – 1 – sp Bibl Santa Ana [920]
PEDRO DE VALDIVIA CONQUITADOR DE CHILE / Rusula, Jose de & Solar y Taboada, Antonio del – Badajoz: La Minerva Extremena, 1928 – 1 – sp Bibl Santa Ana [946]
PEDRO DE VALDIVIA. INTERROGANTES PARA SU BIOGRAFIA / Manzano de Garias, Antonio – Badajoz: Dip. Provincial, 1956. Sep. REE – sp Bibl Santa Ana [920]
PEDRO DE VALENCIA. ESTUDIO BIOGRAFICO Y CRITICO / Serrano Sanz, Manuel – Badajoz: Tip. y Lib. Antonio Arqueros, 1910. Biblioteca Archivo Extremeno – sp Bibl Santa Ana [920]
Pedro de Vitoria, Fray *see* DOS OBRAS...FIEL CRISTIANO
Pedro Pascual, Saint, Bp. of Jaen *see* OBRAS. EN SU LENGUA ORIGINAL CON LA TRADUCCION LATINA Y ALGUNAS ANOTACIONES POR PEDRO ARMENGOL VALENZUELA
Pedroso de Acin. Ayuntamiento *see* MEMORIA QUE SUSCRIBE EL ALCALDE-PRESIDENTE Y EL...PARA DAR A CONOCER CON DETTALE LA LABOR EXTRAORDINARIA...HASTA FINALES DE 1958
Pedroso, Nicolas Ignacio *see* TRATADO DE ARMAS Y EXPLOSIVOS
PEDWAR CYFLWR DYN...WEDI EI GHFIEITHU O'R SAESONEG GAN I. PARRY / Boston, Thomas – Caerlleon, 1821. 438p – 1 – us U.W. Library [100]
PEE DEE ADVOCATE – Bennettsville. S.C. 1903-1914; 1915-1939 – 1 – us UMI [071]
PEEBLESHIRE NEWS – 1 – £42.00r – uk Scot News [072]
PEEBLES-SHIRE, 1837 : BRITISH ISLES CENSUS DIRECTORIES PROJECT, SCOTLAND. VOL 49 – 1mf – 9 – A$9.00 – at Vine [941]
PEEBLES-SHIRE, 1915 : BRITISH ISLES CENSUS DIRECTORIES PROJECT, SCOTLAND. VOL 11 – 1mf – 9 – A$9.00 – at Vine [941]
Peeke, Hewson L *see* HISTORY OF ERIE COUNTY
PEEL BIBLIOGRAPHY / National Library of Canada – 9 – cn Nat'l Library [971]
PEEL CITY GUARDIAN – Dec 2 1882-Nov 29, Dec 6 1884-Nov 27, Dec 4 1886-Nov 24 1888; May 4-Dec 28 1889; 1890-93; Jan 13-Dec 29 1894; 1895-1904; Jan 5-Dec 23 1905; 1906-64; Jan 9 1965-70; Jan 9-Dec 1971; Jan 8-Dec 1972; 1973-78; Jan 13-Dec 29 1979; 1980-81; Aug-Dec 1986; Mar 10-Dec 12 1987; 1988-Jun, Jul 7-Dec 22 1990; Jan 19-Jun 22, Jul 6-Dec 21 1991; Jan 11-Jun 27, Jul 11-Dec 26 1992; Jan 9-Jun 26, Jul-Dec 1993; Jan 8 1994-Jun 1997 – 76 1/2r – 1 – uk British Libr Newspaper [072]
Peel, Dorothy Constance Bayliff *see* HOW WE LIVED THEN, 1914-1918: A SKETCH OF SOCIAL AND DOMESTIC LIFE IN ENGLAND DURING THE WAR
Peel, Frank *see* THE RISINGS OF THE LUDDITES, CHARTISTS AND PLUGDRAWERS
Peel, Robert *see* CORRESPONDENCE
Peele, Stanton Canfield *see* THE GENERAL PRINCIPLES OF THE LAW OF INSURANCE
Peelle, Will J *see* DIARY
PEER GYNT NO. 1, OP. 46 : SELECTIONS, ARR. FOR ORGAN BY E.H. LEMARE / Grieg, E & LeMare, E H – 1 – us Sibley [780]
PEERAGE AND PEDIGREE : STUDIES IN PEERAGE LAW AND FAMILY HISTORY / Round, J H – London. 2v. 1910 – 15mf – 9 – H-1157/2 – ne IDC [920]
THE PEERLESS PROPHET : OR, THE LIFE AND TIMES OF JOHN THE BAPTIST / McCullagh, Archibald – New York: Anson D F Randolph, c1888 – 1mf – 9 – 0-8370-4173-2 – 1985-2173 – us A.T.L.A. [920]
Peers, A Allison *see* OUR DEBT TO SPAIN. LONDON, 1938
Peery Family *see* PAPERS OF THE PEERY FAMILY
Peet, T E *see*
- THE CEMETERIES OF ABYDOS (MEES VOL 34)
- THE CEMETERIES OF ABYDOS (MEES VOL 35)
- THE CITY OF AKHENATEN (MEES VOL 38)
- A COMPARATIVE STUDY OF THE LITERATURES OF EGYPT, PALESTINE AND MESOPOTAMIA

PEG WOOFINGTON / Reade, Charles L – British Fiction Archive: Unit 2 – 9 – uk Bell [830]
PEGANY – Boston. v. 1-3, no. 4. 1930-Mar 1933 – 1 – us NY Public [073]
PEGAS – Zhurnal iskusstv. v. 1-10. M. 1915-16. B-1110 2 – 8 – ne IDC [073]
PEGASUS – U. S. 1943-57 – 1 – 76.00 – us L of C Photodup [629]
Pegel, Walter *see* OHNE BEFEHL
PEGINAS ESCOGIDAS / Cento, Fernando – Caracas, 1930; Madrid: Razon y Fe, 1932 – 1 – sp Bibl Santa Ana [946]
PEGMA, CUM NARRATIONIBUS PHILOSOPHICIS / Costalius, Petrus – O-587. 1555 – 9 – ne IDC [100]
Pegues, A W *see* OUR BAPTIST MINISTERS AND SCHOOLS
Pegues, T *see*
- DEFENSIONES THEOLOGIAE DIVI THOMAE AQUINATIS
- DEFENSIONES THEOLOGIAE DIVI THOMAE AQUINATIS. VOL 1-7

DIE PEHLEVIVERSION DES ERSTEN CAPITELS DES VENDIDAED / Geiger, W – Erlangen, 1877 – 1mf – NE-20154/1 – ne IDC [490]
P'EI LING YEN CHING HUI (CCC259) – (In Chinese) – [s.l: s.n, 1950] – 1r – 1 – 1984-6598 – us A.T.L.A. [240]
A PEIA : JORNAL CRITICO, HUMORISTICO E NOTICIOSO – Manaos, Amazonas. 1 Jan-26 Dez 1926 – 1,5,6 – bl Biblioteca [072]
PEI-CHING JIH-PAO – Peking, China. Peking Daily. Jan 1954-Oct 1968. 27 reels – 1 – 654.00 – us Chinese Res [072]
PEI-CHING WAN PAO – Peking, China. Feb 26 1959-June 28 1964; June 30 1964-66 – 4r – 1 – us L of C Photodup [072]
Peigne-Delacourt, M *see* CARTULAIRE DE L'ABBAYE DE NOTRE DAME D'OURSCAMP
THE PEIHO AND PEKING / Martin, William A P – 1860 – 1 – $50.00 – us Presbyterian [950]
Peill, J *see* THE BELOVED PHYSICIAN OF TSANG CHOU
Pein, Richard L *see* THE EFFECTS OF AN INDUCED INTERNAL AND EXTERNAL ATTENTIONAL FOCUS UPON UPPER BODY STRENGTH
Pein, Wayne E *see* THE CHANGE IN OXYGEN CONSUMPTION OVER TIME IN DOWNHILL VERSUS LEVEL GRADE RUNNING
Peinado, I *see* DIPUTATIONES IN UNIVERSAM ARISTOTELIS LOGICAM
LA PEINE AUX CHAUMIERES / Guillaumin, Emile – Nevers. 1909. (La Condition Ouvriere. Part Two.) – 9 – 5.00 – fr Bibl Nationale [360]
LE PEINTRE AMATEUR ET CURIEUX / Mensaert, G P – O-988 1. 1763 – 9 – ne IDC [760]
LE PEINTRE-GRAVEUR ILLUSTRE / Delteil, H L – 1906-30.32v – 9 – $148.00 – uk Chadwyck [760]
LA PEINTURE ANGLAISE. 18E ET 19E SIECLES / Reunion des musees nationaux. Paris – 1938. 4 fiches – 9 – fr Réunion [700]
LA PEINTURE INDIENNE A L'EPOQUE DES GRANDS MOGHOLS / Stchoukine, I – Paris. 1929. BI-1140 1 – 9 – ne IDC [750]
LA PEINTURE RELIGIEUSE EN BULGARIE / Grabar, A – Paris. 1928. BR-3822 2 – 8 – ne IDC [240]
PEINTURES DE GOYA DES COLLECTIONS DE FRANCE / Reunion des musees nationaux. Paris – 1938. 19 illus. 1 fiche – 9 – fr Réunion [700]
LES PEINTURES MURALES POSTCLASSIQUES DU QUINTANA ROO, MEXIQUE / Fettweis-Vienot, M – Du catalogue au dechiffrement, recherche d'une methode et application a deux cas: Coba et Xelha – 15 – F140.00 – fr Ethnologie [306]
LES PEINTURES RUPESTRES DE LA "TOCA DO INDIO", ANDRELANDIA, MINAS GERAIS, BRESIL / Prous, A et al – 1987 – 8mf – 9 – F250.00 – fr Ethnologie [750]
PEINTURES RUPESTRES DE VARZEA GRANDE, PIAUI, BRESIL, NO. 2 / Guidon, N – 9 – F50.00 – fr Ethnologie [306]
LES PEINTURES RUPESTRES DU PARC NATIONAL DE SETE CIDADES, ETAT DU PIAUI, BRESIL / Monzon, S – 6mf – 9 – F80.00 – fr Ethnologie [306]
LES PEINTURES RUPESTRES DU PARC NATIONAL DE SETE CIDADES, ETAT DU PIAUI, BRESIL / Monzon, S – Le site no. 10 – 9 – F50.00 – fr Ethnologie [306]
LES PEINTURES RUPESTRES DU PARC NATIONAL DE SETE CIDADES, ETAT DU PIAUI, BRESIL / Monzon, S – Le site no. 4 – 9 – F70.00 – fr Ethnologie [306]
Peip, Albert *see*
- DAS CREDO DER KIRCHE UND DIE INTELLIGENZ DES ZEITGEISTES
- ZUM BEWEIS DES GLAUBENS

Peiping. Institute of Social Research. Academia Sinica *see* SHE-HUI-K' O-HSUEH TSA-CHIH
Peiping. Palace Museum *see*
- KU-KUNG CHOU-K'AN
- KU-KUNG SHU-HUA CHI
- KU-KUNG YUEH-K'AN

Peirce, Bradford Kinney *see* THE WORD OF GOD OPENED: ITS INSPIRATION, CANON, AND INTERPRETATION
Peirce, Charles Sanders *see* STUDIES IN LOGIC
Peirce, W *see*
- THE ECCLESIASTICAL PRINCIPLES AND POLITY OF THE WESLEYAN METHODISTS...
- THE ECCLESIASTICAL PRINCIPLES AND POLITY OF THE WESLEYAN METHODISTS;...

Peirce, William Shannon *see* "REMINISCENCES OF THE BAR"
Peiro, Francisco *see* EL EVANGELIO COMENTADO CONFERENCIAS POR RADIO
Peiser, Felix Ernst *see*
- DIE ASSYRISCHE VERBTAFEL
- KEILSCHRIFTLICHE ACTEN-STUECKE AUS BABYLONISCHEN STAEDTEN

Peiser, Jacob *see* DIE GESCHICHTE DER SYNAGOGEN-GEMEINDE ZU STETTIN
Peiser, Juergen *see* GUSTAV STRUVE ALS POLITISCHER SCHRIFTSTELLER UND REVOLUTIONAER
Peisker, Martin *see* DIE BEZIEHUNGEN DER NICHTISRAELITEN ZU JAHVE
Peixoto, A *see* CASTRO ALVES, O POETA E O POEMA
Peixoto, Alzira Vargas do Amaral *see* GETULIO VARGAS, MEU PAI
PEJMURDE / Ekrem, Recaizade Mahmut – Kostantiniye: Alem Matbaasi, 1312 [1896] – $45.00 – us MEDOC [470]
PEKAN INDUSTRI NASIONAL, 1961 / Tjirebon, Java – "Pekan Industri Nasional," Untuk Menjambut Perajaan Peringatan Hari Ulang Tahun Ke 55 Berdirinja Pemerintahan Kotapradja Tjirebon, Tanggal 1 Djuni S D 30 Djuni 1961 Di Tjirebon. SE 4496 1. 1961 – 9 – ne IDC [950]
PEKAN RAYA WINDU KEMERDEKAAN REPUBLIK INDONESIA / Jogjakarta. Indonesia – 1961. 32p. BSEM-3912/1 – 9 – ne IDC [950]
Pekarskii, E K *see* SLOVAR' IAKUTSKOGO IAZYKA
Pekarskii, P P *see*
- DOPOLNENIIA K ISTORII MASONSTVA V ROSSII V 18 STOLETII
- ISTORIIA IMP. AKADEMII NAUK V PETERBURGE

Pekarskii, V F *see*
- K VOPROSU O MUNITSIPAL'NO-KOOPERATIVNOI ORGANIZATSII NARODNOGO PRODOVOL'STVIIA V SEVERNOI OBLASTI
- ZADACHI I OSNOVNYE PRINTSIPY ORGANIZATSII SOIUZOV KOOPERATIVOV (GLAVNYM OBRAZOM – POTREBITEL'NYKH)

PEKERDJA MINJAK DI INDONESIA. PENJUSUNAN BUKU INI DISELENGGARAKAN / Standard-Vacuum Oil Company – SE 3466 1 – 9 – ne IDC [660]
PEKIN, YEDDO, SAN FRANCISCO. VOYAGE AUTOUR DU MONDE / Beauvoir – Neuvieme ed. Paris, Plon. 1876 – 9 – 12.50 – fr Orientalistes [910]
PEKING – Reich Gottes in China. nos. 1, 2, 7, 8. 1930-36. BCH-1205 1 – 9 – ne IDC [240]
PEKING AND TIENTSIN TIMES – Peking. China. -w. 10 Mar 1894-18 Oct 1902. (4 reels) – 1 – uk British Libr Newspaper [072]
THE PEKING CHRONICLE – Peking, China. 28 Nov 1937-26 Oct 1941. Incomplete. 3 reels – 1 – 42.75 – us Chinese Res [072]
PEKING DAILY NEWS – Peking, 1914-17 – 3r – 1 – us Ross [072]
Peking, Foreign Languages Press *see* FORTY-ONE RED HEARTS ARE WITH CHAIRMAN MAO FOR EVER
PEKING GAZETTE – Peking, 1915-17 – 6r – 1 – us Ross [072]
PEKING GAZETTE – Peking, China. Aug 14 1915-Nov 20 1917 – 1 – us NY Public [072]
PEKING LEADER – Peking, 1918-19 – 1r – 1 – us Ross [072]
THE PEKING LEADER – Peking, China. 27 Sept 1925-10 Jan 1932. Incomplete. 13 reels – 1 – 205.00 – us Chinese Res [072]
THE PEKING LEADER – Peking, China. June 1 1918-Oct 31 1919. Incomplete – 1 – us NY Public [072]
PEKING NEWS – Peking, China. Daily. Feb 20 1914-Oct 31 1917. Incomplete – 1 – us NY Public [072]
PEKING REVIEW – 1973- – 9 – us UMI [073]
PEKING REVIEW : FOREIGN LANGUAGES PRESS – Peking, 1958-67 – 511mf – 9 – CH-167/2 – ne IDC [950]
PEKING REVIEW – v. 1-7. 1958-64 – 1 – 187.00 – us L of C Photodup [950]
PEKINGER DEUTSCHE ZEITUNG *see* THE CHINESE PUBLIC OPINION
PEKINGER TAGEBLATT – Peking. 1900 (no. 599), 1901 (nos. 1-19). BCH-1204 1 – 9 – ne IDC [950]
Peladeau, Pierre *see*
- JOURNAL DE MONTREAL
- LE MONDE DES AFFAIRES

PELADJARAN BAHASA NIPPON : DJILID 3 / JAVA. (Japanese Military Administration 1942-45) – (N.p., n.d.) – 56-57mf – 9 – ne IDC [350]
PELADJARAN BAHASA NIPPON CHUNGHUA INDONESIA. (OLEH) YANG KWONG / Yang, Kuang – (Microfiches Nos 182-185) – Ed 4. Djakarta, Kwong Tay, 2603.-xii/280p, viii – 4mf – 9 – SE-2002/1 – ne IDC [950]

PELADJARAN BAHASA NIPPON OENTOEK OEMOEM : DJILID PERTAMA – Djakarta, Djawa Gunseikanbu, 2605. 165, 3, 39p – 127-129mf – 9 – ne IDC [950]

PELADJARAN BAHASA TIONGHWA, DENGAN KAMOES HARIAN INDONESIA-TIONGHWA, PERKATAAN BIASA DAN SADERHANA. TJETAKAN 1 / Lim, Kwi Tie N – Malang: Paragon Press, 2602. 126p – 99-100mf – 9 – ne IDC [950]

PELADJARAN DARI REVOLUSI / Lenin, Vladimir Ilyich – SE-2959 1. 1960 – 9 – ne IDC [335]

PELADJARAN HUKUM INDONESIA / Simorangkir, J C T – SE 4056 1. 1962 – 9 – ne IDC [950]

PELADJARAN MERANGKAI BUNGA / Rini, K W – 9 – ne IDC [950]

Pelaez, Florentino *see* A EXTREMADURA

Pelaez Lorenzo, Luis *see* DISLEXIAS

PELAGIUS'S EXPOSITIONS OF THIRTEEN EPISTLES OF ST PAUL : 1. INTRODUCTION. 2. TEXT AND APPARATUS CRITICUS. 3. PSEUDO-JEROME INTERPOLATIONS / Souter, A – 3pts in 1v. 1931 – 19mf – 9 – ne Slangenburg [220]

PELAPOERAN. LAPORAN / Bank Negara. Indonesia – Djakarta, 1946-1970. TEN 151 – 22mf – 9 – ne IDC [380]

PELE-MELE : HUMOUR, NOUVELLES, CINEMA – Montreal. v1 no 1 16fev 1930-. SEM35P166 – 1r – 1 – Can$15.00 – cn Bibl Nat [073]

LE PELERIN – Ste-Cunegonde [Quebec]: J.U.A. Geoffrion, [1895] – 9 – cn C.I.H.M. [971]

UN PELERINAGE AU PAYS D'EVANGELINE / Casgrain, Henri-Raymond – Quebec: L. Demers, 1887. 00528. (Pre-1900 Canadiana) – 9 – cn C.I.H.M. [390]

LE PELERINAGE DE VIE HUMAINE / Deguilleville, Guillaume de; ed by Stueirzinger, J J – London. 3v. 1893-1897 – 17mf – 8 – Dfl116.00 – ne Slangenburg [240]

Pelesh, Iuliian *see* GESCHICHTE DER UNION DER RUTHENISCHEN KIRCHE MIT ROM VON DEN ALTESTEN ZEITEN BIS AUF DIE GEGENWART

Peletier du Mans, J *see*
- L'ART POETIQUE
- DIALOGUE DE L'ORTHOGRAPHE E PRONONCIATION FRANCOESE

PELHAM 1709-1849 – (Mf 1T-2T: Births & Deaths 1709-1820. Mf 3T-4T: Births 1769-1844. Mf 4T: Deaths 1817-44; Marriages & Publ 1768-86. Mf 5T: Marriages & Publ 1746-1816) – (mf ed 1998) – 7mf – 9 – 0-87623-313-2 – us Holbrook [920]

PELHAM 1738-1895 – (Mf 1-2: Births & Deaths 1743-1819. Mf 3-5: Proprietors Records 1738-67. Mf 6-10: Town Meetings 1742-84. Mf 10: Marriages & Intentions 1746-80. Mf 11-17: Town Minutes 1784-1815. Mf 17-18: Marriages & Intentions 1786-1815. Mf 19-21: Marriages & Intentions 1815-72. Mf 22-24: Births & Deaths 1820-44. Mf 25: Births, Marriages, Deaths 1843-60. Mf 26-27: Deaths 1861-1905. Mf 28-29: Deaths 1906-88. Mf 30: Marriages 1860-1905. Mf 31: Births 1860-95) – (mf ed 1989) – 31mf – 9 – 0-87623-094-X – us Holbrook [920]

PELHAM ROAD BAPTIST CHURCH. GREENVILLE, SOUTH CAROLINA : CHURCH RECORDS – 1974-75.Missions Committee Minutes, 58p – 1 – 5.00 – us Baptist [240]

PELICULAS DE AVENTURAS / Carrasco, Castulo – Caceres: Imprenta Moderna, 1955. Cuad. Alcantara, no 12 – sp Bibl Santa Ana [946]

PELITA – Djakarta, Indonesia. Apr 1974-1993 – 66r – 1 – us L of C Photodup [072]

Pellan, Alfred *see*
- ALFRED PELLAN ET SON OEUVRE
- OEUVRE

Pellaz y Espinosa, Manuel *see* DEFENSA Y VERDADERO MANIFIESTO DE LA VIA CURATIVA QUE D. MANUEL PELLAZ Y ESPINOSA...

Pellechet, M *see* NOTES SUR LES LIVRES LITURGIQUES DES DIOCESES D'AUTUN, CHALON ET MACON

Pellegrini, Matteo *see*
- DELLE ACVTEZZE, CHE ALTRIMENTI SPIRITI, VIVEZZE, E CONCETTI, VOLGARMENTE SI APPELLANO, TRATTATO. IN QUESTA SECONDA IMPRESSIONE DALL AUTORE RIUISTE, E MIGLIORATE
- POLITICA MASSIMA DIUISA IN DICIASETTE DECLAMATIONI

Pellerin, Joseph-Michel *see*
- 19 OEUVRES MICROFILMEES ENSEMBLE
- CORRESPONDANCE INEDITE(...) 5 MAI 1789 – 29 MAI 1790
- COURS D'ETUDE, OU RECUEIL DES DEVOIRS DONNES DANS LES COURS DE QUATRIEME...

Pelletan, Jean Gabriel *see* MEMOIRE SUR LA COLONIE FRANCAISE DU SENEGAL

Pelletan, Jean-Gabriel *see* MEMOIRE SUR LA COLONIE FRANCAISE DU SENEGAL, AVEC QUELQUES CONSIDERATIONS HISTORIQUES ET POLITIQUES SUR LA TRAITE DES NEGRES, SUR LEUR CARACTERE, ET ...A LA PROSPERITE DE CETTE COLONIE

Pelletier, Albert *see* LES IDEES

Pelletier, Alexis *see* M. L'ABBE SAX ET SES SOUFFLEURS

Pelletier, Carmen *see* BIBLIOGRAPHIE ANALYTIQUE DE L'OEUVRE, 1941-1960, DE MONSIEUR PIERRE-PAUL TURGEON, NOTAIRE

Pelletier, J -Antoine *see* BIO-BIBLIOGRAPHIE DE L'ABBE JOSEPH-WILLIAM-IVANHOE CARON, 1875-1941

Pelletier, J G *see* L'OPINION FRANCAISE ET LA GUERRE DES BOERS

Pelletier, Jacqueline *see* BIBLIOGRAPHIE ANALYTIQUE DE L'OEUVRE DE M. L'ABBE ARTHUR MAHEUX DE LA SOCIETE ROYALE DU CANADA, ARCHIVISTE DU SEMINAIRE DE QUEBEC

Pelletier, Madeleine *see*
- L'EMANCIPATION SEXUELLE DE LA FEMME
- LA FEMME EN LUTTE POUR SES DROITS

Pellett, H A H *see* THE RELATIONSHIP BETWEEN HEALTH-RELATED PHYSICAL FITNESS LEVELS AND ACADEMIC ACHIEVEMENT IN ELEMENTARY STUDENTS

Pellett, Tracy L *see*
- THE EFFECT OF REFINEMENT AND TEACHER FEEDBACK ON FEMALE JUNIOR HIGH SCHOOL STUDENTS' VOLLEYBALL PRACTICE SUCCESS AND ACHIEVEMENT
- VISUAL PRETRAINING EFFECTS ON COINCIDENT TIMING SKILL ACQUISITION AND RETENTION

Pellew, George *see*
- JOHN JAY
- THE LIFE AND CORRESPONDENCE OF THE RIGHT HONOURABLE HENRY ADDINGTON, FIRST VISCOUNT SIDMOUTH

Pelliccia, Alexius Aurelius *see* THE POLITY OF THE CHRISTIAN CHURCH OF EARLY, MEDIAEVAL, AND MODERN TIMES

Pellicer de Tovar, Joseph *see*
- MISSION EVANGELICA AL REYNO DE CONGO POR LA SERAFICA RELIGION DE LOS CAPUCHINOS
- MISSION EVANGELICA AL REYNO DE CONGO POR LA SERAFICA RELIGION DE LOS CAPUCINOS

Pellicer Saforcada, Juan Antonio *see*
- ENSAYO DE UNA BIBLIOTECA DE TRADUCTORES ESPANOLES

Pellicier *see* MEMOIRE QUATRIEME MEMOIRE SUR LA NECESSITE DE FONDER UNE ECOLE POUR FORMER DES MAITRES, SELON LE PLAN D'EDUCATION DONNE PAR LE PARLEMENT

Pelligra, D *see* LE ROLE DES MISSIONNAIRES DANS L'ACCULTURATION EN AMERIQUE DU SUD

Pelliot, P *see*
- LA FILLE DE MO-TCH'O QAGHAN ET SES RAPPORTS AVEC KUL-TEGIN
- L'INSCRIPTION CHINOISE D'IDIQNTSAHRI
- LES MONGOLS ET LA PAPAUTE
- NOTE SUR LES TOU-YU-HOUEN ET LES SOU-P'I
- NOTES SUR LE "TURKESTAN" BARTHOLD, DE M.W.
- L'ORIGINE DU NOM DE "CHINE"
- UN TRAITE MANICHEEN RETROUVE EN CHINE

Pellisson, P *see* REFLEXIONS SUR LES DIFFERENDS DE LA RELIGION

Pelloutier, Fernand L E *see*
- HISTOIRES DES BOURSES DU TRAVAIL
- LA VIE OUVRIERE EN FRANCE

Pelloux, R *see* LIBERALISME, TRADITIONALISME, DECENTRALISATION

Peltchinski, VS *see* LA RUSSIE EN 1844. SYSTEME DE LEGISLATION, D'ADMINISTRATION ET POLITIQUE, PAR UN HOMME D'ETAT RUSSE

Pelton, Joseph N *see* GLOBAL COMMUNICATIONS SATELLITE POLICY: INTELSAT, POLITICS AND FUNCTIONALISM

Pelzeln, A von *see* BEITRAEGE ZUR ORNITHOLOGIE SUEDAFRIKAS

Pelzer, A *see*
- ETUDE SUR LES MANUSCRITS DES QUODLIBETS
- LES QUATRE PREMIERS QUODLIBETS DE GODEFROID DE FONTAINES

Pelzer, Auguste *see* GESKIEDENIS VAN DIE SUID-AFRIKAANSE REPUBLIEK

PEM : PLANT ENGINEERING AND MAINTENANCE – Oakville. v13-17. 1990-94 – 9 – Can$28.00y – cn Micromedia [621]

Peman, Cesar *see* CUANDO PINTO ZURBARAN LOS CUADROS DE LA CARTUJA DE JEREZ DE LA FRONTERA?

PEMANDANGAN SOCIOLOGISCH TENTANG PEROBAHAN DALAM MASJARAKAT / Sunaria, Sanyatavijaya Kalapaking – SE 5460 1. 1946 – 9 – ne IDC [360]

Pematang Siantar, Indonesia *see* GRADUATION DAY FAKULTAS EKONOMI AND AKADEMI PEMIMPIN PERUSAHAAN DAN AKUNTANSI

Pematang Siantar, Indonesia. Universitas H.K.B.P. Nommensen *see* CHARTER NOMMENSEN-UNIVERSITY, INSTITUTION OF THE BATAK PROTESTANT CONGREGATION, SUMATRA, INDONESIA

Pematang Siantar, Sumatra. Fakultas Ekonomi *see* PROGRAMS OF STUDY

PEMBANGOENAN – Djakarta, 1945-1947 – 12mf – 9 – SE-945/1 – ne IDC [950]

PEMBANGUNAN DESA – Djakarta. Incomplete. SE-839 1. 1960-1964 – 9 – ne IDC [073]

PEMBANGUNAN MASJARAKAT DESA DI INDONESIA / Sutomo, S Honggowongso – SE 4491 1. 1961 – 9 – ne IDC [950]

PEMBAROEAN – Djakarta, 1945-1946 – 4mf – 9 – SE-946/1 – ne IDC [950]

PEMBERONTAKAN SILUNGKANG 1927, SUMATRA BARAT / Said, Nawir – SE 4375 1. 1963 – 9 – ne IDC [950]

Pemberton, R B *see*
- REPORTS ON THE EASTERN FRONTIER OF BRITISH INDIA, EXTENDING TO YUNAN IN CHINA
- TOUR IN ARRACAN

Pemberton, Robert L *see* HISTORY OF PLEASANTS COUNTY

Pemberton, S George *see* ICHNOS

Pemberville. Ohio. Bethlehem Lutheran Church *see* RECORDS

Pemberville. Ohio. First United Presbyterian Church *see* RECORDS

Pemberville. Ohio. Salem Evangelical Lutheran Church *see* RECORDS

Pemberville. Ohio. St. Paul's Lutheran Church *see* RECORDS

PEMBIMBING KEFILSAFAT, I: METAFISIKA / Alisjahbana, Sutan Takdir – Djakarta, Poestaka 1946. 104 p., pls, 21 cm. SEM-14763 14764 1 – 9 – ne IDC [110]

PEMBINA NEWS ADVISER – Alberta, CN. Jun 1956-Jan 1965 – 6r – 1 – cn Commonwealth Micro [072]

PEMBROKE 1662-1897 – (Mf 1: Vital Records 1692-1751. Mf 2: Town & Vitals 1711-28. Mf 3-5: Town & Vitals 1711-44. Mf 6: Town & Vitals 1726-44. Mf 7-9: Land Records 1662-1785. Mf 10-15: Town Meetings 1735-91. Mf 16-19: Vital Records 1715-91. Mf 20-30: Town & Vitals 1735-1841. Mf 31-38: Town Records 1824-52. Mf 39-40: Church Record 1748-1803. Mf 41-44: Quaker Record 1658-1854. Mf 45: Deaths 1823-80. Mf 45: Marriages 1712-99. Mf 46-50: Mortgages 1834-78. Mf 50: Marriages 1841-44. Mf 51-52: Rebellion 1861-65. Mf 53-54: Paupers 1912-42. Mf 55-61: Intentions 1808-1906; 62-64: Vitals 1844-1856; 65-68: Births 1856-97. Mf 69-71: Marriages 1857-97. Mf 72-75: Deaths 1856-97) – (mf ed 1992) – 75mf – 9 – 0-87623-150-4 – us Holbrook [920]

PEMBROKE 1692-1849 – (Mf 1T-2T: Births & Deaths 1692-1746. Mf 1T-4T: Marriages 1712-91. Mf 2T-6T: Births 1707-90. Mf 3T-4T: Deaths 1715-85. Mf 7T-8T: Marriages 1790-1830. Mf 8T: Deaths 1771-1843. Mf 8T-11T: Births 1730-1842. Mf 11T: Marriages 1827-44. Mf 11T-12T: Marriage Intentions 1842-49. Mf 12T: Deaths 1833-44 & Marriages 1712-99. Mf 12T-13T: Births 1824-49. Mf 13T: Marriages & Deaths 1824-49. Mf 14T: Births 1813-42 & Marriages 1790-1800) – (mf ed 1998) – 14mf – 9 – 0-87623-314-0 – us Holbrook [920]

PEMBROKE COUNTY GUARDIAN ETC – Solva, Wales, UK. 1901.-w. 1 reel – 1 – uk British Libr Newspaper [072]

PEMBROKE OBSERVER – (1993.-4r; 1910-1975.-116r) – Pembroke, 1976-1992 – 1 – cn Preston [971]

PEMBUKTIAN / Harahap, M – SE-5354 1. 1962 – 9 – ne IDC [950]

PEMELIHARAAN IKAN / Ardiwinata, Odjoh Raden – Bandung, W. van Hoeve, 1952. v1 only. illus. Summary in English. SEM-2607 – 9 – ne IDC [590]

PEMELIHARAAN IKAN, DISUSUN OLEH R. O. ARDIWINATA / Ardiwinata, Odjoh Raden – Tjet. 2. Bandung. SEM-9653-9654 – 9 – ne IDC [590]

Pemell, R *see* DE MORBIS CAPITIS

PEMERINTAH – MASJARAKAT – ANGKATAN PERANG; PIDATO-PIDATO DAN KARANGAN-KARANGAN, 1955-1958 / Simatupang, Tahi Bonar – SE 4647 1. 1960 – 9 – ne IDC [950]

Pemerintah Revolusioner Republik Indonesia *see* THE BIRTH OF NEW INDONESIA (SIX MONTHS P.R.R.I.) COMMEMORATION MONOGRAPH GENESIS AND DEVELOPMENT OF THE REVOLUTIONARY GOVERNMENT OF THE REPUBLIC OF INDONESIA

PEMIMPIN BAHASA NIPPON / Barisan Propaganda – Djakarta, Asia Raya, 2602. 73p – 23mf – 9 – ne IDC [950]

PEMIMPIN SEMBAHJANG / Hadiwijoto, S – SE-5211 1. 1960 – 9 – ne IDC [950]

PEMUNGUTAN HASIL HUTAN / Juta, E H P – Boger?. Timun Mas, 1954. 395p – 9 – BSEM-620-624/1 – ne IDC [630]

THE PEN : A LITERARY, HISTORICAL AND CRITICAL REVIEW – Montreal: J K Foran. v1- 1897-. SEM105P12 – 4mf – 9 – Can$9.00 – cn Bibl Nat [410]

THE PEN – Montreal, Canada. 11 dec 1897; v1 n28. 24 jun 1898 – 1r – 1 – Can$25.00 – cn Can Microfilming [072]

PEN. American Center of PEN International *see* NEWSLETTER

PEN PHOTOGRAPHS OF CELEBRATED MEN AND NOTED PLACES, GHOSTS AND THEIR RELATIONS: TALES, SKETCHES, ESSAYS, ETC., ETC / Clark, Daniel – Toronto: Flint, Morton & Co., 1873. 00662. (Pre-1900 Canadiana) – 9 – cn C.I.H.M. [770]

PEN PICTURES OF REPRESENTATIVE MEN OF OREGON / Hodgkin & Galvin – Portland: Farmer and Dairymen Publ. House, 1882.Oregon reel 2. (Cox Library Collection) – 5 – us Americana [978]

PEN PICTURES OF ST PAUL AND BIOGRAPHICAL SKETCHES OF OLD SETTLERS FROM THE EARLIEST SETTLEMENT OF THE CITY TILL 1857 / Newson, T M – St. Paul, 1886. Minnesota Reel 11. (The Cox Library Collection) – 5 – us Americana [978]

PEN PORTRAITS / Parkinson, R R – San Francisco: Alta California Print., 1878. California Reel 2.(The Cox Library Collection) – 5 – us Americana [978]

PEN SKETCHES OF NEBRASKANS / Edmunds, A C – Omaha: R.J. Wilbur, Stationers, 1871. Nebraska Reel 4. (The Cox Library Collection) – 5 – us Americana [978]

PEN SYMPHONIES / Baker, Maude E – Halifax: T.C. Allen, 1899. 06157. (Pre-1900 Canadiana) – 9 – cn C.I.H.M. [830]

A PENA : ORGAO OFICIAL DO "GREMIO LITTERARIO PEDRO 5. GONTIJO" – Divinopolis, 25 Feb 1934 – 1,5,6 – bl Biblioteca [072]

Pena Camara, Jose de la *see*
- LA COPULATA DE LEYES DE INDIAS Y LAS ORDENANZAS OVANDINAS
- LAS REDACCIONES DEL LIBRO DE LA GOBERNACION ESPIRITUAL. OVANDO Y LA JUNTA DE INDIAS DE 1568

LA PENA DE MUERTE, COMO TEMA LITERARIO / Crehuet, Diego Maria – Madrid: Est. Tip. Jaime Rates, 1917 – sp Bibl Santa Ana [410]

Pena El 27 *see*
- EL 27
- EL 27 JUNIO 1975

PENA EL 27. CORIA JUNIO, 1980 – Coria: Pena el 27, 1980 – 1 – sp Bibl Santa Ana [946]

Pena, J *see* EUKLEIDOU EISAGOGE HARMONIKE. EUCLIDIS RUDIMENTA MUSICES

Pena Marazuela, T de la *see* MADRID. ARCHIVO HISTORICO NACIONAL. SECCION DIVERSOS. PAPELES DE LUIS ARAQUISTAIN

Pena, MT *see* MADRID. ARCHIVO HISTORICO NACIONAL. SECCION DE CODICES. INVENTARIO DE LA SECCION DE CODICES

LA PENA (RETIRO PREDILECTO DE MONTANO) / Doetsch, Carlos – Malaga: Revista Espanola de Estudios Biblicos, 1928 – 1 – sp Bibl Santa Ana [946]

Pena Viva la Gente *see*
- FIESTAS DE SAN JUAN 1976
- FIESTAS DE SAN JUAN 1977

Pena y Camara, J M *see* SEVILLA. ARCHIVO GENERAL DE INDIAS GUIA DEL VISITANTE

THE PENAL CODE FOR THE KINGDOM OF SIAM (DRAFT VERSION.) R.S. 127 (1908) / Thailand. Laws, Statutes, etc – Bangkok, The A.P. Mission, 1908 2 p. l., iii, 1 93 p. LL-10018 – 1 – us L of C Photodup [340]

THE PENAL CODE OF GUAM, 1933 / Robinson, Stephen B – Manila: Bureau of Printing. 2pts. 1933 – 6mf – 9 – $9.00 – LLMC 82-100B Title 18 – us L.L.M.C. [324]

THE PENAL CODE OF GUAM, 1947 / Guam. (Commonwealth). Laws, Statutes, etc – Washington: GPO, 1947 – 3mf – 9 – $4.50 – LLMC 82-100B Title 8 – us L.L.M.C. [324]

THE PENAL CODE OF THE RUSSIAN SOCIALIST FEDERAL SOVIET REPUBLIC; TEXT OF 1926 (WITH AMENDMENTS UP TO DECEMBER 1, 1932) WITH THREE APPENDICES. / Russia. (1917-R.S.F.S.R.). Laws, Statutes, etc – London: H. M. Stationery Office, 1934. 82p. LL-4219 – 1 – us L of C Photodup [340]

THE PENAL CODE OF THE TERRITORY OF GUAM, 1970 / Bohn, John A – (With 1974 pocket pt and suppl covering the Rules of Criminal Procedure) – Agana: n.p, 1970 – 13mf – 9 – $19.50 – LLMC 82-100B Title 14 – us L.L.M.C. [324]

PENALTIES UPON OPINION, OR, SOME RECORDS OF THE LAWS OF HERESY AND BLASPHEMY / Bonner, Hypatia Bradlaugh – London: Issued for the Rationalist Press Association, Ltd., [by] Watts, 1913 – 1mf – us A.T.L.A. [240]

Penalver, Nicolas *see* DISCURSO DE...AUDIENCIA DE CACERES

Penalver y Bachiller, P *see* BOSQUEJO DE LA MATEMATICA ESPANOLA EN LOS SIGLOS DE LA DECADENCIA

THE PENANCE OF JOHN LOGAN; AND TWO OTHER TALES / Black, William – British Fiction Archive: Unit 4 – 9 – uk Bell [830]

PENANG ARGUS – George Town. Malaysia. -w. 8 Aug, 3 Oct 1867-10 Mar 1873. (Imperfect). (2 reels) – 1 – uk British Libr Newspaper [072]

PENANG DAILY EXPRESS – George Town. Malaysia. -d. 5-17 Feb 1879. (Imperfect). (4 ft) – 1 – uk British Libr Newspaper [072]

PENANG GUARDIAN AND MERCANTILE ADVERTISER – George Town. Malaysia. -w. 15 Aug 1873-16 Mar 1874. (25 ft) – 1 – uk British Libr Newspaper [072]

PENANG MARITIME JOURNAL – George Town, Malaysia. 19 Nov 1894-31 Oct 1896 – 3r – 1 – uk British Libr Newspaper [072]

PENANG MARITIME JOURNAL AND GENERAL NEWS *see* STRAITS MARITIME JOURNAL AND GENERAL NEWS

PENANG REGISTER – 1827-28 – 1 – uk Microform Academic [072]

PENARTH TIMES – Jan 19-Dec 21 1901; 1986; Jan 8-Jun 24, Jul 1988-Jun, Jul 3-Dec 23 1992; 1993-Jun 1997 – 20 1/4r – 1 – uk British Libr Newspaper [072]

PENASBEDE: PEMBANGUNAN NASIONAL SEMESTA BERENT JANA DELAPAN TAHUN 1961-1969 DALAM BIDANG KOPERASI INDONESIA / Printono – SE-4643 1. 1960 – 9 – ne IDC [950]

"PENDEKAR HARIMAU." GUBAHAN KWEE OEN KENG – SE-5188 1. v. 1-6 only – 9 – ne IDC [073]

Pendennis, Arthur *see* THE NEWCOMES

PENDER REPUBLICAN – Pender, NE. -w. Aug-Dec 1895; May 1896-May 1898; Dec 1898-Aug 1938 – 1 – us NE Hist [071]

PENDER TIMES – Pender, NE. -w. Jul-Aug 1896; Jan-Sep 1899; Nov 1899; Jan 1900-Jan 1901; Apr 1901 to date – 1 – us NE Hist [071]

Penderghest, Caroline E *see* DOUBLE BLIND CLINICAL EFFICACY STUDY OF DEXAMETHASONE-LIDOCAINE PULSED PHONOPHORESIS ON PERCEIVED PAIN ASSOCIATED WITH SYMPTOMATIC TENDINITIS

PENDIDIKAN DAN PENGADJARAN MUHAMMADIJAH DALAM MASA PEMBANGUNAN SEMESTA / Amir Hamzah Wirjosukarto – SE-5332 1. 1965 – 9 – ne IDC [950]

PENDIDIKAN DI RUMAH TANGGA / Nasution, Amir Taat – SE-3086-1. 1951 – 9 – ne IDC [320]

PENDIDIKAN MENGABDI MANIPOL / Wignjoamidjojo, B – SE 4504 1. 1963 – 9 – ne IDC [950]

PENDIDIKAN OLAHRAGA DAN PEMBANGUNAN MASJARAKAT BARU INDONESIA / Siahaan, A M S – SE 5141 1. 1961 – 9 – ne IDC [950]

Pendit, Njoman Suwandi *see* BALI BERDJUANG

PENDLE HILL PAMPHLETS – v1-307 (complete) – Inquire – 1 – ATLA S0682 – us A.T.L.A. [073]

Pendlebury, JD S *see* THE ARCHEOLOGY OF CRETE

Pendleton, CS *see* THE BIBLE, WHO WROTE IT?

PENDLETON INDEPENDENT – Pendleton OR. Apr 24 1879 + – 1 – us U.O. Library [071]

Pendleton, J M *see*
- COMPENDIO DE TEOLOGIA CRISTIANA
- AN OLD LANDMARK
- THE SOUTHERN PSALMIST
- THREE REASONS WHY I AM A BAPTIST

PENDLETON MERCANTILE REVIEW – Pendleton OR. Apr 1889 – 1 – us U.O. Library [071]

PENDLETON RECORD – Pendleton, OR. -w. 7 Jan 1954-. – 1 – us U.O. Library [071]

PENDLETON REPUBLICAN – Pendleton OR. Jan 20 27 Feb 3 17 24 1900, Mar 3 10 17 31 1900 – 1 – us U.O. Library [071]

PENDLETON REPUBLICAN – Pendleton, OR. -w. 1897-1900. Evening Republican. -d. 1888 – 1 – 41.00 – us Oregon Hist [071]

PENDLETON STREET BAPTIST CHURCH. GREENVILLE COUNTY. SOUTH CAROLINA : CHURCH RECORDS – (Also, WMU 1890-1982, Membership Rolls and Misc. 8,569p) – 1902-July 1985 – 7r – 1 – $385.61 – us Baptist [240]

PENDLETON TIMES – Franklin. West Virginia. 1944-1953 – 1 – us UMI [071]

PENDLETON TRIBUNE – Pendleton, OR. and pred. -w, sw, d. 1885-1910. Incomplete 1914-23 – 1 – 696.00 – us Oregon Hist [071]

PENDLETON TRIBUNE – Pendleton OR. Oct 20 1916, Apr 12 May 18 19 21 1917, Sep 12 13 Oct 26-29 Dec 31 1917, Jan 1 Oct 25 1928, June 26 1920 + – 1 – us U.O. Library [071]

PENDLETON TRIBUNE – Pendleton OR. Sep 1-21 1917, Nov 12 1918, Sep 18 29 21 1920 + – 1 – us U.O. Library [071]

Pendleton, William C *see* HISTORY OF TAZEWELL COUNTY AND THE SOUTHWEST VIRGINIA

PENDLETONIAN – Pendleton OR. Nov 16 23 1902 – 1 – us U.O. Library [071]

PENDUDUK IRIAN BARAT / Kuntjaraningrat – 1963 – 9 – SE-4624 1 – ne IDC [950]

O PENEDENSE – (Cont by: Jornal do Penedo) – Penedo, Alagoas. 8 Jul, 17 Nov 1870 – 1,5,6 – bl Biblioteca [072]

O PENEDENSE *see* JORNAL DO PENEDO

O PENEDO : ORGAM DO PARTIDO REPUBLICANO NO SUL DE ALAGOAS – Penedo, Alagoas. 30 Jul 1899; Jun 1900; Nov 1901; Jan 1904-Dez 1905; Jan-Abr, Jun-Ago, Out 1906; Jan 1909-9 Dez 1911 – 1,5,6 – bl Biblioteca [072]

PENEDO ESPORTIVO – Penedo, Alagoas. 15 Out-Nov 1922; 29 Abr 1923 – 1,5,6 – bl Biblioteca [072]

PENELITIAN LAUT DI INDONESIA – Djakarta. SE-840 1. 1956-1970 – 9 – ne IDC [950]

PENERANGAN RAKJAT – Surabaja. Incomplete. SE-947 1. 1951-1962 – 9 – ne IDC [950]

PENERBIT : GABOENGAN POLITIEK INDONESIA. (G.A.P.I.) / Parlement Indonesia – Djakarta, 1939 – 1mf – 9 – ne IDC [320]

PENETRACION IMPERIALISTA EN LA ARGENTINA / Gutierrez, Guillermo – Buenos Aires: El Cid Editor [distribucion, Capital Federal, Rubbo], 1974 – 1 – CSUXAHZ3666-B – us Hoover Inst Photo [320]

Penev, B *see* NACHALO NA BALGARSKOTO VAZRAZHDANE

PENFIELD BAPTIST CHURCH. PENFIELD, GEORGIA : CHURCH RECORDS – 1839-85 – 1 – 26.73 – us Baptist [240]

Penfield, New York. Penfield Baptist Society *see* RECORDS

P'eng, Ch'ang-lin *see* ELEMENTS OF RELIGIOUS PEDAGOGY (CCC260)

P'Eng, Chen *see* SPEECH AT THE ALIARCHAM ACADEMY OF SOCIAL SCIENCES IN INDONESIA

P'eng, Peter *see* A HISTORY OF CHRISTIAN THOUGHT (CCC261)

PENGAKOEAN MESIR DAN POLITIK ARAB LEAGUE / Banda, Ismail – SE-11,764 1. 1947 – 9 – ne IDC [956]

PENGANTAR ANTHROPOLOGI BUDAJA DAN SOSIALSE-5427/1. 1964 / Rijoatmodjo, Suharto – 9 – ne IDC [950]

PENGANTAR EKONOMI BANK DAN KREDIT / Reksodiprodjo, Susatyo – SE-5890 1. 1965 – 9 – ne IDC [338]

PENGANTAR ILMU POLITIK / Nasution, Basarudin – SE-4164 1. 1961? – 9 – ne IDC [320]

PENGANTAR STUDI ISLAM, MENGANTARKAN PEMBATJA MENGGALI API ISLAM / Sjaf'at – SE 4962 1. 1964 – 9 – ne IDC [260]

PENGANTIN FERGANA / Zaydan, Jirji – SE 5954 1. 1965 – 9 – ne IDC [950]

PENGANTUR ILMU SEDJARAH INDONESIA / Ali, R Moh. – SE-4239 1. 1961 – 9 – ne IDC [950]

PENGERTIAN, KEDUDUKAN DAN PERINTJIAN ILMU ADMINISTRASI / Liang Gie – SE 4319 1. 1963 – 9 – ne IDC [950]

PENGETAHUAN TENTANG TELEVISI / Abdurahman, Fuad – Tjet. 1. Jakarta, 1962-vol. 1 only. Illus. SEM-11096 – 9 – ne IDC [600]

Penggalang rohani. Medan *see* "MADJALAH BULANAN AKSI KATOLIK."SE-5413/1

PENGGEMBALAAN / Abineno, Johannes Ludwig Chrysostomus – SE-10,346 1. 1963 – 9 – ne IDC [950]

PENGHUBUNG – SE-949 1. Pontianak. Not published Nov. 1952-March 1953. Lacking: 1952, v. 2(4-8). 1951-1963 – 9 – ne IDC [073]

PENINSULA – (Weekly Union newspaper) – Jacksonville, FL. Apr 21 1864 – 1r – 1 – us Western Res [071]

PENINSULA HERALD – Monterey. Calif. 1922- – 1 – us UMI [071]

PENINSULA HERALD – Portland, OR. -w. 13 Jul 1923-8 May 1931; 20 Mar-16 Oct 1936; 10,17,30 Dec 1937; 7 Jan-17 June 1933. – 2r – 1 – us U.O. Library [071]

THE PENINSULA HERALD AND SIMONSTOWN GAZETTE – Cape Town, South Africa.12 Apr 1902-5 Dec 1903. 2 reels – 1, 16 diazo available at reduced price – sa SA Libr [072]

PENINSULA METRO REPORTER – East Palo Alto & SF Peninsula area, CA. Aug 1979-Dec 1979 – 1r – 1 – $50.00 – B02192 – us Library Micro [071]

PENINSULA MIRROR – Palo Alto, CA. 1936-1937 – 1r – 1 – $50.00 – C03628 – us Library Micro [071]

PENINSULA MIRROR *see* THE PALO ALTO NEWS

PENINSULA NEWS AND SAN BRUNO PROGRESS *see* SAN BRUNO HERALD

PENINSULA NEWS WHO'S WHO – San Bruno, CA. 1949 – 1r – 1 – $50.00 – B02774 – us Library Micro [071]

PENINSULA TIMES TRIBUNE : 3 EDITIONS – (Cont: Palo Alto Times) – Palo Alto, CA. Apr 1979-93 – 639r – 1 – $31,950.00 – B02602 – us Library Micro [071]

PENINSULA TIMES TRIBUNE : ONE STAR EDITION – (Cont: Redwood City Tribune) – Redwood City, CA. Apr 1979-May 1980 – 28r – 1 – $1,400.00 – B02681 – us Library Micro [071]

PENINSULA TIMES TRIBUNE *see*
- REDWOOD CITY TRIBUNE
- TIMES (DAILY)

PENINSULAIRE – Mont-Joli, Canada. v18 n30. 6 aut 1965-23 jun 1971 – 4r – 1 – Can$50.00r – cn Can Microfilming [072]

PENINSULAR NEWS – Marblehead, Ohio. 1916- – 14r – 1 – $32.50r – us Archival [071]

PENINSULAR WEST – Camborne, England. May 1872-2 Oct 1874 – 2 1/2r – 1 – uk British Libr Newspaper [072]

Penistone. Yorkshire *see* PARISH REGISTERS

Penkina, Z M *see*
- POLES'E
- ZAKASPIISKII KRAI

PENN DENTAL JOURNAL – v69- 1965- 1; 1975- 5,6,9 – us UMI [617]

Penn, J *see* VARIOUS TRACTS

PENN JERSEY BAPTIST – Harrisburg, PA. 1971-1991. 296p – 1 – $85.28 – us Baptist [071]

PENN MONTHLY – Philadelphia. v1-14. 1870-82 – 5r – 1 – us Ross [073]

PENN MONTHLY – v. 1-14. Jan 1870-Jul 1882 – 1 – us UMI [073]

PENN SCHOOL PAPERS – 1861-1964. 33 reels. Guide – 1 – $594.00 – us U.N.C. Southern Hist [240]

Penn, Thomas *see*
- CORRESPONDENCE, 1729-1775
- THE THOMAS PENN PAPERS

Penn, WE *see*
- HARVEST BELLS, 1882, 1884, 1887
- THE LIFE AND LABORS OF MAJOR W.E. PENN, THE TEXAS EVANGELIST

Penn, William *see* WILLIAM PENN PAPERS, 1644-1718

A PENNA – Curitiba, 4 Apr-16 Jul 1897 – 1,5,6 – bl Biblioteca [072]

A PENNA : ORGAO POPULAR – Maceio, Alagoas. 29 Nov-6 Dez 1897 – 1,5,6 – bl Biblioteca [072]

Penna, L *see* PRIMI ALBORI MUSICALI PER LI PRINCIPANTI DELLA MUSICA FIGURATA

Pennant, T *see*
- GENERA OF BIRDS
- INDIAN ZOOLOGY
- SYNOPSIS OF QUADRUPEDS
- TOURS IN WALES
- THE VIEW OF INDIA EXTRA GANGEM, CHINA; AND, JAPAN

PENN-BAPTIST – Philadelphia. Pennsylvania Baptist Convention. 1932-70. Single reels available – 1 – 144.80 – us A.B.H.S. [073]

Pennekamp, Markus *see*
- DIE AUSWIRKUNGEN DES EUROPAEISCHEN BINNENMARKTES AUF DIE WIRTSCHAFTSBEZIEHUNGEN ZUR DRITTEN WELT
- OEKONOMISCHE ANALYSE DES RECHTS AM BEISPIEL DES GEWAESSERSCHUTZES

Pennell, BL *see* A DESCRIPTIVE ANALYSIS OF SPORTS COMMISSIONS IN THE UNITED STATES

Pennell, T L *see* AMONG THE WILD TRIBES OF THE AFGHAN FRONTIER

Penney *see* THE FIRST PUBLISHERS OF TRUTH

Penniman, Alford Brown *see* STUDIES IN OPTIMISM

PENNINE BAPTIST CHURCH. SPRING CITY, TENNESSEE : CHURCH RECORDS – 1895-1973 – 1 – 18.45 – us Baptist [240]

Pennington, Arthur Robert *see*
- THE CHURCH IN ITALY
- JOHN WICLIF
- THE LIFE AND CHARACTER OF ERASMUS
- THE PAPAL CONCLAVES
- PRELUDES TO THE REFORMATION, OR, FROM DARK TO DAY IN EUROPE

PENNINGTON BAPTIST CHURCH. PENNINGTON, TEXAS : CHURCH RECORDS – 1860-1940 – 1 – 36.54 – us Baptist [240]

Pennotto, Gabr. *see*
- FACULA VERITATIS
- GENERALIS TOTIUS ORDINIS CLERICORUM CANONICORUM HISTORIA
- GENERALIS TOTIUS SACRI ORDINIS CLERICORUM CANONICORUM HISTORIA

PENNSYLVANAI SCOTCH-IRISH SOCIETY *see* PROCEEDINGS, 1890-1974

PENNSYLVANIA : PURDON'S PENNSYLVANIA STATUTES ANNOTATED – 1930-Jun 1996 update – 9 – $3,039.00 set – us Hein [340]

PENNSYLVANIA : SESSION LAWS OF AMERICAN STATES AND TERRITORIES – 1776-1994 – 9 – $2,408.00 set – us Hein [340]

Pennsylvania *see*
- COURT REPORTS, COUNTY REPORTS 1885-1921, DISTRICT REPORTS 1892-1921, DISTRICT AND COUNTY REPORTS, 1922-50
- FORMAL OPINIONS (A-G)
- INFORMAL OPINIONS (A-G)
- MISCELLANEOUS NEWSPAPERS
- REPORTS AND OPINIONS (A-G)
- REPORTS, POST-NRS
- REPORTS, PRE-NRS
- SESSION LAWS
- STATE LABOR REPORTS
- STATE REPORTS, POST-NRS

PENNSYLVANIA ABOLITION SOCIETY PAPERS, 1775-1975 – Historical Society of Pennsylvania – 32r – 1 – $2115.00 – us UMI [975]

Pennsylvania Academy of Ophthalmology and Otolaryngology *see* TRANSACTIONS

THE PENNSYLVANIA ARGUS – Greensburg, PA. -w 1889; 1901-1912 – 13 – $25.00r – us I.M.R. [071]

Pennsylvania. Assembly *see* JOURNALS AND MINUTES OF THE PENNSYLVANIA ASSEMBLY, 1776-1790

PENNSYLVANIA ATTORNEY GENERAL REPORTS AND OPINIONS – (6 1889-1978 $525.00. 9 1978-1994 $30.00) – 1889-1994 – 6,9 – $555.00set – us Hein [340]
Pennsylvania. Auditor General's Office *see* REPORT OF THE AUDITOR GENERAL AND OF THE TABULATIONS AND DEDUCTIONS FROM THE REPORTS OF THE RAILROAD, CANAL AND TELEGRAPH COMPANIES
Pennsylvania. Banking Dept *see* REPORTS OF THE COMMISSIONER OF BANKING
PENNSYLVANIA BAR ASSOCIATION QUARTERLY – nos 1-40, v11-40. 1929-69 – 71mf – 9 – $319.00 – LLMC 84-667 – us L.L.M.C. [073]
PENNSYLVANIA BAR ASSOCIATION QUARTERLY – v1-66. 1929-95 – 9 – $741.00 set – us Hein [340]
PENNSYLVANIA BAR ASSOCIATION REPORTS – (Lacking: 43rd to 47th, 56th, & 67th meetings) – 1st-72nd Annual Meetings. 1895-1968 – 130mf – $585.00 – LLMC 84-668 – us L.L.M.C. [073]
PENNSYLVANIA BAR ASSOCIATION REPORTS – (Lacking: 43rd-47th, 56th, 67th meetings) – 1st-72nd annual meetings. 1895-1968 – 130mf – 9 – $585.00 – LLMC 84-668 – us L.L.M.C. [340]
Pennsylvania. Bureau of Employment Security *see* REPORTS
PENNSYLVANIA BUSINESS SURVEY – v1-1938- 1; v11- 5,6; v17- 9 – us UMI [380]
PENNSYLVANIA CHRONICLE – Philadelphia. Pa. 1767-1774 – 1,3 – us Readex [071]
THE PENNSYLVANIA CHRONICLE, 1767-1774 / Philadelphia, PA – 1972 – 4r – 1 – $340.00 – S1715 – us Scholarly Res [978]
Pennsylvania. (Colony). Provincial Council *see* RECORDS
PENNSYLVANIA: COUNTY AND REGIONAL HISTORIES AND ATLASES – 1 – us Primary [978]
Pennsylvania. Court of Common Pleas (Schuykill County) *see* RULES OF PRACTICE IN THE COURTS OF COMMON PLEAS, OYER AND TERMINER, QUARTER SESSIONS OF THE PEACE AND GENERAL JAIL DELIVERY OF SCHUYLKILL COUNTY
Pennsylvania. Court of Intermediate Appeals *see* PENNSYLVANIA SUPERIOR COURT REPORTS
Pennsylvania. Dept. of Community Affairs *see* LOCAL GOVERNMENT FINANCIAL STATISTICS
Pennsylvania. Dept. of Internal Affairs *see* REPORT OF THE BUREAU OF RAILWAYS, DEPT. OF INTERNAL AFFAIRS, PART 4: RAILROAD, CANAL, NAVIGATION, TELEGRAPH AND TELEPHONE COMPANIES
PENNSYLVANIA DISTRICT AND COUNTY COURT REPORTS *see* PENNSYLVANIA DISTRICT COURT REPORTS
PENNSYLVANIA DISTRICT AND COUNTY REPORTS 1825-1983 – (Contained in Pennsylvania Side Reports) – 9 – $3,500.00 set – us Hein [340]
PENNSYLVANIA DISTRICT COURT REPORTS / Pennsylvania. District Courts – (Title ends with v30 1921. Updates planned. Filming of lapsed-copyright vols of its successor: Pennsylvania District and County Court Reports, v1- 1921 will occur on an annual basis) – v1-29. 1892-1920 – 330mf – 9 – $495.00 – LLMC 84-189 – us L.L.M.C. [340]
Pennsylvania. District Courts *see* PENNSYLVANIA DISTRICT COURT REPORTS
PENNSYLVANIA DUTCHMAN – Lancaster, PA. -w Circa 1849 – 13 – $25.00r – us I.M.R. [071]
THE PENNSYLVANIA EVENING POST – Philadelphia. Pa. 1775-1784 – 3 – us Readex [071]
PENNSYLVANIA FARMER – Pittsburgh. Pa. 1929-1956; 1959 – 1 – us UMI [071]
PENNSYLVANIA FREEMAN – Philadelphia. PA. 1836-54 – 1 – us UMI [071]
PENNSYLVANIA GAME NEWS – v2- 1931- 1; v42- 5,6; v47- 9 – us UMI [639]
THE PENNSYLVANIA GAZETTE, 1728-1815 / Philadelphia, PA; ed by Franklin, Benjamin – 1972 – 26r – 1 – $2,210.00 – S1716-7 – us Scholarly Res [978]
PENNSYLVANIA GERMAN ART, 1683-1850 / Philadelphia Museum of ArtThe Henry Francis du Pont Winterthur Museum – (264p accompanying text) – 1984 – 5mf – 15 – $108.00f – 0-226-69535-2 – us Chicago [740]
PENNSYLVANIA HERALD – York. Pa. and York General Advertiser – 1 – us UMI [071]
Pennsylvania Historical and Museum Commission *see*
- BAYNTON, WHARTON, AND MORGAN PAPERS, 1757-1787
- HARMONY SOCIETY RECORDS, 1786-1951
- JOHN NICHOLSON PAPERS, 1772-1819
- MISCELLANEOUS MANUSCRIPTS OF THE REVOLUTIONARY WAR ERA, 1771-1791
- RECORDS OF PENNSYLVANIA'S REVOLUTIONARY GOVERNMENT, 1775-1790
- RECORDS OF PROVINCIAL COUNCIL, 1682-1776
- RECORDS OF THE PROVINCIAL COUNCIL, 1682-1776
- SIMON CAMERON PAPERS 1824-1892

PENNSYLVANIA HISTORY – v.1-38. 1934-71 – 1 – us UMI [073]
Pennsylvania. Human Relations Commission *see* REPORTS
Pennsylvania. Insurance Dept *see* REPORTS OF THE INSURANCE COMMISSIONER
THE PENNSYLVANIA INSURANCE DIGEST / Fowler, John A – Philadelphia: Review Printing House, 1868. 74p. LL-918 – 1 – us L of C Photodup [340]
THE PENNSYLVANIA JOURNAL, 1742-1793 / Philadelphia, PA – 1972 – 25r – 1 – $2,125.00 – S1718 – us Scholarly Res [978]
Pennsylvania. Labor Relations Board *see* REPORTS
PENNSYLVANIA LAW AFFECTING WOMEN AND CHILDREN, 1900 – Philadelphia? Pennsylvania Woman Suffrage Association, 1900. 45p. LL-1393 – 1 – us L of C Photodup [340]
PENNSYLVANIA LAW JOURNAL *see* THE AMERICAN LAW JOURNAL
PENNSYLVANIA LAWYER – v1-16. 1980-94 – 9 – $141.00 set – us Hein [340]
PENNSYLVANIA LEDGER – Philadelphia. Pa. 1775-1778 – 1,3 – us Readex [071]
PENNSYLVANIA MAGAZINE; OR AMERICAN MONTHLY MUSEUM – v.1-2. Jan 1775-Jul 1776 – 1 – us UMI [073]
THE PENNSYLVANIA MERCURY – Philadelphia. Pa. 1784-1792 – 3 – us Readex [071]
PENNSYLVANIA MIRROR – State College. Pa. 1969- – 1 – us UMI [071]
PENNSYLVANIA NEGLIGENCE CASES, STREET AND STEAM RAILWAYS &C., INDEXED / Rickert, Horace – Philadelphia: Johnson & Prince, 1913. LL-1408 – 1 – us L of C Photodup [340]
Pennsylvania. Nisi Prius. Supreme Court *see* BRIGHTLY'S REPORTS
PENNSYLVANIA ORPHANS' COURT COMMON PLACE BOOK / Hunter, David Gilbert – (1952 Cumulative Suppl. Philadelphia, 1952. 682p. LL-653. 1954 Suppl. (directly supplementing 1939-52 Suppl.). Philadelphia, 1954. 90p. LL-653) – Philadelphia: Bisel Co., 1939. 2v. LL-653 – 1 – us L of C Photodup [340]
PENNSYLVANIA PACKET – Philadelphia. Pa. 1771-90. and yPennsylvania Packet. Lancaster. 1777-78. Sold as one unit – 3 – us Readex [071]
THE PENNSYLVANIA PACKET, 1771-1790 / Philadelphia, PA – 1972 – 21r – 1 – $1,785.00 – S1721 – us Scholarly Res [978]
Pennsylvania. Presbytery (Assoc. Ch.) *see* MINUTES, 1762-1798
Pennsylvania. Presbytery (Cum. Pres. Ch.) *see* MINUTES
Pennsylvania. Public Utility Commission *see* DECISIONS
PENNSYLVANIA. RECORDS / U.S. Bureau of the Census – 1850-80 – 1 – us UMI [310]
PENNSYLVANIA REPORTER AND DEMOCRAT STATE – Harrisburg, PA., 1836 – 13 – $25.00r – us I.M.R. [071]
Pennsylvania. Revolutionary Governments *see* RECORD
PENNSYLVANIA SCHOOL JOURNAL – v1-1852- 1; v120- 5,6; v125- 9 – us UMI [370]
PENNSYLVANIA SCHOOL JOURNAL – v. 1-97. 1852-1948 – 1 – us Princeton Micro [370]
Pennsylvania. Second Presbytery. (Assoc. Ref. Ch. of NA) *see* MINUTES, 1793-1802
Pennsylvania. Securities Commission *see* REPORTS
PENNSYLVANIA SIDE REPORTS : OPINIONS OF THE LOWER COURTS OF RECORD IN PENNSYLVANIA – (Updated quarterly ca $828.00y) – Backfile-1996 no 2 update – 9 – $19,225.00 set – 0-89941-423-0 – us Hein [340]
Pennsylvania. State Bar Association *see* PROCEEDINGS
Pennsylvania. State Education Association *see* REPORT OF PROCEEDINGS
PENNSYLVANIA STATE LIBRARY MISC. NEWS – Harrisburg, PA., 1823 – 13 – $25.00r – us I.M.R. [071]
PENNSYLVANIA STATE REPORTS : HIGHEST COURT REPORTS / Pennsylvania. Supreme Court – (Pre-NRS: v1-108 1854-85 692mf $1,038.00. Updates planned) – v1-266. 1845-1920 – 1958mf – 9 – $2,931.00 – LLMC 82-989 – us L.L.M.C. [340]
PENNSYLVANIA STATESMAN – Carlisle, PA. -w 1842-45. 1 roll – 13 – $25.00r – us I.M.R. [071]
PENNSYLVANIA STATESMAN – Harrisburg, PA., 1860 – 13 – $25.00r – us I.M.R. [071]
Pennsylvania. Superior Court *see*
- ADDISON'S REPORTS
- BINNEY'S REPORTS
- DALLAS' REPORTS
- GRANT'S CASES
- MONAGHAN'S REPORTS
- PENNYPACKER'S REPORTS
- PENROSE AND WATTS' REPORTS
- RAWLE'S REPORTS
- SADLER'S REPORTS
- SERGEANT AND RAWLE'S REPORTS
- WALKER'S REPORTS
- WATTS AND SERGEANT'S REPORTS
- WATTS' REPORTS
- WHARTON'S REPORTS
- YEATES' REPORTS

PENNSYLVANIA SUPERIOR COURT REPORTS / Pennsylvania. Court of Intermediate Appeals – (Pre-NRS: v1-101. Updates planned) – v1-71. 1895-1919 – 568mf – 9 – $852.00 – LLMC 84-190 – us L.L.M.C. [340]
Pennsylvania. Supreme Court *see* PENNSYLVANIA STATE REPORTS
PENNSYLVANIAN – Philadelphia. Pa. 1846-1853 – 1 – us UMI [071]
PENNSYLVANISCHE SAMMLUNG VON KIRCHEN-MUSIK – 1840. with Gerhart, Isaac. Choral Harmonie. 1822 – 1 – $50.00 – us Presbyterian [780]
PENNSYLVANNIA LAW JOURNAL *see* AMERICAN LAW JOURNAL
PENNY MOTHERS NEWS – Salem OR. Sep 3 1938 – 1 – us U.O. Library [071]
PENNY NEWS AND WEST OF SCOTLAND OBSERVER : PEOPLE'S PENNY NEWS AND WEEKLY JOURNAL OF POLITICS AND LITERATURE – Dumbarton, Scotland. 5 Jun-21 Aug 1858 – 10ft – 1 – uk British Libr Newspaper [072]
PENNY PAPERS FOR THE PEOPLE – London, UK. 1830-31 – 13ft – 1 – uk British Libr Newspaper [072]
PENNY POST, CONTAINING FRESH NEWS, ADVERTISEMENTS, USEFUL HINTS, ETC – v1-9. Jan 1769-Jan 1769 – 1 – us UMI [073]
PENNY POWER *see* ZILLIONS
PENNY PRESS – Montrose, Scotland, UK. Jul 1865-Mar 1867 – 1r – 1 – uk British Libr Newspaper [072]
PENNY SATIRIST – London. -w. Apr 1837-Apr 1846. (3 reels) – 1 – uk British Libr Newspaper [072]
Pennycuff, Mattie *see* REMINISCENCES OF THE EARLY WEST AND EXPERIENCES OF THE BOWLBY FAMILY
PENNYPACKER'S REPORTS : UNREPORTED / Pennsylvania. Superior Court – (A Pre-NRS title) – v1-4. 1881-84 (all publ) – 28mf – 9 – $42.00 – LLMC 84-205 – us L.L.M.C. [340]
PENRITH HERALD – 1857; Nov 17, Dec 29 1860; Jan 5-26 1861; Jan 3-Feb 28 1874; Apr 4-Dec 26 1874; 1875-90; Jan 3-Dec 26 1891; 1892-95; 1897-1924; Jan 3-Dec 26 1925; 1926-96 – 187r – 1 – uk British Libr Newspaper [072]
PENROSE AND WATTS' REPORTS / Pennsylvania. Superior Court – (A Pre-NRS title) – 1829-32 (all publ) – 19mf – 9 – $28.50 – LLMC 84-199 – us L.L.M.C. [340]
Penrose, John *see* LIVES OF VICE ADMIRAL SIR C.V. PENROSE AND CAPTAIN J. TREVENEN
Penrose, Stephen Beasley Linnard *see* THE REPUTATION AND INFLUENCE OF FRANCIS BACON IN THE SEVENTEENTH CENTURY
Penrose, Valeria Fullerton *see* OPPORTUNITIES IN THE PATH OF THE GREAT PHYSICIAN
Pensa, Mario *see* CONRAD FERDINAND MEYER
O PENSADOR : ORGAO DOS INTERESSES DA SOCIEDADE MODERNA – '(s.l.')-Sao Luis, Brazil. 10 Sep 1880-30 Nov 1881 – 1,5,6 – bl Biblioteca [072]
PENSAMIENTE PROPIO – Managua, NQ. 1982-1985 – 1r – $50.00 – R04228 – us Library Micro [072]
PENSAMIENTO CRITICO – Havana, CU. 1967-1971 – 5r – $250.00 – R04206 – us Library Micro [073]
EL PENSAMIENTO POLITICO HISPANOAMERICANO... / Donoso Cortes, Juan Francisco – Buenos Aires: Ediciones de Palma, 1965 – 1 – sp Bibl Santa Ana [320]
EL PENSAMIENTO POLITICO Y SOCIAL DE JAMES FENIMORE COOPER / Vinuela Angulo, Urbano – 1mf – 9 – Pta1,000.00 – 84-85422-17-1 – sp Pentalfa [420]
PENSAMIENTOS / Sanchez-Arjona, Vicente – Sevilla: Graficas Tirvia, Tomo 3. 1954 – 1 – sp Bibl Santa Ana [810]
PENSAMIENTOS / Sanchez-Arjona, Vicente – Sevilla: Imp. Carlos Acuna, Tomo 2. 1952 – 1 – sp Bibl Santa Ana [810]
PENSAMIENTOS / Sanchez-Arjona, Vicente – Sevilla: Imp. Zambrano, Tomo 1. 1952 – 1 – sp Bibl Santa Ana [810]
PENSAMIENTOS Y SENTIRES / Sanchez-Arjona, Vicente – Sevilla: Imp. Alvarez, Tomo 13-16. 1957 – 1 – sp Bibl Santa Ana [810]
PENSAMIENTOS Y SENTIRES / Sanchez-Arjona, Vicente – Sevilla: Imp. Alvarez, Tomo 1-4. 1957 – 1 – sp Bibl Santa Ana [810]
PENSAMIENTOS Y SENTIRES / Sanchez-Arjona, Vicente – Sevilla: Imp. Alvarez, Tomo 17-20. 1957 – 1 – sp Bibl Santa Ana [810]
PENSAMIENTOS Y SENTIRES / Sanchez-Arjona, Vicente – Sevilla: Imp. Alvarez, Tomo 21-24. 1957 – 1 – sp Bibl Santa Ana [810]
PENSAMIENTOS Y SENTIRES / Sanchez-Arjona, Vicente – Sevilla: Imp. Alvarez, Tomo 24-28. 1957 – 1 – sp Bibl Santa Ana [810]
PENSAMIENTOS Y SENTIRES / Sanchez-Arjona, Vicente – Sevilla: Imp. Alvarez, Tomo 29-32. 1957 – 1 – sp Bibl Santa Ana [810]
PENSAMIENTOS Y SENTIRES / Sanchez-Arjona, Vicente – Sevilla: Imp. Alvarez, Tomo 37-40. 1957 – 1 – sp Bibl Santa Ana [810]
PENSAMIENTOS Y SENTIRES / Sanchez-Arjona, Vicente – Sevilla: Imp. Alvarez, Tomo 41-44. 1957 – 1 – sp Bibl Santa Ana [810]
PENSAMIENTOS Y SENTIRES / Sanchez-Arjona, Vicente – Sevilla: Imp. Alvarez, Tomo 45-48. 1957 – 1 – sp Bibl Santa Ana [810]
PENSAMIENTOS Y SENTIRES / Sanchez-Arjona, Vicente – Sevilla: Imp. Alvarez, Tomo 49-52. 1957 – 1 – sp Bibl Santa Ana [810]
PENSAMIENTOS Y SENTIRES / Sanchez-Arjona, Vicente – Sevilla: Imp. Alvarez, Tomo 5-8. 1957 – 1 – sp Bibl Santa Ana [810]
PENSAMIENTOS Y SENTIRES / Sanchez-Arjona, Vicente – Sevilla: Imp. Alvarez, Tomo 9-12. 1957 – 1 – sp Bibl Santa Ana [810]
PENSAMIENTOS Y SENTIRES / Sanchez-Arjona, Vicente – Sevilla: Imprenta Alvarez, Tomo 33-36. 1957 – 1 – sp Bibl Santa Ana [810]
PENSAMIENTOS...MALOS! / Sanchez-Arjona, Vicente – Sevilla: Imp. Alvarez, Tomos 1-3. 1958 – 1 – sp Bibl Santa Ana [810]
LA PENSEE – Revue independante de litterature, d'art et de science. no. 1-89. Belfort puis Paris. 25 oct 1899-1905. mq no. 21-24; n.s. juil 1913-juin 1914, juin 1920 – 1 – fr A.C.R.P.P. [073]
PENSEE A SON AMI SIGISMOND THALBERG... / Burgmueller, F – Paris: Ms, 13 mars 1843 – 1 – us Sibley [780]
LA PENSEE DE BAGOT – (Cont by the last section of: Le Courrier de St-Hyacinthe under the title: Courrier La Pensee de Bagot 24 fev 1971) – Acton Vale, Canada. 16 mai 1951-17 fev 1971 – 6r – 1 – Can$65.00r – cn Can Microfilming [072]
LA PENSEE SYNDICALE FRANCAISE. MILITANTS ET THEORICIENS / Goetz-Girey, R – 4mf – 9 – F60.00 – fr Ethnologie [320]
PENSEES POLITIQUES ET RELIGIEUSES DU SAINT-SIMONIEN / Desessart – Paris, Johanneau, 1833, 48 p. Les Saint-Simoniens, 1825-1834. 6965 – 9 – fr Hachette [335]
PENSEES RELIGIEUSES PAR UN SAINT-SIMONIEN / Fournier – Angers, impr. E. Le Sourd, 1833, 50 p. Les Saint-Simoniens, 1825-1834. 6913 – 9 – fr Hachette [335]
PENSEES SECRETES ET OBSERVATIONS CRITIQUES ATTRIBUEES A FEU M. DE SAINT-HYACINTHE – (D'Holbach series). 1769 – 9 – fr Hachette [190]

PENSIERO E LINGUAGGIO IN OPERAZIONI – 1970- 1; 1971- 5,6; 1975- 4 x 6 in. 9 – us UMI [400]
PENSIERO ED AZIONE – London, Genoa, Lugano. No1-39, Sept 1858-May 1860 – 5 fiches – 9 – $45.00 – us UPA [945]
IL PENSIERO ITALIANO – Utica, NY, July 3, 1914-April 20, 1929 – 6r – 1 – us I.H.R.C. [978]
PENSIL AMERICANO FLORIDO...MARIA DE GUADALUPE DE MEXICO. 1797 / Carrillo Lopez, Ignacio – 9 – 1.50f – sp Bibl Santa Ana [972]
PENSION AND BOUNTY-LAND CLAIMS DECISIONS / U.S. Department of the Interior – (Occasionally entitled: "Pension and Bounty-Land Decisions" or "Pension and Retirement Claims Decisions". Cont by: Decisions of the Administrator of Veterans' Affairs LLMC 80-522 in Military Law Collection) – v1-22. 1887-1930 (all publ) – 137mf – 9 – $205.00 – LLMC 81-211 – us L.L.M.C. [324]
PENSION AND BOUNTY-LAND DECISIONS *see* PENSION AND BOUNTY-LAND CLAIMS DECISIONS
PENSION AND PROFIT SHARING TAX JOURNAL *see* JOURNAL OF PENSION PLANNING AND COMPLIANCE
PENSION AND RETIREMENT CLAIMS DECISIONS *see* PENSION AND BOUNTY-LAND CLAIMS DECISIONS
PENSION AND WELFARE NEWS – v1-11 1964-75 1; v9-11 5,6; v11 1975- 9 – us UMI [073]
THE PENSION LAWYER'S DIGEST – Washington: Lowell, 1890. LL-1175 – 1 – us L of C Photodup [340]
PENSION PLANS, 1936-1954 : AN ANALYTIC BIBLIOGRAPHY OF THE DEVELOPMENT OF NATIONAL GROUP, PRIVATE AND INDIVIDUAL PENSION PLANS ON THE NORTH AMERICAN CONTINENT / Ho, Alice – 1954. SEM105P4 – 2mf – 9 – cn Bibl Nat [360]
PENSION WORLD – (See also: Pension and Welfare News) – v11- 1975- – 1,5,6,9 – us UMI [336]
PENSIONNAT MONT SAINT-LOUIS / Bellay, A – 1891?. 02325. (Pre-1900 Canadiana) – 9 – cn C.I.H.M. [370]
PENSIONS AND INVESTMENTS – (v. 7- 1979 5,6,9) – 1$ 1973- – 1 – us UMI [332]
PENTAGON – v1- 1941- 1; v34- 5,6; v36- 9 – us UMI [355]
THE PENTAGON PAPERS TRIAL WITH INDEX / Meiklejohn Civil Liberties Institute – 23 reels – 1 – $900.00 – us Trans-Media [340]
DER PENTATEUCH / Klostermann, August – Leipzig: A. Deichert, 1893. 1 fiche – 9 – us A.T.L.A. [240]
THE PENTATEUCH / Hervey, Arthur Charles – (Includes index) – New York: Longmans, Green, 1895 – 1mf – 9 – 0-8370-3577-5 – 1985-1577 – us A.T.L.A. [220]
THE PENTATEUCH / Kennedy, John – 1884 – 9 – us A.T.L.A. [220]
THE PENTATEUCH / Rowland, Adoniram Judson – Philadelphia: Am. Bapt. Pub. Soc., 1893.1 fiche – 9 – us A.T.L.A. [240]
THE PENTATEUCH : TRANSLATED FROM THE VULGATE AND DILIGENTLY COMPARED WITH THE ORIGINAL TEXT – Baltimore: Kelly, Hedian & Piet, 1860 – 2mf – 9 – 0-8370-7396-0 – 1986-1396 – us A.T.L.A. [220]
PENTATEUCH ANALYSIS : THE CODES / Bissell, Edwin Cone – (Includes bibliographical references) – New York: Funk & Wagnalls, 1888, c1887 – 1mf – 9 – 0-8370-5794-9 – 1985-3794 – us A.T.L.A. [220]
THE PENTATEUCH AND ITS ANATOMISTS : OR, THE UNITY AND AUTHENTICITY OF THE BOOKS OF MOSES VINDICATED AND CONFIRMED IN REPLY TO MODERN CRITICISM / Birks, Thomas Rawson – London: Hatchards, 1869 – 1mf – 9 – 0-8370-2346-7 – 1985-0346 – us A.T.L.A. [220]
THE PENTATEUCH AND THE BOOK OF JOSHUA : WITH...CRITICAL AND EXPLANATORY COMMENTARY / Jamieson, Robert – Philadelphia: William S & Alfred Martien, 1860 – 1mf – 9 – 0-8370-3766-2 – 1985-1766 – us A.T.L.A. [220]
THE PENTATEUCH AND THE BOOK OF JOSHUA CRITICALLY EXAMINED / Colenso, John William – pts. 1-7. 1862 – 9 – us A.T.L.A. [240]
THE PENTATEUCH AND THE ELOHISTIC PSALMS / Browne, Edward Harold – 1863 – 1,9 – us A.T.L.A. [240]
THE PENTATEUCH AND THE GOSPELS / Porter, Josias Leslie – London: T. Nelson, 1864.1 fiche – 9 – us A.T.L.A. [240]
PENTATEUCH, IN ITS PROGRESSIVE REVELATIONS OF GOD TO MEN / Cowles, Henry – New York: Appleton, 1874. 1 fiche – 9 – us A.T.L.A. [240]
THE PENTATEUCH, IN ITS PROGRESSIVE REVELATIONS OF GOD TO MEN DESIGNED FOR BOTH PASTORS AND PEOPLE / Cowles, Henry – New York:D Appleton, 1874 – 1mf – 9 – 0-8370-2757-8 – 1985-0757 – us A.T.L.A. [220]
PENTATEUCH LAWS AND THE HIGHER CRITICISM : A SERIES OF QUESTIONS IN REVIEW OF RECENT THEORIES CONCERNING THE ORIGIN OF THE PENTATEUCH LEGISLATION / Bissell, Edwin Cone – Hartford, CT: Case, Lockwood & Brainard, 1885 – 1mf – 9 – 0-8370-3505-8 – 1985-1505 – us A.T.L.A. [220]
THE PENTATEUCHAL NARRATIVE VINDICATED FROM THE ABSURDITIES CHARGED AGAINST IT BY THE BISHOP OF NATAL / Knight, JC – 2nd ed. 1890 – 9 – us A.T.L.A. [240]
PENTATEUCHUS MOYSIS COMMENTARIO ILLUSTRATUS / Bonfrere, J – 2189 2. 1625 – 8 – ne IDC [220]
PENTATEUCHUS, SIVE COMMENTARIUS IN QUINQUE LIBROS MOYSIS / Jansenius, Corn. – Lovanii, 1641 – 12mf – 8 – ne Slangenburg [220]
Pentecost, George Frederick *see*
- IN THE VOLUME OF THE BOOK, OR, THE PROFIT AND PLEASURE OF BIBLE STUDY
- OUT OF EGYPT: BIBLE READINGS ON THE BOOK OF EXODUS

PENTECOSTAL ADVOCATE – (Lacking some issues) – v11-15. 1907-12 – 4r – 1 – ATLA S0418 – us A.T.L.A. [240]
PENTECOSTAL AGGRESSIVENESS, OR, WHY I CONDUCTED THE MEETINGS OF THE CHESAPEAKE HOLINESS UNION AT BOWENS, MARYLAND / Knapp, Martin Wells – Cincinnati, Ohio: M.W. Knapp, 1899 – 1mf – us A.T.L.A. [240]
PENTECOSTAL HERALD – 1889; 1897-1976 (complete) – 36r – 1 – ATLA S0294 – us A.T.L.A. [073]
PENTECOSTAL MISSION HERALD – v1 no1. Dec 1897 (complete) – Inquire – 1 – ATLA S0932 – us A.T.L.A. [073]
PENTECOSTAL UNION HERALD – v3-5. 1902-04 (complete) – Inquire – 1 – ATLA S0933 – us A.T.L.A. [073]
PENTHESILEA : EIN TRAUERSPIEL / Kleist, Heinrich von – [Leipzig: Wildermann, 1927] – 1 – us U.W. Library [820]
"PENTHESILEA" IN DER KLEISTLITERATUR / Schmidt, Werner – (Includes bibliographical references) – Leipzig: Verlagsbuchhandlung von J J Weber, 1934 – 1 – us U.W. Library [430]
PENTHOUSE – v10-. 1978- – 9 – us UMI [790]
PENTICTON HERALD – (1993.-12r; 1906-1920.-4r) – Penticton, 1972-1992 – 136r – 1 – cn Preston [971]
PENTJA – Djakarta. Incomplete. SE-951 1. 1951-1971 – 9 – ne IDC [073]
PENTRU SOCIALISM – Baia Mare, Romania. 1962-Jul 1979 – 25r – 1 – us L of C Photodup [949]
PENUNDJUK TELEPON, DJAKARTA – Incomplete. SE-620 1. 1950-1971 – 9 – ne IDC [073]
PENUNDJUK TELEPON, MEDAN – (Title varies: Telefoongids) – 1948-58 (incomplete) – 9 – SE-623 1 – ne IDC [073]
PENUNTUN DJIWA / Amrullah, Abdul Malik Karim – SE-4910 1. 1962 – 9 – ne IDC [950]
PENUNTUN PRAKTIS UNTUK PEMBUATAN KARET / Thio, Goan Loo – SE 4858 1. 1963 – 9 – ne IDC [950]
PENUNTUN WANITA AND PRIJA MODERN / Adlin, Rina – SE-4869 1. 1960 – 9 – ne IDC [950]
Penwell, L.M. Undertaking Company, Topeka, KS *see* UNDERTAKER'S REGISTER AND ACCOUNT BOOK[S]
Penwill, D J *see* KAMBA CUSTOMARY LAW; NOTES TAKEN IN THE MACHAKOS DISTRICT OF KENYA COLONY
PENYATA TAHUNAN = ANNUAL REPORT FOR 1975-1977 / Sarawak. Education Department – (In English) – Kuching – 6mf – 9 – DE-199/1 – ne IDC [370]
PENZANCE SHOPPER – Falmouth, England. 1985-Nov 1986. -w. 3 reels – 1 – uk British Libr Newspaper [072]
Penzig, A J O *see*
- ICONES FUNGORUM JAVANICORUM
- DIE MYXOMYCETEN DER FLORA VON BUITENZORG...
- PFLANZEN-TERATOLOGIE SYSTEMATISCH GEORDNET

Penzol, Pedro *see* LAS TRADUCCIONES DE "CALILA E DIMNA"
Penzoldt, Ernst *see*
- DER DANKBARE PATIENT
- ETIENNE UND LUISE
- IDOLINO
- DIE LEUTE AUS DER MOHRENAPOTHEKE
- DIE PORTUGALESISCHE SCHLACHT
- ZUGAENGE

PEONAGE FILES, 1901-45 / U.S. Department of Justice – 26 reels with printed guide – 1 – $2,860.00 – 0-89093-991-8 – us UPA [977]
PEOPLE – Merced, CA. May-Jun 1872 – 1r – 1 – $50.00 – B02449 – us Library Micro [071]
PEOPLE – New York. v9-10. 1899-1900 – 1r – 1 – us Ross [071]
PEOPLE : THEIR RIGHTS AND LIBERTIES, THEIR DUTIES AND INTERESTS – (Series 1: 1-3 (all publ). 1848-1851. Series 2: 1-2 (all publ). 1851-1852) – 23mf – 9 – $95.00 – us UPA [360]
PEOPLE – Wexford, Ireland. 1853-61; 1863-96. -w. 60 reels – 1 – uk British Libr Newspaper [072]
THE PEOPLE = DOS FOLK – Montreal, CN. v1 no 14. 1917 – 1r – 1 – Can$30.00 – cn Can Microfilming [072]
THE PEOPLE – Dublin. Ireland. -w. 2 Feb-5 Oct 1833. (45 ft) – 1 – uk British Libr Newspaper [072]
THE PEOPLE – New York. Daily. July 1 1900-Feb 22 1914 – 1 – us NY Public [071]
THE PEOPLE – New York. Rival paper to Weekly People Jan 16 1899-Apr 1 1900. Incomplete – 1 – us NY Public [071]
THE PEOPLE – Norman, OK. 27 Sept-13 Dec 1971 – 1 – us A.J.P.C. [071]
THE PEOPLE – Providence. R.I. 1887- – 1 – us UMI [071]
THE PEOPLE – (Sunday People). London. -w. 1881-1976. (122mqn reels) – 1 – uk British Libr Newspaper [072]
THE PEOPLE – Wexford, Ireland. -d. 1863-1900, 1986.20 reels – 1 – PS27.50r – ie European Micro [072]
THE PEOPLE *see*
- POPULAR NEWSPAPERS DURING WORLD WAR 1
- POPULAR NEWSPAPERS DURING WORLD WAR 2

PEOPLE AND EDUCATION / Zimbabwe. Department of African Education – 1979 – 1mf – 9 – DE-506/1 – ne IDC [370]
THE PEOPLE AND FREEDOM NEWS SHEET – London. -m. Easter 1938-Jul 1953. (53 ft) – 1 – uk British Libr Newspaper [072]
PEOPLE AND TAXES – Riverside, CA. 1976-1985 – 3r – 1 – $150.00 – R03414 – us Library Micro [071]
THE PEOPLE AND WE YONE – The People, June 2, 1972 through April 14, 1973, with April 14, 1973, with scattered issues missing. 1r. $49.50; we Yone: includes both Sunday and Wednesday edition for 1973. 2r. $99.00 – us African Imprint [320]
A PEOPLE AT WAR / ed by Sellers, John R – (With cumulative printed guide & index) – 150r (30r per yr for 5yrs) – 13 – £3,655.00 – uk Chadwyck [976]
THE PEOPLE CALLED METHODISTS *see*
- AN ALPHABETICAL ARRANGEMENT OF ALL THE WESLEYAN METHODIST PREACHERS AND MISSIONARIES, WHO ARE NOW TRAVELLING IN GREAT-BRITAIN AND IN DISTANT PARTS OF THE GLOBE,...
- [GENERAL RULES, 1824]

THE PEOPLE CALLED METHODISTS. A DOCUMENTARY HISTORY OF THE METHODIST CHURCH IN GREAT BRITAIN AND IRELAND, PHASE 1 : REFERENCE TOOLS, 1738-1932 / ed by Field, Clive – (Includes a printed guide. Individual titles also listed separately) – 1993 – 1,134mf coll of 3 phases – 9 – ne IDC [240]
THE PEOPLE CALLED METHODISTS. A DOCUMENTARY HISTORY OF THE METHODIST CHURCH IN GREAT BRITAIN AND IRELAND, PHASE 2 : PRIMARY SOURCES, 1738-1800 / ed by Field, Clive – (Includes printed guide. Individual titles also listed separately) – 1993 – 1,134mf coll of 3 phases – 9 – ne IDC [240]
THE PEOPLE CALLED METHODISTS. A DOCUMENTARY HISTORY OF THE METHODIST CHURCH IN GREAT BRITAIN AND IRELAND, PHASE 3 : PRIMARY SOURCES, 1801-1850 / ed by Field, Clive – (Includes printed guide. Individual titles also listed separately) – 1993 – 1,134mf coll of 3 phases – 9 – ne IDC [240]
PEOPLE CALLED METHODISTS, PHASE 1 *see*
- CATALOGUE OF THE CHARLES WESLEY PAPERS, V1
- CATALOGUE OF THE CHARLES WESLEY PAPERS, V2
- CATALOGUE OF THE HUGH BOURNE AND WILLIAM CLOWES PAPERS
- CATALOGUE OF THE THOMAS COKE PAPERS
- CATALOGUE OF THE WESLEY FAMILY MANUSCRIPTS, V1
- CATALOGUE OF THE WESLEY FAMILY PAPERS, V2
- CATALOGUE OF THE WESLEY FAMILY PAPERS, V3
- CHRONICLES OF WESLEYAN METHODISM, SECOND DEPARTMENT
- HANDLIST OF HARTLEY-VICTORIA COLLEGE COLLECTION
- THE PAPERS OF DR. ADAM CLARKE
- THE PAPERS OF FRANK O. SALISBURY (1874-1962)
- THE PAPERS OF JOSEPH BENSON

PEOPLE CALLED METHODISTS, PHASE 2, 1738-1800 *see*
- AUTOBIOGRAPHIE, 1785
- DIARIES, 1767, 1772-1786, 1788-1791
- DIARIES, 1742-1744 [FRAGMENTS], 1747-1754
- DIARIES, 1777-1815
- DIARIES, 1779-1781, 1784-1797, 1805-1809, 1817-1825
- DIARIES AND POCKET-BOOKS, 1772, 1805, 1809-1810, 1815, 1817, 1822
- DIARY, 1755-1757
- DIARY, 1775-1776
- DIARY, 1794-1805
- DIARY AND MEMORANDA BOOK, 1730-1759
- IN- AND OUT-LETTERS, 1750-1815
- IN- AND OUT-LETTERS, 1776-1826
- IN- AND OUT-LETTERS, 1780-1823
- IN-LETTERS, 1735-1787
- IN-LETTERS, 1737-1786
- IN-LETTERS, 1742-1788
- IN-LETTERS, 1749-1789
- IN-LETTERS, 1749-1810
- IN-LETTERS, 1752-1783
- IN-LETTERS, 1756-1812
- IN-LETTERS, 1775-1820
- IN-LETTERS, 1776-1816
- IN-LETTERS, 1780-1827
- IN-LETTERS, 1789-1828
- IN-LETTERS FROM METHODIST PREACHERS ON RELIGIOUS EXPERIENCE, 1738-1788
- JOURNAL, 1765-1766, AND LETTER-BOOKS, 1772-1776
- JOURNAL, 1773-1819
- JOURNALS, 1764, 1783, 1785, 1788, 1792-1799
- JOURNALS, 1790, 1792, 1794-1795, 1797-1798, 1800-1806
- JOURNALS, 1765-1794
- JOURNALS, 1807-1815
- LETTER-BOOK, 1748-1754, AND SERMONS
- LIFE, BY HIMSELF
- MANUSCRIPT SERMONS, 1710-1723, 1730-1734
- MEMORANDA BOOKS, 1774-1815
- OUT-LETTERS, 1728-1787
- OUT-LETTERS, 1733-1787
- OUT-LETTERS, 1739-1766
- OUT-LETTERS, 1740-1783
- OUT-LETTERS, 1748-1787
- OUT-LETTERS, 1752-1784
- OUT-LETTERS, 1752-1785
- OUT-LETTERS, 1766-1820
- OUT-LETTERS, 1769-1799
- OUT-LETTERS, 1788-1826
- OUT-LETTERS, 1788-1830
- OUT-LETTERS, 1789-1797
- OUT-LETTERS, 1795-1833
- OUT-LETTERS AND MISCELLANEOUS PAPERS, 1754-1816
- OUT-LETTERS AND MISCELLANEOUS PAPERS, 1772-1835
- OUT-LETTERS AND MISCELLANEOUS PAPERS, 1785-1835

- OUT-LETTERS AND POEMS, 1775-1828
- OUT-LETTERS, SERMONS AND MISCELLANEOUS PAPERS, 1779-1815
- SERMON REGISTERS, 1774-1803
- SERMONS
- SHORT ACCOUNT, 1772-1792
- SHORT ACCOUNT AND JOURNAL, 1775-1789

PEOPLE CALLED METHODISTS, PHASE 3, 1801-1850 *see*
- ACCOUNT, 1801-1838, V3-6, 8
- ASSEMBLY. MINUTES...
- AUTOBIOGRAPHY
- AUTOBIOGRAPHY, 1855
- AUTOBIOGRAPHY, 1870
- CONFERENCE
- CONFERENCE. MINUTES ... 1819-1850
- CORRESPONDENCE RELATING TO THE JOSEPH BARKER CASE, 1838-1869
- DIARIES, 1788-1790, 1805, 1810, 1815-1819, 1821-1828, 1831-1836
- DIARIES, 1825-1858
- DIARIES, 1845-1846, 1848, 1850, 1852-1858, 1861, 1863, 1867
- DIARY, 1825-1827, 1831-1834, 1836-1838, 1840, 1842, 1845, 1848, 1855, 1857-1864
- IN- AND OUT-LETTERS, 1795-1799, RELATING TO THE FORMATION OF THE METHODIST NEW CONNEXION
- IN- AND OUT-LETTERS, 1820-1849
- IN-LETTERS, 1836-1848, RELATING TO THE METHODIST NEW CONNEXION IN IRELAND
- JOURNAL
- JOURNAL, 1829-1835
- JOURNAL, 1841-1851, 1853-1859
- JOURNALS, 1796-1807, 1813-1814, 1832-1833, 1837-1842
- JOURNALS, 1803-1804, 1808-1813, 1816-1820, 1842-1852
- NOTEBOOKS, 1836-1838
- NOTES AND MEMORANDA, 1784-1868
- OUT-LETTERS, 1780-1840
- OUT-LETTERS 1785-1832
- OUT-LETTERS, 1802-1841
- POCKET-BOOKS AND DIARIES, 1799, 1801-1812, 1815, 1818-1831
- PRIMITIVE METHODIST MAGAZINE
- WESLEYAN METHODIST ASSOCIATION MAGAZINE

PEOPLE IN VICTORIA – 29mf – 9 – A$80.00 – at State Libr Vic [920]

PEOPLE OF INDONESIA, UNITE AND FIGHT TO OVERTHROW THE FASCIST REGIME / Hung ch'i – SE-6655 1968 – 9 – ne IDC [335]

PEOPLE OF IOWA / Harlan, Edgar R – (Chicago: American Historical Society, Inc., 1931). Vol. 1-2. Iowa Reel 3; Vol. 3-5. Iowa Reel 4. (The Cox Library Collection) – 5 – us Americana [978]

THE PEOPLE OF THE POLAR NORTH : A RECORD / Rasmussen, Knud; ed by Herring, G – London: Kegan Paul, Trench, Truebner, 1908 – 2mf – us A.T.L.A. [305]

PEOPLE PILOT – Rensselaer. Ind. 1893-1897 – 1 – us UMI [071]

PEOPLE SENTINEL – Barnwell. S.C. 1973- – 1 – us UMI [071]

PEOPLE VS. GOETZ : THE SUMMATION AND THE CHARGES TO THE JURY / ed by Roehrenbeck, Carol A – 1v – 9 – $45.00 – 0-89941-657-8 – us Hein [340]

PEOPLE WEEKLY – v1- 1974- 1; v3- 5,6,9 – us UMI [073]

PEOPLE'S ADVOCATE – Anderson. S.C. 1892-1901; 1904-1915 – 1 – us UMI [071]

PEOPLE'S ADVOCATE – Ansley, NE. -w. Jun. 1892-Apr. 1896. Incomplete; May 1896-Feb. 1897; Apr. 1897-Nov. 1898. Incomplete – 1 – us NE Hist [071]

PEOPLE'S ADVOCATE – Chehalis. Wash. -w. 1892-1902 – 1 – us UMI [071]

PEOPLE'S ADVOCATE – Monaghan, Ireland. -w. Feb 1876-April 1906. (1905 imperfect.) 29 1 2 reels – 1 – uk British Libr Newspaper [072]

PEOPLE'S ADVOCATE – Ventura, CA. 1894 – 1r – 1 – $50.00 – B03561 – us Library Micro [071]

PEOPLE'S ADVOCATE – Winnemucca, NV. 1890-99 – 1r – 1 – $50.00 – U04820 – us Library Micro [071]

PEOPLES ADVOCATE – Sydney, 1848-56 – 4r – 1 – A$135.00 silver A$116.00 vesicular – at Pascoe [072]

THE PEOPLE'S ADVOCATE – San Francisco. Calif. 5, 24 Jan 1944 – 1 – us NY Public [071]

PEOPLE'S ADVOCATE AND PRESS – New Bloomfield, PA. -w 1857-1913 – 13 – $25.00r – us I.M.R. [071]

THE PEOPLES' ALMANAC FOR 1878: ...FACTS AND FIGURES CONCERNING THE DOMINION OF CANADA.. – Comp. and ed. by D. Creighton. Montreal: T. & R. White, 1878?. 00072.(Pre-1900 Canadiana) – 9 – cn C.I.H.M. [971]

THE PEOPLE'S CHAMPION – Hebron. Neb. 1896-1916 – 1 – us UMI [071]

PEOPLES' CHARTER – 1836 and 1848. And Chartism. An Address. 1841. From Nuffield College Library, Oxford – 1 – uk Microform Academic [941]

PEOPLE'S CHINA – Beijing, China. Semimonthly. 1950-57. M-E8 – 1 – $60.00r – cc Microforms [073]

PEOPLE'S CHINA – Peking, 1950-57 – 150mf – 9 – CH-168/2 – ne IDC [950]

PEOPLE'S CHINA – v. 1-7. 1950-57. Some supplemental nos. wanting – 1 – 127.00 – us L of C Photodup [950]

PEOPLE'S COMMENTARY ON THE GOSPEL ACCORDING TO MATTHEW / Rice, Edwin Wilbur – Philadelphia: Am. Sun. Sch. Un., 1887. 1 fiche – 9 – us A.T.L.A. [240]

THE PEOPLE'S COMMUNE ON MAINLAND CHINA – Primary source materials dealing with people's communes – 1 – 35.00r – us Hoover Inst Photo [335]

PEOPLE'S COMPUTER COMPANY – (See also: People's Computers and Recreational Computing) – v1-5 1972-1977 1; v5- 5,6,9 – us UMI [000]

PEOPLE'S COMPUTERS – (See also: Recreational Computing and People's Computer Company) – v5-7. 1977-1978 – 1,5,6,9 – us UMI [000]

PEOPLE'S CONSERVATIVE *see* DESTRUCTIVE AND POOR MAN'S CONSERVATIVE

The People's Court of Nam Dinh Province *see* VU AN NGUYEN QUANG ICH VA DONG BON CAN TOI LOI DUNG DANH NGHIA TAP DOAN MIEN NAM THAP MUOI DE AN CAP CMA CONG

People's Court of Quang Ninh Province *see* MOT SO LUAT LE CUA NHA NUOC

PEOPLE'S COURTS IN THE U.S.S.R / Sheinin, Lev Romanovich – Moscow: Foreign Languages Pub. House, 1957. 111p. LL-4213 – 1 – us L of C Photodup [340]

PEOPLE'S DAILY WORLD : 1987-1991 – 9 – $1,830.00 – us UPA [320]

THE PEOPLE'S FRIEND – Worcester. Mass. 1913; 1921; 1924 – 1 – us A.J.P.C. [071]

PEOPLE'S GOVERNMENT – North Platte, NE. -w. Nov 1885-Apr 1887, scattered issues missing – 1 – us NE Hist [071]

THE PEOPLE'S HISTORY: WORKING CLASS AUTOBIOGRAPHIES – Series 1: Working class autobiographies, 1792-1920 – 1 – us Primary [920]

PEOPLE'S JOURNAL – Davenport, NE. -w. Jul. 1892-Sep. 1901. Incomplete; Aug. 1902-Dec. 1906; Feb. 1909-Dec. 1920; Jun. 1923; Jan. 1924-Jul. 1942 – 1 – us NE Hist [071]

THE PEOPLE'S JOURNAL – Hamilton. Toronto. 1869-71 – 1 – 45.00 – cn McLaren [971]

PEOPLE'S JOURNAL OF NEW ZEALAND – Dunedin. New Zealand. -w. 10 Nov 1893-7 Apr 1894. (1 reel) – 1 – uk British Libr Newspaper [072]

THE PEOPLE'S LAWYER, AND CONVEYANCER. COMPRISING, ALL THE FEDERAL AND STATE LAWS OF PARTICULAR INTEREST TO THE FARMING COMMUNITY – Fremont, Neb.: Shutt, 1886. 154p. LL-1326 – 1 – us L of C Photodup [340]

PEOPLE'S MAGAZINE *see* THE PEOPLE'S MAGAZINE AND WEEKLY JOURNAL

THE PEOPLE'S MAGAZINE – (Cont by: The People's Magazine and Weekly Journal) – Montreal: Publ for the Proprietor by R D Wadsworth, 1846 – 9 – cn C.I.H.M. [073]

PEOPLE'S MAGAZINE AND WEEKLY JOURNAL *see* THE PEOPLE'S MAGAZINE

THE PEOPLE'S MAGAZINE AND WEEKLY JOURNAL – (Cont: The People's Magazine) – Montreal: Publ for the Proprietor by R D Wadsworth, [1846-18–?] – 9 – cn C.I.H.M. [073]

PEOPLE'S NEWSPAPER – London, UK. 1847. -w. 28 feet – 1 – uk British Libr Newspaper [072]

PEOPLE'S OBSERVER – Portland OR. June 29 1943-Feb 28 1945 – 1 – us U.O. Library [071]

THE PEOPLES OF SARAWAK / Harrisson, Thomas Harnett – 1911 ed. Distributed by the Curator, Sarawak Museum, 1959 – 1 – us U.W. Library [305]

PEOPLE'S PAPER : CHAMPION OF POLITICAL JUSTICE AND UNIVERSAL RIGHTS – 1-331 (all publ). 1852-1858 – 7r – 1 – $465.00 – us UPA [335]

THE PEOPLE'S PAPER – 1852-58.Organ of Chartist Movement – 1 – uk World [941]

THE PEOPLE'S PAPER – London. -w. May 1852-Sep 1858. (12 reels) – 1 – uk British Libr Newspaper [072]

PEOPLE'S PARTY FARMERS JOURNAL – Portland OR. Aug 18 1893 – 1 – us U.O. Library [071]

PEOPLE'S PARTY POST – Portland, OR. 22 Nov 1894-19 Mar 1896. 1 roll – 1 – us U.O. Library [071]

PEOPLE'S PARTY POST – Portland, OR. -w. 1894-96 – 1 – 17.00 – us Oregon Hist [071]

PEOPLE'S POLITE GAZETTE – London, UK. 1841. -w. 12 reels – 1 – uk British Libr Newspaper [072]

PEOPLE'S PONIARD – Sidney, NE. -w. Sep 1892; Aug 1895-Jan 1899 – 1 – us NE Hist [071]

PEOPLE'S PRESS – Albany, OR. -w. 5 Aug 1898-29 Aug 1901. 1 roll – 1 – us U.O. Library [071]

PEOPLE'S PRESS – Cambridge. Ohio. -w. 1893 – 1 – us UMI [071]

PEOPLE'S PRESS – El Reno. Okl. 1923-29 – 1 – us UMI [071]

PEOPLE'S PRESS – Eugene OR. Mar 8 June 7 1859, Oct 1 Nov 19 Dec 24 1859, Jan 14 21 28 Feb 25 1860, Nov 17 24 1860 – 1 – us U.O. Library [071]

PEOPLE'S PRESS – Owatonna. Minn. 1956- – 1 – us UMI [071]

PEOPLE'S PRESS – Portland OR. July 28 1911 – 1 – us U.O. Library [071]

PEOPLE'S PRESS – Wilmington. N.C. and Wilmington Advertiser. 1835-36 – 1 – us UMI [071]

PEOPLES PRESS – Pioche, NV. 1944 – 1r – 1 – $50.00 – U04647 – us Library Micro [071]

PEOPLES PRESS – Welland, 1899-1908 – 3r – 1 – cn Preston [971]

PEOPLE'S PRESS AND CORK WEEKLY REGISTER – Cork. Ireland. -w. 20 Sep 1834-10 Feb 1836. (1 reel) – 1 – uk British Libr Newspaper [072]

PEOPLE'S REGISTER – Chambersburg, PA. -w 1896-1925 – 13 – $25.00r – us I.M.R. [071]

PEOPLE'S REGISTER – Chambersburg. PA. -w. 1896-97 – 1 – us UMI [071]

PEOPLES REGISTER – York, PA., 1890-1896 – 13 – $25.00r – us I.M.R. [071]

PEOPLE'S REPUBLIC – (Set incl. People's Republic (Wasco)) – Moro, OR. -w. 18 Nov 1898-23 June 1899. – 1r – 1 – us U.O. Library [071]

PEOPLE'S REPUBLIC – Wasco OR. Apr 21-Nov 3 1898 – 1 – us U.O. Library [071]

PEOPLE'S REVIEW *see* RARE RADICAL AND LABOUR PERIODICALS OF GREAT BRITAIN, SERIES 1

THE PEOPLES' RIGHTS / Churchill, Winston S – 1909. 1 fiche (24x) – 9 – 1.00f – at Libertarian Micro [320]

PEOPLE'S RIP-SAW – Crete, NE. -w. Jul. 1885-Oct. 1890; Jul. 1891-Nov. 1891 – 1 – us NE Hist [071]

PEOPLE'S SENTINEL – Trenton, NE. -w. Jul 1892; Nov-Dec 1895; Feb-Jun 1896; Aug 1897 – 1 – us NE Hist [071]

PEOPLE'S SONGS – 9 – $50.00 – us UPA [780]

PEOPLE'S STORIES (CCC178) / Hsieh, Sung-kao – (In Chinese) – Hong Kong: Bible Book and Tract Depot. 2v. 1953-1956 – 1r – 1 – 1984-B500 – us A.T.L.A. [240]

The People's Supreme Court *see*
- LUAT LE VE TU PHAP
- SO TAY NQUOI THAM PHAN

The People's Supreme Procuracy *see* LUAT LE NUOC VIET NAM DAN CHU CONG HOA

THE PEOPLE'S TELEPHONE – Red Oak. Iowa. 1878-1884 – 1 – us UMI [071]

PEOPLE'S TRIBUNE – Hankow, China, 1927 – 1r – 1 – us Ross [072]

PEOPLES TRIBUNE – Hankow. Mar-Aug 1927. Incomplete – 1 – us NY Public [073]

THE PEOPLE'S TRIBUNE – (Tribune Midland Counties Tribune). Nuneaton. England. -w. 1895-1909, 1913-57. (49 reels) – 1 – uk British Libr Newspaper [072]

THE PEOPLE'S TRIBUNE, 1931-1942 : AN ORGAN OF NATIONAL REVOLUTIONARY THOUGHT AND OPINION – (In English) – 6r – 1 – $210.00 in US $40.00r outside – L9300080 – Dist. us Scholarly Res – us L of C Photodup [950]

PEOPLE'S UNION FOR DEMOCRATIC RIGHTS – New Delhi. 70 docs. 1980-1991 – 22mf – 9 – ne IDC [320]

PEOPLE'S VOICE : AMERICA'S GREATEST NEGRO NEWSPAPER – New York. v1-7. 1942-48 – 9r – 1 – us Ross [071]

PEOPLE'S VOICE – Wellington. Kan. 1890-1917 – 1 – us UMI [071]

PEOPLES VOICE – Imperial, NE. -w. Dec 1892; Oct 1895-Aug 1896 – 1 – us NE Hist [071]

PEOPLES' VOICE – Helena. Mont. 1958-1959; 1966- – 1 – us UMI [071]

THE PEOPLE'S VOICE *see* LA VOIX DU PEUPLE

THE PEOPLE'S VOICE (NEW YORK, N.Y.: 1933) – (Library has: v. 1, no. 1 (July 25, 1933)) – New York, N.Y.: People's Voice Publishing Assn., 1933- – 1 – CSUX89-S83 – us Hoover Inst Photo [978]

PEOPLE'S WEEKLY WORLD : 1992-1995 – 9 – $280.00ea yr – us UPA [320]

PEOPLE'S WEEKLY WORLD – San Francisco, CA. 1938-1939; 1940; 1987 – 13+ r – 1 – $650.00 ($135.00y) – C03490 – us Library Micro [071]

THE PEOPLE'S WIT – (New York). 1893-94 – 1 – us A.J.P.C. [071]

PEOPLE'S WORLD – Central edition. v. 1-1938- – 1 – us UMI [071]

PEOPLE'S WORLD – (Cont. see San Francisco) – Berkeley, CA. 1943-86 – 67r – 1 – $3,350.00 – C02060 – us Library Micro [071]

PEOPLE'S WORLD – San Francisco. Calif. 1955-1966 – 1 – us UMI [071]

PEOPLE'S WORLD *see* GUARDIAN

PEORIA CITY AND COUNTY / Rice, James M – Historical and biographical. Chicago: S. J. Clarke Publ. Co., 1912. Vols. 1-2. Illinois Reel 48. (The Cox Library Collection) – 5 – us Americana [978]

PEP – Issue Nos. 11-15 Jan 1941-May 1941 – 5mf – 15 – $31.95 – us Comics [760]

PEP – Issue Nos. 1-5 Jan 1940-Jun 1940 – 5mf – 15 – $31.95 – us Comics [760]

PEP – Issue Nos. 16-20 Jun 1941-Oct 1941 – 5mf – 15 – $31.95 – us Comics [760]

PEP – Issue Nos. 21-25 Nov 1941-Mar 1942 – 5mf – 15 – $31.95 – us Comics [760]

PEP – Issue Nos. 26-30 Apr 1942-Aug 1942 – 5mf – 15 – $31.95 – us Comics [760]

PEP – Issue Nos. 31-35 Sept 1942-Jan 1943 – 5mf – 15 – $31.95 – us Comics [760]

PEP – Issue Nos. 36-40 Feb 1943-Jul 1943 – 5mf – 15 – $31.95 – us Comics [760]

PEP – Issue Nos. 41-45 Aug 1943-Jan 1944 – 5mf – 15 – $31.95 – us Comics [760]

PEP – Issue Nos. 46-50 Feb 1944-Sept 1944 – 5mf – 15 – $31.95 – us Comics [760]

PEP – Issue Nos. 6-10 Jul 1940-Dec 1940 – 5mf – 15 – $31.95 – us Comics [760]

PEPEL / Belyi, A – Spb. 1909. BR-581 2 – 8 – ne IDC [460]

Peperius, Ben. *see* COMMENTARIORUM ET DISPUTATIONUM IN GENESIM

PEPITA JIMENEZ / Valera, Juan – Trans. from the Spanish.Introd. essay on Spanish fiction by Maurice Francis Egan. New York: Collier, c1886. 311p – 1 – us U.W. Library [830]

Pepper, George Hubbard *see* GEORGE HUBBARD PEPPER PAPERS, 1895-1918

Pepper, George Wharton *see* SYNOPSIS OF A COURSE OF LECTURES ON PLEADING AT COMMON LAW, DELIVERED IN THE DEPARTMENT OF LAW, UNIVERSITY OF PENNSYLVANIA, FIRST TERM, 1889-90

Pepper, Robert D *see* FOUR TUDOR BOOKS ON EDUCATION

PEPPERDINE LAW REVIEW – (v1-12 1973-85 on reel $250.00. v13-22 1985-95 on mf $195.00) – v1-22. 1973-95 – 5,6,9 – $444.00 set – us Hein [340]

PEPPERDINE LAW REVIEW – (v.7-. 1979-5,6,9) – v.1-. 1973- – 1 – us UMI [370]

PEPPERELL 1699-1891 – (Mf 1-5: Birth Index 1727-1962. Mf 6-8: Intentions Index 1754-1905. Mf 9-12: Marriage Index 1745-1962. Mf 13-16: Death Index 1729-1962. Mf 17-20: Vital Records 1699-1802. Mf 21: Deaths 1729-77. Mf 22-29: Vital Records 1746-1848. Mf 30-31: Vital Records 1843-52. Mf 32: Marriages 1778-96. Mf 32-35: Marriages 1853-91. Mf 36-41: Births 1853-91. Mf 42-47: Deaths 1853-91) – (mf ed 1983) – 47mf – 9 – 0-931248-41-8 – us Holbrook [920]

PEPPERMINT PRESS SUMMER WEEKLY READER – (v.6-. 1980- 5,6,9) – v.1-. 1975- – 1 – us UMI [800]

PEPPERRELL PAPERS 1689-1764 – 1974 – 2r – 1 – $60.00 – us New England [920]

Pepperrell, William *see* WILLIAM PEPPERRELL PAPERS, 1683-1769

PEPTIDES – v1- 1980- – 1,5,6,9 – us UMI [540]

Pepusch, J C *see*
- THE BEGGAR'S OPERA
- SONATAS (16) COMPOSED FOR A VIOLIN AND A BASS VIOL OR HARPSICHORD
- A TREATISE ON HARMONY
- A TREATISE ON HARMONY: CONTAINING THE CHIEF RULES FOR COMPOSING IN TWO, THREE, AND FOUR PARTS
- TRIOSONATEN FUER 2 VIOLINEN, VIOLONCELLO UND BASSO CONTINUO

PEQUENO JORNAL : ORGAM CRITICO, HUMORISTICO, LITTERARIO, NOTICIOSO E POLITICO – Manaos, Amazonas. 22 Jul 1915 – 1,5,6 – bl Biblioteca [072]

O PEQUENO SEMEADOR : ORGAO DO INSTITUTO PADRE MACHADO – S. Joao Del-Rei, 11 Jun 1933-Dec 1937; Jan-Feb, May-Dec 1939; Mar 1940-Mar 1943; 25 Dec 1944 – 1,5,6 – bl Biblioteca [072]

PER IL DOMINIO DEL MARE / Arena, O – Palermo, 1927 – 4mf – 9 – ILM-2218/1 – ne IDC [340]

PER LA PACE MONDIALE / Assante, A – Napoli, 1936 – 2mf – 9 – ILM-1960/1 – ne IDC [340]

PER LA VITTORIA DELL'ARMATA CHRISTIANA, ... / Adrario, A – N.p. [1571] – 1mf – 9 – H-8311/1 – ne IDC [956]

PER ON Y LA CRISIS ARGENTINA / Irazusta, Julio – Buenos Aires: La Voz del Plata, [1956] – 9 – us Hoover Inst Photo [972]

PERADJOERIT – Simeleongoen; Markas Penerangan Saranan T.R.I. 1946-v1(1) – 1mf – 9 – SE-555/1 – ne IDC [950]

Peragallo, H *see*
- DIATOMEES DU MIDI DE LA FRANCE
- DIATOMEES MARINES DE FRANCE ET DES DISTRICTS MARITIMES VOISINS

Peragallo, M *see* DIATOMEES MARINES DE FRANCE ET DES DISTRICTS MARITIMES VOISINS

PERAHIM – (New York). 1910-11 – 1 – us A.J.P.C. [071]

PERALIHAN KE SOSIALISME. TERDJEMAHAN KAMARUZZAMAN / Roland Holst(van der Schalk), Henriette – SE 5428 1. 1953 – 9 – ne IDC [335]

Peramato, P de *see* PARECERES EN EL ESTADO DE SALUD DE SEVILLA

PERANAN BANGSA INDONESIA DALAM SEDJARAH ASIA TENGGARA / Ali, R Moh. – SE-3528 1. 1963 – 9 – ne IDC [950]

PERANAN DAN TUGAS DEWAN PERUSAHAAN / Sentral Organisasi Buruh Seluruh Indonesia – SE 5138 1. 1963 – 9 – ne IDC [025]

PERANG PARTISAN / Lenin, Vladimir Ilyich – SE-4542 1. 1958 – 9 – ne IDC [335]

Perarskii, P P *see* ZHIZN'I LITERATURNAIA PEREPISKA PETRA IVANOVICHA RYCHKOVA

PERATURAN MENGHANTAR ORANG HUKUMAN (PESAKITAN) / Karjadi, mas – SE-5389 1 – 9 – ne IDC [950]

Perboyre, G *see* MEMOIRES DE LA CONGREGATION DE LA MISSION

Perce, Warren Raymond *see*
- GENESIS AND MODERN SCIENCE

PERCEIVED AND PREFERRED COACH LEADER BEHAVIORS OF HIGH SCHOOL AND COLLEGE FOOTBALL PLAYERS / Schubiger, Scott, P & Murray, Mimi – 1993 – 2mf – $8.00 – us Microform Publ [150]

PERCEIVED BENEFITS OF STRENGTH TRAINING FOR YOUTH PARTICIPANTS AS DETERMINED BY ORTHOPEDIC SURGEONS / Michaud, Peter & Redmond, Charles J – 1993 – 2mf – $8.00 – us Microform Publ [617]

PERCEIVED BODY IMAGE : SELECTED LIFESTYLE PRACTICES AND THEIR RELATIONSHIP TO PHYSICAL SELF-ESTEEM / Norder-Pietrzak, Michelle M & Chase, Lisa A – 1993 – 1mf – $4.00 – us Microform Publ [150]

PERCEIVED COMPETENCE AND INTRINSIC MOTIVATION AMONG JUNIOR TENNIS PLAYERS / Lesko, Stephen J & Murray, Mimi – 1992 – 2mf – $8.00 – us Microform Publ [150]

PERCEIVED EXERTION OF PARAPLEGICS DURING SUBMAXIMAL ARM CRANK ERGOMETRY / Felice, Algernon A D – 1989 – 86p 1mf – 9 – $4.00 – us Microform Publ [612]

THE PERCEIVED IMPORTANCE OF A LEISURE EDUCATION COMPONENT IN OUTPATIENT WEIGHT MANAGEMENT PROGRAMS SERVING ADULT WOMEN / Castille, Cheryl L – 1994 – 1mf – $4.00 – us Microform Publ [370]

THE PERCEIVED INFLUENCE OF PARTICIPATION IN INTRAMURAL SPORTS ON PURPOSE, INTERPERSONAL RELATIONSHIP, AND AUTONOMY / Todaro, R Elaine & Kleinman, S – 1990 – 2mf – 9 – $8.00 – us Microform Publ [150]

PERCEPTION – (Cont: Digeste Social, 1977/78) – Ottawa. v1-18. 1977/78-1994/95 – 9 – Can$20.00y – cn Micromedia [073]

PERCEPTION – v. 1-. 1977- – 1,5,6,9 – us UMI [612]

PERCEPTION *see* DIGESTE SOCIAL

PERCEPTION, PHYSICS, AND REALITY : AN ENQUIRY INTO THE INFORMATION THAT PHYSICAL SCIENCE CAN SUPPLY ABOUT THE REAL / Broad, C D – Cambridge: University Press, 1914 – 1mf – us A.T.L.A. [120]

PERCEPTIONS AND ATTITUDES OF DEAF AND HEARING STUDENTS IN INTEGRATED PHYSICAL EDUCATION CLASSES / Ormsby, K A – 1990 – 2mf – 9 – $8.00 – us Microform Publ [150]

PERCEPTIONS OF AGENCIES THAT MARKET COLLEGIATE EMBLEMATIC MERCHANDISE TOWARD SELECTED FACTORS RELATED TO ROYALTY INCOME / Meyer, Jane C & Hansen, Gary F – 1992 – 4mf – 9 – $16.00 – us Microform Publ [650]

THE PERCEPTIONS OF COLLEGE PHYSICAL EDUCATION TEACHING MAJORS WITH RESPECT TO TEACHER ENTHUSIASM / Bodette, Derek R – Springfield College, 1995 – 2mf – 9 – $8.00 – PE3584 – us Microform Publ [790]

PERCEPTIONS OF LEISURE, RELIGION AND WELL-BEING OF SELECTED WORKING AND NON-WORKING WOMEN AGED 25-45 / Winter, Wilma G – 1981 – 2mf – 9 – $8.00 – us Microform Publ [790]

PERCEPTIONS OF PSYCHOLOGICAL MOMENTUM BY FEMALE COMPETITIVE SWIMMERS : A PHENOMENOLOGICAL INVESTIGATION / Peterson, Kirk – University of Tennessee, 1996 – 1mf – 9 – PSY 1897 – us Microform Publ [150]

THE PERCEPTIONS OF RESIDENTS OF MONROE COUNTY ON THE IMPACT OF TOURISM IN MONROE COUNTY, PA. / Seid, Bradford S – 1994 – 2mf – $8.00 – us Microform Publ [338]

THE PERCEPTIONS OF SPORT MANAGEMENT STUDENTS TOWARD THE MARKET ABILITY OF PROFESSIONAL ATHLETES / Gentile, Dina – 1994 – 2mf – $8.00 – us Microform Publ [150]

PERCEPTIONS OF THE IMPORTANCE AND ACHIEVEMENT OF STUDENT TEACHING OBJECTIVES / Karageorgis, Fevronia & Brockmeyer, Gretchen A – 1993 – 2mf – $8.00 – us Microform Publ [370]

PERCEPTIONS OF "UTILITY" AND "LIKEABILITY" DIMENSIONS OF A PHYSICAL EDUCATION FITNESS CURRICULUM / Richard, Juliana J & Brockmeyer, Gretchen A – 1992 – 2mf – $8.00 – us Microform Publ [790]

PERCEPTUAL AND MOTOR SKILLS – Louisville. v1-4. 1949-52 – 1,5,6 – us Princeton Micro [073]

PERCEPTUAL AND MOTOR SKILLS – (v1-27 1949-68 $272.00 2) – v1-85. 1949-97 – 5 – $4,323.50 – us Perceptual [073]

A PERCEPTUAL COMPARISON OF EXPERTS, PRINCIPALS AND TEACHERS WITH RESPECT TO SCHOOL HEALTH PROGRAMS WITHIN THE ELEMENTARY SCHOOLS UNDER THE JURISDICTION OF BANGKOK METROPOLIS, THAILAND / Rat-rim-chong, A – 1989 – 3mf – 9 – $12.00 – us Microform Publ [370]

PERCEPTUAL ESTIMATION AND PRODUCTION OF EXERCISE INTENSITY USING THE BORG CATEGORY-RATIO SCALE / Smith, D A – 1989 – 2mf – 9 – $8.00 – us Microform Publ [150]

PERCEPTUAL-COGNITIVE DEVELOPMENT – v1-6 1965-70 1; v6- 5,6 – us UMI [150]

IL PERCHE MUSICALE / Berardi, A – 1693 – 9 – us Sibley [780]

PERCHE SE MIO TU SEI. (FROM LA BELLA PESCATRICE) / Tritto, G – (Full score) – London: Goulding/Skillern, 1790 – 1 – us Sibley [780]

Percher, Jules Hippolyte *see* NOS AFRICAINS...

Percheron, A R *see*
- BIBLIOGRAPHIE ENTOMOLOGIQUE, COMPRENANT L'INDICATION PAR ORDRE ALPHABETIQUE DE NOMS D'AUTEURS...
- GENERA DES INSECTES

Percier, Charles *see* RECUEIL DE DECORATIONS INTERIEURES.

Percival, R *see* AN ACCOUNT OF THE ISLAND OF CEYLON

PERCOLATOR – Vale OR. June 27 1940 – 1 – us U.O. Library [071]

PERCUSSIONIST – v1- 1963- 1; v10- 5,6; v15- 9 – us UMI [780]

PERCUSSOR OF UNITY – London, UK. 1844. - irr. 13 feet – 1 – uk British Libr Newspaper [072]

THE PERCY ANECDOTES – (Includes "Anecdotes of the Bar") – New York: Harper & Bros. 2v. 1838 – 8mf – 9 – $12.00 – LLMC 91-054 – us L.L.M.C. [340]

PERCY BYSSHE SHELLEY, POET AND PIONEER : A BIOGRAPHICAL STUDY / Salt, Henry Stephens – London: W. Reeves; New York: C. Scribner's Sons, 1896 – 1 roll – 1 – 1-55879-859-5 – uk Libr Preservation [420]

PERCY GRAINGER'S PERSONAL LIBRARY – 1990 – 9 – 0-7325-0052-4 – at Grainger Mus [780]

Percy Scott Flippin *see* THE ARCHIVES OF THE U.S. GOVERNMENT: A DOCUMENTARY HISTORY, 1774-1934

Percyvall, Richard *see* A DICTIONARIE IN SPANISH AND ENGLISH

PERDAGANGAN LUAR-NEGERI URSS / Alkhimov, V S – SE-4780 1. 1958 – 9 – ne IDC [950]

PERDANA MENTERI PEREMPUAN DALAM PENJAMARAN (BENG LEE KOEN) / Meng, Li-Chuen – SE-4714 1. 1963 – 9 – ne IDC [950]

PERDE – (Sahib-i Imtiyaz: Kirkor, Mueduer-i Mes'ul: A. Sami, Sermuharriri: A. Rifki. Nos. 4, 6, 8 (3 Kanunievvel 1327-5 Kanunisani 1328[1912]) – Istanbul: Asir Matbaasi, 1911-1912 – 1mf – 9 – $12.00 – us MEDOC [949]

PERDIGON Y PERRUNILLA / Alba, Jose – Caceres: Tip. La Minerva Extremena, 1937? – sp Bibl Santa Ana [946]

Perdiguier, Agricol *see* STATISTIQUE DU SALAIRE DES OUVRIERS EN REPONSE A M. THIERS ET AUTRES ECONOMISTES DE LA MEME ECOLE

PERDJUANGAN DAN HATI PEREMPUAN. SE 3830/1. 1962 / Said, Titie – 9 – ne IDC [950]

PERDJUANGAN MELAWAN KESESATAN / Al-Ghazzali, Iman – SE-4779 1963 – 9 – ne IDC [950]

LE PERE : 2 DOCUMENTS MICROFILMES ENSEMBLE / Waldeck-Rousseau, Rene – (Quesnay de Beaurepaire, Jules. – Waldeck-Rousseau (1809-1882) (...). – Paris: Colin, 1898; Aux ouvriers et industriels de la ville de Nantes (formation d'un comite pour la confection d'une plaque de bronze destinee a M. Waldeck-Rousseau. -[Nantes]:[s.n.],[1849]) – fr Armell [910]

LE PERE COULANGE OU ENTRETIENS SUR LA CULTURE ET LA PREPARATION DU TABAC / Cuisset, Octave – Quebec: Imp. A Cote, 1876. SEM105P28 – 1mf – 9 – Can$2.25 – cn Bibl Nat [631]

LE PERE DUCHENE – Le titre varie. no. 1-68. Paris. fevr mars-mai juin 1871 – 1 – fr A.C.R.P.P. [073]

LE PERE LACORDAIRE ET LES JEUNES GENS: LECTURE FAITE AU CERCLE VILLE MARIE DE MONTREAL / Babonneau, F M – Montreal: E. Senecal, 1891. 02210. (Pre-1900 Canadiana) – 9 – cn C.I.H.M. [971]

LE PERE PEINARD – Paris. fevr 1889-avr 1900. Remplace de mai 1895 a oct 1896 par: La Sociale voir a ce titre – 1 – fr A.C.R.P.P. [073]

Perea Romero, M *see* CATALOGO DEL "EL COJO ILUSTRADO", 1892-1915

PERECHEN' (KHRONOLOGICHESKII) ZAKONOV RSFSR DEISTVUIUSHCHIKH NA 1 IANVARIIA 1933 G – Moscow, 1933. BR-9077/1 – 9 – ne IDC [520]

Pereda, Julian *see* LOS TOROS ANTE LA IGLESIA Y LA MORAL. BILBAO, 1945

PEREDUMANNOE I PEREZHITOE DNEVNIKI, PISMA, VOSPOMINANIIA / Alchevskaia, Kh. D – Moscow, 1912. 467p. BR-9214 1 – 9 – ne IDC [240]

Pereferkovich, N *see* TALMUD BAVLI AL PI KITVEI YAD U-DEFUSIM RISHONIM

PEREGRINACION DIOCESANA A FATIMA PRESIDIDA POR...OBISPO – Plasencia: Imp. La Victoria, 1967 – 1 – sp Bibl Santa Ana [240]

PEREGRINAGGIO DE TRE GIOVANI FIGLIVOLI DEL RE DI SERENDIPPO, PER OPRA... – Venetia, 1557 – 2mf – 9 – H-8156/1 – ne IDC [956]

PEREGRINATION D'UN PARIA: 1833-1834 / Tristan, Flore Celestine – Paris: A. Bertrand, 1838. 2v. 10 fiches. (Les Femmes Collection) – 9 – 25.00 – fr Bibl Nationale [920]

PEREGRINATIONS DU S. IEAN PALERNE OU EST TRAICTE DE PLUSIEURS SINGULARITES ET ANTIQUITES REMARQUEES ES PROVINCES D'EGYPTE, ARABIE DESERTE ET PIERREUSE, TERRE SAINCTE, SURIE, ANATOLIE, GRECE / Palerne, Jean – Lyon, I. Pillehotte, 1605, 554-15 p. French Voyagers in the Mediterranean 16th to 18th Centuries. 5959 – 9 – fr Hachette [949]

PEREGRINENRECHT UND IUS GENTIUM / Baron, J – Leipzig, 1892 – 1mf – 9 – ILM-838/1 – ne IDC [340]

LOS PEREGRINOS INMOVILES, NOVELA / Lopez y Fuentes, Gregorio – Mexico: Ediciones Botas, 1944. 287p – 1 – us U.W. Library [830]

Pereira da Silva and Ca., Lisboa *see* LIVROS RAROS E CURIOSOS DE HISTORIA E LITERATURA A VENDA NA LIVRARIA PEREIRA DA SILVA AND CA. ARCHIVO DO BIBLIOPHILO

Pereira da Silva, Antonio *see* A QUESTAO DO...EM PORTUGAL NO SECULO 28

Pereire, Emile *see*
- CONSIDERATIONS SUR LES FINANCES DE FRANCE ET DES ETATS-UNIS
- DE L'ASSIETTE DE L'IMPOT. EXAMEN CRITIQUE
- EXAMEN DU BUDGET DE 1832. REFORMES FINANCIERES. EXAMEN THEORIQUE ET PRATIQUE DE L'AMORTISSEMENT

PEREKONOMIAN INDONESIA DIDALAM MASA 150 TAHUN, 1800-1950 / Sonda, Amir – SE 10,726 1. 1963 – 9 – ne IDC [338]

Perelman, Sidney Joseph *see* DAWN GINSBURGH'S REVENGE

PERELOM V RAZVITII MIROVOGO PROMYSHLENNOGO KRIZISA / Falkner, Semen Anisimovich – Moskva: [Vysshi i Sovet Narodnogo khozi a istva, Otdel Red.-izd.], 1922 – 1 – CSUX91-B2728 – us Hoover Inst Photo [947]

PEREMPUAN ITU BERNAMA BARABAH; SEBUAH NOVEL / Motinggo, Busje – SE-4550 1. 1963 – 9 – ne IDC [950]

PEREPISKA IZ DVUKH UGLOV / Ivanov, V & Gershenson, M – "Alkonost". Spb. 1921. BR-3315 2 – 8 – ne IDC [460]

PEREPISKA MOSKOVSKIKH MASONOV XVIII VEKA. 1780-92 GG / Barskov, I L – Petrograd, 1915. lxii, 399p. BR-5984 2 – 8 – ne IDC [310]

PEREPISKA S LAFATEROM / Karamzin, Nikolai M – Spb. 1893. BR-6048 2 – 8 – ne IDC [460]

Pererius, B *see*
- BENEDICTI PERERII VALENTINI, E SOCIETATE JESU COMMENTARIORUM ET DISPUTATIONUM IN GENESIM
- COMMENTARIUM ET DISPUTATIONUM IN GENESIM, TOMI QUATUOR
- DE COMMUNIBUS OMNIUM RERUM NATURALIUM PRINCIPIIS ET AFFECTIONIBUS

Peretrukhin, IK *see* RUKHOVOD'STVO PO OBLICHENII RATINALISTICHESKIKH SEKT SHTUNDOBAPTIZMA I ADVENTIZMA

Peretts, V N *see*
- ITALIANSKIIA KOMEDII I INTERMEDII, PREDSTAVLENNYIA PRI DVORE IMP. ANNY IOANNOVNY V 1733-1735 GG. TEKSTY

- NOVYE TRUDY PO ISTOCHNIKOVEDENIIU DREVNE-RUSSKOI LITERATURY
Peretz, I L *see* YUDISHE VOKHENSHRIFT
PEREVODY / Remizov, A – St. Petersburg, 1908. 76p. BR-832 2 – 8 – ne IDC [460]
PEREVOROT 1762 GODA – Sochineniia i perepiska uchastnikov i sovremennikov. Ed 3. 1910 – 8 – BR-7761 2 – ne IDC [947]
Pereyra, Carlos *see*
- FRANCISCO PIZARRO Y EL TESORO DE ATAHUALPA
- HOMENAJE A HERNANDO CORTES EN MEJICO
- POSTRERA VOLUNTAD Y TESTAMENTO DE HERNANDO CORTES MARQUES DEL VALLE
Pereyra, L *see*
- THEODICEA O LA RELIGION NATURAL...
- TRATADO COMPLETO DE LAS CALENTURAS FUNDADO SOBRE LAS LEYES DE LA INFLAMACION...
Perez, A *see* BREVE TRATADO DE PESTE CON SUS CAUSAS SENALES Y CURACION...
Perez Angel, Gabriel *see* EL PATRONATO ESPANOL EN EL VIRREYNO DEL PERU DURANTE EL SIGLO 16
Perez Arcas, L *see* INSECTOS NUEVOS O POCO CONOCIDOS DE LA FAUNA ESPANOLA
Perez Bueno, Fernando *see*
- EL DEBER DEL ESTADO CON RELACION A LA RIQUEZA INTELECTUAL DE UN PUEBLO
- ROSMINI. DOCTRINAS ETICO-JURIDICAS (SINTESIS)
Perez Bustamante, Ciriaco *see*
- LA CORRESPONDENCIA DIPLOMATICA ENTRE LOS DUQUES DE PARMA Y SUS AGENTES O AMBAJADORES EN LA CORTE DE MADRID, DURANTE LOS SIGLOS XVI, XVII Y XVIII
- ESPANA EN INDIAS
- ESPANOLES E INGLESES EN AMERICA DURANTE EL SIGLO 17. EL CONDE DE GANDOMAR Y SU INTERVENCION EN EL PROCESO, PRISION Y MUERTE DE SIR WALTER RALEIGH. SANTIAGO DE COMPOSTELA, 1928
- LOS ORIGENES DEL GOBIERNO VIRREINAL EN LAS INDIAS ESPANOLAS. DON ANTONIO DE MENDOZA, PRIMER VIRREY DE LA NUEVA ESPANA (1535-1550)
Perez Casas, B *see* A MI TIERRA! SUITE MUSICANA PARA GRAN ORQUESTRA
Perez Cascales, F *see* LIBER DE AFFECTIONIBUS PUERORUM...
Perez Castro, Pedro A *see* INFORMACION... MARQUES DE PERALES
Perez Coca y Sanchez Matas, Carmen *see* SINODO PLACENTINO DEL OBISPO NORONA (1582)
Perez Comendador, Enrique *see* DE ESCULTURA E IMAGENERIA
Perez Cordoba, Luis *see* INFORME PRONUNCIADO POR...ACUSADOR PRIVADO...CONTRA VICENTE SANCHEZ PEREZ...POR ASESINATO, 1948
Perez Cortes y Garcia Camacho, Angel *see* JUICIO CRITICO DE DONOSO CORTES
Perez de Anaya, Francisco *see* MEMORIA HISTORICA...PUBLICA...DON JAN BRAVO MURILLO
Perez de Barrados, Jose *see*
- ARQUEOLOGIA Y ANTROPOLOGIA DE LA TIERRA
- COLOMBIA DE NORTE A SUR. 2 VOL. MADRID, 1943
Perez de Bustos, D *see* TRATADO BREVE DE FLEBOTOMIA (SANGRIA)
Perez de Egea, M *see* PRECEPTOS MILITARES, ORDEN Y FORMACION DE ESQUADRONES
Perez de Guzman, Juan *see*
- BAJO LOS AUSTRIAS. LA MUJER ESPANOLA EN LA MINERVA LITERARIA CASTELLANA
- CARTAS FAMILIARES DE DON BARTOLOME JOSE GALLARDO
- CRONICA DE LA PROVINCIA DE CACERES
- CRONICA DE LA...CACERES
- DISCURSOS...ACADEMIA SEVILLANA DE BUENAS LETRAS
- DOCUMENTOS PARA LA BIBLIOGRAFIA DE D. MANUEL JOSE QUINTANA
- FALLECIMIENTO
- FALLECIMIENTO DE DON VICENTE PAREDES GUILLEN
- LAS HISTORIAS Y LOS HISTORIADORES DE SEVILLA
- INSCRIPCION...SATURNINO...MERIDA
- NOTA SOBRE DOCUMENTOS INEDITOS DE PIZARRO, DE CUNEO VIDAL
- NOTICIA SOBRE LA SEPULTURA DE PIZARRO, DE CUNEO VIDAL
- LOS PRINCIPES DE LA POESIA ESPANOLA... MARTIN CORTES
- LOS PRINCIPES DE LA...FERNANDO DE VERA Y MENDOZA
- PROCESO DEL MARQUES DE SIETE IGLESIAS. DON RODRIGO CALDERON
- SIETE CARTAS INEDITAS DEL REY D. FELIPE 2
- T'SERCLAES ANUNCIA UN PREMIO
- T'SERCLAES, DUQUE DE. FIRMA LA PROPUESTA DE ACADEMICO DEL DUQUE DE ALBA
Perez de Guzman y Boza, Manuel *see* DISCURSOS LEIDOS ANTE LA REAL ACADEMIA SEVILLANA DE BUENAS LETRAS EL 3 DE ENERO DE 1897
Perez de Herrera, C *see* BREVIS...TRACTATUS DE ESSENTIA...CURATIONE ET PRAECAUTIONE FAUCIUM ET GUTTURIS...
Perez de la Mata, Antonio *see* TRATADO DE METAFISICA
Perez de Urbel, Justo *see*
- SAN EULOGIO DE CORDOBA
- SAN EULOGIO DE CORDOBA. MADRID, 1928
Perez del Pulgar, Jose Agustin *see* LA SOLUCION QUE ESPANA DA AL PROBLEMA DE SUS PRESOS POLITICOS
Perez Embrid, Florentino *see*
- EL ALMIRANTE DE CASTILLA HASTA LAS CAPITULACIONES DE SANTA FE. SEVILLA, 1944
- DE LAS SIETE PALABRAS...DE MANUEL BENITEZ SANCHEZ CORTES
Perez Fadrique, J *see* MODO DE EMBALSAMAR CUERPOS DIFUNTOS...
Perez Fernandez, Manuel *see* YO MATE AL DIABLO
Perez, Fernando *see* CARTA DE PARACUELLOS
Perez Galdos, Benito *see*
- OBRAS INEDITAS, ORDENADAS Y PROLONGADAS POR ALBERTO GHIRALDO
- TRISTANA
- VOLUNTAD: COMEDIA EN TRES ACTOS Y EN PROSA
- VULGARIZACIONES HISTORICAS.
Perez Garcia, Augusto *see* TEORIA Y METODO DEL CONOCIMIENTO DE SISTEMAS POR SU COMPORTAMIENTO
Perez Gimenez, Nicolas *see* PERFILES BIOGRAFICOS DE QUINTANA AYALA, MORENO NIETO, BALMASEDA Y JIMENEZ
Perez Goyena, A *see*
- ARIAS MONTANO Y LOS JESUITAS
- CUARTO CENTENARIO DEL NACIMIENTO DE D. BENITO ARIAS MONTANO
Perez Grille, Ramon *see* DEL ESTADO DE SALUD Y ENFERMEDAD Y SUS CONSECUENCIAS JURIDICO-SOCIALES; MEMORIA DE PRUEBA PARA OPTAR AL GRADO DE LICENCIADO EN LA FACULTAD DE CIENCIAS JURIDICAS Y SOCIALES DE LA UNIVERSIDAD DE CHILE
Perez Guzman J *see* NUNEZ DE BALBOA. CONGRESO DE HISTORIA Y GEOGRAFIA HISPANOAMERICANA, CELEBRADO EN SEVILLA
Perez Hernandez, Justo *see* SEMINARIO DE BADAJOZ. LAS MONEDAS ARABES DE SU MONETARIO
Perez, I *see* LIBRO DE THERIACA...
Perez Iglesias, Jose Manuel *see* ESTUDIO DE LA FUENTE DE IONES GRANDES POSITIVOS EN OVIEDO
Perez Jimenez, Nicolas *see*
- FALLECIMIENTO
- HISTORIA...COMARCA DE LA SERENA... CABEZA DEL BUEY
- MUNOZ TORRERO Y SU EPOCA
- PROBLEMAS DE TOXICOLOGIA...MEDICA
- TERMAS DE SAN HILARIO
Perez Llamazares, Julio *see* LOS PRIORES DE SAN MARCOS (LEON)
Perez, Lorenzo *see*
- ANTONIO DE SANTA MARIA...EN CUSTODIOS Y PROVINCIALES DE LA PROVINCIA DE SAN JOSE
- FR. PEDRO DE JEREZ EN LOS CUSTODIOS Y PROVINCIALES DE LA PROVINCIA DE SAN JOSE
- JUAN DE SAN ESTEBAN O DE SAUCEDILLA. JUAN TORIBIO ARROYA EN LOS CUSTODIOS Y PROVINCIALES DE LA PROVINCIA DE SAN JOSE
Perez Lozano, Jose Maria *see*
- UN CATOLICO VA AL CINE
- CRISIS MATRIMONIALES
- CRISTIANOS CADA DIA
- EL DIALOGO CON LOS HIJOS
- DIARIO DE UN PADRE DE FAMILIA
- FE Y COMPROMISO HUMANO
- LA GRAN NOCHE DEL MUNDO
- PREGONCILLO DE NAVIDAD
- TELEVISION EN EL CUARTO DE ESTAR
Perez, Luintin *see* FR. HERNANDO DE SANTIAGO. SANTANDER, 1929
Perez, Manuel *see* CUATRO MESES DE BARBARIE, MALLORCA BAJO EL TERROR FASCISTA
Perez Martin, Maria Jesus *see* UNA TUMBA HISPANO-VISIGODA EXCEPCIONAL HALLADA EN EL TURUNUELO
Perez Merino, I *see*
- BREVE ANTIPOLOGIA AL DISCURSO NUEVO... MIGUEL FERNANDEZ DE LA PENA...DEL USO DE AGUA DE LA NIEVE EN DIA DE PURGA
- MEDICA CONTROVERSIA...SE AYA DE SANGRAR DEL BRAZO Y VENA PROXIMOS AL DOLOR...
Perez, Miguel *see* DON MANUEL RUIZ ZORRILLA...NOTICIAS SOBRE..
Perez Minguez, Fidel *see*
- EL CASTILLO E LOS MARQUESES DE LAS NAVAS
- UN CASTILLO Y VARIOS CASTELLANOS...
Perez Munoz, Adolfo *see*
- CARTA PASTORAL QUE EL EXCMO...ADOLFO PEREZ MUNOZ DIRIGE AL CLERO Y FIELES DE SU DIOCESIS
- CARTA PASTORAL QUE...OBISPO DE BADAJOZ DIRIGE AL CLERO Y FIELES DE SU DIOCESIS
- LA DEVOCION AL PAPA
- EL DINERO DE SAN PEDRO. CARTA PASTORAL QUE...ADOLFO PEREZ MUNOZ DIRIGE AL CLERO Y FIELES DE SU DIOCESIS
- LA ESPERANZA EN DIOS CARTA PATORAL
- EXHORTACION PASTORAL...CON MOTIVO DE LA EPIDEMIA REINANTE
- LA FAMILIA CRISTIANA
- INSTRUCCION PASTORAL QUE EL EXCMO. E ILTMO. SENOR...DIRIGE A LOS FIELES DE SU DIOCESIS SOBRE LA DEVOCION AL S. CORAZON DE JESUS
- LACARIDAD. CARTA PASTORAL. EXCMO. ADOLFO PEREZ MUNOZ DIRIGE AL CLERO Y FIELES DE SU DIOCESIS
- OBEDIENCIA Y AMOR
Perez, Pedro *see* LOS OBISPOS DE LA ORDEN DE LA MERCED EN AMERICA (1601-1926). SANTIAGO DE CHILE, 1927
Perez Reviriego, Miguel *see*
- POEMA DE CAPPNTEDRICO
- POEMA OCOEDRICO
- POEMAS DE AUSENCIA
Perez Rosales, Vicente *see* RECUERDOS DEL PASADO (1814-1860) 4TH ED. SANTIAGO DE CHILE, 1943
Perez Toro, Augusto *see* LA MILPA
Perez, V *see*
- HISTORICO-CRITICO-MEDICO-PRACTICA EN QUE SE ESTABLECE EL AGUA POR REMEDIO UNIVERSAL DE LAS DEOLENCIAS
- EL SECRETO A VOCES, ARCANIDADES DE LOS POLVOS DE AIX
Perez Valero, Jose *see* MONOGRAFIA HISTORICO-DESCRIPTIVA Y ESTUDIO CRITICO-HISTORICO SOBRE
Perez Villamil, Juan *see* DOCTRINA...ANTONIO GOMEZ...DIEGO GOMEZ CORNEJO
Perez-Embrid, Florentino *see* PIZARRO
Perez-Villamil, Manuel *see* ENSAYO DE CATALOGO DE LOS LUGARES DE SENORIO TEMPORAL, LOS OBISPOS DE ESPANA EN LA EDAD MEDIA
Perez-Vitoria, Silvia *see* IMPACT OF COMMUNICATION TECHNOLOGIES ON WOMEN
PEREZVONY = BELLS CHIMING – Riga, Latvia, 1925-29 – 23mf – 9 – $150.00 – us Ross [073]
PERFECT MAN'S MODEL (CCC135) / Gutzlaff, Karl Friedrich August – (In Chinese) – [s.l: s.n, 1837] – 1r – 1 – 1984-B500 – us A.T.L.A. [240]
A PERFECT SURVEY OF THE ENGLISH TONGUE / Hewes, John – 1624. 184p. (English Linguistics Series 1500-1800) – 9 – us UMI [420]
PERFECTED INTERNATIONAL TREATIES / U.S. Congress – 56r – 1 – M1247 – us Nat'l Archives [327]
PERFECTION : A POETICAL EPISTLE, CALMLY ADDRESSED TO THE GREATEST HYPOCRITE IN ENGLAND / Combe, W – London, 1778 – 1mf – 9 – MP-531/1 – ne IDC [240]
THE PERFECTIONISTS EXAMIN'D : OR, INHERENT PERFECTION IN THIS LIFE NO SCRIPTURE DOCTRINE... / Fleetwood, W – London, 1741 – 2mf – 9 – MP-290/1 – ne IDC [240]
EL PERFECTO CAPITAN, INSTRUIDO EN LA DISCIPLINA MILITAR Y NUEVA CIENCIA DE ARTILLERIA / Alva y Viamont, D – Madrid, 1590 – 10mf – 9 – sp Cultura [355]
PERFECTO PRACTICANTE, CIRUJANO Y DE MORBO GALICO / Trilla y Munoz, A – Toledo, 1679 – 4mf – 9 – sp Cultura [610]
PERFECTO PRACTICANTE MEDICO Y NUEVA LUZ DE FACIL ENSENANZA / Trilla y Munoz, A – Toledo, 1677 – 4mf – 9 – sp Cultura [610]
PERFIL ACTUAL DE DONOSO CORTES / Corts Grau, Jose – Madrid, 1945 – 1 – sp Bibl Santa Ana [920]
PERFILES BIOGRAFICOS DE QUINTANA AYALA, MORENO NIETO, BALMASEDA Y JIMENEZ / Perez Gimenez, Nicolas – Badajoz: La economica, 1889 – 1 – sp Bibl Santa Ana [920]
"PERFILES SACERDOTALES". BARCELONA, EDIT. HERNANDO. 1959... / Alverez, Felix – Madrid: Archivo Ibero-Americano, 1959 – 1 – sp Bibl Santa Ana [946]
Perfilov, B *see* CHERNAIA GODINA
PERFORMANCE BONDS / Ottawa County. Ohio. Carroll Township. Board of Trustees – 1903 – 1r – 1 – $32.50r – us Archival [324]
PERFORMANCE BUDGET 1988/89-1990/91 / India. Department of Education – New Delhi – 9mf – 9 – DE-536/1 – ne IDC [370]
PERFORMANCE EVALUATION – v1-4. 1981-84 – 1,5,6,13 – sz Elsevier [073]
PERFORMANCE EVALUATION OF DEVELOPMENT IN THAILAND FOR 1965 UNDER THE NATIONAL ECONOMIC DEVELOPMENT PLAN, 1961-1966 / Thailand. National Economic Development Board – Bangkok. 1966 – 9 – ne IDC [338]
PERFORMANCE SITES OF THE ANCIENT WORLD : A PHOTOGRAPHIC SURVEY / ed by Ashby, Clifford – (Includes a printed guide) – 11 colour mf – 15 – $319.00 – 1-869934-35-0 – uk Emmett [790]
PERFORMING ARTS AND ENTERTAINMENT IN CANADA – (Cont: Performing Arts in Canada at v26 no 3 1991) – Toronto. v26-30. 1990/91-1994/95 – 9 – cn Micromedia [790]
PERFORMING ARTS AND ENTERTAINMENT IN CANADA *see* PERFORMING ARTS IN CANADA
PERFORMING ARTS CATEGORY / The NewsBank Review of the Arts – 1975-. Monthly index with cumulations – 9 – us NewsBank [790]
PERFORMING ARTS IN CANADA – v1- 1961-1; v10- 5,6; v13- 9 – us UMI [790]
PERFORMING ARTS IN CANADA – (Cont by: Performing Arts and Entertainment in Canada at v26 no 3 1991) – Toronto. v1-25. 1961-1988/89 – 9 – Can$20.00y – cn Micromedia [790]
PERFORMING ARTS IN CANADA *see* PERFORMING ARTS AND ENTERTAINMENT IN CANADA
PERFORMING ARTS REVIEW *see* JOURNAL OF ARTS MANAGEMENT, LAW AND SOCIETY
PERFORMING ARTS REVIEW; THE JOURNAL OF MANAGEMENT AND LAW OF THE ARTS – v4-11 1973-81 1,5,6; v6-11 9 – us UMI [790]
PERFUMER AND FLAVORIST – v1- 1976- – 1,5,6,9 – us UMI [660]
PERFUMERY AND ESSENTIAL OIL RECORD – v1-60 1910-69 – 1,5,6 – us Princeton Micro [660]
Pergamini, Giacomo *see* IL MEMORIALE DELLA LINGUA
PERGAMINOS DEL MUSEO ARQUEOLOGICO PROVINCIAL DE BADAJOZ / Gil Julian, Juan – Badajoz: Dip. Provincial, 1964. Sep. REE – sp Bibl Santa Ana [930]
PERGERAKAN DI INDIA. DENGAN KATA PENGANTAR SOEKARNO / Tjipto Mangunkusomo – Translation of De Beweging in India. SE 10,736 1. 1947 – 9 – ne IDC [360]
PERGERAKAN KAUM BURUH: CAUSERIE TJOA SEK IEN DALAM KONGRES SERIKAT BURUH KEHUTANAN, 16 OKT. 1949 / Tjoa, Sik Ien – SE 3959 1. 1949 – 9 – ne IDC [950]
Pergolesi, G B *see*
- CONFITEBOR A 5 VOIX AVEC DES INSTRUMENTS
- QUATTRO CANTATE DA CAMERA...LA PRIMA PER CIMBALO.
- SYMPHONIA, 2 VIOLINS, VIOLA AND CELLO, B-FLAT MAJOR, F MAJOR, F MINOR

PERGURUAN PARTIKELIR, KEDUDUKAN DAN TUGASNJA DALAM MASARAKAT DULU, SEKARANG DAN DIMASA DATANG / Tauchid, Mochammad – SE 4074 1. 1955? – 9 – ne IDC [950]
DE PERHIMPOENAN INDONESIA EN DE INDONESISCHE NATIONALISTISCHE BEWEGING : GETYPT AFSCHRIFT UIT DE SOCIALIST, 19 OCT. 1929. NO. 55, FOL / Salim, A – 1mf – 9 – SE-1300/1 – ne IDC [320]
Perhimpunan Bank-Bank Nasional Indonesia *see* DASA-WARSA PERDJUANGAN PERBANA, 1952-1962
PERI KIZILE COBAN HIKAVESI / Orhon, Orhan Seyfi – Istanbul: Ahmed Ihsan ve Suerekasi Matbaasi, 1919 – $9.00 – us MEDOC [470]
Periago Morata, Tomas *see* RAMILLETE LITERATO
PERIBAHASA / Pamuntjak, Kasuma gelar Sutan – SE-4040 1. 1961 – 9 – ne IDC [950]
Peric, Zivojin M, 1868-1953 *see* DE LA NATIONALITE SUIVANT LA LEGISLATION SERBE
Pericot y Garcia, Luis *see* LA AMERICA INDIGENA. TOMO 1. EL HOMBRE AMERICANO. LOS PUEBLOS DE AMERICA. BARCELONA, 1935
DAS PERIGORD UND SEINE BEWOHNER IN DEN ROMANEN EUGENE LE ROYS / Rau, Erich – Muenster, 1936 – 1mf – DM48.00 – 3-8267-3091-7 – gw Hänsel [440]
LES PERIGORDINISMES / Lascoux, J B – 1818 – 9 – fr I.C.S. [440]
O PERILAMPO POPULAR – Rio de Janeiro, 24 Nov-18 Dec 1830 – 1,5,6 – bl Biblioteca [072]
A PERILOUS SECRET / Reade, Charles L – British Fiction Archive: Unit 2 – 9 – uk Bell [830]
PERIMBANGAN KEUANGAN ANTARA NEGARA DAN DAERAH2 / Wajong, J – SE 4322 1. 1960 – 9 – ne IDC [950]
PERIMETRES IRRIGABLES ET DEFENDUS; COMPTE RENDU / Algeria. Service de la Colonisation et de l'Hydraulique – 2v. 1953-54. BNE-8664 1 – 9 – ne IDC [338]
PERINATAL PRESS – 1985- – 1 – us UMI [073]
PERINGATAN HARI KO-OPERASI KE-VIII,12 DJULI 1958. SE-2625/1. 1958 / Batik. Nomor Hari Kooperasi – 9 – ne IDC [950]
Peringuey, L *see* FIRST (FOURTH) CONTRIBUTION TO THE SOUTH-AFRICAN COLEOPTEROUS FAUNA. 1884-92). BZ-1538/2
PERINTIS DJALAN : TJETAKAN 2 – (Microfiche No 130) – Djakarta: Gunseikanbu Kokumin Tosyokyoku, 2605 – 1mf – 9 – SE-2002/1 – ne IDC [950]
THE PERIOD – London. -w. 30 Oct 1869-26 Feb 1870. (12 ft) – 1 – uk British Libr Newspaper [072]
PERIODENBAU IN GOETHES UND SCHILLERS GROESSEREN DICHTUNGEN / Pfannkuchen, Wilhelm – 1995 – 1mf – 9 – DM48.00 – 3-8267-3113-1 – gw Hänsel [430]
PERIODIC JEW – Newark, NJ. 1970-78 – 1 – us A.J.P.C. [071]
PERIODICA ISLAMICA – 1992- 3v – 9 – £64.00 – 0128-3715 – uk Carfax [260]
PERIODICAL ACCOUNTS OF THE WORK OF THE MORAVIAN MISSIONS – (Lacking some pgs) – v1-34. 1790-1889; serial 2: v1-12. 1890-1930; v139-169. 1931-61 – 22r – 1 – ATLA S0108 – us A.T.L.A. [073]
PERIODICAL INDEX / Southern Baptist Convention – 1966, 1969, 1973 – 1 – 34.09 – us Baptist [240]
PERIODICAL LIBRARY – v. 1-3. 1833 – 1 – us UMI [073]
A PERIODICAL OVERTURE IN EIGHT PARTS... NO. 1 / Cannabich, Christian – 1779? – 9 – us Sibley [780]
THE PERIODICAL OVERTURE, K. 19, C MAJOR / Ditters von Dittersdorf, C – (8 parts) – London: Bremner, 178- – 1 – us Sibley [780]
PERIODICAL SKETCHES BY AN AMERICAN PATRIOT – v. 1. 1820 – 1 – us UMI [073]
PERIODICALS / Southern Baptist Foreign Mission Board – (Name changes: Commission 1849-51, 1856-61, 1938-53, 1971-75. The Foreign Mission Journal 1874-1916. Home and Foreign Fields 1916-37. Home and Foreign Journal 1851-61, 1868-74. Southern Baptist Mission Journal 1846-51) – 1846-1953 – 1 – $1,286.32 – us Baptist [240]
PERIODICALS / Southern Home Mission Board – 1888-1916, 1930-60. (Name changes: Home Fields. 1909-16; Home Missions. 1955-60; Our Home Fields. 1888-1909; Southern Baptist Home Missions. 1930-54) – 1 – 452.97 – us Baptist [240]
PERIODICALS BY AND ABOUT AMERICAN INDIANS, 1923-81 – $4,855.00 – us UPA [305]
PERIODICALS CATALOGUE – 335mf – 9 – $1,620.00 – 0-907006-94-9 – uk Mindata [305]
PERIODICALS FROM THE NINETEENTH CENTURY READERS' GUIDE, 1890-1899 – (51 American periodicals selected from H.W. Wilson's 19th Century Readers' Guide 1890-99. Cataloging available) – 241r – 1 – $13,370.00 – us UMI [073]
PERIODICALS IN SOUTHERN AFRICAN LIBRARIES / South Africa. State Library. Pretoria – 1985 and updated supplements-1992. Updated twice yearly – 9 – sa State Libr [073]
PERIODICALS ON WOMEN AND WOMEN'S RIGHTS – (Series 1: Forerunner; Liberal Review; Lily; Lowell Offering; Lucifer the Lightbearer; Mother Earth Bulletin; The National Citizen and Ballot Box; The Revolution; Stiletto; Una; Western Woman Voter; Woman's Protest; Woman Voter. $1,330.00 set; Series 2: The Club Woman; The Coming Nation and the Progressive Woman; Equal Rights; Independent Feminist Weekly; The Keystone and Woman's Column; The Ladies Garment Worker; Lady's Friend; Life and Labor; The Woman Patriot; Woman Rebel; Woman Worker. $1,545.00 set. Also avail. separately, see indiv. titles) – 1 – $2,730.00 complete set – us UPA [305]
PERIODICHESKAIA PECHAT' V KITIAE / Polevoi, S A – Vladivostok. 1913. BR-4414 2 – 8 – ne IDC [073]
PERIODICO CDI – (Some issues are missing) – Mexico City, Mexico. n1656 (Feb 21 1993)-n1744 (Dec 18 1994) – 1r – 1 – us A.J.P.C. [073]
PERIODICO OFICIAL / Aguascalientes. Mexico (State) – Aguascalientes. Title varies. 1862-1924, 1937-57. LL-02012 – 1 – us L of C Photodup [340]
PERIODICO OFICIAL – Aguascalientes, Mexico. v13-34. 1949-70 – 4r – 1 – us Ross [324]
PERIODICO OFICIAL / Chihuahua. Mexico. (State) – 1948-1956. Incomplete – 1 – us NY Public [324]
PERIODICO OFICIAL / Coahuila. Mexico. (State) – Saltillo. 1951-1966. Incomplete – 1 – us NY Public [972]
PERIODICO OFICIAL / Colima. Mexico. (State) – 1951-1968. Incomplete – 1 – us NY Public [972]
PERIODICO OFICIAL / Durango. Mexico (State) – Durango. 1950-1970 – 1 – us NY Public [972]
PERIODICO OFICIAL / Guanajuato. Mexico (State) – Jan 1872-Dec 1924 – 1 – 874.00 – us L of C Photodup [324]
PERIODICO OFICIAL – Monterrey, Mexico. v94-104. 1957-67 – 5r – 1 – us Ross [324]
PERIODICO OFICIAL / Morelos. Mexico (State) – Cuernavaca. On film: 1869-1926. LL-02027 – 1 – us L of C Photodup [340]
PERIODICO OFICIAL / New Leon. Mexico – Monterrey. 1950-1967- – 1 – us NY Public [324]
PERIODICO OFICIAL / Oaxaca. Mexico (State) – Oaxaca. On film: 1841-45, 1851, 1858-63, 1865-70, 1872-1924. LL-02030 – 1 – us L of C Photodup [340]
PERIODICO OFICIAL / San Luis Potosi. Mexico (State) – San Luis Potosi. On film: 1851, 1871-74, 1877-1920. LL-02033 – 1 – us L of C Photodup [340]
PERIODICO OFICIAL / Sinaloa. Mexico – Culican. Jun. 24, 1941-Sept. 14, 1950 – 1 – us NY Public [972]
PERIODICO OFICIAL / Tamaulipas. Mexico – Ciudad Victoria. On film: 1880-1913, 1916-66. LL-02037 – 1 – us L of C Photodup [340]
PERIODICO OFICIAL / Tlaxcala. Mexico – 1948-1953 – 1 – us NY Public [972]
PERIODICO OFICIAL / Tlaxcala. Mexico – Tlaxcala. On film: 1887-1924. LL-02038 – 1 – us L of C Photodup [340]
PERIODICO OFICIAL / Tobasco. Mexico – Villahermosa. On film: 1861-1924. LL-02036 – 1 – us L of C Photodup [340]
PERIODICO OFICIAL / Zacatecas. Mexico (State) – Zacatecas. On film: 1900-24, 1927-69. LL-02041 – 1 – us L of C Photodup [340]
PERIODICO OFICIAL DE GOBIERNO – Hidalgo, Mexico. v90-101.1957-68 – 3r – 1 – us Ross [324]
PERIODICO OFICIAL DEL GOBIERNO – Durango, Mexico. v140-143. 1969-70 – 1r – 1 – us Ross [324]
PERIODICO OFICIAL DEL GOBIERNO – Guanajuato, Mexico. v91-107. 1961-69 – 4r – 1 – us Ross [324]
PERIODICO OFICIAL DEL GOBIERNO CONSTITUCIONAL – Chiapas, Mexico. v74-80. 1957-63 – 4r – 1 – us Ross [324]
PERIODICO OFICIAL DEL GOBIERNO CONSTITUCIONAL DEL ESTADO DE CAMPECHE / Campeche. Mexico (State) – Title varies. On film: 1926-61. LL-02015 – 1 – us L of C Photodup [340]
PERIODICO OFICIAL DEL GOBIERNO CONSTITUCIONAL DEL ESTADO DE CHIAPAS / Chiapas. Mexico (State) – Tuxtla Gutierrez. On film: 1830-1950. LL-02016 – 1 – us L of C Photodup [340]
PERIODICO OFICIAL DEL GOBIERNO DEL ESTADO / Chihuahua. Mexico. (State) – Chihuahua. On film: 1840-1952. LL-02017 – 1 – us L of C Photodup [340]
PERIODICO OFICIAL DEL GOBIERNO DEL ESTADO DE DURANGO / Durango. Mexico (State) – Durango. On film: 1843-1951. LL-02020 – 1 – us L of C Photodup [340]
...PERIODICO OFICIAL DEL GOBIERNO DEL ESTADO DE GUERRERO / Guerrero. Mexico (State) – Chilpancingo. On film: 1870-1951. LL-02022 – 1 – us L of C Photodup [340]
PERIODICO OFICIAL DEL GOBIERNO DEL ESTADO DE HIDALGO / Hidalgo. Mexico (State) – Pachucao de Soto. On film: 1869-1969. LL-02023 – 1 – us L of C Photodup [340]
PERIODICO OFICIAL DEL GOBIERNO DEL ESTADO DE MICHOACAN DE OCAMPA / Michoacan. Mexico (State) – Morelia. On film: 1876-1966. LL-02026 – 1 – us L of C Photodup [340]
PERIODICO OFICIAL-GOBIERNO CONSTITUCIONAL DEL ESTADO INDEPENDIENTE, LIBRE Y SOBERANO DE COAHUILA DE ZARAGOZA / Coahuila. Mexico – Saltillo. On film: 1851-1969. LL-02018 – 1 – us L of C Photodup [340]
PERIODICO OFICIAL-GOBIERNO CONSTITUCIONAL DEL ESTADO LIBRE Y SOBERANO DE NUEVO LEON / Nuevo Leon. Mexico (State) – Monterrey. On film: 1826-1969. LL-02029 – 1 – us L of C Photodup [340]
PERIODICO OFICIAL-GOBIERNO CONSTITUCIONAL DEL ESTADO LIBRE Y SOBERANO DE PUEBLA / Puebla. Mexico (State) – Puebla. On film: 1873-1940. LL-02031 – 1 – us L of C Photodup [340]
PERIODICO OFICIAL-GOBIERNO DEL ESTADO DE NAYARIT / Nayarit. Mexico (State) – Tepic. On film: 1878-1969. LL-02028 – 1 – us L of C Photodup [340]
...PERIODICO OFICIEL....MEXICALI. 1949-52 – 1 – us NY Public [324]
PERIODICOS DEL FRENTE – n.p. 1937? Fiche W1104. (Blodgett Collection of Spanish Civil War Pamphlets) – 9 – us H.U. College Libr [946]
PERIODICOS Y PERIODISTAS EXTREMENOS / Rincon Jimenez, Jesus – Badajoz: A.Arqueros, 1915 – 1 – sp Bibl Santa Ana [073]
PERIODIQUES CLANDESTINS 1939-1945 / France – (ACTION. Organe social de la France combattante puis Organe social du Mouvement de la liberation nationale. AURORA (L'). Organe de la resistance republicaine. AVANT-GARDE (L'). Organe central des jeunesses communistes de France puis Journal de la Federation des jeunesses communistes de France; Organe central de la Federation des jeunesses communistes de France. Zone Nord. AVANT-GARDE (L'). Organe central de la Federation des jeunesses communistes de France. Ed. centrale de Zone Sud. AVENIR. Journal provisoirement clandestin destine aux jeunes de France. ARC (L'). Fond. Gaston Teissier, Jules Correard, etc. BULLETIN D'INFORMATION DU FRONT NATIONAL DE LUTTE POUR LA LIBERATION DE LA FRANCE. Destine aux comites departementaux, aux secteurs et sections, aux comites locaux et d'enterprise. BULLETIN DE L'UNION DES SYNDICATS OUVRIERS DE LA REGION PARISIENNE. Francs-tireurs et partisans. BULLETIN INTERIEUR DE l'A.S. Armee secrete. Region de Toulouse) – bobine no. 1 – 1 – fr A.C.R.P.P. [073]
PERIODIQUES CLANDESTINS 1939-1945 / France – (B.I.M.U. Bulletin interieur des Mouvements unis de resistance. BULLETIN D'INFORMATION. Publ. par le Parti communiste francais. Ed. de Zone Nord. BULLETIN D'INFORMATION. Publ. par le Parti communiste francais. Ed. de Zone Sud) – bobine no. 2 – 1 – fr A.C.R.P.P. [073]
PERIODIQUES CLANDESTINS 1939-1945 / France – bobines no. 1-24 – 1 – fr A.C.R.P.P. [073]
PERIODIQUES CLANDESTINS 1939-1945 / France – (BUREAU DE PRESSE DE LA FRANCE COMBATTANTE. Bulletin d'informations generales) – bobine no. 3-5 – 1 – fr A.C.R.P.P. [073]
PERIODIQUES CLANDESTINS 1939-1945 / France – (CAHIERS (LES). Etudes pour une revolution francaise. CAHIERS DE DEFENSE DE LA FRANCE. CAHIERS (LES) DE LIBERATION puis DE LA LIBERATION. CAHIERS DU TEMOIGNAGE CHRETIEN) – bobine no. 6 – 1 – fr A.C.R.P.P. [073]
PERIODIQUES CLANDESTINS 1939-1945 / France – (CAHIERS (LES) POLITIQUES. CEUX DE LA LIBERATION.. CEUX DE LA RESISTANCE. Bulletin d'informations. COMBAT. Organe du Mouvement de liberation francaise puis Organe des Mouvements de resistance unis. COMMUNE DE PARIS. Journal des marraines de la compagnie des Francs-tireurs et partisans. DEFENSE DE LA FRANCE. DOCUMENTS. Edites par le Comite directeur du Front National. ENCHAINE (L'). Organe de la region communiste du Nord. ENCHAINE (L'). Organe de la region communiste du Pas-de-Calais. ESSOR. L'Avenir de l'etudiant. ETUDIANT (L') PATRIOTE) – bobine no. 7 – 1 – fr A.C.R.P.P. [073]
PERIODIQUES CLANDESTINS 1939-1945 / France – (COMBAT ACTUALITES. COMBAT ILLUSTRE. COMBAT. Supplement regional du Languedoc. COMBAT DU LANGUEDOC. Publ. par les Mouvements de resistance unis. COMAT DU LANGUEDOC ET DU ROUSSILLON. Organe regional de la resistance pour la region de Montpellier. COMBAT MEDICAL. Organe des medecins du Mouvement national contre le racisme. COMBAT (LE) NATIONAL REVOLUTIONNAIRE. COMBAT (LE) REGIONAL. Organe regional de Combat. COMBATTANT (LE) DE 39-40. Organe des comites populaires des demobilises de la banlieue Est. COMMUNISTES (LES) ET LA LUTTE ARMEE. Edite par le Comite central du Parti communiste francais. COQ (LE) ENCHAINE. Journal officiel du governement libre de Paris. COQ (LE) ENCHAINE EST LA POUR LIBERER LA FRANCE. COURRIER (LE) D'ALSACE-LORRAINE. Organe du groupe "Erckmann-Chatrian", membre des Mouvements de la liberation nationale. COURRIER (LE) DU PEUPLE. COURRIER FRANCAIS DU TEMOIGNAGE CHRETIEN. Lien du Front de resistance spirituelle contre l'hitlerisme. CRI D'ALARME. Edite par la commission de l'enfance de l'Union des femmes francaises. Region parisienne. DEFENSE (LA). Journal mensuel du Secours populaire de France. DEFENSE (LA) DU PERSONNEL DES SERVICES PUBLICS. devient: La Defense. Organe de l'Union des comites populaires des services publics. DEFENSE (LA) DES PRISONNIERS. Organe des rapatries. DEFENSE (LA) LORRAINE. Organe des cercles "Jeanne d'Arc" et "Barres" de l'Alliance. DELIVRANCE. (Reserve au groupe medical). DELIVRANCE. (Edite par le groupe Cahors-Asturies). DEPARTEMENT (LE). Ed. speciale de La Marseillaise du Berry. DERNIER (LE) QUART D'HEURE. Organe de redressement et d'offensive. DESTIN. Message de la resurrection francaise. ECHO (L') DES TRAVAILLEURS. Journal du Comite populaire (Usine Floquet). VERITAS) – bobine no. 16 – 1 – fr A.C.R.P.P. [073]
PERIODIQUES CLANDESTINS 1939-1945 / France – (FRANCAIS (LE). Organe national. FRANCE (LA) AU COMBAT. Organe regional du Front national de resistance. FRANCE D'ABORD. Organe d'information sur le Mouvement des patriotes francais pour la

liberation du territoire. Organe d'information de liaison et de combat des detachements de Francs-tireurs et partisans. FRANCE (LA) EN ARMES. Bulletin des officiers du cadre de reserve des Francs-tireurs et partisans francais.. FRANCE ET RUSSIE. Ou le Realisme dans l'economique et le social. FRANCE (LA) LIBRE. Journal mensuel de propagande pour la liberation de la France.. FRANCE (LA) LIBRE. Liberte, Egalite Fraternite. Ed. pour la France. – Londres. Exemplaires lances d'avion. FRANCE (LA) LIBRE. Liberte, Egalite, Fraternite. Ed. anthologique pour la France. FRANCE (LA) LIBRE. Organe d'union et de combat pour l'independance de la France. FRANCE (LA) LIBRE. Organe de "Ceux de la liberation-vengeance". FRANCE LIBRE. Organe de l'Association francaise des amis de l'Union sovietique. FRANCE (LA) LIBRE. Organe du Comite breton de la France libre. FRANCE (LA) UNIE. Organe du Front national de lutte pour la liberation et l'independance de la France. Region Bretonne. FRONT NATIONAL. Francs-tireurs et partisans. Ordre du jour du haut-commandement des F.T.P.F. Zone Sud. FRONT NATIONAL. Organe de liaison du Comite directeur du Front national pour la liberation de la France, avec ses comites departementaux, locaux, d'entreprise. GUIDE (LE). HOMME (L') LIBRE. Bulletin d'informations ouvrieres. INDUSTRIE (L') FRANCAISE. Bulletin d'information de l'Union des cadres industriels de la France combattante. INFORMATIONS (LES) SOCIALES. Bulletin d'information a l'usage des militants syndicalistes et des futurs cadres sociaux de la France liberee. INSURGE (L'). Organe socialiste de liberation proletarienne) – bobine no. 9 – 1 – fr A.C.R.P.P. [073]

PERIODIQUES CLANDESTINS 1939-1945 / France – (FRANCE (LA) INTERIEURE. FRANC-TIREUR (LE). Mensuel dans la mesure du possible et par la grace de la police du Marechal puis Organe des Mouvements de la resistance unis. FRANC-TIREUR (LE). Organe des Mouvements unis de resistance. Mensuel malgre la Gestapo et la police de Vichy) – bobine no. 8 – 1 – fr A.C.R.P.P. [073]

PERIODIQUES CLANDESTINS 1939-1945 / France – (Humanite (L'). Faux d'origine allemande. HUMANITE (L'). Organe central du Parti communiste francais. Ed. centrale de Zone Sud. HUMANITE (L') DE L'ALLIER. HUMANITE (L'). Organe central du Parti communiste francais S.F.I.C. Ed. de l'Aveyron.. HUMANITE (L'). Organe central du Parti communiste francais S.F.I.C. Ed. de Bordeaux. HUMANITE (L'). Organe central du Parti communiste francais S.F.I.C. Ed. caennaise. HUMANITE (L'). Organe central du Parti communiste francais S.F.I.C. Ed. havraise. HUMANITE (L'). Ed. speciale de la Loire-inferieure. HUMANITE (L'). Ed. du Lot-et-Garonne. HUMANITE (L'). Ed regionale Normandie du Parti communiste francais. HUMANITE (L'). Regional provencale puis Ed. de la region marseillaise. HUMANITE (L'). Section rennaise du Parti communiste. HUMANITE (L'). Section sarthoise du Parti communiste. HUMANITE (L'). Ed. de Toulouse. HUMANITE (L'). Ed. de Toulouse. Faux d'origine allemande. HUMANITE (L'). Organe central du Parti communiste francais S.F.I.C. Ed. speciale feminine. Zone Nord. HUMANITE (L') DE LA FEMME. Numero special de l'Humanite. Organe central du Parti communiste francais S.F.I.C. Zone Sud. HUMANITE (L') DES PAYSANS. Ed. speciale de l'Humanite. Organe central du Parti communiste francais S.F.I.C. HUMANITE (L') DES PAYSANS. Ed. de la Correze. HUMANITE (L') DU SOLDAT. Trait d'union des soldats, ouvriers, paysans. HUMANITE (L') SANS ROUBLES. Faux d'origine allemande) – bobine no. 19 – 1 – fr A.C.R.P.P. [073]

PERIODIQUES CLANDESTINS 1939-1945 / France – (HUMANITE (L'). Organe central du Parti communiste francais. Ed. centrale de Zone Nord) – bobine no. 18 – 1 – fr A.C.R.P.P. [073]

PERIODIQUES CLANDESTINS 1939-1945 / France – (JACQUES BONHOMME. Journal des paysans patriotes de Seine-et-Oise.. JEUNE (LE) PAYSAN PATRIOTE. Organe paysan du Front patriotique de la jeunesse. LIBERTE, EGALITE, FRATERNITE OU LA MORT. Journal officiel des Forces francaises de l'Interieur. LIBERATION. Organe des Francais libres puis Hebdomadaire des Francais libres; Organe des Mouvements unis de resistance. Ed. zone occupee; Hebdomadaire de la resistance francaise. Ed. Nord. LIBERATION. Organe du directoire des forces de liberation francaises puis Organe des Mouvements de resistance unis. Zone Sud. LIBERATION. Chronique alpine.. LIBERATION. Organe des Mouvements de resistance unis. Ed. speciale pour la region lyonnaise. LIBERATION. Organe central du Secours populaire. LIBERATION DU BAS-LANGUEDOC, DU ROUSSILLON ET DU ROUERGUE. Organe des Mouvements unis de resistance. Res. G. 1470 (215). LIBERATION DU NORD ET DU PAS-DE-CALAIS. Organe du Mouvement de la liberation nationale) – bobine no. 10 – 1 – fr A.C.R.P.P. [073]

PERIODIQUES CLANDESTINS 1939-1945 / France – (LIBERER ET FEDERER. Organe du Mouvement revolutionnaire pour la liberation et la reconstruction de la France. LIBERTE. LIBERTE (LA) SYNDICALE. Organe du Comite de defense des libertes syndicales. LORRAINE. Organe des Groupes de Lorraine de la France combattante. M.O.F. Mouvement ouvrier francais puis Expression cegetiste du Mouvement francais. MARSEILLAISE (LA). Organe de la gendarmerie nationale. Front national. Marseillaise (LA). Organe du Front national de lutte pour la liberation de la France. Region provencale. MARSEILLAISE (LA). Organe du Front national pour la liberte et l'independance de la France. Ile-de-France. METALLO (LE). Organe de defense des ouvriers metallurgistes. NOUVELLE (LA) REPUBLIQUE. Patriam recuperare. PARTI SOCIALISTE. Bulletin interieur de documentation et d'etudes. PETITES (LES) AILES. Tirage de zone libre. PETITES (LES) AILES DE FRANCE. Ed. de Paris. PEUPLE (LE) SYNDICALISTE. Fonde par les syndiques militants de la C.G.T. POPULAIRE (LE). Organe du Comite d'action socialiste. "Socialisme et liberte". Ed. de Zone Nord. POPULAIRE (LE). Organe du Parti socialiste. "Socialisme et liberte". Ed. de la region parisienne. IVe REPUBLIQUE (LA). Organe d'action socialiste et de liberation nationale. refractaire (LE). Organe national de liaison et de coordinationa du Comite d'entraide aux refractaires a la deportation (Zone Nord)) – bobine no. 11 – 1 – fr A.C.R.P.P. [073]

PERIODIQUES CLANDESTINS 1939-1945 / France – (PENSEE (LA) LIBRE. Revue francaise. PERE (LE) DUCHESNE. Haine aux tyrans, la liberte ou la mort. ALSACE (L'). Journal libre. devient: Das Elsass. Freie Zeitung. Cahiers (LES) DU BOLCHEVISME. Organe theorique du Parti communiste francais. Le sous-titre varie) – bobine no. 17 – 1 – fr A.C.R.P.P. [073]

PERIODIQUES CLANDESTINS 1939-1945 / France – (PERIODIQUES CLANDESTINS DIFFUSES A L'ETRANGER. Allemagne- – Belgique – Danemark – Italie – Pays-Bas – Pologne) – bobine no. 20-23 – 1 – fr A.C.R.P.P. [073]

PERIODIQUES CLANDESTINS 1939-1945 / France – (PERIODIQUES CLANDESTINS DIFFUSES EN FRANCE ET DESTINES AUX IMMIGRES. Journaux en langue armenienne – espagnole ou catalane. – italienne – polonaise – roumaine – russe – tcheque) – bobine no. 24 – 1 – fr A.C.R.P.P. [073]

PERIODIQUES CLANDESTINS 1939-1945 / France – (RADIO JOURNAL LIBRE puis Radio-maquis) – bobine no. 16 – fr A.C.R.P.P. [073]

PERIODIQUES CLANDESTINS 1939-1945 / France – (RESISTANCE. Bulletin officiel du Comite national de salut public. RESISTANCE. Ile-de-France. RESISTANCE. Journal de la liberation nationale. RESISTANCE. Le nouveau journal de Paris. RESISTANCE DE BORDEAUX ET DU SUD-OUEST. Bulletin mensuel d'informations. RESISTANCE (LA) OUVRIERE. Organe ouvrier de la France combattante. RESISTANCE (LA) PAYSANNE. Bulletin clandestin de la C.G.A. REVOLUTION (LA) FRANCAISE. Bulletin pour un mouvement national revolutionnaire francais. REVUE (LA) LIBRE. Etudes, temoignages, documents. Ed. du Franc-tireur. ROUGE-MIDI. Organe regional du Parti communiste francais. Ed. de Marseille. RUSSIE D'AUJOURD'HUI. Organe de l'Association francaise des amis de l'Union sovietique. N.s (Ed. de Zone Sud). RUSSIE D'AUJOURD'HUI. Organe de l'Association francaise des amis de l'Union sovietique. N.s. (Ed. de Zone Nord). RUSSIE D'AUJOURD'HUI. Edite par les A.U.S. Amis de l'Union sovietique de la Marne. RUSSIE D'AUJOURD'HUI. Organe mensuel des Amis de l'Union sovietique. Region de Saone-et-Loire. RUSSIE D'AUJOURD'HUI. Association francaise des amis de l'Union sovietique. Region de Toulouse. RUSSIE D'AUJOURD'HUI. Organe de l'Association des amis de l'Union sovietique. Federation varoise. PATRIOTE RUSSE. (Titre francais). En russe. Quelques numeros traduits en francais. SOCIALISME ET LIBERTE. Bulletin du Comite d'action socialiste. TERRE (LA). Organe paysan du Parti communiste francais (Ed. de Zone Nord). TERRE (LA). Organe de defense des interets paysans, edite par le Parti communiste francais S.F.I.C. Ed. de Bretagne) – bobine no. 12 – 1 – fr A.C.R.P.P. [073]

PERIODIQUES CLANDESTINS 1939-1945 / France – (TRAVAILLEUR (LE) ALPIN. Organe regional du Parti communiste francais S.F.I.C. UNION DES CADRES INDUSTRIELS DE LA FRANCE COMBATTANTE. Bulletin d'information. UNION (L') DES COMITES POPULAIRES DE LA REGION PARISIENNE. Ed. de Paris-ville. UNITE (L') DE LA SARTHE. Organe regional du Parti communiste francais. UNITE (L') OUVRIERE ET PAYSANNE. Organe regional du Parti communiste francais. (Sarthe). UNIVERSITE (L') LIBRE. Fond. Jacques Salomon, Jacques Decours, Frederic Joliot-Curie, Paul Langevin, Pierre Manucherat et Georges Politzer. UNIVERSITE (L') LIBRE. Serie mensuelle. UNIVERSITE (L') LIBRE. Organe du Comite national des professeurs. Ed. de la Zone Sud. VERITES. Journal independant) – bobine no. 13 – 1 – fr A.C.R.P.P. [073]

PERIODIQUES CLANDESTINS 1939-1945 / France – (VIE (LA) OUVRIERE. Edite par le Parti communiste francais. Ed. centrale de Zone Nord. VIE (LA) OUVRIERE. Ed. centrale de Zone Sud) – bobine no. 14 – 1 – fr A.C.R.P.P. [073]

PERIODIQUES CLANDESTINS 1939-1945 / France – (VOIX DE FRANCE. VOIX (LA) DU NORD. Organe de la resistance de la Flandre francaise. VOIX (LA) DU NORD ET DU PAS-DE-CALAIS. Organe de la resistance de la Flandre francaise.. VOIX (LA) DU PEUPLE. Organe de l'Union des syndicats ouvriers de la region parisienne. VOIX (LA) DU PEUPLE. Organe regional du Parti communiste francais (Rhone). TOUR D'HORIZON. VERITE (LA) FRANCAISE. Organe des verites francaises, edite quelque part en France. PANTAGRUEL. Feuille d'informations. LETTRES (LES) FRANCAISES. Front national des ecrivains puis Revue des ecrivains groupes au Comite national des ecrivains. ECRAN (L') FRANCAIS. Organe des comites du cinema du Front national de lutte pour la liberation. – Paris. dec 1943 (no. 1). A paru, a dater de mars 1944, en annexe des Lettres francaises. BIR-HAKEIM. Journal republicain mensuel paraissant malgre la Gestapo, malgre le negrier Laval et son gouvernement de Vichy. Ed. de Paris et de province. VALMY. Organe de la resistance francaise a l'oppression. Mensuel. DEMAIN. Liberte, Egalite, Fraternite) – bobine no. 15 – 1 – fr A.C.R.P.P. [073]

EL PERIODISMO POLITICO / Garcia Costa, Victor O – [Buenos Aires: Centro Editor de America Latina, 1972] – 1 – CSUXADJ0985-B – us Hoover Inst Photo [320]

PERIODONTICS – v. 1-6. 1963-68 – 1 – us UMI [617]

Perionius, J *see* DIALOGORUM DE LINGUAE GALLICAE ORIGINE...

PERIOPERATIVE NURSING QUARTERLY – 1985- – 1,5,6,9 – us UMI [610]

PERIPHERAL CHEMORESPONSIVENESS AND EXERCISE INDUCED ARTERIAL HYPOXEMIA IN HIGHLY TRAINED ENDURANCE ATHLETES / Cooper, Trevor K – 1993 – 2mf – $8.00 – us Microform Publ [612]

O PERIQUITO : ORGAO CRITICO E NOTICIOSO – Pilar, Alagoas. 22 Fev-5 Mar 1893 – 1,5,6 – bl Biblioteca [072]

O PERIQUITO : PERIODICO LITTERARIO, CRITICO E NOTICIOSO – Maceio, Alagoas. 25 Mar, 3 Ago 1888 – 1,5,6 – bl Biblioteca [072]

Peris Mencheta, Ramon *see* SINODO DIOCESANO DE CORIA

Peris, Ramon *see* DATO Y SU VIDA

PERISCOOP – (Lacking: 1948(1, 3-8); 1949(10, 13, 15)) – Batavia: Culturele Voorlichting R.V.D., 1948-1949 – 4mf – 9 – SE-785/1 – ne IDC [306]

PERISCOPE – Shorter College. Rome. Georgia. 20 Feb 1920-Feb 1974 – 1 – 50.50 – us Baptist [240]

O PERISCOPIO : JORNAL HUMORISTICO ESPORTIVO – Manaos, Amazonas. 20 Jun-4 Jul 1920 – 1,5,6 – bl Biblioteca [072]

PERJOGI DONTVENYTAR. – Budapest. On film: v1-12; 1916-28. LL-0250 – 1 – us L of C Photodup [340]

PERJUICIOS DE LA SEPARACION DE LA MEDICINA Y LA CIRUJIA.. / Caceres, Rafael de – 1837 – 9 – 1.50f – sp Bibl Santa Ana [610]

PERKEMBANGAN BANK UMUM NASIONAL DALAM TAHUN... / Bank Umum Nasional – (Annual) – Djakarta, 1954 – 1mf – 9 – SE-1341/1 – ne IDC [332]

PERKEMBANGAN SEDJARAH NEGARA MADJAPAHIT (T.M. 1293-1525) DALAM EMPAT DEWASA MENURUT ADJARAN PROF. TOYNBEE / Yamin, Muhammad – SE 4393 1. 1962 – 9 – ne IDC [900]

Perkin *see* WORKS

Perkins, Ann L *see* THE COMPARATIVE ARCHEOLOGY OF EARLY MESOPOTAMIA

Perkins, C C *see*
- TUSCAN SCULPTORS: ...
- TUSCAN SCULPTORS: THEIR LIVES, WORKS AND TIMES

PERKINS COUNTY SENTINEL – Grant, NE. -w. Jun 1892-Dec 1895, scattered issues missing; Feb 1896-Sept 1902 – 1 – us NE Hist [071]

Perkins, D A W *see* HISTORY OF O'BRIEN COUNTY

Perkins, Frederic Beecher *see* CHARLES DICKENS: A SKETCH OF HIS LIFE AND WORKS

Perkins, Henry Martyn *see* LIFE OF REV. JUSTIN PERKINS, D.D.

PERKINS JOURNAL – (1985-. 5,6,9) – v26-. 1972- – 1 – us UMI [240]

Perkins, Justin *see*
- HISTORICAL SKETCH OF THE MISSION TO THE NESTORIANS
- MISSIONARY LIFE IN PERSIA
- OUR COUNTRY'S SIN
- A RESIDENCE OF EIGHT YEARS IN PERSIA AMONG THE NESTORIAN CHRISTIANS

Perkins, Merle L *see* VOLTAIRE'S CONCEPT OF INTERNATIONAL ORDER

Perkins School of Theology *see* PERKINS SCHOOL OF THEOLOGY JOURNAL

PERKINS SCHOOL OF THEOLOGY JOURNAL / Perkins School of Theology – v1-25. 1947-72 – 1 – us UMI [240]

Perkins, Thomas Handasyd *see* THOMAS HANDASYD PERKINS PAPERS, 1789-1892

Perkins, William *see* CATHOLICUS REFORMATUS; HOC EST, EXPOSITIO ET DECLARATIO

Perkonig, Josef Friedrich *see* DER SCHINDERHANNES ZIEHT UEBERS GEBIRGE

PERKUAT PERSATUAN NASIONAL DAN PERSATUAN KOMUNIS / Aidit, Dipa Nusantara – SE-6692 1. 1961 – 9 – ne IDC [950]

Perky, Charles *see* PAST AND PRESENT OF SAUNDERS COUNTY

LA PERLE EVANGELIQUE : NOUVELLEMENT TRADUITE DE LATIN EN FRANCOIS – Paris, 1602 – 17mf – 8 – ne Slangenburg [240]

LA PERLE JAUNE, OU, LA VIERGE DE L'HINDOUSTAN / Desy, Edouard – Montreal?: s.n., 1887, (Montreal: "L'Etenard"). 02671. (Pre-1900 Canadiana) – 9 – cn C.I.H.M. [971]

Perles, Felix *see*
- ANALEKTEN ZUR TEXTKRITIK DES ALTEN TESTAMENTS
- JUEDISCHE SKIZZEN
- ZUR ALTHEBRAEISCHEN STROPHIK
- ZUR ERKLAERUNG DER PSALMEN SALOMOS

Perles, Joseph *see*
- BEITRAEGE ZUR GESCHICHTE DER HEBRAEISCHEN UND ARAMAEISCHEN STUDIEN

Perley, Sidney *see* PRACTICE IN THE PROBATE COURT OF MASSACHUSETTS

Perlini, R *see* FORME DI LEPIDOTTERI ESCLUSIVAMENTE ITALIANE

Perlman, Philip B *see* MARYLAND MANUAL 1923

Perlman, Selig *see* A THEORY OF THE LABOR MOVEMENT
DIE PERLMUSCHELN UND IHRE PERLEN / Hessling, T von – Z-572 2. 1859 – 8 – ne IDC [590]
Perlovagor, M *see* ZAKONY O TRUDEI SOTSIALNOM STRAKHOVANII NA STROITELNYKH RABOTAKH
Perlowski, J *see* POLAND. HER PEOPLE, HISTORY, INDUSTRIES, FINANCE, SCIENCE
PERLYCROSS / Blackmore, Richard Doddridge – British Fiction Archive: Unit 3 – 9 – uk Bell [830]
PERMANENCE OF CHRISTIANITY:...EIGHT LECTURES / Eaton, John Richard Turner – New York: E.P. Dutton, 1879. 1 fiche – 9 – us A.T.L.A. [240]
Permanent Court of International Justice. Hague *see*
- PUBLICATIONS
- SERIES A: JUDGEMENTS. NOS. 1-24. 1922-30

PERMANENT PEOPLES' TRIBUNAL OF THE INTERNATIONAL LEAGUE FOR THE RIGHTS AND LIBERATION OF PEOPLES – Rome. 68 docs. 1979-1990 – 47mf – 9 – ne IDC [320]
PERMANENT VALUE OF THE BOOK OF GENESIS / Body, Charles WE – New York: Longmans, Green, 1894.1 fiche – 9 – us A.T.L.A. [240]
THE PERMESTRA AFFAIR *see* REBELS WITHOUT A CAUSE
PERMSKAIA GUB – Permskaia guberniia v sel'skokhoziaistvennom otnoshenii. Perm'. 1895-1906. BRZ-219 2 – 8 – ne IDC [073]
PERMSKII KOOPERATOR – Perm', 1923-24 n10 – 14mf – 9 – COR-666/1 – ne IDC [334]
PERMSKII SBORNIK; POVREMENNOE IZDANIE – M. 2v. 1859-1860 – 10mf – 9 – RET-13/1 – ne IDC [947]
Pernambuco. Brazil (State) *see* DIARIO OFICIAL
Pernambuco. Brazil (State). Assemblea Legislativo *see* DIARIO DO PODER LEGISLATIVO
Pernambuco. Brazil (State). Courts *see* DIARIO DA JUSTICA
PERON : SINTESIS BIOGRAFICA DE SU VIDA / Giudice, Fiorangel del – Buenos Aires: Sapaleri, [194-?] – 1 – CSUXADP9136-B – us Hoover Inst Photo [320]
Peron *see* MEMOIRES DU CAPITAINE PERON SUR SES VOYAGES AUX COTES D'AFRIQUE EN ARABIE, A L'ILE D'AMSTERDAM, AUX ILES D'ANJOUAN ET DE MAYOTTE
PERON CONTRA PERON / Confalonieri, Orestes D – Buenos Aires: Editorial Antygua, [1956] – 1 – CSUXADP3870-B – us Hoover Inst Photo [320]
PERON, EL EJERCITO Y LA IGLESIA : HOMENAJE AL CORONEL FEDERICO GENTILUOMO / Gentiluomo, Federico A – [Buenos Aires?]: Ediciones LL, 1970 – 1 – CSUCADH9506-B – us Hoover Inst Photo [320]
PERON, EL REGRESO Y LA MUERTE / Peron, Juan Domingo – [Montevideo]: Biblioteca de Marcha, [1974?- – 1 – CSUXADP3182-B – us Hoover Inst Photo [320]
PERON EN 6 [I.E. SEIS] ANOS HISTORICOS / Argentine Republic. Presidencia. Subsecretaria de Informaciones – Buenos Aires, 1952 – 1 – CSUXADH9077-B – us Hoover Inst Photo [320]
THE PERON ERA / Alexander, Robert Jackson – New York: Columbia University Press, 1951 – 1 – CSUXADM9243-B – us Hoover Inst Photo [320]
PERON ERA POLITICAL PAMPHLETS AND MONOGRAPHS – Includes government documents, writings of intellectual, labor and political leaders including Peron – 1,485mf – 9 – $6,430.00 – us UPA [320]
Peron, Eva *see* LA PALABRA, EL PENSAMIENTO Y LA ACCION DE EVA PERON
Peron, F *see* VOYAGE DE DECOUVERTE AUX TERRES AUSTRALES
PERON HABLA A LOS TRABAJADORES, 2 DE NOVIEMBRE DE 1973 *see* SINDICALISMO Y POLITICA
Peron, Juan *see*
- LA ACCION DEL PODER EJECUTIVO DESDE EL 1. DE ABRIL DE 1947 HASTA EL 31 DE MARZO DE 1948
- LOS ANHELOS DE DOS PUEBLOS HERMANOS EN LA PALABRA DE PERON E IBANEZ
- MENSAJE DEL PRESIDENTE DE LA REPUBLICA TENIENTE GENERAL JUAN D. PERON
- LA OBRA DE PERON
- PLAN QUINQUENAL DE GOBIERNO DEL PRESIDENTE PERON, 1947-1951

Peron, Juan Domingo *see*
- 6 ARTICULOS PERIODISTICOS DE PERON
- 17 DE OCTUBRE
- APUNTES DE HISTORIA MILITAR
- EL GOBIERNO, EL ESTADO Y LAS ORGANIZACIONES LIBRES DEL PUEBLO, LA COMUNIDAD ORGANIZADA
- LA LIBERTAD A TRAVES DEL PENSAMIENTO DE PERON
- EL LIBRO ROJO DE PERON; CITAS
- MAXIMAS DE PERON
- OBRAS COMPLETAS
- PERON, EL REGRESO Y LA MUERTE
- PERON SENALA LA MISION UNIVERSALISTA DE LAS NACIONES UNIDAS
- PERON, SU PUEBLO Y EL 20. PLAN QUINQUENAL
- PERON, SU PUEBLO Y EL 20. PLAN QUINQUENAL; DISERTACION, 1-3,5
- PERON Y EVA PERON HABLAN EN EL CABILDO ABIERTO DEL JUSTICIALISMO
- PERON Y EVA PERON HABLAN EN EL DIA DE LOS TRABAJADORES, 1. DE MAYO, 1951
- PERON Y EVA PERON HABLAN EN EL DIA DE LOS TRABAJADORES, 10. DE MAYO DE 1952
- PERON Y EVITA HABLAN EN EL ACTO DE CLAUSURA DEL CONGRESO NACIONAL EXTRAORDINARIO DE LA CONFEDERACION GENERAL DEL TRABAJO 19 DE ABRIL DE 1950
- PERON Y EVITA HABLAN EN LA FIESTA DE LOS TRABAJADORES, 10. DE MAYO, 1950
- PERON Y LA DOCTRINA JUSTICIALISTA
- PERON Y "LA PRENSA" DE LA ERA JUSTICIALISTA
- PERON Y LAS FUERZAS ARMADAS
- PLAN ECONOMICO DE 1952
- POLICY AND STRATEGY
- POLITICA ALIMENTARIA ARGENTINA
- POLITICA Y ESTRATEGIA
- PRINCIPIOS DEL SINDICALISMO JUSTICIALISTA DE PERON
- SE INICIA LA ERA DE LA POLITICA SOCIAL ARGENTINA
- SELECCION DE SUS ESCRITOS, CONFERENCIAS Y DISCURSOS
- SERIE DE SEIS ARTICULOS SOBRE PROBLEMAS POLITICOS, SOCIALES Y ECONOMICOS
- SINDICALISMO Y POLITICA
- UN SOLO INTERES
- SOLO LA VERDAD NOS HARA LIBRES
- TEORIA Y PRACTICA DE LA LIBERCION ECONOMICA, SOCIAL Y POLITICA DE LA REPUBLICA; DISCURSOS PRONUNCIADOS POR EL PRESIDENTE DE LA NACION Y POR MARIA EVA DURATE DE PERON
- LA TERCERA POSICION EN LA PREDICA Y EL EJEMPLO DE PERON
- THE THEORY AND COMPLETE DOCTRINE OF GENERAL PERON
- TODOS SUS DISCURSOS, MENSAJES Y CONFERENCIAS COMPLETOS, 1973-1974
- TOPONIMIA PATAGONICA DE ETIMOLOGIA ARAUCANA
- TRES REVOLUCIONES MILITARES
- THE VOICE OF PERON

PERON, LA IGLESIA Y UN CURA / Badanelli, Pedro – [Buenos Aires]: Editorial Tartessos, 1958 – 1 – CSUXADQ7995-B – us Hoover Inst Photo [320]
PERON, LA IGLESIA Y UN CURA / Badanelli, Pedro – [Buenos Aires?]: Editorial Tartessos, 4th ed 1960 – 1 – CSUXADQ8002-B – us Hoover Inst Photo [320]
PERON NO EST A EXCOMULGADO : UN DESAFIO JURIDICO AL EPISCOPADO MUNDIAL. EL CASO DE MONSENOR PLAZA / Bandanelli, Pedro – [Buenos Aires?]: Editorial Tartessos, [1959?] – 1 – CSUXAHZ3538-B – us Hoover Inst Photo [320]
PERON SENALA LA MISION UNIVERSALISTA DE LAS NACIONES UNIDAS / Peron, Juan Domingo – Buenos Aires: Presidencia de la Nacion, Secretaria de Prensa y Difusion, [1973?] – 1 – CSUXADJ2880-B – us Hoover Inst Photo [320]
PERON, SU PUEBLO Y EL 20. PLAN QUINQUENAL / Peron, Juan Domingo – Buenos Aires: Presidencia de la Nacion, Subsecretaria de Informaciones, 1953 – 1 – CSUXAHZ3492-B – us Hoover Inst Photo [320]
PERON, SU PUEBLO Y EL 20. PLAN QUINQUENAL / Peron, Juan Domingo – [Buenos Aires: Presidencia de la Nacion, Subsecretaria de Informaciones, 1953] – 1 – CSUXAHZ3486-B – us Hoover Inst Photo [320]
PERON, SU PUEBLO Y EL 20. PLAN QUINQUENAL; DISERTACION, 1-3,5 / Peron, Juan Domingo – Buenos Aires: [Presidencial de la Nacion, Subsecretatia de Informaciones], 1953. 5v – 1 – CSUXAGQ4391-B – us Hoover Inst Photo [320]
PERON VISTO POR UN PERIODISTA / Barrios, Americo – Buenos Aires: Ministerio de Educacion, 1955 – 1 – CSUXADM8790-B – us Hoover Inst Photo [320]
PERON Y EL DEPORTE / Argentina. Secretaria de Prensa – [Buenos Aires]: El Secretaria, [197-] – 1 – CSUXAGN2217-B – us Hoover Inst Photo [790]
PERON Y EL JUSTICIALISMO / Ciria, Alberto – Mexico: Siglo Veintiuno Editores, [1971] – 1 – CSUXADH9039-B – us Hoover Inst Photo [320]
PERON Y EL PERONISMO EN LA HISTORIA CONTEMPORANEA / Chavez, Fermin – Buenos Aires: Editorial Oriente, c1975- – 1 – CSUXADJ2864-B – us Hoover Inst Photo [320]
PERON Y ESPANA : POLITICA SOCIAL, INTERNA E INTERNACIONAL / Campano, Jose – Buenos Aires: Editorial Plus Ultra, c1982 – 1 – CSUXADQ7277-B – us Hoover Inst Photo [320]
PERON Y EVA : TRAYECTORIA Y FIN DE UN REGIMEN / Benedetti, Antonio – Mexico: Editores Panamericanos Asociados, 1956 – 1 – CSUXAJA8533-B – us Hoover Inst Photo [320]
PERON Y EVA PERON HABLAN EN EL CABILDO ABIERTO DEL JUSTICIALISMO / Peron, Juan Domingo – Buenos Aires?: Presidencia de la Nacion, Subsecretaria de Informaciones, 1951? – 1 – CSUXADP3548-B – us Hoover Inst Photo [972]
PERON Y EVA PERON HABLAN EN EL DIA DE LOS TRABAJADORES, 1. DE MAYO, 1951 / Peron, Juan Domingo – Buenos Aires?: Presidencia de la Nacion, Subsecretaria de Informaciones, 1951? – 1 – CSUXAGQ4384-B – us Hoover Inst Photo [972]
PERON Y EVA PERON HABLAN EN EL DIA DE LOS TRABAJADORES, 10. DE MAYO DE 1952 / Peron, Juan Domingo – Buenos Aires: [Presidencia de la Nacion, Sub-Secretaria de Informaciones], 1952 – 1 – CSUXAGQ4372-B – us Hoover Inst Photo [972]
PERON Y EVITA HABLAN EN EL ACTO DE CLAUSURA DEL CONGRESO NACIONAL EXTRAORDINARIO DE LA CONFEDERACION GENERAL DEL TRABAJO 19 DE ABRIL DE 1950 / Peron, Juan Domingo – Buenos Aires?: Subsecretaria de Informaciones de la Presidencia de la Nacion], 1950 – 1 – CSUXAHZ2989-B – us Hoover Inst Photo [320]
PERON Y EVITA HABLAN EN LA FIESTA DE LOS TRABAJADORES, 10. DE MAYO, 1950 / Peron, Juan Domingo – [Buenos Aires?: Subsecretaria de Informaciones de la Presidencia de la Nacion, 1950?] – 1 – CSUXAGQ4378-B – us Hoover Inst Photo [972]
PERON Y LA DOCTRINA JUSTICIALISTA / Peron, Juan Domingo – [Buenos Aires]: Presidencia de la Nacion, Secretaria de Prensa y Difusion, [1974] – 1 – CSUXADH9073-B – us Hoover Inst Photo [360]
PERON Y "LA PRENSA" DE LA ERA JUSTICIALISTA / Peron, Juan Domingo – Buenos Aires: Presidencia de la Nacion, Subsecretaria de Informaciones, 1953 – 1 – CSUXAJA7319-B – us Hoover Inst Photo [360]
PERON Y LA SEGUNDA GUERRA MUNDIAL : LA SEGUNDA GUERRA MUNDIAL, REPERCUSIONES Y CONSECUENCIAS EN LA ARGENTINA / Agosti, Hector Pablo – Buenos Aires: Editorial Polemica, 1970 – 1 – CSUXAHZ7784-B – us Hoover Inst Photo [350]
PERON Y LAS FUERZAS ARMADAS / Peron, Juan Domingo – Buenos Aires: Pena Lillo Editor, 1982 – 1 – CSUXADJ2683-B – us Hoover Inst Photo [355]
PERON Y LOS PERONISTAS / Firpo, M Eduardo – [Buenos Aires]: Tall. Graf. Alberdi, 1965] – 1 – CSUXADQ4951-B – us Hoover Inst Photo [320]
PERON-IBANEZ / Argentine Republic. Presidencia. Subsecretaria de Informaciones – [Buenos Aires, 1953] – 1 – CSUXADQ7559-B – us Hoover Inst Photo [920]
EL PERONISMO : 1943-1955 – Montevideo: Marcha, 1973 – 1 – CSUXAJA7278-B – us Hoover Inst Photo [320]
EL PERONISMO / Cardenas, Gonzalo – Buenos Aires: Ediciones Cepe, 2nd ed [1973] – 1 – CSUXADQ2825-B – us Hoover Inst Photo [320]
EL PERONISMO / Floria, Carlos Alberto et al – Buenos Aires: Todo es Historia, 1976- – 1 – CSUXAJA7732-B – us Hoover Inst Photo [320]
EL PERONISMO / Halperin, Leopoldo – Buenos Aires: Centro Editor de America Latina, 1972 – 1 – CSUXADL5938-B – us Hoover Inst Photo [320]
PERONISMO : APUNTES PARA UNA REVALORACION CRITICA MARXISTA / Aldao, Andres – [Buenos Aires], 1969 – 1 – CSUXADH9756-B – us Hoover Inst Photo [320]
PERONISMO : AUTOCRITICA Y PRSPECTIVAS / Gazzera, Miguel & Ceresole, Norberto – [Buenos Aires]: Editorial Descartes, 1970 – 1 – CSUXADQ4956-B – us Hoover Inst Photo [320]
PERONISMO – [Buenos Aires?, 1948?] – 1 – CSUXADP5180-B – us Hoover Inst Photo [320]
PERONISMO : CLAVES / Cairo, Angel – Buenos Aires: Ediciones Centro de Estudios Aporte, [1975] – 1 – CSUXADJ3784-B – us Hoover Inst Photo [320]
PERONISMO : DE LA REFORMA A LA REVOLUCION [POR] NORBERTO CERESOLE, MIGUEL GAZZERA [Y] CARLOS P. MASTRORILLI / Ceresole, Norberto et al – [Buenos Aires]: A. Pena Lillo, [1972] – 1 – CSUXADQ2961-B – us Hoover Inst Photo [320]
PERONISMO : EL EXILIO, 1955-1973 – Buenos Aires: Marcha, 1973 – 1 – CSUXAJA7284-B – us Hoover Inst Photo [320]
PERONISMO : MYTHOLOGY OR IDEOLOY / Ciria, Alberto – Riverside: University of California, 1967 – 1 – CSUXADQ2936-B – us Hoover Inst Photo [320]
EL PERONISMO 1943-1955 = DER PERONISMUS 1943-1955 / Waldmann, Peter – Buenos Aires: Editorial Sudamericana, 1981 – 1 – CSUXADJ7578-B – us Hoover Inst Photo [320]
EL PERONISMO, ANTECEDENTES Y GOBIERNO / Franco, Juan Pablo & Alvarez, Fernando – [Buenos Aires: Tall. Graf. Artex, 1972] – 1 – CSUXADL6466-B – us Hoover Inst Photo [320]
PERONISMO, BUROCRACIA Y BURGUESIA NACIONAL / Alberti, Blas – [Buenos Aires]: Ediciones Rancagua, [1974] – 1 – CSUXADQ1414-B – us Hoover Inst Photo [320]
EL PERONISMO DE LA VICTORIA / Bernetti, Jorge Luis – Buenos Aires: Editorial Legasa, 1983 – 1 – CSUXADQ4924-B – us Hoover Inst Photo [320]
PERONISMO DENTRO DEL PERONISMO / Casco, Marcos – [Santa Fe, Argentina: Editorial Belgrano], 1974 – 1 – CSUXADQ7291-B – us Hoover Inst Photo [320]
PERONISMO E INTEGRACION / Cooke, John William – [Buenos Aires]: Aquarius, [1972] – 1 – CSUXADL7046-B – us Hoover Inst Photo [320]
EL PERONISMO EN LA LITERATURA ARGENTINA / Goldar, Ernesto – Buenos Aires: Editorial Freeland, 1971 – 1 – CSUXADJ1911-B – us Hoover Inst Photo [440]
PERONISMO, GOBIERNO Y PODER (DE LA CRISIS DEL SISTEMA AL SOCIALISMO NACIONAL) / Bortnik, Ruben – [Buenos Aires], Corregidor, [1973] – 1 – CSUXADJ1341-B – us Hoover Inst Photo [320]
PERONISMO, LA MAYORIA PERDIDA / Cordeu, Mora – Buenos Aires, Argentina: Sudamericana/Planeta, 2nd ed 1985 – 1 – CSUXADM8365-B – us Hoover Inst Photo [320]
EL PERONISMO POLEMICO / Alberti, Blas – Buenos Aires: Ediciones Macchi, c1976 – 1 – CSUXADQ4937-B – us Hoover Inst Photo [972]

EL PERONISMO, SOCIALISMO NACIONAL – Cordoba [Argentina]: Z. Mariani, [1st ed 1969] – 1 – CSUXAJB7985-B – us Hoover Inst Photo [320]

PERONISMO Y DICTADURA / Bittel, Deolindo Felipe – Buenos Aires: Editora del Movimento, [1983] – 1 – CSUXADL7492-B – us Hoover Inst Photo [320]

EL PERONISMO Y EL GOLPE DE ESTADO : INFORME A LAS BASES DE MOVIMIENTO / Cooke, John William – [Buenos Aires: Accion Revolucionaria Peronista, 1966] – 1 – CSUXADQ6401-B – us Hoover Inst Photo [320]

EL PERONISMO Y LA IGLESIA / Gamini, Hugo – [Buenos Aires]: Centro Editor de America Latina, [1971] – 1 – CSUXAHZ2512-B – us Hoover Inst Photo [320]

EL PERONISMO Y LA PRIMACIA DE LA POLITICA / Feinmann, Jose Pablo – [Buenos Aires]: Cimarron, Libreria Editorial, [1974] – 1 – CSUXADJ1336-B – us Hoover Inst Photo [320]

PERONISMO Y LIBERACION NACIONAL / Eggers Lan, Conrado – [Buenos Aires]: Ediciones Busqueda, [1973] – 1 – CSUXADQ4967-B – us Hoover Inst Photo [320]

PERONISMO Y PETROLEO : DECLARACIONES ANTE LA COMISION ESPECIAL INVESTIGADORA SOBE PETROLEO DE LA CAMARA DE DIPUTADOS DE LA NACION / Cooke, John William – [Buenos Aires?]: Ediciones Segunda Etapa, 1964 – 1 – CSUXAHZ2389-B – us Hoover Inst Photo [320]

PERONISMO Y SOCIALISMO NACIONAL / Belloni, Alberto – Buenos Aires: [Editorial Coyoac an], 1962 – 1 – CSUXAHZ6140-B – us Hoover Inst Photo [320]

EL PERONISTA – (c.1: v.1:no.1 1946:Apr.4) – 1 – CSUXAJA8058-S – us Hoover Inst Photo [073]

EL PERONISTA – (c.1: v.1:no.1 1974:Apr.19-v.1:no.6 (May 28)) – 1 – CSUXAJA8111-S – us Hoover Inst Photo [073]

Perowne, J J Stewart *see* THE BOOK OF PSALMS

Peroz, Etienne *see* L'EMPIRE DE L'ALMENY-EMIZ LAMORY OU EMPIRE DU OUASSOULOU

Peroz, Marie Etienne *see*
- AU NIGER
- LA TACTIQUE DANS LE SOUDAN; QUELQUES COMBATS ET EPISODES DE GUERRES REMARQUABLES

PERPETUAL DIARY / Martin, Elizabeth (Hosack) Ayres – 1865, Martin lived in Gilead, Ohio, and Edgerton, KS – 1 – us KS Hist [920]

PERPETUAL READY REFERENCE GUIDE TO THE STATUTES OF CANADA: VIZ. THE REVISED STATUTES OF 1886, AND ALL SUBSEQUENT AMENDING, REPEALING, COGNATE AND NEW ACTS / Blatch, F K – Brockville, Ont.: The Times, 1891. 02336. (Pre-1900 Canadiana) – 9 – cn C.I.H.M. [340]

Perpetuel-Secours, Marie-du *see*
- BIBLIOGRAPHIE DE L'OEUVRE DE SA GRANDEUR MONSEIGNEUR PAUL-EUGENE ROY, 1859-1926, DIX-HUITIEME EVEQUE ET HUITIEME ARCHEVEQUE DE QUEBEC
- BIO-BIBLIOGRAPHIE

LA PERPETUITE DE LA FOY DE L'EGLISE CATHOLIQUE TOUCHANT L'EUCHARISTIE / Arnauld, Antoine – Paris, 1669 – 14mf – 9 – CA-96/1 – ne IDC [240]

A PERPLEXED PHILOSOPHER / George, Henry – 1893. With 2 talks on Justice and Poverty; and utterances by Churchill on the land monopoly. 4 fiches (24x) – 9 – 1.00f – at Libertarian Micro [320]

Perraud, Charles-Alexis *see* LA LIBRE-PENSEE ET LE CATHOLICISME

Perrault *see*
- LE CABINET DES BEAUX ARTS

Perrault, C *see* MEMOIRS FOR A NATURAL HISTORY OF ANIMALS

Perrault, Claude *see* ORDONNANCE DES CINQ ESPECES DE COLONNES SELON LA METHODE DES ANCIENS

Perrault, Francais *see* L'ANTIDEMON DE MASCON OU LA RELATION PURE ET SIMPLE DES PRINCIPALES CHARGES QUI ONT ESTE FAITES PAR UN DEMON

Perrault, Joseph Francois *see*
- DICTIONNAIRE PORTATIF ET ABREGE DES LOIX ET REGLES DU PARLEMENT PROVINCIAL DU BAS-CANADA, DEPUIS SON ETABLISSEMENT...JUSQUES ET COMPRIS L'AN DE NOTRE SEIGNEUR, 1805
- EXTRAITS OU PRECEDENTS, TIRES DES REGISTRES DE LA PREVOSTE DE QUEBEC 1726-1756, ET DEDIES AUX HONORABLES JUGES, AUX GENS DU ROI, AUX AVOCATS, PROCUREURS, ET PRATICIENS DE LA PROVINCE DU BAS-CANADA
- QUESTIONS ET REPONSES SUR LE DROIT CIVIL DU BAS-CANADA

Perrault, M *see* LES DIX LIVRES D'ARCHITECTURE DE VITRUVE

PERRAULT'S CONSEIL SUPERIEUR / Canada. Quebec – 1v. 1729-59 (all publ) – 1mf – 9 – $1.50 – LLMC 81-079 – us L.L.M.C. [340]

PERRAULT'S PREVOSTE DE QUEBEC / Canada. Quebec – 1v. 1726-59 (all publ) – 1mf – 9 – $1.50 – LLMC 81-080 – us L.L.M.C. [340]

Perret, E *see* WOUDT VAN WONDERLICKE SINNE-FABULEN DER DIEREN...

Perret, I *see* ARCHITECTURE ET PERSPECTIVE DES FORTIFICATIONS

Perret, Jacques *see* DES FORTIFICATIONS ET ARTIFICES, ARCHITECTURE ET PERSPECTIVES.

Perret, Paul *see* L'AMOUR ET LA GUERRE

Perrett, Jennie *see* BEN OWEN: A LANCASHIRE STORY

Perreymond *see* LE BILAN DE LA FRANCE, OU LA MISERE ET LE TRAVAIL

Perrier, O *see* LE CANADA-FRANCAIS

Perriere, Guillaume de la *see* LA MOROSOPHIE DE GUILLAUME DE LA PERRIERE TOLOSAIN

Perrin, J Nick *see* PERRIN'S HISTORY OF ILLINOIS

Perrin, R *see* IMAGES MALGACHES DU FOKONOLONA TRADITIONNEL

Perrin, William Henry *see*
- HISTORY OF ALEXANDER COUNTY, UNION AND PULASKI COUNTIES
- HISTORY OF BOND AND MONTGOMERY COUNTIES
- HISTORY OF BOURBON, SCOTT, HARRISON AND NICHOLAS COUNTIES
- HISTORY OF CASS COUNTY
- HISTORY OF CRAWFORD AND CLARK COUNTIES
- HISTORY OF EFFINGHAM COUNTY
- HISTORY OF JEFFERSON COUNTY
- HISTORY OF STARK COUNTY
- HISTORY OF SUMMIT COUNTY

Perrin-Dulac, F M *see* DESCRIPTION GENERALE DU DEPARTEMENT DE L'ISERE

PERRIN'S HISTORY OF ILLINOIS / Perrin, J Nick – Springfield: Illinois State Register Printers, 1906. Illinois Reel 1. (The Cox Library Collection) – 5 – us Americana [978]

PERRIS PROGRESS – Perris, CA. 1912- – 41+ r – 1 – $2,050.00 ($50.00y) – R02621 – us Library Micro [071]

Perron, Michel *see* L'ERE NIGERIENNE

Perronet, Charles *see* A SUMMARY VIEW OF THE DOCTRINES OF METHODISM, OCCASIONED BY THE LATE PERSECUTION OF THE METHODISTS AT NORWICH,...

LE PERROQUET : HUMORISTIQUE – Sorel, Canada. 27 aut-7 sep 1878 – 1r – 1 – Can$25.00 – cn Can Microfilming [072]

LE PERROQUET : HUMORISTIQUE ET ILLUSTRE – Montreal, Canada. 7 jan. 1865-12 aut 1865 – 1r – 1 – Can$30.00 – cn Can Microfilming [072]

LE PERROQUET – Montreal. v1 no 1 jan-no 20 juin 1926. SEM35P167 – 1r – 1 – Can$15.00 – cn Bibl Nat [073]

Perrot *see* POISONS DE FLECHES ET POISONS D'EPREUVE

Perrot, Georges *see* MUSEE DU BARDO A TUNIS ET LES FOUILLES DE M. GAUCKLER A CARTHAGE

Perrot, Jean-Claude *see*
- FRANCE: STATISTICAL SOURCES ON THE HISTORY OF FRANCE DURING THE REVOLUTION AND THE EMPIRE
- STATISTICAL SOURCES ON THE HISTORY OF FRANCE. UNDER THE EMPIRE

Perrot, Michelle *see* CONDITION OF THE FRENCH WORKING CLASS IN THE 19TH CENTURY

Perrotta, Christopher *see* CATHOLIC CARE OF THE ITALIAN IMMIGRANT IN THE UNITED STATES

Perroux, Francois *see* NEW CONCEPT OF DEVELOPMENT

Perry *see* HISTORY OF CARROLL AND HARRISON COUNTIES

Perry, A J *see* HISTORY OF KNOX COUNTY

Perry, Alfred Tyler *see* THE PRE-EMINENCE OF THE BIBLE AS A BOOK

Perry, Benjamin F *see* BENJAMIN F. PERRY PAPERS

Perry, Charles *see*
- THE BIBLE: ITS EVIDENCES, CHARACTERISTICS, AND EFFECTS: A LECTURE
- SCIENCE AND THE BIBLE: A LECTURE

Perry, Cicero F *see* PAST AND PRESENT OF THE CITY OF QUNINCY AND ADAMS COUNTY

PERRY COUNTY DEMOCRAT – New Bloomfield, PA. -w 1836-1945 – 13 – $25.00r – us I.M.R. [071]

PERRY COUNTY FREEMAN – New Bloomfield, PA. -w 1841-44; 1858-60; 1885-94; 1895-96 – 13 – $25.00r – us I.M.R. [071]

PERRY COUNTY TIMES – New Bloomfield. Pa. 1958- – 1 – us UMI [071]

THE PERRY COUNTY TIMES – New Bloomfield, PA. -w 1940-1980 – 13 – $25.00r – us I.M.R. [071]

PERRY D. COVINGTON FIELD DIARY – (Field diary of the Captain Perry D. Covington of Co. F, 118th United States Colored Infantry, detailing company personnel, equipment, reports, and remarks regarding the regiment's activities in the American Civil War) – 1864-1866 – 1r – 1 – us Western Res [920]

Perry, G *see* CONCHOLOGY

Perry, George G *see*
- HISTORY OF THE REFORMATION IN ENGLAND
- THE LIFE AND TIMES OF ROBERT GROSSETESTE, BISHOP OF LINCOLN
- THE LIFE OF ST HUGH OF AVALON
- VOX ECCLESIAE ANGLICANAE ON THE CHURCH, MINISTRY, AND SACRAMENTS

Perry, Gideon B *see*
- SERMON DELIVERED AT THE FUNERAL OF MISS SARAH POTTER WILLIAMS: SABBATH, 25 JUL 1824
- A SERMON DELIVERED AT THE FUNERAL OF MR. HENRY G. PALMER, PRECEPTER OF WESTFIELD ACADEMY, N. J., SABBATH, 25 JUL 1824

Perry, Jairus Ware *see* A TREATISE ON THE LAW OF TRUSTS AND TRUSTEES

Perry, James H *see* REPLY TO PROF. MATTISON'S "CALM REVIEW OF DR. PERRY'S LATE ARTICLE IN THE CHRISTIAN ADVOCATE AND JOURNAL"

Perry, Jean *see* CHILGOOPIE THE GLAD

Perry, Matthew C *see*
- LETTER BOOKS
- PRIVATE JOURNALS OF COMMODORE M.C. PERRY, 1853-54

Perry, Ralph Barton *see* THE MORAL ECONOMY

Perry, Thomas E Perry *see* NEVILE AND PERRY'S REPORTS

PERRY TOWNSHIP OHIO TRUSTEE RECORDS, MS 2026 – (Organization of the township, minutes of meetings, lists of householders and copies of indenture and other legal documents) – 1815-48 – 1r – 1 – us Western Res [978]

PERRY TOWNSHIP SCHOOL DISTRICTS 3 AND 5, MS 578 – (Daily register, quarterly reports, and general register, including names of students and attendance records) – 1838-53 – 1r – 1 – us Western Res [978]

Perry, William Stevens *see*
- BISHOP SEABURY AND BISHOP PROVOOST
- THE GENERAL ECCLESIASTICAL CONSTITUTION OF THE AMERICAN CHURCH
- A HANDBOOK OF THE GENERAL CONVENTION OF THE PROTESTANT EPISCOPAL CHURCH
- HISTORICAL COLLECTIONS RELATING TO THE AMERICAN COLONIAL CHURCH
- LIFE LESSONS FROM THE BOOK OF PROVERBS

Perrysburg Grain and Supply Association. Ohio *see* RECORDS AND STOCK REPORTS

PERRYSBURG JOURNAL – Perrysburg, Ohio. 1853-1965 – 34r – 1 – $32.50r – us Archival [071]

PERRYSBURG MESSENGER JOURNAL – Perrysburg, Ohio. 1975-1994 – 17r – 1 – us Archival [071]

Perrysburg. Ohio. Zoar Lutheran Church *see* RECORDS

PERRYSBURG STAR – Perrysburg, Ohio. 1851-52 – 1r – 1 – $32.50r – us Archival [071]

PERS, DE – Pretoria, South Africa. 2 Aug 1889-26 Sept 99. 5 reels – 1, 16 diazo available at reduced price – sa SA Libr [072]

Pers, DP. *see*
- BELLEROPHON, OF LUST TOT WIJSHEYD
- BELLEROPHON OF LUST TOT WYSHEYD
- BELLEROPHON, OF LUST TOT WYSHEYT

PERSATUAN PENGGUNA-PENGGUNA NEGERI = CONSUMERS' ASSOCIATION OF PENANG – Penang. 193 docs. 1980-1991 – 117mf – 9 – ne IDC [380]

PERSC NEWSLETTER – (Ceased publ) – 1973-80 – 1r – 1 – ATLA S0827 – us A.T.L.A. [073]

PER/SE – v. 1-3. 1966-68 – 1 – us UMI [073]

PERSECUTION AND TOLERANCE : BEING THE HULSEAN LECTURES PREACHED BEFORE THE UNIVERSITY OF CAMBRIDGE IN 1893-4 / Creighton, Mandell – London; New York: Longmans, Green,1895 – 1mf – us A.T.L.A. [240]

LA PERSECUTION DES CHRETIENS AU JAPON ET L'AMBASSADE JAPONAISE EN EUROPE / Pages, Leon – Paris: typographie Georges Chamerot. 1973 – 9 – 5.00 – fr Orientalistes [240]

PERSECUTION IN THE EARLY CHURCH : A CHAPTER IN THE HISTORY OF RENUNCIATION / Workman, Herbert Brook – London: C.H. Kelly, [1906?] – 1mf – us A.T.L.A. [240]

PERSECUTION OF DEFENCE LAWYERS IN SOUTH KOREA – 1979 – sz I.C.J. [320]

THE PERSECUTION OF DIOCLETIAN : A HISTORICAL ESSAY / Mason, Arthur James – Cambridge: Deighton, Bell; London: George Bell,1876 – 1mf – us A.T.L.A. [240]

THE PERSECUTION OF PROTESTANTS IN FASCIST SPAIN / American Friends of Spanish Democracy – Washington, DC. 1936? Fiche W 718. (Blodgett Collection of Spanish Civil War Pamphlets) – 9 – us H.U. College Libr [946]

PERSEPOLIS AND ANCIENT IRAN / Schneider, Ursula – (50p accompanying text) – 1976 – 1 color 11 b/w mf – 15,9 – $66.00f – 0-226-69493-3 – us Chicago [930]

PERSEPOLIS TREASURY TABLETS / Cameron, George G – 1948 – 9 – $7.50f – 0-226-09227-5 – us U.C. Orient [930]

PERSEVERANCA – Maceio, Alagoas. 17 Jun, 31 Ago 1890 – 1,5,6 – bl Biblioteca [072]

PERSEVERANCA : REVISTA CONSAGRADA AOS INTERESSES DAS CLASSES PROLETARIAS – Maceio, Alagoas. 30 Jul 1909-Maio, 15 Ago 1910 – 1,5,6 – bl Biblioteca [072]

PERSEVERANCE : A POEM, IN REPLY TO THE REVEREND MR. WESLEY'S POETICAL PERFORMANCE FALSLY CALL'D 'AN ANSWR TO ALL...' / Gurney, T – London, 1755 – 1mf – 9 – MP-368/1 – ne IDC [240]

PERSEVERANCE OF ALL SAINTS / Dayton, A C – 1879 – 1 – 5.00 – us Baptist [240]

PERSEVERANCE WINS: THE CAREER OF A TRAVELLING CORRESPONDENT: ENGLAND, CANADA, UNITED STATES, HAWAIIAN ISLANDS, NEW ZEALAND, AUSTRALIA, EGYPT, ITALY / Cureton, Stephen – Toronto: J. Clougher, 1880?. 02242. (Pre-1900 Canadiana) – 9 – cn C.I.H.M. [910]

LA PERSEVERANZA – Milan, Italy. -d. 20 Nov 1859-31 Dec 1897. 82 reels – 1 – uk British Libr Newspaper [072]

PERSIA : WESTERN MISSION / Wilson, Samuel Graham – (Includes appendix and index) – Philadelphia: Presbyterian Board of Publ and Sabbath-School Work, 1896 – 1mf – 9 – 0-8370-6541-0 – 1986-0541 – us A.T.L.A. [240]

PERSIA, EASTERN MISSION : A NARRATIVE OF THE FOUNDING AND FORTUNES OF THE EASTERN PERSIA MISSION: WITH A SKETCH OF THE VERSIONS OF THE BIBLE AND CHRISTIAN LITERATURE IN THE PERSIAN AND PERSIAN-TURKISH LANGUAGES / Bassett, James – (Includes index) – Philadelphia: Presbyterian Board of Publication and Sabbath-School Work, c1890 – 1mf – 9 – 0-8370-6643-3 – 1986 0643 – us A.T.L.A. [240]

PERSIAN GULF GAZETTE – v1-18. 1953-70 – 4r – 1 – us Ross [324]

PERSIAN MANUSCRIPT / Michaux, Francois Andre – 11th cent. 11 fiches – 9 – us South Carolina Historical [574]

A PERSIAN-ENGLISH GRAMMAR: OR, GRAMMAR OF THE ENGLISH LANGUAGE EXPLAINED IN PERSIAN – Anon. 1790. 180p. (English Linguistics Series 1500-1800) – 9 – us UMI [420]
PERSIDSKIE TADZHIKSKIE RUKOPISI INSTITUTA NARODOV AZII AN SSSR (KRATKII ALFAVITNYI KATALOG) – Moscow, 1964. 2v. BR-10,984/1 – 9 – ne IDC [025]
PERSIMFANS – Moscow, 1926-29 (irregular) – 10mf – 9 – us Ross [780]
DIE PERSISCHE MYSTERIENRELIGION IM ROEMISCHEN REICHE UND DAS CHRISTENTUM : REDE ZUM GEBURTSFEST SEINER MAJESTAET DES KOENIGS WILHELM 2 / Grill, Julius – Tuebingen: Mohr, 1903 – 1mf – us A.T.L.A. [230]
Persius *see* SATIRAE
PERSOALAN-PERSOALAN ORGANISASI EKONOMIS DAN POLITIK EKONOMIS / The, Sian Kie – SE 4494 1. 1959-1960 – 9 – ne IDC [331]
DIE PERSOENLICHE HEILSERFAHRUNG DES CHRISTEN UND IHRE BEDUETUNG FUER DEN GLAUBEN NACH DEM ZEUGNISSE DER APOSTEL : EIN BEITRAG ZUR NEUTESTAMENTLICHEN THEOLOGIE / Bachmann, Philipp – Leipzig: A Deichert, 1899 – 1mf – 9 – 0-8370-2138-3 – 1985-0138 – us A.T.L.A. [220]
DIE PERSOENLICHKEIT JESU CHRISTI: MIT... MYTHOLOGIEN UND MYSTERIEN DER ALTEN VOELKER / Marius, Emanuel – Leipzig: Louis Senf, 1879. 1 fiche – 9 – us A.T.L.A. [240]
PERSOENLICHKEITSENTWICKLUNGEN IN ZERFALLENDER TRADITION : EINE TIEFENPSYCHOLOGISCHE UNTERSUCHUNG UEBER DEN IDENTITAETSKONFLIKT IM WERK VON MONGO BETI / Geiger, Michael – 1992 – 9 – DM98.00 – 3-89349-542-8 – gw Hänsel [150]
PERSON JESU IM STREITE DER MEINUNGEN DER GEGENWART = JESUS IN MODERN CRITICISM : A LECTURE / Schmiedel, Paul Wilhelm – (In English) – London: Adam & Charles Black, 1907 – 1mf – 9 – 0-8370-5118-5 – 1985-3118 – us A.T.L.A. [240]
THE PERSON OF CHRIST : THE MIRACLE OF HISTORY: WITH A REPLY TO STRAUSS AND RENAN, AND A COLLECTION OF TESTIMONIES OF UNBELIEVERS / Schaff, Philip – Boston:American Tract Society, c1865 – 1mf – 9 – 0-8370-5071-5 – 1985-3071 – us A.T.L.A. [240]
LA PERSONA HUMANA / Frutos Cortes, Eugenio – Madrid: Doncel, 1962 – sp Bibl Santa Ana [120]
PERSONAJES DEL SIGLO 18 / Segura Otano, Enrique – Badajoz: Imprenta Diputacion Provincial, 1967 – sp Bibl Santa Ana [946]
PERSONAL AND BUSINESS PAPERS / Mackinnon, William – 1823-93. From the School of Oriental and African Studies at the University of London – 1 – uk Microform Academic [941]
PERSONAL AND CONFIDENTIAL LETTERS FROM SECRETARY OF STATE LANSING TO PRESIDENT WILSON, 1915-18 / U.S. Department of State – M743. Printed guide – 1r – 1 – us Nat'l Archives [324]
THE PERSONAL AND LITERARY RELATIONS OF HEINRICH HEINE TO KARL IMMERMANN / Bacon, Grace Mabel – (Includes bibliographical references) – [S.l.: s.n.], 1910 – 1r – 1 – us U.W. Library [430]
PERSONAL AND PROFESSIONAL – v1-2. 1983-85 – 9 – us UMI [510]
THE PERSONAL AND PROPERTY RIGHTS OF A CITIZEN OF THE UNITED STATES : HOW TO EXERCISE AND HOW TO PRESERVE THEM / Parsons, Theophilus – Hartford: S S Scranton & Co, 1876 – 8mf – 9 – $12.00 – LLMC 92-134 – us L.L.M.C. [320]
PERSONAL COMPUTING – (v.4-. 1980- 5,6,9) – v.1-. 1977- – 1 – us UMI [073]
"A PERSONAL DETOUR INTO THE WAR." / Raymond, Bob – 1 – us KS Hist [978]
PERSONAL DIARY AND SCRAPBOOK / Chastain, J G – (40 years as a missionary in Mexico.) 1672p – 1 – 58.52 – us Baptist [240]
PERSONAL FRIENDSHIPS OF JESUS / Miller, James Russell – New York:Thomas Y Crowell, c1897 – 1mf – 9 – 0-8370-4432-4 – 1985-2432 – us A.T.L.A. [240]
PERSONAL INJURY ANNUAL *see* PERSONAL INJURY REVIEW
PERSONAL INJURY DESKBOOK *see* PERSONAL INJURY REVIEW
PERSONAL INJURY LAW JOURNAL – New York. v1-2. 1910-11 – 1 – $80.00 – us Hein [073]
PERSONAL INJURY REVIEW – (Cont: Personal Injury Annual and Personal Injury Deskbook) – 1961-90 – 1,5,6 – $675.00 – us Hein [073]
PERSONAL INVESTMENT – (Details on Request) – Aug 1983- – 9 – at Pascoe [072]
PERSONAL INVESTMENT IN EXERCISE AND SPORT : A CROSS-CULTURAL ANALYSIS / Chen, Kwan – 1989 – 139p 2mf – 9 – $8.00 – us Microform Publ [150]
PERSONAL INVESTOR – v1-. 1985- – 1,5,6,9 – us UMI [073]
PERSONAL JOURNAL OF EVENTS ABOARD HMS CHALLENGER 1909-1910 / Norton, Charles Basil – 1r – 1 – at Pacific Mss [920]
THE PERSONAL LAW OF THE MAHOMMEDANS, ACCORDING TO ALL THE SCHOOLS / Ali, Ameer – London, Allen, 1880. 430 p. LL-1661 – 1 – us L of C Photodup [340]
PERSONAL NARRATIVE OF EVENTS FROM 1799 TO 1815 / Lovell, William Stanhope – 2nd ed. 1879 – 9 – $20.00 – uk Libr Preservation [941]
PERSONAL NARRATIVES FROM THE SOVIET UNION DURING WORLD WAR 2 PAMPHLET COLLECTION – 1947 – 1 reel – 1 – CSUXANR3113-B – us Hoover Inst Photo [800]
PERSONAL NARRATIVES OF WORLD WAR 1 PAMPHLET COLLECTION – 1914-1920 – 3r – 1 – CSUXANM5026-B – us Hoover Inst Photo [800]
PERSONAL PAPERS OF BENITO MUSSOLINI. ALSO SOME OFFICIAL RECORDS OF THE ITALIAN FOREIGN OFFICE AND THE MINISTRY OF CULTURE, 1922-44 – 316r – 1 – $7,268.00 – T586 – us Nat'l Archives [945]
PERSONAL PAPERS OF "THE FATHER OF SEQUOIA NATIONAL PARK, 1890-1930" / Stewart, George W – 1r – 5,9 – $50.00 – B70017 – us Library Micro [920]
PERSONAL PAPERS RE PNG / Speer, Albert – 1943-94 – PMB1123 – at Pacific Mss [920]
PERSONAL POWER / Thomas, Keith Johnston – New York, London: Funk & Wagnalls Co., 1914. viii,304p – 1 – us U.W. Library [150]
THE PERSONAL PROPERTY LAW OF THE STATE OF NEW YORK BEING CHAPTER FORTY-SEVEN OF THE GENERAL LAWS. / Fowler, Robert Ludlow – New York: Baker, Voorhis, 1900. 186p. LL-320 – 1 – us L of C Photodup [340]
A PERSONAL RECORD / Conrad, Joseph – New York; London: Harper, 1912 – 1 – us U.W. Library [920]
PERSONAL RELIGIOUS LIFE IN THE MINISTRY AND IN MINISTERING WOMEN / Huntington, Frederic Dan – 1900 – 9 – us A.T.L.A. [240]
PERSONAL REMINISCENCES IN BOOK-MAKING / Ballantyne, Robert Michael – London: J. Nisbet, 1893?. 07476. (Pre-1900 Canadiana) – 9 – cn C.I.H.M. [070]
PERSONAL REMINISCENCES OF CARDINAL NEWMAN / Henry, Caroline Vinton – Chicago: J.S. Hyland, 1899 – 1mf – us A.T.L.A. [240]
PERSONAL SOFTWARE – v1-. 1983- – 1,5,6,9 – us UMI [073]
PERSONAL SOURCES FOR THE HISTORY OF RUSSIA IN THE 19TH CENTURY / ed by O'Flaherty, Dennis M – 55 titles – 9 – ne IDC [947]
PERSONAL STUDIES / Holland, Henry Scott – London: Wells Gardner, Darton, 1905 – 1mf – us A.T.L.A. [240]
PERSONAL TESTIMONIES OF / Graves, F A & Graves, Mrs. – 1924 – 1 – $5.00 – us Baptist [240]
PERSONAL- UND REALUNION / Franz, M – Breslau, 1908 – 1mf – 1 – ILM-1688/1 – ne IDC [327]
PERSONAL WAR SKETCHES / Grand Army of the Republic. Norris Post No27 (Fostoria, OH) – 1812-1939 – 1r – 1 – $32.50r – us Archival [920]
PERSONAL WORK : OR, BRINGING MEN TO CHRIST / Broadhurst, Cyrus Napoleon – Cincinnati: Jennings and Graham; New York: Eaton and Mains, c1912 – 1mf – 9 – 0-8370-6165-2 – 1986-0165 – us A.T.L.A. [240]
PERSONAL WORK FOR CHRIST AND SOME EXPERIENCES : WITH A BIOGRAPHICAL SKETCH BY HIS WIFE / Soltau, George; ed by Helps, E A – London: Samuel E Roberts, [ca 1911] – 1mf – 9 – 0-8370-6388-4 – 1986-0388 – us A.T.L.A. [240]
LA PERSONALIDAD JURIDICA DE LOS ENTES MORALES Y DEL ESTADO... / Fiore, P – Madrid, 1895 – 1mf – 1 – ILM-3933/1 – ne IDC [327]
LA PERSONALIDAD Y LA OBRA DE TOMAS FALKNER. BUENOS AIRES, 1929 / Furlong Cardiff, Guillermo – Madrid: Razon y Fe, 1931 – 1 – sp Bibl Santa Ana [420]
PERSONALISM / Bowne, Borden Parker – Boston: Houghton, Mifflin, 1908 – 1mf – us A.T.L.A. [140]
PERSONALISM AND THE PROBLEMS OF PHILOSOPHY : AN APPRECIATION OF THE WORK OF BORDEN PARKER BOWNE / Flewelling, Ralph Tyler – New York: Methodist Book Concern, c1915 – 1mf – us A.T.L.A. [200]
EL PERSONALISMO. APUNTES PARA UNA FILOSOFIA / Campoamor y Campoosorio, Ramon de – 1855. Libros en Microficha no 17 – 1mf – 9 – Pta1,000.00 – 84-85422-44-9 – sp Pentalfa [190]
PERSONALIST UND EMANCIPATOR – Berlin, 1899-1922 – 2r – 1 – Inquire at Mikrofilmarchiv for details – gw Misc Inst [072]
PERSONALIST UND EMANCIPATOR – Duehrings Monatsschrift fuer aktionsfaehige Geisteshaltung und gegen korrupte Wissenschaft. Berlin. nos. 1-422. 1899-1922. Complete. B497 (Leo Baeck Institute. German-Jewish Periodicals, Pt 1) – 2r – 1 – $135.00 – us UPA [270]
LA PERSONALITA GIURIDICA INTERNAZIONALE / Constantino, I – Ferrara, 1926 – 2mf – 1 – ILM-3356/1 – ne IDC [327]
PERSONALITY AND FELLOWSHIP / Bradfield, William – New York: Methodist Book Concern, [1914?] – 1mf – us A.T.L.A. [240]
PERSONALITY AND INDIVIDUAL DIFFERENCES – v1- 1980- – 1,5,9 – us UMI [150]
PERSONALITY AND THE CHRISTIAN IDEAL : A DISCUSSION OF PERSONALITY IN THE LIGHT OF CHRISTIANITY / Buckham, John Wright – Boston: Pilgrim Press, c1909 – 1mf – 9 – 0-8370-2505-2 – 1985-0505 – us A.T.L.A. [240]
PERSONALITY AND THE SOCIAL GROUP / ed by Burgess, Ernest Watson – Chicago: University of Chicago Press, (c1929). xii,230p. (University of Chicago Sociological Series) – 1 – us U.W. Library [300]
PERSONALITY, HUMAN AND DIVINE : BEING THE BAMPTON LECTURES FOR THE YEAR 1894 / Illingworth, John Richardson – (Includes bibliographical references) – London; New York:Macmillan, 1894 – 1mf – 9 – 0-8370-2448-X – 1985-0448 – us A.T.L.A. [210]
THE PERSONALITY OF GOD / Abbott, Lyman – New York: Thomas Y. Crowell, 1905. 1 fiche – 9 – us A.T.L.A. [240]
PERSONALITY OF HAHNEMANN / Campbell, Clarence Thomas – Delivered February 4th, 1892: publ. under the auspices of the Hahnemann Society of the Homeopathic Hospital College, Cleveland, Ohio. Cleveland: The Society, 1892? 00406. (Pre-1900 Canadiana) – 9 – cn C.I.H.M. [610]
PERSONALITY OF JESUS / Barrows, Charles H – Boston: Houghton, Mifflin, 1906.1 fiche – 9 – us A.T.L.A. [240]
THE PERSONALITY OF JESUS / Barrows, Charles Henry – (Includes index) – Boston: Houghton, Mifflin, 1906 – 1mf – 9 – 0-8370-2187-1 – 1985-0187 – us A.T.L.A. [240]
PERSONALITY TRAITS, CARDIOVASCULAR FITNESS, AND MORTALITY IN MEN / Brill, Patricia A – 1989 – 116p 2mf – 9 – $8.00 – us Microform Publ [150]
PERSONALITY TYPES OF NCAA AND NAIA MALE AND FEMALE ADMINISTRATORS : A DESCRIPTIVE STUDY / Holmes, Patricia A – Texas Woman's University, 1993 – 2mf – 9 – $8.00 – PSY 1890 – us Microform Publ [150]
PERSONALS : A CHOREOGRAPHIC EXPLORATION OF SUBJECTIVITY AND GENDER / Bloom, Michele L – University of Oregon, 1994 – 2mf – $8.00 – PE3583 – us Microform Publ [790]
DAS PERSONALSTATUT UND DIE GESCHAEFTSFAEHIGKEIT... / Hahn, G G – Borna, Leipzig, 1909 – 1mf – 1 – ILM-3526/1 – ne IDC [327]
PERSONENKATALOG / Institut fuer Weltwirtschaft. Kiel. Bibliothek – 1966.- 670,000 cards 30 reels.-ISBN: 0-8161-1466-8 – 1 – $3260.00 – uk Hall [330]
DIE PERSONENNAMEN IN DEN URKUNDEN DER HAMMURABIDYNASTIE : EIN BEITRAG ZUR KENNTNIS DER SEMITISCHEN NAMENBILDUNG / Ranke, Hermann – (Includes bibliographical references) – Muenchen: Hermann Lukaschik, 1902 – 1mf – 9 – 0-8370-8607-8 – 1986-2607 – us A.T.L.A. [470]
PERSON-ENVIRONMENT INTERACTION : EFFECTS OF STUDENT-FACULTY CONGRUENCE ON ACADEMIC STATISFACTION AND ACHIEVEMENT OF STUDENTS / Poirot, J L – 1992 – 2mf – 9 – $8.00 – us Microform Publ [150]
LE PERSONNAGE DU LION A TRAVERS QUELQUES CONTES BEMBA RECUEILLIS DANS LA (LUAPALA PROVINCE) ET LA (NORTHERN PROVINCE) (ZAMBIE) / Dauphin-Tinturier, A M – 9 – F130.00 – fr Ethnologie [960]
PERSONNAVNE – 1947 – 1 – us I.U. Libraries [390]
PERSONNEL – (v. 46- 1969- 5,6. v. 52- 1975- 9) – v. 1- 1919- – 1 – us UMI [380]
PERSONNEL – v1-2. 1967-68 – 1 – us UMI [650]
PERSONNEL AND GUIDANCE JOURNAL – (v.47 1968- 5,6; v.49 1970 9) – v.1- 1921- – 1 – us UMI [650]
THE PERSONNEL AND GUIDANCE JOURNAL – (v47-62, no.10. Sept 1979-Jun 1984. 5,6. v49-62, no.10. Sept 1981-Jun 1984. 9) – v1-62, no.10. Aug 1921-Jun 1984 – 1 – us UMI [073]
PERSONNEL EXECUTIVE – 1985-. -m – 1 – us UMI [650]
LE PERSONNEL FEMININ DES P.T.T. PENDANT LA GUERRE / Capus, Alfred – Paris: Impr. Nationale, 1915. 14p. (Les Femmes Collection) – 1mf – 9 – $6.00 – fr Bibl Nationale [331]
PERSONNEL JOURNAL – (v.48- 1969- 5,6; v.54- 1975- 9) – v.1- 1922- – 1 – us UMI [650]
PERSONNEL LIST / Louisiana State University. Cooperative Extension Service – Feb 1975-Nov 1982. 1 reel – 1,5 – us Spaulding [630]
PERSONNEL MANAGEMENT – v1- 1920- 1; v7- 5,6; v8- 9 – us UMI [650]
PERSONNEL MANAGEMENT – v34-49. 1952-67 – 1 – us UMI [650]
PERSONNEL MANAGEMENT MANUAL : VOLUME 9. OVERSEAS ALLOWANCES – (Each additional copy $26.00 for 26 issues) – 9 – $100.00 – at AusInfo [650]
PERSONNEL PSYCHOLOGY – (1983-. 1,5,6,9) – v1-. 1948- – 1 – us UMI [073]
PERSONNEL RETURNS OF THE 6TH MASSACHUSETTS BATTALION / U.S. War Department. Collection of Revolutionary War Records – 1779-80 and returns and accounts of military stores for the 8th and 9th Massachusetts Regiments, 1779-82. 1 roll. M913 – 1 – us Nat'l Archives [324]
PERSONNEL REVIEW – (1981-. 1,5,6,9) – v1-. 1971- – 1 – us UMI [650]
DES PERSONNES MORALES ETRANGERES... / Haladjian, B – Paris, 1901 – 3mf – 1 – ILM-3308/1 – ne IDC [327]
PERSONS GRANTED NZ CITIZENSHIP 1949-68 – (Alphabetical listing containing full name, date and place of birth, date of naturalisation and file number) – 7mf – 9 – NZ$28.00 – nz BAB [980]
PERSONS GRANTED NZ CITIZENSHIP 1969-77 – (Alphabetical listing containing full name, place and date of birth, date of naturalisation and file number) – 9mf – 9 – NZ$36.00 – nz BAB [980]
PERSONS GRANTED NZ CITIZENSHIP 1977-81 – (Alphabetical listing containing full name, date and place of birth, date of naturalisation and file number) – 10mf – 9 – NZ$40.00 – nz BAB [980]
PERSONS NATURALISED IN NZ TO 1948 – (Alphabetical listing containing fullname, age or date of birth, place of birth, previous nationality, occupation, place of residence, date of naturalisation and file number) – 6mf – 9 – NZ$24.00 – nz BAB [980]

Persoon, C H *see*
- COMMENTARIUS D.IAC.CHRI SCHAEFFERI FUNGORUM BAVARIAE INDIGENORUM ICONES PICTAS
- COMMENTATIO DE FUNGIS CLAVAEFORMIBUS
- ICONES ET DESCRIPTIONES FUNGORUM MINUS COGNITORUM
- ICONES PICTAE RARIORUM FUNGORUM
- MYCOLOGIA EUROPAEA
- OBSERVATIONES MYCOLOGICAE
- SYNOPSIS METHODICA FUNGORUM SISTENS ENUMERATIONEM OMNIUM HUCUSQUE DETECTARUM SPECIERUM, CUM BREVIBUS DESCRIPTIONIBUS SELECTIS
- SYNOPSIS PLANTARUM
- TENTAMEN DISPOSITIONIS METHODICAE FUNGORUM IN CLASSES, ORDINES GENERA ET FAMILIAS CUM SUPPLEMENTO ADJECTO

PERSPECTA – 1979- – 1,5,6,9 – us UMI [073]

LA PERSPECTIVA Y ESPECULARIA DE EUCLIDES / Euclides – Madrid, 1585 – 3mf – 9 – sp Cultura [720]

PERSPECTIVAS HUMANAS DE LA TERCERA POSICION / Argentine Republic. Secretaria de Prensa – [Buenos Aires, 1948?] – 1 – CSUXAJA7365-B – us Hoover Inst Photo [972]

PERSPECTIVE – New York, NY. Sept 1969 only. Continued by: Middle East Perspective – 1 – us A.J.P.C. [071]

PERSPECTIVE – (v. 5. 1974. 5,6) – v. 1-5. 1969-74 – 1 – us UMI [073]

LA PERSPECTIVE AVEC LA RAISON DES OMBRES ET MIROIRS / Caus, Salomon de – London, 1612. SEM35P135 – 1r – 1 – Can$15.00 – cn Bibl Nat [760]

A PERSPECTIVE OF SPORT CONSUMER BEHAVIOR IN THE PEOPLE'S REPUBLIC OF CHINA / Geng, Lizhong – Brigham Young University, 1994 – 2mf – 9 – $8.00 – PSY 1887 – us Microform Publ [150]

A PERSPECTIVE ON EDUCATION IN HONG KONG : REPORT BY A VISITING PANEL / Hong Kong – Hong Kong, 1982 – 3mf – 9 – DE-156/1 – ne IDC [370]

PERSPECTIVE ON MYCOTOXINS – 1979 – 171p – it F.A.O. [640]

PERSPECTIVE POLICIES AND PLANNING FOR THE DEVELOPMENT OF CHILDREN / Thailand. National Education Commission and National Youth Bureau – 1983 – 3mf – 9 – DE-590/1 – ne IDC [370]

PERSPECTIVE POLICIES AND PLANNING FOR THE DEVELOPMENT OF YOUTH, AGE 15-25 YEARS / Thailand. National Youth Promotion and Coordination Committee – 1982 – 4mf – 9 – DE-591/1 – ne IDC [370]

PERSPECTIVES – (See now: Interdisciplinary Perspectives) – v1-8 1969-76 1; v4-8 5,6,9 – us UMI [073]

PERSPECTIVES – v12-. 1982- – 1,5,6,9 – us UMI [073]

PERSPECTIVES – (1993-95 1r) – Czech Republic, 1999- – 1r per y standing order – 1 – us Ross [072]

LES PERSPECTIVES DE L'UNIFICATION DU DROIT DE CHANGE DEPUIS 1910 / Franssen, M – Paris, 1930 – 5mf – 1 – ILM-3378/1 – ne IDC [327]

PERSPECTIVES DECENNALES DE DEVELOPPEMENT, 1962-1971 / Tunisia. Secretariat d'Etat au Plan et aux Finances – Tunis. 1962. BD-101 1 – 9 – ne IDC [336]

PERSPECTIVES DECENNALES DE DEVELOPPEMENT, 1965-1974 / Niger. Commissariat General au Plan – 3v. Niamey. 1965. BD-179 1 – 9 – ne IDC [338]

PERSPECTIVES DECENNALES DE DEVELOPPEMENT ECONOMIC, SOCIAL ET CULTUREL (1960-1970) / Ivory Coast. Ministere des Finances – D-1342 1. 4 v. 1964 – 9 – ne IDC [338]

PERSPECTIVES DECENNALES DE DEVELOPPEMENT ECONOMIQUE DE L'ALGERIE / Algeria – D-1240 1. 1957-1966 – 9 – ne IDC [338]

PERSPECTIVES DECENNALES DE DEVELOPPEMENT ECONOMIQUE DE L'ALGERIE / Algeria. Gouvernement General – 1958. BNE-8644 1 – 9 – ne IDC [338]

PERSPECTIVES IN BIOLOGY AND MEDICINE – v1- 1957- 1; v10- 5,6; v21- 1977- 9 – us UMI [574]

PERSPECTIVES IN COMPUTING – (1985-. 5,6,9) – v1-. 1981- – 1 – us UMI [510]

PERSPECTIVES IN OPHTHALMOLOGY – v. 1-. 1977 – 1,5,6,9 – us UMI [617]

PERSPECTIVES IN PSYCHIATRIC CARE – v1-1963- 1; v11- 5,6,9 – us UMI [073]

PERSPECTIVES IN RELIGIOUS STUDIES – (1985-. 5,6,9) – v1-. 1974- – 1 – us UMI [200]

PERSPECTIVES IN RELIGIOUS STUDIES – v9-11. 1982-84 (complete) – 1r – 1 – ATLA S0645 – us A.T.L.A. [073]

PERSPECTIVES NEWSLETTER OF THE AMERICAN HISTORICAL ASSOCIATION *see* AHA PERSPECTIVES

PERSPECTIVES: NEWSLETTER OF THE AMERICAN HISTORICAL ASSOCIATION – v22, no.3-. Mar 1984- – 1,5,6,9 – us UMI [073]

PERSPECTIVES NIGERIENNES – Paris, 1966-69 – 8mf – 9 – A-730/2 – ne IDC [960]

PERSPECTIVES OF THE OLYMPIC GAMES – (Series: The United States Olympic Academy, 1) – University of Illinois at Chicago Circle, 1977 – 3mf – 9 – $12.00 – us Microform Publ [790]

PERSPECTIVES ON DEVELOPMENTAL NEUROBIOLOGY / ed by Lauder, Jean & Prochiantz, Alain – 9,5,1 – us Gordon [616]

PERSPECTIVES ON LITERACY : A SELECTED WORLD BIBLIOGRAPHY / Rassekh, Shapour – (UNESCO has exclusive sales rights in the UK and USA) – 1991 – 300p – 9 – 92-3-102705-0 – Co-published with the Librairie du Liban, Beirut – fr UNESCO [370]

PERSPECTIVES/DIMANCHE-MATIN – (Becomes: Carrefour) – Montreal, Canada. 7 oct 1961-1 avr 1979 – 18r – 1 – Can$70.00r – cn Can Microfilming [072]

PERSPEKTIV – Stockholm. 1950-64 – 4r – 1 – sw Kungliga [410]

DIE PERSPEKTIVE – (Cont by: Bayerische Arbeiter-Zeitung) – Augsburg, jun 15 1921-jan 24 1923 – 1 – Dist. gw Mikrofilm – gw Misc Inst [072]

PERSPEKTIVEN DEUTSCHER DICHTUNG / Meidinger-Geise, Inge – 1. Folge (1957). Nuernberg: Glock und Lutz, 1957- – 1r – 1 – us U.W. Library [430]

PERSPEKTIVNYI PLAN RAZVITIIA ZHELEZNODOROZHNOGO TRANSPORTA NA 1926/27-1930/31 GG : DOKLAD S. V. BERNSHTEIN-KOGANA V PREZIDIUME SOVETA PRAVLENI I TRANSPORTA SSSR 2-GO OKTIABRIA 1926 G / Bernshte in-Kogan, Serge i Vladimirovich – Moskva: Izd. "Transpechati", 1926 – 1 – CSUX91-B55 – us Hoover Inst Photo [380]

PERSPEKTIVPLAN-REDEGORELSE 1972-1987 / Denmark – 5suppls. Kobenhavn. December. 1973. Lacking: suppl. 2. BD-2016 1 – 9 – ne IDC [338]

PERSPEKTIVY GRIADUSHCHEI MEZHDUNARODNOI REVOLIUTSII : K GODOVSHCHINE OKTIABRSKOI REVOLIUTSII / Dzhorov, Stolian – T Sarit syn na Volge: "Soldat revoliutsii", 1918 – 1 – CSUX88-B7666 – us Hoover Inst Photo [947]

PERSPEKTIVY RAZVITIIA POTREBITEL'SKOI KOOPERATSII NA 5 LET : (1926/27-1930/31 GG. – M., 1927 – 3mf – 9 – COR-345/1 – ne IDC [334]

PERSPEKTIVY RAZVITIIA SEL'SKOGO KHOZIAISTVA SSSR : TRUDY ZEMPLANA VYP. 1 / Kondrat'ev, N D & Oganovskii, N P; ed by Teodorovich, I A – M., 1924 – 2mf – 9 – COR-202/1 – ne IDC [334]

Persson, J A *see* AN ENGLISH-TSWA DICTIONARY

PERSUATAN ISLAM – Bandung. Incomplete. SE-403 1. 1962-1971 – 9 – ne IDC [073]

Pertev, Pasa *see* DIVAN

PERTH COURIER – Perth, Canada. 1834-1970. Also called The Bathurst Courier from 1834-45 – 53r – 1 – $3,445.00 – cn Library Assoc [971]

PERTH GAZETTE – Australia. 1864-70. -w. (2mqn reels) – 1 – uk British Libr Newspaper [072]

PERTH HERALD – Stratford, 1863-1864 – 1r – 1 – cn Preston [971]

Perthes, Clemens Theodor *see* POLITISCHE ZUSTAENDE UND PERSONEN IN DEUTSCHLAND ZUR ZEIT DER FRANZOESISCHEN HERRSCHAFT

PERTHSHIRE, 1837 : BRITISH ISLES CENSUS DIRECTORIES PROJECT, SCOTLAND. VOL 50 – 1mf – 9 – A$9.00 – at Vine [941]

PERTHSHIRE ADVERTISER – Perth, Scotland. -w. 1919. 1 reel – 1 – uk British Libr Newspaper [072]

PERTHSHIRE CONSTITUTIONAL AND JOURNAL – 1917-1928 – 1. 335-366 – £42.00r – uk Scot News [072]

PERTHSHIRE (PERTH), 1860 : BRITISH ISLES CENSUS DIRECTORIES PROJECT, SCOTLAND. VOL 1 – 2mf – 9 – A$15.00 – at Vine [941]

Perthuis de Laillevault, L *see* TRAITE D'ARCHITECTURE RURALE

PERTJIKAN FILSAFAT / Drijarkara, N – SE-5058 1. 1964 – 9 – ne IDC [950]

PERTJOBAAN SETIA / Suman, Hasibuan – SE 5205 1 – 9 – ne IDC [950]

Pertsov, P *see* LITERATURNYE VOSPOMINANIIA 1890-1902

Pertsov, V *see*
- MAIAKOVSKII
- REALIZM I MODERNISTICHESKIE TECHENIIA V RUSSKOI LITERATURE NACHALA 20 V. "VOPROSY LITERATURY"

Perty, M *see* OBSERVATIONS NONNULLAE IN COLEOPTERA INDIAE ORIENTALIS

Pertz, G H *see*
- ANNALES IMPERII OCCIDENTIS BRUNSVICENSES (768-1005)
- GESCHICHTLICHE AUFSAETZE UND GEDICHTE

PERU : ANUARIO ESTADISTICO DE PERU 1944/45-1958/66 / Peru. Direccion Nacional de Estadistica y Censos – (1958-66 not available. Coll title: Latin American and Caribbean Official Statistical Serials, 1821-1982) – 104mf – 9 – £5.00 (set £1,460.00 232mf) – uk Chadwyck [972]

PERU : BOLETIN DE ESTADISTICA PERUANA 1958-1962, 1964 / Peru. Direccion Nacional de Estadistica – (1964 not available. Coll title: Latin American and Caribbean Official Statistical Serials, 1821-1982) – 44mf – 9 – £7.00f (set £1,460.00 232mf) – uk Chadwyck [972]

PERU : LA INDEPENDENCIA DEL PODER JUDICIAL – 1989 – sz I.C.J. [340]

Peru *see*
- BUDGET PLANS
- EL PERUANO. DIARIO OFICIAL
- PLAN NACIONAL DE DESARROLLO ECONOMICO Y SOCIAL DEL PERU, 1962-1971
- PLAN NACIONAL DE DESARROLLO PARA 1971-1975

PERU 1742-1849 – (Mf 1T-3T: Intentions & Marriages 1778-1818; Births & Deaths 1742-1842. Mf 4T: Marriages & Intentions 1815-43; Births 1806-33. Mf 5T: Births 1793-1849) – (mf ed 1998) – 5mf – 9 – 0-87623-315-9 – us Holbrook [920]

PERU 1771-1894 – (Mf 1-2: Vital Records 1742-1833. Mf 3-8: Town Records 1774-1819. Mf 9-11: Town Minutes 1796-1843. Mf 9: Births & Deaths 1781-1841; Marriages 1817-46. Mf 10: Deaths 1807-44. Mf 11: Marriage Intnetions 1813-49. Mf 11-12: Births 1793-1848. Mf 12-13: Town Minutes 1840-43. Mf 14-15: Vital Records 1843-73. Mf 16: Vital Records 1873-94) – (mf ed 1985) – 16mf – 9 – 0-87623-066-4 – us Holbrook [920]

Peru. Banco Central de Reserva del Peru *see* PROGRAMACION DEL DESARROLLO

PERU CHALLENGE – Peru, NE. -w. Feb 1973 to date – 1 – us NE Hist [071]

Peru. Comite del Plan *see* PLAN BIENAL DE DESARROLLO PARA 1973-1974

Peru. Direccion Nacional de Estadistica *see* PERU

Peru. Direccion Nacional de Estadistica y Censos *see* PERU

PERU ENTERPRISE – Peru, NE. -w. Jul 1897-Jul 1898 – 1 – us NE Hist [071]

Peru. Instituto Nacional de Planificacion *see*
- PLAN DE DESARROLLO ECONOMICO Y SOCIAL, 1967-1970
- PLAN DE DESARROLLO ECONOMICO Y SOCIAL 1967-1970
- PLAN DE DESARROLLO ECONOMICO Y SOCIAL, 1967-70 PLAN SECTORIAL AGROPECUARIO
- RESUMEN DEL DOCUMENTO "LINEAMENTOS BASICOS DE POLITICA DE DESARROLLO A MEDIANO PLAZO"

Peru. Instituto Nacional de Planificacion. Comission Coordinadora del sistema "Marcopomacocha" *see* INFORME DE LA COMISION, "ESTUDIO DE PRE-FACTIBILIDAD DE UN PROYECTO DE PROPOSITOS MULTIPLES PARA EL SERVICIO DE LA GRAN LIMA"

Peru. Ministerio de Educacion *see* POLITICA EDUCATIVA

Peru. Ministerio de Trabajo y Asuntos Indigenas *see*
- INFORME DEL PLAN NACIONAL DE INTEGRACION DE LA POBLACION ABORIGEN. ENERO 1962-JUNIO 1963
- PLAN NACIONAL DE INTEGRACION DE LA POBLACION ABORIGEN: INFORME. ACTIVIDADES ENERO 1963-JUNIO 1964

Peru. Ministerio de Trabajo y Comunidades. Instituto Indigenista Peruano *see* BIBLIOGRAFIA DEL PLAN NACIONAL DE INTEGRACION DE LA POBLACION ABORIGEN (PNIPA)

PERU POINTER – Peru, NE. -w. Oct 1898-Dec 1961 – 1 – us NE Hist [071]

Peru. Sistema Nacional de Planificacion *see* PLAN NACIONAL DE DEASARROLLO 1971-1975. V. 1: PLAN GLOBAL

PERU TIMES – Peru, NE. -w. Dec 1894-Aug 1896, scattered issues missing – 1 – us NE Hist [071]

EL PERUANO – Lima, 1948-67 – 70r – 1 – us Ross [072]

EL PERUANO. DIARIO OFICIAL / Peru – 1968- – 1 – us L of C Photodup [340]

EL PERUANO. DIARIO OFICIAL / Peru – Noticias de una Semana para una Hora de Lectura. Lima. 1958-Jun. 1961. Ceased publication – 1 – us NY Public [972]

PERUGIA AUGUSTA DESCRITTA / Crispolti, C – O-962 1. 1648 – 9 – ne IDC [945]

PERUN. STIKHOTVORENIIA LIRICHESKIIA I LIRO-EPICHESKIIA / Gorodetskii, S – izd. Ory. Spb. 1907. BR-1128 2 – 8 – ne IDC [460]

Perusse, Claire *see* BIBLIOGRAPHIE ANALYTIQUE DE MONSIEUR L'ABBE ARMAND DUBE, CURE DE KAMOURASKA

PERVAI A RUSSKAI A GOSUDARSTVENNAI A DUMA : POLITICHESKII A VOZZRI ENII A I TAKTIKA EI A CHLENOV / Gere, Vladimir Ivanovich – 2-e izd. Moskva: T-vo "Pechatyi a S.P. I Akovleva", 1906 – 1 – CSUX89-B675 – us Hoover Inst Photo [320]

PERVAIA DUMA : STAT'I, ZAMETKI I VPECHATLENIIA BYVSHEGO CHLENA GOSUDARSTVENNOI DUMY / Lokot, T V – M., 1906. 365p – 4mf – 9 – ne IDC [320]

PERVAIA DUMA I VTORAIA REVOLIUTSIIA : RIECH PO SLUCHAI U GODOVSHCHINY OTKRYTIIA ZANIATII GOSUD. DUMY, 27 APRIELIA 1917 GODA / Bramson, Leontii Moiseevich – Petrograd: Izd. T Sentr. kom-ta Trudovo i gruppy, 1917 – 1 – CSUX88-B1257 – us Hoover Inst Photo [947]

PERVAIA RUSSKAIA GOSUDARSTVENNAIA DUMA : POLITICHESKIE VOZZRENIIA I TAKTIKA EE CHLENOV – 2nd ed. M., 1906. 119p – 2mf – 9 – ne IDC [320]

PERVAIA VSEOBSHCHAIA PEREPIS' NASELENIIA ROSSIISKOI IMPERII, 1897 / Russia. Tsentralnyi Statisticheskii Komitet – (Russian census, 1897). v. 1-89. 1899-1905 – 1 – $379.00 – us L of C Photodup [947]

PERVENTSY SVOBODY / Merezhkovskii, Dimitrii – Istoriia vozstaniia 14-go dekabria 1825 g. Petrograd. 1917. BR-782 2 – 8 – ne IDC [460]

PERVOBYTNAJA RELIGIA V SVETE ETNOGRAFII... / Sternberg, Lev J – Leningrad: Instituta narodov severa C.I.K. S.S.S.R. im P.G. Smidovica, 1936 – 1 – F297.92 – fr Armell [305]

PERVOE MINISTERSTVO SVOBODNOI ROSSII : PORTRETY I BIOGRAFII CHLENOV VREMENNAGO PRAVITELSTVA / Filippov, PO – Moskva: Izd. D.I A. Makovskago, 1917 – 1 – CSUXA89-B3299 – us Hoover Inst Photo [947]

PERVOE POLNOE SOBRANIE SOCHINENII / Dobroliubov, N A – Pod red. i s vstup. statei M. K. Lemke. v. 1-4. Spb. 1912. BR-10.567 2 – 8 – ne IDC [460]

PERVOE SOVESHCHANIE TRAKTORNYKH RABOTNIKOV SEL'SKOKHOZIAISTVENNOI KOOPERATSII, DEK. 1925 G : STENOGR. OTCHET – M., 1926 – 3mf – 9 – COR-499/1 – ne IDC [334]

PERVOE SVIDANIE. POEMA / Belyi, A – Izd. Alkonost. Spb. 1922. BR-583 2 – 8 – ne IDC [460]

PERVOE TREKHLETIE INSTITUTA MEZHDUNARODNOGO PRAVA, 1873-76 / Kamarovskii, L A – Moscow, 1877. 105p. Description of the Institute of International Law's first three years of operation. BR-9702/1 – 9 – ne IDC [340]

Pervol'f, I *see* GERMANIZATSIIA BALTIISKIKH SLAVIAN

PERVYE LITERATURNYE SHAGI – Avtobiografii sovremennykh russkikh pisatelei. F. F. Fidler, Red. M. 1911. BR-1492 2 – 8 – ne IDC [920]
PERVYI GOD SUSHCHESTVOVANIIA PETROGRADSKOGO KOOPERATIVNOGO INSTITUTA / Pazhitnov, K A – Pg., 1918 – 1mf – 9 – COR-270/1 – ne IDC [334]
PERVYI RUSSKII PARLAMENT / Aleksieev, V P – Moskva: Izd. E.V. Kozhevnikovo i i E.A. Kolomi it sevo i, 1906 (Moskva: Tip. G. Lissnera i D. Sobko) – 1 – CSUX89-B2554 – us Hoover Inst Photo [947]
PERVYI S'EZD REVOLIUTSIONNYKH ORGANIZATSII DAL'NEGO VOSTOKA / Congress of the Toilers of the Far East. 1. Moscow and Leningrad. 1922 – Sbornik. Petrograd, 1922 – 1 – $35.00r – us Hoover Inst Photo [335]
PERVYI SOVET RABOCHIKH DEPUTATOV – gorod Ivanovo-Voznesensk, mai-iiul' 1905 G. Iaroslavl', 1965 – 1 – $35.00r – us Hoover Inst Photo [947]
PERVYI VSEROSSIISKII KOOPERATIVNYI S"EZD V MOSKVE 1908 G : DOKLADY – M., 1908 – 2mf – 9 – COR-95/1 – ne IDC [334]
PERVYI VSEROSSIISKII S"EZD PREDSTAVITELEI KOOPERATIVNYKH UCHREZHDENII : SEKTSIIA MELKOGO KREDITA, 16-21 APR 1908 G. V MOSKVE – M., 1908 – 2mf – 9 – COR-96/1 – ne IDC [334]
PERVYI VSEROSSIISKII S"EZD PREDSTAVITELEI KOOPERATIVNYKH UCHREZHDENII V MOSKVE, 16-21 APR. 1908 GODA – M., 1908 – 7mf – 9 – COR-97/1 – ne IDC [334]
Perzl, Irmgard *see* JUNGMAEDEL AUF DEM KOELLINGSHOF
Pesado Blanco, Sergio *see*
- BREVES...AGUAS...BANOS DE MONTAMAYOR
- NOCIONES DE ANATOMIA Y FISIOLOGIA HUMANA PARA USO DE LOS ALUMNOS DE PRIMERA ENSENANZA POR...
- TERMAS DE MONTEMAYOR

PESAN TAHUN BARU POLITBURO CC PKI / Communist Party. Indonesia. Comite Central – SE-6591 1. 1959 – 9 – ne IDC [335]
PESAN TJINTA DAN BELAS-KASIH / Menendez, Josefa, Sister – SE-4813 1. 1963 – 9 – ne IDC [950]
PESAVE DASARANTUNA NIVADALELE KAGADA – (Selections from the Peshwa Daftar) – Bombay: Govt Central Press, 1930-34 – us Res Libr [950]
PESCA MARINA – v. 25- 1973- – 1,5,6. ; 9 – apply; v.27- – us UMI [073]
Pescador del Hoyo, C *see* MADRID. ARCHIVO HISTORICO NACIONAL. SEC. DIVERSOS. DOCUMENTOS DE INDIAS
Pescador del Hoyo, Maria del Carmen *see*
- LA HOSPEDERIA REAL DE GUADALUPE
- LA HOSPEDERIA REAL DE GUADALUPE 2
- EL RETABLO DE SAN VICENTE DE PLASENCIA, SUS AUTORES Y NOTICIAS DE OTROS PINTORES EXTREMENOS DEL SIGLO 16

Pesch, Christian *see* INSTITUTIONES PROPAEDEUTICAE AD SACRAM THEOLOGIAM
Peschel, Emil *see* THEODOR KOERNER UND DIE SEINEN
Peschel, W Emil *see* THEODOR KOERNER'S TAGEBUCH UND KRIEGSLIEDER AUS DEM JAHRE 1813
Peschier, A *see* SUPPLEMENT AU DICTIONNAIRE DES LANGUES FRANCAISE ET ALLEMANDE DE L'ABBE MOZIN
DIE PESCHITTA ZU DEUTEROJESAIA : UND IHR VERHAELTNISS ZU MT., 70. U. TRG / Weisz, Heinrich – Halle: s.n., 1893 – 1mf – 9 – 0-8370-6456-2 – 1986-0456 – us A.T.L.A. [220]
DIE PESCHITTA ZUM BUCHE DER WEISHEIT: EINE KRITISCH-EXEGETISCHE STUDIE / Holtzmann, Joseph – Freiburg im Breisgau: Herder, 1903. 1 fiche – 9 – us A.T.L.A. [240]
Pescow de Cherville, Gaspard Georges de *see* PAUVRES BETES ET PAUVRES GENS
PESHAW DAFTAR *see* PESAVE DASARANTUNA NIVADALELE KAGADA
Peshotan, D D *see* THE DINA I MAINU I KHYRAT, OR THE RELIGIOUS DECISIONS OF THE SPIRIT OF WISDOM
PESNI / ed by Kireevskii, Petr Vasil'evich – v1-10, complete.1864-79. Russian folk-songs – 1 – us I.U. Libraries [390]
PESNI MSTITELIA / Bal'mont, K D – Paris. 1907. BR-527 2 – 8 – ne IDC [460]
PESNI RUSSKAGO NARODA... – Saint-Petersbourg: Bernarda, [1866] – 1 – F84.44 – fr Armell [306]
Pesori, S *see* TOCCATE DI CHITARRIGLIA, PARTE TERZA...OVE CON CINQUE BELLISIMI ORDINI DESCRITTA SI VEDE UNA FACILLISSIMA REGOLA PER APPRENDERE IL MONDO DI SUONARE LA CHITARRIGLIA DI SPAGNE
Pesselier, Charles-Etienne *see* LETTRES SUR L'EDUCATION
DER PESSIMISMUS BEI THOMAS HARDY, G. CRABBE UND J. SWIFT / Bergh, G van den – H-342 2. 1945 – 8 – ne IDC [420]
PESSIMORUM PESSIMUM, ET OPTIMORUM OPTIMUM / Pauwels, Jan Anton Frans – O 396. 1774 – 9 – ne IDC [190]
Pessis, A M *see*
- ETUDE EN COULEUR DES SUPERPOSITIONS DE LA TOCA DO BOQUEIRAO DO SITIO DA PEDRA FURADA, SUD-EST DU PIAUI, BRESIL
- LE SITE TOCA DO BAIXAO DAS MULHERES 2, UN ABRI PEINT DE L'AIRE DE SAO RAIMUNDO NONATO, SUD-EST DU PIAUI, BRESIL

PEST CONTROL – v1-47 1933-79 1; v39-47 5,6; v41-47 9 – us UMI [630]
PEST CONTROL – v52-. Dec 1984- – 1,5,6,9 – us UMI [073]
PEST MEGYEI HIRLAP – Budapest, Hungary. 1962-79 – 35r – 1 – us L of C Photodup [072]
PEST RESISTANCE TO PESTICIDES AND CROP LOSS ASSESSMENT, 2 : REPORT OF THE 2ND SESSION OF THE F.A.O. PANEL OF EXPERTS, ROME, 1978 – 1979 – 47p – it F.A.O. [660]
PEST RESISTANCE TO PESTICIDES AND CROP LOSS ASSESSMENT, 3 : REPORT OF THE 3RD SESSION OF THE F.A.O. PANEL OF EXPERTS, KYOTO, 1980 – 1981 – 42p – it F.A.O. [660]
DIE PEST VON LIANORA / Neumann, Robert – Stuttgart: J Engelhorn, 1927 – 1r – 1 – us U.W. Library [830]
PESTALOZZI AND ELEMENTARY EDUCATION = PESTALOZZI ET L'EDUCATION ELEMENTAIRE / Compayre, Gabriel – (In English) – New York: Thomas Y Crowell, 1907 – 1mf – 9 – 0-8370-7619-6 – 1986-1619 – us A.T.L.A. [370]
Pestalozzi, Johann Heinrich *see* FABELN
PESTE DES PETITS RUMINANTS (PPR) IN SHEEP AND GOATS : PROCEEDINGS OF THE INTERNATIONAL WORKSHOP HELD AT IITA, IBADAN, NIGERIA, 24-26 SEPTEMBER 1980 / ed by Hill, D H – 1983 – 9 – $15.00 – 92-9053-136-3 – et ILRI [630]
Pesteil, P *see* PRATIQUE ET PERCEPTION DE L'ESPACE DANS LA PIEVE DE MURIANI
PESTER LLOYD – Budapest, 1919-oct 23 1943 – 1 – Inquire at Mikrofilmarchiv for details – gw Misc Inst [943]
PESTER LLOYD – Budapest, Hungary. 1908-44 – 89r – 1 – us L of C Photodup [072]
PESTER LLOYD – Budapest, Hungary. Feb 1922-23 Oct 1943 – 133r – 1 – gw Mikrofilm [072]
PESTER LLOYD (ABENDBLATT) – (Scattered issues lacking) – Budapest, Hungary. 1904; 1909-April 15 1944 – 80r – 1 – us L of C Photodup [072]
PESTER ZEITUNG – Budapest, Hungary. Nov 1920-Oct 1921 – 1 – gw Mikrofilm [072]
PESTER ZEITUNG – Budapest, nov 1920-oct 1921 – 1 – Inquire at Mikrofilmarchiv for details – gw Misc Inst [943]
PESTI HIRLAP – [Budapest: s.n., jul 1938-40; feb-apr, jul-sep 1941; jan-jul 1944] – us Res Libr [072]
PESTI NAPLO – Budapest, Hungary. 20 Apr 1930 – 1r – 1 – us L of C Photodup [072]
PESTICIDE APPLICATION EQUIPMENT AND TECHNIQUES – 1979 – 261p – it F.A.O. [660]
PESTICIDE LABELLING LEGISLATION – 1988 – 159p – it F.A.O. [340]
PESTICIDE POINTERS / Nebraska. College of Agriculture. Dept. of Agronomy – n.1-5. 1965-69 – 1, 5 – us Spaulding [630]
PESTICIDE RESIDUES IN FOOD : INDEX AND SUMMARY OF REPORTS OF JOINT MEETINGS OF F.A.O. AND W.H.O. EXPERT BODIES ON PESTICIDE RESIDUES 1965-1978 – 1978 – 41p – it F.A.O. [660]
PESTICIDE RESIDUES IN FOOD : REPORT OF THE JOINT MEETING FAO/WHO. GENEVA, 1983 – 1984 – 75p – it F.A.O. [360]
PESTICIDE RESIDUES IN FOOD : REPORT OF THE JOINT MEETING FAO/WHO. ROME, 1982 – 1983 – 79p – it F.A.O. [360]
PESTICIDE RESIDUES IN FOOD, 1977 : REPORT OF THE JOINT MEETING F.A.O./W.H.O., GENEVA, 1977 – 1979 – 88p – it F.A.O. [660]
PESTICIDE RESIDUES IN FOOD, 1977. SUPPLEMENT : EVALUATIONS – 1978 – 468p – it F.A.O. [660]
PESTICIDE RESIDUES IN FOOD, 1978 : EVALUATIONS. DATA AND RECOMMENDATIONS OF THE JOINT MEETING F.A.O./W.H.O., ROME, 1978 – 1979 – 301p – it F.A.O. [660]
PESTICIDE RESIDUES IN FOOD, 1980. SUPPLEMENT : EVALUATIONS. DATA AND RECOMMENDATIONS OF THE JOINT MEETING F.A.O./W.H.O., ROME, 1980 – 1981 – 469p – it F.A.O. [660]
PESTICIDE RESIDUES IN FOOD – 1988 : EVALUATIONS – it F.A.O. [660]
PESTICIDE RESIDUES IN FOOD – 1989 : EVALUATIONS – it F.A.O. [660]
PESTICIDE RESIDUES IN FOOD – 1990 : EVALUATIONS – it F.A.O. [660]
PESTICIDE RESIDUES IN FOOD – 1991 : EVALUATIONS; PART 1: RESIDUES – 1992 – 662p – it F.A.O. [660]
PESTICIDE RESIDUES IN FOOD – 1991 : REPORT OF THE JOINT MEETING FAO/WHO; GENEVA, 1991 – 1991 – 147p – it F.A.O. [660]
PESTICIDE RESIDUES IN FOOD – 1992 : REPORT OF THE JOINT MEETING FAO/WHO; ROME, 1992 – 1993 – 161p – it F.A.O. [660]
PESTICIDE RESIDUES IN FOOD-1981 : EVALUATIONS – 1982 – 576p – it F.A.O. [360]
PESTICIDE RESIDUES IN FOOD-1982 : EVALUATION. THE MONOGRAPHS – 1983 – 434p – it F.A.O. [360]
PESTICIDE RESIDUES IN FOOD-1983 : EVALUATIONS. THE MONOGRAPHS – 1985 – 515p – it F.A.O. [360]
PESTICIDE RESIDUES IN FOOD-1984 : REPORT OF THE JOINT MEETING FAO/WHO. ROME, 1984 – 1985 – 108p – it F.A.O. [360]
PESTICIDE RESIDUES IN FOOD-1984. THE MONOGRAPHS – 739p – it F.A.O. [360]
PESTICIDE RESIDUES IN FOOD-1985 : EVALUATIONS. PART 1: RESIDUES – 1986 – 384p – it F.A.O. [660]
PESTICIDE RESIDUES IN FOOD-1985 : EVALUATIONS. PART 2: TOXICOLOGY – 1986 – 238p – it F.A.O. [660]
PESTICIDE RESIDUES IN FOOD-1985 : REPORT OF THE JOINT MEETING FAO/WHO. GENEVA, 1985 – 1986 – 87p – it F.A.O. [360]
PESTICIDE RESIDUES IN FOOD-1986 : EVALUATIONS. PART 1-RESIDUES – 1986 – 374p – it F.A.O. [360]
PESTICIDE RESIDUES IN FOOD-1986 : EVALUATIONS. PART 2: TOXICOLOGY – 1987 – 235p – it F.A.O. [360]
PESTICIDE RESIDUES IN FOOD-1986 : REPORT OF THE JOINT MEETING FAO/WHO. ROME, 1986 – 1986 – 77p – it F.A.O. [360]
PESTICIDE RESIDUES IN FOOD-1987 : EVALUATIONS. PART 1: RESIDUES – 1988 – 205p – it F.A.O. [360]
PESTICIDE RESIDUES IN FOOD-1987 : EVALUATIONS. PART 2: TOXICOLOGY – 1988 – 154p – it F.A.O. [360]
PESTICIDE RESIDUES IN FOOD-1987 : REPORT OF THE JOINT MEETING FAO/WHO – 79p – it F.A.O. [360]
PESTICIDES ABSTRACTS *see* HEALTH ASPECTS OF PESTICIDES ABSTRACT BULLETIN
PESTICIDES DOCUMENTATION BULLETIN – v. 1-5. 1965-69 – 1,5,6 – us Princeton Micro [631]
PESTS OF THE COCONUT PALM / Lever, R J A W – 1969 – 190p – it F.A.O. [580]
THE PET PHILATELIST – Berlin [Kitchener], Ont.: E Moyer, [1894] – 9 – cn C.I.H.M. [760]
PET SHOP MANAGEMENT – v.9-26. 1955-72 – 1 – us UMI [636]
PET STOCK JOURNAL – v1-3. 1917-19 – 1 – us UMI [073]
PETA-DJALAN INDONESIA / Standard-Vacuum Oil Company – SE 2457 1. 1958 – 9 – ne IDC [660]
Petagna, V *see*
- INSTITUTIONES ENTOMOLOGICAE
- SPECIMEN INSECTORUM ULTERIORIS CALABRIAE

THE PETAL PAPER – Hattiesburg. Miss. 1956-1964 – 1 – us UMI [071]
PETALUMA ARGUS – Petaluma, CA. Mar-Apr 1920 – 1r – 1 – $50.00 – C02622 – us Library Micro [071]
PETALUMA ARGUS COURIER – Petaluma, CA. 1941- – 227+ r – 1 – $11,350.00 ($225.00y) – B02625 – us Library Micro [071]
PETALUMA COURIER – Petaluma, CA. 1900 – 1r – 1 – $50.00 – B02624 – us Library Micro [071]
PETALUMA DAILY COURIER – Petaluma, CA. Apr 1890-1928 – 73r – 1 – $3,650.00 – B02623 – us Library Micro [071]
PETALUMA WEEKLY ARGUS – Petaluma, CA. 1880-1889 – 3r – 1 – $150.00 – B03392 – us Library Micro [071]
LE PETARD : HUMORISTIQUE / ed by Brazeau, A V – Montreal, Canada. 26 mar-5 mai 1881 – 1r – 1 – Can$25.00 – cn Can Microfilming [072]
LE PETARD – Montreal, 7 jan 1879 – 1r – 1 – Can$25.00 – cn Can Microfilming [072]
Petau, D *see* BREVIARIUM HISTORICUM (CBH 2,2)
PETAUBUN = PEEP OF DAY – Sarnia [Ont.]: T Hurlbert, [1861?-1862?] – 9 – cn C.I.H.M. [971]
Petavel, Emmanuel *see* LA BIBLE EN FRANCE
Petavius, Dion *see* OPUS DE THEOLOGICIS DOGMATIBUS
PETAWAWA INFORMER – Petawawa, Ma1989-1991Au – 3r – 1 – cn Preston [971]
PETENG LELIMENGAN, TJRITA MASJARAKAT – SE-4981 1. 1964 – 9 – ne IDC [950]
Petenyi, S J von *see* ORNITHOLOGISCHE FRAGMENTE
PETER ABAELARD : EIN KRITISCHER THEOLOGE DES ZWOELFTEN JAHRHUNDERTS / Deutsch, S M – Leipzig: S. Hirzel, 1883 – 2mf – us A.T.L.A. [240]
PETER ABELARD / McCabe, Joseph – London: Duckworth, 1901 – 1mf – us A.T.L.A. [240]
PETER B. PORTER PAPERS / ed by Detmers, Arthur C Jr – 1810-1939 – 13r – 1 – $300.00 set $25.00r – us Buffalo [977]
PETER G. KAUTENBERGER DIARY *see* KAUTENBERGER, PETER G., DIARY, MS MICR
Peter, Hartmut Ruediger *see* DIE SOWJETISCHE HISTORIOGRAPHIE ZUR GESCHICHTE DER INTERNATIONALEN SOZIALDEMOKRATIE ZWISCHEN DEM ERSTEN UND DEM ZWEITEN WELTKRIEG
PETER HILLE / Hart, Heinrich – Berlin, Leipzig: Schuster & Loeffler, [1904] – 1r – 1 – us U.W. Library [430]
Peter, Klaus *see* SCHLEGELS AESTHETISCHER INTELLEKTUALISMUS
PETER MOENKEMANN, FREIKORPSKAEMPFER AN DER RUHR : ROMAN / Weller, Tuedel – Muenchen: F Eher nachf, 1938 – 1r – 1 – us U.W. Library [830]
Peter Of Ickham *see* LE LIVERE DE REIS DE BRITTANIE E LE LIVERE DE REIS DE ENGLETERRE (RS42)
Peter Of Langtoft *see* CHRONICLE OF PIERRE DE LANGTOFT (RS47)
PETER RAMUS AND THE EDUCATIONAL REFORMATION OF THE SIXTEENTH CENTURY / Graves, Frank Pierrepont – New York: Macmillan, 1912 – 1mf – us A.T.L.A. [240]
Peter, Robert *see* HISTORY OF FAYETTE COUNTY
Peter, Robert et al *see* ITS ORIGIN, RISE, DECLINE AND FALL
PETER ROSEGGER / Schlossar, Anton – (Includes bibliographical references and index) – Leipzig: P Reclam jun, c1921 – 1r – 1 – us U.W. Library [920]
PETER ROSEGGER : SEIN LEBEN UND SEIN SCHAFFEN / Latzke, Rudolf – (Includes bibliographical references and index) – Weimar: Boehlau, 1943-53 – 1r – 1 – us U.W. Library [920]
Peter, Simone *see* NEUE WEGE IN DER RUSSISCHEN LITERATUR ENDE DES 18./ANFANG DES 19. JAHRHUNDERTS
PETER SMITH PAPERS, 1763-1850; THE GERRIT SMITH PAPERS, 1775-1924 / Smith, Peter & Smith, Gerrit – 89r – 1 – $6580.00 – us UMI [975]
PETER, THE APOSTLE / Taylor, William MacKergo – New York: Harper, 1876. 1 fiche – 9 – us A.T.L.A. [240]
PETER UND ALEXEJ : TRAGOEDIE / Heiseler, Henry von – Berlin: Theaterverlag A Langen/G Mueller, 1940 – 1r – 1 – us U.W. Library [820]

PETER VON AILLI (PETRUS DE ALLIACO) : ZUR GESCHICHTE DES GROSSEN ABENDLAENDISCHEN SCHISMA UND DER REFORMCONCILIEN VON PISA UND CONSTANZ / Tschackert, Paul – Gotha: F.A. Perthes, 1877 – 2mf – us A.T.L.A. [240]

PETERA STUCKAS LATVIJAS VALSTS UNIVERSITATES ZINATNISKA BIBLIOTEKA. VESTURE, FONDI, KATALOGI, LASITAJU APKALPOSANA – Riga, 1963 – 1mf – 9 – ne IDC [370]

Peterboro, New Hampshire. Peterboro Free Will Baptist Church *see* RECORDS

PETERBOROUGH ADVERTISER (WED. ED.) – England.1898-28 Mar 1900; 2 May 1900-18 Dec 1901; 1902; 7 Jan-16 Dec 1911; 13 Jan-Dec 1912.-w. 5 reels – 1 – uk British Libr Newspaper [072]

PETERBOROUGH CITIZEN AND ADVERTISER – England. 1955-62.-w. 29 reels – 1 – uk British Libr Newspaper [072]

PETERBOROUGH EXAMINER – (1993.-24r; 1858-1899.-34r) – Peterborough, 1901-1992 – 712r – 1 – cn Preston [971]

PETERBOROUGH EXPRESS – England.1 Apr 1884-1894; 1907-17. -w.15 1/2 reels – 1 – uk British Libr Newspaper [072]

PETERBOROUGH HERALD – England. -w. 29 June-28 Sept 1850. 9 ft – 1 – uk British Libr Newspaper [072]

PETERBOROUGH MONTHLY ADVERTISER – England. April-Dec 1846 – 1 – uk British Libr Newspaper [072]

PETERBOROUGH PINNACLE – Ontario, CN. 1986-Jun 1988 – 2r – 1 – cn Commonwealth Micro [072]

PETERBOROUGH PSALTER AND BESTIARY – 1 – uk Microform Academic [240]

PETERBOROUGH PSALTER AND BESTIARY: SELECTED ILLUMINATIONS – 14 – uk Microform Academic [240]

PETERBOROUGH TIMES – England. 27 May 1865-14 Mar 1874.-w. 3 reels – 1 – uk British Libr Newspaper [072]

PETERBURG / Belyi, A – ed. 1: Sirin. Peterburg. 1916. BR-3717 2 – 8 – ne IDC [460]

PETERBURG / Belyi, A – ed. 2: Epokha. Berlin. 1922. BR-584 2 – 8 – ne IDC [460]

PETERBURG / Belyi, A – M. 1935. BR-585 2 – 8 – ne IDC [460]

PETERBURGSKAIA KHRONIKA – Organ svobodnago samoupravleniia. Ezhenedel'nyi zhurnal. nr. 1-4. Spb. 1907. BR-2290 2 – 8 – ne IDC [073]

PETERBURGSKIE ZIMY / Ivanov, G – Paris. 1928. BR-1305 2 – 8 – ne IDC [460]

PETERBURGSKIE ZIMY IZD. IMENI CHEKHOVA / Ivanov, G – 1952. BR-1181 2 – 8 – ne IDC [460]

PETERBURGSKII KOMITET BOLSHEVIKOV V GODY VOINY, 1914-1917 / Fleer, Matvei Gustavovich – Leningrad: "Pribo i", [192-?] – 1 – CSUX89-B427 – us Hoover Inst Photo [947]

PETERBURGSKII VESTNIK – Literaturnyi ezhenedel'nyi zhurnal. Spb. 1861-62. B-1831 2 – 8 – ne IDC [073]

PETERHEAD SENTINEL – Scotland, UK. 1858-28 Nov 1914.-w. 47 reels – 1 – uk British Libr Newspaper [072]

Peters *see* HISTORY OF FAYETTE COUNTY

PETERS' ADMIRALTY DECISIONS IN THE DISTRICT COURT FOR PENNSYLVANIA, 1780-1807 / Peters, Richard – Philadelphia: Farrand. v1-2. 1807 (all publ) – 10mf – 9 – $15.00 – LLMC 81-466 – us L.L.M.C. [340]

Peters, Arlene L *see* A DESCRIPTIVE STUDY EXAMINING TWENTY YEARS OF FOOTBALL RELATED INJURY RESEARCH AT THE HIGH SCHOOL AND COLLEGE LEVELS

PETERS' CONDENSED REPORTS OF DECISIONS IN THE SUPREME COURT OF THE U.S. : CONTAINING THE WHOLE SERIES OF DECISIONS OF THE COURT FROM ITS ORGANIZATION TO THE COMMENCEMENT OF PETER'S REPORTS AT THE JANUARY TERM, 1827 / Peters, Richard – Philadelphia: J. Grigg. v1-6. 1830-34 (all publ) – 50mf – 9 – $75.00 – LLMC 81-423 – us L.L.M.C. [340]

PETERS CREEK BAPTIST CHURCH. LIBRARY. PENNSYLVANIA : CHURCH RECORDS – 1773-1908. 564p – 1 – us Baptist [240]

PETER'S CREEK BAPTIST CHURCH. PICKENS COUNTY. EASLEY, SOUTH CAROLINA : CHURCH RECORDS – 1825-1864; 1887-1977 – 1 – 20.48 – us Baptist [240]

Peters, Friedrich Ernst *see*
- KLEINE ERZAEHLUNGEN
- ZWIEGESANG SELIGER GEISTER

Peters, John John Punnett *see* THE OLD TESTAMENT AND THE NEW SCHOLARSHIP

Peters, Karl *see* THE ELDORADO OF THE ANCIENTS

PETER'S LETTERS TO HIS KINSFOLK / Lockhart, John Gibson – 2nd ed. Edinburgh: W. Blackwood, 1819. 3v – 1 – us U.W. Library [941]

Peters, Madison Clinton *see*
- THE JEW AS PATRIOT
- THE JEWS IN AMERICA
- JUSTICE TO THE JEW

Peters, Maria *see* FRIEDRICH WILHELM WEBERS JUGENDLYRIK

Peters, Norbert *see*
- BEITRAEGE ZUR TEXT- UND LITERARKRITIK SOWIE ZUR ERKLAERUNG DER BUECHER SAMUEL
- DIE PROPHETIE OBADJAH'S UNTERSUCHT UND ERKLAERT

PETER'S PRINCE EDWARD ISLAND REPORTS / Prince Edward Island. Canada – 1v. 1850-72 (all publ) – 3mf – 9 – $4.50 – LLMC 81-062 – us L.L.M.C. [340]

PETERS' REPORTS OF CASES IN THE THIRD CIRCUIT, 1803-1818 / Peters, Richard – Philadelphia: Fry. 1v. 1819 (all publ) – 7mf – 9 – $10.50 – LLMC 81-467 – us L.L.M.C. [340]

Peters, Richard *see*
- PETERS' ADMIRALTY DECISIONS IN THE DISTRICT COURT FOR PENNSYLVANIA, 1780-1807
- PETERS' CONDENSED REPORTS OF DECISIONS IN THE SUPREME COURT OF THE U.S.
- PETERS' REPORTS OF CASES IN THE THIRD CIRCUIT, 1803-1818

PETERS' SAX-HORN JOURNAL – A collection of new and beautiful marches, waltzes, polkas, schottisches, etc., intended for a brass band of 13 instruments, or a less number if desirable – 1 – us L of C Photodup [780]

PETERSBURG : ROMAN / Asch, Sholem – Berlin: P Zsolnay, 1929 – 1r – 1 – us U.W. Library [830]

PETERSBURG INDEX – Petersburg, NE. -w. Sep 1892-Jul 1896, scattered issues missing; Dec 1896-Feb 1899; Nov 1900-Jul 1907, scattered issues missing; Sep 1911-Jul 1918; Feb 1919-Dec 1927; Apr-Aug 1928; Oct 1928-Jan 1943 – 1 – us NE Hist [071]

PETERSBURG PRESS – Petersburg, NE. -w. Jan 1950 to date – 1 – us NE Hist [071]

Petersen, Asmus *see* THUNENS ISOLIERTER STAAT

Petersen, B *see* THE TARDIGRADE FAUNA OF GREENLAND

Petersen, C *see* DEN SIDSTE FRANKLIN-EXPEDITION

Petersen, Carl *see* ERNST MORITZ ARNDT

Petersen, Guenter *see* METHODE UND HERMENEUTIK

Petersen, Johannes *see* GEBRUEDER HAGEDORN

Petersen, Julius *see*
- DEUTSCHE FORSCHUNGEN
- DIE ENTSTEHUNG DER ECKERMANNSCHEN GESPRAECHE UND IHRE GLAUBWUERDIGKEIT
- LESSINGS WERKE

Petersen, Marie *see* PRINZESSIN ILSE

Petersen, Peter *see* GOETHE UND ARISTOTELES

Petersen, Richard *see* HENRIK STEFFENS

Petersen, W *see* BEITRAEGE ZUR MORPHOLOGIE DER LEPIDOPTEREN

Petersen, Wilhelm *see* DAS LACHEN DES SERGEANTEN WASSENAAR

PETERSEN'S CB LIFE – v1-2 1977-78 – 1,5,6,9 – us UMI [790]

PETERSEN'S CIRCLE TRACK – (1986-. 1,5,6) – 1983- – 9 – us UMI [790]

PETERSEN'S FOUR WHEEL AND OFF-ROAD – (v.3-. 1980- 5,6,9) – v.1-. 1978- – 1 – us UMI [073]

PETERSEN'S HUNTING – (1986-. 1,5,6) – 1982- – 9 – us UMI [790]

PETERSEN'S KIT CAR – (1986-. 1,5,6) – 1983- – 9 – us UMI [790]

PETERSEN'S SPORTS CAR GRAPHIC – v1-2. 1983-84 – 9 – us UMI [790]

PETERSHAM 1739-1849 – (Mf 1T-2T: Births & Deaths 1739-1837. Mf 2T: Marriages & Intentions 1739-97. Mf 3T: Marriage Intentions 1778-1815. Mf 4T: Births 1774-1831; Marriages & Intentions 1797-1826. Mf 4T-5T: Births & Deaths 1764-1849. Mf 5T-6T: Marriages & Intentions 1820-49. Mf 6T-7T: Births 1844-50. Mf 7T: Marriages & Deaths 1844-49) – (mf ed 1997) – 7mf – 1 – 0-87623-316-7 – us Holbrook [920]

PETERSHAM 1743-1893 – (Mf 1-4: Births, Marriages, Deaths 1735-1841. Mf 4-5,9: Town Records 1754-60. Mf 6: Partial Index; Births 1735-1837. Mf 7: Births, Marriages, Deaths 1739-1839. Mf 7-9: Marriage Intentions 1754-1826. Mf 10: Out-of-Town Marriages 1747-99. Mf 11-13: Marriage Intentions 1826-51. Mf 12: Marriage Intentions 1851-81. Mf 13: Marriage Intentions 1881-1905; Marriages 1820-48. Mf 14: Index, Births & Deaths 1732-1849. Mf 14-15: Marriages & Index 1811-21. Mf 16-17: Vital Records 1844-53. Mf 18-19: Births 1854-93. Mf 20-21: Marriages 1854-93. Mf 22-23: Deaths 1854-93. Mf 24-25: Birth Index 1854-93. Mf 26: Marriage Intentions Index 1826-93. Mf 27-28: Marriage Index 1844-93. Mf 29-30: Death Index 1844-93. Mf 31-32: Paupers 1864-1900) – (mf ed 1987) – 32mf – 9 – 0-87623-024-9 – us Holbrook [920]

PETERSHAM BAPTIST CHURCH. PETERSHAM, MASSACHUSETTS : CHURCH RECORDS – 1768-1822. 344p – 1 – 15.48 – us Baptist [240]

Peterson, Andrew *see* ANDREW PETERSON PAPERS

PETERSON BAPTIST CHURCH. PETERSON, WEST VIRGINIA : CHURCH RECORDS – 1910-66 – 1 – 37.98 – us Baptist [240]

Peterson, CS *see* MEN OF WYOMING 1915

Peterson, Kirk *see* PERCEPTIONS OF PSYCHOLOGICAL MOMENTUM BY FEMALE COMPETITIVE SWIMMERS

PETERSON MAGAZINE – 1-NS.7 1842-97 – 1 – us UMI [073]

Peterson, Paul A *see* AN ASSESSMENT OF THE EFFECTIVENESS OF THE COOL CAPE ON THE RAPID REDUCTION OF EXERCISE-INDUCED, ELEVATED BODY CORE TEMPERATURE

PETFOOD INDUSTRIES – v1- 1959- 1; v16-5,6; 1975- 9 – us UMI [073]

Petgrave, Ezekiel Charles *see* A MANUAL OF THE LAW OF PRINCIPAL AND AGENT

Peth, Wilhelm *see* UEBER LUEFTUNG UND BEFEUCHTUNG VON SCHULRAEUMEN

Pethan, Scott M *see* EFFECTS OF TRAINING IN STRENGTH SHOES(TM) ON SPEED, JUMPING ABILITY, AND CALF GIRTH

PETICION ESCRITO DE CONCLUSIONES AL NUNCIO POR EL P. CACERES CON EL P. JUAN DE LA SERENA Y OTROS / Castro, Antonio de & Bargas, Luis de – S.l., s.i., s.a., 1642 – 1 – sp Bibl Santa Ana [946]

PETICION...AL NUNCIO POR EL P. CACERES.. / Castro, Antonio de – 1642 – 9 – 1.50f – sp Bibl Santa Ana [240]

PETICIONES DE LAS CORTES DE 1588, CON ANOTACIONES DE FELIPE 2 – Cordoba – 1r – 5,6 – sp Cultura [946]

THE PETIE SCHOLE WITH AN ENGLISH ORTHOGRAPHIE / Clement, Francis – 1587. 94p. (English Linguistics Series 1500-1800) – 9 – us UMI [420]

LA PETIMETRA / Fernandez de Moratin, Nicolas – 1762 – 1mf – 9 – Pta1,000.00 – 84-7848-149-4 – sp Pentalfa [820]

PETIR – Singapore: People's Action Party. ill. -q. May/Apr 1983- . Text in English – 1 – us U.W. Library [073]

PETIT – (In Yiddish) – New York City, NY. v1 no4. Apr 1950 – 1r – 1 – $25.00 – cn Can Microfilming [071]

Petit *see* TRAITE SUR LE GOVERNEMENT DES ESCLAVES

LE PETIT ALMANACH DE LA PROVINCE DE QUEBEC, POUR L'ANNEE... – Quebec: N S Hardy & Marcotte, c1869-. SEM105P668 – 3mf – 9 – Can$6.75 – cn Bibl Nat [073]

LE PETIT ALMANACH DU BAS-CANADA POUR L'ANNEE...1863 – Quebec: Librairie du Canadien, c1857-. SEM105P636 – 1mf – 9 – Can$2.25 – cn Bibl Nat [030]

Petit, Andre *see* MON VOYAGE AU SOUDAN FRANCAIS

LE PETIT ANGEVIN – Angers (Maine-et-Loire), Dec. 1881 – Sept. 1883 – 2r – fr Armell [320]

LE PETIT ATLAS MARITIME / Bellin, Jacques N – Paris: L'Amerique Septentrionale et les Isles Antilles. v1. 1764. SEM35P115 – 1r – 1 – Can$15.00 – cn Bibl Nat [910]

LE PETIT AVENIR DE LA MAYENNE – Laval, Nov. 1894 – Nov. 1896 – 2r – fr Armell [944]

LE PETIT BEAUNOIS : JOURNAL POLITIQUE QUOTIDIEN – Quot., Beaune (Cote-d'Or), fevr.-dec. 1890 – 2r – 1 – F668.90 – fr Armell [320]

LE PETIT BLEU – Quebec, Canada. v1 n1. 30 nov 1929-v1 n2. 7 dec 1929 – 1r – 1 – Can$25.00 – cn Can Microfilming [072]

LE PETIT BOURGUIGNON – Dijon (Cote-d'Or), Feb. 1881 – Nov. 1911 – 8r – fr Armell [944]

LE PETIT CALIFORNIEN – San Francisco, CA. Apr 1887-1896 – 2r – 1 – $100.00 – B02837 – us Library Micro [071]

LE PETIT CANADIEN – Montreal: la Societe: la Caisse. v10-15. 1913-18. SEM16P339 – 1r – 5 – Can$23.00 – cn Bibl Nat [073]

LE PETIT CANADIEN : REVUE MENSUELLE, LITTERAIRE ET PITTORESQUE – Quebec, v1 no 1-2. 1904. SEM105P14 – 1mf – 9 – Can$2.25 – cn Bibl Nat [073]

LE PETIT CANADIEN – Sweetsburg, Canada. v1 n12. 5 nov 1941 – 1r – 1 – Can$25.00 – cn Can Microfilming [072]

LE PETIT CATECHISME DU DIOCESE DE QUEBEC – Nouv. ed. Quebec: de la Nouvelle-Imprimerie, Halle des Franc-Macons, 1819. SEM16P239 – 1r – 5 – Can$9.00 – cn Bibl Nat [240]

PETIT CENSEUR, CRITIQUE ET LITTERAIRE; JOURNAL FRANCAIS A NEW YORK – no. 1-17. Jul 1805$ Aug 1805 – 1 – us UMI [410]

PETIT CENSEUR, SEMAINE CRITIQUE ET LITTERAIRE – v. 1-12. Sep 1805-Dec 1805 – 1 – us UMI [410]

PETIT CODE DE RAISON HUMAINE: OU, EXPOSITION SUCCINTE DE CE QUE LA RAISON DICTE A TOUS LES HOMMES, POUR ECLAIRER LEUR CONDUITE ET ASSURER LEUR BONHEUR / Barbeu-Dubourg, Jacques – (D'Holbach series). 1774 – 9 – fr Hachette [120]

PETIT DE BACHAUMONT : HIS CIRCLE AND THE 'MEMOIRES SECRETS' / Tate, R S – (Studies on Voltaire and the eighteenth century, v65) – Oxford. 1968 – 9 – $27.00 – 0-7294-0158-8 – uk Voltaire [440]

Petit de Barancourt *see* DE L'EMANCIPATION DES NOIRS OU LETTRES A M. LE DUC DE BROGLIE SUR LES DANGERS DE CETTE MESURE, SUIVIES DE CONSIDERATIONS SUR LE DROIT DE VISITE

Petit de la Saussaye, S *see* CATALOGUE DES MOLLUSQUES TESTACES DES MERS D'EUROPE

LE PETIT DEMOCRATE – Journal de la democratie populaire. Fond. R. Cornilleau. Paris. nov 1923-mai 1940 – 1 – fr A.C.R.P.P. [073]

PETIT DICTIONNAIRE DU PEUPLE / Desgranges, J – 1821 – 9 – fr I.C.S. [440]

Petit, F *see*
- L'ANCIENNE VERSION LATINE DES QUESTIONS SUR LA GENESE DE PHILON D'ALEXANDRIE

LE PETIT FIGARO – Red. en chef H. de Villemessant. Paris. 1er oct 1867-19 sept 1870, 16 juil-4 sept 1871 – 1 – fr A.C.R.P.P. [073]

LE PETIT GLANEUR – Journal litteraire, commercial, feuille d'annonces judiciaires et d'avis divers de l'arrondissement de Sarreguemines. Sarreguemines. 1868-juin 1870 – 1 – fr A.C.R.P.P. [073]

PETIT GLOSSAIRE POUR SERVIR A L'INTELLIGENCE DES AUTEURS DECADENTS ET SYMBOLISTES / Plowert, J – 1888 – 9 – fr I.C.S. [440]

Petit, J L *see* TRAITE DES MALADIES DES OS

LE PETIT JOURNAL – illustre. Suppl. de: Le Petit journal, quotidien. Paris. juin 1884-86, 1888-aout 1937 – 1 – fr A.C.R.P.P. [073]

LE PETIT JOURNAL / ed by Jos. Dussault & Cie – Quebec, Canada. 24 mai 1881-v4 n101. 2 mai 1885 – 1r – 1 – Can$25.00 – cn Can Microfilming [072]

LE PETIT JOURNAL / ed by Maillet, Roger et al – Montreal, Canada. 23 oct 1926-7jan 1978 – 144r – 1 – Can$55.00r – cn Can Microfilming [072]

LE PETIT JOURNAL : MENSUEL / ed by Simard, G A – Montreal, Canada. avr 1900-nov 1901 – 1r – 1 – Can$35.00 – cn Can Microfilming [072]
LE PETIT JOURNAL – Paris. Red. en chef, H. Marinoni. 1863-26/27 aout 1944 – 1 – fr A.C.R.P.P. [073]
LE PETIT JOURNAL : QUOTIDIEN / ed by Berthiaume, Treffle – Montreal, Canada. 1-22 aut 1878 – 1r – 1 – Can$40.00 – cn Can Microfilming [072]
LE PETIT JOURNAL *see* LE MATIN
PETIT JOURNAL DE LONDRES – London, UK. 25 Jul-25 Sept 1898 – 1 – uk British Libr Newspaper [072]
PETIT LAROUSSE ILLUSTRE (AEL, ABT 2;11) / Auge, Claude – Paris, 1905-06 (mf ed 1997) – 19mf – 9 – DM270.00 – 3-89131-194-X – gw Fischer [440]
LE PETIT LAVALLOIS – Laval, Nov. 1896 – August 1898 – 2r – fr Armell [944]
PETIT MANUEL D'AGRICULTURE A L'USAGE DES ECOLES / Bellerose, L H – Union des Cantons de l'Est, 1883. 00114. (Pre-1900 Canadiana) – 9 – cn C.I.H.M. [370]
PETIT MANUEL DU CULTIVATEUR A L'USAGE DES ECOLES PRIMAIRES / Rousseau, Edmond – Montreal: Cadieux et Derome, 1893. SEM105P49 – 1mf – 9 – Can$2.25 – cn Bibl Nat [630]
PETIT MANUEL FRANCAIS-KANOURI / Noel, P – Paris: P Guethner, 1923 – us Res Libr [490]
LE PETIT MARSEILLAIS – Journal politique quotidien. Marseille. 1868-aout 1944 – 1 – fr A.C.R.P.P. [073]
LE PETIT MESSAGER DES COEURS DE JESUS ET DE MARIE – (Suivi de: Le Messager Canadien du Sacre-Coeur de Jesus. Autre ed de lang: Messenger of the Sacred Heart) – Montreal: College Ste-Marie, [1890?-1891] – 9 – cn C.I.H.M. [240]
LE PETIT MESSAGER DES COEURS DE JESUS ET DE MARIE *see*
- LE MESSAGER CANADIEN DU SACRE-COEUR DE JESUS
- MESSENGER OF THE SACRED HEART

LE PETIT MESSAGER DU TRES SAINT SACREMENT – (Suivi de: Le Messager du T.S. Sacrement. Autre Ed. de Lang.: The Sentinel of the Blessed Sacrament) – Montreal: Bureau des Oeuvres Eucharistiques, [1898?-1920] – 9 – cn C.I.H.M. [240]
LE PETIT MESSAGER DU TRES SAINT SACREMENT *see* THE SENTINEL OF THE BLESSED SACRAMENT
LE PETIT MONTCELLIEN – Organe des interets politiques, industriels, agricoles et commerciaux. Dir. J. Delorme. devenu: Le Socialiste de Saone-et-Loire. Montceau-les-Mines. fevr 1904-janv 1915 – 1 – fr A.C.R.P.P. [073]
LE PETIT MONTLUCONNAIS – Journal republicain socialiste. Red. en chef Eugene Fourniere. Montlucon. mars 1892-janv 1895 – 1 – fr A.C.R.P.P. [335]
Petit, P C M *see* CATALOGUE DES DIATOMEES DE L'ILE CAMPBELL ET DE LA NOUVELLE ZELANDE
LE PETIT PARISIEN – Paris. 15 oct 1876-aout 1944 – 1 – fr A.C.R.P.P. [073]
LE PETIT PARISIEN – Supplement litteraire illustre. Paris. No.1-1090. 10 fevr 1889-1909; 1902-09 – 1 – fr A.C.R.P.P. [073]
LE PETIT PHOTOGRAPHE ECONOME – Paris, France. Le Journal de l'acetylene, etc. -w. March 1896-Dec 1904. 3 reels – 1 – uk British Libr Newspaper [073]
LE PETIT QUEBECOIS : HUMORISTIQUE ILLUSTRE – Quebec, Canada. 27 fev 1909-v4 n8. 3 mai 1913 – 1r – 1 – Can$25.00 – cn Can Microfilming [072]
PETIT QUESTIONNAIRE POUR FACILITER L'ETUDE DE L'ARBRE HISTORIQUE DU CANADA / Congregation de Notre-Dame – Montreal: Senecal, 1875. 00745. (Pre-1900 Canadiana) – 9 – cn C.I.H.M. [971]
PETIT RECUEIL LITTERAIRE – (Filmed with: Le Recueil Litteraire v2 n34 15 jul 1890-v1 n24 25 mar 1892) – Sainte-Cunegonde, Montreal, Canada. v1 n2. dec 1888 – 1r – 1 – Can$35.00 – cn Can Microfilming [073]
PETIT RECUEIL LITTERAIRE – nos 1-4. 1888-89. SEM16P363 – 1r – 5 – Can$11.00 – cn Bibl Nat [073]
LE PETIT SOU – Paris. Dir., Alfred Edwards. 2 sept 1900-14 juil 1914 – 1 – fr A.C.R.P.P. [073]
PETIT TRAITE DE GRAMMAIRE ANGLAISE A L'USAGE DES ECOLES PRIMAIRES / Gosselin, Charles – Montreal: Beauchemin & Valois, 1878. 04378. (Pre-1900 Canadiana) – 9 – cn C.I.H.M. [420]
PETIT TRAITE DE POESIE FRANCAISE / Banville, Th. de – 1872 – 9 – fr I.C.S. [440]
PETIT TRAITE SUR LE DESSECHEMENT ET LE DRAINAGE DES TERRES, POUVANT SERVIR DE TEXTE AUX CONFERENCES DES CERCLES AGRICOLES / Barnard, Edouard Andre – Montreal: E. Senecal, 1887. 03372. (Pre-1900 Canadiana) – 9 – cn C.I.H.M. [630]
LE PETIT VAR – Journal republicain socialiste quotidien. Toulon. sept 1880-89, 1891, 1893-1905 – 1 – fr A.C.R.P.P. [335]
PETIT VOCABULAIRE A L'USAGE DES CANADIENS-FRANCAIS: CONTENANT LES MOTS DONT IL FAUT REPANDRE L'USAGE ET SIGNALANT LES BARBARISMES QU'IL FAUT EVITER POUR BIEN PARLER NOTRE LANGUE / Caron, Napoleon – Trois-Rivieres: Journal des Trois-Rivieres, 1880. 00471. (Pre-1900 Canadiana) – 9 – cn C.I.H.M. [440]
PETIT VOCABULAIRE COMPARATIF DU BON ET DU MAUVAIS LANGAGE / Boinvilliers, J E F – 1829 – 9 – fr I.C.S. [440]
LA PETITE CONVERSATION. SIX TRIOS POUR 2 VIOLINE, ALTO OU BASSE (AD. LIB.) / Bruni, A – (4 pts) – Leipsic: Breitkopf & Hartel, 181- – 1 – us Sibley [780]
PETITE CORRESPONDANCE AUTOGRAPHIEE (D'A. MALLET) – Paris. avr 1853-oct 1854 – 1 – fr A.C.R.P.P. [073]
LA PETITE ECOLE DES PERES / Etienne & Gaugiran-Nanteuil – French Theatre Series. Paris. Mme Masson, an XI. 1803 – 9 – fr Hachette [820]
LA PETITE FEUILLE / ed by Serin, Paul & Moineau, J – Quebec, Canada. 25 fev 1909-v1 n16. 10 jun 1909 – 1r – 1 – Can$25.00 – cn Can Microfilming [072]
LA PETITE FRANCE *see* L'ETINCELLE
LA PETITE GIRONDE – Bordeaux. 1900-44 – 1 – fr A.C.R.P.P. [073]
PETITE HISTOIRE DES MISSIONS CHRETIENNES, PAR UN LAIEQUE – 1923 – 1 – us A.T.L.A. [240]
LA PETITE INDUSTRIE CONTEMPORAINE / Brants, Victor L – Paris. 1902. (La Condition Ouvriere. Part Two.) – 9 – 7.50 – fr Bibl Nationale [360]
LA PETITE INDUSTRIE. SALAIRES ET DUREES DU TRAVAIL / Du Maroussem, P – (Condition of 19th C. French working class series). 1893 – 9 – fr Hachette [331]
PETITE INTRODUCTION A L'ETUDE DE LA MASSORE / Hyvernat, Henri – Mesnil: Revue biblique, 1902. 1 fiche – 9 – us A.T.L.A. [270]
LA PETITE NATION (1972) – Buckingham. v11-18. 1972-79. SEM35P241 – 7r – 1 – Can$342.00 – cn Bibl Nat [971]
LA PETITE NATION (1980) – Saint Andre Avellin: (s.n., s.l.) v23-24. 1980-85. SEM35P245 – 5r – 1 – Can$212.00 – cn Bibl Nat [971]
LA PETITE NATION PLUS – Saint Andre Avellin. v1-2. 1983-85. SEM35P244 – 1r – 1 – Can$48.00 – cn Bibl Nat [072]
LA PETITE NATION/LE BULLETIN – Saint Andre Avellin: (s.n.) v22-23. 1979-80. SEM35P242 – 3r – 1 – Can$98.00 – cn Bibl Nat [073]
LA PETITE PRESSE – Journal quotidien du soir republicain progressiste. Paris. janv-juin 1876, 3 mai 1899-juin 1902, juil-dec 1903, juil-dec 1906, juil-2 sept 1907, 23 aout 1908-09, 1912, 6 janv-16 juil 1914 – 1 – fr A.C.R.P.P. [073]
LA PETITE PRESSE – Sherbrooke, Canada. 15 mar-14 sep 1899 – 1r – 1 – Can$25.00 – cn Can Microfilming [072]
LA PETITE QUINZAINE : REVUE INTERNE DU MINISTERE DES AFFAIRES / Quebec. (Province). Ministere des Affaires Culturelles. Direction des Communications – Quebec: la Direction. v1-3. 1975-77. SEM16P289 – 1r – 5 – Can$9.00 – cn Bibl Nat [971]
LA PETITE REPUBLIQUE – Red. Millerand puis Henri Turot. Paris. avr 1876-sept 1914, dec 1916-oct 1925, fevr-mai 1927 – 1 – fr A.C.R.P.P. [073]
LA PETITE RESISTANCE – Organe socialiste. Dir.-red. en chef Marc Larcher. Fort-de-France. oct-dec 1933 – 1 – fr A.C.R.P.P. [335]
LA PETITE REVUE – Montreal: A Pelletier, [1899-1900] – 9 – cn C.I.H.M. [971]
LA PETITE REVUE – Paris. janv-aout 1870 – 1 – fr A.C.R.P.P. [073]
PETITE REVUE DU TIERS-ORDRE ET DES INTERETS DU COEUR DE JESUS – (Suivi de: Revue du Tiers-ordre et de la Terre Sainte) – Montreal: J Chapleau, 1884-1890 – 9 – cn C.I.H.M. [240]
LA PETITE SOURIS GRISE / Segur, Sophie, Comtesse de – Quebec: Louis-Alexandre Belisle, editeur, [1942?]. SEM105P1292 – 1mf – 9 – Can$2.25 – cn Bibl Nat [971]
LA PETITE TRIBUNE INDIGENE – Saigon. sept 1918-19 – 1 – fr A.C.R.P.P. [073]
LES PETITES AFFICHES DE LA MAYENNE – Laval, June 1894 – August 1914 – 3r – fr Armell [944]
PETITES AFFICHES DE LONDRES – London, UK. Journal-guide des francais a Londres. 18 Nov-16 Dec 1882 – 1 – uk British Libr Newspaper [072]
PETITES AFFICHES (LES) – 1994-1995 – 6 – F3,000.00 – sz Infoprint [072]
PETITES ANNALES DE LA CONGREGATION DES MISSIONAIRES OBLATS DE MARIE IMMACULEE – (Issues for 1903 p120-1904 filmed with: Petites annales des Missionaires oblats de Marie Immaculee (1905), 1905-08) – Paris: La Congregation. v1-14. 1891-1904 – 3r – 1 – us Res Libr [960]
PETITES CANTANDES A SEULE VOIX DE CHANT / Scarlatti, Alessandro – [172-?], MS in ink on paper in 3 copyists's hands – 1 – us Sibley [780]
PETITES CHRONIQUES POUR 1877 / Buies, Arthur – Quebec: C. Darveau, 1878. 00348. (Pre-1900 Canadiana) – 9 – cn C.I.H.M. [971]
LES PETITES LECTURES CANADIENNES / ed by Denault, Amedee – Montreal, Canada. 1894-v1 n17. 31 dec 1895 – 1r – 1 – Can$25.00 – cn Can Microfilming [830]
LES PETITES LECTURES CANADIENNES – Montreal: [s.n.], 1894-96. SEM105P292 – 6mf – 9 – Can$13.50 – cn Bibl Nat [073]
PETITES NOTES SUR LE CANADA / Cazes, Paul de – Quebec: C. Darveau, 1881. c1880. 00525. (Pre-1900 Canadiana) – 9 – cn C.I.H.M. [971]
PETITES NOUVELLES ENTOMOLOGIQUES – (Cont as: Le Naturaliste. Journal des echanges et des nouvelles. Paris v1-9 1879-87) – Paris. v1-2. 1869-79 – 85mf – 9 – Z-983/2 – ne IDC [590]
PETITES PIECES POUR LE CLAVECIN DE C.P.E. BACH / Bach, C P E – Ms, 1777? – 1 – us Sibley [780]
PETITION DES FEDERES A L'ASSEMBLEE NATIONALE / Robespierre, Maximilien de – Reprod. de l'ed., s.l., s.n., 1782. 8p. 1 fiche. (Political Science Collection) – 9 – 6.00 – fr Bibl Nationale [323]
PETITION D'UN PROLETAIRE A LA CHAMBRE DES DEPUTES / Beranger, Charles – Paris, Everat, 1831, 16 p. Les Saint-Simoniens, 1825-1834. 6866 – 9 – fr Hachette [305]
PETITION FROM MONTREAL COMPLAINING OF MALVERSATION OF OFFICE BY JAMES STUART, ESQ. ATTORNEY GENERAL,... – [S.l.: s.n.], 1830. SEM105P1909 – 1mf – 9 – Can$2.25 – cn Bibl Nat [323]
PETITION OF MEMBERS OF THE AMERICAN BAR TO THE PRESIDENT OF THE UNITED STATES – With accompanying memorandum on the embargo against Spain. New York, 1938. Fiche W1105. (Blodgett Collection of Spanish Civil War Pamphlets) – 9 – us H.U. College Libr [946]
A PETITION TO ENGLAND, THE UNITED STATES AND GERMANY : FROM THE ACCREDITED REPRESENTATIVES OF WESTERN SAMOA KNOWN AS THE MAU..., AUGUST 19 1931, APIA, WESTERN SAMOA – n.p., n.d. – 1mf – 9 – $1.50 – LLMC 82-100C Title 41 – us L.L.M.C. [980]
PETITIONS / Ottawa County. Ohio. Carroll Township. Board of Trustees – 1922 – 1r – 1 – $32.50r – us Archival [324]
PETITIONS AND RECORDS OF NATURALIZATION OF THE U.S. DISTRICT COURT AND CIRCUIT COURTS OF THE DISTRICT OF MASSACHUSETTS, 1906-1929 – 330r – 1 – M1368 – us Nat'l Archives [340]
PETITIONS FOR ROAD IMPROVEMENT / Hancock County, Ohio. Biglick Township. Board of Trustees – 1913-1914 – 1r – 1 – $32.50r – us Archival [324]
PETITIONS OF THE EARLY INHABITANTS OF KENTUCKY TO THE GENERAL ASSEMBLY OF VIRGINIA, 1769 TO 1792 – By James Rood Robertson, 1914. Indexed.5 fiches. F-0502 – 9 – us A.G.L.L. [978]
Petitjean-Roget, V *see* LES COMBATS DE COQS DANS LE NORD DE LA FRANCE
Petitot, E *see*
- DICTIONNAIRE DE LA LANGUE DENE-DINDJIE
- LES GRANDS ESQUIMAUX. 6, 307P., ILLUS., MAP
- TRADITIONS INDIENNES DU CANADA NORD-OUE V. 23, XVII, 521P
- VOCUBULAIRE FRANCAIS-ESQUIMAU
- VOCUBULAIRE FRANCAIS-ESQUIMAU. DIALECTE DES TCHIGLIT. 64, 75 P

PETITS CHEFS-D'OEUVRE / Rousseau, Jean-Jacques – Paris: Librairie du Paris, 1762? – 530p – 1 – us U.W. Library [190]
Petity, L'Abbe Jean-Raymond de *see*
- MANUEL DES ARTISTES ET DES AMATEURS, OU
- MANUEL DES ARTISTES ET DES AMATEURS, OU...

PETOFI NEPE – Kecskemet, Hungary. 1962-70 – 17r – 1 – us L of C Photodup [072]
Petonnet, C *see* L'INTEGRATION DES HARKIS DE VANVEY ET DE BAIGNEUX-LES-JUIFS (COTE D'OR) A LA SOCIETE FRANCAISE
PETR ALEKSEEVICH PLAVIL'SHCHIKOV. 1760-1812 / Kulakova, L I – M., L. 1952. BR-6226 2 – 8 – ne IDC [920]
PETR. I. TRAGEDIIA V 5-TI DEISTVIIAKH V STIKHAKH / Pogodin, M P – M. 1873. BR-8324 2 – 8 – ne IDC [460]
PETR VELIKII / Platonov, S F – Paris. 1927. BR-7773 2 – 8 – ne IDC [920]
PETR VELIKII : SBORNIK STATEI / ed by Andreev, A I – Moscow, Leningrad, 1947. 433p – 8 – BR-6075 2 – ne IDC [947]
PETR VELIKII V OTSENKE SOVREMENNIKOV I POTOMSTVA / Shmurlo, E F – NR. 1 (XVIII vek.). Spb. 1912. BR-7886 2 – 8 – ne IDC [920]
PETR VELIKII V RUSSKOI LITERATURE / Shmurlo, E F – Spb. 1889. BR-4028 2 – 8 – ne IDC [460]
PETRA: ITS HISTORY AND MONUMENTS / Kennedy, Sir Alexander B W – Country Life, 1925 – 9 – $10.00 – us I.R.C. [930]
Petraeus, Theodorus *see* NOTAE SEU ELUCIDATIONES BREVES IN PETRI DORLANDI CHRONICI CARTUSIENSIS LIBROS
Petran, Ernst *see* BEITRAEGE ZUR VERSTAENDIGUNG UEBER BEGRIFF UND WESEN DER SITTLICH-RELIGIOESEN ERFAHRUNG
Petrarca *see*
- AFRICA ET BUCOLICA
- RIME Y TRIONFI
- SONETTI AND CANZONI
- TRIONFI

PETRARCH : A SELECTION OF NOTEWORTHY WORKS FROM THE CORNELL PETRARCH COLLECTION – (With guidebook) – 45v. 1475-1899 – 394mf – 9 – $5.00f – us Ross [450]
Petre, Edward *see* NOTICES OF THE ENGLISH COLLEGES AND CONVENTS ESTABLISHED ON THE CONTINENT AFTER THE DISSOLUTION OF RELIGIOUS HOUSES IN ENGLAND
Petre, Maude Dominica *see*
- AETHJOPUM SERVUS
- CATHOLICISM AND INDEPENDENCE

PETREFACTA GERMANIAE... / Goldfuss, G A – Duesseldorf. 3v. 1826-1844 – 25mf – ne IDC [590]
PETRI ABAELARDI OPERA. TOMUS 1,2 / ed by Cousin, V – Parisiis, 1849-1859 – 51mf – 8 – ne Slangenburg [240]
Petri, Friedrich Karl Wilhelm *see* KRITISCHE BEITRAEGE ZUR GESCHICHTE DER DICHTERSPRACHE KLOPSTOCK'S
Petri, Johann S *see*
- ANLEITUNG ZUR PRACTISCHEN MUSIK..
- ANLEITUNG ZUR PRACTISCHEN MUSIK

Petri, K *see* MONOGRAPHIE DES COLEOPTEREN-TRIBUS HYPERINI
PETRI MARTYRIS AB ANGLIERA(...)DE REBUS OCEANICIS ET ORBO NOVO DECADES TRES(...) / Anghiera, Pietro Martire d' – Basilae: J. Bebelium, 1533 – fr Armell [941]
PETRI MOLINAEI NOVI ANATOMICI MALA ENCHEIRESIS SEU CENSURA ANATOMES ARMINIANISMI / Corvinus, J A – Francofurti ad Moenum, 1632 – 19mf – 8 – ne Slangenburg [240]
Petrie, George *see* CHURCH AND STATE IN EARLY MARYLAND

Petrie, William Matthew Flinders *see*
- ANCIENT GAZA
- ANCIENT GAZA: I
- EHNASYA
- LAHUN 2
- MEMPHIS
- MEYDUM AND MEMPHIS (3)
- NEBESHEH AND DEFENNEH
- PREHISTORIC EGYPT
- THE PYRAMIDS AND TEMPLES OF GIZEH
- RESEARCHES IN SINAI
- THE REVOLUTIONS OF CIVILISATION
- ROMAN PORTRAITS AND MEMPHIS (4)
- THE ROYAL TOMBS OF THE FIRST DYNASTIES
- SCARABS AND CYLINDERS
- SYRIA AND EGYPT
- TANIS
- TELL EL AMARNA
- TOMBS OF THE COURTIERS AND OXYRHYNKHOS

DIE PETRINISCHE STROEMUNG DER NEUTESTAMENTLICHEN LITERATUR : UNTERSUCHUNGEN UEBER DIE SCHRIFTSTELLERISCHE EIGENTUEMLICHKEIT DES ERSTEN PETRUSBRIEFS, DES MARCUSEVANGELIUMS UND DER PETRINISCHEN REDEN DER APOSTELGESCHICHTE / Scharfe, Ernst – (Includes bibliographical references) – Berlin:Reuther & Reichard, 1893 – 1mf – 9 – 0-8370-5076-6 – 1985-3076 – us A.T.L.A. [220]

PETROGLIFOS EN LA ALTA EXTREMADURA / Sayans Castanos, Marcelo – Caceres: Dip. Prov. de Caceres, 1956 – 1 – sp Bibl Santa Ana [946]

PETROGRADSKAIA PRAVDA – Leningrad. U.S.S.R. 1918-1925; 1952-53 – 1 – us UMI [072]

Petrogradski i okruzhno i komissariat po voennym delam *see* PRIKAZY, PRIKAZANII A I OBI AVLENII A PETROGRADSKOGO OKRUZHNOGO KOMISSARIATA PO VOENNYM DELAM

PETROGRADSKI I SOVET NARODNOGO KHOZI A ISTVA *see* BIULLETEN PETROGRADSKOGO SOVETA NARODNOGO KHOZI A ISTVA

Petrogradski i sovet narodnogo khozia istva *see* TOPLIVNYI EZHEGODNIK PETROGRADA NA...

PETROGRADSKII KOOPERATOR – Pg., 1914-19 n2 – 39mf – 9 – COR-667/1 – ne IDC [334]

EL PETROLEO DE COLOMBIA / Bayle, Constantino – Madrid: Razon y Fe, 1923 – 1 – sp Bibl Santa Ana [660]

EL PETROLEO EN LA ARGENTINA / Argentina. Direccion General de Relaciones Culturales y Difusion – [Buenos Aires?, 1950?] – 1 – CSUXAHZ2385-B – us Hoover Inst Photo [331]

PETROLEO Y POLITICA : CONTRIBUCION AL ESTUDIO DE LA HISTORIA ECONOMICA ARGENTINA Y DE LAS RELACIONES ENTRE EL IMPERIALISMO Y LA VIDA POLITICA NACIONAL / Frondizi, Arturo – Buenos Aires: Raigal, 2nd ed 1955 – 1 – CSUXAHZ2398-B – us Hoover Inst Photo [320]

PETROLEUM BULLETIN – Orange, CA. 1921 – 1r – 1 – $50.00 – C03376 – us Library Micro [071]

PETROLEUM CHEMISTRY – (Cont: Petroleum Chemistry USSR) – v1- 1962- – 5,6,9 – us UMI [660]

PETROLEUM CHEMISTRY USSR *see* PETROLEUM CHEMISTRY

PETROLEUM COMPANY REVIEW / Arabian Gulf Emirates. Abu-Dhabi – 1970-72 – 9 – ne IDC [660]

PETROLEUM ENGINEER INTERNATIONAL – v1- 1929- 1; v47- 5,6; v48- 9 – us UMI [660]

PETROLEUM ENGINEER INTERNATIONAL – v56- 1984- – 1,5,6,9 – us UMI [660]

PETROLEUM MANAGEMENT – (v. 37-39. 1965-67. 5,6) – v. 36-39. 1964-1967 – 1 – us UMI [660]

PETROLEUM MARKETER – v17- 1949- 1; v38- 5,6; v42- 9 – us UMI [380]

PETROLEUM PRESS – Taft. Calif. 1928-1930 – 1 – us UMI [071]

PETROLEUM PROCESSING – v. 1-12. 1946-57 – 1 – us UMI [660]

PETROLEUM REPORTER – Taft. Calif. 1914-1931 – 1 – us UMI [071]

PETROLEUM REVIEW – v1- 1947- 1; v31- 5,6,9 – us UMI [073]

PETROLEUM TIMES – 1899-1992. Continued annually – 1 – £3,625.00 – uk World [660]

PETROLEUM TODAY – v1-18 1959-77 1; v14-18 5,6; v18- 9 – us UMI [338]

PETROLEUM WEEK – v. 1-12. 1955-61 – 1 – us UMI [338]

PETROLEUM ZEITSCHRIFT – Berlin. Oct 1905-Sep 1910. -w – 6r – 1 – uk British Libr Newspaper [660]

PETROLIA ADVERTISER AND CANADIAN OIL JOURNAL – Petrolia, Canada. -w. Mar 1906-Nov 1910 – 412r – 1 – uk British Libr Newspaper [660]

PETROMIN AND ITS ROLE IN THE INTERNATIONAL OIL INDUSTRY / Saudi Arabia. General Petroleum and Mineral Organization – Boston. Mass. Tuesday, April 26th, 1966 – 9 – ne IDC [338]

PETROS BAPTIST CHURCH. PETROS, TENNESSEE : CHURCH RECORDS – Aug 1896-Jul 1984. Lacking: Oct 1953-Sept 1956.944p – 1 – 42.48 – us Baptist [240]

Petrov, A *see* SOBRANIE KNIG, IZDANNYKH V TSARSTVOVANIE PETRA VELIKAGO

Petrov, F A *see* NAPOLEON – SA FAMILLE – SON ENTOURAGE

Petrov, K *see*
- SISTEMATICHESKII UKAZATEL'K SOCHINENIIAM BELINSKAGO S PRISOEDINENIEM SOOTVETSTVUIUSHCHIKH UKAZANII NA SOCHINENIIA DOBROLIUBOVA
- SLOVAR' K SOCHINENIIAM I PEREVODAM D.I. FONVIZINA

Petrov, M *see* NOVEISHAIA NATSIONAL'NAIA ISTORIOGRAFIIA GERMANII, ANGLII I FRANTSII

Petrov, N I *see* OPISANIE RUKOPISNYKH SOBRANII NAKHODIASHCHIKHSIA V GORODE KIEVE

Petrov, N P *see* BIBLIOGRAFICHESKII UKAZATEL' RUSSKIKH DISSERTATII PO MEDITSINE I VETERINATII

Petrov, P V *see* SUVOROV V RODNOI POEZII

Petrov, SO *see*
- KNIGI GRAZHDANSKOI PECHATI 18 V
- SLAVIANSKIE KNIGI KIRILLOVSKOI PECHATI 15-18 VV

Petrov V A *see* BOLSHEVIKI I ARMII A V 1905-1917 GG

Petrov, Yuri A *see* BANKING AND FINANCE IN RUSSIA, PART 1

Petrova, OP *see* OPISANIE PIS'MENNYKH PAMIATNIKOV KOREISKOI KUL'TURY

Petrova, OP et al *see* OPISANIE IAPONSKIKH RUKOPISEI, KSILOGRAFOV, I STAROPECHATNYKH KNIG

Petrovic, Vojislav M *see* SERBIA; HER PEOPLE, HISTORY AND ASPIRATIONS

Petrovskaia, I F *see*
- ISTOCHNIKOVEDENIE ISTORII RUSSKOGO DOREVOLIUTSIONNOGO DRAMATICHESKOGO TEATRA
- MATERIALY K ISTORII RUSSKOGO TEATRA V GOSUDARSTVENNYKH ARKHIVAKH SSSR

Petrovskii, S A *see* FINLIANDSKAIA OKRAINA ROSSII

Petrovsky, Alexey B *see* PRACTICAL ASPECTS OF SCIENTIFIC AND TECHNOLOGICAL RESEARCH PROGRAMMING

Petrumkevich, I I *see* POLITICHESKII STROI SOVREMENNYKH GOSUDARSTV

Petrus a S Catharina *see* CURSUS PHILOSOPHICUS AD USUM STUDENTIUM TOTIUS ORDINIS MINORAM

PETRUS BOHERIUS : IN REGULAM SANCTI BENEDICTI COMMENTARIUM NUNC PRIMUM EDITUM / Allodi, L – Sublaci, 1908 – Dfl95.00 – ne Slangenburg [240]

PETRUS CANISIUS : DER ERSTE DEUTSCHE JESUIT / Drews, Paul – Halle: Verein fuer Reformationsgeschichte, 1892. ([Schriften des Vereins fuer Reformationsgeschichte; Bd. 38]) – 1mf – us A.T.L.A. [240]

Petrus Cellensis *see* COMMENTARIA IN RUTH

Petrus Chrysologus *see* COLLECTIO SERMONUM (CCSL 24-24A-24B)

Petrus Damiani *see*
- SERMONES
- SERMONES (CCCM 57)

Petrus Pictaviensis *see* [SUMMA DE CONFESSIONE]

PETRUS RAMUS ALS THEOLOGE: EIN BEITRAG ZUR GESCHICHTE DER PROTESTANTISCHEN THEOLOGIE *see* COLLECTED WORKS

PETRUS STIRBT NICHT! : GEDANKEN UEBER DIE UNZERSTOERBARKEIT DES FELSEN PETRI / Moerzinger, Johann – Wien: Heinrich Kirsch, 1902 – 1mf – 9 – 0-8370-6922-X – 1986-0922 – us A.T.L.A. [240]

DIE PETRUS- UND PAULUSACTEN IN DER LITTERARISCHEN UEBERLIEFERUNG DER SYRISCHEN KIRCHE : FESTGRUSS DEM PRIESTERCOLLEGIUM DES DEUTSCHEN CAMPO SANTO ZU ROM ZUR FEIER SEINES 25 JAEHRIGEN BESTEHENS (8 DECEMBER 1901) / Baumstark, Anton – Leipzig: O. Harrassowitz, 1902 – 1mf – us A.T.L.A. [220]

Petrus Venerabilis *see* ADVERSUS LUDAEOS (CCCM 63-63A)

PETRUSBLATT – (Cont by: Katholische Kirchenzeitung) – Berlin, dec 2 1945-dec 23 1990 – 1 – Inquire at Mikrofilmarchiv for details – gw Misc Inst [240]

Petrushevskii, A *see*
- GENERALISIMUS KNIAZ SUVOROV
- KRATKII OBZOR SUVOROVSKOI LITERATURY

Petry, Karl *see* HANDBUCH ZUR DEUTSCHEN LITERATURGESCHICHTE

PETS AND PETSHOP MANAGEMENT – v.1-8. 1947-54 – 1 – us UMI [636]

PETS SUPPLIES MARKETING – (v.35-. 1981-. 5,6,9) – v.27-. 1973- – 1 – us UMI [636]

Petsch, Robert *see* GOETHES FAUST

Petsov, V *see* MAIAKOVSKII

Pettee, James Horace *see* A CHAPTER OF MISSION HISTORY IN MODERN JAPAN

Pettenegg, E G von *see* DIE URKUNDEN DES DEUTSCH-ORDENS-CENTRALARCHIVES ZU WIEN

Petters, Karl Olaf *see* HANS ROTHFELS

Pettigrew, Renee *see* BIBLIOGRAPHIE DES JOURNAUX DE QUEBEC, 1889-1940

Pettigrew, T J *see* MEDICAL PORTRAIT GALLERY

Petty, J *see*
- THE HISTORY OF THE PRIMITIVE METHODIST CONNEXION FROM ITS ORIGIN TO THE CONFERENCE OF 1859
- THE HISTORY OF THE PRIMITIVE METHODIST CONNEXION, FROM ITS ORIGIN TO THE CONFERENCE OF 1860, THE FIRST JUBILEE YEAR OF THE CONNEXION

Petty, W *see*
- AN ESSAY CONCERNING THE MULTIPLICATION OF MANKIND
- THE POLITICAL ANATOMY OF IRELAND
- POLITICAL ARITHMETICK

PETUNDJUK PRACTICUM KIMIA UNTUK S.P.M.A / Supomo – SE 5666 1 – 9 – ne IDC [950]

PETUNDJUK SINGKAT TENTANG "SUMBANGAN WADJIB ISTIMEWA 1962 ATAS BANGUNAN" (S.W.I. BANGUNAN); DILENGKAPI DENGAN TEKS PERATURAN DAN PENDJELASANNJA, SERTA BENTUK2 PORMULIR PELAKSANAAN / Hussein, Kartasasmita – SE-4529 1. 1962 – 9 – ne IDC [950]

PETUNDJUK STATISTIK PERTANIAN RAKJAT / Abdulrachman, Moch – Tjet. 2. Jakarta, 1953. 42p. SEM-3056 – 9 – ne IDC [310]

PETUNDJUK TJANDI.. / Kaelan. Indonesia – 1959. 159p. fold. map.SEM-4787-4788/1 – 9 – ne IDC [950]

Petzet, Christian *see* DIE BLUETEZEIT DER DEUTSCHEN POLITISCHEN LYRIK VON 1840 BIS 1850

Petzet, Erich *see*
- AUGUST GRAF VON PLATENS SAEMTLICHE WERKE IN ZWOELF BAENDEN
- DEUTSCHE SCHRIFTTAFELN DES 9. BIS 16. JAHRHUNDERTS AUS HANDSCHRIFTEN DER K. HOF- UND STAATSBIBL. IN MUENCHEN
- JOHANN PETER UZ
- PAUL HEYSE
- PAUL HEYSE ALS DRAMATIKER

Petzoldt, Julius *see* ANZEIGER FUER LITERATUR DER BIBLIOTHEKSWISSENSCHAFT

Peuchet, Jacques *see*
- DESCRIPTION TOPOGRAPHIQUE ET STATISTIQUE
- ESSAI D'UNE STATISTIQUE GENERALE DE LA FRANCE

Peuchgaric, N *see* COTE OCCIDENTALE D'AFRIQUE. COTE D'OR. GEOGRAPHIE. COMMERCE. MOEURS

Peuckert, Will Erich *see* DEUTSCHES VOLKSTUM IN MAERCHEN UND SAGE, SCHWANK UND RAETSEL

Peugnet, Jeffrey C *see* EFFECT OF DIETARY EDUCATION, EXERCISE, AND TWO DIETARY PROGRAMS ON WOMEN'S BODY COMPOSITION, CALORIC INTAKE, DIETARY COMPOSITION, AND SUBJECTIVE FEELINGS CONCERNING THE PROGRAMS

Peukert, Werner *see* DER ATLANTISCHE SKLAVENHANDEL VON DAHOMEY (1740-1797)

PEULS NOMADES / Dupire, M – 9 – F100.00 – fr Ethnologie [306]

LES PEUPLADES DE LA SENEGAMBIE / Berenger-Feraud, Laurent Jean Baptiste – Histoire, ethnographie, moeurs et coutumes. Legendes, etc. Paris, Ernest Leroux – 9 – 12.50 – fr Orientalistes [306]

LE PEUPLE : 3 CAHIERS ANNUELS – ECONOMIE REGIONALE – Montmagny, Canada. n1. sep 1971-n3. nov 1974 – 1r – 1 – Can$30.00 – cn Can Microfilming [330]

LE PEUPLE – Bruxelles, 1914 (incompl), 1918-40 – 1 – us Hoover Inst Photo [072]

LE PEUPLE / Confederation Generale du Travail – Paris. 16 sept 1944-1986. Suite de: Le Peuple.Quot. du syndicalisme. Voir a ce titre – 1 – fr A.C.R.P.P. [331]

LE PEUPLE – (Cont by: Le Peuple-Courrier 28 dec 1972-28 oct 1986. Cont by: Le Peuple de la Cote-du-Sud 25 mar-oct 1986) – Montmagny, Canada. 21 sep 1900-21 dec 1972 – 57r – 1 – Can$75.00r – cn Can Microfilming [072]

LE PEUPLE – Marseille. mai 1850-51 – 1 – fr A.C.R.P.P. [073]

LE PEUPLE – Montreal, Canada. 2 sep 1922-v1 n10. 4 nov 1922 – 1r – 1 – Can$25.00 – cn Can Microfilming [072]

LE PEUPLE – Montreal, Canada. 21 mai 1911-v1 n41. 10 fev 1912 – 1r – 1 – Can$30.00 – cn Can Microfilming [072]

LE PEUPLE – Montreal, Canada. 22 mai 1880-21 mai 1887 – 1r – 1 – Can$40.00 – cn Can Microfilming [072]

LE PEUPLE – Montreal, Canada. sep 1963-v1 n2. avr 1964 – 1r – 1 – Can$25.00 – cn Can Microfilming [072]

LE PEUPLE – Paris. 2 fevr-juin 1869 – 1 – fr A.C.R.P.P. [073]

LE PEUPLE – Paris. 4 janv 1921-6 juin 1940 – 1 – fr A.C.R.P.P. [073]

LE PEUPLE – Paris, FR. 1944-1950 – 2r – $100.00 – R63568 – us Library Micro [072]

LE PEUPLE – Pointe-a-Pitre. juil 1891-fevr 1895, sept-dec 1899 – 1 – fr A.C.R.P.P. [073]

LE PEUPLE – Sherbrooke, Canada. 18 nov 1890-20 mar 1891 – 1r – 1 – Can$35.00 – cn Can Microfilming [072]

LE PEUPLE AVAIT-IL DES ECOLES AVANT 1789? / Michaud, Gustave – Poitiers. 1910. (La Condition Ouvriere. Part Two.) – 9 – 2.50 – fr Bibl Nationale [360]

LE PEUPLE CONSTITUANT – no. 1-134. Paris. 27 fevr-11 juil 1848 – 1 – fr A.C.R.P.P. [073]

LE PEUPLE COURIER *see* LA TRIBUNE DE LEVIS-METRO

LE PEUPLE DE FRANCE AUX COTES DE L'ESPAGNE REPUBLICAINE; EXTRAITS DES RAPPORTS ET INTERVENTIONS / Parti Communiste. Congres National, 9th, Arles, 1937 – Discours de Camarade Delicado. Paris, 1938. Fiche W1097. (Blodgett Collection of Spanish Civil War Pamphlets) – 9 – us H.U. College Libr [946]

LE PEUPLE DE LA COTE-DU-SUD *see* LE PEUPLE

UN PEUPLE DE L'OUEST AFRICAIN : LES DIAWARA / Boyer, Gaston – Dakar, 1953 – us Res Libr [305]

LE PEUPLE D'ISRAEL ET SES ESPERANCES RELATIVES A SON AVENIR / Vernes, Maurice – Paris: Sandoz et Fischbacher, 1872. 1 fiche – 9 – us A.T.L.A. [270]

PEUPLE ET CULTURE / La Maison de la Culture de Marseille – no. 1-7. Marseille. sept 1936-mars 1937 – 1 – fr A.C.R.P.P. [073]

LE PEUPLE ET LA LANGUE DES MEDES / Oppert, Jules – Paris: Maisonneuve, 1879 – 1mf – 9 – 0-8370-8540-3 – 1986-2540 – us A.T.L.A. [470]

LE PEUPLE FRANCAIS – Paris. Red. en chef, Abbe Garnier. Contient egalement l'ed. hebd. 18 dec 1893-juin 1894, juil 1909-juin 1910 – 1 – fr A.C.R.P.P. [073]

LE PEUPLE INSTRUIT, OU LES ALLIANCES DANS LESQUELLES LES MINISTRES DE LA GRAND BRETAGNE ONT ENGAGE LA NATION... / Shebbeare, John – 1756. SEM16P83 – 1r – 5 – Can$9.00 – cn Bibl Nat [941]

LE PEUPLE LIBRE – Fond. Roger Salengro. Lille. 1936-aout 1939 – 1 – fr A.C.R.P.P. [335]

PEUPLE MARTYR *see* TROIS ETUDES

LE PEUPLE RUSSE ET LE SOCIALISME / Herzen, Aleksandr I – (Russia – 19th C. series). 1852 – 9 – fr Hachette [335]

LE PEUPLE SIENA OU SENOUFO : COTE D'IVOIRE / Delafosse, Maurice – 1 – F66.42 – fr Armell [305]

LE PEUPLE SOUVERAIN – Journal de Lyon puis Journal des interets democratiques et du progres social. no. 1-407. Lyon. 4 avr 1848-17 18 juin 1849. mq no. 1-2, 7, 16, 24, 26-28, 35, 38, 82, 158, 160-161, 406 – 1 – fr A.C.R.P.P. [073]
LE PEUPLE TRAVAILLEUR – Montreal, Canada. v1 n2. 5 fev 1850-v1 n11. 9 avr 1850 – 1r – 1 – Can$25.00 – cn Can Microfilming [072]
LE PEUPLE-COURRIER *see*
- LE COURRIER DE MONTMAGNY
- LE PEUPLE
PEUPLEMENTS DES SEDIMENTS CORALLIENS DE LA REGION DE TULEAR (S.W. DE MADAGASCAR) ET LEUR INSERTION DANS LE CONTEXTE COTIER INDO-PACIFIQUE / Thomassin, B A – 9 – F300.00 – fr Ethnologie [574]
PEUPLEMENTS PISCICOLES ET TEUTHOLOGIQUES DU BASSIN MARITIME DE LA RANCE: IMPACT DE L'AMENAGEMENT MAREMOTEUR / Le Mao, P – 9 – F40.00 – fr Ethnologie [590]
DES PEUPLES DU CAUCASE ET DES PAYS AU NORD DE LA MER NOIRE ET DE LA MER CASPIENNE DANS LE 10E / Ohsson, M C d' – SIECLE ou Voyage d'Abou-el-Cassim. Paris. 1828. BU-536 2 – 8 – ne IDC [910]
LES PEUPLES ORIENTAUX CONNUS DES ANCIENS CHINOIS / Rosny, Leon de – Seconde ed. revue et augmentee. Paris: Ernest Leroux. 1886 – 9 – 10.00 – fr Orientalistes [950]
PEURILES CONFABULATIUNCULAE / Brinsley, John – 1617. 74p. (English Linguistics Series 1500-1800) – 9 – us UMI [420]
PEUTINGERIANA TABULA ITINERARIA 1753 / Scheyb, F C de – 1 – uk Microform Academic [910]
PEUT-ON FERMER LE CANAL DE SUEZ? / Guibal, R – Paris, 1937 – 2mf – 1 – ILM-2333/1 – ne IDC [327]
Peverall, Albert Arthur *see* DEVELOPING A MINISTRY OF LAY EVANGELISM AT THE FIRST BAPTIST CHURCH OF ROANOKE, VIRGINIA
PEVETS VOLGI D.N. SADOVNIKOV / Sadovnikov, Dmitrii Nikolaevich – 1940. Selections from the poet's work – 1 – us I.U. Libraries [810]
Pevsner, Isaiah *see* ISRAEL AND HUMAN RIGHTS
PEWARTA PRIJAJI : SOERAT KABAR BOELANAN, AKEN BERGOENA... – Semarang, 1900-1902.-v1-4 – 16mf – 9 – SE-20,010/1 – ne IDC [950]
Pexenfelder, M *see* ETHICA SYMBOLICA E FABULARUM UMBRIS IN VERITATIS LUCEM VARIA ERUDITIONE, NOVITER EVOLUTA
Peydro, Miguel *see* LA OBRA DE LA REPUBLICA ESPANOLA
Peyerimhoff, H De *see* CATALOGUE DES LEPIDOPTERES D'ALSACE
Peyrat, Alphonse *see* HISTOIRE ELEMENTAIRE ET CRITIQUE DE JESUS
Peyre, Marie Joseph *see* OEUVRES D'ARCHITECTURE
Peyre, Thomas Walter *see* PLANTATION JOURNAL
Peyreleau, Boyer de *see* LES ANTILLES FRANCAISES, PARTICULIEREMENT LA GUADELOUPE, DEPUIS LEUR DECOUVERTE JUSQU'AU 1ER NOVEMBRE, 1825
Peyrere, I de la *see* RELATION DU GROENLAND. 13, 278, 4 P., MAP
Peyret, Alexis *see* UNE VISITE AUX COLONIES DE LA REPUBLIQUE ARGENTINE
Peyrissac, Leon *see* AUX RUINES DES GRANDES CITES SOUDANAISES
Peyritsch, J J *see*
- AROIDEAE MAXIMILIANAE
- SERTUM BENGUELENSE
Peyrony, Denis *see* LA FERRASSIE [SUIVIE DE] LES CUIRASSES HALLSTATIENNES DE ELLINGES...
Peyton, V J *see* THE HISTORY OF THE ENGLISH LANGUAGE
Pez, Bern. *see*
- BIBLIOTHECA ASCETICA ANTIQUO-NOVA
- BIBLIOTHECA BENEDICTINO-MAURIANA
- THESAURUS ANECDOTORUM NOVISSIMUS
Pezron, P[Y] *see* ANTIQUITE DE LA NATION ET DE LA LANGUE DES CELTES, AUTREMENT APPELLEZ GAULOIS
Pezuela y Lobo, Jacobo de la *see* HISTORIA DE ISLA DE CUBA
DER PFAELZER IN BERLIN – Berlin, 1921-41 – 5 – Inquire at Mikrofilmarchiv for details – gw Misc Inst [072]
PFAELZER TAGEBLATT : BA DER RHEINFALZ – Landau-Ludwigshafen, Germany. 1977-1990 – 115r – 1 – gw Mikrofilm [072]
PFAELZISCHE GESCHICHTSBLAETTER – Kaiserslautern. Jahrg. 1-11, Nr. 2; Apr. 1905-Feb. 1915. "Monatliche Beilage zur Pfaelzischen Presse." Film Mas 9402 – 1 – us H.U. Library [073]
PFAELZISCHER MERKUR – Zweibruecken, West Germany. 1978- – ca 5r per yr – 1 – gw Mikrofilm [072]
Pfaff, Friedrich *see* SAMMLUNG VON VORTRAEGEN FUER DAS DEUTSCHE VOLK, ERSTER BAND
DER PFAFFENSPIEGEL : AN ILLUSTRATED MONTHLY JOURNAL FOR THE ADVANCEMENT OF FREETHOUGHT IDEAS – Chicago. v1 no 9-v5 no 10 Mar 1906-Sep 1910. Incomplete – 1 – us NY Public [140]
Pfafflin, J R *see* INTERNATIONAL JOURNAL OF ENVIRONMENTAL STUDIES
DIE PFAFF'SCHEN IRENAEUS-FRAGMENTE ALS FAELSCHUNGEN PFAFFS NACHGEWIESEN : MISCELLEN ZU DEN APOSTOLISCHEN VAETERN, DEN ACTA PAULI, APELLES, DEM MURATORISCHEN FRAGMENT, DEN PSEUDOCYPRIANISCHEN SCHRIFTEN UND CLAUDIANUS MAMERTUS / Harnack, Adolf von – Leipzig: J.C. Hinrichs, 1900. (Texte und Untersuchungen zur Geschichte der altchristlichen Literatur; der ganzen Reihe 20. Bd., [Heft 3]: n.F., 5. Bd., 3. Heft) – 1mf – us A.T.L.A. [240]
DIE PFAFF'SCHEN IRENAEUS-FRAGMENTE ALS FAELSCHUNGEN PFAFFS (T.U.U. 2-20/3A) / Harnack, Adolf von – Leipzig, 1900 – 2mf – 9 – ne Slangenburg [240]
Pfahl, I *see* SAMMLUNG ABENDSMAHLSORDNUNGEN
PFALZGRAF PHILIPP LUDWIG VON NEUBURG, SEIN SOHN WOLFGANG WILHELM UND DIE JESUITEN : EIN BILD AUS DEM ZEITALTER DER GEGENREFORMATION / Sperl, August – Halle: Verein fuer Reformationsgeschichte, 1895. ([Schriften des Vereins fuer Reformationsgeschichte; Bd. 48]) – 1mf – us A.T.L.A. [240]
PFALZGRAF WOLFGANG : HERZOG VON ZWEIBRUECKEN UND NEUBURG / Ney, Julius – (Lazarus von Schwendi : Kaiserlicher General und Geheimer Rat: Seine kirchenpolitische Taetigkeit und seine Stellung zur Reformation / von Rudolf Krone) – Leipzig: Verein fuer Reformationsgeschichte, 1912. (Schriften des Vereins fuer Reformationsgeschichte; Jahrg. 29, 2. u. 3. Stueck, Nr. 106/107) – 1mf – us A.T.L.A. [240]
Pfann, S J *see* THE DEAD SEA SCROLLS ON MICROFICHE
Pfannenschmidt, Heinz *see* DAS FRISIERTE TESTAMENT
Pfannkuchen, Wilhelm *see* PERIODENBAU IN GOETHES UND SCHILLERS GROESSEREN DICHTUNGEN
PFARRER KALENDAR FUER DIE REFORMIERTE SCHWEIZ – 1970-86 (complete) – 3r – 1 – ATLA S0761 – us A.T.L.A. [240]
DER PFARRER VON KIRCHFELD : VOLKSSTUECK MIT GESANG IN VIER AKTEN VON LUDWIG ANZENGRUBER / Anzengruber, Ludwig – Stuttgart: J G Cotta, 1915 – 1r – 1 – us U.W. Library [820]
Pfatteicher, Ernst P H *see* WOMAN AS CONGREGATIONAL VOTER
Pfeffel, Gottlieb Konrad *see* AUSGEWAEHLTE FABELN UND GEDICHTE
Pfeffel, J A *see* GUELDENE AEPFEL IN SILBERBEN SCHAELEN
Pfeffer, Carl *see* DIE PSYCHOLOGIE DER CHARAKTERE IN HEBBELS TRAGOEDIE
Pfefferle, W *see* DIE SCHWEIZERISCHEN GOLDHYPOTHEKEN IN DEUTSCHLAND...
Pfeifer, Thomas *see* SOZIALPSYCHIATRISCHE DIENSTE IN BADEN-WUERTTEMBERG
Pfeiffer, A *see* UEBER DIE MUSIK DER ALTEN HEBRAER..
Pfeiffer, C *see* NATURGESCHICHTE DEUTSCHER LAND- UND SUESSWASSERMOLLUSKEN
Pfeiffer, Eduard *see* DIE AETHIOPISCHE BIBELUEBERSETZUNG...ALT- UND NEUTESTAMENTLICHE WISSENSCHAFT
Pfeiffer, Edward *see* MISSION STUDIES
Pfeiffer, Emilie *see* SHAKESPEARES UND TIECKS MAERCHENDRAMEN
Pfeiffer, Erich *see* DER KREIS ANGERBURG
Pfeiffer, Franz *see*
- BRIEFWECHSEL ZWISCHEN JOSEPH FREIHERRN VON LASSBERG UND LUDWIG UHLAND
- GERMANIA
Pfeiffer, Johannes *see* MATTHIAS CLAUDIUS, DER WANDSBECKER BOTE
Pfeiffer, L K G *see* ABBILDUNG UND BESCHREIBUNG BLUEHENDER CAKTEEN
Pfeiffer, Peter *see* DAS "GRAND MINISTERE" LEON GAMBETTAS 10. NOVEMBER 1881 – 26. JANUAR 1882
Pfeiffer, Richard *see* DIE RELIGIOES-SITTLICHE WELTANSCHAUUNG DES BUCHES DER SPRUECHE
Pfeiffer-Belli, Wolfgang *see* GESCHICHTE DER DEUTSCHEN DICHTUNG
Pfeil, Leopold *see* GOTTFRIED WILHELM SACER'S "REIME DICH, ODER ICH FRESSE DICH...NORTHAUSEN 1673"
DIE PFEILGIFTE / Lewin, L – 8031 1. 1923 – 9 – ne IDC [890]
DAS PFENNIG-MAGAZIN – Leipzig, DE. 1833-55 – 8r – 1 – gw Mikrofilm [072]
DAS PFENNIG-MAGAZIN FUER KINDER – Leipzig, DE. 5 May-28 Jun, 6 Sep-25 Dec 1834; 1835-38 – 1 – gw Mikrofilm [072]
DAS PFERD, DER ESEL UND DER HUND IN DER HEILIGEN SCHRIFT / Zeller, Alwin – Plauen i.V.: Moritz Wieprecht, 1890. 1 fiche – 9 – us A.T.L.A. [240]
PFERDEMUSIK : ROMAN / Tuegel, Ludwig – Muenchen: A Langen, G Mueller, 1935 – 1r – 1 – us U.W. Library [830]
PFI (PIPE FABRICATION INSTITUTE) – Printed index. Updated every 60 days – 6,9 – ne IDC [670]
DER PFINGSTMONTAG : LUSTSPIEL IN STRASSBURGER MUNDART / Arnold, Georges-Daniel – Strassburg: J H E Heitz, 1893 – 1r – 1 – us U.W. Library [820]
DER PFINGSTMONTAG : LUSTSPIEL IN STRASSBURGER MUNDART / Arnold, Georges-Daniel – Strassburg: K J Truebner, 1914 – 1r – 1 – us U.W. Library [820]
Pfister, Friedrich *see*
- DEUTSCHES VOLKSTUM IN GLAUBEN UND ABERGLAUBEN
- DER RELIQUIENKULT IM ALTERTUM
Pfister, L *see*
- CARTES DES PROVINCES ET DES MISSIONS DE LA COMPAGNIE AVANT LA SUPPRESSION (1763-1773)
- NOTICES BIOGRAPHIQUES ET BIBLIOGRAPHIQUES SUR LES JESUITES DE L'ANCIENNE MISSION DE CHINE 1552-1773
Pfister, Oskar *see* DIE FROEMMIGKEIT DES GRAFEN LUDWIG VON ZINZENDORF
Pfitzner, Heinrich *see* DIE PRUEFUNGEN DER BAPTISTEN ZU LITTLEVILLE
PFLANZEN-GATTUNGEN NACH DEM INBEGRIFFE SAEMMTLICHER FRUKTIFIKATIONS-THEILE GEBILDET / Medikus, F K – Mannheim, 1792. 127, 1 pp., 2 pls. B-6061 2 – 8 – ne IDC [580]
PFLANZENKRANKHEITEN DURCH KRYPROGAME PARASITEN VERURSACHT / Tubeuf, C von – Berlin. 1895. B-7489 – 9 – ne IDC [580]
PFLANZEN-PHYSIOLOGISCHE ABHANDLUNGEN / Medikus, F K – 3v. Leipzig. 1803. B-8143 1 – 9 – ne IDC [580]
PFLANZENSOZIOLOGISCHE ANALYSE DER HALBTROCKENRASEN IM SUEDLICHEN RINGGAU (NORDHESSEN) / Boehle, Uta-Regina – 1995 – 2mf – 9 – DM80.00 – 3-8267-2154-3 – gw Hänsel [574]
PFLANZENSOZIOLOGISCH-OEKOLOGISCHE UNTERSUCHUNGEN IN AUSGEWAEHLTEN FEUCHTGEBIETEN IM NATURPARK SCHWALM-NETTE (NORDRHEIN-WESTFALEN) / Schleiter, Ingrid M – 1995 – 2mf – 9 – DM80.00 – 3-8267-2107-1 – gw Hänsel [574]
PFLANZEN-TERATOLOGIE SYSTEMATISCH GEORDNET / Penzig, A J O – Ed. 2. Berlin. 1921-22. B-7383 1 – 9 – ne IDC [580]
DIE PFLANZENTHIERE IN ABBILDUNGEN NACH DER NATUR / Esper, E J C – Nuernberg. 1791. BZ-2245 1 – 9 – ne IDC [590]
Pflaum, H *see* DIE IDEE DER LIEBE. LEONE EBREO
Pfleiderer, Joh Gottlob *see* AMERIKANISCHE REISEBILDER MIT BESONDERER BERUEKSICHTIGUNG DER RELIGIOESEN UND KIRCHLICHEN ZUSTAENDE DER VEREINIGTEN STAATEN
Pfleiderer, Otto *see*
- CHRISTIAN ORIGINS
- DAS CHRISTUSBILD DES URCHRISTLICHEN GLAUBENS IN RELIGIONSGESCHICHTLICHER BELEUCHTUNG
- THE DEVELOPMENT OF THEOLOGY IN GERMANY SINCE KANT AND ITS PROGRESS IN GREAT BRITAIN SINCE 1825
- DIE ENTSTEHUNG DES CHRISTENTUMS
- DIE ENTWICKLUNG DER PROTESTANTISCHEN THEOLOGIE IN DEUTSCHLAND SEIT KANT UND IN GROSSBRITANNIEN SEIT 1825
- GRUNDRISS DER CHRISTLICHEN GLAUBENS- UND SITTENLEHRE
- THE INFLUENCE OF THE APOSTLE PAUL ON THE DEVELOPMENT OF CHRISTIANITY
- THEOLOGIE UND GESCHICHTSWISSENSCHAFT: REDE BEI ANTRITT DES REKTORATS
Pfleiderer, R *see* DIE ATTRIBUTE DER HEILIGEN
DER PFLICHTTEIL IM DEUTSCHEN UND ENGLISCHEN RECHT / Busch, H – Hamburg, 1935 – 1mf – 1 – ILM-2962/1 – ne IDC [327]
PFLUEGERS ARCHIV – v. 249-389. 1947-80 – 1,5,9 – 21,044.00 – us UMI [073]
PFLUGER'S ARCHIV-EUROPEAN JOURNAL OF PHYSIOLOGY – v150-261. 1913-55 – 1,5,6 – us Princeton Micro [073]
Pflug-Harttung, Julius von *see* DIE BULLEN DER PAEPSTE
Pflugk-Harttung, J von *see* LEIPZIG 1813
Pfordten, Hermann Ludwig, Freiherr von der *see* EINFUEHRUNG IN RICHARD WAGNERS WERKE UND SCHRIFTEN
DER PFORZHEIMER BEOBACHTER – (Title changes: General-Anzeiger, 16 Jan 1901; Pforzheimer Neueste Nachrichten, 20 Nov 1918; Pforzheimer Rundschau, 8 Jan 1925; Pforzheimer Zeitung, 1 Oct 1949) – Pforzheim, West Germany. 1976- – ca 8r per yr – 1 – gw Mikrofilm [072]
PFORZHEIMER NEUESTE NACHRICHTEN *see* DER PFORZHEIMER BEOBACHTER
PFORZHEIMER RUNDSCHAU *see* DER PFORZHEIMER BEOBACHTER
PFORZHEIMER ZEITUNG *see* DER PFORZHEIMER BEOBACHTER
Pfuelf, Otto *see* CARDINAL VON GEISSEL
Pfund, Margaret E *see* POST OFFICES AND POSTMASTERS OF OHIO TO 1930
Pfungst, Arthur *see*
- LASKARIS
- NEUE GEDICHTE
P.H. EMERSON'S "LIFE AND LANDSCAPE ON THE NORFOLK BROADS." / U.S. Library of Congress. Prints and Photographs Division – 40 original platinum prints with brief essays. 1 reel. P&P12011 – 1 – 23.00r – us L of C Photodup [080]
P.H. EMERSON'S "PICTURES ON EAST ANGLIAN LIFE." / U.S. Library of Congress. Prints and Photographs Division – 1888. 32 photogravures of East Anglian peasants and watermen. 1 reel. P&P12012 – 1 – 23.00r – us L of C Photodup [080]
PHAEDIN THAI – Chiangmai, Thailand. Jul 1969-Dec 1976 – 8r – 1 – us L of C Photodup [072]
PHAENOMENOLOGIE DES SITTLICHEN BEWUSSTSEINS: PROLEGOMENA ZU JEDER KUNFTIGEN ETHIK / Hartmann, Eduard von – Berlin: Carl Dunckner, 1879. 871p. Includes bibliog – 1 – us U.W. Library [170]
PHAENOMENOLOGIE DES UNGLUECKS : ZU LEBEN UND WERK SIMONE WEILS (1909-1943) / Holthaus, Thomas – 1992 – 9 – DM98.00 – 3-89349-506-1 – gw Hänsel [190]
PHAENOTYPISIERUNG ZYTOMEGALIEVIRUS-INFIZIERTER ZELLEN / Schoener, Juergen Josef – 1995 – 1mf – 9 – DM60.00 – 3-8267-2222-1 – gw Hänsel [612]
LA PHALANGE – Paris. juil 1906-mai 1914 – 1 – fr A.C.R.P.P. [073]
LA PHALANGE – Revue de la science sociale. n.s., I-X. Paris. 1845-49. voir aussi: Le Phalenstere – 1 – fr A.C.R.P.P. [073]
PHALANX; ORGAN OF THE DOCTRINE OF ASSOCIATION – Oct 1843-May 1845 – 1 – us UMI [073]
LE PHALENSTERE – juin-aout 1832. devenu: La Reforme industrielle ou le Phalenstere. SEPT 1832-FEVR 1834. devenu: La Phalange. juil 1836-juil 1843. Paris – 1 – fr A.C.R.P.P. [073]
PHANEROGAMAE CUMINGIANAE PHILIPPINARUM / Vidal y Soler, S – Manila. 1885. B-5789 2 – 8 – ne IDC [580]

PHANTASIE, 2 PIANOS, OP. 11 / Bruch, M – (2 pts) – Leipzig: Breitkopf, 18– – 1 – us Sibley [780]
PHANTASIE D MOLL, OP. 11, FUER 2 KLAVIERE ZU 4 HAENDEN / Bruch, M – Leipzig: Breitkopf & Haertel, 188- – 1 – us Sibley [780]
PHANTASIE UND VERANTWORTUNG : DOKUMENTATION DES DRITTEN SCHRIFTSTELLERKONGRESSES DES VERBANDES DEUTSCHER SCHRIFTSTELLER (VS) IN DER IG DRUCK UND PAPIER / Verband Deutscher Schriftsteller; ed by Pingel, Horst – (Includes bibliographical references) – Frankfurt am Main: Fischer-Taschenbuch-Verlag, 1975 – 1 – us U.W. Library [430]
PHANTASMION / Coleridge, Sara Coleridge – London: W. Pickering, 1837 – 1 roll – 1 – 1-55879-622-3 – uk Libr Preservation [890]
PHANTOM FORTUNE / Braddon, Mary Elizabeth – British Fiction Archive: Unit 5 – 9 – uk Bell [830]
THE PHANTOM 'RICKSHAW : AND OTHER TALES / Kipling, Rudyard – Allahabad: A.H. Wheeler; London: Sampson Low, Marston, Searle & Rivington, [18–?] – 1 roll – 1 – 1-55879-957-5 – uk Libr Preservation [830]
PHAP-VIET NHU'T-GIA – no. 2-28. Saigon. 8 fevr-17 mai 1927. mq no. 27 – 1 – fr A.C.R.P.P. [073]
LE PHARE : BULLETIN PAROISSIAL DE ST-JACQUES – Montreal, Canada. v10 n7. 15 jul 1946 – 1r – 1 – Can$25.00 – cn Can Microfilming [240]
LE PHARE : HEBDO – Chicoutimi, 17 mars 1960-26 avr 1961. La Baie. v2 n7. 3 mai 1961-21 jun 1968 – 5r – 1 – Can$70.00 – cn Can Microfilming [072]
LE PHARE DE LA GUADELOUPE – Organe de defense des principes Schoelcheristes et socialistes. Pointe-a-Pitre. No.1-3. avr 1937 – 1 – fr A.C.R.P.P. [073]
LE PHARE DE LA LOIRE – Journal quotidien, politique, litteraire et commercial. Nantes. juil 1870-71, 1888, 1891 – 1 – fr A.C.R.P.P. [073]
PHARE DE LA ROCHELLE – Journal politique, commercial et litteraire. La Rochelle. 1848-51 – 1 – fr A.C.R.P.P. [073]
LE PHARE DES LACS – Watertown, NY. 28 avr 1859-v1 n9. 23 jun 1859 – 1r – 1 – Can$30.00 – cn Can Microfilming [071]
LE PHARE DU BOUT DU MONDE / Verne, Jules – Paris: J. Hetzel, 1905. 4 fiches. (Literature Collection) – 9 – 10.00 – fr Bibl Nationale [830]
LE PHARE DU NORD *see* THE NORTHERN BEACON – THE BEACON/LE PHARE – LE PHARE DU NORD
LE PHARE LITTERAIRE – Echo de Royan. no. 3-116. Royan. 11 fevr 1877-6 avr 1879 – 1 – fr A.C.R.P.P. [073]
LE PHARILLON – Gaspe, Canada. 23 aut 1973-29 dec 1991 – 20r – 1 – Can$70.00r – cn Can Microfilming [072]
DIE PHARISAEER UND DIE SADDUCAEER : EINE UNTERSUCHUNG ZUR INNEREN JUEDISCHEN GESCHICHTE / Wellhausen, Julius – (Includes bibliographical references) – Greifswald: L Bamberg, 1874 – 1mf – 9 – 0-8370-6457-0 – 1986-0457 – us A.T.L.A. [270]
DIE PHARISAEER UND VERFOLGER DER KIRCHE IN UNSEREN TAGEN : FEST-REDE / Weninger, Francis Xavier – New York: Benziger, [1875?] – 1mf – 9 – 0-8370-6868-1 – 1986-0868 – us A.T.L.A. [240]
THE PHARISEES AND JESUS / Robertson, A T – The Stone lectures for 1915-1916. 1920 – 1 – 6.61 – us Baptist [240]
PHARMACAL NOTES – Detroit: Parke, Davis & Co. bimonthly – 1 – us U.W. Library [073]
PHARMACEUTICAL ABSTRACTS – v. 1-13. 1935-1947 – 1,5,6 – us Princeton Micro [615]
PHARMACEUTICAL CHEMISTRY JOURNAL – v1-27. 1967-93 – 1,5 – $120.00v – us UMI [540]
PHARMACEUTICAL JOURNAL – v. 1-209. 1841-1972 – 1,5,6 – us Princeton Micro [615]
PHARMACEUTICAL MEDICINE – v1-. Dec 1984- – 1,5,6,9 – us UMI [073]
PHARMACEUTICAL NEWS / ed by Triggle, David J – 9,5,1 – us Harwood [615]
PHARMACEUTICAL RESEARCH – (v5-11 1988-94 $150.00v) – v1-4. 1984-87 – 1,5 – $75.00v – us UMI [615]
Pharmaceutical Society of Japan. Tokyo *see* JOURNAL
PHARMACEUTICAL TECHNOLOGY – (v.3-. 1979- 5,6,9) – v.1-. 1977- – 1 – us UMI [615]
PHARMACEUTICE RATIONALIS / Willis, Thomas – M 426. Pars secunda. 1675 – 9 – ne IDC [615]
PHARMACEUTICE RATIONALIS / Willis, Thomas – Oxford, 1674 – 7mf – 9 – ne IDC [615]
LA PHARMACIE LABORIEUSE – Montreal, Canada. 1 jan 1898-v1 n4. 1 avr 1898 – 1r – 1 – Can$25.00 – cn Can Microfilming [615]
LE PHARMACIEN – (Ceased v67 no 7 1993) – Toronto. v64-67. 1990-93 – 9 – Can$20.00y – cn Micromedia [615]
PHARMACIST NEWS – v1- 1993/94- – 1 – Can$85.00y – cn Micromedia [615]
PHARMACOGNOSY TITLES – v5-9 1970-74 1; v7-9 5,6 – us UMI [073]
PHARMACOLOGICAL REVIEWS – v1-48. 1949-96 – 1,5,6,9 – $90.00r – us Williams [615]
PHARMACOLOGICAL TREATMENT OF INTRACOULAR PROLIFERATIVE EMTITIES : NONCARCINOGENIC ANTHRACYCLINES FOR PREVENTION OF PROLIFERATIVE VITREORETINOPATHY (PVR) / Steinhorst, Ulrich H – 1995 – 2mf – 9 – DM80.00 – 3-8267-2239-6 – gw Hänsel [615]
PHARMACOLOGIST – v1- 1959- 1; v14- 5,6; v18- 9 – us UMI [073]
PHARMACOLOGY – v. 1-12. 1968-74 – 1,5,6 – us UMI [615]
PHARMACOLOGY – v13-. 1975- – 1,5,9 – us UMI [615]
PHARMACOLOGY AND THERAPEUTICS – v1-1976- – 5,6,9 – us UMI [615]
PHARMACOLOGY, BIOCHEMISTRY AND BEHAVIOR – v1- 1973- – 5,6,9 – us UMI [540]
PHARMACOLOGY COMMUNICATIONS / ed by Bowery, Norman G & Ruffolo, Robert R Jr – 9,5,1 – us Harwood [615]
PHARMACO-MEDICA DISSERTATIO DE VIPERIIS TROCHISCIS / Alos, J – Barcelona, 1664 – 1mf – 9 – sp Cultura [615]
PHARMACOPEIA / American Institution of Hemoeopathy – Boston: Otis Clap & Sons, 1897. 622p. includes indexes – 1 – us U.W. Library [615]
PHARMACOPOEA NANNETENSIS, SEU SERIES MEDICAMENTORUM... – Nantes: Vve Doriou, 1677 – 1 – F69.26 – fr Armell [615]
PHARMACOPOEIA : BRITISH PHARMACOPOEIA...PERSUANT TO THE MEDICAL ACT 1858 – London, 1864 – 9mf – ne IDC [615]
PHARMACOPOEIA / Royal College of Physicians – M 399. 1668 – 9 – ne IDC [610]
PHARMACOPOEIA LONDINENSIS... / Culpeper, N – London, 1654 – 8mf – ne IDC [615]
PHARMACOPOEIA LONDINENSIS... / Culpeper, N – London, 1659 – 7mf – ne IDC [615]
PHARMACOPOEIA LONDINENSIS... / Culpeper, N – London, 1661 – 6mf – 9 – ne IDC [615]
PHARMACOPOEIA LONDINENSIS... / Culpeper, N – London, 1695 – 7mf – 9 – ne IDC [615]
PHARMACOPSYCHIATRIA – v14-. 1981- – 1,5,6,9 – us UMI [615]
PHARMACOTHERAPY – v.1-. 1981- – 1,5,6,9 – us UMI [615]
PHARMACY INTERNATIONAL – v. 4-5. 1950-51 – 1 – us UMI [615]
PHARMACY INTERNATIONAL – v1-5. 1980-84 – 1,5,6,13 – sz Elsevier [073]
PHARMACY MANAGEMENT *see*
– AMERICAN JOURNAL OF PHARMACY AND THE SCIENCES SUPPORTING PUBLIC HEALTH
PHARMACY PRACTICE – THE CHALLENGE OF ETHICS : A SYMPOSIUM / Buerki, Robert A – Madison, WI.: American Institute of Pharmacy Practice, 1985 – 1mf – 9 – $1.50 – LLMC 91-052 – us L.L.M.C. [170]
PHARMACY TIMES – (v.45-. 1979- 5,6,9) – v.35- 1969-. Continues: American Professional Pharmacist – 1 – us UMI [073]
PHARMAKO-BASANOS / Floyer, J – M 348. 2 v. 1687-1691 – 9 – ne IDC [615]
Pharmakologisches Institut zu Dorpat *see* ARBEITEN
PHARMAKOPSYCHIATRIE NEUROPSYCHOPHARMAKOLOGIE – (v. 9-13. 1976-81. 5,6,9) – v. 1-13. 1968-81 – 1 – us UMI [073]
DIE PHARMAZIE – v1-39. 1946-84 – 1,5,6 – us Princeton Micro [073]
O PHAROL – Curitiba, 23 May-Jun 1898; 25 Sep 1899 – 1,5,6 – bl Biblioteca [072]
O PHAROL – Estancia, Brazil. 22 Jun 1879; Mar-Nov 1880; Apr-Aug 1881; 16 Apr 1882 – 1 – bl Biblioteca [072]
O PHAROL – S. Thomaz de Aquino, 29 Oct 1921 – 1,5,6 – bl Biblioteca [072]
PHAROL – Juiz de Fora, 9 Apr 1870; 10 Feb-Mar, Jun, Oct 1876; Apr 1877-Dec 1878; Jan, May-Jun, Aug-Dec 1879; Feb 1880; Jan-May 1881; Jan 1882-Dec 1885; Jan-Sep, Nov-Dec 1886; Jan-Nov 1887; Jan-Dec 1888; Oct-Dec 1889; Jan-Dec 1890; Jan-Feb, Jul, Dec 1901; Jan 1902-Dec 1904; Apr, Jun, Nov 1912; 7 Oct 1925 – 1,5,6 – bl Biblioteca [072]
PHAROL : PERIODICO LITTERARIO E NOTICIOSO – Maceio, Alagoas. 5 Ago 1888 – 1,5,6 – bl Biblioteca [072]
PHAROS – Logansport. Ind. -d. 1881-1913 – 1 – us UMI [071]
PHAROS – Logansport. Ind. -w. 1913 – 1 – us UMI [071]
PHAROS – Mead, NE. -w. Dec 1896-Oct 1897 – 1 – us NE Hist [071]
PHAROS TRIBUNE AND PRESS – Logansport. Ind. 1920-1939; 1947- – 1 – us UMI [071]
PHAROS-REPORTER – Logansport. Ind. 1913-1919; 1920-1939; 1947-1966 – 1 – us UMI [071]
PHASE TRANSITIONS / ed by Glazer, A M et al – 1,5,9 – us Gordon [530]
PHASES ET CAUSES... / Cussy, F de Cornot – Leipzig, 1856 – 12mf – 1 – ILM-153/1 – ne IDC [327]
PHASES OF FAITH : OR, PASSAGES FROM THE HISTORY OF MY CREED / Newman, Francis William – London: J. Chapman, 1850 – 1 roll – 1 – 1-55879-806-4 – uk Libr Preservation [240]
Phayre, A P *see* HISTORY OF BURMA INCLUDING BURMA PROPER, PEGU, TAUNGU, TENASSERIM, AND ARAKAN
Phelan, Anna Augusta *see* THE SOCIAL PHILOSOPHY OF WILLIAM MORRIS
Phelippes – Beaulieux, Emmanuel *see* RECUEIL FACTICE DE 31 OEUVRES ECRITES OU TRADUITES PAR E. PHELIPPES-BEAULIEUX, TRAITANT SURTOUT D'AGRONOMIEET D'HISTOIRE LOCALE
Phelps *see* THE HISTORY OF ADAMS COUNTY, ILLINOIS
Phelps, Austin *see*
– MEN AND BOOKS
– MY NOTEBOOK
– MY PORTFOLIO
– MY STUDY
– THE NEW BIRTH
– SABBATH HOURS
– STUDIES OF THE OLD TESTAMENT
Phelps, E S *see* A WOMAN'S PULPIT
Phelps, John Wolcott *see* THE ISLAND OF MADAGASCAR
Phelps, W W *see* CHRONOLOGY OF AMERICAN CASE LAW COVERING ALL REPORTED CASES, STATE AND FEDERAL, FROM THE EARLIEST PERIOD TO 1897
Phelps, Winthrop M *see* THE DIAGNOSIS AND TREATMENT OF POSTURAL DEFECTS
PHELPS-STOKES FELLOWSHIP FUND : FELLOWSHIP STUDIES / Georgia. University – 1 – $80.00 – us UPA [976]
PHELPS-STOKES FELLOWSHIP FUND : PUBLICATIONS / Virginia. University. Phelps-Stokes Fellowship Fund – Nos. 1-20 (all publ). 1915-50 – 2r – 1 – $120.00 – us UPA [976]
A PHENIX : ORGAM CRITICO E LITTERARIO – Curitiba, 10 Aug-15 Nov 1907 – 1,5,6 – bl Biblioteca [072]
LE PHENIX – St-Fulgence (Lac St-Jean), Canada. v1 n2. 14 jul 1973 – 1r – 1 – Can$25.00 – cn Can Microfilming [072]
PHENOMENOLOGIE ET PHILOSOPHIE RELIGIEUSE / Hering, J – Paris, 1926 – 3mf – 8 – ne Slangenburg [290]
PHI DELTA KAPPAN – v1- 1915- 1; v50- 5,6; v57- 9 – us UMI [073]
Phi Delta Phi *see*
– BRIEF
– DIRECTORY
PHI KAPPA PHI JOURNAL – (See also: National Forum) – v1 58 1915-78 1; v56-58 5,6,9 – us UMI [370]
PHILABAPTIST – Philadelphia. Baptist Union of Philadelphia and Vicinity. 1947, 1950-66 – 1 – 43.10 – us A.B.H.S. [073]
PHILADELPHIA ALBUM AND LADIES' LITERARY PORTFOLIO – v. 1-8. Jun 1826-Dec 1834 – 1 – us UMI [410]
PHILADELPHIA BAPTIST CHURCH. CHOCTAW NATION INDIAN TERRITORY. BLUE COUNTY. OKLAHOMA : CHURCH RECORDS – Jul 1846-Jun 1954 – 1 – 8.01 – us Baptist [240]
PHILADELPHIA BAPTIST CHURCH. DEVILLE, LOUISIANA : CHURCH RECORDS – May 1918-Sept 1981 – 1 – 49.77 – us Baptist [240]
PHILADELPHIA BAPTIST CHURCH. PAULINE, SOUTH CAROLINA : CHURCH RECORDS – 1803-Oct 1966 – 1 – 80.19 – us Baptist [240]
PHILADELPHIA BAPTIST CHURCH. TAR RIVER ASSOCIATION. NORTH CAROLINA : CHURCH RECORDS – 1871-88 – 1 – 5.00 – us Baptist [240]
Philadelphia. Bar *see* IN MEMORIAM. CONSTANT GUILLOU
Philadelphia Bar Association *see* REPORT OF THE COMMITTEE APPOINTED BY THE LAW ASSOCIATION OF PHILADELPHIA TO CONSIDER THE ADVISABILITY OF ASKING FOR LEGISLATION FOR THE ORGANIZATION OF ONE COURT OF COMMON PLEAS IN LIEU OF THE FOUR COURTS NOW EXISTING IN THE COUNTY OF PHILADELPHIA
Philadelphia Central. Presbytery (Pres. Ch. in the U.S.A.) *see* MINUTES, 1860-1891
PHILADELPHIA FIRST BAPTIST CHURCH. PHILADELPHIA, PENNSYLVANIA : CHURCH RECORDS – 1724-1900. List of items sent on request – 1 – 369.54 – us Baptist [240]
Philadelphia Fourth. Presbytery (Pres. Ch. in the U.S.A. New School) *see* MINUTES, 1845-1870
PHILADELPHIA GAZETTE DEMOCRAT – Philadelphia, PA. 3 May 1975-1984 – 4r – 1 – gw Mikrofilm [071]
PHILADELPHIA GAZETTE-DEMOCRAT – (In German and English) – Philadelphia, PA. 1927-62 – 157r – 1 – $13,345.00 – D3377 – us Scholarly Res [071]
PHILADELPHIA HEROLD – (In German) – Philadelphia, PA. 1928-42 – 11r – 1 – $935.00 – D3378 – us Scholarly Res [071]
THE PHILADELPHIA INDEPENDANT – Philadelphia. Pa. mar. 21, 1937; Dec. 15, 1940; Feb. 20, 1944 – 1 – us NY Public [071]
THE PHILADELPHIA INQUIRER – Philadelphia, PA., 1945 – 13 – $25.00r – us I.M.R. [071]
THE PHILADELPHIA JEWISH AMERICAN – Philadelphia. Pa. 1908-10 – 1 – us A.J.P.C. [071]
PHILADELPHIA JEWISH EVENING POST – Philadelphia. Pa. 1905 – 1 – us A.J.P.C. [071]
PHILADELPHIA JEWISH MORNING NEWS – Philadelphia. Pa. 1907 – 1 – us A.J.P.C. [071]
PHILADELPHIA JEWISH PRESS – Philadelphia. Pa. 1904 – 1 – us A.J.P.C. [071]
PHILADELPHIA JEWISH TIMES – Philadelphia. Pa. 1965-67 – 1 – us A.J.P.C. [071]
PHILADELPHIA JOURNAL OF THE MEDICAL AND PHYSICAL SCIENCES – v. 1-14. 1820-1827 – 1 – us UMI [610]
PHILADELPHIA JOURNAL OF THE MEDICAL AND PHYSICAL SCIENCES *see* AMERICAN JOURNAL OF THE MEDICAL SCIENCES
PHILADELPHIA LAWYER – (Title varies: v1-54 1938-91 as Shingle: Philadelphia Bar Association) – v1-57. 1938-94 – 9 – $295.00 set – us Hein [340]
A PHILADELPHIA LAWYER IN THE LONDON COURTS / Leaming, Thomas – (A treatise aimed at Americans on the British bench, bar and legal institutions) – New York: Henry Holt & Co, 1911 – 3mf – 9 – $4.50 – LLMC 92-104 – us L.L.M.C. [340]
PHILADELPHIA MAGAZINE – v1- 1909- 1; v64-5,6; v67- 9 – us UMI [073]
PHILADELPHIA MAGAZINE AND REVIEW; OR, MONTHLY REPOSITORY OF INFORMATION AND AMUSEMENT – v. 1. Jan-Jun 1799 – 1 – us UMI [073]
PHILADELPHIA MAGAZINE, AND WEEKLY REPERTORY – v. 1. Jan- Nov 1818 – 1 – us UMI [073]
PHILADELPHIA MEDICAL AND PHYSICAL JOURNAL – 1-3. 1804-09 – 1 – us UMI [610]
PHILADELPHIA MEDICAL MUSEUM – 1-n.s. 1. 1804-11 – 1 – us UMI [610]
PHILADELPHIA MINERVA – Containing a variety of fugitive pieces in prose and poetry, original and selected. v. 1-4. Feb 1795-Jul 1798 – 1 – us UMI [410]

PHILADELPHIA MONTHLY MAGAZINE *see* PHILADELPHIA MONTHLY MAGAZINE DEVOTED TO LITERATURE AND FINE ARTS

PHILADELPHIA MONTHLY MAGAZINE DEVOTED TO LITERATURE AND FINE ARTS – 1-ns: 1 Oct 1827-29 – 1 – us UMI [073]

Philadelphia Museum of ArtThe Henry Francis du Pont Winterthur Museum *see* PENNSYLVANIA GERMAN ART, 1683-1850

PHILADELPHIA MUSEUM, OR REGISTER OF NATURAL HISTORY AND THE ARTS – v. 1. Jan 1824 – 1 – us UMI [574]

THE PHILADELPHIA NEGRO : A SOCIAL STUDY / DuBois, WE B – (Together with a Special Report on Domestic Service by Isabel Eaton) – Philadelphia: Published for the University; Boston: Ginn [distributor], 1899 – 2mf – us A.T.L.A. [305]

Philadelphia North. Presbytery (Pres. Ch. in the U.S.A.) *see* MINUTES, 1870-1907

Philadelphia, PA *see*
- THE PENNSYLVANIA CHRONICLE, 1767-1774
- THE PENNSYLVANIA GAZETTE, 1728-1815
- THE PENNSYLVANIA JOURNAL, 1742-1793
- THE PENNSYLVANIA PACKET, 1771-1790
- THE PHILADELPHIA PRICE CURRENT, 1827-1850

Philadelphia, Pennsylvania *see*
- FEDERAL GAZETTE, 1788-1802
- THE MECHANIC'S FREE PRESS, 1829-1831
- MISCELLANEOUS NEWSPAPERS

Philadelphia, Pennsylvania. Lower Dublin/ Pennepek Baptist Church *see* RECORDS

Philadelphia. Pennsylvania. Old Christ Church *see* ARCHIVES

Philadelphia, Pennsylvania. Sansom Street Baptist Church *see* RECORDS

Philadelphia. Pennsylvania. Second Presbyterian Church Corporation *see* MINUTES

THE PHILADELPHIA PHOTOGRAPHER – 1864-88. 25v. 10 reels – 1 – $760.00 – us UPA [700]

THE PHILADELPHIA POLICE, PAST AND PRESENT / Sprogle, Howard O – Philadelphia, 1887. Pennsylvania Reel 36. (The Cox Library Collection) – 5 – us Americana [978]

Philadelphia. Presbytery (Assoc. Ch.) *see* MINUTES, 1801-1861

Philadelphia. Presbytery (Assoc. Ref. Ch.) *see* MINUTES, 1845-1861

Philadelphia. Presbytery (Pres. Ch. in the U.S.A.) *see* MINUTES

Philadelphia. Presbytery (United Pres. Ch. of No. Am.) *see* MINUTES, 1859-1922

THE PHILADELPHIA PRICE CURRENT, 1827-1850 / Philadelphia, PA – 1972 – 9r – 1 – $765.00 – S1722 – us Scholarly Res [978]

PHILADELPHIA PRISM – Philadelphia, Pennsylvania, v1, no. 1 (Apr. 1983); v5, no. 1 (Mar./Apr. 1985); v6, no. 2 (Feb./Mar. 1986); v7, no. 2 (Mar. 1987) – us A.J.P.C. [073]

Philadelphia. Recorder *see* REPORTS OF SOME OF THE CRIMINAL CASES ON PRIMARY HEARING, BEFORE RICHARD VAUX

PHILADELPHIA REPERTORY – v. 1-2. May 1810-May 1812 – 1 – us UMI [073]

Philadelphia Second. Presbytery (Pres. Ch. in the U.S.A. New School) *see* MINUTES, 1883-1870

PHILADELPHIA STADTZEITUNG – Philadelphia. Pa. 1895 – 1 – us A.J.P.C. [071]

Philadelphia Sunday and Adult School Union *see* ANNUAL REPORTS, 1818-1824

PHILADELPHIA TAGEBLATT – (In German) – Philadelphia, PA. 1877-1909; 1911; 1917; 1919-26; 1928-29; 1941 – 109r – 1 – $9,265.00 – D3380 – us Scholarly Res [071]

Philadelphia Third. Presbytery (Pres. Ch. in the U.S.A. New School) *see* MINUTES, 1836-1870

PHILADELPHIA UNIVERSALIST MAGAZINE AND CHRISTIAN MESSENGER, DEVOTED TO DOCTRINE, RELIGION, AND MORALITY – v. 1-10. Aug 1821-Jul 1823 – 1 – us UMI [240]

PHILADELPHIA WEST SCENE – Ardmore. Pa. 1965- – 1 – us UMI [071]

PHILADELPHIA-I FUGGETLENSEIG = INDEPENDENCE – (In Hungarian) – Philadelphia, PA. 1928-1954 – 13r – 1 – $1,105.00 – D3376 – us Scholarly Res [071]

THE PHILADELPHIAN – Philadelphia, PA. -w 1829-1836 – 13 – $25.00r – us I.M.R. [071]

PHILADELPHISCHES MAGAZIN ODER UNTERHALTENDER GESELLSCHAFTER FUER DIE DEUTSCHEN IN AMERIKA – v. 1. May 1798 – 1 – us UMI [073]

Philalethes, Eirenaeus, pseud *see* RIPLEY REVIV'D: OR, AN EXPOSITION UPON SIR GEORGE RIPLEY'S HERMETICO-POETICAL WORKS

Philalethes (Pseud. of R. Fellowes) *see* THE HISTORY OF CEYLON FROM THE EARLIEST PERIOD TO THE YEAR 1815

PHILALETHIE / Basedow, Johann Bernhard – Altona, 1764 – 1 – DM80.00 – gw Mikro Press [190]

Philalethus, Eirenaeus *see* SECRETS REVEAL'D: OR, AN OPEN ENTRANCE TO THE SHUT-PALACE OF THE KING; CONTAINING THE GREATEST TREASURE IN CHYMISTRY..

PHILANDER VON SITTEWALD / Scholtze, Christian Achmed – (Includes bibliographical references) – [S.l.: s.n.], 1877 – 1r – 1 – us U.W. Library [430]

PHILANTHROPIC GAZETTE – London, UK. 1817-Aug 1823. -w.3 reels – 1 – uk British Libr Newspaper [072]

PHILANTHROPIST – 1-7 (all publ). 1811-1819 – 32mf – 9 – $100.00 – us UPA [360]

PHILANTHROPIST – Cincinnati. Ohio. 1841-1843 – 1 – us UMI [071]

PHILANTHROPIST – v. 7, 13-16. Oct 1817-Dec 1817 – 1 – us UMI [073]

THE PHILANTHROPIST – (New York). 1889-91 – 1 – us A.J.P.C. [360]

PHILANTHROPIST, A WEEKLY JOURNAL CONTAINING ESSAYS, ON MORAL AND RELIGIOUS SUBJECTS – v. 1-7. Dec 1818-Apr 1822 – 1 – us UMI [073]

PHILANTHROPIST (NEW RICHMOND, OHIO) *see* CINCINNATI WEEKLY HERALD AND PHILANTHROPIST

PHILANTHROPY IN MISSIONS : ECUMENICAL MISSIONARY CONFERENCE STUDIES 1-5 – New York: Foreign Missions Library, 1901 – 1mf – 9 – 0-8370-7380-4 – 1986-1380 – us A.T.L.A. [240]

PHILANTROPISCHES ARCHIV – Erstes, zweites und drittes stuck. Dessau 1776 – 1 – DM70.00 – gw Mikro Press [025]

Philaret, Metropolitan of Mosow *see* SELECT SERMONS

PHILATELIC ADVOCATE *see*
- THE PHILATELIC MESSENGER
- THE STAMP REPORTER

THE PHILATELIC ADVOCATE *see* THE ONTARIO PHILATELIST

THE PHILATELIC AND ADVOCATE – (Is absorbed by: Canada Stamp Sheet and Energy. Absorbed: The Ontario Philatelist. Absorbed: The Stamp Reporter. Absorbed: The Jubilee Philatelist and Mount Royal Stamp News. Absorbed in part: The Philatelic Messenger) – Berlin [Kitchener], Ont.: Starnaman Bros, [1896-1901] – 9 – cn C.I.H.M. [870]

THE PHILATELIC CANADIAN – Toronto: W McMahon, [1896-1897] – 9 – cn C.I.H.M. [760]

THE PHILATELIC COURIER AND STAMP-COLLECTOR'S JOURNAL – Halifax, NS: H Hechler, [1881-1889] – 9 – cn C.I.H.M. [760]

THE PHILATELIC FRAUD REPORTER *see* THE INTERNATIONAL PHILATELIST

THE PHILATELIC JOURNAL OF CANADA – London, Ont.: Philatelic Journal of Canada Pub Co, [1892-1893] – 9 – cn C.I.H.M. [760]

PHILATELIC MESSENGER *see* THE PHILATELIC MESSENGER AND MONTHLY ADVERTISER

THE PHILATELIC MESSENGER – (Cont in part by: The Philatelic Messenger and Monthly Advertiser. Is absorbed in part by: The Philatelic Advocate) – Oak Hill, NB: M R Knight, [1896-1899] – 9 – cn C.I.H.M. [760]

THE PHILATELIC MESSENGER *see* THE PHILATELIC AND ADVOCATE

PHILATELIC MESSENGER AND MONTHLY ADVERTISER *see* THE PHILATELIC MESSENGER

THE PHILATELIC MESSENGER AND MONTHLY ADVERTISER – (Cont in part: The Philatelic Messenger) – Boiestown, NB: M R Knight, [1899-1902] – 9 – cn C.I.H.M. [760]

PHILATELIC RECORD *see* THE PHILATELIC SPECTATOR

THE PHILATELIC RECORD – (Cont: The Philatelic Spectator) – Montreal: A R Magill, [1901] – 9 – cn C.I.H.M. [760]

PHILATELIC SPECTATOR *see* THE PHILATELIC RECORD

THE PHILATELIC SPECTATOR – (Cont by: The Philatelic Record) – Berlin [Kitchener], Ont.: G E Mueller, [1899-1900] – 9 – cn C.I.H.M. [760]

PHILATELIC TRADER – 1889-1977 1; 1974-77 5,6; 1975-77 4 x 6 in. 9 – us UMI [760]

PHILATELIST – 1866- 1; 1975- 5,6,9 – us UMI [760]

PHILATELIST AND P J G B – v1-. 1981- – 1,5,6,9 – us UMI [760]

PHILATELY : THE CATALOG OF THE COLLECTORS CLUB LIBRARY / Collectors Club Library. New York – 1974.-21,800 cards 1 reel – 1r – 1 – $120.00 export $145.00 – 0-8161-1538-9 – uk Hall [760]

Phile, Philip *see* PRESIDENT'S MARCH

Philelphus, Franciscus *see* SATYRARUM HECATOSTICHON

Philematheon Club, Leavenworth, KS *see* RECORDS

Philidor, F A *see* AIRS DETACHES DE MELIDE, OU LE NAVIGATEUR

LE PHILINTE DE MOLIERE OU LA SUITE DU "MISANTHROPE."(FRENCH THEATRE SERIES). PARIS. PRAULT. 1791 / Fabre, Philippe d'Eglantine – 9 – fr Hachette [820]

A PHILIOSOPHICAL ACCOUNT OF NATURE IN GENERAL, AND OF THE GENERATION OF THE THREE PRINCIPLES OF NATURE, VIZ. MERCURY, SULPHUR, AND SALT, OUT OF THE FOUR ELEMENTS / Sendivogius, Michael – Translated from the French by John Digby. London, 1722 – 1 – us U.W. Library [530]

PHILIP DODDRIDGE, D.D. / Stanford, Charles – New York: A.C. Armstrong, 1881 – 1mf – us A.T.L.A. [240]

PHILIP FRENEAU, THE HUGUENOT PATRIOT-POET OF THE REVOLUTION AND HIS POETRY / De Lancey, Edward Floyd – New York?: s.n., 1891 (New York: J. Little). 04220. (Pre-1900 Canadiana) – 9 – cn C.I.H.M. [971]

Philip, Kaete *see* JULIANUS APOSTATA IN DER DEUTSCHEN LITERATUR

PHILIP LINHART FAMILY HISTORY / Linhart Family – 1812-1928 – 1r – 1 – $32.50r – us Archival [920]

PHILIP MELANCHTON : THE PROTESTANT PRECEPTOR OF GERMANY, 1497-1560 / Richard, James William – New York: G.P. Putnam, 1907, c1898 – 2mf – us A.T.L.A. [240]

Philip, Robert *see*
- THE MARTHAS; OR, THE VARIETIES OF FEMALE PIETY
- THE MARYS; OR, THE BEAUTY OF FEMALE HOLINESS

Philipon de La Madelaine, Louis *see* DE L'EDUCATION DES COLLEGES

Philipon de la Madelaine, Louis *see* VUES PATRIOTIQUES SUR L'EDUCATION DU PEUPLE, TANT DES VILLES QUE DES CAMPAGNES

Philipon-de-la-Madelaine *see* DES HOMONYMES FRANCAIS

PHILIPP MELANCHTHON : EIN LEBENSBILD / Ellinger, Georg – Berlin: R. Gaertners, 1902 – 2mf – us A.T.L.A. [240]

PHILIPP MELANCHTHON, DEUTSCHLANDS LEHRER : EIN BEITRAG ZUR FEIER DES 16. FEBRUAR 1897 / Cohrs, Ferdinand – Halle: Verein fuer Reformationsgeschichte, 14. Jahrg., Schrift 55 – 1mf – us A.T.L.A. [240]

PHILIPP MELANCHTHON UND DIE DEUTSCHE REFORMATION BIS 1531 / Sell, Karl – Halle: Verein fuer Reformationsgeschichte, 1897 (Schriften des Vereins fuer Reformationsgeschichte; 14. Jahrg., Schrift 56) – 1mf – us A.T.L.A. [240]

Philipp, Richard *see* BEITRAEGE ZUR KENNTNIS VON KLINGERS SPRACHE UND STIL IN SEINEN JUGEND-DRAMEN

PHILIPP VON ZESEN : EIN BEITRAG ZUR GESCHICHTE DER SPRACHREINIGUNG IM DEUTSCHEN / Prahl, Karl – (Includes bibliographical references) – [S.l: s.n.] 1890, (Danzig: Druck von E Groening) – 1r – 1 – us U.W. Library [430]

PHILIPP VON ZESEN ALS SPRACHREINIGER / Harbrecht, Hugo – (Includes bibliographical references) – Karlsruhe in Baden: M Gillardon, 1912 – 1r – 1 – us U.W. Library [430]

PHILIPP VON ZESEN ALS SPRACHREINIGER / Harbrecht, Hugo – (Includes bibliographical references) – Karlsruhe: M Gillardon, 1912 – 1 – us U.W. Library [430]

PHILIPP VON ZESEN UND DIE DEUTSCHGESINNTE GENOSSENSCHAFT / Dissel, Karl – (Includes bibliographical references) – Hamburg: Luetcke & Wulff, 1890 – 1r – 1 – us U.W. Library [430]

Philippart, Leon *see* LE BAS-CONGO, ETAT RELIGIEUX ET SOCIAL

PHILIPPE AUBERT DE GASPE / Casgrain, Henri-Raymond – Quebec: L. Brousseau, 1871. 00648. (Pre-1900 Canadiana) – 9 – cn C.I.H.M. [920]

Philippe, B *see* LES ARCHIVES ISRAELITES DE FRANCE DE LEUR CREATION EN 1840 A FEVRIER 1848 OU UN JOURNAL JUIF SOUS LOUIS-PHILIPPE. ETUDE DE MENTALITES

Philippe, J M *see* REPORT TO THE GOVERNMENT OF THE FEDERATION OF SOUTH ARABIA ON EXISTING AND POTENTIAL BANANA PRODUCTION

Philippe, Obbe *see* RECOGNOISSANCE PAR LAQUELLE IL CONFESSE QUE LUY ET CEUX QUI ONT ENSEIGNE ET ENSEIGNENT LES ANABAPTISTES. AVEC UN DISCOURS DES FAICTS EXERABLES DU NOUVEAU ROY DES ANABAPTISTES JAN WILHEMS ET DE SES COMPLICES

DER PHILIPPER-BRIEF AUSGELEGT UND DIE GESCHICHTE SEINER AUSLEGUNG / Weiss, Bernhard – (Includes bibliographical references) – Berlin: Wilhelm Hertz, 1859 – 1mf – 9 – 0-8370-9668-5 – 1986-3668 – us A.T.L.A. [220]

PHILIPPI BAPTIST CHURCH. EDGEFIELD COUNTY. SOUTH CAROLINA : CHURCH RECORDS – 1814-1917 – 1 – 21.24 – us Baptist [240]

Philippi, E *see* SCHILLERS LYRISCHE GEDANKENDICHTUNG IN IHREM IDEELLEN ZUSAMMENHANGE BELEUCHTET

Philippi, Ferdinand *see* DIE NOTWENDIGKEIT UND VERBINDLICHKEIT DES KIRCHLICHEN BEKENNTNISSES

Philippi, Friedrich Adolph *see*
- DER EINGANG DES JOHANNESEVANGELIUMS (KAPITEL 1, 6-18)
- ERKLAERUNG DES BRIEFES PAULI AN DIE GALATER

Philippi, Friedrich Wilhelm Martin *see* WESEN UND URSPRUNG DER STATUS CONSTRUCTUS IM HEBRAEISCHEN

Philippi, R A *see*
- ENUMERATIO MOLLUSCORUM SICILIAE
- HANDBUCH DER CONCHYLIOLOGIE UND MALACOZOOLOGIE
- REISE DURCH DIE WUESTE ATACAMA
- VERZEICHNISS DER VON FRIEDRICH PHILIPPI AUF DER HOCHEBENE DER PROVINZEN ANTOFAGASTA UND TARAPACA. PFLANZEN

PHILIPPINE AGRICULTURAL AND INDUSTRIAL DEVELOPMENT PROGRAM / Philippines. Economic Survey Commission – Rev. Manila. 1950. BD-429 1 – 9 – ne IDC [338]

THE PHILIPPINE CLAIM TO SABAH / Leifer, M – (also available in book-form: 063-932-0) – 256 1. 1968 – 9 – 3.50 – ne IDC [950]

PHILIPPINE DAILY INQUIRER – (Yrly reel count varies) – 1985- – 1 – us Ross [072]

PHILIPPINE EDUCATION INDICATORS 1965-1985 / Philippines. Ministry of Education, Culture and Sports – Manila, 1986 – 1mf – 9 – DE-637/1 – ne IDC [370]

PHILIPPINE ETHNOGRAPHIC SERIES : BISAYAN ETHNOGRAPHY / Diosay, Marian Po – (The H. Otley Beyer Manuscript Collection) – 1983 – A$10.00 – 0-86758-135-2 – at BISA [306]

PHILIPPINE ETHNOGRAPHIC SERIES : TAGALOG ETHNOGRAPHY / Alas, Leonila E de las – (The H. Otley Beyer manuscript collection) – 1985 – A$10.00 – 0-86758-184-0 – at BISA [306]

PHILIPPINE EXAMINER – Stockton, CA. 1943-48 – 1r – 1 – $50.00 – C03015 – us Library Micro [071]

PHILIPPINE EXAMINER – Stockton. CA. -w. 1943-48 – 1 – us UMI [071]

PHILIPPINE GEOGRAPHICAL JOURNAL – v1-1953- 1; v20- 5,6,9 – us UMI [910]

PHILIPPINE INSURGENT RECORDS, 1896-1901, WITH ASSOCIATED RECORDS OF THE U.S. WAR DEPARTMENT, 1900-06 / Philippines – 643 r – 1 – M254. Printed Guide – us Nat'l Archives [324]

PHILIPPINE JOURNAL FOR LANGUAGE TEACHING – v1- 1961- 1; 1975- 5,6,9 – us UMI [370]

PHILIPPINE JOURNAL OF COMMERCE – Manila. v1, 1925-v10, 1934. -m. Title varies – 1 – us U.W. Library [073]
PHILIPPINE JOURNAL OF OPHTHALMOLOGY – v1- 1969- 1; v4- 5,6; v7- 9 – us UMI [617]
PHILIPPINE JOURNAL OF PUBLIC ADMINISTRATION – v1- 1957- 1; v17- 5,6; v20- 9 – us UMI [073]
PHILIPPINE JOURNAL OF SCIENCE – v.7-78. 1912-1949 – 1,5,6 – us Princeton Micro [500]
(PHILIPPINE LABOR PUBLICATIONS) – Collected and filmed by Univ. of Wisconsin, Madison Libraries. 1985- – 1 – us U.W. Library [331]
PHILIPPINE LAW JOURNAL – (v1-59 1914-85 on reel $600.00. v60-65 1985-90 on mf $122.00. Suspended 1920-26, 1942-46) – v1-65. 1914-90 – 5,9,6 – $722.00 set – us Hein [340]
PHILIPPINE LIBERATION THEOLOGY : AN INDEX TO SELECTED MATERIALS / Fabito, Cornelia D – 1987 – 9 – A$10.00 – 0-86758-235-9 – at BISA [240]
THE PHILIPPINE OBSERVER – (Some issues lacking) – v1-31 no 4. Jun 1911-May 1934 – 6r – 1 – ATLA S0277 – us A.T.L.A. [073]
PHILIPPINE OPPOSITION LITERATURE – Oct-Nov 1983. Includes Veritas, no.1-2; selection of tabloids publ. during Oct-Nov 1983 including Mr. and Ms. special suppls. 1 unnumbered, 1-12; Malaya, v2, no.36,39,42, 44-60,62. A collection of broadsides distributed in Manila on 27 Nov 1983 – 1 – us U.W. Library [080]
PHILIPPINE PROSE AND POETRY – Rev. ed.Manila: Bureau of Printing, 1963. ix,483p. illus. Fourth in a series for use of secondary school students – 1 – us U.W. Library [420]
PHILIPPINE STAR – (Yrly reel count varies) – 1987- – 1 – us Ross [072]
PHILIPPINE SUPREME COURT REPORTS / Philippines – v1-124. 1901-66 – 1403mf – 9 – $2,104.00 – LLMC 93-900 – us L.L.M.C. [340]
PHILIPPINE TIMES-JOURNAL – (Yrly reel count varies) – 1972- – 1 – us Ross [072]
THE PHILIPPINE YEARBOOK – 1933-34. Running title: Philippines Herald Year Book – 1 – us U.W. Library [950]
Philippines *see*
- BUDGET PLANS
- GUIA OFICIAL
- GUIA OFICIAL DE FILIPINAS
- OFFICIAL GAZETTE
- PHILIPPINE INSURGENT RECORDS, 1896-1901, WITH ASSOCIATED RECORDS OF THE U.S. WAR DEPARTMENT, 1900-06
- PHILIPPINE SUPREME COURT REPORTS
- THREE-YEAR PRODUCTION PROGRAM(FY 1957-1959). LOCSIN, SENATOR JOSE C. IN: NATIONAL ECONOMIC COUNCIL

THE PHILIPPINES : U.S. POLICY DURING THE MARCOS YEARS, 1965-1986 – (With 2-vol printed guide & index £630.00) – 652mf – 9 – £2,940.00 – uk Chadwyck [327]
PHILIPPINES AGRICULTURAL LAND TENURE STUDY / U.S. Operations Mission to the Philippines – Manila: U.S. Operations Mission, 1954. iv,52 leaves. Bibliographic footnotes – 1 – us U.W. Library [630]
Philippines. Budget Commission *see*
- BUDGET FOR THE FISCAL YEAR 1960
- THE FIVE-YEAR FISCAL PLAN, 1961-1965

Philippines. Bureau of Civil Service *see* OFFICIAL ROSTER OF OFFICERS AND EMPLOYEES..
Philippines. Bureau of Commerce *see* STATISTICAL BULLETIN OF THE PHILIPPINE ISLANDS
Philippines. Census Office *see* CENSUS OF THE PHILIPPINE ISLANDS. 1918
Philippines. (Commonwealth). Commission of the Census *see* CENSUS OF THE PHILIPPINES, 1939
Philippines. Congress. House of Representatives *see* CONGRESSIONAL RECORD
Philippines. Congress. Senate *see* CONGRESSIONAL RECORD
Philippines. Department of Agriculture and Commerce *see* STATISTICAL HANDBOOK..
Philippines. Department of Finance and Justice. Bureau of Customs *see* FOREIGN COMMERCE..
Philippines. Economic Survey Commission *see* PHILIPPINE AGRICULTURAL AND INDUSTRIAL DEVELOPMENT PROGRAM
PHILIPPINES. HISTORICAL DOCUMENTS AND MANUSCRIPTS *see* HISTORICAL DOCUMENTS AND MANUSCRIPTS
Philippines. Legislature *see* DIRECTORIO OFICIAL DE SENADO Y DE LA CAMARA DE REPRESENTATES
Philippines. Mindano Development Authority *see* A FIVE YEAR ECONOMIC DEVELOPMENT PROGRAM FOR THE MINDANO REGION FY 70-71 TO FY 74-75
Philippines. Ministry of Education, Culture and Sports *see* PHILIPPINE EDUCATION INDICATORS 1965-1985
Philippines. National Development Company *see* PROPOSED PROGRAM FOR INDUSTRIAL REHABILITATION AND DEVELOPMENT
Philippines. National Economic and Development Authority *see*
- FOUR-YEAR DEVELOPMENT PLAN FY 1974-1977
- REGIONAL DEVELOPMENT PROJECTS

Philippines. National Economic Council *see*
- FOUR-YEAR DEVELOPMENT PLAN FY 1972-1975
- THREE-YEAR PROGRAM OF ECONOMIC AND SOCIAL DEVELOPMENT (FY 1959-60 TO FY 1961-62)

Philippines. President *see* FIVE-YEAR INTEGRATED SOCIO-ECONOMIC PROGRAM FOR THE PHILIPPINES
PHILIPPINES TODAY – v1,no.1.23 Aug 1983-.Washington: Office of Media Affairs of Government of the Republic of the Philippines, 1983-.-biw – 1 – us U.W. Library [073]
Philippines. U.S. Economic Survey Mission to the Philippines *see* REPORT TO THE PRESIDENT OF THE U.S
Philipps, W B *see* NOTES ON THE SMELTING PROCESSES AT FREIBERG
Philippson, L *see* ISRAELITISCHES PREDIGT- UND SCHULMAGAZIN
Philippson, M *see* FESTSCHRIFT
PHILIPPUS VAN LIMBORCHS VRIENDELIJKE ONDERHANDELING MET EEN GELEERDEN JOOD,. URIELS ACOSTAAS VOORBEELD VAN 'T MENSCHELIJK LEVEN / Limborch, P van – Amsterdam. 1723. BJ-262.53 1 – 9 – ne IDC [900]
PHILIPS COUNTY NEWS – Malta. Mont. 1951-1954; 1956- – 1 – us UMI [071]
Philips, Dirk *see*
- EEN APOLOGIA OFTE VERANTWOORDINGE, DAT WY (DIE VANDER WERELT MET GROOTEN ONRECHT ANABAPTISTEN GHESCHOLDEN WORDEN) GHEEN WEEDERDOOPERS NOCH SECTEMAKERS EN SIJNT
- EEN CORT, DOCH GRONDTLICK VERHAEL VANDEN TWISTIGEN HANDEL ENDE ONSCHRIFTMETIGEN ORDEEL
- EENE CORTE BEKENTENISSE ENDE BELYDINGHE VANDEN EENIGEN, ALMACHTIGEN, LEUENDIGEN GOD, VADER, SOON ENDE HEYLIGE GEST, ENDE VAN DIE SCHEPPINGHE. ENDE TEN LAETSTEN VAN DAT RECHTE GEBRUYCK DES AUONTMAELS ONSES HEEREN
- ENCHIRIDION OFT HANDBOECXKEN VAN DE CHRISTELIJCKE LEERE ENDE RELIGION, IN CORTE SOMMA BEGREPEN
- ENCHIRIDION OFT HANTBOECXKEN VAN DE CHRISTELIJCKE LEERE ENDE RELIGION, IN CORTE SOMMA BEGREPEN
- EEN LIEFLICKE VERMANINGHE WT DES HEEREN WOORT, INDEN WELCKEN
- EEN SCHOONE VERMANINGHE ENDE CORTTE ONDERWYSINGHE VANDER WARACHTIGHER KENNISSEN GODTS
- EEN SEER SCHOON ENDE WAERACHTIGE VERCLARINGE ENDE WTLEGGHINGE DES TABERNAKELS OFT DER HUTTEN MOSI
- EENEN SEER SCHOONEN TROOSTELIJCKEN ENDE CHRISTELIJCKEN SENDTBRIEF
- VAN DE GEESTELIJCKE RESTITUTION, DAT IS, HOE DAT, ALWAT VANDEN BEGHINNE GHESCHIET IS, IN CHRISTO JESU GHEESTELIJCK VERUULT
- VAN DE MENSCHWERDINGHE ONSES HEEREN JESU CHRISTI, DES EENGHEBOOREN SOONS SYNES EEWIGHEN ENDE ALMACHTIGHEN VADERS
- VAN DIE ECHT DER CHRISTENEN, HOE SY VAN GODT BEUOLEN
- VAN DIE GHEMEYNTE GODTS, HOE DIE VANDEN BEGINNE GHEWEEST IS. EEN CORTE BEKENTENISSE
- VAN DIE RECHTE KENNISSE JESU CHRISTI, DES EENIGHEN GHEBOOREN SOONS DES ALMACHTIGEN ENDE LEUENDIGHEN GODS
- VANDE WEDERGEBOORTE ENDE NIEUWE CREATURE EEN CORTE VERMANINGHE ENDE AENWIJSINGHE WT DE HEYLIGHE SCHRIFT
- VANDER DOOPE ONSES HEEREN JESU CHRISTI, BEKENTNISSE DOOR DIERICK PHILIPS
- VANDER SENDINGE DER PREDICANTEN OFT LEERAERS

Philips, Hughes *see* SINTESIS DE HISTORIA DE LA IGLESIA
Philips Oppenheim, E *see* PRODIGALS OF MONTECARLO
PHILIPS RESEARCH REPORTS – v1-17. 1945-62 – 1 – us Princeton Micro [000]
Philips, S J *see* GEDENKBOEK TER GELEGENHEID VAN HET HONDERDJARIG BESTAAN VAN HET NEDERLANDSCH-ISRAELIETISCH ARMBESTUUR, 1825-1925
Philipson, David *see*
- THE REFORM MOVEMENT IN JUDAISM
- SELECTED WRITINGS OF ISAAC M. WISE

Philipsz, Obbe *see* BEKENNTENISSE. WAER MEDE HY VERCLAERT, SIJN PREDICKAMPT SONDER WETTELICKE BEROEPINGHE GEBRUYCKT TE HEBBEN BECLAECHT HEM DIES
PHILISTINE, A PERIODICAL OF PROTEST – 1-41. no.2, 1895-1914 – 1 – 115.00 – us L of C Photodup [073]
PHILISTINE, A PERIODICAL OF PROTEST – v. 1-23, Jun 1895-Nov 1906 – 1 – us UMI [073]
Phillimore, Augustus *see* THE LIFE OF ADMIRAL OF THE FLEET SIR WILLIAM PARKER, BART
Phillimore, William Phillimore Watts *see* CORNWALL PARISH REGISTERS. MARRIAGES
Phillipps, Samuel March *see* A TREATISE ON THE LAW OF EVIDENCE
Phillips, A V *see* SPAIN UNDER FRANCO
PHILLIPS ADVERTISER – Phillips, NE. -bw. Nov 1946-Dec 1966; Feb 1967-Dec 1970; May 1971; Jul 1971-Jun 1972 – 1 – us NE Hist [071]
PHILLIPS BROOKS : A STUDY / Lawrence, William – (Includes bibliographical references) – Boston: Houghton, Mifflin, 1903 – 1mf – 9 – 0-8370-9711-8 – 1986-3711 – us A.T.L.A. [920]
PHILLIPS BROOKS' ADDRESSES / Ward, Julius H – Boston: C.E. Brown, c1893 – 1mf – us A.T.L.A. [240]
Phillips, Charles H *see* THE HISTORY OF THE COLORED METHODIST EPISCOPAL CHURCH IN AMERICA
Phillips Collection *see* A COLLECTION IN THE MAKING
PHILLIPS COUNTY NEWS – Helena. Mont. 1951-1954; 1956-1957 – 1 – us UMI [071]
Phillips, D *see* CHEMISTRY REVIEWS
Phillips, Edward *see*
- THE MYSTERIES OF LOVE AND ELOQUENCE
- THE NEW WORLD OF ENGLISH WORDS

Phillips, George *see* DIE DIOECESANSYNODE
Phillips, George Lemon *see*
- AN EXPOSITION OF THE PRINCIPLES OF CODE PLEADING
- AN EXPOSITION OF THE PRINCIPLES OF PLEADING UNDER THE CODES OF CIVIL PROCEDURE

Phillips, J *see* A MONOGRAPH OF BRITISH BELEMNITIDAE
Phillips, LF March *see* LECTURES ON THE...EVIDENCES OF DIVINE REVELATION: ADDRESSED TO...WOMEN
Phillips, Michael J *see* HISTORY OF SANTA BARBARA COUNTY
PHILLIPS MILL BAPTIST CHURCH. WILKES COUNTY. GEORGIA : CHURCH RECORDS – 1785-1948 – 1 – 43.38 – us Baptist [240]
Phillips, Philip *see*
- HALLOWED SONGS
- OBSERVATIONS ON THE COURT OF CLAIMS
- THE STATUTORY JURISDICTION AND PRACTICE OF THE SUPREME COURT OF THE UNITED STATES.

Phillips, Ray Edmund *see* THE BANTU ARE COMING
Phillips, Ronald C et al *see* SEAGRASS RESEARCH METHODS
Phillips, Samuel Louis *see* AGREEMENT OF EVOLUTION AND CHRISTIANITY
Phillips, Semira A *see* PROUD MAHASKA
Phillips, Thomas Wharton *see* THE CHURCH OF CHRIST
Phillips, W Louis *see*
- CATALOG OF THE MANUSCRIPT AND ARCHIVAL COLLECTIONS AND INDEX TO THE CORRESPONDENCE OF JOHN TORREY
- INDEX TO PLANT DISTRIBUTION MAPS IN NORTH AMERICAN PERIODICALS THROUGH 1972

Phillips, Walter Alison *see* HISTORY OF THE CHURCH OF IRELAND, FROM THE EARLIEST TIMES TO THE PRESENT DAY
Phillips, Wendell *see*
- SELECTED WORKS BY AND ABOUT WENDELL PHILLIPS
- SPEECHES, LECTURES, AND LETTERS
- SPEECHES, LECTURES AND LETTERS

Phillips, Willard *see* A TREATISE ON THE LAW OF INSURANCE
PHILLIPSTON 1762-1849 – (Mf 1T: Births & Deaths 1765-95; Marriages & Intentions 1787-95. Mf 1T-2T: Births 1762-1848. Mf 2T-4T: Marriage Intentions 1794-1849. Mf 4T: Marriages 1793-1844; Out-of-Town Marriages 1787-99. Mf 4T-5T: Deaths 1781-1843. Mf 5T: Marriages 1789-1814; Vital Records 1843-49. Mf 6T: Deaths 1776-1849; Baptisms 1789-1807) – (mf ed 1998) – 6mf – 9 – 0-87623-317-5 – us Holbrook [920]
PHILLIPSTON 1762-1900 – (Mf 1-3: Births 1762-1848. Mf 3-5: Intentions 1794-1852. Mf 5: Marriages 1797-1844. Mf 6: Church Members 1821-22. Mf 6: Deaths 1781-1843. Mf 7: Births 1844-64. Mf 7: Marriages 1844-64. Mf 8: Deaths 1844-64. Mf 9: Births 1864-1900. Mf 9-10: Deaths 1864-1900. Mf 10-11: Marriages 1864-1900. Mf 12: Rebellion 1861-65. Mf 13-20: Town Records 1794-1814. Mf 21-30: Town Records 1814-37. Mf 31-38: Town Records 1838-76. Mf 39-48: Town Records 1876-1917. Mf 49-53: Town Records 1917-40) – (mf ed 1993) – 53mf – 9 – 0-87623-177-6 – us Holbrook [920]
Philly, John *see* THE ARRAINMENT OF CHRISTENDOM
PHILO AND HOLY SCRIPTURE, OR, THE QUOTATIONS OF PHILO FROM...THE OLD TESTAMENT / Ryle, Herbert Edward – London: Macmillan, 1895.1 fiche – 9 – us A.T.L.A. [240]
PHILO JUDAEUS; OR THE JEWISH-ALEXANDRIAN PHILOSOPHY IN ITS DEVELOPMENT AND COMPLETION / Drummond, James – 1888 – 1 – us A.T.L.A. [180]
PHILO UND DIE ALEXANDRINISCHE THEOSOPHIE, ODER, VOM EINFLUSSE DER JUEDISCH-AEGYPTISCHEN SCHULE AUF DIE LEHRE DES NEUEN TESTAMENTS / Gfroerer, August – Stuttgart: E. Schweizerbart, 1831 – 3mf – us A.T.L.A. [240]
PHILO UND DIE HALACHA : EINE VERGLEICHENDE STUDIE UNTER STETER BERUECKSICHTIGUNG DES JOSEPHUS / Ritter, Bernhard – (Includes bibliographical references) – Leipzig: J C Hinrichs, 1879 – 1mf – 9 – 0-8370-6349-3 – 1986-0349 – us A.T.L.A. [270]
PHILO UND JOSEPHUS: ALS APOLOGETEN DES JUDENTUMS / Krueger, Paul – Leipzig: Duerr, 1906. 1 fiche – 9 – us A.T.L.A. [270]
PHILOBIBLION; A MONTHLY BIBLIOGRAPHICAL JOURNAL – v. 1-2. Dec 1861-Dec 1863 – 1 – us UMI [070]
PHILOBIBLON : A TREATISE ON THE LOVE OF BOOKS / Bury, Richard de – (First printed in Latin at Cologne in 1473, this work by the Bishop of Durham and Chancellor of Edward 3rd is mostly famous being the first book written in praise of books. It is included here because of its Chapter 11, which makes the argument that "Laws are, properly speaking, neither Sciences nor Books") – New York: Meyer Bros & Co, 1899 – 2mf – 9 – $3.00 – LLMC 92-106 – us L.L.M.C. [340]
PHILOCHRISTUS: MEMOIRS OF A DISCIPLE OF THE LORD / Abbott, Edwin Abbott – Boston: Roberts, 1878. 1 fiche – 9 – us A.T.L.A. [240]
PHILOCOPHUS / Bulwer, J – M 322. 1648 – 9 – ne IDC [610]
PHILOGOGY – AFRICAN *see* THE LIBRARY OF H.E. SIR GEORGE GREY
PHILO-LEXIKON : HANDBUCH DES JUEDISCHEN WISSENS – 4th ed Berlin, 1937 – 8mf – 8 – ne Slangenburg [270]
PHILOLOGICA SACRA...URGESTALT DER EVANGELIEN UND APOSTELGESCHICHTE / Nestle, Eberhard – Berlin: Reuther & Reichard, 1896. 1 fiche. 8370-4566-5 – 9 – us A.T.L.A. [240]

PHILOLOGICAL INQUIRIES / Harris, James – (Linguistic series). 1801 – 9 – fr Hachette [400]
PHILOLOGICAL QUARTERLY – v1- 1922- 1; v47- 5,6; v54- 9 – us UMI [400]
PHILOLOGICAL QUARTERLY – (Includes Index) – Iowa City. 1922-41. v1-20. – 156mf – 8 – ne IDC [073]
PHILOLOGICAL QUARTERLY – v. 1-33. 1922-1954 – 1 – us Princeton Micro [400]
PHILOLOGICAL SERIALS – 138 titles – 9 – ne IDC [400]
PHILOLOGICAL STUDIES WITH ENGLISH ILLUSTRATIONS / Gibbs, Josiah Willard – 1857 – 9 – us A.T.L.A. [240]
PHILOLOGISCHE WOCHENSCHRIFT – Berlin. v1-23. 1881-1903 – 1 – 207.00 – us L of C Photodup [400]
PHILOLOGISCHER KOMMENTAR ZUR PEREGRINATIO AETHERIAE / Loefstedt, E – H-212 2. 1911 – 8 – ne IDC [450]
PHILOLOGUS – Supplement vols. Leipzig, 1922-39. v15-32. – 162mf – 8 – ne IDC [073]
PHILOLOGUS : ZEITSCHRIFT FUER DAS KLASSISCHE ALTERTUM UND SEIN NACHLEBEN – Leipzig. V76-94. 1920-39 – 115mf – 8 – ne IDC [073]
PHILOLOGY AND LEXICOGRAPHY OF THE NEW TESTAMENT / Robinson, Edward – (The Biblical Repository, v. 4, no. 13, Jan. 1834, p. 154-182) – 9 – us A.T.L.A. [450]
PHILOMATH CRUCIBLE – Philomath, OR. -w. 27 Mar 1879-8 May 1879. 1 roll – 1 – us U.O. Library [071]
Philomathes, V *see*
– VENCESLAI PHILOMANTHIS DE NOVA DOMO MUSICORUM LIVRI QUATUOR
– VENCESLAI PHILOMATHIS DE NOVA DOMO MVSICORVM LIBRI QVATVOR COMPENDIOSO CARMINE ELVOVBRATI
PHILOMATHIA : REVISTA ARTISTICA, SCIENTIFICA E PHILOSOPHICA – '(s.l.')- Sao Luis, Brazil. 2 Oct 1895-15 Jan 1896 – 1,5,6 – bl Biblioteca [072]
DIE PHILOS. ABHANDLUNGEN DES JA'QUB BEN ISHAG AL-KINDI : BGPHMA 2/5 / Nagy, A – Muenster, 1897 – 2mf – 9 – ne Slangenburg [240]
THE PHILOSOPHERS AND THE FRENCH REVOLUTION / Wadia, P A – London: S. Sonnenschein & Co. Ltd., 1904 – 131p – 1 – us U.W. Library [190]
PHILOSOPHIA ACADEMICA... / Frassen, C – Ed.3. Tolosae. 2v. 1686 – 17mf – 9 – CA-16/1 – ne IDC [100]
PHILOSOPHIA AD MENTEM...DIVI THOMAE AQUINATIS...EXPLICATA / Rentz, P – Altdorfii ad Vineas. 3v. 1714 – 26mf – 9 – CA-34/1 – ne IDC [100]
PHILOSOPHIA BOTANICA / Linnaeus, Carl – Stockholmiae. 1751. B-173 2 – 8 – ne IDC [580]
PHILOSOPHIA ENTOMOLOGICA / Fabricius, J C – Z-157 2. 1778 – 8 – ne IDC [590]
PHILOSOPHIA IMAGINUM / Menestrier, Claude-Francois – O-1251 1. 1695 – 9 – ne IDC [190]
PHILOSOPHIA IUXTA INCONCUSSA TUTISSIMAQUE DIVI THOMAE DOGMATA... / Goudin, A – Bononiae, 1686 – 21mf – 9 – CA-17/1 – ne IDC [100]
PHILOSOPHIA MAGNETICA... / Cabeus, N – Ferrariae, 1629 – 8mf – 9 – CA-8/1 – ne IDC [100]
PHILOSOPHIA METAPHYSICAM PHYSICAMQUE COMPLECTENS QUESTIONIBUS CONTEXTA / Aversa, R – Bonaniae. 2v. 1650 – 22mf – 9 – CA-4/1 – ne IDC [100]
PHILOSOPHIA PERENNIS : ABHANDLUNGEN ZU IHRER VERGANGENHEIT UND GEGENWART / ed by Rintelen, Fritz-Joachim von – Regensburg, 1930. 2v – 32mf – 8 – ne Slangenburg [100]
PHILOSOPHIA PERENNIS : ABHANDLUNGEN ZU IHRER VERGANGENHEIT UND GEGENWART / ed by Rintelen, Fritz-Joachim von – Regensburg, 1930.-2v – 32mf – 8 – ne Slangenburg [100]
PHILOSOPHIA PERIPATETICA / Benedictis, J B – Neapoli. 2v. 1687-88 – 14mf – 9 – CA-40/1 – ne IDC [100]
PHILOSOPHIA POLLINGANA AD NORMAM BURGUNDICAE / Amort, E – Augustae Vindelicorum, 1730 – 16mf – 9 – CA-5/1 – ne IDC [100]
PHILOSOPHIA SCOTI A PROLIXITATE ET SUBTILITAS EJUS AB OBSCURITATE LIBERA ET VINDICATA... / Boyvin, J G – Venetiis. 4v. 1701 – 23mf – 9 – CA-7/1 – ne IDC [100]
PHILOSOPHIAE, AC MATHEMATICAE TOTIUS... INSTITUTIO / Galtruchius, P – Cadomi. 2v. 1665 – 10mf – 9 – CA-41/1 – ne IDC [100]
PHILOSOPHIAE AD MENTEM SCOTI CURSUS INTEGER / Poncius, J – Lugduni, 1672 – 18mf – 9 – CA-32/1 – ne IDC [100]
THE PHILOSOPHIC AND SCIENTIFIC ULTIMATUM : WRITTEN IN THE CONSTITUTION AND LAWS OF UNIVERSE BY THE OMNIPOTENT HAND OF DIVINE INTELLIGENCE,... / Allibaco, W A – (Includes appendix) – New York: W A Allibaco, 1864 – 1mf – 9 – 0-8370-2078-6 – 1985-0078 – us A.T.L.A. [210]
PHILOSOPHIC AND SCIENTIFIC ULTIMATUM... FOR THE GUIDE OF NATIONS / Allibaco, W A – New York: W.A. Allibaco, 1864. 1 fiche – 9 – us A.T.L.A. [240]
A PHILOSOPHICAL AND A CHEMICAL DIGEST OF THE MOSAIC CREATION : IN TWO POPULAR LECTURES / Quarterman, James – New York: Folger & Turner, 1868 – 1mf – 9 – 0-8370-4814-1 – 1985-2814 – us A.T.L.A. [220]
PHILOSOPHICAL BOOKS – (1982- 1,5,6,9) – v1- 1960- – 1 – us UMI [073]
A PHILOSOPHICAL ESSAY FOR THE REUNION OF THE LANGUAGES / Besnier, Pierre – 1675. 90p. (English Linguistics Series 1500-1800) – 9 – us UMI [400]
THE PHILOSOPHICAL HISTORY AND MEMOIRES OF THE ROYAL ACADEMY OF SCIENCES AT PARIS / Academie des Sciences. Paris – An abridgment of all the papers relating to natural philosophy...With many curious observations relating to the natural history and anatomy of animals, &c. 1742 – 3 – us Readex [500]
A PHILOSOPHICAL INQUIRY INTO THE ORIGIN OF OUR IDEAS OF THE SUBLIME AND BEAUTIFUL / Burke, Edmund – O-1196 1. 1787 – 9 – ne IDC [110]
PHILOSOPHICAL INVESTIGATIONS – (1982-1,5,6,9) – v1- 1978- – 1 – us UMI [100]
PHILOSOPHICAL MAGAZINE – (London, Edinburgh and Dublin Philosophical Magazine and Journal of Science). Series 1-8. 1798-1974 – 1,5,6 – us Princeton Micro [100]
PHILOSOPHICAL MAGAZINE – London. Series 1 o.s. v1-68 1798-1826; Series 2 n.s. v1-11 1827-32; Series 3 v1-37 1832-50; Series 4 v1-50 1851-75; Series 5 v1-50 1876-1900; Series 6 v1-50 1901-25; Series 7 v1-46 1926-55 – 1 – $2410.00y – uk Dawson [100]
PHILOSOPHICAL PSYCHOLOGY – 1988- 6v – 9 – £169.50 – 0951-5089 – uk Carfax [150]
PHILOSOPHICAL QUARTERLY – v1- 1950- 1; v21- 5,6; v26- 9 – us UMI [100]
PHILOSOPHICAL REVIEW – v1- 1892- 1; v78- 5,6; v84- 9 – us UMI [100]
PHILOSOPHICAL REVIEW – v1-76 1892-1967 – 1 – us Princeton Micro [100]
Philosophical Society of Edinburgh *see* ESSAYS AND OBSERVATIONS, PHYSICAL AND LITERARY, READ BEFORE A SOCIETY IN EDINBURGH, AND PUBLISHED BY THEM
PHILOSOPHICAL STUDIES – (v46- 1984-5,6,9) – v1- 1950- – 1 – us UMI [100]
PHILOSOPHICAL STUDIES IN EDUCATION : PROCEEDINGS OF THE ANNUAL MEETING OF THE OHIO VALLEY PHILOSOPHY OF EDUCATION SOCIETY – 1976- – 1,5,6,9 – us UMI [370]
A PHILOSOPHICAL STUDY OF CHRISTIAN ETHICS / Barbour, G F – Edinburgh: W. Blackwood, 1911 – 2mf – us A.T.L.A. [240]
PHILOSOPHICAL TERMS IN THE MOREH NEBUKHIM / Efros, Il – (Columbia University Oriental Studies, v. 22). New York. 1924. BJ-33-1 1 – 9 – ne IDC [180]
PHILOSOPHICAL TRANSACTIONS / Royal Society of London – Series A v178-287 1887-1977 – 1,5,6 – us Princeton Micro [100]
PHILOSOPHICAL TRANSACTIONS / Royal Society of London – Series B v178-280 1887-1977 – 1,5,6 – us Princeton Micro [100]
PHILOSOPHICAL TRANSACTIONS / Royal Society of London – v1-177 1665-1886 – 1,5,6 – us Princeton Micro [100]
PHILOSOPHICAL TRANSACTIONS OF THE ROYAL SOCIETY OF LONDON : GENERAL INDEX 1665-1780 / Maty, P H – London, 1787. V.1-70 – 18mf – 9 – ne IDC [100]
PHILOSOPHICAL TRANSACTIONS OF THE ROYAL SOCIETY OF LONDON – London, 1665-1886. V.1-177 – 2,919mf – 9 – ne IDC [100]
PHILOSOPHICAL TRANSACTIONS OF THE ROYAL SOCIETY OF LONDON : SERIES A – London, 1887-1940. v178-238 – 1,134mf – 9 – ne IDC [100]
PHILOSOPHICAL TRANSACTIONS OF THE ROYAL SOCIETY OF LONDON : SERIES B – London, 1887-1939/1940. v178-231 – 1,004mf – 9 – ne IDC [100]
A PHILOSOPHICAL VIEW OF REFORM / Shelley, Percy Bysshe – London, New York: Oxford University Press, 1920 – 1 roll – 1 – 1-55879-726-2 – uk Libr Preservation [320]
PHILOSOPHICAL WORKS : WITH A PRELIMINARY ESSAY AND NOTES / Locke, John – Essay and notes by J.A. St. John. London: G. Bell: 1877-82. 2v – 1 – us U.W. Library [190]
THE PHILOSOPHICAL WORKS OF FRANCIS BACON, BARON OF VERULAM, VISCOUNT ST ALBANS. / Bacon, Francis; ed by Ellis & Spedding – Reprinted from the texts and transls. Introd. by John M. Robertson. London: G. Routledge and Sons, Ltd; New York: E.P. Dutton & Co., 1905 – xx/920p – 1 – us U.W. Library [190]
PHILOSOPHIE – Rawdon, 1897. SEM105P13 – 1mf – 9 – Can$2.25 – cn Bibl Nat [100]
PHILOSOPHIE ANATOMIQUE DES ORGANES RESPIRATOIRES SOUS LE RAPPORT DE LA DETERMINATION ET DE L'IDENTITE DE LEURS PIECES OSSEUSES / Geoffroy Saint-Hilaire, Etienne – Paris, 1818, xxxix-517 p. plus 10 pl. Histoire des Sciences XVIIe-XIXe Siecles. 7938 – 9 – fr Hachette [590]
LA PHILOSOPHIE CONDAMNEE / Halleux, Jean – Paris: Desclee, De Brouwer, [1908?] – 1mf – 9 – 0-8370-8431-8 – 1986-2431 – us A.T.L.A. [240]
PHILOSOPHIE CRITIQUE DE LA COMMUNICATION / Villani, Arnaud – 2mf – 9 – 10300 – fr Atelier National [380]
DE LA PHILOSOPHIE DE LA HENRIADE / Tabaraud, M M – Ou supplement necessaire aux divers jugements qui ont ete portes, surtout a celui de M. de la Harpe. Paris. Onfroi. 1805 – 9 – fr Hachette [190]
LA PHILOSOPHIE DE L'AMOUR CHEZ RAYMOND LULLE / Sala-Molins, L – 1mf – 9 – fr Atelier National [180]
LA PHILOSOPHIE DE RURAVEBOHNI, PAYS DONT LA DECOUVERTE SEMBLE D'UN GRAND INTERET POUR L'HOMME, OU RECIT DIALOGUE DES MOEURS PAR LESQUELS LES RURAVEHEUXIS HABITANTS DE CE PAYS ONT ETE CONDUITS AU VRAI ET SOLIDE BONHEUR / Jaunez-Sponville & Pierre-Ignace & Bugnet, Nicolas – Utopias in the Enlightment series. 1809 – 9 – fr Hachette [190]
DIE PHILOSOPHIE DER GRIECHEN / Deussen, Paul – Leipzig, 1920 – 10mf – 8 – ne Slangenburg [180]
DIE PHILOSOPHIE DER KIRCHENVAETER / Huber, Johannes – Muenchen: J.G. Cotta, 1859 – 1mf – us A.T.L.A. [240]
DIE PHILOSOPHIE DER KUNST DENKT SICH ZU ENDE / Frey, Peter – Muenchen, 1977 – 3mf – 9 – DM76.00 – 3-89349-767-6 – gw Hänsel [140]
DIE PHILOSOPHIE DER PERSOENLICHKEIT NACH FRIEDRICH HEINRICH JACOBI / Jacobi, Wilhelm Heinrich – Magdeburg, 1911 – 79p – 9 – DM48.00 – 3-89349-010-8 – gw Hänsel [190]
DIE PHILOSOPHIE DER VORZEIT / Kleutgen, J – (Muenster, 1860.-1st Bd.-19mf; Muenster, 1863.-2nd Bd.-20mf) – 8 – ne Slangenburg [180]
DIE PHILOSOPHIE DES ALANUS DE INSULIS : BGPHMA 2/4 / Baumgartner, M – Muenster, 1896 – 3mf – 9 – ne Slangenburg [240]
PHILOSOPHIE DES DEUX AMPERES – Paris: Didier, 1866. SEM16P2 – 1r – 5 – Can$9.00 – cn Bibl Nat [190]
LA PHILOSOPHIE DES IMAGES / Menestrier, Claude-Francois – O-372. 1682 – 9 – ne IDC [190]
DIE PHILOSOPHIE DES JOSEF (IBN) ZADDIK : BGPHMA 2/2 / Doctor, M – Muenster, 1895 – 2mf – 9 – ne Slangenburg [240]
DIE PHILOSOPHIE DES PETRUS LOMBARDUS : BGPHMA 3/5 / Espenberger, J N – Muenster, 1901 – 3mf – 9 – ne Slangenburg [240]
DIE PHILOSOPHIE DES SALOMON IBN GABIROL / Guttmann, J – Goettingen. 1889. BJ-33-15 1 – 9 – ne IDC [180]
PHILOSOPHIE DES SICHSELBSTBEWUSSTEN / Dahlmann, Friedrich Wilhelm – Chicago: Koelling & Klappenbach, 1901. 1 fiche – 9 – us A.T.L.A. [240]
LA PHILOSOPHIE DU PEUPLE: L'HYGIENE, L'HABITATION / Gache, Ferdinand Pierre – Paris. 1901. (La Condition Ouvriere. Part Two.) – 9 – 7.50 – fr Bibl Nationale [360]
DIE PHILOSOPHIE IM DEUTSCHEN GEISTESLEBEN DES 19 JAHRHUNDERTS / Windelband, Wilhelm – Tuebingen: J.C.B. Mohr (P. Siebeck), 1909 – 120p – 1 – us U.W. Library [190]
PHILOSOPHIE RELIGIEUSE DE LA THEOLOGIE NATURELLE EN FRANCE ET EN ANGLETERRE / Remusat, Charles de – Paris; New York: Germer Bailliere, 1864 – 1mf – 9 – 0-8370-7327-8 – 1986-1327 – us A.T.L.A. [210]
PHILOSOPHIE RELIGIEUSE DE LEVI-BEN-GERSON / Weil, I – Paris. 1868. BJ-33-28 1 – 9 – ne IDC [270]
LA PHILOSOPHIE RELIGIEUSE EN ANGLETERRE : DEPUIS LOCKE JUSQU'A NOS JOURS / Carrau, Ludovic – Paris: F. Alcan, 1888 – 1mf – us A.T.L.A. [240]
PHILOSOPHIE SOCIALE DEDIEE AU PEUPLE FRANCAIS / Frey, Lucius J – Paris, Froulle. 1793 – 9 – fr Hachette [190]
PHILOSOPHIE UND CHRISTENTUM:... HARTMANN'SCHEN WELTANSCHAUUNG FUER JEDEN GEBILDETEN / Schuez, Alfred – Stuttgart: J.B. Metzler, 1884. 1 fiche – 9 – us A.T.L.A. [240]
PHILOSOPHIE UND PSYCHOLOGIE : UNTERSUCHUNGEN ZUM PROBLEM IHRES VERHAELTNISSES SEIT 1880 / Schmidt, Nicole D – 1994 – 5mf – DM118.00 – 3-8267-2024-5 – gw Hänsel [120]
PHILOSOPHIE UND RELIGION: NEUE BEITRAEGE ZUR...GRUNDLEGUNG DER DOGMATIK / Lipsius, Richard Adelbert – Leipzig: J.A. Barth, 1885. 1 fiche – 9 – us A.T.L.A. [240]
PHILOSOPHIE UND THEOLOGIE: EINE STREITSCHRIFT / Kuhn, Johannes von – Tuebingen: H. Laupp, 1860. 1 fiche – 9 – us A.T.L.A. [240]
PHILOSOPHIEAE MAGNI PATRIS ET ECCLESIAE DOCTORIS AUGUSTINI...PARS ALTERA / Nebridius a Muendelheim – [Viennae], 1654 – 6mf – 9 – CA-42/1 – ne IDC [100]
DIE PHILOSOPHIN : SCHAUSPIEL IN VIER AKTEN / Spielhagen, Friedrich – Berlin: Reg London Stat Hall, 1877 – 1r – 1 – us U.W. Library [820]
PHILOSOPHISCHE BOTANIK / Medikus, F K – 2pts. Mannheim. 1789-91. B-8138 1 – 9 – ne IDC [580]
DIE PHILOSOPHISCHE ELEMENTE IN DEN OPUSCULA SACRA DES BOETHIUS / Bruder, K – Naumburg, 1927 – 1mf – 8 – ne Slangenburg [180]
PHILOSOPHISCHE MONATSHEFTE – Berlin, etc. v1-30 Apr 1868-1894. Vol. 30 includes index to v1-30. Superseded by: Archiv fuer systematische Philosophie. Film Mas C 285 – 1 – us H.U. Library [100]
PHILOSOPHISCHE MONATSHEFTE – v1-30. 1868-94 (mf ed 1992) – 79mf – 9 – DM1,360.00 – 3-89131-051-X – gw Fischer [100]
PHILOSOPHISCHE MONATSHEFTE DER KANT-STUDIEN – Berlin: Kant-Gesellschaft. v1-2. 1925-26 – 7mf – 9 – 267/2 – ne IDC [140]
DAS PHILOSOPHISCHE SYSTEM SHAFTESBURYS UND WIELANDS AGATHON / Stettner, Leo – (Includes bibliographical references) – Halle (Saale): M Niemeyer, 1929 – 1r – 1 – us U.W. Library [430]
DIE PHILOSOPHISCHEN ABHANDLUNGEN DES JA'QUB BEN ISHAG AL-KINDI / Nagy, A – Muenster, 1897 – 2mf – 8 – ne Slangenburg [100]
DIE PHILOSOPHISCHEN GRUNDGEDANKEN IN GOETHES WILHELM MEISTER / Schubert, Johannes – Leipzig: C G Naumann, 1896 – 1r – 1 – us U.W. Library [430]
DIE PHILOSOPHISCHEN GRUNDLAGEN UND DIE POLITISCHE ZIELSTELLUNG DER PERSONALISTISCHEN GRUNDKONZEPTION VON KAROL WOJTYLA / Kube, Constanze – 1992 – 298p – 9 – DM98.00 – 3-89349-576-2 – gw Hänsel [150]
PHILOSOPHISCHEN MORALSYSTEME = ETHICAL SYSTEMS / Wundt, Wilhelm Max – (In English) – London: Swan Sonnenschein; New York: Macmillan, 1906 – 1mf – 9 – 0-8370-6634-4 – 1986-0634 – us A.T.L.A. [170]
PHILOSOPHISCHES JAHRBUCH : BD. 27 / ed by Gulberlet, C – Fulda, 1914 – 12mf – 8 – ne Slangenburg [100]

PHILOSOPHISCHES JOURNAL EINER GESELLSCHAFT TEUTSCHER GELEHRTEN / ed by Fichte, J G & Niethammer, F J – Leipzig, etc. v1-10. 1795-1800 – 74mf – 9 – H-538/2 – ne IDC [100]
PHILOSOPHISCHES MAGAZIN – Halle. v1-4. 1788-92 – 36mf – 9 – H-535/2 – ne IDC [100]
PHILOSOPHISCH-HISTORISCHE KLASSE: ABHANDLUNGEN / Akademie der Wissenschaften. Berlin – 1908-1949 – 1 – us Schnase [100]
PHILOSOPHISCH-HISTORISCHE KLASSE: SITZUNGSBERICHTE / Akademie der Wissenschaften. Berlin – 1922-1949 – 1 – us Schnase [100]
PHILOSOPHISCH-KRITISCHE-VERGLEICHUNG UND WURDIGUNG VON VIERZEHN ALTERN UND NEUERN SPRACHENS EUROPENS / Jenish, Daniel – (Linguistic series). 1796 – 9 – fr Hachette [400]
PHILOSOPHY – (1985- 5,6,9) – v6- 1931- – 1 – us UMI [100]
PHILOSOPHY – v1-50 1936-75. London – 9 – $24,190.00; $244.00v – uk Dawson [100]
PHILOSOPHY AND CHRISTIANITY : A SERIES OF LECTURES / Morris, George Sylvester – New York: Robert Carter, 1883 – 1mf – 9 – us A.T.L.A. [240]
THE PHILOSOPHY AND FINANCIAL VALUE OF CORPORATE SIGNAGE AT NCAA DIVISION 1-A ATHLETIC DEPARTMENTS / Pope, Eugene M – 1994 – 1mf – $4.00 – us Microform Publ [650]
PHILOSOPHY AND LIFE : AND OTHER ESSAYS / Muirhead, John Henry – London: S. Sonnenschein, 1902 – 1 roll – 1 – 1-55879-948-6 – uk Libr Preservation [840]
PHILOSOPHY AND POPULAR MORALS IN ANCIENT GREECE : AN EXAMINATION OF POPULAR MORALITY AND PHILOSOPHICAL ETHICS, IN THEIR INTERRELATIONS AND RECIPROCAL INFLUENCE IN ANCIENT GREECE, DOWN TO THE CLOSE OF THE THIRD CENTURY B.C. / Dobbs, Archibald Edward – (Includes bibliographical references and index) – Dublin: Edward Ponsonby; London: Simpkin, Marshall, 1907 – 1mf – 9 – 0-8370-6109-1 – 1986-0109 – us A.T.L.A. [170]
PHILOSOPHY AND THEOLOGY / Stirling, James Hutchison – Edinburgh: T.& T. Clark, 1890. 1 fiche – 9 – us A.T.L.A. [240]
PHILOSOPHY AS SCIENTIA SCIENTIARUM : AND, A HISTORY OF CLASSIFICATIONS OF THE SCIENCES / Flint, Robert – New York: Scribner, 1904 – 1mf – us A.T.L.A. [100]
PHILOSOPHY COLLECTION / Bibliotheque Nationale – (Titles available separately) – 12 titles, 66mf – 9 – $163.00 – fr Bibl Nationale [190]
Philosophy Documentation Center *see* CHARLES S. PEIRCE MICROFICHE COLLECTION
PHILOSOPHY EAST AND WEST – v1- 1951- 1; v25- 5,6; v26- 9 – us UMI [100]
THE PHILOSOPHY OF CHANGE : A STUDY OF THE FUNDAMENTAL PRINCIPLE OF THE PHILOSOPHY OF BERGSON / Carr, H Wildon – London: Macmillan, 1914 – 1mf – us A.T.L.A. [140]
PHILOSOPHY OF CHRISTIAN EXPERIENCE: EIGHT LECTURES / Foster, Randolph Sinks – New York: Hunt & Eaton, 1891. 1 fiche – 9 – us A.T.L.A. [240]
THE PHILOSOPHY OF DON HASDAI CRESCAS / Waxman, M – Columbia University Oriental Studies, v17. New York. 1920. BJ-33-50 1 – 9 – ne IDC [190]
THE PHILOSOPHY OF FRIEDRICH NIETZSCHE / Mencken, H L – 3rd ed. Boston: Luce and Co., 1913 – xiii/304p – 1 – us U.W. Library [190]
THE PHILOSOPHY OF HANDWRITING, BY DON FELIX DE SALAMANCA (PSEUD.)... WITH 135 AUTOGRAPHS / Ingram, John H – London: Chatto & Windus, (1879).153p – 1 – us U.W. Library [150]
THE PHILOSOPHY OF HERBERT SPENCER : BEING AN EXAMINATION OF THE FIRST PRINCIPLES OF HIS SYSTEM / Bowne, Borden Parker – New York: Nelson & Phillips, 1874 – 1mf – us A.T.L.A. [100]
THE PHILOSOPHY OF HISTORY / Schade, A – Cleveland, O[hio]: A. Schade, 1899 – 2mf – us A.T.L.A. [900]
THE PHILOSOPHY OF JESUS CHRIST AS UNFOLDED IN THE PHYSICAL ASPECT OF HIS MIRACLES / Collins, Richard – London: Elliot Stock, 1879 – 1mf – 9 – 0-8370-2716-0 – 1985-0716 – us A.T.L.A. [240]
PHILOSOPHY OF JESUS CHRIST AS UNFOLDED IN...HIS MIRACLES / Collins, Richard – London: Elliot Stock, 1879. 1 fiche – 9 – us A.T.L.A. [240]
PHILOSOPHY OF JEWISH HISTORY / Deutsch, Gotthard – (Includes bibliographical references) – Cincinnati, O[hio]: Bloch, [1900?] – 1mf – 9 – 0-8370-9693-6 – 1986-3693 – us A.T.L.A. [270]
PHILOSOPHY OF LAW / Kohler, Josef – N.Y.: The Maxmillan Co, 1921 – 5mf – 9 – $7.50 – LLMC 95-186 – us L.L.M.C. [340]
THE PHILOSOPHY OF LAW : BEING NOTES OF LECTURES DELIVERED DURING TWENTY-THREE YEARS (1852-1875) IN THE INNER TEMPLE HALL, ADAPTED FOR STUDENTS AND THE PUBLIC – 2nd ed. London: Wm. Maxwell & Son, 1878 – 4mf – 9 – $6.00 – LLMC 95-203 – us L.L.M.C. [340]
THE PHILOSOPHY OF LAW; AN EXPOSITION OF THE FUNDAMENTAL PRINCIPLES OF JURISPRUDENCE AS THE SCIENCE OF RIGHT / Kant, Immanuel – 1887 – 1 – us A.T.L.A. [340]
THE PHILOSOPHY OF LIFE, AND PHILOSOPHY OF LANGUAGE IN A COURSE OF LECTURES / Schlegel, Frederick von – Trans. from the German by A.J.W. Morrison. Bell & Daldy, 1866 – 1 – us U.W. Library [190]
THE PHILOSOPHY OF MIND : A CORRECTIVE FOR SOME ERRORS OF THE DAY / Chandler, Henry William – (Includes bibliographical references) – London: Rivingtons, 1867 – 1mf – 9 – 0-8370-2628-8 – 1985-0628 – us A.T.L.A. [200]
PHILOSOPHY OF MIND: AN INAUGURAL LECTURE / Chandler, Henry William – London: Rivingtons, 1867. 1 fiche – 9 – us A.T.L.A. [240]
THE PHILOSOPHY OF NATURAL THEOLOGY : AN ESSAY IN CONFUTATION OF THE SCEPTICISM OF THE PRESENT DAY,... / Jackson, William – New York: A D F Randolph, 1875 – 1mf – 9 – 0-8370-3742-5 – 1985-1742 – us A.T.L.A. [210]
PHILOSOPHY OF NATURAL THEOLOGY: AN ESSAY IN CONFUTATION OF THE SCEPTICISM / Jackson, William – New York: A.D.F. Randolph, 1875.1 fiche – 9 – us A.T.L.A. [240]
THE PHILOSOPHY OF PLOTINUS / Inge, William Ralph – (London, 1948.-v1.-10mf; London, 1948.-v2.-11mf) – 8 – ne Slangenburg [180]
PHILOSOPHY OF RELIGION (CCC171) / Hsieh, Fu-ya – (In Chinese) – Hong Kong: To Hung Printing Press, 1959 – 1r – 1 – 1984-B500 – us A.T.L.A. [240]
THE PHILOSOPHY OF RELIGION IN ENGLAND AND AMERICA / Caldecott, Alfred – New York: Macmillan, 1901 – 2mf – us A.T.L.A. [240]
THE PHILOSOPHY OF REVELATION : THE STONE LECTURES FOR 1908-1909, PRINCETON THEOLOGICAL SEMINARY / Bavinck, Herman – New York: Longmans, Green, 1909 – 1mf – us A.T.L.A. [240]
PHILOSOPHY OF RHETORIC / Bascom, John – Boston, Chicago: Woolworth, Ainsworth and Co., 1870. 251p – 1 – us U.W. Library [160]
PHILOSOPHY OF RITUAL : APOLOGIA PRO RITU / Gratacap, LP – New York: J. Pott, 1887 – 1mf – us A.T.L.A. [240]
PHILOSOPHY OF SCIENCE – v26- 1959- 1; v37- 5,6; v42- 9 – us UMI [100]
PHILOSOPHY OF SCIENCE – v1-26 1934-59 – 1,5,6 – $22,138.00 – us Princeton Micro [500]
THE PHILOSOPHY OF SECTARIANISM, OR, A CLASSIFIED VIEW OF THE CHRISTIAN SECTS IN THE UNITED STATES : WITH NOTICES OF THEIR PROGRESS AND TENDENCIES / ILLUSTRATED BY HISTORICAL FACTS AND ANECDOTES / Blaikie, Alexander – Boston: Phillips, Sampson, 1854 – 1mf – us A.T.L.A. [240]
THE PHILOSOPHY OF SPINOZA / Wolfson, H A – (Vol 1: 8mf; Vol 2: 8mf) – 1934 – 8 – ne Slangenburg [190]
PHILOSOPHY OF THE SOCIAL SCIENCES – v1- 1971- 1; v4- 5,6; v6- 9 – us UMI [300]
THE PHILOSOPHY OF THE SUPERNATURAL / Platt, William Henry – New York: E.P. Dutton, 1886 – 1mf – 9 – us A.T.L.A. [130]
PHILOSOPHY OF THE UNCONSCIOUS. / Hartmann, Eduard von – Authorized trans. by William Chatterton Coupland. London: Truebner, 1884. 3v. diagrs – 1 – us U.W. Library [120]
PHILOSOPHY OF THEISM / Bowne, Borden Parker – New York: Harper, c1887 – 1mf – 9 – 0-8370-2429-3 – 1985-0429 – us A.T.L.A. [210]
PHILOSOPHY OF THEISM / Fraser, Alexander Campbell – New York: Scribner, 1899 – 1mf – 9 – us A.T.L.A. [140]
PHILOSOPHY OF THEISM (CCC352) = SHEN TI CHE HSUEH / Yuan, Ting-an – (In Chinese) – Shanghai: Christian Literature Society, 1924 – 1r – 1 – 1984-6691 – us A.T.L.A. [210]
THE PHILOSOPHY OF THOMAS HILL GREEN / Fairbrother, William Henry – London: Methuen, 1896. 187p – 1 – us U.W. Library [190]
THE PHILOSOPHY OF THOMAS HILL GREEN / Fairbrother, William Henry – London, New York: Methuen, 1896 – 1mf – us A.T.L.A. [190]
PHILOSOPHY OF TRINITARIAN DOCTRINE : A CONTRIBUTION TO THEOLOGICAL PROGRESS AND REFORM / Pease, Aaron Gaylord – New York: G P Putnam, 1875 – 1mf – 9 – 0-8370-5218-1 – 1985-3218 – us A.T.L.A. [240]
PHILOSOPHY TODAY – v1- 1957- 1; v14- 5,6; v19- 9 – us UMI [100]
PHILOTAS : EIN TRAUERSPIEL / Lessing, Gotthold Ephraim; ed by Zernial, U – 3. Aufl. Leipzig: L Ehlermann, [19–?] – 1r – 1 – us U.W. Library [820]
PHILOTHEI SYMBOLA CHRISTIANA QUIBUS IDEA / Philotheus (Pseud. of Karl Ludwig) – O-715 1. 1677 – 9 – ne IDC [240]
Philotheus *see* SYMBOLA CHRISTIANA QUIBUS IDEA HOMINIS CHRISTIANI EXPRIMITUR
Philotheus (Pseud. of Karl Ludwig) *see* PHILOTHEI SYMBOLA CHRISTIANA QUIBUS IDEA
Philpot, J *see* THE EXAMINATIONS AND WRITINGS
Phin, John *see*
– THE CHEMICAL HISTORY OF THE SIX DAYS OF CREATION
– THE EVOLUTION OF THE ATMOSPHERE...: A...SCIENTIFIC REPLY TO MODERN MATERIALISTIC ATHEISM
Phinot, Dominique *see* LIBER SECUNDUS MUTETARUM QUINQUE VOCUM
Phipps, C J *see* VOYAGE AU POLE BOREAL, FAIT EN 1773 PAR ORDRE DU ROI D'ANGLETERRE, TRAD. DE L'ANGLAIS
PHLAVI TEXTS : PART 5: MARVELS OF ZOROSTRIANISM / ed by Mueller, Friedrich Max – (Translated by E.W. West) – 1897 – 4mf – 8 – ne Slangenburg [290]
PHO THONG – Dir. Dang-Nguyen-Quang. no. 2-182. Hanoi. 1 juil 1930-9 fevr 1931. mq no. 125, 147, 151-152 – 1 – fr A.C.R.P.P. [073]
PHOBIA THERAPY JOURNAL – v1-. 1986- – 1,5,6,9 – us UMI [616]
AN PHOBLACHT – Dublin, Ireland.20 Jun 1925-4 Jul 1936 – 1 – ie Microforms [072]
PHOENICISCHES GLOSSAR / Bloch, Armand – Berlin: Mayer & Mueller, 1890 – 1mf – 9 – 0-8370-7202-6 – 1986-1202 – us A.T.L.A. [470]
DE PHOENIX – Amsterdam. nos1-4. 1930-31 – 1mf – 9 – J-261-105/1 – ne IDC [073]
LE PHOENIX – Montreal, Canada. 23 jun-6 jul 1841 – 1r – 1 – Can$25.00 – cn Can Microfilming [072]
PHOENIX – (1983-. 1,5,6,9) – v1-. 1946- – 1 – us UMI [073]
PHOENIX – Bristol. R.I. -w. 1850- – 1 – us UMI [071]
PHOENIX – Eugene, OR. 24 Sep 1974-31 Aug 1984. – 1r – 1 – us U.O. Library [071]
PHOENIX – (First Black newspaper in Bay Area) – San Jose, CA. Oct 1891-92 – 1r – 1 – $50.00 – B02885 – us Library Micro [071]
PHOENIX – Hernando. Miss. 1842-1846; 1845 – 1 – us UMI [071]
PHOENIX – Irvine, CA. 1986-1989 – 1r – 1 – $50.00 – R04037 – us Library Micro [071]
PHOENIX – London, UK. 1837. -w. 6 feet – 1 – uk British Libr Newspaper [072]
PHOENIX – South Norwalk, Conn. v. 1-6, no. 1. June 1914-Dec 1916 – 1 – us NY Public [073]
PHOENIX – v. 1- 1968- – 1 – us UMI [073]
THE PHOENIX – Ireland.9 Dec 1916-24 Feb 1917 – 1 – ie Microforms [072]
THE PHOENIX – San Francisco, CA: San Francisco State University, 1968-1980; 1985-1986 – 9r – 1 – $450.00 – B03491 – us Library Micro [071]
Phoenix Foundation *see*
– THE AZOREAN FIGHT FOR FREEDOM
– BULLETIN
PHOENIX JEWISH NEWS – Phoenix. Ariz. 1948-49 – 1 – us A.J.P.C. [071]
THE PHOENIX REDSKIN – 1931-47.(American Indian Periodicals in the Princeton University Library). 17 fiches – 9 – $75.00 – us UPA [073]
PHOENIX REVIVISCENS. LIBRI 2 / Henriquez, Chrysostomus – Bruxellae, 1626 – 10mf – 8 – Dfl35.00 – ne Slangenburg [240]
PHOENIXIANA; OR, SKETCHES AND BURLESQUES / Derby, George Horatio – 12th ed.New York: D. Appleton, 1875. 274p, ill – 1 – us U.W. Library [830]
PHOENIXVILLE MESSENGER – Phoenixville, PA. -w 1889-1910 – 13 – $25.00r – us I.M.R. [071]
PHOENIZISCHES WOERTERBUCH / Levy, Moritz Abraham – Breslau: Schletter (H Skutsch), 1864 – 1mf – 9 – 0-8370-7233-6 – 1986-1233 – us A.T.L.A. [470]
PHONE TES ELEUTHERIAS – Athens. Greece. -m. Jan 1954, Dec 1955-Nov 1962, Jan 1963. (1 reel) – 1 – uk British Libr Newspaper [949]
PHONEFICE FOR AT&T CONSUMER 800 DIRECTORY – 9 – $20.00 – us UMI [380]
PHONEFICE FOR ITALY – Italian Yellow Pages – 9 – us UMI [380]
PHONEFICHE – (Ca 2600 US domestic directories covering ca 50,000 communities) – Current Telephone Directories on Microfiche – 9 – us UMI [380]
PHONEFICHE COMMUNITY CROSS-REFERENCE GUIDE – (Also available on paper $415.00) – Helps find telephone directories for smaller communities not listed in official directory titles – 1 – $195.00 – us UMI [380]
PHONEFICHE FOR AT&T BUSINESS-TO-BUSINESS 800 DIRECTORY – 9 – $20.00 – us UMI [380]
PHONEFICHE FOR AUSTRALIA – Telephone directories from 7 Australian cities – 9 – us UMI [380]
PHONEFICHE FOR CANADA – 61 metropolitan areas in Ontario and Quebec – 9 – us UMI [380]
PHONEFICHE FOR CHINA – Telephone and Telex & Fax Directories – 9 – us UMI [380]
PHONEFICHE FOR GREAT BRITAIN – Telephone directories from ca 96 cities – 9 – us UMI [380]
PHONEFICHE FOR PUERTO RICO – Telephone directories from the San Juan Metropolitan Area and 6 other regions – 9 – us UMI [380]
PHONEFICHE FOR SWITZERLAND – Telephone directories from Berne, Geneva and Zurich – 9 – us UMI [380]
PHONEFICHE FOR U.S. NATIONAL ZIP CODE DIRECTORY – 9 – $20.00 – us UMI [380]
PHONEFICHE FOREIGN-LANGUAGE DIRECTORIES – Yellow Pages in Spanish from 7 California cities, Miami and New York City – 9 – us UMI [380]
THE PHONETIC AND TONAL STRUCTURE OF EFIK / Ward, Ida Carolina – Cambridge, England: W Heffer, 1933 – us Res Libr [470]
PHONETICA – (v. 21-30. 1970-74. 5,6) – v. 14-30 1966-74 – 1 – us UMI [400]
PHONETICA – v1-. 1957- – 1,5,9 – us UMI [400]
A PHONETICAL STUDY OF THE ESKIMO LANGUAGE / Thalbitzer, W – Bn 411 2. 1904 – 8 – ne IDC [490]
PHONG HOA – Tuan bao. no. 1-190. Hanoi. juin 1932-5 juin 1936 – 1 – fr A.C.R.P.P. [073]
PHONO TRADER AND RECORDER – London, England. -w. June 1904-Aug 1913. 8 l 2 reels – 1 – uk British Libr Newspaper [072]
PHONOGRAPH MONTHLY REVIEW – v. 1-6. 1926-Mar 1932 – 1 – us Schnase [073]
PHONOGRAPH-HERALD – St. Paul, NE. -w. (-sw 1898). Sept 1878; Sept 1880-Jan 1893; Sept 1895 to date – 1 – us NE Hist [071]
PHONOGRAPHISCHE ZEITSCHRIFT – Berlin, Germany. -w. 15 Aug 1900-1 Nov 1914 – 1 – uk British Libr Newspaper [072]

PHONOGRAPHISCHE ZEITSCHRIFT – (Cont by: PRZ Phonographische und Radiozeitschrift, apr 15, 1935? PRZ Phonographische Radio- und Musikinstrumentenzeitschrift, oct 1, 1937?) – Berlin. aug 15, 1900-mar 15, 1938 – 23r – 1 – gw Mikrofilm [780]

PHONOSCOPE – A Monthly Journal Devoted to Scientific and Amusement Inventions. New York. v. 1-4. Nov 1896-June 1900 – 1 – us NY Public [500]

PHONOSCOPE : A MONTHLY JOURNAL DEVOTED TO SCIENTIFIC AND AMUSEMENT INVENTIONS APPERTAINING TO SOUND AND SIGHT – New York. v1-4. 1896-1900 – 1r – 1 – us Ross [621]

PHOSPHATE DEPOSITS OF TRIPOLITANIA, LIBYA / Libya. Ministry of Industry – 1965. Bulletin no 3. Ayler, M.F. BNE-802 1 – 9 – ne IDC [550]

PHOSPHORUS AND POTASSIUM – 1962- 1; 1969- 5,6; 1976- 4 x 6 in. 9 – us UMI [073]

PHOSPHORUS AND SULFER AND THE RELATED ELEMENTS / ed by Holmes, Robert R – 1970- – 1,5,9 – us Gordon [540]

PHOSPHORYLATION KINETICS OF THE SARCOPLASMIC RETICULUM CA2+-ATPASE FOLLOWING EXERCISE / McCarthy, John J – University of Oregon, 1995 – 2mf – 9 – $8.00 – PH1469 – us Microform Publ [612]

PHOTO ALBUM / South Carolina. State Ports Authority – c1920-c1940. 8 fiches – 9 – us South Carolina Historical [978]

PHOTO CANADA – (v3-5. Mar 1979-82. 5,6,9) – v1-5. Mar 1977-82 – 1 – us UMI [760]

PHOTO COMMUNIQUE – (Ceased v10 no 2 1988) – Toronto. v1-10 1979-1988 – 9 – Can$20.00y – cn Micromedia [770]

PHOTO JAPAN MAGAZINE – v1- 1963- 1; v13- 5,6,9 – us UMI [073]

PHOTO LIFE – Markham. v1-19. 1976-94 – 9 – Can$28.00y – cn Micromedia [770]

PHOTO NEWS – Charlotte Amalie. Virgin Islands. july 27-31, 1948 – 1 – us NY Public [072]

PHOTO OIKOUMENE – 1984-94 (complete) – 1r – 1 – ATLA S0928 – us A.T.L.A. [073]

PHOTO SPORTS ACTUALITE – Montreal, Canada. v12 n3. 3 jan 1965-v12 n10. 28 fev 1965 – 1r – 1 – Can$35.00 – cn Can Microfilming [790]

PHOTO WEEKLY – 1973- – 9 – us UMI [073]

PHOTOADDITION VON APLPHA-MORPHOLINOACRYLONITRIL AN 8-CHINOLINCARBONSAEUREMETHYLESTER / Jung, Andreas – 1995 – 1mf – 9 – DM60.00 – 3-8267-2120-9 – gw Hänsel [540]

DIE PHOTOAKUSTISCHE BESTIMMUNG ABSOLUTER OPTISCHER EXTINKTIONSKOEFFIZIENTEN VON ADSORBIERTEN FARBSTOFFEN / Frank, Uwe – 1991 – 71p – 9 – DM98.00 – 3-89349-402-2 – gw Hänsel [540]

PHOTOAKUSTISCHE UNTERSUCHUNG DES ENERGIETRANSFERS AUF FRAKTALEN OBERFLAECHEN / Frank, Uwe – 1991 – 94p – DM98.00 – 3-89349-404-9 – gw Hänsel [540]

THE PHOTO-AMERICAN – New York: Loeber, 1891-1907. v5-7 1895-96 – us Res Libr [770]

PHOTO-ARCHIV GENERALFELDMARSCHALL GOERING – (photo albums) 1914-42 – 1 – 150.00 – us L of C Photodup [943]

PHOTOBIOCHEMISTRY AND PHOTOBIOPHYSICS – v1-8. 1979-84 – 1,5,6,13 – sz Elsevier [073]

PHOTOCHEMISTRY AND PHOTOBIOLOGY – v.1-. 1968- – 5,6,9 – us UMI [540]

PHOTOELEKTRONENSPEKTROSKOPIE AN ALKALIMETALL/SI-GRENZFLAECHEN MIT SYNCHROTRONSTRAHLUNG / Effner, Ute Antonie – 1993 – 2mf – 9 – DM98.00 – 3-89349-730-7 – gw Hänsel [540]

PHOTO-ERA MAGAZINE : THE AMERICAN JOURNAL OF PHOTOGRAPHY / American Federation of Photographic Societies – 1898-1932 – 9r – 1 – us Ross [770]

PHOTOGRAMMETRIA – v20-39. 1965-84 – 1,5,6,13 – sz Elsevier [530]

PHOTOGRAPH ALBUMS OF SULTAN 'ABDULHAMID 2 IN THE BRITISH LIBRARY / ed by Waley, Muhammad Isa – (Includes a printed list of contents and plastic binder) – 126mf – 9 – ne IDC [770]

PHOTOGRAPH COLLECTION / Jackson, Sheldon – 1 – $100.00 – us Presbyterian [978]

THE PHOTOGRAPHER – Montreal: [s.n., 1868?-18– or 19–] (Montreal: Witness Steam Printing House) – 9 – cn C.I.H.M. [770]

PHOTOGRAPHER'S FRIEND – 1871-74 – 1 – uk World [760]

THE PHOTOGRAPHER'S FRIEND – 1871-74. 4v. 1 reel – 1 – $80.00 – us UPA [700]

PHOTOGRAPHIC ABSTRACTS – v. 1-51. 1921-1971 – 1,5,6 – us Princeton Micro [770]

THE PHOTOGRAPHIC AND FINE ART JOURNAL *see* PHOTOGRAPHIC ART-JOURNAL

PHOTOGRAPHIC ART-JOURNAL – 1851-60 – 1 – uk World [760]

PHOTOGRAPHIC ART-JOURNAL – (Cont by: The Photographic and Fine-Art Journal) – 12v. 1851-Aug 1860 – 3r – 1 – $225.00 – us UPA [770]

THE PHOTOGRAPHIC JOURNAL *see*
- THE JOURNAL OF PHOTOGRAPHIC SCIENCE
- THE JOURNAL OF THE PHOTOGRAPHIC SOCIETY

THE PHOTOGRAPHIC NEWS – 1859-1908 – 1 – £1,100.00 – uk World [700]

THE PHOTOGRAPHIC NEWS – 1859-1908. v1-35. 21 reels – 1 – $1,590.00 – us UPA [700]

PHOTOGRAPHIC PERIODICALS OF THE DAGUERREIAN ERA – (See also indiv. titles: Daguerreian Journal/Humphrey's Journal; Photographic Art-Journal; Philadelphia Photographer; Photographer's Friend; Photographic News) – $2,795.00 set – us UPA [770]

THE PHOTOGRAPHIC PORTFOLIO / McLaughlin, S – [Quebec?: s.n., 1859?-1860?] – 9 – cn C.I.H.M. [770]

PHOTOGRAPHIC SOCIETY OF AMERICA – JOURNAL OF PHOTOGRAPHIC SOCIETY OF AMERICA *see* PSA JOURNAL

PHOTOGRAPHIC TIMES – (Issues for 1877-80 filmed with: Photographic Times and American Photographer) – New York: Scovill Manufacturing, v1 n1-v10. 1871-80 – 2r – 1 – us Res Libr [770]

PHOTOGRAPHIC TIMES – New York: Photographic Times Publ Assoc, 1895-1902; 1895-1900 (4r) – 1 – us Res Libr [770]

PHOTOGRAPHIC TIMES AND AMERICAN PHOTOGRAPHER *see* PHOTOGRAPHIC TIMES

PHOTOGRAPHIC VIEWS : OR, RELIGIOUS AND MORAL TRUTHS REFLECTED IN THE UNIVERSE / Weninger, Francis Xavier – New York: P O'Shea, 1873 – 1mf – 9 – 0-8370-6869-X – 1986-0869 – us A.T.L.A. [210]

PHOTOGRAPHIC VIEWS OF NEW YORK CITY, 1870S TO 1970S – From New York Public Library's Local History and Genealogy Division – 1481mf – 9 – $4025.00 – us UMI [978]

PHOTOGRAPHICA / ed by Kaprelian, Edward K – 1968-93. Monthly journal of the Photographic Historical Society of New York. Continued annually – 1 – £395.00 – uk World [760]

PHOTOGRAPHICA: A SUBJECT CATALOG OF BOOKS ON PHOTOGRAPHY / New York Public Library. Research Libraries – 1983. 5500 entries. 1 reel. ISBN 0-8161-1447-1 – 1 – $110.00 – uk Hall. [770]

LA PHOTOGRAPHIE, SES ORIGINES, SES PROGRES, SES TRANSFORMATIONS / Blanquart-Evrard, Louis-Desire – 1869 – 1 – inquire – us Ross [770]

LA PHOTOGRAPHIE, SES ORIGINES, SES PROGRES, SES TRANSFORMATIONS / Blanquart-Evrard, Louis-Desire – Illustrated treatise, English transl. 1 reel. (Collections of the Department of Prints and Photographs) – 1 – 50.00 – fr Bibl Nationale [770]

PHOTOGRAPHING THE INVISIBLE : PRACTICAL STUDIES IN SUPERNORMAL PHOTOGRAPHY, SCRIPT AND OTHER ALLIED PHENOMENA / Coates, James – new rev ed. London: L N Fowler, [1921] – us Res Libr [770]

PHOTOGRAPHS / New York Times. Paris Bureau – 1900-40. A Series. 1 roll. M1149 – 1 – us Nat'l Archives [324]

PHOTOGRAPHS / New York Times. Paris Bureau – 1900-40. B Series. 21 rolls. M1150 – 1 – us Nat'l Archives [324]

PHOTOGRAPHS / New York Times. Paris Bureau – 1900-40. C Series. 28 rolls. M1152 – 1 – us Nat'l Archives [324]

PHOTOGRAPHS / New York Times. Paris Bureau – 1900-40. Letterless Series. 95 rolls. M1151 – 1 – us Nat'l Archives [324]

PHOTOGRAPHS / New York Times. Paris Bureau – 1924-39. D Series. 7 rolls., M1153 – 1 – us Nat'l Archives [324]

PHOTOGRAPHS / New York Times. Paris Bureau – 1940-45. E Series. 1 roll. M1154 – 1 – us Nat'l Archives [324]

PHOTOGRAPHS AND ACQUISITION RECORDS / William Randolph Hearst Collection – Printed guide – 9 – $2,455.00 – us UPA [770]

PHOTOGRAPHS BY THE WRIGHT BROTHERS – 301 images taken by the Wrights themselves – 9 – us L of C Photodup [770]

PHOTOGRAPHS OF EGYPTIAN ART AND OF EGYPT / ed by Franke, D – (Book includes a printed guide and a plastic binder) – 84mf – 9 – ne IDC [770]

PHOTOGRAPHS OF IRRIGATION PROJECTS OF THE BUREAU OF RECLAMATION – 1902-38. 18 rolls. M1145 – 1 – us Nat'l Archives [324]

PHOTOGRAPHS OF THE COMMISSION OF FINE ARTS – 1901-50. 9 rolls. M1148 – 1 – us Nat'l Archives [324]

PHOTOGRAPHS OF THE EXPLORING PARTIES, 1865-1877 / Palestine Exploration Fund – 1 – uk Microform Academic [910]

PHOTOGRAPHS OF THE FEDERAL EXTENSION SERVICE – 1920-45. SC Series. 11 rolls. M1147 – 1 – us Nat'l Archives [324]

PHOTOGRAPHS OF THE FEDERAL EXTENSION SERVICE – 1920-54. S Series. 13 rolls. M1146 – 1 – us Nat'l Archives [324]

PHOTOGRAPHY – v13- 1958- 1; v10- 5,6,9 – us UMI [770]

PHOTOGRAPHY *see* AMATEUR PHOTOGRAPHER

PHOTOGRAPHY AND FOCUS *see* AMATEUR PHOTOGRAPHER

PHOTOGRAPHY AS ART AND SOCIAL HISTORY – (Part 1: The Francis Bedford Topographical Photographs; Part 2: The Warwickshire Photographic Survey, ca 124mf. $1,100.00) – Marlborough: Adam Matthew Publications, 1993 – 53mf – 9 – $580.00 – uk Matthew [770]

PHOTOGRAPHY, CINEMA : ARCHITECTURE, APPLIED ARTS, STUDIO ARTS – (Individual titles not listed separately) – 47 catalogues on 51mf – 9 – £375.00 – uk Chadwyck [770]

PHOTO-JOURNAL : ABONDAMMENT ILLUSTRE – Montreal, Canada. 17 avr 1937-9 jan 1978 – 73r – 1 – Can$50.00r – cn Can Microfilming [072]

PHOTOLITH – (See also: Photolith, SCM: the Journal for Scholastic Media) – v1-25. 1970-75 – 1 – us UMI [370]

PHOTOLITH, SCM: THE JOURNAL FOR SCHOLASTIC MEDIA – (See also: Photolith) – v26-28. 1975-77 – 1,5,6,9 – us UMI [370]

PHOTOMETHODS *see* PMI PHOTO METHODS FOR INDUSTRY

PHOTO-POLICE – Montreal: Cie Jacmond, v1 no 1(2 Nov 1968)-. SEM35P334 – 48r – 1 – cn Bibl Nat [072]

PHOTOTHERMISCHE UNTERSUCHUNGEN AN KLEINEN SILBERPARTIKELN / Bauer, Martin – 1992 – 78p – DM75.00 – 3-89349-534-7 – gw Hänsel [540]

PHOTO-VEDETTES – Montreal: Publ Quebecor. v1-19. 1963-82. SEM35P102 – 35r – 1 – Can$1,388.00 – cn Bibl Nat [073]

PHOTOVIDEO – (Ceased v7 1990) – Toronto. v1-7. 1984-90 – 9 – Can$20.00y – cn Micromedia [770]

PHOTOVIDEO PROFESSIONAL – (1986- . 5,6,9) – v1- . 1984- – 1 – us UMI [073]

PHOTOVIDEO RETAILER – (1986- . 5,6,9) – v1- . 1984- – 1 – us UMI [073]

PHOTO-WOCHE – (Publ. since sep 5, 1922 in Prerow/Darss) – Berlin-Charlottenburg. sep 23, 1911-oct 3, 1922 – 7r – 1 – gw Mikrofilm [770]

Phrantzes, Georgius et al *see* CORPUS SCRIPTORUM HISTORIAE BYZANTINAE (CSHB 36)

Phranzae, Georgii *see* CHRONICON (CBH 30,2)

PHRASEOLOGISCHE EINHEITEN IN PUBLIZISTISCHEN TEXTEN DES ENGLISCHEN UND RUSSISCHEN / Walbe, Ute – 1993 – 2mf – 9 – DM80.00 – 3-89349-766-8 – gw Hänsel [420]

PHRASES LINGUAE LATINAE / Manuzio, Aldo – 1579. 309p. (English Linguistics Series 1500-1800) – 9 – us UMI [450]

PHRASIS : A TREATISE ON THE HISTORY AND STRUCTURE OF THE DIFFERENT LANGUAGES OF THE WORLD: WITH A COMPARATIVE VIEW OF THE FORMS OF THEIR WORDS AND THE STYLE OF THEIR EXPRESSIONS / Wilson, Jacob – (Includes index) – Albany: J Munsell, 1864 – 1mf – 9 – 0-8370-8559-4 – 1986-2559 – us A.T.L.A. [400]

PHRENOLOGY, OR THE DOCTRINE OF THE MENTAL PHENOMENA / Spurzheim, Johann Gaspar – Introd. by Cyrus Elder. Rev. ed. from the 2nd American ed. Philadelphia, London: J.B. Lippincott Co., 1908. 459p. 14 pl – 1 – us U.W. Library [150]

PHRYNIS MITILENAEUS.. / Printz, Wolfgang C – Erster-Dritter Theil. 1696 – 2,9 – us Sibley [780]

PHTHISIOLOGIA / Morton, R – M 382. 1694 – 9 – ne IDC [610]

PHTHISIOLOGIA, SEU EXERCITATIONES DE PHTHISI / Morton, R – M-71. 1689 – 9 – ne IDC [610]

PHUC QUOC – Organe des revendications des Annamites paraissant en francais annamite et chinois. no. 1-2. Saint-Denis (Seine). sept 1926 – 1 – fr A.C.R.P.P. [073]

PHU-DRAG BKA'-'GYUR – 1697-1705 – 7,698mf – $3,500.00 – us I.A.S.W.R. [280]

PHU-DRAG BKA'-'GYUR – c1700 A.D. From Phu-drag Monastery. 120v – 7,698mf – 9 – $3,500.00 – us I.A.S.W.R. [280]

PHU-NU TAN TIEN – Red. en chef Nguyen-van-Tan. no. 1-24; n.s., no. 1-4. Hue. juil 1932-juil 1933. mq. no. 21-22 – 1 – fr A.C.R.P.P. [073]

PHU-NU' TAN VAN – Saigon. Hebd. Quot. en juin-juil. 1932. Suspendu de janv a mai 1931, mai 1929-34 – 1 – fr A.C.R.P.P. [073]

PHU-NU' THO'I DAM – Dir. Mme Nguyen-van-Da. Hanoi. Quot. jusqu'en janv. 1933 puis hebd. dec 1930-juin 1934 – 1 – fr A.C.R.P.P. [073]

PHYCEAE CAPENSES / Areschoug, J E – 4pts. Upsaliae. 1851. B-7397 1 – 9 – ne IDC [580]

PHYCEAE NOVAE ET MINUS COGNITAE IN MARIBUS EXTRAEUROPAEIS COLLECTAE / Areschoug, J E – (Acta R. Soc. Sci. Ups., S. III, v. 1). Uppsala. 1854. B-1346 2 – 8 – ne IDC [580]

PHYCEAE SCANDINAVICAE MARINAE SIVE FUCACEARUM / Areschoug, J E – Upsaliae. 1850. B-7396 1 – 9 – ne IDC [580]

PHYCOLOGIA – Oxford, Berkeley. v1-12. 1961-72 – 5,9 – Dfl960.00; Dfl80.00v – ne Swets [580]

PHYCOLOGIA – v.1-10. 1961-71 – 1,5,6 – 2235.00 – us Princeton Micro [580]

PHYCOLOGIA GENERALIS / Kuetzing, F T – Leipzig. 1843. B-602 2 – 8 – ne IDC [580]

PHYCOLOGIA GERMANICA / Kuetzing, F T – Nordhausen. 1845. B-618 2 – 8 – ne IDC [580]

PHYCOLOGICA GENERALIS ODER ANATOMIE DER TANGE / Kuetzing, F T – 1843 – 7 – uk Microform Academic [580]

PHYCOLOGICA GERMANICA / Kuetzing, F T – 1845 – 7 – uk Microform Academic [580]

PHYLOGENETISCHE UNTERSUCHUNGEN DER GATTUNG KALANCHOE MITTELS FINGERPRINT-VERFAHREN / Roesicke, Helmut – 1994 – 1mf – DM60.00 – 3-8267-2072-5 – gw Hänsel [574]

PHYLOGENY OF AN ACQUIRED CHARACTERISTIC / Hyatt, A – Z-298 2. 1894 – 8 – ne IDC [150]

PHYLON – (v. 30- 1969- 5,6. v. 37- 1976- 9) – v. 1- 1940- – 1 – us UMI [300]

PHYSICA – v26-78. 1960-74 – 1,5,6,13 – sz Elsevier [073]

PHYSICA SECTION A: THEORETICAL AND STATISTICAL PHYSICS – v79A-128A. 1975-84 – 1,5,6,13 – sz Elsevier [073]

PHYSICA SECTION B AND SECTION C.B: LOW TEMPERATURE AND SOLID STATE PHYSICS. C: ATOMIC, MOLECULAR AND PLASMA PHYSICS, OPTICS – v79B plus C-130B plus C. 1975-84 – 1,5,6,13 – sz Elsevier [530]

PHYSICA SECTION D: NONLINEAR PHENOMENA – v1D-13D.1980-84 – 1,5,6,13 – sz Elsevier [073]

PHYSICAL ACTIVITY, CALCIUM INTAKE, BODY COMPOSITION AND STATURE AS PREDICTORS OF BONE INDICES IN COLLEGE-AGED MEN / Burtt, Scott L – 1988 – 94p 1mf – 9 – $4.00 – us Microform Publ [612]

PHYSICAL ACTIVITY PATTERNS AND CHARACTERISTICS OF HIGH SCHOOL STUDENTS IN A GOVERNOR'S HONORS PROGRAM / Stueck, Patricia MO & Baumgartner, Ted A – 1991 – 2mf – 9 – $8.00 – us Microform Publ [150]
PHYSICAL AGGRESSION AS A FUNCTION OF ANGER IN MEN AND WOMEN / Wood, Ray O & Morris, Harold H – 1992 – 2mf – 9 – $8.00 – us Microform Publ [150]
PHYSICAL AND CHEMICAL METHODS OF SOIL AND WATER ANALYSIS – 1976 – 287p – it F.A.O. [550]
PHYSICAL AND MENTAL REHABILITATION JOURNAL: OFFICIAL PUBLICATION OF THE PHYSICAL AND MENTAL REHABILITATION ASSOCIATION *see* AMERICAN CORRECTIVE THERAPY JOURNAL
PHYSICAL AND OCCUPATIONAL THERAPY IN GERIATRICS : CURRENT TRENDS IN GERIATRIC REHABILITATION / ed by Taira, Ellen Dunleavey – v1- 1980- – 1, 9 ($250.00 in US $350.00 outside hardcopy subsc) – us Haworth [615]
PHYSICAL AND OCCUPATIONAL THERAPY IN PEDIATRICS – v1- . 1980- . q – 1, 9 – $185.00v; $36.00v hardcopy subscribers – us Haworth [615]
THE PHYSICAL CAUSE OF THE DEATH OF CHRI..AND PRACTICE OF CHRISTIANITY / Stroud, William – New York: D. Appleton, 1874. 1 fiche – 9 – us A.T.L.A. [240]
THE PHYSICAL CAUSE OF THE DEATH OF CHRIST, AND ITS RELATION TO THE PRINCIPLES AND PRACTICE OF CHRISTIANITY / Stroud, William – 1871 – 1 – us A.T.L.A. [240]
PHYSICAL DATA / Israel. Prime Minister's Office. Ministry of the Interior. Local Authorities in Israel 1973 74 – Jerusalem, 1975. 25, 239, 27 p. (Special Series no. 488). Text also in Hebrew – 9 – 6.00 – is I.T.T.I. [956]
PHYSICAL DEFECTS: THE PATHWAY TO CORRECTION / Franzen, Raymond H – 1934 – 4mf – 9 – $12.00 – us Microform Publ [370]
A PHYSICAL DICTIONARY / Blancard, S – London, 1684 – 6mf – ne IDC [610]
A PHYSICAL DICTIONARY / Blancard, S – M 303 1684 – 9 – ne IDC [530]
PHYSICAL EDUCATION AND NONPHYSICAL EDUCATION MAJORS : A COMPARISON OF EXERCISE BEHAVIORS / Butler, Stanley B – 1989 – 243p 3mf – 9 – $12.00 – us Microform Publ [150]
PHYSICAL EDUCATION AND SPORT IN THE JEWISH HISTORY AND CULTURE / Israel. Ministry of Education and Culture – Proceedings of the second international seminar, Jul 1977. By Uriel Simri. Netanya, 1977. 170, 44 p. illus. Summary also in Hebrew. Bibliogr – 9 – 5.00 – is I.T.T.I. [790]
PHYSICAL EDUCATION BY MUSCULAR EXERCISE / Gulick, Luther Halsey – 1904 – 2mf – 9 – $6.00 – us Microform Publ [790]
PHYSICAL EDUCATION OBJECTIVES AS PERCEIVED BY MIDDLE SCHOOL STUDENTS / Patke, Kathryn E – 1989 – 92p 1mf – 9 – $4.00 – us Microform Publ [370]
PHYSICAL EDUCATOR – v1- 1940- 1; v30- 5,6; v32- 9 – us UMI [073]
THE PHYSICAL EDUCATOR AND THE COACH: SIMILARITIES AND DISSIMILARITIES / Israel. Ministry of Education and Culture – Proceedings of an international seminar, 1976. By Uriel Simri and Giselher Tiegel. 1977. 223 p. In cooperation with the Deutsche Sporthochschule Koeln – 9 – 5.00 – is I.T.T.I. [324]
PHYSICAL EXERCISE AND ACTIVITY FOR THE AGING / Israel. Ministry of Education and Culture – Proceedings of an international seminar. By Uriel Simri. Nov 1975. 228 p. Diagr – 9 – 5.00 – is I.T.T.I. [324]
PHYSICAL FITNESS OF DEAF AND HEARING ADOLESCENT FEMALES / Williams, Martha A – 1981 – 2mf – 9 – $8.00 – us Microform Publ [790]
PHYSICAL GEOGRAPHY OF THE GLOBE / Herschel, John FW – 5th ed. Edinburgh: Adam & Charles Black, 1875. 448p. maps – 1 – us U.W. Library [910]
THE PHYSICAL GROWTH OF GIRLS / Boynton, B – 1936 – 6mf – 9 – $18.00 – us Microform Publ [612]
PHYSICAL MEASURES OF GROWTH AND NUTRITION / Franzen, Raymond H – 1929 – 5mf – 9 – $15.00 – us Microform Publ [616]
PHYSICAL PRACTICE, MENTAL IMAGERY, AND RELAXATION, RELATED TO MOTOR SKILL ACQUISITION / Turner, Paul E – 1989 – 2mf – 9 – $8.00 – us Microform Publ [150]
PHYSICAL REVIEW : A, B, C, D, AND E – (Apply to publisher for pre-1994 prices) – 1994 – 1,5,6,9 – $6,400.00mf set $5,760.00r set – us A.I.P. [530]
PHYSICAL REVIEW – Series 1. v1-35.1893-1912 – 1,5,6,9 – us A.I.P. [530]
PHYSICAL REVIEW – Series 2. v1-188. 1913-1969 – 1,5,6 – us A.I.P. [530]
PHYSICAL REVIEW A: GENERAL PHYSICS – Series 3. v. 1- Includes index 1970- – 1,5,6,9 – us A.I.P. [530]
PHYSICAL REVIEW B: CONDENSED MATTER – Series 3. v. 1- Includes index 1970- – 1,5,6,9 – us A.I.P. [530]
PHYSICAL REVIEW C: NUCLEAR PHYSICS – Series 3. v. 1- Includes index 1970- – 1,5,6,9 – us A.I.P. [530]
PHYSICAL REVIEW D: PARTICLES AND FIELDS – Series 3. v. 1- Includes index 1970- – 1,5,6,9 – us A.I.P. [530]
PHYSICAL REVIEW E – 1,5,6,9 – us A.I.P. [530]
PHYSICAL REVIEW LETTERS – v. 1- 1958- – 1,5,6,9 – us A.I.P. [530]
PHYSICAL SELF-ESTEEM ACROSS FOUR PHASES OF A CARDIAC REHABILITATION PROGRAM / Boge, Justin – 1993 – 1mf – $4.00 – us Microform Publ [150]
Physical Society. London *see* PROCEEDINGS. SERIES B
Physical Society of Japan *see*
– JOURNAL
– JOURNAL OF THE PHYSICAL SOCIETY OF JAPAN
PHYSICAL THERAPY – v1- 1921- 1; v51- 5,6; v55- 9 – us UMI [615]
A PHYSICAL TREATISE / Russell, W – M 401. 1684 – 9 – ne IDC [610]
PHYSICALISCH-MATHEMATISCHE ABHANDLUNG.. / Mayer, Johann Tobias – Frankfurt: Bey G.P. Monath, 1786. 2+142p. Illus. 1 reel. 1227 – 1 – us U.W. Library [510]
PHYSICIAN AND SPORTSMEDICINE – v1- 1973- 1,5,6; v4- 9 – us UMI [617]
PHYSICIAN ASSISTANT, HEALTH PRACTITIONER – v3- 1979- 1; v4- 1980- 5,6,9 – us UMI [073]
PHYSICIANS' AND SURGEONS' INVESTIGATOR – v. 1-10. 1880-89 – 1 – us UMI [616]
PHYSICIAN'S ASSOCIATE *see* PA JOURNAL
PHYSICIANS' BIRTH RECORDS / Sandusky County. Ohio. Woodville Township. Village Clerk – (Some issues missing) – 1909-1936 – 2r – 1 – $32.50r – us Archival [324]
PHYSICIANS FOR HUMAN RIGHTS – Somerville. 87 docs. 1987-1991 – 27mf – 9 – ne IDC [320]
PHYSICIAN'S MAGAZINE – v. 1. Aug 1885-Mar 1886 – 1 – us UMI [610]
PHYSICIAN'S MANAGEMENT – (v.21-. 1981-. 5,6,9) – v.1-. 1961- – 1 – us UMI [610]
PHYSICIAN'S MANAGEMENT MANUALS – (1985- . 5,6,9) – 1976- – 1 – us UMI [650]
PHYSICIANS MANAGEMENT MANUALS – (1976-88 Can$46.00y. Ceased v18 no 7 1994) – Toronto, 1976-87; v12-18. 1988-94 – 9 – Can$37.00y – cn Micromedia [610]
PHYSICIAN'S MONITOR – v. 1-13. 1870-85 – 1 – us UMI [610]
THE PHYSICIANS OF MYDDVAI; MEDDYGON MYDDFAI / ed by Williams ab Ithel, J W – Llandovery, 1861 – 9mf – 8 – ne Slangenburg [610]
THE PHYSICIANS OF MYDDVAL; MEDDYGON MIDDFAL / ed by Williams ab Ithel, J W – Llandvery, 1861 – 9mf – 8 – Dfl32.00 – ne Slangenburg [610]
PHYSICIAN'S RECORDS: NEW RIEGEL, OHIO / Hermann, Francis – 1857-1866 – 1r – 1 – $32.50r – us Archival [610]
PHYSICIAN'S RECORDS: OTTAWA COUNTY, OHIO / Mapes, Orlo – 1896-1915 – 1r – 1 – $32.50r – us Archival [610]
LA PHYSICIENNE *see*
– VOYAGE AUTOUR DU MONDE. EXECUTE SUR LES CORVETTES DE S.M. L'URANIE ET LA PHYSICIENNE, 1817-1820
– VOYAGE AUTOUR DU MONDE EXECUTE SUR LES CORVETTES DE S.M. L'URANIE ET LA PHYSICIENNE, 1817-1820
– VOYAGE AUTOUR DU MONDE. EXECUTE SUR LES CORVETTES DE S.M. L'URANIE ET LA PHYSICIENNE, 1817-1820
PHYSICOCHEMICAL BIOLOGY REVIEWS / ed by Skulachev, V P – 1,5,9 – us Gordon [574]
PHYSICOCHEMICAL HYDRODYNAMICS. THE INTERNATIONAL JOURNAL – v. 1-. 1980- – 5,6,9 – us UMI [550]
PHYSICS ABSTRACTS : FOUR YEAR CUMULATIVE INDEXES – (With author-subject indexes) – 1957-1992 – 1,5,6,9 – uk INSPEC [530]
PHYSICS ABSTRACTS : SEMI-ANNUAL INDEXES – (With author-subject indexes) – 1898-1995 – 1,5,6,9 – uk INSPEC [530]
PHYSICS ABSTRACTS – v1-94. 1898-1995 – 1,5,6,9 – uk INSPEC [530]
PHYSICS AND CHEMISTRY – v63-81 1959-77 1; v73-81 5,6; v74-81 9 – us UMI [530]
PHYSICS AND CHEMISTRY OF GLASSES – v. 1-13. Sheffield. 1960-72 – 9 – 2478.00; 6.00v – uk Dawson [530]
PHYSICS AND CHEMISTRY OF LIQUIDS / ed by March, N H – 1968- – 1,5,9 – us Gordon [530]
PHYSICS AND CHEMISTRY OF METAL PROCESSING – v1- 1980- – 5,6,9 – us UMI [660]
PHYSICS AND CHEMISTRY OF MINERALS – v1-7, 1977-81. ISSN: 0342-1791 – 1,5,6,9,13 – $155.00v – us UMI [530]
PHYSICS AND CHEMISTRY OF THE EARTH – v1- 1956- – 5,6,9 – us UMI [550]
PHYSICS AND POLITICS, OR, THOUGHTS ON THE APPLICATION OF THE PRINCIPELS OF "NATURAL SELECTION" AND "INHERITANCE" TO POLITICAL SOCIETY / Bagehot, Walter – New York. 1873. 224 p. Includes biblographical references. 1 reel – 1 – us U.W. Library [500]
PHYSICS, CHEMISTRY AND THE MECHANICS OF SURFACES / ed by Osip'yan, Yu.A et al – 1983- – 1,5,9 – us Gordon [073]
PHYSICS – DOKLADY – v1- 1956- – 1,5,6 – us A.I.P. [530]
PHYSICS EDUCATION – v1-. 1966- – 1,5,6,9 – £85.00 – uk I.O.P. [370]
PHYSICS IN CANADA = LA PHYSIQUE AU CANADA – (v42-50 1986-94 Can$20.00y 9) – Ottawa. v8-50. 1952-94 – 5,9 – Price varies – cn Micromedia [530]
PHYSICS IN MEDICINE AND BIOLOGY – v1- . 1956- – 1,5,6,9 – £431.00 – uk I.O.P. [610]
PHYSICS LETTERS – (Section A. v24A-106A. 1967-84. Section B. v24B-147B. 1967-84) – v1-23. 1962-66 – 1,5 – sz Elsevier [073]
PHYSICS OF ATOMIC NUCLEI – 1,5,6,9 – us A.I.P. [530]
PHYSICS OF CONDENSED MATTER *see* ZEITSCHRIFT FUER PHYSIK. B
THE PHYSICS OF FLUIDS – (Formerly: Physics of Fluids A) – v1-31. 1958-88 – 1,5,6,9 – us A.I.P. [530]
PHYSICS OF FLUIDS A *see* THE PHYSICS OF FLUIDS
PHYSICS OF FLUIDS A,B – v1- 1989- – 1,5,6,9 – us A.I.P. [530]
PHYSICS OF FLUIDS/PHYSICS OF PLASMAS – (Apply to publisher for pre-1994 prices) – 1994 – 1,5,6,9 – $1,570.00mf set $1,415.00r set – us A.I.P. [530]
PHYSICS OF METALS / ed by Nemoshkalenko, V V & Molodkin, V B – 1982 – 1,5,9 – us Gordon [530]
PHYSICS OF PARTICLES AND NUCLEI – 1,5,6,9 – us A.I.P. [530]
PHYSICS OF PLASMAS – 1,5,6,9 – us A.I.P. [530]
PHYSICS OF THE EARTH AND PLANETARY INTERIORS – v1-39. 1967-84 – 1,5,6,13 – sz Elsevier [073]
PHYSICS OF THE SOLID STATE – v1- 1959- – 1,5,6 – us A.I.P. [530]
PHYSICS REPORTS – Section C of Physics Letters. v1-118. 1971-84 – 1,5,6,13 – sz Elsevier [530]
PHYSICS REVIEWS / ed by Khalatnikov, I M – 9,5,1 – us Harwood [530]
THE PHYSICS TEACHER – v1- 1963- – 1,5,6 – us A.I.P. [370]
PHYSICS TODAY – v. 1- 1948- – 1,5,6,9 – us A.I.P. [530]
PHYSICS – USPEKHI – v1- 1958- – 1,5,6 – us A.I.P. [530]
PHYSICS WORLD – v1-. 1988- – 1,5,6,9 – £73.00 – uk I.O.P. [530]
PHYSIK IN REGELMASSIGEN BERICHTEN – Berlin. (All published. Supplement to Zeitschrift fuer Technique Physik.) v. 1-12. 1933-1944 – 1,5,6 – us Princeton Micro [530]
PHYSIKALISCHE ABHANDLUNGEN. / Akademie der Wissenschaften. Munich – Munich, 1803-06. v.1-2 – 3 – us Readex [530]
PHYSIKALISCHE BLAETTER : ORGAN DER DPG/MEMBERSHIP JOURNAL OF THE GERMAN PHYSICAL SOCIETY – v1-52. 1944-96 – 1,5,6,13 – us V.C.H. [530]
PHYSIKALISCHE CHARAKTERISIERUNG DES GENOMS THERMOPHILER CLOSTRIDIEN MIT HILFE DER PULSED-FIELD AGAROSE GEL ELECTROPHORESIS / Landmann, Bernhard – 1995 – 1mf – 9 – DM60.00 – 3-8267-2122-5 – gw Hänsel [574]
PHYSIKALISCHE CHARAKTERISIERUNG ULTRAFLEXIBLER LIPID-VESIKEL / Kurze, Volker – 1994 – 1mf – DM60.00 – 3-8267-2047-4 – gw Hänsel [530]
PHYSIKALISCHE UND MEDICINISCHE ABHANDLUNGEN DER KOENIGLICHEN AKADEMIE DER WISSENSCHAFTEN ZU BERLIN – Gotha, 1781-1786. V.1-4 – 36mf – 9 – ne IDC [610]
PHYSIKALISCHE ZEITSCHRIFT – v. 1-45. 1899-1945 – 1,5,6 – us Princeton Micro [530]
PHYSIKALISCHE ZEITSCHRIFT DER SOWYETUNION – v. 1-12. 1932-1937 – 1,5,6 – us Princeton Micro [530]
Physikalischer Verein. Frankfurt am Main *see* JAHRESBERICHT DES PHYSIKALISCHEN VEREINS ZU FRANKFURT AM MAIN
PHYSIKALISCHES WOERTERBUCH ODER ERKLAERUNG DER VORNEHMSTEN ZUR PHYSIK GEHOERENDEN BEGRIFFE UND KUNSTWOERTER / Fischer, Johann Carl – Goettingen. 10v. 1798-1827 – 100mf – 9 – subsc: DM600.00 diazo DM700.00 silver – gw Olms [530]
PHYSIKALISCH-OEKONOMISCHE BIBLIOTHEK / Beckmann, Johann – Goettingen. 23v. 1770-1806 – 160mf – 9 – subsc: DM1000.00 diazo DM1200.00 silver – gw Olms [530]
THE PHYSIOCRATS – Series: French Economists of the 18th Century – $500.00 – us UPA [330]
THE PHYSIOGRAPHIC BASIS OF PIONEER SETTLEMENT IN SOUTHERN SUMATRA / Verstappen, Herman Theodoor – In Indonesian. SE 4231 1. 1956? – 9 – ne IDC [910]
O PHYSIOLATRA : REVISTA CONSAGRADA AOS IDEAES ORTHOLOGICOS – Curitiba, 14 Jul-Oct 1910; Feb-Mar, Jun-Oct 1911; Jun 1912 – 1,5,6 – bl Biblioteca [072]
PHYSIOLOGIA PLANTARUM – Copenhagen, 1948-64. v1-17. 1595/2 – 8 – ne IDC [580]
PHYSIOLOGIA PLANTARUM – v. 1-32. 1948-74 – 1,5,6 – us Princeton Micro [580]
PHYSIOLOGIA PLANTARUM – (v1-3. Dfl70.00v; v4-20. Dfl110.00v) – Copenhagen. v1-20. 1948-67 – 5,9 – Dfl2,080.00 – ne Swets [580]
THE PHYSIOLOGIC RESPONSES TO IN-LINE ROLLER SKATING COMPARED TO TREADMILL RUNNING / Wallick, Mark E & Porcari, John P – 1991 – 1mf – $4.00 – us Microform Publ [612]
THE PHYSIOLOGICAL AND PERCEIVED EFFECTS OF DRAFTING ON A GROUP OF HIGHLY TRAINED DISTANCE RUNNERS / Corvalan-Groessling, Veronica – University of British Columbia, 1995 – 2mf – $8.00 – PE3587 – us Microform Publ [612]
PHYSIOLOGICAL AND PERFORMANCE DETERMINANTS IN MANNED SPACE SYSTEMS – (v5 1960, Science and Technology) – 9 – $20.00 – us Univelt [629]
PHYSIOLOGICAL COMPARISON OF HIGH PERFORMANCE SWIMMERS AND RUNNERS / Contarsy, Steven A – 1979 – 1mf – 9 – $4.00 – us Microform Publ [790]
THE PHYSIOLOGICAL COST OF PLYOMETRIC REBOUND JUMPING AT VARIED INTENSITIES / Zisk, D M – 1991 – 1mf – 9 – $4.00 – us Microform Publ [612]
PHYSIOLOGICAL DISCRIMINATORS OF ROWING PERFORMANCE IN MALE, CLUB ROWERS / Gayer, Christina D & Thorland, William G – 1993 – 1mf – $4.00 – us Microform Publ [612]
PHYSIOLOGICAL DISQUISITIONS : OR, DISCOURSES ON THE NATURAL PHILOSOPHY OF THE ELEMENTS / Jones, William – London: J. Rivington and Sons, 1781 – 627p – 1 – us U.W. Library [500]

PHYSIOLOGICAL MEASUREMENT / ed by Evans, D H – (Co-published with the Institute of Physical Sciences in Medicine) – UK: 10P Publishing, 1993.-v14 – 1,5,6,9 – £122.00 – uk I.O.P. [621]

A PHYSIOLOGICAL PROFILE OF CHAMPION LEVEL FEMALE TRIATHLETES / Greene, Carol – 1989 – 2mf – 9 – $8.00 – us Microform Publ [612]

PHYSIOLOGICAL RESPONSE OF TRAINED CYCLISTS TO VARIOUS CYCLING HANDLEBAR POSTURES / Wagner, Dale R & Berger, Richard A – 1991 – 1mf – 9 – $4.00 – us Microform Publ [612]

PHYSIOLOGICAL RESPONSES OBTAINED DURING EXERCISE ON THE STAIRMASTER GAUNTLET WITH AND WITHOUT THE USE OF HANDS / Heilman, Paula S & Butts, Nancy Kay – 1991 – 1mf – $4.00 – us Microform Publ [612]

THE PHYSIOLOGICAL RESPONSES OF THE ADDITION OF HAND HELD WEIGHTS TO STATIONARY BICYCLING / Gasunas, Geraldine & Wilson, Philip K – 1991 – 1mf – $4.00 – us Microform Publ [612]

THE PHYSIOLOGICAL RESPONSES TO WALKING WITH AND WITHOUT POWER POLES(TM) ON TREADMILL EXERCISE / Hendrickson, Thomas L – 1993 – 1mf – $4.00 – us Microform Publ [612]

PHYSIOLOGICAL REVIEW – v1- 1921- 1; v45- 5,6; v50- 9 – us UMI [612]

PHYSIOLOGICAL REVIEWS – v1-35. 1921-55 – 1,5,6 – us Princeton Micro [612]

PHYSIOLOGICAL ZOOLOGY – v1- 1928- 1; v43- 5,6; v50- 1977- 9 – us UMI [590]

PHYSIOLOGICAL ZOOLOGY – v. 1-16. 1928-1943 – 1 – us Princeton Micro [590]

PHYSIOLOGIE DE L'HOMME ALIENE APPLIQUEE A L'ANALYSE DE L'HOMME SOCIAL / Pinel, Scipion – (French Precursors of Psychiatry Series). Paris. J. Rouvier. 1833 – 9 – fr Hachette [150]

PHYSIOLOGIE DES MOUVEMENTS DEMONTEE A L'AIDE... / Duchenne de Boulogne, G B A – Paris, 1867 – 16mf – 9 – ne IDC [612]

PHYSIOLOGISCHE UND ALGOLOGISCHE STUDIEN / Hansgirg, A – Prag. 1887. B-6369 2 – 8 – ne IDC [580]

PHYSIOLOGIST – v1- 1957- 1; v14- 5,6; v19- 9 – us UMI [612]

PHYSIOLOGY AND BEHAVIOR – (Back issues of journal available from UMI) – 12 issues/y. v53-54. 1993 – 9 – £716.00y – uk Elsevier Sci [612]

PHYSIOLOGY AND BEHAVIOR – v1- 1966- – 5,6,9 – us UMI [150]

PHYSIOLOGY AND GENERAL BIOLOGY REVIEWS / ed by Turpaev, T M – 1,5,9 – us Gordon [574]

PHYSIOLOGY; BEING A COURSE OF LECTURES UPON THE VISCERAL ANATOMY AND VITAL ECONOMY OF HUMAN BODIES / Haller, Albrecht von – H-119 2. 2 v. 1754 – 9 – ne IDC [612]

THE PHYSIOLOGY OF TEETOTALISM: A LECTURE DELIVERED IN THE VESTRY OF THE FREE BAPTIST CHURCH, FREDERICTON, FEBRUARY 23RD, 1883 / Annear, S – Saint John, N.B., Christian Visitor, 1883? 00021. (Pre-1900 Canadiana) – 9 – cn C.I.H.M. [360]

PHYSIOTHERAPY – (v70-. 1984-. 5,6,9) – v34-. 1948- – 1 – us UMI [073]

PHYSIOTHERAPY CANADA-PHYSIOTHERAPIE – (v.33-. 1981-. 5,6,7) – v.24-. 1972- – 1 – us UMI [615]

PHYSIOTHERAPY PRACTICE – v1- . 1985- – 1,5,6,9 – us UMI [073]

PHYTOCHEMISTRY – (Back isssues of journal available from UMI) – 18 issues/y. v32-34. 1993 – 9 – £856.00y – uk Elsevier Sci [580]

PHYTOCHEMISTRY – v1- 1962- – 5,6,9 – us UMI [540]

PHYTOGRAPHIA LUSITANIAE / Brotero, F di Avelar – Olissipone. 1801. B-6437 2 – 8 – ne IDC [580]

PHYTOGRAPHIA LUSITANIAE SELECTIOR SEU NOVARUM ET ALIARUM MINUS COGNITARUM STIRPIUM / Brotero, F di Avelar – Lisboa. 1800. B-5629 2 – 8 – ne IDC [580]

PHYTOGRAPHIA, SEU DESCRIPTIO RARIORUM MINUS COGNITARUM PLANTARUM / Willdenow, C L – Erlangae. 1794. B-353 2 – 8 – ne IDC [580]

LA PHYTOGRAPHIE / Candolle, A P de – Paris. 1880. B-402 2 – 8 – ne IDC [580]

PHYTOGRAPHIE MEDICALE,... / Roques, J – Paris 1821[-1824]. 2v – 24mf – 9 – ne IDC [615]

PHYTOLOGIST – London. v1-6. 1844-62 – 215mf – 9 – 5302/2 – ne IDC [580]

PHYTON. ANNALES REI BOTANICAE – 7701. V. 1-13. 1948-1961 – 9 – ne IDC [580]

PHYTON. INTERNATIONAL JOURNAL OF EXPERIMENTAL BOTANY – 7713. V. 1-25. Lacking: v. 1(2); v. 2(2); v. 3(1); v. 22. 1951-1968 – 9 – ne IDC [580]

PHYTOPATHOLOGISCHE ZEITSCHRIFT – v. 1-15. 1929-1949 – 1,5,6 – us Princeton Micro [580]

PHYTOPATHOLOGY – v1- 1911- 1; v60- 5,6; v66- 9 – us UMI [631]

PHYTOPATHOLOGY – New York, Baltimore. v1-31. 1911-41 – 475mf – 9 – 5394c/2 – ne IDC [580]

PHYTOPATHOLOGY – v1-60. 1911-70 – 1,5,6 – us Princeton Micro [616]

PHYTOPLANKTON MANUAL / ed by Sournia, A – 2nd ed 1981 – xvi+337p – 9 – 92-3-101572-9 – fr UNESCO [580]

PHYTOZOOLOGIE PHILOSOPHIQUE / Necker, N J de – B245 2. 1790 – 8 – ne IDC [580]

PI HSUEH CHIEN / Chin, Yung – Hong Kong: distributed by Ming Pao Daily News Ltd., 1975, 1977 printing. 2v.ill. Title in English in colophon: The Sword Stained with Royal Blood. Appendices – 1 – us U.W. Library [800]

PI MU EPSILON JOURNAL – v1- 1949- 1; v6- 5,6,9 – us UMI [073]

PIA DESIDERIA EMBLEMATIS, ELEGIIS ET AFFECTIBUS / Hugo, H – O 639. 1628 – 9 – ne IDC [240]

PIA DESIDERIA EMBLEMATIS ELEGIIS ET AFFECTIBUS SS. PATRUM / Hugo, H – O 309. 1624 – 9 – ne IDC [240]

PIA DESIDERIA. LIB. 3. AD URBANUM 8 / Hugo, H – Editio 5. emendata. Antwerpen, 1629 – 5mf – 9 – O-3241/1 – ne IDC [760]

PIA DESIDERIA TRIBUS LIBRIS COMPREHENSA : 1. GEMITUS ANIMAE PAENITENTIS: 2. VOTA ANIMAE SANCTAE: 3. SUSPIRIA ANIMAE AMANTIS / Hugo, H – (Engraved titlepage missing?) – Antwerpen, 1676 – 5mf – 9 – O-3230/1 – ne IDC [760]

PIA DESIDERIA TRIBUS LIBRIS COMPREHENSA : 1. GEMITUS ANIMAE PENITENTE 2. VOTA ANIMAE SANCTAE 3. SUSPIRIA ANIMAE AMANTIS / Hugo, H – Antwerpen, [c1657] – 5mf – 9 – O-3229/1 – ne IDC [760]

PIA ET IN VERBO DEI FVNDATA ASSERTIO, DECLARATIO AND CONFESSIO D. PAVLI EBERI...DE SACRATISSIMA COENA... / Eber, P – Vitebergae, 1571 – 5mf – 9 – ne IDC [240]

PIA ET NECESSARIA ADMONITIO DE DECRETIS ET CANONIBVS CONCILII TRIDENTINI, SUB PIO QUARTO ROM. PONTIFICE, ANNO AND C. 62. AND 63. CELEBRATI... / Flacius Illyricus d.A E, M – Francoforti apvd, 1563 – 2mf – 9 – ne IDC [240]

PIA NEWS BULLETIN – Djakarta. Indonesia. June 1947-1950; 1954-1962 – 1 – us UMI [072]

O PIAGA : PERIODICO LITERARIO, COMMERCIAL E NOTICIOSO – Sao Luiz, 3 Nov 1898-17 Dec 1899 – 1,5,6 – bl Biblioteca [072]

Pianciani, G B *see* IN HISTORIAM CREATONIS MOSAICAM COMMENTATIO

PIANGIL AND KOOLOONONG CULTIVATOR – 1921 – 1 – at Corangamite [980]

PIANIST – New York, 1895-98 – 1 – £60.00 – uk Chadwyck [780]

Piano, Frank De *see* PSYCHOTHERAPY IN PRIVATE PRACTICE

PIANO TEACHER – v. 1-8. 1958-65 – 1 – us UMI [780]

THE PIANO TRIO : 1770-1820 – 134mf – 9 – MS-n – ne IDC [780]

PIANO-CANADA – Montreal, Canada. v1 n3. 15 avr 1893-v3 n6. 20 jul 1895 – 1r – 1 – Can$30.00 – cn Can Microfilming [780]

PIANOFORTE – v1-8. 1920-27 – 1 – us Schnase [780]

PIANTE ICONOGRAFICHE E PRO PETTICHE DI ROMA ANTERIORI AL SEC. 16 / Rossi, Giovanni Battista de – O 1202. 1879 – 9 – ne IDC [700]

PIANTO, ET LAMENTO DE SELIN, DRIAN IMPERADOR DE TVRCHI : NELLA ROTTA, & DESTRUTTION DELLA SO ARMADA – Veniexia, 1571 – 1mf – 9 – H-8178/1 – ne IDC [956]

Piast, V *see*
- KNIGA O RUSSKIKH POETAKH POSLEDNIAGO DESIATILETIIA
- VOSPOMINANIIA OB ALEKSANDRE BLOKE
- VSTRECHI

Piat, Clodius *see* DE LA CROYANCE EN DIEU

PIATAIA IAZVA / Remizov, A – Berlin, 1922. 116p. BR-834 2 – 8 – ne IDC [460]

PIATIDESIATIIAZYCHNYI PUSHKIN, T.E. PEREVODY A. S. PUSHKINA NA 50 IAZYKOV I NARECHII MIRA / Draganov, P D – Bibliograficheskii venok. Spb. 1899. BR-5891 2 – 8 – ne IDC [460]

PIATILETNII PLAN NARODNO-KHOZIAISTVENNOGO STROITELSTVA SSSR / U.S.S.R. Gosudarstvennaia Planovaia Komissiia – 2v. in 3. M. 1929. BD-215 1 – 9 – ne IDC [330]

Piatt and Company. Marysville, California *see* RECORD BOOK

Piatt, Emma C *see* HISTORY OF PIATT COUNTY

PIATYI VSEMIRNYI KONGRESS KOMMUNISTI-CHESKOGO INTERNATSIONALA / Communist International. Congress. 5. (1924) – 17 Jun-8 Jul 1924. Moscow. 1925. 2v – 1 – $35.00r – us Hoover Inst Photo [335]

Pic, Josef Ladislav *see* LES ROIS ROUMAINES ET LEUR CONNEXITE AVEC LE DROIT BYZANTIN ET SLAV

PIC NIC – v. 1-2. 8 Jan-9 Apr 1803 – 1 – us UMI [073]

Picard *see*
- LES AMIS DE COLLEGE OU L'HOMME OISIF ET L'ARTISAN
- DUHAUTCOURS OU LE CONTRAT D'UNION
- L'ENTREE DANS LE MONDE
- LE MARI AMBITEUX OU L'HOMME QUI VEUT FAIRE SON CHEMIN
- MEDIOCRE ET RAMPANT OU LE MOYEN DE PARVENIR
- LE PASSE, LE PRESENT, L'AVENIR

Picarda, R P *see* AUTOUR DE MANDERA; NOTES SUR L'OUZIGOUA, L'OUKWERE ET L'OUDOE

LES PICARDS AU CANADA / Lomier, Eugene – Mamers, Paris: Gabriel Enault: Societe d'histoire du Canada, c1926. SEM105P56 – 1mf – 9 – Can$2.25 – cn Bibl Nat [920]

PICARESCA PUNTANA / Oteyza, Luis de – Madrid: J.M. Yaques. Editor, 1931 – sp Bibl Santa Ana [946]

PICAROS ET DREGO, OU LA FOLLE SOIREE : OPERA BOUFFON EN UN ACTE ET EN PROSE / Dalayrac, N – Paris: Pleyel, 1803? – 1 – us Sibley [780]

PICCADILLY : A FRAGMENT OF CONTEMPORARY BIOGRAPHY / Oliphant, Laurence – Edinburgh, London: W. Blackwood, 1870 – 1 roll – 1 – 1-55879-472-7 – uk Libr Preservation [920]

Piccha, G *see* ORATIONE PER LA GVERRA CONTRA TVRCHI A SISTO QVINTO PONT, MASSIMO, ...

Piccini, Alexandre *see* LE JUIF ERRANT

Piccini, Caigniez *see* LE JUIF ERRANT

Piccinni, N *see* SE IL CIEL MI DIVIDE FROM "DIDONE ABDANDONATE"

Piccinni, Nicolo *see* TRE SONATE E UNA TOCCATA PER IL CEMBALO

Piccirelli, Josephus M *see* DE DEO

IL PICCOLO – Naples, Rome. -w. 9 Feb 1885-5 Jan 1888. 6 reels – 1 – uk British Libr Newspaper [072]

IL PICCOLO – Trieste: UPI. nov 3 1968-70 (13r); 1971-74 (24r); jul 1975-81 (39r) – 1 – us Res Libr [072]

Piccolomineus, F *see* UNIVERSA PHILOSOPHIA DE MORIBUS

DIE PICCOLOMINI / Richter, Heinrich Moriz – (Includes bibliographical references) – Berlin: Luederitz, 1874 – 1r – 1 – us U.W. Library [880]

IL PICCONE – Taylorville, NY, 1909 – 1mf or 1r – 1,9 – us I.H.R.C. [978]

Pichard, Pierre *see* INVENTORY OF MONUMENTS AT PAGAN

Piche, Odessa *see* MUNICIPALITES, PAROISSES, CANTONS, ETC. DE LA PROVINCE DE QUEBEC DE 1896 A 1924

Pichler, A *see* GESCHICHTE DER KIRCHLICHEN TRENNUNG ZWISCHEN DEM ORIENT UND OCCIDENT: VON DEN ERSTEN ANFAENGEN BIS ZUR JUENGSTEN GEGENWART

Pichler, Adolf *see* NEUE MARKSTEINE

Pichler, Aloys *see* DIE WAHREN HINDERNISSE UND DIE GRUNDBEDINGUNGEN EINER DURCHGREIFENDEN REFORM DER KATHOLISCHEN KIRCHE ZUNAECHST IN DEUTSCHLAND

Pichler, V *see* THEOLOGIA POLEMICA...

Pichot, Amedee *see* CHARLES 5...VIE POLITIQUE

Picitone, Angelo da *see* FIOR ANGELICO DI MUSICA NOUAMENTE DAS R.P. FRATE ANGELO DA PICITONO, CONUENTUALE, DELL' ORDINE MINORE, ORGANISTA PRECLARISSIMO, COMPOSTO;....

THE PICK – New York, 1852 – 1r – 1 – us Ross [073]

THE PICK – New York. v. 1, no. 10-43. Apr 24-Dec 11 1852. Incomplete – 1 – us NY Public [071]

Pick, Bernhard *see*
- THE EXTRA-CANONICAL LIFE OF CHRIST
- INDEX TO LANGE'S COMMENTARY ON THE OLD TESTAMENT: 1. HEBREW. 2. TOPICAL
- THE LIFE OF JESUS ACCORDING TO EXTRA-CANONICAL SOURCES
- THE TALMUD
- THE TALMUD: WHAT IT IS AND WHAT IT KNOWS ABOUT JESUS AND HIS FOLLOWERS

Pick, Hermann *see* ASSYRISCHES UND TALMUDISCHES: KULTURGESCHICHTLICHE UND LEXIKALISCHE NOTIZEN

Pickard-Cambridge, O *see* THE SPIDERS OF DORSET

Pickbourn, James *see* A DISSERTATION ON THE ENGLISH VERB

Pickens, Andrew *see*
- PAPERS ANDREW PICKENS
- TRADITIONARY STORIES OF OLD FAMILIES, AND LEGENDARY ILLUSTRATIONS OF FAMILY HISTORY

Pickens County. South Carolina. Crescent Hill Baptist Church *see* COVENANT, CONSTITUTION, BY-LAWS, CERTIFICATE OF INCORPORATION, DEED

PICKENS FIRST BAPTIST CHURCH. PICKENS, SOUTH CAROLINA : CHURCH RECORDS – 1891-1941 – 1 – 18.50 – us Baptist [240]

Pickens, Francis W *see*
- ACCOUNTS
- PAPERS

Pickerill, Ronald K *see* ICHNOS

Pickering, Danby *see*
- STATUTES AT LARGE FROM MAGNA CHARTA TO THE END OF THE ELEVENTH PARLIAMENT OF GREAT BRITAIN, ANNO 1761
- THE STATUTES AT LARGE (PICKERING'S STATUTES), 1225-1869

PICKERING NEWS – Pickering, 1887-1964 – 35r – 1 – cn Preston [971]

Pickering, Timothy *see* TIMOTHY PICKERING PAPERS, 1758-1829

Pickersgill *see* HISTORY OF MIDDLESEX COUNTY 1664-1920

PICKET – Red Lodge. Mont. 1891-1892 – 1 – us UMI [071]

THE PICKET LINE OF MISSIONS : SKETCHES OF THE ADVANCED GUARD / McDowell, William Fraser – New York: Eaton & Mains; Cincinnati: Curts & Jennings, 1897 – 1mf – 9 – 0-8370-6278-0 – 1986-0278 – us A.T.L.A. [240]

PICKUP, VAN AND 4WD – v1- 1972- 1; v3- 5,6; v4- 9 – us UMI [629]

PICOLA BIBLIOGRAFIA DELL'AFRICA ORIENTALE : CON SPECIALE RIGUARDO ALL'ERITREA E PAESI CONFINANTI / Pollera, Alberto – Asmara, Eritrea: Stab Tip Coloniale Ditta M Fioritti, 1933 – us Res Libr [960]

Picon, F R *see* CONTACT ET ADAPTATION

Picon, Jacinto O *see* LA HONRADA

Picon La Res, Eduardo *see* ESCRITURAS COMPLETAS. REVELACIONES DE ANTANO

Picrochole *see* LE SENEGAL DROLATIQUE

THE PICTISH NATION, ITS PEOPLE & ITS CHURCH / Scott, Archibald Black – Edinburgh, London: T.N. Foulis, 1918. xiii,560p. tables, maps – 1 – us U.W. Library [941]

PICTON ADVOCATE – May 29 1896-Dec 24 1897 – 9 – at Pascoe [072]

PICTON ARGUS – Feb 13 1896-Mar 25 1896 – 9 – at Pascoe [072]

PICTON GAZETTE – Picton, Canada. 1860-73 – 2r – 1 – $136.00 – cn Library Assoc [971]

Picton, James Allanson *see* PANTHEISM: ITS STORY AND SIGNIFICANCE

PICTON PENNY POST – May 27 1896-Dec 22 189Picton Post-Jan 4 1911-Dec 31 1969 – 9 – at Pascoe [072]

PICTON POST AND ADVOCATE – Jan 11 1899-Dec 23 1908 – 9 – at Pascoe [072]

PICTORIAL AND BIOGRAPHICAL MEMOIRS OF INDIANAPOLIS AND MARION COUNTY – Chicago, 1893. Indiana Reel 21. (The Cox Library Collection) – 5 – us Americana [978]

PICTORIAL AND BIOGRAPHICAL RECORD OF LAPORTE, PORTER, LAKE AND STARKE COUNTIES – Chicago: 1894. Indiana Reel 19. (The Cox Library Collection) – 5 – us Americana [978]

A PICTORIAL COMMENTARY ON THE GOSPEL ACCORDING TO MARK / Rice, Edwin Wilbur – Philadelphia: Am. Sun. Sch. Un., 1881. 1 fiche – 9 – us A.T.L.A. [240]

PICTORIAL DESCRIPTION OF THE TABERNACLE IN THE WILDERNESS : ITS RITES AND CEREMONIES / Dilworth, John – rev ed. London: Sunday School Union, 1878 – 1mf – 9 – 0-8370-2920-1 – 1985-0920 – us A.T.L.A. [240]

PICTORIAL EDUCATION – 1927- – 1 – us UMI [073]

PICTORIAL EDUCATION QUARTERLY – Superseded by Pictorial Education Special – 1931-78 1; 1972-78 5,6; 1975-78 4 x 6 in. 9 – us UMI [073]

PICTORIAL EDUCATION SPECIAL – v.1- 1978- – 1,5,6,9 – us UMI [073]

A PICTORIAL HISTORY OF ARKANSAS FROM EARLIEST TIME TO THE YEAR 1890 / Hempstead, Fay – 1900. 18 fiches. F-0009 – 9 – us A.G.L.L. [978]

PICTORIAL HISTORY OF TEXAS / Thrall, Homer S – St. Louis: N.D. Thompson Publ. Co., 1885. Texas Reel 1.(The Cox Library Collection) – 5 – us Americana [978]

A PICTORIAL HISTORY OF THE FAMILY / Miller, Nyle and Esther (Pennock) Family – 1930-1980s – 1 – us KS Hist [920]

PICTORIAL REVIEW COMBINED WITH DELINEATOR – v. 1-8. 1899-1906 – 1 – us UMI [073]

A PICTORIAL REVIEW OF INDONESIA'S HISTORY OF INDEPENDENCE / Abdulsalam – (Indonesian and English) SE-4868 1. 1964 – 9 – ne IDC [950]

PICTORIAL TIMES – Montreal, Canada. 15 jan 1887-v1 n11. 26 mar 1887 – 1r – 1 – Can$25.00 – cn Can Microfilming [072]

PICTORICAL RECORDS AND TRACES OF THE SOCIETY... / Repeti, N CS – Madrid: Razon y Fe, 1940 – 1 – sp Bibl Santa Ana [306]

PICTORICAL RECORDS AND TRACES OF THE SOCIETY... / Repeti, N CS – Madrid: Razon y Fe, 1940 – sp Bibl Santa Ana [306]

THE PICTURE OF DORIAN GRAY / Wilde, Oscar – London, New York: Ward, Lock, 1891 – 1 roll – 1 – 1-55879-769-6 – uk Libr Preservation [830]

PICTURE POST – London, UK. 1938-57. -w. 39 reels – 1 – uk British Libr Newspaper [072]

PICTURE POST – (Part 2: 1948-57) – Great Britain. 1938-57.Part 1: 1938-47 – 1 – us Primary [073]

PICTUREGOER, 1913-1960 – oct 1913-apr 1960 – 656mf – 9 – £2,200.00 – uk Chadwyck [790]

PICTURES – Reno, NV. 1919 – 1r – 1 – $50.00 – B06067 – us Library Micro [071]

PICTURES IN NATIONAL TRUST PROPERTIES / National Trust. London – (Over 7,500 reproductions of paintings; Artist index; Siter index; extensive additional information on fiche) – 1991 – 211mf – 9 – $1,200.00 – 0-907006-38-8 – uk Mindata [750]

PICTURES OF ZION, TERRESTRIAL AND CELESTIAL:...SCRIPTURE AND EMBLEMS / Gould, Mark – Boston: Noyes, Snow, 1878 – 9 – us A.T.L.A. [240]

PICTURESQUE QUEBEC – Sherbrooke, Quebec: G H Bradford, [1894-189- or 19-] – 9 – cn C.I.H.M. [910]

PIDATO DALAM SIDANG SOVJET TERTINGGI URSS, 21 DESEMBER 1957 / Khrushchev, Nikita Sergeevich – SE-5391 1 – 9 – ne IDC [335]

Pidge, John B Gough *see* THE PROPHETICAL BOOKS OF THE OLD TESTAMENT

Pidge, John Bartholomew Gough *see* THE INSPIRATION OF THE HOLY SCRIPTURES

PIDO LA PALABRA : RESPONDIENDO A: EZEQUIEL MARTINEZ ESTRADA, MARIO AMADEO Y ERNESTO SABATO / Ferraris, Agustin – [Buenos Aires]: Editorial Capricornio, [1957] – 1 – CSUXADJ0120-B – us Hoover Inst Photo [972]

LA PIE : HUMOURISTIQUE – Montreal. n131. 1953?-n857. 17 jun 1969 – 1r – 1 – Can$25.00 – cn Can Microfilming [072]

PIE 6 : SA VIE, SON PONTIFICAT (1717-99): D'APRES LES ARCHIVES VATICANES ET DE NOMBREUX DOCUMENTS INEDITS / Gendry, Jules – (Includes bibliographical references and indexes) – Paris: Alphonse Picard. 2v. [1906] – 4mf – 9 – 0-8370-8507-1 – 1986-2507 – us A.T.L.A. [920]

PIE 6 ET LA PRIMIERE COALITION : A PROPOS DE QUELQUES DOCUMENTS DES ARCHIVES DU SAINT-SIEGE / Madelin, Louis – (Includes bibliographical references) – [S.l.: s.n., between 1900 and 1914] – 1mf – 9 – 0-8370-8592-6 – 1986-2592 – us A.T.L.A. [240]

PIECES A UNE ET A DEUX VIOLES.. / Marais, Marin – Premier livre. 2 v.. 1686 & 1689 – 9 – us Sibley [780]

PIECES ANNEXES AU RAPPORT SUR L'AFFAIRE DU MARECHAL BAZAINE. / Bazaine, Achille Francois – Paris, 1873? 34 p. LL-4064 – 1 – us L of C Photodup [340]

PIECES DE CLAVECIN. PREMIER LIVRE / Couperin, Francois – Paris: L'autuer; Belange: Foucaut, 1713 – 1 – us Sibley [780]

PIECES DE CLAVECIN...AVEC LA MANIERE DE LES JOUER...ET AUTRES AIRS DE MONSIEUR DE LULLY.. / Anglebert, Jean H d' – 1703 – 9 – us Sibley [780]

PIECES DE VIOLES.. / Marais, Marin – Second livre. 2 v.. 1701 – 9 – us Sibley [780]

PIECES DIVERSES MANUS. OU IMPR. REUNIES PAR M. COUANIER DE LAUNAY ET CONCERNANT L'HISTOIRE DE LAVAL / Launay, Couanier de – 18-19th cent – 32r – 1 – F12,478.62 – fr Armell [944]

PIECES ET DOCUMENTS RELATIFS A LA TENURE SEIGNEURIALE, DEMANDES PAR UNE ADRESSE DE L'ASSEMBLEE LEGISLATIVE, 1851 – Quebec: Imp. E R Frechette, 1852. SEM105P251 – 8mf – 9 – Can$18.00 – cn Bibl Nat [971]

PIECES EXTRAITES DU RECUEIL PERIODIQUE INTITULE LE REPUBLICAIN / Condorcet, Marie Jean Antoine Nicolas de – Paris: Imp. du Cercle social, 1792 – 9 – fr Hachette [321]

PIECES IMPRIMEES PAR ORDRE DE LA CONVENTION / France. Parlement. Convention Nationale – 1792 – 1 – fr A.C.R.P.P. [324]

PIECES PHILOSOPHIQUES, CONTENANT: 1. PARITE DE LA VIE ET DE LA MORT. 2. DIALOGUES SUR L'AME PAR LES INTERLOCUTEURS EN CE TEMPS LA. 3. JUNIUS REDIVIDUS OU TRAITE DES ERREURS POPULAIRES – (D'Holbach series). 1771 – 9 – fr Hachette [120]

LE PIED DE MOUTON / Ribie & Martainville – French Theatre Series. Paris. Mme Masson. 1807 – 9 – fr Hachette [820]

LA PIEDAD (DOLOROSA A ANGUSTIAS). GRUPO ESCULTORICO EXISTENTE EN LA IGLESIA DE NUESTRA SENORA DE LA GRANADA, DE LLERENA / Lepe de la Camara, Jose Maria – Badajoz: Dip. Provincial, 1970. Sep. REE – 1 – sp Bibl Santa Ana [240]

PIEDAD HEROYCA DE DON HERNANDO CORTES / Siguenza y Gongora, Carlos – Madrid: Jose Porrua T. Editor, 1960 – sp Bibl Santa Ana [946]

PIEDMONT – Greenville. S.C. 1927- – 1 – us UMI [071]

PIEDMONT BAPTIST CHURCH. KINGS MOUNTAIN, NORTH CAROLINA : CHURCH RECORDS – 1955-63 – 1 – 5.00 – us Baptist [240]

PIEDMONT BAPTIST CHURCH. PICKENS COUNTY. EASLEY, SOUTH CAROLINA : CHURCH RECORDS – 1947-76 – 1 – 19.13 – us Baptist [240]

THE PIEDMONTER – Oakland, CA. 1889 – 5+ r – 1 – $250.00 ($50.00y) – B05044 – us Library Micro [071]

PIEDMONT/MONTCLAIR – 1992- – 3+ r – 1 – $150.00 – P00086 – us Library Micro [910]

PIEDRA DE SACRIFICIOS Y ANTIGUEDADES DE MAYORALGUILLO DE VARGAS / Sanguino y Michel, Juan – Madrid: Fortanet, 1917. B.R.A.H. 70, pp. 312-319 – sp Bibl Santa Ana [946]

LA PIEDRA PINTADA *see* THE PAINTED ROCK OF CALIFORNIA

PIEDRAS AREMERAS DE LA PROVINCIA DE BADAJOZ / Solar y Taboada, Antonio et al – 1 – sp Bibl Santa Ana [946]

PIEGE POUR UN LION / Dauphin-Tinturier, A M – Etude ethnolinguistique de Contes Bemba (Zambie) – 9 – F160.00 – fr Ethnologie [306]

PIEGES ET CHARLATANISME DES DEUX SECTES SAINT-SIMON ET OWEN QUI PROMETTENT L'ASSOCIATION ET LE PROGRES / Fourier, Charles – Paris, Bossange, 1831, viii-72 p. Les Saint-Simoniens, 1825-1834. 6980 – 9 – fr Hachette [335]

Piehl, K *see* SPHINX

Pielat, B *see* L'ANTI-GRAMMAIRE

Pielat, J Ch *see* MEMOIR LEFT BY PIELAT TO HIS SUCCESSOR, DIEDERIK VAN DOMBURG, 1734

Pielert, Charles *see* PUBLIC SERVICE CORPORATIONS OF BALTIMORE CITY

Pientini da Corsignano, A *see* DELLE DEMOSTRATIONI DEGLI ERRORI DELLA SETTA MACOMETTANA LIBRI CINQUE

Pientka, Ludger *see* DIE BEDEUTUNG FUNKTIONALER PROBLEME FUER DIE MEDIZINISCHE VERSORGUNG AELTERER MENSCHEN

Piepenbring, Charles *see*
- JESU HISTORIQUE
- THEOLOGY OF THE OLD TESTAMENT

Piepers, M C *see* DE RECHTSZEKERHEID VAN DEN INLANDER IN NED: -INDIE, OP HET GEBIED VAN HET STRAFRECHT

Piepkorn, M B *see* AN EXAMINATION OF THE MOTIVATIONAL DIFFERENCES BETWEEN ADULTS IN STRUCTURED AND UNSTRUCTURED EXERCISE PROGRAMS

Piera, M da *see* SHIRIM

Pierce Beaver, R *see* THE GOSPEL AND FRONTIER PEOPLES

PIERCE COUNTY CALL – Pierce, NE. -w. Oct 1877-Dec 1884; Apr 1887-Dec 1917; Jan 1920-Jan 1948 – 1 – us NE Hist [071]

PIERCE COUNTY LEADER – Pierce, NE. -w. Jul 1892-Dec 1896, scattered issues missing; Jan 1897-Jul 1902; Sep 1902-May 1909, scattered issues missing; Oct 1909-Nov 1918; Apr 1925 to date – 1 – us NE Hist [071]

Pierce, Edward B *see*
- DIGEST OF DECISIONS OF THE COURTS AND THE INTERSTATE COMMERCE COMMISSION...UNDER THE ACT TO REGULATE COMMERCE
- PIERCE'S DIGEST OF I.C.C. DECISIONS AND THE COURTS

Pierce, Edward Lillie *see* A TREATISE ON THE LAW OF RAILROADS

PIERCE EGAN'S LIFE IN LONDON AND SPORTING GUIDE – London. -w. 1 Feb 1824-28 Oct 1827. (2 reels) – 1 – uk British Libr Newspaper [073]

Pierce, Franklin *see* PAPERS

Pierce, Gilbert A *see* DICKENS DICTIONARY

Pierce, James Oscar *see* FRAUDULENT MORTGAGES OF MERCHANDISE

PIERCE TIMES – Pierce, NE. -w. Jul 1884-Jul 1885; Jan 1887-Apr 1887 – 1 – us NE Hist [071]

Pierce, William *see*
- THE DOMINION OF CHRIST
- AN HISTORICAL INTRODUCTION TO THE MARPRELATE TRACTS

PIERCE'S DIGEST OF I.C.C. DECISIONS AND THE COURTS : UNDER THE ACT TO REGULATE COMMERCE / Pierce, Edward B – Chicago: E B Pierce, 1908 (all publ) – 4mf – 9 – $18.00 – LLMC 84-392 – us L.L.M.C. [340]

Pierer, Heinrich A *see* PIERERS UNIVERSAL-CONVERSATIONS-LEXIKON

Pierer, Johann Friedrich *see* MEDIZINISCHES REALWOERTERBUCH ZUM HANDGEBRAUCH PRACTISCHER AERZTE UND WUNDAERZTE..(AEL, ABT.3;6)

PIERERS ENZYKLOPAEDISCHES WOERTERBUCH *see*
- ENCYKLOPAEDISCHES WOERTERBUCH DER WISSENSCHAFTEN, KUENSTE UND GEWERBE (AEL, ABT.1;6.1)
- UNIVERSAL-LEXIKON DER GEGENWART UND VERGANGENHEIT ODER NEUESTES ENCYKLOPAEDISCHES WOERTERBUCH DER WISSENSCHAFTEN, KUENSTE UND GEWERBE BEARBEITET VON 220 GELEHRTEN (AEL, ABT.1;6.6)

PIERER'S JAHRBUECHER DER WISSENSCHAFTEN, KUENSTE UND GEWERBE (AEL, ABT.1;6.8) : ERGAENZUNGSWERK ZU SAEMMTLICHEN AUFLAGEN DES UNIVERSAL-LEXIKONS – Altenburg. 3v. 1865-72 (mf ed 1993) – 25mf – 9 – DM260.00 – 3-89131-101-X – gw Fischer [030]

PIERER'S KONVERSATIONS-LEXIKON (AEL, ABT.1;6.7) : MIT UNIVERSAL-SPRACHEN-LEXIKON NACH PROF. JOSEPH KUERSCHNERS SYSTEM / ed by Kuerschner, Joseph – 7th ed. 1993. Berlin, Stuttgart. 12v. 1888-93 (mf ed 1993) – 72mf – 9 – DM1,100.00 – 3-89131-150-8 – gw Fischer [030]

PIERER'S UNIVERSAL-CONVERSATIONS-LEXIKON : NEUESTES ENCYKLOPAEDISCHES WOERTERBUCH ALLER WISSENSCHAFTEN, KUENSTE UND GEWERBE (AEL, ABT.1;6.6) – 6th rev ed. Oberhausen, Leipzig. 18v. 1875-79 (mf ed 1993) – 113mf – 9 – DM1,320.00 – 3-89131-149-4 – gw Fischer [030]

PIERERS UNIVERSAL-CONVERSATIONS-LEXIKON / Pierer, Heinrich A – Oberhausen. v. 1-18. 1875-80 – 1 – 109.00 – us L of C Photodup [050]

PIERER'S UNIVERSAL-LEXIKON DER VERGANGENHEIT UND GEGENWART ODER NEUESTES ENCYKLOPAEDISCHES WOERTERBUCH DER WISSENSCHAFTEN, KUENSTE UND GEWERBE (AEL, ABT.1;6.4) – 4th rev ed. Altenburg. 19v. 1857-65 (mf ed 1993) – 95mf – 9 – DM1,640.00 – 3-89131-147-8 – gw Fischer [030]

PIERER'S UNIVERSAL-LEXIKON DER VERGANGENHEIT UND GEGENWART ODER NEUESTES ENCYKLOPAEDISCHES WOERTERBUCH DER WISSENSCHAFTEN, KUENSTE UND GEWERBE (AEL, ABT.1;6.5) – 5th rev ed. Altenburg. 19v. 1867-72 (mf ed 1993) – 95mf – 9 – DM1,640.00 – 3-89131-148-6 – gw Fischer [030]

Piermay, J L *see* LA ROUTE BANGUI-KAGA BANDERO, REPUBLIQUE CENTRAFRICAINE.STRUCTURES HERITEES ET MUTATIONS CONTEMPORAINES DANS UNE REGION DE LA SAVANE CENTRAFRICAINE

Pierne, G *see* LES CATHEDRALS. PRELUDE POUR ORCHESTRE; VERSION AVEC OU SANS CHOEURS

Pierotti, Ermete *see* CUSTOMS AND TRADITIONS OF PALESTINE: ILLUSTRATING THE MANNERS OF... ANCIENT HEBREWS

LA PIERRE DE TOUCHE, OU LA VRAYE METHODE POUR DESABUSER LES ESPRITS / Gontery, J – Bourdeaus. 3v. 1614-15 – 14mf – 9 – CA-101/1 – ne IDC [240]

Pierre, Frere *see* BIBLIOGRAPHIE SUR LA METHODOLOGIE DU CATECHISME

Pierre, J B L *see* FLORE FORESTIERE DE LA COCHINCHINE

PIERRE MENARD COLLECTION / Illinois State Historical Society – Personal and business papers (1741-1910) from two generations of French and English settlers in Illinois. Printed guide (including index) Seineke and available separately ($2.00). 28 reels. Single reels available – 1 – $600.00; $22.00r – us IL Hist [920]

PIERRE QUI ROULE / Tremblay, Remi – Montreal: Librairie Beauchemin limitee, [1923?]. SEM105P1407 – 3mf – 9 – Can$6.75 – cn Bibl Nat [971]

PIERRE ROSEGGER : L'HOMME ET L'OEUVRE / Vulliod, Amedee – (Includes bibliographical references) – Paris: Felix Alcan, 1912 – 1r – 1 – us U.W. Library [920]

PIERRE ROUSSEAU AND THE PHILOSOPHES OF BOUILLON / Birn, Raymond F – (Studies on Voltaire and the eighteenth century, v29) – 1964 – 9 – $27.00 – 0-7294-0080-8 – uk Voltaire [190]

PIERRE VIRET, LE REFORMATEUR VAUDOIS : BIOGRAPHIE POPULAIRE / Cart, J – Lausanne: L. Meyer, 1864 – 1mf – us A.T.L.A. [240]

Pierre-de-la-Croix, Soeur *see* BIBLIOGRAPHIE DE L'OEUVRE DE MONSIEUR L'ABBE ADRIEN BOUFFARD, PTRE, SECRETAIRE NATIONAL DE L'UNION PONTIFICALE MISSIONNAIRE DU CLERGE...

Pierre-Ignace *see* LA PHILOSOPHIE DE RURAVEBOHNI, PAYS DONT LA DECOUVERTE SEMBLE D'UN GRAND INTERET POUR L'HOMME, OU RECIT DIALOGUE DES MOYENS PAR LESQUELS LES RURAVEHEUXIS HABITANTS DE CE

PAYS ONT ETE CONDUITS AU VRAI ET SOLIDE BONHEUR
PIERRE-LE-GRAND / Carrion-Nisas – (French Theatre Series). Paris. Baudouin, an XII. 1804 – 9 – fr Hachette [820]
Pierret, G *see* TRANSPORTATION ET COLONISATION PENALE
Pierrot, Marc *see*
- LE PARLEMENTARISME CONTRE L'ACTION OUVRIERE
- TRAVAIL ET SURMENAGE

Pierson, A *see* DE MODERNE RICHTING EN DE KRISTELIJKE KERK
Pierson, Arthur Tappan *see*
- THE CRISIS OF MISSIONS
- THE DIVINE ENTERPRISE OF MISSIONS
- GEORGE MUELLER OF BRISTOL AND HIS WITNESS TO A PRAYER-HEARING GOD
- THE GORDIAN KNOT, OR, THE PROBLEM WHICH BAFFLES INFIDELITY
- THE GREATEST WORK IN THE WORLD
- IN CHRIST JESUS
- THE INSPIRED WORD: A SERIES OF PAPERS...AT THE BIBLE-INSPIRATION CONFERENCE
- KEYS TO THE WORD, OR, HELP TO BIBLE STUDY
- LIFE-POWER
- MANY INFALLIBLE PROOFS,...OR, THE WRITTEN AND LIVING WORD OF GOD
- THE MODERN MISSION CENTURY...A REVIEW
- THE PACIFIC ISLANDERS...FAMOUS MISSIONARIES AND NATIVE CONVERTS
- SELECTED PAPERS AND PUBLICATIONS OF ARTHUR T. PIERSON
- SEVEN YEARS IN SIERRA LEONE...THE WORK OF WILLIAM A.B. JOHNSON...FROM 1816 TO 1823
- SHALL WE CONTINUE IN SIN?
- STUMBLING STONES REMOVED FROM THE WORD OF GOD

Pierson, Arthur Tappan et al *see* THE MIRACLES OF MISSIONS
Pierson, Donald *see* BRANCOS E PETROS NA BAHIA
Pierson, Edgar *see* GUSTAV KUEHNE
Pierson, Leslie Cook *see* DIRECTORY OF THE BAR OF NEW JERSEY
Pierson, Thomas *see* EXCELLENT ENCOURAGEMENTS AGAINST AFFLICTIONS
Pierson, Ward W *see* SELECTED CASES ON CONTRACTS
PIERWSZE ZASADY GRAMMATYKI JEZYKA POLSKIEGO / Mrozinski, J – Warszawa. 1822. BR-4844 2 – 8 – ne IDC [460]
LOS PIES DE CARLOS / Sanchez-Arjona, Vicente – Sevilla: Imp. Alvarez, 2nd ed 1958 – 1 – sp Bibl Santa Ana [810]
LOS PIES DE CARLOS / Sanchez-Arjona, Vicente – Sevilla: Imp. y Pap. Casa Vega, 1935 – 1 – sp Bibl Santa Ana [810]
PIETAS OXONIENSIS : OR, A FULL AND IMPARTIAL ACCOUNT OF THE EXPULSION OF SIX STUDENTS FROM ST. EDMUND HALL, OXFORD,... / Hill, Richard – London, 1768 – 1mf – 9 – MP-447/1 – ne IDC [240]
LA PIETE AFFLIGEE OU DISCOURS HISTORIQUE ET THEOLOGIQUE DE LA POSSESSION DES RELIGIEUSES DITTES DE SAINCTE ELIZABETH DE LOUVRIERS / Esprit du Bosroger, Le P – Rouen. 1652 – 9 – fr Hachette [360]
LA PIETE REFORMEE D'APRES CALVIN / Doumergue, Emile – Paris: Editions de foi et vie, [1907?] – 1mf – us A.T.L.A. [240]
Pieter Cornelisz *see* GRONDIGHE WEDERLEGGINGHE, VAN SEKER GHESCHRIFT, EERST BY JACOB JANSZ. GHESTELT
PIETERMARITZBURG COMMERCIAL ADVERTISER – Pietermaritzburg, South Africa. 1883-88 – 1 – sa State Libr [072]
PIETISTEN / Juengst, Johannes – Tuebingen: J.C.B. Mohr, 1906 (Religionsgeschichtliche Volksbuecher fuer die deutsche christliche Gegenwart; 4. Reihe, 1. Heft) – 1mf – us A.T.L.A. [240]
PIETISTEN – v1-77. 1842-1918 (complete) – 13r – 1 – ATLA S0086 – us A.T.L.A. [073]
Pietrasancta, S *see*
- DE SYMBOLIS HEROCIS. LIBRI
- SYMBOLA HEROICA

Pietre, Simon *see* TRAICTE DES MARQUES DE POSSEDEZ ET LA PREUVE DE LA VERITABLE POSSESSION DES RELIGIEUSES DE LOUVIERS
Pietremont, Maria *see* LE BONHEUR AU FOYER DOMESTIQUE
Pietri, Camille *see* LES FRANCAIS AU NIGER
Pietruska, Reinhard *see* STATISTISCHES VERFAHREN UND NEURONALE NETZE ZUR DATENANALYSE IM MARKETING
Pietry *see* STATISTIQUE DU DEPARTEMENT DU GOLO
Pietsch, Otto *see* SCHILLER ALS KRITIKER
PIETY HONORED AFTER DEATH...ON THE DEATH OF ROBERT PORTER / Gilbert, E W – 1838 – 9 – $50.00 – us Presbyterian [920]
Pieyre, Jean *see* STATISTIQUE DU DEPARTEMENT DE LOT-ET-GARONNE
PIG INTERNATIONAL – v1- 1971- 1; v7- 5,6,9 – us UMI [636]
PIG WARTA BERITA – Djakarta. Indonesia. 1960-1961 – 1 – us UMI [072]
Pigafetta, Philippe *see* LE CONGO
Pigarev, K V *see* TVORCHESTVO FONVIZINA
Pigault-Lebrun *see*
- CHARLES ET CAROLINE OU LES ABUS DE L'ANCIEN REGIME
- LE MAJOR PALMER

Pigeaud, T *see* JAVAANSE VOLKSVERTONINGEN, BIJDRAGE TOT DE BESCHRIJVING VAN LAND EN VOLK
THE PIGEON FANCIER – (Contained in: The Canadien Poultry Review) – Toronto: Fancier Pub. Co., 1894 – 9 – cn C.I.H.M. [636]
THE PIGEON FONCIER *see* CANADIAN POULTRY REVIEW
PIGEON FORGE FIRST BAPTIST CHURCH. PIGEON FORGE, TENNESSEE : CHURCH RECORDS – Sept 1914-Nov 1933; Sept 1936-Aug 1942; Jul 1943-Aug 1960 – 1 – 31.14 – us Baptist [240]
PIGEON FORK BAPTIST CHURCH. FRANKFORT, KENTUCKY : CHURCH RECORDS – 1825-1968 – 1 – 52.29 – us Baptist [240]
PIGEON VALLEY BAPTIST CHURCH. HARTFORD, TENNESSEE : CHURCH RECORDS – 1889-1982. Lacking: 1890-Oct 1893; Oct 1895-Oct 1900 – 1 – 45.09 – us Baptist [240]
PIGEONS AND PETS – Toronto: H B Donovan, [1888-18– or 19–] – 9 – cn C.I.H.M. [636]
Piggott, Isaac N *see* DRAPER MANUSCRIPT, 24 NOV. 1842-27 OCT. 1869
PIGMALIONE. OPERA IN UN ATTO... MANUSCRIPT / Federici, F – 179- – 1 – us Sibley [780]
Pigott, George M *see* JOURNAL OF AQUATIC FOOD PRODUCT TECHNOLOGY
Pigou, Arthur Cecil *see* THE PROBLEM OF THEISM AND OTHER ESSAYS
Pigulevskaia, N V *see* KATALOG SIRIISKIKH RUKOPISEI LENINGRADA
PII QUINTI PONT. MAX., APOSTOLICARUM EPISTOLARUM LIBRI QUINQUE : NUNC PRIMUM IN LUCEM EDITI OPERA ET CURA FRANCISCI GOUBAU – Antverpiae, 1640 – Dfl32.00 – ne Slangenburg [240]
Piis et al *see* VOLTAIRE OU UNE JOURNEE DE FERNEY
Pijper, F *see* BIBLIOTHECA REFORMATORIA NEERLANDICA
Pike and Fisher, Inc *see* RADIO REGULATION
PIKE BAPTIST CHURCH. BLUE RIDGE, TEXAS : CHURCH RECORDS – 1866-1956 – 1 – 30.60 – us Baptist [240]
PIKE COUNTY DISPATCH – Milford, PA. -d 1962-1970; 1971-1980 – 13 – $25.00r – us I.M.R. [071]
PIKE COUNTY DISPATCH – Milford. Pa. -w. 1955- – 1 – us UMI [071]
PIKE COUNTY HERALD – Magnolia. Miss. 1940-1946 – 1 – us UMI [071]
PIKE COUNTY PRESS – Milford, PA. -w 1904-1923 – 13 – $25.00r – us I.M.R. [071]
Pike, Douglas *see* HISTORY OF THE VIETNAM WAR
Pike, Edward Carey *see* THE STORY OF THE ANABAPTISTS
Pike, G D *see* THE JUBILEE SINGERS AND THEIR CAMPAIGN FOR TWENTY THOUSAND DOLLARS
Pike, Granville Ross *see* THE DIVINE DRAMA: THE MANIFESTATION OF GOD IN THE UNIVERSE
Pike, L O *see*
- A CONSTITUTIONAL HISTORY OF THE HOUSE OF LORDS
- YEAR BOOKS OF THE REIGN OF KING EDWARD 3 (RS31B)

Pike, S *see*
- FREE GRACE INDEED
- SIMPLE TRUTH VINDICATED, IN SUNDRY IMPORTANT THEOLOGICAL QUERIES WHICH ARE EXAMINED AND RESOLVED BY THE SCRIPTURES ONLY, UNDER FOUR HEADS,...

Pike, W *see* THE BARREN GROUND OF NORTHERN CANADA
PIKE WAYNE EAGLE – Hawley. Pa. -sw. 1956- – 1 – us UMI [071]
Pike, Zebulon Montgomery *see* LETTERS, MS 2150
Pikhoia, Rudolf G et al *see* ARCHIVES OF THE SOVIET COMMUNIST PARTY AND SOVIET STATE. THE OPISI SERIES
PIKIRAN RAKJAT – Bandung. Indonesia. 1950-1963 – 1 – us UMI [072]
Piksanov, N K *see* STARORUSSKAIA POVEST'
O PILAR : PERIODICO LITTERARIO E NOTICIOSO – Pilar, Alagoas. 15 Jan 1902 – 1,5,6 – bl Biblioteca [072]
O PILARENSE : PERIODICO COMMERCIAL, NOTICIOSO E LITTERARIO – Pilar, Alagoas. 1 Jun-20 Jul 1870 – 1,5,6 – bl Biblioteca [072]
LOS PILARES DE LA HISPANIDAD SE FORJARON EN GUADALUPE / Alvarez, Arturo – Caceres: Diputacion Provincial, 1959 – sp Bibl Santa Ana [946]
O PILARINO : ORGAO NOTICIOSO E JOCO-SERIO – Pilar, Alagoas. 13 Dez 1896 – 1,5,6 – bl Biblioteca [072]
PILEGESH BE-GIVAH / Mekler, I L – Warsaw. 1898. BJ-422-60 1 – 9 – ne IDC [270]
PILEGESH BE-GIVAH / Zamosc, D – Breslau. 1818. BJ-422-99 1 – 9 – ne IDC [470]
Piles, Roger de *see* COURS DE PEINTURE PAR PRINCIPES
Pilet, Otto *see* EIN RUCKBLICK AUF MEIN LEBEN: INBESONDERE ANF DIE ENTWICKLUNG DES HANDELS IN DEN LETZTEN FUNFZIG JAHREN
DER PILGER – (In German) – Reading, PA. 1871; 1873-81 – 3r – 1 – $255.00 – D3386 – us Scholarly Res [071]
PILGER ENTERPRISE – Pilger, NE. -w. Dec 1951-Aug 1968 – 1 – us NE Hist [071]
PILGER HERALD – Pilger, NE. -w. Jul 1970 to date – 1 – us NE Hist [071]
PILGERKLAENGE / Herzberger, FW – Chicago: L Lange, [1889?] – 1r – 1 – us U.W. Library [830]
PILGRIM – Cortland, NE. -w. Nov. 1923-Mar. 1926. Incomplete; Feb. 1927-Apr. 1934 – 1 – us NE Hist [071]
THE PILGRIM CHURCH / Broadbent, E H – London, 1931 – Dfl30.00 – ne Slangenburg [240]
THE PILGRIM FAITH / Davis, Ozora S – Boston: Pilgrim Press, c1913 – 1mf – us A.T.L.A. [240]
THE PILGRIM FATHERS OF NEW ENGLAND : A HISTORY / Martyn, W Carlos – New York: American Tract Society, c1867 – 1mf – us A.T.L.A. [240]
THE PILGRIM FATHERS OF NEW ENGLAND AND THEIR PURITAN SUCCESSORS / Brown, John – London: Religious Tract Society, 1897 – 1mf – us A.T.L.A. [240]
PILGRIM HOLINESS ADVOCATE – (Title varies) – 25 Jun 1920-1968 (complete) – 27r – 1 – ATLA S0326 – us A.T.L.A. [240]
PILGRIM LIFE IN THE MIDDLE AGES / Heath, Sidney – London: T.F. Unwin, 1911 – 1mf – us A.T.L.A. [306]
THE PILGRIM PSALMS : AN EXPOSITION OF THE SONGS OF DEGREES / Cox, Samuel – London:Daldy, Isbister, 1874 – 1mf – 9 – 0-8370-2764-0 – 1985-0764 – us A.T.L.A. [220]
PILGRIM PSALMS: AN EXPOSITION OF THE SONGS OF DEGREES / Cox, Samuel – London: Daldy, Isbister, 1874. 1 fiche – 9 – us A.T.L.A. [240]
THE PILGRIM REPUBLIC / Goodwin, John A – 1888. Item J. Historical review of the colony of New Plymouth, sketches of the rise of other NE settlements, history of Congregationalism, and the creeds of the period. Indexed, 662p. SW16-0102 – 5 – us A.G.L.L. [978]
PILGRIM SONGS: BEING A RENDERING INTO ENGLISH OF FIFTEEN HEBREW LYRICS / Watkins, Arthur Charles – Hannibal: A.C. Watkins, 1899. 1 fiche – 9 – us A.T.L.A. [460]
PILGRIM TRUST: SURVEY OF ECCLESIASTICAL ARCHIVES – 1952. Bodleian Library, Oxford. Ms. R3.150 – 1 – uk Microform Academic [240]
PILGRIMAGE – (v.4-. 1976- 5,6,9) – v.1$. 1972- – 1 – us UMI [073]
THE PILGRIMAGE OF THE LIFE OF MAN / Deguilleville, Guillaume de – (English by John Lydgate) – A.D. 1426. London, 1899-1904 – 17mf – 8 – Dfl60.00 – ne Slangenburg [240]
THE PILGRIMAGE TO KEVLAAR: A PARAPHRASE FROM HEINE / Chapman, Edward John – Toronto: Lovell Bros., 1877. 02853. (Pre-1900 Canadiana) – 9 – cn C.I.H.M. [971]
PILGRIMAGES IN THE PYRENEES AND LANDES / Lawlor, Denys Shyne – (Includes bibliographical references) – London: Longmans, Green, 1870 – 2mf – 9 – 0-8370-6206-3 – 1986-0206 – us A.T.L.A. [240]
PILGRIMS AND SABIE NEWS – Pilgrims Rest, South Africa. 1924-1927 – 1 – sa State Libr [072]
THE PILGRIMS OF IOWA / Douglass, Truman O – (Boston, Chicago: The Pilgrim Press, 1911). Iowa Reel 2. (The Cox Library Collection) – 5 – us Americana [978]
PILGRIMS OF THE LONELY ROAD / Atkins, Gaius Glenn – New York: F.H. Revell, c1913 – 1mf – us A.T.L.A. [240]
THE PILGRIM'S PROGRESS *see* PUBLICATIONS
PILIHAN TJERPEN; TERDJEMAHAN SHANNU / Chou, Shu-jen – SE-4917 1. 1963 – 9 – ne IDC [950]
Pillai, T Ramalingam *see* A DICTIONARY OF MALAYALAM PHRASES AND IDIOMS
THE PILLAR – Oneonta, New York, v1, no. 1 (Apr. 1982); v2, no. 1 (Dec. 1982) – us A.J.P.C. [073]
PILLAR OF FIRE – v9 no33-v93. Aug 1908-Oct 1992 (complete) – Inquire – 1 – ATLA S0935 – us A.T.L.A. [073]
PILLAR OF FIRE MAGAZINE – v93 no 12-v95 Nov 1992-94 (complete) – Inquire – 1 – ATLA S0936 – us A.T.L.A. [073]
Pillay, A Mootootamby *see* A DICTIONARY OF THE ENGLISH LANGUAGE CONTAINING ALL ENGLISH WORDS AND PHRASES NOW IN USE, WITH THEIR MEANINGS, SYNONYMS, AND TAMIL EQUIVALENTS
Piller, M *see* ITER PER POSEGANAM SCLAVONIAE PROVINCIAM
Piller, Pedro R *see* NUESTRO PROGRAMA DE RECONSTRUCCION POR GASTON LEVAL (PSEUD.); CONFERENCIA PRONUNCIADA EN EL CINE COLISEUM DE BARCELONA, EL DIA 10 DE ENERO DE 1937
Pillion, Lori A *see* THE RELATIONSHIP BETWEEN IDENTITY STATUS AND CONTRACEPTIVE PRACTICES OF COLLEGE STUDENTS
PILLOW GAZETTE – Pillow, PA., 1931-1941 – 13 – $25.00r – us I.M.R. [071]
Pillsbury, Albert Enoch *see* THE LEGAL RELATIONS BETWEEN BENCH AND BAR; AN ADDRESS BEFORE THE SOUTHERN NEW HAMPSHIRE BAR ASSOCIATION, AT CONCORD. FEB 26, 1898
Pilone, Jorge *see* ESTADO Y RELACIONES OBRERO-PATRONALES EN LOS ORIGENES DE LA NEGOCIACION COLECTIVA EN ARGENTINA
PILOT – Blair. Neb. 1876-1929 – 1 – us UMI [071]
PILOT – Bronson. Kan. 1883-1930 – 1 – us UMI [071]
PILOT – Montreal, Canada. 1844-62 – 22r – 1 – $1,430.00 – cn Library Assoc [971]
PILOT – Panama City. Fl. 1910, 1912-1915, 1916 July-Oct., 1917-1936 – 1 – us P.K. Yonge [071]
PILOT – Panama City. Fl. 1939-41 – 1 – us UMI [071]
PILOT – Whitefish. Mont. 1904-1959; 1966- – 1 – us UMI [071]
THE PILOT – Birmingham, England. 28 Sep 1844-25 Apr 1846.-w. 1 reel – 1 – uk British Libr Newspaper [072]
THE PILOT : DISCOURS DE D'ARCY MCGEE RE PONT VICTORIA – Montreal, Canada. v1 n3. 21 dec 1883 – 1r – 1 – Can$25.00 – cn Can Microfilming [072]
THE PILOT – Dublin. Ireland. -w. 24 Nov 1828-16 Feb 1849. (22 reels) – 1 – uk British Libr Newspaper [072]
THE PILOT / ed by Hincks, Francis & Campbell, Rollo – Montreal, Canada. v2 n264. 23 dec 1845-v15 n39. 16 jun 1858 – 1r – 1 – Can$40.00 – cn Can Microfilming [072]
THE PILOT – Ritchey. Mont. 1922-1945 – 1 – us UMI [071]
THE PILOT; A MANUAL OF DIRECTIONS / Spanish Refugee Relief Campaign Program Bureau – N.Y., n.d. Fiche W1210. (Blodgett Collection of Spanish Civil War Pamphlets) – 9 – us H.U. College Libr [946]

A PILOT ASSESSMENT OF NONNEUTRAL POSTURES AND WORKER DISCOMFORT IN VDT OPERATORS / Vatland, Howard W – University of Wisconsin-La Crosse, 1995 – 1mf – 9 – $4.00 – HE560 – us Microform Publ [360]

PILOT ROCK – Ashland, OR. 21 Jun 1975-1 Dec 1975. 1 roll – 1 – us U.O. Library [071]

PILOT ROCK NEWS – Pilot Rock, OR. -w. 17 May 1951-. – 1 – us U.O. Library [071]

PILOT ROCK RECORD – Pilot Rock, OR. 26 Dec 1902-30 May 1929. 1 roll – 1 – us U.O. Library [071]

PILOTAGE ACT AND REGULATIONS / Canada. Laws, Statutes, etc – (Amendment Service. YX76-P14EM) – Basic set. YX76-P14-1-EM – 9 – Can$7.50 – cn Communication [340]

PILOTE – London, UK. 7 Jun-22 Sept 1881 – 1 – uk British Libr Newspaper [072]

PILOTE DE LONDRES – London, UK. Moniteur de l'Exposition universelle. 26 Apr-20 Sep 1851 – 1 – uk British Libr Newspaper [900]

LE PILOTE DU DANUBE / Verne, Jules – Paris: J. Hetzel, 1908. 4 fiches. (Literature Collection) – 9 – 10.00 – fr Bibl Nationale [830]

Pilote, F *see* RAPPORT DE LA FERME-PILOTE DE STE. ANNE DE LA POCATIERE MONTRANT DE QUELLE MANIERE...

LE PILOTE GERMANIQUE – Paris. No.1-20.21 juil 1844-3 mai 1846. Mq: 1844, no.5-8,14; 1845, no.14 – 1 – fr A.C.R.P.P. [073]

PILOT-TRIBUNE – Blair, NE. -w. Sep. 1872-Jun. 1892. Incomplete; Oct. 1895-Dec. 1897. Incomplete; Feb. 1898-Aug. 1899; Nov. 1900-Dec. 1918; Jan. 1921- – 1 – us NE Hist [071]

PILOT-TRIBUNE – Blair. Neb. 1872-1961 – 1 – us UMI [071]

Pilsbry, H A *see* MANUAL OF CONCHOLOGY

PILSUDSKI I PILSUDCZYCY / Wrzos, Conrad – Warszawa: Nakl. Glownej..., 1936. 231p.illus – 1 – us U.W. Library [920]

Piltz, E *see* POLAND. HER PEOPLE, HISTORY, INDUSTRIES, FINANCE, SCIENCE

DIE PILZE DER OBSTGEWAECHSE / Thuemen, F K A von – Wien. 1887. B-6325 1 – 9 – ne IDC [580]

DIE PILZE DES WEINSTOCKES / Thuemen, F K A von – Wien. 1878. B-6322 1 – 9 – ne IDC [580]

DIE PILZE IN MEDIZINISCH-POLIZEILICHER BEZIEHUNG / Horaninow, P – In Russian. 6276 1. 1848 – 9 – ne IDC [615]

DIE PILZE UND SCHWAEMME DEUTSCHLANDS MIT BESONDERER RUECKSICHT AUF DIE ANWENDBARKEIT ALS NAHRUNGS-UND HEILMITTEL, SOWIE AUF DIE NACHTHEILE DERSELBEN / Ebbinghaus, J – Ed. 2. Leipzig. 1868. B-6267 2 – 8 – ne IDC [580]

A PIMENTA : ORGAO CRITICO E HUMORISTICO – Manaus, Amazonas. 11 Abr 1915-31 Dez 1916 – 1,5,6 – bl Biblioteca [072]

Pimenta, Alfredo *see* ESTE E O LIVRO DAS CHYMERAS

Pimentel, M H *see* GESCHIEDKUNDIGE AANTEEKENINGEN BETREFFENDE DE PORTUGESCHE ISRAELIETEN IN DEN HAAG EN HUNNE SYNAGOGEN ALDAAR

Pimentel y Donaire, Miguel *see*
- ALMANAQUE DEL MAESTRO
- COLECCION LEGISLATIVA DE PRIMERA ENSENANZA
- COLECCION LEGISLATIVA...ENSENANZA

EL PIMENTON DE LA VERA EN SU COCINA / Gremio Oficial de Exportadores de Pimenton – Plasencia: Imp. Sanchez Rodrigo, 1976 – 1 – sp Bibl Santa Ana [946]

Pimmer, Hans *see*
- KREATIVITAETSFORSCHUNG UND JOY PAUL GUILFORD (1897-1987) – MATERIALIEN ZU EINER ERSTBEGEGNUNG
- REDEMOKRATISIERUNG DES KONZERTLEBENS IN OSTBAYERN NACH DEM 2. WELTKRIEG IN DREI STADTKREISEN

O PIMPAO : HUMORISTICO – Manaos, Amazonas. 13 Ago-15 Out 1911 – 1,5,6 – bl Biblioteca [072]

O PIMPAO : SEMANARIO CRITICO E NOTICIOSO – Manaos, Amazonas. 26 Dez 1915 – 1,5,6 – bl Biblioteca [072]

Pinamonti, G P *see* SPIEGEL SONDER BEDROGH OFTE KENNISSE SYNS SELFS...

Pinar, Blas *see* TRES DICURSOS DE...CACERES

Pinart, Desire *see* THE NOURISHMENT OF THE CHRISTIAN SOUL

PINAUD, MR. PROGRAMA...FISICA / Martin y Castro, Florencio – 1847 – 9 – $1.50f – sp Bibl Santa Ana [530]

PINAX THEATRI BOTANICI / Bauhin, C – Basiliae. 1623. B-5324 2 – 8 – ne IDC [580]

PINCELADAS EN CUADROS DE AYER, DE HOY Y DESIEMPRE / Tinoco de Castilla & Liano, Antonia – Badajoz: Arqueros, 1958 – sp Bibl Santa Ana [946]

DIE PINCELLIADE : EIN POEM IN FUENF GESAENGEN / Saar, Ferdinand von – Heidelberg: Georg Weiss, 1897 – 1r – 1 – us U.W. Library [810]

Pinchard, Marguerite M *see* THE NEW SOCIETY BLUE BOOK

PINCHER CREEK ECHO – Alberta. Canada. Aug-Dec 1906 – 1 – cn Commonwealth Micro [072]

PIN-CH'UAN CHOU-CHIH – 1727, 4-6. BCH-674 2 – 8 – ne IDC [950]

Pinckert, J *see* HYMNEN UND GEBETE AN NEBO

Pinckney, Charles Cotesworth *see* PAPERS OF CHARLES COTESWORTH PINCKNEY

Pinckney Family *see* PAPERS OF THE PINCKNEY FAMILY

Pinckney, Thomas, Jr. *see* ACCOUNTS

Pinczower, E *see* HEBRAICA ET RABBINICA

Pindar, Peter [pseud] *see* A COMPLIMENTARY EPISTLE TO JAMES BRUCE, ESQ, THE ABYSSINIAN TRAVELLER

Pindaro *see* OLIMPICAS Y PITICAS (GRIEGO) (SIECLE 15)

Pinder, Wilhelm *see* GOETHE UND DIE BILDENDE KUNST

Pinderi, MauR *see* ANNALES (CSHB 42, 43)

PINE BLUFF BAPTIST CHURCH. RICHLAND COUNTY. SOUTH CAROLINA : CHURCH RECORDS – (Includes WMU Records, 1949-1982. 1,348p) – 1955-1987 – 1 reel – 1 – $60.66 – us Baptist [240]

PINE BLUFF COMMERCIAL – Pine Bluff. Arkansas. 1912- – 1 – us UMI [071]

PINE CONE – Carmel. Calif. -w. 1915-66 – 1 – us UMI [071]

PINE EAGLE HERALD – Halfway, OR. -w. 14 Jan 1932-15 Dec 1932. 1 roll – 1 – us U.O. Library [071]

PINE GROVE BAPTIST CHURCH. COLLINS, GEORGIA : CHURCH RECORDS – 1921-6 Apr 1960 – 1 – $25.84 – us Baptist [240]

PINE GROVE BAPTIST CHURCH. LOUDON, TENNESSEE : CHURCH RECORDS – Dec 1938-Feb 1951 – 1 – 8.64 – us Baptist [240]

PINE GROVE BAPTIST CHURCH. MADISON, FLORIDA : CHURCH RECORDS – 1887-1985 (incomplete) – 1r – 1 – $61.56 – us Baptist [240]

PINE GROVE BAPTIST CHURCH, NO. 1. COLLETON COUNTY. SOUTH CAROLINA : CHURCH RECORDS – 1959-78 – 1 – 5.00 – us Baptist [240]

PINE GROVE HERALD – Pine Grove, PA. 1879-1937. 17 rolls – 13 – $25.00r – us I.M.R. [071]

PINE LEVEL BAPTIST CHURCH. HAMPTON COUNTY. SOUTH CAROLINA : CHURCH RECORDS – 1872-1982. Deacons' Minutes. 570p – 1 – 25.65 – us Baptist [240]

PINE, ROSE AND FLEUR DE LIS / Harrison, Susie Frances – Toronto: Hart, 1891. 05387. (Pre-1900 Canadiana) – 9 – cn C.I.H.M. [830]

PINE TREE AND RAP / Lefevre, Robert – All four issues of these 2 jounals. 1970. 2 fiches (24x) – 9 – 1.00f – at Libertarian Micro [320]

PINE VALLEY HERALD – Halfway, OR. -w. 11 Oct 1917-11 Apr 1929. – 2r – 1 – us U.O. Library [071]

Pineau, L *see* L'EVOLUTION DU ROMAN EN ALLEMAGNE AU XIE SIECLE

Pineau, Leon *see* LES VIEUX CHANTS POPULAIRES SCANDINAVES

Pineda, Ramon *see*
- DE LO PASADO
- MENUDENCIAS

Pinel, P *see* TRAITE MEDICO-PHILOSOPHIQUE SUR L'ALIENATION MENTALE OU LA MANIE

Pinel, Philippe *see* NOSOGRAPHIE PHILOSOPHIQUE. OU LA METHODE DE L'ANALYSE APPLIQUEE A LA MEDECINE

Pinel, Scipion *see* PHYSIOLOGIE DE L'HOMME ALIENE APPLIQUEE A L'ANALYSE DE L'HOMME SOCIAL

PINELANDS NEWS – Pinelands, South Africa. 8 Feb 1946-11 Oct 1946 – 1r – 1, 16 diazo available – sa SA Libr [960]

Pinell, J *see* LAS ORACIONES DEL SALTERIO "PER ANNUM" EN EL NUEVO LIBRO DE LA LITURGIA DE LAS HORAS

Pinero, Arthur Wing *see*
- THE GAY LORD QUEX
- HIS HOUSE IN ORDER
- IRIS
- LETTY
- MID-CHANNEL
- THE NOTORIOUS MRS. EBBSMITH
- THE SECOND MRS. TANQUERAY
- THE THUNDERBOLT
- TRELAWNEY OF THE "WELLS"

Pines, Y M *see*
- AL DEVAR AVODAH U-MELAKHAH VE-YISHUV HA-AREZ
- MIKHTAV GALUY LE-AHAD HA-AM
- MIKHTAV LI-VENEI ZIYYON BE-ROHATYN

THE PINE-TREE COAST / Drake, Samuel Adams – Boston: Estes & Lauriat, 1891, c1890. 02757. (Pre-1990 Canadiana) – 9 – cn C.I.H.M. [910]

THE PINETUM BRITANNICUM / Ravenscroft, E J – 3v. London-Edinburgh. 1863-84. B-5655 1 – 9 – ne IDC [580]

PINEY GROVE BAPTIST CHURCH. CHOWAN ASSOCIATION. GATES COUNTY. NORTH CAROLINA : CHURCH RECORDS – 1827-78 – 1 – 18.72 – us Baptist [240]

PINEY GROVE BAPTIST CHURCH. PEE DEE ASSOCIATION. RICHMOND COUNTY. NORTH CAROLINA : CHURCH RECORDS – 1836-65 – 1 – 5.00 – us Baptist [240]

PINEY WOODS PLANTER – Liberty. Miss. 1838-1840 – 1 – us UMI [071]

PING TING CHUN-KO-ERH FANG LUEH – 1772. 100v. 6 reels. Chronicles of the Dzungari Rebellion. Primary source material for the study of the Mongols during the Ching dynasty – 1 – $200.00 – us L of C Photodup [025]

Pinganaud, G *see* ORGANISATION MORPHOGENETIQUE DU SYSTEME VISUEL DE LA TRUITE SALMO GAIRDNERI

Pingat, Henri *see* HYGIENE INFANTILE ET MODERNE

Pingel, Horst *see* PHANTASIE UND VERANTWORTUNG

Pinger, Wilhelm Robert Richard *see* LAURENCE STERNE AND GOETHE

PINGLUN BAO – The Commentator.1946-47. 5 fiches. F/C 79 – 9 – $27.50 – cc Microforms [073]

P'ING-LUN PAO – Shanghai. v1-21. 1946-47 – 8 – BCH-805 2 – ne IDC [920]

Pingrey, Darius Harlan *see*
- A TREATISE ON THE LAW OF CHATTEL MORTGAGES
- A TREATISE ON THE LAW OF EXTRAORDINARY, INDUSTRIAL AND INTERSTATE CONTRACTS

Pinheiro d'Almeida da Camara Manuel, Jeronymo *see* MISSOES DOS JESUITAS NO ORIENTE NOS SECULOS 16 E 17

PINHEIRO MACHADO – Manaos, Amazonas. 10 Out 1915 – 1,5,6 – bl Biblioteca [072]

PINKAS MEDINAT LITA / ed by Dubnov, S – Berlin, 1928 – 7mf – 9 – ne IDC [947]

PINKASIM : FROM THE MUSEUM OF ETHNOGRAPHY, ST PETERSBURG – 1r – 1 – us Ross [060]

Pinkerton, John J *see* A PRACTICAL GUIDE TO ADMINISTRATORS, GUARDIANS AND ASSIGNEES, CONTAINING FULL AND COMPLETE INSTRUCTIONS FOR THE SETTLEMENT OF ESTATES.

PINNEBERGER TAGEBLATT – Pinneberg, West Germany. 1976- – ca 7r per yr – 1 – gw Mikrofilm [072]

Pinner, M *see* PROSPECTUS DER ODESSAER GESELLSCHAFT FUER GESCHICHTE UND ALTERTUEMER GEHOERENDEN AELTESTEN HEBRAEISCHEN UND RABBINISCHEN MANUSCRIPTE

Pinney, John B *see*
- JOURNALS OF TRIP TO LIBERIA, 1868
- MESSAGE BROUGHT TO THE NEW YORK COLONIZATION SOCIETY

PINNEY'S REPORTS / Wisconsin. Supreme Court – (A Pre-NRS title) – v1-3. 1839-1852 (all publ) – 22mf – 9 – $33.00 – LLMC 91-304 – us L.L.M.C. [340]

PINNEY'S REPORTS *see*
- BURNETT'S REPORTS
- CHANDLER'S REPORTS

Pinnock, Samuel G *see* THE YORUBA COUNTRY, ITS PEOPLE, CUSTOMS, AND MISSIONS

Pinnock, William Henry *see*
- AN ANALYSIS OF NEW TESTAMENT HISTORY
- AN ANALYSIS OF SCRIPTURE HISTORY
- ICONOLOGY, OR EMBLEMATIC FIGURES EXPLAINED

Pino y Caza, Gabriel *see* EL MUY MAGNIFICO SENOR DON GONZALO PIZARRO

Pinque, Tracey E *see* LONG LASTING TRAINING EFFECTS

Pinsker, L *see*
- AUTO-EMANCIPATION
- SEFER PINSKER

Pinsoneault, A R *see* ATLAS OF THE ISLAND AND CITY OF MONTREAL AND ILE BIZARD

Pinta Llorente, Miguel de la *see* PROCESOS INQUISITORIALES CONTRA FRANCISCO SANCHEZ DE LAS BROZAS

Pintado, Vincente Sebastian *see* PAPERS OF VINCENTE SEBASTIAN PINTADO

Pinto Corraliza, Maria del Carmen *see* APORTACION AL ESTUDIO DE LOS ACIDOS L(-) MALICO, D(-) Y L(+) LACTICO EN MOSTOS Y VINOS DE TIERRA DE BARROS

Pinto, Estevao *see* OS INDIGENAS DO NORDESTE

Pinto, Isaac de *see* REFLEXOENS POLITICAS, TOCANTE A CONSTITUICAO DE NACAO JUDAICA

Pinto, J de A *see*
- DICCIONARIO DE BOTANICA BRASILEIRA...
- ERNSTIGE OVERDENKINGEN OVER DE GEWAANDEN VOORUITGANG DER ISRAELIETEN

PINTO OU LA JOURNEE D'UNE CONSPIRATION / Lemercier – (French Theatre Series). Paris. Huet et Charon, an VIII. 1800 – 9 – fr Hachette [820]

Pinto, S *see* HOW I CROSSED AFRICA

Pinto Sanchez, Evaristo *see* MEMORIA... CLASE OBRERA...PLACENTINA

EL PINTOR EUGENIO HERMOSO / Garcia Vazquez, Sebastian – Badajoz: Imp. Diputacion Provincial, 1968. Sep. REE – sp Bibl Santa Ana [946]

EL PINTOR EUGENIO HERMOSO / Pantorba, Bernardino de – Badajoz: Imprenta Diputac. P., 1965 – sp Bibl Santa Ana [946]

UN PINTOR QUITENO Y UN CUADRO ADMIRABLE DEL SIGLO 16 EN EL MUSEO ARQUEOLOGICO NACIONAL, 1929 / Bayle, Constantino – Madrid: Razon y Fe, 1931 – 1 – sp Bibl Santa Ana [930]

UNA PINTURA DE VELAZQUEZ (EL LOBO DE CORIA) / Martin Gil, Tomas – Caceres: Tip. Minerva Cacerena S.A., 1934 – sp Bibl Santa Ana [946]

LA PINTURA MILITAR / Barado, Francisco – 1890 – 9 – 1.50f – sp Bibl Santa Ana [946]

LA PINTURA. POEMA DIDACTICO / Rejon de Silva, Diego A – 1786 – 1mf – 9 – Pta1,000.00 – 84-7848-353-5 – sp Pentalfa [810]

PINTURAS PREHISTORICAS Y DOLMENES DE LA REGION DE ALBURQUERQUE / Hernandez Pacheco, Eduardo – Madrid: Fortanet – 1 – sp Bibl Santa Ana [946]

Pio 12. *see* DISCURSO DEL PAPA A 20000 OBREROS EL 13 DE JUNIO, DIA DE PENTECOSTES. PLASENCIA

Piolin, D Pauli *see*
- PROV. ALBIENSIS-AUSCIENSIS (GC 1)
- PROV. BITURICENSIS-BURDIGALENSIS (GC 2)
- PROV. CAMERACENSIS-COLONIENSIS-EBREDUNENSIS (GC 3)
- PROV. MECHLIENSIS ET MOGUNTINENSIS (GC 5)
- PROVINCIA LUGDUNENSIS (GC 4)
- PROVINCIA ROTOMAGENSIS (GC 11)
- PROVINCIAE TOLOSANA ET TREVIRENSIS (GC 13)

Pioloet, Jean Baptiste *see* MADAGASCAR ET LES HOVA

PIONEER : BEING THE ORGAN OF THE SOCIAL PURITY ALLIANCE AND THE MORAL REFORM UNION – (Missing: 1893 (32, Jan-Dec?)) – London, 1887-98 – 15mf – 9 – W-36/1 – ne IDC [360]

PIONEER – Big Rapids. Mich. -d. 1881-1915, 1924- – 1 – us UMI [071]

PIONEER – Big Rapids. Mich. -w. 1885-1914 – 1 – us UMI [071]

PIONEER – Big Timber. Mont. -w. 1891-1917; 1923-50; 1956-58; 1966-69 – 1 – us UMI [071]

PIONEER – Fort Scott. Kan. 1876-1878 – 1 – us UMI [071]

PIONEER – (Irregular: English: Lacking: 1930-1941, V.1-12(1-44); 1941-1948, V.12-14?; 1952 (Jan.-Oct.)) – Bandung: Indonesian Mission of the Christian and Missionary Alliance, 1930-1955 (April) – 7mf – 9 – SE-760/1 – ne IDC [240]
PIONEER – London. 1903-04 – 1 – uk Microform Academic [073]
PIONEER – Niobrara. Neb. 1874-1904 – 1 – us UMI [071]
PIONEER – Olympia. Or. and Democrat. 1858-61 – 1 – us UMI [071]
PIONEER – Olympia.WA. -w. 1858-61. Also: Democrat – 1 – us UMI [071]
PIONEER – Pendleton OR. Dec 8 1897-Sep 1902 – 1 – us U.O. Library [071]
PIONEER – Ronan. Mont. 1948-1958; 1966- – 1 – us UMI [071]
PIONEER – v1-41. 1951-90 (complete) – 12r – 1 – ATLA S0377 – us A.T.L.A. [073]
PIONEER – Vale, OR. -w. Aug 1953-Dec 1959. 1 roll – 1 – us U.O. Library [071]
THE PIONEER – Allahabad and Lucknow. India. -d. Jan 1865-Dec 1869; Jan 1886-Dec 1889. (28 reels) – 1 – uk British Libr Newspaper [072]
THE PIONEER – Allahabad and Lucknow. India. In English. 1919-22, 1924-26, 1933-48. 1924-26, 1933-48 – 1 – us UMI [072]
THE PIONEER – Allahabad, India. 1870-1888 – 1 – uk Microform Academic [072]
THE PIONEER – Allahabad, India: Printed by G A Savielle at Pioneer Press, jan 6-feb 20, feb 24-mar 29, apr 7-jun 30, jul 14-aug 4, aug 9, aug 16 1865-dec 29 1869; jan 11-sep 22, sep 27-30, oct 7-dec 30 1870 – 15r – 1 – us Res Libr [072]
THE PIONEER – Hayward, CA: CSU Hayward, 1960-1987 – 10r – 1 – $500.00 – B02290 – us Library Micro [370]
THE PIONEER / ed by Ignotus – London. Jan 1903-May 1904.-m. 14 ft – 1 – uk British Libr Newspaper [072]
THE PIONEER – Ireland.Feb 1924-Mar 1925 – 1 – ie Microforms [072]
THE PIONEER – New London. Ind. -w. 1848-50 – 1 – us UMI [071]
THE PIONEER – Omaha. Neb. 1874-1883 – 1 – us UMI [071]
THE PIONEER: A LITERARY MAGAZINE – 1843 – 9 – 15.00 – us Scholars' Facs [073]
PIONEER AND DEMOCRAT – Olympia, WA. -w. 1857-61 – 1 – 24.00 – us Oregon Hist [071]
PIONEER AND GENERAL HISTORY OF GEAUGA COUNTY / Historical Society of Geauga County – Biographical sketches. 1880. Ohio Reel 34. (The Cox Library Collection) – 5 – us Americana [978]
PIONEER AND WEEKLY RECORD OF MOVEMENTS – London, UK. 1851. -w. 15 feet – 1 – uk British Libr Newspaper [072]
THE PIONEER BISHOP, OR, THE LIFE AND TIMES OF FRANCIS ASBURY / Strickland, William Peter – New York: Carlton & Porter, c1858 – 2mf – us A.T.L.A. [240]
THE PIONEER (CCC245) / King, Man – (In Chinese) – 1st ed. Hong Kong: Council on Christian Literature for Overseas Chinese, 1960 – 1r – 1 – 1984-6584 – us A.T.L.A. [920]
PIONEER FAMILIES OF CRAWFORD COUNTY / Ohio Genealogical Society. Crawford County Chapter – 17??-1994 – 6r – 5 – $32.50r – us Archival [920]
PIONEER GRIP – Alliance, NE. -w. Jun. 1892; Oct. 1893-Sep. 1905 – 1 – us NE Hist [071]
PIONEER GRIP – Alliance. Neb. 1892-1905 – 1 – us UMI [071]
PIONEER HISTORY OF BANDERA COUNTY / Hunter, J Marvin – Bandera: Hunter's Printing House, 1922. Texas Reel 10. (The Cox Library Collection) – 5 – us Americana [978]
A PIONEER HISTORY OF BECKER COUNTY / West, Mrs. Jessie C & Wilcox, Alvin H – St. Paul: Pioneer Press, 1907. Minnesota Reel 4. The Cox Library Collection – 5 – us Americana [978]
PIONEER HISTORY OF COOS COUNTY AND CURRY COUNTY / Dodge, Orvil – Salem: Capital Printing Co., 1898. Oregon reel 7. (Cox Library Collection) – 5 – us Americana [978]
PIONEER HISTORY OF CUSTER COUNTY / Butcher, SD – Broken Bow: Solomon D. Butcher and Ephraim L. Finch, 1901. Nebraska Reel 7. (The Cox Library Collection) – 5 – us Americana [978]
THE PIONEER HISTORY OF ILLINOIS / Reynolds, John – 1673-1818 – 1 – 12.25 – us Baptist [240]
PIONEER HISTORY OF INGHAM COUNTY / Adams, Franc L – Lansing: Wynkoop Hallenbeck Crawford Co., 1923. Michigan Reel 12. (The Cox Library Collection) – 5 – us Americana [978]
PIONEER HISTORY OF ORLEANS COUNTY / Thomas, Arad – Albion: H. A. Burner, Orleans American Steam Press Print, 1871. New York Reel 29. (The Cox Library Collection) – 5 – us Americana [978]
PIONEER HISTORY OF POCAHONTAS COUNTY / Flickinger, Robert E – Fonda: George Sanborn, The Times Print, 1904. Iowa Reel 33. (The Cox Library Collection) – 5 – us Americana [978]
PIONEER HISTORY OF TURNER COUNTY / Stoddard, W H – Sioux Falls: Brown and Saenger, 1931. South Dakota Reel 5. (The Cox Library Collection) – 5 – us Americana [978]
PIONEER MAIL – Allahabad. India. 1911-31. Also: Indian Weekly News – 1 – us UMI [072]
PIONEER MEMORIAL LIBRARY RECORDS / Colby. Kansas. Public Library. Board of Directors – 1926-75 – 1 – us KS Hist [025]
PIONEER MISSIONARIES OF THE CHURCH / Creegan, Charles Cole – New York: American Tract Society, 1903 – 1mf – 9 – 0-8370-6099-0 – 1986-0099 – us A.T.L.A. [920]
PIONEER; OR, GRAND NATIONAL CONSOLIDATED TRADES' UNION MAGAZINE – 1-44 (all publ). 1833-1834 – 5mf – 9 – $55.00 – us UPA [335]
PIONEER PARSON / Sowell, Benjamin Luther – Unpub. mss. 120p – 1 – 5.00 – us Baptist [240]
THE PIONEER PASTOR: SOME REMINISCENCES OF THE LIFE AND LABORS OF THE REV. GEO. BUCHANAN, M.D., THE FIRST PRESBYTERIAN MINISTER OF BECKWITH, LANARK COUNTY, UPPER CANADA / Campbell, Jessie Buchanan – Toronto: J. Campbell, 1900. (Pre-1900 Canadiana) – 9 – cn C.I.H.M. [240]
PIONEER PITH, THE GIST OF LECTURES ON RATIONALISM / Adams, Robert Chamblet – New York: Truth Seeker, c1889. 04415. (Pre-1900 Canadiana) – 9 – cn C.I.H.M. [140]
PIONEER PREACHER IN THE TREASURE STATE / Dosker, Nina Ellis – 1 – $50.00 – us Presbyterian [240]
PIONEER PRESS – Ashland. Mont. 1921-1927 – 1 – us UMI [071]
PIONEER PRESS – Cut Bank. Mont. 1966-1967 – 1 – us UMI [071]
PIONEER PRESS – Fort Jones, CA. 1983 – 6+ r – 1 – $300.00 ($50.00y) – B03220 – us Library Micro [071]
Pioneer Publishing Co *see*
- THE FOOTPRINTS OF THE PIONEERS
- HISTORY OF DE WITT COUNTY
- HISTORY OF EMMETT AND DICKINSON COUNTIES
- PAST AND PRESENT OF BUREAU COUNTY

PIONEER STORIES OF CUSTER COUNTY / Purcell, E R – Broken Bow: Custer County Chief, 1936. Nebraska Reel 7.(The Cox Library Collection) – 5 – us Americana [978]
PIONEER STORIES OF FURNAS COUNTY, NEBRASKA / Beaver City Times-Tribune – University Place: Claflin Printing Co., 1914. Nebraska Reel 8. (The Cox Library Collection) – 5 – us Americana [978]
PIONEER TALES OF THE OREGON TRAIL / Dawson, Charles – Topeka: Crane and Co., 1912. Nebraska Reel 10. (The Cox Library Collection) – 5 – us Americana [978]
PIONEER WOMAN – (New York). 1960 – 1 – us A.J.P.C. [073]
PIONEER WORK IN HUNAN BY ADAM DORWARD : AND OTHER MISSIONARIES OF THE CHINA INLAND MISSION / Broomhall, Marshall – Philadelphia: China Inland Mission; London: Morgan & Scott, 1906 – 1mf – 9 – 0-8370-6246-2 – 1986-0246 – us A.T.L.A. [240]
PIONEER-GAZETTE – Wibaux. Mont. 1948-1959; 1966- – 1 – us UMI [071]
PIONEERING IN BOLIVIA / Stillwell, H E – 258p – 1 – 9.03 – us Baptist [240]
PIONEERING IN MOROCCO : A RECORD OF SEVEN YEARS' MEDICAL MISSION WORK IN THE PALACE AND THE HUT / Kerr, Robert – London, [1894] – 3mf – 9 – ne IDC [610]
PIONEERING IN THE SAN JUAN : PERSONAL REMINISCENCES OF WORK DONE IN SOUTHWESTERN COLORADO DURING THE "GREAT SAN JUAN EXCITEMENT" / Darley, George Marshall – Chicago: Fleming H Revell, 1899 – 1mf – 9 – 0-8370-6102-4 – 1986-0102 – us A.T.L.A. [920]
PIONEERS AND BUSINESSMEN OF TODAY / Hartwick & Tuller – Pentwater: Pentwater News Steam Print., 1890. Michigan Reel 20. (The Cox Library Collection) – 5 – us Americana [978]
PIONEERS AND MAKERS OF ARKANSAS / Shinn, Josiah H – 1908. Item B. 410p. Includes index. SW16-0011 – 5 – us A.G.L.L. [978]
PIONEERS AND MAKERS OF ARKANSAS / Shinn, Josiah H – 1967. Orig. publ., 1908. Biog. and hist. sketches. Indexed. 7 fiches. F-0862 – 9 – us A.G.L.L. [978]
PIONEERS AND MAKERS OF ARKANSAS / Shinn, Josiah H – (Chicago: Genealogical and Historical Publ. Co., 1908). Arkansas Reel 3. (The Cox Library Collection) – 5 – us Americana [978]
PIONEERS OF AMERICAN FREEDOM / Rocker, Rudolf – 1949. Together with: The Philosophy of Rudolf Rocker. Together, 270p. 1 fiche (24x) – 9 – 1.00f – at Libertarian Micro [320]
THE PIONEERS OF BEVERLY, SERIES OF SKETCHES / Cornell, John A – With supplementary articles on the municipal history by Wallace McDonald; educational matters by Robert McQueen; the Agricultural Society by David Bell. Dundas Ont?: Printed by R. Somerville at the office of the True Banner, 1889. 03613. (Pre-1900 Canadiana) – 9 – cn C.I.H.M. [971]
THE PIONEERS OF MAINE & NEW HAMPSHIRE / Pope, Charles Henry – 1623-1660. Drawn from records of colonies, towns, Churches, courts & other contemporary sources. 1965. Orig. publ., 1908.Indexed. 4 fiches. F-0876 – 9 – us A.G.L.L. [978]
THE PIONEERS OF MORGAN COUNTY / Esarey, Logar – Indianapolis: Indiana Historical Society Publs., 1915. Indiana Reel 23. (The Cox Library Collection) – 5 – us Americana [978]
THE PIONEERS OF NEW FRANCE IN NEW ENGLAND: WITH CONTEMPORARY LETTERS AND DOCUMENTS / Baxter, James Phinney – Albany: J. Munsell, 1894. 03507. (Pre-1900 Canadiana) – 9 – cn C.I.H.M. [971]
THE PIONEERS OF OUTAGAMIE COUNTY, WISCONSIN / Spencer, Elihu – Appleton: Post Publ. Co., 1895. Wisconsin Reel 16. (The Cox Library Collection) – 5 – us Americana [978]
PIONEERS OF POLK COUNTRY / Andrews, L F – Des Moines: Baker-Trisler Co., 1908. Vols. 1-2. Iowa Reel 34. (The Cox Library Collection) – 5 – us Americana [978]
PIONEERS OF THE CHUNG HUA SHEN KUNG HUI (CCC263) = CH'UAN TAO WEI JEN CHI : LESSONS OF THE WOMEN'S MISSIONARY SERVICE LEAGUE, 1925 / ed by Pott, F H L, Mrs – (In Chinese) – [S.l.]: Church Literature Committee, Chung Hua Shen Kung Hui by the help of the Society for Promoting Christian Knowledge, 1926 – 1r – 1 – 1984-6602 – us A.T.L.A. [305]
THE PIONEERS OF THE KLONDYKE: BEING AN ACCOUNT OF TWO YEARS POLICE SERVICE ON THE YUKON / Hayne, MH E – London: Low, Marston, 1897. 05522. (Pre-1900 Canadiana) – 9 – cn C.I.H.M. [971]
PIONEERS OF THE PROTESTANT CHURCH IN CHINA (CCC100) / Chien, Yu-wan – (In Chinese) – 1st ed. Hong Kong: Council on Christian Literature for Overseas Chinese, 1956 – 1r – 1 – 1984-B500 – us A.T.L.A. [240]
PIONEERS OF UTICA / Bagg, M M – Utica: Curtiss and Childs, 1877. New York Reel 24. (The Cox Library Collection) – 5 – us Americana [978]
THE PIONEERS, PREACHERS AND PEOPLE OF THE MISSISSIPPI VALLEY / Milburn, William Henry – New York: Derby & Jackson, 1860 – 2mf – us A.T.L.A. [978]
O PIONEIRO : JORNAL PAUTADO NA SOCIALDEMOCRACIA – Benfica, 10 Oct-Dec 1951; Apr, Dec 1952; Jun, Oct 1953; Feb, Apr, Sep, Nov 1954; Aug 1955; Dec 1956; Apr, Jun, Aug-Sep 1957; 10 Aug 1960 – 1,5,6 – bl Biblioteca [072]
EL PIONERO – Havana. Saturday children's supplement to Juventud Rebelde. July Aug. 1962-Dec. 25, 1971. Missing: no. 359; 1971 – 1 – $35.00r – us Hoover Inst Photo [320]
PIONERSKAI A PRAVDA – (Library has: 1933, Apr. 14, 1936, 1945-1954 (incomplete), 1960-1967, 1984) – [Moskva: s.n.], 1925- – 1 – CSUX87-S253 – us Hoover Inst Photo [947]
PIONERSKAYA PRAVDA – Moscow. U.S.S.R. -sw. 1968- – 1 – us UMI [072]
DER PIONIER – Berlin, Germany. Oct 1911-25 Dec 1912; 7 Jan-5 Aug 1914 – 1r – 1 – gw Mikrofilm [072]
DER PIONIER – Berlin, oct 1911-dec 25 1912, jan 7-aug 5 1914 – 1r – 1 – Inquire at Mikrofilmarchiv for details – gw Misc Inst [072]
DER PIONIER – Berlin. v. 1-2. Oct 1911-1912 – 1 – us NY Public [073]
PIONIER-LEITER – Dresden, East Germany. Sept 1963-77 – 1 – gw Mikrofilm [072]
PIONIERLEITER – Berlin, 1963-84 – 8r – 1 – Inquire at Mikrofilmarchiv for details – gw Misc Inst [370]
PIONIERLEITER – East Berlin, Germany. Sep 1963-Dec 1984 – 8r – 1 – gw Mikrofilm [072]
LE PIONNIER / ed by Denault, Amedee – Montreal, Canada. v35 n1. 12 mai 1901-28 mar 1903 – 1r – 1 – Can$65.00 – cn Can Microfilming [072]
LE PIONNIER – Sherbrooke, 4 mar 1886-3 mai 1901f – 3r – 1 – Can$65.00 – cn Can Microfilming [072]
LE PIONNIER *see* L'AMI DU COLON
LE PIONNIER CANADIEN / ed by Bran, T – Montreal, Canada. 1 mar; 16 avr 1887 – 1r – 1 – Can$25.00 – cn Can Microfilming [072]
LE PIONNIER CANADIEN – Hull, Canada. v3 n1. 3 fev 1904-v3 n78. 2 mar 1905 – 1r – 1 – Can$40.00 – cn Can Microfilming [072]
LE PIONNIER DE SHERBROOKE – Sherbrooke, Canada. 13 oct 1866-25 fev 1886 – 4r – 1 – Can$35.00r – cn Can Microfilming [072]
LE PIONNIER DE SHERBROOKE – Sherbrooke, Canada. 1866-1902 – 13r – 1 – $845.00 – cn Library Assoc [971]
LES PIONNIERS CANADIENS ET LE TABLEAU DE LA RIVIERE-QUELLE: LEGENDES / Casgrain, Henri-Raymond – Montreal: C. Beauchemin, 1875. 00993. (Pre-1900 Canadiana) – 9 – cn C.I.H.M. [390]
LES PIONNIERS DU SOUDAN, AVANT, AVEC ET APRES ARCHINARD, 1879-1894 / Meniaud, Jacques – Paris. 1931 – 1 – us Res Libr [960]
Piontkovskii, A A *see* UGOLOVNOE PRAVO RSFSR
Piontkovskii, S *see* GRAZHDANSKAIA VOINA V ROSSII (1918-1921 G.G.)
Piorters, A *see* HET DUYFKEN IN DE STEEN-ROTSE...
Piot, Ch. *see* CARTULAIRE DE L'ABBAYE DE SAINT TROND
Piotrowski, Rufin *see* SOUVENIRS D'UN SIBERIEN
THE PIOUS INCENDIARIES : OR, FANATICISM DISPLAY'D: A POEM / O'Brien, Mary – London, 1785 – 2mf – 9 – MP-549/1 – ne IDC [810]
THE PIOUS MONTHLY OF ST JOSEPH'S DEATH – v1-2. 1927-29 (complete) – 1r – 1 – ATLA S909 – us A.T.L.A. [073]
Piozzi, Hester Lynch *see* BRITISH SYNONYMY
PIPELINE AND GAS JOURNAL – v1- 1859- 1; v201- 5,6; v203- 9 – us UMI [660]
PIPELINE AND GAS JOURNAL – v211- Dec 1984- – 1,5,6,9 – us UMI [660]
Piper, F *see* MYTHOLOGIE DER CHRISTLICHEN KUNST
Piper, Richard *see* DIARY AND FINANCIAL ACCOUNTS
PIPISTRELLO / Ouida – British Fiction Archive: Unit 3 – 9 – uk Bell [830]
Piquer, Andres *see*
- FILOSOFIA MORAL PARA LA JUVENTUD ESPANOLA
- FISICA MODERNA RACIONAL Y EXPERIMENTAL. 1ER T.
- LOGICA MODERNA O ARTE DE HALLAR LA VERDAD...

- MANIFESTACION DE LAS RAZONES Y FUNDAMENTOS QUE TUVO EL DR. ANDRES PIQUER...PARA INZGAR Y DE CLARA SU HETICO VICENTE NAVARRO
- MEDICINA VETUS ET NOVA...CONTINENS PHARMACIAM GALENICO-CHIMICAM
- REFLEXIONES CRITICAS SOBRE LOS ESCRITOS QUE HAN PUBLICADO...MANUEL MORERA (Y OTROS) RESPECTO DE LA ULTIMA ENFERMEDAD DE VICENTE NAVARRO
- TRATADO DE CALENTURAS
- TRATADO DE LAS CALENTURAS SEGUN LA OBSERVACION Y EL MECANISMO

O PIRACICABA : FOLHA IMPARCIAL – Sao Paulo, 1 Apr 1876-23 Dec 1877 – 1,5,6 – bl Biblioteca [072]

Pirandello, Luigi *see*
- ENRICO 4; TRAGEDIA IN TRE ATTI
- IL FU MATTIA PASCAL, ROMANZO
- THE ONE-ACT PLAYS..

O PIRAPORA : ORGAO LITTERARIO, NOTICIOSO E COMMERCIAL – Pirapora, 15 Nov-Dec 1911; Jan-Apr, Jun-Dec 1912; Jan-Mar, Jun-Dec 1913; Jan-1 Nov 1914 – 1,5,6 – bl Biblioteca [072]

LOS PIRATAS LOFITTE... / Mane, Ignacio Rubio – Madrid: Razon y Fe, 1940 – sp Bibl Santa Ana [946]

THE PIRATES OF MALABAR; AND AN ENGLISHWOMAN IN INDIA TWO HUNDRED YEARS AGO / Biddulph, John – London: Smith, Elder, 1907. xx,327p. illus. map – 1 – us U.W. Library [950]

PIRHEI ZAFON – Vilna, 1841-1844 – 3mf – 9 – ne IDC [470]

Pirich, Hermann *see* DIE VERRUFENE INSEL

Pirie, James *see* SCHOOL MANUAL OF THE LAW OF MOSES

Pirie-Gordon, Charles Harry Clinton *see*
- INNOCENT THE GREAT
- INNOCENT THE GREAT, AN ESSAY ON HIS LIFE AND TIMES

PIRINSKO DELO – Blagoyevgrad, Bulgaria. 1951-92 – 41r – 1 – us L of C Photodup [949]

PIRKEI AVOT – Cracow. c.1590. BJ-43-73 1 – 9 – ne IDC [956]

PIRKET AVOT – Cracow. 1617. BJ-43-74 1 – 9 – ne IDC [956]

PIRMASENSER ZEITUNG – Pirmasens, West Germany. 1976- – ca 5r per yr – 1 – gw Mikrofilm [072]

PIRMIEJI AMERIKOS LIETUVIU PROFESIJONALAI IR KRONIKA / Milukas, Antanas – Philadelphia, PA, 1929-1931 – 2r – 1 – us I.H.R.C. [305]

Pirngadie, Rudy *see*
- THE PRRI AFFAIR AS SEEN IN THE LIGHT OF THE INDONESIAN ARMED FORCES
- REBELS WITHOUT A CAUSE

O PIROLITO : ORGAM CRITICO SOCIAL – Itacoatiara, Amazonas. 5 Mar-9 Jul 1915 – 1,5,6 – bl Biblioteca [072]

Piron, Alexo *see* HERNANDO CORTES

Pirot et al *see* DICTIONNAIRE DE LA BIBLE

Pirotta, R *see* ANNUARIO DEL R. ISTITUTO BOTANICO DI ROMA

PIRQUET BULLETIN OF CLINICAL MEDICINE *see* VIRCHOW-PIRQUET MEDICAL SOCIETY

O PIRRALHO – Maceio, Alagoas. 3 Abr 1886 – 1,5,6 – bl Biblioteca [072]

O PIRRALHO ; ORGAM DE ALUMNOS DO INSTITUTO UNIVERSITARIO – Manaus, Amazonas. 5 Out 1915-Maio 1916 – 1,5,6 – bl Biblioteca [072]

O PIRRALHO – Sao Paulo, 12 Aug 1911-23 Feb 1918 – 1,5,6 – bl Biblioteca [072]

PIRU NEWS – Piru, CA. 1927-1946 – 6r – 1 – $300.00 – B03631 – us Library Micro [071]

PIS' MA K M.A. MAKSIMOVICHU / Pogodin, M P – Sbornik Otdel. Russkago iazyka i slov. Imp. Ak. nauk, 31 (2). Spb. 1882. BR-8321 2 – 8 – ne IDC [947]

PIS' MA K TRUDIASHCHEISIA MOLODEZHI / Kollontai, A – Pis' mo 3-e. O"Drakone" i "Beloi ptitse". Molodaia Gvardiia. nr. 2. 1923. BR-3667 2 – 8 – ne IDC [460]

THE PISACA LANGUAGES OF NORTH WESTERN INDIA / Grierson, G A – 1906 – 1 – uk Microform Academic [490]

Pisador, Diego *see* LIBRO DE MUSICA DE VIHUELA AGORA NUEUMENTE COMPUESTO POR DIEGO PISADOR

PISATELI SOVREMENNOI EPOKHI / Koz'min, B – M. 1928. BR-1347 2 – 8 – ne IDC [460]

DIE PISCATORBIBEL: EIN BEITRAG ZUR GESCHICHTE DER DEUTSCHEN BIBELUEBERSETZUNG / Schlosser, Heinrich – Heidelberg: Carl Winter, 1908. 1 fiche – 9 – us A.T.L.A. [240]

PISCES / Pallas, Peter Simon – (In Spicilegia Zoologica)Z-260 2. v. 1. 1769 – 8 – ne IDC [590]

PISCHEBUMAZHNOE DELO – Izdanie Soiuza pischebumazhnykh fabrikantov v Rossii. Spb. 1904-17. Lacking: 1904 (2, 6, 11); 1905 (8, 10-12); 1906 (1); 1915 (9). BR-2355 2 – 8 – ne IDC [073]

Pishchevich, A S *see* ZHIZN' (1764-1805)

PISHGAM – (Sal-i 1, shumarah-'i 1-9, 11-14 (20 Isfand 1359-Tir 1360[11 Mar 1981-Sep 1981])) – [S.l.]: Sazman-i Chirik'ha-yi Fada'i-i Khalq-i Iran – 1 reel – 1 – $25.00 – us MEDOC [950]

PISHUSHCHII AMUR – St Petersburg. n1-13. 1914-16 – 4mf – 9 – $25.00 – us Ross [780]

PISHUSHCHII AMUR I GRAMMOFONNYE NOVOSTI – Moscow, dec 1910; feb, apr 1911 – 2mf – 9 – $25.00 – us Ross [780]

PISHUSHCHII AMUR I GRAMMOFONNYE NOVOSTI – Moscow, dec 1910; feb, apr 1911 – 2mf – 9 – $25.00 – us Ross [780]

PISHUSHCHII AMUR I GRAMMOFONNYE NOVOSTI *see* OFITSIAL'NYE IZVESTIIA AKTSIONERNOGO OBSHCHESTVA GRAMMOFON

Pishvanova, V I *see* KATALOG RUKOPISEI

Piskunov, F M *see* SLOVNYTSIA UKRAINS'KOI (ABO IUGOVOI-RUSS'KOI) MOVY. (SLOVAR' UKRAINSKOGO IAZYKA)

PISLANETS' PRAVDY = THE MESSENGER OF TRUTH – 1927-1939. Organ of the Ukrainian Evangelical Baptist Churches in Poland. Publ. in Poland. 3268p – 1 – us Baptist [240]

PISLANETS' PRAVDY = THE MESSENGER OF TRUTH – 1947-84.Organ of the Ukrainian Evangelical Baptist Convention (USA). 5584p – 1 – us Baptist [240]

PIS'MA IMPERATRITSY EKATERINY 2 K DATSKOI KOROLEVE IULIANE MARII / Shelkunov, I – Copenhagen. 1914. BR-10,529 2 – 8 – ne IDC [947]

PIS'MA K ARKHIMANDRITU ANTONIIU, 1831-1867 / Filaret, Mitropolit M – v. 1-4. M. 1877-84. BR-10,084 1 – 9 – ne IDC [240]

PIS'MA K VYSOCHAISHIM OSOBAM I RAZNYM DRUGIM LITSAM / Filaret, Mitropolit M – v. 1-2. Tver's. 1888. BR-10,083 1 – 9 – ne IDC [240]

PIS'MA M.P. POGODINA, S.P. SHEVYZEVA I M.A. MAKSIMOVICHA K KNIAZIU P.A. VIAZEMSKOMU, 1825-1874 / Pogodin, M P – Spb. 1901. BR-8322 2 – 8 – ne IDC [947]

PIS'MA O RUSSKOI POEZII / Gumilev, Nikolai Sepanovich – Izd. "Mysl". Petrograd. 1923. BR-1291 2 – 8 – ne IDC [460]

PIS'MA OTTSA K SYNU (STARAGO PRAVOVEDA K NOVOMU) I SYNA (MINISTRA) K OTTSU (IZ PROSHLAGO) / Meshcherskii, Vladimir P – Spb. 1897. BR-10.605 2 – 8 – ne IDC [947]

PIS'MA PO POVODU POYAVLENIYA V" S.-PETERBURGE NOVAGO UCHETELYA VERY I EGO UCHENIYA = LETTERS ON THE OCCASION OF THE APPEARANCE IN ST. PETERSBURG OF A NEW TEACHER OF FAITH AND HIS TEACHING – Simferopol, 1881 – 1r – 1 – $7.20 us Baptist [240]

PIS'MA V. S. SOLOV'EVA. POD. RED. E. L. RADLOVA / Solov'ev, Vsevolod S – v. 1-4. Spb.,-Pb. 1908-23. BR-9205 1 – 9 – ne IDC [920]

PIS'MENNYE ISTOCHNIKI V SOBRANII GOSUDARSTVENNOGO ISTORICHESKOGO MUZEIA, PT. 1 – Moscow, 1958. 110p. BR-11,021/1 – 9 – ne IDC [947]

PISMENNYE PAMIATNIKI VOSTOKA. ISTORIKO-FILOLOGICHESKIE ISSLEDOVANIIA – Ezhegodnik, Moscow. 1970-74. 3v. (yearbooks for 1968-70). BR-11,058 1 – 9 – ne IDC [460]

Piso, G *see* DE INDIAE UTRIUSQUE RE NATURALI ET MEDICA

PISOGOH *see* HA-PISOGOH

Pissanos, B W *see* CONTINUED PROFESSIONAL LEARNING AND THE EXPERIENCED ELEMENTARY SCHOOL PHYSICAL EDUCATION SPECIALIST

Pissin, Raimund *see* FRANK WEDEKIND

LA PISTE: MAROC-SENEGAL / Du Puigaudeau, Odette – Paris, 1954 – 1 – us Res Libr [910]

Pita y Pizarro, P *see* MEMORIA...SOBRE LA LIBERTAD DE COMERCIO Y EL PUERTO DE CADIZ

O PITANGUY : FOLHA NOTICIOSA E POPULAR – Pitanguy, 2 Oct 1907; Feb 1908; Nov 1912; Dec 1923; 30 Nov 1924 – 1,5,6 – bl Biblioteca [072]

O PITANGUY : PERIODICO LITTERARIO, CRITICO E NOTICIOSO – Pitanguy, 25 Apr 1886; 1 Jul 1888 – 1,5,6 – bl Biblioteca [072]

Pitard, J *see* LES ILES CANARIES: FLORE DE L'ARCHIPEL

PITCHON PEH – Amsterdam. nos1-8. 1939-40 – 2mf – 9 – J-261-106/1 – ne IDC [073]

PITEATIDNINGEN – Pitea, Sweden. 1915-78 – 216r – 1 – sw Kungliga [072]

PITEATIDNINGEN – Pitea, Sweden. 1979- 1 – sw Kungliga [072]

Pitezel, John H *see* LIGHTS AND SHADES OF MISSIONARY LIFE...IN THE REGION OF LAKE SUPERIOR

PITFALLS IN BIBLE ENGLISH / Clapperton, John Alexander – (Includes index) – London: Charles H Kelly, 1899 – 1mf – 9 – 0-8370-2663-6 – 1985-0663 – us A.T.L.A. [220]

Pithois, P Claude Le *see* LA DESCOUVERTE DES FAUX POSSEDEZ

PITHY BIT ARITHMETIC APPLIED TO THE COMPUTATION OF SOME ELEMENTARY TRANSCENDENTAL AND SPECIAL FUNCTIONS / Walster, G W & Tretter, M J – Nov 1979 – 9 – Can$20.00 – 0-88769-006-8 – cn Nash Info [510]

THE PITIFUL ROLE OF THE GERMANS – n.p. 1936. Fiche W1109. (Blodgett Collection of Spanish Civil War Pamphlets) – 9 – us H.U. College Libr [946]

LA PITITA – Madrid, Spain. 2 Mar-4 May 1873.-w. 4 ft – 1 – uk British Libr Newspaper [072]

Pitkin, Gary M *see* TECHNICAL SERVICES QUARTERLY

Pitman, Emma Raymond *see*
- CENTRAL AFRICA, JAPAN, AND FIJI: A STORY OF MISSIONARY ENTERPRISE, TRIALS AND TRIUMPHS
- HEROINES OF THE MISSION FIELD: BIOGRAPHICAL SKETCHES OF FEMALE MISSIONARIES WHO HAVE LABORED IN VARIOUS LANDS AMONG THE HEATHEN

Pitra, J -B *see*
- ANALECTA NOVISSIMA SPICILEGIO SOLESMENSI PARATA
- ANALECTA SACRA SPICILEGIO SOLESMENSI PARATA

Pitra, J B *see*
- ANALECTA SACRA SPICILEGIO SOLESMENSI PARATA
- HYMNOGRAPHIE DE L'EGLISE GRECQUE
- IURIS ECCLESIASTICI GRAECORUM HISTORIA ET MONUMENTA
- SPICILEGIUM SOLESMENSE

PITT MEADOWS JAPANESE FARMERS' ASSOCIATION COLLECTION – Vancouver, BC: University of British Columbia Library, Facilities and Preservation Office, 1996 – 1r – 1 – Can$100.00r – cn U.B.C. Preserve [971]

PITT NEWS – Pittsburgh. Pa. -w. 1910- – 1 – us UMI [071]

Pittman, Nancy *see* STRESS AND JOB SATISFACTION OF NURSE MANAGERS IN HOSPITAL SETTINGS

Pittman, R H *see* BIOGRAPHICAL HISTORY OF PRIMITIVE OR OLD SCHOOL BAPTIST MINISTERS OF THE UNITED STATES

Pitts, F E *see* A BOOK ON BAPTISM

PITTSBURG DISPATCH – Pittsburg, PA. -d. 24 Aug 1894-20 Feb 1895. 3 reels – 1 – uk British Libr Newspaper [071]

PITTSBURGH CHRISTIAN HERALD – Pittsburgh, PA. -w. 31 Jan 1829-6 Apr 1837. Incomplete – 1 – us Western Res [071]

PITTSBURGH CHRISTIAN HERALD – (Title varies) – v1-10. 1829-38 (complete) – 4r – 1 – ATLA S0156 – us A.T.L.A. [073]

PITTSBURGH CHRISTIAN HERALD AND WESTERN MISSIONARY REPORTER *see* PITTSBURGH CHRISTIAN HERALD

PITTSBURGH POST-GAZETTE *see* ALLEGHENY BULLETIN

Pittsburgh. Presbytery (Cum. Pres. Ch.) *see* MINUTES, 1899-1906

Pittsburgh. Presbytery (Pres. Ch. in the U.S.A.) *see* RECORDS, 1839-1908

PITTSBURGH PRESS *see* ALLEGHENY BULLETIN

PITTSBURGHER VOLKSBLATT – Pittsburgh. Pa. -w. 1859-69 – 1 – us UMI [071]

PITTSFIELD 1761-1899 – (Mf 1-28: Birth Index 1761-1938 (WPA copy). Mf 29-49: Marriage Index 1761-1938, (WPA copy). Mf 50-69: Death Index 1778-1938 (WPA copy). Mf 70-72: Birth Index 1761-1849. Mf 73-77: Birth Index 1845-91. Mf 78-81: Intentions Index 1850-89. Mf 82-85: Marriage Index 1761-1849. Mf 85-87: Marriage Index 1845-71. Mf 87-92: Marriage Index 1871-1904. Mf 93-94: Death Index 1761-1849. Mf 94-98: Death Index 1845-94. Mf 99-115: Vital Records 1761-1850. Mf 116-122: Vital Records 1845-65. Mf 123- 128: Births 1865-84. Mf 129-137: Births 1884-99. Mf 138-163: Births 1844-99 (WPA copy). Mf 164-167: Marriage Intentions 1850-61. Mf 168-173: Marriage Intentions 1861-79. Mf 174-178: Marriage Intentions 1879-89. Mf 179-184: Marriages 1854-71. Mf 185-190: Marriages 1871-87. M'f 191-197: Marriages 1887-99. Mf 198-226: Marriages 1844-1909 (WPA copy). Mf 227-233: Deaths 1862-79. Mf 234-239: Deaths 1880-94. Mf 240-246: Deaths 1894-1900) – (mf ed 1983) – 246mf – 9 – 0-931248-39-6 – us Holbrook [920]

PITTSFIELD FIRST BAPTIST CHURCH. PITTSFIELD, MASSACHUSETTS : CHURCH RECORDS – 1800-c1830 – 1 – 5.00 – us Baptist [240]

Pittsfield, Massachusetts. Pittsfield Baptist Church *see* RECORDS

Pittsfield, New Hampshire. Pittsfield Baptist Church *see* RECORDS

PITTSTON GAZETTE – Pittston, PA. -d 1850-1921. (Missing dates) – 13 – $25.00r – us I.M.R. [071]

PITTURE NELLE QUALI SI MOSTRA DI NUOVA INVENTIONE: AMORE, FORTUNA, TEMPO, CASTITA, RELIGIONE, SDEGNO, RIFORMA, MORTE, SONNO E SOGNO, HUOMO, REPUBLICA, E MAGNANIMITA / Doni, A F – Padova. 1564. BO-1032 1 – 9 – ne IDC [700]

PITUDUH PAWULANG BASA / Supjan, Iskandar – Contents: v. 1, A-B: Anggoeun Guru Nu Ngawulan Basa Sunda Di Kelas Dua Sakola Handap. SE 5930 v. 1 A-B only. 1950 – 9 – ne IDC [950]

Pitween. Fifeshire, Scotland *see* REGISTER OF BURIALS

O PIUM : JORNAL HUMORISTICO INOFFENSIVO – Rio Branco, Acre. 20 Fev 1913 – 1,5,6 – bl Biblioteca [072]

O PIUMHY – Piumhy, 10 May 1908 – 1,5,6 – bl Biblioteca [072]

Piurko, A M *see* HASKALAH MEDUMMAH

Pius, 2nd, Pope *see* ASIAE EVROPAE' Q ELEGANTISS. DESCRIPTIO, ...

Pius 9, Pope *see* LE SYLLABUS

Pius 9th, Pope *see* ACTA SS. D.N. PII PP. 9

PIUS 10TH / Sentzer, Bonifaz – Graz: Styria, 1908 – 1mf – 9 – 0-8370-7262-X – 1986-1262 – us A.T.L.A. [920]

Pius 11, Pope *see* THE POPE ON THE SPANISH TERROR

Pius, Father *see* LIFE OF FATHER IGNATIUS OF ST. PAUL, PASSIONIST (THE HON. AND REV. GEORGE SPENCER)

Pius, N H *see* AN OUTLINE OF BAPTIST HISTORY, NEGRO

Pivarnik, James M *see* THE EFFECTS OF ENDURANCE EXERCISE ON METABOLIC WATER PRODUCTION AND PLASMA VOLUME CHANGES

Pixberg, Hermann *see* NOVALIS ALS NATURPHILOSOPH

Pixerecourt *see* COELINA OU L'ENFANT DU MYSTERE

PIZARRE. THE FAVORITE GRAND BALLET PERFORMED AT THE KING'S THEATRE HAYMARKET COMPOSED BY MON. GATLET / Mazzinghi, J – (Adapted for the pianoforte by Joseph Mazzinghi) – London, [1797] – 1 – us Sibley [780]

PIZARRO / Armas Medina, Fernando – Madrid: Publicaciones Espanolas, 1959. Col. Temas Espanoles, no 84 (2nd ed.) – sp Bibl Santa Ana [920]

PIZARRO / Perez-Embrid, Florentino – Barcelona: Editorial Gustavo Gili, S.A. Sep. de Los Descubridores Celebres – sp Bibl Santa Ana [920]

Pizarro, A *see* SPORT SOCIALIZATION OF URBAN COSTA RICAN CHILDREN

PIZARRO BIOGRAFIA DEL CONQUISTADOR DEL PERU / Arciniega, Rosa – Madrid: Editorial Cenit S.A., 1936 – sp Bibl Santa Ana [350]

Pizarro de Aragon, Juan *see* DISCURSO DE LA RAZON

PIZARRO EL FUNDADOR / Porras Barrenechea, Paul – Lima: Academica Peruana de la Lengua, 1941 – sp Bibl Santa Ana [920]

PIZARRO ET SES FRERES. CONQUERANTS DE L'EMPIRE DES INCAS / Huber, Siegfried – Traduit par Roger Olivier: Plan, 1964 – sp Bibl Santa Ana [350]

Pizarro, Francisco *see* PIZARRO Y ALMAGRO Y LA CONQUISTA DEL PERU

PIZARRO O LA CONQUISTA DEL PERU / Bartholomin, Mr – 1843 – 9 – 1.50f – sp Bibl Santa Ana [946]

PIZARRO Y ALMAGRO Y LA CONQUISTA DEL PERU / Pizarro, Francisco – Valencia: Editorial Guerri, S.A – sp Bibl Santa Ana [350]

Pizzati, G *see* LA SCIENZA DE' SUONI E DELL'ARMONIA

Pizzo, Piero *see* DIE FRANZOESISCHE TRAGOEDIE DER ERSTEN HAELFTE DES 17. JAHRHUNDERTS IM URTEILE IHRER ZEITGENOSSEN

P.J. PROUDHON, LEBEN UND WERKE / Muelberger, Arthur – 1898, 1979. Mit einem Nachwort der Mackay Gesellschaft. 254p. 1 fiche (24x) – 9 – $1.00f – at Libertarian Micro [320]

PKI DAN PERWAKILAN – (Lacking: 1961-63. 1956-64) – Djakarta – 9 – SE-393 1 – ne IDC [950]

PLA NEWSLETTER – Public Library Association. v.9-16. 1970-77. Superseded by Public Libraries – 1 – us UMI [073]

PLA UNIT HISTORY / U.S. Office of the Chief of Military History – 1 – 18.00 – us L of C Photodup [950]

Pla y Deniel, Enrique *see* LAS DOS CIUDADES

Plaatje, Solomon Tshekisho *see* NATIVE LIFE IN SOUTH AFRICA, BEFORE AND SINCE THE EUROPEAN WAR AND THE BOER REBELLION

PLACAAT V. DEN RAAD VAN STRAATSBURG TEGEN DE WEDERDOOPERS – 27 Jul 1527. Plano. BME-12 1 – 9 – ne IDC [270]

PLACCAET ENDE EDICT TEGENT CONCEPT ENDE VOORNEMEN DER ANABAPTISTEN ENDE ANDERE QUAETWILLIGE – Antwerpen, Jacob van Liesveldt. 1541. BME-174 1 – 9 – ne IDC [240]

Place, Francis *see* PAPERS

Place, Jean-Michel *see*
– BIBLIOGRAPHIE DES REVUES ET JOURNAUX LITTERAIRES DES 19E ET 20E SIECLES

Place, Jean-MichelVasseur, Andre *see* BIBLIOGRAPHIE DES REVUES ET JOURNAUX LITTERAIRES DES XIXE ET XXE SIECLES

THE PLACE OF AUTHORITY IN MATTERS OF RELIGIOUS BELIEF / Stanton, Vincent Henry – London: Longmans, Green, 1891. 1 fiche – 9 – us A.T.L.A. [240]

THE PLACE OF CHRIST IN MODERN THEOLOGY / Fairbairn, Andrew Martin – (Includes bibliographical references and index) – New York: Charles Scribner, 1893 – 2mf – 9 – 0-8370-9467-4 – 1986-3467 – us A.T.L.A. [240]

PLACE OF INFORMATION IN EDUCATIONAL DEVELOPMENT / Fernig, L – 1980 – 135p – 9 – 92-3-101822-1 – fr UNESCO [370]

THE PLACE OF MONEY IN A FREE SOCIETY / Dowe, WA – 1965, 1p – 9 – 1.00f – at Libertarian Micro [335]

PLACEME DE...AL EXCMO.SR.SECRETARIO DE ESTADO Y DEL DESPACHO D. JOSE M^A CALATRAVA... / Noche, Diego de – 1 – sp Bibl Santa Ana [946]

LE PLACEMENT DES EMPLOYES, OUVRIERS ET DOMESTIQUES EN FRANCE. SON HISTOIRE. SON ETAT ACTUEL. AVEC UN APPENDICE RELATIF AU PLACEMENT DANS LES PAYS ETRANGERS / France. Ministere du Commerce et de l'Industrie. Office du travail – (Condition of 19th C. French working class series). 1893 – 9 – fr Hachette [360]

LE PLACEMENT DES TRAVAILLEURS / Bailacq, Charles Jules – Bordeaux. 1912. (La Condition Ouvriere. Part Two.) – 9 – 6.00 – fr Bibl Nationale [360]

PLACENTIA NEW-TIMES – Placentia, CA. 1992 – 7+ r – 1 – $350.00 ($100.00y) – R04089 – us Library Micro [071]

THE PLACER ARGUS – Auburn, CA. 1872-88; 1889-97 – 14r – 1 – $700.00 – B02028 – us Library Micro [071]

PLACER COUNTY, 1861; 1875 – 2r – 1 – $100.00 – D074 – us Library Micro [978]

PLACER COUNTY LEADER – Auburn, CA. 1898-1902 – 1r – 1 CB02029 – $50.00 – us Library Micro [071]

PLACER COUNTY REPUBLICAN – Auburn, CA. 1855-98; 1903-18 – 15r – 1 CB02030 – $750.00 – us Library Micro [071]

PLACER HERALD – Auburn. Calif. -w. 1873-1906, 1945-66 – 1 – us UMI [071]

PLACER HERALD – Rocklin, CA. 1947-82; 1984-87 – 1r – 1 BC02725 – $1,250.00 – us Library Micro [071]

PLACER HERALD-ROCKLIN *see* WEEKLY PLACER HERALD

PLACER PRESS – Auburn, CA. 1857-1858 – 1r – 1 – $50.00 – C03146 – us Library Micro [071]

PLACER TIMES – Sacramento, CA. Apr 1849-Jun 1850 – 1r – 1 – $50.00 – C02738 – us Library Micro [071]

PLACER TIMES – Sacramento. Calif. -w. 1849-50 – 1 – us UMI [071]

PLACERVILLE CITY DIRECTORIES – El Dorado Co, CA. 1862; 1947 – 2r – 1 – $100.00 – D016 – us Library Micro [910]

PLACERVILLE HERALD – Placerville, CA. 1853 – 1r – 1 – $50.00 – C03399 – us Library Micro [071]

PLACERVILLE REPUBLICAN – Placerville, CA. 1924-1943 – 37r – 1 – $1,850.00 – C03399a – us Library Micro [071]

PLACERVILLE TIMES – Placerville, CA. 1936-58 – 14r – 1 – $700.00 – C02632 – us Library Micro [071]

PLACES – v1-. 1983- – 1,5,6,9 – us UMI [073]

PLACETS ADRESSES AU ROI ET A LA REINE : REQUETE (DU 1ER NOV. 1788) AUX OFFICIERS MUNICIPAUX DE LA VILLE DE NANTES ET ARRETE DU 6 NOV. 1788... – Nantes: [s.n.], 1788 – 1 – F50.00 – fr Armell [350]

PLACITORUM IN DOMO CAPITULARI WESTMONASTERIENSI ASSERVATORUM ABREVIATIO : TEMPORIBUS REGUM RIC. 1, JOHANN., HENR. 3, EDW. 1, EDW.2 – 1811 – Dfl91.00 – ne Slangenburg [240]

LE PLACOTEUX – Saint-Pascal. v1 no 1 (12 Sept 1978)-. SEM35P297 – 19r – 1 – Can$1,300.20 – cn Bibl Nat [072]

PLADNE – Sofia. 1928-34. Complete – 1 – 35.00r – us Hoover Inst Photo [073]

LA PLAGA SOCIAL DE LA BLASFEMIA / Bayle, Constantino – Madrid: Razon y Fe, 1920 – 1 – sp Bibl Santa Ana [240]

Plaid Cymru *see* ARCHIVES

PLAIDOYER DE M. O. DESMARAIS L'AFFAIRE DE NAPOLEON DEMERS / Desmarais, Odilon – Preface par Henri Roullaud. s.l.: s.n., 1896 (Montreal: L. Belair). 02646. (Pre-1900 Canadiana) – 9 – cn C.I.H.M. [971]

PLAIDOYERS ET DISCOURS DU BATONNAT / Favre, Jules – Paris: Chevalier-Marescq, 1893. 2v. 14 fiches.(Law Collection) – 9 – 35.00 – fr Bibl Nationale [340]

A PLAIN AND COMPENDIOUS METHOD OF TEACHING THOROUGH BASS / Lampe, J F – 1737 – 9 – us Sibley [780]

A PLAIN AND COMPLETE GRAMMAR OF THE ENGLISH LANGUAGE / Bayly, Anselm – 1772. 159p. (English Linguistics Series 1500-1800) – 9 – us UMI [420]

A PLAIN ARGUMENT FOR GOD / Fullerton, George Stuart – Philadelphia: J.B. Lippincott, 1889 – 1mf – us A.T.L.A. [210]

PLAIN DEALER – Alberta, CN. 1936-40 – 1r – 1 – cn Commonwealth Micro [072]

PLAIN DEALER – Atkinson. Neb. 1895-1897 – 1 – us UMI [071]

PLAIN DEALER – Burchard, NE. -w. Jun. 1884-Feb. 1885 – 1 – us NE Hist [071]

PLAIN DEALER – Cleveland. Ohio. 1845- – 1 – us UMI [071]

PLAIN DEALER – Cleveland. Ohio. 1914- – 1 – us UMI [071]

PLAIN DEALER – Dunsmuir, CA. Mar-Dec 1912 – 1r – 1 – $50.00 – B02188 – us Library Micro [071]

PLAIN DEALER – London. -d. 1 Jan-19 Feb 1832. (1 reel) – 1 – uk British Libr Newspaper [072]

PLAIN DEALER – Mt. Vernon. IN.1935- – 1 – us UMI [071]

PLAIN DEALER – Paulding, Ohio. 1870-74 – 1r – 1 – $32.50r – us Archival [071]

PLAIN DEALER – Wabash. Ind. 1972- – 1 – us UMI [071]

PLAIN DEALER – Waukesha. Wis. 1865-73 – 1 – us UMI [071]

THE PLAIN DEALER – North Vernon. Ind. Also: The Sun. -w.1870- – 1 – us UMI [071]

PLAIN ENGLISH – London, England. -w. 10 July 1920-18 March 1922. 1 1 2 reels – 1 – uk British Libr Newspaper [072]

PLAIN FACTS FOR FAIR MINDS : AN APPEAL TO CANDOR AND COMMON SENSE / Searle, George Mary – New York: Columbus Press, 1906 – 1mf – 9 – 0-8370-8383-4 – 1986-2383 – us A.T.L.A. [230]

PLAIN FRANCES MOWBRAY; AND OTHER TALES / Lawless, Emily – British Fiction Archive: Unit 4 – 9 – uk Bell [830]

A PLAIN INTRODUCTION TO THE CRITICISM OF THE NEW TESTAMENT FOR THE USE OF BIBLICAL STUDENTS / Scrivener, Frederick Henry Ambrose – 4th ed. Ed. by Edward Miller. London, New York: G. Bell, 1894.2v – 1 – us U.W. Library [240]

PLAIN LECTURES ON THE GROWTH OF THE PAPAL POWER / Robertson, James Craigie – London: S.P.C.K.; New York: Pott, Young, [1876?] – 1mf – us A.T.L.A. [240]

A PLAIN MAN'S WORKING VIEW OF BIBLICAL INSPIRATION / Lyman, Albert Josiah – New York: Y.M.C.A. Press, 1907. 1 fiche – 9 – us A.T.L.A. [240]

THE PLAIN PEOPLE – Ireland.9 Apr-2 Jul 1922 – 1 – ie Microforms [072]

A PLAIN, RATIONAL ESSAY ON ENGLISH GRAMMAR / Mackintosh, Duncan – 1797. 250p. (English Linguistics Series 1500-1800) – 9 – us UMI [420]

PLAIN SPEAKER – Hazleton. Pa. 1935-1961 – 1 – us UMI [071]

PLAIN TALES FROM THE HILLS / Kipling, Rudyard – Calcutta: Thacker, Spink; London: W. Thacker, 1888 – 1 roll – 1 – 1-55879-788-2 – uk Libr Preservation [830]

PLAIN TALK / Hogan, Benedict – [Chicago]: Chicago Legal News, 1882 – 1mf – 9 – 0-8370-6577-1 – 1986-0577 – us A.T.L.A. [240]

A PLAIN TREATISE ON THE LAW OF MARRIAGE AND DIVORCE / Hayes, Everand A – Buffalo: Fries, 1889. 40 8p. LL-84 – 1 – us L of C Photodup [340]

PLAIN WORDS ABOUT FOOD: THE RUMFORD KITCHEN LEAFLETS / Richards, Ellen Henrietta – 1899. Boston: Home Science Publishing, 1899. 176p. 10 leaves of plates. ill – 1 – us U.W. Library [640]

PLAINDEALER – Alturas, CA. Apr 1906-Dec 1940 – 11r – 1 – $550.00 – B02010 – us Library Micro [071]

PLAINDEALER – McHenry.Ill. 1875- – 1 – us UMI [071]

PLAINDEALER – Roseburg, OR. 25 Mar 1870-23 Nov 1905. 11 rolls – 1 – us U.O. Library [071]

THE PLAINDEALER – Reno, NV. 1881-89 (broken series) – 7r – 1 – $350.00 – U04708 – us Library Micro [071]

PLAINDEALER AND MODOC COUNTY TIMES – Alturas, CA. 1913-52 – 23r – 1 – $1,150.00 – C02011 – us Library Micro [071]

PLAINDEALER AND MODOC COUNTY TIMES – Alturas. Calif. 1941-52 – 1 – us UMI [071]

A PLAINE AND EASIE INTRODUCTION TO PRACTICALL MUSICKE / Morley, Thomas – 1597 – 9 – us Sibley [780]

A PLAINE AND EASIE INTRODUCTION TO PRACTICALL MUSICKE.. / Morley, Thomas – 1608 – 9 – us Sibley [780]

A PLAINE PATHWAY TO THE FRENCH TONGUE – Anon. 1575. 149p. (English Linguistics Series 1500-1800) – 9 – us UMI [440]

THE PLAINESMAN – Plains. Mont. 1958-1959; 1966- – 1 – us UMI [071]

PLAINFIELD 1785-1863 – (Mf 1: Birth Index 1785-1983, A-P. Mf 2: Birth Index 1785-1983, R-Z. Mf 3: Marriage Index 1785-1983, A-R. Mf 4: Marriage Index 1785-1983, R-Z. Mf 5: Intentions Index 1785-1983, A-S. Mf 6: Intentions Index, s-Z. Mf 7: Death Index 1785-1983, A-S. Mf 8: Death Index 1785-1983, S-W. Mf 9: Births 1782-1824. Mf 10: Intentions 1785-1824. Mf 11: Marriages 1815-22; Deaths 1792-1824. Mf 12: Intentions 1824-44; Marriages 1824-44. Mf 13: Births & Deaths 1814-44. Mf 14: Marriage Intentions 1844-81; Out-Town Marriages 1777-1858. Mf 15: Births; Marriages: 1844-63. Mf 16: Deaths 1844-63) – (mf ed 1983) – 16mf – 9 – 0-931248-27-2 – us Holbrook [929]

Plainfield, New Hampshire. Plainfield Baptist Church *see* RECORDS

THE PLAINS AND THE ROCKIES – 537v., including books, articles, federal documents relating to the early history of the West – 9 – us Primary [978]

PLAINSDEALER – Kansas City. Kan. sept. 20, 1940; Oct. 10, 1941 – 1 – us NY Public [071]

PLAINVIEW GAZETTE – Plainview, NE. -w. Sep 1887; Jan 1889; May-Jun 1890; Jan-Sep 1891; Dec 1891-Dec 1899 – 1 – us NE Hist [071]

PLAINVIEW NEWS – Plainview, NE. -w. Apr 1895; Sep 1895-Aug 1903; Oct 1903-Jun 1904; Oct 1904-Apr 1907; Jul-Aug 1907; Nov 1907 to date – 1 – us NE Hist [071]

PLAINVIEW REPUBLICAN – Plainview, NE. -w. (-sw 1903-05). Sep 1887-Mar 1919, scattered issues missing – 1 – us NE Hist [071]

Plaisance, Carli de *see* RELATION CURIEUSE ET NOUVELLE D'UN VOYAGE DE CONGO

Plaisance, D de *see* RELATION D'UN VOYAGE AU CONGO FAIT LES ANNEES 1666 ET 1667

Plaisance, Guattini de *see* RELATION CURIEUSE ET NOUVELLE D'UN VOYAGE DE CONGO

Plaisant, Marcel *see* TRAITE DE DROIT CONVENTIONNEL INTERNATIONAL CONCERNANT LA PROPRIETE INDUSTRIELLE

DAS PLAKAT – Berlin. jan-oct 1910. jan-oct 1911. jan-oct 1912. jan-nov 1913. jan-nov 1914. jan-jul 1915. jan-sep, nov 1916. jan-may, jul, sep-nov 1917. jan-sep, nov 1918. jan-may, jul-nov 1919. 1920-21 – 1 – gw Mikrofilm [760]

PLAKATSAMMLUNG DES INSTITUTS FUER ZEITUNGSFORSCHUNG DER STADT DORTMUND = POSTER COLLECTION IN THE INSTITUT FUER ZEITFORSCHUNG DER STADT DORTMUND / Posthoff, Barbara – (Part A: German Posters. Part B: German Posters. Part C: Foreign Posters.-includes 2 index volumes) – 1988-1992 – 111 colour fiches (1:24) – 15 – silver DM3,980.00 – 3-598-32563-0 – gw Saur [760]

PLAMEN – 1959-1969 – 1 – us I.U. Libraries [073]

PLAMENNYI KRUG / Sologub, F – Stikhi. Kniga. M. 1908. BR-871 2 – 8 – ne IDC [460]

Plamondon, Jocelyne *see* BIO-BIBLIOGRAPHIE ANALYTIQUE DE REINE MALOUIN

Plamondon, Louis *see* ALMANACH DES DAMES, POUR L'ANNEE 1807

PLAN / Gosudarstvennaia Planovaia Komissiia – Moscow, 1933-37 – 2r – 1 – us Ross [335]

PLAN / Gosudarstvennaia Planovaia Komissiia – (n13-14 never publ. Cont: Narodnoe Khozialistvo SSR) – Moscow, 1933-37 – 2r – 1 – us Ross [335]

PLAN – Moscow. 1933-1937 – 1 – us NY Public [338]

PLAN 1969-1972 / Tunisia – Ajustement des previsions pour les annees 1971-1972. Secr. d'Etat au Plan. Apr 1970. Bd-1564 1 – 9 – ne IDC [338]

PLAN ANUAL 1971 / Chile. Oficina de Planificacion Nacional – (Annual plan for 1971). Santiago. Mar 1971 – 9 – ne IDC [338]

EL PLAN BADAJOZ, 1966 / Secretaria Gestora del Plan Badajoz – Madrid: Imp. en Escuelas Profesionales Sagrado Corazon de Jesus, 1964 – sp Bibl Santa Ana [307]

PLAN BIENAL DE DESARROLLO ECONOMICO Y SOCIAL, 1963-64 / Bolivia. Secretaria Nacional de Planificacion y Coordinacion – La Paz. 1963 – 9 – ne IDC [338]

PLAN BIENAL DE DESARROLLO ECONOMICO Y SOCIAL, 1965-1966 / Bolivia. Secretaria Nacional de Planificacion y Coordinacion – D-957 1. 1965 – 9 – ne IDC [338]

PLAN BIENAL DE DESARROLLO PARA 1973-1974 / Peru. Comite del Plan – 3v. 1973. BD-2015 1 – 9 – ne IDC [336]

PLAN BIENNAL D'EQUIPEMENT 1958-1959 RAPPORT GENERAL / Morocco. Division de la Coordination Economique et du Plan – Rabat. 1958 – 9 – ne IDC [338]

PLAN CUATRIENAL, 1960-1964 / Venezuela – Version preliminar. Rev. 1. v. 1. Caracas. 1960 – 9 – ne IDC [338]

PLAN CUATRIENAL DE INVERSIONES PUBLICAS NACIONALES, 1961-1964 / Colombia. Departamento Administrativo de Planeacion.. – Bogota. 1960 – 9 – ne IDC [338]

PLAN D'ACTION ECONOMIQUE ET SOCIAL 1970-1971 / Haiti. Conseil National de Developpement et de Planification – D-1091 1. 1970 – 9 – ne IDC [338]

PLAN D'ACTION ECONOMIQUE ET SOCIALE, 1968-1969 / Haiti. Conseil National de Developpement et de Planification – D-1090 1. 1968 – 9 – ne IDC [338]

PLAN DE ACCION 1970 / Argentine Republic. Secretaria del Consejo Nacional de Desarrollo. Consejo Federal de Inversiones – (Action Plan 1970). (Buenos Aires). 1970. BD-1608 1 – 9 – ne IDC [338]

EL PLAN DE BADAJOZ. RESUMEN INFORMATIVO DE SU SITUACION EN FIN DE 1962 / Instituto Nacional de Industria – Madrid: Secretaria Gestora del Plan Badajoz, 1962? – 1 – sp Bibl Santa Ana [338]

EL PLAN DE BADAJOZ. SU REALIDAD ACTUAL / Instituto Nacional de Industria – Madrid, 1956 – 1 – sp Bibl Santa Ana [338]

PLAN DE BOYACA, INVERCIONES 1954-1958 / Colombia. Direccion Nacional de Planeacion.. – Bogota. 1953. BD-196 1 – 9 – ne IDC [330]

PLAN DE COLONISATION DES POSSESSIONS FRANCAISES DANS L'AFRIQUE OCCIDENTALE, AU MOYEN DE LA CIVILISATION DES NEGRES INDIGENES / Hautefeuille, Laurent B – (African Library). Paris. Levavasseur. 1830 – 9 – fr Hachette [960]

PLAN DE CONSTANTINE: 2 ANS DE REALISATIONS / Algeria. Caisse d'Equipement pour le Developpement de l'Algerie – 1961. BNE-8615 1 – 9 – ne IDC [338]

PLAN DE CONSTANTINE, 1959-1963: RAPPORT GENERAL / Algeria. Delegation generale du Gouvernement en Algerie – 1960? BNE-8628 1 – 9 – ne IDC [338]

EL PLAN DE DESAROLLO COLOMBIANO EN MARCHA / Colombia. Departamento Nacional de Planeacion – Bogota. March. 1974. BD-1795 1 – 9 – ne IDC [338]

PLAN DE DESARROLLO / Colombia. Departamento Nacional de Planeacion – 4pts. Bogota. 1971. Lacking: pt. 1-2. BD-2007 1 – 9 – ne IDC [338]

PLAN DE DESARROLLO 1971-1975 / Guatemala. Sec. General del Con. Nac. De Plan. Econ – D-1088 1. 2v 1970 – 9 – ne IDC [338]

PLAN DE DESARROLLO AGRICOLA Y DE TRANSPORTE 1954-1961 / Chile. Corporacion de Fomento de la Produccion – D-1264 1 – 9 – ne IDC [330]

PLAN DE DESARROLLO DE LA 4 REGION VALPAIRASO-ACONCAGUA, 1971-1976 / Chile. Oficina de Planificacion Nacional – Santiago. 1971. BD-1839 1 – 9 – ne IDC [338]

PLAN DE DESARROLLO ECONOMICO DE GUATEMALA, 1955-1960 / Guatemala – 2a ed. Guatemala. 1957 – 9 – ne IDC [338]

PLAN DE DESARROLLO ECONOMICO Y SOCIAL, 1962-1971 / Bolivia. Junta Nacional de Planeamiento – (Plan for Economic and Social Development, 1962-1971). La Paz. Sep 1961. BD-1622 1 – 9 – ne IDC [338]

PLAN DE DESARROLLO ECONOMICO Y SOCIAL. 1964-1967 / Spain. Comisaria del Plan de Desarrollo Economico – Madrid. 1963. BD-117 1 – 9 – ne IDC [338]

PLAN DE DESARROLLO ECONOMICO Y SOCIAL 1967-1970 / Peru. Instituto Nacional de Planificacion – (Economic and Social Development Plan 1967-1970). Lima. 1966. BD-1730 1 – 9 – ne IDC [338]

PLAN DE DESARROLLO ECONOMICO Y SOCIAL, 1967-1970 / Peru. Instituto Nacional de Planificacion – 4v. Lima. 1967. BD-415 1 – 9 – ne IDC [338]

PLAN DE DESARROLLO ECONOMICO Y SOCIAL, 1967-70 PLAN SECTORIAL AGROPECUARIO / Peru. Instituto Nacional de Planificacion – 2v. Lima. 1967 – 9 – ne IDC [338]

PLAN DE DESARROLLO ECONOMICO Y SOCIAL 1968-1972 / El Salvador. Consejo Nacional de Planificacion y Coordinacion Economica – D-1040 1. 3v 1968 – 9 – ne IDC [338]

PLAN DE DESARROLLO ECONOMICO Y SOCIAL 1970-73 / Colombia. Departamento Nacional de Planeacion – Volumen general. 2v. D-1530-1 – 9 – ne IDC [338]

PLAN DE DESARROLLO ECONOMICO Y SOCIAL 1973-1977 / El Salvador. Consejo Nacional de Planificacion y Coordinacion Economica – Economic and Social Development Plan 1973-1977. 4 v. San Salvador. 1972. BD-1647 1 – 9 – ne IDC [338]

PLAN DE DESARROLLO ECONOMICO Y SOCIAL DE CORTO PLAZO, 1967-70 / Guatemala – Guatemala. 1967. Bd-703 1 – 9 – ne IDC [338]

PLAN DE DESARROLLO ECONOMICO Y SOCIAL DE COSTA RICA. VERSION PRELIMINAR REVISADA, JUN 1965 / Costa Rica. Oficina de Planificacion – 4v. San Jose. 1965. BD-185 1 – 9 – ne IDC [338]

PLAN DE DEVELOPPEMENT / Cameroon – 1960 – 1 – 39.50 – us African Imprint [338]

PLAN DE DEVELOPPEMENT, 1964-1968 / Lebanon. Ministere du Plan – Texte approuve par le Conseil des ministres en date du 20 mai 1964. BNE-9677 1 – 9 – ne IDC [338]

PLAN DE DEVELOPPEMENT, 1965-1969 / Lebanon. Ministere du Plan – Beirut. 1965. BD-410 1 – 9 – ne IDC [338]

PLAN DE DEVELOPPEMENT 1972-1977 / Lebanon. Ministere du Plan – (Development Plan 1972-1977). BD-1687 1 – 9 – ne IDC [338]

PLAN DE DEVELOPPEMENT ECONOMICQUE ET SOCIAL POUR LA DECENNIE 1971-1980 / Chad. Ministere du Plan et des Aides Exterieures – 1972. BD-2009 1 – 9 – ne IDC [338]

PLAN DE DEVELOPPEMENT ECONOMIQUE / French Guiana. Comite departmental d'action economique de la Guyane – D-1056 1. Ed. 2. 1960 – 9 – ne IDC [380]

PLAN DE DEVELOPPEMENT ECONOMIQUE ET SOCIAL / Burundi – D-997 1. 2 v. 1968-1972 – 9 – ne IDC [338]

PLAN DE DEVELOPPEMENT ECONOMIQUE ET SOCIAL / Tunisia. Secretariat d'Etat au Plan et a l'Economie Nationale – D 1222 1. 2 v. 1969-1972 – 9 – ne IDC [338]

PLAN DE DEVELOPPEMENT ECONOMIQUE ET SOCIAL, 1947-1952 / French Cameroons – D-1297 1. 1952 – 9 – ne IDC [338]

PLAN DE DEVELOPPEMENT ECONOMIQUE ET SOCIAL, 1961-1963 (PLAN INTERIMAIRE) / Niger – 2v. Niamey. 1961. BD-160 1 – 9 – ne IDC [338]

PLAN DE DEVELOPPEMENT ECONOMIQUE ET SOCIAL, 1966-1970 / Dahomey – Cotonou. 1966. BD-593 1 – 9 – ne IDC [338]

PLAN DE DEVELOPPEMENT ECONOMIQUE ET SOCIAL, 1966-1970 / Gabon – Libreville. 1966 – 9 – ne IDC [338]

PLAN DE DEVELOPPEMENT ECONOMIQUE ET SOCIAL 1966-1970. EDITION PROVISOIRE. PROJET SOUMISA L'ASSEMBLEE NATIONALE / Dahomey – (Economic and social development plan. Provisional edition. Draft submitted to the national assembly). 2 v. 15 Nov 1965 – 9 – ne IDC [338]

PLAN DE DEVELOPPEMENT ECONOMIQUE ET SOCIAL, 1967-1970 / Central African Republic – Bangui. 1968. BD-653 1 – 9 – ne IDC [338]

PLAN DE DEVELOPPEMENT ECONOMIQUE ET SOCIAL, 1973-1977 / Morocco. Secretariat d'Etat au Plan, au Developpement regional et a la Formation des Cadres – 3v. Rabat. 1973. BD-1796 1 – 9 – ne IDC [956]

PLAN DE DEVELOPPEMENT ECONOMIQUE ET SOCIAL DU DAHOMEY, 1962-65 / Dahomey. Societe Generale d'Etudes et de Planification, Paris – 6v. 1962 – 9 – ne IDC [338]

PLAN DE DEVELOPPEMENT ECONOMIQUE ET SOCIAL DU TERRITOIRE, 1947-1952 / French Cameroons – D-1296 1. 1946 – 9 – ne IDC [338]

PLAN DE DEVELOPPEMENT ECONOMIQUE ET SOCIAL PROBLEME, VOTES A SUIVRE, ORGANISATION / Congo. Leopoldville. Ministere du Plan.. – 1962 – 9 – ne IDC [338]

PLAN DE DEVELOPPEMENT ECONOMIQUE ET SOCIAL RAPPORT D'EXECUTION, 1 JUILLET 1954-30 JUIN 1955 / Madagascar – Tananarive. 1956. BD-435 1 – 9 – ne IDC [338]

PLAN DE DEVELOPPEMENT ECONOMIQUE ET SOCIAL RAPPORT D'EXECUTION, 1ER JUILLET 1955-30 JUIN 1956 / Madagascar – Tananarive. 1957 – 9 – ne IDC [338]

PLAN DE DEVELOPPEMENT ECONOMIQUE ET SOCIAL RAPPORT D'EXECUTION, 1ER JUILLET 1958-30 JUIN 1959 / Malagasy Republic – Tananarive. 1960 – 9 – ne IDC [338]

PLAN DE DEVELOPPEMENT ECONOMIQUE ET SOCIAL-TRAVAUX PREPARATOIRE / Cameroon. Societe Generale d'Etudes et de Planification, Paris – 3v. 1960 – 9 – ne IDC [338]

PLAN DE DEVELOPPEMENT ET SOCIAL, 1959/64 / Laos – Vientiane. 1959. BD-220 1 – 9 – ne IDC [338]

EL PLAN DE FOMENTO DE LA ECONOMIA NACIONAL / Colombia. Ministerio de la Economia Nacional – D-1268 1 – 9 – ne IDC [338]

PLAN DE FOMENTO DE LA PRODUCCION / Ecuador. Ministerio de Economia – D-1287 1. 1948 – 9 – ne IDC [338]

PLAN DE FOMENTO ECONOMICO / Costa Rica. Banco de Costa Rica – D-1275 1. 1954-1958 – 9 – ne IDC [338]

PLAN DE FORMACION-ACCION (REUNIONES DE EQUIPO). PRIMER CICLO-GUIONES / Consejo Diocesano de los hombres de Accion Catolica – Badajoz: Graficas Jimenez, 1962 – sp Bibl Santa Ana [240]

PLAN DE GOBIERNO, 1947-1951 / Argentine Republic – Buenos Aires, 1946. 2v – 1 – CSUXADH9365-B – us Hoover Inst Photo [350]

PLAN DE GOBIERNO, 1947-1951 / Argentine Republic. Presidencia de la Nacion – v. 1. Buenos Aires. 1946. BD-351 1 – 9 – ne IDC [324]

PLAN DE INVERSIONES PUBLICAS / Costa Rica. Oficina de Planificacion – D-1536 1. 1971-1973 – 9 – ne IDC [338]

PLAN DE INVERSIONES PUBLICAS, 1960-1964 / Guatemala. Con. Nac. de Plan. Econ – D-1318 1. 1961 – 9 – ne IDC [338]

PLAN DE LA ECONOMIA NACIONAL 1971-1976 / Chile. Oficina de Planificacion Nacional – Antecedentes sobre el Desarrollo Chileno. 1960-1970. Santiago. 1971. BD-1836 1 – 9 – ne IDC [338]

PLAN DE LA NACION, 1960-1964 / Venezuela. Coordination and Economic Planning Office – D 1514 1. 1960 – 9 – ne IDC [338]

PLAN DE LA NACION, 1963-1966 / Venezuela. Oficina Centrale de Coordinacion y Planificacion – Caracas. 1963. BD-636 1 – 9 – ne IDC [338]

PLAN DE LA NACION, 1965-1968 / Venezuela. Oficina Central de Coordinacion y Planificacion – Caracas. 1967. BD-170 1 – 9 – ne IDC [338]

PLAN DE MEJORAS...CACERES / Osuna, Candido – 1841 – 9 – 1.50f – sp Bibl Santa Ana [600]

PLAN DE OBRAS PUBLICAS NACIONALES PARA EL PERIODO PRESIDENCIAL, 1941 A 1946 / Venezuela. Presidente – D 1513 1. 1942 – 9 – ne IDC [360]

PLAN DE RECONSTRUCCION 1971-1973, DE LA PROVINCIAS DE COQUIMBO, ACONCAGUA, SANTIAGO, VALPARASIO Y O'HIGGINS, AFECTADAS POR EL SISMO DEL 8 DE JULIO DE 1971 / Chile. Oficina de Planificacion Nacional – Santiago. 1971. BD-1838 1 – 9 – ne IDC [338]

PLAN DE REFORMATION DES ETUDES ELEMENTAIRES / Borrely, Jean-Alexis – La Haye. P. F. Gosse. 1776. 6736 – 9 – fr Hachette [360]

PLAN DE SANTANDER, INVERSIONES 1954-1958 / Colombia. Direccion Nacional de Planeacion.. – Bogota. 1955 – 9 – ne IDC [338]

PLAN DE TRABAJO DE EDUCACION PRELIMINAR PARA LOS MESES DE FEBRERO Y MARZO / Delegacion Provincial del Frente de Juventudes – Caceres: Imprenta Garcia Floriano, s.a. – 1 – sp Bibl Santa Ana [370]

PLAN DE UNA BIBLIOTECA DE AUTORES ARABES ESPANOLES / Fernandez Gonzalez, Francisco – Madrid, 1861. 73p. 1 fiche. Libros en Microficha no.05 – 9 – Pta1,000.00 – 84-85422-30-9 – sp Pentalfa [020]

LE PLAN DECENNAL APRES 6 ANS D'EXISTENCE / Congo. Belgian – Leopoldville. 1956 – 9 – ne IDC [338]

PLAN DECENNAL D'EQUIPEMENT ECONOMIQUE ET SOCIAL RAPPORT D'EXECUTION, 1 JUILLET 1950-30 JUIN 1951 / Madagascar – Tananarive. 1952. BD-712 1 – 9 – ne IDC [338]

PLAN DECENNAL D'EQUIPEMENT ECONOMIQUE ET SOCIAL RAPPORT D'EXECUTION, 1 JUILLET 1952-30 JUIN 1953 / Madagascar – Tananarive. 1954. BD-434 1 – 9 – ne IDC [338]

PLAN DECENNAL D'EQUIPEMENT ECONOMIQUE ET SOCIAL RAPPORT D'EXECUTION 1ER JUILLET 1947-30 JUIN 1950 / Madagascar – Tananarive. 1951 – 9 – ne IDC [338]

PLAN DECENNAL D'EQUIPEMENT ECONOMIQUE ET SOCIAL RAPPORT D'EXECUTION, 1ER JUILLET 1951-30 JUIN 1952 / Madagascar – Tananarive. 1953 – 9 – ne IDC [338]

PLAN DECENNAL D'EQUIPEMENT ECONOMIQUE ET SOCIAL RAPPORT D'EXECUTION 1ER JUILLET 1953-30 JUIN 1954 / Madagascar – Tananarive. 1955 – 9 – ne IDC [338]

PLAN DECENNAL ETUDE SUR L'EVOLUTION ECONOMIQUE DU RUANDA-URUNDI DE 1949 A 1955 / Ruanda-Urundi – Usumbura. 1956. BD-452 1 – 9 – ne IDC [338]

PLAN DECENNAL POUR LE DEVELOPPEMENT ECONOMIQUE ET SOCIAL / Belgium. Ministere des Colonies – Ed. by de Visscher. 2 v. Bruxelles. 1949. BD-173 1 – 9 – ne IDC [338]

PLAN DECENNAL POUR LE DEVELOPPEMENT ECONOMIQUE ET SOCIAL / Ruanda-Urundi. Belgium. Ministere des Colonies – Ed. by de Visscher. Bruxelles. 1951 – 9 – ne IDC [338]

PLAN D'EDUCATION EN REPONSE AUX ACADEMIES DE MARSEILLE ET DE CHALONS / Gosselin, Charles-Robert – Amsterdam. 1785 – 9 – fr Hachette [370]

PLAN D'EDUCATION ET LES MOYENS DE L'EXECUTER / Devienne, Jean Baptiste d'Agneaux, dit Dom – London, 1775. 36p. 1 fiche. (Education Collection) – 9 – 6.00 – fr Bibl Nationale [370]

PLAN D'EDUCATION NATIONALE / DuCasteleier – Paris: Laurens, 1791. 25p. 1 fiche. (Education Collection) – 9 – 6.00 – fr Bibl Nationale [370]

PLAN D'EDUCATION NATIONALE, ADRESSE AUX ETATS GENERAUX PAR UN PERE DE FAMILLE DAUPHINOIS / Mounier, Jean-Joseph – de Berry. 1789. 6776 – 9 – fr Hachette [305]

PLAN D'EDUCATION NATIONALE CONSIDEREE SOUS LE RAPPORT DES LIVRES ELEMENTAIRES / Barruel, Etienne – Paris. Desenne. 1791. 6734 – 9 – fr Hachette [305]

PLAN D'EDUCATION NATIONALE, EN FAVEUR DES PAUVRES ENFANS DE LA CAMPAGNE / Thelis, Claude-Antoine de – s.l. 1779 – 9 – fr Hachette [370]

PLAN D'EDUCATION, PRESENTE A L'ASSEMBLEE NATIONALE, AU NOM DES INSTITUTEURS PUBLICS DE L'ORATOIRE / Daunou, Pierre Claude Francois – Paris. Volland. 1790. 6747 – 9 – fr Hachette [324]

PLAN D'EDUCATION PUBLIQUE / Coyer, Gabriel-Francois – Paris. Duchesne. 1770 – 9 – fr Hachette [370]

PLAN D'EDUCATION PUBLIQUE PAR LE MOYEN DUQUEL ON REDUIT A CINQ ANNEES LE COURS DES ETUDES ORDINAIRES / Wandelaincourt, Hubert – Paris. Durand. 1777 – 9 – fr Hachette [370]

PLAN D'EQUIPEMENT BIENNAL, 1956-1957 / Cambodia – Phnom-Penh. 1956 – 9 – ne IDC [338]

PLAN DETAILLE DE TOPOGRAPHIE / Dralet – (French Socialist Congresses Series). Paris. Huzard, an IX – 9 – fr Hachette [944]

PLAN DETAILLE DE TOPOGRAPHIE, SUIVI DE LA TOPOGRAPHIE DU DEPARTEMENT DU GERS / Dralet – An IX – 9 – fr Hachette [944]

PLAN D'ETUDES ET D'EDUCATION, AVEC UN DISCOURS SUR L'EDUCATION / Sutaine, Ger – Paris. Impr. Lottin. 1764 – 9 – fr Hachette [370]

PLAN D'ORIENTATION POUR LE DEVELOPPEMENT ECONOMIQUE ET SOCIAL 1989-1995 (HUITIEME PLAN) / Senegal. Ministere du Plan et de la Cooperation – Dakar, 1989 – 5mf – 9 – ne IDC [338]

PLAN D'UN EDUCATOIRE NATIONAL / Fauleau – Orleans. impr. Jacob-Sion. 1789. 6754 – 9 – fr Hachette [944]

PLAN D'UN ESTABLISSEMENT D'EDUCATION NATIONALE / Bourdon de la Crosniere, Louis Jean Joseph Leonard – Orleans: Couret de Villeneuve, 1788. 1 fiche. (Education Collection) – 9 – 6.00 – fr Bibl Nationale [370]

PLAN D'UNE STATISTIQUE GENERALE POUR LES SIX DEPARTEMENTS DE LA 27E DIVISION MILITAIRE (CI-DEVANT PIEMONT) / Labouliniere, Pierre – An XI – 9 – fr Hachette [944]

PLAN ECONOMICO DE 1952 : CONFERENCIAS PRONUNCIADAS EL 18 DE FEBRERO ANUNCIANDO EL PLAN ECONOMICO DE 1952 Y LOS PRECIOS DE LA COSECHA, Y EL 5 DE MARZO REFIRI ENDOSE A LA EJECUCION Y CONTRODEL PLAN / Peron, Juan Domingo – [Buenos Aires?]: Consejo Economico Nacional, 1952 – 1 – CSUXAJB7971-B – us Hoover Inst Photo [330]

EL PLAN ECONOMICO DE 1952 Y LA CONSOLIDACION DE LA PROSPERIDAD NACIONAL : CONFERENCIA PRONUNCIADA EN EL SALON DE ACTOS DE LA BOLSA DE COMERCIO DE BUENOS AIRES, EL 24 DE MARZO DE 1952 / Cereijo, Ramon Antonio – [Buenos Aires?]: Consejo Economico Nacional, 1952 – 1 – CSUXADM9647-B – us Hoover Inst Photo [330]

LE PLAN ECONOMIQUE QUINQUENNAL TCHECOSLOVAQUE TEXTE DE LA LOI / Czechoslovakia – Prague. 1948. BD-517 1 – 9 – ne IDC [338]

PLAN EXPERIMENTAL DE EDUCACION FISICO-DEPORTIVA ESCOLAR : PROGRAMA DE EDUCACION FISICA PARA LA E.G.B. SEGUNDO PERIODO 3RD Y 4TH CURSOS, TERCER PERIODO 5TH Y 6TH CURSOS, CUARTO PERIODO 7TH Y 8TH CURSOS / Lozano Pino, Manuel – Caceres: Imp. Extremadura, 1980 – sp Bibl Santa Ana [370]

PLAN EXPERIMENTAL DE EDUCACION FISICO-DEPORTIVA ESCOLAR : PROGRAMAS DE EDUCACION FISICA PARA LA E.G.B. PRIMER PERIODO 1ST Y 2ND CURSOS / Lozano Pino, Manuel – Caceres: Ed. Extremadura, 1980 – sp Bibl Santa Ana [370]

PLAN FINANCIER DES PROGRAMMES DE DEVELOPPEMENT 1969-1970 / Haiti. Conseil National de Developpement et de Planification – (Financial plan for development program 1969-1970). Port-au-Prince – 9 – ne IDC [338]

PLAN FINANCIER DES PROGRAMMES DE DEVELOPPEMENT 1971-72 / Haiti. Conseil National de Developpement et de Planification – (Financial Plan for Development Program 1971-72). Port-au-Prince. BD-1663 1 – 9 – ne IDC [338]

A PLAN FOR BETTER RELIGIOUS INSTRUCTION IN THE SOUTHERN METHODIST CHURCH / Cuninggim, J L – Nashville, TN: Methodist Episcopal Church, South: Barbee & Smith, agents, 1901 – 1mf – 9 – 0-8370-7538-6 – 1986-1538 – us A.T.L.A. [370]

A PLAN FOR MAURITIUS PROGRAMME FOR CAPITAL EXPENDITURE FOR THE PERIOD 1 JUL 1957 TO 30 JUN 1962 / Mauritius – (Sessional Paper No. 4 of 1958). Port Louis. 1958. BD-664 1 – 9 – ne IDC [338]

A PLAN FOR PREPARING A CONGREGATION FOR THE CONSTRUCTION OF A CHURCH BUILDING / Thomas, Joe Milton – 1982 – 1 – 6.72 – us Baptist [240]

A PLAN FOR PREVENTING ROBBERIES WITHIN TWENTY MILES OF LONDON: WITH AN ACCOUNT OF THE RISE AND ESTABLISHMENT OF THE REAL THIEFTAKERS; TO WHICH IS ADDED, ADVICE TO PAWNBROKERS, STABLEKEEPERS, AND PUBLICANS / Fielding, John – London: A. Millar, 1755 – 1 – us U.W. Library [941]

A PLAN FOR SEYCHELLES / Seychelles – Victoria. 1959 – 9 – ne IDC [338]

PLAN FUER DIE WIRTSCHAFTLICHE UND SOZIALE ENTWICKLUNG, 1966-1970 / Togo. Europaeischer Wirtschaftsgemeinschaft – Soziologischer Teil, "Baeuerliche Bevolkerung," von J. O. Muller. (Institut fuer Auslandische Bandwirtschaft). Gottingen. 1966. BD-1830 1 – 9 – ne IDC [338]

PLAN GARUDA INDONESIAN AIRWAYS, 1951-1955 (TRAFFIC ANALYSIS AND PRODUCTION PLAN) / Garuda Indonesian Airways – SE-6644 1. 1952? – 9 – ne IDC [380]

PLAN GENERAL DE DESARROLLO ECONOMICO Y SOCIAL / Colombia. Departamento Administrativo de Planeacion.. – 2v. Bogota. 1962 – 9 – ne IDC [338]

PLAN GENERAL DE DESARROLLO ECONOMICO Y SOCIAL / Ecuador. Junta Nacional de Planificacion y Coordinacion Economica – Version preliminar (1964-1973). D-1038 6v. 1963 – 9 – ne IDC [338]

PLAN GENERAL D'INSTITUTION PARTICULIEREMENT DESTINE POUR LA JEUNESSE DU PARLEMENT DE BOURGOGNE – Dijon. impr. Causse. 1763. 6782 – 9 – fr Hachette [305]

PLAN INMEDIATO DE POLITICA ECONOMICA DEL GOBIERNO DE LA REVOLUCION NACIONAL / Bolivia. Ministerio de Relaciones Exteriores y Culto – Memorandum 2, por W. Guevara Arze. La Paz. 1954 – 9 – ne IDC [330]

PLAN INTERIMAIRE, 1964 / Niger. Commissariat General au Plan – (Interim plan, 1964). Niamey. 1964. BD-1388 1 – 9 – ne IDC [338]

PLAN INTERIMAIRE, 1963-1964 / Upper Volta – Ouagadougou. 1964. BD-168 1 – 9 – ne IDC [338]

PLAN INTERIMAIRE DE DEVELOPPEMENT ECONOMIQUE ET SOCIAL / Congo. (Brazzaville) – D-1026 1. 1964-1968 – 9 – ne IDC [338]

PLAN INTERMEDIAIRE, 1960-61 / France – Paris. 1960. BD-638 1 – 9 – ne IDC [338]

PLAN INTERMEDIAIRE 1965-66 / Central African Republic. Presidence du Gouvernement. Haut Commissariat au Plan et a l'Assistance Technique – (Interim Plan 1965-1966). BD-1629 1 – 9 – ne IDC [338]

PLAN INTERMEDIAIRE BIENNAL, 1965-66 / Central African Republic. Haut Commissariat – Bangui. 1966 – 9 – ne IDC [338]

PLAN MEROPRII ATI I PO SELSKOMU KHOZI A ISTVU UKRAINY NA... : U.S.S.R. NARODNY I KOMISSARIAT ZEMLEDELII A – (Includes c.1: 1925/1926) – Kharkov: Radi anskky i seli anyn, -[1925] – 1 – CSUXAKZ6786-S – us Hoover Inst Photo [947]

PLAN NACIONAL DE DEASARROLLO 1971-1975. V. 1: PLAN GLOBAL / Peru. Sistema Nacional de Planificacion – Lima. 1971. BD-1847 1 – 9 – ne IDC [338]

PLAN NACIONAL DE DESAROLLO / Costa Rica. Oficina de Planificacion – 4v. 1973-74. BD-1809 1 – 9 – ne IDC [338]

PLAN NACIONAL DE DESARROLLO / Dominican Republic. Oficina Nacional de Planificacion – D-1285 1. 1970-1974 – 9 – ne IDC [338]

PLAN NACIONAL DE DESARROLLO, 1965-1969 / Argentine Republic. Consejo Nacional de Desarrollo – Buenos Aires. 1965. BD-346 1 – 9 – ne IDC [338]

PLAN NACIONAL DE DESARROLLO, 1974-1978. ESTRATEGIA Y PLAN GLOBAL / Costa Rica. Oficina de Planificacion – Version Preliminar. San Jose. 1974. BD-1840 1 – 9 – ne IDC [338]

PLAN NACIONAL DE DESARROLLO ECONOMICO Y SOCIAL, 1965-1969 / Nicaragua. Cons. Nac. de Econ. Oficina de Plan – D-1139 1. 5v 1965 – 9 – ne IDC [338]

PLAN NACIONAL DE DESARROLLO ECONOMICO Y SOCIAL, 1965-1974 / Uruguay. Comision de Inversiones y Desarrollo Economico – 5v. in 6. Montevideo. 1965. BD-210 1 – 9 – ne IDC [338]

PLAN NACIONAL DE DESARROLLO ECONOMICO Y SOCIAL DE GUATEMALA 1965-1969 / Guatemala. Con. Nac. de Plan. Econ – D-1420 1. 2v – 9 – ne IDC [338]

PLAN NACIONAL DE DESARROLLO ECONOMICO Y SOCIAL DE HONDURAS, 1965-1969 / Honduras. Consejo Nacional de Economia – D-879 1. 4v. 1965 – 9 – ne IDC [338]

PLAN NACIONAL DE DESARROLLO ECONOMICO Y SOCIAL DEL PERU, 1962-1971 / Peru – Tomo 1. Lima, Banco Central de Reserva del Peru. 1962 – 9 – ne IDC [338]

PLAN NACIONAL DE DESARROLLO PARA 1971-1975 / Peru – Republica Peruama. Tomo 1-5, v. 1-11. Lima. 1971-72. BD-1572 1 – 9 – ne IDC [338]

PLAN NACIONAL DE EDUCACION / Chile. Oficina de Planificacion Nacional – Santiago, 1987 – 1mf – 9 – DE-650/1 – ne IDC [370]

PLAN NACIONAL DE EDUCACION PARA LA REP. DE GUATEMALA / Guatemala – (Cuadrienio 1969-72). Oficina de Plan. 1969. BD-1566 1 – 9 – ne IDC [324]

PLAN NACIONAL DE INTEGRACION DE LA POBLACION ABORIGEN: INFORME. ACTIVIDADES ENERO 1963-JUNIO 1964 / Peru. Ministerio de Trabajo y Asuntos Indigenas – Lima. 1964. BD-1843 1 – 9 – ne IDC [310]

THE PLAN OF A DICTIONARY OF THE ENGLISH LANGUAGE / Johnson, Samuel – 1747. 41p. (English Linguistics Series 1500-1800) – 9 – us UMI [420]

PLAN OF A SETTLEMENT TO BE MADE NEAR SIERRA LEONE ON THE GRAIN COAST OF AFRICA : INTENDED MORE PARTICULARLY FOR THE SERVICE AND HAPPY ESTABLISHMENT OF BLACKS AND PEOPLE OF COLOUR, TO BE SHIPPED AS FREEMEN... / Smeathman, Henry – London, 1786 – us Res Libr [960]

PLAN OF DEVELOPMENT, 1966-1970 IMPLEMENTATION PROGRAMME AND TARGETS FOR 1967-68 / Ceylon. Ministry of Land, Irrigation and Power – Colombo. 1967 – 9 – ne IDC [307]

A PLAN OF DEVELOPMENT FOR MALAYA 1956-60 / Malaya. Economic Secretariat – Kuala Lumpur. 1956. BD-1690 1 – 9 – ne IDC [338]

A PLAN OF DEVELOPMENT FOR THE COLONY OF ST VINCENT / St. Vincent. Development Committee – Port-of-Spain. 1947 – 9 – ne IDC [338]

PLAN OF DEVELOPMENT OF MINISTRY OF LAND, IRRIGATION AND POWER, 1966-1970 / Ceylon. Ministry of Land, Irrigation and Power – Colombo. 1966 – 9 – ne IDC [307]

A PLAN OF ECONOMIC DEVELOPMENT FOR SIERRA LEONE / Sierra Leone – Freetown. 1949 – 9 – ne IDC [338]

PLAN OF OPERATION : AN IMPLEMENTATION OF THE THIRD NATIONAL DEVELOPMENT PLAN (1972-1976) / Thailand. Ministry of Education. Department of Secondary Education – Bangkok, 1972 – 1mf – 9 – DE-277/1 – ne IDC [370]

THE PLAN OF UNION, OR, A HISTORY OF THE PRESBYTERIAN AND CONGREGATIONAL CHURCHES OF THE WESTERN RESERVE : WITH BIOGRAPHICAL SKETCHES OF THE EARLY MISSIONARIES / Kennedy, William S – Hudson, O[hio]: Pentagon, 1856 – 1mf – us A.T.L.A. [240]

PLAN OPERATIVO ANUAL 1988 / Costa Rica. Ministerio de Education Publica – San Jose, [1987] – 1mf – 9 – DE-613/1 – ne IDC [370]

PLAN OPERATIVO DE GOBIERNO NACIONAL PARA 1974 / Panama. Ministerio de Planificacion y Politica Economica – 1974. BD-2010 1 – 9 – ne IDC [338]

PLAN QUADRENNIAL, 1970-1973 / Algeria. Direction Generale du Plan et des Etudes Economiques – 1970. BNE-8630 1 – 9 – ne IDC [338]

PLAN QUADRIENNAL 1963-1966 / Mauritania. Ministere des Affaires Etrangeres et du Plan – Bilan de 3 annees d'execution. Nouakchott. n.d. BD-1871 1 – 9 – ne IDC [338]

PLAN QUADRIENNAL, 1965-1968 / Niger – 2v. Niamey. 1965 – 9 – ne IDC [338]

PLAN QUADRIENNAL, 1965-1968 / Tunisia. Secretariat d'Etat au Plan – 3v. Tunis. 1965. BD-177 1 – 9 – ne IDC [338]

PLAN QUADRIENNAL, 1970-1973 / Algeria. Ministere de l'Agriculture – Rapport sur le secteur agricole. 1971? BNE-8659 1 – 9 – ne IDC [630]

PLAN QUADRIENNAL 1970-1973 RAPPORT GENERAL / Algeria – D-908 1 – 9 – ne IDC [338]

PLAN QUADRIENNAL DE DEVELOPPEMENT, 1961-1964 / Senegal. Ministere du Plan, du Developpement – Dakar. 1961. BD-161 1 – 9 – ne IDC [338]

PLAN QUADRIENNAL DE DEVELOPPEMENT ECONOMIQUE ET SOCIAL, 1963-1966 / Mauritania – Nouackchott. 1963 – 9 – ne IDC [338]

PLAN QUINGUENNAL, 1968-1972: RAPPORT SUR L'EXECUTION DU PLAN. ET PROGRAMME D'ACTION / Morocco. Division du Plan et des Etudes Economiques – 1969. BNE-3045 1 – 9 – ne IDC [338]

PLAN QUINQUENAL DE GOBIERNO DEL PRESIDENTE PERON, 1947-1951 / Peron, Juan – [Buenos Aires]: Editorial Primicias, [194-?] – 1 – CSUXADH8416-B – us Hoover Inst Photo [320]

EL PLAN QUINQUENAL DE PERON Y LOS COMUNISTAS / Filippo, Virgilio – Buenos Aires: Lista Blanca, 2nd ed 1947 – 1 – CSUXADQ3398-B – us Hoover Inst Photo [320]

EL PLAN QUINQUENAL EXPLICADO A LOS NINOS / Ianantuoni, Domingo Rafael – Buenos Aires, 1947 – 1 – CSUXAHZ5801-B – us Hoover Inst Photo [947]

PLAN QUINQUENNAL 1960-1964 / Morocco. Conseil Superieur du Plan – 1960. BNE-3027 1 – 9 – ne IDC [330]

PLAN QUINQUENNAL, 1960-1964 / Morocco. Division de la Coordination Economique et du Plan – Rabat. 1964 – 9 – ne IDC [330]

PLAN QUINQUENNAL 1960-1964 LE DEVELOPPEMENT INDUSTRIEL / Morocco. Ministere de l'Economie Nationale et des Finances – Rabat. 1961. BD-430 1 – 9 – ne IDC [338]

LE PLAN QUINQUENNAL 1972-1976 / Upper Volta – Summary in French. Bulletin de l'Afrique Noire. numero special 3rd ed. Paris. 1975. BD-1860 1 – 9 – ne IDC [338]

LE PLAN QUINQUENNAL 1974-1978 DE DEVELOPPEMENT / Mali – Summary in French. Bulletin de l'Afrique Noire. Numero special 3rd. ed. Paris. 1975. BD-1862 1 – 9 – ne IDC [338]

PLAN QUINQUENNAL 1982-1986 : BLOCKS PROGRAMMES ET PROJETS 1983-1986 / Congo (People's Republic). Ministere du Plan ... Ministere du Travail. Ministere de l'Education Nationale – Brazzaville, 1981 – 2mf – 9 – DE-316/1 – ne IDC [370]

PLAN QUINQUENNAL DE DEVELOPPEMENT, 1966-1970 / Togo – Paris, SIMAG. 1965 – 9 – ne IDC [338]

PLAN QUINQUENNAL DE DEVELOPPEMENT ECONOMIQUE ET SOCIAL 1972-1976 / Upper Volta. Assemblee Nationale – BD-1807 1 – 9 – ne IDC [960]

PLAN QUINQUENNAL DE DEVELOPPEMENT ECONOMIQUE ET SOCIAL 1972-1976 / Upper Volta. Ministere du Plan – Ouagadougou. 1972. BD-2001 1 – 9 – ne IDC [960]

PLAN QUINQUENNAL DE DEVELOPPEMENT ECONOMIQUE ET SOCIAL DU BURUNDI, 1968-1972 / Burundi – (Five Year Economic and Social Development Plan for Burundi, 1968-1972). Bujumbura. 1970. BD-1625 – 9 – ne IDC [338]

PLAN QUINQUENNAL DE DEVELOPPEMENT ECONOMIQUE ET SOCIAL. PRINCIPES GENERAUX 1965-1969 / Congo. (Kinshasa). Ministere du Plan et du Developpement Industriel – D-1025 1 – 9 – ne IDC [338]

PLAN QUINQUENNAL DE DEVELOPPEMENT ECONOMIQUE, SOCIAL ET CULTUREL 1971-1975 / Ivory Coast. Ministere du Plan – D-1555 1. 1971 – 9 – ne IDC [338]

LE PLAN QUINQUENNAL POUR LE DEVELOPPEMENT ECONOMIQUE ET SOCIAL, 1960-1965 RESUME / United Arab Republic – Cairo. 1960. BD-635 1 – 9 – ne IDC [338]

PLAN QUINQUENNEL 1960-1964: LE DEVELOPPEMENT INDUSTRIEL / Morocco. Division de la Coordination Economique et du Plan – 1961. BNE-3042 1 – 9 – ne IDC [338]

PLAN QUINQUENNEL: 1960-1964: MEMENTO DES OBJECTIFS DE L'INDUSTRIE, 1961 / Morocco. Division de la Coordination Economique et du Plan – BNE-3041 1 – 9 – ne IDC [338]

PLAN QUINQUENNEL; INDUSTRIALISATION ET CROISSANCE ECONOMIQUE GLOBAL / Morocco. Division de la Coordination Economique et du Plan – 1962. BNE-3040 1 – 9 – ne IDC [338]

PLAN QUIQUENNAL, 1964-1968 / Malagasy Republic. Commissariat General au Plan – Tananarive. 1964. BD-219 1 – 9 – ne IDC [338]

PLAN RABOTY GLAVPOLITPROSVETA NA SENTI ABRDEKABR 1921 G / Glavpolitprosvet (RSFSR) – Moskva: Glavpolitprosvet, 1921 – 1 – CSUX90-B6161 – us Hoover Inst Photo [947]

PLAN RABOTY GLAVPOLITPROSVETA NA SENTIABRDEKABR 1921 G / Glavpolitprosvet (RSFSR) – Moskva: Glavpolitprosvet, 1921 – 1 – CSUX90-B6160 – us Hoover Inst Photo [947]

PLAN REGIONAL DE DEV. ECON. ET SOCIAL ET D'AMENAGEMENT DU TERRITOIRE POUR LA CIRCONSCR. DE PROVENCE-COTE D'AZUR / France. Ministere des Finances et des Affaires Economiques – Paris. 1961 – 9 – ne IDC [336]

PLAN ROBAT / Kommunisticheskaya Akademiya. Moscow – Moscow. 1927-28, 1928-29, 1929-30 – 1 – us NY Public [335]

LE PLAN SECTORIEL ET LA REFORME DE L'EDUCATION AUX SEYCHELLES 1982-1986 / Seychelles. Ministere de l'Education et de l'Information – Victoria, 1982 – 3mf – 9 – DE-461/1 – ne IDC [370]

PLAN SEPTENNAL 1964-1970 / Guinea. Ministere du Plan – D-1089 1. 1965 – 9 – ne IDC [338]

PLAN SEXENAL DEL PARTIDO NACIONAL REVOLUCIONARIO / Mexico – Mexico. 1937. BD-402 1 – 9 – ne IDC [335]

PLAN SOCIAL DE DEVELOPPEMENT ECONOMIQUE DE LA YOUGOSLAVIE, 1961-1965 / Yugoslavia – Beograd. 1961. BD-604 1 – 9 – ne IDC [324]

PLAN TRIENAL DE CUBA / Cuba – Habana, 1938 – 9 – ne IDC [338]

PLAN TRIENAL PARA LA RECONSTRUCCION Y LA LIBERACION NACIONAL 1974-1977 / Argentine Republic. Poder Ejecutivo Nacional – Buenos Aires. 1973. BD-2008 1 – 9 – ne IDC [972]

PLAN TRIENNAL, 1962-1964 / Tunisia. Secretariat d'Etat aux Plan et aux Finances – Tunis. 1962 – 9 – ne IDC [336]

PLAN TRIENNAL, 1965-1967 / Morocco. Division de la Coordination Economique et du Plan – Rabat. 1965. BD-199 1 – 9 – ne IDC [338]

PLAN TRIENNAL 1965-1967: TRAVAUX / Morocco. Conseil superieur du Plan – 1965. BNE-3026 1 – 9 – ne IDC [330]

PLAN TRIENNAL 1967-1969, PROGRAMME D'EQUIPEMENT, NOMENCLATURE / Algeria. Direction Generale du Plan et des Etudes Economiques – 2v. in 2. 1967-69. BNE-8634 1 – 9 – ne IDC [338]

PLAN TRIENNAL DE DEVELOPPEMENT ECONOMIQUE ET SOCIAL DE LA REPUBLIQUE DE GUINEE / Guinea – Conakry. 1960 – 9 – ne IDC [338]

PLAN TRIENNAL TABLEAU DETAILLE DES INVESTISSEMENTS, 1962-1964 / Tunisia. Secretariat d'Etat au Plan et aux Finances – Tunis. 1965. BD-693 1 – 9 – ne IDC [336]

PLAN ZAKHODIV U SILSKOMU KOSPODARSTVI NA... : U.S.S.R. NARODNI I KOMISARII AT ZEMELNYKH SPRAV – (Includes c.1: 1926/1927) – Kharkiv: Radi ansky i seli anyn, 1926- – 1 – CSUXAKZ6774-S – us Hoover Inst Photo [947]

PLANADA ENTERPRISE – Planada, CA. 1912-1918 – 1r – 1 – $50.00 – B06048 – us Library Micro [071]

O PLANALTO – Januaria, Brazil. Oct 1923; May 1925 – 1 – bl Biblioteca [072]

PLAN-CADRE DE DEVELOPPEMENT, 1967-1970 / Upper Volta – 1v. Ouagadougou. 1967 – 9 – ne IDC [338]

PLAN-CADRE DE HAUTE-VOLTA. ANNEE INTERIMAIRE 1971 / Upper Volta – D 1512 1. 1970 – 9 – ne IDC [338]

Planche, J R *see* AN INTRODUCTION TO HERALDRY: WITH NEARLY ONE THOUSAND ILLUSTRATIONS, INCLUDING THE ARMS OF ABOUT FIVE HUNDRED DIFFERENT FAMILIES

PLANCHES – Paris. 1902. 3v in 1 – 1 – us NY Public [380]

PLANCHES DE L'ARMORIAL GENERAL DE J.-B. RIETSTAP, 6 [TA A ZY] / Rolland, Henri – La Haye: Nijhoff, 1926 – 1 – F218.22 – fr Armell [920]

Planchet, Regis *see* EL COLONIAJE Y SUS DETRACTORES. EL PASO, 1927

Planchon, [F]G *see*
- DES GLOBULAIRES AU POINT DE VUE BOTANIQUE ET MEDICAL
- LES DROGUES SIMPLES D'ORIGINE VEGETALE
- MATERIAUX POUR LA FLORE MEDICALE DE MONTPELLIER...
- LES PRINCIPES DE LA METHODE NATURELLE

Planchon, J E *see* TROISIEME VOYAGE DE J. LINDEN

Planchon, L *see* ETUDES SUR LES PRODUITS DE LA FAMILLE DES SAPOTEES

Planchon, LD *see* LES ARISTOLOCHES

Planck, G J *see* GESCHICHTE DER PROTESTANTISCHEN THEOLOGIE

Plancquaert, M *see* LES JAGA ET LES BAYAKA DU KWANGO

Plancquaert, S J *see* LES SOCIETES SECRETES CHEZ LES BAYAKA

Plancus, J *see* DE CONCHIS MINUS NOTIS LIBER

Planelli, A *see* DELL'OPERA IN MUSICA TRATTATO

PLANES Y PROGRAMAS DE DESARROLLO 1969-72 / Colombia. Departamento Nacional de Planeacion – (Development Plans and Programs 1969 72). Dic 1969 – 9 – ne IDC [338]

PLANET – Richmond. Va. 1890-1894; 1896-1897; 1899-1938 – 1 – us UMI [071]

PLANET COMICS – Issue Nos. 11-15 Nov 1940-Nov 1941 – 5mf – 15 – $31.95 – us Comics [760]

PLANET COMICS – Issue Nos. 1-5 Jan 1940-May 1940 – 5mf – 15 – $31.95 – us Comics [760]

PLANET COMICS – Issue Nos. 16-20 Jan 1942-Sept 1942 – 5mf – 15 – $31.95 – us Comics [760]

PLANET COMICS – Issue Nos. 21-25 Nov 1942-Jul 1943 – 5mf – 15 – $31.95 – us Comics [760]

PLANET COMICS – Issue Nos. 26-30 Sept 1943-May 1944 – 5mf – 15 – $31.95 – us Comics [760]

PLANET COMICS – Issue Nos. 31-35 Jul 1944-Mar 1945 – 5mf – 15 – $31.95 – us Comics [760]

PLANET COMICS – Issue Nos. 36-42 May 1945-May 1946 – 5mf – 15 – $31.95 – us Comics [760]

PLANET COMICS – Issue Nos. 43-47 Jul 1946-Mar 1947 – 5mf – 15 – $31.95 – us Comics [760]

PLANET COMICS – Issue Nos. 48-52 May 1947-Jan 1948 – 5mf – 15 – $31.95 – us Comics [760]

PLANET COMICS – Issue Nos. 53-57 Mar 1948-Nov 1948 – 5mf – 15 – $31.95 – us Comics [760]

PLANET COMICS – Issue Nos. 58-63 Jan 1949-Winter 1949 – 5mf – 15 – $31.95 – us Comics [760]

PLANET COMICS – Issue Nos. 6-10 Jun 1940-Oct 1940 – 5mf – 15 – $31.95 – us Comics [760]

PLANET COMICS – Issue Nos. 64-73 Spring 1950-Winter 1953 – 5mf – 15 – $31.95 – us Comics [760]

PLANET IN PERIL? : MAN AND THE BIOSPHERE TODAY / Dasmann, R F – 1972 – 135p – 9 – 92-3-100947-8 – fr UNESCO [360]

Planet. (Ship) *see* DIE FORSCHUNGSREISE S.M.S. " PLANET" 1906-1907

PLANET STORIES – v1-2. 1939-1945 – 2r – 1 – $190.00 – us UPA [830]

PLANETARY AND SPACE SCIENCE – v1-1959- – 5,6,9 – us UMI [520]

PLAN...FUNCIONES A LA...FREGENAL... REMEDIOS / Martin Carnes Moreno, Rafael – 1825 – 9 – 1.50f – sp Bibl Santa Ana [946]

PLANIFICACION PERONISTA : CONTRIBUCION A SU ESTUDIO DOCTRINARIO Y METODOLOGICO / Garcia, Lorenzo A – Santa Fe: Libreria y Editorial Catellvi, 1953 – 1 – CSUXAJB7750-B – us Hoover Inst Photo [320]

LA PLANIFICATION ECONOMIQUE ET SOCIALE AU MAROC / Morocco. Ministere de l'Economie Nationale – (Assouline, A.) 1962. BNE-3072 1 – 9 – ne IDC [338]

PLANIFICATION ET DEVELOPPEMENT RURAL AU MAROC / Morocco. African Training and Research Centre in Administration for Development – (Articles chosen by W. Teller). Tanger. 1969. BNE-3200 1 – 9 – ne IDC [324]

LA PLANIFICATION URBAINE ET LE POUVOIR LOCAL : ETUDE DE LA PARTICIPATION POPULAIRE DANS LA GESTION URBAINE A RECIFE (BRESIL) / Souto-Maior Fontes, Breno Augusto – 2mf – 9 – 10382 – fr Atelier National [307]

PLANIROVANIE KHOZIAISTVENNOI DEIATEL'NOSTI SOIUZOV I NIZOVOI SETI PROMYSLOVOI KOOPERATSII / Berezin, M M – M., 1930 – 2mf – 9 – COR-412/1 – ne IDC [334]

PLANIROVANIE NARODNOGO KHOZIAISTVA MONGOLII (SBORNIK MATERIALOV) / Mongolia. U.S.S.R – Moskva, izd.-vo inostrannoi literatury. 1951. BD-769 1 – 9 – ne IDC [340]

THE PLANKTONIC DIATOMS OF NORTHERN SEAS / Lebour, M V – 1930 – 1 £35.00 7 £24.50 – uk Microform Academic [580]

A PLANNED PREACHING PROGRAM UTILIZING CONGREGATIONAL INVOLVEMENT AT FIRST BAPTIST CHURCH, MCDONOUGH, GEORGIA. 1982 / Bradshaw, James Daniel – 1 – 6.64 – us Baptist [240]

Planner-Petelin, Rose *see*
- DER FAEHRMANN AN DER WEICHSEL
- DAS HEILIGE BAND
- UND DENNOCH BLUEHT DIE ERDE

PLANNERS JOURNAL *see* JOURNAL OF THE AMERICAN INSTITUTE OF PLANNERS

PLANNERS NOTEBOOK – (See also: Practicing Planner) – v1-5. 1971-1975 – 1 – us UMI [300]

PLANNING – v1- 1935- 1; v41- 5,6,9 – us UMI [073]

PLANNING A FOREST INVENTORY / Husch, B – 1978 – 121p – it F.A.O. [634]

PLANNING AGRICULTURE : FAO SUPPORT TO AGRIGULTURAL PLANNING IN DEVELOPING COUNTRIES – 1984 – 39p – it F.A.O. [350]

PLANNING AN AQUACULTURE FACILITY : GUIDELINES FOR BIOPROGRAMMING AND DESING – 1988 – 46p – it F.A.O. [639]

Planning and Administrative Division, Ministry of Education and Community Development *see* EDUCATIONAL STATISTICS IN THE NORTH-WESTERN STATE, NIGERIA

PLANNING AND CHANGING – v1- 1970- 1; v6- 5,6,9 – us UMI [073]

PLANNING AND CIVIC COMMENT *see*
- PARKS AND RECREATION

PLANNING AND EVALUATION OF APPLIED NUTRITION PROGRAMMES / Latham, M C – 3rd printing 1978 – 125p – it F.A.O. [640]

PLANNING AND MANAGING FORESTRY RESEARCH : GUIDELINES FOR MANAGERS – 1990 – 190p – it F.A.O. [634]

PLANNING AND PROGRAMMING OF AGRICULTURAL RESEARCH / Arnon, I – 1978 – 122p – it F.A.O. [630]

PLANNING AND RESOURCE DEVELOPMENT SERIES / Massachusetts. College of Agriculture. Holdsworth Natural Resources Center – v. 1, 14, 15A-I. 1964-69 – 1,5,6 – us Spaulding [333]

PLANNING CHALLENGES OF THE 70'S IN SPACE – (Suppl to v26, Advances) – 1970 – 13mf – 9 – $20.00 – 0-87703-130-4 – us Univelt [629]

PLANNING CHALLENGES OF THE 70'S IN THE PUBLIC DOMAIN – (Suppl to v22, Space and Technology) – 1970 – 15mf – 9 – $20.00 – 0-87703-131-2 – us Univelt [629]

PLANNING FOR ACTION IN AGRICULTURAL DEVELOPMENT – 1974 repr 1984 – 53p – it F.A.O. [630]

PLANNING FOR HIGHER EDUCATION – v1-1972- 1; v7- 5,6,9 – us UMI [370]

PLANNING FOREST ROADS AND HARVESTING SYSTEMS – 1979 – 158p – it F.A.O. [634]

PLANNING HUMAN RESOURCES : METHODS, EXPERIENCES AND PRACTICES / Bertrand, Olivier – 1992 – 9 – 92-803-1142-5 – fr UNESCO [333]

PLANNING IN MOROCCO: ORGANIZATION AND IMPLEMENTATION / Waterson, A – (IBRD). 1962. BNE-3109 1 – 9 – ne IDC [338]

PLANNING INTEGRATED DEVELOPMENT : METHODS USED IN ASIA – 1986 – 271p – 9 – 92-3-102390-X – fr UNESCO [338]

PLANNING METHODS AND THE HUMAN ENVIRONMENT / Gallopin, Gilberte C – 1981 – 9 – 92-3-101894-9 – fr UNESCO [333]

PLANNING OF ECONOMIC DEVELOPMENT IN THE UNITED ARAB REPUBLIC / El-Morshidy, A M – 1962. BNE-4628 1 – 9 – ne IDC [338]

PLANNING PRACTICE AND RESEARCH – 1995, Vol 10 – £122.00 – uk Carfax [650]

PLANNING REVIEW – v1- 1972- 1; v5- 5,6,9 – us UMI [650]

PLANO BASICO DE DESENVOLVIMENTO CIENTIFIO E TECHNOLOGICO 1973-1974 / Brazil – BD-1813 1 – 9 – ne IDC [600]

PLANO DE APROVEITAMENTO DE CAMARATUBA, MAMANGUAPE, PARAIBA / Brazil. Superintendencia do Desenvolvimento do Nordeste – Recife. 1962. BD-1833 1 – 9 – ne IDC [338]

PLANO DE DESENVOLVIMENTO DO NORDESTE. (1972-1974) / Brazil. Superintendencia do Desenvolvimento do Nordeste – (Recife). Agosto. 1971. BD-1835-1 – 9 – ne IDC [338]

PLANO DE FOMENTO / Angola. Ministerios da. Economia e do Ultramar – (Plano de Fomento 1959-64. D-936-1. 9. Plano de Fomento 1968-73. D-887-1. 9) – 1953-1958. D-934 1 – 9 – ne IDC [330]

PLANO DE FOMENTO, 3, PARA 1968-1973 / Portugal. Presidencia do Conselho – 4v. Lisboa. 1968 – 9 – ne IDC [338]

PLANO DE FOMENTO 3" – PROGRAMA DE EXECUCAO PARA 1969 / Portugal. Presidencia do Conselho – D 904 1 – 9 – ne IDC [338]

PLANO DE FOMENTO (1953-1958) / Mozambique. (Portugal). Ministerios da Economia e do Ultramar – D-1128 1. 1953 – 9 – ne IDC [338]

PLANO DE FOMENTO 1953-1958 / Goa. India – D-1083 1. 1953 – 9 – ne IDC [338]

PLANO DE FOMENTO 1953-1958 / Macao. (Portugal). Ministerios da Economia e do Ultramar – D-1370 1. 1953 – 9 – ne IDC [330]

PLANO DE FOMENTO 1959-1964 / Goa. India – D-1084 1. 1959 – 9 – ne IDC [338]

PLANO DE FOMENTO (LEI NO. 2058) REVISAO DE 1955 (LEI NO. 2077) / Mozambique – (Development Plan (Law No. 2058) Revision of 1955 (Law No. 2077)). Lisboa. 1955. BD-1696 1 – 9 – ne IDC [338]

PLANO DE FOMENTO (LEI NO. 2058) REVISAO DE 1955 (LEI NO. 2077) / Sao Tome and Principe Islands. (Portugal) – (Development Plan (Law No. 2058) Revision of 1955 (Law No. 2077). Lisboa. 1955. BD-1743 1 – 9 – ne IDC [338]

PLANO DE FOMENTO REVISAO DE 1955 / Portugal. Fundo de Fomento Nacional – Lisboa. 1955. BD-513 1 – 9 – ne IDC [338]

PLANO DE VALORIZACAO ECONOMICA DE COLONIA DE MOCAMBIQUE / Portugal. Ministerio das Colonias – 28th May. 1947. BD-1798 1 – 9 – ne IDC [946]

PLANO DECENAL DE DESENVOLVIMENTO ECONOMICO E SOCIAL / Brazil. Ministerio do Planjamento e Coordenacao Economica – Versao Preliminar. Rio. 1967- BD-186 1 – 9 – ne IDC [338]

PLANO DO FOMENTO, 3, PROGRAMA DE EXECUCAO PARA 1968 / Portugal. Presidencia do Conselho – Lisboa. 1968. BD-671 1 – 9 – ne IDC [338]

PLANO DO FOMENTO PARA 1953-1958 / Portugal. Ministerio da Economia – 2v. Lisboa. 1953 – 9 – ne IDC [338]

PLANO INTEGRADO DE DESENVOLVIMENTO, REGIAO NORDESTE / Minas Gerais. Brazil – Belo Horizonte. 1966. BD-368 – 9 – ne IDC [338]

PLANO INTERCALAR DE FEMENTO PARA 1965-1967 PROGRAMA DE EXECUCAO PARA 1965 / Portugal. Direccao de Servicos de Planeamento – Lisboa. 1965 – 9 – ne IDC [338]

PLANO INTERCALAR DE FOMENTO PARA 1965-1967 / Angola. Presidencia do Conselho – (Interim Development Plan for 1965-1967). Lisboa. v. 2. 1964. BD-1607 1 – 9 – ne IDC [960]

PLANO INTERCALAR DE FOMENTO PARA 1965-1967 / Goa. India. Presidencia do Conselho – (Interim Development Plan for 1965-1967). Lisboa. 1964. BD-1659 1 – 9 – ne IDC [338]

PLANO INTERCALAR DE FOMENTO PARA 1965-1967 / Macao. (Portugal). Presidencia do Conselho – (Interim Development Plan for 1965-1967). Lisboa. v. 2. 1964. BD-1688 1 – 9 – ne IDC [330]

PLANO INTERCALAR DE FOMENTO PARA 1965-1967 / Mozambique. Presidencia do Conselho – (Interim Development Plan for 1965-1967). Lisboa. v. 2. 1964. BD-1697 1 – 9 – ne IDC [338]

PLANO INTERCALAR DE FOMENTO PARA 1965-1967 / Portugal. Presidencia do Conselho – 1v. Lisboa. 1964. BD-188 1 – 9 – ne IDC [338]

PLANO INTERCALAR DE FOMENTO PARA 1965-1967 PROGRAMA DE EXECUCAO PARA 1966 / Portugal. Presidencia do Conselho – Lisboa. 1966. BD-598 1 – 9 – ne IDC [338]

PLANO INTERCALAR DE FOMENTO PARA 1965-1967 PROGRAMA DE EXECUCAO PARA 1967 / Portugal. Presidencia do Conselho – Lisboa. 1967 – 9 – ne IDC [338]

PLANO QUINQUENNALE PER LO SVILUPPO ECONOMICO E SOCIALE DELLA SICILIA / Sicily – Palermo. 1956 – 9 – ne IDC [338]

PLANO TRIENAL DE DESENVOLVIMENTO ECONOMICO E SOCIAL, 1963-1965 / Brazil. Presidencia de Republica – (Sintese). Rio de Janeiro. 1962. BD-617 1 – 9 – ne IDC [338]

Plano y Garcia, Pedro *see* AMPLIACIONES...HISTORIA DE MERIDA DE MORENO...FERNANDEZ

PLANO-GUIA / Caceres. Junta Provincial del Turismo. Caceres – Madrid: Rivadeneyra, s.a. – 1 – sp Bibl Santa Ana [338]

PLANO-GUIA DE LOS MONUMENTOS DE MERIDA – Merida: Imp. Rodriguez, 1975 – 1 – sp Bibl Santa Ana [910]

PLANO-GUIA-CALLEJERO DE CACERES / Garcia Figueroa, Fernando – Caceres: Imp. Rodriguez, 1968 – 1 – sp Bibl Santa Ana [946]

PLANOVOE KHOZIAISTVO – Moscow. (Planned Economy). 1923-1953 – 3 – us Readex [330]

PLANOVOE KHOZIAISTVO – Moscow. Subtitle varies. 1924, nos. 7-10; 1925, nos. 1-7, 9, 10, 12; 1926-1940; 1941, nos. 1-7; 1944, nos. 1-3; 1945-1970 – 1 – 35.00r – us Hoover Inst Photo [072]

PLANOVOE KHOZIAISTVO / Russia. (1923- U.S.S.R.). Gosudarstvennaia Planovaia Komissiia.State Planning Commission – (Planned economy). 1923-53 – 3 – us Readex [947]

PLANOVOIE KHOZIAISTVO – Moscow. no. 1-3. Jan-Mar 1928 – 1 – us NY Public [335]

PLANOVOYE KHOZYAIUNIONSTVO / U.S.S.R. – (Planned Economy). Moscow. U.S.S.R. 1961- – 1 – us UMI [330]

PLANS – Revue mensuelle. Organe de doctrine et d'action., V. devenu: Bulletin des groupes Plans. Paris. 1931-avr 1933 – 1 – fr A.C.R.P.P. [073]

PLANS, COUPES, ELEVATIONS DES PLUS BELLES MAISONS ET DES HOTELS CONSTRUITS A PARIS ET DANS LES ENVIRONS / Krafft, Johann Karl – Reproduction en facsimile par J. Mayor et L. Derobert; Preface de Paul Marmottan. Paris: Librairie d'Art decoratif et industriel, G. Hue, 1909. 120 plates (inc. plans). 1 reel. 1183 – 1 – us U.W. Library [720]

PLANS D'ASSURANCES DE VILLES DU QUEBEC / Bibliotheque Nationale. Quebec – (A collection of 464 maps) – Montreal: La Bibliotheque, 1977. SEM35P151 – 1r – 1 – Can$51.00 – cn Bibl Nat [910]

PLANS DE DEVELOPPEMENT ECONOMIQUE DE LA SOMALIE, 1954-1960 / Somalia. Italian Administration – Roma. 1954 – 9 – ne IDC [338]

PLANS DES DIFFERENTS LACS ET RIVIERES ENTRE LE LAC HURON ET LA RIVIERE DES OUTAOUAIS, POUR ACCOMPAGNER LES RAPPORTS GEOLOGIQUES DU CANADA POUR LES ANNEES 1853, 54, 55, 56 / Canada. Exploration Geologique – Toronto: Imp. John Lovell, 1857. SEM35P192 – 1r – 1 – Can$15.00 – cn Bibl Nat [550]

PLANS D'INSTRUCTIONS SUR LES SACREMENTS D'APRES LE CATECHISME DU CONCILE DE TRENTE / Hallez, D-G – 2e rev et corr ed. Paris: H Casterman, 1863 – 3mf – 9 – 0-8370-7149-6 – 1986-1149 – us A.T.L.A. [240]

PLANS, ELEVATIONS, SECTIONS, AND PERSPECTIVE VIEWS OF THE GARDENS AND BUILDINGS AT KEW IN SURREY / Chambers, W – O-200 1. 1763 – 9 – ne IDC [700]

PLANS OF HOLKHAM / Holkham Hall. Norfolk. England – 18th cent. By Matthew Brettingham, the younger – 1 – uk Microform Academic [720]

PLANS OF PARIS FROM THE ARCHIVES NATIONALES / Archives Nationales, Paris – (Over 200 maps. With printed index) – 1988 – 60 colour mf – 15 – $1,310.00 – 0-907716-54-7 – uk Mindata [910]

PLANS OF VARIOUS LAKES AND RIVERS BETWEEN LAKE HURON AND THE RIVER OTTAWA, TO ACCOMPANY THE GEOLOGICAL REPORTS FOR 1853, 54, 55, 56 / Canada. Exploration Geologique – Toronto: Printed by John Lovell, 1857. SEM35P193 – 1r – 1 – Can$15.00 – cn Bibl Nat [550]

PLANS OFFICIELS DE LA PAROISSE DE MONTREAL / Sicotte, Louis W – Montreal: Departement des Travaux Publics. 1v. 1878. SEM35P119 – 1r – 1 – Can$15.00 – cn Bibl Nat [910]

PLANS OFFICIELS DES COMTES DE HOCHELAGA AND JACQUES CARTIER, L.-W. SICOTTE / Canada – Montreal, Canada. 1878 – 1r – 1 – Can$25.00 – cn Can Microfilming [910]

PLANS OFFICIELS DES COMTES D'HOCHELAGA ET DE JACQUES-CARTIER / Sicotte, Louis W – Canada: Ministere de l'Agriculture. 1v. 1876. SEM35P88 – 1r – 1 – Can$15.00 – cn Bibl Nat [910]

PLANT – (v47 1988/89 Can$60.00y. Cont: Plant Management and Engineering at v47 no 8 1988/89) – Willowdale. v47-53. 1988/89-1994 – 1 – Can$85.00y – cn Micromedia [621]

PLANT *see* PLANT MANAGEMENT AND ENGINEERING

PLANT AND CELL PHYSIOLOGY – v1-18. 1959-77 – 1,5,6 – us Princeton Micro [580]

PLANT BREEDING ABSTRACT – (Includes Index 1930-35) – Cambridge. 1930-41. v1-11. – 67mf – 9 – ne IDC [580]

PLANT BREEDING AND THE NUTRITIVE VALUE OF CROP RESIDUES : PROCEEDINGS OF A WORKSHOP HELD AT ILCA, ADDIS ABABA, ETHIOPIA, 7-10 DECEMBER 1987 / ed by Reed, J D et al – 1988 – 9 – $24.00 – 92-9053-142-8 – et ILRI [631]

PLANT CELL REPORTS – v.1, 1981. ISSN:0721-085X – 1,5,6,9,13 – $100.00v – us UMI [580]

PLANT COLLECTING AND HERBARIUM DEVELOPMENT : A MANUAL – 1981 – 148p – it F.A.O. [630]

PLANT DISEASE REPORTER / U.S. Department of Agriculture – v. 1-60. w supplements. nos. 1-261. 1917-1976 – 1,5,6 – us Princeton Micro [630]

PLANT DISEASE REPORTER BULLETIN / U.S. Department of Agriculture – Nos.1-261. 1919-59 – 1,5,6 – us Princeton Micro [580]

PLANT ENGINEERING – v1- 1947- 1; v19- 5,6; v29- 9 – us UMI [621]

PLANT MANAGEMENT AND ENGINEERING – v1- 1941- 1; v35- 5,6,9 – us UMI [650]

PLANT MANAGEMENT AND ENGINEERING – (v1-29 1941-69 Can$990.00 1. v30-45 1970-86 Can$550.00 1. Cont by: Plant at v47 no 8 1988/89) – Willowdale. v1-46. 1941-1987/88 – 1,9 – Can$28.00y – cn Micromedia [620]

PLANT MANAGEMENT AND ENGINEERING *see* PLANT

PLANT OPERATING MANAGEMENT *see* FACTORY

PLANT PATHOLOGY PAMPHLET / South Dakota. State University. Agricultural Experiment Station – nos.1-12. 1942-62 – 1,5,6 – us Spaulding [580]

PLANT PHYSIOLOGY – v1-73. 1926-83 – 1,5,6 – us Princeton Micro [631]

PLANT PROTECTION BULLETIN *see* FAO PLANT PROTECTION BULLETIN

PLANT PROTECTION LEGISLATION – 1984 – 171p – it F.A.O. [340]

PLANT SCIENCE CATALOG : BOTANY SUBJECT INDEX / U.S. Department of Agriculture. Library. Washington, D.C. – (Available on microfilm by request) – 1958. 315,000 cards – 9 – $1,485.00 export $1,795.00 – uk Hall [580]

PLANT SCIENCE LETTERS – v1-37. 1973-84 – 1,5,6,13 – sz Elsevier [580]

PLANT SCIENCE LITERATURE: SELECTED REFERENCES / U.S. Department of Agriculture – v. 1-15. 1935-1942 – 1,5,6 – us Princeton Micro [630]

PLANT TAXONOMIC LITERATURE : MICROFICHE COLLECTION / ed by Mears, James – (Available by phytogeographic region: America, Latin America, North America, Indian sub-continent, Continental Asia, Australasia, Africa, Europe and the Near East. Includes guide £105.00) – 2nd ed – 13,047mf – 9 – £33,795.00 – uk Chadwyck [580]

PLANT WORLD : A MONTHLY JOURNAL OF POPULAR BOTANY – Baltimore. v1-22. 1897-1919 – 110mf – 9 – 7420/1 – ne IDC [580]

PLANTA : ARCHIV FUER WISSENSCHAFTLICHE BOTANIK – Berlin. v1-31. 1926-41 – 445mf – 9 – 259c/2 – ne IDC [580]

PLANTA – v. 1-150. 1926-80 – 1,5,9 – 32,063.00 – us UMI [580]

PLANTA: ARCHIV FUER WISSENSCHAFTLICHE BOTANIK – v1-46. 1925-55 – 1,5,6 – us Princeton Micro [580]

Planta, Joseph *see* AN ACCOUNT OF THE ROMANSH LANGUAGE

PLANTAE ARABIAE IN DITIONIBUS HEDSCHAS / Kotschy, T – (Sitzungsber. Kais. Akad. Wissensch. Mathem.-Naturw. Klassw, v. 52, 1866). Wien. 1866. B-1045 2 – 8 – ne IDC [580]

PLANTAE ASIATICAE RARIORES / Wallich, N – 3v. London. 1829, 1830-32. B-514 2 – 8 – ne IDC [580]

PLANTAE CANTABRIGIENSES / Martyn, T – London, 1763. 114 pp. B-6057 1 – 9 – ne IDC [580]

PLANTAE CRYPTOGAMICAE, QUAS IN PLAGA ORBIS NOVI AEQUINOCTIALI COLLEGERUNT A. DE HUMBOLDT ET A. BONPLAND / Hooker, W J – Londini. 1816. B-5960 2 – 8 – ne IDC [580]

PLANTAE DAVIDIANAE / Franchet, A R – 2v. Paris. 1884-88. B-882 2 – 8 – ne IDC [580]

PLANTAE E FAMILIA ASPERIFOLIARUM NUCIFERAE / Lehmann, J G C – 2pts. Berolini. 1818. B-8315 1 – 9 – ne IDC [580]

PLANTAE ET PAPILIONES RARIORES DEPICTAE ET AERI INCISAE / Ehret, G D – 5918 2. 1748-1759 – 8 – ne IDC [580]

PLANTAE EUROPEAE / Richter, K – 5678. V. 1-2. FASC. 3. 1890-1897 – 9 – ne IDC [580]

PLANTAE INDIAE BATAVAE ORIENTALIS... / Vriese, W H de – Lugduni-Batavoru, 1856[-1857] – 6mf – 9 – 5795/2 – ne IDC [580]

PLANTAE INDICAE / Zenker, J C – 2v. Jena. 1835-37. B-360 2 – 8 – ne IDC [580]

PLANTAE JAVANICAE RARIORES.. / Bennett, J J & Brown, Robert – London. 1838-52. viii. 258p. 50 pls. B-5845/2 – 8 – ne IDC [580]

PLANTAE JAVANICAE RARIORES... / Hasskarl, J K – Berolini, 1848 – 9mf – 9 – ne IDC [580]

PLANTAE JUNGHUHNIANAE / Miquel, F A W – Lugduni Batavorum, 1851 -1857. 570 pp. Second title, for pages 523-570 reads: R. B. van den Bosch, Hymenophyllaceae. B-636 2 – 8 – ne IDC [580]

PLANTAE LORENZIANAE / Grisebach, A – 1874 – 7 – uk Microform Academic [580]

PLANTAE MELITAE LECTAE / Grech Delicata, G C – Holmiae. 1849. B-5132 2 – 8 – ne IDC [580]

PLANTAE NOVAE HISPANIAE... : JARDIN BOTANICO, 4-11 BIS / Sesse y Lacasta, Martin de & Mocino, Jose Mariano – 6mf – 9 – sp Cultura [580]

PLANTAE NOVAE TURCICAE EX BALCANO / Frivaldszky von Frivald, I – (Magyar Tudos Tarsasag Evkoenyvei). v. 2. 1835; v. 3. 1837; v. 4. 1840. B-5528 2 – 8 – ne IDC [580]

PLANTAE NOVAE VEL MINUS NOTAE OPUSCULIS DIVERSIS / Parlatore, F – Parisiis. 1842. B-8319 1 – 9 – ne IDC [580]

PLANTAE PREISSIANAE SIVE ENUMERATIO PLANTARUM QUAS IN AUSTRALASIA OCC. ET ANNIS 1838-1841 COLLEGIT / Lehmann, J G C – 2v. Hamburgi. 1844, 1845-1847-48. B-6011 2 – 8 – ne IDC [580]

PLANTAE RARIORES AFRICANAE / Linnaeus, Carl – Holmiae. 1760. B-5505 2 – 8 – ne IDC [580]

PLANTAE RARIORES HORTI ACADEMICI MONACENSIS / Schrank, F von & Paula, A von – Monachii. 1817-19-22. B-771 2 – 8 – ne IDC [580]

PLANTAE RARIORES, QUAS IN ITINERE PER ORAS JONII AC ADRIATICI / Gussone, G – Neapoli. 1826. B-5046 2 – 8 – ne IDC [580]

PLANTAE RARIORES, QUAS MAXIMAM PARTEM IPSE IN HORTO DOMESTICO COLUIT / Trew, C J – Norimbergae. 1763-84. B-5778 1 – 9 – ne IDC [580]

PLANTAE RARIORES VIVIS COLORIBUS DEPICTAE / Meerburgh, N – Lugduni Batavorum, 1789. B-6062 prSF 16,00 IDC 9 – ne IDC [580]

PLANTAE SELECTAE. PINXIT G. D. EHRET / Trew, C J – Norimbergae. 1750-73. B-488 2 – 8 – ne IDC [580]

PLANTAE VERTICILLATAE UNILABIATAE / Schreber, J C D von – Lipsiae. 1774. B-5728 2 – 8 – ne IDC [580]

PLANTAE WRIGHTIANAE REVISITED *see* CHARLES WRIGHT ON THE BOUNDARY, 1849-1852

PLANTAE WRIGHTIANAE TEXANO-NEO-MEXICANAE / Gray, A – 7547 1. 2 v. 1852-1853 – 9 – ne IDC [580]

PLANTARUM AEGYPTIARUM DECADES 4 / Viviani, D – Genuae, 1830 – 8 – B-717 2 – ne IDC [580]

PLANTARUM AMERICANARUM / Plumier, C – Lugduni Batavorum. 1755-60. B-1002 2 – 8 – ne IDC [580]

PLANTARUM BRASILIAE ICONES ET DESCRIPTIONES / Pohl, J B E – 2v. Viennae. 1826-1827-1831-33. B-933 2 – 8 – ne IDC [580]

PLANTARUM BRASILIENSIUM / Thunberg, C P – Decas 1-3. Upsaliae. 1817-21. B-5260 2 – 8 – ne IDC [580]

PLANTARUM CRYPTOGAMICARUM BRITANNIAE / Dickson, J – London. 1785-1801. B-1257 2 – 8 – ne IDC [580]

PLANTARUM GUIANAE RARIORUM ICONES ET DESCRIPTIONES HACTENUS INEDITAE / Rudge, E – Londini. 1805-06. B-5698 2 – 8 – ne IDC [580]

PLANTARUM HISTORIA SUCCULENTARUM PARIS / Candolle, A P de – (Ill. P. J. Redoute). 1799-1805. Lacking: Pt. 29-32, pls. 160-182. B-5055 2 – 8 – ne IDC [580]

PLANTARUM HORTI ACADEMICI ERLANGENSIS / Martius, Karl Friedrich Philipp von – Erlangae, 1814. 209 pp. B-887 2 – 8 – ne IDC [580]

PLANTARUM ICONES HACTENUS INEDITAE, PLERUMQUE AD PLANTAS IN HERBARIO LINNEANO CONSERVATAS DELINEATAE / Smith, J E – Londini, 1789-1791. 75 pls., with descriptive letterpress. B-5485 2 – 8 – ne. IDC [580]

PLANTARUM IMAGINES ET DESCRIPTIONES FLORAM RUSSICAM ILLUSTRATES / Trautvetter, E R – Monachii. 1844-46-1847. B-5774 2 – 8 – ne IDC [580]

PLANTARUM MINUS COGNITARUM PUGILLUS PRIMUS ET SECUNDUS / Sprengel, K P J – Halae, 1813 -1815. 2 pts. B-701 2 – 8 – ne IDC [580]

PLANTARUM NOVARUM VEL MINUS COGNIATRUM IN HORTO BOTANICO HERBARIOQUE REGIO MONACENSI / Zuccarini, J G – Monachi. 1837-40. B-416 2 – 8 – ne IDC [580]

PLANTARUM NOVARUM VEL MINUS COGNITARUM QUAS IN ITINERE CASPIO-CAUCASICO / Eichwald, C E von – Fasc. 1-2. Lipsiae. 1831-33. B-408 2 – 8 – ne IDC [580]

PLANTARUM RARIORUM HORTI CAESAREI SCHOENBRUNNENSIS / Jacquin, N J von – 4v. Vienna. 1797-1804. B-129 2 – 8 – ne IDC [580]

PLANTARUM RARIORUM REGNI NEAPOLITANI / Cyrillus, D – Neapoli. 1788-92 – 8 – ne IDC [580]

PLANTARUM RARIORUM SICILIAE MINUS COGNITARUM / Tineo, V – Palermo. 1846. B-326a 2 – 8 – ne IDC [580]

PLANTARUM RARIORUM SICILIAE PUGILLUS PRIMUS / Tineo, V – Panormi. 1817. B-720 2 – 8 – ne IDC [580]

PLANTARUM SELECTARUM ICONES PICTAE / Meerburgh, N – Lugduni Batavorum, 1798. 12 pp., 28 pls. B-6063 1 – 9 – ne IDC [580]

PLANTARUM SEU STIRPIUM ICONES / Lobelius, M – Antverpiae. 1581. B-7676 2 – 8 – ne IDC [580]

PLANTARUM SPECIES, QUAS IN INTENERE PER AEGYPTYM, ARABIAM ET SYRIAM / Schenk, J A von – Monachi. 1840. B-414 2 – 8 – ne IDC [580]

PLANTARUM UMBELLIFERARUM / Sprengel, K P J – Halae. 1813. B-5166 2 – 8 – ne IDC [580]

PLANTARUM VASCULARIUM GENERA SECUNDUM ORDINES NATURALES / Meisner, C F – Lipsiae, 1836-1843. 2 vols. B-5015 2 – 8 – ne IDC [580]

PLANTAS HARTWEGIANAS IMPRIMIS MEXICANAS / Bentham, G – Londini. 1839-57. B-5847 2 – 8 – ne IDC [580]

LAS PLANTAS MEDICINALES DE MEXICO / Martinez, M – Mexico, D.F., 1933 – 8mf – 9 – ne IDC [615]

PLANTATION ACCOUNT BOOKS / Aimar, C P – 1876-1904. Record of debits and credits of plantation on Toogoodoo River, Charleston County. 7 fiches – 9 – us South Carolina Historical [978]

PLANTATION BOOK / Bluff. (Plantation) – 1755-59, 1770-74. 2 fiches – 9 – us South Carolina Historical [978]
PLANTATION DIARY – 1840-80.Owner of Windsor and Kensington Plantations, Berkeley County, SC. 1 fiche – 9 – us South Carolina Historical [978]
PLANTATION JOURNAL / Chaplin, Thomas B – 1845-86. Tombee Plantation, St. Helona Island, Beaufort County. Daily entries record weather, planting, family affairs, local events, and rental and treatment of slaves. 12 fiches – 9 – us South Carolina Historical [978]
PLANTATION JOURNAL / Middleton, Henry Augustus – 1841-61.Georgetown County (SC) planter. 2 fiches – 9 – us South Carolina Historical [978]
PLANTATION JOURNAL / Peyre, Thomas Walter – 1834-50. 8 fiches – 9 – us South Carolina Historical [978]
PLANTATION RECORDS / Coffin, Thomas Aston – 1800-1813. 2 fiches – 9 – us South Carolina Historical [978]
PLANTATION RECORDS / Weston, Plowden Charles Jennett – 1802-19 (1827). Lowcountry planter and merchant. 5 fiches – 9 – us South Carolina Historical [978]
PLANTATION REGISTERS / Liverpool – 1744-1773 and 1779-1784. BRRAM – 1 – uk Microform Academic [630]
PLANTATION SERMONS.. / Dickson, Andrew F – 1856; Lessons about Salvation. 1860 – 1 – $50.00 – us Presbyterian [240]
PLANTATION SERMONS, OR, PLAIN AND FAMILIAR DISCOURSES FOR THE INSTRUCTION OF THE UNLEARNED / Dickson, Andrew F – Philadelphia: Presbyterian Board of Publication, c1856 – 1mf – us A.T.L.A. [240]
Plante, Therese *see* BIBLIOGRAPHIE ANALYTIQUE DU MAJOR LOUIS-ALEXANDRE PLANTE
DE PLANTEN, DOOR DEN HEER NORONHA,...OPGESPOORD,... / Hasskarl, J K – Amsterdam, 1844 – 1mf – 9 – ne IDC [580]
Planters and Mechanics Bank. Charleston, South Carolina *see* LETTERBOOK
THE PLANTERS OF THE COMMONWEALTH: A STUDY OF THE EMIGRANTS AND EMIGRATION IN COLONIAL TIMES, 1620-1640 / Banks, Charles Edward – Item K. Ships' names, passengers to Boston & the Bay Colony, their English homes and their places of settlement in Mass. 231p, indexed. SW16-0076 – 5 – us A.G.L.L. [920]
THE PLANTERS OF THE COMMONWEALTH; A STUDY OF THE EMIGRANTS AND EMIGRATION...LISTS OF PASSENGERS TO BOSTON...SHIPS...ENGLISH HOMES...PLACES OF SETTLEMENT IN MASSACHUSETTS – 1620-1640. By Charles Edward Banks, 1967. Orig. publ., 1930. Indexed, 5 fiches. F-0869 – 9 – us A.G.L.L. [978]
PLANTES CELLULAIRES / Montagne, J P F C – Paris, 1838-1842. 549 pp., 21 pls. Botanie. 10ea6me Partie de Sagra: R. de la Histoire physique, politique et naturelle de l'ile de Cuba. B-5707-J 2 – 8 – ne IDC [580]
PLANTES DE LA FRANCE / Jaume Saint-Hilaire, J H – Paris. 1805-24. B-815 2 – 8 – ne IDC [580]
LES PLANTES MEDICINALES DE LA GUINEE / Pobeguin, C H O – Paris, 1912 – 1mf – 9 – ne IDC [615]
PLANTES MEDICINALES DU CHILI / Murillo, A – Paris, 1889 – 3mf – 9 – ne IDC [615]
LES PLANTES MEDICINALES ET TOXIQUES DE LA GUYANE FRANCAISE / Heckel, E M – Macon, 1897 – 1mf – 9 – ne IDC [615]
LAS PLANTES MEDICINALES ET USUELLES... / Rodin, H – Paris, 1872 – 5mf – 9 – ne IDC [615]
PLANTES NOUVELLEMENT DECOUVERTES, RECEMMENT DENOMMEES ET CLASSEES, REPRESENTEES EN GRAVURES AVEC LEURS DESCRIPTIONS; POUR SERVIR D'INTELLIGENCE A L'HISTOIRE GENERALE ET ECONOMIQUE DES TROIS REGNES / Buchoz, P J – Paris. 1779. B-42 2 – 8 – ne IDC [580]
PLANTES NOUVELLES D'AMEA1RIQUE / Moricand, M E – Genea6ve, 1833-1846 -1847. 176 pp. 100 pls. B-6082 2 – 8 – ne IDC [580]
PLANTES RARES DU JARDIN DE GENEVE / Candolle, A P de – Geneve. 1825-27. B-5876 2 – 8 – ne IDC [580]
PLANTES RECUILLIES PENDANT LE VOYAGE DES RUSSES AUTOUR DU MONDE / Langsdorff & Fischer – 1810 – 1 – uk Microform Academic [910]
PLANTES USUELLES DES BRASILIENS / Saint-Hilaire, A F C P de – Paris. 1824-28. B-5708 2 – 8 – ne IDC [580]
PLANTES VASCULAIRES / Richard, Achille – Paris. 1839. 1845. Botanie. (89eme Partie de: Sagra, R. de la. Histoire physique, politique et nat. de l'ile de Cuba). B-5707-I 2 – 8 – ne IDC [580]
Plantier, Claude Henri Augustin *see* UEBER DIE ALLGEMEINEN KIRCHENVERSAMMLUNGEN
PLANTING AND PROGRESS OF THE BAPTISTS' CAUSE IN TENNESSEE / Inman, W G – 1422p – 1 – 49.77 – us Baptist [240]
PLANTKUNDE VOOR HET VOORTGEZET ONDERWIJS IN INDONESIE / Uit de Bos, T – Ed 8. Groningen, Batavia, 1948 – 4mf – 9 – SEM-10,217 – 10,220/1 – ne IDC [950]
PLANT/OPERATIONS PROGRESS – v1-. 1982- – 1,5,6,9 – us UMI [073]
PLANTS AND PLANT PRODUCTS OF ECONOMIC IMPORTANCE – 1974 – it F.A.O. [338]
THE PLANTS INDIGENOUS AROUND SHARKS BAY AND ITS VICINITY / Mueller, Ferdinand Jakob Heinrich von – Perth, 1883. 24 pp. B-6467 1 – 9 – ne IDC [580]
THE PLANTS OF NEW SOUTH WALES / Dixon, W A – Sydney. 1906. B-5122 2 – 8 – ne IDC [580]
PLANTS OF THE COAST OF COROMANDEL / Roxburgh, W – 3v. London. 1795-1820. B-5228 2 – 8 – ne IDC [580]
Plantz, Samuel *see* THE CHURCH AND THE SOCIAL PROBLEM
PLANUNG ALS DURCHSETZUNGSSTRATEGIE : ZUR INTERESSENSELEKTIVITAET PLANENDER VERWALTUNG. KOORDINATION, KONFLIKT UND KONSENSBILDUNG AM BEISPIEL EINES FACHPLANUNGSPROJEKTES / Bohnert, Werner – Frankfurt a.M., 1976 – 3mf – 9 – DM76.00 – 3-89349-717-X – gw Hänsel [650]
PLANZEN-ATLAS NACH DEM LINNE'SCHEN SYSTEM... / Hoffmann, C – Stuttgart, 1881 – 2mf – ne IDC [580]
Plasencia. Asociacion Cultural Placentina Pedro de Trejo *see* FERIAS Y FIESTAS EN 1974
Plasencia. Aula Medica *see* ESTATUTOS
Plasencia. Ayuntamiento *see*
– FERIA Y FIESTAS EN LA CIUDAD DE ALFONSO 8, 1965
– FERIA Y FIESTAS. JUNIO, 1965
– FERIAS Y FIESTAS DE PLASENCIA. JUNIO, 1959
– FERIAS Y FIESTAS DURANTE...8, 9 Y 10 DE JUNIO, 1960
– FERIAS Y FIESTAS EN PLASENCIA, 1958
– FIESTA DE LA HISPANIDAD. 1972
– PLASENCIA. CIUDAD TURISMO. GUIA OFICIAL
PLASENCIA. CIUDAD TURISMO. GUIA OFICIAL / Plasencia. Ayuntamiento – Plasencia: Imp. La Victoria, 1961 – 1 – sp Bibl Santa Ana [338]
Plasencia. Diocesis *see*
– MEMORIA DEL EJERCICIO MISIONAL 1974
– MEMORIA DEL EJERCICIO MISIONAL 1976
– ORDO DIVINI OFFICCI RECITANDI
PLASENCIA DURANTE LA INVASION NAPOLEONICA. CATALOGO DE DOCUMENTOS QUE SE CONSERVAN EN EL ARCHIVO HISTORICO DE CACERES / Martinez Quesada, Juan – Madrid, 1965. Sep. Rev. Archivos. Bibliotecas y Museos. pp. 77-110 – 1 – sp Bibl Santa Ana [350]
PLASENCIA EN FERIAS 1977 / Centro de Iniciativas Turisticas – Plasencia: Imp. Sanchez Rodrigo S.A., 1977 – 1 – sp Bibl Santa Ana [060]
PLASENCIA EN LA...EJECUCION / Sanchez Garrido, Eduardo – 1867 – 9 – 1.50f – sp Bibl Santa Ana [946]
PLASENCIA. FERIAS Y FIESTAS – 1945, 1946 – 1 – sp Bibl Santa Ana [946]
Plasencia. Guia *see* GUIA TURISTICA DE PLASENCIA
Plasencia, Juan de *see*
– CARTAS Y MEMORIAL AL REY. MANILA, 23 JUNIO 1584
– EL COLEGIO DE LA CONSTANCIA. ROBO DE CUATRO RUILLONES
PLASENCIA. NAVIDAD-76 / Centro de Iniciativas Turisticas – Plasencia: Imp. Sanchez Rodrigo, S.A. 1976 – 1 – sp Bibl Santa Ana [338]
PLASENCIA PLAZA DE TOROS 1960 / Plaza de Toros – Plasencia: Imp. Victoria, 1960 – 1 – sp Bibl Santa Ana [946]
PLASENCIA POR JESUS SACRAMENTADO. TRADICION EUCARISTICA (19 OCTUBRE 1488) POR... / Polo Benito, Jose – Madrid: Imp. San Francisco de Sales, 1911 – sp Bibl Santa Ana [240]
Plasencia. Secretariado Catequistico *see* CANTEMUS DOMINO
Plasencia. Seminario *see* MI SEMINARIO
Plasencia. Seminario Diocesano *see* DIA DEL SEMINARIO
Plasencia. (Spain). Ayuntamiento *see*
– ORDENANZAS MUNICIPALES
– REGLAMENTO...SECRETARIA...PLASENCIA
Plasencia. (Spain). Circulo de las Artes *see* REGLAMENTO
Plasencia. (Spain). Diocesis *see* SYNODO... OBISPADO DE PLASENCIA
PLASMA AND ERYTHROCYTE LACTATE CONCENTRATIONS IN HUMANS AFTER SUBMAXIMAL EXERCISE / Kime, J – 1990 – 1mf – 9 – $4.00 – us Microform Publ [612]
PLASMA CHEMISTRY AND PLASMA PROCESSING – v1-14. 1981-94 – 1,5 – $65.00v – us UMI [540]
PLASMA DEVICES AND OPERATIONS / ed by Glukhikh, V A – 9,5,1 – us Gordon [660]
PLASMA FREE FATTY ACIDS AT REST AND EXHAUSTION FOLLOWING THEOBROMINE INGESTION / Durham, Timothy L & Miller, Wayne C – 1992 – 1mf – 9 – $4.00 – us Microform Publ [613]
PLASMA PHYSICS – v1- 1959- – 5,6,9 – us UMI [530]
PLASMA PHYSICS AND CONTROLLED FUSION / ed by Stott, Peter – UK: 10P Publishing, 1993.-v35 – 1,5,6,9 – £573.00 – uk I.O.P. [621]
PLASMA PHYSICS REPORTS – 1,5,6,9 – us A.I.P. [530]
PLASMA SOURCES SCIENCE AND TECHNOLOGY – 1992. v1 – 1,5,6,9 – £134.00 – uk I.O.P. [530]
PLASTE UND KAUTSCHUK – v2-23 1955-76 – 1,5,6 – us Princeton Micro [660]
PLASTIC AND RECONSTRUCTIVE SURGERY – v1-98. 1946-96 – 1,5,6,9 – $120.00r – us Williams [617]
PLASTIC GREENHOUSES FOR WARM CLIMATES – 1982 – 52p – it F.A.O. [631]
PLASTIC MAN – Issue Nos. 1-5 1943-Autumn 1946 – 5mf – 15 – $31.95 – us Comics [760]
PLASTIC MAN – Issue Nos. 6-10 Winter 47-Winter 48 – 5mf – 15 – $31.95 – us Comics [760]
PLASTICS – Chicago.v1-9. 1944-49 – 1,5,6 – us Princeton Micro [073]
PLASTICS AND RUBBER PROCESSING AND APPLICATIONS – v1-4. 1981-84 – 1,5,6,13 – sz Elsevier [073]
PLASTICS BUSINESS – (Mf available to v10 only) – Don Mills. v110. 1980-89 – 1 – Can$60.00y – cn Micromedia [660]
PLASTICS COMPOUNDS – v. 1- 1978- – 1,5,6,9 – us UMI [660]
PLASTICS DESIGN FORUM – v.1- 1976- – 1,5,6,9 – us UMI [660]
PLASTICS ENGINEERING – (See also: SPE Journal) – v29- 1973- 1,5,6; v33- 9 – us UMI [660]
PLASTICS INDUSTRY NEWS – 1977- – 1,5,6,9 – us UMI [660]
Plastics Institute. London *see*
– TRANSACTIONS AND JOURNAL
– TRANSACTIONS AND JOURNALS
PLASTICS MACHINERY AND EQUIPMENT – v. 1- 1972- – 1,5,6,9 – us UMI [660]
PLASTICS TECHNICAL EVALUATION CENTER (PLASTEC) – (Updated Every 60 Days) – Information Handling Services – 5 – us Info Handling [660]
PLASTICS TECHNOLOGY – v1- 1955- 1; v14- 5,6; v21- 9 – us UMI [660]
PLASTICS WORLD – (1984-. 5,6,9) – v1-. 1943- – 1 – us UMI [660]
PLASTIZITAET UND ANELASTIZITAET NANOKRISTALLINER MATERIALIEN / Laun, Uwe – 1995 – 1mf – 9 – DM60.00 – 3-8267-2248-5 – gw Hänsel [530]
PLAT MAPS / Huron County. Ohio. Recorder – 1890-1952 – 1r – 1 – $32.50r – us Archival [324]
PLATAFORMA PARA EL DESARROLLO ECONOMICO Y SOCIAL DE LA REPUBLICA DOMINICANA (1968-1985) / Dominican Republic. Oficina Nacional de Planificacion – Santo Domingo. 1968. BD-587 1 – 9 – ne IDC [338]
PLATE MAKERS' CRITERION, 1907-1909 : AMERICAN PHOTO-ENGRAVER, 1908-1955 / International Photoengravers Union of North America – (Coll title: Labor Union Periodicals, Pt 2) – 28r – 1 – $3,780.00 – 1-55655-310-2 – us UPA [680]
PLATE PRINTER, 1902-1932 / International Plate Printers', Die Stampers' and Engravers' Union of North America – (Coll title: Labor Union Periodicals, Pt 2) – 4r – 1 – $540.00 – 1-55655-311-0 – us UPA [680]
Plate, WE *see* A GRAMMAR OF THE VULGATE
A PLATEA – Manaos, Amazonas. 9 Abr-1 Jun 1907 – 1,5,6 – bl Biblioteca [072]
A PLATEA : ORGAO CRITICO E HUMORISTICO – Manaos, Amazonas. 23 Out 1898; 15 Nov 1899 – 1,5,6 – bl Biblioteca [072]
LE PLATEAU CENTRAL NIGERIEN / Desplagnes, Louis – Une mission archeologique et ethnographique au Soudan francais. Paris, Emile Larose. 1907 – 9 – 17.50 – fr Orientalistes [306]
PLATEAU TONGA OF NORTHERN RHODESIA: STUDIES / Colson, E – 7 – uk Microform Academic [910]
Platen, August, Graf von *see*
– AUGUST GRAF VON PLATENS WERKE
– MISCELLANEOUS SONNETS
– PLATENS WERKE
– SONNETS FROM VENICE
– SONNETS TO LITERARY PERSONAGES
– DIE TAGEBUECHER DES GRAFEN AUGUST VON PLATEN
PLATEN POLITISCHES DENKEN UND DICHTEN / Renck, Heinrich – (Includes bibliographical references) – Breslau: F Hirt, 1910 – 1 – us U.W. Library [943]
PLATENS LITTERATUR-KOMOEDIEN : EINE LITTERAR-HISTORISCHE UNTERSUCHUNG / Greulich, Oskar – (Includes bibliographical references (p. 129-131)) – Bern: Schmid & Francke, 1901 – 1r – 1 – us U.W. Library [430]
PLATENS POLITISCHES DENKEN UND DICHTEN / Renck, Heinrich – (Includes bibliographical references) – Breslau: F Hirt, 1910 – 1 – us U.W. Library [430]
PLATENS WERKE = WORKS / Platen, August, Graf von; ed by Wolff, G A & Schweizer, V – (Includes bibliographical references and index) – Leipzig: Bibliographisches Institut, [1895?] – 1 – us U.W. Library [810]
Plater, Emily *see* THE LIFE OF COUNTESS EMILY PLATER
EL PLATERESCO EN LA LITERATURA EXTREMENA / Segura Covarsi, Enrique – Badajoz: Imp. Dip. Provincial, 1958 – sp Bibl Santa Ana [440]
PLATFORM – Kohima, India. 21 Dec 1976-1981 – 1r – 1 – us L of C Photodup [072]
PLATFORM ECHOES, OR, LIVING TRUTHS FOR HEAD AND HEART:...DRAWN FROM THE HUMOR AND PATHOS OF LIFE / Gough, John B – Toronto: W. Briggs, 1885. 03487. (Pre-1900 Canadiana) – 9 – cn C.I.H.M. [360]
Plath, J H *see* GESCHICHTE DES OESTLICHEN ASIENS. V. 1 DIE MANDSCHUREY: V. 2 DIE VOELKER DER MANDSCHUREY
Plath, Karl Heinrich Christian *see*
– GOSSNERS MISSION UNTER HINDUS UND KOLHS UM NEUJAHR 1878
– THE SUBJECT OF MISSIONS CONSIDERED UNDER THREE NEW ASPECTS
– WAS MACHEN WIR CHRISTEN MIT UNSERN JUDEN!?
PLATICA MANUAL DE ARTILLERIA / Collado, L – Milan, 1592 – 5mf – 9 – sp Cultura [355]
Plato *see*
– SELECT DIALOGUES
– TALKS WITH SOCRATES ABOUT LIFE
PLATO AND PAUL / Mendenhall, James William – 1886 – 9 – us A.T.L.A. [240]
PLATO AND PLATONISM : A SERIES OF LECTURES / Pater, Walter – London, New York: Macmillan, 1893 – 1 roll – 1 – 1-55879-916-8 – uk Libr Preservation [180]
Platon, Metropolitan of Moscow *see* THE FAITH OF THE EASTERN CHURCH
Platonis *see* OPERA OMNIA...MARSILIO FICINO INTERPRETE
PLATONIS OPERA OMNIA... / Ficino, Marsilio – Marsilio Ficino interprete. Lugd., 1590 – 38mf – 8 – ne Slangenburg [180]

PLATONIS OPERA OMNIA... / Ficinus, Marsilius – Marsilio Ficino interprete. Francof., 1602 – 60mf – 8 – ne Slangenburg [180]
Platonov, S F *see* PETR VELIKII
PLATS OF POTTAWATOMIE RESERVE AND POTTAWATOMIE ROLL – 1863 – 1 – us KS Hist [910]
PLATT BOOK OF LA SALLE COUNTY / Ottawa Printing Co – Roster of county soldiers, sailors, nurses of World War I. Ottawa, 1921. (Illinois Reel 38). (The Cox Library Collection) – 5 – us Americana [978]
Platt, Isaac L *see* A COMPARATIVE VIEW OF THE GOSPELS
Platt, L *see* DICTIONNAIRE CRITIQUE ET RAISONNE DU LANGAGE VICIEUX
Platt, T *see* MATHEMATICAL MODELS IN BIOLOGICAL OCEANOGRAPHY
Platt, Ward *see* THE FRONTIER
Platt, William Henry *see* THE PHILOSOPHY OF THE SUPERNATURAL
PLATTDEUTSCHE VOLKSMAERCHEN : AUSGABE FUER ERWACHSENE / Wisser, Wilhelm – Jena: E Diederichs, 1919 – 1r – 1 – us U.W. Library [390]
PLATTDUETSCHE POST – Staten Island, NY. 1972-1979; 1981-1984 – 1 – gw Mikrofilm [071]
PLATTE CENTER SIGNAL – Platte Center, NE. -w. Oct-Dec 1895; Apr 1896-Aug 1898; Mar 1908-Jul 1923 – 1 – us NE Hist [071]
PLATTE COUNTY ARGUS – Columbus, NE. -w. Jul. 1892; Nov. 1895-May 1898; Nov. 1898;Jun. 1899-Dec. 1905 – 1 – us NE Hist [071]
PLATTE RIVER ZEITUNG – Fremont, NE. -w. 5 Nov 1892-11 Jan 1917. In German – 1 – us NE Hist [071]
PLATTE VALLEY DAILY STAR HERALD – Scottsbluff, NE. Jun 1916-Jun 1917 – 1 – us NE Hist [071]
PLATTE VALLEY DEMOCRAT – Columbus, NE. -w. Jul 1879-Feb 1880 – 1 – us NE Hist [071]
PLATTE VALLEY NEWS – Bridgeport, NE. -w. Oct. 1902-Aug. 1903 – 1 – us NE Hist [071]
Plattensteiner, Richard *see* "LIEBE IN VERKLAERUNG"
DIE PLATTFORM : INFORMATIONSDIENST DER FDP – Duesseldorf, 1949-51 – 1r – 1 – DM100.00 – gw Mikro Press [072]
DIE PLATTFORM : INFORMATIONSDIENST DER FDP VON NORDRHEIN-WESTFALEN – Duesseldorf, West Germany. 1949-1951 – 1r – 1 – gw Mikrofilm [072]
Plattner, Felix Alfredo *see* JESUITAS EN EL MAR...
PLATTSMOUTH COURANT – Plattsmouth, NE.-w. Apr 1880-6 Jul 1880; 21-28 Oct 1880 – 1 – us NE Hist [071]
PLATTSMOUTH DAILY HERALD – Plattsmouth, NE. Mar-Oct 1883; May-Oct 1884; Sept 1887-Jun 1889; Jun 1890; Feb 1891-Jul 1892 – 1 – us NE Hist [071]
PLATTSMOUTH DAILY JOURNAL – Plattsmouth, NE. Dec 1884-Jan 1885; Nov 1890-Jun 1894, scattered issues missing; Jul 1897-Jun 1898, scattered issues missing – 1 – us NE Hist [071]
PLATTSMOUTH DAILY TRIBUNE – Plattsmouth, NE. Oct 1895-Feb 1896; Apr-Sept 1896 – 1 – us NE Hist [071]
PLATTSMOUTH EVENING JOURNAL – Plattsmouth, NE. -d. Jun 1905-May 1942, scattered issues missing – 1 – us NE Hist [071]
PLATTSMOUTH JOURNAL – Plattsmouth, NE. -sw. Nov 1890-Oct 1902, scattered issues missing; Dec 1902-Sept 1904; Jan-Dec 1905, scattered issues missing; Feb 1906 to date – 1 – us NE Hist [071]
PLATTSMOUTH NEWS-HERALD – Plattsmouth, NE. -w. (-sw 1895-1910). Apr 1865-Jan 1868; Aug 1868-Mar 1882; Nov 1882-Dec 1896, scattered issues missing; Dec 1901-Oct 1904, scattered issues missing; Dec 1908-May 1911; Aug 1911-Nov 1912 – 1 – us NE Hist [071]
PLATTSMOUTH TRIBUNE – Plattsmouth, NE. -w. Jan 1899-Jun 1901, scattered issues missing; Aug 1901-Jan 1904 – 1 – us NE Hist [071]
Plautus *see* COMEDIAE 18
PLAVAIUSHCHIE PUTESHESTVUIUSHCHIE / Kuzmin, M – Roman. Petrograd. 1915. BR-1196 2 – 8 – ne IDC [460]
THE PLAY – London. -w. Oct 1881-Jan 1884. (1 reel) – 1 – uk British Libr Newspaper [790]
PLAY IN PHYSICAL EDUCATION AND SPORT / Israel. Ministry of Education and Culture – Proceedings of an international seminar. Dec 1975. 191 p – 9 – 3.00 – is I.T.T.I. [790]
PLAY MATERIALS FOR PRE-SCHOOL CHILDREN / National College of Education. Evanston, IL – 17p. Bibliography. 1935 – 1 – us U.W. Library [790]
THE PLAY OF MAN / Groos, Karl – Elizabeth L. Baldwin, trans. New York: D. Appleton and Company, 1901. ix,412p – 1 – us U.W. Library [820]
PLAY PARADE / Coward, Noel Pierce – London: Heineman. 1954. vol. IV. 554 p. includes: Tonight at 8:30; Present Laughter; This Happy Breed. 1 reel – 1 – us U.W. Library [790]
PLAY THERAPY IN CHILDHOOD / Rogerson, Cuthbert Harry – London: Oxford University Press, Humphrey Milford, 1939. 63p – 1 – us U.W. Library [150]
PLAYBACK – v1-4, no. 29 (all publ). Jan 1948-Mar Apr 1952. (Title varies). (Jazz Periodicals) – 1 reel – 1 – $85.00 – us UPA [073]
PLAYBACK STRATEGY – (Cont by: Strategy at v2 no 23 1991) – Toronto. v1. 1989/90 – 1 – Can$85.00y – cn Micromedia [650]
PLAYBACK STRATEGY *see* STRATEGY
PLAYBILL – (1979- 5,6,9) – 1884- – 1 – us UMI [410]
PLAYBILL – Subscription ed. v1-. 1982- – 1,5,6,9 – us UMI [410]
PLAYBILLS : NORTH AMERICAN NONPROFIT REPERTORY THEATRES, 1958-1975 – From the collection of the Theatre Communications Group, New York City – 394mf – 9 – $1,440.00 – us UPA [790]
PLAYBILLS AND PROGRAMMES FROM LONDON THEATRES, 1801-1900 / Theatre Museum. London – (100,000 playbills & programmes from 75 London Theatres. Arranged by theatre in chronological order. Theatres also listed individually) – 2997mf – 9 – £8,215.00 – uk Chadwyck [790]
PLAYBILLS FROM THE HARVARD THEATRE COLLECTION – British playbills from the mid-18th century to the 20th century – 1 – us Primary [790]
PLAYBOY – (black white) – v1- 1953- 1,5,6; v22- 9 – us UMI [073]
PLAYBOY – (color). v.1- 1953- – 1,4 – us UMI [073]
Playfair, R L *see* THE FISHES OF ZANZIBAR
Playfair, William *see* ELEMENS DE STATISTIQUE: OU L'ON DEMONTRE... LES RESSOURCES DE CHAQUE ROYAUME, ETAT ET REPUBLIQUE DE L'EUROPE.
Playford, J *see*
– AN INTRODUCTION TO THE SKILL OF MUSICK: IN THREE BOOKS
– AN INTRODUCTION TO THE SKILL OF MUSICK IN THREE BOOKS
PLAYGIRL – (1985-. 1,5,6) – v10-. 1982- – 9 – us UMI [073]
PLAYGROUND NEWS – Fort Walton Beach. Fl. -w. 1946- – 1 – us UMI [071]
THE PLAYGROUND OF EUROPE / Stephen, Leslie – London, New York: Longmans, Green and Co., 1904 – 1 roll – 1 – 1-55879-925-7 – uk Libr Preservation [190]
PLAYHOUSE IMPRESSIONS / Walkley, Arthur Bingham – London: T. Unwin, 1892 – 1 roll – 1 – 1-55879-580-4 – uk Libr Preservation [790]
PLAYMATE *see*
– HAPPY DAYS
– THE SUNBEAM
A PLAYNE TREATISE TO LEARNE IN A SHORT SPACE THE FRENCHE TONGUE / La Pichonnaye, Guillaume de – 1576. 128p. (English Linguistics Series 1500-1800) – 9 – us UMI [440]
PLAYS / Robinson, Emmett – 1937. 4 fiches – 9 – us South Carolina Historical [820]
PLAYS / Strindberg, August – Includes: The Dream Play; The Link; The Dance of Death, pts.1-2.Trans. by Edwin Bjorkman. New York: Scribners, 1912 – 1 – us U.W. Library [820]
PLAYS – (v. 28- 1968-. 5,6. v. 29- 1969-. 9) – v. 1- 1941- – 1 – us UMI [820]
THE PLAYS OF GEORG BUECHNER / Buechner, Georg – (Includes bibliographical references) – New York: Viking Press, 1928 – 1 – us U.W. Library [820]
Playter, George F *see* THE HISTORY OF METHODISM IN CANADA
Plaza, A de la *see* VALLADOLID. ARCHIVO GENERAL DE SIMANCAS GUIA DEL INVESTIGADOR
Plaza de Toros *see*
– PLASENCIA PLAZA DE TOROS 1960
– PLAZA DE TOROS DE PLASENCIA
– PLAZA DE TOROS PLASENCIA 1972
PLAZA DE TOROS DE PLASENCIA / Plaza de Toros – Plasencia: La Victoria, 1959 – 1 – sp Bibl Santa Ana [946]
PLAZA DE TOROS PLASENCIA 1972 / Plaza de Toros – Plasencia: Imp. La Victoria, 1972 – 1 – sp Bibl Santa Ana [946]
Plazuelos, Fr. Gabriel *see* SENTIMIENTOS... VIRTUDES DE FRANCISCO DE SAN MIGUEL
A PLEA FOR LIBERTY : WITH CONTRIBUTIONS BY HERBERT SPENCER, AUBERON HERBERT ET AL / ed by Mackay, T – 414p 1 fiche (36x) – 9 – $1.00f – at Libertarian Micro [320]
A PLEA FOR PIONEERS / Bell, Robert – 18–?. 03561. (Pre-1900 Canadiana) – 9 – cn C.I.H.M. [971]
A PLEA FOR SUPPORT / Catalonia. Comissariat de Propaganda – Barcelona, 1936. Fiche W 784. (Blodgett Collection of Spanish Civil War Pamphlets) – 9 – us H.U. College Libr [946]
A PLEA FOR THE AUGSBURG CONFESSION : IN ANSWER TO THE OBJECTIONS OF THE DEFINITE PLATFORM: AN ADDRESS TO ALL MINISTERS AND LAYMEN OF THE EVANGELICAL CHURCH OF THE UNITED STATES / Mann, William J – Philadelphia: Lindsay & Blakiston, 1856 – 1mf – us A.T.L.A. [240]
A PLEA FOR THE BIBLE / Kirkwood, Robert – NY: Sheldon, 1860 – 1mf – 9 – 0-8370-3909-6 – 1985-1909 – us A.T.L.A. [220]
A PLEA FOR THE CONSTITUTION OF THE UNITED STATES, WOUNDED IN THE HOUSE OF ITS GUARDIANS / Bancroft, George – From 1983 reprint. 89p – 9 – 1.00f – at Libertarian Micro [335]
A PLEA FOR THE GOSPEL / Herron, George D – 1892 – 1 – us A.T.L.A. [240]
A PLEA FOR YOUNG MEN OF MONTREAL / Carmichael, James – Montreal, 1889? 02042. (Pre-1900 Canadiana) – 9 – cn C.I.H.M. [240]
PLEA IN DEFENCE OF LOEB AND LEOPOLD : AUGUST 22, 23 AND 25 1924 / Darrow, Clarence S – Girard, Kansas: Haldeman-Julius Co, 1926 – 1mf – 9 – $1.50 – LLMC 91-060 – us L.L.M.C. [340]
THE PLEA OF THE MIDSUMMER FAIRIES : HERO AND LEANDER, LYCUS THE CENTAUR, AND OTHER POEMS / Hood, Thomas – London: Printed for Longman, Rees, Orme, Brown, and Green, 1827 – 1 roll – 1 – 1-55879-432-8 – uk Libr Preservation [810]
PLEADING AND FORMS...NOW IN USE IN THE STATE OF WEST VIRGINIA / Hogg, Charles Edgar – (2nd ed. rev. enl. and annotated. Cincinnati: Clarke Co., 1901. 719 (i.e. 729)p. LL-647. 3rd ed. Cincinnati: Clarke Co., 1908. 719 (i.e. 729)p. LL-877) – 2nd ed. Cincinnati: Clarke Co., 1899. 719p. LL-505 – 1 – us L of C Photodup [340]
PLEADING AND PRACTICE IN COURTS OF COMMON LAW / Poe, John Prentiss – (4th ed. Baltimore: King, 1906. 2v. LL-1308. 5th ed. Baltimore: Curlander, 1925. 2v. LL-1299) – 3rd ed. Baltimore: King, 1897. 2v. Title-page wanting in v2. LL-1297 – 1 – us L of C Photodup [340]
PLEADING AND PRACTICE UNDER THE CIVIL CODE / Nash, Simeon – 3rd ed. Cincinnati: Clarke, 1864. 844p. LL-837 – 1 – us L of C Photodup [340]
PLEAS FOR PROGRESS / Haygood, Atticus Greene – Nashville, Tenn.: Publishing House of the M.E. Church, South, 1889 – 1mf – us A.T.L.A. [240]
PLEASANT DALE BAPTIST CHURCH. LANCASTER COUNTY. SOUTH CAROLINA : CHURCH RECORDS – 1946-56; 1975-78. 150p – 1 – 6.75 – us Baptist [240]
PLEASANT DALE QUIZ – Pleasant Dale, NE. -w. Jul 1890-Mar 1893; Jan 1896-Feb 1899; May 1899-Apr 1900, scattered issues missing – 1 – us NE Hist [071]
PLEASANT GROVE BAPTIST CHURCH. CHATTOOGA COUNTY. GEORGIA : CHURCH RECORDS – Sept 1872 – Feb 1892 – 1 – 10.71 – us Baptist [240]
PLEASANT GROVE BAPTIST CHURCH. GREENVILLE COUNTY. SOUTH CAROLINA : CHURCH RECORDS – (481p) – 1956-1984 – 1 reel – 1 – $21.65 – us Baptist [240]
PLEASANT GROVE BAPTIST CHURCH. GREER, SOUTH CAROLINA : CHURCH RECORDS – 1833-1955 – 1 – 60.93 – us Baptist [240]
PLEASANT GROVE BAPTIST CHURCH. NEWPORT, TENNESSEE : CHURCH RECORDS – 1838-Sept 1982. Lacking: Aug 1929-Aug 1936 – 1 – 32.40 – us Baptist [240]
PLEASANT GROVE BAPTIST CHURCH. PICKENS COUNTY. PICKENS, SOUTH CAROLINA : CHURCH RECORDS – 1946-1972 – 1 – 6.80 – us Baptist [240]
PLEASANT GROVE BAPTIST CHURCH. STANLY ASSOCIATION. NORTH CAROLINA : CHURCH RECORDS – 1853-74 – 1 – 5.28 – us Baptist [240]
PLEASANT GROVE BAPTIST CHURCH. STEWART COUNTY. INDIAN MOUND, TENNESSEE : CHURCH RECORDS – 1919-Jul 1968 – 1 – 5.00 – us Baptist [240]
PLEASANT GROVE CHURCH. FALLSTON, NORTH CAROLINA : CHURCH RECORDS – 1877-1963 – 1 – 5.00 – us Baptist [240]
PLEASANT GROVE MISSIONARY BAPTIST CHURCH. FAIRFIELD, ILLINOIS : CHURCH RECORDS – 1853-1958 – 1 – 37.98 – us Baptist [240]
PLEASANT GROVE "PINEY" BAPTIST CHURCH. NEW MARKET, TENNESSEE : CHURCH RECORDS – 1903-73 – 1 – 43.11 – us Baptist [240]
Pleasant, Hazen Hayes *see* A HISTORY OF CRAWFORD COUNTY
PLEASANT HILL BAPTIST CHURCH. CAMPBELLSVILLE, KENTUCKY : CHURCH RECORDS – April 1837-January 1989, lacking 1870-1871. 1,532p – 1 – $68.94 – us Baptist [240]
PLEASANT HILL BAPTIST CHURCH. ORLINDA, TENNESSEE : CHURCH RECORDS – 1849-1979. Lacks 1933-40; WMU Minutes, 1906-35 (lacks May 1920-Sep 1924). 1312p – 1 – 59.04 – us Baptist [240]
PLEASANT HILL BAPTIST CHURCH. PICKENS COUNTY. CENTRAL, SOUTH CAROLINA : CHURCH RECORDS – 1860-83, 1907-66 – 1 – $19.89 – us Baptist [240]
PLEASANT HILL BAPTIST CHURCH. SHELBY, NORTH CAROLINA : CHURCH RECORDS – 1906-63 – 1 – 19.80 – us Baptist [240]
Pleasant Hill Church of the Nazarene, Sylvia, KS *see* RECORDS
PLEASANT HILL FIRST BAPTIST CHURCH. PLEASANT HILL, ILLINOIS : CHURCH RECORDS – Pleasant Hill, Illinois. First Baptist Church, 1847-1989, lacking 1889-1914 . 1,548p – 1 – $69.66 – us Baptist [240]
PLEASANT HILL NEWS – Pleasant Hill, CA. 1957-Oct 1963 – 4r – 1 – $200.00 – B02633 – us Library Micro [071]
Pleasant Hill Union Sunday School, Reno County, KS *see* RECORDS
PLEASANT HOURS – (Biweekly (1881-between 1890 and 1892); weekly (between 1890 and 1892-1929)) – Toronto: W Briggs, [1881-1929] – 9 – cn C.I.H.M. [240]
PLEASANT RIDGE BAPTIST CHURCH. SHELBY, NORTH CAROLINA : CHURCH RECORDS – 1957-63 – 1 – 5.00 – us Baptist [240]
PLEASANTON BAPTIST CHURCH. TEXAS : CHURCH RECORD BOOK. WOMAN'S MISSIONARY SOCIETY – 1885-1908 – 1 – $8.82 – us Baptist [240]
PLEASANTON TIMES – (Also known as: The Valley Times. Cont by: The Times, Livermore) – Pleasanton, CA. 1975-78 – 37r – 1 – $1,850.00 – B02635 – us Library Micro [071]
PLEASANTRIES OF ENGLISH COURTS AND LAWYERS / Jeaffreson, John C – Jersey City: Fredercik D Linn & Co, n.d. – 4mf – 9 – $6.00 – LLMC 95-207 – us L.L.M.C. [340]
PLEASANTS COUNTY LEADER – St. Mary's. West Virginia. 1932-44; 1958-69 – 1 – us UMI [071]
Pleasants, Frank *see*
– THE COMPARISON OF AEROBIC FITNESS LEVELS IN REPECT TO VISUAL-PERCEPTUAL PERFORMANCE AT REST AND DURING EXERCISE
– THE RELATIONSHIP BETWEEN ASYMMETRICAL LEG POWER AND CHANGE OF RUNNING DIRECTION
Pleasants, J E *see* HISTORY OF ORANGE COUNTY
PLEASURE AND PROFIT IN BIBLE STUDY / Moody, Dwight Lyman – New York: Fleming H. Revell, 1895. 137p. 1 fiche – 9 – us A.T.L.A. [240]

THE PLEASURES OF HOPE : WITH OTHER POEMS / Campbell, Thomas – Edinburgh: Printed for Mundell and Son; London: Longman & Rees, and J. Wright, 1799 – 1 roll – 1 – 1-55879-297-X – uk Libr Preservation [810]

LA PLEBE : PERIODICO DEMOCRATICO, 1868-1883 / ed by Bignami, Enrico – (See also series: Important Periodicals of Italian and International Socialism, 1868-1917) – Lodi and Milan. v1-16, 1868-83. A principal document in the history of the Italian Socialist Movement. – 1 – $305.00 – us UPA [335]

LA PLEBE – Philadelphia, PA, August 24, 1907-Sep. 26, 1908 – 3r – 1 – us I.H.R.C. [978]

PLEDGE OF FRIENDSHIP – 1826-28 – 14mf – 9 – £118.00 – uk Chadwyck [800]

PLEGTIGE INHULDIGING VAN. WILLEM KAREL HENDRIK FRISO. ALS MARKGRAAF VAN VERE / Andriessen, A J – Amsterdam, 1751 – 9 – BO-121 1 – ne IDC [920]

LA PLEIADE – Paris. mars-nov 1886, avr mai-sept oct 1889 – 1 – fr A.C.R.P.P. [073]

LA PLEIADE FRANCOISE. LA LANGUE DE LA PLEIADE / Marty-Laveaux, Charles Joseph – 1896-98 – 9 – fr I.C.S. [440]

PLEIN-JOUR – Forestville, Canada. 25 sep 1968; v4 n44. 9 aut 1972 – 1r – 1 – Can$25.00 – cn Can Microfilming [072]

PLEIN-JOUR SUR CHARLEVOIX – La Malbaie, Canada. 24 jul 1974 – 1r – 1 – Can$25.00 – cn Can Microfilming [072]

LE PLEIN-JOUR SUR LA MANICOUAGAN – Manicouagan, 11 fev 1976-29 dec 1991 – 32r – 1 – Can$75.00 – cn Can Microfilming [072]

LE PLEIN-JOUR SUR LA MANICOUAGAN *see* LE NORDIC

PLEINS POUVOIRS – Montreal, Canada. 25 jan-30 mai 1968 – 1r – 1 – Can$30.00 – cn Can Microfilming [072]

PLEITO CELEBRE. ANTECEDENTES. INFORMES. SENTENCIA DICTADA...EN EL PLEITO PROMOVIDO POR DON SATURNINO SUDON CONTRA LA RESOLUCION DEL GOBERNADOR CIVIL CONFIRMANDO UN ACUERDO DEL AYUNTAMIENTO DE ALBURQUERQUE... / Badajoz. Tribunal Provincial de lo Contencioso-Administrativo de Badajoz – Badajoz: Tip. y Lib. de Antonio Arqueros, 1905 – 1 – sp Bibl Santa Ana [350]

EL PLEITO DE "LA ESPERANZA DE LAS HURDES" FOLLETO HISTORICO-DOCUMENTADO QUE DEDICAN A LOS SOCIOS PROTECTORES DE LA MISMA, LOS INDIVIDUOS DE LA JUNTA DIRECTIVA... / Martin, Francisco et al – Plasencia: Imp. y Libreria de Generoso Montero, s.a. (1909) – sp Bibl Santa Ana [946]

PLEITO DE ORELLANA LA VIEJA, PEDRO DE ORELLANA CONTRA MARQUES DE ORELLANA Y CATALINA DE ORELLANA – S.l., s.i., s.a. Hacia 1650 – 1 – sp Bibl Santa Ana [946]

PLEITOS. INSTRUCCIONES A LOS LETRADOS DEFENSORES DE LOS SENORES PAREDES. ESCRITURA DE CESION DEL ANO 1861 Y OTROS DOCUMENTOS – Caceres: Est. Tip. El Noticiero, 1906 – 1 – sp Bibl Santa Ana [946]

Plekhanov, Georgi Valentinovich *see* SOCHINENIIA

Plemp, CG *see* AMSTERODAMUM MONOGRAMMON

Plenkers, H *see*
- TEXTGESCHICHTE DER REGULA S. BENEDICTI
- UNTERSUCHUNGEN ZUR UEBERLIERFERUNGSGESCHICHTE DER AELTESTEN LATEINISCHEN MOENCHSREGELN

UN PLENO HISTORICO / Ibarruri, Dolores – n.p. 1937. Fiche W955. (Blodgett Collection of Spanish Civil War Pamphlets) – 9 – us H.U. College Libr [946]

Plenzat, Karl *see* KAMPF UM IRLAND

Pleske, Th. D *see* ORNITHOGRAPHIA ROSSICA. ORNITHOLOGICESKAJA ROSSIJSKOJ IMPERII. DIE VOGEL-FAUNA DES RUSSISCHEN REICHS

Plessen, Kerstin von *see* DIE "STRUKURIERTE BIOGRAPHISCHE ANAMNESE FUER SCHMERZPATIENTEN" BEI PATIENTEN MIIT LUMBAGO-ISCHIALGIE-SYNDROMEN

PLEWNA : ROMAN / Samarow, Gregor – Stuttgart: Deutsche Verlags-Anstalt, [18–] – 1r – 1 – us U.W. Library [830]

PLEXUS – Berkeley, CA. 1974-1986 – 3r – 1 – $150.00 – C03583 – us Library Micro [071]

Pleyel, Ignaz J *see*
- GRANDES SONATAS, TROIS, POUR LE FORTEPIANO AVEC ACCOMPAGNEMENT DE VIOLON ET VIOLONCELLE, OP. 33. 3E LIVRE
- NEW GRAND QUARTETS, TWO
- QUARTETS, STRING, OP. 20
- QUARTETS, STRINGS, KING OF PURSSIA NO 1. BOOK 1
- QUARTETTI, SEI, OP. 6, NO. 2
- QUATUORS, DOUZE NOUVEAUX 4E LIVRAISON
- QUATUORS, TROIS, ARR. PIANO, VIOLIN, CELLO
- QUATUORS, TROIS, OP. 42
- QUINTETTI, DEUX, OP. 5
- QUINTETTI, TROIS, OP. 8, 2E LIVRE
- SIX TRIOS POUR DEUX VIOLONS ET VIOLONCELLE: 3E OEUVRE E TRIOS...
- THREE ORIGINAL DUETTS FOR TWO PERFORMERS ON THE PIANO-FORTE OR HARPSICHORD
- TROIS SONATAS, A QUATRE MAINS POUR CLAVECIN OU FORTE-PIANO ARR. FROM "DUETS, VIOLINS, B. 519-21"

Pleyer, Wilhelm *see*
- KAEMPFEN UND LACHEN
- MUTTERS SCHLEIER

Pleyte, W *see*
- MANUSCRITS COPTES DUMUSEE D'ANTIQUITES DES PAYS-BAS A LEYDE
- PAPYRUS DE TURIN. FACSIMILES

Pliester, Hans *see* DIE WORTHAEUFUNG IM BAROCK

Plinguet, Jacques-A *see* LA CANADIENNE

Pliny *see*
- EPISTOLAE
- HISTORIA NATURALIS

Pliny, Virgil, etc *see* VARIOUS MSS

Plisko, N *see* FUTURISM

Plitt, Gustav Leopold *see* DIE REVISION DER LUTHERISCHEN BIBELUEBERSETZUNG UND DIE...PROBEBIBEL VON 1883

Ploechl, W M *see* GESCHICHTE DES KIRCHENRECHTS

Ploegaerts, Th. *see* LES MONIALES CISTERCIENNES DANS L'ANCIEN ROMAN-PAYS DU BRABANT

Ploeger, Robin *see* THE EFFECTS OF THREE SELECTED TRAINING PROGRAMS ON SHOULDER EXTERNAL ROTATION STRENGTH, FLEXIBILITY, AND THROWING VELOCITY IN COLLEGIATE BASEBALL PLAYERS

Plomer, William *see* ALI THE LION: ALI OF TEBELENI, PASHA OF JANNINA, 1741-1822

Plopper, C H *see* HISTORY OF THE EASTERN CHURCH (CCC262)

PLOSHCHADI SADOV, OGORODOV I BAKHCHE I V SELSKIKH KHOZI A ISTVAKH SAMARSKO I GUBERNII V...GODU : SAMARSKOE GUBERNSKOE STATISTICHESKOE BI URO – (Includes c.1: 1919) – Samara: [Bi uro], 1920 – 1 – CSUXAKZ1219-S – us Hoover Inst Photo [947]

Ploss, H *see* MEDICINISCH-CHIRURGISCHE ENCYKLOPAEDIE FUER PRAKTISCHE AERZTE (AEL, ABT.3;7)

PLOTINI ENNEADES CUM MARSILII FICINI INTERPRETATIONE CASTIG / ed by Creuzer, F & Moser, G H – Paris, 1896 – 17mf – 8 – ne Slangenburg [180]

PLOTINS STELLUNG ZUM GNOSTICISMUS UND KIRCHLICHEN CHRISTENTUM / Schmidt, Carl – Leipzig: J.C. Hinrichs, 1901. (Texte und Untersuchungen zur Geschichte der altchristlichen Literatur; der ganzen Reihe Bd. 20, [Heft 4]: n.F., 5. Bd., Heft 4) – 1mf – us A.T.L.A. [240]

PLOTIN'S STELLUNG ZUM GNOSTICISMUS UND KIRCHLICHEN CHRISTENTUM (T.U.U. 2-20/4A) / Schmidt, Carl – Leipzig, 1901 – 2mf – 9 – ne Slangenburg [240]

Plotke, Georg J *see* HEINRICH HEINE ALS DICHTER DES JUDENTUMS

Plotkin, L *see* RUSSKAIA SOVETSKAIA LITERATURA

Ploucquet, W G *see*
- INITIA BIBLIOTHECAE MEDICOPRACTICAE ET CHIRUGICAE REALIS SIVE REPERTORII MEDICINAE PRACTICAE ET CHIRURGIAE
- INITIA BIBLIOTHECAE MEDICOPRACTICAE ET CHIRURGICAE REALIS SIVE REPERTORII MEDICINAE PRACTICAE ET CHIRURGIAE

THE PLOUGH – A monthly magazine for Scottish ploughmen, small holders, and crofters. Edinburgh. Scotland. -m. Apr 1893-Nov 1895. (1 reel) – 1 – uk British Libr Newspaper [630]

PLOUGH, THE LOOM, AND THE ANVIL *see* AMERICAN FARMERS' MAGAZINE

Ploughe, Sheridon *see* HISTORY OF RENO COUNTY

THE PLOUGHMAN'S SONG (CCC264) / Price, P F – (In Chinese) – Hankow: Religious Tract Society, 1938 – 1r – 1 – 1984-6603 – us A.T.L.A. [780]

Plourde, Marthe *see* M. L'ABBE LOUIS-EUGENE OTIS

PLOW AND HAMMER – Tiffin, Ohio. 1890-93 – 1r – 1 – $32.50r – us Archival [071]

Plowden, Trevor Chichele *see* TRAVELS IN ABYSSINIA AND THE GALLA COUNTRY

Plowden, Walter Chichele *see* TRAVELS IN ABYSSINIA AND THE GALLA COUNTRY

Plowert, J *see* PETIT GLOSSAIRE POUR SERVIR A L'INTELLIGENCE DES AUTEURS DECADENTS ET SYMBOLISTES

PLOWSHARE AND PRUNING HOOK – Winchester, CA. 1892-1893 – 1r – 1 – $50.00 – R04141 – us Library Micro [071]

Pluche, Antoine *see* HISTOIRE DU CIEL: CONSIDEREE SELON LES IDEES DES POETES, DES PHILOSOPHES ET DE MOISE

Pluche, Manuel *see*
- ESPECTACULO DE LA NATURALEZA. TOMO 1
- ESPECTACULO DE LA NATURALEZA. TOMO 2
- ESPECTACULO DE LA NATURALEZA. TOMO 3
- ESPECTACULO DE LA NATURALEZA. TOMO 4
- ESPECTACULO DE LA NATURALEZA. TOMO 5
- ESPECTACULO DE LA NATURALEZA. TOMO 6
- ESPECTACULO DE LA NATURALEZA. TOMO 7
- ESPECTACULO DE LA NATURALEZA. TOMO 8
- ESPECTACULO DE LA NATURALEZA. TOMO 9
- ESPECTACULO DE LA NATURALEZA. TOMO 10
- ESPECTACULO DE LA NATURALEZA. TOMO 11
- ESPECTACULO DE LA NATURALEZA. TOMO 12
- ESPECTACULO DE LA NATURALEZA. TOMO 13
- ESPECTACULO DE LA NATURALEZA. TOMO 14
- ESPECTACULO DE LA NATURALEZA. TOMO 15
- ESPECTACULO DE LA NATURALEZA. TOMO 16

Pluche, N A *see* LA MECANIQUE DES LANGUES ET L'ART DE LES ENSEIGNER

Plugge, Heinrich *see* BEITRAEGE ZUR CARITATIVEN TAETIGKEIT DES GALLITZINKREISES

Plukenet, L *see*
- ALMAGESTUM BOTANICUM MANTISSA
- OPERA OMNIA BOTANICA

LA PLUMA : REVISTA MENSUAL DE CIENCIAS, ARTES Y LETRAS – Montivideo: [s.n.]. v1-4 n1-19. aug 1927-sep 1931 – us Res Libr [073]

PLUMA Y PINCEL – Santiago, CL. 1992- – 2+ r – $100.00 ($50.00y) – R04157 – us Library Micro [072]

Plumard de Dangeul *see* ANMAERKNINGER OVER FRANKRIGES OG ENGELLANDS FORDEELE OG MANGELERI HENSEENDE TIL HANDELEN OG ANDRE KILDER TIL LANDES MAGT OG STYRKE: OVERSATTE AF DET FRANSKE MED NOGLE FAA AF OVERSAETTEREN TILLAGDE NOTER

PLUMAS INDEPENDENT – Quincy. Calif. 1908-1945 – 1 – us UMI [071]

PLUMAS NATIONAL BULLETIN – Quincy, CA. 1970-1872; 1890-1931 – 16r – 1 – $800.00 – C03401 – us Library Micro [071]

PLUMAS/LASSEN COUNTIES – 1941-50 – 9r – 1 – $450.00 – P00045 – us Library Micro [910]

PLUMAZOS / Trivino y Forte, Rogelio – 1892 – 9 – 1.50f – sp Bibl Santa Ana [810]

PLUMB BRANCH BAPTIST CHURCH. MCCORMICK, SOUTH CAROLINA : CHURCH RECORDS – 1965-82.556p – 1 – 25.02 – us Baptist [240]

Plumb, Henry B *see* HISTORY OF HANOVER TOWNSHIP

Plumb, Josiah Burr *see* CANADIAN PUBLIC LANDS: SPEECH...HOUSE OF COMMONS... MONDAY, 5TH APRIL, 1880

PLUMBING ENGINEER – v1- 1973- 1; v4-5,6,9 – us UMI [690]

LA PLUME – no. 1-376. Apr 1889-Aug 1905 – 1 – 152.00 – us L of C Photodup [800]

LA PLUME – Revue de litterature, de critique et d'art independant. Paris. avr 1889-juil aout 1905, dec 1911-janv 1914, 1946 – 1 – fr A.C.R.P.P. [073]

Plumer, William *see* WILLIAM PLUMER PAPERS, 1778-1854

Plumer, William Swan *see* TRUTHS FOR THE PEOPLE

Plumier, C *see*
- DESCRIPTION DES PLANTES DE L'AMERIQUE
- FILICETUM AMERICANUM SEU FILICUM
- NOVA PLANTARUM AMERICANARUM GENERA
- PLANTARUM AMERICANARUM
- TRAITE DES FOUGERES DE L'AMERIQUE

Plumlee, Linda K *see* ACTING THE DANCE

Plummer, Alfred *see*
- THE CHURCHES IN BRITAIN BEFORE A.D. 1000
- THE CONTINENTAL REFORMATION IN GERMANY, FRANCE AND SWITZERLAND
- ENGLISH CHURCH HISTORY FROM THE DEATH OF ARCHBISHOP PARKER TO THE DEATH OF KING CHARLES I
- ENGLISH CHURCH HISTORY FROM THE DEATH OF CHARLES 1ST TO THE DEATH OF WILLIAM 3RD
- ENGLISH CHURCH HISTORY FROM THE DEATH OF KING HENRY 8TH TO THE DEATH OF ARCHBISHOP PARKER
- THE EPISTLES OF ST. JOHN
- THE GENERAL EPISTLES OF ST JAMES AND ST JUDE
- THE GOSPEL ACCORDING TO ST JOHN: WITH MAPS, NOTES AND INTRODUCTION
- THE GOSPEL ACCORDING TO ST MARK
- PASTORAL EPISTLES

Plummer, Ch *see*
- BETHADA NAEM NERENN
- VITAE SANCTORUM HIBERNIAE

Plummer, Charles *see*
- IRISH LITANIES
- LIFE AND TIMES OF ALFRED THE GREAT
- THE LIFE AND TIMES OF ALFRED THE GREAT

Plummer, P E *see* A COMPARISON OF ATHLETIC ANKLE TAPING TECHNIQUES WITH RESPECT TO ANKLE INVERSION

Plumpe, J C *see* MATER ECCLESIA

Plumptre, Edward Hayes *see*
- CHRIST AND CHRISTENDOM
- THE GENERAL EPISTLE OF ST JAMES
- THE GOSPEL ACCORDING TO ST. LUKE
- A POPULAR EXPOSITION OF THE EPISTLES TO THE SEVEN CHURCHES OF ASIA
- THE SECOND EPISTLE TO THE CORINTHIANS

PLUMSTED LETTER BOOK, 1756-58 – Cambridge University Library ADD. Ms 2798. BRRAM – 1 – uk Microform Academic [920]

Plunkett, Horace *see* DIARIES, 1881-1932

A PLURALISTIC UNIVERSE : HIBBERT LECTURES AT MANCHESTER COLLEGE... / James, William – (Includes index) – New York: Longmans, Green, 1909 – 1mf – 9 – 0-8370-9796-7 – 1986-3796 – us A.T.L.A. [190]

PLURALITE DES MONDES HABITES CONSIDEREE AU POINT DE VUE NEGATIF / Burque, Francois Xavier – Montreal: Cadieux & Derome. 1898. 00349. (Pre-1900 Canadiana) – 9 – cn C.I.H.M. [971]

LA PLUS ANCIENNE DECRETALE / Babut, E C – Paris: Societe nouvelle de librairie et d'edition, 1904 – 1mf – us A.T.L.A. [240]

LA PLUS ANCIENNE VERSION LATINE DE LA VIE DE ST ANTOINE / Hoppenbrouwers, H – Nijmegen, 1960 – 7mf – 8 – ne Slangenburg [240]

LES PLUS BELLES HISTOIRES D'AMOUR – Montreal: Ed. Police journal, 1958-. SEM16P333 – 1r – 5 – Can$24.00 – cn Bibl Nat [073]

PLUS ULTRA / Glanvill, Joseph – 1668 – 9 – 15.00 – us Scholars' Facs [500]

PLUS ULTRA...ERSTER ZWEETER VORRATH....1754-55 / Mattheson, J – 9 – us Sibley [780]

O PLUTAO – Maceio, Alagoas. 28 Maio 1879 – 1,5,6 – bl Biblioteca [072]

PLUTARCO / Infante, Modesto – 1869 – 9 – 1.50f – sp Bibl Santa Ana [920]

Plutarco *see* VIDAS PARALELAS (GRIEGO) (SIECLE 14)

EL PLUTARCO EXTREMENO / Diaz Perez, Nicolas – 1890 – 9 – 1.50f – sp Bibl Santa Ana [946]

PLUTOT LA MORT : ROMAN JAPONAIS / Tokutoml, Kenjiro – Quebec: Imprimerie de l'Action sociale, ltee, 1910. SEM105P1582 – 4mf – 9 – Can$9.00 – cn Bibl Nat [830]

PLUTOT LA MORT QUE LE DESHONNEUR : APPEL AUX ANCIENS CATHOLIQUES DE FRANCE CONTRE LES REVOLUTIONNAIRES ROMANISTES / Michaud, Eugene – Paris: Sandoz et Fischbacher, 1872 – 1mf – 9 – 0-8370-8535-7 – 1986-2535 – us A.T.L.A. [240]

PLYMOUTH 1663-1890 – (Mf 1-3: Births & Deaths 1638-1807. Mf 3-5: Marriages 1662-1759. Mf 4: Deaths 1669-1759. Mf 4-5, 10-11: Marriage Intentions 1719-54. Mf 5: Vital Records Index 1638-1807. Mf 6-10: Births & Index 1661-1826. Mf 8-9,10: Marriages 1662-1759. Mf 12-17: Vital Records Index 1661-1826. Mf 18-19, 21-24: Births & Deaths 1723-1863. Mf 19-21: Marriage Intentions 1755-1822. Mf 21-25: Marriages 1753-1842. Mf 25: Deaths 1824-43. Mf 25-35: Vital Records Index 1723-1863. Mf 36-43: Vital Records 1783-1887. Mf 44-50: Vital Records Index 1783-1887. Mf 51-58: Vital Records 1843-57. Mf 59-65: Vitals Index 1843-57. Mf 66-70: Births 1856-73. Mf 71-80: Marriages 1853-84; Deaths 1855-75. Mf 81-85: Births 1874-93. ;f 86-87: Marriages 1885-97. Mf 88-92: Deaths 1875-94. Mf 93-97: Birth Index 1783-1908. Mf 98-102: Marriage Index 1783-1917. Mf 103-107: Death Index 1783-1908. Mf 108-118: Deaths 1895-1910) – (mf ed 1984) – 107mf – 9 – 0-931248-60-4 – us Holbrook [920]

PLYMOUTH CHRONICLE – England.30 May 1809; 13 Oct, 10,17,24 Nov, 1-15 Dec, 29 Dec 1812; 5 Jan, 23 Feb, 8 Dec 1813. -w. 15 feet – 1 – uk British Libr Newspaper [072]

PLYMOUTH COURT RECORDS, 1686-1859 / ed by Konig, David Thomas – (With printed guide) – 1994 – 5r – 1 – $425.00 – S3303 – us L of C Photodup [340]

PLYMOUTH NEWS – Plymouth, NE. -w. Jun 1893; Oct-Dec 1895; Feb 1896-May 1898; Oct 1898; Dec 1898-Jul 1956 – 1 – us NE Hist [071]

PLYMOUTH WEEKLY JOURNAL – Plymouth, England. 24 Nov 1721-8 Feb 1724. -w.1/4 reel – 1 – uk British Libr Newspaper [072]

PLYMOUTH-BRETHRENISM : A REFUTATION OF ITS PRINCIPLES AND DOCTRINES / Croskery, Thomas – London: William Mullan, 1879 – 1mf – us A.T.L.A. [240]

PLYMPTON 1649-1900 – (Mf 1-4: Town & Vitals 1679-1762. Mf 5-19: Town & Vitals 1649-1854. Mf 20-21: Vitals Index 1731-1815. Mf 21: Marrs & Intents 1731-90. Mf 22-26: Town Records 1813-25. Mf 27-33: Parish Recs 1695-1865. Mf 34-35: Town Records 1832-86. Mf 36-42: Town Records 1822-38. Mf 43-50: Town Records 1835-50. Mf 51-52: Town Records 1746-1916. Mf 53-59: Mortgages 1838-1924. Mf 60-64: Vital Records 1709-1901. Mf 65-69: Town Records 1851-62. Mf 70-74: Accounts 1785-1831. Mf 75-82: Tax Valuation 1783-1809. Mf 83-91: Tax Valuation 1810-31. Mf 92: Vitals Index 1841-1851+; 93-94: Vital Records 1841-1859; 95: Birth Index 1851-1900. Mf 96: Marriage Index 1851-1900. Mf 97: Death Index 1851-1900. Mf 98-99: Births 1857-1900. Mf 100-101: Marriages 1852-1900. Mf 102-104: Deaths 1860-1900) – (mf ed 1993) – 104mf – 9 – 0-87623-167-9 – us Holbrook [920]

PLYMPTON 1679-1849 – (Mf 1T-2T: Vital Records 1679-1762. Mf 2T-7T: Vital Records 1682-1850. Mf 8T: Births & Deaths 1732, 1781-1838; Marriages & Intentions 1731-46, 1783-1815. Mf 9T: Marriages 1746-67; Deaths 1732-39, 1822-23. Mf 9T-16T: Marriages & Intents 1815-40. Mf 9T-15T: Births & Deaths 1717-1875. Mf 17T: Marriage Intentions 1839-45. Mf 16T-17T: Births & Deaths 1777-1857. Mf 18T-19T: Marriages 1845-49. Mf 19T-20T: Out-of-Town Marriages 1709-97. Mf 20T: Intentions 1739-48, 1765-79; Church Marriages 1732-53, 1780-90; Deaths 1828, 1841-43. Mf 20T-21T: Marriages 1842-49; Births 1842-49. Mf 22T: Deaths 1843-49) – (mf ed 1998) – 22mf – 9 – 0-87623-318-3 – us Holbrook [920]

PLYOMETRIC TRAINING AND ITS EFFECTS ON SPEED, STRENGTH, AND POWER OF INTERCOLLEGIATE ATHLETES / Conroy, Theresa R & Bowers, Richard – 1992 – 2mf – $8.00 – us Microform Publ [617]

PLYWOOD, FIBREBOARD AND PARTICLE BOARD – 1980 – 211p – it F.A.O. [670]

PM – New York. N.Y. 1940-1948 – 1 – us UMI [071]

P.M DAILY – New York. June 18 1940-June 22 1948 – 1 – us NY Public [071]

PM DAILY – New York, 1940-48 – 60r – 1 – us Ross [071]

PM ENGINEER – Troy. v1-3. 1995-97+ – 1,5,9 – D21299 – us UMI [620]

PMI PHOTO METHODS FOR INDUSTRY – (Cont by: Photomethods) – New York. v1-17. 1958-aug 1974 1; v13-16. 1970-73 5 – 1,5 – D2556 – us UMI [770]

PMLA – (v. 81- 1966- 5,6. v. 85- 1970-9) – (Publications of the Modern Language Association of America). v. 1- 1884- – 1 – us UMI [400]

PNCC, Western Diocese, Sacred Hearth Church *see* PARISH COMM. MINUTES 1914-1930, FINANCIAL REPORTS, 1923-1934

PNEUMA – 1979-91 (complete) – 3r – 1 – ATLA S0626 – us A.T.L.A. [073]

PNEUMA IN THE GOSPELS / Crump, J, Fr. – SST 2nd series nr. 82. Washinton, DC, 1954 – Dfl9.00 – ne Slangenburg [220]

PNG COLLECTION : RECORDS OF FISHERIES RESEARCH, SURVEYS AND MANAGEMENT P1-P360 / Papua New Guinea National Fisheries Authority. Kanudi Research Station Library – r1-11 – 1 – PMB1116 – at Pacific Mss [639]

PNP NEWS LETTER 1950-52 AND PNP NEWS 1955-57 FROM THE RICHARD HARK COLLECTION – 5mf – 9 – uk Microform Academic [320]

PO KONIU I PO OGLOBLIAM / Bednyi, Demian – Moskva: Gos. izd-vo, 1920 – 1 – CSUX88-B6768 – us Hoover Inst Photo [947]

PO KOOPERATIVNOMU PUTI : ISTORIIA KOOP. STROITEL'STVA SELA GAN'KINA / Makhov, V N – M., 1928 – 1mf – 9 – COR-490/1 – ne IDC [334]

PO POVODU NASHEI SMUTY I VYSOCHAISHAGO UKAZA 12 DEKABRIA 1904 G / Demchenko, I Akov Grigorevich – Kiev: Lito-tip. T-va I.N. Kushnerev, 1905 – 1 – CSUX89-B679 – us Hoover Inst Photo [947]

PO POVODU SOBRANIIA SOCHINENII OSIPA MANDEL'SHTAMA / Adamovich, G – Opyty, VI, New York, 1956. p.92-94. BR-3635 2 – 8 – ne IDC [460]

PO PROSTU – Warsaw. Poland. -w. 22 Sep 1950-30 Jun 1957. (7 reels) – 1 – uk British Libr Newspaper [947]

PO TIURMAM I ETAPAM / Genkin, Iosif Isaevich – Peterburg: Gos. izd-vo, 1922 – 1 – CSUX89-B7325 – us Hoover Inst Photo [947]

PO ZEMSKIM VOPROSAM / Skalon, V Iu – I: V perekhodnoe vremia 1880-1882. Spb. 1905 – 8 – BR-10 619 2 – ne IDC [947]

PO ZHURNALNYM OKOPAM / Lelevich, G – Molodaia Gvardiia. n7-8. 1924 – 8 – BR-3671 2 – ne IDC [947]

PO ZVEZDAM / Ivanov, V – Stat'i i aforizmy. Izd. "Ory". Spb. 1909. BR-739 2 – 8 – ne IDC [460]

POBEDA – Plovdiv, Bulgaria. Aug 1945-Jan 1946 – 1r – 1 – us L of C Photodup [949]

POBEDA SMERTI / Sologub, F – Tragediia. Spb. 1908. BR-873 2 – 8 – ne IDC [460]

Pobedonostsev, K P *see* ISTORIKO-IURIDICHESKIE AKTY PEREKHODNOI EPOKHI XVII-XVIII VEKOV

Pobedonoszew, K P *see* K.P. POBEDONOSZEWS SAMMLUNG MOSKOWITISCHER STUDIEN UEBER DAS...LEBEN DER GEGENWART

Pobeguin, C H O *see* LES PLANTES MEDICINALES DE LA GUINEE

POBJEDA – Cetinje, Yugoslavia. Apr 1945-Jun 1954 – 4r – 1 – us L of C Photodup [949]

POBJEDA – Titograd, Yugoslavia. Jun 1954-1979; 1981-86 – 66r – 1 – us L of C Photodup [949]

POBLACHT NA H-EIREANN (SCOTTISH EDITION) – Scotland. 16 Aug 1922-13 Jan 1923 – 1 – ie Microforms [072]

POBLACHT NA H-EIREANN (SOUTHERN EDITION) – Ireland.14 Aug-25 Oct 1922 – 1 – ie Microforms [072]

POBLACHT NA H-EIREANN WAR NEWS – Ireland.28 Jun 1922-7 Mar 1923 – 1 – ie Microforms [072]

POBLACION DE VENEZUELA SEGUN EL CENSO DE 1881, TOMOS 1 Y 2 – Caracas, 1883 – 15mf – 9 – sp Cultura [972]

Poblaclon, Juan Martinez *see* DE USU ASTROLABI COMPENDIUM, SCHEMATIBUS COMMODISSIMIS ILLUSTRATUM

POBLACION Y VIVIENDA / Honduras. Direccion General de Estadistica y Censos – v.1-9 – 1 – 46.00 – us L of C Photodup [310]

O POBRE : JORNAL DA UNIAO CATHOLICA PAO DE SANTO ANTONIO – Juiz de Fora, 25 Dec 1899; Jan-May, Jul-Aug 1900; 20 Feb 1901 – 1,5,6 – bl Biblioteca [072]

POBRES CANTOS / Rubio Diaz, Felix – Caceres: Tip. El Noticiero, s.l. s.a. – 1 – sp Bibl Santa Ana [780]

POCAHONTAS TIMES – Marlinton. West Virginia. 1897-1968 – 1 – us UMI [071]

Poch Noguer, Jose *see* CRISTOBAL COLON

Pochedly, Carl *see* INTERNATIONAL JOURNAL OF PEDIATRIC HEMATOLOGY/ONCOLOGY

POCHEMU MY POBEDILI V GRAZHDANSKOI VOINE / Baz, I – Moskva: Gos. voen. izd-vo, 1930 – 1 – CSUX88-B7533 – us Hoover Inst Photo [947]

POCHEMU OSNOVANO VSEROSSIISKOE OBSHCHESTVO KNIZHNAGO DELA / Lemke, M K – Spb, 1912 – 8 – BR-4578 2 – ne IDC [070]

POCHEMU U NAS V ROSSII GOLOD I KAK S NIM BOROTSIA? : PROSTAIA BESEDA S KRESIANAMI / Aroslavskii, Emelian – Moskva: Gos. izdvo, Moskovskoe otd-nie, 1921 – 1 – CSUX88-B9794 – us Hoover Inst Photo [947]

Pochhammer, Margarete Cauer *see* DIE MODERNE GESELLSCHAFT, IHRE GESELLIGKEIT UND IHRE MORAL

Pochhammer, Paul *see* WIE STEHT GOETHE ZU DANTE?

POCHITO VERSUS ALBERTO BATILANA (EX VICE) CAIGA QUIEN CAIGA / Fernando, Hugo – [Buenos Aires: Editorial Tiorilo, 195-?] – 1 – CSUXADL6476-B – us Hoover Inst Photo [972]

POCHODEN – Hradec Kralove, Czechoslovakia. 1956-61 – 5r – 1 – us L of C Photodup [072]

POCHTOVO-TELEGRAFNY I ZHURNAL : CHAST OFIT SIALNAI A – (Includes c.1: v.31:no.32/34 1918:Sept.23-; v.31:no.35/36 1918:Oct.5) – Moskva: Komissariat pocht i telegrafov, 1888 – 1 – CSUXAKY9876-S – us Hoover Inst Photo [947]

THE POCKET ATLAS AND GAZETTEER OF THE DOMINION OF CANADA / Bartholomew, John George – Ed. by J. M. Harper. London: J. Walker, 1890. 03007. (Pre-1900 Canadiana) – 9 – cn C.I.H.M. [971]

POCKET-BOOKS AND DIARIES, 1799, 1801-1812, 1815, 1818-1831 / Tooth, M – (Coll title: The People Called Methodists, Phase 3: Primary Sources, 1801-1850) – 48mf – 9 – MP-681/1 – ne IDC [240]

A POCKET-SYSTEM OF THEOLOGY / Reid, John – 1884 – 9 – us A.T.L.A. [240]

Pococke, R *see* A DESCRIPTION OF THE EAST AND SOME OTHER COUNTRIES

POCOS DE CALDAS : ORGAM DA SOCIEDADE DE PROPAGANDA DE POCOS DE CALDAS (S.P.P.C.) – Pocos de Caldas, 1 Jan, 10 Jul 1927 – 1,5,6 – bl Biblioteca [072]

POCZATKI PISMIENNICTWA POLSKIEGO / Los, J – 2d rev. ed. Lwow. 1922. B-1479 2 – 8 – ne IDC [947]

POD CHERNYM ZNAMENEM : ZAPISKI ANARKHISTA / Chudnov, MN – [Moskva]: Molodai a gvardii a, 1930 – 1 – CSUX88-B3959 – us Hoover Inst Photo [460]

POD GNETOM RELIGII = UNDER THE WEIGHT OF RELIGION / Reinmarus, A & Frizen, F – Moscow, Leningrad, 1931.One of 13 titles by Soviet authors on reel – 1 – 74.32 – us Baptist [240]

POD NOVYM SERPOM. ROMAN / Bal'mont, K D – Berlin. 1923. BR-528 2 – 8 – ne IDC [460]

POD STIAGOM PROLETARSKOI BORBY : OTRYVKI IZ VOSPOMINANII O RABOTE V SARATOVE ZA VREMIA S 1915 G. DO 1918 G / Antonov, Vladimir Pavlovich – Moskva: Gos. izd-vo, 1925- – 1 – CSUX88-B1648 – us Hoover Inst Photo [947]

POD ZNAMENEM BOLSHEVIZMA : ZAPISKI PODPOLSHCHIKA / Degot, Vladimir Aleksandrovich – Moskva: Izd-vo Vses. ob-va politkatorzhan i ssylno-poselent sev, 1927 – 1 – CSUX88-B1841 – us Hoover Inst Photo [460]

POD ZNAMENEM MARKSIZMA – Moscow. Jan. Feb. 1922-May 1944 gaps – 1 – 35.00r – us Hoover Inst Photo [947]

POD ZNAMENEM MARKSIZMA – Moscow. U.S.S.R. 1922-44 – 1 – us UMI [073]

POD ZNAMENEM MARKSIZMA – (Under the Banner of Marxism). 1921-44 – 3 – us Readex [335]

PODER EJECUTIVO NACIONAL PERIODO 1932-38 / Argentine Republic. Presidente, 1932-38 (Justo) – 10v. 1938 – 1 – 46.00 – us L of C Photodup [972]

PODER IMPERIALISTA Y LIBERACION NACIONAL : (LAS LUCHAS DEL PERONISMO CONTRA LA DEPENDENCIA) / Carri, Roberto – [Buenos Aires]: Efece Ediciones, 1973 – 1 – CSUXADP8806-B – us Hoover Inst Photo [320]

PODER POLITICO Y EDUCACION : EL PERONISMO Y LA COMISION NACIONAL DE APRENDIZAJE Y ORIENTACION PROFESIONAL / Winar, David L – Buenos Aires: Centro de Investigaciones en Ciencias de la Educacion, 1970 – 1 – CSUXAGN1662-B – us Hoover Inst Photo [320]

PODER POLITICO Y POPULISMO : DEL PERONISMO A LA SUBVERSION Y OTROS ENSAYOS / Calello, Hugo – [Caracas]: Ediciones de la Biblioteca, Universidad Central de Venezuela, 1973 – 1 – CSUXAHZ3265-B – us Hoover Inst Photo [320]

EL PODER TEMPORAL DE LOS PAPAS EN EL S. 19 / Diaz Perez, Nicolas – 1885 – 9 – 1.50f – sp Bibl Santa Ana [240]

PODER Y CLASSES SOCIALES EN EL DESARROLLO DE AMERICA LATINA / Graciarena, Jorge – Buenos Aires: Paidos, 1972 – 1 – CSUXAHZ3584-B – us Hoover Inst Photo [972]

Podewils, Clemens, Graf *see* SOEHNE DER HEIMAT

Podgotovil k pechati I. Mints *see* APONSKAI A INTERVENTSII A 1918-1922 GG. V DOKUMENTAKH

Podlech, Alfred *see* LEITFADEN DER DEUTSCHEN LITERATURGESCHICHTE

Podmore, Frank *see* MODERN SPIRITUALISM

Podol'skii, IM *see* OTVETY NA VOPROSY UCHREZHDENII MELKOGO KREDITA

PODOROZHIE / Remizov, A – St. Petersburg, 1913. 254p. BR-837 2 – 8 – ne IDC [460]

PODOROZHNIK / Akhmatova, A – Petrograd. 1921. BR-1100 2 – 8 – ne IDC [460]

PODRECZNIK PALEOGRAFII RUSKIEJ / Horodyski, B – Krakow, 1951. BR-10,024 1 – 9 – ne IDC [410]

PODROBNAIA OPIS' 142 RUKOPISIAM 17 DO NACHALA 19 STOLETII TRET'IAGO (LOSEVSKAGO) SOBRANIIA LINEVSKAGO ARKHIVA / Selifontov, N N – St. Petersburg, 1893, 81p. BR-7325/2 – 8 – ne IDC [947]

PODROBNAIA OPIS' 272 RUKOPISIAM KONSTA 16 DO NACHALA 19 STOLETII VTORAGO (SHEVLIAGINSKAGO) SOBRANIIA LINEVSKAGO ARKHIVA / Selifontov, N N – St. Petersburg, 1892, 183p. BR-7326/2 – 8 – ne IDC [947]

PODROBNAIA OPIS' 440 RUKOPISIAM 17, 18 I NACHALA 19 STOLETII PERVAGO SOBRANIIA LINEVSKAGO ARKHIVA / Selifontov, N N – St. Petersburg, 1891, 132p. BR-7327/2 – 8 – ne IDC [947]

PODROBNAIA OPIS 962 RUKOPISIAM NACHALA 17 DO NACHALA 19 STOLETIJ DOLMATOVSKAGO ARKHIVA / Preobrazenskii, ID & Albitskii, N A – St. Petersburg, 1895. 326p. BR-7320/2 – 8 – ne IDC [460]

PODSTRIZHENNYMI GLAZAMI. KNIGA UZLOV I ZAKRUT PAMIATI / Remizov, A – YMCA Press: Paris, 1951. 301, (3)p. BR-836 2 – 8 – ne IDC [460]

POE BAPTIST CHURCH. GREENVILLE, SOUTH CAROLINA : CHURCH RECORDS – 1903-1965 – 1 – $34.33 – us Baptist [240]

Poe, Edgar Allen *see*
- LETTERS AND DOCUMENTS IN THE ENOCH PRATT FREE LIBRARY
- WORKS

Poe, John Prentiss *see* PLEADING AND PRACTICE IN COURTS OF COMMON LAW

Poebel, A *see* GRUNDZUEGE DER SUMERISCHEN GRAMMATIK

Poebel, Arno *see* "ANCIENT BABYLONIAN TABLETS"

Poel, J. van der *see* RAILWAY AND CUSTOMS POLITICS IN SOUTH-AFRICA. 1885-1910

POELAU DARAH : KEBOEASAN BANGSA BELANDA MEMBOENOEH BANGSA METAWAI / Arifin, Hassan Noel – Medan, Poestaka "Antara" (2604). 32p. 1st ed – 7mf – 9 – ne IDC [950]

Poelnitz, Goetz Freiherr von *see* JOSEPH GOERRES UND DIE PRESSEPOLITIK DER DEUTSCHEN REAKTION
Poelnitz, Goetz, Freiherr von *see* JOSEPH GOERRES UND DIE PRESSEPOLITIK DER DEUTSCHEN REAKTION
Poels, Henricus Andreas *see*
- EXAMEN CRITIQUE DE L'HISTOIRE DU SANCTUAIRE DE L'ARCHE
- LE SANCTUAIRE DE KIRJATH-JEARIM
POEMA BEZ GEROIA. TRIPTIKH. VOZDUSHNYE PUTI / Akhmatova, A – New York. 1960. BR-1101 2 – 8 – ne IDC [460]
POEMA DE CAPPNTEDRICO / Perez Reviriego, Miguel – (Fregenal: Imp. Angel Verde, 1978) – sp Bibl Santa Ana [810]
UN POEMA INEDITO SOBRE HERNAN CORTES : "LAS CORTESIADAS..." / Lopez de Toro, Jose – Madrid: Revista de Indias, 1948 – 1 – sp Bibl Santa Ana [972]
POEMA. LA MUJER FELIZ. TOMO 1 / Merino de Jesucristo, Andres – 1786 – 1mf – 9 – Pta1,000.00 – 84-7848-290-3 – sp Pentalfa [810]
POEMA. LA MUJER FELIZ. TOMO 2 / Merino de Jesucristo, Andres – 1786 – 1mf – 9 – Pta1,000.00 – 84-7848-291-1 – sp Pentalfa [810]
POEMA. LA MUJER FELIZ. TOMO 3 / Merino de Jesucristo, Andres – 1786 – 1mf – 9 – Pta1,000.00 – 84-7848-292-X – sp Pentalfa [810]
POEMA OCOEDRICO / Perez Reviriego, Miguel – (Fregenal: Imprenta de Angel Verde, 1978) – sp Bibl Santa Ana [810]
POEMAS / Belloso Rodriguez, Pedro – 1977 – 1 – sp Bibl Santa Ana [810]
POEMAS A LA MUERTE DE COVARSI – Badajoz: Alor, Hojas de poesias, 1952 – 1 – sp Bibl Santa Ana [810]
POEMAS DE AUSENCIA / Perez Reviriego, Miguel – Badajoz: Tipografia clasica, 1978 – 1 – sp Bibl Santa Ana [810]
POEMAS DE CAMPO Y PUEBLO (MECANOGRAFIADO) / Belloso Rodriguez, Pedro – 1976 – 1 – sp Bibl Santa Ana [810]
POEMAS DE JUVENTUD (ANTOLOGIA 1913-1922) / Martin de Caceres y Cruz, Emilio – Caceres: Cuadernos Alcantara, 1954. no 11 – sp Bibl Santa Ana [810]
POEMAS DEL CANTE JONDO. FRAGMENTO MANUSCRITO / Garcia Lorca, Federico – 1mf – 9 – sp Cultura [810]
POEMAS INMEDIATOS / Montaner, Joaquin – Barcelona, 1913-1916 – 1 – sp Bibl Santa Ana [810]
POEMAS MARIANOS / Corredor Garcia, Antonio – Caceres: Edic. Cruzada Mariana, 1954 – 1 – sp Bibl Santa Ana [810]
POEMAS RECOPILADOS Y ORDENADOS POR EL PROF. IRVING A. LEONARD / Siguenza y Gongora, Carlos – Madrid, 1931; Madrid: Razon y Fe, 1932 – 1 – sp Bibl Santa Ana [810]
POEMAS Y EPISODIOS / Moreno Torrado, Luis – 1892 – 9 – 1.50f – sp Bibl Santa Ana [810]
POEMATA ET INSCRIPTIONES / Landor, Walter Savage – Londini: impensis Edwardi Moxon, 1847 – 1 roll – 1 – 1-55879-286-4 – uk Libr Preservation [810]
POEME ET DRAME – Paris. nov 1912-janv mars 1914 – 1 – fr A.C.R.P.P. [073]
POEMES DE PROVENCE / Aicard, Jean – Paris: A. Lemerre, 1873.182p. 2 fiches. (Literature Collection) – 9 – 6.00 – fr Bibl Nationale [810]
POEMES ET LEGENDES / Heine, Heinrich – (Prose translation by Heine himself, done partly in collaboration with friends) – Nouvelle ed. Paris: Calmann Levy, [1855?] – 1 – us U.W. Library [800]
DES POEMES LATINS ATTRIBUES A SAINT BERNARD / Haureau, B – Paris: C. Klincksieck, 1890 – 1mf – us A.T.L.A. [240]
POEMS : 2ND SERIES / Arnold, Matthew – London: Longman, Brown, Green, and Longmans, 1855 – 1 roll – 1 – 1-55879-190-6 – uk Libr Preservation [810]
POEMS / Allen, Jacob D – London: Ont.. 1869. 02396. (Pre-1900 Canadiana) – 9 – cn C.I.H.M. [810]
POEMS : BALLADS, STUDIES FROM NATURE, SONNETS, ETC / Scott, William Bell – London: Longmans, Green, 1875 – 1 roll – 1 – 1-55879-691-6 – uk Libr Preservation [810]
POEMS / Brooke, John – Toronto: Hunter, Rose and Co., 1882. 00286. (Pre-1900 Canadiana) – 9 – cn C.I.H.M. [810]
POEMS / Chilton, Robert S – Goderich, Ont.: McGillicuddy, 1885. 00609. (Pre-1900 Canadiana) – 9 – cn C.I.H.M. [810]
POEMS / Clough, Arthur Hugh – Cambridge: Macmillan and Co., 1862 – 1 roll – 1 – 1-55879-322-4 – uk Libr Preservation [810]
POEMS / Clough, Arthur Hugh – London: Macmillan and Co., 2nd ed 1863 – 1 roll – 1 – 1-55879-300-3 – uk Libr Preservation [810]
POEMS / Coleridge, Samuel Taylor – London: Printed by N. Biggs for T.N. Longman and O. Rees, 3rd ed 1803 – 1 roll – 1 – 1-55879-307-0 – uk Libr Preservation [810]
POEMS / Cowper, William – London: J. Johnson, 1782 – 1 roll – 1 – 1-55879-352-6 – uk Libr Preservation [810]
POEMS / Crabbe, George – London: Printed for J. Hatchard, 1807 – 1 roll – 1 – 1-55879-283-X – uk Libr Preservation [810]
POEMS / Dickinson, Emily; ed by Todd, Mabel Loomis & Higginson, T W – Boston: Roberts Brothers, 1892 (c1890). xii,152p – 1 – us U.W. Library [810]
POEMS / Dickinson, Emily; ed by Todd, Mabel Loomis & Higginson, T W – Second Series. Boston: Roberts Brothers, 1893. 230p – 1 – us U.W. Library [810]
POEMS / Domett, Alfred – London: Henry Leggat, 1833 – 1 roll – 1 – 1-55879-858-7 – uk Libr Preservation [810]
POEMS / Hoelderlin, Friedrich – (Translated by Michael Hamburger. German and English on opposite pages; introduction in English. Includes bibliographical references) – [London]: Nicholson & Watson, 1943 – 1 – us U.W. Library [810]
POEMS / Johnson, Lionel Pigot – London: Elkin Mathews; Boston: Copeland & Day, [n.d.] – 1 roll – 1 – 1-55879-582-0 – uk Libr Preservation [810]
POEMS / Lydgate, Chaucer et al – Longleat Mss. 257, 258 – 1 – uk Microform Academic [810]
POEMS / Patmore, Coventry Kersey Dighton – London: Edward Moxon, 1844 – 1 roll – 1 – 1-55879-594-4 – uk Libr Preservation [810]
POEMS : SELECTIONS / Zschokke, Emil; ed by Weber, Robert – Aarau: H R Sauerlaender, 1886 – 1r – 1 – us U.W. Library [810]
POEMS / Smith, Alexander – London: D. Bogue, 1853 – 1 roll – 1 – 1-55879-303-8 – uk Libr Preservation [810]
POEMS / Werfel, Franz – (German and English on opposite pages) – Princeton, NJ: Princeton University Press, 1945 – 1r – 1 – us U.W. Library [810]
POEMS / Wilde, Oscar – London: D. Bogue, 1881 – 1 roll – 1 – 1-55879-422-0 – uk Libr Preservation [810]
POEMS : WITH BIOGRAPHICAL INTRODUCTION BY JOHN MITCHEL / Mangan, James Clarence – New York: P.M. Haverty, 1859 – 1 roll – 1 – 1-55879-843-9 – uk Libr Preservation [810]
THE POEMS : TOGETHER WITH A BIOGRAPHICAL NOTICE OF THE AUTHOR AND NECESSARY NOTES BY ALEXANDER PLATT / Uhland, Ludwig – (Includes bibliographical references) – Leipzig: F Volckmar, 1848 – 1r – 1 – us U.W. Library [810]
POEMS AND BALLADS / Quiller-Couch, Arthur Thomas – London: Methuen, 1896 – 1 roll – 1 – 1-55879-877-3 – uk Libr Preservation [810]
THE POEMS AND BALLADS OF SCHILLER / Schiller, Friedrich von – Leipzig: Bernhard Tauchnitz, 1844 – 1r – 1 – us U.W. Library [810]
POEMS AND HYMNS / Cameron, Charles Innes – Geelong, Australia: J. Purdie, 1870. 00907. (Pre-1900 Canadiana) – 9 – cn C.I.H.M. [810]
POEMS AND LETTERS TO WALTER SAVAGE LANDOR / Southey, Robert – 1 – uk Microform Academic [810]
POEMS AND PLAYS / Hayley, William – London: T. Cadell, 1785 – 2 rolls – 1 – 1-55879-161-2 – uk Libr Preservation [810]
POEMS AND SONGS ON VARIOUS SUBJECTS / Bannantyne, William – Toronto: J. Campbell, 1875. 03362. (Pre-1900 Canadiana) – 9 – cn C.I.H.M. [810]
POEMS AND TRANSLATIONS / Linton, W J – London: J.C. Nimmo, 1889 – 1 roll – 1 – 1-55879-185-X – uk Libr Preservation [810]
THE POEMS AND VERSES OF CHARLES DICKENS / Dickens, Charles; ed by Kitton, F G – New York, London: Harper & Brothers, 1903 – 1 roll – 1 – 1-55879-864-1 – uk Libr Preservation [810]
POEMS BY THE WAY / Morris, William – Hammersmith: Kelmscott Press; London: Sold by Reeves & Turner, 1891 – 1 roll – 1 – 1-55879-170-1 – uk Libr Preservation [810]
POEMS, CHARADES, INSCRIPTIONS OF POPE LEO 13 : INCLUDING THE REVISED COMPOSITIONS OF HIS EARLY LIFE IN CHRONOLOGICAL ORDER / ed by Henry, Hugh Thomas – (Discussion and translations in English. Texts in English, Latin, Italian) – New York: Dolphin Press, 1902 – 1mf – 9 – 0-8370-8443-1 – 1986-2443 – us A.T.L.A. [080]
POEMS, CHIEFLY OF EARLY AND LATE YEARS : INCLUDING THE BORDERERS, A TRAGEDY / Wordsworth, William – London: Edward Moxon, 1842 – 1 roll – 1 – 1-55879-870-6 – uk Libr Preservation [810]
THE POEMS OF HEINE, COMPLETE : TRANSLATED INTO THE ORIGINAL METRES WITH A SKETCH OF HIS LIFE / Heine, Heinrich; ed by Bowring, Edgar Alfred – London: G Bell, 1916 – 1 – us U.W. Library [810]
THE POEMS OF JOHN C. COLGAN / Colgan, John C – Toronto: Hunter, Rose, 1873. 00707. (Pre-1900 Canadiana) – 9 – cn C.I.H.M. [810]
THE POEMS OF OLIVER GOLDSMITH / Goldsmith, Oliver; ed by Robert Aris Willmott – London: New York: Routledge – 1 – us U.W. Library [810]
THE POEMS OF SCHILLER / Schiller, Friedrich von – [2nd. rev. ed.] New York: T Crowell, [between 1871 and 1881] – 1 – us U.W. Library [810]
POEMS OF THE HUZAILIS / Hudail. (Tribe) – 1854 – 1 – uk Microform Academic [810]
POEMS OF THE PAST AND THE PRESENT / Hardy, Thomas – [London, New York: Harper, 1902] – 1 roll – 1 – 1-55879-818-8 – uk Libr Preservation [810]
THE POEMS OF WALTER SAVAGE LANDOR / Landor, Walter Savage – London: Printed for T. Cadell, junr. and W. Davies, (Successors to Mr. Cadell) in the Strand, 1795 – 1 roll – 1 – 1-55879-447-6 – uk Libr Preservation [810]
POEMS OF WORDSWORTH. CHOSEN AND EDITED BY MATTHEW ARNOLD / Wordsworth, William; ed by Arnold, Matthew – London: Macmillan, 1879 – 1 roll – 1 – 1-55879-301-1 – uk Libr Preservation [810]
POEMS ON VARIOUS OCCASIONS:... / Gurney, T – Sudbury, 1790 – 1mf – 9 – MP-567/1 – ne IDC [810]
POEMY / Kamenskii, V – M. 1958. BR-943 2 – 8 – ne IDC [460]
POEMY ALEKSANDRA BLOKA / Remenik, G – M. 1959. BR-2086 2 – 8 – ne IDC [460]
POEMY MAIAKOVSKOGO KUIBYSHEV, 1960 / Mashbits-Verov, I – BR-1413 2 – 8 – ne IDC [460]
Poeppig, E F *see* NOVA GENERA AC SPECIES PLANTARUM QUAS IN REGNO CHILENSI PERUVIANO
Poertner, B *see*
- AEGYPTISCHE GRABSTEINE UND DENKSTEINE AUS ATHEN UND KONSTANTINOPEL
- AEGYPTISCHE GRABSTEINE UND DENKSTEINE AUS SUEDDEUTSCHEN SAMMLUNGEN
Poerwadarminta, W J S *see*
- BAOESASTRA INDONESIA-DJAWI. TJAP-TJAPAN KAPING TIGA
- KAMOES HARIAN. NIPPON-INDONESIA; INDONESIA-NIPPON
- KAMOES HARIAN. NIPPON-INDONESIA; INDONESIA-NIPPON. TJETAKAN KETIGA, DITAMBAH DAN DIPERBAIKI
- KAWI-DJARWA. DAMELANIPOEN W.J.S. POERWADARMINTA
- LATIHAN PERTJAKAPAN NIPPON
POESARA : JOGJAKARTA, PERSATOEAN TAMAN-SISWA – (Lacking: 1930-1934 v1-5(6). 1938 v8(2,10,12). 1939 v9(2,6 12). 1940 v4(3,6-12). 1941 v11(5-6,9,12). 1942-1948 v12(2-6,8-12)) – Jogjakarta. v1-41 n10. 1930-1972 – 123mf – 9 – SE-763/1 – ne IDC [950]
POESIA – Rassegna internazionale. Milano. fevr 1905-aout oct 1909, juil-aout sept 1920 – 1 – fr A.C.R.P.P. [073]
Poesia *see* POESIA CRISTIANA. ANTOLOGIA DE POESIA ROMANO-CRISTIANA Y LATINO-MEDIEVAL
A POESIA AFRO-BRASILEIRA / Bastide, Roger – [Sao Paulo]: Livraria Martins Editora, [1943] – us Res Libr [810]
POESIA CRISTIANA. ANTOLOGIA DE POESIA ROMANO-CRISTIANA Y LATINO MEDIEVAL (SIGLOS 4-15) TOLEDO, 1946 / Errandonea, Ignacio & Sanchez Aliseda, C – Madrid: Razon y Fe, 1947 – 1 – sp Bibl Santa Ana [810]
POESIA CRISTIANA. ANTOLOGIA DE POESIA ROMANO-CRISTIANA Y LATINO-MEDIEVAL / Poesia – Toledo: Vol. 4. 1946 – 1 – sp Bibl Santa Ana [240]
POESIA EXTREMENA ACTUAL 1^A PARTE : ANTOLOGIA – Badajoz: Edit. Esquina Viva, 1977 – 1 – sp Bibl Santa Ana [440]
POESIA EXTREMENA ACTUAL 2^A PARTE : ANTOLOGIA – Badajoz: Editorial Esquina Viva, 1978 – 1 – sp Bibl Santa Ana [810]
POESIA NAVIDENA – Badajoz: Imprenta Campini, 1966 – sp Bibl Santa Ana [810]
POESIA...INMACULADA / Rodriguez Soriano y Alvarez, Rafael – 1881 – 9 – 1.50f – sp Bibl Santa Ana [810]
POESIAS / Alvarez del Vayo, Juan – 1886 – 9 – 1.50f – sp Bibl Santa Ana [810]
POESIAS / Alvarez Medina, Felipe – Madrid: Graf. Espana, 1943 – 1 – sp Bibl Santa Ana [810]
POESIAS / Calvo Flores, Josquin – Badajoz: Escuela del Magisterio, 1967 – 1 – sp Bibl Santa Ana [810]
POESIAS / Coronado, Carolina – (1853; $1.50f; 9) – 1843 – 9 – $1.50f – sp Bibl Santa Ana [810]
POESIAS / Espronceda, Jose de – (1840 ed.1.50f; 9. 1957 ed.1.50f; BSA; 9. 1874 ed.1.50f; BSA; 9) – 1848 ed – 9 – 1.50f – sp Bibl Santa Ana [810]
POESIAS / Gabriel y Ruiz de Apodaca, Fernando de – (1865 ed.1.50f; 9) – 1884 – 9 – 1.50f – sp Bibl Santa Ana [810]
POESIAS / Garcia de la Huerta, Vicente – Madrid: Pantaleon Aznar, 1786 – 1 – sp Bibl Santa Ana [810]
POESIAS / Gonzalez, Fray Diego – 1796 – 1mf – 9 – Pta1,000.00 – 84-7848-041-2 – sp Pentalfa [810]
POESIAS / Malendez Valdes, Juan – 1797. Tomos 1-3 – 9 – 1.50f – sp Bibl Santa Ana [810]
POESIAS / Malendez Valdes, Juan – 1832. Tomos 1-4 – 9 – 1.50f – sp Bibl Santa Ana [810]
POESIAS / Malendez Valdes, Juan – 1838 – 9 – 1.50f – sp Bibl Santa Ana [810]
POESIAS / Martinez Abeytia, Mateo – 1838 – 9 – 1.50f – sp Bibl Santa Ana [810]
POESIAS / Melendez Valdes, Juan – 1785 – 1mf – 9 – Pta1,000.00 – 84-7848-269-5 – sp Pentalfa [810]
POESIAS / Salas, Francisco Gregorio de – Tomos I-II. 1797 – 9 – 1.50f – sp Bibl Santa Ana [810]
POESIAS / Sanchez-Arjona, Vicente – Sevilla: I. Mejias, s.a. – 1 – sp Bibl Santa Ana [810]
POESIAS / Solis y Willancourt, Alfonso – 1790 – 9 – 1.50f – sp Bibl Santa Ana [810]
POESIAS / Torreorgaz, Marques de – 1850 – 9 – 1.50f – sp Bibl Santa Ana [810]
POESIAS A...NTR. SRA. REMEDIOS...FREGENAL DE LA SIERRA / Real, Enrique – 1885 – 9 – 1.50f – sp Bibl Santa Ana [810]
POESIAS COMPLETAS / Coronado, Carolina – 1884 – 9 – 1.50f – sp Bibl Santa Ana [810]
POESIAS DE DONA CATALINA CLARA RAMIREZ DE GUZMAN / Entrambasaguas Pena, Joaquin – Badajoz: Arqueros, 1929 – 1 – sp Bibl Santa Ana [810]
POESIAS ELEGIDAS / Espronceda, Jose de – 1958 – 1 – sp Bibl Santa Ana [810]
POESIAS ESCOGIDAS / Malendez Valdes, Juan – 1811. Tomos 1-2 – 9 – 1.50f – sp Bibl Santa Ana [810]
POESIAS ESPIRITUALES / Carvajal y Mendoza, Luisa de – 1885 – 9 – $1.50f – sp Bibl Santa Ana [810]
POESIAS JUVENILES. TOMO 1 / Arriaza, Juan Bautista – (1816) – 1mf – 9 – Pta1,000.00 – 84-7848-038-2 – sp Pentalfa [810]
POESIAS JUVENILES. TOMO 2 / Arriaza, Juan Bautista – 1816 – 1mf – 9 – Pta1,000.00 – 84-7848-039-0 – sp Pentalfa [810]

POESIAS LIRICAS / Sanchez Arjona y Sanchez Arjona, Francisco – 1878 – 9 – 1.50f – sp Bibl Santa Ana [810]
POESIAS LIRICAS Y LA VIRGEN DE LA SERVILLETA / Sanchez Arjona y Sanchez Arjona, Jose – 1874 – 9 – 1.50f – sp Bibl Santa Ana [810]
POESIAS PATRIOTICAS / Arriaza, Juan Bautista – 1810 – 1mf – 9 – Pta1,000.00 – 84-7848-037-4 – sp Pentalfa [440]
POESIAS POSTUMAS. TOMO 1 / Iglesias de la Casa, Jose – 1793 – 1mf – 9 – Pta1,000.00 – 84-7848-042-0 – sp Pentalfa [810]
POESIAS POSTUMAS. TOMO 2 / Iglesias de la Casa, Jose – 1793 – 1mf – 9 – Pta1,000.00 – 84-7848-043-9 – sp Pentalfa [810]
POESIAS SELECTAS / Justiniano Arribas, Juan – 1891 – 9 – 1.50f – sp Bibl Santa Ana [810]
POESIAS SERIAS / Moreno Torrado, Luis – 1900 – 9 – 1.50f – sp Bibl Santa Ana [810]
POESIAS. TOMOS 1 Y 2 / Salas, Francisco Gregorio de – 1797 – 2mf – 9 – Pta1,500.00 – 84-7848-275-X – sp Pentalfa [810]
POESIAS VARIAS / Marco Rintro, Diego – Madrid: Imp. de Antonio Sanz – 1 – sp Bibl Santa Ana [810]
POESIAS VARIAS / Miguel Romero, Antonio – 1898 – 9 – 1.50f – sp Bibl Santa Ana [810]
POESIE – Paris. Dir., Pierre Seghers. No.1-41. 1939-nov 1947. En 1939-1940 a paru sous le titre de: Poetes casques – 1 – fr A.C.R.P.P. [073]
POESIE DER DEMOKRATIE : LITERARISCHE WIDERSPRUECHE ZUR DEUTSCHEN WIRKLICHKEIT VOM 18. ZUM 20. JAHRHUNDERT / Scherpe, Klaus Ruediger – (Includes bibliographical references and index) – Koeln: Pahl-Rugenstein, 1980 – 1 – us U.W. Library [430]
DIE POESIE DES ALTEN TESTAMENTS / Koenig, Eduard – (Includes bibliography) – Leipzig: Quelle & Meyer, 1907 – 1mf – 9 – 0-8370-3971-1 – 1985-1971 – us A.T.L.A. [220]
DIE POESIE DES EVANGELIUMS JESU: EIN VERSUCH / Frommel, Otto – Berlin: Gebr. Paetel, 1906. 1 fiche – 9 – us A.T.L.A. [240]
LA POESIE GNOMIQUE CHEZ LES HEBREUX ET CHEZ LES GRECS : SALOMON ET THEOGNIS / Bois, Henri – (Includes bibliographical references) – Toulouse: A Chauvin, 1886 – 1mf – 9 – 0-8370-9445-3 – 1986-3445 – us A.T.L.A. [230]
LA POESIE LATINE RYTHMIQUE DU HAUT MOYEN-AGE / Norberg, D – Stockholm, 1954 – 2mf – 8 – Dfl9.00 – ne Slangenburg [450]
POESIE LITURGIQUE DES EGLISES DE FRANCE AUX 17 ET 18E SIECLES, OU, RECUEL D'HYMNES ET DE PROSES : USITEES A CETTE EPOQUE ET DISTRIBUEES SUIVANT L'ORDRE DU BREVIAIRE ET DU MISSEL / Chevalier, Ulysse – Paris: Alphonse Picard, 1913 – 1mf – us A.T.L.A. [240]
POESIE LITURGIQUE DU MOYEN AGE : RYTHME ET HISTOIRE: HYMNAIRES ITALIENS / Chevalier, Ulysse – Paris: A. Picard; Lyon: E. Vitte, 1893 – 1mf – us A.T.L.A. [240]
DIE POESIE UND DIE POETISCHEN BUECHER DES ALTEN TESTAMENTS : SECHS VORTRAEGE / Kautzsch, Emil – (Includes bibliographical references) – Tuebingen: J C B Mohr (Paul Siebeck), 1902 – 1mf – 9 – 0-8370-9161-6 – 1986-3161 – us A.T.L.A. [220]
POESIE UND PROSA AUS DEM LITERARISCHEN NACHLASS / Wolff, Albert – St. Paul, MI: Druck der Volkszeitung, 1894 – 1r – 1 – us U.W. Library [800]
LES POESIES / Bonneville, Nicolas de – Paris. Imp. du Cercle Social. 1793 – 9 – fr Hachette [321]
LES POESIES / Chatillon, Auguste de – Paris: Librairie du Petit Journal, 1866.342p. 4 fiches. (Literature Collection) – 9 – 10.00 – fr Bibl Nationale [810]
POESIES / Garneau, Alfred – Montreal: Beauchemin, 1906. SEM16P141 – 1r – 5 – Can$9.00 – cn Bibl Nat [810]
POESIES CHOISIES / Frechette, Louis-Honore – Quebec?: s.n., 1879 (Quebec: C. Darveau). 03240. (Pre-1900 Canadiana) – 9 – cn C.I.H.M. [810]
POESIES CHOISIES / Hugues, Clovis – Avec Introd. par Alexandre Zevaes et Preface par Gusta e Kahn. Paris: A. Lemerre, 1935. 252p. With: La sape xGeorges Leneveu. Paris: P. Ollendorff, 1899 – 1 – us U.W. Library [810]
POESIES DE MARIE DE FRANCE, POETE ANGLO-NORMAND DU XIIIE SIECLE. / Marie, de France – Par B. de Roquefort...Paris, 1819-20. 2v – 1 – us U.W. Library [440]
POESIES GALLIQUES. / Ossian – Paris: Husier, 1777. 2v in 1. 9 fiches. (Literature Collection) – 9 – 22.00 – fr Bibl Nationale [810]
POESIES GALLIQUES EN VERS FRANCAIS / Ossian (supposed author) – Trans. by P.M.F.L. Baour-Lormian. Paris: P.J. Gayet, 1827. xviii,431p. 5 fiches.(Literature Collection) – 9 – 12.00 – fr Bibl Nationale [810]
POESIES RUSTIQUES / Theuriet, Claude Adhemar, dit Andre – Paris: A. Lemerre, 1920. 117p. 2 fiches. (Literature Collection) – 9 – 6.00 – fr Bibl Nationale [810]
POESIJA NARODNA / Sipovskij, V V – R 2130 1924 – 8 – ne IDC [460]
Poespowijoto, Soetojo *see* PORT ADMINISTRATION IN INDONESIA
Poestion, J C (Josef Calasanz) *see* AUS HELLAS, ROM UND THULE
Poestion, Josef Calasanz *see* LAPPLAENDISCHE MAERCHEN, VOLKSSAGEN, RAETHSEL UND SPRICHWOERTER
POET – Ezhemesiachnyi zhurnal. Spb. 1907-08. B-1540 2 – 8 – ne IDC [460]
THE POET OF GALILEE / Leonard, William Ellery – New York: B.W. Huebsch, 1909. 1 fiche – 9 – us A.T.L.A. [240]
EL POETA / Fernandez de Moratin, Nicolas – 1764 – 1mf – 9 – Pta1,000.00 – 84-7848-145-1 – sp Pentalfa [820]
POETA EN NUEVA YORK. MANUSCRITO / Garcia Lorca, Federico – 2mf – 9 – sp Cultura [810]
POETA LATINI AEVI CAROLINI (MGH ANTIQUITATES 1: 2.BD) – 1884 – Dfl67.00 – ne Slangenburg [240]
EL POETA VERDAGUER Y EL MARQUES DE COMILLAS / Bayle, Constantino – Madrid: Razon y Fe, 1928 – 9 – sp Bibl Santa Ana [440]
POETAE LATINI AEVI CAROLINI (MGH ANTIQUITATES 1: 1.BD) – 1881 – Dfl60.00 – ne Slangenburg [240]
POETAE LATINI AEVI CAROLINI (MGH ANTIQUITATES 1: 3.BD) – 1886-1896 – Dfl77.00 – ne Slangenburg [240]
POETAE LATINI AEVI CAROLINI (MGH ANTIQUITATES 1: 4.BD. 1.TEIL) – 1899 – Dfl42.00 – ne Slangenburg [240]
POETAE LATINI AEVI CAROLINI (MGH ANTIQUITATES 1: 4.BD. 2.UND 3.TEIL) – 1914-1923 – Dfl67.00 – ne Slangenburg [240]
POETES ARMENIENS, BEDROS TOURIAN, GAMAR-KATHIPA, SAIATH-NOVA, GUEVORK DOKOKHIANTZ, MIKAEL NALBANDIANTZ CORENE DE LUSIGNAN / Tcheraz, M – Paris, 1913 – 2mf – ne IDC [460]
LES POETES CONTRE LA GUERRE. ANTHOLOGIE DE LA POESIE FRANCAISE 1914/1919. – Geneva. 1920 – 1 – us Res Libr [810]
LES POETES ILLUSTRES DE XIXE SIECLE: LEMARTINE-VICTOR HUGO: ESQUISSES BIOGRAPHIQUES, NOTICES LITTERAIRES, MORCEAUX CHOISIS, RECUEILS ET ANNOTES. / Andre, Frederic – Montreal: Librairie Saint Joseph, 1885. 02444. (Pre-1900 Canadiana) – 9 – cn C.I.H.M. [810]
POETIC COMMONPLACE BOOKS AND MANUSCRIPTS OF THOMAS GRAY, 1716-1771, FROM PEMBROKE COLLEGE, CAMBRIDGE – Marlborough: Adam Matthew Publications, 1991 – 14r – 1 – $1,700.00 – uk Matthew [810]
POETIC GENESIS: SEBASTIEN MERCIER INTO VICTOR HUGO / Patterson, H Temple – (Studies on Voltaire and the eighteenth century, 11) – Oxford. 1960 – 9 – $36.00 – 0-7294-0066-2 – uk Voltaire [440]
LA POETICA DE ARISTOTELES / Florez Canseco, Casimiro – 1778 – 1mf – 9 – Pta1,000.00 – 84-7848-140-0 – sp Pentalfa [810]
POETICAL LEISURE HOURS AND TORONTONIAN DESCRIPTIONS: IN FRENCH VERSE AND ENGLISH ESSAYS, FOLLOWED BY A TOKEN OF AFFECTION TO A DEPARTED AND FOND SISTER, AND A CURRICULUM VITAE / Coulon, Emile – Toronto: s.n., 1897 (Toronto: Rowsell and Hutchison). 00619. (Pre-1900 Canadiana) – 9 – cn C.I.H.M. [810]
THE POETICAL RECREATIONS OF THE CHAMPION, AND HIS LITERARY CORRESPONDENTS. WITH A SELECTION OF ESSAYS, LITERARY AND CRITICAL, WHICH HAVE APPEARED IN THE CHAMPION NEWSPAPER / Thelwall, John – London: Printed at the Champion Press by and for J. Thelwall, sold by Sir R. Phillips, 1822 – 1 roll – 1 – 1-55879-743-2 – uk Libr Preservation [810]
THE POETICAL WORKS OF CAROLINE BOWLES SOUTHEY / Southey, Caroline Bowles – Edinburgh, London: William Blackwood, 1867 – 1 roll – 1 – 1-55879-178-7 – uk Libr Preservation [810]
THE POETICAL WORKS OF CHARLES MACKAY : NOW FOR THE FIRST TIME COLLECTED; COMPLETE IN ONE VOLUME / Mackay, Charles – London: F. Warne; New York: Scribner, Welford, and Armstrong, 1876 – 1 roll – 1 – 1-55879-398-4 – uk Libr Preservation [810]
THE POETICAL WORKS OF HENRY KIRKE WHITE AND JAMES GRAHAME / White, Henry Kirke & Grahame, James – Edingburgh: J. Nichol; London: James Nisbet; Dublin: W. Robertson, 1856 – 1 roll – 1 – 1-55879-615-0 – uk Libr Preservation [810]
THE POETICAL WORKS OF JOHN AND CHARLES WESLEY / Wesley, John & Wesley, Charles – 1868-72 – 1 – $100.00 – us Presbyterian [810]
THE POETICAL WORKS OF JOHN GODFREY SAXE – New York: Houghton, Mifflin & Co, 1892? – 4mf – 9 – $6.00 – LLMC 91-013 – us L.L.M.C. [810]
THE POETICAL WORKS OF JOHN KEATS / Keats, John – London: Edward Moxon, 1854 – 1 roll – 1 – 1-55879-648-7 – uk Libr Preservation [810]
THE POETICAL WORKS OF MISS SUSANNA BLAMIRE : "THE MUSE OF CUMBERLAND" / Blamire, Susanna – Edinburgh: John Menzies, 1842 – 1 roll – 1 – 1-55879-292-9 – uk Libr Preservation [810]
THE POETICAL WORKS OF MRS. FELICIA HEMANS... / Hemans, Felicia Dorothea Browne; ed by Rossetti, William Michael – London, New York: Ward, Lock & Co., 1873? – 1 roll – 1 – 1-55879-308-9 – uk Libr Preservation [810]
THE POETICAL WORKS OF PERCY BYSSHE SHELLEY : INCLUDING VARIOUS ADDITIONAL PIECES FROM MS. AND OTHER SOURCES / Shelley, Percy Bysshe – London: E. Moxon, 1870 – 2 rolls – 1 – 1-55879-256-2 – uk Libr Preservation [810]
THE POETICAL WORKS OF REGINALD HEBER, LORD BISHOP OF CALCUTTA / Heber, Reginald – London: John Murray, 1842 – 1 roll – 1 – 1-55879-314-3 – uk Libr Preservation [320]
THE POETICAL WORKS OF ROBERT SOUTHEY / Southey, Robert – London: Longman, Orme, Brown, Green, and Longmans, [1837-1838] – 5 rolls – 1 – 1-55879-011-X – uk Libr Preservation [810]
THE POETICAL WORKS OF ROBERT STEPHEN HAWKER... / Hawker, Robert Stephen; ed by Wallis, Alfred – London, New York: John Lane, 1899 – 1 roll – 1 – 1-55879-438-7 – uk Libr Preservation [810]
THE POETICAL WORKS OF SAMUEL TAYLOR COLERIDGE / Coleridge, Samuel Taylor; ed by Campbell, James Dykes – London, New York: Macmillan, 1898 – 1 roll – 1 – 1-55879-449-2 – uk Libr Preservation [810]
THE POETICAL WORKS OF SIR WALTER SCOTT / Scott, Walter – Edinburgh, etc.,: Robert Cadell & Whittaker & Co., 1833-34 – 7 rolls – 1 – 1-55879-489-1 – uk Libr Preservation [810]
THE POETICAL WORKS OF THOMAS CAMPBELL / Campbell, Thomas; ed by Hill, W Alfred – London: George Bell and Sons, 1900 – 1 roll – 1 – 1-55879-279-1 – uk Libr Preservation [810]
THE POETICAL WORKS OF THOMAS HIGGINSON / Higginson, Thomas – 1888. 05566. (Pre-1900 Canadiana) – 9 – cn C.I.H.M. [810]
THE POETICAL WORKS OF THOMAS LOVELL BEDDOES / Beddoes, Thomas Lovell; ed by Gosse, Edmund – London: J.M. Dent and Co., 1890 – 1 roll – 1 – 1-55879-239-2 – uk Libr Preservation [810]
THE POETICAL WORKS OF THOMAS MOORE / Moore, Thomas – London: Longman, Orme, Brown, Green, and Longmans, 1840-1841 – 5 rolls – 1 – 1-55879-047-0 – uk Libr Preservation [810]
POETICES / Scaliger, Julius Caesar – Apud Antonium Vincentium. 1561. B-540 2 – 8 – ne IDC [450]
POETICHESKII OBRAZ U MAIAKOVSKOGO / Papernyi, Z – M. 1961. BR-1482 2 – 8 – ne IDC [460]
POETICHESKOE ISKUSSTVO BLOKA / Nikitina, E & Shuvalov, S – Izd. "Nikitinskie subbotniki". 1926. BR-1460 2 – 8 – ne IDC [460]
POETICHESKOE TVORCHESTVO ANNY AKHMATOVOI / Mochul'skii, K – Russkaia Mysl'. (Sophia). v. 3-4. 1921. BR-3684 2 – 8 – ne IDC [460]
POETICS – v1-13. 1972-84 – 1,5,6,13 – sz Elsevier [410]
POETIKA – Sborniki po teorii poeticheskogo iazyka. Spb. 1919. B-928 2 – 8 – ne IDC [460]
LA POETIQUE / La Mesnardiere, H J P de – 1639 – 9 – fr I.C.S. [410]
POETIQUE FRANCOISE / Marmontel, Jean Francois – 1763 – 9 – fr I.C.S. [440]
DAS POETISCHE GENUS PERSONFIZIERTER SUBSTANTIVA BEI JAMES THOMSON UND EDWARD YOUNG BETRACHTET IM ZUSAMMENHANG DER GESCHICHTLICHEN ENTWICKLUNG VOM MITTEL-ENGLISCHEN BIS AUF LORD TENNYSON / Brandenburg, Werner – Kiel, 1914 – 2mf – DM62.00 – 3-8267-3045-3 – gw Hänsel [420]
DIE POETISCHE STAATS- UND GESCHICHTSAUFFASSUNG FRIEDRICH VON HARDENBERGS (NOVALIS) : STUDIEN ZUR ROMANTISCHEN GESCHICHTSPHILOSOPHIE / Samuel, Richard H – (Includes bibliographical references) – Frankfurt am Main: M Diesterweg, 1925 – 1 – us U.W. Library [430]
DIE POETISCHE THEORIE GOTTSCHED'S UND DER SCHWEIZER / Braitmaier, Friedrich – Tuebingen: H Laupp, 1879 – 1r – 1 – us U.W. Library [430]
POETISCHE UND DRAMATISCHE WERKE = SELECTIONS / Lessing, Gotthold Ephraim – Leipzig: P Reclam jun, [1867?] – 1 – us U.W. Library [800]
POETISCHE WERKE / Voss, Johann Heinrich – Berlin: G Hempel. 3v. [1867] – 1 – us U.W. Library [810]
POET-LORE – v1-58. 1889-1963 – 1,5,6 – us Princeton Micro [410]
POETRY – (Chicago). A magazine of verse. v. 1-66. 1912-1945 – 1 – us Princeton Micro [410]
POETRY – v.1-. 1912- – 1,5,6,9 – us UMI [410]
POETRY AND DRAMA – London. v. 1-2, no. 4. Mar 1913-Dec 1914 – 1 – us NY Public [810]
POETRY AND LETTERS IN EARLY CHRISTIAN GAUL / Chadwick, Nora (Kershaw) – London: Bowes & Bowes, (1955). 342p – 1 – us U.W. Library [450]
THE POETRY AND THE RELIGION OF THE PSALMS / Robertson, James Craigie – (Includes bibliographical references) – Edinburgh:William Blackwood, 1898 – 1mf – 9 – 0-8370-4925-3 – 1985-2925 – us A.T.L.A. [220]
POETRY CANADA REVIEW – (v1-3 1979-82 Can$115.00. v4-13 1982/83-1993 Can$60.00y. 1994 Can$80.00. Con Poesie 1979/80) – Kingston. v1- 1979- – 1 – Price varies – cn Micromedia [410]
POETRY CANADA REVIEW *see* POETRY WINDSOR POESIE
POETRY CHAP-BOOK – New York. v1-11 Oct 1942-Summer 1953 – 1 – us NY Public [800]
POETRY JOURNAL – Boston. v. 1-8. Dec 1912-Mar 1918 – 1 – us NY Public [810]
POETRY NOW – Eureka, CA. v2. 1975 – 1r – 1 – $50.00 – R02224 – us Library Micro [420]
THE POETRY OF ROBERT BURNS / Burns, Robert; ed by Henley, William Ernest & Henderson, Thomas F – Edinburgh: T.C. and E.C. Jack, 1896-97 – 3 rolls – 1 – 1-55879-260-0 – uk Libr Preservation [810]

THE POETRY OF THE PERIOD / Austin, Alfred – London: R. Bentley, 1870 – 1 roll – 1 – 1-55879-930-3 – uk Libr Preservation [810]
POETRY OF TO-DAY – London. v1-2; ns: v1-10. 1919-47 – 3r – 1 – us Ross [420]
POETRY OF TODAY – London. 1919-1920, n.s. 1924-1947 – 1 – us NY Public [800]
THE POETRY PALISADE – Indianola, Iowa. v. 1-2. 1942-1943 – 1 – us NY Public [810]
THE POETRY REVIEW OF AMERICA – Cambridge, Mass. v. 1-2, no. 4. May 1916-Feb 1917 – 1 – us NY Public [410]
Poetry Society of South Carolina *see* MINUTES
POETRY VENTURE – St. Petersburg, FL. v1-3. 1968-70 – 5mf – 9 – $5.00f – us Ross [420]
POETRY VENTURE QUARTERLY ESSAYS – St. Petersburg, FL. v1-2. 1968-70 – 2mf – 9 – $5.00f – us Ross [420]
POETRY WINDSOR POESIE – (Cont by: Poetry Canada Review 1979/80) – Kingston. v1-3. 1974/75-1977/78 – 9 – Can$20.00y – cn Micromedia [410]
POETRY WINDSOR POESIE *see* POETRY CANADA REVIEW
POETS AND NOVELISTS / Smith, George Barnett – London: Smith, Elder, 1875 – 1 roll – 1 – 1-55879-571-5 – uk Libr Preservation [420]
THE POETS AND POETRY OF ENGLAND : IN THE NINETEENTH CENTURY / Griswold, Rufus Wilmot – Philadelphia: Carey & Hart, 3rd ed 1846, c1844 – 1 roll – 1 – 1-55879-857-9 – uk Libr Preservation [420]
POETS OF THE YOUNGER GENERATION / Archer, William – London, New York: John Lane, The Bodley Head, 1902 – 1 roll – 1 – 1-55879-203-1 – uk Libr Preservation [420]
POETY I POETESSY / Aikhenvald, Iu – M. 1922. BR-1960 2 – 8 – ne IDC [460]
POETY I VREMIA. SOV. PISATEL / Antokol'skii, P – M. 1957. BR-3248 2 – 8 – ne IDC [460]
POETY-SIMVOLISTY VO FRANTSII "VESTNIK EVROPY" / Vengerova, Z – v. 9. 1892. BR-3305 2 – 8 – ne IDC [440]
Poetzl, Eduard *see*
– IN SPIRITUS AUFBEWAHRT
– UEBER DEN UMGANG MIT WIENERN
O POEZII FUTURIZMA / Chizhevskii, D – Novyi Zhurnal 73. 1963. BR-3591 2 – 8 – ne IDC [460]
O POEZII GEORGIIA IVANOVA / Markov, V – Opyty, VIII. New York. 1957. BR-3680 2 – 8 – ne IDC [460]
POEZIIA / Pasternak, B – Izbrannoe. Frankfurt a M. 1960. BR-1016 2 – 8 – ne IDC [460]
POEZIIA BURZHUAZNOGO UPADKA / Stepanov, N – Istoriia russkoi literatury. Akademiia Nauk SSSR. v. 10. M., L. 1954. BR-3582 2 – 8 – ne IDC [460]
POEZIIA BURZHUAZNOGO UPADKA / Volkov, A – Akmeizm. Istoriia russkoi literatury. v. 10. M., L. 1954. BR-3713 2 – 8 – ne IDC [460]
POEZIIA I POETIKA / Vygodskii, D – v. 1. Letopis'. 1917. BR-3714 2 – 8 – ne IDC [460]
POEZIIA PERVYKH LET REVOLIUTSII 1917-1920 / Men'sutin, A & Siniavskii, A – M. 1964. BR-1428 2 – 8 – ne IDC [460]
POEZIIA RUSSKOGO IMPERIALIZMA / Volkov, A – M. 1935. Index. BR-2210 – 8 – ne IDC [460]
POEZIIA SLOVA / Belyi, A – Epokha. Berlin. 1922. BR-587 2 – 8 – ne IDC [460]
POEZIIA VALERIIA BRIUSOVA / Maksimov, D – L. 1940. BR-1406 2 – 8 – ne IDC [460]
POEZOANTRAKT. PIATAIA KNIGA POEZ / Severianin, I – M. 1915. BR-1036 2 – 8 – ne IDC [460]
POEZYE = POETRY / Goodelman, E DH – (Monthly) – Bronx, NY, 1919 – 1r – Can$25.00 – cn Can Microfilming [073]
POEZYE / Slowacki, J – v. 1-3. Paris. 1832-33. BR-8020 2 – 8 – ne IDC [460]
Poffadas, Francisco de *see* VIA Y VIRTUDES DEL VENERABLE...PADRE CHRISTOBAL DE SANTA CATHALINA
Poggendorff, J C *see* BIOGRAPHISCH-LITERARISCHES HANDWOERTERBUCH ZUR GESCHICHTE DER EXACTEN WISSENSCHAFTEN
Poggi, Alfredo *see* SOCILISMO E CULTURA
POGLAD NA WROST LUDNOSCI ZIEM POLSKICH W WIEKU 19-TYM / Buzek, Jozef – Krakow, 1915 – 1r – 1 – us I.H.R.C. [947]
Pogodin, M P *see*
– ALEKSEI PETROVICH ERMOLOV
– BOR'BA NE NA ZHIVOT, A NA SMERT', S NOVYMI ISTORICHESKIMI ERESIAMI
– CHERNAIA NEMOCH'
– DREVNIAIA RUSSKAIA ISTORIIA DO MONGOL'SKAGO IGA
– DREVNIIA RUSSKIIA KNIAZHESTVA S 1054 PO 1240 GOD
– ISTOCHNIKI DLIA UDEL'NAGO PERIODA RUSSKOI ISTORII
– ISTORICHESKIE AFORIZMY
– ISTORIIA V LICHAKH O TSARE BORISE FEODOROVICHE GODUNOVE
– ISTORIKO POLITICHESKIE PIS'MA I ZAPISKI V PRODOLZHENII KRYMSKOI VOINY, 1853-1856
– ISTORIKO-KRITICHESKIE OTRYVKI
– IZSLEDOVANIIA, ZAMECHANIIA I LEKTSII O RUSSKOI ISTORII
– KIRILLO-MEFODIEVSKII SBORNIK
– KRATKOE NACHERTANIE RUSSKOI ISTORII
– LEKTSII PO GERENU O POLITIKE, SVIAZI I TORGOVLE GLAVNYKH NARODOV DREVNIAGO MIRA
– MARFA POSADNITSA NOVGORODSKAIA
– NACHERTANIE RUSSKOI ISTORII
– NIKOLAI MIKHAILOVICH KARAMZIN, PO EGO SOCHINENIIAN, PIS'MAM I OTZYVAM SOVREMENNIKOV
– NORMANSKII PERIOD RUSSKOI ISTORII
– OFFENER BRIEF AN HERRN PROFESSOR SCHIRREN UEBER DESSEN BUCH "LIVLAENDISCHE ANTWORT VON PROF. POGODIN"
– OSTZEISKII VOPROS
– PETR. I. TRAGEDIIA V 5-TI DEISTVIIAKH V STIKHAKH
– PIS' MA K M.A. MAKSIMOVICHU
– PIS'MA M.P. POGODINA, S.P. SHEVYZEVA I M.A. MAKSIMOVICHA K KNIAZIU P.A. VIAZEMSKOMU, 1825-1874
– POL'SKII VOPROS
– POVESTI
– O PROIZKHOZDENII RUSI
– PSKOV (IZ DOROZHNYKH ZAMETOK)
– RECHI, PROIZNESENNYIA. V TORZHESTVENNYKH I PROCHIKH SOBRANIIAKH, 1830-1872
– RUSSKII ISTORICHESKII AL'BOM
– SEMNADTSAT' PERVYKH LET V ZHIZNI IMPERATORA PETRA VELIKAGO, 1672-1689
– SOBRANIE DOKUMENTOV PO DELU CAREVICA ALEKSEJA
– SOBRANIE STATEI, PISEM I RECHEI PO POVODU SLAVIANSKAGO VOPROSA
– SOCHINENIIA
– TSAREVICH ALEKSEI PETROVICH PO SVIDETEL'STVAM' VNOV' OTKRYTYM
Pogorelov, V *see* CHUDOVSKAIA PSALTYR'
Pogrebetskii, A I *see* DENEZHNOE OBRASHCHENIE I DENEZHNYE ZNAKI DAL'NEGO VOSTOKA ZA PERIOD VOINY I REVOLIUTSII (1914-1924)
POGRUND JUDGEMENT AND APPEAL – (Case history. Includes evidence in Van Schalkwyk trial) – 1 reel – 1 – sa Microfile [960]
POHJOLA – Haparanda, Sweden. 1896-98 – 1 reel – 1 – sw Kungliga [072]
POHJOLAN SANOMAT – Calumet, Michigan. 22 Jun 1957-11 Apr 1959. 1 reel – 1 – us I.H.R.C. [071]
POHJOLAN SANOMIA – Haparanda, Sweden. 1886-88 – 1 reel – 1 – sw Kungliga [072]
Pohl, Ernst *see* DIE LOHN- UND WIRTSCHAFTSVERHALTNISSE IN MASUREN IN DEN LETZTEN JAHRZEHNTEN
Pohl, J B E *see*
– PLANTARUM BRASILIAE ICONES ET DESCRIPTIONES
– TENTAMEN FLORAE BOHEMIAE
Pohlenz, M *see* KLEMENS VON ALEXANDREIA UND SEIN HELLENISCHES CHRISTENTUM
POHNPEI – PONAPE DISTRICT CODE, 1978 : PUBLIC LAW NO 6-130; AS AMENDED BY P.L. NO 7-124, WITH AMENDMENTS BY THE HIGH COMMISSIONER OF THE TRUST TERRITORY OF THE PACIFIC ISLANDS THRU JANUARY 22 1979 / Federated States of Micronesia – Saipan: Office of the High Commissioner, 1979 – 1mf – 9 – $1.50 – LLMC 82-100H Title 5 – us L.L.M.C. [324]
THE POHPEI CONSTITUTION AND THE LEGISLATURE RULES OF ORDER, 1984 / Federated States of Micronesia – (In Pohnpeian and English language versions) – Agana, Guam: Star Press Publ Inc, Jan 1989 – 4mf – 9 – $6.00 – LLMC 82-100H Title 11 – us L.L.M.C. [324]
POIA : OPERA IN 3 ACTS / Nevin, AF & Hartley, R – (Vocal score in English and German) – Berlin: Furstner, 1909 – 1 – us Sibley [780]
LES POIDS MESURES ET MONNAIES DES MERS DU SUD AUX XVI ET XVIIE SIECLES / Ferrand, G – Paris. 1921. B-773 2 – 8 – ne IDC [338]
Poille, G *see* LE GRAND DICTIONNAIRE FRANCOIS-LATIN
Poincelot, Raymond P *see* JOURNAL OF SUSTAINABLE AGRICULTURE
LE POINT – 1976- – 3r per y – 1 – inquire – us Ross [072]
LE POINT – Colmar, 1936-62 – 2r – 1 – £115.00 – uk Chadwyck [760]
LE POINT – Dolbeau, jan 1976-26 dec 1979 – 5r – 1 – Can$75.00 – cn Can Microfilming [072]
LE POINT – Ville LaSalle et Ville St-Pierre, Canada. 27 aut 1975 – 1r – 1 – Can$25.00 – cn Can Microfilming [072]
POINT – (Chicago, Ill.) v1 n2-n5; n7; n9-n11; n13-n14 – us A.J.P.C. [270]
POINT – France. 1976-1995 – 3 times per yr – 6 – F2,600.00 – sz Infoprint [944]
POINT – Toledo, Ohio. 1978-79 – 1r – 1 – $32.50r – us Archival [071]
POINT AND SHORELAND – Toledo, Ohio. 1979-80 – 1r – 1 – $32.50r – us Archival [071]
POINT AND SHORELAND JOURNAL – Toledo, Ohio. 1980- – 1r – 1 – $32.50r – us Archival [071]
POINT ARENA RECORD – Point Arena, CA. 1877-1930 – 4r – 1 – $200.00 – B03632 – us Library Micro [071]
POINT DE MIRE – Montreal: Solibec. v1-3. 1970-72. SEM35P140 – 1r – 1 – Can$66.00 – cn Bibl Nat [073]
POINT DE MIRE : REVUE POLITIQUE QUEBECOISE – (Becomes: Espace et Vie) – Montreal. v1 n1. fev 1970-v3 n14. mai 1972 – 2r – 1 – cn Can Microfilming [072]
LE POINT DU JOUR – ou Resultat de ce qui s'est passe la veille a l'Assemblee nationale. Par Barere. Paris. juin 1789-oct 1791 – 1 – fr A.C.R.P.P. [073]
POINT PLACE HERALD – Toledo, Ohio. 1954-81 – 6r – 1 – $32.50r – us Archival [071]
POINT PLEASANT BAPTIST CHURCH. BUCHANAN, TENNESSEE : CHURCH RECORDS – 1843-54 – 1 – 6.48 – us Baptist [240]
POINT REYES LIGHT – (Also known as: Synanon Expose Feb 1978-May 1979) – Point Reyes Station, CA. Jul 1976- – 21+ r – 1,5,9 BC02639 – $1,050.00 ($90.00y) – us Library Micro [071]
POINT RICHMOND PROGRESS – Richmond, CA. 1927; 1929; 1933-42 – 5r – 1 – $250.00 – B02696 – us Library Micro [071]
LE POINT SUR LE VIRAGE TECHNOLOGIQUE – Quebec: Ministere, 1983. SEM105P487 – 1mf – 9 – Can$2.25 – cn Bibl Nat [600]
LE POINT (VERSION NAT.) – (Also available on CD-ROM) – 1976-1995 – 3r per yr – 5,6 – Sfr642.00 – sz Infoprint [072]
POINTE-CLAIRE RECORD – (Includes: Lakeshore Press Record 16 mai 1925. Lakeshore Press 2 jan 1926-v18 n8. 12 avr 1940. Cont by: The Lakeshore News) – Pointe-Claire, Quebec. v1 n?. 11 dec 1924 – 2r – 1 – Can$100.00 – cn Can Microfilming [072]
POINTED BARK CANOES OF THE KUTENAI AND AMUR / Mason, Otis Tufton – BN 312 2. 1899 – 8 – ne IDC [306]
THE POINTER – Chicago. Ill. 1907-1934; 1936-1941; 1944; 1945-1946; 1951-1954; 1959-1961; 1966-1968 – 1 – us UMI [071]
POINTERS BEING A BRIEF DIGEST OF DEBT, INTEREST, USURY, MORTGAGE AND FORECLOSURE, WITH COMMENTS AND CHAPTER ON EQUITY / Hart, H A – Winfield, KS: Vincent, 1889. 76p. LL-336 – 1 – us L of C Photodup [340]
Pointier, J P *see* MOLLUSQUE VECTEUR ET SCHISTOSOMOSE INTESTINALE EN GUADELOUPE
POINTS DE VENTE – (Also available on CD-ROM) – 1988-1995 – 3r per y – 5,6 – Sfr775.00 – sz Infoprint [072]
POINTS DE VUE / ed by Chaput-Rolland, Solange et al – Montreal, Canada. sep 1955-oct 1961 – 2r – 1 – Can$55.00r – cn Can Microfilming [072]
Poiret, J L M *see*
– ENCYCLOPEDIE METHODIQUE BOTANIQUE
– HISTOIRE PHILOSOPHIQUE, LITTERAIRE, ECONOMIQUE DES PLANTES DE L'EUROPE
– TABLEAU ENCYCLOPEDIQUE ET METHODIQUE DES TROIS REGNES DE LA NATURE BOTANIQUE
– VOYAGE EN BARBARIE, OU LETTRES ECRITES DE L'ANCIENNE NUMIDIE PENDANT 1785 ET 1786
Poirier, Jules *see*
– CAMPAGNE DU DAHOMEY 1892-1894
– DE L'OUBANGHI A FACHODA
Poirier, O *see* L'ASBESTOS
Poirier, Osias *see* LE JOURNAL DE RICHMOND
Poirot, J L *see* PERSON-ENVIRONMENT INTERACTION
Poirters, Adrianus *see*
– DEN ALDERHEIJLICHSTEN NAEM VOOR EEN NIEUJAER-GIFT
– HET DUYFKEN IN DE STEEN-ROTSE DAT IS, EENE MEDE-LYDENDE SIELE OP DE BITTERE PASSIC JESU CHRISTI MEDITERENDE GEMAECKT DOOR EENEN PRIESTER DER SOCIETEYT JESU 7. DRUCK RYCKER VAN STOFFE, VAN BEELDEN, EN VAN POESIE
– HET DUYFKEN IN DE STEEN-ROTSE DAT IS, EENE MEDE-LYDENDE ZIELE, OP DE BITTERE PASSIE JESU CHRISTI MEDITERENDE
– HET HEYLICH HERTE VER-EERT AEN ALLE GODT-VRUGHTIGHE HERTEN VOOR EEN NIEU-IAER
– HEYLIGH HOF VANDEN KEYSER THEODOSIUS VERCIERT MET SINEBEELDEN, RYMDICHTEN, EN SEDELEERINGEN
– HET MASKER VAN DE WERELD
– HET MASKER VAN DE WERELD, AFGETROKKEN
– HET MASKER VANDE WERELDT AFGETROCKEN
– HET MASKER VANDE WERELDT AFGETROCKEN DOOR P. ADRIANUS POIRTERS S.I.
– HET MASKER VANDE WERELDT AFGHETROCKEN DOOR P. ADRIANUS POIRTERS S.I.
– NIEUWE AFBELDINGHE VAN DE VIER UYTERSTEN BESCHREVEN IN HET LATYN DOOR DEN EERWEERDIGHEN PATER GUILLIELMUS STANIHURSTUS PRIESTER DER SOCIETEYT IESU
– YDELHEYD DES WERELDS VERCIERT MET ZINNEBEELDEN, RYM-DIGHTEN EN ZEDE-LEERINGEN
– YDELHEYT DES WERELTS
POISINDEX SYSTEM – Poison identification and treatment system for over 650,000 domestic and foreign substances. Republished quarterly – 9 – us Micromedex [616]
POISONS DE FLECHES ET POISONS D'EPREUVE / Perrot & Vogt – 8032 1. 1913 – 9 – ne IDC [610]
Poisson *see* MEMOIRE SUR LA PROPORTION DES NAISSANCES DES FILLES ET DES GARCONS
Poisson, Albert *see* HISTOIRE DE L'ALCHIMIE: 19E SIECLE: NICHOLAS FLAMEL
Poisson, C *see* METEOROLOGIE DE MADAGASCAR
Poisson, Leonard *see* NOUVELLE METHODE..
Poisson, R *see* ALFABET NOUVEAU DE LA VREE ET PURE ORTOGRAFE FRANSOIZE
POISSONS, CATALOGUE DES PRINCIPALES ESPECES DE POISSONS / Valenciennes, M – 2627 2. v. 5, pt. 2. 1847 – 8 – ne IDC [590]
POISSONS DES COTES DU LIBAN (MEDITERRANEE ORIENTALE): BIOLOGIE ET PECHE / Mouneimne, N – Paris. 1978. 490p – 9 – F130.00 – fr Ethnologie [590]
POISSONS. ZOOLOGIE. VOYAGE. 1826-1829 / Quoy, J R C & Quoy, G – 2607 2. v. 3. 1834 – 8 – ne IDC [590]
Poiteau, P A *see* FLORE PARISIENNE
Poiters, A *see* HET MASKER VANDE WERELDT AFGETROCKEN
Poitevin, C *see* LES SPOLIATIONS COLONIALES EN TUNISIE
Poitevin, P *see* NOUVEAU DICTIONNAIRE UNIVERSEL DE LA LANGUE FRANCAISE
Poitou *see* ARCHIVES HISTORIQUES DU POITOU
DER POJAZ / Franzos, Karl Emil – 4e. Auf. Stuttgart und Berlin. 1905 – 1 – us Res Libr [830]
POKER – Toronto. 1858-59 – 1 – 45.00 – cn McLaren [971]

O POKLONENII BOGO OTTSTU V" VUKHE I ISTINE = ON THE WORSHIP OF GOD THE FATHER IN SPIRIT AND TRUTH / Il'in, Valilii – Kursk, 1909, part 1 – 1r – 1 – $5.00 – us Baptist [240]

POKOK DASAR CONTRACT BRIDGE. MENURUT POINT COUNT METHOD DARI CHARLES H. GOREN / Tan, Eng Kie – SE 5153 1. 1961 – 9 – ne IDC [790]

POKOK-POKOK HUKUM PERNIAGAAN / Tirtaamidjaja, Husein – SE 4321 1. 1962 – 9 – ne IDC [950]

POKROK – Clarkson, NE. -w. 29 Sep 1904-17 Jun 1909. In Bohemian – 1 – us NE Hist [071]

POKROK : TRIWEEKLY CZECH LANGUAGE FREE THINKER NEWSPAPER – Cleveland, Oh. 15 Aug 1874-11 Nov 1876 – 1r – 1 – us Western Res [071]

POKROK ZAPADU – Omaha, NE. -w. Sep 1871; Mar 1872; May 1875-Apr 1880; Nov 1881-Apr 1883; Jul 1891-Dec 1920 – 1 – us NE Hist [071]

Pokrovksii, M M *see* BOR'BA KLASSOV I PARTII VO VTOROI GOSUDARSTVENNOI DUME

Pokrovskii, Iosif Alekseevich *see* ISTORIIA RIMSKOGO PRAVA

Pokrovskii, Ivan Mikhailovich *see* RUSSKIIA EPARKHII V 16-19 VV, IKH OTKRYTIE, SOSTAV I PREDIELY

Pokrovskii, Mikhail N *see* HISTORY OF RUSSIA, FROM EARLIEST TIMES TO THE RISE OF COMMERCIAL CAPITALISM

Pokrovskii, MN et al *see* INTELLIGENTSIIA I REVOLIUTSIIA

Pokrovskii, Serafim Aleksandrovich *see* POLITICHESKIE I PRAVOVYE VZGLIADY S. E. DESNITSKOGO

Pokrovskij, M N *see* OCERK ISTORII RUSSKOJ KUL'TURY

Pokrovskogo et al *see* INTELLIGENTSIIA I REVOLIUTSIIA

POKRYVALO IZIDY / Chulkov, G I – Kriticheskie Ocherki. (Izd. Zolotoe ryno). M. 1909. BR-2040 2 – 8 – ne IDC [460]

POKUSHENIE NA V.I. LENINA V MOSKVE 30-GO AVGUSTA 1918 GODA : PO LICHNYM VOSPOMINANIIAM / Bonch-Bruevich, Vladimir Dmitrievich – Moskva: Izd. Komissii po uluchshenii u zhizni dete i pri VT SIK i Koopratívnogo izd-va "Zhizn i znanie", 1924 – 1 – CSUX88-B9275 – us Hoover Inst Photo [947]

POLA BIMBINGAN KEPARIWISA TAAN DAERAH CHUSUS IBUKOTA DJAKARTA / Indonesia – D-1004/1 – 9 – ne IDC [950]

POLA PEMBANGUNAN DAERAH BAGIAN / Indonesia – 1964-69.D-1007/1 – 9 – ne IDC [950]

POLA PEMBANGUNAN DAERAH KABUPATEN PURWOREDJO / Indonesia – 1964-68.D-1006/1 – 9 – ne IDC [950]

POLA PEMBANGUNAN PROPINSI DJAWA-TENGAH / Indonesia – 1963-68.7v. D-1002/1 – 9 – ne IDC [950]

[POLACCA] ARIA CONSOLA AMATI BENE. CAVATA NEL 'OPERA LA COSA RARA / Viotti, Giovanni B – Ms, 1791 – 1 – us Sibley [780]

POLACY W AMERYCE / Iciek, X.A – Poznan, 1921 – 1r – 1 – us I.H.R.C. [947]

Polak, GI *see* HOTAM TOKHNIT

Polak, J E *see* HET JOODSCH IN NEDERLAND

Polak, Jacques Jacobus *see* THE NATIONAL INCOME OF THE NETHERLANDS INDIES, 1921-1939. SE-11,679/1

Polanco, J A de *see* MONUMENTA HISTORICA SOCIETATIS JESU

POLAND : ROCZNIK STATYSTYCZNY 1920/21-1965 / Poland. Glowny Urzad Statystyczny – (Coll title: European Official Statistical Serials, 1841-1984) – 141mf – 9 – £890.00 – uk Chadwyck [947]

Poland *see*
- DZIENNIK USTAV POLSKIEJ RZECZYPOSPOLITEJ LUDOWEJ
- MONITOR POLSKI
- SPRAWOZDANIE

Poland. (1918-). Senat *see* SPRAWOZDANIE STENOGRAFICZNE

Poland. Centralny Urzad Planowania *see*
- POLISH NATIONAL ECONOMIC PLAN JANUARY 1, 1946 DECEMBER 31, 1949
- RESOLUTION DU CONSEIL NATIONAL (K.R.N.) DU 21 SEPTEMBRE 1946 CONCERNANT LE PLAN DE RECONSTRUCTION ECONOMIQUE
- UCHWALA KRAJOWEJ RADY NARODOWEJ Z DNIA 21.9.1946 R. W SPRAWIE PLANU ODBUDOWY GOSPODARCZEJ

Poland. Glowny Urzad Statystyczny *see* POLAND

POLAND. HER PEOPLE, HISTORY, INDUSTRIES, FINANCE, SCIENCE / ed by Piltz, E & Woroniecki, E & Zaleski, S S & Perlowski, J – London. 1919. BR-5443 2 – 8 – ne IDC [943]

Poland. Instytut Geologiczny *see* PRACE POLSKIOGO INSTYTUTU GEOLOGICZNEGO

Poland, Jocelyn *see* INDEX TO OBITUARIES AND DEATH NOTICES IN THE NEW ZEALAND MEDICAL JOURNAL 1886-FEBRUARY 1981

Poland, Maine. First Free Will Baptist Church *see* RECORDS

POLAND, OHIO, TAXES, MS V.F.O. – (List of taxable property in the township taken May 15 1805) – 1805 – 1r – 1 – us Western Res [978]

POLARIS – Portland OR. Mar 25 Apr 1 1883, Apr 15 July 22 29 1883 – 1 – us U.O. Library [071]

POLARIZED LAW / Baty, T – London, 1914 – 3mf – 9 – ILM-426/1 – ne IDC [340]

POLARIZED LAW : THREE LECTURES ON CONFLICTS OF LAW,... / Baty, T – London, 1914 – 3mf – 9 – ILM-718/1 – ne IDC [340]

DIE POLARVOELKER / Byhan, A – BN-153 1909 – 8 – ne IDC [306]

POLATA KNIGOPIS'NAJA – (Supplemented: 1984-1989. V.10-24. 17mf) – Nijmegen, 1978-1989. v1-24 – 29mf – 9 – R-17130/1 – ne IDC [947]

Polavieja, Marques de *see* HERNANDO CORTES (ESTUDIO DE UN CARACTER)

DOS POLCKER LEBEN = LIFE – (In Yiddish) – Plock, PL. v1 no1 1 Aug 1937-no2 Sep 1937 – 1r – 1 – $25.00 – cn Can Microfilming [072]

POLEMIQUES ET DOCUMENTS TOUCHANT LE NORD-OUEST ET L'EXECUTION DE LOUIS RIEL / Riel, Louis – Montreal: L'Etendard, 1886. SEM35P76 – 1r – 1 – Can$15.00 – cn Bibl Nat [920]

POLEMISCHE UND APOLOGETISCHE LITERATUR IN ARABISCHER SPRACHE, ZWISCHEN MUSLIMEN, CHRISTEN UND JUDEN... / Steinschneider, M – Leipzig, 1877 – 5mf – ne IDC [270]

DIE POLEMISCHEN SCHRIFTEN DES GEORG NIGRINUS GEGEN JOHANN NAS : EIN BEITRAG ZUR GESCHICHTE DER KONFESSIONELLEN POLEMISCHEN LITERATUR IM ZEITALTER DER GEGENREFORMATION / Venn, Arthur – Heidelberg, 1931 – 1mf – 9 – DM48.00 – 3-89349-787-0 – gw Hänsel [240]

Polemologisch Instituut Rijksunivers. Groningen *see* NIEUWE LITERATUUR OVER OORLOG EN VREDE

DIE POLEN IM RHEINISCH-WESTFALISCHEN STEINKOHLENBEZIRKE – Munchen 1901 – 1 – DM30.00 – gw Mikro Press [943]

POLENS PALAEONTOLOGIE / Pusch, G G – 2539 2. 1837 – 8 – ne IDC [560]

Polenz, Wilhelm von *see*
- GLUECKLICHE MENSCHEN
- LIEBE IST EWIG

POLES IN CANADA – v. 1. 1938-43 – 1 – 65.00 – cn McLaren [305]

POLES OF CLEVELAND MANUSCRIPT, MS 3552 – 1941 – 1 reel – 1 – us Western Res [978]

POLES'E / Penkina, Z M – Bibliograficheskie materialy. Spb. 1883. BR-7206 2 – 8 – ne IDC [010]

POLESER SZTYME = SZTYME – (In Yiddish) – Brzesc, PL. v1 no13 14 Dec 1923-v4 no-17 Feb 1926 – 1r – 1 – $25.00 – cn Can Microfilming [072]

POLESER VOKHENBLAT = POLESER VOICE – (In Yiddish) – Brzesc, PL. no1 24 Apr 1925-no36 25 Dec 1925 – 1r – 1 – $35.00 – cn Can Microfilming [072]

Polevitskii, K A *see* PROKATNYE PUNKTY SEL'SKOKHOZIAISTVENNYKH MASHIN I ORUDII

POLEVO I TSENTR "PLAMIA" / Rein, Rikard Petrovich – Moskva: Izdvo politkatorzhan, 1927 – 1 – CSUX88-B1542 – us Hoover Inst Photo [947]

Polevoi, Petr *see* RUSSIAN FAIRY TALES FROM THE SKAZKI OF POLEVOI

Polevoi, S A *see* PERIODICHESKAIA PECHAT' V KITIAE

POLGARIJOGI HATAROZATOK TARA, A KIR. KURIANAK HIVATALOS KIADVANYA. / Hungary. Kuria – Budapest. On film: v1-8; 1918-38. LL-0264 – 1 – us L of C Photodup [340]

Polge, Abbe *see* DEMONSTRATION PHILOSOPHIQUE DU CATHOLICISME

POLGODA V ZAKLI UCHENII : DNEVNIK 1920-1921 / Davydova, Natalia – Berlin: N. Davydova, 1923 – 1 – CSUX88-B4578 – us Hoover Inst Photo [920]

Poli, G S *see* TESTACEA UTRIUSQUE SICILIAE EORUMQUE HISTORIA ET ANATOME

Polianin, A *see* V POISKAKH PUTI ISKUSSTVA

Polianskaia, L *see*
- ARKHIVNYI FOND GLAVNOGO UPRAVLENIIA PO DELAM PECHATI. OBZOR
- OBZOR FONDA TSENTRAL'NOGO KOMITETA TSENZURY INOSTRANNOI

POLIANTEIA-COMEMORATIVA DAS BODAS DE OURO SACERDOTAIS... – Manaus, Amazonas. 2 Jul 1949 – 1,5,6 – bl Biblioteca [072]

POLIARNAIA ZVEZDA – Ezhemesiachnyi literaturnoistoricheskii zhurnal. v. 1-6. Spb. 1881. B-1835 2 – 8 – ne IDC [073]

POLIARNAIA ZVEZDA – Ezhenedel'noe obshchestvennopoliticheskoe i kul'turno-filosofoskoe izd. v. 1-14. Spb. 1905-06. Cont. as: Svoboda i kultura. v. 1-8. Spb. 1906. B-1442 2 – 8 – ne IDC [100]

POLIBILION – Ezhenedel'nyi illiustrirovannyi zhurnal, posviashchennyi knizhnomu, zhurnal'nomu i pechatnomy delu. M. 1903. Available: 1903 (1). BR-4329 2 – 8 – ne IDC [073]

LA POLICE – Montreal, Canada. 26 sep 1865-v1 n3. 30 sep 1865 – 1r – 1 – Can$25.00 – cn Can Microfilming [072]

POLICE CHIEF – v.46-. 1953- – 1,5,6,9 – us UMI [360]

POLICE CHIEFS NEWSLETTER – 1934-47 – 1,5,6,9 – us UMI [360]

A POLICE CODE, AND MANUAL OF THE CRIMINAL LAW. 3D ED / Vincent, Charles Edward Howard – London, Cassell, Petter, Galpin 1881. 454 p. LL-132 – 1 – us L of C Photodup [340]

POLICE DOCKET / Caldwell. Kansas – 1879-96 – 1 – us KS Hist [025]

POLICE GAZETTE – Montreal, Canada. v1 n2. 9 nov 1924-v1 n9. 28 dec 1924 – 1r – 1 – Can$30.00 – cn Can Microfilming [072]

THE POLICE GAZETTE – (Part 1: The Police Gazette, 1866-78, 1882-97, 1899-1900 from the Cambridgeshire Police Archives) – Marlborough: Adam Matthews Publications, 1993 – 12r – 1 – $1,450.00 – uk Matthew [360]

POLICE JOURNAL – Lincoln, NE. -w. Jun-Dec 1897, scattered issues missing; Jan 1898-Oct 1899 – 1 – us NE Hist [071]

POLICE MAGAZINE – v.1-. 1978- – 1,5,6,9 – us UMI [073]

POLICE OFFICER-EMPLOYEE RIGHTS LAW BULLETIN – Jun 1984- – 1,5,6,9 – us UMI [073]

THE POLICE POWER OF THE STATE AND DECISIONS THEREON AS ILLUSTRATING THE DEVELOPMENT AND VALUE OF CASE LAW / Russell, Alfred – Chicago: Callaghan, 1900. 204p. LL-1237 – 1 – us L of C Photodup [340]

POLICE RESEARCH (SLIM) / U.S. National Institute of Justice NCJRS – Full-text copies of 437 documents with printed indexes – 9 – $285.00 – us N.C.J.R.S. [360]

POLICE & SECURITY BULLETIN – v1-19. 1969-88.-m – 1 – 36.00y – us UMI [360]

POLICE STUDIES – v. 1-. 1978- – 1,5,6,9 – us UMI [360]

THE POLICEMAN'S POCKET LAWBOOK / McTigue, Thomas – Boston: Fort Hill Press 1922. 99 2p. LL-572 – 1 – us L of C Photodup [360]

POLICHINELLE – Montreal, Canada. 22 jan 1858 – 1r – 1 – Can$25.00 – cn Can Microfilming [072]

O POLICHINELLO – Sao Paulo, 16 Apr-31 Dec 1876 – 1,5,6 – bl Biblioteca [072]

POLICIES AND PROVISIONS FOR ADAPTED PHYSICAL EDUCATION IN THE ORDINARY SCHOOL: A CROSS-CULTURAL COMPARISON BETWEEN THE UNITED STATES OF AMERICA AND ENGLAND AND WALES / Cutforth, Nicholas J – 1983 – 2mf – 9 – $8.00 – us Microform Publ [790]

POLICING AND SOCIETY : AN INTERNATIONAL JOURNAL OF RESEARCH AND POLICY / ed by Morgan, Rod & Reiner, Robert – 9,5,1 – us Harwood [350]

POLICY ANALYSIS – v1- 1975- 1; v4- 1978- – us UMI [073]

POLICY AND STRATEGY = POLITICA Y ESTRATEGIA : WITHOUT ATTACKING ANYBODY, I OFFER MY CRITICISM / Peron, Juan Domingo – Buenos Aires: [s.n.], 1951 – 1 – CSUXADQ4388-B – us Hoover Inst Photo [320]

POLICY IN PALESTINE / Great Britain. Colonial Office – Despatch dated 23 Dec 1937 from the Secretary State for the Colonies to the High Commissioner for Palestine. London. Jan 1938. BJ-28-83 1 – 9 – ne IDC [956]

A POLICY OF FREE EXCHANGE / ed by Mackay, Thomas – 1894. With his essay: The Interest of the Working Class in Free Exchange. 1 fiche (29x) – 9 – 1.00f – at Libertarian Micro [320]

POLICY OF PUBLIC EDUCATION : OFFICIAL DOCUMENT 1971(3) / Nigeria. East Central State. Ministry of Education – Enugu, 1971 – 1mf – 9 – DE-103/1 – ne IDC [370]

THE POLICY OF SELF HELP: SUGGESTIONS TOWARDS THE CONSOLIDATION OF THE EMPIRE AND THE DEFENCE OF ITS INDUSTRIES AND COMMERCE: TWO LETTERS / Ecroyd, William Farrer – London: Hamilton, Adams, 1879. 05215. (Pre-1900 Canadiana) – 9 – cn C.I.H.M. [971]

THE POLICY OF THE TURKISH EMPIRE – London, 1597 – 1mf – 9 – H-8217/1 – ne IDC [956]

THE POLICY OF THE UNIONIST ASSOCIATION OF CEYLON – [n.p.], 1927 – us Res Libr [360]

POLICY OF THE U.S. TOWARD MARITIME COMMERCE IN WAR : WITH DOCUMENTS, 1776-1918 / Savage, Carlton – Washington: GPO. 2v. 1919 (all publ) – 16mf – 9 – $24.00 – LLMC 80-913 – us L.L.M.C. [340]

POLICY, PLANNING AND MANAGEMENT IN TECHNICAL AND VOCATIONAL EDUCATION : A COMPARATIVE STUDY – 1984 – 208p – 9 – 92-3-102169-9 – fr UNESCO [370]

POLICY PLANNING STAFF NUMBERED PAPERS, 1-63, 1947-49 / U.S. Department of State – RG 59. M1171. 71 fiches – 9 – us Nat'l Archives [324]

POLICY REPORTS – v1,no.1-3. Feb-Jun 1985 – 9 – 1.00f – at Libertarian Micro [335]

POLICY REVIEW – v. 1-. 1977- – 1,5,6,9 – us UMI [073]

POLICY REVIEW AND OUTLOOK – (No issues publ in 1981 or 1989) – Toronto, 1974-94 – 9 – Can$20.00y – cn Micromedia [350]

POLICY SCIENCES – v1-17. 1970-84 – 1,5,6,13 – sz Elsevier [300]

POLICY STUDIES JOURNAL – (v.8-. 1979- 5,6,9) – v.1-. 1972- – 1 – us UMI [073]

POLICY STUDIES REVIEW – v.1-. 1981- – 1,5,6,9 – us UMI [320]

Polidori, John William *see* THE DIARY OF DR. JOHN WILLIAM POLIDORI, 1816

Polier, Marie Elisabeth *see* MYTHOLOGIE DES INDOUS

LA POLIGLOTA DE ARIAS MONTANO / Ramos Frechilla, Domicio – Malaga: Revista Espanola de Estudios Biblicos, 1928 – 1 – sp Bibl Santa Ana [946]

Polikarpov, F *see* LEKSIKON TREIAZYCHNYI

Polipodio de Salamanca (Seud. Doncel y Ordaz) *see* LA SOLTERONA

DIE POLIS IN KIRCHE UND WELT : EINE LEXIKOGRAPHISCHE UND EXEGETISCHE STUDIE / Schmidt, Karl Ludwig – Basel, 1939 – 2mf – 9 – DM62.00 – 3-89349-315-8 – gw Hänsel [240]

DIE POLIS IN KIRCHE UND WELT / Schmidt, Karl Ludwig – H 287 2. 1939 – 8 – ne IDC [240]

POLISH AMERICAN JOURNAL – Scranton, PA. -w. 4 Nov 1950-23 July 1955. 2 reels – 1 – uk British Libr Newspaper [073]

Polish Association of Ohio *see* PAPERS

POLISH DAILY NEWS – Cleveland. Ohio. 1917-1919 – 1 – us UMI [071]

POLISH INDEPENDENT PUBLICATIONS, 1976- – (Uncensored periodicals: 1976-12 Dec 1981 598mf Dfl4,640.00. Solidarnosc periodicals: 1980-12 Dec 1981 993mf Dfl8,245.00. Martial law and underground periodicals: Dec 1981- 2,002mf Dfl18,070.00. Monographs: Dec 1981- 142mf Dfl1,860.00.) – 9 – ne IDC [943]

POLISH MEDICAL JOURNAL – (English translation). v. 1-8. 1962-1969 – 1,5,6 – us Princeton Micro [610]

POLISH NATIONAL ECONOMIC PLAN JANUARY 1, 1946 DECEMBER 31, 1949 / Poland. Centralny Urzad Planowania – Warzawa. 1946. BD-455 1 – 9 – ne IDC [943]

POLISH NEWS BULLETIN / U.S. British Embassies.Warsaw, Poland – (Some issues missing) – Jan 1960-Jun 1984 – ca 127r – 1 – us L of C Photodup [943]

POLISH PERSPECTIVES – v1- 1958- 1; v18-5,6; v19- 9 – us UMI [460]

POLISH PIONEERS OF VIRGINIA AND KENTUCKY : WITH NOTES ON GENEALOGY OF THE SADOWSKI FAMILY / Haiman, Miecislaus – 1937 – 1r – 1 – us Ross [920]

POLISH SINGERS ALLIANCE RECORDS, MS 4072 – (Records, in Polish, recording the activities of the Cleveland chapter of the Polish Singers Alliance of America, a national fraternal order promoting Polish music and culture) – Cleveland, Cuyahoga, OH. 1939-52 – 1r – 1 – us Western Res [780]

POLISH-CATHOLIC BOOK PUBLISHING IN THE U.S. AND ITS DISTRIBUTION DURING THE PERIOD 1871-1900 / Samsel, N Ancilla – May 1957 – 1r – 1 – us I.H.R.C. [070]

POLITCHESKAYA ROL' TSERKOVNIKOV I SEKTANTOV V SSSR / Chudnovtsev, M – The Political Role of Churchmen and Sectarians in the USSR. Moscow, 1930. One of 13 titles by Soviet authors on reel – 1 – 74.32 – us Baptist [240]

Politi, Ambr. Cathar. *see* ENARRATIONES IN QUINQUE PRIORA CAPITA LIBRI GENESEOS, ET ALII TRACTATUS

LA POLITICA AGRARIA DEL PARTIDO COMUNISTA / Uribe, Vicente – Conferencia pronunciada el domingo 4 de julio de 1937 en el Cine Olympia, de Valencia. Barcelona, 1937. Fiche W1242. (Blodgett Collection of Spanish Civil War Pamphlets) – 9 – us H.U. College Libr [946]

POLITICA AGRARIA Y REGULACION ECONOMICA / Horne, Bernardino C – Buenos Aires: Losada, 2nd ed 1945 – 1 – CSUXAHZ2684-B – us Hoover Inst Photo [320]

POLITICA ALIMENTARIA ARGENTINA : CONFERENCIA INAUGURAL DEL CURSO SOBRE POLITICA ALIMENTARIA ARGENTINA / Peron, Juan Domingo – Buenos Aires: [s.n.], 1949 – 1 – CSUXADN4018-B – us Hoover Inst Photo [320]

LA POLITICA COMO CONCIENCIA : MEDITACION SOBRE LA ARGENTINA DE 1955 / Cossio, Carlos – Buenos Aires: Abeledo-Perrot, 1957 – 1 – CSUXADJ1326-B – us Hoover Inst Photo [320]

POLITICA DE DESARROLLO NAC DIRECTIVAS NAC. Y REG / Chile. Oficina de Planificacion Nacional – D-888 1. 1968 – 9 – ne IDC [330]

LA POLITICA DE LOS MILITARES ARGENTINOS : 1900-1971 / Canton, Dario – [Buenos Aires]: Siglo Veintiuno Argentino Editores, [1st ed 1971] – 1 – CSUXADJ1829-B – us Hoover Inst Photo [320]

POLITICA DEL FRENTE POPULAR EN AGRICULTURA; LEYES MAS IMPORTANTES DE AGRICULTURA DESDE EL ADVENIMIENTO DE LA REPUBLICA EN 1931 – Madrid, 1937. Fiche W1111. (Blodgett Collection of Spanish Civil War Pamphlets) – 9 – us H.U. College Libr [946]

POLITICA ECONOMICA PERONISTA / Gomez Moralos, Alfredo – Buenos Aires: Escuela Superior Peronista, [1951] – 1 – CSUXAHZ2073-B – us Hoover Inst Photo [330]

POLITICA EDUCATIVA : PARA LA DEMOCRACIA, LA CONCIENCIA HISTORICA Y EL DESARROLLO / Peru. Ministerio de Educacion – Lima, 1988 – 1mf – 9 – DE-640/1 – ne IDC [370]

LA POLITICA EXTERIOR ARGENTINA / Frondizi, Arturo – 2a ed. Buenos Aires, Transici on 1963 – 1 – CSUXADL7037-B – us Hoover Inst Photo [320]

POLITICA EXTERIOR ARGENTINA, 1930-1962 / Conil Paz, Alberto A & Ferrari, Gustavo – Buenos Aires: Editorial Huemul, [1964] – 1 – CSUXADL7006-B – us Hoover Inst Photo [320]

LA POLITICA EXTERIOR PERONISTA / Escipion – [Buenos Aires]: Editorial Descartes, [1974] – 1 – CSUXADQ4962-B – us Hoover Inst Photo [320]

POLITICA EXTERNA INDEPENDENTE – Rio de Janeiro, BL. 1965-1966 – 1r – $50.00 – R04179 – us Library Micro [072]

POLITICA INDIANA, CORREGIDA POR...FRANCISCO RAMIRO DE VALENZUELA. 5 TOMOS / Solorzano Pereira, Juan de – Madrid: Razon y Fe, 1930 – 1 – sp Bibl Santa Ana [320]

POLITICA MASSIMA DIUISA IN DICIASETTE DECLAMATIONI / Pellegrini, Matteo – Genoua, Presso G.B. Ferroni, 1641 – 1 – us U.W. Library [320]

POLITICA MONETARIA Y FINANCIERA / Bogliolo, Romulo – [Buenos Aires]: Editorial "La Vanguardia", 1949 – 1 – CSUXAHZ6167-B – us Hoover Inst Photo [320]

POLITICA PARA COREGIDORES Y SENORES DE VASSALOS EN TIEMPOS DE PAZ Y DE GUERRA... / Castillo de Bovadilla, J – Madrid, 1597 – 47mf – 9 – sp Cultura [320]

POLITICA PLANIFICADA PARA EL DESARROLLO RESUMEN DEL PLAN GENERAL DE DESARROLLO ECONOMICO Y SOCIAL / Ecuador. Junta Nacional de Planificacion y Coordinacion Economica – Quito. 1966 – 9 – ne IDC [338]

POLITICA SOCIAL DEL EMPERADOR CARLOS 5 A TRAVES DE DOCUMENTOS DEL ARCHIVO DE MONTEMOLIN / Mota Arevalo, Horacio – Badajoz: (Imprenta de la Diputacion Provincial). Badajoz, 1958. Sepr. Revista Estudios Extremenos – 1 – sp Bibl Santa Ana [320]

LA POLITICA SOCIAL EN LA ZONA MARXISTA / Montero Diaz, Santiago – Bilbao, 1938. Fiche W 1056. (Blodgett Collection of Spanish Civil War Pamphlets) – 9 – us H.U. College Libr [946]

POLITICA Y ESTRATEGIA : APUNTES PARA UNA DOCTRINA DE LA GUERRA / Peron, Juan Domingo – Buenos Aires: Aquarius, [1973] – 1 – CSUXAGP9709-B – us Hoover Inst Photo [320]

POLITICA Y ESTRATEGIA : EFECTOS ECONOMICOS DE LA GUERRA; NO ATACO, CRITICO / Peron, Juan Domingo – Buenos Aires, 1951 – 1 – CSUXADL5921-B – us Hoover Inst Photo [320]

POLITICA Y ESTRATEGIA : LAS IDEOLOGIAS MODERNAS: NO ATACO, CRITICO / Peron, Juan Domingo – Buenos Aires: [s.n.], 1952 – 1 – CSUXADQ4341-B – us Hoover Inst Photo [320]

POLITICA Y ESTRATEGIA : NO ATACO, CRITICO / Peron, Juan Domingo – Buenos Aires: Editorial Pleamar, 2nd ed [1973] – 1 – CSUXADQ4351-B – us Hoover Inst Photo [320]

POLITICA Y ESTRATEGIA : NO ATACO, CRITICO / Peron, Juan Domingo – Buenos Aires: [s.n.], 1951 – 1 – CSUXAJA8453-B – us Hoover Inst Photo [320]

POLITICA Y ESTRATEGIA : NO ATACO, CRITICO / Peron, Juan Domingo – Buenos Aires: [s.n.], 1951 – 1 – CSUXADQ4370-B – us Hoover Inst Photo [320]

POLITICA Y ESTRATEGIA : NO ATACO, CRITICO / Peron, Juan Domingo – Buenos Aires: [s.n.], 1952 – 1 – CSUXAJA8444-B – us Hoover Inst Photo [320]

POLITICA Y ESTRATEGIA : NO ATACO, CRITICO / Peron, Juan Domingo – Buenos Aires: [s.n.], 1952 – 1 – CSUXAGP9694-B – us Hoover Inst Photo [320]

POLITICA Y ESTRATEGIA : NO ATACO, CRITICO: AL INSULTO DEL VIL, EL SABIO CALLA / Peron, Juan Domingo – Buenos Aires: [s.n.], 1952 – 1 – CSUXADQ4363-B – us Hoover Inst Photo [320]

POLITICA Y ESTRATEGIA : NO ATACO, CRITICO: LA POLITICA INTERNACIONAL Y LA JUSTICIA / Peron, Juan Domingo – Buenos Aires: [s.n.], 1952 – 1 – CSUXAJA8438-B – us Hoover Inst Photo [320]

POLITICA Y ESTRATEGIA : NO ATACO, CRITICO: PACTOS BILATERALES Y AYUDA TECNICA / Peron, Juan Domingo – Buenos Aires: [s.n.], 1952 – 1 – CSUXADQ4383-B – us Hoover Inst Photo [320]

POLITICA Y JUSTICIA ARGENTINAS / Bertotto, Jose Guillermo – Montevideo, Editorial Ceibo, 1945 – 1 – CSUXAHZ7754-B – us Hoover Inst Photo [320]

POLITICA Y LITERATURA / Ramirez, Alfonso Francisco – Mexico, 1931; Madrid: Razon y Fe, 1932 – 1 – sp Bibl Santa Ana [320]

LA POLITICA Y LOS PARTIDOS / Galletti, Alfredo – Mexico: Fondo de Cultura Economica, [1st ed 1961] – 1 – CSUXADP4624-B – us Hoover Inst Photo [320]

THE POLITICAL ACTIVITIES OF THE BAPTISTS AND FIFTH MONARCHY MEN IN ENGLAND DURING THE INTERREGNUM / Brown, Louise Fargo – Washington, D.C.: American Historical Association; London: Oxford University Press, 1912, c1913. (Prize essays of the American Historical Association; 1911) – 1mf – us A.T.L.A. [240]

POLITICAL ACTIVITIES OF THE JOHNSON WHITE HOUSE, 1963-69 – Part 1: White House Central and Confidential Files. With printed guide.47 reels – 1 – $5,175.00 – 0-89093-924-1 – us UPA [025]

POLITICAL ACTIVITIES OF THE JOHNSON WHITE HOUSE, 1963-69 – Part 2: White House Aides. Series A: Office Files of Marvin Watson. 20 reels. With printed guide – 1 – $2,200.00 – 0-89093-926-8 – us UPA [025]

THE POLITICAL ANATOMY OF IRELAND / Petty, W – London, 1691 – 3mf – 9 – ne IDC [320]

THE POLITICAL AND LEGISLATIVE HISTORY OF LIBERIA / Huberich, C H – 2v. New York. 1947. BA-314 2 – 8 – ne IDC [960]

POLITICAL AND MILITARY EPISODES IN THE LATTER HALF OF THE EIGHTEENTH CENTURY: DERIVED FROM THE LIFE AND CORRESPONDENCE OF THE RIGHT. HON. JOHN BURGOYNE, GENERAL, STATESMAN, DRAMATIST / De Fonblanque, Edward Barrington – London: MacMillan, 1876. 02701. (Pre-1900 Canadiana) – 9 – cn C.I.H.M. [971]

THE POLITICAL AND OCCASIONAL POEMS OF WINTHROP MACKWORTH PRAED / Praed, Winthrop Mackworth; ed by Young, George – London: Ward, Lock, & Bowden, 1888 – 1 roll – 1 – 1-55879-626-6 – uk Libr Preservation [810]

POLITICAL AND SATYRICAL POEMS / Holkham Hall. Norfolk. England – (English). 1688 to 1698 – 1 – uk Microform Academic [810]

POLITICAL AND SOCIAL CHANGES IN CATALONIA DURING THE REVOLUTION, JULY 19-DECEMBER 31, 1936 / Martin, J G – Barcelona, 1936. Fiche W 1029. (Blodgett Collection of Spanish Civil War Pamphlets) – 9 – us H.U. College Libr [946]

POLITICAL AND SOCIAL SIGNIFICANCE OF THE LIFE AND TEACHINGS OF JESUS / Jenks, Jeremiah W – New York: Y.M.C.A. Press, 1907. 1 fiche – 9 – us A.T.L.A. [240]

POLITICAL APPOINTMENTS, PARLIAMENTS AND THE JUDICIAL BENCH IN THE DOMINION OF CANADA, 1867 TO 1895 / Cote, Narcisse Omer – Ottawa: Thoburn, 1896. 00255. (Pre-1900 Canadiana) – 9 – cn C.I.H.M. [971]

POLITICAL ARITHMETICK / Petty, W – M-389 2. 1690 – 8 – ne IDC [320]

POLITICAL BEHAVIOR – v.1-. 1979- – 1,5,6,9 – us UMI [073]

POLITICAL BEHAVIOR – v1-16. 1979-94 – 1,5 – $65.00v – us UMI [150]

POLITICAL CHANGE IN LATIN AMERICA : THE EMERGENCE OF THE MIDDLE SECTORS / Johnson, John J – Stanford, Calif.: Stanford University Press, [1964] – 1 – CSUXAJL9697-B – us Hoover Inst Photo [320]

POLITICAL COMMUNICATIONS AND PERSUASION – v.1-. 1980- – 1,5,6,9 – us UMI [073]

THE POLITICAL DYNAMICS OF THE CHINESE MILITARY ELITE, PART 2, THE ROLE OF THE MILITARY ELITE IN THE CULTURAL REVOLUTION (1966-1968) / U.S. Office of the Chief of Military History – 1 – 18.00 – us L of C Photodup [950]

THE POLITICAL ECONOMY OF ART : BEING THE SUBSTANCE (WITH ADDITIONS) OF TWO LECTURES DELIVERED AT MANCHESTER, JULY 10TH AND 13TH, 1857 / Ruskin, John – London: Smith, Elder, and Co., 1857 – 1 roll – 1 – 1-55879-919-2 – uk Libr Preservation [700]

POLITICAL EMPIRICISM : A LETTER TO THE REV. MR. JOHN WESLEY – London, 1776 – 1mf – 9 – MP-510/1 – ne IDC [240]

POLITICAL ESSAY ON THE KINGDOM OF NEW SPAIN / Humboldt, Alexander von – London. 4v. 1822 – 1r – 1 – us Ross [972]

POLITICAL ESSAYS : WITH SKETCHES OF PUBLIC CHARACTERS / Hazlitt, William – London: Printed for William Hone, 1819 – 1 roll – 1 – 1-55879-349-6 – uk Libr Preservation [320]

POLITICAL FORUM – Holdrege, NE. -w. Jun 1892; Dec 1892; Aug 1895-Feb 1897 – 1 – us NE Hist [071]

THE POLITICAL FUTURE OF THE INDONESIAN ARCHIPELAGO; A MANIFESTO / Tiro, Hasan Muhammad – SE 11,144 1. 1965 – 9 – ne IDC [320]

POLITICAL GEOGRAPHY AND THE CYPRUS CONFLICT : 1963-1971 / Patrick, Richard A; ed by Bater, James & Preston, Richard – 1975 – 481p – 9 – $8.00 – 0-921083-05-X – cn Geography [320]

A POLITICAL HISTORY OF EUROPE SINCE 1814 / Seignobos, Charles – New York: Henry Holt, 1900 – 10mf – 9 – $15.00 – LLMC 92-236 – us L.L.M.C. [327]

THE POLITICAL HISTORY OF GUJARAT / Ali Muhammad Khan – 1835 – 1 – uk Microform Academic [950]

POLITICAL HISTORY OF PALESTINE UNDER BRITANNIC ADMINISTRATION / Great Britain – Memorandum submitted to U.N.S.C.O.P. Jerusalem. 1947. BJ-28-154 1 – 9 – ne IDC [956]

A POLITICAL HISTORY OF SLAVERY : BEING AN ACCOUNT OF THE SLAVERY CONTROVERSY FROM THE EARLIEST AGITATIONS IN THE EIGHTEENTH CENTURY TO THE CLOSE OF THE RECONSTRUCTION PERIOD IN AMERICA / Smith, William Henry – New York. 2v. 1903 – 1r – 1 – us Ross [976]

A POLITICAL INDEX TO THE HISTORIES OF GREAT BRITAIN & IRELAND: OR, A COMPLETE REGISTER OF THE HEREDITARY HONOURS, PUBLIC OFFICES, AND PERSONS IN OFFICE, FROM THE EARLIEST PERIODS TO THE PRESENT TIME / Beatson, Robert – 3rd ed., corr. and enl. London: Longman, Hurst, Rees, and Orme, 1806. 3v – 1 – us U.W. Library [941]

POLITICAL INTELLIGENCER – New Brunswick. N.J. 1783-86 – 1 – us UMI [071]

POLITICAL INVESTIGATOR – London, UK. 1832. -irr. 3 feet – 1 – uk British Libr Newspaper [072]

POLITICAL LEADERS OF LATIN AMERICA : CHE GUEVARA; ALFREDO STROESSNER; EDUARDO FREI MONTALVA; JUSCELINO KUBITSCHEK; CARLOS LACERDA; EVA PERON / Bourne, Richard – Harmondsworth: Penguin, 1969 – 1 – CSUXADJ4212-B – us Hoover Inst Photo [320]

POLITICAL LETTERS AND PAMPHLETS BY WILLIAM CARPENTER / Carpenter, William – 1-34 (all publ). 1830-1831 – 6mf – 9 – $65.00 – us UPA [335]

POLITICAL MANIFESTO OF THE GOVERNMENT OF THE REPUBLIC OF INDONESIA / Indonesia – SE-10,760 1. 1945 – 9 – ne IDC [324]

POLITICAL MANIFESTOS IN THE POST-WAR ERA 1945-1981 / ed by European Consortium for Political Research Manifestos Group – (Distribution Rights for German-Speaking Europe and Eastern Europe) – 1992 – 114 fiches (1:24) – 9 – DM2,280.00 silver – 0-86291-800-6 – gw Saur [320]

POLITICAL OBSERVER – London. -w. 28 Nov 1819-30 Jan 1820. (10 feet) – 1 – uk British Libr Newspaper [072]

POLITICAL OLIO *see* CHENANGO WEEKLY ADVERTISER

POLITICAL OPINION POLLS AND SOCIAL SURVEYS – Family Expenditure Survey, 1957-74 – 1 – us Primary [360]

POLITICAL ORGANIZATION, CULTS AND CEREMONIES OF THE PLAINS-CREE / Skinner, A – BN 390 2. 1916 – 8 – ne IDC [306]

POLITICAL PAMPHLETS / Tolson Memorial Museum. Huddersfield – 1 – uk Microform Academic [941]

POLITICAL PAMPHLETS FROM THE INDIAN SUBCONTINENT – (Pt 1. Political Parties and Special Interest Groups. 462mf. $3,175.00; Pt 2. Internal Indian Politics. 312mf. $2,170.00; Pt 3. State and Regional Politics. 119mf. $830.00; Pt 4. Pakistan, Bangladesh, and Indian Foreign Affairs. 140mf. $1,200.00) – 1 – $7,010.00 set – us UPA [320]

POLITICAL PARTIES, ARMED GROUPS, LABOUR UNIONS AND YOUTH ORGANIZATIONS IN INDONESIA / Indonesia. Kementerian Penerangan – SE-6861 1. 1950 – 9 – ne IDC [950]

THE POLITICAL, PERSONAL AND PROPERTY RIGHTS OF A CITIZEN OF THE UNITED STATES / Parsons, Theophilus – Hartford, Scranton, 1874. 744p. LL-1402 – 1 – us L of C Photodup [340]

POLITICAL POEMS AND SONGS RELATING TO ENGLISH HISTORY : COMPOSED DURING THE PERIOD FROM THE ACCESSION OF EDWARD 3 TO THAT OF RICHARD 3(RS14) – v1-2. 1859-1862 – Dfl63.00 – ne Slangenburg [941]

POLITICAL POWER AND POLITICAL CULTURE IN INDONESIA / Maryanov, Gerald Seymour – SE-4885 1. 1962? – 9 – ne IDC [320]

POLITICAL PSYCHOLOGY – v1-13. 1979-92 – 1,5 – $90.00v – us UMI [320]

POLITICAL QUARTERLY – v1-26. 1930-55 – 1,5,6 – us Princeton Micro [073]

THE POLITICAL QUARTERLY – Great Britain. 1980-1985 – 1 – us Primary [320]

POLITICAL RECORDS FILMED SPRING 1969 / Barrier, N G – (List of contents available upon request) – New Delhi: National Archives of India, 1968 – us Res Libr [950]

POLITICAL RELATIONS BETWEEN THE UNITED STATES AND EGYPT / U.S. Department of State – 1910-29. 1 roll. M572 – 1 – us Nat'l Archives [327]

POLITICAL RELATIONS BETWEEN THE UNITED STATES AND URUGUAY / U.S. DEPARTMENT OF STATE RECORDS. – (1930-1944 1r $85.00 S3159. Political Relations between Uruguay and Other States 1930-1944 2r $170.00 S3160) – 1810-1959 – 1 – us Scholarly Res [972]

THE POLITICAL REORIENTATION OF JAPAN, 1945-48 / Supreme Command for the Allied Powers. Headquarters – 1983 – 1r – 1 – $85.00 – S1663 – Co-publ with the Center of Military History – us Scholarly Res [950]

POLITICAL RESEARCH, ORGANIZATION AND DESIGN *see* AMERICAN BEHAVIORAL SCIENTIST

THE POLITICAL REVIEW – Montreal?: G Bemister, 1878-18– or 19– – 9 – cn C.I.H.M. [320]

POLITICAL SCIENCE COLLECTION / Bibliotheque Nationale – Includes writings by Fourier, Benoit Malon, de Condorcet, Abbe Constant, Thomas Paine, Quetelet and Robespierre. In French. 36 titles on 112 fiches. Titles available separately – 9 – 277.00 – fr Bibl Nationale [080]

POLITICAL SCIENCE IN ASIA AND THE PACIFIC : STATUS REPORT ON TEACHING AND RESEARCH IN TEN COUNTRIES / ed by Uchida, Takeo – 1985 – 9 – 92-3-102394-2 – fr UNESCO [370]

POLITICAL SCIENCE MICRO REVIEW – Issues 1-4. Oct 1982-1983 – 1 – us UMI [073]

THE POLITICAL SCIENCE OF JOHN ADAMS : A STUDY IN THE THEORY OF MIXED GOVERNMENT AND THE BICAMERAL SYSTEM / Walsh, Correa M – New York/ London: G P Putnam's Sons, 1915 – 4mf – 9 – $6.00 – LLMC 95-067 – us L.L.M.C. [323]

POLITICAL SCIENCE QUARTERLY – v. 1-55. 1886-1940 – 1 – us Princeton Micro [320]

POLITICAL SCIENCE QUARTERLY – (v. 84-1969- 5,6. v. 90- 1975- 9) – v. 1- 1886- – 1 – us UMI [320]

POLITICAL SCIENCE TEACHER *see* PS

THE POLITICAL SITUATION: SPEECH DELIVERED BY THE HON. GEO. E. FOSTER, MINISTER OF FINANCE, IN THE MECHANICS INSTITUTE, ST JOHN, N.B., ON DECEMBER 15TH, 1891 / Foster, George Eulas – St. John, N.B.: s.n., 1891?. 05593. (Pre-1900 Canadiana) – 9 – cn C.I.H.M. [971]

THE POLITICAL SITUATIONS: A LETTER TO THE HONORABLE JAMES FERRIER, SENATOR / Galt, Alexander Tilloch – Montreal?: s.n., 1875 (Montreal: D. Bentley). 04189. (Pre-1900 Canadiana) – 9 – cn C.I.H.M. [971]

POLITICAL SOPHISTRY DETECTED : OR, BRIEF REMARKS ON THE REV. MR. FLETCHER'S LATE TRACT ENTITLED 'AMERICAN PATRIOTISM', IN A LETTER TO A FRIEND / Evans, C – Bristol, 1776 – 1mf – 9 – MP-514/1 – ne IDC [240]

Political Status Commission of the Marshall Islands *see* ANALYSIS OF THE PROPOSED CONSTITUTION OF THE FEDERATED STATES OF MICRONESIA

Political Status Delegation of the Congress of Micronesia *see* REPORT TO THE 3RD CONGRESS

POLITICAL STATUS DIGEST : 3RD REG SESS, JUL-AUG 1970 / Congress of Micronesia – (Various pagination) – n.p, n.d. – 3mf – 9 – $4.50 – LLMC 82-100F, Title 38 – us L.L.M.C. [323]

POLITICAL STATUS DIGEST : 4TH CONG, 1971 / Congress of Micronesia – (Various pagination) – n.p, n.d. – 2mf – 9 – $3.00 – LLMC 82-100F, Title 41 – us L.L.M.C. [323]

POLITICAL STATUS DIGEST : 4TH CONG, 1972 / Congress of Micronesia – (Various pagination) – n.p, n.d. – 3mf – 9 – $4.50 – LLMC 82-100F, Title 47 – us L.L.M.C. [323]

POLITICAL STUDIES – v1- 1953- 1; v19- 5,6; v23- 9 – us UMI [320]

POLITICAL STUDIES – (v. 1-11. 246.00v; 9. v. 12-16. 247.50v; WDS; 9) – v. 1-16. Oxford. 1953-68 – 9 – 24100.00 – uk Dawson [320]

POLITICAL SURVEY, 1946-1947 / Jewish Agency for Palestine. Jerusalem – Memorandum submitted to the United Nations Special Committee on Palestine. 1947. BJ-28-148 1 – 9 – ne IDC [956]

THE POLITICAL THEORIES OF MARTIN LUTHER / Waring, Luther Hess – New York: Putnam, 1910 – 1mf – us A.T.L.A. [320]

POLITICAL THEORIES OF THE MIDDLE AGE / Gierke, Otto – Cambridge: University Press; New York: Macmillan, 1900 – 1mf – us A.T.L.A. [320]

POLITICAL THEORY – (v.7-. 1979- 5,6,9) – v.1-. 1973- – 1 – us UMI [073]

POLITICAL TROUBLE IN INDIA *see* POLITICO-CRIMINAL WHO'S WHO

POLITICAL TROUBLE IN INDIA, 1907-1917 / Ker, James Campbell – (Filmed with: India, Intelligence Bureau: Politico-criminal Who's Who, and Terrorism in India, 1917-36) – [S.l: s.n.], 1917 – us Res Libr [950]

THE POLITICAL UNIFICATION OF THE UNITED STATES AND CANADA: AN ADDRESS / Ellison, William Bruce – New York?: s.n., 1891?. 05237. (Pre-1900 Canadiana) – 9 – cn C.I.H.M. [971]

POLITICAL UNIONIST – London, UK. 1832. -irr. 2 feet – 1 – uk British Libr Newspaper [072]

POLITICAL WORLD – London, England. -w. July 1888-May 1890. 2 reels – 1 – uk British Libr Newspaper [072]

POLITICHESKAIA SISTEMA PETRA 3 / Shchebal'skii, P K – 1870 – 8 – BR-7835 2 – ne IDC [947]

POLITICHESKIE DVIZHENIIA RUSSKOGO NARODA / Morodovtsev, D – Istoricheskie monografii. v. 1-2. Spb. 1871. BR-7710 2 – 8 – ne IDC [947]

POLITICHESKIE I PRAVOVYE VZGLIADY S. E. DESNITSKOGO / Pokrovskii, Serafim Aleksandrovich – Moskva: Gos. Izd-vo iurid. lit-ry, 1955. 166p. LL-4012 – 1 – us L of C Photodup [340]

POLITICHESKIE PARTII I GRUPPY V GOSUDARSTVENNOI DUME / Lokot, T V – M., 1907. 111p – 4mf – 9 – ne IDC [320]

POLITICHESKIE PARTII V ROSSII / Martov, L – 2nd ed. M., 1917. 36p – 1mf – 9 – ne IDC [320]

POLITICHESKIE PROTSESSY V ROSSII (1901-1917) : PT. 1 (1901-1905) / ed by Gol'dman, L I – M., 1932. 248p – 3mf – 9 – ne IDC [320]

POLITICHESKII STROI I MEZHDUNARODNO-PRAVOVYE POLOZHENIE TANNUTUVY V PROSHLOM I NASTOIASHCHEM / Shostakovich, S – Irkutsk. 1929 – 9 – ne IDC [320]

POLITICHESKII STROI SOVREMENNYKH GOSUDARSTV / ed by Dolgorukov, P D & Petrumkevich, I I – v1-2. Spb. 1905-06. BR-3524 2 – 8 – ne IDC [320]

POLITICHESKII ZHURNAL – M. 1790-1802. B-1834 2 – 8 – ne IDC [073]

POLITICHESKIIA SKAZOCHKI / Sologub, F – Spb. 1906. BR-874 2 – 8 – ne IDC [321]

POLITICHESKIIA SKAZOCHKI. IZD. "RODNAIA RECH'" / Sologub, F – M. 1916. BR-875 2 – 8 – ne IDC [321]

POLITICHESKOYE SAMOOBRAZOVANIYE – (Political Self-Education). Moscow. U.S.S.R. 1961- – 1 – us UMI [335]

POLITICIAN AND FREE TRADE JOURNAL – London, UK. Nov 1906. -irr. 7 feet – 1 – uk British Libr Newspaper [072]

LE POLITICIEN – Dakar, Senegal. July 24-Dec 24 1987 – 1r – 1 – us L of C Photodup [072]

POLITICKE STRANY PO UNORU. / Pavlicek, Vaclav – Praha: Svobodne slovo, 1966- – 1 – us U.W. Library [943]

POLITICO-CRIMINAL WHO'S WHO – (Filmed with: India, Intelligence Bureau: Political Trouble in India, 1907-17, and Terrorism in India) – [S.l: s.n.], 1914 ([Simla: G M Press]) – us Res Libr [950]

POLITICO-CRIMINAL WHO'S WHO *see* POLITICAL TROUBLE IN INDIA, 1907-1917

POLITICS – 1-6 2+1 (all publ). 1944-1949 – 18mf – 9 – $105.00 – us UPA [320]

POLITICS : HEBDO – Montreal, Canada. 6 mars-8 jun 1896 – 1r – 1 – Can$30.00 – cn Can Microfilming [072]

THE POLITICS.. / Aristotle – With introd., two prefatory essays and notes critical and explanatory by W.L. Newman. Oxford: Clarendon Press, 1887-1902. 4v. With: Domostrafi- A.S. Orlov. 1 reel. 1264 – 1 – us U.W. Library [180]

POLITICS AND ADMINISTRATION OF TUDOR AND STUART ENGLAND – The most important volumes selected from the Landsdowne Collection in the British Library, London. Part 1: Lord Burghley's Papers. Part 2: The Papers of Sir Julius Caesar, Elizabethan Minister. Part 3: Selection from Vols. 187-554. Part 4: Selections from Vols. 555-1036. Part 5: Selections from Vols 1037-1238 – 1 – us Primary [941]

POLITICS AND DISEASE / Levy, J H – 1906. Together with: Short Studies in Economic Subjects (1903); and Individualism and the Land Question, by J. H. Levy et al (1912). 1 fiche (29x) – 9 – 1.00f – at Libertarian Micro [320]

POLITICS AND EDUCATION – 1977- – 1,5,6,9 – us UMI [320]

POLITICS AND RELIGION; A STUDY IN SCOTTISH HISTORY FROM THE REFORMATION TO THE REVOLUTION / Mathieson, William Law – Glasgow: J. Maclehose, 1902. 2v – 1 – us U.W. Library [941]

POLITICS AND RELIGION IN ANCIENT ISRAEL : AN INTRODUCTION TO THE STUDY OF THE OLD TESTAMENT / Todd, James Cameron – (Includes indexes) – London: Macmillan, 1904 – 1mf – 9 – 0-8370-5545-8 – 1985-3545 – us A.T.L.A. [220]

POLITICS AND SOCIETY IN INTER-WAR BRITAIN / Great Britain. Public Record Office – Protest movements, civil disorder and the police in inter-war Britain. (PRO Class Mepo 2) – 1 – us Primary [941]

POLITICS AND STATECRAFT IN EARLY MODERN ENGLAND: THE MAIN PAPERS OF THE HOUSE OF LORDS / Great Britain. Parliament. House of Lords – (Part 1: 1509-1641. Part 2: Protestation Returns, 1641-42. Part 3: 1642-22 Dec 1645. Part 4: 23 Dec 1645-48. Part 5: Nov 1648-78. Part 6: 25 Jun 1678-Mar 1696. Part 7: Apr 1696-Jan 1704. Part 8: Feb 1704-3 Feb 1709. Part 9: 10 Feb 1709-Jun 1715) – 1 – us Primary [941]

POLITICS FOR THE PEOPLE – 1-2 (all publ). 1794-1795 – 10mf – 9 – $65.00 – us UPA [320]

POLITICS FOR THE PEOPLE – London, UK. 1848. -irr. 11 feet – 1 – uk British Libr Newspaper [072]

POLITICS IN REVIEW – London. 1934-1939 – 1 – us Primary [320]

POLITICS IN THE AGE OF REVOLUTION, 1715-1848 – (Part 1: The Papers of Edmund Burke, 1729-97, from Sheffield City Libraries) – Marlborough: Adam Matthew Publications, 1994 – 25r – 1 – $2,950.00 – uk Matthew [320]

THE POLITICS OF CONSCIENCE : T.H. GREEN AND HIS AGE / Richter, W – London, 1964 – 11mf – 8 – ne Slangenburg [170]

POLITICS, RELIGION AND SOCIETY IN ENGLAND, 1650-1750 – Ballard Collection of correspondence and papers in the Bodleian Library, Oxford – 1 – us Primary [941]

POLITIEK VERSLAG 1852 : BUITENBEZITTINGEN – (Microfiche Nos 26-50) – Arch Kol. Geh. Exh. 9 juni 1855, 303 – 25mf – 9 – SD-100/1 – ne IDC [320]

POLITIEK VERSLAG 1852,1 : CORRESPONDENTIE MET DE RAAD VAN INDIE OVER HET POLITIEK VERSLAG – (Microfiche Nos 8-13) – Arch. Kol. Geh. Exh. 9 juni 1855, 303 – 6mf – 9 – SD-100/1 – ne IDC [320]

POLITIEK VERSLAG 1852,2 : ALGEMEEN OVERZICHT VAN DE STAATKUNDIGE GESTELDHEID VAN NEDERL. INDIE – (Microfiche Nos 14-25) – Arch. Kol. Geh. Exh. 9 juni 1855, 303 – 12mf – 9 – SD-100/1 – ne IDC [320]

POLITIEKE GROEPERINGEN IN INDONESIE : EEN OVERZICHT VAN DE IN DE LAATSTE TIJD OP DE VOORGROND TREDENDE POLITIEKE ORGANISASTIES – Batavia, 1948 – 3mf – 9 – SE-1617/1 – ne IDC [320]

POLITIK / Tan Malaka – SE 4578 1. 1945 – 9 – ne IDC [320]

POLITIK BAHASA NASIONAL / Slametmuljana, R B – SE 2203 1. 1959 – 9 – ne IDC [320]

POLITIK FUER DEUTSCHLAND / Saenger, Fritz & Selbmann, Eugen – Sozialdemokratische Beitrage 1962-1964. Bonn, 1964 – 1 – DM30.00 – gw Mikro Press [320]

POLITIKA – Belgrade, Yugoslavia. Mar 1930-Mar 1941; Oct 1944-1948; 1950-Oct 1970; 1984-92 – 179r – 1 – us L of C Photodup [949]

POLITIKA – Beograd: Politika, sep 20 1939-apr 5 1941; 1949 – 26r – 1 – us Res Libr [072]

POLITIKA : THE INTERNATIONAL WEEKLY – Belgrade, Yugoslavia. Apr-Dec 1990 – 1r – 1 – us L of C Photodup [072]

POLITIKA – Prague. Czechoslovakia. -w. 19 Sep 1968-26 Apr 1969. (1 reel) – 1 – uk British Libr Newspaper [072]

POLITIKA – Sofia, Bulgaria. Oct 1944-Feb 1945 – 1r – 1 – us L of C Photodup [949]

POLITIKA EKSPRES – Belgrade, Yugoslavia. Nov 1963-1968; Apr 1969-1970 – 30r – 1 – us L of C Photodup [949]

POLITIKEN – Kobenhavn: [s.n, 1952-54] – 36r – 1 – us Res Libr [072]

POLITIKEN – (Yrly reel count varies) – 1991- – 1 – inquire – us Ross [072]

POLITIKEN *see* FOLKETS DAGBLAD

POLITIKO-EKONOMICHESKIE VZAIMOOTNOSHENII A MEZHDU SSSR I PRIBALTIKO I ZA DESI AT LET 1917-1927 / Bakh, MG – Moskva: Izd-vo Kommunistichesko i akademii, 1928 – 1 – CSUX88-B8755 – us Hoover Inst Photo [320]

POLITIKON – (v.6-. 1979- 5,6,9) – v.1-. 1974- – 1 – us UMI [073]

POLITIQUE – Revue de doctrine et d'action. Paris. 1927-mai 1940, juin 1945-oct 1948 – 1 – fr A.C.R.P.P. [073]

LA POLITIQUE AFRICAINE DE LA LYBIE DU 1ER SEPTEMBRE 1969 / Otayek, R W – 9 – F70.00 – fr Ethnologie [306]

LA POLITIQUE COLONIALE – Paris, France. -w. 23 Jan 1892-19 April 1909. 29 reels – 1 – uk British Libr Newspaper [072]

UNE POLITIQUE COLONIALE : LE SALUT PAR LES COLONIES / Hubert, Lucien – Paris: F Alcan, 1918 – us Res Libr [960]

LA POLITIQUE CRIMINELLE IRANIENNE A L'EPREUVE DES CHANGEMENTS POLITIQUES / Nadjafi Abrandabadi, Ali Hossein – 2mf – 9 – 10358 – fr Atelier National [320]

POLITIQUE DE CONSERVATION DU PATRIMOINE DOCUMENTAIRE / Bibliotheque Nationale. Quebec – Montreal: Ministere des Affaires Culturelles, 1979. SEM105P421 – 2mf – 9 – Can$4.50 – cn Bibl Nat [025]

LA POLITIQUE DES TRAVAUX PUBLICS DU SECOND EMPIRE / Girard, Louis – Paris: A. Colin, 1952. xxxii,415p – 1 – us U.W. Library [944]

LA POLITIQUE DU CLERGE DE FRANCE / Jurieu, P – La Haye, 1682 – 4mf – 9 – CA-135/1 – ne IDC [240]

LA POLITIQUE ECONOMIQUE DE LA FRANCE EN AFRIQUE NOIRE DE 1936 A 1946 / Cotte, C – 6mf – 9 – F90.00 – fr Ethnologie [320]

LA POLITIQUE ETRANGERE D'INDONESIE. INDONSIA'S FOREIGN POLICY / Subandrio – SE 10,974 1. 1964 – 9 – ne IDC [950]

LA POLITIQUE ETRANGERE ET SES FONDEMENTS / Duroselle, J -B – F80.00 – fr Ethnologie [327]

POLITIQUE MONETAIRE ET CROISSANCE ECONOMIQUE EN FRANCE, 1950-1966 / Guillaumont-Jeanneney, S – 4mf – 9 – F60.00 – fr Ethnologie [332]

LA POLITIQUE NATURELLE. OU DISCOURS SUR LES VRAIS PRINCIPES DU GOUVERNEMENT / Holbach, Paul-Thiry d' – (D'Holbach series). 1773 – 9 – fr Hachette [321]
POLITISCHE ANNALEN – Berlin, 1793-94 – 4r – 1 – gw Mikrofilm [072]
POLITISCHE ANNALEN – Berlin, 1793-94 – 4r – 1 – Inquire at Mikrofilmarchiv for details – gw Misc Inst [943]
POLITISCHE BETRACHTUNGEN UEBER DIE GROSSEN VORTHEILE / Baumgartner, F G – Leipzig, 1814 – 2mf – 9 – ILM-2557/1 – ne IDC [327]
POLITISCHE FLUGBLAETTER, 1814-1816 / ed by Kotzebue, August von – 1814-16 (mf ed 1997) – 4mf – 9 – DM140.00 – 3-89131-238-5 – gw Fischer [305]
POLITISCHE INFORMATION : ZEITSCHRIFT DER DEUTSCHEN ANTIFASCHISTEN IN SCHWEDEN – Stockholm. 15 Jul 1943-15 Nov 1945 – 1r – 1 – gw Mikrofilm [072]
DER POLITISCHE SCHNEIDERUND DER PHLEGMATISCHE SCHUELER : EINE KOMISCHE SCENE AUS DEM WIENER VOLKSLEBEN / Moser, J B – [Wien?: s. n., 18–?] – 1r – 1 – us U.W. Library [890]
DAS POLITISCHE SYSTEM DER BUNDESREPUBLIK DEUTSCHLAND NACH DER WIEDERVEREINIGUNG / Moellers, Martin – 1993 – 2mf – 9 – DM98.00 – 3-89349-710-2 – gw Hänsel [320]
POLITISCHE UND HUMANISTISCHE IDEEN DER MEDICI IN DER VILLA POGGIO A CAIANO : UNTERSUCHUNGEN ZU DEN FRESKEN DER SALA GRANDE / Kliemann, Julian-Matthias – Heidelberg, 1976 – 4mf – 9 – DM90.00 – 3-89349-384-0 – gw Hänsel [750]
POLITISCHE UND KIRCHENGESCHICHTE ARMENIENS UNTER ASOT 1. UND SMBAT 1. : NACH ARMENISCHEN, ARABISCHEN, SYRISCHEN, UND BYZANTINISCHEN QUELLEN / Thopdschian, Hagob – (Includes bibliographical references) – Berlin: Reichsdruckerei, 1905 – 1mf – 9 – 0-8370-8871-2 – 1986-2871 – us A.T.L.A. [930]
POLITISCHE UND RELIGIOESE VOLKSBEWEGUNGEN VOR DER REFORMATION / Gothein, Eberhard – Breslau: W. Koebner, 1878 – 1mf – us A.T.L.A. [940]
POLITISCHE WAHRHEITEN IM GEWANDE DER DICHTUNG – Hamburg: Hoffmann und Campe, 1848 – 1r – 1 – us U.W. Library [943]
POLITISCHE ZUSTAENDE UND PERSONEN IN DEUTSCHLAND ZUR ZEIT DER FRANZOESISCHEN HERRSCHAFT : DAS SUEDLICHE UND WESTLICHE DEUTSCHLAND / Perthes, Clemens Theodor – Gotha, 1862 – 9 – DM98.00 – 3-89349-257-7 – gw Hänsel [320]
DIE POLITISCHEN BERICHTE DES FUERSTEN BISMARCK AUS PETERSBURG UND PARIS (1859-1862) / Bismarck, Otto, Fuerst von; ed by Raschdau, L – Berlin: R Hobbing. 2v. 1920 – 1r – 1 – us U.W. Library [943]
DIE POLITISCHEN BEZIEHUNGEN NORDKOREAS ZUR VR CHINA UND ZUR SOWJETUNION IM HINBLICK AUF DIE WIEDERVEREINIGUNG KOREAS : EINE UNTERSUCHUNG FUER DIE ZEIT VON DER TEILUNG BIS ZUM GESPRAECH UEBER EINE WIEDERVEREINIGUNG KOREAS, 1945-1975 / Yong-Kil, Chung – Heidelberg, 1977 – 2mf – 9 – DM62.00 – 3-89349-745-5 – gw Hänsel [320]
DIE POLITISCHEN FUEHRUNGSSCHICHTEN IN DEN NEUEN STAATEN SCHWARZ-AFRIKAS / Hauck, Gerhard – Heidelberg, 1965 – 2mf – 9 – DM62.00 – 3-89349-783-8 – gw Hänsel [320]
POLITISCHES PFENNIG-MAGAZIN – Leipzig, DE. 1850 – 1r – 1 – gw Mikrofilm [072]
POLITISCHES WOCHENBLATT FUER DIE FREIE HANSESTADT BREMEN – Bremen, 1832 – 1r – 1 – Inquire at Mikrofilmarchiv for details – gw Misc Inst [943]
POLITISCH-RELIGIOESE TEXTE AUS DER SARGONIDENZEIT / Klauber, E G – Leipzig. 1913. BNE-472 1 – 9 – ne IDC [290]
POLITISCH-RELIGIOESE TEXTE AUS DER SARGONIDENZEIT / Klauber, Ernst Georg; ed by Klauber, Ernst Georg – (Text in German and Akkadian; introduction and notes in German. Includes indexes) – Leipzig: Eduard Pfeiffer, 1913 – 1mf – 9 – 0-8370-9164-0 – 1986-3164 – us A.T.L.A. [470]
POLITISK REVY – Kobenhavn. Selvejende institution politisk revy. -biw.1 Sept 1963- . New serial titles, 1950-70 – 1 – us U.W. Library [073]
Politus, Ambrosius C *see* IN OMNES DIVI PAULI APOSTOLI, ET ALIAS SEPTEM CANONICAS EPISTOLAS...COMMENTARIA..
THE POLITY OF THE CHRISTIAN CHURCH OF EARLY, MEDIAEVAL, AND MODERN TIMES / Pelliccia, Alexius Aurelius – London: J. Masters, 1883 – 2mf – us A.T.L.A. [240]
POLITYKA – (1990-92 1r per y $85y. 1993-95 2r per y $170y. 1996 4r $340. 1997-98 6r per y $510y) – Poland, 1999- – 6r per y – 1 – $480.00 standing order – us Ross [072]
POLIZEI UND FREMDENBLATT DER STADT BRESLAU – Breslau (Wroclaw), Poland. 1853-1862 – 11r – 1 – gw Mikrofilm [943]
POLIZEI- UND FREMDENBLATT DER STADT BRESLAU – (Cont: Polizeiblatt der Stadt Breslau, -oct 1853?) – Breslau, 1853-56, 1857-58 (incomplete), 1859-62 – 1 – Inquire at Mikrofilmarchiv for details – gw Misc Inst [943]
POLIZEIBLATT DER STADT BRESLAU *see* POLIZEI- UND FREMDENBLATT DER STADT BRESLAU
Poliziano, Angelo *see* ANGEL POLICIANO-SILVAE NUTRITIA
LA POLIZZA DI CARICO ... / Berlingieri, F – Genova, 1932 – 4mf – 9 – ILM-3671/1 – ne IDC [327]
Polk *see*
- OREGON AND WASHINGTON GAZETTEER AND BUSINESS DIRECTORY 1909-1910
- UTAH STATE GAZETTEER 1922-1923
- UTAH STATE GAZETTEER 1930-1931

POLK COUNTY DEMOCRAT – Bartow. Fl. 1946- – 1 – us P.K. Yonge [071]
POLK COUNTY DEMOCRAT – Osceola, NE. -w. Oct 1895-Sept 1897; Dec 1897-Dec 1898, scattered issues missing; Apr 1901-Dec 1917; Feb 1918-Feb 1926; Apr 1926; Jun 1926-Dec 1944 – 1 – us NE Hist [071]
POLK COUNTY FARMER'S ADVOCATE – Osceola, NE. -w. Apr-Oct 1882 – 1 – us NE Hist [071]
POLK COUNTY INDEPENDENT – Osceola, NE. -w. Apr 1895-Dec 1900, scattered issues missing – 1 – us NE Hist [071]
POLK COUNTY ITEMIZER – (Set incl. Itemizer (Dallas)) – Dallas, OR. -w. 26 Feb 1876-30 Dec 1926. – 7r – 1 – us U.O. Library [071]
POLK COUNTY ITEMIZER-OBSERVER – Dallas, OR. -w. 2 Jun 1927-.;7 Jan-25 Feb 1976 – 1 – us U.O. Library [071]
POLK COUNTY OBSERVER – Dallas, OR. -w, -d. 7 Apr 1888-26 May 1927. 9 rolls – 1 – us U.O. Library [071]
POLK COUNTY POST – Independence, OR. -w. 26 May 1918-16 Dec 1921. – 1r – 1 – us U.O. Library [071]
POLK COUNTY RECORD – Bartow. Fl. 1919-1925, 1930-1946 – 1 – us P.K. Yonge [071]
POLK COUNTY REPUBLICAN – Osceola, NE. -w. Dec 1900-May 1902, scattered issues missing – 1 – us NE Hist [071]
POLK COUNTY SIGNAL – Dallas, OR. -w. 6 Apr 1868-23 Feb 1869. 1 roll – 1 – us U.O. Library [071]
POLK COUNTY TIMES – Dallas, OR. -w. 1 May 1869-12 Feb 1870. 1 roll – 1 – us U.O. Library [071]
Polk, James K *see* PAPERS
POLK PROGRESS – Polk, NE. -w. Aug 1909-24 (scattered issues missing); 1927- – 1 – us NE Hist [071]
POLK SUN – Monmouth, OR. -w. 5 Nov 1970-9 May 1979. 5 rolls – 1 – us U.O. Library [071]
POLKA – Scranton, PA: Zjednoczone Towarzystwa Niewiast Polskich Adoracyi Natswietszego Sakramentu. v1-40. may 1935-1974 – us Res Libr [073]
POLKVILLE BAPTIST CHURCH. SHELBY, NORTH CAROLINA : CHURCH RECORDS – 1950-60 – 1 – 11.70 – us Baptist [240]
POLL BOOK AND TALLY SHEETS / Erie County. Ohio. Vermilion. City Clerk – 1921-1929 – 1r – 1 – $32.50r – us Archival [324]
POLL BOOK OF THE BOROUGH ELECTION 1868 / Wakefield. Yorkshire – 7 – uk Microform Academic [941]
POLL BOOKS AND TALLY SHEETS / Defiance County, Ohio. Board of Elections – (Some issues missing) – 1839-1883 – 1r – 1 – $32.50r – us Archival [324]
POLL BOOKS AND TALLY SHEETS / Hancock County. Ohio. Biglick Township. Township Clerk – 1873-1929 – 1r – 1 – $32.50r – us Archival [324]
POLL BOOKS AND TALLY SHEETS / Lucas County, Ohio. Sylvania Township Township Clerk – 1835-1929 – 3r – 1 – $32.50r – us Archival [324]
POLL BOOKS AND TALLY SHEETS / Ottawa County. Ohio. Carroll Township. Board of Elections – 1914-1929 – 1r – 1 – $32.50r – us Archival [324]
POLL BOOKS AND TALLY SHEETS / Wyandot County. Ohio. Clerk of Courts – 1858 – 1r – 1 – $32.50r – us Archival [324]
POLL BOOKS/TALLY SHEETS / Hancock County. Ohio. Biglick Township. Township Clerk – 1876-1890 gaps in holdings – 1r – 1 – $32.50r – us Archival [978]
Poll, G Jv.d. *see* MARTIN BUCER'S LITURGICAL IDEAS
POLL LISTS / Wyandot County. Ohio. Board of Elections – 1933-1939 – 1r – 1 – $32.50r – us Archival [324]
Pollak-Eltz, A *see* PANORAMA DE ESTUDIOS AFROAMERICANOS
Pollard, AF *see*
- ENGLAND UNDER PROTECTOR SOMERSET
- HENRY 8

Pollard, Albert Frederick *see* THOMAS CRANMER AND THE ENGLISH REFORMATION, 1489-1556
Pollard, Alfred William *see* ENGLISH MIRACLE PLAYS, MORALITIES, AND INTERLUDES; SPECIMENS OF THE PRE-ELIZABETHAN DRAMA
Pollard, Edward B *see* LUTHER RICE, PIONEER IN MISSIONS AND EDUCATION
Pollard, John Garland *see* A GUIDE TO MAGISTRATES AND CONSTABLES.
Pollard, Willard Lacy *see* DIGEST OF DECISIONS OF LAW AND PRACTICE IN THE PATENT OFFICE AND THE UNITED STATES COURTS IN PATENTS, TRADEMARKS, COPYRIGHTS AND LABELS, 1912-1919
Polle, Friedrich *see* WIE DENKT DAS VOLK UEBER DIE SPRACHE?
Pollen, FPL *see* RECHERCHES SUR LA FAUNE DE MADAGASCAR
Pollen, John Hungerford *see*
- ACTS OF ENGLISH MARTYRS
- THE LIFE AND LETTERS OF FATHER JOHN MORRIS, OF THE SOCIETY OF JESUS, 1826-1893

Pollera, Alberto *see* PICOLA BIBLIOGRAFIA DELL'AFRICA ORIENTALE
Pollich, J A *see* HISTORIA PLANTARUM IN PALATINATU ELECTORALI
Pollini, F *see* VARIATIONS ET RONDEAUX POUR LE PIANOFORTE
Pollitt, Ernesto *see* MALNUTRITION AND INFECTION IN THE CLASSROOM
Pollitt, Harry *see*
- POLLITT VISITS SPAIN; HARRY POLLITT'S STORY OF HIS VISIT TO SPAIN IN DECEMBER, 1937
- SAVE SPAIN FROM FASCISM

POLLITT VISITS SPAIN; HARRY POLLITT'S STORY OF HIS VISIT TO SPAIN IN DECEMBER, 1937 / Pollitt, Harry – London, 1938. Fiche W1112. (Blodgett Collection of Spanish Civil War Pamphlets) – 9 – us H.U. College Libr [946]
Pollock, F *see* THE HISTORY OF ENGLISH LAW BEFORE THE TIME OF EDWARD I
Pollock, Frederick *see*
- ESSAYS IN JURISPRUDENCE AND ETHICS
- LECTURES AND ESSAYS BY WILLIAM KINGDON CLIFFORD

Pollock, Frederick et al *see* THE REVISED REPORTS
Pollock, Louise *see* NATIONAL KINDERGARTEN MANUAL
Pollock, Richard Leo *see* TAX DEPRECIATION AND THE NEED FOR THE RESERVE RATIO TEST
POLLUTING BRITAIN: A REPORT / Bugler, Jeremy – Harmondsworth: Penguin, 1972. 182p. illus., map – 1 – us U.W. Library [360]
POLLUTION : AN INTERNATIONAL PROBLEM FOR FISHERIES – 1978 – 85p – it F.A.O. [360]
POLLUTION : MAJOR SOURCES FOR RESEARCH, 1800-1950 / ed by Moscato, Michael – (Pt 1, Environmental Pollution: ISBN 0-89093-193-3. $1,830.00; Pt 2, Pollution and Health: ISBN 0-89093-194-1. $1,635.00) – 1980 – $3,285.00 set – us UPA [360]
POLLUTION ATMOSPHERIQUE – Paris. 1959-72 – 5 – fr A.C.R.P.P. [073]
POLLUTION PREVENTION REVIEW – v1-3. 1990-93 – 9 – $73.00 set – us Hein [360]
POLNAIA ENTSIKLOPEDIIA RUSSKAGO SEL'SKAGO KHOZIAISTVA = ENCYCLOPEDIA OF RUSSIAN AGRICULTURE / ed by Rudzkii, A – St Petersburg: A F Devrien ed. v1-12. 1900-12 – 133mf – 9 – $750.00 – us Ross [630]
DIE POLNISCHE ZUWANDERUNG IM RUHRREVIER UND IHRE WIRKUNGEN / Schulze, Franz – Muenchen – 1 – DM30.00 – gw Mikro Press [943]
POLNOE SOBRANIE RUSSKICH LETOPISEJ, IRDANNOE ARCHEOGRAFICESKOJU KOMISSIEJU – v. 1-32. BR-10.307 1 – 9 – ne IDC [930]
POLNOE SOBRANIE RUSSKIKH LETOPISEI – (Complete Collection of Russian Chronicles). 27 v. 1841-1918 – 3 – us Readex [947]
POLNOE SOBRANIE RUSSKIKH LETOPISEI / Russia – St. Petersburg. 1841-1959 – 1 – us UMI [947]
POLNOE SOBRANIE RUSSKIKH LETOPISEI IZDANNOE ARKHEOGRAFICHESKOIU KOMISSIEIU – St. Petersburg, 1847-1968. v1- . BR-10,307/1 – 9 – ne IDC [020]
POLNOE SOBRANIE SOCHINENII / Aksakov, I S – Moscow, 1886-87. v1-7. BR-10,543 1 – 9 – ne IDC [947]
POLNOE SOBRANIE SOCHINENII / Aksakov, K S – Moscow, 1861-80. v1-3. BR-10,544 1 – 9 – ne IDC [947]
POLNOE SOBRANIE SOCHINENII / Lomonosov, Mikhail V – 10 v. 1950-59. BR-7659 2 – 8 – ne IDC [460]
POLNOE SOBRANIE SOCHINENII / Merezhkovskii, Dimitrii – 17v. 1911-14 – 1 – 46.00 – us L of C Photodup [460]
POLNOE SOBRANIE SOCHINENII / Mikhailovskii, N K – 4th ed. 8v. Spb. 1906-14. BR-10.606 2 – 8 – ne IDC [460]
POLNOE SOBRANIE SOCHINENII TOM 4, CHAST'I / Maiakovskii, Vladimir – 1937 – 8 – BR-989 2 – ne IDC [460]
POLNOE SOBRANIE SOCHINENII V 13 TOMAKH / Maiakovskii, Vladimir – Gosudarstvennoe izdatel'stvo khudozhestvennoi literatury. v. 1-13. M. 1955-61. BR-991 2 – 8 – ne IDC [460]
POLNOE SOBRANIE SOCHINENII V DVUKH TOMAKH / Kirevskii, IV – Moscow, 1911. BR-10,587/2 – 8 – ne IDC [947]
POLNOE SOBRANIE SOCHINENII V PIATNADTSATI TOMAKH / Chernyshevskii, Nikolai Gavrilovich – Moscow, 1939-53.BR-10,563/1 – 9 – ne IDC [947]
POLNOE SOBRANIE ZAKONOV ROSSIISKOJ IMPERII – 1649-1913 – 7,530mf – 8 – ne IDC [073]
POLNYI SLOVAR' RUSSKIKH RIFM / Abramov, N – Spb., 1912 – 3mf – 9 – 1152/2 – ne IDC [460]
POLNYI SPRAVOCHNYI UKAZATEL' KNIG, BROSHIUR, GAZET ZHURNALOV, AREST NA KOTORYE UTVERZHDEN SUBDEBNYMI USTANOVLENIIAMI PO 1-E IANVARIA 1912 GODA / Nikol'skii, A A – Kiev. 1912. BR-7178 2 – 8 – ne IDC [460]
POLNYI TSERKOVNO-SLAVIANSKII SLOVAR' / D'iachenko, G – M., 1900 – 31mf – 9 – 982/2 – ne IDC [290]
Polo Benito, Jose *see*
- PLASENCIA POR JESUS SACRAMENTADO. TRADICION EUCARISTICA (19 OCTUBRE 1488) POR...
- EL PROBLEMA SOCIAL DEL CAMPO EN EXTREMADURA

Polo, J *see* PRO VALENTINA MEDICORUM SCHOLA ADVERSUS BERNARDUM CAXANES BARCINONENSEM MEDICUM...
POLONIA – Chicago, 1918-nov 2 1944 – us Res Libr [071]
Polonskii, V *see* OCHERKI LITERATURNOGO DVIZHENIIA REVOLIUTSIONNOI EPOKHI, 1917-1927
POLOVOI VOPROS, GOSUDARSTVO, KULTURA / Fridlender, P – Peterburg: Gos. izd-vo, Peterburgskoe otd-nie, 1920 – 1 – CSUX91-B4083 – us Hoover Inst Photo [947]
Polovtsov, A A et al *see* THE RUSSIAN BIOGRAPHICAL DICTIONARY
POLOZHENIE O PROMYSLOVOI KOOPERATSII : POSTANOVLENIE VTSIK I SNK RSFRSR OT 11 IULIIA 1928 G. – M., 1929 – 1mf – 9 – COR-182/1 – ne IDC [334]
POLOZHENIE O SELSKIKH SOVETAKH – 3rd ed., rev. Moscow, 1929. 320p. BR-8677/1 – 9 – ne IDC [947]

POLOZHENIE O TOVARISHCHESKIKH SUDAKH / Azerbaijan S.S.R. – Baku: Verkhovny i Sovet Azerba idzhansko i SSR, 1964 – 1 – CSUX91-B2242 – us Hoover Inst Photo [947]

POLOZHENIE O VYBORAKH RAIONNYKH (GORODSKIKH) NARODNYKH SUDOV BELORUSSKOI SSR : UTVERZHDENO UKAZOM PREZIDIUMA VERKHOVNOGO SOVETA BELORUSSKOI SSR OT 25 OKTIABRIA 1960 GODA / Byelorussian S.S.R. – Minsk: Belarus, 1964 – 1 – CSUX91-B2004 – us Hoover Inst Photo [947]

POLOZHENIE O VYBORAKH V OBLASTNYE, RAIONNYE, GORODSKIE, SELSKIE I POSELKOVYE SOVETY DEPUTATOV TRUDI ASHCHIKHSIA BELORUSSKOI SSR : UTVERZHDENO UKAZOM PREZIDIUMA VERKHOVNOGO SOVETA BELORUSSKOI SSR OT 5 OKT. 1950 G. S IZMENENIIAMI ...OT 23 I 29 DEK. 1958 G., 6 II UNI A 1962 G. I 5 I ANV. 1963 G / Byelorussian S.S.R. – Minsk: "Belarus", 1965 – 1 – CSUX91-B1595 – us Hoover Inst Photo [947]

POLOZHENIE O VYBORAKH V RAIONNYE, GORODSKIE, POSELKOVYE I SELSKIE SOVTY DEPUTATOV TRUDI ASHCHIKHSIA ESTONSKOI SSR – Tallin: E esti raamat, 1965 – 1 – CSUX91-B1957 – us Hoover Inst Photo [947]

POLOZHENIE O VYBORAKH V VEKHOVNYI SOVET BELORUSSKOI SSR / Byelorussian S.S.R. – Minsk: Gos. izd-vo, Red. polit. lit-ry, 1940 – 1 – CSUX91-B2356 – us Hoover Inst Photo [947]

POLOZHENIE ROSSII V MIROVOM KHOZIAISTVE : ANALIZ RUSSKOGO EKSPORTA DO VOINY: STATISTICHESKII OCHERK / Den, Vladimir Eduardovich – Petrograd: 25-i a Gos. tip., 1922 – 1 – CSUX89-B3558 – us Hoover Inst Photo [380]

POLOZHENIIA O KUSTARNOI IM MELKOI PROMYSHLENNOSTI I PROMYSLOVOI KOOPERATSII : SBORNIK DEKRETOV, POSTANOVLENNII I INSTRUKTSII PO DEKABR' 1921 G. VKLIUCHITEL'NO – M., 1922 – 2mf – 9 – COR-439/1 – ne IDC [334]

POLSKA BAJKA LUDOWA W UKADZIE SYSTEMATYCZNYM / ed by Krzyzanowski, K – 2v. Warsaw. 1947. B-1276 2 – 8 – ne IDC [943]

POLSKA I AUTONOMIA / Filipowicz, Tytus – Warszawa: [Nak. Wydawn. "Zycie"], 1908 – 1 – CSUX89-B258 – us Hoover Inst Photo [320]

POLSKA LUDOWA – Poznan, Poland. May 1946-Nov 1949 (scattered issues) – 2r – 1 – us L of C Photodup [943]

POLSKA LUDOWA *see* PRZEBUDOWA

Polska Partia Socjalistyczna *see* ROBOTNIK

POLSKA ZBROJNA – Warsaw. Poland. -w. 26 Jul-30 Dec 1945, 22 Jun 1946-21 Jul 1950. (Imperfect). (17 reels) – 1 – uk British Libr Newspaper [943]

POLSKA ZBROJNA *see* ZOLNIERZ WOLNOSCI

POLSKI SLOWNIK ARCHIWALNY / Grygier, T et al; ed by Maciejewska, W – Warszawa, 1974 – 2mf – 9 – R-9884/1 – ne IDC [460]

Polskie Towarzystwo Jezykoznawcze *see* BIULETYN

POL'SKII VOPROS / Pogodin, M P – Sobranie razsuzhdenii, zapisok i zamechanii 1831-1867. M. 1867. BR-8323 2 – 8 – ne IDC [943]

Polstorff, Friedrich *see* DER SUBJEKTIVISMUS IN DER MODERNEN THEOLOGIE UND SEIN ANRECHT

POLTAVSKAIA POBEDA – Iz istorii mezhdunarodnykhotnoshenii nakune i posle Poltavy. M. 1959. BR-7780 2 – 8 – ne IDC [947]

Polunin, F *see* GEOGRAFICHESKII LEKSIKON ROSSIISKOGO GOSUDARSTVA

POLUTORAGLAZYI STRELETS / Livshich, B – L. 1933. BR-963 2 – 8 – ne IDC [999]

POLVEKA DLIA KNIGI – (1866-1916). Literaturnokhudozhestvennyi sbornik posviashchennyi piatidesiatiletiiu izdatel'skoi deiatel'nosti. I.D. Sytina. M. 1916. BR-4605 2 – 8 – ne IDC [460]

POLVO DE SUS SANDALIAS / Castro Albarran, A de – Salamanca, 1931; Madrid: Razon y Fe, 1932 – 1 – sp Bibl Santa Ana [830]

Polwhele, R *see*
- THE HISTORY OF DEVONSHIRE
- A LETTER TO THE REV. ROBERT HAWKER, D.D., VICAR OF THE PARISH OF CHARLES, PLYMOUTH, OCCASIONED BY HIS LATE EXPEDITION INTO CORNWALL

POLYANHEA MARIANA : HOMENAGEM A IMMACULADA CONCEICAO – Manaos, Amazonas. 8 Dez 1916 – 1,5,6 – bl Biblioteca [072]

POLYANTHEA : AO EXMO SR. CORONEL ANTONIO GUERREIRO ANTONY – Manaos, Amazonas. 5 Set 1912 – 1,5,6 – bl Biblioteca [072]

POLYANTHEA : AO EXMOR SR. CORONEL JOSE H. DE OLIVEIRA AMARAL – Manaos, Amazonas. 2 Set 1907 – 1,5,6 – bl Biblioteca [072]

POLYANTHEA : COMMEMORATIVO DAS FESTAS DA INSTRUCAO NA ESCOLA NORMAL – Manaos, Amazonas. 21 Nov 1906 – 1,5,6 – bl Biblioteca [072]

POLYANTHEA : EM BENEFICIO DA CRUZ VERMELHA BRASILEIRA – Manaos, Amazonas. Nov 1917 – 1,5,6 – bl Biblioteca [072]

POLYANTHEA : HOMENAGEM A SAUDOSA MEMORIA DO BARAO DO RIO BRANCO – Manaos, Amazonas. 1912 – 1,5,6 – bl Biblioteca [072]

POLYANTHEA : HOMENAGEM DA CONGREGACAO DO GYMNASIO AMAZONENSE E ESCOLA NORMAL – Manaos, Amazonas. 28 Abr 1898 – 1,5,6 – bl Biblioteca [072]

POLYANTHEA : HOMENAGEM DOS FILHOS DOS PAIZES ALLIADOS RESIDENTES NO AMAZONAS AO EXMO SR. DR. GASPAR GUIMARAES – Manaos, Amazonas. 20 Set 1916 – 1,5,6 – bl Biblioteca [072]

POLYANTHEA : J. ROCHA DOS SANTOS – Manaos, Amazonas. 24 Out 1903 – 1,5,6 – bl Biblioteca [072]

POLYANTHEA : JURACY – Manaos, Amazonas. 23 Jun 1910 – 1,5,6 – bl Biblioteca [072]

POLYANTHEA : LEOPOLDO DE MATTOS – Manaos, Amazonas. 11 Dez 1912 – 1,5,6 – bl Biblioteca [072]

POLYANTHEA – Manaos, Amazonas. 10 Fev 1917 – 1,5,6 – bl Biblioteca [072]

POLYANTHEA – Manaos, Amazonas. 20 Set, 17 Nov 1916 – 1,5,6 – bl Biblioteca [072]

POLYANTHEA MEDICIS SPECIOSA CHIRURGIS MIRIFICA MYREPSICIS VALDE UTILIS ET NECESSARIA / Gomez de la Parra, A – Madrid, 1625 – 7mf – 9 – sp Cultura [617]

POLYCHETES ERRANTES. FAUNE DE FRANCE / Fauvel, P – 2785 2. v. 5. 1923 – 8 – ne IDC [590]

POLYCHRONICON RANULPHI HIGDEN MONACHI CESTRENSIS (RS41) : TOGETHER WITH THE ENGLISH TRANSLATION OF JOHN OF TREVISA AND OF AN UNKNOWN WRITER IN THE 15TH CENTURY / Ranulf Higden; ed by Babington, C (v1-2) & Lumby, J R (v3-9) – (v1 1865 v2 1869 v3 1871 Dfl35.00v. v4 1872 v5 1874 Dfl32.00v. v6 1876 Dfl35.00. v7 1879 Dfl39.00. v8 1882 Dfl42.00. v9 1886 Dfl39.00) – ne Slangenburg [240]

POLYCHRONIUS : BRUDER THEODORS VON MOPSUESTIA UND BISCHOF VON APAMEA: EIN BEITRAG ZUR GESCHICHTE DER EXEGESE / Bardenhewer, Otto – Freiburg im Breisgau, St. Louis, Mo.: Herder, 1879 – 1mf – us A.T.L.A. [240]

POLYCYCLIC AROMATIC COMPOUNDS : AN INTERNATIONAL AND INTERDISCIPLINARY JOURNAL / ed by Zander, Maximilian – 1,5,9 – us Gordon [540]

POLYDAKTYLIEN DER HAENDE : EIN BEITRAG ZUR SPEZIELLEN ANATOMIE, ENTWICKLUNGSGESCHICHTE, KLASSIFIKATION UND OPERATIVE BEHANDLUNG / Schrader, Marianne – 1993 – 5mf – 9 – DM125.00 – 3-89349-640-8 – gw Hänsel [611]

Polydorus, Vergilius *see* DE RERUM INVENTORIBUS LIBRI 8

LA POLYGINIE SORORALE ET LE SORORAT DANS LA CHINE FEODALE / Granet, Marcel – Paris: Leroux, 1920. 93p. (Les Femmes Collection) – 2mf – 9 – $6.00 – fr Bibl Nationale [360]

POLYGLOT LIST OF BIRDS IN TURKI, MANCHU AND CHINESE / Denison Ross, E – (Asiatic society of Bengal, v. 2, no. 9). Calcutta. 1909. BU-483 2 – 8 – ne IDC [590]

THE POLYGLOTT : OR, HOPE OF ETERNAL LIFE ACCORDING TO THE VARIOUS SENTIMENTS OF THE PRESENT DAY,... – London, 1761 – 1mf – 9 – MP-406/1 – ne IDC [240]

POLYGLOTTA AFRICANA, OR A COMPARATIVE VOCABULARY... / Koelle, Sigismund W – London: Church Missionary House, 1854 – 1 – F130.93 – fr Armell [400]

POLYGRAM *see* THE MUSTANG

POLYHEDRON – (Back issues of journal available from UMI) – Incorp. Journal of inorganic & Nuclear Chemistry and its suppl. Inorganic & Nuclear Chemistry Letters. 24 issues/y. v12. 1993 – 9 – £1,130.00y – uk Elsevier Sci [540]

POLYMER – (1982-. 1,5,6,9) – v1-. 1960- – 1 – us UMI [073]

POLYMER COMMUNICATIONS – v24-. 1983- – 1,5,6,9 – us UMI [073]

POLYMER DEGRADATION AND STABILITY – v1-9. 1979-84 – 1,5,6,13 – sz Elsevier [073]

POLYMER NEWS – 1,5,9 – us Gordon [540]

POLYMER NEWS / ed by Kirshenbaum, G S – 9,5,1 – us Gordon [540]

POLYMER PHOTOCHEMISTRY – v1-5. 1981-84 – 1,5,6,13 – sz Elsevier [073]

POLYMER PROCESS ENGINEERING – v1-. 1983- – 1,5,6,9 – us UMI [073]

POLYMER SCIENCE USSR – v.1-. 1960- – 5,6,9 – us UMI [073]

POLYMER TESTING – v1-4. 1980-84 – 1,5,6,13 – sz Elsevier [073]

POLYMER-PLASTICS TECHNOLOGY AND ENGINEERING – (1984-. 5,6,9) – v2-. 1973- – 1 – us UMI [073]

THE POLYMORPHIAN – Saint John, NB: South End Polymorphian Club, [1897] – 9 – cn C.I.H.M. [941]

Polynesia. French *see* JOURNAL OFFICIEL DE LA POLYNESIE FRANCAISE

POLYNESIAN – Honolulu. Hawaii. -w. 1840-63 – 1 – us UMI [071]

POLYPETALAE THALAMIFLORAE ET DISCIFLORAE REHMANNIANAE. ROZPRAWY I SPRAWOZDANIA / Szyszylowicz, I – (Akademy umiejetnoa1scie w Krakowie, 1888, v. 17, p. 96-167; 1888, v. 18, p. 1-75). B-216 2 – 8 – ne IDC [580]

DIE POLYPHEMSAGE IN DER VOLKSUEBERLIEFERUNG / Hackmann, Oskar – 1904 – 1 – uk Microform Academic [390]

POLYPODIORUM ASPLENIORUM SPECIES NOVAE ET NON SATIS NOVAE AND OTHER ITEMS / Hieronymus, G – Hedwigia. 1904 – 7 – uk Microform Academic [580]

POLYTECHNIC CALIFORNIAN *see* THE MUSTANG

POLYTECHNIC HIGH SCHOOL YEARBOOK – Caerulea, Long Beach, CA. 1908- – 22r – 1 – $1,100.00 – R60014 – us Library Micro [370]

POLYTECHNISCHES JOURNAL / Dingler, Johann Gottfried – Stuttgart. 318v. 1820-1900 – 2160mf – 9 – subsc: DM10,800.00 – gw Olms [500]

POLYTECHNISCHES JOURNAL 1. 1820-211. 1874. DINGLERS POLYTECHNISCHES JOURNAL 212.1874-346. 1931 / ed by Dingler, Johann Gottfried – Stuttgart, Berlin, 1820-1931 (mf ed 1994) – 1,167mf – 9 – DM15,000.00 – 3-89131-169-9 – gw Fischer [600]

POLYTHECON – 1990 – 5mf – 9 – Bf1,400.00 – 2-503-63932-1 – be Brepols [240]

Polz, Marianne *see* ZUR PROZESSKONZEPTION MUENDLICHEN DARSTELLENS IM AUSDRUCKSUNTERRICHT UNTER BESONDERER BERUECKSICHTIGUNG DER SUBJEKT-OBJEKT-DIALEKTIK

Polzer, Claudia *see* ZWISCHEN FLUCHT UND MIGRATION

Pomel, A *see* NOUVEAUX MATERIAUX POUR LA FLORE ATLANTIQUE

POMEROY ABBEY / Wood, Ellen – British Fiction Archive: Unit 1 – 9 – uk Bell [830]

Pomeroy, Dwight Abel *see* BUSINESS LAW

Pomeroy, Henry H *see* DIARY

Pomeroy, John Norton *see* CODE REMEDIES AND REMEDIAL RIGHTS BY THE CIVIL ACTION ACCORDING TO THE REFORMED AMERICAN PROCEDURE.

POMESHCHIKI I IKH ORGANIZATSII V 1917 G. / Chaadaeva, O N – M., L., 1928. 176p – 2mf – 9 – ne IDC [320]

Pomier, M *see* MANUEL DES LOCUTIONS VICIEUSES

POMMERELLER TAGEBLATT – Dirschau (Tczew)-Simonsdorf, Poland. 10 Jul 1924-28 Mar 1937 – 1 – gw Mikrofilm [943]

POMMERN-BRIEF – Hamburg. Germany. -w. 20 Jul 1953-24 Dec 1955. (2 reels) – 1 – uk British Libr Newspaper [072]

DIE POMMERSCHE ZEITUNG – Hamburg, West Germany. Oct 1951-17 Dec 1975 – 1 – gw Mikrofilm [072]

POMMERSCHE ZEITUNG – Szczecin, Poland. Jun 1936-Sept 1937; Mar 1943-Mar 1945 (scattered issues – 2r – 1 – us L of C Photodup [943]

POMNIKI GISTORYI I KUL'TURY BELARUSI – (Only backfile available) – Belarus, 1970-89 – 20r – 1 – $85.00r – us Ross [072]

POMOC – Pueblo, CO, 1929-1931 – 2mf or 1 reel – 1,9 – us I.H.R.C. [978]

POMOGA I STROIT SOVETSKUIU VLAST : NAPUTSTVIE OTPUSKNOMU KRASNOARME IT SU / Divilkovskii, A – Moskva: Gos. izd-vo, 1921 – 1 – CSUX88-B7212 – us Hoover Inst Photo [947]

POMONA BULLETIN – (Also known as: Pomona Progress) – Pomona, CA. 1912-1927; 1954-1959 – 37r – 1 – 1,850.00 – CH03400 – us Library Micro [071]

POMONA DAILY REVIEW – Pomona, CA. 1902-1914 – 20r – 1 – $1,000.00 – H04035 – us Library Micro [071]

POMONA NEWS *see* NEWSPAPERS PUBLISHED IN INTERNMENT CAMPS

POMONA PROGRESS *see* POMONA BULLETIN

POMONA VALLEY / Brackett, FP – Los Angeles: Historic Record Co., 1920. California Reel 19. (The Cox Library Collection) – 5 – us Americana [978]

POMOSHCH AVIATSII DEISTVIIAM PARTIZANOV / Atsuk, N A – Moskva: Gos. izdvo, 1921 – 1 – CSUX89-B1033 – us Hoover Inst Photo [355]

POMOTROPIC – Azusa. Calif. 1910-1929 – 1 – us UMI [071]

POMOTROPICS – Azusa, CA. Jun 1900-1914 (incomplete) – 4r – 1 – $200.00 – C02038 – us Library Micro [071]

Pompecki, Josef Felix *see* DIE BODENSCHAETZE DER KAMPFGEBIETE IN IHRER BEDEUTUNG FUER UNS UND UNSERE FEINDE

POMPEIANISCHE WANDINSCHRIFTEN UND VERWANDTES / Diehl, Ernst – Bonn: A. Marcus und E. Weber, 1910. 60p – 1 – us U.W. Library [410]

POMPEII / Maiuri, Amedeo – 1951 – 9 – $10.00 – us I.R.C. [930]

POMPEII A.D. 79 : TREASURES FROM THE NATIONAL ARCHAEOLOGICAL MUSEUM, NAPLES, AND THE POMPEII ANTIQUARIUM / Ward-Perkins, John Bryan – Boston: Boston Museum of Fine Arts, c1978. 2v. ill – 1 – us U.W. Library [930]

Pompigny *see* L'EPOUS REPUBLICAIN

POMURSKI VESTNIK – Murska Sobota, Yugoslavia. 1961-62 – 1r – 1 – us L of C Photodup [949]

PONCA GRIT – Ponca, NE. -w. Jul 1892; Aug 1895-May 1898; Dec 1898-Aug 1900 – 1 – us NE Hist [071]

THE PONCA TRIBE / Howard, James Henri – (In collaboration with Peter LeClaire, tribal historian, and other members of the tribe) – 1965 – 5mf – 9 – $5.00f – us Ross [307]

Ponce de Santa Cruz, A *see*
- DE IMPEDIMENTIS MAGNORUM AUXILIORUM IN MORBORUM CURATIONE, LIBRI 3
- PRAELECTIONES VALLISOLETANAE IN LIBRO MAGNI HIPPOCRATIS. DE MORBO SACRO

Ponce, M *see* DESCRIPTION DES BAINS DE TITUS, OU COLLECTION DES PEINTURES TROUVEES DANS LES RUINES DES THERMES DE CET EMPEREUR

Poncelet, E *see* ACTES DES PRINCES-EVEQUES DE LIEGE

Poncet, Charles J *see* RELATION ABREGEE DU VOYAGE. EN ETHIOPIE

Poncius, J *see* PHILOSOPHIAE AD MENTEM SCOTI CURSUS INTEGER

POND CONSTRUCTION FOR FRESHWATER FISH CULTURE – BUILDING EARTHEN PONDS – it F.A.O. [639]

POND CONSTRUCTION FOR FRESHWATER FISH CULTURE : POND-FARM STRUCTURES AND LAYOUTS – 1992 – 214p – it F.A.O. [639]

Pond, Enoch *see*
- THE AUTOBIOGRAPHY OF THE REV. ENOCH POND, D.D.
- THE SEALS OPENED, OR, THE APOCALYPSE EXPLAINED
- SKETCHES OF THE THEOLOGICAL HISTORY OF NEW ENGLAND

PONDELNI RANNI NOVINY – Prague, Czechoslovakia. 29 Nov 1937; 24 Jan-1 Aug 1938 – 1r – 1 – us L of C Photodup [072]

PONDELNIK – Bratislava, Czechoslovakia. 23 Jul; 22,29 Oct; 5 Nov 1951 – 1r – 1 – us L of C Photodup [072]
PONDELNIK – Prague, Czechoslovakia. May 1949-Jan 1952 (scattered issues) – 2r – 1 – us L of C Photodup [072]
PONDELNIK (SUPPLEMENT) – Prague, Czechoslovakia. Feb, Apr 1926 – 1r – 1 – us L of C Photodup [072]
PONDERS COUNTY NEWS – Conrad. Mont. 1929-1946 – 1 – us UMI [071]
Pondicherry. India *see* LA GAZETTE DE L'ETAT
PONDS CREEK BAPTIST CHURCH. MONROE COUNTY. TENNESSEE : CHURCH RECORDS – 1824-Oct 1860 – 1 – 5.85 – us Baptist [240]
PONEDELJAK – Belgrade, Yugoslavia. 1942-Jun 1943 – 1r – 1 – us L of C Photodup [949]
PONENCIA ACERCA DE "PROCEDIMIENTOS DE ELABORACION DE ACEITES DE OLIVAS EN SUS DISTINTOS ASPECTOS" / Cruz Valero, Antonio – Badajoz: Imp. La Minerva Extremena, 1927 – 1 – sp Bibl Santa Ana [946]
PONENCIA PARA LA ASAMBLEA DE COLEGIO (DE PRACTICANTES DEL DIA 22 DE NOVIEMBRE DE 1944 PRESENTADA PRO EL PRESIDENTE... / Orozco Avelianeda, Agustin J – Caceres: Imp. Garcia Floriano, s.a. – sp Bibl Santa Ana [320]
Pongratz, Alfons *see* XEUVERL
PONOKA HERALD – Alberta. Canada. 1902-23 – 1 – cn Commonwealth Micro [072]
Ponomarev, A I *see* PAMIATNIKI DREVNERUSSKOI TSERKOVNOI-UCHITEL'NOI LITERATURY
Ponomarev, A I, red *see* PAMIATNIKI DREVNERUSSKOI TSERKOVNOI-UCHITEL'NOI LITERATURY
Ponomareva, S *see* IERUSALIM I PALESTINA V RUSSKOI LITERATURE, NAUKE, ZHIVOPISI I PEREVODAKH (MATERIALY DLIA BIBLIOGRAFII)
PONOVYM VIEKHAM / Bielov, Vadim – Revel: "Novai a zemli a", 1922 – 1 – CSUX88-B8739 – us Hoover Inst Photo [947]
Pons, F *see* MEMORIA PRACTICA SOBRE LAS CALENTURAS PUTRIDAS DEL AMPURDAN
Pons, Jaime *see* VIDA DE SAN BERNARDO ABAD DE CLARAVAL
Pons, Jean Francois de *see* OEUVRES
Ponsonby, Arthur Ponsonby *see* DEMOCRACY AND DIPLOMACY
LE PONT – Berlin-Charlottenburg, 1943 – 1 – Inquire at Mikrofilmarchiv for details – gw Misc Inst [072]
Pont, Pierre-Samuel du *see* JOURNAL DE L'AGRICULTURE, DU COMMERCE, DES ARTS ET DES FINANCES
PONTANI OPERA / Pontano, Giovanni Gioviano – Vrania, Siue de stellis libri quing;, Meteorum liber unus. De hortis Hesperidum libri duo. Lepidina, siue Postorales sic pompae septem. Item Meliseus. Maeon. Acon. Hendecasyllaborum libri duo. Tumulorum liber unus. Neniae duodecim. Epigrammata duodecim...Colophon: Venetiis, in aedibvs Aldi, et Andreae Asvlani Soceri, M.D. XIII – 1 – us U.W. Library [890]
Pontano, Giovanni Gioviano *see* PONTANI OPERA
Pontanus, J *see*
– HISTORIARUM LIBRI 4 (CBH 17)
– HISTORIARUM LIBRI 8 (CBH 2,1)
IL PONTE D'ALCANTARA / Huebner, E – Roma: Tip. Tiberina, 1863 – 1 – sp Bibl Santa Ana [946]
Ponte e Horta, Jose Maria da *see* TRATADO DE LOURENCO MARQUES
Ponten, Josef *see*
– AUF ZUR WOLGA
– ROEMISCHES IDYLL
– DIE STUNDE HEIDELBERGS
Pontes, Eloy *see*
– A VIDA CONTRADICTORIA DE MACHADO DE ASSIS
– A VIDA DRAMATICA DE EUCLYDES DA CUNHA
PONTIAC ADVANCE – Portage-du-Fort Canada. v17 n24. 27 dec 1888; v17 n25. 2 jan 1889 – 1r – 1 – Can$25.00 – cn Can Microfilming [072]
THE PONTIAC ADVANCE – Quyon, Canada. v37 n32. 19 avr 1907 – 1r – 1 – Can$25.00 – cn Can Microfilming [072]
PONTIAC, CHIEF OF THE OTTAWAS: A TALE OF THE SIEGE OF DETROIT / Ellis, Edward Sylvester – By H. R. Gordon. New York: E. P. Dutton, c1897. 05234. (Pre-1900 Canadiana) – 9 – cn C.I.H.M. [971]
PONTIAC NEWS – Bryson, Canada. v3 n7. 20 avr 1882-v3 n36. 9 nov 1882 – 1r – 1 – Can$35.00 – cn Can Microfilming [072]
PONTIAC PIONEER AND PORTAGE-DU-FORT ADVERTISER – Portage-du-Fort, Canada. v3 n48. 14 oct 1864 – 1r – 1 – Can$25.00 – cn Can Microfilming [072]
Pontiac-Monroeville. Ohio. St. Peter Lutheran Church *see*
– RECORDS
PONTIAC-PRESSE – Fort-Coulonge, Canada. v1 n2. 14 jun 1973-28 aut 1973 – 1r – 1 – Can$25.00 – cn Can Microfilming [072]
PONTIFICAL DE CHARFE – v1-2. 1950 – 18mf – 8 – Dfl63.00 – ne Slangenburg [240]
Pontifical Institute of Mediaeval Studies. Toronto *see*
– DICTIONARY CATALOG OF THE LIBRARY
– DICTIONARY CATALOGUE OF THE LIBARY OF THE PONTIFICAL INSTITUTE OF MEDIAEVAL STUDIES
THE PONTIFICAL OF MAGDALEN COLLEGE, OXFORD / Wilson, H Austin – 1910 – 6mf – 8 – ne Slangenburg [240]
PONTIFICALE ECCLESIAE S. ANDREAE – Edinburgh, 1885 – 6mf – 8 – Dfl25.00 – ne Slangenburg [240]
PONTIFICALE IUXTA RITUM ECCLESIAE SYRORUM ORIENTALIUM ID EST CHALDAEORUM : VERSIO LATINA – Romae, 1937 – 13mf – 8 – Dfl46.00 – ne Slangenburg [240]
PONTIFICALE LANALETENSE / Doble, G H – 1937 – 3mf – 8 – ne Slangenburg [240]
LE PONTIFICAT DE PIE 19, 1846-1878 (21) – Paris, 1952 – Dfl49.00 – ne Slangenburg [240]
LES PONTIFICAUX. MANUSCRITS DES BIBLIOTHEQUES PUBLIQUES DE FRANCE / Leroquais, Victor – (Tome 1, 15mf; Tome 2, 15mf; Tome 3, 6mf; Planches, 5mf) – Paris. Tom 1-3, Planches. 1937 – 8 – Dfl144.00 – ne Slangenburg [240]
Pontones, P *see* ARCHITECTURA HYDRAULICA EN LAS FABRICAS DE PUENTES METHODO DE PROYECTARLOS Y REPARLOS
PONTOS NOS 2 : HEBDOMADARIO HUMORISTICO, CRITICO, IMPOLITICO E REBARBATIVO – Manaos, Amazonas. 14 Jul-8 Set 1906 – 1,5,6 – bl Biblioteca [072]
Pontotoc, Mississippi *see* MISCELLANEOUS EARLY NEWSPAPERS
LES PONTS DE L'AMERIQUE DU NORD: ETUDE, CALCUL, DESCRIPTION DE CES PONTS: COMPARAISON DES SYSTEMES AMERICAIN ET EUROPEEN / Comolli, Louis Antoine – Paris: A. Lefevre, 1879. 00727. (Pre-1900 Canadiana) – 9 – cn C.I.H.M. [970]
PONTYPRIDD OBSERVER. (THE OBSERVER) – Wales. Mar 1897-Dec 1977.-w. 73 reels – 1 – uk British Libr Newspaper [072]
Ponz, Antonio *see*
– VIAJE DE ESPANA. TOMO 1
– VIAJE DE ESPANA. TOMO 2
– VIAJE DE ESPANA. TOMO 3
– VIAJE DE ESPANA. TOMO 4
– VIAJE DE ESPANA. TOMO 5
– VIAJE DE ESPANA. TOMO 6
– VIAJE DE ESPANA. TOMO 7
– VIAJE DE ESPANA. TOMO 8
– VIAJE DE ESPANA. TOMO 9
– VIAJE DE ESPANA. TOMO 10
– VIAJE DE ESPANA. TOMO 11
– VIAJE DE ESPANA. TOMO 12
– VIAJE POR ESPANA
POOLE AND BOURNEMOUTH HERALD *see* POOLE AND SOUTH WESTERN HERALD
POOLE AND SOUTH WESTERN HERALD – (Poole and Bournemouth Herald. 5 Jul 1877-18 Apr 1895. Poole, Parkstone & East Dorset Herald. 25 Apr 1895-24 Jun 1937) – England. 1852-65; 1874-77; 1879; 1882; 1937. -w – 15r – 1 – uk British Libr Newspaper [072]
Poole, John E *see* PAPERS
Poole, Joshua *see*
– THE ENGLISH ACCIDENCE: OR, A SHORT, PLAINE AND EASIE WAY FOR THE MORE SPEEDY ATTAINING TO THE LATINE TONGUE
– THE ENGLISH PARNASSUS: OR, A HELP, TO ENGLISH POESIE
– PRACTICAL REHTORICK
Poole, Karen L *see* USE OF THE EXERCISE BENEFITS/BARRIERS SCALE IN NORTH CAROLINA DEPARTMENT OF CORRECTION EMPLOYEES
POOLE, PARKSTONE AND EAST DORSET HERALD *see* POOLE AND SOUTH WESTERN HERALD
Poole, Ralph J *see* SIND FRAUEN ESSBAR?
Poole, Reginald Lane *see*
– A HISTORY OF THE HUGUENOTS OF THE DISPERSION
– ILLUSTRATIONS OF THE HISTORY OF MEDIAEVAL THOUGHT
– LECTURES ON THE HISTORY OF THE PAPAL CHANCERY
– WYCLIFFE AND MOVEMENTS FOR REFORM
POONA OBSERVER – India. -d. March 1876-Feb 1877; 1878-1906. 103 reels – 1 – uk British Libr Newspaper [072]
POONA SARVAJNIK SABHA – (Missing: v19 1915/16. v21(2) 1917/18. v23(1) 1919/20. v24(3-4) 1920) – Poona. v1-24. 1878-1920 – 136mf – 9 – I-106/2 – ne IDC [073]
Poona Sarvajnik Sabha *see* QUARTERLY JOURNAL
POOR MAN'S ADVOCATE AND WORKMAN'S GUIDE – 1-50 (all publ). 1832-1833 – 5mf – 9 – $55.00 – us UPA [335]
THE POOR MAN'S CATECHISM : OR, THE CHRISTIAN DOCTRINE EXPLAINED / Mannock, John – (Includes index) – New York: Catholic Publ Society, [ca 1815] – 1mf – 9 – 0-8370-7332-4 – 1986-1332 – us A.T.L.A. [240]
POOR MAN'S GUARDIAN – 1-238 (all publ). 1831-1835 – 21mf – 9 – $80.00 – us UPA [335]
POOR MAN'S GUARDIAN – England. 1847 – 1 – uk Microform Academic [072]
POOR MAN'S GUARDIAN – London. -w. Jul 1831-Dec 1835. (2 reels) – 1 – uk British Libr Newspaper [072]
Poot, H K zn *see* HET GROOT NATUUR-EN ZEDEKUNDIGH WERELTTONEEL
O POP – Rio Branco, Acre. 6 Jun 1971; 1 Jan 1973 – 1,5,6 – bl Biblioteca [072]
THE POPE = DU PAPE : CONSIDERED IN HIS RELATIONS WITH THE CHURCH, TEMPORAL SOVEREIGNTIES, SEPARATED CHURCHES, AND THE CAUSE OF CIVILIZATION / Maistre, Joseph Marie, Comte de – (Includes bibliographical references) – London: C Dolman, 1850 – 1mf – 9 – 0-8370-7166-6 – 1986-1166 – us A.T.L.A. [240]
Pope, A *see* THE DUNCIAD, IN FOUR BOOKS, PRINTED ACCORDING TO THE COMPLETE COPY FOUND IN THE YEAR 1742, WITH THE PROLEGOMENA OF SCRIBLERUS AND NOTES VARIORUM;...
THE POPE AND ITALY / Parsons, Wilfrid – New York: The American Press, 1929. 134p. Illus. 1 reel. 1293 – 1 – us U.W. Library [945]
THE POPE AND THE COUNCIL = PAPST UND DAS CONCIL / Doellinger, Johann Joseph Ignaz von – (In English. Includes bibliographical references) – Boston: Roberts, 1870 – 1mf – 9 – 0-8370-9137-3 – 1986-3137 – us A.T.L.A. [240]
Pope, Charles Henry *see* THE PIONEERS OF MAINE & NEW HAMPSHIRE
Pope, Eugene M *see* THE PHILOSOPHY AND FINANCIAL VALUE OF CORPORATE SIGNAGE AT NCAA DIVISION 1-A ATHLETIC DEPARTMENTS
Pope, G D *see* OCMULGEE NATIONAL MONUMENT, GEORGIA
Pope, Howard Walter *see* 2. TIMOTHY 2:15
POPE JOHN THE TWENTY-THIRD AND MASTER JOHN HUSS OF BOHEMIA / Kitts, Eustace J – London: Constable, 1910 – 2mf – us A.T.L.A. [240]
POPE LEO 13 : HIS LIFE AND LETTERS, FROM RECENT AND AUTHENTIC SOURCES / ed by Talbot, James F – (Includes glossary of terms) – Boston: Martin Garrison, 1886 – 2mf – 9 – 0-8370-8948-4 – 1986-2948 – us A.T.L.A. [920]
POPE LEO 13 : HIS LIFE AND WORK / Narfon, Julien de – London: Chapman & Hall; Philadelphia; J B Lippincott, 1899 – 1mf – 9 – 0-8370-8599-3 – 1986-2599 – us A.T.L.A. [920]
POPE LEO 13 / McCarthy, Justin – 2nd enl ed. New York: Frederick Warne, c1899 – 1mf – 9 – 0-8370-8595-0 – 1986-2595 – us A.T.L.A. [920]
THE POPE ON THE SPANISH TERROR / Pius 11, Pope – London, 1936. Fiche W1110. (Blodgett Collection of Spanish Civil War Pamphlets) – 9 – us H.U. College Libr [946]
POPE, OR PRESIDENT : STARTLING DISCLOSURES OF ROMANISM AS REVEALED BY ITS OWN WRITERS: FACTS FOR AMERICANS – New York: R L Delisser, 1859, c1858 – 1mf – 9 – 0-8370-8860-7 – 1986-2860 – us A.T.L.A. [240]
Pope Pius 9 *see* INEFFABILIS DEUS
Pope, R Martin *see* THE LETTERS OF JOHN HUS
Popek, A (Anton) *see* DER FALSCHE DEMETRIUS IN DER DICHTUNG
POPERY : ITS CHARACTER AND ITS CRIMES / Tayler, William Elfe – (Includes bibliographical references) – 2nd rev enl ed. London: Partridge and Oakey, 1851 – 1mf – 9 – 0-8370-8474-1 – 1986-2474 – us A.T.L.A. [240]
POPERY : THE MAN OF SIN AND THE SON OF PERDITION: BEING A PRIZE ESSAY OF THE EVANGELICAL ALLIANCE / Gault, Robert – New York: American and Foreign Christian Union, 1855 – 2mf – 9 – 0-8370-8425-3 – 1986-2425 – us A.T.L.A. [240]
POPERY AS OPPOSED TO THE KNOWLEDGE, THE MORALS, THE WEALTH AND THE LIBERTY OF MANKIND – London: J. Brooks, 1833.571p – 1 – us U.W. Library [240]
Popham, A E *see* OLD MASTERS DRAWINGS AT HOLKHAM HALL
Popham, Home Riggs *see* TELEGRAPHIC SIGNALS, OR MARINE VOCABULARY; WITH OBSERVATIONS ON SIGNAL FLAGS, AND THE BEST MODE OF APPLYING THEM
LE POPIL, OBJET RITUEL CAMBODGIEN / Thierry, S – 9 – F30.00 – fr Ethnologie [306]
POPLAR CREEK BAPTIST CHURCH. FLAT RIVER BAPTIST ASSOCIATION. GRANSVILLE COUNTY. NORTH CAROLINA : CHURCH RECORDS – 1863-1914 – 1 – 13.14 – us Baptist [240]
POPLAR SPRINGS BAPTIST CHURCH. LAURENS COUNTY. SOUTH CAROLINA : CHURCH RECORDS – 1895-1984 – 1 – $52.02 – us Baptist [240]
POPLAR SPRINGS BAPTIST CHURCH. SHELBY, NORTH CAROLINA : CHURCH RECORDS – 1898-1963 – 1 – 8.55 – us Baptist [240]
POPLAR SPRINGS BAPTIST CHURCH. SPARTANBURG COUNTY. SOUTH CAROLINA : CHURCH RECORDS – 1874-1972 – 1 – 37.72 – us Baptist [240]
POPLAR SPRINGS BAPTIST CHURCH. TAR RIVER ASSOCIATION. NORTH CAROLINA : CHURCH RECORDS – 1788-1877. (Dead, 1882) – 1 – 8.73 – us Baptist [240]
POPLAR SPRINGS BAPTIST CHURCH. WEBSTER COUNTY. GEORGIA : CHURCH RECORDS – 1877-1912 – 1 – 29.32 – us Baptist [240]
POPLARS AND WILLOWS – 1980 – 360p – it F.A.O. [634]
POPOLNENIE FONDOV TSENTRAL'NOGO PARTIINOGO ARKHIVA IML PRI TSK KPSS / U.S.S.R. Moscow – (In Voprosy istorii KPSS, 1958-66, 1968, 1972). Article titles vary. BR-9890 1 – 9 – ne IDC [335]
IL POPOLO – New York, NY. 1921(?)-1922 – us I.H.R.C. [071]
IL POPOLO – New York, NY. 1938 – us I.H.R.C. [071]
IL POPOLO – Philadelphia, PA. Sept 1905-Apr 1906 – 3r – 1 – us I.H.R.C. [978]
IL POPOLO *see* LA VOCE DEL POPOLO
POPOLO – 1946-1947 – 1r per y – 5,6 – Sfr481.00 – sz Infoprint [072]
POPOLO – 1948-1995 – 3r per y – 5,6 – Sfr936.00 – sz Infoprint [072]
IL POPOLO DI ROMA – Italy. -d. 8 Dec 1940-4 Sep 1943. (Imperfect). (10 reels) – 1 – uk British Libr Newspaper [072]
IL POPOLO D'ITALIA – Milan, Italy. 1914-43. 50 reels – 1 – $4,160.00 – us UPA [945]
IL POPOLO D'ITALIA – Milan. Italy. -d. 24 Aug 1916-8 Aug 1919; 28 May 1932-25 Jul 1943. (Imperfect). (39 reels) – 1 – uk British Libr Newspaper [072]
POPOLO D'ITALIA – 1936-1943 – 3 times per yr – 1 – L240,000 – sz Infoprint [072]
Popov, AN *see*
– OPISANIE RUKOPISEI KATALOG KNIG TSERKOVNOI PECHATI BIBLIOTEKI A.I. KHLUDOVA
– RUKOPISI MOSKOVSKOI SINODALNOI PATRIARSHEI BIBLIOTEKI
Popov, K *see*
– SISTEMATICHESKII KATALOG KNIG BIBLIOTEKI MOSKOVSKOI DUKHOVNOI AKADEMII
– VOSPOMANINIIA KAVKAZKAGO GRENADERA, 1914-1920
Popov, N I *see* TEORIIA KOOPERATSII

Popova, K A *see* DISKUSSII A 1925 GODA

Popovich, Charles J *see* JOURNAL OF BUSINESS AND FINANCE LIBRARIANSHIP

Poppe, G H M von *see* AUSFUHRLICHE VOLKS-GEWERBSLEHRE ODER ALLGEMEINE UND BESONDERE TECHNOLOGIE

Poppe, Johann Heinrich Moritz von *see* AUSFUHRLICHE VOLKS-GEWERBSLEHRE; ODER, ALLGEMEINE UND BESONDERE TECHNOLOGIE ZUR BELEHRUNG UND ZUM NUTZEN FUR ALLE STENDE

Poppe, N N *see* MONGOL'SKII SLOVAR' MUKADDIMAT AL-ADAB

Popper, Julius *see* DER BIBLISCHE BERICHT UEBER DIE STIFTSHUETTE...COMPOSITION UND DIASKEUE DES PENTATEUCH

Popruzhenko, M *see* BIBLIOGRAFISKI PREGLED NA SLAVIANSKITE KIRILSKI IZTOCHNISTSI ZA ZHIVOTA I DEINOSTTA NA KIRILA I METODIIA

POPSI – (Annual) – 9 – £23.00 + VAT UK E.U. £28.00 overseas – uk British Libr Docs [780]

POPULACOES PAULISTAS / Ellis, Alfredo – Sao Paulo, 1934 – 7mf – 8 – ne Slangenburg [240]

LE POPULAIRE – Montreal, Canada. 10 avr 1837-3 nov 1838 – 1r – 1 – Can$35.00 – cn Can Microfilming [072]

LE POPULAIRE – (Remplace par: Bulletin socialiste voir a ce titre) – Paris, mai 1916-juin 1940, aout 1944-fevr 1970 – 1 – fr A.C.R.P.P. [335]

LE POPULAIRE DE 1841 – Journal de reorganisation sociale et politique, dirige par M. Cabet, ancien depute. devenu: Le Republicain populaire et social. Paris. mars 1841-nov 1851 – 1 – fr A.C.R.P.P. [073]

LE POPULAIRE (DE PARIS) – (In mf 1916-38, 1958 (incompl)) – Paris, 1939-40, 1944-55, 1966, 1967 (all incompl) – 1 – us Hoover Inst Photo [335]

LE POPULAIRE ROYALISTE – Journal des interets moraux et materiels du peuple. Dir. M. Magnant. Paris. 1837-20 avr 1839 – 1 – fr A.C.R.P.P. [073]

O POPULAR – Cuiaba, 17 Oct-28 Dec 1868 – 1,5,6 – bl Biblioteca [072]

O POPULAR – East Providence. R.I. 1933-1936 – 1 – us UMI [071]

O POPULAR : FOLHA DEMOCRATICA – Cataguazes, 4 Sep 1890 – 1,5,6 – bl Biblioteca [072]

O POPULAR : ORGAM GENUINAMENTE IMPARCIAL – Lima Duarte, 1 Nov 1914 – 1,5,6 – bl Biblioteca [072]

O POPULAR : ORGAO POLITICO, LITERARIO E NOTICIOSO, ARAUTO DAS ASPIRACOES ALVINOPOLENSES – Alvinopolis, 4 Mar-May, Jul-Sep, Dec 1934; Jan-Mar, Nov 1935; Apr-31 May 1936 – 1,5,6 – bl Biblioteca [072]

POPULAR AMUSEMENTS / Mattison, Hiram – 1867 – 9 – us A.T.L.A. [790]

A POPULAR ARGUMENT FOR THE UNITY OF ISAIAH : WITH AN EXAMINATION OF THE OPINIONS OF CANONS CHEYNE AND DRIVER, DR DELITZSCH, THE REV G A SMITH AND OTHERS / Kennedy, John – (Includes bibliographical references) – London: James Clarke, 1891 – 1mf – 9 – 0-8370-3885-5 – 1985-1885 – us A.T.L.A. [220]

POPULAR ASTRONOMY – v. 1-59. 1893-1959 – 1 – us UMI [520]

POPULAR ASTRONOMY – v1-48. 1893-1940 – 590mf – 9 – 1112c/1 – ne IDC [520]

POPULAR BALLADS OF THE OLDEN TIME – 1903-06 – 1 – us I.U. Libraries [390]

POPULAR BIOGRAPHY: EMBRACING THE MOST EMINENT CHARACTERS OF EVERY AGE, NATION, AND PROFESSION. / Goodrich, Samuel G – New York: Leavitt & Allen, c1832. 526p – 1 – us U.W. Library [920]

POPULAR BRITISH CONCHOLOGY / Sowerby, G B – Z 799 2 – 8 – ne IDC [590]

POPULAR BRITISH ENTOMOLOGY / Catlow, M E – London, 1848. Z-1129/2 – 8 – ne IDC [590]

POPULAR BULLETIN / Washington. Agricultural Experiment Station – nos.1-200. 1908-50 – 1,5,6 – us Spaulding [630]

POPULAR BULLETIN / Washington. Western Washington Research and Extension Center. Puyallup. Agricultural Experiment Station – n.s. nos.1-19. 1926-31 – 1,5,6 – us Spaulding [630]

POPULAR CERAMICS – 1976- – 9 – us UMI [660]

A POPULAR COMMENTARY ON THE NEW TESTAMENT, 3 *see* AN ILLUSTRATED COMMENTARY ON THE GOSPEL ACCORDING TO ST. JOHN

POPULAR COMPUTING – v.1-. 1981- – 1,5,6,9 – us UMI [510]

POPULAR CONTROL OF THE LIQUOR TRAFFIC / Gould, Elgin Ralston Lovell – London: Cassell, 1894. 03488. (Pre-1900 Canadiana) – 9 – cn C.I.H.M. [360]

Popular Culture Association. Fifth National Convention. March 20-22, 1975 *see* PROCEEDINGS

Popular Culture Association. Sixth National Convention. April 22-24, 1976 *see* PROCEEDINGS

POPULAR CULTURE IN LIBRARIES / ed by Harnsberger, R Scott et al – v4 n1. 1996- – 1,9 – $75.00 in US $105.00 outside hardcopy subsc – us Haworth [020]

THE POPULAR EDUCATION OF FRANCE : WITH NOTICES OF THAT OF HOLLAND AND SWITZERLAND / Arnold, Matthew – London: Longman, Green, Longman, and Roberts, 1861 – 1 roll – 1 – 1-55879-191-4 – uk Libr Preservation [370]

POPULAR ELECTRONICS – v1-20 1954-82 1; v10-20 5,6,9 – us UMI [621]

POPULAR ELECTRONICS *see* HANDS-ON ELECTRONICS

A POPULAR EXPOSITION OF THE EPISTLES TO THE SEVEN CHURCHES OF ASIA / Plumptre, Edward Hayes – London: Hodder & Stoughton, 1877. 1 fiche – 9 – us A.T.L.A. [240]

POPULAR EXPOSITOR OF THE GOSPELS AND ACTS : FOR PULPIT, SUNDAY-SCHOOL, AND FAMILY: MATTHEW / Nevin, Alfred – Philadelphia, PA: Ziegler & McCurdy, c1872 – 1mf – 9 – 0-8370-4573-8 – 1985-2573 – us A.T.L.A. [220]

POPULAR FALLACIES, ADAPTION FROM SOPHISMES ECONOMIQUES / Bastiat, Frederic – 1fiche (29x) – 9 – 1.00f – at Libertarian Micro [320]

POPULAR FALLACIES REGARDING TRADE AND FOREIGN DUTIES / Pearce Edcumbe, E R – 1885. An Adaption of Bastiat's Economic Sophisms. 1 fiche (29x) – 9 – 1.00f – at Libertarian Micro [320]

A POPULAR HANDBOOK OF METHODIST LAW AND USAGE / Grubb, A P – London, 1913. 128p – 2mf – 9 – ne IDC [240]

A POPULAR HAND-BOOK OF THE NEW TESTAMENT / McWhorter, George Cumming – New York: Harper, 1864. 1 fiche – 9 – us A.T.L.A. [240]

A POPULAR HANDBOOK OF USEFUL AND INTERESTING INFORMATION FOR BEGINNERS IN THE ELEMENTARY STUDY OF ASSYRIOLOGY / Norton, Francis Collins – Comp. by F.C. Norton. 1908. 201p. fold. map – 1 – us U.W. Library [470]

A POPULAR HISTORY OF FRANCE, FROM THE EARLIEST TIMES / Guizot, M Francois – Boston: D. Estes and C.E. Lauriat, 187?. 6v. illus., maps – 1 – us U.W. Library [944]

A POPULAR HISTORY OF THE BRITISH FERNS AND THE ALLIED PLANTS / Moore, T – London, 1851. 354 pp., 20 pls. B-7234 1 – 9 – ne IDC [580]

A POPULAR HISTORY OF THE CHURCH OF ENGLAND : FROM THE EARLIEST TIMES TO THE PRESENT DAY / Carpenter, William Boyd – New York: E.P. Dutton, London: J. Murray, 1900 – 2mf – us A.T.L.A. [240]

A POPULAR HISTORY OF THE FREE CHURCHES / Horne, C Silvester – London: J. Clarke, 1903 – 2mf – us A.T.L.A. [240]

A POPULAR HISTORY OF THE MOLLUSCA / Roberts, M – Z 750 2. 1851 – 8 – ne IDC [590]

POPULAR HISTORY OF THE TRANSLATION OF THE HOLY SCRIPTURES INTO THE ENGLISH TONGUE / Conant, H C – New York: Funk, 1881. 1 fiche – 9 – us A.T.L.A. [240]

POPULAR INDIAN PAINTINGS IN THE INDIAN OFFICE LIBRARY / India Office Library. London – (Almost 800 paintings in colour. With printed index) – 1985 – 12 colour 4 bw mf – 15,9 – $495.00 – 0-907716-04-0 – uk Mindata [750]

A POPULAR INTRODUCTION TO THE HISTORY OF CHRISTIAN DOCTRINE / Crippen, T G – Edinburgh: T. & T. Clark, 1883 – 1mf – us A.T.L.A. [240]

A POPULAR INTRODUCTION TO THE NEW TESTAMENT / Lumby, Joseph Rawson – London: Hodder & Stoughton, 1883 – 1mf – 9 – us A.T.L.A. [240]

POPULAR LAW LIBRARY. / Putney, Albert Hutchinson – 2nd ed. Chicago: Cree, 1910. 12v. LL-1479 – 1 – us L of C Photodup [340]

POPULAR LAW LIBRARY. / Putney, Albert Hutchinson – Minneapolis: Cree, 1908. 12v. LL-796 – 1 – us L of C Photodup [340]

POPULAR LITERATURE IN EIGHTEENTH AND NINETEENTH CENTURY BRITAIN – (Unit 2: The Sabine Baring-Gould and Thomas Crampton Collections from the British Library. Unit 3: The Barry Ono Collection. Unit 4: The Barry Ono Collection. Unit 5: The Barry Ono Collection. Unit 6: The Barry Ono Collection; Units 7-10: The Barry Ono Collection) – Unit 1: The Robert White Collection from University Library – 1 – us Primary [800]

POPULAR MECHANICS – (v. 123- 1965- 5,6. v. 133- 1970- 9) – v. 1- Jan 1902- – 1 – us UMI [600]

POPULAR MISCONCEPTIONS AS TO CHRISTIAN FAITH AND LIFE / Lee, Frank Theodosius – Boston: Pilgrim Press, [1900] – 1mf – 9 – 0-8370-4366-2 – 1985-2366 – us A.T.L.A. [240]

POPULAR NEWSPAPERS DURING WORLD WAR 1 : DAILY EXPRESS, DAILY MIRROR, NEWS OF THE WORLD, THE PEOPLE AND SUNDAY EXPRESS – (Pt 1: 1914-1915 26r $2,950.00. Pt 2: 1916-1917 19r $2,200.00. Pt 3: 1918-1919 19r $2,200.00. Includes guides) – Marlborough: Adam Matthew Publications, 1996 – 1 – uk Matthew [072]

POPULAR NEWSPAPERS DURING WORLD WAR 2 : DAILY EXPRESS, DAILY MIRROR, NEWS OF THE WORLD, THE PEOPLE, AND SUNDAY EXPRESS – (Pt 1: 1939 26r $2,950.00. Pt 2: 1940 16r $1,900.00. Pt 3: 9r $1100.00. Pt 4: 1942-1943 16r $1,900.00. Pt 5: 1944-1945 16r $1,900.00. Guide to Pts 1-5) – Marlborough: Adam Matthew Publications, 1993 – 1 – uk Matthew [072]

POPULAR OBJECTIONS TO REVEALED TRUTH / Christian Evidence Society – New York: A.D.F. Randolph, 1873.1 fiche. 8370-4779-X – 9 – us A.T.L.A. [240]

POPULAR PHOTOGRAPHY – (v. 62- 1968- 5,6. v. 66- 1970- 9) – v. 1- 1937- – 1 – us UMI [770]

THE POPULAR PREACHERS OF THE ANCIENT CHURCH : THEIR LIVES, THEIR MANNER, AND THEIR WORK / Wilson, William – London: J. Hogg, [1859?] – 1mf – us A.T.L.A. [240]

POPULAR SCIENCE – (v. 186- 1965- 5,6. v. 196- 1970- 9) – v. 1- 1872- – 1 – us UMI [500]

POPULAR SCIENCE MONTHLY – (Issued as: Appleton's Popular Science Monthly 1895-1900. v. 1-87. 1872-1915 – 1,5,6 – us Princeton Micro [073]

POPULAR SCIENCE NEWS – v. 1-36. 1866-1902. All pub – 1,5,6 – us Princeton Micro [500]

POPULAR SINS: A SERIES OF SERMONS AGAINST THE SINS OF THE TIMES / Austin, Benjamin Fish – Toronto: Hunter, Rose, 1880. 06582. (Pre-1900 Canadiana) – 9 – cn C.I.H.M. [240]

POPULAR SPORTS – 1974- – 1. 1978-; ; 56,9 – us UMI [790]

THE POPULAR STAGE: DRAMA IN NINETEENTH CENTURY ENGLAND : SERIES 1: MANUSCRIPT AND TYPESCRIPT PLAYS – (Part 1: Arbarbanel the Hebrew to Exit by Mistake. Part 2: A Fable of the Fenians to My Uncle's Pet. Part 3: Naomi the Gypsy Girl to The Swindler. Part 4: The Taylor of Eisback to Zulema, the Circassian Beauty. Part 5: Typescript and outsize manuscript plays: Across the Continent to Work Girls of London) – Frank Pettingell Collection of Plays in the Library of the University of Kent at Canterbury – 1 – us Primary [790]

THE POPULAR STAGE: DRAMA IN NINETEENTH CENTURY ENGLAND : SERIES 2: PANTOMIMES – Frank Pettingell Collection of Plays in the Library of the University of Kent at Canterbury – 1 – us Primary [790]

THE POPULAR STAGE: DRAMA IN NINETEENTH CENTURY ENGLAND : SERIES 3: RARE PRINTED PLAYS – Frank Pettingell Collection of Plays in the Library of the University of Kent at Canterbury – 1 – us Primary [420]

POPULAR WISSENSCHAFTLICHE MONATSBLATTER = POPULAR SCIENCE MONTHLY – (In German) – Frankfurt, DE. v6 no2 1 Feb 1886-v8 no4 1 Apr 1886 – 1r – 1 – $25.00 – cn Can Microfilming [072]

POPULATION – it F.A.O. [304]

POPULATION – v. 1-13. Paris. 1946-58. BH-1816 1 – 9 – ne IDC [073]

POPULATION AND AGRICULTURAL DEVELOPMENT : SELECTED RELATIONSHIPS AND POSSIBLE PLANNING USES – 1979 – 136p – it F.A.O. [338]

POPULATION AND AGRICULTURE IN THE DEVELOPING COUNTRIES – 1980 – 56p – it F.A.O. [304]

POPULATION AND BUILDING IN ISRAEL 1948-1973 / Haber, Aliza – Jerusalem, Sep 1975. 67, 141p. Text also in Hebrew – 9 – 3.00 – is I.T.T.I. [310]

POPULATION AND DEVELOPMENT: A STUDY ON THE POPULATION INCREASE AND ITS CHALLENGE TO DEVELOPMENT IN EGYPT / United Arab Republic. Central Agency for Public Mobilisation and Statistics – Cairo. 1973. BNE-4683 1 – 9 – ne IDC [310]

POPULATION AND DEVELOPMENT REVIEW – v. 1-. 1975- – 1,5,6,9 – us UMI [310]

POPULATION AND ENVIRONMENT – v3-. 1980- – 1,5,6,9 – us UMI [304]

POPULATION AND LABOUR FORCE IN THE AGRICULTURE SECTOR, 1967 / Jordan. Department of Statistics – 1968. BNE-9777 1 – 9 – ne IDC [310]

POPULATION AND THE LABOUR FORCE IN RURAL ECONOMIES – 1986 – 175p – it F.A.O. [331]

POPULATION AND VITAL STATISTICS REPORT / United Nations. Statistical Office – (1986-. 1,5,6) – 1975- – 9 – us UMI [073]

LA POPULATION BELGE DEPUIS 1830: TOME I, ETAT DE LA POPULATION / Rutten, Adolphe – Louvain: C. Peeters, 1899. 122p. illus. 3 fiches. (Statistics Series: Demography) – 9 – 8.00 – fr Bibl Nationale [310]

POPULATION CENSUS 1961 / Indonesia. Biro Pusat Statistik – SE-3897 1. 1962 – 9 – ne IDC [310]

POPULATION CENSUS 1961; THE RESULT OF HOUSEHOLD LISTING IN MARCH, 1961, ALL INDONESIA / Indonesia. Biro Pusat Statistik – SE-5837 1. 1965 – 9 – ne IDC [310]

POPULATION CENSUS AND INTERNAL MIGRATION FOR AMMAN, JERUSALEM, ZARQA RUSEIFA, IRBID AND AQABA, 1967 / Jordan. Department of Statistics – 1969? BNE-9775 1 – 9 – ne IDC [310]

POPULATION CENSUS OF EGYPT, 1937 / Egypt. Ministry of Finance – 1942. BNE-4661 1 – 9 – ne IDC [336]

POPULATION CENSUS OF EGYPT, 1947: GENERAL TABLES / Egypt. Ministry of Finance – 1954 – 9 – ne IDC [336]

POPULATION CENSUS OF THE NORTHERN REGION OF NIGERIA, 1952 / Nigeria. Department of Statistics – Lagos, [1953] – us Res Libr [310]

POPULATION CENSUS PAPER NR.(1): LITERACY IN LIBYA / Libya. Ministry of Economy and Trade. Census and Statistical Department – Tripoli. BNE-704 1 – 9 – ne IDC [304]

POPULATION CENSUS SCHEDULES / Minnesota – 1865-1905 – 164r – 1 – $30.00r – us M.H.S. [324]

POPULATION CONCEPTS IN AGRICULTURAL COOPERATIVE TRAINING COURSES – 1981 – 60p – it F.A.O. [370]

Population Council. New York *see* CATALOGUE OF THE POPULATION COUNCIL LIBRARY

POPULATION DE PARIS: REMARQUES DEMOGRAPHIQUES SUR L'HABITAT URBAIN / Lagneau, Gustave – Reprod. d'un extrait du Bulletin de l'Academie de Medecine, 1893, p740-60. 1 fiche. (Statistics Series: Demography) – 9 – 6.00 – fr Bibl Nationale [310]

LA POPULATION DE TROYES AU DIX-HUITIEME SIECLE / Babeau, Albert – Troyes, Dufour-Bouquet, 1873. 23 p. 1 fiche. (Statistics Series: Demography) – 9 – 6.00 – fr Bibl Nationale [310]

POPULATION EDUCATION : A CONTEMPORARY CONCERN / UNESCO. International Study of the Conceptualization and Methodology of Population Education (ISCOMPE) – 1978 – 120p – 9 – 92-3-101553-2 – fr UNESCO [360]

POPULATION ET HABITAT DES VILLES ET CHEFS-LIEUX AU RECENSEMENT DE 1966. POPULATION NON ALGERIENNE L'HABITAT DANS LES CHEFS-LIEUX URBANS / Algeria. Commissariat National aux Recensements et Enquetes Statistiques – 1970. BNE-8708 1 – 9 – ne IDC [310]

POPULATION GROWTH AND ITS CONTROL, FOOD REQUIREMENTS AND FOOD PRODUCTION / Gunawan, Kartono – (From: NAS-LIPI workshop on food, Djakarta, May 27-June 1, 1968). SE-6647 1 – 9 – ne IDC [304]

POPULATION GROWTH AND MANPOWER IN THE SUDAN: A JOINT STUDY BY THE UNITED NATIONS AND THE GOVERNMENT OF THE SUDAN / Sudan. U.N. Bureau of Social Affairs – 1964. BNE-7692 1 – 9 – ne IDC [360]

POPULATION IN INDONESIA, THE SHORT AND LONG RUN / Keyfitz, Nathan – SE-4677 1. 1964 – 9 – ne IDC [310]

POPULATION INCREASE IN INDONESIA / Indonesia. Biro Pusat Statistik – Vaino Kannisto. 1963. SE-8465-1 – 9 – ne IDC [310]

POPULATION INDEX – v1- 1935- 1; v37- 5,6; v43- 9 – us UMI [304]

POPULATION INDEX BIBLIOGRAPHY CUMULATED 1935-1968 BY AUTHORS AND GEOGRAPHICAL AREAS / Princeton University. Office of Population Research – (By Author, Separately, 81,800 entries 4 reels. $435.00 export $525.00. – ISBN 0-8161-1437-4; By Geographical Area, Separately, 1971. 91,400 entries 5 reels. $455.00 export $550.00. – ISBN 0-8161-1398-X) – 1971. 173,000 entries on 9 reels – 1 – $890.00 export $1,075.00 – 0-8161-0880-3 – uk Hall [304]

POPULATION INDEX BIBLIOGRAPHY / Princeton University. Office of Population Research – (By author.-81,800 entries 4 reels. $480.00 US; $580.00 elsewhere ISBN: 0-8161-1437-4; By geographical area.-91,400 entries 5 reels. $500.00 US; $605.00 elsewhere ISBN: 0-8161-1398-X) – Cumulated 1935-68 by authors and geographical areas, 1971.-173,000 entries 9 reels – 1,979.00; 1 – $890.00 – uk Hall [304]

POPULATION LEGALE DU MAROC D'APRES LE RECENSEMENT GENERAL DE LA / Morocco. Secretariat d'Etat au Plan – Serie E. v. 1. 1971. BNE-3113 1 – 9 – ne IDC [310]

POPULATION LEGALE DU MAROC D'APRES LE RECENSEMENT GENERAL DE LA POPULATION ET DE L'HABITAT / Morocco. Direction des Statistiques – 1971. BNE-3204 1 – 9 – ne IDC [310]

POPULATION NOTE / Wisconsin. College of Agricultural and Life Sciences. Dept. of Rural Sociology – no.1-12. Sep 1961-Aug 1, 1970 – 1,5 – us Spaulding [630]

POPULATION OF ENGLAND AND WALES, 1911 / Great Britain. Parliament. House of Commons – 2v in 1. Chiefly tables – 1 – us U.W. Library [310]

THE POPULATION OF INDONESIA, 1930-1968: A BIBLIOGRAPHY / Singarimbun, Masri – (Draft). SE 6676 1. 1968? – 9 – ne IDC [304]

THE POPULATION OF INDONESIA, 1930-1968; A BIBLIOGRAPHY / Singarimbun, Masri – SE 6906 1. 1969 – 9 – ne IDC [304]

THE POPULATION OF ISRAEL / Bach, Robert – 428p. In co-op. with the Hebrew Univ. of Jerusalem and the Instit. of Contemporary Jewry – 9 – 8.00 – is I.T.T.I. [310]

THE POPULATION OF SUDAN : REPORT ON THE SIXTH ANNUAL CONFERENCE HELD IN THE UNIVERSITY OF KHARTOUM / Sudan. Philosophical Society of the Sudan – 16th and 17th Jan, 1958. BNE-7681 1 – 9 – ne IDC [310]

POPULATION OF THE PHILIPPINE ISLANDS IN 1916 / Beyer, Henry Otley – Manila: Philippine Education Co., 1917. 95p. English-Spanish ed. With: Lo que Fuimos y lo que Somas by J.M. de la Torre. 1 reel. 1262 – 1 – us U.W. Library [310]

THE POPULATION PROBLEM IN EGYPT / Egypt. Permanent Council of Public Service – 1955. BNE-4675 1 – 9 – ne IDC [310]

POPULATION PROJECTIONS (NATIONAL FIGURES) OPCS SERIES PP2 1970-1977 – (Coll title: British Government Publications...1801-1977, Demography) – 14mf – 9 (£2,110.000 demography set of 38r + 14mf) – uk Chadwyck [310]

POPULATION: RECENCEMENT ET MOUVEMENTS DE LA POPULATION DES VOSGES / Charton, Charles – Nancy: Peiffer, 1845. p695-729.1 fiche. (Statistics Series: Demography) – 9 – 6.00 – fr Bibl Nationale [310]

POPULATION SERIES: WISCONSIN'S POPULATION / Wisconsin. College of Agricultural and Life Sciences. Dept. of Rural Sociology – Feb 1961-Jul 1970,n.1-24 – 1,5 – us Spaulding [630]

POPULATION, SOCIETY AND AGRICULTURAL PLANNING – 1987 – 170p – it F.A.O. [300]

POPULATION STUDIES / United Nations – 373 fiches – 9 – 720.00; 1.90f – uk UNIMICRO [324]

POPULATION STUDIES / United Nations – (Nos. 1-10; 13-54. ST/SOA/Ser.A/1-10; 13-54. E.149 F.142 S.115; Nos. 11-12. ST/SOA/Ser.A/11-12. E/F/R/S.12; Nos. 55-56; 58-115. ST/ESA/Ser.A/55-56; 58-115. E.300 F.98 S.93; No. 57. ST/ESA/Ser.A/57. E/F/R/S.27; Many of the publications were not issued neither in French nor Spanish) – 9 – us U.N. Pubs [304]

POPULATION STUDY AND DEMOGRAPHIC RESEARCH IN INDONESIA (RECOMMENDATIONS) / Indonesia. Lembaga Ekonomi dan Kemasjarakatan Nasional – 1964. SE-11,381-1 – 9 – ne IDC [310]

POPULATION-ENVIRONMENT RELATIONS IN TROPICAL ISLANDS : THE CASE OF EASTERN FIJI / ed by Brookfield, H C – 1980 – 228p – 9 – 92-3-101821-3 – fr UNESCO [304]

LES POPULATIONS DANGEREUSES ET LES MISERES SOCIALES / Cere, Paul – (Condition of 19th C. French working class series). 1872 – 9 – fr Hachette [360]

LES POPULATIONS OUVRIERES ET LES INDUSTRIES DE LA FRANCE. ETUDES COMPARATIVES SUR LE REGIME ET LES RESSOURCES DES DIFFERENTES INDUSTRIES, SUR L'ETAT MORAL ET MATERIEL DES OUVRIERS DANS CHAQUE BRANCHE DU TRAVAIL ET LES INSTITUTIONS QUI LES CONCERNENT / Audiganne, A – (Condition of 19th C. French working class series). 1860 – 9 – fr Hachette [331]

LE POPULAZIONI INDIGENE DELLA SOMALIA ITALIANA / Puccioni, Nello – Bologna. 1937 – 1 – us Res Libr [301]

POPULI – v. 3-. 1976- – 1,5,6,9 – us UMI [073]

POPULIARNYE OCHERKI PO TEORII KOOPERATSII / Pazhitnov, K A – Pg., 1917 – 1mf – 9 – COR-91/1 – ne IDC [334]

POPULIST – New York. v1. 1894-95 – 1r – 1 – us Ross [071]

THE POPULIST – New York. v. 1, no. 1, 9. Dec 15 1894, Feb 9 1895 – 1 – us NY Public [073]

POPULUS – Journal democratique de l'arrondissement de Narbonne et du departement des Pyrenees-Orientales. no. 1-38. Narbonne. 25 aout 1849-18 mai 1850. mq no. 5, 13, 21-22, 32 – 1 – fr A.C.R.P.P. [073]

POR ANTONIO DE VALENCIA GODOY, OYDOR DE LA REAL CHANCILLERIA DE GRANADA Y SACRISTAN MAYOR DE LA ORDEN DE ALCANTARA CONTRA PEDRO MANZANO... – S.l., s.i., s.a. Hacia 1617 – 1 – sp Bibl Santa Ana [350]

POR D. JOAQUIN TOPETE, AFRONTE...POR SI Y POR SUS HIJOS... / Diez Coronel, Diego Manuel – s.l., s.i., 1735 – 1 – sp Bibl Santa Ana [946]

POR DON JUAN DE OVANDO...LAVADERO LANAS DE ALMENDRALEJO / Gaspar de Segovia, Jose M – 1721? – 9 – $1.50f – sp Bibl Santa Ana [946]

POR DON LUIS PACHECO...CON DONA MARIANA DE CARDENAS / Mendoza Jordan, Lorenzo – 1741 – 9 – $1.50f – sp Bibl Santa Ana [946]

POR DON LUIS PACHECO...DON CRISTOBAL DE PORTOCARRERO...MAYORAZGO / Mendoza Jordan, Lorenzo – 1740 – 9 – $1.50f – sp Bibl Santa Ana [946]

POR DONDE VAMOS...HISTORIA DE UN FETO POLITICO / Leon, Ramon David – Madrid: Razon y Fe, 1940 – 1 – sp Bibl Santa Ana [320]

POR EL ESCAPULARIO VERDE HASTA LA CUNA DE LA SANTIDAD – Plasencia: Imp. La Victoria, 1960 – sp Bibl Santa Ana [946]

POR EL...JUAN DE LA SERENA...DEFINIDORES.. / Palma y Freites, Luis de la – 1641 – 9 – 1.50f – sp Bibl Santa Ana [440]

POR EUZKADI HACIA LA VICTORIA BILBAO NO HA SIDO TOMADO POR FRANCO, SINO POR LOS EJERCITOS ALEMAN E ITALIANO QUE COMBATEN EN ESPANA EN NOMBRE DE BERLIN Y DE ROMA – Madrid, 1937. Fiche W1114. (Blodgett Collection of Spanish Civil War Pamphlets) – 9 – us H.U. College Libr [946]

POR LA GEOGRAFIA CACERENA : BERZOCANA / Gutierrez Macias, Valeriano – Badajoz: Dip. Provincial, 1969. Sep. REE – 1 – sp Bibl Santa Ana [900]

POR LA GEOGRAFIA CACERENA : CASATEJADA / Gutierrez Macias, Valeriano – Badajoz: Imp. Dip. Provincial, 1963. Sep. REE – sp Bibl Santa Ana [910]

POR LA GEOGRAFIA CACERENA : CORIA Y VIANDAR DE LA VERA / Gutierrez Macias, Valeriano – Badajoz: Imp. Dip. Provincial, 1965. Sep. REE – sp Bibl Santa Ana [910]

POR LA GEOGRAFIA CACERENA : GARCIAZ, POZUELO DE ZARZON, ROBLEDILLO DE GATA, CADALSO DE GATA, VALDEOBISPO, BERZOCANA / Gutierrez Macias, Valeriano – Badajoz: Imp Dip. Provincial, 1964. Sep. REE – sp Bibl Santa Ana [910]

POR LA GEOGRAFIA CACERENA : JARAICEJO / Gutierrez Macias, Valeriano – Badajoz: Dip. Provincial, 1967. Sep. REE – sp Bibl Santa Ana [910]

POR LA GEOGRAFIA CACERENA : TRUJILLO, VILLANUEVA DE LA VERA, CUACOS, TORREORGAZ, VALVERDE DEL FRESNO / Gutierrez Macias, Valeriano – Badajoz: Imp. Dip. Provincial, 1962. Sep. REE – sp Bibl Santa Ana [910]

POR LA GEOGRAFIA CACERENA. (BANOS DE MONTEMAYOR) / Gutierrez Macias, Valeriano – Badajoz: Diputacion Provincial de Badajoz, 1966 – sp Bibl Santa Ana [946]

POR LA GEOGRAFIA CACERENA (FIESTAS POPULARES) / Gutierrez Macias, Valeriano – Madrid: Imp. Juan Bravo, 1968 – 1 – sp Bibl Santa Ana [946]

POR LA INDEPENDENCIA DE ESPANA, POR LA LIBERTAD, POR LA REPUBLICA / Ibarruri, Dolores – Madrid, 1938. Fiche W1759. (Blodgett Collection of Spanish Civil War Pamphlets) – 9 – us H.U. College Libr [946]

POR LA REPUBLICA Y LA LEGALIDAD CONSTITUCIONAL: TODOS UNIDOS A LA LUCHA / Carrillo, Santiago – Toulouse? 1945. Fiche W 777. (Blodgett Collection of Spanish Civil War Pamphlets) – 9 – us H.U. College Libr [946]

POR LA UNIDAD, HACIA LA VICTORIA / Diaz, Jose – Discurso pronunciado en el pleno del C.C. ampliado del partido comunista de espana.Espana, 1937. Fiche W 834. (Blodgett Collection of Spanish Civil War Pamphlets) – 9 – us H.U. College Libr [946]

POR LA VENTANA DE LA PREHISTORIA... / Martinez del Rio, Pablo – Madrid: Razon y Fe, 1940 – sp Bibl Santa Ana [930]

POR LA VIEJA EXTREMADURA-PROVINCIA DE CACERES / Blazquez Marcos, Jose – Caceres: Tip. Extremadura, 1929 – 1 – sp Bibl Santa Ana [946]

POR LO QUE LUCHA LA REPUBLICA ESPANOLA – Mexico, 1940? Fiche W1115. (Blodgett Collection of Spanish Civil War Pamphlets) – 9 – us H.U. College Libr [946]

POR LOS BLANCOS CAMINOS DEL MARGEN. NOTAS PARA UNA PSICOLOGIA DEL LECTOR / Carrasco, Castulo – Caceres: Imp. Moderna, 1952. Cuad. Alcantara, no 2 – sp Bibl Santa Ana [150]

POR LOS CAMINOS DEL JUSTICIALISMO : APORTE A LA DOCTRINA PERONISTA / Freire, Jose Maria – Buenos Aires: [s.n.], 1951 – 1 – CSUXADJ2568-B – us Hoover Inst Photo [360]

POR LOS FUEROS DE LA VERDAD / Garcia Morgado, Jose – Caceres: Editorial Extremadura, 1932 – 1 – sp Bibl Santa Ana [946]

POR LOS...MONASTERIOS DE... / Encina y la Carrera, Juan Ignacio de la & Gaspar de Segovia, Joseph Manuel – Madrid, s.i. 1727 – 1 – sp Bibl Santa Ana [240]

POR MIS SENDEROS / Spinola de Gironza, Araceli – Madrid: Graf. Nebrija, 4th ed 1958 – sp Bibl Santa Ana [946]

POR MIS SOLEDADES VOY... / Sanchez-Arjona, Vicente – Sevilla: Imp. Alvarez, 1959 – 1 – sp Bibl Santa Ana [810]

POR NUESTROS CAMINOS / Juez Nieto, Antonio – Badajoz: Argueros, 1951 – 1 – sp Bibl Santa Ana [946]

POR QUE ESTA EN CRISIS LA ECONOMIA ARGENTINA / Gonzalez Alberdi, Paulino – Buenos Aires: Editorial Anteo, 1949 – 1 – CSUXAHZ2038-B – us Hoover Inst Photo [330]

POR QUE HICIMOS LA REVOLUCION / Nelken, Margarita – Barcelona: Ediciones Europa. America S.A., 3rd ed 1936? – 1 – sp Bibl Santa Ana [946]

POR QUE MOTIVOS O CAUSAS LAS TERCIANAS SE HAN HECHO TAN COMUNES Y GRAVES... / Cibat, A – Madrid, 1806 – 3mf – 9 – sp Cultura [610]

POR QUE NO VAS A LA CONFERENCIA? / El Avisador – 1890 – 9 – 1.50f – sp Bibl Santa Ana [946]

POR QUE SE CREY O EN PERON : POLITICOS, MILITARES, Y PERONISTAS / Baquerizas, Jose Manuel – Buenos Aires, 1957 – 1 – CSUXADJ1893-B – us Hoover Inst Photo [320]

POR QUE SOY PERONISTA / Consoli, Maximiliano – [Argentina?: s.n., 1946] – 1 – CSUXADQ2801-B – us Hoover Inst Photo [320]

POR QUE VOLVEMOS A DONOSO CORTES / Armas, Gabriel – Las Palmas de Gran Canaria: Imp. Lezcano, 1956 – sp Bibl Santa Ana [946]

POR UNA JUSTICIA POPULAR, HUMANA Y DEMOCRATICA / Spain. Ministerio de Justicia – Barcelona, 19?? Fiche W1116. (Blodgett Collection of Spanish Civil War Pamphlets) – 9 – us H.U. College Libr [946]

POR UNA SOLUCION NACIONAL : DISCURSO PRONUNCIADO E 21 DE DICIEMBRE DE 1962 / Amadeo, Mario – Buenos Aires, [1962?] – 1 – CSUXAJA7592-B – us Hoover Inst Photo [320]

PORADNIK JEZYKOWY – v. 1-12. Warszawa. 1901-12. BR-8019 – 8 – ne IDC [073]

Porcari, John P *see*
- COMPARISON OF HYDROSTATIC WEIGHING TO BIOELECTRICAL IMPEDANCE ANALYSIS IN WOMEN GREATER THAN THIRTY PERCENT BODY FAT
- THE EFFECT OF THE MENSTRUAL CYCLE ON BIOIMPEDANCE RELIABILITY
- THE EFFECTS OF A TEN-WEEK STEP AEROBIC TRAINING PROGRAM ON AEROBIC CAPACITY OF COLLEGE-AGED FEMALES
- THE EFFECTS OF A TEN-WEEK STEP AEROBIC TRAINING PROGRAM ON THE BODY COMPOSITION OF COLLEGE-AGED WOMEN
- THE EFFECTS OF TWELVE WEEKS OF WALKING OR EXERSTRIDING ON UPPER BODY MUSCULAR STRENGTH AND ENDURANCE
- THE PHYSIOLOGIC RESPONSES TO IN-LINE ROLLER SKATING COMPARED TO TREADMILL RUNNING
- STRENGTH GAINS CONSEQUENT TO TEN WEEKS OF UNIVERSAL OR BOWFLEX TRAINING

PORCELAINES DE SAXE / Reunion des musees nationaux. Paris – 1952. 8 illus. 1 fiche – 9 – fr Réunion [730]

Porcell, G *see* LIEUX D'EAU. L'EAU ET L'HOMME DANS LE COMARCA DU RIPOLLES (PYRENEES CATALANES)

Porcell, J *see* INFORMACION Y CURACION DE LA PESTE EN ZARAGOZA Y PERSERVACION CONTRA LA PESTE

Porcell, M *see* LA VANNERIE DU PAYS NDUT, REPUBLIQUE DU SENEGAL

LES PORCELLANIDES ET DES BRACHYURES / Edwards, A M & Bouvier, E L – Z-233 2. 1923 – 8 – ne IDC [590]

Porcher, Elizabeth L *see* HISTORY OF THE CHARLESTON LIBRARY SOCIETY

PORCUPINE – Gold Circle, NV. 20 May 1914 – 1r – 1 – $50.00 – U04547 – us Library Micro [071]

PORCUPINE – v.1-20. 1860-1879. (all pub.) – 1 – 22112.00 – us Princeton Micro [073]

PORCUPINE ADVANCE – Timmins, 1912-1950 – 25r – 1 – cn Preston [971]

PORCUPINE ADVANCE – Timmins, Canada. -w. Dec 1915-Dec 1921. 3 1 2 reels – 1 – uk British Libr Newspaper [072]

PORCUPINE'S GAZETTE – Philadelphia. Pa. 1797-1800 – 1,3 – us Readex [071]

Poree, Charles Gabriel *see* LE POUR ET CONTRE DE LA POSSESSION DES FILLES DE LA PAROISSE DE LANDES, DIOCESE DE BAYEUX

Porete, Margareta *see* SPECULUM SIMPLICIUM ANIMARUM
Porfir'ev, Ila *see* APOKRIFICHESKIIA SKAZANIIA O VETKHOZAVETNYKH LITSAKH I SOBYTIIAKH PO RUKOPISIAM SOLOVETSKOI BIBLIOTEKI (SBORNIK OTDELENIIA RUSSKOGO IAZYKA I SLOVESNOSTI IMP. AK. NAUK, TOM XVII, NO. 1)
POR...FR. DIEGO DE CACERES, GENERAL...DE S. GERONIMO...Y DEMAS DIPUTADOS QUE SE CONFIRMA LA SENTENCIA / Castro, Antonio de – 1641 – 9 – 1.50f – sp Bibl Santa Ana [240]
Porges, Heinrich *see* TRISTAN UND ISOLDE
Porges, N *see* HEBRAICA ET RABBINICA
"PORGY" DRAFTS / Heyward, DuBose – ca.1924. 8 fiches – 9 – us South Carolina Historical [410]
Porier, Jules *see* LE TRANSVAAL (1652-1899).
Poritzky, J E *see* WIE SOLLEN WIR HEINE VERSTEHEN
Porkel, J N *see* MUSIKALISCHER ALMANACH FUER DEUTSCHLAND AUF DAS JAHR, 1782-1784
PORKORNEISHEE KHODATAISTVO = A MOST HUMBLE PETITION / Fetler, V A – St. Petersburg, 1913. 20p – 1 – 5.00 – us Baptist [240]
PORODICNO PRAVO NASLEDA U DANASNJIM ROMANSKIM I GERMANSKIM DRZAVAMA / Dordevic, Andra – Beograd, Shtamparja "Dositje Obradovih," 1908. 53 p. LL-4098 – 1 – us L of C Photodup [340]
Poroshin, S A *see* ZAPISKI
Porphyrogenneti, Constantini *see* LIBRI DUO DE CEREMONIIS AULAE BYZANTINAE (CBH 33)
PORQUE ME UFANO DO MEU PAIZ; RIGHT OR WRONG, MY COUNTRY / Affonso Celso, Affonso Celso de Assis Figueiredo, Conde de – 2nd ed. rev. Rio de Janeiro: Laemmert & Co., 1901. 202p – 1 – us U.W. Library [972]
Porras Barrenechea, Paul *see*
– CEDULARIO DEL PERU
– PIZARRO EL FUNDADOR
– LA PRIMERA COPLA DE LA CONQUISTA
– EL TESTAMENTO DE FRANCISCO PIZARRO, CONQUISTADOR DE PERU
– EL TESTAMENTO DE PIZARRO
– EL TESTAMENTO DE PIZARRO DE 1539
Porres, M *see* BREVES ADVERTENCIAS PARA BEBER FRIO CON NIEVE...
Porritt, Edward *see* THE ENGLISHMAN AT HOME, HIS RESPONSIBILITIES AND PRIVILEGES
Porro, P J *see* ENTRENNES DE GUITARE. 4E ANNEE 1787. ENTIEREMENT COMPOSEES D'AIRS NOUVEAUS CHANSONS, ROMANCES ....
Porsild, M P *see* STUDIES ON THE MATERIAL CULTURE OF THE ESKIMO IN WEST GREENLAND
Porsius, H *see*
– BRIEVE HISTOIRE DE LA GVERRE DE PERSE, FAITE L'AN MIL CINQ CENS SEPTANTE HUIT
– HISTORIA BELLI PERSICI, GESTI INTER MVRATHEM 3
Porson, Richard *see*
– THE CORRESPONDENCE OF RICHARD PORSON, M.A. FORMERLY REGIUS PROFESSOR OF GREEK IN THE UNIVERSITY OF CAMBRIDGE
– TRACTS AND MISCELLANEOUS CRITICISMS OF THE LATE RICHARD PORSON, ESQ. REGIUS GREEK PROFESSOR IN THE UNIVERSITY OF CAMBRIDGE
PORT ADELAIDE NEWS, AND LEFEVRE'S PENINSULA ADVERTISER – Australia. 2 Jan 1885-7 Oct 1887.-sw. 2 reels – 1 – uk British Libr Newspaper [072]
PORT ADMINISTRATION IN INDONESIA / Poespowijoto, Soetojo – Material submitted to ECAFE Regional Port Seminar, to be held in Singapore, Oct. 7 to 16th, 1968. SE-8490 1. 1968 – 9 – ne IDC [380]
PORT ALBERT BOND STORE JOURNAL – 1854-55 – 7mf – 9 – A$30.00 – at State Libr Vic [380]
PORT ALBERT MUSEUM MSS – 34mf – 9 – A$65.00 – at State Libr Vic [060]
THE PORT AND TRADE OF LONDON, HISTORICAL, STATISTICAL, LOCAL, AND GENERAL / Capper, Charles – London: Smith, Elder, 1862. x,507p – 1 – us U.W. Library [941]
PORT ARTHUR NEWS – Port Arthur. Texas. 1921- – 1 – us UMI [071]
PORT CAMPBELL CEMETERY REGISTER – 1877-1993 – 9 – at Corangamite [920]
Port Clinton Literary and Social Club. Ohio *see* RECORDS
Port Clinton. Ohio. Neidecker and Crosser Funeral Home *see* FUNERAL RECORDS
Port Clinton. Ohio. St. John's Lutheran Church *see* RECORDS
Port Clinton. Ohio. St. Thomas Episcopal Church *see* RECORDS
Port Clinton. Ohio. Trinity United Methodist Church *see* RECORDS
PORT COLBORNE NEWS – (1956-1992.-35r) – Port Colborne, 1993 – 1r – 1 – cn Preston [971]
PORT COLBORNE PROGRESS REPORT – Port Colborne, 1951-1961 – 1r – 1 – cn Preston [971]
PORT CRESCENT – Appleton. Wis. 1850-66; 1928-1932; 1937-40; 1958- – 1 – us UMI [071]
PORT DARWIN PASSENGER LISTS (COMPILED FROM NT NEWSPAPERS) NOVEMBER 1873-DECEMBER 1914 – 6mf – 9 – A$30.00 – 0-949124-54-0 – item 22 – at G.S.N.T. [920]
PORT DARWIN SHIPPING, 1887, 1898, 1899 AND 1900 – (1887 Departures from Port Darwin. ISBN: 0-949124-40-0; 1887 Inward Shipping for the Northern Territory. ISBN: 0-949124-44-3; 1889 Shipping to Port Darwin. ISBN: 0-949124-57-5; 1898 Inward Shipping for the Northern Territory. ISBN: 0-949124-42-7; 1899 Inward/Outward Shipping for the Northern Territory. ISBN: 0-949124-43-5; 1900 Shipping to Port Darwin. ISBN: 0-949124-47-8) – 1988 – 1mf – 9 – A$4.00 – item 16 – at G.S.N.T. [920]
LE PORT DE SAIGON. / Texier, Paul – Bordeaux, Trenit, 1909.198 p. LL-10014 – 1 – us L of C Photodup [340]
PORT DOVER MAPLE LEAF – 1889-1986 – cn Commonwealth Micro [072]
THE PORT ELIZABETH ADVERTISER – (Merged with: Saturday Post to become: Evening Post) – Port Elizabeth, South Africa. 1 Jan 1870-31 Dec 1910. – 37r – 1, 16 diazo available at reduced price – sa SA Libr [072]
PORT ELIZABETH ARGUS – Port Elizabeth, South Africa. 20 Nov 1896-26 Nov 1897. 1 reel – 1, 16 diazo available at reduced price – sa SA Libr [072]
PORT ELIZABETH TELEGRAPH *see* THE CAPE DAILY TELEGRAPH
PORT FAIRY AND KORDIT NEWS – 3-6/1991. PFKN1 – 1r – 1 – at Corangamite [910]
PORT FAIRY BOROUGH MINUTE BOOKS – 1984-1989. PFBM21-22 – 2r – 5 – at Corangamite [910]
PORT FAIRY BOROUGH RATE BOOKS – 1856-1901. 1861-78, 79-87. PFB1 – 1r – 1 – at Corangamite [910]
PORT FAIRY CEMETERY REGISTER – 1869-1984. PFC1-6 – 6r – 1 – at Corangamite [920]
PORT FAIRY GAZETTE – 1901-1989 – 65r – 1 – at Corangamite [072]
PORT FAIRY MECHANICS INSTITUTE – 1864-1985. Records. PFMI1 – 1r – 1 – at Corangamite [910]
PORT FAIRY NEWS – 1910-1912. PFN1-2 – 2r – 1 – at Corangamite [072]
PORT FAIRY TIMES AND MACARTHUR NEWS – 1917-1918. PFTMN1 – 1r – 1 – at Corangamite [072]
PORT FOWO – 1989-1994 – 1r – 1 – at Corangamite [072]
PORT GARDNER NEWS – Everett. Wash. 1891-1896 – 1 – us UMI [071]
Port Gibson, Mississippi *see* MISCELLANEOUS EARLY NEWSPAPERS
PORT HOPE EVENING GUIDE – Port Hope, Ju1990-1992Jn – 8r – 1 – cn Preston [971]
PORT HUENEME HARBOR BULLETIN – Port Hueneme, CA. 1938-1941 – 1r – 1 – $50.00 – B03633 – us Library Micro [071]
PORT HUENEME HERALD – Port Hueneme, CA. 1941-1942 – 1r – 1 – $50.00 – B03634 – us Library Micro [071]
PORT HUENEME HERALD EXPRESS – Port Hueneme, CA. 1948-1951 – 2r – 1 – $100.00 – B03635 – us Library Micro [071]
PORT HUENEME PILOT – Port Hueneme, CA. 1951-1963 – 8r – 1 – $400.00 – B03636 – us Library Micro [071]
PORT INFORMATION / U.S. Operations Mission to Indonesia – SE 5467 1. 1960 – 9 – ne IDC [324]
PORT LAVACA FIRST BAPTIST CHURCH. PORT LAVACA, TEXAS : CHURCH RECORDS – 1854-84 – 1 – 7.38 – us Baptist [240]
PORT MACQUARIE NEWS – July 8 1882-Dec 31 1898; Jan 28 1899-Dec 28 1907; Jan 4 1913-Oct 6 1950 – 1 – at Pascoe [072]
THE PORT OF QUEBEC: ITS FACILITIES AND PROSPECTS: THE PAST, PRESENT AND FUTURE OF QUEBEC'S SHIPPING TRADE / Chambers, Edward Thomas Davies – Quebec: "Morning Chronicle", 1890. 02345. (Pre-1900 Canadiana) – 9 – cn C.I.H.M. [971]
PORT OF SPAIN GAZETTE – Port of Spain. May 12 1947; Mar 9-11 1948; Feb 1-3 1949 – 1 – us NY Public [073]
PORT OF SPAIN GAZETTE – Port of Spain. Trinidad. -d. 22 Feb 1941-30 Jun 1956. (67 reels) – 1 – uk British Libr Newspaper [072]
PORT OF SPAIN GAZETTE – Trinidad. 1825-1956 – 1 – us UMI [072]
PORT OF TANDJONG PRIOK – SE 5120 1 – 9 – ne IDC [950]
PORT OREGON TRIBUNE – Warrenton, OR. -w. 24 Jul 1896-23 May 1902. 1 roll – 1 – us U.O. Library [071]
PORT ORFORD BULLETIN – Port Orford OR. Oct 10 17 24 Nov 6 1935 – 1 – us U.O. Library [071]
PORT ORFORD NEWS – Port Orford, OR. -w. 30 May 1961-. – 1 – us U.O. Library [071]
PORT ORFORD NEWS – Port Orford, OR. -w. 9 Nov 1926-21 Mar 1933. 2 rolls – 1 – us U.O. Library [071]
PORT ORFORD PILOT – Port Orford OR. Oct 8 1931 – 1 – us U.O. Library [071]
PORT ORFORD POST – Port Orford, OR. 30 Apr 1937-10 Apr 1942 – 1r – 1 – us U.O. Library [071]
PORT ORFORD POST – Port Orford, OR. -w. 27 May 1880-25 May 1882. 1 roll – 1 – us U.O. Library [071]
PORT ORFORD TRIBUNE – Port Orford, OR. -w. 17 May 1892-29 Jul 1925; 17 May 1892-2 Dec 1903 – 1r – 1 – us U.O. Library [071]
PORT ORFORD TRIBUNE – Port Orford, OR. -w. 1901-20, 1924 – 1 – 113.00 – us Oregon Hist [071]
PORT PERRY STAR – (1993.-3r) – Port Perry, 1984-1992 – 20r – 1 – cn Preston [971]
PORT PHILIP HERALD – Melbourne, Australia. Melbourne Morning Herald Melbourne Herald The Herald. -d. 1840-50; 1852; 1855; Jan 1857-Jan 1869; 20 Nov 1883; 1 March, 3 May 1884; 23 Aug 1910-20 May 1922; 27 Nov 1922-10 Feb 1928; June 1928-Feb 1940; Nov 1953-Sept 1970. 764 reels – 1 – uk British Libr Newspaper [072]
PORT PHILLIP GAZETTE – Melbourne, Australia. -w. Oct 1838-Dec 1841; April 1844-March 1845. 1845 imperfect. 3 reels – 1 – uk British Libr Newspaper [072]
PORT PHILLIP GOVERNMENT GAZETTE – 1843-1851 – 58mf – 9 – A$80.00 – at State Libr Vic [072]
PORT PHILLIP PATRIOT – Melbourne, 1838-42 – 2r – 1 – A$58.00 silver A$50.00 vesicular – at Pascoe [072]
PORT PHILLIP PATRIOT – Melbourne, Australia. -w. 14 Feb 1845-5 March 1847. 2 reels – 1 – uk British Libr Newspaper [072]
PORT PHILLIP/VICTORIA DIRECTORIES – 1839-1867. 39v – 64mf and hard copy contents list – 9 – A$70.00 – at State Libr Vic [980]
PORT ROYAL : A CONTRIBUTION TO THE HISTORY OF RELIGION AND LITERATURE IN FRANCE / Beard, Charles – London: Longman, Green, Longman, and Roberts. 2v. 1861 – 4mf – 9 – 0-8370-8966-2 – 1986-2966 – us A.T.L.A. [944]
PORT ROYAL BAND BOOKS – Manuscript collection of band music used by the 3rd New Hampshire Volunteer Infantry during the Civil War at Port Royal Island, South Carolina. ca. 1861. About 50 compositions, including: "Hail Columbia," "Hail to the Chief," "Listen to the Mocking Bird," "Star Spangled Banner," and "Garry Owen." MUSIC 654 – 1 – us L of C Photodup [780]
PORT STEPHENS PILOT – July 16 1926-Febr 7 1930 – 1 – at Pascoe [072]
PORT UMPQUA BELL BOUY – Gardiner OR. July 30 1921 – 1 – us U.O. Library [071]
PORT UMPQUA COURIER – Gardiner OR. Apr 10 1915-Oct 20 1917 – 1 – us U.O. Library [071]
PORT UMQUA COURIER – Reedsport, OR. 25 Apr 1914-23 May 1963 – 1 – us U.O. Library [071]
Porta, B *see* TROIS QUATUORS POUR FLUTE, VIOLON, ALTO, ET BASSE, OP. 1
PORTA LINGUARUM TRILINGUIS / Comenius, Johann Amos – 1631. 261p. (English Linguistics Series 1500-1800) – 9 – us UMI [400]
PORTA SION: LEXIKON ZUM LATEINISCHEN PSALTER / Ecker, Jakob – Trier: Paulinus Druckerei, 1903.1 fiche – 9 – us A.T.L.A. [240]
PORTABLE COMPUTER – v1-. 1983- – 1,5,6,9 – us UMI [073]
O PORTACOLLO : JORNAL QUE INTERESSA A TODOS OS BRASILEIROS NATOS, E LIVRES – '(s.l.')-Bahia, Brazil. 29 Aug 1832 – 1,5,6 – bl Biblioteca [072]
PORTADOWN EXPRESS & COUNTY ARMAGH ADVERTISER – Ireland. -w. 9 Nov 1906-25 June 1920. 11 reels – 1 – uk British Libr Newspaper [072]
PORTADOWN & LURGAN NEWS – Ireland.1887. -w. 1 reel – 1 – uk British Libr Newspaper [072]
PORTADOWN RECORDER *see* ADVERTISER ETC
PORTADOWN TIMES – Oct 13 1922-Dec 28 1923; 1924-25; Jan 29 1926-41; 1986-87; Jan 8-Mar 25, Apr 1988-89; Jul 1990-96 – 56 1/2r – 1 – uk British Libr Newspaper [072]
PORTADOWN WEEKLY NEWS – Ireland. Portadown News Portadown & Lurgan News. -w. 1859-1974. Lacking 1926. 101 reels – 1 – uk British Libr Newspaper [072]
LE PORTAGE – (Cont by: Information) – L'Assomption, Canada. 15 jul 1949-29 dec 1971 – 14r – 1 – Can$60.00r – cn Can Microfilming [072]
LE PORTAGE *see* INFORMATION
PORTAGE COUNTY GAZETTE – Stevens Point. Wis. 1878-1922 – 1 – us UMI [071]
THE PORTAGE DISPATCH – Portage, PA. 1954-72. 10 rolls – 13 – $25.00r – us I.M.R. [071]
PORTAGE FIRST BAPTIST CHURCH. PORTAGE, MICHIGAN : CHURCH RECORDS – 1959-68 – 1 – 29.43 – us Baptist [240]
PORTAGE LA PRAIRIE DAILY GRAPHIC – Portage La Prairie, Manitoba, CN. 1910- – 6r per yr – 1 – Can$53.00r – cn Commonwealth Micro [072]
PORTAGE LA PRAIRIE HERALD LEADER PRESS – Portage La Prairie, Manitoba, CN. 1948- – 2r per yr – 1 – Can$57.00r – cn Commonwealth Micro [072]
PORTAGE LAKE AND LAKE SUPERIOR CANALS COLLECTION / Institute for Great Lakes Research – 1891-1929 – 1r – 1 – $32.50r – us Archival [380]
Portage. Ohio. Presbytery *see* CHURCH RECORDS, MS 501
Portage. Presbytery (Pres. Ch. in the USA. New School) *see* MINUTES, 1843-1863
Portal y Canton, Salustiano *see* SENTENCIA...PLEITO...MONTIJO...MERIDA
PORTALES NEWS-TRIBUNE – Portales. New Mexico. Jul 1976- – 1 – us UMI [071]
Portalin Garcia, A *see* GUIA PARA EL TRABAJADOR ESPANOL EN FRANCIA, 1977
PORTA-VOZ : PELA PROSPERIDADE DO MUNICIPIO EM TODOS OS RAMOS DA ACTIVIDADE – Divinopolis, 25 Feb 1934 – 1,5,6 – bl Biblioteca [072]
Porte, Albert *see* PAPERS
LE PORTEFEUILLE – Revue critique, historique et litteraire. no. 1-15. Paris. mai-aout 1855 – 1 – fr A.C.R.P.P. [073]
LE PORTE-FEUILLE D'UN PHILOSOPHE, OU MELANGE DE PIECES PHILOSOPHIQUES, POLITIQUES, CRITIQUES, SATYRIQUES ET GALANTES / Du Laurens, Henri-Joseph – (D'Holbach series). 1770 – 9 – fr Hachette [190]
Portenschlag-Ledermayer, F von *see* ENUMERATIO PLANTARUM IN DALMATIA LECTARUM
Porter Academy. Charleston, South Carolina *see* TRUSTEE MINUTES
Porter, Andrew *see* LETTERS
Porter, Catharine Wiggins *see* REMINISCENCES
Porter, Charles Talbot *see* MECHANICS AND FAITH: A STUDY OF SPIRITUAL TRUTH IN NATURE
PORTER COUNTY VIDETTE – Valparaiso. Ind. 1874-1885 – 1 – us UMI [071]
Porter, George P *see* FROM ATHEISM TO CHRISTIANITY
Porter, Howard N *see* PAPERS, 1936-1952
Porter, J W *see* WHY AM I A BAPTIST?

Porter, James *see*
– REVIVALS OF RELIGION
Porter, James Gray *see* LETTERBOOK
Porter, James M *see* EXPERIMENTS AND DEMONSTRATIONS IN PSYCHOLOGY
Porter, John Scott *see*
– LECTURES ON THE DOCTRINE OF ATONEMENT
– PRINCIPLES OF TEXTUAL CRITICISM
– UNITARIANISM: A DEVOTIONAL FAITH
– UNITARIANISM: THE DOCTRINE OF OUR LORD JESUS CHRIST
– UNITARIANISM: THE FAITH OF THE APOSTLES
Porter, Josias Leslie *see*
– THE GIANT CITIES OF BASHAN
– THE LIFE AND TIMES OF HENRY COOKE
– THE PENTATEUCH AND THE GOSPELS
– SCIENCE AND REVELATION:...IN REPLY TO...TYNDALL, HUXLEY, DARWIN, SPENCER
Porter, Noah *see*
– AGNOSTICISM
– THE EDUCATIONAL SYSTEMS OF THE PURITANS AND JESUITS COMPARED
– KANT'S ETHICS
– THE SCIENCES OF NATURE VERSUS THE SCIENCE OF MAN
Porter, Samuel Thomas *see* THE SILVER RUSH AT MINERAL KING, CALIFORNIA 1873-1882
Porter, Scott T *see* ANALYSIS OF IN-VIVO MENISCAL KINEMATIC MOTION OF THE NON-INJURED KNEE
Porter, T *see* EPIGRAMMATA
Porter, T C *see*
– FLORA OF PENNSYLVANIA
– SYNOPSIS OF THE FLORA OF COLORADO
Porter, Will *see* ANNALS OF POLK COUNTY AND THE CITY OF DES MOINES
Porter, William Dennison *see* THE CONSTITUTIONALITY OF THE LAWYERS TEST OATH; ARGUMENT OF W. D. PORTER, IN THE DISTRICT COURT OF THE UNITED STATES
PORTER'S REPORTS / Alabama. Supreme Court – (A Pre-NRS title) – Alabama. v1-9. 1834-39 (all publ) – 64mf – 9 – $96.00 – LLMC 91-046 – us L.L.M.C. [340]
THE PORTERVILLE ENTERPRISE – Porterville, CA. 1889-1901 – 2r – 1 – $100.00 – C02642 – us Library Micro [071]
PORTERVILLE PAPERS – (Consists of: Evening Recorder; Weekly Review Jul 1898. Enterprise Jul 1903. Daily Recorder 1916-33 (scattered issues)) – Porterville, CA. – 1r – 1 – $50.00 – B02644 – us Library Micro [071]
PORTERVILLE RECORDER – Porterville, CA. 1910-14; 1959-62; 1985- – 59+ r – 1 – $2,950.00 ($280.00y) – B02645 – us Library Micro [071]
PORTFEULLE FUR MUSIKLIEBHABER / Junker, K – Leipziger Ostermesse, 1792 – 1 – us Sibley [780]
THE PORTFOLIO – Hamilton, Ont.: Literary Society of the Wesleyan Female College, [1879?-189- or 19–] – 9 – cn C.I.H.M. [370]
THE PORTFOLIO / Northern Congregational Church (Toronto, Ont.). Young Men's Association – Toronto: Young Men's Association, [1886-18– or 19–] – 9 – cn C.I.H.M. [240]
PORTIA LAW JOURNAL *see* NEW ENGLAND LAW REVIEW
Portier, J *see* CONVERGENCE DES SYSTEMES ET COEXISTENCE PACIFIQUE
THE PORTIFORIUM OF ST WULSTAN / Hughes, A – Vol 1, 1958; Vol 2, 1960 – 6mf – 8 – ne Slangenburg [240]
Portillo, Rodrigo de *see* LIBRO DE LOS TRATADOS DE..
PORTLAND ADVERTISER – Portland, ME, 1831-63 – us Res Libr [071]
PORTLAND AND VICINITY – Chicago, 1903. Oregon reel 5. (Cox Library Collection) – 5 – us Americana [978]
PORTLAND BULLETIN – Portland OR. June 29 1928-Mar 21 1935 + – 1 – us U.O. Library [071]
PORTLAND BUSINESS TODAY – Portland OR. May 15 1985-Oct 30 1987 – 1 – us U.O. Library [071]
PORTLAND CHALLENGER – Portland OR. Nov 28 Dec 12 1952, Jan 23-Aug 7 1953 – 1 – us U.O. Library [071]
PORTLAND CHALLENGER – Portland, OR. -sw. 1952-54 – 1 – 17.00 – us Oregon Hist [071]
PORTLAND CHRONICLE – Portland, OR. -w. 1 Jun 1894-5 Nov 1904. 1 roll – 1 – us U.O. Library [071]
PORTLAND COMMERCIAL – Portland OR. Mar 24 28 31 Apr 28 1853 – 1 – us U.O. Library [071]
PORTLAND COMMERCIAL AND GENERAL ADVERTISER – Portland OR. Aug 25 Sep 5 8 1853, Jan 27 1854 – 1 – us U.O. Library [071]
PORTLAND COMMONER – Portland OR. May 10 1930 – 1 – us U.O. Library [071]
PORTLAND DAILY ABSTRACT – Portland OR. June 2 1906-May 31 1916 – 1 – us U.O. Library [071]
PORTLAND DAILY ABSTRACT AND OREGON BUILDING RECORD – Portland OR. June 1-June 30 1916 – 1 – us U.O. Library [071]
PORTLAND DAILY ADVERTISER – Portland OR. Aug 19 Oct 13 1859, Jan 16 1860-Nov 25 1861, Jan 6 Feb 1 1862 – 1 – us U.O. Library [071]
PORTLAND DAILY BEE – Portland, OR. 1875-79 – 1 – 120.00 – us Oregon Hist [071]
PORTLAND DAILY DRAMATIC CHRONICLE AND HOTEL GAZETTE – Portland OR. Sep 15 Nov 10 16 22 Dec 3 1883, Jan 3 12 May 24 1884 – 1 – us U.O. Library [071]
PORTLAND DAILY EXAMINER – Portland OR. Apr 6 1891 – 1 – us U.O. Library [071]
PORTLAND DAILY EXAMINER – Portland OR. Mar 20 1912-Dec 31 1913 – 1 – us U.O. Library [071]
PORTLAND DAILY NEWS – Portland, OR. 1859-60. Incomplete – 1 – 17.00 – us Oregon Hist [071]
PORTLAND DAILY NEWS – Portland, OR. 1884-87 – 1 – 120.00 – us Oregon Hist [071]
PORTLAND DAILY PLAINDEALER – Portland OR. May 23 1862 – 1 – us U.O. Library [071]
PORTLAND DAILY UNION – Portland OR. Jan 2 Feb 9 23 1864 – 1 – us U.O. Library [071]
Portland Directory Co *see* EASTERN OREGON DIRECTORY 1899-1900
PORTLAND EVENING JOURNAL – Portland OR. May 23 26 1902 – 1 – us U.O. Library [071]
PORTLAND EXAMINER – Portland OR. Apr 15-May 27 1926 – 1 – us U.O. Library [071]
PORTLAND FORUM – Portland, OR. -w. 5 Jan 1940-26 Dec 1941. 1 roll – 1 – us U.O. Library [071]
PORTLAND GAZETTE – Portland, ME: Elezer A Jenks, mar-jul 16 1805 – us Res Libr [071]
PORTLAND GAZETTE, AND MAINE ADVERTISER – Portland, ME: I Adams & W Jenks, jul 23 1805-mar 1818 – us Res Libr [071]
PORTLAND GUARDIAN – 1902-1964 – 27mf – 1 – at Corangamite [980]
PORTLAND GUARDIAN – Australia. -w. Jan 1848-Nov 1850; 1856-58. 4 1 2 reels – 1 – uk British Libr Newspaper [072]
PORTLAND GUARDIAN – Portland, 1842-49 – 2r – 1 – A$62.00 silver A$54.00 vesicular – at Pascoe [072]
PORTLAND INDUSTRIAL EXPOSITION DAILY – Portland OR. Oct 10 1891 – 1 – us U.O. Library [071]
PORTLAND INQUIRER – Portland, OR. -w. 12 Jul 1944-22 Mar 1946. 1 roll – 1 – us U.O. Library [071]
PORTLAND LABOR NEWS – Portland, OR. 1919 – 1 – 17.00 – us Oregon Hist [071]
PORTLAND LABOR NEWS – Portland OR. Aug 22-Oct 31 1919 – 1 – us U.O. Library [071]
PORTLAND LABOR PRESS – Portland, OR. 6 Sept 1900-25 Aug 1905. 1 roll – 1 – us U.O. Library [071]
PORTLAND LABOR PRESS – Portland, OR. -w. 1900-13. Incomplete – 1 – 72.00 – us Oregon Hist [071]
PORTLAND LEADER – Portland OR. June 1945 – 1 – us U.O. Library [071]
PORTLAND LIVE STOCK REPORTER – Portland OR. May 10 1917 – 1 – us U.O. Library [071]
PORTLAND MESSENGER – Portland OR. Apr 1916 – 1 – us U.O. Library [071]
PORTLAND NEWS – Portland, OR. -d. 1906-31. And pred – 1 – 1440.00 – us Oregon Hist [071]
PORTLAND NEWS – Portland OR. Sep 3 1918 – 1 – us U.O. Library [071]
PORTLAND NEWSPAPER UNION – Portland OR. May 23 Aug 1-29 Sep 12 1914, Oct 3-Dec 26 1914, Jan 23 Feb 6-Apr 3 May 8 1915, June 2 July 10-Aug 21 Dec 4 1915 – 1 – us U.O. Library [071]
PORTLAND NEWS-TELEGRAM – Portland, OR. -d. 1931-39 – 1 – 744.00 – us Oregon Hist [071]
PORTLAND OBSERVER – 1890-1968 – 32r – 1 – at Corangamite [980]
PORTLAND OBSERVER – Portland, OR. 1 Oct 1970-. – 1 – us U.O. Library [071]
PORTLAND OBSERVER – Portland OR. Dec 16 1938-May 5 1939 – 1 – us U.O. Library [071]
PORTLAND, OREGON, ITS HISTORY AND BUILDERS / Gaston, Joseph – (v2-3. Oregon reel 6) – Portland: S.J. Clarke Publ. Co., 1911. v1. Oregon reel 5. (Cox Library Collection) – 5 – us Americana [978]
PORTLAND PAPERS / Bath. Archives (Marquess). Longleat – v. 1-24. Boxes 1-3, Misc. vol. 1-4 – 1 – uk Microform Academic [920]
PORTLAND PAYROLL NEWS – Portland OR. Apr 10 July 24 1931 – 1 – us U.O. Library [071]
PORTLAND REALTY INDEX – Portland OR. Mar 9 May 18 1912 – 1 – us U.O. Library [071]
PORTLAND REPORTER – Portland, OR. -d. 11 Feb 1960-1 Oct 1964. 32 rolls – 1 – us U.O. Library [071]
PORTLAND SCRIBE – Portland, OR. 1972 – 1 – 24.00 – us Oregon Hist [071]
PORTLAND SHIRE COUNCIL MINUTES – 1986-1988 – 2r – 5 – at Corangamite [910]
PORTLAND SHIRE COUNCIL RECORDS – 1856-1967 – 13r – 1,5 – at Corangamite [910]
PORTLAND SHIRE RATES – 1864-1940 – 10r – 1 – at Corangamite [910]
PORTLAND SPORTOGRAM – Portland OR. Jan 25 Feb 15 Mar 29 1946, Apr 12 19 May 10 1946 – 1 – us U.O. Library [071]
PORTLAND STATESMAN – Portland, OR. -w. 3 Nov 1944-Jul 1952. 1 roll – 1 – us U.O. Library [071]
PORTLAND TELEGRAM – (Set incl. Evening Telegram (Portland)) – Portland, OR. -d. 2 Dec 1918-5 May 1931. – 156r – 1 – us U.O. Library [071]
PORTLAND TODAY – Portland OR. Dec 1 1976-Sep 1977 – 1 – us U.O. Library [071]
PORTLAND WEEKLY DISPATCH – Portland, OR. 17 June 1891-28 Aug 1902 – 1 – us U.O. Library [071]
PORTLAND WEEKLY NEWS – Portland, OR. 1883-87. Incomplete – 1 – 48.00 – us Oregon Hist [071]
Portmann, J G *see* LEICHTES LEHRBUCH DER HARMONIE, COMPOSITION UND DES GENERALBASSES, ZUM GEBRAUCHT FUR LIEBHABER DER MUSIK, ANGEHANDE UND FORTSCHREITENDE MUSICI UND COMPONISTEN...
PORTNEUF-PRESSE *see* L'ECHO DE PORTNEUF-PRESSE
PORTO ACRE : DEPARTAMENTO DO ACRE – Porto Acre, Acre. 7 Set 1913-Jan 1915; Mar-Jul, Set-Nov 1916; Fev, Ago, Dez 1917; Jan-16 Jun 1918 – 1,5,6 bl Biblioteca [072]
PORTO LIVRE : JORNAL POLITICO, COMMERCIAL E NOTICIOSO – '(s.l.')-Sao Luis, Brazil. 26 Aug-Sept 1861. Jan 1862-20 Sept 1965 – 1,5,6 – bl Biblioteca [072]
PORTO RICO FEDERAL REPORTS : UNITED STATES DISTRICT COURT FOR THE DISTRICT OF PORTO RICO – 1900-18. Rochester: Lawyers' Coop. v1-10. 1906-19 (mf ed all publ) – 76mf – 9 – $114.00 – LLMC 91-029 – us L.L.M.C. [340]
THE PORTO RICO REVIEW – 6V. 1906-12 – 1 – 138.00 – us L of C Photodup [972]
PORTOBELLO ADVERTISER – Scotland, UK. 1890. -w. 1 reel – 1 – uk British Libr Newspaper [072]
Portocarrero, Francisco *see* LIBRO DE LA DESCENSION...TOLEDO Y VIDA DE SAN ILDEFONSO
PORTOLA REPORTER – Portola, CA. 1943-59; 1972; 1977 – 10r – 1 BC02648 – $500.00 – us Library Micro [071]
PORTOLA SENTINEL – Portola, CA. 1916-1917 – 1r – 1 – $50.00 – C03637 – us Library Micro [071]
A PORTRAIT *see* CANADA HANDBOOK
PORTRAIT AND BIOGRAPHICAL ALBUM OF BENTON COUNTY – Chicago: 1887. Iowa Reel 6. (The Cox Library Collection) – 5 – us Americana [978]
PORTRAIT AND BIOGRAPHICAL ALBUM OF CALHOUN COUNTY – Chicago, 1891. Michigan Reel 7.(The Cox Library Collection) – 5 – us Americana [978]
PORTRAIT AND BIOGRAPHICAL ALBUM OF CHAMPAIGN COUNTY – Chicago, 1887. Illinois Reel 14. (The Cox Library Collection) – 5 – us Americana [978]
PORTRAIT AND BIOGRAPHICAL ALBUM OF CLINTON AND SHIAWASSEE COUNTIES – Chicago, 1891. Michigan Reel 8.(The Cox Library Collection) – 5 – us Americana [978]
PORTRAIT AND BIOGRAPHICAL ALBUM OF DE KALB COUNTY – Chicago, 1885. Illinois Reel 21. (The Cox Library Collection) – 5 – us Americana [978]
PORTRAIT AND BIOGRAPHICAL ALBUM OF DES MOINES COUNTY – Chicago: 1888. Iowa Reel 13. (The Cox Library Collection) – 5 – us Americana [978]
PORTRAIT AND BIOGRAPHICAL ALBUM OF FAYETTE COUNTY / Lake City Publishing Co – Chicago: 1891. Iowa Reel 16. (The Cox Library Collection) – 5 – us Americana [978]
PORTRAIT AND BIOGRAPHICAL ALBUM OF FOND DU LAC COUNTY – Chicago: 1889. Wisconsin Reel 11. (The Cox Library Collection) – 5 – us Americana [978]
PORTRAIT AND BIOGRAPHICAL ALBUM OF FULTON COUNTY – Chicago, 1890. Illinois Reel 25. (The Cox Library Collection) – 5 – us Americana [978]
PORTRAIT AND BIOGRAPHICAL ALBUM OF GAGE COUNTY – Chicago, 1888. Nebraska Reel 8.(The Cox Library Collection) – 5 – us Americana [978]
PORTRAIT AND BIOGRAPHICAL ALBUM OF GRATIOT COUNTY – Chicago: 1884. Michigan Reel 10. (The Cox Library Collection) – 5 – us Americana [978]
PORTRAIT AND BIOGRAPHICAL ALBUM OF GREENE AND CLARK COUNTIES – Chicago: 1890. Ohio Reel 34. (The Cox Library Collection) – 5 – us Americana [978]
PORTRAIT AND BIOGRAPHICAL ALBUM OF HENRY COUNTY – Chicago, 1885. (Illinois Reel 27). (The Cox Library Collection) – 5 – us Americana [978]
PORTRAIT AND BIOGRAPHICAL ALBUM OF HENRY COUNTY – Chicago: 1888. Iowa Reel 20. (The Cox Library Collection) – 5 – us Americana [978]
PORTRAIT AND BIOGRAPHICAL ALBUM OF HILLSDALE COUNTY – Chicago: 1888. Michigan Reel 11. (The Cox Library Collection) – 5 – us Americana [978]
PORTRAIT AND BIOGRAPHICAL ALBUM OF HURON COUNTY – Chicago: 1884. Michigan Reel 12. (The Cox Library Collection) – 5 – us Americana [978]
PORTRAIT AND BIOGRAPHICAL ALBUM OF INGHAM AND LIVINGSTON COUNTIES – Chicago: 1891. Michigan Reel 12. (The Cox Library Collection) – 5 – us Americana [978]
PORTRAIT AND BIOGRAPHICAL ALBUM OF IONIA AND MONTCALM COUNTIES – Chicago: 1891. Michigan Reel 13. (The Cox Library Collection) – 5 – us Americana [978]
PORTRAIT AND BIOGRAPHICAL ALBUM OF JACKSON COUNTY – Chicago: 1889. Iowa Reel 21. (The Cox Library Collection) – 5 – us Americana [978]
PORTRAIT AND BIOGRAPHICAL ALBUM OF JACKSON COUNTY – Chicago: 1890. Michigan Reel 14. (The Cox Library Collection) – 5 – us Americana [978]
PORTRAIT AND BIOGRAPHICAL ALBUM OF JACKSON, JEFFERSON AND POTTAWATOMIE COUNTIES – Chicago, 1890. Kansas Reel 8. (The Cox Library Collection) – 5 – us Americana [978]
PORTRAIT AND BIOGRAPHICAL ALBUM OF JEFFERSON AND VAN BUREN COUNTIES / Lake City Publishing Co – Chicago: 1890. Iowa Reel 23. (The Cox Library Collection) – 5 – us Americana [978]
PORTRAIT AND BIOGRAPHICAL ALBUM OF JO DAVIESS AND CARROLL COUNTIES – Chicago, 1889. (Illinois Reel 30). (The Cox Library Collection) – 5 – us Americana [978]

PORTRAIT AND BIOGRAPHICAL ALBUM OF KNOX COUNTY – Chicago, 1886. (Illinois Reel 34). (The Cox Library Collection) – 5 – us Americana [978]

PORTRAIT AND BIOGRAPHICAL ALBUM OF LANCASTER COUNTY – Chicago, 1888. Nebraska Reel 10. (The Cox Library Collection) – 5 – us Americana [978]

PORTRAIT AND BIOGRAPHICAL ALBUM OF LEE COUNTY – Chicago: 1887. Iowa Reel 25. (The Cox Library Collection) – 5 – us Americana [978]

PORTRAIT AND BIOGRAPHICAL ALBUM OF LENAWEE COUNTY – Chicago: 1888. Michigan Reel 17. (The Cox Library Collection) – 5 – us Americana [978]

PORTRAIT AND BIOGRAPHICAL ALBUM OF LINN COUNTY – Chicago: 1887. Iowa Reel 26. (The Cox Library Collection) – 5 – us Americana [978]

PORTRAIT AND BIOGRAPHICAL ALBUM OF LOUISA COUNTY – Chicago: 1889. Iowa Reel 27. (The Cox Library Collection) – 5 – us Americana [978]

PORTRAIT AND BIOGRAPHICAL ALBUM OF MAHASKA COUNTY – Chicago: 1887. Iowa Reel 28. (The Cox Library Collection) – 5 – us Americana [978]

PORTRAIT AND BIOGRAPHICAL ALBUM OF MARSHALL COUNTY – Chicago, 1889. Kansas Reel 9. (The Cox Library Collection) – 5 – us Americana [978]

PORTRAIT AND BIOGRAPHICAL ALBUM OF MCLEAN COUNTY – Chicago: 1887. Illinois Reel 44. (The Cox Library Collection) – 5 – us Americana [978]

PORTRAIT AND BIOGRAPHICAL ALBUM OF MIDLAND COUNTY – Chicago: 1884. Michigan Reel 19. (The Cox Library Collection) – 5 – us Americana [978]

PORTRAIT AND BIOGRAPHICAL ALBUM OF MUSCATINE COUNTY – Chicago: 1889. Iowa Reel 30. (The Cox Library Collection) – 5 – us Americana [978]

PORTRAIT AND BIOGRAPHICAL ALBUM OF NEWAYCO COUNTY – Chicago: 1884. Michiagn Reel 19. (The Cox Library Collection) – 5 – us Americana [978]

PORTRAIT AND BIOGRAPHICAL ALBUM OF OGLE COUNTY – Chicago, 1886. (Illinois Reel 47). (The Cox Library Collection) – 5 – us Americana [978]

PORTRAIT AND BIOGRAPHICAL ALBUM OF OSCEOLA COUNTY – Chicago: 1884. Michigan Reel 20. (The Cox Library Collection) – 5 – us Americana [978]

PORTRAIT AND BIOGRAPHICAL ALBUM OF OTOE AND CASS COUNTIES – Chicago, 1889. Nebraska Reel 12. (The Cox Library Collection) – 5 – us Americana [978]

PORTRAIT AND BIOGRAPHICAL ALBUM OF PEORIA COUNTY – Chicago, 1890. (Illinois Reel 48). (The Cox Library Collection) – 5 – us Americana [978]

PORTRAIT AND BIOGRAPHICAL ALBUM OF POLK COUNTY / Lake City Publishing Co – Chicago: 1890. Iowa Reel 33. (The Cox Library Collection) – 5 – us Americana [978]

PORTRAIT AND BIOGRAPHICAL ALBUM OF RACINE AND KENOSHA COUNTIES / Lake City Publishing Co – Chicago: 1892. Wisconsin Reel 17. (The Cox Library Collection) – 5 – us Americana [978]

PORTRAIT AND BIOGRAPHICAL ALBUM OF ROCK COUNTY – Chicago: 1889. Wisconsin Reel 18. (The Cox Library Collection) – 5 – us Americana [978]

PORTRAIT AND BIOGRAPHICAL ALBUM OF ROCK ISLAND COUNTY – Chicago, 1885. (Illinois Reel 51). (The Cox Library Collection) – 5 – us Americana [978]

PORTRAIT AND BIOGRAPHICAL ALBUM OF SANGAMON COUNTY – Chicago, 1891. (Illinois Reel 53). (The Cox Library Collection) – 5 – us Americana [978]

PORTRAIT AND BIOGRAPHICAL ALBUM OF SEDGWICK COUNTY – Chicago, 1888. Kansas Reel 11. (The Cox Library Collection) – 5 – us Americana [978]

PORTRAIT AND BIOGRAPHICAL ALBUM OF ST JOSEPH COUNTY – Chicago: 1889. Michigan Reel 21. (The Cox Library Collection) – 5 – us Americana [978]

PORTRAIT AND BIOGRAPHICAL ALBUM OF STEPHENSON COUNTY – Chicago, 1888. (Illinois Reel 56). (The Cox Library Collection) – 5 – us Americana [978]

PORTRAIT AND BIOGRAPHICAL ALBUM OF SUMNER COUNTY – Chicago, 1890. Kansas Reel 12. (The Cox Library Collection) – 5 – us Americana [978]

PORTRAIT AND BIOGRAPHICAL ALBUM OF VERMILION COUNTY – Chicago, 1889. (Illinois Reel 57). (The Cox Library Collection) – 5 – us Americana [978]

PORTRAIT AND BIOGRAPHICAL ALBUM OF WAPELLO COUNTY – Chicago, 1887. Iowa Reel 41. (The Cox Library Collection) – 5 – us Americana [978]

PORTRAIT AND BIOGRAPHICAL ALBUM OF WARREN COUNTY – Chicago, 1886. (Illinois Reel 59). (The Cox Library Collection) – 5 – us Americana [978]

PORTRAIT AND BIOGRAPHICAL ALBUM OF WASHINGTON, CLAY AND RILEY COUNTIES – Chicago, 1890. Kansas Reel 13. (The Cox Library Collection) – 5 – us Americana [978]

PORTRAIT AND BIOGRAPHICAL ALBUM OF WASHINGTON COUNTY – Chicago, 1887. Iowa Reel 42. (The Cox Library Collection) – 5 – us Americana [978]

PORTRAIT AND BIOGRAPHICAL ALBUM OF WASHTENAW COUNTY – Chicago: 1891. Michigan Reel 22. (The Cox Library Collection) – 5 – us Americana [978]

PORTRAIT AND BIOGRAPHICAL ALBUM OF WHITESIDE COUNTY – Chicago, 1885. (Illinois Reel 60). (The Cox Library Collection) – 5 – us Americana [978]

PORTRAIT AND BIOGRAPHICAL ALBUM OF WILL COUNTY – Chicago, 1890. (Illinois Reel 62). (The Cox Library Collection) – 5 – us Americana [978]

PORTRAIT AND BIOGRAPHICAL ALBUM OF WOODFORD COUNTY – Chicago, 1889. (Illinois Reel 64). (The Cox Library Collection) – 5 – us Americana [978]

PORTRAIT AND BIOGRAPHICAL RECORD OF ADAMS COUNTY, ILLINOIS – Chicago, 1892. Illinois Reel 11. (The Cox library collection) – 5 – us Americana [978]

PORTRAIT AND BIOGRAPHICAL RECORD OF ALLEGAN, VAN BUREN AND KALAMAZOO COUNTIES – Chicago, 1892. Michigan Reel 4.(The Cox Library Collection) – 5 – us Americana [978]

PORTRAIT AND BIOGRAPHICAL RECORD OF ALLEN AND VAN WERT COUNTIES / A.W. Bowen and Co – Chicago, 1896. Ohio Reel 12. The Cox Library Collection – 5 – us Americana [978]

PORTRAIT AND BIOGRAPHICAL RECORD OF AUGLAIZE, LOGAN AND SHELBY COUNTIES – Chicago, 1892. Ohio Reel 14. (The Cox Library Collection) – 5 – us Americana [978]

PORTRAIT AND BIOGRAPHICAL RECORD OF BARRY AND EATON COUNTIES – Chicago, 1891. Michigan Reel 4.(The Cox Library Collection) – 5 – us Americana [978]

PORTRAIT AND BIOGRAPHICAL RECORD OF BERRIEN AND CASS COUNTIES – Chicago, 1893. Michigan Reel 5. (The Cox Library Collection) – 5 – us Americana [978]

PORTRAIT AND BIOGRAPHICAL RECORD OF BOONE, CLINTON AND HENDRICKS COUNTIES / A.W. Bowen and Co – Chicago, 1895. Indiana Reel 6. The Cox Library Collection – 5 – us Americana [978]

PORTRAIT AND BIOGRAPHICAL RECORD OF BUCHANAN AND CLINTON COUNTIES – Chicago, 1893. Missouri Reel 10. (The Cox Library Collection) – 5 – us Americana [978]

PORTRAIT AND BIOGRAPHICAL RECORD OF CITY OF TOLEDO, LUCAS AND WOOD COUNTIES – Chicago: 1895. Ohio Reel 44. (The Cox Library Collection) – 5 – us Americana [978]

PORTRAIT AND BIOGRAPHICAL RECORD OF CLAY, RAY CARROL, CHARITON AND LINN COUNTIES – Chicago, 1893. Missouri Reel 13. (The Cox Library Collection) – 5 – us Americana [978]

PORTRAIT AND BIOGRAPHICAL RECORD OF COOK AND DU PAGE COUNTIES / Lake City Publishing Co – Chicago, 1894. Illinois Reel 16. (The Cox Library Collection) – 5 – us Americana [978]

PORTRAIT AND BIOGRAPHICAL RECORD OF DE WITT AND PIATT COUNTIES – Chicago, 1891. Illinois Reel 22. (The Cox Library Collection) – 5 – us Americana [978]

PORTRAIT AND BIOGRAPHICAL RECORD OF DELAWARE AND RANDOLPH COUNTIES / A.W. Bowen and Co – Chicago, 1894. Indiana Reel 10. The Cox Library Collection – 5 – us Americana [978]

PORTRAIT AND BIOGRAPHICAL RECORD OF DENVER AND VICINITY – Chicago, 1898. Colorado reel 4.(Cox Library Collection) – 5 – us Americana [978]

PORTRAIT AND BIOGRAPHICAL RECORD OF DICKINSON, SALINE, MCPHERSON AND MARION COUNTIES – Chicago, 1893. Kansas Reel 8. (The Cox Library Collection) – 5 – us Americana [978]

PORTRAIT AND BIOGRAPHICAL RECORD OF DUBUQUE, JONES AND CLAYTON COUNTIES – Chicago: 1894. Iowa Reel 15. (The Cox Library Collection) – 5 – us Americana [978]

PORTRAIT AND BIOGRAPHICAL RECORD OF EFFINGHAM, JASPER AND RICHLAND COUNTIES / Lake City Publishing Co – Chicago, 1893. Illinois Reel 24. (The Cox Library Collection) – 5 – us Americana [978]

PORTRAIT AND BIOGRAPHICAL RECORD OF FAYETTE, PICKAWAY AND MADISON COUNTIES – Chicago, 1892. Ohio Reel 31. (The Cox Library Collection) – 5 – us Americana [978]

PORTRAIT AND BIOGRAPHICAL RECORD OF FORD COUNTY / Lake City Publishing Co – Chicago, 1892. Illinois Reel 24. (The Cox Library Collection) – 5 – us Americana [978]

PORTRAIT AND BIOGRAPHICAL RECORD OF GENESEE, LAPEER AND TUSCOLA COUNTIES – Chicago: 1892. Michigan Reel 9. (The Cox Library Collection) – 5 – us Americana [978]

PORTRAIT AND BIOGRAPHICAL RECORD OF IROQUOIS COUNTY / Lake City Publishing Co – Chicago, 1893. (Illinois Reel 29). (The Cox Library Collection) – 5 – us Americana [978]

PORTRAIT AND BIOGRAPHICAL RECORD OF JASPER, MARSHALL, AND GRUNDY COUNTIES – Chicago: 1894. Iowa Reel 22, (The Cox Library Collection) – 5 – us Americana [978]

PORTRAIT AND BIOGRAPHICAL RECORD OF JO DAVIESS COUNTY – Chicago, 1889. (Illinois Reel 30). (The Cox Library Collection) – 5 – us Americana [978]

PORTRAIT AND BIOGRAPHICAL RECORD OF JOHNSON AND PETTIS COUNTIES – Chicago, 1895. Missouri Reel 21. (The Cox Library Collection) – 5 – us Americana [978]

PORTRAIT AND BIOGRAPHICAL RECORD OF KANE AND KENDALL COUNTIES / Beers, Leggett and Co – Chicago, 1888. (Illinois Reel 31). (The Cox Library Collection) – 5 – us Americana [978]

PORTRAIT AND BIOGRAPHICAL RECORD OF KANKAKEE COUNTY / Lake City Publishing Co – Chicago, 1893. (Illinois Reel 32). (The Cox Library Collection) – 5 – us Americana [978]

PORTRAIT AND BIOGRAPHICAL RECORD OF LACKAWANNA COUNTY – New York, 1897. Pennsylvania Reel 25. (The Cox Library Collection) – 5 – us Americana [978]

PORTRAIT AND BIOGRAPHICAL RECORD OF LAFAYETTE AND SALINE COUNTIES – Chicago, 1893. Missouri Reel 23. (The Cox Library Collection) – 5 – us Americana [978]

PORTRAIT AND BIOGRAPHICAL RECORD OF LEAVENWORTH, DOUGLAS AND FRANKLIN COUNTIES – Chicago, 1899. Kansas Reel 9. (The Cox Library Collection) – 5 – us Americana [978]

PORTRAIT AND BIOGRAPHICAL RECORD OF LEE COUNTY – Chicago, 1892. (Illinois Reel 38). (The Cox Library Collection) – 5 – us Americana [978]

PORTRAIT AND BIOGRAPHICAL RECORD OF LEHIGH, NORTHAMPTON, AND CARBON COUNTIES – Chicago, 1894. Pennsylvania Reel 28. (The Cox Library Collection) – 5 – us Americana [978]

PORTRAIT AND BIOGRAPHICAL RECORD OF LIVINGSTON COUNTY – Chicago, 1888. (Illinois Reel 39). (The Cox Library Collection) – 5 – us Americana [978]

PORTRAIT AND BIOGRAPHICAL RECORD OF MACON COUNTY / Lake City Publishing Co – Chicago, 1893. (Illinois Reel 40). (The Cox Library Collection) – 5 – us Americana [978]

PORTRAIT AND BIOGRAPHICAL RECORD OF MACOUPIN COUNTY – Chicago, 1891. (Illinois Reel 41). (The Cox Library Collection) – 5 – us Americana [978]

PORTRAIT AND BIOGRAPHICAL RECORD OF MADISON COUNTY – Chicago, 1894. (Illinois Reel 42). (The Cox Library Collection) – 5 – us Americana [978]

PORTRAIT AND BIOGRAPHICAL RECORD OF MARION AND HARDIN COUNTIES – Chicago: 1895. Ohio Reel 47. (The Cox Library Collection) – 5 – us Americana [978]

PORTRAIT AND BIOGRAPHICAL RECORD OF MONTGOMERY AND BOND COUNTIES – Chicago, 1892. (Illinois Reel 46). (The Cox Library Collection) – 5 – us Americana [978]

PORTRAIT AND BIOGRAPHICAL RECORD OF MONTGOMERY, PARKE, AND FOUNTAIN COUNTIES – Chicago, 1893. Indiana Reel 22.(The Cox Library Collection) – 5 – us Americana [978]

PORTRAIT AND BIOGRAPHICAL RECORD OF OKLAHOMA – Chicago, 1901. Oklahoma Reel 2.(The Cox Library Collection) – 5 – us Americana [978]

PORTRAIT AND BIOGRAPHICAL RECORD OF PORTAGE AND SUMMIT COUNTIES / A.W. Bowen and Co – Logansport, 1898. Ohio Reel 53. The Cox Library Collection – 5 – us Americana [978]

PORTRAIT AND BIOGRAPHICAL RECORD OF QUEENS COUNTY – New York, 1896. New York Reel 30. (The Cox Library Collection) – 5 – us Americana [978]

PORTRAIT AND BIOGRAPHICAL RECORD OF RALLS, MARION AND PIKE COUNTIES / C.O. Owen and Co – Chicago, 1895. Missouri Reel 25. The Cox Library Collection – 5 – us Americana [978]

PORTRAIT AND BIOGRAPHICAL RECORD OF RANDOLPH, MONROE, PERRY AND JACKSON COUNTIES – Chicago, 1894. (Illinois Reel 50). (The Cox Library Collection) – 5 – us Americana [978]

PORTRAIT AND BIOGRAPHICAL RECORD OF SANILAC COUNTY – Chicago: 1884. Michigan Reel 21. (The Cox Library Collection) – 5 – us Americana [978]

PORTRAIT AND BIOGRAPHICAL RECORD OF SHELBY AND MOULTRIE COUNTIES – Chicago, 1891. (Illinois Reel 55). (The Cox Library Collection) – 5 – us Americana [978]

PORTRAIT AND BIOGRAPHICAL RECORD OF SHEYBOYGAN COUNTY / Excelsior Publishing Co – Chicago: 1894. Wisconsin Reel 19. (The Cox Library Collection) – 5 – us Americana [978]

PORTRAIT AND BIOGRAPHICAL RECORD OF SOUTHEASTERN KANSAS – Chicago, 1894. Kansas Reel 6. (The Cox Library Collection) – 5 – us Americana [978]

PORTRAIT AND BIOGRAPHICAL RECORD OF ST CHARLES, LINCOLN AND WARREN COUNTIES – Chicago, 1895. Missouri Reel 28. (The Cox Library Collection) – 5 – us Americana [978]

PORTRAIT AND BIOGRAPHICAL RECORD OF ST CLAIR COUNTY – Chicago: 1892. Illinois Reel 52. (The Cox Library Collection) – 5 – us Americana [978]

PORTRAIT AND BIOGRAPHICAL RECORD OF STARK COUNTY – Chicago: 1892. Ohio Reel 59. (The Cox Library Collection) – 5 – us Americana [978]

PORTRAIT AND BIOGRAPHICAL RECORD OF TAZEWELL AND MASON COUNTIES – Chicago, 1894. (Illinois Reel 56). (The Cox Library Collection) – 5 – us Americana [978]

PORTRAIT AND BIOGRAPHICAL RECORD OF THE SCIOTO VALLEY – Chicago, 1894. Ohio reel 11. (The Cox Library Collection) – 5 – us Americana [978]

PORTRAIT AND BIOGRAPHICAL RECORD OF THE SIXTH CONGRESSIONAL DISTRICT – New York, 1898. Maryland Reel 1. (The Cox Library Collection) – 5 – us Americana [978]

PORTRAIT AND BIOGRAPHICAL RECORD OF THE STATE OF COLORADO – Chicago: 1899. Colorado reel 2.(Cox Library Collection) – 5 – us Americana [978]

PORTRAIT AND BIOGRAPHICAL RECORD OF WESTERN OREGON – Chicago, 1904. Oregon reel 4. (Cox Library Collection) – 5 – us Americana [978]

PORTRAIT AND BIOGRAPHICAL RECORD OF WILLAMETTE VALLEY – Chicago, 1903. Oregon reel 6. (Cox Library Collection) – 5 – us Americana [978]

PORTRAIT AND BIOGRAPHICAL RECORD OF WINNEBAGO AND BOONE COUNTIES – Chicago, 1892. (Illinois Reel 63). (The Cox Library Collection) – 5 – us Americana [978]

PORTRAIT AND BIOGRAPHICAL RECORDS OF ARIZONA – Chicago, 1901. Arizona Reel 3. (The Cox Library Collection) – 5 – us Americana [978]

PORTRAIT AND BIOGRAPHICAL REVIEW OF MORGAN AND SCOTT COUNTIES – Chicago, 1889. (Illinois Reel 47). (The Cox Library Collection) – 5 – us Americana [978]

PORTRAIT CATALOG / New York Academy of Medicine. Library – 1960.-95,800 cards 10 reels.-ISBN: 0-8161-1391-2 – 1 – $360.00 – uk Hall [610]

LE PORTRAIT DANS L'ART FLAMAND DE MEMLING A VAN DYCK / Reunion des musees nationaux. Paris – 1952. 70 illus. 2 fiches – 9 – fr Réunion [700]

UN PORTRAIT DU CANADA – (1986 Can$22.00. English version: Canada: a portrait. Cont: Le Canada, 1986) – Ottawa, 1986- – 9 – Can$20.00y – cn Micromedia [971]

PORTRAIT D'UN MISSIONNAIRE APOSTOLIQUE / Ciquard, Francois – Quebec: Nouvelle Imprimerie, 1810. SEM16P15 – 1r – 5 – Can$9.00 – cn Bibl Nat [240]

LE PORTRAIT FRANCAIS DE WATTEAU A DAVID / Reunion des musees nationaux. Paris – 1957. 43 illus. 2 fiches – 9 – fr Réunion [700]

PORTRAIT HISTORIQUE DE L'EMPEREUR DE LA CHINE,... / Bouvet, J – Paris, 1698 – 3mf – 9 – ne IDC [950]

PORTRAIT MINIATURES IN THE NATIONAL MUSEUM OF AMERICAN ART / Bolton-Smith, Robin – (80p accompanying text) – 1984 – 4mf – 9 – $72.00f – 0-226-68857-7 – us Chicago [700]

PORTRAITS : SUBJECT COLLECTIONS – (Individual titles not listed separately) – 40 catalogues on 67mf – 9 – £490.00 – uk Chadwyck [700]

PORTRAITS DE VICTOR HUGO ET DE SES FAMILIERS – A family collaboration chronicle of the author, his family and friends during the early years of his exile. 1 reel. (Collections of the Department of Prints and Photographs) – 1 – $50.00 – fr Bibl Nationale [920]

PORTRAITS D'OYSEAUX, ANIMAUX, SERPENTS, HERBES, ARBRES, HOMMES ET FEMMES, D'ARABIE ET D'EGYPTE PLUS Y EST ADIOUSTE LA CARTE DU MONT ATTOS ET DU MONT SINAY, POUR L'INTELLIGENCE DE LEUR RELIGION / Belon, Pierre – Paris, G. Cavellat, 1557, xviii p.-122 ff. French Voyagers in the Mediterranean 16th to 18th Centuries. 5956 – 9 – fr Hachette [956]

PORTRAITS ET DOSSIERS PARLEMENTAIRES DU PREMIER PARLEMENT DE QUEBEC / Achintre, Auguste – Montreal, Ateliers Typographiques de Duvernay. 1871. 00006. (Pre-1900 Canadiana) – 9 – cn C.I.H.M. [971]

PORTRAITS ET FIGURES DE FEMMES. PASTELS ET DESSINS / Reunion des musees nationaux. Paris – 1935. 21 illus. 1 fiche – 9 – fr Réunion [740]

PORTRAITS LITTERAIRES – Paris, 1891-92. 2v. 6 fiches. (Literature Collection) – 9 – 15.00 – fr Bibl Nationale [840]

PORTRAITS OF AMERICANS – (From the permanent coll of the National Portrait Gallery, Smithsonian Institute set up to collect and exhibit nearly 2,000 portraits of the key figures in American history. With catalogue £37) – 35 colour mf – 15 – £800.00 – uk Chadwyck [700]

PORTRAITS OF COMPOSERS AND MUSICIANS / ed by Hul, Dick van den – (Includes printed guide) – 33mf – 9 – P-748/1 – ne IDC [780]

PORTRAITS OF RARE AND CURIOUS BIRDS / Hayes, W – 2091 2. 1794 – 8 – ne IDC [760]

PORTRAITS OF THE WESLEYAN METHODIST MINSTERS : WITH BIOGRAPHICAL MEMOIRS – London, 1837 – 1mf – 9 – ne IDC [240]

A PORTRAITURE OF METHODISM : BEING AN IMPARTIAL VIEW OF THE RISE, PROGRESS, DOCTRINES, DISCIPLINE AND MANNERS OF THE WESLEYAN METHODISTS...LETTERS,...TO A LADY / Nightingale, J – London, 1807. xvi/496p – 6mf – 9 – ne IDC [240]

A PORTRAITURE OF METHODISM; OR, THE HISTORY OF THE WESLEYAN METHODISTS, SHOWING THEIR RISE, PROGRESS AND PRESENT STATE; BIOGRAPHICAL SKETCHES... / Crowther, J – London, 2nd enl ed 1815 – 6mf – 9 – ne IDC [240]

THE PORTRAYAL OF WOMEN IN SPORT ADVERTISING IN TWO WOMEN'S FITNESS MAGAZINES / Incantalupo, Patricia & Murray, Mimi – 1992 – 2mf – $8.00 – us Microform Publ [650]

PORTRET BEZ SKHODSTVA / Ivanov, G – Stikhi. Paris. 1950. BR-1182 2 – 8 – ne IDC [460]

PORTRETY RUSSKIKH POETOV / Erenburg, I – Berlin. 1922. Index (3). BR-3653 2 – 8 – ne IDC [460]

PORTRETY SOVREMENNIKOV / Makovskii, S K – New York. 1955. BR-3275 2 – 8 – ne IDC [460]

PORT-ROYAL / Sainte-Beuve, Charles Augustin – Extraits. Avec notice biographique, notice historique et litteraire, notes explicatives, jugements, questionnaire. Paris: Librairie Larousse, 1936. 95p – 1 – us U.W. Library [320]

PORT-ROYAL EDUCATION / Saint-Cyran, abbe de et al – (Includes bibliographical references and index) – New York: Chas Scribner, 1898 – 1mf – 9 – 0-8370-7583-1 – 1986-1583 – us A.T.L.A. [370]

PORT-ROYAL ET MAGNY : FONDATION DE L'ABBAYE, LA REFORME, LES SOLITAIRES, LES PETITES ECOLES, LE JANSENISME, L'AUGUSTINUS... / Finot, Ed – Paris: Georges Chamerot, 1888 – 1mf – 9 – 0-8370-9144-6 – 1986-3144 – us A.T.L.A. [240]

Portsmouth, New Hampshire. First Baptist Church *see* RECORDS

PORTSMOUTH ORACLE – Portsmouth. N.H. 1803-1820 – 3 – us Readex [071]

PORTSMOUTH PROMOTER – England.Apr 1971-72. -w. 1 reel – 1 – uk British Libr Newspaper [072]

PORTSMOUTH TELEGRAPH. (HAMPSHIRE TELEGRAPH) – Portsmouth, England. Oct 1799-1849, 1881-1976 (missing 1897-98, 1911).-w. 138 reels – 1 – uk British Libr Newspaper [072]

PORTSMOUTH TIMES ETC – England.1899; 1911. -w. 2 reels – 1 – uk British Libr Newspaper [072]

LES PORTUGAIS ET L'AFRIQUE DU NORD DE 1521-1557 / Sousa, L de – Trans. by R. Richard. Paris. 1940. Index. B-1341 2 – 8 – ne IDC [946]

PORTUGAL. ANUARIO ESTATISTICO DE PORTUGAL : ANNUAIRE STATISTIQUE 1875-1970 / Portugal. Instituto Nacional de Estatistico – (Coll title: European Official Statistical Serials, 1841-1984) – 344mf – 9 – £1,800.00 – uk Chadwyck [946]

Portugal. Assembleia Nacional *see* 2 PLAN DE FOMENTO (1959-1964)

Portugal. Cortes. Camara dos deputados *see* DIARIO

Portugal. Direccao de Servicos de Planeamento *see* PLANO INTERCALAR DE FEMENTO PARA 1965-1967 PROGRAMA DE EXECUCAO PARA 1965

Portugal. Direccao Geral das Alfandegas *see* BOLETIM OFICIAL

Portugal. Fundo de Fomento Nacional *see* PLANO DE FOMENTO REVISAO DE 1955

Portugal. Instituto Nacional de Estatistico *see* PORTUGAL. ANUARIO ESTATISTICO DE PORTUGAL

Portugal. Ministerio da Economia *see* PLANO DO FOMENTO PARA 1953-1958

Portugal. Ministerio das Colonias *see* PLANO DE VALORIZACAO ECONOMICA DE COLONIA DE MOCAMBIQUE

Portugal. Presidencia do Conselho *see*
- 3 PLANO DE FOMENTO. PROGRAMA DE EXECUCAO, 1970
- 3 PLANO DE FOMENTO. PROGRAMA DE EXECUCAO, 1971
- 3 PLANO DE FOMENTO. PROGRAMA DE EXECUCAO, 1972
- PLANO DE FOMENTO, 3, PARA 1968-1973
- PLANO DE FOMENTO 3" – PROGRAMA DE EXECUCAO PARA 1969
- PLANO DO FOMENTO, 3, PROGRAMA DE EXECUCAO PARA 1968
- PLANO INTERCALAR DE FOMENTO PARA 1965-1967
- PLANO INTERCALAR DE FOMENTO PARA 1965-1967 PROGRAMA DE EXECUCAO PARA 1966
- PLANO INTERCALAR DE FOMENTO PARA 1965-1967 PROGRAMA DE EXECUCAO PARA 1967
- PROJECTO DE PLANO DE FOMENTO PARA 1959-1964
- PROJECTO DO 3 PLANO DE FOMENTO PARA 1968-1973
- PROJECTO DO 4. PLANO DE FOMENTO
- RELATORIO DA EXECUCAO DO PLANO INTERCALAR DE FOMENTO METROPOLE, 1965
- RELATORIO DA EXECUCAO DO PLANO INTERCALAR DE FOMENTO-ULTRAMAR
- RELATORIO FINAL PREPARATORIO DO 2 PLANO DE FOMENTO
- REVISAO DO 3. PLANO DE FOMENTO PROGRAMA PARA 1971-73

Portugal. Presidencia do Conselho. Secreteriado Tecnico *see* 3 PLANO DE FOMENTO, PROGRAM DE EXECUCAO 1973

DIE PORTUGALESISCHE SCHLACHT : KOMOEDIE DER UNSTERBLICHKEIT / Penzoldt, Ernst – Berlin: Propylaeen-Verlag, c1930 – 1r – 1 – us U.W. Library [870]

Portugalov, A V *see* UKAZATEL' KNIG DLIA CHTENIIA PO VOPROSAM KOOPERATSII

PORTUGEESCHE JODEN TE MAARSSEN EN MAARSSEVEEN IN DE 17DE EEUW / Zwarts, J – (Jaarboekje van het Oudheidkundig Genootschap Niftarlake). 1922. BJ-262-79 1 – 9 – ne IDC [949]

PORTUGESE MANUSCRIPTS MICROFILMED FOR HMML : BIBL. NACIONAL DE LISBOA, FUNDO ALCOBACA – (not for bulk or commercial purchase or resale) – Descriptive Inventories for the Fundo Alcobaca in 3 printed vols available from HMML – 1 – $35.00r + $10.00 per owning library – us H.M.M.L. [090]

PORTUGUESE AFRICA / ed by Chilcote, Ronald – Documentary collection on emerging nationalism, including both published material and ephemera through 1965 – 1 – 35.00r – us Hoover Inst Photo [960]

PORTUGUESE EURASIANS IN MALAYSIA : A SUBJECT APPROACH / Mukhtiar, Kaur – 1987 – 9 – A$10.00 – 0-86758-232-4 – at BISA [305]

Portuguese Guinea. (Portugal) *see* ECONOMIC PLANS

THE PORTUGUESE IN ASIA 1498-C. 1800 – (Individual titles available. Includes printed bibliography "The Portuguese in Asia, an Annotated Bibliography of Studies on Colonial History in Asia 1498-c. 1800" by D. de Silva) – 1237mf – 9 – ne IDC [950]

PORTUGUESE PAMPHLETS – 1 – 1700.00 – us L of C Photodup [946]

PORTUGUESE REVOLUTION OF 1974 – Various newspapers from Portugal published from 21 Feb 1971 to 15 Feb 1980, collected and filmed by the University of Wisconsin-Madison libraries – 1 – us U.W. Library [080]

OS PORTUGUESES EM ANGOLA... / Sousa Dias, Gastao – Madrid: Arch. Ibero Americano, 1960 – 1 – sp Bibl Santa Ana [946]

OS PORTUGUESES NA COLONICAO...LISBOA, 1929 / Villas, Gaspar do Couto Ribeiro – Madrid: Razon y Fe, 1930 – 1 – sp Bibl Santa Ana [946]

OS PORTUGUESES NO MUNDO. AGRANDES TRAVESSIA AFRICANA DE CAPELO E IVERIS POR... / Bayle, Constantino – Madrid: Missionalia Hispanica, 1949 – 1 – sp Bibl Santa Ana [946]

O PORTUGUEZ : JORNAL HISTORICO, POLITICO E LITTERARIO – Salvador, Dec 1838 – 1,5,6 – bl Biblioteca [072]

Portus, Garnet V *see* CARITAS ANGLICANA, OR, AN HISTORICAL INQUIRY INTO THOSE RELIGIOUS AND PHILANTHROPICAL SOCIETIES THAT FLOURISHED IN ENGLAND BETWEEN THE YEARS 1678 AND 1740

EL PORVENIR DE EXTREMADURA – Caceres, 1871 – 5 – sp Bibl Santa Ana [073]

PORVENIR DE EXTREMADURA – Caceres.1871, no. suelto 34 – 9 – 1.50f – sp Bibl Santa Ana [072]

O PORVIR – Curvello, 2 Jun-May 1902; Jun-Jul 1904; Jan, May 1905; 2 Dec 1907 – 1,5,6 – bl Biblioteca [072]

O PORVIR : ORGAM LITTERARIO, NOTICIOSO E COMMERCIAL – Manaos, Amazonas. 5 Set 1906 – 1,5,6 – bl Biblioteca [072]

O PORVIR : ORGAO DA CLASSE ESTUDANTAL – '(s.l.')-Sao Luis, Brazil. 15 Jun, 20 Aug 1895 – 1,5,6 – bl Biblioteca [072]

O PORVIR : PERIODICO LITTERARIO E NOTICIOSO – Maceio, Alagoas. 20 Maio-1 Jun 1884 – 1,5,6 – bl Biblioteca [072]

O PORVIR : PERIODICO NOTICIOSO, RECREATIVO E LITTERARIO – Cuiaba, 28 Jun-Dec 1877; Jan, Mar-May, 9 Jul 1878 – 1,5,6 – bl Biblioteca [072]

PORZIA : EINE ZEITSCHRIFT ZUR FOERDERUNG DES SCHOENEN UND GUTEN – Bremen, 1837-39 (single issues only), 1842-47, 1849-50, 1852-55 (all incomplete) – 1r – 1 – Inquire at Mikrofilmarchiv for details – gw Misc Inst [072]

LA PORZIENCULA NEI PIU ANTICHI DOCUMENTI FRANCESCANI... / Canonici, Luciano – Madrid: Arch. Ibero Americano, 1960 – 1 – sp Bibl Santa Ana [240]

POS NEWS – (Cont by: Debit Card News) – Chicago. v1-11. 1984-jun 1995* – 1 – D18379 – us UMI [073]

POS. REPORT / Bank Tabungan. Djakarta – SE-271 1. 1937-39, 1941-46, and 1955 – 9 – ne IDC [336]

Posada, Eduardo *see* APOSTILLAS...

LAS POSADAS DEL AMOR. MI PRIMA ME ODIA. ADEMAS DEL FRAC. MI MEDIA NARANJA / Trigo, Felipe – Madrid: Renacimiento, 4th ed 1920 – sp Bibl Santa Ana [946]

Posadas, Francisco de *see*
- RESUMEN DE LA VIDA Y VIRTUDES DEL V.P. CRISTOBAL DE SANTA CATALINA
- VIDA DEL PADRE CRISTOBAL DE SANTA CATALINA
- VIDA Y VIRTUDES DEL VENERABLE SIERVO DE DIOS EL PADRE
- VIDA Y...CRISTOBAL DE SANTA CATALINA

POSADSKAIA OBSHCHINA V ROSSII 18 ST / Kizevetter, A A – M. 1903. BR-6052 2 – 8 – ne IDC [460]

Poschwitz, Hartmut *see* RENATURIERUNGSMASSNAHMEN AN EINEM KLEINEN FLIESSGEWAESSER AM BEISPIEL DES WICKERBACHES

POSEIDONIOS METAPHYSISCHE SCHRIFTEN / Heinemann, F – 116 2. v. 1-2. 1921-1928 – 8 – ne IDC [110]

POSEIDONIOS UND DIE JUEDISCH-CHRISTLICHE GENESISEXEGESE / Gronau, K – Leipzig, 1914 – 6mf – 8 – ne Slangenburg [220]

Posen, I Sheldon *see* INDEX TO HOOSIER FOLKLORE BULLETIN (1942-45) AND HOOSIER FOLKLORE (1946-50)

POSENER NEUESTE NACHRICHTEN – Posen (Poznan), Poland. 23 Mar 1922-31 Oct 1923; 22 Jan 1924-12 Feb 1926 – 5r – 1 – gw Mikrofilm [943]

POSENER TAGEBLATT – Posen (Poznan), Poland. 1920; 10 May 1921-29 Jun 1929; 1 Oct 1929-29 Aug 1939 – 38r – 1 – gw Mikrofilm [943]

POSENER TAGEBLATT – Poznan, Poland. May 12 1912 – 1r – 1 – us L of C Photodup [072]

POSENER ZEITUNG – Posen (Poznan), Germany. 29 Oct 1914-24 Jan 1915; Aug-26 Oct 1916 – 2r – 1 – gw Mikrofilm [943]

POSESIAS SERIAS / Moreno Torrado, Luis – Merida: Imprenta y Estereotipia de Plano y Corchero, 1900 – 1 – sp Bibl Santa Ana [810]

POSEV : EZHENEDEL'NIK OBSHCHESTVENNO-POLITICHESKOI MYSLI – Moenchehof, Limburg, Frankfurt, 1945-67 – 7r – 1 – us Ross [072]

POSEY'S UNREPORTED CASES / Texas. Supreme Court – (A Pre-NRS title) – v1-2. 1879-1884 (all publ) – 8mf – 9 – $12.00 – LLMC 92-409 – us L.L.M.C. [340]

LA POSGUERRA : PROGRAMA PARA LA RECONSTRUCCION Y EL DESARROLLO ECONOMICO DE LA ARGENTINA / Ferrer, Aldo – Buenos Aires, Argentina: El Cid Editor: Fundaci on para la Democracia en Argentina, 1982 – 1 – CSUXADQ4295-B – us Hoover Inst Photo [330]

POSHCHESHINA OBSHCHESTVENNOMU VKUSU – V zashchitu, svobodnago iskusstva. Stikhi, proza, stat'i. M. 1912. BR-1902 2 – 8 – ne IDC [460]

THE POSING OF THE PARTS / Brinsley, John – 1612. 139p. (English Linguistics Series 1500-1800) – 9 – us UMI [420]

POSITION AND PROSPECTS OF THE CHURCH OF SCOTLAND / Tulloch, John – Edinburgh: W. Blackwood, 1878 – 1mf – us A.T.L.A. [240]

POSITION CARDS OF LEADERS IN COMMUNIST CHINA / U.S. Consulate General. Hong Kong – Text in English. Includes Master Index 16 mm. 1956-1968. (2259.9 17.1) – 1 – 35.00r – us Hoover Inst Photo [335]

THE POSITION OF CHRISTIANITY IN THE UNITED STATES : IN ITS RELATIONS WITH OUR POLITICAL INSTITUTIONS, AND SPECIALLY WITH REFERENCE TO RELIGIOUS INSTRUCTION IN THE PUBLIC SCHOOLS / Colwell, Stephen – Philadelphia: Lippincott, Grambo, 1854 – 1mf – 9 – 0-8370-7613-7 – 1986-1613 – us A.T.L.A. [370]

THE POSITION OF FOREIGN CORPORATIONS IN AMERICAN CONSTITUTIONAL LAW / Henderson, G C – Cambridge, 1918 – 3mf – 1 – ILM-3301/1 – ne IDC [327]

THE POSITION OF GREEK IN THE THEOLOGICAL EDUCATION OF TODAY / Dickey, Samuel – [S.l.: s.n., 1907?] – 1mf – us A.T.L.A. [240]

THE POSITION OF THE PROVINCE OF QUEBEC IN THE DOMINION OF CANADA: DELIVERED IN THE HOUSE OF COMMONS ON THE RESOLUTIONS PROVIDING FOR SUBSIDIES TO LOCAL RAILWAY, 12TH APRIL, 1884 / Chapleau, Joseph Adolphe – Montreal: Gazette, 1884. 02858. (Pre-1900 Canadiana) – 9 – cn C.I.H.M. [971]

THE POSITION OF THE RIGHT REV. SAMUEL WILBERFORCE, D.D., LORD BISHOP OF OXFORD, IN REFERNCE TO RITUALISM : TOGETHER WITH A PREFATORY ACCOUNT OF THE ROMEWARD MOVEMENT IN THE CHURCH OF ENGLAND IN THE DAYS OF ARCHBISHOP LAUD / Golightly, Charles Portales – London: Hatchard; Oxford: Slatter and Rose, 1867 – 1mf – us A.T.L.A. [240]

POSITION PAPER ON THE MALAYSIAN PROBLEM / Indonesia – SE-4993 1. 1964 – 9 – ne IDC [950]

POSITIONS – Hebdomadaire de culture chretienne. no. 1-81. Lyon. 23 mai 1942-29 juil 1944 – 1 – fr A.C.R.P.P. [073]

POSITIONS LUTHERIENNES – 1(1953)-18(1970) – 90mf – 9 – Dfl315.00 – ne Slangenburg [073]

POSITIVE UNION – Kirchliche monatsschrift, Organ der Landeskirchlichen Vereinigung der Freunde der Positiven Union. v. 1-15, 21-31, 1904-19, 1925-35. (Lacks v. 22, 1926, no. 3) – 1 – us A.T.L.A. [073]

POSITIVES CHRISTENTUM – Berlin, 1935-36 – 1r – 1 – Inquire at Mikrofilmarchiv for details – gw Misc Inst [240]

POSITIVES CHRISTENTUM – Berlin, Germany. 1935-36 – 1r – 1 – gw Mikrofilm [072]

POSITIVISME ET CATHOLICISME : A PROPOS DE "L'ACTION FRANCAISE" / Laberthonniere, Lucien – (Includes bibliographical references and index) – Paris: Bloud, 1911 – 1mf – 9 – 0-8370-8917-4 – 1986-2917 – us A.T.L.A. [240]

POSLEDNIAIA SKAZKA PUSHKINA / Akhmatova, A – (Skazka o zolotom petushke). Zvezda. 1933. BR-3722 2 – 8 – ne IDC [490]

POSLEDNIE DNI KOLCHAKOVSHCHINY / Konstantinov, M M – Moscow, 1926 – 1 – 35.00r – us Hoover Inst Photo [947]

POSLEDNIE DNI TSENZURY V MINISTERSTVE NARODNAGO PROSVESHCHENIIA / Rudakov, V E – Spb, 1911 – 9 – BR-10 095 1 – ne IDC [947]

POSLEDNIE GODY TVORCHESTVA PUSHKINA / Pushkinskoye Obshchestvo. Leningrad – Leningrad. v. 1-2. 1933-1934 – 1 – us NY Public [460]

POSLEDNIE NOVOSTI – Paris, 1920-40 – 35r – 1 – us Ross [072]

POSLEDNIE NOVOSTI – Paris. Apr 27 1920-June 10 1940. Incomplete – 1 – us NY Public [072]

POSLEDNIE STIKHI / Gippius, Z N – 1914-1918. Spb. 1918. BR-723 2 – 8 – ne IDC [460]

POSLEDNIIA IZVESTIIA : IZDANIE ZAGRANITSNOGO KOMITETA VSEOBSHCHEGO EVREISKOGO RABOCHEGO SOIUZA V LITVE, POL'SHE I ROSSII – London, Geneva. n1-256. 1901-1906 – 16mf – 9 – ne IDC [947]

POSLEDNIJA NOVOSTI – Paris. 27 avr 1920-juin 1940 – 1 – fr A.C.R.P.P. [073]

O POSLEDNIKH STIKHAKH MANDEL'SHTAMA / Veidle, V – Vozdushnye puti, al'manakh. v. 2. 1961. BR-3712 2 – 8 – ne IDC [460]

POSLEDNYI TSAR : KONETS ROMANOVYKH: ISTORIIA REVOLIUTSIONNOGO DVIZHENIIA V ROSSII PO NEOPUBLIKOVANNYM NEMETSKIM ISTOCHNIKAM – Pg., 1918. 190p – 3mf – 9 – ne IDC [320]

POSLEVOENNYE PERSPEKTIVY RUSSKOI PROMYSHLENNOSTI / Grinevetskii, Vasilii Ignatevich – 2-e izd. / s predisloviem V. Sarabianova. Moskva: Izd. Vseros. t sentr. soiuza potrebitelnykh ob-v, 1922 – 1 – CSUX89-B1302 – us Hoover Inst Photo [670]

POSLI EDNII A IZVI ESTII A (TALLINN, ESTONIA) – Revel, 19uu – 1 – CSUXAMG6387-S – us Hoover Inst Photo [947]

POSLIEVOENNYIA PERSPEKTIVY RUSSKOI PROMYSHLENNOSTI / Grinevetskii, Vasilii Ignatevich – Moskva: Sklad izd. Vserros. [sic] t sentr. soiuz potrebitelnykh ob-v, 1919 – 1 – CSUX88-B8926 – us Hoover Inst Photo [670]

POSMERTNYI SBORNIK. RAZSKAZY, STIKHI, PUTEVYE OCHERKI / Solov'ev, Vsevolod S – Spb. 1901. BR-888 2 – 8 – ne IDC [190]

POSOLON' / Remizov, A – Moscow, 1907. BR-838 2 – 8 – ne IDC [460]

POSOLON' / Remizov, A – (Volshebnaia Rossiia). Paris, 1930. 234p. BR-839 2 – 8 – ne IDC [460]

POSOSHKOV / Kafengauz, B B I T – Zhizn' i deiatel'nost'. Ed. 2. M. 1951. BR-6192 2 – 8 – ne IDC [460]

Pospelov, Poitr N *see* THE HISTORY OF THE GREAT PATRIOTIC WAR OF THE SOVIET UNION, 1941-1945

POSREDNIK – Spb. 1906. Available: 1906 (13-14, 17-61). BR-4330 2 – 8 – ne IDC [073]

POSREDNIK PECHATNOGO DELA – Ezhem, illiustrirovannyi zhurnal izdatel'skoi deiatel'nosti i graficheskikh iskusstv. M. 1892. Available: 1892 (1-7). BR-4331 2 – 8 – ne IDC [073]

Posse, V A *see*
- IDEALY KOOPERATSII
- OSNOVY KOOPERATIVNOGO DVIZHENIIA

POSSIBILITIES OF CREATION, OR, WHAT THE WORLD MIGHT HAVE BEEN: A BOOK OF FANCIES – London: Simpkin Marshall, 1863. 1 fiche – 9 – us A.T.L.A. [240]

POSSIBILITIES OF PROCESSING AND MARKETING OF PRODUCTS MADE FROM ANTARCTIC KRILL – 1985 – 51p – it F.A.O. [660]

Possinus, P *see*
- ANNAE COMMENAE PORPHYROGENITAE CAESARISSAE ALEXIAS SIVE DE REBUS AB ALEXIO IMPERATORE VEL EJUS TEMPORE GESTIS (CBH 10)
- HISTORIA RERUM A MICHAELE PALAEOLOGO (CBH 28,1)
- HISTORIA RERUM AB ANDRONICO SENIORE (CBH 28,2)

Possinus, P, *see* COMMENTARII DE REBUS BYZANTINIS (CBH 3,4)

DIE POST – (Also suppl available: Zweite Beilage, 1897; Aus grosser Zeit, jan 1-mar 31 1915, may 9-dec 31 1915, jan 1-jun 30 1918) – Berlin, aug 1866-jun 1871, jul 1874-jun 1893, 1894-mar 1898, jul 1898-mar 1904, jul 1904-oct 1910, jan-apr 1911, jul 1911-jun 1914, sep-dec 1914, feb 1915-jun 1921 – 210r – 1 – Inquire at Mikrofilmarchiv for details – gw Misc Inst [072]

DIE POST – Berlin, 1866-1921 (incomplete) – 210r – 1 – gw Mikrofilm [072]

DIE POST – Berlin, Germany. -d. 20 Jan 1916-7 Aug 1919. Imperfect. 13 reels – 1 – uk British Libr Newspaper [072]

POST – Daly City, CA. 1963-67 – 8r – 1 – $400.00 – B02157 – us Library Micro [071]

POST – Durban, South Africa. 14 Nov. 1971- – 49r – 1 – sa Microfile [960]

POST – Henderson, NV. 1964 – 1r – 1 – $50.00 – U04846 – us Library Micro [071]

POST – Late Reef ed. Johannesburg, 1965-69 – 7r – 1 – us Ross [072]

POST – Manhattan, NV. 1910-14 – 1r – 1 – $50.00 – U04632 – us Library Micro [071]

POST : NORTH COUNTY EDITION, WESTLAKE – San Mateo, CA. 1963-75; 1977-80 – 66r – 1 – $3,300.00 – B02920 – us Library Micro [071]

POST – Palm Beach. Fl. 1916-1942 – 1 – us P.K. Yonge [071]

POST – San Mateo, CA. 1946-76; 1977-87 – 127r – 1 – $6,350.00 – B02921 – us Library Micro [071]

POST – Silver Peak, NV. 6 Jun 1906 – 1r – 1 – $50.00 – U04741 – us Library Micro [071]

THE POST – Berkeley Springs. West Virginia. 1907-1916 – 1 – us UMI [071]

THE POST – Ellicottville. N.Y. 1885-1969 – 1 – us UMI [071]

THE POST – Goldfield, NV. 25 May 1912 – 1r – 1 – $50.00 – U04559 – us Library Micro [071]

POST AMERICAN – (Cont by: Sojourners) – v1-4. Fall 1971-1975 (complete) – 1r – 1 – ATLA S0280 – us A.T.L.A. [073]

POST AMERICAN – v1-4. 1971-75 – 1,5,6,9 – us UMI [073]

POST AMERICAN *see* SOJOURNERS

THE POST (BUCKINGHAM, QUEBEC) – Buckingham. v79-89. 1974-83. SEM35P268 – 5r – 1 – Can$274.00 – cn Bibl Nat [072]

POST DISPATCH – Pittsburg, CA. Nov 1978-90 – 155r – 1 – $7,750.00 – B02627 – us Library Micro [071]

Post, George Edward *see* THE BOTANICAL GEOGRAPHY OF SYRIA AND PALESTINE

POST INDEPENDENCE DEVELOPMENT PLAN / Swaziland – D 869 1. 1969 – 9 – ne IDC [338]

POST INTELLIGENCER – Seattle. Wash. 1901-1947; 1955- – 1 – us UMI [071]

POST- OCH INRIKES TIDNINGAR – Stockholm, Sweden. 1979- – 1 – sw Kungliga [072]

POST OFFICES / Baughman, Robert Williamson – May 1960 – 1 – us KS Hist [380]

POST OFFICES AND POSTMASTERS OF OHIO TO 1930 / Pfund, Margaret E – 1 – us Ohio Hist [380]

Post, Pierre *see* LES OUVRAGES D'ARCHITECTURE

POST RECORD – San Jose, CA. Jan 1967-89; Jan-Mar 1990 – 74r – 1 – $3,700.00 – C02886 – us Library Micro [071]

POST RETURNS.. / U.S. Army. Fort Leavenworth – 1827-1919 – 1 – us KS Hist [324]

POST RUNNING, POST-CYCLING, AND POST TRAINING RUNNING ECONOMY IN DUATHLETES / Springer, Judy B – Northern Illinois University, 1995 – 2mf – 9 – $8.00 – PH 1510 – us Microform Publ [612]

POST SCRIPT – Palm Desert, CA. 1980-81 – 2r – 1 – $100.00 – R02594 – us Library Micro [071]

POST (TRANSVAAL) *see* BANTU WORLD

POST TRIBUNE – Dallas. Tex. 1965- – 1 – us UMI [071]

POST WORLD WAR 2 FOREIGN POLICY PLANNING : STATE DEPARTMENT RECORDS OF HARLEY A. NOTTER, 1939-45 – (Printed index available separately: $1,755.00) – 5,313mf – 9 – $21,840.00 – us UPA [327]

POSTA REHBERI / Ihsan, Mustafa – Istanbul: Mahmud Bey Matbaasi, 1308 [1892] – 9 – $50.00 – us MEDOC [380]

POST-ADVOCATE – (Also known as: Advocate and Valley Vista, Daily Alhambra Advocate, Alhambra Progress) – Alhambra, CA. 1898-1902; 1903-1915; 1916-1918; 1919-1965; 1965-1966; 1966; 1968-1970; 1970-1974; 1975 – 396+ r – 1 – $19,800.00 ($50.00y) – H03133 – us Library Micro [071]

POSTAL CARD – Eustis, NE. -w. Aug. 1902-Jan. 1905 – 1 – us NE Hist [071]

POSTAL TECHNOLOGY AND MANAGEMENT / Mustafa, Husain – 1971. 240p. ISBN: 0-912338-02-4 – 9 – 9.50 – us Lomond [380]

POSTANOVLENII A I RASPORI AZHENII A NARODNOGO KOMISSARIATA FINANSOV R.S.F.S.R. – (Library has: July 22, 1929) – [Moskva]: NKF R.S.F.S.R., 1928-1936. 9v – 1 – CSUX89-S769 – us Hoover Inst Photo [947]

POSTANOVLENIIA PO SEL'SKOKHOZIAISTVENNOI KOOPERATSII – M., 1930 – 2mf – 9 – COR-304/1 – ne IDC [334]

POST-APOLLO EXPLORATION – (V20 1 and 2 1966, Advances) – 1966 – 9 – $65.00 – us Univelt [629]

THE POST-APOSTOLIC AGE / Waterman, Lucius – New York: Scribner, 1898 – 2mf – us A.T.L.A. [240]

DIE POSTBAPTISMALE SALBUNG / Welte, B – Freiburg i.Br., 1939 – 3mf – 8 – Dfl13.00 – ne Slangenburg [240]

POST-BIBLICAL HEBREW LITERATURE, AN ANTHOLOGY / Harper, B – 9 – $10.00 – us I.R.C. [800]

POST-BIBLICAL HEBREW LITERATURE: AN ANTHOLOGY / Halper, B – Philadelphia. 1921. BJ-421-40 1 – 9 – ne IDC [800]

POST-BOY – Windsor, VT. 1803-07 – 1,3 – us Readex [071]

POST-BULLETIN – Rochester. Minn. 1952- – 1 – us UMI [071]

THE POST-CAPTAIN; OR, THE WOODEN WALLS WELL MANNED, COMPREHENDING A VIEW OF NAVAL SOCIETY AND MANNERS / Davis, John – 3rd ed., corrected – 9 – $20.00 – uk Libr Preservation [941]

POSTCARDS OF WARRNAMBOOL – Early – 10mf – 9 – at Corangamite [910]

POST-DISPATCH – Houston.TX. 1924-31 – 1 – us UMI [071]

POST-DISPATCH – Pittsburg. Calif. 1930- – 1 – us UMI [071]

POST-DISPATCH – St. Louis. MO. 1874- – 1 – us UMI [071]

POST-DISPATCH INDEX – St. Louis. MO. 1979- – 1 – us UMI [071]

LA POSTE – Red. en chef Henri des Houx. Paris. 20 aout 1895-2 juin 1896 – 1 – fr A.C.R.P.P. [073]

LA POSTE / ed by Rousseau, Jean-Jacques – Berthier, Canada. 17 oct 1908-29 jul 1909 – 1r – 1 – Can$30.00 – cn Can Microfilming [072]

POSTE PER DIVERSE PARTI DEL MONDO, ... / Stella, C di – Venetia, 1598 – 1mf – 9 – H-8402/1 – ne IDC [956]

Postel, G *see*
- ALCORANI SEU LEGIS MAHOMETI ET EVANGELISTARUM COCORDIAE LIBER, IN QUO DE CALAMITATIBUS ORBI CHRISTIANO IMMINENTIBUS TRACTATUR
- DE LA REPVBLIQUE DES TURCS
- DE ORBIS TERRAE CONCORDIA LIBRI QUATUOR, ...
- ...DE ORIGINIBUS SEU DE HEBRAICAE LINGUAE ET GENTIS ANTIQUITATE, ...
- DE ORIGINIBUS SEU DE HEBRAICAE LINGUAE ET GENTIS ANTIQUITATE, ATQUE VARIARUM LINGUARUM AFFINITATE
- DE ORIGINIBUS, SEV, DE VARIA ET POTISSIMUM ORBI LATINO AD HANC DIEM INCOGNITA, AUT INCOSYDERATA HISTORIA, QUU TOTIUS ORIENTIS, TUM MAXIME TARTARORUM, PERSARUM, TURCARUM
- DELA REPVBLIQUE DES TURCS, ...
- GRAMMATICA ARABICA
- DES HISTOIRES ORIENTALES ET PRINCIPALEMENT DES TURKES OU TURCHIKES ET SCHITIQUES OU TARTARESQUES ET AULTRES QUI EN SONT DESCENDUES, ...
- LINGUARUM 12 CHARACTERIBUS DIFFERENTIUM INTRODUCTIO AC LEGENDI METHODUS
- LINGVARUM DUODECIM CHARACTERIBVS DIFFERENTIVM ALPHABETVM, INTRODVCTIO, AC LEGENDI MODUS LONGE FACILIMUS
- SYRIAE DESCRIPTIO

Postel, Guillaume *see* LES TRES-MERVEILLEUSES VICTOIRES DES FEMMES DU NOUVEAU MONDE

Postels, A *see* ILLUSTRATIONES ALGARUM

POSTEN – Lindsborgs. Kan. 1898-1930 – 1 – us UMI [071]

POSTEN OGVED ARNEN – Decorah.Iowa. 1874- – 1 – us UMI [071]

POST-ENQUIRER – Oakland. Calif. 1945-50 – 1 – us UMI [071]

POSTER – Portland OR. Apr 18 May 31 July 26 1938, Nov 29 Dec 20 1938, Jan 25 Mar 1 Apr 12 1939, June 14 Sep 20 1939 – 1 – us U.O. Library [071]

THE POSTER – London, 1898-1901 – 1r – 14 – £110.00 – uk Chadwyck [760]

POSTERS, PROGRAMS, PLAYBILLS, PHOTOGRAPHS AND PICTURES *see* SHAKESPEARE AT STRATFORD-UPON-AVON

LA POSTESCENA DEL TEATRO ROMANO DE MERIDA / Melida, Jose Ramon & Macias, Maximiliano – 1 – sp Bibl Santa Ana [946]

THE POST-EXERCISE BLOOD PRESSURE RESPONSE TO ACUTE EXERCISE IN BORDERLINE HYPERTENSIVE WOMEN / Inbar, Galit & Wallace, Janet P – 1992 – 3mf – 9 – $12.00 – us Microform Publ [613]

THE POST-EXILIAN PROPHETS : HAGGAI, ZECHARIAH, MALACHI / Dods, Marcus – (With introduction & notes) – Edinburgh: T &T Clark, 1879 – 1mf – 9 – 0-8370-2941-4 – 1985-0941 – us A.T.L.A. [220]

POST-EXPRESS – Rochester. N.Y. 1859-1925; 1926-1927 – 1 – us UMI [071]

Postgate, Richmond *see* OPEN LEARNING

POST-GAZETTE – Hudson. Mich. 1968- – 1 – us UMI [071]

POST-GAZETTE – Pittsburgh. Pa. 1927- – 1 – us UMI [071]
POSTGRADUATE MEDICAL JOURNAL – v61-. 1985- – 1,5,6,9 – us UMI [073]
POST-HARVEST AND PROCESSING TECHNOLOGIES OF AFRICAN STAPLE FOODS : A TECHNICAL COMPENDIUM – 1991 – 360p – it F.A.O. [338]
POST-HARVEST LOSSES IN QUALITY OF FOOD GRAINS – 1984 – 110p – it F.A.O. [630]
POST-HERALD – Beckley. West Virginia. 1924-1966 – 1 – us UMI [071]
POST-HERALD – Beckley. West Virginia. and Raleigh Register. 1966- – 1 – us UMI [071]
POST-HERALD – Birmingham. Ala. 1945-1950 title varies; 1950- – 1 – us UMI [071]
Posthoff, Barbara *see* PLAKATSAMMLUNG DES INSTITUTS FUER ZEITUNGSFORSCHUNG DER STADT DORTMUND
POSTHUMOUS POEMS OF PERCY BYSSHE SHELLEY / Shelley, Percy Bysshe – London: Printed for John and Henry L. Hunt, 1824 – 1 roll – 1 – 1-55879-633-9 – uk Libr Preservation [810]
Posthumus, O *see*
- THE FERNS OF SURINAM AND OF FRENCH AND BRITISH GUIANA
- VARENFLORA VOOR JAVA...

POSTILLA... / Arndt, Johann – Jehna, 1616 – 32mf – 9 – ne IDC [240]
POSTILLA... / Eber, P – Franckfurt am Mayn, 1578 – 12mf – 9 – ne IDC [240]
POSTILLA DAS IST AUSSLEGUNG DER EUANGELIEN AUFF ALLE FEST VND APOSTEL TAGE DURCHS GANTZE JAR / Hesshusen, T – Helmstadt, 1581. 2 pts – 8mf – ne IDC [240]
POSTILLA DAS IST AVSZLEGUNG DER EUANGELIEN DURCHS GANTZE JAHR... / Gedik, S – [Wittenberg], 1593. 3v – 31mf – ne IDC [240]
POSTILLA DEUDSCH VBER ALLE FEST VND GEMEINE FEYERTAG DER HEYLIGEN DURCHS GANTZE IAR / KURTZE VND NUTZLICHE AUSSLEGUNG / Huberinus, Caspar – Frankfurt a.d. Oder: Johann Eichhorn, 1554. V.3. [G.F.: 20.7] – 9mf – 9 – HUB-48/1 – ne IDC [240]
POSTILLA ODER AUSSLEGUNG DER EUANGELIEN... / Chemnitz, Martin – Magdeburg, 1594 – 16mf – 9 – ne IDC [240]
POSTILLA ODER AUSSLEGUNG DER SONTAGS EUANGELIEN UBER DAS GANTZE JAR / Mathesius, Johannes – Nuernberg, 1565 – 7mf – ne IDC [240]
POSTILLA ODER AVSSLEGUNG DER EPISTELN VND EUANGELIEN AUFF ALLE SONTAG FEST VND FEYERTAGE DURCH DAS GANTZE JAHR / Hunnius, A – Frankfort am Mayn, 1593-1594. 3v – 15mf – ne IDC [240]
POSTILLA SUPER ECCLESIASTICUM (SIECLE 15) / San Victor, Hugo de – Barcelona – 1r – 5,6 – sp Cultura [240]
POSTILLA TEUETSCH VBER ALLE SONTAEGLICHE EUANGELIEN VOM ADUENT BISS AUF OSTERN / KURTZE... / Huberinus, Caspar – [Augsburg: Philipp Uhart, AB 1545]. 2v. [G.F.: 20.1] – 16mf – 9 – HUB-47/1 – ne IDC [240]
LE POSTILLON – Angers (Maine-et-Loire), Oct 1883 – May 1884 – 1r – fr Armell [320]
DER POSTILLON VON LONJUMEAU / Adam, Adolf – German: Ms, 186-? – 1 – us Sibley [780]
POSTIMEES – (Backfile $85r) – Estonia, 1999- – 6r per y – 1 – $480.00 standing order – us Ross [072]
POSTITIVE EINLEITUNG / Hermes, Georg – Muenster, 1829. x/626p – DM98.00 – 3-89349-150-3 – gw Hänsel [240]
POST-JOURNAL – Jamestown. N.Y. 1942- – 1 – us UMI [071]
Postlethwayt, M *see* GREAT-BRITAIN'S TRUE SYSTEM
THE POSTMAN'S KNOCK – Saint John, NB: Excelsior Stamp Assoc, [1866-1870] – 9 – cn C.I.H.M. [760]
POSTMASTER OR ROYAL MERCURY – Exeter, England.11 Nov 1720-14 Sept 1722; 24 May-13 Sept 1723; 24 Sept 1724-23 Apr 1725.-w. 1 reel – 1 – uk British Libr Newspaper [072]
POSTMASTERS' ACCOUNT BOOK / Wyandot County. Ohio. Lovell. City Post Office – 1906-1908 – 1r – 1 – $32.50r – us Archival [324]
POST-MEDIAEVAL PREACHERS : SOME ACCOUNT OF THE MOST CELEBRATED PREACHERS OF THE 15TH, 16TH, AND 17TH CENTURIES : WITH OUTLINES OF THEIR SERMONS, AND SPECIMENS OF THEIR STYLE / Baring-Gould, Sabine – London: Rivingtons, 1865 – 1fm – us A.T.L.A. [240]
POSTNATALE ENTWICKLUNG DES MITTELOHRS BEI PACHYUROMYS DUPRASI / Franz, Martin – 1994 – 1mf – DM60.00 – 3-8267-2002-4 – gw Hänsel [573]
Postnov, I U S *see* ISTORIIA RUSSKOI LITERATURY SIBIRI V DVUKH TOMAKH
POST-OCH INRIKES TIDNINGAR – (Suppl: Tidning for Leveranser till Staten, 1889-1978) – Stockholm, Sweden. 1844-1978 – 351r – 1 – sw Kungliga [072]
POST-PRANDIAL PHILOSOPHY / Allen, Grant – London: Chatto & Windus, 1894. 05061. (Pre-1900 Canadiana) – 9 – cn C.I.H.M. [190]
POST-PRIMARY SCHOOL DIRECTORY OF MIDWESTERN STATE OF NIGERIA 1971 (SECONDARY LEVEL) / Nigeria. Mid-Western State. Ministry of Education. Planning Division – Benin City, 1972 – 1mf – 9 – DE-113/1 – ne IDC [370]
POST-PRIMARY STATISTICS 1980-1981 / Nigeria. Sokoto State. Ministry of Education. Statistics Section – Sokoto – 1mf – 9 – DE-124/1 – ne IDC [370]
POST-RECORD – San Jose. Calif. 1967- – 1 – us UMI [071]
POST-REGISTER – Washington. Kan. 1895-1905 – 1 – us UMI [071]
POSTRERA VOLUNTAD Y TESTAMENTO DE HERNANDO CORTES / Bayle, Constantino – Madrid: Razon y Fe, 1940 – sp Bibl Santa Ana [946]
POSTRERA VOLUNTAD Y TESTAMENTO DE HERNANDO CORTES MARQUES DEL VALLE / Pereyra, Carlos & Conwray, G R G – Madrid: Revista de Indias, 1940 – 1 – sp Bibl Santa Ana [920]
POST-STANDARD – Syracuse. N.Y. 1953- – 1 – us UMI [071]
POST-STAR – Glens Falls. N.Y. 1964- – 1 – us UMI [071]
POST-TELEGRAM – Camden. N.J. 1899-1920 – 1 – us UMI [071]
POSTTIDNINGAR – Stockholm, Sweden. Title varies. 1645-51; 1655-60; 1663-64; 1666-68; 1670; 1672-90; 1692-1718; 1720-21. – 8r – 1 – sw Kungliga [072]
POST-TRIBUNE – Jefferson City. Mo. 1925-1944; 1947; 1949- – 1 – us UMI [071]
POSTUP PROGRESS-UKRAINIAN WEEKLY – Winnipeg, Canada 27 Feb 1959-Dec 1975.-w. 17 reels – 1 – uk British Libr Newspaper [072]
POSTURAL ADJUSTMENT FOR VOLUNTARY LEG MOVEMENT IN DANCERS / Monasterio, Rita A – University of Oregon, 1994 – 1mf – 9 – $4.00 – PE3613 – us Microform Publ [790]
POSTWAR AGRICULTURE IN MINNESOTA / Minnesota. University. Agricultural Experiment Station. St. Paul – nos.1-4. 1943-46 – 1,5,6 – us Spaulding [630]
POST-WAR DEVELOPMENT IN ORISSA / Orissa. India (State) – Cuttack. 1946 – 9 – ne IDC [360]
POSTWAR EUROPE / U.S. Office of Strategic Services – 1977. Series: US State Department Intelligence and Research Reports, Pt 5 – 1 – $965.00 – 0-89093-121-6 – us UPA [940]
POSTWAR JAPAN, KOREA AND SOUTHEAST ASIA : 1945-49 / U.S. Office of Strategic Services – 1977. Series: US State Department Intelligence and Research Reports, Pt 2 – 1 – $580.00 – 0-89093-118-6 – us UPA [950]
POSTZEITUNG *see* AUGSPURGISCHE ORDINARI-POST-ZEITUNG
[/POSTZEITUNGSLISTEN/] : DDR – Berlin. 1958, 1961-71, 1973-91 – 8r – 1 – gw Mikrofilm [073]
[/POSTZEITUNGSLISTEN/] : DEUTSCHES REICH UND BUNDESREPUBLIK – Berlin. 1894. 1900. 1923. 1930-31. 1933. 1935. 1938. 1940-45. 1948-54. 1958-66. 1968-90 – 38r – 1 – gw Mikrofilm [073]
LE POT AU NOIR, ET LE POT AU BLANC OU LA VERITE DEVOILEE, LA FOURBERIE DEMASQUEE ET LA RELIGION PAPISTE RENVERSEE – (D'Holbach series). 1787 – 9 – fr Hachette [240]
POT POURRI – Seattle, WA. 1964-68 – 1r – 1 – $50.00 – R04154 – us Library Micro [071]
LE POTAGER, JARDIN DU CULTIVATEUR / Santerre, Alec – Quebec: Darveau, Jos. Beauchamp..., 1902. SEM105P477 – 2mf – 9 – Can$4.50 – cn Bibl Nat [631]
Potain *see* TRAITE DES ORDRES D'ARCHITECTURE
POTATO PRODUCTION AND CONSUMPTION IN DEVELOPING COUNTRIES – 1991 – 52p – it F.A.O. [338]
POTCHEFSTROOM BUDGET – Potchefstroom. South Africa. 1888-99 – 1 – sa State Libr [072]
POTCHEFSTROOM HERALD – Potchefstroom. South Africa. 1908-1981 – 1 – sa State Libr [072]
POTCHEFSTROOMER – Potchefstroom. South Africa. 1883-1907 – 1 – sa State Libr [072]
Potekhin, I I *see* AFRIKA 1956-1961
DE POTENTATU / Hartmann, J M – Vitembergae, 1737 – 1mf – 1 – ILM-961/1 – ne IDC [327]
POTENTIAL FOR IMPACT : ILCA LOOKS TO THE FUTURE / ILCA – 1992 – 9 – 92-9053-239-4 – et ILRI [333]
POTENTIAL OF FORAGE LEGUMES IN FARMING SYSTEMS OF SUB-SAHARAN AFRICA : PROCEEDINGS OF A WORKSHOP HELD AT ILCA, ADDIS ABABA, ETHIOPIA, 16-19TH SEPTEMBER 1985 / ed by Haque, I et al – 1986 – 9 – $22.00 – 92-9053-141-X – et ILRI [630]
POTENTIAL POPULATION SUPPORTING CAPACITIES OF LANDS IN THE DEVELOPING WORLD – 1982 – 169p – it F.A.O. [304]
POTENTIAL POPULATION SUPPORTING CAPACITIES OF LANDS IN THE DEVELOPING WORLD – 1983 – 150p – it F.A.O. [304]
POTENTIAL YIELD OF FISH STOCKS – 1983 – 56p – it F.A.O. [639]
POTENTIEL D'IMPACT : LE CIPEA FACE A L'AVENIR / CIPEA – 1992 – 9 – 92-9053-240-8 – et ILRI [333]
LA POTERIE DE CARNARU, NORD-EST DU BRESIL / Moraes Sequeira, V M – 9 – F30.00 – fr Ethnologie [306]
Poth, Joseph *see* NATIONAL LANGUAGES AND TEACHER TRAINING IN AFRICA
Potier de la Varde, R *see*
- CONTRIBUTION A LA FLORE BRYOLOGIQUE DE L'ANNAM
- MUSCINEES ANNAMITES RECOLTEES PAR M. POILANE

Potier, Le P *see* FACONS DE PARLER PROVERBIALES, TRIVIALES, FIGUREES DES CANADIENS AU XVIIIE
LES POTIERS DE GRES. PERMANENCES ET CHANGEMENTS TECHNO-ECONOMIQUES DANS UNE COMMUNAUTE ARTISANALE RURALE / Massion, A – 9 – F70.00 – fr Ethnologie [306]
POTOMAC INTEREST – Colonial Beach. Va. -w. 1947- – 1 – us UMI [071]
Potomac Press *see* AMERICAN BIOGRAPHICAL DIRECTORIES
Potonie, R *see* TASCHENATLAS ZUR FLORA VON NORD- UND MITTELDEUTSCHLAND
POTPOURRI FRANCOIS DE CONTRE-DANSE ANCIENNE / Landrin – 1785? – 9 – us Sibley [780]
POT-POURRI POPUR VIOLON AVEC ACCOMPAGNEMENT DE VIOLON ET BASSE / Kreutzer, R – (Parts) – Amsterdam: A Kuntze, [189-?] – 1 – us Sibley [780]
POTREBITEL' – Khar'kov, 1912-13 n12 – 5mf – 9 – COR-668/1 – ne IDC [334]
POTREBITEL'NYE OBSHCHESTVA : ISTORIIA, TEORIIA I PRAKTIKA / Totomiants, V F – Ed 2. Spb., 1908 – 5mf – 9 – COR-120/1 – ne IDC [334]
POTREBITEL'SKAIA KOOPERATSIIA : (TSENTR I PERIFERIIA). MESTNYE TORGOVYE ORGANY (GUBTORGI I PAITORGI) – M., 1923 – 2mf – 9 – COR-735/1 – ne IDC [334]
POTREBITEL'SKAIA KOOPERATSIIA NA VSESOIUZNOI SEL'SKOKHOZIAISTVENNOI I KUSTARNO-PROMYSHLENNOI VYSTAVKE 1923 GODA V G. MOSKVE – M., 1923 – 1mf – 9 – COR-736/1 – ne IDC [334]
POTREBITEL'SKAIA KOOPERATSIIA PERED 14 S"EZDOM RKP (B) : SBORNIK STATEI – M., 1926 – 2mf – 9 – COR-737/1 – ne IDC [334]
POTREBITEL'SKAIA KOOPERATSIIA SSSR – M., 1924 – 2mf – 9 – COR-351/1 – ne IDC [334]
POTREBITEL'SKAIA KOOPERATSIIA SSSR, 1927/28 GOD – PERVAIA POLOVINA 1928/29 GG. : STATISTIKO-EKONOMICHESKII OBZOR – M., 1929 – 2mf – 9 – COR-353/1 – ne IDC [334]
POTREBITEL'SKAIA KOOPERATSIIA SSSR MEZHDU PERVYM I VTORYM KOOPERATIVNYMI S"EZDAMI : OBZOR RABOTY ZA 1928/29 G. – 1-E POLUGODIE 1929/30 KHOZ. G. – M., 1930 – 3mf – 9 – COR-356/1 – ne IDC [334]
POTREBITEL'SKAIA KOOPERATSIIA V 1925/26 I 1926/27 GODAKH – M., 1928 – 4mf – 9 – COR-349/1 – ne IDC [334]
POTREBITEL'SKAIA KOOPERATSIIA V LENINGRADE, MAI-DEK. 1924 G – L., 1925 – 4mf – 9 – COR-347/1 – ne IDC [334]
POTREBITEL'SKAIA KOOPERATSIIA V SIBIRI V PROTSESSE EE RAZVITIIA : MATERTIALY PO ISTORII KOOPERATSII (1898-1920 GG.) / Makhov, V N – Novonikolaevsk, 1923 – 3mf – 9 – COR-334/1 – ne IDC [334]
POTREBITEL'SKAIA KOOPERATSIIA ZA 10 LET SOVETSKOI VLASTI / Makerova, N Ia. – Ed 2. M., 1927 – 1mf – 9 – COR-332/1 – ne IDC [334]
POTSDAM CONFERENCE DOCUMENTS / Truman, Harry S – 1980. (Presidential Documents Series) – 1 – $210.00 – 0-89093-353-7 – us UPA [977]
POTSDAMER KIRCHE – (Lacking: 1971-72. nos 16-20 1981) – 1970-91 – Inquire – 1 – ATLA S0478 – us A.T.L.A. [073]
POTSDAMER NEUESTE NACHRICHTEN *see* BRANDENBURGISCHE NEUESTE NACHRICHTEN
POTSDAMER NEUESTE NACHRICHTEN, STADTAUSGABE BRANDENBURG *see* BRANDENBURGISCHE NEUESTE NACHRICHTEN
Pott, August *see* DER ABENDLAENDISCHE TEXT DER APOSTELGESCHICHTE UND DIE WIR-QUELLE: EINE STUDIE
Pott, F H L, Mrs *see* PIONEERS OF THE CHUNG HUA SHEN KUNG HUI (CCC263)
Pott, Johann Heinrich *see* CHYMISCHE UNTERSUCHUNGEN WELCH FURNEHMLICH VON..
Pott, P *see*
- CHIRURGICAL OBSERVATIONS RELATIVE TO THE CATARACT, THE POLYPUS OF THE NOSE, THE CANCER OF THE SCROTUM,...
- OBSERVATIONS ON THE NATURE AND CONSEQUENCES OF WOUNDS AND CONTUSIONS OF THE HEAD,...
- REMARKS IN THAT KIND OF PALSY OF THE LOWER LIMBS, WHICH IS FREQUENTLY FOUND TO ACCOMPANY CURVATURE OF THE SPINE
- SOME FEW GENERAL REMARKS ON FRACTURES AND DISLOCATIONS
- A TREATISE ON RUPTURES

POTTER AND CLAY: A SERMON PREACHED IN THE BRIXTON INDEPENDENT CHURCH, LONDON, ENGLAND / Brown, James Baldwin – Montreal: Milton Publishing League, 1876. 00973. (Pre-1900 Canadiana) – 9 – cn C.I.H.M. [240]
Potter, Burton Willis *see* THE ROAD AND THE ROADSIDE
POTTER COUNTY JOURNAL – Coudersport. Pa. 1958-1966 – 1 – us UMI [071]
POTTER DEMOCRAT – Coudersport, PA. -w 1893-1896; 1899-1919 – 13 – $25.00r – us I.M.R. [071]
POTTER ENTERPRISE – Coudersport, PA. -tri-w 1880-1983 – 13 – $25.00r – us I.M.R. [071]
Potter, Jacqueline S *see* LEISURE PARTICIPATION AMONG INDIVIDUALS WITH TRAUMATIC BRAIN INJURY FOLLOWING DISCHARGE FROM A TRANSITIONAL FACILITY
Potter, James *see* NARRATION OF THE EXPERIENCE, TRAVELS AND LABOURS OF ELDER JAMES POTTER, MINISTER OF THE GOSPEL, AND PASTOR OF THE BAPTIZED CHURCH IN BOWDOIN, COMMONWEALTH OF MASSACHUSETTS
Potter, Joseph Lewis *see* AN ENGLISH-HEBREW LEXICON
THE POTTER JOURNAL – Coudersport, PA. 1867-71. 1 roll – 13 – $25.00r – us I.M.R. [071]
Potter, Platt *see* TREATISE ON THE LAW OF CORPORATIONS: GENERAL AND LOCAL, PUBLIC AND PRIVATE; AGGREGATE AND SOLE
POTTER REVIEW – Potter, NE. -w. Mar 1912-Oct 1942 – 1 – us NE Hist [071]

Potter, William J *see* THE FREE RELIGIOUS ASSOCIATION...AN ADDRESS
POTTERIES ADVERTISER AND NORTH STAFFORDSHIRE CHRONICLE – Stoke-on-Trent, England. -w. 14 March 1908-24 Aug 1912. 1 1 2 reels – 1 – uk British Libr Newspaper [072]
POTTERIES EVENING ECHO – Stoke-on-Trent, England. -d. 29 Nov 1886-12 Feb 1887. 39 ft – 1 – uk British Libr Newspaper [072]
POTTERIES EXAMINER – (Staffordshire and Potteries Examiner). Stoke-on-Trent. England. -w. 17 Mar 1871-11 Jun 1881 – 9r – 1 – uk British Libr Newspaper [941]
POTTERIES FREE PRESS – Stoke-on-Trent. England. -w. 12 Feb-16 Apr 1853 – 1r – 1 – uk British Libr Newspaper [941]
POTTER'S AMERICAN MONTHLY – v1-9. Jan 1872-Sep 1882 – 1 – $101.00 – us L of C Photodup [073]
POTTERS BAR PRESS – 1990-Jun, Jul 2-Dec 24 1992; 1993-Jun, Jul 5-Dec 20 1995; 1996-Jun 1997 – 16r – 1 – uk British Libr Newspaper [072]
POTTER'S EXAMINER AND WORKMAN'S ADVOCATE – 1843-45. BRRAM – 1 – uk Microform Academic [072]
POTTERSFIELD PORTFOLIO – Fredericton. v8- 1986/87- – 9 – Can$20.00y – cn Micromedia [800]
POTTERY AND GLASS TRADES JOURNAL – (Pottery Gazette). London. -m. Jan 1878-Dec 1894 – 24r – 1 – uk British Libr Newspaper [660]
POTTERY TECHNIQUES OF NATIVE NORTH AMERICA : AN INTRODUCTION TO TRADITIONAL TECHNOLOGY / White, John – (52p accompanying text) – 4 color mf – 15 – $46.00f – 0-226-69815-7 – us Chicago [730]
Potthast, A *see* BIBLIOTHECA HISTORICA MEDII AEVI
Pottinger, I *see* THE METHODIST
Potts, Robert Alfred *see* EPIPSYCHIDION
Potts, Thomas *see* A COMPENDIOUS LAW DICTIONARY
Potvin, D *see* LE TRAVAILLEUR
Potvin, Micheline *see* BIO-BIBLIOGRAPHIE DU DOCTEUR LOUIS PAUL DUGAL
Potvin, Patrick J *see* STATISTICAL POWER FOR REPEATED MEASURES ANOVA
Potwin, Lemuel Stoughton *see* HERE AND THERE IN THE GREEK NEW TESTAMENT
Potwin Place. Kansas *see* RECORDS OF THE CITY OF POTWIN PLACE, SHAWNEE COUNTY
Pou Marti, Jose *see* EMBAJADA DEL OBISPO DE CARTAGENA FR. ANTONIO TREJO PIDIENDO AL PAPA LA DEFINICION DE LA INMACULADA
POUCHENYA V OGRAZHDENIE PRAVOSLAVNYKH OT SHTUNDISTSKIKH ZABLUZHDENI / Dankevich, Vladimir – Sermons on the protection of the Orthodox from Stundist errors. Moscow, 1893. One of 13 titles on reel – 1 – 86.44 – us Baptist [240]
Poudra, Jean-G *see* TESTAMENT DE MARIE-ANTOINETTE, REINE DE FRANCE(...)
Poughkeepsie, New York *see* MISCELLANEOUS EARLY NEWSPAPERS
Poujol, D F *see* HISTOIRE ET INFLUENCE DES EGLISES WALLONNES DANS LES PAYS-BAS
Poujoulat, M *see* HISTOIRE DE SAINT AUGUSTIN
Poulain, I *see* ANTHOLOGIE FRANCOISE
Poulain, Marc *see* AUSSENPOLITIK ZWISCHEN MACHTPOLITIK UND DOGMA
Poulain-Josien, Th. *see* LES ANIMAUX DOMESTIQUES ET SAUVAGES EN FRANCE DU NEOLITHIQUE AU GALLO-ROMAIN
Poulet, Georges *see* AUTOUR D'UNE FEMME SOUS LES TROPIQUES
Poulin, Henri *see* SAMEDI-DIMANCHE
Pouliot, Aline *see* BIBLIOGRAPHIE ANALYTIQUE DE L'OEUVRE DE L'ABBE ROCH DUVAL, LICENCIE EN ORIENTATION, DEBUT A SEPTEMBRE 1964
Pouliot, Ghislaine *see* BIBLIOGRAPHIE ANALYTIQUE DE MONSIEUR FRANCIS DESROCHES
Pouliot, Marcelle *see* BIO-BIBLIOGRAPHIE DE MONSIEUR JEAN-CHARLES BONENFANT ATTACHE A LA BIBLIOTHEQUE DE LA LEGISLATURE PROVINCIALE, CHARGE DE COURS D'HISTOIRE POLITIQUE A L'UNIVERSITE LAVAL
Poulot, DP Denis *see* QUESTION SOCIALE. LE SUBLIME OU LE TRAVAILLEUR COMME IL EST EN 1870 ET CE QU'IL PEUT ETRE
POULSON'S AMERICAN DAILY ADVERTISER – Philadelphia, 1801-37 – 2r – 1 – us Ross [071]
POULSON'S AMERICAN DAILY ADVERTISER – Philadelphia. Pa. 1800-1820 – 3 – us Readex [071]
POULTNEY BAPTIST CHURCH. POULTNEY, VERMONT : CHURCH RECORDS – 1802-1919 – 1 – 66.15 – us Baptist [240]
POULTRY DAY / South Dakota. State University. Agricultural Experiment Station – nos.1-6. 1969-74 – 1,5,6 – us Spaulding [636]
POULTRY INTERNATIONAL – v1- 1962- 1; v16- 5,6,9 – us UMI [636]
POULTRY MEAT – (See now: Broiler Business and P P M: Poultry Processing and Marketing) – v1-26. 1950-75 – 1 – us UMI [636]
POULTRY PELLETS / Virginia. Polytechnic Institute. Extension Division – v. 1-12. 1958-69 – 1,5,6 – us Spaulding [636]
POULTRY POINTERS / Washington. Agricultural Extension Service, Pullman – nos.1-43 and revisions. 1930-53 – 1,5,6 – us Spaulding [636]
POULTRY PROGRESS REPORT / Louisiana State University. Agricultural Experiment Station. North Louisiana Experiment Station, Calhoun – No.2. 1976. 1 reel – 1,5 – us Spaulding [636]
POULTRY RESEARCH SERIES / Clemson University. Agricultural Experiment Station – No.29-42. 1969-82. 1 reel – 1,5 – us Spaulding [636]
POULTRY SCIENCE – (v.58-. 1979- 5,6,9) – v.1-. 1921- – 1 – us UMI [073]
POULTRY SCIENCE *see* JOURNAL
POULTRY SCIENCE DEPARTMENTAL SERIES 1 / Alabama. Agricultural Experiment Station – 1964 – 1,5,6 – us Spaulding [636]
POULTRY TRIBUNE – v1- 1895- 1; v83- 5,6,9 – us UMI [636]
Pound, Roscoe *see*
- CASES ON EQUITABLE RELIEF AGAINST DEFAMATION AND INJURIES TO PERSONALITY. SUPPLEMENTARY TO AMES'S CASES IN EQUITY JURISDICTION
- THE ROSCOE POUND PAPERS

POUND'S CASES ON PRACTICE / Nebraska. Supreme Court – 1v. 1904 (all publ) – 2mf – 9 – $3.00 – LLMC 90-007 – us L.L.M.C. [340]
Poupardin, C *see* COMMENT SONT PRESENTES LES PREDETERMINANTS DU SUBSTANTIF DANS LES OUVRAGES DES GRAMMAIRIENS DU 17E ET 18E SIECLE
LES POUPEES DES INDIENS KARAJA / Chiara, V – 9 – F80.00 – fr Ethnologie [740]
LES POUPEES KARAJA DU MUSEE DE L'HOMME / Vellard, Jet al – 9 – Fr60.00 – fr Ethnologie [306]
LE POUR ET CONTRE – Ouvrage periodique d'un gout nouveau. Par l'Abbe A.F. Prevost. Paris. 1733-40 (I-XX) – 1 – fr A.C.R.P.P. [073]
LE POUR ET CONTRE DE LA POSSESSION DES FILLES DE LA PAROISSE DE LANDES, DIOCESE DE BAYEUX / Poree, Charles Gabriel – 1738 – 9 – fr Hachette [360]
LE 'POUR ET CONTRE' ET SON TEMPS / Labriolle, Marie-Rose de – (Studies on Voltaire and the eighteenth century, v34-35) – Oxford. 1965 – 9 – $122.00 – 0-7294-0128-6 – uk Voltaire [440]
LE POUR ET LE CONTRE – no. 1-41. 16 juin-26 juil 1830. devenu: La Revolution puis La Revolution de 1830. no. 42. 27 juil 1830. devenu: Le Bien public. no. 1-109. 5 oct 1832 (prosp.) Paris. 16 juin-9 oct 1930. mq no. 99, 104. no. 142-382. 11 nov 1830-15 aout 1831. 5 oct 1832 – 1 – fr A.C.R.P.P. [073]
POUR LA FEMME – Montreal. v1 n10. 18 mar 1956 – 1r – 1 – Can$25.00 – cn Can Microfilming [072]
POUR LA FEMME: ETUDES FEMINISTES / Naudet, Paul Antoine – Paris: Fontemoing, 1903. ii,330p. (Les Femmes Collection) – 4mf – 9 – $10.00 – fr Bibl Nationale [305]
POUR LA NORMALISATION DE LA DESCRIPTION DES POTERIES. ESSAI DE NOMENCLATURE DES FORMES / Balfet, H et al – 9 – F20.00 – fr Ethnologie [740]
POUR LA SOCIETE DES NATIONS / Bourgeois, L – Paris, 1910 – 5mf – 9 – ILM-4075/1 – ne IDC [327]
POUR LA VICTOIRE – IV, no. 1-52. New York. 1945 – 1 – fr A.C.R.P.P. [073]
POUR LA VICTOIRE – New York City, NY. v1 n13. 4 avr 1942-v1 n29. 25 jul 1942 – 1r – 1 – Can$25.00 – cn Can Microfilming [071]
POUR LA VICTOIRE – NY City, NY. 1942-1943 – 1r – 1 – $50.00 – R04928 – us Library Micro [071]
POUR LE PAPE... / Bessieres, A; ed by Bayle, Constantino – Madrid: Razon y Fe, 1928 – 9 – sp Bibl Santa Ana [240]
POUR L'HISTOIRE DU PROBLEME DE L'AMOUR AU MOYEN-AGE / Rousselot, P – Muenster, 1907. 2mf; idem, Muenster, 1908 – 2mf – 8 – ne Slangenburg [110]
POUR SEDUIRE LES FEMMES / Amans, Georges – Paris, 1923 ed. 62p. (Les Femmes Collection) – 1mf – 9 – $6.00 – fr Bibl Nationale [150]
POUR SORTIR DU CHAOS MONETAIRE / Zander, Walter – 5fiches (24x) – 9 – 1.00f – at Libertarian Micro [320]
POUR UNE PAIX DURABLE, POUR UNE DEMOCRATIE POPULAIRE – Belgrade, puis Bucarest.No.1-389. nov 1947-avr 1956 – 1 – fr A.C.R.P.P. [073]
POURQUOI JE NE SUIS PAS FEMINISTE / Vallette, Marguerite Eymery – Paris: Editions de France, 1928. 87p. (Les Femmes Collection) – 1mf – 9 – $6.00 – fr Bibl Nationale [305]
POURQUOI NOUS SOMMES FRANCAIS / Dunn, Oscar – Montreal: La Minerve, 1870. 05197. (Pre-1900 Canadiana) – 9 – cn C.I.H.M. [306]
POURQUOI SE BAT L'ARMEE ESPAGNOLE; UN DISCOURS DU GENERAL ROJO / Rojo, Vincente – Paris, 193? Fiche W1148. (Blodgett Collection of Spanish Civil War Pamphlets) – 9 – us H.U. College Libr [946]
POUSO ALEGRENSE : ORGAM POLITICO E NOTICIOSO – Pouso Alegre, 20 Dec 1906 – 1,5,6 – bl Biblioteca [072]
O POUSO ALTO : ORGAO DOS INTERESSES DOS MUNICIPIOS DE POUSO ALTO E VILLA DE PASSA QUATRO – Pouso Alto, 30 Jun 1912; 26 Dec 1920 – 1,5,6 – bl Biblioteca [072]
O POUSO-ALEGRENSE : SEMANARIO LITTERARIO, COMMERCIAL E NOTICIOSO – Pouso Alegre, 10 Apr 1881 – 1,5,6 – bl Biblioteca [072]
Pouvillon, Emile *see* CESETTE, HISTOIRE D'UNE PAYSANNE
LE POUVOIR : BULLETIN D'INFORMATION DU P.Q. – Montreal. v1 n2. jul 1969-v1 n3. sep 1969 – 1r – 1 – Can$30.00 – cn Can Microfilming [072]
POUVOIR ET SOCIETE DANS LE PEROU CONTEMPORAIN / Bourricaud, F – 1967 – F90.00 – fr Ethnologie [972]
LE POUVOIR EXECUTIF AUX ETATS-UNIS, ETUDE DE DROIT CONSTITUTIONNEL / Chambrun, Charles Adolphe de Pineton – 2me ed. Paris: Fontemoing, 1896. 336p. LL-314 – 1 – us L of C Photodup [340]
LE POUVOIR JUDICIAIRE AUX ETATS-UNIS; SON ORGANISATION ET SES ATTRIBUTIONS / Helbronner, Horace – Paris: Parent, 1872. 39p. LL-1214 – 1 – us L of C Photodup [340]
POUVOIRS ET SOCIETE AGRA-PASTORALE DANS LES HAUTES PLAINES STEPPIQUES DE L'ALGERIE : LES COMMUNES PASTORALES DE L'ALGERIE CENTRALE / Chellig, Nadia – 3mf – 9 – 10096 – fr Atelier National [306]
Pouw, Boen Seng *see* BUKU PENUNTUN SERAT NIPA
Pouw, Peng Hong *see* SEDIKIT DARI HAL HOMILETIK ATAU ILMU BERI WAJAT
Pouyanne, Lydie *see* UNE PRISON DE FEMMES
Povah, C *see* A HANDY DIGEST OF WESLEYAN RULES AND USAGES
O POVEIRO : ORGAM DE PROPAGANDA DA POVOA DE VARZIM – Manaos, Amazonas. 25 Nov-Dez 1915; Jan-Jul, Set-25 Nov 1917 – 1,5,6 – bl Biblioteca [072]
POVERI BIMBI; LA BARBARIE DEI RIBELLI SPAGNUOLI / Gaddi, Giuseppe – Paris, 1936. Fiche W 902. (Blodgett Collection of Spanish Civil War Pamphlets) – 9 – us H.U. College Libr [946]
POVERKH BAR'EROV / Pasternak, B – Vtoraia kniga stikhov. M. 1917. BR-1017 2 – 8 – ne IDC [460]
LA POVERTA A CURA DI...ASSISI, 1967 / Melani, Gaudezio – Madrid: Graf. Calleja, 1967 – 1 – sp Bibl Santa Ana [946]
POVERTY, PROGRESS AND DEVELOPMENT / ed by Henry, Paul-Marc – 1991 – 9 – 92-3-102617-8 – Co-published with Kegan Paul International, London – fr UNESCO [339]
POVERTY, WORK AND MIGRATION IN MODERN BRITAIN – Series 1: The Westminster Parish Examinations, 1708-1835, from Westminster City Libraries, London – 1 – us Primary [360]
Povesa *see* MODERNISTY I IKH PREDSHESTVENNIKI I KRITICHESKAIA LITERATURA O NIKH
POVEST' O DVUKH ZVERIAKH. IKHNELAT / Remizov, A – Paris, 1950. 60, (2)p. BR-840 2 – 8 – ne IDC [460]
POVEST O IVANE SEMENOVICHE STRATILATOVE-NEUEMNYI BUBEN / Remizov, A – Berlin, 1922. 78p. BR-841 2 – 8 – ne IDC [460]
POVESTI / Pogodin, M P – v. 1-3. M. 1832. BR-8325 2 – 8 – ne IDC [947]
POVEST'O ROZHDENII MOEM, PROISKHOZDENII I VSEI ZIZNI, 1764-1800 / Dolgorukov, I M – Spb. 1916. BR-6019 2 – 8 – ne IDC [947]
O POVO – Bicas, 11 Jan 1903 – 1,5,6 – bl Biblioteca [072]
O POVO : ORGAM DO PARTIDO E LITTERARIA – Pitanguy, 30 Nov 1924 – 1,5,6 – bl Biblioteca [072]
O POVO : ORGAM DOS INTERESSES DO PARTIDO REPUBLICANO DO 9O. DISTRICTO – Cataguazes, 7 Jan-Feb, Apr-Jun, Sept 1888; 6 Apr 1889 – 1,5,6 – bl Biblioteca [072]
O POVO : ORGAO CRITICO, LITTERARIO E NOTICIOSO – Maceio, Alagoas. 26 Mar, 4 Nov 1900 – 1,5,6 – bl Biblioteca [072]
O POVO : ORGAO NEUTRAL DOS INTERESSES MORAES E MATERIAES DA PROVINCIA – Cuiaba, 12 Jan-Aug 1879; Mar-Jul, Nov 1880; 12 Jan 1882 – 1,5,6 – bl Biblioteca [072]
O POVO – Ouro Preto, 13 May-21 Oct 1849 – 1,5,6 – bl Biblioteca [072]
O POVO : SEMANARIO IMPARCIAL – Sacramento, 20 Jan 1889 – 1,5,6 – bl Biblioteca [072]
O POVO DE LORIGA : ORGAM DA COLONIA LORIGUENSE EM MANAOS – Manaos, Amazonas. 5 Jun-20 Ago 1910 – 1,5,6 – bl Biblioteca [072]
Povolotskii, LI *see*
- KOOPERATIVNOE ZAKONODATEL'STVO S PRILOZHENIEM DEKRETOV O VSEKH VIDAKH KOOPERATSII
- OSNOVNYE NACHALA KOOPERATIVNOGO PRAVA SSSR
- PRAVOVOI SPRAVOCHNIK DLIA RABOTNIKOV POTREBITEL'SKOI KOOPERATSII
- RUSSKOE KOOPERATIVNOE ZAKONODATEL'STVO

Povorinskii, A F *see* SISTEMATICHESKII UKAZATEL' RUSSKOI LITERATURY PO GRAZHDANSKOMU PRAVU
POVREMENNYIA IZDANIIA V ROSSII V 1860-M I 1861-GODAKH / Mezhov, VI – Spb, 1861 – 8 – BR-7168 2 – ne IDC [947]
POW WOW – Kamloops, BC: [s.n., 1900-190-?] – 9 – cn C.I.H.M. [590]
POWDER METALLURGY – v1- 1958- – 1,5,6,9 – us UMI [660]
POWDER METALLURGY AND METAL CERAMICS – (Continues: Soviet Powder Metallurgy and Metal Ceramics) – v1-32. 1962-93 – 1,5 – $120.00v – us UMI [660]
POWDER RIVER EXAMINER – Broadus. Mont. 1954; 1956-1959; 1966- – 1 – us UMI [071]
POWDER TECHNOLOGY – v1-39. 1967-84 – 1,5,6,13 – sz Elsevier [073]
Powderly, Terence Vincent *see* TERENCE VINCENT POWDERLY PAPERS, 1864-1937; THE JOHN WILLIAM HAYES PAPERS, 1880-1921
THE POWELL COUNTY CALL – Deer Lodge. Mont. 1906-1907; 1917-1918; 1920-1924 – 1 – us UMI [071]
POWELL COUNTY POST – Deer Lodge. Mont. 1917-1918; 1920-1921; 1922-1924 – 1 – us UMI [071]
POWELL COUNTY RECORD – Elliston. Mont. 1902-1904 – 1 – us UMI [071]
Powell, Edward Payson *see* LIBERTY AND LIFE
Powell, Frederick James *see* PARENT AND SUBSIDIARY CORPORATIONS
Powell, Henry Montefiore *see* THE TAXATION OF CORPORATIONS AND PERSONAL INCOME IN NEW YORK
Powell, Herbert Harry *see* THE SUPPOSED HEBRAISMS IN THE GRAMMAR OF THE BIBLICAL ARAMAIC

Powell, J W *see* INTRODUCTION TO THE STUDY OF INDIAN LANGUAGES WITH WORDS, PHRASES, AND SENTENCES TO BE COLLECTED

Powell, Jehu Z *see* HISTORY OF CASS COUNTY

Powell, John William *see* THE CHINA WEEKLY REVIEW

Powell, Lyman P *see*
- CHRISTIAN SCIENCE
- THE EMMANUEL MOVEMENT IN A NEW ENGLAND TOWN
- HISTORY OF EDUCATION IN DELAWARE

Powell, Ransom Judd *see* RANSOM JUDD POWELL PAPERS

POWELL RIVER CITIZEN – Powell River, British Columbia, CN. May 1945-Jul 1949 – 1r – 1 – cn Commonwealth Micro [072]

POWELL RIVER NEWS – (Ju1991-1992De) – Powell River, 1993 – 1r – 1 – cn Preston [971]

POWELL RIVER NEWS – Powell River, Britsh Columbia, CN. Nov 1927-1989 – 56r – 1 – cn Commonwealth Micro [072]

POWELL RIVER TOWN CRIER – Powell River, British Columbia, CN. Jan 1937-Jul 1949 – 1r – 1 – cn Commonwealth Micro [072]

Powell, Robert S *see* THE NEW JERSEY OFFICE OF CONSUMER PROTECTION: A PROMISE UNFULFILLED

Powell, Roberta B *see* WOMEN AND SPORT IN VICTORIAN AMERICA

Powell, Steven W *see* A CINEMATOGRAPHICAL ANALYSIS AND FORCE MEASURE OF THREE STYLES OF THE KARATE BACK PUNCH AND SIDE KICK

POWELL VALLEY NEWS – Pennington Gap. Va. 1931-46; 1950- – 1 – us UMI [071]

Powell, William H *see* POWELL'S RECORDS OF LIVING OFFICERS OF THE UNITED STATES ARMY

POWELL'S RECORDS OF LIVING OFFICERS OF THE UNITED STATES ARMY / Powell, William H – Philadelphia: L.R. Hamersly and Co., n.d. Military Books, reel 4. (Cox Library Collection) – 5 – us Americana [920]

POWER – v5- 1884- 1; v109- 5,6; v119- 9 – us UMI [600]

THE POWER AND BEAUTY OF SUPERB WOMANHOOD. / Macfadden, Bernarr Adolphus – New York: The Physical Culture Pub. Co., 1901. 273p. illus – 1 – us U.W. Library [790]

POWER AND THE SOVIET ELITE / Nicolaevsky, Boris I – 1965. 275p – 1 – 35.00r – us Hoover Inst Photo [947]

POWER ENGINEERING – v6- 1902- 1; v75- 5,6; v79- 9 – us UMI [600]

POWER EQUIPMENT – 1953-56. Continued by Transmission and distribution – 1 – us UMI [600]

POWER EQUIPMENT FOR GENERATION, TRANSMISSION DISTRIBUTION – 1949-52. Continued by Power equipment – 1 – us UMI [600]

POWER FARMING *see* AMJ

POWER HOUSE – Toronto, Canada. Devoted to the generation of steam, gas, electric, air and water power. -m. Apr 1909-Jul 1914 – 512r – 1 – uk British Libr Newspaper [621]

Power, J C *see* DIRECTORY AND SOLDIER'S REGISTER OF WAYNE COUNTY

Power, John C *see* HISTORY OF THE EARLY SETTLERS OF SANGAMON COUNTY

THE POWER OF CHRISTIAN BENEVOLENCE: ILLUSTRATED IN THE LIFE AND LABORS OF MARY LYON / Hitchcock, Edward – 1852 – 9 – us A.T.L.A. [240]

THE POWER OF CONGRESS / Lefevre, Robert – Ed. by R. S. Radford. 1976. 2 fiches (24x) – 9 – 1.00f – at Libertarian Micro [320]

THE POWER OF CONSCIENCE EXEMPLIFIED IN THE GENUINE AND EXTRAORDINARY CONFESSION OF THOMAS BEDWORTH. / Bedworth, Thomas – London, Hone, 1815. 18p. LL-2242 – 1 – us L of C Photodup [340]

THE POWER OF FAITH: EXEMPLIFIED IN THE LIFE AND WRITINGS OF THE LATE MRS. ISABELLA GRAHAM / Graham, Isabella Marshall – 1843 – 9 – us A.T.L.A. [240]

THE POWER OF PRAYER : ILLUSTRATED IN THE WONDERFUL DISPLAYS OF DIVINE GRACE AT THE FULTON STREET AND OTHER MEETINGS IN NEW YORK AND ELSEWHERE, IN 1857 AND 1858 / Prime, Samuel Irenaeus – New York: Scribner; London: Sampson, Low, 1859, c1858 – 1mf – us A.T.L.A. [240]

THE POWER OF THE POPE DURING THE MIDDLE AGES, OR, AN HISTORICAL INQUIRY INTO THE ORIGIN OF THE TEMPORAL POWER OF THE HOLY SEE, AND THE CONSTITUTIONAL LAWS OF THE MIDDLE AGES RELATING TO THE DEPOSITION OF SOVEREIGNS / Gosselin, M – Baltimore: J. Murphy; London: C. Dolman, 1853 – 2mf – us A.T.L.A. [240]

POWER STRUGGLE IN SOUTHEAST ASIA[E] / Oey, Hong Lee – 1977 – ix/614p + 11 microfiches – hb (book + microfiche Sfr89.00) – 3-85750-018-2 – ne IDC [320]

POWERS AND DUTIES OF SHERIFFS, CONSTABLES, TAX COLLECTORS, AND OTHER OFFICERS IN THE NEW ENGLAND STATES / Hitchcock, Loranus Eaton – (2nd. ed. Boston: Little, Brown, 1904. 472p. LL-175) – Boston: Little, Brown, 1889. 460p. LL-176 – 1 – us L of C Photodup [340]

Powers, Carl J *see* THE PSYCHOPHYSIOLOGICAL EFFECTS OF BIOFEEDBACK OPEN FOCUS SELF-REGULATION TRAINING UPON HOMEOSTATIC EFFICIENCY DURING EXERCISE

THE POWERS, DUTIES AND LIABILITIES OF CORONERS AND CONSTABLES. / Smith, Borden Dodge – Albany, N.Y.: Little, 1897. 288p. LL-1135 – 1 – us L of C Photodup [340]

Powers, Grant *see* ESSAY UPON THE INFLUENCE OF THE IMAGINATION ON THE NERVOUS SYSTEM CONTRIBUTING TO A FALSE HOPE IN RELIGION

POWERS OF THE ARBITRATION COMMITTEE...AND THE FORMS OF SUBMISSION, AWARDS, ETC / New York. Chamber of Commerce of the State of New York – New York: Craighead, 1864. 10p. LL-931 – 1 – us L of C Photodup [340]

THE POWERS OF THE EXECUTIVE DEPARTMENT OF THE GOVERNMENT OF THE UNITED STATES, AND THE POLITICAL INSTITUTIONS AND CONSTITUTIONAL LAW OF THE UNITED STATES / Conkling, Alfred – Albany, N.Y., Little, 1882. 195 p. LL-159 – 1 – us L of C Photodup [340]

POWERS OF THE UNITED STATES SUPREME COURT / Gavagan, Joseph Andrew – Washington: GPO, 1936. 16p. LL-1636 – 1 – us L of C Photodup [340]

Powers, Otero, Lowe and Company. Kansas *see* LETTERS

POWERS PATRIOT – Powers, OR. -w. 26 Apr 1918-25 May 1923. 1 roll – 1 – us U.O. Library [071]

Powicke, F J *see* HENRY BARROW, SEPARATIST (1550?-1593), AND THE EXILED CHURCH OF AMSTERDAM (1593-1622)

Powicke, Frederick J *see*
- DAVID WORTHINGTON SIMON
- A HISTORY OF THE CHESHIRE COUNTY UNION OF CONGREGATIONAL CHURCHES
- ROBERT BROWNE, PIONEER OF MODERN CONGREGATIONALISM

Powles, Francis *see* THE AFRICAN MAGICIAN

POWNAL BAPTIST CHURCH. VERMONT : CHURCH RECORDS – 1782-1791 – 1 – 5.00 – us Baptist [240]

POWROT OWIDIUSZA. TRISTIA OSIPA MANDELSZTAMA / Przybylski, R – Zycie literackie. Krakow. 1961. BR-3697 2 – 8 – ne IDC [460]

POWSZECHNY ZJAZD HISTORYKOW POLSKICH – Added title page title: Travaux du...Congres des historiens polonais – 1 – us U.W. Library [943]

Poyart, AF *see* FLANDRICISMES, WALLONISMES

Poyas, Elizabeth A *see* CAROLINA IN THE OLDEN TIME

Poynting, F *see* EGGS OF BRITISH BIRDS

POZARNI OCHRANA – Prague, Czechoslovakia. 1957-60 – 1r – 1 – us L of C Photodup [072]

POZNAI SVOI KRAIE – Pskov. v. 1-4. 1924-1929 – 1 – us NY Public [073]

POZNANIE ROSSII – Ezhemesiachnyi literaturnyi i obshchestvenno-ekonomicheskii zhurnal. v. 1-3. Spb. 1909. BR-3784 2 – 8 – ne IDC [330]

Poznanski, S A *see*
- SEFER ZIKKARON. LIVRE D'HOMMAGE A. S. POZNANSKI
- ZUR GESCHICHTE DER PALAESTINAENSISCHEN GEONIM

Poznyshev, S V *see* UCHEBNIK UGOLOVNOGO PRAVA

Pozos, Emmanuel R de *see* PATRE ANTONIO LLINAS, COLLEGIORUM MISSIONARIUM IN HISPANIA ET AMERICA FUNDATORE 1635-1693

Pozzo, Andrea *see*
- PROSPETTIVA DE PITTORI E ARCHITETTI
- PROSPETTIVA DE PITTORI E ARCHITETTI, PARTE PRIMA

Pozzo di Borgo, Carlo Andrea, Comte *see* CORRESPONDANCE DIPLOMATIQUE DU COMTE POZZO DI BORGO, AMBASSADEUR DE RUSSIE EN FRANCE, ET DU COMTE DE NESSELRODE DEPUIS LA RESTAURATION..., 1814-18

Pozzo, FB Dal. *see* LE VITE DE' PITTORI, DEGLI SCULTORI ET ARCHITETTI VERONESI

PPA / University of Kentucky. Department of Plant Pathology – No.1-21.1972-83. 3 fiches – 9 – us Spaulding [630]

THE PPA IN ONTARIO: BEING EXTRACTS FROM SPEECHES AND TWO LETTERS OF MR. J. D. EDGAR, M.P / Edgar, James David – s.l.: s.n., 1893?. 05218. (Pre-1900 Canadiana) – 9 – cn C.I.H.M. [971]

PPI : PULP AND PAPER INTERNATIONAL – (Former title: Pulp and Paper International 1959-jan 1970) – San Francisco. v1-14. 1959-72* 1; v15-39 1973-97+ 1,5,9 – 1,5,9 – D9665 – us UMI [670]

PPI (PLASTIC PIPE INSTITUTE) – Printed index. Updated every 60 days – 6,9 – us Info Handling [660]

PPM: POULTRY PROCESSING AND MARKETING – (See also: Broiler Business and Poultry Meat) – v28- 1977- – 1,5,6,9 – us UMI [636]

PR PAMPHLET-THE PROPORTIONAL REPRESENTATION SOCIETY – Westminster: The Society. -irr.1905?-. Each no. has a distinctive title – 1 – us U.W. Library [073]

Praag, S van *see* HET GHETTO

PRABA – Jogjakarta. Incomplete. SE-953 1. 1949?-1971 – 9 – ne IDC [073]

Prabhajasa, S *see* WIRIT BUDI PEKERTI (IRAMA KEBATHINAN)

Prabhubhai Bhikhabhai Patel *see* CITTAVISUDDHIPRAKARANA: SANSKRIT AND TIBETAN TEXTS

PRABUDDA BHARATA – (Lacking some issues) – v73-97. 1968-92 – Inquire – 1 – ATLA S0766 – us A.T.L.A. [280]

PRACA – Bratislava, Czechoslovakia. -d. Aug 1956-June 1967. 32 reels – 1 – uk British Libr Newspaper [072]

PRACA – Bratislava, Czechoslovakia. Feb 1948-49; Aug 1952-84; 1988-90; 1992 – 68r – 1 – us L of C Photodup [072]

PRACE = THE ADVANCE – May 9 1925-Dec 24 1927 – 1r – 1 – us I.H.R.C. [073]

PRACE – Prague, Czechoslovakia. -d. 18 July-26 Aug 1945; 2 Oct 1951-Dec 1970. 48 reels – 1 – uk British Libr Newspaper [072]

PRACE – Prague, Czechoslovakia. Jun 1945-1992 – 88r – 1 – us L of C Photodup [072]

PRACE FILOLOGICZNE – v. 1-17. Warszawa. 1885-1937. B-786 2 – 8 – ne IDC [073]

PRACE POLSKIOGO INSTYTUTU GEOLOGICZNEGO / Poland. Instytut Geologiczny – Warsaw. tom. 3-10. 1938-1953 – 1 – us NY Public [550]

PRACHATHIPATAI – Bangkok, Thailand. 1961 – 4r – 1 – us L of C Photodup [072]

PRACHUM PHONGSAWADAN PHAKTHI 56: WADUAI HETKAN MUANG KHAMN TON SADET SONGKHRAM THAI KAP YUAN – In Thai.1932. 34p – 1 – us U.W. Library [950]

PRACTICA DE BOTICARIOS : GUIA DE ENFERMOS. REMEDIO PARA POBRES / Gutierrez de Arevalo, P – Madrid, 1634 – 6mf – 9 – sp Cultura [615]

PRACTICA MUSICA / Finck, H – 1556 – 9 – us Sibley [780]

PRACTICA MUSICAE UTRIUSQUE CANTUS / Gaffurio, Franchino – 1512 – 9 – us Sibley [780]

PRACTICA MUSICAE VTRIUSQUE CATUS EXCELLETIS FRACHINI GAFFORI LAUDESIS / Gaffurius, F – P 679. 1512 – 9 – ne IDC [780]

PRACTICA MUSICE / Gaffurio, Franchino – 1496 – 9 – us Sibley [780]

PRACTICA POLITICA Y ECONOMICA DE EXPOSITOS... / Montalvo, T – Granada, 1701 – 5mf – 9 – sp Cultura [360]

PRACTICA SAVONAROLE DE FEBRIBUS... / Optatus, C – Venecia, 1517 – 5mf – 9 – sp Cultura [610]

PRACTICA Y TEORICA DE LAS APOSTEMAS... CUESTIONES Y PRACTICAS DE CIRUGIA... / Lopez de Leon, P – Sevilla, 1628 – 13mf – 9 – sp Cultura [617]

PRACTICABLE SOCIALISM : ESSAYS ON SOCIAL REFORM / Barnett, Samuel & Barnett, Henrietta – London; New York: Longmans, Green, 1894 – 1mf – us A.T.L.A. [335]

PRACTICAE MUSICAE PRAECEPTA / Zanger, Johann – P 524 2. 1554 – 8 – ne IDC [780]

PRACTICAL AND EXPLANATORY COMMENTARY ON THE NEW TESTAMENT / Bickersteth, Edward Henry – London: Virtue, 18–. 1 fiche – 9 – us A.T.L.A. [240]

A PRACTICAL APPROACH TO PATENTS, TRADEMARKS AND COPYRIGHTS – (An int. journal of proprietary property rights) – An int. journal of proprietary property rights. v1-2. 1979-83 – 1,5,9 – us Harwood [340]

PRACTICAL ASPECTS OF SCIENTIFIC AND TECHNOLOGICAL RESEARCH PROGRAMMING : CASE STUDIES FROM THE USSR / Larichev, Oleg I & Petrovsky, Alexey B – 1991 – 38p – 9 – 92-3-102759-X – fr UNESCO [500]

THE PRACTICAL BEE-KEEPER – Tilbury Centre [Tilbury], Ont.: C A Ouelette, [1893-1895] – 9 – cn C.I.H.M. [630]

THE PRACTICAL BOLSHEVIK: A. I. RYKOV AND RUSSIAN COMMUNISM 1881-1938 / Oppenheim, Samuel A – 1979. 600p – 1 – 35.00r – us Hoover Inst Photo [335]

PRACTICAL BUILDER – v1-32 1936-67 – 1 – us UMI [690]

PRACTICAL CONVEYANCING / Oliver, Benjamin Lynde – Hallowell Me.: Glazier, Masters & Smith, 1836. 635p. LL-710 – 1 – us L of C Photodup [340]

PRACTICAL DIABETOLOGY – v1-. 1982- – 1,5,6,9 – us UMI [616]

A PRACTICAL DIRECTORY FOR YOUNG CHRISTIAN FEMALES : BEING A SERIES OF LETTERS FROM A BROTHER TO A YOUNGER SISTER / Newcomb, Harvey – 1833 – 9 – us A.T.L.A. [240]

A PRACTICAL DISCUSSION OF THE PARLOR DANCE, THE THEATRE, THE CARDS / Crossley, Hugh Thomas – Toronto: W. Briggs, c1895. 02135. (Pre-1900 Canadiana) – 9 – cn C.I.H.M. [971]

PRACTICAL ENTOMOLOGIST – Philadelphia. v1-2. 1865/66-1866/67 – 9mf – 9 – Z-990/2 – ne IDC [590]

PRACTICAL ETHICS : A COLLECTION OF ADDRESSES AND ESSAYS / Sidgwick, Henry – London: Swan Sonnenschein; New York: Macmillan, 1898 – 1mf – 9 – 0-8370-6379-5 – 1986-0379 – us A.T.L.A. [170]

PRACTICAL EXPOSITIONS OF THE WHOLE BOOK OF RUTH AND ESTHER / Lawson, George – Edinburgh: James Gemmell, 1869. 1 fiche – 9 – us A.T.L.A. [240]

PRACTICAL FARM NEWS – Smithfield, NE. -w. Apr 1896-Apr 1897, scattered issues missing – 1 – us NE Hist [071]

PRACTICAL FORMS OF THE SUPREME COURT, TAKEN FROM TIDD'S APPENDIX OF THE FORMS OF THE COURT OF KING'S BENCH. / Caines, George – New York: Alsop, Brannan and Alsop, 1808. 526p. LL-857 – 1 – us L of C Photodup [340]

PRACTICAL FORMS, WITH NOTES AND REFERENCES EXPLANATORY OF THE LAW GOVERNING THE CASES TO WHICH THEY ARE APPLICABLE. / Aikens, Asa – (A supplement to Aikens' Practical forms, adapting that work to the present state of the statutes of Vermont. By Peter T. Washburn. Clarement? N.H. Clarement Manufacturing, 1847. 110, 2 p. LL-1434) – 2nd ed. Windsor, Vt., Goddard, 1836. 447 p – 1 – us L of C Photodup [340]

PRACTICAL GASTROENTEROLOGY – v.4-. Oct 1980- – 1,5,6,9 – us UMI [616]

A PRACTICAL GRAMMAR OF THE AVISTA LANGUAGE, COMPARED WITH SANSKRIT, WITH A CHAPTER SYNTAX AND A CHAPTER ON THE GATHA DIALECT – Bombay, 1891 – 4mf – NE-20163/1 – ne IDC [490]

A PRACTICAL GRAMMAR OF THE ENGLISH TONGUE / Gough, James – 1754. 153p. (English Linguistics Series 1500-1800) – 9 – us UMI [420]

A PRACTICAL GRAMMAR OF THE LATIN TONGUE / Milner, John – 1729. 93p. (English Linguistics Series 1500-1800) – 9 – us UMI [450]

A PRACTICAL GUIDE TO ADMINISTRATORS, GUARDIANS AND ASSIGNEES, CONTAINING FULL AND COMPLETE INSTRUCTIONS FOR THE SETTLEMENT OF ESTATES. / Pinkerton, John J – West Chester: Moore, 1870. 115p. LL-1355 – 1 – us L of C Photodup [340]

A PRACTICAL GUIDE TO POLICE MAGISTRATES AND JUSTICES OF THE PEACE: WITH AN ALPHABETICAL SYNOPSIS OF THE CRIMINAL LAW AND AN ANALYTICAL INDEX / Crankshaw, James – Montreal: Whiteford & Theoret, 1895. 00512. (Pre-1900 Canadiana) – 9 – cn C.I.H.M. [971]

A PRACTICAL GUIDE TO REVISION OF LOCAL COURT RULES / Bowden, Jeanne J – Washington: FJC, 1988 – 1mf – 9 – $1.50 – LLMC 95-399 – us L.L.M.C. [340]

A PRACTICAL GUIDE TO THE ENGLISH KINDERGARTEN / Ronge, Johann & Ronge, Bertha – 19th ed.London: A.N. Myers, 1896. 68p – 1 – us U.W. Library [370]

A PRACTICAL GUIDE TO THOROUGHBASS / Kollman, A – London: Author, 1801 – 1 – us Sibley [780]

A PRACTICAL HANDBOOK OF THE NYANJA LANGUAGE / Hetherwick, Alexander – 3rd enl ed. [Mandala, Blantyre, Nyasaland]: The African Lakes Corp, 1914 – us Res Libr [470]

PRACTICAL INSTRUCTIONS FOR THE DETERMINATION BY FURNACE ASSAY OF GOLD AND SILVER IN ROCKS AND ORES / Chapman, Edward John – Toronto: Copp, Clark, 1881. 05406. (Pre-1900 Canadiana) – 9 – cn C.I.H.M. [622]

PRACTICAL INTELLECT : COMPUTER AND SKILLS / Goeranzon, Bop – 1992 – 113p – 9 – 92-3-102757-3 – Co-published with Springer-Verlag, Berlin and New York – fr UNESCO [000]

A PRACTICAL INTRODUCTORY HEBREW GRAMMAR / Bissell, Edwin Cone – 2nd ed. Hartford, CT: Hartford Theological Seminary, 1892, c1890 – 1mf – 9 – 0-8370-9205-1 – 1986-3205 – us A.T.L.A. [470]

PRACTICAL KEY TO THE CANARESE LANGUAGE / Ziegler, Friedrich – 2nd ed. Bangalore: Basel Mission Book & Tract Depository, 1892 – us Res Libr [490]

PRACTICAL LAWYER (ALI-ABA) – v1-41. 1955-95 – 9 – $757.00 set – us Hein [340]

PRACTICAL LITIGATOR (ALI-ABA) – v1-6. 1990-95 – 9 – $102.00 set – us Hein [340]

PRACTICAL NURSING – (See also: Journal of Practical Nursing) – v1-13. 1955-1963 – 1 – us UMI [610]

PRACTICAL OBSERVER – Valparaiso. Ind. w. 1849-57 – 1 – us UMI [071]

THE PRACTICAL OPERATION OF THE MASSACHUSETTS LAW REQUIRING THE PSYCHIATRIC EXAMINATION OF CERTAIN PERSONS ACCUSED OF CRIME (THE "BRIGGS LAW") / Overholser, Winfred – Boston, 1928. 16p. LL-974 – 1 – us L of C Photodup [340]

PRACTICAL PARASITOLOGY : GENERAL LABORATORY TECHNIQUES AND PARASITIC PROTOZOA; NOTES FOR STUDENTS OF ANIMAL HUSBANDRY / Price, C J & Reed, J E – 1970 – 112p – it F.A.O. [574]

PRACTICAL PATENT PROCEDURE / Andrew, Lucy Brett – New ed. New York? 1950. 35 p. LL-565 – 1 – us L of C Photodup [340]

PRACTICAL PHILOSOPHY OF THE MUHAMMADAN PEOPLE / Dawani, Jalal-al-Din – 1839 – 1 – uk Microform Academic [180]

PRACTICAL PHONOGRAPHY / Jones, John – 1701. 157p. (English Linguistics Series 1500-1800) – 9 – us UMI [420]

PRACTICAL PUBLIC SPEAKING : A TEXT-BOOK FOR COLLEGES AND SECONDARY SCHOOLS / Clark, S H & Blanchard, F M – (An anthology of famous speeches, many by legal figures) – New York: Charles Scribner's Sons, 1901 – 4mf – 9 – $6.00 – LLMC 92-224 – us L.L.M.C. [340]

PRACTICAL QUESTIONS AND ANSWERS ON WILLS; HOW TO MAKE YOUR WILL / Rockwood, Albert S – New York: Electric, 1914. 16p. LL-1003 – 1 – us L of C Photodup [340]

PRACTICAL REAL ESTATE LAWYER (ALI-ABA) – v1-11. 1985-95 – 9 – $176.00 set – us Hein [340]

THE PRACTICAL REALIZATION OF THE MILHAUD PROPOSALS / Beckerath, Ulrich von – 2fiches. 24x – 9 – 1.00f – at Libertarian Micro [320]

PRACTICAL REFLECTIONS ON THE BOOK OF RUTH / Horine, M C – Philadelphia: Lutheran Publ Society, c1892 – 1mf – 9 – 0-8370-3655-0 – 1985-1655 – us A.T.L.A. [220]

PRACTICAL REFLECTIONS UPON EVERY VERSE OF THE BOOK OF GENESIS – London: Longmans, Green, 1892. 1 fiche – 9 – us A.T.L.A. [240]

PRACTICAL REHTORICK / Poole, Joshua – 1663. 230p. English Linguistics Series 1500-1800) – 9 – us UMI [400]

PRACTICAL REMARKS ON INSANITY: TO WHICH IS ADDED A COMMENTARY ON THE DISSECTION OF THE BRAINS OF MANIACS; WITH SOME ACCOUNT OF DISEASES INCIDENT TO THE INSANE / Crowther, Bryan – London, 1811. viii,130p – 1 – us U.W. Library [616]

PRACTICAL REMARKS ON THE PROCEEDINGS OF GENERAL COURTS MARTIAL / Kennedy, Vans – London: J & W T Clarke, 1825 – 4mf – 9 – $6.00 – LLMC 96-090 – us L.L.M.C. [340]

PRACTICAL RULES FOR LEARNING COMPOSITION / Fux, J J – C.1800 – 9 – us Sibley [780]

PRACTICAL SPACE APPLICATIONS – (v21 1967, Advances) – 9 – $40.00 – us Univelt [629]

PRACTICAL STUDENT – Delaware, Ohio. 1888-91 – 1r – 1 – $32.50r – us Archival [071]

PRACTICAL TALKS ON IMPORTANT THEMES: TO YOUNG CONVERTS, OLDER CHRISTIANS AND THE UN-CONVERTED / Crossley, Hugh Thomas – Toronto: W. Briggs, 1895. 02136. (Pre-1900 Canadiana) – 9 – cn C.I.H.M. [971]

A PRACTICAL TAMIL READING BOOK FOR EUROPEAN BEGINNERS / Jensen, Herman – Madras; Memorial Press, 1882 – us Res Libr [490]

PRACTICAL TAX LAWYER (ALI-ABA) – v1-9. 1986-95 – 9 – $214.00 set – us Hein [340]

PRACTICAL THEOLOGY / Oosterzee, Johannes Jacobus van – A manual for theological students. 1878 – 1 – us A.T.L.A. [240]

A PRACTICAL TREATISE OF POWERS / Sugden, Edward Burtneshaw – 1st American ed. from the 3rd London ed. Philadelphia: Small, 1823. 703 – 1 – us L of C Photodup [340]

A PRACTICAL TREATISE ON CRIMINAL LAW, AND PROCEDURE IN CRIMINAL CASES...IN THE STATE OF ILLINOIS. / Moore, Ira M – 2nd ed. Chicago: Callaghan, 1890. 987p. LL-547 – 1 – us L of C Photodup [340]

A PRACTICAL TREATISE ON FINES AND RECOVERIES IN THE COURT OF COMMON PLEAS; WITH PRECEDENTS / Hands, William – 3d ed. London: Butterworth, 1817. 432p. LL-139 – 1 – us L of C Photodup [340]

A PRACTICAL TREATISE ON MINERAL OILS AND THEIR BY-PRODUCTS / Redwood, Iltyd I – 1897 – 1 – us Res Libr [660]

A PRACTICAL TREATISE ON PARTIES TO BILLS AND OTHER PLEADINGS IN CHANCERY: WITH PRECEDENTS / Edwards, Charles – New York, Gould, Banks, 1832. 360 p. LL-1289 – 1 – us L of C Photodup [340]

A PRACTICAL TREATISE ON SINGING AND PLAYING WITH JUST EXPRESSION AND REAL ELEGANCE.. / Bayly, Anselm – 1771 – 9 – us Sibley [780]

A PRACTICAL TREATISE ON THE CODE SUMMONS AND THE MODE OF SERVING IT AS PRESCRIBED BY THE CIVIL CODES OF COLORADO, WYOMING, KANSAS, NEVADA, NEBRASKA AND OTHER STATES. / Fitnam, John Christopher – Denver: Denver Law Journal, 1883. 144p. LL-1268 – 1 – us L of C Photodup [340]

A PRACTICAL TREATISE ON THE CRIMINAL LAW : COMPRISING THE PRACTICE, PLEADINGS AND EVIDENCE WHICH OCCUR IN THE COURSE OF CRIMINAL PROSECUTIONS, WHETHER BY INDICTMENT OR INFORMATION, WITH A COPIOUS COLLECTION OF PRECEDENTS / Chitty, Joseph – v1-4. 1819 – 1 – $95.00 – 0-89093-035-X – us UPA [941]

A PRACTICAL TREATISE ON THE LAW OF CONVENANTS FOR TITLE / Rawle, William Henry – 4th ed. Boston, Little, Brown, 1873. 754 p. LL-95 – 1 – us L of C Photodup [340]

A PRACTICAL TREATISE ON THE LAW OF MARRIAGE, DIVORCE, AND LEGITIMACY, AS ADMINISTERED IN THE DIVORCE COURT AND IN THE HOUSE OF LORDS / Macqueen, John Fraser – 2nd ed. London, Maxwell, 1860. 521 p. LL-118 – 1 – us L of C Photodup [340]

A PRACTICAL TREATISE ON THE LAW OF MUNICIPAL BONDS. / Coler, William Nichols – New York, 1873. 2 v. LL-635 – 1 – us L of C Photodup [340]

A PRACTICAL TREATISE ON THE LAW OF NATIONS... / Chitty, J – London, 1812 – 4mf – 1 – ILM-924/1 – ne IDC [327]

A PRACTICAL TREATISE ON THE LAW OF PARTNERSHIP; WITH AN APPENDIX OF FORMS / Collyer, John – 5th Amer. from the 2d Eng. ed. Boston, Little, Brown, 1861. 1148 p. LL-1161 – 1 – us L of C Photodup [340]

A PRACTICAL TREATISE ON THE MANUFACTURE OF PAPER IN ALL ITS BRANCHES / Hofmann, Karl – Philadelphia: H C Baird, 1873 – us Res Libr [670]

A PRACTICAL TREATISE ON THE POWERS AND DUTIES OF JUSTICES OF THE PEACE. / Haines, Elijah Middlebrook – (7th ed., Chicago, Myers, 1876. 1013 p. LL-80. 14th rev. ed. Chicago, Myers, 1893. 1464 p. LL-1704. 15th rev. ed. Chicago, Myers, 1896. 1464 p. LL-448) – 6th ed. Chicago, Myers, 1873. 850 p. LL-79 – 1 – us L of C Photodup [340]

A PRACTICAL TREATISE UPON THE AUTHORITY AND DUTY OF JUSTICES OF THE PEACE IN CRIMINAL PROSECUTIONS. / Davis, Daniel – 3d ed. Boston, Little, Brown, 1853. 753 p. LL-1470 – 1 – us L of C Photodup [340]

A PRACTICAL TREATISE UPON THE JURISDICTION OF, AND PRACTICE IN, THE COUNTY AND PROBATE COURTS OF ILLINOIS. / Jones, William Caswell – (3rd ed. Chicago, Flood, 1903. 956 p. LL-737) – 2d ed. Chicago, Flood, 1892. 703 p. LL-809 – 1 – us L of C Photodup [340]

PRACTICARUM QUAESTIONUM / Gutierrez, Juan – (Liber II. 1730.1.50f; 9. Liber III. 1730. 1.50f; BSA; 9. Liber IV. 1730.1.50f; BSA; 9. Liber I y II. 1593. 1.50f; BSA; 9) – Liber I.1730 – 9 – 1.50f – sp Bibl Santa Ana [240]

PRACTICARUM...REAGIAS HISPANIAE / Gutierrez, Juan – 1589. I y II – 9 – 1.50f – sp Bibl Santa Ana [946]

PRACTICARUM...TRACTATUS DE BABELLIS / Gutierrez, Juan – 1619 – 9 – 1.50f – sp Bibl Santa Ana [240]

PRACTICAS ECLESIATICA PARA EL USO Y EJERCICIOS DE NOTARIOS PUBLICOS / Arias, Juan – Madrid: Imp. Licenciado.Cafbre, 1596 – 1 – sp Bibl Santa Ana [240]

PRACTICAS ELEMENTALES DE FISIOLOGIA E HIGIENE / Rodriguez Rosillo, Abilio – Caceres: Tip. y Lib. Luciano Jimenez Merino, 1923 – 1 – sp Bibl Santa Ana [612]

PRACTICAS PEDAGOGICAS. TERCER CURSO / Sanchez Yusta, Urbano – Caceres: Tip. El Noticiero, 1953 – 1 – sp Bibl Santa Ana [370]

PRACTICE AND BELIEF BARRIERS TO DIABETES MANAGEMENT IN CAMBODIAN NON-INSULIN-DEPENDENT DIABETES MELLITUS PATIENTS / Bond, Carol – Brigham Young University, 1995 – 1mf – 9 – HE 563 – us Microform Publ [613]

PRACTICE AND PLEADING IN CIVIL ACTIONS AND PROCEEDINGS AT LAW IN ALL COURTS OF MASSACHUSETTS / Mason, Joseph – Boston: Little, Brown, 1883. 662p. LL-696 – 1 – us L of C Photodup [340]

PRACTICE AND PROCEDURE OF THE GOVERNMENT OF INDIA – Calcutta: Superintendent Govt Printing, 1913 1913 – us Res Libr [340]

PRACTICE COURSE, UNIVERSITY OF CHICAGO LAW SCHOOL / Tenney, Horace Kent – Chicago, Chicago Legal News Co., 1909. 81 p. LL-1190 – 1 – us L of C Photodup [340]

PRACTICE COURT AND CHAMBER REPORTS *see* ONTARIO PRACTICE REPORTS

PRACTICE DIGEST – v. 1- 1978$ – 1,5,6,9 – us UMI [360]

THE PRACTICE IN CIVIL ACTIONS AND PROCEEDINGS AT LAW IN THE COMMON LAW COURTS OF THE NEW ENGLAND STATES / Mason, Joseph – Boston: Little, Brown, 1880. 754p. LL-193 – 1 – us L of C Photodup [340]

THE PRACTICE IN INDIANA UNDER THE LAWS FOR CONSTRUCTING DITCHES AND DRAINS / Kenner, James B – Huntington, Herald Printing Co., 1880. 73, 2 p. LL-926 – 1 – us L of C Photodup [340]

PRACTICE IN SURROGATES' COURTS. / McClellan, Robert Henry – 2nd ed. Albany, N.Y., Little, 1880. 1024 p. LL-813 – 1 – us L of C Photodup [340]

PRACTICE IN THE PROBATE COURT OF MASSACHUSETTS / Perley, Sidney – 2d ed. Boston: Reed, 1907. 507p. LL-1400 – 1 – us L of C Photodup [340]

PRACTICE IN THE UNITED STATES PATENT OFFICE; A TABLE OF CASES. / Stoddard, Elliott Joseph – Detroit, Drake, 1907. 167 p. LL-1093 – 1 – us L of C Photodup [340]

THE PRACTICE OF ANARCHIST REVOLUTION: THE POSITION OF WOMEN IN SPANISH ANARCHIST COLLECTIVES / Ackelsberg, Martha A – 1980 – 9 – 1.00f – at Libertarian Micro [320]

THE PRACTICE OF COURTS-MARTIAL : ALSO THE LEGAL EXPOSITION OF THE MUTINY ACT AND ARTICLES OF WAR... / Hough, William – 2nd ed. London: Kingsbury, Parbury & Allen, 1825 – 11mf – 9 – $16.50 – LLMC 89-025 – us L.L.M.C. [340]

THE PRACTICE OF COURTS-MARTIAL AND OTHER MILITARY COURTS : WITH CHAPTERS ON INQUEST, COURTS OF REQUESTS, THREE TRIALS, RULES OF EVIDENCE, AND OTHER USEFUL MATTER AND TABLES / Hough, William – London/ Calcutta: Parbury, Allen & Co/Thacker & Co, 1834 – 4mf – 9 – $6.00 – LLMC 90-032 – us L.L.M.C. [340]

THE PRACTICE OF HUMILITY = PRACTICA DELL'UMILITA : A TREATISE / Leo 13, Pope – London: Burns & Oates; New York: Catholic Publ Society Co, 1888 – 1mf – 9 – 0-8370-7165-8 – 1986-1165 – us A.T.L.A. [240]

THE PRACTICE OF INTEREST / Jones, W F R S – 1 – uk Microform Academic [900]

THE PRACTICE OF NAVIGATION AND NAUTICAL ASTRONOMY / Raper, Henry – Enlarged by Commander T.A. Hull. 19th ed. 1891 – 9 – $60.00 – uk Libr Preservation [623]

THE PRACTICE OF THE PARLIAMENT OF CANADA UPON BILLS OF DIVORCE: INCLUDING AN HISTORICAL SKETCH OF PARLIAMENTARY DIVORCE AND SUMMARIES OF ALL THE BILLS OF DIVORCE PRESENTED TO PARLIAMENT FROM 1867 TO 1888, ALSO NOTES ON THE PROVINCIAL DIVORCE COURTS, &C / Gemmill, John Alexander – Toronto: Carswell, 1889. 03037. (Pre-1900 Canadiana) – 9 – cn C.I.H.M. [971]

THE PRACTICE OF THE SUPREME COURT OF CANADA / Cassels, Robert – Toronto: Carswell, 1888. 00760. (Pre-1900 Canadiana) – 9 – cn C.I.H.M. [971]

PRACTICE ON ATTACHMENT AND GARNISHMENT OF PROPERTY IN THE STATE OF OHIO / Kerr, James Manford – Norwalk, O., Laning, 1898. 400 p. LL-829 – 1 – us L of C Photodup [340]

PRACTICE TEACHING : CLASS 1 GROUPS / Papua New Guinea. Department of Education – Konedobu, 1972 – 1mf – 9 – DE-241/1 – ne IDC [370]

PRACTICING LAW, WHEN, WHERE AND HOW / Quindry, Sylvester Eugene – Washington, D.C., Washington Law Book, 1938. 567 p. LL-1245 – 1 – us L of C Photodup [340]

THE PRACTICING MIDWIFE – 1985-. -q – 1 – us UMI [618]

PRACTICING PLANNER – (See also: Planners Notebook) – v6-9 1976-1979 1; v8-9 5,6,9 – us UMI [300]

PRACTICO DE MORBO GALICO, EN EL QUE SE CONTIENE EL ORIGEN Y CONOCIMIENTO DE ESTA ENFERMEDAD... / Leon, A – Valladolid, 1605 – 5mf – 9 – sp Cultura [610]

LA PRACTIQUE DE L'ORTHOGRAPHE FRANCOISE / Mermet, Cl – 1608 – 9 – fr I.C.S. [440]

LA PRACTIQVE LVDICIAIRE: TANT CIVILE QVE CRIMINELLE, RECEVE ET OBSERUEE PAR TOUT DE ROYAUME DE FRANCE / Imbert, Jean – Illvstree et enrichie de plvsievrs doctes commentaires, interpretations et annotations, extraictes tant du mesme autheur, que des docteurs et practiciens, tant anciencs due modernes, edicts ordonnances, et arrests des cours de Parlements, par M. Pierre Gvenois. Cologny: I. Arnavld, 1615 – 1 – us U.W. Library [944]

PRACTISCHER CURSUS UEBER DIE FORMENLEHRE DER HEBRAEISCHEN SPRACHE : ODER, ANALYSIERUEBUNGEN ZUR METHODISCHEN EINFUEHRUNG DES SCHOLARS IN DIE HEBRAEISCHE FORMENLEHRE / Maurer, Franz Joseph Valentin Dominik – (Texts in Hebrew. Introduction in German) – Leipzig: Friedrich Volckmar, 1837 – 1mf – 9 – 0-8370-9256-6 – 1986-3256 – us A.T.L.A. [470]

THE PRACTISE OF. PHISICKE / Gesner, C – M354. 1599 – 9 – ne IDC [616]

PRACTITIONER – v154-175. 1945-55 – 1,5,6 – us Princeton Micro [610]

PRADJOERIT – (Lacking: 1944(1-2). Microfiche Nos 390-407) – Djakarta: Kantor Besar Badan Pembantoe Pembelaan (with the assistance of Booei Giyugun Siddobu and Gun-Hoodoobu), 1944-1945 – 18mf – 9 – SE-2002/1 – ne IDC [950]

Prado, Eladio del *see* CORRESPONDIENTE DE LA REAL ACADEMIA DE LA HISTORIA

Prado, Pedro *see* ALSINO, NOVELA

Pradt, D G F de *see*
- PARALLELE DE LA PUISSANCE ANGLAISE ET RUSSE RELATIVEMENT A L'EUROPE, SUIVI D'UN APERCU SUR LA GRECE
- VOYAGE AGRONOMIQUE EN AUVERGNE

[P]RAECURSOR LOGICUS...; CUIUS PARTES TRES : METHODICA, METRICA, CRITICA / Caramuel, J – Francofurti, 1654-55 – 24mf – 9 – CA-10/1 – ne IDC [100]

Praed, Winthrop Mackworth *see*
- ESSAYS
- THE POLITICAL AND OCCASIONAL POEMS OF WINTHROP MACKWORTH PRAED

PRAELECTIONES ACADEMICAE DE ANALOGIS LINGUAE GRAECAE, SIVE RATIONUM ANALOGICARUM LINGUAE GRAECAE EXPOSITIO / Lennep, J D van – In French. (Linguistic series). 1805 – 9 – fr Hachette [450]

PRAELECTIONES ACADEMICAE IN HUGONIS GROTII DE IURE BELLI ET PACIS LIBROS III / Heineck, I G – Berolini, 1744 – 11mf – 1 – ILM-2600/1 – ne IDC [327]

PRAELECTIONES IN LIBRUM SAPIENTIAE / Robertus Holkot – Coloniae: Conrad Winters de Homborch, ca 1479 – 36mf – 8 – ne Slangenburg [200]

PRAELECTIONES VALLISOLETANAE IN LIBRO MAGNI HIPPOCRATIS. DE MORBO SACRO / Ponce de Santa Cruz, A – Madrid, 1631 – 4mf – 9 – sp Cultura [610]

PRAELUDIEN : EIN ESSAYBUCH / Servaes, Franz – Berlin: Schuster & Loeffler, 1899 – 1r – 1 – us U.W. Library [430]

PRAELUDIUM AND ALLEGRO / Kreisler, F – New York: C Fisher, 1910 – 1 – us Sibley [780]

PRAEMISSA IN FLORA CRYPTOGAMICAM JAVAE INSULAE / Junghuhn, F W – Batavia, 1838.86p. 15 pls. B-5981/2 – 8 – ne IDC [580]

DIE PRAERIE AM JACINTO / Sealsfield, Charles – Stuttgart: Verlag Deutsche Volksbuecher, 1942 – 1r – 1 – us U.W. Library [830]

Praesidium und vom wissenschaftlichen Ausschuss der Platen-Gesellschaft e.V. *see* BLAETTER DER PLATEN-GESELLSCHAFT

Praetorius, Michael *see*
- SYNTAGMA MUSICUM EX VETERUM ET RECENTIORUM ECCLESIASTICORUM AUTOREM LECTIONE
- SYNTAGMA MUSICUM EX VETERUM ET RECENTIORUM. MUSICAE ARTIS OBSERVATIONE

UN PRAETRE MARIE : CHARLES PERRAUD, CHANOINE HONORAIRE D'AUTUN, 1831-92 / Houtin, Albert – (Includes bibliographical references and index) – 2e rev ed. Paris: A Houtin, 1908 – 1mf – 9 – 0-8370-8681-7 – 1986-2681 – us A.T.L.A. [920]

DER PRAEZEPTORATSVIKARI : AUS HEBELS JUGEND-JAHREN / Albrecht, Hermann – Karlsruhe: F Gutsch, c1921 – 1r – 1 – us U.W. Library [943]

PRAGER BORSEN-COURIER – Prague, Czechoslovakia. Aug 1932-Aug 1937 (scattered issues) – 2r – 1 – us L of C Photodup [072]

DER PRAGER ILLUSTRIERTE MONTAG – Prague, Czechoslovakia. Jan-Sept 1938 (scattered issues) – 1r – 1 – us L of C Photodup [072]

PRAGER MITTAG – Prague, Czechoslovakia. Jan-Sept 1938 (scattered issues) – 1r – 1 – us L of C Photodup [072]

PRAGER MONTAGSBLATT – Prague, Czechoslovakia. Apr 1933-Sept 1938 (scattered issues) – 1r – 1 – us L of C Photodup [072]

PRAGER PRESSE – Prague, Czechoslovakia. Aug 1921-1938 – 47r – 1 – us L of C Photodup [072]

PRAGER PRESSE – Prague, Czechoslovakia. -d. April 1921-Dec 1926; July 1935-Dec 1938. Imperfect. 35 reels – 1 – uk British Libr Newspaper [072]

PRAGER PRESSE – Prague. Sept 1931-Dec 1932; July-Dec 1938 – 1 – us NY Public [073]

PRAGER TAGBLATT – Prague, Czechoslovakia. -d. 9 Feb-31 March 1915; 1 Aug-25 Oct 1916; 2 Jan 1917-29 July 1919; 1-30 June 1938. Imperfect. 10 reels – 1 – uk British Libr Newspaper [072]

PRAGER TAGBLATT – Prague, Czechoslovakia. Jul 1914-Mar 1919; 1935-Oct 1938 – 31r – 1 – us L of C Photodup [072]

PRAGER VOLKSZEITUNG : DAS WOCHENBLATT DER DEUTSCHEN WERKTAETIGEN IN DER CSSR – (To be cont) – Prag, 1979-82 – 4r – 1 – DM300.00 – gw Mikro Press [072]

PRAGMATIC AND ADMINISTRATIVE FACTORS RELATED TO A SUCCESSFUL WRESTLING PROGRAM / Manning, Mark, M – 1986 – 63p 1mf – 9 – $4.00 – us Microform Publ [370]

PRAGMATISCHE GESCHICHTE DER DEUTSCHEN CONCILIEN VOM 4. JAHRHUNDERT BIS ZUM CONCILIUM VON TRIENT / Binterim, Anton Joseph – (1. Band: 3 Fiche. DM75.00. ISBN: 3-89349-286-0; 2. Band: 3 Fiche. DM75.00. ISBN: 3-89349-287-9; 3. Band: 3 Fiche. DM75.00. ISBN: 3-89349-288-7; 4. Band: 3 Fiche. DM75.00. ISBN: 3-89349-289-5; 5. Band: 2 Fiche. DM75.00. ISBN: 3-89349-290-9; 6. Band: 3 Fiche. DM75.00. ISBN: 3-89349-291-7; 7. Band: 3 Fiche. DM75.00. ISBN: 3-89349-292-5) – Mainz, 2nd ed 1851 – 7pts 20mf – 9 – DM500.00 – 3-89349-293-3 – gw Hänsel [943]

PRAGMATISME, MODERNISME, PROTESTANTISME / Leclere, Albert – Paris: Librairie Bloud, 1909. 1 fiche – 9 – us A.T.L.A. [240]

THE PRAGUE POST – 1991-1994 – 2r – 1 – F1,397.00 – sz Infoprint [947]

THE PRAGUE POST – (1992 (incl oct-dec 1991) 1r $85. 1993-98 2r per y $170) – Czech Republic, 1999- – 2r per y – 1 – $160.00 standing order – us Ross [072]

PRAGUE SPRING 1968 / ed by Obrman, Jan – Munich – 2,032mf – 9 – ne IDC [943]

PRAHA-MOSKVA – 1955-1959 inc. – 1 – us I.U. Libraries [073]

PRAHA-MOSKVA – Prague, Czechoslovakia: 1936. v1-4. 1936-1949 – 1 – us I.U. Libraries [073]

Prahl, Karl *see* PHILIPP VON ZESEN

Prain, D *see* BENGAL PLANTS: A LIST OF THE PHANEROGAMS, FERNS AND FERN ALLIES

PRAIRE FORUM – Regina. v1-19. 1976-94 – 9 – Can$20.00y – cn Micromedia [971]

THE PRAIRIE CHIEF: A TALE / Ballantyne, Robert Michael – 10th ed.London: J.Nisbet, 1886?. 07477. (Pre-1900 Canadiana) – 9 – cn C.I.H.M. [830]

PRAIRIE CHILDREN / Thomas, Augusta (Dodge) – ca1934, Access Closed – 1 – us KS Hist [920]

PRAIRIE DEPOT OBSERVER – Wayne, Ohio. 1908-27. 9 reels – 1 – us Archival [071]

Prairie Farmer *see* PRAIRIE FARMER'S RELIABLE DIRECTORY OF FARMERS AND BREEDERS OF BOONE COUNTY

PRAIRIE FARMER'S DIRECTORY – ROCK COUNTY – 1919. Wisconsin Reel 18. (The Cox Library Collection) – 5 – us Americana [978]

PRAIRIE FARMER'S RELIABLE DIRECTORY OF FARMERS AND BREEDERS OF BOONE COUNTY / Prairie Farmer – Chicago. Indiana Reel 6. (The Cox Library Collection) – 5 – us Americana [630]

PRAIRIE HILL BAPTIST CHURCH. HUNT COUNTY. TEXAS : CHURCH RECORDS – 1892-2 Jan 1903 – 1 – 5.00 – us Baptist [240]

PRAIRIE LEA BAPTIST CHURCH. PRAIRIE LEA, TEXAS : CHURCH RECORDS – May 1850-Oct 1977. 1858p – 1 – 83.61 – us Baptist [240]

PRAIRIE MEDICAL JOURNAL *see* MANITOBA MEDICINE

THE PRAIRIE MISSIONARY – Philadelphia: American Sunday-School Union, c1853 – 1mf – 9 – 0-8370-7280-8 – 1986-1280 – us A.T.L.A. [240]

PRAIRIE NEWS – Okolona. Miss. 1858-1859 – 1 – us UMI [071]

PRAIRIE SCHOONER – (v.54-. 1980-. 5,6,9) – v.36-. 1962- – 1 – us UMI [800]

THE PRAISE OF PARIS / Child, Theodore – New York: Harper, 1893. viii,299p. illus. plates – 1 – us U.W. Library [910]

PRAJAMITRA – Bangkok, Thailand. 1939-43 – 9r – 1 – us L of C Photodup [072]

PRAJAMITRA DAILY NEWS – Bangkok, Thailand. 1938-41 – 26r – 1 – us L of C Photodup [072]

PRAJASAKTI – (Telugu language) – Vijayawada, India. Nov 1981-1994 – 34r – 1 – us L of C Photodup [072]

PRAJATANTRA – (Manpuri language) – Imphal, India. 1962-90 – 44r – 1 – us L of C Photodup [072]

PRAJATANTRA DAILY – (Oriya language) – Cuttack, India. Jul 1966-Jun 1971 – 20r – 1 – us L of C Photodup [072]

PRAJAVANI – Bangalore, India. 1962-1993 – 128r – 1 – us L of C Photodup [072]

PRAJAVANI – (Oriya language) – Jeypore, India. 22 Mar 1944-29 Dec 1952 – 1r – 1 – us L of C Photodup [072]

Prakhov, A *see* KHUDOZHESTVENNYE SOKROVISHCHA ROSSII

PRAKRITARUPAVATARA / Simharaja – 1909 – 1 – uk Microform Academic [280]

PRAKTICHESKII KOMMENTARII K USTAVU VNUTRENNEGO VODNOGO TRANSPORTA / Khodunov, M E – 2nd ed. Moscow, 1955. 181p. Commentary to the statute on Internal Water Transport. BR-9117/1 – 9 – ne IDC [340]

PRAKTICHESKII KURS IZUCHENIIA DREVNEI RUSSKOI SKOROPISI DLIA CHTENIIA RUKOPISEI XV-XVIII STOLETII / Beliaev, IS – Moscow, 1911. BR-10,314/1 – 9 – ne IDC [947]

PRAKTICHESKOE RUKOVODSTVO PO PROPAGANDA PRAVA / ed by Alimov, P – Moscow, 1928. 132p. BR-9605 1 – 9 – ne IDC [340]

PRAKTIKA ARBITRAZHNOI KOMISSII VSNKH SSSR I RSFSR / Ignat'ev, A I & Begaks, A I – Moscow, 1926-28. 3v. Collection of typical awards by the RSFSR and YSSR arbitral commission, with commentary. BR-8461/1 – 9 – ne IDC [947]

DER PRAKTIKUS / ed by "Der Kinematograph" – (Cont by: Der Kino-Praktikus, 1909) – Duesseldorf. 1908-10 – 1 – gw Mikrofilm [790]

PRAKTISCHE ANAESTHESIE, WIEDERBELEBUNG UND INTENSIVTHERAPIE *see* ZEITSCHRIFT FUER PRAKTISCHE ANAESTHESIE, WIEDERBELEBUNG UND INTENSIVTHERAPIE

DER PRAKTISCHE LANDWIRTH – Bremen, jun 17 1882 – 1 – Inquire at Mikrofilmarchiv for details – gw Misc Inst [630]

PRAKTISCHE THEOLOGIE / Harnack, T – Erlangen: A. Deichert, 1877-1878 – 3mf – us A.T.L.A. [240]

PRAKTISCHE THEOLOGIE – v1-19. 1974-92 (complete) – 7r – 1 – ATLA S0830 – us A.T.L.A. [073]

PRAKTISCHE WINKE FUER MISSIONAERE : ZUR ABHALTUNG DER MISSIONEN UND FUER DEN CURAT-CLERUS / Weninger, Francis Xavier – Cincinnati: [s.n.], 1885 – 1mf – 9 – 0-8370-6796-0 – 1986-0796 – us A.T.L.A. [240]

PRAKTISCHES HANDBUCH DER PAPIER-FABRIKATION / Hofmann, Carl – 2. umgearb. vergross. Ausg. Berlin: Verlag der Papier-Zeitung, 1891-97 – us Res Libr [670]

Pralle, Elka *see* KULTURARBEIT ALS BESTANDTEIL SOZIALISTISCHER ERWACHSENENBILDUNG IN DER DDR

Pramita, Sal *see* MENGOLAH KUE, PENGANAN DAN MINUMAN

PRAMUAN RATSADAKON CHABAB SOMBUN: PHAK L WA DUAI TUABOTKOTMAI / Thailand – Phra Nakhon: Rongphim 'Amphonphitthaya, 1957. 4p,330p – 1 – us U.W. Library [336]

Prankard, Graffin *see* THE PAPERS

Prantl, Carl *see* GESCHICHTE DER LOGIK IM ABENDLANDE

Prantl, K *see*
- DIE NATUERLICHEN PFLANZENFAMILIEN DIE NATURLICHEN PFLANZENFAMILLIEN

Prasad, Ishwari *see* THE LIFE AND TIMES OF HUMAYUN

Prasad, N *see* INDIAN MUSIC, SCIENTIFIC AND PRACTICAL

Prasad, Navln *see* THE RELATIONSHIP BETWEEN AEROBIC AND ANAEROBIC EXERCISE CAPACITIES IN PRE-PUBERTAL CHILDREN

Prasch, J L *see* DISSERTATIO DE ORIGINE GERMANICA LATINAE LINGUAE

PRASIOLAE GENERIS ALGARUM MONOGRAPHIA / Jessen, C F G – Kiliae. 1848. B-6378 2 – 8 – ne IDC [580]

Prat, Ferdinand *see* ORIGENE, LE THEOLOGIEN ET L'EXEGETE

PRATAP – New Delhi, India. 29 Aug 1946-1953; 1961-1993 – 123r – 1 – us L of C Photodup [072]

PRATAPARUDRIYAMU: ANU ALANKARASASTRAMU; RATNAPANA MANEDU VYAKHYANAMUTONGUDA.. / Vidyanatha – Cennapuri: Vankayala Krsnasvami Setti, 1888 – 1 – us U.W. Library [470]

O PRATEANO : FOLHA DEDICADA AOS INTERESSES DO MUNICIPIO – Sao Domingos do Prata, 25 Jun 1893-18 Aug 1895 – 1,5,6 – bl Biblioteca [072]

O PRATEANO : ORGAO OFICIAL DA CAMARA MUNICIPAL – Sao Domingos do Prata, 3 Nov 1912; 20 Apr 1913 – 1,5,6 – bl Biblioteca [072]

PRATER'S CREEK BAPTIST CHURCH. PICKENS COUNTY. PICKENS, SOUTH CAROLINA : CHURCH RECORDS – 1875-1977 – 1 – 55.88 – us Baptist [240]

LA PRATICA DELLA PERSPETTIVA / Barbaro, D – O-1000 1. 1569 – 9 – ne IDC [323]

Pratikto, Herman *see* GADJAH MADA

PRATIQUE ET PERCEPTION DE L'ESPACE DANS LA PIEVE DE MURIANI / Pesteil, P – 9 – F90.00 – fr Ethnologie [306]

PRATIQUES ET CROYANCES MEDICALES DES MALGACHES / Ramisiray, Gershon – Paris: A Maloine, 1901 – us Res Libr [306]

Prato, Stanislau *see*
- LA BEAUTE DES FEMMES
- L'ORMA DEL LEONE

Pratomo, R *see* THE AGENCY CONTRACT AND THE POWER OF ATTORNEY APPLIED TO BUSINESS IN INDONESIA

PRATSI NAUKOVO-PEDAGOGICHNOJI' KOMISIJI' – Vseukrajins'ka akademiia nauk. Kiew. 1929. BR-3437 2 – 8 – ne IDC [947]

PRATSYA PRACIA – Prudentopolis, Brazil. Dec 1948-Dec 1975.-w. 13 reels – 1 – uk British Libr Newspaper [072]

Pratt, Edwin A *see* LEADING POINTS IN SOUTH AFRICAN HISTORY, 1486 TO MARCH 30, 1900, ARRANGED CHRONOLOGICALLY, WITH DATE-INDEX

Pratt, Henry F A *see* THE GENEALOGY OF CREATION...FROM THE UNPOINTED HEBREW TEXT OF... GENESIS

Pratt, Hilton *see* FINANCIAL RECORDS

Pratt, J H *see* SONGS OF THE CHURCH

Pratt, John Gill *see* JOHN GILL PRATT PAPERS

Pratt, Samuel Wheeler *see*
- THE DEITY OF JESUS CHRIST ACCORDING TO THE GOSPEL OF ST JOHN
- THE LIFE AND EPISTLES OF SAINT PAUL

Pratt, Walter E *see* THE HOUSE OF EDWARD WINSLOW

PRATTICA DI MUSICA UTILE ET NECESSARIA SI AL COMPOSITORE PER COMPORRE I CANTI SUOI REGOLATAMENTE / Zacconi, L – 1596 – 9 – us Sibley [780]

PRATTICA DI MVSICA VTILE ET NECESSARIA SI ALCOMPOSITORE PER COMPORRE I CANTI SUO REGOLATAMENTE / Zacconi, L – Venetia. 1596. BP-777 1 – 9 – ne IDC [780]

PRATZI / Ukrayin'skyi Naukovyi Instytut – Warsaw. 1931-1939. v1-48 – 1 – us NY Public [500]

Praud de la Nicolliere-Teijeiro, Stephane *see*
- 32 DOC. MANUSCRITS INTERESSANT L'HISTOIRE BRETONNE, MICROFILMES ENSEMBLE
- JOYEULSE ADVENUE ET NOUVELLE ENTREE DES ROY ET ROYNE...EN CESTE VILLE DE NANTES (1518)

PRAVA I OBIAZANNOSTI CHLENA KREDITNOGO KOOPERATIVA / Kil'chevskii, V A – Ed.3. M., 1918 – 1mf – 9 – COR-385/1 – ne IDC [334]

O PRAVAKH INOSTRANTSEV V ROSSII DO VSTUPLENIIA IOANA 3 VASIL'EVICHA NA PRESTOL VELIKOGO KNIAZHESTVA MOSKOVSKAGO / Andreevskii, I – St. Petersburg, 1854. 142p BR-8544 1 – 9 – ne IDC [340]

PRAVDA – 1917-1994 – 1 – Sfr240.00 – sz Infoprint [947]

PRAVDA – 1993-1995 – 1 – F1,397.00 – sz Infoprint [072]

PRAVDA – (Backfile 1917-98 $85r) – Russia, 1999- – 2r per y – 1 – $160.00 standing order – us Ross [072]

PRAVDA – Banska Bystrica, Czechoslovakia. Sept-Oct 1944 – 1r – 1 – us L of C Photodup [072]

PRAVDA – Bratislava, Czechoslovakia. -d. Aug 1951-Dec 1970. 73 reels – 1 – uk British Libr Newspaper [072]

PRAVDA – Bratislava, Czechoslovakia. Jun 1945-1971; 1973-1991 – 111r – 1 – us L of C Photodup [072]

PRAVDA – Ezhemesiachnyi zhurnal iskusstva, literatury, obshchestvennoi zhizni. M. 1904-06. Lacking: 1906 (6-10). B-1838 2 – 8 – ne IDC [073]

PRAVDA – Moscow, RU – 1r – $50.00 – R04230 – us Library Micro [072]

PRAVDA – Moscow. U.S.S.R. 1961- – 1 – us UMI [072]

PRAVDA – Moscow, USSR. 1961-1979 – 56r – $2,800.00 – B63591 – us Library Micro [072]

PRAVDA – Moscow, U.S.S.R. -d. 1917-32. Imperfect. 29 1 2 reels – 1 – uk British Libr Newspaper [072]

PRAVDA – Moscow, USSR. Mar 1917-Jun 1938 – 45r – 1 – us L of C Photodup [072]

PRAVDA – Moskau, 1954-1993ff – 79r – 1 – DM11,850.00 – gw Mikro Press [072]

PRAVDA – New York: Pravda Pub Co, [dec 1917-nov 10 1922] (3r); [1923-51] (13r) – 1 – us Res Libr [071]

PRAVDA – Plzen, Czechoslovakia. Jun 1945-Oct 1948; 1953-1969 (scattered issues) – 20r – 1 – us L of C Photodup [072]

PRAVDA – St Petersburg/Moskva, 1917-38, 1941-47, 1951-53, 1960-89 – 1 – us Hoover Inst Photo [072]

PRAVDA : TSENTRALNYI ORGAN ROSSIISKOI SOTSIAL-DEMOKRATICHESKOI RABOCHEI PARTII – Petrograd: RS-DRP, 1917- ; jul 1938-jun 1991, 1992 – us Res Libr [072]

PRAVDA – Vienna, Austria. In Russian. -m. 5 Nov 1909-1 Aug 1910; 20 Nov 1910-23 April 1912. 11 ft – 1 – uk British Libr Newspaper [072]

PRAVDA OB II ULSKIKH DNI AKH : K PREDSTOI ASHCHEMU PROT SESSU INTERNATSIONALISTOV / Bezrabotnyi, I – Petrograd: "Pribo i", 1917 – 1 – CSUX88-B6975 – us Hoover Inst Photo [947]

PRAVDA UKRAINE – Kiev, USSR. Aug 1944-Dec 1952 – 17r – 1 – us L of C Photodup [943]

PRAVDA UKRAINY – (Backfile through 1998 $85r) – Ukraine, 1999- – 2r per y – 1 – $160.00 standing order – us Ross [072]

PRAVDA UKRAINY – Kiev. Ukraine. U.S.S.R. 1955- – 1 – us UMI [072]

PRAVDA VOSTOKA – Tashkent, USSR. Jan 1930-31 Dec 1954 – 43r – 1 – us L of C Photodup [072]

PRAVDA VOSTOKA – Tashkent. Uzbek. U.S.S.R. 1955- – 1 – us UMI [072]

PRAVILA PRIEMA I PROGRAMMY PRIEMNYKH EKZAMENOV DLI A POSTUPAI USHCHIKH V VYSSHIE UCHEBNYE ZAVEDENII A SSSR V...GODU : MINISTERSTVO VYSSHEGO OBRAZOVANII A SSSR – (Includes c.1: 1957) – Moskva: Sovetskai a nauka, 19uu – 1 – CSUXALJ6404-S – us Hoover Inst Photo [947]

PRAVILA PRIEMA I PROGRAMMY PRIEMNYKH EKZAMENOV DLI A POSTUPAI USHCHIKH V VYSSHIE UCHEBNYE ZAVEDENII A SSSR V...GODU : MINISTERSTVO VYSSHEGO OBRAZOVANII A SSSR – (Includes C.1: 1957) – Moskva: Sovetskai a nauka, 19uu – 1 – CSUXALJ6394-S – us Hoover Inst Photo [947]

PRAVILA SOSTAVLENIIA KATALOGOV, ALFAVITNAGO, SISTEMATICHESKAGO I PREDMETNAGO – Petrograd. 1915. BR-4650 2 – 8 – ne IDC [010]

PRAVITEL'STVENNYI VESTNIK – Petrograd. 1914 complete; scattered issues, 1915-1917 – 1 – 35.00r – us Hoover Inst Photo [072]

PRAVITEL'STVENNYI VIESTNIK – Leningrad, 1869-1917 – 72r – 1 – us Ross [072]

PRAVITEL'STVENNYI VIESTNIK – Leningrad, USSR. Jan 1901-Dec 1906 – 12r – 1 – us L of C Photodup [947]

PRAVITEL'STVENNYI VIESTNIK / Russia – St. Petersburg. v. 1-49. 1869-1917. (Wanting scattered numbers) – 1 – $1,639.00 – us L of C Photodup [324]

PRAVITELSTVENNYJ VESTNIK – Saint-Petersbourg. 1905-06 – 1 – fr A.C.R.P.P. [073]

PRAVITEL'STVO I OBSHCHESTVO V IKH OTNOSHENIIAKH / Firsov, N N – Kazan. 1902. BR-254 2 – 8 – ne IDC [320]

PRAVITESTVENNY VESTNIK – St Petersburg. 1869-1916. Not collated – 1 – us NY Public [073]

PRAVLENIE / Soiuz rabochikh poligraficheskogo proizvodstva S SS R Leningradskii gubernskii otdel – Kollektivn'ii dogovor i tarifnoe polo zhenie, Leningrad, 1928. 110 p. LL-4011 – 1 – us L of C Photodup [340]

PRAVLENIE GENERALA DENIKINA / Sokolov, K N – Sofia, 1921 – 1 – 35.00r – us Hoover Inst Photo [335]

PRAVLENIE SAKHAROTRESTA SSSR *see* BIULLETEN SAKHAROTRESTA

PRAVO – 1898-1917 – 1 – 334.00 – us L of C Photodup [947]

PRAVO – Cleveland. Ohio. 1912-1915 – 1 – us UMI [071]

PRAVO – Ezhenedel'naia iur dicheskaia gazeta. Spb. 1898-1917. Lacking: 1898 (1-52); 1905 (1-52); 1913 (1-26); 1917 (40-52). BR-4160 2 – 8 – ne IDC [072]

PRAVO : EZHENEDEL'NAIA IURIDICHESKAIA GAZETA – (Systematic index 1898-1909. Spb., 1910) – Spb., 1898-1917 – 906mf – 9 – R-4160/1 – ne IDC [072]

PRAVO – (jan 1 1991-98 6r per y $510y) – Czech Republic, 1999- – 6r per y – 1 – $480.00 standing order – us Ross [072]

PRAVO I GOSUDARSTVO V IKH OBOIUDNYKH OTNOSHENIIAKH / Khlebnikov, N I – Warsaw, 1874. 494p. Relationships between law and the state as expounded by various schools of philosophy. BR-8608- – 9 – ne IDC [340]

PRAVO I MIR V MEZHDUNARODNYKH OTNOSHENIIAKH / Kamarovskii, L A & Bogaevskii, P M – Moscow, 1899. 11, 545p. Collected essays on various aspects of state independence, peaceful settlement of disputes, and international organization; dedicated to the Institute of International Law. BR-9153/1 – 9 – ne IDC [320]

PRAVO I ZHIZN' – 1922-28 – 1 – 40.00 – us L of C Photodup [947]

PRAVO KNIGI / Grinevskaia, I – Spb. 1907. BR-4616 2 – 8 – ne IDC [010]

PRAVO LIDU – Prague, Czechoslovakia. Jul 1945-May 1947 – 6r – 1 – uk British Libr Newspaper [072]

PRAVO LIDU – (Some issues missing) – Prague, Czechoslovakia. 30 Dec 1924; Nov 1937-Aug 1938; May 1945-Jun 1948 – 5r – 1 – us L of C Photodup [072]

PRAVO ZENY – v1, no.1-6. 1910 – 1 – us I.U. Libraries [073]

PRAVOE DELO – Zhurnal posviashchennyi istorii Bakinskago rabochego dvizheniia. v. 1-3. Spb. 1907-08. BR-2340 2 – 8 – ne IDC [947]

PRAVOSLAVNAIA BOGOSLOVSKAIA ENTSIKLOPEDIIA – Pg., 1900-1911. v1-12 – 113mf – 9 – R-10538/1 – ne IDC [290]

PRAVOSLAVNOE OBOZRENIE – M. 1860-91. Lacking: (5) 1873. BR-4159 2 – 8 – ne IDC [073]

PRAVOSLAVNYI AMERIKANSKII VIESTNIK – New York, NY, Sep. 1896-Sep. 1897 – 1r – 1 – us I.H.R.C. [978]

PRAVOSLAVNYI SOBESEDNIK, IZDAVAEMYI PRI KAZANSKOI DUCHOVNOI AKADEMII – Kazan'. 1855-1917. Tables. 1855-91. Lacking: 1864 (2, 3, 9, 11, 12); 1865 (4, 6, 8); 1879 (2, 8); 1880 (6, 12); 1881 (12); 1882 (11); 1883 (4); 1884-91; 1894; 1895; 1896 (6, 11); 1897-1900; 1901 (3, 6); 1902 (1); 1906 (11); 1910 (6); 1912 (1-2). BR-8347 2 – 8 – ne IDC [073]

PRAVOSLAVNYI SOBESEDNIK – 1876-1909 (complete) – 8r – 1 – ATLA S0193E – us A.T.L.A. [073]

PRAVOVAIA ORGANIZATSIIA SOVETSKOI KOOPERATSII : PO ISTOCHNIKAM SSSR I RSFSR / Ozeretskovskii, N E – M., 1927 – 3mf – 9 – COR-730/1 – ne IDC [334]

PRAVOVOE POLOZHENIE IUNOSHESKOGO TRUDA V SSSR / Grishin, Zin – Moskva: Gos. izd vo Voprosy truda "Gostrudizdat", 1929 – 1 – CSUX89-B1663 – us Hoover Inst Photo [360]

PRAVOVOE POLOZHENIE PROFESSIONALNYKH SOIUZOV SSSR : OCHERKI PROFSOIUZNOGO PRAVA / Dogadov, Vasilii Mikhailovich – Moskva: Gos. izd-vo, 1928 – 1 – CSUX89-B7317 – us Hoover Inst Photo [947]

PRAVOVOI SPRAVOCHNIK DLIA RABOTNIKOV POTREBITEL'SKOI KOOPERATSII / Povolotskii, Ll – Ed 2. M., 1927 – 3mf – 9 – COR-302/1 – ne IDC [334]

PRAVOVYE FORMY MONOPOLII VNESHNEI TORGOVLI SSSR V IKH ISTORICHESKOM RAZVITII / Kaliuzhnaia, G P – Moscow, 1951. 149p. History of the state monopoly of foreign trade in the USSR. BR-9116/1 – 9 – ne IDC [947]

PRAVOVYE OSNOVY KHOZIAISTVENNOGO STROIA SSSR / Kantorovich, Ia. A – Leningrad, 1925.231p. Basic outline of the legal bases of the Soviet economic system in the mid-NEP period.Subject index.BR-9404/1 – 9 – ne IDC [340]

PRAVOVYE OSNOVY PROMYSLOVOINOGO KONTROLIA / D"iakov, FB – Tiflis, 1926 – 2mf – 9 – COR-294/1 – ne IDC [334]

PRAWDA – 1954-1994 – 2 times per yr – 1 – DM140.00 – sz Infoprint [072]

PRAWDA – London, UK. 1 Oct 1917-1 Jun 1918 – 1 – uk British Libr Newspaper [072]

PRAWDA – London, UK. 24 Sept-13 Dec 1873 – 1 – uk British Libr Newspaper [072]

PRAWDA – Warsaw. 1893-1895; 1904-1908. Not collated – 1 – us NY Public [073]

PRAWDA – Warsaw, 1893-95; 1904-07 – 2r – 1 – us Ross [072]

Prawer, J *see* LE-VIKKORET IGGAROT YERUSHALMIYYOT MIN HA-MEAH HA-15 VE-HA-16

Prawirangara, R I *see* OEBAR KAMPOENG. TJITAKAN 1

Prawirasumantri, Kosasih *see* DIRECTORY OF SPECIAL LIBRARIES IN INDONESIA, INCLUDING PROVINCIAL LIBRARIES

PRAWO NARODOW 1927 / Ehrlich, L – Lwow, 1927 – 7mf – 1 – ILM-1764/1 – ne IDC [327]

PRAXIS – v37-68. 1948-79 – 1,5,6 – us Princeton Micro [073]

PRAXIS CRIMINALIS CIVILIS Y CANONICA / Gutierrez, Juan – 1730. Liber XIV – 9 – 1.50f – sp Bibl Santa Ana [240]

PRAXIS DER PSYCHOTHERAPIE UND PSYCHOSOMATIK – v.1-4; 6-12; 16-19; 20-26. 1956-81 – 1,5,6,9,13 – 52.00v – us UMI [616]

PRAXIS DES NEUSPRACHLICHEN UNTERRICHTS – 1953- 1; 1976- 5,6,9 – us UMI [370]

PRAXIS FRANCISCI CLERKE, TAM JUS DICENTIBUS QUAM ALIIS OMNIBUS QUI IN FORO ECCLESIASTICO VERSANTUR APPRIME UTILIS / Clerke, Francis – Londini: Sawbridge, 1684. 428p. LL-2349 – 1 – us L of C Photodup [340]

PRAXIS GRAMMATICA / Harmar, John – 1623. 68p. (English Linguistics Series 1500-1800) – 9 – us UMI [400]

PRAXIS IN MANUSCRIPTS OF THE GREEK TESTAMENT / Sitterly, Charles Fremont – New York: Eaton & Mains, 1898. 1 fiche – 9 – us A.T.L.A. [240]

PRAXIS INTERNATIONAL – v1-. 1981- – 1,5,6,9 – us UMI [616]

PRAXIS, THEORIE... / Bulmerincq, A von – Leipzig, 1874 – 3mf – 1 – ILM-140/1 – ne IDC [327]

Pray, G *see* HISTORIA CONTROVERSIARUM DE RITIBUS SINICIS

Pray, Lewis G *see* THE HISTORY OF SUNDAY SCHOOLS AND OF RELIGIOUS EDUCATION FROM THE EARLIEST TIMES

PRAYER AND ITS ANSWER : ILLUSTRATED IN THE FIRST TWENTY-FIVE YEARS OF THE FULTON STREET PRAYER MEETING / Prime, Samuel Irenaeus – New York: Scribner, 1882 – 1mf – us A.T.L.A. [240]

PRAYER AS A THEORY AND A FACT / Faunce, Daniel Webster – 1890 – 9 – us A.T.L.A. [240]

A PRAYER FOR GUIDANCE / Clarke, Bella – Toronto: Toronto Willard Tract Depository, 1888. 00665. (Pre-1900 Canadiana) – 9 – cn C.I.H.M. [240]

PRAYER MANUAL FOR THE INDONESIAN MISSION / Christian and Missionary Alliance – SE-5224 1. 1955 – 9 – ne IDC [240]

THE PRAYER MEETING HYMN BOOK / Weishampel, John F, Jr – 1858 – 1 – $9.17 – us Baptist [780]

PRAYER-MEETING THEOLOGY : A DIALOGUE / Morris, Ebenezer Joseph – New York: G P Putnam, 1892 – 1mf – 9 – 0-8370-4034-5 – 1985-2034 – us A.T.L.A. [240]

PRAYERS AND INSTRUCTIONS, WITH FORMS / Thomas, Armstrong – Baltimore, Lord Baltimore, 1908. 539 p. LL-1167 – 1 – us L of C Photodup [340]

PRAYERS FOR THE DAILY TASK (CCC226) : A COLLECTION OF PRAYERS FOR WOMEN / Liu, Mary – (In Chinese) – 1st ed. Hong Kong: Council on Christian Literature for Overseas Chinese, 1955 – 1r – 1 – 1984-B500 – us A.T.L.A. [240]

PRAYING AND WORKING : BEING SOME ACCOUNT OF WHAT MEN CAN DO WHEN IN EARNEST / Stevenson, William Fleming – New York: Thomas Whittaker, [1892?] – 1mf – 9 – 0-8370-6780-4 – 1986-0780 – us A.T.L.A. [240]

PRAZHSKIE NOVOSTI – v3-5, 1948-50 – 1 – us I.U. Libraries [073]

PRAZSKE LIDOVE NOVINY – Prague, Czechoslovakia. 27 Sept-2 Oct 1938 – 1r – 1 – us L of C Photodup [072]

PRAZSKE NOVINY – Prague, Czechoslovakia. Oct 1932-1938 – 12r – 1 – us L of C Photodup [072]

PRE- AND POST-KNOWLEDGE OF RESULTS INTERVALS AND MOTOR PERFORMANCE OF MENTALLY RETARDED INDIVIDUALS / Yun, Chi-Hong – 1989 – 69p 1mf – 9 – $4.00 – us Microform Publ [150]

PRE-1900 ANNUALS COLLECTION – 16,595mf – 9 – cn C.I.H.M. [020]

PRE-1900 CANADIANA – (53,000 monographs and pamphlets of primary research material printed prior to 1900. Cataloging available. Individual subject segments available: History and Geography $74,355; Native American Studies $6450; Sociology, Psychology and Anthropology $9375; Economics $22,355; Religion and Phlosophy $43,660; Science, Technology, Agriculture and Medicine $31,010; Canadian-English Literature and Language $7105; French-Canadian Literature and Language $2285; Political Science $16,590; Law $12,500; Education $7975; Music and Fine Arts $5510; Literature, General Works, and Bibliography $27,285) – 76,083mf – 9 – $218,493.00 complete – us UMI [971]

PRE-1900 PERIODICALS COLLECTION – (Units 1 to 7 (completed) 42,850 issues; Units 8 and 9 (completed in 1993) ca. 6,000 issues each) – 9 – cn C.I.H.M. [073]

PRE-1949 KUOMINTANG PARTY ORGANS AND NATIONALIST CHINESE GOVERNMENT GAZETTES – (In Chinese) – 7r – 1 – $245.00 in US $40.00r outside US – L9300043 – Dist. us Scholarly Res – us L of C Photodup [320]

THE PREACHER, OR METHODE OF PREACHING / Hemmingsen, Neils – 1574. 156p. (English Linguistics Series 1500-1800) – 9 – us UMI [420]

THE PREACHER, OR THE ART AND METHOD OF PREACHING / Chappell, William – 1656. 233p. (English Linguistics Series 1500-1800) – 9 – us UMI [420]

A PREACHER'S AND A BANKER'S VIEWS ON IMPORTANT SUBJECTS / Weaver, Joseph Myrtle – Louisville, KY: Baptist Book Concern, 1906 – 1mf – 9 – 0-8370-5712-4 – 1985-3712 – us A.T.L.A. [240]

A PREACHER'S BOOK OF RELIGIOUS EDUCATION (CCC182) = TSUNG CHIAO CHIAO YU TS'UNG SHU / Hsieh, Sung-kao – (In Chinese) – [s.l: s.n, 1924] – 1r – 1 – 1984-B500 – us A.T.L.A. [240]

PREACHERS DESCRIBED AND THE PEOPLE ADVISED / Manners, N – [Hull, 1788] – 1mf – 9 – MP-556/1 – ne IDC [240]

PREACHER'S MAGAZINE = TAO SHENG – (In Chinese) – 1931-35 (complete) – 1r – 1 – ATLA S0314 – us A.T.L.A. [073]

THE PREACHERS OF SCOTLAND : FROM THE SIXTH TO THE NINETEENTH CENTURY : TWELFTH SERIES OF THE CUNNINGHAM LECTURES / Blaikie, William Garden – Edinburgh: T.& T. Clark, 1888 – 1mf – us A.T.L.A. [240]

PREACHER'S PILGRIMAGE: A STUDY OF THE BOOK OF ECCLESIASTES / Cooke, John Hunt – London: Elliot Stock, 1887. 1 fiche – 9 – us A.T.L.A. [240]

PREACHING HELPS – v1-13. 1974-86 (complete) – 1r – 1 – ATLA S0857 – us A.T.L.A. [073]

PREACHING TO THE TIMES : IN ST. MARGARET'S WESTMINISTER, DURING THE CORONATION YEAR / Henson, H Hensley – London: J. Clarke, 1902 – 1mf – us A.T.L.A. [240]

THE PRE-ARGUMENT CONFERENCE PROGRAM IN THE SIXTH CIRCUIT COURT OF APPEALS / Eaglin, James B – Washington: FJC, 1990 – 1mf – 9 – $1.50 – LLMC 95-366 – us L.L.M.C. [340]

Prebendado de la Catedral, un sudonimo de Eugenio Escobar Prieto *see* COMPRENDIO HISTORIAL DE CORIA PARA USO DEL COLEGIO DE NINAS DEL SAGRADO CORAZON DE DICHA CIUDAD ESCRITO POR...

Preble, William Pitt *see*
– PATENT CASE INDEX.
– PREBLE'S PATENT CASE INDEX

PREBLE'S PATENT CASE INDEX / Preble, William Pitt – (Covers state and federal reports: the Patent Office Gazette, and Robb's Patent Cases) – 1st ed. Boston: Little-Brown, 1880 (all publ) – 4mf – 9 – $6.00 – LLMC 84-335 – us L.L.M.C. [340]

PRECAMBRIAN RESEARCH – v1-26. 1974-84 – 1,5,6,13 – sz Elsevier [560]

PRECEDENTS AND FORMS OF INDICTMENTS, INFORMATIONS, COMPLAINTS. / Pagan, Oliver Elwood – Chicago: Callaghan, 1894. 570p. LL-1185 – 1 – us L of C Photodup [340]

PRECEDENTS IN CONVEYANCING, WITH DISSERTATIONS ON ITS LAW AND PRACTICE / Prideaux, Frederick – 12th ed. London: Stevens, 1883. 2v. LL-124 – 1 – us L of C Photodup [340]

PRECEDENTS OF EQUITY PLEADINGS / Heard, Franklin Fiske – Boston: Little, Brown, 1884. 247p. LL-467 – 1 – us L of C Photodup [340]

LES PRECEPTEURS / Fabre, Philippe d'Eglantine – (French Theatre Series). Paris. Impr. de la Republique, an VIII. 1799 – 9 – fr Hachette [820]

PRECEPTIVA LITERARIA / Sanchez Castanar, Eduardo – 1895 – 9 – 1.50f – sp Bibl Santa Ana [410]

PRECEPTOS MILITARES, ORDEN Y FORMACION DE ESQUADRONES / Perez de Egea, M – Madrid, 1632 – 6mf – 9 – sp Cultura [355]

PRECES – Caceres: Edit. Extremadura, 1975 – 1 – sp Bibl Santa Ana [946]

THE PRECINCT OF RELIGION IN THE CULTURE OF HUMANITY / Shaw, Charles Gray – London: Swan Sonnenschein, 1908.1 fiche – 9 – us A.T.L.A. [240]

PRECINCT REPORTER – San Bernardino, CA. 1965- – 28+ r – 1 – $1,400.00 ($180.00y) – R02767 – us Library Micro [071]

PRECIOS Y SALARIOS EN BADAJOZ DURANTE EL BIENIO 1775-76 / Guerra Guerra, Arcadio – Badajoz: Dip. Provincial, 1976. Sep. REE – 1 – sp Bibl Santa Ana [946]

PRECIOUS SONGS : AND SONGS OF DEVOTION FOR CHRISTIAN ASSOCIATIONS / Stockton, Kirkpatrick & Stockton, Doane – 1 – 11.41 – us Baptist [240]

PRECIOUS STONES FOR ZION'S WALLS: A RECORD OF PERSONAL EXPERIENCE IN THINGS CONNECTED WITH THE KINGDOM OF GOD ON EARTH / Bentley, Eliza – Introd. by Wesley F. Campbell. Toronto, W. Briggs, 1897. 03573. (Pre-1900 Canadiana) – 9 – cn C.I.H.M. [240]

PRECIOUS STONES OF THE BIBLE...A TREATISE ON THE BREASTPLATE OF THE HIGH PRIEST / Clapton, Edward – London: Simkin, Marshall, 1899. 1 fiche – 9 – us A.T.L.A. [240]

THE PRECIOUS THINGS OF ST PETER / Rogers, Ebenezer Platt – New York: A.D.F. Randolph, 1874.1 fiche – 9 – us A.T.L.A. [240]

PRECIOUS WATERS : PHOTOGRAPHS BY DOMINIQUE ROGER – (English, French and Spanish) – 1981 – 9 – 92-3-001963-1 – fr UNESCO [770]

THE PRECIPICE / Goncharov, Ivan – Translated...by M. Bryant. New York, 1916 – 1 – us Res Libr [460]

PRECIS DE DROIT ANNAMITE ET DE JURISPRUDENCE EN MATIERE INDIGENE / Miraben, A – Paris: Plon, Nourrit, 1896. 351p. LL-10012 – 1 – us L of C Photodup [340]

PRECIS DE LA LANGUE MALTAISE / Mizzi, L – 9 – F60.00 – fr Ethnologie [440]

PRECIS DE L'ART ARABE / Bourgoin, J – 1800 – 1 – uk Microform Academic [700]

PRECIS DE L'ART DE LA GUERRE, OU NOUVEAU TABLEAU ANALYTIQUE DES PRINCIPALES COMBINAISONS DE LA STRATEGIE / Jomini, A H de – Paris. Anselin. 1838. v.1, 415p. maps; v.2. 342. 32p., maps. (Strategy of War Series) – 9 – fr Hachette [355]

PRECIS DE MANUEL OPERATOIRE. / Farabeuf, Louis Hubert – Paris: G. Masson, 1872-81. 2v. 9 fiches. (Statistics Series: Medical Studies) – 9 – 22.00 – fr Bibl Nationale [310]

PRECIS DE MEDICINE VETENNAIRE: A L'USAGE DES CULTIVATEURS / Couture, Joseph Alphonse – s.l.: s.n., 1895, c1896 (Quebec: Erousseau). 00263. (Pre-1900 Canadiana) – 9 – cn C.I.H.M. [971]

PRECIS DE PHILOSOPHIE SCIENTIFIQUE ET DE PHILOSOPHIE MORALE / Sortais, Gaston – (Includes bibliographies and index) – Paris: P Lethielleux, [1904?] – 2mf – 9 – 0-8370-6389-2 – 1986-0389 – us A.T.L.A. [100]

PRECIS DES LECONS D'ARCHITECTURE DONNEA1ES A L'ECOLE POLYTECHNIQUE / Durand, Jean Nicolas Louis – Paris, 1802-05. 2v. in 4 fol., pl. (Architecture Series) – 9 – fr Hachette [720]

PRECIS DU DROIT DES GENS... / Funck-Brentano, Th & Sorel, A – Paris, 1900 – 6mf – 1 – ILM-176/1 – ne IDC [327]

PRECIS DU MOUVEMENT CATHOLIQUE-LIBERAL DANS LE JURA BERNOIS, 1873-74 / Deramey, J-P – Delemont: J Boechat, 1875 – 1mf – 9 – 0-8370-8335-4 – 1986-2335 – us A.T.L.A. [240]

PRECIS D'UN CODE DU DROIT INTERNATIONAL / Domin-Petrushevecz, A de – Leipzig, 1861 – 2mf – 1 – ILM-1698/1 – ne IDC [327]

PRECIS D'UN VOYAGE AU CAP DE BONNE-ESPERANCE / Delalande, P – Paris, A. Belin. 1822 – 9 – 5.00 – fr Orientalistes [910]

PRECIS ELEMENTAIRE DE DROIT COMMERCIAL. / Cator, Leonce – Paris: Foucher 1947. 104p. LL-4092 – 1 – us L of C Photodup [340]

PRECIS HISTORIQUE... / Cussy, F de Cornot – Leipzig, 1859 – 5mf – 1 – ILM-159/1 – ne IDC [327]

PRECIS HISTORIQUE DE LA TRAITE DES NOIRS ET DE L'ESCLAVAGE COLONIAL, CONTENANT L'ORIGINE DE LA TRAITE, SES PROGRES, SON ETAT ACTUEL ET UN EXPOSE DES HORREURS PRODUITES PAR LE DESPOTISME DES COLONS / Morenas, Joseph-Elzear – (Slave Trade and Abolitionism in France series). 1828 – 9 – fr Hachette [305]

PRECIS HISTORIQUE DE LA TRAITE DES NOIRS ET DE L'ESCLAVAGE COLONIAL, CONTENANT L'ORIGINE DE LA TRAITE, SES PROGRES, SON ETAT ACTUEL, ET UN EXPOSE DES HORREURS PRODUITES PAR LE DESPOTISME DES COLONS / Morenas, Joseph-Elzear – (African Library). Paris. L'Auteur. 1828 – 9 – fr Hachette [960]

PRECIS HISTORIQUE ET STATISTIQUE DU DEPARTEMENT DE LA LOIRE (FOREST) / Du Lac de La Tour d'Aurec, Hector – 1807 – 9 – fr Hachette [944]

PRECIS HISTORIQUE, OU, ABREGE DE L'HISTOIRE DU CANADA: AVEC APERCU SUR LES PRINCIPAUX PERSONNAGES DU PAYS – Montreal: E. Senecal, 1867. 00263. (Pre-1900 Canadiana) – 9 – cn C.I.H.M. [971]

PRECIS OF INFORMATION CONCERNING THE COLONY OF THE GOLD COAST AND ASHANTI / Climo, V C – (Filmed with: Precis of the Ashanti Expedition, 1895-96; Military Report on the Gold Coast, Ashanti and the Northern Territories, and Route Book of the Gold Coast Colony, Ashanti and the Northern Territories) – [London: s.n.], 1904 – us Res Libr [960]

PRECIS OF THE ASHANTI EXPEDITION, 1895-1896 / Reade, R N R – (Filmed with: Great Britain War Office: Precis of Information Concerning the Colony of the Gold Coast and Ashanti) – London: Harrison, 1897 – us Res Libr [960]

PRECIS TOUCHANT LA COLONIE DU LORD SELKIRK SUR LA RIVIERE ROUGE / Halkett, John – Montreal: James Lane, 1818. SEM35P77 – 1r – 1 – Can$15.00 – cn Bibl Nat [971]

PRECISION MACHINERY INCORPORATING LIFE SUPPORT TECHNOLOGY : AN INTERNATIONAL JOURNAL OF SYSTEMICS / ed by Funakubo, Hiroyasu – 1,5,9 – us Gordon [621]

PRE-COLUMBIAN ART / Dumbarton Oaks Collection; ed by Benson, Elizabeth P – (16p accompanying text) – 1976 – 1 color mf – 15 – $30.00f – 0-226-68981-6 – us Chicago [730]

PRE-COLUMBIAN PEOPLES OF NORTH AMERICA – 1995 – 36p – 9 – 92-3-102694-1 – fr UNESCO [970]

Preconcise l'independance du Canada *see* L'AMI DU PEUPLE

PRE-CONFEDERATION STATUTES, 1774-1871 / Canada – (Subsets available by province) – 5 – cn Micromedia [971]

PRECOTT JOURNAL – 1866-1986 – cn Commonwealth Micro [073]

LES PRECURSEURS DE LA REFORME ET DE LA LIBERTE DE CONSCIENCE DANS LES PAYS LATINS DU XIIE AU XVE SIECLE / Bonet-Maury, Gaston – Paris: Fischbacher, 1904 – 1mf – us A.T.L.A. [944]

O PRECURSOR FEDERAL – '(s.l.')-Bahia, Brazil. 14 Apr-5 May 1832 – 1,5,6 – bl Biblioteca [072]

LOS PRECURSORES DEL CONGRESO EUCARISTICO DE BUENOS AIRES. LA DEVOCION AL SANTISIMO DE LOS CONQUISTADORES Y POBLADORES DE AMERICA / Bayle, Constantino – Madrid: Razon y Fe, 1934 – 1 – sp Bibl Santa Ana [240]

LOS PRECURSORES IDEOLOGICOS DE LA GUERRA DE LA INDEPENDENCIA 1789-1794 / Bayle, Constantino – Mexico, 1929; Madrid: Razon y Fe, 1932 – 1 – sp Bibl Santa Ana [320]

Preczang, Ernst *see* ROETE DICH JUNGER TAG

PREDATOR-PREY RELATIONSHIPS, POPULATION DYNAMICS AND FISHERIES PRODUCTIVITIES OF LARGE AFRICAN LAKES – 1988 – 157p – it F.A.O. [639]

LES PREDECESSEURS DE DANIEL: RECHERCHES SUR LA TRACE DE FAITS ET D'IDEES / Dujardin, Edouard – Paris: Librairie Fischbacher, 1908. 1 fiche – 9 – us A.T.L.A. [270]

PREDECESSORS TO THE CONGRESSIONAL RECORD ON MICROFICHE / U.S. Congress – (Provides access to historical congressional debate. Available separately as: The Annals of Congress 1789-1824 $850.00. The Register of Debates in Congress 1824-37 $720.00. The Congressional Globe 1833-73 $2,250.00) – 1st-42nd Congresses. 1789-1873 – 9 – $3,245.00 set – us CIS [324]

PREDESTINATION AND FREEWILL AND THE WESTMINSTER CONFESSION OF FAITH : WITH EXPLANATION OF ROMANS 9. / Forbes, John – (Includes bibliographical references) – Edinburgh: T & T Clark, 1878 – 1mf – 9 – 0-8370-4968-7 – 1985-2968 – us A.T.L.A. [210]

PREDESTINATION CONSISTENT, PRESBYTERIAN CHURCH *see* THEOLOGICAL MISCELLANY 1

LA PREDICACION SAGRADA SEGUN LOS DOCUMENTOS PONTIFICIOS Y DOCTRINA DE LOS SANTOS PADRES / Bayle, Constantino – Barcelona: Tip. Catolica, Casals, s.a. 2nd ed – 1 – sp Bibl Santa Ana [240]

UN PREDICATEUR DE LA COUR DE POLOGNE SOUS SIGISMOND 3, PIERRE SKARGA (1536-1612) / Berga, A – Paris. 1916. BR-5466 2 – 8 – ne IDC [240]

PREDICTING BLOOD PRESSURE FROM ACTIVITY, FITNESS, AND BODY COMPOSITION OF BORDERLINE HYPERTENSIVE INDIVIDUALS / Brown, DE – 1991 – 1mf – 9 – $4.00 – us Microform Publ [613]

PREDICTING BODY COMPOSITION OF HEALTHY FEMALES BY B-MODE ULTRASOUND : COMPARISON WITH ANTHROPOMETRY AND BIOELECTRICAL IMPEDANCE / Garzarella, L – 1991 – 2mf – 9 – $8.00 – us Microform Publ [790]

PREDICTING ECOLOGY AND FISH YIELDS IN AFRICAN RESERVOIRS FROM PREIMPOUNDMENT PHYSICO-CHEMICAL DATA – 1984 – 42p – it F.A.O. [639]

PREDICTING EFFECTS OF POWER PLANT ONCE-THROUGH COOLING ON AQUATIC SYSTEMS : A STATE-OF-THE-ART REPORT... / ed by Majewski, W & Miller, D C – 1979 – 171p – 9 – 92-3-101704-7 – fr UNESCO [621]

PREDICTING MUSCLE FIBER TYPE THROUGH SELF-REPORTING / Foran, Joseph F – 1993 – 1mf – $4.00 – us Microform Publ [612]

PREDICTING SUCCESSFUL ADJUSTMENT TO DISENGAGEMENT FROM COLLEGIATE ATHLETICS / Cramer-Hamman, Buffy – 1994 – 1mf – $4.00 – us Microform Publ [150]

PREDICTION OF FAT FREE MASS IN AFRICAN AMERICAN WOMEN / Mussulman, Laura M – University of North Carolina at Chapel Hill, 1995 – 2mf – 9 – $8.00 – PE3614 – us Microform Publ [612]

PREDICTION OF INJURY IN HIGH SCHOOL VOLLEYBALL PLAYERS WITH PERCEIVED LEADERSHIP BEHAVIOR OF THE COACH / Ernst, Stacey L & Redmond, Charles J – 1993 – 1mf – $4.00 – us Microform Publ [150]

PREDICTION OF ONE REPETITION MAXIMUM BENCH PRESS FROM PUSH-UPS IN ACTIVE YOUNG MALES / Xi, Jianwei – 1993 – 1mf – $4.00 – us Microform Publ [612]

PREDICTION OF RUNNING PERFORMANCE FROM SELECTED VARIABLES MEASURED DURING BICYCLE ERGOMETRY / Seljevold, Peter J – 1989 – 95p 1mf – 9 – $4.00 – us Microform Publ [612]

PREDICTION OF THE PHYSICAL ABILITY REQUIREMENT EVALUATION (PARE) SCORES USING STANDARD MEASURES OF PHYSICAL FITNESS / Stanish, Heidi I – Dalhousie University, 1994 – 2mf – 9 – $8.00 – PH1479 – us Microform Publ [611]

PREDICTION OF THE WORLD MEN'S BEST PERFORMANCES IN HIGH JUMP AND LONG JUMB BY THE TOP AVERAGE PERFORMANCE / Fang, J – 1991 – 2mf – 9 – $8.00 – us Microform Publ [790]

PREDICTION OF TRIATHLON PERFORMANCE FROM VENTILATORY THRESHOLD MEASUREMENTS / Langill, Robert H & Rhodes, E C – 1993 – 1mf – 9 – $4.00 – us Microform Publ [617]

PREDICTIVE FISH YIELD MODEL FOR LAKES AND RESERVOIRS OF THE PHILIPPINES, SRI LANKA AND THAILAND – 1991 – 47p – it F.A.O. [639]

PREDICTORS OF OVERALL JOB SATISFACTION AMONG PUBLIC SCHOOL PHYSICAL EDUCATORS / Davis, Frederick W – 1981 – 2mf – 9 – $8.00 – us Microform Publ [790]

PREDICTORS OF RESPONSIBLE ENVIRONMENTAL BEHAVIOR AMONG BOATERS ON THE CHESAPEAKE BAY : AN EXPLORATORY ANALYSIS / Cottrell, Stuart P – 1993 – 2mf – $8.00 – us Microform Publ [150]

PREDICTORS OF SUCCESS ON THE HUMAN ANATOMY-RELATED PORTIONS OF THE NATIONAL ATHLETIC TRAINERS' ASSOCIATION CERTIFICATION EXAMINATION / Huntington, Mark W – 1994 – 2mf – $8.00 – us Microform Publ [370]

PREDICTORS OF SUCCESS ON THE NATIONAL ATHLETIC TRAINERS ASSOCIATION CERTIFICATION EXAMINATION / Harrelson, Gary L & Larson, Bill – 1992 – 1mf – 9 – $4.00 – us Microform Publ [790]

PREDICTORS OF UPHILL RIDING PERFORMANCE IN TRAINED CYCLISTS / Rollings, Anne T – University of Wisconsin-La Crosse, 1995 – 1mf – 9 – $4.00 – PH1473 – us Microform Publ [611]

PREDIG (EIN CHRISTLICH) WIDER DIE VNCHRISTLICHEN EMPOERUNG VNND VNGEHORSAM, ETLICHER VNTERTHANEN – 1538. BME-131 1 – 9 – ne IDC [240]
EIN PREDIG VON DEM WIDERTAUFF. SAMPT ANGEHENCKTER HISTORIEN, WELCHER GESTALT SICH DIE WIDERTAEUFFER / Osiander, Lucas – Tuebingen, A. Hock. 1582. BME-163 1 – 9 – ne IDC [240]
DIE PREDIGEN SO VONN DEN FROEMBDEN PREDICANTEN / Schmid, C – Zureich, Chr. Froschouer. 1528. BME-92 1 – 9 – ne IDC [240]
DER "PREDIGER SALMONIS" IN HISTORISCHER BELEUCHTUNG / Leimdoerfer, David – 1892 – 1 – us A.T.L.A. [240]
PREDIGER UND HOHESLIED / Siegfried, Carl – Goettingen: Vandenhoeck, 1898. 126p. 1 fiche – 9 – us A.T.L.A. [240]
PREDIGT BEI DER FUENFTEN HAUPT-VERSAMMLUNG DES VEREINS FUER REFORMATIONSGESCHICHTE : IN DER BARFUESSER-KIRCHE ZU ERFURT AM 13. APRIL 1898 / Loofs, Friedrich – Halle: In Commissionsverlag von Max Niemeyer, 1898 – 1mf – us A.T.L.A. [240]
DIE PREDIGT JESU VOM REICHE GOTTES / Weiss, Johannes – (Includes bibliographical references and index) – 2., voellig neubearb Aufl. Goettingen: Vandenhoeck & Ruprecht, 1900 – 1mf – 9 – 0-8370-6455-4 – 1986-0455 – us A.T.L.A. [220]
DIE PREDIGT UND DAS BRIEFFRAGMENT DES ARISTIDES (T.U.U. 1-12/2B) / Pape, P – Leipzig, 1894 – 1mf – 9 – ne Slangenburg [240]
PREDIGTEN / Tauler, Johannes; ed by Hofmann, Georg – Freiburg, 1961 – 11mf – 8 – ne Slangenburg [290]
DIE PREDIGTEN TAULERS / Vetter, Ferdinand – Berlin, 1910 – 11mf – 8 – ne Slangenburg [290]
PREDISPOSING, REINFORCING, AND ENABLING FACTORS IDENTIFIED BY DIVISION 1 COACHES OF WOMEN'S CROSS-COUNTRY TEAMS AND THE RELATIONSHIP TO THE PERCEIVED ONSET OF EATING DISORDERS / Ross, Carolyn K – Purdue University, 1995 – 1mf – 9 – $4.00 – PSY1861 – us Microform Publ [150]
PREDSTAVITELI PECHATI V KOMMISII / Voronich, K I – Spb. 1880. BR-10,097 1 – 9 – ne IDC [947]
PREDUVEDOMLENIE / U.S.S.R. Komitet Flotskoi Biblioteki.. – Katalog Russkich knig, sochinitelei perevodchikov i izdatelei po azbuchnomu i sistematicheskomu poriadku. Spb. 1840. BR-4524 2 – 8 – ne IDC [070]
PREDVARITELNYE DANNYE [PO] TEKUSHCHE I PROMYSHLENNO I STATISTIKE ZA... : STATISTICHESKI I OTDEL SOVETA NARODNOGO KHOZI A ISTVA SEVERNOGO RA IONA – (Includes c.1: 1918:Aug., Sept.) – Petrograd: Sovet, 1918 – 1 – CSUXAKZ0484-S – us Hoover Inst Photo [947]
PREDVARITEL'NYE ITOGI VSEROSSIISKOI SEL'SKOKHOZIASTVENNOI PEREPISI 1916 G – Evrepeiskaia Rossiia. v. 1. Petrograd. 1916. BR-264 2 – 8 – ne IDC [947]
PREDVARITEL'NYIA IURIDICHESKIIA SVEDENIIA DLIA POLNAGO OB IASNENIIA RUSSKOI PRAVDY / Kalachov, N V – 2nd ed. Saint Petersburg, 1880.277p. v1. A comparison of the various texts of Russkaia Pravda. BR-9089/1 – 9 – ne IDC [340]
PRE-DYNASTIC CEMETARY AT EL-MAHASNA / Ayrton, Edward R – 9 – $10.00 – us I.R.C. [930]
PRE-DYNASTIC CEMETERY AT AL MAHASNA (MEES VOL 31) / Ayrton, Edward R & Loat, W L S – London, 1911 – 6mf – 8 – Dfl25.00 – ne Slangenburg [930]
THE PRE-EMINENCE OF THE BIBLE AS A BOOK : INAUGURAL ADDRESS OF ALFRED TYLER PERRY, FEB 10, 1899 / Perry, Alfred Tyler – (Includes bibliographical references) – Hartford, CT: Hartford Seminary Press, [1899?] – 1mf – 9 – 0-8370-9727-4 – 1986-3727 – us A.T.L.A. [220]
THE PREFACE: A POEM OF THE PERIOD / Albyn – Halifax: J. Bowes, 1876.06132.(Pre-1900 Canadiana) – 9 – cn C.I.H.M. [810]
PREFACE TO LA MORALE DES JESUITES / Bert, Paul – Montreal: W. Drysdale, 1889. 03577. (Pre-1900 Canadiana) – 9 – cn C.I.H.M. [240]
PREFACES TO CONTEMPORARIES / Howells, William Dean – 1882-1920 – 9 – 15.00 – us Scholars' Facs [840]
PRE-FEDERAL ADMIRALTY COURT REPORTS, PROVINCE AND STATE OF SOUTH CAROLINA, 1716-89 / U.S. District Courts. South Carolina – RG 21. 3 rolls – 1 – M1180 – us Nat'l Archives [340]
Prefontaine, Chevalier de *see* MAISON RUSTIQUE A L'USAGE DES HABITANS DE LA PARTIE DE LA FRANCE EQUINOXIALE CONNUE SOUS LE NOM DE CAYENNE
Preger, Konrad *see* PANKRAZ VON FREYBERG AUF HOHENASCHAU
Preger, W *see* GESCHICHTE DER DEUTSCHEN MYSTIK IM MITTELALTER
O PREGO – Rio Branco, Acre. 12 Dez 1915 – 1,5,6 – bl Biblioteca [072]
O PREGOEIRO CONSTITUCIONAL – Arraial de Pouso-Alegre, 7 Sept 1830-4 Jun 1831 – 1,5,6 – bl Biblioteca [072]
PREGON DE LA FIESTAS PATRONALES DE L'ERENA, 11 DE AGOS TO DE 1968 / Cienfuegos Linares, Julio – 1 – sp Bibl Santa Ana [650]
PREGON DE LA SANTISIMA VIRGEN DE LA VICTORIA / Gonzalez Ramos, Vicente – Caceres: Edit. Extremadura, 1963 – 1 – sp Bibl Santa Ana [240]
PREGON DE LA SEMANA SANTA CACERENA / Elviro Meseguer, Francisco – Caceres: Diputacion Provincial. Servicios Culturales, 1958 – sp Bibl Santa Ana [946]
PREGON DE LA SEMANA SANTA CACERENA / Floriano Cumbreno, Antonio C – Caceres: Tip. Edit. Extremadura, 1957 – 1 – sp Bibl Santa Ana [946]
PREGON DE LA SEMANA SANTA CACERENA, 1976 / Crespo Marquez, Jose Maria – Caceres: Diputacion Provincial, 1977 – sp Bibl Santa Ana [946]
PREGON DE LA SEMANA SANTA CACERENA. MARZO 1972 / Lucas Verdu, Antonio – Caceres: Excma. Dip. Provincial, 1972 – 1 – sp Bibl Santa Ana [946]
PREGON DE LAS FIESTAS PATRONALES DE TRUJILLO, PRONUNCIADO EN SEPTIEMBRE DE 1970, POR EL EXCMO. SR. D. ALFONSO DE FIGUEROA Y MELGAR, DUQUE DE TOVAR / Figueroa y Melgar, Alfonso de – Badajoz: Dip. Provinicial, 1971. Sep. REE – 1 – sp Bibl Santa Ana [390]
PREGON DEL CONCEJO SOBRE LA DEMOLICION DE LA MEZQUITA (ANNO 1253) – Cordoba – 1r – 5,6 – sp Cultura [946]
PREGON PRONUNCIADO POR D. JOSE GARCIA NIETO...EN LA MUY NOBLE Y MUY LEAL CIUDAD DE TRUJILLO / Garcia Nieto, Jose – Caceres: Imp. Provincial, 1969 – sp Bibl Santa Ana [946]
PREGON PRONUNCIADO...EN LA 6 FIESTA DE LA VENDIMIA LOS SANTOS DE MAIMONA / Sanchez de Leon Perez, Enrique – Los Santos de Maimona: Imp. Los Santos, 1972 – 1 – sp Bibl Santa Ana [390]
PREGONCILLO DE NAVIDAD / Perez Lozano, Jose Maria – Madrid: PPC, 1967 – 1 – sp Bibl Santa Ana [946]
PREGON...EN LAS FIESTAS DEL CINCUENTENARIO DE LA CORONACION DE NTRA. SRA. DE LA MONTANA PATRONA DE CACERES / Quintana, Manuel Jose – Caceres, 1974 – 1 – sp Bibl Santa Ana [390]
LA PREHISTOIRE : ORIGINE ET ANTIQUITE DE L'HOMME / Mortillet, Gabriel de & Mortillet, Adrien de – Paris: Schleicher Fres, [1910] – 1 – F352.95 – fr Armell [572]
LA PREHISTOIRE NEO-CALEDONIENNE / Frimigacci, D – 9 – F180.00 – fr Ethnologie [930]
PREHISTORIA DE LA REGION NORTE DE MARRUECOS / Blasquez y Delgado-Aquilera, Antonio – (Filmed with: Barahona e Costa, Henrique Cesar da Silva: Apontamentos para a historia de querra de Zambezia 1871-75, and others) – Madrid: Patronato de Huerfanos de Intendencia e Intervencion Militares, 1913 – us Res Libr [900]
PREHISTORIC AND PRESENT COMMERCE AMONG THE ARCTIC COAST ESKIMO / Stefansson, Vilhjalmur – BN 405 2. 1914 – 8 – ne IDC [306]
PREHISTORIC ARCHAEOLOGY AND THE OLD TESTAMENT / Astley, Hugh John Dukinfield – Edinburgh: T. & T. Clark, 1908. 1 fiche – 9 – us A.T.L.A. [220]
THE PREHISTORIC ARCHAEOLOGY OF NORTH WEST AFRICA / Wulsin, F R – (Papers of the Peabody Museum of Am. Arch. and Ethn. V. XIX, no. 1). 1941. BA-637 2 – 8 – ne IDC [930]
PREHISTORIC EGYPT / Petrie, William Matthew Flinders – 1920 – 9 – $10.00 – us I.R.C. [930]
PREHISTORIC ROCK ART – 34p – 9 – 92-3-102599-6 – Co-Published with Childrens Press, Chicago, who have exclusive sales rights in the USA and Canada – fr UNESCO [930]
PREHISTORIC STONE MONUMENTS – 1993 – 36p – 9 – 92-3-102686-0 – fr UNESCO [930]
PREHISTORIC SURVEY OF EGYPT AND WESTERN ASIA : FICHE MAPS / Sandford, K S & Arkell, W J – 1973 – 9 – $5.00f – 0-226-73469-2 – us U.C. Orient [930]
PREHISTORIC SURVEY OF EGYPT AND WESTERN ASIA, VOL 2 : PALEOLITHIC MAN AND THE NILE VALLEY IN NUBIA AND UPPER EGYPT. A STUDY OF THE REGION DURING PLIOCENE AND PLEISTOCENE TIMES / Sandford, K S & Arkell, W J – 1933 – 9 – $5.00f – 0-226-73472-2 – us U.C. Orient [930]
PREHISTORIC SURVEY OF EGYPT AND WESTERN ASIA, VOL 3 : PALEOLITHIC MAN AND THE NILE VALLEY IN UPPER AND MIDDLE EGYPT. A STUDY OF THE REGION DURING PLIOCENE AND PLEISTOCENE TIMES / Sandford, K S & Arkell, W J – 1934 – 9 – $5.00f – 0-226-73470-6 – us U.C. Orient [930]
PREHISTORIC SURVEY OF EGYPT AND WESTERN ASIA, VOL 4 : PALEOLITHIC MAN AND THE NILE VALLEY IN LOWER EGYPT WITH SOME NOTES UPON A PART OF THE RED SEA LITTORAL. A STUDY OF THE REGION DURING THE PLIOCENE AND PLEISTOCENE TIMES / Sandford, K S & Arkell, W J – 1939 – 9 – $5.00f – 0-226-73471-4 – us U.C. Orient [930]
Preisendanz, K *see* PAPYRUSFUNDE UND PAPYRUSFORSCHUNG
Preiser, Rosa C *see* IN AND OUT OF THE BARRIO: ADAPTED FROM BOOK TWO
Preisner, Rio *see* ASPEKTE EINER PROVOKATIVEN TSCHECHISCHEN GERMANISTIK
Preissig, E von *see* DICTIONARY AND GRAMMAR OF THE CHAMORRO LANGUAGE OF THE ISLAND OF GUAM
Preiswerk, Samuel *see* GRAMMAIRE HEBRAEIQUE
PREITO : DE ALGUNS DISCIPULOS E AMIGOS – Maceio, Alagoas. 29 Out 1884 – 1,5,6 – bl Biblioteca [072]
Preitz, Max *see*
- GOTTFRIED KELLERS DRAMATISCHE BESTREBUNGEN
- WERKE

PREJUGEZ LEGITIMES CONTRE LE PAPISME / Jurieu, P – Amsterdam. 2v. 1685 – 11mf – 9 – CA-136/1 – ne IDC [240]
PREJUGEZ LEGITIMES CONTRE LES CALVINISTES / Nicole, P – Paris, 1671 – 6mf – 9 – CA-104/1 – ne IDC [240]
PRELIMINARES DEL DERECHO PUBLICO ECLESTIASTICO / Pulido y Espinosa, Jose – 1849 – 9 – 1.50f – sp Bibl Santa Ana [240]
PRELIMINARY BIBLIOGRAPHY ON LONGEVITY DRUGS, WITH 2 PAPERS ON CRYONICS / Donaldson, Thomas – 1 fiche – 9 – 1.00f – at Libertarian Micro [615]
A PRELIMINARY BIBLIOGRAPHY RELATING TO CHURCHES IN WEST VIRGINIA, VIRGINIA, KENTUCKY, & SOUTHERN OHIO – 1940. 1 fiche. F-1122 – 9 – us A.G.L.L. [240]
PRELIMINARY CLASSIFIED INDEX OF TECHNICAL OIL MISSION REPORTS / U.S. Bureau of Mines – 5v. 1949-51 – 1 – $23.00 – us L of C Photodup [660]
PRELIMINARY COMPILATION OF STATISTICAL DATA ON NATIONAL ACCOUNTING IN LIBYA IN THE PERIOD FROM 1962 TO 1968 / Libya. Census and Statistical Department. National Accounts Section – Draft. Tripoli. 1970. BNE-625 1 – 9 – ne IDC [310]
PRELIMINARY FIVE YEAR PROGRAMME FOR THE ECONOMIC DEVELOPMENT OF GREECE / Greece. Ministry of Coordination – Athens. 1959. BD-527 1 – 9 – ne IDC [338]
PRELIMINARY FIVE-YEAR PROGRAMME FOR ECONOMIC DEVELOPMENT OF GREECE (1959-1963) / Greece – D-1311 1. 1959 – 9 – ne IDC [338]
PRELIMINARY INVENTORY OF NON-SEMINARY-RELATED MSS IN THE A.R. WENTZ LIBRARY. (MIMEO.) / Lutheran Theological Seminary – Gettysburg, PA. 1976 – 1mf – 9 – ne IDC [240]
PRELIMINARY NATIONAL ACCOUNTS OF LIBYA. 1962-1968 / Libya – Preliminary compilation of statistical data on national accounting in Libya. (Draft). Tripoli. 1970. BNE-525 1 – 9 – ne IDC [339]
PRELIMINARY REPORT OF AN UNOFFICIAL ORGANIZATION UPON THE VICE CONDITIONS IN MONTREAL... – [Montreal ?]: [s.n.], 1918. SEM105P1477 – 1mf – 9 – Can$2.25 – cn Bibl Nat [360]
PRELIMINARY REPORT OF THE FIFTH THULE EXPEDITION / Birket-Smith, K – (Physical anthropology, linguistics, and material culture) – 1925 – 8 – BN 129 2 – ne IDC [910]
PRELIMINARY REPORT ON ECONOMIC AND ENGINEERING SURVEY OF BURMA FOR BURMA ECONOMIC COUNCIL / Burma. Knappen-Tippetts-Abbett Engineering Co., et al – D-1256 1. 1952-1959 – 9 – ne IDC [950]
PRELIMINARY REPORT ON KALI BRANTAS OVERALL PROJECT / Indonesia. Kementerian Pekerdjaan Umum dan Tenaga – SE-5371 1. 1960 – 9 – ne IDC [624]
PRELIMINARY REPORT ON THE GEOLOGY OF A PORTION OF CENTRAL ONTARIO SITUATED IN THE COUNTIES OF VICTORIA / Adams, Frank Dawson – Peterborough and Hastings: together with the results of an examination of certain ore deposits occurring in the region. Ottawa? 1894. 02426. (Pre-1900 Canadiana) – cn C.I.H.M. [550]
PRELIMINARY REPORTS OF THE IRAQ EXPEDITIONS, 1-5 / Frankfort, Henri – 1932-1936 – 9 – $30.00 – us I.R.C. [930]
PRELIMINARY REPORTS ON THE ECOLOGICAL SURVEY OF THE VEGETATION TYPES IN FOREST AND GRAZING LANDS OF JORDAN / United Nations. Food and Agriculture Organization – B. Kasapligil. 1955. BNE-9788 1 – 9 – ne IDC [324]
PRELIMINARY RESULT OF THE GENERAL POPULATION CENSUS 1964 / Libya. Ministry of National Economy – May 1955. BNE-504 1 – 9 – ne IDC [304]
PRELIMINARY RESULTS OF THE GENERAL POPULATION CENSUS 1964 / Libya. Ministry of National Economy – Tripoli. BNE-511 1 – 9 – ne IDC [304]
PRELIMINARY REVIEW OF SELECTED LEGISLATION GOVERNING AQUACULTURE – 1989 – 87p – it F.A.O. [340]
A PRELIMINARY STUDY OF THE EAST SUMBANESE SOCIAL ORGANIZATION AND RELIGION / Kana, Nicodemus Lulu – (Thesis). SE-5239 1. 1966 – 9 – ne IDC [360]
PRELIMINARY SURVEY OF EGYPT / Egypt. Middle East Supply Centre – 1945. BNE-4645 1 – 9 – ne IDC [330]
A PRELIMINARY SURVEY OF LUVALE RURAL ECONOMY / White, C M N – 7 – uk Microform Academic [960]
A PRELIMINARY SURVEY OF THE FRESHWATER FOOD FISHES OF ECUADOR / International Center for Aquaculture – Jul 1972. 1 reel – 1, 5 – us Spaulding [639]
Preller, Ludwig *see* GRIECHISCHE MYTHOLOGIE
Prellwitz, Walther *see* ETYMOLOGISCHES WOERTERBUCH DER GRIECHISCHEN SPRACHE
THE PRELUDE : OR, GROWTH OF A POET'S MIND; AN AUTOBIOGRAPHICAL POEM / Wordsworth, William – London: E. Moxon, 1850 – 1 roll – 1 – 1-55879-638-X – uk Libr Preservation [810]
PRELUDE, SCHERZION, IMPROMPTU / Dopper, C – (Holograph) – Manuscript, 190- – 1 – us Sibley [780]
LES PRELUDES DE L'HARMONIE UNIVERSELLE / Mersenne, Marin – 1634 – 9 – us Sibley [780]
PRELUDES TO THE REFORMATION, OR, FROM DARK TO DAY IN EUROPE / Pennington, Arthur Robert – London: Religious Tract Society, 1886 – 1mf – us A.T.L.A. [940]
O PRELUDIO : PERIODICO LITTERARIO, CRITICO, HUMORISTICO E NOTICIOSO – Manaos, Amazonas. 11-31 Ago 1913 – 1,5,6 – bl Biblioteca [072]
Prem, Ma Ananda *see* DYNAMICS OF MEDITATION: (TWELVE INTERVIEW-DISCOURSES ON THE VARIOUS ASPECTS OF MEDITATION)
Premaray, Jules de *see* PROMENADES SENTIMENTALES DANS LONDRES ET LE PALAIS DE CRISTAL
Premare, J H *see* LETTRE INEDITE DU P. PREMARE SUR LE MONOTHEISME DES CHINOIS

LE PREMIER CENTENAIRE DE "LA REVUE CANADIENNE" – [Quebec (Province): s.n., 1887?]. SEM105P1647 – 1mf – 9 – Can$2.25 – cn Bibl Nat [440]

PREMIER ESSAI (SUIVI DE SECOND ESSAI) SUR LE DEPARTEMENT DE LA SEINE-INFERIEURE / Noel de la Moriniere, Simon B J – An III – 9 – fr Hachette [944]

PREMIER ET SECOND RAPPORTS / Canada. Province. Assemblee legislative. Comite pour s'enquirir des causesqui retardent la colonisation des townships de l'Est du Bas-Canada – 1851. SEM105P563 – 1mf – 9 – Can$2.25 – cn Bibl Nat [324]

PREMIER ETABLISSEMENT DE LA FOY DANS LA NOUVELLE FRANCE / LeClercq, Ch – Paris, France. 2v. 1691 – 1r – 1 – cn Can Microfilming [240]

PREMIER JOURNAL DE LA CONVENTION NATIONALE – ou Le Point du jour. Paris. nov 1792-juin 1793 – 1 – fr A.C.R.P.P. [073]

PREMIER LIVERE D'AIRS SPIRITUELS DE DIFFERENTS AUTHEURS, A DEUX PARTIES – A Paris: chez Christophe Ballard, seul Imprimeur du Roy pour la musique, 1679. SEM105P2020 – 1mf – 9 – Can$2.25 – cn Bibl Nat [780]

PREMIER LIVRE DE PIECES POUR LA FLUTE TRAVERSIERE AVEC LA BASSE CONTINUE / Barre – 18th c. – fr Armell [780]

LE PREMIER LIVRE DES PROVERBES EPIGRAMMATIZEZ / Estienne, Henri – 1594 – 9 – fr I.C.S. [880]

LE PREMIER LIVRE...A QUATRE VOIX. / Jannequin, C – 1550. SECONDO LIBRO DI CANZON FRANCESE, A QUATRO VOCI...1549. Two books bound together, tenor part only – 9 – us Sibley [780]

PREMIER MEMOIRE SUR GUILLAUME DE MACHAUT; POETE ET MUSICIEN DANS LE XIV SIECLE / Caylus, A C P de – 1770. P 662 – 9 – ne IDC [780]

PREMIER NEGRIN'S ADDRESS TO THE LEAGUE OF NATIONS ASSEMBLY ON SEPT. 18, 1937 / Negrin, Juan – n.p., 1937. Fiche W 1072. (Blodgett Collection of Spanish Civil War Pamphlets) – 9 – us H.U. College Libr [946]

PREMIER PLAN QUINQUENNAL, (1960-1964) / Cambodia. Ministere du Plan – Phnom-Penh. 1960. D-423 1 – 9 – ne IDC [338]

PREMIER PLAN QUINQUENNAL DE DEVELOPPEMENT ECONOMIQUE ET SOCIAL / Cameroon. Ministere des Finances et du Plan – Yaounde. 1961 – 9 – ne IDC [338]

PREMIER PLAN QUINQUENNAL DE DEVLOPPEMENT ECONOMIQUE ET SOCIAL, 1966-1970 / Chad. Ministere du Plan et de la Cooperation – Fort Lamy. 1966 – 9 – ne IDC [338]

LE PREMIER PLAN QUINQUENNAL POUR LE DEVELOPPEMENT DE L'ECONOMIE NATIONALE. (1953-1957) / China. People's Republic – 1v. Pekin, Editions en Langues Etrangeres. 1956. Illus. BD-515 1 – 9 – ne IDC [338]

PREMIER RAPPORT DE LA COMMISSION CHARGEE DE LA REVISION ET DE LA MODIFICATION DU CODE DE PROCEDURE CIVILE DU BAS-CANADA / Quebec Province – [s.n.], 1893. SEM105P1510 – 1mf – 9 – Can$2.25 – cn Bibl Nat [340]

PREMIER RAPPORT DE LA COMMISSION DE MODERNISATION DES TERRITOIRES D'OUTRE-MER / France. Commissariat General du Plan – Paris. 1948 – 9 – ne IDC [338]

PREMIER RAPPORT DE LA SOUS-COMMISSION DE MODERNISATION DE L'INDOCHINE / Indochina. French – Paris, Commissariat General du Plan. 1948 – 9 – ne IDC [330]

PREMIER RAPPORT DU COMITE SPECIAL SUR LES COMMUNICATIONS INTERIEURES / Bas-Canada. Parlement...Comite Special sur... – [S.l.]: [s.n.], [1830] – 1mf – 9 – Can$2.25 – cn Bibl Nat [340]

PREMIER (-SECOND) LIVRE DE SONATES / Leclair, Jean-Marie – 1723-25? – 1 – us Sibley [780]

LE PREMIER TOME DE L'ARCHITECTURE / Delorme, Philibert – O 223. Facs. ed. 1894 – 9 – ne IDC [720]

LE PREMIER TOME DE L'ARCHITECTURE / Delorme, Philibert – Paris. F. Morel. 1567. 285 f. ill. Incompl. (Architecture Series) – 9 – fr Hachette [720]

PREMIERE CONFERENCE, 15 MARS 1882 / Conferences pour la negociation d'une convention regulant les relations commerciales entre la France et le Canada – 1882? 05603. (Pre-1900 Canadiana) – 9 – cn C.I.H.M. [971]

PREMIERE DECADE DU ORBE NOVO / Angleria, Pedro Martir – 1893 – 9 – 1.50f – sp Bibl Santa Ana [970]

LA PREMIERE FAMILLE FRANCAISE AU CANADA, SES ALLIES ET SES DESCENDANTS / Couillard-Despres, Azarie – Montreal: Imp. de l'Ecole catholique des sourds-muets, 1906. SEM105P1588 – 5mf – 9 – Can$11.25 – cn Bibl Nat [971]

LA PREMIERE INTERNATIONALE, RECUEIL DE DOCUMENTS / Freymond, Jacques – Geneve: E. Droz, 1962-1971 – 1 – us U.W. Library [073]

PREMIERE LECTURE DU BILL CONCERNANT LA MILICE ET LA DEFENSE DE LA PUISSANCE DU CANADA – 1868? SEM105P651 – 1mf – 9 – Can$2.25 – cn Bibl Nat [971]

PREMIERE LITURGIE DES EGLISES REFORMEES DE FRANCE / Baum, J C – Paris, 1859 – 1mf – 8 – Dfl6.00 – ne Slangenburg [944]

PREMIERE RETRAITE SOUS LES AUSPICES DU CERCLE VILLE-MARIE: DANS L'EGLISE DE NOTRE-DAME DE BONSECOURS / Barbezieux, Alexis de – Montreal, decembre 1890. Prechee par le Rev. Pere Alexis. 03982. (Pre-1900 Canadiana) – 9 – cn C.I.H.M. [240]

PREMIERES POESIES : 1876-1878 / Evanturel, Eudore – Quebec: Augustin Cote et cie, 1878. SEM105P20 – 3mf – 9 – Can$6.75 – cn Bibl Nat [810]

PREMIERS MEMOIRES MATHEMATIQUES / Alembert, Jean Le Rond d' – Histoire de l'Academie de Berlin, 1746-1750 Berlin. Histoire des Sciences XVIIe-XIXe Siecles. 7972 – 9 – fr Hachette [510]

LES PREMIERS RESULTATS DU DENOMBREMENT DE 1881, AFIN QU'ON PUISSE JUGER DU MOUVEMENT DE LA POPULATION – Reprod. d'un extrait du Journal de la Societe de Statistique de Paris, 1882. p62-65.1 fiche. (Statistics Series: Demography) – 9 – 6.00 – fr Bibl Nationale [310]

PREMIER'S (SHIRLEY BAKER'S) LETTERBOOKS / Government of Tonga – 1873-74; 1880-90 – 3r – 1 – PMB1089 – at Pacific Mss [920]

PREMIO A LA VIRTUD / T'Serclaes, Duque de & Ballesteros Beretta, Antonio – Ano de 1926. Madrid: Tip. Arch., Bibl. y Mus, 1928. B.R.A.H. 92. p. 829 – sp Bibl Santa Ana [946]

PREMIO A LA VIRTUD 1923 / T'Serclaes, Duque de – Madrid: Tip. Arch. Bibl. y Mus, 1923. B.R.A.H. 82, pp. 499-503 – sp Bibl Santa Ana [946]

PREMIO DE LA FUNDACION LOUBAT 1929 / T'Serclaes, Duque de et al – Madrid, 1934. B.R.A.H. 104, pp. 686-688 – sp Bibl Santa Ana [060]

PREMIUM LIST CATALOG / Louisiana State University. Agricultural Extension Service. Junior Livestock Show – No.41. 1976. 1 reel – 1,5 – us Spaulding [630]

PREMIUM LIST CATALOG / Louisiana State University. Agricultural Extension Service. National Quarterhorse Show – 1973-77.1 reel – 1,5 – us Spaulding [630]

PREMIUM LIST CATALOG / Louisiana State University. Agricultural Extension Service. Open Livestock Show – 1974-82.No.39-47. 1 reel – 1,5 – us Spaulding [630]

Premo, Mary C *see* REPRODUCTIVE ENDOCRINE RESPONSE FOLLOWING ANAEROBIC AND AEROBIC EXERCISE

PRENATAL DIAGNOSIS – v.1-. 1981- – 1,5,6,9 – us UMI [618]

Prenner, Manuel *see* CONCURRENCE AND DISSENT; SOME RECENT SUPREME COURT CASES

PRE-NRS NOMINATIVE EQUITY REPORTS *see*
- BAILEY'S CASES IN EQUITY
- CHEVES' CASES IN EQUITY
- DESAUSSURE'S CASES IN EQUITY
- DUDLEY'S CASES IN EQUITY
- HARPER'S CASES IN EQUITY
- HILL'S CASES IN EQUITY
- MCMULLAN'S CASES IN EQUITY
- MCORD'S CASES IN EQUITY
- RICE'S CASES IN EQUITY
- RICHARDSON'S CASES IN EQUITY
- RILEY'S CASES IN EQUITY
- SPEER'S CASES IN EQUITY
- STROBHART'S CASES IN EQUITY

PRE-NRS NOMINATIVE LAW REPORTS *see*
- BAILEY'S LAW REPORTS
- BAY'S LAW REPORTS
- BREVARD'S LAW REPORTS
- CHEVES' LAW REPORTS
- DUDLEY'S LAW REPORTS
- HARPER'S LAW REPORTS
- HILL'S LAW REPORTS
- MCMULLAN'S LAW REPORTS
- MCORD'S LAW REPORTS
- MILL'S CONSTITUTIONAL REPORTS
- NOTT AND M'CORD'S LAW REPORTS
- RICE'S LAW REPORTS
- RICHARDSON'S LAW REPORTS
- RICHARDSON'S LAW REPORTS, N.S.
- RILEY'S LAW REPORTS
- SPEER'S LAW REPORTS
- STROBHART'S LAW REPORTS
- TREADWAY'S LAW REPORTS

PRE-NRS NOMINATIVE REPORTS *see*
- ADDISON'S REPORTS
- BINNEY'S REPORTS
- BRIGHTLY'S REPORTS
- DALLAS' REPORTS
- GRANT'S CASES
- MONAGHAN'S REPORTS
- PENNYPACKER'S REPORTS
- PENROSE AND WATTS' REPORTS
- RAWLE'S REPORTS
- SADLER'S REPORTS
- SERGEANT AND RAWLE'S REPORTS
- WALKER'S REPORTS
- WATTS AND SERGEANT'S REPORTS
- WATTS' REPORTS
- WHARTON'S REPORTS
- YEATES' REPORTS

LA PRENSA – Buenos Aires. Argentina. 1970- – 1 – us UMI [072]

LA PRENSA – Buenos Aires: [s.n.] 1869- ; 1938-may 1970 – us Res Libr [072]

LA PRENSA – Don Benito. 1886-88, no. sueltos – 9 – 1.50f – sp Bibl Santa Ana [072]

LA PRENSA – Los Angeles, CA. 1917-22; 1967-70 – 3r – 1 BR02388 – $150.00 – us Library Micro [071]

LA PRENSA – Managua, Nicaragua: [s.n.] 1956-jun 25 1986 – us Res Libr [072]

LA PRENSA – Netherlands Antilles. 1940-1957 – 1 – us UMI [072]

LA PRENSA – San Antonio, Texas: La Prensa, [dec 20 1916-jan 17 1928] – 62r – 1 – us Res Libr [071]

LA PRENSA – (Some missing issues) – Buenos Aires, Argentina. 31 Jul 1857-1937 – 415r – 1 – us L of C Photodup [072]

LA PRENSA – Toledo, Ohio, 1989-1993 – 1r – 1 – $32.50r – us Archival [978]

LA PRENSA : EL UNICO DIARIO ESPANOL E HISPANO-AMERICANO DE NUEVA YORK – New York: La Prensa, [jul 19-aug 19, 25 1919; 1922-jan 12 1933; 1945-50] – 52r – 1 – us Res Libr [071]

LA PRENSA COMO AGENTE DE EDUCACION / Vega y Relea, Juvenal de – Caceres: Tip. La Minerva, 1924 – 1 – sp Bibl Santa Ana [370]

LA PRENSA LIBRE – Berkeley, CA. 1969 – 1r – 1 – $50.00 – R03157 – us Library Micro [071]

LA PRENSA LIBRE – Guatemala: P J Garcia, [jan 3 1973-mar 1979] (154r); apr 2 1979-oct 1982] (124r); [nov 1982-may 10 1986] (124r); [may 11 1986-may 10 1991] (180r); [may 11 1991-sep 30 1992] (43r) – 1 – us Res Libr [072]

LA PRENSA LIBRE – San Jose, Costa Rica: [s.n., jan 2 1964-aug 1975]; [sep 1975-1988] – us Res Libr [072]

LA PRENSA LITERARIA – Managua, D.N. 14 Mayo 1977-. -w. illus – 1 – us U.W. Library [440]

LA PRENSA LITERARIA CENTROAMERICANA – Managua, D.N. no1-. Feb 1976-. -m. Absorbed by: Prensa Literaria, 14 Mayo 1977- – 1 – us U.W. Library [440]

LA PRENSA MADRILENA A TRAVES DE LOS SIGLOS / Asenso, Antonio – (Apuntes para su historia desde el ano 1661, al 1925) – Madrid: Artes Graficas Municipales, 1933 – 1 – sp Bibl Santa Ana [946]

Prensa Obrera *see* EL PARTIDO OBRERO Y EL PERONISMO

LA PRENSA/THE PRESS – (Has more recent copies under LOC Np 2758) – Panama City, Panama. 1908-1916 (incomplete) – 7r – 1 – us L of C Photodup [072]

Prentice, William E *see*
- AN ASSESSMENT OF THE EFFECTIVENESS OF THE COOL CAPE ON THE RAPID REDUCTION OF EXERCISE-INDUCED, ELEVATED BODY CORE TEMPERATURE
- THE EFFECTS OF EXERCISE ON THE STRENGTH OF THE LOW BACK

Prentiss, Elizabeth Payson *see* THE LIFE AND LETTERS OF ELIZABETH PRENTISS, AUTHOR OF STEPPING HEAVENWARD

Prentiss, George L *see* THE AGREEMENT BETWEEN UNION SEMINARY AND THE GENERAL ASSEMBLY

Prentiss, George Lewis *see*
- THE UNION THEOLOGICAL SEMINARY IN THE CITY OF NEW YORK

PRENZLAUER ZEITUNG UND KREIS-BLATT – Prenzlau, Germany. 1920 (Nrn.1-77) – 1 – gw Mikrofilm [072]

Preobrazenskii, ID *see* PODROBNAIA OPIS 962 RUKOPISIAM NACHALA 17 DO NACHALA 19 STOLETIJ DOLMATOVSKAGO ARKHIVA

Preobrazhenskii, E *see*
- AZBUKA KOMMUNIZMA

PREOCCUPATIONS STATISTIQUES, GEOGRAPHIQUES, PITTORESQUES ET SYNOPTIQUES DU DEPARTEMENT DES HAUTES-ALPES / Chaix, Barthelemy – 9 – 226.00 – fr Bibl Nationale [944]

PREOCUPACIONES SOCIALES / Gonzalez Serrano, Urbano – 1882 – 9 – 1.50f – sp Bibl Santa Ana [300]

PRE-ORGANIC EVOLUTION AND THE BIBLICAL IDEA OF GOD : AN EXPOSITION AND A CRITICISM / Chapman, Charles – (Includes bibliographical references) – Edinburgh: T & T Clark, 1891 – 1mf – 9 – 0-8370-3202-4 – 1985-1202 – us A.T.L.A. [210]

PREP. FEODOR, ISPOVEDNIK I IGUMEN STUDIISKII / Dobroklonskii, Aleksandr Pavlovich – 1913-14 – 1 – us A.T.L.A. [240]

PRE-PALEOZOIC DECAY OF CRYSTALLINE ROCKS NORTH OF LAKE HURON / Bell, Robert – Rochester, NY: Geological Society of America, 1894. 03562. (Pre-1900 Canadiana) – 9 – cn C.I.H.M. [560]

PREPARATION AND NEGOTIATION : THE TRANSFER OF POWER FROM AUSTRALIA TO PAPUA NEW GUINEA, 1970-1975 / Goode, Christine Mary – 1r – 1 – PMB Doc410 – at Pacific Mss [320]

PREPARATION DU PLAN DE DEVELOPPEMENT, 1968-1972; NOTE D'ORIENTATION POUR LA COMMISSION DE LA POLITIQUE FINANCIERE / Morocco. Ministere du Developpement – 1966. BNE-3081 1 – 9 – ne IDC [338]

PREPARATION FOR CHURCH GROWTH IN THE MIAMI SPRINGS BAPTIST CHURCH, MIAMI SPRINGS, FLORIDA / Campbell, William Cecil – 1982 – 1 – 5.00 – us Baptist [240]

THE PREPARATION FOR THE GOSPEL (CCC86) / Ch'en, Chi-yun – (In Chinese) – Shanghai: Christian Literature Society, 1949 – 1r – 1 – 1984-B500 – us A.T.L.A. [220]

PREPARATION OF SAMPLING SURVEY REPORTS *see* SAMPLE SURVEYS OF CURRENT INTEREST

PREPARATION OF THE DRAFT HANDBOOK ON THE PEACEFUL SETTLEMENT OF DISPUTES BETWEEN STATES / United Nations – 9 – in prep – us U.N. Pubs [327]

PREPARATORY MATERIAL FOR THE REVISION OF JAPANESE CIVIL LAW PREPARED IN THE HEADQUARTERS OF THE AMERICAN MILITARY GOVERNMENT FOR JAPAN / Supreme Commander for the Allied Powers – Tokyo? 1947 Collation of the original: 1 v. LL-10025 – 1 – us L of C Photodup [340]

PREPAREDNESS – Portland OR. Easter and Decoration Day 1916 – 1 – us U.O. Library [071]

PREPARING A U.S. COURT FOR AUTOMATION / Bermant, Gordon – Washington: FJC, 1985 – 1mf – 9 – $1.50 – LLMC 95-325 – us L.L.M.C. [340]

PREPARING AGRICULTURAL INVESTMENT PROJECTS – 1985 2nd print 1988 – 64p – it F.A.O. [332]

PREPARING FOR TRIALS INVOLVING FORGERY. / M'Govern, Chauncey – San Francisco, M'Govern, 1922. 32 p. LL-799 – 1 – us L of C Photodup [340]

PREPRINTS OF PAPERS / American Chemical Society – v1- 1956- – 1,5,6 – us A.C.S. [660]

PREPRINTS OF PAPERS / American Chemical Society – v1- 1957- – 1,5,6 – us A.C.S. [660]
PREPROGRAMMING VS. ON-LINE PREPARATION IN SIMPLE MOVEMENT SEQUENCES / Van Donkelaar, Paul & Franks, Ian – 1990 – 2mf – 9 – $8.00 – us Microform Publ [150]
PRE-RAPHAELITE PAINTINGS AND DRAWINGS / Birmingham Museum and Art Gallery – (With printed catalogues) – 29 colour mf – 15 – $551.00 – 1-869934-17-2 – uk Emmett [700]
PRE-RAPHAELITE PAINTINGS AND DRAWINGS IN THE BIRMINGHAM MUSEUM AND ART GALLERY – (Printed index and list of sources) – 1990 – A635.00 – 0-8161-1760-8 – uk Hall [750]
PRE-REVOLUTIONARY DIARIES AT THE MASSACHUSETTS HISTORICAL SOCIETY, 1635-1774 – Massachusetts Historical Society – 13r – 1 – $965.00 – us UMI [920]
PRE-REVOLUTIONARY RECORD COMPANY CATALOGS FROM RUSSIA – (Inquire for complete listing) – 49mf – 9 – inquire – us Ross [780]
PRE-ROMAN AND EARLY ROMAN GLASS IN THE CORNING MUSEUM OF GLASS / Goldstein, Sidney M – 1979. 312p., 919 illus. incl. 36 color plates, 144 profile drawings. 7 fiches. Fiche no. 5377 – 9 – $11.25 – us Corning Mus [740]
Presber, Rudolf *see*
- DER GUTEN FRAUEN ALLERSCHOENSTER KRAN
- NEUE KRIEGSGEDICHTE
- DER TAG DES DEUTSCHEN

Presbitero Secular *see* NOVENARIO DEL GLORIOSO APOSTOL Y MARTIR SAN BARTOLOME...
Presbyter Anglicanus *see* ECCE HOMO: A CRITIQUE ON BEHALF OF...FREE ENQUIRY AND FREE EXPRESSION
THE PRESBYTERIAFR. *see* THE PRESBYTERIAN RECORD FOR THE DOMINION OF CANADA
DIE PRESBYTERIALE SYNODALVERFASSUNG DER EVANGELISCHEN KIRCHE IN NORDDEUTSCHLAND / Heppe, Heinrich – Iserlohn: J. Baedeker, 1874 – 1mf – us A.T.L.A. [240]
THE PRESBYTERIAN – (Is absorbed by: The Presbyterian Record for the Dominion of Canada) – Montreal: A H Armour, [1848-1875] – 9 – cn C.I.H.M. [240]
THE PRESBYTERIAN – v1-118. 1831-1948 (complete) – 88r – 1 – ATLA P0001 – us A.T.L.A. [073]
PRESBYTERIAN AND REFORMED REVIEW – v1-13 nos 1-52. 1890-1902 (complete) – 5r – 1 – ATLA S0207 – us A.T.L.A. [073]
PRESBYTERIAN BANNER – (Lacking: v1-83) – v84-124. 1897-1937 – 41r – 1 – ATLA S0179 – us A.T.L.A. [073]
PRESBYTERIAN BANNER – Philadelphia, PA., 1865 – 13 – $25.00r – us I.M.R. [071]
THE PRESBYTERIAN BANNER – Pittsburgh, PA. Cont. Thru York. Circa 1865-1867 – 13 – $25.00r – us I.M.R. [071]
THE PRESBYTERIAN CHURCH : A BRIEF ACCOUNT OF ITS DOCTRINE, WORSHIP, AND POLITY / Macphail, W M – (Includes bibliographical references and index) – London: Hodder and Stoughton, 1908 – 1mf – 9 – 0-8370-8695-7 – 1986-2695 – us A.T.L.A. [240]
PRESBYTERIAN CHURCH IN CANADA *see*
- FOREIGN MISSIONARY TIDINGS
- MONTHLY LETTER LEAFLET
- WFM SOCIETY
- WOMAN'S FOREIGN MISSIONARY SOCIETY

Presbyterian Church in Canada. Woman's Foreign Missionary Society *see* WFM SOCIETY
Presbyterian Church in Canada. Woman's Foreign Missionary Society. Western Division *see*
- MONTHLY LETTER LEAFLET
- WOMAN'S FOREIGN MISSIONARY SOCIETY

Presbyterian Church in Canada. Woman's Foreign Missionary Society. Western Divison *see* FOREIGN MISSIONARY TIDINGS
Presbyterian Church in the United States *see* MINUTES OF THE GENERAL ASSEMBLY, 1861-1983
Presbyterian Church in the U.S.A. Northern Kansas Presbytery *see* RECORDS OF THE UNITED PRESBYTERIAN CHURCH IN JAMESTOWN, MUNDEN AND SCOTTSVILLE
PRESBYTERIAN CHURCH IN THE U.S.A. : BOARD OF FOREIGN MISSIONS CORRESPONDENCE AND REPORTS, 1833-1911 – 292r – 1 – $24,820.00; $85.00r – Co-publ with the Presbyterian Historical Society, Dept of History, Presbyterian Church (U.S.A.) 1995 – us Scholarly Res [240]
Presbyterian Church in the U.S.A. *see*
- THE HOME AND FOREIGN RECORD
- THE PRESBYTERIAN MONTHLY RECORD
- THE RECORD

Presbyterian Church in the U.S.A. Board of Aid for Colleges and Academies. Henry Kendall College-University of Tulsa *see* CORRESPONDENCE AND REPORTS
Presbyterian Church in the U.S.A. Board of Christian Education *see*
- ANNUAL REPORTS, 1924-1958
- GRADED BIBLE LESSONS AND MATERIALS

Presbyterian Church in the U.S.A. Board of Church Erection *see* ANNUAL REPORTS, 1855-1923
Presbyterian Church in the U.S.A. Board of Church Extension (Old School) *see* ANNUAL REPORTS, 1856-1870
Presbyterian Church in the U.S.A. Board of Domestic Missions (Old School) *see* ANNUAL REPORTS, 1857-1870
Presbyterian Church in the U.S.A. Board of Education *see*
- ANNUAL REPORTS, 1820-1918
- MINUTES, 1819-1897

Presbyterian Church in the U.S.A. Board of Foreign Missions *see*
- ANNUAL REPORTS, 1833-1958
- MANUAL FOR THE USE OF MISSIONARIES
- MINUTES, 1837-1918
- MISSIONS TO CHINESE IN CALIFORNIA

Presbyterian Church in the U.S.A. Board of Foreign Missions. Executive Committee *see* MINUTES, 1837-1870
Presbyterian Church in the U.S.A. Board of Foreign Missions. Furrukhabad Mission *see* CORRESPONDENCE
Presbyterian Church in the U.S.A. Board of Foreign Missions. Korea, Conspiracy Case, Japanese Colonial government *see* CORRESPONDENCE, REPORTS
Presbyterian Church in the U.S.A. Board of Foreign Missions. Korea, Independence movement *see* CORRESPONDENCE AND REPORTS
Presbyterian Church in the U.S.A. Board of Foreign Missions. Korea, Japanese Colonial Government, Religious education controversy *see* CORRESPONDENCE AND REPORTS
Presbyterian Church in the U.S.A. Board of Home Missions *see*
- ANNUAL REPORTS, 1871-1923
- MINUTES, 1870-1919

Presbyterian Church in the U.S.A. Board of Ministerial Relief and Sustenation *see* ANNUAL REPORTS, 1913-1927
Presbyterian Church in the U.S.A. Board of Missions *see*
- ANNUAL REPORTS, 1817-1856
- MINUTES, 1815-1856

Presbyterian Church in the U.S.A. Board of Missions for Freedmen *see* ANNUAL REPORTS, 1866-1923
Presbyterian Church in the U.S.A. Board of National Missions *see* ANNUAL REPORTS, 1924-1957
Presbyterian Church in the U.S.A. Board of Publication and Sabbath School Work *see*
- ANNUAL REPORTS, 1839-1923
- MINUTES, 1833-1924

Presbyterian Church in the U.S.A. Board of Relief for Disabled Ministers and the Widows and Orphans of Deceased Ministers *see*
- ANNUAL REPORTS, 1876-1912
- MINUTES, 1876-1918

Presbyterian Church in the U.S.A. Board of Temperance *see* ANNUAL REPORTS, 1882-1923
Presbyterian Church in the U.S.A. College Board *see*
- ANNUAL REPORTS, 1884-1918
- MINUTES, 1883-1916

Presbyterian Church in the U.S.A. General Assembly *see*
- CONSTITUTION, 1786-1956
- DIGEST OF ACTS AND DELIVERANCES
- MINUTES AND REPORTS

Presbyterian Church in the U.S.A. General Assembly. Committee on Home Missions (New School) *see* ANNUAL REPORTS, 1862-1870
Presbyterian Church in the U.S.A. General Assembly. Permanent Committee on Education for the Ministry (New School) *see* MINUTES, 1856-1870
Presbyterian Church in the U.S.A. General Assembly. Trustees. Committee on the Relief Fund for Disabled Ministers and the Widows and Orphans of Deceased Ministers *see* ANNUAL REPORTS, 1855-1875
Presbyterian Church in the U.S.A. General Board of Education *see* ANNUAL REPORTS, 1919-1923
Presbyterian Church in the U.S.A. Synods. Virginia *see* THE SPHERE AND RIGHTS OF WOMAN IN THE CHURCH
Presbyterian Church in the U.S.A. Woman's Board of Foreign Missions *see*
- ANNUAL REPORTS, 1871-1923
- RECORDS, 1876-1914

Presbyterian Church in the U.S.A. Woman's Board of Home Missions *see*
- ANNUAL REPORTS, 1898-1927
- RECORDS, 1896-1911

Presbyterian Church in the U.S.A. Woman's Foreign Missionary Society *see*
- ANNUAL REPORTS, 1872-1923
- RECORDS, 1870-1922

Presbyterian Church in the U.S.A. Woman's North Pacific Presbyterian Board of Missions *see* ANNUAL REPORTS, 1887-1920
Presbyterian Church in the U.S.A. Woman's Presbyterian Board of Foreign Missions of the Southwest *see* ANNUAL REPORTS, 1883-1920
Presbyterian Church in the U.S.A. Woman's Presbyterian Board of Missions of the Northwest *see* ANNUAL REPORTS, 1872-1920
PRESBYTERIAN CHURCH OF ENGLAND 1847-1950 / School of Oriental and African Studies, London – (Includes printed guide) – 2,850mf – 9 – ne IDC [240]
PRESBYTERIAN CHURCH OF NEW SOUTH WALES : SYDNEY MINUTE BOOKS – (Apply to publ for details) – 1840-1919 – 9 – at Pascoe [240]
PRESBYTERIAN CHURCH OF NEW ZEALAND : PROCEEDINGS – 1959-68 (complete) – 4r – 1 – ATLA S0556 – us A.T.L.A. [240]
PRESBYTERIAN CHURCH OF NEW ZEALAND : PROCEEDINGS – 1970-84 (complete) – 2r – 1 – ATLA S0555 – us A.T.L.A. [240]
PRESBYTERIAN CHURCH OF NEW ZEALAND : REPORTS – 1969-88 (complete) – Inquire – 1 – ATLA S0553 – us A.T.L.A. [240]
PRESBYTERIAN CHURCH OF NEW ZEALAND : YEARBOOK – 1962-69 (complete) – 1r – 1 – ATLA S0554 – us A.T.L.A. [240]
THE PRESBYTERIAN CHURCHES : DIVISIONS AND UNIONS IN SCOTLAND, IRELAND, CANADA AND AMERICA / Stephens, John Vant – (Includes index) – Philadelphia: Presbyterian Board of Publ, 1910 – 1mf – 9 – 0-8370-8714-7 – 1986-2714 – us A.T.L.A. [240]
THE PRESBYTERIAN CHURCHES : THEIR PLACE AND POWER IN MODERN CHRISTENDOM / Ogilvie, James Nicoll – New York: Fleming H Revell, c1897 – 1mf – 9 – 0-8370-8776-7 – 1986-2776 – us A.T.L.A. [240]
PRESBYTERIAN COLLEGE JOURNAL – Montreal: Alma Mater Society of the Presbyterian College, [1880?-19–] – 9 – cn C.I.H.M. [370]
PRESBYTERIAN FOREIGN MISSIONS : AN ACCOUNT OF THE FOREIGN MISSIONS OF THE PRESBYTERIAN CHURCH IN THE USA / Speer, Robert Elliott – (Includes bibliographical references) – Philadelphia: Presbyterian Board of Publ and Sabbath-School Work, 1901 – 1mf – 9 – 0-8370-6523-2 – 1986-0523 – us A.T.L.A. [240]
PRESBYTERIAN HERALD: THE RECORD OF THE PRESBYTERIAN CHURCH IN IRELAND – (1986- . 5,6,9) – 1944- – 1 – us UMI [073]
PRESBYTERIAN HISTORICAL ALMANAC.. / Wilson, Joseph M – 10v. 1858-68 – 1 – $50.00 – us Presbyterian [240]
Presbyterian Historical Society *see*
- AMERICAN INDIAN CORRESPONDENCE
- PRESBYTERIAN KEY

PRESBYTERIAN HOME MISSIONARY – (Title varies) – v1-15. Mar 1872-1886 (complete) – 3r – 1 – ATLA S0120 – us A.T.L.A. [073]
PRESBYTERIAN HOME MISSIONS / Doyle, Sherman Hoadley – Philadelphia: Presbyterian Board of Publishing, 1902. xiv, 318p. 1 fiche – 9 – us A.T.L.A. [240]
PRESBYTERIAN HOME MISSIONS *see* PRESBYTERIAN HOME MISSIONARY
PRESBYTERIAN KEY / Presbyterian Historical Society – v1-39. 1945-1982 – 1 – $50.00 – us Presbyterian [240]
THE PRESBYTERIAN LAYMAN – (Lacking some pgs. Some pgs of original damaged) – v1-20. 1968-1987 – 2r – 1 – ATLA S0344 – us A.T.L.A. [073]
PRESBYTERIAN LIFE *see* AD
THE PRESBYTERIAN MAGAZINE – London, C.W. [Ont.]: J Norval, [1843?-184-] – 9 – cn C.I.H.M. [240]
THE PRESBYTERIAN MONTHLY – Philadelphia, PA. v1-5. 1866-1870 – 3r – 1 – $150.00 – us Presbyterian [240]
THE PRESBYTERIAN MONTHLY RECORD / Presbyterian Church in the U.S.A. – Philadelphia, PA. v21-37. 1870-1886 – 3r – 1 – $150.00 – us Presbyterian [240]
PRESBYTERIAN OF OUR UNION *see* ST. LOUIS PRESBYTERIAN
THE PRESBYTERIAN QUARTERLY – v-17. 1887-04 (complete) – 6r – 1 – ATLA 1994-S508 – us A.T.L.A. [073]
PRESBYTERIAN QUARTERLY AND PRINCETON REVIEW – (Cont by: The Princeton Review) – v1-6. 1872-77 (complete) – 2r – 1 – ATLA S0206 – us A.T.L.A. [073]
PRESBYTERIAN RECORD – (Cont: The Presbyterian Record for the Dominion of Canada) – Montreal: E Scott, [1892?-19–] – 9 – cn C.I.H.M. [240]
PRESBYTERIAN RECORD – Don Mills. v104-118. 1980-94 – 9 – Can$28.00y – cn Micromedia [240]
PRESBYTERIAN RECORD *see* THE PRESBYTERIAN RECORD FOR THE DOMINION OF CANADA
THE PRESBYTERIAN RECORD *see* THE PRESBYTERIAN RECORD FOR THE DOMINION OF CANADA
THE PRESBYTERIAN RECORD FOR THE DOMINION OF CANADA – (Cont: The Home and Foreign Record of the Canada Presbyterian Church. Cont by: Presbyterian Record. Is absorbed by: The Presbyterian) – Montreal: Printed for the General Assembly by A A Stevenson, [1876?-1891] – 9 – cn C.I.H.M. [240]
THE PRESBYTERIAN RECORD FOR THE DOMINION OF CANADA *see*
- THE HOME AND FOREIGN RECORD OF THE CANADA PRESBYTERIAN CHURCH
- THE HOME AND FOREIGN RECORD OF THE PRESBYTERIAN CHURCH OF THE LOWER PROVINCES OF BRITISH NORTH AMERICA
- THE PRESBYTERIAN
- PRESBYTERIAN RECORD

PRESBYTERIAN REUNION : A MEMORIAL VOLUME, 1837-1871 / Miller, Samuel, DD – New York: De-Witt C. Lent, 1870 – 2mf – us A.T.L.A. [240]
PRESBYTERIAN REVIEW – New York. N.Y. 1880-1888 – 1 – us UMI [071]
THE PRESBYTERIAN REVIEW – Toronto: Presbyterian News Pub Co, [1855?-18– or 19–] – 9 – cn C.I.H.M. [240]
THE PRESBYTERIAN REVIEW – Toronto. v1 n36. 3 sep 1885 – 1r – 1 – Can$25.00 – cn Can Microfilming [072]
THE PRESBYTERIAN REVIEW – v1-10. 1880-89 (complete) – 4r – 1 – ATLA S0212 – us A.T.L.A. [073]
PRESBYTERIAN SENTINEL – v1-2. 1859-60 – 1 – $50.00 – us Presbyterian [071]
THE PRESBYTERIAN TREASURY : OF EDUCATION, RELIGION, AND GENERAL INTELLIGENCE – Philadelphia, PA. v1-2. 1848-49 – 4r – 1 – $200.00 – us Presbyterian [240]
THE PRESBYTERIAN WITNESS *see* THE WITNESS
PRESBYTERIANISM AND EDUCATION / Schaff, David Schley – (Includes bibliographical references) – [S.l.: s.n., 1893?] – 1mf – 9 – 0-8370-7584-X – 1986-1584 – us A.T.L.A. [230]
PRESBYTERIANISM IN THE COLONIES : WITH SPECIAL REFERENCE TO THE PRINCIPLES AND INFLUENCE OF THE FREE CHURCH OF SCOTLAND : THE FIFTH SERIES OF THE CHALMERS LECTURES / Balfour, Robert Gordon – Edinburgh: Macniven & Wallace, 1899 – 1mf – us A.T.L.A. [240]
PRESBYTERIANISM IN THE OZARKS *see* AMERICAN PRESBYTERIANA 1
PRESBYTERIANISM THREE HUNDRED YEARS AGO / Breed, William Pratt – Philadelphia: Presbyterian Board of Publ, c1872 – 1mf – 9 – 0-8370-8725-2 – 1986-2725 – us A.T.L.A. [240]

THE PRESBYTERIANS / Thompson, Charles L – New York: Baker & Taylor, 1903 – 1mf – us A.T.L.A. [240]

PRESBYTERIANS AND THE REVOLUTION / Breed, William P – 1876 – 1 – $50.00 – us Presbyterian [240]

Presbyteries of Lorain and Elyria, Ohio *see* CHURCH RECORDS, 1836-1839, MS 444

PRESBYTERION – (1985-. 5,6,9) – v1-. 1975- – 1 – us UMI [240]

PRESBYTERION : COVENANT THEOLOGICAL SEMINARY REVIEW – v1-16. 1975-90 (complete) – 3r – 1 – ATLA S0798 – us A.T.L.A. [073]

PRESBYTERS AND DEACONS NOT COMMISSIONED TO PREACH WITHOUT THE BISHOP'S ALLOWANCE : A DISCOURSE ADDRESSED TO A CERTAIN METHODIST CLERGYMAN / N, N – London, 1761 – 1mf – 9 – MP-408/1 – ne IDC [240]

PRESBYTERY OF KANSAS CITY, 1821-1901 / Hill, John B – 1901 – 1 – $50.00 – us Presbyterian [240]

PRESBYTERY REPORTER – v1-8. May 1845-Jun 1871 (complete) – 3r – 1 – ATLA S0190 – us A.T.L.A. [073]

Preschez, P *see* LES RELATIONS ENTRE LA FRANCE ET LA BIRMANIE AU 18TH ET AU 19TH SIECLES

PRESCHOOL CHILDREN'S ASSESSMENT OF HEALTH VALUE RELATED TO SELECTED NONHEALTH VALUES / Wood, Martin L & Torabi, Mohammad R – 1992 – 3mf – 9 – $12.00 – us Microform Publ [613]

PRESCOT REPORTER – England.1873-75. -w. 2 reels – 1 – uk British Libr Newspaper [072]

PRESCOTT 1795-1890 – (Mf 1-4: Vital Records 1816-1900. Mf 5-6: Births, Marriages, Deaths 1843-61. Mf 7: Deaths 1862-90. Mf 8: Births 1862-90. Mf 9: Marriages 1862-90. Mf 10-19: Birth Index 1795-1928. Mf 20-29: Intentions Index 1822-1937. Mf 30-38: Marriage Index 1822-1937. Mf 39-46: Death Index 1822-1933) – (mf ed 1984) – 46mf – 9 – 0-931248-75-2 – us Holbrook [920]

Prescott, Guillermo H *see*
- HISTORIA DE LA CONQUISTA DEL PERU... INCAS
- HISTORIA...MEJICO...HERNANDO CORTES

Prescott, Thomas H *see* AMERIKANISCH DEUTSCHE ENCYCLOPAEDIE (AEL, ABT 1;13)

THE PRESCRIPTION: THERAPEUTICALLY, PHARMACEUTICALLY, GRAMMATICALLY AND HISTORICALLY CONSIDERED / Wall, Otto Augustus – 2nd rev. ed. St. Louis: Mosby, 1890. 206p. ill – 1 – us U.W. Library [615]

LA PRESCRIZIONE NEL DIRITTO INTERNAZIONALE PRIVATO / Cavarretta, G – Palermo, 1908 – 2mf – 1 – ILM-3341/1 – ne IDC [327]

PRESENCA – -irr. num. 1-54 (ano I-II), 10. marco 1927-. nov. 1938; ser. 2, num. 1- (ano 12-), nov. 1939-. Coimbra, Lisboa – 1 – us U.W. Library [073]

PRESENCE / Brent, Charles H – New York: Longmans, Green, 1914 – 1mf – us A.T.L.A. [240]

PRESENCE – Montreal, Quebec, Canada. 1973-75 – 1 – us A.J.P.C. [072]

PRESENCE CONGOLAISE – Kinshasa, 1956(Dec 22)-1967 – 4r – 1 – AF-100/3 – ne IDC [960]

PRESENCE UNIVERSITAIRE : ORGANE DES ETUDIANTS CATHOLIQUES DU CONGO ET DU RUANDA-URUNDI – Leopoldville, 1959-65 – 31mf – 9 – A-695/1 – ne IDC [370]

LE PRESENT – (Cont by: Echo de Drummondville 3,11 avr 1914) – Drummondville, Canada. 7 sep 1912-v2 n16. 28 fev 1914 – 1r – 1 – Can$35.00 – cn Can Microfilming [072]

LE PRESENT – no. 1-15. Paris. juil-nov 1857 – 1 – fr A.C.R.P.P. [073]

THE PRESENT – (New York). 1920 – 1 – us A.J.P.C. [071]

THE PRESENT – Philadelphia. Pa. The gegenwart. 1896-98 – 1 – us A.J.P.C. [071]

THE PRESENT CONDITION OF THE CHURCH OF ENGLAND : SEVEN ADDRESSES / Campbell, Archibald – London: Macmillan, 1872 – 1mf – us A.T.L.A. [240]

PRESENT CONDITIONS IN SPAIN, JANUARY 1938 / Forbes, William Cameron – Baltimore, MD. 1938. Fiche W 888. (Blodgett Collection of Spanish Civil War Pamphlets) – 9 – us H.U. College Libr [946]

PRESENT ET AVENIR DES OUVRIERS PAR UN TYPOGRAPHE / Burgy, Jules – Paris. 1847. (La Condition Ouvriere. Part Two.) – 9 – 2.50 – fr Bibl Nationale [360]

A PRESENT HEAVEN : ADDRESSED TO A FRIEND / Greenwell, Dora – Edinburgh: A. Strahan, 1862 – 1mf – us A.T.L.A. [240]

THE PRESENT METHOD OF INOCULATING FOR THE SMALL-POX / Dimsdale, T – M-96. 1767 – 9 – ne IDC [616]

THE PRESENT PROBLEMS OF NEW TESTAMENT STUDY / Hill, William Bancroft – New York: Edwin S Gorham, 1903 – 1mf – 9 – 0-8370-3587-2 – 1985-1587 – us A.T.L.A. [220]

THE PRESENT RELATIONS OF SCIENCE AND RELIGION / Bonney, Thomas G – New York: F. H. Revell, 1913 – 1mf – us A.T.L.A. [240]

THE PRESENT STATE OF MUSIC IN FRANCE AND ITALY / Burney, Charles – or, the journal of a tour through those countries. P 653. 1771 – 9 – ne IDC [780]

THE PRESENT STATE OF MUSIC IN FRANCE AND ITALY.. / Burney, Charles – The second edition corrected. 1773 – 9 – us Sibley [780]

THE PRESENT STATE OF MUSIC IN GERMANY, THE NETHERLANDS, AND UNITED PROVINCE / Burney, Charles – P 655. Ed. 2. 1775 – 9 – ne IDC [780]

THE PRESENT STATE OF MUSIC IN GERMANY, THE NETHERLANDS, AND UNITED PROVINCES / Burney, Charles – P 654. 2 v. 1773 – 9 – ne IDC [780]

THE PRESENT STATE OF MUSIC IN GERMANY, THE NETHERLANDS, AND UNITED PROVINCES.. / Burney, Charles – Second edition, corrected. 2 v. 1775 – 9 – us Sibley [780]

THE PRESENT STATE OF THE CHURCH IN ENGLAND : SEVENTEEN PARAGRAPHS / Braye, Alfred Thomas Townshend Verney-Cave – London: R Washbourne, 1884 – 1mf – 9 – 0-8370-7366-9 – 1986-1366 – us A.T.L.A. [240]

THE PRESENT STATE, PROSPECTS, AND RESPONSIBILITIES OF THE METHODIST EPISCOPAL CHURCH / Bangs, Nathan – 1850 – 9 – us A.T.L.A. [240]

THE PRESENT STATUS OF ALL THE PROJECTS OF DEVELOPMENT IN SYRIA AND ALL NECESSARY FIGURES AND STATISTICS AS IN MAY 1970 / Syria. Syrian Documentation Papers – 1970. BNE-9738 1 – 9 – ne IDC [338]

PRESENT STATUS OF INDONESIAN AGRICULTURE / Indonesia. Agriculture – Se-10,961 1. 1956 – 9 – ne IDC [630]

THE PRESENT STATUS OF THE INQUIRY CONCERNING THE GENUINENESS OF THE PAULINE EPISTLES / Weiss, Bernhard – Chicago: University of Chicago Press, 1897 – 1mf – 9 – 0-8370-9669-3 – 1986-3669 – us A.T.L.A. [220]

THE PRESENT TENSES OF THE BLESSED LIFE / Meyer, Frederick Brotherton – Chicago: Fleming H Revell, c1892 – 1mf – 9 – 0-8370-7176-3 – 1986-1176 – us A.T.L.A. [240]

PRESENT TO MY CHRISTIAN FRIEND: ON ENTIRE DEVOTION TO GOD / Palmer, Phoebe Worrell – 1859 – 9 – us A.T.L.A. [240]

THE PRESENT WORLD SITUATION : WITH SPECIAL REFERENCE TO THE DEMANDS MADE UPON THE CHRISTIAN CHURCH IN RELATION TO NON-CHRISTIAN LANDS / Mott, John Raleigh – New York: Student Volunteer Movement for Foreign Missions, 1915 – 1mf – us A.T.L.A. [900]

PRESENTACION DE LA FEDERACION EMPRESARIAL CACERENA. BORRADOR PARA EXAMEN / Federacion Empresarial Cacerena – Caceres: Imp. Extremadura, 1976 – 1 – sp Bibl Santa Ana [946]

PRESENTATION DES BAHNAR-JOLONG, PROTO-INDOCHINOIS DE LANGUE AUSTROASIATIQUE, PROVINCE DE KONTUM, VIETNAM DU SUD / Leger, D – 9 – F120.00 – fr Ethnologie [490]

PRESENTATION OF PORTRAIT OF HONORABLE ASA BIGGS TO UNITED STATES DISTRICT COURT / Biggs, Asa – Address by F. S. Spruill. Raleigh: Uzzell, 1915. 24p. LL-1196 – 1 – us L of C Photodup [340]

PRESENT-DAY EVANGELISM / Chapman, John Wilbur – (Includes bibliographical references) – New York: Bakor & Taylor, [1903] – 1mf – 9 – 0-8370-6251-9 – 1986-0251 – us A.T.L.A. [240]

PRESENT-DAY INDONESIAN-AMERICAN RELATIONSHIP / Subandrio – Speech at American Association. SE 2219 1. Sept. 4, 1958 – 9 – ne IDC [335]

PRESENT-DAY PROBLEMS OF CHRISTIAN THOUGHT / McKim, Randolph Harrison – (Includes bibliographical references) – New York: Thomas Whittaker, 1900 – 1mf – 9 – 0-8370-9168-3 – 1986-3168 – us A.T.L.A. [240]

PRESENT-DAY RATIONALISM CRITICALLY EXAMINED / Henslow, George – (Includes bibliographical references & index) – Cincinnati: Jennings & Graham; New York: Eaton & Mains, [1905?] – 1mf – 9 – 0-8370-4897-4 – 1985-2897 – us A.T.L.A. [210]

PRESENT-DAY THINKERS AND THE NEW SKOLASTICISM... / Zybura, John S – Madrid: Razon y Fe, 1927 – 1 – sp Bibl Santa Ana [180]

O PRESENTE – Aracaju, 25 Aug, Dec 1877; 5 Jan 1878 – 1,5,6 – bl Biblioteca [072]

O PRESENTE : PERIODICO LITTERARIO, CRITICO E NOTICIOSO – Maceio, Alagoas. 23 Jul 1887 – 1,5,6 – bl Biblioteca [072]

PRESENTE – Lima. nos. 1-112. 7 Dec 1956-Mar 1969 – 1 – 35.00r – us Hoover Inst Photo [073]

PRESENTMENTS OF THE COURT LEET / Neath Burgage – 1677-87. Survey of the Manor of Cadoxton Juxta Neath. 1602. Ms – 1 – uk Microform Academic [941]

PRESENTO...NUEVAS INSCRIPCIONES ROMANAS QUE ACABAN DE HACER EN PLASENICA...EXTENSION DE LA PENINSULA / Fita, Fidel & Rodriguez Villa, Antonio – Madrid: Est. Tip. Fortanet, 1898. B.R.A.H. 32, 1898, pp. 255-256 – 1 – sp Bibl Santa Ana [946]

A PRESERVATIVE IN PERILOUS TIMES, IN THREE LETTERS : 1. TO MR. JAMES RELLY,...2. TO MR. JOHN WESLEY,...3. TO MR. JOHN WESLEY,... / Cudworth, W – London, [1758] – 2mf – 9 – MP-376/1 – ne IDC [240]

PRESERVICE TEACHERS AS MENTORS DURING AN EARLY FIELD EXPERIENCE THROUGH ELECTRONIC COMMUNICATION (E-MAIL) / LaMaster, Kathryn J – Ohio State University, 1996 – 2mf – 9 – $8.00 – PE 3660 – us Microform Publ [370]

LA PRESIDENCIA DE CARLOS PILLEGINI; POLITICA DE ORDEN, 1890-92 / Carcano, Miguel Angel – Buenos Aires: EUDEBA, 1968. 118p. Bibliog – 1 – us U.W. Library [972]

Presidencia de la Nacion, Secretaria de Prensa y Difusion *see* CONSTRUCCION NACIONAL

LE PRESIDENT DU CONSEIL DE LA SOCIETE DES NATIONS / Avramoff, D – Bordeaux, 1932 – 2mf – 9 – ILM-4016/1 – ne IDC [340]

PRESIDENT DWIGHT D. EISENHOWER'S OFFICE FILES, 1953-1961, PART 1 : EISENHOWER ADMINISTRATION SERIES – 9 – $3,520.00 – 1-55655-165-7 – us UPA [324]

PRESIDENT DWIGHT D. EISENHOWER'S OFFICE FILES, 1953-1961, PART 2 : INTERNATIONAL SERIES – 9 – $3,520.00 – 1-55655-166-5 – us UPA [324]

PRESIDENT EISENHOWER'S MEETINGS WITH LEGISLATIVE LEADERS, 1953-61 – 2 reels with printed guide – 1 – $220.00 – 0-89093-980-2 – us UPA [977]

PRESIDENT FRANKLIN D. ROOSEVELT'S OFFICE FILES, 1933-1945 / ed by Leuchtenburg, William E – (Pt 1: "Safe" and Confidential Files 22r $2,750.00 ISBN 1-55655-265-3. Pt 2: Diplomatic Correspondence File 36r $4,395.00 ISBN 1-55655-266-1. Pt 3 Departmental Correspondence File 39r $4,505.00 ISBN 1-55655-267-X. Pt 4 Subject Files 45r $5,630.00 ISBN 1-55655-495-8. Pt 5 The John Franklin Carter Files on German Nazi Party Members 25r $3,130.00 ISBN: 1-55655-496-6) – 1 – $19,390.00 coll – us UPA [320]

PRESIDENT HARRY S. TRUMAN'S OFFICE FILES : COMPLETE COLLECTION: 1945-1953 – 9 – $9,055.00 – us UPA [324]

PRESIDENT HARRY S. TRUMAN'S OFFICE FILES, PART 1 : POLITICAL FILE – 9 – $795.00 – 1-55655-150-9 – us UPA [324]

PRESIDENT HARRY S. TRUMAN'S OFFICE FILES, PART 2 : CORRESPONDENCE FILE – 9 – $2,955.00 – 1-55655-151-7 – us UPA [324]

PRESIDENT HARRY S. TRUMAN'S OFFICE FILES, PART 3 : SUBJECT FILE – 9 – $4,765.00 – 1-55655-152-5 – us UPA [324]

PRESIDENT HARRY S. TRUMAN'S OFFICE FILES, PART 4 : KOREAN WAR FILES – 9 – $795.00 – 1-55655-153-3 – us UPA [324]

PRESIDENT HARRY S. TRUMAN'S OFFICE FILES, PART 5 : TRUMAN DIARIES AND HANDWRITTEN NOTES FILES – 9 – $225.00 – 1-55655-154-1 – us UPA [324]

PRESIDENT JOHN F. KENNEDY'S OFFICE FILES : COMPLETE COLLECTION: 1961-1963 – 9 – $10,765.00 – us UPA [324]

PRESIDENT JOHN F. KENNEDY'S OFFICE FILES, PART 1 : SPECIAL CORRESPONDENCE, SPEECH, LEGISLATIVE AND PRESS CONFERENCE FILES – 9 – $2,530.00 – 1-55655-089-8 – us UPA [324]

PRESIDENT JOHN F. KENNEDY'S OFFICE FILES, PART 2 : STAFF MEMORANDA FILE – 9 – $990.00 – 1-55655-090-1 – us UPA [324]

PRESIDENT JOHN F. KENNEDY'S OFFICE FILES, PART 3 : DEPARTMENTS AND AGENCIES FILE – 9 – $3,190.00 – 1-55655-091-X – us UPA [324]

PRESIDENT JOHN F. KENNEDY'S OFFICE FILES, PART 4 : SUBJECTS FILES – 9 – $1,540.00 – 1-55655-092-8 – us UPA [324]

PRESIDENT JOHN F. KENNEDY'S OFFICE FILES, PART 5 : COUNTRIES FILE – 9 – $3,080.00 – 1-55655-093-6 – us UPA [324]

PRESIDENT KENNEDY AND THE PRESS (1961-1963) / Kennedy, John F – 1982. (Presidential Documents Series) – 1 – $1,920.00 – 0-89093-358-8 – us UPA [977]

PRESIDENT OF THE PHILIPPINES *see* THE FIVE-YEAR FISCAL PLAN, 1961-1965

PRESIDENT SUKARNO'S MESSAGE TO THE NATION ON THE SIXTH ANNIVERSARY OF INDONESIAN INDEPENDENCE / Sukarno, Pres. Indonesia – SE 6196 1. Aug. 17, 1951 – 9 – ne IDC [324]

PRESIDENT TRUMAN'S COMMITTEE ON CIVIL RIGHTS – (With printed guide) – 10r – 1 – $1,280.00 – 0-89093-657-9 – us UPA [323]

PRESIDENTE OLEGARIO : ORGAO OFICIAL DOS PODERES DO MUNICIPIOS – Presidente Olegario, 15 Apr, Jun-17 Jul 1943 – 1,5,6 – bl Biblioteca [072]

PRESIDENTIAL ADDRESS AT THE MEETING OF THE MARITIME MEDICAL ASSOCIATION: HELD IN ST JOHN, N.B., JULY 22ND AND 23RD 1891 / Bayard, William – 1891?. 05976. (Pre-1900 Canadiana) – 9 – cn C.I.H.M. [610]

THE PRESIDENTIAL CAMPAIGNS OF 1928 AND 1960: THE RELIGIOUS ISSUE / McClerren, Beryl F – 288p – 1 – 10.08 – us Baptist [240]

PRESIDENTIAL DIARIES OF HENRY MORGENTHAU JR. (1938-45) / Morgenthau, Henry Jr. – (With printed guide. Series: Presidential Documents Series) – 1980 – 2r – 1 – $220.00 – 0-89093-350-2 – us UPA [977]

PRESIDENTIAL DIRECTIVES ON NATIONAL SECURITY FROM TRUMAN TO CLINTON – (Printed guide & index £630.00 ISBN: 0-89887-111-5) – 1994 – 441mf – 9 – £2,940.00 coll – 0-89887-110-7 – uk Chadwyck [327]

PRESIDENTIAL DOCUMENTS SERIES *see* PRESIDENTIAL DIARIES OF HENRY MORGENTHAU JR. (1938-45)

PRESIDENTIAL ELECTION CAMPAIGN BIOGRAPHIES, 1824-1976 – (465v. Cataloging available. Price together with "Presidential Election Campaign Documents, 1868-1900" $4,985.00) – 1367mf – 1 – $4,175.00 – us UMI [975]

PRESIDENTIAL ELECTION CAMPAIGN DOCUMENTS, 1868-1900 – (Materials from Dartmouth College Library collection of pamphlets. Price together with "Presidential Election Campaign Biographies, 1824-1976" $4,985.00) – 14r – 1 – $1,075.00 – us UMI [975]

PRESIDENTIAL ELECTION CAMPAIGN DOCUMENTS FOR THE YEARS 1868-1900 – 14r – 1 – $225.00 set – us Dartmouth [320]

PRESIDENTIAL ELECTIONS – 1900-68 – 21r – 1 – us Ross [977]

PRESIDENTIAL ELECTIONS IN MARYLAND / Willis, John T – 1984. 315p. ISBN: 0-912338-46-6 – 9 – 12.50 – us Lomond [975]

PRESIDENTIAL EXECUTIVE ORDERS / U. S. President – 26 Jun 1845-26 Jun 1936.11 reels – 1 – $475.00 – us Trans-Media [340]
PRESIDENTIAL EXECUTIVE ORDERS RELATING TO THE PANAMA CANAL : MARCH 8 1904 TO DECEMBER 30 1931 / Panama Canal Zone – (With suppls 1-28 1922-35) – Washington(?): GPO(?), n.d. – 6mf – 9 – $9.00 – LLMC 82-100D Title 11 – us L.L.M.C. [340]
PRESIDENTIAL MESSAGES AND PAPERS OF THE CONFEDERACY / Confederate States of America – 1 reel – 1 – $50.00 – us Trans-Media [340]
PRESIDENTIAL PROCLAMATIONS / U. S. President – 1-2160. 1789-1936. 11 rolls – 1 – T1223 – us Nat'l Archives [975]
PRESIDENTIAL PROCLAMATIONS / U. S. President – 1789-1936. From the files of the National Archives of the United States. 12 reels with indexes – 1 – $475.00 – us Trans-Media [340]
PRESIDENTIAL STUDIES QUARTERLY – (v. 5-1975- 5,6,9) – v. 4- 1974- – 1 – us UMI [320]
PRESIDENT'S CLOSING ADDRESS AT THE FIFTH ANNUAL MEETING OF THE NATIONAL COUNCIL OF WOMEN OF CANADA / Aberdeen and Temair, Ishbel Gordon, Marchioness of – 1898?. 06572. (Pre-1900 Canadiana) – 9 – cn C.I.H.M. [971]
PRESIDENT'S COMMISSION ON IMMIGRATION AND NATURALIZATION : "PERLMAN COMMISSION HEARINGS – (App by President Harry S. Truman) – Washington: GPO, 1952 – 22mf – 9 – $33.00 – LLMC 81-508 – us L.L.M.C. [324]
PRESIDENT'S COMMISSION ON IMMIGRATION AND NATURALIZATION : REPORT: WHOM SHALL WE WELCOME – (Contains President Truman's veto message of the McCarran-Walter Act) – Washington: GPO, 1952 – 4mf – 9 – $6.00 – LLMC 81-509 – us L.L.M.C. [324]
PRESIDENT'S COMMISSION ON THE ASSASSINATION OF PRESIDENT JOHN F. KENNEDY : "WARREN COMMISSION" HEARINGS AND REPORT – (App by President Lyndon B. Johnson) – Washington: GPO. v1-26 (hearings) + report, 1964 (all publ) – 208mf – 9 – $312.00 – LLMC 80-515 – us L.L.M.C. [324]
PRESIDENT'S COUNCIL ON INTEGRITY AND EFFICIENCY REPORTS – 1981-88 – 9 – us L.L.M.C. [340]
PRESIDENT'S MARCH / Phile, Philip – Philadelphia: G. Willig c.1798. For the piano, followed by an arrangement for the flute. MUSIC 3082, Item 9 – 1 – us L of C Photodup [780]
PRESIDENT'S OFFICE FILES, SERIES A : WILLIAM GREEN PAPERS, 1934-52 / American Federation of Labor – From holdings of State Historical Society of Wisconsin. (AFL Records, Pt 2) – 38r – 1 – $3,715.00 – 0-89093-896-2 – us UPA [331]
PRESIDENT'S PRIVATE SECTOR SURVEY OF COST CONTROL : "GRACE COMMISSION" – v1-3. Spring/Fall 1983 – 61mf – 9 – $91.00 – LLMC 90-377 – us L.L.M.C. [340]
PRESIDENTS' REPORTS / Lucas County. Ohio. Toledo, City Board of Education – 1879 – 1r – 1 – $32.50r – us Archival [324]
Presl, C B *see*
- EPIMELIAE BOTANICAE
- SUPPLEMENTUM TENTAMINIS PTERIDOGRAPHIAE
- TENTAMEN PTERIDOGRAPHIAE

Presl, J S *see*
- DELICIAE PRAGENSES, HISTORIAM NATURALEM SPECTANTES
- FLORA CECHICA
- WSEOBECNY ROSTLINOPIS

Presl, K B *see*
- BOTANISCHE BEMERKUNGEN
- CYPERACEAE ET GRAMINEAE SICULAE
- DELICIAE PRAGENSES, HISTORIAM NATURALEM SPECTANTES
- EPIMELIAE BOTANICAE
- FLORA CECHICA
- FLORA SICULA, EXHIBENS PLANTAS VASCULOSAS
- DIE GEFAESSBUENDEL IM STIPES DER FARRN
- HYMENOPHYLLACEAE
- PRODROMUS MONOGRAPHIAE LOBELIACEARUM
- RELIQUIAE HAENKEANAE
- SYMBOLAE BOTANICAE
- TENTAMEN PTERIDOGRAPHIAE, SEU GENERA FILICACEARUM

PRESLIA : VESTNIK CESKE BOTANICKE SPOLECNOSTI – (In French and Russian) – Praha. v1-11. 1914-32 – 21mf – 9 – 8636/1 – ne IDC [073]
LA PRESPECTIVE CVRIEVSE: OU, MAGIE ARTIFICIELLE DES EFFETS MERVEILLEVX / Niceron, Jean Francois – Paris: chez Pierre Billaine, 1638 – 1 – us U.W. Library [530]
PRESPEVKY K DEJINAM HNUTIA POLNOHOSPODARSKYCH ROBOTNIKOV / Merci, J – Bratislava, 1952 – 1r – 1 – us I.H.R.C. [947]
LA PRESQU'ILE – Dorion, Canada. 1 fev 1952; v5 n1. 3 fev 1956-v6 n34. 26 nov 1956 – 1r – 1 – Can$55.00 – cn Can Microfilming [072]
LA PRESQU'ILE DU CAP-VERT. / Institut Francais d'Afrique Noire – Dakar, 1949 – 1 – us Res Libr [960]
PRESS – Blair, NV. 1908-10 – 1r – 1 – $50.00 – U04421 – us Library Micro [071]
PRESS – Kenton, Ohio. 1897-1904 – 1r – 1 – $32.50r – us Archival [071]
PRESS : NORTH CLACKMAS – (Set incl. North Clackamas News (Milwaukie, OR)) – Portland, OR. -w. 1 Mar 1967-12 Feb 1969. – 4r – 1 – us U.O. Library [071]
PRESS – Pittsburgh, CA. 1972-78 – 18r – 1 – $900.00 – B02628 – us Library Micro [071]
PRESS – Pretoria. South Africa. 1889-99 – 1 – sa State Libr [072]
PRESS : SUBURBAN EAST – (Set incl. Greater Enterprise News (Portland)) – Portland, OR. -w. 1 Mar 1967-26 Dec 1973+. – 12r – 1 – us U.O. Library [071]
THE PRESS – Bakersfield. Calif. 1955-1958 – 1 – us UMI [071]
THE PRESS – Bedford, Canada. v1 n15. 6 dec 1899 – 1r – 1 – Can$25.00 – cn Can Microfilming [072]
THE PRESS – Christchurch, 1987- – 36r per y – 1 – inquire – us Ross [072]
THE PRESS – Dublin. Ireland. -w. 19 Feb 1849-22 Feb 1850. (1 reel) – 1 – uk British Libr Newspaper [072]
THE PRESS – Dublin. Ireland. -w. 25 Jan-8 Mar 1833. (13 ft) – 1 – uk British Libr Newspaper [072]
THE PRESS – Philadelphia: J W Forney, 1857-80. jan-dec 1858; jan-dec 1876 (4r) – 1 – us Res Libr [071]
THE PRESS – Philadelphia, PA. -d 1857-64. 16 rolls – 13 – $25.00r – us I.M.R. [071]
THE PRESS – Santa Monica, CA. 1953-1954 – 2r – 1 – $100.00 – R03524 – us Library Micro [071]
THE PRESS – Wilmington, CA. 1928-1938 – 33r – 1 – $1,650.00 – R04137 – us Library Micro [071]
THE PRESS *see* LA PRENSA/THE PRESS
PRESS AND BROADCAST RELEASES ISSUED BY THE DEPARTMENT OF INFORMATION / Indonesia – In English. SE-4995 1 – 9 – ne IDC [950]
PRESS AND HORTICULTURIST – Riverside. Calif. -tri wkly. 1885-86 – 1 – us UMI [071]
PRESS AND LEADER – Bryan, Ohio. 1862-63 – 1r – 1 – $32.50r – us Archival [071]
PRESS BANQUET AT TORONTO: SPEECHES OF PREMIER BOWELL AND MR. DAVIN: SPLENDID RECEPTION TO THE PREMIER – 1895?. 00419. (Pre-1900 Canadiana) – 9 – cn C.I.H.M. [971]
PRESS BULLETIN / Colorado. Agricultural Experiment Station. Fort Collins – nos.1-100. 1900-45 – 1,5,6 – us Spaulding [630]
PRESS BULLETIN / Georgia. Experiment Station. Experiment – v. 1-60. 1893-1907 – 1,5,6 – us Spaulding [630]
PRESS BULLETIN / Georgia. Experiment Station. Experiment – v. 1-651. 1905-54 – 1,5,6 – us Spaulding [630]
PRESS BULLETIN / Iowa State University. Agricultural Experiment Station – No.1-38.1906-20. 1 reel – 1,5 – us Spaulding [630]
PRESS BULLETIN / Nebraska. Agricultural Experiment Station. Lincoln – n.1-46. 1887-1915 – 1,5 – us Spaulding [630]
PRESS BULLETIN / Tennessee. University. Agricultural Experiment Station – v.1-50. Apr 1889-Apr 1925 – 1,5 – us Spaulding [630]
PRESS BULLETINS / Minnesota. University. Agricultural Experiment Station. St. Paul – nos.1-46. 1894-1915 – 1,5,6 – us Spaulding [630]
PRESS BULLETINS / North Dakota. Agricultural Experiment Station. Fargo – nos.1-59. 1893-1913 – 1,5,6 – us Spaulding [630]
PRESS CIRCULAR / Mississippi. Agricultural Experiment Station. State College – v. 45-275. 1923-27 – 1,5,6 – us Spaulding [630]
PRESS CONFERENCES OF FRANKLIN D. ROOSEVELT / U. S. President – (Index. 1933-45. 1 roll. 1) – 1933-45. 12 rolls – 1 – us Roosevelt [323]
PRESS CONFERENCES OF THE U.S. SECRETARIES OF STATE, 1922-1974 – (Harding-Coolidge-Hoover Eras 3 Jan 1922-3 Mar 1933 5r. Roosevelt-Truman Eras 6 Mar 1933-14 Jan 1953 7r. Eisenhower-Kennedy-Johnson-Nixon-Ford Eras 18 Feb 1953-Sept 1974 3r) – 1974 – 15r – 1 – $1,275.00 – S1866 – us Scholarly Res [327]
PRESS CUTTING FILES, 1956-1967 / South African Institute of Race Relations – (Inventory available) – Johannesburg: Microfile, [19–?] – reels 1-25 only – 1 – us Res Libr [070]
PRESS CUTTINGS, PAMPHLETS AND ARTICLES ON KANAKA LABOUR TRAFFIC AND MISSIONARY LIFE IN THE NEW HEBRIDES / Gray, William – PMB Doc404 – at Pacific Mss [980]
PRESS DEMOCRAT – Santa Rosa, CA. 1980-1982 – 4r – 1 – $200.00 – B02980 – us Library Micro [071]
THE PRESS DEMOCRAT – Santa Rosa, CA. 1896- – 847+ r – 1 – $42,350.00 ($780.00y) – B02978 – us Library Micro [071]
PRESS DIGEST – (Issues for apr 29 1943-44 filmed with: Press Reports (Johannesburg, South Africa), 1936-apr 15 1943) – [Johannesburg: South African Jewish Board of Deputies], apr 29 1943-44; feb 14,28-may 9,22-jun 13,27-dec 1946; sep 15, nov 10-11 1949; jan 12 1950-52; 1953-dec 1967 – us Res Libr [070]
PRESS ENTERPRISE – (Also known as: The Daily Enterprise. Morning and evening combined Oct 1983) – Riverside, CA. 1878- – 1309+ r – 1 – $65,450.00 ($565.00y) – R02721 – us Library Micro [071]
PRESS ENTERPRISE AND HORTICULTURIST – Riverside, CA. 1880-1905 – 11r – 1 – $550.00 – R04095 – us Library Micro [071]
PRESS GAZETTE – Milton. Fl. 1953- – 1 – us P.K. Yonge [071]
PRESS HERALD – Portland. Maine. 1921- – 1 – us UMI [071]
THE PRESS HERALD – Ravine, PA., 1980-1985 – 13 – $25.00r – us I.M.R. [071]
THE PRESS HERALD – Tyrone, PA., 1977-1980 – 13 – $25.00r – us I.M.R. [071]
PRESS INDEPENDENT – (Cont: Native Press at v20 no 32 1990. Cont by: Northern Star at v23 no 17 1993) – Yellowknife. v20-22. 1990-92 – 1 – Can$115.00y – cn Micromedia [070]
PRESS INDEPENDENT *see*
- NATIVE PRESS
- NORTHERN STAR

PRESS JOURNAL – Sacramento, CA. 1969-77; Jan-Mar 1979 – 12r – 1 – $600.00 – C02739 – us Library Micro [071]
PRESS JOURNAL – Vero Beach. Fl. -w. 1937-1939, 1946-1973 – 1 – us P.K. Yonge [071]
PRESS LIST OF ANCIENT DOCUMENTS PRESERVED IN THE IMPERIAL RECORD ROOM OF THE GOVERNMENT OF INDIA 1748-1800 – Calcutta. v1-17. 1900-16 – 337mf – 9 – I-313/2 – ne IDC [025]
PRESS LIST OF "MUTINY PAPERS", 1857 / India. Imperial Record Office – Calcutta. 1921. BI-326 2 – 8 – ne IDC [950]
PRESS LISTS OF THE PUBLIC DEPARTMENT RECORDS, 1748-1800 / India. Imperial Record Office – Calcutta. 1924. BI-313 2 – 8 – ne IDC [310]
PRESS RELEASE FOR FAVOUR OF PUBLICATION PR : INDONESIAN REPUBLIC, 1945-1949. OFFICE, LONDON – (Lacking: 1949 (1-5, 27-29, 31-34, 37-39)) – London, 1949 – 5mf – 9 – SE-1517/1 – ne IDC [070]
PRESS RELEASES / Ridgecrest. North Carolina. Ridgecrest Baptist Assembly – 1949-51. 288p – 1 – 10.08 – us Baptist [240]
PRESS RELEASES / U. S. President – 1953- – 1 – us L of C Photodup [977]
PRESS RELEASES / U.S. Department of State. U.S. Mission to the United Nations – 1946- – 1 – $20.00y – us L of C Photodup [977]
PRESS RELEASES ISSUED BY AND SPEECHES BY OFFICIALS OF THE U.S. DEPARTMENT OF HOUSING AND URBAN DEVELOPMENT – (Press Release Collection complete 436mf $1360 – Base Collection 1934-78 407mf $1270 – 1979 update 29mf $90; Speeches 1934-79 complete 420mf $1235 – Base Collection 1934-78 395mf $1150 – 1979 update $85) – 9 – us UMI [360]
PRESS RELEASES N1-116 – (Various pagination) – Saipan, n.p, 1975 – 7mf – 9 – $10.50 – LLMC 82-100F, Title 94 – us L.L.M.C. [323]
PRESS RELEASES OF THE ADVISORY COMMISSION TO THE COUNCIL OF NATIONAL DEFENSE, JUNE 3, 1940-JAN. 15, 1941 / U.S. War Production Board – 1 roll. M185. Printed guide – 1 – us Nat'l Archives [324]
PRESS REPORTS – (Issues for 1936-apr 15 1943 filmed with: Press Digest (Johannesburg, South Africa), apr 29 1943-44; issues for 1936-apr 15 1943 also filmed with an untitled press report called: no 1 (8/8/38)) – [Johannesburg: South African Jewish Board of Deputies], n1-22,24-130,135-151,153-338 (jul 31? 1936-apr 15 1943 (2r) – 1 – us Res Libr [070]
PRESS SUMMARIES OF THE U.S. CONSULATE GENERAL, HONG KONG – (Survey of China Mainland Press, Nov 1950-Sep 1977 L9300058 158r. Supplement to Survey of China Mainland Press, May 1960-1977 L9300059 8r. Index to Survey of China Mainland Press, Selections from China Mainland Magazines and Current Background, Nov 1950-Sep 1977 L9300060 18r. Review of Hongkong Chinese Press, Jul 1947-May 1961 L9300061 10r. Extracts from China Mainland Publications, Apr 1962-Aug 1964 L9300062 3r. Current Background, Jun 1950-Jul 1977 L9300063 26r. Selections from China Mainland Magazines, Aug 1955-Sep 1977 L9300064 30r. Supplement to Selections of China Mainland Magazines, 1965-1975 L9300065 4r. In English) – 257r – 1 – $40.00r outside US – Dist. us Scholarly Res – us L of C Photodup [320]
PRESS TELEGRAM AND LONG BEACH SUN – Long Beach, CA. 1938-47 – 105r – 1 – $5,250.00 – C02364 – us Library Micro [071]
PRESS TIMES – (Also known as: Rawhide Times) – Rawhide, NV. 1908-11 – 1r – 1 – $50.00 – U04655 – us Library Micro [071]
THE PRESS TRIBUNE – Roseville, CA. 1945- – 194+ r – 1 – $9,700.00 ($420.00y) – C02727 – us Library Micro [071]
PRESS-CHRONICLE – Johnson City. Tenn. 1948- – 1 – us UMI [071]
PRESS-CITIZEN – Iowa City. Iowa. 1965- – 1 – us UMI [071]
PRESS-COURIER – Oxnard. Calif. 1935- – 1 – us UMI [071]
PRESS-DEMOCRAT – Santa Rosa. Calif. 1901- – 1 – us UMI [071]
DI PRESSE = THE PRESS – (In Yiddish) – Buenos Aires, AG. v19 no7006. 28 May 1936 – 1r – 1 – $25.00 – cn Can Microfilming [072]
DIE PRESSE – 1986-1995 – 12 times per yr – 1 – F4,800.00 – sz Infoprint [072]
DIE PRESSE : TAGESZEITUNG DER DEUTSCHEN PRESSE-AUSSTELLUNG DUESSELDORF – Bielefeld, oct 22-nov 30 1947 – 1r – 1 – Inquire at Mikrofilmarchiv for details – gw Misc Inst [070]
DIE PRESSE – Vienna, 1979- – 9 – inquire – us Ross [072]
DIE PRESSE – Vienna. 1979- – 22310.00y; CPC; 9 – gw Alpha Com [072]
DIE PRESSE – Vienna, 1989- – 12r per y – 1 – inquire – us Ross [072]
DIE PRESSE – Wien, 1860-62 – 8r – 1 – DM640.00 – gw Mikro Press [072]
DIE PRESSE – Wien, sep 1 1953-66 – 51r – 1 – gw Mikrofilm [072]
LA PRESSE – (avr 1973-31 dec 1992 451r) – Montreal, Canada. 20 oct 1884-mar 1973 – 704r – 1 – cn Can Microfilming [072]
LA PRESSE : EDITION BI-HEBDOMADAIRE / ed by Lanctot, Mederic – Montreal, Canada. 15 sep 1863-5 sep 1864 – 1r – 1 – Can$40.00 – cn Can Microfilming [072]
LA PRESSE – Fond. Emile de Girardin. no. 1. Paris. 1er juil 1836-85, 21 mai 1886; no. 1. 17 mars 1887; n.s., no. 1. 6 juin 1888; 13 oct 1929, mai-dec 1930, mai-juin 1932, fevr 1934-juil 1935 – 1 – fr A.C.R.P.P. [073]

LA PRESSE – Montreal, Canada. 3 Jan 1922-16 Aug 1928. -d. 112 reels – 1 – uk British Libr Newspaper [072]
LA PRESSE – Montreal, Quebec, Canada. 1884- – 1 – cn Commonwealth Micro [072]
LA PRESSE : NUMERO ILLUSTRE DU 25IEME ANNIVERSAIRE – Montreal, Canada. 3 sep 1910 – 1r – 1 – Can$25.00 – cn Can Microfilming [072]
LA PRESSE – Port-au-Prince. Sept 21 1929-Nov 25 1931. Incomplete – 1 – us NY Public [072]
LA PRESSE – Quebec, 1951-1953 – 22r – 1 – cn Preston [971]
LA PRESSE – Quebec, Canada. 23 avr 1883; v1 n1. 1 mai 1883 – 1r – 1 – Can$25.00 – cn Can Microfilming [072]
LA PRESSE – Revue de toutes les branches de l'activite humaine. Paris. nov 1887-avr 1888 – 1 – fr A.C.R.P.P. [073]
LA PRESSE *see* LE NOUVEAU MONDE
PRESSE AFRICAINE – (29 Jul 1960-3 Aug 1963 not publ) – [Bukavu], 1958(Oct 25)-1967 – 4r – 1 – AF-120/3 – ne IDC [960]
PRESSE CAMPUS *see* LE JOURNAL DES ETUDIANTS DE L'UNIVERSITE DE SHERBROOKE
LA PRESSE COLONIALE – Organe de defense des interets coloniaux. Dir. G. Boussenot, P. Vivien. Paris. 1914-24 – 1 – fr A.C.R.P.P. [073]
LA PRESSE DAHOMEENNE FACE AUX ASPIRATIONS DES "EVOLUES" / Codo, B C – "La Voix du Dahomey". 1927-57 – 9 – F120.00 – fr Ethnologie [306]
LA PRESSE DE FARNHAM – Farnham, Canada. v1 n21. 13 fev 1885; v1 n25. 13 mar 1885 – 1r – 1 – Can$25.00 – cn Can Microfilming [072]
LA PRESSE DE FRANCO / Comite de Vigilance des Intellectuels Antifascistes – Paris, 1937? Fiche W 808. (Blodgett Collection of Spanish Civil War Pamphlets) – 9 – us H.U. College Libr [946]
PRESSE DE LONDRES – London, UK. 20 Sept 1857-9 May 1863 – 1 – uk British Libr Newspaper [072]
PRESSE DER SOWJETUNION – 1952-1989 – 3,842mf – 1 – DM21,899.40 – gw Mikro Press [070]
LA PRESSE EN COTE-D'IVOIRE: LA COLONISATION, L'AUBE DE LA DECOLONISATION (1906-1952) / Guillaneuf, R – 9 – F160.00 – fr Ethnologie [306]
LA PRESSE INDOCHINOISE – Saigon. mai 1924-janv 1941 – 1 – fr A.C.R.P.P. [073]
PRESSE KATANGA – Elisabethville. 5v. 1960-63 – 39mf – 9 – A-690/1 – ne IDC [960]
LA PRESSE LIBRE – Feuilles belges-germaniques publiees sans censure. no. 1-70. Bruxelles. 1840-6 mai 1841 – 1 – fr A.C.R.P.P. [073]
LA PRESSE LIBRE – Journal politique quotidien. spec juin 1868, no. 1-124. 16 dec 1868-5 mai 1869. devient: La Reforme. Politique et sociale. 9 mai 1869-19 fevr 1870. Paris – 1 – fr A.C.R.P.P. [073]
LA PRESSE LIBRE : REDIGEE PAR LES GREVISTES DE "LA PRESSE" – Montreal, Canada. 28 sep 1964-10 dec 1964 – 1r – 1 – Can$35.00 – cn Can Microfilming [070]
LA PRESSE MEDICALE – Paris. v58-79. 1950-71 – 1,5,6 – us Princeton Micro [616]
PRESSE POP – Montreal-Nord, 21 sep 1971 – 1r – 1 – Can$25.00 – cn Can Microfilming [072]
LA PRESSE REGIONALE / ed by Cote, J-P – Repentigny, Canada. v1 n24. 5 nov 1964-v1 n38. 18 mar 1965 – 1r – 1 – Can$35.00 – cn Can Microfilming [072]
PRESSE RIVIERA CHABLAIS – 1994-1995 – 3r per y – 6 – F4,400 – sz Infoprint [944]
LA PRESSE SYNDICALE : GREVISTES DE "LA PRESSE" – Montreal, Canada. 3 oct-15 oct 1958 – 1r – 1 – Can$35.00 – cn Can Microfilming [072]
LA PRESSE THEATRALE ET MUSICALE – Musique, theatres, sciences, litterature, beaux-arts. Paris. 1860-61 – 1 – fr A.C.R.P.P. [073]
PRESSEARCHIV ZUR GESCHICHTE DEUTSCHLANDS SOWIE ZUR INTERNATIONALEN POLITIK VON 1949-60 / Horn-Sauder, Erdmute; ed by Fachbereich Politische Wissenschaft der Freien Universitaet Berlin, Pressearchiv des Bibliotheks- und Informationssystem – (incl. Erschliessungsband) – 1995 – 4681mf (1:24) – 9 – diazo DM18,800.00 – 3-598-33850-3 – gw Saur [320]
PRESSEBERICHT – Berlin, 1920-22 – 2r – 1 – Inquire at Mikrofilmarchiv for details – gw Misc Inst [072]
LA PRESSE-BULLETIN – Montreal, Canada. 4 jan 1900 – 1r – 1 – Can$25.00 – cn Can Microfilming [072]
PRESSED GLASS: 1825-1925 – 1983. 48p. 30 color illus. 2 fiches. Fiche No.7378 – 9 – $5.00 – us Corning Mus [740]
PRESSEDIENST DES REICHSSENDERS BRESLAU *see* REICHSSENDER BRESLAU: NACHRICHTENDIENST
PRESSEDIENST: DEUTSCHLANDSENDER UND REICHSSENDER *see* NACHRICHTENDIENST DES DEUTSCHLANDSENDERS
Pressel, Wilhelm *see*
- DIE STIMMEN DER VOELKER UEBER DIE URGESCHICHTE
- DER THALMUD VOR DEM SCHWURGERICHT AM ENDE DES XIX. JAHRHUNDERTS

Pressense, Edmond de *see*
- LE CONCILE DU VATICAN
- CONTEMPORARY PORTRAITS
- DISCOURS RELIGIEUX
- REDEMPTEUR
- DAS VATICANISCHE CONCIL

Pressense, Edmond Dehault de *see*
- THE EARLY YEARS OF CHRISTIANITY
- THE MYSTERY OF SUFFERING
- RELIGION AND THE REIGN OF TERROR
- ROME AND ITALY AT THE OPENING OF THE OECUMENICAL COUNCIL
- A STUDY OF ORIGINS

Pressey, W Benfield *see*
- AN INDEX TO ILLUSTRATIONS OF SHAKESPEARE'S PLAYS
- INDEX TO ILLUSTRATIONS OF SHAKESPEARE'S PLAYS

DER PRESSEZUSTAND IN INDONESIEN / Djojoadhiningrat, Abdulmadjid – Haag, 1928. 23p – 1mf – 9 – ne IDC [070]
PRESS-GAZETTE – Green Bay. Wis. 1872- – 1 – us UMI [071]
PRESS-GAZETTE – Hillsboro. Ohio. -w. 1939- – 1 – us UMI [071]
PRESS-HERALD – Torrance. Calif. 1964- – 1 – us UMI [071]
PRESS-REGISTER – Clarksdale. Miss. 1949- – 1 – us UMI [071]
PRESS-REGISTER *see* UNIT-REGISTER
PRESS-REPUBLIC – Springfield. Ohio. 1901-05 – 1 – us UMI [071]
PRESS-REPUBLICAN – Plattsburg. N.Y. 1954-57 – 1 – us UMI [071]
PRESS-SCIMITAR – Memphis. Tenn. 1945- – 1 – us UMI [071]
PRESS-TELEGRAM – Long Beach. CA.1948-. Southland magazine section – 1 – us UMI [071]
PRESS-TELEGRAM – Long Beach. Calif. 1946- – 1 – us UMI [071]
PRESS-TRIBUNE – Auburn. Neb. 1955-1961 – 1 – us UMI [071]
PRESS-TRIBUNE – Roseville. Calif. 1918-1919; 1920-1941; 1945- – 1 – us UMI [071]
PRESSURE SORE PREVENTION SELF-EFFICACY AND OUTCOME EXPECTATIONS IN THE SPINAL CORD-INJURED : A VALIDITY AND RELIABILITY STUDY / Basta, Susan M & Chen, Moon S – 1992 – 5mf – 9 – $20.00 – us Microform Publ [612]
PRESTATYN WEEKLY – Wales. -w. 1908-33. 13 reels – 1 – uk British Libr Newspaper [072]
Preston *see* HISTORY OF HARTFORD COUNTY 1608-1812
PRESTON COUNTY JOURNAL – Kingwood. West Virginia. 1866-1968 – 1 – us UMI [071]
PRESTON COUNTY NEWS – Terra Alta. West Virginia. 1962-1964; 1966-1968 – 1 – us UMI [071]
Preston, Henry *see* BRIEF DIRECTIONS FOR TRUE-SPELLING
PRESTON REPUBLICAN – Terra Alta. West Virginia. 1914-1944 – 1 – us UMI [071]
Preston, Richard *see* POLITICAL GEOGRAPHY AND THE CYPRUS CONFLICT
Preston, Richard E *see*
- APPLIED GEOGRAPHY AND THE HUMAN ENVIRONMENT
- ESSAYS ON CANADIAN URBAN PROCESS AND FORM 2

Preston, Thomas Scott *see*
- GOD AND REASON: LECTURES UPON THE PRIMARY TRUTHS OF NATURAL RELIGION
- LECTURES ON REASON AND REVELATION

PRESUPONESE...PEDRO DE TAPIA...DE CONSEJO REAL... – S.l., s.i., s.a. Hacia 1621 – 1 – sp Bibl Santa Ana [946]
PRESUPUESTO DE GASTOS E INGRESOS PARA EL ANO / Caceres – Caceres: Imprenta Garcia Floriano, 1936, 1938, 1939, 1940, 1943, 1946, 1947 – 1 – sp Bibl Santa Ana [946]
PRESUPUESTO GENERAL DE GASTOS E INGRESOS DE LAS ISLAS FILIPINAS / Spain. Ministerio de ultramar – v. 1-20. 1859-96 – 1 – 92.00 – us L of C Photodup [950]
PRESUPUESTO MUNICIPAL ORDINARIO DE INGRESOS Y GASTOS (CON UN APENDICE CONTENIENDO LAS ORDENANZAS MUNICIPALES. ANO 1930 / Villafranca de los Barros – Villafranca de los Barros: Juan J. Bolanos, Impresor, 1930 – 1 – sp Bibl Santa Ana [946]
PRESUPUESTO ORDINARIO DE GASTOS E INGRESOS. EJERCICIO 1966 / Diputacion Provincial – Badajoz: Dip. Prov., 1965 – sp Bibl Santa Ana [946]
PRESUPUESTO ORDINARIO DE GASTOS E INGRESOS EJERCICIO DE 1961 / Badajoz – Badajoz: Imp. Provincial, 1961 – sp Bibl Santa Ana [946]
PRESUPUESTO ORDINARIO DE GASTOS E INGRESOS. EJERCICIO DE 1963 / Diputacion Provincial – Badajoz: Imp. Dip. Provincial, 1963 – sp Bibl Santa Ana [946]
PRESUPUESTO ORDINARIO DE GASTOS E INGRESOS. EJERCICIO DE 1967 / Diputacion Provincial – Badajoz: Imp. de la Dip. Provincial, 1967 – sp Bibl Santa Ana [946]
PRESUPUESTO ORDINARIO DE GASTOS E INGRESOS. EJERCICIO DE 1968 / Diputacion Provincial – Badajoz: Dip. Prov., 1968 – sp Bibl Santa Ana [946]
PRESUPUESTO ORDINARIO DE GASTOS E INGRESOS PARA 1948. MEMORIA JUSTIFICADA ORDENANZAS Y TARIFAS NUEVAS O MODIFICADAS. BASES DE EJECUCION / Caceres – Caceres: Imprenta Moderna, 1949, 1950, 1952, 1953, 1954, 1955, 1956, 1957, 1958, 1959, 1960, 1961, 1962, 1963, 1964, 1966, 1972 – 1 – sp Bibl Santa Ana [340]
PRESUPUESTO ORDINARIO DE GASTOS E INGRESOS PARA 1951 / Caceres. Ayuntamiento – Caceres: Tip. El Noticiero, 1951 – sp Bibl Santa Ana [946]
PRESUPUESTO ORDINARIO DE INGRESOS Y GASTOS ANO / Caceres – Caceres: Tip. La Minerva, 1915, 1916, 1917, 1918, 1919, 1920-21, 1924-25, 1927, 1930, 1931, 1932, 1933, 1934, 1935 – 1 – sp Bibl Santa Ana [946]
PRESUPUESTO ORDINARIO DE INGRESOS Y GASTOS. EJERCICIO DE 1960 / Diputacion Provincial – Badajoz: Dip. Provincial, 1960 – sp Bibl Santa Ana [946]
PRESUPUESTO ORDINARIO DE INGRESOS Y GASTOS. EJERCICIO DE 1969 / Diputacion Provincial – Badajoz: Diputacion Provincial, 1909 – sp Bibl Santa Ana [946]
PRESUPUESTO ORDINARIO DE INGRESOS Y GASTOS. EJERCICIO DE 1971 / Diputacion Provincial – Badajoz: Imp. Dip. Provincial, 1971 – sp Bibl Santa Ana [946]
PRESUPUESTO ORDINARIO DE INGRESOS Y GASTOS PARA EL ANO / Caceres – Caceres: Tip. La Minerva, 1911, 1912, 1913, 1914 – 1 – sp Bibl Santa Ana [946]
PRESUPUESTO ORDINARIO DE INGRESOS Y GASTOS PARA EL EJERCICIO DE 1972 / Caceres. Diputacion Provincial – Caceres: Imp. Dip. Provincial, 1972 – 1 – sp Bibl Santa Ana [946]
PRESUPUESTO ORDINARIO DE INGRESOS Y GASTOS PARA EL EJERCICIO DE 1973... / Diputacion Provincial – Caceres: Imp. Diputacion, 1973 – 1 – sp Bibl Santa Ana [946]
PRESUPUESTO ORDINARIO DEL INTERIOR CORRESPONDIENTE AL ANO 1951...BADAJOZ / Badajoz – Tipografia Vda. de Antonio Argueros, 1951 – sp Bibl Santa Ana [946]
PRESUPUESTO ORDINARIO PARA INGRESOS Y GASTOS PARA EL ANO 1910 / Caceres – Caceres: Tip. El Noticiero, 1910 – 1 – sp Bibl Santa Ana [946]
PRESUPUESTO ORDINARIO Y ESPECIAL DE URBANISMO PARA EL EJERCICIO DE 1971 – Caceres: Tip. Rodriguez Santano, 1972 – 1 – sp Bibl Santa Ana [946]
PRESUPUESTOS GENERAL DE GASTOS E INGRESOS DE LA ISLA DE CUBA EN 1883-1886 – Madrid, 1883-85 – 11mf – 9 – sp Cultura [972]
PRESUPUESTOS GENERALES DE GASTOS E INGRESOS DE LAS ISLAS FILIPINAS EN 1880-1881 – Madrid, 1880 – 6mf – 9 – sp Cultura [950]
PRESUPUESTOS GENERALES DE LA ISLA DE PUERTO RICO. ANO 1874-1886 – Madrid, 1874-1885 – 14mf – 9 – sp Cultura [972]
PRESUPUESTOS GENERALES DE LA ISLA FILIPINAS / Instituto Geografico – Madrid, 1878-1879, 1885-1886 – 11mf – 9 – sp Cultura [950]
PRET BAPTISTU SEKTI / Walter, C – Riga: Ernst Plates, 1885. Publ. No. 6298 c. One of five items on a reel – 1 – us Baptist [240]
PRETASK ORDER REPORTS / Development Projects Consulting Service (Indonesia) – SE-6458 1. 1964 – 9 – ne IDC [380]
Pretasky, Barbara J *see* THE IMPACT OF "WINNING WEIGHS" WEIGHT CONTROL PROGRAM ON PERCEIVED BODY IMAGE
LES PRETENDUS REFORMEZ CONVAINCUS DE SCHISME... / Nicole, P – Paris, 1684 – 7mf – 9 – CA-105/1 – ne IDC [240]
PRETENSIONES DE LA VILLA DE POTOSI (ANNO 1639). FF. 542-685 – Madrid – 1r – 5,6 – sp Cultura [910]
THE PRETENSIONS EXPOSED OF MESSRS. LANG, BURNET & CO. TO BE "THE PRESBYTERIAN CHURCH IN CANADA IN CONNEXION WITH THE CHURCH OF SCOTLAND" / Campbell, Robert, 1835-1921 – Montreal: W. Drysdale; Toronto: Hart and Rawlinson, 1878. 00401. (Pre-1900 Canadiana) – 9 – cn C.I.H.M. [240]
PRETORIA FRIEND – Pretoria. South Africa. Jun-Jul 1900 – 1 – sa State Libr [072]
PRETORIA NEWS – Pretoria, South Africa. 13 Jun 1898- – 786r – 1 – sa Microfile [960]
Pretoria State Library. South Africa *see* SOUTH AFRICAN LIBRARY AFRICANA CATALOGUE
LE PRETRE, LA FEMME ET LA FAMILLE: LES JESUITES / Michelet, Jules – Paris: Calmann Levy, 1900. (Les Femmes Collection) – 6mf – 9 – $15.00 – fr Bibl Nationale [305]
LE PRETRE, LA FEMME ET LE CONFESSIONNAL / Chiniquy, Charles – Montreal: Librarie evangelique, 1875. 00611. (Pre-1900 Canadiana) – 9 – cn C.I.H.M. [240]
LES PRETRES DEMASQUES OU DES INIQUITES DU CLERGE CHRETIEN – (D'Holbach series). 1768 – 9 – fr Hachette [240]
THE PRETTY WAYS O' PROVIDENCE / Pearse, Mark Guy – 1906 – 9 – us A.T.L.A. [240]
Preuschen, Erwin *see*
- EUSEBIUS KIRCHENGESCHICHTE BUCH 6 UND 7 AUS DEM ARMENISCHEN UEBERSETZT (T.U.U. 2-22/3)
- MOENCHTUM UND SARAPISKULT
- PALLADIUS UND RUFINUS

Preuss, Arthur *see* THE FUNDAMENTAL FALLACY OF SOCIALISM
Preuss, Eduard *see* DIE RECHTFERTIGUNG DES SUENDERS VOR GOTT
Preuss, Edward *see* THE ROMISH DOCTRINE OF THE IMMACULATE CONCEPTION TRACED FROM ITS SOURCE
Preuss, K Th *see* VORLAGE DER ESKIMO-SAMMLUNG DES FORSCHUNGSREISENDEN BERNARD HANTZSCH
Preuss, Th *see* DIE BEGRAEBNISARTEN DER AMERIKANER UND NORDOSTASIATEN
PREUSSEN UND DER KONGRESS VON VERONA : EINE STUDIE ZUR POLITIK DER HEILIGEN ALLIANZ IN DER SPANISCHEN FRAGE / Schmieder, Ulrike – 1993 – 3mf – 9 – DM98.00 – 3-89349-824-9 – gw Hänsel [320]
PREUSSEN UND ROM AN DER WENDE DES 18. JAHRHUNDERTS / Westerburg, Hans – Stuttgart, 1908 – 2mf – 9 – DM62.00 – 3-89349-739-0 – gw Hänsel [943]
PREUSSEN, WEIMAR UND DIE UNGARISCHE KOENIGSKRONE, MIT DEM FAKSIMILE EINES GOETHE-BRIEFES / Gragger, Robert – Berlin, Leipzig: W. de Gruyter & Co., 1923. x,158p – 1 – us U.W. Library [943]
PREUSSENLAND UND DEUTSCHER ORDEN : FESTSCHRIFT FUER KURT FORSTREUTER ZUR VOLLENDUNG SEINES 60. LEBENSJAHRES – Wuerzburg: Holzner-Verlag, 1958 – 10r – 1 – us U.W. Library [943]
PREUSSEN-PARTEITAG / Sozialdemokratische Partei Deutschlands – Berlin, 3-5 Jan 1910 – 1 – DM80.00 – gw Mikro Press [335]

PREUSSEN-PARTEITAG / Sozialdemokratische Partei Deutschlands – Berlin, 6-8 Jan 1913 – 1 – DM80.00 – gw Mikro Press [335]
PREUSSISCHE JAHRBUECHER – v. 1-240. 1858-1935. V. 198 Wanting – 1 – 1,023.00 – us L of C Photodup [073]
PREUSSISCHE KRIEGSLIEDER IN DER FELDZUGEN 1756 UND 1757 VON EINEM GRENADIER / Telemann, G M – Berlin, 1778 – 1 – us Sibley [780]
PREUSSISCHE LEHRER-ZEITUNG – (Later publ in Magdeburg) – Berlin-Spandau, 1877-89, 1893, apr 1 1913-18, 1920-33 – 1 – Inquire at Mikrofilmarchiv for details – gw Misc Inst [370]
PREUSSISCHE MERKWUERDIGKEITEN – Koenigsberg (Kaliningrad), Russia. 1741-1742 – 8r – 1 – gw Mikrofilm [943]
PREUSSISCHE PROVINZIAL-BLAETTER – Koenigsberg (Kaliningrad), Russia. 1829-1830 – 4r – 1 – gw Mikrofilm [943]
PREUSSISCHE REBELLION : DIE ENTSCHEIDENDE TAT DES GENERALLEUTNANTS VON YORCK / Helke, Fritz – Stuttgart: Union Deutsche Verlagsgesellschaft, [1935?] – 1r – 1 – us U.W. Library [830]
PREUSSISCHE SPINNEN. SCHRIFTEN NATURF / Menge, A – Z-2186 2. 11 pts. 1866-1879 – 8 – ne IDC [590]
DAS PREUSSISCHE STAATSSCHULDENWESEN UND DIE PREUSSISCHEN STAATSPAPIERE / Richter, Eugen – Breslau: Maruschke & Berendt, 1869. xiii,431p. Includes index – 1 – us U.W. Library [336]
PREUSSISCHE STATISTIK / ed by Treue, William & Kaufhold, Karl Heinrich – Berlin: Royal Statistical Bureau, 1861-1934. 368v – 1049mf – 9 – DM9,100.00 – gw Keip [324]
PREUSSISCHE STATISTIK. (AMTLICHES QUELLENWERK) / Prussia. Statistisches Landesamt – v. 1-298. 1861-34. 7 V. and 1861-80 index wanting – 1 – 1,382.00 – us L of C Photodup [943]
PREUSSISCHE UND OESTERREICHISCHE ACTEN ZUR VORGESCHICHTE DES SIEBENJAEHRIGEN KRIEGES / ed by Volz, G B & Kuentzel, G – Leipzig, 1899 – 11mf – 9 – HQ-73/1 – ne IDC [943]
DIE PREUSSISCHEN LANDWIRTSCHAFTLICHEN VERSUCHS- UND FORSCHUNGSANSTALTEN, LANDSBERG/W. : OSTBRANDENBURGS LANDBAU ALS PARTNER DER WISSENSCHAFT / ed by Koenekamp, Alfred Heinrich – (Includes bibliographical references and indexes) – Wuerzburg: Holzner Verlag, 1968 – 1 – us U.W. Library [330]
PREUSSISCHER STAATS-ANZEIGER *see*
– ALLGEMEINE PREUSSISCHE STAATS-ZEITUNG
– ALLGEMEINE PREUSSISCHE ZEITUNG
PREUSSISCHER VOLKSFREUND – Berlin, jul-dec 1836, jul-dec 1838 – 1r – 1 – Inquire at Mikrofilmarchiv for details – gw Misc Inst [072]
LA PREUVE DE LA NATIONALITE D'ORIGINE / Guiraudou, R – Montpellier, 1936 – 2mf – 1 – ILM-3405/1 – ne IDC [327]
PREUVE TESTIMONIALE DANS L'AFFAIRE DES SYNDICS DE LA VILLE DE LONGUEUIL.. / Gingras, Isaie – Montreal: Imp. W F Daniel, 1897. SEM105P381 – 2mf – 9 – Can$4.50 – cn Bibl Nat [323]
PREUVES PSYCHOLOGIQUES DE L'EXISTENCE DE DIEU / Broglie, Paul de – Paris: Librairie Bloud, 1905. 1 fiche – 9 – us A.T.L.A. [240]
Prevel *see* NOTICE SUR MISSILLAC ET SUR LA BARONNIE DE LA ROCHE-BERNARD
PREVENCION DE ACCIDENTES Y SOCORRISMO EN EL TRABAJO / Obra Sindical – Badajoz: Imprenta Inca, 1966 – sp Bibl Santa Ana [331]
PREVENIR : LA REVUE DE LA SANTE NATURELLE – Montreal. v1 n1. mai 1971-v1 n17. automne 1974 – 1r – 1 – cn Can Microfilming [072]
PREVENTION IN HUMAN SERVICES *see* JOURNAL OF PREVENTION AND INTERVENTION IN THE COMMUNITY
THE PREVENTION OF DEFECTIVE AND SLIPSHOD LEGISLATION / Sterne, Simon – Philadelphia, Harris, 1884. 31 p. LL-1385 – 1 – us L of C Photodup [340]
PREVENTION OF POST-HARVEST FOOD LOSSES : A TRAINING MANUAL – 1985 – 120p – it F.A.O. [630]
PREVENTION OF POST-HARVEST FOOD LOSSES, FRUITS, VEGETABLES AND ROOT CROPS : A TRAINING MANUAL – 1989 – 157p – it F.A.O. [630]
PREVIEWS OF HEAT AND MASS TRANSFER – v1- 1974- 1,5,6; v2- 9 – us UMI [530]
PREVISION Y REFUTACION DEL ATEISMO COMUNISTA EN LOS ULTIMOS ESCRITOS DE JUAN DONOSO CORTES : 1848-1853 / Leturia, Pedro S – Roma: Pontificie Universitate Gregoriana, 1937 – 1 – sp Bibl Santa Ana [320]
Prevorsek, D C *see* INTERNATIONAL JOURNAL OF POLYMERIC MATERIALS
Prevost, Abbe *see*
– MANUEL LEXIQUE DES MOTS FRANCAIS
– SUPPLEMENT A LA PREMIERE EDITION DU MANUEL LEXIQUE
Prevost, AF *see* OEUVRES CHOISIES
Prevost, Antoine F *see* VOYAGES DU CAPITAINE ROBERT LADE EN DIFFERENTES PARTIES DE L'AFRIQUE, DE L'ASIE ET DE L'AMERIQUE
Prevost, Augustine *see* THE JOURNAL OF... IN PENNSYLVANIA, 1774
Prevost, Gustave Amable *see* L'EGLISE ET LES CAMPAGNES AU MOYEN AGE
Prevost, J-E *see* L'AVENIR DU NORD
Prevost, Marcel *see* FEMMES
Prevost, Paul E *see* TRAITE ELEMENTAIRE D'ANATOMIE, DE PHYSIOLOGIE ET D'HYGIENE PRIVEE
Prevost, Pierre *see* L'AVENIR DU NORD
PREVOSTS "MANON LESCAUT" IN DEUTSCHEN UEBERSETZUNGEN DES 18., 19. UND 20. JAHRHUNDERTS / Hampel, Beate – 1994 – 4mf – DM112.00 – 3-8267-2078-4 – gw Hänsel [440]
Prezel, L de *see*
– DICTIONNAIRE ICONOLOGIQUE...
– DICTIONNAIRE ICONOLOGIQUE
– DICTIONNAIRE ICONOLOGIQUE...
– IKONOLOGISCHES WOERTERBUCH...
Prezzolini, Giuseppe *see* IL CATTOLICISMO ROSSO: STUDIO SUL PRESENTE MOVIMENTO DE RIFORMA NEL CATTOLICISMO
PRI SVETE SOVESTI / Minskii, N – Mysli i mechty o tseli zhizni. Ed. 2. Spb. 1897. BR-812 2 – 8 – ne IDC [460]
PRI SVETE SOVESTI / Minskii, N – (Mysli i mechty o tseli zhizni). Spb. 1890. BR-811 2 – 8 – ne IDC [460]
PRIAMOI PUT' – Zhurnal politicheskii ekonomicheskii i literaturnyi. Spb. 1909-14. Lacking: (1-12) 1909; (5-8) 1910; (6-9) 1911; (2-3, 6-9) 1912; (9) 1914. B-1839 – 8 – ne IDC [330]
PRIAMURSKIE (KHABAROVSK) GUBERNSKIE VEDOMOSTI, 1894-1917, RUSSIA – 48r – 1 – $4,300.00 coll $100.00r – us Ross [072]
PRIBAVLENIE K IZDANNOMU V 1845 I 1847 GODOV SOBRANIIU TRAKTATOV, KONVENTSII I DRUGIKH AKTOV – 5v. Spb, 1858-82 – 8 – BR-9490 2 – ne IDC [947]
Price, C J *see* PRACTICAL PARASITOLOGY
Price, Edward *see* SICK CALLS
Price, Ezekiel *see* EZEKIEL PRICE PAPERS, 1754-1785
Price, George McCready *see* ILLOGICAL GEOLOGY: THE WEAKEST POINT IN THE EVOLUTION THEORY
Price, Henry E *see* DIARY
Price, Ira Maurice *see*
– THE ANCESTRY OF OUR ENGLISH BIBLE... VERSIONS, TEXTS, AND MANUSCRIPTS
– THE MONUMENTS AND THE OLD TESTAMENT
– A SYLLABUS OF OLD TESTAMENT HISTORY
Price, J M *see* THE GREAT CYLINDER INSCRIPTIONS A AND B OF GUDEA
Price, Kathleen M *see* A BIOMECHANICAL AND PHYSIOLOGICAL ANALYSIS OF EFFICIENCY DURING DIFFERENT RUNNING PACES
Price, Langford Lovell *see* A SHORT HISTORY OF ENGLISH COMMERCE AND INDUSTRY
Price, Lawrence Marsden *see* ENGLISH-GERMAN LITERARY INFLUENCES
PRICE LIST OF THE BARLOW LIBRARY / J.O. Wright & Co – New York: J.O. Wright, 1890?. 03497. (Pre-1900 Canadiana) – 9 – cn C.I.H.M. [070]
Price, Monroe E *see* EXECUTIVE CONTROL OF RULEMAKING
THE PRICE OF PRICE CONTROLS / Olds, Irving S – 3fiches (29x) – 9 – 1.00f – at Libertarian Micro [320]
THE PRICE OF VISION : THE DIARY OF HENRY A. WALLACE, 1942-1946 / Wallace, Henry Agard; ed by Blum, John Morton – Boston: Houghton Mifflin, 1973 – 1 – CSUXADM8880-B – us Hoover Inst Photo [920]
Price, Owen *see*
– ENGLISH ORTHOGRAPHIE
– THE VOCAL ORGAN, OR A NEW ART OF TEACHING THE ENGLISH ORTHOGRAPHIE
Price, P F *see*
– THE ABC CATECHISM (CCC265)
– INTRODUCTORY CATECHISM, VOL 2 (CCC344)
– THE PLOUGHMAN'S SONG (CCC264)
– SCRIPTURE CATECHISM (CCC266)
– SHORT SHORT STEPS (CCC267)
– SHORT STEPS TO GREAT TRUTHS (CCC268)
PRICE PARITY TABLES FOR THE NETHERLANDS EAST INDIES / Chda, Kok Hong – In English and Chinese. Reel 4002. 1921 – 1 – ja CEACS [338]
Price, Pattie *see* BANTU TALES
Price, R *see*
– ADDITIONAL OBSERVATIONS ON THE NATURE AND VALUE OF CIVIL LIBERTY, AND THE WAR WITH AMERICA
– AN APPEAL TO THE PUBLIC, ON THE SUBJECT OF NATIONAL DEBT
– A DISCOURSE ON THE LOVE OF OUR COUNTRY, DELIVERED ON NOV. 4, 1789,...
– THE GENERAL INTRODUCTION AND SUPPLEMENT TO THE TWO TRACTS ON CIVIL LIBERTY, THE WAR WITH AMERICA, AND THE FINANCES OF THE KINGDOM
– OBSERVATIONS ON THE NATURE OF CIVIL LIBERTY,...
Price, Realto E *see* HISTORY OF CLAYTON COUNTY
Price, Richard W *see* JOURNAL OF NEURO-AIDS
Price, S *see* ILLUSTRATIONS OF THE FUNGI OF OUR FIELDS AND WOODS
Price, W P *see* SIXTY YEARS OF THE LIFE OF A COUNTRY VILLAGE BAPTIST CHURCH, DAHLONEGA, GEORGIA
Price, William *see* PARAGRAPHS ON THE SUBJECT OF JUDICIAL REFORM IN MARYLAND.
Price, William T *see* HISTORICAL SKETCHES OF POCAHONTAS COUNTY
Price, Wm H *see* THE LIFE AND LABORS OF THE REV. CHRISTIAN FREDERICK SCHWARTZ
PRICES CURRENT AND SHIPPING LIST – San Francisco, CA. 1854-1859 – 1r – 1 – $50.00 – C03673 – us Library Micro [071]
Prichard, James Cowles *see*
– DISPUTATIO INAUGURALIS DE GENERIS HUMANI VARIETATE
– THE NATURAL HISTORY OF MAN; COMPRISING INQUIRIES INTO THE MODIFYING INFLUENCE OF PHYSICAL AND MORAL AGENCIES ON THE DIFFERENT TRIBES OF THE HUMAN FAMILY
– RESEARCHES INTO THE PHYSICAL HISTORY OF MANKIND
O PRICHINAKH UPADKA I O NOVYKH TECHENIIAKH SOVREMENNOI RUSSKOI LITERATURY / Merezhkovskii, Dimitrii – Spb. 1893. BR-778 2 – 8 – ne IDC [460]
PRICHINY SUSCHESTVOVANIYA I PUTI PREODOLENIYA RELIGIOZNYKH PEREZHITKOV = THE CAUSES OF THE EXISTENCE AND THE PATH OF OVERCOMING RELIGIOUS SURVIVALS – Minsk: "Nauka i tekhnika", 1965. 264p. Publ. No. 6300 – 1 – $10.56 – us Baptist [240]
THE PRICK OF CONSCIENCE / Rolle, Richard – c1400. Sir Kenelm Digby, Observations on "Religio Medici". 1642. Holkham mss. 668, 688.Holkham Hall, Norfolk, England – 1 – uk Microform Academic [880]
PRICKLY PEAR – Bloomington, NE. -w. Jun. 1899-May 1901 – 1 – us NE Hist [071]
THE PRIDE OF URHOBO NATION / Numa, Yamu – Lagos: Ribway Press, [1950] – us Res Libr [960]
Prideaux, Frederick *see* PRECEDENTS IN CONVEYANCING, WITH DISSERTATIONS ON ITS LAW AND PRACTICE
Pridham, C *see* AN HISTORICAL, POLITICAL AND STATISTICAL ACCOUNT OF CEYLON AND ITS DEPENDENCIES
Priegel, F *see* DIE CHRISTIANISIERUNG DER FUERSTENTUEMER REUSS
PRIEKOPNIK – Kosice, Czechoslovakia. Oct 1954-1957 (scattered issues) – 2r – 1 – us L of C Photodup [072]
PRIEMY LENINSKOI RECHI. K IZUCHENIIU IAZYKA LENINA / Kruchenykh, A – ed. 3. M. 1928. BR-956 2 – 8 – ne IDC [335]
PRIEPORETS – Sofia, Bulgaria. Jul 1898-Apr 1903 – 1r – 1 – us L of C Photodup [949]
Prieras, S *see* SUMMAE SYLVESTRINAE PARS 1-2
Pries, A *see* SYSTEMATIC CARD CATALOGUE
Pries, Anne *see*
– THE COOPERATIVE MOVEMENT IN RUSSIA
– RUSSIAN AND SOVIET STATISTICS
– RUSSIAN POLITICAL PARTIES
– RUSSIAN SYMBOLISM
– RUSSIAN/SOVIET LAW CARD CATALOGUE
– ZEMSTVO STATISTICS
THE PRIEST : A TALE OF MODERNISM IN NEW ENGLAND / Sullivan, William – Boston: Sherman, French, 1911 – 1mf – 9 – 0-8370-8389-3 – 1986-2389 – us A.T.L.A. [240]
PRIEST AND NUN / Wright, Julia McNair – (Includes bibliographical references) – Philadelphia: Crittenden & McKinney; Springfield, MA: D E Fisk, c1869 – 2mf – 9 – 0-8370-8637-X – 1986-2637 – us A.T.L.A. [240]
Priest, George Madison *see* A BRIEF HISTORY OF GERMAN LITERATURE
THE PRIEST, THE WOMAN, AND THE CONFESSIONAL / Chiniquy, Charles – Kankakee County, IL: St Anne, 1884, c1880 – 1mf – 9 – 0-8370-8892-5 – 1986-2892 – us A.T.L.A. [240]
PRIEST WHO SAW PLANE ATTACK TELLS OF GUERNICA "MASSACRE." / Onaindia, Alberto – n.p., 1937? Fiche W 1086. (Blodgett Collection of Spanish Civil War Pamphlets) – 9 – us H.U. College Libr [946]
PRIESTCRAFT DEFENDED : A SERMON OCCASIONED BY THE EXPULSION OF SIX YOUNG GENTLEMEN FROM THE UNIVERSITY OF OXFORD FOR PRAYING, READING AND EXPOUNDING THE SCRIPTURES,... / MacGowan, John – London, 8th ed 1768 – 1mf – 9 – MP-452/1 – ne IDC [240]
DIE PRIESTER UND DER CULTUS IM LETZTEN JAHRZEHNT DES JERUSALEMISCHEN TEMPELS / Buechler, Adolf – Wien: Alfred Hoelder, 1895 – 1mf – 9 – 0-8370-2504-4 – 1985-0504 – us A.T.L.A. [270]
DAS PRIESTERTHUM DES ALTEN BUNDES / Kueper, Lic – (Includes bibliographical references and index) – Berlin: Wilhelm Hertz, 1866 – 1mf – 9 – 0-8370-7399-5 – 1986-1399 – us A.T.L.A. [220]
THE PRIESTHOOD OF CHRIST : A RESTATEMENT OF VITAL TRUTH / Parker, Joseph – (Includes bibliographical references) – 2nd corr ed. London: R D Dickinson, 1877 – 1mf – 9 – 0-8370-6294-2 – 1985-0294 – us A.T.L.A. [240]
Priestley, Joseph *see*
– A COURSE OF LECTURES ON ORATORY AND CRITICISM
– A COURSE OF LECTURES ON THE THEORY OF LANGUAGE, AND UNIVERSAL GRAMMAR
– THE HISTORY AND PRESENT STATE OF ELECTRICITY, WITH ORIGINAL EXPERIMENTS
– LETTERS
– MISCELLANEOUS PAPERS
– THE RUDIMENTS OF ENGLISH GRAMMAR
PRIESTLY ELEMENT IN THE OLD TESTAMENT / Harper, William Rainey – Chicago: University of Chicago, 1905. 1 fiche – 9 – us A.T.L.A. [220]
Priestly, J *see* ORIGINAL LETTERS BY THE REV. JOHN WESLEY AND HIS FRIENDS, ILLUSTRATIVE OF HIS EARLY HISTORY,...
THE PRIEST'S STUDIES / Scannell, Thomas Bartholomew – London: Longmans, Green, 1908. 1 fiche – 9 – us A.T.L.A. [240]
Prieto, Adolfo *see* LITERATURA Y SUBDESARROLLO; NOTAS PARA UN ANALISIS DE LA LITERATURA ARGENTINA
Prieto del Rio, LF *see* DICCIONARIO BIOGRAFICO DEL CLERO SECULAR DE CHILE, 1535-1918
Prieto Gonzalvez, Pedro *see* NUEVE MESES DE ACTUACION DE LA CORPORACION MUNICIPAL DE ALJUCEN
Prieto, Ignacio *see* MISA RECITADA Y CANTADA
Prieto, Indalecio *see*
– EL AUXILIO DE AMERICA PARA LA RECONSTRUCCION DE ESPANA; TEXTO TAQUIGRAFICO DE LA CONFERENCIA PRONUNCIADA EN LA SALA STUDIUM DE BARCELONA, EL DIA 9 DE OCTUBRE DE 1938

- A FIRST OF MAY IN THE MIDST OF TRAGEDY
- INTRIGAS DE LOS RUSOS EN ESPANA; COMO Y POR QUE SALI DEL MINISTERIO DE DEFENSA NACIONAL
- REMEMBRANCES AND PERSPECTIVES; A SPEECH, BARCELONA, 28TH AUGUST 1938
- SOUVENIRS ET PERSPECTIVES; UNE DISCOURS, BARCELONE, 28 AOUT, 1938

Prieur, Leon *see* LES ORIGINES FRANCAISES DU JURY. LES ASSISES FEODALES

Prieur, P Claude Le *see* DIALOGUE DE LA LYCANTHROPIE OU TRANSFORMATION D'HOMMES EN LOUP

Prijono *see* GLIMPSES OF INDONESIAN EDUCATION AND CULTURE

Prijono, R *see* SEDIKIT TENTANG SEDJARAH ASIA TIMOER RAJA DAN SEDJARAH TANAH DJAWA

PRIKARPATSKAI A RUS : EZHEDNEVNAI A POLITICHESKAI A, OBSHCHESTVENNAI A I LITERATURNAI A GAZETA. ORGAN RUSSKO I NARODNO I ORGANIZAT SII V GALICHINI E – (Includes c.1: 1915:Apr.13) – Lvov: Russkoe izdatelskoe ob-vo vo Lvovie e, 19uu – 1 – CSUXANS3522-S – us Hoover Inst Photo [947]

PRIKARPATSKAI A RUS : ORGAN RUSSKAGO ISPOLNITELNAGO KOMITETA VO LVOVI E – (Includes c.1: 1920:Jan.23) – Lvov: Kirill Mikh. Valnit ski i, 1919 – 1 – CSUXANS3531-S – us Hoover Inst Photo [947]

PRIKARPATSKAI A RUS (RUSSKAI A NARODNAI A OGANIZAT SII A V GALICHINI E) *see* PRIKARPATSKAI A RUS

PRIKARPATSKAI A RUS (RUSSKI I ISPOLNITELNY I KOMITET VO LVOVI E) *see* PRIKARPATSKAI A RUS

PRIKAZ MINISTRA VOORUZHENNYKH SIL SOIUZA SSR / Soviet Union, Ministerstvo vooruzhennykh sil; ed by Stalin, Iosif – (Includes c.1: no.7 1946:May 1, no.10 (1947:Feb.23)) – [Moskva]: Gospolitizdat, 19uu – 1 – CSUXAKZ1546-S – us Hoover Inst Photo [355]

PRIKAZY, PRIKAZANII A I OBI AVLENII A PETROGRADSKOGO OKRUZHNOGO KOMISSARIATA PO VOENNYM DELAM / Petrogradski i okruzhno i komissariat po voennym delam – (Includes c.1: no.8, no.11) – [Petrograd]: Komissariat, 191u – 1 – CSUXAKZ3645-S – us Hoover Inst Photo [947]

PRIKLIUCHENIIA POCHERPNUTYIA IZ MORIA ZHITEISKAGO / Veltman, A F – Moscow, 1856. 2v. B-1465/2 – 8 – ne IDC [460]

PRILOZHENIIA K SOCHINENIIAM A.S. PUSHKINA, IZDANNYM A.A. ISAKOVYM / Gennadi, G – Bibliograficheskii, spisok vsech proizvedenii A. S. Pushkina, dop., chernovye otryvki, nevozhedshie v tekst i primechaniia. Spb. 1860. BR-5898 2 – 8 – ne IDC [010]

PRIMA COMUNICAZIONE – 1985-1995 – 1r per y – 5,6 – Sfr401.00 – sz Infoprint [072]

PRIMA QUATUOR CAPITA GENESEOS – Constance. 1543. Cowley. BJ-43-75 1 – 9 – ne IDC [220]

THE PRIMACY OF THE APOSTOLIC SEE VINDICATED / Kenrick, Francis Patrick – Baltimore: J. Murphy, 1855 – 1mf – us A.T.L.A. [240]

PRIMARY AND SECONDARY CARDIOVASCULAR DISEASE RISK FACTORS AND THEIR CORRELATIONS WITH WAIST-TO-HIP RATIO AND BODY MASS INDEX IN NORTH CAROLINA DEPARTMENT OF CORRECTION EMPLOYEES / Thomas, Anita C – 1994 – 1mf – $4.00 – us Microform Publ [616]

PRIMARY CARDIOLOGY – (v.6-. 1980- 5,6,9) – v.1-. 1975- – 1 – us UMI [073]

PRIMARY CARE: CLINICS IN OFFICE PRACTICE – v1- 1974- 1; v4- 5,6,9 – us UMI [616]

PRIMARY CARE: PHYSICIAN'S GUIDE TO PRACTICAL GASTROENTEROLOGY – (v.4. 1980. 5,6,9) – v.2-. 1978- – 1 – us UMI [616]

THE PRIMARY CAUSE OF ANTISEMITISM: AN ANSWER TO THE JEWISH QUESTION / Schomer, Abraham Shaikewitz – New York: Israel Publ. Co., 1909. xiii,162p – 1 – us U.W. Library [300]

PRIMARY CONVICTIONS : BEING DISCUSSIONS OF WHICH THE GREATER PART WERE DELIVERED IN THE CHURCH OF THE HEAVENLY REST... / Alexander, William – New York: Harper, 1893 – 1mf – 9 – 0-8370-2066-2 – 1985-0066 – us A.T.L.A. [230]

PRIMARY CURRICULUM SEMINAR. HOUSE OF ASSEMBLY, PORT MORESBY 1971 : REPORT / Papua New Guinea. Department of Education – Konedobu, 1971 – 1mf – 9 – DE-244/1 – ne IDC [370]

PRIMARY CURRICULUM SEMINAR. HOUSE OF ASSEMBLY, PORT MORESBY 1971 : RESOLUTIONS / Papua New Guinea. Department of Education – Konedobu, 1971 – 1mf – 9 – DE-245/1 – ne IDC [370]

PRIMARY EDUCATION – v.1-34. 1893-1926 – 1 – us UMI [073]

PRIMARY EDUCATION AND PRE-PRIMARY SERVICES 1981 / Hong Kong – Hong Kong – 1mf – 9 – DE-157/1 – ne IDC [370]

PRIMARY EDUCATION IN BOTSWANA 198?-1988(1-23) / Botswana. Department of Education and Teacher Training – (Missing: 198?-1983(1-10)) – Gaborone – 7mf – 9 – DE-417/1 – ne IDC [370]

PRIMARY EDUCATION IN SINGAPORE / Singapore. Ministry of Education – Singapore, 1977 – 1mf – 9 – DE-266/1 – ne IDC [370]

PRIMARY EDUCATION IN THE RURAL VILLAGES OF PAKISTAN 1976-1977 / Pakistan. Ministry of Education. Bureau of Educational Planning and Management – Islamabad. 2v. 1977 – 6mf – 9 – DE-580/1 – ne IDC [370]

PRIMARY EDUCATION NEWS 1988-1989 / Lesotho. Ministry of Education – (Missing: v1(1-3) 1988) – Maseru – 3mf – 9 – DE-693/1 – ne IDC [370]

PRIMARY EDUCATION TEACHER'S GUIDE / Great Britain. Ministry of Education – 9 – uk Microform Academic [941]

PRIMARY EDUCATION TEACHERS' GUIDE / Northern Ireland. Ministry of Education – 1974 – 9 – uk Microform Academic [370]

PRIMARY PUPIL – 1915-61. (Name change: Children's Quarterly. 1915-35; Pupil's Primary Quarterly. Jul 1935-49; Primary Pupil. 1950) – 1 – 253.26 – us Baptist [240]

PRIMARY QUARTERLY *see* SESSION PROGRAMME FOR THE PRIMARY DEPARTMENT

THE PRIMARY QUARTERLY – (Cont: Session Programme for the Primary Department) – Toronto: Published under authority of the General Assembly, [1899-19–] – 9 – cn C.I.H.M. [240]

PRIMARY SOURCES AND ORIGINAL WORKS / ed by McCrank, Laurence J – v1- 1981- – 1, 9 ($95.00 in US $133.00 outside hardcopy subsc) – us Haworth [080]

PRIMARY SOURCES FOR THE HISTORY OF PHARMACY IN THE UNITED STATES – (Filmed at University of Wisconsin in cooperation with American Institute of the History of Pharmacy. Colonial period to 1940) – 450mf – 9 – $1,520.00 – us UMI [615]

PRIMARY TEACHER'S AND PUPIL BOOK, YEARS 1-3 – 1 – 70.07 – us Baptist [240]

PRIMARY TRUTHS OF RELIGION / Clark, Thomas March – New York: D Appleton, 1870 – 1mf – 9 – 0-8370-2669-5 – 1985-0669 – us A.T.L.A. [230]

Primasius *see* COMMENTARIUS IN APOCALYPSIN

PRIMATE AND PRIEST / Lobo, Leocadio – London, 1937. Fiche W1005. (Blodgett Collection of Spanish Civil War Pamphlets) – 9 – us H.U. College Libr [946]

LA PRIMAUTE ET L'INFAILLIBILITE DES SOUVERAINS PONTIFES: LECONS D'HISTOIRE DONNEES A L'UNIVERSITE LAVAL / Begin, Louis Nazaire – Quebec: L. Huot 1873. 02333. (Pre-1900 Canadiana) – 9 – cn C.I.H.M. [240]

A PRIMAVERA : LITTERARIO, HUMORISTICO E NOTICIOSO – Santa Maria, Alagoas. 8 Out 1911 – 1,5,6 – bl Biblioteca [072]

PRIMAVERA – (v.6-. 1980- 5,6,9) – v.1-. 1975- – 1 – us UMI [073]

LA PRIMAVERA DE LA VIDA / Guibert, J; ed by Bayle, Constantino – Madrid: Razon y Fe, 1928 – 9 – sp Bibl Santa Ana [946]

PRIME AREAS – Garibaldi Highlands. v33-36. 1990/91-1993/94 – 9 – Can$20.00y – cn Micromedia [370]

Prime, Edward Dorr Griffin *see* FORTY YEARS IN THE TURKISH EMPIRE, OR, MEMOIRS OF REV. WILLIAM GOODELL

THE PRIME MINISTER / Trollope, Anthony – London: Chapman & Hall, 1876 – 2 rolls – 1 – 1-55879-228-7 – uk Libr Preservation [830]

Prime Minister, Great Britain *see* PAPERS OF THE PRIME MINISTERS OF GREAT BRITAIN, SERIES 8

LE PRIME PAGINE DEL PONTIFICATO DI PAPA PIO 9 / Ballerini, Raffaele – Roma: Civita Cattolica, 1909 – 1mf – us A.T.L.A. [240]

Prime, Samuel Irenaeus *see*
- FIFTEEN YEARS OF PRAYER IN THE FULTON STREET MEETING
- FIVE YEARS OF PRAYER, WITH THE ANSWERS
- LETTERS FROM SWITZERLAND
- MEMOIRS OF THE REV. NICHOLAS MURRAY, D.D. (KIRWAN)
- THE POWER OF PRAYER
- PRAYER AND ITS ANSWER
- THOUGHTS ON THE DEATH OF LITTLE CHILDREN
- WALKING WITH GOD

Prime, T *see* CHECK LIST OF THE SHELLS OF NORTH AMERICA

PRIMECHANIYA K EVANGELIYU V OBLICHENIE SHTUNDISTOV I PODOBNYKH IM SEKTANTOV / Kokhomskii, S V – Kiev, 1899. One of 13 titles on reel – 1 – 86.44 – us Baptist [240]

O PRIMEIRO DE MAIO : ORGAM DO PROLETARIADO AMAZONENSE – Manaos, Amazonas. 1 Maio 1928 – 1,5,6 – bl Biblioteca [072]

PRIMEIRO PLANO DE FOMENTO, 1953-58 / Cape Verde Islands – D-1262 1 – 9 – ne IDC [338]

PRIMEIRO PLANO DIRECTOR, 1967-1969 / Brazil. Superintendencia do Desenvolvimento da Fronteira Sudoeste-Sudesul – Porto Alegre. 1967 – 9 – ne IDC [338]

EL PRIMER BERGSON EN ANTONIO MACHADO / Frutos Cortes, Eugenio – sp Bibl Santa Ana [946]

PRIMER CENSO DE LA REPUBLICA DE ARGENTINA...DE 1869 – Buenos Aires, 1872 – 14mf – 9 – sp Cultura [972]

PRIMER CENTENARIO DE LA MUERTE DE DONOSO CORTES – Madrid: Arbor, 1953 – 1 – sp Bibl Santa Ana [320]

PRIMER CONCURSO FOTOGRAFICO CATALOGO MAYO 1927 / Ateneo – (Caceres): Tip. Minerva de Castor Moreno, s.a. – 1 – sp Bibl Santa Ana [770]

PRIMER CONCURSO PROVINCIAL DE GANADO LANAR : MERIDA / Junta Provincial de Fomento Pecuario. Badajoz – Madrid: Talleres Espasa-Calpe, 1948 – sp Bibl Santa Ana [946]

PRIMER CONGRESO PEDAGOGICO DE CACERES. 1929 – Serradilla (Caceres): Edit. Sanchez Rodrigo, 1930 – 1 – sp Bibl Santa Ana [370]

PRIMER CONSEJO COMARCAL SINDICAL DE OLIVENZA. CONCLUSIONES DEFINITIVAS / Delegacion Provincial de Sindicatos – Badajoz: Tip. Martinez Rengifo, 1959 – sp Bibl Santa Ana [946]

PRIMER CONSEJO SINDICAL COMARCAL DE DON BENITO / Delegacion Provincial de Sindicatos – Badajoz: Imprenta Inca, 1960 – sp Bibl Santa Ana [946]

PRIMER CONSEJO SINDICAL COMARCAL. DELEGACION COMARCAL DE FREGENAL DE LA SIERRA / Delegacion Provincial de Sindicatos – Fregenal de la Sierra: Imp. Angel Verde, 1959 – sp Bibl Santa Ana [946]

PRIMER CONSEJO SINDICAL COMARCAL. DELGACION COMARCAL DE CASTUERA / Delegacion Provincial de Sindicatos de FET y de las JONS – Badajoz: Imp. Inca, 1959 – sp Bibl Santa Ana [946]

PRIMER DISCURSO DE LA FALANGE A CATALUNA / Falange Espanola Tradicionalista y de las Juntas Ofensivas Nacional-Sindicalistas – n.p., 1938? Fiche W 872. (Blodgett Collection of Spanish Civil War Pamphlets) – 9 – us H.U. College Libr [946]

PRIMER LIBRO DE ODAS / Montaner, Joaquin – Villanueva de la Serena, 1915 – 1 – sp Bibl Santa Ana [810]

EL PRIMER MOLINO DE RODILLOS FUE INVENTO DE...? / Redonet, Luis – Madrid: Tip. Rev. Arch., Bibl. y Mus, 1931. B.R.A.H. 98, pp. 68-82 – sp Bibl Santa Ana [946]

A PRIMER OF ASSYRIOLOGY / Sayce, Archibald Henry – New York: Fleming H Revell; London: Religious Tract Society, 1894 – 1mf – 9 – 0-8370-8379-6 – 1986-2379 – us A.T.L.A. [930]

PRIMER OF CHRISTIAN EVIDENCE / Redford, Robert Ainslie – American ed. Boston: Congregational Sunday-School and Publ Society, c1885 – 1mf – 9 – 0-8370-4852-4 – 1985-2852 – us A.T.L.A. [230]

A PRIMER OF HEBREW / Fagnani, Charles Prospero – New York: Charles Scribner, 1903 – 1mf – 9 – 0-8370-9231-0 – 1986-3231 – us A.T.L.A. [470]

A PRIMER OF HEBREW ANTIQUITIES / Whitehouse, Owen Charles – New York: Fleming H. Revell, 1895. 1 fiche – 9 – us A.T.L.A. [270]

PRIMER OF KANURI GRAMMAR / Duisberg, Adolf von – London, New York: Oxford Press, 1917 – us Res Libr [490]

A PRIMER OF PHONETICS / Sweet, Henry – 3rd rev ed. Oxford: Clarendon, 1906 – 1mf – 9 – 0-8370-8390-7 – 1986-2390 – us A.T.L.A. [420]

A PRIMER OF ROMAN CATHOLICISM : OR, THE DOCTRINES OF THE CHURCH OF ROME BRIEFLY EXAMINED IN THE LIGHT OF SCRIPTURE / Wright, Charles Henry Hamilton – (Includes index) – New York: Fleming H Revell, [1896?] – 1mf – 9 – 0-8370-8399-0 – 1986-2399 – us A.T.L.A. [240]

A PRIMER OF SPOKEN ENGLISH / Sweet, Henry – Oxford: Clarendon press, 3rd rev ed 1900 – 1 roll – 1 – 1-55879-904-4 – uk Libr Preservation [420]

A PRIMER ON THE JURISDICTION THE U.S. COURTS OF APPEALS / Baker, Thomas E – Washington: FJC, 1989 – 2mf – 9 – $3.00 – LLMC 95-377 – us L.L.M.C. [340]

PRIMER PLAN DE DESARROLLO ECONOMICO Y SOCIAL, 1965-1969 / El Salvador. Consejo Nacional de Planificacion y Coordinacion Economica – 2v. San Salvador. 1964. BD-1291 1 – 9 – ne IDC [338]

PRIMER PLAN DE LA NACION PARA EL DESARROLLO ECONOMICO Y SOCIAL, 1965-1969 / El Salvador. Consejo Nacional de Planificacion – 2a parte, version preliminar. San Salvador. 1964 – 9 – ne IDC [338]

EL PRIMER REGRESO DE HERNAN CORTES A ESPANA / Lopez de Meneses, Amada – Sep. Revista de Indias. Ano 14. Enero-Junio 1954. no 55-56 – sp Bibl Santa Ana [946]

EL PRIMER VIAJE DE CRISTOBAL COLON. MADRID, 1942 / Guillen, Julio F – Madrid: Razon y Fe, 1946 – 1 – sp Bibl Santa Ana [910]

PRIMERA ANTOLOGIA DE POETAS PACENSES / Angelus – Zafra: Teologado Claretiano, 1960 – 1 – sp Bibl Santa Ana [810]

LA PRIMERA COPLA DE LA CONQUISTA / Porras Barrenechea, Paul – Badajoz: Imprenta Diputacion Provincial, 1971 – sp Bibl Santa Ana [946]

PRIMERA Y...DE LA CHRISTI VICTORIA / Sanchez Galindo, Benito – 1576 – 9 – 1.50f – sp Bibl Santa Ana [240]

PRIMERA Y...GRANDEZAS...ESPANA / Medina, Pedro de – 1595 – 9 – 1.50f – sp Bibl Santa Ana [920]

PRIMERAS JORNADAS DE COMERCIO EXTERIOR. CAMARA OFICIAL DE COMERCIO E INDUSTRIA DE CACERES. PONENTE D. ... / Carmona Alonso, Miguel – Caceres: Tip. Extremadura, 1977 – 1 – sp Bibl Santa Ana [946]

PRIMERAS NOCIONES DE CRONOLOGIA / Florez, Jose Segundo – 1841 – 9 – 1.50f – sp Bibl Santa Ana [946]

PRIMERA...VEINTIUN LIBROS RITUALES...INDIANA / Torquemada, Juan de – (Segunda.... 1723. Tercero.... 1723) – 1723 – 9 – 1.50f – sp Bibl Santa Ana [946]

PRIMERNAIA REVIZIIA I PLAN DEIATEL'NOSTI SEL'SKOGO KOOPERATIVA / Dneprovskii, S P – M., 1926 – 2mf – 9 – COR-472/1 – ne IDC [334]

EL PRIMERO DE LOS EDUCADORES DE LA NUEVA ESPANA, FR. PEDRO DE GANTE. MEJICO, 1934 / Chavez, A Ezequiel – Madrid: Razon y Fe, 1935 – 1 – sp Bibl Santa Ana [972]

LOS PRIMEROS FRUTOS DE MI HUERTA. (VERSOS MUY MALOS) / Cascales Munoz, Jose – Sevilla: Imp. E. Rasco, 1897 – 1 – sp Bibl Santa Ana [810]

PRIMEVAL MAN UNVEILED, OR, THE ANTHROPOLOGY OF THE BIBLE / Gall, James – London: Hamilton, Adams, 1880. 1 fiche – 9 – us A.T.L.A. [240]

PRIMEVAL REVELATION : STUDIES IN GENESIS 1-8 / Jones, John Cynddylan – New York: American Tract Society, 1897 – 1mf – 9 – 0-8370-3796-4 – 1985-1796 – us A.T.L.A. [220]
THE PRIMEVAL WORLD OF HEBREW TRADITION / Hedge, Frederic Henry – Boston: Roberts, 1870, c1869 – 1mf – 9 – 0-8370-3544-9 – 1985-1544 – us A.T.L.A. [220]
PRIMI ALBORI MUSICALI PER LI PRINCIPANTI DELLA MUSICA FIGURATA / Penna, L – 1679 – 9 – us Sibley [780]
PRIMI TUONI OVERO INTRODUZIONE DEL CANTO FERMO CON L'AGGIUNTA D'ALTRI TUONI DEL SIGNOR DOTTOR MARCO DIONIGI... / Dionigi, M – Parma: Per Mario Vigna, 1667 – 3mf – 9 – us Sibley [780]
PRIMICIAL (LA DESGRACIA PUDO MAS... ODISEA...EL DOCTOR AMORES...!PERO NO AL AXILO!) / Gonzalez y Gonzalez, Valeriano – Caceres: Tip. Extremadura, 1928 – 1 – sp Bibl Santa Ana [946]
PRIMITAIE FLORAE WERTHEMENSIS / Wibel, A W E C – Jenae. 1799. B-7386 1 – 9 – ne IDC [580]
PRIMITIAE ESSEQUEBOENSIS / Meyer, G F W – Goettingae. 1818. B-5480 2 – 8 – ne IDC [580]
PRIMITIAE FLORAE GALICIAE AUSTRIACAE / Besser, W S JG von – 2v. Viennae. 1809. B-902 2 – 8 – ne IDC [580]
PRIMITIAE FLORAE HOLSATICAE / Wiggers, F H – Kiliae. 1780. B-5809 2 – 8 – ne IDC [580]
PRIMITIAE FLORAE SALISBURGENSIS / Schrank, F von & Paula, A von – Francofurti a M. 1792. B-1127 2 – 8 – ne IDC [580]
LES PRIMITIFS ET LEURS SIGNATURES / Mely, Fernand de – O-370. 1913 – 9 – ne IDC [306]
LES PRIMITIFS FLAMANDS / Reunion des musees nationaux. Paris – 1947. 72 illus. 2 fiches – 9 – fr Réunion [700]
PRIMITIVE AND CATHOLIC CHRISTIANITY : AN ADDRESS / McGiffert, Arthur Cushman – (Together with the charge on behalf of the board of directors by James M. Ludlow) – New York: J.C. Rankin, 1893 – 1mf – us A.T.L.A. [240]
PRIMITIVE BAPTIST – North Carolina. 1835-79 – 1 – 182.00 – us Baptist [240]
THE PRIMITIVE BAPTIST – The Throgmorton-Potter debate, held at Fulton, Ky., 12 Jul 1887 – 1 – 12.25 – us Baptist [240]
PRIMITIVE CHRISTIAN – Meyersdale. Pa. 1876-1878 – 1 – us UMI [071]
THE PRIMITIVE CHRISTIAN'S ESTIMATE OF WAR AND SELF-DEFENSE / Leeds, Josiah Woodward – New Vienna, O.: Peace Association of Friends in America.58p – 1 – us U.W. Library [240]
THE PRIMITIVE CHURCH AND THE PRIMACY OF ROME / Bartoli, Giorgio – London: Hodder and Stoughton, 1909 – 1mf – us A.T.L.A. [240]
PRIMITIVE CONCEPTS OF DISEASE / Clement, F E – BN 175 2. 1932 – 8 – ne IDC [306]
THE PRIMITIVE CULTURE OF INDIA / Hodson, T C – 1922 – 1 – uk Microform Academic [301]
THE PRIMITIVE DOCTRINE OF BAPTISMAL REGENERATION / Mozley, James Bowling – London: J. Murray, 1856 – 1mf – us A.T.L.A. [240]
THE PRIMITIVE HYMNS / Lloyd, Benjamin – 1841 – 1 – 20.79 – us Baptist [240]
PRIMITIVE MAN *see* ANTHROPOLOGICAL QUARTERLY
P[RIMITIVE] M[ETHODIST] CIRCUITS ABROAD / Leary, William – 1981 – 1mf – 9 – ne IDC [240]
PRIMITIVE METHODIST CIRCUITS [AND THEIR MINISTERS, TO 1932] / Leary, William – 1980 – 5mf – 9 – ne IDC [240]
Primitive Methodist Connexion *see*
– CONFERENCE
– [GENERAL RULES, 1824]
PRIMITIVE METHODIST MAGAZINE – (Coll title: The People Called Methodists, Phase 3: Primary Sources, 1801-1850) – Leicester, Derby. v1-10. 1819-1829; N.S. v1-11. 1830-1841; S.2. v12. 1842; S.3. v1-8. 1843-1850 – 182mf – 9 – H-2739/1 – ne IDC [240]
PRIMITIVE METHODIST MINISTERS, FROM THE COMMENCEMENT TO THE YEAR 1932 / Leary, William – 1981 – 4mf – 9 – ne IDC [240]
Primitive Methodist World *see* AN INDEX TO THE PRIMITIVE METHODIST WORLD, 1883 [AND] THE PRIMITIVE METHODIST, 1870, 1 AND 2 WILLIAM LEARY
PRIMITIVE PIETY REVIVED, OR, THE AGGRESSIVE POWER OF THE CHRISTIAN CHURCH : A PREMIUM ESSAY / Fish, Henry Clay – Boston: Congregational Board of Publication, 1855 – 1mf – us A.T.L.A. [240]
PRIMITIVE TRAITS IN RELIGIOUS REVIVALS : A STUDY IN MENTAL AND SOCIAL EVOLUTION / Davenport, Frederick Morgan – New York: Macmillan, 1905 – 1mf – us A.T.L.A. [200]
PRIMITIVE TRAITS IN RELIGIOUS REVIVALS: A STUDY IN MENTAL AND SOCIAL EVOLUTION / Davenport, Frederick Morgan – New York: Macmillan Co., 1905. xii,323p – 1 – us U.W. Library [240]
PRIMITVE METHODIST CIRCUITS AND BRANCHES – [1983] – 1mf – 9 – ne IDC [240]
PRIMIZIE DI CANTO FERMO DEL PADRE FRANCESCO MARIA VALLARA DA PARMA / Vallara, F M – 1700 – 9 – us Sibley [780]
PRIMO CENSIMENTO GENERALE DELIE AZIENDE AGRARIE METROPOLITANE DELLA LIBIA AL 21 APRILE 1937 XV / Libya – 9 – ne IDC [338]
Primo de Rivera, Jose Antonio *see*
– 3 DISCURSOS.
– BAJO EL TIEMPO DIFICIL
Primo de Rivera, Pilar *see* 4 DISCURSOS.
IL PRIMO LIBRO DI MADRIGALI A QUARTO VOCI. / Palestrina, Giovanni Pierluigi – Cantus part only. 1555 – 9 – us Sibley [780]
IL PRIMO LIBRO ORATIONI NEL GENERE DELIBERATIVO... : SCRITTE DA LUI A DIUERSI PRENCIPI PER LA GUERRA CONTRA IL TURCO / Frachetta, G – Roma, 1598 – 3mf – 9 – H-8430/1 – ne IDC [956]
PRIMORSKAI A ZHIZN – (Includes c.1: 1918:July 25) – Vladivostok: T-vo "Trudovai a pechat", 1918- – 1 – CSUXAKP2778-S – us Hoover Inst Photo [947]
PRIMROSE LEAGUE GAZETTE – London, England. -m. Oct 1887-Dec 1926. 13 reels – 1 – uk British Libr Newspaper [072]
PRIMROSE PRESS – Primrose, NE. -w. Jan 1925-Aug 1940 – 1 – us NE Hist [071]
PRIMROSE RECORD – Primrose, NE. -w. May 1908-Nov 1909 – 1 – us NE Hist [071]
PRIMUS : PROBLEMS, RESOURCES, AND ISSUES IN MATHEMATICS UNDERGRADUATE STUDIES – West Point. v1-4 1991-94*. v5-7 1995-97+ – 1,5,9 – D18236 – us UMI [510]
Primus, J H *see* THE VESTMENTS CONTROVERSY
PRINCE ALBERT DAILY HERALD – (1993.-12r; 1934-1935.-5r) – Prince Albert, 1976-1992 – 197r – 1 – cn Preston [971]
Prince, Albert Happoldt *see* HISTORY OF THE BROOKS ARTILLERY
PRINCE ALBERT TIMES – Prince Albert, Canada. 1882-95 – 4r – 1 – $260.00 – cn Library Assoc [971]
Prince, Benjamin F *see* A STANDARD HISTORY OF SPRINGFIELD AND CLARK COUNTY
Prince, Carl E *see* THE PAPERS OF ALBERT GALLATIN
Prince Edward Island *see*
– ROYAL GAZETTE
– ROYAL GAZETTE AND MISCELLANY OF THE ISLAND OF SAINT JOHN
Prince Edward Island. Canada *see*
– HAZZARD AND WARBURTON'S PRINCE EDWARD ISLAND CASES
– PETER'S PRINCE EDWARD ISLAND REPORTS
– PRINCE EDWARD ISLAND STATUTES, SESSION LAWS AND REVISIONS
PRINCE EDWARD ISLAND, GARDEN PROVINCE OF CANADA: ITS HISTORY, INTERESTS AND RESOURCES, WITH INFORMATION FOR TOURISTS, ETC / Crosskill, William Hay – Charlottetown, P. E. Island: Published by the Provincial government, 1899 (Charlottetown, P. E. Island: Murley & Garnham). 03629. (Pre-1900 Canadiana) – 9 – cn C.I.H.M. [971]
PRINCE EDWARD ISLAND GAZETTE – (v95-108 1969-82 5. v109- 1983- 9) – Charlottetown. v83- 1957- – 1,5,9 – Price varies – cn Micromedia [910]
Prince Edward Island. House of Assembly *see* JOURNALS
PRINCE EDWARD ISLAND: HOW IT WAS BOUGHT BACK FROM THE LANDLORDS / Childers, Hugh Culling Eardley – Illus. by Herbert Railton. 1895? 00608. (Pre-1900 Canadiana) – 9 – cn C.I.H.M. [971]
Prince Edward Island. Laws, Statutes, etc *see*
– GENERAL INDEX TO THE STATUTES... ,PUBLIC AND PRIVATE, PASSED DURING THE YEARS 1869-1919 (BOTH INCLUDED)
– INDEX TO THE STATUTES OF PRINCE EDWARD ISLAND, IN FORCE IN THE YEAR 1845
PRINCE EDWARD ISLAND MAGAZINE – v1-7. Mar. 1899-Jan. 1905 – 1 – cn Precision [971]
THE PRINCE EDWARD ISLAND PHILATELIST – Charlottetown, PEI: P.E.I. Philatelist, [1888] – 9 – cn C.I.H.M. [760]
PRINCE EDWARD ISLAND REGISTER – Charlottetown, Canada. 1823-30 – 2r – 1 – $136.00 – cn Library Assoc [971]
PRINCE EDWARD ISLAND STATUTES, SESSION LAWS AND REVISIONS / Prince Edward Island. Canada – (For after 1945, materials will be filmed and offered periodically as they fall out of copyright) – 1901-1945 – 140mf – 9 – $210.00 – LLMC 90-180 – us L.L.M.C. [324]
PRINCE GEORGE CITIZEN – (1916-78 inquire. 1979-84 24r per yr) – Prince George, British Columbia, CN. May 1916- – 12r per yr – 1 – cn Commonwealth Micro [072]
PRINCE GEORGE LEADER – Prince George, British Columbia, CN. Mar 1921-1923 – 1r – 1 – cn Commonwealth Micro [072]
PRINCE GEORGE POST – Prince George, British Columbia, CN. Nov 1914-Oct 1915 – 1r – 1 – cn Commonwealth Micro [072]
PRINCE GEORGE STAR – Prince George, British Columbia, CN. Oct 1916-May 1917 – 1r – 1 – cn Commonwealth Micro [072]
Prince, J E *see* UN PROCES SOUS LA RESTAURATION; L'AFFAIRE DU MARECHAL NEY
Prince, John Dyneley *see*
– A CRITICAL COMMENTARY ON THE BOOK OF DANIEL...FOR STUDENTS OF THE ENGLISH BIBLE
– MENE MENE TEKEL UPHARSIN
LE PRINCE JOSEPH PONIATOWSKI. MARECHAL DE FRANCE (1763-1813) / Askenazy, S – Paris. 1921. BR-5489 2 – 8 – ne IDC [920]
Prince, Le Baron Bradford *see* SPANISH MISSION CHURCHES OF NEW MEXICO
PRINCE LUCIFER / Austin, Alfred – London, New York: Macmillan, 1887 – 1 roll – 1 – 1-55879-458-1 – uk Libr Preservation [890]
Prince, Madeleine *see* BIO-BIBLIOGRAPHIE ANALYTIQUE DE GERARD LANGLOIS, JOURNALISTE-DIRECTEUR DES EDITIONS DU CACTUS
PRINCE OF LIGHT AND THE PRINCE OF DARKNESS IN CONFLICT / Grosart, Alexander Balloch – London: James Nisbet, 1864. 1 fiche – 9 – us A.T.L.A. [240]
THE PRINCE OF LIGHT AND THE PRINCE OF DARKNESS IN CONFLICT : OR, THE TEMPTATION OF CHRIST / Grosart, Alexander Balloch – London:James Nisbet, 1864 – 1mf – 9 – 0-8370-3406-X – 1985-1406 – us A.T.L.A. [220]
PRINCE OF THE KINGS OF THE EARTH / Cornish, Louisa S – Worthing:Charles E Thomas, [c1902] – 1mf – 9 – 0-8370-2747-0 – 1985-0747 – us A.T.L.A. [240]
PRINCE OF WALES ISLAND GAZETTE – Georgetown. Penang. 1806-30 – 1 – uk Microform Academic [072]
THE PRINCE OF WALES SARABAND / L'Abbe, A – London: Pemberton, 1731 – 1 – us Sibley [780]
PRINCE OTTO : A ROMANCE / Stevenson, Robert Louis – London: Chatto & Windus, 1885 – 1 roll – 1 – 1-55879-563-4 – uk Libr Preservation [830]
PRINCE RUPERT DAILY NEWS – Prince Rupert. B.C. Canada. May 1914- – 1 – cn Commonwealth Micro [072]
THE PRINCE SOCIETY – 36v. of source materials on early American history published by the Boston society, 1865-1920 – 9 – us Primary [975]
PRINCELIICKE DEVIISEN VAN CLAUDE PARADIN, GABRIEL SIMEON, ENDE MEER ANDER / Paradin, Claude & Simeoni, G – Leiden, 1615 – 5mf – 9 – ne IDC [700]
PRINCELY MEN IN THE HEAVENLY KINGDOM / Beach, Harlan Page – (Includes appendix) – Boston: American Board of Commissioners for Foreign Missions, Young Peoples' Dept, c1903 – 1mf – 9 – 0-8370-6562-3 – 1986-0562 – us A.T.L.A. [920]
THE PRINCESS : A MEDLEY / Tennyson, Alfred, Lord – London: Edward Moxon, 1850 – 1 roll – 1 – 1-55879-950-8 – uk Libr Preservation [810]
PRINCESS NAPRAXINE / Ouida – British Fiction Archive: Unit 3 – 9 – uk Bell [830]
A PRINCESS OF THULE / Black, William – British Fiction Archive: Unit 4 – 9 – uk Bell [830]
PRINCESS & POET / Bell, Lallah – Halifax, 1897. 05939. (Pre-1900 Canadiana) – 9 – cn C.I.H.M. [810]
Princeteau, T *see* CORNELIE OU LA PUPILLE DE VOLTAIRE
PRINCETON 1676-1900 – (Mf 1-8: Vital Records 1676-1881. Mf 9: Vital Records 1744-87. Mf 9-15: Town Meetings 1761-86. Mf 16: Residents 1767-1807. Mf 16-18: Marriages 1761-1844. Mf 17: Intentions: 1816-21. Mf 19-25: Proprietors 1686-1770. Mf 26-55: Town Records 1786-1853. Mf 56-61: Selectmen 1838-70. Mf 62-63: Pews & Roads 1805-65. Mf 62-63: Dog Tags 1858-84. Mf 64-68: Treasurer 1817-64. Mf 69-71: Fences 1818-87. Mf 72-75: Mortgages 1832-42. Mf 76-79: Poor House 1838-87. Mf 80: Rebellion Recs 1861-65. Mf 81-83: Cemetery 1695-1942. Mf 84-90: Intentions 1821-1906; 91: Birth Index 1842-1900; 92: Marriage Index 1844-1900. Mf 93: Death Index 1844-1900. Mf 94-95: Vital Recs 1842-52. Mf 96-97: Births 1853-1900. Mf 98-99: Marriages 1853-1900. Mf 99-101: Deaths 1853-1900) – (mf ed 1993) – 101mf – 9 – us Holbrook [920]
PRINCETON 1742-1849 – (Mf 1T-4T: Births & Deaths 1742-1879. Mf 4T: Marriages 1783-91, 1804. Mf 5T-6T: Vital Records 1779-1882. Mf 6T-7T: Marriage Intentions 1760-1816. Mf 7T-8T: Births & Deaths 1815-59. Mf 7T-9T: Marriages 1772-1844. Mf 9T-10T: Marriage Intentions 1816-49. Mf 10T-11T: Births 1843-49. Mf 11T: Marriages & Deaths 1844-49) – (mf ed 1998) – 11mf – 9 – 0-87623-319-1 – us Holbrook [920]
PRINCETON BAPTIST CHURCH. LAURENS COUNTY. SOUTH CAROLINA : CHURCH RECORDS – 1901-72 – 1 – 21.78 – us Baptist [240]
PRINCETON FIRST BAPTIST CHURCH. PRINCETON, WEST VIRGINIA : CHURCH RECORDS – 1840-1960. (History of church included) – 1 – 49.46 – us Baptist [240]
PRINCETON REVIEW – 1878-84 (complete) – 4r – 1 – ATLA S0208 – us A.T.L.A. [073]
THE PRINCETON REVIEW *see* PRESBYTERIAN QUARTERLY AND PRINCETON REVIEW
PRINCETON SEMINARY BULLETIN – 1907- 1; 1973- 5,6; 1975- 4 x 6 in. 9 – us UMI [240]
PRINCETON THEOLOGICAL REVIEW – (Includes index 1900-29) – v1-27. 1903-1929 (complete) – 9r – 1 – ATLA S0211 – us A.T.L.A. [073]
Princeton University. Firestone Library. Plasma Physics Laboratory Library *see* DICTIONARY CATALOG OF THE PRINCETON UNIVERSITY PLASMA PHYSICS LABORATORY LIBRARY
PRINCETON UNIVERSITY LATIN AMERICAN MICROFILM COLLECTION – (Argentina 29r $2,465. Bolivia 16r $1,360. Brazil 62r $5,270. Chile 72r $6,120. Colombia 8r $680.00. Cuba 63r $5,355. Mexico 35r $2,975. Nicaragua 22r $1,870. Peru 38r $3,230. Puerto Rico 11r $935. Canary Islands 1r $85. Central America/Panama 4r $340. Costa Rica 1r $85. Ecuador 4r $340. El Salvador 3r $255. Guadaloupe 1r $85. Guatemala 2r $170. Haiti 3r $255. Honduras 2r $170. Latin America (general) 4r $340. Panama 1r $85. Paraguay 1r $85. Uruguay 9r $765. Venezuela 2r $170. The West Indies 1r $85. Printed guide available separately $25.00 P0000.G) – 395r – 1 – $33,575.00 – P0000 – us Scholarly Res [972]
PRINCETON UNIVERSITY LIBRARY LATIN AMERICAN MICROFILM COLLECTION : SUPPLEMENT 1 – (Argentina 2r $170. Bolivia 5r $425. Brazil 11r $935. Chile 39r $3,315. Colombia 1r $85. Cuba 2r $170. Latin America 2r $170. Mexico 8r $680. Nicaragua 1r $85. Peru 5r $425.

Guide to suppl 1 only sold separately $25 P0001.G) – 1996 – 76r – 1 – $6,460.00 – P0001 – us Scholarly Res [972]

Princeton University. Office of Population Research *see*
- POPULATION INDEX BIBLIOGRAPHY CUMULATED 1935-1968 BY AUTHORS AND GEOGRAPHICAL AREAS
- POPULATION INDEX BIBLIOGRAPHY

DAS PRINCIP DES KATHOLICISMUS UND DIE WISSENSCHAFT : GRUNDSAETZLICHE EROERTERUNGEN AUS ANLASS EINER TAGESFRAGE / Hertling, Georg Freiherr von – Freiburg im Breisgau, St. Louis, Mo.: Herder, 1899 – 1mf – us A.T.L.A. [240]

PRINCIPAL ENGLISH WRITINGS OF THE LATE REV. P. J. DOHERTY: PREFACED BY A SKETCH OF HIS LIFE / Doherty, Patrick John – L.H.P.. Quebec: s.n., 1873 (Quebec: L. Huot). 02731. (Pre-1900 Canadiana) – 9 – cn C.I.H.M. [971]

PRINCIPAL GRANT'S LETTERS ON PROHIBITION: AS THEY APPEARED IN THE TORONTO DAILY GLOBE, DECEMBER 1897, JANUARY, 1898 / Grant, George Monro – 1898?. 05122. (Pre-1900 Canadiana) – 9 – cn C.I.H.M. [971]

PRINCIPAL RULES OF THE ITALIAN GRAMMAR / Thomas, William – 1550. 267p. (English Linguistics Series 1500-1800) – 9 – us UMI [440]

PRINCIPAL TOWNS EAST OF THE CASCADE MOUNTAINS – West Coast. 1865 – 1r – 1 – $50.00 – D122 – us Library Micro [978]

PRINCIPAL WOMEN OF THE EMPIRE – London: Mitre Press, 1940 – 2mf – 9 – A$10.00 – at State Libr Vic [920]

PRINCIPALITY – Cardiff, Wales, UK. Sept 1847-1850. -w. 2 1/2 reels – 1 – uk British Libr Newspaper [072]

LES PRINCIPAUX MANUSCRITS A PEINTURES CONSERVES DANS L'ANCIENNE BIBLIOTHEQUE IMPERIALE PUBLIQUE DE SAINT-PETERSBOURG / Laborde, A de – (Describes illuminated mss in Saltykov-Shchedrin) – Paris. 2v. 1936-38 – 9mf – 9 – R-10860/1 – ne IDC [090]

LE PRINCIPE DE LA FOI / Abravanel, I – Trans. by B. Mosse. Avignon. 1884. BJ-33-33 1 – 9 – ne IDC [240]

LE PRINCIPE DE L'UNANIMITE / Eles, G T – Paris, 1935 – 3mf – 1 – ILM-4008/1 – ne IDC [327]

LE PRINCIPE DES NATIONALITES : LECTURE PUBLIQUE FAITE DEVANT L'INSTITUT CANADIEN, A MONTREAL / Doutre, Gonzalve – Montreal: Press of le Pays, 1864. SEM16P132 – 1r – 5 – Can$9.00 – cn Bibl Nat [971]

LE PRINCIPE DES NATIONALITES... / Hauser, Henri – Paris, 1916 – 1mf – 1 – ILM-1984/1 – ne IDC [327]

PRINCIPES DE GRAMMAIRE GENERALE MIS A LA PORTEE DES ENFANTS, AN 7 / Sacy, I Silvestre de – 1799 – 9 – fr I.C.S. [400]

PRINCIPES DE GRAMMAIRE GENERALE MIS A LA PORTEE DES ENFANTS, ET PROPRES A SERVIR D'INTRODUCTION A L'ETUDE DE TOUTES LES LANGUES / Sacy, I Sylvestre de – (Linguistic series). 1799 – 9 – fr Hachette [400]

PRINCIPES DE J.J. ROUSSEAU POUR L'EDUCATION DES ENFANTS / Thiery, Avocat – Ou instruction sur leur education physique et morale depuis leur naissance jusqu'a l'epoque de leur entree dans les ecoles nationales. Paris, Aubry – 9 – fr Hachette [190]

PRINCIPES DE LA FLUTE TRAVERSIERE / Hotteterre, J – 1722 – 9 – us Sibley [780]

PRINCIPES DE LA GRAMMAIRE FRANCOISE / Antonini – 1753 – 9 – fr I.C.S. [440]

PRINCIPES DE LA GUERRE DE MONTAGNES. / Bourcet – Paris. Impr. Nationale. 1888. iii, 322p. (Strategy of War Series) – 9 – fr Hachette [355]

PRINCIPES DE LA LANGUE WOLOFE / Missionnaires de la Congregation du Saint-Esprit – Dakar, Imprimerie de la Mission. 1855 – 9 – $5.00 – fr Orientalistes [490]

LOS PRINCIPES DE LA LITERATURA... / ed by Bayle, Constantino – Madrid: Razon y Fe, 1926 – 1 – sp Bibl Santa Ana [440]

LES PRINCIPES DE LA METHODE NATURELLE / Planchon, [F]G – Montpellier, 1860 – 2mf – 9 – ne IDC [615]

LOS PRINCIPES DE LA POESIA ESPANOLA... MARTIN CORTES / Perez de Guzman, Juan – 1890 – 9 – $1.50f – sp Bibl Santa Ana [440]

PRINCIPES DE LA STRATEGIE DEVELOPPES PAR LES RELATIONS DE LA CAMPAGNE DE 1796 EN ALLEMAGNE / Charles, Archduke of Austria – Paris. Magimel. 1818. 3v., 1v. of pl. (Strategy of War Series) – 9 – fr Hachette [355]

LOS PRINCIPES DE LA...FERNANDO DE VERA Y MENDOZA / Perez de Guzman, Juan – 1891 – 9 – 1.50f – sp Bibl Santa Ana [440]

PRINCIPES DE L'ART DE LA GUERRE, DEVELOPPES D'APRES LES MEILLEURS EXEMPLES / Leroy de Bosroger – Paris. Cellot et Jombert fils jeune. 1779. viii, 426p., pl. (Strategy of War Series) – 9 – fr Hachette [355]

LES PRINCIPES DE L'HON. M. MERCIER / Mercier, Honore – Quebec, 1890. 02576. (Pre-1900 Canadiana) – 9 – cn C.I.H.M. [971]

PRINCIPES DE MORALE RATIONNELLE / Landry, Adolphe – (Includes bibliographical references and index) – Paris: Felix Alcan, 1906 – 1mf – 9 – 0-8370-6136-9 – 1986-0136 – us A.T.L.A. [230]

PRINCIPES DE MUSIQUE.. / Monteclair, Michel P – 1736 – 2 – us Sibley [780]

PRINCIPES DE STYLE / Herissant, LT – 1779 – 15 – fr I.C.S. [440]

PRINCIPES DE VIOLON PAR DEMANDES.. / Dupont, P – 1740 – 9 – us Sibley [780]

LES PRINCIPES DU BLAZON / Dangeau, L de Courcillon de – 1715 – 9 – fr I.C.S. [920]

PRINCIPES DU DROIT DE LA NATURE ET DES GENS / Burlamaqui, J J – rev ed. Paris. 5v. 1820-1821 – 30mf – 1 – ILM-141/1 – ne IDC [327]

PRINCIPES DU DROIT DE LA NATURE ET DES GENS / Formey – Amsterdam, 1758 – 4mf – 1 – ILM-2711/1 – ne IDC [327]

PRINCIPES DU DROIT NATUREL... / Burlamaqui, J J – rev ed. Geneva, Copenhagen, 1756 – 4mf – 1 – ILM-792/1 – ne IDC [327]

PRINCIPES D'UN BON GOUVERNEMENT OU REFLEXIONS MORALES ET POLITIQUES TENDANTES A PROCURER LE BONHEUR DE L'HOMME ET CELUI DES SOCIETES POLITIQUES / Campagne, Alexandre Auguste de – Berlin: G.L. Winter, 1768. 6 fiches. (Political Science Collection) – 9 – 15.00 – fr Bibl Nationale [320]

PRINCIPES ELEMENTAIRES... / Audinet, E L A – Paris, 1906 – 8mf – 9 – ILM-320/1 – ne IDC [340]

PRINCIPES ESSENTIELS POUR LA CONDUITE DE LA GUERRE. CLAUZEWITZ INTERPRETE / Dragomirov, M I – Paris, L. Baudoin. 1889. 102p. (Strategy of War Series) – 9 – fr Hachette [355]

PRINCIPES FONDAMENTAUX DE SOMIOLOGIE / Rafinesque-Schmaltz, Constantine S – Palermo. 1814. B-5650 1 – 9 – ne IDC [580]

PRINCIPES GENERAUX DE GRAMMAIRE POUR TOUTES LES LANGUES / Condillac, E B de – (Linguistics series). 1798 – 9 – fr Hachette [400]

PRINCIPES GENERAUX DE GRAMMAIRE. POUR TOUTES LES LANGUES. PARIS, (AN 6) / Condillac, E B de – 9 – fr I.C.S. [400]

PRINCIPES GENERAUX DU DROIT INTERNATIONAL EN MATIERE CRIMINELLE / Deloume, A – Paris, Toulouse, 1882 – 2mf – 1 – ILM-2002/1 – ne IDC [327]

PRINCIPES GENERAUX ET RAISONNES DE LA GRAMMAIRE FRANCOISE / Restaut, P – 1730 – 9 – fr I.C.S. [440]

PRINCIPES GUIDANT L'ELABORATION D'UNE METHODE D'ENSEIGNEMENT DU FRANCAIS ORAL POUR DES ETUDIANTS ANGLOPHONES / Drach, Margaret – 2mf – 9 – 10404 – fr Atelier National [440]

LES PRINCIPES INFAILLIBLES DE LA PRONONCIATION / Lartigaut, A – 1670 – 9 – fr I.C.S. [440]

LES PRINCIPES MODERNES DU DROIT PENAL INTERNATIONAL / Donnedieu de Vabres, H – Paris, 1928 – 5mf – 1 – ILM-2076/1 – ne IDC [327]

PRINCIPES REGENERATEURS DU SYSTEME SOCIAL / Billaud-Varenne, Jacques N – Paris: R. Vatar, Pluviose an III. 1795 – 9 – fr Hachette [190]

PRINCIPES TRES FACILES POUR BIEN APPRENDRE LA MUSIQUE / L'Affillard, M – Paris. 1717. BP-108 1 – 9 – ne IDC [780]

PRINCIPI DI SCIENZA NUOVA D'INTORNO ALLA COMUNE NATURA DELLE NAZIONI / Vico, Giambattista – (Linguistic series). 1744 – 9 – fr Hachette [321]

PRINCIPIA JURIS CIVILIS TUM ROMANI TUMGALLICI... / Dupin, M – Parisiis: A A Everat, 1806-1812. SEM105P873 – 5mf – 9 – Can$11.25 – cn Bibl Nat [971]

PRINCIPIA LATINE LOQUENDI / Cicero, Marcus Tullius – 1575. 341p. (English Linguistics Series 1500-1800) – 9 – us UMI [450]

PRINCIPIEN DER SITTLICHKEIT = THE PRINCIPLES OF MORALITY AND THE DEPARTMENTS OF THE MORAL LIFE / Wundt, Wilhelm Max – (In English. Includes bibliographical references and index) – London: Swan Sonnenschein; New York: Macmillan, 1901 – 1mf – 9 – 0-8370-6636-0 – 1986-0636 – us A.T.L.A. [230]

PRINCIPII DI MUSICA TEORICO-PRATTICA.. / Bertezen, Salvatore – 1780 – 9 – us Sibley [780]

IL PRINCIPIO DELLA SCUOLA ITALIANA... / Fusinato, G – Macerata, 1884 – 1mf – 1 – ILM-1977/1 – ne IDC [327]

IL PRINCIPIO DI NAZIONALITA / Gasparotto, L – Torino, 1898 – 2mf – 1 – ILM-1979/1 – ne IDC [327]

IL PRINCIPIO DI NAZIONALITA... / Esperson, P – N.p., 1868 – 3mf – 1 – ILM-2485/1 – ne IDC [327]

PRINCIPIO Y ORIGEN DE LA CRISTO DE LA VICTORIA – 1849 – 9 – $1.50f – sp Bibl Santa Ana [240]

PRINCIPIOS ... / [Bello, A] – Santiago de Chile, 1832 – 3mf – 9 – ILM-129/1 – ne IDC [327]

PRINCIPIOS BASICOS Y ESTRUCTURAS DE LA ORGANIZACION SINDICAL; NOTAS ACERCA DE "LO SINDICAL" / Pedret de Falgas, Ramon – Huesca, 1941. Fiche W1101. (Blodgett Collection of Spanish Civil War Pamphlets) – 9 – us H.U. College Libr [946]

PRINCIPIOS DE DERECHO PENAL INTERNACIONAL / Alcorta, C A – Buenos Aires, 1931 – 5mf – 9 – ILM-2040/1 – ne IDC [340]

PRINCIPIOS DE LA GRAMMATICA LATINA / Sanchez, Juan – Sevilla: En la inprenta de Alonso de la Barrera, 1589. 99 leaves. With: de constructione octo partium orationis liber. xEmmanuelis Alvari – 1 – us U.W. Library [450]

PRINCIPIOS DE RETORICA Y POETICA / Sanchez de las Brozas, Francisco – 1845 – 9 – 1.50f – sp Bibl Santa Ana [410]

PRINCIPIOS DEL PERONISMO : CURSO BASICO / Buenos Aires. Escuela Superior Peronista – Buenos Aires, 1951- – 1 – CSUXADL6512-B – us Hoover Inst Photo [320]

PRINCIPIOS DEL SINDICALISMO JUSTICIALISTA DE PERON / Peron, Juan Domingo – Buenos Aires: [Presidencia de la Nacion, Subsecretaria de Informaciones], 1951 – 1 – CSUXAHZ5322-B – us Hoover Inst Photo [360]

PRINCIPIOS DEL SINDICALISMO JUSTICIALISTA DE PERON / Peron, Juan Domingo – Buenos Aires: Presidencia de la Nacion, Subsecretaria de Informaciones, 1953 – 1 – CSUXAGN1578-B – us Hoover Inst Photo [360]

PRINCIPIOS FUNDAMENTALES DE LA RELIGION, 1 / Allezt, Agustin – 1783 – 1mf – 9 – Pta1,000.00 – 84-7848-172-9 – sp Pentalfa [200]

PRINCIPIOS FUNDAMENTALES DE LA RELIGION, 2 / Allezt, Agustin – 1783 – 1mf – 9 – Pta1,000.00 – 84-7848-173-7 – sp Pentalfa [200]

PRINCIPLE DI DIRITTO CONSUETUDINARIO DELLA SOMALIA, ITALIANA MERIODINALE / Colucci, M – Firenze, 1924 – 8 – BA-394 2 – ne IDC [960]

PRINCIPLE IN ART, ETC / Patmore, Coventry Kersey Dighton – London: G. Bell and Sons, 1889 – 1 roll – 1 – 1-55879-174-4 – uk Libr Preservation [410]

THE PRINCIPLE OF AUTHORITY : IN RELATION TO CERTAINTY, SANCTITY AND SOCIETY: AN ESSAY IN THE PHILOSOPHY OF EXPERIMENTAL RELIGION / Forsyth, Peter Taylor – New York: Hodder and Stoughton, [1912?] – 2mf – us A.T.L.A. [240]

THE PRINCIPLE OF PROGRESSION IN TAXATION / Mallet, Bernard – 1894. 1 fiche (29x) – 9 – 1.00f – at Libertarian Micro [320]

THE PRINCIPLES AND OBJECTS OF THE RELIGIOUS REFORMATION URGED BY A. CAMPBELL AND OTHERS / Richardson, R – Bethany, Va.: A. Campbell, 1853 – 1mf – us A.T.L.A. [240]

PRINCIPLES AND POLICIES / The Australian Rights Movement (Georgist) – Jul 1987 – 16p – 9 – $41.00f – at Libertarian Micro [335]

PRINCIPLES AND PRACTICE OF NAVAL AND MILITARY COURTS-MARTIAL : WITH AN APPENDIX ILLUSTRATIVE OF THE SUBJECT / McArthur, John – 4th ed. London: A Strahan. 2v. 1813 – 12mf – 9 – $18.00 – LLMC 88-129 – us L.L.M.C. [340]

THE PRINCIPLES AND PREACHING OF THE METHODISTS CONSIDERED IN A LETTER TO THE REVEREND MR. **** / Cruttenden, R – London, 1753 – 1mf – 9 – MP-365/1 – ne IDC [240]

PRINCIPLES AND STANDARDS OF PURCHASING PRACTICE : WITH ACCOMPANYING GUIDELINES / National Association of Purchasing Management – 1992 – 1mf – 9 – $1.50 – LLMC 92-195 – us L.L.M.C. [170]

PRINCIPLES IN CHILD TRAINING (CCC3) / Barbour, Dorothy Dickinson – (In Chinese) – 2nd ed. Shanghai: Christian Literature Society, 1932 – 1r – 1 – 0-8370-1703-3 – 1984-6094 – us A.T.L.A. [240]

PRINCIPLES OF AGNOSTICISM APPLIED TO EVIDENCES OF CHRISTIANITY : NINE SERMONS TO WHICH IS ADDED A TENTH, ON THE CHRISTIAN DOCTRINE OF THE TRINITY / Harris, John Andrews – New York: Thomas Whittaker, 1883 – 1mf – 9 – 0-8370-3497-3 – 1985-1497 – us A.T.L.A. [230]

PRINCIPLES OF ANGLICANISM / Kinsman, Frederick Joseph – (Includes bibliographical references) – New York: Longmans, Green, 1910 – 1mf – 9 – 0-8370-8684-1 – 1986-2684 – us A.T.L.A. [240]

THE PRINCIPLES OF ARGUMENTATION / Baker, George Pierce – Boston/London: Ginn & Co, 1898 – 5mf – 9 – $7.50 – LLMC 96-066 – us L.L.M.C. [340]

PRINCIPLES OF BIBLICAL CRITICISM / Lias, John James – London: Eyre & Spottiswoode, 1893. 1 fiche – 9 – us A.T.L.A. [240]

THE PRINCIPLES OF CHRISTIANITY / Sharpe, Alfred B – London: Sands; St Louis, MO: B Herder, 1906 – 1mf – 9 – 0-8370-7508-4 – 1986-1508 – us A.T.L.A. [230]

PRINCIPLES OF COMEDY AND DRAMATIC EFFECT / Fitzgerald, Percy Hetherington – London: Tinsley Brothers, 1870 – 1 roll – 1 – 1-55879-403-4 – uk Libr Preservation [790]

THE PRINCIPLES OF ECCLESIASTICAL UNITY : FOUR LECTURES / Mason, Arthur James – London; New York: Longmans, Green, 1896 – 1mf – us A.T.L.A. [240]

PRINCIPLES OF EDUCATION, DRAWN FROM NATURE AND REVELATION, AND APPLIED TO FEMALE EDUCATION IN THE UPPER CLASSES / Sewell, Elizabeth Missing – New York: D. Appleton, 1866. 2v in 1 – 1 – us U.W. Library [370]

THE PRINCIPLES OF EQUITY AND EQUITY PLEADING / Merwin, Elias – Boston: Houghton, Mifflin, 1895. 658p. LL-841 – 1 – us L of C Photodup [340]

THE PRINCIPLES OF EQUITY, INTENDED FOR THE USE OF STUDENTS AND THE PROFESSION / Snell, Edmund Henry Turner – 1st Amer. ed., from the 6th English ed. St. Louis, Stevenson, 1884. 550 p. LL-128 – 1 – us L of C Photodup [340]

THE PRINCIPLES OF ETHICS / Bowne, Borden Parker – New York: Harper, 1892 – 1mf – 9 – 0-8370-6087-7 – 1986-0087 – us A.T.L.A. [170]

PRINCIPLES OF FEDERAL APPROPRIATIONS LAW – 1st ed. Washington: US General Accounting Office, June 1982 – 11mf – 9 – $16.50 – LLMC 96-068 – us L.L.M.C. [340]

PRINCIPLES OF GEOLOGY, BEING AN ATTEMPT TO EXPLAIN THE FORMER CHANGES OF THE EARTH'S SURFACE, BY REFERENCE TO CAUSES NOW IN OPERATION / Lyell, Charles – London: John Murray, 1830-33 – 2 rolls – 1 – 1-55879-218-X – uk Libr Preservation [550]

THE PRINCIPLES OF GEOLOGY EXPLAINED, AND VIEWED IN THEIR RELATIONS TO REVEALED AND NATURAL RELIGION / King, David – (Includes bibliographical references and index) – New York: Robert Carter, 1851 – 1mf – 9 – 0-8370-7397-9 – 1986-1397 – us A.T.L.A. [230]

PRINCIPLES OF HINDU ASTROLOGY: OR, THE BOOK OF FATE / Guru Dutt, K – Calcutta: R.P. Dutt, 1901. vi,269p – 1 – us U.W. Library [150]

PRINCIPLES OF HYDRAULIC MANAGEMENT OF COASTAL LAGOONS FOR AQUACULTURE AND FISHERIES – 1990 – 95p – it F.A.O. [639]

THE PRINCIPLES OF IDOMA / Abraham, Roy Clive – [Lagos?], 1935 – us Res Libr [470]

PRINCIPLES OF INTERPRETATION : THE LAWS OF INTERPRETATION TREATED AS A SCIENCE, DERIVED INDUCTIVELY FROM AN EXEGESIS OF MANY IMPORTANT PASSAGES OF SCRIPTURE / Lockhart, Clinton – (Includes indexes) – Des Moines, IA: Christian Index Pub Co, 1901 – 1mf – 9 – 0-8370-9487-9 – 1986-3487 – us A.T.L.A. [210]

THE PRINCIPLES OF LOGIC / Bradley, Francis Herbert – London: K. Paul, Trench, 1883 – 2mf – us A.T.L.A. [160]

THE PRINCIPLES OF LOGIC / Bradley, Francis Herbert – London: K. Paul, Trench, 1883 – 1 roll – 1 – 1-55879-576-6 – uk Libr Preservation [160]

PRINCIPLES OF LOVE TO GOD : IN FOUR DISCOURSES – Utica: R Northway, 1850 – 1mf – 9 – 0-8370-7259-X – 1986-1259 – us A.T.L.A. [240]

THE PRINCIPLES OF METAPHYSICAL AND ETHICAL SCIENCE : APPLIED TO THE EVIDENCES OF RELIGION / Bowen, Francis – Boston: Hickling, Swan and Brown, 1855 – 2mf – us A.T.L.A. [240]

THE PRINCIPLES OF MONEY APPLIED TO THE PRESENT STATE OF THE COIN OF BENGAL / Steuart, J – 1772 – 2mf – 9 – ne IDC [332]

THE PRINCIPLES OF MORAL SCIENCE / McDonald, Walter – (Includes bibliographical references and index) – Dublin: Browne and Nolan; St Louis, MO: B Herder, 1904 – 1mf – 9 – 0-8370-6332-9 – 1986-0332 – us A.T.L.A. [230]

THE PRINCIPLES OF MUSIK, IN SINGING AND SETTING.. / Butler, Charles – 1636 – 2 – us Sibley [780]

THE PRINCIPLES OF NATURE, HER DIVINE REVELATIONS, AND A VOICE TO MANKIND. / Davis, Andrew Jackson – 2nd American ed.New York: S.S. Lyon, 1863. xxii,786p – 1 – us U.W. Library [150]

PRINCIPLES OF NEW TESTAMENT QUOTATION : ESTABLISHED AND APPLIED TO BIBLICAL CRITICISM AND SPECIALLY TO THE GOSPELS AND PENTATEUCH / Scott, James – (Includes index) – 2nd ed. Edinburgh: T&T Clark, 1877 – 1mf – 9 – 0-8370-5191-6 – 1985-3191 – us A.T.L.A. [220]

PRINCIPLES OF PASTURE IMPROVEMENT AND RANGE MANAGEMENT AND THEIR APPLICATION IN SOMALIA – 1985 – 229p – it F.A.O. [634]

THE PRINCIPLES OF PLANT TERATOLOGY / Wordsell, W C – 1915 and 1916 – 1,7 – uk Microform Academic [580]

THE PRINCIPLES OF PLEADING IN CIVIL ACTIONS / Heard, Franklin Fiske – Boston: Little, Brown, 1880. 352p. LL-481 – 1 – us L of C Photodup [340]

PRINCIPLES OF POLITICAL ECONOMY : WITH SOME OF THEIR APPLICATIONS TO SOCIAL PHILOSOPHY / Mill, John Stuart – London: Longmans, Green, Reader, and Dyer, 7th ed 1871 – 2 rolls – 1 – 1-55879-233-3 – uk Libr Preservation [320]

THE PRINCIPLES OF PROTESTANTISM : AN EXAMINATION OF THE DOCTRINAL DIFFERENCES BETWEEN THE PROTESTANT CHURCHES AND THE CHURCH OF ROME / Lilley, James Philip – (Includes bibliographical references and index) – Edinburgh: T & T Clark, 1911 – 1mf – 9 – 0-8370-8760-0 – 1986-2760 – us A.T.L.A. [240]

THE PRINCIPLES OF SOCIOLOGY / Spencer, Herbert – New York: Appleton, 1886-97 – 3 rolls – 1 – 1-55879-208-2 – uk Libr Preservation [300]

THE PRINCIPLES OF SOCIOLOGY / Spencer, Herbert – Part II. 1882. 472p. 1 fiche (29x) – 9 – 1.00f – at Libertarian Micro [320]

PRINCIPLES OF SURVEYING / Gaillard, Thomas – 1813 – 6mf – 9 – us South Carolina Historical [520]

THE PRINCIPLES OF SYRIAC GRAMMAR = GRAMMATICA SYRIACA / Hoffmann, Andreas Gottlieb – London: Williams and Norgate; Leipzig: F A Brockhaus, 1858 – 1mf – 9 – 0-8370-7545-9 – 1986-1545 – us A.T.L.A. [470]

PRINCIPLES OF TEXTUAL CRITICISM / Porter, John Scott – 1848 – 9 – us A.T.L.A. [240]

THE PRINCIPLES OF THE AMERICAN LAW OF CONTRACTS AT LAW AND IN EQUITY / Lawson, John Davison – St. Louis, Thomas, 1893. 640 p. LL-339 – 1 – us L of C Photodup [340]

PRINCIPLES OF THE CONSTITUTIONAL LAW OF THE UNITED STATES / Willoughby, Westel Woodbury – New York, Baker, Voorhis, 1912. 576 p. LL-1552 – 1 – us L of C Photodup [340]

PRINCIPLES OF THE ENGLISH LAW OF CONTRACT AND OF AGENCY : IN ITS RELATION TO CONTRACT / Anson, William; ed by Huffcut, Ernest Wilson – (2nd American ed from the 11th English ed with American notes) – New York: Banks Law Publ, 1907 – 6mf – 9 – $9.00 – LLMC 94-268 – us L.L.M.C. [340]

PRINCIPLES OF THE LAW OF CONTRACTS / Leake, Stephen Martin – 8th ed. London, Stevens, 1931. 1088 p. LL-115 – 1 – us L of C Photodup [340]

PRINCIPLES OF THE LAW OF CONTRACTS, AS APPLIED BY COURTS OF LAW / Metcalf, Theron – (?rid., Cambridge: Houghton, 1872. 357p. LL-294. Ibid., Boston: Houghton, Osgood, 1880. 357p. LL-346. Ibid., 2nd ed., Boston: Soule, 1888. 433p. LL-820) – New York: Hurd and Houghton, 1868. 357p. LL-309 – 1 – us L of C Photodup [340]

PRINCIPLES OF THE LAW OF PRIVATE AND PUBLIC CORPORATIONS. / Chadman, Charles Erehart – Chicago: Drake 1905. 271p. LL-508 – 1 – us L of C Photodup [340]

PRINCIPLES OF THE LAW OF REAL PROPERTY. / Warvelle, George William – 2d ed. Chicago, Callaghan, 1900. 483 p. LL-859 – 1 – us L of C Photodup [340]

THE PRINCIPLES OF THE LAW OF REAL PROPERTY / Patterson, Christopher Stuart – Philadelphia: Allen, Lane & Scott, 1894. 83p. LL-1030 – 1 – us L of C Photodup [340]

PRINCIPLES OF THE LAW OF REAL PROPERTY AND THE LAW OF PLEADING AND PRACTICE AT COMMON LAW / Chadman, Charles Erehart – Chicago: Drake 1906. 331p. LL-743 – 1 – us L of C Photodup [340]

THE PRINCIPLES OF THE LAW RELATING TO CORPORATE LIABILITY FOR ACTS OF PROMOTERS / Lloyd, Malcolm – Philadelphia, Bisel, 1897. 92 p. LL-495 – 1 – us L of C Photodup [340]

PRINCIPLES OF THE YOUNG MEN'S CHRISTIAN ASSOCIATION (CCC167) = CHI TU CHIAO CH'ING NIEN HUI YUAN LI : SPECIALLY ADAPTED TO THE USE OF ASSOCIATIONS IN CHINA / Hsieh, Fu-ya – (In Chinese) – Shanghai: Association Press of China, 1923 – 1r – 1 – 1984-B500 – us A.T.L.A. [360]

THE PRINCIPLES OF TIV / Abraham, Roy Clive – (Filmed with the author's: A Dictionary of the Tiv Language, 1940) – London, 1940 – us Res Libr [470]

PRINCIPLES OF WAR / Clausewitz, Karl von – Harrisburg, Pa.: Stackpole, 1942. Translation of the 1936 edition of Die Wichtigsten Grundsatze des Kriegfuhrens – 1 – us U.W. Library [355]

PRINEVILLE NEWS – Prineville OR. Jan 1 1915-Feb 13 1917 – 1 – us U.O. Library [071]

PRINEVILLE NEWS AND PRINEVILLE REVIEW – Prineville OR. Apr 2-Nov 13 1914 – 1 – us U.O. Library [071]

PRINEVILLE REVIEW – Prineville OR. Dec 30 1894-June 20 1912, May 26 1904-Mar 26 1914 – 1 – us U.O. Library [071]

Pringle, J *see* OBSERVATIONS ON THE DISEASES OF THE ARMY

Pringle, Patrick *see* HUE AND CRY

Pringsheim, N *see*
- BEITRAEGE ZUR MORPHOLOGIE DER MEERES-ALGEN
- JAHRBUECHER FUER WISSENSCHAFTLICHE BOTANIK
- UEBER DIE BEFRUECHTUNG UND KEIMUNG DER ALGEN UND DAS WESEN DES ZEUGUNGSACTES
- ZUR KRITIK UND GESCHICHTE DER UNTERSUCHUNGEN UEBER DAS ALGENGESCHLECHT

Prinsep, C C *see* RECORDS OF SERVICES OF MADRAS CIVILIANS, 1741-1838

Prinsep, H T *see* A GENERAL REGISTER OF H.E.I.C. CIVIL SERVANTS

PRINT – v1- 1940- 1; v29- 5,6; v30- 9 – us UMI [070]

PRINT – v.5-. 1968- – 1 – us UMI [760]

PRINT *see* PACKAGING DESIGN

THE PRINT OF MY REMEMBRANCE / Thomas, Augustus – New York, London: C Scribner's Sons, 1922 – 1r – 1 – us U.W. Library [420]

PRINTED BOOKS TO 1700 *see* SHAKESPEARE AT STRATFORD-UPON-AVON

PRINTED CATALOGUE / Trinity College. Dublin. Library – 1872. 63 fiches in set – 9 – PS200.00 – ie European Micro [010]

PRINTED CIRCUIT DESIGN *see* PC DESIGN

THE PRINTED ENGLISH BIBLE, 1525-1885 / Lovett, Richard – London:Religious Tract Society, 1894 – 1mf – 9 – 0-8370-4185-6 – 1985-2185 – us A.T.L.A. [220]

PRINTED MATERIALS / National Nonpartisan League – 1910-28 – 4r – 1 – $120.00 $35.00r – us M.H.S. [025]

PRINTED MINUTES / Ohio. Cleveland Baptist Association/Rocky River Association – 1832-1911, 1958 – 1 – 49.00 – us A.B.H.S. [240]

PRINTED MINUTES / Rhode Island. Warren Baptist Association – 1767-1800 – 1 – us A.B.H.S. [240]

PRINTED MUSIC BEFORE 1800 – (Unit One: Individual composers. Unit Two: Anthologies and tract volumes) – Series One: British Printed Music, Period A: Music before 1650 – 1 – us Primary [780]

PRINTED MUSIC BEFORE 1800 – (Unit Three: Individual Composers, A-H and tract volumes A-H; Unit Four: Individual Composers I-S; Unit Five: Individual composers T-Y, tract volumes I-Y and anthologies 1650-1700; Unit Six: Anthologies 1700-1750; Unit Seven: Handel operas, oratories, masques and odes; Unit Eight: Handel duets, trios, arias, and songs, church music and instrumental music) – Series One: British Printed Music, Period B: Music 1650-1750 – 1 – us Primary [780]

THE PRINTED RECORDS OF THE PARLIAMENT OF IRELAND, 1613-1800 / Ireland. Parliament – 46 reels – 1 – $1,800.00 – us Trans-Media [941]

PRINTER AND PUBLISHER – Toronto: J B MacLean Co, [1892-19–] – 9 – cn C.I.H.M. [680]

PRINTER REVIEW – Barstow. Calif. -w. 1943-58 – 1 – us UMI [071]

PRINTER'S CIRCULAR AND STATIONERS' AND PUBLISHERS' GAZETTE, 1866-1888 : AMERICAN MODEL PRINTER, 1879-1882 : CRAFTSMAN, 1884-1888 – (Coll title: Labor Union Periodicals, Pt 2) – 4r – 1 – $540.00 – 1-55655-312-9 – us UPA [680]

THE PRINTER'S MISCELLANY – Saint John, NB: H Finlay, 1876-1882 – 9 – cn C.I.H.M. [680]

PRINTING AND ENGRAVING : ARCHITECTURE, APPLIED ARTS, STUDIO ARTS – (Individual titles not listed separately) – 243 catalogues on 297mf – 9 – £1,485.00 – uk Chadwyck [760]

PRINTING AND PUBLISHING – (v13-23, no.1. 1972-Spring 1982. 5,6. v17-23, no.1. 1976-Spring 1982. 9) – v1-23, no.1. 1959-Spring 1982 – 1 – us UMI [073]

PRINTING AND PUBLISHING HISTORY, SERIES 1 – (Part One: Printing Ledgers, Cost Books, Accounts and Memoranda 1739-1815 (Additional MSS. 48800-48861). Part Two: Accounts, Inventories, Correspondence, Lists of Employers, Notes on a Strike of 1836 and Other Papers, 1815-55 (Additional MSS, 48862-48918)) – The Strahan Archive from the British Library, London – 1 – us Primary [070]

PRINTING AND PUBLISHING HISTORY, SERIES 2 – The Chiswick Press Archive, from the British Library – 1 – us Primary [010]

PRINTING MANAGEMENT – v42-105 1931-75 1; v101-105 5,6 – us UMI [070]

PRINTING NEWS – MIDWEST *see* PV

PRINTING TRADES JOURNAL – v1-1094 1887-1978 1; v1055-1094 5,6,9 – us UMI [070]

Printono *see* PENASBEDE: PEMBANGUNAN NASIONAL SEMESTA BERENT JANA DELAPAN TAHUN 1961-1969 DALAM BIDANG KOPERASI INDONESIA

Printz, Wolfgang C *see*
- COMPENDIUM MUSICAE SIGNATORIAE ET MODULATORIAE VOCALIS
- EXERCITATIONES MUSICAE THEORETICO-PRACTICAE CURIOSAE DE CONCORDANTIIS SINGULIS
- HISTORISCHE BESCHREIBUNG DER EDELEN SING- UND KLING-KUN.
- HISTORISCHE BESCHREIBUNG DER EDELEN SING-UND KLING-KUN VON WOLFGANG CASPAR PRINTZEN
- PHRYNIS MITILENAEUS..
- WOLFFGANG CASPAR PRINTZENS VON WALDTHURN PHRYNIS MITILENAEUS, ODER SATYRISCHER COMPONIST, WELCHER

Prinz, E L *see* TASHLUM ABUDRAHAM

PRINZ FRIEDRICH VON HOMBURG : FUER SCHULGEBRAUCH UND SELBSTUNTERRICHT HERAUSGEGEBEN / Kleist, Heinrich von; ed by Gaudig, H – Leipzig: B G Teubner, 1908 – 1 – us U.W. Library [820]

PRINZ FRIEDRICH VON HOMBURG / Kleist, Heinrich von; ed by Scholte Nollen, John – (Includes bibliographical references) – Boston: Ginn, c1899 – 1 – us U.W. Library [820]

PRINZ FRIEDRICH VON HOMBURG / Kleist, Heinrich von; ed by Windel, H – Bielefeld: Velhagen & Klasing, 1905 – 1 – us U.W. Library [820]

PRINZ, ODER, SCHLOSSERGESELLE / Muehlbach, Luise – Berlin: Delta-Verlag, c1921 – 1r – 1 – us U.W. Library [830]

PRINZ UND DERWISCH / Meisel, W A – Stettin. 1847. BJ-421-68 1 – 9 – ne IDC [470]

PRINZ UND DERWISCH / Weisslovits, N – Ein indischer Roman. in hebr. Darstellung. Munich. 1890. BJ-421-69 – 9 – ne IDC [830]

PRINZ WIEDUWITT : ERZAEHLUNG / Strauss, Emil – Muenchen: A Langen, G Mueller, 1943, c1939 – 1r – 1 – us U.W. Library [830]

PRINZESSIN ILSE : EIN MAERCHEN AUS DEM HARZGEBIRGE / Petersen, Marie – Leipzig: P Reclam, [19–?] – 1r – 1 – us U.W. Library [390]

PRINZESSIN PUMPHIA / Kurz, Joseph Felix, Freiherr von – (1st ed publ in 1767 under title: Die getreue Prinzessin Pumphia, und Hanns-Wurst, der tyrannische Tartar-Kulikan) – Wien: C Konegen, 1883 – 1r – 1 – us U.W. Library [830]

DAS PRINZIP DES MYTHUS IM DIENST DER CHRISTLICHEN POSITION / Bagge, Oskar – Leipzig: Friedrich Fleischer, 1865. 1 fiche – 9 – us A.T.L.A. [240]

PRINZIPIEN DER INFORMATIONSUE-BERTRAGUNG UEBER ELEKTRISCHE ENERGIEVERSORGUNGSNETZE / Dostert, Klaus – 1991 – 306p – DM98.00 – 3-89349-414-6 – gw Hänsel [621]

PRINZIPIEN DES INTERNATIONALEN STRAFRECHTS / Hegler, A – Breslau, 1906 – 3mf – 1 – ILM-2406/1 – ne IDC [327]

DIE PRINZIPIENERKLAERUNG DES SYNDIKALISMUS / Rocker, Rudolf – Berlin: Der Syndikalist, 1920. 20p – 1 – us U.W. Library [943]

Prior, E S *see* A HISTORY OF GOTHIC ART IN ENGLAND

Prior, John V *see* A TREATISE ON THE CONSTRUCTION OF LIMITATIONS IN WHICH THE WORDS "ISSUE" AND "CHILD" OCCUR, AND ON THE STATUTE 1 VICTORIA, C. 26, S. 29

Prior, Matthew *see* PAPERS

LOS PRIORES DE SAN MARCOS (LEON) / Perez Llamazares, Julio – Madrid, s.i., 1957 – 1 – sp Bibl Santa Ana [946]

Prioris, Cartusiae *see* CHRONICON CARTUSIENSE

Priscianus *see*
- DE CONSTRUCTIONE LIBRI 2
- GRAMMATICA, ETC

PRISCILLIEN ET LE PRISCILLIANISME / Babut, E C – Paris: H. Champion, 1909. (Bibliotheque de l'Ecole des Hautes Etudes: Sciences historiques et philologiques, v169.) – 1mf – us A.T.L.A. [240]

Prisco, Jose *see* ELEMENTOS DE FILOSOFIA

LA PRISE ET SAC DE PATRAS CITE PRINCIPALE DE LA MOREE EN GRECE, NOUUELLEMENT ADUENUE PAR LES CHRESTIENS – Liege, 1595 – 1mf – 9 – H-8213/1 – ne IDC [960]

LOS PRISIONEROS DEL CERRO ROJO – Madrid?, 1937. Fiche W1122. (Blodgett Collection of Spanish Civil War Pamphlets) – 9 – us H.U. College Libr [946]
PRISLOWA A PRISLOWNE HRONCKA A WUSLLOWA HORNJOLUZISKICH SERBOW / ed by Radyserb-Wjela, Jan – 1902. Serbian proverbs – 1 – us I.U. Libraries [390]
PRISM INTERNATIONAL – Vancouver. v6-17. 1966-78 – 9 – Can$20.00y – cn Micromedia [073]
PRISMA : REVISTA ILISTRADA DE ARTES, LETRAS, ETC – (Prospecto: aug 16 1905) – Lima: M Moral. v1-3. sep 15 1905-dec 28 1908 – us Res Libr [073]
A PRISMATIC APPROACH TO THE ANALYSIS OF STYLE IN DANCE / Gibbons, Ruth E G – 1989 – 237p 3mf – 9 – $12.00 – us Microform Publ [790]
THE PRISMS OF ESARHADDON AND ASHURBANIPAL FOUND AT NINEVEH 1927 AND 1928 / Thompson, R C – Oxford, 1931 – 9 – $10.00 – us I.R.C. [930]
PRISOEDENENIE KRYMA K ROSII / Dubrovin, N F – Reskripty, pis'ma, reliatsii i doneseniia. 4 v. Spb. 1885-89. BR-10,552 1 – 9 – ne IDC [947]
THE PRISON CHAPLAINCY AND ITS EXPERIENCES / Quinby, Hosea – Concord, N.H.: D.L. Guernsey, 1873 – 1mf – us A.T.L.A. [240]
UNE PRISON DE FEMMES / Pouyanne, Lydie – Montpellier: Manufacture de la Charite, 1928. (Les Femmes Collection) – 2mf – 9 – $6.00 – fr Bibl Nationale [360]
PRISON JOURNAL *see* JOURNAL OF PRISON DISCIPLINE AND PHILANTHROPY (1845-1920) AND THE PRISON JOURNAL (1921-1986)
THE PRISON JOURNAL – (1983-. 1,5,6,9) – v1-. 1921- – 1 – us UMI [073]
PRISON LAW REPORTER (ABA) – (With bibliography) – v1-3. 1971-74 – 9 – $49.00 set – us Hein [340]
PRISON MIRROR – Stillwater, MN. v1-57. 1887-1944 – 5r – 1 – us Ross [071]
PRISON WORLD – v.2-16. 1940-54 – 16 – apply; photocopies of articles – us UMI [360]
PRISON WORLD *see* AMERICAN JOURNAL OF CORRECTION
PRISONER HALM = PRISONNIER HALM / Wilke, Karl – 1st Am ed. Indianapolis: Bobbs-Merrill, [1931] – 1r – 1 – us U.W. Library [890]
THE PRISONER LEAPS; A DIARY OF MISSIONARY LIFE IN JAVA / Overseas Missionary Fellowship – By David Bentley-Taylor. SE-10,863 1. 1965 – 9 – ne IDC [240]
A PRISONER OF THE GERMANS IN SOUTHWEST AFRICA / Close, Percy L – London: T.F. Unwin, 1916. 318p – 1 – us U.W. Library [940]
THE PRISONER OF ZENDA : BEING THE HISTORY OF THREE MONTHS IN THE LIFE OF AN ENGLISH GENTLEMAN / Hope, Anthony – Bristol: J.W. Arrowsmith, [18–?] – 1 roll – 1 – 1-55879-476-X – uk Libr Preservation [830]
PRISONERS / Cholmondeley, Mary – British Fiction Archive: Unit 3 – 9 – uk Bell [830]
PRISONERS AND PRISONS IN GERMANY DURING WORLD WAR 1 PAMPHLET COLLECTION – 1914-1922 – 2r – 1 – CSUXANL3533-B – us Hoover Inst Photo [355]
PRISONERS AND PRISONS IN GREAT BRITAIN DURING WORLD WAR 1 PAMPHLET COLLECTION – 19??-1918 – 1 reel – 1 – CSUXANL3542-B – us Hoover Inst Photo [355]
PRISONERS AND PRISONS IN ITALY DURING WORLD WAR 2 PAMPHLET COLLECTION – 1943-1978 – 2r – 1 – CSUXANN0313-B – us Hoover Inst Photo [355]
PRISONERS AND PRISONS IN ITALY DURING WORLD WAR 2 PAMPHLET COLLECTION – 1947 – 1 – CSUXANN0317-B – us Hoover Inst Photo [355]
PRISONERS AND PRISONS IN RUSSIA DURING WORLD WAR 1 PAMPHLET COLLECTION – 1915-19?? – 1 reel – 1 – CSUXANL3550-B – us Hoover Inst Photo [355]
PRISONERS AND PRISONS IN THE UNITED STATES DURING WORLD WAR 2 PAMPHLET COLLECTION – 1943-1946 – 1 reel – 1 – CSUXANN0322-B – us Hoover Inst Photo [355]
PRISONERS OF HOPE AND OTHER SERMONS / Brent, Charles H – New York: Longmans, Green, 1915 – 1mf – us A.T.L.A. [240]
THE PRISONERS OF THE FORTY-FIVE / Seton, BG & Arnot, JG – 1928 – 1 – uk Microform Academic [941]
PRISONNIER DE GUERRE : EDITION SPECIALE DE LA CROIX-ROUGE CANADIENNE – Montreal: Bureau provincial d'investigation de la Croix-rouge, 1943?-45? SEM105P799 – 2mf – 9 – Can$4.50 – cn Bibl Nat [360]
PRISONS AND PRISONERS DURING WORLD WAR 1 PAMPHLET COLLECTION – 1914-1940 – 3r – 1 – CSUXANL3518-B – us Hoover Inst Photo [355]
LES PRISONS DE FEMMES / Letellier, Albert – Paris: Riviere, 1923. 102p. (Les Femmes Collection) – 2mf – 9 – $6.00 – fr Bibl Nationale [360]
PRISONS DE FEMMES / Carco, Francis – Paris: Edition de France, 1931. 269p. (Les Femmes Collection) – 3mf – 9 – $8.00 – fr Bibl Nationale [360]
LES PRISONS DE NANTES PENDANT LA REVOLUTION / Lallie, Alfred – (Microf. avec Les Prisons de Nantes... – 2e ed. rev. et augm. – Nantes: Durance, 1912) – Nantes: Forest et Grimaud, 1883 – 1 – F178,37 – fr Armell [360]
Pritchard, Charles *see* OCCASIONAL THOUGHTS OF AN ASTRONOMER ON NATURE AND REVELATION
Pritchard, Fred Eills *see* THE ADMISSIBILITY OF EVIDENCE OF "SYSTEM" IN CRIMINAL CASES; A READING DELIVERED IN THE HALL OF THE HONOURABLE SOCIETY OF THE MIDDLE TEMPLE BY THE AUTUMN READER, SIR FRED E. PRITCHARD, ON THURSDAY, 21 NOVEMBER, 1957
Pritchard, Helen M *see* FRIENDS AND FOES IN THE TRANSKEI
PRITEL LIDU – Wilber, NE. -w. Aug 1895-Sep 1896; Nov 1896-Dec 1898, scattered issues missing; Mar 1899-Mar 1904 – 1 – us NE Hist [071]
PRITOMNOST – Prague. 1928-1932; 1936-1939. Not collated – 1 – us NY Public [073]
PRITOMNOST – Prague, 1928-39 – 2r – 1 – us Ross [072]
Pritzel, G A *see*
- DIE DEUTSCHEN VOLKSNAMEN DER PFLANZEN
- ICONUM BOTANICARUM INDEX LOCUPLETISSIMUS
- THESAURUS LITERATURAE BOTANICAE...
- THESAURUS LITERATURAE BOTANICAE

Pritzker, David M *see* NEGOTIATED RULEMAKING SOURCEBOOK
PRIVACY AND HUMAN RIGHTS : AN INTERNATIONAL AND COMPARATIVE STUDY, WITH SPECIAL REFERENCE TO DEVELOPMENTS IN INFORMATION TECHNOLOGY / Michael, James – 1994 – 194p – 9 – 92-3-102808-1 – Co-publ with Dartmouth/UNESCO Publishing – fr UNESCO [320]
PRIVACY JOURNAL – v1- 1974- 1; v5- 5,6,9 – us UMI [321]
Privat de Fontanilles *see* MALTHE OU LISLE-ADAM: DERNIER GRAND-MAITRE DE RHODES ET PREMIER GRAND-MAITRE DE MALTHE: POEME
PRIVATE ACTS / Great Britain. Laws, Statutes, etc – 1708-97 – 1 – 345.00 – us L of C Photodup [324]
PRIVATE AND GENERAL LAWS RELATING TO THE CHICAGO, BURLINGTON AND QUINCY RAILROAD, 1867 / Illinois. Laws, Statutes, etc – Chicago: Garden City Print. and Blank Book Co., 1867. 137p. LL-1679 – 1 – us L of C Photodup [340]
PRIVATE CORRESPONDENCE, COMPETITION OR MONOPOLY IN AUSTRALIA'S POSTAL SERVICES? / Albon, Robert – 1985. 78p – 9 – 1.00f – at Libertarian Micro [320]
PRIVATE EMPLOYMENT AGENCIES; LAWS RELATING TO THEIR REGULATION AS OF SEPTEMBER 1, 1943 / Mcl, Marian Louise – Washington U.S. Dept. of Labor, Division of Labor Standards 1943. 514p. LL-236 – 1 – us L of C Photodup [340]
PRIVATE EYE *see* THE UNDERGROUND AND ALTERNATIVE PRESS IN BRITAIN
A PRIVATE JOURNAL KEPT DURING THE NIGER EXPEDITION : FROM THE COMMENCEMENT IN MAY 1841, UNTIL THE RECALL OF THE EXPEDITION IN JUNE 1842 / Simpson, William – London: J F Shaw, 1843 – us Res Libr [910]
THE PRIVATE JOURNAL OF H.M.S. HECLA / Lyon, G F – BN 299 2. 1824 – 8 – ne IDC [910]
PRIVATE JOURNALS OF COMMODORE M.C. PERRY, 1853-54 / Perry, Matthew C – 1roll. T1097 – 1 – us Nat'l Archives [920]
PRIVATE LAND GRANT CASES / U.S. Circuit Court. California. Northern District – 1852-1910. 28 rolls – 1 – T1207 – us Nat'l Archives [340]
THE PRIVATE LIFE OF HENRY MAITLAND / Roberts, Morley; ed by Roberts, Morley – London: Eveleigh Nash, 1912 – 1 roll – 1 – 1-55879-481-6 – uk Libr Preservation [920]
PRIVATE MARKETING ENTREPRENEUR AND RURAL DEVELOPMENT : CASE STUDIES AND COMMENTARY – 1982 – 119p – it F.A.O. [650]
PRIVATE PILOT – 1976- – 9 – us UMI [073]
THE PRIVATE WAR JOURNAL OF GENERALOBERST FRANZ HALDER, CHIEF OF THE GENERAL STAFF OF THE SUPREME COMMAND OF THE GERMAN ARMY, 14 AUGUST 1939 TO 24 SEPTEMBER 1942 / Halder, Franz – 1 – $200.00 – 0-89093-021-X – us UPA [940]
DIE PRIVATISIERUNG DER BRITISH TELECOM VERSUS POSTREFORM – MEHR WETTBEWERB AUF DEN TELEKOMMUNIKATIONSMAERKTEN / Reinkemeyer, Lars – 1994 – 2mf – DM80.00 – 3-89349-900-8 – gw Hänsel [338]
PRIVILEGES DE L'ORDRE DE CISTEAUX – Paris, 1713 – 12mf – 8 – Dfl42.00 – ne Slangenburg [240]
PRIVILEGES ET ELECTIONS – Quebec, 1871? SEM105P634 – 1mf – 9 – Can$2.25 – cn Bibl Nat [320]
PRIVILEGIA SELECTIORA MILITIAE SANCTI IULIANI.. / Calderon de Robles, Juan – 1662 – 9 – 1.50f – sp Bibl Santa Ana [240]
PRIVILEGIOS A FAVOR DE LA CATEDRAL (ANNO 1239-1351) – Calahorra – 1r – 5,6 – sp Cultura [240]
PRIVILEGIOS CONCEDIDOS A LA CIUDAD DE VALENCIA (ANNO 1230-1301) – Barcelona – 1r – 5,6 – sp Cultura [946]
PRIVILEGIOS CONCEDIDOS A MONTEMOLIN POR LOS MAESTROS DE LA ORDEN DE CABALLERIA DE SANTIAGO / Mota Arevalo, Horacio – Badajoz: (Imprenta de la Diputacion Provincial), 1962. Sep. Rev. Estudios Extremenos – 1 – sp Bibl Santa Ana [350]
PRIVILEGIOS DE CASTELLON (SIECLE 15-16) – Castellon – 1r – 5,6 – sp Cultura [946]
PRIVILEGIOS DE CHINCHILLA (SIECLE 14-15). COPIA (SIECLE 15-16) – Alabacete – 1r – 5,6 – sp Cultura [946]
PRIVILEGIOS REALES (ANNO 1210-1455). OTROS DOCUMENTOS (SIECLE 13-16) – Agreda – 1r – 5,6 – sp Cultura [946]
PRIVILEGIOS REALES DE FERNANDO 3 Y ALFONSO 10 (SIECLE 13) – Cordoba – 1r – 5,6 – sp Cultura [946]
PRIVILEGIOS Y ACUERDOS DEL CONCEJO (SIECLE 16-17) – Albarracin – 1r – 5,6 – sp Cultura [946]
PRIVILEGIRTE HILDESHEIMISCHE ZEITUNG *see* HILDESHEIMER RELATIONS-COURIER
PRIVILEGIRTE SCHLESISCHE ZEITUNG *see* SCHLESISCHE ZEITUNG
PRIVILIGIRTE LISTE DER BOERSENHALLE – (Title change: Liste der Boersen-Halle, Hamburgische Abend-Zeitung, 1825; Boersen-Halle, 1827; Hamburgische Boersen-Halle, 1869; Neue Hamburgische Boersen-Halle, 1903) – Hamburg, Germany. 1848-49 – 2r – 1 – gw Mikrofilm [072]
PRIVREDNI PREGLED – Belgrade, Yugoslavia. 1954-Feb 1992 – 77r – 1 – us L of C Photodup [949]
PRIX OFFERTS PAR LA SOCIETE D'AGRICULTURE DE QUEBEC, 1829-30 / Societe d'Agriculture de Quebec – 1829? SEM16P205 – 1r – 5 – Can$9.00 – cn Bibl Nat [630]
PRIZE AND RELATED RECORDS FOR THE WAR OF 1812 OF THE U.S. DISTRICT COURT FOR THE SOUTHERN DISTRICT OF NEW YORK / U.S. Circuit and District Courts. New York – 1812-16. 9 rolls – 1 – M928 – us Nat'l Archives [324]
PRIZE CASES IN NEW YORK / New York. (State) – 1v. 1863-64 – 7mf – 9 – $10.50 – LLMC 80-044 – us L.L.M.C. [340]
THE PRIZE LAW, PARTICULARLY WITH REFERENCE TO THE DUTIES AND OBLIGATIONS OF BELLIGERENTS AND NEUTRALS / Kachenovskii, D I – London, 1867. 189p. English version, with revisions by the author. BR-9458/1 – 9 – ne IDC [340]
PRIZE LIST / Agricultural and Industrial Provincial Exhibition (1885: Kentville, Nova Scotia) – 1885. 07190. (Pre-1900 Canadiana) – 9 – cn C.I.H.M. [630]
PRIZRENIE I BLAGOTVORITEL'NOST' V ROSSII – Spb. 1913-17. Lacking: (2,3) 1917. BR-9279 2 – 8 – ne IDC [073]
PRM DE PALMA : ORGAO OFFICIAL DO PARTIDO REPUBLICANO MINEIRO DE PALMA – Palma, 7 Oct 1934 – 1,5,6 – bl Biblioteca [072]
PRO ACRE : ORGAM DOS INTERESSES DO POVO – Xapury, Acre. 18 Dez 1910 – 1,5,6 – bl Biblioteca [072]
PRO- AND ANTI-GERMAN PROPAGANDA IN BRITAIN DURING WORLD WAR 2 PAMPHLET COLLECTION – 1939-1944 – 1 reel – 1 – CSUXANN2819-B – us Hoover Inst Photo [941]
PRO- AND ANTI-GERMAN PROPAGANDA IN FRANCE DURING WORLD WAR 2 PAHMPHLET COLLECTION – 1941-1945 – 1 reel – 1 – CSUXANN2597-B – us Hoover Inst Photo [944]
PRO- AND ANTI-GERMAN PROPAGANDA IN NORWAY DURING WORLD WAR 2 PAMPHLET COLLECTION – 1940-1942 – 1 reel – 1 – CSUXANN2823-B – us Hoover Inst Photo [948]
PRO ARMENIA – Paris. nov 1900-sept 1908, dec 1913-juin juil 1914 – 1 – fr A.C.R.P.P. [073]
PRO BAPTISMO ET FIDE PARVULORUM ADUERSUS ANABAPTISTAS. ITEM. EPIPHANIA CRUCIS THEOPHILI / Venatorius, Th – Norembergae, Io. Petreius. 1527. BME-107 1 – 9 – ne IDC [240]
PRO BELGICA – Montreal. v1 n12. 31 mai 1916-v1 n38. 29 nov 1916; v3 n35. 15 nov 1918 – 1r – 1 – Can$30.00 – cn Can Microfilming [072]
PRO CHRISTO ET ECCLESIA / Dougall, Lily – London, New York: Macmillan, 1900 – 1mf – 9 – 0-8370-3631-3 – 1985-1631 – us A.T.L.A. [240]
PRO MUNDI VITA DOSSIERS: AFRICA – (1979-5,6,9) – 1976- – 1 – us UMI [073]
PRO MUNDI VITA DOSSIERS: ASIA AUSTRALASIA – (1979- 5,6,9) – 1976- – 1 – us UMI [073]
PRO MUNDI VITA DOSSIERS: EUROPE/NORTH AMERICA – 1976- – 1 – us UMI [073]
PRO MUSICA – Organ fuer neue Musik. v. 1-2. 1932-1933 – 1 – us Schnase [780]
PRO SANCTISSIMO LIBRO CHRISTIANAE CONCORDIAE DISPVTATIO PRIMA SEX CAPITVM:... / Gesner, S – Wittebergae, 1593 – 1mf – ne IDC [240]
PRO THEOLOGICA MYSTICA CLAVIS / Sandaeus, M – Keulen, 1640 – 8mf – 8 – ne Slangenburg [290]
PRO VALENTINA MEDICORUM SCHOLA ADVERSUS BERNARDUM CAXANES BARCINONENSEM MEDICUM... / Polo, J – Valencia, 1594 – 5mf – 9 – sp Cultura [610]
PROBA FIDEI. OFT, DE PROEVE DES GHELOOFS – Amst., By N. Biestkens de jonghe voor W. J. Buys. 1595. BME-173 1 – 9 – ne IDC [240]
PROBA FIDEI. OFT. DE PROEVE DES GHELOOFS – 1569. BME-172 1 – 9 – ne IDC [240]
PROBABILITY THEORY AND RELATED FIELDS *see* ZEITSCHRIFT FUER WAHRSCHEINLICHKEITSTHEORIE UND VERWANDTE GEBIETE
PROBATE AND PROPERTY (ABA) – v1-9. 1987-95 – 9 – us Hein [340]
THE PROBATE CODE OF GUAM, 1947 : IN 4 DIVISIONS / Guam. (Commonwealth). Laws, Statutes, etc – Washington: GPO, 1947 – 2mf – 9 – $3.00 – LLMC 82-100B Title 12 – us L.L.M.C. [324]
THE PROBATE JURISDICTION AND PRACTICE IN THE COUNTY COURTS, ACCORDING TO THE STATUTES AND DECISIONS IN THE STATE OF ILLINOIS. / Hill, Edward Judson – 2d ed. Chicago: Myers, 1875. 407p. LL-673 – 1 – us L of C Photodup [340]

THE PROBATE JURISDICTION AND PRACTICE IN THE COURTS OF THE STATE OF ILLINOIS. / Hill, Edward Judson – 4th ed. Chicago: Myers, 1880. 407p. LL-513 – 1 – us L of C Photodup [340]

PROBATE LAW / Chatterton, Mason Daniel – Lansing, MI: Smith, 1901. 2v. LL-61 – 1 – us L of C Photodup [340]

THE PROBATE LAW AND PRACTICE AND THE LAWS OF SUCCESSION OF THE STATE OF INDIANA. / Henry, George Adams – Indianapolis: Bowen-Merrill, 1896. 1496p. LL-786 – 1 – us L of C Photodup [340]

PROBATE LAW AND PRACTICE OF THE STATE OF IOWA.. / Holmes, Calvin Pratt – Chicago: Flood, 1900. 474p. LL-728 – 1 – us L of C Photodup [340]

PROBATE PROCEEDINGS AND ADMINISTRATION OF ESTATES / Goodmann, Gustav – New York? 1909. 22p. LL-879 – 1 – us L of C Photodup [340]

PROBATE RECORDS-ULSTER COUNTY / Anjou, Gustave – Dutch, English Wills, letters of administration after intestates, and inventories from 1665, with genealogical and historical notes. New York, 1906. Vols. 1-2. New York Reel 36. (The Cox Library Collection) – 5 – us Americana [920]

PROBATE REPORTS ANNOTATED – (Cont: American Probate Reports) – New York: Baker & Voorhis. v1-14. 1903-09 (all publ) – 120mf – 9 – $180.00 – LLMC 82-408 – us L.L.M.C. [340]

PROBATE REPORTS ANNOTATED *see* AMERICAN PROBATE REPORTS

PROBE – (Incorporates: Music Scene in v1 1990. Ceased v4 1993) – Toronto. v1-4. 1990-93 – 9 – Can$20.00y – cn Micromedia [780]

PROBE – v1-16. 1970-88 (complete) – 2r – 1 – ATLA S0408 – us A.T.L.A. [073]

PROBE – v.27-. 1980- – 1,5,6,9 – us UMI [073]

PROBE MAGAZINE *see* MUSIC SCENE

PROBE. PROBING RESOURCES OF BETTER EDUCATION – v1- 1971- 1; 1977- 5,6,9 – us UMI [370]

PROBIR HITAISHI/ BANGLADESH JOURNAL OF GERIATRICS – v. 1-. 1977- – 1,5,6,9 – us UMI [618]

DAS PROBLEM DER ANALYTISCHEN FORTSETZBARKEIT IN DER THEORIE DER LAPLACE-TRANSFORMATION / Boche, Holger – 1993 – 1mf – 9 – DM48.00 – 3-89349-664-5 – gw Hänsel [510]

DAS PROBLEM DER ERZIEHUNG BEI GOTTFRIED KELLER / Toegel, Friedrich – (Includes bibliographical references) – Leipzig: A Haase, 1917 – 1r – 1 – us U.W. Library [430]

DAS PROBLEM DER FREIHEIT / Mann, Thomas – Stockholm: Bermann-Fischer, 1939 – 1r – 1 – us U.W. Library [840]

DAS PROBLEM DER MEERESFREIHEIT... / Calker, W van – Jena, 1917 – 1mf – 9 – ILM-2192/1 – ne IDC [327]

DAS PROBLEM DER THEODICEE IN DER AELTEREN JUEDISCHEN RELIGIONSPHILOSOPHIE / Goitein, Hirsch – Berlin: Mayer & Mueller, 1890 – 9 – us A.T.L.A. [270]

A PROBLEM IN NEW TESTAMENT CRITICISM : THE STONE LECTURES FOR 1897-1898 / Jacobus, Melancthon Williams – (Includes bibliographical references and index) – New York: Charles Scribner, 1900 – 1mf – 9 – 0-8370-3751-4 – 1985-1751 – us A.T.L.A. [220]

PROBLEM IN NEW TESTAMENT CRITICISM / Jacobus, Melancthon Williams – New York: Charles Scribner, 1900. 1 fiche – 9 – us A.T.L.A. [240]

PROBLEM OF CITY GOVERNMENT / Allen, Thomas – Halifax, 1893. 05824. (Pre-1900 Canadiana) – 9 – cn C.I.H.M. [971]

THE PROBLEM OF DIVINE ANGER IN ARNOBIUS AND LACTANTIUS / Micka, E F – 1943 – 4mf – 9 – ne Slangenburg [240]

THE PROBLEM OF EVIL : A CRITICISM OF THE AUGUSTINIAN POINT OF VIEW / Burton, Marion Le Roy – (Includes index) – Chicago: Open Court; London: Kegan Paul, Trench, Truebner [distributor], 1909 – 1mf – 9 – 0-8370-9766-5 – 1986-3766 – us A.T.L.A. [210]

THE PROBLEM OF EVIL IN PLOTINUS / Fuller, B A G – Cambridge: University Press, 1912 – 1mf – us A.T.L.A. [170]

THE PROBLEM OF FINAL DESTINY / Brown, William Bryant – New York: Thomas Whittaker, 1900. 1 fiche – 9 – us A.T.L.A. [240]

THE PROBLEM OF FRANCO SPAIN; STATEMENT MADE ON APRIL 17 AT THE MEETING OF THE SECURITY COUNCIL / Lange, Oscar Richard – N.Y., 1946. Fiche W989. (Blodgett Collection of Spanish Civil War Pamphlets) – 9 – us H.U. College Libr [946]

THE PROBLEM OF HUMAN DESTINY / Dewey, Orville – 1864 – 9 – us A.T.L.A. [240]

THE PROBLEM OF INDIVIDUALITY : A COURSE OF FOUR LECTURES / Driesch, Hans – London, New York: Macmillan, 1914 – 1mf – us A.T.L.A. [240]

THE PROBLEM OF INFLATION / Libya. UNO. United Nations Mission in Libya – Tripoli. BNE-602 1 – 9 – ne IDC [960]

THE PROBLEM OF KRAKATAO AS SEEN BY A BOTANI.. / Backer, C A – The Hague, Weltevreden, [1929] – 4mf – 9 – ne IDC [580]

THE PROBLEM OF LAY LEADERSHIP / Elliott, Ernest Eugene – New York: Revell, c1914 – 1mf – us A.T.L.A. [240]

THE PROBLEM OF LAY-ANALYSES / Freud, Sigmund – Introd. by Dr. S. Ferenczi. New York: Brentano's, 1927. 316p – 1 – us U.W. Library [150]

THE PROBLEM OF MALAYSIA / Indonesia. Kedutaan Besar. Great Britain – 1964. SE-10,876-1 – 9 – ne IDC [950]

THE PROBLEM OF OLD TESTAMENT CRITICISM / Orr, James – 1906 – 9 – us A.T.L.A. [240]

THE PROBLEM OF POSITIVE THEOLOGY : THE CATHOLIC UNIVERSITY OF AMERICA STUDIES IN SACRED THEOLOGY / Salm, C L – Washington, D.C., 1955 – 3mf – 8 – ne Slangenburg [240]

THE PROBLEM OF PROOF, ESPECIALLY AS EXEMPLIFIED IN DISPUTED DOCUMENT TRIALS. / Osborn, Albert Sherman – New York: Bender, 1922. 526p. LL-937 – 1 – us L of C Photodup [340]

THE PROBLEM OF RELIGIOUS PROGRESS / Dorchester, Daniel – New York: Eaton & Mains; Cincinnati: Jennings & Pye, c1900 – 2mf – us A.T.L.A. [200]

THE PROBLEM OF SIMILARITY IN ANCIENT NEAR EASTERN RELIGIONS / Frankfort, Henri – 1951 – 9 – $10.00 – us I.R.C. [230]

THE PROBLEM OF SPACE IN JEWISH MEDIAEVAL PHILOSOPHY / Efros, Il – Columbia University Oriental Studies. v. 11. New York. 1917. BJ-33-8 1 – 9 – ne IDC [180]

THE PROBLEM OF SUFFERING IN THE OLD TESTAMENT: THE HARTLEY LECTURE / Peake, Arthur Samuel – London: Robert Bryant, 1904. 1 fiche – 9 – us A.T.L.A. [220]

THE PROBLEM OF THE BOOK OF JONAH / Aalders, G – 1948 – 9 – $10.00 – us I.R.C. [220]

THE PROBLEM OF THE CHURCHLESS AND POOR IN OUR LARGE TOWNS : WITH SPECIAL REFERENCE TO THE HOME MISSION WORK OF THE CHURCH OF SCOTLAND / Milne, Robert – Edinburgh: W. Blackwood, 1884 – 1mf – us A.T.L.A. [240]

THE PROBLEM OF THE PENTATEUCH...RESULTS OF THE HIGHER CRITICISM / McKim, Randolph Harrison – New York: Longmans, Green, 1906.1 fiche – 9 – us A.T.L.A. [240]

THE PROBLEM OF THEISM AND OTHER ESSAYS / Pigou, Arthur Cecil – London: Macmillan, 1908.1 fiche – 9 – us A.T.L.A. [240]

THE PROBLEM OF THEOLOGY IN MODERN LIFE AND THOUGHT / Miller, Andrew – (Includes bibliographical references and index) – London:Hodder and Stoughton, 1909 – 1mf – 9 – 0-8370-4429-4 – 1985-2429 – us A.T.L.A. [240]

PROBLEM TERRITORIES OF SOUTHERN AFRICA : BASUTOLAND, BECHUANALAND PROTECTORATE, SWAZILAND / Dundas, Charles & Ashton, Hugh – [Cape Town]: South African Institute of International Affairs, [1952] – us Res Libr [327]

DAS PROBLEM "VOLKSTUM UND DICHTUNG" BEI HERDER / Schmitz, Reta – (Includes bibliographical references) – Berlin: Junker und Duennhaupt, 1937 – 1r – 1 – us U.W. Library [430]

PROBLEM Y EKONOMIK – Moscow. 1929. Complete; 1930, nos. 3, 7-12; 1931-4 complete; 1941, no. 1 – 1 – 35.00r – us Hoover Inst Photo [947]

EL PROBLEMA CAMPESINO IN ANDALUCIA / Gallego, Ignacio – n.p. 193? Fiche W 903. (Blodgett Collection of Spanish Civil War Pamphlets) – 9 – us H.U. College Libr [946]

EL PROBLEMA DE LA DEFENSA DE LOS DERECHOS E INTERESES LEGITIMOS DE LAS MINORIAS DE ACCIONISTAS EN LAS SOCIEDADES MERCANTILES / Cuellar Grajera, Antonio – Badajoz: Imp. Dip. Provincial, 1964. Sep. REE – sp Bibl Santa Ana [320]

EL PROBLEMA DE LA DOBLE NACIONALIDAD / Fonseca Hermes, J S da – Santiago, 1932 – 1mf – 1 – ILM-3169/1 – ne IDC [327]

EL PROBLEMA DE LA VIVIENDA : CONFERENCIAS Y DEBATES PUBLICOS ORGANIZADOS POR LA CAMARA ARGENTINA DE LA CONSTRUCCION / Camara Argentina de la Construccion – [Buenos Aires], 1950 – 1 – CSUXADQ0942-B – us Hoover Inst Photo [972]

EL PROBLEMA DE LAS LIMITACIONES DE LA SOBERANIA... / Goicoechea, A – Madrid, 1923 – 3mf – 1 – ILM-2137/1 – ne IDC [327]

EL PROBLEMA DE LAS NACIONALIDADES EN ESPANA A LA LUZ DE LA GUERRA POPULAR POR LA INDEPENDENCIA DE LA REPUBLICA ESPANOLA / Uribe, Vicente – n.p., n.d. Fiche W1511. (Blodgett Collection of Spanish Civil War Pamphlets) – 9 – us H.U. College Libr [946]

IL PROBLEMA DELLA PACE PERPETUA / Ballerini, G – Torino, 1885 – 2mf – 9 – ILM-822/1 – ne IDC [340]

EL PROBLEMA RELIGIOSO EN AMERICA / Bayle, Constantino – Madrid: Razon y Fe, 1922 – 1 – sp Bibl Santa Ana [240]

EL PROBLEMA SOCIAL DEL CAMPO EN EXTREMADURA / Polo Benito, Jose – Salamanca: Tip.Calatrava, 1919 – 1 – sp Bibl Santa Ana [360]

EL PROBLEMA UNIVERSITARIO ARGENTINO (BASES PARA SU SOLUCION) – Santa Fe: Editorial Colmegna, 1945 – 1 – CSUXAJL9754-B – us Hoover Inst Photo [370]

PROBLEMAS – Rio de Janeiro, BL. 1947-1956 – 5r – $250.00 – R04180 – us Library Micro [320]

PROBLEMAS DE ARITMETICA / Luna y Gomez, Sergio – Badajoz: Tip. Lib. y Enc. de Antonio Argueros, 1931 – 1 – sp Bibl Santa Ana [510]

PROBLEMAS DE GOVERNO / Calogeras, Pandia – Sao Paulo, 1936 – 5mf – 8 – ne Slangenburg [350]

LOS PROBLEMAS DE LA FABRICACION DEL QUESO / Corrales Vicente, Manuel – Caceres: Tip. Garcia Floriano, 1943 – sp Bibl Santa Ana [946]

PROBLEMAS DE LA REVOLUCION Y LA DEMOCRACIA / Caril, Bonifacio del. – [Buenos Aires]: Emece Editores, [1956] – 1 – CSUXAGP8760-B – us Hoover Inst Photo [320]

PROBLEMAS DE ORIENTACI ON Y TACTICA DEL MOVIMIENTO SINDICAL / Iscaro, Rubens – Buenos Aires: Editorial Anteo, 1965 – 9 – us Hoover Inst Photo [972]

LOS PROBLEMAS DE SU RECONQUISTA Y DE SU NOMBRE / Floriano Cumbreno, Antonio C – Oviedo: Imp. La Gruz, 1956 – 1 – sp Bibl Santa Ana [946]

PROBLEMAS DE TOXICOLOGIA...MEDICA / Perez Jimenez, Nicolas – 1888 – 9 – 1.50f – sp Bibl Santa Ana [615]

LOS PROBLEMAS DEL CAMPO ESPANOL Y LA SUBLEVACION MILITAR – n.p., 193? Fiche W1123. (Blodgett Collection of Spanish Civil War Pamphlets) – 9 – us H.U. College Libr [946]

PROBLEMAS ECONOMICOS DE CHILE / Valdes Vergara, Francisco – Valparaiso: Sociedad Imprenta y Litografia universo, 1913. 368p. With: El clero en la independencia by Roberto Taramillo. Antioquia: revista Universidad, 1946 – 1 – us U.W. Library [339]

PROBLEMAS ESCOLARES : POR LA LIBERTAD DE ENSENANZA / Tobar Donoso, Julio – Quito, 1930; Madrid: Razon y Fe, 1931 – 1 – sp Bibl Santa Ana [370]

PROBLEMAS O PREGUNTAS PROBLEMATICAS ANSI DE AMOR...Y ACERCA DEL VINO / Jarava, J – Alcala de Henares, 1546 – 6mf – 9 – sp Cultura [440]

DIE PROBLEMATIK DES ENGLISCHEN SCHAUERROMANS : EIN KRITISCHES MODELL ZUR BEHANDLUNG DISKRIMINIERTER LITERATUR / Bierwirth, Gerhard – Frankfurt a.M., 1970 – 3mf – 9 – DM76.00 – 3-89349-645-9 – gw Hänsel [420]

LE PROBLEME COLONIAL DU POINT DE VUE INTERNATIONAL / Louwers, O – Brussels. 1936 – 1 – us Res Libr [940]

LE PROBLEME DE LA FEMME / Braun, Lily – Paris: Cornely, 1908. viii,419p. (Les Femmes Collection) – 5mf – 9 – $12.00 – fr Bibl Nationale [305]

LE PROBLEME DE LA JUSTIFICATION DANS SAINT PAUL : ETUDE DE THEOLOGIE BIBLIQUE / Tobac, Edouard – (Includes index) – Lovanii: Josephus van Linthout, 1908 – 1mf – 9 – 0-8370-7109-7 – 1986-1109 – us A.T.L.A. [220]

LE PROBLEME DE LA POPULATION EN FRANCE: PRECEDE D'UNE HISTOIRE GENERALE DE LA POPULATION: ETUDE DE SOCIOLOGIE DE LA POPULATION / Rabinowicz, Leon – Paris: Marcel Riviere, 1929. 429p. 1 reel. 1296 – 1 – us U.W. Library [310]

LE PROBLEME DE LA SCISSION ET SON DEPASSEMENT DANS L'OEUVRE DU JEUNE HEGEL (1785-1802) / Leydet, Dominique – 2mf – 9 – 10060 – fr Atelier National [190]

PROBLEME DE L'ANCIENNE THEOLOGIE: À PROPOS DE LA DOGMATIQUE DE M. GRETILLAT *see* COLLECTED WORKS

LE PROBLEME DE L'AUTORITE / Monod, Leopold – Paris: Librairie Fischbacher, 1891. 1 fiche – 9 – us A.T.L.A. [240]

LE PROBLEME DE L'EAU EN SYRIE ET AU LIBAN. LECON DONNEE A LA 3. SEMAINE SOCIALE DE BEYROUTH EN 1942 / Mazloum, S – L'Agriculture, richesse nationale". 1942. BNE-9711 1 – 9 – ne IDC [333]

PROBLEME DER BEGRIFFSBILDUNG IN DER HANDLUNGSKONTROLL-THEORIE VON J. KUHL : VERSUCH EINER NEUINTERPRETATION UND OPERATIONALISIERUNG DES KONSTRUKTS "HANDLUNGS- UND LAGERORIENTIERUNG" / Schroeder, Kerstin – 1993 – 5mf – 9 – DM125.00 – 3-89349-668-8 – gw Hänsel [150]

PROBLEME DER INTERNATIONALEN ORGANISATION / Erich, R – Breslau, 1914 – 2mf – 1 – ILM-3138/1 – ne IDC [327]

PROBLEME DER UMSETZUNG DER RICHTLINIEN DER EUROPAEISCHEN GEMEINSCHAFT IN DAS NATIONALE RECHT PORTUGALS AM BEISPIEL DER WASSERRICHTLINIEN / Xavier, Humberto Flavio – 1994 – 3mf – DM98.00 – 3-8267-2067-9 – gw Hänsel [340]

PROBLEME DES APOSTOLISCHEN ZEITALTERS / Dobschuetz, Ernst von – Leipzig: J C Heinrichs, 1904 – 1mf – 9 – 0-8370-2933-3 – 1985-0933 – us A.T.L.A. [240]

PROBLEME DES FRIEDENS UND DES SOZIALISMUS – 1958-1989 – 1,048mf – 1 – DM5,973.60 – gw Mikro Press [320]

LE PROBLEME DES MINORITES ETHNIQUES ET SA SOLUTION PAR L'AUTONOMIE ET LA PERSONNIFICATION / Friedman, S – Toulouse, 1927 – 3mf – 1 – ILM-1566/1 – ne IDC [327]

LE PROBLEME DU LOGEMENT OUVRIER EN FRANCE / Morenne, Daniel – Paris. 1942. (La Condition Ouvriere. Part Two.) – 9 – 5.00 – fr Bibl Nationale [360]

LE PROBLEME FINANCIER ET LE PROBLEME ECONOMIQUE AU CONGO BELGE EN 1932 / Louwers, O – Brussels. 1933 – 1 – us Res Libr [960]

LE PROBLEME POLITIQUE SYRIEN / Aboussouan, B – Paris, 1925 – 4mf – 9 – ILM-1925/1 – ne IDC [340]

PROBLEMES AFRICAINS – (Missing: nos1-266) – Bruxelles. nos1-539. 1966-70 – 168mf – 9 – A-727/2 – ne IDC [960]

PROBLEMES ECONOMIQUES – 1992-1995 – 51 times per yr – 9 – F8,160.00 – sz Infoprint [330]

PROBLEMES ET CONCLUSIONS DE L'HISTOIRE DES RELIGIONS / Broglie, L'Abbe de – Paris: Putois-Crette, 1886 – 2mf – us A.T.L.A. [240]

LES PROBLEMES FONDAMENTAUX DU DROIT / Coste-Floret, Alfred – Paris: Dalloz, 1946. 208p. LL-4094 – 1 – us L of C Photodup [340]
LES PROBLEMES FONDAMENTAUX DU DROIT INTERNATIONAL PUBLIC / Akzin, B – Paris, 1929 – 2mf – 9 – ILM-1725/1 – ne IDC [340]
PROBLEMES POLITIQUES ET SOCIAUX – 1992-1995 – 24 times per yr – 9 – F3,848.00 – sz Infoprint [320]
PROBLEMS AND PERSONS / Ward, Wilfrid Philip – London, New York: Longmans, Green, 1903 – 1mf – us A.T.L.A. [240]
PROBLEMS AND QUIZ. BILLS AND NOTES / Fisher, S B – St. Paul: West, 1895. 44p. LL-273 – 1 – us L of C Photodup [340]
PROBLEMS AND QUIZ ON COMMON-LAW PLEADING / Fisher, S B – St. Paul: West, 1895. 52p. LL-1225 – 1 – us L of C Photodup [340]
PROBLEMS AND QUIZ ON CRIMINAL PROCEDURE / Hopkins, Earl Palmer – St. Paul: West, 1895. 64p. LL-519 – 1 – us L of C Photodup [340]
PROBLEMS AND SOLUTIONS IN EQUITY. / Harvey, Zola Emile – Brooklyn, NY: Academy Publications 1937. 120p. LL-431 – 1 – us L of C Photodup [340]
PROBLEMS AND SOLUTIONS IN PERSONAL PROPERTY. / Harvey, Zola Emile – Brooklyn, NY: Academy Publications 1936. 52p. LL-279 – 1 – us L of C Photodup [340]
PROBLEMS AND SOLUTIONS IN TORTS. / Harvey, Zola Emile – Brooklyn, NY: Academy Publications 1936. 73p. LL-244 – 1 – us L of C Photodup [340]
THE PROBLEMS BEFORE LIBERIA : A LECTURE DELIVERED IN THE SENATE CHAMBER AT MONROVIA, JANUARY 18 1909 / Blyden, Edward Wilmot – London: C M Phillips, 1909 – us Res Libr [960]
PROBLEMS IN AMERICAN SOCIETY : SOME SOCIAL STUDIES / Crooker, Joseph Henry – Boston: G.H. Ellis – 1mf – us A.T.L.A. [303]
PROBLEMS IN GENERAL SURGERY – v1-. 1984- – 1,5,6,9 – us UMI [617]
PROBLEMS IN SPACE BIOLOGY / Sisakyan, N M – 1,5,9 – us Gordon [580]
PROBLEMS IN THE NEW TESTAMENT: CRITICAL ESSAYS / Wood, William Spicer – London: Rivingtons, 1890. 1 fiche – 9 – us A.T.L.A. [240]
PROBLEMS OF CHRISTIANITY AND SCEPTICISM: LESSONS FROM TWENTY YEARS EXPERIENCE / Harrison, Alexander James – London: Longmans, Green, 1891. 1 fiche – 9 – us A.T.L.A. [240]
PROBLEMS OF COMMUNISM – v1- 1952- 1; v20- 5,6; v24- 9 – us UMI [335]
PROBLEMS OF CONDUCT : AN INTRODUCTORY SURVEY OF ETHICS / Drake, Durant – Boston, etc: Houghton Mifflin Co, 1914? – 5mf – 9 – $7.50 – LLMC 96-048 – us L.L.M.C. [170]
PROBLEMS OF CONTROL AND INFORMATION THEORY – v.8-. 1979- – 5,6,9 – us UMI [020]
PROBLEMS OF ECONOMIC GROWTH AND PLANNING: THE SUDAN EXAMPLE; SOME ASPECTS AND IMPLICATIONS OF THE CURRENT TEN YEAR PLAN / Guesten, R – Berlin. 1966 – 9 – ne IDC [338]
PROBLEMS OF FISH CULTURE ECONOMICS WITH SPECIAL REFERENCE TO CARP CULTURE IN EASTERN EUROPE – 1981 – 107p – it F.A.O. [639]
PROBLEMS OF HEMATOLOGY AND BLOOD TRANSFUSION – v. 2-4. 1957-59 – 1,5,6 – us Princeton Micro [610]
PROBLEMS OF ICHTHYOLOGY – v8-9. 1968-69 – 1 – us UMI [073]
PROBLEMS OF IMMANENCE : STUDIES CRITICAL AND CONSTRUCTIVE / Warschauer, Joseph – (Includes bibliographical references) – London: James Clarke, 1909 – 1mf – 9 – 0-8370-5699-3 – 1985-3699 – us A.T.L.A. [230]
PROBLEMS OF INFORMATION TRANSMISSION – v1-30. 1965-94 – 1,5 – $65.00v – us UMI [000]
PROBLEMS OF LIFE : SELECTIONS FROM THE WRITINGS OF LYMAN ABBOTT / Abbott, Lyman – New York: Dood, Mead, 1900 – 1mf – us A.T.L.A. [240]
PROBLEMS OF SOCIOLOGY IN EDUCATION / Girod, Roger – 1990 – 159p – 9 – 92-3-102582-1 – Co-published with Jessica Kingsley Publishers, London – fr UNESCO [370]
PROBLEMS OF THE AGE : WITH, STUDIES IN ST. AUGUSTINE IN KINDRED TOPICS / Hewit, Augustine Francis – (Includes bibliographical references and glossary) – New York: Catholic Publ House, 1868 – 1mf – 9 – 0-8370-6742-1 – 1986-0742 – us A.T.L.A. [230]
PROBLEMS OF THE AMERICAN NEGRO : POPULARLY KNOWN AS THE CARNEGIE-MYRDAL STUDY OF THE NEGRO IN AMERICA – New York, 1940 – 13r – 1 – us Ross [305]
PROBLEMS OF THE FUTURE STATE: A SERIES OF SERMONS DELIVERED IN EMMANUEL REFORMED EPISCOPAL CHURCH OTTAWA, ONTARIO / Cooper, William H – s.l.: s.n., 1882 (Ottawa: C. Mitchell). 00053. (Pre-1900 Canadiana) – 9 – cn C.I.H.M. [971]
PROBLEMS OF THE HEBREW VERBAL SYSTEM / Driver, G R – 1937 – 9 – $10.00 – us I.R.C. [470]
PROBLEMS OF THE INDONESIAN REVOLUTION / Aidit, Dipa Nusantara – SE-10,891 1. 1963 – 9 – ne IDC [335]
PROBLEMY ARKHIVOVEDENIIA I ISTOCHNIKOVEDENIIA – Materialy nauchnoi konferentsii arkhivistov Leningrada, 4-6 fevralia 1964 g. Leningrad, 1964. 283p. BR-10,761/1 – 9 – ne IDC [025]
PROBLEMY ARKHIVOVEDENIIA I ISTORII ARKHIVNYKH UCHREZHDENII – Materialy iubileinoi nachnoi konferentsii arkhivistov Leningrada 13-14 iiunia 1968 g.Leningrad, 1970. 256p. BR-10,763/1 – 9 – ne IDC [025]
PROBLEMY ISTOCHNIKOVEDENIIA. SBORNIK – Moscow, 1933-63. v1-11. -irr. BR-10,753/1 – 9 – ne IDC [073]
PROBLEMY KITAIA – Moscow. 1929-1933, nos. 1-14 – 1 – 35.00r – us Hoover Inst Photo [073]
PROBLEMY REALIZMA V RUSSKOI LITERATURE XVIII VEKA / Akademiia Nauk. SSSR Institut mirovoi literatury im. A M – Sbornik statei. Gor'kogo izd. M., L. 1940. B-1547 2 – 8 – ne IDC [460]
PROBLEMY SOTSIALISTICHESKOGO PRAVA – Moscow, 1937-39. -irr. 1938 available. BR-9375 1 – 9 – ne IDC [335]
PROBLEMY VOSTOKOVEDENIA NARODY AZII I AFRIKI – Moscow, 1959-70.Lacking: 1961 (1-3). BR-10,440/1 – 9 – ne IDC [073]
Probst, Ferdinand *see*
– DIE ABENDLAENDISCHE MESSE
– DIE AELTESTEN ROEMISCHEN SACRAMENTARIEN UND ORDINES
– KIRCHLICHE DISCIPLIN
– LEHRE UND GEBET IN DEN DREI ERSTEN CHRISTLICHEN JAHRHUNDERTEN
– LITURGIE DER DREI ERSTEN CHRISTLICHEN JAHRHUNDERTE
– LITURGIE DES VIERTEN JAHRHUNDERTS UND DEREN REFORM
– SAKRAMENTE UND SAKRAMENTALIEN IN DEN DREI ERSTEN CHRISTLICHEN JAHRHUNDERTEN
PROBUZHDENIE – Literaturnyi khudozhestvennyi i nauchnyi zhurnal. Spb. 1906-17. Lacking: v. 1, 1915. B-1228 2 – 8 – ne IDC [500]
Proby, William Henry Baptist *see* ANNALS OF THE "LOW-CHURCH" PARTY IN ENGLAND
LES PROCEDES DE REDACTION DES TROIS PREMIERS EVANGELISTES / Nicolardot, Firmin – (Includes index) – Paris: Librairie Fischbacher, 1908 – 1mf – 9 – 0-8370-4588-6 – 1985-2588 – us A.T.L.A. [220]
PROCEDIMIENTOS DE LA INQUISICION / Melgares, Marin, Julio – Madrid: Libreria de L. P. Villaverde, 1886 – 1 – us U.W. Library [946]
PROCEDIMIENTOS PRACTICOS MODERNOS PARA LAFABRICACION DE VINOS EN EXTREMADURA / Garcia Romero, Diego – Almendralejo: Imp. de Juan Bote, 1915 – 1 – sp Bibl Santa Ana [946]
PROCEDURAL ISSUANCES...: ORDERS AND CIRCULARS, 1854-1960 / U.S. Bureau of Indian Affairs – 17 rolls. M1121 – 1 – us Nat'l Archives [975]
PROCEDURAL MANUAL OF THE CODEX ALIMENTARIUS COMMISSION / Codex Alimentarius Commission – 6th ed 1986 – 182p – it F.A.O. [640]
PROCEDURE ACT OF 1887, AND SECTION FIVE OF ACT OF MARCH 21ST, 1806. / Higgins, George Henry – Erie, Pa.: Dispatch Printing and Engraving Co., 1896. 82p. LL-726 – 1 – us L of C Photodup [340]
PROCEDURE AND FORMS COMMON LAW PLEADING, COVERING ALL COMMON LAW ACTIONS / O'Donnell, Roger – Washington, D.C.: National Law Book Co., 1934. 821p. LL-727 – 1 – us L of C Photodup [340]
PROCEDURE AND METHODS OF THE COURTS OF FINAL RESORT OF THE REPUBLIC OF MEXICO, THE UNITED STATES OF AMERICA, AND OF THE SEVERAL STAGES AND TERRITORIES OF THE UNION / Kinne, La Vega George – Chicago, Rogers & Wells, 1896. 55 p. LL-733 – 1 – us L of C Photodup [340]
A PROCEDURE FOR DETERMINING AND MEETING THE FACILITY NEEDS OF BROOKS BAPTIST CHURCH / Marston, Bruce Steven – 1982 – 1 – 5.12 – us Baptist [240]
PROCEDURE IN INTERSTATE COMMERCE CASES, WITH ILLUSTRATIVE PRECEDENTS AND FORMS / Daish, John Broughton – Washington, Lowdermil, 1909. 494 p. LL-1052 – 1 – us L of C Photodup [340]
PROCEDURE, ITS THEORY AND PRACTICE / Hughes, William Taylor – Chicago: Callaghan, 1905. 2v. LL-1425 – 1 – us L of C Photodup [340]
LA PROCEDURE PARLEMENTAIRE EN EUROPE : ETUDE COMPAREE / Campion, Lord & Lidderdale, D W S – F50.00 – fr Ethnologie [320]
PROCEDURES AND CONVERSATION STANDARDS FOR MUSEUM COLLECTIONS IN TRANSIT AND ON EXHIBITION – 1981 – 56p – 9 – 92-3-101913-9 – fr UNESCO [060]
PROCEEDING HAD IN THE LEGISLATURE OF UPPER CANADA DURING THE YEARS 1831-2... / Haut-Canada. Parliament. House of Assembly – Montreal: printed by Desbarats & Derbishire, 1845. SEM105P151 – 1mf – 9 – Can$2.25 – cn Bibl Nat [370]
PROCEEDING. JUDGEMENT / International Military Tribunal for the Far East – Tokyo. On film: v1-49, v858; 1946-49. LL-042 – 1 – us L of C Photodup [340]
PROCEEDING OF THE AMERICAN CONGRESS ON SURVEYING AND MAPPING ANNUAL MEETING *see* TECHNICAL PAPERS
PROCEEDING OF THE HOUSE OF ASSEMBLY UPON THE PETITION OF THE ELECTORS OF THE COUNTRY OF BEDFORD / Canada. Bas-Canada. Parlement. Chambre d'Assemblee – s.l., s.n, 1821. SEM105P97 – 1mf – 9 – Can$2.25 – cn Bibl Nat [324]
PROCEEDINGS – 1948- 1; 1972- 5,6; 1975- 9 – us UMI [650]
PROCEEDINGS : 3RD SPEC SESS AND 4TH SESS, MAR-NOV 1963 / Council of Micronesia – Saipan, n.d. – 3mf – 9 – $4.50 – LLMC 82-100F, Title 29 – us L.L.M.C. [980]
PROCEEDINGS / Academy of Political Science – (1970- . 5,6. 1975- . 9) – 1-1910- – 1 – us UMI [320]
PROCEEDINGS / Academy of Sciences of the USSR Section: Geochemistry – (v111-123. Nov 1956-1958) – v106-109. Jan 1956-Aug 1956 – 1 – us UMI [540]
PROCEEDINGS / Academy of Sciences of the U.S.S.R. Section: Geological Sciences – v112-113. Jan 1957-Dec 1958 – 1 – us UMI [550]
PROCEEDINGS / AFL-CIO (American Federation of Labor-Congress of Industrial Organizations) – 1955- 1; 1971- 5,6; 1975- 4 x 6 in9 – us UMI [330]
PROCEEDINGS / Alabama. State Bar Association – 1878-1949. 6 reels – 1 – $38.00r – us Trans-Media [340]
PROCEEDINGS / American Antiquarian Society – (1969- 5,6; 1977- 9) – v1-1880- – 1 – us UMI [975]
PROCEEDINGS / American Association for Cancer Research – v. 1-13. 1953-72 – 1,5,6 – us Princeton Micro [610]
PROCEEDINGS / American Association for the Advancement of Science – 1st (Sept 1848)-62nd (Dec 1910).(s.l., s.n.), 1849-1912. (Philadelphia: John C. Clark).-irr – 1 – us U.W. Library [500]
PROCEEDINGS / American Association of Equine Practitioners – Lexington, dec 1956- – 1 – D5967 – us UMI [636]
PROCEEDINGS / American Congress on Surveying and Mapping – (Cont by: Papers from the annual meeting- American Congress on Surveying and Mapping annual meeting. Cont by: Technical papers of the Annual Meeting of the American Congress on Surveying and Mapping) – Falls Church. v32-39. 1972-79* – 1 – D12486.01 – us UMI [520]
PROCEEDINGS / American Congress on Surveying and Mapping – v32-39 1972-79. Continued by: Technical Papers – 1 – us UMI [520]
PROCEEDINGS / American Historical Association – (1977- . 5,6,9) – 1976- – 1 – us UMI [970]
PROCEEDINGS / American Mathematical Society – (1982- 1,5,6,9) – v1- 1950- – 1 – us UMI [510]
PROCEEDINGS / American Philosophical Society – (1970- 5,6; 1976- 9) – v1-1838- – 1 – us UMI [100]
PROCEEDINGS / American Physical Education Association – 1-10. 1885-1895 – 24mf – 9 – $72.00 – us Microform Publ [790]
PROCEEDINGS / American Political Science Association – (1979-. 5,6,9) – 1904- – 1 – us UMI [320]
PROCEEDINGS / American Society For Engineering Education – v56-73 1948-66 – 1 – us UMI [620]
PROCEEDINGS / American Society for Testing and Materials – v1-81 1899-1981 1; 1965-81 5,6; 1977-81 9 – us UMI [999]
PROCEEDINGS / American Society for Testing and Materials – v1-76 1901-76 – 1,5,6 – us Princeton Micro [620]
PROCEEDINGS / American Society of Pension Actuaries – (1977- 5,6,9) – 1974- – 1 – us UMI [360]
PROCEEDINGS / American Society of Safety Engineers – 1968-73 – 1 – us UMI [620]
PROCEEDINGS / American Society of Safety Engineers – (1979- 5,6,9) – 1974- – 1 – us UMI [620]
PROCEEDINGS / American Statistical Association – (1974- . 5,6. 1976- . 9) – 1958- – 1 – us UMI [310]
PROCEEDINGS / American Statistical Association – v. 1-. 1978- – 1,5,6,9 – us UMI [310]
PROCEEDINGS / American Statistical Association – (v3- , 1977- . 5,6,9) – v. 1-. 1975 – 1 – us UMI [310]
PROCEEDINGS / Annual Convention of the Christian Association for Psychological Studies – v.4-9. 1957-62. Continued by: Christian Association for Psychological Studies. Proceedings of the Annual Convention – 1 – us UMI [150]
PROCEEDINGS / Arizona. State Bar Association – 1906-12 – 1r – 1 – $38.00r – us Trans-Media [340]
PROCEEDINGS / Arkansas. State Bar Association – 1838-1947. 3 reels – 1 – $38.00r – us Trans-Media [340]
PROCEEDINGS / Association of American Railroads. Telegraph and Telephone Section – 1921-35 – 1,5,6 – us Princeton Micro [380]
PROCEEDINGS / Association of Military Surgeons of the United States. Annual Meeting – v.4-9. 1894-1901. Continued by: Journal of The Assoc. of Military Surgeons of the United States – 1 – us UMI [610]
PROCEEDINGS / Baptist Brazilian Convention – 1907-70 – 1 – 307.79 – us Baptist [240]
PROCEEDINGS / Baptist Congress – 1882-1912 (lacking 1891, not pub.) – 1 – 227.43 – us Baptist [240]
PROCEEDINGS / Baptist State Conventions. (Southern Baptist). Tennessee – 1834, 1838-40; General Association of the Baptists of East Tenn., 1845-1885; East Tenn. Assn. of United Baptists, 1843-1872; Proceedings of General State Conv. of Tenn., North Alabama and South Kentucky, 1876; Minutes of Baptist State Convention for West Tenn., 1837-1874 – 1 – 93.87 – us Baptist [240]
PROCEEDINGS / Baptist Triennial Convention – 1814-46 – 1 – 60.83 – us Baptist [240]
PROCEEDINGS / Basutoland. National Council. Maseru – 1910-54 (10r); 1955 (1r) – 1 – us Res Libr [324]
PROCEEDINGS / Bristol Naturalist's Society – (v34- . 1975- . 5,6,9) – 1863- – 1 – us UMI [580]
PROCEEDINGS / Burma. Legislative Council – v. 1-32. Rangoon. 1923-36; Index. v. 1-32. 1923-36. BI-39 2 – 8 – ne IDC [324]
PROCEEDINGS / California. State Bar Association – 1890-1950. 5 reels – 1 – $38.00r – us Trans-Media [340]
PROCEEDINGS / Calvinistic Conference on Psychology and Psychiatry – v.1-3. 1954-56. Continued by: Annual Convention of the Christian Assoc. for Psychological Studies. Proceedings – 1 – us UMI [240]

PROCEEDINGS / Cambridge Philosophical Society – v1-64 1843-1968 – 1 – us Princeton Micro [100]
PROCEEDINGS / Casualty Actuarial Society – (v.67-. 1980- 5,6,9) – v.7-. 1921- – 1 – us UMI [310]
PROCEEDINGS / Chemical Society – 1885-1914, 1957-1964. For the years 1915-1956 see Chemical Society. JOURNAL – 1 – us UMI [540]
PROCEEDINGS / Chemical Society. Analytical Division – (See also: Society for Analytical Chemistry. Proceedings) – v12-. 1975- – 1,5,6,9 – us UMI [999]
PROCEEDINGS / Chemical Society. London – 1885-1914; 1957-1964 – 1,5,6 – us Princeton Micro [540]
PROCEEDINGS / China. National Financial Conference – Shanghai. July 1928. 1 reel – 1 – 20.00 – us Chinese Res [950]
PROCEEDINGS / China. Second National Financial Conference – Nanking. 1934. 1 reel – 1 – 20.00 – us Chinese Res [950]
PROCEEDINGS / China. Third National Financial Conference – ChungKing. 1941. 1 reel – 1 – 12.00 – us Chinese Res [950]
PROCEEDINGS / Classical Association – (v74-. 1977- . 5,6,9) – v. 1-. 1904- – 1 – us UMI [930]
PROCEEDINGS / Connecticut. State Bar Association – 1910-26 – 1r – 1 – $38.00r – us Trans-Media [340]
PROCEEDINGS / Deutscher Arbeitsnachweis-Kongress – v5, 1908. (Serial Publications of German trade unions in the Memorial Library, University of Wisconsin-Madison.) – 1 – us U.W. Library [073]
PROCEEDINGS : FIRST IOC WORLD CONGRESS ON SPORT SCIENCES, OCT 28-NOV 3 1989 / IOC World Congress on Sport Sciences – Colorado Springs, 1989 – 5mf – 9 – $20.00 – us Microform Publ [790]
PROCEEDINGS / Florida. State Bar Association – 1907-27 – 1r – 1 – $38.00r – us Trans-Media [340]
PROCEEDINGS / Governors' Conference – 1908-76. 84-475 – 9 – $140.00 – us L.L.M.C. [977]
PROCEEDINGS / Hearn Academy. Board of Trustees. (Cave Spring, Georgia) – 1858-1920. 398p – 1 – us Baptist [240]
PROCEEDINGS / Human Factors Society. Annual Meeting – v16- 1972- – 1,5,6,9 – us UMI [300]
PROCEEDINGS / Idaho. State Bar Association – 1921-69 – 2r – 1 – $38.00r – us Trans-Media [340]
PROCEEDINGS / Indiana. State Bar Association – 1897-1924 – 3r – 1 – $38.00r – us Trans-Media [340]
PROCEEDINGS / Institute of Electrical Engineers – v1- 1872- – 1. – apply; v122-1975- 5,6 – us UMI [621]
PROCEEDINGS / Institution of Mechanical Engineers – v1- 1847- – 1,5,6,9 – us UMI [621]
PROCEEDINGS / International Association of Factory Inspectors – 1st-28th (all publ). 1887-1914 – 44mf – 9 – $160.00 – us UPA [360]
PROCEEDINGS / International Association of Officials of Bureaus of Labor. Factory Inspection and Industrial Commissions – 1st-30th. (all publ). 1883-1914 – 55mf – 9 – $185.00 – us UPA [360]
PROCEEDINGS / International Conference on the Peaceful uses of Atomic Energy – v. 1-16. 1955 – 1,5,6 – us Princeton Micro [500]
PROCEEDINGS / International Conference on the Peaceful Uses of Atomic Energy. Geneva. 1955. (First). "Atoms for Peace" – 16v 1955 – 3 – us Readex [621]
PROCEEDINGS / Japan. Imperial Academy – (v.26-53. 1950-77. 22311.00; PHC; 1,5,6) – v.2-21. 1926-46 – 1,5,6 – us Princeton Micro [500]
PROCEEDINGS / Kansas. State Bar Association – 1885-1931. 3 reels – 1 – $38.00r – us Trans-Media [340]
PROCEEDINGS / Kentucky. State Bar Association – 1882-1942. 4 reels – 1 – $38.00r – us Trans-Media [340]
PROCEEDINGS / London Mathematical Society – Series 2, v. 1-54. 1904-52 – 1,5,6 – us Princeton Micro [510]
PROCEEDINGS / London Mathematical Society – v1-54 1904-52 – 1,5,6 – us Princeton Micro [510]
PROCEEDINGS / London Mathematical Society – (v48- 1984- 5,6,9) – v1- 1865- – 1 – us UMI [510]
PROCEEDINGS / Louisiana. State Bar Association – 1898-1952 – 3r – 1 – $38.00r – us Trans-Media [340]
PROCEEDINGS / Maine. State Bar Association – 1892-1968 – 3r – 1 – $38.00r – us Trans-Media [340]
PROCEEDINGS / Maryland. State Bar Association – 1897-1970. 8 reels – 1 – $38.00r – us Trans-Media [340]
PROCEEDINGS / Massachusetts. State Bar Association – 1910-14 – 1r – 1 – $38.00r – us Trans-Media [340]
PROCEEDINGS / Mayo Clinic – v. 2-52. 1927-1977 – 1,5,6 – us Princeton Micro [610]
PROCEEDINGS / Mayo Clinic – (v.54-. 1979- 5,6,9) – v.39-. 1964- – 1 – us UMI [073]
PROCEEDINGS / Medical Society of London – v1-12 1872-89 – 1 – us UMI [610]
PROCEEDINGS / Michigan. State Bar Association – 1891-1920 – 2r – 1 – $38.00r – us Trans-Media [340]
PROCEEDINGS / Middle States Association of Colleges and Secondary Schools – 1887-1; 1970- 5,6; 1974- 4 x 6 in. 9 – us UMI [370]
PROCEEDINGS / Minnesota. State Bar Association – 1901-48 – 3r – 1 – $38.00r – us Trans-Media [340]
PROCEEDINGS / Mississippi. State Bar Association – 1886-1927 – 2r – 1 – $38.00r – us Trans-Media [340]
PROCEEDINGS / Mississippi Valley Historical Association – v. 1-11. 1907-1924. All pub – 1,5,6 – us Princeton Micro [978]
PROCEEDINGS / Mississippi Valley Historical Association – v. 1-11. 1907-24 – 1 – us UMI [975]
PROCEEDINGS / Missouri. State Bar Association – 1880-1930 – 4r – 1 – $38.00r – us Trans-Media [340]
PROCEEDINGS / Montana. Forest and Conservation Experiment Station. Missoula – Apr 28-29, 1966 – 1,5,6 – us Spaulding [630]
PROCEEDINGS / Montana. State Bar Association – 1885-1947. 1 reel – 1 – $38.00 – us Trans-Media [340]
PROCEEDINGS / Mumps Users' Group Meeting – (1979- 9) – 1973- – 1,5,6 – us UMI [380]
PROCEEDINGS / National academy of science – v1- 1915- 1,5,6; v74- 9 – us UMI [500]
PROCEEDINGS / National Academy of Sciences of the United States of America – (v35-. 1949- 5,6; v73-. 1976- 9) – v1-. 1915- – 1 – us UMI [500]
PROCEEDINGS / National Academy of Sciences. Washington – v1-74. 1915-77 – 1,5,6 – us Princeton Micro [500]
PROCEEDINGS / National Arbitration Peace Congresses – 1907, 1909, 1911, 1913, 1915 – 28mf – 9 – $120.00 – us UPA [320]
PROCEEDINGS / National Paint, Varnish and Lacquer Association. Scientific Section – Nos. 1-568. 1911-1938 – 1,5,6 – us Princeton Micro [540]
PROCEEDINGS / National Science Council. Taiwan – 1965-84.192 fiches – 9 – 180.00 – ch Transmission [500]
PROCEEDINGS / National Speech Arts Association – v. 1-24. 1892-1916 – 1 – us UMI [410]
PROCEEDINGS / Nebraska. State Bar Association – 1900-37 – 2r – 1 – $38.00r – us Trans-Media [340]
PROCEEDINGS / Nevada. State Bar Association – 1912-35 – 1r – 1 – $38.00r – us Trans-Media [340]
PROCEEDINGS / New Hampshire. State Bar Association – 1882-1963 – 5r – 1 – $38.00r – us Trans-Media [340]
PROCEEDINGS / New Jersey. State Bar Association – 1899-1951 – 4r – 1 – $38.00r – us Trans-Media [340]
PROCEEDINGS / New Mexico. State Bar Association – 1886-1961 – 2r – 1 – $38.00r – us Trans-Media [340]
PROCEEDINGS / New Mexico State University – Statewide conference economic development for rural New Mexico. 30-31 Oct 1973. 1 reel – 1,5 – us Spaulding [630]
PROCEEDINGS / New York. (City). State Bar Association – 1870-1947. 7 reels – 1 – $38.00r – us Trans-Media [340]
PROCEEDINGS / New York. Public Service Commission. First District – v.1-20, Jul 1, 1907-Apr 25, 1921. 238 fiches. (Harvard Law School Library Collection.) – 9 – 1.50f – us H.U. Law [336]
PROCEEDINGS / New York. (State). State Bar Association – 1876-1968. 17 reels – 1 – $38.00r – us Trans-Media [340]
PROCEEDINGS / New York University. Annual National Conference on Labor – 1948- 1; 1977- 5,6,9 – us UMI [380]
PROCEEDINGS / North American Metalworking Research Conference – 1973-76 – 1 – us UMI [670]
PROCEEDINGS / North Carolina. State Bar Association – 1885-1948; State Bar: 1934-43 – 5r – 1 – $38.00r – us Trans-Media [340]
PROCEEDINGS / North Central Weed Control Conference – 1944- 1; v24- 5,6; v30- 9 – us UMI [631]
PROCEEDINGS / North Dakota. State Bar Association – 1899-1925. 1 reel – 1 – $38.00r – us Trans-Media [340]
PROCEEDINGS / Nova Scotian Institute of Science – 1863-1954 – 5r – 1 – $325.00 – cn Library Assoc [500]
PROCEEDINGS / Nutrition Society. London – v12-42 1953-83 – 1,5,6 – us Princeton Micro [612]
PROCEEDINGS / Ohio. State Bar Association – 1880-1927 – 4r – 1 – $38.00r – us Trans-Media [340]
PROCEEDINGS / Oklahoma Baptist State B.Y.P.U. Conventions – 1919-25 – 1 – 13.44 – us Baptist [240]
PROCEEDINGS / Oklahoma. State Bar Association – 1902-32 – 3r – 1 – $38.00r – us Trans-Media [340]
PROCEEDINGS / Oregon. State Bar Association – 1891-1917. 1 reel – 1 – $38.00r – us Trans-Media [340]
PROCEEDINGS / Pennsylvania. State Bar Association – 1895-1968. 12 reels – 1 – $38.00r – us Trans-Media [340]
PROCEEDINGS / Popular Culture Association. Fifth National Convention. March 20-22, 1975 – 1r – 1 – $32.50r – us Archival [390]
PROCEEDINGS / Popular Culture Association. Sixth National Convention. April 22-24, 1976 – 1r – 1 – $32.50r – us Archival [390]
PROCEEDINGS / Rhode Island. State Bar Association – 1898-1929 – 1r – 1 – $38.00r – us Trans-Media [340]
PROCEEDINGS / Royal Anthropological Institute of Great Britain and Ireland – 1966-73 – 1 – us UMI [306]
PROCEEDINGS / Royal Geographic Society – London. (Supersedes Geographical Magazine.) v1-21 1855-1871 – 1,5,6 – us Princeton Micro [910]
PROCEEDINGS / Royal Institution of Great Britian – v38- 1960- 1; v43- 5,6; v50- 9 – us UMI [941]
PROCEEDINGS / Royal Irish Academy – v1-23 1840-1902 – 1,5,6 – $22,242.00 – us Princeton Micro [500]
PROCEEDINGS / Royal Meteorological Society – London. v1-5. 1863-71 – 3 – us Readex [550]
PROCEEDINGS / Royal Netherlands Academy of Science – v. 1-53. 1899-1950 – 1,5,6 – us Princeton Micro [500]
PROCEEDINGS / Royal Philosophical Society of Glasgow – v10-60 1875-1932 – 1,5,6 – us Princeton Micro [100]
PROCEEDINGS / Royal Society of Edinburgh – v1-60 1841-1940 – 1,5,6 – us Princeton Micro [500]
PROCEEDINGS / Royal Society of London – Series A. v. 1-364. 1800-1978 – 1,5,6 – us Princeton Micro [500]
PROCEEDINGS / Royal Society of London – Series B, Biological Sciences. v. 76-203. 1905-78 – 1,5,6 – us Princeton Micro [500]
PROCEEDINGS / Royal Society of Medicine – See also: Royal Society of Medicine Journal – 1,5,6,9 – us UMI [610]
PROCEEDINGS / Rudolf Virchow Medical Society in the City of New York – v1-29 1942-73. Continued by Virchow-Pirquet Medical Society, Proceedings – 1 – us UMI [610]
PROCEEDINGS / Scottish Anthropological and Folklore Society – 1936, v2, no.1-1956 – 1 – us I.U. Libraries [390]
PROCEEDINGS / Scottish Anthropological and Folklore Society – v1, no.1-3. Oct 1934-Sept 1935. -irr – 1 – us I.U. Libraries [390]
PROCEEDINGS / Seventh Day Baptist General Conference – 1800-1964 – 1 – 943.11 – us Baptist [240]
PROCEEDINGS / Socialist Labor Party – 1900-1901 – 1 – us UMI [335]
PROCEEDINGS / Society for Analytical Chemistry – v1-11. 1964-74 – 1 – us UMI [540]
PROCEEDINGS / Society for Experimental Biology and Medicine – v. 1-75. 1903-49 50 – 3 – us Readex [610]
PROCEEDINGS / Society for Experimental Biology and Medicine – v1-89. 1903-55 – 1,5,6 – us Princeton Micro [580]
PROCEEDINGS / Society for Experimental Stress Analysis – v3-40. 1945-83 – 1 – us UMI [073]
PROCEEDINGS / Soil Science Society of America – v11-20 1946-56 – 1 – us Princeton Micro [630]
PROCEEDINGS / South Carolina. State Bar Association – 1894-1947 – 2r – 1 – $38.00r – us Trans-Media [340]
PROCEEDINGS / South Dakota. State Bar Association – 1897-1931 – 2r – 1 – $38.00r – us Trans-Media [340]
PROCEEDINGS / Southern Baptist Convention – 1845-63. 206p – 1 – us Baptist [240]
PROCEEDINGS / Tennessee. State Bar Association – 1882-1935 – 4r – 1 – $38.00r – us Trans-Media [340]
PROCEEDINGS / Texas. State Bar Association – 1882-1948 – 4r – 1 – $38.00r – us Trans-Media [340]
PROCEEDINGS / United Nations. Conference on International Organization, 1945. San Francisco – 7r – 1 – $350.00 – us Trans-Media [900]
PROCEEDINGS / U.S. Anthracite Coal Strike Commission 1902-1903 – v. 1-56. 1902-03 – 1 – 142.00 – us L of C Photodup [330]
PROCEEDINGS / U.S. National Museum – (1972- 5,6; 1975- 9) – v1- 1878- – 1 – us UMI [060]
PROCEEDINGS / U.S. Naval Institute – v1-1874- 1; v99- 5,6; v101- 9 – us UMI [355]
PROCEEDINGS / U.S. Naval Institute – v1-83 1874-1963. Index, 1878-1957 – 1 – $1546.00 – us L of C Photodup [355]
PROCEEDINGS / U.S. State Bar Association – 190 reels – 1 – $7,000.00 – us Trans-Media [340]
PROCEEDINGS / Utah. State Bar Association – 1904-28.1 reel – 1 – $38.00 – us Trans-Media [340]
PROCEEDINGS – v.1-38. 1926-63 – 1 – us UMI [073]
PROCEEDINGS – v1-7 1881-1905 – 1 – 25.00 – us L of C Photodup [331]
PROCEEDINGS / Vermont. State Bar Association – 1878-1966. 5 reels – 1 – $38.00r – us Trans-Media [340]
PROCEEDINGS / Virchow-Pirquet Medical Society – (v34- 1980- 5,6,9) – v30-34 1976-80 – 1 – us UMI [610]
PROCEEDINGS / Virginia. State Bar Association – 1888-1970. 11 reels – 1 – $38.00r – us Trans-Media [340]
PROCEEDINGS / Washington. State Bar Association – 1894-1927. 2 reels – 1 – $38.00r – us Trans-Media [340]
PROCEEDINGS / Washington State Potato Conference – 1961-69. 1961, unnumbered 1-8 – 1,5,6 – us Spaulding [630]
PROCEEDINGS / West Virginia. State Bar Association – 1886-1967 – 6r – 1 – $38.00r – us Trans-Media [340]
PROCEEDINGS / Wisconsin. State Bar Association – 1878-1946. 4 reels – 1 – $38.00r – us Trans-Media [340]
PROCEEDINGS / Wyoming. State Bar Association – 1915-36 – 1r – 1 – $38.00r – us Trans-Media [340]
PROCEEDINGS / Zoological Society of London. Committee of Science and Correspondence – 1830-32 – 3 – us Readex [590]
PROCEEDINGS / American Academic of Deans – Washington. 1945-1978 1; 1971-1978 5* – 1,5 – D5754 – us UMI [370]
PROCEEDINGS / American Bar Association, Section of Insurance Negligence and Compensation Law – (Ceased publ) – Chicago. 1933-1972* – 1 – D7711 – us UMI [340]
PROCEEDINGS / American Mathematical Society – Providence. cum index v1-30 1950-nov 1971; v1-131 feb 1950- 1,5; v1-131 feb 1950- 9 – 1,5,9 – D13412 – us UMI [510]

PROCEEDINGS, 1ST-2ND SESSIONS 1944, 4TH-8TH SESSIONS NOV 1944-1948 / Advisory Council for the Northern Sudan. Khartoum – us Res Libr [324]

PROCEEDINGS, 1851-1983 / Society of Antiquaries of Scotland – Edinburgh. 46 reels – 1 – $3,835.00 – us UPA [941]

PROCEEDINGS 1874-1968 / Iowa. State Bar Association – 6 reels – 1 – $38.00r – us Trans-Media [340]

PROCEEDINGS 1877-1939 / Illinois. State Bar Association – 8 reels – 1 – $38.00r – us Trans-Media [340]

PROCEEDINGS 1882-1940 / Colorado. State Bar Association – 4 reels – 1 – $38.00r – us Trans-Media [340]

PROCEEDINGS 1884-1962 / Georgia. State Bar Association – 9 reels – 1 – $38.00r – us Trans-Media [340]

PROCEEDINGS, 1890-1974 / Scotch-Irish Society of the U.S.A – (1890-1960 as Pennsylvania Scotch-Irish Society) – 1 – $200.00 – us Presbyterian [970]

PROCEEDINGS 1957-63 – (v1-5, 7-8, Advances) – 9 – $20.00v – us Univelt [629]

PROCEEDINGS, ACADEMY OF MANAGEMENT *see* ACADEMY OF MANGEMENT

PROCEEDINGS – AMERICAN ASSOCIATION OF COLLEGES OF PHARMACY TEACHERS' SEMINAR / American Association of Colleges of Pharmacy Teachers' Seminar – (Ceased publ) – Alexandria. cum index 1959-1963; jun 1950-jul 1963 – 1 – D1657 – us UMI [615]

PROCEEDINGS AND ADDRESSES / American Philosophical Association – (1970- 5,6; 1976-9) – 1- 1927- – 1 – us UMI [100]

PROCEEDINGS AND BULLETIN / National Conference on Social Welfare – v3-60. 1876-1933 – 1 – us Princeton Micro [360]

PROCEEDINGS AND ORDINANCES OF THE PRIVY COUNCIL OF ENGLAND / ed by Harris, N – London. 6v. 1834-37 – 64mf – 9 – H-913/2 – ne IDC [323]

PROCEEDINGS AND ORDINANCES OF THE PRIVY COUNCIL OF ENGLAND, 1385-1422 / Nicolas – 1 – uk Microform Academic [323]

PROCEEDINGS AND REPORTS / John S Slater Fund – New York. 1882-1936 37. (Wanting 1890, 1936 37) – 1 – 26.00 – us L of C Photodup [977]

PROCEEDINGS AND REPORTS OF SELECT COMMITTEES / Transkei (South Africa). Territorial Authority – Umtata, 1957-63 – us Res Libr [324]

PROCEEDINGS AND REPORTS OF SELECT COMMITTEES / Transkeian Territories. General Council – Umtata, [1908-30] – us Res Libr [324]

PROCEEDINGS AND REPORTS OF SELECT COMMITTEES / United Transkeian Territories. General Council – Umtata, [1931-56] – us Res Libr [324]

PROCEEDINGS AND RESEARCH SUMMARIES / Virginia Feed Convention and Nutrition Conference – 1949-50. 13 fiches – 9 – us Spaulding [630]

PROCEEDINGS AND TRANSACTIONS / Royal Society of Canada – Series 1. v. 1-12. 1882-94; Series 2. v. 1-12. 1895-1906; Series 3. v. 1-42. 1907-48 – 1,5,6 – us Princeton Micro [500]

PROCEEDINGS AND TRANSACTIONS OF THE AMERICAN ENTOMOLOGICAL SOCIETY OF PHILADELPHIA – v1-6. 1861/63-1867; v1-46. 1867-1920 – 407mf – 9 – 2779/2 – ne IDC [590]

PROCEEDINGS: ANIMAL SCIENCES / Indian Academy of Sciences – v89 1980 – 1,5,6,9 – us UMI [636]

PROCEEDINGS (CCC337) = MA TE LA SSU TA HUI YIN HSIANG CHI / 4th International Missionary Council; ed by Wu, Yao-tsung – (In Chinese) – [s.l: s.n, 1939?] – 1r – 1 – 1984-6676 – us A.T.L.A. [240]

PROCEEDINGS: CHEMICAL SCIENCES / Indian Academy of Sciences – v89 1980 – 1,5,6,9 – us UMI [540]

PROCEEDINGS: DEBATES OF THE SENATE / Canada. Parliament. Senate – 1st-28th. 1871-1972 – 1 – us Princeton Micro [324]

PROCEEDINGS: EARTH AND PLANETARY SCIENCES / Indian Academy of Sciences – v89 1980 – 1,5,6,9 – us UMI [550]

PROCEEDINGS FOR AFRICA AND THE EAST / Church Missionary Society – 1801-1921 – 1 – uk Microform Academic [240]

PROCEEDINGS FROM THE AASCB ANNUAL MEETING – (American Assembly of Collegiate Schools of Business) – 1,5,6,9 – us UMI [380]

PROCEEDINGS HAD IN THE LEGISLATURE OF UPPER CANADA DURING THE YEARS 1831-2 AND 3 ON THE SUBJECT OF THE LANDS / Canada. Haut-Canada. Chambre d'Assemblee – Montreal: Printed by Desbarats & Derbishire, 1845. SEM105P151 – 1mf – 9 – Can$2.25 – cn Bibl Nat [324]

PROCEEDINGS: HANSARD DEBATES / Canada. Parliament. House of Commons – 3rd-28th. 1875-1972 – 1 – us Princeton Micro [324]

PROCEEDINGS IN CHAMBER / International Military Tribunal for the Far East – Tokyo. On film: 1946-48. LL-024 – 1 – us L of C Photodup [340]

PROCEEDINGS IN CONGRESS – Attending the reception of the statue of Roger Williams, Founder of the State of Rhode Island, 1872 – 1 – 5.00 – us Baptist [978]

PROCEEDINGS IN CONGRESS ATTENDING THE RECEPTION OF THE STATUE OF ROGER WILLIAMS, FOUNDER OF THE STATE OF RHODE ISLAND – 1872 – 1 – $5.00 – us Baptist [240]

PROCEEDINGS IN MEMORY OF JUDGE EDWARD LEES / Minnesota. Supreme Court – St. Paul? 1928? 13p. LL-1199 – 1 – us L of C Photodup [340]

PROCEEDINGS... IN RELATION TO THE GREAT SOUTHERN RAILWAY / Canada. Parliament. Legislative Assembly. Committee – s.l: s.n, 1857. SEM105P363 – 1mf – 9 – Can$2.25 – cn Bibl Nat [380]

PROCEEDINGS IN THE ASSEMBLY OF LOWER-CANADA, ON THE ACCUSATIONS AGAINST PIERRE BEDARD, ESQ. PROVINCIAL JUDGE FOR THE DISTRICT OF THREE-RIVERS / Bas-Canada. Parliament. House of Assembly – [Quebec: s.n.], 1819. SEM105P1227 – 5mf – 9 – Can$11.25 – cn Bibl Nat [971]

PROCEEDINGS IN THE NORTH ATLANTIC COAST FISHERIES ARBITRATION... – Washington, D.C., 1912 – 85mf – 9 – ILM-699/1 – ne IDC [639]

PROCEEDINGS. INSTITUTE OF INDUSTRIAL ENGINEERS *see* TECHNICAL PAPERS, INSTITUTE CONFERENCE AND CONVENTION

PROCEEDINGS, INSTITUTION OF BRITISH AGRICULTURAL ENGINEERS *see* AGRICULTURAL ENGINEER

PROCEEDINGS: JOURNAL / Canada. Parliament. Senate – 1st-28th. 1867-1970 – 1 – us Princeton Micro [324]

PROCEEDINGS: JOURNALS / Canada. Parliament. House of Commons – 1st-28th. 1867-1970 – 1 – us Princeton Micro [324]

PROCEEDINGS: JOURNALS / Canada. Parliament. Legislative Assembly – 1st-8th.1841-1866 – 1 – us Princeton Micro [324]

PROCEEDINGS: MATHEMATICAL SCIENCES / Indian Academy of Sciences – v89 1980 – 1,5,6,9 – us UMI [510]

PROCEEDINGS OF A CONFERENCE BETWEEN THE SECRETARY OF STATE FOR THE COLONIES AND THE PREMIERS OF THE SELF-GOVERNING COLONIES...LONDON, JUNE AND JULY 1897 – London: H.M.S.O., 1897. 00718. (Pre-1900 Canadiana) – 9 – cn C.I.H.M. [941]

PROCEEDINGS OF A COURT OF INQUIRY CONCERNING THE CONDUCT OF MAJ. MARCUS A. RENO AT THE BATTLE OF THE LITTLE BIG HORN RIVER ON JUNE 25 AND 26, 1876 / U.S. Army. Judge Advocate General – 2rolls. M592 – 1 – us Nat'l Archives [324]

PROCEEDINGS OF A MILITARY COURT HELD AT MANUS ISLAND, JUNE 1950-APRIL 1951 / Australia. Army. Military Court – On film: Ju. 5, 1950-Ap. 9, 1951, index. LL-025 – 1 – us L of C Photodup [340]

PROCEEDINGS OF INTERNATIONAL CONFERENCE... – Washington, D.C. 6v. 1910-16 – 23mf – 9 – ILM-4004/1 – ne IDC [327]

PROCEEDINGS OF THE 3RD CONVENTION / General Organization of the Jewish Workers of Palestine. (Histadrut) – 1927. BJ-28-32 1 – 9 – ne IDC [330]

PROCEEDINGS OF THE 6TH ROUND OF FUTURE POLITICAL STATUS NEGOTIATIONS : HELD AT BARBERS POINT, OAHU, HI, SEP-OCT 1972 / Cong of Micronesia. Joint Committee on Future Status – Saipan: Joint Committee on Future Status, 1972 – 1mf – 9 – $1.50 – LLMC 82-100F, Title 84 – us L.L.M.C. [323]

PROCEEDINGS OF THE 6TH ROUND OF FUTURE POLITICAL STATUS NEGOTIATIONS : HELD AT BARBERS POINT, OAHU, HI, SEP-OCT 1972 / Off of Micronesian Status Negotiations – Washington: Office of Micronesian Status Negotiations, 1972 – 1mf – 9 – $1.50 – LLMC 82-100F, Title 48 – us L.L.M.C. [323]

PROCEEDINGS OF THE AMERICAN ANTIQUARIAN SOCIETY / American Antiquarian Society – Worcester. cum index 1-15 1880-1903; v1- oct 1880- 1; v79- apr 1969- 5; v87- apr 1977- 9 – 1,5,9 – D186 – us UMI [000]

PROCEEDINGS OF THE AMERICAN CONGRESS ON SURVEYING AND MAPPING ANNUAL MEETING *see* PAPERS FROM THE ANNUAL MEETING

PROCEEDINGS OF THE AMERICAN CONGRESS ON SURVEYING AND MAPPING FALL CONVENTION *see* JOINT PROCEEDINGS

PROCEEDINGS OF THE AMERICAN FISH CULTURISTS' ASSOCIATION *see* TRANSACTIONS

PROCEEDINGS OF THE AMERICAN FISHERIES SOCIETY *see* TRANSACTIONS

PROCEEDINGS OF THE AMERICAN PHILOSOPHICAL SOCIETY – Philadelphia. v1-59. 1838-1920 – 564mf – 9 – H-174/2 – ne IDC [100]

PROCEEDINGS OF THE AMERICAN SOCIETY OF AGRONOMY / American Society of Agronomy – (Cont. as JOURNAL OF THE AMERICAN SOCIETY OF AGRONOMY. Washington. 1914-1941 . v5-33) – Washington. 1907-1913, v1-40 – 279mf – 9 – ne IDC [630]

PROCEEDINGS OF THE AMERICAN SOCIETY OF CIVIL ENGINEERS – New York. v46-54. 1920-28 – 354mf – 9 – 219/2 – ne IDC [624]

PROCEEDINGS OF THE AMERICAN SOCIETY OF INTERNATIONAL LAW AT THE MEETING OF THE EXECUTIVE COUNCIL *see* AMERICAN JOURNAL OF INTERNATIONAL LAW

PROCEEDINGS OF THE AMERICAN SOCIETY OF PHOTOGRAMMETRY FALL TECHNICAL MEETING *see* JOINT PROCEEDINGS

PROCEEDINGS OF THE ANNUAL CONFERENCE / Auburn University. Extension Service – 1960-67 – 1,5,6 – us Spaulding [630]

PROCEEDINGS OF THE ANNUAL CONVENTION / Catholic Theological Society of America – (v35- 1980- 5,6,9) – v1- 1946- – 1 – us UMI [240]

PROCEEDINGS OF THE ANNUAL CONVENTION / Christian Association for Psychological Studies – 1963-67 – 1 – us UMI [150]

PROCEEDINGS OF THE ANNUAL MEETING / American Society of International Law – (v76- 1982- 1,5,6,9) – v68-75 1974-81 – 1 – us UMI [340]

PROCEEDINGS OF THE ANNUAL MEETING, 1974 *see* AMERICAN JOURNAL OF INTERNATIONAL LAW

PROCEEDINGS OF THE ANNUAL STAFF CONFERENCE / Alabama. Agricultural Experiment Station – 1951-65 – 1,5,6 – us Spaulding [630]

PROCEEDINGS OF THE ASIATIC SOCIETY OF BENGAL / Asiatic Society of Bengal – 1866-1905. v1-40. Calcutta. – 213mf – 8 – ne IDC [950]

PROCEEDINGS OF THE ASSAM LEGISALTIVE COUNCIL – v1-11. 1937-47 – 69mf – 9 – I-64/2 – ne IDC [950]

PROCEEDINGS OF THE ASSAM LEGISLATIVE COUNCIL – (Index 1921-35) – Shillong. v1-16. 1921-36 – 411mf – 9 – I-63/2 – ne IDC [950]

PROCEEDINGS OF THE BAR OF THE NEW YORK ON OCCASION OF THE DEATH OF HON. LEWIS B. WOODRUFF. – New York, Browne, 1875. 28p. LL-1364 – 1 – us L of C Photodup [340]

PROCEEDINGS OF THE BENCH AND BAR OF THE CIRCUIT COURT OF THE UNITED STATES, DISTRICT OF MASSACHUSETTS, UPON THE DECEASE OF HON. BENJAMIN ROBBINS CURTIS, SEPTEMBER AND OCTOBER, 1874 / U.S. Circuit Court. First Circuit – Boston, 1875. 60 p. LL-367 – 1 – us L of C Photodup [340]

PROCEEDINGS OF THE BENGAL LEGISLATIVE COUNCIL *see* PROCEEDINGS OF THE COUNCIL OF THE LIEUTENANT-GOVERNOR OF BENGAL FOR THE PURPOSE OF MAKING LAWS AND REGULATIONS

PROCEEDINGS OF THE BETHEL CHURCH / Cape Girardeau. Missouri – 1806-67 – 1 – 5.00 – us Baptist [240]

PROCEEDINGS OF THE CALIFORNIA ACADEMY OF NATIONAL SCIENCES – (Botany, Geology: v1-2; Mathematics, Physics, Zoology: v1-4) – San Francisco. S1 1854-1906; S2 v1-7; S3 v1-6 – 36mf – 9 – H-175/2 – ne IDC [500]

PROCEEDINGS OF THE CAMBRIDGE PHILOLOGICAL SOCIETY / Cambridge Philological Society – london. 1882-1940 – 36mf – 8 – ne IDC [400]

PROCEEDINGS OF THE CANADIAN INSTITUTE / Canadian Institute – Toronto: Printed for the Canadian Institute by Copp, Clark, [1879?-19–] – 9 – cn C.I.H.M. [971]

PROCEEDINGS OF THE CASUALTY ACTUARIAL AND STATISTICAL SOCIETY OF AMERICA – v.1-7. 1914-20 – 1 – us UMI [310]

PROCEEDINGS OF THE CENTENNIAL CELEBRATION OF THE INCORPORATION OF THE TOWN OF LONGMEADOW, OCTOBER 17, 1883 – 1884. Published by the Secretary of the Centennial Committee. Massachusetts Reel 5. (The Cox Library Collection – 5 – us Americana [978]

PROCEEDINGS OF THE CONSTITUTIONAL CONVENTION OF THE CONGRESS OF INDUSTRIAL ORGANIZATIONS *see* AFL-CIO PROCEEDINGS

PROCEEDINGS OF THE COORG LEGISLATIVE COUNCIL – (Index 1924-26) – Bangalore, 1924-38 – 150mf – 9 – I-53/2 – ne IDC [960]

PROCEEDINGS OF THE COUNCIL OF THE CHIEF COMMISSIONER OF ASSAM... – Shillong, 1919-21 – 47mf – 9 – I-62/2 – ne IDC [960]

PROCEEDINGS OF THE COUNCIL OF THE GOVERNOR OF BOMBAY ASSEMBLED FOR THE PURPOSE OF MAKING LAWS AND REGULATIONS – Bombay. v1-58. 1865-1920 – 624mf – 9 – I-26/2 – ne IDC [960]

PROCEEDINGS OF THE COUNCIL OF THE GOVERNOR OF FORT SAINT GEORGE FOR THE PURPOSE OF MAKING LAWS AND REGULATIONS – Madras. v1-48. 1862-1920 – 734mf – 9 – I-32/2 – ne IDC [960]

PROCEEDINGS OF THE COUNCIL OF THE LIEUTENANT-GOVERNOR OF BENGAL FOR THE PURPOSE OF MAKING LAWS AND REGULATIONS – (Cont as: Proceedings of the Bengal Legislative Council. Calcutta v42-52 1911-20) – Calcutta. v1-41. 1865-1910 – 814mf – 9 – I-20/2 – ne IDC [960]

PROCEEDINGS OF THE COUNCIL OF THE LIEUTENANT-GOVERNOR OF THE PUNJAB / Punjab. India (State). Council of the Lieut. Governor – v. 1-9. Lahore. 1897-1918. – 132mf – 8 – ne IDC [324]

PROCEEDINGS OF THE ENTOMOLOGICAL SOCIETY OF LONDON – London. SA: v11-16. 1936-41; SB: v5-10. 1936-41 – 49mf – 9 – 2577c/2 – ne IDC [590]

PROCEEDINGS OF THE ENTOMOLOGICAL SOCIETY OF LONDON – London. v1-10. 1926-35 – 41mf – 9 – 2576/2 – ne IDC [590]

PROCEEDINGS OF THE FAO EXPERT CONSULTATION ON FISH TECHNOLOGY IN AFRICA : ABIDJAN, 1988 – 1990 – 355p – it F.A.O. [639]

PROCEEDINGS OF THE FAO EXPERT CONSULTATION ON THE GENETIC ASPECTS OF TRYPANOTOLERANCE : ROME, 1991 – 1992 – 143p – it F.A.O. [575]

PROCEEDINGS OF THE FAO EXPERT CONSULTATION ON THE SUBSTITUTION OF IMPORTED CONCENTRATE FEEDS IN ANIMAL PRODUCTION SYSTEMS IN DEVELOPING COUNTRIES – 1987 – 246p – it F.A.O. [636]

THE PROCEEDINGS OF THE FIRST GENERAL PEACE CONVENTION: ...1843,... – London, 1843 – 2mf – 9 – ILM-681/1 – ne IDC [327]

PROCEEDINGS OF THE FIRST HOUSE OF REPRESENTATIVES BURMA LEGISLATURE / Burma. Senate – v. 1-9. Rangoon. 1937-41. – 241mf – 8 – ne IDC [324]

PROCEEDINGS OF THE FIRST LEGISLATIVE ASSEMBLY OF BIHAR DEBATES – Bihar, Patna. v1-5. 1937-39 – 220mf – 9 – I-47/2 – ne IDC [960]

PROCEEDINGS OF THE FIRST LEGISLATIVE ASSEMBLY OF THE GOVERNOR OF ORISSA – v1-10. 1937-44 – 152mf – 9 – I-51/2 – ne IDC [960]

PROCEEDINGS OF THE GENERAL CONFERENCE OF THE PROTESTANT MISSIONARIES OF JAPAN : HELD AT OSAKA, JAPAN, APRIL, 1883 / ed by General Conference of the Protestant Missionaries of Japan – Yokohama: R. Meiklejohn, 1883 – 2mf – us A.T.L.A. [240]

PROCEEDINGS OF THE GENEVA CONFERENCE.. / Evangelical Alliance – 1861 – 1 – $50.00 – us Presbyterian [240]

PROCEEDINGS OF THE GEOLOGICAL SOCIETY OF LONDON / Geological Society of London – 1826-1845 – 3 – us Readex [550]

PROCEEDINGS OF THE GEOLOGICAL SOCIETY OF LONDON / Geological Society of London – no.1-1664; Nov. 1826-1971. London – 1 – us U.W. Library [550]

PROCEEDINGS OF THE GERMAN REICHSTAG, 1871-1933 – 10,287mf (1:18) – 9 – $23,590.00 – us UPA [943]

PROCEEDINGS OF THE GRAFTON COUNTY BAR, ON THE DEATH OF THE HON. HARRY HIBBARD. / Grafton County. New Hampshire. Bar – Concord, N.H.: Woodbury & Batchelder, 1873. 18p. LL-560 – 1 – us L of C Photodup [340]

PROCEEDINGS OF THE HAWAIIAN ENTOMOLOGICAL SOCIETY – Honolulu. v1-11. 1905-42 – 98mf – 9 – Z-996c/2 – ne IDC [590]

PROCEEDINGS OF THE HOUSE OF ASSEMBLY UPON THE PETITION OF THE ELECTORS OF THE COUNTY OF BEDFORD AGAINST THE LEGALITY OF THE ELECTION FOR THE SAID COUNTY / Canada. Parliament. House of Assembly – [s.l.]: [s.n.], 1821. SEM105P97 – 1mf – 9 – Can$2.25 – cn Bibl Nat [323]

PROCEEDINGS OF THE INDIAN HISTORICAL RECORDS COMMISSION / Indian Historical Records Commission – v. 1-36. 1919-61. – 273mf – 8 – ne IDC [073]

PROCEEDINGS OF THE INDIAN HISTORY CONGRESS 1938-41, 1945-63 / Indian History Congress – Patna. 1939-64. Lacking: 1957, Session 20; 1959-62, Session 22-24. – 169mf – 8 – ne IDC [950]

PROCEEDINGS OF THE INSTITUTION OF MECHANICAL ENGINEERS / Institution of Mechanical Engineers – London. 1936-49. v132-161. – 184mf – 8 – ne IDC [620]

PROCEEDINGS OF THE INTERNATIONAL CONFERENCE ON PEACEFUL USES OF ATOMIC ENERGY / United Nations – (First International Conference, Geneva, 1955: Vols 1-16. A/Conf.8/1-16. E.151 F.175 S.172; Vol 17. A/Conf.8/17. E.3; Second International Conference, Geneva, 1958: Vols 1-13. A/Conf.15/1-13. E.159 F.202 S.179; Vols 14-33. English A/Conf.15/14-33. E.175; Third International Conference, Geneva, 1964: Vols 1-16. A/Conf.28/1-16. E/F/R/S.157; Fourth International Conference, Geneva, 1971: Vols 1-15. A/Conf.49/1-15. E.157) – 9 – us U.N. Pubs [333]

PROCEEDINGS OF THE INTERNATIONAL MILITARY TRIBUNAL FOR THE FAR EAST – (In English) – 36r – 1 – $1,260.00 set in US $40.00r outside – L9400092 – Dist. us Scholarly Res – us L of C Photodup [340]

PROCEEDINGS OF THE ISRAEL-FRANCE SYMPOSIUM ON BEHAVIOR OF PESTICIDES IN SOIL / Israel. Prime Minister's Office. Ministry of Agriculture – 10-13 Nov 1975. By M. Bet-Dagan Horowitz. 1977. 98 p. Diagr. Special Pub. no. 82 – 9 – 2.00 – is I.T.T.I. [631]

PROCEEDINGS OF THE LEGISLATIVE ASSEMBLY OF THE CENTRAL PROVINCES AND BERAR – Nagpur. v1-7. 1937-39 – 123mf – 9 – I-58/2 – ne IDC [950]

PROCEEDINGS OF THE LEGISLATIVE COUNCIL OF EASTERN BENGAL AND ASSAM – Shillong. 1v. 1906-17 – 34mf – 9 – I-60/2 – ne IDC [950]

PROCEEDINGS OF THE LEGISLATIVE COUNCIL OF INDIA 1854-61 / India. Legislative Council – v. 1-7. Calcutta. 1856-62 – 66mf – 8 – ne IDC [324]

PROCEEDINGS OF THE LEGISLATIVE COUNCIL OF THE CHIEF COMMISSIONER OF THE CENTRAL PROVINCES / Central Provinces. India. Legislative Council – v. 1-3. Nagpur. 1914-20. – 129mf – 8 – ne IDC [324]

PROCEEDINGS OF THE LEGISLATIVE COUNCIL OF THE GOVERNOR OF THE CENTRAL PROVINCES – (Index included) – Nagpur. v1-13. 1921-36 – 537mf – 9 – I-56/2 – ne IDC [950]

PROCEEDINGS OF THE LEGISLATIVE COUNCIL OF THE LIEUTENANT-GOVERNOR OF BIHAR AND ORISSA / Bihar and Orissa. India (States). Legislative Council – v. 1-6. Patna. 1914-20. – 163mf – 8 – ne IDC [324]

PROCEEDINGS OF THE LEGISLATIVE COUNCIL OF THE STRAITS SETTLEMENTS FOR THE YEARS 1901-1938, WITH APPENDIX – (Index 1896-1913) – Singapore, 1902-39 – 691mf – 9 – SE-102/2 – ne IDC [950]

PROCEEDINGS OF THE LEGISLATIVE COUNCIL OF THE UNITED PROVINCES – (Index included) – Allahabad. v1-73. 1921-36 – 877mf – 9 – I-80/2 – ne IDC [950]

PROCEEDINGS OF THE LEGISLATIVE COUNCIL OF THE UNITED PROVINCES / United Provinces. India. Legislative Council – (Includes Index 1937-39) – 1938-1941. V. 1-6. Allahabad. – 105mf – 8 – ne IDC [324]

PROCEEDINGS OF THE LEGISLATIVE COUNCIL OF UPPER CANADA, ON THE BILL SENT UP FROM THE HOUSE OF ASSEMBLY ENTITLED, AN ACT TO AMEND THE JURY LAWS OF THIS PROVINCE / Haut-Canada. Parliament. Legislative Council – [s.l.]: R Stanton..., 1836. SEM105P160 – 1mf – 9 – Can$2.25 – cn Bibl Nat [340]

PROCEEDINGS OF THE LINNEAN SOCIETY OF LONDON – London, 1849-1934 – 97mf – 9 – 13259/1 – ne IDC [590]

PROCEEDINGS OF THE LONDON ELECTRICAL SOCIETY, DURING THE SESSIONS 1841-2 AND 1842-3 / London Electrical Society – London, 1843 – 3 – us Readex [621]

PROCEEDINGS OF THE MALACOLOGICAL SOCIETY OF LONDON – London. v1-24. 1895-1940/1942 – 173mf – 9 – 2801c/2 – ne IDC [590]

PROCEEDINGS OF THE MASSACHUSETTS HISTORICAL SOCIETY – 67r – 1 – us UMI [978]

PROCEEDINGS OF THE MASSACHUSETTS HISTORICAL SOCIETY / Massachusetts Historical Society – Annual – 17r – 1 – $1285.00 – us UMI [978]

PROCEEDINGS OF THE MEETINGS FOR THE YEARS 1908, 1909 AND 1910 / International Association of Instructors and Investigators in Poultry Husbandry – v1 1908-10 – 1 – us UMI [636]

PROCEEDINGS OF THE MEN'S NATIONAL MISSIONARY CONGRESS OF THE UNITED STATES OF AMERICA, CHICAGO, ILLINOIS, MAY 3-6 1910 – (Includes index) – New York: Laymen's Missionary Movement, 1910 – 2mf – 9 – 0-8370-6405-8 – 1986-0405 – us A.T.L.A. [240]

PROCEEDINGS OF THE NATIONAL ARBITRATION AND PEACE CONGRESS. NEW YORK, 1907 – New York. 5v. 1907-15 – 27mf – 9 – ILM-4003/1 – ne IDC [320]

PROCEEDINGS OF THE NATIONAL CONFERENCE ON ADULT EDUCATION 23-25 SEPTEMBER 1971 SINGAPORE / Singapore. Adult Education Board – Singapore, 1971 – 1mf – 9 – DE-259/1 – ne IDC [370]

PROCEEDINGS OF THE NATIONAL EMERGENCY COUNCIL, DEC. 19, 1933-APRIL 28, 1936 / U.S. Office of Government Reports – 1roll – 1 – T38 – us Nat'l Archives [324]

PROCEEDINGS OF THE NEW JERSEY HISTORICAL SOCIETY – v.1-84. 1845-1966. Continued by New Jersey History – 1 – us UMI [073]

PROCEEDINGS OF THE NINTH CONGRESS / Israel. Prime Minister's Office. International Council of the Aeronautical Sciences (ICAS) – Haifa, Aug 25-30, 1974. R. R. Dexter and J. Singer, eds. Jerusalem. v. 1: Fluid Dynamics. Aerodynamics. Gas dynamics. v. 2: Structure, Materials. Dynamic Propulsion design. Noise and pollution. Diagr., illus – 9 – 15.00 – is I.T.T.I. [324]

PROCEEDINGS OF THE PUNJAB LEGISLATIVE COUNCIL – (Index included) – Lahore. v1-29. 1921-36 – 565mf – 9 – I-75/2 – ne IDC [950]

PROCEEDINGS OF THE ROUND TABLE 1961-1964 / Sudan. Institute of Public Administration – 4v. in 1. BNE-7651 1 – 9 – ne IDC [330]

PROCEEDINGS OF THE ROYAL COLONIAL INSTITUTE / Royal Colonial Institute – v1-40. London. 1869-1909. – 163mf – 8 – ne IDC [941]

PROCEEDINGS OF THE ROYAL SOCIETY OF LONDON – (Index included) – OS. London. v1-75. 1800-1905 – 4mf – 9 – H-626/2 – ne IDC [500]

PROCEEDINGS OF THE ROYAL SOCIETY OF LONDON : S.A. MATHEMATICAL AND PHYSICAL SCIENCES – v76-177. 1905-40/41 – 1323mf – 9 – H-625c/2 – ne IDC [500]

PROCEEDINGS OF THE ROYAL SOCIETY OF LONDON *see* ABSTRACTS OF THE PAPERS PRINTED IN THE PHILOSOPHICAL TRANSACTIONS OF THE ROYAL SOCIETY

PROCEEDINGS OF THE SECTION ON STATISTICAL EDUCATION / American Statistical Association – 1979- – 1,5,6,9 – us UMI [310]

PROCEEDINGS OF THE SEMINAR TO IDENTIFY PRIORITIES FOR FISHERIES MANAGEMENT AND DEVELOPMENT IN THE SOUTHWEST INDIAN OCEAN : ALBION, MAURITIUS, 1991 – 1991 – 200p – it F.A.O. [338]

PROCEEDINGS OF THE SIND ADVISORY COUNCIL – (Missing: v23. 1945) – Karachi. v1-24. 1936-46 – 400mf – 9 – I-72/2 – ne IDC [950]

PROCEEDINGS OF THE SOCIETY FOR EXPERIMENTAL BIOLOGY AND MEDICINE – New York. v1-41. 1903-39 – 456mf – 9 – 6146/2 – ne IDC [619]

PROCEEDINGS OF THE SOCIETY FOR EXPERIMENTAL MECHANICS – (1986- . 5,6,9) – v41- . 1984- – 1 – us UMI [073]

PROCEEDINGS OF THE SOCIETY OF BIBLICAL ARCHAEOLOGY – (Index v1-32) – London. 40v. 1879-1918 – 302mf – 9 – H-629/2 – ne IDC [220]

PROCEEDINGS OF THE STANDING COMMITTEE ON RAILROADS, AND C. IN RELATION TO THE GREAT SOUTHERN RAILWAY / Canada. Parlement. Assemblee legislative. Standing Committee on Railroads – [s.l.]: [s.n.], 1857. SEM105P363 – 1mf – 9 – Can$2.25 – cn Bibl Nat [380]

PROCEEDINGS OF THE SYMPOSIUM ON POST-HARVEST FISH TECHNOLOGY – 1992 – 122p – it F.A.O. [639]

PROCEEDINGS OF THE TENTH NATIONAL SYMPOSIUM ON DESALINATION / Israel. Prime Minister's Office. National Council for Research and. Development. Desalination and Technical Forecasting – Arad 26-27. 3. 1973. By A. Levite, A. Gideon and Ariel Dickman. 243 p. Diagr – 9 – 5.00 – is I.T.T.I. [324]

PROCEEDINGS OF THE UNION MISSIONARY CONVENTION: HELD IN NEW YORK, MAY 4TH & 5TH, 1854 : TOGETHER WITH THE ADDRESS OF THE REV. DR. DUFF, AT THE PUBLIC MEETING IN THE BROADWAY TABERNACLE / Union Missionary Convention – New York: Taylor & Hogg, 1854 – 1mf – us A.T.L.A. [240]

PROCEEDINGS OF THE UNITED NATIONS CONFERENCE ON NEW SOURCES OF ENERGY / United Nations – (Information Bulletin. E/CONF.35/1. E.1 F.1 S.1; Vols 1-7. E/CONF.35/2-8. E/F.61) – 9 – us U.N. Pubs [333]

PROCEEDINGS OF THE WORKSHOP ON THE PHENOMENON KNOWN AS "EL NINO", GUAYAQUIL, ECUADOR – 1980 – 284p – 9 – 92-3-101509-5 – fr UNESCO [550]

PROCEEDINGS OF THE ZOOLOGICAL SOCIETY OF LONDON – (Index 1848-1928) – London. v1-97. 1833-1929 – 962mf – 9 – Z-2220/1 – ne IDC [590]

PROCEEDINGS OF THE...MEETING OF THE SHAREHOLDERS OF THE GRAND TRUNK RAILWAY COMPANY OF CANADA...1854 / Chemin de Fer du Grand Tronc – Montreal: James Potts – 1mf – 9 – Can$2.25 – cn Bibl Nat [380]

PROCEEDINGS OF TRIENNIAL CONVENTION / Baptist General Missionary Convention. Board of Foreign Missions – 1814-46. 1,738p – 1 – 60.83 – us Baptist [240]

PROCEEDINGS OF U.S. ARMY COURTSMARTIAL AND MILITARY COMMISSIONS OF UNION SOLDIERS EXECUTED BY U.S. MILITARY AUTHORITIES, 1861-1866 – 8r – 1 – M1523 – us Nat'l Archives [355]

PROCEEDINGS, PART B / Institution of Mechanical Engineers – Management and engineering manufacture. v197- 1983- – 1,5,6,9 – us UMI [621]

PROCEEDINGS, PART C / Institution of Mechanical Engineers – Mechanical engineering science. v197- 1983- – 1,5,6,9 – us UMI [621]

PROCEEDINGS, PART D / Institution of Mechanical Engineers – Transport engineering. v198- 1984- – 1,5,6,9 – us UMI [625]

PROCEEDINGS: PHYSICAL SCIENCES / National Academy of Sciences of the United States of America – v77- 1980- – 1,5,6,9 – us UMI [530]

PROCEEDINGS: PLANT SCIENCES / Indian Academy of Sciences – v.89. 1980 – 1,5,6,9 – us UMI [580]

PROCEEDINGS. SECTION A. MATHEMATICAL AND PHYSICAL SCIENCES / Royal Society of Edinburgh – v. 61-69. 1941-1972 – 1,5,6 – us Princeton Micro [510]

PROCEEDINGS. SECTION B. BIOLOGY / Royal Society of Edinburgh – v61-70 1941-1969 – 1,5,6 – us Princeton Micro [574]

PROCEEDINGS. SERIES A: MATHEMATICAL, ASTRONOMICAL AND PHYSICAL SCIENCE / Royal Irish Academy – v24-77 1902-1977 – 1,5,6 – $22,138.00 – us Princeton Micro [500]

PROCEEDINGS. SERIES B / Physical Society. London – v62-70 no 2. 1949-57. 1532/2 – 8 – ne IDC [530]

PROCEEDINGS. SERIES B: BIOLOGICAL, GEOLOGICAL, AND CHEMICAL SCIENCE / Royal Irish Academy – v24-77 1902-77 – 1,5,6 – $22,242.00 – us Princeton Micro [500]

PROCEEDINGS. SERIES C: ARCHEOLOGY, CELTIC STUDIES, HISTORY, LINGUISTICS AND LITERATURE / Royal Irish Academy – v24-77 1902-77 – 1,5,6 – $22,242.00 – us Princeton Micro [400]

PROCEEDINGS: SESSIONAL PAPERS / Canada. Parliament – 1st-14th. 1867-1925 – 1 – us Princeton Micro [324]

PROCEEDINGS: SESSIONAL PAPERS / Canada. Parliament – 6th-8th.1860-66 – 1 – us Princeton Micro [324]

PROCEEDINGS TURKEY INDUSTRY DAY / Texas A & M University. Agricultural Extension Service – 1967-82.10 fiches – 9 – us Spaulding [636]

PROCEEDINGS UN CONFERENCE ON NEW SOURCES OF ENERGY / United Nations – 63 fiches – 9 – 110.00; 1.90f – uk UNIMICRO [621]

PROCEEDINGS, UNITED STATES OLYMPIC ACADEMY 12 – (Series: United States Olympic Academy, 12) – Pennsylvania State University, 1988 – 3mf – 9 – $12.00 – us Microform Publ [790]

PROCEEDINGS UPON THE OCCASION OF THE PRESENTATION OF PORTRAITS OF FEDERAL JURISTS TO THE UNITED STATES COURTS FOR THE SOUTHERN DISTRICT OF ILLINOIS, AT SPRINGFIELD, ON JUNE SECOND, NINETEEN HUNDRED AND THREE. – Springfield? 1903?. 124p. LL-1096 – 1 – us L of C Photodup [340]

PROCEEDINGS: WHO WERE THE LIBYANS? / Society of Biblical Archaeology – P. LePage Renouf. Jun 1891. BA-626 2 – 8 – ne IDC [930]

PROCEEDINGS...BIOLOGICAL SCIENCES / Cambridge Philosophical Society – v1-. 1923-25 – 1 – us UMI [574]

PROCEEDINGS...IN DETERMINING STATE EQUALIZED VALUATIONS / Michigan. State Tax Commission – Session of 1871-1970. 84 fiches. (Harvard Law School Library Collection.) – 9 – 1.50f – us H.U. Law [336]

PROCEEDINGS...IN RELATION TO IMPERIAL POSTAL AND TELEGRAPHIC COMMUNICATIONS THROUGHOUT CANADA – Ottawa: Printed by order of Parliament by B. Chamberlin, 1888. 03397. (Pre-1900 Canadiana) – 9 – cn C.I.H.M. [971]

PROCEEDINGS...MILDMAY PARK, LONDON, OCTOBER 5TH TO 7TH 1886 : ADDRESSES / Conference on Foreign Missions...London, 1886 – London: John F Shaw, 1886 – 1mf – 9 – 0-8370-6037-0 – 1986-0037 – us A.T.L.A. [240]

UN PROCER EXTREMENO DESCONOCIDO. EL ILUSTRISIMO SENOR DON BENITO CRESPO DE SOLIS, OBISPO DE PUEBLADE LOS ANGELES/MEXICO / Ramirez Ramirez, Tomas – Badajoz: Imp. Diputacion Provincial, 1974 – sp Bibl Santa Ana [240]

PROCES BAZAINE. / Bazaine, Achille Francois – Paris, Librairie du Moniteur universel, 1873. 804 p. LL-4064 – 1 – us L of C Photodup [340]

PROCES COMPLET DES SAINT-SIMONIENS AVEC LES PORTRAITS DES ACCUSES – Paris, B. Waree, 1832, 45 p. Les Saint-Simoniens, 1825-1834. 6999 – 9 – fr Hachette [335]

LE PROCES DAUTRICHE / Dautriche, Gregoire – Compte-rendu stenographique in extenso. Paris, Societe nouvelle de librairie et d'edition, 1905. 705p. LL-4033 – 1 – us L of C Photodup [340]

PROCES DE JOSEPH N. CARDINAL ET AUTRES, AUQUEL ON A JOINT LA REQUETE ARGUMENTATIVE EN FAVEUR DES PRISONNIERS ET PLUSIEURS AUTRES DOCUMENTS PRECIEUX,... / Cherrier, Andre R – Montreal: Lovell, 1839. SEM16P253 – 1r – 5 – Can$9.00 – cn Bibl Nat [971]

PROCES DE M. LE COMTE CH. D'AUTICHAMP ET DE M. L'ABBE LEGAULT / Autichamp, Charles, Cte d' – Paris: Pihan de la Forest, 1838 – 1 – F50.00 – fr Armell [340]

PROCES DE MARIE ANTOINETTE, DE LORRAINE D'AUTRICHE, VEUVE CAPET, DU 23 DU PREMIER MOIS, L'AN 2 DE LA REPUBLIQUE, OCTOBRE 14, 1793 – Londres: Chez J de Boffe, 1793. SEM105P951 – 2mf – 9 – Can$4.50 – cn Bibl Nat [944]

PROCES DES SAINT-SIMONIENS – Paris, Pihan Delaforet, 1832, 35 p. Les Saint-Simoniens, 1825-1834. 6998 – 9 – fr Hachette [335]

HET PROCES SNEEVLIET. DE SOCIAAL-DEMOCRATIE IN NEDERLANDSCH-INDIE / Baars, A & Sneevliet, H – Semarang, 1917. 368p – 5mf – 9 – ne IDC [320]

UN PROCES SOUS LA RESTAURATION; L'AFFAIRE DU MARECHAL NEY / Prince, J E – Quebec: L J Demers & frere..., 1901. SEM105P488 – 1mf – 9 – Can$2.25 – cn Bibl Nat [944]

DER PROCES UND DIE ACTA APOLLONII (T.U.U. 1-15/2) / Klette, E T – Leipzig, 1897 – 3mf – 9 – ne Slangenburg [240]

PROCES VERBAL DE MR. LE PENITENCIER D'EVREUX, DE CE QUI LUY EST ARRIVE DANS LA PRISON / Delangle – Paris. 1643 – 9 – fr Hachette [360]

PROCES VERBAL DU CRIME DETESTABLE DE TROIS SORCIERES SURPRISES ES FAULX-BOURGS SAINCT GERMAIN DES PREZ – Paris. 1619 – 9 – fr Hachette [360]

PROCES VERBAL, RAPPORTS, RESOLUTIONS, LOIS – 1972-73 – 1r – 1 – $49.50 – us African Imprint [324]

PROCES-D.D. MET OFFICIELE BESCHEIDEN INZAKE ZIJN [E.F.E. DOUWES DEKKER'S] VERVOLGING... – Bandoeng, 1937.-2v – 3mf – 9 – SE-1299/1 – ne IDC [950]

PROCESO A LOS TRIBUNALES / Aradillas Agudo, Antonio – Barcelona: Juan Flors, editor, 1959 – 1 – sp Bibl Santa Ana [946]

PROCESO DE ALBARRACIN CONTRA LA VILLA DE MOYA (ANNO 1525) – Albarracin – 1r – 5,6 – sp Cultura [340]

PROCESO DE PEDRO DE VALDIVIA Y.. / Barros Arana, Diego – 1873 – 9 – $1.50f – sp Bibl Santa Ana [360]

PROCESO DEL MARQUES DE SIETE IGLESIAS. DON RODRIGO CALDERON / Perez de Guzman, Juan – Madrid: Fortanet, 1918. B.R.A.H. lxxii/pp. 194-200 – 1 – sp Bibl Santa Ana [360]

UN PROCESO, DOS JUICIOS ORALES Y UN RECURSO DE CASACION / Pantoja Idrovo de Castaneda, W – Madrid: Ricardo Fe, 1905 – 1 – sp Bibl Santa Ana [340]

PROCESO ENTRE LA CATEDRAL Y LA IGLESIA DE SAN VICENTE (SIECLE 16) – Calahorra – 1r – 5,6 – sp Cultura [240]

PROCESO PLEBISCITARIO, 1989-1991 = POLITICAL STATUS REFERENDUM, 1989-1991 : CORRESPONDENCE OF THE POLITICAL LEADERSHIP AND LEGISLATIVE DOCUMENTS – (Mixed Spanish & English in both vols) – Washginton: Puerto Rico Fed Affairs Admin, dec 1992 – 12mf – 9 – $18.00 – LLMC 95-042 – us L.L.M.C. [324]

PROCESOS DE CORTES. COMPROMISO DE CASPE (ANNO 1410) – Barcelona – 1r – 5,6 – sp Cultura [355]

PROCESOS INQUISITORIALES CONTRA FRANCISCO SANCHEZ DE LAS BROZAS / Tovar, Antonio & Pinta Llorente, Miguel de la – Madrid: Instituto Antonio de Nebrija, 1941 – 1 – sp Bibl Santa Ana [946]

PROCESS: ARCHITECTURE – v1-. 1983- – 1,5,6,9 – us UMI [073]

PROCESS BIOCHEMISTRY – (1971-. 5,6. 1973-. 9) – v1-. 1966- – 1 – us UMI [073]

PROCESS ENGINEERING INDEX – 1964. 1v. 5 sections. Updated twice per yr – 5 – uk Tech [660]

PROCESS INDUSTRIES CANADA – (Cont: Canadian Chemical Processing at v60 1976. Incorporated in: Water and Pollution Control at v130 no 2 1992) – Unionville. v60-76. 1976-92 – 9 – Can$20.00y – cn Micromedia [660]

PROCESS INDUSTRIES CANADA *see*
- CANADIAN CHEMICAL PROCESSING
- WATER AND POLLUTION CONTROL

PROCESS OF WATER RESOURCES PROJECT PLANNING : A SYSTEMS APPROACH – 1987 – 196p – 9 – 92-3-102476-0 – fr UNESCO [333]

PROCESS STUDIES – (v.10-. 1980- 5,6,9) – v.1-. 1971- – 1 – us UMI [073]

PROCESS VERBAUX DES SEANCES / Lyons. France. Conseil Municipal – Oct 20, 1940-1968 – 1 – us NY Public [130]

PROCESS, WIE ES SOLL GEHALTEN WERDEN MIT WIDERTAEUFFERN – Wormbs, P.u. Ph. Koepflein, 1557. BME-137 1 – 9 – ne IDC [240]

A PROCESS-DESCRIPTIVE STUDY OF THE DRUG AFTERCARE PROGRAM FOR DRUG-DEPENDENT FEDERAL OFFENDERS / Eaglin, James B – Washington: FJC, August 1984 – 2mf – 9 – $3.00 – LLMC 95-386 – us L.L.M.C. [340]

PROCESSED FRUIT AND VEGETABLES : TRENDS IN WORLD PRODUCTION AND TRADE OF CITRUS PRODUCTS, CANNED PEACHES AND APRICOTS, AND TOMATO PRODUCTS – 1970 – 76p – it F.A.O. [338]

PROCESSED PREPARED FOOD – v146- 1977- – 1,5,6,9 – us UMI [660]

PROCESSI VERBALI / Societa Toscana di Scienze Naturali – (Missing: v33-34. 1924-25) – Pisa. v1-50. 1878-1941 – 190mf – 9 – Z-255c/2 – ne IDC [500]

PROCESSING – v. 21-. 1975- – 1,5,6,9 – us UMI [073]

PROCESSING AND STORAGE OF FOODGRAINS BY RURAL FAMILIES – 1983 – 134p – it F.A.O. [631]

PROCESSING OF NATURAL RUBBER – 1973 repr 1979 – 200p – it F.A.O. [670]

PROCESSING OF OCEANOGRAPHIC STATION DATA / Joint Panel on Oceanographic Tables and Standards Editorial Panel – 1991 – 138p – 9 – 92-3-102756-5 – fr UNESCO [550]

THE PROCESSIONAL OF THE NUNS OF CHESTER / Wickham Legg, J – 1899 – 2mf – 8 – Dfl9.00 – ne Slangenburg [240]

PROCESSIONALE AD USUM INSIGNIS AC PRAECLARAE ECCLESIAE SARUM / Henderson, W – Leeds, 1882 – 4mf – 8 – Dfl19.00 – ne Slangenburg [240]

PROCESSIONALE ROMANUM CUM OFFICIO – 1513 – 9 – us Sibley [780]

PROCESSIONARIUM ORDINIS FRATRUM PREDICATORUM – 1494 – 9 – us Sibley [240]

O PROCESSO – Conselheiro Lafaiete, Brazil. Jul 1972-Jan 1979. Very incomplete – 1 – bl Biblioteca [072]

PROCESSUS POLITIQUES A TLAYACAPAN, MORELOS, MEXIQUE / Varela, R – 9 – F70.00 – fr Ethnologie [306]

PROCES-VERBAL / France. Parlement. Assemblee Nationale – avec une table des matieres contenant les seances. 1 oct 1791-21 sept 1792 – 1 – fr A.C.R.P.P. [324]

PROCES-VERBAL / France. Parlement. Convention Nationale – 1792 a l'an IV – 1 – fr A.C.R.P.P. [324]

PROCES-VERBAL DES SEANCES / France. Parlement. Chambre de l'Ordre de la noblesse aux Etats Generaux a Versailles – 1789 – 1 – fr A.C.R.P.P. [324]

PROCES-VERBAL HISTORIQUE DES ACTES DU CLERGE DISPUTE A L'ASSEMBLEE DES ETATS GENERAUX DES ANNEES 1789 ET 1790 / France. Parlement. Assemblee des Etats generaux – 1 – fr A.C.R.P.P. [324]

PROCES-VERBAUX / Reunion. Conseil general – 1870-1911, 1913-20. MQ 1894, 1903 – 1 – fr A.C.R.P.P. [073]

PROCES-VERBAUX DE LA SOCIETE DES MISSIONS EVANGELIQUES DE PARIS – Paris. 1822-1935 – 327mf – 9 – H-2102/1 – ne IDC [240]

PROCES-VERBAUX ET MEMOIRES / Academie des Sciences, Belles-lettres et arts. Besancon – 1891-1942 – 1 – $92.00 – us L of C Photodup [944]

Prochaska, Bruno *see* HEITERER GUCKKASTEN

PROCHE-ORIENT CHRETIEN – Jerusalem, 1951-68 – 93mf – 9 – H-2508/1 – ne IDC [240]

Prochiantz, Alain *see* PERSPECTIVES ON DEVELOPMENTAL NEUROBIOLOGY

Procksch, Otto *see* GESCHICHTSBE-TRACHTUNG UND GESCHICHTLICHE UEBERLIEFERUNG...PROPHETEN

PROCLAMATION AUX FEMMES SUR LA NECESSITE DE FONDER UNE SOCIETE DES DROITS DE LA FEMME / Saint Amand, Adele de – Paris, H. Fournier, s.d., 4 p. Les Saint-Simoniens, 1825-1834. 6909 – 9 – fr Hachette [305]

PROCLAMATION OF THE U.S. PRESIDENT PLACING INTO FULL FORCE AND EFFECT THE COVENANT WITH THE COMMONWEALTH OF THE NORTHERN MARIANA ISLANDS, AND THE COMPACTS OF FREE ASSOCIATION WITH THE FEDERATED STATES OF MICRONESIA AND THE REPUBLIC OF THE MARSHALL ISLANDS : ISSUED ON NOV 3, 1986 BY PRESIDENT RONALD REAGAN, WITH ACCOMPANYING WHITE HOUSE STATEMENT AND THE EXECUTIVE ORDER PLACING RESPONSIBILITY FOR RELATIONS WITH THE COMMONWEALTH OF THE NORTHERN MARIANA ISLANDS ... / U.S. President – (Typescript; various pagination) – n.p, n.d. – 1mf – 9 – $1.50 – LLMC 82-100F, Title 65 – us L.L.M.C. [324]

PROCLAMATIONS / Great Britain. General Officer Commanding Forces in Palestine – Published by the Authority of the General Officer Commanding His Britannic Majesty's Forces in Palestine. Jerusalem. 1948. BJ-28-104 1 – 9 – ne IDC [324]

PROCLAMATIONS AND EXECUTIVE ORDERS / Hoover, Herbert – Washington: GPO. 2v. 1974 – 18mf – 9 – $27.00 – LLMC 94-295 – us L.L.M.C. [340]

PROCLAMATIONS AUX FEMMES SUR LA NECESSITE DES DROITS DE LA FEMME / Saint Amand, Adele de – Paris: H. Fournier, n.d. 4p. (Les Femmes Collection) – 1mf – 9 – $6.00 – fr Bibl Nationale [305]

PROCLAMATIONS, BROADSIDES, BALLADS AND POEMS : THE HALLIWELL-PHILIPPS COLLECTION IN CHETHAM'S LIBRARY, MANCHESTER / Snape, Anne – 1990 – 7r – 13 – IrL£505.00 – uk Mansell Publ [800]

PROCLAMATIONS, ORDINANCES AND NOTICES / Egypt. Occupied Enemy Territory Administration (OETA) South – Aug 1919. Cairo. 1920. BJ-28-163 1 – 9 – ne IDC [324]

O PRO-COIO : VESPERTINO SEMANAL – [s.l.] 29 Set-15 Nov 1912 – 1,5,6 – bl Biblioteca [072]

Procopius *see* CORPUS SCRIPTORUM HISTORIAE BYZANTINAE (CSHB 18-20

Procopius, of Caeserea *see*
- DE LA GVERRA DI GIUSTINIANO IMPERATORE CONTRA I PERSIANI...
- DE LA LONGA ET ASTRA GUERRA DE GOTHI

PROCOPIUS VON GAZA : EINE LITERARHISTORISCHE STUDIE / Eisenhofer, Ludwig – Freiburg im Breisgau, St. Louis, Mo.: Herder, 1897 – 1mf – us A.T.L.A. [240]

Procter, Adelaide Anne *see* LEGENDS AND LYRICS

Procter, F *see* THE MARTILOGE IN ENGLYSSHE AFTER THE USE OF THE CHURCH OF SALISBURY AND AS IT REDDE IN SYON. WITH ADDICYONS

Proctor *see* MEN OF PROGRESS IN WISCONSIN

Proctor, Lucien Brock *see*
- BENCH AND BAR OF NEW YORK
- THE BENCH AND BAR OF NEW YORK
- LAWYER AND CLIENT
- LAWYER AND CLIENT; OR, THE TRIALS AND TRIUMPHS OF THE BAR

PROCULTURA. TRABAJOS DE EXTENSION PEDAGOGICA / Colegio San Jose de Azuaga – Badajoz: Tip. y Lib. de Antonio Arqueros, 1920 – sp Bibl Santa Ana [946]

EL PROCURADOR GENERAL – Ano 1814 (16-i/31-XII) – 52mf – 9 – sp Cultura [946]

PROCURADORES DE LOS TRIBUNALES EJERCIENTES EN ESPANA / Themudo Quiros, Florencio & Gragera Vega, Silverio – Badajoz: Tip. Clasica, 1946 – sp Bibl Santa Ana [946]

PROCUREMENT SUPPORT IN VIETNAM, 1966-1968 – n.p., n.d. – 3mf – 9 – $4.50 – LLMC 96-067 – us L.L.M.C. [975]

PROD – Political Research, Organization and Design. v. 1-3. New York. 1957-59; cont. as: American Behavioral Scientist. v. 4-13. New York. 1960-70. Lacking: v. 3 (1) 1959. BH-1811 1 – 9 – ne IDC [073]

THE PRODIGAL SON : A MONOGRAPH:WITH AN EXCURSUS ON CHRIST AS A PUBLIC TEACHER / Willcox, Giles Buckingham – (Includes bibliographical references) – New York:American Tract Society, c1890 – 1mf – 9 – 0-8370-5852-X – 1985-3852 – us A.T.L.A. [220]

THE PRODIGAL SON / Mott, George Scudder – Philadelphia: Presbyterian Board of Educ, c1863 – 1mf – 9 – 0-8370-4503-7 – 1985-2503 – us A.T.L.A. [220]

PRODIGALS OF MONTECARLO : LEIPZIG, 1928 / Philips Oppenheim, E – Madrid: Razon y Fe, 1928 – 9 – sp Bibl Santa Ana [943]

THE PRODIGAL'S RETURN : ITS LESSONS OF PENITENCE AND PARDON / Ritchie, William – Edinburgh:William Oliphant ; London:Hamilton, Adams, 1868 – 1mf – 9 – 0-8370-4913-X – 1985-2913 – us A.T.L.A. [220]

O PRODNALOGE / Aroslavskii, Emelian – [Moskva]: Gos. izdvo, 1921 – 1 – CSUX91-B2421 – us Hoover Inst Photo [336]

Prodnigg, Heinrich *see* GOETHES WILHELM MEISTER UND DIE AESTHETISCHE DOCTRIN DER AELTEREN ROMANTIK

PRODOVOLSTVENNAI A GAZETA : IZDANIE NARODNOGO KOMISSARIATA PRODOVOLSTVII A – (Includes c.1: 1921:Jan.13-1922:May 27) – Moskva: Komissariat, 1921-1924. 4v – 1 – CSUXAKY5282-S – us Hoover Inst Photo [947]

PRODOVOL'STVENNO-KOOPERATIVNYI I SEL'SKOKHOZIAISTVENNYI VESTNIK – (Missing: 1921 n1-7) – Tula, 1921 – 1mf – 9 – COR-669/1 – ne IDC [334]

PRODOVOLSTVENNO-SEMENNOI I FURAZHNYI BIUDZHET UFIMSKOI GUBERNII NA 1921-22 GOD, PO PREDVARITELNYM DANNYM OB UROZHAE KHLEBOV I TRAV / Bragin, A – Ufa: [Gubispolkom], 1921 – 1 – CSUX91-B1227 – us Hoover Inst Photo [339]

PRODOVOL'STVENNYI VOPROS / Chaianov, A V – M., 1917 – 1mf – 9 – COR-238/1 – ne IDC [334]

PRODROBNYI KATALOG IZDANII ARKHEOGRAFICHESKOI KOMISSII VYSHEDSHIKH V SVET S 1836 PO 1918 GOD – Ed. 6. Petrograd, 1918.116p. BR-11,047/1 – 9 – ne IDC [930]

PRODROME DE FAMILLE DES FOUGERES / Desvaux, A N – (Paris). 1827 – 8 – ne IDC [580]

PRODROME DE LA FLORE ALGOLOGIQUE DES INDES NEERLANDAISES / Wildeman, E de – Batavia, 1897.-VIII, 193p. Suppl. Batavia, 1899. VII/277pp – 14mf – 9 – 6423/2 – ne IDC [580]

PRODROME DE LA FLORE DES ALGUES MARINES DES ILES ANGLO-NORMANDES ET DES COTES NORD-OUEST DE LA FRANCE / Heurck, H F van – Jersey. 1908. B-6376 2 – 8 – ne IDC [580]

PRODROME DE LA MONOGRAPHIE DES ESPECES ET VARIETES CONNUES DU GENRE ROSIER / Thory, C A – Paris. 1820. B-5764 2 – 8 – ne IDC [580]

PRODROME DES CINQUIEME ET SIXIEME FAMILLES DE L'AETHEOGAMIE / Palisot de Beauvois, A M F J – Les mousses, les lycopodes. Paris. 1805. B-5003 2 – 8 – ne IDC [580]

PRODROMI CATOPTRICORVM ET DIOPTRICORVM: SIVE, CONICORVM OPERIS AD ABDITA RADII REFLEXI ET REFRACTI MYSTERIA PRAEUIJ ET FACEM PRAEFERENTIS: LIBRI PRIMVS ET SECVNDVS / Mydorge, Claude – Parisiis: I. Dedin, 1631 – 1 – us U.W. Library [530]

PRODROMI DI UNA MONOGRAFIA DELLE SPECIE DEL GENERE MORUS / Moretti, G – Milano, 1842. 18 pp. B-6461 2 – 8 – ne IDC [580]

PRODROMI FLORAE STARGARDIENSIS SUPPLEMENTUM PRIMUM / Schultz, K F – Neobrandenburgi. 1819. B-5732 2 – 8 – ne IDC [580]

PRODROMO DELLA FLORA TOSCANA / Caruel, T – Firenze. 1860. B 5582 2 – 8 – ne IDC [580]

PRODROMO DI UN'OPERA DA IMPRIMIRSI SOPRA LE RIPRODUZIONI ANIMALI / Spallanzani, Lazzaro – Modena: Nello stamperia de G. Montanari, 1768. 102p – 1 – us U.W. Library [590]

PRODROMOS: OR, OBSERVATIONS ON ENGLISH LETTERS / Rudd, Sayer – 1755. 65p. (English Linguistics Series 1500-1800) – 9 – us UMI [420]

PRODROMUS BRYOLOGIAE MEDIOLANENSIS / Balsamo, G G & DeNotaris, G – Mediolani. 1834. B-5314 2 – 8 – ne IDC [580]

PRODROMUS DER FLORA VON BOEHMEN / Celakovsky, L – 4v. Prag. 1867-81 – 8 – ne IDC [580]

PRODROMUS DES ISLANDISCHEN ORNITHOLOGIE, ODER GESCHICHTE DER VOEGEL ISLANDS / Faber, F – Kopenhagen. 1822. B-2080 2 – 8 – ne IDC [590]

PRODROMUS DESCRIPTIONIS GRATIOLAE / Colsmann, J – Hafniae. 1793 – 8 – ne IDC [580]

PRODROMUS D'UNE MONOGRAPHIE DE LA FAMILLE DES HYPERICINEES / Choisy, J D – Geneve, Paris. 1821 – 8 – ne IDC [580]

PRODROMUS FAUNAE ZEYLANICAE / Kelaart, E F – 2048 2. 1852 – 8 – ne IDC [590]

PRODROMUS FLORAE HISPANICAE / Willkomm, H M & Lange, J M C – 3v. Stuttgartiae. 1861-80; suppl. Stuttgartiae. 1893. B-5247 2 – 8 – ne IDC [580]

PRODROMUS FLORAE MOSQUENSIS / Martius, Karl Friedrich Philipp von – ed. 2. Lipsiae, 1817. 288 pp. B-6459 2 – 8 – ne IDC [580]

PRODROMUS FLORAE NEOMARCHICAE / Rebentisch, J F – Berolini. 1804. B-5246 1 – 9 – ne IDC [580]

PRODROMUS FLORAE NEPALENSIS / Don, D – 1825 – 7 – uk Microform Academic [580]

PRODROMUS FLORAE NEPALENSIS / Don, D – London. 1825. B-5298 2 – 8 – ne IDC [580]

PRODROMUS FLORAE NORFOLKICAE / Endlicher, S L – Vindobonae. 1833. B-5921 2 – 8 – ne IDC [580]

PRODROMUS FLORAE NOVAE HOLLANDIAE / Brown, Robert – 1810 – 7 – uk Microform Academic [580]

PRODROMUS FLORAE NOVAE HOLLANDIAE ET INSULAE VAN DIEMEN / Brown, Robert – v. 1. Londini. 1810. B-231 2 – 8 – ne IDC [580]

PRODROMUS FLORAE PENINSULAE BALCANICAE / Hayek, A – 1927-33 – 7 – uk Microform Academic [580]

PRODROMUS FLORAE PENINSULAE INDIAE ORIENTALIS / Walker-Arnott, G A – London. 1834. B-5812 2 – 8 – ne IDC [580]

PRODROMUS FLORAE STARGARDIENSIS, CONTINENS PLANTAS IN DUCATU MEGAPOLITANO-STARGARDIENSI SEU STRELITZENSI SPONTE PROVENIENTES / Schultz, K F – Berolini. 1806. B-631 2 – 8 – ne IDC [580]

PRODROMUS GENERUM, SPECIERUMQUE PHYCEARUM NOVARUM / Montagne, J P F C – Parisiis, 1842. 16 pp. B-212 2 – 8 – ne IDC [580]

PRODROMUS HYMENOPTEROLOGIAE SCANDINAVICAE / Dahlbom, A G – Lundae, 1836. 104 4p., 2 pls. Z-1167 2 – 8 – ne IDC [590]

PRODROMUS MONOGRAPHIAE CASTNIAE, GENERIS LEPIDOPTERORUM / Dalman, J W – Holmiae, 1825. vi,26p. 1 pl.Z-1175/2 – 8 – ne IDC [590]

PRODROMUS MONOGRAPHIAE LOBELIACEARUM / Presl, K B – Prag. 1836. B-261 2 – 8 – ne IDC [580]

PRODROMUS PLANTARUM CAPENSIUM, QUAS IN PROMONTORIO BONAE SPEI AFRICES, ANNIS 1772-1775 COLLEGIT / Thunberg, C P – Upsaliae. 1794-1800. B-325 2 – 8 – ne IDC [580]

PRODROMUS PLANTARUM INDIAE OCCIDENTALIS / Hamilton, W – Londini. 1825. B-5947 2 – 8 – ne IDC [580]

PRODROMUS STIRPIUM IN HORTO AD CHAPEL ALLERTON VIGENTIUM / Salisbury, R A – Londini. 1796. B-2322 2 – 8 – ne IDC [580]

PRODROMUS SYSTEMATIS AROIDEARUM / Schott, H W – Vindobonae. 1860. B-1035 2 – 8 – ne IDC [580]

PRODROMUS SYSTEMATIS NATURALIS REGNI VEGETABILIS / Candolle, A P de – v. 1-17. Index. Paris. 1823-73 – 8 – ne IDC [580]

PRODROMUS SYSTEMATIS NATURALIS REGNI VEGITABILIS / Candolle, A P de – 1824-45 – 5 – uk Microform Academic [580]

Prodromus, Theodore *see* THEODORI PRODROMI COMMENTARIOS IN CARMINA SACRA MELODORUM COSMAE HIEROSOLYMITANI ET IOANNIS DAMASCENI

PRODUCER *see* AMERICAN BEEF PRODUCER

PRODUCER VS. CONSUMER / Benn, Ernest J P – 1928. 1 fiche (29x) – 9 – 1.00f – at Libertarian Micro [320]

PRODUCER-GAS TECHNOLOGY FOR RURAL APPLICATIONS – 1985 – 153p – it F.A.O. [621]

PRODUCER'S CALL – Oregon City OR. Jan 4-Mar 15 1922 – 1 – us U.O. Library [071]

PRODUCER'S CALL – (Set incl. Producer's Call (Oregon City)) – Portland, OR. -w. 22 Mar 1922-27 Mar 1925. – 1r – 1 – us U.O. Library [071]

PRODUCT DESIGN AND DEVELOPMENT – v1-1946- 1; v33- 5,6,9 – us UMI [680]

PRODUCT ENGINEERING – (v37- 1966- 5,6; v41- 1970- 9) – v1- 1930- – 1 – us UMI [670]

PRODUCT FINISHING – Cincinnati. v1-15 1936-50 – 1,5,6 – us Princeton Micro [670]

PRODUCT FINISHING – London. v1-29 1948-76 – 1,5,6 – us Princeton Micro [670]

LE PRODUCTEUR – Journal de l'industrie, des sciences et des beauxarts. Parait a Paris, chaque semaine, a partir du 1er oct 1825. Devient mensuel le 1er mai 1826. Dernier livraison: oct 1826. Forme cinq volumes in 8: 16 et 636 p, 622 p. 586 p, 547 p, 160 p. Les volumes 1 et 3 sont precedes d'un propectus. Les Saint-Simoniens, 1825-1834. 6841-6846 – 9 – fr Hachette [500]

LE PRODUCTEUR – Paris. Fond., Saint Simon. Red., Aug. Comte. 1825-26 (I-V) – 1 – fr A.C.R.P.P. [073]

LE PRODUCTEUR – Revue de culture generale appliquee. Credit, assurance, industrie, agriculture, sciences, lettres. Paris. juin 1920-juin 1922 (I-VII) – 1 – fr A.C.R.P.P. [073]

PRODUCTION – it F.A.O. [338]

PRODUCTION AND PROCESSING OF MILK FROM CATTLE IN SUB-SAHARAN AFRICA : A BIBLIOGRAPHY / O'Connor, C & Sahlu, Marcos – 1990 – 9 – $15.00 – 92-9053-155-X – et ILRI [636]

PRODUCTION AND UTILIZATION OF PRODUCTS FROM COMMERCIAL SEAWEEDS – 1987 – 194p – it F.A.O. [338]

PRODUCTION CALENDAR / National Catholic Theatre Conference – 1937-59 – 1 – us UMI [240]

PRODUCTION ET ECHANGES CHEZ LES TOUAREG KEL GRESS DU NIGER / Bonte, P – 9 – F130.00 – fr Ethnologie [960]

PRODUCTION OF FISH MEAL AND OIL – 1981 rev ed 1986 – 64p – it F.A.O. [660]

PRODUCTION OF PRINCIPAL FOODSTUFFS IN INDONESIA / Indonesia. Biro Pusat Statistik – SE-2823 1. Lacking: 1961, 1962 – 9 – ne IDC [630]

PRODUCTION RECORDS. 1946-1960 *see* SHAKESPEARE AT STRATFORD-UPON-AVON

PRODUCTION RESEARCH REPORTS / U.S. Department of Agriculture – Nos. 1-184. 1956-85. 183 fiches – 9 – 230.00 – us Updata [630]

LES PRODUCTIONS DE L'AFRIQUE OCCIDENTALE FRANCAISE / France. Office Colonial – Melun, 1918 – 1 – us Res Libr [960]

PRODUCTIVIDAD ANEXO AL PLAN. 1964/67 / Spain. Comisaria del Plan de Desarrollo Economico y Social – Madrid. 1964. BD-343 1 – 9 – ne IDC [338]

LA PRODUCTIVITE DES PETITS RUMINANTS DANS LES STATIONS DE RECHERCHE DE L'INSTITUT DES SCIENCES AGRONOMIQUES DU RWANDA / Murayi, T et al – 1987 – 9 – $10.00 – 92-9053-185-1 – et ILRI [636]

PRODUCTIVITY OF BORAN CATTLE MAINTAINED BY CHEMOPROPHYLAXIS UNDER TRYPANOSOMIASIS RISK = PRODUCTIVITE DE BOVINS BORAN PROTEGES PAR CHIMIOPROPHYLAXIE CONTRE LA TRYPANOSOMIASE / Trail, J C M et al – 1985 – 9 – $10.00 – 92-9053-113-4 – et ILRI [636]

PRODUCTIVITY OF TRANSHUMANT FULANI CATTLE IN THE INNER NIGER DELTA OF MALI = PRODUCTIVITE DE BOVINS PEULS TRANSHUMANTS DANS LE DELTA INTERIEUR DU NIGER AU MALI / Wagenaar, K T et al – 1986 – 9 – $10.00 – 92-9053-117-7 – et ILRI [636]

PRODUCTO E INGRESO DE LA REPUBLICA ARGENTINA EN EL PERIODO 1935-54 / Argentine Republic. Secretaria de Asuntos Economicos – Buenos Aires, 1955 – 1 – CSUXADJ1081-B – us Hoover Inst Photo [338]

PRODUCTS FINISHING – v1- 1936- 1; v35-5,6; v41- 9 – us UMI [680]

PROEFSTUKKEN VAN HEILIGE SINNE-BEELDEN / Outrein, J D' – O-824. 1700 – 9 – ne IDC [760]

PROEKT ARKHIVNOI REFORMY I SOVREMENNOE SOSTOIANIE OKONCHATEL'NYKH ARKHIVOV V ROSSII / Samokvasov, D Ia – M. 1902. PKG-A-88a BR-11,125 1 – 9 – ne IDC [025]

PROEKT NOVOGO UGBLOVNOGO KODEKSKA RSFSR – Moscow, 1930. 65p. BR-9806/1 – 9 – ne IDC [340]

PROEKT UGOLOVNO-PROTSESSUAL'NOGO KODEKSA RSFSR – Moscow, 1931. 40p. BR-9805/1 – 9 – ne IDC [340]

PROEKT USTAV KHAR'KOVSKAGO...EVANGEL SKIKH KHRISTIAN – Draft regulations of the Kharkov Youth Circles of Evangelical Christian Believers. Kharkov, 1910. 15p – 1 – 5.00 – us Baptist [240]

PROEKT USTAVA O PECHATI I TSENZURE – b.m., b.g. but Spb. 1871. BR-9249 1 – 9 – ne IDC [324]

PROEKT VTOROGO PIATILETNEGO PLANA RAZVITIIA NARODNOGO KHOZIAISTVA SSSR, 1933-1937 GG / U.S.S.R. Gosudarstvennaia Planovaia Komisiia – 2v. M. 1934. BD-214 1 – 9 – ne IDC [330]

O PROEKTE OBSHCHEGO KOOPERATIVNOGO ZAKONA / Ushakov, I I – M., 1915 – 1mf – 9 – COR-128/1 – ne IDC [334]

Proell, Karl *see* SIND DIE REICHSDEUTSCHEN BERECHTIGT UND VERPFLICHTET, DAS DEUTSCHTHUM IM AUSLANDE ZU STUETZEN?

Proelss, Johannes Moritz *see* SCHEFFEL

Proemsa *see* PROGRAMA FUNDACIONAL Y PROYECTO DE ESTATUTOS

PROEVE EENER KRITIEK VAN DE LEER DER GODDELIJKE VOORZIENIGHEID / Hamel, Anton Gerard van – (Includes bibliographical references) – Groningen: P Noordhoff, 1879 – 1mf – 9 – 0-8370-5082-0 – 1985-3082 – us A.T.L.A. [210]

PROF. J. W. CROUTER'S NEW AND IMPROVED PHRENOLOGICAL CHART / Crouter, John Wesley – s.l.: s.n., 1896. 02226. (Pre-1900 Canadiana) – 9 – cn C.I.H.M. [971]

PROFANGRAECITAET UND BIBLISCHER SPRACHGEIST : EINE VORLESUNG UEBER DIE BIBLISCHE UMBILDUNG HELLENISCHER BEGRIFFE BESONDERS DER PSYCHOLOGISCHEN / ed by Zezschwitz, Gerhard von – (Includes bibliographical references) – Leipzig: J C Hinrichs, 1859 – 1mf – 9 – 0-8370-9357-0 – 1986-3357 – us A.T.L.A. [450]

PROFESSION DE FOI DES SAINT-SIMONIENS / Mission Saint-Simonienne – Le Chevalier, J. Metz, impr. P. Wittersheim, 1831, 8 p. Les Saint-Simoniens, 1825-1834. 6932 – 9 – fr Hachette [335]

PROFESSIONAL AGENT – (v.48-. 1979- 5,6,9) – v.45-. 1976-. Continues Mutual Review – 1 – us UMI [073]

PROFESSIONAL BUILDER – v33-37 1968-72 – 1 – us UMI [690]

PROFESSIONAL BUILDER – v50- 1985- – 1,5,6,9 – us UMI [690]

PROFESSIONAL BUILDER & APARTMENT BUSINESS – v38-42 1973-77 – 1 – us UMI [690]

PROFESSIONAL BUILDER, APARTMENT BUSINESS – v42-50 1977-85 – 1,5,6,9 – us UMI [690]

PROFESSIONAL COMPUTING – v1- .1984- – 1,5,6,9 – us UMI [073]

THE PROFESSIONAL CORRESPONDENCE OF FRANZ BOAS / Boas, Franz – (With printed guide) – 1858-1942 – 44r – 1 – $3,740.00 – S1845 – us Scholarly Res [306]

PROFESSIONAL GEOGRAPHER – n.s. v1-1949- 1; n.s. v27- 1975- 5,6,9 – us UMI [910]

PROFESSIONAL HORTICULTURE – v1- . 1987- – 1,5,6,9 – us UMI [073]

PROFESSIONAL MEMOIRS / U.S. Army. Corps of Engineers – v1-11, no.1-60. 1909-19 – 1 – 200.00 – us L of C Photodup [355]

PROFESSIONAL PAPERS / U. S. Geological Survey – n.1-1000. 1902-76 – 1,5,6 – us Princeton Micro [550]

PROFESSIONAL PSYCHOLOGY – v. 1-10. 1969-79 – 1,5,6 – us Princeton Micro [150]

PROFESSIONAL PSYCHOLOGY, RESEARCH AND PRACTICE – v14-. 1983- – 1,5,6,9 – us UMI [073]

PROFESSIONAL RECOLLECTIONS ON POINTS OF SEAMANSHIP, DISCIPLINE, ETC / Liardet, Francis – 1849 – 9 – $20.00 – uk Libr Preservation [623]

PROFESSIONAL REMODELING – v1- 1979- – 1,5,6,9 – us UMI [690]

PROFESSIONAL REPORT – (v.10-. 1980-. 5,6,9) – v.1-. 1971- – 1 – us UMI [073]

THE PROFESSIONAL UPHOLSTERER – 1985-. -m – 1 – us UMI [640]

PROFESSIONALNOE DVIZHENIE : IZDANIE VSEROSSI ISK T SENTRALNOGO I MOSKOVSKOGO SOVETOV PROFESSIONALNYKH SOI UZOV – (Includes c.1: no.22(1919:Aug.1)) – Moskva: Vser. t sentr. sov., 19uu – 1 – CSUXANS3546-S – us Hoover Inst Photo [947]

PROFESSIONALNOE DVIZHENIE RABOTNIKOV SVIAZI, 1917-18 / Bazilevich, K V – Moskva: Izd. T SK Soi uza svi azi, 1927 – 1 – CSUX88-B1388 – us Hoover Inst Photo [947]

PROFESSIONALNOE DVIZHENIE SLUZHASHCHIKH 1917-1924 GG / Antoshkin, Dimitrii – Moskva: Izd. T SK Sovtorgsluzhashchikh, 1927 – 1 – CSUX89-B7284 – us Hoover Inst Photo [947]

PROFESSIONALNOE DVIZHENIE V ROSSII V 1905-1907 GG : SZHATY I OCHERK / Ainzaft, Samuil Semenovich; ed by Milonova, U. – Moskva: "Trud i kniga", 1925 – 1 – CSUX89-B7264 – us Hoover Inst Photo [947]

PROFESSIONALNO-TEKHNICHESKOE OBRAZOVANIE V ROSSII ZA 1917-1921 GG : IUBILEINY I [SIC] SBORNIK / Glavprofobr (RSFSR) – Moskva: Gos. izd-vo, 1922 – 1 – CSUX90-B5935 – us Hoover Inst Photo [947]

PROFESSIONELLES BEWUSSTSEIN VON GEWERBE- UND GYMNASIALLEHRAMTSKANDIDATEN IN DER ERSTEN AUSBILDUNGSPHASE / Ommerborn, Rainer – 1994 – 3mf – DM98.00 – 3-8267-2045-8 – gw Hänsel [370]

LES PROFESSIONNELS DE L'ENSEIGNEMENT LUTTENT POUR LA LIBERATION DU PEUPLE ESPAGNOLE / Federacion Espanola de Trabajadores de la Ensenanza – Paris? 1937? Fiche W 1124. (Blodgett Collection of Spanish Civil War Pamphlets) – 9 – us H.U. College Libr [946]

PROFESSOR CHAPMAN'S REPORT ON COLLINS COAL AREA, CAPE BRETON / Chapman, Edward John – Toronto, 1873. 02424. (Pre-1900 Canadiana) – 9 – cn C.I.H.M. [622]

PROFESSOR GEORGE BARKER STEVENS, D.D., LL.D. : AN ADDRESS / Walker, Williston – [S.l.: s.n., 1907?] (Tuttle, Morehouse & Taylor Press) – 1mf – us A.T.L.A. [240]

DIE PROFETEN ISRAELS IN SOZIALER BEZIEHUNG / Kleinert, Paul – Leipzig: J.C. Hinrichs, 1905. 1 fiche – 9 – us A.T.L.A. [240]

PROFETIA DE I TVRCHI, DELLA LORO ROUINA, O LA CONUERSIONE ALLA FEDE DI CHRISTO PER FORZA DELLA SPADA CHRSTIANA / Bartholomaeus, G – Roma, 1553 – 1mf – 9 – H-8285/1 – ne IDC [945]

Proffatt, John *see*
- THE CURIOSITIES AND LAW OF WILLS
- A TREATISE ON THE LAW RELATING TO THE OFFICE AND DUTIES OF NOTARIES PUBLIC THROUGHOUT THE UNITED STATES.
- A TREATISE ON TRIAL BY JURY, INCLUDING QUESTIONS OF LAW AND FACT
- WOMAN BEFORE THE LAW

PROFILAXIS DE LA FIEBRE CARBUNCOSA : TESIS DOCTORAL / Diaz Villar Martinez, Juan Manuel – Madrid: Hijos de R. Alvarez, 1907 – 1 – sp Bibl Santa Ana [616]

PROFILAXIS DE LAS ENFERMEDADES INFECCIOSAS DEL GANADO DE CERDA / Diaz Villar Martinez, Juan Manuel – Madrid: T Hijos de R Ramirez, 1908 – 1 – sp Bibl Santa Ana [616]

PROFILE : CURRENT CANADIAN PROVINCIAL DOCUMENTS / (Canada) – 1973-1978 – 9 – cn Micromedia [971]

PROFILE OF EDUCATION IN NEW BRUNSWICK – Fredericton. v1-12. 1962-73 – 5 – Can$100.00 – cn Micromedia [370]

PROFILES IN COURAGE / Kennedy, John F – In Indonesian. SE-11,669 1. 1964 – 9 – ne IDC [920]

PROFILS ET TYPES DE LA LITTERATURE ALLEMANDE / Combes, Ernest – (Includes bibliographical references and index) – Paris: Librairie Fischbacher, 1888 – 1r – 1 – us U.W. Library [430]

PROFIT : THE MAGAZINE FOR CANADIAN ENTREPRENEURS – (Cont: Small Business at v9 1990) – Toronto. v9-13. 1990-94 – 9 – Price varies – cn Micromedia [650]

THE PROFIT MOTIVE / Flew, Anthony – 2fiches (29x) – 9 – 1.00f – at Libertarian Micro [320]

PROFIT: THE MAGAZINE FOR CANADIAN ENTREPRENEURS *see* SMALL BUSINESS

A PROFITABLE AND NECESSARIE BOOKE OF OBSERVATIONS / Clowes, William – M 326. 1596 – 9 – ne IDC [610]

PROFITABLE AND NECESSARIE BOOKE OF OBSERVATIONS / Clowes, William – 1596 – 9 – 15.00 – us Scholars' Facs [616]

PROFITS : BILINGUE; PUBLICATION POUR PROMOUVOIR LES SERVICES DE LA BANQUE FEDERALE DE DEVELOPPEMENT – Montreal. v1 n1. Jul 1981-dec 1991 – 1r – 1 – cn Can Microfilming [072]

PROFITS, DIVIDENDS AND THE LAW. / Reiter, Prosper, jr – New York: Ronald Press Co., 1926. 260p. LL-1061 – 1 – us L of C Photodup [340]

PROFSOIUZYI KHOZIAISTVENNOE STROITELSTVO / Gornberg, B – Moskva: Kn-vo VT SSPS, 1928 – 1 – CUX89-B7333 – us Hoover Inst Photo [947]

PROFYTELYCK CABINET, VOOR DEN CHRISTELIJCKEN JONGELINGH / Biens, C P – 2nd ed. C.P.B. Enkhuizen, 1642 – 2mf – 9 – ne IDC [700]

PRO-GERMAN PROPAGANDA DURING WORLD WAR 1 PAMPHLET COLLECTION – 1914-1924 – 5r – 1 – CSUXANL5395-B – us Hoover Inst Photo [943]

PRO-GERMAN PROPAGANDA IN SPAIN DURING WORLD WAR 1 PAMPHLET COLLECTION – 1914-1918 – 1 reel – 1 – CSUXANL9119-B – us Hoover Inst Photo [946]

PROGESS : A MONTHLY MAGAZINE OF ADVANCED THOUGHT – v1-7 (all publ). 1883-1887 – 2r – 1 – $120.00 – us UPA [335]

PROGETTO DI PROGRAMMA DI SVILUPPO ECONOMICO PER IL QUINQUENNIO 1965-1969 / Italy. Ministero del Bilancio – Roma. 1965 – 9 – ne IDC [338]

DIE PROGNOSE DER RAUSCHGIFTSUCHTEN / Riechert, Traugott – 1995 – 1mf – 9 – DM48.00 – 3-8267-3167-0 – gw Hänsel [616]

PROGNOSIS AND MONITORING OF SALINITY AND SODICITY – PRINCIPLES AND THEIR APPLICATION – it F.A.O. [631]

PROGNOSIS OF SALINITY AND ALKALINITY – 1976 – 272p – it F.A.O. [631]

A PROGRAM FOR ESTABLISHING THE PRIMARY OPERATIVE ROLES OF THE PASTOR AT THE FIRST BAPTIST CHURCH OF BENTON, KENTUCKY / Morgan, Herschel Darrell – 1981 – 1 – 6.24 – us Baptist [240]

PROGRAM FOR INCREASING PRODUCTION OF FOOD AND FOREST PRODUCTS FOR THE YEAR 1967 / Indonesia. Departemen Pertanian – SE-6939 1 – 9 – ne IDC [630]

PROGRAM NOTES / Association of University Programs In Health Administration – (1977-5,6,9) – 1966- – 1 – us UMI [370]

A PROGRAM OF CHURCH GROWTH FOR EUTAW BAPTIST CHURCH, EUTAW, ALABAMA / Smith, Jimmy Ray – 1982 – 1 – 5.00 – us Baptist [240]

A PROGRAM OF NEW CHURCH MEMBER ORIENTATION IN THE FAIRFAX BAPTIST CHURCH, VALLEY, ALABAMA / Brooks, Michael John – 1982 – 1 – 5.00 – us Baptist [240]

A PROGRAM OF OUTREACH THROUGH RECREATION AT THE HUFFMAN BAPTIST CHURCH / Dorris, Charles Ellis – 1982 – 1 – 5.68 – us Baptist [240]

A PROGRAM OF PREPARATION FOR MARRIAGE FOR THE YOUTH OF THE RICH POND BAPTIST CHURCH / Browning, Robert Franklin – 1982 – 1 – $5.68 – us Baptist [240]

PROGRAM OF RECONSTRUCTION / Greece. Greek Board of Reconstruction – D-1307 1. 1947 – 9 – ne IDC [330]

PROGRAM OF THE ANNUAL MEETING / American Historical Association – v. 1-90. 1886-1975. With 91 (1976)+, this material is included in the micro-edition of AMERICAN HISTORICAL ASSOCIATION. PROCEEDINGS – 1 – us UMI [970]

A PROGRAM OF VISITATION FOR A CHURCH IN A SUBURBAN METROPOLIS / Langham, E James – 1981 – 1 – 5.36 – us Baptist [240]

PROGRAM OPERATIONS STATUS REPORT AS OF JUNE 10, 1964 / U.S. Agency for International Development – SE 5685 1. 1964 – 9 – ne IDC [337]

PROGRAM PERSPECTIVES – New York, NY. May 1975-Oct 1985 – 1 – us A.J.P.C. [071]

PROGRAM TUNTUTAN SOBSI UNTUK SANDANG PANGAN DAN DEMOKRASI / Sentral Organisasi Buruh Seluruh Indonesia. Kongres Nasional. 3d Solo Surakarta, 1960 – SE 4475 1. 1960 – 9 – ne IDC [025]

PROGRAMA CUATRIENAL DE INVERSIONES PUBLICAS, 1962-1965 / Honduras. Consejo Nacional de Economia – D-1322 1. 1961 – 9 – ne IDC [338]

PROGRAMA DE 2ND CURSO DE RELIGION (3RD DEL BACHILLERATO) HISTORIA DE LA IGLESIA Y LITURGIA 1937-1938 / Garcia y Garcia, Casimiro – Caceres: Tip. La Minerva, s.a. – sp Bibl Santa Ana [240]

PROGRAMA DE ACAO ECONOMICA DO GOVERNO, 1964-1966 (SINTESE) / Brazil. Ministerio do Planjamento e Coordenacao Economica – Rio de Janeiro. 1964 – 9 – ne IDC [338]

PROGRAMA DE ACCION COMUN PARA LA CREACION DEL PARTIDO UNICO DEL PROLETARIADO / Partido Comunista de Espana. Comite Central – n.p. 1937? Fiche W1100. (Blodgett Collection of Spanish Civil War Pamphlets) – 9 – us H.U. College Libr [946]

PROGRAMA DE ACTOS QUE SE CELEBRARAN CON MOTIVO DEL 10TH ANIVERSARIO DE LA IMPLANTACION DE LA ENSENANZA LABORAL EN TRUJILLO / Instituto Laboral "Garcia de Paredes". Trujillo – Trujillo: S.B. Pena, 1960 – 1 – sp Bibl Santa Ana [331]

PROGRAMA DE CUADROS DE HISTORIA NATURAL / Aguas Monreal, Mariano – 1894 – 9 – 1.50f – sp Bibl Santa Ana [574]

PROGRAMA DE DESARROLLO ECONOMICO Y SOCIAL. 1963-1970 / Panama. Direccion General de Planificacion y Administracion – Panama. 1963. BD-205 1 – 9 – ne IDC [338]

PROGRAMA DE ENCICLOPEDIA FILOSOFICA / Nieto y Serrano, M – Madrid; 1877 – 3mf – 9 – sp Cultura [100]

PROGRAMA DE EXAMEN DE GEOGRAFIA / Arenas Lopez, Anselmo – 1893 – 9 – 1.50f – sp Bibl Santa Ana [370]

PROGRAMA DE FERIAS Y FIESTAS EN HONOR DEL SANTISIMO CRISTO DE LA PAZ. SEPTIEMBRE 1976 / Cheles. Ayuntamiento – Olivenza: Imp. Suc. de Martinez Rengifo, 1975 – 1 – sp Bibl Santa Ana [390]

PROGRAMA DE FESTEJOS DE...FERIA DE AGOSTO 1980 – Miajadas: Imp. Gexme 2, 1980 – 1 – sp Bibl Santa Ana [390]

PROGRAMA DE FESTEJOS EN HONOR DE SAN MARCOS 1976 – Caceres: Tip. La Minerva, 1976 – 1 – sp Bibl Santa Ana [240]

PROGRAMA DE FESTEJOS EN HONOR DE SU SANTO PATRON SANTIAGO APOSTOL. JULIO, 1972 – Zorita: Imp. Carrasco, 1972 – 1 – sp Bibl Santa Ana [240]

PROGRAMA DE FESTEJOS EN HONOR DEL EMIGRANTE 1972 / Torrejoncillo. Ayuntamiento – Caceres: Imp. La Minerva, 1972 – 1 – sp Bibl Santa Ana [390]

PROGRAMA DE FESTEJOS QUE EN HONOR DE SU PATRONA LA SANTISIMA VIRGEN DEL ROSARIO, CELEBRA LA BARRIADA DE HUERTAS DE ANIMAS 1971 / Trujillo. Ayuntamiento – Caceres: Imp. Rodriguez, 1971 – sp Bibl Santa Ana [390]

PROGRAMA DE FIESTAS DURANTE LOS DIAS...1971 – Jaraiz de la Vera: Imp. La Verata, 1971 – 1 – sp Bibl Santa Ana [390]

PROGRAMA DE GEOGRAFIA / Gonzalez Cuadrado, Antonio – 1894 – 9 – 1.50f – sp Bibl Santa Ana [910]

PROGRAMA DE LA ASIGNATURA DE CASTELLANO.(PRIMO CURSO) / Castillo, Manuel – 1898 – 9 – 1.50f – sp Bibl Santa Ana [440]

PROGRAMA DE LAS LECCIONES DE DERECHO INTERNACIONAL PUBLICO / Dios Trias, D J de – Barcelona, 1890 – 1mf – 1 – ILM-2534/1 – ne IDC [327]

PROGRAMA DE LATIN 1ER.CURSO / Duque Fuentes, Martin – Caceres: Tip. La Minerva, s.a. – sp Bibl Santa Ana [370]

PROGRAMA DE LATIN 2ND CURSO / Duque Fuentes, Martin – Caceres: Tip. La Minerva, s.a. – sp Bibl Santa Ana [370]

PROGRAMA DE LATIN 3RD CURSO / Duque Fuentes, Martin – Caceres: Tip. La Minerva, s.a. – sp Bibl Santa Ana [370]

PROGRAMA DE METAS / Brazil. Conselho do Desenvolvimento – 3V. D-1243 1. 1957-1961 – 9 – ne IDC [338]

PROGRAMA DE RELIGION Y MORAL PARA LOS CURSOS 2ND, 4TH, 5TH Y 6TH DE BACHILLERATO 1937-1938 / Garcia y Garcia, Casimiro – Caceres: Tip. La Minerva, sa. – sp Bibl Santa Ana [240]

PROGRAMA DE UN CURSO ELEMENTALDE FISICA. TRADUCIDO DE A MARTA EDICION FRANCESA POR DON FLORENCIO MARTIN Y CASTRO / Martin y Castro, Florencio – Caceres: Imp. de Concha y Compania, 1847 – 1 – sp Bibl Santa Ana [370]

PROGRAMA DE UNIDAD DE ACCION ENTRE LA U.G.T. Y LA C.N.T / Union General de Trabajadores de Espana – Barcelona, 1938? Fiche W1125. (Blodgett Collection of Spanish Civil War Pamphlets) – 9 – us H.U. College Libr [946]

PROGRAMA DEFESTEJOS EN HONOR DE SU SANTO PATRON SANTIAGO APOSTOL. JULIO, 1973 – Zorita: Im. Xarrasco, 1973 – 1 – sp Bibl Santa Ana [240]

PROGRAMA DEL CURSO...FORMACION PARA MIEMBROS DE COMITE DE SEGURIDAD...Y VIGILANTES DE SEGURIDAD DE LA OBRA DEL SALTO DE CEDILLO (CACERES) / Hidroelectrica Espanola – Caceres: Imp. La Minerva, 1972 – 1 – sp Bibl Santa Ana [946]

PROGRAMA DEL PRIMER CONSEJO PROVINCIAL DE LA... / Seccion Femenina de Falange Espanola...Caceres – Caceres: Imprenta Moderna, 1939 – sp Bibl Santa Ana [946]

PROGRAMA ECONOMICO DE 4 ANOS, ANOS FISCALES 1964-1967 / Puerto Rico. Planning Board – San Juan. 1963 – 9 – ne IDC [338]

PROGRAMA ECONOMICO DE CUATRO ANOS, 1967 A 1970 / Puerto Rico. Junta de Planificacion – San Juan. 1966 – 9 – ne IDC [338]

PROGRAMA ECONOMICO DE CUATRO ANOS ANOS FISCALES 1966 A 1969 / Puerto Rico. Junta de Planificacion – San Juan. 1965. BD-355 1 – 9 – ne IDC [338]

PROGRAMA ECONOMICO DE CUATRO ANOS ANOS FISCALES 1969 A 1972 / Puerto Rico. Junta de Planificacion – San Juan. 1968. BD-380 1 – 9 – ne IDC [338]

EL PROGRAMA ECONOMICO DE CUBA / Cuba. Programa Nacional de Accion Economica. (Primera Revision) – D-1279 1. 1955 – 9 – ne IDC [338]

PROGRAMA FUNDACIONAL Y PROYECTO DE ESTATUTOS / Proemsa – Badajoz: Doncel, I.G., 1970 – sp Bibl Santa Ana [946]

PROGRAMA GENERAL DEL CONCURSO HIPICO INTERNACIONAL / Concurso hipico internacional (No oficial) – (No oficial) ... Badajoz: Tip. A. Mangas, 1952 – 1 – sp Bibl Santa Ana [946]

PROGRAMA NACIONAL DE ACCION ECONOMICA / Cuba. Consejo Nacional de Economica – D-1278 1. 1951 – 9 – ne IDC [338]

PROGRAMA NACIONAL DE DESARROLLO ECONOMICO, 1961-1970 / Chile. Corporacion de Fomento de la Produccion – Santiago. 1964 – 9 – ne IDC [330]

PROGRAMA NACIONAL DE DESARROLLO ECONOMICO Y SOCIAL DE HONDURAS, 1965-69 VERSION PRELIMINAR / Honduras. Consejo Nacional de Economia – Tegucigalpa. 1965 – 9 – ne IDC [338]

PROGRAMA OFICIAL DE CULTOS Y FESTEJOS EN HONOR DE LA SANTA CRUZ / Don Alvaro – Merida: Imp. Vadillo, 1970 – sp Bibl Santa Ana [390]

PROGRAMA OFICIAL DE CULTOS Y FESTEJOS EN HONOR DE LA SANTA CRUZ...1971 – Merida: Tip. Vadillo, 1971 – 1 – sp Bibl Santa Ana [390]

PROGRAMA OFICIAL DE CULTOS Y FESTEJOS EN HONOR DE LA VIRGEN DE LA CONSOLACION DEL CASTILLO...1977 / Montanchez. Ayuntamiento – Caceres: Tip. Extremadura, 1977 – 1 – sp Bibl Santa Ana [390]

PROGRAMA OFICIAL DE FERIA Y FIESTAS. AGOSTO, 1960 / Valencia de Alcantara. Ayuntamiento – Valencia de Alcantara: Tip Avila, 1960 – 1 – sp Bibl Santa Ana [390]

PROGRAMA OFICIAL DE FERIA Y FIESTAS EN HONOR DE LA SANTISIMA VIRGEN DE PIEDRA-ESCRITA / Campanario – Campanario: Tip. R. Castillo, 1958 – sp Bibl Santa Ana [240]

PROGRAMA OFICIAL DE FERIA Y FIESTAS QUE SE CELEBRARAN EN CAMPANARIO (BADAJOZ) LOS DIAS 27, 28, 29 Y 30 DE ABRIL DE 1954 – (Tambien 1956) – Don Benito: Tip. de Trejo. s.a., 1954? – 1 – sp Bibl Santa Ana [390]

PROGRAMA OFICIAL DE FERIAS Y FIESTAS EN HONOR DE LA STMA. VIRGEN DE BARBANOS. SEPTIEMBRE 1966 / Montijo. Ayuntamiento – (Tambien 1980) – Badajoz: Tip. Clasica, 1966 – 1 – sp Bibl Santa Ana [390]

PROGRAMA OFICIAL DE FESTJOS QUE...CON MOTIVO DE LAS FIESTAS DE SAN JUAN 1969 / Badajoz – Badajoz: Tip. Barrena, 1969 – sp Bibl Santa Ana [946]

PROGRAMA OFICIAL DE LAS FIESTAS DE SAN JUAN QUE...SE CELEBRARAN...1968 / Badajoz – Badajoz: Tip. Manuel Barrena, 1968 – sp Bibl Santa Ana [946]

PROGRAMA OFICIAL DE LAS FIESTAS DE SAN JUAN...1973 / Badajoz – Badajoz: Tip. Antonio Barrena, 1973 – sp Bibl Santa Ana [390]

PROGRAMA QUINQUENAL, 1961-1965 / El Salvador. Instituto Salvadoreno de Fomento de la Produccion – D-1039 1. 2v 1961 – 9 – ne IDC [338]

PROGRAMA VENEZOLANO DE EDUCACION-ACCION EN DERECHOS HUMANOS = VENEZUELAN PROGRAM ON HUMAN RIGHTS EDUCATION AND ACTION – Caracas. 45 docs. 1988-1991 – 13mf – 9 – ne IDC [320]

PROGRAMA Y TEXTO PARA UN CURSILLO DE AUXILIARES DE PRACTICANTES / Sanidad Militar Divisionaria de la 74 Division – Caceres: Tip. Extremadura, 1939 – 1 – sp Bibl Santa Ana [355]

PROGRAMA...CASTELLANO / Montanchez, Enrique y – 1898 – 9 – 1.50f – sp Bibl Santa Ana [440]

PROGRAMACION DEL DESARROLLO / Peru. Banco Central de Reserva del Peru – 2v. Lima. 1963. BD-1841 1 – 9 – ne IDC [336]

PROGRAMACION IDEOLOGICA DEL BIMILENARIO DE MERIDA / Becerro de Bengoa, Ricardo – Caceres – 1 – sp Bibl Santa Ana [946]

PROGRAMAOFICIAL DE LAS FIESTAS DE SAN JUAN 1962 – Badajoz: Tip. Barrena, 1962. Tambien Anos: 1966, 1967 – 1 – sp Bibl Santa Ana [390]

PROGRAMAS ASIGNATURAS DE DERECHO INTERNACIONAL PUBLICO... / Bustamente, A S de – Madrid, 1891 – 3mf – 1 – ILM-2107/1 – ne IDC [327]

PROGRAMAS Y PROTECTOS DE INVERSIONES PUBLICAS 1971-1975 / Panama. Direccion General de Planificacion y Administracion. Departemento de Planificacion – Preliminary. D-1422 1. 1971 – 9 – ne IDC [338]

PROGRAMAS Y PROYECTOS DE INVERSIONES PUBLICAS 1972-1975 / Panama. Direccion General de Planificacion y Administracion – (Public Investment Programs and Projects 1972-1975). 1971. BD-1728 1 – 9 – ne IDC [338]

PROGRAMM DER HOEHEREN BUERGERSCHULE ZU QUAKENBRUECK DEN 26 MAERZ 1874...RATHHAUSES / Gessner, Th – 1874?. 1 fiche – 9 – us A.T.L.A. [240]

PROGRAMM DER K.K. DEUTSCHEN STAATS-REALSCHULE IN BUDWEIS – 1875 – 1 – us I.U. Libraries [370]

DAS PROGRAMM DER OPPOSITION : DIE DREI VORSITZENDEN DER SOZIALDEMOKRATISCHEN BUNDESTAGSFRAKTION UEBER DIE ZIELE DER OPPOSITION. / Schumacher, Kurt & Ollenhauer, Erich & Schmid, Carlo – Hannover 1949 – 1 – DM30.00 – gw Mikro Press [943]

PROGRAMM DER REALSCHULE ERSTER ORDNUNG ZU QUAKENBRUECK – S.l.: s.n., 1879 (Quakenbrueck: Heinrich Buddenberg) – 1mf – 9 – 0-8370-3260-1 – 1985-1260 – us A.T.L.A. [220]

PROGRAMM UND ORGANISATIONS-STATUT / Demokratisch-Zionistische Fraktion – Berlin. 1902. BJ-28-29 1 – 9 – ne IDC [956]

PROGRAMMA DI SVILUPPO ECONOMICO 1965-1969 PER IL QUINQUENNIO 1966-1970. PRESENTATA DEL MINISTERIO DEL BILANCIO ON. PIERACCINI, E APPROVATA DA CONSIGLIO DEI MINISTRI IL 29 OTT 1965 / Italy. Ministero del Bilancio – (Additional Note to the economic development program 1965 1969 for the five-year period 1966-70. Presented by the Minister of the Budget, Hon. Pieraccini, and approved by the Council of Ministers on 29 Oct 1965). Roma. Ott 1965. BD-1676 1 – 9 – ne IDC [338]

PROGRAMMA DI SVILUPPO ECONOMICO PER IL QUINQUENNIO 1965-69 / Italy. Ministero del Bilancio – Roma. 1965. BD-197 1 – 9 – ne IDC [338]

PROGRAMMA DI SVILUPPO ECONOMICO PER IL QUINQUENNIO 1966-70 / Italy. Ministero del Bilancio – Roma. 1967 – 9 – ne IDC [338]

PROGRAMMA ECONOMICO NAZIONALE PER IL QUINQUENNIO 1966-70 / Italy – (Gazzetta Ufficiale, 14 Agosto 1967, Supplemento Ordinario). Roma. 1967 – 9 – ne IDC [338]

PROGRAMMA KOMMUNISTOV (BOLSHEVIKOV) / Bukharin, Nikolai Ivanovich – Gamburg: Izd. "Krasnago nabata", 1920 – 1 – CSUX89-B3168 – us Hoover Inst Photo [335]

PROGRAMMA KOMMUNISTOV (BOLSHEVIKOV) / Bukharin, Nikolai Ivanovich – Minsk: Izd-vo "Zvezda", 1919 – 1 – CSUX89-B3872 – us Hoover Inst Photo [320]

PROGRAMMA KOMMUNISTOV (BOLSHEVIKOV) / Bukharin, Nikolai Ivanovich – Moskva: Izd-vo "Kommunist", 1918 – 1 – CSUX89-B4532 – us Hoover Inst Photo [320]

PROGRAMMABLE CONTROLLERS DIRECTORY – 1985- – 1 – us UMI [073]

PROGRAMMABLE CONTROLS *see* PC USER

PROGRAMMATION 1971-1974 / Niger. Commissariat General au Developpement – D-1393 1 – 9 – ne IDC [338]

THE PROGRAMME – Toronto: [s.n., 1862-18–?] – 9 – cn C.I.H.M. [700]

PROGRAMME DE EQUIPEMENT / Algeria. Caisse d'Equipement pour le Developpement de l'Algerie – 1959-62. (lacking 1962, v. 2). BNE-8617 1 – 9 – ne IDC [330]

PROGRAMME DE REFORME DE L'EGLISE D'OCCIDENT : PROPOSE AUX ANCIENS CATHOLIQUES ET AUX AUTRES COMMUNIONS CHRETIENNES / Michaud, Eugene – Paris: Sandoz et Fischbacher, 1872 – 1mf – 9 – 0-8370-8536-5 – 1986-2536 – us A.T.L.A. [240]

PROGRAMME DECENNAL DES INVESTISSEMENTS PUBLICS, 1948-1957 / Belgium. Ministere de la Coordination Economique et du Reequipement National – (Ten-Year Public Investment Program, 1948-1957). Bruxelles. 1948? BD-1618 1 – 9 – ne IDC [336]

PROGRAMME D'EDUCATION CIVIQUE ET MORALE DANS L'ENSEIGNEMENT PRIMAIRE / Ivory Coast. Ministere de l'Education Nationale et de la Recherche Scientifique – [Abidjan], 1983 – 1mf – 9 – DE-639/1 – ne IDC [370]

PROGRAMME D'EQUIPEMENT A LONG TERME, 1949-1952 / Morocco. Division du Commerce et de la Marine Marchande – Rabat. 1949 – 9 – ne IDC [380]

PROGRAMME D'EQUIPEMENT A LONG TERME RESULTAT DU 2EME / Morocco. Division du commerce et de la Marine Marchande – semestre 1949. Rabat. 1950 – 9 – ne IDC [380]

PROGRAMME D'EQUIPEMENT A LONG TERME RESULTATS DU 1ER / Morocco. Division du Commerce et de la Marine Marchande – Semestre 1949, Previsions pour le 2emeSemestre 1949. Rabat. 1949. BD-724 1 – 9 – ne IDC [380]

PROGRAMME D'EQUIPEMENT: NOMENCLATURE DU PROGRAMME D EQUIPEMENT PUBLIC; CONCOURS A TITRE DEFINITIF. 4 V. IN 5. 1963-66. BNE-8610/1 / Algeria. Caisse Algerienne de Developpement – 9 – ne IDC [338]

PROGRAMME DES NATIONS UNIES POUR LE DEVELOPPEMENT. RAPPORT DE MISSION D'EVALUATION / Morocco. ILO. Institute National de Formation des Cadres Techniques – Casablanca. 1970. BNE-3209 1 – 9 – ne IDC [338]

PROGRAMME D'EXPANSION ECONOMIQUE, 1962-1965 / Belgium. Ministere des Affaires Economiques – Bruxelles. 1962. BD-406 1 – 9 – ne IDC [338]

PROGRAMME DU COURS DE DROIT DES GENS... / Arntz, E R N – Bruxelles, 1882 – 3mf – 9 – ILM-1965/1 – ne IDC [340]

PROGRAMME DU COURS DE LANGUE ET DE LITTERATURE CHINOISE ET DE TARTARE MANDCHOU, PREC. DU DISCOURS PRONONCE A LA PREMIERE SEANCE DE CE COURS. LE 16 JANV / Remusat, J P A – Paris. 1815. BCH-830 2 – 8 – ne IDC [480]

PROGRAMME D'UN PRIX DE 500 FRANCS POUR LA MEILLEURE REFUTATION DE LA DOCTRINE SAINT-SIMONIENNE / Societe de la morale chretienne – Paris, impr. de Sellegue, 1832, 4 p. Les Saint-Simoniens, 1825-1834. 6987 – 9 – fr Hachette [335]

PROGRAMME EKA DASA RUDRA. CENTENARY TEMPLE FESTIVAL AT PURA BESAKIH BALI, MARCH-APRIL 1963 / Indonesia. Departemen Penerangan – SE-4346 1 – 9 – ne IDC [324]

PROGRAMME FOR ECONOMIC EXPANSION / Ireland – Dublin. 1958 – 9 – ne IDC [338]

PROGRAMME FOR ECONOMIC EXPANSION PROGRESS REPORT FOR SIX MONTHS ENDED 30 SEP 1960 / Ireland – Dublin. 1960. BD-568 1 – 9 – ne IDC [338]

PROGRAMME FOR ECONOMIC EXPANSION PROGRESS REPORT FOR SIX MONTHS TO 31 MAR 1960 / Ireland – Dublin. 1960 – 9 – ne IDC [338]

PROGRAMME FOR ECONOMIC EXPANSION PROGRESS REPORT FOR THE PERIOD TO SEP 1959 / Ireland – Dublin. 1959. BD-566 1 – 9 – ne IDC [338]

PROGRAMME FOR THE CONTROL OF AFRICAN TRYPANOSOMIASIS AND RELATED DEVELOPMENT : ECOLOGICAL AND TECHNICAL ASPECTS – 1992 – 209p – it F.A.O. [630]

A PROGRAMME FOR THE IMMEDIATE ABOLITION OF UNEMPLOYMENT / Beckerath, Ulrich von – 7p – 9 – 1.00f – at Libertarian Micro [335]

PROGRAMME GLOBAL INTEGRE / Lebanon. Ministere du Plan – (Premier document). 1970. BNE-19.710 1 – 9 – ne IDC [337]

PROGRAMME OF CHRISTIANITY: AND OTHER ADDRESSES / Drummond, Henry – New York: James Pott, 1897. 1 fiche – 9 – us A.T.L.A. [240]

PROGRAMME OF DEVELOPMENT PROJECTS FOR THE YEAR 1963 / Trinidad and Tobago – Port of Spain. 1963. BD-397 1 – 9 – ne IDC [338]

A PROGRAMME OF HIGHLAND DEVELOPMENT / Scotland. Home Department – Edinburgh. 1950 – 9 – ne IDC [338]

PROGRAMME OF LAW STUDIES. / Knox, Peter – Rockford, Ill., Register Book and Job Printing House, 1868. 21 p. LL-433 – 1 – us L of C Photodup [340]

THE PROGRAMME OF MODERNISM : A REPLY TO THE ENCYCLICAL OF PIUS 10, PASCENDI DOMINICI GREGIS / Buonaiuti, Ernesto – London: T. Fisher Unwin, 1908 – 1mf – us A.T.L.A. [240]

PROGRAMME OF SOCIAL AND ECONOMIC DEVELOPMENT IN THE ZANZIBAR PROTECTORATE FOR THE FIVE YEAR PERIOD 1STJAN. 1955 TO 31STDEC. 1959 – D 1522 1. 1955 – 9 – ne IDC [360]

PROGRAMME OF SOCIAL AND ECONOMIC DEVELOPMENT IN THE ZANZIBAR PROTECTORATE FOR THE TEN-YEAR PERIOD, 1946-1955 – Sessional Paper No. 1 of 1946. Zanzibar. 1946. BD-694 1 – 9 – ne IDC [338]

PROGRAMME QUINQUENNAL DE DEVELOPPEMENT DES TRAVAUX STATISTIQUES ET ETUDES ECONOMETRIQUES ET DEMOGRAPHIQUES AU MAROC / Morocco. Service Central des Statistiques – 1961. BNE-3101 1 – 9 – ne IDC [310]

PROGRAMME QUINQUENNAL D'EXPANSION ECONOMIQUE / Belgium – (Belgium. Parl. Chambre des Repres. Documents Parlementaries, no. 687, Session 1960-1961). Bruxelles. 1960 – 9 – ne IDC [338]

PROGRAMME QUINQUENNAL D'EXPANSION ECONOMIQUE, 1961-1965 / Belgium – D-952 1 – 9 – ne IDC [338]

LE PROGRAMME TRIENNAL DE DEVELOPPEMENT 1975-1977 / Congo – Summary in French. Bulletin de l'Afrique Noire. numero special 3rd ed. Paris. 1975. BD-1863 1 – 9 – ne IDC [338]

PROGRAMME TRIENNAL DE DEVELOPPEMENT ECONOMIQUE ET SOCIAL, 1959-1962 / Malagasy Republic. Ministere de l'Industrie et du Plan – Tananarive. 1959. BD-318 1 – 9 – ne IDC [338]

PROGRAMME TRIENNAL DE REDRESSEMENT ECONOMIQUE ET FINANCIER 1970-1972 / Mali. Direction Generale du Plan et de la Statistique – (Three-year program of economic and financial recovery 1970-1972). 3 v. Jun 1970 – 9 – ne IDC [338]

PROGRAMME TRIENNAL INTERIMAIRE 1963-1965 PREPARATOIRE AU PLAN QUINQUENNAL DE DEVELOPPEMENT 1966-1970 / Gabon – D-1068 1. 1962 – 9 – ne IDC [338]

PROGRAMMED LEARNING AND EDUCATIONAL TECHNOLOGY – v1- 1964- 1; v13- 5,6,9 – us UMI [370]

PROGRAMMES AND POLICIES FOR THE ECONOMIC DEVELOPMENT OF PAPUA AND NEW GUINEA / Papua-New Guinea. (Territory) – D-868 1. 1968 – 9 – ne IDC [338]

PROGRAMMES DE COOPERATION TECHNIQUE. / Congo. Nations Unies – Leopoldville, 1964-65. 2v. BA-702/1 – 9 – ne IDC [960]

PROGRAMMES OF INDUSTRIAL DEVELOPMENT, 1951-56 / India. Planning Commission – New Delhi. 1953 – 9 – ne IDC [338]

PROGRAMMES OF INDUSTRIAL DEVELOPMENT, 1956-61 / India. Planning Commission – Delhi. 1956. BD-277 1 – 9 – ne IDC [330]

PROGRAMMES OF INDUSTRIAL DEVELOPMENT, 1961-66 / India. Planning Commission – Delhi. 1962. BD-525 1 – 9 – ne IDC [338]

PROGRAMMES-HORAIRES DE RADIO-COLLEGE – Montreal, Canada. 1941-42; 1955-56 – 1r – 1 – Can$50.00 – cn Can Microfilming [073]

PROGRAMMING AND COMPUTER SOFTWARE – v1-20. 1975-94 – 1,5 – $65.00v – us UMI [000]

PROGRAMMING FOR AGRICULTURAL DEVELOPMENT – 1976 – 57p – it F.A.O. [338]

PROGRAMMY IMPERATORSKIKH TEATROV = PROGRAMS OF THE RUSSIAN IMPERIAL THEATERS FROM THE RUSSIAN NATIONAL LIBRARY, ST PETERSBURG : 1809, 1813-1831, 1847, 1850-1880 – 64r – 1 – $4,900.00 coll – us Ross [790]

PROGRAMMY RADIO I TELEVIDENIYA. I RADIOVESHEHANIYA – Moscow. U.S.S.R. 1969- – 1 – us UMI [380]

PROGRAMS OF STUDY / Pematang Siantar, Sumatra. Fakultas Ekonomi – SE-3491 1. 1959 – 9 – ne IDC [370]

LE PROGRES : 1ER JOURNAL FRANCAIS PUBLIE EN ONTARIO – Ottawa, Ontario. 20 mai 1858-v1 n24. 8 dec 1858 – 1r – 1 – Can$40.00 – cn Can Microfilming [072]

LE PROGRES : AGRICOLE, INDUSTRIEL, POLITIQUE ET COMMERCIAL / ed by Belanger, Louis Charles – Sherbrooke, Canada. 26 sep 1874-25 avr 1878 – 1r – 1 – Can$45.00 – cn Can Microfilming [072]

LE PROGRES – Ed. Lyon-ville. Lyon. 1970-1991 – 1 – fr A.C.R.P.P. [073]

LE PROGRES – Hull, Canada. 7 jan 1911 – 1r – 1 – Can$20.00 – cn Can Microfilming [072]

LE PROGRES : JOURNAL DE COMMERCE – Montreal, Canada. 20 jun-15 jul 1846 – 1r – 1 – Can$35.00 – cn Can Microfilming [380]

LE PROGRES – Kinshasa, Aug 1 1962-Jan 1 1968 – 17r – 1 – AF-101/3 – ne IDC [960]

LE PROGRES – Lyon. 1933-juin 1940 – 1 – fr A.C.R.P.P. [073]

LE PROGRES – Lyon, [France]: L DeLaroche, 1953-69 – us Res Libr [072]

LE PROGRES – Macon (Saone-et-Loire), Nov. 1842 – August 1843 – 1r – fr Armell [320]

LE PROGRES – Manchester, NH. v20 n20. 26 aut 1931; 9 sep 1931 – 1r – 1 – Can$25.00 – cn Can Microfilming [071]

LE PROGRES – Montreal, Canada. v1 n3. 16 nov 1907-v1 n32. 6 jun 1908 – 1r – 1 – Can$25.00 – cn Can Microfilming [072]

LE PROGRES – Morinville, Alberta. v1 n11. 29 avr 1909-27 nov 1913 – 1r – 1 – Can$50.00 – cn Can Microfilming [072]

LE PROGRES – Nicolet, Canada. 17 aut 1900 – 1r – 1 – Can$25.00 – cn Can Microfilming [072]

LE PROGRES / Parti Republicain Democrate et Socialiste de la Guyane – Cayenne. 1924-26 – 1 – fr A.C.R.P.P. [335]

LE PROGRES = THE PROGRESS : HEBDO – Montreal, Canada. v1 n1. 26 nov 1898 – 1r – 1 – Can$25.00 – cn Can Microfilming [072]

LE PROGRES – Ste-Therese, Canada. v27 n41. 4 oct 1967; v27 n42. 11 oct 1967 – 1r – 1 – Can$25.00 – cn Can Microfilming [072]

LE PROGRES – Windsor, Ontario. 6 sep 1888-v15 n23. 3 jun 1897 – 1r – 1 – Can$25.00 – cn Can Microfilming [072]

PROGRES – Revue culturelle algerienne. Dir. A. Valero. no. 1-5. Alger. mars 1953-fevr 1954 – 1 – fr A.C.R.P.P. [073]

LE PROGRES AGRICOLE DE L'OUEST – Journal hebdomadaire absolument independent. Agriculture, viticulture, elevage. Le sous-titre varie. Red. en chef H. Dorgeres. Rennes. juil 1925-juin 1940 – 1 – fr A.C.R.P.P. [073]

LE PROGRES ALBERTAIN – Edmonton, Alberta. v5 n40. 4 dec 1913-v7 n25. 19 aut 1915 – 1r – 1 – Can$50.00 – cn Can Microfilming [072]

LE PROGRES CIVIQUE – Journal de critique politique et de perfectionnement social. Dir. Henri Dumay. no. 1-689. Paris. mai 1919-oct 1932; n.s., no. 2, 4-5. juil 1939 – 1 – fr A.C.R.P.P. [073]

LE PROGRES DE COATICOOK – Coaticook, Canada. 9 mar 1950-v11 n52. 23 fev 1961 – 4r – 1 – Can$60.00r – cn Can Microfilming [072]

LE PROGRES DE FRASERVILLE *see* LE JOUR

LE PROGRES DE LA MAURICIE *see* L'HISTOIRE

LES PROGRES DE LA RAISON, DANS LA RECHERCHE DU VRAI / Helvetius, Claude-Adrien – (D'Holbach series). 1775 – 9 – fr Hachette [190]

LE PROGRES DE LA RIVE SUD : HEBDO-INDEPENDANT – Nicolet, Canada. 12 oct 1950-7 jun 1951 – 1r – 1 – Can$35.00 – cn Can Microfilming [072]

LES PROGRES DE LA VERITABLE ORTOGRAFE / Lartigaut, A – 1669 – 9 – fr I.C.S. [440]

LE PROGRES DE L'EST / ed by Belanger, Louis Charles & Belanger, L A – Sherbrooke, Canada. v1 n2. 1 sep 1883-15 fev 1924 – 12r – 1 – Can$45.00r – cn Can Microfilming [072]

LE PROGRES DE LEVIS – Levis, Canada. 11 nov 1867-23 jul 1869 – 1r – 1 – Can$50.00 – cn Can Microfilming [072]

LE PROGRES DE LIMOILOU – Quebec, Canada. v3 n8. jun 1974 – 1r – 1 – Can$20.00 – cn Can Microfilming [072]

LE PROGRES DE LOUISEVILLE – Louiseville, Canada. v3 n24. 26 sep 1899; 3 oct 1899; v5 n40. 12 nov 19O1 – 1r – 1 – Can$25.00 – cn Can Microfilming [072]

LE PROGRES DE MAGOG / ed by Beaudry, R et al – Magog, Canada. 17 aut 1949-31 dec 1991 – 33r – 1 – Can$70.00r – cn Can Microfilming [072]

LE PROGRES DE MAISONNEUVE – Montreal, Canada. 26 oct 1907 – 1r – 1 – Can$25.00 – cn Can Microfilming [072]

LE PROGRES DE QUEBEC : CAMPAGNE POLITIQUE MUNICIPALE / ed by LaFerriere, Philippe – Quebec, Canada. 28 mai 1938-23 dec 1938 – 1r – 1 – Can$25.00 – cn Can Microfilming [971]

LE PROGRES DE ROCK FOREST – Rock Forest. v1 n1. 23 mai 1979-14 nov 1979f – 1r – 1 – Can$35.00 – cn Can Microfilming [072]

LE PROGRES DE ROSEMONT – Rosemont, Canada. v2 n43. 12 jan 1956-30 dec 1991 – 23r – 1 – Can$75.00r – cn Can Microfilming [072]

LE PROGRES DE ROUYN-NORANDA / ed by Bonneville, Jean-Pierre – Rouyn-Noranda. v1 n9. 18 nov 1954-26 dec 1957 – 1r – 1 – Can$60.00 – cn Can Microfilming [072]

LE PROGRES DE SAINT-GEORGES – (Merges with: L'Eclaireur to become: L'Eclaireur-Progres 15 nov 1960) – St-Georges (Beauce), Canada. v4 n20. 1 oct 1947-10 nov 1960 – 5r – 1 – Can$60.00r – cn Can Microfilming [072]

LE PROGRES DE SAINT-LOUIS – Montreal, Canada. v1 n8. 21 dec 1907 – 1r – 1 – Can$25.00 – cn Can Microfilming [072]

LE PROGRES DE SILLERY – Sillery. v1 n10. dec 1951-avr 1956 – 1r – 1 – Can$50.00 – cn Can Microfilming [072]

LE PROGRES DE VALLEYFIELD – Valleyfield, Canada. 29 aut 1878-17 oct 1979 – 48r – 1 – Can$65.00r – cn Can Microfilming [072]

LE PROGRES DE VILLERAY – Montreal. v9 n38. 22 avr 1943-12 mai 1960 – 1r – 1 – Can$60.00 – cn Can Microfilming [072]

LE PROGRES DU GOLFE – (Merges with: L'Echo du Bas St-Laurent to become: Le Progres-Echo 6 mai 1970) – Rimouski, Canada. 15 avr 1904-1 mai 1970 – 31r – 1 – Can$70.00r – cn Can Microfilming [072]

LE PROGRES DU NORD *see* JOURNAL LE NORD

LE PROGRES DU RICHELIEU – Sorel, Canada. v2 n1. 13 dec 1945-11 mar 1965 – 6r – 1 – Can$80.00r – cn Can Microfilming [072]

LE PROGRES DU SAGUENAY / ed by Guay, A & Guay, J D – (Becomes: Le Progres-Dimanche) – Chicoutimi, Canada. 18 aug 1887-21 fev 1965 – 45r – 1 – Can$85.00r – cn Can Microfilming [072]

LE PROGRES DU SAGUENAY *see* LE PROGRES-DIMANCHE

PROGRES DU TEMISCAMINGUE – Ville-Marie, Canada. v2 n23. 24 fev 1956 – 1r – 1 – Can$25.00 – cn Can Microfilming [072]

LES PROGRES DU XIXE SIECLE / Baillairge, Charles – 1901?. 02491. (Pre-1900 Canadiana) – 9 – cn C.I.H.M. [624]

LE PROGRES MUNICIPAL – Montreal, Canada. 29 jan 1891; v1 n2. 5 fev 1891 – 1r – 1 – Can$25.00 – cn Can Microfilming [072]

LE PROGRES OUVRIER – (La Peche au Canada; abondamment illustre) – Montreal, 6 mar 1915; supp – 1r – 1 – Can$25.00 – cn Can Microfilming [072]

LE PROGRES REGIONAL *see* LE REGIONAL

LE PROGRES SOCIAL – French West Indies. 1957-1962 – 1 – us UMI [072]

DU PROGRES SOCIAL AU PROFIT DES CLASSES POPULAIRES OU INDIGENTES, SUIVI DE: PLAN D'UNE REORGANISATION DISCIPLINAIRE DES CLASSES INDUSTRIELLES EN FRANCE / La Farelle, FF de – (Condition of 19th C. French working class series). 1847 – 9 – fr Hachette [360]

LE PROGRES-DIMANCHE / ed by Vachon, Gaston – (Cont: Le Progres du Saguenay) – Chicoutimi, Canada. 7 mar 1965-29 nov 1992 – 184r – 1 – Can$85.00r – cn Can Microfilming [072]

LE PROGRES-DIMANCHE *see* LE PROGRES DU SAGUENAY

LE PROGRES-ECHO – Rimouski, Canada. v67 n5. 6 mai 1970-29 dec 1991 – 62r – 1 – Can$80.00r – cn Can Microfilming [072]

LE PROGRES-ECHO *see*
– L'ECHO DU BAS SAINT-LAURENT
– LE PROGRES DU GOLFE

PROGRES-LAURENTIDES – Mont-Laurier, Canada. 29 aut 1973-v2 n14. 3 avr 1974 – 1r – 1 – Can$25.00 – cn Can Microfilming [072]

El Progreso *see* EL PROGRESO. SOCIEDAD DE SOCORROS MUTUOS DE TORREMOCHA

EL PROGRESO. SOCIEDAD DE SOCORROS MUTUOS DE TORREMOCHA / El Progreso – Caceres: Tip. La Minerva de Serafin Rodas, sa.a 1906 – 1 – sp Bibl Santa Ana [946]

LE PROGRESS – Providence. R.I. 1898-1913 – 1 – us UMI [071]

PROGRESS : 1882-1885 / Cigar Makers Progressive Union of America – (Coll title: Labor Union Periodicals, Pt 3) – 1996 – 1r – 1 – $135.00 – 1-55655-623-3 – us UPA [331]

PROGRESS – Anacortes. Wash. -w. 1889-92 – 1 – us UMI [071]

PROGRESS = THE BROOKLYN JEWISH PROGRESS – Brooklyn, NY. 1917 – 1 – us A.J.P.C. [071]

PROGRESS = CHIN-PU – (In Chinese) – v1-11. 1911-16 (complete) – 3r – 1 – ATLA S0301 – us A.T.L.A. [073]

PROGRESS – Claremore. Okl.-w. 1893-94; 1897-1926 – 1 – us UMI [071]

PROGRESS – Clearfield. Pa. 1913- – 1 – us UMI [071]

PROGRESS – Indiana. Pa. 1870-1881; 1889-1903 – 1 – us UMI [071]

PROGRESS – (Local neighbourhood editions) – San Francisco, CA. 1949-55 – 70r – 1 – $3,500.00 – B02854 – us Library Micro [071]

PROGRESS – London. 1883-87 – 1 – uk Microform Academic [073]

PROGRESS – New York. N.Y. 1865-66 – 1 – us A.J.P.C. [071]

PROGRESS : THE OFFICIAL ORGAN OF THE NATIONAL AMERICAN WOMAN SUFFRAGE ASSOCIATION – (Monthly Suffragist newspaper) – New York, Feb 1910 – 1r – 1 – us Western Res [071]

PROGRESS – Petersburg. Va. and Index Appeal. 1879-1922 – 1 – us UMI [071]

PROGRESS – Pontotoc. Miss. 1942-1953 – 1 – us UMI [071]

PROGRESS – Water Valley. Miss. 1902-1906; 1915-1917 – 1 – us UMI [071]

PROGRESS – Wells. Nev. -w. 1949- – 1 – us UMI [071]

PROGRESS – Wells, NV. 1937-89 – 44r – 1 – $2,200.00 – UN04809 – us Library Micro [071]

THE PROGRESS – (Also known as: Encinitas Coast Dispatch) – Encinitas, CA. 1925-1926; 1927-1982 – 51r – 1 – $2,550.00 – H03211 – us Library Micro [071]

THE PROGRESS – Fredericton, NB: Boys of the Collegiate School, [1874?-18– or 19–] – 9 – cn C.I.H.M. [370]

THE PROGRESS – St-Andrews, Canada. v1 n2. 14 aut 1874-v1 n25. 22 jan 1875 – 1r – 1 – Can$25.00 – cn Can Microfilming [072]

PROGRESS AND MINING REVIEW – Basin. Mont. 1904-1908 – 1 – us UMI [071]

THE PROGRESS AND PROSPECTS OF CHRISTIANITY IN THE UNITED STATES OF AMERICA : WITH REMARKS ON THE SUBJECT OF SLAVERY IN AMERICA : AND ON THE INTERCOURSE BETWEEN BRITISH AND AMERICAN CHURCHES / Baird, Robert – London: Partridge and Oakey, [1851?] – 1mf – us A.T.L.A. [240]

PROGRESS DE LA GUADELOUPE – French West Indies. Guadeloupe. 1880, 1883-84, 1886, 1891, 1893-95 – 1 – us UMI [072]

LE PROGRESS DE L'ISLET/LE COURRIER DE L'ISLET *see* LE COURRIER DE L'ISLET

PROGRESS IN AEROSPACE SCIENCES – v1-1961- – 5,6,9 – us UMI [629]

PROGRESS IN BIOPHYSICS AND MOLECULAR BIOLOGY – v10- 1960- – 5,6,9 – us UMI [573]

PROGRESS IN BORON CHEMISTRY – v.1-3. 1964-70 – 5,6,9 – us UMI [073]

PROGRESS IN CARDIOVASCULAR NURSING – v1- . 1986- – 1,5,6,9 – us UMI [073]

PROGRESS IN CERAMIC SCIENCE – v.1-4. 1961-66 – 5,6,9 – us UMI [660]

PROGRESS IN CRYSTAL GROWTH AND CHARACTERIZATION OF MATERIALS – v1-1978- – 5,6,9 – us UMI [530]

PROGRESS IN ENERGY AND COMBUSTION SCIENCE – v1- 1975- – 5,6,9 – us UMI [621]

PROGRESS IN FOOD AND NUTRITION SCIENCE – v1- 1975- – 5,6,9 – us UMI [660]

PROGRESS IN GROWTH FACTOR RESEARCH – 1,5,69 – us UMI [610]

PROGRESS IN HEAT AND MASS TRANSFER – v.1-8. 1969-77 – 5,6,9 – us UMI [073]

PROGRESS IN LIPID RESEARCH – (Cont: Progress in the Chemistry of Fats and Other Liquids) – v1- 1952- – 5,6,9 – us UMI [540]

PROGRESS IN MATERIALS SCIENCE – (Cont: Progress in Metals Physics) – v1- 1949- – 5,6,9 – us UMI [620]

PROGRESS IN METALS PHYSICS *see* PROGRESS IN MATERIALS SCIENCE

PROGRESS IN NEUROBIOLOGY – v1- 1973- – 5,6,9 – us UMI [574]

PROGRESS IN NEURO-PSYCHOPHARMACOLOGY AND BIOLOGICAL PSYCHIATRY – v1- 1977- – 5,6,9 – us UMI [615]

PROGRESS IN NUCLEAR ENERGY : ANALYTICAL CHEMISTRY – v1- 1959- – 1,5 $633.60 $76.80v; 9 $396.00 $48.00v – us UMI [621]

PROGRESS IN NUCLEAR MAGNETIC RESONANCE SPECTROSCOPY – v1- 1966- – 5,6,9 – us UMI [621]

PROGRESS IN NUCLEAR PHYSICS *see* PROGRESS IN PARTICLE AND NUCLEAR PHYSICS

PROGRESS IN OCEANOGRAPHY – v1- 1963- – 5,6,9 – us UMI [550]

PROGRESS IN ORGANIC COATINGS – v1-12. 1972-84 – 1,5,6,13 – sz Elsevier [073]

PROGRESS IN PARTICLE AND NUCLEAR PHYSICS – (Formerly: Progress in Nuclear Physics) – v1- 1963- – 5,6,9 – us UMI [530]

PROGRESS IN PLANNING – v1- 1973- – 5,6,9 – us UMI [338]

PROGRESS IN POLYMER SCIENCE – v.1-1967- – 5,6,9 – us UMI [073]

PROGRESS IN QUANTUM ELECTRONICS – v1-1971- – 5,6,9 – us UMI [621]

PROGRESS IN REACTION KINETICS – v1-1961- – 5,6,9 – us UMI [530]

PROGRESS IN RELIGIOUS AND MORAL EDUCATION / Hall, Charles Cuthbert – [S.l.: s.n., 1904?] – 1mf – 9 – 0-8370-8518-7 – 1986-2518 – us A.T.L.A. [230]

PROGRESS IN RETINAL RESEARCH – v1-1982- – 5,6,9 – us UMI [610]

PROGRESS IN SOLID STATE CHEMISTRY – v1- 1964- – 5,6,9 – us UMI [621]

PROGRESS IN SOLVING FARM PROBLEMS OF ILLINOIS REPORT / Illinois. Agricultural Experiment Station – n.1-61. 1887-1948 – 1, 5 – us Spaulding [630]

PROGRESS IN SURFACE SCIENCE – v1-1971- – 5,6,9 – us UMI [530]

PROGRESS IN THE CHEMISTRY OF FATS AND OTHER LIQUIDS *see* PROGRESS IN LIPID RESEARCH

PROGRESS IN THE SCIENCE AND TECHNOLOGY OF THE RARE EARTHS – v1-3 1964-68 – 5,6,9 – us UMI [540]

PROGRESS IN WATER TECHNOLOGY *see* WATER SCIENCE AND TECHNOLOGY

PROGRESS INDEX – Petersburg. Va. 1923- – 1 – us UMI [071]

THE PROGRESS MAGAZINE – Summerside, PEI: T Kirwan, [1866?-18–?] – 9 – cn C.I.H.M. [073]

PROGRESS MEDICAL – (1981-. 1,5,6,9) – 1973- – 1 – us UMI [073]

THE PROGRESS OF DOCTRINE IN THE NEW TESTAMENT : CONSIDERED IN EIGHT LECTURES / Bernard, Thomas Dehany – 3rd ed. London: Macmillan, 1873 – 1mf – 9 – 0-8370-2294-0 – 1985-0294 – us A.T.L.A. [220]

PROGRESS OF EDUCATION OF SCHEDULED CASTES AND SCHEDULED TRIBES 1976-1977 / India. Ministry of Education and Culture – New Delhi, 1980 – 3mf – 9 – DE-540/1 – ne IDC [370]

THE PROGRESS OF METHODISM IN BRISTOL : OR, THE METHODIST UNMASK'D... – Bristol, 2nd ed 1743 – 1mf – 9 – MP-303/1 – ne IDC [240]

PROGRESS OF RELIGIOUS THOUGHT IN SCOTLAND / Tulloch, John – (The Contemporary Review, v. 29, March, 1877, p. 535-551) – 9 – us A.T.L.A. [240]

THE PROGRESS OF ROMANCE, THROUGH TIMES, COUNTRIES, AND MANNERS : WITH REMARKS ON THE GOOD AND BAD EFFECTS OF IT, ON THEM RESPECTIVELY, IN A COURSE OF EVENING CONVERSATIONS / Reeve, Clara – Colchester: Printed for the author by W. Keymer, 1785 – 1 roll – 1 – 1-55879-344-5 – uk Libr Preservation [410]

THE PROGRESS OF SOCIALISM : A LECTURE / Webb, Sidney – The Hampstead Society for the Study of Socialism. Tract n1. 1888 – 1r – 1 – us Ross [335]

PROGRESS OF THE CATHOLIC CHURCH IN AMERICA : AND THE GREAT COLUMBIAN CATHOLIC CONGRESS OF 1893 – 4th ed. Chicago: J S Hyland, c1897 – 2mf – 9 – 0-8370-7115-1 – 1986-1115 – us A.T.L.A. [240]

PROGRESS OF THE PLAN A SHORT SURVEY OF THE WORKING OF THE FIVE YEAR PLAN FROM APR 1951 TO SEP 1953 / India. Planning Commission – New Delhi. 1954. BD-442 1 – 9 – ne IDC [338]

PROGRESS OF THEORETICAL PHYSICS – v. 1-52. 1946-74 – 1,5,6 – us Princeton Micro [530]

PROGRESS OF THEORETICAL PHYSICS: SUPPLEMENTS – Osaka. Supp. nos.1-54. 1955-73 – 1,5,6 – us Princeton Micro [530]

PROGRESS REPORT / Colorado. Agricultural Experiment Station. Fort Collins – PR1-242; PR68 to PR69-79. 1962-69 – 1,5,6 – us Spaulding [630]

PROGRESS REPORT / Connecticut. Agricultural Experiment Station. Storrs – v. 1-57. 1954-64 – 1,5,6 – us Spaulding [630]

PROGRESS REPORT / Louisiana State University. Agricultural Experiment Station. Southeast Louisiana Dairy and Pasture Experiment Station, Franklinton – 1978-82.1 reel – 1,5 – us Spaulding [630]

PROGRESS REPORT / Louisiana State University. Agricultural Experiment Station. Sweet Potato Research Center – 1978-82.1 reel – 1,5 – us Spaulding [630]

PROGRESS REPORT / Louisiana State University. Agricultural Experiment Station. West Louisiana Experiment Station, Rosepine – 1970-82.1 reel – 1,5 – us Spaulding [630]

PROGRESS REPORT / Massachusetts. Agricultural Experiment Station – v. 1-6. 1962-66 – 1,5,6 – us Spaulding [630]

PROGRESS REPORT / Minnesota. College of Agriculture – Development and use of shortwave transmitter to trace animal movements. Nos.1-5. 1960-65 – 1,5,6 – us Spaulding [630]

PROGRESS REPORT / Minnesota. College of Agriculture. Chemical Products from Peat Project – 1954-58 – 1,5,6 – us Spaulding [630]

PROGRESS REPORT / Nebraska. College of Agriculture. Dept. of Agricultural Education – n.1-15. 1938-46 – 1,5 – us Spaulding [630]

PROGRESS REPORT / New Hampshire. Agricultural Experiment Station – v. 1-8. 1961-69 – 1,5,6 – us Spaulding [630]

PROGRESS REPORT / New Hampshire. Agricultural Experiment Station – v. 1-9. 1955-63 – 1,5,6 – us Spaulding [630]

PROGRESS REPORT / North Carolina. Agricultural Experiment Station. Raleigh – n.1-53. Jul 1943-68 – 1,5 – us Spaulding [630]

PROGRESS REPORT / North Carolina State University.Department of Sociology and Anthropology – No.69. 1979-82.1 reel – 1,5 – us Spaulding [630]

PROGRESS REPORT / Texas A & M University. Agricultural Experiment Station – No.2708-4057. 1970-82 – 1,5 – us Spaulding [630]

PROGRESS REPORT / University of Kentucky. Agricultural Experiment Station – No.187-275. 1970-83 – 1,5 – us Spaulding [630]

PROGRESS REPORT (ADMINISTRATIVE REPORTS) / Mississippi. Agricultural Experiment Station. State College – 1950-69 – 1,5,6 – us Spaulding [630]

PROGRESS REPORT FASE REHABILISASI TAHUN 1967; SUB-BIDANG PEKERDJAAN UMUM / Indonesia. Departemen Pekerdjaan Umum dan Tenaga – SE-8463 1. 1967? – 9 – ne IDC [324]

PROGRESS REPORT IN SOCIOLOGY AND RURAL LIFE / Mississippi. State University. Division of Sociology and Rural Life – v. 1-34. 1954-69 – 1,5,6 – us Spaulding [307]

PROGRESS REPORT NO. 1 / Development Projects Consulting Service (Indonesia) – SE-5051 1. June 1962- – 9 – ne IDC [338]

PROGRESS REPORT OF THE ARCHAEOLOGICAL SURVEY DEPARTMENT, SOUTHERN CIRCLE, FOR THE YEAR... / India. Archaeological Survey. Southern Circle – (Issues for 1906/07-1908/09 filmed with several other reports. Enquire for details) – Madras: Printed by the Govt Press, -1909 – 1 – us Res Libr [930]

A PROGRESS REPORT ON ECONOMIC AND SOCIAL DEVELOPMENT, 27 APR 1961-31 MAR 1965 / Sierra Leone – Freetown. 1965 – 9 – ne IDC [338]

PROGRESS REPORT ON EPIGRAPHICAL WORK, ACCOMPLISHED FROM 1887 TO 1917 / Madras. Home Department (Education) – BI-579 2 – 8 – ne IDC [410]

PROGRESS REPORT ON EPIGRAPHICAL WORK, FOR THE YEARS 1918/1919-1922 / Madras. Home Department (Education) – Madras. 1919-23. BI-581 2 – 8 – ne IDC [410]

PROGRESS REPORT ON THE DEVELOPMENT OF FISHERIES IN NORTHEAST BRAZIL / International Center for Aquaculture – No.1-2. 1972. 1 reel – 1, 5 – us Spaulding [639]

PROGRESS REPORT ON THE DEVELOPMENT OF THE WESTERN REGION OF NIGERIA, 1955-60 / Nigeria. Western – (Sessional Paper No. 4 of 1959). Ibadan. 1959. BD-755 1 – 9 – ne IDC [338]

PROGRESS REPORT ON THE DEVELOPMENT PROGRAMME FOR 1947 / Sierra Leone - Freetown. 1947. BD-538 1 - 9 - ne IDC [338]
PROGRESS REPORT ON THE DEVELOPMENT PROGRAMME FOR 1948 / Sierra Leone - Freetown. 1948 - 9 - ne IDC [338]
PROGRESS REPORT ON THE DEVELOPMENT PROGRAMME FOR 1949 / Sierra Leone - Freetown. 1949. BD-540 1 - 9 - ne IDC [338]
PROGRESS REPORT ON THE DEVELOPMENT PROGRAMME FOR 1951 / Sierra Leone - Freetown. 1951. BD-541 1 - 9 - ne IDC [338]
PROGRESS REPORT ON THE PROGRAMME FOR ECONOMIC EXPANSION FOR SIX MONTHS TO 30 SEP 1960 / Ireland - Dublin. 1962. BD-572 1 - 9 - ne IDC [338]
PROGRESS REPORT ON THE PROGRAMME FOR ECONOMIC EXPANSION FOR SIX MONTHS TO 30 SEP 1961 / Ireland - Dublin. 1961. BD-570 1 - 9 - ne IDC [338]
PROGRESS REPORT ON THE PROGRAMME FOR ECONOMIC EXPANSION FOR SIX MONTHS TO 30 SEP 1963 / Ireland - Dublin. 1963. BD-574 1 - 9 - ne IDC [338]
PROGRESS REPORT ON THE PROGRAMME FOR ECONOMIC EXPANSION FOR SIX MONTHS TO 31 MAR 1961 / Ireland - Dublin. 1961 - 9 - ne IDC [338]
PROGRESS REPORT ON THE PROGRAMME FOR ECONOMIC EXPANSION FOR SIX MONTHS TO 31 MAR 1962 / Ireland - Dublin. 1962 - 9 - ne IDC [338]
PROGRESS REPORT ON THE PROGRAMME FOR ECONOMIC EXPANSION FOR SIX MONTHS TO 31 MAR 1963 / Ireland - Dublin. 1963 - 9 - ne IDC [338]
PROGRESS REPORT ON THE THREE-AND-A-HALF-YEAR DEVELOPMENT PLAN / Kenya - (Sessional Paper No. 97 of 1955). Nairobi. 1955. BD-531 1 - 9 - ne IDC [338]
PROGRESS REPORT SERIES / Alabama. Agricultural Experiment Station - v. 1-92. 1944-69 - 1,5,6 - us Spaulding [630]
PROGRESS REPORT SOC / North Carolina State University. Agricultural Experiment Station - No. 54-68. 1971-78. 1 reel - 1,5 - us Spaulding [630]
PROGRESS REPORTS / Auburn University. Agricultural Experiment Station - No.93-116. 1971-82. 1 reel - 1, 5 - us Spaulding [630]
PROGRESS REPORTS / Kentucky. Agricultural Experiment Station - v. 1-186. 1954-69 - 1,5,6 - us Spaulding [630]
PROGRESS REPORTS / Mississippi. Agricultural Experiment Station. State College - 1938-69 - 1,5,6 - us Spaulding [630]
PROGRESS REPORTS IN SOCIOLOGY AND RURAL LIFE / Mississippi State University. Agricultural Experiment Station - 1970. No.35. 1 reel - 1,5 - us Spaulding [307]
PROGRESS REPORTS OF THE ADVISORY COMMISSION TO THE COUNCIL OF NATIONAL DEFENSE, JULY 24, 1940-MAY 28, 1941 / U.S. War Production Board - 1 roll. M186. Printed guide - 1 - us Nat'l Archives [324]
PROGRESS REVIEW - Paradise. Calif. 1925-1956 - 1 - us UMI [071]
PROGRESS WARDEN - Europa. Miss. 1905-1917 - 1 - us UMI [071]
O PROGRESSISTA - Carangola, 11 Oct 1903; Nov 1905; 8 Nov 1906 - 1,5,6 - bl Biblioteca [072]
O PROGRESSISTA : JORNAL POLITICO, COMMERCIAL E NOTICIOSO - Maceio, Alagoas. 5 Nov 1866; 25 Out 1867 - 1,5,6 - bl Biblioteca [072]
O PROGRESSISTA : ORGAM DO PARTIDO REPUBLICANO PROGRESSISTA, DEDICADO AOS INTERESSES DO MUNICIPIO - Villa Nepomuceno, 2 Jul 1922; Jun, Aug, Nov-Dec 1924; Mar-Jul, Sep-Nov 1925; 18 Feb 1945 - 1,5,6 - bl Biblioteca [072]
O PROGRESSISTA - Rio Pomba, Brazil. Apr-Jul, Sept 1935 - 1 - bl Biblioteca [072]
LE PROGRESSISTE - Journal republicain liberal. Paris. 12 juil 1896-2 juin 1914 - 1 - fr A.C.R.P.P. [073]
PROGRESSIVE - NSV. v1- 1929- 1; v35- 5,6; v39- 9 - us UMI [073]
PROGRESSIVE - 1975- - 9 - us UMI [073]
PROGRESSIVE - Chester, CA. 1955-57; 1972; 1977 - 3r - 1 - $150.00 - B02106 - us Library Micro [071]
PROGRESSIVE - Chester. Calif. W. 1946-1954; 1961-1967 - 1 - us UMI [071]
PROGRESSIVE - Portland OR. Apr 8 22 May 10 17 1938, June 24 Dec 23 1949, Apr 21 May 12 June 9 Oct 1950, June 1954, May 1956 - 1 - us U.O. Library [071]
THE PROGRESSIVE - Saskatchewan. Canada. Apr 1923-Sept 1924 - 1 - cn Commonwealth Micro [072]
PROGRESSIVE ARCHITECTURE - v1- 1920- 1; v52- 5,6; v56- 9 - us UMI [720]
PROGRESSIVE CHRISTIAN - Berlin. Pa. and Gospel Preacher. 1881-1882 - 1 - us UMI [071]
PROGRESSIVE CITIZEN - Lumberton. Miss. 1943-1947; 1949-1954 - 1 - us UMI [071]
PROGRESSIVE COMMUNIST - Cedar Vale, KS. v1. 1875 - 1r - 1 - us Ross [335]
PROGRESSIVE ENTERPRISE - Portland, OR. -w. 30 Aug 1935-11 Nov 1938. 1 roll - 1 - us U.O. Library [071]
A PROGRESSIVE GRAMMAR OF THE MALAYALAM LANGUAGE FOR EUROPEANS / Frohnmeyer, Ludwig Johannes - Mangalore: Basel Mission Book & Tract Depository, 1889 - us Res Libr [490]
PROGRESSIVE GROCER - (1983-. 1,5,6,9) - v1-. 1922- - 1 - us UMI [073]
PROGRESSIVE MEN OF IOWA / Cure, B F - (Des Moines: Conaway and Shaw Publ., 1899). Vols. 1-2. Iowa Reel 3. (The Cox Library Collection) - 5 - us Americana [978]
PROGRESSIVE MEN OF THE STATE OF MONTANA / A.W. Bowen and Co - Chicago, 1886. Montana reel 3. The Cox Library Collection - 5 - us Americana [920]
PROGRESSIVE MEN OF THE STATE OF WYOMING / A.W. Bowen and Co - Chicago, 1903. Wyoming Reel 2. The Cox Library Collection - 5 - us Americana [978]
PROGRESSIVE MEN OF WESTERN COLORADO / A.W. Bowen and Co - Chicago, 1905. Colorado Reel 3. The Cox Library Collection - 5 - us Americana [978]
Progressive National Baptist Convention *see* MISCELLANEOUS REPORTS AND PAMPHLETS
PROGRESSIVE ORTHODOXY : A CONTRIBUTION TO THE CHRISTIAN INTERPRETATION OF CHRISTIAN DOCTRINES - Boston: Houghton, Mifflin, 1892, c1885 - 1mf - 9 - 0-8370-5128-2 - 1985-3128 - us A.T.L.A. [240]
PROGRESSIVE REVIEW - London, UK. 1896-97. -irr. 1/2 reel - 1 - uk British Libr Newspaper [072]
PROGRESSIVE SCHOOLS DON'T HAVE TO BE RADICAL, JUST DIFFERENT / Byrnes, Michael - 1973, 2p - 9 - 1.00f - at Libertarian Micro [335]
THE PROGRESSIVE STUDENT - Quebec, Canada: Wallace College. v1 n2. fev 1899 - 1r - 1 - Can$25.00 - cn Can Microfilming [370]
PROGRESSIVE TIMES - Port Clinton, Ohio. 1922-31 - 2r - 1 - $32.50r - us Archival [071]
THE PROGRESSIVE WOMAN *see* THE COMING NATION
THE PROGRESSIVENESS OF MODERN CHRISTIAN THOUGHT / Lindsay, James - Edinburgh: William Blackwood, 1892. 1 fiche - 9 - us A.T.L.A. [240]
O PROGRESSO - Araxa, 1 Feb, Jun-2 Jul 1892 - 1,5,6 - bl Biblioteca [072]
O PROGRESSO - Cidade do Rio Preto, 16 Apr 1939 - 1,5,6 - bl Biblioteca [072]
O PROGRESSO : FOLHA IMPARCIAL - Varginha, 12 Oct 1913 - 1,5,6 - bl Biblioteca [072]
O PROGRESSO : JORNAL INDEPENDENTE, LITTERARIO E NOTICIOSO - Alvinopolis, 17 May 1959-3 Jan 1960 - 1,5,6 - bl Biblioteca [072]
O PROGRESSO : JORNAL POLITICO, LITTERARIO E COMMERCIAL - '(s.l.')-Sao Luis, Brazil. 4 Jan 1847-Jun 1852. Jan 1853-Dec 1855. Jul 1856-May 1857. Mar 1861-31 Jan 1862 - 1,5,6 - bl Biblioteca [072]
O PROGRESSO - Manacapuru, Amazonas. 1 Jan-Dez 1911; Jan, Mar-14 Abr 1912 - 1,5,6 - bl Biblioteca [072]
O PROGRESSO : ORGAO DO PARTIDO CONSERVADOR DO BAIXOS. FRANCISCO - Penedo, Alagoas. 19 Set 1882 - 1,5,6 - bl Biblioteca [072]
O PROGRESSO - Penedo, Alagoas. 20 Nov 1922-Jan 1923; Ago-31 Dez 1926 - 1,5,6 - bl Biblioteca [072]
O PROGRESSO : PERIODICO CRITICO, NOTICIOSO, LITTERARIO E FEDERALISTA - Maceio, Alagoas. 10 Out 1888 - 1,5,6 - bl Biblioteca [072]
O PROGRESSO - Rio Jurua, Acre. 7 Set-5 Out 1904 - 1,5,6 - bl Biblioteca [072]
O PROGRESSO - Santa Rita do Jacutinga, Brazil. Feb 1927-Dec 1954. Widely scattered issues except 1948 and 1953 complete - 1 - bl Biblioteca [072]
O PROGRESSO - Uberlandia, Brazil. Aug 1912 - 1 - bl Biblioteca [072]
IL PROGRESSO ITALO-AMERICANO - New York, 1886-1950 - 157r - 1 - us Ross [071]
IL PROGRESSO ITALO-AMERICANO - New York. Daily, Italian. Jan 1886-Dec 1950. Incomplete - 1 - us NY Public [071]
PROGRESSOR-TIMES - Carey, Ohio, 1971-1995 - 16r - 1 - $32.50r - us Archival [071]
PROGRESSUS REI BOTANICAE / Lotsy, J P - Jena, 1907-1917. v. 1-5. B-7342 1 - 9 - ne IDC [580]
PROGULKA PO S.-PETERBURGSKOI IMP. PUBLICHNOI BIBLIOTEKA / Mintslof - Spb. 1872. BR-4625 2 - 8 - ne IDC [020]
LA PROHIBITION : L'UNION PROHIBITIONNISTE DES CITOYENS DE QUEBEC - (Quebec, Canada. 22 sep-3 oct 1917) - 1r - 1 - Can$25.00 - cn Can Microfilming [360]
PROHIBITION: GREAT SPEECH OF SIR A. T. GALT, G.C.M.G / Galt, Alexander Tilloch - Ottawa?: s.n., 1867?. 04229. (Pre-1900 Canadiana) - 9 - cn C.I.H.M. [971]
PROHIBITION IN KANSAS AND THE KANSAS PROHIBITORY LAW / Bradford, Simeon Briggs - Topeka, Crane, 1889. 36, 28 p. LL-585 - 1 - us L of C Photodup [340]
Prohibition Party *see* PAPERS
THE PROHIBITION PLEBISCITE: IS IT TO BE UNTRAMMELLED AND FAIR? - 1898?. 05163. (Pre-1900 Canadiana) - 9 - cn C.I.H.M. [360]
THE PROHIBITION PLEBISCITE: VOTING SEPTEMBER 29TH, 1898: AN APPEAL - Toronto: Office of the Dominion Alliance, 1898?. 05162. (Pre-1900 Canadiana) - 9 - cn C.I.H.M. [360]
PROHIBITION STAR - Ord, NE. -w. Jun 1878; Apr 1881-Mar 1885; Mar 1886 - 1 - us NE Hist [071]
PROHIBITION STAR - Salem OR. May 13 1886, May 13 20 June 3 10 1886, Feb 10 Mar 3 1887 - 1 - us U.O. Library [071]
PROHIBITORY LEGISLATION IN THE UNITED STATES / McCarthy, Justin - London, Tinsley, 1872. 60 p. LL-1048 - 1 - us L of C Photodup [340]
PROIA - Athens, Greece. -d. 2 May 1940-5 April 1941. 3 reels - 1 - uk British Libr Newspaper [949]
PROIZKHOD I ZNACHENIE NA IMENATA NA NASHITE GRADOVE I SELA, REKI, PLANINI I MESTA / Mikov, V - (Nauka izd., nr. 1). Soffia, 1943 - 8 - BR-3952 2 - ne IDC [947]
O PROIZKHOZDENII RUSI / Pogodin, M P - Razsuzhdenie. M. 1825. BR-8318 2 - 8 - ne IDC [947]
PROIZVODSTVENNAI A PROPAGANDA : RECH NA MOSKOVSKO I GUBERNSKO I KONFERENTSII / Bukharin, Nikolai Ivanovich - Moskva: Gos. izd-vo, 1920 - 1 - CSUX89-B3820 - us Hoover Inst Photo [303]
PROIZVODSTVENNAIA KOOPERATSIIA I ELEKTRIFIKATSIIA SEL'SKOGO KHOZIAISTVA / Chizhikov, OL - M., 1924 - 2mf - 9 - COR-526/1 - ne IDC [334]
PROJECT ANNOUNCEMENT / University of Missouri. Agricultural Experiment Station - 1915-35.No.1-33. 1 reel - 1,5 - us Spaulding [630]
PROJECT ANNUAL REPORT / Auburn University. Extension Service - 1963 - 1,5,6 - us Spaulding [630]
PROJECT AUDIT REPORT: MALARIA ERADICATION, DEC. 20, 1957 THROUGH DEC. 31, 1961 / U.S. Agency for International Development - SE 11,628 1. 1962 - 9 - ne IDC [324]
PROJECT "BLUEBOOK." - 94 rolls. T1206 - 1 - us Nat'l Archives [975]
PROJECT CYCLE - 1986 - 99p - it F.A.O. [300]
PROJECT DE LOI PORTANT APPROB. DU 1ER PROGR. D'EXP. ECONOMIQUE / Belgium - (Belgium. Parl. Senat. Documents Parlementaires, no. 238, Session 1962-1963, 28 Mai 1963). Bruxelles. 1963 - 9 - ne IDC [338]
PROJECT EVALUATION : METHODOLOGIES AND TECHNIQUES / Soumelis, Constantin G - 2nd ed 1980 - 137p - 9 - 92-3-101456-0 - fr UNESCO [000]
PROJECT EVALUATION : PROBLEMS OF METHODOLOGY - 1984 - 141p - 9 - 92-3-102132-X - fr UNESCO [650]
PROJECT HISTORIES AND REPORTS OF RECLAMATION BUREAU PROJECTS, 1905-25 / U.S. Bureau of Reclamation - 141 rolls. M96 - 1 - us Nat'l Archives [324]
PROJECT IDENTIFICATION IN SMALL PELAGIC FISHERIES : INDONESIA, INDIA, THAILAND, MOROCCO - 1987 - 74p - it F.A.O. [338]
PROJECT REPORT CONCERNING WORKERS EDUCATION IN LIBYA / International Labour Organisation - Report to the Government of Libya on Workers Education. Geneva. 1971. Ed. by A. Abualam. BNE-711 1 - 9 - ne IDC [331]
PROJECT REPORT ON A MANPOWER INFORMATION PROGRAMME IN LIBYA / ed by Rijn, C P van - Report to the Government of the United Kingdom of Libya on a manpower information programme. Geneva. 1962. 24 pp. BNE-910 1 - 9 - ne IDC [331]
PROJECT REPORT ON LABOUR LEGISLATION AND LABOUR ADMINISTRATION IN LIBYA / ed by Joukhadar, I - Report to the Government of Libya on Labour Legislation and Labour Administration. Geneva. 1968. III, 104 pp., tables. BNE-911 1 - 9 - ne IDC [331]
PROJECT SOUTH / Stanford University. KZSU Radio Station - Transcribed interviews with civil rights workers in the South during the "Freedom Summer" of 1965. 2 reels or 68 fiches - 1. 21.00; 9 - 34.00; 17.00r; set - us S.U. Libraries [323]
PROJECT. THE SCIENCE JOURNAL / United World College of the Atlantic - n. 6-. 1979- - 5,6,9 - us UMI [370]
PROJECTED PULP AND PAPER MILLS IN THE WORLD, 1985-1995 - 1986 - 118p - it F.A.O. [338]
PROJECTED PULP AND PAPER MILLS IN THE WORLD, 1987-1997 - 1988 - 137p - it F.A.O. [670]
PROJECTED PULP AND PAPER MILLS IN THE WORLD, 1990-2000 - 1991 - 158p - it F.A.O. [680]
A PROJECTION OF SCHOOL ENROLMENTS AND TEACHER REQUIREMENTS FOR SINGAPORE 1971 TO 1980 / Singapore. Ministry of Education. Research and Statistics Unit - Singapore, 1970 - 1mf - 9 - DE-256/1 - ne IDC [370]
PROJECTO DE PLANO DE FOMENTO PARA 1959-1964 / Portugal. Presidencia do Conselho - Lisboa. 1958 - 9 - ne IDC [338]
PROJECTO DO 3 PLANO DE FOMENTO PARA 1968-1973 / Portugal. Presidencia do Conselho - (Draft of the Third Development Plan for 1968-1973). 3 v., 4 pts. Lisboa. 1967. BD-1736 1 - 9 - ne IDC [338]
PROJECTO DO 4. PLANO DE FOMENTO / Portugal. Presidencia do Conselho - 3v. Lisbon. 1973. BD-2013 1 - 9 - ne IDC [338]
PROJEKT : STADTBILD UND RECHT. EINE EXKURSION AUS HISTORISCHER, GEOGRAPHISCHER, THEOLOGISCHER UND RECHTLICHER SICHT, INHALTLICH MIT FOTOS, SCHAUBILDERN SOWIE TAFELN DARGESTELLT / Moellers, Martin - 1993 - 1mf - 9 - DM60.00 - 3-89349-742-0 - gw Hänsel [650]
PROJEKTMANAGEMENT INTERNATIONALER KOOPERATIONSVORHABEN MITTLERER UNTERNEHMEN IN DER EUROPAEISCHEN GEMEINSCHAFT : DIE ROLLE DES PROJEKTLEITERS UND DIE ORGANISATORISCHE PROJEKTEINBINDUNG / Wiesner, Iris - 1994 - 2mf - 9 - DM80.00 - 3-89349-868-0 - gw Hänsel [650]
PROJET CONCERNANT DE NOUVEAUX SIGNES POUR LA MUSIQUE / Rousseau, Jean-Jacques - 1781 - 9 - us Sibley [780]
PROJET DE BUDGET DES RECETTES ET DES DEPENSES DEPARTEMENTALES AND DECISION MODIFICATIVE / Aube. France (Department) - Bar-sur-Aube. no. 1-2. 1948-1949 - 1 - us NY Public [330]

PROJET DE CHARTE DE LA REVOLUTION AGRAIRE / Algeria. Presidence du Conseil de la Revolution – 1969. BNE-8740 1 – 9 – ne IDC [630]
PROJET DE CODE CIVIL POUR L'EMPIRE DU JAPON / Boissonnade, Gustave – 2eme ed. Paris, E. Thorin. 1882, 1883, 1888, 1889 – 9 – 100.00 – fr Orientalistes [340]
PROJET DE CODE DE PROCEDURE CRIMINELLE POUR L'EMPIRE DU JAPON / Boissonnade, Gustave – Tokyo. 1882 – 9 – 25.00 – fr Orientalistes [340]
PROJET DE CODE NOIR POUR LES COLONIES FRANCAISES / Billiard, Auguste – Briere. 1829 – 9 – 5.00 – fr Orientalistes [960]
PROJET DE LA CONSTITUTION FRANCAISE DE 1791 / Robespierre, Maximilien de – Notes manuscrites et inedites de Robespierre. Aix: A. Makaire, 1894. 14p. 1 fiche.(Political Science Collection) – 9 – 6.00 – fr Bibl Nationale [323]
PROJET DE PLAN QUINQUENNAL, 1963-67 / Upper Volta – 2v. Ouagadougou. 1962. Bd-339 – 9 – ne IDC [338]
LE PROJET DE REFORME DE LA PROCEDURE PENALE, RAPPORT / Besson, Antonin – Paris, Librairie Dalloz, 1956. 75 p. LL-4198 – 1 – us L of C Photodup [340]
PROJET DE REVISION DE LA LITURGIE DES EGLISES REFORMEES DE FRANCE PREPARE SUR L'INVITATION DU SYNODE GENERAL OFFICIEUX / Bersier, E – Paris, 1888 – 6mf – 8 – Dfl25.00 – ne Slangenburg [240]
PROJET DE STATUT D'UNE COUR DE JUSTICE CRIMINELLE INTERNATIONALE / Association Internationale de Droit Penal – Paris, n.d. – 1mf – 9 – ILM-3930/1 – ne IDC [340]
PROJET DE TRAITE POUR RENDRE LA PAIX PERPETUELLE ENTRE LES SOUVERAINS CHRETIENS, POUR MAINTENIR TOUJOURS LE COMMERCE LIBRE ENTRE LES NATIONS / Castel de Saint Pierre, Charles Irenee – Utrecht. A. Schouten. 1717. xxxiv, 455p. (Strategy of War Series) – 9 – fr Hachette [940]
PROJET DE TROISIEME PLAN QUADRIENNAL, SECTION TERRITORIALE / Congo. Middle – 1958-62.D-1272-1 – 9 – ne IDC [338]
PROJET D'EDUCATION NATIONALE PRESENTE A L'ASSEMBLEE NATIONALE / Ferlus, Francois – Paris. Belin. 1791. 6755 – 9 – fr Hachette [944]
PROJET DU PLAN QUINQUENNAL (1957-1961) / Vietnam. South. Direction Generale du Plan – (Draft Five-Year Plan (1957-1961)). Saigon. 1957. BD-1521 1 – 9 – ne IDC [338]
PROJET DU PLAN QUINQUENNAL 1964-1968 / Lebanon. Ministere du Plan – (Draft Four-Year Plan 1964-1968). May 1964. BD-1686 1 – 9 – ne IDC [338]
PROJET DU PLAN QUINQUENNAL 1968-1972 / Morocco. Division du Plan et des Statistiques – D-1382 1. 3 v. 1968 – 9 – ne IDC [310]
PROJET DU REGLEMENT...NAVIGATION DU RHIN,... / Eichhoff, J J – Mayence, 1817 – 2mf – 1 – ILM-854/1 – ne IDC [327]
PROJET D'UNE ECOLE GRATUITE DES SCIENCES POUR TOUTES LES PROVINCES DU ROYAUME OU TOUS LES CITOYENS, DE QUELQUE ORDRE QU'ILS SOIENT, TROUVERAIENT LES SECOURS DE L'EDUCATION / Fleury, Nicolas-Marie de – France. 1761. 6758 – 9 – fr Hachette [944]
PROJET POUR RENDRE LA PAIX PERPETUELLE EN EUROPE / Castel de Saint Pierre, Charles Irenee – Utrecht. A. Schouten. 1713. xxiv, 400, 423p. (Strategy of War Series) – 9 – fr Hachette [940]
PROJET POUR UN PLAN DE DEVELOPPEMENT ECONOMIQUE DECENNIE 1971-1980 / Chad. Haut Commissariat Charge du Plan et des Aides Exterieures – (Draft economic development plan for the decade 1971-1980). Fort Lamy. Jul 1971 – 9 – ne IDC [338]
PROJETS ET FRAGMENTS D'UN DICTIONNAIRE CRITIQUE / Bayle, P – 1692 – 9 – fr I.C.S. [440]
PROJETS PROPOSES POUR UN FINANCEMENT EXTERIEUR AU GROUPE CONSULTATIF / Morocco. Ministere de Finances – 1970. BNE-3077 1 – 9 – ne IDC [336]
Prokanov, Ivan S *see* TRI SVETOCHA
PROKATNYE PUNKTY SEL'SKOKHOZIAISTVENNYKH MASHIN I ORUDII / Polevitskii, K A – M., L., 1925 – 2mf – 9 – COR-500/1 – ne IDC [334]
Prokesch von Osten, A *see*
– AUS DEM NACHLASSE FRIEDRICHS VON GENTZ
– AUS DEN TAGEBUECHERN DES GRAFEN PROKESCH VON OSTEN...1830-1834
– ZUR GESCHICHTE DER ORIENTALISCHEN FRAGE
Prokhanov, A *see* ZAVTRA
Prokhanov, IS *see* KRATKOE UCHENIE O PROPOVEDI
Prokopovich, SN *see*
– KOOPERATIVNAIA ORGANIZATSIIA MELKOGO KREDITA
– KOOPERATIVNOE DVIZHENIE V ROSSII
– KOOPERATIVNYE TOVARISHCHESTVA I IKH KLASSIFIKATSIIA
– KREDITNAIA KOOPERATSIIA V ROSSII
– SEL'SKOKHOZIAISTVENNAIA KOOPERATSIIA I BIUDZHET KREST'IANSKOGO KHOZIAISTVA
Prokushev, I *see* SERGEI ESENIN
PROLEGOMENA TO ST. PAUL'S EPISTLES TO THE ROMANS AND THE EPHESIANS / Hort, Fenton John Anthony – (Includes bibliographical references) – London, New York: Macmillan, 1895 – 1mf – 9 – 0-8370-3663-1 – 1985-1663 – us A.T.L.A. [220]
PROLEGOMENA TO ST PAUL'S EPISTLES TO THE ROMANS AND THE EPHESIANS / Hort, Fenton John Anthony – 1895 – 9 – $10.00 – us I.R.C. [240]
PROLEGOMENA TO SYSTEMATIC THEOLOGY : A STUDY OF AUTHORITY / Davies, Edward Owen – (Sequel to: Theological Encyclopaedia) – London: Hodder & Stoughton, 1909 – 1mf – 9 – 0-8370-2838-8 – 1985-0838 – us A.T.L.A. [200]
PROLEGOMENA TO THE HISTORY OF ANCIENT ISRAEL / Wellhausen, Julius – 1885 – 9 – $18.00 – us I.R.C. [270]
PROLEGOMENA ZU EINER NEUEN AUSGABE DER IMITATIO CHRISTI NACH DEM AUTOGRAPH DES THOMAS VON KEMPEN / Hirsche, K – Berlin. bd 1-3. 1873-1894 – Dfl98.00 – ne Slangenburg [240]
PROLEGOMENA ZU MOSES IBN ESRA'S BUCH DER 'TEGNIS.' PT. 1. HALLE. 1893. BJ-421-49/1 / Lewenstein, T – 9 – ne IDC [270]
PROLEPSIS PHILOLOGIAE ANGLICANAE / Dawson, Benjamin – 1797. 57p. (English Linguistics Series 1500-1800) – 9 – us UMI [420]
EIN PROLET ERZAEHLT : LEBENSSCHILDERUNG EINES DEUTSCHEN ARBEITERS / Turek, Ludwig – 2. Aufl. Berlin: Dietz, c1947 – 1r – 1 – us U.W. Library [920]
LE PROLETAIRE – nov 1878-mars 1884. devenu: Le Proletariat. 5 avr 1884-90. devenu: Le Proletaire. 1891-15 avr 1894, 11 fevr-23 avr 1900. Paris – 1 – fr A.C.R.P.P. [073]
LE PROLETAIRE – Organe hebdomadaire du Parti ouvrier francais du bassin houiller du Pas-de-Calais. Avion. (P.-d.-C.). nov 1900-nov 1901 – 1 – fr A.C.R.P.P. [073]
LE PROLETAIRE ET LE BOURGEOIS, DIALOGUE SUR LA QUESTION DES SALAIRES / Leroux, Jules – Paris. 1840. (La Condition Ouvriere. Part Two.) – 9 – 2.50 – fr Bibl Nationale [360]
PROLETAREC – Chicago, IL, 1906-1918, 1929-1952 – 12r – 1 – us I.H.R.C. [975]
PROLETAREN – Goteborg, Sweden. 1979- – 1 – sw Kungliga [072]
PROLETARIAN – Detroit. v. 2, no. 1-v. 14, no. 7. May 1919-July 1931. Incomplete – 1 – us NY Public [331]
PROLETARIAN / Proletarian Party of America – v2-14. 1919-31 – 1r – 1 – us Ross [335]
THE PROLETARIAN: ITALIAN WEEKLY OF THE INDUSTRIAL WORKERS OF THE WORLD *see* IL PROLETARIO
Proletarian Party of America *see* PROLETARIAN
LE PROLETARIAT : ORGANE OFFICIEL DE LA FEDERATION DES TRAVAILLEURS SOCIALISTES DE FRANCE – Paris, 1884-94 – 1 – fr A.C.R.P.P. [335]
PROLETARIAT : MONATSSCHRIFT FUER KOMMUNISMUS – Berlin, 1920-22 – 1 – Inquire at Mikrofilmarchiv for details – gw Misc Inst [335]
PROLETARIAT : MONATSSCHRIFT FUER KOMMUNISMUS – Berlin, Germany. 1920-1922 – 1 – gw Mikrofilm [073]
PROLETARIAT FINLIANDII V GODY PERVOI RUSSKOI REVOLIUTSII / Vlasova, M N – 1905-1907. Petrozavodsk, 1961 – 1 – 35.00r – us Hoover Inst Photo [335]
PROLETARIAT, TRUDOVOE KRESTI ANSTVO I REVOLIUTSII A / Chernov, Viktor Mikhailovich – Petrograd: Revoliutsionnai a Mysl, 1917 – 1 – CSUX89-B2829 – us Hoover Inst Photo [320]
PROLETARIAT V 1917 G. V BORBE ZA VLAST / Gorin, Pavel Osipovich – Moskva: Gos. izd-vo, 1927 – 1 – CSUX88-B5120 – us Hoover Inst Photo [320]
PROLETARIER : MONATSSCHRIFT FUER KOMMUNISMUS – Berlin, 1920-21 (incomplete), 1922-23 (many issues missing), 1924-25 (incomplete), 1926, 1927 (incomplete), 1933 (many issues missing) – 11r – 1 – Inquire at Mikrofilmarchiv for details – gw Misc Inst [335]
PROLETARIER I – Berlin, Germany. 1920-1927 (incomplete); 1933 – 1r – 1 – gw Mikrofilm [073]
PROLETARIERJUGEND – Leipzig, DE. 1920 – 1r – 1 – gw Mikrofilm [072]
PROLETARII – Geneva. 1905, nos. 1-26 – 1 – 35.00r – us Hoover Inst Photo [335]
IL PROLETARIO / Industrial Workers of the World – New York etc. v. 9-46. no. 4. 1905-1942. Incomplete – 1 – us NY Public [331]
IL PROLETARIO – (Library has: v.27,no.17,22,24-31,33,37-38,40,47,49-50; v.28,no.4,15,19,25,31-32,34-35,37-28,40-42; Apr. 28.1923-Oct. 25, 1924; a few issues are mutilated) – [New York, Chicago: Italian Socialist Federation: Industrial Workers of the World, 1896- – 1 – CSUX87-S421 – us Hoover Inst Photo [332]
IL PROLETARIO – New York, NY, 1899-1946 – 3r – 1 – us I.H.R.C. [978]
IL PROLETARIO – New York, NY, 1903 – 8mf or 1r – 1,9 – us I.H.R.C. [978]
O PROLETARIO : ORGAO DO PARTIDO OPERARIO DO ESTADO DE ALAGOAS – Maceio-Jaragua, Alagoas. 12 Nov 1893 – 1,5,6 – bl Biblioteca [072]
IL PROLETARIO (INDUSTRIAL WORKERS OF THE WORLD) *see* IL PROLETARIO
PROLETARISCHE PARTEI UND BUERGERLICHES ERBE : STUDIEN ZU GESCHICHTE UND THEORIE DES LITERARISCHEN ERBES IN DER VOLKSFRONTSTRATEGIE DER KPD / Schwarze, Michael – Frankfurt a.M., 1976 – 2mf – 9 – DM62.00 – 3-89349-681-5 – gw Hänsel [320]
PROLETARISCHE SOZIALPOLITIK – Berlin, 1928-31 – 2r – 1 – Inquire at Mikrofilmarchiv for details – gw Misc Inst [360]
PROLETARISCHE SOZIALPOLITIK – Berlin, Germany. 1928-1931 – 2r – 1 – gw Mikrofilm [073]
DI PROLETARISHE SHTIME = THE PROLETARIAN VOICE – New York City, NY. v2 no3 15 Dec 1922-v2 no15 18 May 1923 – 1r – 1 – $25.00 – cn Can Microfilming [071]
DER PROLETARISHER GEDANK = PROLETARIAN THOUGHT – (In Yiddish) – Moscow, RU. no43-45 Dec 1926-no46-48 Mar 1927 – 1r – 1 – $25.00 – cn Can Microfilming [072]
DER PROLETARISHER GEDANK = THE PROLETARIAN THOUGHT – (In Yiddish) – Vilnius, LT. no1 Jan-no3 28 Feb 1907 – 1r – 1 – $25.00 – cn Can Microfilming [072]
PROLETARISHER GEDANK = PROLETARIAN THOUGHT – (In Yiddish) – New York City, NY. v2 no1 1926-v4 no1 1929 – 1r – 1 – $25.00 – cn Can Microfilming [071]
PROLETARISHER GEDANK = PROLETARIAN THOUGHT – New York, NY. 1941-47 – 1 – us A.J.P.C. [071]
PROLETARSKAI A PRAVDA : EZHEDNEVNAI A GAZETA KIEVSKOGO GUBKOMA KPBU I GUBPROFSOVETA – (Includes c.1: v.2:no.56=no.169 1922:Mar.11) – Kiev: Gubkom i Gubprofsovet, 1921 – 1 – CSUXAKB0393-S – us Hoover Inst Photo [947]
PROLETARSKAI A REVOLIUTSII A I KULTURA / Bukharin, Nikolai Ivanovich – Petrograd: "Pribo i", 1923 – 1 – CSUX88-B9823 – us Hoover Inst Photo [320]
PROLETARSKAIA KUL'TURA – Moscow. July 1918-June 1921 – 1 – 35.00r – us Hoover Inst Photo [335]
PROLETARSKAIA KUL'TURA = PROLETARIAN CULTURE – Moscow. n1-19. 1918-21 – 15mf – 9 – $100.00 – us Ross [790]
PROLETARSKAIA REVOLIUTSIIA – Moscow. 1921-31, suspended during 1932. Missing: no. 8, 1937; no. 3, 1940. Index – 1 – 35.00r – us Hoover Inst Photo [947]
PROLETARSKAIA REVOLIUTSIIA – Moscow. Istoricheskii Zhurnal (Proletarian Revolution: An historical journal). 1921-40 – 3 – us Readex [947]
PROLETARSKAIA REVOLIUTSIIA I BURZHUAZNAIA KULTURA : STATI 1918-1919 G.G / Chudakov, Gerasim – Kazan: Otd-nie Gos. izd-va, 1920 – 1 – CSUX88-B4454 – us Hoover Inst Photo [335]
PROLETARSKAIA REVOLIUTSIIA. ISTORICHESKI ZHURNAL – Moscow. U.S.S.R. 1921-40 – 1 – us UMI [073]
PROLETARSKAIA REVOLUTSIIA I PRAVO – 1918-21 – 1 – 20.00 – us L of C Photodup [947]
PROLETARSKI I SUD : ORGAN MOSKOVSK. GUBERNSK. SOVETA NAROD. SUDE I – (Library has: Oct.-Nov./Dec. 1922) – Moskva: Prezidium M.G.S.N.S., 1922-1928 – 1 – CSUX89-S525 – us Hoover Inst Photo [947]
PROLETARSKII MUZYKANT – Moscow, 1926-32 (monthly) – 27mf – 9 – us Ross [780]
PROLETARY – Geneva. Switzerland. -w. 27 May-25 Nov 1905. (28 ft) – 1 – uk British Libr Newspaper [072]
PROLETARY – Moscow, Geneva and Paris. -f. 29 Oct 1906-2 May 1907, 26 Feb 1908-28 Dec 1909. (28 ft) – 1 – uk British Libr Newspaper [072]
PROLETCULT (PROLETARIAN CULTURE) / Paul, Eden – New York: Thomas Seltzer Inc., 1921. 159p – 1 – us U.W. Library [305]
PROLIFIC TROPICAL SHEEP – 1980 – 130p – it F.A.O. [636]
PROLIT – Montreal, CN, 1935 – 1r – 1 – Can$25.00 – cn Can Microfilming [072]
PROLOG – St. Petersburg. v. 1-2. 1895-1896 – 1 – us NY Public [073]
DER PROLOG DES JOHANNESEVANGELIUMS : NACH DEM EVANGELIUM / Meyer, Konrad – Leipzig: A Deichert (Georg Boehme), 1902 – 1mf – 9 – 0-8370-4419-7 – 1985-2419 – us A.T.L.A. [220]
DER PROLOG DES VIERTEN EVANGELIUMS : SEIN POLEMISCH-APOLOGETISCHER ZWECK / Baldensberger, Wilhelm – Freiburg: J C B Mohr (Paul Siebeck), 1898 – 1mf – 9 – 0-8370-2160-X – 1985-1060 – us A.T.L.A. [220]
PROLOGO GALEATO.RELACION...DE AGREDA / Jimenez Samaniego, Jose – 1720 – 9 – 1.50f – sp Bibl Santa Ana [830]
PROLOGUE: THE JOURNAL OF THE NATIONAL ARCHIVES – 2 rolls. T1195 – 1 – us Nat'l Archives [025]
PROLUSIONS, OR, SELECT PIECES OF ANCIENT POETRY – 1760 – 1 – us I.U. Libraries [800]
PROMEA1THEA1E – Paris. v. 1-7. no. 73. Nov 1926-Dec 1936. Incomplete – 1 – us NY Public [073]
PROMENADE AUTOUR DU MONDE / Hubner, Joseph A de – Ileme partie: Le Japon. Paris, Hachette. 1873 – 9 – 12.50 – fr Orientalistes [910]
PROMENADE DE NANTES... *see* GUIDE DU VOYAGEUR A NANTES ET AUX ENVIRONS...
PROMENADE DE NANTES A LA MER : GUIDE A PAIMBOEUF... – Nantes: Forest, 1841 – fr Armell [910]
PROMENADES ARCHEOLOGIQUES / Paris, Pierre – Bordeaux: Feret, Tome 16, No 3. 1914 – 1 – sp Bibl Santa Ana [930]
PROMENADES JAPONAISES / Guimet, Emile – Paris: G. Charpentier. 1878 – 9 – 7.50 – fr Orientalistes [950]
PROMENADES JAPONAISES, TOKIO-NIKKO / Guimet, Emile – Paris: G. Charpentier. 1880 – 9 – 10.00 – fr Orientalistes [950]
PROMENADES SENTIMENTALES DANS LONDRES ET LE PALAIS DE CRISTAL / Premaray, Jules de – Paris. 1851. x,343p. (Travel series) – 9 – 12.00 – fr Bibl Nationale [910]
IL PROMESSI SPOSI (LOS NOVIOS) / Manzoni, Alejandro – 3rd ed. castellana. Tomo 1. Madrid: Imp. Tejado, 1859. Tambien Tomo 2, 3 – 1 – sp Bibl Santa Ana [946]
PROMETEI / Ivanov, V – Tragediia. "Alkonost". Spb. 1919. BR-741 2 – 8 – ne IDC [460]
PROMETHEAN OR COMMUNTERIAN APOSTLE – London, UK. 1842. -Irr. 6 feet – 1 – uk British Libr Newspaper [072]

PROMETHEUS BOUND / Browning, Elizabeth Barrett – London: A.J. Valpy, 1833 – 1 roll – 1 – 1-55879-429-8 – uk Libr Preservation [810]
PROMINENT AND PROGRESSIVE PENNSYLVANIANS OF THE NINETEENTH CENTURY / Record Publishing Co – Philadelphia, 1898. Vols. 1-2, Pennsylvania Reel 6. (The Cox Library Collection) – 5 – us Americana [978]
PROMINENT MEN OF CANADA: A COLLECTION OF PERSONS DISTINGUISHED IN PROFESSIONAL AND POLITICAL LIFE, AND IN THE COMMERCE AND INDUSTRY OF CANADA / ed by Adam, Graeme Mercer – Toronto: Canadian Biographical Pub. Co. 1892. 00030. (Pre-1900 Canadiana) – 9 – cn C.I.H.M. [971]
PROMINENT MEN OF CARBONDALE, SCRANTON, WILKES-BARRE, PITTSTON, HAZELTON, AND MONTROSE / Stoddard, Dwight J – Photographs only for some. 1906. Pennsylvania Reel 25. (The Cox Library Collection) – 5 – us Americana [978]
PROMINENT MEN OF WEST VIRGINIA / Atkinson & Gibbens – Biographical sketches. Wheeling, W. L. Callin, 1890. West Virginia Reel 2. (The Cox Library Collection) – 5 – us Americana [978]
PROMINENT PEOPLE / Jerusalem Post. Jerusalem. Clippings Archive – 1933-77. BJ-95-1 1 – 9 – ne IDC [072]
PROMISE OF THE FATHER, OR, A NEGLECTED SPECIALITY OF THE LAST DAYS: ADDRESSED TO THE CLERGY AND LAITY OF ALL CHRISTIAN COMMUNITIES / Palmer, Phoebe Worrell – 1859 – 9 – us A.T.L.A. [240]
PROMISES AND AFTERTHOUGHTS / Jewish Agency for Palestine. London – Notes on Certain White Papers relating to the Palestine Conferences. (L. Stein). 1939. BJ-28-140 – 9 – ne IDC [956]
PROMO-SERVICES / LE NORDIC *see* LE NORDIC
PROMO-SERVICES LE NORDIC *see* LE MEILLEUR JOURNAL
PROMOTER – Pendleton, OR. -w. 23 May 1906-29 Aug 1906. 1 roll – 1 – us U.O. Library [071]
PROMOTER – Shelby. Mont. 1958-1959; 1966- – 1 – us UMI [071]
THE PROMOTER – Willows, CA. 1897-98 – 1r – 1 – $50.00 – B03107 – us Library Micro [071]
PROMOTER (PORTSMOUTH ED.) – Chichester, England. 1973-Jul 1975. -w. 1 reel – 1 – uk British Libr Newspaper [072]
LE PROMOTEUR – Montreal, Canada. v1 n2. mai 1934 – 1r – 1 – Can$25.00 – cn Can Microfilming [072]
PROMOTING AGRICULTURAL TRADE AMONG DEVELOPING COUNTRIES – 1984 – 188p – it F.A.O. [380]
PROMOTING THE READING HABIT / Bamberger, Richard – 2nd ed 1982 – 52p – 9 – 92-3-101218-5 – fr UNESCO [400]
PROMOTION – us UMI [380]
PROMOTION – v. 22. 1974 – 1,5,6 – us UMI [380]
PROMOTION *see*
– ADVERTISING AGE
– ADVERTISING AND SALES PROMOTION
LA PROMOTION AU MAROC / Morocco. Delegation Generale a la Promotion. Nationale et au Plan – 1963? BNE-3031 1 – 9 – ne IDC [338]
LA PROMOTION DES TRAVAILLEURS NATIONAUX A L'INTERIEUR DES ENTERPRISES INDUSTRIELLES DES PAYS EN VOIE DE DEVELOPPEMENT / Charles, P – Rabat. 1961. BNE-3022 1 – 9 – ne IDC [338]
LA PROMOTION NATIONALE: REPONSES AU QUESTIONNAIRE DE LA F.A.O. RELATIF A LA MOBILISATION DE LA MAIN-D'OEUVRE – 1965. BNE-3203 1 – 9 – ne IDC [338]
PROMOTION OF SMALL FARMERS' COOPERATIVES IN ASIA – 1980 – 74p – it F.A.O. [334]
EL PROMOTOR DE EDUCACION CRISTIANA – 1949. 156p – 1 – 5.46 – us Baptist [240]
PROMPT BOOKS IN THE THEATRE MUSEUM, LONDON / Theatre MuseumVictoria & Albert Museum. London – (260 prompt books and actor's copies with library index cards and printed guide) – 1983 – 486mf – 9 – $2,625.00 – 1-900853-65-5 – uk Mindata [790]
PROMPTER – London, UK. 1830-31. -irr. 1/2 reel – 1 – uk British Libr Newspaper [072]
PROMPTORIUM PARVULORUM – Anon. 1499. 233p. (English Linguistics Series 1500-1800) – 9 – us UMI [420]
PROMPTUAIRE D'UNISONS / Le Gaygnard, P – 1585 – 9 – fr I.C.S. [999]
PROMPTUARIO LLENERENSE GRAMATICO-LATINO / Cayetano, Luis – 1746 – 9 – 1.50f – sp Bibl Santa Ana [400]
PROMPTUARIUM CATHOLICUM... / Stapleton, Thomas – Lugduni, 1591 – 7mf – 9 – CA-59/1 – ne IDC [240]
DAS PROMPTUARIUM EXEMPLORUM DES ANDREAS HONDORFF : VOLKSKUNDLICHE STUDIEN ZUM PROTESTANTISCHEN PREDIGTEXEMPEL IM 16. JAHRHUNDERT / Schade, Heidemarie – Frankfurt a.M., 1966 – 2mf – 9 – DM62.00 – 3-89349-396-4 – gw Hänsel [240]
PROMUISHLENNOST STROITELNUIKH MATERIALOV – Moscow, U.S.S.R. -w. Jan 1950-Dec 1951; Jan 1953-Aug 1954. 3 reels – 1 – uk British Libr Newspaper [947]
THE PROMULGATOR – Metropolis. Ill. 1866-1870 – 1 – us UMI [071]
PROMYSHELENNYE PRAVA I IKH KHOZIAISTVENNOE ZNACHENIE V SOIUZE SSR I NA ZAPADE / Kheifets, Ila – Moscow, 1930. 248p. Patent rights for Soviet industry, comparison of Soviet law and practice with that of western Europe. BR-9800/1 – 9 – ne IDC [340]
PROMYSHLENNAIA ORGANIZATSIIA / Dembovskii, Kazimir Bronislavovich – Petrograd: Tip. K.P. Shrader, 1917 – 1 – CSUX88-B7537 – us Hoover Inst Photo [330]
PROMYSHLENNOST, RUSSIA – 1861-63 – 210mf – 9 – $1,390.00 – us Ross [330]
PROMYSHLENNYI MIR, RUSSIA : RUSSKII EKONOMIST – 1899-1907 – 11r – 1 – $880.00 – us Ross [330]
PROMYSLOVAIA KOOPERATSIIA – M., 1919 n1 – 2mf – 9 – COR-670/1 – ne IDC [334]
PROMYSLOVAIA KOOPERATSIIA LENINGRADA I LENINGRADSKOI OBLASTI – L., M., 1932 – 1mf – 9 – COR-440/1 – ne IDC [334]
PROMYSLOVOE KOOPERATIVNOE TOVARISHCHESTVO (ARTEL') : CHTO NADOZNAT' CHLENU PROMYSLOVOGO TOVARISHESTVA (ARTELI) O ZAKONE O PROMYSLOVOI KOOPERATSII 11 IIUNIA 1928 GODA / Filatov, VB – M., 1929 – 2mf – 9 – COR-453/1 – ne IDC [334]
PROMYSLOVOE KREDITNOE TOVARISHCHESTVO : VOPROSY ORGANIZATSIIA / Iakhontov, P V – M., 1928 – 2mf – 9 – COR-459/1 – ne IDC [334]
PROMYSLY I REMESLA – M., 1927-31 n12 – 19mf – 9 – COR-671/1 – ne IDC [334]
A PRONOUNCING AND SPELLING DICTIONARY / Johnston, William – 1764. 262p. (English Linguistics Series 1500-1800) – 9 – us UMI [420]
A PRONOUNCING DICTIONARY OF THE ENGLISH LANGUAGE – Anon. 1796. 361p. (English Linguistics Series 1500-1800) – 9 – us UMI [420]
A PRONOUNCING DICTIONARY OF THE ENGLISH LANGUAGE / Burn, John – 1786. 439p. (English Linguistics Series 1500-1800) – 9 – us UMI [420]
A PRONOUNCING ENGLISH-TAMIL DICTIONARY WITH ABBREVIATIONS / Anketell, Cyrus P – Madras: SPCK Press, 1888 – us Res Libr [040]
A PRONOUNCING VOCABULARY OF THE ENGLISH LANGUAGE / Angus, William – 1800. 127p. (English Linguistics Series 1500-1800) – 9 – us UMI [420]
PRONTUARIO DE DECENTO DEL REY JOSE 1 – 1808-1811, TOMOS 1 Y 2 – 23mf – 9 – sp Cultura [320]
PRONTUARIO DE LEGISLACION Y PRACTICA LABORAL / Mata Jimeno, Amador – Badajoz: Imp. Graf. Jimenez 1965 – sp Bibl Santa Ana [350]
PRONTUARIO DE ORTOGRAFIA / Fernandez, Francisco – 1853 – 9 – 1.50f – sp Bibl Santa Ana [440]
PRONTUARIO LEGISLATIVO DE VIVIENDAS SUBVENCIONADAS / Ministerio de la Vivienda. Delegacion Provincial de Badajoz – Badajoz: Imprenta Arqueros, 1959 – sp Bibl Santa Ana [946]
LA PRONUNCIACION DEL LATIN / Santos Coco, Francisco – Badajoz: Tip. Antonio Arqueros, 1929 – sp Bibl Santa Ana [450]
THE PRONUNCIATION OF THE ENGLISH LANGUAGE VINDICATED FROM IMPUTED ANOMALY AND CAPRICE / Adams, James – 1799. 175p. (English Linguistics Series 1500-1800) – 9 – us UMI [420]
DIE PROOEMIEN DES ALTEN JUEDISCHEN HOMILIE : BWAT / Bacher, Wilhelm – Leipzig. Heft 12. 1913 – Dfl13.00 – ne Slangenburg [220]
PROOF AND PLEADINGS IN ACCIDENT CASES. / Black, Charles Clarke – Jersey City, N.J., Linn, 1886. 301 p. LL-544 – 1 – us L of C Photodup [340]
PROOFS OF CHRIST'S RESURRECTION: FROM A LAWYER'S STANDPOINT / Morrison, Charles Robert – Andover: Warren F. Draper, 1882.1 fiche – 9 – us A.T.L.A. [240]
PROOFTEXTS – v.1-. 1981- – 1,5,6,9 – us UMI [070]
A PROOVED PRACTISE FOR ALL YOUNG CHIRURGIANS, CONCERNING BURNINGS WITH GUNPOWDER, AND WOUNDES MADE WITH GUNSHOT / Clowes, William – M 232. 1588 – 9 – ne IDC [617]
O PROPAGADOR DAS SCIENCIAS MEDICAS, OU ANNAES DE MEDICINA, CIRURGIA, E PHARMACIA – Rio de Janeiro, Jan-Dec 1827 – 1,5,6 – bl Biblioteca [073]
DIE PROPAGANDA : IHRE PROVINZEN UND IHR RECHT: MIT BESONDERER RUECKSICHT AUF DEUTSCHLAND / Mejer, Otto – Goettingen: Dieterich; Leipzig: F. C. W. Vogel, 1852-1853 – 3mf – us A.T.L.A. [302]
LA PROPAGANDA – Chicago, IL, 1908 – 3mf or 1r – 1,9 – us I.H.R.C. [978]
PROPAGANDA – Berlin. oct 1897-sep 1900 – 2r – 1 – gw Mikrofilm [073]
PROPAGANDA / Bernays, Edward L – New York: H. Liveright, 1928. 159p – 1 – us U.W. Library [380]
PROPAGANDA : ORGAO CONSAGRADO AOS INTERESSES DO POVO, IMPARCIAL E NOTICIOSO – Diamantina 10 Jul-20 Dec 1888 – 1,5,6 – bl Biblioteca [072]
PROPAGANDA, ETHICS AND PSYCHOLOGICAL ASSUMPTIONS IN CAESAR'S WRITINGS / Collins, John H – Frankfurt a.M., 1952 – 2mf – 9 – DM62.00 – 3-89349-719-6 – gw Hänsel [450]
PROPAGANDA I AGITAT SII A : ZHURNAL LENINGRADSKOGO OBLASTNOGO I GORODSKOGO KOMITETOV VKP (B) – (Library has: 1939, nos. 5, 7-8, 11-12, 16; 1940, nos. 2, 4-7, 12; 1941, nos. 1-11) – Leningrad: Lenizdat, 1936-1952. 17v – 1 – CSUX90-S459 – us Hoover Inst Photo [947]
DIE PROPAGANDA IN ENGLAND : ZUR KIRCHENRECHTLICHEN BELEUCHTUNG DER BISTHUMSFRAGE / Mejer, Otto – Leipzig: B. Tauchnitz, 1851 – 1mf – us A.T.L.A. [240]
A PROPAGANDA OF PHILOSOPHY : HISTORY OF THE AMERICAN INSTITUTE OF CHRISTIAN PHILOSOPHY, 1881-1914 / MacCracken, Henry Mitchell – New York: F.H. Revell, 1914 – 1mf – us A.T.L.A. [240]
LA PROPAGANDA PROTESTANTE EN LA AMERICA ESPANOLA / Bayle, Constantino – Madrid: Razon y Fe, 1923 y 1924 – 1 – sp Bibl Santa Ana [240]
LA PROPAGANDE PHILOSOPHIQUE DANS LES TRAGEDIES DE VOLTAIRE / Ridgway, Ronald S – (Studies on Voltaire and the eighteenth century, v15) – Oxford. 1961 – 9 – $27.00 – 0-7294-0069-7 – uk Voltaire [440]
DER PROPAGANDIST – Berlin, 1931, jan-sep 1932 – 1r – 1 – Inquire at Mikrofilmarchiv for details – gw Misc Inst [072]
DER PROPAGANDIST – Berlin, Germany. 1931; Jan-Sept 1932 – 1r – 1 – gw Mikrofilm [072]
PROPAGANDIST I AGITATOR RKKA : ORGAN POLITICHESKOGO UPRAVLENII A RKKA – (Library has: 1938, no. 1-11, 13-18, 21-24; 1939, no. 7-8, 10-11, 14-16, 20-24; 1940, no. 1-3, 6, 9-24) – Moskva: Voenizdat, 1936-1940. 5v – 1 – CSUX89-S839 – us Hoover Inst Photo [947]
LE PROPAGATEUR – (Fait suite a: Le Propagateur des bons livres) – Montreal: Cadieux & Derome, [1890-1913?] – 9 – cn C.I.H.M. [240]
LE PROPAGATEUR – Martinique. French West Indies. 1855, 1868-93 with omission – 1 – us UMI [072]
LE PROPAGATEUR DE LA DEVOTION A STE PHILOMENE AU CANADA – Quebec: C Darveau, [1880?-1889?] – 9 – cn C.I.H.M. [240]
LE PROPAGATEUR DES BONS LIVRES – Montreal, Canada. 19 mar 1884-1 fev 1890 – 1r – 1 – Can$45.00 – cn Can Microfilming [072]
LE PROPAGATEUR HAITIEN – Journal politique et litteraire. no. 1-9. Port-au-Prince. juin-oct 1822 – 1 – fr A.C.R.P.P. [073]
PROPALLADIA AND OTHER WORKS... / Torres Naharro, Bartolome; ed by Guillet, Joseph E – Menasha: Pub. G. Banta, v2. 1946 – 1 – sp Bibl Santa Ana [946]
PROPALLADIA AND OTHER WORKS OF... / Torre Naharro, Bartolome de; ed by Gillet, Joseph E – Philadelphia: Univ. of Pennsylvania, (1961) – 1 – sp Bibl Santa Ana [830]
PROPALLADIA AND OTHER WORKS OF... / Torres Naharro, Bartolome; ed by Gillet, Joseph E – Menasha: (G. Banta), v1. 1943 – 1 – sp Bibl Santa Ana [946]
PROPALLADIA AND OTHER WORKS OF... / Torres Naharro, Bartolome; ed by Gillet, Joseph H E – Philadelphia: (Anthoensen Press Portland), v3. 1951 – 1 – sp Bibl Santa Ana [830]
PROPELLANTS, EXPLOSIVES, PYROTECHNICS : AN INTERNATIONAL JOURNAL DEALING WITH SCIENTIFIC AND TECHNOLOGICAL ASPECTS OF ENERGETIC MATERIALS – v1-21. 1976-96 – 1,5,6,13 – us V.C.H. [660]
THE PROPER ATTITUDE OF YOUNG MINISTERS TOWARD ISSUES OF THE DAY / Sampey, John R – 1887 – 1 – 5.00 – us Baptist [240]
PROPERTIUS / Propertius, Sextus – Trans. by J.S. Phillimore. Oxford: The Clarendon Press, 1906. xi,183p – 1 – us U.W. Library [450]
Propertius, Sextus *see* PROPERTIUS
PROPERTY – Montreal: H Bragg, [1895-189- or 19–] – 9 – cn C.I.H.M. [333]
PROPERTY AND ECONOMIC PROGRESS; SCHOOLS CAN PAY DIVIDENDS / Clark, Colin – 1945 – 9 – 1.00f – at Libertarian Micro [335]
PROPERTY AND PRIVILEGE IN MEDIEVAL AND EARLY MODERN ENGLAND AND WALES: CARTULARIES AND OTHER REGISTERS – (Part 2: Cotton Otho-Cotton Roll. Part 3: Egerton-Lansdowne. Part 4: Royal -Addit. Rolls) – Series 1; Part 1: Arundel-Cotton Nero – 1 – us Primary [025]
PROPERTY IN LAND / Sommer, Frank Henry – Newark, N.J., Soney & Sage, 1899. 188 p. LL-28 – 1 – us L of C Photodup [340]
PROPERTY INSURANCE : COMPRISING FIRE AND MARINE INSURANCE, CORPORATE SURETY BONDING, TITLE INSURANCE AND CREDIT INSURANCE / Huebner, Solomon S – New York, London: D Appleton & Co, 1913 – 5mf – 9 – $7.50 – LLMC 92-169 – us L.L.M.C. [360]
PROPERTY; ITS RIGHTS AND DUTIES IN OUR LEGAL AND SOCIAL SYSTEMS / Dillon, John Forrest – Albany, N.Y., Banks, 1895. 30 p. LL-429 – 1 – us L of C Photodup [340]
PROPERTY RECORDS / Allen County. Ohio. Coroner – 1897-1926 – 1r – 1 – $32.50r – us Archival [324]
THE PROPERTY RIGHTS OF HUSBAND AND WIFE UNDER THE LAW OF CONNECTICUT / Peck, Epaphroditus – Hartford: Dissell, 1904. 277p. LL-935 – 1 – us L of C Photodup [340]
PROPERTY TAX JOURNAL – v1-. 1982- – 1,5,6,9 – us UMI [073]
THE PROPHECIES OF BALAAM (NUMBERS 22 TO 24) : OR, THE HEBREW AND THE HEATHEN / Kalisch, Marcus Moritz – (Includes bibliographical references, appendix on the original form of the book of Balaam, and Hebrew text of Nos 22-24) – London: Longmans, Green, 1877 – 1mf – 9 – 0-8370-3836-7 – 1985-1836 – us A.T.L.A. [220]
THE PROPHECIES OF DANIEL / Terry, Milton Spenser – New York: Hunt & Eaton, 1893. 1 fiche – 9 – us A.T.L.A. [240]
THE PROPHECIES OF ISAIAH / Orelli, Conrad von – Edinburgh: T. & T. Clark, 1889. 1 fiche – 9 – us A.T.L.A. [240]

THE PROPHECIES OF ISAIAH : AN OUTLINE STUDY OF ISAIAH'S WRITINGS IN THEIR CHRONOLOGICAL ORDER IN CONNECTION WITH THE CONTEMPORARY ASSYRIO-BABYLONIAN RECORDS / Kellner, Maximilian – Cambridge, MA: [s.n.], 1895 – 1mf – 9 – 0-8370-6193-8 – 1986-0193 – us A.T.L.A. [220]

THE PROPHECIES OF ISAIAH: A NEW TRANSLATION WITH COMMENTARY / Cheyne, Thomas Kelly – New York: Thomas Whittaker, 1892. 2 fiches – 9 – us A.T.L.A. [240]

THE PROPHECIES OF ISAIAH: A NEW TRANSLATION WITH COMMENTARY AND APPENDICES – By the Rev. T.K. Cheyne.5th ed. rev. New York: Thomas Whittaker, 1890. 2v in 1 – 1 – us U.W. Library [240]

PROPHECIES OF JEREMIAH / Ball, Charles James – New York: A.C. Armstrong, 1890. 1 fiche – 9 – us A.T.L.A. [240]

THE PROPHECIES OF JEREMIAH / Orelli, Conrad von – Edinburgh: T. & T. Clark, 1889. 1 fiche – 9 – us A.T.L.A. [240]

PROPHECIES OF JESUS CHRIST RELATING TO HIS DEATH, RESURRECTION... SECOND COMING / Schwartzkopff, Paul – Edinburgh: T.&T. Clark, 1897. 1 fiche – 9 – us A.T.L.A. [240]

PROPHECIES OF OUR LORD AND HIS APOSTLES: A SERIES OF DISCOURSES / Hoffmann, Wilhelm – London: Hodder & Stoughton, 1869. 1 fiche – 9 – us A.T.L.A. [240]

THE PROPHECIES OF ZECHARIAH / Robinson, George Livingstone – Chicago: University of Chicago Press, 1896. 1 fiche – 9 – us A.T.L.A. [240]

PROPHECY : OR, SPEAKING FOR GOD / Stackpole, Everett Schermerhorn – New York:Thomas Y. Crowell, c1896 – 1mf – 9 – 0-8370-5362-5 – 1985-3362 – us A.T.L.A. [220]

PROPHECY : A PREPARATION FOR CHRIST: EIGHT LECTURES / Payne Smith, Robert – (Includes indexes) – 2nd corr rev ed. London: Macmillan, 1871 – 1mf – 9 – 0-8370-5303-X – 1985-3303 – us A.T.L.A. [220]

PROPHECY AND DIVINATION AMONG THE HEBREWS AND OTHER SEMITES / Guillaume, Alfred – London: Hodder and Stoughton Ltd. 1938. xviii,434p. (The Bampton Lectures, 1938) – 1 – us U.W. Library [270]

PROPHECY AND HISTORY IN RELATION TO THE MESSIAH / Edersheim, Alfred – London: Longmans, Green, 1885. 1 fiche – 9 – us A.T.L.A. [240]

PROPHECY AND POETRY: STUDIES IN ISAIAH AND BROWNING / Rogers, Arthur Kenyon – New York: Longmans, Green, 1909.1 fiche – 9 – us A.T.L.A. [410]

PROPHECY: ITS NATURE AND EVIDENCE / Redford, Robert Ainslie – London: Religious Tract Society, 1882. 1 fiche – 9 – us A.T.L.A. [240]

PROPHECY – NOT "FORECAST" / Burgon, John William – 1880 – 9 – us A.T.L.A. [240]

THE PROPHECY OF HAGGAI : INTERPRETED AND APPLIED IN SUNDRY SERMONS / Rainolds, John – Edinburgh: James Nichol, 1864 – 1mf – 9 – 0-8370-5918-6 – 1985-3918 – us A.T.L.A. [220]

THE PROPHECY OF OBADIAH OPENED AND APPLIED IN SUNDRY SERMONS / Rainolds, John – Edinburgh: James Nichol, 1864 – 1mf – 9 – 0-8370-4669-6 – 1985-2669 – us A.T.L.A. [220]

PROPHECY, OR, SPEAKING FOR GOD / Stackpole, Everett Schermerhorn – New York: Thomas Y. Crowell, 1896. 1 fiche – 9 – us A.T.L.A. [240]

THE PROPHESYING OF WOMEN; A POPULAR AND PRACTICAL EXPOSITION OF THE BIBLE DOCTRINE / Wilkin, G F – c1895 – 9 – us A.T.L.A. [240]

PROPHET – London, UK. 1894. -irr. 1 foot – 1 – uk British Libr Newspaper [072]

DER PROPHET AMOS: NACH DEM GRUNDTEXTE / Hartung, K – Freiburg i.B.: Herder, 1898. 1 fiche – 9 – us A.T.L.A. [220]

PROPHET DANIEL = THE BOOK OF THE PROPHET DANIEL / Zoeckler, Otto; ed by Strong, James – (In English) – New York: Charles Scribner, 1890, c1876 – 1mf – 9 – 0-8370-6879-7 – 1986-0879 – us A.T.L.A. [220]

DER PROPHET EZECHIEL : FUER DIE ZWEITE AUFL / Smend, Rudolf – 2. Aufl. Leipzig: S Hirzel, 1880 – 1mf – 9 – 0-8370-7339-1 – 1986-1339 – us A.T.L.A. [220]

DER PROPHET EZECHIEL / Hitzig, Ferdinand – Leipzig: Weidmann, 1847 – 1mf – 9 – 0-8370-2253-3 – 1985-0253 – us A.T.L.A. [220]

DER PROPHET JEREMIA / Hitzig, Ferdinand – Leipzig: Weidmann, 1841 – 2mf – 9 – 0-8370-3597-X – 1985-1597 – us A.T.L.A. [220]

DER PROPHET JEREMIA / Volz, Paul – 2. Aufl. Tuebingen, Mohr, 1921. 55 p. Film Mas 8375 – 1 – us H.U. Library [240]

DER PROPHET JEREMIAS / Lazarus, Moritz – Breslau [Wroclaw]: S Schottlaender, 1894 – 1mf – 9 – 0-8370-4062-0 – 1985-2062 – us A.T.L.A. [220]

DER PROPHET JESAIA / Bredenkamp, Conrad Justus – Erlangen: Andreas Deichert, 1887 – 1mf – 9 – 0-8370-2441-2 – 1985-0441 – us A.T.L.A. [220]

DER PROPHET JESAIA / Dillmann, August – 5. Aufl. Leipzig: S Hirzel, 1890 – 2mf – 9 – 0-8370-9462-3 – 1986-3462 – us A.T.L.A. [220]

THE PROPHET JOEL : AN EXPOSITION / Gaebelein, Arno Clemens – (Includes indexes) – New York: Publ Office "Our Hope", c1909 – 1mf – 9 – 0-8370-3221-0 – 1985-1221 – us A.T.L.A. [220]

PROPHET JOEL: AN EXPOSITION / Gaebelein, Arno Clemens – New York: Our Hope, 1909. 1 fiche – 9 – us A.T.L.A. [240]

THE PROPHET JONAH: HIS CHARACTER AND MISSION TO NINEVEH / Martin, Hugh – London: Alexander Strahan, 1866.1 fiche – 9 – us A.T.L.A. [240]

DER PROPHET MALACHIAS / Isopescul, Octavian – Czernowitz: s.n., 1908. 1 fiche – 9 – us A.T.L.A. [220]

DER PROPHET MALEACHI, MIT AUSZLEGUNG. VERDEUETSCHT D. L. HAETZER / Oecolampad, J & Ecolampadius, J – 1526. BME-54 1 – 9 – ne IDC [220]

DER PROPHET MICAH : EINLEITUNG, GRUNDTEXT UND UEBERSETZUNG: NEBST EINEM VOLLSTAENDIGEN PHILOLOGISCH-KRITISCHEN UND HISTORISCHEN COMMENTAR / Reinke, Laurenz – Giessen: Emil Roth, 1874 – 1mf – 9 – 0-8370-9729-0 – 1986-3729 – us A.T.L.A. [220]

THE PROPHET OF NAZARETH / Schmidt, Nathaniel – (Includes bibliographical references and indexes) – New York:Macmillan, 1905 – 1mf – 9 – 0-8370-5112-6 – 1985-3112 – us A.T.L.A. [240]

THE PROPHET OF SORROW : OR, THE LIFE AND TIMES OF JEREMIAH / Smith, Thornley – (Includes index) – London: Wesleyan Conference Office, 1875 – 1mf – 9 – 0-8370-9305-8 – 1986-3305 – us A.T.L.A. [920]

DER PROPHET SACHARJA / Bredenkamp, Conrad Justus – Erlangen: Andreas Deichert, 1879 – 1mf – 9 – 0-8370-2442-0 – 1985-0442 – us A.T.L.A. [220]

PROPHETAE CHALDAICE : PAULUS DE LAGARDE E FIDE CODICIS REUCHLINIANI EDIDIT – Lipsiae: B G Teubneri, 1872 – 2mf – 9 – 0-8370-9484-4 – 1986-3484 – us A.T.L.A. [220]

LE PROPHETE AGGE : INTRODUCTION CRITIQUE ET COMMENTAIRE / Andre, Louis Edouard Tony – (Tables on the texts of Haggai) – Paris: Librairie Fischbacher, 1895 – 1mf – 9 – 0-8370-2100-6 – 1985-0100 – us A.T.L.A. [220]

LE PROPHETE OSEE / Mercier, Charles – Lausanne: Georges Bridel, 1900. 1 fiche – 9 – us A.T.L.A. [240]

DIE PROPHETEN DES ALTEN BUNDES / Ewald, Heinrich – 3V. 1867-68 – 5 – us A.T.L.A. [220]

DIE PROPHETEN IN IHREM SOZIALEN BERUF UND DAS WIRTSCHAFTSLEBEN IHRER ZEIT : EIN BEITRAG ZUR GESCHICHTE DER SOZIALETHIK / Walter, Franz – (Includes index) – Freiburg i.B.; St Louis, MO: Herder, 1900 – 1mf – 9 – 0-8370-9339-2 – 1986-3339 – us A.T.L.A. [220]

PROPHETEN- UND APOSTELLEGENDEN : NEBST JUENGERKATALOGEN DES DOROTHEUS UND VERWANDTER TESTE / Schermann, Theodor – Leipzig: J.C. Hinrichs, 1907. (Texte und Untersuchungen zur Geschichte der altchristlichen Literatur; der ganzen Reihe 31. Bd., Heft 3: 3. Reihe, 1. Bd., Heft 3) – 1mf – us A.T.L.A. [220]

PROPHETEN- UND APOSTELLEGENDEN (T.U.U.3-31-/3) / Schermann, Theodor – Leipzig, 1907 – 6mf – 9 – ne Slangenburg [240]

DIE PROPHETEN UND IHRE WEISSAGUNGEN : EINE APOLOGETISCH-HERMENEUTISCHE STUDIE / Tholuck, August – (Includes bibliographical references) – Gotha: Friedrich Andreas Perthes, 1860 – 1mf – 9 – 0-8370-9314-7 – 1986-3314 – us A.T.L.A. [220]

PROPHETENIDEAL JUDENTUM UND CHRISTENTUM : DAS HAUPTPROBLEM DER SPAETISRAELITISCHEN RELIGIONSGESCHICHTE / Koenig, Eduard – (Includes bibliographies) – Leipzig: J C Hinrichs, 1906 – 1mf – 9 – 0-8370-3972-X – 1985-1972 – us A.T.L.A. [220]

LES PROPHETES D'ISRAEL / Darmester, James – Paris: Calmann Levy, 1892. 1 fiche – 9 – us A.T.L.A. [240]

PROPHETIA DE MAOMETANI, ET ALTRE COSE TURCHESCHE, ... / Bartholomaeus, G – Firenze, 1548 – 2mf – 9 – H-8279/1 – ne IDC [956]

THE PROPHETIC ELEMENT IN THE OLD TESTAMENT : AN AID TO HISTORICAL STUDY: FOR USE IN ADVANCED BIBLE CLASSES / Harper, William Rainey – Chicago: University of Chicago Press, 1905 – 1mf – 9 – 0-8370-9390-2 – 1986-3390 – us A.T.L.A. [220]

PROPHETIC IDEAS AND IDEALS:...PROPHETIC LITERATURE OF THE HEBREW PEOPLE / Jordan, William George – Chicago: Fleming H. Revell, 1902. 1 fiche – 9 – us A.T.L.A. [240]

PROPHETIC RELIGION *see* SOUTHERN CHURCHMAN / PROPHETIC RELIGION

PROPHETIC RELIGION / SOUTHERN CHURCHMAN – 1937-55 (complete) – 1r – 1 – ATLA S0616 – us A.T.L.A. [073]

PROPHETIC TIMES – v. 1-2. 1863-1864 – 1 – us UMI [240]

THE PROPHETIC TIMES AND WATCH TOWER – v7-12. ns: v1-3. 1869-77 (incomplete) – 1 – $50.00 – us Presbyterian [240]

PROPHETIC TIMES AND WATCHTOWER : DEVOTED TO SACRED LITERATURE AND CURRENT EVENTS – (Lacking: v1-6) – v1-12. ns: v1-4. 1875-78 – 3r – 1 – ATLA S0196 – us A.T.L.A. [073]

THE PROPHETICAL BOOKS OF THE OLD TESTAMENT / Pidge, John B Gough – (Includes index) – Philadelphia:American Baptist Publication Society, 1897 – 1mf – 9 – 0-8370-4744-7 – 1985-2744 – us A.T.L.A. [220]

DIE PROPHETIE OBADJAH'S UNTERSUCHT UND ERKLAERT / Peters, Norbert – (Includes index) – Paderborn:Ferdinand Schoeningh, 1892 – 1mf – 9 – 0-8370-4717-X – 1985-2717 – us A.T.L.A. [220]

DIE PROPHETIEN DER PROPHETEN / Jacobszoon, Mattheus – 1554. BME-57 1 – 9 – ne IDC [240]

DIE PROPHETISCHE OFFENBARUNG : NACH WESEN, INHALT UND GRENZEN:UNTER DEM GESICHTSPUNKTE DER ALTTESTAMENTLICHEN WEISSAGUNG / Schwartzkopff, Paul – (Includes bibliographical references) – Giessen: J Ricker, 1896 – 1mf – 9 – 0-8370-5180-0 – 1985-3180 – us A.T.L.A. [220]

DER PROPHETISMUS DER HEBRAEER UND DIE MANTIK DER GRIECHEN / Koehler, Karl – Darmstadt: Eduard Zernin, 1860. 1 fiche – 9 – us A.T.L.A. [270]

THE PROPHETS AND KINGS OF THE OLD TESTAMENT : A SERIES OF SERMONS / Maurice, Frederick Denison – Boston: Crosby, Nichols; New York: Charles S Francis, 1853 – 2mf – 9 – 0-8370-9489-5 – 1986-3489 – us A.T.L.A. [220]

PROPHETS AND PROPHECY: A COMPILATION...OF THE LECTURES BEFORE THE SENIOR CLASS / Green, William Henry – Princeton: Princeton University Press, 1895. 1 fiche – 9 – us A.T.L.A. [240]

THE PROPHETS AND PROPHECY...IN ISRAEL TO THE CLOSE OF THE EIGHTH CENTURY B.C / Wilson, Alexander – Edinburgh: William Blackwood, 1903. 1 fiche – 9 – us A.T.L.A. [270]

PROPHETS AND THE PROMISE / Beecher, Willis Judson – New York: Thomas Y. Crowell, 1905. 1 fiche – 9 – us A.T.L.A. [240]

PROPHETS AS STATESMEN AND PREACHERS / Fowler, Henry T – Boston: Pilgrim Press, 1904. 1 fiche – 9 – us A.T.L.A. [240]

THE PROPHETS AS STATESMEN AND PREACHERS / Fowler, Henry Thatcher – Boston:Pilgrim Press, c1904 – 1mf – 9 – 0-8370-3174-5 – 1985-1174 – us A.T.L.A. [220]

THE PROPHETS OF ISRAEL / Smith, William Robertson – 2nd ed. 1897 – 9 – us A.T.L.A. [220]

THE PROPHETS OF ISRAEL AND THEIR PLACE IN HISTORY / Smith, William Robertson – 1895 – 9 – us A.T.L.A. [220]

THE PROPHET'S RAVEN / Pearse, Mark Guy – 1908 – 9 – us A.T.L.A. [240]

LA PROPIA HONRA. BOCETO DRAMATICO EN UN ACTO ORIGINAL DE... / Romero Munoz, Manuel – Madrid: Sociedad de Autores Espanoles (Villafranca de los Barros) Imp. Juan J. Bolanos, 1927 – sp Bibl Santa Ana [946]

LA PROPIEDAD DE LAS MINAS Y SU ADQUISICION POR EXTRANJEROS / Gomez Gomez, P A – Bogota, 1930 – 1mf – 1 – ILM-3371/1 – ne IDC [327]

LA PROPIEDAD EN ALBURQUERQUE / Duarte Insua, Lino – Badajoz: Tip.Enc.A.Arqueros, 1932 – 1 – sp Bibl Santa Ana [910]

PROPIUM FESTORUM QUAE IN...PACENSIS / Badajoz – 1822 – 9 – 1.50f – sp Bibl Santa Ana [946]

PROPORTIONS OF EUROPEANS AND NATIVES IN THE PUBLIC SERVICE / India. Home Department – (Filmed with: India. Memoranda of Native States in India, together with a list of independent ruling chiefs...1907 and 1912) – Calcutta: Office of Supt of Govt Printing, India, 1904 – us Res Libr [350]

PROPOS MISSIONAIRES : BULLETIN DE CULTURE ET DE CORRESPONDANCE INTERMISSIONAIRE – v1-13. Jun 1927-Apr 1940 (complete) – 1r – 1 – ATLA B0275 – us A.T.L.A. [073]

PROPOSAL FOR ADVOCATING TAXATION METHODS. / Ferguson, John R – Georgist, 1982. 21p – 9 – 1.00f – at Libertarian Micro [336]

A PROPOSAL FOR CORRECTING, IMPROVING AND ASCERTAINING THE ENGLISH TONGUE / Swift, Jonathan – 1712. 52p. (English Linguistics Series 1500-1800) – 9 – us UMI [420]

A PROPOSAL FOR PERFECTING A LATIN GRAMMAR / Lowe, Solomon – 1722. 93p. (English Linguistics Series 1500-1800) – 9 – us UMI [450]

PROPOSALS FOR AN AMERICAN BIMETALLIC UNION / Brown, William – Montreal: W. Brown, 1882. 00279. (Pre-1900 Canadiana) – 9 – cn C.I.H.M. [336]

PROPOSALS FOR SOME URGENT FUTURE SOCIOLOGICAL STUDIES IN INDONESIA / Heeren, H J – SE-1165 1 – 9 – ne IDC [300]

PROPOSALS OF THE 8TH NATIONAL CONGRESS OF THE COMMUNIST PARTY OF CHINA FOR THE 2ND FIVE-YEAR PLAN (1958-62) / China. People's Republic – Peking: Foreign Language Press, 1956. BD-519-1 – 9 – ne IDC [335]

PROPOSALS OF THE GOVERNMENT OF PALESTINE FOR THE PROTECTION OF SMALL OWNERS BY THE RESERVATION OF SUBSISTENCE AREAS / Great Britain. Colonial Office. Palestine Royal Commission – Memorandum. BJ-28-80 1 – 9 – ne IDC [324]

PROPOSED AMENDMENTS OF THE JUDICIAL SYSTEM, OF THE STATE OF NEW YORK – n.p., 186?. 8p. LL-1386 – 1 – us L of C Photodup [340]

PROPOSED AMENDMENTS TO THE CODE OF PROCEDURE / New York. (State). Laws, Statutes, etc – New York Bar Association of the City of New York. 1871. 16p. LL-4205 – 1 – us L of C Photodup [340]

THE PROPOSED CODIFICATION OF OUR COMMON LAW / Carter, James Coolidge – New York: Evening Post Job Printing Office, 1884. 117p. LL-533 – 1 – us L of C Photodup [340]

PROPOSED CONSTITUTION FOR GUAM : HEARING BEFORE THE SENATE COMMITTEE ON ENERGY AND NATURAL RESOURCES, 22 MAY 1978 / Guam. US Congress – Washington: GPO, 1978 – 4mf – 9 – $6.00 – LLMC 82-100B Title 26 – us L.L.M.C. [323]

PROPOSED CONSTITUTION FOR GUAM : HEARING BEFORE THE SENATE COMMITTEE ON INTERNATIONAL AND INSULAR AFFAIRS / Guam. US Congress – (Also covers the Puerto Rico Federal Relations Act and a proposed constitution for the Virgin Islands) – 94th Congress 2nd sess. 12 Apr 1976. Washington: GPO, 1976 – 2mf – 9 – $3.00 – LLMC 82-100B Title 34 – us L.L.M.C. [323]

PROPOSED DEVELOPMENTAL PLAN FOR THE PERIOD 1971-1975 / Malaysia. University of Penang. Centre for Educational Services – 1mf – 9 – DE-217/1 – ne IDC [370]

PROPOSED DIRECTIVES FOR PREPARING A FIVE-YEAR DEVELOPMENT PLAN FOR THE NATIONAL ECONOMY, 1965-70 / Israel. Economic Planning Authority – Jerusalem. 1963. BD-335 1 – 9 – ne IDC [338]

PROPOSED EDUCATION FIVE YEAR PLAN SEPTEMBER 1973 / Papua New Guinea. Department of Education – (Draft document for the plan period 1974-1979. Missing: pt2 (too tightly bound)) – Port Moresby. 3pts. 1973 – 4mf – 9 – DE-227/1 – ne IDC [370]

PROPOSED FORMATION OF AN ARAB AGENCY / Great Britain. Colonial Office. Palestine – Correspondence with the High Commissioner for Palestine. London. Nov 1923. Cmd. 1989. BJ-28-70 1 – 9 – ne IDC [956]

PROPOSED NEW CONSTITUTION FOR PALESTINE, PRESENTED BY THE SECRETARY OF STATE FOR THE COLONIES TO PARLIAMENT BY COMMAND OF HIS MAJESTY / Great Britain. Colonial Office – London. Mar 1936. BJ-28-77 1 – 9 – ne IDC [956]

PROPOSED PROGRAM FOR INDUSTRIAL REHABILITATION AND DEVELOPMENT / Philippines. National Development Company – Manila. 1947 – 9 – ne IDC [338]

PROPOSED REVISED CONSTITUTION OF AMERICAN SAMOA, 1986 / American Samoa. Constitutional Convention – 1mf – 9 – $1.50 – LLMC 82-100C Title 12 – us L.L.M.C. [324]

THE PROPOSED REVISION OF THE WESTMINSTER STANDARDS / Shedd, William Greenough Thayer – (Includes bibliographical references) – New York: Charles Scribner, 1890 – 1mf – 9 – 0-8370-8867-4 – 1986-2867 – us A.T.L.A. [240]

PROPOSED SCHEME OF IMPERIAL COMMERCIAL UNION / Crawford, J Law – Ottawa: The Flag, 1897? 03624. (Pre-1900 Canadiana) – 9 – cn C.I.H.M. [380]

A PROPOSED TRIBUNAL: IS IT CONSTITUTIONAL? / Otis, Merrill Edward – Kansas City, Mo.: University of Kansas City, 1939?. 53p. LL-477 – 1 – us L of C Photodup [340]

PROPOSICION DEL DOCTOR...SOBRE LA ENFERMEDAD QUE ANDA EN SEVILLA... / Sanchez, F – Sevilla, 1599 – 1mf – 9 – sp Cultura [610]

DAS DIE PROPOSITIO "GUTE WERCK SIND ZUR SELIGKEIT SCHEDLICH" EIN RECHTE WARE CHRISTLICHE PROPOSITION SEY... / Amsdorff, N von – [Magdeburg], 1559 – 1mf – 9 – ne IDC [240]

PROPOSITIONES MATHEMATICO-MUSICAE / Gibelius, O – P 296. 1666 – 9 – ne IDC [780]

PROPOSITIONS AND CONCLUSIONS CONCERNING TRUE CHRISTIAN RELIGION / Smyth, John – York Minster Library – 1 – uk Microform Academic [240]

PROPOSITIONS POUR LE PROJECT DE PLAN DE DEVELOPPEMENT 1964-1968 / Lebanon. Ministere du Plan – Texte approuve par le Conseil des ministres en date du 20 Mai 1964. BNE-9674 1 – 9 – ne IDC [338]

PROPOSITIONS POUR UN CADRE REGIONAL DE PLANIFICATION EN COTE D'IVOIRE TRAVAUX PREPARATOIRES AU PLAN, 1971-1975 / Trouchaud, J P – (Africa series). 1970 – 9 – fr Hachette [960]

PROPOSTA DI UN CODICE DI... / Farnese, L – Roma, 1873 – 3mf – 1 – ILM-1699/1 – ne IDC [327]

PROPRIETA TERRITORIALE / Bon, A del – Padova, 1867 – 3mf – 9 – ILM-1539/1 – ne IDC [327]

LE PROPRIETAIRE : LIGUE DES PROPRIETAIRES – (Filmed with: Le Proprio – Organe de la Ligue des proprietaires de Montreal jan 1940) – Montreal, Canada. v2 n16. mar 1935-v13 n145. jan 1946 – 1r – 1 – Can$25.00 – cn Can Microfilming [072]

LE PROPRIETAIRE DE LAVAL / ed by Belanger, Fernand – Ville de Laval, Canada. v3 n10. 22 jun 1971-v9 n16. 27 avr 1977 – 1r – 1 – Can$25.00 – cn Can Microfilming [072]

LE PROPRIETAIRE ET L'OUVRIER – Montreal: J Chabert, [1875-18-19–] – 9 – cn C.I.H.M. [331]

LA PROPRIETE COMMUNALE AU TONKIN (CONTRIBUTION A L'ETUDE HISTORIQUE, JURIDIQUE ET ECONOMIQUE DES CONG-DIEN ET CONG-THO EN PAYS D'ANNAM) / Vu-van-Hien – Paris, Les Presses modernes, 1939. 200 p. LL-10022 – 1 – us L of C Photodup [340]

LA PROPRIETE FONCIERE EN A.O.F. REGIME EN DROIT PRIVE / Doublier, Roger – Saint-Louis, 1952 – 1 – us Res Libr [323]

LA PROPRIETE IMMOBILIERE DES ETRANGERS EN FRANCE / Devin, J – Paris, 1926 – 3mf – 1 – ILM-3191/1 – ne IDC [327]

LA PROPRIETE PRIVEE... / Auzillon, C – Paris, 1897 – 3mf – 9 – ILM-325/1 – ne IDC [340]

LE PROPRIO *see* LE PROPRIETAIRE

UNA PROPUESTA JUSTICIALISTA / Amadeo, Eduardo – Buenos Aires: El Cid Editor-Fundaci on para la Democracia en Argentina, 1982 – 1 – CSUXAHZ5799-B – us Hoover Inst Photo [320]

PROPUESTAS DEL 8 CONGRESO NACIONAL DEL PARTIDO COMMUNISTA DE CHINA PARA EL 2 PLAN QUINQUENAL (1958-1962) / China. People's Republic – Pekin, Ediciones en Lenguas Extranjeras. 1956. BD-520 1 – 9 – ne IDC [335]

PROPUGNACULUM ECCLESIAE ADVERSUS LUTERANOS... / Clichtove, J – [Coloniae Agrippinae], 1526 – 7mf – 9 – CA-81/1 – ne IDC [240]

O PROPUGNADOR – Rio de Janeiro, 13 Jul 1824 – 1,5,6 – bl Biblioteca [072]

PROROCHESKOE SVITLO = THE PROPHETIC LIGHT – Proctor, VT: C Skuda, 1921-jan/mar 1953 – us Res Libr [073]

PROROK RUSSKOI REVOLIUTSII / Merezhkovskii, Dimitrii – K iubilieu Dostoevskago. Spb. 1906. BR-784 2 – 8 – ne IDC [335]

PROS AND CONS, A GUIDE TO THE CONTROVERSIES OF THE DAY / Askey, J B – 10th ed. 1940. 1 fiche (29x) – 9 – 1.00f – at Libertarian Micro [320]

PROS AND CONS, A GUIDE TO THE CONTROVERSIES OF THE DAY / ed by White, M I – 10th ed. 1940. (First was 1896 by J. B. Askey). 1 fiche. (29x) – 9 – 1.00f – at Libertarian Micro [320]

A PROSA : PERIODICO LITTERARIO, HUMORISTICO E NOTICIOSO – Maceio, Alagoas. 13 Maio 1900 – 1,5,6 – bl Biblioteca [072]

PROSA SELECTA DE AUTORES ESPANOLES PARA LECTURA Y ANALISIS LITERARIO / Gomez Bravo, Vicente – Madrid: Razon y Fe, 2nd ed 1942 – 1 – sp Bibl Santa Ana [440]

PROSA SELECTA DE AUTORES ESPANOLES PARA LECTURA Y ANALISIS LITERARIO / Gomez Bravo, Vicente – Madrid: Razon y Fe, 3rd ed 1949 – 1 – sp Bibl Santa Ana [440]

PROSAISCHE UND POETISCHE WERKE / Seume, Johann Gottfried – Berlin: G. Hempel, (1867-76). 10v in 4.1 reel. 1283 – 1 – us U.W. Library [800]

Prosch, Heinrich *see* MEDICINISCH-CHIRURGISCHE ENCYKLOPAEDIE FUER PRAKTISCHE AERZTE (AEL, ABT.3;7)

PROSE WORKS / Wagner, Richard – London. 1893-99. 8v – 1 – 23.00 – us L of C Photodup [780]

PROSE WORKS. / Wordsworth, William – Ed. by William Knight. Eversley ed. London; New York: Mcmillan, 1896. 2v – 1 – us U.W. Library [880]

PROSE WORKS OF WILLIAM WORDSWORTH. EDITED BY WILLIAM KNIGHT / Wordsworth, William – London, New York: MacMillan, 1896 – 1 roll – 1 – 1-55879-269-4 – uk Libr Preservation [880]

PROSECUTION EXHIBITS SUBMITTED TO THE INTERNATIONAL MILITARY TRIBUNAL / International Military Tribunal – T988 – 54r – 1 – us Nat'l Archives [940]

PROSECUTOR: A JOURNAL OF THE NATIONAL DISTRICT ATTORNEYS ASSOCIATION – (1984-. 5,6,9) – 1967- – 1 – us UMI [340]

PROSEDURE PRAKTIS DALAM BALIK NAMA / Sena, I Gusti Ktut – SE 4298 1. 1961? – 9 – ne IDC [950]

PROSERPINA : STUDIES OF WAYSIDE FLOWERS, WHILE THE AIR WAS YET PURE AMONG THE ALPS, AND IN THE SCOTLAND AND ENGLAND WHICH MY FATHER KNEW, VOLUME 1 / Ruskin, John – Sunnyside, Orpington, Kent: G. Allen, 1879 – 1 roll – 1 – 1-55879-411-5 – uk Libr Preservation [580]

PROSOPIS TAMARUGO : FODDER TREE FOR ARID ZONES – 1981 – 119p – it F.A.O. [634]

PRO-SOVIET PROPAGANDA PAMPHLET COLLECTION – 1919-1952 – 1 reel – 1 – CSUXANR3174-B – us Hoover Inst Photo [947]

PROSPECT BAPTIST CHURCH. ROANE COUNTY. TENNESSEE : CHURCH RECORDS – Jul 1826-62 – 1 – 11.70 – us Baptist [240]

PROSPECTIVES – (Ceased v25 1989) – Montreal. v23-24. 1988-89 – 9 – Can$20.00y – cn Micromedia [370]

PROSPECTO...COLEGIO...SAN MARTIN / Tobia, Manuel Maria – 1858 – 9 – 1.50f – sp Bibl Santa Ana [946]

PROSPECTOR – Winston. Mont. 1897-1899 – 1 – us UMI [071]

THE PROSPECTOR – Caliente, NV. 1909-13 – 7r – 1 – $350.00 – U04432 – us Library Micro [071]

PROSPECTS – v1- 1969- 1; v5- 5,6,9 – us UMI [073]

PROSPECTS – v1- 1947- 1; v161- 5,6,9 – us UMI [330]

PROSPECTS FOR BIOCHEMICAL ENGINEERING AND TECHNOLOGY IN ISRAEL / Israel. Prime Minister's Office – By Zvi Bohak, Leon Goldstein, and Mordechai Sokolovsky. 69 p. In co-op. with the Dept. of Biophysics, Weizmann Inst., and Dept. of Biochemistry, George S. Wise Center for Life Sciences, Tel Aviv Univ – 9 – 2.00 – is I.T.T.I. [324]

PROSPECTS OF COAL AND LIGNITE IN NORTHERN NEGEV : A REVIEW OF WELL LOGGING TECHNIQUES / Kuslansky, Gerald – Jerusalem. May 1975. 18p – 9 – $2.00 – is I.T.T.I. [550]

PROSPECTUS / Acadia Provident Association – Halifax, N.S.: Nova Scotia Print. Co., 1874. 05935. (Pre-1900 Canadiana) – 9 – cn C.I.H.M. [971]

PROSPECTUS *see* UNIVERSITY OF MICHIGAN JOURNAL OF LAW REFORM

PROSPECTUS.. / Great Northern Railway of Canada – Quebec: L. Demers, 1894.04385.(Pre-1900 Canadiana) – 9 – cn C.I.H.M. [971]

PROSPECTUS AND CONSTITUTION. / Canada Land Law Amendment Association – Toronto: Printed by order of the Association by Globe Print. Co., 1883. 02021. (Pre-1900 Canadiana) – 9 – cn C.I.H.M. [971]

PROSPECTUS, AND OTHER DOCUMENTS / Chicago and Canada Southern Railway Company – New York: E. Sackett, 1872. 02992. (Pre-1900 Canadiana) – 9 – cn C.I.H.M. [380]

PROSPECTUS DE L'HISTOIRE DES PLANTES DE DAUPHINE / Villars, D – Grenoble. 1779. B-719 2 – 8 – ne IDC [580]

PROSPECTUS DER ODESSAER GESELLSCHAFT FUER GESCHICHTE UND ALTERTUEMER GEHOERENDEN AELTESTEN HEBRAEISCHEN UND RABBINISCHEN MANUSCRIPTE / Pinner, M – Oessa, 1845 – 2mf – ne IDC [220]

PROSPECTUS DU CHEMIN DE FER DE MONTREAL ET BYTOWN – Montreal, 1853. SEM105P637 – 1mf – 9 – Can$2.25 – cn Bibl Nat [380]

PROSPECTUS OF COURSE OF STUDIES / College of Ottawa – Ottawa: "Citizen", 1874. 03043. (Pre-1900 Canadiana) – 9 – cn C.I.H.M. [370]

PROSPECTUS OF NEW KINCARDINESHIRE COLONY OF NEW BRUNSWICK: WITH REPORTS OF DIRECTORS REGARDING SITUATION, SOIL, CLIMATE, ETC. ETC., AND A STATEMENT OF CONDITIONS CONCERNING FREE HOUSES, FREE GRANTS OF LAND, AND ASSISTED PASSAGES / Brown, William – Glasgow: W. Macrone, 1872. 00969. (Pre-1900 Canadiana) – 9 – cn C.I.H.M. [971]

PROSPECTUS, REPORTS AND STATISTICS. / Alpha Gold Mining Company – Ottawa?, 1868. 00786. (Pre-1900 Canadiana) – 9 – cn C.I.H.M. [380]

PROSPECTUS: THE BANK OF AGRICULTURE – Hamilton, Ont., 1868. 00916. (Pre-1900 Canadiana) – 9 – cn C.I.H.M. [971]

PROSPECTUS...WITH REPORTS UPON THEIR PROPERTY SITUATED IN MADOC, ONTARIO / Anglo-Saxon Gold Mining Company – By Charles Robb and Andrew Whyte. Montreal: J. Lovell, 1868. 00019. (Pre-1900 Canadiana) – 9 – cn C.I.H.M. [380]

LA PROSPERITE *see* LE LAISSEZ-PASSER

PROSPETTIVA DE PITTORI E ARCHITETTI / Pozzo, Andrea – Roma: Nella stamperia di G G Komarek Boemo, 1693. SEM105P793 – 3mf – 9 – Can$6.75 – cn Bibl Nat [720]

PROSPETTIVA DE PITTORI E ARCHITETTI, PARTE PRIMA : IN TRCUI INSEGNA IL MODO PIU SBRIGATO DI METTERE IN PROSPETTIVA TUTTI I DISEGNI D'ARCHITETTURA / Pozzo, Andrea – Roma, 1693. SEM105P793 – 3mf – 9 – Can$6.75 – cn Bibl Nat [720]

PROSROMUS MOLLET: SUPPLEMENT / Brown, Robert – 5 – uk Microform Academic [580]

Prosser, William Farrand *see* HISTORY OF THE PUGET SOUND COUNTRY

Prost, Albert *see* L'IMMIGRATION EN FRANCHE-COMTE

Prost, Andre *see* LA LANGUE BISA; GRAMMAIRE ET DICTIONNAIRE

PROSTAGLANDINS – (1982-. 1,5,6,9) – v1-. 1972- – 1 – us UMI [073]

PROSTAGLANDINS – v1-8. 1972-74 – 1,5,6 – us Princeton Micro [073]

PROSTAGLANDINS AND MEDICINE – v1-7. 1978-81 – 1 – us UMI [073]

PROSTAGLANDINS, LEUKOTRIENES, AND MEDICINE – v8-. 1982- – 1,5,6,9 – us UMI [073]

DE LA PROSTITUTION DANS LA VILLE DE PARIS, CONSIDEREE SOUS LE RAPPORT DE L'HYGIENE PUBLIQUE, DE LA MORALE ET DE L'ADMINISTRATION; OUVRAGE APPUYE DE DOCUMENTS STATISTIQUES PUISES DANS LES ARCHIVES DE LA PREFECTURE DE PARIS / Parent-Duchatelet, A J B – (Condition of 19th C. French working class series). 1857 – 9 – fr Hachette [360]

Prost-Leroy, C *see* L'INDUSTRIE OSSEUSE DE L'AURIGNACIEN

PROSTO Z MOSTU – Warsaw, 1936-39 – 1r – 1 – us Ross [947]

PROSTOE KAK MYCHANIE / Maiakovskii, Vladimir – Stikhi. Petrograd. 1916. BR-993 2 – 8 – ne IDC [460]

PROSTONARODNI CESKE PISNE A RIKADLA. NAPEVY PROSTONARODNICH PISNI CESKYCH / ed by Erben, K J – v. 1-2. Praha. 1862-64. HO-ECE-1155. BR-5173 2 – 8 – ne IDC [943]

PROSTOR – 1960-73 – 1 – us I.U. Libraries [073]

PROSVESCENIE – (See also series: Important Periodicals of Italian and International Socialism, 1868-1917) – Education. St. Petersburg. v1,no1-v4,no2. Dec 1911-Oct 1917. Social, political, and literary review with Bolshevik tendencies – 9 – $80.00 – us UPA [335]

PROSVESHCHENIE – Ezhemesiachnyi zhurnal. Spb. 1911-14. Lacking: (10-12) 1912; (7-12) 1914. B-1840 2 – 8 – ne IDC [073]

PROSVETA – Chicago, IL, 1916-1967 – 35r – 1 – us I.H.R.C. [975]

PROSVETA = ENLIGHTENMENT – Chicago, IL: [Narodna tiskarna, jul 1916-dec 7 1967] – us Res Libr [071]

PROSVETA – Skopjle, Yugoslavia. -f. 11 Jan 1966-13 Dec 1968. 1 reel – 1 – uk British Libr Newspaper [949]

PROSVETITEL 18 VEKA : IA. P. KOZELSKII / Kogan, Iu. Ia – 1958 – 8 – BR-6214 2 – ne IDC [947]

PROSVETITELNYI VEK I ALEKSANDROVSKAIA PORA / Veselovskii, A N – 1916 – 8 – BR-7950 2 – ne IDC [947]

PROSVETNI GLASNIK / Yugoslavia. Ministarstvo prosvete – v. 1-35, no. 5. 1880-1914. Several scattered issues wanting – 1 – 260.00 – us L of C Photodup [370]

PROSVETNI PREGLED – Belgrade, Yugoslavia. Apr 1945-1953; 1955-68 – 6r – 1 – us L of C Photodup [949]

PROSVITA = ENLIGHTMENT – McKeesport, PA: United Societies of Gr C Religion of the USA, 1943-sep 1975 – us Res Libr [071]

PROSVJETNI LIST – Sarajevo. Yugoslavia. -f. 1 Jan 1960-1 Nov 1961. (1 reel) – 1 – uk British Libr Newspaper [949]

Protas'eva, T N *see* OPISANIE RUKOPISEI SINODAL'NOGO SOBRANIIA (NE VOSHEDSHIKH V OPISANIE A.V. GORSKOGO I K.I. NEVOSTRUEVA)

PROTECCION DE LA DOCTRINA DE HIPOCRATES Y GALENO, ACERCA DEL METHODO DE CURAR... / Valverde Horosco, D – Sevilla, 1653 – 2mf – 9 – sp Cultura [615]

LA PROTECCION DEL ABORIGEN EN EL 20. PLAN QUINQUENAL / Abregu Virreira, Carlos – [Buenos Aires]: Presidencia de la Nacion, 1953 – 1 – CSUXAJA7146-B – us Hoover Inst Photo [320]

PROTECTED CULTIVATION IN THE MEDITERRANEAN CLIMATE – 1990 – 333p – it F.A.O. [631]

LE PROTECTEUR – Montreal: Societe de protection des malades, [1895] – 9 – cn C.I.H.M. [360]

LE PROTECTEUR : SOCIETE DE PROTECTION DES MALADES – Montreal, Canada. 15 jun 1895; 15 jul 1895 – 1r – 1 – Can$25.00 – cn Can Microfilming [610]

LE PROTECTEUR DE SAGUENAY – Chicoutimi, Canada. 17 sep 1896-29 avr 1899 – 1r – 1 – Can$50.00 – cn Can Microfilming [072]

LE PROTECTEUR DU PEUPLE : REDIGE PAR UN COMITE DE MEDECINS ANTI-VACCINATEURS – Montreal, Canada. nov 1885 – 1r – 1 – Can$25.00 – cn Can Microfilming [610]

PROTECTING THE LAMBS / Davis, Abraham N – New York, Judicial Printing Co., 1938 14 p. LL-662 – 1 – us L of C Photodup [340]

PROTECTION AND FREE TRADE / Faucet, Henry – 40p – 9 – 1.00f – at Libertarian Micro [380]

LA PROTECTION AU CANADA: CONFERENCE LE 14 MARS 1895 AUX SALLES DU CLUB CARTIER-MACDONALD / Amyot, Guillaume – 1895. 02400. (Pre-1900 Canadiana) – 9 – cn C.I.H.M. [971]

LA PROTECTION DES MINORITES... / Fouques Duparc, J – Paris, 1922 – 4mf – 1 – ILM-1569/1 – ne IDC [327]

LA PROTECTION DES MINORITES DANS LES PAYS BALTIQUES... / Villecourt, L – Bordeaux, 1925 – 2mf – 9 – ILM-1558/1 – ne IDC [350]

PROTECTION DES OEUVRES LITTERAIRES ET ARTISTIQUES ETRANGERES AUX ETATS-UNIS, LES FORMALITES / Serrero, Andre – Paris: Librairie generale de droit et de jurisprudence, 1953. 157p. LL-1128 – 1 – us L of C Photodup [340]

LA PROTECTION DU SAVANT ET DE L'ARTISTE / Argentina. Direccion General de Relaciones Culturales y Difusion – [Buenos Aires?: Direction Generale des Relations Culturelles et de Diffusion, 1950?] – 1 – CSUXADP5172-B – us Hoover Inst Photo [972]

PROTECTION ECOLOGY – v1-7. 1979-84 – 1,5,6,13 – sz Elsevier [574]

PROTECTION ECOLOGY *see* AGRICULTURE, ECOSYSTEMS AND ENVIRONMENT

PROTECTION ET UTILISATION DE LA MAIN-D'OEUVRE FEMININE DANS LES USINES DE GUERRE – Paris. 1919. (La Condition Ouvriere. Part Two.) – 9 – 7.50 – fr Bibl Nationale [360]

LA PROTECTION INTERNATIONALE DES MINORITES / Balogh, A de – Paris, 1930 – 3mf – 9 – ILM-1568/1 – ne IDC [340]

PROTECTION MANAGEMENT – 1971- 1; 1977-5,6,9 – us UMI [360]

PROTECTION OF METALS – v1-29. 1965-93 – 1,5 – $120.00v – us UMI [660]

PROTECTION OF MOVABLE CULTURAL PROPERTY : COMPENDIUM OF LEGISLATIVE TEXTS – 1984 – 9 – fr UNESCO [340]

PROTECTION OR FREE TRADE / George, Henry – 1fiche (24x) – 9 – 1.00f – at Libertarian Micro [320]

LE PROTECTIONNISTE / ed by Rouillard, Eugene – Quebec, Canada. 19-21 fev 1887 – 1r – 1 – Can$25.00 – cn Can Microfilming [072]

LE PROTECTIONNISTE – Saint-Jean, Canada. 7 jul 1882-v2 n17. 9 oct 1883 – 1r – 1 – Can$30.00 – cn Can Microfilming [072]

PROTECTIVE AND REORGANIZATION COMMITTEES REPORTS / U.S. Securities and Exchange Commission – pts 1-8 + index. 1937-1940 (all publ) – 52mf – 9 – $78.00 – LLMC 80-519 – us L.L.M.C. [324]

PROTECTIVE BULLETIN / American Bankers Association – (Earlier reports of the Protective Dept of the Association are publ as a section of: Banking, American Bankers Association Journal. Cont by: Bank Protection Bulletin) – Washington. 1934-1971* – 1 – D20200 – us UMI [332]

PROTECTIVE MECHANISM OF ESTRADIOL ON ECCENTRICALLY INDUCED MUSCLE DAMAGE / Dumke, Charles L – University of Montana, 1995 – 1mf – 9 – PE 3636 – us Microform Publ [617]

THE PROTECTOR / ed by Larkin, Thomas – (Bilingual) – Montreal, Canada. v7 n10. 1 oct 1903 – 1r – 1 – Can$25.00 – cn Can Microfilming [072]

EL PROTECTOR DE INDIOS / Merino, M & Bayle, Constantino – Sevilla, 1945; Madrid: Missionalia Hispanica, 1946 – 1 – sp Bibl Santa Ana [240]

LE PROTECTORAT EN AFRIQUE OCCIDENTALE FRANCAISE ET LES CHEFS INDIGENES / Forgeron, Jean Baptiste – Bordeaux: l'Universite, 1920. 95p. LL-12008 – 1 – us L of C Photodup [340]

LE PROTECTORAT INTERNATIONAL / Gairal, F – Paris, n.d. – 4mf – 1 – ILM-1953/1 – ne IDC [327]

Protectorate of Annam and Tonkin *see* BULLETIN OFFICIEL

LES PROTECTORATS ANCIENS ET MODERNES / Engelhardt, E – Paris, 1896 – 3mf – 1 – ILM-1956/1 – ne IDC [327]

PROTEIN QUALITY EVALUATION : REPORT OF THE JOINT FAO/WHO EXPERT CONSULTATION, BETHESDA, USA, 1989 – 1991 – 70p – it F.A.O. [660]

PROTEIN-ENERGY REQUIREMENTS UNDER CONDITIONS PREVAILING IN DEVELOPING COUNTRIES : CURRENT KNOWLEDGE AND RESEARCH NEEDS – 1979 – 73p – $4.00 – 92-808-0018-3 – ja U.N. Univ [613]

LA PROTESIS DELLA LITURGIA NEL RITO BIZANTINO-GRECO / Mandala, M – Grottaferrata, 1935 – 4mf – 8 – Dfl19.00 – ne Slangenburg [240]

PROTEST LITERATURE OF NAMIBIA AND SOUTH AFRICA – 1984- . London: various publishers – 1 – us U.W. Library [960]

LA PROTESTA UMANA – Chicago, IL, 1902-1903 – 1r – 1 – us I.H.R.C. [978]

LA PROTESTA UMANA – San Francisco, CA, 1900-1904 – 1r – 1 – us I.H.R.C. [978]

DER PROTESTAND – Switzerland. v71-89. 1968 (complete) – 1r – 1 – ATLA S0875 – us A.T.L.A. [073]

THE PROTESTANT / Bray, Anna Eliza – British Fiction Archive: Unit 2 – 9 – uk Bell [830]

THE PROTESTANT – Montreal, Canada. fev 1874 – 1r – 1 – Can$25.00 – cn Can Microfilming [240]

THE PROTESTANT – Saint John, NB: G W Day, [1858-1859?] – 9 – cn C.I.H.M. [240]

THE PROTESTANT – Toronto: A B Demill, [1891-189- or 19–] – 9 – cn C.I.H.M. [200]

PROTESTANT AND EVANGELICAL WITNESS – Charlottetown, Canada. 1862-65 – 1 reel – 1 – $68.00 – cn Library Assoc [971]

THE PROTESTANT CHURCH IN GERMANY : A GENERAL SURVEY / Schodde, George H – Philadelphia, Pa.: Lutheran Publication Society, c1901 – 1mf – us A.T.L.A. [240]

PROTESTANT DEFENDER – Belfast, Ireland. 22 Nov 1848-16 Jun 1849. -w.1/2 reel – 1 – uk British Libr Newspaper [072]

Protestant Episcopal Church in the U.S.A. Kansas (Diocese) *see* RECORDS

Protestant Episcopal Church in the U.S.A. Western Kansas (Diocese) *see* PARISH RECORDS

Protestant Episcopal Church in the U.S.A. Western Kansas (Missionary District) *see* – PARISH RECORDS OF VARIOUS TOWNS

PROTESTANT EPISCOPAL CHURCH IN THE U.S.A., NEW YORK DIOCESE : JOURNAL OF THE CONVENTION – 1787-91 (complete) – 1r – 1 – ATLA S0253 – us A.T.L.A. [240]

PROTESTANT EPISCOPAL CHURCH IN THE U.S.A., NEW YORK DIOCESE : JOURNAL OF THE PROCEEDINGS – v13-117. 1796-1900 (complete) – 9r – 1 – ATLA S0256 – us A.T.L.A. [240]

PROTESTANT EPISCOPAL CHURCH IN THE U.S.A., NEW YORK DIOCESE : JOURNALS OF THE CONVENTION – 1844 (complete) – 1r – 1 – ATLA S0254 – us A.T.L.A. [240]

PROTESTANT EPISCOPAL CHURCH IN THE U.S.A., NEW YORK DIOCESE : PROCEEDINGS – 1785; 1787 (complete) – 1r – 1 – ATLA S0252 – us A.T.L.A. [240]

PROTESTANT EPISCOPAL CHURCH IN THE U.S.A., NEW YORK DIOCESE : PROCEEDINGS – 1845 (complete) – 1r – 1 – ATLA S0255 – us A.T.L.A. [240]

Protestant Episcopal Church. South Carolina (Diocese) *see* TRANSACTIONS

PROTESTANT EXILES FROM FRANCE.. / Agnew, David C A – 1871. with Samuel Smiles. The Huguenots, Their Settlements... 1867 – 1 – $50.00 – us Presbyterian [240]

THE PROTESTANT FAITH, OR, SALVATION BY BELIEF : AN ESSAY UPON THE ERRORS OF THE PROTESTANT CHURCH / Olmstead, Dwight Hinckley – (Includes bibliographical references) – new ed. New York: G P Putnam, 1885 – 1mf – 9 – 0-8370-8848-8 – 1986-2848 – us A.T.L.A. [240]

PROTESTANT FOREIGN MISSIONS: THEIR PRESENT STATE = GEGENWAERTIGE STAND DER EVANGELISCHEN HEIDENMISSION : A UNIVERSAL SURVEY / Christlieb, Theodor – (In English. Includes index) – Authorized American ed. Boston: Congregational Pub Society, c1880 – 1mf – 9 – 0-8370-6658-1 – 1986-0658 – us A.T.L.A. [240]

PROTESTANT LAWYERS LEAGUE OF THE PHILIPPINES – Metro Manila, Philippines. 17 docs. 1981-1991 – 9mf – 9 – ne IDC [340]

PROTESTANT MERCURY OR EXETER POST BOY – London, UK. 7 Oct 1715-Sept 1717. -w. 1 reel – 1 – uk British Libr Newspaper [072]

PROTESTANT MINISTERS IN HUNGARY: MEMORIAL OF SUFFERINGS – 1676 – 1 – uk Microform Academic [240]

PROTESTANT MISSION WORK AMONG ITALIANS IN BOSTON / DeBillo, Francis D – 1949 – 1r – 1 – us I.H.R.C. [240]

PROTESTANT MISSIONS : THEIR RISE AND EARLY PROGRESS: LECTURES / Thompson, Augustus Charles – (Includes bibliographical references, appendix and index) – New York: Charles Scribner, 1894 – 1mf – 9 – 0-8370-6424-4 – 1986-0424 – us A.T.L.A. [240]

PROTESTANT MISSIONS IN PAGAN LANDS : A MANUAL OF MISSIONARY FACTS AND PRINCIPLES RELATING TO FOREIGN MISSIONS THROUGHOUT THE WORLD / Storrow, Edward – London: J. Snow, 1888 – 1mf – us A.T.L.A. [240]

PROTESTANT MISSIONS IN SOUTH AMERICA / Beach, Harlan Page et al – (Includes appendixes and indexes) – New York: Student Volunteer Movement for Foreign Missions, 1907, c1900 – 1mf – 9 – 0-8370-6563-1 – 1986-0563 – us A.T.L.A. [240]

PROTESTANT PRINCIPLES / Gibson, John Monro – New York: A C Armstrong; London: Hodder and Stoughton, 1901 – 1mf – 9 – 0-8370-8508-X – 1986-2508 – us A.T.L.A. [230]

THE PROTESTANT REVIEW – (Cont: The Monthly Rose) – St. John, NB: D F Hutchinson, [1870?-18– or 19–] – 9 – cn C.I.H.M. [240]

THE PROTESTANT REVIEW – (Some original pgs damaged) – v1-22. 1969-91 – 5r – 1 – ATLA S0364 – us A.T.L.A. [073]

THE PROTESTANT REVIEW *see* THE MONTHLY ROSE

PROTESTANT SEARCHLIGHT – Cleveland, OH, 16 Dec 1916-14 July 1917 – 1 reel – 1 – us Western Res [240]

PROTESTANT THOUGHT BEFORE KANT / McGiffert, Arthur Cushman – New York: Scribner, 1911 – 1mf – us A.T.L.A. [240]

PROTESTANT VANGUARD – Glasgow, Scotland. Vanguard. -w, -m. Aug 1931-May 1947. 3 reels – 1 – uk British Libr Newspaper [072]

PROTESTANT WEEKLY LETTER – nos 1-111. 1914-Jan 1917 (complete) – 1r – 1 – ATLA B0276 – us A.T.L.A. [073]

PROTESTANT WITNESS – West Bromwich. England. -m. Jan 1916-Oct 1919. (38 ft) – 1 – uk British Libr Newspaper [072]

PROTESTANTENBLATT : WOCHENSCHRIFT FUER DEN DEUTSCHEN PROTESTANTISMUS – v44-74. 1911-41 (complete) – 8r – 1 – ATLA S0062 – us A.T.L.A. [073]

PROTESTANTESIMO – 11(1956)-27(1972) – 83mf – 9 – Dfl291.00 – ne Slangenburg [073]

DIE PROTESTANTISCHE FREIHEIT IN IHREM GEGENWAERTIGEN KAMPFE MIT DER KIRCHLICHEN REAKTION : EINE SCHUTZSCHRIFT / Schenkel, Daniel – 2. unver. Aufl. Wiesbaden: C W Kreidel, 1865 – 1mf – 9 – 0-8370-5085-5 – 1985-3085 – us A.T.L.A. [240]

DIE PROTESTANTISCHE KIRCHE FRANKREICHS VON 1787 BIS 1846 / Gieseler, Johann Carl Ludwig – Leipzig: Breitkopf und Haertel, 1848 – 2mf – us A.T.L.A. [240]

PROTESTANTISCHE MONATSHEFTE – v1-25. 1897-1921 (complete) – 7r – 1 – ATLA 1994-S539 – us A.T.L.A. [073]

DIE PROTESTANTISCHEN CENTRALDOGMEN / Schweitzer, Alexander – 1854-56.2v – 1 – us A.T.L.A. [240]

PROTESTANTISK TIDENDE – v24-88. 1928-92 (complete) – Inquire – 1 – ATLA S0858 – us A.T.L.A. [073]

PROTESTANTISM : ITS ULTIMATE PRINCIPLE / Dale, Robert William – London: Hodder and Stoughton, 1874 – 1mf – 9 – 0-8370-8807-0 – 1986-2807 – us A.T.L.A. [240]

PROTESTANTISM AND PROGRESS = BEDEUTUNG DES PROTESTANTISMUS FUER DIE ENTSTEHUNG DER MODERNEN WELT : A HISTORICAL STUDY OF THE RELATION OF PROTESTANTISM TO THE MODERN WORLD / Troeltsch, Ernst – (In English. Includes bibliographical references and index) – London: Williams & Norgate; New York: G P Putnam, 1912 – 1mf – 9 – 0-8370-9433-X – 1986-3433 – us A.T.L.A. [240]

LE PROTESTANTISME JUGE ET CONDAMNE PAR LES PROTESTANTS:.. / Guillaume, C – Montreal?, 1870.05130.(Pre-1900 Canadiana) – 9 – cn C.I.H.M. [240]

PROTESTANTISME LIBERAL = LIBERAL CHRISTIANITY : ITS ORIGIN, NATURE, AND MISSION / Reville, Jean; ed by Leuliette, Victor – (In English) – 1mf – 9 – 0-8370-5285-8 – 1985-3285 – us A.T.L.A. [240]

EL PROTESTANTISMO EN LA AMERICA ESPANOLA / Bayle, Constantino – Madrid: Razon y Fe, 1923 – 1 – sp Bibl Santa Ana [240]

DER PROTESTANTISMUS IN POLEN AUF GRUND DER EINHEIMISCHEN GESCHICHTSSCHREIBUNG / Voelker, Karl – Leipzig: J.C. Hinrichs, 1910 – 1mf – us A.T.L.A. [240]

DER PROTESTANTISMUS IN POLEN AUF GRUND DER EINHEIMISCHEN GESCHICHTSSCHREIBUNG DARGESTELLT / Voelker, Karl – Leipzig. 1910. BR-5562 2 – 8 – ne IDC [240]

DER PROTESTANTISMUS IN STEIERMARK, KAERNTEN UND KRAIN : VOM 15. JAHRHUNDERT BIS IN DIE GEGENWART / Ilwof, Franz – Graz: Leykam, 1900 – 1mf – us A.T.L.A. [240]

PROTESTANTISMUS UND TOLERANZ IM 16. JAHRHUNDERT / Paulus, Nikolaus – Freiburg im Breisgau: Herder, 1911 – 1mf – us A.T.L.A. [240]

LES PROTESTANTS ANGLAIS REFUGIES A GENEVE AU TEMPS DE CALVIN 1555-1560 : LEUR EGLISE, LEURS ECRITS / Martin, Charles – Geneve: A. Julien, 1915 – 1mf – us A.T.L.A. [949]

PROTESTANTS OF THE EAST / Gill, Everett – 322p – 1 – 11.27 – us Baptist [240]

Protestantsche Kerk in Indonesie *see* DE PROTESTANTSCHE KERK IN INDONESIE TIJDENS BEZETTING EN TERREUR

DE PROTESTANTSCHE KERK IN INDONESIE TIJDENS BEZETTING EN TERREUR / Protestantsche Kerk in Indonesie – SE-3323 1946 – 9 – ne IDC [240]

PROTESTATION DE MOSEIGNEUR LE PRINCE DE CONDE / Conde, Louis 1 de Bourbon – s.l.: s.n., 1567?. Filmed with: Advertissement a tous bons et loyaux subiectz du roy – 1 – us U.W. Library [944]

PROTESTATION ODDER EMPIETUNG / Muentzer, T – Alstedt. 1524. BME-27 1 – 9 – ne IDC [240]

PROTESTATION SAMUEL HUBERS PROFESSORN DER H. SCHRIFFT ZU WITTEMBERG. WIDER JOHAN WILHELM STUCK ZU ZUERICH D. JOHANN JACOB GRYNEUM ZU BASEL VND JOHAN JETZLERN (WELCHER SICH SEITHERO HAT GRATIANUM SERLEYU TAUFFENM LASSEN) ZU SCHAFFHAUSEN... / Huber, S – Wittemberg, 1593 – 1mf – ne IDC [240]

PROTEUS OFTE MINNE-BEELDEN VERANDERT IN SINNE-BEELDEN / Cats, J – Den Haag, 1629 – 6mf – 9 – ne IDC [700]

PROTEUS OFTE MINNE-BEELDEN VERANDERT IN SINNEBEELDEN / Cats, J – O 194. 1627 – 9 – ne IDC [760]

PROTEUS VINCTUS / Willis, Thomas – 1655. 517p. (English Linguistics Series 1500-1800) – 9 – us UMI [400]

Prothero, George Walter *see* A MEMOIR OF HENRY BRADSHAW, FELLOW OF KING'S COLLEGE

PROTHESEZ-VOUS – Montreal: Assoc. des denturologistes du Quebec. v1 no 1(juin 1983)- v1 no 2(dec 1983). SEM105P1298 – 1mf – 9 – Can$2.25 – cn Bibl Nat [617]
PROTIDES OF THE BIOLOGICAL FLUIDS – v16- 1969- – 5,6,9 – us UMI [574]
PROTIV RELIGII ZA SOTSIALIZM VO VTORI PYATILETKE / Gulenkov, S & Sobolev, A – Against Religion for Socialism in the Second Five Year Plan. Samara, 1932. – 1 – $74.32 – us Baptist [240]
PROTIV RELIGII ZA VOINSVUYUSHCHEE BEZBOZHIE = AGAINST RELIGION FOR MILITANT ATHEISM / Uzkov, Ivan – Khabarovsk, 1931. One of 13 titles by Soviet authors on reel – 1 – 74.32 – us Baptist [240]
PROTIVORIECHIIA I NESOOBRAZNOSTI V NASHEI VNUTRENNEI POLITIKIE / Demchenko, I Akov Grigorevich – Kiev: Tip. t-va I.N. Kushnerev, 1907 – 1 – CSUX89-B5469 – us Hoover Inst Photo [947]
PROTOCOL – Dat is: alle Handelinge der Tsamensprekinghe tot Franckenthal. gehouden metten genen diemen Wederdoopers noemet. wt de Ouerlantsche sprake. ouergestelt. By my Hans Bruynincx. 1571. BME-235 1 – 9 – ne IDC [240]
PROTOCOL – Dat is, alle handelinge des gesprecks tot Embden in Oostvrieslant met den Wederdooperen, die hen Vlamingen noemen, gehouden. Embden, G. Goebens. 1579. BME-240 1 – 9 – ne IDC [240]
PROTOCOL – Dat is de gansche Handelinge des Gesprecks, te Franckenthal. met dien, welcke men Wederdoopers noemt. Wt den Ouerlantschen Duytsche, in Nederlantsduytsch ouergheset door Gaspar van der Heyden. 1571. BME-237 1 – 9 – ne IDC [240]
PROTOCOL – Dat is, de gantsche handelinge des ghesprecx ghehouden tot Leeuwarden. tusschen Ruardum Aeronium. ter eenre, ende Peter van Ceulen. ter ander syden: Aug-Nov 1596. Franeker, G. Van den Rade. 1597. BME-250 1 – 9 – ne IDC [240]
PROTOCOL – Dath is, alle handelinge des gesprecks tho Embden in Oisfrieszlandt mit den Wedderdoeperen, de sick Flaminge noemen, geholden Febr.-Maij 1578. Embden, G. Goebens. 1579. BME-239 1 – 9 – ne IDC [240]
PROTOCOLES DE LA COMMISSION. PROCES VERBAUX DE LA SOUS-COMMISSION / Egypt. Commission Internationale du Canal de Suez – Avril-mai-juin. 1885. Paris. 1885. BNE-4617 1 – 9 – ne IDC [330]
PROTOCOLES NOTARIALES DE JERONIMO GUTIERREZ (ANNO 1532-1534). CAJA – Caceres – 1r – 5,6 – sp Cultura [340]
PROTOCOLL – Das ist, alle Handlung des gesprechs zu Franckenthal. mit denen so man Widertaeuffer nennet, May, Junij 1571. Heidelb., J. Mayer. 1571. BME-233 1 – 9 – ne IDC [240]
PROTOCOLL – Das ist, alle Handlung des gesprechs zu Franckenthal. mit denen so man Widertaeuffer nennet, May, Junij 1571. Heidelb., J. Mayer. 1573. BME-234 1 – 9 – ne IDC [240]
PROTOCOLO / Gobierno Civil – Badajoz: Graficas Iberia de Bartolome Garcia, 1966 – sp Bibl Santa Ana [946]
PROTOCOLO DEL NOTARIO MARCO HERRERA (ANNO 1566) – Badajoz – 1r – 5,6 – sp Cultura [340]
PROTOCOLO NOTARIAL DE GARCIA ALVAREZ DE AGUILAR (ANNO 1514) – Caceres – 1r – 5,6 – sp Cultura [340]
PROTOCOLOS NOTARIALES (ANNO 1516-1565) – Oviedo – 1r – 5,6 – sp Cultura [340]
PROTOHISTORIA EXTREMENA / Roso de Luna, Mario – Madrid: Est. Tip. Fortanet, 1908. B.R.A.H. Tomo 52, 1908, pp. 140-152 – 1 – sp Bibl Santa Ana [946]
PROTOKOL DES VEREINIGUNG SPARTEITAGES DER SOZIALDEMOKRATISCHEN PARTEI DEUTSCHLANDS (SPD) UND DER KOMMUNISTISCHEN PARTEI DEUTSCHALNDS (KPD) AM 21. UND 22, APRIL 1946 IN DER STAATSOPER "ADMIRALSPALAST" IN BERLIN / Sozialdemokratische Partei Deutschlands – Berlin, JHW Dietz nachf. c1946 – 1 – us U.W. Library [943]
PROTOKOLL / Deutscher Maschinensetzerkongress – Berlin. v2. 1924. Congresses...sponsored by the Zentralkommission der Maschinensetzer Deutschlands. (Serial publications of German trade unions in the Memorial Library, University of Wisconsin-Madison.) – 1 – us U.W. Library [330]
PROTOKOLL / Reichskonferenz der Tucharbeiter und tucharbeiterinnen Deutschlands. Forst in der Lausitz, 1928 – 1928. 104p. (Serial publications of German trade unions in the Memorial Library, University of Wisconsin-Madison.) – 1 – us U.W. Library [330]
PROTOKOLL / Verband der Hut- und Filzwarenarbeiter und arbieterinnen Deutschlands – v11. 1913. Altenburg. (Serial publications of German trade unions in the Memorial Library, University of Wisconsin-Madison.) – 1 – us U.W. Library [330]
PROTOKOLL / Verband der Maler, Lackierer, Anstreicher, Tuencher und Weissbinder Deutschlands – v13,21. 1910-28. Hamburg. (Serial publications of German trade unions in the Memorial Library, University of Wisconsin-Madison.) – 1 – us U.W. Library [330]
PROTOKOLL / Zentralverband der Angestellten – v3. 1927. Berlin. (Serial publications of German trade unions in the Memorial Library, University of Wisconsin-Madison.) – 1 – us U.W. Library [330]
PROTOKOLL / Zentralverband der Hotel-, Restaurant-, und Cafeangestellten – v13, 1929. Berlin. (Serial publications of German trade unions in the Memorial Library, University of Wisconsin-Madison.) – 1 – us U.W. Library [330]
PROTOKOLL / Zentralverband der Lederarbeiter und Arbeiterinnen Deutschlands – v15. 1914. Berlin. (Serial publications of German trade unions in the Memorial Library, University of Wisconsin-Madison.) – 1 – us U.W. Library [330]
PROTOKOLL / Zentralverband der Maurer Deutschlands – v10-11. 1908-10. Hamburg. Continued as: Deutscher Bauarbeiterverband. (Serial publications of German trade unions in the Memorial Library, University of Wisconsin-Madison.) – 1 – us U.W. Library [330]
PROTOKOLL / Zentralverband der Zimmerer und verwandten Berufsgenossen Deutschlands – v19. 1911. (Serial publications of German trade unions in the Memorial Library, University of Wisconsin-Madison.) – 1 – us U.W. Library [330]
PROTOKOLL / Zentralverein fuer alle in der Hut- und Filzwareindustrie beschaeftigten Arbeiter und Arbeiterinnen – Altenburg. v10. 1910. (Serial publications of German trade unions in the Memorial Library, University of Wisconsin-Madison.) – 1 – us U.W. Library [330]
PROTOKOLL.. / Verband der Schneider, Schneiderinnen und Waeschearbeiter Deutschlands – v12. 1912. Berlin. (Serial publications of German trade unions in the Memorial Library, University of Wisconsin-Madison.) – 1 – us U.W. Library [330]
PROTOKOLL... / Deutscher Holzarbeiter-Verband – Berlin. v1-2, 4, 10, 13-16. 1895-1917. illus. (Serial publications of German trade unions in the Memorial Library, University of Wisconsin-Madison.) – 1 – us U.W. Library [330]
PROTOKOLL... / Deutscher Holzarbeiter-Verband – Berlin. v2. 1912. Second Congress has title: Die Korbmacher auf dem Vormarsch. (Serial publications of German trade unions in the Memorial Library, University of Wisconsin-Madison.) – 1 – us U.W. Library [330]
PROTOKOLL... / Deutscher Lederarbeiter-Verband – Berlin. v18, 20. 1925-32. (Serial publications of German trade unions in the Memorial Library, University of Wisconsin-Madison.) – 1 – us U.W. Library [330]
PROTOKOLL... / Gewerkverein christlicher Bergarbeiter Deutschlands – Essen. v14, 17-18, 20. 1913-30. (Serial publications of German trade unions in the Memorial Library, University of Wisconsin-Madison.) – 1 – us U.W. Library [330]
PROTOKOLL... / Verband der Gemeinde- und Staatsarbeiter. Reichssektion Kammereibetriebe. Reichskonferenz – v1. 1929. Berlin. (Serial publications of German trade unions in the Memorial Library, University of Wisconsin-Madison.) – 1 – us U.W. Library [330]
PROTOKOLL DER ERSTEN KONFERENZ.. / Verband der Fabrikarbeiter Deutschlands – 1913. Hannover. Only conference proceedings published. (Serial publications of German trade unions in the Memorial Library, University of Wisconsin-Madison.) – 1 – us U.W. Library [330]
PROTOKOLL DER GENERALVERSAMMLUNG / Allgemeiner deutscher Arbeiter-Verein – v1-4. 1871-74. Berlin. (Serial publications of German trade unions in the Memorial Library, University of Wisconsin-Madison) – 1 – us U.W. Library [073]
PROTOKOLL DER GENERALVERSAMMLUNG / Deutscher Eisenbahner-Verband – v3. 1925. (Serial publications of German trade unions in the Memorial Library, University of Wisconsin-Madison.) – 1 – us U.W. Library [330]
PROTOKOLL DER GENERALVERSAMMLUNG / Verband der Bergbauindustriearbeiter Deutschlands – Bochum. v22,24,26-27. 1920-30. Before 1928, known as Verband der Bergarbeiter Deutschlands. (Serial publications of German trade unions in the Memorial Library, University of Wisconsin-Madison.) – 1 – us U.W. Library [330]
PROTOKOLL DER GENERALVERSAMMLUNG / Verband der deutschen Buchdrucker – Berlin. v3,5-14 & supp. 1899-1929. Title varies: Protokoll des Verbandstages. (Serial publications of German trade unions in the Memorial Library, University of Wisconsin-Madison.) – 1 – us U.W. Library [330]
PROTOKOLL DER GENERALVERSAMMLUNG / Zentralverband der Schiffszimmerer Deutschlands – v13. 1913. Hamburg. (Serial publications of German trade unions in the Memorial Library, University of Wisconsin-Madison.) – 1 – us U.W. Library [330]
PROTOKOLL DER KONFERENZ DES REICHSBEIRATS DER PETRIEBSRATE UND KONZERNVERTRETER DER METALLINDUSTRIE. BERLIN. V10. 1931. (SERIAL / Deutscher Metallarbeiterverband – (Serial Publications of German Trade Unions in the Memorial Library, University of Wisconsin-Madison) – 1 – us U.W. Library [331]
PROTOKOLL DER KONFERENZ...19-23 FEBRUAR 1906 / Konferenz der Gewerkschaftsvorstaende – 3rd Konferenz, Berlin. 48p. (Serial publications of German trade unions in the Memorial Library, University of Wisconsin-Madison.) – 1 – us U.W. Library [330]
PROTOKOLL DER ORDENTLICHEN GENERALVERSAMMLUNG / Zentralverband der Glasarbeiter und -Arbeiterinnen Deutschlands – 1st-. Berlin. v8. 1907. (Serial publications of German trade unions in the Memorial Library, University of Wisconsin-Madison.) – 1 – us U.W. Library [330]
PROTOKOLL DER VERHANDLUNGEN / Allgemeiner Schutzkongress fuer alle in der Schiffahrt und im Schiffbau Beschaeftigten – v1. 1906. Hamburg. Only 1st conference proceedings ever published. (Serial publications of German trade unions in the Memorial Library, University of Wisconsin-Madison) – 1 – us U.W. Library [331]
PROTOKOLL DER VERHANDLUNGEN / Deutscher Transportarbeiter-Kongress. First – Berlin. v1. 1904. (Serial publications of German trade unions in the Memorial Library, University of Wisconsin-Madison.) – 1 – us U.W. Library [330]
PROTOKOLL DER VERHANDLUNGEN / Verband der Buchbinder und Papierverarbeiter Deutschlands – Berlin, v9-10, 13-14, 16-17. 1904-29. (Serial publications of German trade unions in the Memorial Library, University of Wisconsin-Madison.) – 1 – us U.W. Library [330]
PROTOKOLL DER VERHANDLUNGEN / Zentralverband der Schuhmacher Deutschlands. Betriebsrate-Kongress fuer die Schuhindustrie – 1st. 1920. v2. 1922. (Serial publications of German trade unions in the Memorial Library, University of Wisconsin-Madison.) – 1 – us U.W. Library [330]
PROTOKOLL DER VERHANDLUNGEN.. / Allgemeiner Heimarbeiterschutz-Kongress. 1st, Berlin. 1904 – 7-9 Marz 1904. Berlin. 228p. illus. (Serial publications of German trade unions in the Memorial Library, University of Wisconsin-Madison) – 1 – us U.W. Library [331]
PROTOKOLL DER VERHANDLUNGEN.. / Konferenz der Strassenwarter – v1. 1926. (Serial publications of German trade unions in the Memorial Library, University of Wisconsin-Madison.) – 1 – us U.W. Library [330]
PROTOKOLL DER VERHANDLUNGEN.. / Kongress der Gewerkschaften Deutschlands – Hamburg. v1-11, 12, 15. 1892-1932. (Serial publications of German trade unions in the Memorial Library, University of Wisconsin-Madison.) – 1 – us U.W. Library [330]
PROTOKOLL DER VERHANDLUNGEN... / Sozialistische Einheitspartei Deutschlands. Parteitag – 1947-76. Berlin: Dietz – 1 – us U.W. Library [073]
PROTOKOLL DER VERHANDLUNGEN DER.. / Sozialistische Einheitspartei Deutschlands. Parteikonferenz – Jan 1949-64. Berlin: Dietz Verlag. 4v. Title varies slightly – 1 – us U.W. Library [073]
PROTOKOLL DER VERHANDLUNGEN DES 1-23 ZIONISTEN CONGRESSES / Zionist Congresses. 1897-1951 – Basel. London. Haag. Hamburg etc. BJ-72-201 1 – 9 – ne IDC [956]
PROTOKOLL DER VERHANDLUNGEN DES AUSSERORDENTLICHEN KONGRESSES DER GEWERKSCHAFTEN DEUTSCHLANDS / Kongress der Gewerkschaften Deutschlands – Berlin. 1932. (Serial publications of German trade unions in the Memorial Library, University of Wisconsin-Madison.) – 1 – us U.W. Library [331]
PROTOKOLL DER VERHANDLUNGEN DES VERBANDSTAGES / Verband der Steinsetzer, Pflasterer und Berufsgenossen Deutschlands. Berlin – v9. 1913. Berlin. (Serial publications of German trade unions in the Memorial Library, University of Wisconsin-Madison.) – 1 – us U.W. Library [330]
PROTOKOLL DES DELEGIERTENTAGES / Allgemeiner Eisenbahnerverband – Berlin. 1918-19. (Serial publications of German trade unions in the Memorial Library, University of Wisconsin-Madison) – 1 – us U.W. Library [331]
PROTOKOLL DES INTERNATIONALEN ARBEITER-CONGRESSES ZU PARIS / International Socialist Congress. 1st. 1889 – Nuremberg, Worlein & Comp. 1890 – 1 – $35.00r – us Hoover Inst Photo [335]
PROTOKOLL DES KONGRESSES.. / Deutscher Holzarbeiter-Verband. Berlin – Stuttgart. 1893. (Serial publications of German trade unions in the Memorial Library, University of Wisconsin-Madison.) – 1 – us U.W. Library [330]
PROTOKOLL DES KONGRESSES SAECHSISCHER BERG.. / Saechsischer Berg- und Huettenarbeiter-Verband – 13-14 Mai 1876. 32p. (Serial publications of German trade unions in the Memorial Library, University of Wisconsin-Madison.) – 1 – us U.W. Library [331]
PROTOKOLL DES ORDENTLICHEN BUNDESTAGES / Bund der technisch-industriellen Beamten. Berlin – v1 1905 v2 1907. Berlin. (Serial publications of German trade unions in the Memorial Library, University of Wisconsin-Madison) – 1 – us U.W. Library [943]
PROTOKOLL DES ORDENTLICHEN VERBANDSTAGES / Verband der Nahrungsmittel- und Getraenkearbeiter – 1st. v2. 1930. Berlin. Sometimes includes Rechenschaftsbericht. (Serial publications of German trade unions in the Memorial Library, University of Wisconsin-Madison.) – 1 – us U.W. Library [330]
PROTOKOLL DES ORDENTLICHEN VERBANDSTAGES / Verband der Tapezierer und verwandten Berufsgenossen Deutschlands – v2. 1903. Hamburg. Title varies slightly. Meetings held trienneially. (Serial publications of German trade unions in the Memorial Library, University of Wisconsin-Madison.) – 1 – us U.W. Library [330]
PROTOKOLL DES PARTEITAGES / Sozialdemokratische Arbeiterpartei Deutschoesterreichs – Vienna, 1888-1926 – 2r – 1 – us Ross [320]
PROTOKOLL DES VERBANDSTAGES / Zentralverband der Fleischer und Berufsgenossen Deutschlands – v6,9. 1913-25. Title varies slightly. 9th, 1925 includes Bericht. 1922 24. (Serial publications of German trade unions in the Memorial Library, University of Wisconsin-Madison.) – 1 – us U.W. Library [330]
PROTOKOLL DES VERBANDSTAGES / Zentralverband der Stukkateure Gipser, Pliesterer und Verwandten Berufsgenossen Deutschlands – v6. 1908. Hamburg. (Serial publications of German trade unions in the

Memorial Library, University of Wisconsin-Madison.) – 1 – us U.W. Library [330]
PROTOKOLL UEBER DIE KONFERENZ...IM VOLKSHAUS ZU LEIPZIG AM SONNTAG, 28 JUNI. BERLIN. 1925. 77P. (SERIAL PUBLICATIONS OF GERMAN TRADE UNIONS IN THE MEMORIAL LIBRARY, UNIVERSITY OF WISCONSIN-MADISON.) / Deutscher Textilarbeiter-Verband – 1 – us U.W. Library [330]
PROTOKOLL UEBER DIE VERHANDLUNGEN / Reichskonferenz der Arbeitnehmer der Gas-, Elektrizitats-, und Wasserwerk – v1-2. 1922-27. (Serial publications of German trade unions in the Memorial Library, University of Wisconsin-Madison.) – 1 – us U.W. Library [330]
PROTOKOLL UEBER DIE VERHANDLUNGEN.. / Deutscher Bauarbeiterverband. Hamburg – v2. 1918. (Serial publications of German trade unions in the Memorial Library, University of Wisconsin-Madison.) – 1 – us U.W. Library [330]
PROTOKOLL UEBER DIE VERHANDLUNGEN DER GENERALVERSAMMLUNG / Deutscher Tabakarbeiter-Verband – Bremen. v14-15, 19. 1910-25. (Serial publications of German trade unions in the Memorial Library, University of Wisconsin-Madison.) – 1 – us U.W. Library [330]
PROTOKOLL UEBER DIE VERHANDLUNGEN DES ERSTEN AUSSERORDENTLICHEN VERBANDSTAGES / Verband der Fabrikarbeiter Deutschlands – 1917. Hannover. 110p. Only congress held. (Serial publications of German trade unions in the Memorial Library, University of Wisconsin-Madison.) – 1 – us U.W. Library [330]
PROTOKOLL UEBER DIE VERHANDLUNGEN DES ORDENTLICHEN VERBANDSTAGES / Zentralverband der Schuhmacher – v20-22. 1924-28. Nurnberg. (Serial publications of German trade unions in the Memorial Library, University of Wisconsin-Madison.) – 1 – us U.W. Library [330]
PROTOKOLL UEBER DIE VERHANDLUNGEN DES PARTEITAGES / Sozialdemokratische Partei Deutschlands. Parteitag – Zuerich. 1880-1960. Incomplete – 1 – us NY Public [335]
PROTOKOLL UEBER DIE VERHANDLUNGEN DES VERBANDSTAGES / Deutscher Nahrungs- und Genussmitterlarbeiter-verband – v17. 1927. Hamburg. (Serial publications of German trade unions in the Memorial Library, University of Wisconsin-Madison.) – 1 – us U.W. Library [330]
PROTOKOLL UEBER DIE VERHANDLUNGEN DES VERBANDSTAGES / Verband der Gaswirtsgehilfen – Berlin. v6,8-9. 1910-19. (Serial publications of German trade unions in the Memorial Library, University of Wisconsin-Madison.) – 1 – us U.W. Library [330]
PROTOKOLL UEBER DIE VERHANDLUNGEN DES VERBANDSTAGES / Verband der Gemeinde- und Staatsarbeiter – v5-6,11. 1909-28. Berlin. (Serial publications of German trade unions in the Memorial Library, University of Wisconsin-Madison.) – 1 – us U.W. Library [330]
PROTOKOLL UEBER DIE VERHANDLUNGEN DES VERBANDSTAGES / Zentralverband der Backer, Konditoren und verwandten Berufsgenossen Deutschlands – v16. 1924. Hamburg. Continued by: Deutscher Nahrungs- und Genussmitteilarbeiter-Verband. Includes Bericht des Vorstandes. (Serial publications of German trade unions in the Memorial Library, University of Wisconsin-Madison.) – 1 – us U.W. Library [330]
PROTOKOLL UEBER DIE VERHANDLUNGEN VOM KONGRESS.. / Freie Vereinigung Deutscher Gewerkschaften – Berlin. v8. 1908. (Serial publications of German trade unions in the Memorial Library, University of Wisconsin-Madison.) – 1 – us U.W. Library [330]
PROTOKOLL VOM AFA-GEWERKSCHAFTKONGRESS / Allgemeiner Freier Angestelltenbund – Hamburg. v1, 3-4. 1921-31. (Serial publications of German trade unions in the Memorial Library, University of Wisconsin-Madison) – 1 – us U.W. Library [331]
PROTOKOLL VOM KONGRESS.. / Deutscher Textilarbeiter-Verband – Berlin. v1. 1926. (Serial publications of German trade unions in the Memorial Library, University of Wisconsin-Madison.) – 1 – us U.W. Library [330]
PROTOKOLL...DES ERSTEN KULTURTAGES.. / Sozialistische Einheitspartei Deutschlands – 5-7 Mai 1948, Berlin. Berlin: Dietz, 1948 – 1 – us U.W. Library [073]
PROTOKOLLE, BERICHTE.. / Sozialdemokratische Partei Deutschlands – Berlin: 1914-19.15 pamphlets – 1 – us U.W. Library [335]
PROTOKOLLE DER DEUTSCHEN BUNDESVERSAMMLUNG 1816-1866 – Frankfurt a.M., 1816-66. Hildesheim, 1986 – 577mf – 9 – DM3,750.00 diazo DM4,300.00 silver – gw Olms [943]
PROTOKOLLE DER GENERALVERSAMMLUNGEN DES DEUTSCHEN METALLARBEITERVERBAN-DES – Stuttgart, 1915; 1917; 1919; 1921 – 1r – 1 – DM75.00 – gw Mikro Press [331]
PROTOKOLLE DES VERMITTLUNGSAUSS-CHUSSES DES DEUTSCHEN BUNDESTAGES UND DES BUNDESRATES, 1.-11. WAHLPERIODE 1949-1990 – 1986- – 32mf – 9 – diazo DM798.00 (silver DM878.00 ISBN: 3-598-30245-2) – 3-598-30244-4 – Co-published with C.H. Beck Verlag, Munich – gw Saur [943]
PROTOKOLLE PARTEITAGE, PARTEIAUSSCHUSS / Sozialdemokratische Partei Deutschlands – 1914-20 (inkl. Reichskonferenz 1920) – 1 – DM80.00 – gw Mikro Press [335]
PROTOKOLLE UND AUSSCHUSS-BERICHTE / Hamburg.Burgerschaft – Hamburg.1859-1926. 23 reels – 1 – 23.00r – us L of C Photodup [943]
PROTOKOLLID / Estonia. Riigikogu – 1921-34. Five scattered numbers wanting – 1 – 287.00 – us L of C Photodup [947]
PROTOKOLS/PROTOKOLI (MINUTES) – 1905-1908, 1910, 1913, 1923-1928, 1930-1938. Publ. No. 6348a. One of two items on reel. Total Pages 1,228 – 1 – us Baptist [240]
PROTOKOLS/PROTOKOLI (MINUTES) / ed by Latvian Baptist Churches. Baltic Association – 1884-1886. Publ. No. 6347a. One of three items on reel. 146p – 1 – us Baptist [240]
PROTOKOLY / Rossiiskaia Sotsial' Demokraticheskaia Rabochaia Partiia – Moscow, 1903-07 – 1r – 1 – us Ross [335]
PROTOKOLY / Rossiiskaia Sotsial' Demokraticheskaia Rabochaia Partiia – Moscow. v2-6. 1903-1907 – 1 – us NY Public [947]
PROTOKOLY I STENOGRAFICHESKIE OTCHETY S"EZDOV I KONFERENTSII KOMMUNISTICHESKOI PARTII SOVETSKOGO SOIUZA. S"EZDY 1-26 – M., 1958-1981 – 287mf – 9 – ne IDC [320]
PROTOKOLY TS. I. K. P.-T. SOIUZA *see* PROTOKOLY TSENTRALNAGO ISPOLNITELAGO KOMITETA VSEROSSIISKAGO
PROTOKOLY TSENTRALNAGO ISPOLNITELAGO KOMITETA VSEROSSIISKAGO / Vserossiiskii pochtovo-telegrafnyi soiuzTsentralny i komitet – (Includes c.1: no.9/10 1918) – [S.l.]: Komitet, 191u – 1 – CSUXAKZ2688-S – us Hoover Inst Photo [380]
PROTOKOLY ZASEDANII ISPOLNITEL'NOGO KOMITETA I BIURO I. K / Leningrad. Sovet rabochikh i soldatskikh deputatov – Moscow, 1925 – 1 – 35.00r – us Hoover Inst Photo [947]
PROTOKOLY ZASEDANII KONFERENTSII IMP. AKADEMII NAUK S 1725 PO 1803 G – St Petersburg, 1897-1911. 4v. BR-7790 2 – 8 – ne IDC [500]
PROTOKOLY ZASEDANII OBSHCHESTVA ESTESTVOISPYTATELEI PRI IMPERATORSKOM KAZANSKOM UNIVERSITETIE / Kazan Universitet. Russia – Kazan – 1 – us U.W. Library [073]
PROTOPLASMA – v1-46. 1927-55 – 1 – us Princeton Micro [574]
PROTOPLASMA – v.39-109, 1949-81. ISSN:0033-183X – 1,5,6,9,13 – 160.00v – us UMI [073]
PROTOPLASMA MONOGRAPHIEN – v1-21. 1928-54.Publ. suspended: 1942-48 – 1,5,6 – us Princeton Micro [574]
PROTOZOOLOGY, A MANUAL FOR MEDICAL MEN / Wenyon, C M – 2359 2. 2 v. 1926 – 8 – ne IDC [590]
PROTRACTED CIVIL TRIALS : VIEWS FROM THE BENCH AND BAR / Bermant, George et al – Washington: GPO, 1982 – 2mf – 9 – $3.00 – LLMC 95-311 – us L.L.M.C. [340]
PROTREPTICUS STUDIOSORUM POETICES / Murmellius, J – Loannis Murmellii Ruremundensis. Vitebergae. 1517. BP-414 1 – 9 – ne IDC [780]
PROTSESS" EKSKUZOVICHA, FIKHGENDLERA I DAINA ZASIEDANIE UGOLOVNOGO DEPARTAMENTA ODESSKOI SUDEBNOI PALATY, S" UCHASTIEM" PRISIAZHNYKH" ZASIEDATELEI. STENOGRAFICHESKII OTCHET" I IZD. A. S. KARFUNKELIA / Ekskuzovich, Nikolai, defendent – Odessa. Tip. "Odesskogo listka", 1887. 144 p. LL-4038 – 1 – us L of C Photodup [340]
PROTSESSUAL'NYE VOPROSY SOTRUDNICHESTVA ORGANOV IUSTITSII SOTSIALISTICHESKIKH. / Averin, D D – Moscow, 1963. 57p. BR-9132 1 – 9 – ne IDC [340]
Protti, Maria *see* WEBSTER V. REPRODUCTIVE HEALTH SERVICES
Prou, M *see* MANUEL DE PALEOGRAPHIE LATINE ET FRANCAISE
PROUD MAHASKA / Phillips, Semira A – Oskalossa: Herald Print, 1900. Iowa Reel 28. (The Cox Library Collection) – 5 – us Americana [978]
PROUDHON AND HIS BANK OF THE PEOPLE / Dana, Charles A – 1849. Introd. by B.R. Tucker, 1896. Free Banking Series – 9 – $1.00f – at Libertarian Micro [336]
Proudhon, Pierre-Joseph *see*
- DU PRINCIPE FEDERATIF
- GENERAL IDEA OF THE REVOLUTION IN THE NINETEENTH CENTURY
- SYSTEM OF ECONOMIC CONTRADICTIONS
- THEORIE DE LA PROPRIETE

Prous, A et al *see*
- LA LAPA DO CABOCLO, JANUARIA, BRESIL
- LES PEINTURES RUPESTRES DE LA "TOCA DO INDIO", ANDRELANDIA, MINAS GERAIS, BRESIL

Proust, L *see* LES ILES CANARIES: FLORE DE L'ARCHIPEL
Prouvost, Leon *see* LE CODE BOLCHEVIK DU MARIAGE
PROV. ALBIENSIS-AUSCIENSIS (GC 1) / ed by Piolin, D Pauli – Editio Altera. Parisiis, 1870 – Dfl207.00 – ne Slangenburg [240]
PROV. BITURICENSIS-BURDIGALENSIS (GC 2) / ed by Piolin, D Pauli – Editio Altera. Parisiis, 1873 – Dfl231.00 – ne Slangenburg [240]
PROV. CAMERACENSIS-COLONIENSIS-EBREDUNENSIS (GC 3) / ed by Piolin, D Pauli – Editio Altera. Parisiis, 1876 – Dfl179.00 – ne Slangenburg [240]
PROV. MECHLIENSIS ET MOGUNTINENSIS (GC 5) / ed by Piolin, D Pauli – Editio Altera. Parisiis, 1877 – Dfl147.00 – ne Slangenburg [240]
Provancher, Leon A *see*
- ADDITIONS ET CORRECTIONS A LA FAUNE COLEOPTEROLOGIQUE DE LA PROVINCE DE QUEBEC, 1879
- LE VERGER, LE POTAGER ET LE PARTERRE DANS LA PROVINCE DE QUEBEC OU CULTURE RAISONNEE DES FRUITS.

LE PROVENCAL – (Ed. Marseille-ville. 27 aout 1944-59, 1969-81. 1) – Marseille. Toutes eds. 1960-1993 – 1 – fr A.C.R.P.P. [073]
LES PROVENCALISMES CORRIGES / Reynier, J B – 2e ed. 1878 – 9 – fr I.C.S. [440]
PROVERBES ABYSSINS, TRADUITS, EXPLIQUES ET ANNOTES / Faitlovitch, J – Paris, 1907 – 1mf – ne IDC [400]
PROVERBES ET CRITIQUE SOCIALE CHEZ LES FON DU BENIN: UNE APPROCHE ANTHROPOLOGIQUE / Fadairo, D – 9 – F250.00 – fr Ethnologie [306]
PROVERBI, STROFE E RACCONTI ABISSINI / Guidi, I – Roma, 1894 – 2mf – ne IDC [400]
PROVERBIAL PHILOSOPHY. IN FOUR SERIES, NOW FIRST COMPLETE : INCLUDING THE FIFTIETH EDITION OF THE TWO FIRST SERIES / Tupper, Martin Farquhar – London: Ward, Lock, [1880?] – 1 roll – 1 – 1-55879-946-X – uk Libr Preservation [100]
THE PROVERBS OF SOLOMON / Zoeckler, Otto – New York: Charles Scribner, 1870. v,260p. 1 fiche – 9 – us A.T.L.A. [240]
PROVERBS OR ADAGES, GATHERED OUT OF THE "CHILIADES" AND ENGLISHED BY RICHARD TAVERNER / Erasmus, Desiderius – 1569 – 9 – 10.00 – us Scholars' Facs [450]
Providence Association *see* AMERIKA
PROVIDENCE BAPTIST CHURCH. CHESTERFIELD COUNTY. PAGELAND, SOUTH CAROLINA : CHURCH RECORDS – 1894-1960 – 1 – 5.00 – us Baptist [240]
PROVIDENCE BAPTIST CHURCH. CHOCTAW COUNTY. ALABAMA : CHURCH RECORDS – Jul 1836-Nov 1874. 298p – 1 – 13.41 – us Baptist [240]
PROVIDENCE BAPTIST CHURCH. FRANKLIN, KENTUCKY : CHURCH RECORDS – 1895-1926. Records very incomplete – 1 – 13.23 – us Baptist [240]
PROVIDENCE BAPTIST CHURCH. FRANKLIN, KENTUCKY : CHURCH RECORDS – 1928-4 Nov 1964 – 1 – 13.23 – us Baptist [240]
PROVIDENCE BAPTIST CHURCH. GREENWOOD COUNTY. SOUTH CAROLINA : CHURCH RECORDS – 1845-97, 1907-43, 1947-72 – 1 – 22.55 – us Baptist [240]
PROVIDENCE BAPTIST CHURCH. JEFFERSON COUNTY. GEORGIA : CHURCH RECORDS – 1828-1926 – 1 – 40.80 – us Baptist [240]
PROVIDENCE BAPTIST CHURCH. KANSAS CITY, MISSOURI : CHURCH RECORDS – 1848-1966 – 1 – 56.16 – us Baptist [240]
PROVIDENCE BAPTIST CHURCH. SEVIERVILLE, TENNESSEE : CHURCH RECORDS – 1829-Oct 1904 – 1 – 14.22 – us Baptist [240]
PROVIDENCE BAPTIST CHURCH. SHADY DALE, GEORGIA : CHURCH RECORDS – Mar 1851-Sep 1882 – 1 – 5.40 – us Baptist [240]
PROVIDENCE COUNTY TIMES – Olneyville. R.I. 1918-1924; 1926-1932; 1936-1937 – 1 – us UMI [071]
PROVIDENCE GAZETTE – Providence. R.I. 1762-1825 – 1,3 – us Readex [071]
PROVIDENCE ISLAND VENTURE 1630-1641 – 1990 – 2r – 1 – uk Microform Academic [975]
PROVIDENCE JOURNAL – Providence, RI. 1779-1801 – 1,3 – us Readex [071]
PROVIDENCE LEDGER – Providence. RI.1890-92 – 1 – us UMI [071]
PROVIDENCE PATRIOT – Providence. R..I. 1814-1820 – 3 – us Readex [071]
PROVIDENCE PHOENIX – Providence. R.I. 1802-1808. yColumbian Phoenix. 1808-1814. Sold as one unit – 3 – us Readex [071]
LA PROVIDENCE, POEME / Richard de la Vergne, Pierre – 1815 – 1 – F59.77 – fr Armell [810]
PROVIDENCE VISITOR – Providence. R.I. -w. 1884- – 1 – us UMI [071]
PROVIDENCIAS PUBLICADAS PELO COMMISSARIO REGIO NA PROVIDENCIA DE MOCAMBIQUE / Ennes, Antonio Jose – (Filmed with: Barahons e Costa, Henrique Cesar da Silva: Apontamentos para a historia de guerra de Zambezia 1871-75; and others) – Lisboa: Impr Nacional, 1896 – us Res Libr [960]
PROVIDENTIAL EPOCHS / Bristol, Frank Milton – Cincinnati: Cranston & Curts, 1894. 1 fiche – 9 – us A.T.L.A. [240]
THE PROVIDENTIAL ORDER OF THE WORLD / Bruce, Alexander Balmain – (Includes index) – New York: Scribner's, 1897 – 1mf – 9 – 0-8370-2439-0 – 1985-0439 – us A.T.L.A. [210]
PROVIDING FOR THE ESTABLISHMENT OF A CONSTITUTION FOR GUAM : REPORT OF THE HOUSE COMMITTEE ON INTERNATIONAL AND INSULAR AFFAIRS / Guam. US Congress – 94th Congress 1st sess. rept no 94-508. 24 Sept 1975 – 1mf – 9 – $1.50 – LLMC 82-100B Title 33 – us L.L.M.C. [324]
A PROVILE OF ECOTOURISTS AND THE BENEFITS DERIVED FROM THEIR EXPERIENCE : A COSTA RICAN CASE STUDY / Fennell, D A – 1990 – 2mf – 9 – $8.00 – us Microform Publ [790]
LA PROVINCE : ALLIANCE LIBERALE NATIONALE – Montreal, Canada. 5 avr 1935-5 fev 1938 – 1r – 1 – Can$60.00 – cn Can Microfilming [072]
LA PROVINCE – Montreal, Canada. 16 mar 1946-10 sep 1946 – 1r – 1 – Can$40.00 – cn Can Microfilming [072]
LA PROVINCE – Quebec, Canada. 4 mai-7 sep 1917 – 1r – 1 – Can$35.00 – cn Can Microfilming [072]
THE PROVINCE – Vancouver, Mar 1894- – 36r per yr – 1 – Can$53.00r – cn Commonwealth Micro [072]
THE PROVINCE – Victoria, Canada. -w. March 1894-April 1902. 10 1 2 reels – 1 – uk British Libr Newspaper [072]
LA PROVINCE DE QUEBEC: DOCUMENTS EMPRUNTES A LA BROCHURE OFFICIELLE.. / Vekeman, Gustave – Sherbrooke, Quebec: Pionnier, 1882. 02186. (Pre-1900 Canadiana) – 9 – cn C.I.H.M. [971]
PROVINCE OF LOWER CANADA, COUNTY OF BONAVENTURE : TO THE HONORABLE THE KNIGHTS, CITIZENS AND BURGESSES... – [S.l.: s.n., 1832 ?]. SEM105P1382 – 1mf – 9 – Can$2.25 – cn Bibl Nat [971]

PROVINCE OF LOWER-CANADA, DISTRICT OF QUEBEC : COMMITTEE NAMED...AGAINST THE PASSING OF THE BILL FOR THE UNION OF THE LEGISLATURES OF UPPER AND LOWER CANADA,... – [S.l.]: [s.n.], [1822 ?]. SEM105P1402 – 1mf – 9 – Can$2.25 – cn Bibl Nat [323]

PROVINCE OF MUNSTER – Cork, Ireland. 1849-Aug 1853. -w. 5 reels – 1 – uk British Libr Newspaper [072]

THE PROVINCE OF QUEBEC AND THE EARLY AMERICAN REVOLUTION: A STUDY IN ENGLISH-AMERICAN COLONIAL HISTORY / Coffin, Victor – Madison, Wis.: Published by the University, 1896. 00695. (Pre-1900 Canadiana) – 9 – cn C.I.H.M. [971]

Province of Quebec Crown Lands Department see SETTLER'S GUIDE, PROVINCE OF QUEBEC

THE PROVINCE OF REASON : A CRITICISM OF THE BAMPTON LECTURE ON "THE LIMITS OF RELIGIOUS THOUGHT" / Young, John – New York: Robert Carter, 1860 – 1mf – 9 – 0-8370-5937-2 – 1985-3937 – us A.T.L.A. [210]

THE PROVINCE OF REASON: A CRITICISM OF...THE LIMITS OF RELIGIOUS THOUGHT / Young, John – New York: Robert Carter, 1860. 1 fiche – 9 – us A.T.L.A. [240]

UNE PROVINCE PROCURATORIENNE AU DEBUT DE L'EMPIRE ROMAIN: LE PROCES DE JESUS CHRIST / Regnault, Henri – Paris: Librairie A. Picard, 1909. 1 fiche – 9 – us A.T.L.A. [240]

THE PROVINCES OF THE ROMAN EMPIRE FROM CAESAR TO DIOCLETIAN / Mommsen, Theodor – Trans. with the author's sanction and additions by William P. Dickson. London: Richard Bentley, 1886.2v. maps – 1 – us U.W. Library [930]

PROVINCETOWN 1620-1890 – (Mf 1-2: Marriages Index 1779, 1811-44. Mf 2-4: Births & Index 1620-1845. Mf 5-6: Deaths & Index 1729-1843. Mf 7: Births & Deaths 1696-1802. Mf 8-9: Births & Deaths 1750-1850. Mf 10-11: Births & Deaths 1780-1846. Mf 12-13: Births 1843-66. Mf 13-14: Marriages 1844-54. Mf 14: Deaths 1843-61. Mf 15: Marriages 1855-72. Mf 16: Marriages 1872-85. Mf 17: Marriages 1885-90. Mf 18-19: Deaths 1862-90. Mf 20-21: Births 1867-90. Mf 22-24: Birth Index 1843-1976. Mf 25-27: Death Index 1843-1976. Mf 28-30: Marriage Index 1844-1976. Mf 30-32: Marriages 1891-1908. Mf 33: Deaths 1891-1903. Mf 34: Deaths 1903-14. Mf 35: Deaths 1914-23. Mf 36: Births 1891-1902) – (mf ed 1986) – 36mf – 9 – 0-87623-000-1 – us Holbrook [920]

A PROVINCIA : ORGAO DAS IDEIAS DEMOCRATICAS E DOS INTERESSES DO COMMERCIO – Manaos, Amazonas. 29 Out 1878; Mar 1879; 18 Out 1885 – 1,5,6 – bl Biblioteca [072]

A PROVINCIA : ORGAO DO PARTIDO NACIONAL – Maceio, Alagoas. 14 Jan, Maio 1877; 23 Maio 1878 – 1,5,6 – bl Biblioteca [072]

LA PROVINCIA – Badajoz, 1900 y 1901. 2 numeros – 5 – sp Bibl Santa Ana [073]

PROVINCIA DAS ALAGOAS : PERIODICO DEDICADO ESPECIALMENTE A LAVOURA E AO COMMERCIO – Maceio, Alagoas. 1, 10, 28 Ago 1888 – 1,5,6 – bl Biblioteca [072]

PROVINCIA DE GOYAS : MATUTINA MEYAPONTENSE – Meyaponte, 5 Mar 1830-24 Maio 1834 – 1,5,6 – bl Biblioteca [072]

A PROVINCIA DE MATTO-GROSSO : PERIODICO LITTERARIO,NOTICIOSO E DEDICADO AOS INTERESSES DA PROVINCIA – Cuiaba, 9 Jan-Mar, May-Oct 1879; Jan, Apr 1880; Feb 1881-Dec 1882; Jun-Jul, Nov 1884; Nov 1885; Mar, Sep 1886; Jul 1887-Dec 1888; Mar, Jul-8 Dec 1889 – 1,5,6 – bl Biblioteca [072]

A PROVINCIA DE MINAS : ORGAO DO PARTIDO CONSERVADOR – (Cont of: A Ordem) – Ouro Preto, 10 Jul 1880- 13 Nov 1889 – 1,5,6 – bl Biblioteca [072]

A PROVINCIA DE MINAS see A ORDEM

PROVINCIA DE SAN FRANCISCO SOLANO Y SUS MISIONES... / Maestu, Luisa Maria – Madrid: Arch. Ibero Americano, 1964 – 1 – sp Bibl Santa Ana [240]

LA PROVINCIA DESCALZA DE SAN GABRIEL Y SUS LIBROS DE PATENTES (1722-1746) / Barrado Manzano, Arcangel – Madrid: Graf. Calleja, 1967 – 1 – sp Bibl Santa Ana [946]

LA PROVINCIA DESCALZA DE SAN GABRIEL Y SUS LIBROS DE PATENTES (1824-1835) / Barrado Manzano, Arcangel – Madrid: Graf. Calleja, 1968 – 1 – sp Bibl Santa Ana [240]

A PROVINCIA DO AMAZONAS – Manaos, Amazonas. 5 Set 1886 – 1,5,6 – bl Biblioteca [072]

A PROVINCIA DO AMAZONAS : ORGAM ESPECIAL DO COMMERCIO – Manaos, Amazonas. 2 Nov 1887-27 Dez 1888 – 1,5,6 – bl Biblioteca [072]

A PROVINCIA DO PARA – Brazil, Belem (Paraguay). 22 Jul 1907-31 Dec 1911 – 18r – 1 – us L of C Photodup [072]

LA PROVINCIA FRANCISCANA DE SAN MIGUEL INFRA TAGUM (1774-1815) / Barrado Manzano, Arcangel – Madrid: Graficas Canales, 1966 – 1 – sp Bibl Santa Ana [946]

PROVINCIA LUGDUNENSIS (GC 4) / ed by Piolin, D Pauli – Editio Altera. Parisiis, 1876 – Dfl158.00 – ne Slangenburg [240]

PROVINCIA NARBONENSIS (GC 6) – Parisiis, 1739 – Dfl175.00 – ne Slangenburg [240]

PROVINCIA ROTOMAGENSIS (GC 11) / ed by Piolin, D Pauli – Editio Altera. Parisiis, 1874 – Dfl154.00 – ne Slangenburg [240]

PROVINCIA TURONENSIS (GC 14) / ed by Haureau, A B – Parisiis, 1856 – Dfl158.00 – ne Slangenburg [240]

PROVINCIA VESUNTIONENSIS (GC 15) / ed by Haureau, A B – Parisis, 1860 – Dfl116.00 – ne Slangenburg [240]

PROVINCIA VIENNENSIS (GC 16) / ed by Haureau, A B – Parisiis, 1865 – Dfl112.00 – ne Slangenburg [240]

Provinciaal Utrechts genootschap van kunsten en wetenschappen see VERHANDELINGEN VAN HET PROVINCIAAL UTRECHTSCH GENOOTSCHAP VAN KUNSTEN EN WETENSCHAPPEN

PROVINCIAE SENONENSIS ET TARENTASIENSIS (GC 12) – Parisiis, 1770 – Dfl161.00 – ne Slangenburg [240]

PROVINCIAE TOLOSANA ET TREVIRENSIS (GC 13) / ed by Piolin, D Pauli – Editio Altera. Parisiis, 1874 – Dfl217.00 – ne Slangenburg [240]

LE PROVINCIAL – St-Sauveur, Quebec, Canada. 2 dec 1879-v2 n163. 12 nov 1881 – 1r – 1 – Can$40.00 – cn Can Microfilming [072]

PROVINCIAL AND MUNICIPAL LAWS OF PUERTO RICO, 1896 : ROYAL DECREE OF DECEMBER 31 1896 – Washington: GPO, 1899 – 1mf – 9 – $1.50 – LLMC 92-308 – us L.L.M.C. [340]

Provincial Archives. Victoria, British Columbia see DICTIONARY CATALOGUE OF THE LIBRARY OF THE PROVINCIAL ARCHIVES OF BRITISH COLUMBIA

PROVINCIAL EXAMINATION PAPERS, 1988-95 / British Columbia. Ministry of Education – Victoria, BC: The Ministry, 1988-95 – 11r – 1 – Can$60.00r – cn U.B.C. Preserve [370]

A PROVINCIAL GLOSSARY / Grose, Francis – 1787. 376p. (English Linguistics Series 1500-1800) – 9 – us UMI [420]

Provincial Government of India see LEGISLATIVE SERIES

THE PROVINCIAL LAW OF THE CUSTOMS, AND A COLLECTION OF THOSE PARTS OF THE IMPERIAL ACTS ON THE SAME SUBJECT / Canada. Laws, Statutes, etc – Montreal: Printed by S Derbishire and G Desbarats, 1844. SEM105P303 – 3mf – 9 – Can$6.75 – cn Bibl Nat [340]

THE PROVINCIAL LAWS OF THE CUSTOMS, AND A COLLECTION OF THOSE PARTS OF THE IMPERIAL ACTS ON THE SAME SUBJECT. / Canada. Laws, Statutes, etc – Montreal: Derbishire & Desbarats, 1844. 2p 1., 214p. LL-2371 – 1 – us L of C Photodup [340]

PROVINCIAL NEWSPAPERS, MARCH 1959-DECEMBER 1960 – (In Chinese. Apply for complete listing) – 130r – 1 – $40.00r outside US – Dist. us Scholarly Res – us L of C Photodup [950]

THE PROVINCIAL, OR, HALIFAX MONTHLY MAGAZINE – Halifax, NS: J Bowes, 1852-[1853] – 9 – cn C.I.H.M. [073]

PROVINCIAL PARLIAMENT OF LOWER-CANADA / Bas-Canada. Parlement – [S.l.: s.n., 1826 ?]. SEM105P1368 – 1mf – 9 – Can$2.25 – cn Bibl Nat [323]

PROVINCIAL PATRIOT – St. Stephen, Canada. 1853-54 – 1 reel – 1 – $68.00 – cn Library Assoc [971]

PROVINCIAL REPORTS / Great Britain. Indian Education Commission Report (Hunter Commission). 1883 – In full. Statistical tables. BI-518 2 – 8 – ne IDC [324]

PROVINCIAL STANDARD – Calgary, Canada. Calgary Standard. -w. June 1911-Feb 1913. 2 reels – 1 – uk British Libr Newspaper [072]

Provine, D Marie see SETTLEMENT STRATEGIES FOR FEDERAL DISTRICT JUDGES

PROVINSTIDNINGEN DALSLAND – Amal, Sweden. 1911-36; 1977-78 – 34r – 1 – sw Kungliga [072]

PROVINSTIDNINGEN DALSLAND – Amal, Sweden. 1979- – 1 – sw Kungliga [072]

DIE PROVINZEINTEILUNG DES ASSYRISCHEN REICHES / Forrer, E – Leipzig. 1920. BNE-438 1 – 9 – ne IDC [340]

PROVINZIAL-CORRESPONDENZ – Berlin, 1869-sep 20 1876 – 1 – Inquire at Mikrofilmarchiv for details – gw Misc Inst [072]

PROVINZIALZEITUNG – (Cont by: Wesermuender Neueste Nachrichten, jan 1 1926) – Bremerhaven, jul 2 1859-1941 (incomplete) – 108r – 1 – Inquire at Mikrofilmarchiv for details – gw Misc Inst [943]

PROVINZIAL-ZEITUNG FUER SCHLESIEN – Breslau, jan 1-jun 30 1865 – 1 – Inquire at Mikrofilmarchiv for details – gw Misc Inst [943]

PROVINZMAEDEL / Rose, Felicitas – Berlin: R Bong, [1902?-] – 1r – 1 – us U.W. Library [890]

THE PROVISIONAL CONSTITUTION OF THE REPUBLIC OF INDONESIA / Indonesia. Constitution – 1956. Act No. 7, 1950. Gazette No. 37, 1950. SE-4796-1 – 9 – ne IDC [323]

PROVISIONAL ECONOMIC PLAN / Iraq. Ministry of Guidance – Baghdad. 1959 – 9 – ne IDC [338]

PROVISIONAL METHODOLOGY FOR ASSESSMENT AND MAPPING OF DESERTIFICATION – 1983 – 100p – it F.A.O. [550]

PROVISIONAL METHODOLOGY FOR SOIL DEGRADATION ASSESSMENT – 1979 – 94p – it F.A.O. [631]

PROVISIONES, CEDULAS, INSTRUCCIONES DE SU MAGESTAD PARA...GOBERNACION DESTA NUEVA ESPANA / Puga, V – Mejico, 1563 – 8mf – 9 – sp Cultura [946]

PROVISOR'S LEIDEN : POSSE MIT GESANG IN 4 AKTEN / Wallner, Franz – Berlin: Reg. London Stat Hall, 1887 – 1r – 1 – us U.W. Library [820]

Provolovich, I A see ZAKONODATEL'STVO O TRUDOVYKH ARTELIAKH

PROVREMENNYIA IZDANIIA V ROSSII V 1858-M GODU / Mezhov, VI – M. 1858. BR-7167 2 – 8 – ne IDC [947]

EL PROXIMO CONGRESO DE LAS JUVENTUDES HISPANO-AMERICANAS / Bayle, Constantino – Madrid: Razon y Fe, 1920 – 1 – sp Bibl Santa Ana [270]

Proyart, Abbe see HISTOIRE DE LOANGO ET D'AUTRES ROYAUMES D'AFRIQUE, REDIGEE D'APRES LES MEMOIRES DES PREFETS APOSTOLIQUES DE LA MISSION FRANCAISE

Proyart, Lievin-Bonaventure see
– DE L'EDUCATION PUBLIQUE, ET DES MOYENS D'EN REALISER LA REFORME PROJETEE DANS LA DERNIERE ASSEMBLEE DU CLERGE
– HISTOIRE DE LOANGO, KARONGO ET AUTRES ROYAUMES D'AFRIQUE

PROYECTO DE CODIGO POSTAL DE LOS ESTADOS UNIDOS-MEXICANOS. / Mexico. Comision de reformas en el sistema postal – Mexico: Imprenta de gobierno, en Palacio, 1882. 140p. LL-8030 – 1 – us L of C Photodup [340]

PROYECTO DE LAS ORDENANZAS DE LA COMUNIDAD DE LABRADORES DEL TERMINO MUNICIPAL DE BARCARROTA. ANO DE 1921 – Badajoz: Imp. Emilio Hernandez – 1 – sp Bibl Santa Ana [340]

PROYECTO DE LEY SOBRE ESTADOS EXCEPCIONALES / Donoso Cortes, Juan Francisco – Madrid: Tip. R. Rodriguez de Rivera, Tomo 2. 1848 – 1 – sp Bibl Santa Ana [340]

PROYECTO DE ORDENANZAS MUNICIPALES / Fregenal de la Sierra. Spain – 1887 – 9 – 1.50f – sp Bibl Santa Ana [324]

PROYECTO DE PAZ UNIVERSAL / Mendoza, Luis de – 1820 – 9 – $1.50f – sp Bibl Santa Ana [320]

PROYECTO DE REGLAMENTO DE LAS CASAS SINDICALES COMARCALES DEPENDIENTES DE LA DELEGACION PROVINCIAL SINDICAL DE CACERES / Delegacion Provincial de Sindicatos – Caceres: Tip. El Noticiero, s.a. – 1 – sp Bibl Santa Ana [060]

PROYECTO DE UNA NUEVA VIA ENTRE BOLIVIA Y EL OCEANO PACIFICO / Aramayo, Avelino – London: W & A Webster, 1863 – us Res Libr [972]

PROYECTO DEL 2 PLAN DE DESARROLLO ECONOMICO Y SOCIAL Y ANEXO / Spain. Comisaria del Plan de Desarrollo Economico y Social – 2v. Madrid. 1968 – 9 – ne IDC [338]

PROYECTO ECONOMICO Y OBRA PIA / Ward, Bernardo – 1779 – 2mf – 9 – Pta1,500.00 – 84-7848-343-8 – sp Pentalfa [330]

PROYECTO EDUCATIVO 1977-78 / Colegio Maristas San Calixto – Plasencia: Imp. Sanchez Rodrigo, 1977 – sp Bibl Santa Ana [370]

PROYECTO EDUCATIVO CURO 1980-1981 / Colegio Maristas San Calixto – Plasencia: Imp. Sanchez Rodrigo, 1980 – 1 – sp Bibl Santa Ana [370]

PROYECTO EDUCATIVO. CURSO 1976-77 / Colegio Maristas San Calixto – Plasencia: Imp. Sanchez Rodrigo, 1976 – 1 – sp Bibl Santa Ana [370]

PROYECTO...PAGAR LAS CONTRIBUCIONES / Garcia, Jose – 1834 – 9 – 1.50f – sp Bibl Santa Ana [946]

PROZEMLIU, PRO VOLIU, PRO RABOCHUIU DOLIU : POVEST V PIATI CHASTIAKH / Bednyi, Demian – Znachitelno dop. izd. Moskva: Gos. izd-vo, 2nd ed 1920 – 1 – CSUX88-B7096 – us Hoover Inst Photo [947]

PROZEMLIU, PRO VOLIU, PRO RABOCHUIU DOLIU : POVIEST V 2-KH CHASTIAKH / Bednyi, Demian – Peterburg: Pribo i, 1917 – 1 – CSUX88-B5902 – us Hoover Inst Photo [947]

PROZESS GEGEN ERNST HARMENING WEGEN BELEIDIGUNG DES HERZOGS VON COBURG-GOTHA – Leipzig: J G Findel, 1890 – 1r – 1 – us U.W. Library [943]

Prozorov, P see SISTEMATICHESKII UKAZATEL' KNIG I STATEI PO GRECHESKOI FILOLOGII. NAPECHATANNYKH V ROSSI S 17 STOLETIIA PO 1892 GOD NA RUSSKOM I INOSTRANNYKH IAZYKAKH, S PRIBAVLENIEM ZA 1893-1895 GODY

Prozorovskii, D I see OPIS DREVNIKH RUKOPISEI

PROZRACHNOST' / Ivanov, V – Vtoraia kniga liriki. M. 1904. BR-742 2 – 8 – ne IDC [460]

THE PRRI AFFAIR AS SEEN IN THE LIGHT OF THE INDONESIAN ARMED FORCES / Pirngadie, Rudy – SE-1192 1. 1958 – 9 – ne IDC [355]

PRRI BULLETIN – SE-731 1. 1958-1959 – 9 – ne IDC [073]

PRS JOURNAL – (Former title: Horizon aug 1941-spr 1958) – Los Angeles. v1-35 1941-spr 1975*. v36-47 1976-87. v48 1998*. v49 1989. v50 1990* 1; v36-38 1976-78*. v39 1979. v40-48 1980-88*. v49 1989. v50 1990* 5; v36 1976*. v37 1977. v38 1978*. v39 1979. v40 1980*. v41-47 1981-87. v48 1988*. v49 1989. v50 1990* 9 – 1,5,9 – D8175 – us UMI [073]

PRUBEH PLNENI HOSPODARSKEHO PLANU 1948 / Czechoslovakia. Hospodarske Rady – 3pts. Praha. 1948. BD-363 1 – 9 – ne IDC [330]

PRUBEH PLNENI HOSPODARSKEHO PLANU ROK 1947 / Czechoslovakia. Hospodarske Rady – Praha. 1948. BD-362 1 – 9 – ne IDC [338]

PRUBOJ – Usti Nad Labem, Czechoslovakia. 1954-68; 1971-79; 1981-87; 1989-Mar 1990 – 54r – 1 – us L of C Photodup [072]

PRUD / Remizov, A – Roman. 1908. BR-842 2 – 8 – ne IDC [460]

PRUDENTIA – 1969-88 (complete) – 3r – 1 – ATLA S0653 – us A.T.L.A. [073]

Prudnikov, A P see INTEGRAL TRANSFORMS AND SPECIAL FUNCTIONS

PRUEBA HISTORICA DE LA INOCENCIA DE D. HERNANDO CORTES EN LA MUERTE DE SU ESPOSA, DE JUAN PALACIOS. INFORME / Altolaguirre, Angel de – Madrid: Fortanet, 1920. B.R.A.H. 76. pp. 105-110 – 1 – sp Bibl Santa Ana [946]

PRUEBA QUE NO SE DEVE SANGRAR EN EL SARAMPION / Saavedra, J – Malaga, 1625 – 1mf – 9 – sp Cultura [610]

UNAS PRUEBAS DE LABORES EN TERRENOS INFESTADOS CONCANUTOS DE LANGOSTA / Moreno Marquez, Victor – Madrid: Direccion General de Agricultura. Seccion de Plagas del Campo y Fitopatologia. Servicio de lucha contra la langosta, 1941 – 1 – sp Bibl Santa Ana [630]
DER PRUEFSTEIN / Meisel, W A – Budapest. 1878. BJ-421-80 1 – 9 – ne IDC [470]
DIE PRUEFUNGEN DER BAPTISTEN ZU LITTLEVILLE : HUMORISTISCHE BLAETTER AUS DEM MODERNEN PROVINZLEBEN DER NORDAMERIKANISCHEN UNION / Pfitzner, Heinrich – 2. Aufl. Minden in Westf.: J C C Brun, [18–?] – 1r – 1 – us U.W. Library [830]
Pruemm, Karl *see* RELIGIONS-GESCHICHTLICHES HANDBUCH FUER DEN RAUM DER ALTCHRISTLICHEN UMWELT: HELLENISTISCH-ROEMISCHE GEISTRESSTROEMMGEN UND KULTE MIT BEACHTUNG DES EIGENLEBENS DER PROVINZEN
Prugavin, Aleksandr Stepanovich *see*
- RASKOL "VVERKHY: OCHERKI RELIGIOZNYKH" ISKANII V PRIVILEGIROVANOI SREDE
- RASKOL-SEKTANTSTVO. MATERIALY DLIA IZUCHENIIA RELIGIOZNO-BYTOVYKH DVIZHENII RUSSKOGO NARODA

Prugner, N *see* ACHT U. DREYSSIG SCHLUSZREDE
Pruneau de Pommegorge, Antoine E *see*
- DESCRIPTION DE LA NIGRITIE

Prunetti, M A *see*
- L'OSSERVATORE DELLE BELLE ARTI IN ROMA OSSIA ESAME ANALITICO DE' MONUMENTI ANTICHI, E MODERNI
- SAGGIO PITTORICO ED ANALISI DELLE PITTURE PIU FAMOSE ESISTENTI IN ROMA...

Prussia. Landtag. Haus der Abgeordneten *see*
- SAMMLUNG DER DRUCKSACHEN
- SAMMLUNG SAMMTLICHER DRUCKSACHEN
- STENOGRAPHISCHE BERICHTE UEBER DIE VERHANDLUNGEN

Prussia. Landtag. Herrenhaus *see*
- SITZUNGS-PROTOKOLLE
- STENOGRAPHISCHE

Prussia. Landtag. Zweite Kammer *see* STENOGRAPHISCHE BERICHTE UBER DIE VERHANDLUNGEN
Prussia. Statistisches Landesamt *see*
- PREUSSISCHE STATISTIK. (AMTLICHES QUELLENWERK)
- ZEITSCHRIFT

PRUSSIA: ZEITSCHRIFT DER ALTERTUMSGESELLSCHAFT PRUSSIA – Koenigsberg. v. 1-33; 1875-1939. v. 1-25 issued as Sitzungsberichte der Altertumsgesellschaft Prussia. v. 1, 3-4 lacking. Film Mas C 733 – 1 – us H.U. Library [900]
PRUSSIAN MOBILIZATION RECORDS, 1866-1918 / Germany – 5r – 1 – M962 – us Nat'l Archives [324]
Prutz, Robert Eduard *see*
- AUS DER HEIMAT
- GEDICHTE
- MORITZ VON SACHSEN

Pryce, William *see* ARCHAEOLOGIA CORNU-BRITANNICA
Pryor, Charles Foster *see* NINETY-NINE YEAR LEASES AND FORTUNES MADE THEREIN.
Pryor, Roger Atkinson *see* THE FOUNDATION OF PROFESSIONAL SUCCESS
PRZ PHONOGRAPHISCHE RADIO- UND MUSIKINSTRUMENTENZEITSCHRIFT *see* PHONOGRAPHISCHE ZEITSCHRIFT
PRZ PHONOGRAPHISCHE UND RADIOZEITSCHRIFT *see* PHONOGRAPHISCHE ZEITSCHRIFT
PRZEBUDOWA – (Cont as: Polska Ludowa 1943-44) – 1941-43 – 1r – 1 – inquire – us Ross [072]
PRZEBUDZENIE = THE AWAKENING – Chicago, IL: Przebudzenie Pub Co, [nov 6 1927-33; 1935-40; 1943-46; 1948-51; 1953-54] – 14r – 1 – us Res Libr [071]
PRZEDSWIT – London, UK. 4, 11 Jul 1891 – 1 – uk British Libr Newspaper [072]
PRZEGLAD ARCHEOLOGICZNY – v1- . 1919- . illus. -irr, annual. Suspended 1940-45. Articles in Polish, English or German. Summaries in French, English or Polish. Table of Contents in French. Instytut Historii Kultury Materialnej, 1973- – 1 – us U.W. Library [073]
PRZEGLAD EMIGRACYJNY – (Includes Index for 1926-1927 plus articles) – Warsaw, 1926-1927, 1928 – 1r – 1 – us I.H.R.C. [947]
PRZEGLAD EMIGRACYJNY – Lwow/Lemberg, 1892-1895 – 1r – 1 – us I.H.R.C. [947]
PRZEGLAD HISTORYCZNY – Warsaw. v. 1-2, no. 1, 3; v. 3-39, no. 1-2; v. 40-54. 1905-1963 – 1 – us NY Public [947]
PRZEGLAD KULTURALNY – Warsaw. Poland. -w. Nov 1952-Jun 1963. (11 reels) – 1 – uk British Libr Newspaper [947]
PRZEGLAD POWSZECHNY – v1, no.173-222. 1884, 1927 – 1 – us I.U. Libraries [073]
PRZEGLAD SOCJOLOGICZNY – Poznan-Warszawa, 1936 – 1r – 1 – us I.H.R.C. [947]
PRZEGLAD SOCJOLOGICZNY, VOL 3 – 1935 – 1r – 1 – us I.H.R.C. [947]
PRZEGLAD SPORTOWY – Lodz, Poland. Jul-Aug 1945 – 1r – 1 – us L of C Photodup [947]
PRZEGLAD SPORTOWY – Warsaw, Poland. -w. Aug 1952-Dec 1958. 9 reels – 1 – uk British Libr Newspaper [073]
PRZEGLAD WARSZAWSKI – No.1-51, 1921-25 – 1 – us I.U. Libraries [073]
PRZEGLAD WIECZORNY – Warsaw, Poland. Jan-Feb 1919 – 1r – 1 – us L of C Photodup [947]
PRZEGLAD WSPOLCZESNY – Cracow. v. 1-18. no. 1. May 1922-Jan 1939. Incomplete – 1 – us NY Public [073]
PRZEGLAD WSPOLCZESNY – Krakow, 1922-33 – 2r – 1 – us Ross [072]
PRZEGLAD WSZECHPOLSKI – Lwow/Lemberg, 1895 – 1r – 1 – us I.H.R.C. [947]
PRZEGLAD ZAGADNIEN SOCJALNYCH : POLSKIE WYDAWNICTWA GOSPODARCZE – Warsaw, 1951-56 – 2r – 1 – us Ross [330]
PRZEGLAD ZAGADNIENA1 SOCJALNYCH – Warsaw. v. 1-6, no. 12. July Aug 1951-Dec 1956 – 1 – us NY Public [073]
PRZEKROJ – No.91-820. 1947-60 – 1 – us I.U. Libraries [073]
PRZELOM – (In Polish) – Warsaw & Lwow, PL. v3 no17 19 Apr 1948; v4 no20 30 Mar 1949 – 1r – 1 – $25.00 – cn Can Microfilming [072]
PRZEMYSLOWA DEMOKRACJA = INDUSTRIAL DEMOCRACY – New York, NY, Jan. 4, 1925-Dec. 19, 1926 – 1r – 1 – us I.H.R.C. [331]
PRZEWALSKI HORSE AND RESTORATION TO ITS NATURAL HABITAT IN MONGOLIA – 1986 – 188p – it F.A.O. [636]
PRZEWODNIK KATOLICKI = THE CATHOLIC LEADER – New Britain, CT: Rev L Bojnowski, [1921-sep 2 1932] (19r); 1943-45 (3r) – 1 – us Res Libr [071]
Przybylski, R *see*
- ARKADIA OSIPA MANDELSZTAMA
- KLASYCYZM OSIPA MANDEL'SZTAMA
- POWROT OWIDIUSZA. TRISTIA OSIPA MANDELSZTAMA

PRZYSLOWIA POLSKIE / Bystron, J S – Krakow, 1933 – 8 – B-1236 2 – ne IDC [943]
Przywara, Erich *see* HOELDERLIN
PS – 1976- – 9 – us UMI [073]
PS : POLITICAL SCIENCE AND POLITICS – (Absorbed: Political Science Teacher, mar 1991. Former title: PS, win 1968-fal 1987) – Washington. v1-30. 1968-97+ 1; v3-30 1970-97+ 5; v9-30 1976-97+ 9 – 1,5,9 – D2989 – us UMI [320]
PS *see* PS
PSA BULLETIN – (Photographic Society of America). 1933 – 1 – us UMI [760]
PSA JOURNAL – (Former title: Photographic Society of America. Journal of Photographic Society of America, mar 1935-dec 1946) – Philadelphia. v1-14 1935-48*. v15-63 1949-97+ 1; v37-39 1971-73. v41-63 1975-97+ 5; v41-63 1975-97+ 9 – 1,5,9 – D46 – us UMI [770]
Psacharopoulos, G *see* THE DESTINATION AND EARLY CAREER PERFORMANCE OF SECONDARY SCHOOL GRADUATES IN COLOMBIA
Psacharopoulos, George *see* INFORMATION
DIE PSALMEN / Baethgen, Friedrich – 2. neubearb. Aufl. Goettingen: Vandenhoeck & Ruprecht, 1895 – 2mf – 9 – 0-8370-2154-5 – 1985-0154 – us A.T.L.A. [220]
DIE PSALMEN / Duhm, Bernhard – Freiburg i.B: J C B Mohr, 1899 – 1mf – 9 – 0-8370-2996-1 – 1985-0996 – us A.T.L.A. [220]
DIE PSALMEN / Kessler, Hans – (Kurzgefasster Kommentar zu den Heiligen Schriften Alten und Neuen Testamentes sowie zu den Apokryphen. A, Altes Testament ; 6. Abt., 1. Haelfte. Bibliography: p.xix-xx) – 2. neubearb. Aufl. Muenchen: C H Beck, 1899 – 1mf – 9 – 0-8370-3893-6 – 1985-1893 – us A.T.L.A. [220]
DIE PSALMEN: NEU UEBERSETZT UND ERKLAERT / Ehrlich, Arnold B – Berlin: M. Poppelauer, 1905. 1 fiche – 9 – us A.T.L.A. [240]
DIE PSALMEN SALOMO'S (T.U.U. 1-13/2) / Gebhardt, Oscar von – Leipzig, 1895 – 3mf – 9 – ne Slangenburg [240]
DIE PSALMEN: UEBERSETZT UND ERKLAERT / Baethgen, Friedrich – Goettingen: Vandenhoeck & Rup., 1895. 1 fiche – 9 – us A.T.L.A. [240]
PSALMEN UND CHRISTLICHE GESAENGE MIT VIER STIMMEN AUF DE MELODIEN FUGENWEISS COMPONIRT / Hassler, Hans Leo – Leipzig: J G I Breitkopfs Buchdruckerey, 1777 – 1 – us Sibley [780]
PSALMENPROBLEME : UNTERSUCHUNGEN UEBER METRIK, STROPHIK UND PASEQ DES PSALMENBUCHES / Grimme, Hubert – Freiburg [Fribourg], Switzerland: Kommissionsverlag der Universitaetsbuchhandlung, 1902 – 1mf – 9 – 0-8370-3401-9 – 1985-1401 – us A.T.L.A. [220]
PSALMI DAVIDIS / Genebrardus, Gilb. – Ed. 4a. Parisiis, 1588 – 12mf – 8 – ne Slangenburg [220]
THE PSALMIST AND THE SCIENTIST, OR, MODERN VALUE OF THE RELIGIOUS SENTIMENT / Matheson, George – New York: A.D.F. Randolph, 1894.1 fiche. 8370-4311-5 – 9 – us A.T.L.A. [240]
PSALMIST OR CHOIR MELODIES / Hastings, Thomas & Bradbury, William Batchelder – 1852 – 1 – 12.95 – us Baptist [240]
EL PSALMO : MISERERE MEI DEUS... / Salas, Francisco Gregorio de – Madrid: Andres Ramirez, 1774 – 1 – sp Bibl Santa Ana [240]
EL PSALMO: MISERERE MEI DEUS / Salas, Francisco Gregorio de – 1774 – 9 – 1.50f – sp Bibl Santa Ana [810]
PSALMODIA, HOC EST, CANTICA SACRA VETERIS ECCLESIAE SELECTA / Lossius, L – VVitebergae, 1561 – 8mf – ne IDC [240]
PSALMODIA SACRA, DAS IST, DES KOENIGS AND PROPHETEN DAVIDS GEISTREICHE PSALMEN... / Crueger, J – (Tenor partbook) – Berlin: Gedruckt bey Christoff Runge, 1658 – 1 – us Sibley [780]
THE PSALMODY REFORMER – Halifax, NS: Printed (for the Conductors), by W Cunnabell, [1853-18–?] – 9 – cn C.I.H.M. [780]
THE PSALMS / Alexander, Joseph Addison – Translated and explained. 3 v. in 2. 1853-69 – 1 – us A.T.L.A. [240]
THE PSALMS / Maclaren, Alexander – New York: A.C. Armstrong, 1893 – 2mf – 9 – us A.T.L.A. [240]
THE PSALMS / Meyer, Frederick Brotherton – (Includes index) – London:Morgan & Scott, [1891] – 1mf – 9 – 0-8370-4406-5 – 1985-2406 – us A.T.L.A. [220]
THE PSALMS : THEIR HISTORY, TEACHINGS, AND USE / Binnie, William – (Includes bibliographical references & indexes) – rev enl ed. London: Hodder & Stoughton, 1886 – 1mf – 9 – 0-8370-2344-0 – 1985-0344 – us A.T.L.A. [220]
THE PSALMS: A NEW TRANSLATION WITH INTRODUCTORY ESSAY AND NOTES / De Witt, John – New York: A.D.F. Randolph, 1891.1 fiche – 9 – us A.T.L.A. [240]
PSALMS AND HYMN TUNES OF DR. WATTS / Rippon, John – London. 1820 – 1 – $11.27 – us Baptist [780]
PSALMS, HYMNS AND SPIRITUAL SONGS / Campbell, A. et al – 1841 – 1 – $50.00 – us Presbyterian [240]
THE PSALMS IN HUMAN LIFE / Ernle, Rowland Edmund Prothero – (Includes index) – New ed. New York: E P Dutton, 1904 – 1mf – 9 – 0-8370-4628-9 – 1985-2628 – us A.T.L.A. [220]
THE PSALMS IN THE JEWISH CHURCH / Oesterley, William Oscar Emil – London: Skeffington, 1910 – 1mf – 9 – 0-8370-9260-4 – 1986-3260 – us A.T.L.A. [780]
THE PSALMS OF SOLOMON : WITH THE GREEK FRAGMENTS OF THE BOOK OF ENOCH / ed by Swete, Henry Barclay – (Texts in Greek; introduction in English) – Cambridge: University Press, 1899 – 1mf – 9 – 0-8370-9748-7 – 1986-3748 – us A.T.L.A. [220]
PSALMS OF THE PHARISEES, COMMONLY CALLED THE PSALMS OF SOLOMON = PSALMOI SOLOMONTOS : THE TEXT NEWLY REVISED FROM ALL THE MSS. / ed by Ryle, Herbert Edward & James, Montague Rhodes – (In English and Greek. Includes indexes) – Cambridge: University Press; New York: [Macmillan], 1891 – 1mf – 9 – 0-8370-9814-9 – 1986-3814 – us A.T.L.A. [220]
THE PSALMS TRANSLATED AND EXPLAINED / Alexander, J A – Scribner & Armstrong, 1873 – 9 – $36.00 – us I.R.C. [220]
PSALTER – 11th and 12th cents. Holkham mss. 4, 25. Holkham Hall, Norfolk, England – 1 – uk Microform Academic [025]
PSALTER: A WITNESS TO THE DIVINE ORIGIN OF THE BIBLE / Chambers, Talbot Wilson – New York: A.D.F. Randolph, 1876.1 fiche – 9 – us A.T.L.A. [240]
THE PSALTER AND MARTYROLOGY OF RICEMARCH / Lawlor, Hugh Jackson – 2v. 1914 – 5mf – 8 – ne Slangenburg [200]
THE PSALTER COLLECTS – FROM 5-6TH CENTURY SOURCES / Brou, L – 1949 – 5mf – 8 – ne Slangenburg [240]
THE PSALTER OF THE CHURCH : THE SEPTUAGINT PSALMS COMPARED WITH THE HEBREW, WITH VARIOUS NOTES / Mozley, Francis Woodgate – (Includes indexes) – Cambridge: University Press; New York: Macmillan [dist], 1905 – 1mf – 9 – 0-8370-4516-9 – 1985-2516 – us A.T.L.A. [220]
PSALTERIUM FOLCHARDI – Stiftsbibliothek St. Gallen, Cod 23 – 41p + 4 color mf – DM580.00 – 3-89219-011-9 – gw Lengenfelder [700]
PSAUTIER DE DAVID : AVEC LES CANTIQUES A L'USAGE DES ECOLES – Quebec: Guillaume Brown, 1785. SEM16P78 – 1r – 5 – Can$9.00 – cn Bibl Nat [240]
LES PSAUTIERS : MANUSCIRTS LATINS DES BIBLIOTHEQUES PUBLIQUES DE FRANCE / Leroquais, Victor – Paris/Macon. Tom 1-2, Plances. 1940-1941 – 36mf – 8 – Dfl126.00 – ne Slangenburg [240]
LES PSAUTIERS, MANUSCRITS LATINS DES BIBLIOTHEQUES PUBLIQUES DE FRANCE / ed by Leroquais, Victor – Paris. 2v. 1940-41 – 24mf – 9 – O-479/1 – ne IDC [090]
PSEUDEPIGRAPHA : AN ACCOUNT OF CERTAIN APOCRYPHAL SACRED WRITINGS OF THE JEWS AND EARLY CHRISTIANS / Deane, William John – (Includes index) – Edinburgh:T. & T. Clark, 1891 – 1mf – 9 – 0-8370-2856-6 – 1985-0856 – us A.T.L.A. [220]
PSEUDO-CRITICISM : OR, THE HIGHER CRITICISM AND ITS COUNTERFEIT / Anderson, Robert – (Includes index) – NY: Fleming H Revell, c1904 – 1mf – 9 – 0-8370-2097-2 – 1985-0097 – us A.T.L.A. [220]
DER PSEUDOCYPRIANISCHE TRACTAT DE ALEATORBUS (T.U.U. 1-5/1) / Harnack, Adolf von – Leipzig, 1888 – 3mf – 9 – ne Slangenburg [240]
DER PSEUDOCYPRIANISCHE TRAKTAT DE SINGULARITATE CLERICORUM : EIN WERK DES DONATISCHEN BISCHOFS MACROBIUS (T.U.U. 2-24/3A) / Harnack, Adolf von – Leipzig, 1903 – 2mf – 9 – ne Slangenburg [240]
PSEUDO-CYPRIANUS DE 12 ABUSIVES SAECULI (T.U.U. 3-34/1A) / Hellman, S – Leipzig, 1909 – 1mf – 9 – ne Slangenburg [240]
PSEUDO-DIONYSIUS AREOPAGITA IN SEINEN BEZIEHUNGEN ZUM NEUPLATONISMUS UND MYSTERIENWESEN : EINE LITERARHISTORISCHE UNTERSUCHUNG / Koch, Hugo – Mainz: F. Kirchheim, 1900 (Forschungen zur christlichen Literatur- und Dogmengeschichte, v1 issue 2/3) – 1mf – us A.T.L.A. [240]
PSEUDODOXIA EPIDEMICA / Browne, T – M316. 1646 – 9 – ne IDC [610]
DIE PSEUDOKLEMENTINEN : HOMILIEN UND REKOGNITIONEN (T.U.U. 2-25/4) / Waltz, Hans – Leipzig, 1904 – 6mf – 9 – ne Slangenburg [240]

DIE PSEUDOKLEMENTINEN HOMILIEN UND REKOGNITIONEN : EINE QUELLENKRITISCHE UNTERSUCHUNG / Waitz, Hans - Leipzig: J.C. Hinrichs, 1904. (Texte und Untersuchungen zur Geschichte der altchristlichen Literatur; der ganzen Reihe 25. Bd., Heft 4: n.F., 10. Bd., Heft 4) - 1mf - us A.T.L.A. [240]

PSEUDOMORPHOSEN DES MINERALREICHS / Blum, J R - 4v. G-133 2. 1847-1879 - 8 - ne IDC [550]

PSEUDOSCHALLWELLEN-LASERSPEKTROSKOPIE AN NIEDERDRUCKPLASMEN / Franzke, Joachim - 1994 - 2mf - DM80.00 - 3-89349-916-4 - gw Hänsel [530]

DAS PSEUDOTERTULLIANISCHE GEDICHT ADVERSUS MARCIONEM : EIN BEITRAG ZUR GESCHICHTE DER ALTCHRISTLICHEN LITERATUR SOWIE ZUR QUELLENKRITIK DES MARCIONITISMUS / Waitz, Hans - Darmstadt: J. Waitz, 1901 - 1mf - us A.T.L.A. [240]

LA PSICOLOGIA CON LA ONTOLOGIA / Garcia Romero de Tejada, Jose - 1879 - 9 - 1.50f - sp Bibl Santa Ana [110]

LA PSICOLOGIA DEL AMOR / Gonzalez Serrano, Urbano - 1897 - 9 - 1.50f - sp Bibl Santa Ana [150]

LA PSICOLOGIA FISIOLOGICA / Gonzalez Serrano, Urbano - 1886 - 9 - 1.50f - sp Bibl Santa Ana [150]

PSICOLOGIA GENERAL Y DIFERENCIAL DEL NINO / Pacios Lopez, Arsenio - Caceres: Tip. El Noticiero, 1948 - 1 - sp Bibl Santa Ana [150]

LA PSICOLOGIA Y SU RELACION CON LA ONTOLOGIA / Garcia Romero de Tejada, Julio - Madrid: Imp. El Imparcial, 1879 - 1 - sp Bibl Santa Ana [946]

PSIKHOLOGIIA BEZ VSIAKOI METAFIZIKI / Vvedenskii, A I - Ed. 2. Petrograd. 1915. BR-5806 2 - 8 - ne IDC [150]

PSIKHOTERAPIIA - 1910-14 - 35mf - 9 - $240.00 - us Ross [073]

PSIKHOTERAPIIA - 1910-14 - 35mf - 9 - $240.00 - us Ross [073]

PSKOV (IZ DOROZHNYKH ZAMETOK) / Pogodin, M P - Pskov. 1881. BR-8328 2 - 8 - ne IDC [947]

PSKOVSKAIA SUDNAIA GRAMATA - Sostavlennaia na veche v 1467 godu. Odessa, 1847. 27p.BR-11,139/1 - 9 - ne IDC [340]

PSKOVSKAIA SUDNAIA GRAMOTA / St. Petersburg. Imp. Arkheograficheskoi Kommissii - 1914. BR-10, 311 1 - 9 - ne IDC [930]

PSKOVSKI I NABAT : ORGAN OKRUZHKOMA VKP (B), OKRISPOLKOMA I OKRPROFBI URO - (Includes c.1: 1928:Nov.15-16, 18, 20, 29-30, Dec. 21-22, 28) - Pskov: "Pskovski i nabat", 191u - 1 - CSUXALC2558-S - us Hoover Inst Photo [947]

PSRO LETTER - (Cont by: McGraw-Hill's Medical Utilization Review) - Washington. v1-10. 1973-jul 1982* - 1 - D21692 - us UMI [610]

PSYCH NURSE - v.1-7. 1961-May 1966. Continued by Canadian Journal of Psychiatric Nursing - 1 - us UMI [610]

PSYCHE : ORGAN OF THE CAMBRIDGE ENTOMOLOGICAL CLUB - (Cont as: Psyche. A Journal of Entomology. Cambridge, (Mass.). v4-27. 1883-1920) - Cambridge, (Mass.). v1-3. [1874-]1877-1880/1882 - 173mf - 9 - Z-997/2 - ne IDC [590]

PSYCHE : SEELENKULT UND UNSTERBLICHKEITSGLAUBE DER GRIECHEN / Rohde, Erwin - Tuebingen, 1921 - 20mf - 8 - ne Slangenburg [180]

PSYCHE : A STUDY OF THE SOUL / Huntington, William Reed - New York: T. Whittaker, 1899 - 1mf - us A.T.L.A. [210]

PSYCHE. A JOURNAL OF ENTOMOLOGY *see* PSYCHE

PSYCHIATRIA CLINICA - v101-132. 1939-56 - 1,5,6 - us Princeton Micro [616]

PSYCHIATRIC CLINICS OF NORTH AMERICA - (1980- 5,6,9) - 1978- - 1 - us UMI [073]

PSYCHIATRIC DEVELOPMENTS - v1-. 1983- - 1,5,6,9 - us UMI [616]

PSYCHIATRIC HOLOCAUST / Breggin, Peter R - LA Libertarian Reprints, No.5. 4p - 9 - 1.00f - at Libertarian Micro [335]

PSYCHIATRIC OPINION - v1- 1964- 1; v11- 5,6; v13- 9 - us UMI [616]

PSYCHIATRIC QUARTERLY - (v. 39- 1965- 5,6. v. 44- 1970- 9) - v. 1- 1927- - 1 - us UMI [616]

PSYCHIATRY RESEARCH - v1-13. 1979-84 - 1,5,6,13 - sz Elsevier [616]

PSYCHIC RESEARCH *see* JOURNAL OF THE AMERICAN SOCIETY FOR PSYCHICAL RESEARCH

PSYCHIC WORLD AND THE OCCULT - v. 7$8. 1976-1977 - 1,5,6,9 - us UMI [130]

PSYCHISCH KRANKE ALTE MENSCHEN UND SOZIALE UNTERSTUETZUNG : VOM BUERGER ZUM HEIMBEWOHNER ODER WARUM PSYCHISCH KRANKE ALTE MENSCHEN IN EIN HEIM UEBERSIEDELN / Netz, Peter - 1995 - 3mf - 9 - DM98.00 - 3-8267-2153-5 - gw Hänsel [616]

PSYCHOANALYTIC REVIEW - v1- 1913- 1; v57- 5,6; v63- 9 - us UMI [150]

PSYCHOANALYTISCHE BEWEGUNG - Wien. 1929-33 (t. I-V) - 1 - fr A.C.R.P.P. [073]

PSYCHOANALYTISCHE SOZIALTHERAPIE PSYCHOGENER ERKRANKUNGEN / Weidkuhn, Wilmar - 1993 - 1mf - 9 - DM60.00 - 3-89349-772-2 - gw Hänsel [150]

PSYCHOCULTURAL REVIEW - v. 1-. 1977- - 1,5,6,9 - us UMI [150]

PSYCHOENERGETIC SYSTEMS - 1974- - 1,5,9 - us Gordon [150]

PSYCHOHISTORY REVIEW - v.5-. 1976- - 1,5,6,9 - us UMI [150]

PSYCHOLOGI DAN MASJARAKAT / Danziger, Kurt - SE-10,009 1. 1960 - 9 - ne IDC [950]

PSYCHOLOGICAL ABSTRACTS - (v. 39- 1965- 5,6. v. 53- 1975- 9) - v. 1- 1927- - 1 - us UMI [150]

PSYCHOLOGICAL ABSTRACTS: CUMULATED SUBJECT INDEX - (First Suppl., 1961-65.-1 reel. $340.00 ISBN: 0-8161-1295-9; Second Suppl., 1966-68.-2 reels. $450.00 ISBN: 0-8161-1289-4) - 1927-60.-2 reels.-ISBN: 0-8161-1352-1 - 1 - $820.00 US; $990.00 elsewhere - uk Hall [150]

PSYCHOLOGICAL AFFECT OF THE INJURED ATHLETE / McDonald, Susan A - 1988 - 137p 2mf - 9 - $8.00 - us Microform Publ [150]

PSYCHOLOGICAL AND PHYSIOLOGICAL CHANGES ASSOCIATED WITH A PERIOD OF INCREASED TRAINING / Caruso, Christina M & Gill, Diane L - 1993 - 2mf - $8.00 - us Microform Publ [150]

PSYCHOLOGICAL AND THEOLOGICAL RELATIONSHIPS IN THE MULTIPLE STAFF MINISTRY / Mitchell, Kenneth R - 1966 - 1 - us A.T.L.A. [240]

PSYCHOLOGICAL ANTECEDENTS OF THE FREQUENCY AND INTENSITY OF FLOW IN GOLFERS / Catley, Delwyn & Duda, Joan L - 1992 - 2mf - 9 - $8.00 - us Microform Publ [150]

PSYCHOLOGICAL BULLETIN - (v. 63- 1965- 5,6. v. 73- 1970- 9) - v. 1- 1904- - 1 - us UMI [150]

PSYCHOLOGICAL BULLETIN - v1-94. 1904-83 - 1,5,6 - us Princeton Micro [150]

PSYCHOLOGICAL DESCRIPTORS OF PREDICTED ROS EXPERIENCES : THE EFFECT OF TIME AND ORDER / Mayer, Peter M & Udd, Edward - 1993 - 2mf - 9 - $8.00 - us Microform Publ [150]

THE PSYCHOLOGICAL ELEMENTS OF RELIGIOUS FAITH : LECTURES / Everett, Charles Carroll; ed by Hale, Edward - New York: Macmillan, 1902 - 1mf - us A.T.L.A. [240]

PSYCHOLOGICAL FACTORS THAT PREDISPOSE ATHLETES TO INJURY / Fritts, Suzanne M & Sachs, Michael L - 1992 - 1mf - 9 - $4.00 - us Microform Publ [150]

PSYCHOLOGICAL PROFILES BEFORE AND AFTER 12 WEEKS OF WALKING OR EXERSTRIDER TRAINING IN ADULT WOMEN / Stoughton, Laurie J & Butts, Nancy Kay - 1992 - 1mf - $4.00 - us Microform Publ [150]

PSYCHOLOGICAL REPORTS - (v1-23 1955-68 $270.00 2) - v1-81. 1955-97 - 5 - $4,230.50 - us Psychological [150]

PSYCHOLOGICAL RESEARCH - v. 1-42. 1921-80 - 1,5,9 - 3,087.00 - us UMI [073]

PSYCHOLOGICAL REVIEW - (v.72- 1965- 5,6. v.77- 1970- 9) - v. 1- 1894- - 1 - us UMI [150]

PSYCHOLOGICAL REVIEW - Washington. v. 1-86. 1894-1979 - 1,5,6 - us Princeton Micro [150]

PSYCHOLOGIE / Gondokusumo, Djody - SE-10,659 1. 1946 - 9 - ne IDC [150]

PSYCHOLOGIE / Woodworth, R S & Marquis, D G - Utrecht, 1954 - 14mf - 8 - ne Slangenburg [150]

PSYCHOLOGIE / Woodworth, R S & Marquis, D G - Utrecht, 1954 - 14mf - 8 - ne Slangenburg [150]

DIE PSYCHOLOGIE BEI DEN JUEDISCHEN RELIGIONSPHILOSOPHEN DES MITTELALTERS VON SAADJA BIS MAIMUNI / Horovitz, S - Breslau. 1898-1900, 1906-12. BJ-33-7 1 - 9 - ne IDC [270]

LA PSYCHOLOGIE DE LA CONVERSION CHEZ LES PEUPLES NONCIVILISES / Allier, R - Paris. v1-2. 1925 - 1r - 1 - us Ross [240]

DIE PSYCHOLOGIE DER CHARAKTERE IN HEBBELS TRAGOEDIE / Pfeffer, Carl - (Includes bibliographical references) - [S.l.: s.n.], 1907 (Borna-Leipzig: Buchdruckerei R Noske) - 1r - 1 - us U.W. Library [430]

DIE PSYCHOLOGIE DES APOSTELS PAULUS / Simon, Theodor - (Includes index) - Goettingen: Vandenhoeck & Ruprecht, 1897 - 1mf - 9 - 0-8370-5262-9 - 1985-3262 - us A.T.L.A. [220]

DIE PSYCHOLOGIE DES HUGO VON S. VIKTOR : BGPHMA 6/1 / Ostler, H - Muenster, 1906 - 4mf - 9 - ne Slangenburg [240]

DIE PSYCHOLOGIE DES NEMESIUS : BGPHMA 3/1 / Domanski, B - Muenster, 1900 - 4mf - 9 - ne Slangenburg [240]

PSYCHOLOGIE ET MORALE AUX 12 ET 13 SIECLKE / Lottin, O - 68mf - 8 - ne Slangenburg [170]

PSYCHOLOGISCHE ABHANDLUNG UEBER DEN EINFLUSS DER TOENE UND INS BESONDERE DER MUSIK AUF DIE SEELE / Kausch, J J - 1782 - 9 - us Sibley [780]

PSYCHOLOGISCHE ASPEKTE DES DARSTELLENDEN SPIELS / Barz, Andre - 1992 - 138p - DM98.00 - 3-89349-442-1 - gw Hänsel [150]

DAS PSYCHOLOGISCHE PROBLEM DER FRAU IN KLEISTS DRAMEN UND NOVELLEN / Fueller, Franziska - Leipzig: H Haessel, 1924 - 1r - 1 - us U.W. Library [430]

PSYCHOLOGISCHE UNTERSUCHUNGEN UEBER DAS LESEN AUF EXPERIMENTELLER GRUNDLAGE / Erdman, B & Dodge, R - Halle a.S., 1898 - 7mf - 9 - ne IDC [616]

PSYCHOLOGY AND ATHLETICS / Griffith, Coleman R - 1928 - 5mf - 9 - $15.00 - us Microform Publ [790]

PSYCHOLOGY AND HEALTH / ed by Kaptein, A - 9,5,1 - us Harwood [150]

PSYCHOLOGY AND MARKETING - v1-. 1984- - 1,5,6,9 - us UMI [650]

PSYCHOLOGY, CRIME, AND LAW / ed by Hollin, Clive et al - 9,5,1 - us Harwood [150]

PSYCHOLOGY IN THE SCHOOLS - v1- 1964- 1; v9- 5,6,9 - us UMI [370]

THE PSYCHOLOGY OF COACHING / Griffith, Coleman R - 1928 - 3mf - 9 - $9.00 - us Microform Publ [790]

THE PSYCHOLOGY OF JESUS : A STUDY OF THE DEVELOPMENT OF HIS SELF-CONSCIOUSNESS / Hitchcock, Albert Wellman - Boston:Pilgrim Press, 1907 - 1mf - 9 - 0-8370-3595-3 - 1985-1595 - us A.T.L.A. [150]

PSYCHOLOGY OF JESUS: A STUDY OF THE DEVELOPMENT OF HIS SELF-CONSCIOUSNESS / Hitchcock, Albert Wellman - Boston: Pilgrim Press, 1907. 1 fiche - 9 - us A.T.L.A. [240]

THE PSYCHOLOGY OF LAUGHTER / Sidis, Boris - New York, London: D. Appleton, 1913. ix,300p - 1 - us U.W. Library [150]

THE PSYCHOLOGY OF RELIGION (CCC5) = TSUNG CHIAO HSIN LI HSUEH / Cady, Lyman van Law - (In Chinese) - Hong Kong: Bible Book and Tract Depot, 1953 - 1r - 1 - 0-8370-1705-X - 1984-6099 - us A.T.L.A. [200]

THE PSYCHOLOGY OF RELIGIOUS EXPERIENCE / Ames, Edward Scribner - Boston: Houghton Mifflin, 1910 - 1mf - us A.T.L.A. [200]

PSYCHOLOGY OF THE MORAL SELF / Bosanquet, Bernard - London, New York: Macmillan, 1897 - 1mf - us A.T.L.A. [150]

PSYCHOLOGY TODAY - May- 1967- - 9 - us UMI [073]

PSYCHOLOGY TODAY - (v.4- 1970- 9) - v.1- 1967- - 1,5,6 - us UMI [073]

PSYCHOLOGY USSR - v. 1-. 1980- - 5,6,9 - us UMI [150]

PSYCHOMETRIC ASSESSMENT OF THE CAROLINA SPORT CONFIDENCE INVENTORY / Manzo, Luis G - 1994 - 2mf - $8.00 - us Microform Publ [150]

PSYCHOMETRIKA - v1- 1936- 1; v42- 5,6,9 - us UMI [073]

PSYCHONEUROENDOCRINOLOGY - v.1- 1976- - 5,6,9 - us UMI [616]

PSYCHOPATHOLOGIE AFRICAINE : BULLETIN DE LA SOCIETE DE PSYCHOPATHOLOGIE ET D'HYGIENE MENTALE DE DAKAR - (Vol 1 1965. F130.00. Vol 2 1966. F130.00. Vol 3 1967. F120.00. Vol 4 1968. F130.00. Vol 5 1969. F120.00. Vol 6 1970. F90.00. Vol 7 1971. F120.00. Vol 8 1972. F120.00. Vol 9 1973. F120.00. Vol 10 1974. F120.00) - F950.00 set - fr Ethnologie [616]

PSYCHOPATHOLOGY - v8-. 1975- - 1,5,9 - us UMI [616]

PSYCHOPHARMACOLOGIA - v. 1-72. 1959-80 - 1,5,9 - 12,366.00 - us UMI [073]

THE PSYCHOPHYSIOLOGICAL EFFECTS OF BIOFEEDBACK OPEN FOCUS SELF-REGULATION TRAINING UPON HOMEOSTATIC EFFICIENCY DURING EXERCISE / Powers, Carl J - 1980 - 3mf - 9 - $12.00 - us Microform Publ [790]

PSYCHOPHYSIOLOGIE VON EMOTIONEN : KORTIKALE UND PERIPHERPHYSIOLOGISCHE PARAMETER AFFEKTIVER ZUSTAENDE / Schupp, Harald Thomas - 1994 - 2mf - DM80.00 - 3-8267-2071-7 - gw Hänsel [150]

PSYCHOSOCIAL FACTORS IN THE DEVELOPMENT OF BREAST CANCER / Fox, Cyndy M & Hyner, Gerald G - 1992 - 1mf - 9 - $4.00 - us Microform Publ [150]

PSYCHOSOCIAL PROCESS - us UMI [150]

PSYCHOSOCIAL PROCESS - v1-4 1970-76 1; v4- 5,6,9 - us UMI [150]

PSYCHOSOCIAL REHABILITATION JOURNAL - v5-. 1982- - 1 - us UMI [073]

PSYCHOSOMATIC MEDICINE : JOURNAL OF THE AMERICAN PSYCHOSOMATIC SOCIETY - v51-58. 1989-96 - 1,5,6,9 - $80.00r - us Williams [616]

PSYCHOSOMATIC MEDICINE - v1-46. 1939-84 - 1,5,6,13 - sz Elsevier [616]

PSYCHOTHERAPY AND PSYCHOSOMATICS - v25-. 1975- - 1,5,9 - us UMI [616]

PSYCHOTHERAPY AND SOCIAL SCIENCE REVIEW - New York. v1-4. 1967-70 - 53mf - 9 - $5.00f - us Ross [150]

PSYCHOTHERAPY IN PRIVATE PRACTICE : INNOVATIONS IN CLINICAL METHODS AND ASSESSMENT, CONSULTATION AND PRACTICE MANAGEMENT / ed by Piano, Frank De - v1- 1983- - 1, 9 ($200.00 in US $280.00 outside hardcopy subsc) - us Haworth [616]

THE PSYCHOTHERAPY PATIENT : A JOURNAL OF ATTRIBUTE-FOCUSED PRACTICE / ed by Stern, E Mark - v1- 1984- - 1, 9 ($135.00 in US $189.00 outside hardcopy subsc) - us Haworth [615]

PTA MAGAZINE - 1960-74 - 9 - us UMI [073]

PTA MAGAZINE - (1968-74. 5,6. 1969-74. 9) - 1-69 1906-74 - 1 - us UMI [370]

PTA MAGAZINE - (Former titles: National Congress of Mothers Magazin, 1906-nov 1909. Child Welfare Magazine, dec 1909-sep 1928. Child Welfare, oct 1928-jun/jul 1934. National Parent-teacher Magazine, sep 1934-jan 1937. National Parent-teacher, feb 1937-jan 1961) - Chicago. v1-69. nov 1906-nov 1974 1; v63-69. sep 1968-nov 1974 5; v54-64 sep 1959-jun 1970*. v65-69 sep 1970-nov 1974 9 - 1,5,9 - D854 - us UMI [370]

PTA TODAY - (v9-. Oct 1984-. 5,6,9) - v1-. May 1974- - 1 - us UMI [073]

Ptashitskii, S L *see* SBORNIK SNIMKOV S SLAVIANORUSSKIKH STAROPECHATNYKH IZDANII

Ptaszycki, S *see* ENCYKLOPEDJA NAUK POMOCNICZYCH HISTORJI I LITERATURY POLSKIEJ

PTITSEVODNOE KHOZIAISTVO - M. 1899-1917. Lacking: 1899-1912; 1914; v. 2-3, 14, 1915; v. 1-18, 21-24, 1916; v. 4-5, 8-24, 1917. BR-8158 2 - 8 - ne IDC [073]

PTITSEVODSTVO - (Cont as: Kooperativnoe Ptitsevodstvo) - M., 1928-29 n23 - 27mf - 9 - COR-672/1 - ne IDC [334]

PTITSY V VOZDYKHE. STROKI NAPEVNYIA / Bal'mont, K D - Spb. 1908. BR-532 2 - 8 - ne IDC [460]

PTOLEMAIS CYRENAICA / Nasgowitz, David - (76p accompanying text) - 1980 - 2 color 4 b/w mf - 15,9 - $60.00f - 0-226-69474-7 - us Chicago [700]

PTOLEMY'S GEOGRAPHY : A BRIEF ACCOUNT OF ALL THE PRINTED EDITIONS DOWN TO 1730 / Stevens, H N – London, 1908 – 2mf – 9 – 1598/2 – ne IDC [019]
Pu, Hua-jen *see* MY LIFE DECISIONS (CCC269)
Puaux, F *see* ETUDES SUR LA REVOCATION DE L'EDIT DE NANTES
Puaux, Francois *see* VIE DE CALVIN
Puaux, Frank *see* HISTOIRE DE L'ETABLISSEMENT DES PROTESTANTS FRANCAIS EN SUEDE
Pub, Emerson W *see* FORGOTTEN HEROES OF DELAWARE
LE PUBLIC – Journal du soir, politique et quotidien. Dir. Ernest Dreolle. no. 1-658. Paris. 15 nov 1868-14 sept 1870 – 1 – fr A.C.R.P.P. [073]
THE PUBLIC – v. 1-22. 1898-1919. V. 12-14 wanting – 1 – 227.00 – us L of C Photodup [073]
PUBLIC ACCOUNTS / Canada. Department of Finance – 1925- – 9 – cn Micromedia [336]
PUBLIC ACCOUNTS FOR... COMPTES PUBLICS POUR... / Bas-Canada – Quebec: s.n, 18–?-. SEM105P1226 – 8mf – 9 – Can$18.00 – cn Bibl Nat [336]
A PUBLIC ADDRESS TO THE BAPTIST SOCIETY OF THE BAPTIST BOARD OF FOREIGN MISSIONS / Parker, Daniel – 1820 – 1 – 5.00 – us Baptist [240]
PUBLIC ADMINISTRATION – v1- 1923- 1; v49- 5,6; v54- 9 – us UMI [323]
PUBLIC ADMINISTRATION – v.1-53. 1923-75. London – 9 – 24180.00; 244.00v – uk Dawson [350]
PUBLIC ADMINISTRATION AND DEVELOPMENT – v.1-. 1981- – 1,5,6,9 – us UMI [073]
PUBLIC ADMINISTRATION AND SOCIAL CHANGES IN ARGENTINA, 1943-1955 / Garcia Zamor, Jean Claude – Rio de Janeiro, [1968] – 1 – CSUXADP4030-B – us Hoover Inst Photo [320]
PUBLIC ADMINISTRATION REVIEW – v1- 1940- 1; v31- 5,6; v35- 9 – us UMI [323]
PUBLIC ADVERTISER – New York, NY. 1807-1813 – 3 – us Readex [071]
PUBLIC AND ACCESS SERVICES QUARTERLY / ed by Blake, Virgil – v2 n1. 1996- – 1,9 – $60.00 in US $84.00 outside hardcopy subsc – us Haworth [020]
PUBLIC ARCHITECTURE IN THE NETHERLANDS, 1850-1950 – (Price includes inventory and multilingual terminology lists. Available separately: inventory Dfl175.00, terminology lists Dfl104.50) – Plans and Drawings from the Government Buildings Agency General State Archives, The Hague – 6,069mf – 9 – Dfl27,625.00 – ne MMF Publ [720]
PUBLIC BUDGETING AND FINANCE – 1985- – 1 – us UMI [073]
PUBLIC CHARACTERS – v1-10.1798-1809. 10v. -ann. Title varies.No more published – 1 – us U.W. Library [920]
PUBLIC CONTRACT LAW JOURNAL (ABA) – v1-20. 1967-1992 – 9 – $200.00 set – us Hein [340]
PUBLIC DEBTS AND STATE SUCCESSION / Feilchenfeld, E H – New York, 1931 – 10mf – 1 – ILM-1545/1 – ne IDC [327]
THE PUBLIC DOMAIN, ITS HISTORY...AND DISPOSITION TO 1880 / Donaldson, Thomas – Washington: GPO, 1884 – 17mf – 9 – $25.50 – LLMC 82-101-6 – us L.L.M.C. [340]
PUBLIC EDUCATION EDICT 1970 : EDICT NO. 2 OF 1971 / Nigeria. East Central State – 1971 – 1mf – 9 – DE-100/1 – ne IDC [370]
PUBLIC ELEMENTARY EDUCATION IN ENGLAND AND WALES. BILL 33 / Great Britain. Laws, Statutes, etc – 1870 – 1 £35.00 7 £3.50 – uk Microform Academic [324]
PUBLIC ELEMENTARY SCHOOL: SUGGESTIONS FOR THE CONSIDERATION OF TEACHERS AND OTHERS CONCERNED IN THE WORK / Great Britain. Ministry of Education – 1905 – 9 – uk Microform Academic [370]
PUBLIC ELEMENTARY SCHOOLS / Great Britain. Departmental Committee for the Training of Teachers – 1925. Cmd. 2409 – 9 – uk Microform Academic [370]
THE PUBLIC EVIDENCE PRESENTED TO THE ROYAL COMMISSION ON LEGAL SERVICES, 1979 / Great Britain. Royal Commission on Legal Services – 9 reels with reel guide-index – 1 – $400.00 – us Trans-Media [340]
PUBLIC FIGURES IN THE CIS AND THE BALTIC STATES : A BIOGRAPHICAL INDEX, 1984-JUNE 1993 / Radio Free Europe-Radio Liberty Inc – 1984 – 137mf – 9 – £660.00 – uk Chadwyck [947]
PUBLIC FINANCE FOR STABILITY AND GROWTH IN THE UNDERDEVELOPED EXPORT ECONOMY: A CASE STUDY OF THE REPUBLIC OF THE SUDAN / International Bureau of Fiscal Documentation – Kubinski, Z. M. 1961. BNE-7657 1 – 9 – ne IDC [336]
PUBLIC FINANCE QUARTERLY – (v.7-. 1979- 5,6,9) – v.1-. 1973- – 1 – us UMI [073]
PUBLIC FINANCE, TRADE AND STATE FORMATION : THE ARCHIVE OF THE STATES OF HOLLAND, C.1445-1572 – 1993 – 83r – 1 – Dfl16,650.00 – ne MMF Publ [336]
PUBLIC FORESTRY ADMINISTRATION IN LATIN AMERICA – 1981 – 185p – it F.A.O. [634]
PUBLIC GAZETEER – Dublin, Ireland.23 Sept 1758-16 Sept 1760. -w. 2 reels – 1 – uk British Libr Newspaper [072]
PUBLIC GENERAL ACTS, 1714-1933 / Great Britain. Laws, Statutes, etc – 98 reels. Segments available – 1 – $4,000.00 – us Trans-Media [340]
PUBLIC GENERAL ACTS, 1801-1922 / Great Britain – (The complete authentic official Sessional (later annual) volumes as issued by Authority, The King's-Queen's Printers' Copies. Pt 1: 1801-45. Pt 2: 1846-1922) – 9 – us Primary [941]
PUBLIC HEALTH ECONOMICS – v1-21. Sept 1944-Feb 1964 – 1 – us UMI [073]
PUBLIC HEALTH ECONOMICS AND MEDICAL CARE ABSTRACTS – v21-23 Mar 1964 – 1966 – 1 – us UMI [610]
PUBLIC HEALTH ENGINEER – v1- 1973- 1; v13- 5,6,9 – us UMI [610]
PUBLIC HEALTH ENGINEERING ABSTRACTS – v.47. 1967 – 1,5,6 – 2235.00 – us Princeton Micro [614]
PUBLIC HEALTH MAGAZINE – Montreal, Canada. jul 1875-v1 n10. jun 1876 – 1r – 1 – Can$25.00 – cn Can Microfilming [610]
PUBLIC HEALTH REPORTS – (See also: Health Services Reports) – v89- 1974- – 1,5,6,9 – us UMI [610]
PUBLIC HEALTH REPORTS – v1-95. 1878-1980. Continues: Health Services Reports – 1,5,6 – us Princeton Micro [610]
PUBLIC HEALTH REVIEW – v1-11. 1972-82 – 1 – us UMI [073]
PUBLIC HEARINGS / Great Britain. Foreign Office. Anglo-American Committee of Enquiry, 1945-1948 – London. BJ-28-94 1 – 9 – ne IDC [324]
PUBLIC HEARINGS OF THE COMMISSION ON WARTIME RELOCATION AND INTERNMENT OF CIVILIANS – 6r – 1 – M1293 – us Nat'l Archives [324]
PUBLIC HISTORIAN – (1982-. 1,5,6,9) – v1-. 1978- – 1 – us UMI [073]
PUBLIC INSURANCE AND COMPENSATION MONEY / Beckerath, Ulrich von – 2fiches. (24x) – 9 – 1.00f – at Libertarian Micro [320]
PUBLIC INTEREST ACCOUNTING NEWSLETTER *see* API NEWSLETTER
PUBLIC INTERNATIONAL DEVELOPMENT FINANCING IN SUDAN / Meagher, R F – 1965. BNE-7662 1 – 9 – ne IDC [338]
PUBLIC INTERNATIONAL LAW – v1-6 1975-80 – 1,5,9 – $171.00 – us UMI [340]
PUBLIC LAND LAW REVIEW – University of Montana. v1-16. 1980-95 – 9 – $150.00 set – us Hein [340]
PUBLIC LAND LAWS OF THE UNITED STATES / Keener, John – Washington: GPO, 1916 – 6mf – 9 – $9.00 – LLMC 82-101-8 – us L.L.M.C. [340]
PUBLIC LAND LAWS OF THE UNITED STATES / Keener, John – Washington: GPO, 1923 – 8mf – 9 – $12.00 – LLMC 82-101-9 – us L.L.M.C. [340]
THE PUBLIC LAND LAWS OF THE UNITED STATES, 1796-1869. / Zabriskie, James C – (Supplement. Being the public land laws of the United States, from 1869 to 1876. San Francisco, 1877. 104 p) – San Francisco, Bancroft, 1870. 1168 p. LL-1602 – 1 – us L of C Photodup [340]
PUBLIC LAND LAWS OF THE UNITED STATES, 1869-1882 / Copp, Henry Norris – (1869-1875 in 1 bk and 1875-1882 in 2 bks) – Henry N. Copp, 1875, 1883 – 27mf – 9 – $40.50 – LLMC 82-101-3 – us L.L.M.C. [340]
PUBLIC LAND LAWS OF THE UNITED STATES, 1882-1890 / Copp, Henry Norris – Washington: Published by the compiler. 2v. 1890 – 15mf – 9 – $22.50 – LLMC 82-101-4 – us L.L.M.C. [340]
PUBLIC LAND STATUTES AND REGULATIONS IN FORCE JUNE 1, 1938 – (Part of Code of Federal Regulations, Title 43) – Washington: GPO, 1940 – 13mf – 9 – $19.50 – LLMC 82-101-11 – us L.L.M.C. [340]
PUBLIC LAND STATUTES OF THE UNITED STATES / Greene, Daniel – Washington: GPO, 1931 – 9mf – 9 – $13.50 – LLMC 82-101-10 – us L.L.M.C. [340]
PUBLIC LAW 414 (ACT OF JUNE 27, 1952; 66 STAT. 163) / U.S. Congress. Senate. Committee on the Judiciary – Comparative print of the texts of the Imm. and Natur. Act and Imm. and Natur. Laws existing prior to enactment of Pub. Law 414. Washington: GPO. 1952. 81-500 – 9 – 4.00 – us L.L.M.C. [340]
PUBLIC LAW FORUM *see* SAINT LOUIS UNIVERSITY PUBLIC LAW REVIEW
PUBLIC LAWS PASSED BY CONGRESS FROM APRIL 1, 1882 TO JANUARY 1, 1890. / Copp, Henry Norris – Washington, DC, 1890. 2v. LL-1443 – 1 – us L of C Photodup [340]
PUBLIC LEDGER – Norfolk. Va. 1876-1906 – 1 – us UMI [071]
PUBLIC LEDGER – Philadelphia. Pa. 1836-1934 – 1 – us UMI [071]
PUBLIC LEDGER AND NEWFOUNDLAND GENERAL ADVERTISER – St. John's, Canada. 1827-82 – 32r – 1 – $2,080.00 – cn Library Assoc [971]
PUBLIC LIBRARIES – v.17-. 1978- – 1,5,6,9 – us UMI [073]
THE PUBLIC LIBRARY OF NEW SOUTH WALES: DICTIONARY CATALOG OF PRINTED BOOKS / Mitchell Library. Sydney, Australia – (First Suppl., 1970.-17,500 cards 2 reels. $155.00 ISBN: 0-8161-1323-8) – 1968.-603,000 cards 76 reels.-ISBN: 0-8161-1362-9 – 1 – $4110.00 – uk Hall [010]
PUBLIC LIBRARY QUARTERLY / ed by Waters, Richard L – v1- 1979- – 1, 9 ($125.00 in US $175.00 outside hardcopy subsc) – us Haworth [020]
PUBLIC LIBRARY TRUSTEE – (1979- 5,6,9) – 1958- – 1 – us UMI [073]
THE PUBLIC LIFE OF CHRIST / Kephart, Cyrus Jeffries – (Includes appendix and index) – New York: Fleming H Revell, [1892] – 1mf – 9 – 0-8370-3888-X – 1985-1888 – us A.T.L.A. [240]
PUBLIC MANAGEMENT – v1- 1919- 1; v50- 5,6; v57- 9 – us UMI [323]
PUBLIC MEN IN ALABAMA FOR 30 YEARS / Garrett, William – Atlanta: Plantation Publ. Co., 1872. Alabama Reel 1. (The Cox Library Collection) – 5 – us Americana [978]
THE PUBLIC MINISTRY AND PASTORAL METHODS OF OUR LORD / Blaikie, William Garden – London: James Nisbet, 1883 – 1mf – 9 – 0-8370-2362-9 – 1985-0362 – us A.T.L.A. [240]
PUBLIC NEWSPAPER = KUNG PAO – (In Chinese) – v2-3. 1930-31; v15. 1943; v21-26. 1949-54 (complete) – 1r – 1 – ATLA S0296N – us A.T.L.A. [073]
PUBLIC OPINION – A comprehensive summary of the press throughout the world on all important current topics. v. 1-40. 1886-1906 – 1,5,6 – us Princeton Micro [073]
PUBLIC OPINION – Bayonne. N.J. 1923-25 – 1 – us UMI [071]
PUBLIC OPINION – Bombay: R K Karanjia, sep 3 1952-feb 25 1953 – 2r – 1 – us Res Libr [072]
PUBLIC OPINION – Chambersburg. Pa. 1901- – 1 – us UMI [071]
PUBLIC OPINION – Chambersburg, PA. -w 1869-1912 – 13 – $25.00r – us I.M.R. [071]
PUBLIC OPINION – Chambersburg. Pa. -w. 1869-71 – 1 – us UMI [071]
PUBLIC OPINION – San Francisco, CA. 1890-99 – 2r – 1 – $100.00 – B02855 – us Library Micro [071]
PUBLIC OPINION – (Set incl. Mapleton Bee; Lane County Bee (Mapleton)) – Eugene, OR. -w. 5 Oct 1934-22 Mar 1935 – 1r – 1 – us U.O. Library [071]
PUBLIC OPINION – v. 1-179. 5 Oct 1861-22 Jun 1951 – 1 – 1,512.00 – us L of C Photodup [073]
PUBLIC OPINION – Westerville. Ohio. -w. 1880- – 1 – us UMI [071]
PUBLIC OPINION *see*
– AEI ECONOMIST
– AMERICAN ENTERPRISE
PUBLIC OPINION QUARTERLY – (v. 33- 1969- 5,6. v. 39- 1975- 9) – v. 1- 1937- – 1 – us UMI [073]
PUBLIC ORDER, DISCONTENT AND PROTEST IN NINETEENTH CENTURY ENGLAND, 1820-1850 (PRO CLASS HO 52) / Great Britain. Public Record Office – (Pt 1: 1820-30 (PRO HO 52, Boxes 1-11). Pt 2: 1831-36 (PRO HO 52, Boxes 12-32). Pt 3: 1837-50 (PRO HO 52, Boxes 33-47)) – 1 – us Primary [941]
THE PUBLIC PAPERS OF LOUIS DEMBITZ BRANDEIS IN THE JACOB AND BERTHA GOLDFARB LIBRARY OF BRANDEIS UNIVERSITY / Sachar, Abram L & Goldsmith, William M – 6 sections. 1978 – 8r – 1 – $395.00 – us OmniSys [323]
PUBLIC PAPERS OF THE PRESIDENTS, 1929-1993 – (Series does not cover presidency of Franklin D. Roosevelt. Updates planned) – Washington: GPO. Hoover v1-Clinton v1 – 874mf – 9 – $1,311.00 – LLMC 80-514 – us L.L.M.C. [324]
PUBLIC PAPERS OF THE PRESIDENTS, 1929-1993 *see* PROCLAMATIONS AND EXECUTIVE ORDERS
PUBLIC PERSONNEL MANAGEMENT – (v.4- 1975- 9) – v.2- 1973- – 1,5,6 – us UMI [650]
PUBLIC POLICY – v. 1-. 1940- – 1,5,6,9 – us UMI [320]
PUBLIC POLICY – v1-29. 1940-81 – 1,5,6 – us Princeton Micro [073]
Public Record Office *see* CURRENT GUIDE
PUBLIC RELATIONS JOURNAL – v1- 1945- 1; v27- 5,6; v31- 9 – us UMI [300]
PUBLIC RELATIONS OF THE COMMISSION FOR RELIEF IN BELGIUM: DOCUMENTS / ed by Gay, George I & Fisher, Harold H – 2v. 1935. 606, 539p – 1 – $35.00r – us Hoover Inst Photo [360]
PUBLIC RELATIONS REVIEW – (v.5-. 1979- 5,6,9) – v.1-. 1975- – 1 – us UMI [073]
PUBLIC ROADS – v1- 1918- 1; v36- 5,6; v39- 9 – us UMI [625]
THE PUBLIC SCHOOL – Montreal: The Montreal Catholic School Commission. v1-7. 1969-1976. SEM35P33 – 1r – 1 – Can$20.00 – cn Bibl Nat [370]
PUBLIC SCHOOL HISTORY OF ENGLAND AND CANADA: WITH INTRODUCTION, HINTS TO TEACHERS, AND BRIEF EXAMINATION QUESTIONS / Adam, Graeme Mercer – Toronto: Copp, Clark, 1886. 00746. (Pre-1900 Canadiana) – 9 – cn C.I.H.M. [971]
PUBLIC SCHOOLS AND THE GENERAL EDUCATION SYSTEM: REPORT OF THE COMMITTEE ON PUBLIC SCHOOLS / Great Britain. Committee on Public Schools – 1944. Fleming Report – 9 – uk Microform Academic [324]
PUBLIC SCHOOLS ENQUIRY: MINUTES OF EVIDENCE AND REPORT / Great Britain. Clarendon Committee – 1864 – 9 – uk Microform Academic [324]
THE PUBLIC SCHOOLS OF CHICAGO: A SOCIOLOGICAL STUDY / Clark, Hannah Belle – Chicago: The University of Chicago Press, 1897. (3)-117p – 1 – us U.W. Library [370]
PUBLIC SECTOR DEVELOPMENT PROGRAMME, 1966-70 / Mauritius – (Sessional Paper no. 4 of 1966). Port Louis. 1966 – 9 – ne IDC [360]
PUBLIC SECTOR INVESTMENT PROGRAMME, 1969-1972 / Rhodesia – Bd-1462 1 – 9 – ne IDC [336]
PUBLIC SECTOR INVESTMENT PROGRAMME, 1970-1973 / Rhodesia – 9 – ne IDC [336]
PUBLIC SERVICE CORPORATIONS OF BALTIMORE CITY / Pielert, Charles – Baltimore: King, 1908. 1316p. LL-1709 – 1 – us L of C Photodup [340]
PUBLIC SPIRIT – Hatboro. Pa. 1958-1959 – 1 – us UMI [071]
PUBLIC STATEMENTS BY THE SECRETARIES OF DEFENSE / US. Department of Defense – (Pt 1: The Truman Administration (1947-53) 6r ISBN: 0-89093-529-7 $670. Pt 2: The Eisenhower Administration (1953-61) ISBN: 0-89093-530-0 $860. Pt 3: The Kennedy and Johnson Administrations (1961-69) ISBN: 0-89093-531-9 $1,830. Pt 4: The Nixon and Ford Administrations (1969-77) ISBN: 0-89093-532-7 $2,410. Pt 5: The Carter Administration (1977-81) ISBN: 0-89093-533-5 $1,150. All with printed guides) – 1983 – 1 – us UPA [324]

PUBLIC TELEVISION TRANSCRIPTS – (Backfiles from 1973-1996 for various Public TV news programs including MacNeil/Lehrer NewsHour) – 9 – us Primary [070]

PUBLIC UNDERSTANDING OF SCIENCE – 1992-. v1 – 1,5,6,9 – £76.00 – uk I.O.P. [500]

PUBLIC UTILITIES, 1886-1990 – (Guide only $325.00) – 481mf – 9 – $2,860.00 – 1-55655-476-1 – us UPA [338]

PUBLIC UTILITIES FORTNIGHTLY – v1- 1928- 1; v87- 5,6; v95- 9 – us UMI [305]

PUBLIC UTILITIES REPORTS, ANNOTATED – (Add vols planned) – Rochester, NY: Lawyers' Co-op. 1915-1920 – 382mf – 9 – $573.00 – LLMC 90-353 – us L.L.M.C. [340]

PUBLIC UTILITIES REPORTS ANNOTATED, CONTAINING DECISIONS OF THE PUBLIC SERVICE COMMISSIONS AND OF STATE AND FEDERAL COURTS / New York. (State). Public Service Commission – Rochester, N.Y. 1915-1933; n.s. v. 1-55. 1934-1944 – 1 – us NY Public [336]

PUBLIC WELFARE – v1- 1943- 1; v32- 5,6; v33- 9 – us UMI [073]

PUBLIC WORKS – v1- 1896- 1; v102- 5,6; v107- 9 – us UMI [600]

PUBLIC WORKS – v95-112 1964-81 – 1,5,6 – us Princeton Micro [624]

PUBLIC WORSHIP : A STUDY IN THE PSYCHOLOGY OF RELIGION / Hylan, John P – Chicago: Open Court; London: Kegan Paul, Trench, Truebner, 1901. ([Religion of science library; no. 50]) – 1mf – us A.T.L.A. [240]

THE PUBLIC WORSHIP OF PRESBYTERIAN SCOTLAND : HISTORICALLY TREATED / M'Crie, Charles Greig – Edinburgh: William Blackwood, 1892. (The Fourteenth series of the Cunningham lectures) – 2mf – us A.T.L.A. [240]

[PUBLICACIONES] / Partido Socialista (Argentine Republic) – (Includes c.1: v.1-6, 8-9) – Buenos Aires, [1946?] – 1 – CSUXADQ3244-S – us Hoover Inst Photo [320]

PUBLICACIONES DE LA REAL SOCIEDAD GEOGRAFICA CRISTOBAL COLON...GENOVES – Madrid: Razon y Fe, 1926 – 1 – sp Bibl Santa Ana [946]

O PUBLICADOR MARAHENSE – '(s.l.')-Sao Luis, Brazil. 9 Jul 1842-Dec 1851. Jan-Apr, Jun-Dec 1852. Jan 1853-Jul 1857. Jan-Dec 1858. Jan-Feb, May-Dec 1859. Jan 1860-Jul 1864. Jan 1865- Jun 1869. Jul 1870-Dec 1871. Jan 1874-Jun 1875. Jan-Jun 1876. Jan 1877-31 Dec 1885 – 1,5,6 – bl Biblioteca [072]

O PUBLICADOR OFFICIAL – '(s.l.')-Sao Luis, Brazil. 22 Oct-Dec 1831. Jan-Apr, Dec 1832. Jan-Nov 1833. Apr-Dec 1834. Jan-Apr, Jul 1835. May 1836. Jan 1837-Apr 1839. Feb, Apr-May, Nov 1840. Jan, 6 Mar 1841 – 1,5,6 – bl Biblioteca [072]

PUBLICAN – 1978- – 1 – us UMI [640]

PUBLICAT : CURRENT CANADIAN FEDERAL DOCUMENTS / (Canada) – 1977-78 – 9 – cn Micromedia [324]

LE PUBLICATEUR DES COTES-DU-NORD – (8 missing numbers) – Saint-Brieuc (Cotes d'Armor), June 1836 – Feb. 1916 – 16r – fr Armell [073]

PUBLICATIEEN IN DE HOLLANDSCHE HOOGDUITSCHE ISRAELIETISCHE KERKEN GEDAAN BETREKKELIJK HET OPRIGTEN VAN EEN CORPS TROEPEN TE AMSTERDAM – Amsterdam. 1809. BJ-262-52 1 – 9 – ne IDC [305]

PUBLICATION / Florida. Agricultural Experiment Station – v. 1-7. 1966-69 – 1,5,6 – us Spaulding [630]

PUBLICATION / Louisiana State University. Cooperative Extension Service – 1001-2238 – 1,5 – us Spaulding [630]

PUBLICATION / Massachusetts. Agricultural Extension Service – n.s. v. 1-40. 1967-69 – 1,5,6 – us Spaulding [630]

PUBLICATION / Massachusetts. Agricultural Extension Service – v. 1-446. 1921-66 – 1,5,6 – us Spaulding [630]

PUBLICATION / Mississippi State University. Cooperative Extension Service – No.692-1299 – 1,5 – us Spaulding [630]

PUBLICATION / Mississippi. State University. Cooperative Extension Service – v. 146-691 – 1,5,6 – us Spaulding [630]

PUBLICATION / Tennessee. University. Agricultural Extension Service – n.1-589. Jul 1914-May 1969 – 1,5 – us Spaulding [630]

PUBLICATION / Texas A & M University. Forest Service – No.104-130. 1969-82. 7 fiches – 9 – us Spaulding [630]

PUBLICATION / Virginia. Polytechnic Institute. Extension Division – v. 1-324. 1968-69 – 1,5,6 – us Spaulding [630]

PUBLICATION: AN INDEX / Clemson University. South Carolina Agricultural Experiment Station – 1888-1975. 5 fiches – 9 – us Spaulding [630]

PUBLICATION NEC / New England Cooperative Extension – v. 1-65. 1947-69 – 1,5,6 – us Spaulding [630]

PUBLICATION NEC / Vermont. New England Cooperative Extension – n.1-65. 1947-69 – 1,5 – us Spaulding [630]

PUBLICATION OF THE AMERICAN ECONOMIC ASSOCIATION *see* AMERICAN ECONOMIC ASSOCIATION QUARTERLY

PUBLICATIONS / AFL-CIO (American Federation of Labor-Congress of Industrial Organizations) – 1956- 1; 1973- 5,6; 1977- 4 x 6 in. 9 – us UMI [330]

PUBLICATIONS / Arkansas Historical Association – v1-2. 1906, 1908. Ed. by John High Reynolds. Items C & D. Includes indexes. SW16-0011 – 5 – us A.G.L.L. [978]

PUBLICATIONS / Atlanta University – n1-20. 1888-1917 – 1 – 1 – us Ross [370]

PUBLICATIONS / Canada. Dominion Bureau of Statistics – (Statistics Canada Publications, 1851.-9) – 1841- – 9 – cn Micromedia [971]

PUBLICATIONS / Canada. Statistics Canada – 1841- – 9 – cn Micromedia [971]

PUBLICATIONS / Catholic Record Society. London – v. 1-64. 1905-73 – 9 – 24480.00; 7.50v – uk Dawson [240]

PUBLICATIONS / Ecole Francaise d'Extreme-Orient – Hanoi. v1-28. 1900-36 – 265mf – 8 – ne IDC [950]

PUBLICATIONS / Great Britain. Joint Select Committee on Closer Union in East Africa – v. 1, 11, 111. 1931 – 1 – uk Microform Academic [324]

PUBLICATIONS / Hanserd Knollys Society for the Publication of the Works of Early English and other Baptist Writers – Braght, Martyrology of Churches of Christ, v. 1, 1850; Braght, Martyrology of Churches of Christ, v. 2, 1853; Bristol, Records of a Church of Christ,1640-87; Bunyan, Pilgrim's Progress, 1678; Canne, Necessity of Separation from the Church of England, 1849; Underhill, Confessions of faith, 1611-88; Underhill, Tracts on Liberty of Conscience, 1614-61; Underhill, Records of the Churches of Christ,1644-1720; Veil, Commentary of the Acts of the Apostles, 1685; Williams, Bloudy tenent of Persecution, 1848 – 1 – $164.01 – us Baptist [240]

PUBLICATIONS / Hanserd Knollys Society for the Publication of the Works of Early English and other Baptist Writers – (Includes: Underhill, E.B., comp. Tracts on Liberty of Conscience; Records of the Churches of Christ Gathered at Fenstanton, Warboys and Hexam, 1644-1720; Confessions of Faith and other Public Documents Illustrative of the History of the Baptist Churches of England in the 17th Century. Bristol, England. Broadmead Church: The Records. Bunyan, John. The Pilgrim's Progress. Williams, Roger. The Bloudy Tenent of Persecution. Canne, John. A Necessity of Separation from the Church of England. Bracht, T.J. van. A Martyrology of the Churches of Christ Commonly Called Baptists. 2v. Veil, C.M. du. A Commentary on the Acts of the Apostles) – 10v – 1 – us A.T.L.A. [240]

PUBLICATIONS / Harleian Society. London – v. 1-60. 1877-1930 – 1 – 155.00 – us L of C Photodup [941]

PUBLICATIONS / Hayne, Robert Y – 1814-ca.1913. 40 fiches – 9 – us South Carolina Historical [025]

PUBLICATIONS / Israel. Ministry of Agriculture – 1976. Bet-Dagan. 1977. 7 p – 9 – 2.00 – is I.T.T.I. [630]

PUBLICATIONS / Kingman Park Civic Association – Washington, D.C. 1938-1954 – 1 – us NY Public [073]

PUBLICATIONS / Lancashire Parish Register Society – v1-9 1898-1901 – 1 – 23.00 – us L of C Photodup [920]

PUBLICATIONS / Lebanon. Societe Nouvelle de la Banque de Syrie et du Liban. Assemblee generale ordinaire, 1964-1977 – Beirut. Lacking: 1973. Not published: 1976. BNE-9686 1 – 9 – ne IDC [336]

PUBLICATIONS / Luxembourg. (Grand Duchy). Service de la Publications. Geologique – Luxembourg. Bd.1-15. 1927-65 – 1 – us NY Public [500]

PUBLICATIONS / Minnesota. Agricultural Experiment Station. St. Paul. Northeast Experiment Station. Duluth – 1,5,6 – us Spaulding [630]

PUBLICATIONS / Missouri Historical Society – v1-15 1880-99 – 1 – us UMI [978]

PUBLICATIONS / Nebraska State Historical Society – Nebraska newspapers 1854-; public records and manuscripts relating to the history of Nebraska and the Great Plains region – 1 – us NE Hist [978]

PUBLICATIONS / Paris Peace Conference – (E.S.H. Bulletin.Publ. by U.S. Embassy.Nos. 1-1358. 12 Dec 1919-3 Jan 1921. 15v. Minutes of Proceedings of the Supreme Economic Council. Paris: Imp. nationale, 1920. 2v. Processed Minutes. Nos. 1-327. 26 Jan 1920-12 Jan 1931; Conferences of Ambassadors, Paris, 1920-31. 99v. Recueil des Actes de la Conference. Paris: Imprimerie nationale, 1922-34. 45v. S.H. Bulletin of the American Commission to Negotiate Peace. Nos. 6-1428. 10 Feb-7 Dec 1919. 30v. Catalog of Paris Peace Conference Delegation Propaganda in the Hoover War Library; Introduction to a Bibliography of the Paris Peace Conference; Collections of Sources; Archive Publications; Source Books. By Nina Almond and Ralph Lutz. Guide to Proceedings of the Paris Peace Conference and the Conference of Ambassadors) – 1 – $35.00r – us Hoover Inst Photo [940]

PUBLICATIONS / Permanent Court of International Justice. Hague – Leyden, 1922-46. Judgements, orders, opinions, statutes, rules, index – 24r – 1 – $1000.00 – us Trans-Media [340]

PUBLICATIONS / Ray Society – 1,7 – uk Microform Academic [580]

PUBLICATIONS / Royal Architectural Institute of Canada – v1-5 Jan 1924 – Apr 1928 – 1 – cn Precision [720]

PUBLICATIONS / Royal Asiatic Society – Monographs, Forlong Fund Publications, Oriental Translation Fund Publications and Prize Publication Fund Publications – 1 – uk Microform Academic [950]

PUBLICATIONS / Smithsonian Institution – 1958- – 3 – us Readex [324]

PUBLICATIONS / Southern Baptist Convention. Education Commission – (1) Baptist Education Bulletin. v. 1, no. 1-V. 2, no. 4, Jul 1919-Sep 1924; (2) College News and Views. v. 1, no. 1-V. 2, no. 9, Oct 1936-Jun 1947; (3) Southern Baptist Educator. v. 12, no. 1-V. 20, no. 9, Oct 1947-Aug 1968 – 1 – 205.55 – us Baptist [240]

PUBLICATIONS / U. S. Environmental Science Services Administration – 1966-71 – 3 – us Readex [580]

PUBLICATIONS / U. S. Geological Survey – 1958-81 – 3 – us Readex [550]

PUBLICATIONS / U. S. Naval Material Command – 1967-81 – 3 – us Readex [355]

PUBLICATIONS / U.S. Agency for International Development – 1962-78 – 3 – us Readex [330]

PUBLICATIONS / U.S. Army – 1958-81 – 3 – us Readex [324]

PUBLICATIONS / U.S. Army. Air Force – 1958-81 – 3 – us Readex [324]

PUBLICATIONS / U.S. Army. Corps of Engineers – 1958-81 – 3 – us Readex [623]

PUBLICATIONS / U.S. Atomic Energy Commission – 1958-76 – 3 – us Readex [621]

PUBLICATIONS / U.S. Board of Governors of the Federal Reserve System – 1958-81 – 3 – us Readex [336]

PUBLICATIONS / U.S. Bureau of Aeronautics (Navy Dept.) – 1958-59 – 3 – us Readex [629]

PUBLICATIONS / U.S. Bureau of Domestic Commerce (formerly Business and Defense Services Administration) – 1971-81 – 3 – us Readex [380]

PUBLICATIONS / U.S. Bureau of International Business Operations, International Programs and International Commerce – 1962-81 – 3 – us Readex [380]

PUBLICATIONS / U.S. Bureau of Labor Standards (now Occupational Safety and Health Administration) – 1958-69 – 3 – us Readex [330]

PUBLICATIONS / U.S. Bureau of Labor Statistics – 1958-81 – 3 – us Readex [310]

PUBLICATIONS / U.S. Bureau of Medicine and Surgery (Navy) – 1958-81 – 3 – us Readex [610]

PUBLICATIONS / U.S. Bureau of Mines – 1958-81 – 3 – us Readex [622]

PUBLICATIONS / U.S. Bureau of Naval Weapons – 1960-66 – 3 – us Readex [355]

PUBLICATIONS / U.S. Bureau of the Census – 1958-81 – 3 – us Readex [310]

PUBLICATIONS / U.S. Bureau of the Census – No. 4-58. (incomplete). 1933-1941 – 1 – us NY Public [310]

PUBLICATIONS / U.S. Business and Defense Services Administration – 1958-70 – 3 – us Readex [324]

PUBLICATIONS / U.S. Children's Bureau. Dept. of Health, Education and Welfare – 1958-81 – 3 – us Readex [324]

PUBLICATIONS / U.S. Civil Aeronautics Board – 1958-81 – 3 – us Readex [629]

PUBLICATIONS / U.S. Civil Service Commission – 1958-81 – 3 – us Readex [324]

PUBLICATIONS / U.S. Coast and Geodetic Survey – 1958-70 – 3 – us Readex [550]

PUBLICATIONS / U.S. Coast Guard – 1958-81 – 3 – us Readex [360]

PUBLICATIONS / U.S. Court of Claims – 1958-81 – 3 – us Readex [324]

PUBLICATIONS / U.S. Department of Agriculture – 1958-81 – 3 – us Readex [630]

PUBLICATIONS / U.S. Department of Agriculture – From inception to present – 9 – us Updata [630]

PUBLICATIONS / U.S. Department of Defense – 1958-81 – 3 – us Readex [324]

PUBLICATIONS / U.S. Department of Health, Education and Welfare – 1958-81 – 3 – us Readex [360]

PUBLICATIONS / U.S. Department of Labor – 1958-81 – 3 – us Readex [330]

PUBLICATIONS / U.S. Department of State – 1958-81 – 3 – us Readex [324]

PUBLICATIONS / U.S. Department of the Interior – 1958-81 – 3 – us Readex [324]

PUBLICATIONS / U.S. Federal Aviation Agency – 1958-81 – 3 – us Readex [629]

PUBLICATIONS / U.S. Federal Communications Commission – 1958-81 – 3 – us Readex [380]

PUBLICATIONS / U.S. Federal Supply Service – 1958-79 – 3 – us Readex [324]

PUBLICATIONS / U.S. Federal Trade Commission – 1958-81 – 3 – us Readex [380]

PUBLICATIONS / U.S. Fish and Wildlife Service – 1958-70 – 3 – us Readex [590]

PUBLICATIONS / U.S. Forest Service – 1958-81 – 3 – us Readex [634]

PUBLICATIONS / U.S. General Accounting Office – 1958-81 – 3 – us Readex [380]

PUBLICATIONS / U.S. Internal Revenue Service – 1958-81 – 3 – us Readex [336]

PUBLICATIONS / U.S. Interstate Commerce Commission – 1958-81 – 3 – us Readex [380]

PUBLICATIONS / U.S. Library of Congress – 1958-81 – 3 – us Readex [020]

PUBLICATIONS / U.S. Marine Corps (Navy) – 1958-81 – 3 – us Readex [355]

PUBLICATIONS / U.S. National Aeronautics and Space Administration – 1958-81 – 3 – us Readex [629]

PUBLICATIONS / U.S. National Archives and Records Service – 1958-81 – 3 – us Readex [025]

PUBLICATIONS / U.S. National Archives and Records Service – 24 rolls. M248. Printed guide – 1 – us Nat'l Archives [025]

PUBLICATIONS / U.S. National Bureau of Standards – 1958-81. Includes the Journal of Research – 3 – us Readex [380]

PUBLICATIONS / U.S. National Institutes of Health – 1959-81 – 3 – us Readex [610]

PUBLICATIONS / U.S. National Labor Relations Board – 1958-81 – 3 – us Readex [330]

PUBLICATIONS / U.S. National Library of Medicine – 1958-81 – 3 – us Readex [610]

PUBLICATIONS / U.S. National Marine Fisheries Service (NOAA) – 1971-81 – 3 – us Readex [324]

PUBLICATIONS / U.S. National Monetary Commission – 23v. 1909-11 – 9 – $445.00 – us UPA [330]

PUBLICATIONS / U.S. National Ocean Survey – 1971-81 – 3 – us Readex [550]

PUBLICATIONS / U.S. National Oceanic and Atmospheric Administration – 1971-81.Includes Weather Bureau – 3 – us Readex [324]

PUBLICATIONS / U.S. National Science Foundation – 1958-81 – 3 – us Readex [500]

PUBLICATIONS / U.S. Naval Oceanographic Office – 1963-81 – 3 – us Readex [550]

PUBLICATIONS / U.S. Navy – 1958-81 – 3 – us Readex [355]

PUBLICATIONS / U.S. Nuclear Regulatory Commission – 1976 – 3 – us Readex [324]

PUBLICATIONS / U.S. Occupational Safety and Health Administration – 1970-81 – 3 – us Readex [610]

PUBLICATIONS / U.S. Office of Education – 1958-81 – 3 – us Readex [370]

PUBLICATIONS / U.S. Office of the Federal Register – 1958-81 – 3 – us Readex [324]

PUBLICATIONS / U.S. Patent Office – 1958-81 – 3 – us Readex [340]

PUBLICATIONS / U.S. Public Health Service – 1958-81 – 3 – us Readex [610]

PUBLICATIONS / U.S. Securities and Exchange Commission – 1958-81 – 3 – us Readex [336]

PUBLICATIONS / U.S. Soil Conservation Service – 1958-81 – 3 – us Readex [630]

PUBLICATIONS / U.S. Supreme Court – 1958-81 – 3 – us Readex [340]

PUBLICATIONS / U.S. Tariff Commission – 1958-75 – 3 – us Readex [380]

PUBLICATIONS / U.S. Tax Court – 1958-81 – 3 – us Readex [340]

PUBLICATIONS / University of Tennessee.Agricultural Extension Service – No.590-750. 1970-82 – 1,5 – us Spaulding [630]

PUBLICATIONS / U.S. Treasury Department – 1958-81 – 3 – us Readex [336]

PUBLICATIONS / Walpole Society. London – v1-42. 1912-70 – 9 – $4,250.00; $6.00v – uk Dawson [420]

PUBLICATIONS; 2ND SERIES. NO. 1-99. 1893-1915. (NOS. 19 AND 35 WANTING) / Indian Rights Association – 1 – 35.00 – us L of C Photodup [970]

PUBLICATIONS...: 1790 CENSUS, PRINTED SCHEDULES / U.S. Bureau of the Census – 3 rolls.T498 – 1 – us Nat'l Archives [324]

PUBLICATIONS, 1790-1916 / U.S. Bureau of the Census – 42 rolls. T825 – 1 – us Nat'l Archives [324]

PUBLICATIONS 1907-1914 / Washington State Historical Society – Olympia, 1915. Washington reel 8. (Cox Library Collection) – 5 – us Americana [978]

PUBLICATIONS CATALOG AND INDEXES / U.S. Department of Commerce – 1790-1982. The basic volume, 1790-1950, and 27 supplements. 54mf – 9 – $90.00 – us Updata [380]

PUBLICATIONS CATALOGUE / Food and Agriculture Organization of the United Nations – (Write to the F.A.O. for this catalogue of all publications on microfiche. Subscription for all documents produced in a given year on mf by the F.A.O is available for $2,000 per year) – ca 220p – it F.A.O. [340]

PUBLICATIONS DE LA SOCIETE D'ARCHEOLOGIE : DANS LE DUCHE DE LIMBOURG – 1(1864)-49(1913) – 431mf – 9 – Dfl1,509.00 – ne Slangenburg [073]

PUBLICATIONS DE L'ECOLE FRANCAISE D'EXTREME ORIENT – Paris, Hanoi. v1-28. 1900-1936 – 265mf – 9 – ne IDC [950]

PUBLICATIONS DE L'INSTITUT SUPERIEUR OUVRIER – no. 1-26, 28-36. Paris. 1932 33-1939 – 1 – fr A.C.R.P.P. [073]

PUBLICATIONS DE L'OBSERVATOIRE CENTRAL NICOLAS – Serie 2, v1-32?.St. Petersburg: Impr. de l'Academie imperiale des Sciences. 1893-. Continued by: Trudy Glavnoi rossiiskoi astronomicheskoi observatorii v Pulkove – 1 – us U.W. Library [520]

PUBLICATIONS: DEPOSITORY / U.S. Government Printing Office – Also sold by departments, agencies, etc. 1956-81 – 3 – us Readex [324]

PUBLICATIONS FILED BY NEW MEXICO STATE AGENCIES WITH THE NEW MEXICO STATE LIBRARY / Higgins, Katherine – New Mexico State Library, 1996 – 2y – 5,9 – $0.35f – us NM Archives [978]

PUBLICATIONS INDEX / U.S. National Bureau of Standards – 1901-86 – 137mf – 9 – $240.00 – us Updata [380]

PUBLICATIONS INDEX OF THE GEOLOGICAL SURVEY / U. S. Geological Survey – 1879-1986. Title, subject, area, and author. 58 fiches – 9 – 110.00 – us Updata [550]

PUBLICATIONS LIST / Auburn University. Extension Service – 1964-69 – 1,5,6 – us Spaulding [630]

PUBLICATIONS LIST / U.S. Department of State – 1929-60 – 9 – $20.00 – us Updata [977]

PUBLICATIONS MATHEMATIQUES – v.1-3, 5-7, 9-10, 12-16, 18-19, 21-54. ISSN:0073-8301 – 1,5,9 – us UMI [073]

PUBLICATIONS, NO. 3 / Kentucky Baptist Historical Society – 1913 – 1 – 5.00 – us Baptist [240]

PUBLICATIONS: NON-DEPOSITORY / U.S. Government Printing Office – Also sold by departments, agencies, etc. 1953-81 – 3 – us Readex [324]

PUBLICATIONS OF MUSIC / Coleman, Robert H – List sent by request – 1 – 252.49 – us Baptist [240]

PUBLICATIONS OF THE ASSOCIATION OF COLLEGIATE ALUMNAE *see* AAUW JOURNAL

PUBLICATIONS OF THE CUMBERLAND AND WESTMORELAND ANTIQUARIAN AND ARCHAEOLOGICAL SOCIETY – (Missing: v10, 14, 17; Record Series v1, 3) – London. v9-18. 1893-1937; Record Series. London. v1-8. 1906-32 – 96mf – 9 – H-819/2 – ne IDC [930]

PUBLICATIONS OF THE ENGLISH RECORD SOCIETIES... *see*
- BEDFORDSHIRE HISTORICAL RECORD SOCIETY
- BRADFORD HISTORICAL AND ANTIQUARIAN SOCIETY
- BRISTOL RECORD SOCIETY
- BUCKINGHAMSHIRE RECORD SOCIETY
- CANTILUPE SOCIETY
- CHETHAM SOCIETY
- DEVON AND CORNWALL RECORD SOCIETY
- DEVON AND CORNWALL RECORD SOCIETY NEW SERIES
- HAMPSHIRE RECORD SOCIETY
- HISTORIC SOCIETY OF LANCASHIRE AND CHESHIRE
- INDEX LIBRARY
- KENT ARCHAEOLOGICAL SOCIETY
- LANCASHIRE AND CHESHIRE RECORD SOCIETY
- LINCOLN RECORD SOCIETY
- MANX SOCIETY
- MIDDLESEX COUNTY RECORD SOCIETY
- NEWCASTLE UPON TYNE RECORDS COMMITTEE
- NORFOLK RECORD SOCIETY
- OXFORDSHIRE RECORD SOCIETY
- QUARTO MEMOIRS
- SOCIETE JERSIAISE
- SOUTHAMPTON RECORD SOCIETY
- SOUTHAMPTON RECORD SOCIETY RECORD SERIES
- STAFFORDSHIRE RECORD SOCIETY
- SURTEES SOCIETY
- SUSSEX RECORD SOCIETY
- THORESBY SOCIETY
- THOROTON SOCIETY
- WILTS RECORD SOCIETY
- WORCESTERSHIRE HISTORICAL SOCIETY

PUBLICATIONS OF THE ENGLISH RECORD SOCIETIES, 1835-1972, AND THE INDEX LIBRARY – (Individual titles also listed separately) – 5136mf – 9 – £17,640 complete coll – uk Chadwyck [941]

PUBLICATIONS OF THE ENGLISH RECORDS SOCIETIES... *see* NORTH RIDING RECORD SOCIETY

PUBLICATIONS OF THE FIELD (COLUMBIAN) MUSEUM : BOTANICAL SERIES – Chicago (Ill.). v1-11. 1895-1936 – 64mf – 9 – 8572/1 – ne IDC [580]

PUBLICATIONS OF THE HARLEIAN SOCIETY – London. v1-92. 1869-1939 – 532mf – 9 – H-773c/2 – ne IDC [941]

PUBLICATIONS OF THE LINCOLN RECORD SOCIETY – Lincoln. v1-38. 1911-41 – 267mf – 9 – H-832c/2 – ne IDC [941]

PUBLICATIONS OF THE METROPOLITAN MUSEUM OF ART ON MICROFICHE, 1870 TO THE PRESENT / Metropolitan Museum of Art – (Includes Publications of the Museum of Primitive Art on Microfiche, 1957-1975 which is also available separately) – Boston: G.K. Hall & Co., 1990 – 2045 black and white mf – 9 – $4,950.00 export $5,500.00 – 0-8161-1747-0 – uk Hall [700]

PUBLICATIONS OF THE MUSEUM OF PRIMITIVE ART ON MICROFICHE, 1957-1975 / Metropolitan Museum of Art – Boston: G.K. Hall & Co., 1990 – 113mf – 9 – $495.00 export $550.00 – 0-8161-1770-5 – uk Hall [700]

PUBLICATIONS OF THE NAVY RECORDS – (Missing: v34. 1908/1909) – London. v1-80. 1894-1940 – 649mf – 9 – H-777c/2 – ne IDC [355]

PUBLICATIONS OF THE ORGANISATION FOR SCIENTIVIC RESEARCH IN INDONESIA – Djakarta, 1949(1-41) – 13mf – 9 – SE-499/1 – ne IDC [500]

PUBLICATIONS OF THE PIPE ROLE SOCIETY – London. v1-57. 1883-1941 – 335mf – 9 – H-779c/2 – ne IDC [941]

PUBLICATIONS OF THE SELDEN SOCIETY – (Missing: v37(p182-200). 1920) – Publications. London. v1-57. 1888-1938 – 744mf – 9 – H-781c/2 – ne IDC [941]

PUBLICATIONS OF THE SOCIETY OF LIBERIAN AUTHORS / Society of Liberian Authors – 1973 – 1r – 1 – $49.50 – us African Imprint [390]

PUBLICATIONS OF THE SOMERSET RECORD SOCIETY – London. v1-56. 1887-1941; Extra Series. v1. 1931 – 421mf – 9 – H-840c/2 – ne IDC [910]

PUBLICATIONS OF THE SUSSEX RECORD SOCIETY – Lewes. v1-25. 1902-17 – 143mf – 9 – H-843/2 – ne IDC [910]

PUBLICATIONS OF THE THORESBY SOCIETY – Leeds. v1-39. 1891-1940 – 292mf – 9 – H-851c/2 – ne IDC [941]

PUBLICATIONS OF THE UNITED STATES DEPARTMENT OF JUSTICE / U.S. Department of Justice – 1958-81 – 3 – us Readex [324]

PUBLICATIONS OF THE U.S. COURT OF CUSTOMS AND PATENT APPEALS / U.S. Court of Customs and Patent Appeals – 1958-81. 1973, 1978 not available – 3 – us Readex [340]

PUBLICATIONS OF THE VENICE BIENNALE 1895-1977 *see*
- ART, ARCHITECTURE AND PHOTOGRAPHY WITH ART PERIODICALS 1895-1972 (PVB 1895-1977, PT 1)
- FILM, TELEVISION AND MASS COMMUNICATION 1949-1977 (PVB 1895-1977, PT 2)
- GENERAL PUBLICATIONS OF THE VENICE BIENNALE WITH LA BIENNALE DI VENEZIA (PVB 1895-1977, PT 5)
- MUSIC 1930-1972 (PVB 1895-1977, PT 4)
- THEATRE 1948-1972 (PVB 1895-1977, PT 3)

PUBLICATIONS OF THE VENICE BIENNALE, 1895-1977 (PVB) / Venice. Biennale D'Arte – (With printed bibliography & subject index. Pts also listed separately) – (mf ed 1982) – 1105mf – 9 – £3,960.00 coll – Archivio Storico delle Arti Contemporanee – uk Chadwyck [700]

PUBLICATIONS ON BOTANY – 98mf – 9 – ne IDC [580]

PUBLICATIONS ON INDIANS – US Govt Printing Office, 1927-70 – 168mf – 9 – $5.00f – us Ross [975]

PUBLICATIONS (P.M.L.A.) / Modern Language Association of America – v. 1-80. 1884-1965 – 1 – us Princeton Micro [420]

PUBLICATIONS PROSCRIBED BY THE GOVERNMENT OF INDIA – 1600 titles banned by British government in India – 1 – us Primary [950]

PUBLICATIONS SLIM / U.S. National Institute of Justice NCJRS – (1979-82 suppl. 318 documents, indexed. $193.00) – 1972-78. Full-text copies of 501 documents, indexed – 9 – $275.00 – us N.C.J.R.S. [360]

PUBLICAZIONI / Universita di Firenze. Facolta di Lettere e Filosofia – v1-40, 1875-1918, n.s. v1-14, 1920-31, s.3 v1-.1934-. ill – 1 – us U.W. Library [400]

PUBLICHNAIA BIBLIOTEKA SSSR IM. V.I. LENINA – 10 let. bibliotechnogo stroitel'tstva. M. 1917. BR-4638 2 – 8 – ne IDC [020]

LA PUBLICIDAD – Barcelona, Spain. -d. 16 Oct 1916-31 Dec 1917; 7 June 1918-9 Aug 1919. Very imperfect. 10 reels – 1 – uk British Libr Newspaper [072]

Publicidad Cos *see* GUIA DEL ESPECTADOR

Publicidad Fefa *see* FERIAS Y FIESTAS. CACERES, TRUJILLO, LOGROSAN

DER PUBLICIST : EINE ZEITSCHRIFT FUER FREIHEIT UND GESETZ, FUER OEFFENTLICHES RECHT UND GERICHTSVERFAHREN – Berlin, DE. Jan 1848-Aug 1849 – 1r – 1 – gw Mikrofilm [072]

DER PUBLICIST : EINE ZEITSCHRIFT FUER FREIHEIT UND GESETZ, FUER OEFFENTLICHES RECHT UND GERICHTSVERFAHREN – Berlin, jan 19 1848-aug 30 1849 – 1r – 1 – Inquire at Mikrofilmarchiv for details – gw Misc Inst [943]

LE PUBLICISTE – Paris. 22 mars-22 sept 1800, 23 sept 1801-21 mars 1802, 23-24 sept 1802-nov 1810 – 1 – fr A.C.R.P.P. [073]

LE PUBLICISTE PARISIEN – Journal politique, libre et impartial. Redige par M. Marat. Paris. No.1-5, 12-15 sept 1789. Devenu: l'Ami du Peuple ou Le Publiciste parisien. No.6-105, 16 sept 1789-22 janv 1790. No.106-685, 18 mai 1790-21 sept 1792. Devenu: Journal de la Republique francaise. No.1-143, 25 sept 1792-11 mars 1793. Devenu: Le Publiciste de la Republique francaise. No.144-242, 14 mars-14 juil 1793. Continuation apocryphe: no.243-271, juil-aout 1793 – 1 – fr A.C.R.P.P. [073]

PUBLICITY – Wichita. Kan. 1930-42 – 1 – us UMI [071]

O PUBLICOLA BRASILEIRO – '(s.l.')-Sao Luis, Brazil. 6 Feb 1834 – 1,5,6 – bl Biblioteca [072]

DE PUBLIJKE INTREDE VAN WILLIAM DE 3., 5 FEBRUARIJ 1691 / Bidloo, G – O-1154 1. 1691 – 9 – ne IDC [949]

PUBLIKATIONEN DER GESELLSCHAFT FUER RHEINISCHE GESCHICHTSKUNDE – (Titles also listed individually) – ne Slangenburg [943]

DAS PUBLIKUM DER MITTELHOCHDEUTSCHEN DICHTUNG / Fechter, Werner – (Includes bibliographical references and index) – Frankfurt am Main: M Diesterweg, 1935 – 1r – 1 – us U.W. Library [430]

PUBLISH – 1986- – 1,5,6,9 – us UMI [073]

PUBLISHED AND UNPUBLISHED RESEARCH MATERIAL / Amnesty International – 1962-79 – 1 – ne IDC [323]

PUBLISHED COLONIAL RECORDS OF THE AMERICAN COLONIES – 1 – us Primary [975]

PUBLISHED MANUSCRIPTS / Hastings, Robert J & Hastings, Bessie – 1948-64. 1,996p – 1 – 69.86 – us Baptist [920]

PUBLISHED SEARCHES – More than 2500 bibliographies available. Citations to technical reports and journal articles announced by more than 30 international information sources. Each bibliography includes full abstracts, title list, and subject index – 9 – $65.00 – us N.T.I.S. [600]

PUBLISHED UNEXAMINED PATENT APPLICATIONS IN NUMERICAL ORDER, 1990 / Japan. Patent Office – 1971- . Full set as published before examination during 1990 under annually arranged serial numbers, all classes. 684 reels containing over 312,000 applications – 5,6,9 – Y4,788,000.00 – ja Nippon Tech [340]

PUBLISHED UNEXAMINED UTILITY MODEL APPLICATIONS IN NUMERICAL ORDER, 1990 / Japan. Patent Office – 1971- . Full set as published before examination during 1990 under annually arranged serial numbers, all classes. 122 reels containing over 150,000 applications – 5,6,9 – Y854,000.00 – ja Nippon Tech [340]

PUBLISHED WORKS / McKinney, BB – 1 – 23.45 – us Baptist [240]

THE PUBLISHED WORKS / McKinney, BB – 1 – 23.45 – us Baptist [240]

A PUBLISHER AND HIS FRIENDS : MEMOIR AND CORRESPONDENCE OF THE LATE JOHN MURRAY, WITH AN ACCOUNT OF THE ORIGIN AND PROGRESS OF THE HOUSE, 1768-1843 / Smiles, Samuel – London: John Murray, 1891 – 2 rolls – 1 – 1-55879-961-3 – uk Libr Preservation [860]

PUBLISHERS' CIRCULAR 1837-1900 : [INCLUDING THE ENGLISH CATALOGUE OF BOOKS] / ed by Eliot, Simon & Sutherland, John – (Excluding The English Catalogue of Books 785mf £3;035. Guide £26) – 892mf – 9 – £3,375.00 – uk Chadwyck [070]

THE PUBLISHERS' INDEX – Saint John, NB: Index Pub Co, [1874-1875?] – 9 – cn C.I.H.M. [070]

PUBLISHERS' TRADE LISTS ANNUAL 1903-80 – (Includes 2 printed and 1 fiche index) – 9 – $14,750.00 – us Mecklermedia [070]

PUBLISHER'S WEEKLY – (v. 195- 1969- 5,6. v. 197- 1970- 9) – v. 1- 1872- – 1 – us UMI [070]

PUBLISHERS WEEKLY see AMERICAN LITERARY GAZETTE AND PUBLISHERS' CIRCULAR
PUBLISHING, ENTERTAINMENT, ADVERTISING AND ALLIED FIELDS LAW QUARTERLY – v11- 1972- 1; v14- 5,6,9 – us UMI [340]
PUBLISHING, THE BOOKTRADE AND THE DIFFUSION OF KNOWLEDGE SPECIALIST COLLECTION / ed by Alston, R C & Fellner, H – 2519mf – 9 – £7,900.00 – uk Chadwyck [070]
PUBLIUS – (v.9-. 1979- 5,6,9) – v.1-. 1971- – 1 – us UMI [073]
PUBLIZISTIK UND JOURNALISTIK UND IHRE ERSCHEINUNGSFORMEN BEI JOSEPH GOERRES (1798-1814) : EIN BEITRAG ZUR METHODE DER PUBLIZISTISCHEN WISSENSCHAFT / Spael, Wilhelm – Koeln, 1928 – 91p – 9 – DM48.00 – 3-89349-018-3 – gw Hänsel [070]
PUBLIZISTISCHE SAMMLUNGEN ZUM ACACIANISCHEN SCHISMA / Schwartz, E – (ABAW.PH N.F. Heft 10). Muenchen, 1934 – Dfl35.00 – ne Slangenburg [240]
Puccini, G see
- EDGAR. ACT 3, SCENE 4
- EDGAR; DRAMMA LIRICO IN TRE ATTI...
- EDGAR. LIBRETTO. DRAMMA LIRICO IN QUATTRO ATTI
- LA RONDINE

Puccioni, Nello see LE POPULAZIONI INDIGENE DELLA SOMALIA ITALIANA
Puchner, Rudolph see AGLAJA
PUCK – New York. v1-83. 1877-1918 – 17r – 1 – us Ross [073]
PUCK / Ouida – British Fiction Archive: Unit 3 – 9 – uk Bell [830]
PUCK – v. 1-83. 1877-1918 – 1 – us Princeton Micro [410]
PUCKER ZEITUNG – Puck (Putzig), Poland. 15 Sept-31 Dec 1925 (incomplete); 1926-18 Aug 1939 – 5r – 1 – gw Mikrofilm [943]
Puckree, T see DOES INTERCOSTAL STRETCH AFFECT RESPIRATORY MUSCLE ACTIVITIES
PUDJANGGA BARU – Djakarta, Pustaka Rakjat. 1933-1953. TEN 867. SE 805/1. Lacking: 1933-1940, v1-8 – 42mf – 9 – ne IDC [073]
PUDJANGGA SANUSI PANE / Nasution, Jahja Udin – SE-5403 1. 1963 – 9 – ne IDC [950]
Pudjosubroto, R Santoso see JURIESPRUDENSI INDONESIA, AGIAN PERDATA
Puebla de Argeme. Ayuntamiento see FIESTAS POPULARES EN HONOR DE LA VIRGEN DE ARGEME, PATRONA DE...
Puebla. Mexico (State) see PERIODICO OFICIAL-GOBIERNO CONSTITUCIONAL DEL ESTADO LIBRE Y SOBERANO DE PUEBLA
EL PUEBLO – Mexico. -d. 23 Oct-2 Nov 1914; 12 May 1916-7 April 1917. Imperfect. 3 reels – 1 – uk British Libr Newspaper [072]
PUEBLO – Madrid. Spain. -d. 2 Aug 1941-28 May 1945. (Imperfect). (14 reels) – 1 – uk British Libr Newspaper [072]
EL PUEBLO AL PODER / Garcia Della Costa, Fernando – Buenos Aires: Ediciones Tematica SRL, 1986 – 1 – CSUXAJA7707-B – us Hoover Inst Photo [972]
EL PUEBLO DE GALICIA, CONTRA EL FASCISMO / Alvarez, Santiago – Discurso pronunciado en el pleno ampliado del C. C. del Partido Comunista de Espana, celebrado en Valencia los dias 5, 6, 7 y 8 de marzo de 1937. Valencia, 1937. Fiche W 710. (Blodgett Collection of Spanish Civil War Pamphlets) – 9 – us H.U. College Libr [946]
EN EL PUEBLO DORMIDO / Vargas Zuniga, Rodrigo – Madrid: Imp. Hispano-Africana, 1915 – 1 – sp Bibl Santa Ana [946]
UN PUEBLO EN MARCHA : BASES E IDEARIO DEL MOVIMIENTO OBRERO DE LA REVOLUCION / Defilippo, Rodolfo Antonio – Buenos Aires: Franceschi y Vassallo, 1946 – 1 – CSUXAHZ1944-B – us Hoover Inst Photo [320]
EL PUEBLO ESPANOL EN ARMAS / Minelli, Pablo M – Madrid, 1937. Fiche W 1051. (Blodgett Collection of Spanish Civil War Pamphlets) – 9 – us H.U. College Libr [946]
LOS PUEBLOS DE ESPANA. ENSAYO DE ETNOLOGIA / Caro Baroja, Julio – Barcelona. 1946 – 1 – us Res Libr [306]
LOS PUEBLOS TRAS SU HISTORIA. BIENVENIDA / Carrasco Lianes, Virgilio – Badajoz: Dip. Prov., 1974 – sp Bibl Santa Ana [946]
PUEBLSKE NOVICE – Pueblo, CO, 1916 – 1mf or 1 reel – 9,1 – us I.H.R.C. [975]
Puech, H- see LE TRAITE CONTRE LES BOGOMILES
PUEHAJOGI. ESTLIANDSKIIA POEZY / Severianin, I – Jur'ev, 1919 – 1mf – 9 – ne IDC [460]
PUEHAJOGI. ESTLIANDSKIIA POEZY / Severianin, I – Jur'ev. 1919. BR-1037 2 – 8 – ne IDC [460]
Puel, T see CATALOGUE DE L'HERBIER DE SYRIE
Pueltz, Wilhelm see DIE HOLK'SCHEN JAEGER
Puenjer, G C Bernhard see FRIEDRICH SCHLEIERMACHER'S REDEN UEBER DIE RELIGION
Puenjer, Georg Christian Bernhard see
- DE MICHAELIS SERVETI DOCTRINA
- GRUNDRISS DER RELIGIONSPHILOSOPHIE

EL PUENTE DE ALCANTARA / Corraliza, Jose V – Badajoz: Dip. Provincial, 1974 – 1 – sp Bibl Santa Ana [946]
EL PUENTE DE ALCANTARA / Melida, Jose Ramon – Madrid, 1924 – 1 – sp Bibl Santa Ana [946]
EL PUENTE DE ALCANTARA / Sanchez Loro, Domingo – Caceres: Garcia Floriano, 1947 – 1 – sp Bibl Santa Ana [946]
Puente, Francisco de la see TRATADO... LINAJE DE LA VERA
LA PUENTE JOURNAL – La Puente, CA. 1976 – 33+ r – 1 – $1,650.00 ($135.00y) – R03271 – us Library Micro [071]
LA PUENTE VALLEY HERALD – La Puente, CA. 1961-1962 – 1r – 1 – $50.00 – H04019 – us Library Micro [071]
LA PUENTE VALLEY JOURNAL – La Puente, CA. 1975 – 2r – 1 – $100.00 – H04020 – us Library Micro [073]
PUERILES CONFABULATIUNCULAE, OR CHILDRENS TALKE / Webbe, Joseph – 1627. 189p. (English Linguistics Series 1500-1800) – 9 – us UMI [450]
Puerto Reyna, Juan Antonio see
- ALANGE
- ALANGE. NOTICIAS HISTORICAS ACERCA DE ESTA VILLA Y DE SUS FAMOSOS BANOS

PUERTO RICO : LAWS OF PUERTO RICO ANNOTATED – Superseded vols. Includes latest Pocket Parts supplement – 9 – Inquire – us Hein [340]
PUERTO RICO : SESSION LAWS OF AMERICAN STATES AND TERRITORIES – 1900-1989 – 9 – $1,168.50 set – us Hein [340]
PUERTO RICO = STATISTICAL YEARBOOK 1848/49-1970 : ANUARIO ESTADISTICO 1848/49-1970 / Puerto Rico. Bureau of Economics and Statistics – (Coll title: Latin American and Caribbean Official Statistical Serials, 1821-1982) – 65mf – 9 – £480.00 – uk Chadwyck [972]
Puerto Rico see
- ECONOMIC DEVELOPMENT OF PUERTO RICO, 1940-1950, 1951-1960
- REPORTS AND OPINIONS (A-G)
- REPORTS, PRE-NRS

PUERTO RICO ATTORNEY GENERAL REPORTS AND OPINIONS – (6 1901-1991 $175.00. 9 1901-1958 $325.00) – v30-62. 1901-1991 – 6,9 – $500.00set – us Hein [340]
Puerto Rico. Bureau of Economics and Statistics see PUERTO RICO
PUERTO RICO FEDERAL RELATIONS ACT : HEARING BEFORE THE SENATE COMMITTEE ON INTERNATIONAL AND INSULAR AFFAIRS / U.S. Congress – 94th Cong. 2nd sess. apr 12 1976. Washington: GPO, 1976 (mf ed) – 2mf – 9 – $3.00 – LLMC 82-100B Title 34 – us L.L.M.C. [327]
PUERTO RICO JOURNAL OF PUBLIC HEALTH AND TROPICAL MEDICINE – v. 6-25. 1930-1950 – 1,5,6 – us Princeton Micro [610]
Puerto Rico. Junta de Planificacion see
- THE FOUR YEAR ECONOMIC AND SOCIAL DEVELOPMENT PLAN OF PUERTO RICO, 1969-1972
- PROGRAMA ECONOMICO DE CUATRO ANOS, 1967 A 1970
- PROGRAMA ECONOMICO DE CUATRO ANOS ANOS FISCALES 1966 A 1969
- PROGRAMA ECONOMICO DE CUATRO ANOS ANOS FISCALES 1969 A 1972

Puerto Rico. Junta de Planificacion, Urbanizacion y Zonificacion see FIFTH SIX-YEAR FINANCIAL PROGRAM, 1948-49 TO 1953-54
Puerto Rico. Planning Board see PROGRAMA ECONOMICO DE 4 ANOS, ANOS FISCALES 1964-1967
Puerto Rico. Planning, Urbanizing and Zoning Board see DEVELOPMENT PLAN FOR PUERTO RICO, TECHNICAL PAPER NO. 1
Puerto Rico. Secretaria del Gobierno Superior Civil see REGISTRO CENTRAL DE ESCLAVOS
Puerto Rico. Spanish Governors see
- EXPEDIENTE SOBRE LA REBELION DE LARES, 1868-69 (CASE FILE ON THE REBELLION OF LARES)
- REALES ORDENES, 1792-93, Y REALES ORDENES Y DECRETOS, 1767-1854 (ROYAL ORDERS AND DECREES)
- REGISTRO CENTRAL DE ESCLAVOS, 1872 (SLAVE SCHEDULES)

PUE'S OCCURANCES – Ireland.5 reels – 1 – ie Microforms [072]
PUESKUELUE BELA – (Sahib-i Imtiyaz: Hueseyin Huesnue. Nos. 1-3, 5-7 (11 Subat 1324-25 Mart 1325[1908-1909])) – Istanbul: A. Servicen Matbaasi, 1908-1909 – 1mf – 9 – $12.00 – us MEDOC [949]
Puetzfeld, Carl see HEINRICH HEINES RELIGIOESE ENTWICKLUNG BIS ZUM ABSCHLUSS SEINER UNIVERSITAETSJAHRE
Puffendorf, Samuel von see LE DROIT DE LA NATURE ET DES GENS
Puga, V see PROVISIONES, CEDULAS, INSTRUCCIONES DE SU MAGESTAD PARA...GOBERNACION DESTA NUEVA ESPANA
PUGACHEV I EGO SOOBSHCHNIKI / Dubrovin, N F – 3v. Spb. 1884. BR-6022 2 – 8 – ne IDC [947]
PUGACHEVSHCHINA – Moscow, Leningrad, 1926-31. v1-3. maps. BR-7792/2 – 8 – ne IDC [947]
PUGACHEVSKII BUNT V ZAURAL'E I SIBIRI / Dmitriev-Mamanov, A I – Spb. 1907. BR-6016 – 8 – ne IDC [947]
PUGACHOV / Esenin, Sergei – Berlin. 1922. BR-1057 2 – 8 – ne IDC [460]
Puget, H et al see LA MODERNISATION DES INSTRUMENTS DE TRAVAIL ET DES METHODES DANS LES ADMINISTRATIONS PUBLIQUES
PUGET SOUND ARGUS – Port Townsend. Wash. 1870-1889 – 1 – us UMI [071]
PUGET SOUND COURIER – Steilacoom. Wash. -w. 1855-56 – 1 – us UMI [071]
PUGET SOUND DISPATCH – Seattle. Wash. -w. 1871-80 – 1 – us UMI [071]
PUGET SOUND EXPRESS – Steilacoom. Wash. -w. 1872-80 – 1 – us UMI [071]
PUGET SOUND GAZETTE – Seattle. Wash. -w, sw. 1863-67 – 1 – us UMI [071]
PUGET SOUND HERALD – Steilacoom. WAsh. -w. 1858-64 – 1 – us UMI [071]
PUGET SOUND POSTEN – Tacoma, Washington. 1907-35 – 15r – 1 – sw Kungliga [071]
PUGET SOUND WEEKLY COURIER – Olympia. Wash. 1872-1884 – 1 – us UMI [071]
Pugh, Edward Fox see FORMS OF PROCEDURE IN THE COURTS OF ADMIRALTY OF THE UNITED STATES OF AMERICA
Pugh, Edwin William see CHARLES DICKENS, THE APOSTLE OF THE PEOPLE
PUGH FLAT BAPTIST CHURCH. DOVER, TENNESSEE : CHURCH RECORDS – 1905-65. Roll of membership. 1925-52 – 1 – 7.83 – us Baptist [240]
PUGH'S HEREFORD JOURNAL – Hereford, Great Britain. 1770-1774; 1783-1786. etc – 1 – uk Microform Academic [072]
PUGH'S HEREFORD JOURNAL see HEREFORD JOURNAL
PUGILLUS PLANTARUM INDIAE ORIENTALIS / Walker-Arnott, G A – (Nova Acta Leopoldini-Carolinae Naturae Curiosorum, v. 18, pt. 1, 1836). B-5828 2 – 8 – ne IDC [580]
PUGILLUS PLANTARUM NOVARUM AFRICAE BOREALIS HISPANIAEQUE AUSTRALIS / Boissier, E P & Reuter, G F – Geneve. 1852. B-5854 2 – 8 – ne IDC [580]
PUGILLUS PLANTARUM NOVARUM PRAESERTIUM GALLICARUM / Jordan, A. – Paris. 1852. B-753 2 – 8 – ne IDC [580]
PUGILLUS PLANTARUM NOVARUM SYRIAE ET TAURI OCCIDENTALIS / Fenzl, E – Viennae. 1842. B-657 2 – 8 – ne IDC [580]
Pugin, A WN see ARCHITECTURAL AND DESIGN HISTORY
Pugliese, Ari see THE EFFECTS OF 90 DAYS OF KM SUPPLEMENTATION ON AEROBIC CAPACITY AND GENERAL WELL-BEING OF HEALTHY ADULTS
Puig, Francois see ETUDE SUR LES COUTUMES DES CABRAIS (TOGO)
Puig, S see COMPENDIO INSTRUCTIVO SOBRE EL MEJOR METODO DE CURAR LAS TERCIANAS Y QUARTANAS...
Pujol Puiguehi, Ana see LAPIDA FUNERARIA DE MONROY (CACERES) CON S. SOLAR
Pujol, Thomas J see THE EFFECTS OF EXERCISE ON LOW-DENSITY-LIPOROTEIN-RECEPTOR MEDIATED CLEARANCE AND ATHEROSCLEROTIC LESIONS IN DIETARY INDUCED HYPERLIPIDEMIC NZW RABBITS
Pujolas, J see THE KEY OF THE FRENCH TONGUE
Pujoulx see LES MODERNES ENRICHIS
Pukhov, G E see ENGINEERING SIMULATION
PUL MECMUASI – Istanbul: Alem Matbaasi. Sahib-i Imtiyaz ve Mueduer-i Mes'ul: Mehmed Ekrem, 1897-1899. Nos. 1-28 (Agustos 1313-Mart 1315 [1897-1899]) – 5mf – 9 – $75.00 – us MEDOC [949]
Pulido y Espinosa, Jose see PRELIMINARES DEL DERECHO PUBLICO ECLESTIASTICO
PULITZER PRIZES IN JOURNALISM, 1917-1985 – 56r – 1 – $3360.00 – us UMI [070]
PULKOVO.GLAVNAIA ASTRONOMICHESKAIA OBSERVATORIIA – v1-14. 1869-88.series 2,v1-.1893-. -irr.Unnumbered suppls. accompany some volumes – 1 – us U.W. Library [073]
Pullen, Henry William see MODERN CHRISTIANITY
Pullen, W J S see JOURNAL OF THE PROCEEDINGS OF THE PARTY FROM THE RIVER MACKENZIE TOWARDS CAPE BATHURST
Puller, Christopher see
- BOSANQUET AND PULLER'S NEW REPORTS
- BOSANQUET AND PULLER'S REPORTS

Pulling see SURNAMES OF THE UNITED KINGDOM
Pulling, Alexander see THE ORDER OF THE COIF
PULMONARY DIFFUSING CAPACITY AND EXERCISE-INDUCED HYPOXEMIA IN HIGHLY TRAINED ATHLETES / Lama, Iris L – University of British Columbia, 1996 – 1mf – 9 – PH 1499 – us Microform Publ [612]
PULP AND PAPER – v1- 1927- 1; v45- 5,6; v49- 9 – us UMI [670]
PULP AND PAPER see PAPER TRADE JOURNAL
PULP AND PAPER CANADA – (v88-96 1987-95 9) – Don Mills. v76-96. 1974-1995 – 5,9 – Price varies – cn Micromedia [670]
PULP AND PAPER CANADA see
- JOURNAL OF PULP AND PAPER SCIENCE
- PULP AND PAPER MAGAZINE OF CANADA

PULP AND PAPER CAPACITIES : SURVEY 1983-1988 – 1983 – 247p – it F.A.O. [338]
PULP AND PAPER CAPACITIES : SURVEY 1984-1989 – 1985 – 247p – it F.A.O. [338]
PULP AND PAPER CAPACITIES : SURVEY 1985-1990 – 1986 – 256p – it F.A.O. [338]
PULP AND PAPER CAPACITIES : SURVEY 1986-1991 – 1987 – 248p – it F.A.O. [338]
PULP AND PAPER CAPACITIES : SURVEY 1990-1995 – 1991 – 256p – it F.A.O. [680]
PULP AND PAPER CAPACITIES : SURVEY 1991-1996 – 1992 – 237p – it F.A.O. [680]
PULP AND PAPER CAPACITIES-SURVEY 1987-1992 – 1988 – 251p – it F.A.O. [670]
PULP AND PAPER INTERNATIONAL see PPI
PULP AND PAPER JOURNAL – v35- 1982- – 1,5,6,9 – us UMI [670]
PULP AND PAPER JOURNAL – (v43 1990 Can$37.00y. Cont: Mill edition of Canadian Pulp and Paper Industry at v35 1982. Cont by: Canadian Papermaker at v45 no 7 1992) – Toronto. v35-44. 1982-91 – 9 – Can$28.00y – cn Micromedia [670]
PULP AND PAPER JOURNAL see
- CANADIAN PAPERMAKER
- CANADIAN PULP AND PAPER INDUSTRY

PULP AND PAPER MAGAZINE OF CANADA – (v 1-42 1903-41, 44-45 1943-44, 47-48 1946-47 Can$100.00. v43 1942,46 1945, 49-75 1948-74 Can$50y) – Don Mills. v1-75. 1903-1973/74 – 5 – Price varies – cn Micromedia [670]
PULP AND PAPER MAGAZINE OF CANADA see PULP AND PAPER CANADA
PULPING AND PAPER-MAKING PROPERTIES OF FAST-GROWING PLANTATION WOOD SPECIES – it F.A.O. [660]
THE PULPIT AND THE PEW : LYMAN BEECHER LECTURES DELIVERED 1913, BEFORE THE DIVINITY SCHOOL OF YALE UNIVERSITY / Parkhurst, Charles H – New Haven, Conn.: Yale University Press, 1913 – 1mf – us A.T.L.A. [240]

PULPIT CRITICISM / Edwards, David – (Merged with: Medical Criticism; Merged to become: The Critic) – Toronto: [s.n., 1882?-1883] – 9 – cn C.I.H.M. [240]
PULPIT CRITICISM *see*
- THE CRITIC
- MEDICAL CRITICISM
PULPIT DIGEST – v1-15 no 160. 1936-51 (complete) – Inquire – 1 – ATLA 1994-S506 – us A.T.L.A. [073]
PULPIT ELOQUENCE OF THE NINETEENTH CENTURY / Fish, Henry Clay – 1857 – 9 – us A.T.L.A. [240]
PULPIT NOTES / Parker, Joseph – 1873 – 9 – us A.T.L.A. [240]
PULPITS LECTERNS AND ORGANS IN ENGLISH CHURCHES / Cox, John Charles – London; New York: Humphrey Milford, 1915. (Church art in England) – 1mf – us A.T.L.A. [700]
PULPSMITH – 1985- – 1,5,6,9 – us UMI [073]
PULSE – 1967-69 – 1 – us UMI [073]
PULSE – v19-. 1984- – 1,5,6,9 – us UMI [073]
PULSE OF PUBLIC CONTINUING AND ADULT EDUCATION – v23, no.6-. Sept 1982- – 1,5,6,9 – us UMI [073]
Pulsford, John *see*
- CHRIST AND HIS SEED: CENTRAL TO ALL THINGS...IN PAUL'S EPISTLE TO THE EPHESIANS
- INFOLDINGS AND UNFOLDINGS OF THE DIVINE GENIUS, IN NATURE AND MAN
- QUIET HOURS
Pulsiano, Philip *see* ANGLO-SAXON MANUSCRIPTS IN MICROFICHE FACSIMILE, VOL 4
Pulsiano, Phillip *see* ANGLO-SAXON MANUSCRIPTS IN MICROFICHE FACSIMILE, VOL 2
PULT UND TAKTSTOCK – 1-7, Apr 1924-30 – 1 – 23.00 – us L of C Photodup [780]
PULT UND TAKTSTOCK – v. 1-7. no. II. 1924-1930 – 1 – us Schnase [780]
Pultenay, William *see* CONSIDERATIONS ON THE QUESTION...WHETHER THE PROCEEDINGS OF COMMANDERS IN CHIEF OF FLEETS AND ARMIES...ARE SUBJECT TO THE REVIEW OF THE CIVIL COURTS OF LAW...
Pulteney, R *see*
- CATALOGUES OF THE BIRDS, SHELLS AND SOME OF THE MORE RARE PLANTS OF DORSETSHIRE
- A GENERAL VIEW OF THE WRITINGS OF LINNAEUS
Pulver, Max *see*
- AUFFAHRT
- IGERNES SCHULD
"THE PUMPKIN PAPERS": MICROFILM EVIDENCE USED IN UNITED STATES V. ALGER HISS, 1948-1951 – 1r – 1 – M1491 – us Nat'l Archives [340]
PUNA – Tirana, Albania. 1962-88; 4 Jul 1989-1990 – 20r – 1 – us L of C Photodup [949]
PUNCH – v1- 1841- 1; v262- 5,6; v268- 9 – us UMI [073]
PUNCH – London. England. 1841-1900 – 1 – us UMI [072]
THE PUNCH : ILLUSTRE – Montreal, Canada. 17-26 oct 1878 – 1r – 1 – Can$25.00 – cn Can Microfilming [072]
PUNCH IN CANADA – 1849-50 – 1 – 60.00 – cn McLaren [073]
PUNCH IN CANADA : CARICATURES – Montreal, Canada. 1 jan 1849-v? n6. 16 fev 1850 – 1r – 1 – Can$40.00 – cn Can Microfilming [760]
PUNCH OR THE NORTHERN LIGHT : CARICATURES – Montreal, Canada. v1 n2. 11 avr 1868 – 1r – 1 – Can$25.00 – cn Can Microfilming [072]
Punchard, G *see* A VIEW OF CONGREGATIONALISM
PUNCHINELLO – New York. v. 1-2, no. 39. April-Dec 24 1870 – 1 – us NY Public [073]
PUNCHINELLO – New York. v1-2. 1870 – 1r – 1 – us Ross [071]
Puner, Helen Walker *see* CHILDREN IN COURT
PUNGOTEAGUE BAPTIST CHURCH. ACCOMAC COUNTY. VIRGINIA : CHURCH RECORDS – 1833-1956 – 1 – 18.00 – us Baptist [240]
PUNISHMENTS FOR FEDERAL CRIMES / Partridge, Anthony et al – Washington: FJC, 1986 – 1mf – 9 – $1.50 – LLMC 95-332 – us L.L.M.C. [340]
PUNJAB / Punjab. India. Superintendent of Census Operations – Lahore. pt 4. 1911 – us Res Libr [310]
THE PUNJAB A HUNDRED YEAR AGO AS DESCRIBED BY V. JACQUEMONT (1831) & A. SOLTYKOFF (1842) / ed by Garrett, Herbert Leonard Offley – Lahore: Punjab Government Record Office, 1935 – 1 – us U.W. Library [950]
PUNJAB GOVERNMENT GAZETTE / Punjab. India – Chandigarh. 1952-1966 – 1 – us NY Public [324]
Punjab Historical Society *see* JOURNAL OF THE PUNJAB HISTORICAL SOCIETY
PUNJAB HUMAN RIGHTS ORGANISATION – Ludhiana. 37 docs. 1988-1992 – 10mf – 9 – ne IDC [320]
Punjab. India *see* PUNJAB GOVERNMENT GAZETTE
Punjab. India. Education Department *see* REPORT ON POPULAR EDUCATION IN THE PUNJAB AND ITS DEPENDENCIES
Punjab. India (State). Council of the Lieut. Governor *see* PROCEEDINGS OF THE COUNCIL OF THE LIEUTENANT-GOVERNOR OF THE PUNJAB
Punjab. India. Superintendent of Census Operations *see*
- CODE OF CENSUS PROCEDURE
- PUNJAB
PUNJAB LEGISLATIVE ASSEMBLY DEBATES – Lahore. v1-25. 1937-46 – 445mf – 9 – I-76/2 – ne IDC [950]
PUNJAB PLANTS, COMPRISING BOTANICAL AND VERNACULAR NAMES AND USES OF MOST OF THE TREES, SHRUBS AND HERBS OF ECONOMICAL VALUE / Stewart, J L – Lahore. 1869. B-7318 1 – 9 – ne IDC [580]
Punjab University. Historical Society *see* JOURNAL OF THE PUNJAB UNIVERSITY HISTORICAL SOCIETY
Punnett, R C *see* JOURNAL OF GENETICS
Punshon, William Moreley *see* THE HUGUEONOTS
Puntis, Malcolm *see* HPB SURGERY
PUNTO CRITICO – Santiago, CL. 1972-1984 – 4r – $200.00 – R04192 – us Library Micro [072]
PUNTO FINAL – Santiago, CL. 1966-1973 – 7r – $350.00 – R04193 – us Library Micro [072]
PUNTOS DE LA SENTENCIA QUE DIO EL SENOR NUNCIO DE SU SANTIDAD CONTRA LOS TRES DIPUTADOS DEL CAPITULO PRIVADO DE LA ORDEN DE SAN JERONIMO EN TRES DE ABRIL DE 1642 / Fachenetti, Cesar – S.l., s.i., s.a., 1642 – 1 – sp Bibl Santa Ana [946]
PUNTUALIZACIONES HISTORICAS SOBRE EL LINAJE DE MONROY / Munoz de San Pedro, Miguel – Badajoz: (Imp. Diput. Provincial), 1965. Sep. Revistas de Estudios Extremenos – 1 – sp Bibl Santa Ana [920]
PUNXSUTAWNEY PLAINDEALER – Punxsutawney, PA., 1868-1871 – 13 – $25.00r – us I.M.R. [071]
PUPIL STATISTICAL BULLETIN : GOVERNMENT AND GOVERNMENT - AIDED SCHOOLS, AS ON DECEMBER 1982 / Singapore. Ministry of Education – 8mf – 9 – DE-253/1 – ne IDC [370]
Puranas *see* VISHNU PURANA
PURANAS.VISHNUPURANA – A prose English trans. based on Prof. H.H. Wilson's trans. Ed. and pub. by Manmatha Nath Dutt.Calcutta: H.C. Dass, 1894. xii,464p – 1 – us U.W. Library [280]
Purcell, E R *see* PIONEER STORIES OF CUSTER COUNTY
Purcell, Henry *see*
- AMPHITRYON
- [BESS OF BEDIAM] MAD BESS
- [THE TEMPEST] COME UNTO THESE YELLOW SANDS
- [TRIO SONATAS, Z.790-810] SONATAS OF THREE PARTS, TWO VIOLINS AND BASSE, TO THE ORGAN OR HARPSICHORD
- WORKS OF HENRY PURCELL
Purchas, H T *see*
- A HISTORY OF THE ENGLISH CHURCH IN NEW ZEALAND
- JOHANNINE PROBLEMS AND MODERN NEEDS
Purchas, S *see* A DISCOURSE OF THE KINGDOM OF CHINA...
PURCHASE OF ALASKA – 1 – us Ross [977]
THE PURCHASING AGENT – New York etc.. v. 1-23. Oct 1915-Jan 1933 – 1 – us NY Public [331]
PURCHASING (CPI EDITION) – 1982-83 – 1 – us UMI [380]
PURDUE AGRICULTURAL REPORT / Purdue University. Agricultural Experiment Station and Cooperative Extension Service. School of Agriculture – No.1-9. 1971-80. 1 reel – 1,5 – us Spaulding [630]
Purdue University. Agricultural Experiment Station *see*
- ANNUAL REPORT
- BULLETIN
- CIRCULAR
- INSPECTION REPORT
- RESEARCH BULLETIN
- RESEARCH PROGRESS REPORT
- STATION BULLETIN
Purdue University. Agricultural Experiment Station and Cooperative Extension Service. School of Agriculture *see* PURDUE AGRICULTURAL REPORT
Purdue University. Cooperative Extension Service *see*
- ANNUAL REPORT
- CROPS AND LIVESTOCK REPORT
- EXTENSION BULLETIN
- EXTENSION CIRCULAR
- MIMEO AE (AGRICULTURAL ENGINEERING)
- MIMEO AH AND AS (ANIMAL HUSBANDRY AND ANIMAL SCIENCE)
- MIMEO AY (AGRONOMY)
- MIMEO BP (BOTANY AND PLANT PATHOLOGY)
- MIMEO DH (DAIRY HUSBANDRY)
- MIMEO E (ENTOMOLOGY)
- MIMEO EC (AGRICULTURAL ECONOMICS)
- MIMEO F (FORESTRY)
- MIMEO FH (4-H)
- MIMEO HE (HOME ECONOMICS)
- MIMEO HO (HORTICULTURE)
- MIMEO ID (INTERDEPARTMENTAL)
- MIMEO PIH (PORK INDUSTRY HANDBOOK)
Purdy, James Hart *see* A TREATISE ON THE LAW OF PRIVATE CORPORATIONS...ENLARGEMENT, REVISION AND RECONSTRUCTION OF BEACH ON PRIVATE CORPORATIONS
PURE AND APPLIED CHEMISTRY – v.1- 1960- – 5,6,9 – us UMI [073]
PURE AND APPLIED OPTICS : JOURNAL OF THE EUROPEAN OPTICAL SOCIETY, PART A – v1. 1992 – 1,5,6,9 – £146.00 – uk I.O.P. [530]
PURE-BRED DOGS, AMERICAN KENNEL GAZETTE *see* AKC GAZETTE
Purefoy, George W *see* A HISTORY OF THE SANDY CREEK BAPTIST ASSN., NORTH CAROLINA, FROM ITS ORGANIZATION, 1758-1858
PURI LUKISAN / Ubud, Indonesia – In Indonesian and English. SE 5682 1 – 9 – ne IDC [950]
Purificacion y Tornavacas, Pedro de *see* CAMINO DEL CIELO
Purify, John *see* A SELECTION OF HYMNS AND SPIRITUAL SONGS
Purinton, Daniel Boardman *see* CHRISTIAN THEISM
THE PURITAN AGE AND RULE IN THE COLONY OF THE MASSACHUSETTS BAY, 1629-1685 / Ellis, George E – Boston: Houghton, Mifflin, 1888 – 2mf – us A.T.L.A. [240]
PURITAN AND ANGLICAN: : STUDIES IN LITERATURE / Dowden, Edward – London: K. Paul, Trench, Truebner, 1900 – 1mf – us A.T.L.A. [240]
THE PURITAN AS A COLONIST AND REFORMER / Byington, Ezra Hoyt – Boston: Little, Brown, 1899 – 1mf – us A.T.L.A. [240]
PURITAN MANIFESTOES : A STUDY OF THE ORIGIN OF THE PURITAN REVOLT : WITH A REPRINT OF THE ADMONITION TO THE PARLIAMENT AND KINDRED DOCUMENTS, 1572 / ed by Frere, Walter H & Douglas, C E – London: S.P.C.K.; New York: E.S. Gorham, 1907. (The Church Historical Society; 72) – 1mf – us A.T.L.A. [940]
PURITAN PREACHING IN ENGLAND : A STUDY OF PAST AND PRESENT / Brown, John – New York: Charles Scribner, 1900. (The Lyman Beecher lectures on preaching at Yale University; October, 1899) – 1mf – us A.T.L.A. [240]
THE PURITAN REPUBLIC / Howe, Daniel Wait – Indianapolis, 1899. Massachusetts Reel 1. (The Cox Library Collection) – 5 – us Americana [978]
THE PURITAN REPUBLIC OF THE MASSACHUSETTS BAY IN NEW ENGLAND / Howe, Daniel Wait – Indianapolis: Bowen-Merrill, c1899 – 1mf – us A.T.L.A. [240]
THE PURITAN SCHEME OF NATIONAL GROWTH : AN ORATION / Storrs, Richard Salter – New York: John F. Trow, 1858 – 1mf – us A.T.L.A. [320]
THE PURITAN SPIRIT / Storrs, Richard Salter – Boston: Congregational Sunday-school and Pub. Society, c1890 – 1mf – us A.T.L.A. [240]
PURITANISM AND ART : AN INQUIRY INTO A POPULAR FALLACY / Crouch, Joseph – London; New York: Cassell, 1910 – 1mf – us A.T.L.A. [240]
PURITANISM IN ENGLAND / Henson, H Hensley – London, New York: Hodder and Stoughton, 1912 – 1mf – us A.T.L.A. [941]
THE PURITANS IN POWER : A STUDY IN THE HISTORY OF THE ENGLISH CHURCH FROM 1640 TO 1660 / Tatham, G B – Cambridge: University Press, 1913 – 1mf – us A.T.L.A. [941]
PURITANS IN THE BALKANS / Hall, W, Jr – The American board mission in Bulgaria, 1878-1918: a study in purpose and procedure. Sofia. 1938. BR-3823 2 – 8 – ne IDC [949]
PURNAMA – Djakarta, Aneka. Incomplete. SE-954 1. 1963-1967 – 9 – ne IDC [073]
PURPLE AND GOLD – Ashland, Ohio, 1900-1922 – 3r – 1 – $32.50r – us Archival [978]
THE PURPLE AND SCARLET WOMAN AND HER RELATIVES : A BOOK FOR THE TIMES / King, Albert Barnes – Boston: James H Earle, 1900 – 1mf – 9 – 0-8370-8754-6 – 1986-2754 – us A.T.L.A. [230]
PURPORT LISTS FOR THE DEPARTMENT OF STATE DECIMAL FILE, 1910-1944 / U.S. Department of State – 654r – 1 – M973 – us Nat'l Archives [975]
PURPOSE – London. v. 8-11. 1936-1940 – 1 – us NY Public [073]
PURPOSE : A QUARTERLY MAGAZINE – London, 1936-40 – 1r – 1 – us Ross [073]
THE PURPOSE OF THE PAPACY / Vaughan, John Stephen – London: Sands; St Louis, MO: Herder, 1910 – 1mf – 9 – 0-8370-7112-7 – 1986-1112 – us A.T.L.A. [240]
PURPOSES, PRINCIPLES AND CONTRADICTIONS OF THE OLYMPIC MOVEMENT – (Series: United States Olympic Academy, 6) – Pepperdine University, 1982 – 2mf – 9 – $8.00 – us Microform Publ [790]
Purry, Jean-Pierre *see*
- MEMOIRE SUR LE PAIS DES CAFRES ET LA TERRE DE NUYTS
- SECOND MEMOIRE SUR LE PAIS DES CAFRES ET LA TERRE DE NUYTS
Purschke, Marie Sidonie *see* HOCH OESTERREICH
Purser, W C B *see* CHRISTIAN MISSIONS IN BURMA
PURSE-SEINING WITH SMALL BOATS / Ben-Yami, M – 1987 – 97p – it F.A.O. [639]
Pursh, F T *see* FLORA AMERICAE SEPTENTRIONALIS
Purton, T *see* A BOTANICAL DESCRIPTION OF BRITISH PLANTS IN THE MIDLAND COUNTIES
O PURUS – Labrea, Amazonas. 22 Jul 1888; 1892 – 1,5,6 – bl Biblioteca [072]
Purves, George Tybout *see*
- CHRISTIANITY IN THE APOSTOLIC AGE
- THE TESTIMONY OF JUSTIN MARTYR TO EARLY CHRISTIANITY
Purvis, John Bremner *see* THROUGH UGANDA TO MOUNT ELGON
Purwono, P H *see* SEGERING KEMBANG ALUM
Purysburg Colony-Bourquin Family *see* COLLECTION
PUSAKA RIMBA HIDJAU (BU LIM TIAP) – Dituturkan by Tse Yung. SE-5123 1. 3 v – 9 – ne IDC [950]
Pusch, G G *see* POLENS PALAEONTOLOGIE
PUSCHKINIANA / Mezhov, VI – Bibliograficheskii ukazatel' statei o zhizni A. S. Pushkina, ego sochinenii i vyzvannykh imi proizvedenii literatury i iskusstva. Spb. 1886. BR-7162 2 – 8 – ne IDC [460]
Puschmann, Theodor *see* DIE MEDICIN IN WIEN WAEHREND DER LETZTEN 100 JAHRE
Pusey, E B *see* DANIEL AND THE PROPHET: NINE LECTURES DELIVERED IN THE DIVINITY SCHOOL OF THE UNIVERSITY OF OXFORD
Pusey House *see* TRACTARIAN PAMPHLETS AT PUSEY HOUSE: THE HALIFAX AND CHURCH SUB-COLLECTIONS

PUSEYISM TRACED TO ITS ROOT : IN A VIEW OF THE PAPAL AND HIERARCHICAL SYSTEM, AS COMPARED WITH THE RELIGION OF THE NEW TESTAMENT / Gurney, Joseph John – Norwich: Josiah Fletcher; London: Charles Gilpin, 1848 – 1mf – us A.T.L.A. [240]
PUSH – Truro, NS: Truro Public School, [1894] – 9 – cn C.I.H.M. [370]
Pushkin, Alexander Sergevich *see* VREMENNIK PUSHKINSKOI KOMISSI
PUSHKIN I DANTES / Kamenskii, V – Roman. Berlin. 1928. BR-944 2 – 8 – ne IDC [460]
O PUSHKINE / Khodasevich, V – Berlin. 1937. BR-698 2 – 8 – ne IDC [920]
PUSHKINIST – Istoriko-literaturnyi sbornik. Spb., 1914-1918. v. 1-3. B-1550 2 – 8 – ne IDC [460]
Pushkinskii dom *see* 50 LET PUSHKINSKOGO DOMA
Pushkinskoye Obshchestvo. Leningrad *see* POSLEDNIE GODY TVORCHESTVA PUSHKINA
Pusponegoro, Sudjono Djuned *see* ADDRESS AT NINTH PLENARY MEETING OF UNESCO 13TH GENERAL CONFERENCE
PUSTAKA DAN BUDAJA – Djakarta. Incomplete. SE-641 1. 1959-1964 – 9 – ne IDC [073]
Pustardos, C *see* CATHOLIC HYMNS
PUT' – Ezhemesiachnyi literaturnyi i obshchestvennyi zhurnal. M. 1911-14. B-1841 2 – 8 – ne IDC [073]
PUT BEDNI AKA – (Includes c.1: no.31 1921:Nov.7) – Elnia: N.A. Morozov, 19uu – 1 – CSUXALC2630-S – us Hoover Inst Photo [947]
PUT' K OKTYABRYU – Moscow. v. 1-5. 1923-1926 – 1 – us NY Public [335]
PUT K SOTSIALIZMU I RABOCHE-KRESTIANSKII SOIUZ / Bukharin, Nikolai Ivanovich – Moskva: Gos. izd-vo, 1925 – 1 – CSUX89-B4270 – us Hoover Inst Photo [947]
PUT OKTI ABRI A – (Includes c.1: 1930:May 24) – St.-Oskol: "Put Okti abri a", 1929 – 1 – CSUXALC3332-S – us Hoover Inst Photo [947]
PUT REVOLI UT SII : ORGAN ALATYRSKOGO UISPOLKOMA I UKOMA R.K.P. (BOLSH.) – (Includes c.1: 1921:Nov.6) – Alatyr: Uispolkom, 191u – 1 – CSUXALC2584-S – us Hoover Inst Photo [947]
PUT YOURSELF IN HIS PLACE / Reade, Charles L – British Fiction Archive: Unit 2 – 9 – uk Bell [830]
PUTERA SAMUDERA – Djakarta. Incomplete. SE-595 1. 1950-1959 – 9 – ne IDC [073]
Puterbaugh, Sabin D *see*
- PUTERBAUGH'S COMMON LAW PLEADING AND PRACTICE
- PUTERBAUGH'S MICHIGAN CHANCERY PLEADING AND PRACTICE

PUTERBAUGH'S COMMON LAW PLEADING AND PRACTICE / Puterbaugh, Sabin D – 5th ed. Peoria, Ill.: Franks 1880. 867p. LL-782 – 1 – us L of C Photodup [340]
PUTERBAUGH'S MICHIGAN CHANCERY PLEADING AND PRACTICE / Puterbaugh, Sabin D – 3rd ed. Chicago: Callaghan, 1898. 889p. LL-1303 – 1 – us L of C Photodup [340]
PUTESHESTVIE IZ PETERBURGA V MOSKVU / Radishchev, A N – Tom I: Fotolitograficheskoe vosproizvedenie "Puteshestviia" 1790. Tom II: Materialy k izucheniiu Puteshestviia. M., L. 1935. Lacking: v. 1. BR-7800 2 – 8 – ne IDC [760]
PUTESHESTVIIA RUSSKIKH LIUDEI ZA GRANITSU V 18 V / ed by Sivkov, K V – Spb, 1914 – 8 – BR-7869 2 – ne IDC [947]
PUTEVODITEL' / Tsentral'nyi Gosudarstvennyi Arkhiv Drevnikh Aktov – Moscow. 2 pts., 1946,1947. BR-10,706/1 – 9 – ne IDC [947]
PUTEVODITEL' / Tsentral'nyi Gosudarstvennyi Arkhiv Krasnoi Armii – Moscow, 1945. 470p. BR-10,678/1 – 9 – ne IDC [947]
PUTEVODITEL' / Tsentral'nyi Gosudarstvennyi Arkhiv Literatury i Iskusstva SSSR – Moscow, 1963. 810p. BR-10,681/1 – 9 – ne IDC [025]
PUTEVODITEL' / Tsentral'nyi Gosudarstvennyi Arkhiv Literatury i Isskusstva SSSR – Moscow, 1959. 445p. BR-10,680/1 – 9 – ne IDC [025]
PUTEVODITEL' / Tsentral'nyi Gosudarstvennyi Arkhiv Oktiabr'skoi Revoliutsii i Sotsialisticheskogo Stroitel'stva – Moscow, 1946. BR-10,676/1 – 9 – ne IDC [947]
PUTEVODITEL' / Tsentral'nyi Gosudarstvennyi Istoricheskii Arkhiv SSSR v Leningrade – Leningrad, 1956. 607p. BR-10,722/1 – 9 – ne IDC [025]
PUTEVODITEL' / Tsentral'nyi Gosudarstvennyi Literaturnyi Arkhiv SSSR – Moscow, 1951. 626p. BR-10,683/1 – 9 – ne IDC [025]
PUTEVODITEL' / Tsentral'nyi Gsudarstvennyi Arkhiv Literatury i Iskusstva S SS R – Moscow, 1968. 484p. BR-10,682/1 – 9 – ne IDC [025]
PUTEVODITEL' PO ISTORICHESKOMU ARKHIVU MUZEIA / Leningrad. Artilleriskii istoricheskii muzei; ed by Lebedianskaia, A P, et al – L. 1957. BR-10,932 1 – 9 – ne IDC [355]
PUTEVODITEL PO SOVREMENNOJ RUSSKOJ LITERATURE / Rozanov, I N – 1163. Ed. 2. 1929 – 9 – ne IDC [460]
PUTEVODITEL'PO ARKHIVU LENINGRADSKOGO OTDELENIIA INSTITUTA ISTORII – Moscow, Leningrad, 1958. 603p. BR-10,957/1 – 9 – ne IDC [947]
PUTEVODITEL'PO FONDAM / Arkhivy SSSR Leningradskoe otdelenie Tsentral'nogo istoricheskogo arkhiva – Leningrad, 1933. 280p. BR-10,816/1 – 9 – ne IDC [947]
PUTEVODITEL'PO FONDAM LICHNOGO PROISKHOZHDENIIA OTDELA PIS'MENNYKH ISTOCHNIKOV GOSUDARSTVENNOGO ISTORICHESKOGO MUZEIA – Moscow, 1967. 388p. BR-11,022/1 – 9 – ne IDC [947]
PUTEVYE ZAMETKI / Belyi, A – Izd. Gelikon. Berlin. 1922. BR-588 2 – 8 – ne IDC [460]
Puthiadam, I *see* COME, LET US CELEBRATE
PUTI I NAVYKI LITERATUROVEDCHESKOGO TRUDA / Bel'chikov, N F – Moscow, 1965. 333p. Introd. to literary studies includes survey of mss. holdings in USSR.BR-10,675/1 – 9 – ne IDC [410]
PUTI I SUD'BY / Orlov, V N – Sovetskii Pisatel'. M., L. 1963. BR-1472 2 – 8 – ne IDC [460]
PUTI INDUSTRIALIZATSII – 1928-31 – 9 – 55.00 – us L of C Photodup [338]
PUTI K PODNIATIIU UROZHAINOSTI OZIMYKH KHLEBOV / Doiarenko, A G – M., 1922 – 1mf – 9 – COR-196/1 – ne IDC [334]
PUTI RABOCHEI KOOPERATSII NA ZAPADE I U NAS / Ezhov, V – Pg., 1917 – 1mf – 9 – COR-27/1 – ne IDC [334]
PUTI REVOLI UT SII : ISTORICHESKI I ZHURNAL TATBI URO ISPARTA – Kazan: Komissii a po istorii Okti abrsko i revoli ut sii i R.K.P.(b), 1922-1923. 2v – 1 – CSUX89-S783 – us Hoover Inst Photo [947]
PUTI ROSSII / Bielotsvietov, N A – Berlin: [s.n.], 1921 (Berlin: "Presse") – 1 – CSUX89-B693 – us Hoover Inst Photo [947]
PUTI RUSSKO I REVOLIUTSII, 28 FEV. 1917 G.-28 FEV. 1919[SIC] G / Arskii, R – Niulork: Izd. Russko i sotsialistichesko i federatsii, 1918 – 1 – CSUX88-B6763 – us Hoover Inst Photo [320]
PUTI TVORCHESTVA – (Library has: 1919, no. 4) – Kharkov: Izd. pod/Otdela iskusstv Otdela narodnogo obrazovanii a Kharkovskogo Gub/Ispolkoma, 1919-1920. 2v – 1 – CSUX89-S636 – us Hoover Inst Photo [947]
PUT-IN-BAY GAZETTE – Put-in-Bay, Ohio. 1937-38 – 1r – 1 – $32.50r – us Archival [071]
Put-in-Bay. Ohio. St. Paul's Episcopal Church *see* RECORDS
Putintsev, Fedor Maksimovich *see* SETANTI I PEREVYBORY SOVETOV
PUT'K OKTIABRIU – Moscow. v1-5. 1923-26 – 1r – 1 – us Ross [947]
Putman *see* HISTORY OF THE TOWN OF WILTON
Putnam, Alfred P *see* SINGERS AND SONGS OF THE LIBERAL FAITH
THE PUTNAM BAFFIN ISLAND EXPEDITION / Putnam, G Palmer – BN 116. 2. 1928 – 8 – ne IDC [910]
PUTNAM COUNTY CITIZEN – Kalida, Ohio. 1855 – 1r – 1 – $32.50r – us Archival [071]
PUTNAM COUNTY DEMOCRAT – Winfield. West Virginia. 1876-87; 1958-1968 – 1 – us UMI [071]
Putnam County District Library (Ottawa, Ohio) *see* BOARD OF TRUSTEES MINUTES
PUTNAM COUNTY GAZETTE – Ottawa, Ohio. 1892-1949 – 14r – 1 – $32.50r – us Archival [071]
Putnam County. Ohio. Auditor *see*
- ABSTRACTS OF TAX
- ACCOUNT BOOK
- AGRICULTURAL STATISTICS
- ASSESSMENT LISTS
- INDIGENT SOLDIERS' BURIALS
- QUADRENNIAL ENUMERATIONS
- REAPPRAISEMENTS
- TRANSFER RECORDS

Putnam County. Ohio. Board of County Commissioners *see* COMMISSIONERS' JOURNALS
Putnam County. Ohio. Board of Education *see*
- ANNUAL STATISTICAL REPORTS
- CLASS REGISTERS

Putnam County. Ohio. Common Pleas. Civil Division *see*
- ANNUAL STATISTICAL REPORTS
- NATURALIZATION RECORDS
- RECORD OF ESTRAYS

Putnam County. Ohio. Common Pleas. Juvenile Div *see* MOTHERS' PENSION RECORDS
Putnam County. Ohio. Common Pleas. Probate Division *see*
- DECLARATIONS OF INDENTION
- MARRIAGE RECORDS

Putnam County. Ohio. County Home *see*
- MINUTES
- REGISTERS
- SEMI-ANNUAL REPORTS

Putnam County, Ohio. General Health District *see*
- BIRTH CERTIFICATES
- CERTIFICATES OF BIRTHS
- CERTIFICATES OF STILLBIRTHS
- DEATH CERTIFICATES
- RECORD OF BIRTHS

Putnam County. Ohio. Probate Court *see*
- BIRTH REGISTRATION RECORDS
- BONDS AND LETTERS
- CRIMINAL JOURNALS
- DEATH RECORDS
- GENERAL INDEXES
- INDEX TO DEATH RECORDS
- JOURNALS
- MISCELLANEOUS RECORDS
- NURSES RECORD
- RECORD OF MINISTERS' LICENSES
- STATEMENTS OF BIRTHS AND DEATHS
- VITAL AND SOCIAL STATISTICS
- WILL RECORDS
- WITNESS RECORD

Putnam County. Ohio. Recorder *see*
- CEMETERY PLOT MAPS (VETERANS)
- INDEX TO CEMETERY LOTS
- MILITARY DISCHARGE INDEX
- SOLDIERS' DISCHARGE RECORDS
- SOLDIER'S GRAVE RECORD
- SOLDIERS' GRAVE RECORD INDEX

Putnam County. Ohio. Soldiers Relief Commission *see*
- CASE FILES
- RELIEF ORDERS

Putnam County, Ohio. Treasurer *see* RECORDS OF OFFICIALS' BONDS
PUTNAM COUNTY SENTINEL – Ottawa, Ohio. 1885-1988 – 16r – 1 – $32.50r – us Archival [071]
PUTNAM COUNTY VIDETTE – Columbus Grove, Ohio. 1875- – 27r – 1 – $32.50r – us Archival [071]
Putnam, Edward *see* AN EXPOSITION OF THE APOCALYPSE OF ST. JOHN THE APOSTLE
Putnam, G Palmer *see* THE PUTNAM BAFFIN ISLAND EXPEDITION
Putnam, George Haven *see*
- AUTHORS AND THEIR PUBLIC IN ANCIENT TIMES
- THE QUESTION OF COPYRIGHT

Putnam, Kelly *see* EFFECTS OF POSITIVE REINFORCEMENT ON INFLUENCING GRIP STRENGTH PERFORMANCE OF COLLEGE-AGED FEMALES
Putnam, Mary B *see* THE BAPTIST AND SLAVERY
PUTNAM MEMORIAL BAPTIST CHURCH. SHELBY, NORTH CAROLINA : CHURCH RECORDS – 1949-63 – 1 – 8.28 – us Baptist [240]
Putnam, Rufus *see* RUFUS PUTNAM PAPERS AND MEMOIRS
Putnam, Samuel Porter *see* FOUR HUNDRED YEARS OF FREETHOUGHT
Putney, Albert Hutchinson *see*
- POPULAR LAW LIBRARY.

Puton, A *see* CATALOGUE DES HEMIPTERES D'EUROPE ET DU BASSIN DE LA MEDITERRANEE
Putsillo, M P *see* UKAZATEL' DELAM I RUKOPISIAM, OTNOSIASHCHIMSIA DO SIBIRI I PRINADLEZHASHIKH MOSKOVSKOMU GLAVNOMU ARKHIVU MINISTERSTVA INOSTRANNYKH DEL
Putt, SN H et al *see* VETERINARY EPIDEMIOLOGY AND ECONOMICS IN AFRICA
Putte, F van de *see*
- ANNALES ABBATIAE
- CHRONIQUE DU MONASTERE D'OUDENBOURG DE L'ORDRE DE S. BENOIT

Putte, Fvan de *see* CRONICA ET CARTULARIUM MONASTERII DE DUNIS
Puttenham, George *see* THE ARTE OF ENGLISH POESIE
Putterlick, A *see* SYNOPSIS PITTOSPOREARUM
PUTTING LAWS OVER WINGS / Davis, Warren Jefferson – Whittier, Calif., Newsprint, 1926 96, 12 p. LL-654 – 1 – us L of C Photodup [340]
PUTTING THE POPULATION EXPLOSION IN PERSPECTIVE / Clark, Colin – 1fiche (29x) – 9 – 1.00f – at Libertarian Micro [320]
Puttkammer, Ernst Wilfred *see* A MANUAL OF CRIMINAL LAW AND CRIMINAL PROCEDURE FOR POLICE
Putzel, Charles *see* COMMERCIAL PRECEDENTS
PUVIS DE CHAVANNES / Reunion des Musees Nationaux. Paris – 1977 – 9 – fr Réunion [750]
PUXBAUM : DRAMATISCHES GEDICHT / Scherer, F E – Leipzig: Wilhelm Engelmann, 1836 – 1r – 1 – us U.W. Library [810]
PUYALLUP VALLEY TRIBUNE – Puyallup. Wash. -w. 1903-57 – 1 – us UMI [071]
Puydt, P E de *see* PANARCHIE, REVUE TRIMESTRIELLE
Puyol, Julio *see*
- BIBLIOGRAFIA DE R. FOULCHE-DELBOSC NEW YORK
- MONASTERIO DE GUADALUPE
- EL MONASTERIO DE GUADALUPE

Puysegur, J de Chastenet de *see* ART DE LA GUERRE PAR PRINCIPES ET PAR REGLES
Puysegur, Jacques C de *see* RECHERCHES, EXPERIENCES ET OBSERVATIONS PHYSIOLOGIQUES SUR L'HOMME DANS L'ETAT DE SOMNAMBULISME
PV : PRINTING VIEWS – (Cont by: PrintingNews, Midwest) – Skokie. v1-55. 1934-89* – 1 – D7070 – us UMI [680]
P.V. ANNENKOV I EGO DRUZ'IA / Annenkov, P V – St. Petersburg, 1892. BR-9053 2 – 8 – ne IDC [920]
PVBLICA LETITIA DELLA MIRACOLOSA VITTORIA OTTENVTA DALLA ARMATE CHRISTIANE CONTRA QUELLA DEL TURCO, ... – Venetia, [1571] – 1mf – 9 – H-8184/1 – ne IDC [956]
PWLLHELI CHRONICLE – Wales. -w. Dec 1889-Sept 1893. (imperfect). 1 1 2 reels – 1 – uk British Libr Newspaper [072]
PYIDWATHA, THE NEW BURMA: REPORT ON LONG-TERM PROGRAMME FOR ECONOMIC AND SOCIAL DEVELOPMENT 1952-1960? / Burma. Economic and Social Board – D1258 1 – 9 – ne IDC [338]
PYKE'S LOWER CANADA REPORTS : KING'S BENCH / Canada. Quebec – 1v. 1809-10 (all publ) – 1mf – 9 – $1.50 – LLMC 81-081 – us L.L.M.C. [340]
Pyle, Howard *see* THE BUCCANEERS AND MAROONERS OF AMERICA
Pyliaev, M I *see*
- STARAIA MOSKVA
- STAROE ZHIT'E
- STARYI PETERBURG. RAZSKAZY IZ BYLOI ZHIZNI STOLITSY

PYLON – Concordance to the novel – 8mf – 9 – us UMI [420]
PYMBLE NEWS – Febr 21 1901-May 14 1903 – 1 – at Pascoe [072]
Pypin, A N *see* SOCHINENIIA IMPERATRITSY EKATERINY 2. NA OSNOVANII PODLINNYKH RUKOPISEI
Pypin, AN *see*
- ISTORIIA RUSSKOI ETNOGRAFII
- OCHERK LITERATURNOI ISTORII STARINNYKH POVESTEI I SKAZOK RUSSKIKH
- PANSLAVIZM V PROSHLOM I NASTOIASHCHEM, 1878
- RUSSKOE MASONSTVO. (28 I PERVAIA CHETVERT' 19 V.)

THE PYRAMIDS AND TEMPLES OF GIZEH / Petrie, William Matthew Flinders – New and rev. ed.London: Field, (1885).12p,95p. pl – 1 – us U.W. Library [930]

A PYRAUSTA – Penedo, Alagoas. 15 Ago 1888 – 1,5,6 – bl Biblioteca [072]
O PYRAUSTA – Maceio, Alagoas. 7 Fev-30 Maio 1917 – 1,5,6 – bl Biblioteca [072]
PYRENOCARPAE CUBENSES / Mueller, J A – (Engler, Bot. Jahrbuch, 1885, v. 4., p. 374-421). B-623 2 – 8 – ne IDC [580]
PYRENOCARPEAE FEEANAE / Mueller, J A – Geneа6ve, 1888, 45 pp. (Mea1m. Soc. Phys. Hist. Nat. Gen., Gen. v. 30). B-626 2 – 8 – ne IDC [580]
O PYRILAMPO : PERIODICO LITTERARIO, JOCO-SERIO E NOTICIOSO – Maceio, Alagoas. 26 Jan, 4 Maio 1873 – 1,5,6 – bl Biblioteca [072]
PYRILAMPO : LITTERARIO, NOTICIOSO E CRITICO – Cuiaba, 1 Jan, 16 Mar 1882 – 1,5,6 – bl Biblioteca [072]
Pyrker, Johann Ladislav *see* LIEDER DER SEHNSUCHT NACH DEN ALPEN
PYROMETRIE ODER VOM MAASSE DE FEUERS UND DER WARME BERLIN / Lamberts, J H – 1779 – 7 – uk Microform Academic [530]
PYROTECHNY ASSERTED AND ILLUSTRATED, TO BE THE SUREST AND SAFEST MEANS FOR ARTS TRIUMPH OVER NATURES INFIRMITIES / Starkey, George – London, 1658 – 1 – us U.W. Library [610]
PYTHAGORAS : ORGAM DA L.T. – Curitiba, Jan-Dec 1920 – 1,5,6 – bl Biblioteca [072]
Q. AURELII SYMMACHI QUAE SUPERSUNT (MGH 1: 6.BD. 1.TEIL) / ed by Seeck, O – Dfl53.00 – ne Slangenburg [240]
Q. BIBLIA SACRA (REGIA). TOMO 1 / Arias Montano, Benito – 1569 – 9 – 1.50f – sp Bibl Santa Ana [240]
Q. HORATII FLACCI EMBLEMATA / Veen, O van – O 783. 1607 – 9 – ne IDC [740]
Q. HORATII FLACCI EMBLEMATA / Veen, O van – O 784. 1612 – 9 – ne IDC [740]
QANUN – Numrah 1-41 (Rajab 1307-? [Feb 1890-1993?]) – 1 reel – 1 – $50.00 – us MEDOC [950]
Qanungo, Kalika-Ranjan *see* DARA SHUKOH
Qatar *see* AL-JARIDAH AL-RASMIYAH
Qatar. Ministry of Education *see* DEVELOPMENT OF EDUCATION IN QATAR (1982/83-1983/84)
Qatar. National Bank *see* ANNUAL REPORT AND REPORT OF THE DIRECTORS
Qatar. National Commission for Education, Culture and Science *see* THE EDUCATIONAL POLICY OF QATAR
QAUMI AWAZ – Lucknow, India. 1946-Mar 1986; Jun/Jul 1986 – 106r – 1 – us L of C Photodup [072]
QAWANIN DAWLAT ISRA'IL / Israel – (1972-. approx.20.00y; 1) – 1970-71 – 1 – 23.00 – us L of C Photodup [324]
QBS HANDY GUIDE TO HALIFAX AND ENVIRONS: WITH MAPS AND ILLUSTRATIONS / Frye, E M – Halifax, N.S.: Frye & Kellaher, 1899. 03266. (Pre-1900 Canadiana) – 9 – cn C.I.H.M. [971]
QIAN FENG – Magazine of the Communist Party of China. Jul 1923-Feb 1924. 6 ill. DL49f – 9 – 30.00 – cc Globe [073]
QIANFANG RIBAO = FRONT DAILY – Jian ed. Jiangxi, China. May-Oct, Dec 1939; 1940-Nov 1944. 6 reels. M-B24 – 1 – $300.00 – cc Microforms [072]
QIANFENG = THE VANGUARD – Jul 1923-Feb 1927. 4 fiches. F-C70 – 9 – $22.00 – cc Microforms [073]
QIANXIAN RIBAO = FRONTLINE DAILY – Shanghai, China.Dec 1945-Sept 1946; 1947-48. 5 reels.M-B26 – 1 – $325.00 – cc Microforms [072]
QIANXIAN RIBAO = FRONTLINE DAILY – Shangrao ed. Jiangxi, China. May 1939-1944; Jan, Apr-Oct 1945.12 reels.M/B25 – 1 – $600.00 – cc Microforms [072]
QICHE GONGCHENG – Automobile Engineering. In Chinese but English abstracts to the main articles. F p97 – 9 – 4.00 – cc Microforms [073]
QING ZHONGQI WUSHENG BAILIANJIAO QIYI ZILIAO, 1-5 – Source materials on the uprising of the White Lotus Society in five provinces during the mid-Qing Dynasty.Comp. by the Institute of History, Chinese Academy of Social Sciences. I reel. M-H77 – 5 – $40.00 – cc Microforms [950]
QINGBAO KEXUE = INFORMATION SCIENCE – 1982-. F-P240 – 9 – $4.50f – cc Microforms [500]
QINGCHU NONGMIN QIYI ZILIAO JILU – Collection of materials on peasant uprisings at the beginning of the Qing Dynasty. Comp. by Xie Guozhen. 5 fiches. F-H75 – 9 – 4.00f – cc Microforms [950]
QINGDAI DANGAN SHILIAO CONGBIAN, DIERJI – (v1 3f $12.00 F/H1; v2 2f F/H2 $8.00; v3 4f F/H3 $16.00; v4 4f F/H4 $16.00; v5 4f F/H5 $16.00; v6 4f F/H6 $16.00; v7 5f F/H7 $20.00; v8 6f F/H8 $24.00) – Archival materials of the Qing Dynasty – 9 – cc Microforms [950]
QINGDAI DIZHEN DANGAN ZILIAO – Archival materials on earthquakes of the Qing Dynasty. Comp. by the First Chinese Archive of History. 5 fiches. F-H198 – 9 – $13.50 – cc Microforms [550]
QINGDAI HAIHE LUANHE HONGLAO DANGAN SHILIAO – Archival materials on floods and waterloggings along the Haihe and Luanhe rivers during the Qing Dynasty.Comp. by the Scientific Research Institute of Water Conservancy. 7 fiches. F-H199 – 9 – $52.50 – cc Microforms [550]
QINGDAI ZHIGUAN NIANBIAO – Chronological tables of high officials of the Qing Dynasty. Comp. by Qian Shifu. 2 reels. M-J26 – 5 – $80.00r; $175.50f – cc Microforms [520]
QINGDAO RIBAO = QUINGDAO DAILY – China. 1983-. M-D44 – 1 reel/y – 1 – $55.00r – cc Microforms [072]
QINGDAO SHIBAO = QUINGDAO TIMES – China. May 1932-Jun 1948. M/B9 – 30r – 1 – $1.350.00 – cc Microforms [072]
QINGHAI RIBAO – China. Qinghai Daily. 1984-. M-D91 – 1 – $55.00r – cc Microforms [072]
QINGHUA DAXUE XUEBAO – Journal of Qinghua University. In Chinese but English abstracts to the main articles. F p171 – 9 – $4.50f – cc Microforms [073]
QINGMO CHOUBEI LIXIAN DANGAN SHILIAO – Archival materials relating to the preparation of constitutionalism at the end of the Qing Dynasty. Comp. by the First Chinese Archive of History. 1 reel. M-H191 – 5 – $35.00 – cc Microforms [950]
QINGSHI ZILIAO DIYICE – (v2. 3 fiches. F-H10) – Historical materials of the Qing Dynasty. v1. Comp. by the Institute of History, Chinese Academy of Social Sciences. 3 fiches. F-H9 – 9 – $13.50 – cc Microforms [950]
QINGYI BAO = JOURNAL OF POPULAR OPINION – Oct 1898-Dec 1901. 4 reels. M-C27 – 1 – $180.00 – cc Microforms [073]
QISHILIU NIAN SHIXUE SHUMU – Historical works of 76 years. Comp. by the reference room of the Institute of History, Chinese Academy of Social Sciences. 6 fiches. F-J7 – 9 – $22.50 – cc Microforms [950]
QISSEH I KAMRUP VA KALA (ADVENTURES DE KAMRUP) / Tahsin-Al-Din – 1834-35 – 1 – uk Microform Academic [470]
QIU SHI XUEKAN – Seeking Truth-Journal of Heilongjiang University. In Chinese but Table of Contents in English in each issue. F p217 – 9 – $4.50f – cc Microforms [073]
QIXIANG XUEBAO – Acta Meteorologica Sinica. In Chinese but English abstracts to the main articles. F p33 – 9 – 4.00f – cc Microforms [073]
QIXIN YANGHUI GONGSI SHILIAO – Historicial materials on Qixin Cement Company Ltd. Comp. by the Institute of Economics, Nankai University. 5 fiches. F-H177 – 9 – 4.00f – cc Microforms [950]
QIYAM-I IRAN – (Shawra-yi Nivisandigan. Shumarah-'i 14-280. Missing issues: Shumarah-'i 15-24, 26, 28-46, 55, 61-62, 65-66, 72-73, 77, 84, 89-91, 94-103, 106, 158-265) – Paris – 1 reel – 1 – $50.00 – us MEDOC [950]
QIZIL UZBEKISTON : UZBEKISTON KOMMUNIST (BOLSHEVIK) LAR PARTII ASI MARKAZI I KOMITETI, TOSHKENT OBLAST, SHAKHAR KOMITETLARI VA UZBEKISTON SSR OLI I SOVETINING ORGANI – (Includes c.1: 1947:Apr.18, 1949:July 23) – [Toshkent]: "Pravda Vostoka", 1918 – 1 – CSUXAKE9838-S – us Hoover Inst Photo [947]
QOVEZ HA-TAGGNOT / Israel. Ministry of Justice – (State records-ordinance). 1949-76. BJ-81-31 1 – 9 – ne IDC [320]
QST – (v. 55- 1971- 5,6. v. 54- 1970- 9) – v. 1- 1915- – 1 – us UMI [610]
QST MAGAZINE – 1915- – over 1600mf – 9 – $490.00 – us Buckmaster [621]
QUABBIN PARK 1741-1984 – (Mf 1: Ab-Al. Mf 2: Al-Ay. Mf 3: Bab-Bar. Mf 4Bar-Bl. Mf 5: Bl-Bra. Mf 6: Bre-Bu. Mf 7: Bu-Ch. Mf 8: Ch-Coi. Mf 9Coi-Coo. Mf 10: Coo-Cu. Mf 11: Cu-Do. Mf 12: Do-Dy. Mf 13: Dy-Fel. Mf 14: Fel-For. Mf 15: For-Gar. Mf 16: Gar-Gle. Mf 17: Gle-Gri. Mf 18: Gri-Ham. Mf 19: Ham-Has. Mf 20: Has-Ho. Mf 21: Ho-Hu. Mf 22: Hu-Joh. Mf 23: Joh-Jon. Mf 24: Jon-Ki. Mf 25: Ki-Le. Mf 26: Le-Li. Mf 27: Li-Me. Mf 28: Me-Mo. Mf 29: Mc,Mo-Ne. Mf 30: Ne-Pa. Mf 31: Pa-Pi. Mf 32: Pi-Po. Mf 33: Po-Ra. Mf 34: Ra-Ri. Mf 35: Ri-Ry. Mf 36: Ry-Sha. Mf 37: Sha-Slo. Mf 38: Slo-Sob; Mf 39: Sod-Sti. Mf 40: Sti-Str. Mf 41: Str-Th. Mf 42: Th-To. Mf 43: To-Tr. Mf 44: Tu-Wa. Mf 45: Wa-We. Mf 46: We-Wh. Mf 47: Wh-Wo. Mf 48: Wo-Y,Z. Mf 48-58: Unknowns: Greenwich, Enfield, Prescott, Dana, Petersham, New Salem, Belchertown. Mf 60-63,77-79: Dana cemeteries. Mf 64-71,78-79: Enfield cemeteries. Mf 72-73: Greenwich cemeteries. Mf 74-79: Prescott cemeteries. Mf 77: New Salem & Petersham cemeteries. Mf 77-79: Belchertown cemeteries) – (mf ed 1985) – 79mf – 9 – 0-931248-81-7 – us Holbrook [920]
QUADERNS D'ESTUDIS POLITICS, ECONOMICS I SOCIALS – v.1-24. 1945-47 – 1 – us UMI [300]
QUADRAGESIMALE... / Maillard, O – (Missing: Title page) – [Paris, 1498] – 3mf – 9 – CA-94/1 – ne IDC [240]
QUADRANT – (Details on Request) – 1956- – 9 – at Pascoe [072]
QUADRENNIAL ENUMERATIONS / Fulton County, Ohio. Common Pleas. Civil Division – 1907 – 1r – 1 – $32.50r – us Archival [978]
QUADRENNIAL ENUMERATIONS / Hancock County. Ohio. Common Pleas. Civil Division – 1887 – 1r – 1 – $32.50r – us Archival [324]
QUADRENNIAL ENUMERATIONS / Ottawa County. Ohio. Common Pleas. Civil Division – 1887-1907 – 3r – 1 – $32.50r – us Archival [324]
QUADRENNIAL ENUMERATIONS / Putnam County. Ohio. Auditor – (Some issues missing) – 1859-1907 – 5r – 1 – $32.50r – us Archival [324]
QUADRENNIAL ENUMERATIONS / Wyandot County. Ohio. Common Pleas. Civil Division – 1887-1907 – 3r – 1 – $32.50r – us Archival [324]
QUADRENNIEL ENUMERATIONS / Defiance County. Ohio. Clerk of Courts – 1907 – 1r – 1 – $32.50r – us Archival [324]
QUADRINS HISTORIQUES DE LA BIBLE [SUIVIS DE] LA VIE DE MOISE, REPRESENTEE PAR FIGURES [SUIVIE DE] LES DOUZE MOIS DE L'ANNEE, REPRESENTES PAR FIGURES / Paradin, Claude – Lyon: Jean de Tournes, [s.d.], 1560, 1565 – 1 – F139.47 – fr Armell [220]
Quadrotta, Guglielmo *see* IL PAPA, L'ITALIA E LA GUERRA
THE QUADRUPEDS OF NORTH AMERICA / Audubon, John James & Bachman, John – New York. v1-3. 1851-54 – 1r – 1 – us Ross [636]
QUAE HOC IN VOLUMINE TRUCTANTUR / Bessarion, Ioannes – Bessarionis Cardinalis niceni. in calumniatore Platonis Libri quator. Venetiis. 1503. BH-330 2 – 8 – ne IDC [180]
QUAERIS QUID SIT AMOR, QUID AMARE, CUPIDINIS ET QUID CASTRA SEQUI? CHARTAM HANC INSPICE, DOCTUS ERIS : HAEC TIBI DELICIAS HORTUMQ, OSTENDIT AMORUM: INSPICE; SCULPTORI EST INGENIOSA MANUS / Heinsius, D – Amsterdam, c1605 – 1mf – 9 – O-3180/1 – ne IDC [760]
QUAERIS QUID SIT AMOR, QUID AMARE, CUPIDINIS ET QUID CASTRA SEQUI? CHARTAM HANC INSPICE, DOCTUS ERIS : HAEC TIBI DELICIAS HORTUMQ, OSTENDIT AMORUM: INSPICE; SCULPTORI EST INGENIOSA MANUS / Heinsius, D – (Titlepage and prints colored and heightened with gold) – [Amsterdam, 1601] – 1mf – 9 – O-3179/1 – ne IDC [760]
QUAESTIO MEDICA DE MUSICES UTILITATE IN MORBIS CURANDIS.. / Virmontois, Petrus – 1787 – 9 – us Sibley [780]
QUAESTIONES CELEBERRIMAE IN GENESIM / Mersenne, Marin – Lutetiae Parisiorum, 1623 – 44mf – 8 – ne Slangenburg [220]
QUAESTIONES DE DUODECIM QUODLIBET ITALIE AU 25 SIECLE / Aquinas, Thomas – 23mf – 8 – ne Slangenburg [240]
QUAESTIONES DISPUTATAE DU B. GAUTHIER DE BRUGES / Longpre, E – 1928 – 8mf – 8 – ne Slangenburg [190]
QUAESTIONES GRAMMATICAE AD THUCYDIDEM PERTINENTES / Stahl, Johann Matthias – (Includes bibliographical references) – Lipsiae: In Aedibus B G Teubner, 1886 – 1mf – 9 – 0-8370-9184-5 – 1986-3184 – us A.T.L.A. [250]
QUAESTIONES IN LIBROS DE COELO ET MUNDO ARISTOTELIS STAGIRITAE / Joannes, de Janduno – 1501 – 1 – us U.W. Library [190]
QUAESTIONES IN PENTATEUCHUM (SIECLE 8) / Isidore de Seville, Saint – Autun – 1r – 5,6 – sp Cultura [240]
QUAESTIONES MUSICAE IN USUM SCHOLAE NORTHUSIANAE, PER IOANN. SPANG. HERDESS. COLLECTAE... / Spangenberg, Johann – [Lipsiae: M Blum], 1542 – 1 – us Sibley [780]
QUAESTIONES THEOLOGICAE, PHILOSOPHICAE ET MORALES (SIECLE 13) – Madrid – 1r – 5,6 – sp Cultura [200]
QUAESTIONES VULGATIORES IN MUSICAN, PRO MAGDEBURGENSIS SCHOLAE PUERIS DIGESTAE / Agricola, Martin – P-114. 1543 – 9 – ne IDC [780]
Quaglia, Armando *see* L'ORIGINALITA DELLA REGOLA FRANCISCANA
LE QUAI DE LA FOSSE A NANTES / Elder, Marc – Paris: Keltia, 1932 – 1 – F50.00 – fr Armell [910]
QUAINT SAYINGS AND DOINGS CONCERNING LUTHER / Morris, John G – Philadelphia: Lindsay & Blakiston, 1859, c1858 – 1mf – us A.T.L.A. [240]
Quaireau, A *see*
– REGLES TONALES EN ANYI ET EN BAOULE
– SIX VEILLEES DE CONTES EN PAYS AGNI
– LES TROIS NIVEAUX DE L'ANALYSE PHONEMATIQUE DE L'AGNI DU MORONOU: LANGUE KWA DE LA COTE D'IVOIRE
THE QUAKER AND METHODIST COMPARED IN AN ABSTRACT OF GEORGE FOX'S JOURNAL,... / Grey, Z – London, 1740 – 2mf – 9 – MP-282/1 – ne IDC [240]
QUAKER DIGEST REGISTERS OF BIRTHS, MARRIAGES AND BURIALS FOR ENGLAND AND WALES / Library of the Society of Friends, London – c.17thc.-1837. 32 reels with printed guide – £1,350.00 – uk World [920]
THE QUAKER IDEAL / Frith, Francis – London: Edward Hicks, 1894 – 1mf – 9 – 0-8370-8900-X – 1986-2900 – us A.T.L.A. [240]
THE QUAKER IN THE FORUM / Gummere, Amelia Mott – (Includes bibliographical references and index) – Philadelphia: John C Winston, c1910 – 1mf – 9 – 0-8370-8675-2 – 1986-2675 – us A.T.L.A. [240]
THE QUAKER INVASION OF MASSACHUSETTS / Hallowell, Richard P – Boston: Houghton, Mifflin, 1883 – 1mf – us A.T.L.A. [978]
QUAKER MANUSCRIPTS COLLECTION / The Society of Friends. Library – Part A. With printed index – 1 – £595.00 – uk World [240]
QUAKER MONTHLY – (Cont and filmed with: Wayfarer) – v43 no 4-v63. 1964-84 (complete) – 4r – 1 – ATLA S0374A – us A.T.L.A. [073]
QUAKER MONTHLY *see* THE WAYFARER
QUAKER NECROLOGY / Haverford College. Pennsylvania – 1961.-50,000 cards 2 reels.-ISBN: 0-8161-1343-2 – 1 – $255.00 – uk Hall [920]
QUAKER OFFICIAL CORRESPONDENCE : HOME AND ABROAD 1681-1881 / The Religious Society of Friends (Quakers) – 7r – 1 – £350.00 – 1-897955-09-X – uk Academic [240]
QUAKER PIONEERS IN RUSSIA / Benson, Jane – London: Headley, 1902 – 1mf – us A.T.L.A. [240]
QUAKER POEMS : A COLLECTION OF VERSE RELATING TO THE SOCIETY OF FRIENDS / Jenkins, Charles Francis – (Includes indexes) – Philadelphia: John C Winston, 1893 – 1mf – 9 – 0-8370-8911-5 – 1986-2911 – us A.T.L.A. [240]
QUAKER RECORDS: ABSTRACTS OF THE RECORDS OF THE SOCIETY OF FRIENDS IN INDIANA / Society of Friends – Early 1800s. 6v plus index – 9 – us A.G.L.L. [978]
QUAKER RELIGIOUS THOUGHT – (1985-. 5,6,9) – v1-. 1959- – 1 – us UMI [240]
QUAKER WOMEN'S DIARIES: 18TH-19TH – Centuries. 2nd ed. With printed index – 1 – £375.00 – uk World [240]
QUAKER WOMEN'S TRACTS – (With printed guide) – 4r – 1 – $340.00 – us UMI [305]

QUAKER WRITINGS (EARLY) – 1650-1750. With printed index – 1 – £995.00 – uk World [240]

QUAKER WRITINGS (EARLY) – Second series. With printed index – 1 – £425.00 – uk World [240]

THE QUAKERS : FROM THEIR ORIGIN TILL THE PRESENT TIME: AN INTERNATIONAL HISTORY / Cunningham, John – Edinburgh: J. Menzies, 1868 – 1mf – us A.T.L.A. [305]

THE QUAKERS : A STUDY HISTORICAL AND CRITICAL / Turner, Frederick Storrs – (Includes bibliographical references and index) – London: Swan Sonnenschein, 1889 – 1mf – 9 – 0-8370-8872-0 – 1986-2872 – us A.T.L.A. [240]

THE QUAKERS IN GREAT BRITAIN AND AMERICA : THE RELIGIOUS AND POLITICAL HISTORY OF THE SOCIETY OF FRIENDS FROM THE SEVENTEENTH TO THE TWENTIETH CENTURY / Holder, Charles Frederick – New York: Neuner, 1913 – 2mf – us A.T.L.A. [305]

THE QUAKERS IN THE AMERICAN COLONIES / Jones, Rufus M – London; New York: Macmillan, 1911 – 2mf – us A.T.L.A. [240]

Qualalou, F *see* L'ASSISTANCE ETRANGERE FACE AU DEVELOPPEMENT ECONOMIQUE DU MAROC

QUALIFIZIERUNG STUDENTISCHER TUTOREN FUER DAS "PRAKTIKUM ZUR EINFUEHRUNG IN DIE KLINISCHE MEDIZIN" (EKM) / Schwarz, Petra – 1994 – 3mf – DM98.00 – 3-89349-906-7 – gw Hänsel [610]

DIE QUALITAET VON CONJOINT ANALYSEN : EINE EMPIRISCHE ANALYSE ZUM EINFLUSS VON VARIATIONEN DES UNTERSUCHUNGSDESIGNS / Ikels, Marion – 1995 – 1mf – 9 – DM60.00 – 3-8267-2175-6 – gw Hänsel [650]

QUALITAETSMANAGEMENT IN DER UNTERNEHMUNGSBERATUNG / Zimmermann, Thomas – 1994 – 2mf – 9 – DM80.00 – 3-8267-2065-2 – gw Hänsel [650]

QUALITAETSSICHERUNG IN DER KRANKENPFLEGE : SICHERUNG DER QUALITAET DURCH OPTIMIERUNG DER ARBEITSBEDINGUNGEN / Vogler, Martin – 1995 – 2mf – 9 – DM80.00 – 3-8267-2206-X – gw Hänsel [360]

A QUALITATIVE EVALUATION OF CHILDBIRTH EDUCATION BOOKLETS / Riddell, Janet M – Dalhousie University, 1994 – 2mf – 9 – $8.00 – HE558 – us Microform Publ [360]

QUALITATIVE NOUNS IN THE PAULINE EPISTLES AND THEIR TRANSLATION IN THE REVISED VERSION / Slaten, Arthur Wakefield – Chicago: University of Chicago Press, 1918. vii,70p – 1 – us U.W. Library [450]

QUALITATIVE SOCIOLOGY – v.1-. 1978- – 1,5,6,9 – us UMI [073]

QUALITATIVE UND QUANTITATIVE UNTERSUCHUNGEN DER DYNAMIK VON MEHRKOERPERSYSTEMEN MITTELS STOERUNGSGLEICHUNGEN UND 1. INTEGRALEN / Hendel, Klaus – 1993 – 2mf – 9 – DM98.00 – 3-89349-688-2 – gw Hänsel [510]

QUALITE DE L'EAU DE CONSOMMATION AU QUEBEC / Larue, Michel – Quebec: Ministere de l'environment, direction du controle, 1983. SEM105P484 – 2mf – 9 – Can$4.50 – cn Bibl Nat [628]

QUALITY AND QUANTITY – v. 1-4. 1967-70. BH-1798 1 – 9 – ne IDC [073]

QUALITY AND QUANTITY – v1-18. 1967-84 – 1,5,6,13 – sz Elsevier [500]

QUALITY AND RELIABILITY ENGINEERING INTERNATIONAL – v1- 1985- – 1,5,6,9 – us UMI [620]

QUALITY ASSURANCE – v1- 1975 – 1,5,6,9 – us UMI [650]

QUALITY ASSURANCE IN HEALTH CARE – 1,5,69 – us UMI [613]

QUALITY BASIC EDUCATION : THE DEVELOPMENT OF COMPETENCE / Freeman, Joan – 1992 – 243p – 9 – 92-3-102788-3 – fr UNESCO [370]

QUALITY CONTROL IN FRUIT AND VEGETABLE PROCESSING – 1988 – 67p – it F.A.O. [360]

THE QUALITY OF ADVOCACY IN THE FEDERAL COURTS / Partridge, Anthony & Bermant, Gordon – Washington: FJC, 1978 – 3mf – 9 – $4.50 – LLMC 95-303 – us L.L.M.C. [340]

QUALITY OF LIFE : PROBLEMS OF ASSESSMENT AND MEASUREMENT – 1983 – 177p – 9 – 92-3-102096-X – fr UNESCO [301]

QUAN DOI NHAN DAN – Hanoi: [s.n., jul 1962-63; 1966-82; jul-dec 1986] – us Res Libr [072]

QUAN SHANGGU SANDAI QINHAN SANGUO LIUCHAO WEN PIANMING MULU JI ZUOZHE SUOYIN – Complete catalog of articles and authors index from Legendary Period through the Six Dynasties. Comp. by Zhonghua Shuju. 3 fiches. F-J19 – 9 – 4.00f – cc Microforms [950]

QUAND LA VENDEE RESISTA : LES SABOTS A LA GUERRE / Le Govec, Vincent – Paris: Tequi, 1925 – 1 – F161.30 – fr Armell [944]

Quandt, Clara *see*
– GERTRUD VON LODEN
– JOHANNES KNADES SELBSTERKENNTNIS

QUANG-DAT-BAO – Journal d'annonces de l'Indochine. Dir. Vu-Tran. no. 1-5. Hanoi. 28 janv-16 avr 1927. mq no. 3-4 – 1 – fr A.C.R.P.P. [073]

QUANGUO TUSHUGUAN SHUMU HUIBIAN – Bibliography of bibliographies of Chinese libraries. Comp. by Feng Bingwen. 2 fiches. F-J3 – 9 – 4.00 – cc Microforms [020]

QUANGUO ZHONGWEN QIKAN LIANHE MULU, 1833-1949 – Joint national bibliography of Chinese periodicals, 1833-1949. 1 reel. M-J12 – 5 – 20.00 – cc Microforms [073]

Quanrud, Audrey M *see* STAGES OF CHANGE FOR SMOKING CESSATION, ALCOHOL MODERATION, DIETARY FAT REDUCTION, AND EXERCISE ADOPTION IN A RURAL MINNESOTA COUNTY

QUANTICO SENTRY – Richwood. Va. 1935-1944 – 1 – us UMI [071]

QUANTIFICATION FACTORS DESCRIBING PHYSICAL ACTIVITY INVOLVEMENT AND THEIR RELATIONSSHIP TO CURRENT CRITERION REFERENCE STANDARDS FOR AEROBIC CAPACITY IN CHILDREN AND YOUTH / Confessore, R J – 1990 – 4mf – 9 – $16.00 – us Microform Publ [790]

Quantin, Maximilen *see* DICTIONNAIRE TOPOGRAPHIQUE DE DEPARTEMENT DE L'YONNE: COMPRENANT LES NOMS DE LIEU ANCIENS ET MODERNES

A QUANTITATIVE APPROACH TO PLANNING AGRICULTURAL RESEARCH: THE CASE OF CITRUS / Israel. Ministry of Agriculture – By Y. Sapharim and Y. Vaadia. Bet-Dagan. 1976. 84 p. (Special publication no. 76). Diagr – 9 – 2.00 – is I.T.T.I. [634]

QUANTITATIVE ELASTIZITAETSMESSUNG DER HAUT UND IHRE AUSWERTUNG / Diepenbrock, Irmgard – 1995 – 2mf – 9 – DM80.00 – 3-8267-2142-X – gw Hänsel [616]

QUANTITATIVE STRATIGRAPHY / Gradstein, F M et al – 1985 – xi/598p – 9 – 92-3-102336-5 – Co-published with D. Reidel Publishing Company, Dordrecht, Netherlands, who have worldwide exclusive sales rights of the hardback edition. Paperback edition available from Unesco – fr UNESCO [550]

QUANTITATIVE UND QUALITATIVE PROGNOSE DES ZUKUENFTIG ANFALLENDEN AUFKOMMENS AN ELEKTRONIKSCHROTT / Schrauf, Torsten – 1995 – 6mf – 9 – DM125.00 – 3-8267-2157-8 – gw Hänsel [650]

QUANTUM AND SEMICLASSICAL OPTICS : JOURNAL OF EUROPEAN OPTICAL SOCIETY, PART B – v1. 1988 – 1,5,6,9 – £169.00 – uk I.O.P. [530]

QUANTUM ELECTRONICS – 1,5,6,9 – us A.I.P. [530]

Quantz, Johann Joachim *see*
– AUSGEWAHLTE SONATEN. SONATA 1, 2, 3, 4, 5, 6, PER FLAUTO TRAVERSO CON CEMBALO O CON BASSO
– SOLOS FOR A GERMAN FLUTE, A HOBOY OR VIOLIN WITH A THOROUGH BASS FOR THE HARPSICHORD OR BASS VIOLIN
– VERSUCH EINER ANWEISUNG DIE FLOTE TRAVERSIERE ZU SPIELEN

Qu'appelle Association *see* OCCASIONAL PAPERS

QU'APPELLE PROGRESS – Qu'Appelle Station, Canada. 1885-1900 – 5r – 1 – $325.00 – cn Library Assoc [971]

QU'APPELLE VIDETTE – Fort Qu'Appelle, Canada. 1884-99 – 5r – 1 – $325.00 – cn Library Assoc [971]

Quaque, Philip *see* LETTERS

QUARE IMPEDIT. IN TWO PARTS / Mallory, John – London Nutt and Gosling, 1737. Various pagings. LL-978 – 1 – us L of C Photodup [340]

Quarelli, Elena *see* SOCRATES AND THE ANIMALS

IL QUARESIMALE / Segneri, Paolo – (Includes indexes) – Torino: Giacinto Marietti, 1883 – 2mf – 9 – 0-8370-6947-5 – 1986-0947 – us A.T.L.A. [240]

QUARESIMALE = THE QUARESIMALE OF P. PAOLO SEGNERI. FIRST SERIES / Segneri, Paolo – (In English) – 4th ed. London: Joseph Masters, 1869 – 1mf – 9 – 0-8370-6775-8 – 1986-0775 – us A.T.L.A. [240]

QUARRY – Kingston. v1-44. 1965-95 – 9 – Can$20.00y – cn Micromedia [800]

QUARRY AND MINING NEWS – 1976- – 1,5,6,9 – us UMI [622]

QUARTER HORSE JOURNAL – 1986- – 1,5,6,9 – us UMI [790]

QUARTER SESSIONS ORDER BOOKS, 1639-1872 / Suffolk. England – 1 – uk Microform Academic [324]

QUARTERLY / California. Youth Authority – (v30- 1977- 5,6,9) – v1- 1948- – 1 – us UMI [350]

QUARTERLY / Concordia Historical Institute. St. Louis – v59-. 1986- – 1,5,6,9 – us UMI [900]

QUARTERLY / Creation Research Society – (1985-. 5,6,9) – v1-. 1964- – 1 – us UMI [240]

QUARTERLY / Federal Reserve Bank of Minneapolis. Ninth District – v1- 1977- 1; v3- 5,6,9 – us UMI [330]

QUARTERLY / Mountain-Plains Library Association – v. 18-19. 1973-74 – 1,5,6 – us UMI [020]

QUARTERLY / National Genealogical Society – v. 1-36. 1912-48 – 1,5,6 – us Princeton Micro [580]

QUARTERLY / National Institute of Animal Health. Tokyo – v. 6-16. 1966-76 – 1,5,6 – us Princeton Micro [636]

QUARTERLY / Nebraska. Agricultural Experiment Station. Lincoln – n.1-16. 1952-69 – 1,5 – us Spaulding [630]

THE QUARTERLY – (Cont by: The School Magazine) – Hamilton [Ont.: s.n., 1875?-1879] – 9 – cn C.I.H.M. [800]

THE QUARTERLY *see* THE SCHOOL MAGAZINE

QUARTERLY ABSTRACTS OF PASSENGER LISTS OF VESSELS ARRIVING AT BALTIMORE, 1820-69 / U.S. Bureau of the Customs – 6 rolls.M596. Printed guide – 1 – us Nat'l Archives [324]

QUARTERLY ABSTRACTS OF PASSENGER LISTS OF VESSELS ARRIVING AT NEW ORLEANS, 1820-75 / U.S. Bureau of the Customs – 17 rolls. M272 – 1 – us Nat'l Archives [324]

QUARTERLY, AIR FORCE ENGINEERING AND SERVICES *see* AIR FORCE ENGINEERING AND SERVICES QUARTERLY

QUARTERLY ARCHITECTURAL REVIEW *see* CALIFORNIA ARCHITECT AND BUILDING NEWS

QUARTERLY BULLETIN / Association of Food and Drug Officials – v10-42 1946-1978 – 1,5,6 – us Princeton Micro [615]

QUARTERLY BULLETIN / Hamilton Public Library (Ont.) – Hamilton, Ont.?: s.n., 18— 18– or 19– – 9 – cn C.I.H.M. [010]

QUARTERLY BULLETIN OF CHINESE BIBLIOGRAPHY – Shanghai. v1-4. 1934-37; ns: v1-7. 1940-47 – 48mf – 9 – CH-938/2 – ne IDC [950]

QUARTERLY BULLETIN OF NORTHWESTERN UNIVERSITY MEDICAL SCHOOL – v. 23-36. 1949-1962 – 1 – us UMI [610]

QUARTERLY BULLETIN OF STATISTICS / Libya. Technical Planning Body. Census and Statistical Department. – Jan Mar 1970-Oct Dec 1971. (lacking 1972 (Jul Sep)). BNE-536 1 – 9 – ne IDC [310]

QUARTERLY CUMULATIVE INDEX MEDICUS – (See also: Cumulated Index Medicus) – v1-60. 1927-56 – 1 – us UMI [610]

QUARTERLY CUMULATIVE INDEX MEDICUS – v. 1-60. 1927-56. Ceased with v. 60. 1956. Now: Cumulated Index Medicus – 1,5,6 – us Princeton Micro [610]

QUARTERLY CUMULATIVE INDEX TO CURRENT MEDICAL LITERATURE – (Ceased publication. United with Index Medicus to form Quarterly Cumulative Index Medicus.) v. 1-12. 1916-1926 – 1,5,6 – us Princeton Micro [610]

QUARTERLY CUMULATIVE INDEX TO CURRENT MEDICAL LITERATURE – v1-12. 1916-26 – 1 – us UMI [610]

QUARTERLY DIGEST OF STATISTICS *see* ST. VINCENT

QUARTERLY ECONOMIC REPORT / Indian Institute of Public Opinion – 1954- – 1; 1975- 5,6,9 – us UMI [330]

QUARTERLY ECONOMIC REVIEWS – 1952-91. With printed index. Continued annually – 5. ; 9 – £9,750.00 – uk World [330]

QUARTERLY JOURNAL / Geological Society of London – v. 1-133. 1845-1977 – 1,5,6 – us Princeton Micro [580]

QUARTERLY JOURNAL / Poona Sarvajnik Sabha – v1-24. Poona. 1878-1920. (lacking: 1915-16, v19; 1917-18, v21(2); 1919-20, v23(1); 1920, v24(3-4). BI-106 2 – 8 – ne IDC [073]

QUARTERLY JOURNAL OF CONCHOLOGY – (Cont as: Journal of Conchology. London. v2-20. 1879-1934/37) – London. v1. 1874-78 – 156mf – 9 – Z-901c/2 – ne IDC [590]

QUARTERLY JOURNAL OF ECONOMICS – v1-99. 1886-1984 – 1 – us Princeton Micro [330]

QUARTERLY JOURNAL OF EXPERIMENTAL PHYSIOLOGY AND COGNATE MEDICAL SCIENCES – v. 1-57. 1908-1972 – 1,5,6 – us Princeton Micro [619]

QUARTERLY JOURNAL OF MANAGEMENT DEVELOPMENT – v. 1-4. 1970-73 – 1 – us UMI [650]

QUARTERLY JOURNAL OF MATHEMATICS – (Oxford Second Series). v. 1-19. Oxford. 1950-68 – 9 – 24120.00; 6.00v – uk Dawson [510]

QUARTERLY JOURNAL OF MATHEMATICS – (v. 1-10. 246.00v; 9. v. 11-20. 242.50v; WDS; 9) – (Oxford First Series). v. 1-20. Oxford. 1930-49. All pub – 9 – 24105.00 – uk Dawson [510]

QUARTERLY JOURNAL OF MECHANICS AND APPLIED MATHEMATICS – v1-21. 1948-68. Oxford – 9 – 24185.00; 9.00v – uk Dawson [510]

QUARTERLY JOURNAL OF MEDICINE – v. 1-24. 1907-1931. New Series, v. 1-24. 1932-1955 – 1,5,6 – us Princeton Micro [610]

QUARTERLY JOURNAL OF MICROSCOPICAL SCIENCE – 1853-1920 – 1 – uk Microform Academic [578]

QUARTERLY JOURNAL OF MICROSCOPICAL SCIENCE – orig. s. v. 1-8. 1853-60. London. All pub – 9 – 2448.00; 6.00v – uk Dawson [576]

QUARTERLY JOURNAL OF MICROSCOPICAL SCIENCE – (v. 1-20. 246.00v; 9. v. 21-82. 2410.00v; WDS; 9. v. 83-106. 248.00v; WDS; 9) – New and third series. v. 1-106. London. 1861-1965. All pub – 9 – 24930.00 – uk Dawson [576]

QUARTERLY JOURNAL OF PHARMACY AND ALLIED SCIENCES *see* QUARTERLY JOURNAL OF PHARMACY AND PHARMACOLOGY

QUARTERLY JOURNAL OF PHARMACY AND PHARMACOLOGY – (Formerly: Quarterly Journal of Pharmacy and Allied Sciences) – v1-21. 1928-48 (all publ) – 1,5,6 – us Princeton Micro [615]

QUARTERLY JOURNAL OF PURE AND APPLIED MATHEMATICS – Oxford Series. v1-50. 1855-1927 – 5,9 – Dfl3,000.00; Dfl60.00v – ne Swets [510]

QUARTERLY JOURNAL OF SCIENCE AND ARTS / Royal Institution – 1816-30 – 1 – uk Microform Academic [500]

QUARTERLY JOURNAL OF SPEECH – v. 1-29. 1918-1943 – 1 – us Princeton Micro [400]

QUARTERLY JOURNAL OF SPEECH – (v. 55- 1969- 5,6. v. 61- 1975- 9) – v. 1- 1915- – 1 – us UMI [370]

QUARTERLY JOURNAL OF STUDIES ON ALCOHOL – (See now: Journal of Studies on Alchohol) – v1-35 1940-74 1; v28-35 5,6,9 – us UMI [073]

QUARTERLY JOURNAL OF THE ANDHRA HISTORICAL RESEARCH SOCIETY / Andhra Historical Research Society – (Cont. as JOURNAL OF THE ANDHRA HISTORICAL RESEARCH SOCIETY. Rajahmundry. 1929-63. v4-29) – Rajahmundry. 1926-28. v1-3 – 139mf – 8 – ne IDC [950]

THE QUARTERLY JOURNAL OF THE ANDHRA HISTORICAL RESEARCH SOCIETY – (Cont as: Journal of the Andhra Historical Research Society. Rajahmundry. v4-29. 1929-63) – Rajahmundry. v1-3. 1926-28 – 139mf – 9 – I-214/2 – ne IDC [950]

QUARTERLY JOURNAL OF THE MYTHIC SOCIETY – (Missing: v4(3); v33(2-3)) – (Bangalore). Madras. v1-58. 1909-70 – 228mf – 9 – I-1170/1 – ne IDC [390]
QUARTERLY JOURNAL OF THE SOCIETY OF AMERICAN INDIANS *see* AMERICAN INDIAN MAGAZINE
THE QUARTERLY LAW JOURNAL – Richmond. v1-4. 1856-59 (all publ) – 27mf – 9 – $40.50 – LLMC 82-955 – us L.L.M.C. [073]
THE QUARTERLY LAW REVIEW – Richmond. v1-2. 1860-61 (all publ) – 5mf – 9 – $7.50 – LLMC 84-669 – us L.L.M.C. [073]
QUARTERLY MUSICAL MAGAZINE AND REVIEW – Repertoire International de la Presse Musicale Collection – 1 reel – 1 – us UMI [780]
QUARTERLY NOTES ON CHRISTIANITY AND CHINESE RELIGION – v1-7. 1957-63 – 1 – us UMI [240]
THE QUARTERLY OF THE DEPARTMENT OF ANTIQUITIES IN PALESTINE – (Index included) – Jerusalem. v1-14. 1931-50 – 54mf – 9 – H-2528/1 – ne IDC [930]
QUARTERLY REPORT OF THE DOMINION SECRETARY OF THE PATRONS OF HUSBANDRY FOR THE QUARTER ENDING... / Patrons of Husbandry. Dominion Grange – Welland [Ont.]: The Grange, [18—18– or 19–] – 9 – cn C.I.H.M. [630]
QUARTERLY REPORT OF THE SUB-COMMITTEE OF THE BOARD OF ARTS AND MANUFACTURES FOR LOWER CANADA / Board of Arts and Manufactures for Lower Canada – (Cont by: Board of Arts and Manufactures for Lower Canada. Report of the Sub-Committee of the Board of Arts and Manufactures for Lower Canada) – [Montreal]: The Board, [18—1858] (Montreal: Owler & Stevenson) – 9 – cn C.I.H.M. [700]
QUARTERLY REVIEW / Federal Reserve Bank of New York – v. 1. 1976- – 1,5,6,9 – us UMI [336]
QUARTERLY REVIEW – Nashville. Tenn. 1941-61 – 1 – 300.16 – us Baptist [240]
QUARTERLY REVIEW / National Westminster Bank – 1968- 1; 1977- 5,6,9 – us UMI [332]
QUARTERLY REVIEW – v. 1-278. Years: 1809-1942 – 1 – us Princeton Micro [073]
QUARTERLY REVIEW / Vancouver. Planning Department – (Ceased v14 no 3 1987. See also: Vancouver Planning Dept, Quarterly Review) – v1-14. 1974-87 – 9 – Can$20.00y – cn Micromedia [350]
QUARTERLY REVIEW *see* UNITED BRETHREN REVIEW
QUARTERLY REVIEW OF BIOLOGY – (v. 40- 1965- 5,6. v. 45- 1970- 9) – v. 1- 1926- – 1 – us UMI [574]
QUARTERLY REVIEW OF BIOLOGY – v1-30. 1926-55 – 1,5,6 – us Princeton Micro [611]
QUARTERLY REVIEW OF ECONOMICS AND BUSINESS – (v.10- 1970- 5,6. v.15- 1975- 9) – v.1- 1961- – 1 – us UMI [330]
QUARTERLY REVIEW OF FILM AND VIDEO / ed by Renov, Michael – 9,5,1 – us Harwood [790]
QUARTERLY REVIEW OF FILM STUDIES – v1- 1976- 1; v3- 5,6,9 – us UMI [790]
QUARTERLY REVIEW OF HIGHER EDUCATION AMONG NEGROES / Johnson C. Smith University – 1-28. 1933-1960 – 78mf – 9 – $205.00 – us UPA [370]
QUARTERLY REVIEW OF HIGHER EDUCATION AMONG NEGROES / Johnson C Smith University – Charlotte, NC. v1-8. 1933-40 – 2r – 1 – us Ross [370]
THE QUARTERLY REVIEW OF MARKETING – 1978- – 1 – us UMI [073]
QUARTERLY REVIEW: QR – v.1-. 1980- – 1,5,6,9 – us UMI [073]
QUARTERLY REVIEWS / Chemical Society. London – v. 1-25. 1947-1971 – 1,5,6 – us Princeton Micro [540]
QUARTERLY REVIEWS – Chemical Society, London. v1-15. 1947-61. H-205/2 – 8 – ne IDC [073]
QUARTERLY REVIEWS OF BIOPHYSICS – v1- 1968- 1; v9- 5,6,9 – us UMI [574]
QUARTERLY STATISTICAL BULLETIN – 1963-1971 – 1r – $49.50 – us African Imprint [310]
QUARTERLY STEEL REVIEW – 1956-58 – 7 – uk Microform Academic [338]
QUARTERLY/CHRISTIAN LEGAL SOCIETY – (1986- . 5,6,9) – v2- . 1981- – 1 – us UMI [073]
Quarterman, James *see* A PHILOSOPHICAL AND A CHEMICAL DIGEST OF THE MOSAIC CREATION
QUARTERMASTER REPORTS / U.S. Army. Hilton Head Island – 1862. 2 fiches – 9 – us South Carolina Historical [976]
QUARTET NO. 2, OP. 29, IN F, FUR CORNETT, TROMBA, TENORHORN UND TUBA / Ramsoe, W – (Miniature score) – Kopenhagen: W Hansen, 1888 – 1 – us Sibley [780]
QUARTET NO. 44 FOR 2 VIOLINS, VIOLA AND CELLO / Boccherini, Luigi – Manuscript, ca 1780 – 1 – us Sibley [780]
QUARTET, STRINGS, NO. 11, OP. 60 / Romberg, B – (Pts.) – Leipzig: Kistner, 180-? – 1 – us Sibley [780]
QUARTETS, STRING, OP. 20 / Pleyel, Ignaz J – (4 pts) – London: Preston, 18– – 1 – us Sibley [780]
QUARTETS, STRING, OP. 32 / Kozeluch, L – London: J Bland, 179- – us Sibley [780]
QUARTETS, STRINGS, H. 3: 31-36 [NOS. 32-37, OP. 20] / Haydn, Joseph – London: Blundell, 1778 – 1 – us Sibley [780]
QUARTETS, STRINGS, H. 3: 47-49 [NOS. 48-50, NOS. 4-6] OP. 29 LIBRO 2 / Haydn, Joseph – (4 parts) – Berlin: J J Hummel, 1788-9 – 1 – us Sibley [780]
QUARTETS, STRINGS, H. 3: 69-71. TROIS QUATOURS POUR DEUX VIOLONS, ALTO ET VIOLONCELLE, OEUVRE 71... / Haydn, Joseph – (4 parts) – Paris: Pleyel, [179-] – 1 – us Sibley [780]
QUARTETS, STRINGS, H. 3: 75-77 [NOS. 76-78, OP. 76, NOS. 1-3] / Haydn, Joseph – (Parts) – London: Clementi & Co, 1799 – 1 – us Sibley [780]
QUARTETS, STRINGS, H. 3: 78-80 [NOS. 79-81, OP. 76, NO. 4-6] / Haydn, Joseph – (Parts) – London: Clementi & Co, 1799 – 1 – us Sibley [780]
QUARTETS, STRINGS, KING OF PURSSIA NO 1. BOOK 1 / Pleyel, Ignaz J – (4 pts) – London: Preston, 18– – 1 – us Sibley [780]
QUARTETS, STRINGS, NO. 10, OP. 59 / Romberg, B – (Pts.) – Leipzig: Kistner, 1836? – 1 – us Sibley [780]
QUARTETS, STRINGS, SELECTIONS / Haydn, Joseph – (4 parts) – Paris: de la Chevardiere – 1 – us Sibley [780]
QUARTETS, TWO / Wanhal, J B – London: Babbs, 1780 – 1 – us Sibley [780]
A QUARTETTE OF LOVERS / Currie, John Allister – Toronto: Williamson, 1892. 00245. (Pre-1900 Canadiana) – 9 – cn C.I.H.M. [971]
QUARTETTI, 6, OP. 6A. [G. 165-170] / Boccherini, Luigi; ed by Boyer – Paris: Naderman et al, 1785? – 1 – us Sibley [780]
QUARTETTI CONCERTANTI, SEI, OP. 27 / Boccherini, Luigi – Paris: Sieber Sr, ca 1785 – 1 – us Sibley [780]
QUARTETTI, SEI, OP. 6, NO. 2 / Pleyel, Ignaz J – (Parts) – Vienna: Czerny, 182- – 1 – us Sibley [780]
QUARTI SAECULI...JUVENCI...OPERA OMNIA / Migne, Jacques-Paul – 1846 – 9 – 1.50f – sp Bibl Santa Ana [450]
QUARTI...AURELII PRUDENTII / Migne, Jacques-Paul – 1862 – 9 – 1.50f – sp Bibl Santa Ana [450]
LE QUARTIER DE LA PORTE D'AIX A MARSEILLE / Carreno, J.-A. et al – Essai d'ethnologie d'un centre urbain – 9 – F50.00 – fr Ethnologie [306]
Quartieri, Pietro Paolo *see* MADRIGALI A CINQUE VOCI...LIBRO PRIMO
LE QUARTIER-LATIN *see* LE JOURNAL DES ETUDIANTS
QUARTO – London, UK. 1979-1982 – 1r – $50.00 – R63607 – us Library Micro [073]
THE QUARTO – London, 1896-98 – 1r – 1 – £60.00 – uk Chadwyck [760]
QUARTO MEMOIRS – (Coll title: Publications of the English Record Societies, 1835-72...) – v1-3. 1922-29 – 5mf – 9 – £42.00 – uk Chadwyck [941]
QUARTO TOMO DE LAS ESCRITURAS DE TAPIA – 1621 – 1 – sp Bibl Santa Ana [946]
QUARTZ MOUNTAIN MINER – Quartz Mountain, NV. 16 Jun 1926 – 1r – 1 – $50.00 – U04651 – us Library Micro [071]
QUATEMBER : EVANGELISCHE JAHRESBRIEFE – 18(1953)-37(1973) – 88mf – 9 – Dfl308.00 – ne Slangenburg [073]
QUATERNARY INTERNATIONAL – 1,5,69 – us UMI [073]
QUATERNARY SCIENCE REVIEWS – v1- 1982- – 5,6,9 – us UMI [500]
QUATORS, TROIS, OP. 7 / Danzi, F – (Parts) – Maience: B Schott, ca 1790 – 1 – us Sibley [780]
QUATORZE JUILLET – London, UK. 14 Jul 1940 – 1 – uk British Libr Newspaper [072]
QUATOUR, PREMIER GRAND, OP. 2 / Garnier, L – Paris: Pascal, Taskin, 179- – 1 – us Sibley [780]
QUATOURS CONCERTANS, OBOE AND STRINGS, OP. 92 / Amon, J A – Bonn et Cologne: N. Simrock, 1824/1828 – 1 – us Sibley [780]
QUATRE ANS CHEZ LES ACHANTIS / Ramseyer et Kuhne – Paris, Sandoz et Fischbacher. 1876 – 9 – 15.00 – fr Orientalistes [305]
QUATRE ANS D'EXECUTION DU PLAN DE MODERNISATION ET D'EQ1906-1920/21 / France. Commissariat general du plan de modernisation et d'equipement – 9 – ne IDC [338]
QUATRE CENTS AFORISMES CATHALANS... / Amat, Juan Carlos – Barcelona, S.A. – 1mf – 9 – sp Cultura [440]
QUATRE ETUDES DE LINGUISTIQUE BERBERE / Basset, Andre – (Filmed with the author's Le berere a Ecole nationale des langues oreintales vivantes, Paris 1948) – Paris: Impr Nationale, 1945 – us Res Libr [470]
QUATRE MORCEAUX, OP. 38 / Moszkowski, M – Breslau: Hainauer, 188- – 1 – us Sibley [780]
LES QUATRE PREMIERS QUODLIBETS DE GODEFROID DE FONTAINES / Wulf, M de & Pelzer, A – 1904 – 12mf – 8 – ne Slangenburg [100]
QUATRE VOYAGES DANS LE PAYS DES HOTTENTOTS ET LA CAFRERIE / Paterson, William – Traduction de l'anglais. Paris, Plassan. 1791 – 9 – 7.50 – fr Orientalistes [910]
Quatremere de Quincy, A C *see* ENCYCLOPEDIE METHODIQUE: ARCHITECTURE
QUATRES LECTURES TALMUDIQUES / Levinas, Emmanuel – Paris, 1968 – 4mf – 8 – ne Slangenburg [270]
LES QUATRES LIVRES DE L'ARCHITECTURE / Palladio, Andre – Paris, E. Martin, 1650. 4, 329p., 5 pl. (Architecture Series) – 9 – fr Hachette [720]
QUATRIEME CONFERENCE INTERNATIONAL SUR L'EDUCATION DES ADULTES, PARIS, 19-29 MARS 1985 : LE DEVELOPPEMENT DE L'EDUCATION DES ADULTES, ASPECTS ET TENDANCES / UNESCO – Paris, 1985 – 2mf – 9 – DE-136/1 – ne IDC [370]
QUATRI'EME INTERNATIONALE / Fourth International. International Executive Committee – [Paris]: Comite executif international de a IVe International, 19uu – 1 – CSUXALM4281-S – us Hoover Inst Photo [944]
QUATRIEME INTERNATIONALE – no. 1-17. Paris. oct 1936-mai 1939. Reprend les elements de: La Lutte de classes voir a ce titre – 1 – fr A.C.R.P.P. [073]
QUATRIEME PLAN DE DEVELOPPEMENT ECONOMIQUE ET SOCIAL (1962-1965) / France – Paris. 1962 – 9 – ne IDC [338]
QUATRIEME PLAN DE DEVELOPPEMENT ECONOMIQUE ET SOCIAL. 1973-1976 / Tunisia – 2v. Tunis. 1973. BD-1806 1 – 9 – ne IDC [338]
QUATRIEME RAPPORT DE LA COMMISSION CHARGEE DE REVISER ET DE MODIFIER LE CODE DE PROCEDURE CIVILE DU BAS-CANADA / Quebec Province – Quebec: imprime par Leger Brousseau, 1896. SEM105P1516 – 5mf – 9 – Can$11.25 – cn Bibl Nat [340]
QUATRO ELEGANTISIMAS Y GRAVISSIMAS ORATIONES DE M.T. CICERON CONTRA CATILINA... / Laguna, A de – Amberes, 1557 – 4mf – 9 – sp Cultura [440]
LAS QUATROCIENTAS RESPUESTAS A OTRAS TANTAS PREGUNTAS / Escobar, L – Zaragoza, 1545 – 5mf – 9 – sp Cultura [440]
QUATTRO CANTATE DA CAMERA...LA PRIMA PER CIMBALO. / Pergolesi, G B – 1750? – 9 – us Sibley [780]
QUATTRO E QUATTROTTO. CANZONETTA CON CORO – London: Longman & Broderip, 179- – 1 – us Sibley [780]
QUATTRO SONATE NOTTURNE...A 2 VIOLINI, 2 BASSO, A PIU TOSTO VIOLA. OP. 4, NO 1-4 / Bach, Johann Christian – (3 parts) – Markordt, 178- – us Sibley [780]
QUATUOR / Borowski, F – (2nd and 3rd movements only. Parts) – Ms – 1 – us Sibley [780]
QUATUOR BRILLIANT, OP. 20, NO. 1 / Dufresne, F – (Parts) – Paris: Boieldieu, 18– – 1 – us Sibley [780]
QUATUOR BRILLIANT, TROISIEME, POUR DEUX VIOLONS, ALTO ET VIOLONCELLE / Mancourt, C – (Separate parts) – Offenbach S/M: Andre [183-?] – 1 – us Sibley [780]
QUATUOR CONCERTANS, TROIS, OP. 17 / Davaux, J B – (Parts) – Paris: Imbault, 1795 – 1 – us Sibley [780]
QUATUOR CONCERTANT, 3ME, POUR PIANO, VIOLON ALTO ET VIOLONCELLE / Jadin, L – (Separate parts) – Paris: Erard [180-?] – 1 – us Sibley [780]
QUATUOR DIALOQUE / Woldemar, M – (Parts) – Paris: Cochet, 179- – 1 – us Sibley [780]
QUATUOR ECCLESIAE PARISIACAE SUFFRAGANEAE (GC 8) – Parisiis, 1744 – Dfl161.00 – ne Slangenburg [240]
QUATUOR POUR LE CLAVECIN, OU FORTEPIANO, DEUX VIOLONS / Albrechtsberger, Johann G – Vienne: Hoffmeister, [1875?] – 1 – us Sibley [780]
QUATUOR POUR LE CLAVECIN OU PIANO FORTE / Hoffmeister, Franz A – (179? Score & parts) – 9 – us Sibley [780]
QUATUOR POUR LE CLAVECIN, OU PIANO-FORTE AVEC VIOLIN, VIOLA ET VIOLONCELLE / Hoffmeister, Franz A – (1788? Score & parts) – 9 – us Sibley [780]
QUATUOR POUR LE CLAVECIN OU PIANOFORTE, VIOLA ET VIOLONCELLE. OEUVRE 25 / Mozart, Wolfgang Amadeus – Amsterdam: J Schmitt, [180-?] – 1 – us Sibley [780]
QUATUOR POUR LE PIANOFORTE ACCOMPAGNE D'UN VIOLON, VIOLA ET VIOLONCELLE, OP 7 / Fodor, A – Berlin: Hummel, ca 1795 – 1 – us Sibley [780]
QUATUOR POUR TROIS VIOLONS ET VIOLONCELLE / Franklin, Benjamin – Transcription de Guillaume de Van. Paris: O. Lieutier, 1946. Critical notes, printed score, and facsimile of late 18th century copyist's ms. in the library of the Paris Conservatory (Res. 1808). MUSIC 3093 – 1 – us L of C Photodup [780]
QUATUOR, TROIS, OP. 6, LIV. 2 / Fauvel, A J – Paris: Pollet, 179- – 1 – us Sibley [780]
QUATUORS, 3, POUR DEUX VIOLONS, ALTO ET VIOLONCELLE, OEUVRE 7 / Hoffman, H A – (Separate parts) – Bonn: Simrock, 179-? – 1 – us Sibley [780]
QUATUORS, DEUX / Kreutzer, R – Leipsic: Breitkopf & Hartel, 179- – 1 – us Sibley [780]
QUATUORS, DEUX, POUR FLUTE, VIOLON, ALTO, ET VIOLONCELLE / Rolla, A – (Pts.) – Paris: Sieber pere, 17– – 1 – us Sibley [780]
QUATUORS, DOUZE NOUVEAUX 4E LIVRAISON / Pleyel, Ignaz J – (Separate parts) – Paris: Le Duc, [18–?] – 1 – us Sibley [780]
QUATUORS, SIX, 3E LIVRE / Gyrowetz, Adalbert – (Parts) – Paris: Janet et Cotelle, 179- – 1 – us Sibley [780]
QUATUORS, SIX, OP. 1 / Gyrowetz, Adalbert – Paris: Janet et Cotelle, 179- – 1 – us Sibley [780]
QUATUORS, SIX, OP. 98, LIV. 1 ET 2 [FL, VLN, VLA, VC] / Reicha, A – (Pts.) – Paris: Boieldieu, 182- – 1 – us Sibley [780]
QUATUORS, TROIS / Kreutzer, R – Zurich: J G Naigneli, between 1802-1814 – 1 – us Sibley [780]
QUATUORS, TROIS, ARR. PIANO, VIOLIN, CELLO / Pleyel, Ignaz J – (Parts) – Paris: Pleyel, 182- – 1 – us Sibley [780]
QUATUORS, TROIS GRANDS, POUR DEUX VIOLINS, ALTO ET VIOLONCELLE / Jadin, L – (Separate parts) – Paris: J Frey [180-?] – 1 – us Sibley [780]
QUATUORS, TROIS, OP. 6 / Danzi, F – (Parts) – Munic: Falter, ca 1790 – 1 – us Sibley [780]
QUATUORS, TROIS, OP. 42 / Pleyel, Ignaz J – (Parts) – Offenbach s/M: Andre, ca 1792 – 1 – us Sibley [780]
QUATUORS, TROIS, OP. 44 / Danzi, F – (Parts) – Leipzig: Kuhnel, ca 1811 – 1 – us Sibley [780]
QUATUORS, TROIS, OP. 55 / Danzi, F – (Parts) – Offenbach s/M: Andre, ca 1812 – 1 – us Sibley [780]

QUATUORS, TROIS, POUR DEUX VIOLONS, ALTO ET BASSE, OEUVRE 17 / Gyrowetz, Adalbert – (4 parts) – Paris: Sieber fils, 1793 – 1 – us Sibley [780]
QUATUORS, TROIS, POUR FLUTE, VIOLON, ALTO ET VIOLONCELLE, OP. 56 / Danzi, F – (Parts) – Offenbach s/M: Andre, ca 1812 – 1 – us Sibley [780]
LES QUAT'Z'ARTS – Litteraire, hebdomadaire, illustre puis Chansons, revues, ombres. Red. en chef Emile Goudeau. Paris. nov 1897-janv 1908 – 1 – fr A.C.R.P.P. [073]
QUE ES EL PERONISMO / Bittel, Deolindo Felipe – Buenos Aires: Editorial Sudamericana, 1983 – 1 – CSUXAHZ2304-B – us Hoover Inst Photo [320]
QUE ES EL SERVICIO DE ADMINISTRACION LOCAL (LA FALANGE Y EL AYUNTAMIENTO RURAL) / Falange Espanola Tradicionalista y de la Jons – Caceres: Tip. La Minerva, 1940 – sp Bibl Santa Ana [350]
QUE ES UN PLAN QUINQUENAL? / Argentine Republic. Presidencia. Subsecretaria de Informaciones – Buenos Aires, 1953 – 1 – CSUXAHZ5790-B – us Hoover Inst Photo [320]
QUE ES Y QUE REPRESENTA LA UNION NACIONAL DE LOS ESPANOLES / Uribe, Vicente – Mexico? 1945? Fiche W1243. (Blodgett Collection of Spanish Civil War Pamphlets) – 9 – us H.U. College Libr [946]
LO QUE ESTA EN EL CORAZON / Reyes Huertas, Antonio – Madrid: Imprenta Clasica Espanola, 1918 – 1 – sp Bibl Santa Ana [946]
QUE FAIRE? – no. 1 2-53 54. Paris. nov dec 1934-juil 1939. mq no. 31-33, 39, 41-42, 44-46 – 1 – fr A.C.R.P.P. [073]
LO QUE FUIMOS Y LO QUE SOMOS: O, LA HABANA ANTIGUA Y MODERNA / Torres, Jose Maria de la – Habana: Impr. de Spencer y Compania, 1857. 184p. Fold. map. 1 reel. 1262 – 1 – us U.W. Library [910]
QUE LE MONDE CIVILISE EN JUGE – Let the civilized world judge. n.p., 193? Fiche W1126. (Blodgett Collection of Spanish Civil War Pamphlets) – 9 – us H.U. College Libr [946]
LO QUE LOS FACCIOSOS QUIEREN QUE SE OLVIDE – Madrid, 1936. Fiche W1004. (Blodgett Collection of Spanish Civil War Pamphlets) – 9 – us H.U. College Libr [946]
LOS QUE MANDAN / Imaz, Jose Luis de – Buenos Aires: Editorial Universitaria de Buenos Aires, 8th ed 1969, c1964 – 1 – CSUXADJ0077-B – us Hoover Inst Photo [972]
LOS QUE MUEVEN LAS PALANCAS / Alende, Oscar – [Buenos Aires]: A. Pena Lillo, [1971] – 1 – CSUXAHZ3656-B – us Hoover Inst Photo [999]
QUE PASA EN ESPANA? A LOS CATOLICOS DE MUNDO / Bayle, Constantino – Salamanca, 1937. Fiche W 751. (Blodgett Collection of Spanish Civil War Pamphlets) – 9 – us H.U. College Libr [946]
QUE PASA EN ESPANA? A LOS CATOLICOS DEL MUNDO / Bayle, Constantino – Salamanca: Delegacion del Estado para Prensa y Propaganda, 1937 – 1 – sp Bibl Santa Ana [240]
QUE PASA EN MEJICO : SEGUNDO CUADRO / ed by Bayle, Constantino – Madrid: Razon y Fe, 1926 – 1 – sp Bibl Santa Ana [972]
QUE PASA EN MEJICO? / Bayle, Constantino – Madrid: Razon y Fe, 1925 – 1 – sp Bibl Santa Ana [972]
LO QUE PUEDE LA PERRA-CHICA / Leuman Ziur Orelau. Seud. de Benigno Lopez – Badajoz: Imp. Arqueros, 1959 – sp Bibl Santa Ana [830]
LO QUE QUIEREN LOS ESPANOLES DE BUENA VOLUNTAD... / Bayle, Constantino & Sandoval, Adolfo de – Madrid: Razon y Fe, 1941 – sp Bibl Santa Ana [946]
LO QUE SE PIENSA,...SONANDO! / Sanchez-Arjona, Vicente – Sevilla: Imp. Carlos Acuna, 1951 – 1 – sp Bibl Santa Ana [810]
QUE SE PUEDE HACER? / Largo Caballero, Francisco – Mexico, 1940? Fiche W992. (Blodgett Collection of Spanish Civil War Pamphlets) – 9 – us H.U. College Libr [946]
LO QUE SE VA / Sanchez-Ocana y Acedo-Rico, Pedro – Madrid: Editorial Voluntad, S.A. 1928 – sp Bibl Santa Ana [946]
LO QUE SE VA. MADRID, 1928 / Leturia, Rafael & Sanchez Ocana, Pedro – Madrid: Razon y Fe, 1930 – 1 – sp Bibl Santa Ana [946]
LO QUE VI EN RUSIA. MADRID, 1935 / Montero, Eloy – Madrid: Razon y Fe, 1936 – 1 – sp Bibl Santa Ana [947]
QUEANBEYAN AGE – Jan 17 1891-Dec 29 1900 – 9 – at Pascoe [072]
LE QUEBEC : PRO-OUVRIER – Quebec, Canada. 28 oct-29 nov 1889 – 1r – 1 – Can$35.00 – cn Can Microfilming [330]
QUEBEC : LE CANADA FRANCAIS D'AUJOURD'HUI / Quebec. (Province). Ministere des Affaires Culturelles – Paris: le Ministere. nos 1-24. 1964-72. SEM16P287 – 1r – 5 – Can$27.00 – cn Bibl Nat [971]
Quebec *see*
- CURRENT PUBLICATIONS
- OFFICIAL GAZETTE

QUEBEC 9 / ed by Laliberte, Gerard & Huot, M-G – Quebec, 15 nov 1968-v4 n14. fev 1971 – 1r – 1 – Can$35.00 – cn Can Microfilming [072]
THE QUEBEC ACT, 1774 / Hart, Gerald Ephraim – Montreal: Gazette Print. Co., 1891. 02441. (Pre-1900 Canadiana) – 9 – cn C.I.H.M. [971]
Quebec. Archbishop. Archives *see* DIVERS, RE: RIVIERE ROUGE (1820) (MANITOBA)
THE QUEBEC ARGUS – Quebec, Canada. v1 n5. 17 nov 1841-v1 n66. 18 jun 1842 – 1r – 1 – Can$28.00 – cn Can Microfilming [072]
QUEBEC AT A GLANCE / Quebec. (Province). Office d'Information et de Publicite – Quebec, 1970-80. SEM16P292 – 1r – 5 – Can$32.00 – cn Bibl Nat [971]
QUEBEC AUJOURD'HUI *see* QUEBEC
Quebec Benevolent Society *see* GENERAL RULES OF THE QUEBEC BENEVOLENT SOCIETY, PASSED 7TH AUG 1805
Quebec. Bibliotheque de la legislature *see* CATALOGUE DE LA BIBLIOTHEQUE DE LA LEGISLATURE DE LA PROVINCE DE QUEBEC
THE QUEBEC BRIDGE – Montreal: issued by the Canadian National Railways, 1926. SEM105P1792 – 1mf – 9 – Can$2.25 – cn Bibl Nat [624]
Quebec. Canada *see* JUDGMENT DE CONSEIL SUPERIEUR
THE QUEBEC CHRONICLE – Quebec: Chronicle Printing Co. v52-160. 1898-1924. SEM35P237 – 65r – 1 – Can$3,471.00 – cn Bibl Nat [072]
THE QUEBEC CHRONICLE AND QUEBEC GAZETTE – Quebec: Quebec Chronicle Printing Co. v160. 1924-25. SEM35P238 – 3r – 1 – Can$159.00 – cn Bibl Nat [971]
QUEBEC CHRONICLE TELEGRAPH – (Centenary number 21 jun 1864. 175th anniversary 21 jun 1939. 200th anniversary 20 jun 1964. 100th anniversary of Confederation 28 avr 1967 1r Can$50.00) – Quebec, Canada. v22 n1. 2 jan 1946-v23 n302. 31 dec 1947; v190. 2 jul 1953-v207 n156. 31 dec 1970 – 78r – 1 – Can$130.00r – cn Can Microfilming [072]
QUEBEC CHRONICLE-TELEGRAPH – Quebec: Chronicle-Telegraph Pub Co, v9- 1934-. SEM35P240 – 96r – 1 – cn Bibl Nat [072]
Quebec. (City). Canada. Comite des Chemins *see* RAPPORT...POUR LES ANNEES 1882-83..
THE QUEBEC COLONIST – Quebec, Canada. v1 n186. 23 mar 1855-v3 n178. 30 dec 1856 – 1r – 1 – Can$40.00 – cn Can Microfilming [072]
Quebec. Comite des chemins *see* RAPPORT DU COMITE DES CHEMINS SUR LES TRAVAUX DU DEPARTEMENT POUR LES ANNEES 1882-1883...
THE QUEBEC COMMERCIAL LIST – Quebec: printed for Office of the Quebec Gazette, 1816-. SEM35P34 – 1r – 1 – Can$15.00 – cn Bibl Nat [338]
THE QUEBEC COUP D'ETAT: ELOQUENT SPEECH / Chapleau, Joseph Adolphe – Montreal?, 1878? 02857. (Pre-1900 Canadiana) – 9 – cn C.I.H.M. [971]
QUEBEC DAILY MERCURY – Quebec, Canada. 5 jan 1805-17 oct 1903 – 64r – 1 – Can$50.00r – cn Can Microfilming [072]
QUEBEC DAILY NEWS – Quebec, Canada. 1862-67 – 6r – 1 – $390.00 – cn Library Assoc [971]
QUEBEC DAILY NEWS – Quebec, Canada. v1 n8. 9 mai 1862-v6 n135. 11 oct 1867 – 1r – 1 – Can$35.00 – cn Can Microfilming [072]
THE QUEBEC DAILY TELEGRAPH – Quebec, Canada. v13 n253. 2 nov 1888-v14 n9. 26 avr 1889 – 1r – 1 – Can$25.00 – cn Can Microfilming [072]
THE QUEBEC DIOCESAN GAZETTE – Quebec: Publ for the Lord Bishop at the Quebec Chronicle Office, [1894-1945?] – 9 – cn C.I.H.M. [240]
QUEBEC EN 1900: CONFERENCE DONNEE A L'ACADEMIE DE MUSIQUE DE QUEBEC, LUNDI LE 29 MAI, 1893 / Buies, Arthur – Quebec: L. Brousseau, 1893. 00350. (Pre-1900 Canadiana) – 9 – cn C.I.H.M. [971]
LE QUEBEC EN BREF / Quebec. (Province). Office d'Information et de Publicite – Quebec, 1967-80. SEM16P291 – 2r – 5 – Can$54.00 – cn Bibl Nat [073]
QUEBEC ET LEVIS A L'AURORE DU 20E SIECLE / Routhier, Adolphe-Basile – Montreal: Samuel de Champlain, 1900. SEM105P920 – 6mf – 9 – Can$13.50 – cn Bibl Nat [971]
QUEBEC EVENING CHRONICLE – Quebec, Canada. 22 oct 1900 – 1r – 1 – Can$25.00 – cn Can Microfilming [072]
QUEBEC GAZETTE – 1764-1817 – 14r – 1 – cn Library Assoc [971]
QUEBEC GAZETTE – 1862-1873 – 12r – 1 – cn Library Assoc [971]
QUEBEC GAZETTE *see* MORNING CHRONICLE AND COMMERCIAL AND SHIPPING GAZETTE
QUEBEC GAZETTE OFFICIEL – v83-94. 1957-68 – 1 – Can$2,800.00 – cn Micromedia [971]
QUEBEC GAZETTE OFFICIEL PARTIE 2 FRENCH – Quebec. v111-113. 1979-1981 – 9 – Can$120.00y – cn Micromedia [350]
THE QUEBEC GOOD TEMPLAR – Montreal: Kneeland Print. & Pub Co, [1880?-18– or 19–] – 9 – cn C.I.H.M. [360]
THE QUEBEC HERALD AND COMMERCIAL CHRONICLE – Quebec, Canada. v1 n8. 20 mai 1858 – 1r – 1 – Can$25.00 – cn Can Microfilming [072]
QUEBEC HERALD AND UNIVERSAL MISCELLANY – Quebec, Canada. 1778-91 – 1 reel – 1 – $68.00 – cn Library Assoc [971]
QUEBEC INTERNATIONAL – Quebec, 1 mai 1973-v4 n3. mar 1976 – 1r – 1 – Can$40.00 – cn Can Microfilming [072]
QUEBEC ISSUES DISCUSSED AT NICOLET BY THE MINISTERS: HON. MR. FLYNN ON FINANCES, TELLS WHAT HAS BEEN DONE TO RESTORE RIGHT CONDITIONS: WORK ON AGRICULTURE, HON. MR. BEAUBIEN DELIVERS A MOST INTERESTING ADDRESS ON AN INTERESTING SUBJECT / Flynn, Edmund James – s.l.: s.n., 1896?. 05577. (Pre-1900 Canadiana) – 9 – cn C.I.H.M. [971]
THE QUEBEC LAND SLIDE OF 1889 / Baillairge, Charles – 1893. 00807. (Pre-1900 Canadiana) – 9 – cn C.I.H.M. [971]
QUEBEC LAW REPORTS / Canada. Quebec – v1-17. 1875-91 (all publ) – 85mf – 9 – $127.00 – LLMC 81-082 – us L.L.M.C. [340]
Quebec. Laws, Statutes, etc *see*
- ORDINANCES MADE AND PASSED BY THE GOVERNOR AND LEGISLATIVE COUNCIL OF THE PROVINCE OF QUEBEC
- ORDINANCES, MADE FOR THE PROVINCE OF QUEBEC, BY THE GOVERNER AND LEGISLATIVE COUNCIL OF THE SAID PROVINCE, SINCE THE ESTABLISHMENT OF THE CIVIL GOVERNMENT

Quebec. Legislature. Assemblee legislative. Comite... *see*
- RAPPORT DU COMITE SPECIAL, DE L'ASSEMBLEE LEGISLATIVE, CHARGE DE S'ENQUERIR DE LA TENURE DES TERRES AUX ILES DE LA MAGDELEINE, COMTE DE GASPE
- REPORT OF THE SELECT COMMITTEE OF THE LEGISLATIVE ASSEMBLY, QUEBEC ON THE WINTER NAVIGATION OF THE RIVER AND GULF ST LAWRENCE

Quebec. Library *see*
- CATALOGUE OF ENGLISH AND FRENCH BOOKS IN THE QUEBEC LIBRARY
- CATALOGUE OF ENGLISH AND FRENCH BOOKS IN THE QUEBEC LIBRARY, AT THE BISHOP'S PALACE, WHERE THE RULES MAY BE SEEN

QUEBEC LIBRARY ASSOCIATION BULLETIN – 1939-52 – 1r – 1 – $68.00 – cn Library Assoc [020]
LE QUEBEC LIBRE / ed by Lucques, Jacques – Montreal, Canada. avr 1964-sep 1965 – 1r – 1 – Can$35.00 – cn Can Microfilming [072]
Quebec. Lois, etc. Extrait *see* STATUTS DE LA PROVINCE DE QUEBEC PASSES DANS LA PREMIERE ANNEE DU REGNE DE SA MAJESTE LE ROI GEORGE 6...
THE QUEBEC MAGAZINE = LE MAGASIN DE QUEBEC : OR USEFUL AND ENTERTAINING REPOSITORY OF SCIENCE, MORALS,.... – Quebec: Samuel Neilson, 1792-94. SEM105P792 – 17mf – 9 – Can$38.25 – cn Bibl Nat [073]
THE QUEBEC MAGAZINE = LE MAGAZIN DE QUEBEC – Quebec, Canada. aut 1792-sep 1793 – 1r – 1 – Can$35.00 – cn Can Microfilming [073]
QUEBEC MERCURY – Quebec, Canada. 1805-20; 1862-73 – 29r – 1 – $1,885.00 – cn Library Assoc [971]
THE QUEBEC MINER – Toronto, Canada. v20 n1. 10 dec 1954 – 1r – 1 – Can$25.00 – cn Can Microfilming [072]
LE QUEBEC MINIER – Montreal, Canada. 13 aut 1926-22 mar 1929 – 1r – 1 – Can$60.00 – cn Can Microfilming [072]
QUEBEC, MONTMORENCY FALLS AND ST ANNE DE BEAQUPRE / Quebec Railway, Light & Power Co – [Quebec]: Quebec Railway, Light & Power Co, [1937 ?]. SEM105P1836 – 1mf – 9 – Can$2.25 – cn Bibl Nat [380]
QUEBEC MORNING CHRONICLE – Quebec: John J Foote. v42-52. 1888-98. SEM35P236 – 21r – 1 – Can$996.00 – cn Bibl Nat [072]
QUEBEC MORNING CHRONICLE *see*
- THE CHRISTMAS CHIMES AND NEW YEAR'S CALL
- MORNING CHRONICLE (1888)

THE QUEBEC NEWS – Quebec, Canada. v1. 23 fev 1935 – 1r – 1 – Can$25.00 – cn Can Microfilming [072]
QUEBEC NOUVEAU – Montreal, nov 1972 – 1r – 1 – Can$25.00 – cn Can Microfilming [072]
QUEBEC OFFICIAL GAZETTE PART 2 ENGLISH – Quebec. v111-113. 1979-1981 – 9 – Can$120.00y – cn Micromedia [350]
QUEBEC PASSE SIC, PRESENT, FUTUR / Baillairge, Charles – Quebec: J. G. Gingras, 1885. 02490. (Pre-1900 Canadiana) – 9 – cn C.I.H.M. [971]
"THE QUEBEC POLITICAL CRISIS" – Quebec: s.n., 1879. SEM105P457 – 1mf – 9 – Can$2.25 – cn Bibl Nat [320]
THE QUEBEC POLITICAL CRISIS: NOTES AND PRECEDENTS – 1879?. 02265. (Pre-1900 Canadiana) – 9 – cn C.I.H.M. [971]
QUEBEC PRACTICE REPORTS / Canada. Quebec – v1-48. 1897-1944; 35bks. 1945-79 (all publ) – 485mf – 9 – $727.00 – LLMC 81-063 – us L.L.M.C. [340]
Quebec Province *see*
- CODE MUNICIPAL DE LA PROVINCE DE QUEBEC ANNOTE 1898-1902
- CODE MUNICIPAL DE LA PROVINCE DE QUEBEC ANNOTE MIS AU COURANT DE LA LEGISLATION ET DE LA JURISPRUDENCE
- CODE MUNICIPAL DE LA PROVINCE DE QUEBEC MIS AU COURANT DE LA LEGISLATION ET DE LA JURISPRUDENCE
- DEUXIEME RAPPORT DE LA COMMISSION CHARGEE DE REVISER ET DE MODIFIER LE CODE DE PROCEDURE CIVILE DU BAS-CANADA
- PREMIER RAPPORT DE LA COMMISSION CHARGEE DE LA REVISION ET DE LA MODIFICATION DU CODE DE PROCEDURE CIVILE DU BAS-CANADA
- QUATRIEME RAPPORT DE LA COMMISSION CHARGEE DE REVISER ET DE MODIFIER LE CODE DE PROCEDURE CIVILE DU BAS-CANADA
- RAPPORT DES COMMISSAIRES NOMMES POUR S'ENQUERIR DES AFFAIRES DES CHEMINS A BARRIERES DE LA RIVE NORD ET DE LA RIVE SUD A QUEBEC
- RAPPORT DU COMITE SPECIAL NOMME POUR EXAMINER LES LOIS MUNICIPALES ET LES LOIS CONCERNANT LES ABUS PREJUDICIABLES A L'AGRICULTURE, AVEC LES AMENDEMENTS PROPOSES
- REPORT OF THE COMMISSION APPOINTED TO REVISE AND CONSOLIDATE THE STATUTES OF THE PROVINCE OF QUEBEC
- SECOND REPORT OF THE COMMISSION CHARGED WITH THE REVISION AND AMENDMENT OF THE CODE OF CIVIL PROCEDURE OF LOWER CANADA

- THIRD REPORT OF THE COMMISSION CHARGED WITH THE REVISION AND AMENDMENT OF THE CODE OF CIVIL PROCEDURE OF LOWER CANADA
- TROISIEME RAPPORT DE LA COMMISSION CHARGEE DE REVISER ET DE MODIFIER LE CODE DE PROCEDURE CIVILE DU BAS-CANADA

Quebec. Province. Asile d'Aliens de Quebec *see* REPORT OF THE QUEBEC LUNATIC ASYLUM ADDRESSED TO THE...PRIME MINISTER OF THE PROVINCE OF QUEBEC BY THE MEDICAL SUPERINTENDANTS

Quebec. (Province). Assemblee nationale. Commission parlementaire speciale sur les Problemes de la Liberte de Presse *see* LA LIBERTE DE PRESSE

Quebec. (Province). Canada *see*
- LOI DES MINES DE QUEBEC
- QUEBEC STATUTES, SESSION LAWS AND REVISIONS

Quebec. (Province). Canada. Commission... Revision et de la refonte des statuts generaux.. *see* REPORT

Quebec. (Province). Commissaires pour s'enquerir...des chemins a barrieres de la rive nord et de la rive sud a Quebec *see* RAPPORT

Quebec. (Province). Commission de Colonisation *see* RAPPORT

Quebec Province. Commission provinciale d'enquete sur les hopitaux *see* RAPPORT DE LA COMMISSION PROVINCIALE D'ENQUETE SUR LES HOPITAUX

Quebec Province. Commission royale sur les asiles d'alienes *see* RAPPORT DE LA COMMISSION DES ASILES D'ALIENES

Quebec. (Province). Commission royale sur les asiles d'alienes *see* RAPPORT

Quebec. (Province). Commission to Consolidate the General Statutes *see* JUDICIAL REFORMS PROPOSED BY THE COMMISSION FOR THE CODIFICATION OF THE STATUTES. FIRST REPORT.

Quebec (Province). Departement des Terres de la Couronne *see* LE GUIDE DU COLON, PROVINCE DE QUEBEC

Quebec. (Province). Direction Generale de l'Education Permanente *see* LE TEVECOIS

Quebec. (Province). Direction generale des Bois et Forets *see* REVISED REGULATIONS

Quebec. (Province). Laws, Statutes, etc *see*
- CODE CIVIL DU BAS CANADA.
- CODE MUNICIPAL DE LA PROVINCE DE QUEBEC, ANNOTE; COMPRENANT TOUS LES AMENDEMENTS JUSQU'AU 1 JANVIER 1888.
- INDEX GENERAL DES STATUTS DE LA PROVINCE DE QUEBEC DE 1899 A 1928 INC
- LOI DE LA BIBLIOTHEQUE NATIONALE DU QUEBEC
- ORDINANCES MADE FOR THE PROVINCE OF QUEBEC.

Quebec Province. Legislature. Assemblee legislative *see*
- RAPPORT DU COMITE SPECIAL AUQUEL ONT ETE RENVOYES LA CORRESPONDANCE ET LES DOCUMENTS RELATIFS AUX INCENDIES QUI ONT EU LIEU SUR LA COTE DU GOLFE ST LAURENT...
- REPORT OF THE SELECT COMMITTEE OF THE LEGISLATIVE ASSEMBLY OF THE PROVINCE OF QUEBEC ON PUBLIC LANDS AND FORESTS

Quebec. (Province). Legislature. Assemblee legislative. Comite *see*
- RAPPORT...POUR EXAMINER LES LOIS MUNICIPALES ET LES LOIS CONCERNANT... LES ABUS PREJUDICIABLES A L'AGRICULTURE..
- RAPPORT...POUR PRENDRE EN CONSIDERATION LES MEILLEURS MOYENS DE DEVELOPPER L'INDUSTRIE DANS CETTE PROVINCE
- RAPPORT...S'ENQUIRER DE LA TENURE DES TERRES AUX ISLES DE LA MAGDELEINE, COMTE DE GASPE
- REPORT...ON THE WINTER NAVIGATION OF THE RIVER AND GULF OF ST LAWRENCE

Quebec. (Province). Legislature. Assemblee legislative. Comite... relatifs aux incendies...sur la cote du golfe St. Laurent...1867 & 1868 *see* RAPPORT

Quebec. (Province). Legislature. Assemblee legislative. Select Committee on Public Lands and Forests *see* REPORT

Quebec. (Province). Ministere des Affaires Culturelle *see* QUEBEC-AMERIQUE

Quebec. (Province). Ministere des Affaires Culturelles *see*
- CULTURE VIVANTE
- QUEBEC
- VIE MUSICALE

Quebec. (Province). Ministere des Affaires Culturelles. Direction des Communications *see* LA PETITE QUINZAINE

Quebec. (Province). Ministere des communications. Service des communications *see* ANTENNES

Quebec. (Province). Office de la prevention et du traitement de l'alcoolisme et des autres toxicomanies *see* TOXICOMANIES

Quebec. (Province). Office de Planification et de Developpement du Quebec *see* DEVELOPPEMENT-QUEBEC

Quebec. (Province). Office des Communications Sociales *see* NOS LIVRES

Quebec. (Province). Office d'Information et de Publicite *see*
- QUEBEC AT A GLANCE
- LE QUEBEC EN BREF

Quebec. (Province). Secretariat provincial. Bureau de Statistiques *see* ANNUAIRE STATISTIQUE

Quebec. (Province). Syndicat national du rachat des rentes Seigneuriales *see* RELEVES DES TITRES DES RENTES CONSTITUTES DES ANCIENNES SEIGNEURIES DU QUEBEC

Quebec. (Province). Syndicat national du rachat des rentes seigneuriales *see* RAPPORT DES TITRES DES RENTES CONSTITUES DES ANCIENNES SEIGNEURIES DU QUEBEC

Quebec Railway, Light & Power Co *see* QUEBEC, MONTMORENCY FALLS AND ST ANNE DE BEAUPRE

QUEBEC REVISED REPORTS / Canada. Quebec – (Includes 2 index vols) – v1-29. 1726-1891 (all publ) – 208mf – 9 – $312.00 – LLMC 81-083 – us L.L.M.C. [340]

QUEBEC ROUGE : JOURNAL REVOLUTIONNAIRE – Montreal, Canada. n4. 21 nov 1971 – 1r – 1 – Can$25.00 – cn Can Microfilming [072]

THE QUEBEC SPECTATOR – Quebec, Canada. 22 avr-30 oct 1848 – 1r – 1 – Can$35.00 – cn Can Microfilming [072]

THE QUEBEC STAR – (Together with: The Quebec Star/L'Etoile de Quebec 24 aut 1878) – Quebec, Canada. 27 nov 1875-30 sep 1876 – 1r – 1 – Can$35.00 – cn Can Microfilming [072]

QUEBEC STATUTES, SESSION LAWS AND REVISIONS / Quebec. (Province). Canada – (Updates planned) – 1867/68-1945. 1st Parliament to 1940 – 651mf – 9 – $976.00 – LLMC 90-190 – us L.L.M.C. [324]

QUEBEC, SUMMER AND WINTER – 6th ed. Chateau Frontenac, 1896, c1894.04127.(Pre-1900 Canadiana) – 9 – cn C.I.H.M. [910]

QUEBEC TELEGRAPH – Canada. -d. Jan 1922-June 1925. 18 reels – 1 – uk British Libr Newspaper [072]

THE QUEBEC TELEGRAPH / ed by Christie, Robert – Quebec, Canada. 29 avr 1816; 11 mai 1816-14 jul 1817 – 1r – 1 – Can$35.00 – cn Can Microfilming [072]

THE QUEBEC TRANSCRIPT AND GENERAL ADVERTISER – (Cont: The Literary Transcript and General Intelligencer) – Quebec: W Cowan and H Cowan, [1839-18–?] – 9 – cn C.I.H.M. [070]

THE QUEBEC TRANSCRIPT AND GENERAL ADVERTISER *see* THE LITERARY TRANSCRIPT AND GENERAL INTELLIGENCER

QUEBEC YACHTING : REVUE – Montreal, jun/jul 1978-dec 1991 – 4r – 1 – Can$70.00 – cn Can Microfilming [073]

QUEBEC-AMERIQUE : SERVICE DU CANADA FRANCAIS D'OUTRE-FRONTIERES / Quebec. (Province). Ministere des Affaires Culturelle – Quebec, 1967-70. SEM16P293 – 1r – 5 – Can$17.00 – cn Bibl Nat [073]

QUEBEC-CANADA – Montreal, Canada. v1 n1. 1978-v2 n1. jan 1979; jul-aut 1979 – 1r – 1 – Can$25.00 – cn Can Microfilming [072]

QUEBEC-CANADA – Quebec, Canada. v2 n5. jul 1974-v7 n3. mar 1978 – 1r – 1 – Can$40.00 – cn Can Microfilming [072]

THE QUEBEC-CHRONICLE-TELEGRAPH *see* THE CHRONICLE-TELEGRAPH

QUEBEC-FRANCAIS : JOURNAL DE L ASSOCIATION QUEBECOISE DES PROFESSEURS DE FRANCAIS / Association Quebecoise des Professeurs de Francais – Quebec: l'Association, 1970-. SEM35P108 – 9r – 1 – cn Bibl Nat [073]

QUEBEC-FRANCAIS – Montreal, nov 1970 – 1r – 1 – Can$25.00 – cn Can Microfilming [072]

QUEBEC-HISTOIRE : FEDERATION DES SOCIETES D'HISTOIRE DU QUEBEC – Montmagny, Canada. fev/mar 1971-hiver 1973 – 1r – 1 – Can$25.00 – cn Can Microfilming [073]

LE QUEBECOIS : JOURNAL OFFICIEL DU P.Q. – Montreal, 1 sep 1972 – 1r – 1 – Can$25.00 – cn Can Microfilming [073]

LE QUEBECOIS : POLITIQUE ET CULTUREL – Rouyn, Canada. v1 n2. nov 1967 – 1r – 1 – Can$25.00 – cn Can Microfilming [072]

LE QUEBECOIS – Quebec, Canada. 13 sep 1880-v1 n18. oct 1880 – 1r – 1 – Can$25.00 – cn Can Microfilming [072]

LE QUEBECOIS – Quebec, Canada. 20 nov 1909-v1 n15. 19 fev 1910 – 1r – 1 – Can$30.00 – cn Can Microfilming [072]

LE QUEBECOIS LIBRE – Montreal, jun-oct 1972 – 1r – 1 – Can$25.00 – cn Can Microfilming [072]

LA QUEBECOISE / Pare, Emile E – Quebec: Lavigeur and Hutchison, 1904. SEM105P906 – 1mf – 9 – Can$2.25 – cn Bibl Nat [971]

QUEBEC-PRESSE : INDEPENDANT HEBDO – Montreal, 19 oct 1969-10 nov 1974 – 7r – 1 – Can$60.00r – cn Can Microfilming [072]

LES QUEBECQUOISES / Chapman, William – 1876. Quebec: C. Darveau, 1876. 00578. (Pre-1900 Canadiana) – 9 – cn C.I.H.M. [971]

Quecedo, Francisco *see*
- HALLAZGO Y DESCRIPCION DE UNA AUTOBIOGRAFIA DEL PRIMER OBISPO DE MAINAS, DON FRAY HIPOLITO SANCHEZ RANGEL
- EL ILUSTRISIMO FRAY HIPOLITO SANCHEZ RANGEL, PRIMER OBISPO DE MAYNAS

QUEEN ANNA'S NEW WORLD OF WORDS / Florio, John – 1611. 731p. (English Linguistics Series 1500-1800) – 9 – us UMI [420]

"THE QUEEN ANNE CHURCHES" / Lambeth Palace Library – With printed index and published catalogue – 1 – £595.00 – uk World [941]

QUEEN ELIZABETH / Creighton, Mandell – London, New York: Longmans, Green, 1896 – 1mf – us A.T.L.A. [941]

QUEEN ELIZABETH AND HER TIMES : A SERIES OF ORIGINAL LETTERS / ed by Wright, Thomas – London: H. Colburn, 1838. 2v. 1 reel. 1258 – 1 – us U.W. Library [941]

QUEEN MAB : A PHILOSOPHICAL POEM, WITH NOTES / Shelley, Percy Bysshe – London: Printed by P.B. Shelley, 1813 – 1 roll – 1 – 1-55879-851-X – uk Libr Preservation [810]

QUEEN MARY / Tennyson, Alfred, Lord – London: Henry S. King, 1875 – 1 roll – 1 – 1-55879-502-2 – uk Libr Preservation [820]

A QUEEN OF QUEENS AND THE MAKING OF SPAIN / Hare, Christopher pseud – New York: Scribner, 1906. xii,371p., illus – 1 – us U.W. Library [920]

THE QUEEN OF THE AIR : BEING A STUDY OF THE GREEK MYTHS OF CLOUD AND STORM / Ruskin, John – London: Smith, Elder, 1869 – 1 roll – 1 – 1-55879-920-6 – uk Libr Preservation [390]

THE QUEEN'S BIRTH-DAY IN MONTREAL, 24TH MAY, 1879: ORDERS FOR THE MILITARY REVIEW AND SHAM-FIGHT. / Bacon, Thomas – Montreal: Dawson, 1879. 00812. (Pre-1900 Canadiana) – 9 – cn C.I.H.M. [971]

Queens' College. Cambridge *see* MEDIAEVAL MANUSCRIPT COLLECTION

QUEENS COUNTY SENTINEL – Hempstead. N.Y. -w. 1858-98 – 1 – us UMI [071]

QUEEN'S LAW JOURNAL – (Suspended Apr 1974-Spring 1976. Supersedes Intramural Law Journal) – v1-21. 1971-96 – 9 – $303.00 set – us Hein [340]

QUEEN'S NURSING JOURNAL – v. 16-19. 1973-77 – 1,5,6 – us UMI [610]

QUEEN'S QUARTERLY – v1- 1893- 1; v77-5,6; v82- 9 – us UMI [073]

QUEEN'S QUARTERLY – (Current vols available from University Microfilms Inc.) – Kingston. v1-62. 1893/94-1955 – 5 – Can$100.00 – cn Micromedia [073]

Queen's University. Canada. Dept. of History and Political and Economic Science *see* BULLETINS

QUEENS VOICE – Jamaica. N.Y. 1967-1970 – 1 – us UMI [071]

Queensland *see* GOVERNMENT GAZETTE

Queensland. Australia. Parliament *see*
- LEGISLATIVE ASSEMBLY
- LEGISLATIVE COUNCIL
- PARLIAMENTARY DEBATES

QUEENSLAND COUNTRY LIFE – Brisbane, Australia. -m. June 1904-May 1907. 1 reel – 1 – uk British Libr Newspaper [073]

QUEENSLAND FIGARO – Brisbane, Australia. Queensland Figaro and Punch Queensland Punch. -w. May 1883-April 1893. 8 1 2 reels – 1 – uk British Libr Newspaper [072]

QUEENSLAND GOVERNMENT MINING JOURNAL – v1-41. 1900-1940 – 1 – us Princeton Micro [622]

QUEENSLAND GRAZIER AND WOOL AND PRODUCE JOURNAL. (QUEENSLAND GRAZIER AND FARMER) – Brisbane, Australia. 16 May 1902-29 Jun 1922. (Imperfect).-w. 16 reels – 1 – uk British Libr Newspaper [630]

QUEENSLAND INDUSTRIAL GAZETTE – Brisbane, Australia. 11 Mar 1916-23 Dec 1933. (Imperfect).-w. 16 reels – 1 – uk British Libr Newspaper [338]

QUEENSLAND LAW SOCIETY JOURNAL – (1980- 5,6,9) – 1971- – 1 – us UMI [073]

Queensland Legislative Assembly *see* PARLIAMENTARY PAPERS RELATING TO THE PROPOSAL TO SEND MEMBERS OF THE QUEENSLAND DEFENCE FORCE TO THE TRANSVAAL, 1899-1899

QUEENSLAND MERCANTILE GAZETTE – Brisbane, Australia. Aug 1890-Oct 1905.-m. 8 reels – 1 – uk British Libr Newspaper [073]

QUEENSLAND TIMES – Ipswich, Australia. May 1869-Sep 1887.-w. 21mqn reels – 1 – uk British Libr Newspaper [072]

THE QUEENSLANDER – Brisbane, Australia. 4 Feb 1871-29 Oct 1904; 27 May 1905-17 June 1922 (imperfect).-w. 116 reels – 1 – uk British Libr Newspaper [072]

QUEENSTON HEIGHTS: A THRILLING NARRATIVE OF THE FAMOUS BATTLE WHERE GENERAL BROCK DIED DEFENDING HIS COUNTRY: A LECTURE DELIVERED AT DRUMMONDVILLE, ONT., DEC 18, 1889 / Cruikshank, Ernest Alexander – s.l.: s.n., 1890 (Welland Ont.: W. T. Sawle). 03636. (Pre-1900 Canadiana) – 9 – cn C.I.H.M. [971]

QUEENSTOWN FREE PRESS – Queenstown, South Africa. 19 Jan 1859-30 Sept 1901. 39 reels – 1, 16 diazo available at reduced price – sa SA Libr [072]

QUEER PEOPLE AND THEIR KWEER KAPERS: BIRDS THAT TALK, GIANTS THAT FLEE, BEASTS THAT THINK, INSECTS THAT FLIRT, SPRITES THAT DANCE, WITH THEIR VARIOUS ANTICS ILLUSTRATED / Cox, Palmer – Toronto: Rose, 1888. 00271. (Pre-1900 Canadiana) – 9 – cn C.I.H.M. [971]

Quek, Jin-Jong *see* CODING AND DEVELOPMENT OF MOVEMENT RECALL IN LABORATORY AND FIELD SETTINGS

QUEL BUT SE PROPOSENT LES SAINT-SIMONIENS? / Lemonnier, Charles – Montpellier, impr. A. Ricard, 1832, 4 p. Vidal, Edmond. Au peuple de Montpellier. Castelnaudary, L. Groc, 1833, 4 p. Les Saint-Simoniens, 1825-1834. 6933 – 9 – fr Hachette [335]

Quelet, L *see* CLAVIS SYNOPTICA HYMENOMYCETUM EUROPAEORUM

DIE QUELLE DER KANONISCHEN KINDHEITSGESCHTICHTE JESUS' / Conrady, Ludwig – Goettingen: Vandenhoeck & Rup., 1900. 1 fiche – 9 – us A.T.L.A. [240]

DIE QUELLEN DER AELTESTEN KETZERGESCHICHTE / Lipsius, Richard Adelbert – Leipzig: J.A. Barth, 1875 – 1mf – us A.T.L.A. [240]

DIE QUELLEN DER APOSTELGESCHICHTE / Juengst, Johannes – (Includes bibliographical references & appendix) – Gotha: F A Perthes, 1895 – 1mf – 9 – 0-8370-3814-6 – 1985-1814 – us A.T.L.A. [220]

QUELLEN DER BYZANTINISCHEN KUNSTGESCHICHTE / Richter, Jean Paul – O 517w. 1897 – 9 – ne IDC [700]

QUELLEN DER BYZANTINISCHEN KUNSTGESCHICHTE / Unger, Friedrich Wilhelm – O 517 1. 1878 – 9 – ne IDC [700]

DIE QUELLEN DER CHEVY CHASEBALLADE / Sauer, Oskar – Halle-Wittenberg, 1912 – 1mf – DM48.00 – 3-8267-3051-8 – gw Hänsel [420]

DIE QUELLEN DER ROEMISCHEN PETRUSSAGE / Lipsius, Richard Adelbert – (Includes bibliographical references) – Kiel: Schwers, 1872 – 1mf – 9 – 0-8370-5663-2 – 1985-3663 – us A.T.L.A. [920]

DIE QUELLEN DER SOGENANNTEN APOSTOLISCHEN KIRCHENORDNUNG (T.U.U. 1-2/5) / Harnack, Adolf von – Leipzig, 1886 – 2mf – 9 – ne Slangenburg [240]

DIE QUELLEN DER SYNOPTISCHEN UEBERLIEFERUNG (T.U.U. 3-32/3) / Weiss, Bernhard – Leipzig, 1908 – 4mf – 9 – ne Slangenburg [240]

DIE QUELLEN DES JOSEPHUS FUER DIE ZEIT VOM EXIL BIS ZUM JUEDISCHEN KRIEGE / Hoelscher, Gustav – Leipzig: B.G. Teubner, 1904. 1 fiche – 9 – us A.T.L.A. [240]

QUELLEN DES LEBENS JESU = THE SOURCES OF OUR KNOWLEDGE OF THE LIFE OF JESUS / Wernle, Paul – (In English) – London: Philip Green, 1907 – 1mf – 9 – 0-8370-5796-5 – 1985-3796 – us A.T.L.A. [240]

DIE QUELLEN DES LUKASEVANGELIUMS / Weiss, Bernhard – (Includes bibliographical references) – Stuttgart: J G Cotta, 1907 – 1mf – 9 – 0-8370-6452-X – 1986-0452 – us A.T.L.A. [220]

DIE QUELLEN UND DIE ENTSTEHUNGSZEIT VON THOMAS HEYWOOD'S "IRON AGE" / Goebel, Kaete – Jena, 1916 – 1mf – DM48.00 – 3-8267-3068-2 – gw Hänsel [420]

DIE QUELLEN ZU HEINRICH VON KLEISTS MICHAEL KOHLHAAS / ed by Schloesser, Rudolf – Bonn: A Marcus/E Weber, 1913 – 1r – 1 – us U.W. Library [430]

QUELLEN ZUR GESCHICHTE DER DEUTSCHEN KAISERPOLITIK OESTERREICHS WAEHREND DER FRANZOESISCHEN REVOLUTIONSKRIEGE 1790-1801 / Vievento, A & Zeissberg, H von – Wien. 5v. 1873-1890 – 31mf – 9 – ne IDC [943]

DIE QUELLEN ZUR GESCHICHTE DER ENTSTEHUNG DES KIRCHENSTAATES / Haller, Johannes – Leipzig: B.G. Teubner, 1907. (Quellensammlung zur deutschen Geschichte) – 1mf – us A.T.L.A. [240]

QUELLEN ZUR GESCHICHTE DES BAUERNKRIEGS IN DEUTSCHTIROL 1525 / ed by Wopfner, H – (Missing: Pt2) – Innsbruck. 2pts. 1908 – 3mf – 9 – ne IDC [943]

QUELLEN ZUR GESCHICHTE DES CHRISTLICHEN GOTTESDIENSTES / Beckman, J – Guetersloh, 1956 – 6mf – 8 – Dfl25.00 – ne Slangenburg [240]

DIE QUELLEN ZUR GESCHICHTE DES HL. FRANZ VON ASSISI : EINE KRITISCHE UNTERSUCHUNG / Goetz, Walter – Gotha: F.A. Perthes, 1904 – 1mf – us A.T.L.A. [240]

QUELLEN ZUR GESCHICHTE DES PAPSTTUMS / Mirbt, Carl – Freiburg i.B.: J.C.B. Mohr, 1895 – 1mf – us A.T.L.A. [240]

QUELLEN ZUR GESCHICHTE DES PAPSTTUMS UND DES ROEMISCHEN KATHOLIZISMUS / Mirbt, Carl – 1995 – 6mf – 9 – DM118.00 – 3-8267-3158-1 – gw Hänsel [240]

QUELLEN ZUR GESCHICHTE DES ZEITALTERS DER FRANZOESISCHEN REVOLUTION / ed by Hueffer, H – Leipzig, Innsbruck. 2v. 1900-1907 – 22mf – 9 – ne IDC [944]

QUELLENBEITRAEGE U. UNTERS. Z. GESCH. DER GOTTESBEWEISE IM DREIZEHNTEN JAHRHT. / Daniels, A – Muenster, 1909 – 4mf – 8 – ne Slangenburg [120]

DIE QUELLENBERICHTE IN JOSUA 1-12 : BEITRAG ZUR QUELLENKRITIK DES HEXATEUCHS / Albers, Emanuel – Bonn: Otto Paul, 1891 – 1mf – 9 – 0-8370-2058-1 – 1985-0058 – us A.T.L.A. [220]

QUELLENBUCH ZUR GESCHICHTE DER INNEREN MISSION / Hennig, M – Hamburg: Agentur des Rauhen Hauses, 1912 – 2mf – us A.T.L.A. [240]

QUELLENBUCH ZUR KUNSTGESCHICHTE DES ABENDLAENDISCHEN MITTELALTERS / Schlosser, Julius von – O 517v. 1896 – 9 – ne IDC [940]

QUELLENKRITISCHE UNTERSUCHUNGEN ZU PLUTARCHS ALEXANDERBIOGRAPHIE / Rabe, Inge – Hamburg, 1964 – 1 – DM30.00 – gw Mikro Press [920]

QUELLENMAESSIGE DARLEGUNG DER LEHRE VON DER WILLENSFREIHEIT BEI THOMAS VON AQUIN : MIT BERUECKSICHTIGUNG DERSELBEN LEHRE BEI DUNS SKOTUS / Schieefferens, Matthias – Muenster i. W: Johannes Bredt, 1904 – 1mf – 9 – 0-8370-5302-1 – 1985-3302 – us A.T.L.A. [210]

QUELLENSCHRIFTEN FUER KUNSTGESCHICHTE UND KUNSTTECHNIK DES MITTELALTERS UND DER RENAISSANCE – (Cont as: Quellenschriften ... und der Neuzeit. NS. v1-15. 1888-1908) – Wien. v1-18. 1871-82 – 154mf – 9 – O-517/1 – ne IDC [700]

QUELLENSCHRIFTEN ... UND DER NEUZEIT *see* QUELLENSCHRIFTEN FUER KUNSTGESCHICHTE UND KUNSTTECHNIK DES MITTELALTERS UND DER RENAISSANCE

QUELLENSTUDIEN ZU JOH. H. VOSS' ODEN / Meyenburg, Erwin – (Includes bibliographical references) – Berlin: E Ebering, [1916?] – 1r – 1 – us U.W. Library [430]

QUELLENSTUDIEN ZUR HOLLAENDISCHEN KUNSTGESCHICHTE – Haag. v1-15. 1893-1928 – 72mf – 9 – O-518/1 – ne IDC [700]

QUELLENVERHAELTNISS VON WIELANDS OBERON / Koch, Max – (Includes bibliographical references) – Marburg: N G Elwert, 1880 – 1r – 1 – us U.W. Library [430]

QUELLES RESSOURCES DOCUMENTAIRES POUR L'EDUCATION AU DEVELOPPEMENT ET A LA FRANCOPHONIE? : COMMUNICATION ET INTERACTIONS DANS LE SYSTEME EDUCATIF / Tiran, Michel – 1mf – 9 – 10254 – fr Atelier National [440]

QUELQUES ERREURS HISTORIQUES A CORRIGER / Dugas, Georges – s.l.: s.n., 1896?. 05194. (Pre-1900 Canadiana) – 9 – cn C.I.H.M. [971]

QUELQUES LETTRES SUR DES QUESTIONS ACTUELLES ET SUR DES EVENEMENTS RECENTS / Loisy, Alfred Firmin – Ceffonds: A Loisy, 1908 – 1mf – 9 – 0-8370-8691-4 – 1986-2691 – us A.T.L.A. [240]

QUELQUES MOTS SUR LA LITTERATURE CANADIENNE-FRANCAISE : CAUSERIE LUE DEVANT L'OTTAWA LITERARY AND SCIENTIFIC SOCIETY, LE 14 JA / St Aubin, Emmanuel Blain de – Montreal: E. Senegal, 1871. 00150. (Pre-1900 Canadiana) – 9 – cn C.I.H.M. [440]

QUELQUES OBSERVATIONS A PROPOS DE L'ORGANIZATION DU TRAVAIL / Fraysse, C B – Paris. 1845. (La Condition Ouvriere. Part Two.) – 9 – 2.50 – fr Bibl Nationale [360]

QUELQUES OBSERVATIONS SUR L'ANTIQUITE DE LA DECLINAISON DANS LES LANGUES SEMITIQUES / Derenbourg, Hartwig – (Includes bibliographical references) – Paris: Imprimerie Imperiale, 1868 – 1mf – 9 – 0-8370-7135-6 – 1986-1135 – us A.T.L.A. [470]

QUELQUES PAGES D'HISTOIRE EXACTE : SOIT LES PROCES CRIMINELS INTENTES A GENEVE, EN 1547, POUR HAUTE TRAHISON CONTRE NO. AMI PERRIN / Galiffe, J BG – Geneve: [s.n.], 1862 – 1mf – us A.T.L.A. [340]

QUELQUES PARTICULARITES SUR LE MOUVEMENT DE LA POPULATION DANS LE DEPARTEMENT DE L'YONNE / Duche, Emile – Reprod. d'un extrait du Bulletin de la Ste. medicale de l'Yonne. Auxerre: C. Gallot, 1864. 26p. tabl.1 fiche. (Statistics Series: Demography) – 9 – 6.00 – fr Bibl Nationale [310]

QUELQUES RECHERCHES SUR LE DIALECTE FLAMAND EN FRANCE / Carnel, D & Coussemaker, Charles Edmond Henri de – Proverbes et Locutions proverbiale chez les Flamands de France. Dunkerque: B. Kien, 1859. 68p. 1 fiche. (Language Collection) – 9 – 6.00 – fr Bibl Nationale [430]

QUELQUES REFLEXIONS SUR L'EMPLOI DES ENFANTS DANS LES FABRIQUES ET SUR LES MOYENS D'EN PREVENIR LES ABUS / Gillet – (Condition of 19th C. French working class series). 1840 – 9 – fr Hachette [331]

QUELUZ DE MINAS – Queluz de Minas, 10-24 Sep 1931; Jan, Apr, Jun-Jul, Sep-Dec 1932; Jan-Apr, Jun-Sep, Nov-Dec 1933; Jan-Dec 1934; Jan, Mar-May, Aug, Oct, Dec 1935; Jan-6 Feb 1936 – 1,5,6 – bl Biblioteca [072]

O QUELUZIANO – Queluz, 10 Jul-Nov 1910; 11-25 Apr 1912 – 1,5,6 – bl Biblioteca [072]

Quemada, Bernard *see* ARCHIVE OF FRENCH LINGUISTICS: 1500-1900

Quennell, Marjorie (Courtney) *see* EVERYDAY LIFE IN THE OLD STONE AGE

Quenstedt, F A von *see* HANDBUCH DER PETRE FAKTENKUNDE

Quentel, P *see* EIN NEW KUNSTLICH MODELBUCH

Quentin, Henri *see* JEAN-DOMINIQUE MANSI ET LES GRANDES COLLECTIONS CONCILIAIRES

Quer y Martinez, J *see* FLORA ESPANOLA

Queral, Maria A *see* INDUSTRIAS PALEOLITICAS EN EL TRAMO EXTREMENO DEL TAJO

LA QUERELA PACIS / Erasmus, Desiderius – 1924 – 1 – us A.T.L.A. [240]

QUERELA PACIS... / Erasmus of Rotterdam – N.p., [1519] – 1mf – 1 – ILM-711/1 – ne IDC [327]

Queretaro. Mexico (State) *see* LA SEMBRA DE ARTEAGA

Queri, Georg *see* SCHNURREN UDN SPAESSE

Quero, J C et al *see* CHECKLIST OF THE FISHES OF THE EASTERN TROPICAL ATLANTIC (CLOFETA)

LA QUERRA SEPARATISTA DE CUBA... / Casas, J B – Madrid, 1896 – 6mf – 1 – ILM-1694/1 – ne IDC [327]

DER QUERSCHNITT – Dusseldorf, 1921-36 – 9r – 1 – £520.00 – uk Chadwyck [760]

Quesada, Alba Alonso de *see* TOWARDS A CULTURAL POLICY FOR HONDURAS

QUESNAY ET LA PHYSIOCRATIE / Guyot, Yves – Paris: Guillaumin, 1896. lxxix,98p – 1 – us U.W. Library [330]

Quesnel, Joseph *see* COLAS ET COLINETTE OU LE BAILLI DUPE

QUEST – (v. 17- 1972- 5,6. v. 23- 1975- 9) – v. 1-. 1963- – 1 – us UMI [073]

QUEST – (v1-9 1972-80 Can$28.00y. v10-13 1981-84 Can$37.00y) – Toronto. v1-13. 1972-84 – 9 – cn Micromedia [073]

THE QUEST FOR THE HISTORICAL JESUS / Schweitzer, Albert – 1911 – 9 – $15.00 – us I.R.C. [240]

THE QUEST OF FAITH: BEING NOTES ON THE CURRENT PHILOSOPHY OF RELIGION / Saunders, Thomas Bailey – London: A.& C. Black, 1899. 1 fiche – 9 – us A.T.L.A. [240]

THE QUEST OF THE INFINITE : OR, THE PLACE OF REASON AND MYSTERY IN RELIGIOUS EXPERIENCE / Millard, Benjamin Albert – New York:Eaton & Mains; Cincinnati:Jennings & Graham, 1907 – 1mf – 9 – 0-8370-4428-6 – 1985-2428 – us A.T.L.A. [240]

A QUESTAO DAS MISSOES ESTUDADA A LUZ DOS DOCUMENTOS HISTORICOS – Rio de Janeiro, 1891 – 3mf – 9 – ILM-1783/1 – ne IDC [340]

QUESTAO DE SUCCESSAO / Aflalo, S – Lisboa, 1886 – 1mf – 9 – ILM-3832/1 – ne IDC [340]

A QUESTAO DO...EM PORTUGAL NO SECULO 28 / Pereira da Silva, Antonio – Braga, 1964; Madrid: Graficas Calleja, 1966 – 1 – sp Bibl Santa Ana [946]

QUESTION – (1974-80. 1,5,6. 1975-80. 1,5,6,9) – 1884-1980 – 1 – us UMI [073]

LA QUESTION ACADIENNE ET LE RAPPORT SUR LES ARCHIVES DU CANADA POUR 1894 / Casgrain, Henri-Raymond – Quebec, 1895. 02542. (Pre-1900 Canadiana) – 9 – cn C.I.H.M. [971]

LA QUESTION BIBLIQUE CHEZ LES CATHOLIQUES DE FRANCE AU 19E SIECLE / Houtin, Albert – (Includes index) – 2e ed. Paris: Alphonse Picard, 1902 – 1mf – 9 – 0-8370-3676-3 – 1985-1676 – us A.T.L.A. [220]

LA QUESTION CHINOISE... / Cailleux, E – Paris, 1898 – 3mf – 1 – ILM-349/1 – ne IDC [327]

LA QUESTION DE BOSPHORE... / Dascovici, N – Geneve, 1915 – 4mf – 1 – ILM-2194/1 – ne IDC [327]

QUESTION DE DROIT MARITIME / Courcy, A de – Paris. 4v. 1877-1888 – 21mf – 1 – ILM-3247/1 – ne IDC [327]

LA QUESTION DE L'EMPLOYE EN FRANCE: ETUDE SOCIALE ET PROFESSIONNELLE / Artaud, Adrien Jean Marie – Paris. 1909. (La Condition Ouvriere. Part Two.) – 9 – 6.00 – fr Bibl Nationale [360]

LA QUESTION DES HUISSIERS : LES AFFAIRES COMMERCIALES / Xau, Fernand-Arthur-Pierre – Paris: A. Savine, 1890 – fr Armell [340]

LA QUESTION DES NEUTRES... / Campet, E – Paris, 1910 – 2mf – 9 – ILM-360/1 – ne IDC [327]

LA QUESTION DES REGLEMENTS D'ATELIER / Lalle, Henri – Paris. 1904. (La Condition Ouvriere. Part Two.) – 9 – 5.00 – fr Bibl Nationale [360]

LA QUESTION DU BOSPHORE... / Dascovici, N – Geneve, 1915 – 4mf – 1 – ILM-466/1 – ne IDC [327]

LA QUESTION DU DANUBE / Geffcken, F H – Berlin, 1883 – 1mf – 1 – ILM-1827/1 – ne IDC [327]

LA QUESTION DU DANUBE,... / Demorgny, G – Paris, 1911 – 5mf – 1 – ILM-501/1 – ne IDC [327]

LA QUESTION DU JOUR, RESTERONS-NOUS FRANCAIS / Faucher de Saint-Maurice, Narcisse – s.l.: s.n., 1890 (Quebec: Belleau). 03073. (Pre-1900 Canadiana) – 9 – cn C.I.H.M. [971]

LA QUESTION DU VASE DE SANG / Trochon, Charles – Paris: A. Franck, 1872. 1 fiche – 9 – us A.T.L.A. [240]

LA QUESTION ELECTORALE: DEUX LETTRES A PAUL DEROULEDE AVEC LA REPONSE DE CELUI-CI DE CANADA-TRANSVAAL / Arou, Joseph – Paris?, 1900? 04103. (Pre-1900 Canadiana) – 9 – cn C.I.H.M. [971]

QUESTION EN LA QUAL SE INTENTA AVERIGUAR COMO Y DE QUE VENAS Y DE QUE PARTE...SE DEBA SANGRAR / Ahumada, P – Sevilla, 1653 – 1mf – 9 – sp Cultura [610]

A QUESTION IN BAPTIST HISTORY : WHETHER THE ANABAPTISTS IN ENGLAND PRACTICED IMMERSION BEFORE THE YEAR 1641? / Whitsitt, William H – Louisville, Ky.: Chas. T. Dearing, 1896 – 1mf – us A.T.L.A. [240]

A QUESTION IN BAPTIST HISTORY / Whitsitt, William H – 1896 – 1 – 5.95 – us Baptist [240]

THE QUESTION OF A DOMINION PROHIBITORY LAW: CONSIDERED IN ITS FINANCIAL, MORAL AND RELIGIOUS ASPECTS / Hardgrave, Wakefield – Toronto: Authors' Publ., 1897. 05357. (Pre-1900 Canadiana) – 9 – cn C.I.H.M. [971]

THE QUESTION OF COPYRIGHT : COMPRISING THE TEXT (OF THE U.S. LAW) AND A SUMMARY OF THE LAWS OF (MAJOR FOREIGN COUNTRIES) / Putnam, George Haven – 3rd rev ed. New York: Putnam, 1904 – 6mf – 9 – $9.00 – LLMC 82-310 – us L.L.M.C. [340]

THE QUESTION OF DIVORCE / Gore, Charles – New York: Scribner, 1911 – 1mf – us A.T.L.A. [240]

THE QUESTION OF WEST IRIAN / Indonesia. Kementerian Luar Negeri – SE-4009 1. 1955 – 9 – ne IDC [324]

LA QUESTION OUVRIERE / Du Maroussem, P – (Condition of 19th C. French working class series). 1891-96 – 9 – fr Hachette [360]

LA QUESTION PERSANE... / Demorgny, G – Paris, 1916 – 4mf – 1 – ILM-502/1 – ne IDC [327]

LA QUESTION POLONAISE / Dmowski, R – Trans. by Gasztowtt. Paris. 1909. BR-5491 2 – 8 – ne IDC [943]

LA QUESTION SIAMOISE... / Debect, H – La Rochelle, 1904 – 2mf – 1 – ILM-483/1 – ne IDC [327]

LA QUESTION SICILIANA / Gennuso, Giuseppo – 1945 – 1 – us Res Libr [945]

LA QUESTION SOCIALE – Paris. janv-juil 1885, oct 1891-92, mai 1894, 1896-avr 1898 – 1 – fr A.C.R.P.P. [073]

LA QUESTION SOCIALE – Revue mensuelle de sociologie anarchiste. Brussels. Belgium. -m. Jun Jul, Sep Oct 1890, Jan Feb, May Aug 1894. (14 ft) – 1 – uk British Libr Newspaper [073]

QUESTION SOCIALE. LE SUBLIME OU LE TRAVAILLEUR COMME IL EST EN 1870 ET CE QU'IL PEUT ETRE / Poulot, DP Denis – (Condition of 19th C. French working class series). 1872 – 9 – fr Hachette [360]

THE QUESTION WHETHER IT BE RIGHT TO TURN METHODIST CONSIDERED IN A DIALOGUE BETWEEN TWO MEMBERS OF THE CHURCH OF ENGLAND – London, 1745 – 1mf – 9 – MP-324/1 – ne IDC [240]

THE QUESTION-BOX ANSWERS : REPLIES TO QUESTIONS RECEIVED ON MISSIONS TO NON-CATHOLICS / Conway, Bertrand Louis – (Includes indexes) – New York: Catholic Book Exchange, 1903 – 2mf – 9 – 0-8370-8329-X – 1986-2329 – us A.T.L.A. [230]

LA QUESTIONE DELLA RIFORMA DEL CALENDARIO NEL QUINTO CONCILIO LATERANENSE / Marzi, D – Firenze, 1896 – Dfl28.00 – ne Slangenburg [240]
LA QUESTIONE DI PAPA LIBERIO / Savio, Fedele – (Includes bibliographical references) – Roma: Federico Pustet, 1907 – 1mf – 9 – 0-8370-8547-0 – 1986-2547 – us A.T.L.A. [240]
LA QUESTIONE SOCIALE – Organo comunista anarchico. Florence. Italy. -w. Dec 1883-Aug 1884. (1 reel) – 1 – uk British Libr Newspaper [072]
LA QUESTIONE SOCIALE – Paterson, NJ, July 15, 1895-Nov. 4, 1916 – 5r – 1 – us I.H.R.C. [978]
QUESTIONES MUSICAE IN USUM SCHOLAE NORTHUSIANAE / Spangenberg, Johann – P 762. 1536 – 9 – ne IDC [780]
QUESTIONES PHISICALES / Lax, Gaspar – Zaragoza, 1527 – 1 – us U.W. Library [530]
QUESTIONI DI DIRITTO INTERNAZIONALE ... / Bonolis, G – Pisa, 1908 – 3mf – 9 – ILM-3634/1 – ne IDC [327]
QUESTIONI INTERNAZIONALI... / Bufalini, F – Milano, 1879 – 7mf – 1 – ILM-3673/1 – ne IDC [327]
LE QUESTIONNAIRE ANNOTE DU CODE CIVIL DU BAS-CANADA / Beaudry, Edouard Alexis – Montreal: C.O. Beauchemin & Valois, 1872. 06697. (Pre-1900 Canadiana) – 9 – cn C.I.H.M. [340]
QUESTIONS ADAPTED TO THE LECTURES OF REV. A.A. HODGE, D.D. ON DIDACTIC, HISTORICAL AND POLEMICAL THEOLOGY IN THE WESTERN THEOLOGICAL SEMINARY, ALLEGHENY CITY, PENNSYLVANIA : ILLUSTRATED BY QUOTATIONS FROM THE PRINCIPAL CREEDS OF THE CATHOLIC, LUTHERAN AND REFORMED CHURCHES – Pittsburgh: Davis, Clarke, 1867 – 1mf – 9 – 0-8370-7277-8 – 1986-1277 – us A.T.L.A. [240]
QUESTIONS AND ANSWERS ON CRIMINAL LAW AND PROCEDURE. / Shipp, Eli Richard – Washington, D.C.: Byrne, 1902. 81p. LL-589 – 1 – us L of C Photodup [340]
QUESTIONS AND ANSWERS ON LAW / Kinne, Asa – New York, Cornish, Lamport, 1852-55. 11 v. LL-825 – 1 – us L of C Photodup [340]
QUESTIONS AND ANSWERS ON PARTNERSHIP. / Shipp, Eli Richard – Washington, D.C.: Byrne, 1905. 90p. LL-284 – 1 – us L of C Photodup [340]
QUESTIONS AND ANSWERS ON TWENTY-FIVE OF THE MOST IMPORTANT LEGAL SUBJECTS / Owen, Wilber Allen – 2d ed. St. Paul: West, 1900. 613p. LL-306 – 1 – us L of C Photodup [340]
QUESTIONS AND ANSWERS TO PAST BAR EXAMINATION QUESTIONS / Ginsberg, Hyman – Baltimore 1934. LL-617 – 1 – us L of C Photodup [340]
QUESTIONS AND ANSWERS TO THE CIVIL CODE OF LOUISIANA – New Orleans Andree, 1923. 112 p. LL-1354 – 1 – us L of C Photodup [340]
QUESTIONS AND ANSWERS WITH PROBLEMS AND ILLUSTRATIVE MATTER ON CONFLICT OF LAWS. / Henderson, James Max – Chicago: Callaghan, 1932. 59p. LL-845 – 1 – us L of C Photodup [340]
QUESTIONS AND ANSWERS WITH PROBLEMS AND ILLUSTRATIVE MATTER ON THE LAW OF DOMESTIC RELATIONS / Henderson, James Max – Chicago: Callaghan, 1932. 102p. LL-415 – 1 – us L of C Photodup [340]
QUESTIONS AND ANSWERS WITH PROBLEMS AND ILLUSTRATIVE MATTER ON THE LAW OF EQUITY. / Henderson, James Max – Chicago: Callaghan, 1932. 112p. LL-396 – 1 – us L of C Photodup [340]
QUESTIONS AND ANSWERS WITH PROBLEMS AND ILLUSTRATIVE MATTER ON THE LAW OF SALES. / Henderson, James Max – Chicago: Callaghan, 1933. 80p. LL-271 – 1 – us L of C Photodup [340]
QUESTIONS AND PHASES OF MODERN MISSIONS / Ellinwood, Frank Field – New York: Dodd, Mead, 1899 – 1mf – 9 – 0-8370-6114-8 – 1986-0114 – us A.T.L.A. [240]
LES QUESTIONS BRULANTES DU JOUR: ELECTEURS, PRENEZ ET LISEZ – Quebec: Belleau, 1891. 03181. (Pre-1900 Canadiana) – 9 – cn C.I.H.M. [971]
QUESTIONS COLONIALES / Regismanset, Charles – Paris: E Larose, 1912-23 – us Res Libr [960]
QUESTIONS DE DROIT MARITIME... / Hautefeuille, L B – Paris, 1868 – 5mf – 1 – ILM-194/1 – ne IDC [327]
LES QUESTIONS DE NATIONALITE EN EGYPTE / Assabghy, A & Bey, E Colombani – Le Caire, 1926 – 3mf – 9 – ILM-3912/1 – ne IDC [340]
QUESTIONS DE TACTIQUE APPLIQUEE TRAITEES DE 1858 A 1882 AU GRAND ETAT-MAJOR ALLEMAND: THEMES, SOLUTIONS ET CRITIQUES DU MARECHAL / Moltke, Helmuth Karl Bernhard von – Paris. L. Baudoin. 1895. ix, 299p. Atlas de 27 cartes and 11 croquis. (Strategy of War Series) – 9 – fr Hachette [355]
QUESTIONS D'ECONOMIQUE POLITIQUE ET DE DROIT PUBLIQUE,II / Molinari, Gustave de – 1854-65. 4 fiches (24x) – 9 – 1.00f – at Libertarian Micro [320]
QUESTIONS DES TRAVAILLEURS: L'AMELIORATION DU SORT DES OUVRIERS. LES SALAIRES, L'ORGANISATION DU TRAVAIL / Chevalier, Michel – (Condition of 19th C. French working class series). 1848 – 9 – fr Hachette [360]
QUESTIONS D'HISTOIRE ET D'ARCHEOLOGIE CHRETIENNE / Guiraud, Jean – Paris: V. Lecoffre, 1906 – 1mf – us A.T.L.A. [930]
QUESTIONS D'HISTOIRE LITTERAIRE MISES EN RAPPORT AVEC LE PROGRAMME DE L'UNIVERSITE LAVAL / Charland, Paul Victor – Quebec: Mercier, 1884. 00581. (Pre-1900 Canadiana) – 9 – cn C.I.H.M. [410]
QUESTIONS D'HISTOIRE SOCIALE ET RELIGIEUSE : EPOQUE FEODALE / Imbart de la Tour, Pierre – Paris: Hachette, 1907 – 1mf – us A.T.L.A. [940]
QUESTIONS DIPLOMATIQUES ET COLONIALES : REVUE DE POLITIQUE EXTERIEURE – Paris. 37v. 1897-1914 – 316mf – 9 – ILM-3900/1 – ne IDC [327]
QUESTIONS DU JOUR – no. 1-9. Paris. 1934-avr 1936 – 1 – fr A.C.R.P.P. [073]
QUESTIONS ET REPONSES SUR LE DROIT CIVIL DU BAS-CANADA / Perrault, Joseph Francois – 1810. SEM16P77 – 1r – 5 – Can$9.00 – cn Bibl Nat [971]
QUESTIONS FOR LAW STUDENTS ON COOLEY'S CONSTITUTIONAL LIMITATIONS / Farwell, William Washington – Chicago, Legal News Company, 1886. 83 p. LL-168 – 1 – us L of C Photodup [340]
QUESTIONS FOR LAW STUDENTS ON STORY'S EQUITY PLEADINGS / Farwell, William Washington – Chicago, Chicago Legal News Co., 1883. 98 p. LL-17 – 1 – us L of C Photodup [340]
QUESTIONS FOR THE USE OF STUDENTS IN THE JUNIOR LAW CLASS OF COLUMBIAN UNIVERSITY / Cox, Walter Smith – Washington, D.C., Morrison, 1894. 174 p. LL-400 – 1 – us L of C Photodup [340]
THE QUESTIONS OF KING MILINDA : PART 1 / ed by Mueller, Friedrich Max – (Translated from the Pali by T.W. Rhys Davids) – 1890 – 7mf – 8 – ne Slangenburg [280]
THE QUESTIONS OF KING MILINDA : PART 2 / ed by Mueller, Friedrich Max – (Translated from the Pali by T.W. Rhys Davids) – 1894 – 7mf – 8 – ne Slangenburg [280]
QUESTIONS OF MODERN THOUGHT : OR, LECTURES ON THE BIBLE AND INFIDELITY / McCosh, James et al – Philadelphia: Ziegler & McCurdy, 1871 – 1mf – 9 – 0-8370-4816-8 – 1985-2916 – us A.T.L.A. [220]
QUESTIONS OF THE SOUL / Hecker, Isaac Thomas – 6th ed. New York: Catholic Publ House, 1868, c1855 – 1mf – 9 – 0-8370-6740-5 – 1986-0740 – us A.T.L.A. [230]
QUESTIONS SEIGNEURIALES : COMPILATION CONTENANT L'ACTE SEIGNEURIAL DE 1854, L'AMENDEMENT A L'ACTE SEIGNEURIAL DE 1855 (1854).. – Quebec: Imp. Augustin Cote. Montreal: Bureau de la Minerve, 1856. SEM105P244 – 13mf – 9 – Can$29.25 – cn Bibl Nat [340]
QUESTIONS SUBMITTED BY A SPECIAL COMMITTEE ON THE HOUSE OF ASSEMBLY OF LOWER CANADA TO THE CURATES OF THE DIOCESE OF QUEBEC / Canada. Bas-Canada. Parlement. Chambre d'Assemblee – Quebec: Printed by Neilson's Cowan, 1832. SEM105P129 – 5mf – 9 – Can$11.25 – cn Bibl Nat [324]
QUESTIONS SUR LE GOUVERNEMENT ECCLESIASTIQUE DU DISTRICT DE MONTREAL / Chaboillez, Augustin – Montreal: de l'imprimerie de Thos. A Turner, 1823. SEM16P122 – 1r – 5 – Can$9.00 – cn Bibl Nat [240]
QUESTIONS SUR LESQUELLES LES COMMUNES DE LA REPUBLIQUE SONT PRIEES DE FOURNIR DES SOLUTIONS AU MINISTRE DE L'INTERIEUR / France – S. 1 – 9 – fr Hachette [944]
QUESTOES AFRICANAS : FORNECIMENTO D'ARMAS AOS MATABELLES, ZAMBEZIA BRITANICAE E O TERRITORIO DOS SWASIS... / Machado, Joaquim Jose – (Filmed with Barahona e Costa, Henrique Cesar da Silva: Apontamentos para a historia de guerra de Zambezia 1871-75; and others) – Lisboa: Typ do Commercio de Portugal, 1889 – us Res Libr [960]
THE QUESTYONARY OF CYRURGYENS / Guido (Chauliac, Gui de) – Trans. by R. Copland. M 364. 1541 – 9 – ne IDC [610]
Quetelet, Adolphe Lambert Jacques *see*
– DE L'INFLUENCE DES SAISONS SUR LA MORTALITE AUX DIFFERENS AGES DANS LA BELGIQUE
– DU SYSTEME SOCIAL ET DES LOIS QUI LE REAGISSENT
– MEMOIRE SUR LES LOIS DES NAISSANCES ET DE LA MORTALITE A BRUXELLES
– RECHERCHES SUR LA POPULATION, LES NAISSANCES, LES DECES, LES PRISONS, LES DEPOTS DE MENDICITE, ETC...DANS LE ROYAUME DES PAYS-BAS
– SUR LES ANCIENS RECENSEMENTS DE LA POPULATION BELGE
– SUR L'HOMME ET LE DEVELOPPEMENT DE SES FACULTES OU ESSAI DE PHYSIQUE SOCIALE
Quetif, J *see*
– SCRIPTORES ORDINIS PRAEDICATORUM
Quetineau, Pierre *see* MEMOIRE JUSTIFICATIF POUR P. QUETINEAU, COMMANDANT EN CHEF LES TROUPES REUNIES A THOUARS
Quevedo y Quintano, Pedro *see*
– MANIFIESTO...ORENSE A LA..
– REPRESENTACION...DIRIGIDA...CONSEJO DE REGENCIA
QUFU KONGFU DANGAN SHILIAO XUABIAN, DISANBIAN: QINGDAI DANGAN SHILIAO, DISANCE: GONGFU ZUZHINYU ZHIZHANG, SHANG – Selection of archival materials in the Confucian Mansion at Qufu, Part 3: Materials of the Qing Dynasty, v3: Governmental organizations and duties, part 1. Comp. by the History Department of Shandong University. 11 fiches. F-H183 – 9 – $27.00 – cc Microforms [950]
QUFU KONGFU DANGAN SHILIAO XUANBIAN, DIERBIAN: MINGDAI DANGAN SHILIAO – Selection of archival materials in the Confucian Mansion at Qufu, Part 2: Materials of the Ming Dynasty. Comp. by the Institute of History, Chinese Academy of Social Sciences. 4 fiches.F-H179 – 9 – $18.00 – cc Microforms [950]
QUFU KONGFU DANGAN SHILIAO XUANBIAN, DISANBIAN: QINGDAI DANGAN, DI SHIWU CE: SHANGYE,GAOLIDAI, GONG, NONG, WUJIA – Selection of archival materials in the Confucian Mansion at Qufu, Part: 3: Materials of the Qing Dynasty, v15: Commerce, usury, labour, food, prices. Comp. by the History Department of Shandong University. 4 fiches. F-H181 – 9 – $18.00 – cc Microforms [950]
QUFU KONGFU DANGAN SHILIAO XUANBIAN, DISANBIAN: QINGDAI DANGAN, DIERCE: SHENGXIAN HOUYI – Selection of archival materials in the Confucian Mansion at Qufu, Part 3: Materials of the Qing Dynasty, v2: Descendants of sages and wise men. Comp. by the History Department of Shandong University. 4 fiches. F-H182 – 9 – $18.00 – cc Microforms [950]
QUFU KONGFU DANGAN SHILIAO XUANBIAN, DISANBIAN: QINGDAI DANGAN, DILIUCE: GONGFU TIANCHAN, SHANG – Selection of archival materials in the Confucian Mansion at Qufu, Part 3: Archives of the Qing Dynasty, v6: Public estates, part 1. Comp. by the Institute of History, Chinese Academy of Social Sciences. 7 fiches. F-H185 – 9 – $31.50 – cc Microforms [950]
QUFU KONGFU DANGAN SHILIAO XUANBIAN, DISANBIAN: QINGDAI DANGAN DIWUCE – Selection of archival materials in the Confucian Mansion at Qufu, Part 3: Archives of the Qing Dynasty, v5. Comp. by the History Department of the Qufu Normal College. 4 fiches. F-H184 – 9 – $18.00 – cc Microforms [950]
QUFU KONGFU DANGAN SHILIAO XUANBIAN, DISANBIAN: QINGDAI DANGAN SHILIAO, DIYICE – Selection of archival materials in the Confucian Mansion at Qufu, Part 3: Materials of the Qing Dynasty, v1. Comp. by the History Department of the Qufu Normal College. 4 fiches. F-H180 – 9 – $31.50 – cc Microforms [950]
QUFU KONGFU DANGAN SHILIAO XUANBIAN, DIYIBIAN: QUANZONG LEI MULU SUOYIN – Selection of archival materials in the Confucian Mansion at Qufu, Part 1: A general index to the complete holdings. Comp. by the Qufu Management Board for Cultural Relics. 10 fiches. F-H178 – 9 – $45.00 – cc Microforms [950]
QUI? : REVUE MUSICALE, LITTERAIRE ET DES ARTS – Montreal, printemps 1949-jun 1954 – 1r – 1 – Can$35.00 – cn Can Microfilming [073]
QUI VEULENT DONC CES FEMINISTES? – Paris: Giard, 1926. viii,75p. (Les Femmes Collection) – 1mf – 9 – $6.00 – fr Bibl Nationale [305]
QUI VIVE – London, UK. Organe de la Democratie universelle. 3 Oct-11 Dec 1871 – 1 – uk British Libr Newspaper [072]
QUI VIVE – no. 1-60. Londres. 3 oct-11 dec 1871 – 1 – fr A.C.R.P.P. [073]
Quicherat, L M *see* TRAITE DE VERSIFICATION FRANCAISE
Quick, Birney McNabb *see* PAPERS
QUICK FROZEN FOODS – Aug 1938-Mar 1941 – 1 – us UMI [660]
QUICK FROZEN FOODS – (v44- 1981- 5,6,9) – v15- 1952- – 1 – us UMI [660]
QUICK FROZEN FOODS AND THE LOCKER PLANT – Apr 1941-Aug 1952 – 1 – us UMI [660]
Quick, Robert Hebert *see* ESSAYS ON EDUCATIONAL REFORMERS
Quick, S P *see* WORLD SERIES CRICKET, TELEVISION AND AUSTRALIAN CULTURE
THE QUICK YEARS / Arliss, Jean – Napa Co, 1958 – 1r – 1 – $50.00 – B40242 – us Library Micro [978]
Quickert, Carl *see* PAST AND PRESENT OF WASHINGTON COUNTY
QUID INTERSIT INTER CONFOEDERATIONEM CIVITATUM... / Cohn, G – Gryphiae, 1868 – 1mf – 1 – ILM-1508/1 – ne IDC [327]
QUID NUNC – Wellington. Kan. -w. 1887-88 – 1 – us UMI [071]
QUIEN ES EL GENERAL PERON : LA DOCTRINA DEL SINDICALISMO JUSTICIALISTA: SU MISI ON EVOLUTIVA: LOS SABOTEADORES / Caviglia, Hector – Buenos Aires: Caviglia, 1954 – 1 – CSUXADM8817-B – us Hoover Inst Photo [320]
QUIEN ES QUIEN EN LA ARGENTINA – (Includes c.1: 1947, 1958/59, 1969) – Buenos Aires: G. Kraft, 1939- – 1 – CSUXAHZ2488-S – us Hoover Inst Photo [920]
Quien, M Le, OP *see* ORIENS CHRISTIANUS
QUIEN MATO A ROSENDO / Walsh, Rodolfo J – [Buenos Aires]: Editorial Tiempo Contempor aneo, [1969] – 1 – CSUXADP1185-B – us Hoover Inst Photo [972]
QUIENES DERROCARON A ISABEL PERON / Deheza, Jose A – [Argentina]: Ediciones Cuenca del Plata, 1st ed 1981 – 1 – CSUXADJ7771-B – us Hoover Inst Photo [320]
QUIENES SON LOS RESPONSABLES? LIBERALES EL MUNDO / Espanol, Juan – Veracruz, 1939? Fiche W 862. (Blodgett Collection of Spanish Civil War Pamphlets) – 9 – us H.U. College Libr [946]
QUIENES SON LOS TESTIGOS DE JEHOVA / Corcho Asenjo, Leopoldo – Caceres: Ed. Sanchez Rodrigo, 1975 – 1 – sp Bibl Santa Ana [240]
QUIET HOURS / Pulsford, John – 6th ed. London: Hamilton, Adams, 1863 – 1mf – 9 – 0-8370-6932-7 – 1986-0932 – us A.T.L.A. [240]
QUIET TALKS ABOUT JESUS / Gordon, Samuel D – New York: A.C. Armstrong, 1906 – 9 – us A.T.L.A. [240]
Quigley, Brian *see* EVALUATION OF THE SET-POINT AND PROPORTIONAL CONTROL MODELS OF HUMAN THERMOREGULATION DURING EXERCISE
Quigley, Dr *see* THE IRISH RACE IN CALIFORNIA, AND ON THE PACIFIC COAST

Quigley, John B *see* BASIC LAWS ON THE STRUCTURE OF THE SOVIET STATE

Quigley, Richard F *see* IPSE, IPSA–IPSE, IPSA, IPSUM, WHICH?

Quijano Quijano, Adolfo *see* CANTO A EXTREMADURA

QUILL – v1- 1912- 1; v59- 5,6; v63- 9 – us UMI [410]

QUILL – Schuyler, NE. -w. Apr 1890; Jun 1892; Oct-Dec 1895; Mar-Aug 1896; Nov 1896-May 1898; Jul 1898; Oct 1898-Jan 1901; Apr 1901-Jan 1908 – 1 – us NE Hist [071]

THE QUILL – A Magazine of Greenwich Village. New York. v. 1-20. June 1917-May 1929 – 1 – us NY Public [800]

QUILL AND QUIRE – Toronto, 1935- – 1 – Price varies – cn Micromedia [073]

QUILL AND QUIRE: THE MAGAZINE OF THE CANADIAN BOOK TRADE – v1- . 1935- . Includes printed index – 1 – 70.00y – cn McLaren [070]

Quiller-Couch, Arthur Thomas *see*
- ADVENTURES IN CRITICISM
- GREEN BAYS
- HETTY WESLEY
- POEMS AND BALLADS

Quilliam, John *see* LA GAZETTE CANADIENNE

Quimby, Phineas P *see* PAPERS

LA QUIMERA / Pardo Bazan, Condesa Emilia de – Madrid, 191-?.557p – 1 – us U.W. Library [830]

Quinby, Hosea *see*
- A LETTER TO THE REV. J. BUTLER
- THE PRISON CHAPLAINCY AND ITS EXPERIENCES

QUINCENARIO PARA HONRARA LA IMMACULADA CONCEPCION BAJO EL TITULO DE NUESTRA SEÑORA DE LOURDES : VA PRECEDIDO DE UNA SUCINTA HISTORIA DE LAS APARICIONES Y SEGUIDO DE UN TRIDUO DE ACCION DE GRACIAS POR LOS FAVORES ALCANZADOS DE TAN MISERICORDIOSA SENORA / Palles, Jose – Barcelona: Libreria de la Immaculada Concepcion, 1880 – 1mf – 9 – 0-8370-8369-9 – 1986-2369 – us A.T.L.A. [240]

QUINCY – 1941-50; 1992- – 12+ r – 1 – $600.00 – P00087 – us Library Micro [910]

QUINCY 1792-1889 – (Mf 1-5: Birth Index 1850-88. Mf 6-12: Index to Marriage Intentions 1792-1906. Mf 13-16: Marriage Index 1792-1889. Mf 17-20: Index to Deaths 1792-1888. Mf 21-25: Births, Marriages, Intentions 1792-1850. Mf 26-27: Deaths 1793-1843. Mf 28-30: Births, Marriages, Deaths 1844-52. Mf 31-46: Births, Marriages, Deaths 1852-75. Mf 47-60: Births, Marriages, Deaths 1875-89) – (mf ed 1983) – 60mf – 9 – 0-931248-37-X – us Holbrook [920]

QUINCY, WENDELL, HOLMES, AND UPHAM FAMILY PAPERS, 1633-1910 – Massachusetts Historical Society – 67r – 1 – $5130.00 – us UMI [920]

QUINCY'S REPORTS / Massachusetts. Supreme Court – (A Pre-NRS title) – Superior Court of Judicature. 1v. 1761-72 (all publ) – 7mf – 9 – $10.50 – LLMC 84-154 – us L.L.M.C. [340]

Quindry, Sylvester Eugene *see* PRACTICING LAW, WHEN, WHERE AND HOW

Quinet, E *see* ULTRAMONTANISM, OR, THE ROMAN CHURCH AND MODERN SOCIETY

Quinlan *see* HISTORY OF SULLIVAN COUNTY

Quinlan, Aloysius Stanislaus *see* CHRISTIAN SCIENCE BEFORE THE BAR OF REASON

Quinn, Eugene F *see* A SURVEY OF THE PRINCIPLES OF CONTEMPORARY AMERICAN NONLITURGICAL CHURCH MUSIC

Quinn, John Philip *see* FOOLS OF FORTUNE

Quinn, M William *see* RAPPORT SUR LE COMMERCE DES BOIS

Quinn, Ronald W *see* SPORT ADMINISTRATION PROGRAM DIRECTORS AT INSTITUTIONS OF HIGHER EDUCATION

QUINNIPAC LAW REVIEW – (Title varies: v1-12 no 1 1980-1991 as University of Bridgeport Law Review. v12 no 2-13 1992-93 as Bridgeport Law Review. v1-5 1980-84 in reel $64.00. v6-14 1985-94 in mf $168.00) – v1-14. 1980-94 – 5,6,9 – $232.00 – us Hein [340]

QUINOLOGIA, O TRATADO DEL ARBOL DE LA QUINA O CASCARILLA, CON SU DESCRIPCION Y LA DE OTROS ESPECIES... / Ruiz Lopez, Hipolito – Madrid, 1792 – 2mf – 9 – ne IDC [580]

QUINQUAGENA SYMBOLORUM HEROICA IN... SANCTAE REGULAE BENEDICTI / Hanthaler, Chrysostomus – Augustae, 1741 – 5mf – 8 – Dfl22.00 – ne Slangenburg [240]

QUINQUE PRUDENTES VIRGINES / Henriquez, Chrysostomus – Antwerpen, 1633 – 9mf – 8 – Dfl53.00 – ne Slangenburg [240]

QUINTA PARTIDA, COM. DE GREGORIO LOPEZ / Alfonso 10 el Sabio, Rey de Castilla – 1610 – 9 – 1.50f – sp Bibl Santa Ana [946]

Quintana, Manuel Jose *see*
- FRANCISCO PIZARRO
- PREGON...EN LAS FIESTAS DEL CINCUENTENARIO DE LA CORONACION DE NTRA. SRA. DE LA MONTANA PATRONA DE CACERES

Quintanilla, Condessa de *see* CONTESTACION...PLEITO...FALSEDAD Y NULIDAD

Quintanilla, Guillermo *see* CASTILLA AGRICOLA PARA LA ENSENANZA DE LA AGRICULTURA...CACERES

QUINTE QUILL – Belleville, Fe1979-1979No – 2r – 1 – cn Preston [971]

QUINTE WEEKLY NEWS – Belleville, Au1986-1992Ma – 5r – 1 – cn Preston [971]

Quintero Carrasco, J *see* CON LA VOZ DEL CORAZON

QUINTET FOR CLARINET AND STRINGS, OP. 34 / Straesser, E – Berlin: N Simrock, 1920 – 1 – us Sibley [780]

QUINTETS, FLUTE AND STRINGS, "OP. 21E", G. 419-424 / Boccherini, Luigi – (Parts) – Paris: Sieber, 1800? – 1 – us Sibley [780]

[QUINTETS] OP. 20, G. 277-282 / Boccherini, Luigi – 1st ed. Paris: Venier. 5pts. 1776 – 1 – us Sibley [780]

QUINTETS, SIX. OP. 18, G. 283-288 / Boccherini, Luigi – (Parts) – Paris: Sieber, 1800? – 1 – us Sibley [780]

[QUINTETS] THIRD SET OF SIX. OP. 20, G. 277-282 / Boccherini, Luigi – (5 pts) – London: Preston, 1790? – 1 – us Sibley [780]

QUINTETS, THREE. OP. 36, G. 295-297 / Boccherini, Luigi – (Cello part is defective) – 1st ed. Vienna: Artaris Comp. 5pts. 1785? – 1 – us Sibley [780]

QUINTETS, TWO CAPITAL, FOR VIOLIN, VIOLA, 2 HORNS [AD LIB], AND BASS / Wanhal, J B – London: Babbs, 1780 – 1 – us Sibley [780]

QUINTETT FUR 2 VIOLINER, 2 ALTAR OCH VIOLONCELL / Lindblad, A – Stockholm: Musikaliska Konstfoereningen, 1885 – 1 – us Sibley [780]

QUINTETTE, TROIS, OP. 66 / Danzi, F – (5 parts) – Offenbach: Andre, ca 1824 – 1 – us Sibley [780]

QUINTETTI, DEUX, OP. 5 / Pleyel, Ignaz J – (Parts) – Paris: Imbault, 179- – 1 – us Sibley [780]

QUINTETTI, NOUVEAUS, POUR DEUX VIOLONS, DEUX ALTOS ET VIOLONCELLO / Krammer, F – (Separate parts) – Paris: Sieberpere, [181-?] – 1 – us Sibley [780]

QUINTETTI, TROIS GRANDS, OP. 92, NO. 2 [2VLN,2VLA,VC] / Reicha, A – (Pts.) – Paris: Pacini, 182- – 1 – us Sibley [780]

QUINTETTI, TROIS GRANDS, OP. 92, NO. 3. [2VLN,2VLA,VC] / Reicha, A – (Pts.) – Paris: Pacini, 182- – 1 – us Sibley [780]

QUINTETTI, TROIS, OP. 8, 2E LIVRE / Pleyel, Ignaz J – (Parts) – Paris: Sieber, 179- – 1 – us Sibley [780]

QUINTETTOS, SIX, OP. 9 / Davaux, J B – (Parts) – London: W Forster, 180- – 1 – us Sibley [780]

QUINTUOR POUR PIANOFORTE, VIOLIN, ALTO, VIOLONCELLE ET BASSE, OP. 69 / Cramer, Johann Baptist – (5 parts) – Leipzig: H A Probst, [1823?] – 1 – us Sibley [780]

QUINTUOR POUR TROIS VIOLONS, ALTO ET BASSE, CONTENANT UNE FUGUE A QUATRE SUJETS... / Albrechtsberger, Johann G – Vienne: Bureau d'Art d'Industrie, [1798?] – 1 – us Sibley [780]

LA QUINZAINE – no. 1-196. Paris. oct 1894-1902 – 1 – fr A.C.R.P.P. [073]

LA QUINZAINE – Paris, FR. 1978-1986 – 8r – $400.00 – R63567 – us Library Micro [072]

LA QUINZAINE COLONIALE / Union coloniale francaise. Paris – Jan 1897-Jul 1914 – 1 – 35.00r – us Hoover Inst Photo [072]

LA QUINZAINE LITTERAIRE – Paris, France. -f. March 1966-Dec 1970. 3 reels – 1 – uk British Libr Newspaper [800]

QUINZAINE LITTERAIRE – (Also available on CD-ROM) – 1989-1995 – 2r per y – 5,6 – Sfr428.00 – sz Infoprint [072]

QUINZE DE AGOSTO : COMEMORACAO DO DIA – Manaos, Amazonas. 15 Ago 1881; 15 Ago 1882 – 1,5,6 – bl Biblioteca [072]

QUINZE DE NOVEMBRO : ORGAO DO PARTIDO REPUBLICANO FEDERAL DE ALAGOAS – Maceio, Alagoas. 3-5 Set 1897 – 1,5,6 – bl Biblioteca [072]

O QUINZE DE NOVEMBRO DO SEXO FEMININO : PERIODICO QUINZENAL, LITTERARIO, RECREATIVO E NOTICIOSO – Rio de Janeiro, 15 Dec 1889; Mar-Apr, Jul-Sep, 6 Dec 1890 – 1,5,6 – bl Biblioteca [072]

QUIRINDA ADVOCATE – Jan 6 1933-Dec 19 1947 – 9 – at Pascoe [072]

QUIRINDI GAZETTE – Jan 5 1909-June 26 1925 – 1 – at Pascoe [072]

QUIRINDI MAGPIE/HERALD – Jan 3 1899-Dec 31 1907 – 1 – at Pascoe [072]

Quirke, N *see* MOLECULAR SIMULATION

Quirnheim, Christoph Emanuel Hermann Ritter Mertz von *see* PAPERS

Quiroga, Adan *see* LA CRUZ EN AMERICA, CON NOTICIA BIOGRAFICA DEL AUTOR POR ERNESTO MORALES ET PROLOGO DE SAMUEL A. LAFONE QUEVEDO

Quiroga, F *see*
- ESTUDIO PETROGRAFICO DEL METEORITO DE GUARENA
- METEORITO DE GUARENA

Quiros y Benavides, Felipe Bernardo *see*
- HISTORIA DE LA VIDA Y MARTIRIO DE LA SANTA EULALIA DE MERIDA
- TIMBRE ASTURIANO. HISTORIA...VIDA...SANTA EULALIA DE MERIDA

QUIS CUSTODIET *see* LAW AND JUSTICE

LA QUISTIONE INTERNAZIONALE DELL' AUNIS / Gionnais Gianquinto, G de – Pavai, 1863 – 1mf – 1 – ILM-1778/1 – ne IDC [327]

QUITAQUE FIRST BAPTIST CHURCH. QUITAQUE, TEXAS : CHURCH RECORDS – 1940-59 – 1r – 1 – 14.60 – us Baptist [240]

Quitard, P M *see* DICTIONNAIRE ETYMOLOGIQUE, HISTORIQUE, ET ANECDOTIQUE DES PROVERBES

QUITMAN COUNTY DEMOCRAT – Marks. Miss. 1936-1953 – 1 – us UMI [071]

Quitschreiber, G *see* MUSICBUECHLEIN FUER DIE JUGEND IN DEUTSCHEN UND LATEINISCHEN SCHULEN ZU GEBRAUCHEN

DIE QUITZOWS : SCHAUSPIEL IN 4 AKTEN / Wildenbruch, Ernst von – Berlin: G Grote, 1902 – 1r – 1 – us U.W. Library [820]

THE QUIVER – Quebec, Canada. v1 n5. 9 jan 1868 – 1r – 1 – Can$25.00 – cn Can Microfilming [072]

QUIZ BOOK: QUESTIONS AND ANSWERS ON THE SUBJECT OF BAILMENTS AND CARRIERS. / Edwards, Thomas, jr – Washington, D.C., Columbian Correspondence College 1900 39 p. LL-335 – 1 – us L of C Photodup [340]

QUIZ BOOK; QUESTIONS AND ANSWERS ON THE SUBJECT OF EQUITY PLEADING. / Ray, Charles Andrew – Washington, Columbian, Correspondence College, 1900 87 p. LL-595 – 1 – us L of C Photodup [340]

QUIZ MANUAL ON PERSONAL PROPERTY / Ingler, Francis Marion – Chicago, Flood, 1900. 120 p. LL-1626 – 1 – us L of C Photodup [340]

QUIZ ON CRIMINAL LAW, 1896-1897 / Morris, Robert – n.p. 1896. LL-444 – 1 – us L of C Photodup [340]

QUIZ ON INTERNATIONAL LAW / Fisher, S B – St. Paul, 1895 – 1mf – 1 – ILM-1976/1 – ne IDC [327]

QUIZZER NO. 1...BEING QUESTIONS AND ANSWERS ON DOMESTIC RELATIONS. / Sprague, William Cyrus – Detroit, Collector 1894 48 p. LL-1201 – 1 – us L of C Photodup [340]

QUIZZER NO. 2...BEING QUESTIONS AND ANSWERS ON CRIMINAL LAW. / Ellis, Griffith Ogden – 2d ed. Detroit, The Collector 1895 31 p. LL-1230 – 1 – us L of C Photodup [340]

QUIZZER NO. 2...BEING QUESTIONS AND ANSWERS ON CRIMINAL LAW. / Snyder, Emil William – Detroit, Mich., Sprague 1904 37 p. LL-590 – 1 – us L of C Photodup [340]

QUIZZER NO. 4...BEING QUESTIONS AND ANSWERS ON REAL PROPERTY...2ND ED / Sprague, William Cyrus – Detroit, Collector 1895 58 p. LL-1035 – 1 – us L of C Photodup [340]

QUIZZER NO. 10...BEING QUESTIONS AND ANSWERS ON BILLS, NOTES, AND CHEQUES. / Ellis, Griffith Ogden – Detroit, The Collector 1894 55 p. LL-385 – 1 – us L of C Photodup [340]

QUIZZER NO. 14...BEING QUESTIONS AND ANSWERS ON SALES OF PERSONAL PROPERTY...5TH ED / Sprague, William Cyrus – Detroit, Sprague 1910 38 p. LL-274 – 1 – us L of C Photodup [340]

QUIZZER NO. 20; BEING QUESTIONS AND ANSWERS ON INSURANCE. / Kelland, Clarence Budington – Detroit, Sprague Publishing Co. 1911 40 (i.e. 74) p. LL-901 – 1 – us L of C Photodup [340]

Qulsum Nani *see* CUSTOMS AND MANNERS OF THE WOMEN OF PERSIA

QUN ZHONG – China. A newspaper published by the party during the period of Guo Ming Tang's power. Dec 1937-Mar 1947. 103 ill. DL54f – 9 – 435.00 – cc Globe [072]

QUO ORDINE SERMO FIERI DEBEAT. DE BUCELLA IUDAE DATA ET DE VERITATE DOMINI CORPORIS. DE SANCTIS ET EORUM PIGNERIBUS / Novigenti, Guibertus – 1993 – 5mf – 9 – Bf1,700.00 – 2-503-64272-1 – be Brepols [450]

QUO VADIS? : ORGAM DE INTERESSES POPULARES – Manaus, Amazonas. 19 Nov 1902-20 Mar 1904 – 1,5,6 – bl Biblioteca [072]

"QUO VADIS."IN ENGLISH. SE 3460/1. 3E ED. 1958 / Sardjito, K – 9 – ne IDC [950]

QUOC DAN DIEN DAN – no. 1-47. Saigon. 28 oct 1918-20 oct 1919. mq no. 11 – 1 – fr A.C.R.P.P. [073]

QUOD NIHIL SCITUR / Sanchez, Francisco – 16th Century – 1 – uk Microform Academic [140]

LE QUODLIBET 15 ET TROIS QUESTIONS ORDINAIRES DE GODEFROID DE FONTAINE / Lottin, O – 8 – ne Slangenburg [100]

LES QUODLIBET CINQ, SIX ET SEPT DE GODEFROID DE FONTAINES / Wulf, M de & Hoffmans, J – 1914 – 14mf – 8 – ne Slangenburg [140]

LES QUODLIBETS ONZE ET DOUZE DE GODEFROID DE FONTAINES / Hoffmans, J – 1932 – 14mf – 8 – ne Slangenburg [100]

QUOSEGO – Helsinki, Finland. 1928-29 – 1 – sw Kungliga [490]

QUOTATIONS IN THE NEW TESTAMENT / Toy, Crawford Howell – New York: Scribner's, 1884. 1 fiche – 9 – us A.T.L.A. [220]

THE QUOTATIONS OF THE NEW TESTAMENT FROM THE OLD / Johnson, Franklin – (Includes bibliographical references) – Philadelphia: American Baptist Publ Society, 1896, c1895 – 1mf – 9 – 0-8370-3788-3 – 1985-1788 – us A.T.L.A. [220]

QUOTATIONS OF THE OLD TESTAMENT IN THE NEW TESTAMENT / Osgood, Howard – Rochester, NY: E.R. Andrews, 1889. 1 fiche – 9 – us A.T.L.A. [240]

LE QUOTIDIEN / ed by Larouche, J et al – Chicoutimi, Canada. 1 oct 1973-31 dec 1992 – 139r – 1 – Can$85.00r – cn Can Microfilming [072]

LE QUOTIDIEN – Paris. 8 fevr 1923-sept 1936 – 1 – fr A.C.R.P.P. [073]

LE QUOTIDIEN / ed by Roy, P-G – Levis, Canada. 28 jun 1879-18 mai 1937 – 21r – 1 – Can$170.00r – cn Can Microfilming [072]

LE QUOTIDIEN DE PARIS – 1988-1994 – 3r per y – 5,6 – Sfr1,123.00 – sz Infoprint [944]

LE QUOTIDIEN ILLUSTRE – Paris. 11 dec 1894-15 juil 1895 – 1 – fr A.C.R.P.P. [073]

QUOTIDIEN PARIS – 1988-1995 – 3 times per yr – 6 – F4,200.00 – sz Infoprint [072]

LE QUOTIDIEN POPULAIRE : GREVISTES DE "LA PRESSE" ET LA C.S.N. – Montreal, 2 nov-16 nov 1971 – 1r – 1 – Can$40.00 – cn Can Microfilming [072]

LE QUOTIDIEN POPULAIRE – Montreal. v1 no 1-no 13. 1971. SEM35P8 – 1r – 1 – Can$19.00 – cn Bibl Nat [072]

QUOTIDIEN ROUGE *see* ROUGE (PARIS, FRANCE: 1968)

LA QUOTIDIENNE – Montreal, Canada. 30 nov 1837-3 nov 1838 – 1r – 1 – Can$30.00 – cn Can Microfilming [072]

LA QUOTIDIENNE – Paris. 1er juin 1814-1 fev 1847 – 1 – fr A.C.R.P.P. [073]

QUOTLIBETA SEPTEM : TRACTATUS DE SACRAMENTI ALTARIS / Occam, Guillelmus de – 1491 – 7mf – 8 – ne Slangenburg [290]

Quoy *see* VOYAGE AUTOUR DU MONDE. EXECUTE SUR LES CORVETTES DE S.M. L'URANIE ET LA PHYSICIENNE, 1817-1820

Quoy, G *see* POISSONS. ZOOLOGIE. VOYAGE. 1826-1829

Quoy, J R C *see* POISSONS. ZOOLOGIE. VOYAGE. 1826-1829
Quraeshi, Zahir A *see* JOURNAL OF ASIA-PACIFIC BUSINESS
THE QUR'AN : PART 1 / ed by Mueller, Friedrich Max – (Translated by E.H. Palmer) – 1880 – 7mf – 8 – ne Slangenburg [260]
THE QUR'AN : PART 2 / ed by Mueller, Friedrich Max – (Translated by E.M. Palmer) – 1880 – 7mf – 8 – ne Slangenburg [260]
THE QUR'AN AS SCRIPTURE / Jeffery, A – New York, 1952 – 3mf – 8 – ne Slangenburg [260]
QURRAT 'UYUN AL-AKHYAR / Ibn Abidin, Muhammad ibn Muhammad Amin – Egypt, 1882. 2 v. LL-12027 – 1 – us L of C Photodup [340]
QVAESTIO : DE LIBERO ARBITRIO, QVATENVS ILLA QVIBVSDAM NUNC DISCEPTATUR IN ECCLESIJS AUGUSTANAE CONFESSIONIS / Gallus, N – [Ratisponae], 1559 – 1mf – 9 – ne IDC [240]
QVAESTIONES LVCAE LOSSII IN EVANGELIA DOMINICALIA ET PRAECIPUORUM FESTORUM...EXPRAELECTIONIBUS ET SCRIPTIS PHILIP. MELANTHONIS,... / Lossius, L – VVitebergae, 1560 – 7mf – ne IDC [240]
QVESTIVNCVLAE METHODICAE DE CHRISTIANO CATECHISMO, IN FORMAM DIALOGI... / Lossius, L – [Magdeburgae], 1539 – 1mf – ne IDC [240]
QVINTA ESSENTIA / Thurneisser zum Thurn, Leonard – Leipzig, 1574 – 1 – us U.W. Library [190]
R AND D MANAGEMENT – (1982-. 1,5,6,9) – v1-. 1970- – 1 – us UMI [650]
R AND D MANAGEMENT DIGEST – 1 – 36.00y – us UMI [629]
R AND D MANAGEMENT DIGEST – v1- 1971- 1; v6- 5,6,9 – us UMI [650]
R. BRADFORD VS MESSRS TAYLOR AND OATES : FRAUDULENT TRANSACTIONS EXPOSED: AN APPEAL TO GET JUSTICE / Bradford, Robert – 1884? 00234. (Pre-1900 Canadiana) – 9 – cn C.I.H.M. [971]
R. DORSEY MOHAN PAPERS, 1892-1913 / Mohan, R Dorsey – 3rolls. T294. (Records of the Belgium Ministry of Foreign Affairs) – 1 – us Nat'l Archives [920]
R, H *see* ABREGE DE LA VIE DE BERNADETTE, SOEUR MARIE BERNARD
R. Hoe and Company *see* RECORDS
LE R. P. LOUIS SACHE DE LA COMPAGNIE DE JESUS / Duguay, P H Ernest – s.l.: s.n., 1890. 02793. (Pre-1900 Canadiana) – 9 – cn C.I.H.M. [971]
R. PATRIS THOMAE SANCHEZ...DE SANCTO MATRIMONII SACRAMENTO DISPVTATIONVM / Sanchez, Tomas Antonio – Lvgdvni: apud Ioannem Pavhle Typographum in vico Paradifi, 1669. SEM35P230 – 1r – 1 – Can$42.00 – cn Bibl Nat [240]
LE R. PERE VINCENT ROUTIER DE L'ORDRE DES FRERES PRECHEURS / Fortier, Onesime Laurent – Quebec?: s.n., 1885 (Quebec: L. J. Demers). 03157. (Pre-1900 Canadiana) – 9 – cn C.I.H.M. [971]
R, R *see* AN ENGLISH GRAMMAR: OR, A PLAIN EXPOSITION OF LILIES GRAMMAR IN ENGLISH
R. Sutton and Co *see* HISTORY OF VAN WERT AND MERCER COUNTIES
Raab, Karl *see*
– ANNETTE VON DROSTE-HUELSHOFF IM SPIEGEL DER ZEITGENOESSISCHEN KRITIK
– STUDIEN ZU WIELANDS ROMANE "PEREGRINUS PROTEUS"
Raab, Walter *see* TECHNISCHE HOCHSCHULE DARMSTADT
Raabe, Andreas *see* DIE KLAGELIEDER DES JEREMIAS UND DER PREDIGER DES SALOMON
Raabe, Julie L *see* DANCE IS...?: A LECTURE DEMONSTRATION FOR CHILDREN
Raabe, R *see* DIE APOLOGIE DES ARISTIDES (T.U.U. 1-9/1B)
RAABE UND JENSEN : DENKMAL EINER LEBENSFREUNDSCHAFT / Fehse, Wilhelm – Berlin: G Grote, 1940 – 1r – 1 – us U.W. Library [920]
Raabe, Wilhelm Karl *see*
– ABU TELFAN, ODER, DIE HEIMKEHR VOM MONDGEBIRGE
– DIE AKTEN DES VOGELSANGS
– ALTE NESTER
– CHRISTOPH PECHLIN
– DEUTSCHER ADEL
– DER DRAEUMLING
– DREI FEDERN
– ELSE VON DER TANNE
– FERNE STIMMEN
– EIN FRUEHLING
– GESAMMELTE ERZAEHLUNGEN
– GUTMANNS REISEN
– HALB MAER, HALB MEHR
– DER HEILIGE BORN
– HORACKER
– KLEINERE ERZAEHLUNGEN
– DER LAR
– RAABENWEISHEIT
– UNRUHIGE GAESTE
– VERWORRENES LEBEN
– VILLA SCHOENOW
RAABENWEISHEIT / Raabe, Wilhelm Karl; ed by Wolzogen, Hans von – Berlin: Otto Janke, 1901 – 1r – 1 – us U.W. Library [800]
RAADSELACHTIGE VERHALEN UIT HET OUDE EN HET NIEUWE VERBOND / Meijboom, Louisa Susan Pedro – Groningen: J.B. Wolters, 1870. 1 fiche – 9 – us A.T.L.A. [240]
RA'ASH ZEFAT BI-SHENAT 5520 / Yaari, A – v. 28. Sinay. 1941. BJ-27-28 1 – 9 – ne IDC [550]
RABANARA DANCES; PIANO SOLO / Pasaribu, Amir – SE-11,408 1. 1961 – 9 – ne IDC [780]
Rabate, M R *see* LES BIJOUX DU SUD MAROCAIN: ESSAI D'INTERPRETATION DE LEURS FORMES ET DE LEURS DECORS
Rabaud, Camille *see* SIRVEN
RABAUKEN! : PETER MOENKEMANN HAUT SICH DURCH: ROMAN / Weller, Tuedel – 5. Aufl. Muenchen: F Eher Nachf, 1942 – 1r – 1 – us U.W. Library [830]
RABAUL NEWS *see* PAPUA AND NEW GUINEA VILLAGER
Rabaut, Paul *see* DEUX SERMONS
RABBENU MOSHE BEN MAIMON = MOSES MAIMONIDES – (In Hebrew) – Tel Aviv, IS. no4788 1935-(no4797) 1935 – 1r – 1 – $25.00 – cn Can Microfilming [072]
RABBI SHELOMOH BEN GABIROL / Simchoni, J N H – (Ha-Tekufah, v. 10; v. 12; v. 17). Warsaw. 1921-23. BJ-421-44 1 – 9 – ne IDC [470]
A RABBINIC ANTHOLOGY / Montefiore, CG & Loewe, H – 1938 – 25mf – 8 – ne Slangenburg [270]
RABBINIC MSS. CATALOG / Brumer, Judah – 34mf – 9 – $145.00 – us UPA [270]
RABBINICAL COUNCIL QUARTERLY/RECORD – New York, NY. 1953-83 – 1 – us A.J.P.C. [071]
DER RABBINISCHE RATIONALISMUS: EINE UNTERREDUNG / Oxenstirn, Johann Turesson – Wien: S. Modlinger, 1889. 1 fiche – 9 – us A.T.L.A. [270]
Rabbinovicz, R N N *see* DIKDUKEI SOFERIM
Rabbinowitz, J *see* STUDIES IN JEWISH THEOLOGY
LES RABBINS FRANCAIS DU COMMENCEMENT DU 11 SIECLE / Renan, M E – Paris, 1877 – 10mf – ne IDC [270]
LES RABBINS FRANCAIS DU COMMENCEMENT DU 14E / Renan, M E – SIECLE. Histoire litteraire de la France. v. 27. Paris. 1877. BJ-33-29 1 – 9 – ne IDC [270]
RABBIT : HUSBANDRY, HEALTH AND PRODUCTION / Lebas, F et al – 1986 – 225p – it F.A.O. [636]
RABBIT WORLD – v55-56. 1971-72 – 1 – us UMI [073]
RABBITCRAFT AND AMERICAN BREEDERS' REVIEW – v5-9. 1921-25 – 1 – us UMI [073]
RABBITCRAFT AND SMALL STOCK JOURNAL – v3-5. 1919-21 – 1 – us UMI [073]
Rabe, Inge *see* QUELLENKRITISCHE UNTERSUCHUNGEN ZU PLUTARCHS ALEXANDERBIOGRAPHIE
LE RABELAIS – Nice. nov 1880-98 – 1 – fr A.C.R.P.P. [073]
LE RABELAIS REFORME PAR LES MINISTRES,... / Garasse, F – Brusselle, 1619 – 3mf – 9 – CA-132/1 – ne IDC [240]
Rabener, Justus Gotthard et al *see* DEUTSCHE ACTA ERUDITORUM, ODER GESCHICHTE DER GELEHRTEN, WELCHE DEN GEGENWAERTIGEN ZUSTAND DER LITTERATUR IN EUROPA BEGREIFFEN
Rabenhorst, G L *see*
– BEITRAG ZUR NAEHEREN KENNTNISS UND VERBREITUNG DER ALGEN
– FLORA EUROPAEA ALGARUM AQUAE DULCIS ET SUBMARINAE
– KRYPTOGAMEN FLORA VON DEUTSCHLAND, OESTERREICH UND DER SCHWEIZ
– KRYPTOGAMEN-FLORA VON DEUTSCHLAND
– MYCOLOGIA EUROPAEA
– DIE SUESWASSER-DIATOMACEEN
Rabenlechner, Michael Maria *see* DIE ERSTEN POETISCHEN VERSUCHE HAMERLINGS
Rabia, Ali *see* LA COOPERATION AUDIOVISUELLE FRANCO-ALGERIENNE DE 1975 A NOS JOURS
Rabinovich, L *see*
– HA-GAN
– HA-GAT
– ME'ASSEF
Rabinovich, S E *see* ISTORIIA GRAZHDANSKOI VOINY
Rabinovitz, A S *see*
– HAFTARAH
– AL HA-PEREK
– KOL KITVEI
Rabinovitz, A Z *see* HA-GALIL
Rabinovitz, AZ *see* SEFER ZIKKARON
Rabinowicz, Leon *see* LE PROBLEME DE LA POPULATION EN FRANCE: PRECEDE D'UNE HISTOIRE GENERALE DE LA POPULATION: ETUDE DE SOCIOLOGIE DE LA POPULATION
Rabinowitz, Z W *see* SHA'AREI TORAT EREZ YISRA'EL
Rabinsohn, Marcus *see* LE MESSIANISME DANS LE TALMUD ET LES MIDRASCHIM
Rabl, Hans *see* DIE DRAMATISCHE HANDLUNG IN GERHART HAUPTMANNS WEBERN
RABOCHAI A GAZETA (MOSCOW, R.S.F.S.R.: 1922) – (Includes c.1: 1923:Sept.20; 1926:Dec.1-5, 7-12, 14-19, 21-25, 28-31; 1927:Jan.1, 4-9, 11-16, 18-19, 21-22, 26-30, Feb.2-3) – Moskva: T Sentralny i komitet Rossi isko i kommunistich. partii, 1922 – 1 – CSUXALC2046-S – us Hoover Inst Photo [947]
RABOCHAI A MOSKVA : ORGAN MOSKOVSKOGO KOMITETA R.K.P.(B) I MOSKOVSKOGO SOVETA R. I K.D. – (Library has holdings (incomplete) from between Feb. 7, 1922 and July 12, 1923) – Moskvaa: Mosk. kom-t R.K.P., Mosk. Sovet R.Kr. i K.D., 1922-1939 – 1 – CSUX87-S282 – us Hoover Inst Photo [947]
RABOCHAI A ZHIZN (MOSCOW, R.S.F.S.R.) – (Includes c.1: 1918:Sept.16) – [Moskva]: Gruppa rabotnikov proletarskikh organizat si i, 1918 – 1 – CSUXALC2058-S – us Hoover Inst Photo [947]
RABOCHAIA GAZETA – Kiev. U.S.S.R. 1959- – 1 – us UMI [072]
RABOCHAIA KOOPERATSIIA I EE ZADACHI / Ezhov, V – Pg., 1916 – 1mf – 9 – COR-28/1 – ne IDC [334]
RABOCHAIA KOOPERATSIIA I PROFSOIUZY / Kozhanyi, P M – M., 1928 – 3mf – 9 – COR-327/1 – ne IDC [334]
RABOCHAIA KOOPERATSIIA LENINGRADA – L., 1926 – 3mf – 9 – COR-358/1 – ne IDC [334]
RABOCHAIA KOOPERATSIIA ZA 10 LET SOVETSKOI VLASTI / Kozhanyi, P M – M., 1927 – 1mf – 9 – COR-326/1 – ne IDC [334]
RABOCHAIA MOSKVA – (Cont as: Kommunisticheskii Trud, then Moskovskii Bol'shevik) – Moscow, USSR. Dec 9 1920-Aug 2 1924 – 9r – 1 – us L of C Photodup [072]
RABOCHAIA TRIBUNA – (Backfile through 1998 $85r) – Russia, 1999- – 2r per y – 1 – $160.00 standing order – us Ross [072]
RABOCHAIA TRIBUNA – Moscow: Gazeta sotsial;nogo partnerstva i sotsial'noi zashchity, 1990- – 2mf – 9 – $199.95y – us East View [320]
RABOCHAYA MUISL – Leningrad. USSR. -irr. Oct 1898-Apr 1901. (12 ft) – 1 – uk British Libr Newspaper [947]
RABOCHEE DELO – Geneva. no. 1-12. Apr 1899-Feb 1902 – 1 – us NY Public [073]
RABOCHEE DELO / Soiuza Russkikh Sotsial'-Demokratov – v. 1-12. Geneva. 1899-1902. Lacking: v. 4, 5. BR-2339 2 – 8 – ne IDC [073]
RABOCHEE DVIZHENIE V ROSSII V GODY IMPERIALISTICHESKOI VOINY / Fleer, Matvei Gustavovich – Leningrad: "Pribo i", 1926 – 1 – CSUX89-B254 – us Hoover Inst Photo [947]
RABOCHE-KRESTIANSKAIA REVOLIUTSIIA V ROSSII V OTSENKE BURZHUAZNO I PUBLITSISTIKI / Bystrianskii, Vadim – [Petrograd]: Izd. Petrogradskogo Soveta rabochikh i krasnoarm. deputatov, 1919 – 1 – CSUX88-B6735 – us Hoover Inst Photo [947]
RABOCHI I : ORGAN T SENTRALN. BI URO PROF. SOI UZOV G. VLADIVOSTOKA – (Includes c.1: 1918:July 14, 21, 23) – Vladivostok: Bi uro, 1918 – 1 – CSUXALC3294-S – us Hoover Inst Photo [947]
RABOCHI I I ISKUSSTVO : MASSOVAI A GAZETA PO VOPROSAM ISKUSSTVA – (Library has: Nov. 6,15,23,30, Dec. 21-27, 1929) – Moskva: Teakinopechat, 1929-1930. 1v – 1 – CSUX87-S273 – us Hoover Inst Photo [947]
RABOCHI I KLASS I REVOLIUTSIONNOE DVIZHENIE V ROSSII / Akselrod, Pavel Borisovich & Panina, M – S.-Peterburg: Tip. "Obshchestvennai a polza", 1907 – 1 – CSUX89-B5424 – us Hoover Inst Photo [320]
RABOCHI I (PARIS, FRANCE) = L'OUVRIER – (Includes c.1: no.1(1911:Nov.)) – [Paris: s.n., 1911] – 1 – CSUXANS0789-S – us Hoover Inst Photo [947]
RABOCHI I PUT : ORGAN OMSKOGO GUBISPOLKOMA I GUBKOMA R.K.P. (BOLSHEVIKOV) – (Includes c.1: 1921:Nov.6; 1922:Mar.12) – Omsk: T Sentr. gos. tip., 1921 – 1 – CSUXANS0984-S – us Hoover Inst Photo [947]
RABOCHI I (VLADIVOSTOK, R.S.F.S.R.) *see* RABOCHI I
RABOCHIE DEPUTATY V I-OI GOSUDARSTVENNOI DUME / Bogdanov, M & Dan, F – Spb., n.d. 175p – 2mf – 9 – ne IDC [320]
RABOCHIE KOOPERATIVY I PROFESSIONAL'NYE SOIUZY / Lindov, G D – Pg., [1917] – 1mf – 9 – COR-61/1 – ne IDC [334]
RABOCHII GOLOS : SOTSIAL-DEMOKRATICHESKAIA-RABOCHAIA GAZETA – (In Russian and Polish) – London. v5(25). 1901 – 1mf – 9 – ne IDC [947]
RABOCHII I ISKUSSTVO – Moscow, USSR. Apr-Dec 1930 – 1r – 1 – us L of C Photodup [072]
RABOCHII I KOOPERATSIIA / Tatarchukov, O N – M., 1917 – 1mf – 9 – COR-114/1 – ne IDC [334]
RABOCHII I TEATR – Moscow, sep 1924-dec 1937 – 310mf – 9 – $2,000.00 – us Ross [790]
RABOCHII I ZRITEL' = WORKER AND SPECTATOR – Moscow. n1-33 dec 1923-dec 1924; n1-18 jan-may 1925 – 29mf – 9 – $200.00 – us Ross [790]
RABOCHII KLASS I KOOPERATSIIA : SBORNIK / ed by Kheisin, M L – Pg., 1918 – 2mf – 9 – COR-359/1 – ne IDC [334]
RABOCHII VOPROS V KOOPERATSII : STAT'I, TEKSTY DOGOVOROV, INSTRUKTSII, USTAVY, FORMY I PR.: SBORNIK / ed by Kheisin, M L – Pg., 1918 – 2mf – 9 – COR-272/1 – ne IDC [334]
RABOCHII VOPROSI ZEMELNAIA REFORMA / Grei, I – Moskva: "Molodaia Rossiia", 1906 – 1 – CSUX89-B7337 – us Hoover Inst Photo [630]
RABOCHY GOLOS = VOICE OF LABOR – (In Russian) – New York, 1919-23 – 1r – 1 – $85.00 – D3370 – us Scholarly Res [071]
RABOTNICESKI VESTNIK : ORGAN NA RABOTNICESKATA SOCIAL-DEMOKRATICESKATA PARTIJA I OBSCIJA RABOTNICESKI SINDIKALEN SAJUZ – Sofia, 1915-16 – 1 – us Hoover Inst Photo [335]
RABOTNICESKO DELO – (Duma 1990) – Sofia, 1976-1991ff – 32r – 1 – DM2,400.00 – gw Mikro Press [949]
RABOTNICHESKA PROSVETA – (Weekly Bulgarian language socialist newspaper publ in Detroit, MI 1967-69) – Granite City, IL. 1 Jan 1911-20 June 1969 – 12r – 1 – us Western Res [071]
RABOTNICHESKO DELO – Sofia, Bulgaria. -d. 1953-70. 50 reels – 1 – uk British Libr Newspaper [949]
RABOTNICHESKO DELO – Sofia, Bulgaria. Sept 1944-1976 – 64r – 1 – us L of C Photodup [949]
RABOTNICHESKO DELO *see* DUMA
RABOTNIK – Neperiodicheskii sbornik. v. 1-6. Geneva. 1896-99. BR-3796 2 – 8 – ne IDC [073]

RABOTNIK KOOPERATSII – Vologda, 1918 n1 – 1mf – 9 – COR-673/1 – ne IDC [334]
RABOTNIK PROSVESHCHENIIA – Moscow. 1920-1926. Missing: no. 8, 1921; nos. 2, 4, 5, 1923 – 1 – 35.00r – us Hoover Inst Photo [073]
RABOTNITSA – (Backfile through 1998 $85r) – Russia, 1999- – 1r per y – 1 – $80.00 standing order – us Ross [072]
RABOTNITSA – Moscow, 1914, 1917, 1923-72 – 589mf – 9 – $2,890.00 coll – us Ross [331]
RABOTNITSA I KREST'IANKA – St Petersburg, 1922-41 – 249mf – 9 – $1,490.00 – us Ross [305]
RABOTNITSA, K TEBE NASHE SLOVO! : S PRILOZHENIEM LOZUNGOV / Bukharin, Nikolai Ivanovich – Moskva: Gos. izd-vo, 1919 – 1 – CSUX89-B1636 – us Hoover Inst Photo [947]
RABOTNITSY V INTERNATSIONALE / Blonina, El – Moskva: Gos. izd-vo, 1920 – 1 – CSUX89-B3212 – us Hoover Inst Photo [947]
RABOTY IMPERATORSKAGO MOSKOVSKAGO TEKHNICHESKAGO UCHILISHCHA NA OBORONU / Imperatorskoe moskovskoe tekhnicheskoe uchilishche – [Moscow?: s.n., 1916] – 1 – CSUX89-B3505 – us Hoover Inst Photo [600]
RABULAE EPISCOPI EDESSENI, BALAEI ALIORUMQUE. OPERA SELECTA E CODICIBUS MSS. IN MUSEO BRITANNICO ET BIBLIOTHECA BODLEIANA ASSERVATIS / Ephraemi Syri; ed by Overbeck, J J – Oxford, 1865 – 8mf – 8 – ne Slangenburg [240]
Raby, F J E *see* A HISTORY OF CHRISTIAN-LATIN POETRY FROM THE BEGINNINGS TO THE CLOSE OF THE M.A
Racan, Honorat de Bueil, Mis de *see* OEUVRES COMPLETES DE RACAN
RACCOLTA DELLE MEGLIORE SINFONIA DE PIN CELEBRI, COMPOSITORI DE NOSTRO TEMPI, ACCOMODAT ALL'CLAVECEMBALO RACCOLTA 1-4 – (Sinfonia 10 lacking) – Lipsia: G G I Breitkopf, 1761-1762 – 1 – us Sibley [780]
RACCOLTA DI LE PIV ILLVSTRI ET FAMOSE CITTA DI TVTTO IL MONDO – Venice, [1595] – 3mf – 9 – H-8214/1 – ne IDC [956]
RACCOLTA DI STATUE ANTICHE E MODERNE DATA IN LUCE SOTTO I GLORIOSI AUSPICJ, DELLA SANTITA DI N.S. PAPA CLEMENTE 11... / Rossi, D de & Maffei, P A – Roma, 1704 – 12mf – ne IDC [730]
RACCOLTA DI VARIJ BALLI IN OCCORRENZE DI NOZZE, E FESTINI DA NOBILI CAVALIERI, E DAME DI DIUERSE NATIONI / Caraoso, Fabrito – Roma: Appresso Guglielmo Facciotti, 1630 – 1 – us Sibley [780]
RACCOLTA FERRARESE DI OPUSCOLI SCIENTIFICI E LETTERARI DI CH. AUTORI ITALIANI – Ferrara.1779-96 – 3 – us Readex [500]
RACCOLTA UFFICIALE DELLE LEGGI E DEI DECRETI DEL REGNO D'ITALIA / Italy. Laws, Statutes, etc – Roma. On film: v1-481; 1861-1966; supplemento: v482-531; 1861-1910. LL-0282 – 1 – us L of C Photodup [340]
RACE – Devoted to Social, Political and Economic Equality. Nos. 1-2 (all publ). 1935-1936 – 2mf – 9 – $55.00 – us UPA [975]
RACE AND CLASS IN POST-COLONIAL SOCIETY : A STUDY OF ETHNIC GROUP RELATIONS IN THE ENGLISH-SPEAKING CARIBBEAN, BOLIVIA, CHILE AND MEXICO – 1977 – 9 – 92-3-101445-5 – fr UNESCO [305]
RACE AS NEWS – 1974 – 176p – 9 – 92-3-101191-X – fr UNESCO [306]
RACE ATTITUDES IN SOUTH AFRICA : HISTORICAL, EXPERIMENTAL AND PSYCHOLOGICAL STUDIES / MacCrone, Ian Douglas – London, New York [etc]: Publ by OUP for Uni of Witwatersrand, 1937 – us Res Libr [305]
RACE, CLASS AND THE APARTHEID STATE / Wolpe, Harold – 1988 – 9 – 92-3-102510-4 – Co-production James Curry, London (rights UK); OAU, Interafrican Cultural Fund, Addis Ababa (rights Africa); UNESCO – fr UNESCO [320]
RACE MIXTURE / Shapiro, Harry L – 3rd ed 1965 – 58p – 9 – 92-3-100416-6 – fr UNESCO [572]
THE RACE OF CASTLEBAR : A NARRATIVE / Lawless, Emily – British Fiction Archive: Unit 4 – 9 – uk Bell [830]
RACE RELATIONS – A Monthly Summary of Events and Trends. 1-5 (all publ). 1943-1948 – 23mf – 9 – $65.00 – us UPA [975]
RACE RELATIONS LAW REPORTER – v.1-12. 1956-67. Continued by Race relations law survey – 1,5,6,9 – us UMI [323]
RACE RELATIONS NEWS – Johannesburg, SA. 1979-1984 – 2r – $100.00 – R63580 – us Library Micro [072]
RACE RELATIONS REPORTER – Riverside, CA. 1970 – 1r – 1 – $50.00 – R02723 – us Library Micro [071]
RACES AND IMMIGRANTS IN AMERICA / Commons, John R – New York: Macmillan, 1907 – 1mf – us A.T.L.A. [305]
LES RACES DU HAUT-TONKIN DE PHONG-THO A LANG-SON / Abadie, M – Paris, 1924. SE-20,018 1 – 9 – ne IDC [300]
THE RACES OF THE OLD TESTAMENT / Sayce, Archibald Henry – (Includes bibliographical references and index) – London: Religious Tract Society, 1891 – 1mf – 9 – 0-8370-9817-3 – 1986-3817 – us A.T.L.A. [240]
RACHEGEISTER, ODER, DAEMON UNS'RER ZEIT : ORIGINALDRAMA IN DREI AKTEN / Wolff-Kassel, Ludwig – Berlin: G R Kruse, 1884 – 1r – 1 – us U.W. Library [820]
RACHEL DYER / Neal, John – 1828 – 9 – $15.00 – us Scholars' Facs [830]
RACHEL RAY : A NOVEL / Trollope, Anthony – London: Chapman and Hall, 1863 – 1 roll – 1 – 1-55879-969-9 – uk Libr Preservation [830]
Rachman, Asj'ari, Abd *see* KEBUDAJAAN DALAM PEMBANGUNAN SEMESTA
Rachman, R A *see* TATA NEGARA REPUBLIK INDONESIA
RACIAL SEGREGATION IN SOUTH AFRICA, AN APPEAL / Cotton, Walter Aidan – London: The Sheldon Press, 1931.v,(6),158p. With: Lehrbuch der Mechanischen Naturlehre by E.G. Fisher. 1 reel. 1292 – 1 – us U.W. Library [305]
Racicot, Ernest *see* E. RACICOT'S SPEECH TO HIS CONSTITUENTS: AT WEST FARNHAM, SATURDAY, NOV. 1ST, 1879
RACINE ET PORT-ROYAL / Reunion des musees nationaux. Paris – 1955. 2 fiches – 9 – fr Réunion [700]
RACINE VENGE OU EXAMEN DES REMARQUES GRAMMATICALES DE M. L'ABBE D'OLIVET SUR LES OEUVRES DE RACINE / Desfontaines, Pierre-Francois Guyot – 1739 – 9 – fr I.C.S. [440]
LA RACIONALIDAD DEL PERONISMO : CONTRA LA IDEOLOGIA DE LA REPUBLICA PERDIDA / Bordon, Jose Octavio – Buenos Aires: El Cid Editor, 1986 – 1 – CSUXAHZ7346-B – us Hoover Inst Photo [320]
RACISM, SCIENCE AND PSEUDO-SCIENCE – 1983 – 158p – 9 – 92-3-101993-7 – fr UNESCO [305]
EL RACISMO. BREVE HISTORIA DE SUS DOCTRINAS / Truyol Serra, A & Elias de Tejada, F – Madrid: Razon y Fe, 1946 – 1 – sp Bibl Santa Ana [301]
Rackemann, Charles Sedgwick *see* DRAFT OF AN ACT DESIGNED TO SIMPLIFY AND IMPROVE TRANSFERS OF LAND AND TITLES IN MASSACHUSETTS AND TO ENLARGE THE JURISDICTION OF THE LAND COURT
Rackl, M *see* DIE CHRISTOLOGIE DES H. IGNATIUS VON ANTIOCHIEN
Racquet and Tennis Club. Library of Sports, New York *see* A DICTIONARY CATALOGUE OF THE LIBRARY OF SPORTS IN THE RACQUET AND TENNIS CLUB, WITH SPECIAL COLLECTIONS ON TENNIS, LAWN TENNIS, AND EARLY AMERICAN SPORT
Racquet and Tennis Club.New York. Library of Sports *see* DICTIONARY CATALOG
Raczynski, A *see*
- LES ARTS EN PORTUGAL
- DICTIONNAIRE HISTORICO-ARTISTIQUE DU PORTUGAL...

RAD – Belgrade, Yugoslavia. 1945-50 – 5r – 1 – us L of C Photodup [949]
RAD – Belgrade, Yugoslavia. -w. 1960-1970. 16 reels – 1 – uk British Libr Newspaper [949]
RAD – Jugoslawien, 1976-1990 – 15r – 1 – DM1,125.00 – gw Mikro Press [949]
Rada Delgado, Juan de Dios de la *see*
- ANTIGUEDADES DE MERIDA RECIENTEMENTE REMITIDAS AL MUSEO ARQUEOLOGICO NACIONAL POR LA COMISION DE MONUMENTES DE AQUELLA CIUDAD
- UNA VIRIAO TORQUES, EXTREMENA DE ORELLANA DE LA SIERRA

Rada, Juan F *see* IMPACT OF MICROELECTRONICS AND INFORMATION TECHNOLOGY
Rada, Rodrigo Jimenez de *see* CHRONICON HISPANIAE (SIECLE 15)
RADAME : PREMIER ROI DE MADAGASCAR / Harry, Myriam – [Paris]: Ferenczi, [c1949] – us Res Libr [960]
RADAR : REPERTOIRE ANALYTIQUE D'ARTICLES DE REVUES DU QUEBEC / Bibliotheque Nationale. Quebec – Montreal: Ministere des affaires culturelles, 1972-83. SEM105P382 – 360mf – 9 – Can$405.00 – cn Bibl Nat [971]
Radau, Hugo *see* THE CREATION-STORY OF GENESIS 1
Radbertus, Pascasius *see*
- DE BENEDICTIONIBUS PATRIARCHARUM JACOB ET MOYSI
- DE FIDE, SPE ET CARITATE
- EXPOSITIO IN LAMENTATIONES HIEREMIAE
- EXPOSITIO IN PSALMUM 44
- IN MATHEO

Radbertus, Paschasius *see* DE PARTU VIRGINIS
Radcliffe, Ann Ward *see* THE ITALIAN
Radcliffe, James C *see* RELATIONSHIPS BETWEEN LOWER EXTREMITY LOADING AND DEPTH JUMP PERFORMANCE
Radcliffe, Joseph *see* THE LUDDITE PAPERS
Raddatz, Fritz J *see*
- DIE DEUTSCHE KLASSIK UND DIE FRANZOESISCHE REVOLUTION
- DIE DEUTSCHE LITERATUR UND DIE REVOLUTION VON 1848
- MEHRING WERKAUSWAHL
- ZUR PHILOSOPHIE UND POESIE DES KAPITALISMUS

Radde, G FR *see* ORNIS CAUCASICA
Rade, Martin *see* DIE RELIGION IM MODERNEN GEISTESLEBEN
LE RADEAU – no. 1-2. Paris. 31 janv-28 fevr 1925 – 1 – fr A.C.R.P.P. [073]
Radecki, Sigismund von *see* AUSGEWAEHLTE SCHRIFTEN
Radek, Karl *see* HANDSCHRIFTLICHE BRIEFE
Rademaker, A *see* KABINET VAN NEDERLANDSCHE EN KLEEFSCHE OUDHEDEN...
RADEN, DIAGNOSA-KIMIA DAN TAFSIR-KLINIKNJA. OLEH R.D. ASIKIN W.K. DAN AHMAD RAMALI / Asikin Widjaja Kusumah, D – Djakarta, Gunseikanbu Kokumin Tosyokyoku, 2605. v1. 235p – 17-19mf – 9 – ne IDC [616]
Radet *see* IDA OU QUE DEVIENDRA-T-ELLE
Radet et Barre *see* LA NEGRESSE OU LE POUVOIR DE LA RECONNAISSANCE, COMEDIE EN UN ACTE. MELEE DE DIVERTISSEMENTS
Radetzky, J J W *see* DENKSCHRIFTEN MILITAERISCH-POLITISCHEN INHALTS...
RADI ANSKA UKRAINA = SOVETSKAI A UKRAINA: ORGAN NARODNOGO KOMISSARIATA VNUTRENNIKH DEL : ORGAN NARODNOGO KOMISSARII ATA VNUTRISHNYKH SPRAV – (Library has: July 1920) – Kharkiv: Komissariat, 1920. 1v – 1 – CSUX89-S665 – us Hoover Inst Photo [947]
RADIAKALDEMOKRATISCHE BLAETTER – Berlin, Germany. 1931-1932 (incomplete); Apr 1932-Feb 1933 – 1 – gw Mikrofilm [072]
RADIANS'KA UKRAINA – Kiev. U.S.S.R. 1961- – 1 – us UMI [072]
RADIANS'KA UKRAINA *see* KOMUNIST
RADIANS'KE LITERATUROZNAVSTVO – Kiev, 1957-72 (1-6). BR-10,442/1 – 9 – ne IDC [460]
RADIATION AND ENVIRONMENTAL BIOPHYSICS – v. 1-18. 1963-80 – 1,5,9 – 1796.00 – us UMI [073]
RADIATION BOTANY *see* ENVIRONMENTAL AND EXPERIMENTAL BOTANY
RADIATION CONTROL FOR HEALTH AND SAFETY ACT, 1968 : LEGISLATIVE HISTORY / FDA-HEW – Washington: GPO. 2bks. 1975 – 16mf – 9 – $24.00 – LLMC 90-356 – us L.L.M.C. [340]
RADIATION EFFECTS AND DEFECTS IN SOLIOS / ed by Biersack, J P – 1969- – 1,5,9 – us Gordon [530]
RADIATION PHYSICS AND CHEMISTRY – v1-1969- – 5,6,9 – us UMI [530]
LE RADICAL – Liberte, Egalite, Fraternite. Dir. Jules Mottu. Paris. oct 1871-juin 1872 – 1 – fr A.C.R.P.P. [073]
LE RADICAL – Paris. aout 1881-6 dec 1931 – 1 – fr A.C.R.P.P. [073]
O RADICAL – Muriae, Brazil. Dec 1902; Oct 1910 – 1 – bl Biblioteca [072]
RADICAL – Boston, 1865-67 – 1r – 1 – us Ross [320]
RADICAL – London. 1886-97. Irreg – 1 – uk Microform Academic [073]
THE RADICAL – London. -w. 13 Mar-17 Jul 1836 – 1 reel – 1 – uk British Libr Newspaper [072]
RADICAL ABOLITIONIST – 1-4 2+5 (all publ). 1855-1858 – 4mf – 9 – $65.00 – us UPA [335]
RADICAL ABOLITIONIST *see* AMERICAN JUBILEE
RADICAL AND ANTI-RADICAL LITERATURE OF THE PHILIPPINES, 1930S-1941 – Collected and filmed by University of Wisconsin, Madison Libraries. 1985- – 1 – us U.W. Library [950]
RADICAL LEADER – London. 1888 – 1 – uk Microform Academic [073]
RADICAL LEADER – London, 4 Aug-17 Nov 1888 – 15ft – 1 – uk British Libr Newspaper [072]
RADICAL PAMPHLET LITERATURE : A COLLECTION FROM THE TAMIMENT LIBRARY, 1817-1970 – (8600 pamphlets on growth and impact of socialist thought in America) – 90r – 1 – $6680.00 – us UMI [335]
RADICAL PERIODICALS IN THE UNITED STATES, SERIES 1 – (Alternative; Amerasia; America Appeal; American Fabian; American Socialist; American Spectator; Black & White; Blast; Catholic Worker; Challenge: A Libertarian Weekly; Challenge YPSL; Champion Labor Monthly; China Today; Clarity; Class Struggle (Communist League of Struggle); Class Struggle; Clipper; Common Sense; Communist; Communist International; Comrade; Conscientious Objector; Debs Magazine; Dialectics; Dr. Robinson's Voice in the Wilderness; Enquiry; Equal Justice; Equality; Forerunner; Freedom: An Anarchist Monthly; Good Morning; Hour; In Fact; Industrial Democracy; Industrial Pioneer; Industrial Union Bulletin; Industrial Unionist (E.P.B. of the I.W.W.); Industrial Unionist (Industrial Union Party); Industrial Worker; International Class Struggle; International Review; International Socialist Review; International Socialist Review (Socialist Workers Party); Labor Action; Labor Action; Labor Age; Labor Bulletin; Labor Power; League for Industrial Democracy, New York L.I.D. Monthly; Liberty; Man; Marxian; Marxist; Marxist Quarterly; Marxist Review; Militant; Modern Quarterly; Modern Review; Modern Socialism; Monthly Review; Monthly Review (An Independent Socialist Magazine); Mother Earth Bulletin; National Issues; Nationalist; New Day; New Essays; New Foundations; New International; New Justice; New Militant; New Nation; New Review; New Student; New Trends; New World Review; New York Communist; One Big Union Monthly; Pacifica Views; Party Builder; Party Organizer; Politics; Radical Review; Rebel; Retort; Revolutionary Age (C.L.P); Revolutionary Age (C.P.); Road to Communism; Road to Freedom; Socialist; Socialist Appeal; Socialist Review; Socialist Spirit; Spanish Revolution (United Libertarian Org.); Spanish Revolution (Workers' Party of Marxist Unification); Student Advocate; Student Review; Syndicalist; U.S. Week; Upton Sinclair's; Vanguard; Weekly Review; Why?; Wilshire's; Workers Age; Workers' Council; Workers' League for a Revolutionary Party; Bulletin; World Survey; Young Spartacus; Young Worker) – 108 titles. 1880-1960 – 1,9 – $12,985.00; Titles available individually see under title for price – us UPA [335]
RADICAL PERIODICALS IN THE UNITED STATES, SERIES 2 – 1880-1960. AFL Rank and File Federationist; Alarm; California Social Democrat; Clarion; Demonstrator; Fighting Worker; Industrial Union News; International News; Revolt; Social Democrat; Social Democratic Herald; Soviet Russia Pictorial; Spotlight; Toiler; Vanguard; Western Comrade; Western Worker – 1 – $2,085.00 – us UPA [330]

RADICAL PERIODICALS OF GREAT BRITAIN, PERIOD 1 – (Titles available individually: Black Dwarf; British Labourer's Protector and Factory Child's Friend; Carpenter's Monthly Political Magazine; Chartist Circular; Cobbett's Political Register; Cooper's Journal; Crisis and National Co-operative Trades Union Gazette; Diplomatic Review; Economist, A Periodical Paper; Fleet Papers; Free Enquirer; Gauntlet; Gorgon; Herald to the Trades' Advocate and Co-operative Journal; Labourer; Lancashire and Yorkshire Co-operator and Useful Classes' Advocate; Lion; London Co-operative Magazine; London Phalanx; McDouall's Chartist Journal and Trades' Advocate; Movement; National; National Reformer and Manx Weekly Review of Home and Foreign Affairs; New Moral World; Northern Tribune; People, Their Rights and Liberties; People's Paper; Philanthropist; Pioneer; Political Letters and Pamphlets by William Carpenter; Politics for the People; Poor Man's Advocate and Workman's Guide; Poor Man's Guardian; Republican; Reynold's Political Instructor; Union; Working Man) – Protest Literature of the Industrial Revolution. 37 Titles. 1794-1881 – 1,9 – $4,260.00 – us UPA [335]

RADICAL PERIODICALS OF GREAT BRITAIN, PERIOD 2 – Marxism and the Machine Age. 1867-1914. British Socialist; Commonweal; Herald of Revolt; International Herald; International Review; Labour Elector; Labour Standard; Labour World; Liberty; Our Corner; Progress; S.D.P. News; Social Democrat; Social Economist; Socialist Record; Today; Voice of Labour; Worker – 1 – $2,025.00 – us UPA [335]

RADICAL PERIODICALS SERIES – 1813-1980 – 1,5,9 – uk World [073]

RADICAL POLITICS AND THE WORKING MAN IN ENGLAND, SERIES 1 – (The Francis Place Papers in the British Library, Department of Manuscripts. Pt 1: 1791-1854 add mss. 27789-27830. Pt 2: 1791-1854 add mss. 27831-27859 and others) – 1 – us Primary [941]

RADICAL POLITICS AND THE WORKING MAN IN ENGLAND, SERIES 2 – (Pt 1: 1770-1853 Sets 7-11, 13-21, 23-32 and 34-46. Pt 2: 1805-1852 Sets 47-49, 51-53, 55-63 and 65-72) – The Francis Place Papers in the British Library, Department of Printed Books – 1 – us Primary [941]

RADICAL PROBLEMS / Bartol, Cyrus Augustus – Boston: Roberts, 1872 – 1mf – 9 – 0-8370-2559-1 – 1985-0559 – us A.T.L.A. [200]

RADICAL REFORMATION PROJECT: SIXTEENTH CENTURY SOURCES – Ed. by I. B. Horst. 338 titles – 9 – ne IDC [240]

RADICAL REGISTER AND LIBERAL GAZETTE – London, UK. 1835 – 1ft – 1 – uk British Libr Newspaper [072]

RADICAL RELIGION – v1-5. 1973-81 – 1 – us UMI [200]

RADICAL REVIEW – 1-2 2+3 (all publ). 1917-1919 – 9mf – 9 – $60.00 – us UPA [335]

RADICAL REVIEW – 1vol. 1877-78. Ed. by B.R. Tucker before he started Liberty – 9 – 1.00f – at Libertarian Micro [320]

THE RADICAL RIGHT AND PATRIOTIC MOVEMENTS IN BRITAIN – (Updates for 1975, 1976, 1977, 1978, 1979 available) – 1942-74. Series: Harvester Primary Social Sources. A case-bound bibliographical guide is supplied – 9 – us Primary [941]

RADICAL THERAPIST – Riverside, CA. 1970-88 – 7r – 1 – $350.00 – R02724 – us Library Micro [071]

RADICAL THERAPY – Oakland, CA. 1970-76 – 1r – 1 – $50.00 – R02551 – us Library Micro [071]

RADICAL TIMES – London, UK. 1887 – 8ft – 1 – uk British Libr Newspaper [072]

RADICALISM, ANTI-RADICALISM AND REFORM IN ENGLAND, 1769-1861 – Original papers and Minute Books from the British Library, London – 1 – us Primary [941]

RADICALISMO, LIBERACION Y CAMBIA / Girardi, Rene Ulises – Buenos Aires: C.E.P.E., 1972 – 1 – CSUXADQ0997-B – us Hoover Inst Photo [320]

Radics, P v *see* ANASTASIUS GRUEN

RADIKAL – (Lacking: 1946, V.1(1-2, 9-12(?)) – Kabandjahe, 1946-1947.-v1-2 – 4mf – 9 – SE-103/1 – ne IDC [073]

RADIKAL – Sofia, Bulgaria. Oct 1945-Feb 1948 (scattered issues) – 2r – 1 – us L of C Photodup [949]

RADIKALDEMOKRATISCHE BLAETTER – Berlin, 1931-mar 1932 (many issues missing), apr 1932-feb 1933 – 1 – Inquire at Mikrofilmarchiv for details – gw Misc Inst [943]

RADIKALE LIEDER / Gollenperger, Dr. – Leipzig: Gebhardt und Reisland, 1847 – 1r – 1 – us U.W. Library [780]

Radiks Purba *see* MODERN BUSINESS ADMINISTRATION

RADIO – Berlin. 1923-sep 16, 1933 – 8r – 1 – gw Mikrofilm [380]

RADIO ALMANACH – Frankfurt/Main. jun 1, 1947-may 7, 1955 – 8r – 1 – gw Mikrofilm [073]

RADIO BROADCAST – v. 1-16. 1922-1930 – 1,5,6 – us Princeton Micro [621]

RADIO CIRCULAR / Wisconsin. Agricultural Extension Service – 1930-37 – 1,5 – us Spaulding [630]

RADIO COMMUNICATIONS – v1- 1925- 1; v52- 5,6,9 – us UMI [621]

RADIO CONTROL BOAT MODELER *see* AMERICAN BOAT MODELER

RADIO CORRIERE – 1988-1995 – 2r per y – 5,6 – Sfr588.00 – sz Infoprint [380]

RADIO DEL ESTADO *see* LRA

RADIO ENGINEERING AND ELECTRONICS – v1-6. 1956-61 – 1 – us UMI [073]

RADIO ENGINEERING & ELECTRONIC PHYSICS – (1984-. 5,6,9) – v7-29. 1962-84 – 1 – us UMI [073]

RADIO EVANGEL – Portland OR. Sep 8 1938 – 1 – us U.O. Library [071]

RADIO FREE EUROPE : BACKGROUND REPORTS. COUNTRY SERIES – Baltic, 16.4.1986-30.3.1989 – 2mf – 9 – ne IDC [380]

RADIO FREE EUROPE : EAST EUROPEAN LEADERSHIP LISTS:.... – 36mf – 9 – ne IDC [320]

RADIO FREE EUROPE : SITUATION REPORTS – Baltic Area, 4.12.1984-11.9.1989 – 16mf – 9 – ne IDC [380]

RADIO FREE EUROPE / RADIO LIBERTY / ed by Robinson, William F – (79 series) – 9 – ne IDC [380]

Radio Free Europe-Radio Liberty Inc *see* PUBLIC FIGURES IN THE CIS AND THE BALTIC STATES

RADIO ILLUSTRIERTE – Bremen, Germany. Jun 1947-Aug 1949 – 1r – 1 – gw Mikrofilm [073]

RADIO ILLUSTRIERTE – Bremen, jun 1947-aug 1949 – 1r – 1 – Inquire at Mikrofilmarchiv for details – gw Misc Inst [790]

RADIO MERCHANT – New York. v1-26. 1905-30 – 18r – 1 – us Ross [380]

RADIO NEWS – v.7-. 1981- – 1,5,6,9 – us UMI [073]

RADIO REGULATION / Pike and Fisher, Inc – 40 reels – 1 – $1,600.00 – us Trans-Media [380]

RADIO REVUE – Berlin. dec 22, 1946-55 – 7r – 1 – gw Mikrofilm [073]

RADIO SCIENCE, BI MONTHLY – (v4-11 1969-76 $30.00y 1,5,6,13 $50.00y 9. v12 1977 $30.00 1,5,6,13 $70.00 9. v13 1978 $30.00 1,5,6,13 $80.00 9. v14 1979 $30.00 1,5,6,13 $90.00 9. v15 1980 $35.00 1,5,6,13 $90.00 9. v16 1981 $35.00 1,5,6,13 $110.00 9. v17 1982 $45.00 1,5,6,13 $120.00 9. v27 1992 $250.00. v28 1993 $250.00. v29 1994 $265.00. v30 1995 $320.00) – v4-17 1969-82. v1-3 publ. by U.S. Dept. of Commerce – us A.G.U. [530]

Radio Singapore Special News Service *see* MONITORING DIGEST OF NEWS FROM PEKING, VIETMINH, AND MOSCOW

RADIO SPEECH DELIVERED ON SEPT. 19, 1948 ON THE MADIUM COUP / Sukarno, Pres. Indonesia – SE 4692 1. 1948 – 9 – ne IDC [324]

RADIO TIMES 1923- – (v1-225 1923-79 97r 1. v226-283 1980-94 1050mf 9) – 1923-98 – 1,9 (1923-95 £6,185.00; 1996 £120; 1997 £150 1998 – enquire) – uk Chadwyck [073]

RADIO VJESNIK – Sisak. Aug. 11, 1943-Feb. 2, 1944. Missing: 4 scattered issues – 1 – 35.00r – us Hoover Inst Photo [380]

RADIOACTIVE FALLOUT IN SOILS, CROPS AND FOOD – 1989 – 84p – it F.A.O. [360]

RADIOACTIVE WASTE MANAGEMENT – (An intl journal. Cont as Radioactive Waste Management and the Nuclear Fuel Cycle) – 1980-81 – 1,5,9 – us Harwood [628]

RADIOACTIVE WASTE MANAGEMENT AND ENVIRONMENTAL RESTORATION : A MULTINATIONAL JOURNAL / ed by Anderson, D R & Girardi, Francesco – 9,5,1 – us Harwood [628]

RADIOACTIVE WASTE MANAGEMENT AND THE NUCLEAR FUEL CYCLE *see* RADIOACTIVE WASTE MANAGEMENT

RADIOACTIVE WASTE MANAGEMENT AND THE NUCLEAR FUEL CYCLE: AN INTERNATIONAL JOURNAL – 1983- – 1,5,9 – us Harwood [628]

RADIOCHEMICAL AND RADIOANALYTICAL LETTERS – v1-59. 1969-83 – 1,5,6,13 – sz Elsevier [073]

RADIOCHEMISTRY – (Cont: Soviet Radiochemistry) – v4-36. 1962-94 – 1,5 – $80.00v – us UMI [540]

Radiodifusora XELA. Mexico City *see* BOLETIN

RADIO-ELECTRONICS – (v. 40- 1969- 5,6. v. 41- 1970- 9) – v. 1- 1929- – 1 – us UMI [621]

RADIO-ELECTRONICS SPECIAL PROJECTS – v1-1. 1981-84 – 1,5,6,9 – us UMI [073]

RADIO-ELECTRONICS SPECIAL PROJECTS *see* HANDS-ON ELECTRONICS

RADIOGRAPHICS – (1985-. 5,6,9) – v1-. 1981- – 1 – us UMI [600]

RADIO-INFORMATION : REVUE CONSACREE AUX ACTIVITES RADIOPHONIQUES – Montreal, Canada. v3 n16. 27 avr 1940; v3 n20. 25 mai 1940 – 1r – 1 – Can$25.00 – cn Can Microfilming [073]

DIE RADIOLARIEN / Haeckel, Ernst Heinrich Philipp August – Z-210 2. 1862 – 8 – ne IDC [590]

DER RADIOLOGE – v. 1-20. 1961-80 – 1,5,9 – 2190.00 – us UMI [073]

RADIOLOGIA MEDICA – v1- 1914- 1; v61- 5,6,9 – us UMI [610]

RADIOLOGIE: JOURNAL DE CEPUR – College d'enseignement post universitaire de radiologie.v.1, 1981. ISSN:0720-3322 – 1,5,6,9,13 – 70.00v – us UMI [616]

RADIOLOGY – v1- 1923- 1; v114- 5,6 – us UMI [616]

RADIOLOGY-CUMULATIVE INDEX – 1987- – 1,5,6,9 – us UMI [610]

RADIO-MONDE – (Cont by: Radio-Monde et Tele-Monde 6 sep 1952-29 jan 1955) – Montreal, Canada. 1 jan 1939-30 aut 1952 – 10r – 1 – Can$50.00r – cn Can Microfilming [380]

RADIO-MONDE ET TELE-MONDE *see* RADIO-MONDE

RADIOPHYSICS AND QUANTUM ELECTRONICS – v8-36. 1965-93 – 1,5 – $120.00v – us UMI [530]

RADIO-PROGRAMMY VSESOI UZNOGO RADIOKOMITETA PRI SOVNARKOME SOI UZA SSR – (c.1 Library lacks some issues; c.1: 1938:Jan.5-1939:Apr.11) – Moskva: Radioizdat, 193u – 1 – CSUXANQ9617-S – us Hoover Inst Photo [621]

RADIOPROGRAMMY VSESOIUZNOGO RADIOKOMITETA PRI SOVNARKOME SOI UZA SSR *see* RADIO-PROGRAMMY VSESOI UZNOGO RADIOKOMITETA PRI SOVNARKOME SOI UZA SSR

RADIO-SPIEGEL – Stuttgart, 1946-48 – 1r – 1 – gw Mikrofilm [790]

RADIO-UMSCHAU – Frankfurt/Main. 1924-27. jan 4-mar 28, 1931 – 4r – 1 – gw Mikrofilm [073]

Radishchev, A N *see* PUTESHESTVIE IZ PETERBURGA V MOSKVU

RADISHCHEV I EGO VREMIA / Makogonenko, G P – M. 1956. BR-7678 2 – 8 – ne IDC [460]

RADIUM – Wedderburn, OR. -w. 1904-08 – 1 – 17.00 – us Oregon Hist [071]

RADIUM – Wedderburn, OR. -w. Jan 1904-3 Dec 1908. 1 roll – 1 – us U.O. Library [071]

THE RADIUM – Wedderburn. Or. 1904-1908 – 1 – us UMI [071]

Radjab, Muhammad *see* TJATATAN DI SUMATERA

RADLETT AND BOREHAMWOOD ADVERTISER – London, St Albans, England, 1981- – 58+ r – 1 – uk British Libr Newspaper [072]

Radlkofer, LA T *see* UEBER DIE SAPINDACEEN HOLLAENDISCH-INDIENS...

Radloff, Carl Adolf *see* DIE MORPHOLOGISCHEN VERAENDERUNGEN DURCH RADIUM AN LEBER UND MILZ

Radloff, Hans-Henning *see*
- MESSUNG DER WIRKUNGSQUERSCHNITTE FUER DEPOLARISATION DES 6^3P_1 YB-ZUSTANDS DURCH EDELGASSTOESSE MIT HILFE DER QUANTUM-BEAT-METHODE UNTER VERWENDUNG EINES GEPULSTEN FARBSTOFFLASERS
- EIN SYSTEM ZUR ERFASSUNG UND AUSWERTUNG PERIODISCH WIEDERKEHRENDER SIGNALE BEI PHYSIKALISCHEN EXPERIMENTEN

[Radlov, V V] *see*
- AUS SIBIRIEN. LOZE BLAETTER AUS DEM TAGEBUCHE EINES REISENDE LINGUISTEN
- UEBER DIE FORMEN DER GEBUNDENE REDE BEI DEN ALTAISCHEN TARTAREN
- UIGURISCHE SPRACHDENKMAELER

Radlspeck, Carl *see* DIE NATIONALKIRCHLICHE IDEE I.H.V. WESSENBERGS IM URTEIL DER FLUGSCHRIFTENLITERATUR 1803-1821

RADNICKE NOVINE : ORGAN SRPSKE SOCIJAL-DEMOKRAKSKE PARTIJE I GLAVNOG RADNICKOG-SAVEZA – Belgrade, 1903, 1905, 1913-15 (incompl), 1920 (missing Oct 26) – 1 – $35.00r – us Hoover Inst Photo [335]

Radnor, Michael *see* TECHNOLOGY ASSESSMENT

Radnorshire Society *see* TRANSACTIONS

RADOMER-KELTSER LEBEN = LIFE – (In Yiddish) – Radom, PL. v4 no16 24 Apr 1927-v6 no39 4 Oct 1929 – 1r – 1 – $25.00 – cn Can Microfilming [072]

Radoslavoff, V *see* BULGARIEN UND DIE WELTKRISE

Radtmann, B *see* INTRODVCTIO IN LINGVAM ARABICAM...

RADUGA – Illiustrirovannyi semeinyi zhurnal. M. 1883-88. Lacking: v. 1-3, 1883-85; v. 5-6, 1887-88. B-1842 2 – 8 – ne IDC [073]

RADUGA – Zhurnal literaturno-nauchnyi. v. 1. Odessa. 1909. BR-3781 2 – 8 – ne IDC [073]

RADUGA – Zhurnal ucheno-literaturnyi i pedagogicheskii. Odessa. 1860-62. BR-3795 2 – 8 – ne IDC [370]

RADULPH DE RIVO DER LETZTE VERTRETER DER ALTROEMISCHEN LITURGIE / Mohlberg, C – (Band 1: Studien, Louvain 1911. 7mf. Dfl28.00; Band 2: Texte, Louvain 1915. 9mf. Dfl 32.00) – 8 – ne Slangenburg [240]

Radulphi de Coggenshall *see* CHRONICON ANGLICANUM (RS66)

RADY SZKOLNEJ KRAJOWEJ / Sprawozdanie, C K – 1890-1912 – 3r – 1 – us I.H.R.C. [947]

RADYANSKA UKRAIENA – Kiev, U.S.S.R. -d. 18 March 1952-Dec 1970. 32 reels – 1 – uk British Libr Newspaper [947]

Radyserb-Wjela, Jan *see* PRISLOWA A PRISLOWNE HRONCKA A WUSLLOWA HORNJOLUZISKICH SERBOW

Radziwill, Ekaterina Rzewuska Kniagina *see* RUSSIA'S DECLINE AND FALL, THE SECRET HISTORY OF THE GREAT DEBACLE

Radziwill, Ekaterina Rzewuska kniagina *see* THE AUSTRIAN COURT FROM WITHIN

Rae, A *see* LIST OF ANCIENT MONUMENTS SELECTED FOR CONSERVATION IN THE MADRAS PRESIDENCY

Rae, Colin *see* MALABOCH

Rae, J *see*
- ARCTIC EXPLORATION, WITH INFORMATION RESPECTING SIR JOHN FRANKLIN'S MISSING PARTY
- NARRATIVE OF AN EXPEDITION TO THE SHORES OF THE ARCTIC SEA IN 1846 AND 1847
- RECENT EXPLORATIONS ALONG THE SOUTH AND EAST COAST OF VICTORIA LAND

Rae, John *see*
- CONTEMPORARY SOCIALISM

Rae, William Fraser *see* THE BUSINESS OF TRAVEL: A FIFTY YEARS' RECORD OF PROGRESS

Raebiger, Julius Ferdinand *see* ZUR THEOLOGISCHEN ENCYKLOPAEDIE: KRITISCHE BETRACHTUNGEN

Raedeke, Thomas D *see* IS ATHLETE BURNOUT MORE THAN JUST STRESS? A SPORT COMMITMENT PERSPECTIVE

DAS RAESONNIRENDE DORFKONVENT – Erfurt, 1786-1788 – 3r – 1 – DM225.00 – gw Mikro Press [240]

DAS RAESONNIRENDE DORFKONVENT – Erfurt, Germany. 1786-1788 (incomplete) – 2r – 1 – gw Mikrofilm [072]

RAESTDZINAD – Ordzhonikidze, USSR. May-Nov 11 1991; Jan 21-Nov 19 1992 – 2r – 1 – us L of C Photodup [072]

RAETE ZEITUNG – Berlin. Apr. 1919-Dec. 1920 (complete) – 1 – 35.00r – us Hoover Inst Photo [073]
RAETE-ZEITUNG – Berlin, 1919-20 – 1r – 1 – Inquire at Mikrofilmarchiv for details – gw Misc Inst [335]
RAETE-ZEITUNG – Berlin, DE. 1919-20 – 1r – 1 – gw Mikrofilm [072]
DAS RAETSEL DES DEUTEROJESAJANISCHEN BUCHES / Sellin, Ernst – Leipzig: A Deichert, 1908 – 1mf – 9 – 0-8370-5227-0 – 1985-3227 – us A.T.L.A. [220]
DAS RAETSEL DES FUENFBUCHES MOSE UND SEINE FALSCHE LOESUNG / Rupprecht, Eduard – Guetersloh: C. Bertelsmann, 1894. 1 fiche – 9 – us A.T.L.A. [240]
DIE RAEUBER : EIN SCHAUSPIEL IN FUENF AKTEN / Schiller, Friedrich von – Leipzig: P Reclam, [194-?] – 1r – 1 – us U.W. Library [820]
Raeuschel, E A *see* NOMENCLATOR BOTANICUS
RAEVSKIE / Arkhiv Raevskikh – Izdanie P.M. Raevskogo. Red. i primechaniia B.L. Modzalevskogo. v. 1-5. Spb., Petrograd. 1908-15. BR-9201 1 – 9 – ne IDC [920]
Rafal, Marques de *see* DATOS INEDITOS PARA LA BIOGRAFIA DEL CAPITAN ARMANDO DE MONTENEGRO, COMPANERO DE PIZARRO EN LA CONQUISTA DEL PERU
Raff, J *see*
- CONCERT FUR DAS PIANOFORTE
- SINFONIE NO. 6, D MINOR, FUR GROSSES ORCHESTER, OP. 18

Raffenel, Anne *see*
- NOUVEAU VOYAGE DANS LE PAYS DES NEGRES
- VOYAGE DANS L'AFRIQUE OCCIDENTALE EN 1843 ET 1844

Raffenel, Jean-Baptiste A *see*
- NOUVEAU VOYAGE DANS LE PAYS DES NEGRES SUIVI D'ETUDES SUR LA COLONIE DU SENEGAL
- VOYAGE DANS L'AFRIQUE OCCIDENTALE

Rafferty, A C *see* VISIONS OF GOD: THE APOCALYPSES OF OUR SAVIOR, JESUS CHRIST, GIVEN TO JOHN, THE LAST OF THE TWELVE APOSTLES
Raffles, T S *see* THE HISTORY OF JAVA
RAFINESQUE / Fitzpatrick, T J – A sketch of his life with bibliography. Des Moines. 1911. B-8314 1 – 9 – ne IDC [900]
RAFINESQUE, A SKETCH OF HIS LIFE WITH BIBLIOGRAPHY / Fitzpatrick, T J – Des Moines, 1911 – 4mf – ne IDC [580]
Rafinesque-Schmaltz, Constantine S *see*
- ALSOGRAPHIA AMERICANA
- AMERICAN MANUAL OF THE MULBERRY TREES
- ANALYSE DE LA NATURE OU TABLEAU DE L'UNIVERS ET DES CORPS ORGANISES
- ANNALS OF NATURE
- ATLANTIC JOURNAL, AND FRIEND OF KNOWLEDGE
- AUTIKON BOTANIKON
- BULLETIN OF THE HISTORICAL AND NATURAL SCIENCES
- CARATTERI DI ALCUNI NUOVI GENERI
- CHLORIS AETNENSIS, ETC
- CIRCULAR ADDRESS ON BOTANY AND ZOOLOGY
- COLLECTED PAPERS. ZOOLOGY
- COLLECTED PAPERS-BOTANY
- THE COMPLETE WRITINGS OF C.S. RAFINESQUE ON RECENT AND FOSSIL CONCHOLOGY
- FIRST CATALOGUES AND CIRCULARS OF THE BOTANICAL GARDEN OF TRANSYLVANIA UNIVERSITY AT LEXINGTON IN KENTUCKY, FOR THE YEAR 1824
- FIRST CATALOGUES AND CIRCULARS OF THE BOTANICAL GARDEN OF TRANSYLVANIA UNIVERSITY AT LEXINGTON KENTUCKY, FOR THE YEAR 1824
- FLORA TELLURIANA
- FLORULA LUDOVICIANA
- HERBARIUM RAFINESQUANUM
- MANUAL OF THE MEDICAL BOTANY OF THE UNITED STATES
- MEDICAL FLORA...
- A MONOGRAPH OF THE FLUVIATILE BIVALVE SHELLS OF THE RIVER OHIO
- NEOGENYTON
- NEOPHYTON NO. 3
- NEW FLORA AND BOTANY OF NORTH AMERICA
- NOTICE ON THE MEDICAL PROPERTIES OF SOME NORTH-AMERICAN PLANTS
- NOTICES OF MATERIA MEDICA
- PRINCIPES FONDAMENTAUX DE SOMIOLOGIE
- SYLVA TELLURIANA
- WESTERN MINERVA
- THE WORLD, OR INSTABILITY

RAFT SWAMP BAPTIST CHURCH. ROBESON ASSOCIATION. NORTH CAROLINA : CHURCH RECORDS – 1868-91 – 1 – 8.82 – us Baptist [240]
RAFTSMANS JOURNAL – Clearfield, PA. -w 1893-1934 – 13 – $25.00r – us I.M.R. [071]
RAGAN NEWS – Ragan, NE. -w. Sept 1895-Feb 1896; Apr 1896-May 1898; Jul 1898-Jan 1901; Apr 1901-Sept 1902 – 1 – us NE Hist [071]
Ragatz, Lowell J *see*
- BIBLIOGRAPHY OF ARTICLES ON COLONIES APPEARING IN AMERICAN GEOGRAPHICAL AND KINDRED JOURNALS THROUGH 1934
- BIBLIOGRAPHY OF ARTICLES... ON COLONIES... APPEARING IN AMERICAN GEOGRAPHICAL AND KINDRED JOURNALS THROUGH 1934
- CARIBBEAN – GENERAL

Ragg, Lara *see* THE GOSPEL OF BARNABAS
Ragg, Lonsdale *see*
- THE CHURCH OF THE APOSTLES
- EVIDENCES OF CHRISTIANITY
- THE GOSPEL OF BARNABAS

Ragg, Thomas *see* CREATION'S TESTIMONY TO ITS GOD: THE ACCORDANCE OF SCIENCE, PHILOSOPHY, AND REVELATION
RAGGUAGLIO DELLA SOLENNE COMPARSA FATTA IN ROMA GLI OTTO DI GENNAIO MDCLXXXVII, DALL ILLUSTRISSIMO, ET ECCELLEMTISSIMO SIGNOR CONTE DI CASTELMAINE AMBASCIADORE... / Michele Writ Maggiordomo, G – Roma, 1687 – 9 – BO-1103 1 – ne IDC [945]
IL RAGGVAGLIO DELLE MARAUIGLIOSE POMPE CON LE QUALI MEHEMET SETTERGI GENERALE DI MEHEMET 3. IMPERATOR DE' TURCHI E VSCITO FUORI DI CONSTATINOPOLI / Frachetta, G – Venetia, 1597 – 1mf – 9 – H-8394/1 – ne IDC [956]
Raghavan, V *see* NEW CATALOGUS CATALOGORUM
RAGHUVANSA/KUMARA SAMBHAVA / Kalidasa – 1832 and 1838 – 1 – uk Microform Academic [280]
RAGI BUANA – Djakarta. SE-404 1. Lacking: v. 1(6). 1964. v. 1-8. 1964-1971 – 9 – ne IDC [073]
RAGING INFLATION FORCES ISRAELI CURRENCY CHANGE / Davis, Douglas – 1985, 1p – 9 – 1.00f – at Libertarian Micro [332]
RAGIONAMENTI MUSICALI COMPOSTI DAL SIG D. ANGELO BERARDI / Berardi, A – 1681 – 9 – us Sibley [780]
RAGIONAMENTO. SOPRA UNA STANZA DIPINTA DAL. A. ALLEGRI DA CORREGGIO NEL MONISTERO DI S. PAOLO IN PARMA / Affo, I – Parma. 1794. BO-1065 1 – 9 – ne IDC [760]
RAGLAND'S SUPERIOR COURT DECISIONS / California – v1-2. 1924-1929 – 4mf – 9 – $6.00 – LLMC 91-024 – us L.L.M.C. [340]
RAGNAROK: THE AGE OF FIRE AND GRAVEL / Donnelly, Ignatius – New York: D. Appleton and Company, 1883.vi,452p. Illus. With: 35 Mois de Campagne en Chine by E.C.E. Duboc. 1 reel. 1267 – 1 – us U.W. Library [390]
Ragoss, Silvia *see* GEWALT AN FRAUEN
Ragozin, Zenaide A *see* THE STORY OF CHALDEA FROM THE EARLIEST TIMES TO THE RISE OF ASSYRIA,.
Ragsdale, Bruce A *see* BLACK AMERICANS IN CONGRESS 1870-1989
RAGTIME REVIEW – v1-4, no. 1 (all publ). Dec 1914-Jan 1918. (Title varies). (Jazz Periodicals) – 1 reel – 1 – $70.00 – us UPA [073]
Ragueau, F *see* GLOSSAIRE DU DROIT FRANCAIS
RAHA'I – (Cont: Raha'i:nashriyah-'i Guruh-i Ittihad-i Kumunisti. Solna, Sweden: Guruh-i Ittihad-i Kumunisti. Dawrah-'i 2: sal-i 1, shumarah-'i 1–sal-i 3, shumarah-'i 111 (26 Tir 1358-8 Bahman 1360[17 Jul 1979-28 Jan 1982]). Missing issues 92, 98) – [S.I.]: Sazman-i Vahdat-i Kumunisti, 1979- – 2r – 1 – $100.00 – us MEDOC [950]
RAHA'I:NASHRIYAH-'I GURUH-I ITTIHAD-I KUMUNISTI *see* RAHA'I
RAHEL VARNHAGEN : EIN LEBENS- UND ZEITBILD / Berdrow, Otto – 2. verän. Aufl. Stuttgart: Greiner & Pfeiffer, 1902 – 1 – us U.W. Library [920]
RAH-I FADA'I – (Shumarah-'i 1-29 (Shahrivar 1358-Azar 1362[Aug 1979-Nov 1983])) – [S.I.]: Rah-i Fada'i – 1 reel – 1 – $90.00 – us MEDOC [950]
RAH-I FADA'I-MAQALAT – (Shumarah-'i 1-5 (Bahman 1361-Farvardin 1963[Jan/Feb 1983-Mar/Apr 1984])) – [S.I.]: Rah-i Fada-'i – 1 reel – 1 – $25.00 – us MEDOC [950]
RAH-I KARGAR – (Shumarah-'i 1-79 (7 Azar 1358-1 Tir 1360[28 Nov 1979-22 Jun 1981]). Missing issues: 3, 8, 22, 27, 30, 35, 37, 38, 41, 45-47, 49, 51, 57, 68-69, 75) – [S.I.]: Rah-i Kargar, 1979- – 1 reel – 1 – $75.00 – us MEDOC [950]
RAH-I TUDAH – Chicago: Hizb-i Tudah-i Iran Dar Kharij Az Kishvar. Shumarah-i 1, 3, 21, 39 (8 Murdad 1361, 22 Murdad 1361, 26 Azar 1361, 9 Urdibihisht 1362 [31 Jul 1982, 15 Aug 1982, 17 Dec 1982, 29 Apr 1983]) – 9 – $25.00 – us MEDOC [956]
Rahidy, Basilide, R P *see* COURS PRATIQUE DE LANGUE MALGACHE
Rahlfs, Alfred *see*
- 'ANI UND 'ANAV IN DEN PSALMEN
- SEPTUAGINTA

Rahlwes, F *see*
- DIE BUECHER DER BIBEL

Rahmani, Ignace Efraem 2 *see* TESTAMENTUM DOMINI NOSTRI JESU CHRISTI
Rahmdohr, FW B von *see* UEBER MAHLEREI UND BILDHAUERARBEIT IN ROM
DER RAHMEN DES DEUTERONOMIUMS / Steuernagel, Carl – Halle a.S.: J. Krause, 1894. 1 fiche – 9 – us A.T.L.A. [240]
Rahmer, M *see*
- DIE HEBRAEISCHEN TRADITIONEN IN DEN WERKEN DES HIERONYMUS
- ISRAELITISCHE WOCHEN-SCHRIFT

Rahmer, Sigismund *see* HEINRICH VON KLEIST ALS MENSCH UND DICHTER
Rahn, Konstanze *see* ERNST PENZOLDT UND DAS THEATER
RAHNUMA-E-DECCAN – Hyderabad, India. 1961; Jan-Apr 1966 – 3r – 1 – us L of C Photodup [072]
RAHVA HAEAEL – Tallinn, U.S.S.R. -d. April-Dec 1947; Sept-Dec 1951; March 1952-Dec 1953; Jan 1955-Dec 1962. 1947-1953 imperfect. 23 reels – 1 – uk British Libr Newspaper [947]
Raid, Fenian *see* THE CANADIAN MAIL AND MONTREAL WEEKLY GAZETTE
Raige-Delorme, J *see* DICTIONNAIRE ENCYCLOPEDIQUE DES SCIENCES MEDICALES (AEL, ABT 3;15)
Raikes, Robert *see* HIS SUNDAY SCHOOLS AND HIS FRIENDS
Raikov, BE *see* AKADEMIK VASILII ZUEV, EGO ZHIZN' I TRUDY
Raillet, Ph.M *see* LE TRIOMPHE DE LA LANGUE FRANCOISE
RAILROAD / Australian Railways Union – Sydney, Australia. Official organ of the Australian Railways Union. 10 Feb 1934-14 Nov 1969; Jan 1974-Dec 1975.-w. 9 reels – 1 – uk British Libr Newspaper [072]
RAILROAD APPRAISEMENT RECORDS / Allen County. Ohio. Board of Railroad Appraisers – 1903-1910 – 1r – 1 – $32.50r – us Archival [324]
RAILROAD APPRAISEMENT RECORDS / Fulton County. Ohio. Board of Railroad Appraisers – 1873-1903 – 1r – 1 – $32.50r – us Archival [324]
RAILROAD APPRAISEMENT RECORDS / Ottawa County. Ohio. Board of Railroad Appraisers – 1906 – 1r – 1 – $32.50r – us Archival [324]
RAILROAD APPRAISEMENT RECORDS / Wyandot County. Ohio. Board of Railroad Appraisers – 1904-1909 – 1r – 1 – $32.50r – us Archival [324]
RAILROAD CAR DESIGN AND PULLMAN CAR DATA / Anderson, Gene – 1 – us KS Hist [625]
RAILROAD COLLECTION / Barnes, Lela – 1855-1959, Information on all railroads incorporated to do business in Kansas including street railways and roads that never progressed beyond incorporation – 1 – us KS Hist [380]
RAILROAD LABOR BOARD DECISIONS / U.S. Railroad Labor Board – (With indexes) – v1-7. 1920-26 (all publ) – 68mf – 9 – $102.00 – LLMC 81-239 – us L.L.M.C. [324]
RAILROAD MONTHLY – 1978- – 9 – us UMI [380]
RAILROAD REPORTS *see* AMERICAN AND ENGLISH RAILROAD CASES
THE RAILROADS AND THE COMMERCE CLAUSE / Hartshorne, Francis Cope – Philadelphia: University of Pennsylvania Press, 1893. 165p. LL-391 – 1 – us L of C Photodup [340]
RAILWAY ACCIDENTS / Drummond, Andrew Thomas – Montreal?: s.n., 1888?. (Montreal: J. Lovell). 02770. (Pre-1900 Canadiana) – 9 – cn C.I.H.M. [971]
RAILWAY AND CUSTOMS POLITICS IN SOUTH-AFRICA. 1885-1910 / Poel, J. van der – (Imperial Studies, no. 8). London. 1933. B-270 – 8 – ne IDC [380]
THE RAILWAY AND MARINE WORLD *see* THE RAILWAY AND SHIPPING WORLD
RAILWAY AND SHIPPING WORLD – Canada. Canadian Railway & Marine World. -w. Jan 1899-Feb 1903; Feb 1912-Dec 1921. 12 reels – 1 – uk British Libr Newspaper [073]
THE RAILWAY AND SHIPPING WORLD – (Absorbed: The Western World. Cont by: The Railway and Marine World) – Toronto: Railway & Shipping World Co, [1898-1905] – 9 – cn C.I.H.M. [380]
RAILWAY AND STEAMBOAT GUIDE AND TOURISTS' HANDBOOK FOR NOVA SCOTIA, NEW BRUNSWICK AND PRINCE EDWARD ISLAND – Halifax, N.[S.]: Harrington & O'Flaherty, [1873?-18– or 19–] – 9 – cn C.I.H.M. [910]
RAILWAY AND STEAMBOAT TIMES – Montreal, Canada. 11 oct 1880; v12 n21. 25 mai 1891 – 1r – 1 – Can$25.00 – cn Can Microfilming [380]
RAILWAY AND TRAMWAY EXPRESS / Tramway Institute – London. -w. 3 May 1884-1 Dec. 1886. 2 reels – 1 – uk British Libr Newspaper [073]
RAILWAY CLAUSES CONSOLIDATION ACTS AND ACTS RELATING TO THE GRAND TRUNK RAILWAY OF CANADA / Canada. Laws, Statutes, etc – Quebec: Stewart Derbishire & George Desbarats, 1853. SEM105P1763 – 2mf – 9 – Can$4.50 – cn Bibl Nat [380]
RAILWAY COMMISSION / Credit Valley Railway Company – s.l.: s.n., 1879? (Toronto: Globe). 04188. (Pre-1900 Canadiana) – 9 – cn C.I.H.M. [971]
RAILWAY CONSTRUCTION AND WORKING...: WITH AN ABSTRACT OF THE DISCUSSION UPON THE PAPERS / ed by Forrest, James – London: The Institution, 1886. 05584. (Pre-1900 Canadiana) – 9 – cn C.I.H.M. [625]
RAILWAY ENGINEER – v1-3 1976-78 – 1,5,6,9 – us UMI [625]
RAILWAY ENGINEER INTERNATIONAL – (See also: Railway Engineer) – v3- 1978- – 1,5,6,9 – us UMI [625]
RAILWAY INTELLIGENCE, 1849-1879 – 7r – 1 – uk Microform Academic [941]
THE RAILWAY JOURNAL – Montreal, Canada. v2 n2. mar 1882 – 1r – 1 – Can$25.00 – cn Can Microfilming [380]
RAILWAY LAW IN ILLINOIS / Gilbert, Frank – Chicago: Callaghan, 1873. 337p. Imperfect: t.-p. wanting. LL-651 – 1 – us L of C Photodup [340]
RAILWAY LIFE – Toronto: W B Campbell, [1886-1888?] – 9 – cn C.I.H.M. [380]
RAILWAY LOCOMOTIVES AND CARS – 1832-1900 – 1 – $1016.00 – us L of C Photodup [625]
RAILWAY MAGAZINE – London, England. Herapath's Railway Magazine – Herapath's Railway & Commercial Journal – Herapath's Railway Journal. -w. 1 May 1835-24 Dec 1903. 100 reels – 1 – uk British Libr Newspaper [073]
RAILWAY NEWS – London. -w. 1864-1918. (100 reels) – 1 – uk British Libr Newspaper [072]
Raimund, Ferdinand *see* FERDINAND RAIMUNDS SAEMTLICHE WERKE IN DREI TEILEN
Raimundo, Jacques *see* VOCABULARIOS INDIGENAS DE VENEZUELA.
RAIMUNDO RIVA. LECTURAS HISTORICAS / Bayle, Constantino – Madrid: Razon y Fe, 1926 – 1 – sp Bibl Santa Ana [946]
RAIN FOREST REGENERATION AND MANAGEMENT / ed by Gomez-Pompa, A et al – 1991 – 9 – 92-3-102647-X – fr UNESCO [634]
RAIN: ROYAL ANTHROPOLOGICAL INSTITUTE NEWS – v. 1-. 1974- – 1,5,6,9 – us UMI [301]
RAINBARREL ECHOE – LaGrande OR. Mar 5 1913 – 1 – us U.O. Library [071]

RAINBOW ARGUS – 1951-1962 – 4r – 1 – at Corangamite [072]
Raine, J *see*
- THE HISTORIANS OF THE CHURCH OF YORK AND ITS ARCHBISHOPS (RS71)
- HISTORICAL PAPERS AND LETTERS FROM THE NORTHERN REGISTERS (RS61)

RAINER MARIA RILKES FRUEHE LYRIK : ENTWICKLUNGSGESCHICHTLICHE ANALYSE DER DICHTERISCHEN FORM / Berger, Kurt – (Includes bibliographical references) – Marburg a.L.: Elwert, 1931 – 1r – 1 – us U.W. Library [430]
RAINGAN KANPRACHOOM SAPHA PHUTAEN RASADON / Thailand. Sapha Phutaen Rasadon – Bangkok. On film: 1932-75. LL-0262 – 1 – us L of C Photodup [340]
RAINIER GAZETTE – Rainier OR. Dec 17 24 1901, Jan 3-17 1902 – 1 – us U.O. Library [071]
RAINIER NEWS – Rainier OR. Nov 3 1927-Jan 5 1928 – 1 – us U.O. Library [071]
RAINIER REVIEW – Rainier, OR. -w. 3 Aug 1905-30 Jun 1976+. 20 rolls – 1 – us U.O. Library [071]
Rainolde, Richard *see* A BOOKE CALLED THE FOUNDACION OF REHTORIKE
Rainolds, John *see*
- THE PROPHECY OF HAGGAI
- THE PROPHECY OF OBADIAH OPENED AND APPLIED IN SUNDRY SERMONS

Rainville, Lucie *see* BIBLIOGRAPHIE ANALYTIQUE DES RECUEILS BIOGRAPHIQUES CANADIENS, FRANCAIS ET ANGLAIS
A RAINY JUNE / Ouida – British Fiction Archive: Unit 3 – 9 – uk Bell [830]
Rainy, Robert *see*
- THE ANCIENT CATHOLIC CHURCH
- THE BIBLE AND CRITICISM
- DELIVERY AND DEVELOPMENT OF CHRISTIAN DOCTRINE
- EPISTLE TO THE PHILIPPIANS
- LIFE OF WILLIAM CUNNINGHAM, D.D.
- THE SUPERNATURAL IN CHRISTIANITY
- THREE LECTURES ON THE CHURCH OF SCOTLAND

O RAIO : JORNAL DEMOCRATA – Aracaju, 28 Nov 1875-Dec 1876; Jan-Mar, Jun, Nov 1877; Jan-Apr, Aug 1878; Jan-Mar, May-Oct, Dec 1879; Jan-May, Jul-Dec 1880; Jan-Jun 1881; Sep-Dec 1884; Feb-22 Mar 1885 – 1,5,6 – bl Biblioteca [072]
RAIO – Manaos, Amazonas. 8, 11 Dez 1912 – 1,5,6 – bl Biblioteca [072]
O RAIO 10 : JORNAL HUMORISTICO – [s.l.] 21 Nov 1912 – 1,5,6 – bl Biblioteca [072]
O RAIO 10 : ORGAO LITERARIO, CRITICO E HUMORISTICO – Itacoatiara, Amazonas. 1 Jan-17 Abr 1915 – 1,5,6 – bl Biblioteca [072]
Rais, Gilles de *see* GILLES DE RAIS
RAISING CHILDREN FOR FUND AND PROFIT / Lefevre, Robert – 4fiches (24x) – 9 – 1.00f – at Libertarian Micro [320]
RAISING DUCKS, 1 : HOW TO BEGIN – 1990 – 73p – it F.A.O. [639]
LA RAISON – (D'Holbach series) – 9 – fr Hachette [120]
LA RAISON ET LE RATIONALISME / Ollelaprune, Leon – Paris: Perrin, 1906. liii,212p.4 fiches. (Philosophy Collection) – 9 – 10.00 – fr Bibl Nationale [140]
RAISONNEMENTS HASARDEZ SUR LA POESIE FRANCOISE / Longue, LP de – 1737 – 9 – fr I.C.S. [440]
LES RAISONS DES FORCES MOUVANTES AVEC DIVERSES MACHINES / Caus, Salomon de – Francfort. 1615. BH-1825 1 – 9 – ne IDC [530]
Rait, R S *see* ENGLISH EPISCOPAL PALACES
Rait, Robert Sangster *see*
- ENGLISH EPISCOPAL PALACES
- THE HISTORY OF THE UNION BANK OF SCOTLAND
- LIFE IN THE MEDIEVAL UNIVERSITY
- MARY QUEEN OF SCOTS, 1542-1587

Raithel, Hans *see* ANNAMAIG
LA RAIZ ROTA / Barea, Arturo – Buenos Aires: Santiago Rueda, editor, 1955 – sp Bibl Santa Ana [946]
RAJA *see* AL-RAJA
Rajaobelina, Prosper *see* GRAMERA MALAGASY
RAJARSHI RAM MOHAN ROY / Parekh, Manilal Chhotalal – Rajkot: Kathiawad, Oriental Christ House, 1927. viii,186p. (Makers of New Hindustan Series).1 reel. 1258 – 1 – us U.W. Library [920]
Rajasthan. India (State). Directorate of Economics and Statistics *see*
- SECOND FIVE YEAR PLAN PROGRESS REPORT, 1958-59
- SECOND FIVE YEAR PLAN PROGRESS REPORT, 1959-60
- SECOND FIVE YEAR PLAN PROGRESS REPORT FOR 1956-57
- SECOND FIVE YEAR PLAN PROGRESS REPORT FOR 1957-58
- THIRD FIVE YEAR PLAN PROGRESS REPORT, 1961-66
- THIRD FIVE YEAR PLAN PROGRESS REPORT, 1962-63
- THIRD FIVE YEAR PLAN PROGRESS REPORT, 1963-64
- THIRD FIVE YEAR PLAN PROGRESS REPORT, 1964-65

Rajasthan. India (State). Planning and Development Department *see* SECOND FIVE YEAR PLAN
Rajneesh, Bhagwan Shree *see* DYNAMICS OF MEDITATION: (TWELVE INTERVIEW-DISCOURSES ON THE VARIOUS ASPECTS OF MEDITATION)
RAJNEESH TIMES – Rajneeshpuram OR. Sep 3 1982-Nov 29 1985 – 1 – us U.O. Library [071]
RAJPUTANA / Rajputana. India. Superintendent of Census Operations – Lucknow. pt 4. 1901 – us Res Libr [310]
Rajputana. India. Superintendent of Census Operations *see* RAJPUTANA
RAK – RASSENPOLITISCHE AUSLANDS-KORRESPONDENZ – Berlin, 1935 n5, 1936-40 (incomplete) – 1 – Inquire at Mikrofilmarchiv for details – gw Misc Inst [320]
RAKETAKA : TABLEAU DE MOEURS FEMININES MALGACHES, DRESSE A L'AIDE DE PROVERBES ET DE FADY / Mondain, G – Paris: E Leroux, 1925 – us Res Libr [390]
Rakhvalov, E A *see* RASTRATY, KHISHCHENIIA, NEDOCHETY, ZLOUPOTREBLENIIA S OBOROTNYMI SREDSTVAMI
Rakovski, G S *see* SACHINENIIA
Rakow, Juliette K *see* CAMEO GLASS, MASTERPIECES FROM 2000 YEARS OF GLASSMAKING
Rakow, Leonard S *see* CAMEO GLASS, MASTERPIECES FROM 2000 YEARS OF GLASSMAKING
Raleigh, Alexander *see* THE BOOK OF ESTHER: ITS PRACTICAL LESSONS AND DRAMATIC SCENES
RALEIGH HERALD – Beckley. West Virginia. 1907-18 – 1 – us UMI [071]
THE RALEIGH INDEPENDENT – Raleigh. N.C. Aug. 30, Sept. 6, 20, 27, 1919; Mar. 20, 1920 – 1 – us NY Public [071]
RALEIGH REGISTER – Beckley. West Virginia. 1922-1966 – 1 – us UMI [071]
RALEIGH REGISTER – Beckley. West Virginia. -w. 1907-22 – 1 – us UMI [071]
RALEIGH SUN – Bellingen, Jan 7 1898-Dec 21 1906 – 1 – at Pascoe [072]
Raleigh, Walter *see* DISCOVERY OF THE EMPIRE OF GUIANA
Ralfs, J *see* THE BRITISH DESMIDIEAE
Raliby, Osman *see* KAMUS INTERNASIONAL
LE RALLIEMENT – Clarence Creek, Ontario. v1 n1. 11 avr 1895; v2 n19. 27 aut 1896; v2 n46. 11 mar 1897 – 1r – 1 – Can$35.00 – cn Can Microfilming [072]
LE RALLIEMENT : JOURNAL OUVRIER – Quebec, Canada. 3 sep 1910 – 1r – 1 – Can$25.00 – cn Can Microfilming [073]
LE RALLIEMENT – Montreal, Canada. 17 fev 1940-v1 n5. 1 mai 1940 – 1r – 1 – Can$25.00 – cn Can Microfilming [072]
LE RALLIEMENT : ORGANE DES GROUPES FRANCAIS DE LA VALLEE D'OTTAWA – Clarence Creek: Prescott et Russell, v1-1895-. SEM35P35 – 1r – 1 – Can$26.00 – cn Bibl Nat [073]
LE RALLIEMENT – St-Joseph de Beauce, Canada. 29 fev 1912-v1 n5. 28 mar 1912 – 1r – 1 – Can$25.00 – cn Can Microfilming [072]
RALLY *see* AMERICAN GIRL
RALPH DARNELL / Taylor, Philip Meadows – British Fiction Archive: Unit 5 – 9 – uk Bell [830]
Ralph De Diceto *see* THE HISTORICAL WORK OF MASTER RALPH DE DICETO, DEAN OF LONDON (RS68)
RALPH FITCH, ENGLAND'S PIONEER TO INDIA AND BURMA; HIS COMPANIONS AND CONTEMPORARIES.. / Ryley, John Horton – London: T.F. Unwin, 1899. xvi, 264p – 1 – us U.W. Library [950]
Ralph, James *see*
- THE FASHIONABLE LADY; OR HARLEQUIN'S OPERA..
- HISTORY OF ENGLAND DURING THE REIGNS OF KING WILLIAM, QUEEN ANNE, AND KING GEORGE 1

Ralph M. Parsons Company *see* ENGINEERING SERVICES AND PERSONNEL TRAINING FOR THE REPUBLIC OF INDONESIA, MINISTRY OF PUBLIC WORKS AND POWER
Ralph, T S *see* ICONES CARPOLOGICAE
RALPH THE BAILIFF; AND OTHER TALES / Braddon, Mary Elizabeth – British Fiction Archive: Unit 5 – 9 – uk Bell [830]
RALPH THE HEIR / Trollope, Anthony – London: Hurst and Blackett, 1871 – 2 rolls – 1 – 1-55879-970-2 – uk Libr Preservation [830]
RALSTON RECORDER – Ralston, NE. -w. Apr 1940 to date – 1 – us NE Hist [071]
Ram Raz *see* ESSAY ON THE ARCHITECTURE OF THE HINDUS
Rama Murthy, V *see* AMERICAN EXPRESSIONISTIC DRAMA; CONTAINING ANALYSES OF THREE OUTSTANDING AMERICAN PLAYS..
Ramakrishnan, P S *see* SHIFTING AGRICULTURE AND SUSTAINABLE DEVELOPMENT
O RAMALHETE : JORNAL LITTERARIO E RECREATIVO – '(s.l.')-Sao Luis, Brazil. 25 May-Jun, Aug-Nov 1863. Feb, 15 Apr 1864 – 1,5,6 – bl Biblioteca [072]
RAMANCERO DE LA CONQUISTA Y LA COLONIA... / Arciniegas, Ismael Enrique – Madrid: Razon y Fe, 1940 – 1 – sp Bibl Santa Ana [946]
RAMAROW : A TALE OF THE RAJAHMUNDRY MISSION / Kuder, F C – Rock Island, IL: Augustana Book Concern, [19–?] – 1mf – 9 – 0-8370-6746-4 – 1986-0746 – us A.T.L.A. [240]
RAMAYAN / Valmiki – With three commentaries called Tilaka, Shiromani and Bhooshana. Ed. by Shastri Shrinivasa Katti Mudholkara. Bombay: Gujarati Printing Press, 1912-20 – 1 – us U.W. Library [950]
THE RAMAYANA BALLET FESTIVAL : REVIVAL OF THE GLORIOUS AND MIGHTY NATIONAL CULTURE IN SIX EPISODES – Bandung, Badan Penjelenggara Pesta Balet Ramayana, 1900 – 26p – 9 – ne IDC [790]
THE RAMAYANA BALLET FESTIVAL – (Revival of the glorious and mighty national culture in six episodes). SE-3624 1 – 9 – ne IDC [790]
RAMAYANA; OUR NATIONAL READER / Sunardjo Haditjaroko – SE 4774 1. 1961 – 9 – ne IDC [800]
Rambau, A-X *see* LA PATRIE
Rambaud, H *see* LA DECLARATION DES ABUS QUE L'ON COMMET EN ESCRIVANT
Rambaud, J B *see* LA LANGUE MANDE
Rambitan, M H *see* BAHASA INDONESIA; EENVOUDIGE LEEPGANG VOOR DE INDONESISCHE TAAL
RAMBLES ROUND REFORMED LANDS / Good, James Isaac – Reading, PA: Daniel Miller, 1889 – 1mf – 9 – 0-8370-8674-4 – 1986-2674 – us A.T.L.A. [910]
RAMBLINGS IN BEULAH LAND: A CONTINUATION OF EXPERIENCES IN THE LIFE OF JENNIE SMITH / Smith, Jennie – 1886-1888 – 9 – us A.T.L.A. [240]
Rameau, Jean-Philippe *see*
- CODE DE MUSIQUE PRATIQUE
- DEMONSTRATION DU PRINCIPE DE L'HARMONIE
- DISSERTATION SUR LES DIFFERENTES METHODES D'ACCOMPAGNEMENT POUR LE CLAVECIN OU POUR L'ORGUE
- ERREURS SUR LA MUSIQUE DANS L'ENCYCLOPEDIE
- EXTRAIT D'UNE REPONSE DE M. RAMEAU A M. EULER, SUR L'IDENTITE DES OCTAVES
- GENERATION HARMONIQUE, OU TRAITE DE MUSIQUE THEORIQUE ET PRATIQUE
- NOUVEAU SYSTEME DE MUSIQUE THEORIQUE
- NOUVELLES REFLEXIONS DE M. RAMEAU SUR SA DEMONSTRATION DU PRINCIPE DE L'HARMONIE
- OBSERVATIONS SUR NOTRE INSTINCT POUR LA MUSIQUE
- REPONSE DE M. RAMEAU A MM. LES EDITEURS DE L'ENCYCLOPEDIE SUR LEUR DERNIER AVERTISSEMENT
- [SIBARIS] FRAGMENTS DE SIBARIS; BALLET AJOUTE AUX SUPRISES DE L'AMOUR
- TRAITE DE L'HARMONIE REDUITE A SES PRINCIPES NATURELS
- A TREATISE OF MUSIC, CONTAINING THE PRINCIPLES OF COMPOSITION
- ZOROASTRE

Rameau, Marcel *see* DE LA CONDITION SOCIALE DES FEMMES AU TEMPS PRESENT
Rameau, Pierre *see* THE DANCING-MASTER: OR, THE WHOLE ART AND MYSTERY OF DANCING EXPLAINED; AND THE MANNER OF PERFORMING ALL STEPS IN BALL-DANCING MADE SHORT AND EASY
LES RAMEZAY ET LEUR CHATEAU / Morin, Victor – Montreal, 1939. SEM105P759 – 1mf – 9 – Can$2.25 – cn Bibl Nat [971]
LES RAMEZAY ET LEUR CHATEAU / Morin, Victor – Montreal, 1955. SEM105P760 – 2mf – 9 – Can$4.50 – cn Bibl Nat [971]
Ramiere, Henri *see* THE APOSTLESHIP OF PRAYER
Ramiew, H *see* DIE SYMBOLIK IN GERH. HAUPTMANNS MAERCHENDRAMA DIE VERSUNKENE GLOCKE
RAMILLETE LITERATO / Periago Morata, Tomas – 1891 – 9 – 1.50f – sp Bibl Santa Ana [440]
RAMING – (Some missing issues) – Chiangmai, Thailand. 1975; 1979-85 – 30r – 1 – us L of C Photodup [072]
Ramirez, A *see* EXAMEN CHIMICO-MEDICO...DE LAS AGUAS TERMALES Y BANO DE FITERO
Ramirez, Alfonso Francisco *see*
- HERNANDO CORTES
- POLITICA Y LITERATURA

Ramirez de Arellano, Rafael *see* GEOGRAFIA ANTIGUA
Ramirez, J F *see* CODICES MEJICANOS DE FR. BERNARDINO DE SAHAGUN
Ramirez, Juan *see* EXPOSITIO ALEXANDRI... ORDINIS...SAN JACOBI
Ramirez Lopez Uria, Jose *see* LAS TIERRAS PARDAS. CANTOS A EXTREMADURA POR...
Ramirez, Pedro *see* MEMORIA Y...EJERCITO DE ESTREMADURA (SIC)
Ramirez Ramirez, Enrique *see* HACIA UN MEJOR CONOCIMIENTO HISTORICO CIENTIFICO DE EXTREMADURA
Ramirez Ramirez, Tomas *see* UN PROCER EXTREMENO DESCONOCIDO. EL ILUSTRISIMO SENOR DON BENITO CRESPO DE SOLIS, OBISPO DE PUEBLADE LOS ANGELES/MEXICO
Ramirez Sadaba, Jose Luis *see* GASTOS SUNTUARIOS Y RECURSOS ECONOMICOS EN EL AFRICA ROMANA
Ramirez, Santiago *see* NOTICIA HISTORICA DE LA RIQUEZA MINERA DE MEXICO...
Ramirez Vazquez, Fernando *see*
- CARTA DE A...AL PARTIR PARA ROMA
- CARTA PASTORAL QUE...AL...DEAN Y CABILDO
- CARTA PASTORAL...AL CLERO
- EL OBISPO DE BADAJOZ...A LOS CATOLICOS

Ramisiray, Gershon *see* PRATIQUES ET CROYANCES MEDICALES DES MALGACHES
Ramler, Karl Wilhelm *see* ALLEGORISCHE PERSONEN ZUM GEBRAUCHE DER BILDENDEN KUENSTLER
RAMO DE ACACIA : ORGAM DA MACONARIA NO PARANA – Curitiba, Nov 1908-dec 1912 – 1,5,6 – bl Biblioteca [072]
Ramon de Moncada y Calderon, Jesus *see* DISCURSO INAUGURAL PRONUNCIADO POR D. JESUS REUNION DE MONCADA Y CALDERON
Ramon Fernandez Oxea, Jose *see* SEIS INSCRIPCIONES ROMANAS EN TIERRAS CACERENAS
RAMON L. GOMEZ. LOS PRIVILEGIOS DE LA AMERICA LATINA EN SU PARTE HISTORICO-CRONOLOGICA / Bayle, Constantino – Burgos: Razon y Fe, 1939 – 1 – sp Bibl Santa Ana [972]
RAMON MENDEZ PIDAL, FILOLOGO E HISTORIADOR DE LA LITERATURA ESPANOLA MEDIEVAL / Moral OSB Tomas – Badajoz: (Imprenta de la Diputacion Provincial), 1969. Sep. Revista Estudios Extremenos – 1 – sp Bibl Santa Ana [440]
Ramon, Vives *see* LAS NAVAS DEL MARQUES

RAMON Y CAJAL, TOMO 1 : VIDA Y OBRA / Duran Munoz Garcia y, Alonso Buron Francisco – Zaragoza: Institucion Fernando el Catolico, 1960 – 1 – sp Bibl Santa Ana [612]
Ramon y Fernandez, Jose *see*
– ANTIGUEDADES CACERENAS
– COSTUMBRES CACERENAS. MADRID
– LAPIDAS SEPULCRALES DE LA EDAD DEL BRONCE EN EXTREMADURA
– NUEVAS ESCULTURAS ZOOMORFAS PREHISTORICAS EN EXTREMADURA
RAMONA ACRES PROGRESS *see* MONTEREY PARK PROGRESS
RAMONA NEWS – Ramona, CA. 1983 – 1r – 1 – $50.00 – R03403 – us Library Micro [071]
RAMONA PAGENT SPECIAL EDITIONS – Hemet, CA. 1906-1985 – 12r – 1 – $600.00 – R03240 – us Library Micro [071]
RAMONA SENTINEL – Ramona, CA. 1893-1904; 1927-58; 1979-84 – 29r – 1 RC02652 – $1,450.00 – us Library Micro [071]
Ramond, John S *see* BAPTIST BUILDERS IN LOUISIANA
Ramoneda, Ignacio *see* ARTE DE CANTO-LLANO EN COMPENDIO BREVE.
Ramons Sanguino, Joaquin *see* HISTORIA COMICA DE TRUJILLO DESDE LOS TIEMPOS MAS REMOTOS HASTA EL FINAL DEL SIGLO 18
Ramos, Antonio *see* DESCRIPCION...CASA DE AGUALLO
Ramos Aparicio, Juan *see*
– A SOLAS CON MI ALMA
– EL ULTIMO BRIDIS. ROMANCERO A LA MUERTE DE MANOLETE
RAMOS DE...!ORTIGAS! / Sanchez-Arjona, Vicente – Sevilla: Imp. Alvarez, Tomo 2. 1954 – 1 – sp Bibl Santa Ana [810]
RAMOS DE...!ORTIGAS! / Sanchez-Arjona, Vicente – Sevilla: Imp. J. Zambrano, Tomo 1. 1954 – 1 – sp Bibl Santa Ana [810]
Ramos Frechilla, Domicio *see* LA POLIGLOTA DE ARIAS MONTANO
Ramos Sanguino, Joaquin *see* LOS CORDEROS DE LA PASCUA Y NINGUNA TRUJILLANA ES GUAPA
Ramos Yebes, Jose M *see* ELEMENTOS GRIEGOS Y LATINOS QUE ENTRAN EN LA COMPOSICION DE NUMEROSOS TECNICISMOS ESPANOLES, FRANCESES E INGLESES. MADRID, 1929
Ramos-Oliveira, Antonio *see*
– THE DRAMA OF SPAIN FROM THE PROCLAMATION OF THE REPUBLIC TO THE CIVIL WAR, 1931-36
– ON THE EVE OF CIVIL WAR IN SPAIN
Ramos-Olivera, Antonio *see* HERNANDO CORTES Y SUS PARIENTES LOS JUAREZ
RAMPARTS – (v. 7-13. 1968-75. 5,6. v. 9-13. 1970-75. 9) – v. 1-13. 1962-75 – 1 – us UMI [073]
RAMP'S; THE RECOVERY AND REPATRIATION OF LIBERATED PRISONERS OF WAR / U.S. Army. Office of the Chief Historian, European Command – 1947 – 1 – 18.00 – us L of C Photodup [940]
Ramsay, Andrew Michael *see* VOYAGES DE CYRUS. DISCOURS SUR LA MYTHOLOGIE
Ramsay, David *see*
– THE HISTORY OF THE INDEPENDENT OR CONGREGATIONAL CHURCH IN CHARLESTON, S.C
– LETTERS
Ramsay, M A *see* SEIN LEBEN, SEIN WERKEN UND SEINE MITTHEILUNGEN UBER DIE FREYMAUREREY
Ramsay, Michael C *see* GROUP COHESION AND PERCEPTIONS OF PRESSURE TO CONFORM IN A UNIVERSITY RESIDENCE
Ramsay, Thomas Kennedy *see* NOTES SUR LA COUTUME DE PARIS INDIQUANT LES ARTICLES ENCORE EN FORCE, AVEC TOUT LE TEXTE DE LA COUTUME..
Ramsay, William Mitchell *see*
– THE CITIES AND BISHOPRICS OF PHRYGIA, VOL 1 PTS 1 AND 2
– THE EDUCATION OF CHRIST
– A HISTORICAL COMMENTARY ON ST. PAUL'S EPISTLE TO THE GALATIANS
– PAULINE AND OTHER STUDIES IN EARLY CHRISTIAN HISTORY
– THE REVOLUTION IN CONSTANTINOPLE AND TURKEY
– ST. PAUL, THE TRAVELLER AND THE ROMAN CITIZEN
– WAS CHRIST BORN AT BETHLEHEM?
RAMSAY'S APPEAL CASES / Canada. Quebec – 1v. 1873-86 (all publ) – 7mf – 9 – $11.50 – LLMC 81-084 – us L.L.M.C. [340]
Ramsey Abbey *see*
– CARTULARIUM MONASTERII DE RAMESEIA (RS79)
– CHRONICON ABBATIAE RAMESIENSIS (RS83)
Ramsey, Alexander *see* PAPERS AND RECORDS
RAMSEY CHRONICLE – Nov 7-Dec 19 1987; Jan 16-Dec 1988; Jan 14-Jun 17, Jul-Dec 16 1989; Jan-Jun, Jul 14-Dec 15 1990; Jan-Jun, Jul 13-Dec 14 1991; Jan 18-Jun 20, Jul 4-Dec 19 1992; Jan 16-Jun 19, Jul 3-Dec 4 1993; Jan 15-Jun 18, Jul 2-Dec 17 1994; Jan 14-Jun 17, Jul-Dec 16 1995; 1996-Jun 1997 – 4 3/4r – 1 – uk British Libr Newspaper [072]
RAMSEY COURIER AND NORTHERN ADVERTISER – (Also known as: Isle of Man Courier) – 1889; 1891-96; 1898-99; Jan 5-Dec 29 1900; 1901-52; Jan 9-Dec 24 1953; 1954-69; Jan 2-Jun 26 1970; Jul 1970-Jun 1980; Jul 4-Dec 19 1980; 1981; 1986-87; Jan 8-Mar 25 1988; Apr 1988-96 – 154 1/2r – 9 – uk British Libr Newspaper [072]
RAMSEY CREEK BAPTIST CHURCH. CLARKSVILLE, MISSOURI : CHURCH RECORDS – 1823-1959 – 1 – 33.84 – us Baptist [240]
Ramsey, Jill K *see* INFLUENCE OF THE STRENGTH SHOE AND THREE PLYOMETRIC DRILLS ON THE STRENGTH, VELOCITY, AND JUMPING ABILITY OF HIGH SCHOOL FOOTBALL PLAYERS
Ramseyer et Kuhne *see* QUATRE ANS CHEZ LES ACHANTIS
Ramseyer, Friedrich August *see*
– ALBUM DER BASLER MISSIONSGESELLSCHAFT..
– FOUR YEARS IN ASHANTEE
– FOUR YEARS IN ASHANTEE BY THE MISSIONARIES RAMSEYER AND KUEHNE.
RAMSEY'S WATERFORD CHRONICLE – (Waterford Chronicle). Ireland. -w. 1 Jan 1811-31 Dec 1812, 29 May 1813, 2 Jan 1816-30 Dec 1817, 2 Jan 1819-31 Dec 1822, 14 Jul-22 Sep 1827, 1 Jan 1829-1 Feb 1844. (19 reels) – 1 – uk British Libr Newspaper [072]
Ramsoe, W *see* QUARTET NO. 2, OP. 29, IN F, FUR CORNETT, TROMBA, TENORHORN UND TUBA
RAMURI – Craiova, Romania. -w. 1966-70. 2 reels – 1 – uk British Libr Newspaper [949]
Ramus, Peter *see*
– LA DIALECTIQUE
– GRAMERE
– GRAMMAIRE
– GRAMMATICA LATINO-FRANCICA
Ramusio, Giovanni Battista *see* DELLE NAVIGATIONI ET VIAGGI RACCOLTE DA M. GIO. BATTISTA RAMUSIO IN TRE VOLUMI DIVISE
Rana, Swadesh *see* OBSTACLES TO DISARMAMENT AND WAYS OF OVERCOMING THEM
RANAVALO ET SON AMANT BLANC : HISTOIRE A PEINE ROMANCEE... / Harry, Myriam – Paris: Flammarion, [c1939] – us Res Libr [830]
RANCH – v1-35,no.11. 1895-1 Jun 1914 – 1 – us UMI [636]
RANCHO CALIFORNIA NEWS – Rancho, CA. 1968-1993 – 24r – 1 – $1,200.00 – R03404 – us Library Micro [071]
RANCHO CALIFORNIA NEWS – Rancho Mirage, CA. 1968-84 – 10R – 1 – $500.00 – R02654 – us Library Micro [071]
RANCHO CORDOVA GRAPEVINE – Rancho Cordova, CA. 1974-1989 – 8r – 1 – $400.00 – B06050 – us Library Micro [071]
RANCHO CORDOVA GREENSHEETS – Rancho Cordova, CA. 1974-1980 – 6r – 1 – $300.00 – B05045 – us Library Micro [071]
RANCHO MIRAGE CHRONICLE – Rancho Mirage, CA. Mar 1981-83 – 6r – 1 – $300.00 – R02653 – us Library Micro [071]
RANCHO SANTA MARGARITA NEWS – South Co, CA. 1993 – 4r – 1 – $200.00 – R04121 – us Library Micro [071]
RANCHO TODAY – San Bernardino, CA. 1983 – 1r – 1 – $50.00 – R03456 – us Library Micro [071]
Rancon, Andre *see* DANS LA HAUTE-GAMBIE
Rancourt, J-C *see* L'AMI DU PEUPLE
RANCUNE: COMEDIE EN UN ACTE ET EN PROSE / Dandurand, Josephine – Montreal: C. Beauchemin, 1896. 02260. (Pre-1900 Canadiana) – 9 – cn C.I.H.M. [820]
RAND AND THE MICMACS / Clark, Jeremiah Simpson – (Charlottetown: Examiner), 1899. 00663. (Pre-1900 Canadiana) – 9 – cn C.I.H.M. [971]
Rand, Benjamin *see* THE CLASSICAL MORALISTS...SOCRATES TO MARTINEAU
RAND DAILY MAIL – Johannesburg, South Africa. -d. Oct 1905; Nov 1906-June 1931; Aug 1931-Dec 1932. 167 reels – 1 – uk British Libr Newspaper [072]
Rand, Ivan Cleveland *see* SOME ASPECTS OF CANADIAN CONSTITUTIONALISM
RAND MCNALLY BANKER'S MONTHLY *see* BANKERS MONTHLY
DE RAND POST – Johannesburg. South Africa. 1898-1900 – 1 – sa State Libr [072]
Randall, E O *see* OHIO CENTENNIAL ANNIVERSARY CELEBRATION AT CHILLICOTHE, 20-21 MAY 1903
Randall, Henry Edward *see* A TREATISE ON THE LAW OF INSTRUCTIONS TO JURIES IN CIVIL AND CRIMINAL CASES.
Randall, Peter *see*
– ANATOMY OF APARTHEID
– DIRECTIONS OF CHANGE IN SOUTH AFRICAN POLITICS
– FROM 'COOLIE LOCATION' TO GROUP AREA
Randall-Maciver, D *see* EL ANRAH AND ABYDOS (MEES VOL 23)
RANDERS FJORDS NATURHISTORIE / Johansen, A C J – Z-207 2. 1918 – 8 – ne IDC [580]
RANDOLF AND BARRADALL'S REPORTS / Virginia. Supreme Court. Colonial Court – (A Pre-NRS title) – v1-2. 1727-1753 (all publ) – 10mf – 9 – $15.00 – LLMC 90-313 – us L.L.M.C. [340]
RANDOLPH 1731-1890 – 78mf – 9 – us Holbrook [920]
Randolph, Carman Fitz *see*
– THE INSULAR CASES
– NOTES ON SUITS BETWEEN STATES; INTERSTATE WATERS IRRIGATION
RANDOLPH ENTERPRISE – Beverly. West Virginia. 1894-1912 – 1 – us UMI [071]
RANDOLPH ENTERPRISE – Elkins. West Virginia. 1894-1900; 1904-1956 – 1 – us UMI [071]
RANDOLPH ENTERPRISE REVIEW – Elkins. West Virginia. -w. 1956-58; 1961-64 – 1 – us UMI [071]
Randolph, John *see* REMARKS ON MICHAELIS'S INTRODUCTION TO THE NEW TESTAMENT
Randolph, Joseph Fitz *see* A TREATISE ON THE LAW OF COMMERCIAL PAPER.
Randolph. Ohio. First Congregational Church *see* CHURCH RECORDS, MS 40
RANDOLPH REPORTER – Randolph, NE. -w. (-sw 1904). Oct 1895-Jan 1901; Apr 1901-Nov 1903; Jan 1904-Mar 1906; Dec 1908-May 1909 – 1 – us NE Hist [071]
RANDOLPH REVIEW – Elkins. West Virginia. 1913-1949; 1951-1955 – 1 – us UMI [071]
Randolph, T *see* THE WITNESS OF THE SPIRIT
RANDOLPH TIMES – Randolph, NE. -w (-sw 1896). Oct 1895-Feb 1896; Jun 1896-Jan 1901; May-Dec 1901; Feb 1902; May 1902-May 1904; Nov 1909 to date – 1 – us NE Hist [071]
Randolph, Vance *see* OZARK MOUNTAIN FOLKS
RANDOM AND DETERMINISTIC (NONRANDOM) ASPECTS OF ATHLETIC BEHAVIOR WITH SPECIAL REFERENCE TO THE NATIONAL HOCKEY LEAGUE / Macdonald, Neil W & Schutz, R W – 1990 – 3mf – 9 – $12.00 – us Microform Publ [790]
RANDSBURG TIMES – Randsburg, CA. 1924-1929 – 3r – 1 – $150.00 – C03640 – us Library Micro [071]
RANENY I KRASNOARMEET S – (Library has: 1920, no. 8; 1921, no. 2-3) – Moskva: Ra evakpunkt, 1920-1921. 2v – 1 – CSUX89-S663 – us Hoover Inst Photo [947]
Rang, Bernhard *see* GOETHES "SELIGE SEHNSUCHT"
DER RANG DER "ALLGEMEIN ANERKANNTEN REGELN..." / Dencker, K – Greifswald, 1933 – 2mf – 1 – ILM-1729/1 – ne IDC [327]
Rang, Florens Christian *see* GOETHES "SELIGE SEHNSUCHT"
Rang, PKS L *see*
– HISTOIRE NATURELLE DES MOLLUSQUES PTEROPODES
– MANUEL DE L'HISTOIRE NATURELLE, DES MOLLUSQUES ET DE LEURS COQUILLES
Rangachari, K *see* CASTES AND TRIBES OF SOUTHERN INDIA
Rangacharya, V *see* A TOPOGRAPHICAL LIST OF THE INSCRIPTIONS OF THE MADRAS PRESIDENCY
Ranganath, H K *see* USING FOLK ENTERTAINMENTS TO PROMOTE NATIONAL DEVELOPMENT
RANG-DONG TAP-CHI – Revue annamite illustree puis Revue illustree pour l'elite annamite. Saigon. dec 1926-sept 1929 – 1 – fr A.C.R.P.P. [073]
RANGE MAGAZINE – Carson City, NV. 1994 – 2+ r – 1 – $100.00 ($90.00y) – U04836 – us Library Micro [071]
THE RANGE OF CHRISTIAN EXPERIENCE : BEING THE TWENTY-EIGHTH FERNLEY LECTURE / Moss, Richard Waddy – (Includes bibliographical references & index) – London: Charles H Kelly, 1898 – 1mf – 9 – 0-8370-4019-1 – 1985-2019 – us A.T.L.A. [240]
'RANGEHEN IST ALLES! : ROMAN UM GESCHICHTLICHES GESCHEHEN / Goote, Thor – Berlin: H Reichel, c1938 – 1r – 1 – us U.W. Library [830]
RANGER – Glendive. Mont. 1952-1961 – 1 – us UMI [071]
RANGER RICK'S NATURE MAGAZINE – v1-1967- 1; v8- 5,6; v9- 9 – us UMI [574]
Ranggawarsita, Raden Ngabehi *see* SAPTA DHARMA, DENING PUDJANGGA RANGGAWARSITA
RANGKAIAN TJERITA DALAM AL-QUR'AN / Arifin, Bey – SE-5035 1. 1963 – 9 – ne IDC [950]
Rangkuti, A D *see* SEDJARAH INDONESIA UNTUK SEKOLAH MENENGAH
Rangoni, J B de *see* ESSAI SUR LE GOUT DE LA MUSIQUE, AVEC LE CARACTERE DES TROIS CELEBRES JOUERS DE VIOLON
RANGOON DIOCESAN MAGAZINE – (Some original pgs damaged) – 1922-41 – 1r – 1 – ATLA S0725E – us A.T.L.A. [073]
RANGOON GAZETTE WEEKLY BUDGET – Burma. 26 Nov 1906-22 Oct 1928.-w. 46 reels – 1 – uk British Libr Newspaper [072]
THE RANGOON GAZETTE WEEKLY BUDGET – Burma. Jan 1887-Dec 1900 – 1 – uk Microform Academic [072]
RANGOON TIMES – Burma, 24 Nov 1906-11 Mar 1916 (imperfect) – 18r – 1 – uk British Libr Newspaper [072]
RANGOON TIMES – Burma. -d. Jan 1901-Sept 1941. 75 reels – 1 – uk British Libr Newspaper [072]
RANGSTREITLITERATUR / Steinschneider, M – Ein Beitrag zur vergleichenden Literatur- und Kulturgeschichte. Vienna. 1908. BJ-421-2 1 – 9 – ne IDC [410]
RANJBAR – (Sal-i 1, dawrah-'i 1, shumarah-'i 22 – sal-i 1, dawrah-'i 2, shumarah-'i 103 (24 Murdad 1358-27 Shahrivar 1359[15 Aug 1979-18 Sep 1980]). Missing issues: dawrah-'i 1, shumarah-'i 40; dawrah-'i 2, shumarah-'i 50-52, 58, 62-88, 90-91, 93-94, 96, 101-102) – Tehran: Sazman-i Inqilabi-i Hizb-i Tudah-'i Iran, 1979- – 1 reel – 1 – $45.00 – us MEDOC [950]
RANK AND FILE – London, England. Oct 1921 – 3ft – 1 – uk British Libr Newspaper [072]
RANK AND FILE REPORTER *see* NORTH COAST RIPSAW; RANK AND FILE REPORTER; HUMBOLDT INDEPENDENT NEWS
Rank, Josef *see* AUS DEM BOEHMERWALDE
Ranke, Ernst *see* CODEX FULDENSIS
Ranke, Ernst Constantin *see* FESTGABE ZUM NEUNZIGSTEN GEBURTSTAG LEOPOLDS VON RANKE
Ranke, Hermann *see* DIE PERSONENNAMEN IN DEN URKUNDEN DER HAMMURABIDYNASTIE
Ranke, Leopold von *see*
– DIE ERHEBUNG PREUSSENS IM JAHRE 1813 UND DIE REKONSTRUKTION DES STAATES
– HISTORISCH-BIOGRAPHISCHE STUDIEN
– THE HISTORY OF SERVIA AND THE SERVIAN REVOLUTION
– HISTORY OF THE REFORMATION IN GERMANY
Rankin, Earl *see* EARL RANKIN COLLECTION ON CLOZE PROCEDURE
Rankin, F Harrison *see* THE WHITE MAN'S GRAVE

Rankin, John *see* A HISTORY OF OUR FIRM; SOME ACCOUNT OF THE FIRM OF POLLOK, GILMOUR AND CO., AND ITS OFF-SHOOTS AND CONNECTIONS
Rankin, Melinda *see* TWENTY YEARS AMONG THE MEXICANS
Rankin, OS *see* ISRAEL'S WISDOM LITERATURE
Rankin, Robert Stanley *see* WHEN CIVIL LAW FAILS: MARTIAL LAW AND ITS LEGAL BASIS IN THE UNITED STATES
Rankin, William *see*
- HANDBOOK AND INCIDENTS OF FOREIGN MISSIONS OF THE PRESBYTERIAN CHURCH, USA
- MEMORIALS OF FOREIGN MISSIONARIES OF THE PRESBYTERIAN CHURCH USA

RANLIAO HUAXUE XUEBAO – Journal of Fuel Chemistry Technology. In Chinese, with English abstracts to the main articles – 9 – $4.00f – cc Microforms [660]
Rann, W S *see* HISTORY OF CHITTENDEN COUNTY
RANNEE UTRO (NEW YORK, N.Y.) – (Includes c.1: 1932:Dec.28-1933:Feb.1) – New York: [Izd-vo "Rannee utro"], 1932- – 1 – CSUXANS0746-S – us Hoover Inst Photo [947]
RANNII MAIAKOVSKII / Cheremin, G S – Put' poeta k oktiabriu. M., L. 1962. BR-2017 2 – 8 – ne IDC [460]
Ranolder, Joannes *see* HERMENEUTICAE BIBLICAE GENERALIS PRINCIPIA RATIONALIA CHRISTIANA ET CATHOLICA: SELECTIS EXEMPLIS ILLUSTRATA
Ransohoff, Georg *see* UEBER JOHANN GEORG JACOBIS JUGENDWERKE
RANSOM JUDD POWELL PAPERS / Powell, Ransom Judd – 1843, 1896-1938. 15 rolls including filmed inventory – 1 – $450.00 $30.00r – us M.H.S. [920]
Ransom, William Lynn *see* A REPRESENTATIVE AND IMPROVED ORGANIZATION OF THE LEGAL PROFESSION IN THE UNITED STATES; ADDRESS OF WILLIAM L. RANSOM...BEFORE THE STATE BAR OF CALIFORNIA AT SAN FRANCISCO, CALIFORNIA, ON SEPTEMBER 19, 1935
Ransome, David *see* THE FERRAR PAPERS, 1590-1790
Ransonet, Michel F *see* LA VIE DE LA SOEUR MARGUERITE BOURGEOIS
RANTHORPE / Lewes, George Henry – London: Chapman and Hall, 1847 – 1 roll – 1 – 1-55879-530-8 – uk Libr Preservation [999]
Ranulf Higden *see* POLYCHRONICON RANULPHI HIGDEN MONACHI CESTRENSIS (RS41)
O RANZINZA – Manaos, Amazonas. 15 Abr 1922; Ago, 14 Nov 1923 – 1,5,6 – bl Biblioteca [072]
Rao, R *see* FLOWERING PLANTS OF TRAVANCORE
Raomandahy *see* LA GRANDE COMORE
RAOUL GLABER. LES CINQ LIVRES DE SES HISTOIRES (900-1044) / Rodulfus Glaber – Paris: A. Picard, 1886. xv,143p – 1 – us U.W. Library [940]
Raoult, Francois Marie *see*
- CRYOSCOPIE
- TONOMETRIE

RAPALJE AND MACK'S DIGEST OF RAILROAD DECISIONS : U.S., ENGLAND AND CANADA / Rapalje, Stewart & Mack, William – Northport, NY: Thompson Co. v1-8. 1895-1898 (all publ) – 9 – LLMC 95-136 – us L.L.M.C. [340]
Rapalje, Stewart *see*
- A DIGEST OF FEDERAL DECISIONS AND STATUTES, FROM THE EARLIEST PERIOD 1789 TO THE YEAR 1880
- THE LAW RELATING TO REAL ESTATE BROKERS, AS DECIDED BY THE AMERICAN COURTS
- RAPALJE AND MACK'S DIGEST OF RAILROAD DECISIONS
- RAPALJE'S DIGEST OF THE AMERICAN DECISIONS AND REPORTS
- A TREATISE ON CONTEMPT INCLUDING CIVIL AND CRIMINAL CONTEMPTS OF JUDICIAL TRIBUNALS, JUSTICES OF THE PEACE.
- A TREATISE ON CRIMINAL PROCEDURE

RAPALJE'S DIGEST OF THE AMERICAN DECISIONS AND REPORTS / Rapalje, Stewart – San Francisco: Bancroft-Whitney. v1-3. 1891 (all publ) – 41mf – 9 – $61.00 – LLMC 78-032/36 – us L.L.M.C. [340]
RAPAT BESAR KAOEM MOESLIMIN SOEMATERA BAROE DI MEDAN, PADA 20-6-2603 / Moeslimin Soematera Baroe – Disoesoen oleh Badan Penjiaran Bunka-ka, Medan. (Medan, 2603) 62p – 110-111mf – 9 – ne IDC [260]
LE RAPATRIEMENT / ed by Tessier, A – Roberval, Canada. v1 n1. 25 mai 1899-v1 n23. 23 dec 1899 – 1r – 1 – Can$35.00 – cn Can Microfilming [072]
Raper, Henry *see* THE PRACTICE OF NAVIGATION AND NAUTICAL ASTRONOMY
RAPID BIMANUAL MOVEMENT: EFFECTS OF DIRECTION CHANGES ON COORDINATION / Hughes, Barry G – 1981 – 1mf – 9 – $4.00 – us Microform Publ [616]
RAPIDS GAZETTE – Alexandria. La. 1872-1873; 1876-1877 – 1 – us UMI [071]
Rapin, R *see*
- LES ARTIFICES DES HERETIQUES
- LES REFLEXIONS SUR LA POETIQUE D'ARISTOTE

Rapoport, S J L *see* DIVREI SHALOM VE-EMET
Rapp, Adolf *see* DIE ENTWICKELUNG UNSERER ORIENTPOLITIK
Rapp, R R *see* INTERNATIONAL SYMPOSIUM ON EARTH GRAVITY MODELS AND RELATED PROBLEMS
RAPP. SUR UN VOYAGE D'EXPL. FAIT DANS LA REGION DU YUKON. EN 1887 / Dawson, George M – BN 191 2. 1889 – 8 – ne IDC [910]
RAPPAHANNOCK NEWS – Washington. Va. -w. 1950- – 1 – us UMI [071]
RAPPAHANNOCK RECORD – Kilmarnock. Va. 1949- – 1 – us UMI [071]
RAPPAHANNOCK TIMES – Tappahannock. Va. 1939-46; 1950-51; 1953- – 1 – us UMI [071]
LE RAPPEL / ed by Fauteux, Aegidius – Montreal, Canada. 14 sep 1902-19 jun 1904 – 1r – 1 – Can$50.00 – cn Can Microfilming [072]
LE RAPPEL – Organe de la jeunesse socialiste. Dir. Th. Jubel. no. 1-3. Cayenne. avr-mai 1910 – 1 – fr A.C.R.P.P. [073]
LE RAPPEL – Paris. 4 mai 1869-30 sept 1928, fevr 1929-fevr 1933, 6 no – 1 – fr A.C.R.P.P. [073]
LE RAPPEL : REPUBLICAINS FRANCAIS AU CANADA – Montreal, Canada. v1 n6. 1 avr 1914-v1 n10. 1 aut 1914 – 1r – 1 – Can$25.00 – cn Can Microfilming [072]
RAPPEL / Donoso Cortes, Juan Francisco – Conde-sur-Noireau, 1978 – sp Bibl Santa Ana [946]
LE RAPPEL DE LA HAUTE-LOIRE – Organe hebdomadaire d'union des gauches. Le Puy. 7 mars-27 juin 1936, 19 mars-4 mai 1938 – 1 – fr A.C.R.P.P. [073]
Rappoport, Angelo Solomon *see*
- HISTORY OF EGYPT FROM 330 B.C. TO THE PRESENT TIME
- THE LOVE AFFAIRS OF THE VATICAN, OR THE FAVOURITES OF THE POPES

RAPPORT / Belgium. Commission Gouvernementale pour l'Etude des Problemes de Financement de l'Expansion Economique – 2v. Bruxelles. 1962 – 9 – ne IDC [330]
RAPPORT / Canada. Bas-Canada. Commissaires nommes pour l'exploration du pays entre les rivieres St. Maurice et Outaouais – (SEM105P590 1mf Can$2.25 9) – Can$2.25 – cn Bibl Nat [550]
RAPPORT / Canada. Bas-Canada. Commissaires nommes pour l'exploration...borne par les rivieres Saguenay, Saint-Maurice et Saint-Laurent – Quebec, 1831. SEM105P596 – 1mf – 9 – Can$2.25 – cn Bibl Nat [550]
RAPPORT / Canada. Bas-Canada. Parlement. Chambre d'Assemblee. Comite choisi sur le Gouvernement civil du Canada – Quebec: Chez Neilson & Cowan, 1829. SEM105P106 – 5mf – 9 – Can$11.25 – cn Bibl Nat [324]
RAPPORT / Canada. Commissaires de l'Amerique Britannique du nord nommes pour s'enquerir du commerce des Antilles, Mexique et Bresil – Ottawa: Imp. Hunter, Rose et Lemieux, 1866. SEM105P304 – 2mf – 9 – Can$4.50 – cn Bibl Nat [380]
RAPPORT / Canada. Commissaires nommes pour preparer un projet afin de mieux organiser le Departement de l'Adjudant-General de la milice – Quebec. Imp. Stewart Derbishire et Georges Desbarats. 1862. SEM105P315 – 1mf – 9 – Can$2.25 – cn Bibl Nat [355]
RAPPORT / Canada. Commissaires nommes pour s'enquerir de l'origine et des causes de l'incendie qui a consume l'Hospice des Soeurs de la Charite – Quebec: Imp. Louis Perrault, 1854. SEM105P348 – 1mf – 9 – Can$2.25 – cn Bibl Nat [324]
RAPPORT / Canada. Commissaires nommes pour s'enquirer et faire rapport des meilleurs moyens de reorganiser la milice en Canada – Quebec. Imp. Stewart Derbishire and George Desbarats. 1855. SEM105P314 – 1mf – 9 – Can$2.25 – cn Bibl Nat [355]
RAPPORT / Canada (Province). Assemblee Legislative. Comite...comptes publics – c186? SEM105P571 – 1mf – 9 – Can$2.25 – cn Bibl Nat [336]
RAPPORT / Canada (Province). Assemblee legislative. Comite...le sujet de la Formation d'un pont de glace sur le Saint-Laurent devant Quebec – 1853. SEM105P550 – 1mf – 9 – Can$2.25 – cn Bibl Nat [324]
RAPPORT / Canada (Province). Assemblee legislative. Comite...petitions relatives au travail, le dimanche dans le Departement des postes et sur les canaux – 1853. SEM105P572 – 1mf – 9 – Can$2.25 – cn Bibl Nat [324]
RAPPORT / Canada. (Province). Commissaires nommes pour s'enquerir de la Cause de l'incendie qui a detruit l'Hotel du Parlement – Quebec: Louis Perrault, 1854. SEM105P588 – 1mf – 9 – Can$2.25 – cn Bibl Nat [971]
RAPPORT / Canada (Province). Commissaires nommes pour s'enquirer de la conduite des autorites de police.. – 1854. SEM105P541 – 2mf – 9 – Can$4.50 – cn Bibl Nat [360]
RAPPORT / Canada. Province. Legislature. Assemblee legislative. Comite... des causes et de l'importance de l'emigration qui a lieu tous les ans du Bas-Canada vers les Etats Unis – 1849. SEM105P597 – 2mf – 9 – Can$4.50 – cn Bibl Nat [324]
RAPPORT / Canada. (Province). Parlement. Assemblee legislative. Comite... Acte pour amender la loi relative a la pratique de la medecine, ...la chirurgie et de l'art obstetrique...dans le Bas-Canada – Quebec: John Lovell, 1852. SEM105P551 – 1mf – 9 – Can$2.25 – cn Bibl Nat [610]
RAPPORT / Canada. (Province). Parlement. Assemblee legislative. Comite charge...des circonstances relatives a la reduction recente des droits sur le pin rouge – Quebec: John Lovell, 1852? SEM105P639 – 1mf – 9 – Can$2.25 – cn Bibl Nat [971]
RAPPORT / Canada. (Province). Parlement. Assemblee legislative. Comite... des desastres eprouves par les batiments et paquebots transportant les passagers du Royaume-Uni et d'ailleurs au Canada – Quebec: Thompson et cie, 1860. SEM105P660 – 1mf – 9 – Can$2.25 – cn Bibl Nat [971]
RAPPORT / Canada (Province). Parlement. Assemblee Legislative. Comite pour s'enquerir du tarif d'honoraire de la Cour d'Amiraute – 1853. SEM105P569 – 1mf – 9 – Can$2.25 – cn Bibl Nat [971]
RAPPORT / Canada. (Province). Parlement. Assemblee legislative. Comite... prendre en consideration l'opportunite d'attirer l'emigration de la France, de la Belgique et de la Suisse en Canada – Quebec: Thompson et cie, 1860. SEM105P663 – 1mf – 9 – Can$2.25 – cn Bibl Nat [971]
RAPPORT / Canada. (Province). Parlement. Assemblee legislative. Comite... quelle maniere ont ete depenses les Fonds votes en 1855 pour l'achat de grains de semence dans le Bas-Canada et du montant rembourse – Quebec: Hunter, Rose & Lemieux, 1863. SEM105P600 – 1mf – 9 – Can$2.25 – cn Bibl Nat [971]
RAPPORT / Canada. (Province). Parlement. Assemblee legislative. Comite... s'enquerir de la possibilite de cultiver la vigne dans ce pays – Quebec: Hunter, Rose & Lemieux, 1864. SEM105P599 – 1mf – 9 – Can$2.25 – cn Bibl Nat [971]
RAPPORT / Canada. (Province). Parlement. Assemblee legislative. Comite... sur l'etat de l'agriculture du Bas-Canada – Toronto: Louis Perrault, 1850. SEM105P662 – 2mf – 9 – Can$4.50 – cn Bibl Nat [971]
RAPPORT / Canada. (Province). Parlement. Assemblee legislative. Comite...le bill pour regler le pilotage dans le port de Quebec et au dessous – Quebec: John Lovell, 1853. SEM105P574 – 1mf – 9 – Can$2.25 – cn Bibl Nat [971]
RAPPORT / Canada. (Province). Parlement. Assemblee legislative. Comite...l'etat du Bureau du surintendant des mesureurs de bois – Quebec: Hunter, Rose et Lemieux, 1865. SEM105P583 – 1mf – 9 – Can$2.25 – cn Bibl Nat [971]
RAPPORT / Comite Executif nomme pour venir en aide aux victimes de l'incendie du 9 mai 1886 en la cite de Hull – Hull: l'Alliance, 1887. SEM105P829 – 1mf – 9 – Can$2.25 – cn Bibl Nat [971]
RAPPORT : LE COMITE SPECIAL NOMME POUR FAIRE RAPPORT DES MEILLEURS MOYENS DE RENDRE PUBLICS LES RENSEIGNEMENTS DEJA RECUEILLIS PAR L'EXPLORATION GEOLOGIQUE / Canada. Parliament. Legislative Assembly. Special Committee – s.l, s.n, s.d. SEM105P209 – 1mf – 9 – Can$2.25 – cn Bibl Nat [550]
RAPPORT / Comite...pour venir en aide aux victimes de l'incendie du 5 juin 1888 en la cite de Hull – 1888. SEM105P640 – 1mf – 9 – Can$2.25 – cn Bibl Nat [971]
RAPPORT / Commission du Chemin de Fer de Quebec, Montreal, Ottawa et Occidental – 1878. SEM105P549 – 2mf – 9 – Can$2.25 – cn Bibl Nat [380]
RAPPORT – Johannesburg, SA. Nov 1970-1995 – 1 – sa State Libr [072]
RAPPORT / Lebanon. Banque de Liban – 9v. in 4. 1964-72. BNE-9642 1 – 9 – ne IDC [330]
RAPPORT / Morocco. Banque Marocaine du Commerce Exterieur – 1959 -1977. (lacking 1966). BNE-3008 1 – 9 – ne IDC [330]
RAPPORT / Morocco. Caisse de Depot et de Gestion – 1959 60-1972. (lacking 1965-67). BNE-3017 1 – 9 – ne IDC [330]
RAPPORT / Morocco. Caisse Nationale de Credit Agricole – 1962 63-1968 69. BNE-3018 1 – 9 – ne IDC [324]
RAPPORT : ORDONNE PAR LA CHAMBRE D'ASSEMBLEE A ETRE IMPRIME, LE 14 JANVIER 1829 / Canada. Bas-Canada. Commissaires pour Explorer le Saguenay – Quebec: Imprime par Neilson & Cowan, 1829. SEM16P99 – 1r – 5 – Can$9.00 – cn Bibl Nat [971]
RAPPORT / Quebec. (Province). Commissaires pour s'enquerir...des chemins a barrieres de la rive nord et de la rive sud a Quebec – Quebec: Leger Brousseau, 1876. SEM105P587 – 1mf – 9 – Can$2.25 – cn Bibl Nat [971]
RAPPORT / Quebec. (Province). Commission de Colonisation – (Report 1904 8mf Can$18.00. SEM105P42) – Quebec: Impr. Charles Pageau, 1904. SEM105P41 – 24mf – 9 – Can$54.00 – cn Bibl Nat [971]
RAPPORT / Quebec. (Province). Commission royale sur les asiles d'alienes – Quebec, 1888. SEM105P570 – 3mf – 9 – Can$6.75 – cn Bibl Nat [971]
RAPPORT / Quebec. (Province). Legislature. Assemblee legislative. Comite... relatifs aux incendies...sur la cote du golfe St. Laurent...1867 & 1868 – Montreal: Minerve, 1869. SEM105P582 – 1mf – 9 – Can$2.25 – cn Bibl Nat [971]
RAPPORT / Syria. Banque Centrale de Syrie – 1956-57. BNE-9689 1 – 9 – ne IDC [330]
RAPPORT A M. LE MINISTRE DE L'INTERIEUR SUR LA SITUATION ADMINSTRATIVE, MORALE ET FINANCIERE DU SERVICE DES ENFANTS TROUVES ET ABANDONNES EN FRANCE, PAR AD DE WATTEVILLE, INSPECTEUR GENERAL DES ETABLISSEMENTS DE BIENFAISANCE – (Condition of 19th C. French working class series). 1849 – 9 – fr Hachette [360]
RAPPORT A M. LE MINISTRE, SECRETAIRE D'ETAT DE L'INTERIEUR, CONCERNANT LES INFANTICIDES ET LES MORT-NES DANS LEUR RELATION AVEC LA QUESTION DES ENFANTS TROUVES, PAR M. RENACLE – (Condition of 19th C. French working class series). 1845 – 9 – fr Hachette [360]
RAPPORT ANNUEL / Algeria. Banque Industrielle d l'Algerie et de la Mediterranee – 2v. in 1. 1965-66. BNE-8604 1 – 9 – ne IDC [338]
RAPPORT ANNUEL / Algeria. Compagnie Francaise des Petroles. (Algerie) – 1968-69. 2v. BNE-8625-1 – 9 – ne IDC [380]
RAPPORT ANNUEL / Lebanon. Banque Al-Ahli – 11 v. in 8. 1964-64. (lacking 1964). BNE-9639 1 – 9 – ne IDC [330]
RAPPORT ANNUEL / Lebanon. Banque de la Mediterranee – 2v. in 1. 1970-71, 1973-74. BNE-9644 1 – 9 – ne IDC [330]

RAPPORT ANNUEL / Morocco. Banque Nationale pour le Developpement Economique - 1963-66. BNE-3013 1 - 9 - ne IDC [330]

RAPPORT ANNUEL / Morocco. Societe Cherifienne des Petroles - 4v. 1965 $76. Incomplete. BNE-3102 1 - 9 - ne IDC [330]

RAPPORT ANNUEL ADRESSE PAR LE GOUVERNEMENT FRANCAIS AU CONSEIL DE LA SOCIETE DES NATIONS CONFORMEMENT A L'ARTICLE 22 DU PACTE SUR L'ADMINISTRATION SOUS LE MANDAT DU TERRITOIRE DU CAMEROUN - Paris: Impr generale du Lahure, 1927-39 - us Res Libr [960]

RAPPORT ANNUEL ADRESSE PAR LE GOUVERNEMENT FRANCAIS AU CONSEIL DE LA SOCIETE DES NATIONS SUR L'ADMINISTRATION SOUS MANDAT DU TERRITOIRE DU TOGO - Paris: Impr generale Lahure, 1925-38 - us Res Libr [960]

RAPPORT ANNUEL D'ACTIVITE / Algeria. Societe Nationale de Recherche et d'Exploitation des Petroles en Algerie - 11v. 1960-70 (lacking 1962, 1967). BNE-8668 1 - 9 - ne IDC [660]

RAPPORT ANNUEL DE LA PRISON DE REFORME, BAS-CANADA, POUR L'ANNEE 185?-186? - 1860 ed only. SEM105P595 - 1mf - 9 - Can$2.25 - cn Bibl Nat [360]

RAPPORT ANNUEL DU GOUVERNEMENT FRANCAIS A L'ASSEMBLEE GENERALE DES NATIONS UNIES SUR L'ADMINISTRATION DU CAMEROUN PLACE SOUS LA TUTELLE DE LA FRANCE - Paris, 1950-57 - us Res Libr [960]

RAPPORT ANNUEL SUR L'EXECUTION DU PLAN DE MODERNISATION ET D'EQUIPEMENT / France. Commissariat General du Plan - 2v. Paris. 1961. BD-626 1 - 9 - ne IDC [338]

RAPPORT AU GOUVERNEMENT DE LA REPUBLIQUE ALGERIENNE SUR LA SITUATION ET LE DEVELOPPEMENT DU MOUVEMENT COOPERATIF / International Labour Organisation - 1966. Tulou, J. BNE-8729 1 - 9 - ne IDC [334]

RAPPORT AU GOUVERNEMENT DE LA REPUBLIQUE ALGERIENNE SUR LE DEVELOPPEMENT DU MOUVEMENT COOPERATIF / Algeria. Institut pour l'Etude et le Developpement de l'Industrie en Algerie - 1967. BNE-8654 1 - 9 - ne IDC [338]

RAPPORT AU GOUVERNEMENT DE LA REPUBLIQUE ALGERIENNE SUR LE DEVELOPPEMENT DU MOUVEMENT COOPERATIF RESEAU COOPERATIF D'APPROVISIONNEMENT DANS LE SECTEUR AGRICOLE / International Labour Organisation - 1967. Chotard, A. BNE-8727 1 - 9 - ne IDC [334]

RAPPORT AU GOUVERNEMENT DE LA REPUBLIQUE ALGERIENNE SUR LES STATISTIQUES DU TRAVAIL / International Labour Organisation - 1966. Helger, B. BNE-8728 1 - 9 - ne IDC [331]

RAPPORT AU GOUVERNEMENT DE LA REPUBLIQUE LIBANAISE SUR LE DEVELOPPEMENT DE L'ARTISANAT / International Labour Organisation - 1967. Bonete, Y. BNE-19.708 1 - 9 - ne IDC [338]

RAPPORT AU GOUVERNEMENT DE LA REPUBLIQUE LIBANAISE SUR LE DEVELOPPEMENT DU MOUVEMENT COOPERATIF ET LE DEVELOPPEMENT RURAL / International Labour Organisation - 1967. Louis, R. BNE-19.709 1 - 9 - ne IDC [334]

RAPPORT AU GOUVERNEMENT DE LA REPUBLIQUE LIBANAISE SUR L'ORGANISATION ADMINISTRATIVE ET LA MECANISATION DE LA CAISSE NATIONALE DE SECURITE SOCIALE / International Labour Organisation - 1968. Thomas, J. BNE-19.707 1 - 9 - ne IDC [336]

RAPPORT AU GOUVERNEMENT DE L'ALGERIE SUR LA READAPTION PROFESSIONNELLE ET L'EMPLOI DES INVALIDES / International Labour Organisation - 1964. Berlioz, L. BNE-8730 1 - 9 - ne IDC [331]

RAPPORT AU GOUVERNEMENT DE L'ALGERIE SUR L'ADMINISTRATION DU TRAVAIL / International Labour Organisation - Diderich, M. A. BNE-8725 1 - 9 - ne IDC [331]

RAPPORT AU GOUVERNEMENT DE L'ALGERIE SUR L'ORGANISATION ET L'EQUIPEMENT DU CENTRE DU TRAVAIL DU CUIR DE DJIDJELLI / International Labour Organisation - 1963. Rama, L. BNE-8724 1 - 9 - ne IDC [331]

RAPPORT AU GOUVERNEMENT DU LIBAN SUR UNE CONTRIBUTION DU B.I.T. A UN PROGRAMME DE FORMATION DES AGENTS DE L'ADMINISTRATION DU TRAVAIL FORMATION EN MATIERE D'INSPECTION DU TRAVAIL (JANVIER-JUILLET 1964) / International Labour Organisation - 1964. Abdeljaouad, A. BNE-19.705 1 - 9 - ne IDC [331]

RAPPORT AU GOUVERNEMENT DU MAROC SUR LA SECURITE SOCIALE / International Labour Organisation - 1959. Aretaios, D. BNE-3214 1 - 9 - ne IDC [360]

RAPPORT AU GOUVERNEMENT DU ROYAUME DU MAROC SUR LA CREATION D'UN CENTRE DE PERFECTIONNEMENT DE CADRES DIRIGEANTS / Morocco. ILO - 1965. BNE-3219 1 - 9 - ne IDC [338]

RAPPORT AU GOUVERNEMENT DU ROYAUME DU MAROC SUR LA FORMATION, L'EDUCATION ET LA VULGARISATION COOPERATIVES DANS LE SECTEUR ARTISANAL / International Labour Organisation - 1961. Renaud, A. BNE-3213 1 - 9 - ne IDC [334]

RAPPORT AU GOUVERNEMENT DU ROYAUME DU MAROC SUR LA FORMATION PROFESSIONNELLE RURALE / International Labour Organisation - 1967. Haeren, R. van. BNE-3216 1 - 9 - ne IDC [331]

RAPPORT AU GOUVERNEMENT DU ROYAUME DU MAROC SUR LA MECANISATION ET L'AUTOMATION AU SIEN DE LA CAISSE NATIONALE DE SECURITE SOCIALE / International Labour Organisation - 1965. Velimsky, V. BNE-3220 1 - 9 - ne IDC [960]

RAPPORT AU GOUVERNEMENT DU ROYAUME DU MAROC SUR LA SITUATION ET LE DEVELOPPEMENT DU MOUVEMENT COOPERATIF / International Labour Organisation - 1966. Marsan, J. BNE-3218 1 - 9 - ne IDC [334]

RAPPORT AU GOUVERNEMENT DU ROYAUME DU MAROC SUR LES POSSIBILITES D'AMELIORATION DE L'ORGANISATION ADMINISTRATIVE DE LA CAISSE NATIONALE DE SECURITE SOCIALE / International Labour Organisation - 1964. Proust, A. BNE-3221 1 - 9 - ne IDC [332]

RAPPORT AU GOUVERNEMENT DU ROYAUME DU MAROC SUR L'ORGANISATION ADMINISTRATIVE DE LA CAISSE NATIONALE DE SECURITE SOCIALE / International Labour Organisation - 1963. Proust, A. BNE-3212 1 - 9 - ne IDC [332]

RAPPORT AU GOUVERNEMENT DU ROYAUME DU MAROC SUR L'ORIENTATION ET LA SELECTION PROFESSIONELLES / International Labour Organisation - 1968. Voge, F. BNE-3217 1 - 9 - ne IDC [303]

RAPPORT AU ROI SUR LES HOPITAUX, LES HOSPICES ET LES SERVICES DE BIENFAISANCE PAR M. DE GASPARIN / Gasparin, de - (Condition of 19th C. French working class series). 1837 - 9 - fr Hachette [360]

RAPPORT D'ACTIVITE / Algeria. Caisse Algerienne de Developpement - 3v. 1963-68. (lacking 1964, 1966, 1967). BNE-8608 1 - 9 - ne IDC [338]

RAPPORT D'ACTIVITE SUR L'OPERATION CIVILE DES NATIONS UNIES (ORGANISATION ET TRAVAUX) / Congo - Leopoldville, 1960-64. - 18mf - 9 - ne IDC [960]

RAPPORT DE A.C. BUCHANAN, ECUYER, AGENT PRINCIPAL DES EMIGRES, POUR L'ANNEE 1855 / Buchanan, A C - [Quebec?]: [s.n.], [1856]. SEM105P1274 - 1mf - 9 - Can$2.25 - cn Bibl Nat [307]

RAPPORT DE DRS. NELSON ET MACDONNELL, ET ZEPHIRIN PERRAULT, ECR., AVOCAT, SUR L'HOPITAL DE MARINE ET DES EMIGRES DE QUEBEC ET CORRESPONDANCE RELATIVE AUX SERVICES DU DR. ROBITAILLE DANS LE DIT HOPITAL / Nelson, Wolfred - Quebec: imprime par John Lovell, [1853]. SEM105P585 - 2mf - 9 - Can$4.50 - cn Bibl Nat [360]

RAPPORT DE E.S. DE ROTTERMUND, ECUYER, CHIMISTE DE L'EXPLORATION GEOLOGIQUE DE LA PROVINCE / Rottermund, E S, Comte de - Montreal: imprime par Lovell et Gibson, 1846. SEM105P1319 - 1mf - 9 - Can$2.25 - cn Bibl Nat [550]

RAPPORT DE LA COMMISSION DE COLONISATION DE LA PROVINCE DE QUEBEC / Commission de colonisation de la province de Quebec - Quebec: Charles Pageau..., 1904. SEM105P41 - 24mf - 9 - Can$54.00 - cn Bibl Nat [971]

RAPPORT DE LA COMMISSION DE CONCILIATION DES NATIONS UNIES POUR LE CONGO / Congo - Leopoldville, 1961. BA-704/1 - 9 - ne IDC [960]

RAPPORT DE LA COMMISSION DES ASILES D'ALIENES / Quebec Province. Commission royale sur les asiles d'alienes - [Quebec]: [la Commission], [1888]. SEM105P570 - 3mf - 9 - Can$6.75 - cn Bibl Nat [305]

RAPPORT DE LA COMMISSION PROVINCIALE D'ENQUETE SUR LES HOPITAUX / Quebec Province. Commission provinciale d'enquete sur les hopitaux - [Quebec: la Commission, 1943?]. SEM105P1893 - 2mf - 9 - Can$4.50 - cn Bibl Nat [360]

RAPPORT DE LA FERME-PILOTE DE STE. ANNE DE LA POCATIERE MONTRANT DE QUELLE MANIERE... / Pilote, F - Quebec: imprime par E R Frechette, 1860. SEM105P1349 - 1mf - 9 - Can$2.25 - cn Bibl Nat [630]

RAPPORT DE LA MISSION D'ASSISTANCE PRELIMINAIRE DE L'AGENCE INTERNATIONALE DE L'ENERGIE ATOMIQUE AU MAROC / International Atomic Energy Agency - 1960. BNE-3058 1 - 9 - ne IDC [338]

RAPPORT DE LA MISSION SANITAIRE DE LA SOCIETE DES NATIONS EN ESPAGNE, 28 DECEMBRE 1936-15 JANVIER 1937 / League of Nations. Health Mission to Spain - Paris, 1937? Fiche W964.1. (Blodgett Collection of Spanish Civil War Pamphlets) - 9 - us H.U. College Libr [946]

RAPPORT DE LA REUNION DES MISSIONNAIRES AGRICOLES TENUE A OKA LES 9, 10, 11 ET 12 JUILLET, 1895 / Congres des missionnaires agricoles. 1895: Oka - Trois Rivieres Quebec: P. Ayotte, 1895. 00094. (Pre-1900 Canadiana) - 9 - cn C.I.H.M. [971]

RAPPORT DE L'AGENT EN CHEF DE L'IMMIGRATION, POUR L'ANNEE 1860 / Buchanan, A C - Quebec: Hunter, Rose et cie, 1861. SEM105P1464 - 1mf - 9 - Can$2.25 - cn Bibl Nat [320]

RAPPORT DE L'ASSOCIATION DE LA PROPAGATION DE LA FOI POUR LE DIOCESE DE MONTREAL / Association de la propagation de la foi (Diocese de Montreal) - (Fait suite a: Association de la Propagation de la foi (Diocese de Montreal). Rapport de l'Association de la Propagation de la foi. Suivi de: Annales de la propagation de la foi pour le diocese de Montreal) - Montreal: Nouveau-Monde, [1871?]-1873 - 9 - cn C.I.H.M. [240]

RAPPORT DE L'ASSOCIATION...POUR LE DIOCESE DE MONTREAL / Society for the Propagation of the Faith - 1839-73.(American Indian Periodicals in the Princeton University Library). 24 fiches - 9 - $100.00 - us UPA [240]

RAPPORT DE L'EX-INGENIEUR DE LA CITE, DES TRAVAUX FAITS SOUS LE MAIRE...ET DURANT LE DERNIER TIERS DE SIECLE, 1866 A 1899 / Baillairge, Charles - Quebec: C. Darveau, 1900? 02139. (Pre-1900 Canadiana) - 9 - cn C.I.H.M. [971]

RAPPORT DE L'EXPLORATION A LA BAIE GEORGIENNE / Compagnie du chemin a lisses de colonisation du nord de Montreal - (Montreal: La Minerve), 1874. 00730. (Pre-1900 Canadiana) - 9 - cn C.I.H.M. [910]

RAPPORT DE L'INSPECTEUR DES ASSURANCES DE LA PROVINCE DE QUEBEC POUR L'EXERCICE.. - 1885-9? SEM105P620 - 2mf - 9 - Can$4.50 - cn Bibl Nat [336]

RAPPORT DE M. BAILLAIRGE, INGENIEUR DE LA CITE SUR LA 5EME SECTION DU CHEMIN DE FER QUEBEC & LAC ST JEAN...18 DECEMBRE 1885 / Baillairge, Charles - Quebec: G. Vincent, Impr. de la cite, 1886. 02217. (Pre-1900 Canadiana) - 9 - cn C.I.H.M. [625]

RAPPORT DE M. BAILLAIRGE, INGENIEUR DU NOUVEL AQUEDUC DE QUEBEC...30 OCT 1885 / Baillairge, Charles - 1885?. 04240. (Pre-1900 Canadiana) - 9 - cn C.I.H.M. [628]

RAPPORT DE M. BAILLAIRGE SUR LA 3EME SECTION DU CHEMIN DE FER DE QUEBEC & LAC ST JEAN...24 SEPT 1885 / Baillairge, Charles - 1885. 02216. (Pre-1900 Canadiana) - 9 - cn C.I.H.M. [625]

RAPPORT DE PROGRAMMATION DU SYSTEME BIP : BALAYAGE A L'INTERIEUR D'UN POLYGONE / Vollering, Andre - Quebec: La Direction, cop 1984. SEM105P482 - 2mf - 9 - Can$4.50 - cn Bibl Nat [510]

RAPPORT DE PROGRES DEPUIS SON COMMENCEMENT JUSQU'A 1863 / Canada. Exploration Geologique - Montreal: Dawson Freres; Londres, Paris et New York: Balliere, 1864-65. SEM105P340 - 13mf - 9 - Can$29.25 - cn Bibl Nat [550]

RAPPORT D'ENSEMBLE SUR LA PACIFICATION, L'ORGANISATION ET LA COLONISATION DE MADAGASCAR (OCTOBRE 1896 A MARS 1899) / Gallieni, Joseph-Simon - Paris: H Charles-Lavauzelle, [1900] - us Res Libr [960]

RAPPORT... DES COMMISSAIARES...LE 8 SEPTEMBRE 1856 / Canada. Commission speciale nommee pour s'enquirer des Affaires sauvages en Canada - Toronto: Imprime par Stewart Derbishire & George Desbarats, 1858. SEM105P243 - 4mf - 9 - Can$9.00 - cn Bibl Nat [305]

RAPPORT DES COMMISSAIRES ENQUETEURS DANS L'AFFAIRE DU MEURTRE DE CORRIGAN / Canada. Commissaires nommes pour... - Toronto: John Lovell, [1857]. SEM105P648 - 2mf - 9 - Can$4.50 - cn Bibl Nat [360]

RAPPORT DES COMMISSAIRES NOMMES. POUR EXPLORER CETTE PARTIE DE LA PROVINCE QUI SE TROUVE ENTRE LES RIVIERES SAINT-MAURICE ET OTTAWA / Canada. Bas-Canada. Commissaires pour l'Exploration du Pays Situe entre les Rivieres Saint-Maurice et Ottawa - Quebec: Neilson and Cowan, 1830. SEM35P117 - 1r - 1 - Can$15.00 - cn Bibl Nat [971]

RAPPORT DES COMMISSAIRES NOMMES POUR FAIRE UNE ENQUETE SUR LA CONDUITE DES AUTORITES DE POLICE LORS DE L'EMEUTE DE L'EGLISE CHALMERS, LE 6 JUIN 1853... / Canada. Commissaires nommes pour s'enquerir... - Quebec: Louis Perrault, 1854. SEM105P541 - 2mf - 9 - Can$4.50 - cn Bibl Nat [360]

RAPPORT DES COMMISSAIRES NOMMES POUR FAIRE UNE ENQUETE SUR LES AFFAIRES DU DEPARTEMENT DES POSTES DANS L'AMERIQUE SEPTENTRIONALE BRITANNIQUE / Canada. Commissaires nommes pour faire une enquete sur les affaires du departement des postes dans l'Amerique septentrionale britannique - Montreal: Lovell et Gibson, 1846. SEM105P1735 - 1mf - 9 - Can$2.25 - cn Bibl Nat [380]

RAPPORT DES COMMISSAIRES NOMMES POUR PREPARER UN PROJET AFIN DE MIEUX ORGANISER LE DEPARTEMENT DE L'ADJUDANT-GENERAL DE LA MILICE ET RECHERCER... / Canada Province - Quebec: imprime par Stewart Derbishire and George Desbarats..., 1862. SEM105P315 - 1mf - 9 - Can$2.25 - cn Bibl Nat [355]

RAPPORT DES COMMISSAIRES NOMMES POUR S'ENQUERIR DE L'ETAT DES LOIS ET AUTRES CIRCONSTANCES QUI SE RATTACHENT A LA TENURE SEIGNEURIALE DANS LE BAS-CANADA ET APPENDICE / Canada. Commissaires nommes pour s'enquerir de l'etat des lois et autres circonstances qui se rattachent a la tenure seigneuriale dans le Bas-Canada - Montreal: Desbarats et Derbishire, 1844. SEM105P246 - 4mf - 9 - Can$9.00 - cn Bibl Nat [333]

RAPPORT DES COMMISSAIRES NOMMES POUR S'ENQUERIR DE L'ORIGINE ET DES CAUSES DE L'INCENDIE QUI A CONSUME L'HOSPICE DES SOEURS DE LA CHARITE, LE TROIS MAI DERNIER, AINSI QUE DES CIRCONSTANCES QUI S'Y RATTACHENT / Canada Province - Quebec: imprimerie de Louis Perrault..., 1854. SEM105P348 - 1mf - 9 - Can$2.25 - cn Bibl Nat [360]

RAPPORT DES COMMISSAIRES NOMMES POUR S'ENQUERIR DES AFFAIRES DES CHEMINS A BARRIERES DE LA RIVE NORD ET DE LA RIVE SUD A QUEBEC / Quebec Province - Quebec: imprime par Leger Brousseau, 1876. SEM105P587 - 1mf - 9 - Can$2.25 - cn Bibl Nat [324]

RAPPORT DES COMMISSAIRES NOMMES POUR S'ENQUERIR ET FAIRE RAPPORT DES MEILLEURS MOYENS DE REORGANISER LA MILICE EN CANADA, ET POUR RAPPORTER UN PLAN

PERFECTIONNE DE POLICE / Canada Province – Quebec: imprime par Stewart Derbishire and George Desbarats..., 1855. SEM105P314 – 1mf – 9 – Can$2.25 – cn Bibl Nat [355]

RAPPORT DES DIRECTEURS DE L'ECOLE DE REFORME A MONTREAL POUR LA PROVINCE DE QUEBEC – Quebec: C Darveau, 1874. SEM105P586 – 1mf – 9 – Can$2.25 – cn Bibl Nat [971]

RAPPORT DES INSPECTEURS DES PORTS FRANCS DE GASPE ET DU SAULT-STE-MARIE, ACCOMPAGNES DE DIVERS TABLEAUX STATISTIQUES DES IMPORTATIONS – Quebec: Hunter, Rose et Lemieux..., 1865. SEM105P305 – 1mf – 9 – Can$2.25 – cn Bibl Nat [380]

RAPPORT DES TITRES DES RENTES CONSTITUES DES ANCIENNES SEIGNEURIES DU QUEBEC / Quebec. (Province). Syndicat national du rachat des rentes seigneuriales – Montreal: Bibliotheque nationale du Quebec, 1971. SEM35P9 – 1r – 1 – Can$44.00 – cn Bibl Nat [336]

RAPPORT DES TRAVAUX DE COLONISATION DE L'ANNEE 1855 / Boutillier, T – Toronto: imprime par John Lovell, 1856. SEM105P1299 – 1mf – 9 – Can$2.25 – cn Bibl Nat [971]

RAPPORT D'EXECUTION DU PLAN TRIENNAL, 1962-1964 / Tunisia. Secretariat d'Etat au Plan et a l'Econ. Nationale – Tunis, 1965 – 9 – ne IDC [338]

RAPPORT DU BUREAU CENTRAL DE LA SANTE, EN REPONSE A L'ADRESSE CI-ANEXEE DE L'ASSEMBLEE LEGISLATIVE, 1854 / Canada. Bureau Central de la Sante – Quebec: Imprime par John Donaghue & cie, 1855. SEM105P229 – 1mf – 9 – Can$2.25 – cn Bibl Nat [324]

RAPPORT DU BUREAU CENTRAL DE LA SANTE, EN REPONSE A L'ADRESSE CI-ANNEXEE DE L'ASSEMBLEE LEGISLATIVE, 1854 / Canada Province. Bureau central de la sante – Quebec: imprime par John Donaghue & cie..., 1855. SEM105P229 – 1mf – 9 – Can$2.25 – cn Bibl Nat [360]

RAPPORT DU COMITE CHARGE DE S'ENQUERIR DE LA CAUSE DES DESASTRES EPROUVES PAR LES BATIMENTS ET PAQUEBOTS TRANSPORTANT... / Canada (Province). Parlement. Assemblee legislative – Quebec: imprime par Thompson et cie, 1860. SEM105P660 – 1mf – 9 – Can$2.25 – cn Bibl Nat [355]

RAPPORT DU COMITE DES CHEMINS SUR LES TRAVAUX DU DEPARTEMENT POUR LES ANNEES 1882-1883... / Quebec. Comite des chemins – Quebec: [s.n.], 1884. SEM105P632 – 1mf – 9 – Can$2.25 – cn Bibl Nat [625]

RAPPORT DU COMITE NOMME POUR S'ENQUERIR DU TARIF D'HONORAIRES DE LA COUR D'AMIRAUTE / Canada. Parliament. Legislative Assembly. Committee – Quebec: Imprime par John Lovell, s.d. SEM105P206 – 1mf – 9 – Can$2.25 – cn Bibl Nat [324]

RAPPORT DU COMITE NOMME POUR S'ENQUIRER DES TRANSACTIONS DE LA COMPAGNIE DU CHEMIN DE FER DE MONTREAL ET BYTOWN / Canada. Parliament. Legislative Assembly. Committee – Toronto: Imp. John Lovell, 1856. SEM105P360 – 1mf – 9 – Can$2.25 – cn Bibl Nat [336]

RAPPORT DU COMITE SPECIAL AUQUEL A ETE REFERE CETTE PARTIE DE LA HARANGUE DE SON EXCELLENCE RELATIVE A L'ORGANIZATION [SIC] DE LA MILICE / Bas-Canada. Parlement. Chambre d'assemblee – Quebec: imprime chez Nei[l]son and Cowan, 1829. SEM105P93 – 3mf – 9 – Can$6.75 – cn Bibl Nat [355]

RAPPORT [DU] COMITE SPECIAL AUQUEL A ETE RENVOYE LE BILL, INTITULE, "ACTE POUR AMENDER LA LOI RELATIVE A LA PRATIQUE DE LA MEDECINE, DE LA CHIRURGIE ET DE L'ART OBSTETRIQUE DANS LE BAS-CANADA"... / Canada. Parlement. Assemblee legislative. Comite special... – Quebec: John Lowell, [1852]. SEM105P551 – 1mf – 9 – Can$2.25 – cn Bibl Nat [600]

RAPPORT DU COMITE SPECIAL AUQUEL A ETE RENVOYE LE RAPPORT ANNUEL DU PRINCIPAL AGENT DE L'EMIGRATION.. / Canada. Parliament. Legislative Assembly. Committee – Quebec: Imprime par Thompson et cie, 1860. SEM105P213 – 1mf – 9 – Can$2.25 – cn Bibl Nat [323]

RAPPORT DU COMITE SPECIAL AUQUEL ONT ETE RENVOYES LA CORRESPONDANCE ET LES DOCUMENTS RELATIFS AUX INCENDIES QUI ONT EU LIEU SUR LA COTE DU GOLFE ST LAURENT... / Quebec Province. Legislature. Assemblee legislative – Montreal: des presses a vapeur de la Minerve, 1869. SEM105P582 – 1mf – 9 – Can$2.25 – cn Bibl Nat [630]

RAPPORT DU COMITE SPECIAL DE LA CHAMBRE D'ASSEMBLEE DU BAS-CANADA, NOMME POUR S'ENQUERIR DE L'ETAT ACTUEL DE L'EDUCATION DANS LA PROVINCE DU BAS-CANADA / Bas-Canada. Parlement – [Quebec]: T Cary & Co, [1824]. SEM105P102 – 3mf – 9 – Can$6.75 – cn Bibl Nat [370]

RAPPORT DU COMITE SPECIAL, DE L'ASSEMBLEE LEGISLATIVE, CHARGE DE S'ENQUERIR DE LA TENURE DES TERRES AUX ILES DE LA MAGDELEINE, COMTE DE GASPE : SESSION 1874-75 / Quebec. Legislature. Assemblee legislative. Comite... – Levis: "L'Echo de Levis", 1875. SEM105P553 – 1mf – 9 – Can$2.25 – cn Bibl Nat [333]

RAPPORT DU COMITE SPECIAL DE L'ASSEMBLEE LEGISLATIVE NOMME POUR S'ENQUERIR DE L'ETAT DE L'EDUCATION ET DU FONCTIONNEMENT DE LA LOI DES ECOLES DANS LE BAS-CANADA / Canada (Province). Parlement. Assemblee legislative – Quebec: imprime par John Lovell..., 1853. SEM105P325 – 1mf – 9 – Can$2.25 – cn Bibl Nat [370]

RAPPORT DU COMITE SPECIAL DE L'ASSEMBLEE LEGISLATIVE, NOMME POUR S'ENQUERIR DES CAUSES ET DE L'IMPORTANCE DE L'EMIGRATION QUI A LIEU TOUS LES ANS DU BAS-CANADA VERS LES ETATS-UNIS / Canada. Parlement. Assemblee legislative. Comite special... – Montreal: Louis Perrault, 1849. SEM105P597 – 2mf – 9 – Can$4.50 – cn Bibl Nat [304]

RAPPORT DU COMITE SPECIAL DE L'ASSEMBLEE LEGISLATIVE SUR LA CONVENANCE DE DEFENDRE LE TRAVAIL DU DIMANCHE DANS LES DEPARTEMENTS PUBLICS DE LA PROVINCE / Canada. Parlement. Assemblee legislative. Comite special auquel... – Quebec: John Lovell, 1853. SEM105P572 – 1mf – 9 – Can$2.25 – cn Bibl Nat [971]

RAPPORT DU COMITE SPECIAL DE L'ASSEMBLEE LEGISLATIVE,...POUR REMEDIER AUX MAUX QUI RESULTENT DE L'INTEMPERANCE / Canada. Parliament. Legislative Assembly. Special Committee – Montreal: De l'Imprimerie de Lovell et Gibson, 1849. SEM105P204 – 1mf – 9 – Can$2.25 – cn Bibl Nat [324]

RAPPORT DU COMITE SPECIAL NOMME POUR EXAMINER LES LOIS MUNICIPALES ET LES LOIS CONCERNANT LES ABUS PREJUDICIABLES A L'AGRICULTURE, AVEC LES AMENDEMENTS PROPOSES / Quebec Province – [Quebec]: imprime par ordre de la Chambre, [1868]. SEM105P644 – 1mf – 9 – Can$2.25 – cn Bibl Nat [630]

RAPPORT DU COMITE SPECIAL NOMME POUR PRENDRE EN CONSIDERATION LA COLONISATION DES TERRES INCULTES DU BAS-CANADA / Canada. Parliament. Legislative Assembly. Committee – Quebec: Hunter, Rose et Lemieux, 1862. SEM105P216 – 1mf – 9 – Can$2.25 – cn Bibl Nat [323]

RAPPORT DU COMITE SPECIAL NOMME POUR S'ENQUIRER DES CAUSES DE L'EMIGRATION DU CANADA AUX ETATS-UNIS D'AMERIQUE OU AILLEURS / Canada. Comite special sur l'Immigration – Toronto: Imprime par John Lovell, 1857. SEM105P231 – 2mf – 9 – Can$4.50 – cn Bibl Nat [323]

RAPPORT DU COMITE SPECIAL NOMME POUR S'ENQUIRER ET FAIRE RAPPORT SUR L'ETAT, L'ADMINISTRATION ET L'AVENIR DE LA COMPPAGNIE DU CHEMIN DE FER GRAND TRONC / Canada. Parliament. Legislative Assembly. Committee – Toronto: Imp. John Lovell, 1857. SEM105P361 – 3mf – 9 – Can$6.75 – cn Bibl Nat [336]

RAPPORT DU COMITE SPECIAL SUR LA COLONISATION / Canada. Parliament. Legislative Assembly. Committee – Quebec: Thompson et cie, 1860. SEM105P214 – 1mf – 9 – Can$2.25 – cn Bibl Nat [323]

RAPPORT DU COMITE SPECIAL SUR LA CULTURE DE LA VIGNE AU CANADA / Canada (Province). Parlement. Assemblee legislative – Quebec: Hunter, Rose et Lemieux, [1864]. SEM105P599 – 1mf – 9 – Can$2.25 – cn Bibl Nat [630]

RAPPORT DU COMITE SPECIAL SUR LA LOI POUR PROHIBER LA VENTE DES LIQUEURS FORTES / Canada. Parliament. Legislative Assembly. Special Committee – Toronto: Imprime par John Lovell, 1859. SEM105P207 – 1mf – 9 – Can$2.25 – cn Bibl Nat [324]

RAPPORT DU COMITE SPECIAL SUR L'ETAT DE L'AGRICULTURE DU BAS-CANADA / Canada (Province). Parlement. Assemblee legislative – Toronto: Impr. de Louis Perrault, 1850. SEM105P662 – 2mf – 9 – Can$4.50 – cn Bibl Nat [630]

RAPPORT DU COMITE SPECIAL SUR L'ETAT DE L'AGRICULTURE DU BAS-CANADA / Canada Province. Parlement. Assemblee legislative – Toronto: Imprimerie de Louis Perrault, 1850. SEM105P1846 – 2mf – 9 – Can$4.50 – cn Bibl Nat [630]

RAPPORT DU CONSEIL D'ADMINISTRATION. BILAN ET COMPTE DE PROFITS ET PERTES. 1946-1963 / Egypt. Banque de Port Said – 15 v. in 13. (lacking 1947 48, 1960 61). BNE-4606 1 – 9 – ne IDC [338]

RAPPORT DU CONSEIL D'ADMINISTRATION ET BILAN DU EXERCISE, 1947-1957 / Egypt. Banque Misr – 10 v. (lacking 1949). BNE-4605 1 – 9 – ne IDC [336]

RAPPORT DU DR. WOLFRED NELSON...SUR LA CONDITION, LA DISCIPLINE, L'ADMINISTRATION ET L'ENTRETIEN DES PRISONS DE DISTRICT ET AUTRE PRISONS, DU BAS-CANADA / Nelson, Wolfred – Quebec: Imp. John Lovell, 1852. SEM105P352 – 2mf – 9 – Can$4.50 – cn Bibl Nat [360]

RAPPORT DU GREFFIER DE LA COURONNE EN CHANCELLERIE SUR LES ELECTIONS PARTICULIERE DEPUIS JUIN 1883 – Quebec, 1886. SEM105P625 – 1mf – 9 – Can$2.25 – cn Bibl Nat [971]

RAPPORT DU GREFFIER DE LA COURRONNE EN CHANCELLERIE SUR LES ELECTIONS GENERALES DE... = REPORT OF THE CLERK OF THE CROWN IN CHANCERY, ON THE OCCASION OF THE GENERAL ELECTIONS OF...1871-86 – Quebec: des presses a vapeur d'Augustin Cote et cie, c1872-1887. SEM105P566 – 7mf – 9 – Can$15.75 – cn Bibl Nat [320]

RAPPORT DU MAJOR WILLIAM ROBINSON, CAPITAINE DES INGENIEURS ROYAUX,... / Robinson, William – Ottawa: Hunter, Rose et Lemieux, 1868. SEM105P649 – 1mf – 9 – Can$2.25 – cn Bibl Nat [380]

RAPPORT DU MINISTERE DE L'INTERIEUR / Congres du Parti Socialiste Francais, Jauressistes. Congres National (8e), 1908, Marseille – 8p – 9 – fr Hachette [335]

RAPPORT DU MINISTRE DES FINANCES SUR LE TRAITE DE RECIPROCITE AVEC LES ETATS UNIS. / Canada. Ministere des Finances – Quebec: Imp. Stewart Derbishire and George Desbarats, 1862. SEM105P297 – 1mf – 9 – Can$2.25 – cn Bibl Nat [336]

RAPPORT DU SURINTENDANT DE L'EDUCATION POUR LE BAS-CANADA, POUR... / Canada. Bas-Canada. Bureau de l'Education – Quebec: John Lovell, 1852-67. 1850/51-1866. SEM105P946 – 30mf – 9 – Can$67.50 – cn Bibl Nat [971]

RAPPORT DU SURINTENDANT D'EDUCATION POUR LE BAS-CANADA POUR L'ANNEE 1846 / Canada. Bas-Canada. Bureau de l'Education – Montreal: Lovell et Gibson, 1847. SEM105P1010 – 2mf – 9 – Can$4.50 – cn Bibl Nat [370]

RAPPORT ECONOMIQUE AU GROUPE CONSULTATIF / Morocco – 1967-70. (lacking 1968-69). BNE-3084 1 – 9 – ne IDC [330]

RAPPORT ET DELIBERATIONS DU COMITE SPECIAL SUR LES ACCUSATIONS CONTRE LA DERNIERE ADMINISTRATION – Quebec: Lovell et Lamoureux, 1855. SEM105P269 – 3mf – 9 – Can$6.75 – cn Bibl Nat [323]

RAPPORT ET PLANS SUR DES AMELIORATIONS GENERALES DANS LE HAVRE DE QUEBEC.. / Berlinguet, Francois Xavier – Quebec: F. Berlinguet, 1875. 04042. (Pre-1900 Canadiana) – 9 – cn C.I.H.M. [627]

RAPPORT ET TEMOIGNAGE SUR LA DERNIERE ELECTION POUR LE DISTRICT ELECTORAL DE KAMOURASKA / Canada. Parlement. Chambre des communes. Comite permanent des privileges et elections – Ottawa: Hunter, Rose et Lemieux, 1868. SEM105P659 – 1mf – 9 – Can$2.25 – cn Bibl Nat [320]

RAPPORT FAIT AU NOM DE LA COMMISSION CHARGEE D'EXAMINER LA PROPOSITION DE M. DE TRACY, RELATIVE AUX ESCLAVES DES COLONIES. SEANCE DU 23 JUILLET, 1839 / Tocqueville, Alexis de – (Slave Trade and Abolitionism in France series) – 9 – fr Hachette [360]

RAPPORT FAIT AU NOM DE LA COMMISSION D'ENQUETE PARLEMENTAIRE SUR LES CONDITIONS DE TRAVAIL EN FRANCE. SALAIRES ET RAPPORTS ENTRE OUVRIERS ET PATRONS, PAR M. DUCARRE, DEPUTE DU RHONE – (Condition of 19th C. French working class series). 1877 – 9 – fr Hachette [360]

RAPPORT GENERAL A M. LE MINISTRE DE L'INTERIEUR SUR LE SERVICE DES ALIENES EN 1874 PAR LES INSPECTEURS GENERAUX DU SERVICE / Constans, Augustin & Lunier, Jules Joseph Ludger & Dumesnil, Octave – Paris. 1878 – 9 – fr Hachette [150]

RAPPORT GENERAL DE LA COMMISSION D'ETUDE ET DE COORDINATION DES PLANS DE MODERNISATION ET D'EQUIPEMENT DES TERRITORIES D'OUTRE-MER / French Overseas Territories. Commissariat general au plan de modernisation et d'equipement – D-1301 1. 1954 – 9 – ne IDC [338]

RAPPORT GENERAL DES MISSIONNAIRES AGRICOLES.. – 1896-97. s.l., s.n., c1897. SEM105P490 – 1mf – 9 – Can$2.25 – cn Bibl Nat [630]

RAPPORT GENERAL SUR LE DEUXIEME PLAN QUADRIENNAL DE MODERNISATION ET D'EQUIPEMENT DE L'ALGERIE / Algeria – D-931 1. 1953-1956 – 9 – ne IDC [338]

RAPPORT GENERAL SUR LE DEUXIEME PLAN QUADRIENNAL DE MODERNISATION ET D'EQUIPEMENT DE L'ALGERIE / Algeria. Gouvernement General – 1953-56. 1953. BNE-8646 1 – 9 – ne IDC [338]

RAPPORT GENERAL SUR LE PREMIER PLAN DE MODERNISATION ET D'EQUIPEMENT (1947-1950) / France. Commissariat general du plan de modernisation et d'equipement – (General report on the first modernization and equipment plan). Paris. 1946 – 9 – ne IDC [324]

RAPPORT GENERAL SUR L'EPIDEMIE DU CHOLERA QUI A REGNE A LILLE EN 1832 / Lestiboudois, Themistocle – Lille, L. Daniel, c.1832. 107 p. 2 fiches. (Statistics Series: Medical Studies) – 9 – 6.00 – fr Bibl Nationale [310]

RAPPORT GENERAL SUR LES INVESTISSEMENTS PREVUS EN 1955 AU TITRE DU PLAN DE MODERNISATION ET D'EQUIPEMENT / Algeria. Gouvernement General – 1955 56. BNE-8645 1 – 9 – ne IDC [338]

RAPPORT GENERAL SUR LES OBJECTIFS GENERAUX ET LES ACTIONS PRIORITAIRES DU VIE PLAN / France – (Overall Re Port on the General Objectives and Priority Measures of the Sixth Plan). Paris. 1971. BD1656 1 – 9 – ne IDC [338]

RAPPORT GENERAL SUR LES OBJECTIFS GENERAUX ET LES ACTIONS PRIORITAIRES DU VIE PLAN, 1971-1975 / France – D-1526 1. 2 v. 1971 – 9 – ne IDC [338]

RAPPORT GENERAL SUR LES PERSPECTIVES DE DEVELOPPEMENT DU SENEGAL / Senegal – 2nd ed 2 v. Dakar. 1960 – 9 – ne IDC [338]

RAPPORT GENERAL SUR L'EXECUTION DE L'AN 1 DU PLAN QUINQUENNAL / Cameroon. Direction du Plan et de la Coop. Technique – Yaounde. 1962. BD-727 1 – 9 – ne IDC [338]

RAPPORT GENERAL SUR L'EXECUTION DU PREMIER PLAN QUINQUENNAL (JUSQU AU 30 JUIN 1963) / Cameroon. Ministere des Finances et du Plan – Yaounde. 1963 – 9 – ne IDC [338]

RAPPORT GENERAL SUR L'HISTORIQUE ET LE FONCTIONNEMENT DE L'ECOLE MUNICIPALE DE PHYSIQUE ET DE CHIMIE INDUSTRIELLE / Lauth, Charles – Paris. 1900. (La Condition Ouvriere. Part Two.) – 9 – 5.00 – fr Bibl Nationale [360]

RAPPORT JUI-DEC 1959-1977 / Morocco. Banque du Maroc – BNE-3004 1 – 9 – ne IDC [330]

RAPPORT: LE COMITE SPECIAL AUQUEL A ETE RENVOYE LE BILL "POUR REGLER LE PILOTAGE DANS LE PORT DE QUEBEC ET AU DESSOUS". / Canada. Parliament. Legislative Assembly – Quebec: Imprime par

John Lovell, 1853. SEM105P163 – 1mf – 9 – Can$2.25 – cn Bibl Nat [380]

RAPPORT: LE COMITE SPECIAL AUQUEL A ETE RENVOYEE CETTE PARTIE DU RAPPORT DU PRESIDENT DU BUREAU DES TRAVAUX PUBLICS, QUI CONCERNE LE LAC ST-PIERRE... / Canada (Province). Parlement. Assemblee legislative. Comite special... – Montreal: Lowell et Gibson..., [1846]. SEM105P308 – 1mf – 9 – Can$2.25 – cn Bibl Nat [971]

RAPPORT NATIONAL SUR LE DEVELOPPEMENT DE L'EDUCATION AU CAMEROUN (PERIODE 1981-1984) / Cameroon. Service d'Orientation Scolaire, Universitaire et Professionnelle. Ministere Education Nationale – [Yaounde], 1984 – 4mf – 9 – DE-635/1 – ne IDC [370]

RAPPORT OFFICIEL DU LIEUTENANT-GENERAL GRANT A L'HONORABLE E. M. STANTON / Grant, Ulysses – Paris: Correard, 1866. 181p. (Strategy of War Series) – 9 – fr Hachette [355]

RAPPORT PRELIMINAIRE D'ENQUETE DES ZONES D'EXTENSION DES SECTEURS PILOTES DIABO-BROBO / Le Cour Grand Maison – (Africa series). 1969 – 9 – fr Hachette [960]

RAPPORT PRELIMINAIRE D'ETUDE DES CENTRES SEMI-URBAINS / Chevassu, J – (Africa series). 1967 – 9 – fr Hachette [338]

RAPPORT PRELIMINAIRE DU BUREAU DES INSPECTEURS D'ASILES, PRISONS, ETC., 1859 / Canada. Bureau des inspecteurs d'asiles, prisons, etc. – Quebec: Thompson et cie, 1860. SEM105P1460 – 2mf – 9 – Can$4.50 – cn Bibl Nat [360]

RAPPORT PRELIMINAIRE SUR LA ZONE D'ATTAQUE SAHELA-SRA / Morocco. Office National de la Modernisation Rurale – 2v. 1962. BNE-3090 1 – 9 – ne IDC [338]

RAPPORT PRESENTE A LA COMMISSION D'ENQUETE PARLEMENTAIRE SUR LA SITUATION DES OUVRIERS DE L'AGRICULTURE ET DE L'INDUSTRIE EN FRANCE ET SUR LA CRISE PARISIENNE, PAR M. SPULLER, DEPUTE, PRESIDENT DE LA COMMISSION ET RAPPORTEUR PROVISOIRE – (Condition of 19th C. French working class series). 1885 – 9 – fr Hachette [360]

RAPPORT PRESENTE A LA COMMISSION D'ENQUETE PARLEMENTAIRE SUR LA SITUATION DES OUVRIERS DE L'AGRICULTURE ET DE L'INDUSTRIE EN FRANCE. GREVE D'AMZIN PAR M. CLEMENCEAU – (Condition of 19th C. French working class series). 1885 – 9 – fr Hachette [360]

RAPPORT PRESENTE A LA SOCIETE DE LEGISLATION COMPAREE / Daguin, F – Paris, 1886 – 1mf – 1 – ILM-3685/1 – ne IDC [327]

RAPPORT PRESENTE PAR M. SCHNEIDER, D'AUTUN, AU NOM DE LA COMMISSION CHARGEE D'EXAMINER LA LOI DU 22 MARS 1841, SUR LE TRAVAIL DES ENFANTS DANS LES MANUFACTURES / Conseil General du Commerce. Session de 1845-1846 – (Condition of the 19th C. French working class series). 1846 – 9 – fr Hachette [324]

RAPPORT RELATIF AU REGIME DES ESCLAVES DANS LES COLONIES FRANCAISES / Lasteyrie, Jules de – A. Henry, Imprimerie de la Chambre des Deputes. 1845 – 9 – 5.00 – fr Orientalistes [305]

RAPPORT SUR LA CONSTITUTION MEDICALE ET LA MORTALITE DE LA VILLE DE METZ PENDANT L'ANNEE 1865 / Saunois, Victor – Metz: J. Verronnais, 1866. 50p.1 fiche. (Statistics Series: Medical Studies) – 9 – 6.00 – fr Bibl Nationale [310]

RAPPORT SUR LA FABRICATION DU BEURRE:.. / Barre, SM – Quebec: C.F. Langlois, 1882. 07262. (Pre-1900 Canadiana) – 9 – cn C.I.H.M. [630]

RAPPORT SUR LA LETTRE DE CHANGE INTERNATIONALE / Cerutti, D B – Mons, 1905 – 1mf – 1 – ILM-3772/1 – ne IDC [327]

RAPPORT SUR LA MARCHE ET LES EFFETS DU CHOLERA MOBBUS DANS PARIS ET LES COMMUNES RURALES DU DEPARTMENT DE LA SEINE, ANNEE 1832. PAR LA COMMISSION NOMMEE PAR MM. LES PREFETS DE LA SEINE ET DE POLICE – (Condition of 19th C. French working class series). 1834 – 9 – fr Hachette [360]

RAPPORT SUR LA MISSION MEDICO-SCIENTIFIQUE FRANCO-MALIENNE / Chaventre, A – (2eme Mission. F30.00. 3eme Mission. F30.00. 4eme Mission. F30.00. 5eme Mission. F30.00. 6eme Mission. F30.00. 7eme Mission. F40.00. 8eme Mission. F50.00. 9eme Mission. F30.00. 10eme Mission. F20.00. 11eme Mission. F30.00. 12eme Mission. F30.00) – 1ere Mission – 9 – F20.00 – fr Ethnologie [610]

RAPPORT SUR LA MISSION MEDICO-SCIENTIFIQUE FRANCO-MALIENNE / Chaventre, A & Ag Rhaly, A – 13eme mission – 9 – F30.00 – fr Ethnologie [306]

RAPPORT SUR LA PETITION DE WM. L. MACKENZIE, ECUYER AGISSANT COMME EXECUTEUR TESTAMENTAIRE DE FEU ROBERT RANDALL, ECUYER DE CHIPPAOUAIS / Canada. Parliament. Legislative Assembly. Committee – Quebec: Imprimerie de Louis Perrault, 1853. SEM105P217 – 3mf – 9 – Can$6.75 – cn Bibl Nat [323]

RAPPORT SUR LA PRODUCTION AGRICOLE ALGERIENNE ET SUR L'ACTIVITE DES INSTITUTIONS DE CREDIT MUTUEL ET DE COOPERATION AGRICOLES D'ALGERIE / Algeria. Caisse Algerienne de Credit Agricole Mutuel – 1951-60. BNE-8607 1 – 9 – ne IDC [338]

RAPPORT SUR LA SECTION D'HOCHELAGA ET ST JEROME / Compagnie du chemin a lisses de colonisation du nord de Montreal – (Montreal: Le Nouveau Monde), 1869. 00732. (Pre-1900 Canadiana) – 9 – cn C.I.H.M. [910]

RAPPORT SUR LA STATISTIQUE DES DECES DU TROISIEME ARRONDISSEMENT DE PARIS PENDANT LE PERIODE QUINQUENNALE 1853-57 / Bergeron, Jules – Paris: E. Thunot, 1864. 107p. 2 fiches. (Statistics: Medical Studies Series) – 9 – 6.00 – fr Bibl Nationale [310]

RAPPORT SUR LE 1ER PLAN QUINQUENNAL DE CHINE (1953-57) / China. People's Republic – Li, Fu-Chun. Peking: Editions en Langues etrangeres, 1956. BD-641-1 – 9 – ne IDC [338]

RAPPORT SUR LE BUDGET ECONOMIQUE DE L'ANNEE 1966 / Trust Territory of the Pacific Islands. (U.S.). Secretariat d'Etat au Plan et a l'Economie Nationale – D 1499 1. 1965 – 9 – ne IDC [350]

RAPPORT SUR LE BUDGET ECONOMIQUE DE L'ANNEE 1967 / Trust Territory of the Pacific Islands. (U.S.). Secretariat d'Etat au Plan et a l'Economie Nationale – D 1500 1 – 9 – ne IDC [350]

RAPPORT SUR LE BUDGET ECONOMIQUE DE L'ANNEE 1968 / Tunisia. Secretariat d'Etat au Plan et a l'Economie Nationale – (Report on the 1968 Economic Budget). BD-1760 1 – 9 – ne IDC [350]

RAPPORT SUR LE BUDGET ECONOMIQUE DE L'ANNEE 1969 / Tunisia. Secretariat d'Etat au Plan et a l'Economie Nationale – (Report on the 1969 Economic Budget). BD-1761 1 – 9 – ne IDC [350]

RAPPORT SUR LE BUDGET ECONOMIQUE DE L'ANNEE 1970 / Tunisia. Secretariat d'Etat au Plan et a l'Economie Nationale – (Report on the 1970 Economic Budget). BD-1762 1 – 9 – ne IDC [350]

RAPPORT SUR LE BUDGET ECONOMIQUE DE L'ANNEE 1973 / Tunisia. Ministere du Plan – (Report on the Economic Budget for the Year 1973). Tunis. Oct 1972. BD-1764 1 – 9 – ne IDC [350]

RAPPORT SUR LE COMMERCE / Canada (Province). Parlement...Comite Nomme Pour s'Enquerir des Relations Commerciales Entre le Canada et la Grande-Bretagne... – Quebec: Des Presses a Vapeur de Lovell et Lamoureux, 1855 – 1mf – 9 – Can$2.25 – cn Bibl Nat [380]

RAPPORT SUR LE COMMERCE DES BOIS / Quinn, M William – Quebec: Imp. Augustin Cote, 1861. SEM105P242 – 1mf – 9 – Can$2.25 – cn Bibl Nat [380]

RAPPORT SUR LE COMMERCE EXTERIEUR / Egypt. Customs Dept – 7v. 1956-62. BNE-4624 1 – 9 – ne IDC [380]

RAPPORT SUR LE DEVELOPPEMENT DE MADAGASCAR / Malagasy Republic. Commissariat General au Plan – Tananarive. 1962. BD-437 1 – 9 – ne IDC [338]

RAPPORT SUR LE PLAN ECONOMIQUE QUINQUENNAL / Bulgaria. Ministere des Affaires Etrangeres – Terpeshev, Dobri. Sofia. 1949. BD-642 1 – 9 – ne IDC [949]

RAPPORT SUR LE PLAN QUINQUENNAL DE DEVELOPPEMENT ECONOMIQUE ET SOCIAL DE LA REPUBLIQUE DU MALI, 1961-1965 / Mali. Ministere du Plan et de l'Economie Rurale – Bamako. 1960. BD-426 1 – 9 – ne IDC [338]

RAPPORT SUR LE REALISATION DU PLAN DE MODERNISATION ET D'EQUIPEMENT DE L'UNION FRANCAISE ANNEE 1952 / France. Commissariat General du Plan – Paris. 1953. BD-734 1 – 9 – ne IDC [338]

RAPPORT SUR LE SECTEUR TOURISTIQUE PRESENTE AU GROUPE CONSULTATIF MAROC-BIRD / Morocco. Ministere du Tourisme – Nov 1970. 1970. BNE-3080 1 – 9 – ne IDC [338]

RAPPORT SUR L'ECONOMIE SYRIENNE / Syria. Office Arabe de Presse et de Documentation – 10 v. 1963 64-1973. BNE-9727 1 – 9 – ne IDC [330]

RAPPORT SUR L'EDUCATION DANS LE BAS CANADA SUIVI DE TABLEAUX STATISTIQUES POUR L'ANNEE SCOLAIRE...1849/1850 / Canada. Bas-Canada. Bureau de l'Education – Toronto: Lovell et Gibson, 1851. SEM105P945 – 1mf – 9 – Can$2.25 – cn Bibl Nat [370]

RAPPORT SUR L'EDUCATION OUVRIERE EN REPUBLIQUE ALGERIENNE / International Labour Organisation – 1964. Philip, J. BNE-8731 1 – 9 – ne IDC [331]

RAPPORT SUR L'EDUCATION OUVRIERE EN REPUBLIQUE ALGERIENNE DEMOCRATIQUE ET POPULAIRE / International Labour Organisation – 1967. Defalle, V. BNE-8726 1 – 9 – ne IDC [331]

RAPPORT SUR LES AFFAIRES DE SAINT-DOMINGUE FAIT LES 11 ET 12 OCTOBRE / Barnave, A P J M – (Slave Trade and Abolitionism in France Series). 1790 – 9 – fr Hachette [360]

RAPPORT SUR LES AVANTAGES ET LA NECESSITE D'ETABLIR UN RESEAU DE TELEGRAPHE SOUS-MARIN DANS LE FLEUVE ET LE GOLFE ST LAURENT / Canada. Parlement. Chambre des Communes. Comite.. – 1876. SEM105P658 – 1mf – 9 – Can$2.25 – cn Bibl Nat [324]

RAPPORT SUR LES COLONIES, ET DECRET RENDU SUR CETTE AFFAIRE. LE 28 SEPTEMBRE / Barnave, A P J M – (Slave Trade and Abolitionism in France Series). 1791 – 9 – fr Hachette [360]

RAPPORT SUR LES MISSIONS DU DIOCESE DE QUEBEC / Society for the Propagation of the Faith – 1839-74.(American Indian Periodicals in the Princeton University Library). 31 fiches – 9 – $120.00 – us UPA [240]

RAPPORT SUR LES NEGOCIATIONS CONDUITES A MOSCOU, SUIVI DES THESES PRESENTEES AU 2EME CONGRES DE L'INTERNATIONALE COMMUNISTE / Frossard, LO – Paris. 1920 – 1 – fr A.C.R.P.P. [335]

RAPPORT SUR LES OPERATIONS ET LES RESULTATS FINANCIERS / Algeria. Caisse Centrale des Societes Agricoles de Prevoyance de'Algerie – 3v. 1962-64. BNE-8614 1 – 9 – ne IDC [330]

RAPPORT SUR LES PRINCIPES DE MORALE POLITIQUE QUI DOIVENT GUIDER LA CONVENTION NATIONALE / Robespierre, Maximilien de – Paris: Imp. nat., s.d. 31p. 1 fiche. (Political Science Collection) – 9 – 6.00 – fr Bibl Nationale [321]

RAPPORT SUR LES PROGRES DES TRAVAUX DE COLONISATION DURANT L'ANNEE 1860 – Quebec: Hunter et Rose, 1860. SEM105P584 – 1mf – 9 – Can$2.25 – cn Bibl Nat [971]

RAPPORT SUR LES PROGRES RECENTS DES SCIENCES ZOOLOGIQUES EN FRANCE / Milne-Edwards, Henri – Paris, Imp. imperiale, 1867, 499 p. Histoire des Sciences XVIIe-XIXe Siecles. 7927 – 9 – fr Hachette [590]

RAPPORT SUR LES QUESTIONS COLONIALES / Lechevalier, Jules – v1-2, 1843-44 – 1 – 34.00 – us L of C Photodup [944]

RAPPORT SUR LES RESULTATS DE LA REALISATION DU 1ER PLAN / Albania – Shehu, Mehmet. Tirana. 1956. BD-581 1 – 9 – ne IDC [949]

RAPPORT SUR LES STATISTIQUES DU COMMERCE EXTERIEUR AU MAROC / Morocco. Service Central des Statistiques – Elsayed Hafez, A. R. BNE-3100 1 – 9 – ne IDC [380]

RAPPORT SUR LES TERRAINS AURIFERES DU CANADA, ET LES MEILLEURS MOYENS D'EN DEVELOPPER L'EXPLOITATION / Canada. Parliament. Legislative Assembly. Committee – Quebec: Imprime par Hunter, Rose et Lemieux, 1865. SEM105P211 – 2mf – 9 – Can$4.50 – cn Bibl Nat [910]

RAPPORT SUR LES TROUBLES DE SAINT-DOMINGUE.. / France. Commission des Colonies – 4v. 1797-99 – 1r – 1 – us Ross [944]

RAPPORT SUR L'ETAT ACTUEL DES PRISONS, DES HOSPICES, DES ECOLES, ETC.; CONSIDERATIONS GENERALES SUR CES SORTES D'ETABLISSEMENTS / Appert, B – (Condition of 19th C. French working class series). 1824 – 9 – fr Hachette [360]

RAPPORT SUR L'ETAT DE LA MILICE DE LA PROVINCE / Canada. Departement de la Milice – Toronto: Imp. S Derbishire et G Desbarats, 1857. SEM105P313 – 1mf – 9 – Can$2.25 – cn Bibl Nat [355]

RAPPORT SUR L'ETAT DE LA POLICE PROVINCIALE DE QUEBEC POUR...1870-71 – 1870-71 report. SEM105P622 – 2mf – 9 – Can$4.50 – cn Bibl Nat [350]

RAPPORT SUR L'EVOLUTION ECONOMIQUE ET SOCIALE DE LA COTE D'IVOIRE, 1960-1964 / Ivory Coast. Conseil Economique et Social – Abidjan. 1965. BD-463 1 – 9 – ne IDC [338]

RAPPORT. SUR L'EXEC. DU PROGR. D'EXP. ECON. 1963. PREV. 1964 / Belgium – (Belgium. Parl. Chambres des Repres. Documents Parlementaires, No. 834, Session 1963-1964). Bruxelles. 1964. BD-835 1 – 9 – ne IDC [338]

RAPPORT SUR L'EXECUTION DU PLAN QUADRIENNAL, 1963-1966 / Mauritania. Direction du Plan – Nouackchott. 1967. BD-413 1 – 9 – ne IDC [338]

RAPPORT SUR L'EXECUTION DU PROGRAMME D'EQUIPMENT DE L'ALGERIE EN 1961 / France. Commissariat General du Plan – Paris, Caisse d'Equip. pour Dev. de l'Algerie. 1962 – 9 – ne IDC [338]

RAPPORT SUR L'EXPEDITION A LA BAIE D'HUDSON EN 1886 / Gordon, Andrew R – 1887. SEM105P665 – 2mf – 9 – Can$4.50 – cn Bibl Nat [910]

RAPPORT SUR L'EXPLORATION DE LA CONTREE SITUEE ENTRE LE LAC SUPERIEUR ET LA COLONIE DE LA RIVIERE ROUGE, ET ENTRE CE DERNIER ENDROIT ET LES RIVIERES ASSINIBOINE ET SASKATCHEWAN / Dawson, Simon James – Toronto: John Lovell, 1859. SEM105P282 – 1mf – 9 – Can$2.25 – cn Bibl Nat [971]

RAPPORT SUR L'EXPLORATION DE LA CONTREE SITUEE ENTRE LE LAC SUPERIEUR ET LES ETABLISSEMENTS DE LA RIVIERE ROUGE / Canada. Ministere des Terres de la Couronne – Toronto: John Lovell, 1858. SEM105P281 – 6mf – 9 – Can$13.50 – cn Bibl Nat [910]

RAPPORT SUR L'EXPLORATION DES LACS SUPERIEUR ET HURON / Rottermund, W D de – Toronto: s.n, 1856. SEM105P289 – 1mf – 9 – Can$2.25 – cn Bibl Nat [910]

RAPPORT SUR L'EXPLORATION PRELIMINAIRE DU CHEMIN DE FER INTERCOLONIAL, FAITE EN VERTU D'INSTRUCTIONS DU GOUVERNEMENT CANADIEN EN L'ANNEE 1864 / Fleming, Sandford – Quebec: Imp. Hunter, Rose et Lemieux, 1865. SEM105P359 – 2mf – 9 – Can$4.50 – cn Bibl Nat [380]

RAPPORT SUR L'INDUSTRIE MINIERE / Algeria. Direction des Mines et de la Geologie – 1965-67 – 9 – ne IDC [324]

RAPPORT SUR L'INSTRUCTION PUBLIQUE, FAIT AU NOM DU COMITE DE CONSTITUTION, LES 10, 11 ET 19 SEPTEMBRE 1791 / Talleyrand-Perigord, Charles Maurice de – Paris. Impr. nationale. 1791 – 9 – fr Hachette [370]

RAPPORT SUR UN SYSTEME D'INSTRUCTION ELEMENTAIRE PUBLIQUE POUR LE HAUT CANADA / Ryerson, Adolphus Egerton – Montreal: Lovell et Gibson, 1846. SEM105P327 – 1mf – 9 – Can$2.25 – cn Bibl Nat [370]

RAPPORT SUR UNE MISSION SCIENTIFIQUE AUX ARCHIVES D'AUTRICHE ET D'ESPAGNE : ETUDE ET CATALOGUE CRITIQUES DE DOCUMENTS SUR LE CONCILE DE TRENTE / Constant, G – Paris: Imprimerie nationale, 1910 – 1mf – 9 – 0-8370-8413-X – 1986-2413 – us A.T.L.A. [240]

RAPPORT VAN ONLUSTEN IN SINTANG, CA 1885 – (Microfiche No 47) – 1mf – 9 – SD-102/1 – ne IDC [950]

RAPPORT...DANS L'AFFAIRE DU MEURTRE DE CORRIGAN / Canada. (Province). Commissaires nommes pour s'enquerir des Circonstances...la mort de feu Robert Corrigan – Toronto: John Lovell, 1857. SEM105P648 – 2mf – 9 – Can$4.50 – cn Bibl Nat [971]

RAPPORTEN BETREFFENDE GEHEIME VERENIGINGEN TE SUKABUMI – 1921. Arch. Kol. Mailrap. 626 geh./1921. BSD-101/1 mf. 6 – 9 – ne IDC [950]

RAPPORTEN BETREFFENDE JAVA AFKOMSTIG VAN R.A. KERN, ADVISEUR INLANDSE ZAKEN, 1889-1937 – Met lijst no.42-93. KITLV,H 797. BSD-102/1 mf. 48-78 – 9 – ne IDC [950]

RAPPORTEN, BRIEVEN BETREFFENDE DE TJIMAREMEZAAK, 1919 – KITLV,H 474. BSD-102/1 mf. 79-84 – 9 – ne IDC [950]

RAPPORTEN VAN DE COMMISSIE IN NEDERLANDSCH-INDIE VOOR OUDHEIDKUNDIG ONDERZOEK – (Continues as: Oudheidkundig verslag van de Oudheidkundige Dienst in Nederlandsch-Indie.-Weltevreden, 's-Gravenhage, 1912-1949) – Batavia, 's-Gravenhage, 1901-1913 – 109mf – 9 – SE-20,005/1 – ne IDC [073]

RAPPORT...LES 22, 23 ET 24 NOVEMBRE 1898 / Congres de la Colonisation. 1898: Montreal, Quebec – Publication faite par les soins et sous la direction de la Societe generale de colonisation et de repatriement de la province de Quebec. (Montreal: Impr. de la Patrie), 1898? 00089. (Pre-1900 Canadiana) – 9 – cn C.I.H.M. [971]

RAPPORT...NOMME POUR S'ENQUERIR DE L'ETAT ACTUEL DE L'EDUCATION DANS LA PROVINCE DU BAS-CANADA / Canada. Bas-Canada. Parlement. Chambre d'Assemblee – Quebec: T Cary & Co, 1824. SEM105P102 – 3mf – 9 – Can$6.75 – cn Bibl Nat [370]

RAPPORT...POUR EXAMINER LES LOIS MUNICIPALES ET LES LOIS CONCERNANT... LES ABUS PREJUDICIABLES A L'AGRICULTURE.. / Quebec. (Province). Legislature. Assemblee legislative. Comite – Quebec, 1868. SEM105P644 – 1mf – 9 – Can$2.25 – cn Bibl Nat [630]

RAPPORT...POUR LES ANNEES 1882-83.. / Quebec. (City). Canada. Comite des Chemins – Quebec, 1884. SEM105P632 – 1mf – 9 – Can$2.25 – cn Bibl Nat [380]

RAPPORT...POUR PRENDRE EN CONSIDERATION LES MEILLEURS MOYENS DE DEVELOPPER L'INDUSTRIE DANS CETTE PROVINCE / Quebec. (Province). Legislature. Assemblee legislative. Comite – Quebec, 1872. SEM105P543 – 1mf – 9 – Can$2.25 – cn Bibl Nat [338]

RAPPORT...POUR S'ENQUIRER DE L'ETAT DE L'EDUCATION ET DU FONCTIONNEMENT DE LA LOI DES ECOLES DANS LE BAS-CANADA / Canada. Bureau de l'Instruction Publique pour le Bas-Canada – Quebec: Imp. John Lovell, 1853. SEM105P325 – 1mf – 9 – Can$2.25 – cn Bibl Nat [324]

RAPPORT...QUI CONCERNE LE LAC ST PIERRE / Canada. Ministere des Travaux Publics – Montreal: Imp. par Lovell et Gibson, 1846. SEM105P308 – 1mf – 9 – Can$2.25 – cn Bibl Nat [336]

RAPPORT...RELATIVE A L'ORGANISATION DE LA MILICE / Canada. Bas-Canada. Parlement. Chambre d'Assemblee – Quebec: Imprime Chez Neilson & Cowan, 1829. SEM105P93 – 3mf – 9 – Can$6.75 – cn Bibl Nat [355]

RAPPORT...RELATIVEMENT AUX BIENS DU SEMINAIRE DE MONTREAL / Canada. Bas-Canada. Parlement. Chambre d'Assemblee – SEM105P90 – 1mf – 9 – Can$2.25 – cn Bibl Nat [971]

RAPPORTS.. / Canada. Commission nommee pour s'enquerir d'une serie d'accidents et retardements sur le Grand Chemin de fer occidental – Quebec: des presses a vapeur de Lovell et Lamoureux, 1855. SEM105P357 – 3mf – 9 – Can$6.75 – cn Bibl Nat [380]

RAPPORTS A SON EXCELLENCE LE MINISTRE DE L'INTERIEUR SUR L'EMIGRATION: ANNEES 1857 ET 1858 / Desmaze, Ch – Paris: Imp. Imperiale, 1859. 37p. 1 fiche. (Statistics Series: Demography) – 9 – 6.00 – fr Bibl Nationale [310]

RAPPORTS A SON EXCELLENCE LE MINISTRE DE L'INTERIEUR SUR L'EMIGRATION ANNEES 1859 ET 1860 / Bostelle – Paris: Imp. imperiale, 1861. 43p. 1 fiche. (Statistics Series: Demography) – 9 – 6.00 – fr Bibl Nationale [310]

RAPPORTS DE LA SOCIETE DES MISSIONS EVANGELIQUES CHEZ LES PEUPLES NON CHRETIENS – Paris, 1833-1971 – 188mf – 9 – H-2103/1 – ne IDC [240]

RAPPORTS DE PRATIQUE DE QUEBEC = QUEBEC PRACTICE REPORTS – (Suivi de: Revue de droit judiciare) – Montreal: J Lovell, 1898-[1982] – 9 – cn C.I.H.M. [340]

RAPPORTS DES INSPECTEURS DES PORTS FRANC DE GASPE ET DU SAULT STE-MARIE, ACCOMPAGNES DE DIVERS TABLEAUX STATISTIQUES DES IMPORTATIONS – Quebec: Imp. Hunter, Rose et Lemieux, 1865. SEM105P305 – 1mf – 9 – Can$2.25 – cn Bibl Nat [380]

RAPPORTS DES PROPRIETAIRES ET DIRECTEURS DE L'ASILE DES ALIENES DU BAS CANADA AUX COMMISSAIARES, QUEBEC – Quebec: Imp. Middleton et Dawson, 1858. SEM105P346 – 1mf – 9 – Can$2.25 – cn Bibl Nat [360]

LES RAPPORTS DIPLOMATIQUES DE LEBZELTERN, MINISTRE D'AUTRICHE... (1816-1826) / ed by Mikhailowitch, N – (Index) – Sp., 1913 – 6mf – 9 – ne IDC [943]

RAPPORTS DU COMITE SPECIAL SUR LES CHEMINS ET AUTRES COMMUNICATIONS INTERIEURES / Canada. Bas-Canada. Parlement. Chambre d'Assemblee – Quebec: Imprime par Neilson & Cowan, 1829. SEM105P94 – 2mf – 9 – Can$4.50 – cn Bibl Nat [380]

RAPPORTS D'UNE EXPLORATION, DEPUIS LA CHUTE AUX IROQUOIS DANS LE COMTE D'OTTAWA, JUSQU'A LA BAIE DES PERES DANS LA COMTE DE PONTIAC / Boucherville, J B de – 1894. 03713. (Pre-1900 Canadiana) – 9 – cn C.I.H.M. [971]

LES RAPPORTS ENTRE LES COMMUNAUTES RELIGIEUSES ET L'ETAT EN YOUGOSLAVIE / Canapa, M P – F100.00 – fr Ethnologie [200]

LES RAPPORTS ENTRE LES LANGUES HAMITIQUES, SEMITIQUES ET LA LANGUE EGYPTIENNE / Lexa, F – Prague. 191-? BNE-491 1 – 9 – ne IDC [470]

RAPPORTS ET BILAN / Morocco. Banque Commerciale du Maroc – Casablanca. 1958-71. (lacking 1970). BNE-3009 1 – 9 – ne IDC [330]

RAPPORTS ET RESOLUTIONS / France. Commissariat General du Plan. Banque Industrielle de Financement et de Credit, Paris – 14 v. in 8. 1953-65. BNE-8605 1 – 9 – ne IDC [324]

RAPPORTS ET RESOLUTIONS DES CONGRES OUVRIERS DE 1876 A 1883 / Dormoy, Jean – Paris, H. Oriol. 1883. 79 p. 5650 – 9 – fr Hachette [335]

RAPPORTS ET TEMOIGNAGES.. / Canada. Bas-Canada. Parlement. Chambre d'Assemblee. Comite special – s.l, s.n, 1829. SEM105P91 – 3mf – 9 – Can$6.75 – cn Bibl Nat [360]

RAPPORTS FAITS AU NOM DE LA COMMISSION D'ENQUETE / France. Commission d'enquete sur les actes du gouvernement de la defense nationale – 1872-75 – 1 – 100.00 – us L of C Photodup [324]

RAPPORTS FINALS DES CONFERENCES TECHNIQUES DE L'OCCGE, 1963-1974 / Organization of Coordination and Cooperation for the Fight Against Major Endemic Diseases, West Africa – 12r – 1 – $494.00 – us African Imprint [616]

RAPPORTS JUDICIAIRES DE QUEBEC : BANC DU ROI ET DE LA REINE / Canada. Quebec – (v1-9 are called: Banc de la Reine) – v1-71. 1892-1944; 1945-69 – 613mf – 9 – $919.00 – LLMC 81-066 – us L.L.M.C. [340]

RAPPORTS JUDICIAIRES DE QUEBEC : COUR SUPERIEURE / Canada. Quebec – v1-79. 1892-1941; 1942-79 – 867mf – 9 – $1,300.00 – LLMC 81-067 – us L.L.M.C. [340]

RAPPORTS/COMMISSION DES ASSURANCES SOCIALES DE QUEBEC / Commission des assurances sociales de Quebec – Quebec: la Commission [puis] le Ministere du travail, 1932-1933. SEM105P1915 – 4mf – 9 – Can$9.00 – cn Bibl Nat [350]

RAPPORT...S'ENQUIRER DE LA TENURE DES TERRES AUX ISLES DE LA MAGDELEINE, COMTE DE GASPE : SESSION 1874-75 / Quebec. (Province). Legislature. Assemblee legislative. Comite – Levis, 1875. SEM105P553 – 1mf – 9 – Can$2.25 – cn Bibl Nat [324]

RAPPORT...SUR LA DERNIERE ELECTION POUR LE DISTRICT ELECTORAL DE KAMOURASKA / Canada. Parlement. Chambre des Communes. Comite permanent des Privileges et Elections – Ottawa: Hunter, Rose et Lemieux, 1868. SEM105P659 – 1mf – 9 – Can$2.25 – cn Bibl Nat [971]

RAPPORT...SUR LA LIGNE PROJETEE DU CHEMIN DE FER INTERCOLONIAL / Robinson, William – Ottawa, 1868. SEM105P649 – 1mf – 9 – Can$2.25 – cn Bibl Nat [625]

RAPPORT...SUR L'HOPITAL DE MARINE ET DES EMIGRES DE QUEBEC, ET CORRESPONDANCE RELATIVE AUX SERVICES DU DR. ROBITAILLE DANS LE DIT HOPITAL / Nelson, Wolfred – Quebec: John Lovell, 1853. SEM105P585 – 2mf – 9 – Can$4.50 – cn Bibl Nat [971]

LA RAPPRESENTANZA CONVENZIONALE NEL DIRITTO INTERNAZIONALE CONTEMPORANEO / Cavarretta, G – Padova, 1928 – 2mf – 1 – ILM-2101/1 – ne IDC [327]

Rapson, E J *see* THE SCIENCE OF RELIGIONS

RAQUEL / Garcia de la Huerta, Vicente – 1818 – 9 – 1.50f – sp Bibl Santa Ana [830]

RAQUEL / Garcia de la Huerta, Vicente – (S.L., S.A.) – 1 – sp Bibl Santa Ana [946]

LA RAQUEL. TRAGEDIA / Garcia de la Huerta, Vicente – 1772 – 1mf – 9 – Pta1,000.00 – 84-7848-180-X – sp Pentalfa [830]

RARE 19TH CENTURY AMERICAN ART JOURNALS *see*
- AMERICAN ART UNION BULLETIN
- THE ART COLLECTOR
- THE ART JOURNAL
- BECK'S JOURNAL OF DECORATIVE ART
- BRUSH AND PENCIL
- THE COLLECTOR AND ART CRITIC
- THE CONNOISSEUR
- DICTIONARY OF ARCHITECTURE
- THE ILLUSTRATED MAGAZINE OF ART
- THE MAGAZINE OF ART
- THE MONTHLY ILLUSTRATOR
- NEW PATH

RARE BOOK AND MANUSCRIPT COLLECTION MT ANGEL ABBEY LIBRARY / McCrank, Lawrence J – 5mf – 9 – $22.50 – us Scholarly Res [090]

RARE BOOKS / Royal Botanical Gardens. Kew – 5 – uk Microform Academic [580]

RARE BOOKS CATALOGS / Bibliotheque Nationale – 244mf – 9 – $604.00 – fr Bibl Nationale [090]

RARE BOOKS FROM THE CORNING MUSEUM OF GLASS / Corning Museum of Glass – (Pt 1, 15th-17th Centuries: $2,2275.00; Pt 2, 18th-19th Centuries: $8,290.00) – $9,485.00 set – us UPA [090]

RARE ET CURIEUX DISCOURS DE LA PLANTE APPELEE MANDRAGORE / Catelan, Laurent – Paris. 1638 – 9 – fr Hachette [360]

RARE LOCAL RECORDS IN CHINESE DATING FROM 1420 – 107 titles comp. and published 1420-1507. Titles listed and available separately – 9 – 2820.00 – cc Microforms [950]

RARE OR UNIQUE PERIODICALS AND VOLUMES FROM THE FELTRINELLI ARCHIVES – (See also indiv. titles: Giornale Patriottico di Corsica; Michael Bakunin; Pensiero e Azione; Tutti Han Torto) – 9 – $195.00 set – us UPA [073]

RARE PHILIPPINE NEWSPAPERS AND SERIALS – Collected and filmed by the University of Wisconsin-Madison Libraries. Incl. issues of per. and news. publ. between 1900 and 1946-primarily in Tagalog and also in Spanish, English, Bikol, and Kapampangan – 1 – us U.W. Library [072]

RARE PRINTED MATERIAL RELATING TO MOSCOW, 1887-1923 – From the British Library of Political and Economic Science, London. In Russian – 6r – 1 – £200.00 – uk Altair [335]

RARE PRINTED SOURCES FOR GENEALOGICAL RESEARCH – (Part 1: Collectanea Topographica et Genealogica, 1834-43; Topographer and Genealogist, 1846-58; Herald and Genealogist, 1863-74; Miscellanea Genealogica et Heraldica, 1868-1902. Part 2: The Genealogist, 1877-83 and 1884-1922. Part 3: The Genealogical Magazine, 1898-1904; The Northern Genealogist, 1895-1903; The Patrician, 1846-48; The British Archivist, 1913-20; The Ancestor, 1902-05.) – Series One: Genealogical Journals and Periodicals – 1 – us Primary [073]

RARE RADICAL AND LABOUR PERIODICALS OF GREAT BRITAIN, SERIES 1 – The Nineteenth century. 3 parts – 1 – us Primary [331]

RARE RADICAL AND LABOUR PERIODICALS OF GREAT BRITAIN, SERIES 2 – (Part 1: Includes 54 titles) – The late nineteenth and early twentieth centuries – 1 – us Primary [331]

RARE UKRAINIAN SERIAL PUBLICATIONS – (Contains runs of more than 200 newspapers and journals of Western Ukrainian province publ between 1848 and 1918) – 513r coll – 1 – $34,900.00 coll – us Ross [073]

RARIORUM ALIQUOT STIRPIUM PER HISPANIAS OBSERVATARUM HISTORIA / Clusius, C – Antwerpiae. 1576. B-750 2 – 9 – ne IDC [580]

RARIORUM LIGURIAE PLANTARUM / Bertoloni, A – Decas I-III. Genuae, Decas I. 1803. Pisis, Decas II-III. 1806, 1810. Lacking: Decas III, 1810. B-5333 2 – 8 – ne IDC [580]

RARIORUM PLANTARUM HISTORIA / Clusius, C – Antwerpiae. 1601. B-54 2 – 8 – ne IDC [580]

Rarotonga and Niue. Catholic Church Diocese *see* DIOCESAN ARCHIVES

RASAD *see* AR-RASAD

Rasad, BZ *see*
- ILMOE TOEMBOEH-TOEMBOEHAN. OENTOEK DIPAKAI DI SEKOLAH DJOEROE-OBAT (ASSISTANTAPOTHEKER)
- LANGKAH KE ATOERAN. BOEKOE SOERAT MENJOERAT DAN PIDATO-PIDATO DALAM BAHASA INDONESIA. TJETAKAN JANG KEDOEA

Raschdau, L *see* DIE POLITISCHEN BERICHTE DES FUERSTEN BISMARCK AUS PETERSBURG UND PARIS (1859-1862)

Rasche, Christian *see* LASER IN DER MATERIALBEARBEITUNG

RASD UPDATE (REFERENCE AND ADULT SERVICE DIVISION) – 1980- – 1,5,6,9 – us UMI [020]

DER RASENDE PEGASUS / Twardovski, Hans Heinrich von – (Parodies in prose and verse) – 2., stark verm. Ausg. Berlin: A Juncker, 1919 – 1r – 1 – us U.W. Library [800]

RASGOS BIBLIOGRAFICOS DE SANTA TERESA DE JESUS / Dominguez Peaz, Fidel – 1882 – 9 – 1.50f – sp Bibl Santa Ana [240]

RASGOS DE NUESTRA EPOPEYA (EPISODIOS Y PERSONAJES) / Cascales Munoz, Jose – Madrid: Libreria Fernando Fe, 1918 – 1 – sp Bibl Santa Ana [946]

RASGOS DE PLUMA / Gamarra, Abelardo M – Lima: Libreria francesa cientifica Galland, 1911. Primera serie. v1. 1 reel. 1204 – 1 – us U.W. Library [972]

RASGOS FISIOGRAFICOS Y GEOLOGICOS DEL TERRITORIO DE IFNI Y RASGOS FISIOGRAFICOS Y GEOLOGICOS DEL SAHARA / Hernandez Pacheco, Francisco – Madrid: S. Aguirre, Impresor, 1945 – sp Bibl Santa Ana [550]

Rashdall, Hastings *see* THE THEORY OF GOOD AND EVIL

Rashdall, Hastings et al *see* CONTENTIO VERITATIS

RASHI : HIS LIFE AND HIS WORK / Schloessinger, Max – (Includes bibliographical references) – Baltimore, MD: Lord Baltimore Press, 1905 – 1mf – 9 – 0-8370-5098-7 – 1985-3098 – us A.T.L.A. [920]

Rashi *see* SEFER RASHI, KOVEZ TORANI-MADDA'I

RASHTRA DOOT – Jaipur, India. Jul 1966-1980 – 46r – 1 – us L of C Photodup [072]

RASIAH NU GORENG PATUT; KARNADI ANEMER BANGKONG / Sukria – SE 4210 1. 1963 – 9 – ne IDC [950]

Rask, Rasmus *see* (PAMPHLETS BY AND ABOUT RASMUS RASK)
Raska, Johann *see* DIE CHRONOLOGIE DER BIBEL
Raske, Karl *see* DER BETTLER IN DER SCHOTTISCHEN DICHTUNG
Raskelf. Yorkshire *see* PARISH REGISTERS
RASKOL "VVERKHY: OCHERKI RELIGIOZNYKH" ISKANII V PRIVILEGIROVANOI SREDE / Prugavin, Aleksandr Stepanovich – St. Petersburg: Obschchestvenaya Pol'za, 1909. 280p – 1 – $11.20 – us Baptist [240]
RASKOL'NICHESKAIA BIBLIOGRAFIIA / Liubopytnyi, P – Katalog ili biblioteka starovercheskoi tserkvi. Sobrannyi v Spb: e 1829 goda. M. 1861. BR-7138 2 – 8 – ne IDC [010]
RASKOL'NICH'I DELA 18 STOLETIIA, IZVLECHENNYIA IZ DEL PREOBRAZHENSKOGO PRIKAZA I TAINOI ROZYSKNYKH DEL KANTSELIARII / Esipov, G V – v. 1-2. Spb. 1861-63. BR-6156 2 – 8 – ne IDC [947]
RASKOL-SEKTANTSTVO. MATERIALY DLIA IZUCHENIIA RELIGIOZNO-BYTOVYKH DVIZHENII RUSSKOGO NARODA / Prugavin, Aleksandr Stepanovich – Moscow, 1887. v, 1, xi, 523p. BR-7791 2 – 8 – ne IDC [240]
RASMI JARIDA / Afghanistan – 1975- – 1 – 23.00y – us L of C Photodup [950]
Rasmussen, C *see*
- DANSK-GROENLANDSK ORDBOG
- DANSK-GROENLANDSK ORDBOG, PLUS SUPPL

Rasmussen, Knud *see*
- FRA GRONLAND TIL STILLEHAVET
- GRONLAND LANGS POLHAVET
- GRONLANDSK SPROGLAERE
- IGLULIK AND CARIBOU ESKIMO TEXTS
- INTELLECTUAL CULTURE OF THE COPPER ESKIMO
- INTELLECTUAL CULTURE OF THE IGLULIK ESKIMOS
- MINDEUDGAVE
- MYTER OG SAGN FRA GRONLAND KJOBENHAVN, ETC
- THE NETSILIK ESKIMOS
- NYE MENNESKER
- OBSERVATIONS ON THE INTELLECTUAL CULTURE OF THE CARIBOU ESKIMOS
- THE PEOPLE OF THE POLAR NORTH

Rasonyi, L *see*
- UNGARISCHE BIBLIOGRAPHIE DER TURKOLOGIE UND DER ORIENTALISCH-UNGARISCHEN BEZIEHUNGEN
- UNGARISCHE BIBLIOGRAPHIE DER TURKOLOGIE UND DER ORIENTALISCH-UNGARISCHEN BEZIEHUNGEN 1926-1934

RASPAD, 1918-1922 / Burevii, Kost – Moskva: "Novai a Moskva", 1923 – 1 – CSUX88-B2061 – us Hoover Inst Photo [999]
RASPAD ATOMA / Ivanov, G – Paris. 1938. BR-1183 2 – 8 – ne IDC [460]
Raspe, R E *see* A CRITICAL ESSAY ON OILPAINTING; PROVING THAT THE ART OF PAINTING IN OIL WAS KNOWN BEFORE THE PRETENDED DISCOVERY OF JOHN AND HUBERT VAN EYCK
RASPIATIE / Drozdov, Aleksandr – Berlin: "Mysl", 1921 – 1 – CSUX88-B8408 – us Hoover Inst Photo [947]
RASPROSTRANENIE PECHATI : EZHEMESI ACHNY I ZHURNAL GLAVNOGO UPRAVLENII A SOI UZPECHATI MINISTERSTVA SVI AZI SSSR – (Library has: Jan. 1959-Dec. 1971) – Moskva: Svi azizdat, 1940- – 1 – CSUX89-S632 – us Hoover Inst Photo [947]
RASSE UND JUDENTUM = RACE AND JEWISHISM – (Erganzungshefte zur Neuen Zeit. In German) – Stuttgart, DE. 30 Oct 1934 – 1r – 1 – $25.00 – cn Can Microfilming [072]
RASSEGNA D'ARTE – Milan, 1905-19. 5 reels – 1 – $420.00 – us UPA [700]
RASSEGNA DORICA – v1-13. 1929-42. Missing v9, nos 3,4,8; v12, no 10 – 1 – us Schnase [780]
RASSEGNA GREGORIANA – 1(1902)-12(1914) – 100mf – 9 – Dfl350.00 – ne Slangenburg [073]
RASSEGNA GREGORIANA – Rome. v. 1-13. no. III. 1902-1911 – 1 – us Schnase [240]
RASSEGNA GREGORIANA PER GLI STUDI LITURGICI E PEL CANTO SACRO – Rome. v1-13. 1902-1914 – 100mf – 9 – ne IDC [240]
Rassegna mensuale di botanica *see* MALPIGHIA
RASSEGNA MUSICALE – v. 1-16. 1928-1943 – 1 – us Schnase [780]
Rassekh, Shapour *see*
- CONTENTS OF EDUCATION
- PERSPECTIVES ON LITERACY

LE RASSEMBLEMENT – no. 1-17. Paris. juin-oct 1941 – 1 – fr A.C.R.P.P. [073]
RASSKAZY IZ RUSSKOI ISTORII XVIII VEKA / Barsukov, A P – Spb. 1885. BR-5985 2 – 8 – ne IDC [947]
Rassmann, F *see* KURZGEFASSTES LEXICON DEUTSCHER PSEUDONYMER SCHRIFTSTELLER VON DER AELTERN BIS AUF DIE JUENGSTE ZEIT AUS ALLEN FAECHERN DER WISSENSCHAFTEN
RASSVET (CHICAGO, ILL.) – (Library has holdings (incomplete) from between Jan. 3, 1927 and Dec. 31, 1927; Apr. 2, 1929 and Dec. 30, 1933; Aug. 13, 1940 and Dec. 31, 1940) – Chicago: Directorate of Russian Trade Unions of the United States of America and Canada, 1926-1940. 19v – 1 – CSUX87-S259 – us Hoover Inst Photo [331]
RASSVET (NEW YORK, N.Y.) – (Library has holdings (incomplete) from between Dec. 19, 1924 and May 15, 1926) – New York: Directorate of Russian Trade Unions, 1918-1926. 2v – 1 – CSUX87-S145 – us Hoover Inst Photo [331]
RASSVIET = L'AUBE – (In Russian) – Paris, FR. v29 no15. 14 Dec 1934 – 1r – 1 – $20.00 – cn Can Microfilming [072]
Rast, W *see* CONTROL OF EUTROPHICATION OF LAKES AND RESERVOIRS
RASTAKHIZ-I KARGARAN – No. 1-26, 3 Azar 1354-Bahman 2535 [24 November 1975 – January/February 1978]) – 2r – 1 – $200.00 – us MEDOC [950]
Rastell, William *see* RASTELL'S LES TERMES DE LA LEY
RASTELL'S LES TERMES DE LA LEY : OR, CERTAIN DIFFICULT AND OBSCURE WORDS AND TERMS OF THE COMMON AND STATUTE LAWS... / Rastell, William – London: R Gosling. 1v. 1721 – 7mf – 9 – $10.50 – LLMC 95-421 – us L.L.M.C. [941]
RASTRATY, KHISHCHENIIA, NEDOCHETY, ZLOUPOTREBLENIIA S OBOROTNYMI SREDSTVAMI / Rakhvalov, E A – Ed 2. Omsk, 1925 – 2mf – 9 – COR-305/1 – ne IDC [334]
Rastrelli, M *see*
- ILLUSTRAZIONE ISTORICA DEL PALAZZO DELLA SIGNORIA

Rasulov, Medzhid L *see* METOD KONTURNOGO INTEGRALA E EGO PRIMENENIE L ISSLEDOVANIIU ZADACH DLIIA DIFFERENTSIALNYKH URAVENII
THE RAT PORTAGE WEEKLY NEWS – Rat Portage, Ont. 24 Jun 1899 – 1r – 1 – Can$25.00 – cn Can Microfilming [072]
THE RATE OF TEMPERATURE REDUCTION IN DEEP HUMAN MUSCLE FOLLOWING THERMAL ULTRASOUND / Rose, Shannon – Brigham Young University, 1995 – 1mf – 9 – PE 3668 – us Microform Publ [617]
RATEPAYER – England, 1 Jun 1850-1 Oct 1853 – 1/2r – 1 – uk British Libr Newspaper [072]
RATES OF PAY AND REGULATIONS GOVERNING EMPLOYEES IN TRAIN AND YARD SERVICE: ON THE PRINCIPAL RAILROADS OF THE UNITED STATES, CANADA & MEXICO – E.E. Clark, P.H. Morrisey, colls. & comps. Cedar Rapids, IA: T. Metcalf, 1900.03196.(Pre-1900 Canadiana) – 9 – cn C.I.H.M. [331]
DER RATGEBER – Bremen, apr 2 1910 – 1 – Inquire at Mikrofilmarchiv for details – gw Misc Inst [072]
Rathbun, M J *see* THE SPIDER CRABS OF AMERICA
Rathbun, Nathan *see*
- JOURNAL

Rathke, H *see* IGNATIUS VON ANTIOCHIEN UND DIE PAULUSBRIEFE (T.U.U. 5-99)
Rathkopf, Charles Allan *see* THE LAW OF ZONING AND PLANNING
RATIFIED INDIAN TREATIES, 1722-1869 / U. S. – 16 rolls. Printed guide – 1 – M668 – us Nat'l Archives [324]
RATING IN SOUTH AFRICA: A QUEST FOR STABILITY THROUGH LAND TENURE AND TAXATION / Dunkley, G R A – 1982, 12p – 9 – 1.00f – at Libertarian Micro [336]
RATING OF COLLEGE COURSES BY SPRINGFIELD COLLEGE ELEMENTARY PHYSICAL EDUCATION TEACHER PREPARATION PROGRAM GRADUATES / Campbell, ML – 1991 – 2mf – 9 – $8.00 – us Microform Publ [370]
RATING STANDARDS AND RELATED FACTORS IN HIGH LEVEL AMATEUR SPORTS OFFICIATING / Evenbeck, Elizabeth J – 1983 – 4mf – 9 – $16.00 – us Microform Publ [790]
RATINGS OF PERCEIVED EXERTION AS A DETERMINANT OF PHYSICAL ACTIVITY IN 9 TO 11 YEAR-OLD CHILDREN / Darracott, Charles R 3. & Dishman, Rodney K – 1991 – 2mf – 9 – $8.00 – us Microform Publ [150]
RATINGS OF PERCEIVED EXERTION IN COLLEGE AGE MALES AND FEMALES OF HIGH AND LOW FITNESS LEVELS / Klein, Judy L – 1982 – 2mf – 9 – $8.00 – us Microform Publ [790]
RATIO QUA LOCI VETERIS TESTAMENTI IN EVANGELIO MATTHAEI LAUDANTUR : PART 1, 2, 3 / Anger, Rudolf – Lipsiae, 1861, 1862 – 3mf – 8 – ne Slangenburg [220]
A RATIONAL AND SPEEDY METHOD OF ATTAINING TO THE LATIN TONGUE / Lane, A – 1695. 153p. (English Linguistics Series 1500-1800) – 9 – us UMI [450]
THE RATIONAL BASIS OF ORTHODOXY / Moore, Albert Weston – Boston: Houghton, Mifflin, 1901.1 fiche. 8370-4475-8 – 9 – us A.T.L.A. [240]
RATIONAL DRUG THERAPY – v1- 1967- 1; v11- 5,6,9 – us UMI [615]
RATIONAL RELIGION AND THE RATIONALISTIC OBJECTIONS OF THE BAMPTON LECTURES FOR 1858 / Smith, Goldwin – Oxford: J L Wheeler, 1861 – 1mf – 9 – 0-8370-5287-4 – 1985-3287 – us A.T.L.A. [210]
THE RATIONAL TEST : BIBLE DOCTRINE IN THE LIGHT OF REASON / Keyser, Leander Sylvester – Philadelphia, PA:Lutheran Publication Society, c1908 – 1mf – 9 – 0-8370-4486-3 – 1985-2486 – us A.T.L.A. [230]
A RATIONAL WAY OF TEACHING ...OF THE ENGLISH TONGUE / Osborn, Thomas – 1688. 143p. (English Linguistics Series 1500-1800) – 9 – us UMI [420]
RATIONALE DIVINORUM OFFICIORUM / Durandus, Gulielmus – Antverpiae, 1614 – 19mf – 8 – Dfl67.00 – ne Slangenburg [240]
RATIONALE INVESTITIONSPLANUNG / Offermann, Volker – 1992 – 140p – 9 – DM98.00 – 3-89349-624-6 – gw Hänsel [332]
RATIONALISME DU RABBIN = DER RABBINISCHE RATIONALISMUS : EINE UNTERREDUNG DES GRAFEN GABRIEL (TURESON) VON OXENSTIRN MIT DEM RABBINER ISAC VITA CANTARINI AUS PADUA (1693) / Oxenstirn, Johann Turesson – (Text in German and French) – Wien: S Modlinger, 1889 (Moritz Knoepflmacher) – 1mf – 9 – 0-8370-4654-8 – 1985-2654 – us A.T.L.A. [270]
Ratner, DB *see*
- AHAVAT ZIYYON VI-YRUSHALAYIM

Ratner, G M *see* SET' SEL'SKOKHOZIAISTVENNOI KOOPERATSII SSSR
RATOBORETS – Organ obshchestvennykh iacheek russkoi provintsii i lits, v nikh rabotaiushchikh. nr. 1-24. M. 1915. BR-3738 2 – 8 – ne IDC [460]
Rat-rim-chong, A *see* A PERCEPTUAL COMPARISON OF EXPERTS, PRINCIPALS AND TEACHERS WITH RESPECT TO SCHOOL HEALTH PROGRAMS WITHIN THE ELEMENTARY SCHOOLS UNDER THE JURISDICTION OF BANGKOK METROPOLIS, THAILAND
Ratsimba, Emmanuel *see* HISTOIRE DES ROIS
RATSIONALIZATSIIA KOOPERATIVNOI RABOTY / Vorob'ev-Nabatov, N A – M., 1927 – 1mf – 9 – COR-193/1 – ne IDC [334]
RATTA FADERNESLANDET – Stockholm, Sweden. 1864 – 1 reel – 1 – sw Kungliga [072]
Ratte, Alice *see* BIBLIOGRAPHIE ANALYTIQUE DE LA LITTERATURE PEDAGOGIQUE CANADIENNE-FRANCAISE DEPUIS 1900
DER RATTENFAENGER VON HAMELN : EINE AVENTIURE / Wolff, Julius – 19. Aufl. Berlin: G Grot'sche Verlagsbuchhandlung, 1883 – 1r – 1 – us U.W. Library [810]
DER RATTENFAENGER VON HAMELN : EINE AVENTIURE; SINGUF: RATTENFAENGERLIEDER / Wolff, Julius – Leipzig: P List, c1913 – 1r – 1 – us U.W. Library [390]
Rattray, J M *see* GRASS COVER OF AFRICA
Rattray, R S *see* THE TRIBES OF THE ASHANTI HINTERLAND
RATUSHCHII VINOGRAD – Ezhemesiachnoe sochinenie. Spb. 1785-87. Lacking: (1-3) 1785; (4-12) 1787. BR-3794 2 – 8 – ne IDC [073]
Ratzaby, J *see* LE-FERASHAT HITNAHALUT YEHUDEI TEIMAN BI-YERUSHALAYIM
Ratzeburg, J T C *see* FORSTWISSENSCHAFTLICHES SCHRIFTSTELLER-LEXIKON
Rau, A E *see* CATALOGUE OF NORTH AMERICAN MUSCI
Rau, Eric *see* INSTITUTIONS ET COUTUMES CANAQUES
Rau, Erich *see* DAS PERIGORD UND SEINE BEWOHNER IN DEN ROMANEN EUGENE LE ROYS
RAUBFISCHER IN HELLAS : ROMAN / Helwig, Werner – Leipzig: Bibliographisches Institut Leipzig, [1943?] – 1r – 1 – us U.W. Library [830]
DIE RAUBVOEGEL DEUTSCHLANDS UND DES ANGRENZENDEN MITTELEUROPAS / Riesenthal, O von – Z 1889. 1 v. text; 1 v. atlas. 1876 – 9 – ne IDC [590]
Rauch, Mignone *see* EFFECTS OF STEP HEIGHT VARIATION ON KNEE JOINT MOMENTS OF FORCE DURING LATERAL STEP-UP EXERCISES
Rauer, M *see* FORM UND UEBERLIEFERUNG DER LUKAS-HOMILIEN DES ORIGENES (T.U.U. 4-47/3)
Rauf, Mehmet *see* ASIKANE
Rauh, Frederic *see* ESSAI SUR LE FONDEMENT METAPHYSIQUE DE LA MORALE
Rauh, Sigismund *see* HEBRAEISCHES FAMILIENRECHT IN VORPROPHETISCHER ZEIT
Raulin, G de [pseud] *see* AMOURS CONGOLAISES
Raulin J *see* ITINERARIUM PARADISI...
Rault, L *see* LA CITHARE ZHENG
Raumer, Rudolf von *see* DIE EINWIRKUNG DES CHRISTENTHUMS AUF DIE ALTHOCHDEUTSCHE SPRACHE
Raupach, Ernst Benjamin Salomon *see* CROMWELL
DER RAUPEN WUNDERBARE VERWANDELUNG, UND SONDERBARE BLEUMEN-NAHRUNG / Merian, Maria Sibylla – Nuerenberg & Frankfurt, 1679-1683 – 1 – us U.W. Library [631]
Rauschen, G *see* GRUNDRISS DER PATROLOGIE
Rauschen, Gerhard *see* EUCHARIST AND PENANCE IN THE FIRST SIX CENTURIES OF THE CHURCH
Rauschenberg, L *see* BRITISH REGIONAL CHURCH CARVING (1600-1640) AND FURNITURE (1600-1800)
Rauschenbusch, August *see*
- DIE ENTSTEHUNG DER KINDERTAUFE IM DRITTEN JAHRHUNDERT N.CHR. UND DIE WIEDEREINFUEHRUNG DER BIBLISCHEN TAUFE IM SIEBZEHNTEN JAHRHUNDERT N.CHR.
- IST DER SONNTAG HEIDNISCHEN, PAEPSTLICHEN ODER CHRISTLICHEN URSPRUNGS?
- PAPERS
- SATURDAY OR SUNDAY
- DER URSPRUNG DES SONNTAGS

Rauschenbusch, Walter *see* SOME MORAL ASPECTS OF THE 'WOMAN MOVEMENT'
Rauschenbusch, Wilhelm *see* GEDICHTE
Rauscher, Joseph Othmar *see* DAS ALLGEMEINE CONCIL VON VATICAN
Rautenberg, Hans Juergen *see* DEUTSCHE RUSTUNGSPOLITIK VOM BEGINN DER GENFER ABRUSTUNGSKONFERENZ BIS ZUR WIEDEREINFUEHRUNG DER ALLGEMEINEN WEHRPFLICHT
Rauwenhoff, L W E *see* HISTORIA HUNGARORUM ECCLESIASTICA
Rauwolff, L *see*
- AIGENTLICHE BESCHREIBUNG DER RAISZ, SO ER VOR DISER ZEIT GEGEN AUFFGANG INN DIE MORGENLANDER, FUERNEMLICH SYRIAM, IUDAEAM, ARABIAM, MESOPOTAMIAM, BABYLONIAM, ASSYRIAM, ARMENIAM...
- HERBARIUM

Raux *see* NOS JEUNES DETENUS. ETUDE SUR L'ENFANCE COUPABLE AVANT, PENDANT ET APRES SON SEJOUR AU QUARTIER CORRECTIONNEL
Rauzzini, V *see* TROIS GRANDS DUOS, A QUATRE MAINS

RAV SAADYAH GAON, KOVEZ TORANI-MADDA'I / Gaon, S – Ed. by J. L. Fishman. Jerusalem. 1943. BJ-100-77 1 – 9 – ne IDC [900]

RAV SHERIRA GA'ON / Lewin, B M – Jaffa. 1917. BJ-32-43 1 – 9 – ne IDC [270]

RAVALLI REPUBLICAN – Hamilton. Mont. 1950-1968 – 1 – us UMI [071]

RAVAT UEL-EBRAR / Karacelebizade, Abduelaziz – Cairo: Bulak, 1248 [1832] – 2v 30mf – 9 – $150.00 – us MEDOC [949]

Ravaton, H *see* CHIRURGIE D'ARMEE

Raveau, Paul *see* L'AGRICULTURE ET LES CLASSES PAYSANNES

Ravel, M *see* L'HEURE ESPAGNOL. TRIO SUR L'OPERA...

Ravelsberg, Ferdinand Strobl von *see* LES CONFESSIONS DE THEOROIGNE DE MERICOURT

Raven, J J *see* THE BELLS OF ENGLAND

THE RAVEN SPEAKS – 1968-72. Raven Hail (American Indian Periodicals in the Princeton University Library) – 3mf – 9 – $45.00 – us UPA [073]

RAVENNA NEWS – Ravenna, NE. -w. Mar 1888 to date – 1 – us NE Hist [071]

Ravenna. Ohio. Stage Office *see* RECORDS, MS 44

RAVENSBERGISCHES VOLKSBLATT – Bielefeld, apr 12 1848-oct 27 1849 – 1 – Inquire at Mikrofilmarchiv for details – gw Misc Inst [943]

Ravenscroft, E J *see* THE PINETUM BRITANNICUM

Ravenshaw, T F T *see* A NEW LIST OF THE FLOWERING PLANTS AND FERNS GROWING WILD IN THE COUNTRY OF DEVON

RAVENSHOE / Kingsley, Henry – British Fiction Archive: Unit 2 – 9 – uk Bell [830]

Ravenstein, E G *see* AFRICA

RAVENSWOOD POST – Menlo Park, CA. 1960-79 – 14r – 1 – $700.00 – B02443 – us Library Micro [071]

Raverty, H G *see* THE TABAKAT-U-NASIRI/A GENERAL HISTORY OF THE MUHAMMADAN DYNASTIES OF ASIA INCLUDING HINDUSTAN. FROM A.H. 194(810 A.D.) TO A.H. 658(1260 A.H.) AND THE IRRUPTION...

RAVI BHARATA – New Delhi, India. Jul 1971-Jun 1972 – 1r – 1 – us L of C Photodup [072]

Raviguani, Emilio *see* ASAMBLEAS CONSTITUYENTES ARGENTINAS...

Ravnholt, Henning *see* THE DANISH CO-OPERATIVE MOVEMENT

RAW MATERIALS REPORT – 1985-. -q – 1 – us UMI [670]

Rawes, Henry Augustus *see* THE BREAD OF LIFE

RAWHIDE TIMES *see* PRESS TIMES

RAWICZER ZEITUNG – Rawicz (Rawitsch), Poland. 20 Apr 1926-29 Jun 1932 – 7r – 1 – gw Mikrofilm [943]

Rawle, Francis *see*
- ACTS RELATING TO CAR TRUSTS, AS IN FORCE DOWN TO AUGUST 1, 1893
- CAR TRUST SECURITIES

Rawle, William Henry *see* A PRACTICAL TREATISE ON THE LAW OF CONVENANTS FOR TITLE

Rawlence, E A *see* WHAT IS TRUTH?

RAWLE'S REPORTS / Pennsylvania. Superior Court – (A Pre-NRS title) – v1-5. 1828-35 (all publ) – 26mf – 9 – $39.00 – LLMC 84-198 – us L.L.M.C. [340]

Rawlins, Thomas *see*
- FAMILIAR ARCHITECTURE
- FAMILIAR ARCHITECTURE, CONSISTING OF ORIGINAL DESIGNS OF HOUSES FOR GENTLEMEN AND TRADESMEN...

Rawlinson, George *see*
- EZRA AND NEHEMIAH
- THE HISTORICAL EVIDENCES OF THE TRUTH OF THE SCRIPTURE RECORDS, STATED ANEW, WITH SPECIAL REFERENCE TO THE DOUBTS AND DISCOVERIES OF MODERN TIMES
- MOSES; HIS LIFE AND TIMES

Rawlinson, H C *see* THE CUNEIFORM INSCRIPTIONS FROM WESTERN ASIA

Rawlinson, Henry Creswicke *see*
- NOTES ON THE EARLY HISTORY OF BABYLONIA
- ON THE INSCRIPTIONS OF ASSYRIA AND BABYLONIA

Rawnsley, Hardwicke Drummond *see* MEMORIES OF THE TENNYSONS

Rawson, R W *see* SYNOPSIS FILICUM AFRICAE AUSTRALIS

Ray Ball *see* THE AUSTRALIAN STOCKBROKING CARTEL

Ray, Charles *see* THE LIFE OF CHARLES HADDON SPURGEON

Ray, Charles A *see* AMERICAN PRACTICE REPORTS

Ray, Charles Andrew *see* QUIZ BOOK; QUESTIONS AND ANSWERS ON THE SUBJECT OF EQUITY PLEADING.

Ray, Colin *see* LIBRARY SERVICE TO SCHOOLS AND CHILDREN

Ray, D B *see*
- THE NEW REVOLUTIONARY LANDMARK BAPTIST FACTION
- PAPAL CONTROVERSY INVOLVING THE ROMAN CATHOLIC CHURCH

Ray, Douglas et al *see* EDUCATION FOR HUMAN RIGHTS

Ray, J *see*
- A COLLECTION OF CURIOUS TRAVELS AND VOYAGES
- HISTORIA PLANTARUM
- METHODUS PLANTARUM
- METHODUS PLANTARUM NOVA
- SYNOPSIS METHODICA ANIMALIUM QUADRUPEDUM ET SERPENTINI GENERIS
- SYNOPSIS METHODICA STIRPIUM BRITANNICARUM

Ray, J J *see* AUTHORITARIANISM TODAY

Ray, John *see*
- A COLLECTION OF ENGLISH WORDS NOT GENERALLY USED
- CORRESPONDENCE
- MEMORIALS

THE RAY OF LIGHT – (Chicago). 1889 – 1 – us A.J.P.C. [073]

Ray, P C *see* THE "MAHABHARATA" OF KRISHNA-DWAIPAYANA VYASA INTO ENGLISH PROSE

Ray, P H *see*
- HABITS AND CUSTOMS OF THE INU OF THE WESTERN SHORE AND POINT BARROW
- REPORT OF THE INTERNATIONAL POLAR EXPEDITION TO POINT BARROW, ALASKA

Ray Society *see*
- PUBLICATIONS
- REPORTS ON ZOOLOGY

RAYAS – Albuquerque, NM. 1978-1979 – 1r – 1 – $50.00 – R04985 – us Library Micro [071]

RAYAS. CARTILLA 1ST / Rodriguez Alvarez, Angel – Plasencia: Editorial Sanchez Rodrigo, S.A. 1971 – 1 – sp Bibl Santa Ana [946]

RAYAS METODO DE ENSENANZA PARA LA LECTURA / Rodriguez Alvarez, Angel – Plasencia: Editorial Sanchez Rodrigo, 1971 – 1 – sp Bibl Santa Ana [946]

Raybaut, P *see* CORRESPONDANCE DE GUERRE D'UN RURAL 1914-1917

Raymond, Allen *see* WHAT IS TECHNOCRACY?

Raymond, Andrew Van Vranken *see* UNION UNIVERSITY, ITS HISTORY, INFLUENCE, CHARACTERISTICS AND EQUIPMENT.

Raymond, Bob *see* "A PERSONAL DETOUR INTO THE WAR."

RAYMOND DUCHAMP-VILLON, 1876-1918. MARCEL DUCHAMP, 1887. 1967. 14 ILLUS. 1 FICHE / Reunion des musees nationaux. Paris – 9 – fr Réunion [700]

Raymond, E A *see* FOREIGN STUDENTS: THE SOVIET EDUCATIONAL WEAPON

Raymond, F *see*
- DICTIONNAIRE GENERAL DE LA LANGUE FRANCAISE
- SUPPLEMENT AU DICTIONNAIRE DE L'ACADEMIE FRANCAISE

Raymond, Frere *see* BIO-BIBLIOGRAPHIE DE DAMASE POTVIN, ECRIVAIN ET JOURNALISTE

RAYMOND G MCCARTHY MEMORIAL COLLECTION OF ALCOHOL LITERATURE / Rutgers University. Center of Alcoholic Studies – 1935-76 – 2512mf – 9 – $5.00f – us Ross [360]

Raymond, Henry Hubert *see*
- DIARY
- "DIARY OF A BUFFALO HUNTER, 1872-73."

Raymond, J M *see* DIARY

Raymond, J-Moise *see* L'IMPARTIAL

Raymond, Mississippi *see* MISCELLANEOUS EARLY NEWSPAPERS

Raymond, Paul *see* DICTIONNAIRE TOPOGRAPHIQUE DU DEPARTEMENT DES BASSES-PYRENEES

RAYMOND REVIEW – Raymond, NE. -w. Jul 1892; Nov 1895-Dec 1898; Dec 1901-Dec 1902; Mar 1908-Apr 1917; Jan 1918-Apr 1934 – 1 – us NE Hist [071]

Raymond-Marie, Soeur *see* BIBLIOGRAPHIE DE L'OEUVRE DU DOCTEUR ALBERT JOBIN, M.D., 1867 A 1952

RAYMOND'S DIGESTED CHANCERY CASES / Maryland. Court of Appeals – (Contains digests, arranged in subject order, of all the Chancery cases included in the first 4 titles on this page up thru the 7th vol of Gill & Johnsons's Law Reports) – 1v. 1839 (all publ) – 6mf – 9 – $9.00 – LLMC 94-007 – us L.L.M.C. [340]

RAYMOND'S KERRY HERALD – Tralee, Ireland. 12 Jan-16 Feb 1856 – 3ft – 1 – uk British Libr Newspaper [072]

Raymore, Leslie A *see* THE RELATION OF SELF-ESTEEM TO CONSTRAINTS ON LEISURE AMONG ADOLESCENTS

Raymundo, Francisco J *see* COMO SE INICIO EL GLORIOSO MOVIMIENTO NACIONAL EN VALLADOLID Y LA GESTA HEROICA DEL ALTO DEL LEON

Raynaud, Gaston *see* UN NOUVEAU DIT DES FEMMES PUBLIE POUR LA PREMIERE FOIS

Raynaudus, T *see* THEOLOGIA NATURALIS SIVE ENTIS INCREATI ET CREATI INTRA SUPREMAM ABSTRACTIONEM EX NATURAE LUNINE INVESTIGATIO

RAYNHAM 1699-1895 – (Mf 1-2: Vital Records 1733-1849. Mf 3-4: Deaths 1792-1892. Mf 5-11: Town Records 1731-1810. Mf 12-20: Town Records 1810-51. Mf 21-24: Index to Vital Records 1699-1900. Mf 25-31: Vital Records 1699-1868. Mf 32-37: Marriage Intentions 1807-62. Mf 38-39: Marriage Intentions 1863-1900. Mf 40-44: Index to Vital Records 1843-95. Mf 45-46: Vital Records 1843-61. Mf 47-50: Vital Records 1858-95) – (mf ed 1991) – 50mf – 9 – 0-87623-126-1 – us Holbrook [920]

Raynouard *see*
- LES ETATS DE BLOIS
- LES TEMPLIERS

RAYOS DE LUZ / Pacheco Ortiz, Felix – 1731 – 9 – 1.50f – sp Bibl Santa Ana [810]

Rayzor, James Newton *see* HISTORY OF THE DENTON COUNTY BAPTIST ASSOCIATION AND THE SIXTY CHURCHES ORGANIZED WITHIN ITS JURISDICTION

UNA RAZA DE LOBOS – Merida, 1895 – 1 – sp Bibl Santa Ana [946]

UNA RAZA DE LOBOS / Morales, Antonio y otros – 1896 – 9 – 1.50f – sp Bibl Santa Ana [830]

RAZA ESPANOLA / Juez, Antonio – Badajoz, 1937.Tip.Vda.de A. Arqueros, 1937 – 1 – sp Bibl Santa Ana [301]

LA RAZA EXTREMENA / Hoyos Sainz, Luis de – Madrid, 1950 – 1 – sp Bibl Santa Ana [946]

A RAZAO – Estancia, Brazil. 1898; 1901; 1908-10. Incomplete – 1 – bl Biblioteca [072]

A RAZAO – Pouso Alegre, 13 Mar 1936-2 Dec 1937 – 1,5,6 – bl Biblioteca [072]

A RAZAO – Rio de Janeiro, 19 Dec 1916-30 Jul 1921 – 1,5,6 – bl Biblioteca [072]

RAZBOR DESYATI PRAVIL VEROCHENIYA SHTUNDISTOV / Fomenko, Kliment – Kiev, 1873. An analysis of the ten principles of the Confession of the Stundists. One of 13 titles on reel – 1 – 86.44 – us Baptist [240]

RAZBOR SOCHINENIIAG ANDREEVSKAGO "O NAMESTNIKAKH, VOEVODAKH I GUBERNATORAKH" / Kalachov, N V – Spb. 1867. BR-6196 2 – 8 – ne IDC [460]

RAZDEL AZIATSKOI TURTSII PO... / Adamov, E A – Moscow, 1924 – 5mf – 9 – ILM-811/1 – ne IDC [340]

RAZDUM'IA. STIKHOTVORENIIA / Aseev, N – M. 1955. BR-907 2 – 8 – ne IDC [460]

RAZGLEDI – 1952-1995 – 1 – F2,095 – sz Infoprint [947]

RAZGLEDI – (Backfile 1952-98 $85r) – Slovenia, 1999- – 2r per y – 1 – $160.00 standing order – us Ross [072]

RAZGOVOR MEZHDU CHUZHESTRANNYM CHELOVEKOM I ROSSIISKIM OB ORFOGRAFII STARINNOI I NOVOI I O VSEM CHTO PRINADLEZHIT K SEI MATERII / Trediakovskii, V K – Spb., 1748 – 9mf – 9 – R-9034-2 – ne IDC [460]

RAZGOVOR "PRAVOSLAVNAGO I PASHKOVTSA O SVYASHCHENNOM PISANII I PREDANIYAKH TSERKOVNYKH" = A CONVERSATION OF AN ORTHODOX AND PASHKOVITE ON THE HOLY SCRIPTURE AND CHURCH TRADITIONS / Anotnii – Moscow, 1909 – 1r – 1 – $5.00 – us Baptist [240]

RAZGOVOR PRAVOSLAVNAGO I PASHKOVTSA O SVYASHCHENNOM PISANII I PREDANIYAKH TSERKOVNYKH – St. Petersburg, 1902. With 2 other books about Pashkovites – 1 – 9.96 – us Baptist [240]

RAZGOVOR" PRAVOSLAVNAGO S" STUNDISTOM" OB INSTINNOI VERE = DISCUSSION OF AN ORTHODOX WITH A STUNDIST ON THE TRUE FAITH – Simferopol, 2nd ed 1899 – 1r – 1 – $5.00 – us Baptist [240]

RAZGOVOR PROVOSLAVNOGO S SHTUNCISTOM OB ISTINNOI VERE / Tikhivinskii, Pavel – A Conversation of an Orthodox with a Stundist on the True Faith. Simferopol, 1899. 2nd ed. One of 13 titles on reel – 1 – 86.44 – us Baptist [240]

Razia Begum Mukhtar *see* MALAYSIAN SERIALS

RAZLOZHENIE ARMII V 1917 GODU / Russia. (1917-R.S.F.S.R.). Tsentral'noe arkhivnoe upravlenie – Moscow, 1923 – 1 – 35.00r – us Hoover Inst Photo [324]

Raznogorskii, Mikhail *see* SBORNIK STATEI V OBLICHENIE SHTUNDIZMA I V UTVERZHDENIE NEOPYTNYKH V ISTINAKH PROVOSLAVNOI VERY

RAZNOLET'E. STIKHI / Aseev, N – M. 1950. BR-908 2 – 8 – ne IDC [460]

LA RAZON CONTEMPLATIVA / Marrodan, Mario Angel – Caceres: Imp. Moderna, 1954. Cuadernos Alcantara no 7 – 1 – sp Bibl Santa Ana [301]

RAZONES CONTRA ULTRAJES / Garrido, Eduardo – 1896 – 9 – 1.50f – sp Bibl Santa Ana [946]

Razouls, Claude *see*
- BILAN ACTUEL DES COPEPODES PLANCTONIQUES MARINS ET DES EAUX SAUMATRES
- HISTOIRE ELECTORALE DE BANYULS-SUR-MER
- REPERTOIRE MONDIAL TAXINOMIQUE ET BIBLIOGRAPHIQUE PROVISOIRE DES COPEPODES PLANCTONIQUES MARINS ET DES EAUX SAUMATRES. DIVERS SYSTEMES DE CLASSIFICATION

RAZRIADNYE DIAKI 16 VEKA; OPYT ISTORIKO-IURIDICHESKAGO IZSLEDOVANIIA / Likhachev, N P – Spb. 1888. BR-4272 2 – 8 – ne IDC [340]

RAZRIADNYI PRIKAZ (NACHALO XVI V.-1711 G.) – Opis' stolbtsov dopolnitel'nogo otdela arkhivnogo fonda No.210. Moscow, 1950. 144p. BR-10,714/1 – 9 – ne IDC [025]

RAZSKAZY / Gorodetskii, S – I Kladbische Strastei; II Svetkaia Byl', Volk i dr. Spb. 1909-10. Lacking: 1909, Kladbishche Strastei. BR-1129 1 – 9 – ne IDC [460]

RAZSKAZY / Remizov, A – 1910. BR-843 2 – 8 – ne IDC [460]

RAZSKAZY (4-AIA KNIGA) / Gippius, Z N – Spb. 1906. BR-710 2 – 8 – ne IDC [460]

RAZSVET – Organ russkikh evreev. nr. 1-52. Odessa. 1860-61. BR-3739 2 – 9 – ne IDC [073]

RAZSVET – Sotsial-demokraticheskii listok dlia dektantov. v. 1-9. Geneva. 1904. BR-3793 2 – 8 – ne IDC [335]

RAZSVET – Zhurnal nauk, iskusstv i literatury dlia devits. v. 1-14. Spb. 1859-62. BR-3736 – 8 – ne IDC [073]

RAZVEDCHIK = THE SCOUT : A REFERENCE AND BIBLIOGRAPHICAL JOURNAL FOR THE MILITARY – St Petersburg: V Berezovskii, 1888-1917 – 610mf – 9 – $3,600.00 – us Ross [355]

RAZVITIE KHOZIAISTVA KINESHEMSKOGO ZEMSTVA KOSTROMSKOI GUBERNII / Kondrat'ev, N D – Kineshma, 1915 – 5mf – 9 – COR-49/1 – ne IDC [334]

RAZVITIE KOOPERATSII / Kremnev, G M – Ed 3. L., 1928 – 2mf – 9 – COR-206/1 – ne IDC [334]

R.C. Brown and Co *see*
- HISTORY OF BUTLER COUNTY
- HISTORY OF TIOGA COUNTY

RCA REVIEW – v1- 1936- 1; v31- 5,6; v36- 9 – us UMI [500]

RCDA. RELIGION IN COMMUNIST DOMINATED AREAS – (1985-. 5,6,9) – v11-. 1972- – 1 – us UMI [200]

Re, Edward D *see*
- APPELLATE OPINION WRITING
- STARE DECISIS

IL RE TEODORO IN VENEZIA. ATTO PRIMO / Paisiello, G – Ms, 180- – 1 – us Sibley [780]

Rea, Lilian *see* THE ENTHUSIASTS OF PORT-ROYAL

Rea, Thomas *see* SCHILLER'S DRAMAS AND POEMS IN ENGLAND
A REACAO – Manaos, Amazonas. 4 Jun-5 Set 1920 – 1,5,6 – bl Biblioteca [072]
A REACCAO – Maceio-Jaragua, Alagoas. 24 Set-30 Out 1909 – 1,5,6 – bl Biblioteca [072]
A REACCAO : ORGAM DA UNIAO DE MOCOS CATHOLICOS DE MANAOS – Manaos, Amazonas. 13 Maio 1930-21 Maio 1933 – 1,5,6 – bl Biblioteca [072]
A REACCAO : PELA PATRIA E PELA REPUBLICA – Antonina, 15 Jan-30 Apr 1903 – 1,5,6 – bl Biblioteca [072]
A REACCAO – Uberlandia, Brazil. May 1924; Feb 1925 – 1 – bl Biblioteca [072]
THE REACH : OFFICIAL AMERICAN LEAGUE BASE BALL GUIDE FOR AN ANNUAL COMPENDIUM OF BASE BALL RECORDS – 1883-1900 – 1r – 1 – us Ross [790]
THE REACH: OFFICIAL AMERICAN LEAGUE BASE BALL GUIDE FOR 1883-1900 – Philadelphia, 1883-1900 – 1 – us NY Public [790]
REACH OFFICIAL BASEBALL – 1883-89; 1891-94; 1896; 1898-1907 – 3r – 1 – $150.00 – B70091 – us Library Micro [790]
REACH TO THE STARS A YEAR OF SELF-RELIANCE / Sukarno, Pres. Indonesia – SE 6139 1. Address on 20th anniversary of independence on 17 Aug. 1965 – 9 – ne IDC [324]
REACTION : JOURNAL ANTIALCOOLIQUE – Quebec. v1 n11. 15 jun 1942-v11 n5. 15 dec 1951 – 4r – 1 – Can$40.00 – cn Can Microfilming [072]
REACTION – pour l'ordre. Revue mensuelle. Dir. J. de Fabregues. no. 1-12. Paris. avr 1930-juin juil 1932. devenu: La Revue du siecle voir a ce titre – 1 – fr A.C.R.P.P. [073]
REACTION AND PROGRESS IN PALESTINE / Kaznelson, B – London, 1937. BJ-28-11/1 – 9 – ne IDC [956]
REACTION DE L'ACADEMIE DES BEAUX ARTS CONTRE L'ART GOTHIQUE / Lassus, J B A – Paris: Didron, 1846. 4 fol., 14p. (Architecture Series) – 9 – fr Hachette [720]
REACTION KINETICS AND CATALYSIS LETTERS – v1-26. 1974-84 – 1,5,6,13 – sz Elsevier [073]
REACTOR FUEL PROCESSING – v1-9 1958-1966 – 1 – us UMI [621]
REACTOR SAFETY STUDY OF THE NUCLEAR REGULATORY COMMISSION : "THE RASMUSSEN REPORT" – Main report, summary report + appendices 1-11, 1975 – 36mf – 9 – $54.00 – LLMC 81-236 – us L.L.M.C. [324]
THE READ ALL ABOUT ALL REG'D – Montreal. v1 n2. 8 oct 1938 – 1r – 1 – Can$25.00 – cn Can Microfilming [072]
Read, Benjamin M *see* ILLUSTRATED HISTORY OF NEW MEXICO
Read, Carveth *see*
- MAN AND HIS SUPERSTITIONS
- NATURAL AND SOCIAL MORALS

Read, Eliphalet Allison *see* THE IDEA OF GOD IN RELATION TO THEOLOGY
Read, James Burton *see* THE LAW OF SALES
Read, John Meredith *see* HISTORIC STUDIES IN VAUD, BERNE, AND SAVOY; FROM ROMAN TIMES TO VOLTAIRE, ROUSSEAU, AND GIBBON
Read, Leonard E *see*
- ABCS OF FREEDOM
- ACCENT ON THE RIGHT
- ANYTHING THAT'S PEACEFUL
- AWAKE FOR FREEDOM'S SAKE
- COMES THE DAWN
- THE COMING ARISTOCRACY
- CONSCIENCE ON THE BATTLEFIELD
- ELEMENTS OF LIBERTARIAN LEADERSHIP
- ESSAYS FROM "ESSAYS ON LIBERTY"
- THE FREE MAN'S ALMANACH
- THE FREEDOM FREEWAY
- HAVING MY WAY
- LET FREEDOM REIGN
- LIBERTY: LEGACY OF TRUTH
- THE LOVE OF LIBERTY
- NOTES FROM FEE
- SEEDS OF PROGRESS
- TO FREE OR FREEZE, THAT IS THE QUESTION
- WHY NOT TRY FREEDOM?

Reade, Charles L *see*
- THE AUTOBIOGRAPHY OF A THIEF (ETC.)
- BIBLE CHARACTERS
- CHARLES READE, D.C.L., DRAMATIST, NOVELIST, JOURNALIST
- CHRISTIE JOHNSTONE
- THE CLOISTER AND THE HEARTH
- THE COURSE OF TRUE LOVE
- THE DOUBLE MARRIAGE, OR, WHITE LIES
- FOUL PLAY
- GOOD STORIES
- GRIFFITH GAUNT
- HARD CASH
- IT IS NEVER TOO LATE TO MEND
- THE JILT, (ETC.)
- LOVE ME LITTLE
- PEG WOOFINGTON
- A PERILOUS SECRET
- PUT YOURSELF IN HIS PLACE
- READIANA (AND) BIBLE CHARACTERS
- A SIMPLETON
- SINGLEHEART AND DOUBLE FACE
- A TERRIBLE TEMPTATION
- A WOMAN HATER
- WORKS

Reade, Compton *see* CHARLES READE, D.C.L., DRAMATIST, NOVELIST, JOURNALIST
Reade, R N R *see* PRECIS OF THE ASHANTI EXPEDITION, 1895-1896
Reade, William Winwood *see* THE MARTYRDOM OF MAN
Reade, Winwood *see* THE AFRICAN SKETCH-BOOK
A READER OF AUSTRALIAN ANARCHISM, 1886-96 / ed by James, Bob – 1979. 130p. Together with: The Relevance of Anarchism to Modern Society, by Sam Dolgoff. 1977. 24p; and Peter Kropotkin – His Federalist Ideas, by Camillo Berneri. 20p. 1 fiche (24x) – 9 – 1.00f – at Libertarian Micro [320]
A READER ON THE APOSTLES' CREED (CCC274) = HSIN CHING TU PEN – (In Chinese) – [s.l: s.n, 1932] – 1r – 1 – 1984-6613 – us A.T.L.A. [220]
A READER ON THE LORD'S PRAYER (CCC273) = CHU TAO WEN TU PEN – (In Chinese) – [s.l: s.n, 1932] – 1r – 1 – 1984-6612 – us A.T.L.A. [240]
A READER ON THE TEN COMMANDMENTS (CCC275) = SHIH T'IAO CHISH TU PEN – (In Chinese) – [s.l: s.n, 1932] – 1r – 1 – 1984-6614 – us A.T.L.A. [220]
READER'S DIGEST – (v. 88- 1966- 5,6,9) – v. 1- 1922- – 1 – us UMI [073]
READERS' GUIDE ABSTRACTS – (Publication discontinues with vol 8 No8 1993) – Same coverage as Readers' Guide to Periodical Literature. Abstracts for each article indexed in Readers' Guide. Updated and cumulated every six weeks. Indexing, cross-references. Sept 1984-1993 – 9 – $675.00y; $750.00y – us Wilson [073]
THE READER'S GUIDE IN ECONOMIC, SOCIAL AND POLITICAL SCIENCE: BEING A CLASSIFIED BIBLIOGRAPHY. AMERICAN, ENGLISH, FRENCH AND GERMAN.. – Ed. by R.R. Bowker & George Iles. New York: Society for Political Education, 1891. 03818. (Pre-1900 Canadiana) – 9 – cn C.I.H.M. [013]
READIANA (AND) BIBLE CHARACTERS / Reade, Charles L – British Fiction Archive: Unit 2 – 9 – uk Bell [830]
READING – v1- 1967- 1; v10- 5,6,9 – us UMI [370]
READING ADLER – Reading, PA. -w 1885-1912. 10 rolls – 13 – $25.00r – us I.M.R. [071]
READING CHRONICLE – England, 1771-75; 1825- – 336+ r – 1 – uk British Libr Newspaper [072]
READING GAZETTE *see* EVENING GAZETTE
READING GAZETTE AND DEMOCRAT – Reading, PA., 1840-1878 – 13 – $25.00r – us I.M.R. [071]
READING IMPROVEMENT – v1- 1963- 1; 1971- 5,6; 1975- 4 x 6 in. 9 – us UMI [370]
READING IN THE HOME / South Dakota. Agricultural Extension Service. State College of Agriculture and Mechanic Arts – nos.1-14. 1934-43 – 1,5,6 – us Spaulding [630]
READING OBSERVER, BERKS TELEGRAPH, AND BUCKS, HANTS, OXFORDSHIRE AND SURREY NEWS – (Missing: 1888) – England. 2 Aug 1873-23 Aug 1924 – 53r – 1 – uk British Libr Newspaper [072]
A READING ON ARTICLE 16, SECTION 7, OF THE CONSTITUTION OF PENNSYLVANIA / McMurtie, Richard Coxe – Philadelphia, Matlack & Harvey, 1885. 22 p. LL-497 – 1 – us L of C Photodup [340]
READING POST *see* EVENING POST
READING PRESS – Reading, PA., 1889-1893 – 13 – $25.00r – us I.M.R. [071]
READING PSYCHOLOGY – 1979- – 1,5,6,9 – us UMI [150]
READING RESEARCH QUARTERLY – v1- 1965-1; 1968- 5,6; 1975- 4 x 6 in. 9 – us UMI [370]
READING STANDARD – England. 1891-95; 1897-10 Sep 1965 – 114r – 1 – uk British Libr Newspaper [072]
READING TEACHER – v1- 1948- 1; v24- 5,6; 1975- 9 – us UMI [370]
READING TIMES – Reading, PA. -d 1858-1959. 235 rolls – 13 – $25.00r – us I.M.R. [071]
READING-CANADA-LECTURE – (Cont by: Reflections on Canadian Literacy at v8 1990) – Calgary. v1-7. 1983-1989 – 9 – Can$20.00y – cn Micromedia [420]
READING-CANADA-LECTURE *see* REFLECTIONS ON CANADIAN LITERACY
READINGER ADLER – Reading. Pa. 1796-1820 – 1,3 – us Readex [071]
READINGER POSTBOTHE UND BERKS, SCHUYLKILL UND MONTGOMERY COUNTIES ADVERTISER – (In German) – Reading, PA. 1816-22 – 1r – 1 – $85.00 – D3387 – us Scholarly Res [071]
READINGER ZEITUNG – (In German) – Reading, PA. 1789-1802 – 4r – 1 – $340.00 – D3389 – us Scholarly Res [071]
READINGS FROM THE BIBLE : SELECTED FOR SCHOOLS AND TO BE READ IN UNISON / ed by Onahan, William James et al – (Includes indexes) – Chicago: Scott, Foresman, 1896 – 1mf – 9 – 0-8370-8539-X – 1986-2539 – us A.T.L.A. [220]
READINGS IN ACCOUNTING THEORY / ed by Devine, Carl Thomas – SE-3991 1. 4 v. 1962-1963 – 9 – ne IDC [650]
READINGS IN AMERICAN CONSTITUTIONAL HISTORY, 1776-1876 / ed by Johnson, Allen – Boston, New York: Houghton, Mifflin & Co, 1889 – 7mf – 9 – $10.50 – LLMC 92-179 – us L.L.M.C. [323]
READINGS IN ARABIC LINGUISTICS / ed by Al-Ani, Salman H – Zug, 1976. BNE-20,121 1 – 9 – ne IDC [470]
READINGS IN BUSINESS ADMINISTRATION / ed by Ang, Giok Goen – SE-3677 1. 1963 – 9 – ne IDC [650]
READINGS IN BUSINESS ADMINISTRATION AND ECONOMICS / ed by Johnson, Rossal James – SE-4143 1. 1961 – 9 – ne IDC [338]
READINGS IN BUSINESS ADMINISTRATION AND ECONOMICS / ed by Mears, Leon A – SE-2712 1. v. 1 only. 1962 – 9 – ne IDC [650]
READINGS IN CHURCH HISTORY / Stone, James Samuel – 1889 – 1 – us A.T.L.A. [240]
READINGS IN ECONOMICS / Jakarta. Universitas Indonesia. Fakultas Ekonomi – SE-3881 1. 1960 – 9 – ne IDC [330]
READINGS IN THE HISTORY OF EDUCATION : MEDIAEVAL UNIVERSITIES / Norton, Arthur O – Cambridge: Harvard University, 1909 – 1mf – us A.T.L.A. [370]
READINGS ON POPULATION FOR LAW STUDENTS / ed by Lee, L T & Saney, P – 1977 – 9 – 92-3-101364-5 – fr UNESCO [340]
READINGS ON THE INFERNO OF DANTE / Vernon, William – 2v. 1894 – 1 – us A.T.L.A. [440]
REAGAN BAPTIST CHURCH. REAGAN, TEXAS : CHURCH RECORDS – 1943-1972 – 1 – 13.77 – us Baptist [240]
Real Academia Espanola *see* GRAMATICA DE LA LENGUA ESPANOLA
REAL CAUSE OF BUSINESS STAGNATION IN THE UNITED STATES: A REPLY TO AN ARTICLE IN SAINT JOHN TELEGRAPH, JULY 24TH, 1878 / Baird, Henry Carey – Philadelphia?, 1878?. 00803. (Pre-1900 Canadiana) – 9 – cn C.I.H.M. [338]
REAL CEDULA...LOS SENORES DEL CONSEJO – 1789 – 9 – 1.50f – sp Bibl Santa Ana [440]
Real Cofradia de Nuestra Senora de la Santisima Virgen de la Montana *see* MEMORIA Y CUENTA GENERAL QUE PRESENTA LA JUNTA DIRECTIVA DE LA COFRADIA A LA GENERAL DE HERMANOS. POR LA GESTION...1949
REAL COMPANIA DE GUARDIAS MARINAS Y COLEGIO NAVAL. CATALOGO DE PRUEBAS DE CABALLEROS ASPIRANTES. VOL. 2. MADRID, 1944 / Valgoma Dalmiro y Finestrat, Ramon – Madrid: Razon y Fe, 1947 – 1 – sp Bibl Santa Ana [355]
Real, Cristobal *see*
- EN LAS TIERRAS DEL ORO DEL IMPERIO DEL SOL. MADRID, 1945
- ESPANA Y COLON. MADRID, 1935

REAL DECRETO DE 26 DE MARZO DE 1913 DECLARANDO OFICIAL EL CUARTO CENTENARIO DEL OCEANO PACIFICO / Nunez de Balboa, Vasco – Madrid: Fortanet, 1913. B.R.A.H. 62. pp. 465-467 – 1 – sp Bibl Santa Ana [946]
REAL DECRETO DECLARANDO OFICIAL EL CUARTO CENTENARIO DEL DESCUBRIMIENTO DEL OCEANO PACIFICO Y NOTICIA / Nunez de Balboa – Madrid: Fortanet, 1913. B.R.A.H. 62, pp. 465-467 y 495-496 – sp Bibl Santa Ana [946]
REAL DECRETO E INSTRUCCION PARA FORMAR EL CENSO GENERAL DE POBLACION DE ESPANA – Madrid, 1857 – 1mf – 9 – sp Cultura [304]
REAL DEMOCRACY – v2-18. 1905-21 – 2r – 1 – us Ross [073]
Real, Enrique *see*
- DISCURSO LEIDO POR...ARTES Y OFICIOS DE FREGENAL EN LA SOLEMNE INAUGURACION DE LA MISMA
- HISTORIA DEL PERIODISMO EN FREGENAL DE LA SIERRA
- INTIMAS.POESIAS
- POESIAS A...NTR. SRA. REMEDIOS...FREGENAL DE LA SIERRA

REAL ESTATE ADVERTISER – Chicago. Ill. -w. 1955- – 1 – us UMI [071]
REAL ESTATE AND BUSINESS ATLANTA – v.5-7. 1976-78. Continued by Business Atlanta – 1 – us UMI [073]
REAL ESTATE APPRAISAL RECORDS / Erie County. Ohio. Auditor – 1848-1855 – 1r – 1 – $32.50r – us Archival [324]
REAL ESTATE APPRAISEMENTS / Hancock County. Ohio. Biglick Township. Township Clerk – 1910 – 1r – 1 – $32.50r – us Archival [324]
REAL ESTATE ATLANTA – v.1-5. 1972-76. Continued by yReal Estate and Business Atlanta – 1 – us UMI [073]
REAL ESTATE CATALOGUE : ISSUED FOR DISTRIBUTION IN CANADA AND IN GREAT BRITAIN AND IRELAND AMONG BRITISH EMIGRANTS.. / W.J. Fenton & Co – 1880 – 9 – 05475 (Pre-1900 Canadiana) – cn C.I.H.M. [333]
REAL ESTATE CHRONICLE – Ottawa: J Y Caldwell, [1899?-19–] – 9 – cn C.I.H.M. [333]
REAL ESTATE CIRCULAR – San Francisco, CA. 1868-1942 – 3r – 1 – $150.00 – B02857 – us Library Micro [071]
REAL ESTATE LAW DIGEST – 1976- – 1,5,6,9 – us UMI [336]
REAL ESTATE OWNED BY THE CITY AND COUNTY OF SAN FRANCISCO 1909 / San Francisco. Board of Supervisors – California reel 38. (Cox Library Collection) – 5 – us Americana [978]
REAL ESTATE RECORD – Montreal: J Cradock Simpson & Co., [1888-1916?] – 9 – cn C.I.H.M. [650]
REAL ESTATE RECORD – Pawtucket. R.I. 1886-1890 – 1 – us UMI [071]
REAL ESTATE RECORD – Toronto: McCuaig & Mainwaring, [1891-189- or 19–] – 9 – cn C.I.H.M. [650]
REAL ESTATE REGISTER AND RENTAL GUIDE – Providence. R.I. 1892-1895; 1901-1915 – 1 – us UMI [071]
REAL ESTATE WEEK – Temecula, CA. 1989 – 1+ r – 1 – $50.00 ($50.00y) – R04128 – us Library Micro [071]
THE REAL FOUNDERS OF NEW ENGLAND / Bolton, Charles Knowles – 1929. Item L. Stories of their life along the coast, 1602-1628. Indexed, 192p.SW16-0095 – 5 – us A.G.L.L. [978]
REAL HOSPICIO DE BADAJOZ. FUNDACION / Vargas, Adolfo de – 1896 – 9 – 1.50f – sp Bibl Santa Ana [946]
Real, J C Martini et al *see* HISTORIAS DEL PERONISMO
THE REAL JESUS: A REVIEW OF HIS LIFE, CHARACTER, AND DEATH, FROM A JEWISH STANDPOINT / Vickers, John – London: Williams & Norgate, 1891. 1 fiche – 9 – us A.T.L.A. [270]
THE REAL JESUS: A SERIES OF CONSTRUCTIVE DISCOURSES / Martin, Alfred Wilhelm von – Seattle: A.W. Martin, 1906?. 1 fiche – 9 – us A.T.L.A. [240]
REAL PROPERTY / Graves, Charles Alfred – Indianapolis: Bobbs-Merrill 190-. 534p. LL-750 – 1 – us L of C Photodup [340]

THE REAL PROPERTY LAW OF THE STATE OF NEW YORK: BEING CHAPTER FORTY-SIX OF THE GENERAL LAWS. / Fowler, Robert Ludlow – New York: Baker, Voorhis, 1899. 840p. LL-489 – 1 – us L of C Photodup [340]

REAL PROPERTY PROBATE AND TRUST JOURNAL (ABA) – (Supersedes American Bar Association: Section of Real Property, Probate and Trust Law. Proceedings) – v1-27. 1966-1993 – 9 – $480.00set – us Hein [340]

REAL PROPERTY PROBATE AND TRUST JOURNAL (ABA) – v1-29. 1966-95 – 1,5,6 – $585.00 – us Hein [073]

REAL SALVATION AND WHOLE-HEARTED SERVICE / Torrey, Reuben Archer – 2nd ed. New York: Fleming H Revell, c1905 – 1mf – 9 – 0-8370-5658-6 – 1985-3658 – us A.T.L.A. [240]

REAL-ENCYCLOPAEDIE DER GESAMMTEN HEILKUNDE (AEL, ABT.3;8) / ed by Eulenburg, Albert – Wien und Leipzig, 1894-1901 (mf ed 1993) – 182mf – 9 – DM1,900.00 – 3-89131-144-3 – gw Fischer [610]

REALENCYCLOPAEDIE FUER PROTESTANTISCHE THEOLOGIE UND KIRCHE / ed by Hauck, Albert – Leipzig. 24v. 1869-1913 – 216mf – 9 – ne IDC [240]

REALES CEDULAS – Badajoz: Francisco Barrera, 1789 – 1 – sp Bibl Santa Ana [946]

REALES CEDULAS DE LA REAL Y PONTIFICIA DE LA UNIVERSIDAD DE MEXICO DE 1551 A 1816 / Lanning, John Tate – Madrid: Missionalia Hispanica, 1948 – 1 – sp Bibl Santa Ana [240]

REALES ORDENES, 1792-93, Y REALES ORDENES Y DECRETOS, 1767-1854 (ROYAL ORDERS AND DECREES) / Puerto Rico. Spanish Governors – 1 roll. T1122 – 1 – us Nat'l Archives [324]

Realf, Richard *see* SELECTED DOCUMENTS FROM THE ARCHIVES AND MANUSCRIPTS DEPTS., KSHS, TOPEKA

REALIDAD DE UN CUATRICENTENARIO : MOMENTOS HIST'ORICOS DE LA VIDA VENEZOLANA EON ESPANA. DISCURSO PRONUNCIADO EN EL SALON...CACERES... 1955 / Urdaneta, Ramon – Zaragoza: Imprenta La Acedemia, 1956 – 1 – sp Bibl Santa Ana [972]

REALIDAD Y ESPIRITUALIDAD / Kuprian, Herman – Badajoz: Dip. Provincial, 1974. Sep. REE – 1 – sp Bibl Santa Ana [290]

REALIDAD Y PERSPECTIVA DE LA PLANIFICACION REGIONAL EN ESPANA / Martin Lobo, Manuel – Madrid, 1960-61. Sep. Rev. Est. Agro-sociales, no 33, 1960, no 34, 1961 – sp Bibl Santa Ana [946]

LAS REALIDADES SOCIALES CONTEMPORANEAS / Cotallo, Jose Luis – Caceres: Tip. El Noticiero, 1950 – sp Bibl Santa Ana [946]

REALIGNING KOREA'S NATIONAL PRIORITIES FOR ECONOMIC ADVANCE / Korea (Republic). Presidential Commission on Economic Restructuring – Seoul, 1988 – 2mf – 9 – ne IDC [338]

LES REALISATIONS DE 1959 A 1962 / Algeria. Caisse d'Equipement pour le Developpement de l'Algerie – 1964. BNE-8618 1 – 9 – ne IDC [338]

REALISIERUNG DIGITALER SCHALTUNGEN MIT AND-EXOR-STRUKTUR / Riege, Matthias – 1991 – 100p – DM98.00 – 3-89349-440-5 – gw Hänsel [621]

LE REALISME – Red. Edm. Duranty. no. 1. Paris. juil 1856; n.s., no. 1-6. nov 1856-avr mai 1857 – 1 – fr A.C.R.P.P. [073]

LE REALISME CHRETIEN ET L'IDEALISME GREC / Laberthonniere, Lucien – Paris: P Lethielleux, c1904 – 1mf – 9 – 0-8370-8918-2 – 1986-2918 – us A.T.L.A. [180]

REALISMUS DER ARBEITERLITERATUR : PRAXIS UND THEORIE IM WERKKREIS LITERATUR DER ARBEITSWELT / Deuber, Walter – (Includes bibliographical references) – Zuerich: Verlag Reih W, [1978] – 1r – 1 – us U.W. Library [331]

REALISTISCHE CABINETSTUCKE / Sacher-Masoch – Berlin: J. Gnadenfeld; Wien; L. Steckler distributor, 188-? – 1 – us U.W. Library [320]

REALITATEA ROMANESCA *see* MUNCA

REALITES ALLEMANDES : PUBLICATION DU HAUT-COMMISSARIAT DE LA REPUBLIQUE FRANCAISE EN ALLEMAGNE – Baden-Baden, 1949-52 – 1 – Dist. gw Mikrofilm – fr A.C.R.P.P. [073]

REALITES CAMBODIENNES – Phnom-Penh. Cambodia. 1956- – 1 – us UMI [072]

REALITES CANADIENNES-FRANCAISES – Lovis, Canada. avr 1940; v1 n2. jun 1940 – 1r – 1 – Can$25.00 – cn Can Microfilming [072]

REALITES IVOIRIENNES – Paris. nos1-84. 1965-69 – 13mf – 9 – A-728/1 – ne IDC [960]

REALITIES OF CHRISTIAN THEOLOGY : AN INTERPRETATION OF CHRISTIAN EXPERIENCE / Beckwith, Clarence Augustine – (Includes bibliographical references and index) – Boston: Houghton, Mifflin; Cambridge: Riverside Press, 1906 – 1mf – 9 – 0-8370-2302-5 – 1985-0302 – us A.T.L.A. [240]

THE REALITY OF RELIGION / Van Dyke, Henry – New York: Charles Scribner, 1884 – 1mf – 9 – 0-8370-5644-6 – 1985-3644 – us A.T.L.A. [240]

THE REALITY OF THE MONEY ECONOMY / Bracewell-Milnes, Barry – 1983, LA Economic Notes, No. 4. 2p – 9 – 1.00f – at Libertarian Micro [335]

A REALIZACAO : FOLHA LITTERARIA E NOTICIOSA – Pitanguy, 26 Aug-21 Oct 1883 – 1,5,6 – bl Biblioteca [072]

REALIZACION DEL FUERO DEL TRABAJO 1 CONFERENCIA...18 DE ENERO DE 1950. PRECEDE AL TITULO JEFATURA PROVINCIAL DE FET Y DE LAS JONS / Benavides Llorente, Daniel – Caceres: Tip. El Noticiero, s.a. 1950? – sp Bibl Santa Ana [331]

REALIZACIONES ARGENTINAS EN EL ORDEN SOCIAL – [Buenos Aires?: Servicio Internacional Publicaciones Argentinas, 1951?]. 1v – 1 – CSUXADH4529-B – us Hoover Inst Photo [972]

REALIZACIONES PERONISTAS – Buenos Aires: Editorial Mundo peronista, 1954 – 1 – CSUXAHZ6573-B – us Hoover Inst Photo [320]

REALIZM I MODERNISTICHESKIE TECHENIIA V RUSSKOI LITERATURE NACHALA 20 V. "VOPROSY LITERATURY" / Pertsov, V – NR. 2. 1957. BR-3290 2 – 8 – ne IDC [460]

REALLEXIKON DER DEUTSCHEN LITERATURGESCHICHTE : UNTER MITWIRKUNG ZAHLREICHER FACHGELEHRTER / ed by Merker, Paul & Stammler, Wolfgang – (Issued in parts) – Berlin: W de Gruyter, 1925-31 – 1r – 1 – us U.W. Library [430]

THE REALM – Toronto: Realm, [1898?-19–] – 9 – cn C.I.H.M. [240]

REAL-ZEITUNG *see* CHRISTIAN-ERLANGISCHER ZEITUNGS-EXTRACT

RE'AMIM U-RE'ASHIM / Rokach, nE – (Havazzelet, Jerusalem, 5649). 1889. BJ-27-209 1 – 9 – ne IDC [390]

Reams, Bernard D *see* HUMAN EXPERIMENTATION

Reams, Bernard D Jr *see*
- CONGRESS AND THE COURTS
- FEDERAL LAW OF SCIENCE AND TECHNOLOGY
- HOUSING AND TRANSPORTATION OF THE HANDICAPPED
- INTERNAL REVENUE ACTS OF THE UNITED STATES
- INTERNAL REVENUE ACTS OF THE UNITED STATES 1950-1951
- TAX REFORM 1984

Reams, Bernard N *see* DISABILITY LAW IN THE UNITED STATES

REAPING THE WHIRLWIND : A CHRISTIAN INTERPRETATION OF HISTORY / Gilkey, Langdon – New York, 1976 – 8mf – 8 – ne Slangenburg [240]

REAPPRAISAL OF THE SECOND FIVE YEAR PLAN A RESUME / India. Planning Commission – Delhi. 1958. BD-530 1 – 9 – ne IDC [338]

REAPPRAISEMENT RECORDS / Ottawa County. Ohio. Auditor – 1859-1890 – 3r – 1 – $32.50r – us Archival [324]

REAPPRAISEMENTS / Putnam County. Ohio. Auditor – (Some issues missing) – 1846-1900 – 6r – 1 – $32.50r – us Archival [324]

REAPPRAISMENTS / Van Wert County. Ohio. Auditor – 1853 – 1r – 1 – $32.50r – us Archival [324]

Reardon, George Evett *see* FORMS OF ACKNOWLEDGMENTS FOR DEEDS AND OTHER INSTRUMENTS USED IN THE STATES AND TERRITORIES OF THE UNITED STATES.

REASON – A National News Review – 1 – 55.00 – cn McLaren [971]

REASON – London. 1898 – 1 – uk Microform Academic [073]

REASON AND AUTHORITY IN RELIGION / Sterrett, James Macbride – (Includes bibliographical references) – New York: Thomas Whittaker, 1891 – 1mf – 9 – 0-8370-5403-6 – 1985-3403 – us A.T.L.A. [240]

REASON AND FAITH / Fiske, Asa Severance – Washington: Neale, 1900.1 fiche – 9 – us A.T.L.A. [240]

REASON AND FAITH, OR, THE TWO LIGHTS – Philadelphia: J.B. Lippincott, 1869. 1 fiche – 9 – us A.T.L.A. [240]

REASON AND REVELATION : BEING AN EXAMINATION INTO THE NATURE AND CONTENTS OF SCRIPTURE REVELATION AS COMPARED WITH OTHER FORMS OF TRUTH / Horne, William – London: Henry S King, 1876 – 1mf – 9 – 0-8370-3657-7 – 1985-1657 – us A.T.L.A. [220]

REASON AND REVELATION / Candlish, Robert Smith – London: T. Nelson, 1859.1 fiche – 9 – us A.T.L.A. [240]

REASON AND REVELATION : AN ESSAY IN CHRISTIAN APOLOGY / Illingworth, John Richardson – (Includes bibliographical references) – London: Macmillan, 1903 – 1mf – 9 – 0-8370-3720-4 – 1985-1720 – us A.T.L.A. [230]

REASON AND THE BIBLE : OR, THE TRUTH OF RELIGION / Squier, Miles Powell – (Includes bibliographical references) – New York: Charles Scribner, 1860 – 1mf – 9 – 0-8370-2878-7 – 1985-0878 – us A.T.L.A. [230]

REASON IN BELIEF, OR, FAITH FOR AN AGE OF SCIENCE / Sewall, Frank – London: Elliot Stock, 1906. 1 fiche – 9 – us A.T.L.A. [240]

REASON IN RELIGION / Hedge, Frederic Henry – 1901 – 9 – us A.T.L.A. [240]

THE REASON OF LIFE / DuBose, William Porcher – New York: Longmans, Green, 1911 – 1mf – us A.T.L.A. [240]

REASON, THE ONLY ORACLE OF MAN / Allen, Ethan – 1784 – 9 – $30.00 – us Scholars' Facs [190]

REASON, THOUGHT, AND LANGUAGE : OR, THE MANY AND THE ONE: A REVISED SYSTEM OF LOGICAL DOCTRINE / Macleane, Douglas – London: H. Frowde, 1906 – xv/583p – 1 – us U.W. Library [160]

REASONABLE APPREHENSIONS AND REASSURING HINTS : BEING PAPERS DESIGNED TO ATTRACT ATTENTION TO THE NATURE OF MODERN UNBELIEF, AND TO MEET SOME OF ITS FUNDAMENTAL ASSUMPTIONS / Footman, Henry – (Includes bibliographical references) – New York:James Pott, 1885, c1884 – 1mf – 9 – 0-8370-3160-5 – 1985-1160 – us A.T.L.A. [210]

THE REASONABLE CHRIST: A SERIES OF STUDIES / Merrill, George Edmunds – New York: Silver, Burdett, 1893.1 fiche – 9 – us A.T.L.A. [240]

A REASONABLE HYPOTHESIS OF THE ORIGIN OF THE PENTATEUCH / Osgood, Howard – New York: Funk & Wagnalls, 1888.1 fiche – 9 – us A.T.L.A. [240]

THE REASONER – San Luis Obispo, CA. 1892-96 – 2r – 1 – $100.00 – B02905 – us Library Micro [071]

REASONER SERIES – London. 1846-72 – 1 – uk Microform Academic [073]

REASONS FOR BECOMING A BAPTIST / Alexander, John – 1861. 44p – 1 – 5.00 – us Baptist [240]

REASONS FOR BEING A CHURCHMAN : ADDRESSED TO ENGLISH SPEAKING CHRISTIANS OF EVERY NAME / Little, Arthur Wilde – rev ed. Milwaukee, WI: Young Churchman, 1905 – 1mf – 9 – 0-8370-8588-8 – 1986-2588 – us A.T.L.A. [240]

REASONS FOR BELIEVING IN CHRISTIANITY: ADDRESSED TO BUSY PEOPLE / Row, Charles Adolphus – New York: Thomas Whittaker, 1885. 1 fiche. 8370-4988-1 – 9 – us A.T.L.A. [240]

REASONS FOR CHRISTIAN FAITH (CCC172) : TESTIMONIES OF SOME PROMINENT CHINESE CHRISTIANS AND OTHERS / Hsieh, Hung-lai – (In Chinese) – 2nd ed. Shanghai: Association Press of China, 1918 – 1r – 1 – 1984-B500 – us A.T.L.A. [240]

REASONS FOR FAITH IN THIS NINETEENTH CENTURY / Leavitt, John McDowell – New York: James Pott, 1884. 1 fiche – 9 – us A.T.L.A. [240]

REASONS FOR METHODIST BELIEF AND PRACTICE: RELATIVE TO WATER BAPTISM, EXPRESSED IN PLAIN WORDS AND ARRANGED IN A SUMMARY MANNER / Carroll, John – Toronto: Wesleyan Conference Office, 1870. 00487. (Pre-1900 Canadiana) – 9 – cn C.I.H.M. [240]

REASONS FOR QUITTING THE METHODIST SOCIETY, BEING A DEFENCE OF BARCLAY'S 'APOLOGY', IN ANSWER TO A PRINTED LETTER TO A PERSON JOINED WITH THE PEOPLE CALLED QUAKERS;... / Helton, J – London, 1778 – 1mf – 9 – MP-524/1 – ne IDC [240]

REASONS FOR UNBELIEF / Viardot, Louis – New York: Peter Eckler, 1896. 1 fiche – 9 – us A.T.L.A. [240]

REASONS WHY BRITISH CONSERVATIVES VOTED AGAINST THE BOUCHERVILLE MINISTRY / Bellingham, Sydney – Rouses Point, NY: Lovell, 1875. 02324. (Pre-1900 Canadiana) – 9 – cn C.I.H.M. [971]

A REASSESSMENT OF GUAM'S POLITICAL RELATIONSHIP WITH THE UNITED STATES : SURVEY REPORT AND FINDINGS OF A PUBLIC OPINION POLL, FEB-MAR 1980 / Venture Development Management Resources Inc & 16th Guam Legislature – Agana: Venture Inc. n.d. – 2mf – 9 – $3.00 – LLMC 82-100B Title 28 – us L.L.M.C. [324]

Reavis, LU *see* THE FUTURE GREAT CITY OF THE WORLD

O REBATE : ORGAM DO APOSTOLADO REPUBLICANO – Maceio, Alagoas. 6 Abr 1899-24 Jan 1900 – 1,5,6 – bl Biblioteca [072]

O REBATE : ORGAM INDENPENDENTE – Cruzeiro do Sul, Acre. 19 Jun 1921; Fev 1927-Dez 1929; Jan-Fev, Abr-Maio 1932; Jan 1933; Nov-Dez 1938; Jan-Abr 1939; Out 1943; Mar, Jun-Ago, Out-Dez 1947; Mar 1948; Mar-Abr, Jun, Set, Dez 1949; Fev, Ago-Set 1950; Fev, Ago 1951; Jan-Mar, Maio-Jun, Nov-Dez 1952; Jul 1953; Jan 1958-Juni 1971 – 1,5,6 – bl Biblioteca [072]

O REBATE : ORGAO INDEPENDENTE – Alto Acre, Acre. 8 Set-Nov 1912; Abr-Jun, Ago, Nov 1913 – 1,5,6 – bl Biblioteca [072]

O REBATE – Sao Paulo, Brazil. Jul 1888-Nov 1921. Incomplete except 1903-07, 1909 complete – 1 – bl Biblioteca [072]

REBATE ARQUEOLOGICO EN TORNO A UN BERRACO PROTOHISTORICO / Sanchez Paredes, Antonio – Plasencia: Graf. Sandoval, 1958 – 1 – sp Bibl Santa Ana [930]

REBE UND WEIN IN GOETHES WELTBILD / Christoffel, Karl – Heidelberg: L Schneider, 1948 – 1r – 1 – us U.W. Library [430]

REBECCA AND ROWENA : A ROMANCE UPON ROMANCE BY MR. M.A. TITMARSH / Thackeray, William Makepeace – London: Chapman and Hall, 1850 – 1 roll – 1 – 1-55879-338-0 – uk Libr Preservation [830]

REBECKA – Syracuse. N.Y. 1864 – 1 – us A.J.P.C. [071]

REBEKKA – San Francisco. Calif. 1874 – 1 – us A.J.P.C. [071]

REBEL – 1-6 (all publ). 1895-1896 – 1mf – 9 – $35.00 – us UPA [335]

THE REBEL – Toronto. v. 1-4. 1917-20 – 1 – 55.00 – cn McLaren [335]

THE REBEL POET / ed by Hagglund, B C – v1 1-17 1931-Oct 1932 – 1r – 1 – $5.00 – us M.H.S. [810]

EL REBELDE – Santiago, CL. 1971-1973 – 1r – $50.00 – R04191 – us Library Micro [320]

LOS REBELDES ESPANOLES NO HACEN UNA "GUERRA SANTA." / Maritain, Jacques – Madrid, 1937. Fiche W 1027. (Blodgett Collection of Spanish Civil War Pamphlets) – 9 – us H.U. College Libr [946]

REBELION (BUENOS AIRES, ARGENTINA) – (Includes c.1: 1947:Dec.13,27, 1948:Jan.3) – Buenos Aires: [s.n.], 1965 – 1 – CSUXADP4673-S – us Hoover Inst Photo [978]

LA REBELION DE LOS GENERALES / Garcia Lupo, Rogelio – Buenos Aires: Jamcana, 3rd ed 1963 – 1 – CSUXAHZ7356-B – us Hoover Inst Photo [320]

REBELION DE PIZARRO EN EL PERU / Calvete de Estrella, Juan Cristobal – 1889 – 9 – 1.50f – sp Bibl Santa Ana [946]

DER REBELL : EIN FREIHEITSROMAN AUS DEN BERGEN TIROLS / Trenker, Luis – Berlin: T Knaur, 1935 – 1 – us U.W. Library [830]

Rebell, Hugues *see* ENSEMBLE DES MSS. CONSERVES A LA BIBL. MUN. DE NANTES

LE REBELLE : HISTOIRE CANADIENNE / Trobriand, Philippe R D de K, Comte de – Quebec: N Aubin et W H Rowen, 1842. SEM16P213 – 1r – 5 – Can$9.00 – cn Bibl Nat [971]

REBELLION DE 37-38: PRECIS COMPLET DE CETTE PERIODE: ROLE D'HONNEUR, OU, LISTE COMPLETE DES PATRIOTES DETENUS DANS LES PRISONS DE MONTREAL EN 1837-39: DATE ET LIEUX DES ARRESTATIONS ET AUTRES DETAILS. / Borthwick, John Douglas – Montreal, 1898. 00190. (Pre-1900 Canadiana) – 9 – cn C.I.H.M. [971]

LA REBELLION MILITAIRE EN ESPAGNE ET L'INCOMPREHENSION DES DEMOCRATIES EUROPEENNES DEVANT UN AUSSI GRAVE PROBLEME / Gonzalez, Ceferino – Bruxelles, 1936? Fiche W926. (Blodgett Collection of Spanish Civil War Pamphlets) – 9 – us H.U. College Libr [946]

THE REBELLION RECORD : A DIARY OF AMERICAN EVENTS, WITH DOCUMENTS, NARRATIVES, ILLUSTRATIVE INCIDENTS, POETRY, ETC / ed by Moore, Frank – (With an introductory address on the causes of the struggle and the great issues before the country, by Edward Everett) – New York. v1-9. 1861-68 – 3r – 1 – us Ross [976]

REBELS WITHOUT A CAUSE : THE PERMESTA AFFAIR / Pirngadie, Rudy – 8 – SE-223 – ne IDC [360]

O REBENQUE : LITTERO – CRITICO – SPORTIVO – Manaos, Amazonas. 11 Jan 1913 – 1,5,6 – bl Biblioteca [072]

Rebentisch, J F *see* PRODROMUS FLORAE NEOMARCHICAE

THE REBIRTH OF THE HISTORIC OLD HOLE-IN-THE-ROCK TRAIL AS A RECREATIONAL TRAIL / Black, William L – Brigham Young University, 1995 – 3mf – 9 – $12.00 – RC 495 – us Microform Publ [790]

Rebmann, Georg F *see* COUP-D OEIL SUR LES QUATRE DEPARTEMENTS DE LA RIVE GAUCHE DU RHIN

Rebmann, Johannes *see* A NIKA-ENGLISH DICTIONARY.

Rebollo Parras, Francisco *see* MAR DE FONFO

Rebollo Torio, Miguel Angel *see* ESTUDIOS SOBRE EL VOCABULARIO POLITICO ESPANOL (1931-1971). TESIS DOCTORAL

REBOQUE : CRITICO E NOTICIOSO – Pilar, Alagoas. 9, 22 Set 1891 – 1,5,6 – bl Biblioteca [072]

Reboucas, Andre *see* DIARIO Y NOTAS AUTOBIOGRAFICAS

Recalde, Facundo *see* EVOCACION DE ORTIZ GUERRERO

Recalde, I de *see* ECRITS DES CURES DE PARIS CONTRE LA POLITIQUE ET LA MORALE DES JESUITES (1656) AVEC UNE ETUDE SUR LA QUERELLE DU LAXISME

RECALLED TO LIFE / Allen, Grant – Bristol: J. W. Arrowsmith, 1891?. 05062. (Pre-1900 Canadiana) – 9 – cn C.I.H.M. [830]

RECAPITULATIO MUNDI : DER REKAPITULATIONSBEGRIFF DES HL. IRENAEUS / Scharl, E – Freiburg, 1941 – 3mf – 9 – ne Slangenburg [240]

RECAPITULATION, BY DISTRICTS AND COUNTIES, OF THE RETURNS OF THE ENUMERATION OF THE INHABITANTS OF LOWER CANADA / Canada. Bureau d'Enregistrement et de Statistiques – Montreal: Printed by Stewart & George Desbarats, 1846. SEM105P235 – 2mf – 9 – Can$4.50 – cn Bibl Nat [310]

RECAPITULATION, PAR DISTRICTS ET COMTES, DES RETOURS DU DENOMBREMENT DES HABITANTS DU BAS-CANADA.. / Canada. Bureau d'Enregistrement et de Statistiques – Montreal: Imprime par Stewart & George Desbarats, 1846. SEM105P234 – 2mf – 9 – Can$4.50 – cn Bibl Nat [310]

Recchini de Lattes, Zulma L *see* MIGRACIONES EN LA ARGENTINA

Receb, M ibn-i *see* NEVHAT UEL-'USSAK

RECEIPT BOOK / Brisbane, William – 1800-03, 1809-21. 3 fiches – 9 – us South Carolina Historical [978]

RECEIPT BOOK / Crawford, William – 1793-1802. 2 fiches – 9 – us South Carolina Historical [025]

RECEIPTS / Berkeley County. South Carolina. St. John's Parish – 1932. 2 fiches – 9 – us South Carolina Historical [240]

RECEIPTS AND EXPENDITURES RECORD / Lucas County. Ohio. Toledo, City Park Commission – 1908-1915 – 1r – 1 – $32.50r – us Archival [324]

RECEIPTS AND EXPENDITURES RECORD / Ottawa County. Ohio. Carroll Township. Board of Education – 1914-1928 – 1r – 1 – $32.50r – us Archival [324]

RECEIPTS AND EXPENDITURES RECORD / Ottawa County. Ohio. Carroll Township. Township Clerk – 1914-1928 – 1r – 1 – $32.50r – us Archival [324]

RECEIPTS AND EXPENDITURES RECORD / Van Wert County. Ohio. County Home – 1867-1936 – 2r – 1 – $32.50r – us Archival [324]

RECEIPTS AND EXPENDITURES RECORD / Wyandot County. Ohio. County Home – 1878-1917 – 1r – 1 – $32.50r – us Archival [324]

RECEIPTS JOURNAL / Hancock County. Ohio. Biglick Township. Township Clerk – 1968-1988 – 1r – 1 – $32.50r – us Archival [324]

RECENSEMENT, COMPAGNIE DES INDES (1741) / Montreal. Archives judiciaires – Montreal, Canada – 1r – 1 – cn Can Microfilming [310]

RECENSEMENT D'AGBOVILLE. EXPLOITATION MECANOGRAPHIQUE / Ancey, G – (Africa series). 1968 – 9 – fr Hachette [960]

RECENSEMENT DE LA VILLE DE QUEBEC POUR 1716 / Beaudet, Louis – Quebec: A. Cote, 1887. 02966. (Pre-1900 Canadiana) – 9 – cn C.I.H.M. [971]

RECENSEMENT DE L'INDUSTRIE AU LIBAN RESULTATS POUR 1964 / Lebanon. Direction Centrale de la Statistique – 1964. BNE-19.702 1 – 9 – ne IDC [338]

LE RECENSEMENT DE QUIRINIUS EN JUDEE / Lutteroth, Henri – Paris: Ch. Meyrueis, 1865. 1 fiche – 9 – us A.T.L.A. [240]

RECENSEMENT DEMOGRAPHIQUE DE SAN PEDRO / Chevassu, J – (Africa series). 1970 – 9 – fr Hachette [304]

RECENSEMENT DEMOGRAPHIQUE, JUIN 1960: POPULATION LEGALE DU MAROC / Morocco. Service Central des Statistiques – 2v. 1961. BNE-3094 1 – 9 – ne IDC [304]

RECENSEMENT DEMOGRAPHIQUE, JUIN 1960: POPULATION RURALE DU MAROC / Morocco. Service Central des Statistiques – 1962. BNE-3097 1 – 9 – ne IDC [310]

RECENSEMENT DU CANADA, 1861 : ORIGINE ET RELIGION – Quebec: Imp. S B Foote, a son etablissement de presses a calorique, 1862. SEM105P241 – 2mf – 9 – Can$4.50 – cn Bibl Nat [310]

RECENSEMENT ETHNOLOGIQUE DE LA VALLEE DE HOUAILOU / Leenhardt, Maurice – 9 – F150.00 – fr Ethnologie [980]

RECENSEMENT GENERAL DE LA POPULATION 1966: SITUATION DE RESIDENCE PAR COMMUNE / Algeria. Commissariat National au Recensement de la Population – 1967? BNE-8623 1 – 9 – ne IDC [310]

RECENSEMENT GENERAL DE LA POPULATION ET DE L'HABITAT / Algeria. Commissariat National au Recensement de la Population – 1966. Donnees demographiques complementaires, donnees sur l'habitat. 1968. BNE-8711 1 – 9 – ne IDC [310]

RECENSEMENT GENERAL DE LA POPULATION ET DE L'HABITAT, 1966 / Algeria. Commissariat National au Recensement de la Population – Donnees abregees, resultats du sondage. 1967. BNE-8712 1 – 9 – ne IDC [310]

RECENSEMENT GENERAL DE LA POPULATION ET DE L'HABITAT, 1966: CARACTERISTIQUES SOCIO-ECONOMIQUES DE LA POPULATION; EXPLOITATION PAR SONDAGE / Algeria. Commissariat National au Recensement de la Population – 1967. BNE-8624 1 – 9 – ne IDC [310]

RECENSEMENT GENERAL DE LA POPULATION ET DE L'HABITAT, 1971 / Morocco. Secretariat d'Etat au Plan – Serie "S". Resultats du sondage au 1 10. 1972-74. BNE-3114 1 – 9 – ne IDC [310]

RECENSEMENT GENERAL DE L'EGYPTE : 1ER JUIN 1897 : 1ER MOHARREN 1315 / Egypt. Maslahat al-Ihsa wa-al-Tadad – Le Caire: Impr Nationale, 1898 – us Res Libr [310]

RECENSIO CRITICA ARANEARUM SUECICARUM / Thorell, T T T – Z 2204 2. 1856 – 8 – ne IDC [590]

RECENSIO ORTHOPTERORUM : REVUE CRITIQUE DES ORTHOPTERES DECRITS PAR LINNE, DE GEER ET THUNBERG / ed by Stal, C – Stockholm, 1873-1875 – 3 vols – 8 – ne IDC [590]

RECENSUS OMNIUM LECTIONUM QUIBUS CODEX SINAITICUS DISCREPAT / Buttmann, Philipp Karl – Lipsiae: B.G. Tuebner, 1865. 1 fiche – 9 – us A.T.L.A. [220]

RECENT ACHIEVEMENTS IN ESKIMO RESEARCH / Birket-Smith, K – BN 466 2. 1951 – 8 – ne IDC [306]

RECENT AND PROSPECTIVE DEVELOPMENT IN CANADA: BEING A PAPER READ BEFORE THE FELLOWS OF THE ROYAL COLONIAL INSTITUTE, JANUARY 12, 1886 / Colmer, Joseph Grose – (London: McCorquodale), 1886. 05257. (Pre-1900 Canadiana) – 9 – cn C.I.H.M. [971]

RECENT ARCHAEOLOGICAL DISCOVERIES IN INDIA / Thapar, B K – 1986 – xiii/172p – 9 – 92-3-102385-3 – fr UNESCO [930]

RECENT ARCHAEOLOGICAL DISCOVERIES IN PAKISTAN / Dani, Ahmad Hassan – 1988 – xiv/107p – 9 – 92-3-102466-3 – fr UNESCO [930]

RECENT ARCHAEOLOGICAL DISCOVERIES IN THE REPUBLIC OF KOREA / Won-Yong, Kim – 1983 – 104p – 9 – 92-3-102001-3 – fr UNESCO [930]

RECENT DEVELOPMENTS IN EDUCATION / Papua New Guinea. Department of Education – (In English) – Port Moresby, c1971 – 1mf – 9 – DE-242/1 – ne IDC [370]

RECENT DEVELOPMENTS IN INTERNATIONAL LAW / Garner, J W – Calcutta, 1925 – 9mf – 1 – ILM-2384/1 – ne IDC [327]

RECENT DISCUSSIONS IN SCIENCE, PHILOSOPHY, AND MORALS / Spencer, Herbert – New and enl. ed. New York: Appleton, 1882. 349p. ill – 1 – us U.W. Library [190]

RECENT EXPLORATIONS ALONG THE SOUTH AND EAST COAST OF VICTORIA LAND / Rae, J – N 356. 1852 – 9 – ne IDC [910]

RECENT EXPLORATIONS TO THE SOUTH OF HUDSON BAY / Bell, Robert – London: Clowes, 1897?. 00106. (Pre-1900 Canadiana) – 9 – cn C.I.H.M. [550]

THE RECENT FORAMINIFERA OF GREAT BRITAIN / Williamson, W C – 1858 – 1. 28.00; ; 7 – uk Microform Academic [590]

RECENT INQUIRIES IN THEOLOGY BY EMINENT ENGLISH CHURCHMEN, BEING "ESSAYS AND REVIEWS." / Hedge, Frederic Henry – 1860 – 9 – us A.T.L.A. [240]

RECENT MEMOIRS ON THE CETACEA / Flower, H F – Ray Society. 1866 – 1 £35.00 7 £56.00 – uk Microform Academic [590]

THE RECENT MOVEMENT TOWARD CHRISTIAN UNITY / Vedder, Henry Clay – Chester, Pa.: Seminary Bookstore, 1910 – 1mf – us A.T.L.A. [240]

RECENT RESEARCH IN COOPERATIVE EXTENSION WORK / Wisconsin. Agricultural Extension Service – no.1-64. Nov 1958-Oct 1969 – 1,5 – us Spaulding [630]

RECENT SCHOOL LAW DECISIONS / Smith, Lyndon Ambrose – Washington, D.C.: Govt. Print. Off., 1883. 82p. LL-10947 – 1 – us L of C Photodup [340]

RECENT TRENDS AND DEVELOPMENTS IN EDUCATIONAL PSYCHOLOGY : CHINESE AND AMERICAN PERSPECTIVES – 1995 – 9 – 92-3-102980-0 – fr UNESCO [150]

RECENT TRENDS IN THE FISHERIES AND ENVIRONMENT IN THE GFCM AREA – 1990 – 78p – it F.A.O. [639]

RECEPTION REPORTS AND LETTERS RECEIVED / KFKB Radio, Milford, KS – 1924-1928 – 1 – us KS Hist [380]

RECEPTORS AND CHANNELS : THE INTERNATIONAL JOURNAL OF RECEPTORS, CHANNELS AND TRANSPORTERS / ed by Barnard, Eric A – 9,5,1 – us Harwood [574]

DIE RECESSE UND ANDERE AKTEN DER HANSETAGE, 1256-1430 / Leipzig. Hansetage. Hanserecesse – v1-8. Leipzig. 1870-97. B-2407 2 – 8 – ne IDC [943]

RECESSIONS, DEPRESSIONS, AND ECONOMIC PANICS IN AMERICAN HISTORY: COLLECTION OF SOURCES – An original microform collection which includes documentary, investigative and narrative sources pertaining to economic disturbances throughout American history. 1815-1974. Printed guide – 1 – $675.00 – 0-89093-012-0 – us UPA [970]

RECEUIL DES CHARTES DE L'ABBAYE DE GEMBLOUX / Roland, C-G – Gembloux, 1921 – Dfl28.00 – ne Slangenburg [240]

RECEUIL DES CHARTES DE L'ABBAYE DE STAVELOT-MALMEDY / Halkin, J & Roland, C-G – Bruxelles. v1-2. 1909-30 – 23mf – 8 – Dfl154.00 – ne Slangenburg [240]

RECEUIL DES CHARTES DU PRIEURE DE SAINT-BERTIN A POPERINGHE, ET DE SES DEPENDANCES / ed by d'Hoop, F-G – Bruges, 1870 – Dfl56.00 – ne Slangenburg [240]

RECH / Russia – St. Petersburg. 1906-17 – 1 – us UMI [900]

RECH' – St Petersburg, 1908-09 – 5r – 1 – us Ross [947]

RECHENSCHAFTS-BERICHT / Gewerkschaftskommission. Berlin – 1 Jan-Dec 1897. (Serial publications of German trade unions in the Memorial Library, University of Wisconsin-Madison) – 1 – us U.W. Library [330]

RECHENSCHAFTSBERICHT / Deutsche Angestelltenschaft – Hamburg. Hanseatische Verlagsanstalt. 1927. illus. (Serial publications of German trade unions in the Memorial Library, University of Wisconsin-Madison.) – 1 – us U.W. Library [073]

RECHENSCHAFTSBERICHT / Deutscher Handels- und Industrieangestellten-Verband – Hamburg, Verlegt bei der Hanseatischen Verlagsanstalt Aktiengesellschaft. 1929. illus. (Serial publications of German trade unions in the Memorial Library, University of Wisconsin-Madison.) – 1 – us U.W. Library [330]

RECHENSCHAFTSBERICHT / Generalkommission der Gewerkschaften Deutschlands – Berlin. 1914-19. (Serial publications of German trade unions in the Memorial Library, University of Wisconsin-Madison.) – 1 – us U.W. Library [330]

RECHENSCHAFTSBERICHT DES VORSTANDES / Zentralverband der Handels-, Transport-, und Verkehrsarbeiter und Arbeiterinnen Deutschlands – Berlin. 1905 06. (Serial publications of German trade unions in the Memorial Library, University of Wisconsin-Madison.) – 1 – us U.W. Library [330]

RECHENSCHAFTS-BERICHT UEBER DIE AMTSWIRKSAMKEIT DES MAEHRISCHEN LANDESAUSSCHUSSES / Moravia. Landesausschuss – 1869-1910. 1888-94, 1896-1900 wanting – 1 – 113.00 – us L of C Photodup [943]

RECHENSCHAFTSBERICHTE / Verband der deutschen Buchdrucker – Berlin. 1901-04, 1906, 1909-10, 1914-16, 1918. Title varies: Bericht or Jahresbericht. (Serial publications of German trade unions in the Memorial Library, University of Wisconsin-Madison.) – 1 – us U.W. Library [330]

LE RECHERCHE DES FEUX EN BOURGOGNE AUX 14E ET 15E SIECLES / Garnier, Joseph – Dijon, 1876. 222p. (Historical Studies Series) – 9 – 9.00 – fr Bibl Nationale [944]

RECHERCHE D'UNE DIFFERENCIATION GENETIQUE AU SEIN DE POPULATIONS ICHTHYIQUES MARINES ET LAGUNAIRES DU GOLFE DU LION / Benharrat, K M – Analyse du polymorphisme enzymatique chez Gobius niger, Blennius pavo et Engraulis encrasicolus – 9 – F40.00 – fr Ethnologie [590]

RECHERCHE SUR LA TOXICITE DES PEINTURES ANTISALISSURES A BASE D'ORGANOSTANNIQUES ET DE L'OXYDE DE TRIBUTYLETAIN VIS-A-VIS DE L'HUITRE CRASSOSTREA GIGAS / Gendron, F – 9 – F70.00 – fr Ethnologie [574]

RECHERCHE SUR LE VOCABULAIRE DU GENERAL DE GAULLE / Cotteret, J M et al – Analyse statistique des Allocations radiodiffusées – 5mf – 9 – F70.00 – fr Ethnologie [440]

RECHERCHES AFRICAINES / Institut National de Recherche et de Documentation – NS. Conakry, 1959-63 – 24mf – 9 – A-379/2 – ne IDC [960]

RECHERCHES ANATOMIQUES ET MORPHOLOGIQUES SUR LES MOUSSES / Schimper, W P – Strasbourg. 1848. B-1271 2 – 8 – ne IDC [580]

RECHERCHES ANATOMIQUES ET PHYSIOLOGIQUES SUR LA STRUCTURE INTIME DES ANIMAUX ET DES VEGETAUX, ET SUR LEUR MOTILETE / Dutrochet, R J Henri – Paris. 1824. B-5441 2 – 8 – ne IDC [580]

RECHERCHES ANATOMIQUES SUR LES MELOBESIEES / Rosanoff, S – Paris, Cherbourg. 1866. B-6404 2 – 8 – ne IDC [580]

RECHERCHES ANTOMICO-PATHOLOGIQUES SUR LA PHTHISIE / Louis, P C A – M-67. 1825 – 9 – ne IDC [611]

RECHERCHES ARCHEOLOGIQUES ET HISTORIQUES SUR PEKIN ET SES ENVIRONS / Bretschneider – 1879 – 9 – fr Orientalistes [930]

RECHERCHES CHIMIQUES SUR LES CORPS GRAS D'ORIGINE ANIMALE / Chevreul, Eugene – Paris: Levraut, 1823 – 1 – F257.12 – fr Armell [540]

RECHERCHES CHIMIQUES SUR PLUSIEURS CORPS GRAS ET PARTICULIEREMENT SUR LEURS COMBINAISONS AVEC LES ALCALIS / Chevreul, Eugene – 1 – F184.07 – fr Armell [540]

RECHERCHES CYTOLOGIQUES ET TAXONOMIQUES SUR LES BASIDIOMYCEA6TES / Maire, R – Paris, 1902. 209 pp. (Bull. Soc. Mycologique de France, v. 18). B-5099 2 – 8 – ne IDC [580]

RECHERCHES D'ANTHROPOLOGIE CRIMINELLE CHEZ L'ENFANT. CRIMINALITE ET DEGENERESCENCE / Maupate, Leon – (French Precursors of Psychiatry Series). Lyon. A. Storck. s.d – 9 – fr Hachette [150]

RECHERCHES DE BIONOMIE DESCRIPTIVE ET EXPERIMENTALE (IN VIVO ET IN VITRO) DANS QUELQUES BIOTOPES LITTORAUX SOUMIS A DES VARIATIONS NATURELLES OU ARTIFICIELLES DES CONDITIONS DU MILIEU (NOTAMMENT DANS L'ETANG DE BERRE ET LE GOLFE DE FOS) / Stora, G – 9 – F120.00 – fr Ethnologie [574]

RECHERCHES DE SCIENCE RELIGIEUSE – 1(1910)-42(1954) – 403mf – 9 – Dfl1,411.00 – ne Slangenburg [073]

RECHERCHES DE SCIENCE RELIGIEUSE – Paris. v1-42. 1910-1954 – 403mf – 9 – ne IDC [210]

RECHERCHES DE THEOLOGIE ANCIENNE ET MEDIEVALE – 1(1929)-19(1952) – 147mf – 9 – Dfl515.00 – ne Slangenburg [073]

RECHERCHES DE THEOLOGIE ANCIENNE ET MEDIEVALE – Louvain. v1-19. 1929-1952 – 147mf – 9 – ne IDC [240]

RECHERCHES DES CAUSES DE LA RICHESSE ET DE LA MISERE DES PEUPLES CIVILISES / Morogues, Bigot de – (Condition of 19th C. French working class series). 1834 – 9 – fr Hachette [360]

RECHERCHES ECONOMIQUES. SUR LE DEPARTEMENT DE LA LOIRE-INFERIEURE / Huet de Coetlizan, Jean-Baptiste – an XII – 9 – fr Hachette [944]

RECHERCHES ET DEBATS : DU CENTRE CATHOLIQUE DES INTELLECUELS FRANCAIS – NS: 28 – 3mf – 9 – Dfl13.00 – ne Slangenburg [073]

RECHERCHES ET DOUTES SUR LE MAGNETISME ANIMAL / Thouret, Michel Augustin – Paris: Prault, 1784 – 1 – us U.W. Library [150]

RECHERCHES, EXPERIENCES ET OBSERVATIONS PHYSIOLOGIQUES SUR L'HOMME DANS L'ETAT DE SOMNAMBULISME / Puysegur, Jacques C de – Paris. 1881 – 9 – fr Hachette [150]

RECHERCHES GENEALOGIQUES SUR LES FAMILLES D'ANJOU / Audouys – 1802. 18v, tables – 6r – F2,528.90 – fr Armell [920]

RECHERCHES GENERALES SUR LA MORTALITE ET LA MULTIPLICATION DU GENRE HUMAIN / Euler – Reprod. d'un article de: Memoires de l'Academie royale des Sciences et Belles-Lettres. v16, 1760. p144-64. 1 fiche. (Statistics Series: Medical Studies) – 9 – 6.00 – fr Bibl Nationale [310]

RECHERCHES GEOGRAPHIQUES SUR L'AFRIQUE CENTRALE D'APRES LES ECRITS D'EDRISI ET DE LEON L'AFRICAIN / Latreille – Paris, Mme Veuve Agasse. 1824 – 9 – 5.00 – fr Orientalistes [910]

RECHERCHES GEOGRAPHIQUES SUR L'INTERIEUR DE L'AFRIQUE SEPTENTRIONALE / Walckenaer, C A – Traduction de l'anglais. Paris. 1821 – 9 – 15.00 – fr Orientalistes [910]

RECHERCHES HISTORIQUES – Le Bulletin d'Archea1ologie d'Histoire. Lea1vis Quebec. v. 1-36. 1895-1930 – 1 – us NY Public [930]

RECHERCHES HISTORIQUES SUR CETTE TRADITION QUE LA MORT DANS LA COMPAGNIE DE JESUS EST UN GAGE CERTAIN DE PREDESTINATION / Terrien, Jacques – (Includes bibliographical references and index) – nouv rev augm ed. Poitiers: Imprimerie Oudin, 1883 – 1mf – 9 – 0-8370-9425-9 – 1986-3425 – us A.T.L.A. [240]

RECHERCHES HISTORIQUES SUR LES MAURES ET HISTOIRE DE L'EMPIRE DE MAROC PAR M. DE CHENIER, CHARGE DES AFFAIRES DU ROI AUPRES DE L'EMPEREUR DU MAROC / Chenier, LS de – (African Library series). 1787 – 9 – fr Hachette [960]

RECHERCHES ITALIENNES ET FRANCOISES / Oudin, A – 1640, 1642 – 9 – fr I.C.S. [440]

RECHERCHES LANGUE OUOLOFE, SUIVIES D'UN VOCABULAIRE ABREGE FRANCAIS-OUOLOF / Roger, Jacques F – Paris, Dondey-Dupre. 1829 – 9 – $7.50 – fr Orientalistes [490]

RECHERCHES PHILOSOPHIQUES SUR LES PREMIERS OBJECTS DES CONNAISSANCES MORALES – DEMONSTRATION PHILOSOPHIQUE DU PRINCIPE CONSTITUTIF DE LA SOCIETE – MEDITATIONS POLITIQUES TIREES DE L'EVANGILE / Bonald, Louis Gabriel Ambroise, Vicomte de – Paris: Adrien Le Clere, 1858 – 2mf – 9 – 0-8370-6163-6 – 1986-0163 – us A.T.L.A. [170]

RECHERCHES SOCIOGRAPHIQUES – v1- 1960-1; v17- 5,6,9 – us UMI [300]

RECHERCHES SOCIOGRAPHIQUES / Departement de sociologie, Universite Laval – Quebec: Presses universitaires Laval. v1- 1960-. SEM16P316 – 5r – 5 – Can$194.00 – cn Bibl Nat [300]

RECHERCHES STATISTIQUES SUR LA POPULATION DES 485 COMMUNES DE L'YONNE PENDANT 80 ANS: 1801-81 / Billeau, Fernand – Reprod. de trois extraits de "l'Annuaire historique de Departement de l'Yonne, 1883-85. 1 fiche. (Statistics Series: Demography) – 9 – 6.00 – fr Bibl Nationale [310]

RECHERCHES STATISTIQUES SUR LA POPULATION DES ARDENNES AVANT LE 19EME SIECLE / Collinet, Paul – Reprod. des extraits de la Revue d'Ardenne et d'Argonne, 1900-01. p109-14, 191-98. 1 fiche. (Statistics Series: Demography) – 9 – 6.00 – fr Bibl Nationale [310]

RECHERCHES STATISTIQUES SUR LA VILLE DE PARIS ET LE DEPARTEMENT DE LA SEINE: RECUEIL DE TABLEAUX. – Paris: Imp. Royale, 1833; P. Dupont, 1832-60 pour les v2-6. 26 fiches. (Statistics Series: Demography) – 9 – 64.00 – fr Bibl Nationale [310]

RECHERCHES STATISTIQUES SUR L'ESCLAVAGE COLONIAL ET SUR LES MOYENS DE LE SUPPRIMER / Moreau de Jonnes, Alexandre – Paris, Bourgogne et Martinet. 1842 – 9 – 7.50 – fr Orientalistes [305]

RECHERCHES STATISTIQUES SUR L'ESCLAVAGE COLONIAL ET SUR LES MOYENS DE LE SUPPRIMER / Moreau de Jonnes, Alexandre – (Slave Trade and Abolitionism in France series). 1842 – 9 – fr Hachette [310]

RECHERCHES STATISTIQUES SUR L'HYGIENE ET LA MORTALITE DE LA VILLE DE RENNES / Toulmouche, A – Reprod. de trois extraits des Annales d'Hygiene publique et de Medicine legale. v41-42, 1849, p30-67, 318-353, 21-37. 1 fiche. (Statistics Series: Medical Studies) – 9 – 6.00 – fr Bibl Nationale [310]

RECHERCHES SUR LA CAUSE ET SUR LA VERITABLE TEORIE DE L'ELECTRICITE / Bose, George Mathias – Wittembergue: J. F. Slomac, 1745 – 1 – us U.W. Library [621]

RECHERCHES SUR LA CHALEUR DEVELOPPEE DANS LA COMBUSTION, ET DANS LA CONDENSATION DES VAPEURS / Rumford, Benjamin T – Paris, F. Didot, 1812, 102 p. Histoire des Sciences XVIIe-XIXe Siecles. 7996 – 9 – fr Hachette [530]

RECHERCHES SUR LA FAUNE DE MADAGASCAR / Pollen, FPL & Dam, D C van – Z 218 2. 1866 – 8 – ne IDC [580]

RECHERCHES SUR LA LEGISLATION CRIMINELLE ET LA PROCEDURE DES CAMBODGIENS / Leclere, Adhemard – Paris, Challamel, 1894. 555 p. LL-10011 – 1 – us L of C Photodup [340]

RECHERCHES SUR LA PERSONNALITE INTERNATIONALE DE L'INDIVIDU / Guerry, E – Paris, 1923 – 3mf – 1 – ILM-1538/1 – ne IDC [327]

RECHERCHES SUR LA PHTHISIE PULMONAIRE / Bayle, G L – M-37. 1810 – 9 – ne IDC [610]

RECHERCHES SUR LA POPULATION DES GENERALITES D'AUVERGNE, DE LYON, DE ROUEN, ET DE QUELQUES PROVINCES ET VILLES DU ROYAUME. / Messance, receveur des tailles – s.l., s.d. 4 fiches. (Statistics Series: Demography) – 9 – 10.00 – fr Bibl Nationale [310]

RECHERCHES SUR LA POPULATION, LES NAISSANCES, LES DECES, LES PRISONS, LES DEPOTS DE MENDICITE, ETC...DANS LE ROYAUME DES PAYS-BAS / Quetelet, Adolphe Lambert Jacques – Bruxelles, H. Tarlier, 1827, 90 p., pl. 2 fiches. (Statistics Series: Demography) – 9 – 6.00 – fr Bibl Nationale [310]

RECHERCHES SUR LA PRIORITE DE LA DECOUVERTE DES PAYS SITUES SUR LA COTE OCCIDENTALE D'AFRIQUE / Santarem – Paris, Vve Dondey-Dupre. 1842 – 9 – 12.50 – fr Orientalistes [910]

RECHERCHES SUR LA STRUCTURE DE L'IMAGINAIRE DANS LES CONFESSIONS DE SAINT AUGUSTIN : TOME 1: TEXTE. TOME 2: NOTES. TOME 3: ANNEXES / Cambronne, P – 1982 – 13mf – 9 – Bf800.00 – 2-85121-045-9 – fr Augustiniennes [240]

RECHERCHES SUR LA STRUCTURE DU DISCOURS ORAL SPONTANE / Luzzati, D – 9 – F90.00 – fr Ethnologie [400]

RECHERCHES SUR LA VIE D'UNE COMMUNE DU COTENTIN-BIVILLE (HAGUE) / Navet, E – 9 – F50.00 – fr Ethnologie [305]

RECHERCHES SUR LE PAUPERISME ET SUR LES MOYENS D'Y REMEDIER / Saint Vincent, Philippe de – Metz: S. Lamort, 1847. 61p. 1 fiche. (Political Science Collection). (La Condition ouvriere. Part Two) – 9 – 6.00 – fr Bibl Nationale [360]

RECHERCHES SUR LE RANPORT EXISTANT ENTRE LE NOMBRE DES MORT-NES ET CELUI DES DECES, A PARIS, PENDANT TREIZE ANNEES, DE 1846 A 1858. / Deville, D – Paris, Delarue, 18, 1 fiche. (Statistics Series: Medical Studies) – 9 – 6.00 – fr Bibl Nationale [310]

RECHERCHES SUR LES CAUSES DE L'INDIGENCE / Clement, Ambroise – (Condition of 19th C. French working class series). 1846 – 9 – fr Hachette [360]

RECHERCHES SUR LES CONSOMMATIONS DE TOUT GENRE DE LA VILLE DE PARIS; COMPAREES A CE QU'ELLES ETAIENT EN 1789 / Benoiston de Chateauneuf – (Condition of 19th C. French working class series). 1821 – 9 – fr Hachette [310]

RECHERCHES SUR LES COURBES A DOUBLE COURBURE / Clairaut, Alexis-Claude – Paris, Nyon, Didot et Quillau, 1731, vii plus 122 p. Histoire des Sciences XVIIe-XIXe Siecles. 7967 – 9 – fr Hachette [500]

RECHERCHES SUR LES ENTOZOAIRES DES INSECTES: ORGANISATION ET DEVELOPPEMENT DES OXYURIDES / Galeb, O – Paris, 1879 – 108p, 10 pls. (Archiv.Zool. Exper., v7) – 8 – ne IDC [590]

RECHERCHES SUR LES LANGUES ANCIENNES ET MODERNES DE LA SUISSE, ET PRINCIPALEMENT DU PAYS DE VAUD / Bertrand, E – Geneve, 1758 – 1mf – 9 – ne IDC [440]

RECHERCHES SUR LES MIRACLES – (D'Holbach series). 1773 – 9 – fr Hachette [240]

RECHERCHES SUR LES OSSEMENTS FOSSILES DE QUADRUPEDES / ed by Cuvier, Georges – Ed 4. Paris. 10v. 1834-36; Atlas 2v – 130mf – 9 – 2554/2 – ne IDC [560]

RECHERCHES SUR LES PEUPLEMENTS SCIAPHILES DES RECIFS CORALLIENS DE LA REGION DE TULEAR (S.W. DE MADAGASCAR) / Vasseur, P – 9 – F180.00 – fr Ethnologie [574]

RECHERCHES SUR LES POISSONS FOSSILES / ed by Agassiz, Louis – 5V. Neuchatel. 1833-44 – 102mf – 9 – ne IDC [560]

RECHERCHES SUR LES SYSTEMES DES ZONES ARIDES DU MALI : RESULTATS PRELIMINAIRES / Wilson, R T et al – 1983 – 9 – $12.00 – et ILRI [630]

RECHERCHES SUR LES VOYAGES ET DECOUVERTES DES NAVIGATEURS NORMANDS, DANS LES INDES ORIENTALES ET EN AMERIQUE / Estancelin, Louis – Paris, A. Pinard, Delaunay. 1832 – 9 – 10.00 – fr Orientalistes [910]

RECHERCHES SUR L'ICONOGRAPHIE DE L'EVANGILE, AUX 14E / Millet, G – XVe Et XVIe Siecles. O 374. 1916 – 9 – ne IDC [240]

RECHERCHES SUR L'IDENTITE DES FORCES CHIMIQUES ET ELECTRIQUES / Oersted, Hans – Trad. de l'allemand, Paris, 1813, xx, 259 p., 1 pl. Histoire des Sciences XVIIe-XIXe Siecles. 7994 – 9 – fr Hachette [530]

RECHERCHES SUR L'ORGANISATION, LA FRUCTIFICATION ET LA CLASSIFICATION DE PLUSIEURS GENRES D'ALGUES / Chauvin, J F – Caen. 1842 – 8 – ne IDC [580]

RECHERCHES SUR L'ORIGINE DU DESPOTISME ORIENTAL / Boulanger, Nicolas A – (D'Holbach series). 1761 – 9 – fr Hachette [321]

RECHERCHES...SUR LA MALADIE CONNUE SOUS LES NOMS DE GASTRO-ENTERITE,... / Louis, P C A – (Missing: V.1,p. 1-45) – Paris, 1829. 2v – 19mf – 9 – ne IDC [616]

RECHEUTE DE GENEVE PLAGIAIRE / Coton, P – Lyon, 1619 – 10mf – 9 – CA-123/1 – ne IDC [240]

RECHI I STAT'I / Chuprov, A I – (s prilozheniem: Ukazatel' pechatnykh trudov A.I. Chuprova). Moscow, 1909. v1-3. BR-10,564/1 – 9 – ne IDC [947]

RECHI I STAT'I / Goldshtein, ML – Parizh: Izd. Rodnik, 1929. 211p. 1 reel. 1276 – 1 – us U.W. Library [340]

RECHI KONSERVATORA / Meshcherskii, Vladimir P – Ed. 2. v. 1-2. Spb. 1876. BR-10.603 2 – 8 – ne IDC [460]

RECHI, PROIZNESENNYIA. V TORZHESTVENNYKH I PROCHIKH SOBRANIIAKH, 1830-1872 / Pogodin, M P – M. 1872. BR-8329 2 – 8 – ne IDC [947]

RECHNO I TRANSPORT – (Library has: June-July/Aug. 1945; Feb. 1947; May/June-Nov./Dec. 1948) – Moskva: "Rechizdat", 1941-1953. 13v – 1 – CSUX89-S922 – us Hoover Inst Photo [338]

RECHOWOUS – Amsterdam. nos1-9. 1926-28 – 1mf – 9 – J-261-107/1 – ne IDC [949]

DAS RECHT AUF ARBEIT – Muenchen, may 28 1884-apr 17 1887 – 1r – 1 – gw Mikrofilm [360]

DAS RECHT DER DONAUSCHIFFAHRT... / Buch, F F – Wuerzburg, 1927 – 1mf – 1 – ILM-1826/1 – ne IDC [327]

DAS RECHT DER HAGESTOLZE : EINE HEIRATSGESCHICHTE AUS DEM NECKARTHAL / Wolff, Julius – Berlin: G Grote, 1893 – 1r – 1 – us U.W. Library [830]

DAS RECHT DER LUFTSCHIFFAHRT / Eswein, F L – Frankenthal, 1910 – 1mf – 1 – ILM-1659/1 – ne IDC [327]

DAS RECHT DER STAATSANGEHOERIGKEIT ... SEIT DEM JAHRE 1870 / Binder, W – Schramberg, 1930 – 2mf – 9 – ILM-3460/1 – ne IDC [327]

RECHT GHEBRUYCK ENDE MISBRUYCK, VAN TIJDLICKE HAVE / Coornhert, D V – Amsterdam, 1610 – 1mf – 9 – ne IDC [700]

RECHT GHEBRUYCK ENDE MISBRUYCK VAN TYDLICKE HAVE / Coornhert, D V – Amsterdam, 1620 – 1mf – 9 – ne IDC [700]

RECHT VOOR ALLEN : ORGAAN VAN DE SOCIAALDEMOCRATISCHE PARTIJ VAN NEDERLAND – Amsterdam, 1900-27 – 1 – us Hoover Inst Photo [335]

RECHTE UND PFLICHTEN DER JUGENDLICHEN IM ARBEITSPROZESS / Noack, Ingolf – Berlin: Deutscher Zentralverlag, 1959. 334p. LL-4112 – 1 – us L of C Photodup [340]

RECHTE VND WARE MEINUNG VND VERSTAND GOETTLICHER SCHRIFFT VND DER AUGSPURGISCHEN BEKANDTNUS... / Eitzen, P von – [Hamburg, 1562] – 2mf – 9 – ne IDC [240]

DIE RECHTFERTIGUNG DES SUENDERS VOR GOTT : AUS DER HEILIGEN SCHRIFT / Preuss, Eduard – (Includes bibliographical references and subject and name index) – Berlin: Gustav Schlawitz, 1868 – 1mf – 9 – 0-8370-5127-4 – 1985-3127 – us A.T.L.A. [220]

DIE RECHTFERTIGUNG DES VOELKERRECHTS AUS DEM STAATSWILLEN / Drucker, P – Berlin, 1932 – 1mf – 9 – ILM-3364/1 – ne IDC [327]

DIE RECHTFERTIGUNGSLEHRE CALVINS : UND IHRE BEDEUTUNG FUER SEINE FROEMMIGKEIT / Luettge, Willy – Berlin: Reuther & Reichard, 1909 – 1mf – us A.T.L.A. [240]

DIE RECHTFERTIGUNGSLEHRE DES JOHANNES BRENZ / Kuegelgen, Constantin von – Leipzig: A. Deichert, 1899 – 1mf – us A.T.L.A. [240]

DIE RECHTLICHE NATUR DER NATURALISATION / Baumhoegger, M – Bonn, 1906 – 1mf – 9 – ILM-3149/1 – ne IDC [327]

DIE RECHTLICHE STELLUNG DER EVANGELISCHEN KIRCHE DEUTSCHLAND : IN IHRER GESCHICHTLICHEN ENTWICKELUNG BIS ZUR GEGENWART / Rieker, Karl – Leipzig: C.L. Hirschfeld, 1893 – 2mf – us A.T.L.A. [240]

DIE RECHTLICHE STELLUNG DER KATHOLISCHEN KIRCHE IM LANDESTEIL OLDENBURG UNTER BESONDERER BERUECKSICHTIGUNG DER GESCHICHTLICHEN ENTWICKLUNG / Wehage, Joseph – Vechta, 1928 – 72p – 9 – DM48.00 – 3-89349-050-7 – gw Hänsel [240]

RECHTLICHE UND POLITISCHE ASPEKTE DES GRUNDWASSERSCHUTZES IN DER BUNDESREPUBLIK DEUTSCHLAND / Muehlbauer, Manfred – 1993 – 2mf – 9 – DM98.00 – 3-89349-692-0 – gw Hänsel [332]

DIE RECHTS- UND GESCHAEFTSFAEHIGKEIT... / Frank, R – Giessen, 1908 – 1mf – 1 – ILM-3462/1 – ne IDC [327]

DIE RECHTSBEDINGUNG (CONDICIO IURIS) UNTERSUCHEUNGEN ZUM BURGERLICHEN RECHT UND ZUR ALLGEMEINEN RECHTSLEHRE / Oertmann, Paul Ernst Wilhelm – Leipzig: Deichertsche Verlagsbuchhandlung, 1924. 249p. LL-4113 – 1 – us L of C Photodup [340]

DER RECHTSERWERB VOM NICHTBERECHTIGTEN / Duden, K – Berlin, Leipzig, 1934 – 2mf – 9 – ILM-3038/1 – ne IDC [327]

RECHTSEXTREMISMUS IN DER BUNDESREPUBLIK DEUTSCHLAND – NEUE RECHTE UND REPUBLIKANER / Dudenhofen, Petra – 1994 – 2mf – DM80.00 – 3-8267-2033-4 – gw Hänsel [320]

DE RECHTSGEVOLGEN VAN HET HUWELIJK... / Baak, J M J – Leiden, 1928 – 2mf – 9 – ILM-3017/1 – ne IDC [340]

RECHTSREGLEMENT VOOR BURGERLIJKE- EN STRAFZAKEN IN BORNEO EN DE GROOTE OOST / Allied Forces. Southeast Asia Command. Netherlands Indies Civil Administration – SE-11,729 1. 15 April 1946 – 9 – ne IDC [980]

DER RECHTSSCHUTZ IM SCHWEDISCHEN VERWALTUNGSVERFAHREN / Forstmann, Max Dieter – 1995 – 6mf – 9 – DM118.00 – 3-8267-2091-1 – gw Hänsel [340]

DIE RECHTSSTAATLICHE BEDEUTUNG DER STAATSANWALTSCHAFT UNTER BESONDERER BERUECKSICHTIGUNG IHRER ROLLE IN DER NATIONALSOZIALISTISCHEN ZEIT / Riehle, Gerhard – Frankfurt a.M., 1985 – 5mf – 9 – DM104.00 – 3-89349-372-7 – gw Hänsel [340]

DIE RECHTSSTELLUNG DES VERWALTUNGSRATES NACH DEM AKTIENRECHT DER VEREINIGTEN STAATEN VON NORDAMERIKA / Escher, Andreas – Basel, Verlag fur Recht und Gesellschaft, 1954. 102 p. LL-493 – 1 – us L of C Photodup [340]

DE RECHTSTOESTAND IN NEDERLANDSCH-INDIE... / Lens, A – Leiden, 1889 – 1mf – 9 – ne IDC [950]

RECHTSVERHAELTNISSE DER KRIEGS- UND HANDELSSCHIFFE... / ed by Ferber, D – Kiel, 1895 – 1mf – 1 – ILM-1505/1 – ne IDC [327]

DIE RECHTSVERHAELTNISSE UND DER RECHTSSCHUTZ DES AUSLANDSDEUTSCHTUMS, ... / Bordihn, F – Berlin, 1920 – 1mf – 9 – ILM-1559/1 – ne IDC [327]

RECHTSWISSENSCHAFTLICHE BEITRAGE. JURISTICHE FESTGABE DES AUSLANDES ZU JOSEF KOHLERS SECHZIGSTE GEBURTSTAG 9 MARZ 1909 – Stuttgart, Enke, 1909. 202 p. LL-4083 – 1 – us L of C Photodup [340]

DE RECHTSZEKERHEID VAN DEN INLANDER IN NED: -INDIE, OP HET GEBIED VAN HET STRAFRECHT / Piepers, M C – Amsterdam. 1900. 98p. LL-4191 – 1 – us L of C Photodup [340]

LA RECIENTE ENCICLICA DEL PAPA SOBRE LA UNIDAD RELIGIOSA / Bayle, Constantino – Madrid: Razon y Fe, 1928 – 9 – sp Bibl Santa Ana [240]

Recinos, Adrian et al *see* ESTUDIOS

Recio Veganzones, Alejandro *see* ENSAYO BIBLIOGRAFICO SOBRE SAN PEDRO DE ALCANTARA

RECIPROCAL TRADE AGREEMENT BETWEEN UNITED STATES AND ARGENTINA : COMPLETE TEXT OF THE AGREEMENT AND AN ANALYSIS OF THE GENERAL PROVISIONS AND RECIPROCAL BENEFITS / Boston. First National Bank. Foreign Division – [Boston]: Foreign Division, The First National Bank of Boston, [1941] – 1 – CSUXAJL9763-B – us Hoover Inst Photo [337]

RECIT DE L'ADVENNEMENT DE LA ROYNE D'ALGERE EN LA VILLE DE ROME, ET COMMENT ELLE A ESTE BAPTIZEE AUEC SIX DE SES FILS, ... – Dovay, 1588 – 1mf – 9 – H-8206/1 – ne IDC [956]

RECIT DES DERNIERES VICTOIRES SVR LES TVRCQS, OBTENNVES PAR LES HONGROIS, ALLEMANS, POLAQVES, ET ITALIENS FLORENTINS, ... – Dovay, 1594 – 1mf – 9 – H-8211/1 – ne IDC [956]

RECIT DES FUNERAILLES D'ANNE DE BRETAGNE...AVEC UNE INTROD. ET DES NOTES PAR L. MERLET ET MAX. DE GOMBERT / Choque, Pierre – Paris: Aubry, 1858 – 1 – F82.55 – fr Armell [944]

RECIT D'UNE EXPLORATION COMMERCIALE EN ETHIOPIE... / Soleillet, Paul – Paris: Dreyfous et Dalsace, [1886] – 1 – F166.99 – fr Armell [910]

RECIT VERITABLE DE CE QUI S'EST FAIT ET PASSE A LOUVIERS, TOUCHANT LES RELIGIEUSES POSSEDEES – Paris. 1643 – 9 – fr Hachette [360]

RECIT VERITABLE DE CE QUI S'EST FAIT ET PASSE AUX EXORCISMES DE PLUSIEURS RELIGIEUSES DE LA VILLE DE LOUVIERS / Le Gauffre, Le P Thomas – Paris. 1643 – 9 – fr Hachette [360]

RECIT VERITABLE DE CE QUI S'EST PASSE A LOUDUN CONTRE MAISTRE URBAIN GRANDIER – Paris. 1634 – 9 – fr Hachette [360]

RECIT VERITABLE DE TOUT CE QUI EST ADVENU DIGNE DE MEMOIRE, TANT EN LA VILLE D'ANGERS, PAIS D'ANJOU ET AUTRES LIEUX CONTENUS AU PRESENT MANUSCRIPT... / Louvet, Jehan – (2 missing) – v8. 16th-17th c. – fr Armell [910]

RECIT VERITABLE DES CHOSES ESTRANGES ET PRODIGIEUSES ARRIVEES EN L'EXECUTION DE TROIS SORCIERS ET MAGICIENS DEFFAITS EN LA VILLE DE LYMOGES – Bordeaux. 1630 – 9 – fr Hachette [360]

RECITS DE GUERRE : PARIS ASSIEGE, 1870-1871 / Claretie, Jules – Paris, France. 1870-71 – 1r – 1 – cn Can Microfilming [944]

RECITS DE VOYAGES / Buies, Arthur – Quebec: C. Darveau, 1890. 00354. (Pre-1900 Canadiana) – 9 – cn C.I.H.M. [971]

RECITS DE VOYAGES / Buies, Arthur – Quebec: C Darveau, 1890. SEM105P26 – 3mf – 9 – Can$6.75 – cn Bibl Nat [910]

Reckert, Horst-Walter *see* NLP-ANKER-KOLLABIEREN ALS KURZZEITTHERAPIE VON STUDIERENDEN MIT PRUEFUNGSANST

RECKLINGHAEUSER ZEITUNG – Recklinghausen, West Germany. 1992- – 9r per yr – 1 – gw Mikrofilm [072]

Reckmann, Birgit *see* WELCHE BEDEUTUNG HAT DIE KONNEKTORREGION IN TRYPTOPHAN SYNTHASE AUS SACCHAROMYCES CEREVISIAE? REINIGUNG DES BIFUNKTIONELLEN ENZYMS UEBER EINEN GENTECHNISCHEN ANSATZ UND CHARAKTERISIERUNG DURCH PROTEOLYSE

RECLAMACAO DO BRASIL – Rio de Janeiro, 1822 – 1,5,6 – bl Biblioteca [072]

RECLAMATION AND RELATED LAWS ANNOTATED, 1866-1988 / U.S. Department of the Interior – (Suppl for v1-3 and the Reform Act of 1982. Updates planned) – v1-4. Washington: GPO, 1972; 1988-89 – 51mf – 9 – $76.00 – LLMC 80-502 – us L.L.M.C. [324]

RECLAMATION ERA – (v58-. Feb 1972-Apr 1983. 5,6. v62-. Spring 1976-Apr 1983. 9) – v1-. 1908-Apr 1983 – 1 – us UMI [574]

RECLAMATION REVIEW – v. 1-. 1978- – 5,6,9 – us UMI [574]

Reclus, Elisee *see*
- AFRICA
- DIE ANARCHIE
- RIECHO RUSSKO I REVOLIUTSII

Reclus, Maurice *see* JULES FERRY, 1832-1893

LES RECLUSERIES / Pavy, L-C – Lyon, 1875 – Dfl22.00 – ne Slangenburg [240]

RECOGNITIO MONOGRAPHICA RAMALINARUM / Nylander, W – (Bull. Soc. Linn. Normandie. S. II, v. 4). Caen. 1870. B-1552 2 – 8 – ne IDC [580]

RECOGNITION OF STUDIES AND COMPETENCE : IMPLEMENTATION OF CONVENTIONS DRAWN UP UNDER THE AEGIS OF UNESCO / Guiton, Jean & Charpantier, Jean – 1984 – 63p – 9 – 92-3-102017-X – fr UNESCO [370]

THE RECOGNITION OF THE SUPERNATURAL IN LETTERS AND IN LIFE: AN ORATION / Storrs, Richard Salter – New York: A.D.F. Randolph, 1881.1 fiche – 9 – us A.T.L.A. [130]

THE RECOGNITION POLICY OF THE UNITED STATES SINCE 1901 / Cole, T – N.p., 1928 – 2mf – 1 – ILM-1522/1 – ne IDC [327]

RECOGNOISSANCE PAR LAQUELLE IL CONFESSE QUE LUY ET CEUX QUI ONT ENSEIGNE ET ENSEIGNENT LES ANABAPTISTES. AVEC UN DISCOURS DES FAICTS EXERABLES DU NOUVEAU ROY DES ANABAPTISTES JAN WILHEMS ET DE SES COMPLICES / Philippe, Obbe – Leyde, A. Maire. 1595. BME-320 1 – 9 – ne IDC [240]

Recoleta Dominica, Santiago de Chile, Biblioteca *see* CATALOGO GENERAL POR ORDEN ALFABETICO DE AUTORES DE LA BIBLIOTECA DE LA RECOLECCION DOMINICANA DE SANTIAGO DE CHILE

RECOLLECTIONS / Gladden, Washington – Boston: Houghton Mifflin, 1909 – 2mf – us A.T.L.A. [920]

RECOLLECTIONS / Morley, John – London: Macmillan, 1917 – 1 roll – 1 – 1-55879-971-0 – uk Libr Preservation [420]

RECOLLECTIONS AND SKETCHES OF EARLY LAWYERS AND PUBLIC MEN OF IOWA / Stiles, Edward H – (Des Moines: Homestead Publ. Co., 1916). Iowa Reel 3. (The Cox Library Collection) – 5 – us Americana [978]

RECOLLECTIONS, MS 3143 / Cook, Eveline Bosworth – 1905-06. Hale-Hammond pioneer families of Bath (Summit County), Ohio. 1 reel – 1 – us Western Res [920]

RECOLLECTIONS OF A 48'ER / Mueller, Jakob – (German language history of immigration, and the early German community in Cleveland) – Cleveland, Ohio: Rud, Schmidt Printing Co, 1896 – 1 reel – 1 – us Western Res [304]

THE RECOLLECTIONS OF A BISHOP / Browne, G F – London: Smith, Elder, 1915 – 1mf – us A.T.L.A. [240]

RECOLLECTIONS OF A MISSIONARY IN THE GREAT WEST / Brady, Cyrus Townsend – New York: Charles Scribner, 1901, c1900 – 1mf – us A.T.L.A. [240]

RECOLLECTIONS OF A TOUR MADE IN SCOTLAND A.D. 1803. EDITED BY J.C. SHAIRP / Wordsworth, Dorothy – New York: Putnam, 2nd ed 1874 – 1 roll – 1 – 1-55879-439-5 – uk Libr Preservation [910]

RECOLLECTIONS OF BENCH AND BAR / Alverstone, Viscount – (This is in the nature of autobiography by the Rt. Hon. Viscount Alverstone who was British Lord Chief Justice from 1900-1913) – London: Edward Arnold, 1915 – 4mf – 9 – $6.00 – LLMC 92-136 – us L.L.M.C. [340]

RECOLLECTIONS OF CONFEDERATE SCOUT SERVICE / Gambrell, James Bruton – 342p – 1 – 11.97 – us Baptist [920]

RECOLLECTIONS OF DANTE GABRIEL ROSSETTI / Caine, Hall – London: Elliot Stock, 1882 – 1 roll – 1 – 1-55879-780-7 – uk Libr Preservation [420]

RECOLLECTIONS OF EXPERIENCES ON THE WESTERN PLAINS – 1865 – 1 – us KS Hist [978]

RECOLLECTIONS OF FORTY YEARS / Lesseps, Ferdinand de – Trans. by C.B. Pitman. New York: D. Appleton and Company, 1888. 2v in 1 – 1 – us U.W. Library [920]

THE RECOLLECTIONS OF GEOFFRY HAMLYN / Kingsley, Henry – British Fiction Archive: Unit 2 – 9 – uk Bell [830]

RECOLLECTIONS OF LIFE IN OHIO FROM 1813 TO 1840 / Howells, William Cooper – 1895 – 9 – 15.00 – us Scholars' Facs [978]

RECOLLECTIONS OF MY LIFE AND WORK AT HOME AND ABROAD : IN CONNECTION WITH THE WESLEYAN METHODIST CONFERENCE / Rule, William Harris – London: T. Woolmer, 1886 – 1mf – us A.T.L.A. [240]

RECOLLECTIONS OF MY OWN LIFE AND TIMES / Jackson, Thomas; ed by Frankland, B – London: Wesleyan Conference Office, 1874 – 2mf – us A.T.L.A. [240]

RECOLLECTIONS OF THE EARLY SETTLEMENT OF CARROLL COUNTY, INDIANA / Steward, J H – Cincinnati: Hitchcock and Walden, 1872. Indiana Reel 6. (The Cox Library Collection) – 5 – us Americana [978]

RECOLLECTIONS OF THE LAST FOUR POPES AND OF ROME IN THEIR TIMES / Wiseman, Nicholas Patrick – New York: P O'Shea, [1858?] – 2mf – 9 – 0-8370-7038-4 – 1986-1038 – us A.T.L.A. [240]

RECOLLECTIONS OF THE LIFE OF LORD BYRON, FROM THE YEAR 1808 TO THE END OF 1814... / Dallas, Robert Charles – London: Printed for Charles Knight, 1824 – 1 roll – 1 – 1-55879-639-8 – uk Libr Preservation [420]

RECOLLECTIONS OF THE OLD FOREIGN OFFICE / Hertslet, E – London, 1901 – 4mf – 1 – ILM-737/1 – ne IDC [327]

RECOLLECTIONS OF THE PIONEERS OF LEE COUNTY / Kennedy, Inez A – Dixon: 1893. Illinois Reel 38. (The Cox Library Collection) – 5 – us Americana [978]

A RECOMMENDATION FOR THE REINFORCEMENT OF COMPUTER EDUCATION IN PRIMARY AND SECONDARY SCHOOLS / Korea. Korean Educational Development Institute – Seoul, 1988 – 2mf – 9 – DE-663/1 – ne IDC [370]

RECOMMENDATIONS FOR INSECT CONTROL IN ALABAMA / Auburn University. Extension Service – 1957-71 – 1,5,6 – us Spaulding [660]

RECOMMENDATIONS FOR MODIFICATIONS OF THE INTERNAL REVENUE CODE / New York State Society of Certified Public Accountants. Committee on Federal Taxation – New York, 1953. 37p. LL-754 – 1 – us L of C Photodup [340]

RECOMMENDATIONS FOR THE MARKING OF FISHING GEAR : SUPPLEMENT TO THE REPORT OF THE EXPERT CONSULTATION ON THE MARKING OF FISHING GEAR; VICTORIA, BRITISH COLUMBIA, CANADA, 1991 – 1993 – 55p – it F.A.O. [790]

RECOMMENDATIONS RELATING TO THE ADMINISTRATION OF JUSTICE IN THE U.S. ARMY : REPORT OF THE PROCEEDINGS OF A BOARD OF OFFICERS CONVENED AT THE JUDGE ADVOCATE GENERAL'S SCHOOL, CHARLOTTESVILLE, VIRGINIA, 1-22 NOVEMBER 1952 – n.p., n.d. – 1mf – 9 – $1.50 – LLMC 96-073 – us L.L.M.C. [340]

RECOMMENDED METHODS FOR MEASUREMENT OF PEST RESISTANCE TO PESTICIDES – 1980 – 136p – it F.A.O. [660]

RECOMMENDED PRACTICES FOR THE PREVENTION OF MYCOTOXINS IN FOOD, FEED AND THEIR PRODUCTS – 1979 – 71p – it F.A.O. [660]

RECOMMENDED PROCEDURES FOR HANDLING PRISONER CIVIL RIGHTS CASES IN THE FEDERAL COURTS / FJC Prisoner Civil Rights Committee – Washington: FJC, 1980 – 2mf – 9 – $3.00 – LLMC 95-815 – us L.L.M.C. [340]

RECONCILIATION BY INCARNATION : THE RECONCILIATION OF GOD AND MAN BY THE INCARNATION OF THE DIVINE / Simon, David Worthington – (Includes bibliographical references and index) – Edinburgh: T & T Clark, 1898 – 1mf – 9 – 0-8370-5433-8 – 1985-3433 – us A.T.L.A. [240]

LA RECONCILIATION DES HERETIQUES DANS L'EGLISE LATIN / Saint-Palais D'aussac, Fr de – Paris, 1943 – Dfl19.00 – ne Slangenburg [240]

RECONCILIATION OF RELIGION AND SCIENCE / Fowle, Thomas Welbank – London: Henry S. King, 1873. 1 fiche – 9 – us A.T.L.A. [240]

THE RECONCILIATION OF RELIGION AND SCIENCE : BEING ESSAYS ON IMMORTALITY, INSPIRATION, MIRACLES, AND THE BEING OF CHRIST / Fowle, Thomas Welbank – London:Henry S. King, 1873 – 1mf – 9 – 0-8370-3173-7 – 1985-1173 – us A.T.L.A. [210]

RECONCILIATION OF SCIENCE AND RELIGION / Winchell, Alexander – New York: Harper, 1877 – 9 – us A.T.L.A. [240]

A RECONNAISSANCE IN NORTHERN ALASKA ACROSS THE ROCKY MOUNTAINS, ALONG KOYUKUK, JOHN, ANAKTUVUK, AND COLVILLE RIVERS, AND THE ARCTIC COAST TO CAPE LISBURNE IN 1901 / Schrader, Fr. Ch – BN 382 2. 1904 – 8 – ne IDC [910]

RECONSTRUCTED 1790 CENSUS OF DELAWARE / DeValinger, Leon – Washington, DC, National Gen. Soc., 1962. Delaware Reel 2. (The Cox Library Collection) – 5 – us Americana [920]

RECONSTRUCTION AND DEVELOPMENT PLAN / North Borneo. (United Kingdom). Development Committee – D-1399 1. 1948-1955. 1948 – 9 – ne IDC [338]

RECONSTRUCTION AND DEVELOPMENT PROGRAMME, 1960-65 / Mauritius. Economic Planning Committee – (Sessional Paper no. 2 of 1961). Port Louis. 1961 – 9 – ne IDC [338]

DIE RECONSTRUCTION DER KIRCHLICHEN AUTORITAET / Bunsen, Ernest de – Leipzig: F.A. Brockhaus, 1892. 1 fiche – 9 – us A.T.L.A. [240]

RECONSTRUCTION DURING AND AFTER WORLD WAR 1 PAMPHLET COLLECTION – 1916-1924 – 1 reel – 1 – CSUXANM5421-B – us Hoover Inst Photo [940]

RECONSTRUCTION IN AUSTRIA AS A RESULT OF WORLD WAR 2 PAMPHLET COLLECTION – 19??-1948 – 1 reel – 1 – CSUXANP1521-B – us Hoover Inst Photo [943]

RECONSTRUCTION IN BELGIUM AS A RESULT OF WORLD WAR 2 PAMPHLET COLLECTION – 1940-1945 – 1 reel – 1 – CSUXANP1529-B – us Hoover Inst Photo [943]

RECONSTRUCTION IN DENMARK AS A RESULT OF WORLD WAR 2 PAMPHLET COLLECTION – 1944 – 1 – CSUXANP1537-B – us Hoover Inst Photo [943]

RECONSTRUCTION IN FRANCE AS A RESULT OF WORLD WAR 2 PAMPHLET COLLECTION – 1943-1945 – 1 reel – 1 – CSUXANP1544-B – us Hoover Inst Photo [944]

RECONSTRUCTION IN GERMANY AS A RESULT OF WORLD WAR 2 PAMPHLET COLLECTION – 1941-1982 – 1 reel – 1 – CSUXANP1549-B – us Hoover Inst Photo [943]

RECONSTRUCTION IN GREAT BRITAIN AS A RESULT OF WORLD WAR 2 PAMPHLET COLLECTION – 1941-1948 – 2r – 1 – CSUXANP1553-B – us Hoover Inst Photo [941]

RECONSTRUCTION IN HUNGARY AFTER WORLD WAR 2 PAMPHLET COLLECTION – 1949 – 1 – CSUXANL4364-B – us Hoover Inst Photo [947]

RECONSTRUCTION IN ITALY AS A RESULT OF WORLD WAR 2 PAMPHLET COLLECTION – 1943 – 1 reel – 1 – CSUXANP1561-B – us Hoover Inst Photo [945]

RECONSTRUCTION IN POLAND AFTER WORLD WAR 2 PAMPHLET COLLECTION – 1943 – 1 – CSUXANL4375-B – us Hoover Inst Photo [947]

RECONSTRUCTION IN POLAND FROM 1914-1939 – 1920 – 1 – CSUXANL6542-B – us Hoover Inst Photo [947]

RECONSTRUCTION IN THE NETHERLANDS AS A RESULT OF WORLD WAR 2 PAMPHLET COLLECTION – 1948-1950 – 1 reel – 1 – CSUXANP1563-B – us Hoover Inst Photo [943]

RECONSTRUCTION IN THEOLOGY / King, Henry Churchill – (Includes bibliographical references and index) – New York:Macmillan, 1901 – 1mf – 9 – 0-8370-4473-1 – 1985-2473 – us A.T.L.A. [240]

RECONSTRUCTION IN YUGOSLAVIA AFTER WORLD WAR 2 PAMPHLET COLLECTION – 1947-1973 – 1 reel – 1 – CSUXANL4368-B – us Hoover Inst Photo [947]

THE RECONSTRUCTION OF CHRISTIAN CHURCH IN CHINA (CCC72) = CHUNG-KUO CHI TU CHIAO CHIAO HUI KAI KO TI T'U CHING / Chao, Tzu-ch'en – (In Chinese) – Shanghai: Association Press of China, 1950 – 1r – 1 – 1984-B500 – us A.T.L.A. [240]

RECONSTRUCTION OF FRANCE DURING AND AFTER WORLD WAR 1 PAMPHLET COLLECTION – 1915-1919 – 1 reel – 1 – CSUXANM5429-B – us Hoover Inst Photo [944]

RECONSTRUCTION OF GERMANY DURING AND AFTER WORLD WAR 1 PAMPHLET COLLECTION – 1922 – 1 – CSUXANM5438-B – us Hoover Inst Photo [943]

RECONSTRUCTION OF GREAT BRITAIN DURING AND AFTER WORLD WAR 1 PAMPHLET COLLECTION – 1918 – 1 – CSUXANM5443-B – us Hoover Inst Photo [941]

THE RECONSTRUCTION OF RELIGIOUS BELIEF / Mallock, William Hurrell – New York: Harper, 1905. 1 fiche – 9 – us A.T.L.A. [240]

THE RECONSTRUCTION OF THE ENGLISH CHURCH / Usher, Roland G – New York: D. Appleton, 1910 – 2mf – us A.T.L.A. [941]

RECONTEXTUALIZING EDUCATION THROUGH THE PHYSICAL : A SOMATIC APPROACH / Roth, Robert R – 1990 – 228p 3mf – 9 – $12.00 – us Microform Publ [370]

RECOPILACION DE LAS OBRAS.. / Orozco, Alfonso de – 1570 – 9 – 1.50f – sp Bibl Santa Ana [240]

RECOPILACION DE LEYES, DECRETOS Y CONVENIOS VIGENTES EN MATERIA PESQUERA / Uruguay. Laws, Statutes, etc – Montevideo Servicio Oceanografico y de Pesca, 1972. 48 p. LL-2025 – 1 – us L of C Photodup [324]

RECOPILACION DE SONETOS Y VILLANCICOS A QUATRO Y CINCO / Vasquez, Juan – Barcelona: Imp. Escuela, 1946 – 1 – sp Bibl Santa Ana [810]

RECOPILACION EN METRO / Sanchez de Badajoz, Diego – Badajoz: Graficas Iberia, 1941.-v1 – 1 – sp Bibl Santa Ana [946]

RECOPILACION EN METRO / Sanchez de Badajoz, Diego – (Tomo II.1886. 1.50f; 9) – 1882 – 9 – 1.50f – sp Bibl Santa Ana [810]

RECOPILACION EN METRO DEL BACHILLER...CON UN ESTUDIO DE JOSE LOPEZ PRUDENCIO / Sanchez de Badajoz, Diego – Badajoz: Tip. y Lib. A. Arqueros, Tomo 2. 1910 – 1 – sp Bibl Santa Ana [350]

RECOPILACION EN METRO DEL BACHILLER...CON UN ESTUDIO DE JOSE LOPEZ PRUDENCIO / Sanchez de Badajoz, Diego – Badajoz: Tip. y Lib. de A. Arqueros, Tomo 1. 1910 – 1 – sp Bibl Santa Ana [350]

RECOPILADOR SERGIPANO – Estancia, Brazil. 27 Jul 1833 – 1 – bl Biblioteca [072]

RECOPILLACION EN METRO DEL BACHILLER DIEGO SANCHEZ CON UN ESTUDIO DE DON JOSE LOPEZ PRUDENCIO / Sanchez de Badajoz, Diego – Badajoz: Tip. y Lib. de A. Arqueros, Tomo 2. 1910 – 1 – sp Bibl Santa Ana [370]

RECORD – Alma. Neb. 1896-1925 – 1 – us UMI [071]

RECORD – Angels Camp, CA. 1908-18 – 5r – 1 – $250.00 – B02017 – us Library Micro [071]

RECORD – Battle Creek. Mich. and Lakeview News. 1953-57 – 1 – us UMI [071]

RECORD – Bear Lake. Pa. 1895-1896 – 1 – us UMI [071]

RECORD – Benton. Mo. 1908-1910 – 1 – us UMI [071]

RECORD – Boston. Mass. 1951-1961 – 1 – us UMI [071]

RECORD – Buckhannon. West Virginia. -w.1924-66 – 1 – us UMI [071]

RECORD / Canada. Patent Office – v. 56-97. 1928-69. Formerly: Canadian Patent Office Record – 1,5,6 – us Princeton Micro [340]

RECORD – Cedar Falls. Iowa. 1900-1902; 1954- – 1 – us UMI [071]

RECORD – Central City. Neb. 1895-1905 – 1 – us UMI [071]

RECORD – Chadron. Neb. 1885-1962 – 1 – us UMI [071]

RECORD – Coatsville. Pa. 1934- – 1 – us UMI [071]

RECORD – Colfax. Calif. -w. 1945-58 – 1 – us UMI [071]

RECORD – Colma, CA. 1910-11 – 1r – 1 – $50.00 – B02126 – us Library Micro [071]

RECORD – Columbia. S.C. 1909- – 1 – us UMI [071]

RECORD – Conrad. Iowa. 1946- – 1 – us UMI [071]

RECORD – (Cont by: Lincoln County Record) – Pioche, NV. 1933-68 – 26r – 1 UN04646 – $1,300.00 – us Library Micro [071]

RECORD – (Cont by: Record Messenger and Mill Valley Record) – Mill Valley, CA. 1917-91 – 51r – 1 – $2,550.00 – B02460 – us Library Micro [071]

RECORD – Delano. Calif. 1908-1945; 1955-1967 – 1 – us UMI [071]

RECORD – East Helena. Mont. 1899-1902 – 1 – us UMI [071]

RECORD – Ely. Nev. -w. 1949- – 1 – us UMI [071]

RECORD / First Congregational Church, Emporia, KS – 1858-1988, Record, 1858-1988; Standard church register and record, 1975-1988 – 1 – us KS Hist [240]

RECORD – Gardnerville, NV. 1898-1904 – 1r – 1 – $50.00 – U04534 – us Library Micro [071]

RECORD – Gilbert, NV. 1925-27 – 1r – 1 – $50.00 – U04541 – us Library Micro [071]

RECORD – Greensboro. N.C. 1906- – 1 – us UMI [071]

RECORD – Lansford. Pa. -w. 1911-20 – 1 – us UMI [071]

RECORD – Lawrence. Kan. -d. 1889-93 – 1 – us UMI [071]

RECORD – Lawrence. Kan. -w. 1889-93 – 1 – us UMI [071]

RECORD – Lawrenceville. Ill. 1955- – 1 – us UMI [071]

RECORD – Lompoc. Calif. 1945- – 1 – us UMI [071]

RECORD – Ludington. Mich. 1880-1888; 1895-1897; 1899-1901 – 1 – us UMI [071]

RECORD – Marion. Kan. 1875-1900 – 1 – us UMI [071]

RECORD – Meriden. Conn. 1893- – 1 – us UMI [071]

RECORD – Metamora, Ohio. 1916-73 – 17r – 1 – $32.50r – us Archival [071]

RECORD – National City. Calif. 1882-1903 – 1 – us UMI [071]

RECORD – Neppel. Wash. -w. 1912-15 – 1 – us UMI [071]

RECORD – New London. Ohio. 1873-1890; 1892- – 1 – us UMI [071]

RECORD – Newton. Iowa. -w. 1894-1902 – 1 – us UMI [071]

RECORD – Newton. Miss. 1940-1954 – 1 – us UMI [071]

RECORD – Osceolo. Neb. 1873-1874; 1876-1877; 1880-1883; 1894-1917; 1919- – 1 – us UMI [071]

RECORD / Pennsylvania. Revolutionary Governments – 1775-90. Ed. by R. M. Baumann. (Record Group 27 of the Pa. State Archives). printed guide. 54 reels – 1 – us Penn Hist [975]

RECORD – Philadelphia. Pa. and pred. 1870-71, 1877-1910 – 1 – us UMI [071]

RECORD – Pioche. Nev. -w. 1949-68 – 1 – us UMI [071]

RECORD – Redding. Calif. 1939-41 – 1 – us UMI [071]

RECORD – Rock Hill. S.C. 1904-30 – 1 – us UMI [071]

RECORD – Roseville. Mich. 1926-31 – 1 – us UMI [071]

RECORD – Rossford, Ohio. 1972-80 – 4r – 1 – $32.50r – us Archival [071]

RECORD – St. Augustine. Fl. 1936- – 1 – us UMI [071]

RECORD – St. Augustine. Fl. -w. 1903-04 – 1 – us UMI [071]

RECORD – Statesville. N.C. 1931-1951 – 1 – us UMI [071]

RECORD – Statesville. N.C. and Landmark. 1957- – 1 – us UMI [071]

RECORD – Stockton. Calif. 1891- – 1 – us UMI [071]

RECORD – Troy. N.Y. 1907-08; 1911; 1915; 1919; 1920; 1943- – 1 – us UMI [071]

RECORD – Troy, NY. 1943-72 – 313r – 1 – $15,650.00 – B04918 – us Library Micro [071]

RECORD – v. 1. 1977 – 1,5,6,9 – us UMI [360]

RECORD – v1-. 1981- – 1,5,6,9 – us UMI [073]

RECORD – West Union. West Virginia. -w. 1901-09, 1926, 1929-50, 1951-68 – 1 – us UMI [071]

RECORD – Wilkes-Barre. Pa. 1891-1929; 1944- – 1 – us UMI [071]

RECORD – Woodland. Calif. -w. 1943-56 – 1 – us UMI [071]

RECORD *see* WHEATLAND NEWSPAPERS

THE RECORD – 1968. Item G. Historical Society Yearbook 9th ed. (Arkansas). Includes index. 242p.SW16-0162 – 5 – us A.G.L.L. [978]

THE RECORD – Glossop, England. 1859-29 Apr 1871 – 5r – 1 – uk British Libr Newspaper [072]

THE RECORD – Greenville, CA. 1957-59 – 2r – 1 – $100.00 – B02280 – us Library Micro [071]

THE RECORD – Lansford, PA., 1890-1894 – 13 – $25.00r – us I.M.R. [071]

THE RECORD – London, 1828-1923 – 96r – 1 – uk British Libr Newspaper [072]

THE RECORD – London. 1828-1948 – 1 – uk World [073]

THE RECORD : MISSIONARY MAGAZINE OF THE PRESBYTERIAN CHURCH OF AUSTRALIA – v45-76. Sep 1934-1964 (complete) – 3r – 1 – ATLA S0492 – us A.T.L.A. [073]

THE RECORD – Petaluma, CA. 1936; 1938; 1939 – 1 – B06047 – us Library Micro [071]

THE RECORD / Presbyterian Church in the U.S.A. – Philadelphia, Pa. v19-21. 1868-1870 – 1r – 1 – $50.00 – us Presbyterian [240]

THE RECORD – Quebec. v1 n81. 2 nov 1886 – 1r – 1 – Can$25.00 – cn Can Microfilming [072]

THE RECORD – Stockton, CA. 1890- – 1140+ r – 1 BC03016 – $57,000.00 ($600.00) – us Library Micro [071]

THE RECORD – Stroudsburg, PA., 1930-1943 – 13 – $25.00r – us I.M.R. [071]

THE RECORD – v5-17. 1876-88 (complete) – 2r – 1 – ATLA S0493 – us A.T.L.A. [240]

THE RECORD *see* THE SHERBROOKE RECORD

RECORD AND COURIER – Conneautville, PA., 1865-1876 – 13 – $25.00r – us I.M.R. [071]

RECORD AND COURIER – Lehighton, PA., 1972 – 13 – $25.00r – us I.M.R. [071]

RECORD AND GUIDE – Providence. R.I. -w. 1916- – 1 – us UMI [071]

RECORD AND LINCOLN COUNTY RECORD – Pioche, NV. 1925; 1932 – 2r – 1 – $100.00 – U04648 – us Library Micro [071]

RECORD ARGUS – Greenville. Pa. 1924- – 1 – us UMI [071]

RECORD BOOK / Appanoose Union Sunday School, Franklin County, KS – 1881-1884 – 1 – us KS Hist [240]

RECORD BOOK / COD Cattle Ranch – 1883-91 – 1 – us KS Hist [025]

RECORD BOOK / Hancock County, Ohio. Cass Township. Township Clerk – 1833-1877 – 1r – 1 – $32.50r – us Archival [324]

RECORD BOOK / Hancock County. Ohio. Marion Township. Board of Trustees – 1839-1849 – 1r – 1 – $32.50r – us Archival [324]

RECORD BOOK / Midway Stock Ranch, Osborne County, KS – 1915-1922 – 1 – us KS Hist [978]

RECORD BOOK / Piatt and Company. Marysville, California – 1851-64 – 1 – us KS Hist [978]

RECORD BOOK, 1935-49 / Georgia. New Sunbury Baptist Association. Savannah Extension Board – Also: The Baptist Leader, 1944-65. 982p – 1 – us Baptist [240]

RECORD BOOKS OF THE F.A. HIHN CO., SANTA CRUZ, CALIFORNIA – (Includes indices to deeds, leases, documents, agreements and deeds of Santa Cruz Water Co.) – Santa Cruz Co, 1856-1917 – 9r – 1 – $450.00 – B40327 – us Library Micro [978]

RECORD CARDS TO THE CORRESPONDENCE OF THE WAR COLLEGE DIVISION, RELATED GENERAL STAFF, AND ADJUTANT GENERAL OFFICES / U. S. War Department. Adjutant General's Office – 1902-19. 37 rolls. M1023 – 1 – us Nat'l Archives [324]

RECORD COMPANY CATALOGS FROM RUSSIA ON MICROFICHE – 25 titles 49mf complete coll – 9 – $290.00 coll – us Ross [780]

RECORD COURIER – Haines OR. May 12 1932-Aug 30 1934 – 1 – us U.O. Library [071]

RECORD ENTERPRISE – Mill Valley, CA. 1907-16 – 3r – 1 – $150.00 – B02461 – us Library Micro [071]

RECORD HERALD – Richmond, CA. 1913; 1914-19; 1920-22; 1923-26; 1927-29; 1933; 1935-36 – 35r – 1 – $1,575.00 – B02698 – us Library Micro [071]
RECORD MESSENGER AND MILL VALLEY RECORD – Mill Valley, CA. 1992 – 2+ r – 1 – $100.00 ($50.00y) – B06039 – us Library Micro [071]
RECORD MESSENGER AND MILL VALLEY RECORD *see* RECORD
RECORD OF ADMISSIONS TO CITIZENSHIP. 1790-1906 / U.S. District Courts. South Carolina – RG 21. 1roll – 1 – M1183 – us Nat'l Archives [340]
RECORD OF APPEAL: MANDELA VS. STATE (APPELLATE DIV.) – 1 reel – 1 – sa Microfile [960]
RECORD OF APPOINTMENT OF POSTMASTERS – 1832-Sept 30, 1971. 145 rolls. M841 – 1 – us Nat'l Archives [324]
RECORD OF APPOINTMENT OF POSTMASTERS, OCTOBER 1789-1832 / U.S. Post Office – RG 28. M1131. 4 rolls – 1 – us Nat'l Archives [380]
RECORD OF ARRESTS / Erie County. Ohio. Vermilion. Mayor's Court – 1959-1962 – 1r – 1 – $32.50r – us Archival [324]
RECORD OF BIRTHS / Putnam County, Ohio. General Health District – 1926-1951 – 1r – 1 – $32.50r – us Archival [324]
RECORD OF BUILDING AND OTHER PERMITS ISSUED IN THE CITY OF TOPEKA / Topeka. Kansas. Fire Marshal – 1880-1926 – 1 – us KS Hist [978]
RECORD OF CHATTEL MORTGAGES / Erie County. Ohio. Vermilion Township. Township Clerk – 1877-1891 – 1r – 1 – $32.50r – us Archival [324]
RECORD OF CHEMICAL PROGRESS – v1-15. 1939-54 – 1,5,6 – us Princeton Micro [540]
THE RECORD OF CHRISTIAN WORK / ed by Moody, W R – (Cont: The Evangelistic Record. Absorbed Northfield Echoes; Watchword and Truth. Absorbed by Church Management) – 1881-1933 – 332mf – 9 – $775.00 – us Schnappsburg [240]
RECORD OF EARMARKS AND BRANDS / Van Wert County. Ohio. Pleasant Township. Board of Trustees – 1837-1874 – 1r – 1 – $32.50r – us Archival [324]
RECORD OF ESTRAYS / Putnam County. Ohio. Common Pleas. Civil Division – 1840-1908 – 1r – 1 – $32.50r – us Archival [324]
RECORD OF ESTRAYS / Wyandot County. Ohio. Clerk of Courts – 1885-1920 – 1r – 1 – $32.50r – us Archival [324]
RECORD OF FISHING LICENSES / Wyandot County. Ohio. Clerk of Courts – 1925-1935 – 1r – 1 – $32.50r – us Archival [324]
RECORD OF HUNTERS' LICENSES / Wyandot County. Ohio. Clerk of Courts – 1925-1936 – 1r – 1 – $32.50r – us Archival [324]
RECORD OF INDENTURES / Wood County. Ohio. Common Pleas. Civil Division – 1837-1860s – 1r – 1 – $32.50r – us Archival [324]
RECORD OF INQUESTS / Paulding County, Ohio. Clerk of Courts – 1892-1997 – 1r – 1 – $32.50r – us Archival [920]
RECORD OF JUSTICE'S OATHS / Wyandot County. Ohio. Clerk of Courts – 1914-1957 – 1r – 1 – $32.50r – us Archival [324]
RECORD OF LOTS SOLD / Sumner Town Company. Kansas – n.d – 1 – us KS Hist [978]
RECORD OF MINISTERS' LICENSES / Putnam County. Ohio. Probate Court – 1875-1920 – 1r – 1 – $32.50r – us Archival [324]
RECORD OF MY LIFE-WORK IN ENTOMOLOGY / Osten-Sacken, C R von – Z-175 2. 3 pts. 1903-1904 – 8 – ne IDC [590]
RECORD OF OFFICERS BONDS / Hancock County. Ohio. Biglick Township. Township Clerk – 1980-1989 – 1r – 1 – $32.50r – us Archival [324]
RECORD OF ORDINANCES / Wood County. Ohio. Pemberville. Village Council – 1876-1982 – 2r – 1 – $32.50r – us Archival [324]
RECORD OF PROCEEDINGS / Lucas County. Ohio. Planning Commission – 1916-1953 – 2r – 1 – $32.50r – us Archival [324]
RECORD OF PROCEEDINGS AT JUDICIAL INQUIRY RE SERETSE KHAMA – Serowe, 1949 – us Res Libr [340]
RECORD OF RESOLUTIONS / Wood County. Ohio. Pemberville, Village. Board of Public Affairs – 1953-1985 – 1r – 1 – $32.50r – us Archival [324]
RECORD OF RESOLUTIONS / Wood County. Ohio. Pemberville. Village Council – 1971-1985 – 1r – 1 – $32.50r – us Archival [324]
RECORD OF SCHOOL EXPENDITURES / Wood County. Ohio. Plain Township. Board of Education – 1865 – 1r – 1 – $32.50r – us Archival [324]
RECORD OF SOLDIERS BURIED / U.S. Army. Quartermaster Corps. Fort Wallace, Kansas – 1866 – 1 – us KS Hist [324]
RECORD OF THE ASSOCIATION OF THE BAR OF THE CITY OF NEW YORK – v1-50. 1946-95 – 9 – $766.00 set – us Hein [340]
RECORD OF THE BLUE MOUNTAINS – Katoomba, Feb 1924 – 1 – at Pascoe [072]
RECORD OF THE BUDDHIST RELIGION AS PRACTICED IN INDIA AND THE MALAY ARCHIPELAGO / I-Ching, 635-713. I-Ching – J. Takakusu, trans. Oxford: Clarendon Press, 1896. lxiv,240p – 1 – us U.W. Library [280]
RECORD OF THE FAMILY OF CHARLES BEATTY WHO EMIGRATED FROM IRELAND TO AMERICA IN 1792 / Beatty, Charles C – 1 – $50.00 – us Presbyterian [920]
RECORD OF THE FEDERAL CONVENTION OF 1789 / ed by Farrand, Max – New Haven: Yale UP. 3v. 1911 – 8mf – 9 – $12.00 – LLMC 84-245 – us L.L.M.C. [323]
RECORD OF THE HOME OF HEBREW ORPHANS / Home of Hebrew Orphans – Philadelphia. Pa. 1898 – 1 – us A.J.P.C. [360]
RECORD OF THE SERVICES OF ILLINOIS SOLDIERS IN THE BLACK HAWK WAR, 1831-32 AND IN THE MEXICAN WAR, 1846-48 / Elliott, Isaac H – Springfield: Journal Co. Printers and Binders, 1902. Illinois Reel 10. (The Cox Library Collection) – 5 – us Americana [978]
RECORD OF THE SUFFERINGS OF QUAKERS IN CORNWALL, 1655-86 / Society of Friends. Cornwall, England; ed by Norman Penney – Transcribed and Introd. by Violet Hodgkin. Publ. for the Friends Historical Society. London: Friends Book Centre – 1 – us U.W. Library [240]
RECORD OF THE TIMES – Wilkes-Barre. Pa. 1891-1901 – 1 – us UMI [071]
RECORD OF VOTES / Republican Party. Kansas. State Central Committee – 1896, 1899, 1900, 1902 – 1 – us KS Hist [978]
RECORD OF WINTER SPORTS, 1883-84: SNOWSHOE AND SKATING RACES, HOCKEY AND CURLING MATCHES / Becket, Hugh W – Montreal: Becket, 1884. 03310. (Pre-1900 Canadiana) – 9 – cn C.I.H.M. [790]
RECORD OF ZOOLOGICAL LITERATURE *see* ZOOLOGICAL RECORD
RECORD PILOT – Glen Cove. N.Y. 1953- – 1 – us UMI [071]
Record Publishing Co *see*
– MEMORIAL RECORD OF BUTLER COUNTY
– MEMORIAL RECORD OF LICKING COUNTY
– PROMINENT AND PROGRESSIVE PENNSYLVANIANS OF THE NINETEENTH CENTURY
Record, R *see* THE JUDGMENT OF URINES
RECORD SEARCHLIGHT – Redding, CA. 1945-49 – 18r – 1 – $900.00 – C02673 – us Library Micro [071]
RECORD SERIES OF THE ARCHAEOLOGICAL AND TOPOGRAPHICAL ASSOCIATION – N.p. v1-104. 1885-1941; Extra Series. v1-4. 1935-42 – 526mf – 9 – H-848c/2 – ne IDC [930]
RECORD SOCIETY FOR THE PUBLICATION OF ORIGINAL DOCUMENTS RELATING TO LANCASHIRE AND CHESHIRE – (Missing: v10) – London. v1-95. 1878-1941 – 504mf – 9 – H-830c/2 – ne IDC [941]
RECORD VISITOR – Pawtucket. R.I. 1891-1893 – 1 – us UMI [071]
RECORDACAO : SOCIEDADE PROTETORA DAS ARTES GRAPHICAS DO AMAZONAS – Manaos, Amazonas. 11 Set 1911 – 1,5,6 – bl Biblioteca [072]
RECORDACION FLORIDA. DISCURSO HISTORIAL Y DE DEMOSTRACION NATURAL, MATERIAL, MILITAR Y POLITICA DEL REYNO DE GUATEMALA / Fuentes y Guzman, Francisco Antonio de – Guatemala, 1932-1933. 3v; Madrid: Razon y Fe, 1934 – 1 – sp Bibl Santa Ana [320]
RECORD-AMERICAN – Boston. Mass. 1962- – 1 – us UMI [071]
RECORD-APPEAL – Ludington. Mich. 1901-1906; 1909-1913 – 1 – us UMI [071]
RECORD-CHIEFTAIN – Enterprise. Or. 1911-1943 – 1 – us UMI [071]
RECORD-COURIER – Gardnersville. Nev. 1949- – 1 – us UMI [071]
RECORD-COURIER – (Incl. Record-Courier (Haines)) – Baker, OR. -w. 30 Oct 1931-25 Dec 1975+. – 19r – 1 – us U.O. Library [071]
THE RECORD-COURIER – Gardnerville, NV. 1909- – 88+ r – 1 UN04535 – $4,400.00 ($275.00y) – us Library Micro [071]
RECORD-COURIER-TRIBUNE – Ravenna-Kent. Ohio. 1941-50; 1956- – 1 – us UMI [071]
Recorde, Robert *see* THE WHETSTONE OF WITTE
RECORD-EAGLE – Traverse City. Mich. and pred. 1897-1915, 1917- – 1 – us UMI [071]
RECORDED MUSIC CATALOG : SONG INDEX (1984) – 1984 – 59mf – 9 – $300.00 – us A.J.P.C. [780]
RECORDER – Aiken. S.C. scattered. 1882-1907 – 1 – us UMI [071]
RECORDER – Albion. Mich. -w. 1868-69, 1884-86, 1890-1916 – 1 – us UMI [071]
RECORDER – Bandon. Or. 1901-1916 – 1 – us UMI [071]
RECORDER – Chewelah. Wash. 1909 – 1 – us UMI [071]
RECORDER – Holton. KS. And pred. -w. 1872-1900 – 1 – us UMI [071]
RECORDER – Metuchen. N.J. -w. 1950-51 – 1 – us UMI [071]
RECORDER – Olympia. Wash. -d. 1902-06, 1909-27 – 1 – us UMI [071]
RECORDER – Olympia. Wash. -w. 1903 – 1 – us UMI [071]
RECORDER – Ramsey, NV. 1906-08 – 1r – 1 – $50.00 – U04652 – us Library Micro [071]
RECORDER – San Francisco. Calif. 1946- – 1 – us UMI [071]
RECORDER – v34- 1991/92- – 9 – Can$20.00y – cn Micromedia [971]
RECORDER – Vallejo, CA. Jun 1871-May 1872 – 1r – 1 – $50.00 – B03065 – us Library Micro [071]
RECORDER – York. Pa. 1800-1830 – 1 – us UMI [071]
THE RECORDER – Deer Park, Ontario – 1 – 35.00 – cn McLaren [971]
THE RECORDER – Indianapolis. Ind. 1899- – 1 – us UMI [071]
THE RECORDER – San Francisco, CA. 1906-78; 1979- – 347+ r – 1 BC02858 – $17,350.00 ($450.00y) – us Library Micro [071]
THE RECORDER – San Francisco. On film: 1 Apr 1926-31 Dec 1934; Apr 1935-31 Dec 1945. LL-010 – 1 – us L of C Photodup [340]
RECORDER AND TIMES – (1918-1992.-418r) – Brockville, 1993 – 12r – 1 – cn Preston [971]
RECORDER GAZETTE – Banning, CA. 1972- – 70+ r – 1 – $3,500.00 ($140.00) – R02045 – us Library Micro [071]
RECORDER (MANSFIELD AND SUTTON EDITION) *see* MANSFIELD AND SUTTON RECORDER
The Recorder. San Francisco *see* HISTORICAL AND CONTEMPORARY REVIEW OF BENCH AND BAR IN CALIFORNIA. MARCH, 1926
RECORDER/MENLO ATHERTON RECORDER – Menlo Park, CA. 1924-32; 1933-83 – 48r – 1 – $2,400.00 – B02444 – us Library Micro [071]
RECORD-HERALD – Washington Court House. Ohio. 1858-64; 1911- – 1 – us UMI [071]
RECORD-HERALD – Wausau. Wis. 1907-40; 1951- – 1 – us UMI [071]
RECORD-HERALD – Waynesboro. Pa. 1955- – 1 – us UMI [071]
RECORDI DI CAROVANA : ABISSINIA SETTENTRIONALE 1924 [E] ABISSINIA OCCIDENTALE 1926 / Civinini, Guelfo – [Verona]: Mondadori, [1932] – us Res Libr [910]
...RECORDS : LUFTGAUKOMMANDOS, FLAK, DEUTSCHE LUFTWAFFENMISSION IN RUMANIEN / Germany. Air Force – 64 rolls. T405. Finding Aids: GG25 and T176 roll 24. (Captured German Records Filmed at Alexandria, VA.) – 1 – us Nat'l Archives [324]
RECORDS / 4-H Club, Willing Workers, Reno County, KS – 1927-1934 – 1 – us KS Hist [978]
RECORDS / Ackworth, New Hampshire.First Baptist Church – 1826-83 – 1 – 15.50 – us A.B.H.S. [240]
RECORDS / Addison, Maine. Indian River Baptist Sewing Circle – 1877-1884 – 1 – us A.B.H.S. [240]
RECORDS / Addison, Maine. Second Baptist Church – 1861-99 – 1 – us A.B.H.S. [240]
RECORDS / Adrian, Michigan. First Baptist Church – 1832-1979 – 1 – us A.B.H.S. [240]
RECORDS / Allen County. Kansas. School District 23 – 1 – us KS Hist [370]
RECORDS / All-Union (Russian) Communist Party. Smolensk Archives – 64 rolls. T87. Finding Aid: T87 roll 1. (World War II Collection of Seized Enemy Records) – 1 – us Nat'l Archives [947]
RECORDS / Ambler, Pennsylvania. Mount Pleasant Baptist Church – (Clerk's Records, 1899-1984. Trustee's Minutes, 1926-77. Bible School Minutes, 1893-94. Three Tuns Baptist Mission Records, 1897-1904. Correspondence and Legal Documents) – 1834-1985 – 1 – us A.B.H.S. [240]
RECORDS / American Colonization Society – 1792-1961 – 1 – 6,177.00 – us L of C Photodup [025]
RECORDS / American Federation of Musicians. Local 103, Columbus, Ohio – 1891-1936. 1 reel – 1 – us Ohio Hist [025]
RECORDS / Amherst, Massachusetts. First Baptist Church – 1827-1980 – 1 – us A.B.H.S. [240]
RECORDS / Apprentices Library Society. Charleston, South Carolina – 1872 – 2mf – 9 – us South Carolina Historical [978]
RECORDS / Ashland, Maine. Baptist Church – 1864-75 – 1 – us A.B.H.S. [240]
RECORDS / Ashland University – 1878-1940 – 3r – 1 – $32.50r – us Archival [370]
RECORDS / Atchison. Kansas. Trinity Episcopal Church – 1863-1968 – 1 – us KS Hist [978]
RECORDS / Atchison, Topeka and Santa Fe Railway Company – 1879-1906 – 1 – us KS Hist [380]
RECORDS / Baptist Associations, Maine. Androscroggin Free Will Baptist Quarterly Meeting – 1868-80 – 1 – us A.B.H.S. [240]
RECORDS / Baptist Associations, Maine. Anson Free Will Baptist Quarterly Meeting – 1863-1915 – 1 – us A.B.H.S. [240]
RECORDS / Baptist Associations, Maine. Bowdoinham Free Will Baptist Quarterly Meeting – (Ministers Conference, Records, 1890-1906) – 1895-1914 – 1 – us A.B.H.S. [240]
RECORDS / Baptist Associations, Maine. Bowdoinham Free Will Baptist Yearly Meeting – 1916-23 – 1 – us A.B.H.S. [240]
RECORDS / Baptist Associations, Maine. Cumberland Baptist Association. – 1914-25 – 1 – us A.B.H.S. [240]
RECORDS / Baptist Associations, Maine. Cumberland Baptist Association. – 1925-36 – 1 – us A.B.H.S. [240]
RECORDS / Baptist Associations, Maine. Eastern Free Will Baptist Quarterly Conference – 1845-76 – 1 – us A.B.H.S. [240]
RECORDS / Baptist Associations, Maine. Ellsworth Free Will Baptist Quarterly Meeting – 1851-1917 – 1 – us A.B.H.S. [240]
RECORDS / Baptist Associations, Maine. Exeter Free Will Baptist Quarterly Meeting – 1824-60 – 1 – us A.B.H.S. [240]
RECORDS / Baptist Associations, Maine. Hancock Baptist Association – 1835-39 – 1 – us A.B.H.S. [240]
RECORDS / Baptist Associations, Maine. Kennebec Baptist Association. Woman's Baptist Foreign Missionary Society – 1884-1903 – 1 – us A.B.H.S. [240]
RECORDS / Baptist Associations, Maine. Lincoln Baptist Association. – 1911-13 – 1 – us A.B.H.S. [240]
RECORDS / Baptist Associations, Maine. Maine Central Free Will Baptist Yearly Meeting – 1867-90 – 1 – us A.B.H.S. [240]
RECORDS / Baptist Associations, Maine. Maine Eastern Free Will Baptist Yearly Meeting – 1826-62 – 1 – us A.B.H.S. [240]
RECORDS / Baptist Associations, Maine. Oxford Free Will Baptist Quarterly Meeting – 1866-1956 – 1 – us A.B.H.S. [240]

RECORDS / Baptist Associations, Maine. Oxford Free Will Baptist Yearly Meeting – 1833-1942 – 1 – us A.B.H.S. [240]

RECORDS / Baptist Associations, Maine. Parsonfield Free Will Baptist Quarterly Meeting – 1833-1920, 1902-20 – 1 – us A.B.H.S. [240]

RECORDS / Baptist Associations, Maine. Penobscot Baptist Association. Female Missionary Society – 1843-62 – 1 – 15.50 – us A.B.H.S. [240]

RECORDS / Baptist Associations, Maine. Penobscot Free Will Baptist Yearly Meeting – 1832-90, 1868-90 – 1 – us A.B.H.S. [240]

RECORDS / Baptist Associations, Maine. Penobscot Free Will Baptist Yearly Meeting. Ministers' Conference – 1886-99 – 1 – us A.B.H.S. [240]

RECORDS / Baptist Associations, Maine. South Aroostook Free Will Baptist Quarterly Meeting – 1896-1913 – 1 – us A.B.H.S. [240]

RECORDS / Baptist Associations, Maine. Waterville Free Will Baptist Quarterly Meeting – 1838-1916 – 1 – us A.B.H.S. [240]

RECORDS / Baptist Associations, Maine. Western Free Will Baptist Quarterly Conference – 1843-1905 – 1 – us A.B.H.S. [240]

RECORDS / Baptist Associations, New Hampshire. Belknap Association of Free Will Baptist Churches – 1890-1958 – 1 – us A.B.H.S. [240]

RECORDS / Baptist Associations, New Hampshire. Belknap Association of Free Will Baptist Churches. Woman's Missionary Society – 1888-99 – 1 – us A.B.H.S. [240]

RECORDS / Baptist Associations, New Hampshire. Belknap Free Will Baptist Quarterly Meeting – 1846-90 – 1 – us A.B.H.S. [240]

RECORDS / Baptist Associations, New Hampshire. Portsmouth Baptist Association – 1901-40 – 1 – 15.50 – us A.B.H.S. [240]

RECORDS / Baptist Associations, New Hampshire. Sandwich Free Will Baptist Quarterly Meeting. Ministers Conference – 1845-1911 – 1 – 15.50 – us A.B.H.S. [240]

RECORDS / Baptist State Conventions (American Baptist). Connecticut – 1924-70 – 1 – 50.15 – us A.B.H.S. [240]

RECORDS / Baptist State Conventions (American Baptist). Maine – (Board of Trustees, Minutes, 1863-1909. Executive Committee and Board of Trustees, Minutes, 1891-1915. Board of Education, Minutes, 1915-22) – 1880-91 – 1 – us A.B.H.S. [240]

RECORDS / Baptist State Conventions (American Baptist). New Hampshire. Board of Promotion – (Board of Trustees, Records, 1847-1953. Council on Ordination, Records, 1896-1915; Legacies and Gifts, 1884-1907. Ministers Council, Records, 1940-74) – 1919-52 – 1 – us A.B.H.S. [240]

RECORDS / Baptist State Conventions (American Baptist). South Dakota – 1891-1949 – 1 – us A.B.H.S. [240]

RECORDS / Barnstead, New Hampshire. First Free Will Baptist Church – 1823-74 – 1 – 15.50 – us A.B.H.S. [240]

RECORDS / Barrington, New Hampshire. First Baptist Church – 1816-73 – 1 – 15.50 – us A.B.H.S. [240]

RECORDS / Beaufort. South Carolina. St. Helena's (Episcopal) Church – 1710-1818, 1844-1914. 11 fiches – 9 – us South Carolina Historical [978]

RECORDS / Beaufort. South Carolina. St. Helena's Episcopal Church – 1720-c1830, 1894-1914. 11 fiches – 9 – us South Carolina Historical [978]

RECORDS / Bedford, New Hampshire. Bedford Baptist Church – 1835-48 – 1 – 15.50 – us A.B.H.S. [240]

RECORDS / Bellevue. Ohio.Zion United Church of Christ – 1861-1983 – 1r – 1 – $32.50r – us Archival [240]

RECORDS / Berkeley County. South Carolina. St. Stephen's (Episcopal) Church – 1754-1888. 3 fiches – 9 – us South Carolina Historical [978]

RECORDS / Bethel, Maine. Free Will Baptist Church – 1834-97; 1882-98 – 1 – us A.B.H.S. [240]

RECORDS / Birmingham Ladies' Society for the Relief of Negro Slaves – 1825-1919. BRRAM – 1 – uk Microform Academic [305]

RECORDS / Bloomdale. Ohio. Trinity United Methodist Church – 1881-1973 – 1r – 1 – $32.50r – us Archival [978]

RECORDS / Bloomdale. Ohio. United Brethren Church – 1860-1974 – 1r – 1 – $32.50r – us Archival [240]

RECORDS / Bluff Point, New York. Bluff Point Baptist Church – 1812-32 – 1 – 15.50 – us A.B.H.S. [240]

RECORDS / Boston, Massachusetts. First Baptist Church – 1800-1960 – 1 – us A.B.H.S. [240]

RECORDS / Bourbon County, KS. Public School – 1876-1962 – 1 – us KS Hist [370]

RECORDS / Bowling Green. Ohio. First Presbyterian Church – 1832-1974. 1 reel – 1 – us Archival [240]

RECORDS / Bowling Green. Ohio. Hope Lutheran Church – 1910-85 – 1r – 1 – $32.50r – us Archival [240]

RECORDS / Bowling Green. Ohio. Plain Congregational Church – 1835-1973 – 3r – 1 – $32.50r – us Archival [978]

RECORDS / Bridgewater, New Hampshire. Free Will Baptist Church – 1819-91 – 1 – 15.50 – us A.B.H.S. [240]

RECORDS / Brockport, New York. Brockport Baptist Church – 1875-98; 1916-55 – 1 – us A.B.H.S. [240]

RECORDS / Brownfield, Maine. Brownfield Free Will Baptist Church – (Minutes, 1849-80. Membership Records, 1834-81. Brownfield Free Will Baptist Society, Records, 1822-47, 1854-1914) – 1822-1914 – 1 – 17.95 – us A.B.H.S. [240]

RECORDS / Brunswick, Maine. Baptist Church – 1799-1868 – 1 – 15.50 – us A.B.H.S. [240]

RECORDS / Bryan. Ohio. First Presbyterian Church – 1872-1951 – 1r – 1 – $32.50r – us Archival [240]

RECORDS / Bryan. Ohio. Trinity Episcopal Church – 1870-1982 – 1r – 1 – $32.50r – us Archival [978]

RECORDS / Bryan. Ohio. Trinity Lutheran Church – 1862-1961 – 2r – 1 – $32.50r – us Archival [978]

RECORDS / Bucyrus. Ohio. First Presbyterian Church – 1838-1965 – 1r – 1 – $32.50r – us Archival [240]

RECORDS / Bucyrus. Ohio. Harmony Evangelical Church – 1877-1941 – 1r – 1 – $32.50r – us Archival [240]

RECORDS / Bucyrus. Ohio. St. John's United Church of Christ – 1837-1961 – 1r – 1 – $32.50r – us Archival [240]

RECORDS / Burlington, Vermont. Vermont Baptist Home, Inc – (Hilltop House: Baptist Retirement Community). 1961-75 – 1 – us A.B.H.S. [240]

RECORDS / Caldwell. Kansas – 1884-ca1935 – 1 – us KS Hist [978]

RECORDS / Campton, New Hampshire. Campton Baptist Church – 1826-99 – 1 – us A.B.H.S. [240]

RECORDS / Canada. Indian Dept – v1-16. 1722-1820 – 1 – cn Micromedia [971]

RECORDS / Canterbury, New Hampshire. Canterbury Free Will Baptist Church – 1794-1884 – 1 – us A.B.H.S. [240]

RECORDS / Canterbury, New Hampshire. First Free Will Baptist Society – 1848-1919 – 1 – 15.50 – us A.B.H.S. [240]

RECORDS / Canton. Ohio. First Baptist Church – 1849-1931 – 1r – 1 – $32.50r – us Archival [240]

RECORDS / Canton. Ohio. First United Church of Christ – 1824-1938 – 2r – 1 – $32.50r – us Archival [240]

RECORDS / Carey. Ohio. Memorial United Methodist Church – 1834-1973 – 1r – 1 – $32.50r – us Archival [240]

RECORDS / Carroll, New Hampshire. Carroll Baptist Church – 1845-74 – 1 – 15.50 – us A.B.H.S. [240]

RECORDS / Cecil. Ohio. Immaculate Conception Church – 1868-1982 – 1r – 1 – $32.50r – us Archival [978]

RECORDS / Center Creek. Baptist Church, Jefferson County, Mo. – 1857-61 – 1 – us KS Hist [978]

RECORDS / Central Maine Theological Circle – 1890-1916 – 1 – us A.B.H.S. [240]

RECORDS / Central Old Settlers Union, Jefferson County, KS – 1878-1979 – 1 – us KS Hist [920]

RECORDS / Central United Presbyterian Church, Topeka, KS – 1870-1980 – 1 – us KS Hist [240]

RECORDS / Chadds Ford, Pennsylvania. Brandywine Baptist Church – 1715-1873. Includes church covenant, membership lists and 200th anniversary program, 1915 – 1 – us A.B.H.S. [240]

RECORDS / Charleston Library Society. Charleston, South Carolina – 1758-1811 – 30mf – 9 – us South Carolina Historical [020]

RECORDS / Charleston. South Carolina. Calvary Protestant Episcopal Church – 1848-1984. Burials, 1848-61, 1872-1978; Baptisms, 1848-60, 1872-1978; Confirmations and Communicants, 1849-60, 1872-1984; Marriages, 1849-57, 1872-1974. Founded in 1847 for black communicants. 8 fiches – 9 – us South Carolina Historical [978]

RECORDS / Charleston. South Carolina. Grace (Episcopal) Church – 1846-1977. Includes Parish Registers, Vestry Minutes, Receipt Book, Cash Book, Ledger, Minutes of Woman's Auxiliary, Minutes of Women of Grace, data for slaves and their owners, financial records, etc. 250 fiches – 9 – us South Carolina Historical [978]

RECORDS / Charleston. South Carolina. St. Mark's Protestant Episcopal Church – (1864) 1866-1965. 38 fiches – 9 – us South Carolina Historical [978]

RECORDS / Charleston. South Carolina. St. Michael's Episcopal Church – 1751-1915. 200 fiches. (Courtesy of St. Michael's Church, 1981) – 9 – us South Carolina Historical [978]

RECORDS / Charleston. South Carolina. St. Paul's Stono (Episcopal) Church – 1786-1869. Vestry Minutes, 1786-1864. 6 fiches – 9 – us South Carolina Historical [978]

RECORDS / Charleston. South Carolina. St. Peter's and Christ (Episcopal) Churches – 1834-1958. 42 fiches – 9 – us South Carolina Historical [978]

RECORDS / Charleston. South Carolina. St. Philip's (Episcopal) Church – 1713-1945. 468 fiches – 9 – us South Carolina Historical [978]

RECORDS / Charleston. South Carolina. St. Stephen's (Episcopal) Church – 1822-80.11 fiches – 9 – us South Carolina Historical [978]

RECORDS / Chatfield. Ohio. Evangelical Lutheran Church. Nazareth Congregation – 1840-1972 – 1r – 1 – $32.50r – us Archival [240]

RECORDS / Chatfield. Ohio. Evangelical Lutheran Church. Peace Congregation – 1842-1936 – 1r – 1 – $32.50r – us Archival [240]

RECORDS / Chester, New Hampshire. Chester Baptist Church – 1819-1902 – 1 – us A.B.H.S. [240]

RECORDS / Chesterfield, Massachusetts. Chesterfield Baptist Church – 1789-1848 – 1 – us A.B.H.S. [240]

RECORDS / Chichester, New Hampshire. Chichester Baptist Church and Society – 1827-1950 – 1 – us A.B.H.S. [240]

RECORDS / Chili, New York. Chili Baptist Church – 1834-1949 – 1 – us A.B.H.S. [240]

RECORDS / Church of Seventh Day Adventists (Columbus Grove, Ohio) – 1876-1923 – 1r – 1 – $32.50r – us Archival [978]

RECORDS / Citizens Alliance of Minneapolis – 1903-52 – 22r – 1 – $660.00 $35.00r – us M.H.S. [978]

RECORDS / Claremont, New Hampshire. Claremont Baptist Church and Society – 1821-1968 – 1 – us A.B.H.S. [240]

RECORDS / Clifton Park, New York. Clifton Park Baptist Church – (Clifton Park, First Half Moon Church, Records, 1803-188?. Clifton Park, Second Half Moon Church, Records, 1841-1905) – 1794-1981 – 1 – us A.B.H.S. [240]

RECORDS / Clockmakers Company – From the Guildhall Library, London. MS – 1 – uk Microform Academic [941]

RECORDS / Clyde. Ohio. Clyde Baptist Church – 1863-1926 – 1r – 1 – $32.50r – us Archival [240]

RECORDS / Colleton County. South Carolina. St. Bartholomew's (Episcopal) Parish – 1818-62.8 fiches – 9 – us South Carolina Historical [978]

RECORDS / Columbus Grove. Ohio. First Presbyterian Church – 1836-1987 – 1 – $32.50r – us Archival [240]

RECORDS / Concord, New Hampshire. Concord Baptist Church – 1800-1943 – 1 – us A.B.H.S. [240]

RECORDS / Concordia Luthern Church, Hoisington, KS – 1909-1984, Records pertaining to St. John's, Emmaus, and Concordia Lutheran churches – 1 – us KS Hist [240]

RECORDS / Confederate States of America – 1858-72 – 1 – 1,463.00 – us L of C Photodup [976]

RECORDS / Confederate States of America. Army – 1863. 3 fiches – 9 – us South Carolina Historical [976]

RECORDS / Convocation of Charleston. South Carolina – 1924-42.Minutes, reports, correspondence, lists of members, constitution, etc. Bishops, Presbyters, and Deacons canonically connected with Diocese of South Carolina, Charleston area. 3 fiches – 9 – us South Carolina Historical [978]

RECORDS / Convoy Research Club (Convoy, Ohio) – 1908-1994 – 2r – 1 – $32.50r – us Archival [978]

RECORDS / Corning, Iowa. Corning Baptist Church – 1878-1981 – 1 – us A.B.H.S. [240]

RECORDS / Cornish, New Hampshire. Cornish Baptist Church – 1791-1954 – 1 – us A.B.H.S. [240]

RECORDS / Crawford County.Ohio. St. Paul's Lutheran Church – 1854-1953 – 1r – 1 – $32.50r – us Archival [240]

RECORDS / Crestline. Ohio. First English Lutheran Church – 1854-1935 – 1r – 1 – $32.50r – us Archival [240]

RECORDS / C.T. Mitchell & Co. Charleston, South Carolina – 1850-64 – 134mf – 9 – us South Carolina Historical [025]

RECORDS / Dakota. Territory – (Includes guide) – 1861-89 – 86r – 1 – $2,500.00 (negotiable) – us U.N.D. [978]

RECORDS / Damariscotta Mills, Maine. Damariscotta Mills Baptist Church – (Treasurer's Book, 1921-47) – 1876-1939 – 1 – us A.B.H.S. [240]

RECORDS / Danbury, New Hampshire. Danbury Baptist Church – 1819-1941 – 1 – us A.B.H.S. [240]

RECORDS / Danbury. Ohio. St. Paul Lutheran Church – 1845-1985 – 1r – 1 – $32.50r – us Archival [240]

RECORDS / Danvers, Massachusetts. Danvers Baptist Church – 1793-1818 – 1 – us A.B.H.S. [240]

RECORDS / Delta Woman's Club. Delta, Ohio – 1895-1982 – 3r – 1 – $32.50r – us Archival [978]

RECORDS / Denmark, Maine. First Free Will Baptist Church – 1834-80 – 1 – 15.50 – us A.B.H.S. [240]

RECORDS / Disabled American Veterans. Fulton County Chapter no. 78 – 1939-1958 – 1r – 1 – $32.50r – us Archival [978]

RECORDS / Dodge City. Kansas. City Council – 1875-1928 – 1 – us KS Hist [978]

RECORDS / Dover, New Hampshire. Dover Free Will Baptist Church – 1843-1901 – 1 – us A.B.H.S. [240]

RECORDS / Dunbarton, New Hampshire. Dunbarton Baptist Church – 1829-1907; 1845-96 – 1 – us A.B.H.S. [240]

RECORDS / East Tilton, New Hampshire. East Tilton Free Will Baptist Church – 1830-1920; 1909-34 – 1 – us A.B.H.S. [240]

RECORDS / East Winslow, Maine. East Winslow Baptist Church – 1837-1950 – 1 – 15.50 – us A.B.H.S. [240]

RECORDS / Ebenezer United Methodist Church (Tiffin, Ohio) – 1858-1986 – 2r – 1 – $32.50r – us Archival [240]

RECORDS / Edison Memorial Methodist Church (Milan, Ohio) – 1838-1985 – 2r – 1 – $32.50r – us Archival [240]

RECORDS / Eicholtz, W.H. and Sons – 1881-1951, Funeral home records from Atchison and Abilene – 1 – us KS Hist [920]

RECORDS / Elliston. Ohio. Trinity United Church of Christ – 1862-1974 – 1r – 1 – $32.50r – us Archival [978]

RECORDS / Ellsworth County. Kansas. District Court – 1867-1901 – 1 – us KS Hist [978]

RECORDS / Ellsworth County. Kansas. District Court – 1868-98 – 1 – us KS Hist [324]

RECORDS / Ellsworth. Kansas – 1871-1910 – 1 – us KS Hist [978]

RECORDS / Elmore. Ohio. St. John's United Church of Christ – 1857-1985 – 1r – 1 – $32.50r – us Archival [240]

RECORDS / Emmanuel Lutheran Church, Hoisington, KS – 1900-1983 – 1 – us KS Hist [240]

RECORDS / Emporia Evangelical United Brethren Mission – 1901-64 – 1 – us KS Hist [978]
RECORDS / Emporia. Kansas. St. Andrew's Episcopal Church – 1870-1972 – 1 – us KS Hist [978]
RECORDS / Evangelical Reformirten Schonfeld Gemeinde Kirchenbuch, Barton County, KS – 1883-1978 – 1 – us KS Hist [240]
RECORDS / Exchange National Bank. Atchison, Kansas – 1858-1923 – 1 – us KS Hist [025]
RECORDS / Exeter, New Hampshire. Exeter Baptist Church – 1800-33 – 1 – 15.50 – us A.B.H.S. [240]
RECORDS / Fair Employment Practice Committee – 1941-46 – 212r – 1 – us UMI [330]
RECORDS / Farmingdale, South Dakota. Farmingdale Baptist Church – 1908-48 – 1 – 15.50 – us A.B.H.S. [240]
RECORDS / Findlay. Ohio. Howard Methodist Church – 1887-1968 – 5r – 1 – $32.50r – us Archival [978]
RECORDS / Findlay.Ohio. St. Andrew's United Methodist Church – 1876-1984 – 1r – 1 – $32.50r – us Archival [240]
RECORDS / First Baptist Church, Ottawa, KS – 1871-1948, Membership register, 1871-1948; marriage and funeral registers, 1907-1945 – 1 – us KS Hist [240]
RECORDS / First Congregational and Presbyterian Society (Peru, Ohio) – 1819-1927 – 1r – 1 – $32.50r – us Archival [978]
RECORDS / First Methodist Episcopal Church (Van Wert, Ohio) – 1r – 1 – $32.50r – us Archival [978]
RECORDS / First Presbyterian Church, Topeka, KS – 1859-1983 – 1 – us KS Hist [240]
RECORDS / First United Methodist Church (New Lexington, Ohio) – 1859-1937 – 1r – 1 – $32.50r – us Archival [240]
RECORDS / First United Methodist Church (Oberlin, Ohio) – 1860-1990 – 2r – 1 – $32.50r – us Archival [978]
RECORDS / Ford County. Kansas. District Court – 1874-1910 – 1 – us KS Hist [340]
RECORDS / Ford County. Kansas. Register of Deeds – 1873-1946 – 1 – us KS Hist [978]
RECORDS / Fort Larned. Kansas – 1858-75 – 1 – us KS Hist [025]
RECORDS / Fort Leavenworth. Kansas – 1862-64, 1903-06 – 1 – us KS Hist [025]
RECORDS / Fortnightly Club. Topeka, Kansas – 1899-1943 – 1 – us KS Hist [978]
RECORDS / Fostoria. Ohio. Bethel United Methodist Church – 1843-1991 – 1r – 1 – $32.50r – us Archival [240]
RECORDS / Framingham, Massachusetts. First Baptist Church and Society – 1811-1959 – 1 – us A.B.H.S. [240]
RECORDS / Francistown, New Hampshire. Francistown Baptist Church – 1834-44 – 1 – 15.50 – us A.B.H.S. [240]
RECORDS / Franklin, New Hampshire.East Franklin Baptist Church – 1869-76 – 1 – 15.50 – us A.B.H.S. [240]
RECORDS / Free Will Baptist Foreign Mission Society – 1833-94 – 1 – us A.B.H.S. [240]
RECORDS / Freewill Baptist Church (Ridgefield, Ohio) – 1835-45 – 1r – 1 – $32.50r – us Archival [978]
RECORDS / Fremont. Ohio. Memorial United Methodist Church – 1827-1993 – 1r – 1 – $32.50r – us Archival [240]
RECORDS / Fremont.Ohio. First United Presbyterian Church – 1833-1946 – 2r – 1 – $32.50r – us Archival [240]
RECORDS / Fremont.Ohio. St. John's Evangelical Lutheran Church – 1843-1945 – 2r – 1 – $32.50r – us Archival [240]
RECORDS / Fremont.Ohio. St. Paul's Episcopal Church – 1842-1941 – 1r – 1 – $32.50r – us Archival [240]
RECORDS / Funeral Home, Havana, KS – 1890-1922 – 1 – us KS Hist [920]
RECORDS / Galion. Ohio. First Lutheran Church – 1831-1981 – 1r – 1 – $32.50r – us Archival [240]
RECORDS / Galion. Ohio. First United Methodist Church – 1850-1954 – 1r – 1 – $32.50r – us Archival [240]
RECORDS / Galion. Ohio. Peace United Church of Christ – 1841-1969 – 1r – 1 – $32.50r – us Archival [240]
RECORDS / Garden City, Kansas. Community Congregational Church – 1879-1953 – 1 – us KS Hist [978]
RECORDS / Gardiner, Maine.West Gardiner Free Will Baptist Church/Spears Corner Free Will Baptist Church – 1826-72, 1951 – 1 – us A.B.H.S. [240]
RECORDS / Georgetown County. South Carolina. Church of the Messiah (Episcopal) – 1853-1910. Baptisms, 1855-1906; Marriages, 1873-1907; Burials, 1858-1904; Communicants, 1857-1900; List of Parishioners, 1899-1906. 2 fiches – 9 – us South Carolina Historical [978]
RECORDS / Germany. Armed Forces High Command. Headquarters – 1449 rolls. T77. Finding Aids: GG7, 17-19, and T176 rolls 26, 17. (Captured German Records Filmed at Alexandria, VA.) – 1 – us Nat'l Archives [324]
RECORDS / Germany. Army High Command. Headquarters – 645 rolls. T78. Finding Aids: Gg12, 29, 30 and T176 roll 28. (Captured German Records Filmed at Alexandria, VA.) – 1 – us Nat'l Archives [324]
RECORDS / Germany. Navy High Command. Headquarters – 8rolls. T608. Finding Aids: GG37 and T176 roll 24. (Captured German Records Filmed at Alexandria, VA.) – 1 – us Nat'l Archives [324]
RECORDS / Germany. Office of the Deputy for Serbian Economy – 89 rolls. T75. Finding Aids: T176 roll 32. (Captured German Records Filmed at Alexandria, VA.) – 1 – us Nat'l Archives [324]
RECORDS / Germany. Reich Commissioner for the Strengthening of Germandom – 20 rolls. T74. Finding Aids: GG2. (Captured German Records Filmed at Alexandria, VA.) – 1 – us Nat'l Archives [324]
RECORDS / Germany. Reich Ministry for Armaments and War Production – 193 rolls. T73. Finding Aid: GG10. (Captured German Records Filmed at Alexandria, VA.) – 1 – us Nat'l Archives [324]
RECORDS / Germany. Reich Ministry of Economics – 148 rolls. T71. Finding Aid: GG1 and T176 roll 24. (Captured German Records Filmed at Alexandria, VA.) – 1 – us Nat'l Archives [324]
RECORDS / Germany. Reichsluftfahrtministerium. (Reich Air Ministry) – 52 rolls. T177. Finding Aid: GG13. (Captured German Records Filmed at Alexandria, VA.) – 1 – us Nat'l Archives [324]
RECORDS / Germany. Todt Organization – 7 rolls. T76. Finding Aids: GG4. (Captured German Records Filmed at Alexandria, VA.) – 1 – us Nat'l Archives [324]
RECORDS / Gilmantown, New Hampshire. Gilmantown Baptist Church – 1773-1868 – 1 – 15.50 – us A.B.H.S. [240]
RECORDS / Glen Covenant, New Hampshire. Glen Covenant Free Will Baptist Church – 1901-05 – 1 – 15.50 – us A.B.H.S. [240]
RECORDS / Goffstown, New Hampshire. Goffstown Baptist Church – 1793-1819 – 1 – us A.B.H.S. [240]
RECORDS / Goshen, New Hampshire. Goshen Baptist Church – 1803-54 – 1 – us A.B.H.S. [240]
RECORDS / Grand Army of the Republic. District of Kansas – 1879-1936 – 1 – us KS Hist [976]
RECORDS / Grand Army of the Republic. Robbins Post No91 (Upper Sandusky, OH) – 1881-1927 – 1r – 1 – $32.50r – us Archival [355]
RECORDS / Grand Rapids. Ohio. First Presbyterian Church – 1849-1971 – 1r – 1 – $32.50r – us Archival [240]
RECORDS / Great Britain. Cabinet Office – Cabinet Reports by Prime Ministers to the Crown: Part 1: 1837-1867; Part 2: 1868-1916 – 1 – us Primary [941]
RECORDS / Greece, New York. Greece Baptist Church – 1834-1955 – 1 – us A.B.H.S. [240]
RECORDS / Greene, Maine. Free Will Baptist Church – 1780-1867, 1826-1906 – 1 – us A.B.H.S. [240]
RECORDS / Greenfield Congregational Society Church (Huron County, Ohio) – 1832-1959 – 1r – 1 – $32.50r – us Archival [978]
RECORDS / Gulf, Colorado and Santa Fe Railway Company – 1878-1944, Texas portion of the Atchison, Topeka and Santa Fe Railroad – 1 – us KS Hist [380]
RECORDS / Hampden, Maine. First Baptist Church – 1905 – 1 – us A.B.H.S. [240]
RECORDS / Hancock County. Ohio. Bethlehem United Methodist Church – 1873-1982 – 2r – 1 – $32.50r – us Archival [240]
RECORDS / Harmony Society – 1786-1951. (Ms Group 185 of the PA. State Archives). 311 reels. Printed guide – 1 – us Penn Hist [240]
RECORDS / Harrison, Maine.Harrison Baptist Church – 1827-1908 – 1 – 15.50 – us A.B.H.S. [240]
RECORDS / Hartland Sunday School (Hartland Township, Huron County, Ohio) – 1879-85 – 1r – 1 – $32.50r – us Archival [978]
RECORDS / Haskins,Ohio. Haskins Federated Church – 1867-1941 – 1r – 1 – $32.50r – us Archival [240]
RECORDS / Hebron, New Hampshire. Hebron Baptist Church – 1815-71 – 1 – 15.50 – us A.B.H.S. [240]
RECORDS / Helena, Ohio. Shiloh United Methodist Church – 1822-1895 – 1r – 1 – $32.50r – us Archival [240]
RECORDS / Highland. Kansas. Highland Presbyterian Church – 1843-90 – 1 – us KS Hist [978]
RECORDS / Highland University – 1857-68 – 1 – us KS Hist [025]
RECORDS / Hingham, Massachusetts. Hingham Baptist Church – 1823-1981 – 1 – us A.B.H.S. [240]
RECORDS / Hinsdale, New Hampshire.North Hinsdale Baptist Church – 1800-76 – 1 – 15.50 – us A.B.H.S. [240]
RECORDS / Hodgeman County. Kansas. St. Michael's Evangelical Lutheran Church – 1900-74 – 1 – us KS Hist [978]
RECORDS / Holgate.Ohio. Holgate United Methodist Church – 1891-1916 – 1r – 1 – $32.50r – us Archival [240]
RECORDS / Holgate.Ohio. St. John's Lutheran Church – 1876-1941 – 1r – 1 – $32.50r – us Archival [240]
RECORDS / Hollis, New Hampshire. Hollis Baptist Church – 1837-52 – 1 – 15.50 – us A.B.H.S. [240]
RECORDS / Hudson, New Hampshire. Hudson Baptist Church – 1817-1924 – 1 – us A.B.H.S. [240]
RECORDS / Hyannis, Massachusetts. First Baptist Church and Society – 1772-1945 – 1 – us A.B.H.S. [240]
RECORDS / Immanuel Lutheran Church (Upper Sandusky, Ohio) – 1896-1990 – 1r – 1 – $32.50r – us Archival [978]
RECORDS / Immanuel Lutheran Church (Upper Sandusky, Ohio) – 1896-1990 – 1 reel – 1 – us Archival [240]
RECORDS / International Association of Bridge, Structural and Ornamental Ironworkers. Local 55 (Toledo, Ohio) – 1918-1973 – 3r – 1 – $32.50r – us Archival [978]
RECORDS / International Order of the King's Daughters and Sons. Ohio Branch – 1931-79 – 1r – 1 – $32.50r – us Archival [978]
RECORDS / James Island. Charleston County. South Carolina. St. James Episcopal Church – 1831-1974. 36 fiches. (Courtesy of St. James Church, 1981) – 9 – us South Carolina Historical [978]
RECORDS / Jantzen Hillsboro Creamery – 1899-1903 – 1 – us KS Hist [330]
RECORDS / Jefferson, New Hampshire. Jefferson Baptist Church – 1812-94 – 1 – 15.50 – us A.B.H.S. [240]
RECORDS / Jewell County. Kansas. School District No. 106 – 1874-1947 – 1 – us KS Hist [025]
RECORDS / Jockey Club. South Carolina – 1842-1900. 10 fiches – 9 – us South Carolina Historical [790]
RECORDS / John's Island. South Carolina. St. John's (Episcopal) Church – 1734-1981. 23 fiches – 9 – us South Carolina Historical [978]
RECORDS / Johnson's Island Military Prison. Johnson's Island, Lake Erie – 1862-1864 – 2r – 1 – $32.50r – us Archival [976]
RECORDS / Jonesborough, Maine. Jonesborough and Addison Baptist Church – 1833-61 – 1 – us A.B.H.S. [240]
RECORDS / Junction City. Kansas. First Presbyterian Church – 1868-1967 – 1 – us KS Hist [978]
RECORDS / Kansas. Board of Statehouse Commissioners – 1866-91 – 1 – us KS Hist [978]
RECORDS / Kansas Infantry. 1st Regiment (Colored) – undated – 1 – us KS Hist [350]
RECORDS / Kansas. State Penitentiary – 1871-1906 – 1 – us KS Hist [360]
RECORDS / Kansas State Temperance Union – 1903-16 – 1 – us KS Hist [360]
RECORDS / Knights or Honor. Imperial Lodge No671 (Upper Sandusky, Ohio) – 1877-1884 – 1r – 1 – $32.50r – us Archival [060]
RECORDS / Labour Party. Great Britain. Birmingham – 1909-51 – 1 – uk Microform Academic [360]
RECORDS / Labour Party. Great Britain. Cambridge City and County – 1 – uk Microform Academic [360]
RECORDS / Labour Party. Great Britain. Colne Valley – 1891-1951 – 1 – uk Microform Academic [360]
RECORDS / Labour Party. Great Britain. Conference – 1900-to date – 1 – uk Microform Academic [360]
RECORDS / Labour Party. Great Britain. Doncaster – 1920-51 – 1 – uk Microform Academic [360]
RECORDS / Labour Party. Great Britain. Gloucester – 1899-1951 – 1 – uk Microform Academic [360]
RECORDS / Labour Party. Great Britain. Hamilton – 1918-1951 – 1 – uk Microform Academic [360]
RECORDS / Labour Party. Great Britain. Huddersfield – 1918-51 – 1 – uk Microform Academic [360]
RECORDS / Labour Party. Great Britain. Penistone – 1908-1951 – 1 – uk Microform Academic [360]
RECORDS / Labour Party. Great Britain. Peterborough – 1918-51 – 1 – uk Microform Academic [360]
RECORDS / Labour Party. Great Britain. Pontypridd, Wales – 1897-1951 – 1 – uk Microform Academic [360]
RECORDS / Labour Party. Great Britain. Sheffield – 1903-51 – 1 – uk Microform Academic [360]
RECORDS / Labour Party. Great Britain. South Shields – 1912-51 – 1 – uk Microform Academic [360]
RECORDS / Labour Party. Great Britain. Stockport – 1896-1951 – 1 – uk Microform Academic [360]
RECORDS / Labour Party. Great Britain. Wansbeck – 1914-1951 – 1 – uk Microform Academic [360]
RECORDS / Labour Party. Great Britain. Wolverhampton – 1907-1951 – 1 – uk Microform Academic [360]
RECORDS / Labour Party. Great Britain. Woolwich – 1905-1951 – 1 – uk Microform Academic [360]
RECORDS / Labour Party. Great Britain. Wrexham – 1912-51 – 1 – uk Microform Academic [360]
RECORDS / Laconia, New Hampshire. Laconia Baptist Church – 1888-1915 – 1 – us A.B.H.S. [240]
RECORDS / Lakeside. Ohio.Lakeside United Methodist Church – 1881-1936 – 1r – 1 – $32.50r – us Archival [240]
RECORDS / Lawrence Women's Club. Lawrence, Kansas – 1918-69 – 1 – us KS Hist [978]
RECORDS / Leavenworth County. Kansas. Little Stranger Church – 1852-1938 – 1 – us KS Hist [978]
RECORDS / Leavenworth. Kansas. First Baptist Church – 1864-1942 – 1 – us KS Hist [978]
RECORDS / Leavenworth. Kansas. First Baptist Church – 1942-70 – 1 – us KS Hist [978]
RECORDS / Leavenworth. Kansas. St. Paul Lutheran Church – 1861-1962 – 1 – us KS Hist [978]
RECORDS / Leavenworth. Kansas. Turnverein – 1857-1923 – 1 – us KS Hist [978]
RECORDS / Lexington. Ohio. First United Presbyterian Church – 1832-1983 – 1r – 1 – $32.50r – us Archival [240]
RECORDS / Lima. Ohio. Trinity United Methodist Church – 1960-1981 – 1r – 1 – $32.50r – us Archival [240]
RECORDS / Lindsborg. Kansas. Bethany Lutheran Church – 1869-1954 – 1 – us KS Hist [978]
RECORDS / Lindsey. Ohio. Emmanuel Lutheran Church – 1800-1966 – 1r – 1 – $32.50r – us Archival [240]
RECORDS / Litchfield, Maine. First Baptist Church – 1797-1807 – 1 – 15.50 – us A.B.H.S. [240]
RECORDS / Louisiana and the Floridas. (Diocese) – (Includes guide) – 1576-1803 – 12r – 1 – $480.00 – us U.N.D. Archives [240]

RECORDS / Lyndon. Kansas. First Presbyterian Church – 1870-1954 – 1 – us KS Hist [978]
RECORDS / Lyons. Ohio. East Chesterfield Church of Christ Disciples – 1887-1949 – 1r – 1 – $32.50r – us Archival [240]
RECORDS / McClellanville. South Carolina.St. James, Santee (Episcopal) Church – 1758-1971. 6 fiches – 9 – us South Carolina Historical [978]
RECORDS / McComb Church of Christ (McComb, Ohio) – 1879-1996 – 1r – 1 – $32.50r – us Archival [240]
RECORDS / Madison First Presbyterian Church, Madison, KS – 1882-1982 – 1 – us KS Hist [240]
RECORDS / Maine Baptist Historical Society – 1905-06 – 1 – 15.50 – us A.B.H.S. [240]
RECORDS / Maine Baptist Missionary Society – 1863-70 – 1 – us A.B.H.S. [240]
RECORDS / Maine Baptist Missionary Society – (Board of Trustees, Minutes, 1847-63) – 1805-44 – 1 – us A.B.H.S. [240]
RECORDS / Manchester Center, Vermont. First Baptist Church and Society – 1781-1974. Includes records of Second Baptist Church of Dorset, VT., 1802-12 – 1 – us A.B.H.S. [240]
RECORDS / Manchester, New Hampshire. Peoples Baptist Church – 1887-1930 – 1 – us A.B.H.S. [240]
RECORDS / Manchester, New Hampshire. Pine Street Baptist church – 1868-84 – 1 – 15.50 – us A.B.H.S. [240]
RECORDS / Manhattan. Kansas. First Baptist Church – 1858-78 – 1 – us KS Hist [978]
RECORDS / Manhattan Town Association. Manhattan, Kansas – 1855-77 – 1 – us KS Hist [978]
RECORDS / Mansfield. Ohio. First United Methodist Church – 1868-1982 – 2r – 1 – $32.50r – us Archival [240]
RECORDS / Mariana Islands. Spanish – 1678-1899. Records of the Spanish Colonial Government in the Mariana Islands – 1 – 605.00 – us L of C Photodup [025]
RECORDS / Mason, New Hampshire. Mason Baptist Church – 1788-1802 – 1 – 15.50 – us A.B.H.S. [240]
RECORDS / Maumee. Ohio. First Presbyterian Church – 1820-1969 – 2r – 1 – $32.50r – us Archival [240]
RECORDS / Mechanic Falls, Maine. Mechanic Falls Baptist Church – 1878-1911 – 1 – us A.B.H.S. [240]
RECORDS / Meddybemps, Maine. Meddybemps Baptist Church – 1847-84 – 1 – us A.B.H.S. [240]
RECORDS / Medfield, Massachusetts.Medfield Baptist Church – 1776-1868, 1881-1914 – 1 – us A.B.H.S. [240]
RECORDS / Meredith, New Hampshire.Meredith Baptist Church – 1800-1910 – 1 – us A.B.H.S. [240]
RECORDS / Merrimack Valley, New Hampshire.Merrimack Valley Free Will Baptist Mission Society – 1891-99 – 1 – 15.50 – us A.B.H.S. [240]
RECORDS / Metamora Methodist Church (Metamora, Ohio) – 1850-1946 – 1r – 1 – $32.50r – us Archival [240]
RECORDS / Methodist Episcopal Church. Bowling Green Circuit – 1836-1879 – 1r – 1 – $32.50r – us Archival [240]
RECORDS / Milan. Ohio. First Presbyterian Church – 1828-1954 – 1r – 1 – $32.50r – us Archival [240]
RECORDS / Milan Preparative Meeting of Friends (Erie County, Ohio) – 1879-1940 – 1r – 1 – $32.50r – us Archival [978]
RECORDS / Millbury. Ohio.St. Peter's United Church of Christ – 1884-1966 – 1r – 1 – $32.50r – us Archival [240]
RECORDS / Milo, New York. Second Baptist Church – 1877-1908, 1925-48 – 1 – us A.B.H.S. [240]
RECORDS / Montpelier. Ohio. Saint Paul's United Methodist Church – 1855-1891 – 1r – 1 – $32.50r – us Archival [240]
RECORDS / Moscow, Maine. Bakerston/Moscow Baptist Church – 1812-67 – 1 – 15.50 – us A.B.H.S. [240]
RECORDS / Mount Vernon, Maine. Particular Baptist Church – 1798-1902 – 1 – us A.B.H.S. [240]
RECORDS / Mt. Zion United Methodist Church (Arlington, Ohio) – 1886-1915 – 1r – 1 – $32.50r – us Archival [978]
RECORDS / Mt. Pleasant. South Carolina. Christ (Episcopal) Church – 1674-1865. Births and Baptisms, 1694-1788; Marriages, 1723-51, 1758-85, Deaths and Burials, 1709-89; Church Proceedings, 1708-85. With 2v of transcripts. 36 fiches – 9 – us South Carolina Historical [978]
RECORDS / Mt. Pleasant. South Carolina. St. Andrew's (Episcopal) Church – 1823-1953. 33 fiches – 9 – us South Carolina Historical [978]
RECORDS / Mumford, New York. First Baptist Church – 1852-1956 – 1 – us A.B.H.S. [240]
RECORDS / Muncy, Pennsylvania. Muncy Baptist Church – 1841-54 – 1 – 15.50 – us A.B.H.S. [240]
RECORDS / Munn Memorial Commission. Kansas – 1936-39 – 1 – us KS Hist [978]
RECORDS / Murphy General Store. Tecumseh, Kansas – 1878-86 – 1 – us KS Hist [978]
RECORDS / Nashua, New Hampshire. Crown Hill Baptist Church – 1922-32 – 1 – us A.B.H.S. [240]
RECORDS / National Consumer's League – Selection including Minutes of Executive Committee, Board of Directors, and Annual Meetings. 1898-1952 – 1 – 160.00 – us L of C Photodup [025]
RECORDS / National Socialist German Labor Party – 732 rolls. T81. Finding Aids: GG3, 16, 20-21, 35, and T176 roll 24. (Captured German Records Filmed at Alexandria, VA.) – 1 – us Nat'l Archives [943]
RECORDS / Nelson, New Hampshire. Nelson Baptist Church – 1818-50 – 1 – 15.50 – us A.B.H.S. [240]
RECORDS / Nevada United Methodist Church (Nevada, Ohio) – 1858-1990 – 1r – 1 – $32.50r – us Archival [240]
RECORDS / New Boston, New Hampshire. New Boston Baptist Church and Society – 1819-1940 – 1 – us A.B.H.S. [240]
RECORDS / New Castle. Presbytery (Pres. Ch. in the U.S.A.) – 1716-31, 1759-1909 – 1 – $150.00 – us Presbyterian [240]
RECORDS / New Hampshire Baptist Historical Society – 1881-1929 – 1 – 15.50 – us A.B.H.S. [240]
RECORDS / New Hampshire Charitable Society – 1833-57 – 1 – 15.50 – us A.B.H.S. [240]
RECORDS / New Hampshire. Conference of Baptist Ministers – 1832-1917 – 1 – us A.B.H.S. [240]
RECORDS / New Hampshire Yearly Meeting of Free Will Baptists – (Annual Meeting Records, 1825-1951. Board of Directors Records, 1888-1913. Executive Committee Records, 1900-51) – 1828-1914 – 1 – us A.B.H.S. [240]
RECORDS / New Hartford, New York. New Hartford Baptist Church and Society – 1854-94 – 1 – 15.50 – us A.B.H.S. [240]
RECORDS / New Sharon, Maine. New Sharon Baptist Church – 1815-62 – 1 – 15.50 – us A.B.H.S. [240]
RECORDS / New Washington. Ohio. St. John's Lutheran Church – 1829-1970 – 1r – 1 – $32.50r – us Archival [240]
RECORDS / New York. (Province). Vice Admiralty Court – T842 – 1r – 1 – us Nat'l Archives [340]
RECORDS / Newmarket, New Hampshire. Newmarket Free Will Baptist Church – 1834-1914 – 1 – us A.B.H.S. [240]
RECORDS / Newport, New Hampshire. Newport Baptist Church – 1790-1928 – 1 – us A.B.H.S. [240]
RECORDS / Newton, Massachusetts. First Baptist Church and Society – 1780-1959 – 1 – us A.B.H.S. [240]
RECORDS / North Baltimore. Ohio. Church of the Good Shepherd-United Brethren – 1889-1986 – 1r – 1 – $32.50r – us Archival [240]
RECORDS / North Berwick, Maine. North Berwick Baptist Church – (Treasurer's Book, 1862-67. Great Hill Society Records, 1799-1851. Baptist Society in Berwick Records, 1852-1922) – 1799-1922 – 1 – 18.35 – us A.B.H.S. [240]
RECORDS / North Egremont, Massachusetts. North Egremont Baptist Church – 1789-1975 – 1 – us A.B.H.S. [240]
RECORDS / North Salem Lutheran Church (Wyandot County, Ohio) – 1868-1989 – 2r – 1 – $32.50r – us Archival [978]
RECORDS / North Sanbornton, New Hampshire.Third Baptist Church – 1833-1927 – 1 – 15.50 – us A.B.H.S. [240]
RECORDS / North Yarmouth, Maine. Baptist Religious Society in North Yarmouth and Freeport – 1797-1855 – 1 – 15.50 – us A.B.H.S. [240]
RECORDS / Northborough, Massachusetts. Evangelical Congregational Church – 1833-1948 – 1 – us A.B.H.S. [240]
RECORDS / Northborough, Massachusetts. Northborough Baptist Church – 1827-1948 – 1 – us A.B.H.S. [240]
RECORDS / Northborough, Massachusetts. Trinity Church – 1948-78 – 1 – us A.B.H.S. [240]
RECORDS / Northern Pacific Railway Company. Land Department – 1870-76 – 38r – 1 – $1330.00 $40.00r – us M.H.S. [380]
RECORDS / Northport, Maine. Northport Baptist Church – 1804-29 – 1 – 15.50 – us A.B.H.S. [240]
RECORDS / Northwest Vigilante Committee, Franklin County, KS – undated – 1 – us KS Hist [978]
RECORDS / Northwood, New Hampshire. Northwood Baptist Church – 1829-1939 – 1 – 15.50 – us A.B.H.S. [240]
RECORDS / Norwalk. Ohio. First Presbyterian Church – 1830-1950 – 1r – 1 – $32.50r – us Archival [240]
RECORDS / Norwalk.Ohio. St. Paul's Episcopal Church – 1821-1938 – 1r – 1 – $32.50r – us Archival [240]
RECORDS / Nottingham, New Hampshire. Nottingham Baptist Church – 1805-44 – 1 – 15.50 – us A.B.H.S. [240]
RECORDS / Oak Harbor. Ohio. St. Joseph's Catholic Church – 1811-1972 – 1r – 1 – $32.50r – us Archival [240]
RECORDS / Oak Harbor. Ohio. St. Paul's United Church of Christ – 1879-1979 – 1r – 1 – $32.50r – us Archival [978]
RECORDS / Oak Shade Methodist Church (Fulton County, Ohio) – 1909-1942 – 1r – 1 – $32.50r – us Archival [240]
RECORDS / Oakdale United Methodist Church (Deshler, Ohio) – 1854-1989 – 1r – 1 – $32.50r – us Archival [978]
RECORDS / Occola. Ohio. United Brethren Church – 1850-1927 – 1r – 1 – $32.50r – us Archival [240]
RECORDS / Ohio City. Ohio. Methodist Episcopal Church – 1883-1911 – 1r – 1 – $32.50r – us Archival [240]
RECORDS / Ohio. Grand Army of the Republic. Army & Navy Post No.187 – 1861-65; 1913-20. 1 reel – 1 – us Western Res [380]
RECORDS / Olena Presbyterian Church (Bronson Township, Huron County, Ohio) – 1835-1949 – 1r – 1 – $32.50r – us Archival [978]
RECORDS / Olentangy. Ohio. Emmanuel Lutheran Church – 1902-1935 – 1r – 1 – $32.50r – us Archival [240]
RECORDS / Ontario College of Art. Council – 1912-June 1979 – 1 – 360.00 – cn McLaren [700]
RECORDS / Oregon. Ohio. Saint Mark's Lutheran Church – 1875-1992 – 2r – 1 – $32.50r – us Archival [240]
RECORDS / Osage County. Kansas. Elk Township – 1883-1921 – 1 – us KS Hist [978]
RECORDS / Osage County. Kansas. School District 16 – 1872-1929 – 1 – us KS Hist [978]
RECORDS / Osborne County. Kansas. Superintendent of Schools – 1872-1967 – 1 – us KS Hist [978]
RECORDS / Osborne. Kansas. First Congregational Church – 1872-1946 – 1 – us KS Hist [978]
RECORDS / Ottawa Presbyterian Church (Ottawa, Ohio) – 1864-1995 – 2r – 1 – $32.50r – us Archival [240]
RECORDS / Overbrook Methodist Church – 1892-1944 – 1 – us KS Hist [978]
RECORDS / Oxford, Maine. Baptist Auxiliary Foreign Mission Society – (Northern Baptist). 1826-1928 – 1 – 15.50 – us A.B.H.S. [240]
RECORDS / Pandora United Methodist Chruch (Pandora, Ohio) – 1907-96 – 2r – 1 – $32.50r – us Archival [978]
RECORDS / Patrons of Husbandry. Ohio State Grange. Salem Grange No. 2259. Wood County, Ohio – 1919-68 – 2r – 1 – $32.50r – us Archival [978]
RECORDS / Patrons of Husbandry. Pleasant Hill Grange No. 11, Reno County, KS – 1927-1934 – 1 – us KS Hist [920]
RECORDS / Paulding. Ohio. St. Joseph's Catholic Church – 1900-1983 – 1r – 1 – $32.50r – us Archival [978]
RECORDS / Pemberville. Ohio. Bethlehem Lutheran Church – 1800-1945 – 1r – 1 – $32.50r – us Archival [240]
RECORDS / Pemberville. Ohio. First United Presbyterian Church – 1878-1982 – 3r – 1 – $32.50r – us Archival [978]
RECORDS / Pemberville. Ohio. Salem Evangelical Lutheran Church – 1848-1983 – 1r – 1 – $32.50r – us Archival [978]
RECORDS / Pemberville. Ohio. St. Paul's Lutheran Church – 1881-1939 – 1r – 1 – $32.50r – us Archival [240]
RECORDS / Penfield, New York. Penfield Baptist Society – 1823-85 – 1 – 15.50 – us A.B.H.S. [240]
RECORDS / Pennsylvania. (Colony). Provincial Council – 1682-1776. In PA. State Archives. 26 reels. – 1 – us Penn Hist [975]
RECORDS / Perrysburg. Ohio. Zoar Lutheran Church – 1853-1974 – 1r – 1 – $32.50r – us Archival [240]
RECORDS / Peterboro, New Hampshire. Peterboro Free Will Baptist Church – (Young Ladies Literary and Benevolent Society Records, 1836-64) – 1822-1952; 1840-51 – 1 – us A.B.H.S. [240]
RECORDS / Philadelphia, Pennsylvania. Lower Dublin/Pennepek Baptist Church – 1687-1894 – 1 – 18.30 – us A.B.H.S. [240]
RECORDS / Philadelphia, Pennsylvania. Sansom Street Baptist Church – 1804-24 – 1 – 17.30 – us A.B.H.S. [240]
RECORDS / Philematheon Club, Leavenworth, KS – 1898-1958 – 1 – us KS Hist [920]
RECORDS / Pittsfield, Massachusetts. Pittsfield Baptist Church – 1800-1935 – 1 – us A.B.H.S. [240]
RECORDS / Pittsfield, New Hampshire. Pittsfield Baptist Church – 1791-1854 – 1 – us A.B.H.S. [240]
RECORDS / Plainfield, New Hampshire. Plainfield Baptist Church – 1829-1906 – 1 – 15.50 – us A.B.H.S. [240]
RECORDS / Pleasant Hill Church of the Nazarene, Sylvia, KS – 1920-1968 – 1 – us KS Hist [240]
RECORDS / Pleasant Hill Union Sunday School, Reno County, KS – 1880-1956 – 1 – us KS Hist [240]
RECORDS / Poland, Maine. First Free Will Baptist Church – 1828-87; 1840-84 – 1 – us A.B.H.S. [240]
RECORDS / Pontiac-Monroeville. Ohio. St. Peter Lutheran Church – 1859-1965 – 1r – 1 – $32.50r – us Archival [240]
RECORDS / Pontiac-Monroeville. Ohio. St. Peter Lutheran Church – 1859-1975 – 2r – 1 – us Archival [240]
RECORDS / Port Clinton Literary and Social Club. Ohio – 1881-1980 – 1r – 1 – $32.50r – us Archival [978]
RECORDS / Port Clinton. Ohio. St. John's Lutheran Church – 1875-1977 – 1r – 1 – $32.50r – us Archival [978]
RECORDS / Port Clinton. Ohio. St. Thomas Episcopal Church – 1896-1982 – 1r – 1 – $32.50r – us Archival [978]
RECORDS / Port Clinton. Ohio. Trinity United Methodist Church – 1874-1924 – 1r – 1 – $32.50r – us Archival [978]
RECORDS / Portsmouth, New Hampshire. First Baptist Church – 1832-46; 1851-1915 – 1 – us A.B.H.S. [240]
RECORDS / Protestant Episcopal Church in the U.S.A. Kansas (Diocese) – 1879-1917 – 1 – us KS Hist [978]
RECORDS / Put-in-Bay. Ohio. St. Paul's Episcopal Church – 1865-1962 – 1r – 1 – $32.50r – us Archival [240]
RECORDS / R. Hoe and Company – 1830-1942. 17 reels – 1 – $360.00 – us L of C Photodup [360]
RECORDS / Reece. Kansas – 1886 – 1 – us KS Hist [978]
RECORDS / Rice Township. Sandusky County.Ohio. Trinity Evangelical Lutheran Church – 1892-1987 – 1 – $32.50r – us Archival [240]
RECORDS / Richmond, Maine.Baptist Church in Richmond Village – 1834-73 – 1 – us A.B.H.S. [240]
RECORDS / Richmond, Maine.Bowdoinham Ridge Free Baptist Society – (Treasurer's Records, 1891-1923) – 1841-1926 – 1 – us A.B.H.S. [240]

RECORDS / Richmond, Maine.Bowdoinham Ridge Free Will Baptist Church/Third Free Will Baptist Church – (Membership records, 1836-94) – 1836-1926 – 1 – us A.B.H.S. [240]

RECORDS / Richmond, Maine.Free Will Baptist Church of Bowdoinham Ridge – (Treasurer's Records, 1892-1924. Young People's Social and Literary Guild Records, 1888-96. Women's Missionary Society Records, 1880-88) – 1895-1924 – 1 – us A.B.H.S. [240]

RECORDS / Richmond, Maine.Ridge Meetinghouse Company – 1837-1913 – 1 – us A.B.H.S. [240]

RECORDS / Richmond, New Hampshire.Richmond Baptist Church – 1835-1911 – 1 – 15.50 – us A.B.H.S. [240]

RECORDS / Rochester, New York. Andrews Street Baptist Church – 1851-1944 – 1 – us A.B.H.S. [240]

RECORDS / Rochester, New York. First Baptist Church – 1818-1978 – 1 – us A.B.H.S. [240]

RECORDS / Russell. Kansas. First Congregational Church – 1886-1942 – 1 – us KS Hist [978]

RECORDS / Saint Alphonsus Catholic Church (Peru, Ohio) – 1834-1984 – 2r – 1 – $32.50r – us Archival [978]

RECORDS / St. Anthony's Church (Milan, Ohio) – 1866-1972 – 1r – 1 – $32.50r – us Archival [978]

RECORDS / ST. JOHN CANTIUS R.C. CHURCH – Wilno, MN, 1883-1976 – 5r – 1 – us I.H.R.C. [240]

RECORDS / St. John's Berkeley Parish. South Carolina – 1823-40, 1929-59. 2 fiches – 9 – us South Carolina Historical [978]

RECORDS / St. John's Episcopal Church (Napoleon, Ohio) – 1857-1969 – 1r – 1 – $32.50r – us Archival [240]

RECORDS / St. John's Evangelical Lutheran Church (Sulphur Springs, Ohio) – 1833-1994 – 1r – 1 – $32.50r – us Archival [978]

RECORDS / St. John's Lutheran Church, Herington, KS – undated – 1 – us KS Hist [240]

RECORDS / St. John's Lutheran Church, Russell, KS – undated – 1 – us KS Hist [240]

RECORDS / St. John's United Church of Christ (Holgate, Ohio) – 1860-1990 – 1r – 1 – $32.50r – us Archival [240]

RECORDS / St. John's United Church of Christ (Milan, Ohio) – 1864-1990 – 1r – 1 – $32.50r – us Archival [978]

RECORDS / St. Luke's Episcopal Church (Milan, Ohio) – 1849-1922 – 1r – 1 – $32.50r – us Archival [978]

RECORDS / St. Mark's Episcopal Church (Toledo, Ohio) – 1899-1988 – 2r – 1 – $32.50r – us Archival [978]

RECORDS / St. Paul's American Lutheran Church, Galatia, KS – 1910-1985 – 1 – us KS Hist [240]

RECORDS / Saint Paul's Episcopal Church (Maumee, Ohio) – 1837-1989 – 1r – 1 – $32.50r – us Archival [978]

RECORDS / St. Paul's Evangelical Lutheran Church (Jenera, Ohio) – 1868-1994 – 3r – 1 – $32.50r – us Archival [240]

RECORDS / St. Paul's Lutheran Church, Paradise Twp., Russell County, KS – undated – 1 – us KS Hist [240]

RECORDS / St. Peter's Church (Norwalk, Ohio) – 1851-91 – 1r – 1 – $32.50r – us Archival [978]

RECORDS / St. Peter's Lutheran Church (Lyme Township, Huron County, Ohio) – 1861-1990 – 1r – 1 – $32.50r – us Archival [240]

RECORDS / Saints Peter and Paul Catholic Church (Ottawa, Ohio) – 1872-1980 – 2r – 1 – $32.50r – us Archival [240]

RECORDS / Salisbury, New Hampshire. Salisbury Heights Baptist Church – (Treasurer's Book, 1898-1921) – 1810-69; 1893-1921 – 1 – us A.B.H.S. [240]

RECORDS / Salisbury, New Hampshire. Second Baptist Church – 1831-49 – 1 – 15.50 – us A.B.H.S. [240]

RECORDS / Sanbornton, New Hampshire. First Free Will Baptist Church – 1827-55 – 1 – 15.50 – us A.B.H.S. [240]

RECORDS / Sanbornton, New Hampshire. Sanbornton Baptist Church – 1793-1848 – 1 – 15.50 – us A.B.H.S. [240]

RECORDS / Sandusky. Ohio. First Congregational United Church of Christ – 1819-1986 – 2r – 1 – $32.50r – us Archival [240]

RECORDS / Sandusky. Ohio. First Presbyterian Church – 1852-1951 – 1r – 1 – $32.50r – us Archival [240]

RECORDS / Sandusky. Ohio.Grace Episcopal Church – 1835-1934 – 2r – 1 – $32.50r – us Archival [240]

RECORDS / Sandusky. Ohio.St. John Lutheran Church – 1866-1965 – 1r – 1 – $32.50r – us Archival [240]

RECORDS / Sandusky. Ohio.St. Stephen's United Church of Christ – 1881-1975 – 1r – 1 – $32.50r – us Archival [240]

RECORDS / Sanford, Maine. Sanford Baptist Church – 1772-1887 – 1 – us A.B.H.S. [240]

RECORDS / Scotch Ridge. Ohio. United Presbyterian Church – 1862-1980 – 1r – 1 – $32.50r – us Archival [240]

RECORDS / Sedgwick County. Kansas. District Court – 1870-86 – 1 – us KS Hist [340]

RECORDS / Seneca County. Ohio. Presbyterian Church of Melmore – 1828-1907 – 1r – 1 – $32.50r – us Archival [978]

RECORDS / Seneca County. Ohio. Zion Lutheran Church – 1803-1952 – 1r – 1 – $32.50r – us Archival [978]

RECORDS / Seneca Township.Seneca County. Ohio. Evangelical Jerusalem Church – 1841-1911 – 1r – 1 – $32.50r – us Archival [240]

RECORDS / Shapleigh, Maine. Second Free Will Baptist Church – 1828-69 – 1 – us A.B.H.S. [240]

RECORDS / Shapleigh, Maine. Shapleigh Baptist Church – 1864-1916 – 1 – us A.B.H.S. [240]

RECORDS / Shawnee County. Kansas. Pleasant Hill United Methodist Church – 1885-1978 – 1 – us KS Hist [978]

RECORDS / Shawnee County. Kansas. Pleasant Hill United Methodist Church – 1941-77 – 1 – us KS Hist [978]

RECORDS / Shawnee County. Kansas. Register of Deeds – 1855-98 – 1 – us KS Hist [978]

RECORDS / Shawnee County. Kansas. School District 38 – 1887-1943 – 1 – us KS Hist [978]

RECORDS / Silver Lake Methodist Church – 1869-1965 – 1 – us KS Hist [978]

RECORDS / Society of Friends. Ohio Yearly Meeting – 1760-1965 – 34r – 1 – $32.50r – us Archival [240]

RECORDS / Sorosis Club. Defiance, Ohio – 1894-1977 – 3r – 1 – $32.50r – us Archival [978]

RECORDS / South American Missionary Society. Archives – 1844-1919 – 1 – uk Microform Academic [240]

RECORDS / South Berwick, Maine. South Berwick Baptist Church – 1847-75.Includes membership records, 1847-71 – 1 – us A.B.H.S. [240]

RECORDS / South Carolina. Militia. Fourth Brigade – ca.1877-ca.1884. 6 fiches – 9 – us South Carolina Historical [976]

RECORDS / South Carolina. Militia. Scottish Guard – 1670-1852. 1 fiche – 9 – us South Carolina Historical [978]

RECORDS / South Carolina. St. Thomas and St. Denis Protestant Episcopal Church – 1693-1778. 31 fiches – 9 – us South Carolina Historical [978]

RECORDS / Spanish Government of East Florida – 1737-1821 – 1 – 3,637.00 – us L of C Photodup [975]

RECORDS / Spencerport, New York. Ogden Baptist Church – 1819-1980 – 1 – us A.B.H.S. [240]

RECORDS / Stony Ridge. Ohio. St. John's Evangelical Lutheran Church – 1869-1980 – 2r – 1 – $32.50r – us Archival [978]

RECORDS / Strafford, New Hampshire. Strafford and Barnstead Union Church – (Free Will Baptist). 1873-1915 – 1 – 15.50 – us A.B.H.S. [240]

RECORDS / Sullivan's Island. South Carolina. Chapel of the Holy Cross – 1891-1905. Episcopal. Building expenses, church investments, Vestry minutes. 5 fiches – 9 – us South Carolina Historical [978]

RECORDS / Sulphur Springs. Ohio. St. Paul Lutheran Church – 1838-1927 – 1r – 1 – $32.50r – us Archival [240]

RECORDS / Sulphur Springs.Ohio. Hope United Church of Christ – 1890-1977 – 1r – 1 – $32.50r – us Archival [240]

RECORDS / Sun Grain Association. Risingsun, Ohio – 1912-1954 – 1r – 1 – $32.50r – us Archival [978]

RECORDS / Sylvania United Church of Christ (Sylvania, Ohio) – 1834-1941 – 2r – 1 – $32.50r – us Archival [978]

RECORDS / Taft, Robert – undated, Microfilmed excerpts from a variety of sources relating to his study of western artists and the history of photography – 1 – us KS Hist [920]

RECORDS / Tecumseh. Kansas. Tecumseh Methodist Church – 1855-1965 – 1 – us KS Hist [978]

RECORDS / Temple Church, Saline County, KS – 1886-1969 – 1 – us KS Hist [240]

RECORDS / Thornton, New Hampshire.Thornton Baptist Church – 1835-1924 – 1 – us A.B.H.S. [240]

RECORDS / Thornton, New Hampshire.Thornton Free Will Baptist Church – 1821-43 – 1 – 15.50 – us A.B.H.S. [240]

RECORDS / Tiffin. Ohio. First Lutheran Church – 1870-1956 – 1r – 1 – $32.50r – us Archival [240]

RECORDS / Tiffin. Ohio. First Presbyterian Church – 1831-1930 – 1r – 1 – $32.50r – us Archival [240]

RECORDS / Tiffin. Ohio. St. John's United Church of Christ – 1836-1982 – 1r – 1 – $32.50r – us Archival [978]

RECORDS / Tiffin. Ohio. St. Paul's Methodist Church – 1882-1983 – 1r – 1 – $32.50r – us Archival [240]

RECORDS / Tiffin. Ohio. Trinity United Church of Christ – 1833-1975 – 2r – 1 – $32.50r – us Archival [240]

RECORDS / Tiro. Ohio. Oakland Lutheran Church – 1842-1944 – 1r – 1 – $32.50r – us Archival [240]

RECORDS / Toledo. Ohio. Broadway United Methodist Church – 1892 – 1r – 1 – $32.50r – us Archival [240]

RECORDS / Toledo. Ohio. Epworth United Methodist Church – 1894-1982 – 2r – 1 – $32.50r – us Archival [240]

RECORDS / Toledo. Ohio. First United Church of Christ – 1876-1992 – 1r – 1 – $32.50r – us Archival [240]

RECORDS / Toledo. Ohio. Salem Lutheran Church – 1845-1956 – 1r – 1 – $32.50r – us Archival [240]

RECORDS / Toledo. Ohio. St. Paul's Evangelical Lutheran Church – 1850-1986 – 5r – 1 – $32.50r – us Archival [240]

RECORDS / Tontogany. Ohio. First United Presbyterian Church – 1861-1978 – 1r – 1 – $32.50r – us Archival [978]

RECORDS / Topeka. Kansas. First Baptist Church – 1857-1948 – 1 – us KS Hist [978]

RECORDS / Topeka. Kansas. First Congregational Church – 1855-1927 – 1 – us KS Hist [978]

RECORDS / Topeka. Kansas. First Presbyterian Church – 1859-1931 – 1 – us KS Hist [978]

RECORDS / Topeka, Kansas. John Knox United Presbyterian Church – 1956-70 – 1 – us KS Hist [978]

RECORDS / Topeka. Kansas. Kansas Avenue United Methodist Church – 1870-1973 – 1 – us KS Hist [978]

RECORDS / Topeka. Kansas. Third United Presbyterian Church – 1880-1965 – 1 – us KS Hist [978]

RECORDS / Topeka. Kansas. Wanamaker Road Baptist Church – 1966-78 – 1 – us KS Hist [978]

RECORDS / Trinity Lutheran Church, Bender Hill Community, Russel County, KS – undated – 1 – us KS Hist [240]

RECORDS / Trinity Lutheran Church (Jenera, Ohio) – 1883-1996 – 1r – 1 – $32.50r – us Archival [978]

RECORDS / Trinity Lutheran Church (Middle Point, Ohio) – 1853-1991 – 1r – 1 – $32.50r – us Archival [240]

RECORDS / United Church of Christ (Columbus Grove, Ohio) – 1856-1981 – 2r – 1 – $32.50r – us Archival [240]

RECORDS / United Church of Christ. Kansas. Oklahoma Conference – 1858-1973 – 1 – us KS Hist [978]

RECORDS / United Methodist Women (U.S.). Toledo District – 1976-1991 – 1r – 1 – $32.50r – us Archival [978]

RECORDS / The United Society of Believers in Christ's Second Appearing – (Shaker Papers). 1792-1937 – 1 – $632.00 – us L of C Photodup [240]

RECORDS / U.S. Bureau of Indian Affairs – (Michigan superintendency of indian affairs, 1814-51. x71 rolls. M1. New Mexico superintendency of indian affairs, 1849-80. x30 rolls. T21. Oregon superintendency of indian affairs, 1848-73. x29 rolls. M2. Southern superintendency of indian affairs, 1832-70. x22 rolls. M640. Printed guide. Washington superintendency of indian affairs, 1853-74. x26 rolls. M5) – 1 – us Nat'l Archives [324]

RECORDS / U.S. Congress. Senate. Select Committee on John Brown's Raid at Harper's Ferry, Va. in 1859 – RG 46. M1196. 3 rolls – 1 – us Nat'l Archives [976]

RECORDS / U.S. Court of Commissioners of Alabama Claims – nos. 1-5770. 1882-85 – 1 – 1,068.00 – us L of C Photodup [976]

RECORDS / U.S. Federal Trade Commission – (See also indiv. titles: Minutes of Meetings of the Commission; Economic Investigations) – $9,765.00 set – us UPA [324]

RECORDS / U.S. Indian Claims Commission – (Available by ethnographical region and document type. See individual listings) – 6140 fiches. 2 books. – 9 – $18,975.00 – us UPA [305]

RECORDS / U.S. Life-Saving Service. Point Betsie Life Saving Station. Frankfort, Michigan – 1883-1919 – 1r – 1 – $32.50r – us Archival [978]

RECORDS / U.S. Weather Bureau – 1958-66 – 3 – us Readex [324]

RECORDS / Unity, New Hampshire. Unity Baptist Church – 1806-72 – 1 – 15.50 – us A.B.H.S. [240]

RECORDS / Upper Gilmanton, New Hampshire. Upper Gilmanton Free Will Baptist Church – 1835-1938 – 1 – us A.B.H.S. [240]

RECORDS / Upper Sandusky. Ohio. John Stewart United Methodist Church – 1828-1986 – 2r – 1 – $32.50r – us Archival [240]

RECORDS / Upper Sandusky. Ohio. St. Paul's Lutheran Church – 1861-1986 – 1r – 1 – $32.50r – us Archival [240]

RECORDS / Valley Falls. Kansas. St. Paul's Evangelical Lutheran Church – 1866-1978 – 1 – us KS Hist [978]

RECORDS / Van Wert County.Ohio. Middlepoint Methodist Charge – 1872-1942 – 1r – 1 – $32.50r – us Archival [240]

RECORDS / Van Wert. Ohio. First United Methodist Church – 1889-1984 – 1r – 1 – $32.50r – us Archival [240]

RECORDS / Vermont Baptist Ministers Conference and Aid Society – 1953-65 – 1 – 15.50 – us A.B.H.S. [240]

RECORDS / Wabaunsee County. Kansas. Wabaunsee Township – 1858-1922 – 1 – us KS Hist [978]

RECORDS / Wabaunsee County, KS. School District No. 1 – 1907-1966, Records of the school district and individual teachers – 1 – us KS Hist [370]

RECORDS / Wabaunsee. Kansas. Congregational Christian Community Church – 1914-64 – 1 – us KS Hist [978]

RECORDS / Wabaunsee. Kansas. First Church of Christ – 1857-1917 – 1 – us KS Hist [978]

RECORDS / Waccamaw. South Carolina. All Saints Episcopal Church – 1819-1935. Typed transcripts of the minutes and register. 3 fiches – 9 – us South Carolina Historical [978]

RECORDS / Waldboro, Maine.South Waldboro Baptist Church – 1855-56; 1875-1913; 1926-29 – 1 – 15.50 – us A.B.H.S. [240]

RECORDS / Waterville, Maine. Baptist Sabbath School Society of Waterville – 1842-54 – 1 – us A.B.H.S. [240]

RECORDS / Wayne. Ohio. Wayne United Methodist Church – 1836-1962 – 2r – 1 – $32.50r – us Archival [240]

RECORDS / Webster, New York. Webster Baptist Church – 1830-1955 – 1 – us A.B.H.S. [240]

RECORDS / West Centre Harbor, New Hampshire. West Centre Harbor Sunday School – 1884-93 – 1 – us A.B.H.S. [240]

RECORDS / West Centre Harbor, New Hampshire. West Centre Harbor Union Meeting House Society – 1889-1917 – 1 – us A.B.H.S. [240]

RECORDS / West Millgrove, Ohio. Congregational Church of West Millgrove – 1841-1985 – 1r – 1 – $32.50r – us Archival [240]

RECORDS / West Side Baptist Church, Topeka, KS – 1881-1981 – 1 – us KS Hist [240]

RECORDS / West Sumner, Maine. West Sumner Baptist Church – 1920 – 1 – 15.50 – us A.B.H.S. [240]

RECORDS / Western Reserve Normal School. Milan, Ohio – 1831-1948 – 1r – 1 – $32.50r – us Archival [370]

RECORDS / Westmoreland, New Hampshire. East Westmoreland Baptist Church – 1809-94 – 1 – 15.50 – us A.B.H.S. [240]

RECORDS / Westside Presbyterian Church, Lawrence, KS – 1900-1985 – 1 – us KS Hist [240]

RECORDS / White Cloud. Kansas. Community Church – 1867-1958 – 1 – us KS Hist [978]

RECORDS / Whitefield, Maine. Second Baptist Church at King's Mills – 1834-84 – 1 – us A.B.H.S. [240]

RECORDS / Whitehouse. Ohio. Whitehouse Natural Gas and Oil Company – 1887-1888 – 1r – 1 – $32.50r – us Archival [978]

RECORDS / Wichita. Kansas – 1871-81 – 1 – us KS Hist [978]

RECORDS / William J. Sullivan Collection/21st Ohio Volunteer Infantry – 1863-1866 – 1r – 1 – $32.50r – us Archival [976]

RECORDS / Williams County, Ohio. Pulaski Township. Board of Education – 1853-1954 – 1r – 1 – $32.50r – us Archival [978]

RECORDS / Willmett Family – 1835-1961, Papers of a prominent Potawatomi family in Wabaunsee County, KS – 1 – us KS Hist [920]

RECORDS / Winyaw. South Carolina. Prince Frederick Episcopal Church – 1713-94. 12 fiches – 9 – us South Carolina Historical [978]

RECORDS / Wisconsin Colony. Russell County, Kansas – 1871-84 – 1 – us KS Hist [978]

RECORDS / Wolfeborough, New Hampshire. Wolfeborough Baptist Church – 1833-85 – 1 – 15.50 – us A.B.H.S. [240]

RECORDS / Woman's Relief Corps. Page Corps no. 60 (Sylvania, Ohio) – 1889-1992 – 1r – 1 – $32.50r – us Archival [978]

RECORDS / Woolwich, Maine.Woolwich Baptist Church – 1797-1957 – 1 – us A.B.H.S. [240]

RECORDS / Worcester, Massachusetts. Baptist City Mission Board – 1885-1929 – 1 – us A.B.H.S. [240]

RECORDS / Worden Methodist Episcopal Church – 1906-71 – 1 – us KS Hist [978]

RECORDS / Wright, Beverly and Company. Dodge City, Kansas – 1879-87 – 1 – us KS Hist [978]

RECORDS / Wyandott Indian Council – 1885-1871, Minutes of the Council while the Wyandotts resided in Kansas – 1 – us KS Hist [305]

RECORDS / Zion Lutheran Church (Waterville, Ohio) – 1877-1986 – 2r – 1 – $32.50r – us Archival [240]

RECORDS / Zoar Hunt's Corners United Church of Christ (Huron County, Ohio) – 1854-1981 – 1r – 1 – $32.50r – us Archival [978]

RECORDS, 1691-1820 / Ulster. General Synod. Ireland – 3v. 1890, 1897, 1898; Lecky, A. G. In the days of Laggan Presbytery. 1908; Lecky, A. G. The Laggan and its Presbyterianism. 1905 – 1 – $50.00 – us Presbyterian [240]

RECORDS, 1716-32 / South Carolina. Court of Admiralty – T309 – 1r – 1 – us Nat'l Archives [340]

RECORDS, 1790-1797 / Albany. Presbytery (Pres. Ch. in the U.S.A.) – 1 – $50.00 – us Presbyterian [240]

RECORDS, 1802-67 / Russia. Russian-American Company – M11 – 77r – 1 – us Nat'l Archives [947]

[RECORDS, 1803?-1914] / Church Missionary Society. London – [London]: Kodal Ltd, Recordak Div, 1960 (mf ed) – us Res Libr [240]

RECORDS, 1834-1860 / Church Missionary Society. South India Mission. Madras – London: Kodak Ltd, Recordak Div, 1967 (mf ed) – us Res Libr [240]

RECORDS, 1838-1917 / Dayton. Presbytery (Pres. Ch. in the U.S.A.) – 1 – $100.00 – us Presbyterian [240]

RECORDS, 1838-1918 / Brooklyn, Presbytery (Pres. Ch. in the U.S.A.) – 3r – 1 – $150.00 – us Presbyterian [240]

RECORDS, 1839-1908 / Pittsburgh. Presbytery (Pres. Ch. in the U.S.A.) – 1 – $150.00 – us Presbyterian [240]

RECORDS, 1845-1980, AND MINUTES, 1845-1916 / Charleston. South Carolina. Bethel United Methodist Church – Lists of Members, 1851-55; Baptisms, 1866-1955; Marriages, 1866-1955; Sunday School Society Records, 1859-71; Cashbook, 1848-69. 143 fiches – 9 – us South Carolina Historical [240]

RECORDS, 1855-1906 / Monongahela. Presbytery (United Pres. Ch. of N.A.) – 1 – $50.00 – us Presbyterian [240]

RECORDS, 1856-1882 / Sialkot, India. Associate Church – 1 – $50.00 – us Presbyterian [950]

RECORDS, 1858-1911 / Xenia. Presbytery (United Pres. Ch. of N.A.) – 1 – $50.00 – us Presbyterian [240]

RECORDS, 1862-63 / District of Columbia. Board of Commissioners for the Emancipation of Slaves – 6rolls. M520. Printed guide – 1 – us Nat'l Archives [324]

RECORDS, 1865-89 / Washburn College. Topeka, Kansas – 1 – us KS Hist [370]

RECORDS, 1870-1922 / Presbyterian Church in the U.S.A. Woman's Foreign Missionary Society – 1 – $200.00 – us Presbyterian [240]

RECORDS, 1876-1914 / Presbyterian Church in the U.S.A. Woman's Board of Foreign Missions – 1 – $100.00 – us Presbyterian [240]

RECORDS, 1880-1918 / Chapman, John Wilbur – 1 – $400.00 – us Presbyterian [240]

RECORDS, 1881-1926 / Washburn College. Topeka, Kansas – 1 – us KS Hist [370]

RECORDS, 1893-1923 / Hainan Mission. (Pres. Ch. in the U.S.A.) – 1 – $50.00 – us Presbyterian [240]

RECORDS, 1894-1923 / Minnesota Woman Suffrage Association – 18r – 1 – $540.00 $40.00 – us M.H.S. [360]

RECORDS, 1896-1911 / Presbyterian Church in the U.S.A. Woman's Board of Home Missions – 1 – $100.00 – us Presbyterian [240]

RECORDS, 1936-44 / Germany. Reich Ministry for Public Enlightenment and Propaganda – 125 rolls. T70. Finding Aids: GG22 and T176 roll 24. (Captured German Records Filmed at Alexandria, VA.) – 1 – us Nat'l Archives [324]

RECORDS, 1963-78 / Free Southern Theater – 1 – $1,200.00 – us Amistad [790]

RECORDS AND BRIEFS / U.S. Supreme Court – 1832-1915 – 1 – us UMI [340]

RECORDS AND BRIEFS. / U.S. Emergency Court of Appeals – Washington, DC. On film: Docket nos. 1-676; 1941-61. LL-047 – 1 – us L of C Photodup [340]

RECORDS AND BRIEFS OF CASES SUBMITTED ON APPEAL TO THE PRIVY COUNCIL / Great Britain. Privy Council – 1934-74. Incomplete – 1 – us L of C Photodup [324]

RECORDS AND BRIEFS OF THE U.S. SUPREME COURT, 1832-1915 – (With printed index. 1832-60 42r $3,570 S1311. 1861-70 56r $4,760 S1312. 1871-80 86r $7,310 S1313. 1881-90 170r $14,450 S1314. 1891-96 116r $9,860 S1315. 1897-1900 103r $8,755 S1316. 1901-05 142r $12,070 S1317. 1906-10 154r $13,090 S1318. 1911-15 219r $18,615 S1319) – 1088r – 1 – $92,480.00 complete – us Scholarly Res [340]

RECORDS AND CORRESPONDENCE / Atchison, Topeka and Santa Fe Railroad Company – 1869-80 – 1 – us KS Hist [625]

RECORDS AND DOCUMENTS CONCERNING SERGEANT'S INN, FLEET STREET / King, H C – London: R Flint, 1922 – 3mf – 9 – $4.50 – LLMC 84-299 – us L.L.M.C. [340]

RECORDS AND HISTORY / Biringer Gun Shop. Leavenworth, Kansas – 1859-ca1968 – 1 – us KS Hist [025]

RECORDS AND HISTORY / Biringer Gun Shop. Leavenworth. Kansas – 1859-ca1968, Biography of John Biringer and history of the Biringer Store. It begins with the records of the bill of goods from E.K. Tryon, Philadelphia, Pennsylvania given to Biringer to establish the business. Also included is a centennial history of the Edward K. Tryon Company – 1 – us KS Hist [380]

RECORDS AND LETTERS OF THE APOSTOLIC AGE / Burton, Ernest De Witt – New York: Scribner's, 1901. 1 fiche – 9 – us A.T.L.A. [240]

RECORDS AND PUBLICATIONS / American Civil Liberties Union – 1917-84 – 128r – 1 – us UMI [321]

RECORDS AND SCRAPBOOK / Middle Bass Club. Middle Bass, Ohio – 1891-1977 – 1r – 1 – $32.50r – us Archival [978]

RECORDS AND STOCK REPORTS / Perrysburg Grain and Supply Association. Ohio – 1916-78 – 2r – 1 – $32.50r – us Archival [978]

RECORDS AND VESTRY BOOKS OF THE BOROUGH / Neath. England – 1651-1918 – 1 – uk Microform Academic [941]

RECORDS...: CENTRAL TREASURY RECORDS RELATING TO THE LOAN OF 1790 / U.S. Treasury Department. Bureau of the Public Debt – 1roll. T786 – 1 – us Nat'l Archives [336]

RECORDS CONCERNING APPLICATIONS FOR ADOPTION BY THE QUINAIELT INDIANS, 1910-1919 – 5r – 1 – M1344 – us Nat'l Archives [350]

RECORDS...: CONNECTICUT LOAN OFFICE RECORDS RELATING TO THE LOAN OF 1790 / U.S. Treasury Department. Bureau of the Public Debt – 10 rolls. T654 – 1 – us Nat'l Archives [336]

RECORDS CREATED BY BUREAU OF INDIAN AFFAIRS FIELD AGENCIES HAVING JURISDICTION OVER THE PUEBLO RECORDS, 1874-1900 – 32r – 1 – M1304 – us Nat'l Archives [350]

RECORDS...: DELAWARE LOAN OFFICE RECORDS RELATING TO THE LOAN OF 1790 / U.S. Treasury Department. Bureau of the Public Debt – 1roll. T784 – 1 – us Nat'l Archives [336]

RECORDS...: GEORGIA LOAN OFFICE RECORDS RELATING TO THE LOAN OF 1790 / U.S. Treasury Department. Bureau of the Public Debt – 2rolls. T694 – 1 – us Nat'l Archives [336]

RECORDS...: GEORGIA LOAN OFFICE RECORDS RELATING TO VARIOUS LOANS, 1804-18 / U.S. Treasury Department. Bureau of the Public Debt – 1roll. T788 – 1 – us Nat'l Archives [336]

RECORDS: HOME MISCELLANEOUS SERIES / Great Britain. India Office – 1600-1900. 335 reels – 1 – us UMI [941]

RECORDS IN THE BRITISH PUBLIC RECORD OFFICE RELATING TO SOUTH CAROLINA, 1663-1782 – South Carolina: Department of Archives and History, 1995 – 12r – 1 – $1,020.00 – us Scholarly Res [975]

RECORDS IN THE BRITISH PUBLIC RECORDS OFFICE RELATING TO SOUTH CAROLINA, 1663-1782 / South Carolina. Department of Archives and History – 12r. M-1 – 1 – $75.00r – Out-of-state orders: us Scholarly Res – us SC Archives [978]

RECORDS MANAGEMENT QUARTERLY *see* ARMA RECORDS MANAGEMENT QUARTERLY

RECORDS...: MARYLAND LOAN OFFICE RECORDS RELATING TO THE LOAN OF 1790 / U.S. Treasury Department. Bureau of the Public Debt – 9rolls. T697 – 1 – us Nat'l Archives [336]

RECORDS...: MARYLAND LOAN OFFICE RECORDS RELATING TO VARIOUS LOANS OF 1798 AND 1800 / U.S. Treasury Department. Bureau of the Public Debt – 1 roll. T957 – 1 – us Nat'l Archives [336]

RECORDS...: MASSACHUSETTS LOAN OFFICE RECORDS RELATING TO THE LOAN OF 1790 / U.S. Treasury Department. Bureau of the Public Debt – 7 rolls. T783 – 1 – us Nat'l Archives [336]

RECORDS, MS 44 / Ravenna. Ohio. Stage Office – 1833-66. 1 reel – 1 – us Western Res [380]

RECORDS, MS 91 / Lake County. Ohio. Willoughby Township – 1815-74. 1 reel – 1 – us Western Res [310]

RECORDS, MS 2026 / Lake County. Ohio. Perry Township – 1815-48. 1 reel – 1 – us Western Res [310]

RECORDS, MS 2400 / Ohio. Volunteer Infantry. 105th Regiment – 1862-65 excerpts – 1r – 1 – us Western Res [976]

RECORDS, MS 3106 / Geauga County. Ohio. Russell Township – 1827-50 – 1r – 1 – us Western Res [310]

RECORDS, MS 3546 / Consumer's League of Ohio – 1900-76 – 69r – 1 – us Western Res [360]

RECORDS, MS 3912 / Lakeshore and Michigan Southern Railway System – 1849-1909 – 64r – 1 – us Western Res [380]

RECORDS, MS P.P. / Alliance of Poles of America – 1895-1978 – 5r – 1 – us Western Res [977]

RECORDS, MS P.P. / Czechoslovak Society of America. Cleveland, Ohio – 1870-1978. 16 reels – 1 – us Western Res [025]

RECORDS, MS P.P. / Union of Poles in America – 1898-1968. 3 reels – 1 – us Western Res [306]

RECORDS...: NEW HAMPSHIRE LOAN OFFICE RECORDS RELATING TO THE LOAN OF 1790 / U.S. Treasury Department. Bureau of the Public Debt – 6rolls. T652 – 1 – us Nat'l Archives [336]

RECORDS...: NEW JERSEY LOAN OFFICE RECORDS RELATING TO THE LOAN OF 1790 / U.S. Treasury Department. Bureau of the Public Debt – 2rolls. T698 – 1 – us Nat'l Archives [336]

RECORDS...: NORTH CAROLINA LOAN OFFICE RECORDS RELATING TO THE LOAN OF 1790 / U.S. Treasury Department. Bureau of the Public Debt – 4rolls. T695 – 1 – us Nat'l Archives [336]

RECORDS OF A SCOTTISH VILLAGE : LASSWADE, 1650-1750 / ed by Houston, Rab – (With printed guide) – 6mf – 17 – £52.00 – uk Chadwyck [910]

RECORDS OF AN ENGLISH VILLAGE : EARLS COLNE, 1400-1750 / ed by Macfarlane, Alan et al – (With index and printed guides) – 126mf – 17 – £510.00 – uk Chadwyck [910]

RECORDS OF AND RELATING TO THE C.S.S. FLORIDA, 1862-64 / C.S.S. Florida (Confederate Ship) – (Roll 1. Smooth Logs, Sept 17-Dec 31, 1863; May 1-Oct 3, 1864. Roll 2. Rough Logs, Aug 18, 1862-Jan 22, 1863; Sept 17, 1863-Apr 30, 1864. Roll 3. Engineer, Medical and Court-Martial Records, Dec 28, 1863-Oct 2, 1864. Roll 4. Records relating to the C.S.S. Florida, Mar 3, 1862-Oct 2, 1864) – 4rolls. T716 – 1 – us Nat'l Archives [324]

RECORDS OF ANTE-BELLUM SOUTHERN PLANTATIONS FROM THE REVOLUTION THROUGH THE CIVIL WAR : SERIES A: SELECTIONS FROM THE SOUTH CAROLINIANA LIBRARY, UNIVERSITY OF SOUTH CAROLINA – (With printed guides. Pt 1: The Papers of James Henry Hammond 15r $2,055 ISBN: 0-89093-775-3. Pt 2: Miscellaneous Collections 26r $3,550 ISBN: 0-89093-776-1) – 2pts – 1 – us UPA [976]

RECORDS OF ANTE-BELLUM SOUTHERN PLANTATIONS FROM THE REVOLUTION THROUGH THE CIVIL WAR : SERIES B: SELECTIONS FROM THE SOUTH CAROLINA HISTORICAL SOCIETY – (With printed guide) – 10r – 1 – $1,365.00 – 0-89093-777-X – us UPA [976]

RECORDS OF ANTE-BELLUM SOUTHERN PLANTATIONS FROM THE REVOLUTION THROUGH THE CIVIL WAR : SERIES C: SELECTIONS FROM THE LIBRARY OF CONGRESS – (With printed guides. Pt 1: Virginia 8r $1,090 ISBN: 0-89093-778-8. Pt 2: Alabama, Georgia and South Carolina 5r $685 ISBN: 0-89093-779-6) – 2pts – 1 – us UPA [976]

RECORDS OF ANTE-BELLUM SOUTHERN PLANTATIONS FROM THE REVOLUTION THROUGH THE CIVIL WAR : SERIES D: SELECTIONS FROM THE MARYLAND HISTORICAL SOCIETY – (With printed guide) – 14r – 1 – $1,915.00 – 0-89093-780-X – us UPA [976]

RECORDS OF ANTE-BELLUM SOUTHERN PLANTATIONS FROM THE REVOLUTION THROUGH THE CIVIL WAR : SERIES E: SELECTIONS FROM THE UNIVERSITY OF VIRGINIA LIBRARY – (All with printed guides. Virginia Plantations: Pt 1 39r $5,330 ISBN: 0-89093-781-8. Pt 2 26r $3,550 ISBN: 0-89093-784-2. Pt 3 30r $4,095.00 ISBN: 0-89093-785-0) – 3pts – 1 – us UPA [976]

RECORDS OF ANTE-BELLUM SOUTHERN PLANTATIONS FROM THE REVOLUTION THROUGH THE CIVIL WAR : SERIES F: SELECTIONS FROM THE DUKE UNIVERSITY LIBRARY – (All with printed guides. Pt 1: The Deep South 23r $3,145 ISBN: 0-89093-782-6. Pt 2: South Carolina and Georgia 16r $2,185 ISBN: 0-89093-783-4. Pt 3: North Carolina, Maryland and Virginia 45r $6,150 ISBN: 0-89093-786-9) – 3pts – 1 – us UPA [976]

RECORDS OF ANTE-BELLUM SOUTHERN PLANTATIONS FROM THE REVOLUTION THROUGH THE CIVIL WAR : SERIES G: SELECTIONS FROM THE BARKER TEXAS HISTORY CENTER, UNIVERSITY OF TEXAS AT AUSTIN – (With printed guides. Pt 1: Texas and Louisiana Collections 44r $6,010 ISBN: 0-89093-787-7. Pt 2: William

Massie Collection 45r $5,855 ISBN: 0-89093-799-0. Pt 3: Bank of the State of Mississippi Records 1804-46 18r $2,480. Pt 4: Winchester Family Papers 1783-1906 28r $3,860. Pt 5: Other Plantation Collections ca 45r ca $6,200 ISBN 1-55655-686-1) – 5pts – 1 – us UPA [976]

RECORDS OF ANTE-BELLUM SOUTHERN PLANTATIONS FROM THE REVOLUTION THROUGH THE CIVIL WAR : SERIES H: SELECTIONS FROM THE HOWARD-TILTON LIBRARY, TULANE UNIVERSITY AND THE LOUISIANA STATE MUSEUM ARCHIVES – (With printed guide) – 30r – 1 – $4,095.00 – 1-55655-100-2 – us UPA [976]

RECORDS OF ANTE-BELLUM SOUTHERN PLANTATIONS FROM THE REVOLUTION THROUGH THE CIVIL WAR : SERIES I: SELECTIONS FROM LOUISIANA STATE UNIVERSITY – (All with printed guides. Pt 1: Louisiana Sugar Plantations 15r $2,055 ISBN: 1-55655-101-0. Pt 2: Louisiana and Miscellaneous Southern Cotton Plantations 24r $3,280 ISBN: 1-55655-102-9. Pt 3: The Natchez Area 18r $2,450 ISBN: 1-55655-103-7. Pt 4: Barrow, Bisland, Bowman and Other Collections 38r $5,240 ISBN: 1-55655-646-2. Pt 5: Butler Family Collection 27r $3,720 ISBN: 1-55655-649-7. Pt 6:David Weeks and Family Collection 20r $2,755 ISBN: 155655-680-2) – 6pts – 1 – us UPA [976]

RECORDS OF ANTE-BELLUM SOUTHERN PLANTATIONS FROM THE REVOLUTION THROUGH THE CIVIL WAR : SERIES J: SELECTIONS FROM THE SOUTHERN HISTORICAL COLLECTION, UNIVERSITY OF NORTH CAROLINA, CHAPEL HILL – (All with printed guides. Pt 1: Cameron Family Papers 69r $9,430 ISBN: 1-55655-139-8. Pt 2: Pettigrew Family Papers 29r $3,965 ISBN: 1-55655-140-1. Pt 3: South Carolina 41r $5,595 ISBN: 1-55655-221-1. Pt 4: Georgia and Florida 47r $6,415 ISBN: 1-55655-222-X. Pt 5: Louisiana 19r $2,595 ISBN: 1-55655-223-8. Pt 6: Mississippi and Arkansas 29r $3,965 ISBN: 1-55655-400-1. Pt 7: Alabama 20r $2,730 ISBN: 1-55655-401-X. Pt 8: Tennessee and Kentucky 20r $2,730 ISBN: 1-55655-402-8. Pt 9: Virginia 33r $4,505 ISBN: 1-55655-403-6. Pt 10: Hubard Family Papers, 1741-1865 26r $3,550 ISBN: 1-55655-442-7. Pt 11: Hairston and Wilson Families 22r $3,010 ISBN: 1-55655-443-5. Pt 12: Tidewater and Coastal Plains North Carolina 50r $6,830 ISBN: 1-55655-444-3. Pt 13: Piedmont North Carolina 40r $5,465 ISBN: 1-55655-452-4. Pt 14: Western North Carolina 10r $1,365 ISBN: 1-55655-453-2) – 14pts – 1 – us UPA [976]

RECORDS OF ANTE-BELLUM SOUTHERN PLANTATIONS FROM THE REVOLUTION THROUGH THE CIVIL WAR : SERIES K: SELECTIONS FROM THE COLONIAL WILLIAMSBURG FOUNDATION LIBRARY: THE SHIRLEY PLANTATION COLLECTION, 1650-1888 / ed by Stampp, Kenneth M – (With printed guide) – 26r – 1 – $3,590.00 – 1-55655-484-2 – us UPA [976]

RECORDS OF ANTE-BELLUM SOUTHERN PLANTATIONS FROM THE REVOLUTION THROUGH THE CIVIL WAR : SERIES L: SELECTIONS FROM THE EARL GREGG SWEM LIBRARY, COLLEGE OF WILLIAM AND MARY / ed by Stampp, Kenneth M – (All with printed guides. Pt 1: Carter Papers 1667-1862 18r $2,475 ISBN 1-55655-486-9. Pt 2: Jerdone Family Papers 1736-1918 12r $1,655 ISBN 1-55655-487-7. Pt 3: Skipwith Family Papers 1760-1865 14r $1,935 ISBN 1-55655-488-5. Pt 4: Austin-Twyman Papers 1765-1865 and Charles Brown Papers 1792-1888 35r $4,965 ISBN 1-55655-490-7) – 4pts – 1 – us UPA [976]

RECORDS OF ANTE-BELLUM SOUTHERN PLANTATIONS FROM THE REVOLUTION THROUGH THE CIVIL WAR : SERIES M: SELECTIONS FROM THE VIRGINIA HISTORICAL SOCIETY / ed by Stampp, Kenneth M – (All with printed guides. Pt 1: Tayloe Family 1650-1870 57r $7,860 ISBN 1-55655-525-3. Pt 2: Northern Neck of Virginia, also Maryland 17r $2,340 ISBN 1-55655-526-1. Pt 3: Other Tidewater Virginia 36r $4,965 ISBN 1-55655-527-X. Pt 4: Central Piedmont Virginia 59r $8,130 ISBN 1-55655-560-1. Pt 5: Southside Virginia 50r $6,895 ISBN 1-55655-561-X. Pt 6: Northern Virginia and Valley 14r $1,930 ISBN: 1-55655-562-8) – 6pts – 1 – us UPA [976]

RECORDS OF ARRIVALS AND DEPARTURES, 1920-93 / Cook Islands Collector of Customs – 1r – 1 – PMB1071 – at Pacific Mss [980]

RECORDS OF BAPTISMS, MARRIAGES, BURIALS / St. Paul, Kansas. Osage Mission – 1820-85 – 1 – us KS Hist [978]

THE RECORDS OF BIRTHS, MARRIAGES, AND DEATHS IN THE TOWN OF DEDHAM / Hill, Don Gleason – Dedham, MA. Printed at the "Dedham Transcript," 1886. Massachusetts Reel 7. (The Cox Library Collection) – 5 – us Americana [310]

RECORDS OF CALIFORNIA MEN IN THE WAR OF THE REBELLION 1861-1867 / Orton, Richard H – Sacramento: J.D. Yount Supt. State Printing, 1890. Calif. reel 37. (Cox Library Collection) – 5 – us Americana [978]

RECORDS OF CAPTAIN CLAPPERTON'S LAST EXPEDITION TO AFRICA. WITH SUBSEQUENT ADVENTURES OF THE AUTHOR / Lander, Richard – 2v. London. 1830. BA-331 2 – 8 – ne IDC [910]

RECORDS OF CASES / Harvey County. Kansas. District Court – 1872 – 1 – us KS Hist [340]

RECORDS OF CENTER TOWNSHIP *see* CENTER TOWNSHIP, RECORDS, MS 566

RECORDS OF CLERMONT CO, OHIO *see* CLERMONT CO, OHIO, RECORDS, MSS 1086

RECORDS OF COFFIN PLATES / Sass, Edward George – 1806-51. Charleston, SC. 2 fiches – 9 – us South Carolina Historical [978]

RECORDS OF COLUMBIANA COUNTY *see* COLUMBIANA COUNTY RECORDS, MS 1134

RECORDS OF DEPARTMENT OF STATE RELATING TO INTERNAL AFFAIRS OF YUGOSLAVIA, 1930-1944 / U.S. Department of State – 28r – 1 – M1203 – us Nat'l Archives [949]

RECORDS OF FARMERS' MARKETING AND PURCHASING COOPERATIVES / U.S. Farm Credit Administration – 38 rolls. T947 – 1 – us Nat'l Archives [334]

RECORDS OF FEEBLE MINDED YOUTH / Allen County. Ohio. Probate Court – 1905-1914 – 1r – 1 – $32.50r – us Archival [324]

RECORDS OF GENERAL COURTS-MARTIAL AND COURTS OF INQUIRY OF THE NAVY DEPT., 1799-1867 / U.S. Navy. Judge Advocate General – 200 rolls. M273 – 5 – us Nat'l Archives [340]

RECORDS OF GENERAL SCIENCE – London, 1835-36 – 3 – us Readex [500]

RECORDS OF GERMAN AND JAPANESE EMBASSIES AND CONSULATES, 1890-1945 / Germany – 78r – 1 – T179 – us Nat'l Archives [324]

RECORDS OF GERMAN ARMY AREAS / Germany. Army – 315r – 1 – T79 – us Nat'l Archives [324]

RECORDS OF GERMAN FIELD COMMANDS: ARMIES – 1696r – 1 – T312 – us Nat'l Archives [324]

RECORDS OF GERMAN FIELD COMMANDS: ARMY GROUPS – 304r – 1 – T311 – us Nat'l Archives [324]

RECORDS OF GERMAN FIELD COMMANDS: CORPS – 1670r – 1 – T314 – us Nat'l Archives [324]

RECORDS OF GERMAN FIELD COMMANDS: DIVISIONS – 3256r – 1 – T315 – us Nat'l Archives [324]

RECORDS OF GERMAN FIELD COMMANDS: PANZER ARMIES – 489r – 1 – T313 – us Nat'l Archives [324]

RECORDS OF GERMAN FIELD COMMANDS: REAR AREAS, OCCUPIED TERRITORIES AND OTHERS / Germany. Army – 363r – 1 – $8,349.00 – T501 – us Nat'l Archives [324]

THE RECORDS OF HOLY TRINITY (OLD SWEDES) CHURCH, WILMINGTON, DELAWARE 1697-1773 / Burr, Horace; ed by Burr, Horace – Wilmington, Hist. Soc. of Delaware, 1890. Delaware Reel 2. (The Cox Library Collection) – 5 – us Americana [240]

RECORDS OF INTERMENTS / Memorial Lawn Cemeteries Association. Emporia, Kansas – 1855-1980 – 1 – us KS Hist [025]

THE RECORDS OF JOHN GLASSFORDF AND COMPANY – 71r – 1 – $2,485.00 – Dist. us Scholarly Res – us L of C Photodup [380]

RECORDS OF LATER LIFE / Kemble, Fanny – New York: H. Holt and Company, 1882. 1p,1 leaf,676p – 1 – us U.W. Library [920]

RECORDS OF LIVERY COMPANIES AND RELATED ORGANISATIONS AT THE GUILDHALL LIBRARY, LONDON – (The Worshipful Company of Pewterers 1451-1934. 32 reels. F1,150.00; The Fellowship Porters, The Tacklehouse and Ticket Porters and The Comb-Makers 1566-1895. 13 reels. F495.00; The Worshipful Company of Weavers 1681-1844. 15 reels. F545.00; The Worshipful Company of Musicians 1712-1912; The Watermen and Lightermen's Company 1688-1971; The Worshipful Society of Apothecaries; The Worshipful Company of Haberdashers, Records 1853-1970) – uk World [380]

THE RECORDS OF LIVING OFFICERS OF THE U.S. NAVY AND MARINE CORPS / Hamersly, Lewis R – Philadelphia: L.R. Hamersly and Co., 1890. Military Books, reel 4. (Cox Library Collection) – 5 – us Americana [920]

RECORDS OF MINISTERS' LICENSES / Hancock County. Ohio. Probate Court – 1841-1976 – 1r – 1 – $32.50r – us Archival [324]

RECORDS OF NAZI CULTURAL AND RESEARCH INSTITUTIONS – 548r – 1 – T82 – us Nat'l Archives [943]

RECORDS OF NEGOTIATIONS CONNECTED WITH THE TREATY OF GHENT, 1813-15 / U.S. Department of State – 2rolls. M36 – 1 – us Nat'l Archives [324]

RECORDS OF NEW LISBON, OHIO *see* NEW LISBON, OHIO, RECORDS, MS 1255

RECORDS OF OFFICIALS' BONDS / Putnam County, Ohio. Treasurer – (Some issues missing) – 1834-1900 – 1r – 1 – $32.50r – us Archival [324]

RECORDS OF OFFICIALS' BONDS / Van Wert County. Ohio. Treasurer – 1930-1973 – 1r – 1 – $32.50r – us Archival [324]

RECORDS OF OLDEN TIMES. FIFTY YEARS ON THE PRAIRIES / Home Journal Steam Printing – Lacon, 1880. (Illinois Reel 49). (The Cox Library Collection) – 5 – us Americana [978]

RECORDS OF OXFORD TOWNSHIP, DELAWARE CO., OHIO *see* OXFORD TOWNSHIP, DELAWARE CO., OHIO, RECORDS

RECORDS OF PENNSYLVANIA'S REVOLUTIONARY GOVERNMENT, 1775-1790 / Pennsylvania Historical and Museum Commission – (With printed guide. 4 sections can be purchased separately) – 54r – 1 – $4,590.00 set $85.00r – D3295 – Dist. us Scholarly Res – us Penn Hist [975]

RECORDS OF PERRY TOWNSHIP SCHOOL DISTRICTS 3 AND 5 *see* PERRY TOWNSHIP SCHOOL DISTRICTS 3 AND 5, MS 578

RECORDS OF PICKENS COUNTY, ALABAMA / McGuire, Mrs. C P et al – v1. Item R. Biographies, church records, Confederate War records, War of 1812 and Rev. War Soldiers of Pickens County. Indexed. SW16-0152. v2. Item S. Marriage records, 1881-1892. 45p SW16-0152. v3. Item T. Biography, deeds and cemetery records. 12p SW16-0152 – 5 – us A.G.L.L. [978]

RECORDS OF PICTURES PAINTED IN ITALY, 1781-1798 / Kauffman, Angelica – 1 – uk Microform Academic [700]

RECORDS OF PRIVATE AUSTRIAN, DUTCH, AND GERMAN ENTERPRISES – 109r – 1 – T83 – us Nat'l Archives [940]

RECORDS OF PRIVATE INDIVIDUALS (CAPTURED GERMAN RECORDS) – 58r – 1 – T253 – us Nat'l Archives [943]

RECORDS OF PROVINCIAL COUNCIL, 1682-1776 / Pennsylvania Historical and Museum Commission – (Includes a printed guide) – 26r – 1 – $2,210.00 – D3296 – Dist. us Scholarly Res – us Penn Hist [975]

RECORDS OF PUPILS / Olathe. Kansas. School for the Deaf – 1867-76 – 1 – us KS Hist [978]

RECORDS OF RELIEF DISBURSEMENT / Fulton County. Ohio. Auditor – 1886-1964 – 3r – 1 – $32.50r – us Archival [324]

RECORDS OF RUSSELL TOWNSHIP, OHIO *see* RUSSELL TOWNSHIP, OHIO, RECORDS, MS 3106

RECORDS OF SAMUEL HENDERSON AND E. B. TEAGUE / Henderson, Samuel & Teague, E B – 358p – 1 – 12.53 – us Baptist [240]

RECORDS OF SERVICES OF MADRAS CIVILIANS, 1741-1838 / Prinsep, C C – 1885. BI-353 2 – 8 – ne IDC [950]

RECORDS OF SPECIAL AGENTS FOR SECURING THE FLORIDA ARCHIVES, 1819-35 / U.S. National Archives and Records Service – 6 rolls. T1212 – 1 – us Nat'l Archives [025]

RECORDS OF THE 5TH ROUND OF MICRONESIAN FUTURE POLITICAL STATUS NEGOTIATIONS : HELD IN WASHINGTON, D.C, JUL-AUG 1972 / Off of Micronesian Status Negotiations – Washington, n.p, n.d. – 1mf – 9 – $1.50 – LLMC 82-100F, Title 44 – us L.L.M.C. [323]

RECORDS OF THE 27TH DIVISION OF THE A.E.F. (WORLD WAR I), 1917-19 / U.S. Army. A.E.F. 1917-23 – 60 rolls. M819. Printed guide – 1 – us Nat'l Archives [324]

RECORDS OF THE 1820 CENSUS OF MANUFACTURES / U.S. Bureau of the Census – 27 rolls. M279. Printed guide – 1 – us Nat'l Archives [324]

RECORDS OF THE ALABAMA CLAIMS COMMISSION – 58r – 1 – $2,030.00 – Dist. us Scholarly Res – us L of C Photodup [975]

RECORDS OF THE ALASKAN TERRITORIAL LEGISLATURE / U.S. Department of State – 1913-53. 21 rolls. M1012 – 1 – us Nat'l Archives [324]

RECORDS OF THE ALL-UNION (RUSSIAN) COMMUNIST PARTY (SMOLENSK ARCHIVES), 1917-1941 – 69r – $1,587.00 – T87 – us Nat'l Archives [320]

RECORDS OF THE AMALGAMATED CLOTHING WORKERS OF AMERICA : COMPLETE COLLECTION, 1935-1955 – 9 – $6,235.00 – us UPA [331]

RECORDS OF THE AMALGAMATED CLOTHING WORKERS OF AMERICA, PART 1 : THE PAPERS OF SIDNEY AND BESSIE HILLMAN. CORRESPONDENCE, 1911-1970 – 9 – $3,520.00 – 1-55655-141-X – us UPA [331]

RECORDS OF THE AMALGAMATED CLOTHING WORKERS OF AMERICA, PART 2 : PAPERS OF SIDNEY HILLMAN. NEW DEAL AND WARTIME AGENCIES – 9 – $2,165.00 – 1-55655-142-8 – us UPA [331]

RECORDS OF THE AMALGAMATED CLOTHING WORKERS OF AMERICA, PART 3 : ACWA SCRAPBOOKS AND PRESS RELEASES, 1910-1961 – 9 – $1,250.00 – 1-55655-143-6 – us UPA [331]

RECORDS OF THE AMERICAN COMMITTEE ON AFRICA / ed by Bracey, John H, Jr & Meier, August – (Part 1: ACOA Executive Committee Minutes and National Office Memoranda, 1952-1975. 6r. $660.00. ISBN 1-55655-431-1; Part 2: Correspondence and Subject Files on South Africa, 1952-1985. 45r. $4,950.00. ISBN 1-55655-432-X) – 1 – $5,330.00 set – us UPA [324]

RECORDS OF THE AMERICAN COUNCIL FOR NATIONALITIES SERVICE, 1921-1971 – 25r – 1 – $2,750.00 – 1-55655-063-4 – us UPA [324]

RECORDS OF THE AMERICAN DELEGATION, U.S.-USSR JOINT COMMISSION ON KOREA, AND RECORDS RELATING TO THE UNITED NATIONS TEMPORARY COMMISSION ON KOREA (UNTCOK), 1945-1948 – 23r – 1 – M1243 – us Nat'l Archives [327]

RECORDS OF THE AMERICAN SECTION OF THE SUPREME WAR COUNCIL / U.S. Department of War – 1917-19. 21 rolls. M923 – 1 – us Nat'l Archives [324]

RECORDS OF THE ARIZONA SUPERINTENDENCY OF INDIAN AFFAIRS, 1863-73 / U.S. Bureau of Indian Affairs – 8 rolls.M734. Printed guide – 1 – us Nat'l Archives [324]

RECORDS OF THE ASSISTANT COMMISSIONER, BUREAU OF REFUGEES, FREEDMEN, AND ABANDONED LANDS / U.S. Bureau of Refugees, Freedmen, and Abandoned Lands – (Alabama 1865-70 23r $529 M809. Arkansas 1865-69 52r $1,196 M979. District of Columbia 1865-69 21r $483 M1055. Georgia 1865-69 36r $828 M798. Louisiana 1865-89 36r $828 M1027. Mississippi 1865-70 50r $1,150 M826. North Carolina 1865-70 38r $874 M843. South Carolina 1865-70 44r $1,012 M869. Tennessee 1865-69 34r $782 M999. Texas 1865-69 32r $736 M821. Virginia 1865-69 67r $1,541 M1048) – 1 – us Nat'l Archives [324]

RECORDS OF THE ASSISTANT COMMISSIONER FOR THE DISTRICT OF COLUMBIA / U.S. Bureau of Refugees, Freedmen, and Abandoned Lands – 1865-72. 21 rolls. M1055 – 1 – us Nat'l Archives [324]

RECORDS OF THE ASSISTANT COMMISSIONER FOR THE STATE OF ARKANSAS / U.S. Bureau of Refugees, Freedmen, and Abandoned Lands – 1865-69. 52 rolls. M979 – 1 – us Nat'l Archives [324]
RECORDS OF THE ASSISTANT COMMISSIONER FOR THE STATE OF GEORGIA.. / U.S. Bureau of Refugees, Freedmen, and Abandoned Lands – 36 rolls. M798 – 1 – us Nat'l Archives [324]
RECORDS OF THE ASSISTANT COMMISSIONER FOR THE STATE OF LOUISIANA / U.S. Bureau of Refugees, Freedmen, and Abandoned Lands – 1865-69. 37 rolls. M1027 – 1 – us Nat'l Archives [324]
RECORDS OF THE ASSISTANT COMMISSIONER FOR THE STATE OF MISSISSIPPI / U.S. Bureau of Refugees, Freedmen, and Abandoned Lands – 1865-69. 50 rolls. M826 – 1 – us Nat'l Archives [324]
RECORDS OF THE ASSISTANT COMMISSIONER FOR THE STATE OF NORTH CAROLINA / U.S. Bureau of Refugees, Freedmen, and Abandoned Lands – 1865-70. 38 rolls. M843 – 1 – us Nat'l Archives [324]
RECORDS OF THE ASSISTANT COMMISSIONER FOR THE STATE OF SOUTH CAROLINA / U.S. Bureau of Refugees, Freedmen, and Abandoned Lands – 1865-70. 44 rolls. M869 – 1 – us Nat'l Archives [324]
RECORDS OF THE ASSISTANT COMMISSIONER FOR THE STATE OF TENNESSEE / U.S. Bureau of Refugees, Freedmen, and Abandoned Lands – 1865-69. 34 rolls. M999 – 1 – us Nat'l Archives [324]
RECORDS OF THE ASSISTANT COMMISSIONER FOR THE STATE OF TEXAS / U.S. Bureau of Refugees, Freedmen, and Abandoned Lands – 1865-69. 32 rolls. M821 – 1 – us Nat'l Archives [324]
RECORDS OF THE ASSISTANT COMMISSIONER FOR THE STATE OF VIRGINIA / U.S. Bureau of Refugees, Freedmen, and Abandoned Lands – 1865-69. 67 rolls. M1048 – 1 – us Nat'l Archives [324]
RECORDS OF THE BOARD OF COMMISSIONERS FOR THE EMANCIPATION OF SLAVES IN THE DISTRICT OF COLUMBIA, 1862-1863 – 6r – 1 – M520 – us Nat'l Archives [976]
RECORDS OF THE BOTANICAL SURVEY OF INDIA – Calcutta. v1-14. 1893-1940/1941 – 71mf – 9 – 8573/1 – ne IDC [580]
RECORDS OF THE BROTHERHOOD OF SLEEPING CAR PORTERS – (Part 1: Records of the BSCP, 1925-1969. 30r. ISBN 1-55655-279-3. $3,300.00; Part 2: Records of the Ladies Auxiliary of the BSCP, 1931-1956. 10r. ISBN 1-55655-280-7. $1,105.00; Part 3: Records on the BSCP Relations with the Pullman Company, 1925-1968. 10r. ISBN 1-55655-281-5. $1,105.00; A printed guide accompanies the collection) – Series A: Holdings of the Chicago Historical Society and the Newberry Library, 1925-69 – 1 – $5,230.00 set – us UPA [331]
RECORDS OF THE BUREAU OF INDIAN AFFAIRS CENTRAL CLASSIFIED FILES, 1907-1939 : SERIES C: INDIAN HEALTH AND MEDICAL AFFAIRS, PT 1: REPORTS ON MEDICAL AND NURSING ACTIVITIES – (Guide forthcoming) – (mf ed 1998) – 29r – 1 – $3,805.00 – 1-55655-661-6 – us UPA [306]
RECORDS OF THE BUREAU OF INDIAN AFFAIRS, CENTRAL CLASSIFIED FILES, 1907-1939 : SERIES A: INDIAN DELEGATIONS TO WASHINGTON – (With printed guide) – 25r – 1 – $3,285.00 – 1-55655-550-4 – us UPA [306]
RECORDS OF THE BUREAU OF INDIAN AFFAIRS, CENTRAL CLASSIFIED FILES, 1907-1939 : SERIES B: INDIAN CUSTOMS AND SOCIAL RELATIONS – (With printed guide) – 23r – 1 – $3,020.00 – 1-55655-599-7 – us UPA [306]
RECORDS OF THE BUTLER TOWNSHIP SCHOOL DISTRICT 5 *see* BUTLER TOWNSHIP SCHOOL DISTRICT 5, MS 908
RECORDS OF THE CAPE COLONY : COPIED FOR THE CAPE GOVERNMENT FROM THE MANUSCRIPT DOCUMENTS IN THE PUBLIC RECORD OFFICE, LONDON / ed by Theal, George McCall – [London]: Printed by W Clowes & Sons, 1897-1905 – us Res Libr [324]
RECORDS OF THE CENTRAL SUPERINTENDENCY OF INDIAN AFFAIRS / U.S. Bureau of Indian Affairs – 1813-78. 108 rolls. M856 – 1 – us Nat'l Archives [324]
RECORDS OF THE CHEROKEE INDIAN AGENCY IN TENNESSEE, 1801-35 / U.S. Bureau of Indian Affairs – 14 rolls. M208. Printed guide – 1 – us Nat'l Archives [324]
RECORDS OF THE CHILDREN'S BUREAU, 1912-1969 / U.S. National Archives – (Also available in pts. Not listed individually. With guide £90) – 6pts 294r – 13 – £16,540.00 – uk Chadwyck [305]
RECORDS OF THE CHOCTAW TRADING HOUSE, 1803-24 / U.S. Bureau of Indian Affairs – 6 rolls.T500 – 1 – us Nat'l Archives [324]
RECORDS OF THE CHURCH OF ENGLAND DURING THE COMMONWEALTH PERIOD (1643-61) / Church of England – Lambeth Palace Library. Printed Index – 1 – £1,495.00 – uk World [240]
RECORDS OF THE CHURCHES OF CHRIST GATHERED AT FENSTANTON, WARBOYS AND HEXAM, 1644-1720 *see* PUBLICATIONS
RECORDS OF THE CITY OF GEORGETOWN, DC, 1800-79 / District of Columbia – 49r – 1 – M605. Printed Guide – us Nat'l Archives [324]
RECORDS OF THE CITY OF POTWIN PLACE, SHAWNEE COUNTY / Potwin Place. Kansas – 1888-99 – 1 – us KS Hist [978]
RECORDS OF THE CLERK OF THE COURT / U.S. Circuit and District Courts. New York – 1746-1932. And of the U.S. Commissioners, 1837-60, of the U.S. District Court for the Southern District of New York. 1 roll – 1 – M938 – us Nat'l Archives [324]
RECORDS OF THE COLLECTOR OF CUSTOMS FOR THE COLLECTION DISTRICT OF NEW LONDON, CONNECTICUT, 1789-1938 – 57r – 1 – M1162 – us Nat'l Archives [324]
RECORDS OF THE COLONY OF NEW PLYMOUTH IN NEW ENGLAND – 1857. Item L. Misc. records 1633-1689.Indexed, 210p.SW16-0167 – 5 – us A.G.L.L. [978]
RECORDS OF THE COMMISSIONERS OF CLAIMS (SOUTHERN CLAIMS COMMISSION), 1871-80 / U.S. Treasury Department – 14 rolls. M87 – 1 – us Nat'l Archives [324]
RECORDS OF THE COMMITTEE ON SCIENCE AND THE ARTS OF THE FRANKLIN INSTITUTE 1824-1900 – (Includes printed guide) – 28r – 1 – $2,380.00 – S1852 – us Scholarly Res [500]
RECORDS OF THE CONFEDERATE HISTORIAN – (Roll 1: Roll of Honor, Memorializing South Carolina's Dead Soldiers; Roll 2: Roll of Dead South Carolina Troops and the Roll of South Carolina Volunteers in the Confederate States Provisional Army; Roll 3: Vol 1, Field and Staff Officers; Roll 4: Vols 2 and 3, Infantry; Roll 5: Vol 4, Calvery and Artillery; Roll 6; Vol 5, Miscellaneous and State Troops) – Columbia, South Carolina: Department of Archives and History, 1993 – 6r – 1 – $75.00r – Out-of-state orders: us Scholarly Res – us SC Archives [350]
RECORDS OF THE CONFEDERATE HISTORIAN – South Carolina: Dept of Archives and History, 1995 – 3r – 1 – $255.00 – us Scholarly Res [976]
RECORDS OF THE CONFERENCE FOR REVISION OF THE UNIVERSAL COPYRIGHT CONVENTION, UNESCO, PARIS, 5-24 JULY 1971 – 1973 – 295p – 9 – 92-3-101047-6 – fr UNESCO [340]
RECORDS OF THE CONNECTICUT, NEW HAMPSHIRE, AND RHODE ISLAND CONTINENTAL LOAN OFFICES – 1777-91. 2 rolls. M1005 – 1 – us Nat'l Archives [324]
RECORDS OF THE CONSTITUTIONAL CONVENTION OF 1787 / U.S. Department of State – 1r – 1 – M866 – us Nat'l Archives [324]
RECORDS OF THE COTTON BUREAU OF THE TRANS-MISSISSIPPI DEPARTMENT / Confederate States of America. War Department – 1862-65. 50 rolls. T1129 – 1 – us Nat'l Archives [976]
RECORDS OF THE COUNCIL ON FOREIGN RELATIONS (1921-1951) / US. Council on Foreign Relations – (With printed guide) – 520mf – 9 – $3,490.00 – 1-55655-214-9 – us UPA [327]
RECORDS OF THE COURT OF ARCHES, 1554-1911 : LAMBETH PALACE LIBRARY / Lambeth Palace Library – (Series 1: The Process Books of the Court of Arches 1660-1911 12,437mf £25,800.00 Index 7mf £42.00. Series 2: Proceedings in the Court of Arches 1554-1875 308mf 105r £7,920.00. With index) – 2pts – 9 – £30,870.00 set – uk Chadwyck [340]
RECORDS OF THE CREEK TRADING HOUSE, 1795-1816 / U.S. Bureau of Indian Affairs – 1 roll. M4 – 1 – us Nat'l Archives [324]
RECORDS OF THE DAKOTA SUPERINTENDENCY OF INDIAN AFFAIRS / U.S. Bureau of Indian Affairs – 1861-70, 1877-78. The Wyoming Superintendency, 1870. 13 rolls. M1016 – 1 – us Nat'l Archives [324]
RECORDS OF THE DELAWARE AND MARYLAND CONTINENTAL LOAN OFFICE, 1777-1790 / U.S. Bureau of Public Debt – 1 roll. RG53. M1008 – 1 – us Nat'l Archives [975]
RECORDS OF THE DEPARTMENT OF STATE : COMMUNICATIONS FROM SPECIAL AGENTS, 1794-1906 / U.S. Department of State – M37 – 27r – 1 – us Nat'l Archives [975]
RECORDS OF THE DEPARTMENT OF STATE, RECORDS CODIFICATION MANUAL : CENTRAL DECIMAL FILE, 1950-1963 – 1r – 1 – M1275 – us Nat'l Archives [324]
RECORDS OF THE DEPARTMENT OF STATE RELATING TO GUANO ISLANDS / U.S. Department of State – 1852-1912. 7 rolls. M974 – 1 – us Nat'l Archives [975]
RECORDS OF THE DEPARTMENT OF STATE RELATING TO INTERNAL AFFAIRS OF AFGHANISTAN, 1930-1944 / U.S. Department of State – 7r – 1 – M1219 – us Nat'l Archives [950]
RECORDS OF THE DEPARTMENT OF STATE RELATING TO INTERNAL AFFAIRS OF AUSTRIA, 1930-1944 / U.S. Department of State – 32r – 1 – M1209 – us Nat'l Archives [943]
RECORDS OF THE DEPARTMENT OF STATE RELATING TO INTERNAL AFFAIRS OF BULGARIA, 1910-1944 / U.S.. Department of State – 21r – 1 – M1207 – us Nat'l Archives [949]
RECORDS OF THE DEPARTMENT OF STATE RELATING TO INTERNAL AFFAIRS OF CZECHOSLOVAKIA, 1010-1944 / U.S. Department of State – 32r – 1 – M1218 – us Nat'l Archives [943]
RECORDS OF THE DEPARTMENT OF STATE RELATING TO INTERNAL AFFAIRS OF DENMARK, 1910-1939 – 38r – 1 – M1452 – us Nat'l Archives [324]
RECORDS OF THE DEPARTMENT OF STATE RELATING TO INTERNAL AFFAIRS OF FRANCE, 1930-1939 – 89r – 1 – M1442 – us Nat'l Archives [324]
RECORDS OF THE DEPARTMENT OF STATE RELATING TO INTERNAL AFFAIRS OF HUNGARY, 1930-1944 / U.S. Department of State – 17r – 1 – M1206 – us Nat'l Archives [943]
RECORDS OF THE DEPARTMENT OF STATE RELATING TO INTERNAL AFFAIRS OF ITALY, 1930-1939 – 33r – 1 – M1423 – us Nat'l Archives [324]
RECORDS OF THE DEPARTMENT OF STATE RELATING TO INTERNAL AFFAIRS OF KOREA, 1910-1959 – (1910-1929. 9 rolls. $207.00; 1930-1939. 2 rolls. $150.00; 1940-1944. 3 rolls. $225.00; 1945-1949. 12 rolls. $900.00; 1950-1954. 33 rolls. $2,475.00; 1955-1959. 22 rolls. $1,650.00) – 81 rolls – 9 – Dist. us Scholarly Res – us L of C Photodup [324]
RECORDS OF THE DEPARTMENT OF STATE RELATING TO INTERNAL AFFAIRS OF MEXICO, 1930-1939 – 165r – 1 – M1370 – us Nat'l Archives [324]
RECORDS OF THE DEPARTMENT OF STATE RELATING TO INTERNAL AFFAIRS OF NORWAY, 1910-1939 – 22r – 1 – M1406 – us Nat'l Archives [324]
RECORDS OF THE DEPARTMENT OF STATE RELATING TO INTERNAL AFFAIRS OF PAKISTAN, 1945-1949 – 6r – 1 – M1448 – us Nat'l Archives [324]
RECORDS OF THE DEPARTMENT OF STATE RELATING TO INTERNAL AFFAIRS OF PALESTINE, 1930-1944 / U.S. Department of State – 26r – 1 – M1037 – us Nat'l Archives [956]
RECORDS OF THE DEPARTMENT OF STATE RELATING TO INTERNAL AFFAIRS OF PALESTINE, 1945-1949 – 27r – 1 – M1390 – us Nat'l Archives [324]
RECORDS OF THE DEPARTMENT OF STATE RELATING TO INTERNAL AFFAIRS OF PARAGUAY, 1910-1939 – 22r – 1 – M1470 – us Nat'l Archives [324]
RECORDS OF THE DEPARTMENT OF STATE RELATING TO INTERNAL AFFAIRS OF POLAND, 1916-1944 / U.S. Department of State – 75r – 1 – M1197 – us Nat'l Archives [943]
RECORDS OF THE DEPARTMENT OF STATE RELATING TO INTERNAL AFFAIRS OF ROMANIA, 1910-1944 / U.S. Department of State – 44r – 1 – M1198 – us Nat'l Archives [949]
RECORDS OF THE DEPARTMENT OF STATE RELATING TO INTERNAL AFFAIRS OF SPAIN, 1910-1929 – 38r – 1 – M1369 – us Nat'l Archives [324]
RECORDS OF THE DEPARTMENT OF STATE RELATING TO INTERNAL AFFAIRS OF SWEDEN, 1910-1939 – 44r – 1 – M1424 – us Nat'l Archives [324]
RECORDS OF THE DEPARTMENT OF STATE RELATING TO INTERNAL AFFAIRS OF THE BALKAN STATES, 1910-1939 – 5r – 1 – M1447 – us Nat'l Archives [324]
RECORDS OF THE DEPARTMENT OF STATE RELATING TO INTERNAL AFFAIRS OF THE BALKAN STATES, 1940-1944 / U.S. Department of State – 1r – 1 – M1220 – us Nat'l Archives [949]
RECORDS OF THE DEPARTMENT OF STATE RELATING TO INTERNAL AFFAIRS OF TURKEY, 1930-1944 / U.S. Department of State – 36r – 1 – M1224 – us Nat'l Archives [956]
RECORDS OF THE DEPARTMENT OF STATE RELATING TO POLITICAL RELATIONS BETWEEN BOLIVIA AND OTHER STATES, 1910-1929 / U.S. Department of State – 18r – 1 – M646 – us Nat'l Archives [327]
RECORDS OF THE DEPARTMENT OF STATE RELATING TO POLITICAL RELATIONS BETWEEN CHINA AND JAPAN / U.S. Department of State – 1930-44 – 96r – 1 – M976 – us Nat'l Archives [327]
RECORDS OF THE DEPARTMENT OF STATE RELATING TO POLITICAL RELATIONS BETWEEN THE UNITED STATES AND AUSTRIA-HUNGARY AND AUSTRIA, 1910-1929 – 4r – 1 – M696 – us Nat'l Archives [324]
RECORDS OF THE DEPARTMENT OF STATE RELATING TO POLITICAL RELATIONS BETWEEN THE UNITED STATES AND SIAM / U.S. Department of State – 1909-29. 1 roll. M730 – 1 – us Nat'l Archives [327]
RECORDS OF THE DEPARTMENT OF STATE RELATING TO POLITICAL RELATIONS BETWEEN THE UNITED STATES AND TURKEY / U.S. Department of State – 1930-44. 2 rolls. M1223 – 1 – us Nat'l Archives [327]
RECORDS OF THE DEPARTMENT OF STATE RELATING TO PROPERTY CLAIMS OF U.S. CITIZENS AGAINST POLAND / U.S. Department of State – 1930-44. 8 rolls. T461 – 1 – us Nat'l Archives [943]
RECORDS OF THE DEPARTMENT OF STATE RELATING TO THE INTERNAL AFFAIRS OF ALBANIA, 1910-1944 / U.S. Department of State – 16r – 1 – M1211 – us Nat'l Archives [949]
RECORDS OF THE DEPARTMENT OF STATE RELATING TO THE PROBLEMS OF RELIEF AND REFUGEES IN EUROPE ARISING FROM WORLD WAR 2 AND ITS AFTERMATH, 1938-1949 : RECORD GROUP 59, DECIMAL FILES 840.48 AND 840.48 REFUGEES – 1986 – 70r – 1 – $1,610.00 set in US $30.00r outside – M1284 – us Nat'l Archives [943]
RECORDS OF THE DEPARTMENT OF STATE RELATING TO U.S. CLAIMS AGAINST RUSSIA / U.S. Department of State – 1910-29. 8 rolls. T640 – 1 – us Nat'l Archives [947]
RECORDS OF THE DEPARTMENT OF STATE RELATING TO WORLD WAR 2 / U.S. Department of State – 1939-45. 252 rolls. M982 – 1 – us Nat'l Archives [977]
RECORDS OF THE DEPARTMENT OF STATE SPECIAL INTERROGATION MISSION TO GERMANY, 1945-1946 – 3r – $102.00 – M679 – us Scholarly Res [350]
RECORDS OF THE DEPARTMENT STATE RELATING TO INTERNAL AFFAIRS OF CANADA, 1910-1929 – 54r – 1 – M1435 – us Nat'l Archives [324]
RECORDS OF THE DI OF COLUMBIA COMMISSIONERS AND OF THE OFFICES CONCERNED WITH PUBLIC BUILDINGS, 1791-1867 / U.S. Office of Public Buildings and Grounds – 27r – 1 – M371 – us Nat'l Archives [324]

RECORDS OF THE ECONOMIC ENTERPRISES OF THE SS = ECONOMBETRIEBE, SS WIRTSCHAFTSVERWALTUNGSHAUPTAMT – 1936-45 – 37r – 1 – $851.00 – T976 – us Nat'l Archives [324]

RECORDS OF THE FAIR EMPLOYMENT PRACTICE COMMITTEE, 1941-1946 – 212r – 1 – $12,925.00 – us UMI [331]

RECORDS OF THE FAR EASTERN COMMISSION, 1945-52 – (Sections available separately: Section 1:$3,230.00 38r. Section 2: $10,965.00 129r. Each set includes a printed guide) – 167r – 1 – $14,195.00 – S3274 – us Scholarly Res [975]

THE RECORDS OF THE FEDERAL CONVENTION OF 1787 / ed by Farrand, Max – Yale University Press. 3v. 1911 – 8mf – 9 – $36.00 – LLMC 84-245 – us L.L.M.C. [323]

RECORDS OF THE GAELIC CLUB, CLEVELAND, OHIO *see* GAELIC CLUB, CLEVELAND, OHIO, RECORDS

RECORDS OF THE GENERAL CONFERENCE OF THE PROTESTANT MISSIONARIES OF CHINA : HELD AT SHANGHAI, MAY 10-24, 1877 – Shanghai: Presbyterian Mission Press, 1878 – 2mf – us A.T.L.A. [240]

RECORDS OF THE GENERAL CONFERENCE OF THE PROTESTANT MISSIONARIES OF CHINA : HELD AT SHANGHAI, MAY 7-20, 1890 / General Conference of the Protestant Missionaries of China (1890 : Shangai, China) – Shanghai: American Presbyterian Mission Press, 1890 – 2mf – us A.T.L.A. [240]

RECORDS OF THE GENERAL CONFERENCES / UNESCO – 9 – fr UNESCO [060]

RECORDS OF THE GEOLOGICAL AND GEOGRAPHICAL SURVEY OF THE TERRITORIES "HAYDEN SURVEY", 1867-79 / U. S. Geological Survey – 21 rolls. M623. Printed guide – 1 – us Nat'l Archives [550]

RECORDS OF THE GEOLOGICAL EXPLORATION OF THE FORTIETH PARALLEL ("KING SURVEY"), 1867-81 / U. S. Geological Survey – 3rolls. M622. Printed guide – 1 – us Nat'l Archives [550]

RECORDS OF THE GERMAN FOREIGN MINISTRY PERTAINING TO CHINA, 1919-1935 – 31r – $713.00 – T1141 – us Nat'l Archives [320]

RECORDS OF THE GERMAN FOREIGN OFFICE FILMED FOR THE UNIVERSITY OF LONDON – 25r – $575.00 – T1026 – us Nat'l Archives [320]

RECORDS OF THE GERMAN FOREIGN OFFICE RECEIVED BY THE DEPARTMENT OF STATE – 5026r – $115,598.00 – T120 – us Nat'l Archives [320]

RECORDS OF THE GERMAN FOREIGN OFFICE RECEIVED BY THE DEPARTMENT OF STATE FROM ST ANTONY'S COLLEGE – 144r – $3,312.00 – T136 – us Nat'l Archives [320]

RECORDS OF THE GERMAN FOREIGN OFFICE RECEIVED BY THE DEPARTMENT OF STATE FROM THE UNIVERSITY OF CALIFORNIA (PROJECT 1) – 445r – $10,235.00 – T139 – us Nat'l Archives [320]

RECORDS OF THE GERMAN FOREIGN OFFICER RECEIVED BY THE DEPARTMENT OF STATE FROM THE BRITISH MUSEUM / U.S. Department of State – 2r – 1 – T264 – us Nat'l Archives [324]

RECORDS OF THE GERMAN NAVY, 1850-1945, RECEIVED FROM THE UNITED STATES NAVAL HISTORY DIVISION – 4383r – $100,809.00 – T1022 – us Nat'l Archives [355]

RECORDS OF THE GERMAN NAVY,1850-1945, RECEIVED FROM THE U.S. NAVAL HISTORY DIVISION / Germany. Navy – 1659 rolls. T1022. Finding Aids: T1022 rolls 1, 2. (Captured German Records Filmed at Alexandria, VA.) – 1 – us Nat'l Archives [355]

RECORDS OF THE GOVERNMENT / American Samoa – 1900-58. 62 rolls. T1182 – 1 – us Nat'l Archives [980]

RECORDS OF THE GOVERNOR AND COMPANY OF MASSACHUSETTS BAY IN NEW ENGLAND, 1628-1686 – Boston, 1853-54 – 1r – 1 – us Ross [975]

RECORDS OF THE GOVERNOR AND COMPANY OF THE MASSACHUSETTS BAY IN NEW ENGLAND / Massachusetts. (Colony) – Boston. 1853-54. 5v in 6 – 1 – $46.00 – us L of C Photodup [975]

RECORDS OF THE GREAT PLAYHOUSES, SERIES ONE : THE SADLERS WELLS ARCHIVE – (Pt 1: Scripts, Performer Files, Music, Criticisms, Views, Documents and Programmes, 1720-1981) – From Finsbury Central Library, London – 1 – us Primary [790]

RECORDS OF THE GREAT PLAYHOUSES, SERIES TWO : THE SIR BARRY JACKSON ARCHIVE – (Part One: Prompt Books 1908-1932. Part Two: Prompt Books 1933-1952. Part Three: Prompt Books 1953-1971. Part Four: Programmes, Playbills, Periodicals, Malvern Festival Material, Press Releases and Press Cuttings; Part Five: Production Photos) – Birmingham Central Library – 1 – us Primary [790]

RECORDS OF THE HEADQUARTERS OF THE GERMAN AIR FORCE HIGH COMMAND (OBERKOMMANDO DER LUFTWAFFE-OKL) – 274r – $6,302.00 – T321 – us Nat'l Archives [350]

RECORDS OF THE HEADQUARTERS OF THE GERMAN ARMED FORCES HIGH COMMAND – (Some rolls may be restricted) – 1581r – $36,363.00 – T77 – us Nat'l Archives [355]

RECORDS OF THE HEADQUARTERS OF THE GERMAN ARMY HIGH COMMAND – (Some rolls may be restricted) – 704r – $16,192.00 – T78 – us Nat'l Archives [355]

RECORDS OF THE HEADQUARTERS OF THE GERMAN NAVY HIGH COMMAND (OKM) – 8r – $184.00 – T608 – us Nat'l Archives [355]

RECORDS OF THE HILLSBORO CREAMERY / Jantzen, Peter – 1899-1903 – 1 – us KS Hist [920]

RECORDS OF THE IDAHO SUPERINTENDENCY OF INDIAN AFFAIRS / U.S. Bureau of Indian Affairs – 1863-70. 3 rolls. M832 – 1 – us Nat'l Archives [324]

RECORDS OF THE IMMIGRATION AND NATURALIZATION SERVICE, SERIES A : PART 1: SUBJECT CORRESPONDENCE FILES ON ASIAN IMMIGRATION AND EXCLUSION, 1906-1913 – (Pt 1 Suppl 1898-1941 15r $1,970.00 ISBN 1-55655- 605-5. Both pts with printed guides) – 1991 – 30r – 1 – $3,465.00 – 1-55655-160-6 – us UPA [324]

RECORDS OF THE IMMIGRATION AND NATURALIZATION SERVICE, SERIES A : PART 2: SUBJECT CORRESPONDENCE FILES ON MEXICAN IMMIGRATION, 1906-1930 – (With printed guide) – 17r – 1 – $2,125.00 – 1-55655-492-3 – us UPA [324]

RECORDS OF THE IMMIGRATION AND NATURALIZATION SERVICE, SERIES A : PART 3: SUBJECT CORRESPONDENCE FILES ON ELLIS ISLAND, 1900-1933 – (With printed guide) – 18r – 1 – $2,250.00 – 1-55655-541-5 – us UPA [324]

RECORDS OF THE IMMIGRATION AND NATURALIZATION SERVICE, SERIES A : PART 4: SUBJECT CORRESPONDENCE FILES ON EUROPEAN INVESTIGATIONS, 1898-1936 – (With printed guide) – 1995 – 10r – 1 – $1,250.00 – 1-55655-587-3 – us UPA [324]

RECORDS OF THE IMMIGRATION AND NATURALIZATION SERVICE, SERIES A : PART 5: SUBJECT CORRESPONDENCE FILES ON PROSTITUTION AND "WHITE SLAVERY", 1902-1933 – (With printed guide) – 1995 – 7r – 1 – $875.00 – 1-55655-588-1 – us UPA [324]

RECORDS OF THE INTERGOVERNMENTAL COPYRIGHT CONFERENCE, GENEVA 1952 / UNESCO – (The conference which adopted the Universal Copyright Convention) – New York. 1v – 5mf – 9 – $7.50 – LLMC 82-305 – us L.L.M.C. [340]

RECORDS OF THE INTERNATIONAL CONFERENCE OF STATES ON THE DISTRIBUTION OF PROGRAMMECARRYING SIGNALS TRANSMITTED BY SATELLITE, BRUSSELS, 6-21 MAY 1974 – 1977 – 677p – 9 – Co-published with the World Intellectual Property Organization – fr UNESCO [380]

RECORDS OF THE JOINT BOARD, 1903-1947 – 21r – 1 – M1421 – us Nat'l Archives [324]

RECORDS OF THE JOINT CHIEFS OF STAFF : PART 1, 1942-45 / U.S. Joint Chiefs of Staff – (Pacific Theatre. 1981. 14r. 0-89093-287-5. $1,350.00; European Theatre. 1981. 14r. 0-89093-367-7. $1,350.00; The Soviet Union. 1981. 2r. 0-89093-368-5. $200.00; Meetings of the JCS and CCS. 1980. 0-89093-275-1. $690.00; Strategic Issues. 1982. 0-89093-365-0. $1,250.00) – 1982 – 1 – $4,595.00 set – us UPA [324]

RECORDS OF THE JOINT CHIEFS OF STAFF : PART 2, 1946-53 / U.S. Joint Chiefs of Staff – (The Soviet Union: 1979. 0-89093-290-5. $690.00; The Middle East: 1979. 0-89093-289-1. $200.00; The Far East: 1979. 0-89093-288-3. $1,350.00; Europe and NATO: 1979. 0-89093-291-3. $910.00; The United States: 1980. 0-89093-292-1. $380.00; Meetings of the JCS: 1980. 0-89093-293-X. $770.00; Strategic Issues, Section 1: 1981. 0-89093-369-3. $1,170.00; Strategic Issues, Section 2: 1981. 0-89093-370-7. $1,350.00) – 1981 – 1 – $6,475.00 set – us UPA [324]

RECORDS OF THE KENNEDY ADMINISTRATION, 1961-1963 / John Fitzgerald Kennedy Library – (Records of the US Dept of Agriculture 5r $425 D3269. US Office of Emergency Planning 4r $340 D3272. US Dept of Labor 70r $5,950 D3266. US Dept of the Interior 22r $1,870 D3271. US National Mediation Board 2r $170 D3267. US Dept of Health, Education and Welfare 41r $3,485 D3268. US Housing and Home Finance Agency 8r $680 D3270. Files of Walter W. Heller 1961-1964 49r $4,165 D3273. All with printed guide) – 1991 – 1 – us Scholarly Res [320]

RECORDS OF THE KIRK OF SCOTLAND / Church of Scotland. General Assembly – Alexander Peterkin. v. 1. 1838 – 1 – us A.T.L.A. [240]

RECORDS OF THE KNESSET – (English summary. Ceased after 1969) – Jerusalem, 1949-69 – 101mf – 9 – J-82-41/1 – ne IDC [323]

RECORDS OF THE LOUISIANA STATE GOVT., 1850-88. / U.S. War Department. Confederate Records – 24 rolls. M359. Printed guide – 1 – us Nat'l Archives [324]

RECORDS OF THE MASSACHUSETTS CONTINENTAL LOAN OFFICE – 1777-91. 4 rolls. M925 – 1 – us Nat'l Archives [324]

RECORDS OF THE MEETINGS / Belvoir Literary Society – 1886-89 – 1 – us KS Hist [420]

RECORDS OF THE METHODIST EPISCOPAL CHURCH IN KANSAS / Methodist Episcopal Church. Kansas – 1855-1918 – 1 – us KS Hist [240]

RECORDS OF THE MILITARY ASSISTANCE COMMAND VIETNAM – (Pt 1, The War in Vietnam, 1954-73. MACV Historical Office Documentary Collection: 1-55655-105-3 $5,280.00; Pt 2, Classified Studies from the Combined Intelligence Center Vietnam, 1965-73: 1-55655-106-1 $3,300.00; Pt 3, Progress Reports on Pacification in South Vietnam, 1965-73: 1-55655-155-X $1,320.00) – $9,405.00 – us UPA [355]

RECORDS OF THE MINNESOTA SUPERINTENDENCY OF INDIAN AFFAIRS / U.S. Bureau of Indian Affairs – 1849-56. 9 rolls. M842 – 1 – us Nat'l Archives [324]

RECORDS OF THE MONTANA SUPERINTENDENCY OF INDIAN AFFAIRS / U.S. Bureau of Indian Affairs – 1867-73. 3 rolls. M833 – 1 – us Nat'l Archives [324]

RECORDS OF THE MORAVIAN MISSION AMONG THE INDIANS OF NORTH AMERICA / Moravian Church – 1 – us Primary [240]

RECORDS OF THE NATIONAL ASSOCIATION OF COLORED WOMEN'S CLUBS, 1895-1992 : PART 1: MINUTES OF NATIONAL CONVENTIONS, PUBLICATIONS, AND PRESIDENT'S OFFICE CORRESPONDENCE – (With printed guide. Coll Title: Black Studies Research Sources) – 1993 – 26r – 1 – $3,255.00 – 1-55655-467-2 – us UPA [360]

RECORDS OF THE NATIONAL ASSOCIATION OF COLORED WOMEN'S CLUBS, 1895-1992 : PART 2: PRESIDENT'S OFFICE FILES 1958-68 – (With printed guide. Coll title: Black Studies Research Sources) – 1994 – 15r – 1 – $1,875.00 – 1-55655-504-0 – us UPA [360]

RECORDS OF THE NATIONAL HOME FOR DISABLED SOLDIERS / Illinois – Danville, IL. V146 – 1 – us A.G.L.L. [920]

RECORDS OF THE NATIONAL NEGRO BUSINESS LEAGUE, PART 1 : ANNUAL CONFERENCE PROCEEDINGS AND ORGANIZATIONAL RECORDS, 1900-19 / ed by Hamilton, Kenneth – (With printed guide) – 1994 – 3r – 1 – $375.00 – 1-55655-507-5 – us UPA [360]

RECORDS OF THE NATIONAL NEGRO BUSINESS LEAGUE, PART 2 : CORRESPONDENCE AND BUSINESS RECORDS, 1900-1923 / ed by Hamilton, Kenneth – (With printed guide) – 1994 – 11r – 1 – $1,375.00 – 1-55655-508-3 – us UPA [360]

RECORDS OF THE NATIONAL SOCIALIST GERMAN LABOR PARTY – 732r – $16,836.00 – T81 – us Nat'l Archives [320]

RECORDS OF THE NEVADA SUPERINTENDENCY OF INDIAN AFFAIRS / U.S. Bureau of Indian Affairs – 1869-70. 1 roll. M837 – 1 – us Nat'l Archives [324]

RECORDS OF THE NEW JERSEY AND NEW YORK CONTINENTAL LOAN OFFICES – 1777-90. 2 rolls. M1006 – 1 – us Nat'l Archives [324]

RECORDS OF THE NEW ORLEANS FIELD OFFICES, BUREAU OF REFUGEES, FREEDMEN, AND ABANDONED LANDS, 1865-69 – 10r – 1 – M1483 – us Nat'l Archives [324]

RECORDS OF THE NEW YORK STAGE, FROM 1750 TO 1860 / Ireland, Joseph Norton – 2v. 1866-67 – 1r – 1 – us Ross [790]

RECORDS OF THE NORTHERN SUPERINTENDENCY OF INDIAN AFFAIRS, 1851-1876 – 35r – 1 – M1166 – us Nat'l Archives [350]

RECORDS OF THE OFFICE OF CHINESE AFFAIRS, 1945-1955 – (Guide also sold separately: $15.00) – 1988 – 41 rolls – 9 – $3,075.00 – Dist. us Scholarly Res – us L of C Photodup [324]

RECORDS OF THE OFFICE OF CHINESE AFFAIRS, 1945-55 / U.S. Department of State – (With printed guide) – 1988 – 41r – 1 – $3,485.00 – S3162 – us Scholarly Res [327]

RECORDS OF THE OFFICE OF THE DEPUTY FOR SERBIAN ECONOMY – 89r – $2,047.00 – T75 – us Nat'l Archives [339]

RECORDS OF THE PARLIAMENT HOLDEN AT WESTMINSTER, 28 FEBRUARY IN THE 33RD YEAR OF THE REIGN OF EDWARD 1 (1305) (RS98) / Great Britain. Parliament; ed by Maitland, F W – 1893 – Dfl32.00 – ne Slangenburg [941]

RECORDS OF THE PENNSYLVANIA CONTINENTAL LOAN OFFICE – 1776-88. 3 rolls. M1007 – 1 – us Nat'l Archives [324]

RECORDS OF THE PRESBYTERIAN CHURCH IN THE U.S. OF AMERICA : EMBRACING THE MINUTES OF THE GENERAL PRESYTERY AND GENERAL SYNOD 1706-1788: TOGETHER WITH AN INDEX AND THE MINUTES OF THE GENERAL CONVENTION FOR RELIGIOUS LIBERTY 1766-1775 – Philadelphia: Presbyterian Board of Publication and Sabbath-School Work, 1904 – 2mf – us A.T.L.A. [240]

RECORDS OF THE PROCEEDINGS AND DEBATES AT THE SIXTY-FIRST ANNUAL CONVENTION OF THE PROTESTANT EPISCOPAL CHURCH IN THE DIOCESE OF NEW YORK.. / West, Robert A – 1845 – 1 – us A.T.L.A. [240]

RECORDS OF THE PROVINCIAL COUNCIL, 1682-1776 / Pennsylvania Historical and Museum Commission – (Comes with guide) – 26r – 1 – $2,210.00 – D3296 – us Scholarly Res [320]

RECORDS OF THE PUBLIC TREASURERS OF SOUTH CAROLINA, 1725-1776 – (With printed guide) – South Carolina Department of Archives and History, 1995 – 2r – 1 – $170.00 – D3310 – us Scholarly Res [336]

RECORDS OF THE PUBLIC TREASURERS OF SOUTH CAROLINA, 1725-76 / South Carolina. Department of Archives and History – Printed introd 2r M-3 – 1 – $75.00r – out-of-state orders: us Scholarly Res – us SC Archives [978]

RECORDS OF THE REICH AIR MINISTRY (REICHSLUFTFAHRTMINISTERIUM) – 52r – $1,196.00 – T177 – us Nat'l Archives [350]

RECORDS OF THE REICH COMMISSIONER FOR THE BALTIC STATES, 1941-45 / Germany. Reichskommissar fuer das Ostland – 45r – 1 – $1,035.00 – T459 – us Nat'l Archives [324]

RECORDS OF THE REICH COMMISSIONER FOR THE STRENGTHENING OF GERMANDOM – 20r – $460.00 – T74 – us Nat'l Archives [943]

RECORDS OF THE REICH LEADER OF THE SS AND CHIEF OF THE GERMAN POLICE / Germany. Reich SS. and German Police - 655r - 1 - T175 - us Nat'l Archives [943]

RECORDS OF THE REICH MINISTRY FOR ARMAMENTS AND WAR PRODUCTION - 193r - $4,439.00 - T73 - us Nat'l Archives [355]

RECORDS OF THE REICH MINISTRY FOR PUBLIC ENLIGHTENMENT AND PROPAGANDA, 1936-1944 - 125r - $2,875.00 - T70 - us Nat'l Archives [324]

RECORDS OF THE REICH MINISTRY FOR THE OCCUPIED EASTERN TERRITORIES, 1941-45 = REICHSMINISTERIUM FUER DIE BESETZTEN OSTGEBIETE - 107r - 1 - T454 - us Nat'l Archives [324]

RECORDS OF THE REICH MINISTRY OF ECONOMICS - 148r - $3,404.00 - T71 - us Nat'l Archives [350]

RECORDS OF THE RELATIONS BETWEEN SIAM AND FOREIGN COUNTRIES IN THE 17TH CENTURY - v1-5 1915-21 - 1 - $18.00 - us L of C Photodup [950]

RECORDS OF THE REVOLUTIONARY WAR: CONTAINING THE MILITARY AND FINANCIAL CORRESPONDENCE OF DISTINGUISHED OFFICERS / Saffell, WT R - New York: Pudney and Russell, Publishers, 1858. Military Books reel 3. (Cox Library Collection) - 5 - us Americana [975]

RECORDS OF THE ROYAL BAVARIAN WAR MINISTRY AND OTHER BAVARIAN MILITARY AUTHORITIES, 1866-1913 / Germany - 7r - 1 - M963 - us Nat'l Archives [324]

RECORDS OF THE SECRETARY OF STATE'S STAFF COMMITTEE / U.S. Secretary of State - 1944-47. 5 rolls. M1054 - 1 - us Nat'l Archives [324]

RECORDS OF THE SENATE SELECT COMMITTEE THAT INVESTIGATED JOHN BROWN'S RAID AT HARPER'S FERRY / U.S. Senate - 3r - 1 - M1196 - us Nat'l Archives [324]

RECORDS OF THE SOCIAL AND ECONOMIC HISTORY OF ENGLAND AND WALES - London. v1-9. 1914-35 - 86mf - 9 - H-763/2 - ne IDC [300]

RECORDS OF THE SOUTH CAROLINA TREASURY, 1775-1780 - (With printed guide) - South Carolina Department of Archives and History, 1995 - 3r - 1 - $255.00 - D3311 - us Scholarly Res [332]

RECORDS OF THE SOUTH CAROLINA TREASURY, 1775-80 / South Carolina. Department of Archives and History - M-4 - 6r - 1 - $75.00r - Out-of-state orders: us Scholarly Res - us SC Archives [978]

RECORDS OF THE SOUTHERN CHRISTIAN LEADERSHIP CONFERENCE, 1954-1970 - (Coll title: Black Studies Research Sources. Pt 1: Records of the President's Office 21r $2,625.00 ISBN 1-55655-555-5. Pt 2: Records of the Executive Director and Treasurer 22r $2,750.00 ISBN 1-55655-556-3. Pt 3: Record of the Public Relations Department 10r $1,250.00 ISBN 1-55655-557-1. Pt 4: Records of the Program Department 29r $3,625.00 ISBN 1-55655-558-X) - 1996 - 1 - $9,740.00 coll - us UPA [360]

RECORDS OF THE SPECIAL BOARDS OF INQUIRY, DISTRICT NO. 4 (PHILADELPHIA). IMMIGRATION AND NATURALIZATION SERVICE, 1893-1909 - 18r - 1 - M1500 - us Nat'l Archives [340]

RECORDS OF THE STATIONERS' COMPANY, 1554-1920 / ed by Myers, Robin - (With printed guide) - 115r - 1 - £7,275.00 - uk Chadwyck [070]

RECORDS OF THE STRATEGIC PLANS DIVISION, OFFICE OF THE CNO AND PREDECESSOR ORGANIZATIONS - (With printed guide. Series 3: Miscellaneous Subject File 1917-47 rolls 1-24 $2,040.00. Series 8: Records Summarizing Operations 1939-45 rolls 25-29 $425.00. Series 12: Records of the Pacific, Alaskan and Far Eastern Section 1940-46 rolls 30-50 $1,785.00) - 1991 - 50r - 1 - $4,250.00 set - S3214 - us Scholarly Res [355]

RECORDS OF THE SUBCOMMITTEE FOR THE FAR EAST - 1945-48. T1205 - 14r - 1 - us Nat'l Archives [950]

RECORDS OF THE SUBVERSIVE ACTIVITIES CONTROL BOARD, 1950-1972 : COMPLETE COLLECTION - 9 - $9,335.00 - us UPA [320]

RECORDS OF THE SUBVERSIVE ACTIVITIES CONTROL BOARD, PART 1 : COMMUNIST PARTY USA - 9 - $2,890.00 - 1-55655-050-2 - us UPA [320]

RECORDS OF THE SUBVERSIVE ACTIVITIES CONTROL BOARD, PART 2 : COMMUNIST-ACTION AND COMMUNIST-FRONT ORGANIZATIONS - 9 - $6,935.00 - 1-55655-051-0 - us UPA [320]

RECORDS OF THE SUPERINTENDENT OF EDUCATION, BUREAU OF REFUGEES, FREEDMEN, AND ABANDONED LANDS - (Alabama 1865-70 8r $184 M810. Arkansas 1865-71 5r $115 M980. District of Columbia 1865-72 24r $552 M1056. Georgia 1865-70 28r $644 M799. Louisiana 1864-69 12r $276 M1026. North Carolina 1865-70 16r $368 M844. Tennessee 1865-70 9r $207 M1000. Texas 1865-70 18r $414 M822. Virginia 1865-70 2 0r $460 M1053) - 1 - us Nat'l Archives [370]

RECORDS OF THE SUPERINTENDENT OF EDUCATION FOR THE DISTRICT OF COLUMBIA / U.S. Bureau of Refugees, Freedmen, and Abandoned Lands - 1865-72. 24 rolls. M1056 - 1 - us Nat'l Archives [324]

RECORDS OF THE SUPERINTENDENT OF EDUCATION FOR THE STATE OF ALABAMA / U.S. Bureau of Refugees, Freedmen, and Abandoned Lands - 1865-70. 8 rolls. M810 - 1 - us Nat'l Archives [324]

RECORDS OF THE SUPERINTENDENT OF EDUCATION FOR THE STATE OF ARKANSAS / U.S. Bureau of Refugees, Freedmen, and Abandoned Lands - 1865-71. 5 rolls. M980 - 1 - us Nat'l Archives [324]

RECORDS OF THE SUPERINTENDENT OF EDUCATION FOR THE STATE OF LOUISIANA / U.S. Bureau of Refugees, Freedmen, and Abandoned Lands - 1864-69. 12 rolls. M1026 - 1 - us Nat'l Archives [324]

RECORDS OF THE SUPERINTENDENT OF EDUCATION FOR THE STATE OF NORTH CAROLINA / U.S. Bureau of Refugees, Freedmen, and Abandoned Lands - 1865-70. 16 rolls. M844 - 1 - us Nat'l Archives [324]

RECORDS OF THE SUPERINTENDENT OF EDUCATION FOR THE STATE OF TENNESSEE / U.S. Bureau of Refugees, Freedmen, and Abandoned Lands - 1865-70. 9 rolls. M1000 - 1 - us Nat'l Archives [324]

RECORDS OF THE SUPERINTENDENT OF EDUCATION FOR THE STATE OF TEXAS / U.S. Bureau of Refugees, Freedmen, and Abandoned Lands - 1865-70. 18 rolls. M822 - 1 - us Nat'l Archives [324]

RECORDS OF THE SUPERINTENDENT OF EDUCATION FOR THE STATE OF VIRGINIA / U.S. Bureau of Refugees, Freedmen, and Abandoned Lands - 1865-70. 20 rolls. M1053 - 1 - us Nat'l Archives [324]

RECORDS OF THE SUPT. OF EDUCATION FOR THE STATE OF GEORGIA..., 1865-70 / U.S. Bureau of Refugees, Freedmen, and Abandoned Lands - 28 rolls. M799. Printed guide - 1 - us Nat'l Archives [324]

RECORDS OF THE TENTH MILITARY DEPARTMENT, 1846-51 / U.S. Army - 7 rolls.M210. Printed guide - 1 - us Nat'l Archives [324]

RECORDS OF THE TERRITORIAL COURT OF MICHIGAN, 1815-1836 - 9r - 1 - M1111 - us Nat'l Archives [340]

RECORDS OF THE TODT ORGANIZATION - 7r - $161.00 - T76 - us Nat'l Archives [355]

RECORDS OF THE UNITED PRESBYTERIAN CHURCH IN JAMESTOWN, MUNDEN AND SCOTTSVILLE / Presbyterian Church in the U.S.A. Northern Kansas Presbytery - 1923-78 - 1 - us KS Hist [240]

RECORDS OF THE U. S. DEPARTMENT OF STATE RELATING TO INTERNAL AFFAIRS OF CHINA, 1910-1949 - (1910-1929, 227 rolls $5,221.00; 1930-1939, 167 rolls. $12.525.00; 1940-1944, 43 rolls. $3,225.00; 1945-1949, 69 rolls. $5,175.00) - 9 - Dist. us Scholarly Res - us L of C Photodup [324]

RECORDS OF THE UNITED STATES STRATEGIC BOMBING SURVEY (USSBS) : INTELLIGENCE LIBRARY, 1932-1947 - 1993 - 118r - 1 - $2,714.00 set in US $30.00r outside - M1652 - Dist. us Scholarly Res - us L of C Photodup [355]

RECORDS OF THE UNITED STATES STRATEGIC BOMBING SURVEY (USSBS) : PACIFIC SURVEY REPORTS AND SUPPORTING RECORDS, 1928-1947 - 1993 - 507r - 9 - $23.00r - M1655 - Dist. us Scholarly Res - us L of C Photodup [355]

RECORDS OF THE U.S. CONSULATE IN JERUSALEM, PALESTINE: CONFIDENTIAL CORRESPONDENCE, 1920-35 / U.S. Department of State - 1986 - 3r - 1 - $255.00 - S1591 - us Scholarly Res [327]

RECORDS OF THE U.S. ARMY WAR CRIMES TRIALS : UNITED STATES OF AMERICA V. JOHANN HAIDER ET AL., SEPT. 3-12, 1947 / U.S. Army. Army Commands - RG 338. M1139 - 2r - 1 - us Nat'l Archives [940]

RECORDS OF THE U.S. ARMY WAR CRIMES TRIALS: UNITED STATES OF AMERICA V. ERNEST ANGERER ET AL / U.S. Army. Army Commands - Nov 26-Dec 3, 1946. M1210 - 1r - 1 - us Nat'l Archives [324]

RECORDS OF THE U.S. ARMY WAR CRIMES TRIALS: UNITED STATES OF AMERICA V. FRIEDRICH BECKER ET.AL / U.S. Army. Army Commands - Jul 5, 1945 - Jun 11, 1958. 15 rolls. M1204 - 1 - us Nat'l Archives [324]

RECORDS OF THE U.S. CIRCUIT COURT FOR THE WESTERN DISTRICT OF PENNSYLVANIA / U.S. Circuit and District Courts. Pennsylvania - 1801-02. Minutes and Habeas Corpus and Criminal Case Files of the U.S. District Court for the Eastern District of Pennsylvania, 1789-1843. 3 rolls - 1 - M987 - us Nat'l Archives [324]

RECORDS OF THE U.S. CIVIL COMMISSION AT MEMPHIS, 1863-1864 - 9r - 1 - T410 - us Nat'l Archives [340]

RECORDS OF THE U.S. CONSULATE AT CALLAO-LIMA, PERU, 1825-1912 / U.S. Department of State - T781 - 73r - 1 - us Nat'l Archives [972]

RECORDS OF THE U.S. CONSULATE IN BANGKOK, 1856-1912 / U.S. Department of State - T403 - 14r - 1 - us Nat'l Archives [950]

RECORDS OF THE U.S. CONSULATE IN BOMBAY, 1894-1912 / U.S. Department of State - T307 - 7r - 1 - us Nat'l Archives [950]

RECORDS OF THE U.S. CONSULATE IN KUNMING, 1922-28 / U.S. Department of State - T402 - 19r - 1 - us Nat'l Archives [950]

RECORDS OF THE U.S. CONSULATE IN MADRAS, 1908-12 / U.S. Department of State - T308 - 8r - 1 - us Nat'l Archives [950]

RECORDS OF THE U.S. DEPARTMENT OF STATE RELATING TO COMMERCIAL RELATIONS BETWEEN THE UNITED STATES AND JAPAN, 1910-1949 - (Guide also sold separately: $10.00) - 1987 - 17 rolls - 9 - $1,275.00 - Dist. us Scholarly Res - us L of C Photodup [324]

RECORDS OF THE U.S. DEPARTMENT OF STATE RELATING TO INTERNAL AFFAIRS OF JAPAN, 1910-1959 - (1910-1929. 43 rolls. $989.00; 1930-1939. 33 rolls. $2,475.00; 1940-1944. 20 rolls. $1,500.00; 1945-1949. 39 rolls. $2,925.00; 1950-1954. 51 rolls. $3,825.00; 1955-1959. 48 rolls. $3,600.00) - 234 rolls - 9 - Dist. us Scholarly Res - us L of C Photodup [324]

RECORDS OF THE U.S. DEPARTMENT OF STATE RELATING TO POLITICAL RELATIONS BETWEEN THE UNITED STATES AND JAPAN, 1910-1959 - (1910-1929. 9 rolls. $207.00; 1930-1939. 5 rolls. $375.00; 1940-1944. 8 rolls. $600.00; 1945-1949. 19 rolls. $1,425.00; 1950-1954. 11 rolls. $825.00; 1955-1959. 11 rolls. $825.00) - 63 rolls - 9 - Dist. us Scholarly Res - us L of C Photodup [324]

RECORDS OF THE U.S. DEPARTMENT OF STATE RELATING TO POLITICAL RELATIONS BETWEEN THE UNITED STATES AND KOREA, 1955-1959 - 1955-1959 - 3 rolls - 9 - $225.00 - Dist. us Scholarly Res - us L of C Photodup [324]

RECORDS OF THE U.S. DISTRICT COURT FOR THE DISTRICT OF COLUMBIA RELATING TO SLAVES, 1851-1863 - 3r - 1 - M433 - us Nat'l Archives [976]

RECORDS OF THE U.S. DISTRICT COURT FOR THE DISTRICT OF NEW JERSEY AND PREDECESSOR COURTS, 1790-1950 - 186r - 5 - T928 - us Nat'l Archives [340]

RECORDS OF THE U.S. DISTRICT COURT FOR THE EASTERN DISTRICT OF LOUISIANA / U.S. Circuit and District Courts - 1806-14. 18 rolls - 1 - M1082 - us Nat'l Archives [324]

RECORDS OF THE U.S. DISTRICT COURT... AND PREDECESSOR COURTS, 1790-1950 / U.S. District Courts. New Jersey - 186 rolls. T928 - 5 - us Nat'l Archives [324]

RECORDS OF THE U.S. DISTRICT COURT... AND PREDECESSOR COURTS, 1851-1950 / U.S. District Courts, California, Northern District - 125 rolls - 1 - T717 - us Nat'l Archives [324]

RECORDS OF THE U.S. EXPLORING EXPEDITION UNDER THE COMMAND OF LIEUT. CHARLES WILKES, 1836-42 / U.S. Hydrographic Office (Navy) - 27 rolls. M75 - 1 - us Nat'l Archives [910]

RECORDS OF THE U.S. INDIAN CLAIMS COMMISSION - (With 2-vol printed guide: Index to the Decisions of the Indian Claims Commission; Index to the Expert Testimony Before the Indian Claims Commission) - 6,128mf - 9 - $19,925.00 - us UPA [324]

RECORDS OF THE U.S. JUDICIAL CONFERENCE : COMMITTEES ON RULES OF PRACTICE AND PROCEDURES - (Key documents for discovering the intent of federal court rules. Printed index $2,020.00) - 1935-88 - 4033mf - 9 - $14,175.00 mf + index coll (1989-91 $730.00y mf + index coll) - us CIS [340]

RECORDS OF THE U.S. LEGATION IN CHILE, 1893-1905 / U.S. Department of State - M20 - 14r - 1 - us Nat'l Archives [340]

RECORDS OF THE U.S. LEGATION IN CHINA, 1849-1931 / U.S. Department of State - T898 - 20r - 1 - us Nat'l Archives [340]

RECORDS OF THE U.S. LEGATION IN JAPAN, 1855-1912 / U.S. Department of State - T400 - 94r - 1 - us Nat'l Archives [340]

RECORDS OF THE U.S. LEGATION IN PARIS, 1836-42 / U.S. Department of State - M14 - 10r - 1 - us Nat'l Archives [340]

RECORDS OF THE U.S. LEGATION IN PERU / U.S. Department of State - 1826-1912. 88 rolls. T724 - 1 - us Nat'l Archives [324]

RECORDS OF THE U.S. MARINE CORPS IN THE VIETNAM WAR - (Pt 1, Fleet Marine Force, Pacific Command Histories, 1964-73: 1-55655-254-8 $880.00; Pt 2, 3rd Marine Amphibious Force Command Histories, 1964-71: 1-55655-255-6 $3,300.00; Pt 3, Divisional Command Histories, 1965-71: 1-55655-256-4 $4,400.00) - $8,155.00 set - us UPA [355]

RECORDS OF THE U.S. NUERNBERG WAR CRIMES TRIALS : GUERTNER DIARIES / U.S. Army. Army Commands - Oct 5 1934-Dec 24 1938. M978 - 3r - 1 - us Nat'l Archives [940]

RECORDS OF THE U.S. NUERNBERG WAR CRIMES TRIALS : INTERROGATIONS / U.S. Army. Army Commands - 1946-49. M1019 - 91r - 1 - us Nat'l Archives [940]

RECORDS OF THE U.S. NUERNBERG WAR CRIMES TRIALS : NG SERIES, 1933-1948 - T1139 - 70r - $1,610.00 - us Nat'l Archives [340]

RECORDS OF THE U.S. NUERNBERG WAR CRIMES TRIALS : NM SERIES / U.S. Army. Army Commands - M936 - 1r - 1 - us Nat'l Archives [940]

RECORDS OF THE U.S. NUERNBERG WAR CRIMES TRIALS : NOKW SERIES - T1119 - 47r - $1,081.00 - us Nat'l Archives [340]

RECORDS OF THE U.S. NUERNBERG WAR CRIMES TRIALS : NP SERIES / U.S. Army. Army Commands - 1934-46. M942 - 1r - 1 - us Nat'l Archives [940]

RECORDS OF THE U.S. NUERNBERG WAR CRIMES TRIALS : UNITED STATES OF AMERICA V. ALFONS KLEIN ET AL / U.S. Army. Army Commands - Oct 8-15 1945. Case No. 12-449 and 000-12-31. M1078 - 3r - 1 - us Nat'l Archives [940]

RECORDS OF THE U.S. NUERNBERG WAR CRIMES TRIALS : UNITED STATES OF AMERICA V. ALFRED KRUPP ET AL, CASE 10 / U.S. Army. Army Commands - Aug 16 1947-Jul 31 1948. M896 - 69r - 1 - us Nat'l Archives [940]

RECORDS OF THE U.S. NUERNBERG WAR CRIMES TRIALS : UNITED STATES OF AMERICA V. CARL KRAUCH ET AL, CASE 6 / U.S. Army. Army Commands - Aug 14 1947-Jul 30 1948. M892 - 113r - 1 - us Nat'l Archives [940]

RECORDS OF THE U.S. NUERNBERG WAR CRIMES TRIALS : UNITED STATES OF AMERICA V. ERHARD MILCH / U.S. Army. Army Commands – Case II. Nov 13 1946 – Apr 17 1947. M888 – 13r – 1 – us Nat'l Archives [940]

RECORDS OF THE U.S. NUERNBERG WAR CRIMES TRIALS : UNITED STATES OF AMERICA V. ERNEST DURA ET AL / U.S. Army. Army Commands – Dec 11 1945-Jun 26 1959. RG 338. M1100 – 2r – 1 – us Nat'l Archives [940]

RECORDS OF THE U.S. NUERNBERG WAR CRIMES TRIALS : UNITED STATES OF AMERICA V. ERNST VON WEIZSAECKER ET AL, CASE 11 / U.S. Army. Army Commands – Dec 20 1947-Apr 14 1949. M897 – 173r – 1 – us Nat'l Archives [943]

RECORDS OF THE U.S. NUERNBERG WAR CRIMES TRIALS : UNITED STATES OF AMERICA V. FRANZ AUER ET AL / U.S. Army. Army Commands – Mar 27 1944-Jul 15 1958. RG 338 and 153. M1093 – 13r – 1 – us Nat'l Archives [940]

RECORDS OF THE U.S. NUERNBERG WAR CRIMES TRIALS : UNITED STATES OF AMERICA V. FRIEDRICH FLICK ET AL, CASE 5 / U.S. Army. Army Commands – Mar 3-Dec 22 1947. M891 – 42r – 1 – us Nat'l Archives [940]

RECORDS OF THE U.S. NUERNBERG WAR CRIMES TRIALS : UNITED STATES OF AMERICA V. GOTTFRIED WEISS ET AL / U.S. Army. Army Commands – Nov 15 1945 – Dec 13 1945. RG 338. M1174 – 6r – 1 – us Nat'l Archives [940]

RECORDS OF THE U.S. NUERNBERG WAR CRIMES TRIALS : UNITED STATES OF AMERICA V. HANS JOACHIM GEORG GEIGER ET AL / U.S. Army. Army Commands – Jul 9-Aug 5 1947. RG 338. M1191 – 2r – 1 – us Nat'l Archives [940]

RECORDS OF THE U.S. NUERNBERG WAR CRIMES TRIALS : UNITED STATES OF AMERICA V. JOSEF ALTSTOETTER ET AL, CASE 3 / U.S. Army. Army Commands – Feb 17-Dec 4 1947. M889 – 53r – 1 – us Nat'l Archives [940]

RECORDS OF THE U.S. NUERNBERG WAR CRIMES TRIALS : UNITED STATES OF AMERICA V. JUERGEN STROOP ET AL / U.S. Army. Army Commands – Mar 29 1945-Aug 21 1957. RG 338 and 153. M1095 – 10r – 1 – us Nat'l Archives [940]

RECORDS OF THE U.S. NUERNBERG WAR CRIMES TRIALS : UNITED STATES OF AMERICA V. KARL BRANDT ET AL / U.S. Army. Army Commands – Case I. Nov 21 1946 – Aug 20 1947. M887 – 46r – 1 – us Nat'l Archives [940]

RECORDS OF THE U.S. NUERNBERG WAR CRIMES TRIALS : UNITED STATES OF AMERICA V. KURT GOEBELL ET AL.; UNITED STATES OF AMERICA V. AUGUST HAESIKER / U.S. Army. Army Commands – Jun 4 1945 – Mar 4 1958; May 24 1947 – Dec 3 1963. RG 338 and 153. M1103 – 7r – 1 – us Nat'l Archives [940]

RECORDS OF THE U.S. NUERNBERG WAR CRIMES TRIALS : UNITED STATES OF AMERICA V. MICHAEL VOGEL ET AL. / U.S. Army. Army Commands – May 31 1945-Jun 11 1958. RG 338. M1173 – 2r – 1 – us Nat'l Archives [940]

RECORDS OF THE U.S. NUERNBERG WAR CRIMES TRIALS : UNITED STATES OF AMERICA V. OSWALD POHL ET AL, CASE 4 / U.S. Army. Army Commands – Jan 13 1947 – Aug 11 1948. M890 – 38r – 1 – us Nat'l Archives [940]

RECORDS OF THE U.S. NUERNBERG WAR CRIMES TRIALS : UNITED STATES OF AMERICA V. OTTO OHLENDORF ET AL, CASE 9 / U.S. Army. Army Commands – Sep 15 1947-Apr 10 1948. M895 – 38r – 1 – us Nat'l Archives [940]

RECORDS OF THE U.S. NUERNBERG WAR CRIMES TRIALS : UNITED STATES OF AMERICA V. OTTO SKORZENY ET AL / U.S. Army. Commands – RG 338 and 153. M1106 – 24mf – 9 – us Nat'l Archives [940]

RECORDS OF THE U.S. NUERNBERG WAR CRIMES TRIALS : UNITED STATES OF AMERICA V. ULRICH GREIFELT ET AL, CASE 8 / U.S. Army. Army Commands – Oct 10 1947-Mar 10 1948. M894 – 38r – 1 – us Nat'l Archives [940]

RECORDS OF THE U.S. NUERNBERG WAR CRIMES TRIALS : UNITED STATES OF AMERICA V. WILHELM LIST ET AL, CASE 7 / U.S. Army. Army Commands – Jul 8 1947-Feb 19 1948. M893 – 48r – 1 – us Nat'l Archives [940]

RECORDS OF THE U.S. NUERNBERG WAR CRIMES TRIALS : UNITED STATES OF AMERICA V. WILHELM VON LEEB ET AL, CASE 12 / U.S. Army. Army Commands – Nov 28 1947-Oct 28 1948. M898 – 69r – 1 – us Nat'l Archives [940]

RECORDS OF THE U.S. NUERNBERG WAR CRIMES TRIALS : WA SERIES / U.S. Army. Army Commands – 1940-45. M946 – 1r – 1 – us Nat'l Archives [940]

RECORDS OF THE U.S. NUERNBERG WAR CRIMES TRIALS: NG SERIES, 1933-48 / U. S. – 70 rolls. T1139 – 1 – us Nat'l Archives [940]

RECORDS OF THE U.S. WAR CRIMES TRIALS : NI SERIES, 1933-1948 – T301 – 163r – $3,749.00 – us Nat'l Archives [340]

RECORDS OF THE UTAH SUPERINTENDENCY OF INDIAN AFFAIRS / U.S. Bureau of Indian Affairs – 1853-70. 2 rolls. M834 – 1 – us Nat'l Archives [324]

RECORDS OF THE VICE ADMIRALTY COURT OF THE PROVINCE OF NEW YORK – 1r – 1 – T842 – us Nat'l Archives [340]

RECORDS OF THE VIRGINIA COMPANY OF LONDON, 1606-1626 – 1975 – 2r – 1 – $170.00 – S1875 – us Scholarly Res [975]

RECORDS OF THE VIRGINIA FORCES / U.S. War Department – 1861. 7 rolls. M998 – 1 – us Nat'l Archives [324]

RECORDS OF THE VIVI STATION, 1881-1885 / Association internationale du Haut-Congo. Vivi Station – Eugene, OR: Photographic Bureau, 1966 – us Res Libr [960]

RECORDS OF THE VOCATIONAL INFORMATION : 1908-1932 – 9 – $3,080.00 – 1-55655-104-5 – us UPA [331]

RECORDS OF THE WAR DEPARTMENT'S OPERATIONS DIVISION, PART 1 : WORLD WAR 2 OPERATIONS – (Series A, European and Mediterranean Theaters: 16r. $1,760.00 ISBN 1-55655-272-6; Series B, Pacific Theater: 24r. $2,645.00 ISBN 1-55655-271-8; Series C, Top Secret Files: 24r. $3,100.00 ISBN 1-55655-273-4; All include a printed guide) – $7,130.00 set – us UPA [324]

RECORDS OF THE WAR RELOCATION AUTHORITY / U.S. National Archives – (1: Field Basic Documentation 115r. 2: Headquarters Security-Classified General Files ca 4r. 3: Headquarters Subject-Classified General Files ca 32r) – ca 151r – 1 – £5,680.00 – uk Chadwyck [355]

RECORDS OF THE WICKERSHAM COMMISSION ON LAW OBSERVANCE AND ENFORCEMENT, PART 1 : RECORDS OF THE COMMITTEE ON OFFICIAL LAWLESSNESS / ed by Hall, Kermit – (With printed guide) – 1996 – 15r – 1 – $1,875.00 – 1-55655-631-4 – us UPA [340]

RECORDS OF THE WISCONSIN SUPERINTENDENCY OF INDIAN AFFAIRS / U.S. Bureau of Indian Affairs – 1836-48. And the Green Bay Subagency, 1850. 4 rolls. M951 – 1 – us Nat'l Archives [324]

RECORDS OF THE WOMEN'S CITY CLUB OF NEW YORK, 1916-1980 – Grassroots Women's Organizations Series – 24r – $2,650.00 – 1-55655-095-2 – us UPA [305]

RECORDS OF THE WOMEN'S INTERNATIONAL LEAGUE FOR PEACE AND FREEDOM, US SECTION, 1919-59 / ed by Barr, Eleanor M – (With printed guide) – 97r – 1 – $8,245.00 – S3050 – us Scholarly Res [305]

THE RECORDS OF THE WOMEN'S PEACE UNION, U.S. BRANCH, 1921-1940 / Women's Peace Union – (With printed guide) – 1991 – 26r – 1 – $2,210.00 – D3249 – us Scholarly Res [305]

RECORDS OF ZAGAR INCORPORATED *see* ZAGAR, INCORPORATED, RECORDS

RECORDS...: OLD LOANS RECORDS RELATING TO SELECTED LOANS OF THE PERIOD 1795-1807 / U.S. Treasury Department. Bureau of the Public Debt – 6rolls. T787 – 1 – us Nat'l Archives [336]

RECORDS...: PENNSYLVANIA LOAN OFFICE RECORDS RELATING TO THE LOAN OF 1790 / U.S. Treasury Department. Bureau of the Public Debt – 8rolls. T631 – 1 – us Nat'l Archives [336]

RECORDS RELATING TO AUSTRALIA / Guildhall Library, London – The Papers of Antony Gibbs and Sons, 1853-1930. And, The Records of the Corporation of London Records Office, 1791-1834 – 1 – £1,350.00 – uk World [980]

RECORDS RELATING TO CLAIMS AGAINST BRAZIL UNDER THE CONVENTION OF 1849 / U. S. – T1187 – 19r – 1 – us Nat'l Archives [972]

RECORDS... RELATING TO COMMERCIAL RELATIONS BETWEEN THE UNITED STATES AND JAPAN, 1910-1949 / U.S. Department of State – (With printed guide) – 17r – 1 – $1,445.00 – S3007 – us Scholarly Res [337]

RECORDS... RELATING TO COMMERCIAL RELATIONS BETWEEN THE UNITED STATES AND RUSSIA/THE SOVIET UNION, 1910-1949 / U.S. Department of State – (With printed guide) – 1987 – 22r – 1 – $1,870.00 – S3006 – us Scholarly Res [337]

RECORDS RELATING TO CONFEDERATE NAVAL AND MARINE PERSONNEL / U.S. War Department. Confederate Records – 7rolls. M260. Printed guide – 5 – us Nat'l Archives [324]

RECORDS RELATING TO ENROLLMENT OF EASTERN CHEROKEES BY GUION MILLER, 1908-10 / U.S. Bureau of Indian Affairs – 12 rolls. M685. Printed guide – 1 – us Nat'l Archives [324]

RECORDS... RELATING TO INTERNAL AFFAIRS OF ALBANIA, 1910-1954 / U.S. Department of State – (1910-1944 16r $368.00. 1945-1949 4r $300.00. 1950-1954 3r $225.00. Includes printed guide) – 23r – 1 – $1,725.00 total – us Scholarly Res [327]

RECORDS RELATING TO INTERNAL AFFAIRS OF AUSTRIA-HUNGARY AND AUSTRIA : DECIMAL FILE 863 TO 1950 / U.S. Department of State – (1910-29 69r $2,346 M695. 1930-44 32r $1,088 M1209. 1945-49 16r $1,360 S3046. 1950-54 32r $2,720 S3047. Includes descriptive pamphlet Decimal file 864 1912-29 38r $1,292) – 149r – 1 – $5,923.00 – us Scholarly Res [327]

RECORDS RELATING TO INTERNAL AFFAIRS OF BRAZIL / U.S. DEPARTMENT OF STATE RECORDS. – (1910-1929. 54r $1,242.00, 1930-1939. 48r $1,104.00, 1940-1944. 84r $1,932.00, 1945-1949. 48r $1,104.00, 1950-1954 (Decimal File 732). 14r $322.00, 1950-1954 (Decimal File 832). 34r $782.00, 1955-1959. 8r $184.00; Political Relations between the United States and Brazil: 1910-1929. 1r; 1930-1939. 1r $80.00, 1940-1944. 2r $160.00; Political Relations between Brazil and Other States: 1910-1929. 2r $46.00, 1930-1944. 1r $80.00) – 1810-1959 – 1 – us Nat'l Archives [972]

RECORDS RELATING TO INTERNAL AFFAIRS OF BULGARIA, 1910-1954 / U.S. Department of State – (1910-44 21r $714 M1207. 1945-49 9r $765 S3023. 1950-54 5r $425 S3024. Includes printed guide) – 1 – $1,904.00 – us Scholarly Res [327]

RECORDS RELATING TO INTERNAL AFFAIRS OF CENTRAL AMERICA, 1810-1959 / U.S. Department of State Records – (1910-1929 16r $544 M672. 1930-1949. 6r $204 M1330. Records Relating to Political Relations between the United States and Central America: 1911-1929 1r $34 M673. 1930-1944 1r $85 S3159. Records Relating to Political Relations between Central America and Other States: 1910-1929 2r $68 M674. 1930-1939 2r $170 S3160. 1940-1944 1r $85 S3160. All sets include descriptive pamphlet) – 1 – us Scholarly Res [972]

RECORDS RELATING TO INTERNAL AFFAIRS OF CHILE, 1910-1929 / U.S. Department of State Records – (1910-1929 40r $1,360 M487. Political Relations between the United States and Chile: 1910-1929 1r $34 M489. 1930-1939 1r $85 S3159. 1940-1944 1r $85 S3159. Political Relations between Chile and Other States: 1910-1929 2r $108 M490. 1930-1944 2r $170 S3160. All with descriptive pamphlets) – 1 – us Scholarly Res [972]

RECORDS RELATING TO INTERNAL AFFAIRS OF CHINA, 1910-49 / U.S. Department of State – (1910-29 227r $7,718 M329. 1930-39 167r $14,195 S1411. 1940-44 43r $3,655 S1421. 1945-49 69r $5,865 S1431. Includes printed guides) – 1 – us Scholarly Res [324]

RECORDS RELATING TO INTERNAL AFFAIRS OF COLOMBIA, 1810-1959 / U.S. Department of State Records – (1910-1929 45r $1,530 M1294. Political Relations between the United States and Colombia: 1930-1944 1r $85 S3159 with descriptive pamphlet. Political Relations between Colombia and Other States 1930-1944 12r $1,020 S3160 with dsecriptive pamphlet) – 1 – us Scholarly Res [972]

RECORDS RELATING TO INTERNAL AFFAIRS OF COSTA RICA, 1810-1959 / U.S. Department of State Records – (1910-1929 40r $1,360 M669. Political Relations between the United States and Costa Rica: 1910-1929 1r $34 M670. 1930-1944 1r $85 S3159. Political Relations between Costa Rica and Other States: 1910-1929 10r $340 M671. 1930-1939 1r $85 S3160. 1940-1949 1r $85 S3160. With descriptive pamphlets) – 1 – us Scholarly Res [972]

RECORDS RELATING TO INTERNAL AFFAIRS OF CUBA, 1810-1959 / U.S. Department of State Records – (1910-1929 99r $3,366 M488 Political Relations between the United States and Cuba: 1910-1929 2r $68 M509. 1930-1939 2r $170 S3159. 1940-1944 1r $85 S3159. Political Relations between Cuba and Other States: 1910-1929 1r $34 M510. 1930-1944 1r $85 S3160. With descriptive pamphlets) – 1 – us Scholarly Res [972]

RECORDS RELATING TO INTERNAL AFFAIRS OF CZECHOSLOVAKIA, 1910-1959 / U.S. Department of State – (1910-1944 32r $1,088 M1218. 1945-49 17r $1,445 S3010. 1950-54 15r $1,275 S3011. 1955-1959 8r $680 S3284. With descriptive pamphlets) – 1 – us Scholarly Res [327]

RECORDS RELATING TO INTERNAL AFFAIRS OF EAST GERMANY, 1950-54 : DECIMAL FILES 762B, 862B, 962B / U.S. Department of State – (1955-59 10r $850 S3285. Includes printed guides) – 14r – 1 – $1,190.00 – S3034 – us Scholarly Res [327]

RECORDS RELATING TO INTERNAL AFFAIRS OF ECUADOR, 1810-1959 / U.S. Department of State Records – (1910-1929 27r $918 M1468. Political Relations between the United States and Euador: 1930-1944 1r $85 S3159. Political Relations between Ecuador and Other States: 1930-1939 3r $255 S3160. 1940-1944 10r $850 S3160. Includes descriptive pamphlets) – 1 – us Scholarly Res [972]

RECORDS RELATING TO INTERNAL AFFAIRS OF EL SALVADOR, 1810-1959 / U.S. Department od State Records – (1910-1929 22r $748 M658. Political Relations between the United States and El Salvador: 1910-1929 1r $34 M659. 1930-1944 1r $85 S3159. Political Relations between El Salvador and Other States: 1910-1929 1r $34 M660 1930-1944 1r $85 S3160. Includes descriptive pamphlets) – 1 – us Scholarly Res [972]

RECORDS RELATING TO INTERNAL AFFAIRS OF FINLAND, 1910-1954 / U.S. Department of State – (1910-1944 32r $1,088 T1184. 1945-49 8r $680 S3035. 1950-54 11r $935 S3036. Includes printed guides) – 1 – $2,351.00 – us Scholarly Res [327]

RECORDS RELATING TO INTERNAL AFFAIRS OF GREECE, 1910-1954 / U.S. Department of State – (1910-29 45r $1,530 M443. 1930-39 16r $544 M1179. 1940-44 20r $1,700 S3025. 1945-49 53r $4,505 S3026. 1950-54 29r $2,465 S3027. Includes printed guide) – 1 – us Scholarly Res [327]

RECORDS RELATING TO INTERNAL AFFAIRS OF GUATEMALA, 1810-1959 / U.S. Department of State Records – (1910-1929 40r $1,360 M655. 1930-1944 22r $748 M1280. 1945-1949 12r $408 M1527. Political Relations between the United States and Guatemala: 1910-1929 1r $34 M656. 1930-1944 1r $85 S3159. Political Relations between Guatemala and Other States: 1910-1929 27r $918 M657. 1930-1939 4r $340 S3160. 1940-1944 2r $170 S3160. Includes descriptive pamphlets) – 1 – us Scholarly Res [972]

RECORDS RELATING TO INTERNAL AFFAIRS OF HAITI, 1810-1959 / U.S. Department of State Records – (1910-1929 94r $3,196 M610. 1930-1939 36r $1,224 M1246. Political Relations between the United States and Haiti: 1910-1929 2r $68 M611. 1930-1944 1r $85 S3159. Political Relations between Haiti and Other States: 1910-1929 4r $136 M612. 1930-1939 3r $255 S3160. 1940-1944 1r $85 S3160. Includes descriptive pamphlet) – 1 – us Scholarly Res [972]

RECORDS RELATING TO INTERNAL AFFAIRS OF HONDURAS, 1810-1959 / U.S. Department of State Records – (1910-1929 49r $1,666 M647. Political Relations between the United States and Honduras: 1910-1929 1r $34 M648. 1930-1944 1r $85 S3159. Political Relations between Honduras and Other States: 1930-1939 5r $425 S3160 1940-1944 1r $85 S3160. Includes descriptive pamphlet) – 1 – us Scholarly Res [972]

RECORDS RELATING TO INTERNAL AFFAIRS OF HUNGARY, 1912-1959 / U.S. Department of State – (1912-29 38r $1,292 M708. 1930-44 17r $578 M1206. 1945-49 20r $1,700 S3030. 1950-54 37r $3,145 S3031. 1955-59 25r $2,125 S3286. Includes printed guide) – 57r – 1 – us Scholarly Res [327]

RECORDS RELATING TO INTERNAL AFFAIRS OF JAPAN, 1910-1959 / U.S. Department of State – (1910-29 43r $1,1462 M422. 1930-39 33r $2,805 S1461. 1940-44 20r $1,700 S1471. 1945-49 39r $3,315 S1481. 1950-54 51r $4,335 S3005. 1955-59 48r $4,080 S3195. Includes printed guides) – 1 – us Scholarly Res [327]

RECORDS RELATING TO INTERNAL AFFAIRS OF KOREA, 1910-1959 / U.S. Department of State – (1910-29 9r $306 M426. 1930-39 2r $170 S1508. 1940-44 3r $255 S1509. 1945-49 12r $1,020 S1510. 1950-54 33r $2,805 S1511. 1955-59 22r $1,870 S3205. Includes printed guide) – 1 – us Scholarly Res [327]

RECORDS RELATING TO INTERNAL AFFAIRS OF MEXICO, 1810-1959 / U.S. Department of State Records – (1910-1929 243r $8,262 M274. 1930-1939 165r $5,610 M1370. Political Relations between the United States and Mexico: 1910-1929 29r $986 M314. 1930-1939 44r $3,740 S3159. 1940-1944 3r $255 S3159. Political Relations between Mexico and Other States: 1910-1929 2r $68 M315. 1930-1939 2r $170 S3160. 1940-1944 1r $85 S3160. Includes descriptive pamphlets) – 1 – us Scholarly Res [972]

RECORDS RELATING TO INTERNAL AFFAIRS OF NICARAGUA, 1810-1959 / U.S. Department of State Records – (1910-1929 106r $3,604 M632. 1930-1944 53r $1,802 M1273. Political Relations between the United States and Nicaragua: 1910-1929 2r $68 M633. 1930-1944 1r $85 S3159. Political Relations between Nicaragua and Other States: 1910-1929 3r $102 M634. 1930-1944 1r $85 S3160. Includes descriptive pamphlet) – 1 – us Scholarly Res [972]

RECORDS RELATING TO INTERNAL AFFAIRS OF PALESTINE (ISRAEL), 1910-1949 / U.S. Department of State – (1910-1929 10r $304 M353. 1930-1944 26r $884 M1037. 1945-1949 27r $918 M1390. Includes descriptive pamphlet) – 1 – us Scholarly Res [956]

RECORDS RELATING TO INTERNAL AFFAIRS OF PANAMA, 1810-1959 / U.S. Department of State Records – (1910-1929 58r $1,972 M607. Political Relations between the United States and Panama: 1910-1929. 14r $476 M608. 1930-1939 8r $680 S3159. 1940-1944 1r $85 S3159. Political Relations between Panama and Other States: 1910-1929 3r $102 M609. 1930-1944 1r $85 S3160. Includes descriptive pamphlet) – 1 – us Scholarly Res [972]

RECORDS RELATING TO INTERNAL AFFAIRS OF PARAGUAY, 1810-1959 / U.S. Department of State Records – (1910-1939 22r $748 M1470. Political Relations between the United States and Paraguay: 1930-1944 1r $85 S3159. Political Relations between Paraguay and Other States: 1930-1944 1r $85 S3160. Includes descriptive pamphlet) – 1 – us Scholarly Res [972]

RECORDS RELATING TO INTERNAL AFFAIRS OF PERU, 1810-1959 / U.S. Department of State Records – (1910-1929 30r $1,020 M746. Political Relations between the United States and Peru: 1930-1944 1r $85 S3159. Political Relations between Peru and Other States: 1910-1929 52r $1,768 M748. 1930-1939 1r $85 S3160. 1940-1944 1r $85 S3160. Includes descriptive pamphlet) – 1 – us Scholarly Res [972]

RECORDS RELATING TO INTERNAL AFFAIRS OF POLAND, 1916-1959 / U.S. Department of State – (1916-44 75r $2,550 M1197. 1945-49 23r $1,955 S3008. 1950-54 14r $1,190 S3009. 1955-59 16r $1,360 S3287. Includes printed guides) – 1 – us Scholarly Res [327]

RECORDS RELATING TO INTERNAL AFFAIRS OF ROMANIA, 1910-1959 / U.S. Department of State – (1910-44 44r $1,496 M1198. 1945-49 14r $1,190 S3032. 1950-54 7r $595 S3033. 1955-59 7r $595 S3288. Includes printed guide) – 1 – us Scholarly Res [327]

RECORDS RELATING TO INTERNAL AFFAIRS OF RUSSIA/THE SOVIET UNION, 1910-1944 / U.S. Department of State – (1910-29 177r $6,018 M316. 1930-39 75r $2,550 T1249. 1940-44 35r $1,190 T1250) – 1 – us Scholarly Res [947]

RECORDS RELATING TO INTERNAL AFFAIRS OF THE DOMINICAN REPUBLIC, 1810-1959 / U.S. Department of State Records – (1910-1929 79r $2,686 M626. 1930-1939 37r $1,258 M1272. 1940-1944 20r $680 M1277. Political Relations between the United States and the Dominican Republic: 1930-1944 1r $85 S3159. Political Relations between the Dominican Republic and Other States: 1930-1944 1r $85 S3160. Includes descriptive pamphlet) – 1 – us Scholarly Res [972]

RECORDS RELATING TO INTERNAL AFFAIRS OF VENEZUELA, 1910-1944 / U.S. Department of State Records – (1910-1929 32r $1,088 M366. Political Relations between the United States and Venzuela: 1910-1929 1r $34 M368. 1930-1944 1r $85 S3159. Political Relations between Venezuela and Other States: 1910-1929 2r $68 M369. 1930-1944 1r $85 S3160. Includes descriptive pamphlet) – 1 – us Scholarly Res [972]

RECORDS RELATING TO INTERNAL AFFAIRS OF YUGOSLAVIA, 1910-1959 / U.S. Department of State – (1910-29 27r $918 M358. 1930-44 29r $986 M1203. 1945-49 18r $1,530 S3020. 1950-54 23r $1,955 S3021. 1955-59 18r $1,530 S3289. Includes printed guide) – 1 – us Scholarly Res [327]

RECORDS RELATING TO INVESTIGATIONS OF THE FORT PHIL KEARNEY OR FETTERMAN MASSACRE, 1866-67 / U.S. Bureau of Indian Affairs – 1 roll. M740. Printed guide – 1 – us Nat'l Archives [324]

RECORDS RELATING TO NORTH AMERICA, 1834-99.. / Belgium. Ministry of Foreign Affairs – 9 rolls.T125 – 1 – us Nat'l Archives [324]

RECORDS.... RELATING TO POLITICAL RELATIONS BETWEEN AUSTRIA-HUNGARY AND AUSTRIA AND OTHER STATES, 1910-1929 : DECIMAL FILE 763 / U.S. Department of State – (Decimal File 764: 1920-29 2r $46.00) – 3r – 1 – $69.00 – M697 – us Nat'l Archives [327]

RECORDS RELATING TO POLITICAL RELATIONS BETWEEN GERMANY AND CZECHOSLOVAKIA, 1930-1939 : DECIMAL FILE 760F.62 – 8r – $272.00 – T1243 – us Scholarly Res [327]

RECORDS RELATING TO POLITICAL RELATIONS BETWEEN GERMANY AND FRANCE, 1910-1929 : DECIMAL FILE 751.62 – (Includes descriptive pamphlet) – 2r – $68.00 – M569 – us Scholarly Res [327]

RECORDS RELATING TO POLITICAL RELATIONS BETWEEN GERMANY AND OTHER STATES, 1910-29 : DECIMAL FILE 762 / U.S. Department of State – (Includes descriptive pamphlet) – 4r – 1 – $136.00 – M354 – us Scholarly Res [327]

RECORDS RELATING TO POLITICAL RELATIONS BETWEEN RUSSIA/THE SOVIET UNION AND OTHER STATES, 1910-1944 / U.S. Department of State – (1910-29 20r $680 M340. 1930-39 14r $476 T1247. 1940-44 4r $136 T1248) – 1 – us Scholarly Res [947]

RECORDS RELATING TO POLITICAL RELATIONS BETWEEN SOUTH AMERICA AND OTHER STATES, 1810-1959 / U.S. Department of State Records – (1930-1944 1r $85. Includes descriptive pamphlet) – 1 – S3160 – us Scholarly Res [972]

RECORDS RELATING TO POLITICAL RELATIONS BETWEEN THE AUSTRIA AND THE U.S., 1910-29 : DECIMAL FILE 711.63 / U.S. Department of State – (Decimal file 711.64: 1921-29 1r $34.00 M709. Includes descriptive pamphlet) – 4r – 1 – $136.00 – M696 – us Scholarly Res [327]

RECORDS RELATING TO POLITICAL RELATIONS BETWEEN THE UNITED STATES AND JAPAN, 1910-1959 / U.S. Department of State – (1910-29 9r $306 M423. 1930-39 5r $425 S3041. 1940-44 8r $680 S3042. 1945-49 19r $1,615 S3043. 1950-54 11r $935 S3044. 1955-59 11r $935 S3208. Includes printed guides) – 1 – us Scholarly Res [327]

RECORDS RELATING TO POLITICAL RELATIONS BETWEEN THE UNITED STATES AND KOREA, 1955-1959 / U.S. Department of State – (Includes printed guide) – 3r – $255.00 – S3206 – us Scholarly Res [327]

RECORDS RELATING TO POLITICAL RELATIONS BETWEEN THE UNITED STATES AND LATIN AMERICAN AND CARIBBEAN STATES, 1930-1944 / U.S. Department of State – (Includes printed guide) – 69r – 1 – $5,865.00 – S3159 – us Scholarly Res [327]

RECORDS RELATING TO POLITICAL RELATIONS BETWEEN THE UNITED STATES AND RUSSIA/THE SOVIET UNION, 1910-1944 / U.S. Department of State – (1910-29 7r $238 M333. 1930-39 3r $102 T1241. 1940-44 1r $34 T1242) – 1 – us Scholarly Res [947]

RECORDS RELATING TO POLITICAL RELATIONS BETWEEN THE UNITED STATES AND THE AMERICAN STATES (THE MONROE DOCTRINE) / U.S. Department of State Records – (1910-1949. 30r $690.00; Records Relating to Political Relations between the United States and Latin American and Caribbean States, 1930-1944. 69r $4,830.00; Records Relating to Political Relations of Latin American and Caribbean States, 1930-1944. 90r $6,300.00) – 1810-1959 – 1 – us Nat'l Archives [972]

RECORDS RELATING TO POLITICAL RELATIONS BETWEEN THE U.S. AND GERMANY, 1930-39 : DECIMAL FILE 711.62 / U.S. Department of State – (1910-29 4r $136 M355. Includes printed guide) – 2r – 1 – $68.00 – T1253 – us Scholarly Res [327]

RECORDS RELATING TO POLITICAL RELATIONS OF LATIN AMERICAN AND CARIBBEAN STATES, 1930-1944 / U.S. Department of State – (Includes printed guide) – 90r – 1 – $7,650.00 – S3160 – us Scholarly Res [327]

RECORDS RELATING TO THE 1811 AND 1815 COURTS-MARTIAL OF MAJOR GENERAL JAMES WILKINSON / U.S. Army. Adjutant General's Office – RG 94 and 153. M1136. 2 rolls – 1 – us Nat'l Archives [355]

RECORDS RELATING TO THE APPOINTMENT OF FEDERAL JUDGES, ATTORNEYS, AND MARSHALS FOR: / U.S. Department of Justice – (The territory and state of Idaho, 1861-99. 9 rolls. M681. Printed guide. Oregon, 1853-1903. 3 rolls. M224. Printed guide. The Territory and state of Utah, 1853-1901. 14 rolls. M680. Printed guide. The Territory and State of Washington, 1853-1902. 17 rolls. M198. Printed guide) – 1 – us Nat'l Archives [340]

RECORDS RELATING TO THE APPOINTMENT OF FEDERAL JUDGES, ATTORNEYS AND MARSHALS FOR OREGON / U.S. Department of Justice – 1853-1903. 3 rolls. M224 – 1 – us Nat'l Archives [340]

RECORDS RELATING TO THE ARMY CAREER OF HENRY OSSIAN FLIPPER, 1873-82 / U.S. Army. Judge Advocate General – 1roll. T1027 – 1 – us Nat'l Archives [324]

RECORDS RELATING TO THE DANISH WEST INDIES, 1672-1860, RECEIVED FROM THE DANISH NATIONAL ARCHIVES / Denmark. National Archives – 19 r – 1 – T952 – us Nat'l Archives [324]

RECORDS RELATING TO THE FIRST NORTHWEST BOUNDARY SURVEY COMMISSION, 1853-69 / U. S. – 4 rolls.T606 – 1 – us Nat'l Archives [324]

RECORDS RELATING TO THE INTERNAL AFFAIRS OF ARGENTINA / U.S. Department of State Records – (1910-1929. 44r $1,012.00, 1930-1939. 32r $736.00, 1940-1944. 40r $920.00; Political Relations between the United States and Argentina: 1910-1929. 1r $23.00, 1930-1939. 3r $240.00, 1940-1944. 1r $80.00; Political Relations between Argentina and Other States: 1910-1929. 1r $23.00, 1930-1939. 1r $80.00, 1940-1944. 1r $80.00) – 1810-1959 – 1 – us Nat'l Archives [972]

RECORDS RELATING TO THE INTERNAL AFFAIRS OF BOLIVIA, 1810-1959 / U.S. Department of State Records – (1910-1929 33r $1,122 M644 Political Relations between the United States and Bolivia: 1930-1944 1r $85 S3159. Political Relations between Bolivia and Other States: 1910-1929 18r $612 M646. 1930-1939 32r $2,720 S3160. 1940-1944 2r $170 S3160. With descriptive pamphlets) – 1 – us Scholarly Res [972]

RECORDS RELATING TO THE INTERNAL AFFAIRS OF GERMANY, 1910-1929 : DECIMAL FILE 862 – (Includes descriptive pamphlet) – 182r – $4,186.00 – M336 – us Scholarly Res [320]

RECORDS RELATING TO THE INTERNAL AFFAIRS OF THE FREE CITY OF DANZIG, 1910-1929 : DECIMAL FILE 860K – 11r – $253.00 – M1378 – us Scholarly Res [350]

RECORDS RELATING TO THE JOINT COUNCILS OF EUROPEANS AND NATIVES : CORRESPONDENCE, MEMORANDA, MINUTE BOOKS, ETC, 1929-C1940 / South African Institute of Race Relations – Johannesburg: Microfile, [19-?] – us Res Libr [960]

RECORDS RELATING TO THE U.S. MILITARY ACADEMY, 1812-67 / U.S. War Department. Adjutant General's Office – 29 rolls. M91 – 1 – us Nat'l Archives [324]

RECORDS RELATING TO THE U.S. SURVEYING EXPEDITION TO THE NORTH PACIFIC OCEAN, 1852-63 / U.S. Navy. Office of Naval Records and Library – 27 rolls. M88. Printed guide – 1 – us Nat'l Archives [550]

RECORDS RELATING TO U.S. NAVY FLEET PROBLEMS, 1-22 / U.S. Navy – 1923-41. M964 – 36r – 1 – us Nat'l Archives [355]

RECORDS...: RHODE ISLAND LOAN OFFICE RECORDS RELATING TO THE LOAN OF 1790 / U.S. Treasury Department. Bureau of the Public Debt – 13 rolls. T653 – 1 – us Nat'l Archives [336]

RECORDS...: SOUTH CAROLINA LOAN OFFICE RECORDS RELATING TO THE LOAN OF 1790 / U.S. Treasury Department. Bureau of the Public Debt – 3rolls. T719 – 1 – us Nat'l Archives [336]

RECORDS...: VIRGINIA LOAN OFFICE RECORDS RELATING TO THE LOAN OF 1790 / U.S. Treasury Department. Bureau of the Public Debt – 12 rolls. T696 – 1 – us Nat'l Archives [336]

RECORDS...1863-64 / U.S. Civil Commission at Memphis – 9rolls. T410 – 1 – us Nat'l Archives [324]

RECORDS...1918-65, PART 1 : REPORTS OF THE DIRECTOR, MAJOR CONFERENCES AND SPEECHES AND ARTICLES / U.S. Department of Labor. Women's Bureau – 23 reels with printed guide – 1 – $2,530.00 – 0-89093-870-9 – us UPA [360]

RECORDS...1918-65, PART 2 : WOMEN IN WORLD WAR 2 / U.S. Department of Labor. Women's Bureau – (Series A: Unpublished Studies and Wartime Community Surveys. ISBN 1-55655-297-1. $1,105.00; Series B: Subjects and Correspondence Files on War Industries. ISBN 1-55655-298-X. $3,850.00) – us UPA [360]

RECORDS...CONTAINING STATEMENTS OF FACTS IN FORFEITURE CASES, 1792-1918 / U.S. District Courts. Pennsylvania, Eastern District – 1roll – 1 – T819 – us Nat'l Archives [324]

RECORD-SEARCHLIGHT – Redding. Calif. 1942- – 1 – us UMI [071]

RECORDS...FILMED FOR THE UNIV. OF LONDON / Germany. Foreign Office – 25 rolls. T1026. (World War II Collection of Seized Enemy Records) – 1 – us Nat'l Archives [324]

RECORDS...(OBERKOMMANDO DER LUFTWAFFE-OKL) / Germany. Air Force High Command. Headquarters – 184 rolls. T321. Finding Aids: GG24. (Captured German Records Filmed at Alexandria, VA.) – 1 – us Nat'l Archives [324]

RECORDS...OF THE SPECIAL INTERROGATION MISSION TO GERMANY, 1945-46 / U.S. Department of State – M679 – 3r – 1 – us Nat'l Archives [943]

RECORDS...PERTAINING TO CHINA, 1919-35 / Germany. Foreign Ministry – 31 rolls. T1141 – 1 – us Nat'l Archives [943]

RECORDS...RECEIVED BY THE DEPT. OF STATE (U.S.A.) / Germany. Foreign Office – 5070 rolls. T120. (World War II Collection of Seized Enemy Records) – 1 – us Nat'l Archives [324]

RECORDS...RECEIVED BY THE DEPT. OF STATE (U.S.A.) FROM ANTONY'S COLLEGE / Germany. Foreign Office – 144 rolls. T136. (World War II Collection of Seized Enemy Records) – 1 – us Nat'l Archives [324]

RECORDS...RECEIVED BY THE DEPT. OF STATE (U.S.A.) FROM THE UNIV. OF CALIFORNIA (PROJECT I) / Germany. Foreign Office – 436 rolls. T139. (World War II Collection of Seized Enemy Records) – 1 – us Nat'l Archives [324]

RECORDS...RELATING TO INTERNAL AFFAIRS OF ARGENTINA, 1910-29 / U.S. Department of State – (35) M514. Printed guide – 44r – 1 – us Nat'l Archives [972]

RECORDS...RELATING TO INTERNAL AFFAIRS OF ARMENIA, 1910-29 / U.S. Department of State – 8r – 1 – T1192 – us Nat'l Archives [947]

RECORDS...RELATING TO INTERNAL AFFAIRS OF ASIA, 1910-29 / U.S. Department of State – (With printed guide) – 28r – 1 – M722 – us Nat'l Archives [324]

RECORDS...RELATING TO INTERNAL AFFAIRS OF AUSTRALIA, 1910-1944 / U.S. Department of State – 36r – 1 – T1190 – us Nat'l Archives [980]

RECORDS...RELATING TO INTERNAL AFFAIRS OF AUSTRIA-HUNGARY AND AUSTRIA, 1910-29 / U.S. Department of State – 69 rolls. (63) M695. Printed guide – 1 – us Nat'l Archives [324]

RECORDS...RELATING TO INTERNAL AFFAIRS OF AUSTRIA-HUNGARY AND HUNGARY, 1912-29 / U.S. Department of State – 38 rolls. (64) M708. Printed guide – 1 – us Nat'l Archives [324]

RECORDS...RELATING TO INTERNAL AFFAIRS OF BELGIUM, 1910-29 / U.S. Department of State – 78 rolls. (55) M675 – 1 – us Nat'l Archives [949]

RECORDS...RELATING TO INTERNAL AFFAIRS OF BOLIVIA, 1910-29 / U.S. Department of State – (With printed guide) – 33r – 1 – M644 – us Nat'l Archives [324]

RECORDS...RELATING TO INTERNAL AFFAIRS OF BRAZIL, 1910-29 / U.S. Department of State – 54 rolls. (32) M519 – 1 – us Nat'l Archives [324]

RECORDS...RELATING TO INTERNAL AFFAIRS OF BRITISH AFRICA, 1910-29 / U.S. Department of State – 33 rolls. (48) M583. Printed guide – 1 – us Nat'l Archives [324]

RECORDS...RELATING TO INTERNAL AFFAIRS OF BRITISH ASIA, 1910-29 / U.S. Department of State – 21 rolls. (46) M712. Printed Guide – 1 – us Nat'l Archives [324]

RECORDS...RELATING TO INTERNAL AFFAIRS OF CENTRAL AMERICA, 1910-29 / U.S. Department of State – 16r Printed guide – 1 – M672 – us Nat'l Archives [324]

RECORDS...RELATING TO INTERNAL AFFAIRS OF CHILE, 1910-29 / U.S. Department of State – Printed guide – 40r – 1 – M487 – us Nat'l Archives [324]

RECORDS...RELATING TO INTERNAL AFFAIRS OF CHINA, 1910-29 / U.S. Department of State – Printed guide – 227r – 1 – M329 – us Nat'l Archives [324]

RECORDS...RELATING TO INTERNAL AFFAIRS OF COSTA RICA, 1910-29 / U.S. Department of State – Printed guide – 40r – 1 – M669 – us Nat'l Archives [324]

RECORDS...RELATING TO INTERNAL AFFAIRS OF CUBA, 1910-29 / U.S. Department of State – Printed guide – 99r – 1 – M488 – us Nat'l Archives [324]

RECORDS...RELATING TO INTERNAL AFFAIRS OF EGYPT, 1910-29 / U.S. Department of State – Printed guide – 31r – 1 – M571 – us Nat'l Archives [960]

RECORDS...RELATING TO INTERNAL AFFAIRS OF EGYPT, 1930-39 / U.S. Department of State – 22r – 1 – T1251 – us Nat'l Archives [960]

RECORDS...RELATING TO INTERNAL AFFAIRS OF EL SALVADOR, 1910-29 / U.S. Department of State – Printed guide – 22r – 1 – M658 – us Nat'l Archives [324]

RECORDS...RELATING TO INTERNAL AFFAIRS OF ESTONIA, 1910-44 / U.S. Department of State – 23r – 1 – M1170 – us Nat'l Archives [324]

RECORDS...RELATING TO INTERNAL AFFAIRS OF ETHIOPIA, 1910-29 / U.S. Department of State – Printed Guide – 4r – 1 – M411 – us Nat'l Archives [324]

RECORDS...RELATING TO INTERNAL AFFAIRS OF FINLAND, 1910-44 / U.S. Department of State – 32r – 1 – T1184 – us Nat'l Archives [948]

RECORDS...RELATING TO INTERNAL AFFAIRS OF FRANCE, 1910-29 / U.S. Department of State – 162r – 1 – M560 – us Nat'l Archives [324]

RECORDS...RELATING TO INTERNAL AFFAIRS OF GERMANY, 1910-29 / U.S. Department of State – 182r – 1 – M336 – us Nat'l Archives [324]

RECORDS...RELATING TO INTERNAL AFFAIRS OF GREAT BRITAIN, 1910-29 / U.S. Department of State – Printed Guide – 249r – 1 – M580 – us Nat'l Archives [324]

RECORDS...RELATING TO INTERNAL AFFAIRS OF GREECE, 1910-29 / U.S. Department of State – Printed guide – 45r – 1 – M443 – us Nat'l Archives [949]

RECORDS...RELATING TO INTERNAL AFFAIRS OF GREECE, 1930-39 / U.S. Department of State – 16r – 1 – M1179 – us Nat'l Archives [949]

RECORDS...RELATING TO INTERNAL AFFAIRS OF GUATEMALA, 1910-29 / U.S. Department of State – Printed guide – 40r – 1 – M655 – us Nat'l Archives [324]

RECORDS...RELATING TO INTERNAL AFFAIRS OF HAITI, 1910-29 / U.S. Department of State – Printed guide – 94r – 1 – M610 – us Nat'l Archives [324]

RECORDS...RELATING TO INTERNAL AFFAIRS OF HONDURAS, 1910-29 / U.S. Department of State – Printed guide – 49r – 1 – M647 – us Nat'l Archives [324]

RECORDS...RELATING TO INTERNAL AFFAIRS OF INDIA AND BURMA, 1910-29 / U.S. Department of State – 26r – 1 – M335 – us Nat'l Archives [324]

RECORDS...RELATING TO INTERNAL AFFAIRS OF IRAN, 1930-39 / U.S. Department of State – 24r – 1 – M1202 – us Nat'l Archives [956]

RECORDS...RELATING TO INTERNAL AFFAIRS OF IRAQ, 1930-44 / U.S. Department of State – 18r – 1 – T1180 – us Nat'l Archives [956]

RECORDS...RELATING TO INTERNAL AFFAIRS OF ITALY, 1910-1929 / U.S. Department of State – (With printed guide) – 60r – 1 – M527 – us Nat'l Archives [324]

RECORDS...RELATING TO INTERNAL AFFAIRS OF JAPAN, 1910-29 / U.S. Department of State – 43 rolls. (94) M422. Printed guide – 1 – us Nat'l Archives [324]

RECORDS...RELATING TO INTERNAL AFFAIRS OF KOREA, 1910-1929 / U.S. Department of State – 9r – 1 – M426 – us Nat'l Archives [324]

RECORDS...RELATING TO INTERNAL AFFAIRS OF LATVIA, 1910-1944 / U.S. Department of State – 19r – 1 – M1177 – us Nat'l Archives [947]

RECORDS...RELATING TO INTERNAL AFFAIRS OF LEBANON, 1930-44 / U.S. Department of State – 5 rolls.T1178 – 1 – us Nat'l Archives [956]

RECORDS...RELATING TO INTERNAL AFFAIRS OF LIBERIA, 1910-29 / U.S. Department of State – 34 rolls. (82) M613. Printed guide – 1 – us Nat'l Archives [324]

RECORDS...RELATING TO INTERNAL AFFAIRS OF LITHUANIA, 1910-44 / U.S. Department of State – RG 59. M1178. 22 rolls – 1 – us Nat'l Archives [947]

RECORDS...RELATING TO INTERNAL AFFAIRS OF MEXICO, 1910-29 / U.S. Department of State – 243 rolls. (12) M274. Printed guide – 1 – us Nat'l Archives [324]

RECORDS...RELATING TO INTERNAL AFFAIRS OF MONTENEGRO AND TO POLITICAL RELATIONS BETWEEN THE U.S. AND MONTENEGRO, 1910-29 / U.S. Department of State – (73) M349 – 2r – 1 – us Nat'l Archives [327]

RECORDS...RELATING TO INTERNAL AFFAIRS OF MOROCCO, 1910-29 / U.S. Department of State – 26 rolls. (81) M577. Printed guide – 1 – us Nat'l Archives [324]

RECORDS...RELATING TO INTERNAL AFFAIRS OF NICARAGUA, 1910-29 / U.S. Department of State – 106 rolls. (17) M632. Printed guide – 1 – us Nat'l Archives [324]

RECORDS...RELATING TO INTERNAL AFFAIRS OF PANAMA, 1910-1929 / U.S. Department of State – 58r – 1 – M607 – us Nat'l Archives [324]

RECORDS...RELATING TO INTERNAL AFFAIRS OF PERSIA, 1910-29 / U.S. Department of State – 37 rolls. (91) M715. Printed guide – 1 – us Nat'l Archives [324]

RECORDS...RELATING TO INTERNAL AFFAIRS OF PERU, 1910-29 / U.S. Department of State – 30 rolls. (23) M746. Printed guide – 1 – us Nat'l Archives [324]

RECORDS...RELATING TO INTERNAL AFFAIRS OF PORTUGAL, 1910-29 / U.S. Department of State – 34 rolls. (53) M705. Printed guide – 1 – us Nat'l Archives [324]

RECORDS...RELATING TO INTERNAL AFFAIRS OF RUSSIA AND THE SOVIET UNION, 1910-29 / U.S. Department of State – 177 rolls. (61) M316 – 1 – us Nat'l Archives [947]

RECORDS...RELATING TO INTERNAL AFFAIRS OF SERBIA AND TO POLITICAL RELATIONS BETWEEN THE U.S. AND SERBIA, 1910-29 / U.S. Department of State – 3rolls. (72) M357 – 1 – us Nat'l Archives [327]

RECORDS...RELATING TO INTERNAL AFFAIRS OF SIAM, 1910-29 / U.S. Department of State – 18 rolls. (92) M729. Printed guide – 1 – us Nat'l Archives [324]

RECORDS...RELATING TO INTERNAL AFFAIRS OF SYRIA, 1930-44 / U.S. Department of State – 11 rolls. T1177 – 1 – us Nat'l Archives [956]

RECORDS...RELATING TO INTERNAL AFFAIRS OF THE BALTIC STATES, 1910-1944 / U.S. Department of State – 8r – 1 – M1185 – us Nat'l Archives [947]

RECORDS...RELATING TO INTERNAL AFFAIRS OF THE DOMINICAN REPUBLIC, 1910-29 / U.S. Department of State – 79r – 1 – M626 – us Nat'l Archives [324]

RECORDS...RELATING TO INTERNAL AFFAIRS OF THE NETHERLANDS, 1910-29 / U.S. Department of State – 54 rolls. (56) M682. Printed guide – 1 – us Nat'l Archives [949]

RECORDS...RELATING TO INTERNAL AFFAIRS OF THE PAPAL STATES (HOLY SEE), 1910-29 / U.S. Department of State – 1roll. (66) M561 – 1 – us Nat'l Archives [324]

RECORDS...RELATING TO INTERNAL AFFAIRS OF THE SOVIET UNION, 1930-39 / U.S. Department of State – (1940-44. 2 rolls. T1250) – 75 rolls. T1249 – 1 – us Nat'l Archives [947]

RECORDS...RELATING TO INTERNAL AFFAIRS OF TURKEY, 1910-29 / U.S. Department of State – 88 rolls. (67) M353 – 1 – us Nat'l Archives [956]

RECORDS...RELATING TO INTERNAL AFFAIRS OF VENEZUELA, 1910-29 / U.S. Department of State – 32 rolls. (31) M366. Printed guide – 1 – us Nat'l Archives [324]

RECORDS...RELATING TO INTERNAL AFFAIRS OF YUGOSLAVIA, 1910-29 / U.S. Department of State – 27 rolls. (60h) M358 – 1 – us Nat'l Archives [949]

RECORDS...RELATING TO NAZI INDUSTRIALISTS / U.S. Chief Counsel for War Crimes. Nuremberg Military Tribunals – T301 – 164r – 1 – us Nat'l Archives [943]

RECORDS...RELATING TO POLITICAL RELATIONS BETWEEN ARGENTINA AND OTHER STATES, 1910-29 / U.S. Department of State – (35) M516 – 1r – 1 – us Nat'l Archives [327]

RECORDS...RELATING TO POLITICAL RELATIONS BETWEEN ARMENIA AND OTHER STATES, 1910-29 / U.S. Department of State – 2r – 1 – T1193 – us Nat'l Archives [327]

RECORDS...RELATING TO POLITICAL RELATIONS BETWEEN ASIA AND OTHER STATES (SIC), 1910-1929 / U.S. Department of State – (With printed guide) – 1r – 1 – M724 – us Nat'l Archives [327]

RECORDS...RELATING TO POLITICAL RELATIONS BETWEEN AUSTRIA-HUNGARY AND HUNGARY AND OTHER STATES, 1920-1929 / U.S. Department of State – 2r – 1 – M710 – us Nat'l Archives [327]

RECORDS...RELATING TO POLITICAL RELATIONS BETWEEN BELGIUM AND OTHER STATES, 1910-29 / U.S. Department of State – (With printed guide) – 4r – 1 – M677 – us Nat'l Archives [327]

RECORDS...RELATING TO POLITICAL RELATIONS BETWEEN BOLIVIA AND OTHER STATES, 1910-29 / U.S. Department of State – (24) M646 – 18r – 1 – us Nat'l Archives [327]

RECORDS...RELATING TO POLITICAL RELATIONS BETWEEN BRAZIL AND OTHER STATES, 1910-29 / U.S. Department of State – (32) M526. Printed guide – 2r – 1 – us Nat'l Archives [327]

RECORDS...RELATING TO POLITICAL RELATIONS BETWEEN BRITISH AFRICA AND OTHER STATES, 1910-29 / U.S. Department of State – (48) M585 – 1r – 1 – us Nat'l Archives [327]

RECORDS...RELATING TO POLITICAL RELATIONS BETWEEN BRITISH ASIA AND OTHER STATES, INCLUDING THE U.S., 1910-1929 / U.S. Department of State – (With printed guide) – 1r – 1 – M713 – us Nat'l Archives [327]

RECORDS...RELATING TO POLITICAL RELATIONS BETWEEN CENTRAL AMERICA AND OTHER STATES, 1910-29 / U.S. Department of State – Printed guide – 2r – 1 – M674 – us Nat'l Archives [327]

RECORDS...RELATING TO POLITICAL RELATIONS BETWEEN CHILE AND OTHER STATES, 1910-29 / U.S. Department of State – 2r – 1 – M490 – us Nat'l Archives [327]

RECORDS...RELATING TO POLITICAL RELATIONS BETWEEN CHINA AND OTHER STATES, 1910-29 / U.S. Department of State – Printed guide – 34r – 1 – M341 – us Nat'l Archives [327]

RECORDS...RELATING TO POLITICAL RELATIONS BETWEEN COSTA RICA AND OTHER STATES, 1910-29 / U.S. Department of State – Printed guide – 10r – 1 – M671 – us Nat'l Archives [327]

RECORDS...RELATING TO POLITICAL RELATIONS BETWEEN CUBA AND OTHER STATES, 1910-29 / U.S. Department of State – Printed guide – 1r – 1 – M510 – us Nat'l Archives [327]

RECORDS...RELATING TO POLITICAL RELATIONS BETWEEN EGYPT AND OTHER STATES, 1910-29 / U.S. Department of State – Printed guide – 1r – 1 – M573 – us Nat'l Archives [327]

RECORDS...RELATING TO POLITICAL RELATIONS BETWEEN EL SALVADOR AND OTHER STATES, 1910-29 / U.S. Department of State – Printed guide – 1r – 1 – M660 – us Nat'l Archives [327]

RECORDS...RELATING TO POLITICAL RELATIONS BETWEEN FINLAND AND OTHER STATES, 1910-44 / U.S. Department of State – 8r – 1 – T1186 – us Nat'l Archives [327]

RECORDS...RELATING TO POLITICAL RELATIONS BETWEEN FRANCE AND OTHER STATES, 1910-29 / U.S. Department of State – 7r – 1 – M569 – us Nat'l Archives [327]

RECORDS...RELATING TO POLITICAL RELATIONS BETWEEN GREAT BRITAIN AND OTHER STATES, 1910-29 / U.S. Department of State – Printed guide – 13r – 1 – M582 – us Nat'l Archives [327]

RECORDS...RELATING TO POLITICAL RELATIONS BETWEEN GREECE AND OTHER STATES, 1910-29 / U.S. Department of State – Printed guide – 6r – 1 – M476 – us Nat'l Archives [327]

RECORDS...RELATING TO POLITICAL RELATIONS BETWEEN GUATEMALA AND OTHER STATES, 1910-29 / U.S. Department of State – 27r – 1 – M657 – us Nat'l Archives [327]

RECORDS...RELATING TO POLITICAL RELATIONS BETWEEN HAITI AND OTHER STATES, 1910-29 / U.S. Department of State – 4r – 1 – M612 – us Nat'l Archives [327]

RECORDS...RELATING TO POLITICAL RELATIONS BETWEEN INDIA AND BURMA AND OTHER STATES, 1910-29 / U.S. Department of State – 1r – 1 – M344 – us Nat'l Archives [327]

RECORDS...RELATING TO POLITICAL RELATIONS BETWEEN ITALY AND OTHER STATES, 1910-29 / U.S. Department of State – Printed guide – 8r – 1 – M530 – us Nat'l Archives [327]

RECORDS...RELATING TO POLITICAL RELATIONS BETWEEN JAPAN AND OTHER STATES, 1910-29 / U.S. Department of State – (94) M424. Printed Guide – 1 – us Nat'l Archives [327]

RECORDS...RELATING TO POLITICAL RELATIONS BETWEEN LIBERIA AND OTHER STATES, INCLUDING THE U.S., 1919-29 / U.S. Department of State – (82) M614. Printed guide – 1r – 1 – us Nat'l Archives [327]

RECORDS...RELATING TO POLITICAL RELATIONS BETWEEN MEXICO AND OTHER STATES, 1910-29 / U.S. Department of State – (12) M315. Printed guide – 2r – 1 – us Nat'l Archives [327]

RECORDS...RELATING TO POLITICAL RELATIONS BETWEEN MOROCCO AND OTHER STATES, 1910-29 / U.S. Department of State – (81) M579. Printed guide – 1r – 1 – us Nat'l Archives [327]

RECORDS...RELATING TO POLITICAL RELATIONS BETWEEN NICARAGUA AND OTHER STATES, 1910-29 / U.S. Department of State – (17) M634 – 3r – 1 – us Nat'l Archives [327]

RECORDS...RELATING TO POLITICAL RELATIONS BETWEEN PANAMA AND OTHER STATES, 1910-29 / U.S. Department of State – (19) M609 – 3r – 1 – us Nat'l Archives [327]

RECORDS...RELATING TO POLITICAL RELATIONS BETWEEN PERSIA AND OTHER STATES, 1921-29 / U.S. Department of State – (91) M717. Printed guide – 1r – 1 – us Nat'l Archives [327]

RECORDS...RELATING TO POLITICAL RELATIONS BETWEEN PERU AND OTHER STATES, 1911-29 / U.S. Department of State – (23) M748 – 52r – 1 – us Nat'l Archives [327]

RECORDS...RELATING TO POLITICAL RELATIONS BETWEEN RUSSIA AND THE SOVIET UNION AND OTHER STATES, 1910-29 / U.S. Department of State – (61) M340. Printed guide – 20r – 1 – us Nat'l Archives [327]

RECORDS...RELATING TO POLITICAL RELATIONS BETWEEN SIAM AND OTHER STATES, 1910-29 / U.S. Department of State – (92) M731. Printed guide – 1r – 1 – us Nat'l Archives [327]

RECORDS...RELATING TO POLITICAL RELATIONS BETWEEN THE NETHERLANDS AND OTHER STATES, 1910-29 / U.S. Department of State – (56) M684. Printed guide – 1r – 1 – us Nat'l Archives [327]

RECORDS...RELATING TO POLITICAL RELATIONS BETWEEN THE PAPAL STATES (HOLY SEE) AND OTHER STATES, 1910-29 / U.S. Department of State – (66) M563 – 1r – 1 – us Nat'l Archives [327]

RECORDS...RELATING TO POLITICAL RELATIONS BETWEEN THE SOVIET UNION AND OTHER STATES, 1930-39 / U.S. Department of State – (1940-44. 4 rolls. T1248) – 14 rolls. T1247 – 1 – us Nat'l Archives [327]

RECORDS...RELATING TO POLITICAL RELATIONS BETWEEN THE UNITED STATES AND ASIA, 1920-1929 / U.S. Department of State – (With printed guide) – 1r – 1 – M723 – us Nat'l Archives [327]

RECORDS...RELATING TO POLITICAL RELATIONS BETWEEN THE UNITED STATES AND AUSTRALIA, 1910-1944 / U.S. Department of State – 1r – 1 – T1191 – us Nat'l Archives [327]

RECORDS...RELATING TO POLITICAL RELATIONS BETWEEN THE UNITED STATES AND AUSTRIA-HUNGARY AND HUNGARY, 1921-1929 / U.S. Department of State – (With printed guide) – 1r – 1 – M709 – us Nat'l Archives [327]

RECORDS...RELATING TO POLITICAL RELATIONS BETWEEN THE UNITED STATES AND BELGIUM, 1910-29 / U.S. Department of State – (With printed guide) – 1r – 1 – M676 – us Nat'l Archives [327]

RECORDS...RELATING TO POLITICAL RELATIONS BETWEEN THE U.S. AND ARGENTINA, 1910-29 / U.S. Department of State – (35) M515 – 1r – 1 – us Nat'l Archives [327]

RECORDS...RELATING TO POLITICAL RELATIONS BETWEEN THE U.S. AND BRAZIL, 1910-29 / U.S. Department of State – (32) M525. Printed guide – 1r – 1 – us Nat'l Archives [327]

RECORDS...RELATING TO POLITICAL RELATIONS BETWEEN THE U.S. AND BRITISH AFRICA, 1910-29 / U.S. Department of State – (48) M584 – 1r – 1 – us Nat'l Archives [327]

RECORDS...RELATING TO POLITICAL RELATIONS BETWEEN THE U.S. AND CENTRAL AMERICA, 1911-29 / U.S. Department of State – (13) M673. Printed Guide – 1r – 1 – us Nat'l Archives [327]

RECORDS...RELATING TO POLITICAL RELATIONS BETWEEN THE U.S. AND CHILE, 1910-29 / U.S. Department of State – Printed guide – 1r – 1 – M489 – us Nat'l Archives [327]

RECORDS...RELATING TO POLITICAL RELATIONS BETWEEN THE U.S. AND CHINA, 1910-29 / U.S. Department of State – Printed guide – 2r – 1 – M339 – us Nat'l Archives [327]

RECORDS...RELATING TO POLITICAL RELATIONS BETWEEN THE U.S. AND COSTA RICA, 1910-29 / U.S. Department of State – Printed guide – 1r – 1 – M670 – us Nat'l Archives [327]

RECORDS...RELATING TO POLITICAL RELATIONS BETWEEN THE U.S. AND CUBA, 1910-29 / U.S. Department of State – Printed guide – 2r – 1 – M509 – us Nat'l Archives [327]

RECORDS...RELATING TO POLITICAL RELATIONS BETWEEN THE U.S. AND EGYPT, 1910-29 / U.S. Department of State – Printed guide – 1r – 1 – M572 – us Nat'l Archives [327]

RECORDS...RELATING TO POLITICAL RELATIONS BETWEEN THE U.S. AND EL SALVADOR, 1910-29 / U.S. Department of State – Printed guide – 1r – 1 – M659 – us Nat'l Archives [327]

RECORDS...RELATING TO POLITICAL RELATIONS BETWEEN THE U.S. AND ETHIOPIA, 1910-29 / U.S. Department of State – Printed guide – 1r – 1 – M412 – us Nat'l Archives [327]

RECORDS...RELATING TO POLITICAL RELATIONS BETWEEN THE U.S. AND FINLAND, 1910-44 / U.S. Department of State – 2r – 1 – T1185 – us Nat'l Archives [327]

RECORDS...RELATING TO POLITICAL RELATIONS BETWEEN THE U.S. AND FRANCE, 1910-29 / U.S. Department of State – 5r – 1 – M568 – us Nat'l Archives [327]

RECORDS...RELATING TO POLITICAL RELATIONS BETWEEN THE U.S. AND GREAT BRITAIN, 1910-29 / U.S. Department of State – Printed guide – 15r – 1 – M581 – us Nat'l Archives [327]

RECORDS...RELATING TO POLITICAL RELATIONS BETWEEN THE U.S. AND GREAT BRITAIN, 1930-39 / U.S. Department of State – 6r – 1 – T1252 – us Nat'l Archives [327]

RECORDS...RELATING TO POLITICAL RELATIONS BETWEEN THE U.S. AND GREECE, 1910-29 / U.S. Department of State – Printed guide – 3r – 1 – M475 – us Nat'l Archives [327]

RECORDS...RELATING TO POLITICAL RELATIONS BETWEEN THE U.S. AND GUATEMALA, 1910-29 / U.S. Department of State – 1r – 1 – M656 – us Nat'l Archives [327]

RECORDS...RELATING TO POLITICAL RELATIONS BETWEEN THE U.S. AND HAITI, 1910-29 / U.S. Department of State – 2r – 1 – M611 – us Nat'l Archives [327]

RECORDS...RELATING TO POLITICAL RELATIONS BETWEEN THE U.S. AND HONDURAS, 1910-29 / U.S. Department of State – Printed guide – 1r – 1 – M648 – us Nat'l Archives [327]

RECORDS...RELATING TO POLITICAL RELATIONS BETWEEN THE U.S. AND INDIA AND BURMA, 1910-29 / U.S. Department of State – 1r – 1 – M343 – us Nat'l Archives [327]

RECORDS...RELATING TO POLITICAL RELATIONS BETWEEN THE U.S. AND ITALY, 1910-29 / U.S. Department of State – Printed guide – 3r – 1 – M529 – us Nat'l Archives [327]

RECORDS...RELATING TO POLITICAL RELATIONS BETWEEN THE U.S. AND JAPAN, 1910-29 / U.S. Department of State – (94) M423. Printed guide – 9r – 1 – us Nat'l Archives [327]

RECORDS...RELATING TO POLITICAL RELATIONS BETWEEN THE U.S. AND MEXICO, 1910-29 / U.S. Department of State – (12) M314. Printed guide – 29r – 1 – us Nat'l Archives [327]

RECORDS...RELATING TO POLITICAL RELATIONS BETWEEN THE U.S. AND MOROCCO, 1910-29 / U.S. Department of State – (81) M578. Printed guide – 1r – 1 – us Nat'l Archives [327]

RECORDS...RELATING TO POLITICAL RELATIONS BETWEEN THE U.S. AND NICARAGUA, 1910-29 / U.S. Department of State – (17) M633 – 2r – 1 – us Nat'l Archives [327]

RECORDS...RELATING TO POLITICAL RELATIONS BETWEEN THE U.S. AND PANAMA, 1910-29 / U.S. Department of State – (19) M608 – 14r – 1 – us Nat'l Archives [327]

RECORDS...RELATING TO POLITICAL RELATIONS BETWEEN THE U.S. AND PERSIA, 1921-29 / U.S. Department of State – (91) M716. Printed guide – 1r – 1 – us Nat'l Archives [327]

RECORDS...RELATING TO POLITICAL RELATIONS BETWEEN THE U.S. AND RUSSIA AND THE SOVIET UNION, 1910-29 / U.S. Department of State – (61) M333. Printed guide – 7r – 1 – us Nat'l Archives [327]

RECORDS...RELATING TO POLITICAL RELATIONS BETWEEN THE U.S. AND SIAM, 1909-29 / U.S. Department of State – (92) M730. Printed guide – 1r – 1 – us Nat'l Archives [327]

RECORDS...RELATING TO POLITICAL RELATIONS BETWEEN THE U.S. AND THE NETHERLANDS, 1910-29 / U.S. Department of State – (56) M683. Printed guide – 6r – 1 – us Nat'l Archives [327]

RECORDS...RELATING TO POLITICAL RELATIONS BETWEEN THE U.S. AND THE PAPAL STATES (HOLY SEE), 1910-29 / U.S. Department of State – (66) M562 – 1r – 1 – us Nat'l Archives [327]

RECORDS...RELATING TO POLITICAL RELATIONS BETWEEN THE U.S. AND THE SOVIET UNION, 1930-39 / U.S. Department of State – (1940-44. 1 roll. T1242) – 3 rolls.T1241 – 1 – us Nat'l Archives [327]

RECORDS...RELATING TO POLITICAL RELATIONS BETWEEN THE U.S. AND TURKEY, 1910-29 / U.S. Department of State – (67) M365 – 8r – 1 – us Nat'l Archives [327]

RECORDS...RELATING TO POLITICAL RELATIONS BETWEEN THE U.S. AND VENEZUELA, 1910-29 / U.S. Department of State – (31) M368 – 1r – 1 – us Nat'l Archives [327]

RECORDS...RELATING TO POLITICAL RELATIONS BETWEEN THE U.S. AND YUGOSLAVIA, 1910-29 / U.S. Department of State – (60h) M362 – 1r – 1 – us Nat'l Archives [327]

RECORDS...RELATING TO POLITICAL RELATIONS BETWEEN TURKEY AND OTHER STATES, 1910-29 / U.S. Department of State – (67) M363 – 29r – 1 – us Nat'l Archives [327]

RECORDS...RELATING TO POLITICAL RELATIONS BETWEEN VENEZUELA AND OTHER STATES, 1910-29 / U.S. Department of State – (31) M369 – 2r – 1 – us Nat'l Archives [327]

RECORDS...RELATING TO POLITICAL RELATIONS BETWEEN YUGOSLAVIA AND OTHER STATES, 1910-29 (SIC) / U.S. Department of State – (60h) M361 – 9r – 1 – us Nat'l Archives [327]

RECORDS...RELATING TO POLITICAL RELATIONS OF EASTERN EUROPE / U.S. Department of State – 1930-39; 1940-44 – 46r; 5r – 1 – T1243; T1244 – us Nat'l Archives [327]

RECORDS...RELATING TO POLITICAL RELATIONS OF TURKEY, GREECE, AND THE BALKAN STATES / U.S. Department of State – 1930-39; 1940-44 – 11r; 2r – 1 – T1245; T1246 – us Nat'l Archives [327]

RECORDS...RELATING TO SLAVES,1851-63 / U.S. District Courts. District of Columbia – 3rolls. M433 – 1 – us Nat'l Archives [324]

RECORDS...RELATING TO THE FIRST PANAMA CONGRESS, 1825-27 / U.S. Department of State – M662. Printed guide – 1r – 1 – us Nat'l Archives [972]

RECORDS...RELATING TO THE INTERNAL AFFAIRS OF SAUDI ARABIA / U.S. Department of State – 1930-44.8 rolls. T1179 – 1 – us Nat'l Archives [956]

RECORDS...RELATING TO THE INTERNAL AFFAIRS OF TRANS-JORDAN / U.S. Department of State – 1930-44.1 roll. T1181 – 1 – us Nat'l Archives [956]

RECORDS...RELATING TO THE PARIS PEACE COMMISSION, 1898 / U.S. Department of State – T954 – 3r – 1 – us Nat'l Archives [940]

RECORDS...RELATING TO THE YELLOWSTONE NATIONAL PARK, 1872-86 / U.S. Department of the Interior. Office of the Secretary – 6rolls. M62 – 1 – us Nat'l Archives [324]

RECORDS...RELATING TO WAGON ROADS, 1857-87 / U.S. Department of the Interior. Office of the Secretary – 16 rolls. M95 – 1 – us Nat'l Archives [324]

RECORDS...RELATING TO WORLD WAR I AND ITS TERMINATION, 1914-29 / U.S. Department of State – M367. Printed guide – 518r – 1 – us Nat'l Archives [940]

RECORD-TRIBUNE – Roundup. Mont. 1958-1959; 1966- – 1 – us UMI [071]

Recouvrance, Marie de la *see* BIBLIOGRAPHIE ANALYTIQUE DE MARIE-THERESE 1944-1961 (MLLE MARIE-THERESE CHEVALIER) RESPONSABLE DU SERVICE MARIAL DE MONTREAL ET REDACTRICE DU DIGESTE MARIAL DE 1948 A 1961

THE RECOVERY AND RESTATEMENT OF THE GOSPEL / Osborn, Loran David – (Includes index) – Chicago: Uni of Chicago Press, 1903 – 1mf – 9 – 0-8370-3945-2 – 1985-1945 – us A.T.L.A. [220]

RECREACIONES GEOGRAFICAS...GEOGRAFIA / Machado, Cristobal – 1761 – 9 – 1.50f – sp Bibl Santa Ana [910]

RECREACIONES...FISICA Y QUIMICA / Tissandier, Gaston – 1884 – 9 – 1.50f – sp Bibl Santa Ana [530]

RECREATION – 1-58. 1907-65 – 1 – us UMI [790]

RECREATION *see*
– PARKS AND RECREATION

RECREATION AND ENTERTAINMENT FOR SOLDIERS DURING WORLD WAR 2 PAMPHLET COLLECTION – 1939-1944 – 1 reel – 1 – CSUXANN2547-B – us Hoover Inst Photo [940]

RECREATION CANADA *see* PARKS AND RECREATION CANADA

RECREATION LEGISLATION / Hanmer, Lee Franklin – Rev. ed. New York: Russell Sage Foundation, 1915. 99p. LL-172 – 1 – us L of C Photodup [340]

A RECREATION SURVEY OF THE ROCKFORD PARK DISTRICT, ROCKFORD, ILL / Sapora, Allen V – 1955 – 6mf – 9 – $18.00 – us Microform Publ [790]

RECREATIONAL CHOICE BEHAVIOR : THE INTERRELATIONSHIPS OF SPECIALIZATION LEVELS, MOTIVATIONS, PERCEPTIONS OF SITE ATTRIBUTES AND SPATIAL CHOICE PATTERNS / Lee, Su-Hsin – 1993 – 3mf – $12.00 – us Microform Publ [306]

RECREATIONAL COMPUTING – (See also: People's Computer Company and People's Computers) – v7-10. 1979-81 – 1,5,6,9 – us UMI [510]

RECREATIONS GRAMMATICALES / Daniel, J F – 2nd ed. 1842 – 9 – fr I.C.S. [400]

RECREATIONS WHIRLWINDS – Reno, NV. 1 Dec 1938 – 1r – 1 – $50.00 – U04710 – us Library Micro [071]

RECREATIVE SCIENCE – v. 1-3. 1860-62 – 3 – us Readex [574]

O RECREIO DOS MARANHENSES – '(s.l.')-Sao Luis, Brazil. 20 Oct 1839 – 1,5,6 – bl Biblioteca [072]

RECREIO JUVENIL : ORGAO DO CLUB LITTERARIO DO MESMO NOME – Maceio, Alagoas. 2-20 Jul, 8 Out 1887 – 1,5,6 – bl Biblioteca [072]

RECRUITING FOR CHRIST : HAND TO HAND METHODS WITH MEN / Stone, John Timothy – New York: Fleming H Revell, c1910 – 1mf – 9 – 0-8370-6398-1 – 1986-0398 – us A.T.L.A. [240]

RECRUTEMENT ET BIOLOGIE DES STADES JUVENILES DE MUGILIDAE (POISSONS-TELEOSTEENS) DANS TROIS MILIEUX LAGUNAIRES DU ROUSSILLON ET DU NARBONNAIS (SALSES-LEUCATE, LAPALME, BOURDIGOU) / Cambrony, M – 9 – F70.00 – fr Ethnologie [590]

RECTIFICACIONES Y ADICIONES A LAS ORDENANZAS MINERAS 2, 4, 5, 8, 9, 12, 13, 14 BIS, 16 BIS, 18, 20, 24, 25-26, 28, 31, 35, 47, 48, 51, 52 Y 65 FORMULADAS PARA EL COBRO DE IMPUESTOS Y ARBITRIOS DEL PRESUPUESTO, VIGENTES PARA EL DE – 1958 Y SUCESIVAS / Caceres – Anexo – 1 – sp Bibl Santa Ana [340]

RECTIFICATION DU VOCABULAIRE / Roullaud, Henri; ed by Badreux, Jean – Montreal: A Bouesnel, 1908. SEM105P522 – 3mf – 9 – Can$6.75 – cn Bibl Nat [440]

LE RECUEIL : PREMIER DIGESTE DE LA LANGUE FRANCAISE / ed by Belisle, Louis-Alexandre – (Includes: Index des sommaires nov 1937-sep 1947) – Montreal, Canada. nov 1937-sep 1947 – 5r – 1 – Can$40.00r – cn Can Microfilming [073]

LE RECUEIL – Shipshaw, Canada. v1 n5. 22 aut 1942-v1 n52. 28 aut 1943 – 1r – 1 – Can$40.00 – cn Can Microfilming [072]

RECUEIL / Egypt. Credit Agricole d'Egypte – BNE-4623 1 – 9 – ne IDC [324]

RECUEIL COMPLET DES TRAITES,...DE TOUS LES ETATS DE L'AMERIQUE LATINE... / Calvo, C – Paris, 1862-1868 – 54mf – 1 – ILM-2306/1 – ne IDC [327]

RECUEIL CRITIQUE DE JURISPRUDENCE ET DE LEGISLATION – 1825-1944. (Lacks 1825-44, 1931, 1939-44) – 1 – us L of C Photodup [340]

RECUEIL D'ACTES ET PIECES DIVERSES CONCERNANT DES SEIGNEURIES BRETONNES ET ANGEVINES = COLLECTION OF DEEDS AND DOCUMENTS RELATING TO SOME BRETON AND ANGEVIN SEIGNORIES / Bretagne, Anjou – 1269-1508 – 1 – F198.05 – fr Armell [333]

RECUEIL D'ACTES INTERNATIONAUX DE L'EMPIRE OTTOMAN – (In French und Ottoman) – Paris, 1897-1903 – 4v 36mf – 9 – $700.00 – us MEDOC [949]

RECUEIL D'AIRS. 3 DUETTI AVEC ACCOMPAGNEMENT DE COR HAUBOIS, VIOLON ET VIOLE / Cimarosa, D – Ms – 1 – us Sibley [780]

IL RECUEIL D'AIRS NOUVEAUX SERIEUX ET A BOIRE / Bousset, J B – Paris: Foucault, D Beugnie, C Roussel, 1702 – 1 – us Sibley [780]

RECUEIL D'ARCHITECTURE CIVILE. / Krafft, Jean Charles – Paris. Bance, 1829. 22p., 118 pl. (Architecture Series) – 9 – fr Hachette [720]

RECUEIL D'ARCHITECTURE, DESSINE ET MESURE EN ITALIE... / Seheult, Francois-L – Paris: Bance, 1821 – 1 – F86,34 – fr Armell [720]

RECUEIL D'ARRESTS NOTABLES DES COURS SOUVERAINES DE FRANCE / Papon, J – Coligny, 1616 – 27mf – 8 – Dfl95.00 – ne Slangenburg [240]

RECUEIL D'ARTICLES EXTRAITS DE LA REVUE D'HYGIENE ET DE POLICE SANITAIRE / Bertillon, Jacques – Paris. 1885-98. (La Condition Ouvriere. Part Two.) – 9 – 12.50 – fr Bibl Nationale [360]

RECUEIL DE 22 ACTES ET PIECES CONCERNANT NOTAMMENT : LES DUCS DE BRETAGNE, LES VICOMTES DE ROHAN – 1338-1648 – 1 – F118.60 – fr Armell [920]

RECUEIL DE 28 BROCHURES, SURTOUT HISTORIQUES, PUBL. PAR CET AUTEUR ENTRE 1878 ET 1902 / Granges de Surgeres, Anatole de – 1 – F557.89 – fr Armell [944]

RECUEIL DE 44 ACTES ET PIECES CONCERNANT SURTOUT : CHARLES DE BLOIS ET LE COMTE DE PENTHIEVRE / Blois, Charles de – 1347-1680 – 1 – F224.20 – fr Armell [920]

RECUEIL DE CE QUI S'EST PASSE EN CANADA AU SUJET DE LA GUERRE: TANT DES ANGLAIS QUE DES IROQUOIS DEPUIS L'ANNEE 1682 / Catalogne, Gideon de – Publie sous les auspices de la Societe Litteraire et Historique de Quebec, 18?? 00891. (Pre-1900 Canadiana) – 9 – cn C.I.H.M. [971]

RECUEIL DE CHANTS POPULAIRES DU COMTE NANTAIS ET DU BAS-POITOU, T.1-3 / Gueraud, Armand – 19th cent – 3r – 1 – F1,359.60 – fr Armell [944]

RECUEIL DE CHARTES ET DOCUMENTS DE SAINT-MARTIN-DES-CHAMPS / Depoin, J – Tome 1. 1912 – Dfl28.00 – ne Slangenburg [240]

RECUEIL DE CHARTES ET DOCUMENTS DE SAINT-MARTIN-DES-CHAMPS / Depoin, J – Tome 2. 1913 – Dfl32.00 – ne Slangenburg [240]

RECUEIL DE CHARTES ET DOCUMENTS DE SAINT-MARTIN-DES-CHAMPS / Depoin, J – Tome 4. 1921 – Dfl22.00 – ne Slangenburg [240]

RECUEIL DE CHARTES ET DOCUMENTS DE SAINT-MARTIN-DES-CHAMPS / Depoin, J – Tome 5. 1921 – Dfl13.00 – ne Slangenburg [240]

RECUEIL DE CHARTRES ET DOCUMENTS DE SAINT-MARTIN-DES-CHAMPS : ARCHIVES DE LA FRANCE MONASTIQUE, VOL 13 / Depoin, J – Tom 1. 1912 – 7mf – 8 – Dfl28.00 – ne Slangenburg [240]

RECUEIL DE CIRCULAIRES PREFECTORALES ET DE MODELES DE TABLEAUX CONCERNANT LA STATISTIQUE DES DEPARTEMENTS / France – S. 1. an IX-XI – 9 – fr Hachette [944]

RECUEIL DE CONTES POPULAIRES DE LA SENEGAMBIE / Berenger-Feraud, Laurent Jean Baptiste – Paris, Ernest Leroux. 1885 – 9 – 7.50 – fr Orientalistes [390]

Recueil de Cytologie et d'Histologie Generale *see* CELLULE

RECUEIL DE DECORATIONS INTERIEURES. / Percier, Charles & Fontaine, FP – Paris. 1812. 43p., 72 pl. (Architecture Series) – 9 – fr Hachette [720]

RECUEIL DE DISSERTATIONS, ANCIENNES ET NOUVELLES SUR LES APPARITIONS, LES VISIONS ET LES SONGES. / Lenglet du Fresnoy, Nicolas – Avignon et Paris: J.N. Leloup, 1751-52. 2v in 4. 15 fiches. (Philosophy Collection) – 9 – $37.00 – fr Bibl Nationale [130]

RECUEIL DE DISSERTATIONS PHYSICO-CHYMIQUES, PRESENTEES A DIFFERENTES ACADEMIES / Demachy, Jacques Francois – Amsterdam, 1774 – 1 – us U.W. Library [540]

RECUEIL DE DIVERSES HISTOIRES TOVCHANT LES SITVATIONS DE TOUTES REGIONS ET PAYS CONTENUZ ES TROIS PARTIES DU MONDE, AUEC LES PARTICULIERES MOEURS, LOIX ET CAEREMONIES DE TOUTES NATIONS ET PEUPLES Y HABITAS / Boemus, J – Paris, 1542 – 6mf – 9 – H-8148/1 – ne IDC [900]

RECUEIL DE DIVERSES PIECES POUR SERVIR A L'HISTOIRE / Hay du Chastelet, Paul – [S.l.n.], 1639 – fr Armell [944]

RECUEIL DE DOCUMENTS POUR LE CLERGE DU DIOCESE DE VALLEYFIELD – (Suivi de: Revue ecclesiastique) – Valleyfield, Quebec?: s.n., 1896 – 9 – cn C.I.H.M. [240]

RECUEIL DE DOCUMENTS POUR LE CLERGE DU DIOCESE DE VALLEYFIELD *see* REVUE ECCLESIASTIQUE

RECUEIL DE DOCUMENTS SUR L'ASIE CENTRALE / Imbault-Huart, C – 1881 – 9 – fr Orientalistes [950]

RECUEIL DE DOCUMENTS SUR L'ASIE CENTRALE / Imbault-Huart, C – Pelov. 1st serie. 1881. BU-760 2 – 8 – ne IDC [950]

RECUEIL DE FRAGMENTS DE SCULPTURE ANTIQUE EN TERRE CUITS / Seroux D'Agincourt, J B L G – O 1200 1. 1814 – 9 – ne IDC [930]

RECUEIL DE LA GAZETTE DES TRIBUNAUX: JOURNAL DE JURISPRUDENCE ET DES DEBATS JUDICAIRES – 1898-1935. (lacks 1er semestre, 1933) – 1 – 785.00 – us L of C Photodup [340]

RECUEIL DE L'ORIGINE DE LA LANGUE ET POESIE FRANCOISE / Fauchet, C – 1581 – 9 – fr I.C.S. [440]

RECUEIL DE MEMOIRES, OU, COLLECTION DE PIECES ACADEMIQUES – L'Anatomie et la Chirurgie, la Chymie. Dijon. v1-16. 1754-87 – 3 – us Readex [500]

RECUEIL DE MEMOIRES SUR LA BOTANIQUE / Candolle, A P de – Paris. 1813. B-5873 2 – 8 – ne IDC [580]

RECUEIL DE MEMOIRES TOUCHANT L'EDUCATION DE LA JEUNESSE, SURTOUT PAR RAPPORT AUX ETUDES / Rivard, Dominique-Francois – Paris. 1763. 6784 – 9 – fr Hachette [360]

RECUEIL DE PIECES CHOISIES A UNE ET DEUX FLUTES / Babell, C – (Music for 1 flute with bass or 2 flutes without bass by Marais, Paisibile, Finger, Roziers, Tauvi, C. Stephani, Carissimi, Williams, Courtevill, and Morgan) – 1698 – 1 – us Sibley [780]

RECUEIL DE PIECES ORIGINALES ET AUTHENTIQUES CONCERNANT LA TENUE DES ETATS GENERAUX: D'ORLEANS EN 1560 SOUS CHARLES 9; DE BLOIS EN 1576 SOUS HENRI 3; DE BLOIS EN 1588 SOUS HENRI 3; DE PARIS EN 1614 SOUS LOUIS 13 / Lalource & Duval – Paris (4-12). 1789 – 1 – fr A.C.R.P.P. [324]

RECUEIL DE PLANCHES SUR LES SCIENCES, LES ARTS LIBERAUX ET LES ARTS MECHANIQUES AVEC LEUR EXPLICATION / Diderot, Denis – 9 – fr I.C.S. [000]

RECUEIL DE PLUSIEURS DES OUVRAGES DE MONSIEUR LE PRESIDENT ROLLAND / Rolland d'Erceville, Barthelemy Gabriel – Paris. P. G. Simon et N. H. Nyon. 1783. 6785 – 9 – fr Hachette [370]

RECUEIL DE PLUSIEURS MACHINES MILITAIRES ET FEUX ARTIFICIELS... / Appier, Jean – Pont-a-Mousson: C. Marchand, 1620 – fr Armell [355]

RECUEIL DE PLUSIEURS RELATIONS ET TRAITEZ SINGULIERS ET CURIEUX QUI N'ONT POINT ESTE MIS DANS SES SIX PREMIERS VOYAGES / Tavernier, Jean-Baptiste – Paris, G. Clouzier, 1679, 514 p., cartes et planches. French Voyagers in the Mediterranean 16th to 18th Centuries. 5974 – 9 – fr Hachette [944]

RECUEIL DE POEMES HISTORIQUES EN GREC VULGAIRE – Traduits par Emile Legrand. 1877 – 9 – fr Orientalistes [450]

RECUEIL DE STATISTIQUES LIBANAISES / Lebanon. Ministere du Plan – 8v. 1963-72. BNE-9679 1 – 9 – ne IDC [330]

RECUEIL DE TEXTES / Forestie, Emerand – Reprod. de differents extraits, c1891. 3 fiches. (Miscellaneous Selections) – 9 – 8.00 – fr Bibl Nationale [070]

RECUEIL DE TEXTES ET DE TRADUCTIONS – Publies par les professeurs de l'Ecole des langues orientales vivantes. 1889 – 9 – fr Orientalistes [480]

RECUEIL DE TOUS LES TRAITES,... / [Clausen, H F C] – Berlin, 1796 – 4mf – 1 – ILM-587/1 – ne IDC [327]

RECUEIL DE TRAVAUX RELATIFS A LA PHILOLOGIE ET A L'ARCHEOLOGIE EGYPTIENNES ET ASSYRIENNES – (Index v1-32) – Paris, 1870-1923. v1-40. – 183mf – 9 – ne IDC [930]

RECUEIL DE VOYAGES AU NORD, CONTENANT DIVERS MEM. TRES UTILES AU COMMERCE ET A LA NAVIGATION – BH 496 2. v1-3. 1715 – 8 – ne IDC [910]

RECUEIL D'EMBLEMES DIVERS / Baudouin, J – 2V. O-1233 1. 1646 – 9 – ne IDC [760]

RECUEIL D'ENVIRON 1200 PHRASES FRANCAIS USUELLES AVEC LEUR TRADUCTION. EN OUOLOF DE SAINT-LOUIS / Descemet, Louis – St-Louis, Imprimerie du gouvernement. 1864 – 9 – $5.00 – fr Orientalistes [490]

RECUEIL DES 6. PIECES POUR LE CLAVECIN.. / Sterkel, Johann F X – 1795 – 9 – us Sibley [780]

RECUEIL DES ACTES ADMINISTRATIFS EN ALGERIE / France – puis de la Delegation Generale en Algerie; du Haut-Commissariat en Algerie. 1959-juin 1962; tb. 1958 – 1 – fr A.C.R.P.P. [960]

RECUEIL DES ACTS, ADMINISTRATIFS ET D'INFORMATION DE LA PREFECTURE / Guadeloupe. French West Indies – 1947-1962 – 1 – us UMI [324]

RECUEIL DES ACTES ET ADMINISTRATIFS / Martinique. French West Indies – 1947-1961 – 1 – us UMI [340]

RECUEIL DES ANTIQUITEZ DU PERCHE / Bart des Boullais, Leonard – 1890. 399p. (Historical Studies Series) – 9 – 6.00 – fr Bibl Nationale [930]

RECUEIL DES ARRETES ET DECISIONS DU GRAND LIBAN / Lebanon. Laws, Statutes, etc – Beyrouth, Impr. des lettres J. G., 1925. 321 p. LL-12017 – 1 – us L of C Photodup [340]

RECUEIL DES ARRETS / France. Conseil d'Etat – Paris. 1821-1993 – 1 – fr A.C.R.P.P. [944]

RECUEIL DES CHARTES DE L'ABBAYE DE CLUNY / Bernard, A & Bruel, A – Paris. Tome 1-6. 1876-1903 – Dfl760.00 – ne Slangenburg [240]

RECUEIL DES CRONIQUES ET ANCHIENNES ISTORIES DE LA GRANT BRETAGNE (RS39) : A PRESENT NOMME ENGLETERRE / J EHAN DE WA VRIN; ed by Hardy, H & Hardy E L C P – (v1-3 ed by W Hardy v4-5 by W Hardy and E L C P Hardy. V1 Albina-688 1864 Dfl53.00. v2 1399-1422 1868 Dfl32.00. v3 1422-1431 1880 Dfl32.00. v4 1431-1447 1884 Dfl30.00. v5 1447-1471 1891 Dfl49.00) – ne Slangenburg [941]

RECUEIL DES DECISIONS DES TRIBUNAUX ARBITRAUX MIXTES INSTITUES PAR LES TRAITES DE PAIX / France. Laws, Statutes, etc – no. 1-112. Paris. mars 1921-avr juil 1930 – 1 – fr A.C.R.P.P. [073]

RECUEIL DES ELOGES HISTORIQUES LUS DANS LES SEANCES PUBLIQUES DE FRANCE / Cuvier, Georges – Reprod. de la 2eme ed. en trois tomes: 1800-13, 1814-26, 1827-32. Paris: Firmin Didot. 15 fiches. (Science Collection) – 9 – 37.00 – fr Bibl Nationale [850]

RECUEIL DES ELOGES HISTORIQUES LUS DANS LES SEANCES PUBLIQUES DE L'INSTITUTE DE FRANCE / Cuvier, Georges – Paris, 1819-27, 3 t., 431, 485, 507 p. Histoire des Sciences XVIIe-XIXe Siecles. 7922 4 – 9 – fr Hachette [500]

RECUEIL DES HISTORIENS DES CROISADES : DOCUMENTS ARMENIENS – Paris. 2v. 1869-1906 – 97mf – 9 – H-508/2 – ne IDC [944]

RECUEIL DES HISTORIENS DES CROISADES : HISTORIENS GRECS – Paris. 2v. 1875-81 – 74mf – 9 – H-509/2 – ne IDC [944]

RECUEIL DES HISTORIENS DES CROISADES : HISTORIENS OCCIDENTAUX – Paris. 5v. 1844-95 – 218mf – 9 – H-510/2 – ne IDC [944]

RECUEIL DES HISTORIENS DES CROISADES : HISTORIENS ORIENTAUX – Paris. 5v. 1872-1906 – 138mf – 9 – H-511/2 – ne IDC [944]

RECUEIL DES HISTORIENS DES GAULES ET DE LA FRANCE / Academie des inscriptions et belles lettres, Paris – (Ceased publ) – Paris. v1-24. 1869-1904. – 1 – D3149 – us UMI [944]

RECUEIL DES HISTORIENS DES GAULES ET DE LA FRANCE / Bouquet, D – Paris. v1-24. 1738-1904 – 677mf – 9 – 1569/2 – ne IDC [944]

RECUEIL DES HISTORIENS DES GAULES ET DE LA FRANCE / Danou et al – Paris (20-23). 1226-1328, 1840, 1855, 1865, 1876 – 1 – fr A.C.R.P.P. [944]

RECUEIL DES HISTORIENS DES GAULES ET DE LA FRANCE : RERUM GALLICARUM ET FRANCICARUM SCRIPTORES / Bouquet, Martin et al – Paris, 1738-1904. 24v – 9 – Bf48,000.00 set – 1-799-00602-6 – be Brepols [944]

RECUEIL DES MONOGRAPHIES PEDAGOGIQUES PUBLIEES A L'OCCASION DE L'EXPOSITION UNIVERSELLE DE 1889 / France. Ministere de l'Instruction Publique et des Beaux-Arts – Paris. 1889 – 1 – fr A.C.R.P.P. [324]

RECUEIL DES OEUVRES SPIRITUELLES DU P. ESTIENNE BINET : CONTENANT 8 TRAICTEZ / Binet, Estienne – Rouen: Richard L'Allemant, 1620. SEM35P57 – 1r – 1 – Can$34.00 – cn Bibl Nat [240]

RECUEIL DES PLANCHES, SUR LES SCIENCES ET LES ARTS LIBERAUX, ET LES ARTS MECHANIQUES – 3rd ed. 11v. 1771-73 – 3r – 1 – $225.00 – us OmniSys [500]

RECUEIL DES PRINCIPAUX TRAITES... 1918-1930 / Latvia. Ministere des Affaires Etrangeres – Ed 2. Riga, 1930 – 8mf – 9 – ILM-3927/1 – ne IDC [350]

RECUEIL DES RAPPORTS, DISCOURS ET AUTRES PIECES / France. Parlement. Assemblee nationale constituante – 1789-1876 – 1 – fr A.C.R.P.P. [324]

RECUEIL DES REGLEMENTS CONCERNANT L'ORGANISATION DES REGIES EN INDOCHINE / Indochina. French. Laws, Statutes, etc – Hanoi: Schneider, 1905. 188p. LL-10008 – 1 – us L of C Photodup [340]

RECUEIL DES REGLEMENTS, DECLARATIONS ET ARRETS, CONCERNANT LE COMMERCE, L'ADMINISTRATION DE LA JUSTICE ET LA POLICE DES COLONIES FRANCAISES DE L'AMERIQUE ET LES ENGAGES. AVEC LE CODE NOIR, ET L'ADDITION AUDIT CODE / Duboys, Jacques – (Slave Trade and Abolitionism in France Series). 1744-45 – 9 – fr Hachette [305]

RECUEIL DES STATISTIQUES SYRIENNES COMPAREES, 1928-1968 / Syria. Office Arabe de Presse et de Documentation – 1v. 1970. BNE-9728 1 – 9 – ne IDC [330]

RECUEIL DES SYNODES NESTORIENS *see* SYNODICON ORIENTALE OU RECUEIL DES SYNODES NESTORIENS

RECUEIL DES TEXTES REGLEMENTANT L'ENSEIGNEMENT PRIVE EN COCHINCHINE. / France. Laws, Statutes, etc – Saigon: Impr. de l'Union, 1940. 178p. LL-10004 – 1 – us L of C Photodup [340]

RECUEIL DES TRAITES, CONVENTIONS ET ACTES DIPLOMATIQUES CONCERNANT LA POLOGNE, 1762-1862 PAR LE COMTE D'ANGEBERG / Chodzko, L – Paris. 1862. HO-ECE-2657. BR-5490 2 – 8 – ne IDC [943]

RECUEIL DES TRAITES, CONVENTIONS ET ACTES DIPLOMATIQUES CONCERNANT L'AUTRICHE ET l'ITALIE – Paris, 1859 – 9mf – 9 – HQ-64/1 – ne IDC [943]

RECUEIL DES TRAITES DE LA FRANCE / France. Ministere des Affairs Etrangeres – Traites de 1713-1904. Paris. 1864-1907 (I-XII) – 1 – fr A.C.R.P.P. [073]

RECUEIL DES TRAITES DE LA FRANCE, 1763-1906 / ed by Clercq, E F J de & Clercq, A J H de – Paris. 23v. 1880-1917 – 182mf – 9 – ILM-3899/1 – ne IDC [944]

RECUEIL DES TRAITES DE LA PORTE OTTOMANE – (In French und Ottoman) – Paris, 1864-1898 – 9v 91mf – 9 – $1,600.00 – us MEDOC [949]

RECUEIL DES TRAITES DE LA PORTE OTTOMANE / ed by Testa, I de – Paris. 11v. 1864-1911 – 77mf – 9 – Dfl 471 – ILM-1761/1 – ne IDC [956]

RECUEIL DES TRAITES ET CONVENTIONS CONCLUS PAR LA RUSSIE AVEC LES PUISSANCES ETRANGERES / ed by Martens, F F – Spb. 15v. 1874-1909 – 222mf – 9 – R-3730/2 – ne IDC [947]

RECUEIL DES TRAITES ET CONVENTIONS CONCLUS PAR L'AUTRICHE AVEC LES PUISSANCES ETRANGERS, DEPUIS 1763 JUSQU'A NOS JOURS / Neumann, L – Leipzig. 5v. 1855-1859 – 39mf – 9 – ne IDC [943]

RECUEIL DES TRAVAUX CHIMIQUES DES PAYS-BAS ET DE LA BELGIQUE – v1-74. 1882-1955 – 1,5,6 – us Princeton Micro [540]

RECUEIL D'ITINERAIRES ET DE VOYAGES DANS L'ASIE CENTRALE ET L'EXTREME-ORIENT / Scherzer, F & Leger, L & Schefer, C – 1878 – 9 – fr Orientalistes [950]

RECUEIL D'OEUVRES RELIEES ET MICROFILMEES ENSEMBLE, ENRICHIES DE NOMBREUSES NOTES MANUSCRITES / Cicero, Marcus Tullius – (Audomari Talaei academia. Ejusdem in Academicum Ciceronis fragmentum explicatio[...]. – Parisiis: M. David, 1550. De Divinatione[...] – Parisiis: J.L. Tiletanus, 1544. De Fato liber, Petri Rami praelectionibus explicatus[...]. – Lutetiae: M. Vascosanus, 1550. De Natura deorum[...]. – Parisiis: M. Vascosanus, 1544. Scipionis somnium[...] Petri Rami praelectionibus explicatum[...]. – Parisiis: M. David, 1550. Timeus, sive De Universitate liber[...]. – Parisiis: T. Richard, 1549) – fr Armell [944]

RECUEIL ET PARALLELE DES EDIFICES DE TOUT GENRE ANCIENS ET MODERNES... AVEC UN TEXTE...PAR J.G. LEGRAND / Durand, Jean Nicolas Louis – Paris: Grille, 1800. 52p, 85 pls. (Architecture Series) – 9 – fr Hachette [720]

RECUEIL FACTICE DE 16 OPUSCULES / Gouges, Olympe de – Paris, 1789-1793 – 1 – F155.60 – fr Armell [944]

RECUEIL FACTICE DE 31 OEUVRES ECRITES OU TRADUITES PAR E. PHELIPPES-BEAULIEUX, TRAITANT SURTOUT D'AGRONOMIEET D'HISTOIRE LOCALE / Phelippes – Beaulieux, Emmanuel – Nantes, 1826-1865 – fr Armell [630]

RECUEIL FACTICE DE MEMOIRES DE MEDECINE SOUTENUS A L'UNIVERSITE DE DOUAI, ET DE QUELQUES ACTES ADMINISTRATIFS CONCERNANT CETTE UNIVERSITE / Universite de DOUAI – Douai, Lille, Paris, 1743-1765 – fr Armell [610]

RECUEIL GENERAL DES ANCIENNES LOIS FRANCAISES ... L'AN 420 JUSQU'A LA REVOLUTION DE 1789 / ed by Jourdan et al – (Index included) – Paris. v1-28. 1821-33 – 173mf – 9 – H-1373/1 – ne IDC [944]

RECUEIL GENERAL DES LOIS ET DES ARRETS EN MATIERE CIVILE, CRIMINELLE, COMMERCIALE ET DE DROIT PUBLIC / Sirey, J -B – Paris. 1791 1801-50 – 1 – fr A.C.R.P.P. [073]

RECUEIL HISTORIQUE COMPLET DES TRAITES...DE TOUS LES ETATS DE L'AMERIQUE LATIN, DEPUIS L'ANNEE 1493 JUSQU'A NOS JOURS / Calvo, C – Paris, Madrid, 1864-1867 – 26mf – 1 – ILM-2307/1 – ne IDC [327]

RECUEIL HISTORIQUE DES ARCHEVECHES, EVECHES, ABBAYES ET PRIEURES DE FRANCE / Beaunier, Dom. – (Ed. Besse). Tom. 2: Provinces Ecclesiastiques d'Aix, Avignon et Embrun. 1909 – Dfl25.00 – ne Slangenburg [240]

RECUEIL HISTORIQUE DES ARCHEVECHES, EVECHES, ABBAYES ET PRIEURES DE FRANCE : INTRODUCTION / Beaunier, Dom. – 1906 – Dfl30.00 – ne Slangenburg [240]

RECUEIL HISTORIQUE DES ARCHEVECHES, EVECHES ET PRIEURES DE FRANCE / Beaunier, Dom. – Tom. 1: Province Ecclesiastique de Paris, 1905 – Dfl32.00 – ne Slangenburg [240]

RECUEIL HISTORIQUE SUR L'ANCIENNE PROVINCE D'ANJOU / Berthe, J -A – v2. 1829 – fr Armell [944]

LE RECUEIL LITTERAIRE – Montreal: V Grenier, 1889-92. SEM16P362 – 1r – 5 – Can$23.00 – cn Bibl Nat [073]

LE RECUEIL LITTERAIRE *see* PETIT RECUEIL LITTERAIRE

RECUEIL PHILOSOPHIQUE OU MELANGE DE PIECES SUR LA RELIGION ET LA MORALE – (D'Holbach series). 1770 – 9 – fr Hachette [170]

RECUEIL STATISTIQUE SUR LA PRODUCTION ANIMALE EN AFRIQUE / CIPEA – 1994 – 9 – Gratuit – et ILRI [636]

RECUEIL TIRE DES PROCEDURES CIVILES FAITES EN L'OFFICIALITE DE PARIS, ET AUTRES OFFICIALITEZ DU ROYAUME. / Combes, Pierre de – Paris: Nicolas Le Gras & Louis Josse, 1705. SEM35P295 – 1r – 1 – Can$39.00 – cn Bibl Nat [971]

RECUEILS DOCUMENTAIRES DES ARTS DU SPECTACLE / Bibliotheque Nationale – 2works by Lecomte. Listed and available separately. 11 fiches – 9 – 27.00 – fr Bibl Nationale [490]

UN RECUERDO HISTORICO : LA COLCHA DEL EMPERADOR / Sanchez Ocana & Lopez de Berges, Miguel – Madrid: S.L., 1958 – 1 – sp Bibl Santa Ana [946]

RECUERDO Y PRESENCIA DE FRANCISCO PIZARRO / Balesteros Gaibrais, Manuel – Madrid: Razon y Fe, 1944 – 1 – sp Bibl Santa Ana [910]

RECUERDOS DE AYER : POEMAS DE JUVENTUD / Villalobos Bote, Rufino – D.Benito Secretariodo de Propag.de la Juventud Masc.de Accion Catolica – 1 – sp Bibl Santa Ana [810]

RECUERDOS DE EXTREMADURA / Diaz Perez, Nicolas – 1885 – 9 – 1.50f – sp Bibl Santa Ana [946]

RECUERDOS DE LA CAMPANA DE LOS REPUBLICANOS CONTRA EL IMPERIO, EN EL ESTADO DE YUCATAN / Manzanilla, Yanurario – 1888. xi,229p – 1 – us U.W. Library [972]

RECUERDOS DE MI CAMPANA EN RUSIA / Jimenez Andrades, Ildefonso – Badajoz: Imp. de la Excma. Diputacion Provincial, 1957 – 1 – sp Bibl Santa Ana [947]

RECUERDOS DEL PASADO (1814-1860) 4TH ED. SANTIAGO DE CHILE, 1943 / Perez Rosales, Vicente – Madrid: Razon y Fe, 1948 – 1 – sp Bibl Santa Ana [946]

RECUERDOS. VEINTICINCO ANOS DE AMISTAD INSUSTITUIBLE / Munoz de San Pedro, Miguel – Caceres: Imprenta Provincial, 1970 – 1 – sp Bibl Santa Ana [946]

RECUERDOS Y DATOS HISTORICOS DE LA CIUDAD DE D.BENITO / Torre Isunza de Hita, Pedro – Cabras: Tip.Manuel Cordon, 1916 – 1 – sp Bibl Santa Ana [946]

RECURRING PROBLEMS IN THE TRIAL OF A CRIMINAL ACTION / Voorhees, Donald S – Washington: FJC, 1981 – 2mf – 9 – $3.00 – LLMC 95-838 – us L.L.M.C. [340]

RECURSO DE CASACION...FERROCARRILES EXTREMENOS / Gamazo, German – 1898 – 9 – 1.50f – sp Bibl Santa Ana [380]

RECUSANT HISTORY – v. 1-12. London. 1951 52-1973 74 – 9 – 2470.00; 6.00v – uk Dawson [240]

RED ARCHIVES / U.S.S.R. Krasnyi Arkhiv – Moscow. 106 nos. 1922-41 – 3 – us Readex [025]

RED AS A ROSE IS SHE : A NOVEL / Broughton, Rhoda – London: Richard Bentley, 11th ed 1887 – 1 roll – 1 – 1-55879-373-9 – uk Libr Preservation [830]

RED AS A ROSE IS SHE: A NOVEL / Broughton, Rhoda – British Fiction Archive: Unit 4 – 9 – uk Bell [830]

RED BANK BAPTIST CHURCH. SALUDA, SOUTH CAROLINA : CHURCH RECORDS – 1815-1914 – 1 – 32.22 – us Baptist [240]

RED BOOK OF THE EXCHEQUER (RS99) = LIBER RUBEUS DE SCACCARIO / Great Britain. Exchequer; ed by Hall, H – (v1 1896 Dfl39.00. v2 1896 Dfl32.00. v3 1896 Dfl42.00) – ne Slangenburg [941]

RED CLIFFS CENETERY REGISTER – 1930-1995 – 12r – 9 – at Corangamite [910]

RED CLOUD CHIEF – Red Cloud, NE. -w. Oct 1873-Jul 1875; Sept 1875-Jul 1880; Sept 1880-Sept 1886; Jan 1888-Dec 1891; Mar 1892-Dec 1894; Oct 1894; Jan 1895-Dec 1902; Sept 1903-Oct 1904; Jan 1905-Nov 1923 – 1 – us NE Hist [071]

RED CLOUD CHIEF – Red Cloud, NE. -w (-tw 1902-48; -sw 1948-55). May 1908-Jun 1965; Aug 1965 to date – 1 – us NE Hist [071]

RED CLOUD NATION – Red Cloud, NE. -w (-sw 1903-04). Jul 1892-Feb 1902, scattered issues missing; May 1902-Mar 1908 – 1 – us NE Hist [071]

RED CLOUD REPUBLICAN – Red Cloud, NE. -w. Sept 1889-Aug 1890 – 1 – us NE Hist [071]

THE RED CORD: FROM CREATION TO CHRIST: THE BIBLE...MADE PLAIN TO YOUNG READERS / Rossiter, Stealy Bales – New York: A.D.F. Randolph, 1891.1 fiche. 8370-4975-X – 9 – us A.T.L.A. [240]

RED COTTON NIGHT-CAP COUNTRY, OR, TURF AND TOWERS / Browning, Robert – London: Smith, Elder, 1873 – 1 roll – 1 – 1-55879-885-4 – uk Libr Preservation [840]

THE RED COURT FARM / Wood, Ellen – British Fiction Archive: Unit 1 – 9 – uk Bell [830]

RED DEER ADVOCATE – Red Deer, Alberta, CN. Apr 1904- – 12r per yr – 1 – Can$53.00r – cn Commonwealth Micro [072]

RED DEER NEWS – Alberta, CN. 1906-26 – 7r – 1 – cn Commonwealth Micro [072]

THE RED EXECUTIONER DZIERJINSI, THE GOOD HEART / Jaxa-Roniker, Bogdan H – Trans. from the Polish by Helen Heney. London: Denis Archer, 1935. 316p. illus. Includes index – 1 – us U.W. Library [920]

A RED FLAG – Ireland.20-27 Nov 1919 – 1 – ie Microforms [072]

RED FLAG *see* HUNG CH'I

RED FORK, SALT FORK, AND WICHITA-ARCHER-CLAY BAPTIST ASSOCIATIONS. TEXAS / Baptist Associations. Texas – 1977-87 – 1 – 36.08 – us Baptist [240]

RED GUARD PUBLICATIONS – 8reels – 1 – 200.00 – us Chinese Res [950]

THE RED HAND MAGAZINE – Ireland.Sept-Dec 1920 – 1 – ie Microforms [072]

RED HILL BAPTIST CHURCH. EDGEFIELD COUNTY, SOUTH CAROLINA : CHURCH RECORDS – (Other minutes, 1908-1970) – 1973-July 1991 – 1r – 1 – $54.41 – us Baptist [240]

RED HILL BAPTIST CHURCH. EDGEFIELD COUNTY. SOUTH CAROLINA : CHURCH RECORDS – 1947-73.153p – 1 – 6.89 – us Baptist [240]

Red International of Labour Unions *see* NEGRO WORKER

THE RED MAN; AN ILLUSTRATED MAGAZINE PRINTED BY INDIANS – v. 1-9. Feb 1909-Oct 1917. v. 8, nos. 7-9; v. 9, no. 2 wanting – 1 – 34.00 – us L of C Photodup [360]

RED OAK GROVE BAPTIST CHURCH. EDGEFIELD COUNTY. SOUTH CAROLINA : CHURCH RECORDS – 1812-82, 1890-1982. 1264p – 1 – 56.88 – us Baptist [240]

RED POTTAGE / Cholmondeley, Mary – British Fiction Archive: Unit 3 – 9 – uk Bell [830]

RED RAG – London, UK. 1891. -w. 1 foot – 1 – uk British Libr Newspaper [072]

RED RIVER BAPTIST CHURCH. ROBERTSON COUNTY. TENNESSEE : CHURCH RECORDS – 1791-1826 – 1 – 11.16 – us Baptist [240]

RED SEA, GULD OF ADEN AND SUEZ CANAL : A BIBLIOGRAPHY ON OCEANOGRAPHIC AND MARINE ENVIRONMENTAL RESEARCH / ed by Morcos, Selim A & Varley, Allen – (Bilingual: English/Arabic) – 1990 – xxxiii/198p + 48p – 9 – 92-3-002706-5 – Co-published with ALECSO – fr UNESCO [550]

RED SPRINGS BAPTIST CHURCH. ROBESON ASSOCIATION. NORTH CAROLINA : CHURCH RECORDS – 1881-1920 – 1 – 13.77 – us Baptist [240]

RED WILLOW COUNTY GAZETTE – McCook, NE. -w. Dec 1917-Feb 1925 – 1 – us NE Hist [071]

RED WILLOW COUNTY GAZETTE- McCook. Neb. 1911-1925 – 1 – us UMI [071]

RED WILLOW COUNTY REPORTER – McCook, NE. -w. (-sw 1950-54). Apr 1896-Jul 1898; Sep-Oct 1900; Aug 1901-Jan 1902; Sep 1902-Aug 1904; Jan 1908-Feb 1957 – 1 – us NE Hist [071]

RED WILLOW COUNTY REPUBLICAN – Indianola, NE. -w. Oct 1900-Jan 1901; Apr-Aug 1901 – 1 – us NE Hist [071]

RED WILLOW COUNTY TIMES – Indianola, NE. -w. Dec 1888-Oct 1890 – 1 – us NE Hist [071]

LAS REDACCIONES DEL LIBRO DE LA GOBERNACION ESPIRITUAL. OVANDO Y LA JUNTA DE INDIAS DE 1568 / Pena Camara, Jose de la – Madrid: Revista de Indias, 1941 – 1 – sp Bibl Santa Ana [950]

LA REDACTION DES ARTICLES SCIENTIFIQUES / Tripathi, Bansh R – 1992 – 9 – $6.00 – 92-9053-234-3 – et ILRI [500]

LA REDACTION FRANCAISE : 5E, 6E, 7E ET 8 ANNEE: PRECEPTES, MODELES, EXERCICES ORAUX ET ECRITS – Montreal: les freres du Sacre-Coeur, [1930]. SEM105P1617 – 3mf – 9 – Can$6.75 – cn Bibl Nat [440]

"EL REDACTOR GENERAL DE ESPANA" – Anos 1813-1814 (1-XI/11-V) – 14mf – 9 – sp Cultura [946]

Redaktion der "Lichtbild-Buehne" *see* FILM-EXPRESS

REDBOOK – 1965- – 9 – us UMI [073]

REDBOOK – (v. 132- 1968- 5,6. v. 134- 1969- 9) – v. 1- 1903- – 1 – us UMI [073]

REDBOOK *see* AMERICAN HOME

REDBRIDGE POST – (Also known as: Ilford and Redbridge Post) – Apr 1982-93; Jan 8-Jun 25 1994; Jul 1994-96 – 41r – 9 – uk British Libr Newspaper [072]

REDBRIDGE RECORDER – (Also known as: Ilford Recorder) – 1905; Jan 5-Dec 27 1912; Jan 5-Jun 29 1950; Jul 6-Dec 28 1950; 1973-Dec 19 1974; 1975-96 – 108 1/2r – 9 – uk British Libr Newspaper [072]

REDBRIDGE YELLOW ADVERTISER *see* YELLOW ADVERTISER (REDBRIDGE EDN)

REDCAR AND SALTBURN NEWS – England. -w. 5 Jan 1871-25 Nov 1875; 20 Aug 1892-16 April 1916. 25 reels – 1 – uk British Libr Newspaper [072]

REDCAR AND SALTBURN VISITOR AND MIDDLESBROUGH & STOCKTON GAZETTE – England. -w. 1 Oct 1869-25 June 1870. 48 ft – 1 – uk British Libr Newspaper [072]

REDCAR AND SALTBURN-BY-THE-SEA GAZETTE – England. -w. 9 July 1869-29 Dec 1900. 24 reels – 1 – uk British Libr Newspaper [072]

REDCAR BOROUGH & DISTRICT OBSERVER – England. -w. 10 Nov-29 Dec 1923. 8 ft – 1 – uk British Libr Newspaper [072]

Redcar. Yorkshire *see* COATHAM PARISH CHURCHYARD MONUMENTAL INSCRIPTIONS

Redcar. Yorkshire. St. Peter's *see* MONUMENTAL INSCRIPTIONS

REDCAR-SOUTHBANK FREE PRESS (REDCAR AND DISTRICT FREE PRESS) – England. 11 Jul 1929-16 Feb 1941.-w. 4 reels – 1 – uk British Libr Newspaper [072]

REDCHAISHIIA KNIGI NAPECHATANNYIA V ROSSII NA RUSSKOM IAZYKE / Mintslov, S R – St. Petersburg, 1904. 50p. BR-4661/2 – 8 – ne IDC [460]

Reddemann, Joachim Karl Adolf *see* TERPINEN-4-OL ALS VERHALTENSSTEUERNDER DUFTSTOFF VON FICHTENBORKENKAEFERN

Reddie, James *see* INQUIRIES ELEMENTARY AND HISTORICAL IN THE SCIENCE OF LAW

Reddin, D Thomas *see* 'WINNING THROUGH'

Redding, Cyrus *see* A HISTORY AND DESCRIPTION OF MODERN WINE

REDDITCH INDICATOR – England. -w. 1893; 1933-45; 1959-60. (13 reels) – 1 – uk British Libr Newspaper [072]

REDE AN DIE DEUTSCHE JUGEND, 1945 / Wiechert, Ernst Emil – Muenchen: Zinnenverlag K Desch, [1945] – 1r – 1 – us U.W. Library [943]

REDE AUF GRILLPARZER : GEHALTEN AM 15. JANUAR 1891 IM FESTSAALE DER UNIVERSITAET / Minor, Jacob – Wien: Selbstverlag der k. k. Universitaet, 1891 – 1r – 1 – us U.W. Library [430]

REDE ZU GOETHES HUNDERTSTEM TODESTAG / Gundolf, Friedrich – Berlin: G Bondi, 1932 – 1r – 1 – us U.W. Library [430]

REDEEMED BY THE BLOOD / Duff, Mrs. E S – c.1905 – 9 – us A.T.L.A. [240]

REDEFINING BASIC EDUCATION FOR LATIN AMERICA : LESSONS TO BE LEARNED FROM THE COLOMBIAN ESCUELA NUEVA / Schiefelbein, Ernesto – 1992 – 117p – 9 – 92-803-1143-3 – fr UNESCO [370]

REDEFINING DISCRIMINATION : DISPARATE IMPACT AND THE INSTITUTIONALIZATION OF AFFIRMATIVE ACTION: 4 NOV 1987 – Washington: GPO, 1988 – 2mf – 9 – $3.00 – LLMC 94-364 – us L.L.M.C. [340]

REDEMOKRATISIERUNG DES KONZERTLEBENS IN OSTBAYERN NACH DEM 2. WELTKRIEG IN DREI STADTKREISEN / Pimmer, Hans – 1992 – 474p – 9 – DM125.00 – 3-89349-632-7 – gw Hänsel [780]

REDEMPTEUR = DER ERLOESER : VORTRAEGE / Pressense, Edmond de – (In German) – 1mf – 9 – 0-8370-5123-1 – 1985-3123 – us A.T.L.A. [240]

REDEMPTEUR = THE REDEEMER : A SKETCH OF THE HISTORY OF REDEMPTION / Pressense, Edmond de – (In English) – Boston: American Tract Society, c1867 – 1mf – 9 – 0-8370-5120-7 – 1985-3120 – us A.T.L.A. [240]

REDEMPTION AND REVELATION / Robinson, H Wheeler – Nisbet. 1942 – 9 – $12.00 – us I.R.C. [240]

REDEMPTION AND SOCIAL REFORMATION / Needham, Philip Dennis – 1967 – 1 – us A.T.L.A. [240]

LA REDEMPTION D'APRES JESUS-CHRIST / Vernes, Maurice – Strasbourg: G. Silbermann, 1868.1 fiche – 9 – us A.T.L.A. [240]

REDEMPTION OF OPPRESSED HUMANITY! : CHRIST'S MANIFESTATION BY HIS MESSENGERS FOR THE ABOLITION OF ALL KINDS OF POPERY! / Smolnikar, Andrew B – Cincinnati, Ohio: Ben Franklin Mammoth Steam Press, 1856 – 1r – 1 – us Western Res [240]

THE REDEMPTION OF THE BODY : AN EXAMINATION OF ROMANS 8. 18-23 / Whitehouse, William Fitzhugh – London: Elliot Stock, 1892 – 1mf – 9 – 0-8370-6464-3 – 1986-0464 – us A.T.L.A. [220]

THE REDEMPTION OF THE CITY / Sears, Charles Hatch – Philadelphia: Griffith & Rowland, c1911 – 1mf – us A.T.L.A. [240]

THE REDEMPTION OF THE RED MAN : AN ACCOUNT OF PRESBYTERIAN MISSIONS TO THE NORTH AMERICAN INDIANS OF THE PRESENT DAY / Brain, Belle Marvel – New York: Board of Home Missions of the Presbyterian Church in the USA, 1904 – 1mf – 9 – 0-8370-6649-2 – 1986-0649 – us A.T.L.A. [240]

REDEMPTION: THREE SERMONS 1637-1656 / Hooker, Thomas – 9 – 10.00 – us Scholars' Facs [240]

REDEMPTION TIDINGS – v9-18. Jun 1933-8 May 1942 (complete) – 3r – 1 – ATLA S0490 – us A.T.L.A. [240]

DIE REDEN DES SATAN IN DER HEILIGEN SCHRIFT : EINE EXEGETISCH-RHETORISCHE ANALYSE UND ETHISCHE ZEITSPIEGELUNG / Hoelemann, Hermann Gustav – Leipzig:J.C. Hinrichs, 1875 – 1mf – 9 – 0-8370-3614-3 – 1985-1614 – us A.T.L.A. [220]

REDEN UND AUFSAETZE : GESAMMELT AUS LITTERAERISCHEN MAGAZINEN, UND MIT STETER BEZIEHUNG AUF SEINE UEBRIGEN SCHRIFTEN / Sambuga, Joseph Anton; ed by Schmitter-Hug, Johann Baptist – Lindau, 1834 – 2mf – 9 – DM60.00 – 3-89349-294-1 – gw Hänsel [943]

REDEN UND AUFSAETZE / Stoecker, Adolf – Leipzig: A. Deichert, 1913 – 1mf – us A.T.L.A. [240]

REDEN UND VORLESUNGEN / Hecker, Friedrich – St Louis, MO: C Witter, 1872 – 1 – us U.W. Library [850]

REDEN, VORTRAEGE, ESSAYS / Dietze, Walter – (Includes bibliographical references) – Leipzig: P Reclam, 1972 – 1r – 1 – us U.W. Library [430]

LA REDENCION DEL OBRERO – Manila. Philippine Islands. -w. 8-29 Oct, 12 Nov 1903. (3 ft) – 1 – uk British Libr Newspaper [072]

Redepenning, Ernst Rudolf *see* ORIGENES

Redesdale, John Freeman-Mitford *see* A TREATISE ON THE PLEADINGS IN SUITS IN THE COURT OF CHANCERY, BY ENGLISH BILL. THE 4TH ED. WITH ADDITIONAL REFERENCES AND NOTES, BY GEORGE JEREMY...3RD AMER. ED. WITH NOTES AND REFERENCES, BY CHARLES EDWARDS.

Redewitz, Oskar von *see* HERMANN STARK

Redfern, W *see* MODERN DEVELOPMENTS IN METHODISM

Redfield, Isaac Fletcher *see*
- THE LAW OF CARRIERS OF GOODS AND PASSENGERS.
- THE LAW OF RAILWAYS...3RD ED

Redford, Robert Ainslie *see*
- FOUR CENTURIES OF SILENCE, OR, FROM MALACHI TO CHRIST
- PRIMER OF CHRISTIAN EVIDENCE
- PROPHECY: ITS NATURE AND EVIDENCE
- VOX DEI: THE DOCTRINE OF THE SPIRIT AS...SET FORTH IN THE...TESTAMENTS

REDIA : GIORNALE DI ENTOMOLOGIA – Florence. v1-19. 1903-31 – 157mf – 9 – 2427/2 – ne IDC [590]

Redia *see* GIORNALE DI ENTOMOLOGIA

Reding, A *see* THEOLOGIAE SCHOLASTICAE

THE REDISCOVERY OF OUR REVOLUTION / Sukarno, Pres. Indonesia – In Indonesian.. SE 2184 1. 1959 – 9 – ne IDC [025]

REDISTRIBUTION THROUGH NATIONAL INSURANCE IN ISRAEL BY INCOME AND DEMOGRAPHIC GROUPS / Israel. National Insurance Institute – By Jack Habib. Jerusalem. Nov 1975. 51 p. Diagr. (Discussion Paper 7) – 9 – 2.00 – is I.T.T.I. [310]

REDKIE RUSSKIE KNIGI I LETUCHI IZDANIIA 18 VEKA S BIBLIOGRAFICHESKIMI PRIMECHANIIAMI, UKAZANIEM STEPENI REDKOSTI I TSENAMI.. / Bitovt, Iu – Moscow, 1905. viii,605p. BR-4668/2 – 8 – ne IDC [010]

Red'ko, A M *see* FUTURIZM V LITERATURE. LITERATURNOKHUDOZHESTVENNYE ISKANIIA V KONTSE 19-NACHALE 20 VV

REDLANDS CITROGRAPH – Redlands, CA. 1887-1908 – 12r – 1 – $600.00 – R03406 – us Library Micro [071]

REDLANDS CITY DIRECTORIES INCLUDING MENTONE, LOMA LINDA, MISSION VALLEY AND CRAFTON – San Bernardino Co, CA. 1900; 1902-1936 – 12r – 1 – $600.00 – D081 – us Library Micro [978]

REDLANDS REVIEW – Redlands, CA. 1913-1919 – 19r – 1 – $7,450.00 – C03407 – us Library Micro [071]

Redlich, Christian *see* AUGUST GRAF VON PLATENS WERKE

Redlich, Oswald *see* GRILLPARZER UND DIE WISSENSCHAFT

Redmond, Charles J *see*
- ISOKINETIC EVALUATION OF THE POSTERIOR ROTATOR CUFF MUSCULATURE FOLLOWING A STRENGTHENING PROGRAM UTILIZING RUBBER TUBING
- PERCEIVED BENEFITS OF STRENGTH TRAINING FOR YOUTH PARTICIPANTS AS DETERMINED BY ORTHOPEDIC SURGEONS
- PREDICTION OF INJURY IN HIGH SCHOOL VOLLEYBALL PLAYERS WITH PERCEIVED LEADERSHIP BEHAVIOR OF THE COACH
- THE RELATIONSHIP BETWEEN PERCEIVED STRESSFUL LIFE EVENTS AND OCCURRENCE OF ATHLETIC INJURY AMONG COLLEGE LEVEL GYMNASTS
- STRENGTH GAINS THROUGH AQUATIC EXERCISE

Redmond, Pat H *see* HISTORY OF QUINCY AND ITS MEN OF MARK

Redmond, R A *see* EFFECTS OF STRENGTH TRAINING ON MUSCLE MASS AND MUSCULOSKELETAL INJURY IN MIDDLE AGED AND OLDER MEN

REDMOND SPOKESMAN – Redmond, OR. -w. 14 July 1910-. – 1 – us U.O. Library [071]

REDONDO *see* SOUTH BAY DAILY BREEZE

REDONDO BEACH – 1980-84; 1986 – 7r – 1 – $350.00 – P00088 – us Library Micro [910]

Redondo y Poblacion, Pedro *see*
- DISCURSO...DISTRIBUCION DE PREMIOS
- SEGUNDA PARTE...MONOLOGOS DE LA INFANCIA

Redonet, Luis *see* EL PRIMER MOLINO DE RODILLOS FUE INVENTO DE...?

Redonet y Lopez, Doriga *see* EL AMOR AL LIBRO...

Redoute, P J *see*
- LES LILIACEES

Redpath, H A *see* CONCORDANCE TO THE SEPTUAGINT AND THE OTHER GREEK VERSIONS OF THE OLD TESTAMENT

Redpath, Henry Adeney *see* THE BOOK OF THE PROPHET EZEKIEL

LE REDRESSEMENT FRANCAIS – Bulletin mensuel. Paris. oct 1926-35 – 1 – fr A.C.R.P.P. [073]

REDRUTH TIMES AND CAMBORNE ADVERTISER – Redruth, England. Cornubian and Redruth Times Cornubian and Cornwall County Times Cornubian and Cornwall Mining Times Cornwall County Times. -w. Nov 1867-Oct 1925. Lacking 1873. 46 reels – 1 – uk British Libr Newspaper [072]

Redstone. Presbytery (Pres. Ch. in the U.S.A.) *see* MINUTES, 1781-1902

REDUCING ALCOHOL CONSUMPTION AMONG UNIVERSITY STUDENTS : RECRUITMENT AND PROGRAM DESIGN STRATEGIES BASED ON SOCIAL MARKETING THEORY / Smith, M A – 1992 – 1mf – 9 – $4.00 – us Microform Publ [613]

REDUCING ANTERIOR SHEAR DURING KNEE EXTENSION : EFFECT OF RESISTANCE PAD LOCATION / Giambelluca, Christopher – 1988 – 89p 1mf – 9 – $4.00 – us Microform Publ [617]

REDUCING THE COST OF SPACE TRANSPORTATION – (v21 1967, Advances) – 1969 – 9 – $25.00 – us Univelt [629]

REDUCTION OF SPORTS INJURY MORBIDITY WITH HYPERBARIC OXYGEN TREATMENT / Borromeo, Charles N – Temple University, 1996 – 2mf – 9 – $8.00 – PE 3631 – us Microform Publ [617]

REDUKTION AROMATISCHER NITROVERBINDUNGEN DURCH VERSCHIEDENE PSEUDOMONAS-SPECIES / Schackmann, Archi V – 1992 – 110p – 9 – DM98.00 – 3-89349-568-1 – gw Hänsel [574]

DER REDUPLIZIERTE AORIST IN DEN INDOGERMANISCHEN SPRACHEN / Bendahman, Jadwiga – 1993 – 3mf – 9 – DM98.00 – 3-89349-642-4 – gw Hänsel [430]

REDWOOD CHIPS/REDWOOD NEEDLES – Santa Rosa, CA. 1962-1990 – 1r – 1 – $50.00 – B05066 – us Library Micro [071]

REDWOOD CITY – 1987 – 2r – 1 – $100.00 – P00089 – us Library Micro [910]

REDWOOD CITY DIRECTORY – San Mateo Co, CA. 1916-1917 – 1r – 1 – $50.00 – D092 – us Library Micro [910]

REDWOOD CITY TRIBUNE – (Cont by: Peninsula Times Tribune-One Star Edition) – Redwood City, CA. 1923-79; 1993- – 438+ r – 1 BC02686 – $21,900.00 ($50.00y) – us Library Micro [071]

REDWOOD GUIDE (SHOPPER) – Santa Rosa, CA. Aug 1976-May 1980 – 8r – 1 – $400.00 – B02979 – us Library Micro [071]

Redwood, Iltyd I *see* A PRACTICAL TREATISE ON MINERAL OILS AND THEIR BY-PRODUCTS

REDWOOD JOURNAL PRESS DISPATCH *see* UKIAH DAILY JOURNAL

THE REDWOOD RECORD – Garberville, CA. 1962-91 – 19+ r – 1 – $950.00 ($50.00y) – B02265 – us Library Micro [071]

Reeb, Antoine *see* ESSAI DE GRAMMAIRE DOUMA (HAUT-OGOWE, CONGO FRANCAIS)

Reeb, Georg *see*
- DISTINCTIONES PHILOSOPHICAE
- THESAURUS PHILOSOPHORUM SEU DISTINCTIONES ET AXIOMATA PHILOSOPHICA

Reece. Kansas *see* RECORDS

Reece, R *see* DIARIES, 1788-1790, 1805, 1810, 1815-1819, 1821-1828, 1831-1836

Reed, Andrew *see* A NARRATIVE OF THE VISIT TO THE AMERICAN CHURCHES BY THE DEPUTATION FROM THE CONGREGATIONAL UNION OF ENGLAND AND WALES

Reed, Cathy A *see* ISOKINETIC EVALUATION OF PEAK TORQUE VALUES FOLLOWING CLOSED AND OPEN KINETIC CHAIN EXERCISE TRAINING PROGRAMS

Reed, Charles Edward Baines *see* THE COMPANIONS OF THE LORD: CHAPTERS ON THE LIVES OF THE APOSTLES

Reed, Edward James *see* OUR IRON-CLAD SHIPS; THEIR QUALITIES, PERFORMANCES AND CO WITH CHAPTERS ON TURRET SHIPS, IRONCLAD RAMS, ETC

Reed, G Walter *see* HISTORY OF SACRAMENTO COUNTY

Reed, J D et al *see* PLANT BREEDING AND THE NUTRITIVE VALUE OF CROP RESIDUES

Reed, J E *see* PRACTICAL PARASITOLOGY

Reed, J Eugene *see* THE LIVES OF THE ROMAN EMPERORS AND THEIR ASSOCIATES FROM JULIUS CAESAR (BC 100) TO AUGUSTULUS (AD 476)

Reed, John E *see* HISTORY OF ERIE COUNTY

Reed, Joseph R *see* HISTORY OF POTTAWATAMIE COUNTY

Reed, Mrs. Myron *see* ONE LIFE, ONE LAW

Reed, Parker McCobb *see* BENCH AND BAR OF WISCONSIN

Reed, R C *see* CALVIN MEMORIAL ADDRESSES

Reeder, Robert Patterson *see* THE VALIDITY OF RATE REGULATIONS, STATE AND FEDERAL

REEDLEY CITY DIRECTORIES – Fresno Co, CA. 1933-1936; 1940 – 4r – 1 – $200.00 – D023 – us Library Micro [910]

REEDLEY EXPONENT – Reedley, CA. 1892-1936; 1950- – 50+ r – 1 BC02686 – $2,500.00 ($90.00y) – us Library Micro [071]

REEDY CREEK BAPTIST CHURCH. WARREN COUNTY. NORTH CAROLINA : CHURCH RECORDS – 1789. (List of subscribers) – 1 – 5.00 – us Baptist [240]

REEDY RIVER BAPTIST CHURCH. NORTH GREENVILLE ASSOCIATION. SOUTH CAROLINA : CHURCH RECORDS – 1799-1914 – 1 – 26.91 – us Baptist [240]

REEDY'S MIRROR *see* ALL'S WELL

Reefe, Thomas *see* LUBA DOCUMENTS

REEFS GAZETTE ROLLER – Philadelphia, PA., 1805-1810 – 13 – $25.00r – us I.M.R. [071]

REEMPLAZO DEL EJERCITO Y MILICIAS / Herrero Picado, Manuel F – 1856 – 9 – 1.50f – sp Bibl Santa Ana [355]

Reep, Samuel N *see* SECOND MORTGAGES AND LAND CONTRACTS IN REAL ESTATE FINANCING

Rees, A *see* THE CYCLOPAEDIA

Rees, Byron Johnson *see* HULDA A. REES: THE PENTECOSTAL PROPHETESS

Rees, John Collwyn *see* INTERPRETING THE CONSTITUTION: INAUGURAL LECTURE OF THE PROFESSOR OF POLITICAL THEORY AND GOVERNMENT, DELIVERED AT THE COLLEGE ON 1 DECEMBER 1955

Reese, Gussie *see* THIS THEY REMEMBERED, 1861-1865

REESE RIVER REVEILLE – Austin. Nev. -w. 1949- – 1 – us UMI [071]

REESE RIVER REVEILLE – Austin, NV. 1863-64; May 1867; 1872-1949 (broken series); 1952-93 – 89r – 1 – $4,450.00 – U04404 – us Library Micro [071]

REESE RIVER VALLEY TIMES – Battle Mountain, NV. 1980 – 1r – 1 – $50.00 – N03699 – us Library Micro [071]

Reese, William Miller *see* A TREATISE ON THE LAW OF EXECUTORS, ADMINISTRATORS AND GUARDIANS

REESTR KNIGAM KNIZHNAGO MAGAZINA A. SMIRDINIA. (SYNA), 1856. 148P. BR-5860/2 / Anastasevich, V G – 8 – ne IDC [010]

REESTR ROSSIISKIM KNIGAM, GEOGRAFICHESKIM ATLASAM I KARTAM, PLANAM I MUZYKAL'NYM SOCHINENIIAM, PRODAIUSHCHIMSIA V MOSKVE – u.l. Glazunova. M. 1829; Pribavlenie. v. 1-3. Spb. 1827-31. BR-7232 2 – 8 – ne IDC [910]

REESTR ROSSIISKIM KNIGAM IMP. PUBLICHNOI BIBLIOTEKI / Glazunova, M P – M., 1827. 268 pp. BR-7231 2 – 8 – ne IDC [020]

REESTR ROSSIISKIM KNIGAM, PRODAIUSHCHIMSIA V KNIZHNOM MAGAZINE / Glazunova, M P – M., 1832. 22 pp. Idem. Spb., 1833. 240 pp. Idem, M., 1831. 492 pp., Idem M., 1838. 72 pp., Idem, M., 1845, 278 pp. Pribavleniia. 1-4. M., 1843-1848. 244 pp. – 8 – BR-7230 2 – ne IDC [070]

REESTR RUSSKIM KNIGAM, PRODAIUSHCHIMSIA V KNIZHNOM MAGAZINE / Anastasevich, V G – A. Smirdina. St. Petersburg, 1833. 288, 41p. BR-5861 2 – 8 – ne IDC [010]

Reeth, P van *see* DE ROL VAN DEN MOEDERLIJKEN OOM IN DE INLANDSCHE FAMILIE

A REEVALUATION OF THE CIVIL APPEALS MANAGEMENT PLAN / Partridge, Anthony & Lind, Allan – Washington: FJC, Aug 1983 – 2mf – 9 – $3.00 – LLMC 95-314 – us L.L.M.C. [340]

Reeve, Clara *see*
- THE CHAMPION OF VIRTUE
- THE PROGRESS OF ROMANCE, THROUGH TIMES, COUNTRIES, AND MANNERS

Reeve, Edmund *see* AN INTRODUCTION INTO THE GREEKE TONGUE

Reeve, L A *see* CONCHOLOGIA ICONICA

Reeve, LA *see*
- CONCHOLOGIA SYSTEMATICA, OR
- ELEMENTS OF CONCHOLOGY
- THE LAND AND FRESHWATER MOLLUSKS INDIGENOUS TO

Reeve, Tapping *see*
- THE LAW OF BARON AND FEMME; OF PARENT AND CHILD.
- THE LAW OF HUSBAND AND WIFE, OF PARENT AND CHILD, GUARDIAN AND WARD, MASTER AND SERVANT

Reeve, William *see* A DICTIONARY CARNATACA AND ENGLISH

Reeves, Alfred Gandy *see* A TREATISE ON THE LAW OF REAL PROPERTY

Reeves, Jesse Siddall *see* JEREMY BENTHAM AND AMERICAN JURISPRUDENCE

Reeves, Lynda P *see* MOTOR ABILITY TESTING OF SPEECH HANDICAPPED PRESCHOOL CHILDREN

Reeves, Thomas H *see* DATA BOOK OF THE NOLACHUCKY BAPTIST ASSOCIATION

Reeves, W *see*
- THE CULDEES OF THE BRITISH ISLANDS AS THEY APPEAR IN THE HISTORY
- THE FAVORITE BALLET MUSIC IN THE ENTERTAINMENT OF RAYMOND AND AGNES...

Reeves, Winona E *see* THE BLUE BOOK OF IOWA WOMEN

REFERATE UND DISKUSSIONSBEITRAEGE.. / Zentralvorstandes der Liberal-Demokratischen Partei Deutschlands. Sekretariat – 19 April-10 Mai 1978 – 1 – us U.W. Library [943]

REFERATEDIENST ZUR GERMANISTISCHEN LITERATURWISSENSCHAFT : JAHRG. 1, NR. 1 (1969) – [JAHRG. 2], NR. 7 (1970) – (Index issued annually) – [Berlin]: Deutsche Akademie der Wissenschaften zu Berlin, Institut fuer Deutsche Sprache und Literatur, 1969-1970 – 1r – 1 – us U.W. Library [430]

REFERATIVNYI ZHURNAL. MATEMATIKA – Moscow. 1953-1975 – 1,5,6 – us Princeton Micro [510]

REFEREE – 1886-1939 – 37r – 9 – at Pascoe [072]

THE REFEREE – Sydney, Australia. 17 Mar 1920-16 Jan 1929.-w. 17 reels – 1 – uk British Libr Newspaper [072]

REFERENCE – (Cont by: Business Computing) – 1(Jan-Oct 1983) – 1,5 – $40.80y – D13621 – us UMI [073]

REFERENCE AND RESEARCH MATERIALS / U.S. Central Intelligence Agency. U.S.S.R – 1975- – 9 – us L of C Photodup [947]

THE REFERENCE LIBRARIAN / ed by Katz, Bill – v1- 1981- – 1, 9 ($140.00 in US $196.00 outside hardcopy subsc) – us Haworth [020]

REFERENCE LIST OF WILLS CONSTRUED BY THE SUPREME JUDICIAL COURT OF MASSACHUSETTS (INCLUDING THE CASES IN QUINCY AND FROM VOL. 1 TO VOL. 165 OF THE MASSACHUSETTS REPORTS) / Hall, Prescott Farnsworth – Boston, Reed, 1896. 28 p. LL-718 – 1 – us L of C Photodup [340]

REFERENCE WORKS – 1,031 titles – 9 – ne IDC [020]

REFERENCES TO THE VERSIONS BY THE BRITISH REVISERS COMPARED WITH THE VERSIONS / Osgood, Howard – Rochester, NY: R.W. Lace, 1899. 1 fiche – 9 – us A.T.L.A. [240]

LE REFERENDUM DE SEPTEMBRE ET LES ELECTIONS DE NOVEMBRE 1958 / Dogan, M. et al – L'Etablissement de la Cinquieme Republique – 9 – F120.00 – fr Ethnologie [320]

REFERENTEN-MATERIAL / Sozialistische Einheitspartei Deutschlands – Heft 1- Berlin Sozialistische Einheitspartei Deutschlands, Landesvorstand Gross-Berlin etc., 1946- – 1 – us U.W. Library [943]

REFIERESE POR MENOR, EL ESTADO DE LA PESTE EN NAPOLES – Sevilla, 1657 – 1mf – 9 – sp Cultura [616]

Refi'i, Kalayi *see* DIVAN

REFLECTION – (1985-. 5,6,9) – 1965- – 1 – us UMI [073]

REFLECTIONS / Clarke, Henry Harrison – 9 – $12.00 – us Microform Publ [920]

REFLECTIONS ON CANADIAN LITERACY – (Cont: Reading-Canada-Lecture at v8 1990. Suspended v11 1993) – Calgary. v8-11. 1990-93 – 9 – Can$20.00y – cn Micromedia [420]

REFLECTIONS ON CANADIAN LITERACY *see* READING-CANADA-LECTURE

REFLECTIONS ON DR. SWIFT'S LETTER TO THE EARL OF OXFORD, ABOUT THE ENGLISH TONGUE / Oldmixon, John – 1712. 44p. (English Linguistics Series 1500-1800) – 9 – us UMI [420]

REFLECTIONS ON INDONESIAN ARTS AND CULTURE / Murdowo, Raden – SE-3718 1. 1958 – 9 – ne IDC [700]

REFLECTIONS ON THE ENGLISH LANGUAGE / Baker, Robert – 1770. 219p. (English Linguistic Series 1500-1800) – 9 – us UMI [420]

REFLECTIONS ON THE FUTURE DEVELOPMENT OF EDUCATION – 1984 – 9 – 92-3-102235-0 – fr UNESCO [370]

REFLECTIONS ON THE FUTURE DEVELOPMENT OF EDUCATION – 1985 – 9 – 92-3-102152-4 – fr UNESCO [370]

REFLECTIONS ON THE NATURE AND PROPERTY OF LANGUAGES IN GENERAL / Stackhouse, Thomas – 1731 223p. (English Linguistics Series 1500-1800) – 9 – us UMI [400]

REFLECTIONS SUR LA REVOLUTION INDONESIENNE / Sukarno, Pres. Indonesia – SE 11,227 1. 1964 – 9 – ne IDC [025]

REFLECTIONS UPON THE INDONESIAN REVOLUTION / Sukarno, Pres. Indonesia – Inc. Indonesian foreign policy and foreign economic relations. SE 10,981 1. 1964 – 9 – ne IDC [950]

REFLECTIONS UPON THE INDONESIAN REVOLUTION / Sukarno, Pres. Indonesia – SE 10,982 1. 1964 – 9 – ne IDC [025]

REFLECTIONS UPON THE "MEMORANDUM" OF THE HON. WM. H. WILLIAMS, REGARDING THE COMPENSATION OF JUDGES / Stoughton, John Alden – n.p., 1905? 12 numb. LL-631 – 1 – us L of C Photodup [340]

REFLECTOR – Abilene. Kan. -w. 1883-1935 – 1 – us UMI [071]

REFLECTOR – Everest. Kan. 1884-1887 – 1 – us UMI [071]

REFLECTOR – Greenville. N.C. 1895-1912; 1919- – 1 – us UMI [071]

REFLECTOR – Norwalk. Ohio. -w. 1853-1914 – 1 – us UMI [071]

REFLECTOR – Payne, Ohio, 1895-1967 – 26r – 1 – us Archival [978]

REFLECTOR – Payne, Ohio. 1956-67 – 5r – 1 – $32.50r – us Archival [071]

THE REFLECTOR – Amherst [N.S.: s.n., 1897-189- or 19–] – 9 – cn C.I.H.M. [240]

REFLECTOR-HERALD – Norwalk. Ohio. 1913- – 1 – us UMI [071]

REFLEJOS DE SIETE SIGLOS DE VIDA EXTREMENA EN CIEN DOCUMENTOS NOTARIALES / Munoz de San Pedro, Miguel – Madrid: Junta de Decanos de los Colegios Notariales de Espana, 1965. Sep. Vol 2. Secc. 1ª de Estudios Juridicos varios – sp Bibl Santa Ana [340]

REFLEKSI DJIWA; DJEMPUTAN TJERITA-TJERITA PENDEK DAN DRAMA / Suradji, D – SE 3954 1. 1957 – 9 – ne IDC [950]

LE REFLET – Laprairie, Canada. v2 n32. 20 mar 1967-9 avr 1975 – 1r – 1 – Can$50.00 – cn Can Microfilming [072]

REFLET : LA PRAIRIE, QUEBEC – La Prairie: Composita. v1-9. 1966-1974. SEM35P212 – 3r – 1 – Can$173.00 – cn Bibl Nat [072]

LE REFLET REGIONAL – La Prairie. v9- 1974- . SEM35P330 – 39r – 1 – cn Bibl Nat [072]

REFLEX – Ward, NV. 1883-85 – 1r – 1 – $50.00 – U04803 – us Library Micro [071]

THE REFLEX – Los Angeles, CA. Jun-Sept 1935; Jan, Mar 1936 – 1r – 1 – $50.00 – B02400 – us Library Micro [071]

REFLEXES NOUVELLES = REFLEX NEWS – Ville d'Anjou. v1 n13. 26 mar 1970; v1 n17. 28 avr 1970 – 1r – 1 – Can$25.00 – cn Can Microfilming [072]

REFLEXIONES CRISTIANAS / Isla, Jose Francisco – 1785 – 2mf – 9 – Pta1,500.00 – 84-7848-284-9 – sp Pentalfa [240]

REFLEXIONES CRITICAS SOBRE LOS ESCRITOS QUE HAN PUBLICADO...MANUEL MORERA (Y OTROS) RESPECTO DE LA ULTIMA ENFERMEDAD DE VICENTE NAVARRO / Piquer, Andres – Valencia, 1746 – 3mf – 9 – sp Cultura [610]

REFLEXIONES CRITICO-APOLOGETICAS / Soto y Marne, Francisco de – Salamanca: E. Carcias. Tom. 1 – 1 – sp Bibl Santa Ana [946]

REFLEXIONES CRITICO-APOLOGETICAS / Soto y Marne, Francisco de – Salamanca. Tomo 2 – 1 – sp Bibl Santa Ana [946]

REFLEXIONES CRITICO-APOLOGETICAS. TOMO 1 / Soto Marne, Francisco – 1749 – 1mf – 9 – Pta1,000.00 – 84-7848-013-7 – sp Pentalfa [440]

REFLEXIONES CRITICO-APOLOGETICAS. TOMO 2 / Soto Marne, Francisco – 1749 – 2mf – 9 – Pta1,500.00 – 84-7848-014-5 – sp Pentalfa [440]

REFLEXIONES POLITICAS PARA MILITARES : HACIA UNA POLITICA NACIONAL / Funes, Rafael – Buenos Aires: Ediciones Relevo, 1963 – 1 – CSUXAGP8601-B – us Hoover Inst Photo [320]

REFLEXIONES SOBRE ADUANAS Y EFECTOS DE LA LEY PROHIVITIVA / Inclan, M – Madrid, 1839 – 1/mf – 9 – sp Cultura [946]

REFLEXIONES SOBRE LA HUMANIDAD DE LOS ESPANOLES EN LAS INDIAS / Nuix, Juan & Varela, Pedro – 1782 – 1mf – 9 – Pta1,000.00 – 84-7848-314-4 – sp Pentalfa [946]

REFLEXIONES SOBRE LA LABRO CIENTIFICA DEL R.P. CONFIRMA NAVAS S.J. PROLOGO Y RECOPILACION DE IGNACIO SALA DE CASTELARNAN, S.J. / Gregorio Rocasolano, Antonio del – Zaragoza, 1928. Zaragoza, Acad. Cienc. – 1 – sp Bibl Santa Ana [946]

REFLEXIONES SOBRE LAS ENFERMEDADES QUE AFLIGEN A LAS TROPAS...DEL ROSELLON / Viader, J – Gerona, 1794 – 2mf – 9 – sp Cultura [610]

REFLEXIONES...ESCRIBIR LA HISTORIA DE ESPANA / Forner Segarra, Juan Pablo – 1816 – 9 – 1.50f – sp Bibl Santa Ana [840]

REFLEXIONES...ESPOSA DONA MARIA ROSARIO MENDOZA Y.. / Irisarri, Pantaleon – 1849 – 9 – $1.50f – sp Bibl Santa Ana [920]

REFLEXIONS CRITIQUES SUR LA POESIE ET SUR LA PEINTURE / Du Bos, J B – 1719 – 9 – fr I.C.S. [760]

REFLEXIONS DE M. LE MARQUIS DE CONDORCET SUR L'USUFRUIT DES BENEFICIERS / Condorcet, Marie Jean Antoine Nicolas de – c.1790 Reprod. 8p. (Religion series) – 9 – 3.00 – fr Bibl Nationale [240]

REFLEXIONS D'UN CITOYEN CATHOLIQUE SUR LES LOIX DE FRANCE RELATIVES AUX PROTESTANTS / Condorcet, Marie Jean Antoine Nicolas de – 1778. Reprod. 66p. (Religion series) – 9 – 3.00 – fr Bibl Nationale [240]

REFLEXIONS D'UN CITOYEN SUR LA MARINE / Faure, Pierre-Joseph – [S.l.n.], 1759 – fr Armell [355]

REFLEXIONS D'UN CITOYEN SUR LA REVOLUTION DE 1788 / Condorcet, Marie Jean Antoine Nicolas de – Londres: s.n., 1788. 56p. 1 fiche. (Political Science Collection) – 9 – 6.00 – fr Bibl Nationale [323]

REFLEXIONS D'UN CULTIVATEUR AMERICAIN SUR LE PROJET D'ABOLIR L'ESCLAVAGE ET LA TRAITE DES NEGRES / Jacquemart, Nicolas-Francois – (Slave Trade and Abolitionism in France series). 1788 – 9 – fr Hachette [305]

REFLEXIONS IMPARTIALES SUR LES ELOGES DE VOLTAIRE QUI ONT CONCOURU POUR LE PRIX DE L'ACADEMIE FRANCAISE EN 1779, A FERNEY, ET SE TROUVE A PARIS, CHEZ VALLEYRE, 1780 / Laus de Boissy, L de – 9 – fr Hachette [440]

REFLEXIONS IMPARTIALES SUR L'EVANGILE / Mirabaud, Jean-Baptiste de – (D'Holbach series). 1769 – 9 – fr Hachette [220]

REFLEXIONS SUR LA CAUSE GENERALE DES VENTS / Alembert, Jean Le Rond d' – Piece qui a remporte le prix propose par l'Academie Royale des Science et Belles-Lettres de Prusse pour l'annee 1746. Paris, 1747, 194, 138, xxviii p., ii pl. Histoire des Sciences XVIIe-XIXe Siecles. 7971 – 9 – fr Hachette [510]

REFLEXIONS SUR LA DECADENCE DU THEATRE DE L'OPERA.. – 1798 – 9 – us Sibley [780]

REFLEXIONS SUR LA DOCTRINE DE SAINT-SIMON / Ozanam, Antoine F – (extrait de MELANGES, RELIGION, PHILOSOPHIE, POLITIQUE). Paris, Lecoffre, 1831, pp. 309-409. Les Saint-Simoniens, 1825-1834. 6985 – 9 – fr Hachette [335]

LES REFLEXIONS SUR LA POETIQUE D'ARISTOTE / Rapin, R – 1674 – 9 – fr I.C.S. [450]

REFLEXIONS SUR LA REPONSE DE M. L'ABBE DE LA TRAPPE / Mabillon, Jean – Paris. Tomes 1-2. 1693 – 6mf – 8 – Dfl25.00 – ne Slangenburg [240]

REFLEXIONS SUR LA RHETORIQUE / Gibert, B – 1705-7 – 9 – fr I.C.S. [400]

LES REFLEXIONS SUR L'AME PAR BAHYA BEN JOSEPH IBN PAKOUDA / ed by Broyde, I – 1896. BJ-33-40 1 – 9 – ne IDC [260]

REFLEXIONS SUR L'ANTIMACHIAVEL DE 1740 / Saint-Pierre, Charles Irenee Castel – Rotterdam: J. D. Beman, 1741 – 1 – us U.W. Library [321]

REFLEXIONS SUR LE FACTUM FAIT POUR MARIE BENOIST, DITE LA BUCAILLE – 9 – fr Hachette [360]

REFLEXIONS SUR LE GOUT MUSICAL EN FRANCE / Gail, Jean Francois – 1832 – 9 – us Sibley [780]

REFLEXIONS SUR LE MERVEILLEUX EPIQUE / Bitaube, Paul Jeremie – Reprod. d'un extrait des "Oeuvres completes," Paris: Dentu, 1804. v9, p461-87. 1 fiche. (Literature Collection) – 9 – 6.00 – fr Bibl Nationale [840]

REFLEXIONS SUR LE PREMIER AGE DE L'HOMME, SERVANT DE SUPPLEMENT AUX ELEMENTS ET PROGRES DE L'EDUCATION / Bonneval, Rene de – Paris: Prault, 1751 – 9 – fr Hachette [370]

REFLEXIONS SUR L'ELOGE DE M. DE VOLTAIRE PAR M. D'ALEMBERT / Joly de Saint-Vallier – Francfort. 1780 – 9 – fr Hachette [440]

REFLEXIONS SUR L'ENSEIGNEMENT DE L'ARCHITECTURE EN 1881 / Ruprich-Robert, V – Paris,Morel, 1882. Julien Guadet, L'ENSEIGNEMENT DE L'ARCHITECTURE, CONFERENCE...Paris, Ducher, 1882. 8 fol., 30p. (Architecture Series) – 9 – fr Hachette [720]

REFLEXIONS SUR LES AFFAIRES PUBLIQUES / Condorcet, Marie Jean Antoine Nicolas de – Reprod. d'une ed. s.l., s.n., 1789. 56p. 2 fiches. (Political Science Collection) – 9 – 6.00 – fr Bibl Nationale [323]

REFLEXIONS SUR LES DIFFERENDS DE LA RELIGION / Pellisson, P – Paris, 1686 – 7mf – 9 – CA-142/1 – ne IDC [240]

REFLEXIONS SUR LES LECONS DE MUSIQUE / Bemetzrieder, A – 1778 – 9 – us Sibley [780]

REFLEXIONS SUR LES PROJETS DE CAMPAGNE. / Frederick 2nd, King of Prussia – Tulingue: J.G. Gotta, 1808. 71p. LES PRINCIPES GENERAUX DE LA GUERRE. Berlin: R. Decker, 1856. xxiii/179p. pl. L'ESPRIT DU CHEVALIER FOLARD, TIRE DE SES COMMENTAIRES SUR L'HISTOIRE DE POLYBE... Leipzig. 1761. xvi/240p. pl. Strategy of War Series – 9 – fr Hachette [355]

REFLEXIONS SUR L'ETUDE SOCIOLOGIQUE DES CENTRES SEMI-URBAINS DE LA COTE D'IVOIRE / Soulez – (Africa series). 1967 – 9 – fr Hachette [305]

REFLEXIONS SUR L'USAGE PRESENT DE LA LANGUE FRANCOISE / Andry de Boisregard, N – 1689-93 – 9 – fr I.C.S. [440]

REFLEXOENS POLITICAS, TOCANTE A CONSTITUICAO DE NACAO JUDAICA / Pinto, Isaac de – Amsterdam. 1748. BJ-262-45 1 – 9 – ne IDC [956]

DIE REFORM – Bremen, mar 12-dec 24 1848 – 1r – 1 – Inquire at Mikrofilmarchiv for details – gw Misc Inst [943]

DIE REFORM : EIN COMMUNAL- UND BUERGERBLATT – Hamburg-Altona, Germany. 1848-20 Mar 1850 – 1r – 1 – gw Mikrofilm [072]

DIE REFORM : ORGAN DES ARBEITERBUNDES IN NEW YORK – New York, NY. 12 Mar-Dec 1853 – 1r – 1 – gw Mikrofilm [071]

REFORM – 1972-92 (complete) – Inquire – 1 – ATLA S0628 – us A.T.L.A. [073]

REFORM – (1980- 5,6,9) – 1976- – 1 – us UMI [073]

REFORM – Goeteborg, 1881-87 – 9 – sw Kungliga [072]

THE REFORM ADVOCATE – (Chicago). 1891-1942 – 1 – us A.J.P.C. [360]

REFORM GOVERNMENT IN ONTARIO: EIGHT YEARS' REVIEW: IN AN ADDRESS TO THE ELECTORS OF THE SOUTH RIDING OF OXFORD / Crooks, Adam – Toronto?: s.n., 1879 (Toronto: Hunter, Rose) 02132. (Pre-1900 Canadiana) – 9 – cn C.I.H.M. [971]

REFORM GOVERNMENT IN THE DOMINION: HON. EDWARD BLAKE BEFORE HIS CONSTITUENTS OF THE SOUTH RIDING OF BRUCE: SPEECH DELIVERED BY HIM AT TEESWATER, MONDAY, SEPT. 24TH, 1877 / Blake, Edward – Toronto: Globe Steam Book and Job Press, 1878. 02343. (Pre-1900 Canadiana) – 9 – cn C.I.H.M. [971]

REFORM IN THE EDUCATION OFFICE: A LETTER TO THE HON. OLIVER MOWAT.. / Adam, Graeme Mercer – Toronto: Adam, Stevenson, 1874. 00010. (Pre-1900 Canadiana) – 9 – cn C.I.H.M. [370]

THE REFORM MOVEMENT IN JUDAISM / Philipson, David – New York: Macmillan, 1907 – 2mf – us A.T.L.A. [270]

REFORM OF LOCAL GOVERNMENT STRUCTURES IN THE UNITED STATES – (With guidebook) – 1945-71 – 1177mf – 9 – $5.00f – us Ross [320]

THE REFORM PRESS – Dunnville, Ontario. v37 n28. 14 jul 1909 – 1r – 1 – Can$25.00 – cn Can Microfilming [072]

A REFORMA : ORGAO DO PARTIDO LIBERAL – Aracaju, 1 Jan 1887-29 Dec 1889 – 1,5,6 – bl Biblioteca [072]

A REFORMA – Villa Seabra, Acre. 12 Maio 1918-Set 1932; Nov 1932-Fev, Jun-Ago, Nov 1934 – 1,5,6 – bl Biblioteca [072]

REFORMA – Rio Branco, Acre. 1 Set 1916-5 Jan 1917 – 1,5,6 – bl Biblioteca [072]

REFORMA – Sao Joao del-Rei, Brazil. 1916; Jan, Mar, Jun-Aug, Oct, Dec 1917; 1918-19; Jan-Feb 1920 – 1 – bl Biblioteca [072]

REFORMA AGRARIA Y REFORMA POLITICA : LA SALIDA DE LA CRISIS ARGENTINA / Guido Pastorino, Juan – Buenos Aires: Ediciones Libera, [1971] – 1 – CSUXAHZ2852-B – us Hoover Inst Photo [320]

REFORMA BIBLIOTECHNAGO DELA. BIBLIOTECHNYIA KARTOCHKI PRI VNOV' VYKHODIASHCHIKH KNIGAKH / Kvaskov, Ia. G – M. 1893. BR-4649 2 – 8 – ne IDC [020]

LA REFORMA CONSTITUCIONAL / Borlenghi, Angel G – Buenos Aires: G. Kraft, 1948 – 1 – CSUXAHZ6007-B – us Hoover Inst Photo [340]

LA REFORMA CONSTITUCIONAL, SUS FUNDAMENTOS Y SU ESTRUCTURA / Ibarguren, Carlos – Buenos Aires: V. Abeledo, 1948 – 1 – CSUXADP3985-B – us Hoover Inst Photo [340]

LA REFORMA DE CACERES – Caceres, 1892. 1 numero – 5 – sp Bibl Santa Ana [073]

LA REFORMA DE CACERES – Caceres.1886, no. 48 – 9 – 1.50f – sp Bibl Santa Ana [072]

REFORMA DE LA CONSTITUCION ARGENTINA / ed by Accion Social Universitaria – Buenos Aires: Universidad de Buenos Aires, Accion Social, 1948 – 1 – CSUXADQ6561-B – us Hoover Inst Photo [340]

LA REFORMA DE LA CONSTITUCION NACIONAL : SANCIONADA POR LA CONVENCION NACIONAL CONSTITUYENTE, EL 11 DE MARZO DE 1949, EN LA CIUDAD DE BUENOS AIRES / Argentine Republic. Presidencia. Subsecretaria de Informaciones – Buenos Aires, 1950. 2v – 1 – CSUXADP4993-B – us Hoover Inst Photo [340]

A REFORMA LIBERAL : ORGAO DO PARTIDO LIBERAL DO AMAZONAS – Manaos, Amazonas. 18 Abr 1872; 14 Fev 1880 – 1,5,6 – bl Biblioteca [072]

LA REFORMA MEDICA... / Nieto y Serrano, M – Madrid, 1863 – 8mf – 9 – sp Cultura [610]

REFORMA POLITICA Y REFORMA AGRARIA *see* REFORMA AGRARIA Y REFORMA POLITICA

REFORMA (SAINT PETERSBURG, RUSSIA) – (Includes c.1: 1906:Apr.14, 19, 26-28, May 2, 4, 6, 25) – S.-Peterburg: I U.B. Bak, 1906- – 1 – CSUXANS2042-S – us Hoover Inst Photo [947]

REFORMA SUDEBNYKH USTAVOV V SVIAZI S SOVREMENNYM SOSTOIANIEM PRAVOSDIIA / Karabegov, A I – Saint Petersburg, 1889. 212p. Critique of the 1864 judicial reform in light of 25 years experience with recommendations for changes. BR-9720/1 – 9 – ne IDC [340]

LA REFORMA UNIVERSITARIA 1918-1988 / Argentina. Ministerio de Educacion y JusticiaUniversidad Nacional Cordoba – Buenos Aires, 1989 – 3mf – 9 – DE-655/1 – ne IDC [370]

REFORMA VOLOSTI / Dashkevich, Leonid Viacheslavovich – Moskva: Tip. Russkago t-va, 1912 – 1 – CSUX89-B1753 – us Hoover Inst Photo [947]

REFORMACJA W POLSCE – Warsaw. v1-10. 1921-39 – 1r – 1 – us Ross [943]

LAS REFORMAS Y LA SEGUNDA ENSENANZA / Soler Arques, Carlos – Madrid: Tip. de Manuel Gines Hernandez, 1891 – 9 – $1.50f – sp Bibl Santa Ana [946]

DIE REFORMATION : DEUTSCHE EVANGELISCHE KIRCHEN-ZEITUNG F.D. GEMEINDE – (Lacking: 18(1919)) – 1(1902)-19(1920) – 398mf – 9 – Dfl1,393.00 – ne Slangenburg [073]

DIE REFORMATION : DEUTSCHE EVANGELISCHE KIRCHENZEITUNG FUER DIE GEMEINDE – (Lacking: v22 1928) – v1-35. 1902-41 – 18r – 1 – ATLA S0065 – us A.T.L.A. [073]

THE REFORMATION / Fisher, George Park – New ed. New York: Charles Scribner's sons, 1900,1873. xxxiv,620p – 1 – us U.W. Library [240]

THE REFORMATION / Fisher, George Park – New York: Scribner, 1906 – 2mf – us A.T.L.A. [240]

THE REFORMATION / Walker, Williston – New York: Scribner, 1900 – 2mf – us A.T.L.A. [940]

REFORMATION AND RENAISSANCE : CIRCA 1377-1610 / Stone, Jean Mary – (Includes bibliographical references) – London: Duckworth, 1904 – 2mf – 9 – 0-8370-7024-4 – 1986-1024 – us A.T.L.A. [940]

REFORMATION DER APOTECKEN WELCHE INHALTET VIL QUTER STUCK DIE EYEN YEGLICHEN FA. / Brunfels, Otto – Strassburg? zu strass durch Wend. Kiel, 1536 – 1 – us U.W. Library [615]

DIE REFORMATION IM SPIEGELBILDE DER DRAMATISCHEN LITERATUR DES SECHZEHNTEN JAHRHUNDERTS / Holstein, Hugo – Halle: Verein fuer Reformationsgeschichte, 1886. (Schriften des Vereins fuer Reformationsgeschichte; 14/15) – 1mf – us A.T.L.A. [400]

REFORMATION IN CORNWALL: DOCUMENTS TOWARDS A HISTORY OF THE – 5 – uk Microform Academic [240]

THE REFORMATION IN ENGLAND 1: THE ENGLISH SCHISM HENRY 8TH (1509-1547). LONDON, 1934 / Constant, G – Madrid: Razon y Fe, 1935 – 1 – sp Bibl Santa Ana [320]

THE REFORMATION IN ENGLAND. THE ENGLISH SCHIM. HENRY 7TH 1509-1547. LONDON, 1934 / Constant, G – Madrid: Razon y Fe, 1935 – 1 – sp Bibl Santa Ana [320]

THE REFORMATION IN EUROPE : BY THE AUTHOR OF "THE COUNCIL OF TRENT" / Cramp, John Mockett – New York: American Tract Society, [1840?] – 1mf – us A.T.L.A. [940]

THE REFORMATION IN FRANCE FROM THE DAWN OF REFORM TO THE REVOCATION OF THE EDICT OF NANTES / Heath, Richard – London: Religious Tract Society, 1886. (The Church history series; 2) (The Reformation in France; 1) – 1mf – us A.T.L.A. [240]

THE REFORMATION IN FRANCE FROM THE REVOCATION OF THE EDICT OF NANTES TO THE INCORPORATION OF THE REFORMED CHURCHES INTO THE STATE / Heath, Richard – London: Religious Tract Society, 1888. (The Church history series; 3) (The Reformation in France; 2) – 1mf – us A.T.L.A. [240]

THE REFORMATION IN GERMANY / Vedder, Henry Clay – New York: Macmillan, 1914 – 2mf – us A.T.L.A. [943]

DIE REFORMATION IN KONSTANZ / Issel, Ernst – Freiburg i.B.: J.C.B. Mohr, 1898 – 1mf – us A.T.L.A. [240]

THE REFORMATION IN SCOTLAND : CAUSES, CHARACTERISTICS, CONSEQUENCES : THE STONE LECTURES AT PRINCETON THEOLOGICAL SEMINARY FOR 1907-1908 / Fleming, David Hay – London: Hodder and Stoughton, 1910 – 2mf – us A.T.L.A. [240]

THE REFORMATION IN SWEDEN : ITS RISE, PROGRESS, AND CRISIS, AND ITS TRIUMPH UNDER CHARLES 9 / Butler, Clement Moore – New York: A.D.F. Randolph, c1883 – 1mf – us A.T.L.A. [240]

THE REFORMATION IN SWEDEN; ITS RISE, PROGRESS, AND CRISIS; AND ITS TRIUMPH UNDER CHARLES IX / Butler, Clement Moore – New York: A.D.F. Randolph, (1883). 259p – 1 – us U.W. Library [240]

DIE REFORMATION IN TRIER 1559 UND IHRE UNTERDRUECKUNG / Ney, Julius – Halle a.d.S.: Verein fuer Reformationsgeschichte, 1906-1907. (Schriften des Vereins fuer Reformationsgeschichte; 23. Jahrg., Schrift 88/89; 25. Jahrg., Schrift 94) – 1mf – us A.T.L.A. [240]

REFORMATION KAISER SIEGMUNDS (MGH 10: 6.BD) – 1964 – Dfl39.00 – ne Slangenburg [240]

DIE REFORMATION LUEBECKS / Schreiber, Heinrich – Halle: Verein fuer Reformationsgeschichte, 1902. (Schriften des Vereins fuer Reformationsgeschichte; 20. Jahrg., Schrift 74) – 1mf – us A.T.L.A. [240]

A REFORMATION OF SCHOOLES / Comenius, Johann Amos – 1642. Samuel Hartlib, pub. 102p. (English Linguistics Series 1500-1800) – 9 – us UMI [400]

THE REFORMATION OF THE ECCLESIASTICAL LAWS : AS ATTEMPTED IN THE REIGNS OF KING HENRY 8, KING EDWARD 6, AND QUEEN ELIZABETH / Great Britain. Commissioners on Revision of the Ecclesiastical Laws – Oxford: University Press, 1850 – 1mf – us A.T.L.A. [340]

THE REFORMATION OF THE SIXTEENTH CENTURY IN ITS RELATION TO MODERN THOUGHT AND KNOWLEDGE : LECTURES DELIVERED AT OXFORD AND IN LONDON, IN APRIL, MAI AND JUNE, 1883 / Beard, Charles – London: Williams and Norgate, 1883. (The Hibbert lectures; 1883) – 2mf – us A.T.L.A. [240]

THE REFORMATION PERIOD / Gee, Henry – London: Methuen, 1909 (Handbooks of English church history; 4) – 1mf – us A.T.L.A. [240]

REFORMATION TODAY – Sussex, England.Cuckfield Baptist Church. 1972-78 – 1 – us A.B.H.S. [073]

DIE REFORMATION UND DAS NATURRECHT / Lang, August – Guetersloh: C. Bertelsmann, 1909 – 1mf – us A.T.L.A. [240]

DIE REFORMATION UND DIE AELTEREN REFORMPARTEIEN : IN IHREM ZUSAMMENHANGE / Keller, Ludwig – Leipzig: S. Hirzel, 1885 – 2mf – us A.T.L.A. [240]

DIE REFORMATION UND DIE EHE : EIN BEITRAG ZUR KULTURGESCHICHTE DES SECHZEHNTEN JAHRHUNDERTS / Kawerau, Waldemar – Halle: Verein fuer Reformationsgeschichte, 1892. ([Schriften des Vereins fuer Reformationsgeschichte; Bd. 39]) – 1mf – us A.T.L.A. [240]

REFORMATION UND GEGENREFORMATION / Hermelink, Heinrich – Tuebingen: J.C.B. Mohr, 1911 (Handbuch der Kirchengeschichte fuer Studierende; 3. T.) – 1mf – us A.T.L.A. [940]

REFORMATIONSGESCHICHTE NACH DEM AUTOGRAPHON HRSG. AUF VERANSTALTUNG DER VATERLANDISCH-HISTORISCHEN GESELLSCHAFT IN ZUERICH VON J. J. HOTTINGER UND H. H. VOEGELI / Bullinger, Heinrich – 3v. 1838-40. vWith Wuhrmann, Willy. Register; im Auftrag des Zwingli-Vereins in Zuerich – 1 – us A.T.L.A. [240]

REFORMATIONSGESCHICHTE VON LIPPSTADT : DER ERSTEN EVANGELISCHEN STADT IN WESTFALEN / Niemoeller, Heinrich – Halle a.d.S.: Verein fuer Reformationsgeschichte, 1906. (Schriften des Vereins fuer Reformationsgeschichte; 24. Jahrg., Schrift 91) – 1mf – us A.T.L.A. [240]

REFORMATIONSVERSUCHE IN DER BASLER BISCHOFSSTADT PRUNTRUT / Gauss, Karl – Leipzig: Verein fuer Reformationsgeschichte, 1913. (Schriften des Vereins fuer Reformationsgeschichte; Jahrg. 31, 2. Stueck, Nr. 114) – 1mf – us A.T.L.A. [240]

DIE REFORMATOREN BERNS IM 16. JAHRHUNDERT / Kuhn, G J – Bern: I.R. Walthard, 1828 – 2mf – us A.T.L.A. [240]

DIE REFORMATOREN UND DIE REFORMATION : IM ZUSAMMENHANGE MIT DEN DER EVANGELISCHEN KIRCHE DURCH DIE REFORMATION GESTELLTEN AUSGABEN / Schenkel, Daniel – Wiesbaden: Kreidel und Niedner, 1856 – 1mf – us A.T.L.A. [240]

REFORMATOREN VOR DER REFORMATION VORNEHMLICH IN DEUTSCHLAND UND DEN NIEDERLAENDEN / Ullmann, C – (1.Band: Johann Von Goch und Johann Von Wesel Gotha 1866 Dfl30.00. 2. Band: Johann Von Wesel..Nebst Den Bruedern Vom Gemeinsamen Leben Gotha, 1866 Dfl42.00) – ne Slangenburg [240]

REFORMATORN – Goeteborg, Stockholm. 1887-1965 – 9 – sw Kungliga [072]

THE REFORMATORY PILLAR – St. Cloud. Minn. v. 29-50. 1931-52. Scattered issues wanting – 1 – 141.00 – us L of C Photodup [360]

THE REFORMATORY PRESS – Penetanguishene, Ont.: G E Lloyd, [1889?-18– or 19–] – 9 – cn C.I.H.M. [360]

REFORMATUSOK LAPJA; ORSZAGOS REFORMATUS HETILAP – (Lacking: v1-10) – v11-36. 1967-92 – Inquire – 1 – ATLA S0164 – us A.T.L.A. [073]

LA REFORME / ed by Gagnon, Jean-Louis – Montreal, Canada. 30 mar 1955-dec 1966 – 4r – 1 – Can$65.00 – cn Can Microfilming [072]

LA REFORME – Quebec, Canada. 14 jun; 6 jul 1882 – 1r – 1 – Can$25.00 – cn Can Microfilming [072]

LA REFORME – Quebec, Canada. 9 jun 1860-v3 n109. 10 jul 1863 – 1r – 1 – Can$50.00 – cn Can Microfilming [072]

REFORME – Paris. Dir., Albert Finet. 24 mars 1945-1993 – 1 – fr A.C.R.P.P. [073]

LA REFORME DE L'ENSEIGNEMENT AU SIECLE DES LUMIERES – (Pedagogic Theory in 18th-Century France). Ed. by D. Julia. Complete collection. 66 titles on 163 microfiche – 9 – fr Hachette [370]

LA REFORME DE PARIS – Paris. 2 mai 1882-1er sept 1883 – 1 – fr A.C.R.P.P. [073]

LA REFORME DU BATIMENT – Journal des travaux publics et particuliers pour toute la France. Paris. 1907-fevr 1923 – 1 – fr A.C.R.P.P. [073]

LA REFORME ECONOMIQUE – Paris. v. 1-43. Mar 1892-Dec 1934 – 1 – us NY Public [338]

LA REFORME GREGORIENNE ET LA RECONQUETE CHRETIENNE, 1057-1123 (8) – Paris, 1940 – Dfl46.00 – ne Slangenburg [240]

LE REFORME INTELLECTUELLE DU CLERGE ET LA LIBERTE D'ENSEIGNEMENT / Saintyves, Pierre – Paris: E. Nourry, 1904 – 1mf – us A.T.L.A. [240]

LA REFORME JUDICIAIRE DE 1789 A 1794 D'APRES CAMILLE DESMOULINS ET LA LEGISLATION / Godart, Felix – Paris: Pedone, 1897. 118p. LL-4018 – 1 – us L of C Photodup [340]

LA REFORME MONETAIRE DE 1948 EN ALLEMAGNE OCCIDENTALE ET LE DROIT DES OBLIGATIONS / Pedamon, Michel – Paris: Librairie generale de droit et de jurisprudence, 1956. 311p. LL-4115 – 1 – us L of C Photodup [340]

THE REFORMED BREVIARY OF CARDINAL TOMMASI / Legg, J Wickham – London, 1904 – 2mf – 8 – Dfl9.00 – ne Slangenburg [240]

REFORMED BULLETIN OF MISSIONS – v1 no 1-v7 no 2. Mar 1965-Dec 1972 – 1r – 1 – ATLA S0754 – us A.T.L.A. [073]

REFORMED CHURCH IN AMERICA : THE BOOK OF CHURCH ORDER – 1975-93 – 1r – 1 – ATLA S0897 – us A.T.L.A. [073]

THE REFORMED CHURCH IN AMERICA : ITS ORIGIN, DEVELOPMENT AND CHARACTERISTICS / Demarest, David D – New York: Board of Publication of the Reformed Church in America, 1889. ([Publications / Theological Seminary of the Reformed Church in America]) – 1mf – us A.T.L.A. [240]

THE REFORMED CHURCH IN PENNSYLVANIA : PART 9 OF A NARRATIVE AND CRITICAL HISTORY, PREPARED AT THE REQUEST OF THE PENNSYLVANIA-GERMAN SOCIETY / Dubbs, Joseph Henry – Lancaster, Pa.: [s.n.], 1902 (Lancaster: New Era) – 1mf – us A.T.L.A. [240]

THE REFORMED CHURCH IN THE NETHERLANDS : TRACED FROM A.D. 1340 TO A.D. 1840, IN SHORT HISTORICAL SKETCHES / Hansen, Maurice G – New York: Board of Publication of the Reformed Church in America, 1884 – 1mf – us A.T.L.A. [240]

REFORMED CHURCH REVIEW – (Includes indexes: 1849-1911. 1912-26) – v1-73. 1849-1926 (complete) – 24r – 1 – ATLA S0078 – us A.T.L.A. [073]

Reformed Dissenting Presbytery *see* MINUTES

REFORMED JOURNAL – (1985- . 5,6,9) – v1-1951- – 1 – us UMI [073]

REFORMED JUDAISM AND ITS PIONEERS : A CONTRIBUTION TO ITS HISTORY / Schreiber, Emanuel – (Includes bibliographical references and indexes) – Spokane, WA: Spokane Printing, 1892 – 1mf – 9 – 0-8370-5149-5 – 1985-3149 – us A.T.L.A. [270]

REFORMED LITURGICS *see* REFORMED LITURGY AND MUSIC

REFORMED LITURGY AND MUSIC – (Cont: Reformed Liturgics) – v1-21 (complete) – 4r – 1 – ATLA S0751 – us A.T.L.A. [073]

REFORMED MISSIONARY – v1-7. 1870-76 (complete) – 1r – 1 – ATLA B0072 – us A.T.L.A. [073]

REFORMED MISSIONARY HERALD – v1-10. Aug 1880-90 (complete) – 1r – 1 – ATLA B0071 – us A.T.L.A. [073]

REFORMED, NOT RITUALISTIC, APOSTOLIC, NOT PATRISTIC : A REPLY TO DR. NEVIN'S "VINDICATION," &C / Bomberger, Johann H A – Philadelphia: Rodgers, 1867 – 1mf – us A.T.L.A. [240]

THE REFORMED PASTOR : OR, THE DUTY OF PERSONAL LABORS FOR THE SOULS OF MEN / Baxter, Richard – [rev ed]. New York: American Tract Society, [1850?] – 1mf – 9 – 0-8370-6160-1 – 1986-0160 – us A.T.L.A. [240]

THE REFORMED PRESBYTERIAN ADVOCATE – v1-10. 1867-87 (complete) – 4r – 1 – ATLA S0890 – us A.T.L.A. [073]

Reformed Presbyterian Church in North America. Presbytery *see* MINUTES, 1801-1809

REFORMED PRESBYTERIAN CHURCH OF IRELAND : SYNOD MINUTES – 1969-92 (complete) – Inquire – 1 – ATLA S0648 – us A.T.L.A. [240]

Reformed Presbytery of America *see* MINUTES

REFORMED PROTESTANTISM / ed by Buesser, F – (1: The Swiss Urban Reformation 3,350mf Dfl23,275.00; 2: The Reformation in Geneva Strasbourg and France 1,306mf Dfl8,080.00; 3: The Development of Reformed Protestantism in The Netherlands and Germany 2,532mf Dfl15,960.00) – 9 – ne IDC [240]

REFORMED PROTESTANTISM : SOURCES OF THE 16TH AND 17TH CENTURIES / ed by Balke, W et al – (Switzerland/Geneva 3,350mf Dfl 23,275.00. Strasbourg/France 1,306mf Dfl8,080.00. The Netherlands and Germany 2,552mf Dfl15,960.00. England/Scotland/America in preparation) – 4pts – 9 – ne IDC [240]

THE REFORMED-SCHOOL / Dury, John – 1651. 277p. (English Linguistics Series 1500-1800) – 9 – us UMI [420]

REFORMER – Springdale. Wash. 1908-1917 – 1 – us UMI [071]

THE REFORMER – 1897-1904 – 1 – uk Microform Academic [100]

THE REFORMER – Edinburgh. Scotland. -w. Aug 1868-Feb 1875. (6 reels) – 1 – uk British Libr Newspaper [072]

REFORMER OF PUBLIC ABUSES, AND RAILWAY AND MINING INTELLIGENCE *see* THE WEEKLY EXPOSITOR, OR, REFORMER OF PUBLIC ABUSES, AND RAILWAY AND MINING INTELLIGENCE

THE REFORMER REFORMED / Bangs, Nathan – 1818 – 9 – us A.T.L.A. [240]

THE REFORMER. (THE PHILANTHROPIST) – Birmingham, England. 16 Apr 1835-26 Apr 1838.-w. 1 reel – 1 – uk British Libr Newspaper [072]

THE REFORMERS : JAMES' CHURCH, PAISLEY, BY MINISTERS OF THE UNITED PRESBYTERIAN CHURCH / Joseph, Corbett – Glasgow: J. MacLehose, 1885 – 2mf – us A.T.L.A. [240]

THE REFORMERS AND THE THEOLOGY OF THE REFORMATION / Cunningham, William – Edinburgh: T & T Clark, 1862 – 2mf – 9 – 0-8370-8659-0 – 1986-2659 – us A.T.L.A. [240]

THE REFORMERS OF ENGLAND AND GERMANY IN THE SEXTEENTH CENTURY : THEIR INTERCOURSE AND CORRESPONDENCE: A HISTORICAL SKETCH AND ORIGINAL DOCUMENTS / Heppe, H – London: Hatchard; Edinburgh: Williams & Norgate, 1859 – 1mf – us A.T.L.A. [240]

REFORMIERTE KIRCHENZEITUNG – Erlangen, 1(1851)-3(1853) – 38mf – 9 – Dfl133.00 – ne Slangenburg [073]

REFORMIERTE KIRCHENZEITUNG – Erlangen etc. v1-3. 1851-1853 – 38mf – 9 – ne IDC [240]

REFORMIERTE KIRCHENZEITUNG : ORGAN DES REFORMIERTE BUNDES FUER DEUTSCHLAND – (Lacking: v76-83. 87-89) – v66-75. 1916-25; v84-86. 1934-36; v90-134. 1949-93 – 16r – 1 – ATLA S0057 – us A.T.L.A. [073]

REFORMIERTES KIRCHENBLATT – v43-64. 1969-90 (complete) – 3r – 1 – ATLA S0771 – us A.T.L.A. [073]

DIE REFORMIRTE KIRCHE GENF'S IM NEUNZEHNTEN JAHRHUNDERT : ODER, DER INDIVIDUALISMUS DER ERWECKUNG IN SEINEM VERHAELTNISS ZUM CHRISTLICHEN STAAT DER REFORMATION / Goltz, Hermann, Freiherr von der – Basel: H Georg, 1862 – 2mf – 9 – 0-8370-8817-8 – 1986-2817 – us A.T.L.A. [240]

REFORMISMO CONSERVADOR...ESPANA DE LA RESTAURACION / Montero Garcia, Feliciano – 1890 – 9 – 1.50f – sp Bibl Santa Ana [946]

REFORMISTAS ANTIGUOS ESPANOLES – v1-23. 1843-83 (complete) – 8r – 1 – ATLA S0069 – us A.T.L.A. [073]

DER REFORMKATHOLIZISMUS : FUER DIE GEBILDETEN ALLER BEKENNTNISSE / Mueller, Josef – 2. verm Aufl. Zuerich: Caesar Schmidt. 2v. 1899 – 2mf – 9 – 0-8370-8925-5 – 1986-2925 – us A.T.L.A. [240]

EIN REFORMVERSUCH INNERHALB DER KOPTISCHEN KIRCHE IM 12.JH. / Graf, G – Paderborn, 1923 – Dfl22.00 – ne Slangenburg [240]

REFRACTORIES – v1-35. 1960-94 – 1,5 – $80.00v – us UMI [530]

REFRACTORIES JOURNAL – 1958; 1961-63 – 1 – uk Microform Academic [620]

REFRANERO DEL MAR. MADRID, 1944 / Gella Iturriaga, Jose – Madrid: Razon y Fe, 1947 – 1 – sp Bibl Santa Ana [946]

IL REFRATTARIO – New York, NY, 1919 – 1mf or 1r – 1,9 – us I.H.R.C. [978]

REFRESHER COURSES IN ANESTHESIOLOGY – 1985- – 1,5,6,9 – us UMI [617]

REFRIGERATING ENGINEERING – v. 1-67. 1914-1959 – 1,5,6 – us Princeton Micro [660]

REFRIGERATION AND AIRCONDITIONING BUSINESS *see* AIRCONDITIONING AND REFRIGERATION BUSINESS

REFRIGERATION INDUSTRY *see* AIRCONDITIONING AND REFRIGERATION BUSINESS

LE REFUGE ITALIEN DE GENEVE : AUX XVIME ET XVIIME SIECLES / Galiffe, J BG – Geneve: H. Georg, 1881 – 1mf – us A.T.L.A. [240]

REFUGEE POLICY GROUP – Washington D.C. 70 docs. 1982-1991 – 45mf – 9 – ne IDC [320]

REFUGEE STUDIES PROGRAMME – Oxford. 79 docs. 1984-1991 – 73mf – 9 – ne IDC [320]

REFUGEES – Geneva. United Nations High Commissioner for Refugees. 1981-82 – 1 – us U.W. Library [073]

REFUGEES AND CIVILIAN RELIEF DURING WORLD WAR 2 PAMPHLET COLLECTION – 1939-1949 – 1 reel – 1 – CSUXANN1735-B – us Hoover Inst Photo [360]

REFUGEES AND CIVILIAN RELIEF IN BELGIUM DURING WORLD WAR 2 PAMPHLET COLLECTION – 1940-1945 – 1 reel – 1 – CSUXANN1757-B – us Hoover Inst Photo [360]

REFUGEES AND CIVILIAN RELIEF IN FRANCE AS A RESULT OF WOLRD WAR 2 PAMPHLET COLLECTION – 1941 – 1 – CSUXANN2491-B – us Hoover Inst Photo [360]

REFUGEES AND CIVILIAN RELIEF IN GERMANY AS A RESULT OF WORLD WAR 2 PAMPHLET COLLECTION – 1948-1956? – 1 reel – 1 – CSUXANN2495-B – us Hoover Inst Photo [360]

REFUGEES AND CIVILIAN RELIEF IN GREAT BRITAIN AS A RESULT OF WORLD WAR 2 PAMPHLET COLLECTION – 1940-1943 – 1 reel – 1 – CSUXANN2500-B – us Hoover Inst Photo [360]

REFUGEES AND CIVILIAN RELIEF IN ITALY AS A RESULT OF WORLD WAR 2 PAMPHLET COLLECTION – 1946? – 1 reel – 1 – CSUXANN2504-B – us Hoover Inst Photo [360]

REFUGEES AND CIVILIAN RELIEF IN SWITZERLAND DURING WORLD WAR 2 PAMPHLET COLLECTION – 1943-1946? – 1 reel – 1 – CSUXANN2508-B – us Hoover Inst Photo [360]

REFUGEES AND REPATRIATES FROM THE SOVIET UNION PAMPHLET COLLECTION – 1946-1956 – 1 reel – 1 – CSUXANR3682-B – us Hoover Inst Photo [320]

REFUGEES FROM WORLD WAR 2 PAMPHLET COLLECTION – 1944-1952? – 1 reel – 1 – CSUXANL3538-B – us Hoover Inst Photo [360]

THE REFUGEES IN CATALONIA / Ellis, Richard – London, 1937? Fiche W 856. (Blodgett Collection of Spanish Civil War Pamphlets) – 9 – us H.U. College Libr [946]

REFUGEES IN GREECE AFTER WORLD WAR 1 PAMPHLET COLLECTION – 1924 – 1 – CSUXANL2963-B – us Hoover Inst Photo [360]

LOS REFUGIADOS REPUBLICANOS ESPANOLES EN FRANCIA Y LA SOLIDARIDAD AMERICANA / Mije, Antonio – Mexico, 1940. Fiche W 1049. (Blodgett Collection of Spanish Civil War Pamphlets) – 9 – us H.U. College Libr [946]

REFUTATION DU SYSTEME DE LA RAVALIERE SUR LES ORIGINES DE LA LANGUE FRANCAISE. LEBER, [J.M.]C. COLLECTIONS DES MEILLEURES DISSERTATIONS, NOTICES ET TRAITES PARTICULIERS RELATIFS A L'HISTOIRE DE FRANCE / Rivet, D – Paris. v14(p244-255). 1838 – 1mf – 9 – ne IDC [440]

REFVTATIO INVECTIVAE BRVNI CONTRA CENTURIAS HISTORIAE ECCLESIASTICAE:... / Flacius Illyricus d.A E, M – Basileae, [1566] – 4mf – 9 – ne IDC [240]

REG, URB. WIDDERLEGUNG DER MUENSTERISCHEN NEWEN VALENTINIANER VND DONATISTEN BEKENTNUS, AN DIE CHRISTEN ZU OSNABRUCK, JNN WESTFALEN. MIT EINER VORRHEDE M. LUTHERS / Rhegius, Urbanus – Wittemberg. 1535; Zu Zell inn Saxen. 1534. BME-151 1 – 9 – ne IDC [240]

REGALA MANUSCRITOS DE ALCANTARA A LA REAL ACADEMIA DE LA HISTORIA / Solar y Taboada, Antonio – Madrid: Fortanet, 1919. B.R.A.H. 75, p. 94 – sp Bibl Santa Ana [946]

Regales Serna, Antonio *see* LA TRADUCCION AUTOMATICA

EL REGALO DE BODA / Tomas Navarro, Domingo – Cuadernos Alcantara Caceres, 1953 – 1 – sp Bibl Santa Ana [946]

REGALO DE BODAS / Vargas Zuniga, Rodrigo – Madrid: Imp. y Lit. A. de Angel. Alcoy, 1914 – 1 – sp Bibl Santa Ana [946]

Regamey, Felix *see* LE JAPON PRATIQUE

REGAN REPORT: HOSPITAL LAW FOR HOSPITAL COUNSEL – v.1-8. 1960-67. Continued by regan report on hospital law – 1 – us UMI [340]

REGAN REPORT ON HOSPITAL LAW – (v.21-. 1980- 5,6,9) – v.8-. 1967- – 1 – us UMI [340]

REGAN REPORT ON MEDICAL LAW – (v.13-. 1980- 5,6,9) – v.1-. 1968- – 1 – us UMI [610]

REGAN, ZACHARIAH, PAPERS, MS 4705 – (Land surveys, court records, deeds, contracts, and estate papers, primarily concerning Zachariah Regan's land holdings in Beaver County, PA) – Little Beaver Creek, Beaver, PA. 1808-28 – 1r – 1 – us Western Res [920]

LE REGARD / ed by Duguay, Camille – Drummondville, Canada. 7 avr-2 jun 1927 – 1r – 1 – Can$25.00 – cn Can Microfilming [072]

THE REGARD DUE TO THE VIRGIN MARY : WITH AN EXAMINATION OF THE NEW ROMAN DOGMA: TWO LECTURES / Gallagher, Mason – (Includes bibliographical references and index) – Oswego, NY: Winchester & Ferguson, 1855 – 1mf – 9 – 0-8370-8342-7 – 1986-2342 – us A.T.L.A. [240]

REGARDONS VIVRE UNE TRIBU MALGACHE, LES BETSIMISARAKA. / Cotte, Paul Vincent – nouvelle ed. Paris, [1947] – us Res Libr [306]

REGARDS – no. 1-2. Paris. janv-fevr 1932, fevr 1934-sept 1939 – 1 – fr A.C.R.P.P. [073]

REGARDS – Rouyn. v1 n2. 1 oct 1959-v18 n7-8. jul/aut 1978 – 2r – 1 – Can$65.00 – cn Can Microfilming [072]

REGARDS ET JEUX DANS L'ESPACE : JEUX; ENFANTS; ESQUISSES EN PLEIN AIR; DEUX PAYSAGES; DE GRIS EN PLUS NOIR; SANS TITRE; ACCOMPAGNEMENT / Saint-Denys-Garneau, Hector de – Montreal: Imprimerie Excelsior, 1937. SEM16P202 – 1r – 5 – Can$9.00 – cn Bibl Nat [840]

REGARDS SUR L'ACTUALITE – 1992-1995 – 10 times per yr – 9 – F1,600.00 – sz Infoprint [072]

REGARDS SUR L'ARRONDISSEMENT DE MASCARA / Algeria. Secretariat Social d'Oran – 1967. BNE-8741 1 – 9 – ne IDC [338]

REGARDS SUR L'ART DAHOMEEN / Brand, R – Yesufu Asogha modeleur dahomeen. Approche ethno-esthetique d'une societe – 9 – F70.00 – fr Ethnologie [960]

Rege, J E O *see* AFRICAN ANIMAL GENETIC RESOURCES

DEN REGEL DER VOLMAECTHEYT / Benedictus van Canfield, Ofmcap – Antwerpen, 1623. Den Tweeden Druck – 6mf – 8 – ne Slangenburg [290]

Regel, E A von *see*
- ALLIORUM ADHUC COGNITORUM MONOGRAPHIA
- CATALOGUS PLANTARUM IN HORTO AKSAKOVIANO...
- FLORA TURKESTANICA ELABORATA EX PLANTIS
- TENTAMEN ROSARUM MONOGRAPHIAE

O REGENERADOR : ORGAO LIBERAL – Maceio, Alagoas. 26 Jul, 11 Out 1881 – 1,5,6 – bl Biblioteca [072]

REGENERATION / Anderson, William – [2nd ed]. London: Hodder & Stoughton, 1875 – 1mf – 9 – 0-8370-2500-1 – 1985-0500 – us A.T.L.A. [240]

REGENERATION / Boardman, George Nye – New York: Fleming H Revell, [1891] – 1mf – 9 – 0-8370-2288-6 – 1985-0288 – us A.T.L.A. [210]

REGENERATION : ITS CONDITIONS AND METHODS / Craig, Robert – London: Hamilton, Adams, 1879 – 1mf – 9 – 0-8370-3247-4 – 1985-1247 – us A.T.L.A. [210]

REGENERATION / Sears, Edmund Hamilton – (Includes bibliographical references) – Boston: Crosby, Nichols, 1853 – 1mf – 9 – 0-8370-5145-2 – 1985-3145 – us A.T.L.A. [210]

LA REGENERATION DES BRAS DE SEPIA OFFICINALIS L. (MOLLUSQUE, CEPHALOPODE, COLEOIDE) / Feral, J P – 9 – F60.00 – fr Ethnologie [590]

REGENERATION OR GUIDE TO HAPPINESS – London, UK. 1832. -irr. 1 foot – 1 – uk British Libr Newspaper [072]

REGENERATION STATED AND EXPLAINED ACCORDING TO SCRIPTURE AND ANTIQUITY;... / Waterland, D – London, 1740 – 1mf – 9 – MP-281/1 – ne IDC [240]

DER REGENMACHER VON TURKESTAN : ROMAN / Stratz, Heinz – Dresden: Zwinger-Verlag, c1938 – 1r – 1 – us U.W. Library [830]

REGENSBURGER ANZEIGER – Regensburg, 1918-21 – 11r – 1 – DM880.00 – gw Mikro Press [072]

REGENSBURGER ANZEIGER – Regensburg, Germany. 1918-1921 – 11r – 1 – gw Mikrofilm [072]

REGENSBURGER POST – (Cont by: Mittelbayerische Zeitung, Regensburg) – Regensburg, West Germany. Herausgegeben fuer die deutsche Zivilbevoelkerung von den 12. Amerikanischen Heeresgruppe. 29 Jun-13 Nov 1945 – 1 – gw Mikrofilm [072]

REGENSBURGER POST : FUER DIE DEUTSCHE ZIVILBEVOELKERUNG VON DER 12. AMERIKANISCHEN HEERESGRUPPE – Germany, Jun-Nov 1945 – 1r – 1 – DM75.00 – gw Mikro Press [072]

REGENSBURGER TAGEBLATT – Regensburg, Germany. 1848-1849 – 2r – 1 – gw Mikrofilm [072]

REGENSBURGER UMSCHAU / ed by Mittelbayerischen Zeitung, Regensburg – Regensburg, West Germany. Jul 1952-2 Oct 1962 – 1 – gw Mikrofilm [072]

DIE REGENSBURGER ZEITUNG – Regensburg, Germany. 1848-1849 – 3r – 1 – gw Mikrofilm [072]

REGENT UNIVERSITY LAW REVIEW – v1-6. 1991-95 – 9 – $61.00 set – us Hein [340]

DE REGENTENPOSITIE / Soeria Nata Atmadja, R A A A – Bandoeng, 1940 – 5mf – 9 – SE-1285/1 – ne IDC [950]

Regent's Park College *see* MATERIALS ON THE EARLY EDUCATIONAL LIFE OF THE ENGLISH BAPTISTS

Regent's Park College. Angus Library *see* CATALOG

Regenvolscius, A *see* SYSTEMA HISTORICO-CHRONOLOGICUM ECCLESIARUM SLAVONICARUM

REGESTA PONTIFICUM ROMANORUM / Kehr, PF – v. 1-8. Berlin. 1909-25. B-149 2 – 8 – ne IDC [240]

REGESTA PONTIFICUM ROMANORUM AB CONDITA ECCLESIA AD ANNUM 1198 / ed by Jaffe, Ph – Ed 2. Lipsiae. Tom 1-2. 1885-1888 – Dfl196.00 – ne Slangenburg [240]
DIE REGESTEN ODER DIE CHRONOLOGISCHEN VERZEICHNISSE DER URKUNDEN IN DEN ARCHIVEN ZU IGLAU, TREBITSCH... : SAMMT DEN NOCH UNGEDRUCKTEN BRIEFEN KAISER FERDINAND DES ZWEITEN,... / ed by Chlumecky, P von – Bruenn, 1856 – 7mf – 9 – ne IDC [943]
Regie Nationale de Chemins de Fer du Cameroun *see* LES CHEMINS DE FER DU CAMEROUN
LE REGIME DE L'ASSURANCE-MALADIE AU LIBAN / Lebanon. Centre Beryte de Recherches Orientalis – 2pts. Beirut. 1971. BNE-19.700 1 – 9 – ne IDC [360]
IL REGIME DEGLI STRETTI / Ambrosini, G – Roma, 1936 – 1mf – 9 – ILM-2334/1 – ne IDC [340]
LE REGIME DES BANQUES ETRANGERES DANS LES PRINCIPALES LEGISLATIONS / Barazzetti, P – Paris, 1923 – 1mf – 9 – ILM-3295/1 – ne IDC [340]
LE REGIME DOTAL... / Depinay, J – Paris, 1902 – 7mf – 1 – ILM-3181/1 – ne IDC [327]
LE REGIME DU TRAVAIL AU CONGO BELGE / Heyse, Theodore – 2e ed. Bruxelles: Goemaere, 1924. 248p. LL-12003 – 1 – us L of C Photodup [340]
LE REGIME DU TRAVAIL AU CONGO BELGE. / Heyse, Theodore – 2nd ed. Brussels. 1924 – 1 – us Res Libr [960]
IL REGIME FASCISTA – Cremona. Italy. -d. 2 Apr-4 Jun 1940, 26 Jan 1941-25 Jul 1943, 2 Jan-24 Apr 1945. (Imperfect). (9 reels) – 1 – uk British Libr Newspaper [072]
IL REGIME FASCISTA – Cremona, Italy: [s.n., 1940] – 1r – 1 – us Res Libr [072]
LA REGIME FINANCIER DU GOUVERNEMENT MERCIER: EXPOSE PAR UN CULTIVATEUR / Jean-Louis – Montreal, 1892. 03195. (Pre-1900 Canadiana) – 9 – cn C.I.H.M. [971]
LE REGIME FISCAL DES SOCIETES ETRANGERES EN FRANCE / Duchenois, J – Paris, 1920 – 2mf – 1 – ILM-3292/1 – ne IDC [327]
LE REGIME FISCAL DES VALEURS MOBILIERES... / Guilhot, J – Paris, 1925 – 2mf – 1 – ILM-3257/1 – ne IDC [327]
LE REGIME INTERNATIONAL DE L'ESCAUT / Adanya, S – Paris, 1929 – 2mf – 9 – ILM-1840/1 – ne IDC [340]
THE REGIME OF...DANUBE AND RHINE / Chamberlain, J P – New York, 1923 – 4mf – 1 – ILM-1879/1 – ne IDC [327]
LE REGIME POLITIQUE BRITANNIQUE / Mathiot, A – F70.00 – fr Ethnologie [320]
REGIMEN / Salerno – M 403. 1634 – 9 – ne IDC [610]
REGIMEN DE RECIPROCIDADE... / Flores, L L – Lisboa, 1901 – 2mf – 1 – ILM-3737/1 – ne IDC [327]
REGIMEN JURIDICO DE LAS SOCIEDAS ANONIMAS EXTRANJERAS... / Alta Comision Interamericana – Washington, 1928 – 2mf – 9 – ILM-3808/1 – ne IDC [340]
EL REGIMEN OBLIGATORIO ESPANOL DE SUBSIDIOS FAMILIARES / Leal Ramos, Leon – Bilbao: Imp. Nacional, 1938 – sp Bibl Santa Ana [946]
EL REGIMEN OBLIGATORIO ESPANOL DE SUBSIDIOS FAMILIARES / Leal Ramos, Leon – Madrid: Editorial Vizcaino, 1938 – 1 – sp Bibl Santa Ana [946]
EL REGIMEN PERONISTA, 1946-1955 / Barco, Ricardo del. – Buenos Aires: Belgrano, 1983 – 1 – CSUXADQ7064-B – us Hoover Inst Photo [320]
REGIMEN SANITATIS SALERNI / Salerno – M 404. 1604 – 9 – ne IDC [610]
REGIMENT OF HEALTH / Salerno – M 402. 1575 – 9 – ne IDC [610]
THE REGIMENT OF LIFE / Goeurot, J – M359. 1567 – 9 – ne IDC [999]
REGIMENT REICHSTAG : THE FIGHT FOR BERLIN, JANUARY, 1919 / Lamprecht, Kurt – London: Constable, 1932 – 1r – 1 – us U.W. Library [943]
REGIMENTAL HISTORIES OF THE AMERICAN CIVIL WAR – (Records filmed at U.S. Army Military History Institute, Carlisle Barracks, Pennsylvania. Works and materials previously unpublished or published before 1915. To include 3500 titles) – 9 – us UMI [976]
REGIMENTAL PAPERS, MS 2152 – 1861-64 – 1r – 1 – us Western Res [976]
REGIMENTS IN ITALY DURING WORLD WAR 1 PAMPHLET COLLECTION – 1970 – 1 – CSUXANL2758-B – us Hoover Inst Photo [355]
REGIMENTSTAG / Grabenhorst, Georg – Muenchen: A Langen/ G Mueller, 1937 – 1r – 1 – us U.W. Library [430]
REGIMIENTO CONTRA LA PESTE / Alvarez, Francois – S.L., S.A. ca 1501 – 1mf – 9 – sp Cultura [946]
REGIMIENTO DE SANIDAD DE TODAS LAS COSAS QUE SE COMEN Y BEVEN, CON MUCHOS CONSEJOS / Florez, F – Sevilla, 1541 – 3mf – 9 – sp Cultura [610]
THE REGINA DAILY POST – Regina, Canada. v2 n301. 22 dec 1917-v4 n295. 20 dec 1918 – 1r – 1 – Can$30.00 – cn Can Microfilming [072]
REGINA LEADER – Canada. The Leader. -w. Oct 1886-Sept 1907. Lacking Jan 1893-Nov 1906. 4 reels – 1 – uk British Libr Newspaper [072]
REGINA SEBALDI / Kratzmann, Ernst – Wien: W Frick, c1940 – 1r – 1 – us U.W. Library [830]
REGINA STANDARD – Regina, Canada. 1891-1906 – 13r – 1 – $845.00 – cn Library Assoc [971]
REGINA VS JOHANNES MONYAKI AND OTHERS : [TRIAL RECORD] IN THE COURT OF THE MAGISTRATE FOR THE REGIONAL DIVISION OF THE SOUTH TRANSVAAL – (Filmed with: South Africa. Commission of Enquiry to Enquire into the Events in the Districts of Vereeniging...[Minutes of evidence...1960]) – Vereeniging, 1960-61 – us Res Libr [340]
REGINA VS ROBERT SOBUKWE AND OTHERS – Johannesburg: Microfile, [19–?] – us Res Libr [340]
REGINALD HETHEREGE / Kingsley, Henry – British Fiction Archive: Unit 2 – 9 – uk Bell [830]
REGINALD POLE, CARDINAL ARCHBISHOP OF CANTERBURY / Lee, Frederick George – AN HISTORICAL SKETCH.... 1888 – 1 – us A.T.L.A. [240]
REGINONIS ABBATIS PRUMIENSIS CHRONICON CUM CONTINUATIONE TREVERENSI (MGH 7: 50.BD) – 1890 – Dfl19.00 – ne Slangenburg [240]
Regio, I S *see* BIKKUREI HA-ITTIM HA-HADASHIM
LA REGION – Plasencia, 1914-1915 – 5 – sp Bibl Santa Ana [073]
LA REGION DU LAC SAINT-JEAN: GRENIER DE LA PROVINCE DE QUEBEC: GUIDE DES COLONS / Buies, Arthur – Quebec?: Cie. du chemin de fer de Quebec, 1890. 00356. (Pre-1900 Canadiana) – 9 – cn C.I.H.M. [971]
LA REGION EXTREMENA – Badajoz, 1892-1903 – 5 – sp Bibl Santa Ana [073]
LA REGION EXTREMENA – Badajoz, 1895 y 1904-1917 – 5 – sp Bibl Santa Ana [073]
EL REGIONAL – Plasencia, 1952-1979 – 5 – sp Bibl Santa Ana [073]
LE REGIONAL – Bromont & Granby, 8 nov 1977-31 dec 1991 – 16r – 1 – Can$70.00 – cn Can Microfilming [072]
LE REGIONAL – Farmham, Canada. v1 n24. 18-23 mar 1968 – 1r – 1 – Can$25.00 – cn Can Microfilming [072]
LE REGIONAL – (Filmed with: Le Progres Regional 17 sep 1970-19 mar 1975) – Chicoutimi, Canada. v1 n3. 23 nov 1934 – 10r – 1 – Can$75.00r – cn Can Microfilming [072]
O REGIONAL – Curvello, 3 Jul-30 Oct 1971 – 1,5,6 – bl Biblioteca [072]
O REGIONAL : ORGAO LITTERARIO DA COMPANHIA REGIONAL – Villa Seabra, Acre. 12 Jun-15 Nov 1917 – 1,5,6 – bl Biblioteca [072]
REGIONAL – Plasencia, 1907-1914 – 5 – sp Bibl Santa Ana [073]
REGIONAL ANESTHESIA – (v.5-. 1980$ 5,6,9) – v.1-. 1976- – 1 – us UMI [617]
REGIONAL COMPENDIUM OF FISHERIES LEGISLATION (INDIAN OCEAN REGION), VOL 1 : PROVISIONAL ED. – 1987 – 508p – it F.A.O. [340]
REGIONAL COMPENDIUM OF FISHERIES LEGISLATION (INDIAN OCEAN REGION), VOL 2 : PROVISIONAL ED. – 1987 – 549p – it F.A.O. [340]
REGIONAL COMPENDIUM OF FISHERIES LEGISLATION (WESTERN PACIFIC REGION) – 1984 – 2v 981p – it F.A.O. [340]
REGIONAL DECENTRALIZATION FOR AGRICULTURAL DEVELOPMENT PLANNING IN THE NEAR EAST AND NORTH AFRICA – 1988 – 80p – it F.A.O. [630]
REGIONAL DEVELOPMENT PROJECTS / Philippines. National Economic and Development Authority – Supplement to the Four-Year Development Plan FY 1974-1977. Manila. 1973. BD-2018 1 – 9 – ne IDC [338]
REGIONAL HISTORY : BEGINNING OF COLONIAL PERIOD TO PRESENT – California & the Southwest – 5r – 1 – us Ross [978]
REGIONAL HISTORY : BEGINNING OF COLONIZATION TO PRESENT – New England – 4r – 1 – us Ross [978]
REGIONAL HOUSING CENTRE, BANDUNG, DIRECTORY OF BUILDING RESEARCH AND DEVELOPMENT ORGANIZATIONS IN ECAFE-REGION / United Nations. Economic Commission for Asia and the Far East – SE 6112 1. 1963 – 9 – ne IDC [360]
LE REGIONAL – L'ETINCELLE – Richmond, Canada. 4 dec 1973 – 1r – 1 – Can$25.00 – cn Can Microfilming [072]
REGIONAL SCIENCE AND URBAN ECONOMICS – v1-14. 1971-84 – 1,5,6,13 – sz Elsevier [330]
REGIONAL STATISTICAL HANDBOOKS IN THE USSR : 1. SIBERIA – 47 titles – 9 – ne IDC [304]
REGIONAL STUDIES – (1981-. 1,5,6,9) – v1-. 1967- – 1 – us UMI [073]
REGIONAL STUDIES – 27v – 9 – £206.00 – 0034-3404 – uk Carfax [910]
REGIONAL STUDY ON RAINFED AGRICULTURE AND AGRO-CLIMATIC INVENTORY OF 11 COUNTRIES IN THE NEAR EAST REGION – 1982 – 74p – it F.A.O. [631]
REGIONAL SURVEY OF THE AQUACULTURE SECTOR IN AFRICA SOUTH OF THE SAHARA – 1989 – 66p – it F.A.O. [338]
REGIONAL SURVEY OF THE AQUACULTURE SECTOR IN EAST ASIA – 1989 – 79p – it F.A.O. [338]
REGIONAL SURVEY OF THE AQUACULTURE SECTOR IN ELEVEN MIDDLE EAST COUNTRIES – 1988 – 56p – it F.A.O. [338]
REGIONAL SURVEY OF THE AQUACULTURE SECTOR IN LATIN AMERICA – 1989 – 86p – it F.A.O. [338]
REGIONAL SURVEY OF THE AQUACULTURE SECTOR IN THE CARIBBEAN – it F.A.O. [338]
REGIONAL SURVEY OF THE AQUACULTURE SECTOR IN THE EASTERN AND NORTHWESTERN EUROPE – 1990 – 59p – it F.A.O. [338]
REGIONAL SURVEY OF THE AQUACULTURE SECTOR IN THE MEDITERRANEAN – 1989 – 78p – it F.A.O. [338]
REGIONAL SURVEY OF THE AQUACULTURE SECTOR IN THE PACIFIC – 1989 – 52p – it F.A.O. [338]
REGIONAL SURVEY OF THE AQUACULTURE SECTOR IN WEST ASIA – 1989 – 68p – it F.A.O. [338]
REGIONAL TRAINING COURSE IN AGRICULTURAL PROJECT ANALYSIS, NEW DELHI, 1970 – 1975 – 79p – it F.A.O. [370]
REGIONALISM IN EUROPE PAMPHLET COLLECTION – 1974 – 1 – CSUXANP1985-B – us Hoover Inst Photo [940]
REGIONALISMO : PROBLEMAS DE LA PROVINCIA DE CACERES / Cordero, Juan Luis – Barcelona: Tipografia Maucci, 1917 – 1 – sp Bibl Santa Ana [320]
O REGIONALISTA – Tres Coracoes, 22 Dec 1923 – 1,5,6 – bl Biblioteca [072]
Regis, P S *see* COURS ENTIER DE PHILOSOPHIE, OU SYSTEME GENERAL SELON LES PRINCIPES DE M. DESCARTES
Regismanset, Charles *see*
– L'EXOTISME
– QUESTIONS COLONIALES
REGISTER / Berkeley County. South Carolina. St. Stephen's and St. John's Parishes – 1819-84.1 fiche – 9 – us South Carolina Historical [978]
REGISTER – Chappell. Neb. 1892-1957 – 1 – us UMI [071]
REGISTER / Charleston. South Carolina. Holy Communion (Episcopal) Church – 1849-1913. 5 fiches – 9 – us South Carolina Historical [978]
REGISTER / Charleston. South Carolina. Trinity Methodist Church – 1791-1804. 2 fiches – 9 – us South Carolina Historical [978]
REGISTER – Columbia. S.C. 1875-1887 – 1 – us UMI [071]
REGISTER : COMMUNITY EDITION – Santa Ana, CA. 1943-70; 1984 – 415r – 1 CR02935 – $20,750.00 – us Library Micro [071]
REGISTER – Crown Point. Ind. -w. 1863-1904, 1908-33, 1935- – 1 – us UMI [071]
REGISTER – Danville. Va. 1905- – 1 – us UMI [071]
REGISTER – Des Moines. Iowa. 1871- – 1 – us UMI [071]
REGISTER – Gainesville. Tex. 1915- – 1 – us UMI [071]
REGISTER – Great Bend. KS.1876-1908 – 1 – us UMI [071]
REGISTER – Harrisburg. Ill. 1939- – 1 – us UMI [071]
REGISTER – Indianapolis. Ind. 1875-1884; 1908-1912 – 1 – us UMI [071]
REGISTER – Iola. Kan. 1868- – 1 – us UMI [071]
REGISTER – Iola. Kan. -w. 1875-97 – 1 – us UMI [071]
REGISTER – Keokuk. Iowa. -d. 1847-48 – 1 – us UMI [071]
REGISTER / McPhersonville. South Carolina.Prince William (Episcopal) Parish Church – 1825-76, 1907-32. 2 fiches – 9 – us South Carolina Historical [978]
REGISTER – Napa. Calif. 1883-1888; 1952- – 1 – us UMI [071]
REGISTER – Nehawka. Neb. 1892-1909 – 1 – us UMI [071]
REGISTER – Oconto. Neb. 1908-1920 – 1 – us UMI [071]
REGISTER – Oelwein. Iowa. 1906-1957; 1960- – 1 – us UMI [071]
REGISTER – Oelwein. Iowa. -w. 1881-1917 – 1 – us UMI [071]
REGISTER – Oil City. Pa. 1864-71 – 1 – us UMI [071]
REGISTER – Olathe. Kan. 1898-1928 – 1 – us UMI [071]
REGISTER / Orangeburg. South Carolina. Church of the Redeemer (Episcopal) – 1739-1885. Births and Baptisms, 1739-84; Banns and Marriages, 1740-81; Deaths and Burials, 1744-1885; Confirmations, 1848-82. 4 fiches – 9 – us South Carolina Historical [978]
REGISTER – Orland, CA. 1913-14; 1930-34; 1937-53; 1960-61 – 28r – 1 – $1,400.00 – B02563 – us Library Micro [071]
REGISTER – Oswego. Kan. -w. 1870-74 – 1 – us UMI [071]
REGISTER – Oxford. Kan. 1912-32 – 1 – us UMI [071]
REGISTER / Parker, Matthew – 1 – uk Microform Academic [240]
REGISTER – Point Pleasant. West Virginia. 1862-1923; 1936-1968 – 1 – us UMI [071]
REGISTER – Red Bank. N.J. 1878- – 1 – us UMI [071]
REGISTER – Red Bank. N.J. -w. 1880-1958 – 1 – us UMI [071]
REGISTER – Richmond. Ky. 1958- – 1 – us UMI [071]
REGISTER – Roseville. Calif. 1908-1910 – 1 – us UMI [071]
REGISTER – Sandusky. Ohio. 1957- – 1 – us UMI [071]
REGISTER – Sandusky. Ohio. -w. 1866-1913 – 1 – us UMI [071]
REGISTER – Sheperdstown. West Virginia. 1850-1955 – 1 – us UMI [071]
REGISTER / Summerton. South Carolina. St. Matthias Episcopal Church – 1899-1957. 2 fiches – 9 – us South Carolina Historical [978]
REGISTER – Torrington. Conn. 1914- – 1 – us UMI [071]
REGISTER – Torrington. Conn. -w. 1881-1922 – 1 – us UMI [071]
REGISTER – Valley Falls. Kan. -w. 1881-91 – 1 – us UMI [071]
REGISTER / Van Wert County. Ohio. County Home – 1867-1874 – 1r – 1 – $32.50r – us Archival [324]
REGISTER – Vancouver. Wash. -w. 1865-69 – 1 – us UMI [071]
REGISTER – Washington. Kan. 1881-1895 – 1 – us UMI [071]
REGISTER – Wheeling. West Virginia. 1913-1942 – 1 – us UMI [071]
REGISTER – Whittier. Calif. -w. 1901-02 – 1 – us UMI [071]
REGISTER – Wilbur. Wash. -w. 1889-1920 – 1 – us UMI [071]

REGISTER / Winyaw. South Carolina. Prince George Episcopal Church – 1813-1916. 14 fiches – 9 – us South Carolina Historical [978]

REGISTER / Wood County. Ohio. County Home – 1900-1956 – 1r – 1 – $32.50r – us Archival [324]

REGISTER / Wuerttemberg. Landstande. Kammer der Abgeordneten – Stuttgart. 1855-1918. 1 reel – 1 – 23.00r – us L of C Photodup [943]

REGISTER – Youngstown. Ohio. and Tribune. 1875-80 – 1 – us UMI [071]

THE REGISTER – Helena. Mont. (Western Ed.). 1958-59, 1967 – 1 – us UMI [071]

THE REGISTER – Nevada, NV. 1942 – 1r – 1 – $50.00 – U04872 – us Library Micro [071]

THE REGISTER – Sioux City. Iowa. 1859-1924 – 1 – us UMI [071]

REGISTER, 1294-1313 / Winchelsey, Robert – 1 – uk Microform Academic [240]

REGISTER EN BLADWIJZER OP DE VERHANDELINGEN – Leyden: D. Noothoven van Goor, 1862. 1 fiche – 9 – us A.T.L.A. [240]

DAS REGISTER GREGORS 7 (MGH EPISTOLAE 4: 2.BD. 1.TEIL) : BUCH 1-4 – 1920 – Dfl28.00 – ne Slangenburg [240]

DAS REGISTER GREGORS 7 (MGH EPISTOLAE 4: 2.BD. 2.TEIL) : BUCH 5-9 – 1923 – Dfl28.00 – ne Slangenburg [240]

REGISTER; IM AUFTRAG DES ZWINGLI-VEREINS IN ZUERICH / Wuhrmann, Willy – 1913. With: Bullinger, Heinrich. Reformationsgeschichte. q.v – 1 – us A.T.L.A. [240]

REGISTER OF ARMY LAND WARRANTS ISSUED UNDER THE ACT OF 1788, FOR SERVICE IN THE REVOLUTIONARY WAR: MILITARY DISTRICT OF OHIO / U.S. Bureau of Land Management – 1 roll. T1008 – 1 – us Nat'l Archives [324]

REGISTER OF AUDITS OF "MISCELLANEOUS TREASURY ACCOUNTS" / U.S. Treasury Department. First Auditor's Office – 1roll – 1 – T899 – us Nat'l Archives [336]

REGISTER OF BRITISH SHIPS : APPROPRIATION BOOK FOR OFFICIAL NUMBERS, PORT ADELAIDE, 1855-1982 / Collector of Customs, Adelaide – 1 reel 31486-396607 – 1 – CRS A7510 – at Archives [920]

REGISTER OF BRITISH SHIPS : APPROPRIATION BOOK FOR OFFICIAL NUMBERS, PORT KEMBLA, 1955-1981 / Sub-Collector of Customs, Port Kembla – 1 reel 199281-199189 – 1 – CRS A7578 – at Archives [920]

REGISTER OF BRITISH SHIPS : APPROPRIATION BOOK FOR OFFICIAL NUMBERS, PORT MELBOURNE, 1978-1982 / Collector of Customs, Melbourne – 1 reel 177214-496465 – 1 – CRS A7556 – at Archives [920]

REGISTER OF BRITISH SHIPS : APPROPRIATION BOOK FOR OFFICIAL NUMBERS, PORT OF BRISBANE, 1855-1982 / Collector of Customs, Brisbane – 1 reel 32666-396535 – 1 – CRS A7533 – at Archives [920]

REGISTER OF BRITISH SHIPS : APPROPRIATION BOOK FOR OFFICIAL NUMBERS, PORT OF BURNIE, 1974-1980 / Sub-Collector of Customs, Burnie – 1 reel 355171-385506 – 1 – CRS A7557 – at Archives [920]

REGISTER OF BRITISH SHIPS : APPROPRIATION BOOK FOR OFFICIAL NUMBERS, PORT OF DARWIN, 1968-1982 / Collector of Customs, Darwin – 1 reel 332746-396467 – 1 – CRS A7547 – at Archives [920]

REGISTER OF BRITISH SHIPS : APPROPRIATION BOOK FOR OFFICIAL NUMBERS, PORT OF DEVONPORT, 1968-1981 / Sub-Collector of Customs, Devonport – 1 reel 332421-332426 – 1 – CRS A7559 – at Archives [920]

REGISTER OF BRITISH SHIPS : APPROPRIATION BOOK FOR OFFICIAL NUMBERS, PORT OF FREMANTLE, 1856-1982 / Collector of Customs, Western Australia – 1 reel 40466-396435 – 1 – CRS A7500 – at Archives [920]

REGISTER OF BRITISH SHIPS : APPROPRIATION BOOK FOR OFFICIAL NUMBERS, PORT OF GLADSTONE, 1968-1981 / Sub-Collector of Customs, Gladstone – 1 reel 332401-375221 – 1 – CRS A7520 – at Archives [920]

REGISTER OF BRITISH SHIPS : APPROPRIATION BOOK FOR OFFICIAL NUMBERS, PORT OF HOBART, 1855-1982 / Collector of Customs, Hobart – 1 reel 31916-396500 – 1 – CRS A7561 – at Archives [920]

REGISTER OF BRITISH SHIPS : APPROPRIATION BOOK FOR OFFICIAL NUMBERS, PORT OF MARYBOROUGH, 1870-1981 / Sub-Collector of Customs, Maryborough – 1 reel 46961-385882 – 1 – CRS A7523 – at Archives [920]

REGISTER OF BRITISH SHIPS : APPROPRIATION BOOK FOR OFFICIAL NUMBERS, PORT OF NEWCASTLE, 1855-1982 / Sub-Collector of Customs, Newcastle – 1 reel 32686-385259 – 1 – CRS A7573 – at Archives [920]

REGISTER OF BRITISH SHIPS : APPROPRIATION BOOK FOR OFFICIAL NUMBERS, PORT OF ROCKHAMPTON, 1973-1982 / Sub-Collector of Customs, Rockhampton – 1 reel 196546-385912 – 1 – CRS A7528 – at Archives [920]

REGISTER OF BRITISH SHIPS : APPROPRIATION BOOK FOR OFFICIAL NUMBERS, PORT OF SYDNEY, 1947-1982 / Collector of Customs, Sydney – 1 reel 179706-396544 – 1 – CRS A7580 – at Archives [920]

REGISTER OF BRITISH SHIPS : APPROPRIATION BOOK FOR OFFICIAL NUMBERS, PORT OF TOWNSVILLE, 1886-1981 / Sub-Collector of Customs, Townsville – 1 reel 89881-386155 – 1 – CRS A7519 – at Archives [920]

REGISTER OF BRITISH SHIPS : CERTIFICATES OF BRITISH REGISTRY, PORT ADELAIDE, 1838-1844 / Collector of Customs, Adelaide – 1 reel – 1 – CRS A7507 – at Archives [920]

REGISTER OF BRITISH SHIPS : CONTINUATION REGISTER, PORT ADELAIDE, 1841-1855 / Collector of Customs, Adelaide – 1 reel – 1 – CRS A7506 – at Archives [920]

REGISTER OF BRITISH SHIPS : CONTINUATION REGISTER, PORT MELBOURNE, 1855-1981 / Collector of Customs, Melbourne – 4r – 1 – CRS A7610 – at Archives [920]

REGISTER OF BRITISH SHIPS : CONTINUATION REGISTER, PORT OF BRISBANE, 1856-1927 / Collector of Customs, Brisbane – 1 reel – 1 – CRS A7545 – at Archives [920]

REGISTER OF BRITISH SHIPS : CONTINUATION REGISTER, PORT OF MARYBOROUGH, 1870-1883 / Sub-Collector of Customs, Maryborough – 1 reel – 1 – CRS A7526 – at Archives [920]

REGISTER OF BRITISH SHIPS : CONTINUATION REGISTER, PORT OF NEWCASTLE, 1856-1970 / Sub-Collector of Customs, Newcastle – 1 reel – 1 – CRS A7576 – at Archives [920]

REGISTER OF BRITISH SHIPS : CONTINUATION REGISTER, PORT OF ROCKHAMPTON, 1877-1901 / Sub-Collector of Customs, Rockhampton – 1 reel – 1 – CRS A7530 – at Archives [920]

REGISTER OF BRITISH SHIPS : INDEX BY NAME OF SHIP, PORT ADELAIDE, 1847-1982 / Collector of Customs, Adelaide – 1 reel Augustus – Zora – 1 – CRS A7508 – at Archives [920]

REGISTER OF BRITISH SHIPS : INDEX BY NAME OF SHIP, PORT KEMBLA, 1970-1980 / Sub-Collector of Customs, Port Kembla – 1 reel Apollo X – Kunghah – 1 – CRS A7577 – at Archives [920]

REGISTER OF BRITISH SHIPS : INDEX BY NAME OF SHIP, PORT MELBOURNE, 1965-1982 / Collector of Customs, Melbourne – 1 reel A-Z – 1 – CRS A7555 – at Archives [920]

REGISTER OF BRITISH SHIPS : INDEX BY NAME OF SHIP, PORT OF BRISBANE, 1958-1982 / Collector of Customs, Brisbane – 1 reel Adventure – Zita – 1 – CRS A7534 – at Archives [920]

REGISTER OF BRITISH SHIPS : INDEX BY NAME OF SHIP, PORT OF DARWIN, 1960-1982 / Sub-Collector of Customs, Darwin – 1 reel Aroeta – Zarathustra – 1 – CRS A7546 – at Archives [920]

REGISTER OF BRITISH SHIPS : INDEX BY NAME OF SHIP, PORT OF FREMANTLE, 1968-1981 / Collector of Customs, Western Australia – (Index covers Main Register 1856-1982) – 1 reel Adur – Zaandam – 1 – CRS A7499 – at Archives [920]

REGISTER OF BRITISH SHIPS : INDEX BY NAME OF SHIP, PORT OF NEWCASTLE, 1849-1982 / Sub-Collector of Customs, Newcastle – 1 reel Allyn – Zoroya – 1 – CRS A7572 – at Archives [920]

REGISTER OF BRITISH SHIPS : INDEX BY NAME OF SHIP, PORT OF SYDNEY, 1843-1849 / Collector of Customs, Sydney – Australia – Anna Maria – 1 – CRS C2367 – at Archives [920]

REGISTER OF BRITISH SHIPS : MAIN REGISTER, PORT FAIRY, 1854-1895 / Sub-Collector of Customs, Port Fairy – 1 reel – 1 – CRS A7553 – at Archives [920]

REGISTER OF BRITISH SHIPS : MAIN REGISTER, PORT KEMBLA, 1971-1981 / Sub-Collector of Customs, Port Kembla – 1 reel – 1 – CRS A7579 – at Archives [920]

REGISTER OF BRITISH SHIPS : MAIN REGISTER, PORT OF BUNDABERG, 1899-1981 / Sub-Collector of Customs, Rockhampton – 1 reel – 1 – CRS A7522 – at Archives [920]

REGISTER OF BRITISH SHIPS : MAIN REGISTER, PORT OF BURNIE, 1971-1980 / Sub-Collector of Customs, Burnie – 1 reel – 1 – CRS A7558 – at Archives [920]

REGISTER OF BRITISH SHIPS : MAIN REGISTER, PORT OF CAIRNS, 1951-1982 / Sub-Collector of Customs, Cairns – 1 reel – 1 – CRS A7517 – at Archives [920]

REGISTER OF BRITISH SHIPS : MAIN REGISTER, PORT OF DARWIN, 1886-1982 / Sub-Collector of Customs, Darwin – 1 reel – 1 – CRS A7548 – at Archives [920]

REGISTER OF BRITISH SHIPS : MAIN REGISTER, PORT OF DEVONPORT, 1969-1981 / Sub-Collector of Customs, Devonport – 1 reel – 1 – CRS A7560 – at Archives [920]

REGISTER OF BRITISH SHIPS : MAIN REGISTER PORT OF FREMANTLE, 1856-1982 / Collector of Customs, Western Australia – 7r – 1 – CRS A7498 – at Archives [920]

REGISTER OF BRITISH SHIPS : MAIN REGISTER, PORT OF GEELONG, 1855-1981 / Sub-Collector of Customs, Geelong – 2r – 1 – CRS A7552 – at Archives [920]

REGISTER OF BRITISH SHIPS : MAIN REGISTER, PORT OF GLADSTONE, 1968-1981 / Sub-Collector of Customs, Gladstone – 1 reel – 1 – CRS A7521 – at Archives [920]

REGISTER OF BRITISH SHIPS : MAIN REGISTER, PORT OF MARYBOROUGH, 1868-1982 / Sub-Collector of Customs, Maryborough – 1 reel – 1 – CRS A7527 – at Archives [920]

REGISTER OF BRITISH SHIPS : MAIN REGISTER, PORT OF PORTLAND, 1961-1982 / Sub-Collector of Customs, Portland – 1 reel – 1 – CRS A7554 – at Archives [920]

REGISTER OF BRITISH SHIPS : MAIN REGISTER, PORT OF ROCKHAMPTON, 1866-1982 / Sub-Collector of Customs, Rockhampton – 1 reel – 1 – CRS A7529 – at Archives [920]

REGISTER OF BRITISH SHIPS : MAIN REGISTER, PORT OF TOWNSVILLE, 1884-1982 / Sub-Collector of Customs, Townsville – 2 reel – 1 – CRS A7518 – at Archives [920]

REGISTER OF BRITISH SHIPS : MAIN REGISTER PRIOR TO MERCHANT SHIPPING ACT 1854, PORT ADELAIDE, 1838-1855 / Collector of Customs, Adelaide – 2r – 1 – CRS A7505 – at Archives [920]

REGISTER OF BRITISH SHIPS : MAIN REGISTER PRIOR TO MERCHANT SHIPPING ACT 1854, PORT MELBOURNE, 1839-1855 / Collector of Customs, Melbourne – 2r – 1 – CRS B1231 – at Archives [920]

REGISTER OF BRITISH SHIPS : MAIN REGISTER PRIOR TO MERCHANT SHIPPING ACT 1854, PORT OF NEWCASTLE, 1849-1855 / Sub-Collector of Customs, Newcastle – 1 reel – 1 – CRS A7574 – at Archives [920]

REGISTER OF BRITISH SHIPS : MAIN REGISTER SUBSEQUENT TO MERCHANT SHIPPING ACT 1854, PORT ADELAIDE, 1855-1982 / Collector of Customs, Adelaide – 5 reel – 1 – CRS A7509 – at Archives [920]

REGISTER OF BRITISH SHIPS : MAIN REGISTER SUBSEQUENT TO MERCHANT SHIPPING ACT 1854, PORT MELBOURNE, 1855-1982 / Collector of Customs, Melbourne – 8r – 1 – CRS A7609 – at Archives [920]

REGISTER OF BRITISH SHIPS : MAIN REGISTER SUBSEQUENT TO MERCHANT SHIPPING ACT 1854, PORT OF BRISBANE, 1856-1898 / Collector of Customs, Brisbane – 1 reel – 1 – CRS A7531 – at Archives [920]

REGISTER OF BRITISH SHIPS : MAIN REGISTER SUBSEQUENT TO MERCHANT SHIPPING ACT 1854, PORT OF NEWCASTLE, 1856-1982 / Sub-Collector of Customs, Newcastle – 3r – 1 – CRS A7575 – at Archives [920]

REGISTER OF BRITISH SHIPS : MAIN REGISTER, SUBSEQUENT TO MERCHANT SHIPPING ACT 1894 PORT OF BRISBANE, 1898-1982 / Collector of Customs, Brisbane – 4r – 1 – CRS A7532 – at Archives [920]

REGISTER OF BRITISH SHIPS : MAIN REGISTER (WITH CONTINUATION ENTRIES), PORT OF HOBART, 1855-1982 / Collector of Customs, Hobart – 5r – 1 – CRS A7562 – at Archives [920]

REGISTER OF BRITISH SHIPS : PORT OF SYDNEY, A SERIES, 1888-1916 / Collector of Customs, Sydney – 1 – CRS C3 – at Archives [920]

REGISTER OF BRITISH SHIPS : PORT OF SYDNEY, SINGLE NUMBER SERIES (1), 1827-1855 / Collector of Customs, Sydney – v2-v12 – 1 – CRS C1 – at Archives [920]

REGISTER OF BRITISH SHIPS : PORT OF SYDNEY, SINGLE NUMBER SERIES (2), 1855-1982 / Collector of Customs, Sydney – v1-v39 – 1 – CRS C2 – at Archives [920]

REGISTER OF BRITISH SHIPS : REGISTERS OF TRANSACTIONS SUBSEQUENT TO FIRST REGISTRY, PORT OF SYDNEY, 1856-1949 / Collector of Customs, Sydney – v1-v10 – 1 – CRS C19 – at Archives [920]

REGISTER OF BRITISH SHIPS : REGISTRY OF SHIPPING DEEDS BOOK, PORT ADELAIDE, 1920-1965 / Collector of Customs, Adelaide – 1 reel Alert-Zotitoro – 1 – CRS A7511 – at Archives [920]

REGISTER OF BURIALS / Airdrie. New Monkland Cemetery – 1 – uk Microform Academic [920]

REGISTER OF BURIALS / Alloa, Scotland. Greenside Cemetery – 1814-1955 – 1 – uk Microform Academic [920]

REGISTER OF BURIALS / Ayrshire, Scotland. Newmilns Old Cemetery – 1666-1926 – 1 – uk Microform Academic [941]

REGISTER OF BURIALS / Edinburgh. Greyfriars Graveyard – 1616-1917 – 1 – uk Microform Academic [941]

REGISTER OF BURIALS / Glasgow. North Street Cemetery – 1777-1912 – 1 – uk Microform Academic [941]

REGISTER OF BURIALS / Glasgow. Sighthill – 1773-1915 – 1 – uk Microform Academic [941]

REGISTER OF BURIALS / Kilmarnock. Scotland. St. Andrew's Parish Churchyard – 1 – uk Microform Academic [941]

REGISTER OF BURIALS / Lisburn. Northern Ireland. Cathedral Church Yard – 1 – uk Microform Academic [941]

REGISTER OF BURIALS / Oban. Scotland. Old Parish Church – 1815-1951 – 1 – uk Microform Academic [941]

REGISTER OF BURIALS / Paisley. Scotland. New Street Church – 1 – uk Microform Academic [941]

REGISTER OF BURIALS / Pitween. Fifeshire, Scotland – 1 – uk Microform Academic [941]

REGISTER OF CONFEDERATE SOLDIERS, SAILORS, AND CITIZENS WHO DIED IN FEDERAL PRISONS AND MILITARY HOSPITALS IN THE NORTH / U.S. War Department. Confederate Records – 1861-65. M918 – 1r – 1 – us Nat'l Archives [920]

REGISTER OF CONVEYANCES / Ottawa County. Ohio. Recorder – 1840-1845 – 1r – 1 – $32.50r – us Archival [324]

REGISTER OF CREDENTIALS OF U.S. SENATORS, 1789-1821 / U.S. Senate – 1r – 1 – M1261 – us Nat'l Archives [324]

REGISTER OF CURRENT AUSTRALIAN ORNITHOLOGICAL RESEARCH / Rich et al – 1980 – 9 – A$8.00 – at R.A.O.U. [590]

REGISTER OF DEBATES / U.S. Congress – 1824-27 – 1 – us Princeton Micro [324]

REGISTER OF DEBATES / U.S. Congress – v. 18-25. 1824-37 – 1 – us UMI [324]

REGISTER OF EDUCATION AND TRAINING ACTIVITIES IN LIBRARIANSHIP, INFORMATION SCIENCE AND ARCHIVES – (English, French and Spanish) – 1982 – 61p – 9 – 92-3-002022-2 – fr UNESCO [020]
REGISTER OF ENLISTMENTS IN THE U.S. ARMY, 1798-1914 / U.S. War Department. Adjutant General's Office – 81 rolls. M233 – 1 – us Nat'l Archives [324]
REGISTER OF GRADUATES AND FORMER CADETS, UNITED STATES MILITARY ACADEMY, WEST POINT, NEW YORK 1802-1946 / West Point Alumni Foundation Inc – New York, 1946. Military Books, reel 2. Cox Library Collection – 5 – us Americana [920]
REGISTER OF GUESTS / Delmonico Hotel. Dodge City, Kansas – Aug 1887-Jan 1888 – 1 – us KS Hist [025]
REGISTER OF ISSUE OF MEDALS AND CLASPS, 1903-1911 – 6r – 1 – CRS B5184 – at Archives [920]
REGISTER OF LETTERS RECEIVED, AND LETTERS RECEIVED BY HEADQUARTERS, 9TH MILITARY DEPARTMENT, 1849-1853 / U.S. Army. Continental Commands – RG 393. M1102. 7 rolls – 1 – us Nat'l Archives [355]
REGISTER OF LETTERS RECEIVED BY THE OFFICE OF INDIAN AFFAIRS, 1824-80 / U.S. Bureau of Indian Affairs – 126 rolls. M18 – 1 – us Nat'l Archives [324]
REGISTER OF LETTERS RECEIVED BY THE U.S. GEOLOGICAL SURVEY, 1879-1901 / U. S. Geological Survey – 16 rolls. M157. Printed guide – 1 – us Nat'l Archives [550]
REGISTER OF MARRIAGES, BIRTHS AND DEATHS IN ELLIS COUNTY / Ellis County. Kansas – 1886-1912 – 1 – us KS Hist [324]
REGISTER OF MEDICAL EXAMINATIONS FOR THE 1ST CONTINGENT, QUEENSLAND DEFENCE FORCE, 1899-1899 / Chief Secretary's Office, Queensland – 4r – 1 – CRS B5174 – at Archives [920]
REGISTER OF MEMBERS AND ANCESTORS / Society of Colonial Wars in the State of Minnesota – 1901. Minnesota Reel 17. (The Cox Library Collection) – 5 – us Americana [978]
A REGISTER OF MISSIONARIES, DEPUTATIONS, ETC. FROM 1796 TO 1923 / Sibree, J – London, 1923 – 3mf – 9 – ne IDC [240]
REGISTER OF MONEY ORDERS / Wyandot County. Ohio. Marseilles. City Post Office – 1905-1910 – 1r – 1 – $32.50r – us Archival [324]
REGISTER OF MONEY ORDERS / Wyandot County. Ohio. Upper Sandusky. City Post Office – 1866-1908 – 1r – 1 – $32.50r – us Archival [324]
REGISTER OF MONTHLY REPORTS BY U.S. SECRET SERVICE AGENTS, DEC. 1864-FEB. 1871 / U.S. Treasury Department – 7rolls. T917 – 1 – us Nat'l Archives [336]
REGISTER OF NEGRO SLAVES & MASTERS / Indiana – By June B. Barekman, 1970. Item L. For 1805-1807 Knox County: Indiana Territory Court House at Vincennes. 5p. SW16-0131 – 5 – us A.G.L.L. [920]
REGISTER OF OFFICERS OF THE CONFEDERATE STATES NAVY 1861-1865 / U.S. Government Printing Office – Washington, 1931. Military Books, reel 4. (Cox Library Collection) – 5 – us Americana [920]
REGISTER OF OHIO SOCIETY OF SONS OF THE AMERICAN REVOLUTION 1917-18-19-20-21 / Sherman & Curry & Wirt – Columbus: Published by the Society, 1922. Mississippi Reel 4. (The Cox Library Collection) – 5 – us Americana [978]
REGISTER OF PATENTS / Allen County. Ohio. Probate Court – 1868-1869 – 1r – 1 – $32.50r – us Archival [324]
REGISTER OF PATENTS / Fulton County. Ohio. Probate Court – 1868-1869 – 1r – 1 – $32.50r – us Archival [324]
REGISTER OF PATENTS / Hancock County. Ohio. Probate Court – 1868-1873 – 1r – 1 – $32.50r – us Archival [324]
REGISTER OF PATENTS / Wyandot County. Ohio. Probate Court – 1868-1869 – 1r – 1 – $32.50r – us Archival [324]
REGISTER OF PATENTS AND (FROM 19 FEB. 1851) REGISTER OF CERTIFICATES OF NATURALIZATION VOLUME OF ENROLLED CERTIFICATES WITH INDEX, 1847-1852 / Supreme Court of New South Wales, District Registry, Port Phillip – 1 reel – 1 – CRS A725 – at Archives [600]
REGISTER OF PENNSYLVANIA – DEVOTED TO THE PRESERVATION OF FACTS AND DOCUMENTS, AND EVERY OTHER KIND OF USEFUL INFORMATION RESPECTING THE STATE OF PENNSYLVANIA *see* HAZARD'S REGISTER OF PENNSYLVANIA
REGISTER OF STUDENTS. 1769-1922 / Royal Academy of Arts. London – 1 – uk Microform Academic [025]
REGISTER OF THE ABBEY OF ST THOMAS THE MARTYR, DUBLIN (RS94) / Dublin Abbey Of St Thomas The Martyr; ed by Gilbert, J T – 1889 – Dfl32.00 – ne Slangenburg [240]
REGISTER OF THE MILITARY ORDER OF FOREIGN WARS OF THE UNITED STATES NATIONAL COMMANDERY – New York, 1900. Military Books reel 4. (Cox Library Collection) – 5 – us Americana [350]
REGISTER OF THE PALESTINE PRESS, COMPILED FROM PARTICULARS SUPPLIED BY THE NEWSPAPERS OR PUBLISHED IN THE "PALESTINE GAZETTE" – Jerusalem, [1946] – 1mf – ne IDC [270]
REGISTER OF THE UNIVERSITY OF OXFORD – (Missing: v38 1899; v56 1910: v86 1927) – Oxford. v1-101. 1885-1936; NS. v1-3. 1937-40 – 886mf – 9 – H-839c/2 – ne IDC [370]
REGISTER OF TRANSACTION RELATING TO SHIPS REGISTERED UNDER THE 8TH AND 9TH VICTORIA, CAP. 89, 1855-1862 / Collector of Customs, Sydney – v2-v3 – 1 – CRS C4 – at Archives [920]
REGISTER OVER DE INDISCHE COURANTEN, 1810-1923 / Netherlands. General State Archives – 149mf – 9 – Dfl1340.00 silver – ne MMF Publ [324]
REGISTER PAJARONIAN – Watsonville, CA. 1976- – 211+ r – 1 – $10,550.00 ($625.00y) – R03087 – us Library Micro [071]
REGISTER PAJARONIAN SANTA CRUZ – Santa Cruz, CA 1986-1989 – 36r – 1 – $1,800.00 – R04111 – us Library Micro [071]
The Register Publishing Co *see* REPUBLICAN PARTY
REGISTER TIL FLORA AEGYPTIACO-ARABICA OG HERBARIUM. FORSKALII / Christensen, C F A – Kobenhavn. 1917 – 8 – ne IDC [580]
REGISTER UND NACHTRAEGE ZU DER 1889 ERSCHIENENEN UEBERSICHT UEBER DIE IM ARAMAEISCHEN, ARABISCHEN UND HEBRAEISCHEN UEBLICHE BILDUNG DER NOMINA / Lagarde, Paul de – Goettingen: Dieterich, 1891 – 1mf – 9 – 0-8370-8525-X – 1986-2525 – us A.T.L.A. [470]
REGISTERED OF RETURNED SOLDIERS OF THE QUEENSLAND DEFENCE FORCE WHO SERVED IN THE BOER WAR, 1901-1903 / Chief Secretary's Office, Queensland – 3r – 1 – CRS B5163 – at Archives [920]
REGISTERED PESTICIDES AND LICENSED PESTICIDE APPLICATORS, DEALERS AND CONSULTANTS / New Mexico. Department of Agriculture – 1970-79.1 reel – 1,5 – us Spaulding [630]
REGISTER-LEADER – Mountain View, CA. 1894-1952 – 33r – 1 – $1,650.00 – C02502 – us Library Micro [071]
REGISTER-LEADER – Mountain View. Calif. 1945-52 – 1 – us UMI [071]
REGISTER-LEADER OF THE UNITARIAN-UNIVERSALIST ASSOCIATION – (Includes unnumbered newsletter) – May 1961-Sep 1969 (complete) – 2r – 1 – ATLA S0217 – us A.T.L.A. [073]
REGISTER-MAIL – Galesburg. Ill. 1953- – 1 – us UMI [071]
REGISTER-NEWS – Mount Vernon. Ill. 1921; 1948- – 1 – us UMI [071]
REGISTER-NEWS – Mount Vernon. Ill. (misc titles). 1863-1963 – 1 – us UMI [071]
REGISTER-PAJARONIAN – Watsonville. Calif. 1938- – 1 – us UMI [071]
REGISTERS / Ballyclare. Northern Ireland. Presbyterian Church – 1 – uk Microform Academic [920]
REGISTERS / Charleston Heights (now North Charleston). South Carolina. St. Peter's by-the-Sea (Episcopal) Church – 1919-84.38 fiches – 9 – us South Carolina Historical [978]
REGISTERS / Charleston. South Carolina. Mariner's Church – 1836-99.8 fiches – 9 – us South Carolina Historical [978]
REGISTERS / Clee. Shropshire – 1755-1876 – 1 – uk Microform Academic [920]
REGISTERS / Darlington. South Carolina. St. Matthew's Protestant Episcopal Church – 1888-1982. 5 fiches – 9 – us South Carolina Historical [978]
REGISTERS / Dundee. Balgay Cemetery – 1860-1954 – 1 – uk Microform Academic [920]
REGISTERS / Eutawville. South Carolina. Epiphany Episcopal Church – 1856-1979. 5 fiches – 9 – us South Carolina Historical [978]
REGISTERS / Fulton County. Ohio. County Home – 1874-1926 – 1r – 1 – $32.50r – us Archival [324]
REGISTERS / Huron County. Ohio. County Home – 1849-1913 – 1r – 1 – $32.50r – us Archival [324]
REGISTERS / Kentucky State Historical Society – v5, 1907-v46, 1948. Incomplete – 9 – us A.G.L.L. [920]
REGISTERS / Marion. South Carolina.First United Methodist Church – 1853-96.Marriages, baptisms, pastors, members, and deaths. 3 fiches – 9 – us South Carolina Historical [978]
REGISTERS / Moravian Church. Yorkshire – 1743-1959 – 1 – uk Microform Academic [920]
REGISTERS / Ottawa County. Ohio. County Home – 1872-1968 – 2r – 1 – $32.50r – us Archival [324]
REGISTERS / Putnam County. Ohio. County Home – 1869-1902 – 1r – 1 – $32.50r – us Archival [324]
REGISTERS / Stateburg. South Carolina. Holy Cross Episcopal Church – 1808-1937. 7 fiches – 9 – us South Carolina Historical [978]
REGISTERS / Walterboro. South Carolina. St. Jude's Episcopal Church – 1857-1980. 7 fiches – 9 – us South Carolina Historical [978]
REGISTERS / White House Hotel. Ellsworth, Kansas – 1873-1904 – 1 – us KS Hist [978]
REGISTERS / Wyandot County. Ohio. County Home – 1871-1899 – 1r – 1 – $32.50r – us Archival [324]
REGISTERS AND INDEXES FOR PASSPORT APPLICATIONS, 1810-1906 – 13r – 1 – M1371 – us Nat'l Archives [324]
REGISTERS AND LETTERS RECEIVED BY THE COMMISSIONER..., 1865-72 / U.S. Bureau of Refugees, Freedmen, and Abandoned Lands – 74 rolls. M752. Printed guide – 1 – us Nat'l Archives [324]
REGISTERS, MS / Gloucester Cathedral – 1717-1914 – 1 – uk Microform Academic [240]
REGISTERS OF BIRTHS, MARRIAGES AND DEATHS / Westminster Cathedral. Archives – 1729-1909 – 1 – uk Microform Academic [941]
REGISTERS OF BRITISH SHIPPING, 1846-1982 / Sub-Collector of Customs, Launceston – 2r – 1 – CRS P559 – at Archives [920]
REGISTERS OF BURIALS / Aberdeen. Allenvale Cemetery – 1 – uk Microform Academic [920]
REGISTERS OF BURIALS / Glasgow. Anderston Old Church – 1771-1903 – 1 – uk Microform Academic [920]
REGISTERS OF BURIALS / Glasgow. Ramshorn Churchyard, Ingram Street – 1737-1889 – 1 – uk Microform Academic [920]
REGISTERS OF CERTIFICATES OF NATURALIZATION : VOLUMES OF ENROLLED CERTIFICATES WITH INDEX, 1852-1864 / Supreme Court of Victoria – 6r – 1 – CRS A726 – at Archives [920]
REGISTERS OF CHINESE LABORERS RETURNING TO THE U.S. THROUGH THE PORT OF SAN FRANCISCO, 1882-1888 – 12r – 1 – M1413 – us Nat'l Archives [340]
REGISTERS OF DEAD IN BELGIUM DURING WORLD WAR 2 PAMPHLET COLLECTION – 1953 – 1 – CSUXANM9853-B – us Hoover Inst Photo [920]
REGISTERS OF DOCUMENTS PRESENTED TO THE U.S. SENATE, 1814-1828 / U.S. Senate – 1r – 1 – M1259 – us Nat'l Archives [324]
REGISTERS OF LETTERS RECEIVED, 1812-89 / U.S. War Department. Adjutant General's Office – 85 rolls. M711. Printed guide – 1 – us Nat'l Archives [324]
REGISTERS OF LETTERS RECEIVED, AND LETTERS RECEIVED BY HEADQUARTERS, DEPARTMENT OF NEW MEXICO, 1854-1865 / U.S. Army. Continental Commands – RG 393. M1120. 30 rolls – 1 – us Nat'l Archives [355]
REGISTERS OF LETTERS RECEIVED AND LETTERS RECEIVED BY THE SUPERINTENDENT OF THE U.S. NAVAL ACADEMY / U.S. Naval Academy – 1888-1906. M1018 – 89r – 1 – us Nat'l Archives [355]
REGISTERS OF LETTERS RECEIVED BY HEADQUARTERS, DISTRICT OF NEW MEXICO, SEPTEMBER 1865-AUGUST 1890 / U.S. Army. Continental Commands – RG 393. M1097. 11 rolls – 1 – us Nat'l Archives [355]
REGISTERS OF LETTERS RECEIVED BY THE SECRETARY..., IRREGULAR SERIES, 1861-66 / U.S. War Department. Office of the Secretary – 4rolls. M491. Printed guide – 1 – us Nat'l Archives [324]
REGISTERS OF LETTERS RECEIVED BY THE SECRETARY..., MAIN SERIES, 1800-70 / U.S. War Department. Office of the Secretary – 134 rolls. M22 – 1 – us Nat'l Archives [324]
REGISTERS OF LETTERS RECEIVED BY THE SECRETARY...FROM THE PRESIDENT, EXECUTIVE DEPARTMENTS, AND WAR DEPARTMENT BUREAUS, 1862-70 / U.S. War Department. Office of the Secretary – 12 rolls. M493. Printed guide – 1 – us Nat'l Archives [324]
REGISTERS OF LETTERS RECEIVED BY THE TOPOGRAPHICAL BUREAU OF THE WAR DEPT., 1824-66 / U.S. War Department. Office of the Chief of Engineers – 4 rolls. M505. Printed guide – 1 – us Nat'l Archives [355]
REGISTERS OF LETTERS RELATING TO CLAIMS RECEIVED IN THE OFFICE OF THE SECRETARY OF THE TREASURY, 1864-87 / U.S. Treasury Department – 2rolls. M502. Printed guide – 1 – us Nat'l Archives [336]
REGISTERS OF PAY FOR NEW SOUTH WALES FORCES SERVING IN THE BOER WAR, 1900-1903 – 4r – 1 – CRS B5201 – at Archives [920]
REGISTERS OF SIGNATURES OF DEPOSITORS IN BRANCHES OF THE FREEDMEN'S SAVINGS AND TRUST COMPANY, 1865-74 / U.S. Treasury Department. Office of the Comptroller of the Currency – 27 rolls. M816 – 1 – us Nat'l Archives [332]
REGISTERS OF THE ARCHBISHOPS OF CANTERBURY / Canterbury. Archbishop – 13th-17th centuries. Lambeth Palace Library. With printed index – 1 – £775.00 – uk World [240]
REGISTERS OF THE BISHOPS, 1275-1535 AND / Hereford. England. Diocese – Charters of Hereford Cathedral 1539-1900. Cantilupe Society – 1 – uk Microform Academic [240]
REGISTERS OF THE RECORDS OF THE PROCEEDINGS OF THE UNITED STATES ARMY GENERAL COURTS-MARTIAL, 1809-1890 / U.S. Army. Judge Advocate General – RG 153. M1105. 8 rolls – 1 – us Nat'l Archives [355]
REGISTERS OF VESSELS ARRIVING AT THE PORT OF NEW YORK, NEW YORK FROM FOREIGN PORTS / U.S. Bureau of the Customs – 1789-1919. 27 rolls. M1066 – 1 – us Nat'l Archives [324]
REGISTERS, ROLLS, AND PUBLICATIONS / Delaware and Shawnee Indian Tribes – undated – 1 – us KS Hist [305]
REGISTER-STAR – Hudson. N.Y. 1974- – 1 – us UMI [071]
REGISTER-STAR-NEWS – Sandusky. Ohio. 1941-57 – 1 – us UMI [071]
REGISTO GERAL DA CAMARA DA CIDADE DE SAO PAULO / Sao Paulo. Brazil. Camara Municipal – Sao Paolo: Departamento de cultura. v1-38. 1583/1636-1857/63 – us Res Libr [972]
REGISTRA QUORUNDAM ABBATUM MONASTERII S. ALBANI QUI SAEC. 15 FLORUERE (JOH. WETHAMSTEDE, WILL. ALBON, ETC.) (CHRONIA..6) / St Albans Abbey – (v1 1872 Dfl35.00. v2 1873 Dfl39.00) – ne Slangenburg [240]
REGISTRAR GENERAL'S STATISTICAL REVIEW OF ENGLAND AND WALES 1921-1973 – (Coll title: British Government Publications...1801-1977, Demography) – 20r – 1 (£2,110.00 demography set of 38r +14mf) – uk Chadwyck [310]

REGISTRARS LEDGERS AND INDEX : GRADE BOOKS / Ada. Ohio. Ohio Northern University – 1871-1908 – 2r – 1 – $32.50r – us Archival [370]

REGISTRATION CARDS / Southern Baptist Convention – 1969-1991 – 5 – us Baptist [240]

REGISTRATION CARDS, 1961-68 / Southern Baptist Convention – 5 – us Baptist [240]

REGISTRE DES DELIBERATIONS DU GRAND CONSEIL MANGAREVIEN / Documents Mangareviens – 9 – F100.00 – fr Ethnologie [306]

REGISTRE DES FONDATIONS FAITES DANS LA COMMUNAUTE DES RELIGIEUX CARMES DE NANTES, DEPUIS 1318 JUSQU'EN 1767 / Carmes, Nantes – 18th c. – fr Armell [240]

"REGISTRE DES TREPASSEZ" (1634-1679) / Trois Rivieres. Canada. Bishop. Archives – Trois-Rivieres, Canada – 1r – 1 – cn Can Microfilming [240]

REGISTRE MARITIME : 1829-1974 AND 1976-1987 / Merchant Ship Classification Society – Records of the Society. Antwerp and Paris. 1829-1987. Standing order available. Inquire for indiv. years – 1 – $11,530.00 – us UPA [380]

REGISTRO CENTRAL DE ESCLAVOS / Puerto Rico. Secretaria del Gobierno Superior Civil – Quinto Departmento and Septimo Departmento. 1872 – 7 – 41.00 – us L of C Photodup [025]

REGISTRO CENTRAL DE ESCLAVOS, 1872 (SLAVE SCHEDULES) / Puerto Rico. Spanish Governors – 8 rolls.T1121 – 1 – us Nat'l Archives [324]

REGISTRO DE DOCUMENTOS SIECLE 11-16 (ANNO 1792) / Carracedo, San Salvador de – Astorga – 1r – 5,6 – sp Cultura [946]

REGISTRO DE MATRICULA / Vaquero Mayor, Agustin – Plasencia: Ed. Sanchez Rodrigo S.A., 1970 – 1 – sp Bibl Santa Ana [946]

REGISTRO ESTADISTICO DE LA PROVINCIA DE BUENOS AIRES ANO 1873-1880 – Buenos Aires, 1875-1886 – 58mf – 9 – sp Cultura [304]

REGISTRO ESTADISTICO DE LA REPUBLICA ARGENTINA EN 1864-1871, TOMO 1-6 – Buenos Aires, 1865-1873 – 49mf – 9 – sp Cultura [304]

REGISTRO NACIONAL. / Argentine Republic – Buenos Aires. Jan 1851-Dec 1911; Jan-Jun 1938. LL-0124 – 1 – us L of C Photodup [340]

REGISTRO NACIONAL...QUE COMPRENDE LOS DOCUMENTOS DESDE 1810 HASTA 1891 / Argentine Republic – Buenos Aires. Title varies. On film: v1-14; 1810-91. LL-0130 – 1 – us L of C Photodup [340]

REGISTRO OFICIAL / Ecuador – 1835-1969 – 1 – 3335.00 – us L of C Photodup [324]

REGISTRO OFICIAL / Ecuador – 1970- – 1 – us L of C Photodup [972]

REGISTRO OFICIAL – (Lacks: 1949-53) – Quito, Ecuador, 1883-1970 – 79r – 1 – us Ross [324]

REGISTRO OFICIAL / Paraguay – 1970, 1974- – 1 – us L of C Photodup [972]

REGISTROS (ANNO 1380-1381) – Barcelona – 1r – 5,6 – sp Cultura [946]

REGISTROS (ANNO 1490-1503) – Barcelona – 1r – 5,6 – sp Cultura [946]

LOS REGISTROS DE MATRICULA DE LA ACADEMIA DE SAN FERNANDO DE 1752 A 1815. MADRID, 1967 / Pardo Canalis, E – Madrid: Graf. Calleja, 1968 – 1 – sp Bibl Santa Ana [370]

REGISTROS. PEDRO 4. EL CEREMONIOSO. GRATIARUM INCOMPLETO – Barcelona – 1r – 5,6 – sp Cultura [946]

REGISTRUM EPISTOLARUM FRATRIS JOHANNIS PECKHAM (RS77) : ARCHIEPISCOPI CANTUARIENSIS / John Peckham; ed by Martin, C T – (v1 1882 v2 1884 Dfl32.00. v3 1885 Dfl35.00) – ne Slangenburg [240]

REGISTRUM EPISTULARUM / Gregorius Magnus – 1982 – 20mf – 9 – Bf1,750.00 – 2-503-61402-7 – be Brepols [240]

REGISTRUM MALMESBURIENSE (RS72) = THE REGISTER OF MALMESBURY ABBEY / Malmesbury Abbey; ed by Brewer, J S & Martin, C T – v1 1879 v2 1880 – Dfl35.00v – ne Slangenburg [240]

REGISTRUM PALATINUM DUNELMENSE (RS62) : THE REGISTER OF RICHARD DE KELLAWE, LORD PALATINE AND BISHOP OF DURHAM, 1311-1316 / ed by Hardy, T D – (v1: 1311-1313 1873 Dfl49.00. v2 1314-1316 1874 Dfl49.00. v3 1314-1316 1875 Dfl53.00. v4: Additamenta, Index 1878 Dfl49.00) – ne Slangenburg [240]

REGISTRUM SACRUM ANGLICANUM / Stubbs, William – H 1174 2. Ed. 2. 1907 – 8 – ne IDC [025]

THE REGISTRUM SEDE VACANTE / Worcester Cathedral – 1301-1435 – 1 – uk Microform Academic [240]

THE REGISTRY ACT OF 1865 / Wood, Samuel George – Toronto, Chewett, 1866. 80 p. LL-2216 – 1 – us L of C Photodup [340]

REGISTRY/RETURN OF MARRIAGES / Defiance County, Ohio. Probate Court – 1856-1857 – 1r – 1 – $32.50r – us Archival [324]

REGLA DE LA ORDEN DE LA CABALLERIA DE SANTIAGO / Mendoza, Luis de – Madrid: Sancha, 1791 – 1 – sp Bibl Santa Ana [350]

REGLA DE LAS CINCO ORDENES DE ARCHITECTURA / Vignola, J – Madrid, 1569 – 5mf – 9 – sp Cultura [720]

LA REGLA Y EL...SANTIAGO DEL ESPADA / Garcia de Medrano – 1627 – 9 – 1.50f – sp Bibl Santa Ana [946]

REGLA Y ESTABLECIMIENTO DE LA ORDEN... DE SANTIAGO / Ruiz de Vergara Alava, Francisco – 1655 – 1 – sp Bibl Santa Ana [946]

REGLAMENTACION MUNICIPAL CONTRA EL PARO FORZOSO...1931 / Caceres – Madrid: Imprenta Minuesa de los Rios, 1931 – sp Bibl Santa Ana [340]

REGLAMENTO / La Academia de Musica y Banda Municipal de Caceres – 1892 – 9 – $1.50f – sp Bibl Santa Ana [060]

REGLAMENTO / Hermandad Sindical de Labradores y Ganaderos – Caceres: Imp. El Noticiero, 1943 – 1 – sp Bibl Santa Ana [060]

REGLAMENTO / Madrigalejo. Mercado de Abastos – Caceres: Imp. La Minerva, 1959 – 1 – sp Bibl Santa Ana [060]

REGLAMENTO / Plasencia. (Spain). Circulo de las Artes – 1882 – 9 – 1.50f – sp Bibl Santa Ana [700]

REGLAMENTO / Villafranca de los Barros. Sociedad. Cooperativa de Panificacion de San Jose – Villafranca de los Barros: Imprenta de V. Rodriguez, 1908 – 1 – sp Bibl Santa Ana [350]

REGLAMENTO / Villafranca de los Barros. Sociedad Cultural Recreativa. La Pena – Villafranca de los Barros (Badajoz): Imp. Machuca, 1966 – 1 – sp Bibl Santa Ana [350]

REGLAMENTO ASILO DE MISERICORDIA... BADAJOZ – 1885 – 9 – 1.50f – sp Bibl Santa Ana [360]

REGLAMENTO DE CORO DE LA SANTA CATEDRAL DE BADAJOZ / Badajoz – 1887 – 9 – 1.50f – sp Bibl Santa Ana [946]

REGLAMENTO DE FUTBOL / Colegio Extremeno de Arbitros de Futbol – Plasencia: Imp. Gabriel y Galan, 1972 – 1 – sp Bibl Santa Ana [790]

REGLAMENTO DE GUARDAS DE LA COMUNIDAD DE LABRADORES DE ALMENDRALEJO / Almendralejo. Spain – 1899 – 9 – 1.50f – sp Bibl Santa Ana [946]

REGLAMENTO DE LA... / Camara Privada de Compensacion Bancaria de Caceres – (Tambien: Reglamento de Regimen Interior) – Caceres: Tip. Extremadura, 1976 – 1 – sp Bibl Santa Ana [350]

REGLAMENTO DE LA ACADEMIA DE MUSICA Y BANDA MUNICIPAL DE CACERES (1892) / Caceres – Caceres: Tip. Nicolas M. Jimenez, 1892 – 1 – sp Bibl Santa Ana [370]

REGLAMENTO DE LA ACADEMIA DE MUSICA Y BANDA MUNICIPAL DE CACERES (1935-1949) / Caceres – Caceres: Tip. El Noticiero – 1 – sp Bibl Santa Ana [370]

REGLAMENTO DE LA ASOCIACION DE ANTIGUOS Y ACTUALES ALUMNOS EXTREMENOS DE COLEGIOS DE JESUITAS – Badajoz: Tip. Espanola, 1934 – 1 – sp Bibl Santa Ana [240]

REGLAMENTO DE LA ASOCIACION DE PROPIETARIOS POR RUSTICA Y PECUARIA DE DON BENITO – Don Benito: Tip. Trejo, 1931 – sp Bibl Santa Ana [350]

REGLAMENTO DE LA CAJA COMPENSADORA DE LARGAS FAMILIAS DE CACERES – Caceres: Tip. Garcia Floriano Cumbreno, 1938 – 1 – sp Bibl Santa Ana [946]

REGLAMENTO DE LA CAJA DE AHORROS, PRESTAMOS Y SOCORROS DEL CENTRO CATOLICO DE SAN JOSE DE ALMENDRALEJO – Sevilla: Escuelas Profesionales de Artes Graficas, 1908 – 1 – sp Bibl Santa Ana [946]

REGLAMENTO DE LA CAJA DE CREDITO PROVINCIAL / Diputacion Provincial – Caceres: Imp. Provincial, 1959 – 1 – sp Bibl Santa Ana [060]

REGLAMENTO DE LA CAJA DE PREVISION SOCIAL PARA PRODUCTORES DE FAGSA VILLAFRANCA DE LOS BARROS – Villafranca de los Barros: Imprenta Machuca, 1965 – sp Bibl Santa Ana [946]

REGLAMENTO DE LA CONGREGACION DE MADRES CRISTIANAS, CANONICAMENTE ERIGIDA EN LA IGLESIA DEL I.C. DE MARIA. 1914 / Trivino, Enrique – Almendralejo: Almendralejo, Tip. L. Carballos, 1914 – 1 – sp Bibl Santa Ana [240]

REGLAMENTO DE LA COOPERATIVA DE GANADEROS EXTREMENOS – Merida: A. Rodriguez, 1932 – 1 – sp Bibl Santa Ana [946]

REGLAMENTO DE LA MUTUALIDAD DE PREVISION PARA FUNCIONARIOS DEL AYUNTAMIENTO DE CACERES, 1955 / Caceres – Caceres: Tip. El Noticiero – 1 – sp Bibl Santa Ana [946]

REGLAMENTO DE LA PLAZA DE TOROS DE ALMENDRALEJO – 1873 – 9 – 1.50f – sp Bibl Santa Ana [790]

REGLAMENTO DE LA SOCIEDAD ARTISTICO-MUSICAL DE CACERES – Caceres: Tip. La Elzevirlana, 1903 – 1 – sp Bibl Santa Ana [700]

REGLAMENTO DE LA SOCIEDAD COOPERATIVA Y DE SOCORROS MUTUOS. EL OBRERO EXTREMENO. ALMENDRALEJO / Almendralejo. El Obrero Extremeno – Almendralejo: M. Acosta Imp. y Encuadernacion, 1934 – 1 – sp Bibl Santa Ana [946]

REGLAMENTO DE LA SOCIEDAD DE LABRADORES DE PUEBLA DE LA CALZADA – Badajoz: Tip. La Minerva Extremena, 1912 – sp Bibl Santa Ana [060]

REGLAMENTO DE LA SOCIEDAD DE SOCORROS MUTUOS DEL GLORIOSO PATRIARCA SAN JOSE DE TEJEDA – Caceres: Tip., Enc. y Lib. Jimenez, 1904 – 1 – sp Bibl Santa Ana [060]

REGLAMENTO DE LA SOCIEDAD MUTUA DE CRIADORES DE GANADO VACUNO / Almoharin. Sociedad Mutua de Criadores de Ganado Vacuno – Caceres: Imp. Moderna, 1961 – 1 – sp Bibl Santa Ana [060]

REGLAMENTO DE LA SOCIEDAD...1921 Y 1923 / Fomento de Caceres – Caceres: Imp. de S. Floriano, 1923 – sp Bibl Santa Ana [340]

REGLAMENTO DE LA...OBRA BENEFICO-SOCIAL DE LA CAJA DE AHORROS Y MONTE DE PIEDAD DE CACERES / Residencia Universitaria San Jose. Caceres – Caceres: Imp. Extremadura, 1978 – sp Bibl Santa Ana [060]

REGLAMENTO DE LA...PATRONA DE ALBURQUERQUE / Alburquerque. Hermandad de Ntra. Sra. de Carrion – Valencia de Alcantara: Tip. Avila, 1978 – sp Bibl Santa Ana [240]

REGLAMENTO DE LAS ESCUELAS Y BIBLIOTECA "CONCHA" APROBADO EN EL PATRONATO DE DICHOS CENTROS EN SESION DE 31 DE MARZO DE 1926 – Madrid: Tip. Revista de Archivos, 1926 – 1 – sp Bibl Santa Ana [370]

REGLAMENTO DE LOS SECRETARIOS DE CARIDAD DE ACCION CATOLICA / Junta Diocesano de Accion Catolica. (Coria) – Caceres: Tip. El Noticiero, s.a., 1942 – sp Bibl Santa Ana [240]

REGLAMENTO DE LOS SERVICIOS BENEFICO-SANITARIOS / Diputacion Provincial – Badajoz: Dip. Provincial, 1963 – sp Bibl Santa Ana [946]

REGLAMENTO DE PASTOR HIERBAS Y RASTROJERAS / Espana, Leyes Decretos... – 8 de Eenro de 1954 – sp Bibl Santa Ana [060]

REGLAMENTO DE PRIMERA LINEA / Falange Espanola de las Jons – Caceres: Tip. La Minerva, s.a. (antes de marzo de 1937) – 1 – sp Bibl Santa Ana [060]

REGLAMENTO DE PROCEDIMINETO ADMINISTRATIVO Y DE OBRAS Y SERVICIOS...1955 / Caceres – Caceres: Tip. Extremadura – sp Bibl Santa Ana [340]

REGLAMENTO DE REGIMEN INTERIOR / Club de Tenis Cabeza-Rubia – Caceres: Imp. Moderna, 1976 – 1 – sp Bibl Santa Ana [350]

REGLAMENTO DE REGIMEN INTERIOR DE LA... / Camara Oficial de Comercio e Industria de Caceres – Caceres: Imp. Moderna, 1963 – 1 – sp Bibl Santa Ana [060]

REGLAMENTO DE REGIMEN INTERIOR DELA GUARDIA MUNICIPAL DE LA CIUDAD DE CACERES (1945) / Caceres – Caceres: Imprenta Moderna, 1946 – 1 – sp Bibl Santa Ana [340]

REGLAMENTO DE REGIMEN INTERIOR PARA LAS CENTRALES DE GANADO – Caceres: Tip. El Noticiero, S.A., 1943 – 1 – sp Bibl Santa Ana [060]

REGLAMENTO DE SANIDAD E HIGIENE...1959 / Caceres – Caceres: Tip. El Noticiero S.L., 1960 – sp Bibl Santa Ana [340]

REGLAMENTO DE SUCURSALES Y AGENCIAS ANO, 1940 / Monte de Piedad y Caja General de Ahorros de Badajoz – Badajoz: Imp. Grafica Extremena, s.a. – sp Bibl Santa Ana [340]

REGLAMENTO DE TRABAJO AGRICOLA PARA LA PROVINCIA DE BADAJOZ / Camara Oficial Sindical Agraria – Badajoz: Imp. Inca, 1961 – sp Bibl Santa Ana [630]

REGLAMENTO DE...DENOMINADA "LA REALIDAD" / Montanchez. Sociedad de Seguros de Ganados – Caceres: Imp. Moderna – 1 – sp Bibl Santa Ana [060]

REGLAMENTO DEL CASINO DE BADAJOZ – Badajoz: Tip. F. Uceda, 1921 – 1 – sp Bibl Santa Ana [350]

REGLAMENTO DEL CASINO DE BADAJOZ – Badajoz: Tip. Vda. de A. Arqueros, 1944 – sp Bibl Santa Ana [340]

REGLAMENTO DEL CENTRO DE ESTUDIOS EXTREMENOS / Diputacion Provincial – Badajoz: Imprenta de la Diputacion Provincial, 1943 – sp Bibl Santa Ana [340]

REGLAMENTO DEL CENTRO DE MUJERES DE ACCION CATOLICA – Caceres: Tip. Floriano, 1938 – 1 – sp Bibl Santa Ana [240]

REGLAMENTO DEL CENTRO INSTRUCTIVO FERROVIARIO – Merida: Rodriguez Guillen, 1934 – 1 – sp Bibl Santa Ana [946]

REGLAMENTO DEL CIRCULO DE LA AMISTAD DE LA CIUDAD DE TRUJILLO – Trujillo: Imp.B.Pe, 1901 – 1 – sp Bibl Santa Ana [340]

REGLAMENTO DEL CIRCULO EMERITENSE – Merida: A. Rodriguez, 1941 – 1 – sp Bibl Santa Ana [946]

REGLAMENTO DEL COTO DE PESCA NO 3. LOS POYOS. (RIO GUADIANA) – Badajoz: Graficas Iberia, 1959 – sp Bibl Santa Ana [340]

REGLAMENTO DEL FONDO PARA ATENCIONES DEL CULTO Y CLERO DE LA DIOCESIS DE CORIA – Caceres: Tip. Extremadura, s.a. – 1 – sp Bibl Santa Ana [240]

REGLAMENTO DEL GRUPO SINDICAL DE COLONIZACION NO 2049 DE GABRIEL Y GALAN / Delegacion Nacional de Sindicatos de FET y de las JONS – Plasencia: Imp. La Victoria, 1961 – 1 – sp Bibl Santa Ana [060]

REGLAMENTO DEL MINISTERIO DE HACIENDA DE 17 DE JUNIO DE 1960 / Caceres. Mutua Aseguradora de Transportistas de la Provincia de Caceres – Caceres: Imperenta La Minerva, 1960 – 1 – sp Bibl Santa Ana [380]

REGLAMENTO DEL PATRONATO DEL CENTRO SINDICAL MINERO 9 DE FORMACION PROFESIONAL ACELERADA DE BADAJOZ / Obra Sindical de Formacion Profesional – Badajoz: Imp. INCA, 1967 – 1 – sp Bibl Santa Ana [946]

REGLAMENTO DEL RAMO DE ACCIDENTES APROBADO POR ORDEN DEL MINISTERIO DE HACIENDA DE 17 DE JUNIO DE 1960 / Caceres. Mutua Aseguradora de Transportistas de la Provincia de Caceres – Caceres: Imperenta La Minerva, 1960 – 1 – sp Bibl Santa Ana [380]

REGLAMENTO DEL REGIMEN INTERIOR DEL PERSONAL DE LA EMPRESA "EL GAVILAN", S.A. FABRICA DE CERVEZA Y DE HIELO – Merida: Imp. Rodriguez, 1960 – 1 – sp Bibl Santa Ana [350]

REGLAMENTO DEL SERVICIO MUNICIPAL DE MERCADOS 1955... / Caceres – Caceres: Tip. Editorial Extremena – 1 – sp Bibl Santa Ana [340]

REGLAMENTO DELA SOCIEDAD... / Club Deportivo Cacereno – (Caceres): Tip. La Minerva Cacerena, s.a., (1923) – 1 – sp Bibl Santa Ana [060]

REGLAMENTO DEL...PARA LA EDUCACION DE SENORITAS DIRIGIDO POR LAS RELIGIOSAS CARMELITAS DE LA CARIDAD / Colegio de Santa Cecilia de Caceres – Caceres: Imp. Garcia Floriano, s.a. – 1 – sp Bibl Santa Ana [370]

REGLAMENTO DE...REFORMADO EN 1940 / Asociacion Provincial del Magisterio de Caceres – Caceres: Tip. Floriano, 1941 – 1 – sp Bibl Santa Ana [060]

REGLAMENTO GENERAL DE FUNCINARIOS PROVINCIALES / Badajoz. Diputacion Provincial – Badajoz: Imp. Hospicio Hospital – 1 – sp Bibl Santa Ana [946]

REGLAMENTO GENERAL PARA LA EJECUCION DE LEY HIPOTECARIA DE LA PROVINCIA DE PUERTO-RICO : EDICION OFICIAL – Madrid: Imprenta Nacional, 1879 – 2mf – 9 – $3.00 – LLMC 92-316 – us L.L.M.C. [340]

REGLAMENTO INTERNO. SECCIONES FILIALES NO 1 DE LOS INSTITUTOS NACIONALES DE ENSENANZA MEDIA DE BADAJOZ – Badajoz: Imp. Inca, 1970 – sp Bibl Santa Ana [380]

REGLAMENTO MUNICIPAL CONTRA EL PARO FORZOSO (1931) / Caceres – Caceres: Imprenta de Garcia Floriano – sp Bibl Santa Ana [340]

REGLAMENTO PAEA REGIMEN INTERNO DEL GREMIO FISCAL DEL CORCHO. PROVINCIA DE BADAJOZ – Badajoz, 1961 – 1 – sp Bibl Santa Ana [350]

REGLAMENTO PARA EL COLEGIO DE SENORITAS DIRIGIDO POR LAS HERMANAS DE LA SAGRADA FAMILIA BAJO EL TITULO DE LA INMACULADA CONCEPCION ESTABLECIDO EN PLASENCIA / Colegio de la Inmaculada Concepcion – Plasencia: Imp. F. Ramos y Leon, 1871 – 1 – sp Bibl Santa Ana [240]

REGLAMENTO PARA EL REGIMEN INTERIOR DE LAS OFICINAS DEL EXCMO / Caceres – Ayuntamiento de Caceres: Tip. Luciano Jimenez, 1909 – 1 – sp Bibl Santa Ana [340]

REGLAMENTO PARA EL REGIMEN INTERIOR DE LAS OFICINAS DEL EXCMO. AYUNTAMIENTO DE CACERES / Caceres – Caceres: Tip. Luciano Jimenez Merino, 1921 – sp Bibl Santa Ana [340]

REGLAMENTO PARA EL REGIMEN INTERIOR DE LOS EMPLEADOS SUBALTERNOS DEL AYUNTAMIENTO DE ALMENDRALEJO – Almendralejo: Manuel Soto, 1928 – 1 – sp Bibl Santa Ana [946]

REGLAMENTO PARA EL REGIMEN Y ADMINISTRACION DE LA COFRADIA DE LA SANTISIMA VIRGEN DE NAVELONGA, PATRON MUY QUERIDO DE CILLEROS DE LA DIOCESIS DE CORIA-CACERES / Ballesteros Morientes, Alfredo – S.L., s.i. 1961 – 1 – sp Bibl Santa Ana [240]

REGLAMENTO PARA EL REGIMEN Y FUNCIONAMIENTO DE LAS SECCIONES SOCIALES DE LAS ENTIDADES SINDICALES MENORES, 12 ABRIL, 1950 / Camara Oficial Sindical Agraria. Caceres – Caceres: Tip. El Noticiero, s.a. – sp Bibl Santa Ana [360]

REGLAMENTO PARA ELREGIMEN INTERIOR DEL CEMENTERIO PUBLICO MUNICIPAL DE ESTA CAPITAL / Caceres – Caceres: Tip. de Santos Floriano Gonzalez, 1921 – 1 – sp Bibl Santa Ana [340]

REGLAMENTO PARA LA CONCESION DE BECAS DE ESTUDIOS QUE ESTABLECE ESTA CORPORACION / Diputacion Provincial – Badajoz: Imp. Provincial, 1968 – sp Bibl Santa Ana [338]

REGLAMENTO PARA LA ESCUELA NORMAL... BADAJOZ / Badajoz – 1855 – 9 – 1.50f – sp Bibl Santa Ana [946]

REGLAMENTO PARA LOS ESTABLECIMIENTOS DE BENEFICIENCIA DE LA PROVINCIA DE CACERES – 1873 – 9 – 1.50f – sp Bibl Santa Ana [360]

REGLAMENTO PROVISIONAL DE PROCEDIMIENTO ELECTORAL / Caja Ahorros y Monte de Piedad de Caceres – Caceres: Ed. Extremadura, 1978 – sp Bibl Santa Ana [350]

REGLAMENTO REFORMADO DE LA SOCIEDAD CORAL E INSTRUMENTAL SANTA CECILIA / Villafranca de los Barros. Sociedad Coral e instrumental Santa Cecilia – Villafranca de los Barros: Bolanos Iglesias, impresor, 1929 – 1 – sp Bibl Santa Ana [350]

REGLAMENTO Y ORDENANZAS DE LA COMUNIDAD DE LABRADORES DE ACEUCHAL – Badajoz: Rodriguez y Cordero, 1906 – 1 – sp Bibl Santa Ana [946]

REGLAMENTO Y ORDENANZAS DE LA COMUNIDAD DE LABRADORES DE FUENTE DEL MAESTRE / Fuente del Maestre – Villafranca: S.L., 1904 – 1 – sp Bibl Santa Ana [350]

REGLAMENTO...COLEGIO...INSTITUTO... CACERES – 1871 – 9 – 1.50f – sp Bibl Santa Ana [370]

REGLAMENTO...COMPANIA...PUENTE DE ALMARAZ – 1842 – 9 – 1.50f – sp Bibl Santa Ana [600]

...REGLAMENTO...DEL MATADERO MUNICIPAL DE CACERES...1919 / Caceres – Caceres: Tip Luciano Jim'enez Merino, 1920 – 1 – sp Bibl Santa Ana [340]

REGLAMENTO...ENSENANZA DE BEJAR – 1876 – 9 – 1.50f – sp Bibl Santa Ana [370]

REGLAMENTO...ESCUELA NORMAL...BADAJOZ – 1855 – 9 – 1.50f – sp Bibl Santa Ana [370]

REGLAMENTO...MINERA PODEROSA-CARMEN – 1843 – 9 – 1.50f – sp Bibl Santa Ana [380]

REGLAMENTO...ORDEN DE CABALLERIA DE SANTIAGO – 1791 – 9 – $1.50f – sp Bibl Santa Ana [060]

REGLAMENTO...REGIMEN INTERIO BENIFICENCIA...BADAJOZ – 1879 – 9 – 1.50f – sp Bibl Santa Ana [360]

REGLAMENTO...SECRETARIA...PLASENCIA / Plasencia. (Spain). Ayuntamiento – 1885 – 9 – 1.50f – sp Bibl Santa Ana [946]

REGLAMENTOS...INCLUSA...MATERNIDAD... BADAJOZ – 1885 – 9 – $1.50f – sp Bibl Santa Ana [640]

REGLAMENTO...SOCIEDAD DE AMIGOS DE LA UNION – 1867 – 9 – $1.50f – sp Bibl Santa Ana [060]

REGLAS DE LA HERMANDAD Y COFRADIA DE NAZARENOS DE NUESTRO PADRE JESUS DE LA HUMANIDAD Y MARIA SANTISIMA DE LOS DOLORES – Badajoz: Tip. Grafica Corporativa, 1938 – sp Bibl Santa Ana [240]

REGLAS GENERALES DE ACOMPANAR, EN ORGANO, CLAVICORDIO, Y HARPA, CON SOLO SABER CANTAR LA PARTE, O UN BAXO EN CANTO FIGURADO / Torres Martinez Bravo, Joseph de – 1702 – 9 – us Sibley [780]

REGLAS GENERALES DE ACOMPANAR, EN ORGANO, CLAVICORDIO, Y HARPA, CON SOLO SABER CANTAR LA PARTE, O UN BAXO EN CANTO FIGURADO...ANADIDO AORA UN NUEVO TRATADO.. / Torres Martinez Bravo, Joseph de – 1736 – 9 – us Sibley [780]

REGLAS PARA LA COFRADIA DEL STMO. CRISTO DE LA FE Y DE LA STMA. VIRGEN DE LOS DOLORES / Villafranca de los Barros. Cofradia del Stmo.C. de la Fe – Villafranca de los Barros: Juan J. Bolanos, Impresor, 1938 – 1 – sp Bibl Santa Ana [240]

REGLE DE DROIT PENAL... / Buzea, N T – Paris, n.d. – 1mf – 1 – ILM-2274/1 – ne IDC [327]

LA REGLE DE S. BENOIT MEDITEE / Symphoiren, D – Nevers, 1909 – 12mf – 8 – Dfl42.00 – ne Slangenburg [240]

REGLE DU MONASTERE (DE BEAUMONT-LES-TOURS) / Beaumont – Les-Tours, monastere – 1671? – 1 – F152.00 – fr Armell [240]

REGLE GENERALE DE LA FOY CATHOLIQUE / Veron, F – Lyon, 1674 – 4mf – 9 – CA-153/1 – ne IDC [240]

REGLEMENS DE L'HOTEL-DIEU DE NANTES / Hotel-Dieu. Nantes – Nantes: Vve Vatar, 1760 – 1 – F60.72 – fr Armell [360]

REGLEMENT ANNOTE DE L'ASSEMBLEE LEGISLATIVE CONTENANT LES TEXTES FRANCAIS ET ANGLAIS DU REGLEMENT.. / Geoffrion, Louis Philippe – Quebec: Assemblee legislative. 1941. SEM105P422 – 7mf – 9 – Can$15.75 – cn Bibl Nat [323]

REGLEMENT DE LA SOCIETE DE L'HARMONIE SOCIALE DES SANS-CULOTTES DES DEUX SEXES – Paris, n.d. (Les Femmes Collection) – 1mf – 9 – $6.00 – fr Bibl Nationale [306]

REGLEMENT D'EDUCATION NATIONALE MIS SOUS LES AUSPICES DE BERNARDIN DE SAINT-PIERRE / Hupay De Fuveau, Joseph-Alexandre-Victor d' – (Aix). 1789 – 9 – fr Hachette [370]

REGLEMENT ET CONSTITUTION...FONDE LE 20 NOVEMBRE 1878 / Club de Raquettes 'Le Canadien' – (Montreal: A. Foisy), 1882. 04150. (Pre-1900 Canadiana) – 9 – cn C.I.H.M. [060]

REGLEMENT OP DE BURGERLIJKE RECHTSVORDERING / New Guinea, Dutch. Laws, statutes, etc – SE-5404 1. 3 v. in 1. 1957 – 9 – ne IDC [324]

REGLEMENTATION DES DOUANES ET IMPOTS INDIRECTS / Morocco. Administration des Douanes et Impots Indirects – 1959. BNE-3000 1 – 9 – ne IDC [380]

REGLEMENTS / Association de Tir de Montmagny-L'Islet – Quebec, 1869. 04100. (Pre-1900 Canadiana) – 9 – cn C.I.H.M. [060]

REGLEMENTS CONSULAIRES... / Cussy, F de Cornot – Leipzig, 1851 – 6mf – 1 – ILM-154/1 – ne IDC [327]

...REGLEMENTS CONSULAIRES DE BELGIQUE / Arntz, E R N – Bruxelles, 1876 – 2mf – 9 – ILM-933/1 – ne IDC [340]

REGLEMENTS DE LA LOGE DES COEURS-UNIS, NO. 45, REGISTRE DE QUEBEC – Montreal: s.n., 18–. 04347. (Pre-1900 Canadiana) – 9 – cn C.I.H.M. [060]

REGLEMENTS DE LA SOCIETE DES AMIS DES NOIRS / Condorcet, Marie Jean Antoine Nicolas de – Reprod. de l'edition s.l., s.n., s.d. 46p. 1 fiche. (Political Science Collection) – 9 – 6.00 – fr Bibl Nationale [305]

REGLEMENTS ET CONSTITUTION / Academie de Musique de Quebec – Quebec. s.n. 1869. (Pre-1900 Canadiana) – 9 – cn C.I.H.M. [060]

REGLEMENTS...PASSES LE 26 JANVIER 1875, SANCTIONNES LE 10 AVRIL 1875 / Commissaires du Havre de Montreal – (Montreal: A. Stevenson), 1875. 02154. (Pre-1900 Canadiana) – 9 – cn C.I.H.M. [971]

REGLES DE LA POESIE FRANCOISE / Chalons, V C – 1716 – 9 – fr I.C.S. [440]

REGLES DE LA SOCIETE...ETABLIE DANS L'ARCHDIOCESE DE QUEBEC / Caisse Ecclesiastique St. Joseph. Quebec – Quebec: P.G. Delisle, 1876. 02124. (Pre-1900 Canadiana) – 9 – cn C.I.H.M. [060]

REGLES DE LA TRADUCTION / Tende, G de – 1660 – 9 – fr I.C.S. [400]

REGLES DES CINQ ORDRES D'ARCHITECTURE DE VIGNOLE / Vignola, Giacomo Barozzi – Paris: M. Tavernier, 1632. Revues, augmentees et reduites par Le Muet. 101p. 50 pl. (Architecture Series) – 9 – fr Hachette [720]

LES REGLES DU DESSIN ET DU LAVIS POUR LES PLANS PARTICULIERS DES OUVRAGES ET DES BATIMENTS. / Buchotte – Paris, C. Jombert, 1722. 20, 136p., ill. (Architecture Series) – 9 – fr Hachette [720]

REGLES ET REGLEMENS DE POLICE POUR LA CITE ET LES FAUBOURGS DE MONTREAL / Montreal. Laws, Statutes, etc – Montreal: James Brown, 1821. SEM16P186 – 1r – 5 – Can$9.00 – cn Bibl Nat [360]

REGLES ET REGLEMENS DE POLICE, ADDITIONNELS, POUR LA CITE ET LES FAUBOURGS DE MONTREAL / Montreal. Laws, Statutes, etc – Montreal: Imprime au Bureau de la Gazette de Montreal, 1826. SEM16P187 – 1r – 5 – Can$9.00 – cn Bibl Nat [360]

REGLES ET REGLEMENS DE POLICE POUR LES FAUXBOURGS ET LA CITE DE MONTREAL / Montreal. Laws, Statutes, etc – Montreal: James Lane, 1817. SEM16P70 – 1r – 5 – Can$9.00 – cn Bibl Nat [350]

REGLES ET TRADITIONS, PROVERBES ET CONTES DU ZAMBEZE / Lewanika, Godwin Mbikusita – F100.00 – fr Ethnologie [306]

REGLES GENERALES D'ARCHITECTURE DES CINQ MANIERES DE COLONNES. / Bulland, Jean – Roven, D. Ferrand. 1647. 60p. ill. (Architecture Series) – 9 – fr Hachette [720]

REGLES TONALES EN ANYI ET EN BAOULE / Quaireau, A – 9 – F40.00 – fr Ethnologie [490]

REGLES...ET SOMMAIRES DES INDULGENCES / Association de l'Adoration Perpetuelle du Tres Saint Sacrement – Quebec, 1898. 02202. (Pre-1900 Canadiana) – 9 – cn C.I.H.M. [240]

Regnault, Henri *see* UNE PROVINCE PROCURATORIENNE AU DEBUT DE L'EMPIRE ROMAIN: LE PROCES DE JESUS CHRIST

Regnault-Warin, Jean-Joseph *see* ELEMENTS DE POLITIQUE

LE REGNE ANIMAL / Cuvier, Georges – Ed. 2. 2420 2. 5 v. 1829 – 8 – ne IDC [590]

LE REGNE DE JESUS CHRIST / Gonthier, Dominique C – 1900?. 04376. (Pre-1900 Canadiana) – 9 – cn C.I.H.M. [240]

LA REGNE DE JUSTICE ET DE VERITE – Bordeaux, France. -w. 1975-76. 1 reel – 1 – uk British Libr Newspaper [072]

REGNI CHINENSIS DESCRIPTIO – Lugduni Batavorum, [1639] – 4mf – 9 – ne IDC [950]

REGNI VEGETABILIS SYSTEMA NATURALE / Candolle, A P de – 2v. Paris. 1817 18-1821. B-5058 2 – 8 – ne IDC [580]

Regnier, Adolphe *see* VIE DE SCHILLER

Regnier, Louis-Adolphe *see* DE LA LATINITE DES SERMONS DE SAINT AUGUSTIN

Regnon, T D *see*
– METAPHISIQUE DES CAUSES D'APRES ST THOMAS ET ALB. LE GRAND

Regnon, T de *see* LA SAINTE TRINITE

REGNUM DEI : EIGHT LECTURES ON THE KINGDOM OF GOD IN THE HISTORY OF CHRISTIAN THOUGHT / Robertson, Archibald – (Includes bibliographical references and index) – New York:Macmillan; London:Methuen, 1901 – 1mf – 9 – 0-8370-4919-9 – 1985-2919 – us A.T.L.A. [240]

LA REGOLA DEL CONTRAPONTO, E DELLA MUSICAL COMPOSITIONE / Angleria, Fra. C – 1622 – 9 – us Sibley [780]

REGOLE ARMONICHE / Manfredini – P 386. 1775 – 9 – ne IDC [780]

REGOLE FACILLISSIME PER APPRENDERE IL CANTO FERMO CON UN DIALOGO NUOVAMENTE PER LA SESTA VOLTA RISTAMPE E RICCORRETTE... / Bertalotti, A M – Bologna: Leilo dalle Volpe, 1756 – 1mf – 9 – us Sibley [780]

REGOLE GENERALI DI CANTO FERMO ECCLESIASTICO / Fabbrizi, Pietro – Quarta Impressione. 1689 – 9 – us Sibley [780]

REGOLE PER IL CONTRAPUNTO, E PER L'ACCOMPAGNATURA DEL BASSO CONTINUO COMPENDIATE / Bruschi, A F – 1711 – 9 – us Sibley [780]

Regourd, A *see* DEMONSTRATIONS CATHOLIQUES, OU L'ART DE REUNIR LES PRETENDUS REFORMEZ

REGRAS DE ACOMPANHAR PARA CRAVO OU ORGAO, E AINDA TAMBEM PARA QUALQUER OUTRO INSTRUMENTO DE VOZES, REDUZIDAS A BREVE METHODO, E FACIL PERCEPECAO / Gomes da Silva, A J – Lisboa. 1758. BP-302 1 – 9 – ne IDC [780]

DER REGRESSUS IN INFINITUM IN DER ARISTOTELISCHEN PHILOSOPHIE / Stekla, Herbert – Frankfurt a.M., 1970 – 1mf – 9 – DM48.00 – 3-89349-663-7 – gw Hänsel [180]

REGT IN NEDERLANDSCH-INDIE : REGTSKUNDIG TIJDSCHRIFT – (Continues as: Recht in Nederlandsch-Indie. Batavia, 1883-1914. V.41-103 Continues as: Indisch Tjidschrift van het Recht. Batavia, 1915-1940. V.42-151. Index V.1-134: Continues as: Tijdschrift van het Recht. Batavia, 1947-1950: Lacking: 1949(9-12): Suspended 1868-1874; 1941-1946) – Batavia, 1849-1883.-v1-40 – 1,014mf – 9 – SE-649/1 – ne IDC [073]

REGULA, CONSTITUTIONES ET PRIVILEGIA ORDINIS CISTERCIENSIS / Henriquez, Chrysostomus – Antverpiae, 1630 – Dfl88.00 – ne Slangenburg [240]

REGULA, CONSTITUTIONES ET PRIVILEGIA ORDINIS CISTERCIENSIS / Henriquez, Chrysostomus – Antwerpen, 1630 – 25mf – 8 – Dfl88.00 – ne Slangenburg [240]

REGULA EMBLEMATICA SANCTI BENEDICTI / Gallner, Bonifacius – O-1246 1. 1783 – 9 – ne IDC [240]

REGULA EMBLEMATICA SANCTI BENEDICTI / Gallner, Bonifacius – O-262. 1780 – 9 – ne IDC [240]

REGULA S. BENEDICTI CUM COMMENTARIIS JOH. DE TURRE CREMATA, ET SMARAGDI ABBATIS – Coloniae Agrippinae, 1575 – 21mf – 8 – Dfl74.00 – ne Slangenburg [240]

REGULA...CUM DECLARATIONIBUS CONGREGTIONIS SCI MAURI – s.l., 1663 – 4mf – 8 – Dfl19.00 – ne Slangenburg [240]
REGULA...CUM DECLARATIONIBUS ET CONSTITUTIONIBUS CONGREGATIONIS SS. VITONI ET HYDOLPHI – Tulli Leucorum, 1674 – 3mf – 8 – Dfl13.00 – ne Slangenburg [240]
O REGULADOR BRASILEIRO – (Cont of: O Regulador Brasilico-Luso) – Rio de Janeiro, Oct 1822-Mar 1823 – 1,5,6 – bl Biblioteca [072]
O REGULADOR BRASILICO-LUSO *see* O REGULADOR BRASILEIRO
REGULAE ET CONSTITUTIONES CLERICORUM IN CONGREGATIONE VIVENTIUM / Miraeus, A – Antverpiae, 1638 – Dfl22.00 – ne Slangenburg [240]
REGULAE S. BENEDICTI TRADITIO : CODICUM CASINENSIUM / Morin, G – Montiscasini, 1900 – 7mf – 8 – Dfl28.00 – ne Slangenburg [240]
REGULAERE UND CHAOTISCHE BEWEGUNG EINES ELEKTRONS IM WAKEPOTENTIAL EINES SCHNELLEN IONS IM FESTKOERPER / Mueller, Joerg – 1993 – 1mf – 9 – DM75.00 – 3-89349-712-9 – gw Hänsel [530]
THE REGULAR – (Includes Nov. 1939-Dec. 1941; Jan. 1947-Jan./Feb. 1949; Oct. 1949. Library wants: June-July 1940; Nov. 1947) – Washington, D.C.: Regular Veterans Association, 193u – 1 – CSUX87-S125 – us Hoover Inst Photo [978]
REGULAR BAPTIST MISCELLANY – Zanesville, Ohio. 1828-May 1831. Also: western religious magazine, 1828-Mar 1829, Western miscellany, Feb 1830-Jul 1830. Incomplete. 550p – 1 – 19.25 – us Baptist [240]
REGULAR MEETINGS MINUTES / Typographical Union No 6. New York City – New York. 1870-1917 – 1 – us NY Public [070]
REGULATING TAXI OPERATORS: SOME HISTORICAL INSIGHTS / Aitken, Michael J & Williams, David J – 1984. 18p – 9 – 1.00f – at Libertarian Micro [320]
DIE REGULATION DER GERINNUNG DURCH DAS ENDOTHEL / Nawroth, Peter Paul – 1993 – 4mf – 9 – DM98.00 – 3-89349-658-0 – gw Hänsel [612]
REGULATION DES NAISSANCES: OPINIONS ET ATTITUDES DES COUPLES ALGERIENS / Algeria. Direction Generale du Plan et des Etudes Economiques – 1968. BNE-8714 1 – 9 – ne IDC [360]
REGULATION OF DRIFTNET FISHING ON THE HIGH SEAS : LEGAL ISSUES – 1991 – 92p – it F.A.O. [340]
REGULATIONS APPROVED BY THE HIGH COMMISSIONER / National Council of the Jewish Community. Palestine. (Va'ad Le'umi) – 1927. BJ-28-39 1 – 9 – ne IDC [956]
REGULATIONS FOR SECONDARY SCHOOLS, INCLUDING SUPPLEMENTARY REGULATIONS FOR SECONDARY SCHOOLS / Great Britain. Laws, Statutes, etc – 1907. Cd. 3592, Cd. 3704 – 9 – uk Microform Academic [324]
REGULATIONS MADE UNDER DEFENCE ACT, 1939 AND EMERGENCY POWERS (DEFENCE) ACT, 1940, SEPT. 1ST, 1939, TO FEB. 28TH, 1943 / Newfoundland. Laws, Statutes, etc – St. John's: Office of the King's Printer, 1943. 341p. LL-2396 – 1 – us L of C Photodup [340]
DER REGULATOR – Berlin, DE. 1884-90 – 2r – 1 – gw Mikrofilm [072]
DER REGULATOR – Berlin, sep 5 1884-90, 1921/22 – 2r – 1 – Inquire at Mikrofilmarchiv for details – gw Misc Inst [072]
REGULATORY AGENCY CHAIRMEN AND THE REGULATORY PROCESS / Welborn, David M – Acus: Comm. on Agency Org. & Personell, n.p. nd. 1977? (all publ) – 3mf – 9 – $4.50 – LLMC 94-345 – us L.L.M.C. [340]
REGULATORY BULLETIN / Kentucky. Agricultural Experiment Station – v. 1-204. 1918-69 – 1,5,6 – us Spaulding [630]
REGULATORY BULLETIN / University of Kentucky. Agricultural Experiment Station – No.206-238. 1969-83. 1 reel – 1,5 – us Spaulding [630]
REGULATORY PEPTIDES – v1-10. 1980-84 – 1,5,6,13 – sz Elsevier [073]
REGULIROVANIE PROMYSHLENNOSTI / Arskii, R – [Moskva]: Redaktsionno-izdatelski i otdel V.S.N.Kh., sklad izd. pri T Sentr. knizhnom sklade V.S.N.Kh., [192-] – 1 – CSUX89-B1757 – us Hoover Inst Photo [339]
Regulo Perez, Juan *see*
– CONDADO DE LA GOMERA
– DE NUEVO ACERCA DEL CONDADO DE LA GOMERA
Reh, E *see* MANUAL ON HOUSEHOLD FOOD CONSUMPTION SURVEYS
REHABILITATION AND HANDICAPPED LITERATURE – (Base collection 1950-78 3009mf $7980; 1979 update 503mf $1375; 1980 update 504mf 1375, 1981 update 519mf $1375; 1982-85 update 817mf $1670; 1986-87 update 469mf $430. Cataloging available) – 5821mf complete collection – 9 – $15,225.00 complete collection – us UMI [615]
LA REHABILITATION DE DROIT, COMMENTAIRE DE L'ARTICLE 10 DE LA LOI DU 5 AOUT 1899, MODIFIE PAR LA LOI DU 11 JUILLET 1900 / Le Poitfevin, Gustave – Paris, Rousseau, 1901. 55 p. LL-4044 – 1 – us L of C Photodup [340]
REHABILITATION NURSING – v.6-. 1981-. Continues: A R N Journal (Association of Rehabilitation Nurses) – 1,5,6,9 – us UMI [073]
REHABILITION DIGEST – Toronto. v16-24. 1985-1993/94 – 9 – Can$20.00y – cn Micromedia [360]
REHBER-I MUZAFFERAT-I BAHRIYE / Muhtar, Ahmed – Kostantiniye [Istanbul]: Karabet Matbaasi, 1312 [1896] – 9 – $85.00 – us MEDOC [956]
Rehder, A *see* THE BRADLEY BIBLIOGRAPHY
DAS RE-HEILIGTUM DES KOENIGS NE-WOSER-RE (RATHURES) / Borchardt, L – Bd. 1: Der Bau. H-237 2. 1905 – 8 – ne IDC [720]
Rehfuss, William F *see* A TREATISE ON DENTAL JURISPRUDENCE FOR DENTISTS AND LAWYERS.
Rehm, E *see* DIE ENTWICKLUNGSGESCHICHTE EINES DIE KLEEARTEN ZERSTOERENDEN PILZES
Rehm, Walter *see* AUSGEWAEHLTE SCHRIFTEN UND BRIEFE
REHOBOTH BAPTIST CHURCH. WILKES COUNTY. GEORGIA : CHURCH RECORDS – 1806-1933 – 1 – 25.51 – us Baptist [240]
REHOBOTH BASTARDS, 1916 / Muller, F – 3 fiche – 9 – sa SA Libr [960]
Rehor, Peter R *see* CURRICULUM DEVELOPMENT FOR EXERCISE BEHAVIORAL CHANGE
O REI DE INGLATERRA – Manoas, Amazonas. 20 Maio 1910 – 1,5,6 – bl Biblioteca [072]
O REI DE TIMOR / Duarte, Teofilo – Lisbon, 1931 – 1 – us Res Libr [440]
DAS REICH – Berlin. Germany. -w. 26 May-16 Jun, 21 Jul 1940-18 Mar 1945. (10 reels) – 1 – uk British Libr Newspaper [072]
DAS REICH – Berlin. May 26, 1940-Apr. 15, 1945 – 1 – 35.00r – us Hoover Inst Photo [072]
DAS REICH : GESAENGE / Linke, Johannes – Leipzig: L Staackmann, 1938 – 1r – 1 – us U.W. Library [810]
DAS REICH – (Mit hardcopy-personen- und stichwortregister 2 baende + 4r DM500.00) – Berlin, 26 Mai 1940-22 Apr 1945 – 4r – 1 – DM320.00 – gw Mikro Press [072]
DAS REICH : WOCHENZEITUNG – Berlin, Germany. 26 May 1940-22 Apr 1945 – 4r – 1 – gw Mikrofilm [072]
DAS REICH : WOCHENZEITUNG – Berlin, may 26 1940-apr 22 1945 – 1 – Inquire at Mikrofilmarchiv for details – gw Misc Inst [072]
DAS REICH : WOCHENZEITUNG FUER DEUTSCHE POLITIK – Saarbruecken, Germany. 6 Dec 1934-5 Jan 1935 – 1r – 1 – gw Mikrofilm [072]
Reich, Emil *see*
– THE FAILURE OF THE "HIGHER CRITICISM" OF THE BIBLE
– GRILLPARZERS KUNSTPHILOSOPHIE
Reich, G C *see* MANTISSAE INSECTORUM ICONIBUS ILLUSTRATAE SPECIES NOVAS
DAS REICH GOTTES IN BOEHMEN : TRAGOEDIE EINES FUEHRERS / Werfel, Franz – Berlin: P Zsolnay, 1930 – 1r – 1 – us U.W. Library [890]
DAS REICH GOTTES NACH ALTEM UND NEUEM TESTAMENT, ODER, WEISSAGUNG UND ERFUELLUNG – Jurjew: E.J. Karow, 1897. 1 fiche – 9 – us A.T.L.A. [240]
DAS REICH GOTTES: NACH DEN SYNOPTISCHEN EVANGELIEN / Luetgert, Wilhelm – Guetersloh: C. Bertelsmann, 1895. 1 fiche – 9 – us A.T.L.A. [240]
REICH GOTTES UND MENSCHENSOHN IM BUCHE DANIEL: EIN BEITRAG / Boehmer, Julius – Leipzig: A. Deichert, 1899. 1 fiche – 9 – us A.T.L.A. [240]
REICH OFFICE FOR SOIL EXPLORATION = REICHSAMT FUER BODENFORSCHUNG – 7r – $161.00 – T401 – us Nat'l Archives [550]
REICH UND REFORMATION / Schubert, Hans von – Tuebingen: J.C.B. Mohr, 1911 – 1mf – us A.T.L.A. [943]
Reicha, A *see*
– QUATUORS, SIX, OP. 98, LIV. 1 ET 2 [FL, VLN, VLA, VC]
– QUINTETTI, TROIS GRANDS, OP. 92, NO. 2 [2VLN,2VLA,VC]
– QUINTETTI, TROIS GRANDS, OP. 92, NO. 3. [2VLN,2VLA,VC]
– SIX QUATUORS, OP. 90, LIV. 1
– SONATE POUR LE PIANOFORTE AVEC ACCOMPAGNEMENT DE VIOLON ET VIOLONCELLE, OP. 47
– STRING QUARTETS OP. 49
– TRIOS GRANDS QUINTETTI, OP. 92, NO. 1
Reichard, J J *see* FLORA MOENO-FRANCOFURTANA. FRANCOFURTI AD MOENUM, 1772-1778
Reichardt, Charles August Ludwig *see* GRAMMAR OF THE FULDE LANGUAGE
Reichardt, Johann F *see*
– BRIEFE EINES AUFMERKSAMEN REISENDEN DIE MUSIK BETREFFEND
– GEIST DES MUSIKALISCHEN KUNSTMAGAZINS
– JOH. FRIEDRICH REICHARDT UEBER DIE DEUTSCHE CONISCHE OPER...
– LIEDER, DER LIEBE UND EINSAMKEIT. VOICE AND PIANO
– MUSIKALISCHES KUNSTMAGAZIN..
– SCHREIBEN UEBER DIE BERLINISCHE MUSIK..
– STUDIEN FUER TONKUENSTLER UND MUSIKFREUNDE...IN ZWEI THEILEN
– UEBER DIE DEUTSCHE COSMISCHE OPER
– VERTRAUTE BRIEFE UEBER FRANKREICH
Reichardt, W *see* DIE BRIEFE DES SEXTUS JULIUS AFRICANUS AN ARISTIDES UDN ORIGENES (T.U.U. 3-34/3)
Reichart, Hally M *see* LETTERS
DER REICHE ARME MANN : EINE VOLKS- UND JUGEND-ERZAEHLUNG / Nieritz, Gustav – 5. Aufl. Gütersloh: C Bertelsmann, [between 1900 and 1920?] – 1r – 1 – us U.W. Library [830]
Reiche, C F *see* FLORA DE CHILE
Reiche, Johann Georg *see* COMMENTARIUS CRITICUS IN N.T. QUO LOCA GRAVIORA ET DIFFICILIORA LECTIONIS DUBIAE ACCURATE RECENSENTUR ET EXPLICANTUR
Reichel, Eugen *see*
– GOTTSCHED
– KLEINES GOTTSCHED-DENKMAL
Reichel, Gerhard *see*
– AUGUST GOTTLIEB SPANGENBERG
– CALVIN ALS UNIONSMANN
– ZINZENDORFS FROEMMIGKEIT IM LICHT DER PSYCHOANALYSE
Reichel, Otto *see* DER VERLAG VON MOHR UND ZIMMER IN HEIDELBERG UND DIE HEIDELBERGER ROMANTIK
Reichel-Dolmatoff, I *see* ROCHA, COMMUNAUTE NOIRE DE LA COTE CARAIBE COLOMBIENNE
Reichelt, Johannes *see*
– CHRISTOPH PANZER
– DIETER UND DIE FRAUEN
Reichelt, Kurt *see* RICHARD WAGNER UND DIE ENGLISCHE LITERATUR
Reichelt, Marie W *see* HISTORY OF DEERFIELD
Reichenbach, A *see* DIE LEHRE DES RABBI JESUA VON NAZARETH
Reichenbach, Heinrich G L *see*
– BEITRAEGE ZU EINER ORCHIDEENKUNDE CENTRAL-AMERIKA'S
– BLICKE IN DAS LEBEN DER GEGENWART UND IN DIE HOFFNUNG DER ZUKUNFT
– CONSPECTUS REGNI VEGETABILIS
– DER DEUTSCHE BOTANIKER
– FLORA LIPSIENSIS PHARMACEUTICA...
– HERBARIUM
– ICONES FLORAE GERMANICAE ET HELVETICAE. DEUTSCHLANDS FLORA
– ICONOGRAPHIA BOTANICA
– ICONOGRAPHIA BOTANICA EXOTICA
– ILLUSTRATIO SPECIERUM ACONITI GENERIS
– MAGAZIN DER AESTHETISCHEN BOTANIK
– MONOGRAPHIA GENERIS ACONITI
– UEBERSICHT DER GATTUNG ACONITUM
– XENIA ORCHIDACEA
Reichenbach, Karl Ludwig Friedrich *see*
– ABSTRACT OF RESEARCHES ON MAGNETISM AND ON CERTAIN ALLIED SUBJECTS INCLUDING A SUPPOSED NEW IMPONDERABLE
– RESEARCHES ON MAGNETISM, ELECTRICITY, HEAT, LIGHT, CRYSTALLIZATION, AND CHEMICAL ATTRACTION, IN THEIR RELATIONS TO THE VITAL FORCE
REICHENBERGER ZEITUNG – Liberec, Czechoslovakia. 29,30 Jun 1921; 1935-Nov 1938 (scattered issues) – 10r – 1 – us L of C Photodup [072]
REICHENHALLER TAGBLATT – Bad Reichenhall, West Germany. Sept 1978- – ca 5r per yr – 1 – gw Mikrofilm [072]
Reichenow, A *see*
– ORNITHOLOGISCHES CENTRALBLATT
– VOGELBILDER AUS FERNEN ZONEN
DES REICHES KOMMEN / Kroeger, Timm – Hamburg: Janssen, 1909 – 1r – 1 – us U.W. Library [830]
REICHSARBEITSBLATT : AMTSBLATT DES REICHSMINISTERIUMS – Berlin, 1933-1944 – 34r – 1 – DM2,550.00 – gw Mikro Press [350]
REICHSARBEITSBLATT – v. 1-43. 1903-45. (13 parts wanting) – 1 – 1,116.00 – us L of C Photodup [331]
DAS REICHSBANNER – Magdeburg, Germany. 15 Apr 1925-26 Dec 1931 – 1 – gw Mikrofilm [072]
DER REICHSBOTE – Berlin, 1873-1934 (incomplete) – 219r – 1 – Inquire at Mikrofilmarchiv for details – gw Misc Inst [072]
DER REICHSBOTE – Berlin, DE. 1919-20; 1924-26 (incomplete); 1927 – 13r – 1 – gw Mikrofilm [072]
DER REICHSBOTE – Muenchen, DE. 15 Jul 1848-Jun 1849 – 1r – 1 – gw Mikrofilm [072]
DER REICHSBUERGER – Leipzig, DE. Jun-Sept 1881 (incomplete) – 1r – 1 – gw Mikrofilm [072]
DER REICHSBUERGER – Leipzig, Jun-Sep 1881 – 1r – 1 – DM90.00 – gw Mikro Press [072]
DER REICHSBUND – Hamburg, West Germany. Sept 1949-73 – 1 – gw Mikrofilm [072]
REICHSFILMBLATT – Berlin. apr 28, 1923-35 – 19r – 1 – gw Mikrofilm [790]
REICHSGESETZBLATT – Berlin, 2pts. 1933-11 Apr 1945 – 22r – DM1650.00 – gw Mikro Press [340]
REICHSGESETZBLATT – Germany, 1871-1945 – inquire – us Ross [943]
REICHSGESETZBLATT : TEIL 1 UND TEIL 2 (1871-1945) – (Continues: Gesetzblatt des Norddeutschen Bundes 1867-1870) – 197mf – 9 – ca DM4,800.00 set – 3-406-30234-3 – gw Beck [340]
DIE REICHSGOTTESHOFFNUNG IN DEN AELTESTEN CHRISTLICHEN DOKUMENTEN UND BEI JESUS / Wernle, Paul – Tuebingen: J C B Mohr (Paul Siebeck), 1903 – 1mf – 9 – 0-8370-6462-7 – 1986-0462 – us A.T.L.A. [220]
REICHSHANDBUCH DER DEUTSCHEN GESELLSCHAFT : DAS HANDBUCH DER PERSONLICHKEITEN IN WORT UND BILD. HERAUSGEBER: DEUTSCHER WIRTSCHAFTSVERLAG. BERLIN 1931. EINGELEITET VON FERDINAND TOENNIES – 37mf – 9 – silver DM840.00 – 3-598-30664-4 – gw Saur [943]
REICHSHEROLD – (Incl suppl) – Berlin-Friedenau, 1887-oct 22 1898 – 3r – 1 – Inquire at Mikrofilmarchiv for details – gw Misc Inst [072]
REICHSKANZLEI UND HOFKALLE UNTER HEINRICH 5 UND KONRAD 3 (MGH SCHRIFTEN..: 14.BD) / Hausmann, F – 1956 – Dfl30.00 – ne Slangenburg [240]
Reichskommissar fuer die Ueberwachung der oeffentlichen Ordnung und Nachrichtensammelstelle im Reichsministerium des Innern *see* LAGEBERICHTE (1920-1929) UND MELDUNGEN (1930-1933)
Reichskonferenz der Arbeitnehmer der Gas-, Elektrizitats-, und Wasserwerk *see* PROTOKOLL UEBER DIE VERHANDLUNGEN
Reichskonferenz der Forstarbeiter *see* NIEDERSCHRIFT DER VERHANDLUNGEN AM 15 UND 16 MAI 1921. 104P. (SERIAL PUBLICATIONS OF GERMAN TRADE UNIONS IN THE MEMORIAL LIBRARY, UNIVERSITY OF WISCONSIN-MADISON.)
Reichskonferenz der Tucharbeiter und tucharbeiterinnen Deutschlands. Forst in der Lausitz, 1928 *see* PROTOKOLL

DER REICHSLANDARBEITERBUND – Berlin, 1928 n20-1933 n10 – 1r – 1 – Inquire at Mikrofilmarchiv for details – gw Misc Inst [331]

REICHS-LANDBUND : AGRARPOLITISCHE WOCHENSCHRIFT – Berlin, 1927-33 – 5r – 1 – DM375.00 – gw Mikro Press [320]

REICHS-LANDBUND – Berlin, jan 8 1927-jul 29 1933 – 5r – 1 – Inquire at Mikrofilmarchiv for details – gw Misc Inst [072]

DIE REICHSMINISTERIALITAET DER SALIER UND STAUFER (MGH SCHRIFTEN..: 10.BD) : EIN BEITRAG ZUR GESCHICHTE DES HOCHMITTELALTERLICHEN DEUTSCHEN VOLKES, STAATES UND REICHES TEIL 1 UND 2 / Bosl, K – 1950-1951 – Dfl53.00 – ne Slangenburg [240]

REICHSMINISTERIUM FUER VOLKSAUFKLAERUNG UND PROPAGANDA ALBUM / U.S. Library of Congress. Prints and Photographs Division – 272 press photographs of the 1937 Reichsparteitag celebration in Nuremburg. 1 reel. P&P12001 – 1 – 23.00r – us L of C Photodup [080]

REICHSORGANIZATIONSAMT / Nationalsozialistische Deutsche Arbeiter-Partei – Partei-Statistisk. 1935 – 1 – us U.W. Library [073]

REICHSPOST – Wien: Druck von Umbr Opitz Nachfolger, 1933-34 – 8r – 1 – us Res Libr [072]

REICHS-POST-REUTER *see* RELATIONS-COURIER/HEUSS'SCHE ZEITUNG

REICHSREZESS : DER TEXT DES REICHSDEPUTATIONSHAUPTSCHLUSSES VON 1803 – (Regensburg, 1803) – 1mf – 9 – DM48.00 – 3-89349-209-7 – gw Hänsel [324]

REICHSRUNDFUNK – Berlin. mar 30, 1941-oct 17, 1944 – 2r – 1 – gw Mikrofilm [380]

REICHSSENDER *see* NACHRICHTENDIENST DES DEUTSCHLANDSENDERS

REICHSSENDER BRESLAU: NACHRICHTENDIENST – (Cont: Das Wichtigste der Woche, -1933 n71; Der aktuelle Pressedienst, -1936 n24; Pressedienst des Reichssenders Breslau, -1937 n7) – Breslau, 1933 n51-1942 n3 – 18r – 1 – Inquire at Mikrofilmarchiv for details – gw Misc Inst [790]

REICHSSPORTBLATT – Berlin, 1935-43 – 1 – Inquire at Mikrofilmarchiv for details – gw Misc Inst [790]

REICHSTAEDTISCHE ERZAEHLUNGEN = SHORT STORIES. SELECTIONS / Kurz, Hermann; ed by Narciss, Georg-Adolf – Breslau: W G Korn, 1944 – 1 – us U.W. Library [830]

Reichsverband der Juedischen Kulturbunde in Deutschland *see* MITTEILUNGEN

DER REICHS-WAECHTER – Bielefeld, jul 3-31 1931 – 1 – Inquire at Mikrofilmarchiv for details – gw Misc Inst [072]

REICHSWART – Berlin, 1920-27, 1932-41 – 5r – 1 – Inquire at Mikrofilmarchiv for details – gw Misc Inst [072]

REICHTUM UND EIGENTUM IN DER ALTKIRCHLICHEN LITERATUR / Schilling, O – Freiburg Brsg., 1908 – 5mf – 9 – ne Slangenburg [240]

Reicke, B *see* DIAKONIE, FESTFREUDE UND ZELOS IN VERBINDUNG MIT DER ALTCHRISTLICHEN AGAPENFEIER

REID : THE COLLECTED WRITINGS OF THOMAS MAYNE REID (1818-1883) – (Pt 1: ca 12r plus guide) – Marlborough: Adam Matthew Publications – 1 – $1,450.00 – uk Matthew [420]

REID, ISAAC, PAPERS, MS 4704 – (Ledger/letterbook, receipts, family register and notes, Newburgh, Ohio school register, and transcriptions, of this Presbyterian Irish immigrant to Cleveland, detailing his reactions to American society) – Cleveland, Cuyahoga, OH. 1829-62 – 1r – 1 – us Western Res [920]

Reid, J M *see* DOOMED RELIGIONS

Reid, James Seaton *see* HISTORY OF CONGREGATIONS OF THE PRESBYTERIAN CHURCH IN IRELAND AND BIOGRAPHICAL NOTICES OF EMINENT PRESBYTERIAN MINISTERS AND LAYMEN

Reid, John *see*
- CHRIST AND HIS RELIGION
- FOOTPRINTS OF SORROW
- GREAT THOUGHTS OF THE BIBLE
- A POCKET-SYSTEM OF THEOLOGY
- SORROW
- VOICES OF THE SOUL ANSWERED IN GOD

Reid, John Morrison *see* MISSIONS AND MISSIONARY SOCIETY OF THE METHODIST EPISCOPAL CHURCH

Reid, Michael E *see* THE MOTOR DEVELOPMENT OF INFANTS AND CHILDREN EXPOSED TO COCAINE WHILE IN UTERO

Reid, Struan *see*
- CULTURES AND CIVILIZATIONS
- INVENTIONS AND TRADE
- SILK AND SPICE ROUTES

Reid, Thomas *see* A SYSTEM OF LOGIC

Reid, Thomas Wemyss *see* CHARLOTTE BRONTE

Reid, Whitelaw *see* FAMILY PAPERS

Reid, William *see*
- THE BLOOD OF JESUS
- REVIVAL TRUTH

REIDSVILLE BAPTIST CHURCH. DAN VALLEY ASSOCIATION. ROCKINGHAM COUNTY. NORTH CAROLINA : CHURCH RECORDS – 1850-94 – 1 – 19.62 – us Baptist [240]

REIF STEHT DIE SAAT : NEUE BALLADEN / Strauss und Torney, Lulu von – Jena: E Diederichs, 1921 – 1r – 1 – us U.W. Library [780]

Reifel, August *see* HISTORY OF FRANKLIN COUNTY

Reiffers, Jean-Louis *see* TRANSNATIONAL CORPORATIONS AND ENDOGENOUS DEVELOPMENT

Reifmann, J *see*
- KOL MEVASSER. SEFER HALAKHOT GEDOLOT. AL DEREKH HADASH
- MESHIV DAVAR
- SEFER PESHER DAVAR
- TOLEDOT HA-R. ZERAHYAH HA-LEVI

Reigas, A *see* SBORNIK NORMATIVNYKH AKTOV I INSTRUKTIVNYKH MATERIALOV

Reighard, Frank H *see* A STANDARD HISTORY OF FULTON COUNTY

REIGI RUITEN = COLLECTION OF RECORDS OF VARIOUS CEREMONIES IN IMPERIAL COURT / ed by Tokoro, Isao – In the National Diet Library and The Cabinet Library, 620 books – 63r and 1 colored reel – 1 – Y680,000 (color edition Y50,000) – ja Yushodo [950]

THE REIGN OF GRACE: FROM ITS RISE TO ITS CONSUMMATION / Booth, Abraham – New York: Robert Carter, 1861. 1 fiche – 9 – us A.T.L.A. [240]

THE REIGN OF HENRY 8 FROM HIS ACCESSION TO THE DEATH OF WOLSEY / Brewer, J S; ed by Gairdner, James – London: J. Murray, 1884 – 3mf – us A.T.L.A. [240]

Reilly, Andrew Jackson *see* THE JUROR: BEING A GUIDE TO CITIZENS SUMMONED TO SERVE AS JURORS

Reilly, G F *see* IMPERIUM AND SACERDOTIUM ACCORDING TO ST BASIL THE GREAT

Reilly, Joseph John *see* NEWMAN AS A MAN OF LETTERS

Reimarus, Hermann Samuel *see* VON DEM ZWECKE JESU UND SEINER JUENGER

REIME UND GEDICHTE DES ABRAHAM IBN ESRA / Rosin, David – Breslau. 1885-94. BJ-421-61 1 – 9 – ne IDC [810]

Reimer, Brad W *see* THE EFFECT OF CADENCE ON AEROBIC AND ANAEROBIC CONTRIBUTIONS TO THE TOTAL ENERGY REQUIREMENTS OF CYCLING AT CONSTANT POWER OUTPUT

Reimers, Fernando *see* EDUCATION, ADJUSTMENT AND RECONSTRUCTION

Reimoser, E *see* KATALOG DER ECHTEN SPINNEN (ARANEAE) DES PALAEARKTISCHEN GEBIETES

Rein, G Kurt *see* ABESSINIEN

REIN J. VANDER ZEE, SENATE SERVICE 1961-1964 : ASSISTANT TO THE SENATE DEMOCRATIC WHIP (HUBERT HUMPHREY); ASSISTANT SECRETARY OF THE MAJORITY – 2mf – 9 – $10.00 – us Scholarly Res [320]

Rein, Rikard Petrovich *see* POLEVO I TSENTR "PLAMIA"

REIN ZU DOLLE : NOCH NE MOLLE LUSTIGER DORFGESCHICHTEN / Wiese, Ernst August – Leipzig: Amthorsche Verlagsbuchhandlung, 1940 – 1r – 1 – us U.W. Library [390]

Reinagle, Alexander *see*
- A COLLECTION OF FAVORITE SONGS ARRANGED FOR THE VOICE AND PIANO FORTE
- THE CONSTELLATION (NO. 4 OF MR. FRANCIS'S BALLROOM ASSISTANT)
- FOUR SONATAS FOR THE PIANO
- TWELVE FAVORITE PIECES. ARRANGED FOR THE PIANO FORTE OR HARPSICHORD

Reindahl, E Rullmann *see* BLUETHEN DES GEFUEHLS GESPROSSEN IN MEINEN ERHOLUNGSSTUNDEN

THE REINDEER AND ITS DOMESTICATION / Laufer, B – (Mem. Amer. Anthrop. Ass. v. 4). 1917 – 8 – ne IDC [590]

Reindorf, Carl Christian *see* HISTORY OF THE GOLD COAST AND ASANTE, BASED ON TRADITIONS AND HISTORICAL FACTS

LA REINE DE NAINVILLE : SUIVI DE GRIVETTE, L'AVARE, LE NID AU PIED DU ROCHER, LE PARAPLUIE DE FAMILLE / Lacerte, A B – Montreal: Editions Beauchemin, 1931. SEM105P1301 – 1mf – 9 – Can$2.25 – cn Bibl Nat [971]

LA REINE DE NENNI, NOUVELLE HISTORIQUE / Luchet, Jean-Pierre-Louis de la Roche Du Maine, Mis de – (Utopias in the Enlightment series). 1766 – 9 – fr Hachette [830]

Reine, J *see* THE EUCHARISTIE DOCTRINE AND LITURGY OF THE MYSTAGOGICAL CATECHESE OF THEODORE OF MOPSUESTIA

LA REINE VS LOUIS RIEL – Ottawa: Imprimeur de la Reine, 1886. SEM35P79 – 1r – 1 – Can$15.00 – cn Bibl Nat [971]

Reineck, R *see* COMMENTARIVS DE REGIBVS PERSICIS, SEV FAMILIA ARTAXERXIS MAGVSAEI

Reinecke, C *see* TRIO IN A MOLL, OP. 188, FOR PIANOFORTE, OBOE AND HORN

Reinecker, Virginia M. *see* AN EXAMINATION OF THE UNDERSTANDING OF THE HUMAN PERSON IN THE PHILOSOPHY OF JOHN MACMURRAY

Reiner, Robert *see* POLICING AND SOCIETY

Reiner, Silvain *see* EVA PERON

REINFORCED PLASTICS – v2-7 1963-68. All pub – 1,5,6 – us Princeton Micro [670]

Reinhard, A M *see* MONOCHORDUM ANDREAE REINHARDI, NIVIMONTAMI

REINHARD FLEMMINGS ABENTEUER ZU WASSER UND ZU LANDE / Seidel, Heinrich – Gesamt-Ausg. Stuttgart: J G Cotta, 1920 – 1r – 1 – us U.W. Library [430]

Reinhard, Gustav Edgar *see* SCHILLERS EINFLUSS AUF THEODOR KOERNER

Reinhard, Leonhard *see*
- KURZER UND DEUTLICHER UNTERRICHT VON DEM GENERAL-BASS..

Reinhard, Wilhelm *see* ZUR GESCHICHTE DER SONNTAGSSCHULEN UND KINDERGOTTESDIENSTE IN DEUTSCHLAND

DIE REINHARDSBRUNNER BRIEFSAMMLUNG (MGH EPISTOLAE 4: 5.BD) – 1952 – Dfl13.00 – ne Slangenburg [240]

Reinhardt, O *see* ENUMERATIO MUSCORUM FRONDOSORUM

Reinhart, Caleb S *see* HISTORY OF THE SUPREME COURT OF THE TERRITORY AND STATE OF WASHINGTON.

Reinhart, Herman Francis *see* LIFE AND RECOLLECTIONS

Reinhart, M *see* ANTZEYGUNG WIE DIE GEFALLENE CHRISTENHEIT

REINHOLD: ODER, DIE VERWANDELTEN / Alverdes, Paul – Muenchen: G Mueller, [1931] – 1r – 1 – us U.W. Library [943]

Reinick, Robert *see* EINE SONNIGE WELT

Reinish, Leo *see* DIE SOMALI-SPRACHE

Reinke, J *see*
- ABHANDLUNGEN UEBER FLECHTEN
- ATLAS DEUTSCHER MEERESALGEN
- ENTWICKLUNGSGESCHICHTLICHE UNTERSUCHUNGEN UEBER DIE DICTYOTACEEN UND DIE CUTLERIACEEN DES GOLFES VON NEAPEL
- MEIN TAGEWERK

Reinke, Laurenz *see* DER PROPHET MICAH

Reinkemeyer, Lars *see* DIE PRIVATISIERUNG DER BRITISH TELECOM VERSUS POSTREFORM – MEHR WETTBEWERB AUF DEN TELEKOMMUNIKATIONSMAERKTEN

Reinkens, Joseph Hubert *see*
- HILARIUS VON POITIERS
- DIE LEHRE DES HEIL. CYPRIAN VON DER EINHEIT DER KIRCHE
- DIE PAEPSTLICHEN DECRETE VOM 18. JULI 1870

Reinmarus, A *see* POD GNETOM RELIGII

EL REINO DE DIOS / Juan de los Angeles – Madrid: Espana Editorial, s.a. – 1 – sp Bibl Santa Ana [240]

EL REINO DE DIOS / Juan de los Angeles – Madrid: Imp. de Felipe Marques, s.a. – 1 – sp Bibl Santa Ana [946]

EL REINO DE GALICIA, TOMO 1. VIGO 1966 / Elias de Tejada, Francisco; ed by Pazos, Manuel R – Madrid: Graf. Calleja, 1970 – 1 – sp Bibl Santa Ana [946]

Reinsch, P F *see*
- DIE ALGENFLORA DES MITTLEREN THEILES VON FRANKEN
- CONTRIBUTIONES AD ALGOLOGIAM ET FUNGOLOGIAM
- DE SPECIEBUS GENERIBUSQUE NONNULLIS NOVIS EX ALGARUM ET FUNGORUM CLASSE

Reinsdorf, Otto et al *see* ALLGEMEINE DEUTSCHE MUSIK-ZEITUNG

Reinzer, Franciscus *see* METEOROLOGIA PHILOSOPHICO-POLITICA

Reiper, R *see* ALCIMI ECDICII AVITI VIENNENSIS EPISCOPI OPERA QUAE SUPERSUNT (MGH 1: 6.BD. 2.TEIL)

Reis, F F *see* KATALOG BIBLIOTEKI IMP. MOSKOVSKAGO UNIVERSITETA

Reischer, M *see* SHA'AREI YERUSHALAYIM

Reischke, Gerhard *see* HYDRODYNAMISCHE KENNGROESSEN VON GLEITLAGERN MIT UNTERBROCHENER RINGNUT UND IHRE ANWENDUNG BEI DER BERECHNUNG DYNAMISCH BEANSPRUCHTER RADIALGLEITLAGER

Reischle, Max *see*
- AUFSAETZE UND VORTRAEGE
- CHRISTLICHE GLAUBENSLEHRE IN LEITSAETZEN
- DIE FRAGE NACH DEM WESEN DER RELIGION
- THEOLOGIE UND RELIGIONSGESCHICHTE
- WERTURTEILE UND GLAUBENSURTEILE: EINE UENTERSUCHUNG

REISE DER OESTERREICHISCHEN FREGATTE NOVARA UM DIE ERDE IN DEN JAHREN 1857-1859. GEOLOGISCHER THEIL – 2660 2. 2 v. 1864-1866 – 8 – ne IDC [550]

REISE DURCH DIE WUESTE ATACAMA / Philippi, R A – Halle. 1860. B-5636 2 – 8 – ne IDC [910]

REISE DURCH SIBIRIEN VOM DEM JAHRE 1733 BIS 1743 / Gmelin, J G – (Sammlung neuer und merkwuerdiger Reise zu Wasser und zu Lande, v. 4). v. 1-4. Goettingen. 1751. BU-771 2 – 8 – ne IDC [910]

REISE DURCH VERSCHIEDENE PROVINZEN DES RUSSISCHEN REICHS / Pallas, Peter Simon – 3v. St. Petersburg. 1771-76. B-5016 2 – 8 – ne IDC [910]

REISE IN DAS GEBIET DES WEISSEN NIL, IN DEN JAHREN 1862-1864 / Heuglin, M Th. von – Leipzig. Heidelberg. 1869. BA-190 2 – 8 – ne IDC [910]

REISE IN NORDOST AFRIKA: NEBST ZOOLOGISCHEN SKIZZEN / Heuglin, M Th. von – 2v. Braunschweig. 1877. BA-191 2 – 8 – ne IDC [960]

REISE IN OSTAFRIKA IN DEN JAHREN 1903-1905 : WISSENSCHAFTLICHE ERGEBNISSE / ed by Voeltzkow, A – 5v. Stuttgart. 1906-23. – 119mf – 8 – ne IDC [960]

REISE NACH ABESSINIEN, IN DEN JAHREN 1861 UND 1862 / Heuglin, M Th. von – Jena. 1868. BA-189 2 – 8 – ne IDC [910]

REISE NACH BRASILIEN IN DEN JAHREN 1815-1817 / Wied-Neuwied, M A P zu – 2v. atlas. Frankfurt. 1820-21. B-5808 2 – 8 – ne IDC [580]

REISE NACH DER INSEL KRETA IM GRIECHISCHEN ARCHIPELAGUS IM JAHRE 1817 / Sieber, F W – Leipzig, 1823. 2 vols. B-650 2 – 8 – ne IDC [580]

REISE NACH GUINEA UND DEN CARIBAISCHEN.. / Isert, Paul Erdmann – Kopenhagen, 1788 – 1 – us U.W. Library [910]

DIE REISE NACH RIVA : LUSTSPIEL IN DREI AUFZUEGEN / Wilbrandt, Adolf von – Wien: L Rosner, 1877 – 1r – 1 – us U.W. Library [820]

REISEBERICHTE UND BRIEFE AUS DEN JAHREN 1845-1849 / Castren, M A; ed by Schiefner, A – St. Petersburg, 1856. x/527p. BU-778/2 – 8 – ne IDC [400]

REISEBILDER AUS GRIECHENLAND UND KLEINASIEN / Dalton, Hermann – Bremen: C.Ed. Mueller, 1884. 1 fiche – 9 – us A.T.L.A. [240]

REISEN IM ARCHIPEL DER PHILIPPINEN, THEIL 2, WISSENSCHAFTLICHE RESULTATE / Semper, C G – Leipzig, Wiesbaden, 1868-1905. 10 vols. BZ-217 2 – 8 – ne IDC [574]

REISEN IN AFRIKA; 1875, 1876 / Junker, W – 3v. Wien. 1889-92. BA-175 2 – 8 – ne IDC [910]

REISEN IN OSTAFRIKA: AUSGEFUEHRT IN DEN JAHREN 1837-1855 / Krapf, J L – 2v. Stuttgart. 1858. BA-162 2 – 8 – ne IDC [910]

REISEN UND FORSCHUNGEN IM AMUR-LANDE IN DEN JAHREN 1854-1895 / ed by Schrenk, L von – Spb. 4v. 1858-1900 – 116mf – 9 – Z-202/2 – ne IDC [910]
DAS REISETAGEBUCH EINES PHILOSOPHEN / Keyserlin, Hermann Alexander – Stuttgart, Berlin, 1923 – 16mf – 8 – ne Slangenburg [100]
Reisiger, Hans *see* JOHANN GOTTFRIED HERDER
Reiske, J *see* LIBRI DUO DE CEREMONIIS AULAE BYZANTINAE (CBH 33)
Reiskii, J J *see* ABULFEDAE ANNALES MUSLEMICI ARABICE ET LATINE
Reisner, George A *see*
- HARVARD EXCAVATIONS AT SAMARIA
- ISRAELITE OSTRACA FROM SAMARIA
- SUMERISCH-BABYLONISCHE HYMNEN NACH THONTAFELN GRIECHISCHER ZEIT

Reisner, L *see*
- FRONT 1918-1919
- GAMBURG NA BARRIKADAKH
- IZBRANNYE PROIZVEDENIIA
- UGOL', ZHELEZO I ZHIVOTNYE LIUDI
- V STRANE GINDENBURGA. OCHERKI SOVREMENNOI GERMANII

Reisner, Mikhail Andreevich *see*
- BOG I BIRZHA
- DUKHOVNAIA POLITSIIA V ROSSII

Reissig, Helmut *see* DIE HAFTUNG BEI WECHSELFAELSCHUNGEN
Reissig, Herman F *see*
- SPANISH DEMOCRACY AND ITS REFUGEES: A NARRATIVE OF PERSONAL EXPERIENCE
- TWO MINDS WITH BUT A SINGLE THOUGHT

Reissig, Luis *see* EL FIN DE UN CICLO HISTORICO EN ARGENTINA
Reissinger, Marianne *see* DIE SINFONIEN ERNST EICHNERS (1740-1777)
Reissner, A *see* IERVSALEM, VETVSTISSIMA ILLA ET CELEBERRIMA TOTIVS MVNDI CIVITAS, EX SACRIS LITERIS ET APPROBATIS HISTORICIS AD UNGUEM DESCRIPTA
DER REITER AUF DEM FAHLEN PFERD : EIN BUCH VOM MONGOLEN DSCHINGGIS-KHAN UND SEINEM ABENDLAENDISCHEN GEGENSPIELER / Stickelberger, Emanuel – (Includes bibliographical references) – 7. Aufl. Stuttgart: J F Steinkopf, [1944] – 1r – 1 – us U.W. Library [950]
REITER IM KRIEG : AUS "DAS ABENTEUER" / Mechow, Karl Benno von; ed by Langenbucher, Hellmuth – Muenchen: A Langen/G Mueller, 1933 – 1r – 1 – us U.W. Library [830]
Reiter, Prosper, jr *see* PROFITS, DIVIDENDS AND THE LAW.
Reithmayr, F X *see* DR. J.A. MOEHLER'S, ERNANNTEN DOMDECANS ZU WUERZBURG UND RITTERS, DES KGL. BAYER. ST MICHAEL-ORDENS, EHEDEM ORD. PROFESSORS DER THEOLOGIE AN DER UNIVERSITAET MUENCHEN, PATROLOGIE, ODER, CHRISTLICHE LITERAERGESCHICHTE
Reitler, Marzellin Adalbert *see*
- IHR MITTEL
- STADTRATH DONNING
- DER VATER DER MEDEA
- WER WAR'S?

Reitmeyer, Elisabeth *see* STUDIEN ZUM PROBLEM DER GEDICHTSAMMLUNG MIT EINGEHENDER UNTERSUCHUNG DER GEDICHTSAMMLUNG GOETHES UND TIECKS
Reitsma, A S *see* ACTA DER PROVINCIALE EN PARTICULIERE SYNODEN
Reitsma, J *see* GESCHIEDENIS VAN DE HERVORMING EN DE HERVORMDE KERK DER NEDERLANDEN
Reitsma, Johannes *see* FRANCISCUS JUNIUS
Reitsma, S A *see* BANDOENG
Reitter, E *see* FAUNA GERMANICA
Reitzenstein, R *see* HISTORIA MONACHORUM UND HISTORIA LAUSIACA
REIVINDICACIONES HISTORICAS. VIRIATO NO FUE PORTUGUES, DE ANSELMO ARENAS LOPEZ / T'Serclaes, Duque de – Madrid: Fortanet, 1910. B.R.A.H. 57, 1910, pp. 78-79 – sp Bibl Santa Ana [946]
Reiz, Elizabeth *see* E. T. A. HOFFMANNS ELIXIERE DES TEUFELS UND C. V. BRENTANOS ROMANZEN VOM ROSENKRANZ
Reizabal, Luis *see* MEDICO EN LAS HURDES
REJ; THE RAILWAY ENGINEERING JOURNAL – 1972-75 – 1 – us UMI [380]
A REJOINDER TO DR. HUGHES / Bender, Prosper – Boston, MA?: R. Avery, 1888?. 04176. (Pre-1900 Canadiana) – 9 – cn C.I.H.M. [971]
Rejon de Silva, Diego A *see*
- DICCIONARIO DE LAS NOBLES ARTES
- LA PINTURA. POEMA DIDACTICO

Rekers, Bernard *see*
- BENITO ARIAS MONTANO (1527-1598)

REKISHI CHIRI. "HISTORY AND HISTORICAL GEOGRAPHY OF JAPAN."CH-458. V. 1-82. 1899-1943 – 9 – ne IDC [950]
REKISHIGAKU KENKYU / Historical Science Society – The Journal. v. 1-227. Tokyo. 1933-59. Lacking: v. 1-121, 1933-45; v. 148-149, 1951. BCH-871 2 – 8 – ne IDC [900]
REKLAM – (Supplement to Piyano Gazete. Sahib-i Imtiyaz: Bahaeddin. No. 1 (1326[1910])) – Istanbul Hurriyet Matbaasi, 1910 – 1mf – 9 – $12.00 – us MEDOC [949]
DIE REKLAME – (Cont by: Die deutsche Werbung, dec 1933) – Berlin. 1914-nov 1915. feb, mar 1916. apr 1919-aug 1920. jul-dec 1921. spec iss apr-oct 1924. 1925-28. mar 1929-31. feb 1932- mar 1933. feb 1934-jan 1941 (incomplete) – 12r – 1 – gw Mikrofilm [380]
REKOMENDATE L'NYI SPISOK KNIG DLIA KOMPLEKTOVANIIA I POPOLNENIIA BIBLIOTEK SEL'SKOKHOZIAISTVENNOI, KUST.-PROM. KOOPERATSII I OBSHCHESTV SEL.-KHOZ. KREDITA / Biblioteka Soiuza sel'skokhoziaistvennoi, kreditnoi i kustarno-promyslovoi kooperatsii – Moscow, 1928 – 2mf – 9 – COR-528/1 – ne IDC [334]
Reksodiprodjo, Susatyo *see* PENGANTAR EKONOMI BANK DAN KREDIT
REKVIEM / Akhmatova, A – Izd. Tovarishchestvo Zarubezhnykh Pisatelei. Munich. 1963. BR-1102 2 – 8 – ne IDC [460]
REKVIZITSII A I KONFISKATSII A PO ZAKONODATELSTVU R.S.F.S.R. / ed by Barsegiants, O B – Moskva: "Znanie", 1922 – 1 – CSUX88-B9114 – us Hoover Inst Photo [947]
DIE REL. PHIL. LEHRE SAADJA GAONS UEBER DIE HL. SCHRIFT : BGPHMA 4/4 / Engelkemper, Wilhelm – Muenster, 1903 – 2mf – 9 – ne Slangenburg [240]
DIE REL. PHIL. LEHRE SAADJA GAONS UEBER DIE HL. SCHRIFT / Engelkemper, W – Muenster, 1903 – 2mf – 8 – ne Slangenburg [100]
RELACAM DA ENTRADA...MARTIN ALFONSO DE MELLO – 1641 – 9 – 1.50f – sp Bibl Santa Ana [946]
RELACAO DO NOVO CAMINHO QUE FEZ POR TERRA E MAR VINDO DE INDIA PARA PORTUGAL... / Godinho, Manuel – Madrid: Missionalia Hispanica, 1949 – 1 – sp Bibl Santa Ana [240]
RELACAO DOS DISCOS GRAVADOS DO ESTADO DE CEARA – 1953 – 1 – us I.U. Libraries [390]
RELACAO DOS DISCOS GRAVADOS DO ESTADO DE GOIAS – 1950 – 1 – us I.U. Libraries [390]
RELACAO DOS DISCOS GRAVADOS DO ESTADO DO RIO GRANDE DO SUL – 1959 – 1 – us I.U. Libraries [390]
RELACAO DOS DISCOS GRAVADOS NO ESTADO DE MINAS GERAIS. FEV 1944. 1956 – 1 – us I.U. Libraries [390]
RELACAO E DESCRIPCAO DE GUINE / d'Almada, Andre Alvares – (Filmed with: West African maps, letters and manuscripts from the 17th and 18th centuries) – Lisboa: M Rodrigues, 1733 – us Res Libr [910]
RELACAO VERDADEIRA DOS TRABALHOS QUE O GOVERNADOR D. FERNANDO DE SOUTO E CERTOS FIDALGOS PORTUGUESES PASSARAM NO DESCOBRIMENTO DA PROVINCIA DE FLORIDA – 3rd Edicao prefaciada e anotada e indices por Frederico Gavazzo Perry Vidal. Lisboa: Ed. Atica. 1940 – sp Bibl Santa Ana [946]
RELACIO VERDADERA DEL REBATO... – Seuila, 1562 – 1mf – 9 – H-8160/1 – ne IDC [956]
RELACION ALFABETICA DE LOS ALFERECES PROVISIONALES DE LA PROVINCIA DE CACERES / Caceres. Hermandad Nacional de Alfereces Provisionales – Caceres: Imp. Sanguino, 1960 – sp Bibl Santa Ana [946]
RELACION DE COMO EL PECE NICOLAO SE HA APARECIDO DE NUEVO EN EL MAR... – Barcelona, 1608 – 1mf – 9 – sp Cultura [610]
RELACION DE LA CALIFICACION Y MILAGROS DEL SANTO CRUCIFIJO DE GALAMEA... DIVIDIDA EN DOS LIBROS / Barrantes Maldonado, Francisco – Madrid: Viuda de Alfonso Martin, 1617 – 1 – sp Bibl Santa Ana [240]
RELACION DE LA CONQUISTA DE LA NUEVA ESPANA / Aguilar, Francisco de – Mexico: Jose Porrua e hijos sucs, 1954 – 1 – sp Bibl Santa Ana [350]
RELACION DE LA VISITA GENERAL QUE EN LA DIOCESIS DE CARACAS Y VENEZUELA HIZO EL ILMO. SR. D. MARIANO MARTI, DEL CONSEJO DE S.M. 1771-1784 / Bayle, Constantino – Caracas, 1928; Madrid: Razon y Fe, 1929 – 1 – sp Bibl Santa Ana [240]
RELACION DE LAS EPIDEMIAS...DE CARTAGENA...Y LA EXPOSIXION DEL NUEVO METODO DE JOSE MASDEVALL / Rodon y Bell, M – Cartagena, 1787 – 3mf – 9 – sp Cultura [614]
LA RELACION DE LAS INDIAS DE FRAY ANTONIO / Munoz de San Pedro, Miguel – Vazquez e Espinosa. Madrid: C.S.I.C., 1948 – 1 – sp Bibl Santa Ana [946]
RELACION DE LOS SITIOS Y DEFENSAS DE OLIVENZA, DE BADAJOZ Y DE CAMPO-MAYOR EN 1811 Y 1812 POR LAS TROPAS FRANCESAS DEL – EJERCITO DEL MEDIODIA EN ESPANA. TRADUCIDO POR E. SEGURA / L (Amuse), Coronel – Badajoz: Pub.Cent.E, Extrem., 1934 – 1 – sp Bibl Santa Ana [946]
RELACION DE LOS SUCEDIDO CON LA ENFERMEDAD DE LA PESTE EN LOGRONO – Logrono, 1599 – 1mf – 9 – sp Cultura [616]
RELACION DE LOS SUCESOS DEL REINO DE LA CAMBODJA. MADRID, 1929 / San Antonio, Gabriel de – Madrid: Razon y Fe, 1930 – 1 – sp Bibl Santa Ana [950]
RELACION DE PERO LOPEZ. VISION DE UN CONQUISTADOR DEL SIGLO 16 / Gueenaga de Silva, Rosario – Bahia Blanca: Talleres Graficos Martinez y Rodriguez S.R.L., 1971 – sp Bibl Santa Ana [946]
RELACION DE UN CASO LASTIMOSO QUE SUCEDIO A UNA...DONCELLA...NATURAL DE LA CIUDAD DE TRUJILLO / Rosaura la de Trujillo – Trujillo: Tip. La Perfeccion Trujillana, s.a. – sp Bibl Santa Ana [946]
RELACION DEL DESCUBRIMIENTO DEL REYNO DEL PERU / Trujillo, Diego de – Sevilla: C.S.I.C., Escuela de Estudios Hispanoamericanos, 1948 – 1 – sp Bibl Santa Ana [946]
RELACION DEL FALLECIMIENTO...MOLINA / Ballesteros, Francisco A – 1745 – 9 – 1.50f – sp Bibl Santa Ana [946]
RELACION DEL ORIGEN DE LOS INDIOS QUE HABITAN ESTA NUEVA ESPANA... / Codex Ramirez – Mexico: Leyenda, 1944 – 1 – F157,50 – fr Armell [305]
RELACION DEL VIAGE QUE AMBROSIO DE MORALES...HIZO POR SU MANDADO AL ANO DE 1572 EN GALICIA Y ASTURIAS : SANTA EULALIA / Florez, Enrique – Madrid: Benito Cano, 1792 – 1 – sp Bibl Santa Ana [946]
RELACION DEL VIAJE HECHO A LOS REYNOS DEL PERU Y CHILE POR LOS BOTANICOS DE S.M. / Ruiz Lopez, Hipolito – Madrid: Tip Huelves, 1931; Madrid: Razon y Fe, 1932 – 1 – sp Bibl Santa Ana [580]
UNA RELACION DESCONOCIDA DE LA EXPEDICION A AFRICA DEL REY DON SEBASTIAN / Rodriguez Amaya, Esteban – Vila Nova de Famalicao, Graficas Minerva de Gaspar Pinto de Sousa, 1948. Sep. Bol. A. Historico Militar – sp Bibl Santa Ana [910]
RELACIONES GEOGRAFICAS DE LA GOBERNACION DE VENEZUELA (1767-68) / Altolaguirre, Angel de – Madrid, 1908 – 5mf – 9 – ILM-2112/1 – ne IDC [340]
RELACIONES INTERESANTES Y DATOS HISTORICOS SOBRE LAS MISIONES CATOLICAS DEL CALQUETA Y PUTOMAYO DESDE EL ANO 1632 HASTA EL PRESENTE / Benigno de Canet de Mar, Padre – 1924 – 1r – 1 – us Ross [240]
RELACOES EXTERNAS DE PORTUGAL: REINADO DE D. JOAO V : REINADO DE D. JOAO V / Brazao, Eduardo – 1938. 2v. Bibliographic footnotes. Livraria Civilizacao – 1 – us U.W. Library [946]
O RELAMPAGO : PERIODICO PARA TODAS AS CLASSES: CRITICO, SATYRICO, NOTICIOSO E JOCO-SERIO – Maceio, Alagoas. 19 Ago 1873 – 1,5,6 – bl Biblioteca [072]
THE RELAPSE PREVENTION MODEL AND EXERCISE MAINTENANCE BEHAVIOR / Jacobson, Lynn B & Stein, Gary L – 1992 – 2mf – 9 – $8.00 – us Microform Publ [150]
RELATIO HISTORICA RERUM IN JAPONIAE REGNO GESTARUM ANNO DOMINI 1603 / ed by Pasio, A P Francisco – Moguntiae, 1610 – Dfl19.00 – ne Slangenburg [240]
RELATIO NOVA DE HODIERNO HABESSINIAE STATU, EX INDIA NUPER ALLATA : ADDITIS EPISTOLIS REGLIS AS SOCIETATEM INDIAE ORIENTALIS, EJUSQUE RESPOSIONE CUM NOTIS NECESSARIIS / Ludolfi, Iobi – (Filmed with: his Ad suam Historiam aethiopicam antehac editam Commentarius) – Francofurti ad Moenum: Sumptibus Johannis Davidis Zunner: Typis Martini Jacqueti, 1693 – us Res Libr [960]
RELATION ABREGEE DU VOYAGE. EN ETHIOPIE / Poncet, Charles J – Paris, Nicolas Le Clerc. 1704 – 9 – 7.50 – fr Orientalistes [910]
RELATION CURIEUSE ET NOUVELLE D'UN VOYAGE DE CONGO / Plaisance, Guattini de & Plaisance, Carli de – Lyon, Th. Amaulry. 1680 – 9 – $10.00 – fr Orientalistes [910]
RELATION CURIEUSE ET NOUVELLE D'UN VOYAGE DE CONGO FAIT LES ANNEES 1666 ET 1667 / Gattine, M A de & CarlidePlaisance, D de – Lyon. 1680. BA-104 2 – 8 – ne IDC [910]
RELATION DE CE QUI S'EST PASSE CETTE ANNEE EN CANADA – Paris: Bureau d'Adresse, 1775. SEM105P885 – 1mf – 9 – Can$2.25 – cn Bibl Nat [971]
RELATION DE DIVERS VOYAGES FAITS DANS L'AFRIQUE, L'AMERIQUE ET AUX INDES OCCIDENTALES. LA DESCRIPTION DU ROYAUME DE JUDA ET QUELQUES PARTICULARITES TOUCHANT LA VIE DU ROI REGNANT / Dralse de Grandpierre – (African Library series). 1713 – 9 – fr Hachette [910]
RELATION DE LA MORT DE LOUIS 16, ROI DE FRANCE / Edgeworth De Firmont, Henry E – Montreal: J Brown, 1812. SEM16P27 – 1r – 5 – Can$9.00 – cn Bibl Nat [944]
RELATION DE LA NIGRITIE / Gaby, Jean-Baptiste – Paris, E. Couterot. 1689 – 9 – 5.00 – fr Orientalistes [305]
RELATION DE LA NIGRITIE. CONTENANT UNE EXACTE DESCRIPTION DE SES ROYAUMES ET DE LEURS GOUVERNEMENTS, LA RELIGION, LES MOEURS, COUSTUMES ET RARETES DE CE PAYS / Gaby, Jean-Baptiste – (African Library series). 1689 – 9 – fr Hachette [306]
RELATION DE LA NOUVELLE FRANCE, DE SES TERRES, NATUREL DU PAIS, ET DE SES HABITANTS: ITEM, DU VOYAGE DES PERES JESUITES AUSDICTES CONTREES, ET DE CE QU'ILS Y ONT FAICT JUSQUES A LEUR PRINCE PAR LES ANGLOIS / Biard, Pierre – Albany?, 1871? 03581. (Pre-1900 Canadiana) – 9 – cn C.I.H.M. [971]
RELATION DE LA SORTIE DU DEMON BALAM DU CORPS DE LA MERE PRIEURE DES URSULINES DE LOUDUN – Paris. 1635 – 9 – fr Hachette [360]
RELATION DE L'AMBASSADE AU KHAREZM / Khan, Riza Q. – Texte persan, traduction francaise par Ch. Schefer. 1879 – 9 – fr Orientalistes [950]
RELATION DE L'AMBASSADE AU KHAREZM DE RIZA QOULY KHAN / Schefer, C – Paris. 1879. BU-752 2 – 8 – ne IDC [950]
RELATION DE L'AMBASSADE...SIAM,... / Chaumont, de – La Haye, 1733 – 2mf – 1 – ILM-1047/1 – ne IDC [327]
RELATION DE L'ETAT DE QUELQUES PERSONNES PRETENDUES POSSEDEES / Bayle, Francois & Grangeron, Henri – Toulouse. 1682 – 9 – fr Hachette [360]
RELATION DES COTES D'AFRIQUE APPELEES GUINEE: AVEC LA DESCRIPTION DU PAYS, MOEURS ET FACONS DE VIVRE DES HABITANTS, DES PRODUCTIONS DE LA TERRE ET DES MARCHANDISES QU'ON EN APPORTE, AVEC LES REMARQUES HISTORIQUES SUR LES COTES / Villault, Nicolas – (African Library series). 1669 – 9 – fr Hachette [960]
RELATION DES SIEGES ET DEFENSES DE BADAJOZ, D'OLIVENCA / Lamare, General – Paris: Chez Anselin, 1837 – 1 – sp Bibl Santa Ana [350]
RELATION DU GHANAT ET DES COUTUMES DE SES HABITANTS – (African Library). Traduite litteralement de l'arabe, par M. Amedee Jaubert. s.l.n.d – 9 – fr Hachette [960]
RELATION DU GHANAT ET DES COUTUMES DE SES HABITANTS / Jaubert, Amedee – Traduite litteralement de l'arabe. s.1. n.d. 14 p. (Africa Library) – 9 – fr Hachette [390]

RELATION DU GROENLAND. 13, 278, 4 P., MAP / Peyrere, I de la – BN 293 2. 1647 – 8 – ne IDC [910]

RELATION DU ROYAUME DES FELICIENS / Lassay, Armand-Leon de Madaillon de Lesparre, M de – (Utopias in the Enlightment series). 1756 – 9 – fr Hachette [830]

RELATION DU VOYAGE A LA RECHERCHE DE LA PEROUSE / Labillardiere, J J H de – 2v. Paris. 1800. B-6117 2 – 8 – ne IDC [580]

RELATION DU VOYAGE DE M. EVERT ISBRAND/ENVOYE DE SA MAJESTE SZARIENNE A L'EMPEREUR DE LA CHINE, EN 1692, 93 ET 94 / Brand, A – Amsterdam. 1699. BU-770 2 – 8 – ne IDC [950]

LA RELATION DU VOYAGE D'IBN FADLAN CHEZ LES BULGARES DE LA VOLGA / Canard, M – Annales de l'Institut d'Etudes Orientes.Alger, xvi,1958. p41-146. BU-629/2 – 8 – ne IDC [910]

RELATION DU VOYAGE DU CAP VERT / Saint Lo, Alexis de – (African Library series). 1637 – 9 – fr Hachette [910]

RELATION DU VOYAGE DU CAP-VERD / Saint Lo, Alexis de – Paris, Francois Targa. 1637 – 9 – 7.50 – fr Orientalistes [910]

RELATION DU VOYAGE DU PRINCE DE MONTMERAUD DANS L'ILE DE NAUDELY / Lesconvel, Pierre de – (Utopias in the Enlightment series). 1706 – 9 – fr Hachette [830]

RELATION DU VOYAGE DU ROYAUME D'ISSIGNY, COTE D'OR, PAYS DE GUINEE, EN AFRIQUE. LA DESCRIPTION DU PAYS, LES INCLINATIONS, LES MOEURS ET LA RELIGION DES HABITANTS; AVEC CE QUI S'EST PASSE DE PLUS REMARQUABLE DANS L'ETABLISSEMENT QUE LES FRANCAIS Y ONT FAIT / Loyer, Godefroy – (African Library). 1714 – 9 – fr Hachette [960]

RELATION DU VOYAGE DU SIEUR DE MONTAUBAN EN L'ANNEE 1695. AVEC UNE DESCRIPTION DU ROYAUME DU CAP DE LOPEZ, DES MOEURS, DES COUTUMES, ET DE LA RELIGION DU PAYS / Montauban – (African Library series). 1698 – 9 – fr Hachette [910]

RELATION D'UN VOYAGE A LA COTE DU NORD OUEST DE L'AMERIQUE SEPTENTRIONALE EN 1810, 1811, 1812, 1813 ET 1814 / Franchere, Gabriel – Montreal, Canada. 1820 – 1r – 1 – Can$30.00 – cn Can Microfilming [910]

RELATION D'UN VOYAGE A LA COTE DU NORD-OUEST DE L'AMERIQUE SEPTENTRIONALE, DANS LES ANNEES 1810, 11, 12, 13 ET 14 / Franchere, Gabriel – Montreal: C B Pasteur, 1820. SEM16P42 – 1r – 6 – Can$9.00 – cn Bibl Nat [910]

RELATION D'UN VOYAGE AU CONGO FAIT LES ANNEES 1666 ET 1667 / Gattine, M A de & Plaisance, D de – (African Library series) – 9 – fr Hachette [910]

RELATION D'UN VOYAGE D'EXPLORATION AU NORD-EST DE LA COLONIE DU CAP DE BONNE-ESPERANCE / Arbousset, Jean Thomas – Paris: Arthus Bertrand, 1842 – 9 – 17.50 – fr Orientalistes [960]

RELATION D'UN VOYAGE D'EXPLORATION AU NORD-EST DE LA COLONIE DU CAP DU BONNE-ESPERANCE EN 1836 / Arbousset, Jean Thomas & Daumas, F – Paris. 1842. BA-155 2 – 8 – ne IDC [910]

RELATION D'UN VOYAGE DU LEVANT FAIT PAR ORDRE DU ROY : CONTENANT L'HISTOIRE ANCIENNE ET MODERNE DE PLUSIEURS ISLES DE L'ARCHIPEL, DE CONSTANTINOPLE, DES COTES DE LA MER NOIRE, DE L'ARMENIE, DE LA GEORGIE... / Tournefort, Joseph Pitton de – Paris, Impr. royale, 1717, 2 v., xvi-544 plus ii-526-xxxix p., planches. French Voyagers in the Mediterranean 16th to 18th Centuries. 5987-88 – 9 – fr Hachette [949]

RELATION D'UN VOYAGE FAIT AU LEVANT DANS LAQUELLE IL EST CURIEUSEMENT TRAITE DES ETATS SUJETS AU GRAND SEIGNEUR, DES MOEURS, RELIGIONS, FORCE, GOUVERNEMENTS, POLITIQUES, LANGUE... : ET DE SINGULARITEZ PARTICULIERES DE L'ARCHIPEL, CONSTANTINOPLE, TERRE-SAINTE, EGYPTE, PYRAMIDES, MUMIES, DESERTS D'ARABIE, LA MECQUE / Thevenot, Jean – Paris, L. Billaine, 1665, xvi-576 p. French Voyagers in the Mediterranean 16th to 18th Centuries. 5963 – 9 – fr Hachette [949]

RELATION D'UN VOYAGE FAIT DANS LA MAURITANIE, EN AFRIQUE, DE MARSEILLE EN 1666 / Frejus, Roland – (African Library series). 1670 – 9 – fr Hachette [910]

RELATION D'UN VOYAGE FAIT EN 1695, 1696 ET 1697 AUX COTES D'AFRIQUE DETROIT DE MAGELLAN, BREZIL, CAYENNE ET ANTILLES PAR UNE ESCADRE DES VAISSEAUX DU ROI COMMANDEE PAR M. DE GENNES / Froger, Francois – (African Library). 1698 – 9 – fr Hachette [910]

RELATION D'UNE EXPEDITION. POUR RECONNOITRE LE ZAIRE / Tuckey, James Kingston – Traduction de l'anglais. Paris, Gide Fils. 1818 – 9 – 20.00 – fr Orientalistes [910]

RELATION HISTORIQUE D'ABISSINIE TRADUITE DU PORTUGAIS, CONTINUEE ET AUGMENTEE DE PLUSIEURS DISSERTATIONS, LETTRES ET MEMOIRES / Lobo, Jerome – (African Library). 1728 – 9 – fr Hachette [960]

RELATION HISTORIQUE DE LA REVOLUTION DU ROYAUME D'ITALIE EN 1814 / Guicciardi – Paris, 1822 – 3mf – 1 – ILM-2594/1 – ne IDC [327]

RELATION HISTORIQUE DE L'ETHIOPIE OCCIDENTALE : CONTENANT LA DESCRIPTION DES ROYAUMES DE CONGO, ANGOLLE ET MATAMBA / Cavazzi, Giovanni Antonio – Paris: C J B Delespine. v1-2. 1732 – us Res Libr [960]

RELATION HISTORIQUE DE L'ETHIOPIE OCCIDENTALE – Traduction de l'italien par Pere Jean-Baptiste Labat. Paris: Charles Jean Baptiste Delespine le Fils, 1732 – 9 – 60.00 – fr Orientalistes [960]

RELATION HISTORIQUE DE L'ETHIOPIE OCCIDENTALE: CONTENANT LA DESCRIPTION DES ROYAUMES DU CONGO, ANGOLLE ET MATAMBA / Labat, Jean-Baptiste – (African Library). 5 v. 1732 – 9 – fr Hachette [960]

RELATION IOURNALIERE DU VOYAGE DU LEVANT PAR HAUT ET PUISSANT SEIGNEUR HENRY DE BEAUVAU / Beauvau, Henri – Nancy, I. Garnich, 1615, vi-181 p. French Voyagers in the Mediterranean 16th to 18th Centuries. 5960 – 9 – fr Hachette [944]

RELATION OF A VOYAGE FROM BOSTON TO NEWFOUNDLAND, FOR THE OBSERVATION OF THE TRANSIT OF VENUS, 6 JUN 1761 / Winthrop, John – Boston: Edes and Gill, 1761. SEM35P83 – 1r – 1 – Can$15.00 – cn Bibl Nat [910]

A RELATION OF A VOYAGE TO SAGADAHOE: NOW FIRST PRINTED FROM THE ORIGINAL MANUSCRIPT IN THE LAMBETH PALACE LIBRARY – Edited, with preface notes and appendix by B.F. Decosta.Cambridge, MA: J. Wilson, 1880. 03787. (Pre-1900 Canadiana) – 9 – cn C.I.H.M. [910]

RELATION OF BODY FATNESS AND BLOOD LIPIDS AS RISK FACTORS FOR CORONARY HEART DISEASE IN AFRICAN AMERICAN WOMEN / Brown, Marc A – University of North Carolina at Chapel Hill, 1994 – 2mf – 9 – $8.00 – HE554 – us Microform Publ [616]

THE RELATION OF CHILDREN TO THE FALL, ATONEMENT AND THE CHURCH / Burwash, Nathaniel – Toronto: W. Briggs, 1882. 07208. (Pre-1900 Canadiana) – 9 – cn C.I.H.M. [240]

THE RELATION OF CUSTOM TO LAW / Sadler, Gilbert T – London: Sweet & Maxwell 1919 – 1mf – 9 – $1.50 – LLMC 95-209 – us L.L.M.C. [340]

RELATION OF JESUS TO HIS AGE AND OUR OWN / Carpenter, Joseph Estlin – London: Philip Green, 1895. 1 fiche – 9 – us A.T.L.A. [240]

THE RELATION OF MCGILL UNIVERSITY TO LEGAL EDUCATION: LETTER / Dawson, John William – Montreal?: s.n., 1887?. 04210. (Pre-1900 Canadiana) – 9 – cn C.I.H.M. [971]

THE RELATION OF RELIGION TO CIVIL GOVERNMENT IN THE UNITED STATES OF AMERICA : A STATE WITHOUT A CHURCH, BUT NOT WITHOUT A RELIGION / Cornelison, Isaac A – New York: Putnam, 1895 – 1mf – us A.T.L.A. [240]

THE RELATION OF ST. PAUL TO CONTEMPORARY JEWISH THOUGHT / Thackeray, Henry St John – London: MacMillan, 1900 – 1mf – 9 – us A.T.L.A. [240]

THE RELATION OF SELF-ESTEEM TO CONSTRAINTS ON LEISURE AMONG ADOLESCENTS / Raymore, Leslie A & Godbey, Geoffrey C – 1992 – 1mf – 9 – $4.00 – us Microform Publ [790]

THE RELATION OF THE APOSTOLIC TEACHING TO THE TEACHING OF CHRIST / Drummond, Robert James – Edinburgh: T.& T. Clark, 1900. 1 fiche – 9 – us A.T.L.A. [240]

THE RELATION OF THE BIBLE TO THE SOUL / Parker, Theodore – Western Messenger, 8, 1840-41; with, D.F. Strauss' Das Leben Jesu (Christian Examiner, 28, 1840) – 9 – us A.T.L.A. [240]

THE RELATION OF THE CHURCH OF ENGLAND TO THE OTHER REFORMED CHURCHES / Henson, H Hensley – Edinburgh: W. Blackwood, 1911 – 1mf – us A.T.L.A. [240]

A RELATION OF THE CONFERENCE BETWEEN WILLIAM LAUD, LATE LORD ARCHBISHOP OF CANTERBURY AND MR. FISHER THE JESUIT BY THE COMMAND OF KING JAMES OF EVER BLESSED MEMORY : WITH AN ANSWER TO SUCH EXCEPTIONS AS A.C. TAKES AGAINST IT / Laud, William – new ed. London; New York: Macmillan, 1901 – 2mf – 9 – 0-8370-8834-8 – 1986-2834 – us A.T.L.A. [230]

THE RELATION OF THE LEGAL PROFESSION TO SOCIETY / Brown, George William – Baltimore, Kelly & Piet, 1868. 28 p. LL-371 – 1 – us L of C Photodup [340]

THE RELATION OF THE STATE TO RELIGIOUS EDUCATION : JOHN D. MINOR ET AL. VERSUS THE BOARD OF EDUCATION OF THE CITY OF CINCINNATI ET AL.: ARGUMENT FOR THE DEFENSE / Matthews, Stanley – Cincinnati: Robert Clarke, 1870 – 1mf – 9 – 0-8370-8697-3 – 1986-2697 – us A.T.L.A. [370]

RELATION TIL KONG FREDERIK 3 OM DAVID DANELLS TRE REJSER TIL GRONLAND 1652-54 / Lund, Chr. – BN 298 2. 1916 – 8 – ne IDC [910]

RELATION UNIVERSELLE DE L'AFRIQUE ANCIENNE ET MODERNE, OU L'ON VOIT CE QU'IL Y A DE REMARQUABLE TANT DANS LA TERRE FERME QUE DANS LES ILES, AVEC CE QUE LE ROI A FAIT DE MEMORABLE CONTRE LES CORSAIRES DE BARBARIE / La Croix – (African Library). 4 v. 1688 – 9 – fr Hachette [960]

RELATION VERITABLE DE CE QUI S'EST PASSE AUX EXORCISMES DES RELIGIEUSES URSULINES POSSEDEES DE LOUDUN – Poitiers. 1635 – 9 – fr Hachette [360]

RELATIONE DELLA GRANDE MONARCHIA DELLA CINA / Semmedo, Alvaro – Roma, 1643 – 1 – us U.W. Library [950]

RELATIONER FRA GRONLAND, 1721-36 / Egede, H – N 195. 1738 – 9 – ne IDC [948]

RELATIONI DELLA VENVTA DE GLI AMBASCIATORI GIAPONESI A ROMA, SINO ALLA PARTITA DI LISBONA / Gualtieri, G – Venetia, 1586 – 3mf – 9 – H-8366/1 – ne IDC [956]

RELATIONS AMONG FIGS, FIG WASPS AND SILVEREYES ON HERON ISLAND / Henderson, Leonard – (MSc Thesis) – 1977 – 9 – A$15.00 – at R.A.O.U. [590]

THE RELATIONS BETWEEN RELIGION AND SCIENCE: EIGHT LECTURES / Frederick, Archbishop of Canterbury – New York: Macmillan, 1884. 1 fiche – 9 – us A.T.L.A. [240]

RELATIONS BETWEEN THE DIVINE AND HUMAN ELEMENTS IN HOLY SCRIPTURE: EIGHT LECTURES / Hannah, John – London: John Murray, 1863. 1 fiche – 9 – us A.T.L.A. [240]

LES RELATIONS COMMERCIALES ENTRE LE MAROC ET LES ETATS-UNIS / Morocco. Societe Generale pour favoriser le Developpement du Commerce et de l'Industrie en France – 1963. BNE-3103 1 – 9 – ne IDC [337]

RELATIONS DE PLUSIEURS VOYAGES A LA COTE D'AFRIQUE, AU MAROC, AU SENEGAL EN GOREE, GALAM, ETC. AVEC DES DETAILS INTERSSANTS POUR CEUX QUI SE DESTINENT A LA TRAITE DES NEGRES, L'OR, ET DE L'IVOIRE, ETC / Saugnier – (African Library series). 1791 – 9 – fr Hachette [305]

RELATIONS DES COSTES D'AFRIQUE APPELEES GUINEE / Villault, Sieur de Bellefond N – Paris, Denys Thierre. 1669 – 9 – 12.50 – fr Orientalistes [960]

RELATIONS DES JESUITES CONTENANT CE QUI S'EST PASSE DE PLUS REMARQUABLE DANS LES MISSIONS DES PERES DE LA COMPAGNIE DE JESUS DANS LA NOUVELLE-FRANCE, 1632-1673 / Society of Jesus – Montreal: Bibliotheque Nationale du Quebec, 1975. SEM16P51 – 4r – 5 – Can$139.00 – cn Bibl Nat [240]

LES RELATIONS ENTRE LA FRANCE ET LA BIRMANIE AU 18TH ET AU 19TH SIECLES / Preschez, P – F100.00 – fr Ethnologie [320]

RELATIONS INDUSTRIELLES = INDUSTRIAL RELATIONS – Quebec: Presses universitaires Laval. v6 no 1- 1950-. SEM16P311 – 17r – 5 – Can$397.00 – cn Bibl Nat [331]

RELATIONS INDUSTRIELLES/INDUSTRIAL RELATIONS – v1- 1945- 1; v31- 5,6,9 – us UMI [331]

LES RELATIONS INTERTRIBALES EN HAUTE-GUYANE DU XVIIIEME SIECLE A NOS JOURS / Grenand, P – 9 – F60.00 – fr Ethnologie [305]

THE RELATIONS OF JOHN WESLEY AND OF WESLEYAN METHODISM TO THE CHURCH OF ENGLAND / Rigg, James H – London: Longmans, Green, 1871 – 1mf – us A.T.L.A. [240]

RELATIONS OF SCIENCE AND RELIGION / Calderwood, Henry – New York: Robert Carter, 1881. 1 fiche – 9 – us A.T.L.A. [240]

THE RELATIONS OF THE KINGDOM TO THE WORLD / Dykes, James Oswald – NY: Robert Carter, 1874 – 1mf – 9 – 0-8370-3014-5 – 1985-1014 – us A.T.L.A. [220]

RELATIONS OF THE KINGDOM TO THE WORLD (MATTHEW 6.19-7.27) / Dykes, James Oswald – New York: Robert Carter, 1874. 1 fiche – 9 – us A.T.L.A. [240]

LES RELATIONS PUBLIQUES AU LIBAN, ENTRE LE SECTEUR PUBLIC ET PRIVE, DE 1982 A 1988 / Chouman, Joumana – 2mf – 9 – 10546 – fr Atelier National [650]

LES RELATIONS SOCIALES CHEZ LES LAPONS DE KAUTOKEINO / Roue, M – 9 – F30.00 – fr Ethnologie [305]

RELATIONS-COURIER/HEUSS'SCHE ZEITUNG – (Title changes: Reichs-Post-Reuter, 10 Sep 1700) – Hamburg, Germany. 1696; 1700 (incomplete); 1747, 1750-1758, 1766-1788 – 29r – 1 – gw Mikrofilm [072]

THE RELATIONSHIP BETWEEN ADOLESCENT SMOKING BEHAVIOR AND PEER INFLUENCE / Burwell, Cynthia B – 1981 – 1mf – 9 – $4.00 – us Microform Publ [150]

THE RELATIONSHIP BETWEEN AEROBIC AND ANAEROBIC EXERCISE CAPACITIES IN PRE-PUBERTAL CHILDREN / Prasad, Navin – University of British Columbia, 1996 – 1mf – 9 – PH 1504 – us Microform Publ [612]

THE RELATIONSHIP BETWEEN AEROBIC FITNESS AND DIET COMPOSITION IN ADULT FEMALES / Kano, Marshall – 1991 – 1mf – $4.00 – us Microform Publ [612]

THE RELATIONSHIP BETWEEN ANXIETY AND ATHLETIC PERFORMANCE : A TEST OF THE MULTIDIMENSIONAL ANXIETY AND CATASTROPHE THEORIES / Krane, VI – 1990 – 4mf – 9 – $16.00 – us Microform Publ [150]

THE RELATIONSHIP BETWEEN ASYMMETRICAL LEG POWER AND CHANGE OF RUNNING DIRECTION / Djevalikian, Raffi & Pleasants, Frank – 1992 – 2mf – 9 – $8.00 – us Microform Publ [612]

THE RELATIONSHIP BETWEEN ATTITUDE AND IMPLEMENTATION OF AN ENVIRONMENTAL EDUCATION CURRICULUM IN PENNSYLVANIA PUBLIC ELEMENTARY SCHOOLS / Lovins, Susan – 1989 – 2mf – 9 – $8.00 – us Microform Publ [370]

RELATIONSHIP BETWEEN BIOELECTRICAL CONDUCTANCE AND LEAN BODY MASS FROM THREE ELECTRODE CONFIGURATIONS IN A COLLEGE-AGED POPULATION / McColley, Robin K & Paolone, Vincent J – 1992 – 2mf – $8.00 – us Microform Publ [612]

THE RELATIONSHIP BETWEEN BLOOD TESTOSTERONE LEVELS AND BODY COMPOSITION IN PHYSICALLY ACTIVE, YOUNG ADULT MEN / Johnston, Kelli D & Hackney, Anthony C – 1992 – 1mf – 9 – $4.00 – us Microform Publ [617]

THE RELATIONSHIP BETWEEN BODY ROLL AND HANDPATH DURING THE PULL PHASE IN FREESTYLE SWIMMING / Liu, Qi et al – 1990 – 3mf – 9 – $12.00 – us Microform Publ [612]

THE RELATIONSHIP BETWEEN BONE MINERAL DENSITY AND SELECTED VARIABLES : AN EPIDEMIOLOGICAL PERSPECTIVE / Watson-Bitar, M – 1990 – 1mf – 9 – $4.00 – us Microform Publ [612]

THE RELATIONSHIP BETWEEN CAFFEINE CONSUMPTION AND SYMPTOMS OF PREMENSTRUAL SYNDROME IN COLLEGE AGE FEMALES / Norton, Raquel – 1993 – 1mf – $4.00 – us Microform Publ [612]

THE RELATIONSHIP BETWEEN ELEMENTARY CLASSROOM TEACHERS' PERCEPTIONS OF SCHOOL HEALTH EDUCATION AND THEIR LEVEL OF HEALTH TEACHING / Byrnes, John – 1994 – 3mf – $12.00 – us Microform Publ [370]

THE RELATIONSHIP BETWEEN FINGER FLEXION FORCE PRODUCTION AND SELECTED HAND, FOREARM AND BODY PHYSIQUE MEASUREMENTS / Clasey, Jody Lee – 1987 – 133p 2mf – 9 – $8.00 – us Microform Publ [612]

THE RELATIONSHIP BETWEEN HABITUAL DIET AND BLOOD PRESSURE AMONG BLACK AND WHITE ADULTS / Goldflies, David G – 1988 – 129p 2mf – 9 – $8.00 – us Microform Publ [612]

THE RELATIONSHIP BETWEEN HEALTH-RELATED PHYSICAL FITNESS LEVELS AND ACADEMIC ACHIEVEMENT IN ELEMENTARY STUDENTS / Pellett, H A H – 1990 – 1mf – 9 – $4.00 – us Microform Publ [150]

THE RELATIONSHIP BETWEEN HEART RATE AND RATE OF PERCEIVED EXERTION AMONG PHASE 2 CARDIAC REHABILITATION PATIENTS WITH VARIOUS MODES OF EXERCISE / Donovan, Karen S & Wilson, Philip K – 1992 – 1mf – $4.00 – us Microform Publ [612]

THE RELATIONSHIP BETWEEN IDENTITY STATUS AND CONTRACEPTIVE PRACTICES OF COLLEGE STUDENTS / Pillion, Lori A & Gilbert, Kathleen R – 1991 – 1mf – 9 – $4.00 – us Microform Publ [150]

THE RELATIONSHIP BETWEEN KNOWLEDGE AND EXPERTISE IN BREASTSTROKE SWIMMING / Davis, Cynthia M & Thomas, Jerry R – 1992 – 2mf – 9 – $8.00 – us Microform Publ [150]

THE RELATIONSHIP BETWEEN LACTATE AND VENTILATORY THRESHOLDS IN MEN WITH SPINAL CORD INJURY / Blake, Nancy E – Oregon State University, 1996 – 1mf – 9 – PH 1487 – us Microform Publ [612]

THE RELATIONSHIP BETWEEN LACTATE THRESHOLD, VENTILATORY THRESHOLD, AND HEART RATE THRESHOLD IN CHILDREN / Schulien, C M – 1991 – 1mf – 9 – $4.00 – us Microform Publ [612]

THE RELATIONSHIP BETWEEN MUSCLE FIBER TYPE AND SERUM LACTATE DEHYDROGENASE / Daly, Thomas G – 1988 – 109p 2mf – 9 – $8.00 – us Microform Publ [612]

THE RELATIONSHIP BETWEEN OBESITY MEASUREMENTS WITH SERUM LIPIDS, FAT INTAKE AND PHYSICAL ACTIVITY IN CHILDREN / Strano, Alessandro – 1994 – 1mf – $4.00 – us Microform Publ [612]

RELATIONSHIP BETWEEN PEAK VO2 AND PERFORMANCE ON THE ROCKPORT FITNESS WALKING TEST OF ADOLESCENT MALES WITH MENTAL RETARDATION / Teo-Koh, Sock M – Oregon State University, 1995 – 3mf – 9 – $12.00 – PH 1512 – us Microform Publ [612]

RELATIONSHIP BETWEEN PERCEIVED EXERTION AND REPETITIONS PERFORMED TO EXHAUSTION AT SELECTED PERCENTAGES OF ONE-REPETITION MAXIMUM IN APPARENTLY HEALTHY ADULTS / Madlena, Troy A – University of Wisconsin-La Crosse, 1995 – 1mf – 9 – $4.00 – PE 3610 – us Microform Publ [617]

THE RELATIONSHIP BETWEEN PERCEIVED STRESSFUL LIFE EVENTS AND OCCURRENCE OF ATHLETIC INJURY AMONG COLLEGE LEVEL GYMNASTS / Buonagurio, Joseph J & Redmond, Charles J – 1993 – 1mf – $4.00 – us Microform Publ [150]

THE RELATIONSHIP BETWEEN PERSONALITY HARDINESS, STRESS AND BURNOUT IN SELECTED COLLEGIATE ATHLETES / Flor, Karen K – Ball State University, 1996 – 1mf – 9 – PSY 1886 – us Microform Publ [150]

THE RELATIONSHIP BETWEEN PERSONALITY TYPE PREFERNCES AND LEVELS OF COPING RESOURCES AMONG CARDIAC REHABILITATION PARTICIPANTS AT THE UNIVERSITY OF WISCONSIN-A CROSSE / Lankey, Lori L & Detert, Richard A – 1991 – 1mf – $4.00 – us Microform Publ [150]

THE RELATIONSHIP BETWEEN PHYSICAL ACTIVITY AND SELF-RATED DEPRESSION IN FREE-LIVING WOMEN AGED 60 YEARS AND OLDER / Aenchbacher, L E – 1990 – 2mf – 9 – $8.00 – us Microform Publ [616]

THE RELATIONSHIP BETWEEN PHYSICAL SELF-PERCEPTIONS AND FUNCTIONAL MUSCULAR STRENGTH IN YOUNG ADULT FEMALES / Clark, Tara J – University of Wisconsin-La Crosse, 1995 – 1mf – 9 – PSY 1882 – us Microform Publ [150]

THE RELATIONSHIP BETWEEN PHYSIOLOGICAL MEASUREMENTS AND CROSS-COUNTRY RUNNING PERFORMANCE / Lambert, Gerald P & Costill, David L – 1990 – 1mf – 9 – $4.00 – us Microform Publ [612]

RELATIONSHIP BETWEEN PLAYING POSITION IN FOOTBALL AND SELECTED PSYCHOLOGICAL VARIABLES / Yoo, Ho S – 1989 – 24p 1mf – 9 – $4.00 – us Microform Publ [150]

THE RELATIONSHIP BETWEEN POSITIVE APPROACH METHOD TRAINING AND SELECTED VARIABLES TO LEISURE ACTIVITY SUGGESTIONS BY STAFF MEMBERS OF RESIDENTS IN COMMUNITY LIVING FACILITIES / McCrea, Dawn M – 1993 – 2mf – $8.00 – us Microform Publ [790]

THE RELATIONSHIP BETWEEN PRECOMPETITIVE AFFECT AND COLLEGIATE BASEBALL PERFORMANCE / Whalen, Sean C – University of North Carolina at Chapel Hill, 1995 – 1mf – 9 – $4.00 – PSY1872 – us Microform Publ [150]

THE RELATIONSHIP BETWEEN PRECOMPETITIVE ANXIETY AND TEAM COHESION / McDonald, Kimberley D & Murray, Mimi – 1993 – 2mf – $8.00 – us Microform Publ [150]

THE RELATIONSHIP BETWEEN SEX-ROLE CLASSIFICATION AND ACTIVITY, AND TRAIT AND STATE ANXIETY / Bergh, Christine E – 1980 – 1mf – 9 – $4.00 – us Microform Publ [305]

THE RELATIONSHIP BETWEEN SHARED FAMILY RECREATION TIME AND EXPRESSED PARENT-ADOLESCENT CONFLICT / Kleban, Patricia L & Dattilo, John P – 1991 – 2mf – 9 – $8.00 – us Microform Publ [790]

THE RELATIONSHIP BETWEEN SKELETAL MUSCLE BLOOD FLOW AND BLOOD LACTATE CONCENTRATIONS DURING EXERCISE IN RATS / Mittelstadt, SW – 1990 – 2mf – 9 – $8.00 – us Microform Publ [590]

THE RELATIONSHIP BETWEEN SOCIAL PHYSIQUE ANXIETY AND PHYSICAL ACTIVITY / Belling, Laura R & Ainsworth, Barbara E – 1992 – 2mf – 9 – $8.00 – us Microform Publ [150]

THE RELATIONSHIP BETWEEN SPIRITUALITY AND LEISURE FUNCTIONING IN ADULTS, AS MEASURED BY SPIRITUAL WELL-BEING AND PERCEIVED FREEDOM IN LEISURE / Weight, Brita N – Brigham Young University, 1994 – 1mf – 9 – RC 498 – us Microform Publ [306]

THE RELATIONSHIP BETWEEN SPORT-CONFIDENCE, COMPETITIVE ORIENTATION AND PERFORMANCE ON A MUSCULAR LEG-ENDURANCE TASK / Jacobson, B J – 1989 – 2mf – 9 – $8.00 – us Microform Publ [150]

RELATIONSHIP BETWEEN THE MARITAL SATISFACTION OF THE WIFE AND THE VIEWING OF TELEVISED SPORTS BY THE HUSBAND / Cherrington, Kristy Y – 1993 – 1mf – $4.00 – us Microform Publ [150]

THE RELATIONSHIP BETWEEN THE TIMING OF ARM MOVEMENT AND THE FORCE OF LANDING / Feuer, Willie & Scheuchenzuber, H Joseph – 1993 – 1mf – $4.00 – us Microform Publ [612]

THE RELATIONSHIP BETWEEN TRAIT AND STATE ANXIETY AND TRAIT AND STATE SELF-CONFIDENCE IN HIGH SCHOOL BASEBALL PLAYERS / Shola, J J – 1991 – 1mf – 9 – $4.00 – us Microform Publ [150]

THE RELATIONSHIP OF AEROBIC FITNESS, TYPE A BEHAVIOR PATTERN, AND HOSTILITY TO BAROREFLEX RESPONSES AND CARDIOVASCULAR REACTIVITY TO NONEXERTIONAL STRESSORS / Graham, Ralph E & Dishman, Rodney K – 1990 – 3mf – 9 – $12.00 – us Microform Publ [150]

THE RELATIONSHIP OF ATHLETIC PARTICIPATION AND INACTIVITY TO FATTY FOOD SELECTION IN SENIOR CITIZENS / Kennington, Anna – 1993 – 1mf – $4.00 – us Microform Publ [612]

RELATIONSHIP OF EXCESS POST-EXERCISE OXYGEN CONSUMPTION TO VO2MAX AND RECOVERY RATE / Gitto, Anita T – University of British Columbia, 1995 – 1mf – 9 – PH 1493 – us Microform Publ [612]

THE RELATIONSHIP OF FAT PATTERNING TO PERIPHERAL RESISTANCE FOLLOWING SUPINE SUBMAXIMAL EXERCISE / Darragh, Patricia M – 1988 – 2mf – 9 – $8.00 – us Microform Publ [612]

THE RELATIONSHIP OF HISTORY OF STRESSORS, PERSONALITY, AND COPING RESOURCES, WITH THE INCIDENCE OF ATHLETIC INJURIES / Byrd, B J – 1993 – 2mf – $8.00 – us Microform Publ [150]

THE RELATIONSHIP OF MALE IDENTITY, THE MESOMORPHIC IMAGE, AND ANABOLIC STEROID USE IN BODYBUILDING / Olrich, Tracy W & Ewing, Martha – 1990 – 2mf – 9 – $8.00 – us Microform Publ [150]

THE RELATIONSHIP OF PELVIC GIRDLE ASYMMETRIES AND LOW BACK PAIN / Kelly, Kathryn D – University of North Carolina at Chapel Hill, 1995 – 1mf – 9 – $4.00 – PH1465 – us Microform Publ [611]

THE RELATIONSHIP OF PERCEIVED MOTIVATIONAL CLIMATE TO ACHIEVEMENT-RELATED AFFECT AND COGNITIONS IN A SPORT SETTING / Seifriz, J J – 1991 – 2mf – 9 – $8.00 – us Microform Publ [150]

THE RELATIONSHIP OF PHYSICAL SELF-PERCEPTION TO INJURY POTENTIAL OF COLLEGE FOOTBALL ATHLETES / Janelle, Christopher M & Murray, Mimi – 1993 – 2mf – $8.00 – us Microform Publ [150]

THE RELATIONSHIP OF SPORT INVOLVEMENT AND SEX ROLE CLASSIFICATION OF COLLEGE FEMALES / Kieffer, Patricia E – 1979 – 1mf – 9 – $4.00 – us Microform Publ [790]

THE RELATIONSHIP OF SUBLIMINAL RELAXATION AFFIRMATIONS AND THE DEGREE OF RELAXATION ACHIEVED / Olpin, Michael N – 1993 – 1mf – $4.00 – us Microform Publ [150]

THE RELATIONSHIP OF TASK AND EGO INVOLVEMENT TO SPORTSMANSHIP AND AGGRESSION TENDENDENCIES / Olson, Linda K – 1988 – 1mf – 9 – $4.00 – us Microform Publ [150]

THE RELATIONSHIP OF TRUNK AND HIP MUSCLE STRENGTH TO LOW BACK PAIN / Chacon Miriam E – 1989 – 1mf – 9 – $4.00 – us Microform Publ [617]

RELATIONSHIP OF YIELD TO MORPHO-EDAPHIC INDEX AND NUMBERS OF FISHERMEN IN AFRICAN INLAND FISHERIES – 1979 – 23p – it F.A.O. [338]

RELATIONSHIPS AMONG AGE, COMPETITIVE STRUCTURE, AND MOTIVE STRUCTURES FOR ENGAGING IN REGULAR EXERCISE : AN EXPLORATORY STUDY / Molotsky, E J – 1990 – 2mf – 9 – $8.00 – us Microform Publ [150]

THE RELATIONSHIPS AMONG EXERCISE BLOOD LACTATE RESPONSE, MUSCLE BLOOD FLOW, AND OXIDATIVE ADAPTATION TO ENDURANCE TRAINING IN THE RAT / Basecke, M – 1992 – 3mf – 9 – $12.00 – us Microform Publ [590]

RELATIONSHIPS AMONG PERCEIVED LEADERSHIP STYLES, MEMBER SATISFACTION AND TEAM COHESION IN HIGH SCHOOL BASKETBALL TEAMS / Eichas, Tyler M & Krane, Vikki – 1992 – 2mf – $8.00 – us Microform Publ [150]

RELATIONSHIPS AMONG SELECTED KINETIC PARAMETERS, BAT VELOCITIES, AND THREE METHODS OF STRIDING BY FEMALE SOFTBALL BATTERS / Messier, Stephen P – 1982 – 2mf – 9 – $8.00 – us Microform Publ [790]

RELATIONSHIPS BETWEEN LOWER EXTREMITY LOADING AND DEPTH JUMP PERFORMANCE / Radcliffe, James C & Osternig, Louis R – 1992 – 2mf – 9 – $8.00 – us Microform Publ [612]

RELATIONSHIPS BETWEEN SOCIAL SUPPORT AND GENERAL WELL-BEING IN AN INTRODUCTORY HEALTH, FITNESS, AND RECREATION COURSE / Zins, Wendy S – University of Wisconsin-La Crosse, 1995 – 1mf – 9 – PSY 1903 – us Microform Publ [150]

THE RELATIONSHIPS OF FINANCIAL SUBSIDY TO THE GROWTH AND DEVELOPMENT OF THE LUTHERAN CHURCH IN MALAYSIA / Fisher, Carl Melchior – 1967 – 1 – us A.T.L.A. [240]

THE RELATIVE EFFECTIVENESS OF THREE INSTRUCTIONAL STRATEGIES ON THE LEARNING OF AN OVERARM THROW FOR FORCE / Adams, Deborah – Oregon State University, 1994 – 2mf – 9 – $8.00 – PSY 1877 – us Microform Publ [150]

THE RELATIVE EFFECTS OF A LIVE AND VIDEOTAPED INSTRUCTOR O RATINGS OF PERCEIVED EXERTION AND SUBJECTIVE FEELINGS OF STUDENTS IN AN AEROBIC EXERCISE CLASS / Cook, Yvonne H & Wrisberg, Craig – 1992 – 1mf – 9 – $4.00 – us Microform Publ [150]

DIE RELATIVE HAEUFIGKEIT DES HARNBLASENKARZINOMS AM UNAUSGEWAEHLTEM BIOPSIEGUT DER JAHRE 1977-79... / Kamali, Iris – 1994 – 1mf – DM60.00 – 3-89349-899-0 – gw Hänsel [611]

THE RELATIVE IMPORTANCE OF PROPRIOCEPTION, LIGAMENT LAXITY AND STRENGTH ON FUNCTIONAL PERFORMANCE IN THE ACL DEFICIENT AND ACL RECONSTRUCTED KNEE / Govett, James R – University of British Columbia, 1995 – 2mf – 9 – $8.00 – PE3593 – us Microform Publ [617]

DIE RELATIVITAETSTHEORIE UND IHRE BEZIEHUNG ZUR CHRISTLICHEN WELTANSCHAUUNG / Vortisch, Hermann – Hamburg, 1921 – 1mf – 9 – DM48.00 – 3-89349-316-6 – gw Hänsel [240]

RELATO DE LA CAIDA DE GODOY POR UN TESTIGO PRESENCIAL / Rodriguez Monino, Antonio – Badajoz: Imprenta Diputacion Provincial, 1958 – sp Bibl Santa Ana [946]

RELATO OFICIAL DE LA MENTISIMA EXPEDICION CARLISTA DIRIGIDA POR EL GENERAL ANDALUZ, DON MIGUEL GOMEZ... / Delgado, Jose – San Sebastian: Grafico-Editora S.L., 1943 – 1 – sp Bibl Santa Ana [946]

RELATORIO DA COMPANHIA UNIAO E INDUSTRIA – Rio de Janeiro, Brazil. 1855-? – 1 – bl Biblioteca [072]

RELATORIO DA EXECUCAO DO PLANO INTERCALAR DE FOMENTO METROPOLE, 1965 / Portugal. Presidencia do Conselho – Lisboa. 1967. BD-599 1 – 9 – ne IDC [338]

RELATORIO DA EXECUCAO DO PLANO INTERCALAR DE FOMENTO-ULTRAMAR / Portugal. Presidencia do Conselho – BD-599 1. 1967. 1969 – 9 – ne IDC [338]

RELATORIO FINAL PREPARATORIO DO 2 PLANO DE FOMENTO / Portugal. Presidencia do Conselho – 2v. Lisboa. 1958 – 9 – ne IDC [338]

RELATORIOS DOS PRESIDENTES DAS PROVINCIAS BRASILEIRAS / Brazil – (Alagoas. 1835-89. Amazonas. 1852-89. Bahia. 1823-89. Ceara. 1836-89. Espirito Santo. 1833-88. Goias. 1835-88. Maranhao. 1836-89.. Mato Grosso. 1835-88. Minas Gerais. 1835-89. Para. 1833-89. Paraiba. 1837-88. Parana. 1854-89. Pernambuco. 1838-89. Piaui. 1835-89.. Rio de Janeiro. 1835-89. Rio Grande do Norte. 1835$88. Rio Grande do Sul. 1829-89. Santa Catarina. 1835-89. Sao Paulo. 1836-89. Sergipe. 1835-88) – 1 – bl Biblioteca [324]

RELATORIOS MINISTERIAIS / Brazil – (Agricultura. 1860-89. Fazenda. 1821-90. Guerra. 1827-88. Imperio. 1832-88. Justica. 1825-89. Marinha. 1827-1890. Relacoes exteriores. 1830-88) – 1 – bl Biblioteca [324]

RELATORIOS MINISTERIAIS : EPOCA DO IMPERIO / Brasil – (Ministerio da Fazenda 1821-90. Ministerio da Guerra 1827-88. Ministerio da Justica 1825-89. Ministerio da Marinha 1827-90. Ministerio das Relacoes Exteriores 1830-90. Ministerio do Imperio 1832-88. Ministerio de agricultura 1860-89) – us Res Libr [972]

RELAZIONE SULLA COLONIA ERITREA DE R. COMMISSARIO CIVILE DEPUTATO FERDINANDO MARTINI PER GLIESERCIZI 1902-1907... – Roma: Tip della Camera dei deputati, 1913 – us Res Libr [960]

RELAZIONI INTERNAZIONALI – Milan. Italy. -w. 2 Sep 1939 – 11 May 1940, 30 Nov 1940 – 17 Jul 1943 – 6r – 1 – uk British Libr Newspaper [327]
RELC (REGIONAL LANGUAGE CENTRE) JOURNAL – v1- 1970- 1; v8- 5,6,9 – us UMI [370]
RELEASE / Alabama Committee for Equal Justice – Birmingham. 10, 20, 28 Sep 1945 – 1 – us NY Public [073]
RELEASES / U. S. Federal Services Impasses Panel – no. 1-175. 1970-80. 84-115 – 9 – 44.00 – us L.L.M.C. [324]
RELEASES ISSUED BY THE U.S. SECURITIES AND EXCHANGE COMMISSION, APRIL 2, 1973-DECEMBER 31, 1973 / U.S. Securities and Exchange Commission – A collection of releases, title-by-title, not inseparable intermixed, and originally included in the SEC Docket – 9 – us UMI [336]
RELEASES ISSUED IN SERIES BY THE U.S. SECURITIES AND EXCHANGE COMMISSION, 1933-1976 / U.S. Securities and Exchange Commission – A collection of eighteen titles, with a total of 50,997 releases listed – 9 – us UMI [336]
RELEVES DES TITRES DES RENTES CONSTITUTES DES ANCIENNES SEIGNEURIES DU QUEBEC / Quebec. (Province). Syndicat national du rachat des rentes Seigneuriales – Montreal: Bibliotheque nationale du Quebec, 1971. SEM35P10 – 1r – 1 – Can$48.00 – cn Bibl Nat [336]
Relfe, J *see* LUCIDUS ORDO...
RELF'S PHILADELPHIA GAZZETTE & DAILY ADVERTISER – Philadelphia, PA. -d 1803-11; 1813-18; 1820-22 – 13 – $25.00r – us I.M.R. [071]
Relhan, R *see* FLORA CANTABRIGIENSIS
RELIABILITY ANALYSIS CENTER (RAC) – (Updated Every 60 Days) – Information Handling Services – 5 – us Info Handling [621]
RELIABILITY ENGINEERING – v1-9 1980-84 – 1,5,6,13 – sz Elsevier [620]
RELIABILITY IN THE MEASUREMENT OF MUSCLE FIBER COMPOSITION AND THE HISTOCHEMICAL STAINING FOR GLYCOGEN / Benedict, Michael A & Costill, David L – 1990 – 2mf – 9 – $8.00 – us Microform Publ [612]
THE RELIABILITY OF AN ISOKINETIC MEASUREMENT PROTOCOL FOR THE POSTERIOR ROTATOR CUFF MUSCULATURE / Keskula, DR – 1990 – 1mf – 9 – $4.00 – us Microform Publ [790]
RELIABILITY OF PEAK TORQUE VALUES FOR SHOULDER INTERNAL AND EXTERNAL ROTATION DURING ECCENTRIC AND CONCENTRIC LOADING USING THE KIN-COM 125E ISOKINETIC DYNAMOMETER / Takao, SH – 1991 – 1mf – 9 – $4.00 – us Microform Publ [612]
THE RELIABILITY OF THE DYNAVEC (TM) LVD : A TOOL FOR THE ASSESSMENT OF THREE DIMENSIONAL LUMBAR SPINAL MOTION / Fife, LK – 1991 – 2mf – 9 – $8.00 – us Microform Publ [790]
THE RELIABILITY OF TWO MEASURES OF CARDIAC OUTPUT USING CO2 REBREATHING / Wigglesworth, Janet K et al – 1991 – 3mf – 9 – $12.00 – us Microform Publ [613]
RELIATSII KN. A. D. KANTEMIR IZ LONDONA / Kantemir, A D – 2v. M. 1892-1903. BR-6043 2 – 8 – ne IDC [460]
RELICS OF PRIMEVAL LIFE: BEGINNING OF LIFE IN THE DAWN OF GEOLOGICAL TIME / Dawson, John William – New York: Toronto: F. H. Revell, 1897. 05402. (Pre-1900 Canadiana) – 9 – cn C.I.H.M. [560]
RELIEF AND MEDICAL CARE IN GERMANY DURING WORLD WAR 1 PAMPHLET COLLECTION – 1915-1919 – 2r – 1 – CSUXANL3584-B – us Hoover Inst Photo [360]
RELIEF FOR SPANISH TRADE UNION REFUGEES / Medical Bureau and North American Committee to Aid Spanish Democracy – N.Y., 1939? Fiche W 1038. (Blodgett Collection of Spanish Civil War Pamphlets) – 9 – us H.U. College Libr [946]
RELIEF LEDGERS / Baptist World Alliance – (American Executive Committee, Minutes, 1908-29) – 1923-27 – 1 – us A.B.H.S. [240]
RELIEF LISTS AND REPORTS / Ottawa County. Ohio. Carroll Township. Township Clerk – 1914-1939 – 1r – 1 – $32.50r – us Archival [324]
RELIEF ORDERS / Putnam County. Ohio. Soldiers Relief Commission – 1864-1867 – 1r – 1 – $32.50r – us Archival [324]
RELIEF RECORDS / Wood County. Ohio. Soldiers' Relief Commission – 1940-1947 – 1r – 1 – $32.50r – us Archival [324]
RELIEF WORK AND THE UNITED STATES DURING WORLD WAR 1 PAMPHLET COLLECTION – 1914-1918 – 1 reel – 1 – CSUXANL3591-B – us Hoover Inst Photo [360]
LA RELIGIEUSE / Diderot, Denis; ed by Parrish, J – (Studies on Voltaire and the eighteenth century, v22) – Oxford. 1963 – 9 – $45.00 – 0-7294-0074-3 – uk Voltaire [830]
Religieux Benedictins De La Congregation De S. Maur *see* NOUVEAU TRAITE DE DIPLOMATIQUE
Religieux Benedictins de la Congregation de S. Maur *see* HISTOIRE LITERAIRE DE LA FRANCE
RELIGIIA BUDUSHCHEGO (FILOSOFSKIE RAZGOVORY) / Minskii, N – Spb. 1905. BR-813 2 – 8 – ne IDC [280]
RELIGIO VIATORIS / Edward, Henry – London: Burns & Oates; New York: Catholic Publication Society, [188-?] – 1mf – us A.T.L.A. [240]
DAS RELIGIOESE BEI H.W. LONGFELLOW UND DESSEN STELLUNG ZUR BIBEL / Schulze, Bernhard – Halle, 1913 – 2mf – 9 – DM62.00 – 3-89349-341-7 – gw Hänsel [420]
RELIGIOESE BETRACHTUNGEN UEBER WERKE GERHART HAUPTMANNS : VERSUCH EINER WUERDIGUNG / Mende, Gottfried – Leipzig: Dieterich, 1906 – 1r – 1 – us U.W. Library [430]
DIE RELIGIOESE ENTWICKLUNG GOTTFRIED KELLERS IM HINBLICK AUF DEN NATUR-KULTUR-BEGRIFF SEINES GEREIFTEN WELTBILDES / Derleth, Kurt – (Includes bibliographical references) – Giessen: C Wolf, 1937 – 1r – 1 – us U.W. Library [430]
DIE RELIGIOESE ENTWICKLUNG SCHLEIERMACHERS / Wendland, Johannes – Tuebingen: Mohr, 1916 – 1mf – us A.T.L.A. [240]
RELIGIOESE FRAGEN : MIT BEZUGNAHME AUF UNSERE GEGENWAERTIGE LAGE UND DIE KIRCHLICHEN ZEITKAEMPFE / Engelbach, Georg – Darmstadt: C Koehler, 1869 – 1mf – 9 – 0-8370-5995-X – 1985-3995 – us A.T.L.A. [240]
DIE RELIGIOESE GEDANKENWELT DER JAPANER IM SPIEGEL IHRES SPRICHWORTS / Sudau, Guenter – Leipzig, 1932 – 1mf – 9 – DM48.00 – 3-89349-350-6 – gw Hänsel [290]
DIE RELIGIOESE GEDANKENWELT DES SALOMO IBN GABIROL / Dreyer, Karl – Leipzig, 1929 – 9 – DM48.00 – 3-89349-271-2 – gw Hänsel [270]
DIE RELIGIOESE GEDANKENWELT DES SALOMO IBN GABIROL / Dreyer, Karl – Leipzig. 1930. BJ-421-45 1 – 9 – ne IDC [270]
DER RELIGIOESE GEHALT DES GALATERBRIEFES / Walter, Johann – (Includes bibliographical references) – Goettingen: Vandenhoeck und Ruprecht, 1904 – 1mf – 9 – 0-8370-9340-6 – 1986-3340 – us A.T.L.A. [220]
DIE RELIGIOESE KINDERERZIEHUNG IM DEUTSCHEN REICHE : EINE INTERKONFESSIONELLE STAATSKIRCHENRECHTLICHE STUDIE / Guettler, Wilhelm – Berlin: Dr Walther Rothschild, 1908 – 1mf – 9 – 0-8370-7635-8 – 1986-1635 – us A.T.L.A. [370]
DAS RELIGIOESE LEBEN IN ERFURT BEIM AUSGANGE DES MITTELALTERS : EIN BEITRAG ZUR VORGESCHICHTE DER REFORMATION / Kolde, T – Halle: Verein fuer Reformationsgeschichte, 1898 (Schriften des Vereins fuer Reformationsgeschichte; 16. Jahrg., Schrift 63 – 1mf – us A.T.L.A. [240]
DAS RELIGIOESE MOTIV ALS GESTALTENDE KRAFT DER DEUTSCHEN VOLKSSAGEN DER GEGENWART / Koenigsloew, Eva von – (Includes bibliographical references) – Frankfurt am Main: M Diesterweg, 1935 – 1r – 1 – us U.W. Library [390]
DIE RELIGIOESE POESIE DER JUDEN IN SPANIEN, BERLIN, 1845 / Sachs, M; ed by Bernfeld, Simon – Zum zweiten Male mit biographischer Einleitung und ergaenzenden Anmerkungen herausgegeben. Berlin. 1901. BJ-421-22 1 – 9 – ne IDC [810]
DER RELIGIOESE SOZIALIST IN MANNHEIM *see* DER BOTE AUS KURPFALZ
DIE RELIGIOESE WELTSTELLUNG DES JUEDISCHEN VOLKES / Heman, Friedrich – Leipzig: J C Hinrichs, 1882 – 1mf – 9 – 0-8370-3556-2 – 1985-1556 – us A.T.L.A. [270]
DIE RELIGIOESEN IDEALE DER MODERNEN THEOLOGIE: VIER VORTRAEGE – Frankfurt a.M.: M. Diesterweg, 1908. 1 fiche – 9 – us A.T.L.A. [240]
DIE RELIGIOESEN UND SITTLICHEN ANSCHAUUNGEN DER ALTTESTAMENTLICHEN APOKRYPHEN UND PSEUDEPIGRAPHEN / Couard, Ludwig – (Includes index) – Guetersloh:Bertelsmann, 1907 – 1mf – 9 – 0-8370-2750-0 – 1985-0750 – us A.T.L.A. [220]
RELIGIOESER BOTSCHAFTER – (Lacking: v3 no 7) – v1-3. 1852-55 – 1r – 1 – ATLA 1994-S023 – us A.T.L.A. [073]
DIE RELIGIOES-SITTLICHE WELTANSCHAUUNG DES BUCHES DER SPRUECHE / Pfeiffer, Richard – Muenchen: C.H. Beck, 1897. 1 fiche – 9 – us A.T.L.A. [240]
RELIGION / Bibliotheque Nationale – Collection of 23 titles (available separately). 97 fiches – 9 – approx. 240.00 – fr Bibl Nationale [080]
RELIGION : A CRITICISM AND A FORECAST / Dickinson, Goldsworthy Lowes – New York: McClure, Phillips, 1905 – 1mf – 9 – 0-8370-7214-X – 1986-1214 – us A.T.L.A. [200]
RELIGION / Molinari, Gustave de; ed by Firminger, Walter Kelly – (Includes bibliographical references) – London:Swan Sonnenschein; New York:Macmillan, 1894 – 1mf – 9 – 0-8370-4460-X – 1985-2460 – us A.T.L.A. [200]
RELIGION – no 9-12. 1934-35 (complete) – Inquire – 1 – ATLA 1994-S513 – us A.T.L.A. [073]
RELIGION : A REVELATION AND A RULE OF LIFE / Kirkus, William – New York: Thomas Whittaker, 1886 – 1mf – 9 – 0-8370-7299-9 – 1986-1299 – us A.T.L.A. [240]
DIE RELIGION ALS WILLE ZUM EWIGEN LEBEN: EINE VORTRAG / Weber, Alfred – Strassburg: J.H. Ed. Heitz, 1888. 1 fiche – 9 – us A.T.L.A. [240]
RELIGION AND ART, AND OTHER ESSAYS / Spalding, J L – Chicago: A.C. McClurg, 1905 – 1mf – us A.T.L.A. [200]
RELIGION AND CHEMISTRY: A RE-STATEMENT OF AN OLD ARGUMENT / Cooke, Josiah Parsons – New York: Scribner, 1891. 1 fiche – 9 – us A.T.L.A. [240]
RELIGION AND CULTURE: A CRITICAL SURVEY OF METHODS OF APPROACH TO RELIGIOUS PHENOMENA / Schleiter, Frederick – New York: Columbia University Press, 1919. 206p – 1 – us U.W. Library [200]
RELIGION AND EDUCATION IN AMERICA : WITH NOTICES OF THE STATE AND PROSPECTS OF AMERICAN UNITARIANISM, POPERY, AND AFRICAN COLONIZATION / Lang, John Dunmore – London: T. Ward, 1840 – 2mf – us A.T.L.A. [240]
RELIGION AND ENGLISH SOCIETY : TWO ADDRESSES DELIVERED AT A CONFERENCE HELD IN LONDON, NOVEMBER 9TH AND 10TH, 1910 / Figgis, John Neville – London, New York: Longmans, Green, 1911 – 1mf – us A.T.L.A. [306]
RELIGION AND EXPERIENCE / Brierley, Jonathan – London: James Clarke, 1906. 1 fiche – 9 – us A.T.L.A. [240]
RELIGION AND GERMANY (1945-) PAMPHLET COLLECTION – 1945-1986 – 1 reel – 1 – CSUXAMJ5679-B – us Hoover Inst Photo [200]
RELIGION AND GERMANY (1933-1944) PAMPHLET COLLECTION – 1933-1983 – 1 reel – 1 – CSUXAMJ5656-B – us Hoover Inst Photo [200]
RELIGION AND GERMANY PAMPHLET COLLECTION – 19?? – 1 reel – 1 – CSUXAMJ4583-B – us Hoover Inst Photo [200]
RELIGION AND IMMORTALITY / Dickinson, G Lowes – London: J.M. Dent, 1911 – 1mf – us A.T.L.A. [200]
RELIGION AND ITALY PAMPHLET COLLECTION – 1942 – 1 – CSUXAMJ5686-B – us Hoover Inst Photo [200]
RELIGION AND LEISURE : A CASE STUDY OF THE ROLE OF THE CHURCH AS A PROVIDER OF RECREATION IN SMALL ONTARIO COMMUNITIES / Emard, M R – 1990 – 2mf – 9 – $8.00 – us Microform Publ [790]
RELIGION AND LIFE / Hall, Thomas Cuming – New York: Eaton & Mains; Cincinnati: Jennings & Graham, c1913 – 1mf – us A.T.L.A. [240]
RELIGION AND LIFE (CCC101) : A COMPILATION OF ARTICLES BY EUCKEN, ETC., ETC / Chien, Timothy Yu-wan – (In Chinese) – Shanghai: Publication Dept., National Committee, YMCAs of China, 1923 – 1r – 1 – 1984-B500 – us A.T.L.A. [200]
RELIGION AND LITERATURE – n.s.16-. 1984- – 1,5,6,9 – us UMI [200]
RELIGION AND MIRACLE / Gordon, George A – Boston: Houghton Mifflin, 1909 – 9 – us A.T.L.A. [240]
RELIGION AND MORALITY : THEIR NATURE AND MUTUAL RELATIONS, HISTORICALLY AND DOCTRINALLY CONSIDERED / Fox, James Joseph – New York: William H Young, 1899 – 1mf – 9 – 0-8370-6117-2 – 1986-0117 – us A.T.L.A. [170]
RELIGION AND PHILOSOPHY IN GERMANY: A FRAGMENT / Heine, Heinrich – John Snodgrass, trans. London: Truebner & Co., 1882. (The English and Foreign Philosophical Library, xviii) – x/177p – 1 – us U.W. Library [840]
RELIGION AND PORTUGAL PAMPHLET COLLECTION – 1945 – 1 – CSUXAMJ7755-B – us Hoover Inst Photo [200]
RELIGION AND PUBLIC EDUCATION : A LETTER TO A FRIEND / Canfield, James Hulme – [New York?: Educational Review?], 1906 – 1mf – 9 – 0-8370-8489-X – 1986-2489 – us A.T.L.A. [370]
RELIGION AND REVELATION / Van Horne, D – Dayton: Press Reformed Pub. Co., 1892. 1 fiche – 9 – us A.T.L.A. [240]
RELIGION AND SCIENCE AS ALLIES : OR, SIMILARITIES OF PHYSICAL AND RELIGIOUS KNOWLEDGE / Bixby, James Thompson – Boston: American Unitarian Assoc, 1903, c1889 – 1mf – 9 – 0-8370-2353-X – 1985-0353 – us A.T.L.A. [210]
RELIGION AND SCIENCE (CCC102) : A SYMPOSIUM / ed by Chien, Timothy Yu-wan – (In Chinese) – Shanghai: Association Press of China, 1922 – 1r – 1 – 1984-B500 – us A.T.L.A. [200]
RELIGION AND SCIENCE IN THEIR RELATION TO PHILOSOPHY : AN ESSAY ON THE PRESENT STATE OF THE SCIENCES / Shields, Charles Woodruff – New York: Scribner, Armstrong, 1875 – 1mf – 9 – 0-8370-5248-3 – 1985-3248 – us A.T.L.A. [210]
RELIGION AND SCIENCE: SOME SUGGESTIONS...OF THE RELATIONS BETWEEN THEM / Waggett, Philip Napier – London: Longmans, Green, 1904. 1 fiche – 9 – us A.T.L.A. [240]
RELIGION AND SCIENCE: THE LETTERS OF ALPHA / Allen, Stephen Merrill – Boston: James Campbell, 1875. 1 fiche – 9 – us A.T.L.A. [240]
RELIGION AND SCIENCE...,OR, THE TRUTHS REVEALED IN NATURE AND SCRIPTURE / LeConte, Joseph – New York: D. Appleton, 1891. 1 fiche – 9 – us A.T.L.A. [240]
RELIGION AND SLAVERY : A VINDICATION OF THE SOUTHERN CHURCHES / McNeilly, James Hugh – Nashville, Tenn.: Publishing House of the M.E. Church, South, 1911 – 1mf – us A.T.L.A. [240]
RELIGION AND SOCIETY – (See also: St. Croix Review) – v1-6. 1968-1973 – 1 – us UMI [240]
RELIGION AND SOCIETY – Stillwater, MN. v1-4. 1968-71 – 19mf – 9 – $5.00f – us Ross [230]
RELIGION AND SPAIN PAMPHLET COLLECTION – 1931-1967 – 1 reel. – 1 – CSUXAMJ5688-B – us Hoover Inst Photo [200]
RELIGION AND SWITZERLAND PAMPHLET COLLECTION – 1944-1945 – 1 reel – 1 – CSUXAMJ7762-B – us Hoover Inst Photo [200]
RELIGION AND THE MODERN MIND : AND OTHER ESSAYS IN MODERNISM / Doan, Frank Carleton – Boston: Sherman, French, 1909 – 1mf – 9 – 0-8370-8660-4 – 1986-2660 – us A.T.L.A. [240]

RELIGION AND THE REIGN OF TERROR / Pressense, Edmond Dehault de – 1868 – 9 – us A.T.L.A. [240]

RELIGION AND THE STATE : OR, THE BIBLE AND THE PUBLIC SCHOOLS / Spear, Samuel Thayer – New York: Dodd, Mead, 1876 – 1mf – 9 – 0-8370-8550-0 – 1986-2550 – us A.T.L.A. [370]

RELIGION AND THE STATE : PROTECTION OR ALLIANCE? TAXATION OR EXEMPTION? / Hovey, Alvah – Boston: Estes and Lauriat, 1874 – 1mf – us A.T.L.A. [240]

RELIGION AND WARFARE AMONG THE DANI OF BALIEM-VALLEY / Broekhuijse, Johan Theodorus – In Dutch; summary in English. SE-6454 1. 1967 – 9 – ne IDC [360]

THE RELIGION AND WORSHIP OF THE SYNAGOGUE: AN INTRODUCTION TO THE STUDY OF JUDAISM FROM THE NEW TESTAMENT PERIOD / Oesterley, William Oscar Emil – 2nd and rev. ed.London: I. Pitman, 1911. 474p. ill. Bibliog. footnotes – 1 – us U.W. Library [270]

LA RELIGION ANTIGUA DE LOS FILIPINOS / Reyes y Florentino, Isabelo de los – Manila: Imp. de El Renacimiento, 1909. 249p. ill. Includes bibliog. references – 1 – us U.W. Library [290]

RELIGION AS A CREDIBLE DOCTRINE: A STUDY OF THE FUNDAMENTAL DIFFICULTY / Mallock, William Hurrell – New York: Macmillan, 1903. 1 fiche – 9 – us A.T.L.A. [240]

LA RELIGION CATOLICA VINDICADA DE LAS IMPOSTURAS RACIONALISTAS / Mendive, Jose – 1887. Libros en Microficha no 19 – 3mf – 9 – Pta2,000.00 – 84-85422-62-7 – sp Pentalfa [240]

RELIGION CIVILE PROPOSEE AUX REPUBLIQUES POUR BIEN DES GOUVERNEMENTS REPRESENTATIFS / Lanthenas, Francois X. – Paris, Comminges, an VI. 1795 – 9 – fr Hachette [200]

LA RELIGION DANS LA SOCIETE AUX ETATS-UNIS / Bargy, Henry – Paris: A. Colin, 1902 – 1mf – us A.T.L.A. [306]

LA RELIGION DE JESUS (IASO JA-KYO) RESSUSCITEE AU JAPON DANS LA SECONDE MOITIE DU 19E SIECLE / Marnas, Francisque – Paris: Delhomme et Briguet, [1897?] – 3mf – us A.T.L.A. [240]

LA RELIGION DE L'EMPEREUR JULIEN ET LE MYSTICISME DE SON TEMPS / Farney, Roger – Paris: F. Alcan, 1934. 148p – 1 – us U.W. Library [250]

DIE RELIGION DER BABYLONIER UND ASSYRER.. / Ungnad, Arthur – Jena: E. Diederich, 1921. vii,343p – 1 – us U.W. Library [290]

DIE RELIGION DER GOETHEZEIT / Krueger, Gustav – (Includes bibliographical references) – Tuebingen: Mohr, 1931 – 1r – 1 – us U.W. Library [240]

DIE RELIGION DER PATRI-ARCHENGESCHICHTEN / Zurhellen-Pfleiderer, Else – Tuebingen: J.C.B. Mohr, 1908. 1 fiche – 9 – us A.T.L.A. [240]

DIE RELIGION DES BUDDHA / Koeppen, C F – II. Die lamaische Hierarchie und Kirche. Berlin. 1859. BU-732 2 – 8 – ne IDC [280]

DIE RELIGION DES GEISTES / Hartmann, Eduard von – Berlin: Carl Duncker (C Heymons), 1882 – 1mf – 9 – 0-8370-3508-2 – 1985-1508 – us A.T.L.A. [200]

DIE RELIGION DES NEUEN TESTAMENTS / Weiss, Bernhard – Stuttgart: J G Cotta, 1903 – 1mf – 9 – 0-8370-6453-8 – 1986-0453 – us A.T.L.A. [220]

DIE RELIGION DES VOLKES ISRAEL BIS ZUR VERBANNUNG / Budde, Karl – Giessen: J. Ricker, 1900. 1 fiche – 9 – us A.T.L.A. [270]

DIE RELIGION DES ZWEIFLERS / Schmidt, August – Leipzig:H. Haessel, 1874 – 1mf – 9 – 0-8370-5108-8 – 1985-3108 – us A.T.L.A. [210]

RELIGION DURING WORLD WAR 1 IN GERMANY PAMPHLET COLLECTION – 1914-1918 – 9r – 1 – CSUXANL9137-B – us Hoover Inst Photo [200]

LA RELIGION ET LES SCIENCES DE LA NATURE / Bettex, Frederic – Gen eve: J-H Jeheber, [c1898] – 1mf – 9 – 0-8370-2319-X – 1985-0319 – us A.T.L.A. [210]

RELIGION ET MAGIE / Wing, J van – Bruxelles: G van Campenhout, 1938 – us Res Libr [230]

RELIGION ET NATIONALISME CHEZ LES GALLOIS / Maurer-Avalos, E – 9 – F60.00 – fr Ethnologie [306]

RELIGION ET PATRIE – Quebec: Comite de membres de la ligue des hommes, [1891-189-?] – 9 – cn C.I.H.M. [240]

LA RELIGION FACE AU POUVOIR POLITIQUE AU CAMEROUN / Kengne Pokam, E – 9 – F190.00 – fr Ethnologie [200]

RELIGION FOR A CENTURY *see* MISCELLANEOUS BOOKS AND PAMPHLETS

RELIGION FOR ALL MANKIND: BASED ON FACTS WHICH ARE NEVER IN DISPUTE / Voysey, Charles – London: Longman's, Green, 1903. 1 fiche – 9 – us A.T.L.A. [240]

RELIGION FOR THE TIME: SIX CONFERENCES ON NATURAL RELIGION / Conger, Arthur Bloomfield – Philadelphia: George W. Jacobs, 1902. 1 fiche – 9 – us A.T.L.A. [240]

RELIGION FOR THE TIMES / Clark, Lucien – New York: Hunt & Eaton, 1892 – 1mf – 9 – 0-8370-2667-9 – 1985-0667 – us A.T.L.A. [230]

DIE RELIGION GERHART HAUPTMANNS : EIN BEITRAG ZUR PROBLEMATIK DER RELIGION DER GEGENWART / Langner, Erwin – (Includes bibliographical references) – Tuebingen: J C B Mohr, 1928 – 1r – 1 – us U.W. Library [430]

DIE RELIGION GOETHES UND DAS EVANGELIUM : EIN THEOLOGISCHES WORT ZUM GOETHEJUBILAEUM 1932 / Schanze, Wolfgang – Leipzig: Doerffling & Franke, 1932 – 1r – 1 – us U.W. Library [240]

DIE RELIGION, IHRE PSYCHISCHEN FORMEN UND IHRE ZENTRALIDEE : EIN BEITRAG ZUR LOESUNG DER FRAGE NACH DEM WESEN DER RELIGION / Girgensohn, Karl – (Includes index of authors) – Leipzig: A Deichert, 1903 – 1mf – 9 – 0-8370-3300-4 – 1985-1300 – us A.T.L.A. [200]

DIE RELIGION IM MODERNEN GEISTESLEBEN : MIT EINEM ANHANG UEBER DAS MAERCHEN VON DEN DREI RINGEN IN LESSINGS NATHAN / Rade, Martin – Freiburg i. B: J C B Mohr (Paul Siebeck), 1898 – 1mf – 9 – 0-8370-4821-4 – 1985-2821 – us A.T.L.A. [200]

RELIGION IN AMERICA – (Pt 1 Early Books and Manuscripts 404v 50r $3850; Pt 2 Recent Dissertations (1960-) 242v 47r $3650. Cataloging available) – 97r complete collection – 1 – $7490.00 complete collection – us UMI [240]

RELIGION IN AMERICA, OR, AN ACCOUNT OF THE ORIGIN, RELATION TO THE STATE, AND PRESENT CONDITION OF THE EVANGELICAL CHURCHES IN THE UNITED STATES : WITH NOTICES OF THE UNEVANGELICAL DENOMINATIONS / Baird, Robert – New York: Harper, 1856 – 2mf – us A.T.L.A. [200]

RELIGION IN AMERIKA : BEITRAEGE ZU IHREM VERSTAENDNIS / Bornhausen, Karl – Giessen: Alfred Toepelmann, 1914 – 1mf – us A.T.L.A. [240]

RELIGION IN COMMUNIST DOMINATED AREAS – 1968-83 – 1 – uk World [240]

RELIGION IN COMMUNIST DOMINATED AREAS – v1-10. 1962-71 – 1 – us UMI [200]

RELIGION IN COMMUNIST LANDS – v1- 1973-1; v4- 5,6,9 – us UMI [240]

RELIGION IN CZECHOSLOVAKIA PAMPHLET COLLECTION – 1941 – 1 – CSUXANL2215-B – us Hoover Inst Photo [200]

RELIGION IN ESTONIA PAMPHLET COLLECTION – 194? – 1 reel – 1 – CSUXANL2163-B – us Hoover Inst Photo [200]

RELIGION IN GREEK LITERATURE : A SKETCH IN OUTLINE / Campbell, Lewis – London, New York: Longmans, Green, 1898 – 1mf – us A.T.L.A. [450]

RELIGION IN LIFE – (Cont by: United Methodist Board of Higher Education and Ministry Quarterly) – v1-34. 1932-65 (complete) – 11r – 1 – ATLA S0055 – us A.T.L.A. [073]

RELIGION IN LITERATURE : AND, RELIGION IN LIFE: TWO LECTURES / Brooke, Stopford Augustus – London: P. Green, 1900 – 1mf – us A.T.L.A. [240]

RELIGION IN MONTESQUIEU'S 'LETTRES PERSANES' / Kra, P – (Studies on Voltaire and the eighteenth century, v72) – Oxford. 1970 – 9 – $27.00 – 0-7294-0165-0 – uk Voltaire [440]

RELIGION IN POLAND PAMPHLET COLLECTION – 1939-1949 – 1 reel – 1 – CSUXANL2180-B – us Hoover Inst Photo [200]

RELIGION IN RUSSIA PAMPHLET COLLECTION – 1847-186? – 1 reel – 1 – CSUXANR0958-B – us Hoover Inst Photo [200]

RELIGION IN SOCIAL ACTION / Taylor, Graham – New York: Dodd, Mead, 1913 – 1mf – us A.T.L.A. [240]

RELIGION IN THE LIGHT OF PHILOSOPHY – London: Williams & Norgate, 1882 – 1mf – 9 – us A.T.L.A. [240]

RELIGION IN THE SOVIET UNION PAMPHLET COLLECTION – 1922-1989 – 1 reel – 1 – CSUXANR0983-B – us Hoover Inst Photo [200]

RELIGION IN THE UKRAINE PAMPHLET COLLECTION – 1947-1989 – 1 reel – 1 – CSUXANR1015-B – us Hoover Inst Photo [200]

DE LA RELIGION NATIONALE / Fauchet, Claude – Paris. Bailly. Desenne. 1789 – 9 – fr Hachette [321]

RELIGION OCH KULTUR – 1830-80 (complete) – 6r – 1 – ATLA S0730 – us A.T.L.A. [073]

RELIGION, ODER, REICH GOTTES: EINE GESCHICHTE / Lhotzky, Heinrich – Leipzig: J.C. Hinrichs, 1904. 1 fiche – 9 – us A.T.L.A. [240]

THE RELIGION OF A CHRISTIAN, ETC – 17th Century. Holkham Mss 676, 679, 682 – 1 – uk Microform Academic [240]

THE RELIGION OF A DEMOCRAT / Zueblin, Charles – (Includes bibliographical references) – New York: B W Huebsch, 1908 – 1mf – 9 – 0-8370-6639-5 – 1986-0639 – us A.T.L.A. [240]

THE RELIGION OF ALL GOOD MEN : AND OTHER STUDIES IN CHRISTIAN ETHICS / Garrod, Heathcote William – New York: McClure, Phillips, 1906 – 1mf – 9 – 0-8370-4940-7 – 1985-2940 – us A.T.L.A. [230]

THE RELIGION OF AN EDUCATED MAN / Peabody, Francis Greenwood – (Includes bibliographical references) – New York: Macmillan, 1903 – 1mf – 9 – 0-8370-5251-3 – 1985-3251 – us A.T.L.A. [240]

THE RELIGION OF BABYLONIA AND ASSYRIA / Jastrow, Morris – Boston: Ginn & Co., 1898. xii,780p. map – 1 – us U.W. Library [290]

THE RELIGION OF CHRIST IN THE TWENTIETH CENTURY – (Includes bibliographical references) – New York: G P Putnam, 1906 – 1mf – 9 – 0-8370-5155-X – 1985-3155 – us A.T.L.A. [240]

THE RELIGION OF EVOLUTION / Savage, Minot Judson – Boston: Geo. H. Ellis, 1891. 1 fiche – 9 – us A.T.L.A. [240]

THE RELIGION OF HUMANITY : AN ADDRESS / Balfour, Arthur James – Edinburgh: David Douglas, 1888 – 1mf – us A.T.L.A. [210]

THE RELIGION OF INHUMANITY : A CRITICISM / Harrison, Frederic – New York: A.K. Butts, 1873 – 1mf – us A.T.L.A. [240]

THE RELIGION OF ISRAEL : A MANUAL / Knappert, Jan – Boston: Roberts, 1878 – 1mf – 9 – 0-8370-3940-1 – 1985-1940 – us A.T.L.A. [270]

THE RELIGION OF ISRAEL / Peake, Arthur Samuel – (Includes index) – London: T C & E C Jack, 1908 – 1mf – 9 – 0-8370-4686-6 – 1985-2686 – us A.T.L.A. [220]

THE RELIGION OF JESUS DELINEATED / Reynolds, John – 1726 – 1 – us A.T.L.A. [240]

THE RELIGION OF MOSES / Moses, Adolph – Louisville: Flexner, 1894. 1 fiche – 9 – us A.T.L.A. [270]

THE RELIGION OF NATURE / Robinson, Edward Kay – London: Hodder & Stoughton, 1906. 1 fiche – 9 – us A.T.L.A. [210]

THE RELIGION OF NUMA, AND OTHER ESSAYS ON THE RELIGION OF ANCIENT ROME / Carter, Jesse Benedict – New York: Macmillan Company, 1906. viii,189p – 1 – us U.W. Library [250]

RELIGION OF SCIENCE / Carus, Paul – Chicago: Open Court, 1896. 1 fiche – 9 – us A.T.L.A. [240]

THE RELIGION OF SHAKESPEARE / Simpson, Richard; ed by Bowden, Henry Sebastian – London: Burns & Oates; New York: Benziger, 1899 – 1mf – us A.T.L.A. [240]

THE RELIGION OF THE CHINESE / Groot, J J M de – CH-1006 1. 1910 – 9 – ne IDC [290]

THE RELIGION OF THE CHRIST : ITS HISTORIC AND LITERARY DEVELOPMENT CONSIDERED AS AN EVIDENCE OF ITS ORIGIN / Leathes, Stanley – (Includes bibliographical references) – London: Rivingtons, 1874 – 1mf – 9 – 0-8370-4379-4 – 1985-2379 – us A.T.L.A. [240]

THE RELIGION OF THE FUTURE AND OTHER ESSAYS / Momerie, Alfred Williams – Edinburgh. William Blackwood, 1893. 1 fiche – 9 – us A.T.L.A. [240]

THE RELIGION OF THE INCARNATION DELIVERED BEFORE THE VANDERBILT UNIVERSITY / Hendrix, Eugene Russell – (Includes index) – Nashville: Publ House of the M E Church, South, 1904, c1903 – 1mf – 9 – 0-8370-4900-8 – 1985-2900 – us A.T.L.A. [210]

RELIGION OF THE OLD TESTAMENT / Marti, Karl – New York: G.P. Putnam, 1907. 1 fiche – 9 – us A.T.L.A. [220]

THE RELIGION OF THE POPE AND PRIMITIVE CHRISTIANITY: A CONTRAST / Allen, Joseph Antisell – s.l., s.n., 1891. 00038. (Pre-1900 Canadiana) – 9 – cn C.I.H.M. [240]

RELIGION OF THE POST-EXILIC PROPHETS / Bennett, William Henry – Edinburgh: T. & T. Clark, 1907. 1 fiche – 9 – us A.T.L.A. [270]

THE RELIGION OF TO-MORROW / Crane, Frank – New York:Duffield, 1906, c1899 – 1mf – 9 – 0-8370-3245-8 – 1985-1245 – us A.T.L.A. [240]

THE RELIGION OF WOMAN / McCabe, Joseph – 1905 – 9 – us A.T.L.A. [240]

RELIGION PRODUCTIVE OF JOY AND CONSISTENT WITH POLITENESS : A SERMON PREACHED AT THE ABBEY CHURCH AT BATH, APRIL 16, 1744... / Howdell, W – York, 1744 – 1mf – 9 – MP-316/1 – ne IDC [240]

RELIGION, RADICALISM AND FREETHOUGHT IN VICTORIAN AND EDWARDIAN BRITAIN – Archives, periodicals and pamphlets – 1 – uk Microform Academic [335]

LA RELIGION ROMAINE D'AUGUSTE AUX ANTONINS / Boissier, Gaston – Paris: Hachette, 1874 – 3mf – us A.T.L.A. [240]

LA RELIGION SAINT SIMONIENNE : AUX FEMMES SUR LEUR MISSION RELIGIEUSE DANS LA CRISE ACTUELLE / Bazard, Palmyre – Rouen: D. Briere, 1831. 8p. (Les Femmes Collection) – 1mf – 9 – $2.00 – fr Bibl Nationale [240]

RELIGION SAINT SIMONIENNE: MICHEL A HOLSTEIN – Prison de Sainte-Pelagie, 7 fevrier 1833. Paris, impr. Carpentier Mericourt, 1833, 7 p. Les Saint-Simoniens, 1825-1834. 6960 – 9 – fr Hachette [335]

RELIGION SAINT SIMONIENNE: RETRAITE DE MENILMONTANT, 6 JUIN 1832. PAROLE DU PERE. CHANTS – 12 p. LA FAMILLE SAINT-SIMONIENNE OUVRE POUR LA PREMIERE FOI SES PORTES. (6 juin 1832), 18 p. OUVERTURE DES TRAVAUX DU TEMPLE (1er juillet 1832), 27 p. Les Saint-Simoniens, 1825-1834. 6975 – 9 – fr Hachette [335]

RELIGION SAINT-SIMONIENNE / Bazard, Saint-Amand et Barthelemy-Prosper Enfantin – Lettre a M. le President de la chambre des deputes, Paris, Everat, s. d., 8 p. Les Saint-Simoniens, 1825-1834. 6891 – 9 – fr Hachette [335]

RELIGION SAINT-SIMONIENNE – MICHEL CHEVALIER. La Presse, Paris, le Globe, 1831, 28 p. Les Saint-Simoniens, 1825-1834. 6870 – 9 – fr Hachette [335]

RELIGION SAINT-SIMONIENNE: A BORD DU BATEAU DU CANAL DU LANGUEDOC, LE 5 MAI 1832 – Lemonnier, Ch. Castres, impr Vidal, 1832, 4 p. Les Saint-Simoniens, 1825-1834. 6922 – 9 – fr Hachette [335]

RELIGION SAINT-SIMONIENNE: APERCU DES VUES MORALES ET INDUSTRIELLES DES SAINT-SIMONIENS – Gustave Biard Blois, impr. E. Dezairs, s. d., 16 p. Les Saint-Simoniens, 1825-1834. 6918 – 9 – fr Hachette [335]

RELIGION SAINT-SIMONIENNE: APPEL – Benjamin-Olin-de Rodrigues. Paris, impr. Guiraudet, 1831, 15 p. Les Saint-Simoniens, 1825-1834. 6876 – 9 – fr Hachette [335]

RELIGION SAINT-SIMONIENNE: ASSOCIATION UNIVERSELLE – Fevrier 1831, Paris, impr. de Everat. Degre des Industriels, instructions pour la propagande, s. l. d. Les Saint-Simoniens, 1825-1834. 6897 – 9 – fr Hachette [335]

RELIGION SAINT-SIMONIENNE: AUX CHEFS DES EGLISES DES DEPARTEMENTS – Pereire, Isaac. Paris, impr. de Giraudet, s.d., 4 p. Les Saint-Simoniens, 1825-1834. 6947 – 9 – fr Hachette [335]

RELIGION SAINT-SIMONIENNE: AUX ELEVES DE L'ECOLE POLYTECHNIQUE – Abel-Etienne-Louis Transon. Paris, A. Masnier, 1830, 70 p. Les Saint-Simoniens, 1825-1834. 6859 – 9 – fr Hachette [335]

RELIGION SAINT-SIMONIENNE: AUX FEMMES SUR LEUR MISSION RELIGIEUSE DANS LA CRISE ACTUELLE – Bazard, Palmyre. Rouen, impr. D. Briere, 1831, 8 p. Les Saint-Simoniens, 1825-1834. 6906 – 9 – fr Hachette [305]

RELIGION SAINT-SIMONIENNE: AUX OUVRIERS, PAR UN OUVRIER – Haspot, Emile. Paris, Everat, 1831, 12 p. Les Saint-Simoniens, 1825-1834. 6883 – 9 – fr Hachette [305]

RELIGION SAINT-SIMONIENNE: CEREMONIE DU 27 NOVEMBRE – Paris, impr. de Giraudet, 1831, 24 p. Les Saint-Simoniens, 1825-1834. 6948 – 9 – fr Hachette [335]

RELIGION SAINT-SIMONIENNE: COMMUNION GENERALE DE LA FAMILLE SAINT-SIMONIENNE – Paris, Everat, 1831, 40 p. Les Saint-Simoniens, 1825-1834. 6864 – 9 – fr Hachette [335]

RELIGION SAINT-SIMONIENNE: CORRESPONDANCE – Paris, Guiraudet, 1831, 56 p. Les Saint-Simoniens, 1825-1834. 6875 – 9 – fr Hachette [335]

RELIGION SAINT-SIMONIENNE: DISCUSSIONS MORALES, POLITIQUES ET RELIGIEUSES QUI ONT AMENEES LA SEPARATION QUI S'EST EFFECTUEE EN NOVEMBRE 1831 AU SEIN DE LA SOCIETE SAINT-SIMONIENNE – Premiere partie. RELATION DES HOMMES ET DES FEMMES. MARIAGE, DIVORCE. Paris, Paulin, 1832, xvi-30 p. Les Saint-Simoniens, 1825-1834. 6950 – 9 – fr Hachette [306]

RELIGION SAINT-SIMONIENNE: ECONOMIE POLITIQUE ET POLITIQUE – Enfantin, B,-P. Paris, juillet 1831, xi-176 p. Les Saint-Simoniens, 1825-1834. 6868 – 9 – fr Hachette [330]

RELIGION SAINT-SIMONIENNE: EGLISE DE CASTELNAUDARY. ENSEIGNEMENT POPULAIRE – A. Metge Castelnaudary, impr. L. Groc, 1832, 16 p. Lemonnier, Ch. Religion Saint-Simonienne, Quel but se proposent les Saint-Simoniens? Ibid, s. d., 4 p. Metge, A. A mes Concitoyens. Ibid., s. d., 7 p. Foi Nouvelle. St-Pons, impr. de J. Franc, s. d., 12 p. "Castelnaudary, le 22 fevrier 1933. Les Apotres Rousseau, Massol et Thomas. ". Castelnaudary, impr. L. Groc, 4 p. Toussaint, Gabriel. Foi nouvelle. Paroles prononcees sur la tombe de Jean Izard. Castelnaudary, impr. L. Groc, 1834, 4 p. Toussaint, Marie-Antoine. Au peuple, un croyant de la foi nouvelle. St-Pons, impr. J. Franc, 1836, 4 p. Les Saint-Simoniens, 1825-1834. 6920 – 9 – fr Hachette [335]

RELIGION SAINT-SIMONIENNE: EGLISE DE TOULOUSE. ENSEIGNEMENT DE L'ATHENEE. AVENIR DE LA FEMME – Toulouse. A. Henault, 1831, 18 p. Ch. Lemonnier Present et avenir. Brochure politique. Toulouse, M. Escudier, 1834, 57 p. Les Saint-Simoniens, 1825-1834. 6943 – 9 – fr Hachette [335]

RELIGION SAINT-SIMONIENNE: ENSEIGNEMENT CENTRAL – Lechevalier Jules Saint-Andre. Paris, Everat, 1831, 64 p. et 19 p. Les Saint-Simoniens, 1825-1834. 6861 – 9 – fr Hachette [335]

RELIGION SAINT-SIMONIENNE: ENSEIGNEMENT DES OUVRIERS – Seance du dimanche 18 decembre 1831 (et) du dimanche 25 decembre 1831. Paris, Everat, 1831, 1832, 23 et 26 p. Les Saint-Simoniens, 1825-1834. 6879 – 9 – fr Hachette [335]

LA RELIGION SAINT-SIMONIENNE ET SES PRETRES / Chavard – Paris, impr. de Carpentier Mericourt, 1831, 4 p. Les Saint-Simoniens, 1825-1834. 6979 – 9 – fr Hachette [335]

RELIGION SAINT-SIMONIENNE: EVENEMENTS DE LYON – Michel Chevalier. Paris, Everat, s. d., 16 p. Les Saint-Simoniens, 1825-1834. 6878 – 9 – fr Hachette [335]

RELIGION SAINT-SIMONIENNE: FEUILLES POPULAIRES – 83 brochures publiees par les St-S. durant leur retraite a Menilmontant, de mars a juin 1832, de 2 a 8 p. chacune dans l'ordre de parution. (Fournel "Bibliographie St-Simonienne", en decrit 88, en comptant deux fois les brochures qui ont donne lieu a une seconde edition). Les Saint-Simoniens, 1825-1834. 6954 – 9 – fr Hachette [335]

RELIGION SAINT-SIMONIENNE: L'ANNONCIATION. PROFESSION DE FOI DES SAINT-SIMONIENS – J. Dieppe Lechevalier. impr. Delevoye Barrier, 1831, 8 p. Les Saint-Simoniens, 1825-1834. 6924 – 9 – fr Hachette [335]

RELIGION SAINT-SIMONIENNE: LECONS SUR L'INDUSTRIE ET LES FINANCES PRONONCEES A LA SALLE DE L'ATHENEE. SUIVIES D'UN PROJET DE BANQUE – Isaac Pereire. Paris, Guiraudet, 1832, 105 p. Les Saint-Simoniens, 1825-1834. 6874 – 9 – fr Hachette [336]

RELIGION SAINT-SIMONIENNE: LES SAINT-SIMONIENS DES SPOLIATEURS – Durand. Rodez, impr. Carrere, s.d., 11 p. Les Saint-Simoniens, 1825-1834. 6938 – 9 – fr Hachette [335]

RELIGION SAINT-SIMONIENNE: MISSION DU MIDI – Paris, Everat, s.d., 23 p. Les Saint-Simoniens a Lyon. Lyon, Sauvignet, 1831, 32 p. Doctrine des Saint-Simoniens. Lyon, Sauvignet, 1831, 32 p. Doctrine de Saint-Simonien mise a la portee de toute le monde. Lyon, Louis Babeuf, 1831, 70 p. Compagnonage de la Femme, chant. Paroles de E. Barrault, musique de F. David. Lyon, impr. J. Perret, s.d., 3 p. Cabuchet, Toussaint. Premiere lettre a un Saint-Simonien. Lyon, Louis Babeuf, 1832, 27 p. Religion Saint-Simonienne. Les Apotres a Menilmontant. Lyon, impr. Charvin, 1832, 4 p. Cognat. Les Saint-Simoniens Lyon, impr. Charvin, 1832, 1 p. Les Saint-Simoniens, 1825-1834. 6927 – 9 – fr Hachette [335]

RELIGION SAINT-SIMONIENNE: MORALE. REUNION GENERALE DE LA FAMILLE. ENSEIGNEMENT DU PERE SUPREME – Le Trois Familles. Paris, Everat, 1832, 207 p. Les Saint-Simoniens, 1825-1834. 6955 – 9 – fr Hachette [306]

RELIGION SAINT-SIMONIENNE: PARIS, 15 JUILLET 1833. LE SENTIMENT PROFOND DE NOTRE POSITION ANARCHIQUE – (signe Martin Rose). S. d., 1 p. LETTRES RECUES A PARIS LE 5 NOVEMBRE 1835. Paris, impr. de Malteste, (Lettres d'Egypte de Lambert et Enfantin). 7 p. Les Saint-Simoniens, 1825-1834. 6972 – 9 – fr Hachette [335]

RELIGION SAINT-SIMONIENNE: POLITIQUE EUROPEENNE – Chevalier, Michel. Paris, Everat, 1832, 127 p. Les Saint-Simoniens, 1825-1834. 6877 – 9 – fr Hachette [335]

RELIGION SAINT-SIMONIENNE: POLITIQUE INDUSTRIELLE – et Systeme de la Mediterrannee. Michel Chevalier. Paris, Everat, 1832, 151 p. Les Saint-Simoniens, 1825-1834. 6881 – 9 – fr Hachette [335]

RELIGION SAINT-SIMONIENNE: POURSUITES DIRIGEES CONTRE NOTRE PERE SUPREME ENFANTIN ET CONTRE NOTRE PERE OLINDE RODRIGUES – Paris, Everat, s.d., 40 p. Les Saint-Simoniens, 1825-1834. 6956 – 9 – fr Hachette [335]

RELIGION SAINT-SIMONIENNE: PROCES EN LA COUR D'ASSISES DE LA SEINE LES 27 ET 28 AOUT 1832 – Paris, Librairie Saint-Simonienne, 1832, 405 p., portraits. PAROLE DU PERE A LA COUR D'ASSISES, 8 AVRIL 1833. Paris, Johanneau, 1833, 18 p. Les Saint-Simoniens, 1825-1834. 6958 – 9 – fr Hachette [335]

RELIGION SAINT-SIMONIENNE: PROCES EN POLICE CORRECTIONNELLE LE 19 OCTOBRE 1832 – Paris a la Librairie Saint-Simonienne, 1832, 105 p. portraits. PROCES EN POLICE CORRECTIONNELLE SOUS PREVENTION D'ESCROQUERIE, LE 19 OCTOBRE 1832. Henri Fournel pour le Pere. Paris, impr. de Carpentier Mericourt, 10 p. PLAIDOYER DE M. DUVERGIER POUR M. OLINDE RODRIGUES. Paris, Ibid., 1832, 16 p. Les Saint-Simoniens, 1825-1834. 6959 – 9 – fr Hachette [335]

RELIGION SAINT-SIMONIENNE: PROJET DE DISCOURS DE LA COURONNE POUR L'ANNEE 1831 – Moyens de supprimer immediatement tous les impots. Michel Chevalier. La Vendee, Paris, Giraudet, 1831, 35 p. Les Saint-Simoniens, 1825-1834. 6870 – 9 – fr Hachette [335]

RELIGION SAINT-SIMONIENNE: RAPPORTS ADRESSES AUX PERES SUPREMES, SUR LA SITUATION ET LES TRAVAUX DE LA FAMILLE – F. d'Eichtal, Stephane Flachat et Henri Fournel. Paris, Guiraudet, s. d., 33 p. Les Saint-Simoniens, 1825-1834. 6871 – 9 – fr Hachette [306]

RELIGION SAINT-SIMONIENNE: RECUEIL DE PREDICATIONS – Par Emile Barrault, Abel Transon, Moiese Retouret, et al. Paris, Everat, 1832, 2 vol. 606 plus 419 p. Les Saint-Simoniens, 1825-1834. 6889-6890 – 9 – fr Hachette [335]

RELIGION SAINT-SIMONIENNE: REUNION GENERALE DE LA FAMILLE – Enseignements faits par le Pere supreme. Paris, Everat, 1832, 154 p. Les Saint-Simoniens, 1825-1834. 6946 – 9 – fr Hachette [306]

RELIGION SAINT-SIMONIENNE: REUNION GENERALE DE LA FAMILLE – Seances des 19 et 21 novembre 1831. NOTES SUR LE MARIAGE ET LE DIVORCE. O. Rodrigues. Paris, Everat, 1831, 64 p. Les Saint-Simoniens, 1825-1834. 6945 – 9 – fr Hachette [306]

RELIGION, STATE AND SOCIETY : THE KESTON JOURNAL – 21v – 9 – £135.50 – 0963-7494 – uk Carfax [200]

RELIGION TEACHER'S JOURNAL – (v.14$. 1980- 5,6,9) – v.1-. 1967- – 1 – us UMI [073]

LA RELIGION TRADITIONNELLE DES ABIDJI / Lafargue, Fernand – (Africa series). 1968 – 9 – fr Hachette [290]

DIE RELIGION UND DIE SOZIALE ENTWICKLUNG : VORTRAG AUF DEM ERSTEN RELIGIONSWISSENSCHAFTLICHEN KONGRESS IN STOCKHOLM / Soederblom, Nathan – Freiburg i. B.: J.C.B. Mohr, 1898 – 1mf – us A.T.L.A. [240]

RELIGION UND DOGMA : EIN JAHRHUNDERT INNERER ENTWICKLUNG IM FRANZOESISCHEN PROTESTANTISMUS / Luettge, Willy – Tuebingen: J.C.B. Mohr, 1913. (Zeitschrift fuer Theologie und Kirche; 1913 Ergaenzungsheft) – 1mf – us A.T.L.A. [240]

RELIGION UND GEISTESKULTUR – 1906-14 (complete) – 2r – 1 – ATLA 1994-S520 – us A.T.L.A. [073]

RELIGION UND KIRCHE IN ENGLAND IM FUENFZEHNTEN JAHRHUNDERT / Fueter, Eduard – Tuebingen: J.C.B. Mohr, 1904 – 1mf – us A.T.L.A. [941]

RELIGION UND PRIESTERTHUM / Roth, Julius – Leipzig: Otto Wigand, 1872. 1 fiche – 9 – us A.T.L.A. [200]

RELIGION UND RELIGIONEN : BEI SCHLEIERMACHER UND HEGEL: EINE VERHAELTNISBESTIMMUNG / Vowinckel, Ernst – (Includes bibliographical references) – Erlangen: Rudolf Merkel, 1896 – 1mf – 9 – 0-8370-5916-X – 1985-3916 – us A.T.L.A. [230]

DIE RELIGION UNSERER KLASSIKER LESSING, HERDER, SCHILLER, GOETHE / Sell, Karl – Tuebingen, 1910 – 4mf – DM90.00 – 3-8267-3023-2 – gw Hänsel [430]

LA RELIGION VENGEE, OU REFUTATION DES AUTEURS IMPIES : DEDIEE A MONSEIGNEUR LE DAUPHIN PAR UNE SOCIETE DE GENS DE LETTRES – Paris. 21v. 1757-63 – 126mf – 9 – H-1392/2 – ne IDC [240]

RELIGION Y PATRIOTISMO. POESIAS LIRICAS Y RELIGIOSAS / Lopez Cruz, Lorenzo – Caceres: Imp. Diputacion, 1944 – 1 – sp Bibl Santa Ana [240]

DIE RELIGIONEN DER ERDE: IHR WESEN UND IHRE GESCHICHTE, MIT BEITRAEGEN VON FRANZ RABINGER...ET AL / ed by Clemen, Carl – 2. Aufl. Muenchen, F. Bruckmann, 1949, 480 p. Includes errata slip. Film Mas 8403 – 1 – us H.U. Library [230]

DIE RELIGIONEN DER EUROPAEISCHEN CULTURVOELKER, DER LITAUER, SLAVEN, GERMANEN, GRIECHEN, UND ROEMER, IN IHREM GESCHICHTLICHEN URSPRUNGE / Lippert, Julius – Berlin, 1881. xvi, 496 p. Film Mas 8404 – 1 – us H.U. Library [230]

RELIGIONS – nos13-77. 1935-53 (complete) – Inquire – 1 – ATLA 1994-S514 – us A.T.L.A. [073]

RELIGIONS AND THEOLOGY – v.1-2. 1878-80. Continued by ymennonitische rundschau – 1 – us UMI [240]

RELIGIONS D'AUTHORITE ET LA RELIGION DE L'ESPRIT = RELIGIONS OF AUTHORITY AND THE RELIGION OF THE SPIRIT / Sabatier, Auguste – (In English. Includes bibliographical references and appendix) – 1mf – 9 – 0-8370-5017-0 – 1985-3017 – us A.T.L.A. [200]

RELIGIONS OF MISSION FIELDS AS VIEWED BY PROTESTANT MISSIONARIES – (Includes bibliographies and index) – [S.I.]: Student Volunteer Movement for Foreign Mission, 1905 – 1mf – 9 – 0-8370-6845-2 – 1986-0845 – us A.T.L.A. [230]

RELIGIONSBUECHLEIN FUER DIE UNTERSTUFE EVANGELISCHER SCHULEN : IM ANSCHLUSS AN WENDELS BIBLISCHE GESCHICHTEN / ed by Sperber, Eduard – Breslau: Carl Duelfer, 1908 – 1mf – 9 – 0-8370-8790-2 – 1986-2790 – us A.T.L.A. [240]

RELIGIONSGESCHICHTE-STUDIEN / Guedemann, Moritz – Leipzig. 1876. BJ-100-6 1 – 9 – ne IDC [200]

DIE RELIGIONSGESCHICHTLICHE BEDEUTUNG DER HEBRAEISCHEN EIGENNAMEN DES A.T / Kerber, Georg – Freiburg i.B.: J.C.B. Mohr, 1897. 1 fiche – 9 – us A.T.L.A. [220]

DIE RELIGIONSGESCHICHTLICHE BEDEUTUNG DES DEKALOGS : PROLEGOMENA ZU EINER ALTTESTAMENTLICHEN LEHRE VON DER SUENDE / Lemme, Ludwig – Breslau: Louis Koehler, 1880 – 1mf – 9 – 0-8370-4089-2 – 1985-2089 – us A.T.L.A. [220]

DER RELIGIONSGESCHICHTLICHE RAHMEN DES REICHES GOTTES / Boehmer, Julius – Leipzig: Dieterich, 1909. 1 fiche – 9 – us A.T.L.A. [240]

RELIGIONSGESCHICHTLICHES HANDBUCH FUER DEN RAUM DER ALTCHRISTLICHEN UMWELT: HELLENISTISCH-ROEMISCHE GEISTRESSTROEMMGEN UND KULTE MIT BEACHTUNG DES EIGENLEBENS DER PROVINZEN / Pruemm, Karl – Freiburg im Breisgau, Herder, 1943. xvi, 921 p. Film Mas 8367 – 1 – us H.U. Library [240]

RELIGIONSGESCHICHTLICHES LESEBUCH, IN VERBINDUNG MIT W. GRUBE...R. GELDNER... M. WINTERNITZ...UND A. MEZ. – Ed. by A. Bertholet. Tuebingen: J.C.B. Mohr, 1908. xxviii,401p – 1 – us U.W. Library [200]

DER RELIGIONSGESCHLICHTLICHE GEHALT DER PSALMEN : MIT BEZUG AUF DAS SITTLICH-RELIGIOSE LEBEN DER NACHEXILISCHEN GEMEINDE / Achelis, Johannes – (Wissenschaftliche Beilage zum Jahresbericht der funften Realschule. Ostern, 1904) – Berlin: Weidmann, 1904 – 1mf – 9 – 0-8370-2037-9 – 1985-0037 – us A.T.L.A. [220]

RELIGIONSHISTORIE – 1942 – 1 – us I.U. Libraries [390]

DIE RELIGIONSPHILOSOPHIE DES SAADIA / Guttmann, J – Goettingen. 1882. BJ-33-10 1 – 9 – ne IDC [180]

DIE RELIGIONSPHILOSOPHIE DES SAADIA / Guttmann, J – Goettingen: Vandenhoeck & Rup., 1882. 1 fiche – 9 – us A.T.L.A. [270]

RELIGIONSPHILOSOPHIE IM UMRISS : MIT HISTORISCH-KRITISCHER EINLEITUNG UEBER DIE RELIGIONSPHILOSOPHIE SEIT KANT / Seydel, Rudolf; ed by Schmiedel, Paul Wilhelm – (Includes bibliographical references and index of names) – Freiburg i. B: J C B Mohr (Paul Siebeck), 1893 – 1mf – 9 – 0-8370-5239-4 – 1985-3239 – us A.T.L.A. [210]

DIE RELIGIONSPHILOSOPHIE IN DEUTSCHLAND...RUDOLF EUCKEN ALS FESTGABE / Siebert, Otto – Langensalza: Hermann Beyer, 1906. 1 fiche – 9 – us A.T.L.A. [240]

DIE RELIGIONSPHILOSOPHISCHE BEDEUTUNG DES STOISCH-CHRISTLICHEN EUDAEMONISMUS IN JUSTINS APOLOGIE : STUDIEN UND VORARBEITEN / Clemen, Carl – Leipzig: J.C. Hinrichs, 1890 – 1mf – us A.T.L.A. [240]

DAS RELIGIONSPROBLEM BEI FRIEDRICH NIETZSCHE / Odenwald, Theodor – (Includes bibliographical references) – Leipzig: J C Hinrichs, 1922 – 1r – 1 – us U.W. Library [190]

RELIGIONSPROBLEMET INOM KATOLICISM OCH PROTESTANTISM / Soederblom, Nathan – Stockholm: H. Gebers, 1910 – 2mf – us A.T.L.A. [240]

DIE RELIGIONSVERHANDLUNGEN AUF DEM REICHSTAGE ZU REGENSBURG 1541 / Vetter, Paul – Jena, 1889 – 9 – DM48.00 – 3-89349-276-3 – gw Hänsel [320]

RELIGIONSVIDENSKABELIGT TIDSSKRIFT – 1982-91 (complete) – Inquire – 1 – ATLA S0835 – us A.T.L.A. [073]

RELIGIONZNOST' I PRESTUPNOST' / Sheinman, M – Moscow, 1927. 101p. BR-9442/1 – 9 – ne IDC [240]

Religiosa Concepcionista *see* VIDAS DE DONA FRANCISCA FERNANDEZ DE CORDOBA DE ROMERO Y DE SOR REGLA ROMERO Y FERNANDEZ DE CORDOBA
Una Religiosa Concepcionista *see* LA MARGARITA ESCONDIDA
UNA RELIGIOSA CONCEPCIONISTA. LA MARGARITA ESCONDIDA.VIDA DE LA...SOR JACINTA MARIA TERESA DE JESUS – Romero. Balmaseda Palomeque y Gomez Bravo 2nd Edicion. Madrid. Imp. Helenica, 1922 – 1 – sp Bibl Santa Ana [240]
Religioso de la Orden de San Francisco, Un *see* VIDA DE SAN PEDRO DE ALCANTARA
RELIGIOUS AND MORAL ASPECTS OF WORLD WAR 2 PAMPHLET COLLECTION – 1939-1951 – 2r – 1 – CSUXANM8113-B – us Hoover Inst Photo [200]
RELIGIOUS ART : SUBJECT COLLECTIONS – (Individual titles not listed separately) – 17 catalogues on 27mf – 9 – £230.00 – uk Chadwyck [700]
RELIGIOUS ART AND ARCHITECTURE DESIGN AWARDS – (Also available in mf. Print index available for 1995-98) – 1995-98 – 7r – 1 – $560.00 – us Ross [720]
RELIGIOUS ASPECT OF EVOLUTION / McCosh, James – New York: Scribner's, 1890. 1 fiche – 9 – us A.T.L.A. [240]
THE RELIGIOUS ASPECT OF THE CIVIL WAR IN CHINA / Rule, William Harris – London: Partridge and Oakey, 1853 – 1mf – us A.T.L.A. [950]
RELIGIOUS ASPECTS OF WORLD WAR 1 PAMPHLET COLLECTION – 1914-1920 – 4r – 1 – CSUXANL9127-B – us Hoover Inst Photo [200]
RELIGIOUS BROADCASTING – (1985-. 5,6,9) – v1-. 1969- – 1 – us UMI [380]
RELIGIOUS CHASTITY : AN ETHNOLOGICAL STUDY / Main, John – New York: [s.n.], 1913, c1912 – 1mf – us A.T.L.A. [305]
THE RELIGIOUS CONCEPTION OF THE WORLD : AN ESSAY IN CONSTRUCTIVE PHILOSOPHY / Rogers, Arthur Kenyon – (Includes index) – New York: Macmillan, 1907 – 1mf – 9 – 0-8370-6356-6 – 1986-0356 – us A.T.L.A. [110]
RELIGIOUS CONFESSIONS AND CONFESSANTS : WITH A CHAPTER ON THE HISTORY OF INTROSPECTION / Burr, Anna Robeson – Boston: Houghton Mifflin, 1914 – 2mf – us A.T.L.A. [240]
THE RELIGIOUS CONTROVERSIES OF SCOTLAND / Henderson, Henry F – 1905 – 9 – us A.T.L.A. [240]
THE RELIGIOUS CONTROVERSY BETWEEN THE REV. W.C. BROWNLEE AND THE REV. FELIX VAREGA... – 1833 – 1r – 1 – $50.00 – us Presbyterian [240]
THE RELIGIOUS DEVELOPMENT OF THE NEGRO IN VIRGINIA / Earnest, Joseph B – 1914 (Charlottesville, Va.: Michie) – 1mf – us A.T.L.A. [240]
RELIGIOUS DISCRIMINATION : A NEGLECTED ISSUE / U.S. Commission on Civil Rights – Washington: GPO, 1980. LLMC 94-331 – 6mf – 9 – $9.00 – us L.L.M.C. [200]
RELIGIOUS DISSENSIONS : THEIR CAUSE AND CURE: A PRIZE ESSAY / Church, Pharcellus – New York: Gould and Newman, 1838 – 1mf – us A.T.L.A. [240]
RELIGIOUS EDUCATION – v49- 1954- 1; v66- 5,6; v70- 9 – us UMI [240]
RELIGIOUS EDUCATION – 1934-41 (complete) – 3r – 1 – ATLA S0499 – us A.T.L.A. [073]
RELIGIOUS EDUCATION – Important historical materials on religious education from libraries of University of Pa.; Robert Raikes Historical Soc., London, England; and Angus Library, Oxford. 1814-97, 1933 – 1 – 131.04 – us Baptist [240]
RELIGIOUS EDUCATION = TSUNG-CHIAO-YU CHI-KAN – (In Chinese) – v1-4. 1937-40 (complete) – 1r – 1 – ATLA S0318 – us A.T.L.A. [073]
RELIGIOUS EDUCATION – v. 1-38. 1907-1943 – 1,5,6 – us Princeton Micro [240]
RELIGIOUS EDUCATION – v1-48. Apr 1906-1953 (complete) – 12r – 1 – ATLA S0005 – us A.T.L.A. [073]
RELIGIOUS EDUCATION AND THE PUBLIC SCHOOL : AN AMERICAN PROBLEM / Wenner, George Unangst – new rev enl ed. New York: American Tract Society, c1913 – 1mf – 9 – 0-8370-8633-7 – 1986-2633 – us A.T.L.A. [370]
RELIGIOUS EDUCATION ASSOCIATION : PROCEEDINGS – v1-5. 1903-08 (complete) – 1r – 1 – ATLA S0030 – us A.T.L.A. [240]
Religious Education Association. Southern Baptist Convention *see* PAPERS
RELIGIOUS EDUCATION FELLOWSHIP – Shanghai, Sep 1947-Jun 1948 (complete) – 1r – 1 – ATLA S0696 – us A.T.L.A. [073]
RELIGIOUS EDUCATION FELLOWSHIP (R.E.F) BULLETIN – (Some original pgs damaged) – Shanghai, 1932-50 – 1r – 1 – ATLA S0693 – us A.T.L.A. [073]
RELIGIOUS ENDOWMENTS IN CANADA: THE CLERGY RESERVE AND RECTORY QUESTIONS: A CHAPTER OF CANADIAN HISTORY / Hincks, Sir Francis – London: Dalton & Lucy, 1869. 05624. (Pre-1900 Canadiana) – 9 – cn C.I.H.M. [971]
RELIGIOUS ESTABLISHMENT IN SCOTLAND – 1771 – 1 – $50.00 – us Presbyterian [240]
RELIGIOUS EXPERIENCE AND JOURNAL OF MRS. JARENA LEE: GIVING AN ACCOUNT OF HER CALL TO PREACH THE GOSPEL / Lee, Jarena – 1849 – 9 – us A.T.L.A. [240]
THE RELIGIOUS EXPERIENCE OF THE ROMAN PEOPLE : FROM THE EARLIEST TIMES TO THE AGE OF AUGUSTUS : THE GIFFORD LECTURES FOR 1909-10 / Fowler, William Warde – London; New York: Macmillan, 1911 – 2mf – us A.T.L.A. [240]
RELIGIOUS EXPOSITOR – Eola and Corvallis, OR. 1856 – 1 – 17.00 – us Oregon Hist [071]
THE RELIGIOUS FAITH OF DISTINGUISHED PEOPLE OF THE WORLD (CCC13) = SHENG TAO CHENG YEN: SHIH CHIEH MING JEN TSUNG CHIAO KUAN / Chang, Li-sheng chu – (In Chinese) – Hong Kong: Sheng Tao Press, [19–] – 1r – 1 – 0-8370-1713-0 – 1984-6082 – us A.T.L.A. [240]
THE RELIGIOUS FORCES OF THE UNITED STATES : ENUMERATED, CLASSIFIED, AND DESCRIBED : RETURNS FOR 1900 AND 1910 COMPARED WITH THE GOVERNMENT CENSUS OF 1890 : CONDITION AND CHARACTERISTICS OF CHRISTIANITY IN THE UNITED STATES / Carroll, H K – New York: Charles Scribner, 1912 – 2mf – us A.T.L.A. [200]
RELIGIOUS HERALD – Richmond. Va. 1828-1908 – 1 – us UMI [071]
RELIGIOUS HERALD – Virginia. 1828-1991 – 1 – $5,120.96 – us Baptist [240]
RELIGIOUS HERALD: INDEX TO MARRIAGE AND OBITUARY NOTICES – Richmond. Virginia. 1828-38 – 1 – 38.85 – us Baptist [240]
THE RELIGIOUS HISTORY OF IRELAND, PRIMITIVE, PAPAL AND PROTESTANT.. / Godkin, James – 1873 – 1 – us A.T.L.A. [200]
THE RELIGIOUS INSTRUCTION OF THE NEGROES IN THE UNITED STATES / Jones, Charles C – Savannah: T. Purse, 1842 – 1mf – us A.T.L.A. [370]
RELIGIOUS LEGISLATION: SHALL GOD OR CIVIL RULERS GOVERN THE CONSCIENCE? / Cooke, John T – Toronto: Review and Herald Pub. Co., 1890? 03435. (Pre-1900 Canadiana) – 9 – cn C.I.H.M. [971]
RELIGIOUS LIBERTY : AN HISTORICAL PAPER / King, Henry Melville – Providence, R.I.: Preston & Rounds, 1903 – 1mf – us A.T.L.A. [200]
RELIGIOUS LIBERTY UNDER THE FREE EXERCISE CLAUSE, 13 AUG 1986 – Washington: GPO, 1988 – 2mf – 9 – $3.00 – LLMC 94-362 – us L.L.M.C. [340]
THE RELIGIOUS LIFE AND INFLUENCE OF QUEEN VICTORIA / Walsh, Walter – London: Swan Sonnenschein; New York: E.P. Dutton, 1902 – 1mf – us A.T.L.A. [941]
RELIGIOUS LIFE IN AMERICA : A RECORD OF PERSONAL OBSERVATION / Abbott, Ernest Hamlin – New York: Outlook Company, 1902 – 1mf – us A.T.L.A. [200]
RELIGIOUS LIFE IN GERMANY DURING THE WARS OF INDEPENDENCE : IN A SERIES OF HISTORICAL AND BIOGRAPHICAL SKETCHES / Baur, William – London: Strahan, 1870 – 2mf – us A.T.L.A. [306]
THE RELIGIOUS LIFE OF GOETHE AS ILLUSTRATED IN THE TRAGEDY OF FAUST / Cooledge, Charles Edwin – Boston: Stratford, 1932 – 1r – 1 – us U.W. Library [430]
RELIGIOUS MAGAZINE – Portland/Kennebunk, ME. Free Will Baptists. 1811-12, 1820-22 – 1 – 19.15 – us A.B.H.S. [073]
RELIGIOUS MAGAZINE CONTAINING AN ACCOUNT OF THE UNITED CHURCHES OF CHRIST COMMONLY CALLED FREEWILL BAPTIST / Buzzell, John M G – v. 1. 1811-12; v. 2. no. 2-8. 1820-22 – 1 – us Baptist [240]
RELIGIOUS MOVEMENTS FOR SOCIAL BETTERMENT / Strong, Josiah – New York: Baker and Taylor, c1900 – 1mf – us A.T.L.A. [240]
RELIGIOUS PAMPHLETS / Dearmer, Percy – London: K. Paul, Trench, Truebner, 1898. (The Pamphlet library) – 1mf – us A.T.L.A. [240]
RELIGIOUS PERSECUTION : A STUDY IN POLITICAL PSYCHOLOGY / Haynes, Edmund Sidney Pollck – London: Duckworth, 1904 – 1mf – us A.T.L.A. [320]
RELIGIOUS PERSECUTION; A STUDY IN POLITICAL PSYCHOLOGY / Haynes, Edmund Sidney Pollock – London: Watts and Co., 1906. xi,92p – 1 – us U.W. Library [320]
RELIGIOUS PRACTICES AND HIGH-RISK BEHAVIORS OF COLLEGE STUDENT ATHLETES AND NONATHLETES / Bakker, Debra L – Indiana University, 1995 – 2mf – 9 – $8.00 – PSY1838 – us Microform Publ [300]
THE RELIGIOUS PROBLEM IN SPAIN / Ossorio, Angel – Washington, DC, 1937. Fiche W1183. (Blodgett Collection of Spanish Civil War Pamphlets) – 9 – us H.U. College Libr [946]
RELIGIOUS PROGRESS / Allen, Alexander V G – Boston: Houghton, Mifflin, 1894.1 fiche – 9 – us A.T.L.A. [240]
THE RELIGIOUS REPOSITORY – S.l.: s.n., 1839?-18–? – 9 – cn C.I.H.M. [240]
RELIGIOUS SCEPTICISM AND INFIDELITY : THEIR HISTORY, CAUSE, CURE AND MISSION / Langford, John Alfred – London: J. Chapman, 1850 – 245p – 1 – us U.W. Library [210]
RELIGIOUS SECTARIANS IN RUSSIA – Primarily works by Marxist writers – 1 – us Baptist [240]
RELIGIOUS SOCIETY OF FRIENDS. MEETINGS FOR SUFFERINGS ARCHIVES : THE GREAT BOOKS OF SUFFERINGS, VOLS 1-29, C.1650-1790 – 1990 – 29r/35mm silver positive roll microfilm – 1 – £1,140.00 – uk World [240]
Religious Society of Friends (Quakers) *see* FRIENDS ASSOCIATION FOR ABOLISHING STATE REGULATION OF VICE (1873-1910) AND FRIENDS ASSOCIATION FOR THE PROMOTION OF SOCIAL PURITY (1910-1926)
The Religious Society of Friends (Quakers) *see* QUAKER OFFICIAL CORRESPONDENCE
RELIGIOUS SOCIETY OF FRIENDS. THE LONDON TWO WEEKS MEETING : MINUTES 1672-1789, BOOKS OF CERTIFICATES 1716-1797 AND LIBRARY INDEX OF NAMES – 1990 – 8r/35mm silver positive roll microfilm – 1 – £350.00 – uk World [240]
RELIGIOUS STUDIES NEWS – v1- . 1985- – 1,5,7,9 – us UMI [073]
THE RELIGIOUS SYSTEM OF CHINA / Groot, J J M de – HP 5 5984-5989 2. 6 v. 1892-1910 – 8 – ne IDC [290]
THE RELIGIOUS TEACHERS OF GREECE : BEING GIFFORD LECTURES ON NATURAL RELIGION / Adam, James; ed by Adam, Adele Marion – Edinburgh: T. & T. Clark, 1908 – 2mf – us A.T.L.A. [290]
RELIGIOUS TELESCOPE – (Some pgs lacking. Several mergers) – Dayton, OH. v1-112. 31 Dec 1834-28 Dec 1946 – 77r – 1 – ATLA S0050 – us A.T.L.A. [073]
RELIGIOUS TELESCOPE *see* THE TELESCOPIC MESSENGER
RELIGIOUS THOUGHT IN ENGLAND, FROM THE REFORMATION TO THE END OF LAST CENTURY : A CONTRIBUTION TO THE HISTORY OF THEOLOGY / Hunt, John – London: Strahan, 1870-1873 – 4mf – us A.T.L.A. [240]
RELIGIOUS THOUGHT IN ENGLAND IN THE NINETEENTH CENTURY / Hunt, John – London: Gibbings,1896 – 1mf – us A.T.L.A. [941]
RELIGIOUS THOUGHT IN OLD ENGLISH VERSE / Abbey, Charles J – London: Sampson Low, Marston, 1892 – 2mf – us A.T.L.A. [420]
RELIGIOUS THOUGHT MOVEMENTS IN CHINA DURING THE LAST DECADE (CCC9) = KUO NEI CHIN SHIH NIEN LAI CHIH TSUNG CHIAO SSU CHAO / ed by Chang, Chin-Shih – (In Chinese) – Peking: Yenching School of Chinese Studies, 1927 – 1r – 1 – 0-8370-1709-2 – 1984-6092 – us A.T.L.A. [200]
RELIGIOUS TOLERANCE AND THE CHRISTIAN FAITH; A STUDY CONCERNING THE CONCEPT OF DIVINE OMNIPOTENCE IN THE INDONESIAN CONSTITUTION IN THE LIGHT OF ISLAM AND CHRISTIANITY / Sidjabat, Walter Bonar – SE 5442 1. 1965 – 9 – ne IDC [260]
THE RELIGIOUS USE OF IMAGINATION / Johnson, Elias Henry – (Includes index) – New York: Silver, Burdett, 1901 – 1mf – 9 – 0-8370-3786-7 – 1985-1786 – us A.T.L.A. [240]
THE RELIGIOUS VALUE OF THE OLD TESTAMENT IN THE LIGHT OF MODERN SCHOLARSHIP / Vernon, Ambrose White – New York: Thomas Y Crowell, 1907 – 1mf – 9 – 0-8370-9327-9 – 1986-3327 – us A.T.L.A. [220]
RELIGIOUS WRITINGS / Rolle, Richard – 15th cent. From Bath. Archives (Marquess). Longleat. Ms. 29 – 1 – uk Microform Academic [880]
RELIGIOZNO-OBSHCHESTVENNYE DVIZHENIIA 17-18 VV. V ROSSII / Mel'gunov, S P – M. 1922. BR-7694 2 – 8 – ne IDC [240]
RELIGOUS THOUGHT IN HOLLAND DURING THE NINETEENTH CENTURY / Mackay, James Hutton – London; New York: Hodder and Stoughton, 1911 – 1mf – us A.T.L.A. [200]
LES RELIQUES ET LES IMAGES LEGENDAIRES / Saintyves, Pierre – 1912 – 1 – us I.U. Libraries [390]
RELIQUIAE BOTANICAE, SIVE ENUMERATIO PLANTARUM IN. ASIAE MEDIAE, AB S / Bunge, A A von – (Arb. d. Naturf. Ver. Riga. v. 1, 1847). 1 v. Lehmann. 1839-42. B-421 2 – 8 – ne IDC [580]
RELIQUIAE HAENKEANAE / Presl, K B – 2v. Prague. 1825-30-1835. B-436 2 – 8 – ne IDC [580]
RELIQUIAE IURIS ECCLESIASTICI ANTIQUISSIMAE / Lagarde, P A – Berolini, 1856 – Dfl25.00 – ne Slangenburg [240]
RELIQUIAE RUDBECKIANAE, SIVE CAMPORUM ELYSIORUM LIBRI PRIMI / Smith, J E – Cura J. E. Smith. Londini, 1789. 35 pp. B-5742 2 – 8 – ne IDC [580]
RELIQUIAE SACRAE / Routh, M J – Oxonii. v1-5. 1846 – 43mf – 9 – Dfl151.00 – ne Slangenburg [240]
RELIQUIEN FRIEDRICH LUDWIG WEIDIG'S : GEWESENEN PFARRERS IN OBERGLEEN IM GROSSHERZOGTHUM HESSEN / Weidig, Friedrich Ludwig – Mannheim: H Hoff, 1838 – 1r – 1 – us U.W. Library [240]
DER RELIQUIENKULT IM ALTERTUM / Pfister, Friedrich – H.P. 29. 1909-1912 – 9 – ne IDC [930]
Relly, James *see*
– ANTICHRIST RESISTED IN A REPLY TO A PAMPHLET WROTE BY W. MASON
– REMARKS ON A PAMPHLET INTITLED 'A DIALOGUE BETWEEN A TRUE METHODIST AND AN ERRONEOUS METHODIST'
RELOX DEL ALMA Y ORACION MENTAL / Blazquez del Barco, Juan – 1765 – 9 – 1.50f – sp Bibl Santa Ana [240]
Relton, Frederic *see* THE ENGLISH CHURCH FROM THE ACCESSION OF GEORGE 1 TO THE END OF THE EIGHTEENTH CENTURY (1714-1800)
REMAINS HISTORICAL AND LITERARY CONNECTED WITH THE PALATINE COUNTIES OF LANCASTER AND CHESTER / Chetham Society – os: v1-114. 1844-86; Index v1-30. 1863; Index v31-114. 1893; ns: v1-105. 1883-1941 – 1078mf – 9 – h-831c/2 – ne IDC [941]
REMAINS, IN VERSE AND PROSE, OF ARTHUR HALLAM / Hallam, Arthur Henry – Pall Mall: Printed by W. Nicol, 1834 – 1 roll – 1 – 1-55879-860-9 – uk Libr Preservation [810]
THE REMAINS OF HENRY KIRKE WHITE OF NOTTINGHAM, LATE OF ST JOHN'S COLLEGE, CAMBRIDGE. WITH AN ACCOUNT OF HIS LIFE, BY ROBERT SOUTHEY / White, Henry Kirke – London: Printed for Vernor, Hood, and Sharpe: Longman, Hurst, Rees, Orme; and Brown; and Taylor and Hessey, 5th ed 1811-1822. (London: W. Wilson) – 1 roll – 1 – 1-55879-254-6 – uk Libr Preservation [420]

REMAINS OF JAPHET / Parsons, James – 1767. 455p. (English Linguistics Series 1500-1800) – 9 – us UMI [400]
REMAINS OF PAGAN SAXONDOM / Akerman, J Y – H-1152 2. 1855 – 8 – ne IDC [930]
THE REMAINS OF ROBERT BLOOMFIELD / Bloomfield, Robert – London: Printed by Thomas Davison for Baldwin, Cradock, and Joy, 1824 – 1 roll – 1 – 1-55879-245-7 – uk Libr Preservation [810]
REMAINS OF THE LATE REV. CHARLES WOLFE. WITH A BRIEF MEMOIR OF HIS LIFE BY THE LATE REV. JOHN A. RUSSELL / Wolfe, Charles – London: Hamilton, Adams, and Co., 3rd ed 1827 – 1 roll – 1 – 1-55879-865-X – uk Libr Preservation [240]
REMAINS OF THE LATE REVEREND RICHARD HURRELL FROUDE / Froude, Richard Hurrell – London: J.G. and F. Rivington, 1838-39. 2 pts. in 4v – 1 – us U.W. Library [240]
Remak, Gustavus *see* NEGOTIABLE INSTRUMENTS IN PENNSYLVANIA
REMARKABLE EXAMPLES OF MORAL RECOVERY : SHOWING THE POWER OF RELIGION IN EXTREME CASES / ed by Stevens, Abel – New York: Carlton & Phillips, 1855, c1854 – 1mf – us A.T.L.A. [240]
REMARKABLE FACTS : ILLUSTRATIVE AND CONFIRMATORY OF DIFFERENT PORTIONS OF HOLY SCRIPTURE / Leifchild, John – London: Jackson, Walford & Hodder, 1867 – 1mf – 9 – 0-8370-4085-X – 1985-2085 – us A.T.L.A. [220]
REMARKABLE FACTS: ILLUSTRATIVE AND CONFIRMATORY OF...HOLY SCRIPTURE / Leifchild, John – London: Jackson, Walford, 1867. 1 fiche – 9 – us A.T.L.A. [240]
THE REMARKABLE HISTORY OF SIR THOMAS UPMORE / Blackmore, Richard Doddridge – British Fiction Archive: Unit 3 – 9 – uk Bell [830]
REMARKS AND STATISTICS ON THE OCCASION OF THE THIRD CONFERENCE OF THE CHAMBER OF COMMERCE / Jordan. Chamber of Commerce and Industry. Economic progress in the Hashemite Kingdom of Jordan. Amman – 1953. BNE-9748/1 – 9 – ne IDC [380]
REMARKS IN THAT KIND OF PALSY OF THE LOWER LIMBS, WHICH IS FREQUENTLY FOUND TO ACCOMPANY CURVATURE OF THE SPINE / Pott, P – M 122. 1779 – 9 – ne IDC [610]
REMARKS MADE ON A SHORT TOUR BETWEEN HARTFORD AND QUEBEC, IN THE AUTUMN OF 1819 / Silliman, Benjamin – 2nd ed. New Haven: S Converse, 1824. SEM16P84 – 1r – 5 – Can$9.00 – cn Bibl Nat [910]
REMARKS OF THE HONORABLE DENIS BENJAMIN VIGER, RELATIVE TO THE GRIEVANCES SET FORTH IN THE ADDRESS OF THE COMMONS OF LOWER CANADA – s.l, s.n, 1831. SEM105P400 – 1mf – 9 – Can$2.25 – cn Bibl Nat [971]
REMARKS ON A BOOK INTITLED 'AN EARNEST APPEAL TO MEN OF REASON AND RELIGION', IN A LETTER TO THE REV. MR. JOHN WESLEY / Sharp, T – Newcastle, 1743 – 1mf – 9 – MP-307/1 – ne IDC [240]
REMARKS ON A LATE PAMPHLET INTITLED 'A BRIEF ACCOUNT OF THE LATE PERSECUTION AND BARBAROUS USAGE OF THE METHODISTS AT EXETER,... – Exon, 1745 – 1mf – 9 – MP-322/1 – ne IDC [240]
REMARKS ON A PAMPHLET INTITLED 'A DIALOGUE BETWEEN A TRUE METHODIST AND AN ERRONEOUS METHODIST' / Relly, James – [N.p.], 1751 – 2mf – 9 – MP-344/1 – ne IDC [240]
REMARKS ON M. BUNSEN'S WORK ON ST HIPPOLYTUS : PARTICULARLY ON THE PREFACE OF HIS NEW EDITION / Wordsworth, Christopher – London: Rivingtons, 1855 – 1mf – us A.T.L.A. [240]
REMARKS ON MICHAELIS'S INTRODUCTION TO THE NEW TESTAMENT / Randolph, John – 1802 – 9 – us A.T.L.A. [240]
REMARKS ON MILITARY LAW AND THE PRACTICE OF FLOGGING / Napier, Charles J – London: T & W Boone, 1837 – 3mf – 9 – $4.50 – LLMC 89-032 – us L.L.M.C. [340]
REMARKS ON SYNONYMS OF EUROPEAN SPIDERS / Thorell, T T T – Z 2205 2. 1870-1873 – 8 – ne IDC [590]
REMARKS ON THE ADMINISTRATION OF CRIMINAL JUSTICE IN SCOTLAND. / Alison, Archibald – Edinburgh, Blackwood, 1825. 143 p. LL-2275 – 1 – us L of C Photodup [340]
REMARKS ON THE COUNTRY EXTENDING FROM CAPE PALMAS TO THE RIVER CONGO / Adams, J – London. 1823. BA-266 2 – 8 – ne IDC [910]
REMARKS ON THE FOUR GOSPELS / Furness, William H – 1836 – 1 – us A.T.L.A. [240]
REMARKS ON THE INTERNAL EVIDENCE FOR THE TRUTH OF REVEALED RELIGION / Erskine, Thomas – 3rd Am. from the 5th enl. Edinburgh ed. Andover [Mass.] Warren F Draper, 1871 – 1mf – 9 – 0-8370-3071-4 – 1985-1071 – us A.T.L.A. [210]
REMARKS ON THE LAWS RELATING TO ATTEMPTS AGAINST THE PERSON OF THE SOVEREIGN, INCLUDING THE NEW STATUTE FOR THE BETTER SECURITY OF HER MAJESTY'S PERSON / Rickards, George Kettilby – London: Sweet, 1842. 39p. LL-96 – 1 – us L of C Photodup [340]
REMARKS ON THE OATH, DECLARATIONS AND CONDUCT OF JOHNSON ATKINSON BUSFIELD, ESQ.,... / Baldwyn, E – London, 1791 – 2mf – 9 – MP-576/1 – ne IDC [240]
REMARKS ON THE REPORT OF THE FACULTY OF ADVOCATES, APPOINTED TO CONSIDER THE PROVISIONS OF THE BILL FOR THE BETTER REGULATING OF THE PROCESS OF THE COURTS OF LAW IN SCOTLAND / Erskine, James St. Clair – London, Hunter, 1825. 36 p. LL-2237 – 1 – us L of C Photodup [340]
REMARKS ON THE REVEREND MR. JOHN WESLEY'S LAST JOURNAL, WHEREIN HE GIVES AN ACCOUNT OF THE TENETS AND PROCEEDINGS OF THE MORAVIANS,... / Church, T – London, 1745 – 1mf – 9 – MP-318/1 – ne IDC [240]
REMARKS ON THE WRITINGS OF THE REV. J.W. / Manners, N – Hull, 1788 – 1mf – 9 – MP-555/1 – ne IDC [240]
REMARKS SUGGESTED BY PRESIDENT GARFIELD'S DEATH / Davin, Nicholas Flood – Ottawa: J. Durie, 1881. 02594. (Pre-1900 Canadiana) – 9 – cn C.I.H.M. [971]
REMARKS UPON THE NECESSITY AND EFFECT OF GENERAL BANKRUPT LAW INCLUDING CORPORATIONS – Washington: Polkinhorn, 1858. 16p. LL-1207 – 1 – us L of C Photodup [340]
REMARKS UPON THE REVEREND MR. WHITEFIELD'S LETTER TO THE VICE-CHANCELLOR OF THE UNIVERSITY OF OXFORD,... / C, W – Oxford, 1768 – 1mf – 9 – MP-450/1 – ne IDC [240]
REMARKS UPON THE TRUE LOCATION OF THE INTERNATIONAL BOUNDARY LINE: AT THE MOUTH OF THE RIVER ST CLAIR, WITH REFERENCE TO THE SO-CALLED AMERICAN CANAL / Cameron, DR – Ottawa?, 1870? 00999. (Pre-1900 Canadiana) – 9 – cn C.I.H.M. [971]
REMARQUES CURIEUSES SUR L'ART DE BIEN CHANTER / Bacilly, B de – 1668 – 9 – us Sibley [780]
REMARQUES DE GRAMMAIRE SUR RACINE / Olivet, P J d' – 1738 – 9 – fr I.C.S. [440]
REMARQUES DIVERSES SUR LA PRONONCIATION ET L'ORTHOGRAPHE / Harduin, AX. – 1757 – 9 – fr I.C.S. [440]
REMARQUES ET CONSIDERATIONS SERVANS A LA JUSTIFICATION DU CURE DE LOUDUN – 9 – fr Hachette [360]
REMARQUES ET DECISIONS DE L'ACADEMIE FRANCOISE / Tallemant, P – 1698 – 9 – fr I.C.S. [440]
REMARQUES ET SUGGESTIONS SUR LA REORGANISATION DES TRIBUNAUX: ET AMENDEMENTS PROPOSES AU CODE DE PROCEDURE CIVILE / Amour, Jean d' – Montreal: C.O. Beauchemin, 1894.06506.(Pre-1900 Canadiana) – 9 – cn C.I.H.M. [971]
REMARQUES MORALES / Feydel, Gabriel – 1807 – 9 – fr I.C.S. [170]
REMARQUES NOUVELLES SUR LA LANGUE FRANCOISE / Bouhours, D – 1675 – 9 – fr I.C.S. [440]
REMARQUES SUR LA LANGUE FRANCAISE / Favre de Vaugelas, Cl – (Linguistic series). 1647 – 9 – fr Hachette [440]
REMARQUES SUR LA LANGUE FRANCAISE / Vaugelas, Cl. Favre de – 1647 – 9 – fr I.C.S. [440]
REMARQUES SUR LA LANGUE FRANCAISE AU 19E SIECLE / Wey, Fr – 1845 – 9 – fr I.C.S. [440]
REMARQUES SUR LES PRINCIPES DIFFICULTEZ QUE LES ESTRANGERS ONT EN LA LANGUE FRANCOISE / Saint-Maurice, Alcide de – 1672 – 9 – fr I.C.S. [440]
REMARQUES SUR LES SPHACELARIACEES / Sauvageau, C – 2v. 1900-24. B-1018 2 – 8 – ne IDC [580]
REMARQUES SUR UN LIVRE INTITULE OBSERVATIONS SUR L'ARCHITECTURE / Guillaumot, C A – L'Abbe Laugier. Paris: Hansy, 1768. (Architecture Series) – 9 – fr Hachette [720]
REMBRANDT, 1606-69. TABLEAUX, EAUX-FORTES, DESSINS / Reunion des musees nationaux. Paris – 1947. 8 illus. 1 fiche – 9 – fr Réunion [750]
REMBRANDT. DESSINS ET EAUX-FORTES / Reunion des musees nationaux. Paris – 1937. 1 fiche – 9 – fr Réunion [740]
Remedes *see* NOTE ON 2 PRESCRIPTIONS
REMEDIATION : THE JOURNAL OF ENVIRONMENTAL CLEANUP COSTS, TECHNOLOGIES AND TECHNIQUES – v1-3. 1990-93 – 9 – $92.00 set – us Hein [340]
REMEDIO DE CUERPOS HUMANOS Y SILVA DE LA EXPERIENCIAS Y OTRAS COSAS UTILISSIMAS / Lobera de Avila, L – Alcala, 1542 – 11mf – 9 – sp Cultura [610]
REMEDIOS ESPIRITUALES Y CORPORALES PARA CURAR Y PRESERVAR DEL MAL DE PESTE... / Cabrera, F – Antequera, 1649 – 1mf – 9 – sp Cultura [610]
THE REMEMBRANCER – Toronto: Bible and Tract Depot, 1891?-19– – 9 – cn C.I.H.M. [220]
REMEMBRANCES AND PERSPECTIVES; A SPEECH, BARCELONA, 28TH AUGUST 1938 / Prieto, Indalecio – Barcelona?, 1938. Fiche W1120. (Blodgett Collection of Spanish Civil War Pamphlets) – 9 – us H.U. College Libr [946]
Remenik, G *see* POEMY ALEKSANDRA BLOKA
Remer, Paul *see* DETLEV LILIENCRON
Remesal, Antonio *see* HISTORIA GENERAL DE LAS INDIAS OCCIDENTALES, Y PARTICULAR DE LA GOBERNACION DE CHIAPA Y GUATEMALA TOMO 1 Y 2
REMIDIAL EDUCATION – (Cont by: Support for Learning) – Edinburgh. v1-15. 1966-80. – 5,9 – Dfl900.00; Dfl60.00v – ne Swets [370]
REMIMISCENCES OF THE BOYS IN GRAY 1861-1865 / Yeary, Mamie – Dallas: Smith and Lamar, 1912. Texas Reel 7. (The Cox Library Collection) – 5 – us Americana [978]
REMIN ZHOUKAN – People's Weekly. Feb 1926-Apr 1927. F C22. In Chinese – 9 – $27.00 – cc Microforms [073]
REMINDER – Eugene, OR. -w. 15 July 1970-30 Jun 1971 – 1 – us U.O. Library [071]
REMINDER VALLEY NEWS – Eugene OR. July 8-July 22 1971 – 1 – us U.O. Library [071]
Remington, Frederic *see* LETTERS AND NOTEBOOKS
Remington, Harold *see*
– REMINGTON'S BUSINESS MAN'S MANUAL TO BANKRUPTCY LAW.
– A TREATISE ON THE BANKRUPTCY LAW OF THE UNITED STATES
REMINGTON'S BUSINESS MAN'S MANUAL TO BANKRUPTCY LAW. / Remington, Harold – New York: Bankruptcy 1911. 498p. LL-1057 – 1 – us L of C Photodup [340]
REMINISCENCES / Abbott, Lyman – Boston: Houghton Mifflin, 1915 – 2mf – us A.T.L.A. [240]
REMINISCENCES / Armstrong, John – ca1856-64 – 1 – us KS Hist [978]
REMINISCENCES / Curry, Fred S – 1 – us KS Hist [920]
REMINISCENCES / Lanning, Aaron L – 1848-1934 – 1 – us KS Hist [920]
REMINISCENCES / Porter, Catharine Wiggins – 1888-1902 – 1 – us KS Hist [978]
REMINISCENCES / Wood, Wallace A & Conwell, Effie (Wood) – undated, Miscellaneous titles – 1 – us KS Hist [920]
REMINISCENCES AND LETTERS / West, G M – 1850-62 – 1 – us KS Hist [978]
REMINISCENCES OF A NAVAL OFFICER / Crawford, Abraham – 2v 1851 – 9 – $20.00 – uk Libr Preservation [920]
REMINISCENCES OF ADAMS, JAY AND RANDOLPH COUNTIES. INDIANA REEL 3. (THE COX LIBRARY COLLECTION) – 5 – us Americana [978]
REMINISCENCES OF AN OFFICER OF ZOUAVES / Cler, Jean Joseph Gustave – Tr. from the French. New York, London: D. Appleton and Co., 1860. viii,317p – 1 – us U.W. Library [944]
REMINISCENCES OF BUREAU COUNTY / Matson, N – Princenton: Republic Book and Job Office, 1872. Illinois Reel 12. (The Cox Library Collection) – 5 – us Americana [978]
REMINISCENCES OF CHARLES DURAND OF TORONTO, BARRISTER / Durand, Charles – Toronto?: s.n., 1897 (Toronto: Hunter, Rose). 02807. (Pre-1900 Canadiana) – 9 – cn C.I.H.M. [971]
REMINISCENCES OF DANIEL WEBSTER / Harvey, Peter – Boston: Little, Brown & Co – 6mf – 9 – $9.00 – LLMC 91-057 – us L.L.M.C. [340]
REMINISCENCES OF HIS PUBLIC LIFE / Hincks, Sir Francis – Montreal: W. Drysdale, 1884. 05625. (Pre-1900 Canadiana) – 9 – cn C.I.H.M. [971]
"REMINISCENCES OF JEAN FREDERICK LOBA" / Loba, Jean Frederick – 1 – us KS Hist [920]
REMINISCENCES OF LIFE IN BUTLER COUNTY / Bodecker, Albert – 1 – us KS Hist [978]
REMINISCENCES OF SAMUEL TAYLOR COLERIDGE AND ROBERT SOUTHEY / Cottle, Joseph – London: Houlston and Stoneman, 1847 – 1 roll – 1 – 1-55879-853-6 – uk Libr Preservation [840]
"REMINISCENCES OF THE BAR" / Peirce, William Shannon – An address delivered before the Law Academy, April 17, 1883. Philadelphia: Kay, 1883. 31p. LL-365 – 1 – us L of C Photodup [340]
REMINISCENCES OF THE EARLY BENCH AND BAR OF ILLINOIS / Linder, Usher F – 2nd ed. Chicago, Chicago Legal News Co., 1879. 406 p. LL-1639 – 1 – us L of C Photodup [340]
REMINISCENCES OF THE EARLY BENCH AND BAR OF ILLINOIS / Usher, F Linder – Chicago: The Chicago Legal News Co., 1879. Illinois Reel 7. (The Cox Library Collection) – 5 – us Americana [978]
REMINISCENCES OF THE EARLY WEST AND EXPERIENCES OF THE BOWLBY FAMILY / Pennycuff, Mattie – 1 – us KS Hist [978]
REMINISCENCES OF THE REV. WM. ELLERY CHANNING, D.D / Peabody, Elizabeth Palmer – 1880 – 1 – us A.T.L.A. [240]
REMINISCENCES OF TWELVE YEARS' RESIDENCE IN TASMANIA AND NEW SOUTH WALES, NORFOLK ISLAND AND MORETON BAY, CALCUTTA, MADRAS, AND CAPE TOWN,.. / Atkins, Thomas – Malvern Australia: Advertiser, 1869. 04093. (Pre-1900 Canadiana) – 9 – cn C.I.H.M. [910]
REMINISCENCES OF WINTER IN THE SOUTH OF FRANCE: A LECTURE ON THE PYRENEES, PAU, LOURDES, ETC., DELIVERED AT HALIFAX, N. S. IN AID OF THE FUNDS OF THE SOCIETY OF ST VINCENT DE PAUL / Daly, Malachy Bowes – s.l.: s.n., 1879? (Ottawa: A. Woodburn). 04198. (Pre-1900 Canadiana) – 9 – cn C.I.H.M. [971]
REMINISCENCIAS / Cordovez Moure, J M – Bogata. 8v. 1907-13 – 1 – 46.00 – us L of C Photodup [972]
A REMINISCENT HISTORY OF THE OZARK REGION – Chicago, 1894. Missouri Reel 6.(The Cox Library Collection) – 5 – us Americana [978]
A REMINISCENT HISTORY OF THE OZARK REGION – Condensed general history, brief history of each county and biog. sketches. 12 fiches. F-0010 – 9 – us A.G.L.L. [978]
Remizov, A *see*
– BESNOVATYE. SAVVA GRUDTSYN I SOLOMONIIA
– CHAKKHYGYS-TAASU. SIBIRSKII SKAZ
– CHASY. ROMAN
– CHORTOV LOG I POLUNOSHCHNOE SOLNTSE. RAZSKAZY I POEMY
– DOKUKA I BALAGUR'E. RUSSKIIA SKAZKI
– KRASHENYIA RYLA. TEATR I KNIGA
– KRESTOVYIA SESTRY
– LALAZAR. KAVKAZSKII SKAZ
– LUCH DUKHOVNYI
– MYSHKINA DUKOCHKA
– OBRAZ NIKOLAIA CHUDOTVORSTA. ALATYR'-KAMEN' RUSSKOI VERY
– OGNENNAIA ROSSIIA

- OLIA
- PEREVODY
- PIATAIA IAZVA
- PODOROZHIE
- PODSTRIZHENNYMI GLAZAMI. KNIGA UZLOV I ZAKRUT PAMIATI
- POSOLON'
- POVEST' O DVUKH ZVERIAKH. IKHNELAT
- POVEST O IVANE SEMENOVICHE STRATILATOVE-NEUEMNYI BUBEN
- PRUD
- RAZSKAZY
- ROSSIIA V PIS'MENNAKH
- SHUMY GORODA
- SKAZKI RUSSKAGO NARODNA. DOKUKA I BALAGUR'E. RUSSKIIA ZHENSHCHINY. RUSSKAIA VERA
- SOCHINENIIA
- STRANNITSA. POVEST'
- O SUD'BE OGNENNOI
- TIBETSKII SKAZ
- TRAVA-MURAVA. SKAZ I VELICHANIE
- UKREPA. SLOVO K RUSSKOI ZEMLE O ZEMLE RODNOI, TAINOSTIAKH ZEMNYKH SUD'BE
- V ROZOVOM BLESKE
- VESENNEE POROSH'E
- VZVIKHRENNAIA. RUS'
- ZA SVIATUIU RUS'. DUNY O RODNOI ZEMLE
- ZGA. VOLSHEBNYE RASSKAZY
- ZVENIGOROD OKLIKANNYI. NIKOLINY PRITCHI
- ZVEZDA NEZVEZDNAIA

Remmers, Guido *see* HOCHAUFLOESENDE ABSORPTIONSSPEKTROSKOPIE IM WEICHEN ROENTGENBEREICH AN AUSGEWAEHLTEN ATOMEN UND MOLEKUELEN

O REMO INFORMATIVO – Manaus, Amazonas. Mar-Maio 1982 – 1,5,6 – bl Biblioteca [072]

REMODELING CHARACTERISTICS OF THE RABBIT ACHILLES TENDON COMPLEX FOLLOWING REPAIR WITH SMALL INTESTINAL SUBMUCOSA / Hodde, Jason P – Purdue University, 1994 – 2mf – 9 – $8.00 – PE3598 – us Microform Publ [617]

Remon Camacho, Juan *see* ESTUDIO DE LAS TIERRAS DE LOS NUEVOS REGADIOS DE LA PROVINCIA DE BADAJOZ

Remon de Moncada y Calderon, Jesus *see* DISCURSO INAUGURAL

Remond, R *see* LES ETATS-UNIS DEVANT L'OPINION FRANCAISE 1815-1852

REMONSTRANCE – 1890-1920. 31v – 1 – 23.00 – us L of C Photodup [360]

REMONSTRANTS WEEKBLAD – (Lacking some pgs) – v24-48. 1965-89 – 7r – 1 – ATLA S0353 – us A.T.L.A. [073]

REMOTE SENSING – 1985 – 380p – it F.A.O. [520]

REMOTE SENSING OF ENVIRONMENT – v1-16. 1969-84 – 1,5,6,13 – sz Elsevier [073]

REMOTE SENSING OF SNOW AND ICE : A CONTRIBUTION TO THE INTERNATIONAL HYDROLOGICAL PROGRAMME / Meier, Mark F – 1979 – 54p – 9 – 92-3-101730-6 – fr UNESCO [550]

REMOTE SENSING REVIEWS / ed by Goel, N S et al – 1983- – 1,5,9 – us Harwood [530]

REMOUNT BAPTIST CHURCH. CHARLESTON COUNTY. SOUTH CAROLINA : CHURCH RECORDS – 1948-83 – 1 – $66.96 – us Baptist [240]

REMOVAL OF CAUSES FROM STATE COURTS TO FEDERAL COURTS. / Dillon, John Forrest – 2d ed. St. Louis, Central Law Journal, 1877. 105 p. LL-1267 – 1 – us L of C Photodup [340]

REMOVAL OF CAUSES FROM STATE TO FEDERAL COURTS / Cooper, William Frierson – St. Louis: Jones, 1877. 17p. LL-1224 – 1 – us L of C Photodup [340]

THE REMOVAL OF CAUSES FROM STATE TO FEDERAL COURTS / Desty, Robert – (2nd ed., San Francisco, Bancroft-Whitney, 1888. 346 p. LL-1253) – San Francisco, Whitney, 1882. 283 p. LL-556 – 1 – us L of C Photodup [340]

REMOVAL OF CAUSES FROM THE STATE OF FEDERAL COURTS, AN ANALYSIS OF THE LAW AS CHANGED BY ACT OF CONGRESS OF MARCH 3, 1887 / Speer, Emory – Boston, Little, Brown, 1888. 136 p. LL-1173 – 1 – us L of C Photodup [340]

Remppis, Max *see* DIE VORSTELLUNGEN VON DEUTSCHLAND IM ALTFRANZOESISCHEN HELDENEPOS

REMSCHEIDER GENERAL-ANZEIGER – Remscheid, West Germany. 1992- – 8r per yr – 1 – gw Mikrofilm [072]

Remsen, Daniel Smith *see* INTESTATE SUCCESSION IN THE STATE OF NEW YORK

DER REMSTHALBOTE *see* GEMEINNUETZIGES WOCHENBLATT

REMS-ZEITUNG *see* GEMEINNUETZIGES WOCHENBLATT

Remusat, A *see* HISTOIRE DE LA VILLE DE KHOTAN

Remusat, Charles de *see*
- ABELARD
- PHILOSOPHIE RELIGIEUSE DE LA THEOLOGIE NATURELLE EN FRANCE ET EN ANGLETERRE
- ST. ANSELME DE CANTORBERY

Remusat, J P A *see*
- LE LIVRE DES RECOMPENSES ET DES PEINES
- MELANGES ASIATIQUES
- MEMOIRE SUR LES LIVRES CHINOIS DE LA BIBLIOTHEQUE DU ROI;...
- PROGRAMME DU COURS DE LANGUE ET DE LITTERATURE CHINOISE ET DE TARTARE MANDCHOU, PREC. DU DISCOURS PRONONCE A LA PREMIERE SEANCE DE CE COURS. LE 16 JANV

REN MING RI BAO – China. Published within the party. 15 May 1946-Jul 1987. D1 – 9 – 3990.00 – cc Globe [072]

REN MING RI BAO SUO YING – May 1946-1965, 1977-82. SY – 9 – 235.00 – cc Globe [073]

REN MING WAN BAO – China. Jun-Jul 1949. 5 ill. DL33f – 9 – 30.00 – cc Globe [072]

EL RENACIMIENTO Y PROBLEMAS DE DERECHO INTERNACIONAL... / Aunos y Perez, E – Madrid, 1917 – 3mf – 9 – ILM-3560/1 – ne IDC [340]

LA RENAISSANCE / ed by Asselin, Olivar – Montreal, Canada. 22 jun-14 dec 1935 – 1r – 1 – Can$30.00 – cn Can Microfilming [072]

LA RENAISSANCE – Paris. janv-juil 1896, 23 nov 1897-16 dec 1899 – 1 – fr A.C.R.P.P. [073]

RENAISSANCE : FOR RIGHT, FREEDOM AND PROGRESS – Garden City, Hertfordshire, England. Jul-Oct 1941 – 1r – 1 – gw Mikrofilm [020]

THE RENAISSANCE : STUDIES IN ART AND POETRY / Pater, Walter – London: Macmillan and Co., 2nd rev ed 1877 – 1 roll – 1 – 1-55879-826-9 – uk Libr Preservation [900]

RENAISSANCE AND BAROQUE ART : MAJOR SUBJECT COLLECTIONS – (Individual titles not listed separately) – 82 catalogues on 169mf – 9 – £1,065.00 – uk Chadwyck [700]

RENAISSANCE COMMONPLACE BOOKS FROM THE HUNTINGTON LIBRARY – Marlborough: Adam Matthew Publications, 1994 – 4r – 1 – $490.00 – uk Matthew [941]

LA RENAISSANCE DE LA NATIONALITE FRANCAISE EN ACADIE / Derouet, Camille – s.l.: s.n, 1899?. 02677. (Pre-1900 Canadiana) – 9 – cn C.I.H.M. [306]

LA RENAISSANCE EN FRANCHE-COMTE – 1mf – 15 – F60.00 – fr C.R.D.P. [944]

RENAISSANCE MAN: THE RECONSTRUCTED LIBRARIES OF EUROPEAN SCHOLARS, 1450-1700 / ed by Leedham-Green, Elisabeth & Roberts, Julian – (Series One: The Books and Manuscripts of John Dee, 1527-1608. Pt 1: John Dee's Manuscripts from the Bodleian Library, Oxford 20r $2,400.00. Pt 2: John Dee's Manuscripts from Corpus Christi College, Oxford 20r $2,400.00. Pt 3: John Dee's Manuscripts and Annotated Books from Cambridge University Library ca 20r $2,400.00. Pt 4: John Dee's Annotated Books from the Library of the Royal College of Physicians, London ca 20r $2,400.00) – Marlborough: Adam Matthew Publications, 1991 – 1 – uk Matthew [020]

LA RENAISSANCE MUSICALE – Paris. mars 1881-oct 1883 – 1 – fr A.C.R.P.P. [073]

RENAISSANCE QUARTERLY – New York. v1-35. 1948-82 – 12r or 208mf – inquire – us Ross [410]

LA RENAISSANCE RELIGIEUSE DANS L'ESPAGNE NATIONALISTE – Paris, 1937? Fiche W1132. (Blodgett Collection of Spanish Civil War Pamphlets) – 9 – us H.U. College Libr [946]

RENAISSANCE RHETORIC, 1479-1602 / ed by Murphy, James J – (10,000p of key texts held by the Bodleian Library, Oxford) – 152mf – 9 – $625.00 – us UMI [400]

THE RENAISSANCE, THE PROTESTANT REVOLUTION AND THE CATHOLIC REFORMATION IN CONTINENTAL EUROPE / Hulme, Edward Maslin – New York: Century, c1915 – 2mf – us A.T.L.A. [940]

THE RENAISSANCE; THE REVIVAL OF LEARNING AND ART IN THE FOURTEENTH AND FIFTEENTH CENTURIES / Schaff, Philip – 1891 – 1 – 6.00 – us A.T.L.A. [000]

RENAISSANCE UND HUMANISMUS IN ITALIEN UND DEUTSCHLAND / Geiger, Ludwig – Berlin: G. Grote, 1882 – 2mf – us A.T.L.A. [140]

RENAISSANCE UND REFORMATION : SECHS VORTRAEGE / Wernle, Paul – Tuebingen: J.C.B. Mohr, 1912 – 1mf – us A.T.L.A. [940]

Renan, Ernest *see*
- L'ANTECHRIST
- THE BOOK OF JOB
- LE CANTIQUE DES CANTIQUES
- DE L'ORIGINE DU LANGAGE
- AN ESSAY ON THE AGE AND ANTIQUITY OF THE BOOK OF NABATHAEAN AGRICULTURE
- HISTOIRE GENERALE ET SYSTEME COMPARE DES LANGUES SEMITIQUES. PREMI ERE PARTIE, HISTOIRE GENERALE DES LANGUES SEMITIQUES
- SAINT PAUL
- THE SONG OF SONGS

Renan, M E *see*
- LES ECRIVAINS JUIFS FRANCAIS DU 14 SIECLE
- LES RABBINS FRANCAIS DU COMMENCEMENT DU 11 SIECLE
- LES RABBINS FRANCAIS DU COMMENCEMENT DU 14E

LE RENARD – Montreal, Canada. 5 jun 1921-v1 n15. 11 sep 1921 – 1r – 1 – Can$25.00 – cn Can Microfilming [072]

Renard, A *see*
- ROCK SPECIMENS COLLECTED ON OCEANIC ISLANDS VOYAGE OF H.M.S. CHALLENGER, 1873-1876
- VOYAGE TO OCEANIC ISLANDS, 1873-1876. REPORT ON ROCK SPECIMENS

Renard, Jules *see* L'ESPRIT FRANCAIS

Renard-Casevitz, F M *see* LES ARAWAK DE L'UCAYALI

RENASCENCA : FOLHA POPULAR – S. Joao d'el-Rey, 15 Feb 1890; 26 May 1894 – 1,5,6 – bl Biblioteca [072]

RENASCENCA – Muriae, Brazil. Mar 1914 – 1 – bl Biblioteca [072]

RENASCENCE – (v.33-. 1980$ 5,6,9) – v.1-. 1948- – 1 – us UMI [073]

THE RENASCENCE OF HEBREW LITERATURE (1743-1885) / Slouschz, Nahum – (Includes index) – Philadelphia: Jewish Publ Soc, 1909 – 1mf – 9 – 0-8370-5272-6 – 1985-3272 – us A.T.L.A. [470]

RENATURIERUNGSMASSNAHMEN AN EINEM KLEINEN FLIESSGEWAESSER AM BEISPIEL DES WICKERBACHES / Poschwitz, Hartmut – 1995 – 4mf – 9 – DM112.00 – 3-8267-2095-4 – gw Hänsel [630]

Renaud, A *see* MANIERE DE PARLER LA LANGUE FRANCOISE

Renaudin, Louis Francois Emile *see* ETUDES MEDICO-PSYCHOLOGIQUES SUR L'ALIENATION MENTALE

Renaudin, P *see* LA THEOLOGIE DE S. CYRILLE D'ALEXANDRIE D'APRES S. THOMAS D'AQUIN

Renaudot, E *see* HISTORIA PATRIARCHARUM ALEXANDRINORUM JACOBIUARUM

Renauld, F *see* MOUSSES

Renault, Raoul *see*
- LE BIBLIOPHILE CANADIEN
- LE FRANC-PARLEUR

RENCANA PEMBANGUNAN LIMA TAHUN KEDUA 1974/75-1978/79 / Indonesia – 3v. BD-1817 1 – 9 – ne IDC [324]

Renck, Heinrich *see*
- PLATEN POLITISCHES DENKEN UND DICHTEN
- PLATENS POLITISCHES DENKEN UND DICHTEN

LA RENCONTRE / Berton, Pierre – Paris. 1909 – 1 – us Res Libr [830]

RENCONTRES FRANCO-ALLEMANDES – Paris. nov 1959-65 – 1 – fr A.C.R.P.P. [073]

Rendall, Frederic *see*
- THE ACTS OF THE APOSTLES: IN GREEK AND ENGLISH: WITH NOTES
- THEOLOGY OF THE HEBREW CHRISTIANS

Rendell, E D *see* THE ANTEDILUVIAN HISTORY, AND NARRATIVE OF THE FLOOD

DAS RENDEZVOUS IM ZOO : QUERELLES D'AMOUREUX / Lichnowsky, Mechtilde – Hamburg: M von Schroeder, 1936 – 1r – 1 – us U.W. Library [830]

RENDICONTI / Societa Chimica Italiano Rome – Series 1. v. 1-6. 1903-08. Series 2. v. 1-6. 1909-14 – 1,5,6 – us Princeton Micro [540]

Rendle, A B et al *see* CATALOGUE OF THE PLANTS COLLECTED BY MR. AND MRS. TALBOT IN THE OBAN DISTRICT SOUTH NIGERIA

RENE BAZIN : LA VOZ DE LA SANGRE... / ed by Bayle, Constantino – Madrid: Razon y Fe, 1926 – 1 – sp Bibl Santa Ana [946]

RENE DESCARTES / Bouilly, Jean Nicolas – (French Theatre Series). Paris. Barba, an V. 1796 – 9 – fr Hachette [820]

RENE DESCARTES = MEDITATIONES DE PRIMA PHILOSOPHIA : HIS LIFE AND MEDITATIONS / Descartes, Rene; ed by Lowndes, Richard – London: Frederic Norgate, 1878 – 1mf – 9 – 0-8370-6254-3 – 1986-0254 – us A.T.L.A. [190]

RENE KERVILER : 21 OEUVRES MICROFILMEES ENSEMBLE / Kerviler, Rene – 1 – F634.75 – fr Armell [930]

Renealmus, P *see* SPECIMEN HISTORIA PLANTARUM

LES RENEGATS DU 29 OCTOBRE: PAQUET, CHAUVEAU, FLYNN, RACICOT ET FORTIN / Frechette, Louis-Honore – Montreal: s.n., 1879. 04152. (Pre-1900 Canadiana) – 9 – cn C.I.H.M. [971]

Renesse *see* DICTIONNAIRE DES FIGURES HERALDIQUES

RENEWABLE ENERGY – 1,5,69 – us UMI [333]

THE RENEWAL – New York, NY. 1957-1970(?) – us I.H.R.C. [073]

RENFERME CE QUI RESTOIT A PUBLIER DES MONUMENTS DE LA SECONDE RACE DES ROIS DE FRANCE : DEPUIS LE COMMENCEMENT DU REGNE DE LOUIS LE BEGUE, FILS DE CHARLES LE CHAUVE, JUSQU'AUX PREMIERES ANNEES DU REGNE DE HUGUES CAPET, CHEF DE LA TROISIEME RACE, C.A.D. DEPUIS L'AN 877-991 (RGFS 9) – 1874 – Dfl91.00 – ne Slangenburg [240]

RENFERME LES GESTES DES FILS ET DES PETIT-FILS DE LOUIS LE DEBONNAIRE, DEPUIS L'AN 840-877, AVEC LES CAPITULAIRES DE CHARLES LE CHAUVE, ET AUTRES MONUMENTS HISTORIQUES (RGFS 7) – 1870 – Dfl84.00 – ne Slangenburg [240]

RENFREW JOURNAL – Renfrew, 1910-1913 – 3r – 1 – cn Preston [971]

RENFREW MERCURY – Renfrew, 1900-1991 – 99r – 1 – cn Preston [971]

THE RENFREW MERCURY – Renfrew, Ontario. v46 n2238. 7 jul 1916-v34 n9. 24 mar 1920 – 1r – 1 – Can$30.00 – cn Can Microfilming [072]

RENFREWSHIRE, 1836 : BRITISH ISLES CENSUS DIRECTORIES PROJECT, SCOTLAND. VOL 63 – 4mf – 9 – A$27.00 – at Vine [941]

RENFREWSHIRE, 1837 : BRITISH ISLES CENSUS DIRECTORIES PROJECT, SCOTLAND. VOL 51 – 1mf – 9 – A$9.00 – at Vine [941]

RENFREWSHIRE ADVERTISER – Paisley. Scotland. -w. Jan 1848-Apr 1850. (1 reel) – 1 – uk British Libr Newspaper [072]

RENFREWSHIRE (GREENOCK), 1903 : BRITISH ISLES CENSUS DIRECTORIES PROJECT, SCOTLAND – at Vine [941]

RENFREWSHIRE (GREENOCK AND PAISLEY), 1805 : BRITISH ISLES CENSUS DIRECTORIES PROJECT, SCOTLAND. VOL 22 – 1mf – A$9.00 – at Vine [941]

RENFREWSHIRE INDEPENDENT – Paisley, Scotland. 6 Mar 1858-Dec 1877 (missing 1873).-w. 17men reels – 1 – uk British Libr Newspaper [072]

Renfroe, J J D *see* MANUSCRIPT SERMONS

RENKOU YANJIU – Studies on Population. In Chinese but Table of Contents in English in each issue. F p7 – 9 – $4.50f – cc Microforms [073]

RENKSIZ ISTIRAB / Basar, Suekuefe Nihal – Istanbul: Suehulet Kitabhanesi [1928] – $18.00 – us MEDOC [470]

RENMIN RIBAO : OVERSEAS EDITION – (Yrly reel count varies) – 1985- – 1 – inquire – us Ross [072]

RENMIN RIBAO = PEOPLE'S DAILY – (Yrly reel count varies) – 1977- – 1 – inquire – us Ross [072]

RENMIN RIBAO – People's Daily. China. In Chinese. Current subscriptions. Semi-annual delivery. 1977- . 2 reels per yr. M/D1 – 1 – $55.00r – cc Microforms [072]
RENMIN RIBAO (HAIWAI BAN) – China. People's Daily, Overseas Edition. Jul 1985- . 2 reels per yr. M/D1B – 1 – $55.00r – cc Microforms [072]
RENMIN RIBAO SUOYIN = INDEX TO RENMIN DAILY – 1949-66; 1977- . 5-17mf per yr. F/D1A – 9 – $4.50mf – cc Microforms [072]
RENMIN SHOUCE, 1981 – People's handbook, 1981. Comp. by the editorial board of People's handbook. 1 reel. M-J44 – 5 – $34.00 – cc Microforms [950]
RENMIN TIEDAO – China. People's Railways. Four issues per week. 1986-. M-D102 – 1 – $45.00r – cc Microforms [072]
RENMIN YOUDIAN – China. People's post and telecommunication. 2 issues per week. 1985-. M-D77 – 1 reel/y – 1 – $34.00r – cc Microforms [072]
RENMIN ZHENGXIE BAO – China. Journal of the CPPCC. 2 issues per week. 1984- . M-D56 – 1 reel/y – 1 – $28.00r – cc Microforms [072]
Rennie, Ysabel (Fisk) *see* THE ARGENTINE REPUBLIC
Rennolds, Edwin Hansford *see*
- AUTOBIOGRAPHY
- DIARIES, 1877-8 NOV 1912
Reno, Conrad *see*
- A TREATISE ON THE LAW OF EMPLOYERS' LIABILITY ACTS
- A TREATISE ON THE LAW OF EMPLOYERS' LIABILITY ACTS OF NEW YORK, MASSACHUSETTS, INDIANA, ALABAMA, COLORADO, AND ENGLAND

RENO COURIER – Reno, NV. 1905 – 1r – 1 – $50.00 – U04662 – us Library Micro [071]
RENO EVENING GAZETTE *see* RENO GAZETTE JOURNAL
RENO GAZETTE JOURNAL – (Cont: Reno Evening Gazette, Nevada State Journal) – Reno, NV. 1983 – 775+ r – 1 – $38,750.00 ($1,200.00y) – RB04672 – us Library Micro [073]
RENO GAZETTE JOURNAL *see*
- EVENING GAZETTE
- NEVADA STATE JOURNAL

RENO MAGAZINE – Reno, NV. 1979-1980; 1987-1988 – 2r – 1 – $100.00 – U04891 – us Library Micro [071]
RENO NEVADA WEEKLY – Reno, NV. Jan-Apr 1910; 1994- – 2+ r – 1 – $100.00 ($50.00y) – U04705 – us Library Micro [071]
RENO PACE – Reno, NV. 1952-1953 – 1r – 1 – $50.00 – U04892 – us Library Micro [071]
RENO REMINDER – Reno, NV. Jun-Dec 1945 – 1r – 1 – $50.00 – U04709 – us Library Micro [071]
RENO REPORTER *see* NEVADA INDEPENDENT (AND RENO REPORTER)
RENO REVIEW – Reno, NV. v1. 1942 – 1r – 1 – $50.00 – U04893 – us Library Micro [071]
RENO WHOOPERUP – Reno, NV. 1909-10 – 1r – 1 – $50.00 – U04727 – us Library Micro [071]
RENOIR, 1841-1919 / Reunion des musees nationaux. Paris – 2 catalogues. 1933. 64 illus. 3 fiches – 9 – fr Réunion [700]
DER RENOMIST : EIN KOMISCHES HELDENGEDICHT / Zacharia, Friedrich Wilhelm – Leipzig: Bibliographisches Institut, [1800?] – 1r – 1 – us U.W. Library [810]
LA RENOMMEE – Journal politique. no. 1-137. Paris. 1er juin-16 oct 1836. mq no. 2, 38, 90 – 1 – fr A.C.R.P.P. [073]
LA RENOMMEE – Paris. 15 juin 1819-13 juin 1820. La Minerve francaise voir a ce titre – 1 – fr A.C.R.P.P. [073]
Renouard, G *see* L'OUEST AFRICAIN ET LES MISSIONS CATHOLIQUES
Renov, Michael *see* QUARTERLY REVIEW OF FILM AND VIDEO
RENOVACAO – Rio Branco, Acre. 8 Maio, 28 Ago 1955 – 1,5,6 – bl Biblioteca [072]
RENOVACION – (Includes c.1: v.4:no.29 1945:Apr.6, v. 4:no.33 (1945:Sept.12); v.4:no.36 1946:Apr.26) – Buenos Aires – 1 – CSUXADN3444-S – us Hoover Inst Photo [972]
LE RENOVATEUR – Paris. juil-dec 1835 – 1 – fr A.C.R.P.P. [073]
LA RENOVATION ESTHETIQUE – Paris. Revue de l'art le meilleur. no.1-60. mai 1905-avr 1910 – 1 – fr A.C.R.P.P. [073]
Renschler, Ulrich *see* DAS SCHEITERN DES SUBJEKTS BEI SAMUEL BECKETT
RENSEIGNEMENTS DE L'OFFICE COLONIAL / Belgium. Ministere des Colonies – Jan. 1912-June 1914, 1920-Apr. 1940. Not published July 1912-1919. Missing: no. 12, Dec. 1912 – 1 – 35.00r – us Hoover Inst Photo [323]
RENSEIGNEMENTS HISTORIQUES SUR LES KAZAKS OU KIRGHIZES-KAZAKS, DEPUIS LA FORMATION DE LA HORDE KAZAKE JUSQU' A-LA FIN DU 19E / Majerczak, R – SIECLE. Revue du monde musulman. pt. 43. 1921. BU-754 2 – 8 – ne IDC [947]
RENSEIGNEMENTS POUR SERVIR A L'HISTOIRE DE L'ILE DE FRANCE JUSQU'A L'ANNEE 1810.. / Epinay, Adrien d' – Ile Maurice: Nouvelle imprimerie Dupuy, 1890. SEM35P87 – 1r – 1 – Can$16.00 – cn Bibl Nat [944]
RENSEIGNEMENTS SUR L'AFRIQUE CENTRALE ET SUR UNE NATION D'HOMMES A QUEUE QUI S'Y TROUVERAIT : D'APRES LE RAPPORT DES NEGRES DU SOUDAN, ESCLAVES A BAHIA / Castelnau, Francis de – Paris: Bertrand, 1851 – us Res Libr [960]
RENT ALL – (1981-. 5,6,9) – 1963- – 1 – us UMI [380]
RENT CONTROL, COSTS AND CONSEQUENCES / ed by Albon, Robert – 2fiches (29x) – 9 – 1.00f – at Libertarian Micro [320]
LA RENTA NACIONAL Y EL PRESUPUESTO / Munoz Casillas, Juan – Intituto Edito.Reus.Madrid, 1952 – 1 – sp Bibl Santa Ana [946]
LA RENTE / ed by Asselin, Olivar – Montreal, Canada. v2 n9/10. 1 sep 1921; 1 fev 1922 (supp) – 1r – 1 – Can$25.00 – cn Can Microfilming [072]
LA RENTE : GUIDE DE L'EPARGNE ET DU PLACEMENT – Montreal: Versailles-Vidricaire-Boulais. no 1 (15 nov 1919)-. SEM16P367 – 1r – 5 – Can$14.00 – cn Bibl Nat [332]
RENTJANA EKONOMI / Tan Malaka – SE 5282 1. 1946 – 9 – ne IDC [330]
RENTJANA INDUK DJAKARTA / Indonesia – 1965-85.D-1005/1 – 9 – ne IDC [950]
RENTJANA PEMBANGUNAN LIMA TAHUN / Indonesia – 1969/70-73/74. Djakarta, 1968. v1-3.D-871/1 – 9 – ne IDC [950]
RENTJANA PEMBANGUNAN LIMA TAHUN D.C.I / Indonesia – Djakarta, 1969-73. D-1003/1 – 9 – ne IDC [950]
Rentrop, Klaus W *see* LEBENSQUALITAET, HERZFREQUENZ UND HERZFREQUENZVARIABILITAET NACH AKUTEM MYOKARDINFARKT
Rentz, P *see* PHILOSOPHIA AD MENTEM...DIVI THOMAE AQUINATIS...EXPLICATA
RENUNCIACION / Soriano Diaz, Eloy – Madrid: Sociedad de Autores Espanoles, 1927 – 1 – sp Bibl Santa Ana [440]
RENUNGAN DILEMBAH WAHJU / Aidid, Abdullah – SE-3976 1. 1953 – 9 – ne IDC [950]
LE RENVERSEMENT DE LA MORALE DE JESUS-CHRIST PAR LES ERREURS DES CALVINISTES, TOUCHANT LA JUSTIFICATION / Arnauld, Antoine – Paris, 1672 – 11mf – 9 – CA-97/1 – ne IDC [240]
Renwick, Edward Sabine *see* PATENTABLE INVENTION
LES REORDINATIONS : ETUDE SUR LE SACREMENT DE L'ORDRE / Saltet, Louis – (Includes appendixes) – Paris: J Gabalda, 1907 – 1mf – 9 – 0-8370-6945-9 – 1986-0945 – us A.T.L.A. [240]
REORGANIZACION DEL FRENTE NACIONAL DE EXCOMBATIENTES / Becerro de Bengoa, Ricardo – Caceres: Publicaciones del Departamento Provincial de Seminarios, 1952 – 1 – sp Bibl Santa Ana [360]
REPARACION Y EJEMPLARIDAD... / Gavalda y Cabre, Jose Maria de – Madrid: Razon y Fe, 1926 – 1 – sp Bibl Santa Ana [946]
REPARATEUR DE PORCELAINE / Dardy, Cl. – 9 – F20.00 – fr Ethnologie [740]
LA REPARATION DES DOMMAGES... / Degand, M – Paris, 1919 – 5mf – 1 – ILM-490/1 – ne IDC [327]
REPARATION PAPERS OF THE ALLIED POWERS REPARATION COMMISSION : 1922-30 / Allied Powers. Reparation Commission – An original microform collection which includes the 77 official reports of the Reparation Commission, along with 338 documents prepared by the Economic Service of the Reparations Transfer Committee – 1 – $580.00 – 0-89093-007-4 – us UPA [940]
REPARATIONEN, SOZIALPRODUKT, LEBENSSTANDARD; VERSUCH EINER WIRTSCHAFTSBILANZ / Harmssen, G W – Bremen: F. Trujen, 1948.4v. maps, diagrs – 1 – us U.W. Library [943]
REPARATIONS FOR WORLD WAR 2 PAMPHLET COLLECTION – 1943?-1947 – 1 reel – 1 – CSUXANP1487-B – us Hoover Inst Photo [940]
REPARTIMIENTO DE ALMERIA (SIECLE 15) – Almeria – 1r – 5,6 – sp Cultura [946]
REPARTIMIENTO DEL REINO DE VALENCIA (ANNO 1237-1252) – Barcelona – 2r – 5,6 – sp Cultura [946]
REPARTITION GEOGRAPHIQUE DES GISEMENTS DU PERIGORDIEN SUPERIEUR A BURINS DE NOAILLES EN FRANCE / Leroy, J P – 17mf – 9 – F250.00 – fr Ethnologie [910]
LES REPAS SACRIFICIELS DU VODOU HAITIEN / Montilus, G – Contexte historique et rituel (Essai) – 9 – F60.00 – fr Ethnologie [306]
REPBULICA – Maceio, Alagoas. 24 Fev-27 Mar 1890 – 1,5,6 – bl Biblioteca [072]
REPERTOIRE CHRONOLOGIQUE DU DROIT CAMEROUNAIS, 1956-1972 – 8r – $396.00 – us African Imprint [340]
REPERTOIRE CHRONOLOGIQUE ET ALPHABETIQUE DES LOIS, DECRETS, ARRETES MINISTERIELS PROMULGUES EN INDOCHINE DU 1 JANVIER 1926 AU 1 JANVIER 1935 / Indochina. French. Laws, Statutes, etc – Hanoi: Impr. d'Extreme-Orient, 1935. 565p. LL-10009 – 1 – us L of C Photodup [340]
REPERTOIRE D'EPIGRAPHIE JAINA PRECEDE D'UNE ESQUISSE DE L'HISTOIRE DU JAINISME D'APRES LES INSCRIPTIONS / Guerinot, A – Paris, 1908. BI-1048 2 – 8 – ne IDC [410]
REPERTOIRE D'EPIGRAPHIE SEMITIQUE / Academie des Inscriptions et Belles-Lettres de Paris – (Missing: v2(p1-144) 1906/07; v4(p129-end) 1919) – Paris. v1-7. 1900-1929 – 32mf – 9 – NE-20002/1 – ne IDC [470]
LA REPERTOIRE DES BALS, OU THEORIE-PRACTIQUE DES CONTRADANSES... / La Cuisse, Sr. de – Paris: Cailleau [etc.], 1762- – 1 – us Sibley [780]
REPERTOIRE DES CONNAISSANCES USUELLES. DICTIONNAIRE DE LA CONVERSATION ET DE LA LECTURE – 1832-51 – 9 – fr I.C.S. [440]
REPERTOIRE DES MAITRES EN THEOLOGIE DE PARIS AU 13TH SIECLE / Glorieux, P – (Tome 1.-Paris, 1933.-10mf; Tom. 2.-Paris, 1934.-11mf) – 8 – ne Slangenburg [290]
REPERTOIRE DES SOURCES HISTORIQUES DU MOYEN-AGE : BIO-BIBLIOGRAPHIE ET TOPO-BIBLIOGRAPHIE / Chevalier, Ulysse – Montbeliard, 1894-1899 – Dfl466.00 – ne Slangenburg [240]
REPERTOIRE DES SOURCES HISTORIQUES DU MOYEN-AGE... : BIO-BIBLIOGRAPHIE / Chevalier, Ulysse – (Supplement) – Paris. 2v. 1877-1886 – 27mf – ne IDC [940]
REPERTOIRE DES SYSTEMATICIENS FRANCAIS / Societe Francaise de Systematique – 9 – F40.00 – fr Ethnologie [000]
REPERTOIRE DES TRAITES, CONVENTIONS, ET AUTRES ACTES PRINCIPAUX DE LA RUSSIE AVEC LES PUISSANCES ETRANGERES DEPUIS 1474 JUSQU'A NOS JOURS / Menagios, D de – Paris, 1874 – 1mf – ne IDC [270]
REPERTOIRE GENERAL DE JURISPRUDENCE CANADIENNE...1770-1913 AND SUPPLEMENT 1913-23 / Beauchamp, Joseph – 1 – 30.00 – us L of C Photodup [340]
REPERTOIRE HISTORIQUE DE COMMUNAUTES RURALES DE LA PROVINCE DE TAWA / Echard, N – (Republique du Niger) – 9 – F50.00 – fr Ethnologie [960]
REPERTOIRE INTERNATIONAL DE LA PRESSE MUSICALE *see* THE HARMONICON
REPERTOIRE INTERNATIONAL DE LA PRESSE MUSICALE (RIPM) / ed by Cohen, H Robert et al – (Indexes: Allgemeine Wiener Musik-Zeitung 4v $480; Gazzetta musicale di Firenze 1v $120; The Harmonicon 4v $480; L'Armonia 1v $120; L'Art musical 5v $600; La Chronique musicale 1v $120; Musica (1855, 1857-59) 1v $120; Musica (1876-85) 1v $120; The Quarterly Musical Magazine and Review 2v $240; Strenna teatrale europea 1v $120. Full-text microfilm: Gazzetta musicale di Firenze 1r $95; The Harmonicon 2r $190; La Chronique musicale 1r $95; The Quarterly Musical Magazine and Review 1r $95; Strenna teatrale europea 2r $190) – International Musicological Society and International Association of Music Libraries, Archives, and Documentation Centers – 1; hardbound indexes – us UMI [780]
Repertoire International des Sources Musicales (RISM) *see* LIBRETTI IN DEUTSCHEN BIBLIOTHEKEN
REPERTOIRE INTERNATIONAL D'ICONOGRAPHIE MUSICALE – Zug. 1977. BP-784 1 – 9 – ne IDC [780]
REPERTOIRE METHODIQUE DE L'HISTOIRE MODERNE ET CONTEMPORAINE DE LA FRANCE POUR L'ANNEE 1898-1903 – Paris. v1-6. 1899-1905 – 33mf – 9 – H-450/2 – ne IDC [944]
REPERTOIRE MONDIAL TAXINOMIQUE ET BIBLIOGRAPHIQUE PROVISOIRE DES COPEPODES PLANCTONIQUES MARINS ET DES EAUX SAUMATRES. DIVERS SYSTEMES DE CLASSIFICATION / Razouls, Claude – (v2. Bibliog. and index. F130.00; 9) – Banyuls-sur-mer. 1982. v1. 394p. Bibliog – 9 – F100.00 – fr Ethnologie [590]
REPERTOIRE SUMERIEN (ACCADIEN) / Chossat, Ed de – Lyon: Alf Louis Perrin, 1882 – 1mf – 9 – 0-8370-7208-5 – 1986-1208 – us A.T.L.A. [470]
REPERTOIRE TOPO-BIBLIOGRAPIQUE DES ABBAYES ET PRIEURES / Cottineau, Dom L H – Macon, 1939 – 56mf – 8 – Dfl196.00 – ne Slangenburg [240]
REPERTOIRES ET/OU INDEX DES NOTAIRES / Archives judiciares des Trois-Rivieres – Trois-Rivieres, 1660-1800 – 38r – 1 – cn Can Microfilming [340]
REPERTOIRES ET/OU INDEX DES NOTAIRES (NON-PUBLIES) (1673-1799) / Montreal. Archives Judiciaires – (1800-1902 279r) – Montreal, Canada – 68r – 1 – cn Can Microfilming [340]
REPERTORIO ALFABETICO... / Bufalini, F – Milano, 1879 – 2mf – 1 – ILM-3672/1 – ne IDC [327]
REPERTORIO DE LA BIBLIOGRAFIA VENEZOLANA ECONOMICA Y SOCIAL / Lollett, C C M – Cuernavaca, Mor., Mexico, 1968 – 1mf – 9 – ne IDC [013]
REPERTORIO MUY COPIOSO DEL TEXTO Y LEYES DE LAS SIETE PARTIDAS,...VA POR SU ABECEDARIO / Lopez de Tovar, Gregorio – Valladolid: Diego Fernandez de Cordova, 1588 – 1 – sp Bibl Santa Ana [946]
REPERTORIO...TEXTO DE...PARTIDAS / Lopez de Tovar, Gregorio – (1589. 1.50f; 9. 1588. 1.50f; BSA; 9) – 1611 – 9 – 1.50f – sp Bibl Santa Ana [946]
REPERTORIUM AUREUM, CONTINENS TITULOS QUINQUE LIBORUM DECRETALIUM ET CONCORDANCIAS MATERIARUM, EISDEM IN SEXTO CLEMENTINIS DECRETA... CORRESPONDENTIUM – Coloniae, 1495 – Dfl22.00 – ne Slangenburg [240]
REPERTORIUM BIBLIOGRAPHICUM / Hain, L – (Stuttgart v1, pars 1+2 1826-1827 25mf; v2, pars 1+2 1831-1838 24mf) – 8 – ne Slangenburg [010]
REPERTORIUM BOTANICES SYSTEMATICAE / ed by Walpers, W G – Leipzig. 6v. 1842-1847 – 101mf – ne IDC [580]
REPERTORIUM COMMENTARIORUM IN SENTENTIAS PETRI LOMBARDI / Stegmuller, F – 21mf – 8 – ne Slangenburg [290]
REPERTORIUM DER GESAMMTEN DEUTSCHEN LITERATUR / ed by Gersdorf, F G – Leipzig. 34v. 1834-42 – 276mf – 9 – 8842/1 – ne IDC [430]
REPERTORIUM DER PHYSIK – Munich, 1883-91 – 3 – us Readex [530]
REPERTORIUM FUER EXPERIMENTAL-PHYSIK, FUER PHYSIKALISCHE TECHNIK, MATHEMATISCHE & ASTRONOMISCHE INSTRUMENTENKUNDE – Munich, 1868-82 – 3 – us Readex [530]
REPERTORIUM FUER KUNSTWISSENSCHAFT – (Includes Index v1-16) – Stuttgart und Berlin. v1-45. 1876-1931 – 432mf – 9 – ne IDC [073]
REPERTORIUM FUER PHYSIKALISCHE TECHNIK FUER MATHEMATISCHE UND ASTRONOMISCHE INTRUMENTENKUNDE – Munich, 1866-1867 – 3 – us Readex [530]
REPERTORIUM HYMNOLOGICUM / Chevalier, Ulysse – Louvain. Tom 1-6. 1892-1920 – 56mf – 8 – Dfl196.00 – ne Slangenburg [240]

REPERTORIUM RITUUM : ODER, UEBERSICHTLICHE ZUSAMMENSTELLUNG DER WICHTIGSTEN RITUALVORSCHRIFTEN FUER DIE PRIESTERLICHEN FUNCTIONEN / ed by Hartmann, Philipp – (Includes bibliographical references and index) – 2., vollstaendig umgearb u verm Aufl. Paderborn: Ferdinand Schoeningh, 1866 – 4mf – 9 – 0-8370-7220-4 – 1986-1220 – us A.T.L.A. [240]

REPERTORIUM SPECIERUM NOVARUM REGNI VEGETABILIS / ed by Fedde, F – Berlin, Dahlem. v1-49. 1906-40 – 384mf – 9 – 281c/2 – ne IDC [580]

REPERTORIUM UEBER SAEMMTLICHE, DURCH DIE GESETZ-SAMMLUNG UND DIE AMTS-BLAETTER DER KOENIGLICHEN REGIERUNGEN / Fuerstenthal, Johann August Ludwig – 1995 – 3mf – 9 – DM98.00 – 3-8267-3156-5 – gw Hänsel [943]

REPERTORIUM ZU GOLDFUSS' PETREFAKTEN DEUTSCHLANDS : EIN VERZEICHNISS ALLER SYNONYMEN UND LITERARISCHEN NACHWEISE ZU DEN VON GOLDFUSS ABGEBILDETEN ARTEN / Giebel, C – Leipzig, 1866 – 4mf – 9 – ne IDC [500]

REPERTORIUM...IURIS : BASILEAE APUD AMBROSIUM ET AURELIUM FROBENIOS FRATRES / Bertachinus, Ioan. Firm. – (Pars 3 lacking) – Basileae. Pars 1-5. 1573 – 101mf – 8 – Dfl354.00 – ne Slangenburg [340]

REPERTORIVM LIBRORVM TRIVM... DE OMNIVM GENTIVM RITIBVS / Boemus, J – Augustae Vindelicorum, 1520 – 4mf – 9 – H-8228/1 – ne IDC [010]

REPERTORY OF PRACTICE OF U.N. ORGANS / United Nations – (Table of Contents and Subject Index, Articles 1-111. E.10 F.9 S.5; Vols 1-5, Articles 1-111. E.51 F.53 S.53; Supp. Nos. 1-4, Articles 1-111. E.84 F.79 S.74; Supp. No. 5, Articles 1-54; 92-111. E.14 F.N/A S.N/A) – 9 – us U.N. Pubs [340]

REPERTORY OF PRACTICE OF UNITED NATIONS ORGANS / United Nations – Covers the articles of the United Nations Charter. 270 fiches – 9 – $500.00; $1.90f – uk UNIMICRO [327]

Repeti, N CS *see*
- PICTORICAL RECORDS AND TRACES OF THE SOCIETY...

REPETITIO SANAE DOCTRINAE DE VERA PRAESENTIA... / Chemnitz, Martin – Lipsiae, 1561 – 5mf – 9 – ne IDC [240]

REPETITIONES ET ALLEGATIONES...IURIS / Gutierrez, Juan – 1730. Liber XII – 9 – 1.50f – sp Bibl Santa Ana [946]

REPETITIONES SEX QUATORDECIN... ALLEGATIONES / Gutierrez, Juan – 1592 – 9 – 1.50f – sp Bibl Santa Ana [946]

Repetto, Nicolas *see*
- COMO NACE Y SE DESARROLLA UNA COOPERATIVA
- DE NUEVO EN LA ACCION
- ERRORES Y VICIOS DE NUESTRA DEMOCRACIA
- FOLLETOS
- HOMBRES Y PROBLEMAS ARGENTINOS
- LABOR EN EL EXILIO
- EL SOCIALISMO Y EL ESTADO

REPIN, GOR'KII, MAIAKOVSKII, BRIUSOV / Chukovskii, K – Vospiminaniia. M. 1940. BR-2036 2 – 8 – ne IDC [460]

REPIQUETE – Rio Branco, Acre. Dez 1984-20 Out 1985 – 1,5,6 – bl Biblioteca [072]

REPLACEMENT PARTS FOR AGRICULTURAL MACHINERY – 1981 – 33p – it F.A.O. [631]

REPLICA AL FOLLETO DE DON FRANCISCO GALAN CASTILLO TITULADO "AL PUBLICO" / Castel, Joaquin – Caceres: Tip. Jimenez en testamentario, 1899 – sp Bibl Santa Ana [440]

REPLICA IOAN ECKII ADVERSVS SCRIPTA SECUNDA BUCERI APOSTATAE SUPER ACTIS RATISPONAE.. / Eck, Johann – 1543 – 1 – us A.T.L.A. [240]

REPLIES TO UNITED NATIONS QUESTIONNAIRE ON AGRARIAN REFORM IN THE EGYPTIAN REGION / Egypt. Agrarian Reform General Organization – 1961. BNE-4603 1 – 9 – ne IDC [630]

REPLIQUE A LA RESPONSE DU SERENISSIME ROY DE LA GRANDE BRETAGNE / Du Perron, J D – Ed.2. Paris, 1622 – 19mf – 9 – CA-130/1 – ne IDC [240]

REPLIQUE AUX FURIEUSES DEFENSES DE LOUIS MEIGRET / Des Autels, G – 1551 – 9 – fr I.C.S. [400]

REPLIQUE DE MARIE BUCAILLE A LA REPONSE QU'ON A DONNE A SON FACTUM – Rouen – 9 – fr Hachette [360]

THE REPLY; AN ANTI-SUFFRAGE MAGAZINE – v. 1-2, no. 10. May 1913-May 1915 – 1 – 21.00 – us L of C Photodup [360]

REPLY OF THE DIRECTORS TO THE REPORT OF THE COMMITTEE...30TH OCTOBER 1873:...TO BE SUBMITTED...IN LONDON, WEDNESDAY, 26TH AUGUST, 1874 / Great Western Railway Company of Canada – London: Waterlow, 1874. 04386. (Pre-1900 Canadiana) – 9 – cn C.I.H.M. [971]

A REPLY TO AN APOLOGY FOR PROTESTING AGAINST THE METHODIST EPISCOPAL GOVERNMENT / Snethen, Nicholas – 1900 – 1 – us A.T.L.A. [240]

REPLY TO: BRIEF HISTORICAL SKETCH OF THE WESTERN BAPTIST THEOLOGICAL INSTITUTE IN COVINGTON, KENTUCKY BY THE BOARD OF TRUSTEES, P.S.BUSH, J.M. FROST AND LEWIS ROACH 1850 / Bush, P S et al – 90p – 1 – 5.00 – us Baptist [240]

A REPLY TO DR. LIGHTFOOT'S ESSAYS / Cassels, Walter Richard – London: Longmans, Green, 1889. 1 fiche – 9 – us A.T.L.A. [240]

REPLY TO HARNACK ON THE ESSENCE OF CHRISTIANITY / Cremer, Hermann – New York: Funk & Wagnalls, 1903.1 fiche – 9 – us A.T.L.A. [240]

A REPLY TO MR. LAW'S 'EARNEST AND SERIOUS ANSWER' (AS IT IS CALLED) TO DR. TRAPP'S DISCOURSE OF THE 'FOLLY, SIN AND DANGER OF BEING RIGHTEOUS OVER-MUCH' / Trapp, J – London, 1741 – 2mf – 9 – MP-287/1 – ne IDC [240]

REPLY TO PROF. MATTISON'S "CALM REVIEW OF DR. PERRY'S LATE ARTICLE IN THE CHRISTIAN ADVOCATE AND JOURNAL" / Perry, James H – New York: [s.n.], 1856 – 1mf – us A.T.L.A. [240]

REPLY TO THE GOVERNMENT OF PALESTINE'S MEMORANDUM ON THE ADMINISTRATION OF PALESTINE UNDER THE MANDATE / Jewish Agency for Palestine. Jerusalem – Submitted to the U.N.S.C.O.P. Aug 1947. BJ-28-155 1 – 9 – ne IDC [956]

REPLY TO THE MONTREAL HARBOUR ENGINEER'S REPORT ON THE ST LAWRENCE BRIDGE AND MANUFACTURING SCHEME / Bateman, F Foster – Montreal?, 1882?. 02970. (Pre-1900 Canadiana) – 9 – cn C.I.H.M. [971]

A REPLY TO THE REV. MR. FLETCHER'S VINDICATION OF MR. WESLEY'S 'CALM ADDRESS TO OUR AMERICAN COLONIES' / Evans, C – Bristol, [1775] – 2mf – 9 – MP-506/1 – ne IDC [240]

A REPLY TO THE REV. MR. WESLEY'S 'ADDRESS TO THE CLERGY' / Buller, J – Bristol, 1756 – 1mf – 9 – MP-371/1 – ne IDC [240]

A REPLY TO THE REVEREND MR. JOHN WESLEY'S 'REMARKS ON THE SCRIPTURE-DOCTRINE OF ORIGINAL SIN';... / Taylor, J – London, 1767 – 1mf – 9 – MP-446/1 – ne IDC [240]

REPLY TO THE STATEMENTS MADE AFFECTING THE NORTHERN RAILWAY COMPANY OF CANADA IN THE PETITION OF THE CREDIT VALLEY RAILWAY FOR A RAILWAY COMMISSION / Boulton, George D'Arcy – Toronto?. 1879? 00988. (Pre-1900 Canadiana) – 9 – cn C.I.H.M. [971]

A REPLY TO THE...MILITARY REPUTATION / Long, Charles Edward – 1832 – 9 – 1.50f – sp Bibl Santa Ana [355]

REPLY TO TWO LETTERS ADDRESSED BY MR. VANKOUGHNET TO THE SUPERIOR OF THE SEMINARY OF ST SULPICE: DATED RESPECTIVELY, SEPTEMBER 12TH, 1884, AND JANUARY 13TH, 1885 : ALSO AN EXTRACT FROM A LETTER OF MR. T. WALTON, INDIAN SUPERINTENDENT AT PARRY SOUND, DATED SEPTEMBER 2ND, 1884 / Colin, Frederic Louis de Gonzague – Montreal, 1885. 04156. (Pre-1900 Canadiana) – 9 – cn C.I.H.M. [971]

REPOBLACION DE LA VILLA DE GARROVILLAS / Paredes Guillen, Vicente – Madrid: Fortanet, 1899. pp. 138-146. Boletin de la Academia de la Historia 34, 1899 – 1 – sp Bibl Santa Ana [946]

LA REPOBLACION FORESTAL Y LOS GRUPOS SINDICALES DE COLONIZACION / Martin Lobo, Manuel – Madrid: Obra Sindical de Colonizacion, 1967 – 1 – sp Bibl Santa Ana [630]

REPONSE A DEUX ADRESSES DE L'HONORABLE ASSEMBLEE LEGISLATIVE A SON EXCELLENCE LE GOUVERNEUR-GENERAL, DATES LE 28 FEVRIER 1856,... / Canada. Gouverneur general – [s.l.]: [s.n.], 1856. SEM105P272 – 1mf – 9 – Can$2.25 – cn Bibl Nat [350]

REPONSE A DEUX ADRESSES...POUR 1. "UN ETAT DES DIFFERENTES SOMMES D'ARGENT...POUR VENIR EN AIDE AUX CENSITAIRES..." 2. "COPIES DE TOUTES INSTRUCTIONS...POUR METTRE EN OPERATION LES ACTES DE LA TENURE SEIGNEURIALE DE 1854..." – s.l, s.n, 1856. SEM105P272 – 1mf – 9 – Can$2.25 – cn Bibl Nat [336]

REPONSE A DEUX LETTRES ADRESSEES PAR M. VANKOUGHNET AU SUPERIEUR DU SEMINAIRE DE ST SUPLICE EN DATE DU 12 SEPTEMBRE 1884 ET DU 13 JANVIER 1885 : ET A L'EXTRAIT D'UNE LETTRE DE M.T. WALTON, SURINTENDANT DES SAUVAGES A PARRY SOUND EN DATE DU 2 SEPTEMBRE 1884 / Colin, Frederic Louis de Gonzague – Montreal, 1885. 04304. (Pre-1900 Canadiana) – 9 – cn C.I.H.M. [971]

REPONSE A LA BROCHURE ROUGE: MENSONGES DEVOLES – 1876?. 02583. (Pre-1900 Canadiana) – 9 – cn C.I.H.M. [971]

REPONSE A LA CRITIQUE PUBLIEE PAR M. GUILLET SUR LE VOYAGE DE GRECE DE JACOB SPON / Spon, Jacob – Lyon, T. Amaulri, 1679, xxii-322 p. French Voyagers in the Mediterranean 16th to 18th Centuries. 6008 – 9 – fr Hachette [944]

REPONSE A L'ADRESSE DU CONSEIL LEGISLATIF, DEMANDANT COPIE DU TRAITE FAIT A MANITOULIN EN 1836 ENTRE LE GOUVERNEMENT ET CERTAINES TRIBUS SAUVAGES, ETC / Canada – Quebec: Hunter, Rose et Lemieux, 1863. SEM105P869 – 1mf – 9 – Can$2.25 – cn Bibl Nat [971]

REPONSE A QUELQUES OBSERVATIONS FORMULEES PAR L'HONORABLE L. P. PELLETIER, SECRETAIRE PROVINCIAL DANS L'AUDIENCE DU 29 MARS 1893 / Bernier, Bernard – Quebec?, 1893? 02311. (Pre-1900 Canadiana) – 9 – cn C.I.H.M. [971]

REPONSE A UN ORDRE DE L'ASSEMBLEE LEGISLATIVE...11 DECEMBRE 1890, POUR COPIE DES RAPPORTS DE M. ARTHUR BUIES SUR LES COMTES DE RIMOUSKI, DE MATANE, ET DE TEMISCOUATA / Buies, Arthur – Quebec, 1890. SEM105P610 – 1mf – 9 – Can$2.25 – cn Bibl Nat [971]

REPONSE A UN ORDRE DE L'ASSEMBLEE LEGISLATIVE...DU 20 FEVRIER. POUR COPIE...DE LA BROCHURE DU PREMIER MINISTRE INTITULEE: ESQUISSE GENERALE DE LA PROVINCE DE QUEBEC / Canada – Quebec, 1890. SEM105P611 – 2mf – 9 – Can$4.50 – cn Bibl Nat [971]

REPONSE A UN ORDRE DE L'ASSEMBLEE LEGISLATIVE...DU 30 MAI 1888, POUR UNE COPIE DE LA PRISE DE POSSESSION PAR LE SHERIF...DE QUEBEC,...DES BIENS DES JESUITES. / Canada – Quebec, 1888. SEM105P605 – 1mf – 9 – Can$2.25 – cn Bibl Nat [971]

REPONSE A UN SOPHISTE AU SUJET DE LA QUESTION UNIVERSITAIRE A MONTREAL / St Hilaire, Michel – Montreal: T. Berthiaume, 1879. 02142. (Pre-1900 Canadiana) – 9 – cn C.I.H.M. [370]

REPONSE A UNE ADDRESSE DE L'ASSEMBLEE LEGISLATIVE...DEMANDANT UN ETAT COMPLET, CLAIR ET DETAILLE DES BIENS...DES "ECCLESIASTIQUES".. / Seminaire Saint Sulpice de Montreal. Archives – Quebec: Imp. John Lovell, 1853. SEM105P278 – 1mf – 9 – Can$2.25 – cn Bibl Nat [240]

REPONSE A UNE ADRESSE DE LA CHAMBRE D'ASSEMBLEE, EN DATE DU 7 ULTIMO, DEMANDANT UNE LISTE DES NOMINATIONS QUI ONT ETE FAITES DANS LES DEPARTEMENTS PUBLICS DEPUIS 1855 – Toronto: Louis Perrault, [1858 ?]. SEM105P1850 – 1mf – 9 – Can$2.25 – cn Bibl Nat [350]

REPONSE A UNE ADRESSE DE L'ASSEMBLEE LEGISLATIVE AU GOUVERNEUR-GENERAL, PRIANT SON EXCELLENCE DE VOULOIR BIEN ORDONNER A L'OFFICIER QU'IL APPARTIENT... – [Montreal]: [imprime par Lovell et Gibson], [1845]. SEM105P1064 – 1mf – 9 – Can$2.25 – cn Bibl Nat [370]

REPONSE A UNE ADRESSE DE L'ASSEMBLEE LEGISLATIVE, DATEE LE 29 AVRIL 1857, DEMANDANT COPIE DU RAPPORT DE M. LE SOLLICITEUR GENERAL ROSS SUR L'ENQUETE CONCERNANT LES COMPTES DE LOUIS ARCHAMBAULT... – Toronto: imprime par Louis Perrault, [1857?]. SEM105P1906 – 2mf – 9 – Can$4.50 – cn Bibl Nat [324]

REPONSE A UNE ADRESSE DE L'ASSEMBLEE LEGISLATIVE DEMANDANT COPIE DE CERTAINS DOCUMENTS SEIGNEURIAUX / Canada. Parlement Assemblee legislative – Quebec: John Lovell..., 1853. SEM105P260 – 2mf – 9 – Can$4.50 – cn Bibl Nat [340]

REPONSE A UNE ADRESSE DE L'ASSEMBLEE LEGISLATIVE DU 20 SEPTEMBRE 1852... / Ecclesiastiques du Seminaire de St-Sulpice de Montreal – Quebec: Imprimerie de Louis Perrault, [1853?]. SEM105P1782 – 1mf – 9 – Can$2.25 – cn Bibl Nat [240]

REPONSE A UNE ADRESSE DE L'ASSEMBLEE LEGISLATIVE DU 22 DU COURANT POUR COPIE DE CERTAINE CORRESPONDANCE RELATIVE AU HAVRE DE MONTREAL / Canada – Quebec: Lovell et Lamoureux, 1854. SEM105P633 – 1mf – 9 – Can$2.25 – cn Bibl Nat [971]

REPONSE A UNE ADRESSE DE L'ASSEMBLEE LEGISLATIVE, DU 22 DU MOIS DERNIER... – [S.l.]: [s.n.], [1855]. SEM105P609 – 1mf – 9 – Can$2.25 – cn Bibl Nat [971]

REPONSE A UNE ADRESSE DE L'ASSEMBLEE LEGISLATIVE DU 23 ULTIMO, POUR UN ETAT DES AFFAIRES FINANCIAIRES SIC DE LA PROVINCE. / Canada. Parliament. Legislative Assembly – Quebec: Imprime par John Lovell, 1853. SEM105P161 – 1mf – 9 – Can$2.25 – cn Bibl Nat [336]

REPONSE A UNE ADRESSE DE L'ASSEMBLEE LEGISLATIVE, DU 26 DU MOIS DERNIER... – Quebec: Lovell et Lamoureux, [1855]. SEM105P608 – 2mf – 9 – Can$4.50 – cn Bibl Nat [623]

REPONSE A UNE ADRESSE DE L'ASSEMBLEE LEGISLATIVE DU 28 FEVRIER DERNIER, DEMANDANT UNE LISTE DE TOUTES LES RECLAMATIONS...DEPUIS LE 1ER MARS 1850 – Toronto: Imprime par John Lovell, [1856]. SEM105P1275 – 1mf – 9 – Can$2.25 – cn Bibl Nat [340]

REPONSE A UNE ADRESSE DE L'ASSEMBLEE LEGISLATIVE DU VINGT SEPTEMBRE 1852... / Ecclesiastiques du Seminaire de St-Sulpice de Montreal – Quebec: imprim par John Lovell, [1853]. SEM105P278 – 1mf – 9 – Can$2.25 – cn Bibl Nat [240]

REPONSE A UNE ADRESSE DE L'ASSEMBLEE LEGISLATIVE, EN DATE DU 2 JUIN 1881... – [Quebec]: [s.n.], [1881]. SEM105P593 – 1mf – 9 – Can$2.25 – cn Bibl Nat [324]

REPONSE A UNE ADRESSE DE L'ASSEMBLEE LEGISLATIVE EN DATE DU 16 MARS 1885.... ... – Quebec: Bureau du secretaire, 1887. SEM105P631 – 1mf – 9 – Can$2.25 – cn Bibl Nat [971]

REPONSE A UNE ADRESSE DE L'ASSEMBLEE LEGISLATIVE, EN DATE DU 18 MARS 1885, DEMANDANT UNE LISTE DETAILLEE DES LIVRES ACHETES POUR LA BIBLIOTHEQUE DU PARLEMENT / Dansereau, Clement Arthur – Quebec: Bureau du secretaire, 1885. SEM105P629 – 1mf – 9 – Can$2.25 – cn Bibl Nat [323]

REPONSE A UNE ADRESSE DE L'ASSEMBLEE LEGISLATIVE POUR COPIE DU RAPPORT D'A.C. BUCHANAN, ECUYER, SUR L'EMIGRATION / Canada – 1855. SEM105P607 – 1mf – 9 – Can$2.25 – cn Bibl Nat [971]

REPONSE A UNE ADRESSE DE L'ASSEMBLEE LEGISLATIVE POUR COPIE DU RAPPORT DU COMTE [SIC] DE ROTTERMUND SUR SON EXPLORATION DES LACS SUPERIEUR ET HURON / Rottermund, E S, Comte de – [S.l.: s.n., 1856?]. SEM105P1775 – 1mf – 9 – Can$2.25 – cn Bibl Nat [910]

REPONSE A UNE ADRESSE DE L'ASSEMBLEE LEGISLATIVE SUR L'ETAT DES COLONIES – Quebec: John Lovell, 1853. SEM105P606 – 1mf – 9 – Can$2.25 – cn Bibl Nat [971]

REPONSE A UNE ADRESSE DE L'ASSEMBLEE LEGISLATIVE...DEMANDANT TOUS DOCUMENTS CONCERNANT L'OUVERTURE DU...TERRITOIRE DU NORD-OUE..EN LA POSSESSION DU GOUVERNEMENT DEPUIS LE 1ER JANVIER 1862 / Canada – Quebec: Hunter, Rose et Lemieux, 1863. SEM105P576 – 1mf – 9 – Can$2.25 – cn Bibl Nat [971]

REPONSE A UNE ADRESSE DE L'ASSEMBLEE LEGISLATIVE...DU 2 DU COURANT POUR DES RENSEIGNEMENTS RELATIFS AU CONTRAT...ENTRE LE GOUVERNEMENT ET MM. MCKEAN ET MELARTY, POUR LE SERVICE DES COMMUNICATIONS TRANSATLANTIQUES A VAPEUR / Canada - 1855. SEM105P602 - 1mf - 9 - Can$2.25 - cn Bibl Nat [971]

REPONSE A UNE ADRESSE DE L'ASSEMBLEE LEGISLATIVE...DU 2 JUIN 1881, PRIANT...LE LIEUTENANT-GOUVERNEUR...COPIE DE LA REQUETE EN FAVEUR DE L'ETABLISSEMENT AUX TROIS RIVIERES D'UNE ECOLE NORMALE. / Canada - Quebec, 1881. SEM105P593 - 1mf - 9 - Can$2.25 - cn Bibl Nat [971]

REPONSE A UNE ADRESSE DE L'ASSEMBLEE LEGISLATIVE...DU 4 JUIN 1888, DEMANDANT UN RAPPORT DE TOUTES DECISIONS DU CONSEIL PRIVE FEDERAL, DESAVOUANT TOUS ACTES...DE CETTE LEGISLATURE DEPUIS 1882. / Canada - Quebec, 1888. SEM105P867 - 1mf - 9 - Can$2.25 - cn Bibl Nat [971]

REPONSE A UNE ADRESSE DE L'ASSEMBLEE LEGISLATIVE...DU 6 DECEMBRE 1854, DEMANDANT COPIES DE TOUTES LES PLAINTES PORTEES CONTRE M. MAGUIRE, INSPECTEUR ET SURINTENDANT DE POLICE DE QUEBEC / Canada - Quebec: Lovell et Lamoureux, 1855. SEM105P868 - 1mf - 9 - Can$2.25 - cn Bibl Nat [971]

REPONSE A UNE ADRESSE DE L'ASSEMBLEE LEGISLATIVE...DU 7 MARS 1864, DEMANDANT COPIE DES RAPPORTS DE DIVERSES EXPLORATIONS FAITES DANS LE DISTRICT DU SAGUENAY / Canada - Quebec: Hunter, Rose et Lemieux, 1864. SEM105P603 - 1mf - 9 - Can$2.25 - cn Bibl Nat [971]

REPONSE A UNE ADRESSE DE L'ASSEMBLEE LEGISLATIVE...DU 22 DU MOIS DERNIER, DEMANDANT COPIE DE LA CORRESPONDANCE...RELATIFS AUX ECOLES DU DISTRICT D'OUTAOUAIS. / Canada - 1855. SEM105P609 - 1mf - 9 - Can$2.25 - cn Bibl Nat [971]

REPONSE A UNE ADRESSE DE L'ASSEMBLEE LEGISLATIVE...DU 22 JUIN DERNIER... COPIE DE LA CORRESPONDANCE...ENTRE LUI ET SON EXCELLENCE LE GOUVERNEUR GENERAL RELATIVEMENT AU RENVOI D'OFFICE DU MINISTRE DE BOUCHERVILLE. / Canada - Quebec, 1878. SEM105P592 - 1mf - 9 - Can$2.25 - cn Bibl Nat [971]

REPONSE A UNE ADRESSE DE L'ASSEMBLEE LEGISLATIVE...DU 25 FEVRIER 1889, DEMANDANT COPIES...CONCERNANT LA RECLAMATION DE M.W.P. LOCKWOOD, MENTIONEE A L'ARTICLE 254 DU BUDGET POUR 1889-1890 / Canada - Quebec, 1889. SEM105P575 - 4mf - 9 - Can$9.00 - cn Bibl Nat [971]

REPONSE A UNE ADRESSE DE L'ASSEMBLEE LEGISLATIVE...DU 26 DU MOIS DERNIER POUR COPIE DES DOCUMENTS CONCERNANT LA CONSTRUCTION DES PHARES ET DES QUAIS EN BAS DE QUEBEC ET LES SOUMISSIONS ET CONTRAT POUR LES BATEAUX REMORQUEURS. / Canada - Quebec: Lovell et Lamoureux, 1855. SEM105P608 - 2mf - 9 - Can$4.50 - cn Bibl Nat [971]

REPONSE A UNE ADRESSE DE L'ASSEMBLEE LEGISLATIVE...DU 30 ULTIMO, POUR COPIE...DES RECLAMATIONS DE CERTAINS HABITANTS DE L'ETABLISSEMENT DU RUISSEAU DES SAUVAGES, DANS LES TOWNSHIPS DE L'EST DU BAS-CANADA / Canada - Montreal: John Lovell, 1853. SEM105P601 - 1mf - 9 - Can$2.25 - cn Bibl Nat [971]

REPONSE A UNE ADRESSE DE L'HONORABLE CONSEIL LEGISLATIF, EN DATE DU 2 MARS 1863, DEMANDANT COPIE DU RAPPORT DE LA COMMISSION D'ENQUETE SUR LE BUREAU DE POSTE DE MONTREAL - [S.l.: s.n., 1863 ?]. SEM105P1783 - 1mf - 9 - Can$2.25 - cn Bibl Nat [380]

REPONSE A UNE ADRESSE DU CONSEIL LEGISLATIF, DEMANDANT LA CORRESPONDANCE RELATIVE A LA COMPAGNIE DES VAPEURS-OCEANIQUES DE MONTREAL / Canada - Quebec: Hunter, Rose et Lemieux, 1862. SEM105P580 - 1mf - 9 - Can$2.25 - cn Bibl Nat [971]

REPONSE A UNE ADRESSE EN DATE DU 28 SEPTEMBRE 1863, DEMANDANT DES RENSEIGNEMENTS AU SUJET DES EMPLOYES PUBLICS DESTITUES DEPUIS LE 25 MAI 1862 - Quebec: Hunter, Rose et Lemieux, 1863. SEM105P830 - 1mf - 9 - Can$2.25 - cn Bibl Nat [971]

REPONSE A UNE ADRESSE POUR RENSEIGNEMENTS CONCERNANT LES ILES MANITOULINES / Canada - Quebec: Hunter, Rose et Lemieux, 1863. SEM105P614 - 1mf - 9 - Can$2.25 - cn Bibl Nat [971]

REPONSE A UNE ADRESSE...DEMANDANT COPIE DE CERTAINS DOCUMENTS SEIGNEURIAUX / Canada. Parliament. Legislative Assembly - Quebec: Imprime par John Lovell, 1853. SEM105P260 - 2mf - 9 - Can$4.50 - cn Bibl Nat [323]

REPONSE A UNE ADRESSE...RELATIVE A L'ADMINISTRATION DES AFFAIRES DE LA SEIGNEURIE DE LAUZON / Canada. Parliament. Legislative Assembly - Quebec (sic): Imprime par John Lovell, 1852. SEM105P258 - 1mf - 9 - Can$2.25 - cn Bibl Nat [323]

REPONSE A UNE CRITIQUE SATYRIQUE (CONTRE L'ACADEMIE) / Mallemans de Messanges, Cl - 1696 - 9 - fr I.C.S. [440]

REPONSE AU DERNIER RAPPORT DE L'HON. SURINTENDANT DE L'INSTRUCTION PUBLIQUE DE LA PROVINCE DE QUEBEC / Association des Libraires-Editeurs, Imprimeurs et Relieurs de la Province de Quebec - Montreal? 1880? 00896. (Pre-1900 Canadiana) - 9 - cn C.I.H.M. [370]

REPONSE AU LIVRE DE M. EVEQUE DE CONDOM / La Bastide, M-A de - Ed 2. Quevilly, 1673 - 5mf - 9 - CA-137/1 - ne IDC [240]

REPONSE AU LIVRE DE MONSIEUR DE CONDOM / Brueys, D-A - La Haye, 1681 - 4mf - 9 - CA-119/1 - ne IDC [240]

REPONSE AU "MATIN" DU 2 FEVRIER / Dussault, Joseph - Quebec?: s.n., 1892?. 05205. (Pre-1900 Canadiana) - 9 - cn C.I.H.M. [971]

REPONSE AUX OBSERVATIONS DE M. H.D. SUR L'APPEL AU PEUPLE DU SIEUR VIDAL / Molinie, Louis - St-Pons, impr. J. Franc, 1833, 52 p. Les Saint-Simoniens, 1825-1834. 6921 - 9 - fr Hachette [335]

REPONSE COMPLEMENTAIRE A UNE ADDRESSE DE L'ASSEMBLEE LEGISLATIVE. / Compagnie du Grand Tronc - Quebec: s.n, 1855. SEM105P354 - 1mf - 9 - Can$2.25 - cn Bibl Nat [336]

REPONSE COMPLEMENTAIRE A UNE ADRESSE DE L'ASSEMBLEE LEGISLATIVE DU 21 DU MOIS DERNIER,... / Chemin de Fer du Grand Tronc - Quebec: [s.n.], 1855. SEM105P354 - 1mf - 9 - Can$2.25 - cn Bibl Nat [971]

REPONSE DE LA COMPAGNIE...AU RAPPORT DU COMMISSAIRE SPECIAL.. / Baie des Chaleurs Railway Company - Quebec, 1890. 03223. (Pre-1900 Canadiana) - 9 - cn C.I.H.M. [971]

REPONSE DE M. RAMEAU A MM. LES EDITEURS DE L'ENCYCLOPEDIE SUR LEUR DERNIER AVERTISSEMENT / Rameau, Jean-Phillippe - 1757 - 9 - us Sibley [780]

REPONSE DE MADAME A LA LETTRE QUE M. DE MAIRAN, SECRETAIRE PERPETUEL DE L'ACADEMIE ROYALE DES SCIENCES LUI A ECRITE LE 18 FEVRIER 1741: SUR LA QUESTION DES FORCES VIVES / Du Chatelet-Lomont, Gabrielle Emilie - Bruxelles: Foppens, 1741 - 1 - us U.W. Library [530]

REPONSE DE MONSIEUR MERCI, EVEQUE DE LUCON, A LA LETTRE DE MONSIEUR SERVAN DU VIVIER, NOMME EVEQUE DE LA VENDEE [...] / Mercy, Marie-Ch.-I de - [S.l.: s.n.], [1791] - fr Armell [240]

REPONSE D'UN SAINT-SIMONIEN AU "SPECTATEUR" / Michaud - Dijon, impr. Carion, s. d., 4 p. Les Saint-Simoniens, 1825-1834. 6925 - 9 - fr Hachette [335]

REPONSE PARTIELLE.. / Chemin de Fer du Grand Tronc - 1855. SEM105P547 - 1mf - 9 - Can$2.25 - cn Bibl Nat [380]

REPONSE POUR UN ETAT RELATIF AUX DEMANDES DE LA COMPAGNIE DU GRAND TRONC DE CHEMIN DE FER POUR REMISES DE DEBENTURES PROVINCIALES ET POUR COPIE DE TOUT MEMOIRE DEPUIS LE 1ER JANVIER, 1856 / Canada - 1856. SEM105P612 - 1mf - 9 - Can$2.25 - cn Bibl Nat [971]

REPONSE RELATIVE A L'EXPLORATION FAITE PAR M. BLAIKLOCK DU TERRITOIRE ENTRE QUEBEC ET LE LAC SAINT JEAN / Canada - Toronto: Lovell et Gibson, 1850. SEM105P832 - 1mf - 9 - Can$2.25 - cn Bibl Nat [971]

REPONSE SOMMAIRE POUR LES HERITIERS DE LOUIS DE CORNULIER...AU MEMOIRE PUBLIE AU NOM DE M. MUSSEAU... / Cornulier, Louis de - Nantes: Mellinet, 1844 - 1 - F50.00 - fr Armell [944]

REPONSE...AUX CORRESPONDANCES ET AU PAMPHLET DE ALEXANDRE DUFRESNE.. / Tasse, Didace - Quebec, 1863? SEM105P544 - 1mf - 9 - Can$2.25 - cn Bibl Nat [971]

REPONSE...EN DATE DU 16 MARS 1885,...AU SUJET DE LA CONSTITUTIONALITE DE L'ACTE FEDERAL DES LICENCES - Quebec, 1887. SEM105P631 - 1mf - 9 - Can$2.25 - cn Bibl Nat [323]

REPONSE...EN DATE DU 18 MARS 1885, DEMANDANT...UNE LISTE...DES LIVRES ACHETES POUR LA BIBLIOTHEQUE DU PARLEMENT PAR C.A. DANSEREAU.. - Quebec, 1885. SEM105P629 - 1mf - 9 - Can$2.25 - cn Bibl Nat [340]

REPONSES AUX OBJECTIONS POPULAIRES CONTRE LA RELIGION CATHOLIQUE: CONFERENCE DONNEE A LA CATHEDRALE D'OTTAWA / Damen, Arnold - par R. P. Damen; rapport stenographie de W. H. Waller. s.l.: s.n., 1873 (Ottawa: L. A. Grison). 03642. (Pre-1900 Canadiana) - 9 - cn C.I.H.M. [971]

REPORT / Aberdeen Association - 1898. Ottawa, Paynter & Abbott. 1898. (Pre-1900 Canadiana) - 9 - cn C.I.H.M. [971]

REPORT / Agricultural Education Survey Team - SE-6920 1. Jan. 31, 1968 - 9 - ne IDC [630]

REPORT / Alabama. Agricultural Experiment Station - v. 1-67. 1888-56 - 1,5,6 - us Spaulding [630]

REPORT / Alabama. Canebrake Agricultural Experiment Station - 1888-90,1918. 1 fiche - 9 - us Spaulding [631]

REPORT / Alaska. (Territory). Attorney General's Office - Juneau. Mar 1 1917-Dec 31 1940, 1945-47, 1949-51. LL-066 - 1 - us L of C Photodup [340]

REPORT / American Bar Association. Committee on Canons of Professional Ethics - Chicago. 1907. 13p. LL-1194 - 1 - us L of C Photodup [340]

REPORT / Arizona. Territory. Board of Control - Phoenix.1897-98-1914-15 - 1 - 23.00r - us L of C Photodup [324]

REPORT / Association of Ontario Land Surveyers. Committee on Topographical Surveying - 1899?. 02457. (Pre-1900 Canadiana) - 9 - cn C.I.H.M. [971]

REPORT / Bank Indonesia. Djakarta - SE-262 1. 1953-1967 - 9 - ne IDC [336]

REPORT / California. Dept. of Industrial Relations - 1927-78. 27 fiches. (Harvard Law School Library Collection.) - 9 - $1.50f - us H.U. Law [330]

REPORT / California. Pooled Money Investment Board - First, 1956/57-1979. 12 fiches. (Harvard Law School Library Collection.) - 9 - $1.50f - us H.U. Law [336]

REPORT / California. Pooled Money Investment Board - Monthly. Sept 1957-79. 85 fiches. (Harvard Law School Library Collection.) - 9 - $1.50f - us H.U. Law [336]

REPORT / California. State Banking Department. Superintendant of Banks - First, 1909/10-1979. 337 fiches. (Harvard Law School Library Collection.) - 9 - $1.50f - us H.U. Law [336]

REPORT / Canada. Bas-Canada. Parlement. Chambre d'assemblee. Comite special nomme pour s'enquerir de l'etat...de l'education dans la province. - Quebec: Neilson & Cowan, 1824. SEM105P623 - 3mf - 9 - Can$6.75 - cn Bibl Nat [370]

REPORT / Canada. Commission Appointed to Inquire into Matters Connected with the Public Buildings at Ottawa - Quebec. Joseph Blackburn, 1863. SEM105P311 - 5mf - 9 - Can$11.25 - cn Bibl Nat [350]

REPORT / Canada. Parliament. Legislative Assembly. Select Committee on the Geological Survey - Quebec: Printed by Lovell & Lamoureux, 1855. SEM105P210 - 1mf - 9 - Can$2.25 - cn Bibl Nat [550]

REPORT / Canada. (Province). Commissaires nommes pour s'enquerir de la conduite ..de police lors de l'emeute qui a eu lieu en...Quebec, le 6 juin dernier - Quebec: Rollo Campbell, 1854. SEM105P630 - 2mf - 9 - Can$4.50 - cn Bibl Nat [355]

REPORT / Canada. (Province). Commissaires nommes...de reorganiser la Milice en Canada. - Quebec, 1855. SEM105P594 - 1mf - 9 - Can$2.25 - cn Bibl Nat [355]

REPORT / Canada. (Province). Commissioners Appointed to Enquire as to the Affairs and Financial Condition of Toronto University and University College, Upper Canada - Quebec: Hunter & Rose, 1863. SEM105P573 - 2mf - 9 - Can$4.50 - cn Bibl Nat [370]

REPORT / Canada (Province). Commissioners Appointed to Inquire into the Cause of the Fire at the Parliament Buildings.. - Quebec, 1854. SEM105P552 - 1mf - 9 - Can$2.25 - cn Bibl Nat [324]

REPORT / Canada (Province). Legislative Assembly. Select Committee...State of Education and Working of School Laws in Lower Canada - 1853. SEM105P548 - 1mf - 9 - Can$2.25 - cn Bibl Nat [370]

REPORT / Canada. (Province). Parlement. Assemblee legislative. Comite...le rapport annuel du principal agent de l'emigration...le rapport supplementaire de l'agent allemand a Quebec - Quebec: Thompson & Co, 1860. SEM105P589 - 1mf - 9 - Can$2.25 - cn Bibl Nat [971]

REPORT / Canada. (Province). Parlement. Conseil legislatif. Select Committee on Immigration - Quebec: Hunter, Rose & Lemieux, 1864. SEM105P562 - 1mf - 9 - Can$2.25 - cn Bibl Nat [320]

REPORT / Conference of Bar Association Delegates. Committee on Cooperation of the Press and the Bar - n.p., 1927 11 p. LL-1231 - 1 - us L of C Photodup [340]

REPORT / Egypt. Permanent Council for the Development of National Production - 1v. 1955. BNE-4674 1 - 9 - ne IDC [330]

REPORT / Georgia. Agricultural Experiment Station. Athens - 1914-17 - 1,5,6 - us Spaulding [630]

REPORT / Georgia. Coastal Plain Experiment Station. Tifton - v. 1-30. 1919-50 - 1,5,6 - us Spaulding [630]

REPORT / Georgia. Experiment Station. Experiment - v. 1-63. 1888-1950 - 1,5,6 - us Spaulding [630]

REPORT / Georgia. University. Agricultural Extension Service - 1915-53 - 1,5 - us Spaulding [630]

REPORT / Great Britain. Advisory Council for Education in Northern Ireland on Secondary Education in Northern Ireland - Cmnd. 574. 1973 - 9 - uk Microform Academic [324]

REPORT / Great Britain. Central Advisory Council for Education on Technical Education in Wales - 1961 - 1 - uk Microform Academic [324]

REPORT / Great Britain. Central Advisory Council for Primary Education in Wales - 1967 - 9 - uk Microform Academic [324]

REPORT / Great Britain. Colonial Office. Administration of Palestine and Transjordan - 18v. 1920-38. BJ-28-107 1 - 9 - ne IDC [956]

REPORT / Great Britain. Colonial Office. Palestine Partition Commission - London. 1938. Cmd. 5854. BJ-28-84 1 - 9 - ne IDC [956]

REPORT / Great Britain. Colonial Office. Palestine Royal Commission - London. 1937. Appendixes: 1. Mandate for Palestine, 2. Representations addressed to the High Commissioner by the Higher Arab Officials. 1936. BJ-28-81 1 - 9 - ne IDC [956]

REPORT / Great Britain. Commission on the Palestine Disturbances of August, 1929 - Presented by the Secretary of State for the Colonies to Parliament. London. Mar 1930. BJ-28-72 1 - 9 - ne IDC [956]

REPORT / Great Britain. Commissioners Appointed to Enquire into the State, Discipline, Studies and Revenues of Cambridge University and Colleges - 1852. Command No. 1559, Index 1017 - 1 - uk Microform Academic [324]

REPORT / Great Britain. Commissions Appointed to Enquire into the Property and Income of Oxford and Cambridge Universities - C. 856 I, II 1873 - 1 - uk Microform Academic [324]

REPORT / Great Britain. Committee of Enquiry of the Education of the Visually Handicapped - 9 - uk Microform Academic [941]

REPORT / Great Britain. Committee of Enquiry of the Education of the Visually Handicapped - 1972 - 9 - uk Microform Academic [324]

REPORT / Great Britain. Committee of Inquiry on Teacher Education and Training - Committee of Enquiry into Teacher Education and Training - 9 - uk Microform Academic [324]

REPORT / Great Britain. Committee on Maladjusted Children – 1955 – 9 – uk Microform Academic [324]

REPORT / Great Britain. Committee on Speech Therapy Services – 1972 – 9 – uk Microform Academic [324]

REPORT / Great Britain. Committee on the Limitation of Actions – London: H. M. Stationery Off., 1949. 15p. LL-2 – 1 – us L of C Photodup [340]

REPORT / Great Britain. Committee to consider certain correspondence between Sir Henry McMahon, His Majesty's High Commissioner in Egypt and the Sharif of Mecca in 1915 and 1916 – London. 1939. BJ-28-91 1 – 9 – ne IDC [324]

REPORT / Great Britain. Consultative Committee on Examinations in Secondary Schools – 1911. Cd 6004 – 9 – uk Microform Academic [324]

REPORT / Great Britain. Consultative Committee on the Primary School – 1931 – 9 – uk Microform Academic [324]

REPORT / Great Britain. Departmental Committee for the Enquiry into the Principles which should determine the Construction of the Scales of Salary for teachers in Elementary Schools – 1918.Cd. 8939 and Cd. 8999 – 9 – uk Microform Academic [324]

REPORT / Great Britain. Departmental Committee on Juvenile Education in Relation to Employment after the War – 1916-17. Lewis Report. Cd. 8512 – 9 – uk Microform Academic [324]

REPORT / Great Britain. Foreign Office. Anglo-American Committee of Enquiry regarding the problems of European Jewry and Palestine – Lausanne. 20 Apr, 1946. London. 1946. BJ-28-95 1 – 9 – ne IDC [956]

REPORT / Great Britain. Ministry of Education Committee on Day Release – 1964 – 9 – uk Microform Academic [324]

REPORT / Great Britain. Poor Law Commissioners – 1834 – 1 – uk Microform Academic [360]

REPORT / Great Britain. Royal Commission into Schools in Scotland – 1865-8. (Argyle Report) – 9 – uk Microform Academic [370]

REPORT / Great Britain. Royal Commission on Poor Law – 1909 – 1 – uk Microform Academic [360]

REPORT / Great Britain. Royal Commission on Secondary Education – 1895. Bryce Report; C. 7862 – 1 – uk Microform Academic [324]

REPORT / Great Britain. Royal Commissioners Appointed to Enquire into Popular Education in England. The Newcastle Commission – Command No. 2794 (1-1v). 1861 – 1 – uk Microform Academic [324]

REPORT / Great Britain. Royal Commissioners for Taking a Census of Great Britain on Education – 1852-5 – 9 – uk Microform Academic [370]

REPORT / Great Britain. Royal Commissioners into the Means of Education in Wales – 1847 – 9 – uk Microform Academic [324]

REPORT / Great Britain. Schools Inquiry Commission. Taunton Commission – 1867-68. Command No. 3966 – 1 – uk Microform Academic [324]

REPORT / Great Britain. Select Committee for Giving Instruction in Theoretical and Applied Science to Industrial Classes – 1867-8 – 9 – uk Microform Academic [324]

REPORT / Great Britain. Select Committee on Education in England and Wales – 1835. Command No. 465 – 1 – uk Microform Academic [370]

REPORT / Great Britain. Select Committee on Public Libraries – 1849 – 9 – uk Microform Academic [324]

REPORT / Great Britain. Select Committee on Schools of Art – 1864 – 9 – uk Microform Academic [324]

REPORT / Great Britain. Select Committee on the Education of the Lower Orders – 1817 – 9 – uk Microform Academic [324]

REPORT / Great Britain. Select Committee on the Education of the Poorer Classes – 1837-8 – 9 – uk Microform Academic [324]

REPORT / Great Britain. Select Committee on the State of Education – 1834 – 9 – uk Microform Academic [324]

REPORT / Great Britain. Select Committee on the West Coast of Africa – 1842 – 1 – uk Microform Academic [960]

REPORT / Great Britain. Standing Joint Committee on A Provisional minimum scale of salaries for teachers in Public Elementary Schools – 1919. Cmd. 443 – 9 – uk Microform Academic [324]

REPORT / Great Britain. Study Group on the Government of Colleges of Education – 1966 – 9 – uk Microform Academic [324]

REPORT / India. Famine Commission – London. 1881. Parliamentary Papers nr. 71C, paper C.3086-IV, paper C.3086-V, App. IV, App. V. BI-515 2 – 8 – ne IDC [950]

REPORT / India. Famine Commission – P.P., 1880. v. 52, paper C 2591 and paper C 2735. BI-512 2 – 8 – ne IDC [324]

REPORT / India. Famine Commission – Pt. III. Famine History. P.P., 1881, v. 71. A paper C. 3086, paper C. 3086-I and paper C. 3086-II. App. I., II. BI-513 2 – 8 – ne IDC [950]

REPORT / Indonesia. Bank Negara – SE-265 1. 1956-1964 – 9 – ne IDC [336]

REPORT / International Socialist Congress. 7th. 1907 – Internationaler sozialisten-kongress zu Stuttgart, 18-24 Aug., 1907. Berlin, 1907 – 1 – $35.00r – us Hoover Inst Photo [335]

REPORT / Israel. Prime Minister's Office. Committee for Air Pollution Research in Israel – Jerusalem. Jul 1975. 15p. diagr. (Hebrew Text 204p.) – 9 – $5.00 – is I.T.T.I. [360]

REPORT / Israel. Prime Minister's Office. Israel National Committee on Biosphere and Environment Water Quality in Israel. Committee on Water Quality; ed by Saltiternik, C – Jerusalem, 1973. Summary, conclusions and recommendations in English. 40p. (Hebrew text 226 p) – 9 – $5.00 – is I.T.T.I. [360]

REPORT / Jordan. Currency Board – 1949 51-65 – 9 – ne IDC [336]

REPORT / Jordan. Ministry of Finance – 5v in 1. 1955-60. BNE-9805 1 – 9 – ne IDC [336]

REPORT / Kansas. State University. Agricultural Experiment Station – nos.1-12. 1938-69 – 1,5,6 – us Spaulding [630]

REPORT / Kenya. Kenya Education Commission – Nairobi. 2pts. 1964-1965 – 3mf – 9 – DE-440/1 – ne IDC [370]

REPORT / Knowles, Morris, Inc – 1931 – 2mf – 9 – us South Carolina Historical [380]

REPORT / Lake Mohonk Conference on the Indians – 1ST-35TH. 1883-1929 – 1 – 47.00 – us L of C Photodup [360]

REPORT / Louisiana State University. Agricultural Experiment Station. Department of Dairy Science – 1972, 1982. 1 reel – 1,5 – us Spaulding [630]

REPORT / Louisiana State University. Agricultural Experiment Station. Iberia Livestock Experiment Station. Jeanerette – 1981. 1 reel – 1,5 – us Spaulding [630]

REPORT / Louisiana State University. Agricultural Experiment Station. Livestock Show Open and Juniors – No.36-46. 1971-81. 1 reel – 1,5 – us Spaulding [630]

REPORT / Malaysia. Higher Education Planning Committee – (In Malay and English) – Kuala Lumpur, 1967 – 4mf – 9 – DE-208/1 – ne IDC [370]

REPORT / Minnesota. Agricultural Experiment Station. St. Paul. Northeast Experiment Station – 1896-1919 – 1,5,6 – us Spaulding [630]

REPORT / Minnesota. Agricultural Experiment Station. St. Paul. Northeast Experiment Station. Duluth – 1915-27 – 1,5,6 – us Spaulding [630]

REPORT / Minnesota. Agricultural Experiment Station. St. Paul. Northwest Experiment Station. Crookston – 1900-27 – 1,5,6 – us Spaulding [630]

REPORT / Minnesota. Agricultural Experiment Station. St. Paul. Southeast Experiment Station. Waseca – 1913-23 – 1,5,6 – us Spaulding [630]

REPORT / Minnesota. College of Agriculture. Department of Agricultural Engineering – nos.201-205 – 1,5,6 – us Spaulding [630]

REPORT / National Joint Committee for Spanish Relief – London, 1941. Fiche W1068. (Blodgett Collection of Spanish Civil War Pamphlets) – 9 – us H.U. College Libr [946]

REPORT / Nebraska. College of Agriculture. Dept. of Agricultural Economics – n.1-54. 1952-69 – 1,5 – us Spaulding [630]

REPORT / New Hampshire. College of Agriculture (or N.H. College of Agriculture & Mechanical Arts) – v1-35. 1867-1920 – 1,5,6 – us Spaulding [630]

REPORT / New Jersey. Statistics and records bureau – Trenton (etc.). No1-7, 10-40. 1878-1916/17 – 1 – us NY Public [310]

REPORT / New Mexico Inter-Agency Range Committee – No.5-11.1970-73. 1 reel – 1,5 – us Spaulding [630]

REPORT / New York (City). Board of Alderman, 1902-37. Special Committee to Investigate the Police Dept – 1913. 6v – 1 – $69.00 – us L of C Photodup [360]

REPORT / North Carolina State University.Department of Soil Science. Agronomic-Economic Research on Soils of the Tropics – 1976/77-1981/82.9 fiches – 9 – us Spaulding [630]

REPORT / Ohio. Public Service Commission – 1912. 13 fiches. (Harvard Law School Library Collection.) – 9 – $1.50f – us H.U. Law [336]

REPORT / Palestine. Government of Palestine. Committee for Moslem religious affairs – Jerusalem. 1921. BJ-28-64 1 – 9 – ne IDC [290]

REPORT / Quebec. (Province). Canada. Commission...Revision et de la refonte des statuts generaux.. – 1881. SEM105P624 – 1mf – 9 – Can$2.25 – cn Bibl Nat [323]

REPORT / Quebec. (Province). Legislature. Assemblee legislative. Select Committee on Public Lands and Forests – Quebec, 1895. SEM105P581 – 3mf – 9 – Can$6.75 – cn Bibl Nat [634]

REPORT / Singapore. Commission of Inquiry into Vocational and Technical Education in Singapore – Singapore, 1961 – 2mf – 9 – DE-262/1 – ne IDC [370]

REPORT : THE SPECIAL COMMITTEE TO WHOM WERE REFERRED THE DIVERS ORDERS AND RESOLUTIONS OF YOUR HONORABLE HOUSE... – [S.l.]: [s.n.], [1836]. SEM105P1224 – 5mf – 9 – Can$11.25 – cn Bibl Nat [324]

REPORT / Sudan. Commission on Coordination between Central and Local Government – Ed. 2. 1961? BNE-7605 1 – 9 – ne IDC [324]

REPORT / Sudan. Currency Board – 4v in 1. 1957-59 1960. BNE-7606 1 – 9 – ne IDC [338]

REPORT / Sudan. Forests Department – 3v. 1959-62. BNE-7640 1 – 9 – ne IDC [324]

REPORT / Tennessee. University. Agriculture Department – 1879-1886 – 1,5 – us Spaulding [630]

REPORT / U.N. Visiting Mission to Observe the Referendum in Palau, may-jun 1979 – (Taken from the Official Records of the Trusteeship Council, Suppl n1, jul 1979) – New York: The U.N, 1980 – 2mf – 9 – $3.00 – LLMC 82-100G, Title 18 – us L.L.M.C. [323]

REPORT / United Nations. General Assembly – Geneva, Switzerland. 31 Aug 1947. London. 1947. BJ-28-98 1 – 9 – ne IDC [900]

REPORT / U.S. Bureau of Indian Affairs – 1838-1916 – 1 – 414.00 – us L of C Photodup [324]

REPORT / U.S. Superintendent for the Five Civilized Tribes – v. 1-24. 1893 94-1919 20. w ind. for 1894-1905. 1896 97, 1915 16-1916 17 wanting – 1 – 40.00 – us L of C Photodup [360]

REPORT / University of Missouri. Freedom of Information Center – 1958- 1; 1977- 5,6,9 – us UMI [000]

REPORT / Vermont. Resources Research Center – v. 1-20. 1964-68 – 1,5,6 – us Spaulding [630]

REPORT / Washington. Agricultural Experiment Station – nos.1-80. 1892-1971 – 1,5,6 – us Spaulding [630]

REPORT / Wisconsin. Tax Commission – 1898. 10 fiches. (Harvard Law School Library Collection.) – 9 – $1.50f – us H.U. Law [336]

REPORT / Zambia. Commission of Inquiry University of Zambia – Lusaka, 1986 – 3mf – 9 – DE-499/1 – ne IDC [370]

REPORT. / International Congress for Progressive Thought. 1904: St. Louis – Oct 15-20, 1904.218p. ill – 1 – us U.W. Library [335]

REPORT.. / Believers' Meeting for Bible Study (12th: 1888: Niagara-on-the-Lake) – Toronto, 1888?. 05879. (Pre-1900 Canadiana) – 9 – cn C.I.H.M. [240]

REPORT.. / Canada. Bas-Canada. Parlement. Chambre d'Assemblee. Comite choisi sur le Gouvernement civil du Canada – Quebec: Reprinted by Order of the House of Assembly of Lower Canada, 1829. SEM105P105 – 4mf – 9 – Can$9.00 – cn Bibl Nat [324]

REPORT.. / Rottermund, E S, Comte de – Montreal: Lovell and Gibson, 1846. SEM105P345 – 1mf – 9 – Can$2.25 – cn Bibl Nat [971]

REPORT... / Kenya. National Committee on Educational Objectives and Policies – Nairobi, 1976 – 3mf – 9 – DE-441/1 – ne IDC [370]

REPORT 1908 / Great Britain. Royal Commission upon Decentralisation in India – 7v. London. 1909. Reports and Minutes of Evidence. BI-520 2 – 8 – ne IDC [950]

REPORT 1960 / Malaya (Federation) Education Review Committee – Kuala Lumpur, 1960 – 2mf – 9 – DE-207/1 – ne IDC [370]

REPORT 1963 / Hong Kong. Education Commission – (Includes the report of the Working Party on the Provision of Education for English-speaking Children) – Hong Kong – 4mf – 9 – DE-165/1 – ne IDC [370]

REPORT 1974 / Papua New Guinea. Five Year Education Plan Committee – Konedobu, 1974 – 4mf – 9 – DE-246/1 – ne IDC [370]

REPORT ... 1975 / Swaziland. National Education Commission – Mbabane, 1975 – 2mf – 9 – DE-483/1 – ne IDC [370]

REPORT: 1893-1934 / Independent Labour Party. Great Britain. – 1 – 35.00r – us Hoover Inst Photo [335]

REPORT 1941-53 / Javasche Bank. Batavia – TEN 1140. BSE-295 1 – 9 – ne IDC [950]

REPORT 1960-1972 / Sudan. Bank of Sudan – 13v in 2. BNE-7602 1 – 9 – ne IDC [338]

REPORT 1965-1980 / Tonga. Ministry of Education – (Missing: 1968) – Nuku'alofa – 32mf – 9 – DE-610/1 – ne IDC [370]

REPORT 1972-1988 / South Africa. Bophuthatswana. Department of Education – (Missing: 1986) – 21mf – 9 – DE-468/1 – ne IDC [370]

REPORT 1974-1975 / Gilbert and Ellice Islands. Ministry of Education, Training and Culture – (Cont as: Kiribati. Ministry of Education, Training and Culture. Report 1976-1979. Missing: 1978) – 6mf – 9 – DE-606/1 – ne IDC [370]

REPORT 1975-1976 / Zambia. Adult Education Advisory Board – Lusaka – 1mf – 9 – DE-488/1 – ne IDC [370]

REPORT 1976-79 *see* REPORT 1974-1975

REPORT 1982-1983 / Botswana. Department of Education and Teacher Training – Gaborone – 3mf – 9 – DE-418/1 – ne IDC [370]

REPORT ABOUT THE LOCAL ADMINISTRATION AND THEIR ROLE TOWARDS THE RE-SETTLEMENT OF NOMADS / Libya. Ministry of Interior – Al-Kabeer, S.A. BNE-705 1 – 9 – ne IDC [956]

REPORT AND ACCOUNTS / Kuwait. Commercial Bank – 1962-1976. Lacking: 1974-1975. BNE-9011 1 – 9 – ne IDC [324]

REPORT AND ACCOUNTS, 1966-1977 / Kuwait. Kuwait Investment Company – BNE-9023 1 – 9 – ne IDC [324]

REPORT AND FINDINGS. / Committee of Enquiry into Breaches of International Law Relating to Intervention in Spain – n.p. 1936. Fiche W 929. (Blodgett Collection of Spanish Civil War Pamphlets) – 9 – us H.U. College Libr [946]

REPORT AND PRELIMINARY SURVEY OF FIVE IMPORTANT SERVICE TRADES IN TRIPOLI TOWN / Libya. Ministry of Economy and Trade. Census and Statistical Department – May 1967. BNE-607 1 – 9 – ne IDC [338]

REPORT AND PROCEEDINGS OF THE EXPERT CONSULTATION ON SHARED FISHERY RESOURCES OF THE LESSER ANTILLES REGION. MAYAGUEZ, PUERTO RICO, 1986 – 1987 – 283p – it F.A.O. [639]

REPORT AND PROCEEDINGS OF THE MEETING ON FISHERIES EXPLOITATION WITHIN THE EXCLUSIVE ECONOMIC ZONES OF ENGLISH – SPEAKING CARIBBEAN COUNTRIES : ST. GEORGE'S, GRENADA, 1992 – 1992 – 92-5-103295-5 – it F.A.O. [338]

REPORT AND RECOMMENDATIONS; ATLAS OF INDONESIAN RESOURCES / Howarth, Margery D – SE-5528 1. 1962 – 9 – ne IDC [910]

REPORT AND TABLES / Libya. Ministry of Agriculture. Census of Agriculture – Tripoli. Feb 1962. BNE-1003 – 9 – ne IDC [630]

REPORT APPROVING THE COMPACT OF FREE ASSOCIATION WITH PALAU : 99TH CONG, 2ND SESS / ed by U.S. Congress. The Senate Comm on Energy and Natural Resources – Washington: GPO, 1986 – 4mf – 9 – $6.00 – LLMC 82-100G, Title 31 – us L.L.M.C. [327]

REPORT BOOKS OF THE OFFICE OF INDIAN AFFAIRS, 1838-85 / U.S. Bureau of Indian Affairs – 53 rolls. M348. Printed guide – 1 – us Nat'l Archives [324]

REPORT BY COMMITTEE OF THE FACULTY OF PROCURATORS IN GLASGOW APPOINTED TO CONSIDER AND REPORT UPON A BILL (AS AMENDED IN COMMITTEE) TO CONSOLIDATE AND AMEND THE LAWS RELATING TO PROCEDURE IN THE COURT OF SESSION IN SCOTLAND... / Glasgow. Faculty of Procurators – Glasgow: Graham, 1864. 28p. LL-1453 – 1 – us L of C Photodup [340]

REPORT BY MR. BRYDGES ON HIS INSPECTION OF THE PORTIONS OF THE INTERCOLONIAL RAILWAY NOW IN OPERATION / Brydges, Charles John – Ottawa: MacLean, Roger, 1874. 02086. (Pre-1900 Canadiana) – 9 – cn C.I.H.M. [971]

REPORT BY THE COUNCIL OF THE SOCIETY OF SOLICITORS BEFORE THE SUPREME COURTS, UPON THE BILL (TO ABOLISH FEUDAL AND BURGAGE TENURE, AND TO AMEND THE LAW RELATING TO LAND RIGHTS IN SCOTLAND.) / Society of Solicitors in the Supreme Courts of Scotland. Council – Edinburgh, 1870 11 p. LL-2259 – 1 – us L of C Photodup [340]

REPORT, CONTAINING STATEMENTS RELATIVE TO CUSTOMS-EXCISE REVENUE AND OTHER SERVICES / Canada. Department of National Revenue – 1850-1902 – 1 – 267.00 – us L of C Photodup [336]

REPORT, DEC. 11, 1962 / Indonesia. National Malaria Eradication Assessment Team – SE-11,605 1 – 9 – ne IDC [610]

REPORT ...: EDUACTION FOR 'POPAGANO' : PRELIMINARY REPORT APRIL 1978 / South Africa. Bophuthatswana. National Education Committee – Montshioa, 1978 – 2mf – 9 – DE-469/1 – ne IDC [370]

REPORT FOR THE YEAR 1952 / Rhodesia. Northern. Development Authority – Lusaka. 1953 – 9 – ne IDC [338]

REPORT FOR THE YEAR 1953 / Rhodesia. Northern. Development Authority – Lusaka. 1954 – 9 – ne IDC [338]

REPORT FOR THE YEAR 1954 / Rhodesia. Northern. Development Authority – Lusaka. 1955. Bd-547 1 – 9 – ne IDC [338]

REPORT FOR THE YEAR 1955 / Rhodesia. Northern. Development Authority – Lusaka. 1956 – 9 – ne IDC [338]

REPORT FOR THE YEAR 1973-1977 / British Virgin Islands. Education Department – Road Town – 5mf – 9 – DE-516/1 – ne IDC [370]

REPORT FOR THE YEAR 1977-1986 / Fiji. Ministry of Education – (Missing: 1982-1983) – Suva – 11mf – 9 – DE-603/1 – ne IDC [370]

REPORT FOR THE YEAR ENDING 30TH / Mueller, Ferdinand Jakob Heinrich von – June 1874. Melbourne. 1874. B-8046 1 – 9 – ne IDC [580]

REPORT FOR YEAR 1970/71 / Israel Prime Minister's Office. Negev Research Institute – Beer Sheva, Apr 1971. 98 12p. Text also in Hebrew – 9 – $3.00 – is I.T.T.I. [500]

REPORT FROM SELECT COMMITTEE ON LOWER CANADA / Grande-Bretagne. Parliament. House of Commons. Select Committee on the Affairs of Lower Canada – [London]: [s.n.], [1834]. SEM105P1128 – 1mf – 9 – Can$2.25 – cn Bibl Nat [971]

REPORT FROM SELECT COMMITTEE ON LOWER CANADA / Great Britain. Parliament. House of Commons. Select Committee on the Affairs of Lower Canada – [London]: [s.n.], [1834] – 1mf – 9 – Can$2.25 – cn Bibl Nat [340]

REPORT FROM THE CAPITAL – 1973-88. 2016p – 1 – $80.64 – us Baptist [240]

REPORT FROM THE CAPITAL / The Baptist Joint Committee on Public Affairs – 1946-Sep 1973 – 1 – $54.11 – us Baptist [240]

REPORT FROM THE CLERGY OF A DISTRICT IN THE DIOCESE OF LINOLN, CONVENED FOR THE PURPOSE OF CONSIDERING THE STATE OF RELIGION IN THE SEVERAL PARISHES IN THE SAID DISTRICT... – London, 2nd ed 1800 – 1mf – 9 – MP-599/1 – ne IDC [240]

REPORT FROM THE SELECT COMMITTEE OF THE HOUSE OF ASSEMBLY OF UPPER CANADA, APPOINTED TO REPORT ON THE STATE OF THE PROVINCE / Canada. Haut-Canada. Chambre d'Assemblee – Toronto: Printed at the Patriot Office, 1839. SEM105P159 – 1mf – 9 – Can$2.25 – cn Bibl Nat [324]

REPORT FROM THE SELECT COMMITTEE OF THE HOUSE OF ASSEMBLY OF UPPER CANADA, APPOINTED TO REPORT ON THE STATE OF THE PROVINCE / Haut-Canada. Parliament. House of Assembly. Select Committee Appointed to Report on the State of the Province – Toronto: The Patriot Office, 1839. SEM105P159 – 1mf – 9 – Can$2.25 – cn Bibl Nat [971]

REPORT FROM THE SELECT COMMITTEE OF THE LEGISLATIVE COUNCIL OF UPPER CANADA ON THE STATE OF THE PROVINCE / Canada. Haut-Canada. Conseil Legislatif – s.l: R Stanton, 1838? SEM105P150 – 1mf – 9 – Can$2.25 – cn Bibl Nat [324]

REPORT FROM THE SELECT COMMITTEE OF THE LEGISLATIVE COUNCIL OF UPPER CANADA ON THE STATE OF THE PROVINCE / Haut-Canada. Parliament. Legislative Council. Select Committee on the State of the Province – [s.l.]: R Stanton..., [1838 ?]. SEM105P150 – 1mf – 9 – Can$2.25 – cn Bibl Nat [971]

REPORT FROM THE SELECT COMMITTEE ON THE HUDSON'S BAY COMPANY / Canada. Parlement. Assemblee legislative. Select Committee on the Hudson's Bay Company – [s.l.: s.n.], 1857. SEM105P141 – 7mf – 9 – Can$15.75 – cn Bibl Nat [380]

REPORT FROM THE SPECIAL COMMITTEE... / Taschereau, Jean Thomas – [s.l: s.n, 1826 ?]. SEM105P1413 – 2mf – 9 – Can$4.50 – cn Bibl Nat [350]

REPORT IN RELATION TO THE CRIMINAL BUSINESS OF THE COURTS.. / Connecticut. Comptroller – Hartford. 1879/80-1934/36 – 1 – $23.00r – us L of C Photodup [360]

REPORT OF A JOINT REVIEW OF NEEDS OF THE MARITIME INDUSTRY OF INDONESIA / U.S. Operations Mission to Indonesia – SE 5468 1. 1960 – 9 – ne IDC [380]

REPORT OF A RECENT RELIGIOUS DELEGATION TO SPAIN, APRIL 1937, BY THE DEAN OF CANTERBURY AND OTHERS – London, 1937. Fiche W1133. (Blodgett Collection of Spanish Civil War Pamphlets) – 9 – us H.U. College Libr [946]

REPORT OF A SAMPLE SURVEY OF UNEMPLOYMENT AMONG SCHOOL-LEAVERS 1975 / Nigeria. Ogun State. Ministry of Finance and Economic Development – Abeokuta, 1977 – 1mf – 9 – DE-119/1 – ne IDC [370]

REPORT OF A SAMPLE SURVEY OF UNEMPLOYMENT AMONG SCHOOL-LEAVERS 1977 / Nigeria. Ogun State. Ministry of Economic Planning. Statistics Division – Ibadan, 1979 – 1mf – 9 – DE-117/1 – ne IDC [370]

REPORT OF A SERMON...CHARLOTTETOWN, SABBATH MORNING, AUG. 10TH, 1879 / Beecher, Henry Ward – 1879. 05938. (Pre-1900 Canadiana) – 9 – cn C.I.H.M. [240]

REPORT OF A SPECIAL COMMITTEE OF THE HOUSE OF ASSEMBLY APPOINTED TO ENQUIRE INTO THE STATE OF EDUCATION IN THIS PROVINCE / Bas-Canada. Parlement – Quebec: Neilson & Cowan, 1824. SEM105P623 – 3mf – 9 – Can$6.75 – cn Bibl Nat [370]

REPORT OF A SURVEY OF THE UNIVERSAL PRIMARY EDUCATION SCHEME 1978 / Idowu, A – Abeokuta, 1978 – 2mf – 9 – DE-118/1 – ne IDC [370]

REPORT OF A WORKING PARTY / Great Britain. Teaching Council for England and Wales – 1970 – 9 – uk Microform Academic [324]

A REPORT OF ACTIVITIES, 1940-1946 / American Zionist Emergency Council – (Central Zionist Archives, New York). New York. 1946. BJ-28-28 1 – 9 – ne IDC [956]

REPORT OF AN ENQUIRY INTO HOUSEHOLD EXPENDITURE IN 1953-1954 – (Coll title: British Government Publications...1801-1977, Health and Public Welfare) – 4mf – 9 (£1,080.00 health and public welfare set of 171mf) – uk Chadwyck [360]

REPORT OF ANNIVERSARY / Ohio Anti-Slavery Society – v1-4. 1836-40 – 1 reel – 1 – $65.00 – us UPA [976]

REPORT OF ARGUMENT SUBMITTED TO THE HONORABLE THE EXECUTIVE COUNCIL FOR THE PROVINCE OF QUEBEC: ON PRESENTATION OF A MEMORIAL RESPECTING THE VESTED RIGHTS OF LIMIT HOLDERS IN THEIR LIMITS, MARCH 16TH, 1880 / Church, L. Ruggles – 1880? 03048. (Pre-1900 Canadiana) – 9 – cn C.I.H.M. [336]

REPORT OF CAPT. JAMES BIDDLE, COMMANDING THE U.S.S. ONTARIO – 1817-19. M902 – 1r – 1 – us Nat'l Archives [976]

REPORT OF COMMISSION OF INVESTIGATION INTO THE CONDITIONS AND CIRCUMSTANCES RESULTING IN THE TRAGIC DEATH OF MR. DAG HAMMARSKJOLD. / Congo – 1962. BA-703/1 – 9 – ne IDC [960]

REPORT OF COOPERATIVE AND EXTENSION WORK IN AGRICULTURE IN MIDDLE TENNESSEE / Tennessee. University. Agricultural Experiment Station – 1907-10 – 1,5 – us Spaulding [630]

REPORT OF DR. WOLFRED NELSON,...ON THE PRESENT STATE DISCIPLINE, MANAGEMENT AND EXPENDITURE OF THE DISTRICT AND OTHER PRISONS IN CANADA EAST / Nelson, Wolfred – Quebec: John Lovell, 1852 – 2mf – 9 – Can$4.50 – SEM105P353 – cn Bibl Nat [360]

REPORT OF EXPLORATIONS AND SURVEYS IN PORTIONS OF THE COUNTIES OF CARLETON, VICTORIA, YORK AND NORTHUMBERLAND, NEW BRUNSWICK, 1885 / Bailey, Loring Woart – Montreal: Dawson Bros., 1886. 02214. (Pre-1900 Canadiana) – 9 – cn C.I.H.M. [910]

REPORT OF HON. NOAH DAVIS, REFEREE, TO THE SURROGATE'S COURT, CITY AND COUNTY OF NEW YORK, ON THE AMERICAN SURETY COMPANY, OF NEW YORK / Davis, Noah – New York? 1887? 15 p. LL-474 – 1 – us L of C Photodup [340]

REPORT OF HORTICULTURE RESEARCH PROJECTS / Louisiana State University. Agricultural Experiment Station. Department of Horticulture – 1977-84.1 reel – 1,5 – us Spaulding [580]

REPORT OF INQUEST ON ORIGIN OF FIRE AT THE PACIFIC RAILWAY OFFICES, ON 16TH JANUARY, 1874 – Ottawa: MacLean, Rose, 1874. 02073. (Pre-1900 Canadiana) – 9 – cn C.I.H.M. [971]

REPORT OF MEETING AT GUILDHALL, 3RD DECEMBER, 1896, AND SPEECHES DELIVERED IN THE HOUSE OF LORDS: WITH OPINIONS OF THE PRESS / British Empire League – London, England: The League, 1897. 03724. (Pre-1900 Canadiana) – 9 – cn C.I.H.M. [941]

REPORT OF MEETING OF COUNCIL, JULY 12TH, 1897: TO RECEIVE A DEPUTATION FROM THE LEAGUE IN CANADA / British Empire League – London: Spottiswoode. 00300. (Pre-1900 Canadiana) – 9 – cn C.I.H.M. [941]

REPORT OF MISSIONS / National Indian Association – 1913. 1 fiche. (American Indian Periodicals in the Princeton University Library) – 9 – $45.00 – us UPA [073]

REPORT OF NATIONAL ECONOMIC AND SOCIAL RESEARCH INSTITUTE, 1963 / Indonesia. Lembaga Ekonomi dan Kemasjarakatan Nasional – SE-4622 1. 1964 – 9 – ne IDC [330]

REPORT OF OPERATIONS, UP TO AND INCLUDING DECEMBER, 1954 / Caltex Pacific Petroleum Company – In English and Indonesian. SE-6849 1 – 9 – ne IDC [660]

REPORT OF OUR VISIT TO SPAIN / Atholl, Katharine Marjory – London, 1937? Fiche W 735. (Blodgett Collection of Spanish Civil War Pamphlets) – 9 – us H.U. College Libr [946]

REPORT OF PRESIDENT'S PERSONAL REPRESENTATIVE ON THE STATUS NEGOTIATIONS [TTPI (U.S.)] : HELD IN HANA, MAUI, HI, OCT 1971 / Williams, Franklin H – (Typescript) – n.p, n.d. – 2mf – 9 – $3.00 – LLMC 82-100F, Title 42 – us L.L.M.C. [323]

REPORT OF PROCEEDINGS / Pennsylvania. State Education Association – 63rd-70th meetings. 1912-19 – 1,5,6 – $2238.00 – us Princeton Micro [370]

REPORT OF PROCEEDINGS AT A SPECIAL GENERAL MEETING OF THE SHAREHOLDERS...HELD AT MONTREAL ON THE 3RD AND 6TH DAYS OF MARCH, 1884 / Canadian Pacific Railway Company – Montreal: Gazette, 1884. 02072. (Pre-1900 Canadiana) – 9 – cn C.I.H.M. [380]

REPORT OF PROGRESS FROM ITS COMMENCEMENT TO 1863 / Canada. Exploration Geologique – Montreal: Dawson Bros. London, Paris, and New York. Balliere. 1863-65. SEM105P350 – 12mf – 9 – Can$27.00 – cn Bibl Nat [550]

REPORT OF PROGRESS OF EXPLORATION IN THE COUNTRY BETWEEN LAKE ST JOHN AND JAMES BAY MADE UNDER INSTRUCTIONS FROM THE DEPARTMENT OF COLONIZATION AND MINES, QUEBEC / O'Sullivan, Henry – Quebec: Charles Pageau..., 1898. SEM105P474 – 1mf – 9 – Can$2.25 – cn Bibl Nat [910]

REPORT OF PROJECTS FOR DEPARTMENT OF AGRONOMY / Louisiana State University. Agricultural Experiment Station – 1981-83.1 reel – 1,5 – us Spaulding [630]

REPORT OF SELECT COMMITTEE ON GEORGIAN BAY AND LAKE ONTARIO SHIP CANAL / Canada. Parliament. Legislative Assembly. Committee – Quebec: Printed by Hunter, Rose & Co, 1864. SEM105P221 – 1mf – 9 – Can$2.25 – cn Bibl Nat [380]

REPORT OF SPEECHES DELIVERED AT MEETINGS HELD DURING THE VISIT OF THE PRIME MINISTERS OF THE SELF-GOVERNING COLONIES BETWEEN JUNE 12TH AND JULY 5TH, 1897 / British Empire League – London: The League, 1898. 00302. (Pre-1900 Canadiana) – 9 – cn C.I.H.M. [941]

THE REPORT OF ST BARTHOLOMEW – Gustavia, St. Barthelemy. 1804-07, 1810-12, 1814-19. – 1 reel – 1 – sw Kungliga [072]

REPORT OF SURVEY OF FRENCH RIVER, GEORGIAN BAY, LAKE HURON: MADE FOR THE DEPARTMENT OF RAILWAYS AND CANALS IN 1879 / Bender, E P – Ottawa: Paynter & Abbott, 1900. 02320. (Pre-1900 Canadiana) – 9 – cn C.I.H.M. [910]

REPORT OF THE 1ST SESSION OF THE SUB-COMMITTEE ON FISH TRADE. ROME, 1986 / Committee on Fisheries – 1987 – 36p – it F.A.O. [380]

REPORT OF THE 1ST SESSION OF THE WORKING GROUP ON ARTIFICIAL REEFS AND MARICULTURE : ANCONA, ITALY, 1989 / G.F.C.M. – 1990 – 168p – it F.A.O. [639]

REPORT OF THE 1ST SESSION OF THE WORKING PARTY ON FISHERIES ECONOMICS AND STATISTICS : ROME, 1991 / G.F.C.M. – 1992 – 157p – it F.A.O. [338]

REPORT OF THE 1ST SESSION OF THE WORKING PARTY ON FISHERY ECONOMICS AND PLANNING : ST. GEORGE'S, GRENADA, 1989 / W.E.C.A.F.C. – 1989 – 68p – it F.A.O. [338]

REPORT OF THE 1ST SESSION OF THE WORKING PARTY ON POLLUTION AND FISHERIES. ACCRA, GHANA, 1986 / CIFA – 1987 – 28p – it F.A.O. [338]

REPORT OF THE 2ND F.A.O./UNFPA EXPERT CONSULTATION ON LAND RESOURCES FOR POPULATIONS OF THE FUTURE – 1982 2nd print 1984 – 379p – it F.A.O. [333]

REPORT OF THE 2ND GFCM TECHNICAL CONSULTATION ON RED CORAL OF THE MEDITERRANEAN : TORRE DEL GRECO, ITALY, 1988 / G.F.C.M. – 1989 – 160p – it F.A.O. [639]

REPORT OF THE 2ND SESSION OF THE COMMITTEE FOR THE DEVELOPMENT AND MANAGEMENT OF FISHERIES IN THE LESSER ANTILLES. CASTRIES, SAINT LUCIA, 1985 / W.E.C.A.F.C. – 1986 – 47p – it F.A.O. [639]

REPORT OF THE 2ND SESSION OF THE SUB-COMMITTEE ON FISH TRADE : ROME, 1988 / COFI – 1989 – 68p – it F.A.O. [380]

REPORT OF THE 2ND SESSION OF THE WORKING PARTY ON AQUACULTURE. GUAYAQUIL, ECUADOR, SEPTEMBER 1986 / COPESCAL – 1987 – 42p – it F.A.O. [639]

REPORT OF THE 2ND SESSION OF THE WORKING PARTY ON FISHERIES TECHNOLOGY. SAN SALVADOR, 1985 / COPESCAL – 1986 – 26p – it F.A.O. [639]

REPORT OF THE 2ND SESSION OF THE WORKING PARTY ON POLLUTION AND FISHERIES : NAIROBI, 1989 / CIFA – 1990 – 29p – it F.A.O. [360]

REPORT OF THE 2ND TECHNICAL CONSULTATION ON STOCK ASSESSMENT IN THE CENTRAL MEDITERRANEAN. MAZARA DEL VALLO, ITALY, 1985 / G.F.C.M. – 1985 – 149p – it F.A.O. [639]

REPORT OF THE 2ND TECHNICAL CONSULTATION ON STOCK ASSESSMENT IN THE EASTERN MEDITERRANEAN : ATHENS, 1988 / G.F.C.M. – 1989 – 213p – it F.A.O. [639]

REPORT OF THE 2ND TECHNICAL CONSULTATION ON THE UTILIZATION OF SMALL PELAGIC SPECIES IN THE MEDITERRANEAN AREA. ZADAR, YUGOSLAVIA, 1985 / G.F.C.M. – 1985 2nd print 1986 – 209p – it F.A.O. [639]

REPORT OF THE 2ND WORKSHOP ON THE BIOLOGICAL AND ECONOMICAL MODELLING OF THE SHRIMP RESOURCES ON THE GUYANA-BRAZIL SHELF / W.E.C.A.F.C. – 1989 – 95p – it F.A.O. [333]

REPORT OF THE 3RD SESSION OF THE COMMITTEE FOR THE DEVELOPMENT AND MANAGEMENT OF FISHERIES IN THE LESSER ANTILLES. FORT-DE-FRANCE, MARTINIQUE, JULY 1987 / W.E.C.A.F.C. – 1988 – 64p – it F.A.O. [338]

REPORT OF THE 3RD SESSION OF THE INDO-PACIFIC FISHERY COMMISSION WORKING PARTY OF EXPERTS ON INLAND FISHERIES AND REPORT OF THE WORKSHOP ON STRATEGIES FOR THE MANAGEMENT OF FISHERIES AND AQUACULTURE IN MANGROVE ECOSYSTEMS. BANGKOK, 1986 / IPFC – 1986 – 47p – it F.A.O. [338]

REPORT OF THE 3RD SESSION OF THE SUB-COMMITTEE FOR LAKE TANGANYIKA. LUSAKA, 1985 / CIFA – 1986 – 27p – it F.A.O. [639]

REPORT OF THE 3RD SESSION OF THE SUB-COMMITTEE FOR THE DEVELOPMENT AND MANAGEMENT OF THE FISHERIES OF LAKE VICTORIA, JINJA, UGANDA, 1984 / Committee for Inland Fisheries of Africa – 1985 2nd print 1986 – 150p – it F.A.O. [338]

REPORT OF THE 3RD SESSION OF THE SUB-COMMITTEE FOR THE PROTECTION AND DEVELOPMENT OF THE FISHERIES IN THE SAHELIAN ZONE. ACCRA, 1986 / CIFA – 1987 – 33p – it F.A.O. [338]

REPORT OF THE 3RD SESSION OF THE SUB-COMMITTEE ON FISH TRADE : ROME, 1989 / COFI – 1990 – 64p – it F.A.O. [380]

REPORT OF THE 3RD SESSION OF THE WORKING PARTY ON FISHERY STATISTICS : PAIPA, COLOMBIA, 1984 / W.E.C.A.F.C. – 1985 – 60p – it F.A.O. [338]

REPORT OF THE 3RD SESSION OF THE WORKING PARTY ON POLLUTION AND FISHERIES : ACCRA, 1991 / CIFA – 1992 – 49p – it F.A.O. [360]

REPORT OF THE 3RD TECHNICAL CONSULTATION ON UTILIZATION OF SMALL PELAGIC SPECIES IN THE MEDITERRANEAN AREA : AMALFI, ITALY, 1987 / G.F.C.M. – 1987 – 222p – it F.A.O. [639]

REPORT OF THE 4TH SESSION OF THE COMMISSION FOR INLAND FISHERIES OF LATIN AMERICA. HAVANA, 1986 – 1986 – 48p – it F.A.O. [338]

REPORT OF THE 4TH SESSION OF THE COMMITTEE FOR THE DEVELOPMENT AND MANAGEMENT OF FISHERIES IN THE BAY OF BENGAL : AND THE 10TH MEETING OF THE ADVISORY COMMITTEE FOR THE DEVELOPMENT OF SMALL-SCALE FISHERIES OF THE BAY OF BENGAL PROGRAMME. MALE, MALDIVES, 1986 / I.C.F.C. – 1986 – 33p – it F.A.O. [639]

REPORT OF THE 4TH SESSION OF THE COMMITTEE FOR THE DEVELOPMENT AND MANAGEMENT OF FISHERIES IN THE LESSER ANTILLES : KINGSTOWN, SAINT VINCENT AND THE GRENADINES, 1990 / W.E.C.A.F.C. – 1991 – 105p – it F.A.O. [338]

REPORT OF THE 4TH SESSION OF THE COMMITTEE FOR THE DEVELOPMENT AND MANAGEMENT OF FISHERIES IN THE SOUTH CHINA SEA. KUALA LUMPUR, 1984 / IPFC – 1985 – 22p – it F.A.O. [338]

REPORT OF THE 4TH SESSION OF THE COMMITTEE FOR THE DEVELOPMENT AND MANAGEMENT OF FISHERIES IN THE SOUTHWEST INDIAN OCEAN. ZANZIBAR, TANZANIA, NOV 1986 / IOFC – 1987 – 54p – it F.A.O. [338]

REPORT OF THE 4TH SESSION OF THE INDO-PACIFIC FISHERY COMMISSION WORKING PARTY OF EXPERTS ON INLAND FISHERIES : AND, REPORT OF THE WORKSHOP ON THE USE OF CYPRINIDS IN THE FISHERIES MANAGEMENT OF LARGER INLAND WATER BODIES OF THE INDO-PACIFIC; KATHMANDU, 1988 / IPFC – 1988 – 56p – it F.A.O. [338]

REPORT OF THE 4TH SESSION OF THE SUB-COMMITTEE FOR THE DEVELOPMENT AND MANAGEMENT OF THE FISHERIES OF LAKE VICTORIA. KISUMU, KENYA, APRIL 1987 / CIFA – 1988 – 117p – it F.A.O. [338]

REPORT OF THE 4TH SESSION OF THE SUB-COMMITTEE FOR THE PROTECTION AND DEVELOPMENT OF THE FISHERIES IN THE SAHELIAN ZONE : CONAKRY, 1990 / CIFA – 1990 – 35p – it F.A.O. [338]

REPORT OF THE 4TH SESSION OF THE TECHNICAL CONSULTATION ON STOCK ASSESSMENT IN THE EASTERN MEDITERRANEAN : THESSALONIKI, GREECE, 1991 / G.F.C.M. – 1992 – 178p – it F.A.O. [639]

REPORT OF THE 4TH SESSION OF THE WORKING PARTY ON ASSESSMENT OF MARINE FISHERY RESOURCES. PAIPA, COLOMBIA, 1984 / W.E.C.A.F.C. – 1985 – 37p – it F.A.O. [333]

REPORT OF THE 4TH SESSION OF THE WORKING PARTY ON FISHERY STATISTICS : SANTA CRUZ DE TENERIFE, SPAIN, 1988 / CECAF – 1989 – it F.A.O. [338]

REPORT OF THE 4TH SESSION OF THE WORKING PARTY ON FISHERY STATISTICS. PORT OF SPAIN, TRINIDAD AND TOBAGO, 1986 – 1987 – 65p – it F.A.O. [338]

REPORT OF THE 4TH TECHNICAL CONSULTATION ON STOCK ASSESSMENT IN THE BALEARIC AND GULF OF LIONS STATISTICAL DIVISIONS. SIDI-FEDJ, ALGERIA, 1985 / G.F.C.M. – 1986 – 243p – it F.A.O. [639]

REPORT OF THE 5TH FAO EXPERT CONSULTATION ON FISH TECHNOLOGY IN AFRICA : ACCRA, 1991 – 1992 – 36p – it F.A.O. [636]

REPORT OF THE 5TH SESSION OF THE COMMISSION FOR INLAND FISHERIES OF LATIN AMERICA : PANAMA CITY, 1988 / COPESCAL – 1989 – 65p – it F.A.O. [338]

REPORT OF THE 5TH SESSION OF THE COMMITTEE FOR THE DEVELOPMENT AND MANAGEMENT OF FISHERIES IN THE BAY OF BENGAL. BANGKOK, MARCH 1987 / IOFC – 1988 – 48p – it F.A.O. [338]

REPORT OF THE 5TH SESSION OF THE COMMITTEE FOR THE DEVELOPMENT AND MANAGEMENT OF FISHERIES IN THE SOUTHWEST INDIAN OCEAN : CUREPIPE, MAURITIUS, 1988 / IOFC – 1989 – 83p – it F.A.O. [338]

REPORT OF THE 5TH SESSION OF THE INDO-PACIFIC FISHERY COMMISSION WORKING PARTY OF EXPERTS ON INLAND FISHERIES AND REPORT OF THE WORKSHOP ON TILAPIA IN CAPTURE AND CULTURE-ENHANCED FISHERIES IN THE INDO-PACIFIC FISHERY COMMISSION COUNTRIES : BOGOR, INDONESIA, 1991 / IPFC – 1991 – 46p – it F.A.O. [338]

REPORT OF THE 5TH SESSION OF THE SUB-COMMITTEE FOR THE DEVELOPMENT AND MANAGEMENT OF THE FISHERIES OF LAKE VICTORIA : MWANZA, TANZANIA, 1989 / CIFA – 1990 – 100p – it F.A.O. [338]

REPORT OF THE 5TH SESSION OF THE WESTERN CENTRAL ATLANTIC FISHERY COMMISSION. CASTRIES, SAINT LUCIA, 1985 – 1985 – 30p – it F.A.O. [639]

REPORT OF THE 5TH SESSION OF THE WORKING PARTY ON ASSESSMENT OF MARINE FISHERY RESOURCES. SAINT GEORGE, BERMUDA, 1986 / W.E.C.A.F.C. – 1987 – 31p – it F.A.O. [639]

REPORT OF THE 5TH TECHNICAL CONSULTATION ON STOCK ASSESSMENT IN THE ADRIATIC AND IONIAN SEAS. BARI, ITALY, JUNE 1987 / G.F.C.M. – 1988 – 314p – it F.A.O. [639]

REPORT OF THE 6TH SESSION OF THE COMMITTEE FOR INLAND FISHERIES OF AFRICA. LUSAKA, 1985 – 1986 – 31p – it F.A.O. [338]

REPORT OF THE 6TH SESSION OF THE COMMITTEE FOR THE DEVELOPMENT AND MANAGEMENT OF FISHERIES IN THE BAY OF BENGAL : PENANG, MALAYSIA, 1989 / IOFC – 1989 – 53p – it F.A.O. [338]

REPORT OF THE 6TH SESSION OF THE COMMITTEE FOR THE DEVELOPMENT AND MANAGEMENT OF FISHERIES IN THE SOUTHWEST INDIAN OCEAN : ANTANANARIVO, 1990 / IOFC – 1991 – 90p – it F.A.O. [338]

REPORT OF THE 6TH SESSION OF THE COMMITTEE ON RESOURCE MANAGEMENT. ROME, 1986 / G.F.C.M. – 1986 – 55p – it F.A.O. [639]

REPORT OF THE 6TH SESSION OF THE INDO PACIFIC FISHERY COMMISSION/ INDIAN OCEAN FISHERY COMMISSION JOINT WORKING PARTY OF EXPERTS ON INDIAN AND WESTERN PACIFIC FISHERY STATISTICS. ALBION, MAURITIUS, 1985 – 1985 – 26p – it F.A.O. [310]

REPORT OF THE 6TH SESSION OF THE SUB-COMMITTEE FOR THE DEVELOPMENT AND MANAGEMENT OF THE FISHERIES OF LAKE VICTORIA : JINJA, UGANDA, 1992 / CIFA – 1992 – 65p – it F.A.O. [338]

REPORT OF THE 6TH SESSION OF THE SUB-COMMITTEE ON MANAGEMENT OF RESOURCES WITHIN THE LIMITS OF NATIONAL JURISDICTION. LOME, TOGO, 1985 / CECAF – 1986 – 67p – it F.A.O. [333]

REPORT OF THE 6TH SESSION OF THE WESTERN CENTRAL ATLANTIC FISHERY COMMISSION. MEXICO, D.F., JULY 1987 – 1988 – 30p – it F.A.O. [338]

REPORT OF THE 6TH SESSION OF THE WORKING PARTY ON ASSESSMENT OF MARINE FISHERY RESOURCES : ST. GEORGE'S, GRENADA, 1989 / W.E.C.A.F.C. – 1990 – 133p – it F.A.O. [639]

REPORT OF THE 7TH SESSION OF THE CECAF SUB-COMMITTEE ON MANAGEMENT OF RESOURCES WITHIN THE LIMITS OF NATIONAL JURISDICTION : SANTA CRUZ DE TENERIFE, SPAIN, 1988 / CECAF – 1989 – 89p – it F.A.O. [333]

REPORT OF THE 7TH SESSION OF THE COMMITTEE FOR INLAND FISHERIES OF AFRICA. ACCRA, GHANA, DEC 1987 – 1988 – 57p – it F.A.O. [338]

REPORT OF THE 7TH SESSION OF THE COMMITTEE FOR THE DEVELOPMENT AND MANAGEMENT OF FISHERIES IN THE BAY OF BENGAL : COLOMBO, 1991 / IOFC – 1991 – 52p – it F.A.O. [338]

REPORT OF THE 7TH SESSION OF THE COMMITTEE FOR THE DEVELOPMENT AND MANAGEMENT OF FISHERIES IN THE SOUTH CHINA SEA : KOWLOON, HONG KONG, 1991 / IPFC – 1992 – 31p – it F.A.O. [338]

REPORT OF THE 7TH SESSION OF THE COMMITTEE ON RESOURCES MANAGEMENT : LIVORNO, ITALY, 1989 / G.F.C.M. – 1989 – 84p – it F.A.O. [333]

REPORT OF THE 7TH SESSION OF THE WESTERN CENTRAL ATLANTIC FISHERY COMMISSION : KINGSTOWN, SAINT VINCENT AND THE GRENADINES, 1990 / W.E.C.A.F.C. – 1991 – 53p – it F.A.O. [338]

REPORT OF THE 7TH SESSION OF THE WORKING PARTY OF EXPERTS ON AQUACULTURE : BANGKOK, 1988 / IPFC – 1989 – 41p – it F.A.O. [639]

REPORT OF THE 8TH SESSION OF THE CECAF SUB-COMMITTEE ON MANAGEMENT OF RESOURCES WITHIN THE LIMITS OF NATIONAL JURISDICTION : ABIDJAN, 1991 / CECAF – 1992 – 45p – it F.A.O. [333]

REPORT OF THE 8TH SESSION OF THE COMMITTEE FOR INLAND FISHERIES OF AFRICA : CAIRO, 1990 / CIFA – 1992 – 86p – it F.A.O. [338]

REPORT OF THE 8TH SESSION OF THE COMMITTEE FOR MANAGEMENT OF INDIAN OCEAN TUNA. COLOMBO, SRI LANKA, 1985 / IOFC – 1985 – 29p – it F.A.O. [639]

REPORT OF THE 8TH SESSION OF THE COMMITTEE ON FISHERIES MANAGEMENT : ROME, 1991 / G.F.C.M. – 1991 – 67p – it F.A.O. [338]

REPORT OF THE 8TH SESSION OF THE INDIAN OCEAN FISHERY COMMISSION. BANGKOK, 1985 – 1985 – 29p – it F.A.O. [338]

REPORT OF THE 8TH SESSION OF THE INDO-PACIFIC FISHERY COMMISSION WORKING PARTY ON FISH TECHNOLOGY AND MARKETING : YOGYAKARTA, INDONESIA, 1991 / IPFC – 1992 – 17p – it F.A.O. [639]

REPORT OF THE 8TH SESSION OF THE WORKING PARTY ON RESOURCES EVALUATION : SANTA CRUZ DE TENERIFE, SPAIN, 1988 / CECAF – 1989 – 72p – it F.A.O. [333]

REPORT OF THE 9TH SESSION OF THE COMMITTEE FOR THE MANAGEMENT OF INDIAN OCEAN TUNA. COLOMBO, SRI LANKA, DECEMBER 1986 / IOFC – 1987 – 100p – it F.A.O. [639]

REPORT OF THE 9TH SESSION OF THE INDIAN OCEAN FISHERY COMMISSION : MAHE, SEYCHELLES, 1989 / IOFC – 1990 – 71p – it F.A.O. [338]

REPORT OF THE 9TH SESSION OF THE WORKING PARTY ON RESOURCES EVALUATION : LAGOS, 1990 / CECAF – 1991 – 86p – it F.A.O. [333]

REPORT OF THE 10TH SESSION OF THE COMMITTEE FOR THE MANAGEMENT OF INDIAN OCEAN TUNA : MOKA, MAURITIUS, 1988 / IOFC – 1989 – 64p – it F.A.O. [338]

REPORT OF THE 10TH SESSION OF THE FISHERY COMMITTEE FOR THE EASTERN CENTRAL ATLANTIC (CECAF). PUERTO DE LA CRUZ, TENERIFE, NOV 1986 – 1988 – 88p – it F.A.O. [338]

REPORT OF THE 11TH SESSION OF THE ADVISORY COMMITTEE OF EXPERTS ON MARINE RESOURCES RESEARCH. ROME, ITALY, 1985 – 1985 – 25p – it F.A.O. [639]

REPORT OF THE 11TH SESSION OF THE COMMITTEE FOR THE MANAGEMENT OF INDIAN OCEAN TUNA : BANGKOK, 1990 / IOFC – 1990 – 54p – it F.A.O. [650]

REPORT OF THE 11TH SESSION OF THE FISHERY COMMITTEE FOR THE EASTERN CENTRAL ATLANTIC : DOUALA, CAMEROON, 1988 / CECAF – 1989 – 82p – it F.A.O. [338]

REPORT OF THE 12TH SESSION OF THE FISHERY COMMITTEE FOR THE EASTERN CENTRAL ALTANTIC : ACCRA, 1992 / CECAF – 1992 – 95p – it F.A.O. [338]

REPORT OF THE 13TH SESSION OF THE COORDINATING WORKING PARTY ON ATLANTIC FISHERIES STATISTICS. ROME, 1987 – 1987 – 34p – it F.A.O. [338]

REPORT OF THE 14TH SESSION OF THE COORDINATING WORKING PARTY ON ATLANTIC FISHERY STATISTICS : PARIS 1990, AND REPORT OF THE 2ND AD HOC CONSULTATION ON GLOBAL TUNA STATISTICS; LA JOLLA, CALIFORNIA, USA, 1987 – 1990 – 49p – it F.A.O. [338]

REPORT OF THE 14TH SESSION OF THE EUROPEAN INLAND FISHERIES ADVISORY COMMISSION. BORDEAUX, FRANCE, 1986 – 1986 – 81p – it F.A.O. [338]

REPORT OF THE 15TH SESSION OF THE COORDINATING WORKING PARTY ON ATLANTIC FISHERY STATISTICS : DARTMOUTH, NOVA SCOTIA, CANADA, 1992 – 1992 – 40p – it F.A.O. [338]

REPORT OF THE 15TH SESSION OF THE EUROPEAN INLAND FISHERIES ADVISORY COMMISSION : GOETEBORG, SWEDEN, 1988 / EIFAC – 1988 – 104p – it F.A.O. [338]

REPORT OF THE 15TH SESSION OF THE JOINT F.A.O./WHO CODEX ALIMENTARIUS COMMISSION. ROME. 1983 – 1983 – 141p – it F.A.O. [640]

REPORT OF THE 16TH SESSION OF THE COMMITTEE ON FISHERIES. ROME, 1985 – 1985 – 56p – it F.A.O. [639]

REPORT OF THE 16TH SESSION OF THE EUROPEAN INLAND FISHERIES ADVISORY COMMISSION : PRAGUE, 1990 / EIFAC – 1991 – 97p – it F.A.O. [338]

REPORT OF THE 16TH SESSION OF THE JOINT F.A.O./WHO CODEX ALIMENTARIUS COMMISSION. GENEVA, 1985 – 1985 – 118p – it F.A.O. [640]

REPORT OF THE 17TH SESSION OF THE CODEX ALIMENTARIUS COMMISSION. ROME, JUNE-JULY 1987 – 1987 – 111p – it F.A.O. [630]

REPORT OF THE 17TH SESSION OF THE COMMITTEE ON FISHERIES. ROME, MAY 1987 – 1987 – 59p – it F.A.O. [338]

REPORT OF THE 17TH SESSION OF THE EUROPEAN INLAND FISHERIES ADVISORY COMMISSION : LUGANO, SWITZERLAND, 1992 / EIFAC – 1992 – 73p – it F.A.O. [338]

REPORT OF THE 18TH SESSION OF THE COMMITTEE ON FISHERIES : ROME, 1989 / COFI – 1989 – 59p – it F.A.O. [639]

REPORT OF THE 18TH SESSION OF THE JOINT FAO/WHO CODEX ALIMENTARIUS COMMISSION : GENEVA, 1989 – 1989 – 133p – it F.A.O. [640]

REPORT OF THE 19TH SESSION OF THE JOINT FAO/WHO CODEX : ALIMENTARIUS COMMISSION; ROME, 1991 – 1991 – 123p – it F.A.O. [630]

REPORT OF THE 20TH SESSION OF THE JOINT FAO/WHO COMMITTEE OF GOVERNMENT EXPERTS ON THE CODE OF PRINCIPLES CONCERNING MILK AND MILK PRODUCTS : ROME, 1982 – 1982 – 77p – it F.A.O. [640]

REPORT OF THE 21ST SESSION OF THE INDO-PACIFIC FISHERIES COMMISSION : KUALA LUMPUR, 1984 / IFPC – 1985 – 37p – it F.A.O. [338]

REPORT OF THE 21ST SESSION OF THE JOINT F.A.O./WHO COMMITTEE OF GOVERNMENT EXPERTS ON THE CODE OF PRINCIPLES CONCERNING MILK AND MILK PRODUCTS. ROME, 1986 – 1986 – 84p – it F.A.O. [640]

REPORT OF THE 22ND SESSION OF THE JOINT FAO/WHO COMMITTEE OF GOVERNMENT EXPERTS ON THE CODE OF PRINCIPLES CONCERNING MILK AND MILK PRODUCTS : ROME, 1990 – 1991 – 93p – it F.A.O. [340]

REPORT OF THE AD HOC CONSULTATION ON GLOBAL TUNA STATISTICS. COLOMBO, SRI LANKA, 1985 – 1986 – 98p – it F.A.O. [639]

REPORT OF THE ADVISORY COMMITTEE ON EDUCATION IN PAPUA AND NEW GUINEA 1969 / Papua New Guinea – Canberra, 1969 – 2mf – 9 – DE-229/1 – ne IDC [370]

REPORT OF THE ANNUAL SURVEY: LARGE CONSTRUCTION / Libya – 1969, 1970. BNE-1106 1 – 9 – ne IDC [956]

REPORT OF THE ANNUAL SURVEY OF LARGE MANUFACTURING ESTABLISHMENTS / Libya. Ministry of Trade and Economy, Planning and Development. Census and Statistical Department – 1965-1974. Tripoli. Lacking: 1968. BNE-1203 1 – 9 – ne IDC [338]

REPORT OF THE AUDITOR GENERAL AND OF THE TABULATIONS AND DEDUCTIONS FROM THE REPORTS OF THE RAILROAD, CANAL AND TELEGRAPH COMPANIES / Pennsylvania. Auditor General's Office – 1859-74. 107 fiches. (Harvard Law School Library Collection.) – 9 – $1.50f – us H.U. Law [336]

REPORT OF THE BOARD OF DIRECTORS / Egypt. National Bank – 27v in 7. 1938-64. BNE-4673 1 – 9 – ne IDC [336]

REPORT OF THE BOARD OF DIRECTORS / Lebanon. Banque de Credit Agricole, Industriel et Foncier – 3v. in 1. 1962-66. (lacking 1964, 1965). BNE-9641 1 – 9 – ne IDC [330]

REPORT OF THE BOARD OF DIRECTORS / Sudan. Commercial bank – 7v in 6. 1962-75. (lacking 1963-64, 1966, 1969; 1973 74). BNE-7604 1 – 9 – ne IDC [338]

REPORT OF THE BRITISH TRADE MISSION TO MOROCCO / Morocco. Council for Middle East Trade – London. 1964. BNE-3028 1 – 9 – ne IDC [338]

REPORT OF THE BUREAU OF RAILWAYS, DEPT. OF INTERNAL AFFAIRS, PART 4: RAILROAD, CANAL, NAVIGATION, TELEGRAPH AND TELEPHONE COMPANIES / Pennsylvania. Dept. of Internal Affairs – 1875-1917. 503 fiches. (Harvard Law School Library Collection.) – 9 – $1.50f – us H.U. Law [336]

REPORT OF THE CANADIAN OBSERVATIONS OF THE TRANSIT OF VENUS, 6TH DECEMBER, 1882 / Carpmael, Charles – Toronto?, 1883? 02327. (Pre-1900 Canadiana) – 9 – cn C.I.H.M. [971]

REPORT OF THE CAUSE OF MARTHA BRADSTREET, VERSUS APOLLOS COOPER, ON A WRIT OF RIGHT – Albany, N.Y., Martin and Marshall, 1834. 52 p. LL-55 – 1 – us L of C Photodup [340]

REPORT OF THE CENTRAL BOARD OF HEALTH, IN RETURN TO THE ANNEXED ADDRESS OF THE LEGISLATIVE ASSEMBLY, 1854 / Canada. Bureau Central de la Sante – Quebec: Printed by John Donaghue and Co., 1855. SEM105P230 – 1mf – 9 – Can$2.25 – cn Bibl Nat [610]

REPORT OF THE CHIEF ENGINEER.. / Chemin de fer de Quebec et du Saguenay – 1854. SEM105P546 – 1mf – 9 – Can$2.25 – cn Bibl Nat [380]

REPORT OF THE CHIEF ENGINEER OF THE MEGANTIC JUNCTION RAILWAY, TO THE PROVISIONAL COMMITTEE / MacQuisten, P – Quebec: J.T. Brousseau, 1853. SEM105P591 – 1mf – 9 – Can$2.25 – cn Bibl Nat [971]

REPORT OF THE CHINESE HOSPITAL, AT SHANHAE, FROM JANUARY 1ST, TO DECEMBER 31ST 1849 – Shanhae, 1850 – 1mf – 9 – ne IDC [610]

REPORT OF THE CHINESE HOSPITAL, AT SHANHAE, FROM JULY 1ST 1847, TO DECEMBER 31ST 1848 – Shanhae, 1849 – 1mf – 9 – ne IDC [610]

REPORT OF THE CITY ENGINEER: QUEBEC, ON THE PROPOSED DRY DOCK IN THE MOUTH OF THE RIVER ST CHARLES / Baillairge, Charles – 1876?. 01053. (Pre-1900 Canadiana) – 9 – cn C.I.H.M. [627]

REPORT OF THE COLONIZATION COMMISSION OT THE PROVINCE OF QUEBEC / Commission de colonisation de la province de Quebec – Quebec: Charles Pageau..., 1904. SEM105P42 – 8mf – 9 – Can$18.00 – cn Bibl Nat [971]

REPORT OF THE COMMISSION / Nigeria. Western Region. Commission Appointed to Review the Educational System of Western Nigeria – Ibadan, 1961 – 2mf – 9 – DE-127/1 – ne IDC [370]

REPORT OF THE COMMISSION APPOINTED BY H.M. GOVERNMENT IN THE UNITED KINGDOM OF GREAT BRITAIN AND NORTHERN IRELAND, WITH THE APPROVAL OF THE COUNCIL OF THE LEAGUE OF NATIONS : TO DETERMINE THE RIGHTS AND CLAIMS OF MOSLEMS AND JEWS IN CONNECTION WITH THE WESTERN OR WAILING WALL AT JERUSALEM / Great Britain – London. 1931. BJ-28-73 1 – 9 – ne IDC [956]

REPORT OF THE COMMISSION APPOINTED TO INQUIRE INTO MATTERS CONNECTED WITH THE PUBLIC BUILDINGS AT OTTAWA / Canada. Commission Appointed to Inquire into Matters Connected with the Public Buildings at Ottawa – Quebec: Josiah Blackburn..., 1863. SEM105P311 – 5mf – 9 – Can$11.25 – cn Bibl Nat [350]

REPORT OF THE COMMISSION APPOINTED TO INQUIRE INTO THE AFFAIRS OF THE GRAND TRUNK RAILWAY / Canada. Commission Appointed to Inquire into the Affairs of the Grand Trunk Railway – Quebec: Stewart Derbishire & George Desbarats..., 1861. SEM105P362 – 4mf – 9 – Can$9.00 – cn Bibl Nat [380]

REPORT OF THE COMMISSION APPOINTED TO REVISE AND CONSOLIDATE THE STATUTES OF THE PROVINCE OF QUEBEC / Quebec Province – [S.l.]: [s.n.], 1881. SEM105P624 – 1mf – 9 – Can$2.25 – cn Bibl Nat [340]

REPORT OF THE COMMISSION ON FUTURE POLITICAL STATUS AND TRANSITION / Federated States of Micronesia – 20 June 1980 – 3mf – 9 – $4.50 – LLMC 82-100H Title 6 – us L.L.M.C. [324]

REPORT OF THE COMMISSIONER OF INSURANCE OF NEW JERSEY / New Jersey. Dept. of Insurance – 1891-1978. 459 fiches. (Harvard Law School Library Collection.) – 9 – $1.50f – us H.U. Law [336]

REPORT OF THE COMMISSIONERS / Oxford University – Discipline, studies and revenues of the University and Colleges... together with evidence and appendix. 1852 – 1 – uk Microform Academic [370]

REPORT OF THE COMMISSIONERS APPOINTED TO ENQUIRE INTO THE AFFAIRS AND FINANCIAL CONDITION OF TORONTO UNIVERSITY AND UNIVERSITY COLLEGE, UPPER CANADA / Canada Province. – Quebec: Hunter & Rose & Co, 1863. SEM105P573 – 2mf – 9 – Can$4.50 – cn Bibl Nat [370]

REPORT OF THE COMMISSIONERS APPOINTED TO ENQUIRE INTO THE STATE, DISCIPLINE, STUDIES, AND REVENUES, ETC / Cambridge University – 1852-53. Plus index – 1 – uk Microform Academic [025]

REPORT OF THE COMMISSIONERS APPOINTED TO INQUIRE INTO THE CONDUCT OF THE POLICE AUTHORITIES ON THE OCCASION OF THE RIOT AT CHALMERS CHURCH, ON THE 6TH OF JUNE, 1853... / Canada. Commissaires nommes pour s'enquerir... – Quebec: Rollo Campbell, 1854. SEM105P630 – 2mf – 9 – Can$4.50 – cn Bibl Nat [360]

REPORT OF THE COMMISSIONERS APPOINTED TO INQUIRE INTO THE STATE OF THE LAWS AND OTHER CIRCUMSTANCES CONNECTED... / Canada (Province). Commissaires Nomme Pour s'Enquerir de l'Etat des Lois et Autres Circonstances... – Kingston: Desbarats & Derbishire, 1844 – 4mf – 9 – Can$9.00 – cn Bibl Nat [340]

REPORT OF THE COMMISSIONERS APPOINTED TO INQUIRE INTO THE STATE OF THE LAWS AND OTHER CIRCUMSTANCES CONNECTED WITH THE SEIGNIORIAL TENURE IN LOWER CANADA / Canada. Commissioners of State of Law – Kingston: Desbarats and Derbishire, 1844. SEM105P1186 – 4mf – 9 – Can$9.00 – cn Bibl Nat [333]

REPORT OF THE COMMISSIONERS APPOINTED TO INVESTIGATE AND REPORT UPON THE BEST MEANS OF RE-ORGANIZING THE MILITIA OF CANADA, AND UPON AN IMPROVED SYSTEM OF POLICE / Canada Province – Quebec: Stewart Derbishire and George Desbarats [i.e. Desbarats] 1855. SEM105P594 – 1mf – 9 – Can$2.25 – cn Bibl Nat [355]

REPORT OF THE COMMISSIONERS FOR EXPLORING THE SAGUENAY / Bas-Canada. Commissaires pour explorer le Saguenay – Quebec: printed by Neilson and Cowan, 1829. SEM105P1284 – 3mf – 9 – Can$6.75 – cn Bibl Nat [324]

REPORT OF THE COMMISSIONERS FOR IMPROVEMENT OF THE NAVIGATION OF THE RIVER ST-LAWRENCE / Canada. Haut-Canada. Chambre d'Assemblee – Toronto: Patriot Office, 1836. SEM105P149 – 1mf – 9 – Can$2.25 – cn Bibl Nat [623]

REPORT OF THE COMMISSIONERS OF HER MAJESTY'S CUSTOMS AND EXCISE 1857-1978 – (1940-44 not publ. Coll title: British Government Publications...1801-1977, Finance) – 7r – 1 (£2,260.00 finance set of 93mf + 30r) – uk Chadwyck [336]

REPORT OF THE COMMISSIONERS OF H.M. INLAND REVENUE ON THE INLAND REVENUE 1857-1977 – (Coll title: British Government Publications...1801-1977, Finance) – 8r – 1 (£2,260.00 finance set of 93mf + 30r) – uk Chadwyck [336]

REPORT OF THE COMMISSIONERS UNDER THE PROVINCIAL STATUTES OF THE 58TH OF HIS MAJESTY, CHAP. 10 – [Quebec]: [Chambre d'Assemblee], [1819]. SEM105P1149 – 1mf – 9 – Can$2.25 – cn Bibl Nat [971]

REPORT OF THE COMMISSIONERS UNDER THE PROVINCIAL STATUTES OF THE 58TH OF HIS MAJESTY, CHAP. 10 RAPPORT DES COMMISSAIRES... – [Quebec]: [Chambre d'assemblee], [1819]. SEM105P1149 – 1mf – 9 – Can$2.25 – cn Bibl Nat [971]

REPORT OF THE ... COMMITTEE / Ghana. Education Review Committee – Accra, 1967 – 2mf – 9 – DE-435/1 – ne IDC [370]

REPORT OF THE COMMITTEE APPOINTED BY THE LAW ASSOCIATION OF PHILADELPHIA TO CONSIDER THE ADVISABILITY OF ASKING FOR LEGISLATION FOR THE ORGANIZATION OF ONE COURT OF COMMON PLEAS IN LIEU OF THE FOUR COURTS NOW EXISTING IN THE COUNTY OF PHILADELPHIA / Philadelphia Bar Association – Philadelphia: Allen, Lane & Scott 1899. 32p. LL-1394 – 1 – us L of C Photodup [340]

REPORT OF THE COMMITTEE APPOINTED BY THE LEGISLATIVE ASSEMBLY TO ENQUIRE INTO THE ADMIRALTY TARIFF OF FEES / Canada. Parlement. Assemblee legislative. Comite pour... – Quebec: John Lovell, 1853. SEM105P569 – 1mf – 9 – Can$2.25 – cn Bibl Nat [380]

REPORT OF THE COMMITTEE APPOINTED PURSUANT TO HOUSE RESOLUTIONS NOS. 429 AND 504 TO INVESTIGATE THE CONCENTRATION OF CONTROL OF MONEY AND CREDIT / U.S. Congress. House. Committee on Banking and Currency – 1913 – 4mf – 9 – $5.00f – us Ross [336]

REPORT OF THE COMMITTEE ON PATTERN CRIMINAL JURY INSTRUCTIONS – Washington: FJC, 1987 – 2mf – 9 – $3.00 – LLMC 95-337 – us L.L.M.C. [340]

REPORT OF THE COMMITTEE ON "RELIGION AND PUBLIC EDUCATION" : PRESENTED TO THE SYNOD OF NEW YORK, OF THE PRESBYTERIAN CHURCH IN THE UNITED STATES OF AMERICA, AT ITS MEETING IN AUBURN, N.Y., OCT 20, 1887 – [S.l.: s.n., 1887?] – 1mf – 9 – 0-8370-7575-0 – 1986-1575 – us A.T.L.A. [370]

REPORT OF THE COMMITTEE ON THE RIOTS IN POONA AND AHMEDNAGAR / India. Deccan Riots Commission – 2v. Bombay. 1875-76. BI-519 2 – 8 – ne IDC [324]

REPORT OF THE COMMITTEE TO WHOM HAVE BEEN REFERRED THE PETITION OF THE UNIVERSALISTS OF LOWER CANADA : RAPPORT... / Bas-Canada. Parlement. Chambre d'Assemblee. Comite Auquel ont ete Renvoyees la Petition des Universalistes du Bas-Canada – [Quebec]: [Chambre d'Assemblee], [1833] – 1mf – 9 – Can$2.25 – cn Bibl Nat [971]

REPORT OF THE COMMITTEE...THE PETITION OF AMELIE; EUGENIE DE BEAUMARCHAIS... / Chevallie, J A – Washington, D C, 1814 – 1mf – 1 – ILM-2573/1 – ne IDC [327]

REPORT OF THE CONFERENCE FOR THE ADOPTION OF A DRAFT AGREEMENT FOR THE ESTABLISHMENT OF THE INDIAN OCEAN TUNA COMMISSION : ROME, 1989 – 1989 – 55p – it F.A.O. [338]

REPORT OF THE CONFERENCE FOR THE ADOPTION OF A DRAFT AGREEMENT FOR THE ESTABLISHMENT OF THE INDIAN OCEAN TUNA COMMISSION : ROME, 1992 – 1992 – 86p – it F.A.O. [338]

REPORT OF THE CONFERENCE OF FAO : 26TH SESSION; ROME, 1991 – 1992 – 263p – it F.A.O. [630]

REPORT OF THE CONGRESS DISTRICT AGRICULTURAL SCHOOL OF GEORGIA / Georgia. University. College of Agriculture – n.1-14. 1909-25 – 1,5 – us Spaulding [630]

REPORT OF THE COUNCIL OF F.A.O. – it F.A.O. [630]

REPORT OF THE COUNCIL OF FAO : 100TH SESSION; ROME, 5-8 NOVEMBER 1991 – 1991 – 108p – it F.A.O. [630]

REPORT OF THE COUNCIL OF FAO : 101ST SESSION; ROME, 28 NOVEMBER 1991 – 1991 – 34p – it F.A.O. [630]

REPORT OF THE COUNCIL OF FAO : 102ND SESSION; ROME, NOVEMBER 1992 – 1992 – 132p – it F.A.O. [630]

REPORT OF THE COUNCIL OF FAO : 99TH SESSION; ROME, JUNE 1991 – 1991 – 200p – it F.A.O. [630]

REPORT OF THE DEVELOPMENT COMMITTEE – 1v. BNE-9603 1 – 9 – ne IDC [338]

REPORT OF THE DEVELOPMENT REVISION COMMITTEE, REVISED TEN-YEAR DEVELOPMENT PLAN, 1949-1958 / Fiji – (Legislative Council Paper no. 29, 1949). Suva. 1949 – 9 – ne IDC [338]

REPORT OF THE DIRECTOR, FOR THE YEAR ENDING 1959 / Burma. Archaeological Survey. Director – BI-1008 2 – 8 – ne IDC [930]

REPORT OF THE DIRECTOR-GENERAL, 1992-1993 – 1994 – 291p – 9 – 92-3-103067-1 – fr UNESCO [300]

REPORT OF THE DIVISION OF AGRICULTURE / Iowa State University. Agricultural Experiment Station – 1953/54-1957/58.1 reel – 1,5 – us Spaulding [630]

REPORT OF THE EAST AFRICAN PROTECTORATE / Great Britain. Labour Commission – 1912-13 – 1 – uk Microform Academic [960]

REPORT OF THE EIFAC TECHNICAL CONSULTATION ON GENETIC BROODSTOCK MANAGEMENT AND BREEDING PRACTICE OF FINFISH : LONDON, 1988 – 1988 – 20p – it F.A.O. [639]

REPORT OF THE EIFAC WORKING PARTY ON PREVENTION AND CONTROL OF BIRD PREDATION IN AQUACULTURE AND FISHERIES OPERATIONS – 1989 – 85p – it F.A.O. [639]

REPORT OF THE EIFAC WORKING PARTY ON STOCK ENHANCEMENT. HAMBURG, 1983 – 1984 – 55p – it F.A.O. [639]

REPORT OF THE EVALUATION OF SPECIAL PROPOSALS CONCERNING THE EXPANSION OF THE PRODUCTION OF THE OLIVE OIL INDUSTRY / Libya – 9 – BNE-1210 1 – ne IDC [338]

THE REPORT OF THE EVIDENCE, AND OTHER PROCEEDINGS IN PARLIAMENT RESPECTING THE INVENTION OF THE LIFE-BOAT : WITH PRACTICAL DIRECTIONS FOR THE MANAGEMENT OF LIFE-BOATS / Greathead, Henry – 1804 – 9 – $20.00 – uk Libr Preservation [355]

REPORT OF THE EXPEDITION TO HUDSON BAY AND CUMBERLAND GULF IN THE STEAMSHIP 'DIANA.' BN 443/2. 1898 / Wakeham, W – 8 – ne IDC [910]

REPORT OF THE EXPERT CONSULTATION ON FISHING VESSEL MARKING. HALIFAX, CANADA, 1985 – 1985 – 21p – it F.A.O. [639]

REPORT OF THE EXPERT CONSULTATION ON LARGE-SCALE PELAGIC DRIFTNET FISHING : ROME, 1990 – 1990 – 85p – it F.A.O. [639]

REPORT OF THE EXPERT CONSULTATION ON THE ACQUISITION OF SOCIO-ECONOMIC INFORMATION ON FISHERIES (WITH PARTICULAR REFENCE TO SMALL-SCALE FISHERIES). ROME, 1985 – 1985 – 26p – it F.A.O. [338]

REPORT OF THE EXPERT CONSULTATION ON THE MARKING OF FISHING GEAR : VICTORIA, BRITISH COLUMBIA, CANADA, 1991 – 1993 – 51p – it F.A.O. [790]

REPORT OF THE EXPERT CONSULTATION ON THE TECHNICAL SPECIFICATIONS FOR THE MARKING OF FISHING VESSELS, ROME, 1986 – 1987 – 79p – it F.A.O. [639]

REPORT OF THE EXPERT CONSULTATION ON THE USE OF MICROCOMPUTERS FOR PROCESSING STATISTICAL AND BIOLOGICAL DATA. CHAGUARAMAS, TRINIDAD AND TOBAGO, 1986 / W.E.C.A.F.C. – 1987 – 33p – it F.A.O. [000]

REPORT OF THE EXPERT CONSULTATION ON TRAINING ON THE FISHERIES INVESTMENT PROJECT CYCLE. ROME, 1986 – 1987 – 18p – it F.A.O. [332]

REPORT OF THE FAO AFRICA REGIONAL WORKSHOP ON APPLICATIONS OF GEOGRAPHICAL INFORMATION SYSTEMS AND REMOTE SENSING IN AQUACULTURE AND INLAND FISHERIES IN COOPERATION WITH UNEP/GRID : NAIROBI, 1991 – 1991 – 40p – it F.A.O. [550]

REPORT OF THE FAO ASIAN REGION WORKSHOP ON GEOGRAPHICAL INFORMATION SYSTEMS APPLICATIONS IN AQUACULTURE : BANGKOK, 1988 – 1989 – it F.A.O. [639]

REPORT OF THE FAO EXPERT CONSULTATION ON FISH TECHNOLOGY IN AFRICA : ABIDJAN, 1988 – 1989 – 51p – it F.A.O. [639]

REPORT OF THE F.A.O. EXPERT CONSULTATION ON FISH TECHNOLOGY IN AFRICA. LUSAKA, ZAMBIA, 1985 – 1985 – 24p – it F.A.O. [639]

REPORT OF THE F.A.O. GLOBAL SURVEY OF PESTICIDE SUSCEPTIBILITY OF STORED GRAIN PESTS / Champ, B R & Dyte, C E – 1976 – 297p – it F.A.O. [660]

REPORT OF THE F.A.O. WORLD CONFERENCE ON FISHERIES MANAGEMENT AND DEVELOPMENT. ROME, 1984 – 1984 – 86p – it F.A.O. [650]

REPORT OF THE FAO/DANIDA EXPERT CONSULTATION ON QUALITY ASSURANCE IN THE FISH INDUSTRY : LYNGBY, DENMARK, 1991 – 1992 – 42p – it F.A.O. [338]

REPORT OF THE F.A.O./E.C.A.F.E. EXPERT GROUP ON SELECTED ASPECTS OF AGRICULTURAL PLANNING IN ASIA AND THE FAR EAST – 1975 – 62p – it F.A.O. [338]

REPORT OF THE F.A.O./SEAFDEC WORKSHOP ON SHARED STOCKS IN SOUTHEAST ASIA. BANGKOK, 1985 – 1985 – 103p – it F.A.O. [639]

REPORT OF THE F.A.O./UNEP MEETING ON THE EFFECTS OF POLLUTION ON MARINE ECOSYSTEMS. BLANES, SPAIN, 1985 – 1986 – 25p – it F.A.O. [574]

REPORT OF THE F.A.O./UNEP MEETING ON THE TOXICITY AND BIOACCUMULATION OF SELECTED SUBSTANCES IN MARINE ORGANISM. ROVINJ, YUGOSLAVIA, 1984 – 1985 – 26p – it F.A.O. [639]

REPORT OF THE FAO/UNEP/WHO/IOC/IAEA MEETING ON THE BIOGEOCHEMICAL CYCLE OF MERCURY IN THE MEDITERRANEAN. SIENA, ITALY, 1984 – 1985 – 21p – it F.A.O. [574]

REPORT OF THE FIRST PHASE OF THE HOUSEHOLD SAMPLE SURVEY. REPORT ON THE SECOND PHASE OF HOUSEHOLD SAMPLE SURVEY / Libya. Ministry of Planning. Census and Statistical Department – Tripoli and Benghazi. 5 papers. BNE-613 1 – 9 – ne IDC [339]

REPORT OF THE FULTON COMMISSION 1963 / Hong Kong – Hong Kong, 1963 – 2mf – 9 – DE-163/1 – ne IDC [370]

REPORT OF THE GFCM-ICCAT EXPERT CONSULTATION ON EVALUATION OF STOCKS OF LARGE PELAGIC FISHES IN THE MEDITERRANEAN AREA : BARI, ITALY, 1990 – 1991 – 293p – it F.A.O. [639]

REPORT OF THE GOVERNOR OF BANK INDONESIA FOR THE FINANCIAL YEAR 1953-1967 – Djakarta, 1953-67 – 46mf – 9 – SE-262/1 – ne IDC [336]

REPORT OF THE HACKNEY CHINESE ASSOCIATION, IN AID OF THE MEDICAL MISSIONARY SOCIETY IN CHINA – Hackney, 1845 – 1mf – 9 – ne IDC [610]

REPORT OF THE HIGH COMMISSIONER ON THE ADMINISTRATION OF PALESTINE, 1920-1925 / Great Britain. Colonial Office. Palestine – London. 1925. BJ-28-108 1 – 9 – ne IDC [956]

REPORT OF THE HOME AND FOREIGN MISSIONS OF THE UNITED METHODIST FREE CHURCHES – (Missing: 1868/1869-1874/1875) – London, 1867/1868-1931/1932 – 188mf – 9 – H-2745/1 – ne IDC [240]

REPORT OF THE INAUGURAL MEETING OF THE LEAGUE: HELD ON WEDNESDAY, JANUARY 29TH, 1896, AT THE MANSION HOUSE / British Empire League – London: Spottiswoode, 1892? 00298. (Pre-1900 Canadiana) – 9 – cn C.I.H.M. [941]

REPORT OF THE INDIAN IMMIGRANTS COMMISSION, 1885-87 / Natal. Indian Immigrants Commission – Pietermaritzburg: P Davis, 1887 – us Res Libr [304]

REPORT OF THE INDO-PACIFIC FISHERY COMMISSION EXPERT CONSULTATION ON INLAND FISHERIES OF THE LARGER INDO-PACIFIC ISLANDS. BANGKOK, 1986 / IPFC – 1986 – 27p – it F.A.O. [338]

REPORT OF THE INDUSTRIAL CENSUS, 1964 / Libya. Ministry of Economy and Trade. Census and Statistical Department – Tripoli. BNE-1201 1 – 9 – ne IDC [338]

REPORT OF THE INDUSTRIAL COMMITTEE / Egypt. Ministry of Commerce and Industry – 1948. BNE-4656 1 – 9 – ne IDC [380]

REPORT OF THE INSURANCE COMMISSIONER OF CALIFORNIA / California. Dept. of Insurance – First, 1868-1978. 524 fiches. (Harvard Law School Library Collection.) – 9 – $1.50f – us H.U. Law [336]

REPORT OF THE INTERNATIONAL POLAR EXPEDITION TO POINT BARROW, ALASKA / Ray, P H – BN 367 2. 1885 – 8 – ne IDC [910]

REPORT OF THE IVES MINE: BOULTON TOWNSHIP, P.Q / Chapman, Edward John – Toronto, 1869?. 00626. (Pre-1900 Canadiana) – 9 – cn C.I.H.M. [622]

REPORT OF THE JOINT FAO/WHO TECHNICAL MEETING ON METHODS OF PLANNING AND EVALUATION IN APPLIED NUTRITION PROGRAMS; ROME, 1965 – 1968 – 77p – it F.A.O. [640]

REPORT [OF] THE JOINT HIGHER EDUCATION ENTRANCE EXAMINATION 1967/68-1975/76 / Thailand. Office of the National Education Council – (In Thai and English) – 1967-1979 – 31mf – 9 – DE-275/1 – ne IDC [370]

A REPORT OF THE KINGDOM OF CONGO, AND OF THE SURROUNDING COUNTRIES.. / Lopes, Duarte – Trans. and ed. by Margarite Hutchinson. London: J. Murray, 1881. xxi, 174p. 2 fold. maps – 1 – us U.W. Library [960]

REPORT OF THE LADIES'AUXILIARY OF THE WESLEYAN METHODIST MISSIONARY SOCIETY – (Cont as: Report of the Womens's Auxiliary of the Wesleyan Methodist Missionary Society. London, 1893-1915. Missing: 1898; 1900(p255-End)) – London, 1881-92 – 85mf – 9 – H-275/1 – ne IDC [240]

REPORT OF THE LAND CASES, JUNE 1853-JUNE 1858 : U.S. DISTRICT COURT OF NO. CALIFORNIA / Hoffman, Ogden – San Francisco, CA. 1862 – 1r – 1 – $50.00 – B50526 – us Library Micro [340]

REPORT OF THE MASS EDUCATION DEPARTMENT, INDONESIA / Indonesia. Djawatan Pendidikan Masjarakat – SE-475 1. 1953-1954. Lacking: 1954 – 9 – ne IDC [370]

THE REPORT OF THE MEETING OF WORKINGMEN IN THE CITY OF WHEELING, VA, ON FORMING A SETTLEMENT IN THE STATE OF ILLINOIS – no publisher, 1830 – 1r – 1 – us Western Res [331]

REPORT OF THE MINISTER OF FINANCE ON THE RECIPROCITY TREATY WITH THE UNITED STATES, ALSO... / Canada. Departement des finances – Quebec: Stewart Derbishire and George Desbarats, 1862. SEM105P1520 – 1mf – 9 – Can$2.25 – cn Bibl Nat [380]

REPORT OF THE NATIONAL COMMISSION ON CIVIL DISORDER : KERNER REPORT – Mar 1968 – 1r – 1 – $50.00 – B50560 – us Library Micro [320]

REPORT OF THE OPERATIONS AND DUTIES OF THE SIGNAL DEPARTMENT OF THE ARMY / Myer, Albert James – 1860-65 – 1r – 1 – us Ross [355]

REPORT OF THE ORDINARY GENERAL MEETING / Egypt. Industrial Bank – 5v. in 2. 1955-59. BNE-4635 1 – 9 – ne IDC [330]

REPORT OF THE POST-WAR DEVELOPMENT COMMITTEE (1946-1955) / Nyasaland. Development Committee – D-1405 1. 1946 – 9 – ne IDC [338]

REPORT OF THE PRELIMINARY ASSISTANCE MISSION TO SUDAN / International Atomic Energy Agency – 1960. BNE-7652 1 – 9 – ne IDC [338]

REPORT OF THE PRELIMINARY SURVEY OF WHOLESALE AND RETAIL TRADE IN TRIPOLI TOWN / Libya. Ministry of Economy and Trade. Census and Statistical Department – Jun 1967. BNE-608 1 – 9 – ne IDC [338]

REPORT OF THE PREPARATORY COMMITTEE FOR THE U.N. CONFERENCE ON ENVIRONMENT AND DEVELOPMENT / United Nations – 9 – in prep – us U.N. Pubs [360]

REPORT OF THE PRESIDENT OF THE JAVA BANK ON MARCH 10TH, 1948 AND JULY 9TH, 1949 / Javasche Bank – SE-11,956 1 – 9 – ne IDC [950]

REPORT OF THE PROCEEDINGS AT THE REUNION CONFERENCE : HELD AT BONN ON SEPTEMBER 14, 15, AND 16, 1874 / Reusch – London: Rivingtons, 1875 – 1mf – us A.T.L.A. [240]

REPORT OF THE PROCEEDINGS OF THE 24TH ANNUAL CONVENTION / Zionist Organization of America – New York. 1921. BJ-28-52 1 – 9 – ne IDC [956]

REPORT OF THE PROCEEDINGS... PRESENTATION TO JOHN CRUCE NORTON / Madras Native Association – Madras: Scottish Press, 1860. 99p – 1 – us U.W. Library [950]

REPORT OF THE PUNJAB MISSIONARY CONFERENCE : HELD AT LAHORE IN DECEMBER AND JANUARY, 1862-63 – (Includes index and glossary of Indian words) – Lodiana: American Presbyterian Mission Press, 1863 – 1mf – 9 – 0-8370-6695-6 – 1986-0695 – us A.T.L.A. [240]

REPORT OF THE QUEBEC LUNATIC ASYLUM ADDRESSED TO THE...PRIME MINISTER OF THE PROVINCE OF QUEBEC BY THE MEDICAL SUPERINTENDANTS / Quebec. Province. Asile d'Alienes de Quebec – Quebec Lunatic Asylum, 187-? SEM105P617 – 12mf – 9 – Can$27.00 – cn Bibl Nat [971]

REPORT OF THE REORGANIZATION COMMISSION OF THE EXECUTIVE OF THE ZIONIST ORGANIZATION ON THE WORK OF THE ZIONIST ORGANIZATION IN PALESTINE / World Zionist Organization – New York. 1921. BJ-28-48 1 – 9 – ne IDC [956]

REPORT OF THE SELECT COMMITEE, ON THE PUBLIC ACCOUNTS OF THE PROVINCE, FROM THE COMMENCEMENT OF THE CONSTITUTION IN 1791, UNTIL 1822, INCLUSIVE / Bas-Canada. Parlement. Chambre d'Assemblee. Comite special sur les comptes publics de la Province – [Quebec]: [Chambre d'assemblee], [1823]. SEM105P1162 – 2mf – 9 – Can$4.50 – cn Bibl Nat [336]

REPORT OF THE SELECT COMMITTEE 1909 / Cape of Good Hope. South Africa. Parliament – Cape Town: Printed by S. Solomon. Consists of monographic reports issued by the various select committees appointed by the House – 1 – us U.W. Library [960]

REPORT OF THE SELECT COMMITTEE 1856-1909 / Cape of Good Hope. South Africa. Parliament. Legislative Council – Cape Town: Cape Times Ltd, etc.. Consists of monographic reports issued by the various select committees appointed by the Council – 1 – us U.W. Library [323]

REPORT OF THE SELECT COMMITTEE APPOINTED TO ENQUIRE INTO THE CAUSES OF EMIGRATION FROM CANADA TO THE UNITED STATES OF AMERICA OR ELSEWHERE / Canada. Select Committee on Emmigration – Toronto: John Lovell, [1857]. SEM105P1436 – 2mf – 9 – Can$4.50 – cn Bibl Nat [304]

REPORT OF THE SELECT COMMITTEE APPOINTED TO INQUIRE AND REPORT SIC UPON THE PRESENT SYSTEM OF MANAGEMENT OF THE PUBLIC LANDS / Canada. Parliament. Legislative Assembly. Select Committee – Quebec: Printed by Lovell and Lamoureux, 1855. SEM105P208 – 3mf – 9 – Can$6.75 – cn Bibl Nat [333]

REPORT OF THE SELECT COMMITTEE OF THE LEGISLATIVE ASSEMBLY INTO THE CAUSES AND IMPORTANCE OF THE EMIGRATION... / Select Committee of the Legislative Assembly – Montreal: Rollo Campbell, 1849. SEM105P1635 – 1mf – 9 – Can$2.25 – cn Bibl Nat [304]

REPORT OF THE SELECT COMMITTEE OF THE LEGISLATIVE ASSEMBLY OF THE PROVINCE OF QUEBEC ON PUBLIC LANDS AND FORESTS / Quebec Province. Legislature. Assemblee legislative – [Quebec]: [s.n.], 1895. SEM105P581 – 3mf – 9 – Can$6.75 – cn Bibl Nat [630]

REPORT OF THE SELECT COMMITTEE OF THE LEGISLATIVE ASSEMBLY, QUEBEC ON THE WINTER NAVIGATION OF THE RIVER AND GULF ST LAWRENCE / Quebec. Legislature. Assemblee legislative. Comite... – [Quebec]: [s.n.], [1875]. SEM105P542 – 1mf – 9 – Can$2.25 – cn Bibl Nat [380]

REPORT OF THE SELECT COMMITTEE ON IMMIGRATION / Canada. Parlement. Conseil legislatif. Select Committee on Immigration – Quebec: Hunter, Rose & Lemieux, [1864]. SEM105P562 – 1mf – 9 – Can$2.25 – cn Bibl Nat [304]

REPORT OF THE SELECT COMMITTEE ON THE GEOLOGICAL SURVEY / Canada Province. Parlement – Quebec: printed by Lovell & Lamoureux..., 1855. SEM105P210 – 1mf – 9 – Can$2.25 – cn Bibl Nat [550]

REPORT OF THE SELECT COMMITTEE TO WHOM WAS REFERRED THE ANNUAL REPORT OF THE CHIEF EMIGRATION AGENT, AND SUPPLEMENTARY REPORT OF THE GERMAN ASSISTANT AT QUEBEC / Canada. Select Committee on Emmigration – Quebec: Thompson and Co, 1860. SEM105P589 – 1mf – 9 – Can$2.25 – cn Bibl Nat [323]

REPORT OF THE SELECT COMMITTEE...APPOINTED TO INQUIRE WHETHER ANY, AND WHAT MEASURERS CAN BE ADOPTED, TO REPRESS THE EVILS OF INTEMPERANCE / Canada. Parliament. Legislative Assembly. Select Committee – Montreal: Lovell and Gibson, 1849. SEM105P205 – 1mf – 9 – Can$2.25 – cn Bibl Nat [360]

REPORT OF THE SEMINAR ON AGRICULTURAL PERSPECTIVE PLANNING. ISLAMABAD, 1977 – 1977 2nd print 1983 – 588p – it F.A.O. [350]

REPORT OF THE SPECIAL COMMITTEE, APPOINTED TO CONSIDER AND REPORT WHETHER THE PRESENT DELAY AND UNCERTAINTY IN JUDICIAL ADMINISTRATION CAN BE LESSENED. / American Bar Association – n. p. 1885? 39 p. LL-1218 – 1 – us L of C Photodup [340]

REPORT OF THE SPECIAL COMMITTEE OF THE HOUSE OF ASSEMBLY ON THE POST OFFICE DEPARTMENT IN THE PROVINCE OF LOWER CANADA / Canada. Parliament. House of Assembly – [S.l: s.n, 1832 ?]. SEM105P1788 – 1mf – 9 – Can$2.25 – cn Bibl Nat [380]

REPORT OF THE SPECIAL COMMITTEE ON COLONISATION / Canada. Parlement. Assemblee legislative. Comite special sur la colonisation – Quebec: Thompson & Co, 1860. SEM105P215 – 1mf – 9 – Can$2.25 – cn Bibl Nat [971]

REPORT OF THE SPECIAL COMMITTEE ON COLONIZATION / Canada. Parliament. Legislative Assembly. Committee – Quebec: Thompson & Co, 1860. SEM105P215 – 1mf – 9 – Can$2.25 – cn Bibl Nat [323]

REPORT OF THE SPECIAL COMMITTEE TO WHOM WAS REFERRED THAT PART OF HIS EXCELLENCY'S SPEECH WHICH REFERRED TO THE ORGANIZATION OF THE MILITIA / Bas-Canada. Parlement. Chambre d'assemblee – Quebec: printed by Neilson and Cowan, 1829. SEM105P1790 – 3mf – 9 – Can$6.75 – cn Bibl Nat [355]

REPORT OF THE SPECIAL COMMITTEE TO WHOM WAS REFERRED THE BILL TO REGULATE THE PILOTAGE IS AND BELOW THE PORT OF QUEBEC / Canada. Parliament. Legislative Assembly – Quebec: John Lovell, 1853. SEM105P574 – 1mf – 9 – Can$2.25 – cn Bibl Nat [380]

REPORT OF THE SPECIAL COMMITTEE TO WHOM WAS REFERRED THE PETITION OF WIDOW JACQUES P. SAVEUSE DE BEAUJEU AND GEORGE R. SAVEUSE DE BEAUJEU,... – [Quebec]: [s.n.], [1836] – 3mf – 9 – Can$6.75 – cn Bibl Nat [971]

REPORT OF THE STANDING COMMITTEE OF EDUCATION AND SCHOOLS / Bas-Canada. Parlement. Chambre d'assemblee. Comite permanent sur l'education et des ecoles – [Quebec]: [s.n.], [1831]. SEM105P1151 – 4mf – 9 – Can$9.00 – cn Bibl Nat [370]

REPORT OF THE STATE OF THE PRINCIPAL MUSEUMS IN CANADA AND NEWFOUNDLAND / Ami, Henry Marc – London? 1897? 02397. (Pre-1900 Canadiana) – 9 – cn C.I.H.M. [971]

REPORT OF THE STUDY GROUP ON THE CASELOAD OF THE SUPREME COURT – Washington: Administrative Office of the U.S. Courts, Dec 1972 – 1mf – 9 – $1.50 – LLMC 95-357 – us L.L.M.C. [340]

REPORT OF THE SUPERINTENDANT OF EDUCATION FOR LOWER CANADA, FOR THE YEAR 1846 / Canada. Bas-Canada. Bureau de l'Education – Montreal: Printed by Lovell and Gibson, 1847. SEM105P939 – 1mf – 9 – Can$2.25 – cn Bibl Nat [971]

REPORT OF THE SUPERINTENDENT, FOR THE YEAR ENDING 31ST MARCH, 1924 / Burma. Archaeological Survey. Superintendent – Rangoon. 1924-26 – 7mf – 8 – ne IDC [930]

REPORT OF THE SUPERINTENDENT OF BANKS RELATIVE TO SAVINGS AND LOAN ASSOCIATIONS, SAVINGS AND LOAN BANK OF THE STATE OF NEW YORK AND CREDIT UNIONS / New York. Banking Dept – 1890-1939. 351 fiches. (Harvard Law School Library Collection.) – 9 – $1.50f – us H.U. Law [336]

REPORT OF THE SUPERINTENDENT OF BANKS RELATIVE TO SAVINGS BANKS, INVESTMENT COMPANIES, SAFE DEPOSIT COMPANIES AND LICENSED LENDERS / New York. Banking Dept – 1857-1939. 469 fiches. (Harvard Law School Library Collection.) – 9 – 1.50f – us H.U. Law [336]

REPORT OF THE SUPERINTENDENT OF EDUCATION FOR LOWER CANADA FOR. / Canada. Bas-Canada. Bureau de l'Education – Quebec: John Lovell, 1852-68. 1850/51-1866. SEM105P616 – 25mf – 9 – Can$56.25 – cn Bibl Nat [971]

REPORT OF THE SUPERINTENDENT OF EDUCATION FOR LOWER CANADA, FOR THE YEAR 1846 / Canada Province. Bureau de l'education (Bas-Canada) – [Montreal]: [printed by Lovell and Gibson], [1847]. SEM105P939 – 1mf – 9 – Can$2.25 – cn Bibl Nat [370]

REPORT OF THE SURVEY OF LICENSED CONSTRUCTION UNITS / Libya – 1968. BNE-1105 1 – 9 – ne IDC [333]

REPORT OF THE SYMPOSIUM ON AQUACULTURE IN AFRICA. SUPPLEMENT 1 : REVIEWS AND EXPERIENCE PAPERS, ACCRA, 1975 – 1976 – 794p – it F.A.O. [639]

REPORT OF THE SYMPOSIUM ON HABITAT MODIFICATION AND FRESHWATER FISHERIES. AARHUS, DENMARK, 1984 – 1984 – 43p – it F.A.O. [639]

REPORT OF THE SYMPOSIUM ON NEW DEVELOPMENT IN THE UTILIZATION OF HEATED EFFLUENTS AND OF RECIRCULATION SYSTEMS FOR INTENSIVE AQUACULTURE : STAVANGER, NORWAY, 1980 – 1981 – 44p – it F.A.O. [639]

REPORT OF THE SYMPOSIUM ON PRODUCTION ENHANCEMENT IN STILLWATER POND CULTURE – 1990 – 57p – it F.A.O. [639]

REPORT OF THE SYMPOSIUM ON SELECTION, HYBRIDIZATION AND GENETIC ENGINEERING IN AQUACULTURE OF FISH AND SHELLFISH FOR CONSUMPTION AND STOCKING. BORDEAUX, FRANCE, 1986 – 1987 – 64p – it F.A.O. [639]

REPORT OF THE SYMPOSIUM ON STOCK ENHANCEMENT IN THE MANAGEMENT OF FRESHWATER FISHERIES. BUDAPEST, 1982 – 1982 – 48p – it F.A.O. [636]

REPORT OF THE SYRIAN CHAMBER OF DEPUTIES REGARDING THE FINANCIAL STATE OF THE NATION DURING TEN YEARS / Syria. Ministry of Finance – 4v in 2. 1954-58. BNE-9719 1 – 9 – ne IDC [336]

REPORT OF THE TECHNICAL CONSULTATION ON FISHING TECHNOLOGY AND ITS SOCIO-ECONOMIC ASPECTS. ANCONA, 1986 / G.F.C.M. – 1986 – 96p – it F.A.O. [639]

REPORT OF THE TECHNICAL CONSULTATION ON HIGH SEAS FISHING : ROME, 1992 – 1993 – 95p – it F.A.O. [636]

REPORT OF THE TECHNICAL CONSULTATION ON METHODS OF EVALUATING SMALL-SCALE FISHERIES IN THE EASTERN MEDITERRANEAN. SETE, FRANCE, 1986 / G.F.C.M. – 1986 – 165p – it F.A.O. [639]

REPORT OF THE TECHNICAL CONSULTATION ON OPEN SEA SHELLFISH CULTURE IN ASSOCIATION WITH ARTIFICIAL REEFS. ANCONA, ITALY, 1986 / G.F.C.M. – 1986 – 185p 1630 92-5-002455-X – it F.A.O. [639]

REPORT OF THE TECHNICAL CONSULTATION ON STOCK ASSESSMENT IN THE EASTERN MEDITERRANEAN. ROME, 1986 / G.F.C.M. – 1986 – 142p – it F.A.O. [639]

REPORT OF THE TECHNICAL CONSULTATION ON THE ALLOCATION OF FISHERY RESOURCES : VICHY, FRANCE, 1980 – 1981 – 52p – it F.A.O. [333]

REPORT OF THE TRIAL AND PRELIMINARY PROCEEDINGS IN THE CASE OF THE QUEEN ON THE PROSECUTION OF G. ACHILLI V. DR. NEWMAN : WITH AN INTRODUCTION CONTAINTING COMMENTS ON THE LAW AND ON THE COURSE AND CONDUCT OF THE TRIAL / Finlason, W F – London: C. Dolman, 1852 – 1mf – us A.T.L.A. [340]

A REPORT OF THE TRIALS OF THE CARAVATS AND SHANAVESTS, AT THE SPECIAL COMMISSION, FOR THE SEVERAL COUNTIES OF TIPPERARY, WATERFORD, AND KILKENNY. / Kerwick, Andrew – Dublin, Hibernia Press Office, 1811. 88 p. LL-2253 – 1 – us L of C Photodup [340]

REPORT OF THE WOMEN'S AUXILIARY OF THE WESLEYAN METHODIST MISSIONARY SOCIETY *see* REPORT OF THE LADIES'AUXILIARY OF THE WESLEYAN METHODIST MISSIONARY SOCIETY

REPORT OF THE WORKING PARTY ON PRE-VOCATIONAL EDUCATION OF THE FUNCTIONAL COMMITTEE ON VOCATIONAL TRAINING JANUARY 1970 / Hong Kong. Industrial Training Advisory Committe – Hong Kong, 1972 – 1mf – 9 – DE-178/1 – ne IDC [370]

REPORT OF THE WORKING PARTY SET UP TO REVIEW THE SECONDARY SCHOOL PLACES ALLOCATION SYSTEM 5TH JANUARY 1981 / Hong Kong – Hong Kong, 1981 – 1mf – 9 – DE-186/1 – ne IDC [370]

REPORT OF THE WORKSHOP ON AQUACULTURE PLANNING IN THE SADCC COUNTRIES – 1986 – 27p – it F.A.O. [338]

REPORT OF THE WORKSHOP ON FISHERIES DEVELOPMENT PLANNING IN THE W.E.C.A.F.C. REGION. CASTRIES, SAINT LUCIA, 1985 – 1986 – 23p – it F.A.O. [338]

REPORT OF THE WORKSHOP ON FISHERY CREDIT AND MARKETING DEVELOPMENT : BANGKOK, 1989 – 1990 – 91p – it F.A.O. [332]

REPORT OF THE WORKSHOP ON THE USE OF LENGTH-FREQUENCY DATA FOR THE ASSESSMENT OF FISHERY RESOURCES OF THE CARIBBEAN ISLANDS : TROIS-ILETS, MARTINIQUE, 1991 / W.E.C.A.F.C. – 1992 – 49p – it F.A.O. [639]

REPORT OF UNITED KINGDOM TRADE MISSION TO EGYPT, THE SUDAN AND ETHIOPIA, FEBRUARY 1955 / Great Britain. Board of Trade – BNE-7645 1 – 9 – ne IDC [380]

REPORT OF VISITS PAID BY DR. WALTER T. LORCH TO LIBRAIRIES OF UNIVERSITIES AND SCIENTIFIC INSTITUTES IN DJAKARTA, BOGOR AND BANDUNG, DURING HIS STAY IN INDONESIA / Winarti, Partaningrat – SE 11,368 1. Dec. 29, 1960-Jan. 8, 1961 – 9 – ne IDC [020]

REPORT ON 4TH ROUND OF STATUS NEGOTIATIONS : HELD IN KOROR, PALAU, TO THE 4TH CONG OF MICRONESIA, 2ND SESS / Joint Committee on Future Status [TTPI (U.S.)] – n.p, n.d, submitted apr 1972 – 1mf – 9 – $1.50 – LLMC 82-100F, Title 43 – us L.L.M.C. [323]

REPORT ON 7TH ROUND OF STATUS NEGOTIATIONS : HELD IN WASHINGTON, D.C. / Joint Committee on Future Status [TTPI (U.S.)] – Saipan: Joint Committee on Future Status, jan 1974 – 2mf – 9 – $3.00 – LLMC 82-100F, Title 56 – us L.L.M.C. [323]

REPORT ON 8TH ROUND OF STATUS NEGOTIATIONS : HELD IN SAIPAN, TO THE 6TH CONG OF MICRONESIA, 2ND SPEC SESS / Joint Committee on Future Status [TTPI (U.S.)] – Saipan: Joint Committee on Future Status, jun 1976 – 3mf – 9 – $4.50 – LLMC 82-100F, Title 58 – us L.L.M.C. [323]

REPORT ON A GENERAL SCHEME OF IMPROVEMENTS FOR THE HARBOUR / Harbour Commissioners of Montreal. Commission of Engineers – Montreal?, 1877. 02089. (Pre-1900 Canadiana) – 9 – cn C.I.H.M. [627]

REPORT ON A SOCIAL SURVEY OF SEKONDI-TAKORADI / Busia, Kofi Abrefa – London: Publ by the Crown Agents for the Colonies, 1950 – us Res Libr [960]

REPORT ON A STUDY OF THE PRINTING INDUSTRY OF INDONESIA, INCLUDING THE R.I. GOVERNMENT PRINTING OFFICE AND RELATED RECOMMENDATIONS / McWhorter, Julian H – SE-3511 1. 1961 – 9 – ne IDC [070]

REPORT ON A SURVEY AND RECOMMENDATIONS FOR THE ESTABLISHMENT OF A NATIONAL LIBRARY SERVICE IN INDONESIA / Indonesia. Library service – A.G.W. Dunningham and R. Patah. 1953. SE-2257-1 – 9 – ne IDC [020]

REPORT ON A SYSTEM OF PUBLIC ELEMENTARY INSTRUCTION FOR UPPER CANADA / Ryerson, Adolphus Egerton – Montreal: Lovell and Gibson, 1846. SEM105P328 – 1mf – 9 – Can$2.25 – cn Bibl Nat [370]

REPORT ON A SYSTEM OF PUBLIC ELEMENTARY INSTRUCTION FOR UPPER CANADA / Ryerson, Adolphus Egerton – Montreal: Lovell and Gibson, 1847. SEM105P329 – 3mf – 9 – Can$6.75 – cn Bibl Nat [370]

REPORT ON AGRICULTURAL RESEARCH / Iowa State University. Agricultural Experiment Station – 1915-40 – 1,5 – us Spaulding [630]

REPORT ON AGRICULTURE CENSUS, 1965 / Jordan. Department of Statistics – 1967. BNE-9778 1 – 9 – ne IDC [310]

REPORT ON ALL THE HOLKHAM ESTATES / Keary, W H – 1851 – 1 – uk Microform Academic [650]

REPORT ON AN ILO CONTRIBUTION TO TRAINING PROGRAMMES FOR LABOUR ADMINISTRATION OFFICIALS IN IRAQ, JORDAN, LIBYA AND SYRIA / International Labour Organisation – Training in the field of Labour Inspection (Jul-Dec 1962). Geneva. 1963. Project report in the form of a conference report on a series of I.L.O. meetings on vocational training of public servants concerned with labour inspection in the Near and Middle East Countries of Libya, Syria, Iraq and Jordan. Tripoli, 1962, Oct 3-18, Conf.-Damascus 1962, Oct 21 to Nov 8 Conf.-Bagdad 1962, Nov 15-29, Conf.-Aman 1962, Dec 2-13, Conf. Ed. by A. Abdeljaouad. BNE-907 1 – 9 – ne IDC [331]

REPORT ON BRITISH NORTH BORNEO FROM 1 JUL TO 31 DEC 1882 / Treacher, W H – 1883 – 1 – uk Microform Academic [910]

REPORT ON BUSINESS – (Back Files are available for $85.00r Vesicular $99.00r Negative or Positive Silver) – 1 – $575.00 Vesicular $700.00 Negative or Positive Silver – cn Globe Info [650]

REPORT ON BUSINESS MAGAZINE – (Back Files are available for $85.00r Vesicular $99.00r Negative or Positive Silver) – 1,9 – $70.00y mf; $100.00y reel – cn Globe Info [650]

REPORT ON BUSINESS MANAGEMENT TRAINING IN INDONESIA / Panglaykim, J – SE-2192 1. 1959? – 9 – ne IDC [380]

REPORT ON CERTAIN ECONOMIC QUESTIONS IN THE ENGLISH AND DUTCH COLONIES IN THE ORIENT / U.S. Bureau of Insular Affairs – Reel 4006. 1902 – 1 – ja CEACS [330]

REPORT ON CONDITION OF WOMAN AND CHILD WAGE-EARNERS IN THE UNITED STATES / U.S. Department of Labor – (Studies which "investigate and report on the industrial, social, moral, educational, and physical condition of woman and child workers in the United States.") v1-19. 1910-12 – 1 – $295.00 – 0-89093-002-3 – us UPA [331]

REPORT ON CONVEYANCE / British Association for the Advancement of Science. Canada – Montreal: Gazette, 1884. 02834. (Pre-1900 Canadiana) – 9 – cn C.I.H.M. [971]

REPORT ON CO-OPERATION IN THE FEDERATION OF MALAYA / Surridge, Brewster Joseph – Reel 4001. 1955 – 1 – ja CEACS [950]

REPORT ON COPYRIGHT: ADOPTED AT A MEETING...HELD AT THE CANADIAN INSTITUTE, TORONTO, ON MONDAY EVENING, MARCH 13, 1899 / Canadian Society of Authors – Toronto?, 1899? 00453. (Pre-1900 Canadiana) – 9 – cn C.I.H.M. [070]

REPORT ON DEVELOPMENT AND WELFARE, 1947 / Gambia – Bathurst. 1948. BD-1302 1 – 9 – ne IDC [338]

REPORT ON DEVELOPMENT AND WELFARE, 1948 / Gambia – Bathurst. 1949 – 9 – ne IDC [338]

REPORT ON DEVELOPMENT AND WELFARE, 1949 / Gambia – Bathurst. 1950 – 9 – ne IDC [338]

REPORT ON DOCKYARD MAKASAR / Masduki, W – SE-10,827 1. 1959 – 9 – ne IDC [380]

REPORT ON ECONOMIC DEVELOPMENT PLAN, 1958-1967 / Syria. Economic Development Organization – Syrian region. 1959 – 9 – ne IDC [338]

REPORT ON ECONOMIC UTILISATION OF ENERGY AVAILABLE FROM THE ASWAN DAM AND NILE BARRAGES HYDROELECTRIC SCHEMES / Egypt. Hydro-Electric Power Commission – Abdel Aziz Bey Ahmed. BNE-4632 1 – 9 – ne IDC [333]

REPORT ON EDUCATION FOR THE YEAR 1964-1977 / Rhodesia. Ministry of Education. European, Asian and Coloured Division of Education – Salisbury – 20mf – 9 – DE-503/1 – ne IDC [370]

REPORT ON EDUCATION IN BARBADOS FOR THE PERIOD 1978-1982 / Barbados. Ministry of Education and Culture – Barbados – 4mf – 9 – DE-515/1 – ne IDC [370]

REPORT ON EDUCATION IN LOWER CANADA, FOLLOWED BY STATISTICAL TABLES FOR THE SCHOOL YEAR. / Canada. Bas-Canada. Bureau de l'Education – Toronto: Lovell and Gibson, 1851. SEM105P944 – 1mf – 9 – Can$2.25 – cn Bibl Nat [971]

REPORT ON EGYPT'S FOREIGN TRADE / Egypt. Ministry of Commerce and Industry – 1952. BNE-4655 1 – 9 – ne IDC [380]

REPORT ON ELECTRIC POWER DEVELOPMENT IN SUDAN / MerzMacLellan (Consulting Engineers) – London. 2 v. 1963. BNE-7663 1 – 9 – ne IDC [624]

REPORT ON EXPLORATIONS IN THE LABRADOR PENINSULA / Low, A P – BN-296 2. 1896 – 8 – ne IDC [910]

REPORT ON FIELD WORK IN NORTH-CENTRAL AND NORTH AUSTRALIA 1934-1935 / Stanner, W E H – 1979 – 106p on 2mf – 9 – A$1.50 – at Aboriginal [305]

REPORT ON FIRST YEAR TRIAL OF THE INTEGRATED SCIENCE PROJECT 1973-1974 / Hong Kong. Education Department. Science Subject Section – Hong Kong, 1974 – 5mf – 9 – DE-176/1 – ne IDC [370]

REPORT ON FULFILLMENT OF THE CHINESE NATIONAL ECONOMIC PLAN...IN 1955 / China. People's Republic. Statistical Bureau – Peking, Foreign Language Press. 1956. BD-510 1 – 9 – ne IDC [310]

REPORT ON INDONESIA / Republic of Indonesian Office – (Irregular. Missing v11(Sept-Dec) 1962) – New York, 1949-1964 – 69mf – 9 – SE-1133/1 – ne IDC [950]

REPORT ON INDUSTRIAL DEVELOPMENT FOR INDONESIA,BY RALF W. DUNKLE. SE 11,599/1. 1959 / U.S. Operations Mission to Indonesia – 9 – ne IDC [338]

REPORT ON INSURANCE ACTIVITIES IN THE LIBYAN ARAB REPUBLIC, 1967/1969- / Libya. Ministry of Economy. Insurance Department – Tripoli. 1971? BNE-716 1 – 9 – ne IDC [360]

REPORT ON IRRIGATION IN CEYLON / Keane, John – Colombo: G J A Skeen, 1905 – us Res Libr [333]

REPORT ON LABOUR AND INDUSTRIAL SURVEY IN THE KINGDOM (JORDAN) / Jordan. Department of Statistics – 1957. BNE-9776 1 – 9 – ne IDC [310]

REPORT ON LAND TENURE : NIGER PROVINCE / Cole, C W – [Kaduna, Nigeria, 1952] – us Res Libr [333]

REPORT ON MORAL INSTRUCTION (GENERAL AND DENOMINATIONAL) AND ON MORAL TRAINING : IN THE SCHOOLS OF AUSTRIA, BELGIUM, THE BRITISH EMPIRE, CHINA, DENMARK,... / Spiller, Gustav – London: Watts, 1909 – 1mf – 9 – 0-8370-7590-4 – 1986-1590 – us A.T.L.A. [370]

REPORT ON NATIONAL ECONOMIC DEVELOPMENT AND FULFILLMENT OF THE STATE PLAN IN 1954 / China. People's Republic. Statistical Bureau – Peking, Foreign Language Press. 1956. BD-509 1 – 9 – ne IDC [310]

REPORT ON NATURAL RESOURCES FOR FOOD AND AGRICULTURE IN LATIN AMERICA AND THE CARIBBEAN – 1986 – 108p – it F.A.O. [333]

REPORT ON NATURAL RESOURCES FOR FOOD AND AGRICULTURE IN THE ASIA AND PACIFIC REGION – 1986 – 125p – it F.A.O. [333]

REPORT ON ORGANIZATION AND MANAGEMENT PROBLEMS IN ECONOMIC AND SOCIAL PLANNING IN SYRIA / Melville, L G – Syria. Ministry of Planning. 1963 – 9 – ne IDC [650]

REPORT ON PALESTINE ADMINISTRATION, JUL 1920-DEC 1921 / Great Britain. Colonial Office – London. 1922. BJ-28-124 1 – 9 – ne IDC [956]

REPORT ON POPULAR EDUCATION IN THE PUNJAB AND ITS DEPENDENCIES / Punjab. India. Education Department – Lahore, [1860/61-1885/86] – us Res Libr [370]

REPORT ON POPULATION AND FAMILY LIFE EDUCATION SURVEY IN SCHOOLS AND COLLEGES / Ghana. Ministry of Education, National Family Planning Programme – (Repr of the 1974 ed) – Cape Coast, 1979 – 2mf – 9 – DE-437/1 – ne IDC [370]

REPORT ON RUSSIA / Winterton, Paul – 1945. 1 fiche (29x) – 9 – 1.00f – at Libertarian Micro [320]

REPORT ON SCIENTIFIC RESEARCH IN INDONESIA / Russell, Richard Joel – (Survey conducted between Oct. 1959 and Jan. 1960). SE 6673 1. 1960 – 9 – ne IDC [500]

REPORT ON SEVEN YEAR DEVELOPMENT PLAN FOR THE PLAN ORGANIZATION OF THE IMPERIAL GOVERNMENT OF IRAN / Iran – 5v. New York, Overseas Consultants. 1949 – 9 – ne IDC [338]

REPORT ON SPAIN, OCTOBER 1946 / Spain. Embajada. United States – Washington, DC, 1946. Fiche W1134. (Blodgett Collection of Spanish Civil War Pamphlets) – 9 – us H.U. College Libr [946]

REPORT ON SUGAR BEET TRIALS FOR THE FALL OF 1962-1963 / Libya. Ministry of Agriculture. Experimental Section – Tripoli. Nov 1963. BNE-1034 1 – 9 – ne IDC [630]

REPORT ON THE 3RD ROUND OF STATUS NEGOTIATIONS : HELD IN HANA, MAUI, HI, TO THE 4TH CONG OF MICRONESIA, 2ND REG SESS / Joint Committee on Future Status [TTPI (U.S.)] – (Various pagination) – n.p, n.d., submitted dec 1971 – 2mf – 9 – $3.00 – LLMC 82-100F, Title 40 – us L.L.M.C. [323]

REPORT ON THE 1970 WORLD CENSUS OF AGRICULTURE – 1977 – 289p – it F.A.O. [630]

REPORT ON THE ABYAN SCHEME / Aden. Great Britain Colonial Office – 1951. BNE-9618-1 – 9 – ne IDC [956]

REPORT ON THE ACCOMMODATION FOR RAILWAYS ON THE WATER FRONT OF THE CITY OF TORONTO.. / Gzowski, Casimir Stanislaus – Toronto: J. Reid, 1889?.05137.(Pre-1900 Canadiana) – 9 – cn C.I.H.M. [971]

REPORT ON THE ACCOUNTS OF THE KINGDOM OF LIBYA FOR THE YEARS: 1963/1964; 1964/1965; 1965/1966; 1966/1967 / Libya. Diwan of Audit – BNE-632 1 – 9 – ne IDC [339]

REPORT ON THE AFFAIRS OF BRITISH NORTH AMERICA / Durham, Earl of – s.l: House of Commons, 1839. SEM105P114 – 8mf – 9 – Can$18.00 – cn Bibl Nat [324]

REPORT ON THE AFFAIRS OF BRITISH NORTH AMERICA / Lambton, Earl of Durham, John George – [s.l.]: House of Commons, 1839. SEM105P114 – 8mf – 9 – Can$18.00 – cn Bibl Nat [324]

REPORT ON THE AGRO-ECOLOGICAL ZONES PROJECT, VOL 1 : METHODOLOGY AND RESULTS FOR AFRICA – 1982 – 185p – it F.A.O. [338]

REPORT ON THE AGRO-ECOLOGICAL ZONES PROJECT, VOL 2 : RESULTS FOR SOUTHWEST ASIA – 1978 – 33p – it F.A.O. [338]

REPORT ON THE AGRO-ECOLOGICAL ZONES PROJECT, VOL 3 : METHODOLOGY AND RESULTS FOR SOUTH AND CENTRAL AMERICA – 1981 – 260p – it F.A.O. [338]

REPORT ON THE AGRO-ECOLOGICAL ZONES PROJECT, VOL 4 : RESULTS FOR SOUTHEAST ASIA – 1980 – 40p – it F.A.O. [338]

REPORT ON THE ARCHITECTURAL AND ARCHAEOLOGICAL REMAINS IN THE PROVINCE OF KACHH / India. Archaeological Survey of Western India; ed by Khakbar, Dalpatram Pranjivan – Five papers by the late Sir Alex Burness. Bombay. 1879. BI-701 2 – 8 – ne IDC [930]

REPORT ON THE ASTEROIDEA BY W.P. SLADEN – Zoology.1873-76. Edinburgh, 1889. v30. 42, 893p. 117 pls. Z-2229/1 – 9 – ne IDC [590]

REPORT ON THE AUDIT OF THE ACCOUNTS / Aden. Audit Department – 11 v. in 6. 1954-65. BNE-9606 1 – 9 – ne IDC [338]

REPORT ON THE BIRD'S NEST CAVES OF GOMANTON / Bampflyde, C A – 1882 – 1 – uk Microform Academic [590]

REPORT ON THE CANADIAN GOLD FIELDS AND THE BEST MEANS OF THEIR DEVELOPMENT / Canada. Parliament. Legislative Assembly. Committee – Quebec: Printed by George E. Desbarats, 1865. SEM105P212 – 2mf – 9 – Can$4.50 – cn Bibl Nat [622]

REPORT ON THE CANADIAN PHOSPHATES: CONSIDERED WITH REFERENCE TO THEIR APPLICATION TO AGRICULTURE / Broome, Gordon – Montreal: Dawson, 1870. 00292. (Pre-1900 Canadiana) – 9 – cn C.I.H.M. [550]

THE REPORT ON THE CENSUS OF PRODUCTION 1907-1967 : INCLUDING THE IMPORT DUTIES ENQUIRY 1935 – (Coll title: British Government Publications...1801-1977, Industry) – 13r – 1 – £710.00 – uk Chadwyck [338]

A REPORT ON THE CENSUS OF PUMP SCHEMES, JUN-AUG 1963 / Sudan. Dept. of Statistics – 3v. (lacking 1963, v1, v2 (2-3)). BNE-7622 1 – 9 – ne IDC [310]

A REPORT ON THE CENTRAL PRODUCTION PLANTS OF INDONESIA / Indonesia. Departemen Perindustrian Rakjat – SE-3005 1. 1952 – 9 – ne IDC [338]

REPORT ON THE CLIMATE AND AGRICULTURAL VALUE, GENERAL GEOLOGICAL FEATURES, AND MINERALS OF ECONOMIC IMPORTANCE OF PART OF THE NORTHERN PORTION OF BRITISH COLUMBIA, AND OF THE PEACE RIVER COMPANY / Dawson, George M – s.l.: s.n., 1879?. 02368. (Pre-1900 Canadiana) – 9 – cn C.I.H.M. [550]

REPORT ON THE COMMERCIAL, INDUSTRIAL AND ECONOMIC SITUATION OF CHINA IN JULY 1922 / Fox, Harry Halton – London: His Majesty's Stationery Office, 1922. 64p. illus – 1 – us U.W. Library [950]

REPORT ON THE CUSTOMS AND LIVING HABITS OF THE SOUTH AFRICAN NATIVES AND OF THE ECONOMIC, SOCIAL, AND POLITICAL STRUCTURE OF THEIR SOCIETY – Capetown. v1-5. 1903-05 – 3r – 1 – us Ross [306]

REPORT ON THE DOMINION GOVERNMENT EXPEDITION TO HUDSON BAY AND THE ARCTIC ISLANDS ON BOARD D.G.S. NEPTUNE, 1903-04 / Low, A P – BN 297 2. 1906 – 8 – ne IDC [910]

REPORT ON THE EDUCATION DIVISION 1971-1973 / Antigua and Barbuda. Ministry of Education, Health and Culture – St. John's, 1974 – 3mf – 9 – DE-507/1 – ne IDC [370]

REPORT ON THE ESTABLISHMENT AND PROGRESS OF JOINT INDUSTRIAL COUNCILS SET UP IN ACCORDANCE WITH THE RECOMMENDATIONS OF THE COMMITTEE ON RELATIONS BETWEEN EMPLOYERS AND EMPLOYED "THE WHITLEY" COMMITTEE / Great Britain. Ministry of Labour – 1917-22.London: H.M. Stationery Office, 1923. ii,231p – 1 – us U.W. Library [331]

REPORT ON THE FAMILY BUDGET SAMPLE SURVEY, 1958-1959, AND ON NEW CONSUMER PRICE INDICES IN THE SOUTHERN REGION OF THE UNITED ARAB REPUBLIC (EGYPT) / International Labour Organisation – 1960. BNE-4638 1 – 9 – ne IDC [339]

REPORT ON THE FARMING PROSPECTS IN THE PILOT AREA OF THE FAO-TRIBAL LANDS AND SETTLEMENT PROJECTS TEAM ON THE EASTERN REGION (CYRENAICA) OF LIBYA / United Nations. Food and Agriculture Organization. The Development of the Tribal Lands and Settlement Project – Benghazi. Nov 1966. Singh, H. (Farm Management Expert). BNE-1013 1 – 9 – ne IDC [330]

REPORT ON THE FINANCES OF ADEN COLONY / Tress, R C – Apr 1960. BNE-9630 1 – 9 – ne IDC [330]

REPORT ON THE FIRST FIVE-YEAR PLAN OF CHINA IN 1953-57 / China. People's Republic – Li, Fu-Chun. Peking: Foreign Languages Press, 1955. BD-580-1 – 9 – ne IDC [338]

REPORT ON THE GALWAY MINING LOCATION, COUNTY OF PETERBOROUGH, ONTARIO / Chapman, Edward John – Toronto, 1868?. 00625. (Pre-1900 Canadiana) – 9 – cn C.I.H.M. [622]

REPORT ON THE GEOLOGY OF A PORTION OF THE LAURENTIAN AREA LYING TO THE NORTH OF THE ISLAND OF MONTREAL / Adams, Frank Dawson – Ottawa?: s.n., 1896 (Ottawa: S. E. Dawson). 02427. (Pre-1900 Canadiana) – 9 – cn C.I.H.M. [550]

REPORT ON THE GEOLOGY OF THE COUNTRY NEAR THE FORTY-NINTH PARALLEL OF NORTH LATITUDE WEST OF THE ROCKY MOUNTAINS: FROM OBSERVATIONS MADE IN 1859-1861 / Bauerman, Hilary – Montreal: Dawson, 1884. 07377. (Pre-1900 Canadiana) – 9 – cn C.I.H.M. [550]

REPORT ON THE IMPLEMENTATION OF THE RECOMMENDATIONS OF THE EDUCATION REVIEW COMMITTEE 1960 / Malaysia. Ministry of Education – Kuala Lumpur, 1971 – 1mf – 9 – DE-203/1 – ne IDC [370]

REPORT ON THE INDUSTRIAL AND ECONOMIC SITUATION OF CHINA IN JUNE, 1923 / Brett, H J – London: His Majesty's Stationery Office, 1923. 52p. ill – 1 – us U.W. Library [950]

A REPORT ON THE INDUSTRIAL POSITION IN LIBYA, 1964-1966 / Libya – Delivered at a conference in Kuwait concerning industrial and economic positions in Arabic countries. 1966. BNE-1207 1 – 9 – ne IDC [338]

REPORT ON THE JURY SYSTEM / Cloran, Henry Joseph – Quebec: Printed by order of the Legislative Assembly, 1890. 02151. (Pre-1900 Canadiana) – 9 – cn C.I.H.M. [340]

REPORT ON THE LOCAL ADMINISTRATION OF JERUSALEM / Fitzgerald, W J – 1945. BJ-28-116 1 – 9 – ne IDC [956]

REPORT ON THE LOCATION OF THE BRITISH-ALASKAN BOUNDARY : UNDER THE ANGLO-RUSSIAN CONVENTION OF 1825 / Cameron, DR – London: Printed for H.M.S.O. by Eyre and Spottiswoode 1886?. 00998. (Pre-1900 Canadiana) – 9 – cn C.I.H.M. [971]

REPORT ON THE MANUSCRIPTS OF LORD MIDDLETON, PRESERVED AT WOLLATON HALL, NOTTINGHAMSHIRE / Great Britain. Historical Manuscripts Commission – London: H.M. Stationery Office, 1911. xv,746p – 1 – us U.W. Library [025]

REPORT ON THE MILITARY ACADEMY AT WEST POINT, U.S / Fletcher, Henry Charles – by Lieut.-Colonel Fletcher. s.l.: s.n., 1874?. 05574. (Pre-1900 Canadiana) – 9 – cn C.I.H.M. [355]

REPORT ON THE MILITARY SITUATION IN JAVA, SUMATRA, MADURA, AUG. 4-SEPT. 4, 1947 / Indonesia. Kementerian Luar Negeri – SE-2003 1. 1947 – 9 – ne IDC [324]

REPORT ON THE MINISTRY OF EDUCATION 1978 / Singapore. Education Study Team – Singapore, 1979 – 3mf – 9 – DE-263/1 – ne IDC [370]

REPORT ON THE MOSSES OF THE ABOR EXPEDITION, 1911-1912 / Dixon, H N – (Records of the Bot. Survey of India). v. 6, no. 3. 1914. B-363 2 – 8 – ne IDC [580]

REPORT ON THE NATIONAL ECONOMIC AND SOCIAL RESEARCH INSTITUTE / Indonesia. Lembaga Ekonomi dan Kemasjarakatan Nasional – SE-8498 1. Jan. 1-June 30, 1964 – 9 – ne IDC [330]

REPORT ON THE NATIVES OF SOUTHWEST AFRICA AND THEIR TREATMENT BY GERMANY – London: HMSO, 1918 – us Res Libr [960]

REPORT ON THE NILE VALLEY PLAN / Sudan. Ministry of Irrigation and Hydroelectric power – Morrice, H. A. W. and W. N. Allen. 2 v. 1958. BNE-7679 1 – 9 – ne IDC [630]

REPORT ON THE PHYSICAL CONDITION OF FOURTEEN HUNDRED SCHOOL CHILDREN IN THE CITY, TOGETHER WITH SOME ACCOUNT OF THEIR HOMES AND SURROUNDINGS / City of Edinburgh Charity Organisation Society – London: P.S. King & son, 1906. 44p, fold. tables – 1 – us U.W. Library [360]

REPORT ON THE PLANTS, COLLECTED DURING MR. BABBAGES' EXPEDITION INTO THE N.W. INTERIOR / Mueller, Ferdinand Jakob Heinrich von – Melbourne, 1858. B-6465 1 – 9 – ne IDC [580]

REPORT ON THE PRE-SILURIAN (HURONIAN) AND CAMBRIAN OR PRIMORDIAL SILURIAN ROCKS: OF SOUTHERN NEW BRUNSWICK, 1877-1878 / Bailey, Loring Woart – Montreal: Dawson Bros., 1879. 00918. (Pre-1900 Canadiana) – 9 – cn C.I.H.M. [560]

REPORT ON THE PROPERTY OF THE ST ONGE GOLD MINING COMPANY / Chapman, Edward John – Toronto: Trout & Todd, 1886. 02423. (Pre-1900 Canadiana) – 9 – cn C.I.H.M. [622]

REPORT ON THE PROPOSED EXPANSION OF SECONDARY SCHOOL EDUCATION IN HONG KONG OVER THE NEXT DECADE / Hong Kong. Board of Education – Hong Kong, 1973 – 1mf – 9 – DE-158/1 – ne IDC [370]

REPORT ON THE PROPOSED EXTENSION OF IRRIGATION IN THE JORDAN VALLEY / MacDonald, M – 1951. BNE-9800 1 – 9 – ne IDC [630]

REPORT ON THE P.R.R.I. REBELLION / Djojohadikusumo, Sumitro – SE-2359 1. 1960? – 9 – ne IDC [335]

REPORT ON THE PUTATAN SUB-DISTRICT FOR THE EIGHT MONTHS ENDING 31 DEC 1884 / Dalrymple, S E – 1 – uk Microform Academic [941]

REPORT ON THE QUEBEC COAL, TO HIS WORSHIP THE MAYOR OF QUEBEC / Rottermund, E S, Comte de – Quebec: "Morning Chronicle" office, 1855. SEM105P290 – 1mf – 9 – Can$2.25 – cn Bibl Nat [971]

REPORT ON THE QUESTIONS BETWEEN GREAT BRITAIN AND THE UNITED STATES WITH RESPECT TO THE NORTH AMERICAN FISHERIES / Anglo-American Association – London: Macmillan, 1871. 00819. (Pre-1900 Canadiana) – 9 – cn C.I.H.M. [971]

A REPORT ON THE SAMPLE CENSUS OF AGRICULTURE FOR THE YEAR 1964-1965 IN THE BLUE NILE PROVINCE OF THE SUDAN / Sudan. Dept. of Statistics – 1969. BNE-7620 1 – 9 – ne IDC [324]

A REPORT ON THE SAMPLE CENSUS OF AGRICULTURE FOR THE YEAR 1964/1965 IN THE NORTHERN AND KHARTOUM PROVINCES OF SUDAN / Sudan – 1969. BNE-7623 1 – 9 – ne IDC [630]

REPORT ON THE SETTLEMENT OF THE LAND REVENUE OF THE FYZABAD DISTRICT / Millet, A F – Allahabad: North-Western Provinces & Oudh Govt Press, 1880 – us Res Libr [336]

REPORT ON THE SLAVE TRADE / Great Britain. Commissioners on African Settlements – 1812 – 1 – uk Microform Academic [305]

REPORT ON THE ST LAWRENCE AND ATLANTIC RAIL-ROAD, ITS INFLUENCE ON THE TRADE OF ST LAWRENCE.. / Morton, A C – Montreal: Printed at the Canada Gazette Office, 1849. SEM105P355 – 1mf – 9 – Can$2.25 – cn Bibl Nat [380]

REPORT ON THE STATISTICS OF LABOR / Massachusetts. Dept. of Labor and Industries. Division of Statistics – 1869-1960. 361 fiches. (Harvard Law School Library Collection.) – 9 – 1.50f – us H.U. Law [324]

REPORT ON THE STATISTICS OF MUNICIPAL FINANCES / Massachusetts. Dept. of Corporations and Taxation. Bureau of Accounts – n.1-52, 1906-66. 180 fiches. (Harvard Law School Library Collection.) – 9 – 1.50f – us H.U. Law [324]

REPORT ON THE SURVEY OF INDUSTRY AND THE POSSIBILITIES OF INDUSTRIAL DEVELOPMENT IN THE REPUBLIC OF SUDAN / League of Arab States – 4v. 1969-70. BNE-7659 1 – 9 – ne IDC [338]

REPORT ON THE SURVEY ON EMPLOYERS' ASSESSMENT OF VOCATIONAL TRAINING AND PRE-VOCATIONAL AND SECONDARY MODERN EDUCATION, CONDUCTED IN AUGUST 1976 / Hong Kong. Committee on Vocational Training – (In English and Chinese) – Hong Kong, 1977/78 – 2mf – 9 – DE-164/1 – ne IDC [370]

REPORT ON THE SYSTEM OF ELECTRIC STREET CARS FOR THE CITY OF TORONTO / Cuningham, Granville Carlyle – Toronto?: s.n., 1891?. 00449. (Pre-1900 Canadiana) – 9 – cn C.I.H.M. [971]

REPORT ON THE TRAINING OF MANPOWER IN LIBYA DURING 1965-1966 / Libya. Ministry of Labour and Social Affairs – Tripoli. Sep 1967. BNE-903 1 – 9 – ne IDC [360]

REPORT ON THE U.N. CONFERENCE ON NEW SOURCES OF ENERGY / United Nations – E.2 F.2 S.2 – 62.I.21 ST/ECA/72 – us U.N. Pubs [333]

REPORT ON THE UNITED STATES AND MEXICAN BOUNDARY SURVEY / Emory, W H – v. 2, pt. 1: Botany of the Boundary. Washington. 1850. B-5770 2 – 8 – ne IDC [580]

REPORT ON THE VISIT BY AN ALL PARTY GROUP OF MEMBERS OF PARLIAMENT TO SPAIN / Great Britain. Parliament. House of Commons – London, 1937? Fiche W1135. (Blodgett Collection of Spanish Civil War Pamphlets) – 9 – us H.U. College Libr [946]

REPORT ON TOBACCO VARIETY TRIALS AT SIDI MESRI TRIPOLI / Libya. Administration of Tripolitania – State Tobacco Monopoly. BNE-1019 1 – 9 – ne IDC [338]

REPORT ON TRADE AND COMMERCE / Canada (Province). Parlement. Assemblee legislative – 1855. SEM105P568 – 1mf – 9 – Can$2.25 – cn Bibl Nat [380]

REPORT ON UNITED STATES FOREIGN ASSISTANCE PROGRAMS: JORDAN, LEBANON AND IRAQ / Armstrong, H F – 1957. BNE-9752 1 – 9 – ne IDC [338]

REPORT ON U.S. ASSISTANCE TO MOROCCO, 1957-1963 / U.S. Agency for International Development – 1964. BNE-3105 1 – 9 – ne IDC [337]

REPORT ON WORKERS' EDUCATION IN LIBYA / International Labour Organisation – Geneva. 1966. Ed. by C. Poloni. BNE-709 1 – 9 – ne IDC [331]

THE REPORT ON WORLD AFFAIRS – 1919-80.Continues: Report on Foreign Affairs – 1 – £1,075.00 – uk World [327]

REPORT OR THE SELECT COMMITTEE OF THE LEGISLATIVE ASSEMBLY, APPOINTED TO ENQUIRE INTO THE STATE OF EDUCATION AND THE WORKING OF THE SCHOOL LAWS IN LOWER CANADA / Canada Province. Parlement. Assemblee legislative. Select Committee... – Quebec: John Lowell, [1853] – 1mf – 9 – Can$2.25 – cn Bibl Nat [370]

REPORT PRESENTED BY THE GOVERNMENT OF THE UNION OF SOUTH AFRICA TO THE COUNCIL OF THE LEAGUE OF NATIONS CONCERNING THE ADMINISTRATION OF SOUTHWEST AFRICA TO THE COUNCIL OF THE LEAGUE OF NATIONS CONCERNING THE ADMINISTRATION OF SOUTH-WEST AFRICA – Pretoria, Cape Town, 1918-39 – us Res Libr [960]

REPORT: SAVINGS AND LOAN COMMISSIONER OF CALIFORNIA / California. Dept. of Savings and Loan – Sept 1, 1891-1979. 189 fiches. (Harvard Law School Library Collection.) – 9 – $1.50f – us H.U. Law [336]

REPORT "SERVING GEORGIA THROUGH RESEARCH" / Georgia. Agricultural Experiment Station. Athens – v. 1-21. 1951-69 – 1,5,6 – us Spaulding [630]

REPORT SUBMITTING AN EQUALIZATION AND APPORTIONMENT UPON THE SEVERAL CITIES AND TOWNS / Massachusetts. State Tax Commission – 1872-1977. 21mf. (Harvard Law School Library Collection) – 9 – 1.50f – us H.U. Law [324]

REPORT: THE AIMS OF BRITISH POLICY IN WEST AFRICA / Great Britain. Select Committee on West African Settlements – 1865 – 1 – uk Microform Academic [960]

REPORT. THE SPECIAL COMMITTEE TO WHOM WAS REFERRED THE ANSWER OF HIS EXCELLENCY THE GOVERNOR IN CHIEF, TO THE ADDRESS OF THIS HOUSE OF THE 15TH JANUARY 1834, RELATING TO THE PROPERTY OF THE SEMINARY OF MONTREAL... – [s.l.]: [s.n.], [1834]. SEM105P1313 – 5mf – 9 – Can$11.25 – cn Bibl Nat [971]

REPORT. THE SPECIAL COMMITTEE TO WHOM WAS REFERRED THE MESSAGE OF HIS EXCELLENCY THE GOVERNOR IN CHIEF, OF THE 8TH FEBRUARY 1834, RELATING TO THE ACT 1 WILL. 4. COP. 57... – [Quebec]: [s.n.], [1834]. SEM105P1154 – 2mf – 9 – Can$4.50 – cn Bibl Nat [270]

REPORT. THE SPECIAL COMMITTEE TO WHOM WERE REFERRED THE DIVERS ORDERS AND RESOLUTIONS OF YOUR HONORABLE HOUSE, AND OTHER MATTERS OF REFERENCE, CONCERNING THE ERECTION OF PARISHES... – [s.l.]: [s.n.], [1836]. SEM105P1224 – 5mf – 9 – Can$11.25 – cn Bibl Nat [971]

REPORT. THE SPECIAL COMMITTEE TO WHOM WERE REFERRED THE MESSAGE OF HIS EXCELLENCY THE GOVERNOR IN CHIEF, ACCOMPAGNYING THE DESPATCH FROM VISCOUNT GODERICH, RELATIVE TO THE HONORABLE JUDGE KERR... – [Quebec]: [s.n.], [1833]. SEM105P1155 – 1mf – 9 – Can$2.25 – cn Bibl Nat [324]

REPORT. THE SPECIAL COMMITTEE...THE INHABITANTS OF COTEAU DU LAC, AND OTHERS INTERESTED IN THE TRADE AND NAVIGATION OF THE RIVER ST LAWRENCE... – [Quebec]: [s.n.], [1836]. SEM105P1406 – 2mf – 9 – Can$4.50 – cn Bibl Nat [380]

REPORT TO SECRETARY OF INTERIOR / Central Branch Union Pacific Railroad Company – 1867-79 – 1 – us KS Hist [025]

REPORT TO THE 3RD CONGRESS : 3RD REG SESS, JUL 1970 / Political Status Delegation of the Congress of Micronesia – (Various pagination) – n.p, n.d. – 2mf – 9 – $3.00 – LLMC 82-100F, Title 37 – us L.L.M.C. [323]

REPORT TO THE 3RD CONVENTION (1927), 4TH CONVENTION (1932), 7TH CONVENTION (1948) / General Organization of the Jewish Workers of Palestine (Histadrut) – BJ-28-31 1 – 9 – ne IDC [338]

REPORT TO THE 5TH CONGRESS OF MICRONESIA / Joint Committee on Future Status [TTPI (U.S.)] Eastern Districts Subcommittee – Saipan: The Congress, 1973 – 1mf – 9 – $1.50 – LLMC 82-100F, Title 51 – us L.L.M.C. [323]

REPORT TO THE 5TH CONGRESS OF MICRONESIA / Joint Committee on Future Status [TTPI (U.S.)] Western Districts Subcommittee – Saipan: The Congress, 1973 – 1mf – 9 – $1.50 – LLMC 82-100F, Title 52 – us L.L.M.C. [323]

REPORT TO THE CANADA TEMPERANCE SOCIETY ON THE WORKING AND EFFECTS OF PROHIBITORY LEGISLATION TO SUPPRESS INTEMPERANCE IN THE NEW ENGLAND STATES / Mulkins, Hannibal – Kingston: s.n, 1855. SEM105P451 – 1mf – 9 – Can$2.25 – cn Bibl Nat [360]

REPORT TO THE COMMITTEE ON THE RIOTS IN POONA AND AHMED NAGAR – Bombay, 1875-76 – 29mf – 9 – I-519/2 – ne IDC [360]

REPORT TO THE CONGRESS OF MICRONESIA : 3RD CONG, 2ND SESS, JUL 1969 / Future Political Status Commission [TTPI (U.S.)] – n.p, n.d. – 2mf – 9 – $3.00 – LLMC 82-100F, Title 36 – us L.L.M.C. [323]

REPORT TO THE DIRECTOR GENERAL, CENTRAL WATER AUTHORITY OF JORDAN / U.S. Bureau of Reclamation – 1961. BNE-9817 1 – 9 – ne IDC [333]

REPORT TO THE DIRECTOR OF LAND DEVELOPMENT REGARDING THE AGRICULTURE MECHANIZATION ASPECTS OF THE FOOD BOARD'S EXPANDED LAND DEVELOPMENT PROJECT,BY J.K. GARNER. SE-2495/1. 1959 / Indonesia. Food Board – 9 – ne IDC [630]

REPORT TO THE ECONOMIC COOPERATION ADMINISTRATION OF THE 1949/50 PROGRAMME / Netherlands East Indies. (Netherlands). O.E.E.C – v. 2: Indonesia. D-1385 1. 1949 – 9 – ne IDC [338]

REPORT TO THE ECONOMIC COOPERATION ADMINISTRATION ON 1949/50 PROGRAMME. VOL. 2. SWEDEN / Organization for European Economic Cooperation – Paris. 1949. BD-1748 1 – 9 – ne IDC [948]

REPORT TO THE ECONOMIC COOPERATION ADMINISTRATION ON THE 1949/50 PROGRAMME / Denmark. Organization for European Economic Cooperation – v. II. Denmark. Paris. 1949. BD-1642 1 – 9 – ne IDC [338]

REPORT TO THE ECONOMIC COOPERATION ADMINISTRATION ON THE 1949/50 PROGRAMME / France. Organization for European Economic Cooperation – v. II. France. Paris. 1949. BD-1651 1 – 9 – ne IDC [338]

REPORT TO THE ECONOMIC COOPERATION ADMINISTRATION ON THE 1949/50 PROGRAMME / Iceland. Organization for European Economic Cooperation – v. 2. Iceland. Paris. 1949. BD-1666 1 – 9 – ne IDC [338]

REPORT TO THE ECONOMIC COOPERATION ADMINISTRATION ON THE 1949/50 PROGRAMME. V. 2. UNITED KINGDOM / Great Britain. Organization for European Economic Cooperation – Paris. 1949 – 9 – ne IDC [338]

REPORT TO THE ECONOMIC COOPERATION ADMINISTRATION ON THE 1949/50 PROGRAMME. VOL. 2. AUSTRIA / Organization for European Economic Cooperation – Paris. 1949. BD-1610 1 – 9 – ne IDC [943]

REPORT TO THE ECONOMIC COOPERATION ADMINISTRATION ON THE 1949/50 PROGRAMME. VOL. 2. NETHERLANDS / Organization for European Economic Cooperation – Paris. 1949. BD-1700 1 – 9 – ne IDC [949]

REPORT TO THE ECONOMIC COOPERATION ADMINISTRATION ON THE 1949/50 PROGRAMME. VOL. 2. PORTUGAL / Organization for European Economic Cooperation – Paris. 1949. BD-1734 1 – 9 – ne IDC [946]

REPORT TO THE FOOD AND AGRICULTURE ORGANISATION OF THE UNITED NATIONS / Sudan. FAO – 1v. 1955 57 – 9 – ne IDC [338]

REPORT TO THE GOVERNMENT OF CEYLON ON THE PEARL OYSTER FISHERIES OF THE GULF OF MANAAR WITH SUPPLEMENTARY REPORTS ON THE MARINE BIOLOGY OF CEYLON / Herdman, W A – 5v. London. 1903-06. BZ-2053 – 8 – ne IDC [574]

REPORT TO THE GOVERNMENT OF JORDAN ON SURVEY OF SMALL-SCALE AND HANDICRAFT INDUSTRIES / International Labour Organisation – 1964. BNE-9794 1 – 9 – ne IDC [338]

REPORT TO THE GOVERNMENT OF JORDAN ON THE FURTHER DEVELOPMENT OF THE MANPOWER ASSESSMENT PROGRAM / International Labour Organisation – 1966. BNE-9796 1 – 9 – ne IDC [331]

REPORT TO THE GOVERNMENT OF JORDAN ON THE ORGANISATION OF A MANPOWER ASSESSMENT AND PLANNING PROGRAM / International Labour Organisation – 1964 – 9 – ne IDC [331]

REPORT TO THE GOVERNMENT OF JORDAN ON THE SOILS OF EAST JORDAN / Moormann, F R – 1959 – 9 – ne IDC [333]

REPORT TO THE GOVERNMENT OF LIBYA ON CO-OPERATIVE EDUCATION AND TRAINING / International Labour Organisation – Geneva. 1970. Ed. by G. D. Goswami. BNE-710 1 – 9 – ne IDC [370]

REPORT TO THE GOVERNMENT OF LIBYA ON SOCIAL INSURANCE / International Labour Organisation – Geneva. 1961. Ed. by J. T. Paleologos and G. Zampetti. BNE-1402 1 – 9 – ne IDC [336]

REPORT TO THE GOVERNMENT OF LIBYA ON SOCIAL SECURITY / International Labour Organisation – Geneva. 1970. Ed. by M. Wasfy and G. Zampetti. BNE-1404 1 – 9 – ne IDC [336]

REPORT TO THE GOVERNMENT OF LIBYA ON THE ADMINISTRATION OF THE NATIONAL SOCIAL INSURANCE INSTITUTION AND THE INVESTMENTS OF ITS FUNDS / International Labour Organisation – Geneva. 1964. Ed. by B. Kern and G. Tamburi. BNE-1403 1 – 9 – ne IDC [336]

REPORT TO THE GOVERNMENT OF LIBYA ON THE BRINGING INTO OPERATION OF THE SOCIAL INSURANCE LAW NR. 53 OF 1957 / International Labour Organisation – Geneva. 1959. Ed. by J. T. Paleologos. BNE-1401 1 – 9 – ne IDC [360]

REPORT TO THE GOVERNMENT OF LIBYA ON THE ROLE OF HANDICRAFTS IN A RAPIDLY DEVELOPING ECONOMY / International Labour Organisation; ed by Marsden, K – Geneva. 1967. BNE-1214 1 – 9 – ne IDC [338]

REPORT TO THE GOVERNMENT OF LIBYA ON VOCATIONAL TRAINING / International Labour Organisation – Geneva. 1966. Ed. by A. Figuerda-Colon. BNE-708 1 – 9 – ne IDC [331]

REPORT TO THE GOVERNMENT OF SOUTHERN YEMEN ON THE INTRODUCTION OF HIDE, SKINS AND LEATHER IMPROVEMENT SERVICES AND THE REOPENING OF AN EXISTING TANNERY / South Yemen – Hoorn, G. van. 1969. BNE-9617 1 – 9 – ne IDC [338]

REPORT TO THE GOVERNMENT OF SYRIA ON SOME ASPECTS OF THE GHAB RECLAMATION / Gruyter, P de – 1962. BNE-9700 1 – 9 – ne IDC [333]

REPORT TO THE GOVERNMENT OF THE FEDERATION OF SOUTH ARABIA ON EXISTING AND POTENTIAL BANANA PRODUCTION / Philippe, J M – 1966. BNE-9615 1 – 9 – ne IDC [338]

REPORT TO THE GOVERNMENT OF THE FEDERATION OF SOUTH ARABIA ON EXISTING AND POTENTIAL CITRUS AREAS / Bruno, A – 1966. BNE-9614 1 – 9 – ne IDC [336]

REPORT TO THE GOVERNMENT OF THE REPUBLIC OF THE SUDAN ON A PRODUCTIVITY MISSION / Sudan – Jan-Apr 1959. 1960. BNE-7653 1 – 9 – ne IDC [338]

REPORT TO THE GOVERNMENT OF THE REPUBLIC OF THE SUDAN ON THE DEVELOPMENT OF A SOCIAL INSURANCE SCHEME / Sudan – 1965. BNE-7654 1 – 9 – ne IDC [360]

REPORT TO THE GOVERNMENT OF THE SUDAN ON THE DEVELOPMENT OF CO-OPERATIVES / Sudan – 1959. BNE-7655 1 – 9 – ne IDC [338]

REPORT TO THE GOVERNMENT OF THE SUDAN ON THE REGULATION OF EMPLOYMENT OF DOCK WORKERS: REGULATIONS IN SAFETY AND HEALTH / Sudan – 1960. BNE-7656 1 – 9 – ne IDC [331]

REPORT TO THE GOVERNMENT ON AGRICULTURAL DEVELOPMENT / Manepaard, C H J – 1954 – 9 – ne IDC [338]

A REPORT TO THE KINGDOM OF JORDAN AND THE GOVERNMENT OF THE UNITED STATES OF AMERICA ON THE JOINT POINT 4 ACTIVITIES / Jordan. U.S. Operations Mission to Jordan – 1952-56. BNE-9820 1 – 9 – ne IDC [956]

REPORT TO THE PATHFINDER FUND / McKinnon, Edna R – SE-6075 1. 1963 – 9 – ne IDC [336]

REPORT TO THE PRESIDENT OF THE U.S / Philippines. U.S. Economic Survey Mission to the Philippines – D-1429 1. 1950 – 9 – ne IDC [330]

REPORTAGES – Buckingham, Quebec. v1 no 1(Mai 1963)- v1 no 2(Juin 1963). SEM105P1208 – 2mf – 9 – Can$4.50 – cn Bibl Nat [073]
REPORTAGES – Buckingham, Quebec. v1 nos 1-2. 1963. SEM35P256 – 1r – 1 – Can$15.00 – cn Bibl Nat [073]
REPORT...CONCERNING AN INQUIRY CONDUCTED BY IT IN REFERENCE TO THE ACTIVITIES OF JUDGES IN PARTISAN POLITICS / Chicago Bar Association. Board of Managers – Chicago? 1936. 13p. LL-369 – 1 – us L of C Photodup [340]
REPORTE (SAN SALVADOR, EL SALVADOR) – s.n – 1 – us U.W. Library [073]
O REPORTER – S. Joao del-Rey, 11 Aug, Dec 1908; Mar, Dec 1911; Mar, 24 May 1914 – 1,5,6 – bl Biblioteca [072]
O REPORTER – Uberlandia, Brazil. Mar 1941-1963. Widely scattered issues except 1947 and 1963 complete – 1 – bl Biblioteca [072]
REPORTER – Angelica. N.Y. 1837-1870 – 1 – us UMI [071]
REPORTER – Berlin, 1900 – 1 – Inquire at Mikrofilmarchiv for details – gw Misc Inst [072]
REPORTER – Berlin, Germany.1900 – 1 – gw Mikrofilm [072]
REPORTER – Buttonwillow. Calif. 1953-1955 – 1 – us UMI [071]
REPORTER – Casey. Ill. 1957-1958 – 1 – us UMI [071]
REPORTER – Castro Valley, CA. 1931-51; 1955-79 – 11r – 1 – $550.00 – B02097 – us Library Micro [071]
REPORTER – Chester. Mont. 1922-1936 – 1 – us UMI [071]
REPORTER – Chester. S.C. 1854-1857; 1874-1906 – 1 – us UMI [071]
REPORTER – Cornwall, 1876-1878 – 1r – 1 – cn Preston [971]
REPORTER – Detroit. Mich. 1933-1936; 1955-1956 – 1 – us UMI [071]
REPORTER – Ellsworth. Kan. 1871-1930 – 1 – us UMI [071]
REPORTER – Fayette. Iowa. 1910-1912 – 1 – us UMI [071]
REPORTER – Hamburg. Iowa. -w. 1950- – 1 – us UMI [071]
REPORTER – Holly Springs. Miss. 1905-1918 – 1 – us UMI [071]
REPORTER – Kennewick. Wash. -w. 1908-14 – 1 – us UMI [071]
REPORTER – Lake City. Fl. -sw. 1901- – 1 – us P.K. Yonge [071]
REPORTER – Lamont. Calif. 1954-1967 – 1 – us UMI [071]
REPORTER – Lebanon. Ind. 1974- – 1 – us UMI [071]
REPORTER – Logansport. Ind. -w, sw. 1909-12 – 1 – us UMI [071]
REPORTER – Martinsville. Ind. 1905-08; 1910-1926; 1966- – 1 – us UMI [071]
REPORTER – Norwalk. Ohio. 1827-1830 – 1 – us UMI [071]
REPORTER – Ontario, OR. -w. 11 Nov 1965-6 Oct 1966. 1 roll – 1 – us U.O. Library [071]
REPORTER – Portola. Calif. -w. 1927-53, 1960- – 1 – us UMI [071]
REPORTER – Reno, NV. 1947-50 – 2r – 1 – $100.00 – U04711 – us Library Micro [071]
REPORTER – San Leandro. Calif. -w. 1941-51 – 1 – us UMI [071]
REPORTER – San Marcial. N.M. 1886-89 – 1 – us UMI [071]
REPORTER – Spencer. Iowa. 1880-99; 1954- – 1 – us UMI [071]
REPORTER – Three Rivers. Mich. 1861-62; 1869-85; 1903-05 – 1 – us UMI [071]
REPORTER – Three Rivers. Mich. -w. 1863-76 – 1 – us UMI [071]
REPORTER – Toronto. v14-19. 1988/89-1993/94 – 9 – Can$20.00y – cn Micromedia [070]
REPORTER – Turners Falls. MA. 1872-1922 – 1 – us UMI [071]
REPORTER / University of Tennessee.Institute of Agriculture – No.1-2. 1973-74. y 1 reel – 1,5 – us Spaulding [630]
REPORTER – Vacaville, CA. 1883- – 218+ r – 1 – $10,900.00 ($480.00y) – B03058 – us Library Micro [071]
REPORTER – Wathena. Kan. 1867-1868; 1873-1877 – 1 – us UMI [071]
REPORTER – Wymore, NE. -w. Oct 1881-Jun 1903, scattered issues missing – 1 – us NE Hist [071]
REPORTER *see* LAW AND EQUITY REPORTER
THE REPORTER – (Cont: American Law Times Reports. The Law and Equity Reporter) – Boston: Houghton, Osgood, Houghton, Mifflin. v5-24. 1878-88 (all publ) – 189mf – 9 – $283.00 – LLMC 81-416 – us L.L.M.C. [340]
THE REPORTER : CONTINUING DECISIONS OF THE SUPREME AND CIRCUIT COURTS OF THE UNITED STATES, COURTS OF LAST RESORT OF THE STATES, AND ENGLISH AND IRISH REPORTS – (With digest) – v5-24. 1878-88 – 189mf – 9 – $283.00 – LLMC 81-416 – us L.L.M.C. [340]
THE REPORTER – Long Beach, CA. 1989 – 3+ r – 1 – $150.00 ($50.00y) – R04053 – us Library Micro [071]
THE REPORTER – Montreal, Canada. 5 aut 1899 – 1r – 1 – Can$25.00 – cn Can Microfilming [072]
REPORTER AND NEVADA INDEPENDENT – Reno, NV. Mar-Jun 1950 – 1r – 1 – $50.00 – U04713 – us Library Micro [071]
REPORTER AND STATE JOURNAL – Harrisburg, PA., 1836 – 13 – $25.00r – us I.M.R. [071]
REPORTER (BOX HILL) – 1921-1925. R1-3 – 3r – 1 – at Corangamite [072]
REPORTER (GPO) – v1-17. 1977-90 – 9 – $142.00 set – us Hein [340]
THE REPORTER (TUJUNGA, CALIF.) – (Library has: v.2, no.1, 5, 8; v.3, no.5-7, 17-18, 23-24, 27, 40, 44, 49; v.4, no.6-9 (Sept. 17, 1951-March 2, 1953)) – Tujunga, CA: Standard Pulications, 195u – 1 – CSUX89-S100 – us Hoover Inst Photo [947]
REPORTER-BULLETIN / America's Textiles – (Previously known as American Wool and Cotton Reporter. The Textile Reporter was merged with this September, 1971). v. 14-85. 1900-71. v. 98AT1-98AT7. 1972-78 – 1,5,6 – us Princeton Micro [330]
REPORTER-DISPATCH – White Plains. N.Y. 1939- – 1 – us UMI [071]
REPORTER-NEWS – Abilene. Tex. evening. 1888-93, 1894- – 1 – us UMI [071]
REPORTER-NEWS – Abilene. Tex. morning. 1926- – 1 – us UMI [071]
REPORTER-POINTER – Chicago. Ill. -w. 1969- – 1 – us UMI [071]
REPORTERS SANS FRONTIERES = REPORTERS WITHOUT BORDERS – Montepellier. 37 docs. 1989-1991 – 30mf – 9 – ne IDC [320]
REPORT...IN THE DEPARTMENT OF THE TREASURY / New Jersey. Division of Taxation – 1944-79. 125 fiches. (Harvard Law School Library Collection.) – 9 – 1.50f – us H.U. Law [336]
REPORTING SOUTHERN AFRICA : WESTERN NEWS AGENCIES REPORTING FROM SOUTHERN AFRICA / Harris, Phil – 1981 – 168p – 9 – 92-3-101700-4 – fr UNESCO [910]
REPORT...INTO UNIVERSITY DEVELOPMENT 1974 / Papua New Guinea. Committee of Enquiry – Konedobu, 1974 – 4mf – 9 – DE-236/1 – ne IDC [370]
REPORT...OF THE COMMISSION...APPOINTED BY THE MAYOR, HON. CARTER H. HARRISON, JAN 19TH, 1898 / Chicago. Educational Commission – 2nd ed. Chicago: R.R. Donnelley, 1899. xvi,248p. William R. Harper, Chairman – 1 – us U.W. Library [370]
REPORT...OF THE GRAND TRUNK RAILWAY COMPANY OF CANADA FOR THE YEAR 1859 / Blackwell, Thomas E – London: Waterloo and Sons, 1860. SEM35P202 – 1r – 1 – Can$15.00 – cn Bibl Nat [380]
REPORT...ON THE EXPLORATION MADE OF THE ROUTE OF THE HURON AND OTTAWA RAILWAY FROM OTTAWA CITY TO PARRY SOUND / Bell, Leon G – Ottawa: MacLean, Roger, 1875. 02330. (Pre-1900 Canadiana) – 9 – cn C.I.H.M. [910]
REPORT...ON THE HUDSON'S BAY COMAPNY / Canada. Parliament. Legislative Assembly. Select Committee – s.l, s.n, 1857. SEM105P141 – 7mf – 9 – Can$15.75 – cn Bibl Nat [324]
REPORT...ON THE MAGNETIC NEEDLE / Parker, Charles – 1849-61. 1 fiche – 9 – us South Carolina Historical [520]
REPORT...ON THE OTTAWA SURVEY / Shanly, Walter – Toronto: John Lovell, 1858. SEM105P435 – 1mf – 9 – Can$2.25 – cn Bibl Nat [971]
REPORT...ON THE PETITION OF CERTAINS SIC INHABITANTS OF THE DISTRICT OF GASPE / Canada. Bas-Canada. Parlement. Chambre d'Assemblee. Comite special – s.l: House of Assembly, 1830. SEM105P95 – 2mf – 9 – Can$4.50 – cn Bibl Nat [324]
REPORT...ON THE PRESENT STATE OF DISCIPLINE, MANAGEMENT AND EXPENDITURE OF THE DISTRICT AND OTHER PRISONS IN CANADA EAST / Nelson, Wolfred – Quebec: John Lovell, 1852. SEM105P353 – 2mf – 9 – Can$4.50 – cn Bibl Nat [360]
REPORT...ON THE WINTER NAVIGATION OF THE RIVER AND GULF OF ST LAWRENCE / Quebec. (Province). Legislature. Assemblee legislative. Comite – Quebec, 1875. SEM105P542 – 1mf – 9 – Can$2.25 – cn Bibl Nat [623]
REPORT...PERMANENT RECORD / U.S. Commission of the Role of Gold in the Domestic and International Monetary Systems – Washington, DC. 1982 – 1 – 125.00 – us L of C Photodup [336]
REPORTS / African Institution – 12 v. London. 1808-18. BA-268 2 – 8 – ne IDC [960]
REPORTS / Alabama State Bar Association – Nos 1-35 1880-1912. 29 books. Updates planned. 84-397 – 9 – $56.00 – us L.L.M.C. [340]
REPORTS / American Historical Association – 1889-1975 – 1 – us Princeton Micro [970]
REPORTS / Bahrain. Currency Board – 9v. in 1. 1965 66-1972. BNE-10.009 1 – 9 – ne IDC [956]
REPORTS / Baptist Missionary Society. London – 1792-1957 – 1 – 1023.96 – us Baptist [240]
REPORTS / Bley, Buchner – 1834 and 1837 – 7 – uk Microform Academic [900]
REPORTS / British Broadcasting Corporation. Monitoring Service – (1972-74 9) – v1-758 1939-72 – 1 – us UMI [900]
REPORTS / California. Fair Employment Practice Commission – 1959-78. 8 fiches. (Harvard Law School Library Collection.) – 9 – $1.50f – us H.U. Law [330]
REPORTS / California. Franchise Tax Board – 1950-79. 52 fiches. (Harvard Law School Library Collection.) – 9 – $1.50f – us H.U. Law [336]
REPORTS / California. Public Utilities Commission – 1876-1979. 377 fiches. (Harvard Law School Library Collection.) – 9 – $1.50f – us H.U. Law [336]
REPORTS / California. State Board of Equalization – 1872-1979. 121 fiches. (Harvard Law Shool Library Collection.) – 9 – $1.50f – us H.U. Law [336]
REPORTS / Canada. Chief Electoral Officer – 1841-1974 – 9 – cn Micromedia [324]
REPORTS / Canada. Federal Royal Commission – 1867- – 9 – cn Micromedia [324]
REPORTS / Canada. Federal-Provincial Conferences – 1887-1976 – 9 – cn Micromedia [971]
REPORTS / Canada. Royal Commissions – 1867- – 9 – cn Micromedia [971]
REPORTS / Clemson University. Agricultural Extension Division – 1914-69 – 1,5 – us Spaulding [630]
REPORTS / Connecticut. Board of Compensation Commissioners – 1st-18th, 1913-46. 6 fiches. (Harvard Law School Library Collection.) – 9 – $1.50f – us H.U. Law [336]
REPORTS / Connecticut. Bureau of Labor Statistics – 1st-2nd, 1873-75; 1st-35th, 1885-1932. 136 fiches. (Harvard Law School Library Collection.) – 9 – $1.50f – us H.U. Law [310]
REPORTS / Connecticut. Dept. of Factory Inspection – 1st-20th, 1887-1906; 1st-8th, 1906-22. 47 fiches. (Harvard Law School Library Collection.) – 9 – $1.50f – us H.U. Law [330]
REPORTS / Connecticut. Dept. of Labor and Factory Inspection – 1930-48. 17 fiches. (Harvard Law School Library Collection.) – 9 – $1.50f – us H.U. Law [330]
REPORTS / Connecticut. Office of Bank Commissioner – 1837-1979. 556 fiches. (Harvard Law School Library Collection.) – 9 – $1.50f – us H.U. Law [336]
REPORTS / Connecticut. Public Utilities Commission – 1st-60th, 1911-71. 343 fiches. (Harvard Law School Library Collection.) – 9 – $1.50f – us H.U. Law [336]
REPORTS / Connecticut. Railroad Commissioners – 1st-59th, 1853-1911. 315 fiches. (Harvard Law School Library Collection.) – 9 – $1.50f – us H.U. Law [336]
REPORTS / Connecticut. State Board of Mediation and Arbitration – 1902-79. 10 fiches. (Harvard Law School Library Collection.) – 9 – $1.50f – us H.U. Law [330]
REPORTS / Co-operative Congress – no. 1-4. 1831-2 – 1 – uk Microform Academic [941]
REPORTS / Enfield Waltham Sunday School – 1845 – 1 – 45.50 – us Baptist [240]
REPORTS / Great Britain. Uganda Development Commission, 1920 and Cotton Commissions, 1929, 1938 and 1948 – 1 – uk Microform Academic [960]
REPORTS / Illinois. Commerce Commission – 1916-72. 62 fiches. (Harvard Law School Library Collection.) – 9 – $1.50f – us H.U. Law [336]
REPORTS / Illinois. Department of Insurance – n.1-82, 1869-1949. 1061 fiches. (Harvard Law School Library Collection.) – 9 – $1.50f – us H.U. Law [336]
REPORTS / Illinois. Department of Labor – 1917-79. 71 fiches. (Harvard Law School Library Collection.) – 9 – $1.50f – us H.U. Law [330]
REPORTS / Illinois. Department of Revenue – 1943-79. 30 fiches. (Harvard Law School Library Collection.) – 9 – $1.50f – us H.U. Law [336]
REPORTS / Illinois. Office of Secretary of State. Securities Division – 1954-79. 18 fiches. (Harvard Law School Library Collection.) – 9 – $1.50f – us H.U. Law [336]
REPORTS / Illinois. Office of the Commissioner of Banks and Trust Companies – 1957-79. 23 fiches. (Harvard Law School Library Collection.) – 9 – $1.50f – us H.U. Law [336]
REPORTS / Illinois. Railroad and Warehouse Commission – n.1-16, 1870-86; n.18-43, 1887-1913. 286 fiches. (Harvard Law School Library Collection.) – 9 – $1.50f – us H.U. Law [336]
REPORTS / Illinois. State Public Utilities Commission – n.1-3, 1913-16. 51 fiches. (Harvard Law School Library Collection.) – 9 – $1.50f – us H.U. Law [336]
REPORTS / Illinois. State Tax Commission – n.1-24, 1919-43. 94 fiches. (Harvard Law School Library Collection.) – 9 – $1.50f – us H.U. Law [336]
REPORTS / Lambeth Conference – 1867-1948 – 1 – 41.16 – us Baptist [240]
REPORTS / Maryland. Bank Commissioner – 1910-79. 103 fiches. (Harvard Law School Library Collection.) – 9 – 1.50f – us H.U. Law [324]
REPORTS / Maryland. Bureau of Industrial Statistics and Information – n.1-4, 1884-91. 15 fiches. (Harvard Law School Library Collection.) – 9 – 1.50f – us H.U. Law [324]
REPORTS / Maryland. Bureau of Statistics and Information – n.1-24, 1892-1915. 102 fiches. (Harvard Law School Library Collection.) – 9 – 1.50f – us H.U. Law [324]
REPORTS / Maryland. Commissioner of Labor and Statistics – n.25-49, 1916-41. 62 fiches. (Harvard Law School Library Collection.) – 9 – 1.50f – us H.U. Law [324]
REPORTS / Maryland. Division of Labor and Industry – 1967-79. 13 fiches. (Harvard Law School Library Collection.) – 9 – 1.50f – us H.U. Law [324]
REPORTS / Maryland. Public Service Commission – v.1-, 1910-77. 290 fiches. (Harvard Law School Library Collection.) – 9 – 1.50f – us H.U. Law [324]
REPORTS / Maryland. State Dept. of Assessments and Taxation – 1914-79. 50 fiches. (Harvard Law School Library Collection.) – 9 – 1.50f – us H.U. Law [324]
REPORTS / Maryland. Ten Hour Law Bureau – n.1-2, 1912-15. 1 fiche. (Harvard Law School Library Collection.) – 9 – 1.50f – us H.U. Law [324]
REPORTS / Massachusetts. Board of Conciliation and Arbitration – 1886-1919, n.1-34. 81 fiches. (Harvard Law School Library Collection.) – 9 – 1.50f – us H.U. Law [324]

REPORTS / Massachusetts. Board of Conciliation and Arbitration – 1919-77. 35 fiches. (Harvard Law School Library Collection.) – 9 – 1.50f – us H.U. Law [324]

REPORTS / Massachusetts. Board of Gas and Electric Light Commissioners – n.1-35, 1885-1919. 175 fiches. (Harvard Law School Library Collection.) – 9 – 1.50f – us H.U. Law [324]

REPORTS / Massachusetts. Board of Railroad Commissioners – n.1-44, 1869-1912. 456 fiches. (Harvard Law School Library Collection.) – 9 – 1.50f – us H.U. Law [324]

REPORTS / Massachusetts. Commission Against Discrimination – 1946-73. 31 fiches. (Harvard Law School Library Collection.) – 9 – 1.50f – us H.U. Law [324]

REPORTS / Massachusetts. Commission on Economy and Efficiency – 1912-15. 11 fiches. (Harvard Law School Library Collection.) – 9 – 1.50f – us H.U. Law [324]

REPORTS / Massachusetts. Dept. of Corporations and Taxation – 1866-1976. 240 fiches. (Harvard Law School Library Collection.) – 9 – 1.50f – us H.U. Law [324]

REPORTS / Massachusetts. Dept. of Labor and Industries. Division of Employment Security – 1939-77. 25 fiches. (Harvard Law School Library Collection.) – 9 – 1.50f – us H.U. Law [324]

REPORTS / Massachusetts. Dept. of Labor and Industries. Division of Minimum Wage – 1919-77. 16 fiches. (Harvard Law School Library Collection.) – 9 – 1.50f – us H.U. Law [324]

REPORTS / Massachusetts. Dept. of Public Utilities – 1919-78. 81 fiches. (Harvard Law School Library Collection.) – 9 – 1.50f – us H.U. Law [324]

REPORTS / Massachusetts. Minimum Wage Commission – n.1-7, 1913-19. 10 fiches. (Harvard Law School Library Collection.) – 9 – 1.50f – us H.U. Law [324]

REPORTS / Massachusetts. Public Service Commission – n.1-7, 1913-19. 149 fiches. (Harvard Law School Library Collection.) – 9 – 1.50f – us H.U. Law [324]

REPORTS / Massachusetts. Supervisor of Administration – 1916-22. 7 fiches. (Harvard Law School Library Collection.) – 9 – 1.50f – us H.U. Law [324]

REPORTS / Michigan. Commissioner of Railroads – n.1-35, 1872-1907. 266 fiches. (Harvard Law School Library Collection.) – 9 – $1.50f – us H.U. Law [336]

REPORTS / Michigan. Dept. of Labor – (1947-65. 12 fiches. $1.50f; 9. v.1-10. 1966-75, 20 fiches. $1.50f; HLS; 9) – n.1-37, 1883-1919. 232 fiches. (Harvard Law School Library Collection.) – 9 – $1.50f – us H.U. Law [336]

REPORTS / Michigan. Dept. of Revenue – 1942-66. 34 fiches. (Harvard Law School Library Collection.) – 9 – $1.50f – us H.U. Law [336]

REPORTS / Michigan. Financial Institutions Bureau – n.1-78, 1889-1966. 396 fiches. (Harvard Law School Library Collection.) – 9 – $1.50f – us H.U. Law [336]

REPORTS / Michigan. Financial Institutions Bureau. Bank and Trust Division – 1967-77. 6 fiches. (Harvard Law School Library Collection.) – 9 – $1.50f – us H.U. Law [336]

REPORTS / Michigan. Public Utilities Commission – n.1-7, 1919-25. 9 fiches. (Harvard Law School Library Collection.) – 9 – $1.50f – us H.U. Law [336]

REPORTS / Michigan. Railroad Commission – n.2-12, 1908-18. 51 fiches. (Harvard Law School Library Collection.) – 9 – $1.50f – us H.U. Law [336]

REPORTS / Michigan. State Board of Tax Administration – 1933-41. 2 fiches. (Harvard Law School Library Collection.) – 9 – $1.50f – us H.U. Law [336]

REPORTS / Missouri. Supreme Court – v.1-88. 1821-85 – 1 – us UMI [340]

REPORTS / New Jersey. Board of Equalization of Taxes – n.1-10, 1905-14. 20 fiches. (Harvard Law School Library Collection.) – 9 – $1.50f – us H.U. Law [336]

REPORTS / New Jersey. Board of Public Utility Commissioners – 1910-77. 109 fiches. (Harvard Law School Library Collection.) – 9 – $1.50f – us H.U. Law [336]

REPORTS / New Jersey. Board of Railroad Commissioners – n.1-3, 1907-09. 12 fiches. (Harvard Law School Library Collection.) – 9 – $1.50f – us H.U. Law [336]

REPORTS / New Jersey. Division of Employment Security – n.1-33, 1937-69. 53 fiches. (Harvard Law School Library Collection.) – 9 – $1.50f – us H.U. Law [336]

REPORTS / New Jersey. Division of Savings and Loan Associations – 1899-1976. 297 fiches. (Harvard Law School Library Collection.) – 9 – $1.50f – us H.U. Law [336]

REPORTS / New Jersey. Employment Security Council – 1950-66. 4 fiches. (Harvard Law School Library Collection.) – 9 – $1.50f – us H.U. Law [336]

REPORTS / New Jersey. State Board of Mediation – 1941-79. 11 fiches. (Harvard Law School Library Collection.) – 9 – $1.50f – us H.U. Law [330]

REPORTS / New Jersey. State Board of Taxation – n.1-14, 1891-1904. 31 fiches. (Harvard Law School Library Collection.) – 9 – $1.50f – us H.U. Law [336]

REPORTS / New Jersey. State Board of Taxes and Assessment – n.1-16, 1915-31. 144 fiches. (Harvard Law School Library Collection.) – 9 – $1.50f – us H.U. Law [336]

REPORTS / New Jersey. State Investment Council – 1950-79. 29 fiches. (Harvard Law School Library Collection.) – 9 – $1.50f – us H.U. Law [336]

REPORTS / New Jersey. State Tax Dept – n.1-13, 1931-44. 39 fiches. (Harvard Law School Library Collection.) – 9 – $1.50f – us H.U. Law [336]

REPORTS / New York. Advisory Council on Employment and Unemployment Insurance – 1939-79. 40 fiches. (Harvard Law School Library Collection.) – 9 – $1.50f – us H.U. Law [336]

REPORTS / New York. Advisory Council on the Labor and Management Improper Practices Act – n1-11, 1959-69. 2 fiches. (Harvard Law School Library Collection.) – 9 – $1.50f – us H.U. Law [330]

REPORTS / New York. Banking Dept. Superintendent of Banks – 1851-1978. 680 fiches. (Harvard Law School Library Collection.) – 9 – $1.50f – us H.U. Law [336]

REPORTS / New York. Board of Railroad Commissioners – n.1-24, 1882-1906. 597 fiches. (Harvard Law School Library Collection.) – 9 – $1.50f – us H.U. Law [336]

REPORTS / New York. Dept. of Taxation and Finance – 1964-78. 8 fiches. (Harvard Law School Library Collection.) – 9 – $1.50f – us H.U. Law [336]

REPORTS / New York. Division of the Treasury – 1925-64. 27 fiches. (Harvard Law School Library Collection.) – 9 – $1.50f – us H.U. Law [336]

REPORTS / New York. Division of Water Power and Control – n.1-33, 1927-59. 32 fiches. (Harvard Law School Library Collection.) – 9 – $1.50f – us H.U. Law [336]

REPORTS / New York. Division of Water Resources – 1960-66. 2 fiches. (Harvard Law School Library Collection.) – 9 – $1.50f – us H.U. Law [336]

REPORTS / New York. Public Service Commission – 1921-77. 608 fiches. (Harvard Law School Library Collection.) – 9 – $1.50f – us H.U. Law [336]

REPORTS / New York. Public Service Commission. First District – 1907-20. 367 fiches. (Harvard Law School Library Collection.) – 9 – $1.50f – us H.U. Law [336]

REPORTS / New York. Public Service Commission. Second District – v.1-14, 1907-20. 249 fiches. (Harvard Law School Library Collection.) – 9 – $1.50f – us H.U. Law [336]

REPORTS / New York. State Board of Tax Commissioners – 1896-1914. 138 fiches. (Harvard Law School Library Collection.) – 9 – $1.50f – us H.U. Law [336]

REPORTS / New York. State Tax Commission – 1915-64. 207 fiches. (Harvard Law School Library Collection.) – 9 – $1.50f – us H.U. Law [336]

REPORTS / New York. Transit Commission – n.1-20, 1921-40. 126 fiches. (Harvard Law School Library Collection.) – 9 – $1.50f – us H.U. Law [336]

REPORTS / New York. Unemployment Insurance Appeal Board – n.1-20, 1938-57. 14 fiches. (Harvard Law School Library Collection.) – 9 – $1.50f – us H.U. Law [336]

REPORTS / New York. Water Power Commission – n.1-6, 1921-26. 8 fiches. (Harvard Law School Library Collection.) – 9 – $1.50f – us H.U. Law [336]

REPORTS / Ohio Bar Association – 1928-66 – 1 – us UMI [340]

REPORTS / Ohio. Bureau of Unemployment Compensation. State Advisory Council – May 1939-62. 6 fiches. (Harvard Law School Library Collection.) – 9 – $1.50f – us H.U. Law [336]

REPORTS / Ohio. Dept. of Commerce. Division of Banks – 1908-78. 179 fiches. (Harvard Law School Library Collection.) – 9 – $1.50f – us H.U. Law [336]

REPORTS / Ohio. Dept. of Commerce. Division of Building and Loan Associations – 1891-1979. 418 fiches. (Harvard Law School Library Collection.) – 9 – $1.50f – us H.U. Law [336]

REPORTS / Ohio. Dept. of Industrial Relations – 1921-79. 36 fiches. (Harvard Law School Library Collection.) – 9 – $1.50f – us H.U. Law [336]

REPORTS / Ohio. Dept. of Taxation – 1939-79. 74 fiches. (Harvard Law School Library Collection.) – 9 – $1.50f – us H.U. Law [336]

REPORTS / Ohio. Industrial Commission – 1913-22. 5 fiches. (Harvard Law School Library Collection.) – 9 – $1.50f – us H.U. Law [336]

REPORTS / Ohio. Public Utilities Commission – 1913-79. 233 fiches. (Harvard Law School Library Collection.) – 9 – $1.50f – us H.U. Law [336]

REPORTS / Ohio. Railroad Commission – n.1-6, 1906-11. 37 fiches. (Harvard Law School Library Collection.) – 9 – $1.50f – us H.U. Law [336]

REPORTS / Ohio. Tax Commission – n.1-26, 1910-35. 89 fiches. (Harvard Law School Library Collection.) – 9 – $1.50f – us H.U. Law [336]

REPORTS / Ontario. Royal Commissions – 1867-1983 – 9 – Can$1,045.00 – cn Micromedia [971]

REPORTS / Parkinson, William – (A narrative relating to the reports which have gone abroad concerning William Parkinson, 1810-1811) – 1 – 5.00 – us Baptist [240]

REPORTS / Pennsylvania. Bureau of Employment Security – 1936-78. 26 fiches. (Harvard Law School Library Collection.) – 9 – $1.50f – us H.U. Law [336]

REPORTS / Pennsylvania. Human Relations Commission – 1956-79. 13mf. (Harvard Law School Library Collection) – 9 – $1.50f – us H.U. Law [360]

REPORTS / Pennsylvania. Labor Relations Board – n1-40, 1937-76. 65 fiches. (Harvard Law School Library Collection) – 9 – $1.50f – us H.U. Law [330]

REPORTS / Pennsylvania. Securities Commission – 1923-78. 38 fiches. (Harvard Law School Library Collection.) – 9 – $1.50f – us H.U. Law [336]

REPORTS / Technical Oil Mission – 1945 – 1 – us L of C Photodup [660]

REPORTS / U.S. Atomic Energy Commission – v1-8, 1956-75. 80-499 – 9 – $60.00 – us L.L.M.C. [530]

REPORTS / U.S. Board of Tax Appeals – v1-47. 1924-42. Washington: GPO. 79-420 – 9 – $492.00 – us L.L.M.C. [336]

REPORTS / U.S. Circuit Courts of Appeals – With key-number annots. v1-84, 1892-1908. St. Paul: West. Cited as C.C.A. Title varies. 80-410 – 9 – $496.00 – us L.L.M.C. [340]

REPORTS / U.S. Civil Aeronautics Board – v1-75, 1939-78. 78-204 – 9 – 560.00 – us L.L.M.C. [324]

REPORTS / U.S. Commission on Civil Rights – 1961. Six books in three. 81-205 – 9 – $16.00 – us L.L.M.C. [323]

REPORTS / U.S. Court of International Trade – v1-9. (Nov) 1980-85. Washington: GPO. Updates available. Cite as Ct. Int'l Trade. 78-058B – 9 – 32.00 – us L.L.M.C. [324]

REPORTS / U.S. Department of Agriculture – Nos. 1-117. 1862-1918. 130 fiches – 9 – 200.00 – us Updata [630]

REPORTS / U.S. Federal Communications Commission – Series 1, v. 1-45. 1934-1965. Series 2, v. 1-33. July, 1965-Sept., 1972 – 1,5,6 – us Princeton Micro [323]

REPORTS / U.S. Federal Trade Commission – 1914-38 – 9 – $5.00f – us Ross [380]

REPORTS / U.S. Interstate Commerce Commission – v1-339. 1887-1971 – 1,5,6 – us Princeton Micro [323]

REPORTS / U.S. Joint Publications Research Service – 1958-81. Printed indexes (through 1976) available – 3 – us Readex [324]

REPORTS / U.S. Office of Scientific Research and Development – 1941-47. 487 rolls. T1012 – 1 – us Nat'l Archives [500]

REPORTS / U.S. Securities and Exchange Commission – 9 – us Disclosure [338]

REPORTS / Universities' Mission to Central Africa – 1860-1900 – 1 – uk Microform Academic [240]

REPORTS / Virginia. Dept. of Labor and Industry – 1898-1979. 151 fiches. (Harvard Law School Library Collection.) – 9 – $1.50f – us H.U. Law [336]

REPORTS / Virginia. Dept. of Taxation – 1926-78. 51 fiches. (Harvard Law School Library Collection.) – 9 – $1.50f – us H.U. Law [336]

REPORTS / Virginia. Railroad Commissioner – n.1-26, 1877-1902. 154 fiches. (Harvard Law School Library Collection.) – 9 – $1.50f – us H.U. Law [336]

REPORTS / Virginia. State Corporation Commission – 1903-78. 739 fiches. (Harvard Law School Library Collection.) – 9 – $1.50f – us H.U. Law [336]

REPORTS / Virginia. State Tax Commission – 1924-25. 1 fiches. (Harvard Law School Library Collection.) – 9 – $1.50f – us H.U. Law [336]

REPORTS / Wisconsin. Bank Comptroller – 1853-69. 20 fiches. (Harvard Law School Library Collection.) – 9 – $1.50f – us H.U. Law [336]

REPORTS / Wisconsin. Commissioner of Banking – 1895-1979. 257 fiches. (Harvard Law School Library Collection.) – 9 – $1.50f – us H.U. Law [336]

REPORTS / Wisconsin. Commissioner of Credit Unions – n.11, 1933-79. 37 fiches. (Harvard Law School Library Collection.) – 9 – $1.50f – us H.U. Law [336]

REPORTS / Wisconsin. Commissioner of Savings and Loan – 1897-1979. 161 fiches. (Harvard Law School Library Collection.) – 9 – $1.50f – us H.U. Law [336]

REPORTS / Wisconsin. Commissioner of Securities – 1919-79. 27 fiches. (Harvard Law School Library Collection.) – 9 – $1.50f – us H.U. Law [336]

REPORTS / Wisconsin. Dept. of Industry, Labor and Human Relations – 1883-1977. 155 fiches. (Harvard Law School Library Collection.) – 9 – $1.50f – us H.U. Law [330]

REPORTS / Wisconsin. Dept. of Revenue – 1899-1979. 83 fiches. (Harvard Law School Library Collection.) – 9 – $1.50f – us H.U. Law [336]

REPORTS / Wisconsin. Employment Relations Commission – 1937-75. 32 fiches. (Harvard Law School Library Collection.) – 9 – $1.50f – us H.U. Law [330]

REPORTS / Wisconsin. Public Service Commission – 1930-77. 29 fiches. (Harvard Law School Library Collection.) – 9 – $1.50f – us H.U. Law [336]

REPORTS / Wisconsin. Railroad Commission – 1905-30. 137 fiches. (Harvard Law School Library Collection.) – 9 – $1.50f – us H.U. Law [336]

REPORTS / Wisconsin. Railroad Commissioner – n.1-9, 1874-82; n.1-11, 1882-1904. 95 fiches. (Harvard Law School Library Collection.) – 9 – $1.50f – us H.U. Law [336]

REPORTS / Wisconsin. State Employment Service – 1952-64. 2 fiches. (Harvard Law School Library Collection.) – 9 – $1.50f – us H.U. Law [330]

REPORTS, 1912-15 / U.S. Department of Labor. Commission on Industrial Relations – 15 rolls. T4 – 1 – us Nat'l Archives [330]

REPORTS, 1921-1934 / National Council of the Jewish Community. Palestine. (Va'ad Le'umi) – Lacking: 1921; 1923; 1924; 1926-31; 1933. BJ-28-38 1 – 9 – ne IDC [956]

REPORTS..., 1933-43 / U.S. National Resources Planning Board – 5rolls. M120 – 1 – us Nat'l Archives [324]

REPORTS AND ACCOUNTS / Israel. State Corporations. ZIM Shipping Lines – Available: 1956, nr. 12; 1964, nr. 20; 1966; 1969; 1972. BJ-81-18 1 – 9 – ne IDC [330]

REPORTS AND BULLETINS / Connecticut. Agricultural Experiment Station. New Haven – v1-10. 1922-28 – 1,5,6 – us Spaulding [630]
REPORTS AND CORRESPONDENCE ON THE SUBJECT OF THE CHARGES PREFERRED AGAINST MR. GUGY – [London]: [House of Commons], [1837]. SEM105P1126 – 1mf – 9 – Can$2.25 – cn Bibl Nat [971]
REPORTS AND CORRESPONDENCE RELATING TO THE ARMY INVESTIGATIONS OF THE BATTLE OF WOUNDED KNEE AND TO THE SIOUX CAMPAIGN OF 1890-91 / U.S. Army – 2 rolls.M983 – 1 – us Nat'l Archives [324]
REPORTS AND DECISIONS..., 1863-66 / U.S. Army. Provost Marshal General – 1roll. M621. Printed guide – 1 – us Nat'l Archives [324]
REPORTS AND DOCUMENTS, DJAKARTA / U.S. Operations Mission to Indonesia. Agriculture Division – SE 4973 1. 1958-59 – 9 – ne IDC [630]
REPORTS AND DOCUMENTS IN REFERENCE TO THE LOCATION OF THE LINE AND A WESTERN TERMINAL HARBOUR / Canadian Pacific Railway Company – Ottawa: MacLean, Roger, 1878. 00446. (Pre-1900 Canadiana) – 9 – cn C.I.H.M. [380]
REPORTS AND EVIDENCE OF...THE INHABITANTS OF THE COUNTY OF YORK / Canada. Bas-Canada. Parlement. Chambre d'Assemblee – s.l: House of Assembly of Lower Canada, 1829. SEM105P96 – 3mf – 9 – Can$6.75 – cn Bibl Nat [324]
REPORTS AND JOURNALS OF SCOUTS AND MARCHES / Fort Dodge, KS – 1873-1878 – 1 – us KS Hist [350]
REPORTS AND MEMORANDA / Great Britain. Air Ministry Aeronautical Research Committee – 7 – uk Microform Academic [324]
REPORTS AND OPINIONS (A-G) / Alaska – 1917-1960; 1949-68. 7 reels – 1 – $35.00r – us Trans-Media [340]
REPORTS AND OPINIONS (A-G) / Arizona – 1915-77. 2 reels – 1 – $35.00r – us Trans-Media [340]
REPORTS AND OPINIONS (A-G) / Arkansas – 1877-1943. 3 reels – 1 – $35.00r – us Trans-Media [340]
REPORTS AND OPINIONS (A-G) / California – Reports: 1852-1972, 3 reels. Opinions: 1899-1943, 48 reels – 1 – $35.00r – us Trans-Media [340]
REPORTS AND OPINIONS (A-G) / Colorado – 1887-1966. 4 reels – 1 – $35.00r – us Trans-Media [340]
REPORTS AND OPINIONS (A-G) / Connecticut – 1899-1968. 5 reels – 1 – $35.00r – us Trans-Media [340]
REPORTS AND OPINIONS (A-G) / Florida – 1845-1978. 13 reels – 1 – $35.00r – us Trans-Media [340]
REPORTS AND OPINIONS (A-G) / Georgia – 1878-1979. 7 reels – 1 – $35.00r – us Trans-Media [340]
REPORTS AND OPINIONS (A-G) / Hawaii – Reports: 1845-1928, 1 reel. Opinions: 1915-63, 1 reel – 1 – $35.00r – us Trans-Media [340]
REPORTS AND OPINIONS (A-G) / Idaho – 1893-1978. 2 reels – 1 – $35.00r – us Trans-Media [340]
REPORTS AND OPINIONS (A-G) / Illinois – 1872-1978. 14 reels – 1 – $35.00r – us Trans-Media [340]
REPORTS AND OPINIONS (A-G) / Indiana – 1891-1979. 11 reels – 1 – $35.00r – us Trans-Media [340]
REPORTS AND OPINIONS (A-G) / Iowa – 1896-1978. 7 reels – 1 – $35.00r – us Trans-Media [340]
REPORTS AND OPINIONS (A-G) / Kansas – 1864-1979. 3 reels – 1 – $35.00r – us Trans-Media [340]
REPORTS AND OPINIONS (A-G) / Kentucky – 1908-59.1 reel – 1 – $35.00r – us Trans-Media [340]
REPORTS AND OPINIONS (A-G) / Louisiana – 1854-1969. 12 reels – 1 – $35.00r – us Trans-Media [340]
REPORTS AND OPINIONS (A-G) / Maine – 1840-1972. 4 reels – 1 – $35.00r – us Trans-Media [340]
REPORTS AND OPINIONS (A-G) / Maryland – 1916-79.13 reels – 1 – $35.00r – us Trans-Media [340]
REPORTS AND OPINIONS (A-G) / Massachusetts – 1832-1977. 9 reels – 1 – $35.00r – us Trans-Media [340]
REPORTS AND OPINIONS (A-G) / Michigan – 1890-1978. 11 reels – 1 – $35.00r – us Trans-Media [340]
REPORTS AND OPINIONS (A-G) / Minnesota – 1858-1968. 6 reels – 1 – $35.00r – us Trans-Media [340]
REPORTS AND OPINIONS (A-G) / Mississippi – 1893-1967. 3 reels – 1 – $35.00r – us Trans-Media [340]
REPORTS AND OPINIONS (A-G) / Missouri – Unpublished reports, 1933-75. 43 reels – 1 – $35.00r – us Trans-Media [340]
REPORTS AND OPINIONS (A-G) / Montana – 1900-76.7 reels – 1 – $35.00r – us Trans-Media [340]
REPORTS AND OPINIONS (A-G) / Nebraska – 1877-1978. 6 reels – 1 – $35.00r – us Trans-Media [340]
REPORTS AND OPINIONS (A-G) / Nevada – 1865-1978. 5 reels – 1 – $35.00r – us Trans-Media [340]
REPORTS AND OPINIONS (A-G) / New Hampshire – Reports, 1896-1952; Opinions, 1953-66. 1 reel – 1 – $35.00r – us Trans-Media [340]
REPORTS AND OPINIONS (A-G) / New Jersey – 1878-1978. 4 reels – 1 – $35.00r – us Trans-Media [978]
REPORTS AND OPINIONS (A-G) / New Mexico – 1902-77.6 reels – 1 – $35.00r – us Trans-Media [340]
REPORTS AND OPINIONS (A-G) / New York – 1777-1978. 19 reels – 1 – $35.00r – us Trans-Media [340]
REPORTS AND OPINIONS (A-G) / North Carolina – 1867-1979. 7 reels – 1 – $35.00r – us Trans-Media [340]
REPORTS AND OPINIONS (A-G) / North Dakota – 1889-1979. 4 reels – 1 – $35.00r – us Trans-Media [340]
REPORTS AND OPINIONS (A-G) / Ohio – 1846-1972. 34 reels – 1 – $35.00r – us Trans-Media [340]
REPORTS AND OPINIONS (A-G) / Oklahoma – 1897-1979. 2 reels – 1 – $35.00r – us Trans-Media [340]
REPORTS AND OPINIONS (A-G) / Oregon – 1897-1978. 11 reels – 1 – $35.00r – us Trans-Media [340]
REPORTS AND OPINIONS (A-G) / Pennsylvania – 1989-1978, 1934-56 – 15r – 1 – $35.00r – us Trans-Media [340]
REPORTS AND OPINIONS (A-G) / Puerto Rico – Reports, 1901-71, 2 reels; Opinions, 1903-58, 3 reels – 1 – $35.00r – us Trans-Media [340]
REPORTS AND OPINIONS (A-G) / South Carolina – 1870-1978. 10 reels – 1 – $35.00r – us Trans-Media [340]
REPORTS AND OPINIONS (A-G) / South Dakota – 1889-1978. 8 reels – 1 – $35.00r – us Trans-Media [340]
REPORTS AND OPINIONS (A-G) / Tennessee – 1875-1931, 1 reel. 1971-80, 1 reel – 1 – $35.00r – us Trans-Media [340]
REPORTS AND OPINIONS (A-G) / Texas – 1840-1970. 9 reels – 1 – $35.00r – us Trans-Media [340]
REPORTS AND OPINIONS (A-G) / Utah – 1896-1970. 4 reels – 1 – $35.00r – us Trans-Media [340]
REPORTS AND OPINIONS (A-G) / Vermont – 1904-74.4 reels – 1 – $35.00r – us Trans-Media [340]
REPORTS AND OPINIONS (A-G) / Virgin Islands – 1935-67. 1 reel – 1 – $35.00r – us Trans-Media [340]
REPORTS AND OPINIONS (A-G) / Virginia – 1837-1979. 9 reels – 1 – $35.00r – us Trans-Media [340]
REPORTS AND OPINIONS (A-G) / Washington – 1888-1980. 8 reels – 1 – $35.00r – us Trans-Media [340]
REPORTS AND OPINIONS (A-G) / West Virginia – 1893-1968. 7 reels – 1 – $35.00r – us Trans-Media [340]
REPORTS AND OPINIONS (A-G) / Wisconsin – 1852-1979. 17 reels – 1 – $35.00r – us Trans-Media [340]
REPORTS AND OPINIONS (A-G) / Wyoming – 1888-1970; 1976-82. 4 reels – 1 – $35.00r – us Trans-Media [340]
REPORTS AND OPINIONS OF THE ATTORNEYS-GENERAL OF THE STATES AND UNITED STATES / U. S. Attorney General – 473 reels – 1 – $14,500.00 – us Trans-Media [340]
REPORTS AND PAPERS PRESENTED AT THE INDO-PACIFIC FISHERY COMMISSION ON EXPERT CONSULTATION ON INLAND FISHERIES OF THE LARGER INDO-PACIFIC ISLANDS. BANGKOK, JUNE 1986 / IPFC – 1987 – 263p – it F.A.O. [338]
REPORTS AND PROCEEDINGS IN THE INDIAN NATIONAL CONGRESS / India. National Congress – v. 1-36. 1885-1921. Lacking: 1900, v. 17 (1) – 252mf – 8 – ne IDC [324]
REPORTS AND RECORDS OF PROCEEDINGS OF THE INTERNATIONAL LABOUR CONFERENCE / International Labour Organisation – 1919-92. With printed index. Continued annually – 1 – uk World [331]
REPORTS AND RESOLUTIONS, 1868-1900 / South Carolina – (With a finding aid) – 1784-1900. M-13 – 30r – 1 – $75.00r – Out-of-state orders: us Scholarly Res – us SC Archives [978]
REPORTS AND SUMMARY PROCEEDINGS / International Monetary Fund – 1946-74 – 1 – $580.00 – 0-89093-008-2 – us UPA [336]
REPORTS AND SUMMARY PROCEEDINGS / World Bank. International Bank for Reconstruction and Development – 1946-74 – 1 – $380.00 – 0-89093-009-0 – us UPA [336]
REPORTS BY THE DIRECTOR / Illinois. Department of Insurance – 1930-79. 34 fiches. (Harvard Law School Library Collection.) – 9 – $1.50f – us H.U. Law [336]
REPORTS BY THE NEW JERSEY SECRETARY OF STATE AS COMMISSIONER OF INSURANCE / New Jersey. Commissioner of Insurance – 1876-90. 91 fiches. (Harvard Law School Library Collection.) – 9 – $1.50f – us H.U. Law [336]
REPORTS FROM COMMISSIONERS, INSPECTORS AND OTHERS : EAST INDIA DECENTRALIZATION ROYAL COMMISSION 1908 – London. 7v. 1909 – 63mf – 9 – I-520/2 – ne IDC [950]
REPORTS FROM COMMITTEES OF THE HOUSE OF COMMONS 1715-1801 PRINTED BUT NOT INSERTED IN THE JOURNALS OF THE HOUSE – (With printed general index) – 16v. 1803-06 – 10r – 1 – £710.00 – uk Chadwyck [941]
REPORTS FROM THE LORDS COMMITTEES TOUCHING THE DIGNITY OF A PEER OF THE REALM – (With appendixes and indexes and Parliament-Legislative Assemblies Reports) – 5v. N.p. 1826 repr 1829 – 128mf – 9 – H-916/2 – ne IDC [944]
REPORTS FROM THE SPECIAL COMMITTEE ON ROADS AND OTHER INTERNAL COMUNICATIONS / Bas-Canada. Parlement. Chambre d'Assemblee. Comite Special sur les Chemins et Autres Communications Interieures – Quebec: Printed by Neilson & Cowan, 1829 – 2mf – 9 – Can$4.50 – cn Bibl Nat [380]
REPORTS: INDUSTRIAL WELFARE COMMISSIONERS / California. Division of Industrial Welfare – 1913-54. 26 fiches. (Harvard Law School Library Collection.) – 9 – 1.50f – us H.U. Law [331]
REPORTS OF BANK COMMISSIONER RELATIVE TO LICENSED CREDIT UNIONS / Connecticut. Office of Bank Commissioner – 1953-78. 6 fiches. (Harvard Law School Library Collection.) – 9 – $1.50f – us H.U. Law [336]
REPORTS OF CASES ARGUED AND ADJUDGED IN THE KING'S COURTS AT WESTMINSTER...1742-1774 / Great Britain. Court of King's Bench – 2nd ed. London, 1779-84. 3v in 2. LL-995 – 1 – us L of C Photodup [340]
REPORTS OF CASES ARGUED AND DETERMINED IN THE COURT OF APPEALS OF SOUTH CAROLINA. / South Carolina. Court of Appeals – Columbia, Morgan, 1838. 241, 7 p. LL-629 – 1 – us L of C Photodup [340]
REPORTS OF CASES ARGUED AND DETERMINED IN THE COURTS OF KING'S BENCH AND IN THE PROVINCIAL COURT OF APPEALS OF LOWER CANADA... / Bas-Canada. Cour du Banc du Roi – Quebec: Neilson & Cowan, 1835. SEM105P1383 – 2mf – 9 – Can$4.50 – cn Bibl Nat [324]
REPORTS OF CASES ARISING UPON APPLICATIONS FOR LETTERS-PATENT FOR INVENTIONS DETERMINED IN THE CIRCUIT AND SUPREME COURTS OF THE DISTRICT OF COLUMBIA. / MacArthur, Frank – volume 1. 1841-1859 Washington, D.C., Morrison, 1885. 788 p. LL-461 – 1 – us L of C Photodup [340]
REPORTS OF CASES CONCERNING THE REVENUE, ARGUED AND DETERMINED IN THE COURT OF EXCHEQUER, FROM EASTER TERM 1743, TO HILARY TERM 1767 / Great Britain. Court of Exchequer – London: Strahan and Woodfall, 1776. 283, 10p. LL-994 – 1 – us L of C Photodup [340]
REPORTS OF CASES DECIDED IN COMMON LAW CHAMBERS, CHANCERY CHAMBERS, AND THE MASTER'S OFFICE *see* ONTARIO PRACTICE REPORTS
REPORTS OF CASES DETERMINED IN THE SEVERAL COURTS OF WESTMINSTER-HALL, FROM 1746-1779 / Blackstone, William – 49mf – 9 – LLMC 82-800 Titles 225-228 – us L.L.M.C. [340]
REPORTS OF CASES UPON APPEALS AND WRITS OF ERROR DETERMINED IN THE HIGH COURT OF PARLIAMENT / Brown, Josiah – v1-8. 1803 – 1 – $200.00 – 0-89093-026-0 – us UPA [941]
REPORTS OF CASES...IN THE CONSISTORY COURT OF LONDON: CONTAINING THE JUDGMENTS OF SIR WILLIAM SCOTT / Haggard, John – London, Butterworth, 1822. 2 v. LL-997 – 1 – us L of C Photodup [340]
THE REPORTS OF CHAVONNES AND HIS COUNCIL : AND OF VAN IMHOFF, ON THE CAPE, WITH INCIDENTAL CORRESPONDENCE – Cape Town: Van Riebeeck Society, 1918 – us Res Libr [960]
REPORTS OF CHIEF ENGINEER ON THE SURVEY OF THE NORTH SHORE RAILWAY, AND OF DIRECTORS ON THE PROPER RESOURCES OF THE SAME / North Shore Railway Company – Quebec. Augustin Cote. 1854. SEM105P356 – 1mf – 9 – Can$2.25 – cn Bibl Nat [625]
REPORTS OF CLERKS AND BUREAU OFFICERS OF THE DEPARTMENT OF STATE / U.S. Department of State – 1790-1911. M800 – 8r – 1 – us Nat'l Archives [975]
REPORTS OF COMMISSIONERS FOR ROADS AND OTHER INTERNAL COMMUNICATIONS : RAPPORTS DES... / Bas-Canada. Commissaires Pour les Chemins et Autres Communications Interieures – [Quebec]: [Chambre d'Assemblee], [1830] – 7mf – 9 – Can$15.75 – cn Bibl Nat [380]
REPORTS OF DECISIONS / New York. Public Service Commission. First District – v1-12. Jul 1, 1907-Apr 25, 1921. 77 fiches. (Harvard Law School Library Collection.) – 9 – $1.50f – us H.U. Law [336]
REPORTS OF DECISIONS / New York. Public Service Commission. Second District – v1-9, Jul 1 1907-1920. 67 fiches. (Harvard Law School Library Collection.) – 9 – $1.50f – us H.U. Law [336]
REPORTS OF DECISIONS IN PROBATE / California. Superior Court. San Francisco Probate Department – San Francisco. 6v. 1908-16 – 1 – $46.00 – us L of C Photodup [340]
REPORTS OF EXPLORATIONS AND SURVEYS TO ASCERTAIN THE MOST PRACTICABLE ... FROM THE MISSISSIPPI RIVER TO THE PACIFIC OCEAN IN 1853-1855. – Washington. 12v. 1855-60 – 319mf – 9 – 5772/2 – ne IDC [910]
REPORTS OF EXPLORATIONS PRINTED IN THE DOCUMENTS OF THE UNITED STATES GOVERNMENT – Based on Adelaide R. Hasse's 1899 bibliography – 1 – us Primary [010]
REPORTS OF INSPECTIONS OF THE FIELD JURISDICTIONS OF THE OFFICE OF INDIAN AFFAIRS / U.S. Bureau of Indian Affairs – 1873-1900. 60 rolls M1070 – 1 – us Nat'l Archives [324]
REPORTS OF INTERNATIONAL ARBITRAL AWARDS = RECUEIL DES SENTENCES ARBITRALES / United Nations. Office of Legal Affairs – v1-19. 1920-86. Office of Legal Affairs, Codification Division, 1948?-90 – 129mf – 9 – $193.00 – LLMC 82-978 – us L.L.M.C. [340]
REPORTS OF INTERNATIONAL ARBITRAL AWARDS / United Nations – 197 fiches – 9 – 370.00; 1.90f – uk UNIMICRO [340]
REPORTS OF INVESTIGATIONS / U.S. Bureau of Mines – Nos 3240-8270. 1934-78 – 1,5,6 – us Princeton Micro [622]

REPORTS OF JUDGMENTS, ADVISORY OPINIONS AND ORDERS / United Nations. International Court of Justice – 1947-1989 – E/F.391 – 9 – us U.N. Pubs [340]

REPORTS OF PIERRE FORTIN AND THEOPHILE TETU...IN COMMAND OF THE EXPEDITION FOR THE PROTECTION OF THE FISHERIES IN THE GULF OF ST LAWRENCE... 1867 / Fortin, Pierre & Tetu, Theophile – Ottawa, 1868. SEM105P664 – 1mf – 9 – Can$2.25 – cn Bibl Nat [639]

REPORTS OF SOME OF THE CRIMINAL CASES ON PRIMARY HEARING, BEFORE RICHARD VAUX / Philadelphia. Recorder – Philadelphia: Johnson, 1846. 236p. LL-1351 – 1 – us L of C Photodup [340]

REPORTS OF SPECIES / Peck, C H – New York. 1868-1913 – 5 – uk Microform Academic [580]

REPORTS OF THE ADMINISTRATIVE OFFICE OF THE U.S. COURTS AND U.S. JUDICIAL CONFERENCE / U. S. Courts – 1945-83 – 241MF – 9 – $361.00 – LLMC 80-902 – us L.L.M.C. [340]

REPORTS OF THE ADMINISTRATOR OF THE UNEMPLOYMENT COMPENSATION LAW / Connecticut. Employment Security Division – 1st-9th, 1936-45. 9 fiches. (Harvard Law School Library Collection.) – 9 – $1.50f – us H.U. Law [336]

REPORTS OF THE ANGLO-AMERICAN COMMITTEE OF INQUIRY RE PALESTINE, 1944-1946 – (Includes descriptive pamphlet) – 1988 – 12r – 1 – $1,020.00 – S3049 – us Scholarly Res [956]

REPORTS OF THE ANNUAL MEETINGS OF THE NEW ZEALAND ECOLOGICAL SOCIETY – (Missing: no1) – Wellington. nos1-10. 1953-65 – 27mf – 9 – Z-193/2 – ne IDC [574]

REPORTS OF THE ARCHAEOLOGICAL SURVEY OF INDIA : NEW IMP. SERIES – London, Madras, 1874-1937 – 609mf – 9 – I-301/2 – ne IDC [930]

REPORTS OF THE ATOMENERGIE AB : A1-201, 214, 245 – Stockholm, 1958-66 – 321mf – 9 – 1091/2 – ne IDC [530]

REPORTS OF THE AUDITOR / Indiana. Dept. of Insurance. Audit and Control – 1817-1920. 130 fiches. (Harvard Law School Library Collection.) – 9 – $1.50f – us H.U. Law [336]

REPORTS OF THE BOARDS OF MISSIONS OF THE PROVINCES OF CANTERBURY AND YORK ON THE MISSION FIELD – (Includes bibliographical references and index) – London: SPCK; New York: E & J B Young, 1894 – 1mf – 9 – 0-8370-6362-0 – 1986-0362 – us A.T.L.A. [240]

REPORTS OF THE BUREAU OF APPLIED SOCIAL RESEARCH / Columbia University – (Guide only $75.00) – 1939-77. 510 titles. 810 fiches – 9 – $3,025.00 – us UPA [300]

REPORTS OF THE CIVIL RIGHTS COMMISSION – Bks1-6. 1961 – 20mf – 9 – $30.00 – LLMC 81-205 – us L.L.M.C. [320]

REPORTS OF THE COMMISSION ON HUMAN RIGHTS TO THE ECONOMIC AND SOCIAL COUNCIL : 1ST-41ST SESSIONS / United Nations. Commission on Human Rights – 1947-1989 – E.101 F.97 R.79 S.71 – 9 – us U.N. Pubs [320]

REPORTS OF THE COMMISSIONER OF BANKING / New Jersey. Dept. of Banking – 1891-1979. 205 fiches. (Harvard Law School Library Collection.) – 9 – $1.50f – us H.U. Law [336]

REPORTS OF THE COMMISSIONER OF BANKING / Pennsylvania. Banking Dept – 1891-1917. 447 fiches. (Harvard Law School Library Collection.) – 9 – $1.50f – us H.U. Law [336]

REPORTS OF THE COMMISSIONER OF BANKS / Massachusetts. Dept. of Banking and Insurance. Division of Banks and Loan Agencies – 1838-1974. 890 fiches. (Harvard Law School Library Collection.) – 9 – $1.50f – us H.U. Law [336]

REPORTS OF THE COMMISSIONER OF INSURANCE / Massachusetts. Dept. of Banking and Insurance. Division of Insurance – 1855-1967. 891 fiches. (Harvard Law School Library Collection.) – 9 – 1.50f – us H.U. Law [324]

REPORTS OF THE COMMISSIONER OF INSURANCE / Virginia. Bureau of Insurance – n.1-46, 1906-51. 269 fiches. (Harvard Law School Library Collection.) – 9 – $1.50f – us H.U. Law [336]

REPORTS OF THE COMMISSIONER TO THE FIVE CIVILIZED TRIBES / U.S. Commission to the Five Civilized Tribes – An original microform collection which includes annual and special reports by the Commissioner, along with volumes of statutes and pertinent Congressional hearings. 1893-1920 – 1 – $295.00 – 0-89093-005-8 – us UPA [977]

REPORTS OF THE COMMISSIONERS APPOINTED TO INQUIRE INTO THE GRIEVANCES COMPLAINED OF IN LOWER CANADA – s.l: House of Commons, 1837. SEM105P115 – 5mf – 9 – Can$11.25 – cn Bibl Nat [324]

REPORTS OF THE COMMITTEE / African Institution – 18v. London. 1808-18 – 28mf – 9 – ne IDC [960]

REPORTS OF THE COMMITTEE APPOINTED BY THE GOVERNMENT OF HYDERABAD STATE (NO. 594). PART 2: PRESERVATION AND MAINTENANCE OF THE CAVE-TEMPLES OF ELLORA / India. Preservation of National Monuments – 1949. BI-790 2 – 8 – ne IDC [720]

REPORTS OF THE DIRECTOR OF INSURANCE / Ohio. Dept. of Commerce. Division of Insurance – 1867-1979. 818 fiches. (Harvard Law School Library Collection.) – 9 – $1.50f – us H.U. Law [336]

REPORTS OF THE F.A.O. REGIONAL CONFERENCES – it F.A.O. [630]

REPORTS OF THE GENERAL BOARD, U.S. FORCES, EUROPEAN THEATER : AN ANALYSIS OF U.S. MILITARY ACTIVITIES IN EUROPE, 1944-1945 / U.S. Army. European Theater of Operations – (With printed guide) – US Forces General Board, 1945-46 – 7r – 1 – $595.00 – S1678 – us Scholarly Res [355]

REPORTS OF THE IMMIGRATION COMMISSION, 1907-1910 / U.S. Senate – (With printed guide) – 61st Congress 3rd session, 1993 – 17r – 1 – $1,445.00 – S3037 – us Scholarly Res [320]

REPORTS OF THE INSPECTORS OF THE FREE PORTS OF GASPE AND SAULT STE. MARIE, TOGETHER WITH CERTAIN STATISTICAL TABLES OF IMPORTS – Quebec: Printed by Hunter, Rose and Co, 1865. SEM105P306 – 1mf – 9 – Can$2.25 – cn Bibl Nat [380]

REPORTS OF THE INSURANCE COMMISSIONER / Connecticut. Insurance Dept – 1st-. 1865-1977. 1588 fiches. (Harvard Law School Library Collection.) – 9 – $1.50f – us H.U. Law [336]

REPORTS OF THE INSURANCE COMMISSIONER / Maryland. Insurance Division – 1871-1978. 552 fiches. (Harvard Law School Library Collection.) – 9 – 1.50f – us H.U. Law [324]

REPORTS OF THE INSURANCE COMMISSIONER / Pennsylvania. Insurance Dept – 1873-1979. 1047 fiches. (Harvard Law School Library Collection.) – 9 – $1.50f – us H.U. Law [336]

REPORTS OF THE INTERNATIONAL ARBITRAL AWARDS / United Nations – Vols 1-18 – E/F.207 – 9 – us U.N. Pubs [340]

REPORTS OF THE LOAN FUND ASSOCIATIONS, BY THE INSURANCE COMMISSIONERS / Massachusetts. Insurance Dept – n.1-10, 1856-65. 16 fiches. (Harvard Law School Library Collection.) – 9 – 1.50f – us H.U. Law [324]

THE REPORTS OF THE MAGICIANS AND ASTROLOGERS OF NINEVEH AND BABYLON IN THE BRITISH MUSEUM / Thompson, Reginald Campbell – Orig. text, in cuneiform characters, ed. with trans., notes, vocabulary, index, and introd. London: Luzac and Co., 1900. 2v – 1 – us U.W. Library [150]

REPORTS OF THE MASSACHUSETTS' COMMISSIONER OF BANKS RELATING TO LICENSED SMALL LOAN LENDERS / Massachusetts. Dept. of Banking and Insurance. Division of Banks and Loan Agencies – 1911-75. 62 fiches. (Harvard Law School Library Collection.) – 9 – $1.50f – us H.U. Law [336]

REPORTS OF THE MICHIGAN STATE TAX COMMISSION AND THE STATE BOARD OF ASSESSORS / Michigan. State Tax Commission – n.1-34, 1899-1965. 70 fiches. (Harvard Law School Library Collection.) – 9 – $1.50f – us H.U. Law [336]

REPORTS OF THE NATIONAL RESOURCES PLANNING BOARD, 1936-1943 – 5r – 1 – M120 – us Nat'l Archives [324]

REPORTS OF THE PROGRESS OF APPLIED CHEMISTRY / Society of Chemical Industry – v. 1-39. 1916-1954 – 1,5,6 – us Princeton Micro [540]

REPORTS OF THE RAILROAD CORPORATIONS IN THE STATE OF MASSACHUSETTS / Massachusetts. General Court. Committee on Railways and Canals – 1836-56. 47 fiches. (Harvard Law School Library Collection.) – 9 – 1.50f – us H.U. Law [324]

REPORTS OF THE SCOTTISH ECONOMIC PLANNING DEPARTMENT AND THE SCOTTISH DEVELOPMENT DEPARTMENT / Great Britain. Planning and Development in Scotland 1973 74 – Edinburgh. 1975. BD-2030 1 – 9 – ne IDC [338]

REPORTS OF THE SUPERINTENDENT OF INSURANCE / New York. Insurance Dept – 1859-1978. 3320 fiches. (Harvard Law School Library Collection.) – 9 – $1.50f – us H.U. Law [336]

REPORTS OF THE TRIALS OF COLONEL AARON BURR, (LATE VICE PRESIDENT OF THE UNITED STATES), FOR TREASON. / Burr, Aaron – Philadelphia, Hopkins and Earle, Fry and Kammerer, 1808. 2 v. LL-207 – 1 – us L of C Photodup [340]

REPORTS OF THE U.S. MILITARY GOVERNMENT FOR GERMANY, U.S. ZONE, 1945-1953 / U.S. Army – (With printed guide) – 1984 – 6r – 1 – $510.00 – S1658 – Co-publ with the Center for Military History – us Scholarly Res [355]

REPORTS OF THE U.S. MILITARY GOVERNMENT OF AUSTRIA, 1945-50 / U.S. High Commissioner of Austrian Military Government – (Includes printed guide) – 1984 – 7r – 1 – $595.00 – S1659 – Co-publ with the U.S. Army Center of Military History – us Scholarly Res [943]

REPORTS OF THE U.S. NAVAL TECHNICAL MISSION TO JAPAN, 1945-46 / U.S. Navy – (With printed guide) – 1984 – 13r – 1 – $1,105.00 – S1669 – us Scholarly Res [355]

REPORTS OF THE ZIONIST EXECUTIVE, ITS DEPARTMENTS AND AFFILIATED BODIES TO ZIONIST CONGRESSES / Zionist Congress. (1907-1951) – (Subdivisions:. 8th Zionist Congress, The Hague, 1907. Bericht des zionistischen Zentralblueros. 9th Zionist Congres, Hamburg, 1909. Bericht des Actions-Comites. Taetigkeitsbericht des juedischen Nationalfonds. 10th Zionist Congress, Basle, 1911. Bericht des Actions-Comites. 11th Zionist Congress, Vienna, 1913. Bericht des Actions-Comites) – 1907-51. BJ-72-202 1 – 9 – ne IDC [956]

REPORTS ON ADMINISTRATION OF PALESTINE AND TRANSJORDAN DURING THE PERIOD 1920-1938 – London. v1-18. 1921-39 – 84mf – 9 – J-28-107/1 – ne IDC [956]

REPORTS ON AGRICULTURAL DEVELOPMENT AND LAND SETTLEMENT IN PALESTINE / Palestine. Department of Development – By L. French. Reports: Report on agricultural development. Dec 1931. II. Supplementary report. Jerusalem. Apr 1932. BJ-28-109 1 – 9 – ne IDC [630]

REPORTS ON CLINICAL SIGNIFICANCE OF CATALASE / Herzog, A – Augsburg 1962 2. MS – 9mf – ne IDC [616]

REPORTS ON COMPENSABLE WORK INJURIES IN ILLINOIS / Illinois. Department of Labor. Division of Statistics and Research – 1932-67. 88 fiches. (Harvard Law School Library Collection.) – 9 – $1.50f – us H.U. Law [310]

REPORTS ON CONDITION OF WOMEN AND CHILD WAGE-EARNERS IN THE UNITED STATES / U.S. Bureau of Labor – Washington. 19v. 1910-13 – 91mf – 9 – $5.00f – us Ross [331]

REPORTS ON MATHEMATICAL PHYSICS – v1-1975- – 5,6,9 – us UMI [530]

REPORTS ON MEDICAL CASES / Bright, R – 3V. M 42. 1827-1831 – 9 – ne IDC [610]

REPORTS ON PROGRESS IN PHYSICS – v1-. 1934- – 1,5,6,9 – £500.00 – uk I.O.P. [530]

REPORTS ON THE BOARD OF DIRECTORS / Egypt. Central Bank of Egypt – 11v in 4. 1961-74. BNE-4616 1 – 9 – ne IDC [336]

REPORTS ON THE EASTERN FRONTIER OF BRITISH INDIA, EXTENDING TO YUNAN IN CHINA / Pemberton, R B – Calcutta, 1835. Maps. BSE-66 2 – 8 – ne IDC [910]

REPORTS ON THE MOSSES COLLECTED BY MR. C. E. C. FISCHER A.O. FROM SOUTH INDIA AND CEYLON / Dixon, H N – (Records of the Bot. Survey of India, v. 6). 1914 – 8 – ne IDC [580]

REPORTS ON THE RAILROADS / New York. State Engineer and Surveyor – 1849-82. 336mf. (Harvard Law School Library Collection) – 9 – $1.50f – us H.U. Law [336]

REPORTS ON THE RESULTS OF DREDGING BY THE UNITED STATES COAST SURVEY STEAMER BLAKE, 15 / Dall, W H – Preliminary report on the Mollusca. (Bull. Mus. Comp. Zool., v9, 1881, p33-144). Z-2230/1 – 9 – ne IDC [590]

REPORTS ON THE RESULTS OF DREDGING BY THE U.S. COAST SURVEY STEAMER BLAKE.29 / Dall, W H – 1886. Report on the Mollusca. PT. 1. Brachiopoda and Palecypoda. Bull. Mus. Comp. Zool., 1885-86, v12, p171-318, pls. 1-9. Z-2231/1 – 9 – ne IDC [590]

REPORTS ON THE STATE OF LARGE TOWNS AND POPULOUS DISTRICTS / Great Britain. Commissioners of Health – 1844-45 – 2r – 1 – uk Microform Academic [324]

REPORTS ON U.S. DISBURSEMENTS TO THE INDIANS / U.S. General Accounting Office – (Supplement One to the GAO Reports. 11 titles. 34mf. $130.00) – With printed index. 86 titles. 300mf – 9 – $1,000.00 – us UPA [324]

REPORTS ON ZOOLOGY / Ray Society – 1843-47 – 1 $56.00 7 £35.00 $65.00 – uk Microform Academic [590]

REPORTS ON...ROYAL BANK OF AVRAM / Avram, Duke of – Also reports on the Duchy of Avram, Tasmania, an individual secession, in practice, if not in theory.In: On Panarchy, no.IX. 55p – 9 – 1.00f – at Libertarian Micro [335]

REPORTS, PAPERS, ETC. RELATING TO THE PUBLIC WORKS / Telford, Thomas – 1 – uk Microform Academic [920]

REPORTS, POST-NRS / California – 1885-1922. 34 reels – 1 – $33.50r – us Trans-Media [340]

REPORTS, POST-NRS / Connecticut – 1885-1975. 36 reels – 1 – $33.50r – us Trans-Media [340]

REPORTS, POST-NRS / Delaware – 1894-1968. 21 reels – 1 – $33.50r – us Trans-Media [340]

REPORTS, POST-NRS / Florida – 1886-1948. 46 reels – 1 – $33.50r – us Trans-Media [340]

REPORTS, POST-NRS / Georgia – 1887-1983. 45 reels – 1 – $33.50r – us Trans-Media [340]

REPORTS, POST-NRS / Idaho – 1903-46.21 reels – 1 – $33.50r – us Trans-Media [340]

REPORTS, POST-NRS / Indiana – 1885-1921. 22 reels – 1 – $33.50r – us Trans-Media [340]

REPORTS, POST-NRS / Iowa – 1880-1922. 39 reels – 1 – $33.50r – us Trans-Media [340]

REPORTS, POST-NRS / Kansas – 1883-1974. 52 reels – 1 – $33.50r – us Trans-Media [340]

REPORTS, POST-NRS / Kentucky – 1887-1951. 79 reels – 1 – $33.50r – us Trans-Media [340]

REPORTS, POST-NRS / Louisiana – 1889-1900; 1899-1901; 1900-28. 19 reels – 1 – $33.50r – us Trans-Media [340]

REPORTS, POST-NRS / Maine – 1885-1921. 11 reels – 1 – $33.50r – us Trans-Media [340]

REPORTS, POST-NRS / Maryland – 1886-1922. 19 reels – 1 – $33.50r – us Trans-Media [340]

REPORTS, POST-NRS / Massachusetts – 1885-1974. 61 reels – 1 – $33.50r – us Trans-Media [340]

REPORTS, POST-NRS / Michigan – 1879-1921. 55 reels – 1 – $33.50r – us Trans-Media [340]

REPORTS, POST-NRS / Minnesota – 1887-1976. 66 reels – 1 – $33.50r – us Trans-Media [340]

REPORTS, POST-NRS / Mississippi – 1887-1965. 63 reels – 1 – $33.50r – us Trans-Media [340]

REPORTS, POST-NRS / Missouri – 1886-1957. 82 reels – 1 – $33.50r – us Trans-Media [340]

REPORTS, POST-NRS / Montana – 1881-1977. 38 reels – 1 – $33.50r – us Trans-Media [340]

REPORTS, POST-NRS / Nebraska – 1879-1978. 54 reels – 1 – $33.50r – us Trans-Media [340]

REPORTS, POST-NRS / Nevada – 1882-1974. 15 reels – 1 – $33.50r – us Trans-Media [340]
REPORTS, POST-NRS / New Hampshire – 1886-1980 – 13r – 1 – $33.50r – us Trans-Media [340]
REPORTS, POST-NRS / New Jersey – (1887-1948. Law Reports. 21 reels) – 1885-1948. Equity Reports. 24 reels – 1 – $33.50r – us Trans-Media [340]
REPORTS, POST-NRS / New York. (State) – 1885-1956. 207 reels – 1 – $33.50r – us Trans-Media [340]
REPORTS, POST-NRS / North Carolina – 1887-1975. 61 reels – 1 – $33.50r – us Trans-Media [340]
REPORTS, POST-NRS / Ohio – 1885-1964; 1926-64. 56 reels – 1 – $33.50r – us Trans-Media [340]
REPORTS, POST-NRS / Pennsylvania – 1885-1974 – 71r – 1 – $33.50r – us Trans-Media [340]
REPORTS, POST-NRS / Rhode Island – 1887-1980 – 23r – 1 – $33.50r – us Trans-Media [340]
REPORTS, POST-NRS / South Carolina – 1887-1976. 49 reels – 1 – $33.50r – us Trans-Media [978]
REPORTS, POST-NRS / Tennessee – 1886-1971. 36 reels – 1 – $33.50r – us Trans-Media [340]
REPORTS, POST-NRS / Texas – 1886-1962. 25 reels – 1 – $33.50r – us Trans-Media [340]
REPORTS, POST-NRS / Virginia – 1887-1975. 58 reels – 1 – $33.50r – us Trans-Media [340]
REPORTS, POST-NRS / Washington – 1891-1939. 52 reels – 1 – $33.50r – us Trans-Media [340]
REPORTS, POST-NRS / West Virginia – 1887-1972. 32 reels – 1 – $33.50r – us Trans-Media [340]
REPORTS, POST-NRS / Wisconsin – 1879-1979. 58 reels – 1 – $33.50r – us Trans-Media [340]
REPORTS, POST-NRS / Wyoming – 1883-1959. 16 reels – 1 – $33.50r – us Trans-Media [340]
REPORTS, PRE-1894 / Ireland – 60 reels – 1 – $2,500.00 – us Trans-Media [941]
REPORTS, PRE-NES / Oklahoma – 1890-1893, 1908-1909 – 1 – $35.00 – us Trans-Media [340]
REPORTS PRE-NRS / Alabama – 1820-39.23 reels – 1 – $35.00r – us Trans-Media [340]
REPORTS, PRE-NRS / Arkansas – 1820-26; 1895-1900; 1837-85. 11 reels – 1 – $35.00r – us Trans-Media [340]
REPORTS, PRE-NRS / California – 1855-1910; 1850-83. 21 reels – 1 – $35.00r – us Trans-Media [340]
REPORTS, PRE-NRS / Colorado – 1864-83; 1880-84; 1900-02. 5 reels – 1 – $35.00r – us Trans-Media [340]
REPORTS, PRE-NRS / Connecticut – 1785-89; 1764-98; 1801-13; 1814-85. 12 reels – 1 – $35.00r – us Trans-Media [340]
REPORTS, PRE-NRS / Dakota. Territory – 1867-89.1 reel – 1 – $35.00r – us Trans-Media [340]
REPORTS, PRE-NRS / Delaware – 1832-83; 1814-86; 1856-79. 5 reels – 1 – $35.00r – us Trans-Media [340]
REPORTS, PRE-NRS / District of Columbia – 1801-41; 1863-93; 1893-1920. 16 reels – 1 – $35.00r – us Trans-Media [340]
REPORTS, PRE-NRS / Florida – 1846-86.5 reels – 1 – $35.00r – us Trans-Media [340]
REPORTS, PRE-NRS / Georgia – 1805-37; 1842-43; 1885-86; 1846-87. 21 reels – 1 – $35.00r – us Trans-Media [340]
REPORTS, PRE-NRS / Hawaii – 1847-1961; 1900-17. 14 reels – 1 – $35.00r – us Trans-Media [340]
REPORTS, PRE-NRS / Idaho – 1866-80; 1866-67. 1 reel – 1 – $35.00r – us Trans-Media [340]
REPORTS, PRE-NRS / Illinois – 1819-85; 1877-1936; 1866-1908; 1889-1966. 102 reels – 1 – $35.00r – us Trans-Media [340]
REPORTS, PRE-NRS / Indiana – 1817-47; 1848-49; 1871-74; 1848-84. 24 reels – 1 – $35.00r – us Trans-Media [340]
REPORTS, PRE-NRS / Indiana. Territory – 1896-1907. 2 reels – 1 – $35.00r – us Trans-Media [340]
REPORTS, PRE-NRS / Iowa – 1839-46; 1847-54; 1855-79. 13 reels – 1 – $35.00r – us Trans-Media [340]
REPORTS, PRE-NRS / Kansas – 1862-83; 1858-68. 8 reels – 1 – $35.00r – us Trans-Media [340]
REPORTS, PRE-NRS / Kentucky – 1785-87; 1864-86; 1880-87. 28 reels – 1 – $35.00r – us Trans-Media [340]
REPORTS, PRE-NRS / Louisiana – 1809-88; 1924-28. 32 reels – 1 – $35.00r – us Trans-Media [340]
REPORTS, PRE-NRS / Maine – 1820-85.17 reels – 1 – $35.00r – us Trans-Media [340]
REPORTS, PRE-NRS / Maryland – 1658-1928. 27 reels – 1 – $35.00r – us Trans-Media [340]
REPORTS, PRE-NRS / Massachusetts – 1804-05; 1786-1885; 1936-50. 38 reels – 1 – $35.00r – us Trans-Media [340]
REPORTS, PRE-NRS / Michigan – 1847-78.11 reels – 1 – $35.00r – us Trans-Media [340]
REPORTS, PRE-NRS / Minnesota – 1851-79.5 reels – 1 – $35.00r – us Trans-Media [340]
REPORTS, PRE-NRS / Mississippi – 1818-86.21 reels – 1 – $35.00r – us Trans-Media [340]
REPORTS, PRE-NRS / Missouri – 1821-85; 1876-1902. 42 reels – 1 – $35.00r – us Trans-Media [340]
REPORTS, PRE-NRS / Montana – 1868-80.1 reel – 1 – $35.00r – us Trans-Media [340]
REPORTS, PRE-NRS / Nebraska – 1860-79; 1901-04. 4 reels – 1 – $35.00r – us Trans-Media [340]
REPORTS, PRE-NRS / Nevada – 1865-82.3 reels – 1 – $35.00r – us Trans-Media [340]
REPORTS, PRE-NRS / New Hampshire – 1796-1816; 1816-85. 13 reels – 1 – $35.00r – us Trans-Media [340]
REPORTS, PRE-NRS / New Jersey – 1789-1887; 1830-85. 19 reels – 1 – $35.00r – us Trans-Media [340]
REPORTS, PRE-NRS / New Mexico – 1852-86.1 reel – 1 – $35.00r – us Trans-Media [340]
REPORTS, PRE-NRS / New York – 1847-85; 1874-88; 1889-90. 183 reels – 1 – $35.00r – us Trans-Media [340]
REPORTS, PRE-NRS / North Carolina – 1778-1886. 20 reels – 1 – $35.00r – us Trans-Media [340]
REPORTS, PRE-NRS / Ohio – 1809-1959. 84 reels – 1 – $35.00r – us Trans-Media [340]
REPORTS, PRE-NRS / Oregon – 1853-83.2 reels – 1 – $35.00 – us Trans-Media [340]
REPORTS, PRE-NRS / Panama Canal Zone – 1905-1926. 1 reel – 1 – $35.00 – us Trans-Media [340]
REPORTS, PRE-NRS / Pennsylvania – 1754-1931. 73 reels – 1 – $35.00r – us Trans-Media [340]
REPORTS, PRE-NRS / Puerto Rico – 1900-24; 1899-1937. 20 reels – 1 – $35.00r – us Trans-Media [340]
REPORTS, PRE-NRS / Rhode Island – 1828-87.5 reels – 1 – $35.00r – us Trans-Media [340]
REPORTS, PRE-NRS / South Carolina – 1783-1868; 1784-1816; 1824-68; 1868-87. 23 reels – 1 – $35.00r – us Trans-Media [340]
REPORTS, PRE-NRS / South Dakota – 1867-1889 – 1 reel – 1 – $35.00 – us Trans-Media [340]
REPORTS, PRE-NRS / Tennessee – 1791-1880; 1925-33. 29 reels – 1 – $35.00r – us Trans-Media [340]
REPORTS, PRE-NRS / Texas – 1846-86; 1876-93; 1900-08. 40 reels – 1 – $35.00r – us Trans-Media [340]
REPORTS, PRE-NRS / Utah – 1855-84.1 reel – 1 – $35.00 – us Trans-Media [340]
REPORTS, PRE-NRS / Vermont – 1789-1828; 1826-86. 17 reels – 1 – $35.00r – us Trans-Media [340]
REPORTS, PRE-NRS / Virginia – 1729-72; 1779-1900. 25 reels – 1 – $35.00r – us Trans-Media [340]
REPORTS, PRE-NRS / Washington – 1854-88; 1889-90. 1 reel – 1 – $35.00 – us Trans-Media [340]
REPORTS, PRE-NRS / West Virginia – 1864-86.10 reels – 1 – $35.00r – us Trans-Media [340]
REPORTS, PRE-NRS / Wisconsin – 1839-79.16 reels – 1 – $35.00r – us Trans-Media [340]
REPORTS, PRE-NRS / Wyoming – 1870-82.1 reel – 1 – $35.00 – us Trans-Media [340]
REPORTS REQUIRED BY CONGRESS ON MICROFICHE : CIS GUIDE TO EXECUTIVE COMMUNICATIONS – (1997: index (cd-rom & print) and mf $4,140. 1994-96: mf $3,695.00/yr 1994-96: index $590.00/yr) – 1994- – ca 1300mf per yr – 9 – us CIS [324]
REPORTS, RESOLUTIONS AND SPECIAL NATIONAL CONFERENCE REPORTS, 1914-60 / Independent Labour Party. Great Britain – 1 – uk Microform Academic [360]
REPORTS SHOWING THE CONDITION OF BANKS, SAVINGS AND LOAN ASSOCIATIONS, INDUSTRIAL LOAN ASSOCIATIONS, CREDIT UNIONS / Virginia. Bureau of Financial Institutions. State Corporation Commission – 1904-79. 101mf. (Harvard Law School Library Collection) – 9 – $1.50f – us H.U. Law [336]
REPORTS: SURVEY OF THEOL. EDUCATION / Southern Baptist Convention. Executive Committee – (Account Book of Receipts, 1917-47, for Cooperative Program, Designated Gifts, and Hundred Thousand Club. Reel 3) – Reels 1-2 – 1 – us Baptist [240]
REPORTS TO CONGRESS FROM THE SECRETARY OF WAR, 1803-70 / U.S. War Department. Office of the Secretary – 5rolls. M220. Printed guide – 1 – us Nat'l Archives [324]
REPORTS TO COUNCIL AND CITIZENS / Wood County. Ohio. Bowling Green. City Mayor – 1960-1971 – 2r – 1 – $32.50r – us Archival [324]
REPORT...TO INQUIRE INTO THE AFFAIRS OF THE GRAND TRUNK RAILWAY / Canada. Parliament. Commission – Quebec: Printed by Stewart Derbishire and George Desbarats, 1861. SEM105P362 – 4mf – 9 – Can$9.00 – cn Bibl Nat [336]
REPORT...WITH APPENDICES / Cape of Good Hope. Surveyor-General's Office – Cape Town: W.A. Richards, Govt. Printers. 1894-96, 1898-99, 1901-05, 1907 – 1 – us U.W. Library [960]
LE REPOS DU TRAVAILLEUR : HEBDO DU JOURNAL "LE MONDE" – Montreal, Canada. 1 sep 1890 – 1r – 1 – Can$25.00 – cn Can Microfilming [072]
REPOSITORY – Canton. Ohio. 1876- – 1 – us UMI [071]
REPOSITORY – Canton. Ohio. -w. 1815-1905 – 1 – us UMI [071]
REPOSITORY – Chambersburg. PA. 1847-48. -w. Includes Whig – 1 – us UMI [071]
REPOSITORY – Greensburg. Ind. -w. 1844-48 – 1 – us UMI [071]
THE REPOSITORY OF ARTS, LITERATURE, FASHIONS AND MANUFACTURING / Ackermann, Richard – v1-41. 1809-29 – 9 – 700.00 – us Opus [073]
REPOSITORY OF SACRED MUSIC / Wyeth, John – 1813 – 1 – 5.00 – us Baptist [240]
REPOSITORY OF WIT AND HUMOR : SELECTED AND ARRANGED BY M. LAFAYETTE BYRN – Boston: John P Jewet Co, 1857 – 5mf – 9 – $7.50 – LLMC 91-064 – us L.L.M.C. [870]
REPRESENTACION CONTRA EL VOTO DE SANTIAGO / Robles Vives, Antonio – 1771 – 2mf – 9 – Pta1,500.00 – 84-7848-281-4 – sp Pentalfa [240]
REPRESENTACION... FELIPE V...AUMENTO... ERARIO / Zavala y Aunon, Miguel de – 1732 – 9 – $1.50f – sp Bibl Santa Ana [946]
REPRESENTACION...DIRIGIDA...CONSEJO DE REGENCIA / Quevedo y Quintano, Pedro – 1812 – 9 – 1.50f – sp Bibl Santa Ana [946]
REPRESENTACIONES...AL REY / Moscoso y Montemayor, Cristobal – 1722 – 9 – 1.50f – sp Bibl Santa Ana [946]
LE REPRESENTANT DU PEUPLE – no. 1-3. 27-29 fevr 1848; no. 1-108. 1er avr-21 aout 1848. devenu: La Peuple. no. 1-206. 1er nov 1848-13 juin 1849. devenu: La Voix du peuple. no. 1-223. 1er oct 1849-14 mai 1850. devenu: Le Peuple de 1850. no. 1-33. 15 juin-13 oct 1850. Paris – 1 – fr A.C.R.P.P. [073]
THE REPRESENTATION AND REPRODUCTION OF TWO-DIMENSIONAL MOVEMENT PATTERNS / Hughes, Barry G – 1989 – 2mf – 9 – $8.00 – us Microform Publ [790]
REPRESENTATIONS – (1985- . 5,6,9) – v1- . 1983- – 1 – us UMI [073]
REPRESENTATIONS AND REALITIES : ANALYZING GENDER SYMBOLS IN THE ROMANTIC BALLET / Meglin, Joellen A – Temple University, 1995 – 4mf – 9 – $16.00 – PSY1854 – us Microform Publ [305]
DES REPRESENTATIONS EN MUSIQUE ANCIENNES ET MODERNES / Menestrier, Claude-Francois – 1681 – 9 – us Sibley [780]
REPRESENTATIVE – Barberton, SA. Jan-Feb 1887 – 1 – sa State Libr [072]
THE REPRESENTATIVE – London. -d. 25 Jan-29 Jul 1826. (1 reel) – 1 – uk British Libr Newspaper [072]
A REPRESENTATIVE AND IMPROVED ORGANIZATION OF THE LEGAL PROFESSION IN THE UNITED STATES; ADDRESS OF WILLIAM L. RANSOM...BEFORE THE STATE BAR OF CALIFORNIA AT SAN FRANCISCO, CALIFORNIA, ON SEPTEMBER 19, 1935 / Ransom, William Lynn – Chicago? 1935 20 p. LL-1195 – 1 – us L of C Photodup [340]
REPRESENTATIVE CITIZENS OF NORTHERN CALIFORNIA / Standard Genealogical Publishing Co – Chicago, 1901. California Reel 3. (The Cox Library Collection) – 5 – us Americana [978]
REPRESENTATIVE CITIZENS OF PAULDING COUNTY / Hardesty, W S – Genealogical and biographical. Toledo: 1902., Ohio Reel 53. (The Cox Library Collection) – 5 – us Americana [978]
THE REPRESENTATIVE MEN OF THE BIBLE : FROM ADAM TO JOB / Matheson, George – 4th ed. New York: A C Armstrong, [1902] – 1mf – 9 – 0-8370-4312-3 – 1985-2312 – us A.T.L.A. [220]
REPRESENTATIVE MEN OF THE BIBLE: ADAM TO JOB / Matheson, George – New York: A.C. Armstrong, (1902). 1 fiche – 9 – us A.T.L.A. [220]
REPRESENTATIVE MEN OF THE BIBLE: ISHMAEL TO DANIEL / Matheson, George – New York: A.C. Armstrong, (1903). 1 fiche – 9 – us A.T.L.A. [220]
REPRESENTATIVE MEN OF THE NEW TESTAMENT / Baldwin, George Colfax – New York: Blakeman & Mason, 1860. 1 fiche – 9 – us A.T.L.A. [240]
REPRESENTATIVE MEN OF THE NEW TESTAMENT / Matheson, George – New York: A.C. Armstrong, 1905. 1 fiche – 9 – us A.T.L.A. [240]
THE REPRESENTATIVE MEN OF THE NEW TESTAMENT / Matheson, George – New York:A C Armstrong, 1905 – 1mf – 9 – 0-8370-4314-X – 1985-2314 – us A.T.L.A. [220]
THE REPRESENTATIVE MEN OF THE PHILIPPINES / ed by Frank E – Compiled and Jackson – 1 – us U.W. Library [920]
REPRESENTATIVE PLAYS, BY HENRY ARTHUR JONES / Jones, Henry Arthur; ed by Hamilton, Clayton – London: Macmillan, 1926 – 2 rolls – 1 – 1-55879-212-0 – uk Libr Preservation [820]
REPRESENTATIVE RESPONSIBILITY:...THE DIVINE PROCEDURE IN PROVIDENCE AND REDEMPTION / Wallace, Henry – Edinburgh: T.& T. Clark, 1867. 1 fiche – 9 – us A.T.L.A. [240]
REPRESENTATIVE WOMEN: FROM EVE, THE WIFE OF THE FIRST, TO MARY, THE MOTHER OF THE SECOND ADAM / Baldwin, George Colfax – 1860 – 9 – us A.T.L.A. [240]
REPRESENTATIVE WOMEN OF THE BIBLE / Matheson, George – New York: George H. Doran, 1907.1 fiche – 9 – us A.T.L.A. [220]
THE REPRESENTATIVE WOMEN OF THE BIBLE / Matheson, George – (Includes appendix on Mary Magdalene) – [London]:Hodder & Stoughton; New York:George H. Doran, c1907 – 1mf – 9 – 0-8370-4315-8 – 1985-2315 – us A.T.L.A. [220]
LA REPRESION DE LA BLASFEMIA / Bayle, Constantino – Madrid: Razon y Fe, 1920 – 1 – sp Bibl Santa Ana [240]
THE REPRESSOR OF OVERMUCH BLAMING OF THE CLERGY (RS19) : BY REGINALD PECOCK, SOMETIME BISHOP OF CHICHESTER / Pecock, Reginald; ed by Babington, C – 2v. 1860 – Dfl53.00 – ne Slangenburg [240]
REPRINT / Wisconsin. Land Tenure Center – 1965-69, n.1-63 – 1,5 – us Spaulding [630]

REPRINT OF OFFICIAL REGISTER OF LAND LOTTERY OF GEORGIA / Houston, Martha Lou – (1967 ed. Indexed, 5 fiches. F-0855. 9) – 1928. Item I. Orig. publ. 1827. Includes index. 217p. SW16-0031 – 5 – us A.G.L.L. [920]
REPRINT OF PAPERS ON ELECTROSTATICS AND MAGNETISM / Kelvin, William Thomson – London: Macmillan, 1872 – xv/592p. ill – 1 – us U.W. Library [530]
REPROBACION DEL...ABUSO DE LOS POLVOS DEL QUARANGO... / Colmenero, J – Salamanca, 1697 – 6mf – 9 – sp Cultura [600]
THE REPRODUCIBILITY OF LOW TESTOSTERONE IN ENDURANCE TRAINED MALES / Gulledge, Tracey P – University of North Carolina at Chapel Hill, 1995 – 1mf – 9 – $4.00 – PH1461 – us Microform Publ [612]
REPRODUCTION IN CAMELS – 1990 – 61p – it F.A.O. [590]
REPRODUCTION OF COPYRIGHTED WORKS BY EDUCATORS AND LIBRARIANS – Circular R21 Library of Congress. ED 244-642 – 9 – 0.91 – us EDRS [070]
REPRODUCTION OF THE SECOND MINUTE BOOK OF THE COURT OF QUARTER SESSIONS AND COMMON PLEAS...,1715 / New Jersey. (Colony). Court of General Quarter Sessions of the Peace. (Cape May County) – n.p., 193? 45 numb. LL-939 – 1 – us L of C Photodup [340]
REPRODUCTIONS – (Bilingual) – Montreal, Canada. v1 n2. 16 oct 1909 – 1r – 1 – Can$25.00 – cn Can Microfilming [073]
REPRODUCTIVE ECOLOGY OF TROPICAL FOREST PLANTS / ed by Bawa, K & Hadley, M – 1991 – 9 – 92-3-102669-0 – Co-published with Parthenon Publishing – fr UNESCO [580]
REPRODUCTIVE EFFICIENCY IN CATTLE : A GUIDELINE FOR PROJECTS IN DEVELOPING COUNTRIES – 1982 – 126p – it F.A.O. [636]
REPRODUCTIVE ENDOCRINE RESPONSE FOLLOWING ANAEROBIC AND AEROBIC EXERCISE / Premo, Mary C & Hackney, Anthony C – 1992 – 2mf – 9 – $8.00 – us Microform Publ [612]
REPRODUCTIVE PHYSIOLOGY OF TELFOST FISHES : A REVIEW OF PRESENT KNOWLEDGE AND NEEDS FOR FUTURE RESEARCH – 1981 – 89p – it F.A.O. [580]
REPRODUCTIVE TOXICOLOGY – 1,5,69 – us UMI [616]
REPROGRAPHICS – v19, no.6-. Dec 1981- – 1,5,6,9 – us UMI [073]
REPTILES AND FISHES OF THE SOUTH SEA ISLANDS / Guenther, A C LG – 2621 2. 1873 – 8 – ne IDC [590]
THE REPTILES OF BRITISH INDIA / Guenther, A C LG – Z-270 2. 1864 – 8 – ne IDC [590]
THE REPTILES OF BRITISH INDIA / Gunther, A C L G – Ray Society. 1864 – 1. 100.00; ; 7 – uk Microform Academic [590]
LA REPUBBLICA – (1995 35mm Sfr1,631.00. Also available on CD-ROM) – Italy. 1976-1995 – 4r per y – 5,6 – Sfr1,176.00 – sz Infoprint [945]
LA REPUBBLICA – (Yrly reel count varies) – Italy, 1976- – 1 – inquire – us Ross [072]
REPUBBLICA – 1976-1978 – 1 – F3,500 – sz Infoprint [072]
REPUBBLICA – 1976-1995 – 5 times per yr – 6,1 – F4,600 – sz Infoprint [072]
REPUBBLICA – 1979-1988 – 12 times per yr – 1 – F4,800 – sz Infoprint [072]
REPUBBLICA – 1989 – 18 times per yr – 1 – F6,000 – sz Infoprint [072]
REPUBBLICA – 1990 – 24 times per yr – 1 – L7,500 – sz Infoprint [072]
REPUBBLICA – 1991-1995 – 24 times per yr – 1 – sz Infoprint [072]
REPUBLIC – Brockport. N.Y. 1903-1925 – 1 – us UMI [071]
REPUBLIC – Brockport. N.Y. and Democrat. 1925-53 – 1 – us UMI [071]
REPUBLIC – Brockport. N.Y. -w. 1903-45 – 1 – us UMI [071]
REPUBLIC – Ottawa. Kan. -w. 1902-06 – 1 – us UMI [071]
REPUBLIC – Yakima. Wash. 1903-1967 – 1 – us UMI [071]
REPUBLIC – Yakima. Wash. -w. 1887, 1899-1904 – 1 – us UMI [071]
THE REPUBLIC – Columbus. Ind. 1967- – 1 – us UMI [071]
THE REPUBLIC – Ireland.13 Dec 1906-16 Mar 1907 – 1 – ie Microforms [072]
THE REPUBLIC – Ireland.21 Jun-20 Sept 1919 – 1 – ie Microforms [072]
THE REPUBLIC – Meyersdale, PA., 1978-1988 – 13 – $25.00r – us I.M.R. [071]
Republic Airlines *see* NEWSPAPER CLIPPINGS
Republic Airlines Predecessor Companies *see* NESPAPER CLIPPINGS
THE REPUBLIC OF BELAU : PROFILE OF A NEW PACIFIC ISLAND NATION – Koror: Off of the President, jan 1981 – 1mf – 9 – $1.50 – LLMC 82-100G, Title23 – us L.L.M.C. [980]
REPUBLIC OF BELAU (PALAU) – CONSTITUTION AND LAWS *see*
- THE CONSTITUTION OF THE REPUBLIC OF PALAU, 1979
- CONSTITUTIONAL DEVELOPMENT OF PALAU
- DRAFT CONSTITUTIONS. ALTERNATIVES 1 AND 2
- PALAU'S CONSTITUTIONAL CONVENTION. AN INFORMAL REPORT
- PALAU'S CONSTITUTIONAL TANGLE
- PAPERS OF THE CONSTITUTIONAL CONVENTION
- REPORT
- THE REPUBLIC OF BELAU

REPUBLIC OF BELAU (PALAU) – STATUS NEGOTIATIONS WITH THE U.S. *see*
- ACT TO APPROVE THE COMPACT OF FREE ASSOCIATION WITH PALAU
- COMPACT OF FREE ASSOCIATION
- COMPACT OF FREE ASSOCIATION AND SUBSIDIARY AGREEMENTS
- COMPACT OF FREE ASSOCIATION BETWEEN THE U.S. AND PALAU
- COMPACT OF FREE ASSOCIATION WITH PALAU
- CONCERNED CITIZENS OF PALAU
- DECLARATION OF INTENT
- AN INDEPENDENT REPORT ON THE BELAU PLEBISCITE OF 1984
- MESSAGE TRANSMITTING DRAFT OF PROPOSED LEGISLATION TO APPROVE THE "COMPACT OF FREE ASSOCIATION"
- MESSAGE TRANSMITTING HIS CERTIFICATION OF APPROVAL OF THE COMPACT OF FREE ASSOCIATION BETWEEN THE U.S. AND PALAU
- PALAU INDICATIVE DEVELOPMENT PLAN
- PALAU'S EVOLVING RELATIONSHIP WITH THE U.S.
- PALAU'S STRATEGIC POSITION PLACES DEMOCRACY AT RISK
- PALAU/UNITED STATES AGREEMENTS REGARDING THE COMPACT OF FREE ASSOCIATION ...
- PALAU/U.S. AGREEMENT REGARDING MILITARY USE AND OPERATING RIGHTS OF THE U.S. GOVERNMENT IN PALAU
- REPORT APPROVING THE COMPACT OF FREE ASSOCIATION WITH PALAU
- STATEMENT BY AMBASSADOR PETER R ROSENBLATT
- SUMMARY AND ANALYSIS OF THE 1984 COMPACT OF FREE ASSOCIATION

REPUBLIC OF BELAU (PALUA) – STATUS NEGOTIATIONS WITH THE U.S. *see* SITUATION REPORT
THE REPUBLIC OF CHINA'S TARGETS AND BASIC POLICIES IN THE SIXTH FOUR-YEAR PLAN FOR ECONOMIC DEVELOPMENT OF TAIWAN, 1973-76 / China. Republic. Council for International Economic Cooperation and Development – Taipei, 1973. BD-1637/1 – 9 – ne IDC [338]
THE REPUBLIC OF GOD : AN INSTITUTE OF THEOLOGY / Mulford, Elisha – Boston:Houghton, Mifflin; Cambridge:Riverside Press, 1881 – 1mf – 9 – 0-8370-2417-X – 1985-0417 – us A.T.L.A. [240]
REPUBLIC OF INDONESIA, ECONOMIC PROGRESS / Indonesia. Konsulat. San Francisco. Trade Section – SE-2270 1. 1959 – 9 – ne IDC [339]
Republic of Indonesian Office *see* REPORT ON INDONESIA
THE REPUBLIC OF INDONESIA'S GRAPHIC ARTS AND ALLIED INDUSTRY CONFERENCES, 1961 / Crockett, William D – SE-5498 1 – 9 – ne IDC [760]
REPUBLIC OF KOREA ECONOMIC SUMMATION / U.S. Army. Forces in Korea – nos. 6-36, Mar 1946-Nov Dec 1948 – 1 – 45.00 – us L of C Photodup [339]
THE REPUBLIC OF SEYCHELLES NATIONAL REPORT ON EDUCATION / Seychelles. Ministry of Education and Information – Mahe, 1983 – 2mf – 9 – DE-460/1 – ne IDC [370]
Republic of the Marshall Islands *see* CONSTITUTION OF THE MARSHALL ISLANDS, DECEMBER 1 1978
REPUBLIC OF THE SUDAN GAZETTE – Sudan. n903-1068. 1957-68 – 8r – 1 – us Ross [324]
REPUBLIC OF TURKEY : AN AMERICAN PERSPECTIVE – $6,600.00 – 0-84440-587-6 – us UPA [956]
REPUBLIC REPORTER – Republic, Ohio, 1981-1983 – 1r – 1 – $32.50r – us Archival [978]
A REPUBLICA : HOMENAGEM DOS ALUMNOS DO LYCEU AFFONSO PENNA AO – Cruzeiro do Sul, Amazonas. 15 Nov 1908 – 1,5,6 – bl Biblioteca [072]
A REPUBLICA : JORNAL OFFICIAL DO GOVERNO DO ESTADO DO MARANHAO – '(s.l.')-Sao Luiz, Brazil. 23-31 Dec 1889; Jan-Apr, 4 Dec 1890 – 1,5,6 – bl Biblioteca [072]
A REPUBLICA – Maceio, Alagoas. 30 Jun-26 Out 1894 – 1,5,6 – bl Biblioteca [072]
A REPUBLICA – Manaos, Amazonas. 8 Abr 1894 – 1,5,6 – bl Biblioteca [072]
A REPUBLICA : ORGAM DIARIO, NOCTURNO E DE ABSOLUTA IMPARCIALIDADE – Maceio, Alagoas. 21 Out 1927 – 1,5,6 – bl Biblioteca [072]
A REPUBLICA – Rio de Janeiro, 3 Dec 1870-28 Feb 1874 – 1,5,6 – bl Biblioteca [072]
LA REPUBLICA – Asuncion, PY. 1981 – 1r – $50.00 – R63619 – us Library Micro [072]
LA REPUBLICA – Bogota, [Colombia]: R O Hernandez, [jan 3 1974-aug 1989] – us Res Libr [072]
LA REPUBLICA – Panama City, Panama. 1977, Aug 1978-Jun 1986; Jul 1987-Dec 1988 – 79r – 1 – us L of C Photodup [072]
REPUBLICA – Lisbon, 9,11 Aug 1971-14 Dec 1972. Incomplete. (Portuguese Revolution of 1974. Newspapers from Portugal publ. from 21 Feb 1971 to 15 Feb 1980, collected and filmed by University of Wisconsin-Madison libraries.) – 1 – us U.W. Library [072]
REPUBLICA – Lisbon, Portugal. -d. 1 Jan 1915-14 March 1916. 3 reels – 1 – uk British Libr Newspaper [072]
LA REPUBLICA ARGENTINA ANTE EL "LIBRO AZUL" / Argentina. Ministerio de Relaciones Exteriores y Culto – Buenos Aires: Direccion de informacion al exterior, 1946 – 1 – CSUXAHZ6278-B – us Hoover Inst Photo [972]
LA REPUBLICA DOMINICANA; DIRECTORIO Y GUIA GENERAL / Deschamps, Enrique – Barcelona, 1906?. 336p. illus. fold. map – 1 – us U.W. Library [972]
LA REPUBLICA DOMINICANA, NACION EJEMPLAR – Bogota. 1946 – 1 – us Res Libr [972]
LA REPUBLICA ES LA CULTURA PAR TODOS / Spain. Ministerio de Instruccion Publica y Sanidad – Barcelona, 19?? Fiche W1136. (Blodgett Collection of Spanish Civil War Pamphlets) – 9 – us H.U. College Libr [946]
LA REPUBLICA ES LA REVOLUCION ESPANOLA / Valera, Fernando – Discurso pronunciado a millares de ciudadanos el 11 de febrero de 1937 desde el local social de U. R., Valencia. Valencia, 1937? Fiche W1245. (Blodgett Collection of Spanish Civil War Pamphlets) – 9 – us H.U. College Libr [946]
LA REPUBLICA Y LA POLITICA DE LA IGLESIA / Maumus, Vicente – 1893 – 9 – 1.50f – sp Bibl Santa Ana [240]
REPUBLICA Y POLITICA...REYES Y.. – 1621 – 9 – 1.50f – sp Bibl Santa Ana [946]
LE REPUBLICAIN – Boston, MA. v2 n22. 17 jun 1882 – 1r – 1 – Can$25.00 – cn Can Microfilming [071]
LE REPUBLICAIN / ed by Chaput, Marcel – Montreal, fev 1963; edition speciale 1963f – 1r – 1 – Can$25.00 – cn Can Microfilming [072]
LE REPUBLICAIN – Paris. 16 avr 1798-14 sept 1800 – 1 – fr A.C.R.P.P. [073]
LE REPUBLICAIN = THE REPUBLICAN : SUPPLEMENT TO "LE MADAWASKA" / Chambre de Commerce d'Edmunston – Edmunston, New Brunswick. v1 n1. jul 1970 – 1r – 1 – Can$25.00 – cn Can Microfilming [072]
LE REPUBLICAIN CANADIEN – Montreal, Canada. 9 avr 1867 – 1r – 1 – Can$25.00 – cn Can Microfilming [072]
LE REPUBLICAIN DEMOCRATE DE L'ALLIER – I, no. 1-169; II, no. 1-83. Moulins. 25 avr 1848-24 mars 1850. mq I, no. 1-19, 21-29, 31-34, 41-42, 46-47, 49, 55, 58-59, 66-68, 112; II, no. 22 – 1 – fr A.C.R.P.P. [073]
LE REPUBLICAIN FRANCAIS – Paris. No.1-1856. Nov 1792-3 fevr 1798 – 1 – fr A.C.R.P.P. [073]
LE REPUBLICAIN LORRAIN – Metz. fevr 1945-avr 1981 – 1 – fr A.C.R.P.P. [073]
LE REPUBLICAIN LORRAIN-LUNDI MATIN – suite de: Lundi-matin. Le Republicain lorrain. Metz. 1949, 1951-58, 1961-juin 1971 – 1 – fr A.C.R.P.P. [073]
LE REPUBLICAIN SOCIALISTE DU CENTRE – Red. en chef Vaillant. Vierzon. juil 1883-mai 1884 – 1 – fr A.C.R.P.P. [073]
LE REPUBLICAIN VIENNOIS – Journal de l'arrondissement de Vienne. Dir. Jean Teliet. Vienne. dec 1906-sept 1907 – 1 – fr A.C.R.P.P. [073]
REPUBLICAN – 1-14 2+25 (all publ). 1819-1826 – 115mf – 9 – $380.00 – us UPA [335]
REPUBLICAN – Antelope, OR. -w. 18 Jul 1900-30 Jul 1901. 1 roll – 1 – us U.O. Library [071]
REPUBLICAN – Antigo. Wis. 1888-1908 – 1 – us UMI [071]
REPUBLICAN – Auburn. Wash. 1911-1915 – 1 – us UMI [071]
REPUBLICAN – Axtell. Neb. 1889-1898 – 1 – us UMI [071]
REPUBLICAN – Battle Creek. Neb. 1895-1905 – 1 – us UMI [071]
REPUBLICAN – Baxter Springs. Kan. 1876-1877 – 1 – us UMI [071]
REPUBLICAN – Beatrice. Neb. 1886-1892 – 1 – us UMI [071]
REPUBLICAN – Brandon. Miss. and Eastern Advocate. 1837-38 – 1 – us UMI [071]
REPUBLICAN – Burlington. Kansas. -w. 1882-92, 1894-1915 – 1 – us UMI [071]
REPUBLICAN – Cape Girardeau. Mo. 1904-1918 – 1 – us UMI [071]
REPUBLICAN – Cape Girardeau. Mo. -w. 1910-1921 – 1 – us UMI [071]
REPUBLICAN – Carlisle, PA., 1890 – 13 – $25.00r – us I.M.R. [071]
REPUBLICAN – Central City. Neb. 1896-1959 – 1 – us UMI [071]
REPUBLICAN – Clarion. Pa. -w. 1959-65 – 1 – us UMI [071]
REPUBLICAN – Coldwater. Kan. 1884-86 – 1 – us UMI [071]
REPUBLICAN – Columbus. Ind. -sw. 1894-96 – 1 – us UMI [071]
REPUBLICAN – Columbus. Ind. -w. 1872-77 – 1 – us UMI [071]
REPUBLICAN – Council Grove. Kan. 1879-1924 – 1 – us UMI [071]
REPUBLICAN – Decatur. Ill. -d. 1872-99 – 1 – us UMI [071]
REPUBLICAN – Decatur. Ill. -w. 1867-98 – 1 – us UMI [071]
REPUBLICAN – Dixon. IL. -w.1857-61. Also: Telegraph – 1 – us UMI [071]
REPUBLICAN – Dowagiac. Mich. -w, sw. 1884-92, 1900-08 – 1 – us UMI [071]
REPUBLICAN – El Dorado. Kan. 1883-1929 – 1 – us UMI [071]
REPUBLICAN – Elyria. Ohio. -w. 1875-1917 – 1 – us UMI [071]
REPUBLICAN – Findlay. Ohio. -w, sw. 1889-1890; 1898-1900 – 1 – us UMI [071]
REPUBLICAN – Franklin. Ind. 1856-1857 – 1 – us UMI [071]
REPUBLICAN – Freeport. IL. -w. 1881-83 – 1 – us UMI [071]
REPUBLICAN – Galena. Kan. 1893-1930 – 1 – us UMI [071]
REPUBLICAN – Goodland. Kan. -w. 1886-91 – 1 – us UMI [071]
REPUBLICAN – Hays. Kansas. -w. 1888-1912 – 1 – us UMI [071]
REPUBLICAN – Imperial. Neb. 1899-1964 – 1 – us UMI [071]
REPUBLICAN – Kingsley. Kan. 1878-1881 – 1 – us UMI [071]
REPUBLICAN – Lawrence. Kan. -w. 1857-62 – 1 – us UMI [071]
REPUBLICAN – London. 1880-86 – 1 – uk Microform Academic [073]
REPUBLICAN – London, UK. 1870, 1872.-irr. 16 feet – 1 – uk British Libr Newspaper [072]
REPUBLICAN – McPherson. Kan. 1879-1930 – 1 – us UMI [071]
REPUBLICAN – Martinsville. Ind. -w. 1870-1909 – 1 – us UMI [071]

REPUBLICAN – Meriden.CT. -w. 1892-1917 – 1 – us UMI [071]
REPUBLICAN – Midland. Mich. 1881-1937 – 1 – us UMI [071]
REPUBLICAN – Moline. Kan. 1889-1899 – 1 – us UMI [071]
REPUBLICAN – North Platte. Neb. 1870-1875 – 1 – us UMI [071]
REPUBLICAN – Northport. Wash. 1907-1910 – 1 – us UMI [071]
REPUBLICAN – Omaha. Neb. -w. 1861-83 – 1 – us UMI [071]
REPUBLICAN – Osmond. Neb. 1895-1898; 1899-1900; 1901- – 1 – us UMI [071]
REPUBLICAN – Ottawa. Kan. 1879-1902 – 1 – us UMI [071]
REPUBLICAN – Ottawa. Kan. -w. 1873-1902 – 1 – us UMI [071]
REPUBLICAN – Paola. Kan. -w. 1867-1931 – 1 – us UMI [071]
REPUBLICAN – Partridge. Kan. 1896-1897 – 1 – us UMI [071]
REPUBLICAN – Pawnee City. Neb. 1879-1966 – 1 – us UMI [071]
REPUBLICAN – Pendleton. Or. 1888-1899 – 1 – us UMI [071]
REPUBLICAN – Phillipi. Pa. 1907-1947 – 1 – us UMI [071]
REPUBLICAN – Phillipi. West Virginia. 1907-1947 – 1 – us UMI [071]
REPUBLICAN – Plattsburg, NY. 1811-22 – 3 – us Readex [071]
REPUBLICAN – Poplar Bluff. Mo. -w. 1891-1929, 1933- – 1 – us UMI [071]
REPUBLICAN – Ravenna-Kent. OH. 1855-1928. Also predecessors – 1 – us UMI [071]
REPUBLICAN – Rensselaer. Ind. 1882-1897; 1906- – 1 – us UMI [071]
REPUBLICAN – Rensselaer. Ind. -sw. 1897-1909 – 1 – us UMI [071]
REPUBLICAN – Rushville. Ind. -w, sw. 1888-1903, 1930-40 – 1 – us UMI [071]
REPUBLICAN – Santa Rosa. Calif. 1946-1948 – 1 – us UMI [071]
REPUBLICAN – Scottsbluff. Neb. 1900-1964 – 1 – us UMI [071]
REPUBLICAN – Seattle. Wash. 1908-1913 – 1 – us UMI [071]
REPUBLICAN – (See Corning) – Red Bluff, CA. 1927-56 – 10r – 1 – $500.00 – B02663 – us Library Micro [071]
REPUBLICAN – Seymour. Ind. 1896-1920 – 1 – us UMI [071]
REPUBLICAN – Truckee, CA. 1874-75; 1881-86; 1901-23 – 20r – 1 – $1,000.00 – C03039 – us Library Micro [071]
REPUBLICAN – Tunkhannock. PA. 1962-. Includes New Age – 1 – us UMI [071]
REPUBLICAN – Valentine. Neb. 1888-1963 – 1 – us UMI [071]
REPUBLICAN – Washington. Kan. 1870-1904 – 1 – us UMI [071]
REPUBLICAN – Washington. Miss. 1813-1815 – 1 – us UMI [071]
REPUBLICAN – Waterbury. Conn. 1884- – 1 – us UMI [071]
REPUBLICAN – Wauseon, Ohio. 1894-190 – 4r – 1 – $32.50r – us Archival [071]
REPUBLICAN – Waynesburg. Pa. 1870- – 1 – us UMI [071]
REPUBLICAN – West Point. Neb. 1871-1959 – 1 – us UMI [071]
REPUBLICAN – Weston. West Virginia. 1880-1893 – 1 – us UMI [071]
REPUBLICAN – Willoughby. Ohio. 1917-1927 – 1 – us UMI [071]
REPUBLICAN – Woodville. Miss. 1878-1901; 1954- – 1 – us UMI [071]
REPUBLICAN – Wooster. Ohio. -w. 1873-1908 – 1 – us UMI [071]
REPUBLICAN – York. Neb. 1876-1955 – 1 – us UMI [071]
THE REPUBLICAN – (Also known as: Santa Rosa Republican; Monday Republican; Coast Defender) – Santa Rosa, CA. 1881-82; 1884-1906; 1907-48 – 207r – 1 CB02975 – $10,350.00 – us Library Micro [071]
THE REPUBLICAN – Westfield. N.Y. -w. 1856- – 1 – us UMI [071]
THE REPUBLICAN:... / ed by Harding, C G – London. 2v. 1848 – 4mf – 1 – ILM-1019/1 – ne IDC [327]
REPUBLICAN AND WHIG : WEEKLY WHIG NEWSPAPER – Chardon, OH. 15 June 1847-23 Oct 1849 – 1r – 1 – us Western Res [071]
REPUBLICAN ARGUS – Auburn, CA. 1899-1903 – 3r – 1 – $150.00 – B02031 – us Library Micro [071]
REPUBLICAN ARGUS – Ogallala, NE. -w. Jan 1898-Aug 1899; Nov 1899-Jan 1900; Mar 1900-Jan 1905 – 1 – us NE Hist [071]
REPUBLICAN ARGUS – (Whig campaign paper for the Presidential Election of 1836) – Warren, OH, 4 Aug-28 Oct 1836 – 1 reel – 1 – us Western Res [320]
THE REPUBLICAN ARGUS – Sunbury, PA. 1808-12. 1 roll – 13 – $25.00r – us I.M.R. [071]
REPUBLICAN BAPTIST CHURCH. EDGEFIELD COUNTY. SOUTH CAROLINA : CHURCH RECORDS – 1844-47, 1887-1978, 1978-82. 1887-1978 incomplete; Oct 1978-1982; WMU 1883-1886, WMS Oct 1916-1930; 600p – 1 – 27.00 – us Baptist [240]
REPUBLICAN CARLISLE – Carlisle, PA., 1836-1891 – 13 – $25.00r – us I.M.R. [071]
THE REPUBLICAN CHRONICLE SERIES – London. 1875 – 1 – uk Microform Academic [999]
REPUBLICAN CITY RANGER – Republican City, NE. -w. Jun 1902-Aug 1946 – 1 – us NE Hist [071]
REPUBLICAN CITY REVIEW – Republican City, NE. -w. Mar 1950-May 1952 – 1 – us NE Hist [071]
REPUBLICAN CLARION – Lapeer. Mich. 1901-1904 – 1 – us UMI [071]
REPUBLICAN COMPILER – Gettysburg. Pa. 1818-1857 – 1 – us UMI [071]
REPUBLICAN CONGRESS – Dublin, Ireland.5 May 1934-1 Feb 1936 – 1 – ie Microforms [072]
REPUBLICAN DECREE CONCERNING LAW NO. 4 OF 1971, CONCERNING THE ESTABLISHMENT, FORMATION AND JURISDICTION OF THE CENTRAL BANK OF YEMEN / Yemen. Central Bank of Yemen, Sana'a – 1971. BNE-9611 1 – 9 – ne IDC [332]
REPUBLICAN FILE – Dublin, Ireland.28 Nov 1931-5 Mar 1932 – 1 – ie Microforms [072]
REPUBLICAN FREE PRESS – Redding, CA. 1883-88 – 1r – 1 – $50.00 – B02674 – us Library Micro [071]
REPUBLICAN FREEMAN – Waukesha. Wis. 1888-98 – 1 – us UMI [071]
REPUBLICAN GAZETTE – Lima, Ohio. 1911-25 – 49r – 1 – $32.50r – us Archival [071]
REPUBLICAN GAZETTEER – Boston, MA. 1802-03. Also: Gazetteer, 1803; Democrat, 1804-09.Sold as one unit – 3 – us Readex [071]
REPUBLICAN GROVE BAPTIST CHURCH. OBION COUNTY. TENNESSEE : CHURCH RECORDS – 1838-60 – 1 – 5.00 – us Baptist [240]
REPUBLICAN HERALD – Providence. R.I. 1829-1952 – 1 – us UMI [071]
REPUBLICAN JOURNAL – Lawrence. Kan. -d. 1869-79 – 1 – us UMI [071]
REPUBLICAN LEDGER – Noblesville. Ind. 1881-1887 – 1 – us UMI [071]
REPUBLICAN NEWS-ITEM – Laporte, PA. -w 1898-1901; 1901-1912 – 13 – $25.00r – us I.M.R. [071]
THE REPUBLICAN OF TEHAMA COUNTY – Corning, CA. Aug 1926-Aug 1927 – 1r – 1 – $50.00 – B02142 – us Library Micro [071]
REPUBLICAN PARTY / The Register Publishing Co – Republican League Register of Oregon. Portland, 1896. Oregon reel 8. (Cox Library Collection) – 5 – us Americana [978]
Republican Party *see*
- PAPERS, PART 1
- PAPERS PART 2

Republican Party. Kansas. State Central Committee *see* RECORD OF VOTES
Republican Party. National Convention *see* OFFICIAL REPORT OF THE PROCEEDINGS
REPUBLICAN PRESS – Cambridge. Ohio. and Weekly Guernsey Times. 1909-12 – 1 – us UMI [071]
REPUBLICAN PRESS – Cambridge. Ohio. -w. 1894-98 – 1 – us UMI [071]
REPUBLICAN PRESS – Eureka, NV. 1884-85 – 1r – 1 – $50.00 – U04514 – us Library Micro [071]
REPUBLICAN PRESS – Ukiah, CA. 1891-93; 1895-1919; 1944-49 – 35r – 1 BC03051 – $1,750.00 – us Library Micro [071]
REPUBLICAN PRESS – Ukiah. Calif. -w. 1944-49 – 1 – us UMI [071]
REPUBLICAN PRINCIPALS – Carson City, NV. 1888 – 1r – 1 – $50.00 – U04472 – us Library Micro [071]
REPUBLICAN REGISTER – Aurora, NE. -w. Apr. 1887-Dec. 1889. Incomplete; Jan. 1891-May 1895. Incomplete; Oct. 1895-Nov. 1942 – 1 – us NE Hist [071]
REPUBLICAN REPORTER – Valentine, NE. -w. May 1883-Apr 1884 – 1 – us NE Hist [071]
REPUBLICAN REVIEW – Dublin, Ireland.Jun 1938-Jun 1939 – 1 – ie Microforms [072]
REPUBLICAN SENTINEL – Youngstown. OH.1852-60 – 1 – us UMI [071]
REPUBLICAN STANDARD – Bryan, Ohio. 1857 – 1r – 1 – $32.50r – us Archival [071]
REPUBLICAN STANDARD – Uniontown. Pa. 1870-1888 – 1 – us UMI [071]
REPUBLICAN STATESMAN – Bassett, NE. -w. Oct. 1887-Dec. 1892 – 1 – us NE Hist [071]
REPUBLICAN STATESMAN – Bassett. Neb. 1887-1892 – 1 – us UMI [071]
REPUBLICAN UNION – Aurora. Ill. -w. 1857-58 – 1 – us UMI [071]
REPUBLICAN VALLEY SENTINEL – Orleans, NE. -w. Jan 1876; Sep 1880-Feb 1881; Dec 1885 – 1 – us NE Hist [071]
REPUBLICAN WAR BULLETIN – Ireland.Aug-23 Dec 1922 – 1 – ie Microforms [072]
REPUBLICAN WEEKLY HASTINGS – Hastings, NE. (-sw 1902-05). Sept 1896-Feb 1899; Aug 1899-May 1905 – 1 – us NE Hist [071]
REPUBLICAN-COURIER – Findlay. Ohio. 1886- – 1 – us UMI [071]
REPUBLICAN-DELTA – Buckhannon. West Virginia. 1961-1968 – 1 – us UMI [071]
REPUBLICAN-FREE PRESS – Redding. Calif. 1883-1887 – 1 – us UMI [071]
REPUBLICAN-HERALD – Metropolis. Ill. 1918-1937 – 1 – us UMI [071]
REPUBLICAN-HERALD – Port Clinton, Ohio. 1927-36 – 4r – 1 – $32.50r – us Archival [071]
REPUBLICAN-HERALD – Winona. Minn. 1947-1954 – 1 – us UMI [071]
REPUBLICAN-JEFFERSONIAN – Findlay, Ohio. 1904-11 – 5r – 1 – $32.50r – us Archival [071]
REPUBLICAN-LEADER – Trenton, NE. -w. (-sw 1916-19). May 1898-Nov 1902, scattered issues missing; Jan 1908-Sept 1916; Jan 1920-Mar 1939 – 1 – us NE Hist [071]
REPUBLICAN-NEWS – Mount Vernon. Ohio. 1881-1938 – 1 – us UMI [071]
O REPUBLICANO : DIARIO POLITICO INDEPENDENTE – Manaos, Amazonas. 22 Out 1923 – 1,5,6 – bl Biblioteca [072]
O REPUBLICANO – Lavras, 1 Jan 1901 – 1,5,6 – bl Biblioteca [072]
REPUBLICAN-PRESS – Salamanca. N.Y. 1904- – 1 – us UMI [071]
REPUBLICAN-REGISTER – Aurora. Neb. 1877-1942 – 1 – us UMI [071]
REPUBLICAN-REGISTER – Washington. Kan. 1905-1926 – 1 – us UMI [071]
REPUBLICAN-TIMES – Ottawa. Ill. -w. 1852-1916 – 1 – us UMI [071]
REPUBLICA...ORIGINAL SACADA DEL CUERPO HUMANO... / Merola, J – Barcelona, 1587 – 12mf – 9 – sp Cultura [612]
REPUBLICAS DE INDIAS; IDOLATRIAS Y GOBIERNO EN MEXICO Y PERU ANTES DE LA CONQUISTA. / Roman y Zamora, Jeronimo – Madrid: V. Suarez, 1897.2v – 1 – us U.W. Library [972]
REPUBLICATION OF THE MINUTES OF THE MISSISSIPPI BAPTIST ASSOCIATION, A, 1806-47 / Bond, T M – 272p – 1 – $9.52 – us Baptist [240]
O REPUBLICO – Rio de Janeiro, 2 Oct 1830-Jul 1831; Jun-Jul, Oct-Nov 1832; Jan 1837; Jul 1853-15 Dec 1855 – 1,5,6 – bl Biblioteca [072]
DIE REPUBLIK – Berlin, dec 1918-apr 25 1919, jun 4-24 1919 – 1r – 1 – Inquire at Mikrofilmarchiv for details – gw Misc Inst [943]
DIE REPUBLIK – Berlin. Dec. 3, 1918-June 24, 1919 – 1 – 35.00r – us Hoover Inst Photo [072]
DIE REPUBLIK – Berlin, Germany. Dec 1918-27 Feb 1919 – 1r – 1 – gw Mikrofilm [072]
DIE REPUBLIK – Heidelberg, Germany. 8 Mar 1848-21 Jun 1849 – 1 – gw Mikrofilm [072]
REPUBLIK – Djakarta. Indonesia. 1956-1959 – 1 – us UMI [072]
DIE REPUBLIK DER ARBEITER : ZENTRALBLATT DER PROPAGANDA FUER DIE VERBRUEDERUNG DER ARBEITER. ORGAN DES ALLGEMEINEN ARBEITERBUNDES – New York, NY. 1850-1852 – 1r – 1 – gw Mikrofilm [071]
DIE REPUBLIK DER THIERE : UND, DIE ELFEN-CONSTITUTION / Bauernfeld, Eduard von; ed by Wilhelm, Gustav – (Includes bibliographical references) – Wien; Leipzig: E Strache, c1919 – 1 – us U.W. Library [820]
DIE REPUBLIK, HEIDELBERG *see* DIE DEMOKRATISCHE REPUBLIK
REPUBLIKA – Belgrade, Yugoslavia. Nov 1945-Jun 1956 – 3r – 1 – us L of C Photodup [949]
REPUBLIKANER VON BERKS – (In German) – Reading, PA. 1869-99 – 15r – 1 – $1,275.00 – D3390 – us Scholarly Res [071]
REPUBLIKANISCHE LIEDER : DEM DEUTSCHEN VOLKE GEWIDMET / Holtzendorff, Franz von – Heidelberg: J Groos, 1849 – 1r – 1 – us U.W. Library [780]
DE REPUBLIKEIN – Vryheid. South Africa. 1891-99 – 1 – sa State Libr [072]
DIE REPUBLIKEIN – Pretoria, SA. Jul+Sep 1934; Jul 1938 – 1 – sa State Libr [072]
LA REPUBLIQUE – (1re ed. 26 fev 1848-2 dec 1851. 2eme ed. 21 sept 1849-17 mars 1851) – Red. E. Bareste. Paris – 1 – fr A.C.R.P.P. [073]
LA REPUBLIQUE – Boston (& Fall River), MA. 2 oct 1875-v2 n24. 10 fev 1877 – 1r – 1 – Can$55.00 – cn Can Microfilming [071]
LA REPUBLIQUE – Edmunston, New Brunswick, 30 aut 1978-19 oct 1982f – 4r – 1 – Can$50.00 – cn Can Microfilming [072]
LA REPUBLIQUE – Organe du radicalisme. Journal quotidien. Dir. Emile Roche. Paris. 10 juin 1929-sept 1939 – 1 – fr A.C.R.P.P. [073]
REPUBLIQUE – Toulon. 1954-68 – 1 – fr A.C.R.P.P. [073]
La Republique Autoritaire *see* LA VICTOIRE
LA REPUBLIQUE CUBAINE – En espagnol et en francais. Paris. 1896. mq no. 11-12, 46, 48 – 1 – fr A.C.R.P.P. [073]
LA REPUBLIQUE DEMOCRATIQUE / Parti republicain, democratique et social – Paris. 1921-avr 1930 – 1 – fr A.C.R.P.P. [073]
LA REPUBLIQUE DU CENTRE – Orleans. 1964-1993 – 1 – fr A.C.R.P.P. [073]
LA REPUBLIQUE DU CONGO DEVANT L'CPINION MONDIALE / Congo – Bruxelles, 1960.BA-697/1 – 9 – ne IDC [960]
REPUBLIQUE EXILEE – London, UK. 11 Oct, 1 Nov 1856 – 1 – uk British Libr Newspaper [072]
LA REPUBLIQUE FRANCAISE – Paris. 7 nov 1871-12 juil 1924 – 1 – fr A.C.R.P.P. [073]
LA REPUBLIQUE LIBRE – Paris. 1959-fevr 1961 – 1 – fr A.C.R.P.P. [073]
THE REPUTATION AND INFLUENCE OF FRANCIS BACON IN THE SEVENTEENTH CENTURY / Penrose, Stephen Beasley Linnard – New York: (s.n.), 1934. x,225p – 1 – us U.W. Library [500]
Requadt, Paul *see* LICHTENBERG
Requesens, Francisco de *see*
- EPISODIO DE LA GUERRA DE LA INDEPENDENCIA
- EPISODIO DE LA...INDEPENDENCIA

REQUESTA – 1965-66.244p – 1 – 8.54 – us Baptist [240]
REQUESTE PRESENTEE AU ROY PAR, MONSIEUR LE PRINCE DE CONDE: AC COMPAGNE D'UN GRAND NOMBRE DE SEIGNEURS GENTILS-HOMMES, & AUTRES QUI FONT PROFESSION DE LA RELIGION REFORMEE EN CE ROYAUME / Conde, Louis 1 de Bourbon – s.l.: s.n., 1567?. Filmed with: Advertissement a tous bons et loyaus subiectz du roy – 1 – us U.W. Library [944]
LA REQUETE DES DICTIONNAIRES / Menage, G – 1649 – 9 – fr I.C.S. [440]
REQUIEM FOR A NUN – Concordance to the novel – 6mf – 9 – us UMI [420]
REQUIEM FUER EIN KIND / Andres, Stefan Paul – Hamburg: H Ellermann, 1948 – 1r – 1 – us U.W. Library [810]
REQUIREMENTS OF THE UNITED STATES FOOD, DRUG, AND COSMETIC ACT. REVISION / U.S. Food and Drug Administration – Washington, Govt. Print. Off., 1964 55 p. LL-5 – 1 – us L of C Photodup [340]

REQUIREMENTS OF VITAMIN A, IRON, FOLATE AND VITAMIN B 12 : REPORT OF A JOINT FAO/WHO EXPERT CONSULTATION; GENEVA, 1985 – 1988 – 107p – it F.A.O. [640]
REQUIREMENTS OF VITAMIN A, THIAMINE RIBOFLAVINE AND NIACIN : REPORT OF A JOINT F.A.O./W.H.O. EXPERT GROUP, ROME, 1965 – 1978 – 86p – it F.A.O. [615]
THE RERAL ST FRANCIS OF ASSISI / Robinson, Paschal – London: Catholic Truth Society, 1904 – 1mf – us A.T.L.A. [240]
Reresby, John *see* MEMOIRS OF SIR JOHN RERESBY: THE COMPLETE TEXT AND A SELECTION FROM HIS LETTERS
RERUM A SOCIETATE JESU IN ORIENTO GESTARUM AD ANNUM USQUE / Acosta, E – Dilingae. 1571. B-1004 2 – 8 – ne IDC [240]
RERUM BRITANNICARUM MEDII AEVI SCRIPTORES : OR CHRONICLES AND MEMORIALS OF GREAT BRITAIN AND IRELAND DURING THE MIDDLE AGES. / ed by Master of the Rolls – London. v1-99. 1858-1896 – 9 – Dfl8,750.00 – ne Slangenburg [941]
RERUM BRITTANICARUM MEDII AEVI SCRIPTORES, OR CHRONICLES AND MEMORIALS OF GREAT BRITAIN AND IRELAND DURING THE MIDDLE AGES – London, 1858-1869. 253v – 9 – Bf202,500.00 set – 1-799-00402-3 – be Brepols [941]
RERUM CONCILII OECUMENCI CONSTANTIENSIS / ed by Hardt, H von der – 6v. Francofurti. 1697-1700 – 91mf – 8 – ne IDC [240]
RERUM FAVENTINARUM SCRIPTORES : AD SCRIPTORES RERUM ITALICARUM ACCESSIONES HISTORICAE FAVENTINAE / Mittarelli, J -B – Venetiis, 1771-1775 – 23mf – 9 – Dfl81.00 – ne Slangenburg [220]
RERUM GALLICARUM ET FRANCICARUM SCRIPTORES *see*
- CONTENANT LA 1,2,3,4 (RGFS 20-23)
- CONTIENT CE QUI S'EST PASSE DANS LES GAULES (RGFS 2,3)
- CONTIENT CE QUI S'EST PASSE DEPUIS LE COMMENCEMENT DU REGNE DE LOUIS LE BEGUE, FILS DE CHARLES LE CHAUVE, JUSQU'A LA FIN DU REGNE DE LOUIS 5, DERNIERE ROI DE LA SECONDE RACE, C'EST-A-DIRE DEPUIS L'AN 877-987 (RGFS 8)
- CONTIENT CE QUI S'EST PASSE SOUS LES REGNES DE PEPIN ET DE CHARLEMAGNE (RGFS 5)
- CONTIENT LA SUITE DES MONUMENTS DES TROIS REGNES DE PHILIPPE 1, DE LOUIS 6 ET DE LOUIS VII DEPUIS L'AN 1060-1180 (RGFS 13)
- CONTIENT LA SUITE DES MONUMENTS DES TROIS REGNES...DEPUIS L'AN 1060-1180 (RGFS 14-16)
- CONTIENT LE 1,2,3 (RGFS 17-19)
- CONTIENT LES ENQUETES ADMINISTRATIVES DU REGNE DE SAINT LOUIS ET LA CHRONIQUE DE L'ANONYME DE BETHUNE (RGFS 24)
- CONTIENT LES GESTES DE LOUIS LE DEBONNAIRE, D'ABORD ROI D'AQUITAINE, ET ENSUITE EMPEREUR, DEPUIS L'AN 781-840, AVEC LES LOIS, ETC. DE CE PRINCE, ETC (RGFS 6)
- CONTIENT LES LETTRES HISTORIQUES (RGFS 4)
- CONTIENT PRINCIPALEMENT CE QUI S'EST PASSE SOUS LE REGNE DE HENRI1, FILS DE ROBERT LE PIEUX, C.A.D. DEPUIS L'AN 1031-1060 (RGFS 11)
- CONTIENT SURTOUT CE QUI S'EST PASSE DEPUIS LE COMMENCEMENT DU REGNE DE HUGUES CAPET JUSQU'A CELUI DU ROI HENRI 1, FILS DE ROBERT LE PIEUX (RGFS 10)
- CONTIENT TOUT CE QUI A ETE FAIT PAR LES GAULOIS, ET QUI S'EST PASSE DANS LES GAULOIS AVANT L'ARRIVE DES FRANCOIS (RGFS 1)
- CONTIENT UNE PARTIE DE CE QUI S'EST PASSE SOUS LES TROIS REGNES DE PHILIPPE 1, DE LOUIS 6 DIT LE GROS, ET DE LOUIS 6 SURNOMME LE JEUNE, DEPUIS L'AN 1060-1180 (RGFS 12)
- RENFERME CE QUI RESTOIT A PUBLIER DES MONUMENTS DE LA SECONDE RACE DES ROIS DE FRANCE
- RENFERME LES GESTES DES FILS ET DES PETIT-FILS DE LOUIS LE DEBONNAIRE, DEPUIS L'AN 840-877, AVEC LES CAPITULAIRES DE CHARLES LE CHAUVE, ET AUTRES MONUMENTS HISTORIQUES (RGFS 7)

RERUM GALLICARUM ET FRANCICARUM SCRIPTORES (RGFS) : RECUEIL DES HISTORIENS DES GAULES ET DE LA FRANCE / Bouquet, Martin – (Commence Par Les Benedictins De La Congregation De St. Maur, Continue Par l'Academie Des Inscriptions Et Belles Lettres. Nouv. Edition Publiee Sous La Direction De Leopold Delisle. Vols also listed separately) – Paris: Religieux Benedictins de la Congregation de Saint-Maur. v1-24. 1869-1894 – Dfl2,121.00 coll – ne Slangenburg [240]
RERUM ITALICARUM SCRIPTORES / Antonio Muratori, Ludovico – (Giovani Benedetto Mittarelli, Ad scriptores rerum Italicarum accessiones historicae Faventinae, Venetiis, 1771) – Mediolani, 1723-1751. 26v – 9 – Bf68,200.00 set – 1-799-00302-7 – be Brepols [450]
RERUM ITALICORUM SCRIPTORES / Muratori, Lodovico A – Mediolani. v1-25. 1723-1751 – 819mf – 8 – Dfl2,867.00 – ne Slangenburg [220]
RERUM LITURGICARUM LIBRI DUO : CUM NOTIS E OBSERVATIONIBUS ROB SALA / Bona, Johannes – Aug. Taurinorum. Tom 1-3. 1747-53 – 77mf – 8 – Dfl270.00 – ne Slangenburg [240]
RERUM MUSICORUM OPUSCULUM RARUM AC SIGNE. / Frosch, J – 1535 – 9 – us Sibley [780]
RERUM NOVARUM: HOW TO ABOLISH POVERTY: HOW POVERTY WAS ABOLISHED / Guerin, M – Montreal: A. Pelletier, 1899. 04391. (Pre-1900 Canadiana) – 9 – cn C.I.H.M. [360]
RERVM PRODIGIOSARVM QVAE IN VRBE CONSTANTINOPOLITANA, ... / Laguna, A de – Coloniae, 1543 – 1mf – 9 – H-8151/1 – ne IDC [956]
RES GESTAE ALEXANDRI MAGNI / Curtius, Q. – AND Phalaris. Epistolae. 15th Century. Holkham Mss 365 and 452 – 1 – uk Microform Academic [760]
RES GESTAE (INDIANA STATE BAR ASSOCIATION) – (v1-28 1957-85 on reel or mf $240.00. v29-38 1985-95 on mf $250.00) – Indiana State Bar Association. v1-38. 1957-95 – 5,6,9 – $490.00 set – us Hein [340]
RES IPSA LOQUITUR *see* SAN FRANCISCO LAW REVIEW
RES JUDICATA IN THE CIVIL AND CRIMINAL LAW OF QUEBEC / Colston, J G – Quebec: Le Canadien, 1870. 03403. (Pre-1900 Canadiana) – 9 – cn C.I.H.M. [340]
RES MECHANICA – v1-12. 1980-84 – 1,5,6,13 – sz Elsevier [073]
RES (REFORMED ECUMENICAL SYNOD) NEWS EXCHANGE – 1964-81 (complete) – 2r – 1 – ATLA S0473 – us A.T.L.A. [073]
EN RESA TILL NORRA AMERICA / Kalm, Peter – 3v. Stockholm. 1753-61. B-1000 2 – 8 – ne IDC [910]
RESAPKAN DAN AMALKAM PANTJASILA / Ruslan, Abdulgani – SE 4463 1. 1963 – 9 – ne IDC [320]
RESCATADO / Ruiz-Gonzalez Valero, Manuel – Badajoz: Tip. Viudad de A. Arqueros, 1945 – 1 – sp Bibl Santa Ana [830]
EL RESCATE HUMAN RIGHTS DEPARTMENT – (Missing: Doc. 7) – Los Angeles. 85 docs. 1981-1991 – 86mf – 9 – ne IDC [320]
Resch, A *see*
- AGRAPHA AUSSERCANONISCHE EVANGELIENFRAGMENTE (T.U.U. 1-5/4A)
- AGRAPHA AUSSERCANONISCHE PARALLELTEXTE ZU DEN EVANGELIEN
- AGRAPHA AUSSERCANONISCHE SCHRIFTFRAGMENTE (T.U.U. 2-30/3.4.)
- DAS APOSTELDECRET NACH SEINER AUSSERCANONISCHEN TEXTGESTALT (T.U.U. 2-28/3)
- DER PAULINISMUS UND DIE LOGIA JESU (T.U.U. 2-27)

Resch, Alfred *see*
- DAS FORMALPRINZIP DES PROTESTANTISMUS
- DIE LOGIA JESU

RESCRIPTUM CONTRA LANFRANNUM / Turonensis, Beringerius – 1988 – 6mf – 9 – Bf1,250.00 – 2-503-63842-2 – be Brepols [240]
RESCUED ESSAYS OF THOMAS CARLYLE / Carlyle, Thomas; ed by Newberry, Percy – London: Leadenhall Press, Simpkin, Marshall, Hamilton, Kent & Co.; New York: Charles Scribner's Sons, 1892 – 1 roll – 1 – 1-55879-618-5 – uk Libr Preservation [840]
RESCUING THE ECONOMY IS YOUR CONCERN-YOU ARE THE TRUE ECONOMISTS / Donohue, E B – 12p – 9 – 1.00f – at Libertarian Micro [335]
RESE NA ESTADISTICA DE LA PROVINCIA DE BADAJOZ / Instituto Nacional de Estadistica – Madrid: Instituto Nacional de Estadistica, 1962 – 1 – sp Bibl Santa Ana [304]
RESEARCH AIDS ON THE PEOPLE'S REPUBLIC OF CHINA / U.S. Central Intelligence Agency – 1973- – 1 – us L of C Photodup [950]
RESEARCH AND DEVELOPMENT DOCUMENTS COLLECTIONS ON MICROFICHE *see*
- UPDATA GOVERNMENT DOCUMENTS – RESEARCH AND DEVELOPMENT DOCUMENTS

RESEARCH AND DEVELOPMENT IN AGRICULTURE *see* AGRICULTURAL SYSTEMS
THE RESEARCH AND DEVELOPMENT OF MULTIMEDIA LEISURE-LEARNING PACKAGES FOR THE RURAL ELDERLY / Howe, Laura G – 1980 – 3mf – 9 – $12.00 – us Microform Publ [370]
RESEARCH AND DEVELOPMENT SERIES / International Center for Aquaculture – No.1-29.1972-82. 1 reel – 1,5 – us Spaulding [639]
RESEARCH AND FARMING / North Carolina. Agricultural Experiment Station. Raleigh – n.1-28. 1941-spring 1970 – 1,5 – us Spaulding [630]
RESEARCH AND FARMING / North Carolina State University.Agricultural Experiment Station – No.29-39. 1979-81. 1 reel – 1,5 – us Spaulding [630]
RESEARCH AND INVE ACT. ANNUAL REPORT / Georgia. University. College of Agriculture – n.1-14. 1938-50 – 1,5 – us Spaulding [630]
RESEARCH BULLETIN / Colorado. Agricultural Experiment Station. Fort Collins – nos.1-5. 1936-37 – 1,5,6 – us Spaulding [630]
RESEARCH BULLETIN / Horace Mann-Lincoln Institute – v. 17- 1976- – 1,5,6,9 – us UMI [370]
RESEARCH BULLETIN / I A R (Institute of Administrative Research) – v. 1-16. 1960-76 – 1 – us UMI [370]
RESEARCH BULLETIN / Iowa State University. Iowa Agriculture and Home Economics Experiment Station – Nos 1-589 1911-80 – 1,5 – us Spaulding [630]
RESEARCH BULLETIN / Nebraska. Agricultural Experiment Station. Lincoln – n.1-234. 1913-69 – 1,5 – us Spaulding [630]
RESEARCH BULLETIN / Purdue University. Agricultural Experiment Station – No.653-974. 1957-82 – 1,5 – us Spaulding [630]
RESEARCH BULLETIN / University of Georgia. Agricultural Experiment Station – No.72-291. 1969-82. 84 fiches – 9 – us Spaulding [630]
RESEARCH BULLETIN / University of Missouri. Agricultural Experiment Station – No.1-1053. 1910-84 – 1,5 – us Spaulding [630]
RESEARCH BULLETIN / Wisconsin. Agricultural Experiment Station – no.1-282. 1909-72 – 1,5 – us Spaulding [630]
RESEARCH BULLETIN. HORACE MANN-LINCOLN INSTITUTE – v19, no.2-. Feb 1979- – 1,5,6,9 – us UMI [370]
RESEARCH BULLETIN. V.1-71. 42 FICHES / Georgia. Experiment Station – 9 – us Spaulding [630]
RESEARCH CATALOG OF MAPS OF AMERICA TO 1860 IN THE WILLIAM L. CLEMENTS LIBRARY / University of Michigan. William L. Clements Library – 1972. 43,800 cards on 4 reels – 1 – $270.00 export $325.00 – 0-8161-1227-4 – uk Hall [910]
RESEARCH CATALOGUE OF THE AMERICAN GEOGRAPHICAL SOCIETY / American Geographical Society. Library. New York – (First Supplement Topical Catalogue, 1974. 48,900 cards on 2 reels. $265.00 export $320.00. – ISBN 0-8161-1522-2) – 1 – uk Hall [900]
RESEARCH CENTER FOR RELIGION AND HUMAN RIGHTS IN CLOSED SOCIETIES – New York. 58 docs. 1980-1991 – 28mf – 9 – ne IDC [320]
Research Centre for Monetary and Financial Freedom *see*
- BOOKS, PAMPHLETS; ESSAYS AND ARTICLES
- LITERATURE LIST AND RESEARCH PROGRAMME

RESEARCH COLLECTION IN LABOR STUDIES *see* LABOR UNION PERIODICALS, PART 1
RESEARCH COLLECTIONS IN AMERICAN LEGAL HISTORY *see*
- LETTERS RECEIVED BY THE ATTORNEY GENERAL, 1809-1870
- LETTERS RECEIVED BY THE ATTORNEY GENERAL, 1871-1884
- RECORDS OF THE WICKERSHAM COMMISSION ON LAW OBSERVANCE AND ENFORCEMENT, PART 1

RESEARCH COLLECTIONS IN AMERICAN POLITICS *see*
- THE HARRY S. TRUMAN ORAL HISTORIES COLLECTION
- THE MORGENTHAU DIARIES, 1933-1945

RESEARCH COLLECTIONS IN LABOR STUDIES *see*
- LABOR UNION PERIODICALS, PART 2
- LABOR UNION PERIODICALS, PART 3
- LABOR UNION PERIODICALS, PARTS 1-3

RESEARCH COLLECTIONS IN WOMEN'S STUDIES *see*
- NEW ENGLAND WOMEN AND THEIR FAMILIES IN THE 18TH AND 19TH CENTURIES: PERSONAL PAPERS, LETTERS, AND DIARIES
- SOUTHERN WOMEN AND THEIR FAMILIES IN THE 19TH CENTURY: PAPERS AND DIARIES

RESEARCH COMMUNICATIONS IN CHEMICAL PATHOLOGY AND PHARMACOLOGY – v. 1-12. 1970-1975 – 1,5,6 – us Princeton Micro [616]
RESEARCH FOR AGRICULTURAL DEVELOPMENT IN THE NORTHERN SUDAN TO 1967 / MacLoughlin, P F M – A classified inventory and analysis. 1971. BNE-7661 1 – 9 – ne IDC [338]
THE RESEARCH FOR JOB OPPORTUNITIES IN LIBYA: A COMPARISON BETWEEN THE SITUATION OF EDUCATED AND UNEDUCATED YOUTH / United Nations. Children's Fund – Tripoli, Libya. 5, 6, 7 and 8 Jul 1969. Yasin, M. (Teamleader ILO Manpower Planning and Organisation Project). BNE-905 1 – 9 – ne IDC [331]
RESEARCH IN AFRICAN LITERATURES – v1- 1970- 1; v8- 5,6,9 – us UMI [490]
RESEARCH IN COOPERATIVE EXTENSION WORK / Wisconsin. College of Agriculture. Dept. of Agricultural and Extension Education – Apr 1958-Dec 1966. no. 1-10 – 1,5 – us Spaulding [630]
RESEARCH IN DEVELOPMENTAL DISABILITIES – v1- 1981- – 5,6,9 – us UMI [616]
RESEARCH IN EDUCATION – (1985-. 5,6,9) – no.1-. 1969- – 1 – us UMI [370]
RESEARCH IN EXPERIMENTAL MEDICINE – v. 115-179. 1949-80 – 1,5,9 – 6679.00 – us UMI [073]
RESEARCH IN HIGHER EDUCATION – v1- 1973- 1; v4- 5,6,9 – us UMI [370]
RESEARCH IN INDONESIAN AND REGIONAL LANGUAGES : A BIBLIOGRAPHY / Jumariam – 1985 – A$10.00 – 0-86758-168-9 – at BISA [470]
RESEARCH IN INTERNATIONAL LAW / Harvard Law School – Cambridge, 1929 – 5mf – 1 – ILM-3893/1 – ne IDC [327]
RESEARCH IN INTERNATIONAL LAW / Harvard Law School – Cambridge, 1932 – 11mf – 1 – ILM-3894/1 – ne IDC [327]
RESEARCH IN INTERNATIONAL LAW / Harvard Law School – Cambridge, 1935 – 13mf – 1 – ILM-3895/1 – ne IDC [327]
RESEARCH IN INTERNATIONAL LAW / Harvard Law School – Concord, 1939 – 11mf – 1 – ILM-3891/1 – ne IDC [327]
RESEARCH IN LIFE SCIENCES / Maine. Agricultural Experiment Station – v. 1-17. 1953-70 – 1,5,6 – us Spaulding [570]
RESEARCH IN MINISTRY – 1981-90 (complete) – 3mf – 9 – ATLA 1992-S003 – us A.T.L.A. [073]
RESEARCH IN POPULATION COMMUNICATION / Feliciano, Gloria D – 1978 – 9 – 92-3-101512-5 – fr UNESCO [302]
RESEARCH IN REVIEW / Massachusetts. Agricultural Experiment Station – v. 1-5. 1952-Jun 1956 – 1,5,6 – us Spaulding [630]
RESEARCH IN SCIENCE AND TECHNOLOGICAL EDUCATION – 1983- 11v – 9 – £188.50 – 0263-5143 – uk Carfax [370]
RESEARCH IN TEXAS / Texas A & M University. Agricultural Experiment Station – No.1-8. 1975-82. 3 fiches – 9 – us Spaulding [630]

RESEARCH IN VETERINARY SCIENCE – v. 7-13. 1966-1972 – 1,5,6 – us Princeton Micro [636]
RESEARCH IN VETERINARY SCIENCE – (v.28-. 1980- 5,6,9) – v.1-. 1960- – 1 – us UMI [073]
RESEARCH INTO HIGHER EDUCATION ABSTRACTS – 1968- 26v – 9 – £197.00 – 0034-5326 – uk Carfax [370]
RESEARCH MANAGEMENT – v1- 1958- 1; v19- 5,6,9 – us UMI [650]
RESEARCH MANAGEMENT IN FORESTRY – 1992 – 126p – it F.A.O. [634]
RESEARCH MATERIALS / Institute for the Study of the USSR – Mimeographed ed. Munich. series 2: n1-94. 1953-66 – 151mf – 9 – $5.00f – us Ross [947]
RESEARCH MONOGRAPH / Texas A & M University. Agricultural Experiment Station – No.1-11.1973-81. 12 fiches – 9 – us Spaulding [630]
RESEARCH NEWS / Georgia. Agricultural Experiment Station. Athens – 1947-55 – 1,5,6 – us Spaulding [630]
RESEARCH NOTES / South Carolina Post Offices and Postmasters – No date.Comp. by J.R. Bouknight. 8 fiches – 9 – us South Carolina Historical [380]
RESEARCH NOTES ON THE GILBERT ISLANDS, C. 1952-62 / Maude, Henry Evans – 1r – 1 – PMB1057 – at Pacific Mss [980]
RESEARCH ON AGING – (1983-. 1,5,6,9) – v1-. 1979- – 1 – us UMI [073]
RESEARCH ON CHILDREN'S AND YOUNG ADULT LITERATURE / Cullinan, Bernice E & Dolly Svobodny – 1900-86. 1500 titles on 300mf. Printed card indexes included – 9 – us A.T.B.I. [370]
RESEARCH ON FARM AND LIVESTOCK PRODUCTIVITY IN THE CENTRAL ETHIOPIAN HIGHLANDS = RECHERCHE SUR LA PRODUCTIVITE DEL'AGRICULTURE ET DE L'ELEVAGE DANS LES HAUTS PLATEUX DU CENTRE DE L'ETHIOPIE: RESULTATS DES PREMIERES ANNEES, 1977-1980 : INITIAL RESULTS, 1977-1980 / Gryseels, G & Anderson, F M – 1983 – 9 – $10.00 – 92-9053-109-6 – et ILRI [638]
RESEARCH ON LANGUAGE AND SOCIAL INTERACTION *see* PAPERS IN LINGUISTICS
RESEARCH ON URBAN HYDROLOGY / ed by McPherson, M B – 9 – fr UNESCO [550]
RESEARCH PAMPHLETS / Fabian Society – nos. 1-347 – 1 – uk Microform Academic [335]
RESEARCH PAPER / Wisconsin. Land Tenure Center – 1964-69. n.1-40 – 1,5 – us Spaulding [630]
RESEARCH PAPERS / Kansas. State University. Agricultural Experiment Station – nos.1-27. 1970-77 – 1,5,6 – us Spaulding [630]
RESEARCH PAPERS / U.S. Department of the Treasury. Commission on Private Philanthropy and Public Needs – Washington. 5v in 6bks. 1977 – 9 – Inquire – 0-89941-481-8 – us Hein [360]
RESEARCH PERSPECTIVES / North Carolina State University.Agricultural Research Service – v1,no.1-4. 1981-82. 1 reel – 1,5 – us Spaulding [630]
RESEARCH POLICY – v1-13. 1972-84 – 1,5,6,13 – sz Elsevier [330]
RESEARCH PROGRESS / Illinois. Agricultural Experiment Station – 1948-70 – 1, 5 – us Spaulding [630]
RESEARCH PROGRESS REPORT / Purdue University. Agricultural Experiment Station – No.1-418. 1962-73 – 1,5 – us Spaulding [630]
RESEARCH PUBLICATIONS / Kansas. State University. Agricultural Research Station – nos.1-171. 1916-77 – 1,5,6 – us Spaulding [630]
RESEARCH QUARTERLY / American Alliance for Health, Physical Education and Recreation – v1- 1930- ; v40- ; v46- – 1,5,6,9 – us UMI [073]
RESEARCH QUARTERLY / American Association for Health, Physical Education and Recreation – v. 1-15. 1930-44 – 1 – us Princeton Micro [610]
RESEARCH QUARTERLY – v.1-15. 1930-44 – 1 – 22100.00 – us Princeton Micro [073]
RESEARCH REPORT / Clemson University. Department of Agricultural Economics and Rural Sociology – 1981-82.6 fiches – 9 – us Spaulding [630]
RESEARCH REPORT / Connecticut. Agricultural Experiment Station. Storrs – v. 1-30. 1964-69 – 1,5,6 – us Spaulding [630]
RESEARCH REPORT / Georgia. Agricultural Experiment Station. Athens – v. 1-62. 1967-69 – 1,5,6 – us Spaulding [630]
RESEARCH REPORT / Louisiana State University. Agricultural Experiment Station. Department of Agricultural Engineering – 1971-83.1 reel – 1,5 – us Spaulding [630]
RESEARCH REPORT / Mississippi State University. Agricultural Experiment Station. Agricultural and Forestry Experiment Station – No.1-6. 1975-82. 1 reel – 1,5 – us Spaulding [630]
RESEARCH REPORT / New Mexico State University. Agricultural Experiment Station – 1970-83.No.163-495 – 1,5 – us Spaulding [630]
RESEARCH REPORT / North Carolina. State University. Raleigh. Dept. of Agronomy – v.1-20. Feb. 1953-Dec 1955 – 1,5 – us Spaulding [630]
RESEARCH REPORT / North Carolina. State University. Raleigh. Dept. of Crop Science – v.1-33. Jul 1962-69 – 1,5 – us Spaulding [630]
RESEARCH REPORT / North Carolina. State University. Raleigh. Dept. of Field Crops – v.1-32. Dec 1956-61 – 1,5 – us Spaulding [630]
RESEARCH REPORT / North Carolina State University.Department of Crop Science – No.34-90. 1970-82 – 1,5 – us Spaulding [630]
RESEARCH REPORT / North Dakota. Agricultural Experiment Station. Fargo – nos.1-60. 1960-75 – 1,5,6 – us Spaulding [630]
RESEARCH REPORT / Oklahoma State University. Agricultural Experiment Station – P626-P833. 1970-82 – 1,5 – us Spaulding [630]
RESEARCH REPORT / Timber Development Association – 7 – uk Microform Academic [634]
RESEARCH REPORT / University of Georgia. Agricultural Experiment Station – No.63-418. 1970-82. 125 fiches – 9 – us Spaulding [630]
RESEARCH REPORT / University of Kentucky. Department of Agricultural Economics – No.1-37.1969-83. 18 fiches – 9 – us Spaulding [630]
RESEARCH REPORT / Virginia. Agricultural Experiment Station. Blacksburg – n.1-115. Mar 1956-Nov 1966 – 1,5 – us Spaulding [630]
RESEARCH REPORT / Virginia. Polytechnic Institute. Research Division. Blacksburg – v. 116-139. 1967-69 – 1,5,6 – us Spaulding [630]
RESEARCH REPORT / Wisconsin. Agricultural Experiment Station – no.1-80. May 1957-Jul 1971 – 1,5 – us Spaulding [630]
RESEARCH REPORT. 5. 1-69. 1951-69 (MISCELLANEOUS PUBLICATION) / Vermont. Agricultural Experiment Station – 1,5,6 – us Spaulding [630]
RESEARCH REPORT ON AN EVALUATION OF TEACHER TRAINING CUM EDUCATION EXTENSION PROJECT : ED. IN COLLABORATION WITH UNICEF B.E. 2519-2521 / Thailand. Department of Teacher Training – (In Thai with English abstract) – 6mf – 9 – DE-284/1 – ne IDC [370]
A RESEARCH REPORT ON THE HIGHER EDUCATION : A CASE STUDY OF THAILAND / Thailand. National Education Commission – (In Thai) – 1979 – 3mf – 9 – DE-307/1 – ne IDC [370]
RESEARCH REPORT.DAIRY / Louisiana State University. Agricultural Experiment Station. Hill Farm Experiment Station, Homer – 1983. 1 reel – 1,5 – us Spaulding [636]
RESEARCH REPORTS – North Central Weed Control Conference – 1947- 1; 1975- 5,6,9 – us UMI [630]
RESEARCH REPORTS AERR / Illinois. Department of Agricultural Economics – n.1-102. 1954-69 – 1,5 – us Spaulding [630]
RESEARCH REPORTS ON HISTORY OF SBC AGENCIES / Southern Baptist Convention – Comp. by Historical Comm. for SBC Executive Committee, 1962-63. Home Mission Board and Foreign Mission Board. 324p – 1 – us Baptist [240]
RESEARCH REPORTS ON HISTORY OF SBC AGENCIES / Southern Baptist Convention – Comp. by Historical Commission for SBC Executive Comm., 1845-1962. 585p – 5 – 11.34 – us Baptist [240]
RESEARCH REVIEW (CCF) – v1-3, no. 30. Jun. 1933-Mar. 1936 – 1 – cn Precision [073]
RESEARCH REVIEW OF EQUAL EDUCATION – v. 1-. 1977- – 1,5,6,9 – us UMI [320]
RESEARCH SERIES / South Carolina. Agricultural Experiment Station. Clemson. Dept. of Food Science and Biochemistry – Nos 1-17 1961-69 – 1,5 – us Spaulding [660]
RESEARCH SERIES / South Carolina. Agricultural Experiment Station. Clemson. Dept. of Seed Certification – n.1-3. 1958-69 – 1,5 – us Spaulding [630]
RESEARCH SERIES / South Carolina. Agricultural Experiment Station. Clemson. Horticultural Dept – n.1-125. Apr 1955-69 – 1,5 – us Spaulding [630]
RESEARCH SERIES / South Carolina. Agricultural Experiment Station. Clemson. Poultry Science Dept – n.1-28. 1967 – 1,5 – us Spaulding [630]
RESEARCH SERIES BULLETINS / California. Dept. of Employment – n.1-41, 1941-57. 34 fiches. (Harvard Law School Library Collection.) – 9 – 1.50f – us H.U. Law [331]
RESEARCH STRATEGIES: RS – v1-. Winter 1983- – 1,5,6,9 – us UMI [073]
RESEARCH STUDIES / University of Pennsylvania. Wharton School. Industrial Research Department – Philadelphia. v1-39. 1928-56 – 128mf – 9 – $5.00f – us Ross [330]
RESEARCH SUMMARIES / Clemson University. Agricultural Experiment Station – No.5-13.1970-78. (Ceased). 1 reel – 1,5 – us Spaulding [630]
RESEARCH SUMMARIES / South Carolina. Agricultural Experiment Station. Clemson – n.1-4. 1966-69 – 1,5 – us Spaulding [630]
RESEARCHES IN ANATOLIA : THE ALISHAR HUYUK, SEASONS OF 1930-1932, PART 2 / Osten, Hans Henning von der – 1937 – 9 – $18.00f – 0-226-63939-8 – us U.C. Orient [930]
RESEARCHES IN ANATOLIA, VOL 9 : THE ALISHAR HUYUK SEASONS OF 1930-1932, PART 3 / Osten, Hans Henning von der – 1937 – 9 – $18.00f – 0-226-63940-1 – us U.C. Orient [930]
RESEARCHES IN NON-EUCLIDIAN GEOMETRY AND THE THEORY OF RELATIVITY: A SYSTEMATIC STUDY OF TWENTY FALLACIES IN THE GEOMETRY OF RIEMANN : INCLUDING THE SO-CALLED CURVATURE OF SPACE AND RADIUS OF WORLD CURVATURE, AND OF EIGHTY ERRORS IN THE PHYSICAL THEORIES OF EINSTEIN AND EDDINGTON, SHOWING THE COMPLETE COLLAPSE OF THE THEORY OF RELATIVITY / Jackson, Thomas Jefferson – Mare Island, Calif.: Naval Observatory, 1925 – 1 – us U.W. Library [510]
RESEARCHES IN SINAI / Petrie, William Matthew Flinders – Chaps. by C.T. Currelly.186 illus. 4 maps. London: J. Murray, 1906. 280p. fold. plan – 1 – us U.W. Library [930]
RESEARCHES INTO THE PHYSICAL HISTORY OF MANKIND / Prichard, James Cowles – 2nd. ed. London, 1826 – 1 – us U.W. Library [573]
RESEARCHES OF FUNGI / Buller, A H R – 6v. London. 1909-34. B-5340 2 – 8 – ne IDC [580]
RESEARCHES ON MAGNETISM, ELECTRICITY, HEAT, LIGHT, CRYSTALLIZATION, AND CHEMICAL ATTRACTION, IN THEIR RELATIONS TO THE VITAL FORCE / Reichenbach, Karl Ludwig Friedrich – Tr. and ed., with preface, notes and appendix by William Gregory. 3 plates and 23 woodcuts. London: Taylor, Walton and Maberly; Edinburgh: Maclachlan & Stewart, 1850. xlv,463p.illus., fold. pl., diagrs – 1 – us U.W. Library [530]
RESEARCHES ON PTOLEMY'S GEOGRAPHY OF EASTERN ASIA / Gerini, G E – 1909 – 1 – uk Microform Academic [910]
Resen, Ardis C *see* SPORT AND POETRY: AN EXPLORATION OF THE INTERRELATEDNESS OF WORDS AND ACTIONS
RESENA BIOGRAFICA DEL GENERAL JUAN PERON, PRESIDENTE DE LA NACION ARGENTINA / Argentina. Presidencia. Subsecretaria de Informaciones – [Buenos Aires?, 1950?] – 1 – CSUXADH9029-B – us Hoover Inst Photo [320]
RESENA DE LOS FESTEJOS.. / Caceres. Spain – 1869 – 9 – 1.50f – sp Bibl Santa Ana [390]
RESENA DE VARIOS...MINAS DE VALDELAYEGUA / Gandarias de Colmenares, Eusebio – 1872 – 9 – 1.50f – sp Bibl Santa Ana [622]
RESENA EPIGRAFICA. SAN MARTIN E TREBEJO, MESTANZA, MAZARRON, TOBARRA, ORETO, PERALES DE MILLA, LIRIA RUBI, AMPURIAS Y OLLEROS DE PISUERGA / Fita, Fidel – Madrid: Fortanet, 1891. B.R.A.H. 18, pp. 366-382 – sp Bibl Santa Ana [240]
RESENA ESTADISTICA DE LA PROVINCIA DE BADAJOZ / Instituto Nacional de Estadistica – Madrid: Instituto Nacional de Estadistica, 1954 – 1 – sp Bibl Santa Ana [304]
RESENA GEOGRAFICA Y ESTADISTICA DE ESPANA / Instituto Geografico – Madrid, 1888 – 24mf – 9 – sp Cultura [946]
RESENA HISTORICA...BOTOA / Nougues Secall, Mariano – 1861 – 9 – 1.50f – sp Bibl Santa Ana [946]
RESENA SOBRE LA TRAIDA DE AGUAS A BADAJOZ / Bernaldez, Fernando – 1863 – 9 – 1.50f – sp Bibl Santa Ana [946]
RESENHA JUDAICA – (Sao Paulo: Empresa Jornalistica) – 1 – us U.W. Library [270]
RESENHA SOCIALISTA – Rio de Janeiro, 1 (1956) no 3 – 1 – us Hoover Inst Photo [335]
RESERVOIRS ET AQUEDUCS ANTIQUES DE MERIDA / Lantier, R – (Sep. du Bulletin Hispanique, Tomo 17, nº 2) – Bordeaux, 1915 – 1 – sp Bibl Santa Ana [627]
RESERVOIRS OF SRI LANKA AND THEIR FISHERIES – 1989 – 134p – it F.A.O. [338]
RESHAFIM / ed by Frischmann, D – 2v. Warsaw. 1909-11. BJ-422-71 1 – 9 – ne IDC [470]
RESHETKA – Literaturno-khudozhestvennyi al'manakh. Spb. 1912. BR-1904 2 – 8 – ne IDC [460]
RESHIT HA-SHIMMUSH BI-ZEKHUT HA-KAPITULAZIYYOT AL-YEDEI YEHUDIM BE-EREZ-YISRA'EL / Brawer, A J – v5. Ziyyon. 1940. BJ-27-35 – 8 – ne IDC [956]
RESHIT LIMMUDIM / Lindau, B – Berlin. 1789. BJ-422-53 1 – 9 – ne IDC [470]
RESHUMMOT – Odessa. Berlin. Tel Aviv. 1918-30. BJ-91-71 1 – 9 – ne IDC [470]
RESHUMMOT – Tel Aviv. v. 1-5. 1946-53. BJ-91-92 1 – 9 – ne IDC [470]
RESHUMOT / Israel. Ministry of Justice – Sefer hahuqqim. (State records-law). 1949-75; index. 1948-63. BJ-81-29 1 – 9 – ne IDC [340]
RESHUMOT: HUGGE TAGZIV / Israel. Ministry of Justice – 1953-75. (Budget laws). BJ-81-33 1 – 9 – ne IDC [340]
A RESIDENCE OF EIGHT YEARS IN PERSIA AMONG THE NESTORIAN CHRISTIANS : WITH NOTICES OF THE MUHAMMEDANS / Perkins, Justin – Andover: Allen, Morrill & Wardwell, 1843 – 2mf – us A.T.L.A. [240]
Residencia Universitaria San Jose. Caceres *see* REGLAMENTO DE LA...OBRA BENEFICO-SOCIAL DE LA CAJA DE AHORROS Y MONTE DE PIEDAD DE CACERES
RESIDENTIAL INTERIORS – 1977 – 9 – us UMI [073]
RESIDENTIAL INTERIORS – v. 1-. 1976- – 1,5,6,9 – us UMI [740]
RESIDENTIAL TREATMENT FOR CHILDREN AND YOUTH : THE OFFICIAL JOURNAL OF THE AMERICAN ASSOCIATION OF CHILDREN'S RESIDENTIAL CENTERS / ed by Northrup, Gordon – v4- 1986- – 1, 9 ($200.00 in US $280.00 outside hardcopy subsc) – us Haworth [360]
A RESIDENT'S LIFE IN NIGERIA / Larymore, Constance – London, 1908 – 1 – us Res Libr [960]
A RESIDENT'S WIFE IN NIGERIA / Larymore, Constance – New York: E P Dutton, 1908 – us Res Libr [920]
Residi, Halil *see* OSMANLI KUMANDANLARI
RESIDUES OF SOME VETERINARY DRUGS IN ANIMALS AND FOODS : AZAPERONE, CARAZOLOL, FEBANTEL, FENBENDAZOLE, OXFENDAZOLE, PROPIONYLPROMAZINE, SPIRAMYCIN, TYLOSIN; 38TH MEETING OF JECFA, ROME 1991 – 1991 – 148p – it F.A.O. [636]

RESIDUES OF SOME VETERINARY DRUGS IN ANIMALS AND FOODS : BENZYL PENICILLIN, CARBADOX, CLOSANTEL, IVERMECTIN, LEVAMISOLE, OLAQUINDOX, OXYTETRACYCLINE; 36TH MEETING OF JECFA, ROME 1990 – 1991 – 129p – it F.A.O. [636]
RESIDUES OF SOME VETERINARY DRUGS IN ANIMALS AND FOODS : THIRTY-SECOND MEETING OF THE JOINT F.A.O./WHO EXPERT COMMITTEE ON FOOD ADDITIVES. ROME, JUNE 1987 – 1988 – 56p – it F.A.O. [636]
RESIDUES OF VETERINARY DRUGS IN FOODS : REPORT OF A JOINT F.A.O./WHO EXPERT CONSULTATION. ROME, 1984 – 1985 – 66p – it F.A.O. [360]
RESIGNATIONS AND DECLINATIONS AMONG THE RECORDS OF THE DEPT. OF STATE, 1789-1827 / U.S. Department of State – 1roll. T730 – 1 – us Nat'l Archives [324]
LA RESILIATION DES BAUX RURAUX PAR SUITE DE LA GUERRE, COMMENTAIRE DE LA LOI DU 17 AOUT 1917 / Laurent, M A – Paris, Administration du Recueil general des lois etc., 1917 64 p. LL-4040 – 1 – us L of C Photodup [340]
RESIMLI KITAB – cilt 1-9, nos. 1-51 (1324-1329 1908-1914) – 20mf – 9 – $175.00 – us MEDOC [949]
RESIMLI KITAB – Istanbul: Resimli Kitap Matbaasi, 1924-1329 (1908-1914) – 9 – $250.00 – us MEDOC [956]
RESIMLI KITABIN FIHRISTI – Istanbul. no1-18. 1326 [1910] – $35.00 – us MEDOC [073]
RESIMLI ZAMAN – Konya, 1925-19? – 9 – $10.00 – us MEDOC [956]
RESIST NOT EVIL / Darrow, Clarence S – (Essay on crime and punishment) – Girard, Kansas: Haldeman-Julius Co, 1902 (1925) – 1mf – 9 – $1.50 – LLMC 91-058 – us L.L.M.C. [340]
RESISTANCE WELDER MANUFACTURERS ASSOCIATION (RWMA) – (Updated Every 60 Days) – Information Handling Services – 5,9 – us Info Handling [620]
RESISTENCIA PERONISTA – (Includes c.1: v.1:no.4 1958: Nov. 19) – 1 – CSUXAJA7616-S – us Hoover Inst Photo [073]
O RESISTENTE – S. Joao d'el-Rey, 2 Jan, Jul, Dec 1896; Jul-Aug 1897; Mar-Aug, Oct-Dec 1898; Jan-Mar, May, Jul-Aug, Oct-Nov 1899; May 1900; 20 Feb 1902 – 1,5,6 – bl Biblioteca [072]
Resit, Mustafa *see* BIR CICEK DEMETI
RESMI TEKIRDAG – (No. 66 (29 Mart 1982), no. 82 (19 Temmuz 1928)) – Tekirdag: Vilayet Matbaasi. Cikaran: Tekirdag Vilayeti, 1927-1928 – 1mf – 9 – $10.00 – us MEDOC [949]
Resneli, Niyazi Bey *see* HATIRAT-I NIYAZI
RESNICA – Houghton, MI, 1914 – 1mf or 1 reel – 9,1 – us I.H.R.C. [975]
Resnick, Alan N *see* BANKRUPTCY REFORM ACT OF 1978
RESOLUCION DE LA INCORPORACION DE OLIVENZA.. / Blazquez Prieto, Gabriel R – 1805 – 9 – 1.50f – sp Bibl Santa Ana [946]
RESOLUCION PHILOSOPHICA Y MEDICA...DEL VERDADERO TEMPERAMENTO FRIO Y HUMEDO DE LA NIEVE / Murillo y Velarde Jurado, T – Madrid, 1667 – 2mf – 9 – sp Cultura [610]
RESOLUCION...OLIVENZA Y LAS ALDEAS DE.. / Blazquez Prieto, Gabriel R – 1804 – 9 – 1.50f – sp Bibl Santa Ana [946]
RESOLUSI2 / Sentral Organisasi Buruh Seluruh Indonesia. Kongres Nasional. 3d Solo, 1960 – SE 5139 1. 1965 – 9 – ne IDC [025]
[RESOLUSIES, 1655-1745, SERIES LM 2, 2A, 3, 4, 5, 7] / Leibbrandt, H C V – [s.l: s.n., 19–?] – us Res Libr [960]
RESOLUTIES, RAPPORTEN, BRIEVEN E.D. UITGEWISSELD TUSSEN J. VAN HOORN EN DE KONING VAN BANTAM, 1708 – (Microfiche Nos 12-16) – 5mf – 9 – SD-102/1 – ne IDC [350]
RESOLUTIES VAN DE HEREN ZEVENTIEN DER VERENIGDE OOSTINDISCHE COMPAGNIE, 1602-1796 / Netherlands. General State Archives – (Index available separately for Dfl460.00) – 779mf – 9 – Dfl9350.00 silver – ne MMF Publ [324]
RESOLUTION DU CONSEIL NATIONAL (K.R.N.) DU 21 SEPTEMBRE 1946 CONCERNANT LE PLAN DE RECONSTRUCTION ECONOMIQUE / Poland. Centralny Urzad Planowania – Warsaw. 1946. BD-555 1 – 9 – ne IDC [947]
RESOLUTION RECORD / Seneca County, Ohio. Tiffin, City. City Council – 1933-1989 – 1r – 1 – $32.50r – us Archival [324]
RESOLUTION RECORDS / Crawford County. Ohio. Galion – 1962-1978 – 1r – 1 – $32.50r – us Archival [324]
RESOLUTIONS / Organization of Petroleum Exporting Countries – 1960-78 – 1 – 20.00 – us L of C Photodup [330]
RESOLUTIONS AND DECISIONS / UN – (16th-63rd sess; Year 1978-1988 E/RES/ 1953-87 mf: E.108 F.113 S.109) – 1st-15th sess – E/F29 S.16 – 9 – E/RES/ 1946-53 – us U.N. Pubs [340]
RESOLUTIONS DE MESSIEURS LES DOCTEURS DE SORBONNE, SUR PLUSIEURS QUESTIONS QUI CONCERNENT LE CRIME DE SORTILEGE – Orleans. 1625 – 9 – fr Hachette [360]
RESOLUTIONS OF DISTRICT COUNCILS / Eastern Navajo Council – 1971-78.(American Indian Periodicals in the Princeton University Library). 18 fiches – 9 – $75.00 – us UPA [073]
RESOLUTIONS OF THE BOARD OF GOVERNORS (HEREN ZEVENTIEN) OF THE DUTCH EAST INDIA COMPANY (VOC), 1602-1796 *see* RESOLUTIES VAN DE HEREN ZEVENTIEN DER VERENIGDE OOSTINDISCHE COMPAGNIE, 1602-1796
RESOLUTIONS OF THE CONVENTION OF CHRIST'S MESSENGERS... : ASSEMBLED FROM THE 12TH TO THE 19TH OF AUGUST, 1847, AT THE TRUMBELL PHALANX, OHIO / Smolnikar, Andrew B – 1847 – 1r – 1 – us Western Res [240]
RESOLUTIONS OF THE FOUNDATION CONVENTION / General Organization of the Jewish Workers of Palestine. (Histadrut) – 1920. BJ-28-30 1 – 9 – ne IDC [330]
RESOLVING INDETERMINACY ASSOCIATED WITH JOINT-LEVEL MOTOR EQUIVALENCE IN PLANAR AIMED ARM MOVEMENTS / States, Rebecca A – 1994 – 1mf – $4.00 – us Microform Publ [612]
RESONANCE – Louisville, KY. v1-2. 1969-73 – 5mf – 9 – $5.00f – us Ross [073]
DIE RESORPTION VON AMINOSAEUREN UND PROTEINEN AUS DEM PROXIMALEN TUBULUS DER NIERE : UNTERSUCHUNGEN AM MODELL EINER KLONALEN ZELL-LINIE (OK) / Schwegler, Johann S – 1993 – 3mf – 9 – DM98.00 – 3-89349-652-1 – gw Hänsel [611]
THE RESOUNDING VOICE OF THE INDONESIAN REVOLUTION / Sukarno, Pres. Indonesia – Inc. Manipol – Usdek,BY R. Abdulgani, and The birth of Pantjasila. SE 10,983 1. Independence Day message on Aug. 17, 1963 – 9 – ne IDC [324]
RESOURCE *see* AGRICULTURAL ENGINEERING
RESOURCE CENTER FOR PHILIPPINE CONCERNS – Tokyo. 71 docs. 1980-1991 – 31mf – 9 – ne IDC [950]
RESOURCE DEVELOPMENT NEWSLETTER / University of Tennessee.Agricultural Extension Service – No.72-115. 1970-82. 1 reel – 1,5 – us Spaulding [630]
RESOURCE DEVELOPMENT REPORT / Auburn University. Extension Service – 1965-69 – 1,5,6 – us Spaulding [630]
RESOURCE ECONOMICS RESEARCH MIMEOGRAPH / New Hampshire. Agricultural Experiment Station – v. 1-45. 1947-68 – 1,5,6 – us Spaulding [333]
RESOURCE MANAGEMENT AND OPTIMIZATION / ed by Morgan, W B et al – 1980- – 1,5,9 – us Harwood [333]
RESOURCE PARTITIONING AND THE ROLE OF COMPETITION STRUCTURING IN LICHENOSTOMUS HONEYEATER AND BELL MINER COMMUNITIES IN SOUTHERN VICTORIA / Wykes, Boyd – (PhD Thesis) – 1982 – microfiche – A$15.00 – at R.A.O.U. [590]
RESOURCE RECOVERY – (See also: Resource Recovery and Energy Review) – v1. 1974 – 1,5,6 – us UMI [360]
RESOURCE RECOVERY AND ENERGY REVIEW – v2- 1975- 1,9; v3- 5,6 – us UMI [360]
THE RESOURCE RENT TAX: A PENALTY ON RISK-TAKING / Ball, Ray & Bowers, John – 1984. 20p – 9 – 1.00f – at Libertarian Micro [335]
RESOURCE REPORT / Wisconsin. College of Agricultural and Life Sciences. Cooperative Extension Programs – no.1-17. Aug 1966-Oct 1970 – 1,5 – us Spaulding [630]
RESOURCE SHARING AND INFORMATION NETWORKS / ed by Holley, Robert P – v1- 1983- – 1, 9 ($150.00 in US $210.00 outside hardcopy subsc) – us Haworth [020]
RESOURCES : MENSUEL – (In English) – Montreal, Canada. jun 1903-v3 n12. dec 1905 – 1r – 1 – Can$35.00 – cn Can Microfilming [072]
RESOURCES *see* ACA NEWS
RESOURCES AND CONSERVATION – v1-11. 1975-84. Continues: Resource Recovery and Conservation – 1,5,6,13 – sz Elsevier [333]
RESOURCES AND ENERGY – v1-6. 1978-84 – 1,5,6,13 – sz Elsevier [621]
RESOURCES AND PROGRESS OF THE PROVINCE OF ONTARIO: A PAPER READ BEFORE THE COMMERCIAL UNION CLUB OF ST THOMAS, NOVEMBER 22, 1887 / Blue, Archibald – Toronto: Hunter, Rose, 1888. 00151. (Pre-1900 Canadiana) – 9 – cn C.I.H.M. [971]
RESOURCES FOR AMERICAN LITERARY STUDY – v1- 1971- 1; v6- 5,6; v5- 9 – us UMI [410]
RESOURCES FOR FEMINIST RESEARCH – Toronto. v1-23. 1970-94 – 9 – Can$20.00y – cn Micromedia [305]
RESOURCES IN EDUCATION (RIE) – (1981-82. $112.00 in North America, $115.00 elsewhere. 1983. $112.00y in North America, $115.00y elsewhere) – 1966-80. Main Entry Section – 9 – $869.00 in North America, $886.00 elsewhere. – us Oryx [370]
THE RESOURCES OF BRITISH COLUMBIA – Victoria [B.C.]: A A McArthur, [1883-1885] – 9 – cn C.I.H.M. [910]
RESPEKT – 1991-1994 – 4 times per yr – 1 – F1,397.00 – sz Infoprint [947]
RESPEKT – (nov 1989-dec 1990 2r $170. 1991-92 1r per y $85y. 1993-98 2r per y $170y) – Czech Republic, 1999- – 2r per y – 1 – $160.00 standing order – us Ross [072]
RESPEKT – (Standing order available from De 1994. 2r per year. Sfr225.00y) – 1993 – 2r – 1 – Sfr240.00 – sz Infoprint [947]
RESPIRATION – v32-. 1975- – 1,5,9 – us UMI [616]
RESPIRATION PHYSIOLOGY – v1-58. 1966-84 – 1,5,6,13 – sz Elsevier [073]
RESPOND – 1967-69 (complete) – 1r – 1 – ATLA S0593 – us A.T.L.A. [073]
RESPONDESE AL...DOCTOR CUSPRILLI / Navarrete y Sabogal, P – SL, SA – 1mf – 9 – sp Cultura [610]
LA RESPONSABILITE DES ARMATEURS... / Franck, L – Bruxelles, 1911 – 1mf – 1 – ILM-3445/1 – ne IDC [327]
LA RESPONSABILITE ET LA SOLIDARITE DANS LA LUTTE OUVRIERE / Nettlau, Max – Paris. 1911. (La Condition Ouvriere. Part Two.) – 9 – 2.50 – fr Bibl Nationale [360]
LA RESPONSE A L'APOLOGIE DE JACQUES PELETIER / Meigret, Louis – 1550 – 9 – fr I.C.S. [440]
RESPONSE A L'APOLOGIE DE L'EXAMEN DU SIEUR YVELIN, SUR LA POSSESSION DES RELIGIEUSES DE SAINT LOUYS DE LOUVIERS – Rouen. 1644 – 9 – fr Hachette [360]
RESPONSE A L'EXAMEN DE LA POSSESSION DES RELIGIEUSES DE LOUVIERS A MONSIEUR LEVILIN – Evreux. 1643 – 9 – fr Hachette [360]
RESPONSE AU LIVRE INTITULE LE MYSTERE D'INIQUITE / Coeffeteau, N – Paris, 1614 – 24mf – 9 – CA-120/1 – ne IDC [240]
RESPONSE DE LOUIS MEIGRET / Meigret, Louis – 1551 – 9 – fr I.C.S. [440]
RESPONSE OF WHEAT TO FERTILIZERS – 1971 2nd print 1977 – 134p – it F.A.O. [631]
DIE RESPONSEN DER SPANISCHER LEHRER DES 10. JAHRHUNDERTS / Mueller, J – (Bericht der Lehranstalt fuer die Wiss. des Judentums, nr.7). Berlin. 1889. BJ-421-21 1 – 9 – ne IDC [270]
RESPONSES TO GRADED EXERCISE TESTING IN NORMAL CHILDREN AND ADOLESCENTS WITH HIGH AND LOW LEFT VENTRICULAR MASS / Golden, Jane E et al – 1990 – 4mf – 9 – $16.00 – us Microform Publ [613]
RESPUBLIKA – (Backfile through 1998 $85r) – Belarus, 1999- – 3r per y standing order – 1 – us Ross [072]
RESPUBLIKA – (Backfile through 1998 $85r) – Lithuania, 1999- – 6r per y – 1 – $480.00 standing order – us Ross [072]
RESPUBLIKA BEZPRIZORNYKH (SHKID) / Bielykh, Grigorii & Panteleev, L – Riga: "Gramatu draugs", 1930 – 1 – CSUX89-B3218 – us Hoover Inst Photo [947]
RESPUESTA A LA APROBACION DEL LIBRO DE...LUIS ALDRETE EN QUE SE TRATA DEL AGUA DE LA VIDA / Verdugo, J – Zaragoza, 1695 – 2mf – 9 – sp Cultura [615]
RESPUESTA A LOS PARECERES...ACERCA DEL MAL...EN SEVILLA / Jimenez Guillen, F – Sevilla, 1599 – 1mf – 9 – sp Cultura [610]
RESPUESTA A UNA PREGUNTA INTERESANTE / Bayle, Constantino – Madrid: Razon y Fe, 1924 – 1 – sp Bibl Santa Ana [946]
RESPUESTA AL PARECER QUE DIO CIERTO MEDICO / Valverde Horosco, D – SL, SA – 9 – sp Cultura [610]
RESPUESTA A...MONASTERIOS DE GUADALUPE...ESCORIAL / Oropesa, Manuel, y otros – 1726? – 9 – 1.50f – sp Bibl Santa Ana [240]
RESPUESTA CRITICA DE...AL OPUSCULO DE...CURAR LOS MORBOS / Ocana, H – SL, SA – 1mf – 9 – sp Cultura [610]
RESPUESTA DE ANDRES DAVILA...A LA APOLOGIA EN DEFENSA DE LA MEDICINA SUBSTANCIAL / Amigo y Bertran, L – Zaragoza, 1682 – 1mf – 9 – sp Cultura [610]
RESPUESTA DEL DR. LUIS NICOLAU Y VERGARA...A LA MANIFESTACION DEL DR. ANDRES PIQUER / Nicolau y Vergara, Luis – SL, SA – 9 – sp Cultura [610]
RESPUESTA PARA DESENGANO DEL PUBLICO A LA IMPUGNACION QUE HA DIVULGADO PREMATURAMENTE EL PRESBITERO... : CONTRA EL PRODOMO DE LA FLORA DEL PERU,... / Ruiz Lopez, Hipolito – Madrid, 1796 – 2mf – 9 – ne IDC [580]
LA RESPUESTA PERONISTA / Andino, Armando Walter & Flores, Hector Alberto – Buenos Aires: Grupo Sudamericano de Negocios, 1982 – 1 – CSUXADH2302-B – us Hoover Inst Photo [972]
RESPUESTA QUE DA EL M.R.P...FR. J. TORRUBIA...SOBRE LA LEGITIMIDAD DEL LIBRO DE ORACION.. / Cassar, Francisco del – 1759 – 9 – $1.50f – sp Bibl Santa Ana [440]
RESPUESTA...AL PAPEL DEL DOCTOR LORENCO DE SAN MILLAN / Nunez de Esquivel, G – SL, SA – 9 – sp Cultura [610]
RESPUESTAS CLARA...HACERSE CONTRA LA RELIGION – 1877 – 9 – 1.50f – sp Bibl Santa Ana [240]
RESPUESTAS CLARAS...CONTRA LA RELIGION / Tejado, Gabino – 1877 – 9 – 1.50f – sp Bibl Santa Ana [240]
RESPUESTAS PARTICULARES ALCAZAR DE SAN JUAN (SIECLE 18) – Ciudad Real – 1r – 5,6 – sp Cultura [946]
RESPUESTAS PARTICULARES COLECCION COMPLETA (SIECLE 18) – Ciudad Real – 1r – 5,6 – sp Cultura [946]
RESPUESTAS...D. FELIPE ROSADO DE BELALCAZAR / Garcia de Atocha, Jose – 1839 – 9 – $1.50f – sp Bibl Santa Ana [920]
Ress, Robert *see* ARNO HOLZ UND DIE DEUTSCHE PRESSE
Ressarion, Cardinal *see* LETTERE, ET ORAZIONI...SCRITTE A PRINCIPI D'ITALIA INTORNO AL COLLE GARSI, ET IMPRENDER GUERRA CONTRO AL TURCO
EL RESTABLECIMIENTO DEL CULTO EN LA ESPANA ROJA / Bayle, Constantino – Burgos: Razon y Fe, 1938 – 1 – sp Bibl Santa Ana [240]
A RESTATEMENT OF BAPTIST PRINCIPLES / Jones, Philip Lovering – (Includes bibliographical references) – 3rd ed. Philadelphia: American Baptist Publ Society, c1909 – 1mf – 9 – 0-8370-8912-3 – 1986-2912 – us A.T.L.A. [240]
RESTAURACION DE LA PATRONA DE LOS SANTOS DE MAIMONA. NUESTRA SENORA DE LA ESTRELLA / Fernandez Moreno, Ramon – Badajoz: Dip. Provincial, 1971 – 1 – sp Bibl Santa Ana [240]
O RESTAURADOR : ORGAO DA CLASSE CAIXEIRAL – Manaos, Amazonas. 22 Jun 1890 – 1,5,6 – bl Biblioteca [072]
EL RESTAURADOR JUSTICIALISTA – (c.1: v.1:no.2 1959: Sept. 11) – 1 – CSUXAJA8254-S – us Hoover Inst Photo [360]
RESTAURANT AND HOTEL DESIGN – v5-. 1983- – 1,5,6,9 – us UMI [073]

RESTAURANT BUSINESS *see* FAST FOOD
RESTAURANT DESIGN – v1-4 1979-82 – 1,5,6,9 – us UMI [640]
RESTAURANT EQUIPMENT DEALER – v1-20 1948-67 – 1 – us UMI [640]
RESTAURANT HOSPITALITY – (See also: American Restaurant Hospitality; American Restaurant Magazine; Hospitality: Restaurant) – v61- 1977- – 1,5,6,9 – us UMI [640]
RESTAURANTE BAR EL BURLADERO – Plasencia: Imp. La Victoria, 1960 – sp Bibl Santa Ana [946]
LA RESTAURATION CATHOLIQUE, 1563-1648 (18) – Paris, 1960 – Dfl46.00 – ne Slangenburg [240]
LA RESTAURATION IMPERIALE AU JAPON / Layrle, J – Paris: Armand Colin. 1892 – 9 – 12.50 – fr Orientalistes [950]
Restaut, P *see* PRINCIPES GENERAUX ET RAISONNES DE LA GRAMMAIRE FRANCOISE
RESTENOSIS RATE AFTER PERCUTANEOUS TRANSLUMINAL CORONARY ANGIOPLASTY IN CARDIAC REHABILITATION PROGRAM PARTICIPANTS / Couch, Lorinda C – 1994 – 1mf – $4.00 – us Microform Publ [615]
RESTES DU CULTE DE MITHRA EN ESPAGNE. LE MITHREUM DE MERIDA / Paris, Pierre – Revue Archeologique. Paris, Lercux, 1914 – 1 – sp Bibl Santa Ana [946]
Restier-Melleray, C *see* ATLAS ELECTORAL DE LA GIRONDE
RESTITUTION : RECHTER UND GESUNDER CHRISTLICHER LEHRE: EINE WIEDERTAEUFERSCHRIFT / Rotmann, Bernhard – Halle a.S.: M. Niemeyer, 1888 – 1mf – us A.T.L.A. [240]
RESTO DI CARLINO – 1985-1995 – 4r per y – 5,6 – Sfr989.00 – sz Infoprint [072]
RESTORATION – v. 1-. 1947- – 1 – us UMI [240]
THE RESTORATION OF APOSTLES AND PROPHETS IN THE CATHOLIC APOSTOLIC CHURCH / Norton, Robert – London: Bosworth & Harrison, 1861 – 1mf – us A.T.L.A. [240]
RESTORATION QUARTERLY – (1986- . 5,6,9) – v1- . 1957- – 1 – us UMI [073]
RESTORATIONISM: TWO SERMONS PREACHED IN ST STEPHEN'S CHURCH, TORONTO, ON THE LAST SUNDAY AFTER TRINITY, 1875 / Carry, John – Toronto: Hart & Rawlinson, 1875. 02551. (Pre-1900 Canadiana) – 9 – cn C.I.H.M. [240]
THE RESTORED INNOCENCE / Campbell, Reginald John – New York: Dodd, Mead, 1898. 1 fiche – 9 – us A.T.L.A. [240]
LOS RESTOS DE HERNANDO CORTES (DE LUIS...OBREGON) / Altolaguirre, Angel de – Madrid: Tip. Fortanet, 1906. B.R.A.H. XLVIII, pp. 410-412 – sp Bibl Santa Ana [920]
Restrepo Saenz, Jose Ma. *see* GOBERNADORES DE ANTIOQUIA 1571-1819. BOGOTA, 1932
RESTRICTED/COMMERCIAL OPERATOR HISTORY FILE / U.S. National Technical Information Service – Annual. In operator name sequence. Cross-reference of commercial operators by serial number is included. Contains licenses issued seven or more years ago – 9 – us N.T.I.S. [000]
RESULT OF SOME RESEARCHES AMONG THE BRITISH ARCHIVES...RELATIVE TO THE FOUNDERS OF NEW ENGLAND: MADE IN THE YEARS 1858, 1859, & 1860 – Corr. and enl. by Samuel G. Drake, 1969.Orig. publ. 1860 in The New England Historical & Genealogical Register. Indexed, 2 fiches. F-0865 – 9 – us A.G.L.L. [978]
RESULTADO DE LA VISTA DEL ARTICULO...EN LA CAUSA QUE SIGUE A DON MAURICIO CERESOLES / Ceresoles, Mauricio – 1842 – 9 – $1.50f – sp Bibl Santa Ana [946]
RESULTADO...LIBERTAD...MAURICIO CERESOLES / Rodriguez Leal, Joaquin – 1842 – 9 – 1.50f – sp Bibl Santa Ana [946]
RESULTATEN VAN ONDERZOEK EN ERVARING OP GODSDIENSTIG GEBIED / Muurling, Willem – (Includes bibliographical references) – 2., herziene en vermeerderde uit. Groningen: J B Wolters, 1870 – 1mf – 9 – 0-8370-3904-5 – 1985-1904 – us A.T.L.A. [240]
RESULTATS DE L'ENQUETE A OBJECTIFS MULTIPLES, 1961-1963 / Morocco. Service Central des Statistiques – 1964. BNE-3095 1 – 9 – ne IDC [310]
RESULTATS DE L'ENQUETE ANNUELLE SUR L'INDUSTRIE PETROLIERE. ETUDE MENSUELLE SUR L'ECONOMIE ET LES FINANCES DES PAYS ARABES / Libya. Centre d'Etudes et de Documentation Economiques, Financieres et Sociales. Beirut – Statistics. Dec, 12e annee (18-144). 1969. BNE-624 1 – 9 – ne IDC [338]
LES RESULTATS DE L'EXEGESE BIBLIQUE: L'HISTOIRE, LA RELIGION, LA LITTERATURE / Vernes, Maurice – Paris: Ernest Leroux, 1890. 1 fiche – 9 – us A.T.L.A. [240]
RESULTATS DES GUERRES, ... LA COALITION CONTRE LA FRANCE... / Arnould, A M – Paris, 1803 – 5mf – 9 – ILM-2548/1 – ne IDC [340]
RESULTATS DU RECENSEMENT DE 1960 / Morocco. Service Central des Statistiques – 3v. 1972. BNE-3098 1 – 9 – ne IDC [310]
RESULTATS GENERAUX DE LA RECOLTE EN RUSSIE / Russia. Tsentralnyi Statisticheskii Komitet – 1884-1916. Lacks scattered issues – 1 – $180.00 – us L of C Photodup [310]
RESULTATS PAR CULTURE DE LA CAMPAGNE AGRICOLE 1968-1969 / Morocco. Service Central des Statistiques – 1970. BNE-3099 1 – 9 – ne IDC [310]
RESULTATS STATISTIQUES DE DENOMBREMENT DE 1881 POUR LA VILLE DE PARIS: ET RENSEIGNEMENTS RELATIFS AUX RECENSEMENTS ANTERIEURS / Paris. Service de la Statistique municipale – Paris: Imprimerie Municipale, 1884. 284p. map – 1 – us U.W. Library [310]
RESULTATS STATISTIQUES DU DENOMBREMENT DE 1896 / France. Ministere du Commerce, de l'Industrie, des Postes et des Telegraphes. Statistique generale – Paris: Imp. nationale, 1899. viii,481p – 1 – us U.W. Library [944]
RESULTATS STATISTIQUES DU DENOMBREMENT DE LA POPULATION EFFECTUE LE 13 OCT 1954 / Algeria. Service de la Statistique Generale – 2v. BNE-8667 1 – 9 – ne IDC [310]
RESULTS OF THE ASTRONOMICAL OBSERVATIONS MADE AT THE ROYAL OBSERVATORY, GREENWICH – London: The Observatory, 1847. ill. annual – 1 – us U.W. Library [520]
RESULTS OF THE FULFILLMENT OF THE STATE PLAN OF DEVELOPMENT OF THE NATIONAL ECONOMY FOR THE YEAR 1955 / Czechoslovakia. Statni Urad Statisticky – Prague. 1956. BD-511 1 – 9 – ne IDC [310]
RESULTS OF THE SYNOD OF THE PROTESTANT CHURCH OF THE UNITED BRETHREN, OR UNITAS FRATRUM: HELD AT HERRNHUT IN THE YEAR 1869 / Moravian Church. General Synod, Herrnhut, 1869 – 1870 – 1 – us A.T.L.A. [240]
RESULTS OF WHEAT AND BARLEY TRIALS IN TRIPOLITANIA, 1966-1967 / Libya – BNE-1016 1 – 9 – ne IDC [338]
RESUME DU DISCOURS PRONONCE PAR L'HONORABLE M. FLYNN: LORS DE LA DEUXIEME LECTURE DU PROJET DE LOI CONCERNANT LES MINES / Flynn, Edmund James – s.l.: s.n., 188?. 03119. (Pre-1900 Canadiana) – 9 – cn C.I.H.M. [971]
RESUME DU PLAN DE DEVELOPPEMENT ECONOMIQUE ET SOCIAL DU GABON, 66/70 / Gabon. Presidence – Ed. by Paul Bory. Monaco. 1967. BD-107 1 – 9 – ne IDC [338]
RESUME PHILOSOPHIQUE DE L'HISTOIRE DE LAS MUSIQUE... / Fetis, Francois J – Paris: Fournier, 1835 – 1 – us Sibley [780]
RESUMEN DE GEOGRAFIA / Arenas Lopez, Anselmo – 1883 – 9 – 1.50f – sp Bibl Santa Ana [910]
RESUMEN DE HISTORIA DE ESPANA / Arenas Lopez, Anselmo – 1882 – 9 – 1.50f – sp Bibl Santa Ana [946]
RESUMEN DE LA TEMPORADA TAURINA 1968 EN EXTREMADURA / Garcia Flores, Juan Felipe (Don Felipe) – Badajoz: Tip. Clasica, 1969 – 1 – sp Bibl Santa Ana [790]
RESUMEN DE LA VIDA Y VIRTUDES DEL V.P. CRISTOBAL DE SANTA CATALINA / Posadas, Francisco de – Cordoba: Imp.Colorado, 1945 – 1 – sp Bibl Santa Ana [920]
RESUMEN DE UNA DISCUSION ACERCA DE LOS HIJOS ILEGITIMOS ANTE LA SOCIEDAD Y EL DERECHO / Crehuet, Diego Maria & Corteza Collantes, Alfonso – Madrid: Est. Tip. de Jaime Rates, 1917 – sp Bibl Santa Ana [946]
RESUMEN DEL DOCUMENTO "LINEAMENTOS BASICOS DE POLITICA DE DESARROLLO A MEDIANO PLAZO" / Peru. Instituto Nacional de Planificacion – Lima. 1970. BD-1846 1 – 9 – ne IDC [330]
RESUMEN DEL ESTADO...BADAJOZ / Epalda Guerrero, Juan – 1875 – 9 – 1.50f – sp Bibl Santa Ana [946]
RESUMEN DEL ESTADO...INSTITUTO DE BADAJOZ / Soler Arques, Carlos – (1874 ed.1.50f; 9. 1876 ed.1.50f; BSA; 9. 1877 ed.1.50f; BSA; 9. 1878 ed.1.50f; BSA; 9) – 1872 – 9 – 1.50f – sp Bibl Santa Ana [946]
RESUMEN DEL HISTORICO ESTUDIO DE LA ESCULTURA ESPANOLA. LA ESCULTURA ESPANOLA EN LA ANTIGUEDAD / Tormo, Elias – Madrid: Rev. de Arch. Bibl. y Mus, 1926. B.R.A.H. 88, pp. 397-423, 8 lam – sp Bibl Santa Ana [306]
RESUMEN DEL PLAN ANUAL 1971 / Chile. Oficina de Planificacion Nacional – D-1016 1 – 9 – ne IDC [338]
RESUMEN DEL PLAN ANUAL 1972 / Chile. Oficina de Planificacion Nacional – D-1552 1 – 9 – ne IDC [338]
RESUMEN DEL PLAN DE DESARROLLO ECONOMICO DE CUBA PARA 1962' / Cuba. Junta central de Planificacion – (Summary of the Economic Development Plan of Cuba for 1962). In: El Trimestre Economico. v. 29 (1), no. 113. Mexico, D.F. enero-marzo de 1962. BD-1639 1 – 9 – ne IDC [338]
RESUMEN DEL PLAN DE LA ECONOMICA NACIONAL 1971-1976 / Chile. Oficina de Planificacion Nacional – (Summary of the National Economic Plan 1971-1976). Santiago. Oct 1971. BD-1631 1 – 9 – ne IDC [338]
RESUMEN DEL PLAN GENERAL DE DESARROLLO ECONOMICO Y SOCIAL DEL ECUADOR 1964-1973; VERSION PRELIMINAR / Ecuador. Junta Nacional de Planificacion y Coordinacion Economica – (Outline of the General Plan for Economic and Social Development of Ecuador 1964-1973; preliminary version). Quito. 1963. BD-1644 1 – 9 – ne IDC [338]
RESUMEN GENERAL DEL TERCER CENSO DE LA REPUBLICA DE VENEZUELA. ANO 1890 – Caracas, 1891 – 22mf – 9 – sp Cultura [304]
RESUMEN HISTORICO-CRITICO DE LITERATURA COLOMBIANA / Ruano, Jesus Maria – Bogota: Casa editorial Santafe, 1925. xvi,210p.illus – 1 – us U.W. Library [440]
RESUMEN SACADO DEL INVENTARIO GENERAL...DE LOS ARNESES DE LA REAL ACADEMIA / Abadia, Ignacio – 1793 – 9 – 1.50f – sp Bibl Santa Ana [946]
RESUMEN...HISTORIA UNIVERSAL / Villanueva y Canedo, Luis – 1847 – 9 – 1.50f – sp Bibl Santa Ana [900]
RESUMEN...INSTITUTO PROVINCIAL DE SEGUNDA ENSENANZA DE BADAJOZ...1874 A 1875...POR EL SECRETARIO ACCIDENTAL DON... / Epalza Guerrero, Juan – Badajoz: Imp. Vda. de Arteaga, 1875 – 1 – sp Bibl Santa Ana [946]
RESUMO DAS REGRAS GERAES MAIS IMPORTANTES / Carlos de Jesus Maria – 1741 – 9 – us Sibley [780]
RESURRECTION – no. 1-6. Namur. 1917-18 – 1 – fr A.C.R.P.P. [073]
RESURRECTION AND THE LIFE, OR, LAZARUS REVISITED / Culross, James – London: James Nisbet, 1862. 1 fiche – 9 – us A.T.L.A. [240]
THE RESURRECTION AND THE LIFE, OR, LAZARUS REVIVED : THE GOSPEL OF JOHN, CHAPTER 11 / Culross, James – 3rd ed. London:James Nisbet, 1862 – 1mf – 9 – 0-8370-2785-3 – 1985-0785 – us A.T.L.A. [220]
LA RESURRECTION DE JESU-CHRISTO, NUESTRO SENOR / Geddes, Thomas Edward – Valparaiso: G Helfmann, 1896 – 1mf – 9 – 0-8370-3238-5 – 1985-1238 – us A.T.L.A. [240]
RESURRECTION OF CHRIST: A SERIES OF DISCOURSES / Nott, Eliphalet – New York: Scribner, Armstrong, 1872. 1 fiche – 9 – us A.T.L.A. [240]
THE RESURRECTION OF CHRIST, IS IT A FACT? / Marsh, Gideon William Barker – Edinburgh: Sands, 1905. 1 fiche – 9 – us A.T.L.A. [240]
THE RESURRECTION OF JESUS / Orr, James – Cincinnati: Jennings & Graham, 1909?. 1 fiche – 9 – us A.T.L.A. [240]
THE RESURRECTION OF JESUS / Riggenbach, Eduard – New York: Eaton & Mains; Cincinnati: Jennings & Graham, c1907 – 1mf – 9 – 0-8370-4905-9 – 1985-2905 – us A.T.L.A. [240]
THE RESURRECTION OF JESUS CHRIST HISTORICALLY AND LOGICALLY VIEWED / Dickinson, Richard William – Philadelphia: Presbyterian Bd of Publ, c1865 – 1mf – 9 – 0-8370-2905-8 – 1985-0905 – us A.T.L.A. [240]
THE RESURRECTION OF THE DEAD / Kingsley, Calvin – 1848 – 9 – us A.T.L.A. [240]
THE RESURRECTION OF THE DEAD / Mattison, Hiram – 1886 – 9 – us A.T.L.A. [240]
RESUSCITATIO / Bacon, Francis – Ed. 3. M-294 2. 1671 – 8 – ne IDC [500]
RESUSCITATION – v1-12. 1972-84 – 1,5,6,13 – sz Elsevier [073]
EL RETABLO DE SAN VICENTE DE PLASENCIA, SUS AUTORES Y NOTICIAS DE OTROS PINTORES EXTREMENOS DEL SIGLO 16 / Pescador del Hoyo, Maria del Carmen – Badajoz: Imp. Diputacion Provincial, 1962 – sp Bibl Santa Ana [700]
EL RETABLO DE SANTIAGO DE LOS CABALLEROS DE CACERES Y EL ESCULTOR ALONSO BERRUGUETE / Floriano Cumbreno, Antonio C – Caceres, 1918 – sp Bibl Santa Ana [946]
RETAIL BANKING DIGEST *see* ABA'S CONSUMER BANKING DIGEST
RETAIL CLERKS ADVOCATE – 1896- 1; 1974- 5,6; 1975- 4 x 6 in. 9 – us UMI [650]
RETAIL DELIVERY STRATEGIES *see* PAYMENT SYSTEMS STRATEGIES
RETAIL DIRECTIONS – (Ceased v6 no 2 1993) – Toronto. v1-6. 1988-93 – 9 – Can$20.00y – cn Micromedia [380]
Retail, Leon *see* ROLE ECONOMIQUE DE L'APPRENTISSAGE
A RETAIL LIST OF NEW BEAUTIFUL AND RARE PLANTS,... CATALOGUES 1866-1890 / Bull, W (London) – Number ed issues. Unnumbered: 1891-1894 – 99mf – Dfl603.00 – ne IDC [580]
RETAIL PRICES OF AGRICULTURAL COMMODITIES IN LIBYA IN 1965 / Libya. Ministry of Agriculture and Animal Wealth. Agricultural Planning and Economics Department. Statistics Division – Bulletin nr.2-3. BNE-606 1 – 9 – ne IDC [338]
RETALIATION AND COMMERCIAL FEDERATION: LORD SALISBURY AND SIR CHARLES TUPPER: WITH NOTES ON THE RECENT TARIFF DOCTRINES OF PROTECTIONISTS, FAIR TRADERS, AND COMMERCIAL FEDERATIONISTS / Farrer, Thomas Henry – Written for the Cobden Club by Sir Thomas H. Farrer. London: Printed and published for the Cobden Club by Cassell, 1892?. 02951. (Pre-1900 Canadiana) – 9 – cn C.I.H.M. [971]
Retana, WE *see*
- INDICE DE PERSONAS NOBLES Y OTRAS DE CALIDAD...
- INDICE DE PERSONAS NOBLES Y OTRAS DE CALIDAD QUE HAN ESTADO EN FILIPINAS (1521-1898)

Retcliffe, John *see* UM DIE WELTHERRSCHAFT
RETFORD AND BASSET LAW GAZETTE – England, 4 Sep 1858-11 Jun 1859 – 27ft – 1 – uk British Libr Newspaper [072]
RETFORD, GAINSBOROUGH AND WORKSHOP TIMES – England, 1877; 1880; 1889; Jan-Nov 1896; 1908; Mar-Dec 1910; 1955; 1960- – 86+ r – 1 – uk British Libr Newspaper [072]
RETFORD, WORKSOP ISLE OF AXHOLME AND GAINSBOROUGH NEWS – (Gainsborough News, 1968-) – East Retford, Gainsborough, England. 1954-Apr 1968; May 1968-1983 – 1 – uk British Libr Newspaper [072]
Reticius, FE C *see* ABREGE DE L'EXPOSITION DE LA DOCTRINE CHRETIENNE
Retiere, C *see* CONTRIBUTION A LA CONNAISSANCE DES PEUPLEMENTS BENTHIQUES DU GOLFE NORMANNO-BRETON
Retif de la Bretonne, Nicolas *see*
- LETTRES INEDITES
- LETTRES INEDITES DE RESTIF DE LABRETONE POUR FAIRE SUITE A LA COLLECTION DE SES OEUVRES

Retif de la Bretonne, Nicolas Edme *see* LE THESMOGRAPHE, OU IDEES D'UN HONNETE HOMME SUR UN PROJET DE REGLEMENT, PROPOSE A TOUTES LES NATIONS DE L'EUROPE POUR OPERER UNE REFORME GENERALES DES LOIS; AVEC DES NOTES HISTORIQUES

RETINA – v.1-. 1981- – 1,5,6,9 – us UMI [073]

RETIRO ESPIRITUAL PARA COMUNIDADES RELIGIOSAS... / Bourdalque, Luis; ed by Bayle, Constantino – Madrid: Razon y Fe, 1928 – 9 – sp Bibl Santa Ana [240]

Retor, Georges *see* L'AGNI. VARIETE IALECTALE SANVI

RETORICA. TOMO 1 / Mayans y Siscar, Gregorio – 1786, 2nd ed – 2mf – 9 – Pta1,500.00 – 84-7848-288-1 – sp Pentalfa [440]

RETORICA. TOMO 2 / Mayans y Siscar, Gregorio – 1786, 2nd ed – 2mf – 9 – Pta1,500.00 – 84-7848-289-X – sp Pentalfa [440]

EL RETORNO / Cooke, John William – [Buenos Aires]: Publicaciones de Revolucion Peronista, [1964?] – 1 – CSUXADL7555-B – us Hoover Inst Photo [320]

EL RETORNO AL COLONIAJE : DE PREBISH A KRIEGER VASENA / Jauretche, Arturo – Buenos Aires: Ediciones del Mar Dulce, 1969 – 9 – us Hoover Inst Photo [972]

EL RETORNO DE PERON : ALIENACI ON Y CONTRA-REVOLUCION DE LAS "IZQUIERDAS" / Condor, Tacuara (MNRT) – [Buenos Aires]: Editorial Lanza Seca, 1964 – 1 – CSUXADH9071-B – us Hoover Inst Photo [320]

RETORT – 1-5 2+1 (all publ). 1942-1951 – 10mf – 9 – $65.00 – us UPA [335]

RETORT – Bearsville, N.Y. v. 1-5, no. 1. Winter 1942-Autumn 1951 – 1 – us NY Public [073]

THE RETORT – Billings. Mont. 1949-1967 – 1 – us UMI [071]

RETOUR AU CHRISTIANISME DE LA PART D'UN SAINT-SIMONIEN / Dory, Alphonse – Marseille, Marius Olive, 1834, 383 p. Les Saint-Simoniens, 1825-1834. 6973 – 9 – fr Hachette [335]

LE RETOUR DE L'EMIGRE / Amaron, Calvin E – St-Gabriel de Brandon: [s.n.], 1910. SEM105P1478 – 1mf – 9 – Can$2.25 – cn Bibl Nat [240]

LE RETOUR DE L'EXILE: DRAME EN CINQ ACTES ET HUIT TABLEAUX / Frechette, Louis-Honore – Montreal?: s.n., 1880 (Montreal: Chapleau & Lavigne). 03241. (Pre-1900 Canadiana) – 9 – cn C.I.H.M. [820]

LE RETOUR DU ZOUAVE: ROMANCE / Labelle, Jean Baptiste – Montreal, c1886. SEM105P907 – 1mf – 9 – Can$2.25 – cn Bibl Nat [830]

THE "RETRACTATION" OF ROBERT BROWNE : FATHER OF CONGREGATIONALISM / Browne, Robert – Oxford: Horace Hart; London: Henry Frowde, 1907 – 1mf – us A.T.L.A. [240]

RETRACTATIONES / Augustinus, St – 1984 – 3mf – 9 – Bf750.00 – 2-503-60572-9 – be Brepols [240]

RETRATO DE... / Valdivia, Pedro de – Madrid: Ed. Reus, 1921. B.R.A.H. 79. pp. 70-73 – 1 – sp Bibl Santa Ana [946]

RETRATO DE DON PEDRO DE VALDIVIA. INFORME / Cardecera, Valentin – Madrid: Ed Reus, 1921. B.R.A.H. 79, pp 70-73 – sp Bibl Santa Ana [750]

RETRATO...ALCANTARA / Santibanez, Leandro – 1779 – 9 – 1.50f – sp Bibl Santa Ana [440]

RETRIBUTION: A LITERARY CONTRIBUTION TO THE NOVA SCOTIA DEPARTMENT OF THE PHILADELPHIA EXHIBITION / Albyn – Halifax: W. MacNab, 1875. 06133. (Pre-1900 Canadiana) – 9 – cn C.I.H.M. [830]

RETRIBUTION AND OTHER ADDRESSES / Smith, Samuel George – Cincinnati: Curts & Jennings; New York: Eaton & Mains, c1900 – 1mf – 9 – 0-8370-5178-9 – 1985-3178 – us A.T.L.A. [210]

RETROSPECT OF PHILOSOPHICAL, MECHANICAL, CHEMICAL, AND AGRICULTURAL DISCOVERIES – London. v1-8 1806-15 – 3 – us Readex [500]

RETROSPECTIONS OF AMERICA, 1797-1911 / Bernard, John – Ed. from the manuscript by Mrs. Bayle Bernard. Introd. and notes and index by Lawrence Hutton and Brander Matthews. New York: Harper, 1877. 03575. (Pre-1900 Canadiana) – 9 – cn C.I.H.M. [970]

RETROSPECTIVE HENRI MATISSE / Reunion des musees nationaux. Paris – 1956. 31 illus. 1 fiche – 9 – fr Réunion [700]

RETROSPECTIVE SONIA DELAUNAY / Reunion des musees nationaux. Paris – 1967. 25 illus. 1 fiche – 9 – fr Réunion [700]

RETROSPECTS AND PROSPECTS OF INDIAN POLICY / Bell, Evans – London: Truebner, 1868. 344p – 1 – us U.W. Library [950]

RETTING OF JUTE – 2nd ed 1987 – 64p – it F.A.O. [631]

RETTUNG DES SPRUCHS ROM. 8. DENN WELCHE ER ZUUOR VERSEHEN HAT DIE HAT ER AUCH VERORDNET DAS SIE GLEICH SEIN SOLTEN DEM EBENBILD SEINES SONS,... / Huber, S – Vrsel, 1598 – 3mf – ne IDC [240]

RETTUNG MEINER ALLEZEIT BESTENDIGEN BEKANTNUS VON DER GNADENWAHL DARINNEN AUFF DISMAL HINDAN GESETZT ALLER NEBENSTREITTEN ALLES VND ALLEIN WAS ZUM HAUPTSTREIT GEHOERIG...ERKLERET WIRD... / Huber, S – N.p., 1597 – 7mf – ne IDC [240]

DI RETUNGS AKGYE = EPHEMERIS – (In Yiddish) – Brzesc, PL. 17 Feb 1926 (One-time publication) – 1r – 1 – $25.00 – cn Can Microfilming [072]

THE RETURN FROM THE DEAD IN POPULAR TALES AND BALLADS / Thompson, Stith – 1909 – 1 – us I.U. Libraries [390]

RETURN OF APPOINTMENTS MADE BY THE EARL OF DURHAM SINCE HIS ARRIVAL IN CANADA / Durham, Earl of – [S.l.]: [s.n.], [1838] – 1mf – 9 – Can$2.25 – cn Bibl Nat [320]

RETURN OF ENDOWED GRAMMAR SCHOOLS / Great Britain – 1865 – 9 – uk Microform Academic [941]

THE RETURN OF SHERLOCK HOLMES / Doyle, Arthur Conan – London: G. Newnes, 1905 – 1 roll – 1 – 1-55879-374-7 – uk Libr Preservation [830]

RETURN OF SUMS PAID BY GOVERNMENT, AND CORRESPONDENCE BETWEEN ENGINEERS AND OTHER OFFICERS. RELATIVE TO CERTAIN RAIL-ROADS / Canada. Ministere des Travaux Publics – Quebec: Printed by John Lovell, 1853. SEM105P307 – 1mf – 9 – Can$2.25 – cn Bibl Nat [336]

A RETURN OF THE EXTRA EXPENSE INCURRED IN THE HASTINGS 74, FOR THE PURPOSE OF FITTING HER UP, FOR CARRYING THE EARL OF DURHAM AND HIS SUITE TO CANADA – [London, England: s.n., 1838]. SEM105P1388 – 1mf – 9 – Can$2.25 – cn Bibl Nat [971]

RETURN OF THE NAMES AND QUALITY OR STATION OF THE SEVERAL PERSONS ARRESTED AND PLACED IN CONFINEMENT IN THE PRISONS OF TORONTO / Canada. Parliament. House of Commons – s.l: House of Commons, 1839. SEM105P388 – 1mf – 9 – Can$2.25 – cn Bibl Nat [324]

RETURN STATEMENT OF THE EXPENSE INCURRED BY THE COMMISSION OF ENQUIRY ON THE PUBLIC BUILDINGS AT OTTAWA,...ALLOWANCE PER DIEM TO THE COMMISSIONERS. – Quebec: Hunter, Rose & Lemieux, 1863. SEM105P579 – 1mf – 9 – Can$2.25 – cn Bibl Nat [971]

RETURN TO ADDRESS, RESPECTING ARTHABASKA RAILWAY ROAD, AND SUBSIDIARY LINES TO THE GRAND TRUNK – Quebec: Hunter, Rose & Lemieux, 1863. SEM105P603 – 1mf – 9 – Can$2.25 – cn Bibl Nat [971]

RETURN TO AN ADDRESS DATED 22ND APRIL, 1863, FOR A COPY OF THE REPORT OF THE SUPERINTENDENT OF EDUCATION FOR LOWER CANADA, IN RELATION TO INSPECTORS OF SCHOOLS – Quebec: Hunter, Rose et Lemieux, 1863. SEM105P561 – 1mf – 9 – Can$2.25 – cn Bibl Nat [370]

RETURN TO AN ADDRESS FOR COPIES OF PAPERS CONNECTED WITH THE GRAND TRUNK MAIL SERVICE SINCE 1863 / Canada. Ministere des Postes – Quebec: Imp. Hunter, Rose & Lemieux, 1864. SEM105P320 – 2mf – 9 – Can$4.50 – cn Bibl Nat [380]

RETURN TO AN ADDRESS FROM THE LEGISLATIVE ASSEMBLY TO HIS EXCELLENCY THE GOVERNOR GENERAL DATED THE 2ND INSTANT, PRAYING... TO THE TRIAL AND CONVICTION OF THE AYLWARDS, EXECUTED AT BELLEVILLE ON THE 8TH DECEMBER 1862 / Canada – Quebec: Hunter, Rose et Lemieux, 1863. SEM105P578 – 1mf – 9 – Can$2.25 – cn Bibl Nat [971]

RETURN TO AN ADDRESS FROM...FOR COPIES OF ALL TRANSACTIONS, SALES OR CONTRACTS...CONNECTED WITH THE ALIENATION OF THE ST-MAURICE FORGES. / Canada. Parliament. Legislative Assembly – Quebec: Printed by Rollo Campbell, 1852. SEM105P127 – 1mf – 9 – Can$2.25 – cn Bibl Nat [336]

RETURN TO AN ADDRESS OF THE LEGISLATIVE ASSEMBLY, DATED 9TH JUNE 1853... – Quebec: printed by Rollo Campbell, [1853]. SEM105P1726 – 1mf – 9 – Can$2.25 – cn Bibl Nat [323]

RETURN TO AN ADDRESS OF THE LEGISLATIVE ASSEMBLY DATED 14TH SEPT 1863, FOR INFORMATION RESPECTING MUNICIPAL LOAN FUND – Quebec: Hunter, Rose & Lemieux, 1863. SEM105P628 – 1mf – 9 – Can$2.25 – cn Bibl Nat [336]

RETURN TO AN ADDRESS OF THE LEGISLATIVE ASSEMBLY DATED 16TH MARCH 1863, CONTAINING ...INFORMATION...RESPECTING THE DISTRIBUTION OF COLONIZATION MONEYS, ETC – Quebec: Hunter, Rose and Lemieux, 1863. SEM105P577 – 1mf – 9 – Can$2.25 – cn Bibl Nat [336]

RETURN TO AN ADDRESS OF THE LEGISLATIVE ASSEMBLY FOR COPIES OF CERTAIN SEIGNIORIAL DOCUMENTS / Canada. Parliament. Legislative Assembly – Quebec: Printed by John Lovell, 1853. SEM105P261 – 2mf – 9 – Can$4.50 – cn Bibl Nat [323]

RETURN TO AN ADDRESS OF THE LEGISLATIVE ASSEMBLY, OF 1ST SEPTEMBER, 1863 / Canada. Departement de la Milice – Quebec: Josiah Blackburn, 1863. SEM105P316 – 1mf – 9 – Can$2.25 – cn Bibl Nat [355]

RETURN TO AN ADDRESS OF THE LEGISLATIVE ASSEMBLY,...OF THE INCOME OF THE SEVERAL SEIGNIORIES HELD OR POSSESSED BY THE CROWN IN LOWER CANADA, WITH THE NAMES OF THE AGENTS OF EACH SEIGNIORY,... – Quebec: John Lovell, [1852]. SEM105P1729 – 1mf – 9 – Can$2.25 – cn Bibl Nat [333]

RETURN TO AN ADDRESS TO THE GOVERNOR-GENERAL FOR A STATEMENT OF ALL THE PECUNIARY AND TEMPORAL AFFAIRS OF THE CORPORATION OF THE ECCLESIASTICS OF THE SEMINARY OF ST SULPICE.. / Seminaire Saint Sulpice de Montreal. Archives – Quebec: Printed by John Lovell, 1853. SEM105P279 – 1mf – 9 – Can$2.25 – cn Bibl Nat [240]

THE RETURN TO DEMOCRACY IN SUDAN – 1986 – sz I.C.J. [320]

RETURN TO TWO ADDRESSES OF THE HONORABLE THE LEGISLATIVE ASSEMBLY TO HIS EXCELLENCY THE GOVERNOR GENERAL DATED 28TH FEBRUARY, 1856,... / Canada. Gouverneur general – [s.l.]: [s.n.], 1856. SEM105P273 – 1mf – 9 – Can$2.25 – cn Bibl Nat [971]

RETURN TO TWO ADDRESSES...FOR, FIRST "A STATEMENT OF THE DIFFERENT SUMS OF MONEY...TO AID THE CENSITAIRES....SECONDLY, "COPIES OF ALL INSTRUCTIONS – s.l, s.n, 1856. SEM105P259 – 1mf – 9 – Can$2.25 – cn Bibl Nat [336]

RETURN WITH DESPATCHES AND CORRESPONDENCE RELATIVE TO THE SEIGNIORIAL AND FEUDAL TENURE IN LOWER CANADA – Quebec: John Lovell, 1852. SEM105P259 – 1mf – 9 – Can$2.25 – cn Bibl Nat [333]

RETURNS FOR EACH PUBLIC ELEMENTARY SCHOOL / Great Britain – 1894. 1900 – 9 – uk Microform Academic [941]

RETURNS FROM REGULAR ARMY ARTILLERY REGIMENTS, JUNE 1821-JAN 1901 / U.S. War Department. Adjutant General's Office – 38 rolls. M727. Printed guide – 1 – us Nat'l Archives [324]

RETURNS FROM REGULAR ARMY CAVALRY REQUIREMENTS / U.S. Army – 1833-1916. 117 rolls. M744 – 1 – us Nat'l Archives [355]

RETURNS FROM REGULAR ARMY COAST ARTILLERY CORPS COMPANIES, FEB 1901-JUNE 1916 / U.S. War Department. Adjutant General's Office – 81 rolls. M691. Printed guide – 1 – us Nat'l Archives [324]

RETURNS FROM REGULAR ARMY ENGINEER BATTALIONS, SEP 1846-JUNE 1916 / U.S. War Department. Adjutant General's Office – 10 rolls. M690. Printed guide – 1 – us Nat'l Archives [324]

RETURNS FROM REGULAR ARMY FIELD ARTILLERY BATTERIES AND REGIMENTS / U.S. Army – Feb 1901 – Dec 1916. 14 rolls. M728 – 1 – us Nat'l Archives [355]

RETURNS FROM REGULAR ARMY INFANTRY REGIMENTS, JUNE 1821-DECEMBER 1916 / U.S. War Department. Adjutant General's Office – 300 rolls. M665. Printed guide – 1 – us Nat'l Archives [324]

RETURNS FROM U.S. MILITARY POSTS, 1800-1916 / U.S. War Department. Adjutant General's Office – 1550 rolls. M617. Printed guide – 1 – us Nat'l Archives [324]

RETURNS OF MEMBERS OF THE QUEENSLAND DEFENCE FORCE WHO HAVE BEEN KILLED OR DIED IN SOUTH AFRICA, 1899-1902 / Chief Secretary's Office, Queensland – 5r – 1 – CRS B5178 – at Archives [920]

RETURNS OF QUEENSLAND CONTINGENTS WHICH HAVE PROCEEDED TO SOUTH AFRICA, 1899-1902 / Chief Secretary's Office, Queensland – 5r – 1 – CRS B5175 – at Archives [920]

RETURNS OF THE CAPITAL, TRAFFIC, RECEIPTS AND WORKING EXPENDITURE OF THE RAILWAY COMPANIES OF GREAT BRITAIN 1848-1938 – (1914-18 not publ. Coll title: British Government Publications 1801-1977, Transport) – 6r – 1 (£590.00 transport set of 12mf + 9r) – uk Chadwyck [380]

RETURNS OF THE CORPS OF ENGINEERS / U.S. Army. Corps of Engineers – Apr 1832 – Dec 1916. M851 – 22r – 1 – us Nat'l Archives [623]

RETURNS OF THE CORPS OF TOPOGRAPHICAL ENGINEERS / U.S. Army. Corps of Engineers – Nov 1831 – Feb 1863. M852 – 2r – 1 – us Nat'l Archives [623]

RETURNS OF THE RAILROAD CORPORATIONS IN MASSACHUSETTS / Massachusetts. Secretary of the Commonwealth – 1857-69. 53 fiches. (Harvard Law School Library Collection.) – 9 – 1.50f – us H.U. Law [324]

RETURNS OF TRADE AT THE TREATY PORTS / China. Inspectorate General of Customs – v. 9-23. 1867-82 – 1 – 65.00 – us L of C Photodup [380]

RETURNS RELATING TO ELEMENTARY EDUCATION (CIVIL PARISHES) / Great Britain – 1871 – 9 – uk Microform Academic [941]

RETURNS RELATING TO THE LEGISLATIVE COUNCILS OF LOWER CANADA / Great Britain. Colonial Office – [London]: [s.n.], [1834] – 1mf – 9 – Can$2.25 – cn Bibl Nat [320]

RETURNS: SALES OF LAND IN UPPER AND LOWER CANADA. (MR. HUTT.); RECEIPT AND EXPENDITURE OF THE LAND AND TIMBER FUNDS IN UPPER AND LOWER CANADA. (MR. HUME.) – [London, England: s.n., 1835]. SEM105P1367 – 1mf – 9 – Can$2.25 – cn Bibl Nat [333]

Retzius, A J *see*
- FASCICULUS OBSERVATIONUM BOTANICARUM
- FLORAE SCANDINAVIAE PRODROMUS
- OBSERVATIONES BOTANICAE
- OBSERVATIONUM BOTANICARUM PUGILLUS

Reu, Johann M *see* DR. MARTIN LUTHER'S SMALL CATECHISM

Reuchlin, J *see*
- DE ACCENTIBUS ET ORTHOGRAPHIA, LINGUAE HEBRAICAE
- VOCABULARIOS BREVIOLOQUUS CUM ARTE DIPHTHONGANDI, PUNCTUANDI ET ACCENTUANDI

REUIL D'AIR (6) AVEC ACCOMPAGNEMENT DE VIOLIN, VIOLE, FLUTE ET CORNI / Sarti, G – MS, [178-?] – 1 – us Sibley [780]

Reumont, Alfred von *see* THE CARAFAS OF MADDALONI: NAPLES UNDER SPANISH DOMINION

Reuning, Wilhelm *see* ZUR ERKLAERUNG DES POLYKARPMARTYRIUMS

Reunion. Academie de la Reunion. Service Statistique Rectoral *see* ETUDES STATISTIQUES

REUNION AND INTERCOMMUNION : TWO LECTURES ON THE REPORT OF THE LAMBETH CONFERENCE / Henson, Hensley – London: Hugh Rees, 1909 – 1mf – us A.T.L.A. [240]

Reunion. Conseil general *see* PROCES-VERBAUX
Réunion des Musées Nationaux. Paris *see* LE CABINET DE L'AMOUR DE L'HOTEL LAMBERT
Reunion des Musees Nationaux. Paris *see*
- LE BAIN JURCS D'INGRES
- BAUHAUS
- LA COLLECTION DE FRANCOIS 1ER
- HOMMAGE A COROT
- LA MORT DE GERMANICUS DE POUSSIN
- OR DES SCYTHES
- PUVIS DE CHAVANNES
- LE STUDIOLO D'ISABELLE D'ESTE
- TOUTANKHAMON ET SON TEMPS

Reunion des musees nationaux. Paris *see*
- 7 PEINTRES BELGES
- AFGHANISTAN
- L'AGE D'OR DE LA PEINTURE TOULOUSAINE
- ALBERT GIACOMETTI
- ANTIQUITES ORIENTALES. FOUILLES DE TELLO, DE SUSE ET DE SYRIE
- L'AQUARELLE DE 1400 A 1900
- ART ANCIEN DU TCHAD. BRONZES ET CERAMIQUES
- L'ART DE LA POTERIE EN FRANCE DE RODIN A DUFY
- L'ART DE VERSAILLES ET LES NOUVELLES ACQUISITIONS DU MUSEE
- L'ART DES JARDINS, 1730-1830
- L'ART DES JARDINS CLASSIQUES
- L'ART DU GANDHARA ET DE L'ASIE CENTRALE
- ART SUISSE CONTEMPORAIN DEPUIS HODLER. PEINTURE ET SCULPTURE
- AUTOPORTRAITS DE COURBET
- BONAPARTE EN EGYPTE
- BONNARD
- BONNARD, VUILLARD ET LES NABIS, 1888-1903
- BOURDELLE
- CALDER
- CAMILLE PISSARRO. CENTENAIRE DE SA NAISSANCE
- CATHEDRALES. SCULPTURES, VITRAUX, OBJETS D'ART, MANUSCRITS DES XIIE ET XIIIE SIECLES
- CENTENAIRE DE LA FAYETTE, 1757-1834
- CEZANNE
- CHARLES LE BRUN, PREMIER DIRECTEUR DE LA MANUFACTURE ROYALE DES GOBELINS
- CHEFS-D'OEUVRE DE LA PEINTURE FRANCAISE DANS LES MUSEES DE LENINGRAD ET DE MOSCOU
- CHEFS-D'OEUVRE DE L'ART PALEOLITHIQUE
- CHEFS-D'OEUVRE DES COLLECTIONS PRIVEES FRANCAISES RETROUVEES EN ALLEMAGNE PAR LA COMMISSION DE RECUPERATION ARTISTIQUE ET LES SERVICES ALLIES
- CHRISTIAN BERARD
- CLAUDE MONET. EXPOSITION RETROSPECTIVE
- LE CORBUSIER. OEUVRES PLASTIQUES
- LE DANEMARK. SES TRESORS, SON ART
- DEGAS. PORTRAITISTE-SCULPTEUR
- LE DESSIN FRANCAIS DE FOUQUET A CEZANNE
- DESSINS DE MICHEL-ANGE, 1475-1564
- DESSINS FRANCAIS DU MILIEU DU XVIIE SIECLE
- DESSINS ITALIENS. 14E, 15E ET 16E SIECLES
- DEUX SIECLES DE L'HISTOIRE DE FRANCE ET CENTENAIRE DU MUSEE DE VERSAILLES
- DOMESTIQUES. OBJETS DOMESTIQUES DES PROVINCES DE FRANCE DANS LA VIE FAMILIALE ET LES ARTS MENAGERS
- DONATION PAUL JAMOT
- L'EGYPTE AVANT LES PYRAMIDES, 4E MILLENAIRE
- FAIENCES ROUEN, LILLE, ETC., A DECOR DE "LAMBREQUINS."
- FIGURES DE COROT
- FREDERIC 2. LA PEINTURE FRANCAISE DU 18E SIECLE A LA COUR DE FREDERIC 2
- GAUGUIN. CENTENAIRE
- A LA GLOIRE DE LA MARINE A VOILE DU 16E AU 19E SIECLE. 1935. 16 ILLUS. 3 FICHES
- LES GRANDS SERVICES DE SEVRES
- LA GRAVURE FRANCAISE EN COULEURS AU XVIIIE SIECLE
- GUSTAVE MOREAU
- HENRI MICHAUX
- HOMMAGE A ARISTIDE MAILLOL, 1861-1944. CENTENAIRE DE SA NAISSANCE
- HOMMAGE A CEZANNE
- HOMMAGE A CORREGE. DESSINS DU MAITRE, DE SES ELEVES ET DES ARTISTES QUI ONT SUBI SON INFLUENCE
- HUBERT ROBERT. 2E CENTENAIRE DE SA NAISSANCE
- IMAGES POPULAIRES DU MANS, DE CHARTRES ET D'ORLEANS
- IMPRESSIONNISTES DE LA COLLECTION COURTAULD DE LONDRES. 1955. 92 ILLUS. 2 FICHES
- JACQUES LAFFITTE ET LA REVOLUTION DE 1830
- JEAN ETIENNE LIOTARD, 1702-1789, JOHANN HEINRICH FUESSLI, 1741-1825
- JOSEPHINE. PARURES, DECORS ET JARDINS
- KLEE
- LOUIS 15 ET ROCAILLE
- DES MAITRES DE COLOGNE A ALBERT DURER. PRIMITIFS DE L'ECOLE ALLEMANDE
- MANET, 1832-1883
- MANUSCRITS ET PEINTURES DE TOUEN-HOUANG
- MARIE ANTOINETTE, ARCHIDUCHESSE, DAUPHINE ET REINE
- MARK ROTHKO
- LE MASQUE
- MAURICE DENIS. SES MAITRES, SES AMIS, SES ELEVES
- MAX BECKMANN
- LA NATURE MORTE DE L'ANTIQUITE A NOS JOURS
- LE NEO-CLASSICISME FRANCAIS
- NICOLAS POUSSIN ET SON TEMPS. LE CLASSICISME FRANCAIS ET ITALIEN CONTEMPORAIN DE POUSSIN
- ORIGINES ET DEVELOPPEMENT DE L'ART INTERNATIONAL INDEPENDANT
- LA PAIX D'AMIENS. LE CONCORDAT. LE CONSULAT A VIE
- PASTELS, AQUARELLES ET DESSINS DE PAYSAGISTES FRANCAIS DU XIXE SIECLE
- PAYSAGES DE FRANCOIS DESPORTES, 1661-1743
- LA PEINTURE ANGLAISE. 18E ET 19E SIECLES
- PEINTURES DE GOYA DES COLLECTIONS DE FRANCE
- PORCELAINES DE SAXE
- LE PORTRAIT DANS L'ART FLAMAND DE MEMLING A VAN DYCK
- LE PORTRAIT FRANCAIS DE WATTEAU A DAVID
- PORTRAITS ET FIGURES DE FEMMES. PASTELS ET DESSINS
- LES PRIMITIFS FLAMANDS
- RACINE ET PORT-ROYAL
- RAYMOND DUCHAMP-VILLON, 1876-1918. MARCEL DUCHAMP, 1887. 1967. 14 ILLUS. 1 FICHE
- REMBRANDT, 1606-69. TABLEAUX, EAUX-FORTES, DESSINS
- REMBRANDT. DESSINS ET EAUX-FORTES
- RENOIR, 1841-1919
- RETROSPECTIVE HENRI MATISSE
- RETROSPECTIVE SONIA DELAUNAY
- LA REVOLUTION FRANCAISE. ESTAMPES ET DESSINS
- LE ROLE DU DESSIN DANS L'OEUVRE DE DELACROIX
- RUBENS ET SON TEMPS
- LE SIECLE DE REMBRANDT. TABLEAUX HOLLANDAIS DES COLLECTIONS PUBLIQUES FRANCAISES
- SIX MAITRES DE L'ESTAMPE JAPONAISE AU 18E SIECLE
- LA SOCIETE DU 18E SIECLE. PASTELS DE M. QUENTIN DE LA TOUR, 1704-1788
- SOPHIE TAEUBER-ARP
- SOUTINE
- SOUVENIRS DU ROI DE ROME
- TOULOUSE-LAUTREC. 50E ANNIVERSAIRE DE SA MORT
- TRESORS D'ART SUEDOIS
- TRESORS DE LA PEINTURE ESPAGNOLE
- TRESORS DU MUSEE DE BAGDAD DES ORIGINES A L'ISLAM
- TROIS ARTISTES BRITANNIQUES: ROBERT ADAMS, HUBERT DALWOOD, RICHARDS

REUNION DES PAROISSIENS D'YAMACHICHE, OU, LE 18 OCTOBRE 1876 / Desaulniers, Francois Lesieur – Quebec: Des presses du Canadien, 1876. 02679. (Pre-1900 Canadiana) – 9 – cn C.I.H.M. [971]
LA REUNION DU 10 AOUT OU L'INAUGURATION DE LA REPUBLIQUE FRANCAISE / Bouquier et Moline (musique de Porta) – (French Theatre Series). Paris. R. Vatar, an II. 1793 – 9 – fr Hachette [820]
REUNION ESSAYS : WITH AN APPENDIX ON THE NON-INFALLIBLE DOGMATIC FORCE OF THE BULL APOSTOLICAE CURAE OF POPE LEO 13TH IN CONDEMNATION OF THE HOLY ORDERS OF THE CHURCH OF ENGLAND / Carson, W R – London, New York: Longmans, Green, 1903 – 1mf – us A.T.L.A. [240]
REUNION RECORDS / Burton Family – undated. Minutes and other records of the reunion organization of this Parkerville, KS, family – 1 – us KS Hist [920]
REUNION RECORDS / Rickly-Kunkle Family – 1928-1995 – 1r – 1 – $32.50r – us Archival [920]
Reusch *see* REPORT OF THE PROCEEDINGS AT THE REUNION CONFERENCE
Reusch, Franz Heinrich *see*
- BEITRAEGE ZUR GESCHICHTE DES JESUITENORDENS
- BIBEL UND NATUR; VORLESUNGEN UEBER DIE MOSAISCHE URGESCHICHTE UND IHR VERHAELTNISS ZU DEN ERGEBNISSEN DER NATURFORSCHUNG
- BRIEFE UND ERKLAERUNGEN VON J. VON DOELLINGER UEBER DIE VATICANISCHEN DECRETE, 1869-87
- DAS BUCH TOBIAS
- DIE DEUTSCHEN BISCHOEFE UND DER ABERGLAUBE
- LEHRBUCH DER EINLEITUNG IN DAS ALTE TESTAMENT

Reusner, Esaias *see* HUNDERT GEISTLICHE MELODIEN EVANGELISCHEN LIEDER
Reusner, N *see*
- EMBLEMATA NICOLAI REUSNERI IC. PARTIM ETHICA, ET PHYSICA
- SYMBOLORUM HEROICORUM LIBER SINGULARIS

Reuss, Eduard *see*
- DIE GESCHICHTE DER HEILIGEN SCHRIFTEN NEUEN TESTAMENTS
- HISTORY OF THE CANON OF THE HOLY SCRIPTURES IN THE CHRISTIAN CHURCH

Reuss, J *see*
- JOHANNES-KOMMENTARE AUS DER GRIECHISCHEN KIRCHE (T.U.U. 5-89)
- MATTHAEUS-KOMMENTARE AUS DER GRIECHISCHEN KIRCHE (T.U.U. 5-61)

Reuss, Rodolph *see* UN ECOLIER DU DIX-SEPTIEME SIECLE, OU, L'IDEAL DE L'EDUCATION JESUITIQUE
Reuss, Theodor *see* HEINSE UND HOELDERLIN
Reuter, G F *see*
- DIAGNOSES PLANTARUM NOVARUM HISPANICARUM
- PUGILLUS PLANTARUM NOVARUM AFRICAE BOREALIS HISPANIAEQUE AUSTRALIS

Reuter, Hans Ulrich *see* "DER KOENIG VERDIENT KEIN DENKMAL"
Reuter, Otto *see* LUDWIG JACOBOWSKI
REUTER'S FINANZ-CHRONIK – (Finanz-Chronik, 2 Jul 1898-14 May 1912) – London, UK. 4 Jan 1896-25 Jun 1898 – 1 – uk British Libr Newspaper [072]
Reuther, John G *see* THE DIARI
Reuther, O *see* INDISCHE PALAESTE UND WOHNHAEUSER MIT BEITRAEGEN VON CONRAD PREUSSER UND FRIEDRICH WETZEL
REUTLINGER GENERAL-ANZEIGER – Reutlingen, West Germany. 1976- – ca 9r per yr – 1 – gw Mikrofilm [072]
REUTLINGER GESCHICHTSBLAETTER – Reutlingen. Jahrg. 1-24 25; 1890-1914. "Korrespondenzblatt des Suelchgauer Altertumsvereins". Issued by the Verein fuer Kunst und Altertum in Reutlingen. Ceased with Jahrg. 32 (1921)? Cf. ULS. Film Mas C 359 – 1 – us H.U. Library [930]
REV. JACOB BAILEY, HIS CHARACTER AND WORKS / Allen, Charles Edwin – Lincoln County Historical Society, 1895.06171.(Pre-1900 Canadiana) – 9 – cn C.I.H.M. [240]
REV JOHN BROWNLEE : A VETERAN MISSIONARY AND THE FOUNDER OF KING WILLIAMSTOWN / Rose-Innes, R W – (Filmed with: Souvenir of the Union of South Africa) – [King William's Town, South Africa?]: Lovedale Mission Press, [1905] – us Res Libr [920]
THE REV. OLIVER ARNOLD, FIRST RECTOR OF SUSSEX, N.B. WITH SOME ACCOUNT OF HIS LIFE, HIS PARISH AND HIS SUCCESSORS AND THE OLD INDIAN COLLEGE / Allison, Leonard A – Saint John: Sun Print. Co., 1892. 06079. (Pre-1900 Canadiana) – 9 – cn C.I.H.M. [240]
Reval, Gabrielle *see* UN LYCEE DE JEUNES FILLES, PROFESSEURS-FEMMES
REVALUATIONS: HISTORICAL AND IDEAL / Benn, Alfred William – London: Watts, 1909. 1 fiche – 9 – us A.T.L.A. [240]
REVANCHE / Cladel, Leon – Zuerich, 1880 – 1 – DM30.00 – gw Mikro Press [943]
REVANCHE – London, UK. 30 Jan 1915 – 1 – uk British Libr Newspaper [072]
THE REVEALER – Wichita. Kansas. 1934-1936 – 1 – us UMI [071]
REVEALING INDIA'S PAST / Cumming, Jed – London, 1939. 374p 33 pls. BI-1043 2 – 8 – ne IDC [930]
LE REVEIL – Chicoutimi, 1980-fin jul 1990 – 19r – 1 – Can$75.00 – cn Can Microfilming [072]
LE REVEIL – Dakar. mars 1944-aout 1950 – 1 – fr A.C.R.P.P. [073]
LE REVEIL : EDUCATION PUBLIQUE, – REFORMES / ed by Buies, Arthur – Quebec, Montreal, Canada. 27 mai-23 dec 1876 – 1r – 1 – Can$40.00 – cn Can Microfilming [072]
LE REVEIL – Fort-Coulonge, Canada. 3 mai 1962; v1 n19. 27 sep 1962 – 1r – 1 – Can$25.00 – cn Can Microfilming [072]
LE REVEIL – Fredericton, New Brunswick. 7 aut 1869 – 1r – 1 – Can$25.00 – cn Can Microfilming [072]
LE REVEIL – Hull, Canada. 29 dec 1892 – 1r – 1 – Can$25.00 – cn Can Microfilming [072]
LE REVEIL – Jonquiere, Canada. v1 n27. 20 jun 1946-26 nov 1980 – 42r – 1 – Can$75.00r – cn Can Microfilming [072]
LE REVEIL – Journal litteraire. Toulouse. aout 1864-janv 1865 – 1 – fr A.C.R.P.P. [073]
LE REVEIL – Litteraire, politique, quot. Paris. Red. en chef, E. Le Pelletier. 23 oct 1881-1885 – 1 – fr A.C.R.P.P. [073]
LE REVEIL / ed by Marsil, Tancrede – Montreal, Canada. 3 mai 1915-20 mar 1917 – 4r – 1 – Can$40.00r – cn Can Microfilming [072]
LE REVEIL – Montreal, Canada. 11 mar-13 mai 1871 – 1r – 1 – Can$40.00 – cn Can Microfilming [072]
LE REVEIL – Montreal: [s.n., 1892-189-?] – 9 – cn C.I.H.M. [320]
LE REVEIL – Paris. 2 juil 1868-23 janv 1871 – 1 – fr A.C.R.P.P. [073]
LE REVEIL : REVUE POLITIQUE ET LITTERAIRE – (Cont: Canada-Revue) – Montreal, Canada. 8 sep 1894-14 sep 1901 – 3r – 1 – Can$40.00r – cn Can Microfilming [073]
LE REVEIL – Ste-Foy. v1 n6. jan 1950-v11 n2. 10 sep 1959 – 1r – 1 – Can$25.00 – cn Can Microfilming [072]
LE REVEIL – Ste-Therese Ouest, Canada. mar 1968-v4 n14. 6 sep 1971 – 1r – 1 – Can$50.00 – cn Can Microfilming [072]
LE REVEIL / ed by Tessier, G J – St-Roch, Quebec, Canada. 24 dec 1891-25 fev 1892 – 1r – 1 – Can$35.00 – cn Can Microfilming [072]
REVEIL ANARCHISTE – I, no. 1-13. Paris. 15 fevr-25 oct 1913. mq no. 1-3, 7; II, no. 1-4. 1er avr-16 31 mai 1914 – 1 – fr A.C.R.P.P. [073]
LE REVEIL ARTISTIQUE – Quebec, Canada. v1 n4. 30 oct 1909 – 1r – 1 – Can$25.00 – cn Can Microfilming [700]
LE REVEIL DE CHARLEVOIX – Baie St-Paul, fev 1947-sep 1948 – 1r – 1 – Can$50.00 – cn Can Microfilming [072]
LE REVEIL DE SILLERY – Sillery, Canada. v4 n5. 23 mai 1963 – 1r – 1 – Can$25.00 – cn Can Microfilming [072]
LE REVEIL D'EPIMENIDE A PARIS / Carbon de Flins, Des Oliviers – (French Theatre Series). Paris. Maradan, Nantes, Louis, et Bruxelles, Le Charlier. 1790 – 9 – fr Hachette [820]
LE REVEIL DES GAUCHES – fevr 1922-31. devenu: Le Democrate Savoyard. 1932-40. Chambery – 1 – fr A.C.R.P.P. [073]
LE REVEIL DES MINEURS – Saint-Etienne. 25 oct 1890-91 – 1 – fr A.C.R.P.P. [073]
LE REVEIL DES VERRIERS – Lyon. sept 1892-juil 1899 – 1 – fr A.C.R.P.P. [073]
LE REVEIL DU BEAUJOLAIS – Journal de l'arrondissement de Villefranche. Politique, agricole, litteraire. Villefranche-sur-Saone. 29 mars 1939-28 juin 1944 – 1 – fr A.C.R.P.P. [073]
LE REVEIL DU FORCAT / Parti Ouvrier de la Region Nord – no. 1-43. Roubaix. aout 1885-juin 1886 – 1 – fr A.C.R.P.P. [073]
LE REVEIL DU NORD – Journal socialiste quotidien. Fond. Edmond Delesalle. Lille. 1902, 1906, 1921, 1923-janv 1924 – 1 – fr A.C.R.P.P. [073]
LE REVEIL DU SAGUENAY – Chicoutimi, Canada. 12 aut 1886-4 aut 1887 – 1r – 1 – Can$35.00 – cn Can Microfilming [072]
LE REVEIL ECONOMIQUE – Organe de l'union des interets economiques. Paris. aout 1910-aout 1914, fevr 1917-63 – 1 – fr A.C.R.P.P. [073]

REVEIL JOURNAL – Ville de Laval (Pont Viau). 4 mar 1955-v1 n14. 9 sep 1955 – 1r – 1 – Can$35.00 – cn Can Microfilming [072]

LE REVEIL LAURENTIEN / ed by Brady, Gerard – Montreal, Canada. v3 n17. 30 oct 1936 – 1r – 1 – Can$25.00 – cn Can Microfilming [072]

LE REVEIL LITTERAIRE / ed by Brennan, J J – Quebec, Canada. jan 1887 – 1r – 1 – Can$25.00 – cn Can Microfilming [073]

LE REVEIL OUVRIER / L'Union Departementale des Syndicats Unitaires d'Oran – Journal du syndicalisme et du sport ouvrier. Organe officiel. no. 1. Oran. mai 1924 – 1 – fr A.C.R.P.P. [331]

LE REVEIL SYNDICAL – no. 1-8, 11-12, 20-21, 24-25. Lens, Henin-Lietard. 7 avr-11 oct 1903. devient: L' Action syndicale voir a ce titre – 1 – fr A.C.R.P.P. [073]

Reveillaud, Eugene *see* LA SEPARATION DES EGLISES ET DE L'ETAT

REVEILLE – Bellingham. Wash. 1891-1899; 1901-1907; 1914-1927 – 1 – us UMI [071]

REVEILLE – Jetmore. Kan. 1882-1883; 1885-1892 – 1 – us UMI [071]

REVEILLE – Port Gibson. Miss. 1853-1854; 1890-1896; 1902-1914; 1926-1936; 1937- – 1 – us UMI [071]

THE REVEILLE – Butte. Mont. 1901-1909 – 1 – us UMI [071]

THE REVEILLE – Gloster. Miss. 1942-1943 – 1 – us UMI [071]

THE REVEILLE – Reno, NV. Mar 1908-Arp 1910 (scats) – 1r – 1 – $50.00 – U04712 – us Library Micro [071]

REVEILLE-MATIN A DOUBLE MONTRE / Faverot, I – (Missing: Title page) – Grenoble, 1670 – 5mf – 9 – CA-111/1 – ne IDC [240]

REVELACIONES EXTRAVAGANTES : UTG. AV L. HOLLMAN / Sancta Birgitta – Uppsala, 1956 – 8mf – 8 – ne Slangenburg [240]

REVELATION / Atwood, Isaac Morgan – 2nd ed. Boston: Universalist Publ House, 1891, c1889 – 1mf – 9 – 0-8370-2123-5 – 1985-0123 – us A.T.L.A. [220]

REVELATION / Kelly, William – London: Thomas Weston, 1903. 1 fiche – 9 – us A.T.L.A. [240]

REVELATION AND INSPIRATION / Seeberg, Reinhold – London: Harper, 1909. 1 fiche – 9 – us A.T.L.A. [240]

REVELATION AND RELIGIOUS CERTITUDE / Ritchie, W B – (Includes index) – Edinburgh:J. Gardner Hitt ; London:Marshall, 1907 – 1mf – 9 – 0-8370-4911-3 – 1985-2911 – us A.T.L.A. [220]

REVELATION AND THE BIBLE: AN ATTEMPT AT RECONSTRUCTION / Horton, Robert Forman – New York: Macmillan, (c1892). 1 fiche – 9 – us A.T.L.A. [240]

THE REVELATION AND THE RECORD / Macgregor, James – Edinburgh: T. & T. Clark, 1893. 1 fiche – 9 – us A.T.L.A. [240]

LA REVELATION...: EXPLIQUEE PAR LES ECRITURES ET EXPLIQUANT L'HISTOIRE / Rougemont, Frederic – Neuchatel: Delachaux & Sandoz, 1866. 1 fiche – 9 – us A.T.L.A. [240]

THE REVELATION OF DISCOVERY / Brent, Charles H – New York: Longmans, Green, 1915 – 1mf – us A.T.L.A. [240]

THE REVELATION OF JESUS : A STUDY OF THE PRIMARY SOURCES OF CHRISTIANITY / Gilbert, George Holley – (Includes indexes) – New York: Macmillan, 1899 – 1mf – 9 – 0-8370-3279-2 – 1985-1279 – us A.T.L.A. [240]

THE REVELATION OF JOHN ITS OWN INTERPRETER IN VIRTUE OF THE DOUBLE VERSION IN WHICH IT IS DELIVERED / Cochran, John – New York: D Appleton, 1860 – 1mf – 9 – 0-8370-2696-2 – 1985-0696 – us A.T.L.A. [220]

REVELATION OF JOHN ITS OWN INTERPRETER IN...THE DOUBLE VERSION / Cochran, John – New York: D. Appleton, 1860. 1 fiche – 9 – us A.T.L.A. [240]

REVELATION OF JOHN: WITH NOTES...DESIGNED FOR BOTH PASTORS AND PEOPLE / Cowles, Henry – New York: Appleton, 1871. 1 fiche – 9 – us A.T.L.A. [240]

THE REVELATION OF S. JOHN THE DIVINE / Simcox, William Henry – Cambridge: University Press, 1891. 1 fiche – 9 – us A.T.L.A. [240]

THE REVELATION OF ST. JOHN / Milligan, William – London:Macmillan, 1886 – 1mf – 9 – 0-8370-4440-5 – 1985-2440 – us A.T.L.A. [220]

THE REVELATION OF ST. JOHN THE DIVINE : AN INTERPRETATION / Ames, A H – (Includes index) – New York: Eaton & Mains, c1897 – 1mf – 9 – 0-8370-2089-1 – 1985-0089 – us A.T.L.A. [220]

REVELATION OF ST JOHN THE DIVINE / Ames, A H – New York: Eaton & Mains, 1897. 1 fiche – 9 – us A.T.L.A. [240]

THE REVELATION OF THE RISEN LORD / Westcott, Brooke Foss – [3rd ed]. London, New York: Macmillan, 1884 – 1mf – 9 – 0-8370-5808-2 – 1985-3808 – us A.T.L.A. [240]

A REVELATION OF THE TRUE MINERVA / Blenerhasset, Thomas – 1582 – 9 – 5.00 – us Scholars' Facs [810]

REVELATIONES GERTRUDIANAE AC MECHTILDIANAE – Paris, 1875-1877. 2v – 27mf – 8 – ne Slangenburg [240]

THE REVELATIONES OF SAINT BIRGITTA / ed by Cumming, W P – London, 1929 – 4mf – 8 – ne Slangenburg [240]

REVELATIONES S. BIRGITTAE : TRANSLATIO SUECANA E CODICE BIBL. REG. HOLM / ed by Wessen, Marta – Hafniae, 1949 – 11mf – 8 – ne Slangenburg [240]

REVELATIONES S. BIRGITTAE : TRANSLATIO SUECANA E CODICE BIBL. REG. HOLM. A 5 B... / ed by Wessen, Marta – Hafniae, 1949 – 11mf – 8 – ne Slangenburg [240]

REVELATIONS SUR LA RUSSIE OU L'EMPEREUR NICOLAS ET SON EMPIRE EN 1844, PAR UN RESIDENT ANGLAIS / Henningsen, Charles-Frederick – (Russia-19th C. series). 1845 – 9 – fr Hachette [947]

Revello, Jose Torre *see* EL LIBRO, LA IMPRENTA EL PERIODISMO EN AMERICA DURANTE LA DOMINACION ESPANOLA

Reven, A L *see* A STUDY TO INVESTIGATE THE PSYCHO-SOCIAL REASONS FOR THE TERMINATION OF ORGANIZED SPORT PARTICIPATION AS RELATED TO AGE

LA REVENDICATION / La Ligue Syndicale pour la Defense des Interets du Travail, de l'Industrie et du Commerce – Organe officiel. no. 1-49. Paris. juil 1888-juin 1889 – 1 – fr A.C.R.P.P. [073]

REVENGED / Barr, Robert – New York, London: F. Stokes, c1896. 03352. (Pre-1900 Canadiana) – 9 – cn C.I.H.M. [830]

LE REVENU DES TRAVAILLEURS AGRICOLES AU MAROC / Morocco. ILO – 1969. BNE-3211 1 – 9 – ne IDC [333]

REVENUE BASED ON LAND VALUES / The Association for Good Government – 4p – 9 – $1.00f – at Libertarian Micro [335]

REVERBERO – Lagoa Dourada, 7 Sep 1908 – 1,5,6 – bl Biblioteca [072]

REVERBERO CONSTITUCIONAL FLUMINENSE – Rio de Janeiro, 15 Sep 1821-8 Oct 1822 – 1,5,6 – bl Biblioteca [072]

REVERE FAMILY PAPERS, 1746-1964 – Massachusetts Historical Society – 15r – 1 – $1155.00 – us UMI [920]

THE REVEREND MR. TOPLADY'S DYING AVOWAL OF HIS RELIGIOUS SENTIMENTS / Toplady, Augustus Montague – London, 1778 – 1mf – 9 – MP-527/1 – ne IDC [240]

THE REVEREND OLIVER HEYWOOD, B.A. 1630-1702 : HIS AUTOBIOGRAPHY, DIARIES, ANECDOTE AND EVENT BOOKS...GENERAL AND FAMILY HISTORY OF YORKSHIRE AND LANCASHIR / Heywood, Oliver; ed by Turner, J Horsfall – 4v. geneal. tab – 1 – us U.W. Library [920]

LE REVEREND PERE FRANCOIS DELAPLACE DE LA CONGREGATION DES PERES DU SAINT-ESPRIT... / Marie-Francoise, Soeur – 1959. SEM105P4 – 1mf – 9 – cn Bibl Nat [240]

REVEREND PERE HILAIRE DE LA PERADE, O.F.M., CAP. : BIO-BIBLIOGRAPHIE ANALYTIQUE / Sainte-Therese-d'Alencon, Soeur – 1962. SEM105P4 – 4mf – 9 – cn Bibl Nat [240]

REVEREND PERE UBALD VILLENEUVE, O.M.I., AUMONIER NATIONAL DE L'ASSOCIATION LACORDAIRE ET SAINTE-JEANNE D'ARC DU CANADA / Toussaint, Alice – 1962. SEM105P4 – 2mf – 9 – Can$4.50 – cn Bibl Nat [240]

REVEREND WILLIAM S. WHITE, D.D., AND HIS TIMES (1800-1873) : AN AUTOBIOGRAPHY / White, William S; ed by White, H M – Richmond, Va.: Presbyterian Committee of Publication, 1891 – 1mf – us A.T.L.A. [240]

REVERENDE SOEUR SAINTE-BLANCHE DES SOEURS DE LA CHARITE DE QUEBEC : BIBLIOGRAPHIE ANALYTIQUE / Sainte-Claire-de-la-Trinite, Soeur – 1955. SEM105P4 – 2mf – 9 – Can$4.50 – cn Bibl Nat [240]

REVERENDS PHILIP MULKEY AND JAMES FOWLER / Bailey, J D – Upper South Carolina – 1 – 5.00 – us Baptist [240]

REVERIES D'UN CELIBATAIRE / Mitchell, Donald Grant – Bruxelles et Leipzig: A. Sohnee, 1859. 264p. 3 fiches.(Literature Collection) – 9 – 8.00 – fr Bibl Nationale [830]

REVERSE PAINTINGS ON GLASS : THE RYSER COLLECTION / Ryser, Frieder – Corning, NY: Corning Museum of Glass, 1992. Fiche No. 13,380 – 4mf – 9 – $750 – us Corning Mus [740]

Reverter Delmas, Emilio *see* CUBA ESPANOLA

LES REVEURS D'EAU / Boccara, M – Analyse du mythe de fondation d'un village maya – 9 – F180.00 – fr Ethnologie [306]

DIE REVIDIERTE LUTHERBIBEL DES HALLESCHEN WAISENHAUSES / Lagarde, Paul de – Goettingen: Dieterich, 1885. 1 fiche – 9 – us A.T.L.A. [240]

REVIEL DE J.J. ROUSSEAU. SIXEME FANTASIE POUR PIANO ET COR OU VIOLON / Duvernoy, F – (Score and violin part) – Paris: Richault, 182- – 1 – us Sibley [780]

REVIEW – v1- 1976- 1,5,6; v2- 1977- 9 – us UMI [330]

REVIEW – Alliance. Ohio. 1871- – 1 – us UMI [071]

REVIEW – Branford. Conn. -w. 1928- – 1 – us UMI [071]

REVIEW – Columbia Falls. Mont. 1935-1940 – 1 – us UMI [071]

REVIEW – East Liverpool. OH. And pred. 1885-88; 1892-1920; 1921-22; 1924- – 1 – us UMI [071]

REVIEW – East Liverpool. Ohio. -w. (Saturday Review.) 1879-87 – 1 – us UMI [071]

REVIEW – Elgin. Neb. 1897-1962 – 1 – us UMI [071]

REVIEW – Elkhart. Ind. -sw. 1897-1909 – 1 – us UMI [071]

REVIEW – Elkhart. Ind. -w. 1859-96 – 1 – us UMI [071]

REVIEW – Fayette, Ohio. 1904-42 – 2r – 1 – $32.50r – us Archival [071]

REVIEW / Fernand Braudel Center for the Study of Economies, Historical Systems, and Civilizations – (1983-. 1,5,6,9) – v1-. 1977- – 1 – us UMI [073]

REVIEW – Follansbee. West Virginia. 1958-1966 – 1 – us UMI [071]

REVIEW – Galion. Ohio. -w. 1865-70 – 1 – us UMI [071]

REVIEW – Garden City. Mich. 1932-1967 – 1 – us UMI [071]

REVIEW – Geraldine. Mont. 1913-1950; 1956-1957 – 1 – us UMI [071]

REVIEW – Half Moon Bay. Calif. -w. 1945- – 1 – us UMI [071]

REVIEW – Henderson, NE. -w. Aug 1937-Feb 1940 – 1 – us NE Hist [071]

REVIEW – Inyokern. Calif. 1954-1955 – 1 – us UMI [071]

REVIEW – Las Vegas, NV. Jan-Sep 1926 – 1r – 1 – $50.00 – U04610 – us Library Micro [978]

REVIEW – Laurel. IN. 1857-88 – 1 – us UMI [071]

REVIEW – Lovelock, NV. 1908-11 – 1r – 1 – $50.00 – U04623 – us Library Micro [071]

REVIEW – Miami. Fl. 1926- – 1 – us UMI [071]

REVIEW – Milligan. Neb. 1933-1953 – 1 – us UMI [071]

REVIEW – Milwaukee, OR. -w. 7 Jan 1926-27 Aug 1975. – 1 – us U.O. Library [071]

REVIEW – Moline. IL. -w. 1876-96 – 1 – us UMI [071]

REVIEW / N. J. E. A. (New Jersey Education Association) – v1- 1927- 1; v49- 5,6; v50- 9 – us UMI [370]

REVIEW – Peterborough, 1854-1920 – 92r – 1 – cn Preston [971]

REVIEW – Providence. R.I. -w. 1870-71 – 1 – us UMI [071]

REVIEW – Reidsville. N.C. 1889-1958 – 1 – us UMI [071]

REVIEW – Rosamond. Calif. 1957-1966 – 1 – us UMI [071]

REVIEW – Towanda. Pa. 1958-1968 – 1 – us UMI [071]

REVIEW / Urban League – v. 1-. 1975- – 1,5,6,9 – us UMI [360]

REVIEW – Vernon, NV. Jun-Oct 1907 – 1r – 1 – $50.00 – U04779 – us Library Micro [071]

REVIEW – Whitby, Au1972-1972Oc – 1r – 1 – cn Preston [971]

REVIEW *see* AAESPH REVIEW

THE REVIEW – Goldfield, NV. 1905-09 – 5r – 1 – $250.00 – U04560 – us Library Micro [071]

THE REVIEW – (Lacks: v4 no 7) – v1-5. 1899-1903 – 1r – 1 – ATLA 1994-S021 – us A.T.L.A. [073]

THE REVIEW – Philadelphia. Pa. 1905-64 – 1 – us A.J.P.C. [071]

THE REVIEW – Sydney, Australia. Jul 1910-Jul 1917; Apr 1918-Dec 1921.-m. 11 reels – 1 – uk British Libr Newspaper [072]

THE REVIEW – Valletta, Malta. -f. 27 Jan 1959-31 Oct 1962. Imperfect. 1 reel – 1 – uk British Libr Newspaper [072]

REVIEW ADVERTISER – Alberta, CN. 1919-28 – 3r – 1 – cn Commonwealth Micro [072]

THE REVIEW AND DISTRICT OF BEDFORD INTELLIGENCER – Waterloo, Canada. v1 n9. 3 jun 1881 – 1r – 1 – Can$25.00 – cn Can Microfilming [072]

REVIEW AND EXPOSITOR – 1904-56 – 1 – 1055.53 – us Baptist [240]

THE REVIEW AND EXPOSITOR – (Lacking: 15(1918)-(1919)) – 7(1910)-33(1936) – 240mf – 9 – Dfl840.00 – ne Slangenburg [073]

REVIEW AND EXPOSITOR: INDEX – 1904-54. Covering article titles and authors; 1945-54, covering book reviews – 5 – 265.65 – us Baptist [240]

REVIEW AND RECORD / Organization of Petroleum Exporting Countries – 1967-77 – 1 – 40.00 – us L of C Photodup [330]

REVIEW, FEDERATION OF AMERICAN HOSPITALS – (v.12-. 1979- 5,6,9) – v.9- . 1976- – 1 – us UMI [073]

REVIEW. (GAZETTE) – Atlantic City. N.J. 1884-86, 1907-08, 1910-24 – 1 – us UMI [071]

REVIEW JOURNAL – Las Vegas, NV. 1979-80 – 36r – 1 – $1,800.00 – N04611 – us Library Micro [978]

REVIEW JOURNAL *see* AGE

REVIEW MINER – Lovelock, NV. 1909-86 – 36r – 1 UN04624 – $1,800.00 – us Library Micro [071]

REVIEW OF AFRICAN POLITICAL ECONOMY – (Increased page extent in 1995) – 1995, Vol 22 – £122.00 – uk Carfax [320]

REVIEW OF AGRICULTURAL PLANNING DURING THE SECOND POSTWAR DECADE – 1976 – 31p – it F.A.O. [338]

REVIEW OF AMERICAN CHEMICAL RESEARCH – v.3-12. 1897-1906 – 1,5,6 – 2258.00 – us Princeton Micro [540]

REVIEW OF APPLIED ENTOMOLOGY: SERIES A – (Series B. v.33-45. 1945-57. 2269.00; 1,5,6) – v.33-45. 1945-57 – 1,5,6 – 22104.00 – us Princeton Micro [590]

REVIEW OF BLACK POLITICAL ECONOMY – 1985-. -q – 1 – us UMI [073]

REVIEW OF BLACK POLITICAL ECONOMY – v1-. 1970- – 1,5,6 – us UMI [330]

REVIEW OF BOOKS AND RELIGION – Lexington, KY. 1981-1983 – 1r – 1 – $50.00 – R04145 – us Library Micro [071]

REVIEW OF BOOKS AND RELIGION – v.10-. 1981- – 1,5,6,9 – us UMI [240]

REVIEW OF CHRISTOLOGIE DES ALTEN TESTAMENTES, VON E. W. HENGSTENBERG / Noyes, George Rapall – (The Christian Examiner and General Review, v. 16 (n.s. v. 11) no. 3, July 1834, p. 321-364) – 9 – us A.T.L.A. [240]

REVIEW OF DEVELOPMENT, 1955-1957 / Somaliland – Hargeisa. 1957. BD-551 1 – 9 – ne IDC [338]

REVIEW OF DEVELOPMENT PLAN FOR THE MALTESE ISLANDS, 1959-64 / Malta – Valletta. 1961 – 9 – ne IDC [338]

A REVIEW OF DEVELOPMENT PLANS IN THE SOUTHERN PROVINCE, 1953 / Tanganyika – Dar es Salaam. 1954 – 9 – ne IDC [338]

REVIEW OF ECONOMICS AND STATISTICS – v53-66. 1971-84 – 1,5,6,13 – sz Elsevier [330]

REVIEW OF EDUCATIONAL RESEARCH – v. 1-30. 1931-1960 – 1 – us Princeton Micro [370]

REVIEW OF EDUCATIONAL RESEARCH – (v. 37- 1967- 5,6. v. 40- 1970- 9) – v. 1- 1931- – 1 – us UMI [370]

REVIEW OF EDUCATIONAL RESEARCH – Washington, DC. v19-35.1949-65. H-373/2 – 8 – ne IDC [073]

REVIEW OF EDUCATION/PEDAGOGY/CULTURAL STUDIES / ed by Giroux, Henry & Shannon Patrick – 1,5,9 – us Gordon [370]

REVIEW OF ENGLISH STUDIES – v1- 1925- 1; v22- 5,6; v26- 9 – us UMI [420]

REVIEW OF ENGLISH STUDIES – N.s. v1-19 London 1950-68 – 9 – $24,150.00; $7.50v – uk Dawson [420]

REVIEW OF ENGLISH STUDIES – O.s. v1-25 London 1925-49. All pub – 9 – $24,185.00; $6.00v – uk Dawson [420]

REVIEW OF EXTENSION METHODOLOGIES IN AQUACULTURE – 1990 – 69p – it F.A.O. [639]

REVIEW OF FOOD CONSUMPTION SURVEY 1981 : HOUSEHOLD FOOD CONSUMPTION BY ECONOMIC GROUPS – 1983 – 292p – it F.A.O. [339]

REVIEW OF FOOD CONSUMPTION SURVEYS 1977, VOL 1 : EUROPE, NORTH AMERICA AND OCEANIA – 1981 – 164p – it F.A.O. [640]

REVIEW OF FOOD CONSUMPTION SURVEYS 1977, VOL 2 : AFRICA, LATIN AMERICA, NEAR EAST, FAR EAST – 1981 – 292p – it F.A.O. [640]

REVIEW OF FOOD CONSUMPTION SURVEYS 1985 : HOUSEHOLD FOOD CONSUMPTION BY ECONOMIC GROUPS – 1986 – 236p – it F.A.O. [339]

REVIEW OF FOOD CONSUMPTION SURVEYS, 1988 : HOUSEHOLD FOOD CONSUMPTION BY ECOMONIC GROUPS – 1988 – 223p – it F.A.O. [339]

REVIEW OF FOREST MANAGEMENT SYSTEMS OF TROPICAL ASIA : CASE STUDIES OF NATURAL FOREST MANAGEMENT FOR TIMBER PRODUCTION IN INDIA, MALAYSIA AND THE PHILIPPINES – 1989 – 233p – it F.A.O. [634]

REVIEW OF GASTROENTEROLGY *see* AMERICAN JOURNAL OF GASTROENTEROLOGY

REVIEW OF GHANA LAW – v.11-. 1979- – 1,5,6,9 – us UMI [073]

REVIEW OF HIGHER EDUCATION – (v.4-. 1980$ 5,6,9) – v.2-. 1978- – 1 – us UMI [073]

REVIEW OF HISTORICAL PUBLICATIONS RELATING TO CANADA – Toronto. v1-22. 1896-1917 – 9 – Can$365.00 – cn Micromedia [971]

REVIEW OF HISTORICAL PUBLICATIONS RELATING TO CANADA – v1-22. 1896-1918 – 1 – cn Precision [971]

REVIEW OF HONGKONG CHINESE PRESS / U.S. Consulate General. Hong Kong – 1 Jul 1947-10 May 1961. (ceased publication) – 1 – $193.00 – us L of C Photodup [950]

REVIEW OF INDONESIA – (Available: 1955(1,2,4,6-8,11,12); 1956(9,12); 1957; 1958; 1959; 1960(1-10); 1963(10-12); 1964(5-7); 1965(1)) – Djakarta, 1954-65 – 82mf – 9 – SE2/2 – ne IDC [950]

REVIEW OF LENGTH-BASED APPROACHES TO ASSESSING FISH STOCKS – 1992 – 108p – it F.A.O. [639]

REVIEW OF LITIGATION – (v1-4 1980-85 on reel $60.00. v5-15 1986-96 on mf $187.00) – University of Texas. v1-15. 1980-96 – 5,6,9 – $268.00 set – us Hein [340]

REVIEW OF METAPHYSICS – (v21- 1967- 5,6; v29- 1975- 9) – v1- 1947- – 1 – us UMI [110]

REVIEW OF OPERATION 1950-1974 / Arabian American Oil Company. Saudi Arabia – 20 v. in 4. (lacking 1968, 1969). BNE-6601 1 – 9 – ne IDC [956]

REVIEW OF OPTOMETRY – (See also: Optical Journal and Review of Optometry) – us UMI [617]

REVIEW OF PALAEOBOTANY AND PALYNOLOGY – v1-44. 1967-84 – 1,5,6,13 – sz Elsevier [560]

REVIEW OF POLITICS – v1- 1939- 1; v33- 5,6; v38- 9 – us UMI [320]

REVIEW OF POLITICS – v. 1-28. 1939-1966 – 1 – us Princeton Micro [320]

REVIEW OF PROGRESS : SIXTH FIVE YEAR PLAN 1980-1985 / India. Andhra Pradesh. Finance and Planning (Planning Wing) Department – Hyderabad, 1989 – 9mf – 9 – ne IDC [338]

REVIEW OF PROGRESS IN THE DEVELOPMENT AND WELFARE OF THE COLONY OF BRITISH HONDURAS DURING THE PERIOD 1948-1954 / Honduras. British – Belize. 1954. BD-710 1 – 9 – ne IDC [338]

REVIEW OF REAL PROPERTY / Salvadore, Carlos F – Brooklyn: Americana, 1930. 47 numb. leaves. LL-500 – 1 – us L of C Photodup [340]

REVIEW OF RECENT PUBLICATIONS, REGARDING THE PROPOSED REFORM OF THE BANKRUPTCY LAWS OF SCOTLAND / Douglas, Christopher – Edinburgh, Bell & Bradfute, 1853. 30 p. LL-2288 – 1 – us L of C Photodup [340]

A REVIEW OF REPRODUCTIVE PERFORMANCE OF FEMALE BOS INDICUS (ZEBU) CATTLE / Mukasa-Mugerwa, E – 1989 – 9 – $32.00 – 92-9053-130-4 – et ILRI [636]

REVIEW OF RESEARCH ON MODERN PROBLEMS IN GEOCHEMISTRY / ed by Siegel, F R – 1979 – 290p – 9 – 92-3-101577-X – fr UNESCO [550]

REVIEW OF RESEARCH ON SALT-AFFECTED SOILS / Szabolcs, I & Varallyay, G – 1979 – 137p – 9 – 92-3-101613-X – fr UNESCO [630]

REVIEW OF REVIEWS AND WORLD'S WORK – v. 2-96. 1890-1937 – 1 – us UMI [073]

REVIEW OF REVIEWS AND WORLDS WORK – New York. v. 5-95. 1892-1937 – 1 – us Princeton Micro [073]

REVIEW OF SCIENTIFIC INSTRUMENTS – (Missing: v3(p830-End). 1932; v4(p1-41). 1933) – Wisconsin. v1-12. 1930-41 – 141mf – 9 – 290c/2 – ne IDC [500]

REVIEW OF SCIENTIFIC INSTRUMENTS – v1- 1930- – 1,5,6,9 – us A.I.P. [600]

REVIEW OF "TALES OF MY LANDLORD" : ON THE UNITY OF THE CHURCH; AND, SERMONS / M'Crie, Thomas – Edinburgh: William Blackwood, 1857 – 2mf – us A.T.L.A. [240]

A REVIEW OF THE ARTS AND SCIENCES IN ISRAEL / Israel. Ministry for Foreign Affairs. Cultural Relations Department – Jerusalem, 1962-70.-nos1-27 – 56mf – 9 – J-81-8c/1 – ne IDC [700]

REVIEW OF THE BRITISH PRESS / Indonesia. London office – SE-5998 1 – 9 – ne IDC [070]

REVIEW OF THE CONSTITUTION AND ASSOCIATE STATUTES OF THE THEOLOGICAL SEMINARY IN ANDOVER / Thatcher, Samuel Cooper – (The Monthly Anthology and Boston Review, v. 5, Nov. 1808, p. 602-614) – 9 – us A.T.L.A. [240]

REVIEW OF THE ECONOMY; A SUPPLEMENT TO THE 1967/1968 BUDGET / Sudan. Ministry of Finance and Economics – 1967. BNE-7670 1 – 9 – ne IDC [336]

REVIEW OF THE EVIDENCES OF THE GENUINENESS OF THE GOSPELS / Stuart, Moses – (The American Biblical Repository, v. 11, no. 30, April 1838, p. 265-343) – 9 – us A.T.L.A. [240]

A REVIEW OF THE FERNS OF NORTHERN INDIA / Clarke, C B – 1880 – 7 – uk Microform Academic [580]

A REVIEW OF THE FERNS OF NORTHERN INDIA / Clarke, C B – (Trans. Linn. Soc., London, S.2. Botany). v. 1. 1880 – 8 – ne IDC [580]

REVIEW OF THE FISHERIES RESOURCES OF THE RED SEA AND GULF OF ADEN – 1989 – 144p – it F.A.O. [333]

A REVIEW OF THE LAWS OF THE UNITED STATES OF NORTH AMERICA, THE BRITISH PROVINCES, AND WEST INDIA ISLANDS. – London: Otridge and Otridge, 1790. 259 (i.e. 255)p. LL-2295 – 1 – us L of C Photodup [340]

A REVIEW OF THE POLICY, DOCTRINES AND MORALS OF THE METHODISTS – London, 1791 – 1mf – 9 – MP-573/1 – ne IDC [240]

A REVIEW OF THE PRINCIPLES OF SUCH METHODISTS AS ARE UNDER THE DIRECTION OF THE REV. MR. JOHN WESLEY / Muirhead, J – Kelso, 1784 – 1mf – 9 – MP-547/1 – ne IDC [240]

A REVIEW OF THE QUESTION / Lofton, George A – 1897. 238p – 1 – 8.33 – us Baptist [240]

REVIEW OF THE RATIONALE OF RELIGIOUS ENQUIRY / Ripley, George – (The Christian Examiner and General Review, v. 21 (3d series, v. 3) no. 2, Nov. 1836, p. 225-254) – 9 – us A.T.L.A. [240]

A REVIEW OF THE REFERENCES TO THE HORTUS MALABARICUS / Dillwyn, L W – Swansea. 1839. B-8309 1 – 9 – ne IDC [580]

A REVIEW OF THE REIGN OF GEORGE 2 / Almon, John – 2nd ed. London: J Wilkie, 1762. SEM16P1 – 1r – 5 – Can$9.00 – cn Bibl Nat [941]

A REVIEW OF THE REV. MOSES STUART'S PAMPHLET ON SLAVERY ENTITLED CONSCIENCE AND THE CONSTITUTION / Clark, Rufus W – Boston: C.C.P. Moody, 1850 – 1mf – us A.T.L.A. [320]

REVIEW OF THE RIVER PLATE – Buenos Aires. Argentina. -w. 2 Jul 1892-28 Apr 1894, 15 Nov 1907-4 Dec 1908, 24 Feb 1911-30 Jun 1922; 28 Mar-25 Jul 1930; 9 Jan-27 Mar, 29 May-26 Jun 1931; 1 Jul-30 Sept 1932. (Imperfect). (46mqn reels) – 1 – uk British Libr Newspaper [072]

REVIEW OF THE RIVER PLATE – Buenos Aires. v51-91. 1919-41 – 26r – 1 – us Ross [972]

REVIEW OF THE SECOND SEVEN YEAR PLAN PROGRAM OF IRAN / Iran. Plan Organization – Teheran. 1960. BD-356 1 – 9 – ne IDC [338]

REVIEW OF THE STATE OF AQUATIC POLLUTION OF EAST AFRICAN INLAND WATERS – 1982 – 43p – it F.A.O. [360]

REVIEW OF THE STATE OF AQUATIC POLLUTION OF WEST AND CENTRAL AFRICAN INLAND WATERS – 1985 – 32p – it F.A.O. [360]

REVIEW OF THE STATE OF WATER POLLUTION AFFECTING INLAND FISHERIES IN SOUTHEAST ASIA – 1986 – 30p – it F.A.O. [630]

A REVIEW OF THE SYSTEMS OF ETHICS : FOUNDED ON THE THEORY OF EVOLUTION / Williams, Cora May – (Includes bibliographical references) – New York: Macmillan, 1893, c1892 – 2mf – 9 – 0-8370-6718-9 – 1986-0718 – us A.T.L.A. [170]

REVIEW OF THE TELEGRAPH AND TELEPHONE *see* FACTORY

REVIEW OF THE VIETNAM CONFLICT AND ITS IMPACT ON U.S. MILITARY COMMITMENTS ABROAD: REPORT / U.S. Congress. House. Special Subcommittee on National Defense Posture – Washington, Govt. Print. Off., 1968. 84p. LL-2348 – 1 – us L of C Photodup [340]

A REVIEW OF THE WORKS OF THE ROYAL SOCIETY OF LONDON / Hill, John – London, 1751 – 1 – us U.W. Library [500]

REVIEW OF WORLD AFFAIRS – 1941-45. Continued as: Intelligence Digest – 1 – us UMI [327]

A REVIEW RELATIVE TO THE COURT OF APPEALS OF MARYLAND / Clagett, Charles – Baltimore, 1959. 58p. LL-2252 – 1 – us L of C Photodup [340]

REVIEW (ST. ST ALBANS) – (Also known as: St. Albans and Harpenden Review) – Jul 23-Dec 1981; Jan 7-Jun 24, Jul 1982-Sep, Oct 4-Dec 28 1990; Jan-Jun, Jul 4-Dec 19 1991; 1992-Dec 23 1993; 1994-96 – 53r – 1 – uk British Libr Newspaper [072]

REVIEW (WATFORD EDN) *see* WATFORD AND WEST HERTS REVIEW

REVIEW-ADVERTISER – Forest, Ohio. 1912-23 – 3r – 1 – $32.50r – us Archival [071]

REVIEW-DISPATCH – Moline. IL. -w. 1898, 1903 – 1 – us UMI [071]

THE REVIEWER ANSWERED / Bangs, Nathan – 1830 – 9 – us A.T.L.A. [240]

REVIEW-HERALD – Mammoth Lakes, CA. 1987 – 15+ r – 1 – $750.00 ($160.00y) – B03612 – us Library Micro [071]

REVIEW-MINER – Lovelock. Nev. -w. 1949- – 1 – us UMI [071]

REVIEWS / Chemical Society – (v5- . 5,6,9) – v. 1-. 1972- – 1 – us UMI [540]

REVIEWS AND DISCUSSIONS : LITERARY, POLITICAL, AND HISTORICAL, NOT RELATING TO BACON / Spedding, James – London: C. Kegan Paul, 1879 – 1 roll – 1 – 1-55879-572-3 – uk Libr Preservation [420]

REVIEWS IN ANTHROPOLOGY / ed by Etkin, Nina L – 9,5,1 – us Gordon [301]

REVIEWS IN PURE AND APPLIED PHARMACOLOGICAL SCIENCES – v.1-. 1980- – 1,5,6,9 – us UMI [073]

REVIEWS OF GEOPHYSICS – (v1-14 1963-76 $25.00y 1,5,6,13 1971-76 $25.00y 9. v15 1977 $30.00 1,5,6,13 $60.00 9. v16 1978 $25.00 1,5,6,13 $75.00 9. v17 1979 $50.00 1,5,6,13 $95.00 9. v18 1980 $35.00 1,5,6,13 $95.00 9. v19 1981 $35.00 1,5,6,13 $140.00 9. v20 1982 $45.00 1,5,6,13 $165.00 9. v30 1992 $220.00. v31 1993 $220.00. v32 1994 $220.00. v33 1995 $250.00) – v1-. 1963-. Quarterly – us A.G.U. [520]

REVIEWS OF INFECTIOUS DISEASES – Chicago.v1-8. 1979-86 – 1,5,6 – us Princeton Micro [616]

REVIEWS OF INFECTIOUS DISEASES – v.1-. 1979- – 1,5,6,9 – us UMI [616]

REVIEWS OF MAGNETIC RESONANCE IN MEDICINE *see* MAGNETIC RESONANCE IMAGING

REVIEWS OF MODERN PHYSICS / American Physical Society – v1-11. 1929-39 – 118mf – 9 – 757/2 – ne IDC [530]

REVIEWS OF MODERN PHYSICS – v1- 1929- – 1,5,6,9 – us A.I.P. [530]

REVIEWS OF THE YOKOHAMA CLASS B AND CLASS C WAR CRIMES TRIALS BY THE 8TH ARMY JUDGE ADVOCATE, 1946-1949 / Allied Operational and Occupational Headquarters. World War II – RG 331. M1112. 5 rolls – 1 – us Nat'l Archives [900]

REVIEWS OF U.S. ARMY WAR CRIMES TRIALS IN EUROPE, 1945-1948 – 5r – 1 – M1217 – us Nat'l Archives [340]

REVIEW-TIMES – Fostoria, Ohio, 1981-1990 – 31r – 1 – $32.50r – us Archival [978]

Revilla, L Gonzalez *see* DERECHO MERCANTIL DE ESPANA

Revilla, L Gonzalez Revilla *see* ELEMENTOS DEL DERECHO MERCANTIL DE ESPANA...

Reville, Albert *see*
- HISTOIRE DU DOGME DE LA DIVINITE DE JESU-CHRIST
- JESUS DE NAZARETH, ETUDES CRITIQUES

Reville, Jean *see* PROTESTANTISME LIBERAL

REVISAO DO 3. PLANO DE FOMENTO PROGRAMA PARA 1971-73 / Portugal. Presidencia do Conselho – (Revision of Third Development Plan, Program for 1971). Lisboa. 1971. BD-1738 1 – 9 – ne IDC [338]

THE REVISED AND AUTHENTIC RITES AND CEREMONIES OF THE EPOPTS – 1886?. 03245. (Pre-1900 Canadiana) – 9 – cn C.I.H.M. [971]

REVISED CENTRAL DEVELOPMENT PROGRAMME, 1965-1966 / Pakistan. Planning Commission – Karachi. 1965. BD-873 1 – 9 – ne IDC [338]

REVISED CODE OF AMERICAN SAMOA, 1961 EDITION / American Samoa. Interim Research Section – (Includes 1964 and 1966 suppls) – 27 Dec 1962, n.d.; 18 Jan 1967 – 21mf – 9 – $31.50 – LLMC 82-100C Title 2 – us L.L.M.C. [324]

REVISED CONSTITUTION OF AMERICAN SAMOA, 1967 / American Samoa – n.p, n.d. – 1mf – 9 – $1.50 – LLMC 82-100C Title 11 – us L.L.M.C. [324]

REVISED DEVELOPMENT PLAN, 1964-1966 / British Virgin Islands. Administrator's Office – D-975 1 – 9 – ne IDC [338]

REVISED DEVELOPMENT PROGRAMME, 1958-62 (REVISED APR 1960) / Nigeria. Eastern – (Official Document no. 13 of 1960). Enugu. 1960 – 9 – ne IDC [338]

A REVISED DEVELOPMENT PROGRAMME FOR THE THREE-YEAR PERIOD JUL 1961 TO JUN 1964 – (Sessional Paper No. 3 of 1962). Zanzibar. 1962. Bd-700 1 – 9 – ne IDC [338]

REVISED ENGLISH VERSION OF THE OLD-COVENANT SCRIPTURES: COMPARED / Norton, William – London: W.K. Bloom, 1886. 1 fiche – 9 – us A.T.L.A. [240]

A REVISED KEY TO HEPATICS OF THE BRITISH ISLANDS / Macvicar, S M – Eastbourne, 1906. 19 pp. B-1275 2 – 8 – ne IDC [580]

REVISED LIST OF ANCIENT MONUMENTS IN BENGAL / India – Calcutta, 1887. Bl-721 2 – 8 – ne IDC [720]

REVISED LIST OF THE FERNS OF NATAL / Buchanan, J – (Reprinted from the Natal Colonist). Natal. 1875. B-7169 1 – 9 – ne IDC [580]

REVISED LISTS OF ANTIQUARIAN REMAINS IN THE BOMBAY PRESIDENCY AND THE NAT. STATES OF BARODA, PALANPUR, RADHANPUR, KATHIAWAS, KACHI, KOLHAPUR, AND THE SOUTHERN MARATHA MINOR STATES / India; ed by Burgess, J & Cousens, H – Bombay, 1897. BI-716 2 – 8 – ne IDC [720]

THE REVISED LITURGY : A HISTORY AND CHRITICISM OF THE RITUALISTIC MOVEMENT IN THE GERMAN REFORMED CHURCH / Bomberger, Johann H A – Philadelphia: Jas. B. Rodgers, 1867 – 1mf – us A.T.L.A. [240]

REVISED PHASING, SECTORAL PRIORITIES AND ALLOCATIONS OF THE THIRD FIVE YEAR PLAN (1965-70) / Pakistan. Planning Commission – Karachi. 1967. BD-595 1 – 9 – ne IDC [338]

REVISED REGULATIONS / Quebec. (Province). Direction generale des Bois et Forets – Quebec, 1892. SEM105P650 – 1mf – 9 – Can$2.25 – cn Bibl Nat [634]

REVISED REPORT / Malaysia. Royal Commission on the Teaching Services – Kuala Lumpur, 1971 – 5mf – 9 – DE-213/1 – ne IDC [370]

REVISED REPORT OF THE POST-WAR DEVELOPMENT COMMITTEE (1946-1955) / Nyasaland – D-1406 1. 1947 – 9 – ne IDC [338]

THE REVISED REPORTS : BEING A REPUBLICATION OF SUCH CASES IN THE ENGLISH COURTS OF COMMON LAW AND EQUITY FROM THE YEAR 1785, AS ARE STILL OF PRACTICAL UTILITY / Great Britain. Courts of Common Law and Equity; ed by Pollock, Frederick et al – London: Sweet & Maxwell. v1-149. 1891-1920 (all publ) – 1473mf – 9 – $2,209.00 – LLMC 95-249 – us L.L.M.C. [324]

REVISED ROSTER OF VERMONT VOLUNTEERS AND LISTS OF VERMONTERS WHO SERVED IN THE ARMY AND NAVY OF THE U.S. DURING THE WAR OF THE REBELLION 1861-66 / Peck, Theodore S – Montpelier, Press of the Watchman Publishing Co., 1892. Vermont Reel 5. (The Cox Library Collection) – 5 – us Americana [978]

REVISED SECOND SEVEN-YEAR DEVELOPMENT PLAN, SEPT 1955-SEPT 1962 / Iran. Plan Organization – 1959. D-1097-1 – 9 – ne IDC [338]

THE REVISED STATUTES OF 1875 : COMMISSIONERS' REPORT OF 1872 TO THE CONGRESS AND LEGISLATIVE HISTORY – Washington: GPO. 2v. 1872 – 38mf – 9 – $57.00 – LLMC 81-101 – us L.L.M.C. [340]

THE REVISED STATUTES OF 1875 : PASSED AT THE FIRST SESSION OF THE 43RD CONGRESS, 1873-74 / U. S. Laws, Statutes, etc – (Legal evidence of the law from 1789-1873; also numbered as part of Statutes at Large v18 pt 1) – Washington: GPO, 1875 – 16mf – 9 – $24.00 – LLMC 81-100 – us L.L.M.C. [324]

THE REVISED STATUTES OF 1875 *see* THE REVISED STATUTES OF 1875

THE REVISED STATUTES OF 1878 : SECOND EDITION OF THE REVISED STATUTES OF 1875 / U. S. Laws, Statutes, etc – (Includes 2 suppl vols by Richardson, publ in 1891 and 1985, which carry the work through the 53rd Congress) – 2nd ed. Washington: GPO, 1878 – 43mf – 9 – $64.00 – LLMC 81-102 – us L.L.M.C. [324]

THE REVISED STATUTES OF 1878 *see* NOTES ON THE REVISED STATUTES OF THE U.S.

REVISED STATUTES OF CANADA / Canada. Laws, Statutes, etc – (English and French editions) – 1886-1990 – 5 – cn Micromedia [340]

THE REVISED STATUTES OF MICHIGAN AND MICHIGAN COMPILED LAWS / Michigan Legislature – (The 1838 + 1846 eds are termed "Revised Statutes". Later eds are termed "Compiled Laws") – 1838-1970 – 558mf – 9 – $837.00 – LLMC 81-001 – us L.L.M.C. [340]

REVISED STATUTES OF THE REPUBLIC OF LIBERIA; BEING A REVISION OF THE STATUTES FROM THE ORGANIZATION OF THE GOVERNMENT IN 1848 TO AND INCLUDING THE ACTS OF THE LEGISLATURE OF 1910-1911. / Liberia. Laws, Statutes, etc – Paris, Etablissements Busson, 1928 2 v. LL-12013 – 1 – us L of C Photodup [340]

THE REVISED STATUTES OF THE UNITED STATES / Blodget, Lorin – Philadelphia, Philadelphia Social Science Association 1876. 21 p. LL-379 – 1 – us L of C Photodup [340]

THE REVISED UNIFORM LIFE INSURANCE ACT OF THE PROVINCES OF CANADA (EXCEPT QUEBEC) / Lester, Albert Jeffrey – 3rd ed. Toronto, Stone & Cox 1938? 60 p. LL-2226 – 1 – us L of C Photodup [340]

REVISED VERSION OF THE FIRST THREE GOSPELS / Cook, Frederic Charles – London: John Murray, 1882. 1 fiche – 9 – us A.T.L.A. [240]

THE REVISED VERSION OF THE FIRST THREE GOSPELS : CONSIDERED IN ITS BEARINGS UPON THE RECORD OF OUR LORD'S WORDS AND OF INCIDENTS IN HIS LIFE / Cook, Frederic Charles – London:John Murray, 1882 – 1mf – 9 – 0-8370-2731-4 – 1985-0731 – us A.T.L.A. [220]

THE REVISED VERSION OF THE NEW TESTAMENT : A CRITICAL COMMENTARY, WITH NOTES UPON THE TEXT / Osborne, William Alexander – London: Kegan Paul, Trench, 1882 – 1mf – 9 – 0-8370-4642-4 – 1985-2642 – us A.T.L.A. [220]

REVISIO GENERUM PLANTARUM / Kuntze, C E O – 1891 – 1 – uk Microform Academic [580]

REVISIO GENERUM PLANTARUM VASCULARIUM / Kuntze, C E O – 3v. Leipzig. 1891-98. B-1260 2 – 8 – ne IDC [580]

REVISIO LICHENUM HOFFMANNIANORUM / Wainio, E A – (Meddel. Soc. Fauna et Flora Fennica, v. 14, 1888). B-944 2 – 8 – ne IDC [580]

REVISIO LICHENUM IN HERBARIO LINNAEI OSSERVATORUM / Wainio, E A – (Meddel. Soc. Fauna et Flora Fennica, v. 14, 1888). B-945 2 – 8 – ne IDC [580]

REVISIO SAXIFRAGARUM ICONIBUS ILLUSTRATA / Sternberg, K M von – Ratisbonae, 1810. 60 pp., 31 pls. suppl. 1. Ratisbonae, 1822. 16 pp., 10 pls. suppl. 2. Praha, 1831. 104 pp., 16 pls. B-1095 2 – 8 – ne IDC [580]

UNA REVISION ACTUAL DE LAS IDEAS SOBRE LA DECADENCIA ESPANOLA / Sanchez Montes, Juan – Madrid: Arbor, 1949 – 1 – sp Bibl Santa Ana [946]

REVISION DE LA FAMILLE DES BIGNONIACEES / Kunth, C S – (Journ. Physique, Decembre 1818). B-5990 2 – 8 – ne IDC [580]

REVISION DE LA FAUNE MALACOLOGIQUE DES CANARIES / Mousson, J R A – Z-683 2. 1873 – 8 – ne IDC [590]

LA REVISION DE LA HISTORIA ARGENTINA / Gandia, Enrique de – 1st ed. Buenos Aires: A. Zamora, 1952. 357p – 1 – us U.W. Library [972]

LA REVISION DE LA SENTENCE ARBITRALE / Audry, L – Paris, 1914 – 2mf – 9 – ILM-323/1 – ne IDC [340]

REVISION DE VIDA / Consejo Diocesano de los hombres de Accion Catolica – Badajoz Graficas Jimenez, 1962 – sp Bibl Santa Ana [240]

DIE REVISION DER LUTHERBIBEL / Zittel, Emil – Berlin SW: Carl Habel (C B Luederitz), 1885 – 1mf – 9 – 0-8370-5968-2 – 1985-3968 – us A.T.L.A. [220]

DIE REVISION DER LUTHERISCHEN BIBELUEBERSETZUNG UND DIE...PROBEBIBEL VON 1883 / Plitt, Gustav Leopold – Karlsruhe: Macklot, 1884. 1 fiche – 9 – us A.T.L.A. [240]

REVISION DER ZIONISTISCHEN POLITIK / Lichtheim, R – Berlin. 1930. BJ-28-14 1 – 9 – ne IDC [956]

REVISION DES CULTELLIDAE ET SOLECURTIDAE (MOLLUSQUES LAMELLIBRANCHES) / Fischer-Piette, Edouard – Laboratoire de Biologie des Invertebres marins et Malacologie, Museum d'Histoire naturelle, Paris. 1978. 282p. illus – 9 – F90.00 – fr Ethnologie [590]

REVISION DES GRAMINEES / Kunth, C S – Paris. 1829-34. B-5994 2 – 8 – ne IDC [580]

REVISION DES GRAPHIDEES EXOTIQUES / Mueller, J A – Genea6ve, 1886. (Compt. Rend. Soc. Helv. Sci. 69-e session). B-693 2 – 8 – ne IDC [580]

REVISION DES MAURERISCHEN TASCHENBUCHES AUF DAS JAHR 5802 BIS 5803... / Fessler, I A – Berlin, 1802 – 1mf – ne IDC [943]

REVISION DES PSAMMOBIIDAE / Fischer-Piette, Edouard – Laboratoire de Biologie des Invertebres marins et Malacologie, Museum national d'Histoire naturelle. Paris, 1979. 270p. illus – 9 – F90.00 – fr Ethnologie [590]

REVISION DES ROSES D'ASIE / Boulenger, G A – (Bull. Jard. Bot. Etat Bruxelles, 1931-35, v13, p165-266; 1936-37, v14, p115-221, 274-278. B-8126/1 – 9 – ne IDC [580]

LA REVISION DU PROCES DREYFUS / Dreyfus, Alfred – Paris, Stock, 1899. 2 v. LL-4037 – 1 – us L of C Photodup [340]

REVISION DU SYSTEME DES ORTHOPTERES ET DESCRIPTION DES ESPECES RAPPORTEES PAR...L. FEA DE BIRMANIE / Brunner von Wattenwyl, C – Genova, 1893. 230p. 6 pls. Z-1103/2 – 8 – ne IDC [590]

REVISION MONOGRAPHIQUE DES CLADONIA DU SOUS-GENRE CLADINA / Des Abbayes, H – (Lichens). Rennes. 1939. B-6172 2 – 8 – ne IDC [580]

REVISION MONOGRAPHIQUE DES CLADONIA DU SOUS-GENRE CLADINA (LICHENS) RENNES, 1939 / Abbayes, H des – B-6172 2 – 8 – ne IDC [580]

A REVISION OF THE CHINESE AND SIKKIM HIMALAYAN DRYOPTERIS / Ching, R C – 1935-38 – 10mf – 9 – uk Microform Academic [590]

A REVISION OF THE CHINESE AND SIKKIM-HIMALAYAN DRYOPTERIS / Ching, R C – (Bull. Fan. Mem. Inst. Biol. v.6). 1936 – 8 – ne IDC [580]

A REVISION OF THE COLEOPTEROUS FAMILY COCCINELLIDAE / Crotch, G R – London, 1874. xv,311p. Z-1156/2 – 8 – ne IDC [590]

REVISION OF THE CUCUJIDAE OF AMERICA NORTH OF MEXICO / Casey, Thomas Lincoln – 1884? 02097. (Pre-1900 Canadiana) – 9 – cn C.I.H.M. [580]

REVISION OF THE DEVELOPMENT PROGRAMME, 1964/1967 / Gambia – (Sessional Paper No. 1 of 1966). Bathurst. 1966. BD-657 1 – 9 – ne IDC [338]

REVISION OF THE ENGLISH VERSION OF THE NEW TESTAMENT / Lightfoot, Joseph B et al – New York: Harper, 1873. 2mf – 9 – us A.T.L.A. [240]

A REVISION OF THE GENUS CAPSICUM WITH A SPECIAL REFERENCE TO GARDEN VARIETIES / Irish, H C – (Missouri Bot. Garden, Ninth Ann. Rep. 1898). B-6506 2 – 8 – ne IDC [580]

A REVISION OF THE HEART DISEASE LOCUS OF CONTROL SCALE / Finkel, Robert J – 1988 – 240p 3mf – 9 – $12.00 – us Microform Publ [616]

REVISION OF THE HETEROCEROUS LEPIDOPTERA OF THE FAMILY SPHINGIDAE / Butler, A G – [London], 1876. (Trans. Zool. Soc. London. v9, p 511-644, 5pls) – 8 – ne IDC [590]

REVISION OF THE LAWS GOVERNING THE U.S. COURT OF MILITARY APPEALS AND THE APPEALS PROCESS BEFORE THE MILITARY PERSONNEL SUBCOMMITTEE OF THE COMMITTEE ON ARMED SERVICES – House of Rep. 96th Congress, 2nd session Feb 7, Mar 6 & Sep 23 1980; Hearings. Washington: GPO, 1980 – 2mf – 9 – $3.00 – LLMC 96-084 – us L.L.M.C. [340]

"REVISION OF THE LEAGUE" / Coudert, F R – N.p., 1934 – 1mf – 1 – ILM-4009/1 – ne IDC [327]

REVISION OF THE NORTHERN RHODESIA TEN-YEAR DEVELOPMENT PLAN, NOV 1953 / Rhodesia. Northern – Lusaka. 1953. BD-678 1 – 9 – ne IDC [338]

REVISION OF THE UNITED STATES STATUTES AS DRAFTED BY THE COMMISSIONERS APPOINTED FOR THAT PURPOSE : COMMISSIONER'S REPORT AND LEGISLATIVE HISTORY FOR THE REVISED STATUTES OF 1875 / U. S. Laws, Statutes, etc – Washington: GPO. 2v. 1872 – 38mf – 9 – $57.00 – LLMC 81-101 – us L.L.M.C. [324]

REVISION OF THE UNITED STATES STATUTES AS DRAFTED BY THE COMMISSIONERS APPOINTED FOR THAT PURPOSE / U.S. Congress – 2v – 9 – $68.00 set – us Hein [324]

REVISJON AV LANGTIDSPROGRAMMET 1966-1969 / Norway. Finans- og Toll departementet – D-1144 1. 1966 – 9 – ne IDC [336]

A REVISTA : FOLHA POLITICA E LITTERARIA – '(s.l.')-Sao Luiz, Brazil. 6 Jun 1842; Jan, Mar-May, Aug-Nov 1843; Jan-Jun, Sept, Nov-Dec 1844; Feb, Apr-Dec 1847-6 Dec 1850 – 1,5,6 – bl Biblioteca [073]

REVISTA / Banco de la Nacion Argentina. Buenos Aires – 1-9. no.1. 1937-45 – 1 – 46.00 – us L of C Photodup [336]

REVISTA / Instituto De Salubridad y Enfermedades Tropicales – 1939-59 – 1 – uk Microform Academic [616]

REVISTA / Sociedad de Geografia e Historia de Honduras. Tegucigalpa – v. 1-31. 1904-53. Several scattered missing issues – 1 – 194.00 – us L of C Photodup [972]

REVISTA AGUSTINIANA DE ESPIRITUALIDAD – v1-32. 1960-91 (complete) – 14r – 1 – ATLA S0549 – us A.T.L.A. [073]

REVISTA ALAGOANA : PERIODICO SCIENTIFICO E LITTERARIO DE PROPAGANDA DA EDUCACAO DA MULHER – Maceio, Alagoas. 31 Jan, 30 Jun 1887 – 1,5,6 – bl Biblioteca [072]

REVISTA ANUAL DE CULTURA 1980 / Casatejada. Ayuntamiento – Navalmoral de la Mata: Imp. Rivero, 1980 – 1 – sp Bibl Santa Ana [306]

REVISTA ARGENTINA DE DERECHO INTERNACIONAL – Buenos Aires. v1-2. 1920-22 – 9mf – 9 – IL-12/1 – ne IDC [340]

REVISTA AZUL – Curitiba, Aug-Oct 1893 – 1,5,6 – bl Biblioteca [072]

REVISTA BIMESTRE CUBANA / Sociedad Economica de Amigos del Pais – Havana. v1-76. 1831-1959 – 14r – 1 – us Ross [972]

REVISTA BRASILEIRA : JORNAL DE LITTERATURA, THEATROS E INDUSTRIA – Rio de Janeiro, 1 Jul 1855; 29 Jun 1856 – 1,5,6 – bl Biblioteca [072]

REVISTA BRASILEIRA DE CIENCIAS SOCICAIS – Belo Horizonte, BL. 1961-63 – 1r – $50.00 – R60217 – us Library Micro [300]

REVISTA BRASILEIRA DE ESTATISTICA / Brazil. Conselho nacional de Estatistica – v3-4. 1942-43. Official organ of the Conselho nacional de estatistica – 1 – us U.W. Library [324]

REVISTA BRASILEIRA DE MUSICA – Rio de Janeiro. 1934-44. Lacking: v.7, n.4; v.10. 2 reels – 1 – 44.00 – us L of C Photodup [780]

REVISTA BRASILEIRA DO ESTUDOS POLITICOS – Belo Horizonte, BL. 1956-1979 – 8r – $400.00 – R04163 – us Library Micro [072]

REVISTA BRASILEIRA DO ESTUDOS POLITICOSQ – Belo Horizonte, BL. 1956-79 – 8r – $400.00 – R60218 – us Library Micro [320]

REVISTA BRASILIENSE – Sao Paulo, BL. 1955-1964 – 5r – $250.00 – R04186 – us Library Micro [300]

REVISTA BRAZILEIRA : JORNAL DE SCIENCIAS LETTRAS E ARTES – Rio de Janeiro, 1857-61; 1879-81; 1895-99; 1934-35; 1941-48; 1958; 1960; 1964-66; 1975-76; 1978-80 – 1,5,6 – bl Biblioteca [072]

REVISTA CATOLICA DE FILIPINAS – Manila. Philippine Islands. -w. 26 Dec 1889-28 Dec 1890. (Imperfect). (55 ft) – 1 – uk British Libr Newspaper [072]

REVISTA CHILENA DE HISTORIA Y GEOGRAFIA – 1911-42 – 14r – 1 – us Ross [972]

REVISTA CHILENA DE HISTORIA Y GEOGRAFIA1A – Santiago, Chile. no. 1-100. Jan 1911-1942, and Index to no. 1-100 – 1 – us NY Public [972]

REVISTA CIVILIZACAO BRASILEIRA – Rio de Janeiro, BL. 1965-1968 – 3r – $150.00 – R04181 – us Library Micro [320]

REVISTA COLLEGIAL – Manaos, Amazonas. Ago 1906 – 1,5,6 – bl Biblioteca [072]

REVISTA COMMERCIAL : PERIODICO COMMERCIAL, AGRICOLA, INDUSTRIAL, LITTERARIO E NOTICIOSO – Maceio, Alagoas. 18 Ago 1885; 18, 28 Fev 1886 – 1,5,6 – bl Biblioteca [072]

REVISTA COMMERCIAL DAS ALAGOAS : ORGAM DOS INTERESSES DAS CLASSES COMMERCIAES E INDUSTRIAES DO ESTADO – (Cont by: Revista Commercial e Agricola das Alagoas) – Maceio, Alagoas. 30 Jun 1912-15 Nov 1913 – 1,5,6 – bl Biblioteca [072]

REVISTA COMMERCIAL DAS ALAGOAS *see* REVISTA COMMERCIAL E AGRICOLA DAS ALAGOAS

REVISTA COMMERCIAL E AGRICOLA DAS ALAGOAS : ORGAM DAS CLASSES PRODUCTORAS DO ESTADO – (Cont: Revista Commercial das Alagoas) – Maceio, Alagoas. Jan-31 Dez 1914 – 1,5,6 – bl Biblioteca [072]
REVISTA COMMERCIAL E AGRICOLA DAS ALAGOAS *see* REVISTA COMMERCIAL DAS ALAGOAS
REVISTA CONTEMPORAA1NEA – Madrid. v. 43-134. Jan Feb 1883-June 1907 – 1 – us NY Public [073]
REVISTA CUBANA – Havana. v1-21. 1885-95 – 5r – 1 – us Ross [073]
REVISTA CUBANA – Havana. v1-31. 1935-57 – 3r – 1 – us Ross [073]
REVISTA CUBANA – New York. v1. 1968 – 1r – 1 – us Ross [073]
REVISTA CUBANA : PERIODICO MENSUAL DE CIENCIAS, FILOSOFIA, LITERATURA Y BELLAS ARTES – Habana. v2-6 1885-87; v8-15 1888-92 – 1 – us NY Public [324]
REVISTA DA SOCIEDADE PHARMANEUTICA BRASILEIRA – (Cont of: Revista Pharmaceutica. Cont as: A Abelha) – Rio de Janeiro, Jul 1853-Feb 1856 – 1,5,6 – bl Biblioteca [073]
REVISTA DE AGRICULTURA, INDUSTRIA, Y COMERCIO – 1872. No.1-8 – 9 – 1.50f – sp Bibl Santa Ana [073]
REVISTA DE ALMENDRALEJO – Almendralejo. 1879-85 – 9 – 1.50f – sp Bibl Santa Ana [073]
REVISTA DE ALMENDRALEJO – (Hay que anadir lo ya publicado poniendo como ultimo ano el de 1886) – Almendralejo – 5 – sp Bibl Santa Ana [073]
REVISTA DE AMERICA – Bogata. 1-25 (no.1-83), 1945-57 – 1 – 115.00 – us L of C Photodup [073]
REVISTA DE ARCHIVOS, BIBLIOTECAS Y MUSEOS – Madrid, 1871-1930 – 574mf – 9 – sp Cultura [020]
REVISTA DE CIENCIAS PENALES – v. 1-11. Mar Apr 1935-49. v. 3, no. 12-15, v. 9-10 wanting – 9 – 55.00 – us L of C Photodup [360]
REVISTA DE CUBA – Havana. v1-16. 1877-84 – 4r – 1 – us Ross [073]
REVISTA DE DERECHO INTERNACIONAL – Habana. v1-60. nos1-122. 1922-52 – 262mf – 9 – IL-4/1 – ne IDC [340]
REVISTA DE DERECHO INTERNACIONAL... / ed by Garcia Moreno, A – Madrid. 2v. 1887-88 – 6mf – 1 – ILM-3756/1 – ne IDC [327]
REVISTA DE DERECHO INTERNACIONAL Y POLITICA EXTERIOR – Madrid. v1-4. 1905-10 – 16mf – 9 – IL-5/1 – ne IDC [327]
REVISTA DE DERECHO PUERT ORRIQUENO – Catholic University of Puerto Rico. v1-34. 1961-94 – 9 – $395.00set – us Hein [340]
REVISTA DE DIALECTOLOGIA Y TRADICIONES POPULARES – v1, no. 3-4-v26. 1945-70 – 1 – us I.U. Libraries [390]
REVISTA DE DREPT INTERNATIONAL – Paris. v1. 1930 – 2mf – 9 – ILM-3865/1 – ne IDC [073]
REVISTA DE ESPANA, DE INDIAS – v1. 1845 – 9 – 1.50f – sp Bibl Santa Ana [946]
REVISTA DE ESTUDIOS EXTREMENOS – (Sigue publicandose) – Badajoz, 1945-1992 – 5 – sp Bibl Santa Ana [073]
REVISTA DE EXALTACION A LA TIERRA DE BARROS. FERIAS Y FIESTAS 1952 – S.l., s.i., s.a. 1952 – 1 – sp Bibl Santa Ana [390]
REVISTA DE EXTREMADURA – Caceres, 1899-1911 – 5 – sp Bibl Santa Ana [073]
REVISTA DE FERIA 1969 / Zafra. Ayuntamiento – Zafra: Comision de Feria y Fiestas del Ayuntamiento, 1969 – sp Bibl Santa Ana [946]
REVISTA DE FERIAS, 1943. FESTIVIDAD DE NUESTRA SENORA DE LA PIEDAD / Almendralejo – sp Bibl Santa Ana [390]
REVISTA DE FERIAS Y FIESTAS 1966 / Villafranca de los Barros – Villafranca de los Barros: Ayuntamiento, 1966 – sp Bibl Santa Ana [390]
REVISTA DE FILOLOGIA ESPANOLA – Madrid: Anejos. v1-72. 1926-60 – 10r – 1 – us Ross [440]
REVISTA DE FILOLOGIA ESPANOLA – Madrid: Consejo superior de Investigaciones cientificas, Instituto Antonio de Nebrija. v1-42. 1914-59 – 8R – 1 – us Ross [440]
REVISTA DE INSTRUCCAO E EDUCACAO – Sao Luiz, 11 Aug 1877-27 Jul 1878 – 1,5,6 – bl Biblioteca [073]
REVISTA DE LA FACULTAD DE CIENCIAS ECONOMICAS – Lima: Universidad Mayor de San Marcos, Facultad de Ciencias economicas. v1-30. Continued by: Hevista de la Facultad de Ciencias Economicas y comerciales – 1 – us U.W. Library [330]
REVISTA DE LA FACULTAD DE CIENCIAS ECONOMICAS Y COMERCIALES – Lima: Universidad Mayor de San Marcos, Facultad de Ciencias economicas y comerciales. v32-45. 1947-76 – 1 – us U.W. Library [330]
REVISTA DE LAS FIESTAS QUE SE CELEBRAN EN FUENTE DEL MAESTRE EN HONOR DEL SANTISIMO CRISTO DE LAS MISERICORDIAS / Fuente del Maestre – Villafranca de los Barros: Rodriguez, 1953 – 1 – sp Bibl Santa Ana [390]
REVISTA DE LAS U. B. DE J – 1924. 226p – 1 – 7.91 – us Baptist [240]
REVISTA DE LEGISLACION Y JURISPRUDENCIA DE LA ASOCIACION DE ABOGADOS DE PUERTO RICO – (Text partially in English) – v1-5. 1914-19 (all publ) – 28mf – 9 – $44.00 – LLMC 89-010 – us L.L.M.C. [340]
REVISTA DE LOS ESPARRENSES, NO 5 DEDICADA A LA 2ND SEMANA CULTURAL Y FIESTA DEL EMIGRANTE. AGOSTO 1980 / Esparragalejo. Ayuntamiento – Merida: Tip. Alvarez, 1980 – 1 – sp Bibl Santa Ana [390]
REVISTA DE LOS TRIBUNALES Y DE LEGISLACION UNIVERSAL. – Madrid. On film: v1-69; 1878-1935. Lacking: v53, no39; v54, no11. LL-0228 – 1 – us L of C Photodup [340]
REVISTA DE MUSICA LATINO- AMERICANA. LATIN AMERICAN MUSIC REVIEW – 1980- – 1,5,6,9 – us UMI [073]
REVISTA DE OCCIDENTE – Madrid. v1-20, 23-34. 1923-31 – 1 – 138.00 – us L of C Photodup [073]
REVISTA DE POLITICA INTERNACIONAL – Santiago de Chile. 4v. 1922-25 – 16mf – 9 – ILM-3727/1 – ne IDC [327]
REVISTA DE TELEGRAFOS – Madrid, Spain. -w. 1867-74. 3 reels – 1 – uk British Libr Newspaper [072]
REVISTA DE TRADICIONES POPULARES – v1, no.1-2. 1944 – 1 – us I.U. Libraries [390]
REVISTA DEL CENTRO DE ESTUDIOS EXTREMENOS – (Fue continuada por la siguiente con el nombre de Revista de Estudios Extremenos 149 que sigue publicandose) – Badajoz, 1927-1944 – 5 – sp Bibl Santa Ana [073]
REVISTA DEL COMERCIO DEL PERU – Lima. 1923-59 – 1 – 115.00 – us L of C Photodup [380]
REVISTA DEL PENSAMIENTO CONTROAMERICANA – 1960- 1; 1975- 5,6,9 – us UMI [320]
REVISTA DEL RIO DE LA PLATA; PERIODICO MENSUEL DE HISTORIA Y LITERATURA DE AMERICA – Buenos Aires. v. 1-13. 1871-1877 – 1 – us NY Public [073]
REVISTA DO AMAZONAS : PUBLICACAO MENSAL SOBRE EXPLORACAO DE RIOS, CATECHESE E CIVILSACAO DE INDIOS, COLONISACAO, AGRICULTURA, INDUSTRIA – [s.l.] 5 Abr-15 Set 1876 – 1,5,6 – bl Biblioteca [072]
REVISTA DO BRAZIL – Sao Paulo. Anno 1 v, 1-Anno, v. 28. 1916-1925 – 1 – us NY Public [073]
REVISTA DO INSTITUTO ARCHEOLOGICO E GEOGRAPHICO ALAGOANO – Maceio, Alagoas. Dez 1872-Jun 1881; Dez 1883-Jun 1884; 1901; Jun 1907; Jan-Jun 1915; Jan-Jun 1916; 1924-1932; 1936-1937; 1942-1953; 1968; 1972-1978 – 1,5,6 – bl Biblioteca [072]
REVISTA DO NORTE – Maceio, Alagoas. 12 Jan, Mar-Abr 1888; 13 Maio 1889 – 1,5,6 – bl Biblioteca [072]
REVISTA DO PARANA – Curitiba, 30 Oct-17 Dec 1887 – 1,5,6 – bl Biblioteca [072]
REVISTA DOMINICANA DE DERECHO INTERNACIONAL – Santa Domingo. v1. 1927 – 1mf – 9 – ILM-3866/1 – ne IDC [340]
Revista Espanola de Estudios Biblicos *see* NUEVOS COLABORADORES. DON JUAN FERNANDEZ Y FERNANDEZ
REVISTA EVANGELICA – 1937. 806p – 1 – 28.21 – us Baptist [240]
REVISTA EXTREMENA – Badajoz, 1881 y 1878 – 5 – sp Bibl Santa Ana [073]
REVISTA HISPANO – AMERICANA DE CIENCIAS LETRAS Y ARTES – Madrid. v. 1-15. 15 Apr 1921-Jun 1936 – 1 – us NY Public [073]
REVISTA IBEROAMERICANA – v1- 1939- 1; v70- 5,6; v42- 9 – us UMI [440]
REVISTA ILLUSTRADA – Rio de Janeiro, 1 Jan 1876-1898 – 1,5,6 – bl Biblioteca [073]
REVISTA ITALIANA DI MUSICOLOGIA – v1-1966- 1; v8- 5,6,9 – us UMI [780]
REVISTA ITALIANA PER LE SCIENZE GIURIDICHE. – Roma. Publication suspended, 1922-25 and 1944-46. On film: v1-66, 1886-1921; n.s. anno 1-18, 1926-43; 3 ser. anno 1, 1947. Lacking: v66, 1921. LL-0241 – 1 – us L of C Photodup [340]
REVISTA JAVERIANA – Bogota. v. 2, n. 5-28, n. 140. Feb 1934-Nov 1947. Lacks n. 5 – 1 – 133.00 – us L of C Photodup [972]
REVISTA JURIDICA DE LA UNIVERSIDAD DE PUERTO RICO – v1-63. 1932-94 – 9 – $853.00 set – us Hein [340]
REVISTA JUVENIL – 1924. 260p – 1 – 9.10 – us Baptist [240]
REVISTA JUVENIL : JORNAL LITTERARIO, CRITICO E NOTICIOSO – '(s.l.')-Sao Luis, Brazil. 10 Aug 1876-22 Jun 1877 – 1,5,6 – bl Biblioteca [072]
REVISTA KLAXON – Rio de Janeiro, Brazil. 15 May 1922-Jan 1923 – 1 – bl Biblioteca [073]
REVISTA MEDICA FLUMINENSE *see* SEMANARIO DE SAUDE PUBLICA
REVISTA MENSAL DA SOCIEDADE CLUB LITTERARIO – Maceio, Alagoas. Jul-Set 1876 – 1,5,6 – bl Biblioteca [072]
REVISTA MENSAL DO CLUB LITTERARIO JOSE BONIFACIO – Maceio, Alagoas. Jun 1885 – 1,5,6 – bl Biblioteca [072]
REVISTA MEXICANA DE DERECHO INTERNACIONAL – Mexico, D.F.. v1-5. 1919-23 – 37mf – 9 – IL-6/1 – ne IDC [340]
REVISTA MEXICANA DE SOCIOLOGIA – 1939- 1; 1974- 5,6; 1975- 4 x 6 in. 9 – us UMI [300]
REVISTA MUSICAL CATALANA; BUTLLETI DEL ORFEO CATALA – v. 1-33. 1904-36 – 1 – 186.00 – us L of C Photodup [780]
REVISTA OFICIAL, DE FERIA / Oliva de la Frontera – Badajoz: Imprenta Vda. A. Arqueros, 1949 – 1 – sp Bibl Santa Ana [946]
REVISTA OFICIAL DE LAS FIESTAS DE SAN JUAN 1979 / Badajoz – Los Santos de Maimona: Grafisur, 1979 – 1 – sp Bibl Santa Ana [390]
REVISTA OFICIAL FERIAS Y FIESTAS 1972 / Caceres. Ayuntamiento – Caceres: Edit. Extremadura, 1972 – 1 – sp Bibl Santa Ana [390]
REVISTA PARA UNIONES DE PARVULOS Y PRINCIPLANTES – 1955. 152p – 1 – 5.32 – us Baptist [240]
REVISTA PHARMACEUTICA. A ABELHA *see* REVISTA DA SOCIEDADE PHARMANEUTICA BRASILEIRA
REVISTA PORTUGUESA, COLONIAL E MARITIMA – Lisbon. 1897-Sept. 1910. Complete – 1 – 35.00r – us Hoover Inst Photo [073]
REVISTA PROGRAMA DE FERIA. MERIDA 1927 – 1 – sp Bibl Santa Ana [946]
REVISTA SEMANARIA DOS TRABALHOS LEGISLATIVOS DA CAMARA DOS SENHORES DEPUTADOS DEDICADA A ASSEMBLEA LEGISLATIVA DO BRAZIL – Rio de Janeiro, 1828 – 1,5,6 – bl Biblioteca [073]
REVISTA SUDAMERICANA DE BOTANICA – Montevideo. v1-10. 1934-57 – 49mf – 9 – 7337/2 – ne IDC [580]
REVISTA TECNICA INTEVEP – (1985-. 5,6,9) – v1-. 1981- – 1 – us UMI [600]
REVISTA TEOLOGICA – 1950-67 – 1 – 99.96 – us Baptist [240]
REVISTA TRIMENSAL / Instituto Historico e Geographico Brasileiro. Rio de Janeiro – v1-197. 1839-1947; Index. v1-90. 1839-1921. (Scattered issues wanting) – 1 – $638.00 – us L of C Photodup [972]
REVISTA TRIMESTRAL U. B. DE J – 1937. 174p – 1 – 6.09 – us Baptist [240]
REVISTA-PROGRAMA DE FERIA DE MERIDA. 1932 – Badajoz: La Alianza, 1932 – 1 – sp Bibl Santa Ana [946]
REVISTA-PROGRAMA DE FERIA. MERIDA – Badajoz: La Alianza, 1929 – 1 – sp Bibl Santa Ana [946]
REVISTA-PROGRAMA DE FERIAS. MERIDA – Badajoz: La Alianza, 1930 – 1 – sp Bibl Santa Ana [946]
REVISTAS HISPANO-AMERICANAS – (Based largely on periodicals indexed in S.E. Leavitt's bibliography, Revistas Hispano-Americanas, Indice Bibliografica, 1843-1935) – 391r – 1 – $20,990.00 – us OmniSys [073]
Revius, J *see* DAVENTRIAE ILLUSTRATAE SIVE HISTORIAE URBIS DAVENTRIENSIS, LIBRI SEX
THE REVIVAL : A SYMPOSIUM / McDowell, William Fraser et al – Cincinnati: Jennings & Graham; New York: Eaton & MAins, c1905 – 1mf – 9 – 0-8370-6279-9 – 1986-0279 – us A.T.L.A. [240]
REVIVAL ADDRESSES / Torrey, Reuben Archer – Chicago: Fleming H Revell, c1903 – 1mf – 9 – 0-8370-6427-9 – 1986-0427 – us A.T.L.A. [240]
THE REVIVAL AND THE PASTOR / Peck, Jonas Oramel – New York: Hunt & Eaton; Cincinnati: Cranston & Curts, 1894 – 1mf – 9 – 0-8370-6299-3 – 1985-0299 – us A.T.L.A. [240]
REVIVAL HYMNS / Earle, A B – 1870 – 1 – 5.00 – us Baptist [240]
REVIVAL IN INDIA : "YEARS OF THE RIGHT HAND OF THE MOST HIGH" / Dyer, Helen S – New York: Gospel Publ., 1907 – 1mf – us A.T.L.A. [240]
THE REVIVAL IN ST CATHARINES: A BRIEF HISTORY OF THE GREAT WORK, FROM ITS INCEPTION TO ITS CLOSE, UNDER THE LEADERSHIP OF THE REV. E. P. HAMMOND, AND THE PASTORS OF THE METHODIST, PRESBYTERIAN AND BAPTIST CHURCHES, AIDED BY THE POWER OF THE HOLY SPIRIT / Durham, J H – St. Catharines, Ont.: Burgoyne & Sherwood, 1880. 05204. (Pre-1900 Canadiana) – 9 – cn C.I.H.M. [971]
REVIVAL KINDLINGS / Knapp, Martin Wells – Cincinnati: God's Revivalist Off, c1890 – 1mf – 9 – 0-8370-6072-9 – 1986-0072 – us A.T.L.A. [240]
THE REVIVAL MANUAL / Lee, Luther – 1850 – 9 – us A.T.L.A. [240]
REVIVAL MELODIES, OR SONGS OF ZION – Dedicated to Elder Jacob Knapp. Boston: John Putnam, 1842. MUSIC 907 – 1 – us L of C Photodup [780]
THE REVIVAL OF A DEAD CHURCH / Broughton, Leonard Gaston – Chicago: Fleming H. Revell, 1900. 131p.1 fiche – 9 – us A.T.L.A. [240]
THE REVIVAL OF PRIESTLY LIFE IN THE SEVENTEENTH CENTURY IN FRANCE : A SKETCH / Lear, H L Sidney – London: Rivingtons, 1873 – 1mf – us A.T.L.A. [240]
REVIVAL SKETCHES AND MANUAL / Humphrey, Heman – New York: American Tract Society, c1859 – 2mf – us A.T.L.A. [240]
REVIVAL TORNADOES, OR, LIFE AND LABORS OF REV. JOSEPH H. WEBER : EVANGELIST, THE CONVERTED ROMAN CATHOLIC / Knapp, Martin Wells – Boston, Mass.: McDonald, Gill; Albion, Mich.: Revivalist Publishing, 1889 – 1mf – us A.T.L.A. [240]
REVIVAL TRUTH : BEING SERMONS HITHERTO UNPUBLISHED / M'Cheyne, Robert Murray; ed by Reid, William – London: James Nisbet, 1860 – 1mf – 9 – 0-8370-7237-9 – 1986-1237 – us A.T.L.A. [240]
REVIVALS : HOW AND WHEN? / Newell, William Whiting – New York: A C Armstrong, 1882 – 1mf – 9 – 0-8370-6288-8 – 1985-0288 – us A.T.L.A. [240]
REVIVALS : HOW TO PROMOTE THEM / McIlvaine, C P et al; ed by Doe, Walter P – New York: E B Treat, c1895 – 2mf – 9 – 0-8370-6155-5 – 1986-0155 – us A.T.L.A. [240]
REVIVALS OF RELIGION / Porter, James – 1850 – 1 – $50.00 – us Presbyterian [240]
REVIVALS OF RELIGION : SHOWING THEIR THEORY, MEANS, OBSTRUCTIONS, IMPORTANCE AND PERVERSIONS: WITH THE DUTY OF CHRISTIANS IN REGARD TO THEM / Porter, James – rev enl ed. New York: Nelson & Phillips; Cincinnati: Hitchcock & Walden, 1877 – 1mf – 9 – 0-8370-6931-9 – 1986-0931 – us A.T.L.A. [240]
REVIVIM – Lvov. Jerusalem. v. 1-6. 1908-19. BJ-91-72 1 – 9 – ne IDC [470]
REVIZIIA, ANALIZ BALANSA I OPREDELENIE KREDITOSPOSOBNOSTI KREDITNYKH KOOPERATOROV / Minervin, BM – M., 1927 – 3mf – 9 – COR 395/1 – ne IDC [334]

REVIZIIA KOOPERATIVNYKH TOVARISHCHESTV : INSTRUKTSIONNYE UKAZANIIA / Khizhniakov, V V – Ed 3. M., L., 1926 – 2mf – 9 – COR-281/1 – ne IDC [334]

REVIZIIA SOSTOIANIIA SREDSTV I OBOROTOV KOOPERATIVA / Makhov, V N – Ed 2. Novosibirsk, 1926 – 1mf – 9 – COR-267/1 – ne IDC [334]

REVIZIONNAIA OTSENKA DEIATEL'NOSTI TSENTROSOIUZA ZA VREMIA S 1 OKTIABRIA 1924 G. PO 1 IANVARIA 1936 G : DOKLAD REVIZIONNOI KOMMISSII 40-MU SOBRANIIU UPOLNOMOCHENNYKH TSENTROSOIUZA – M., 1926 – 3mf – 9 – COR-360/1 – ne IDC [334]

LA REVOCATION DE L'EDIT DE NANTES ET MME DE MAINTENON : SA VIE, SON CARACTERE, SON INFLUENCE / Pascal, Cesar – Paris: P. Monnerat, 1885 – 1mf – us A.T.L.A. [944]

Revoil, Georges *see* LA VALLEE DE DARROR; VOYAGES ET PAYS SOMALIS (AFRIQUE ORIENTALE) TYPES, SCENES, PAYSAGES.

REVOLI UT SII A I T SERKOV – (Library has: 1919, no. 1-8; 1920, no. 9-12; 1922, no. 1-3; 1923, no. 1/3; 1924, no. 1/2) – Moskva: Izd. Narodnogo komissariata i ustit sii, 1919-1924. 6v – 1 – CSUX90-S44 – us Hoover Inst Photo [947]

REVOLIUSIONNAIA PROZA – Sbornik pervyi sostavil evg. perlin. Kiev: Gos. izd-vo Ukrainy, 1924. 508p. Illus. No more published. 1 reel. 1185 – 1 – us U.W. Library [460]

REVOLIUTSII A I KULTURA : STATI ZA 1917 G / Gorky, Maksim – Berlin: Izd. T-va I.P. Ladyzhnikova, [1918] – 1 – CSUX88-B3741 – us Hoover Inst Photo [320]

REVOLIUTSIIA 1905 GODA I RUSSKAIA LITERATURA – Pod red. V.A. Desnitskogo i K.D. Muratovoi. M., L. 1956. BR-2088 2 – 8 – ne IDC [460]

REVOLIUTSIIA 1905-1907 GODOV NA TERRITORII MORDOVII / ed by Kotkov, K – Sbornik dokumentov i materialov. Saransk, 1955 – 1 – 35.00r – us Hoover Inst Photo [335]

REVOLIUTSIIA 1905-1907 GODOV V KAZAKHSTANE / Akademiia Nauk Kazakhskoi SSSR – Sbornik documental'nykh materialov. Alma-Ata, 1949 – 1 – 35.00r – us Hoover Inst Photo [335]

REVOLIUTSIIA I GRAZHDANSKAIA VOINA V KRYMU, 1917-1920 GG / Bunegin, Maksim F – Simferopol: Krymgosizdat, 1927 – 1 – CSUX88-B1329 – us Hoover Inst Photo [947]

REVOLIUTSIIA I KUL'TURA / Berdiaev, N A – Poliarnaia zvezda. 1905. BR-3250 2 – 8 – ne IDC [335]

REVOLIUTSIIA I NATSIONAL'NOSTI – Moscow. June-July 1937, nos. 6 7 (88 89) – 1 – 35.00r – us Hoover Inst Photo [335]

REVOLIUTSIIA I NATSIONAL'NOSTI – Moscow. v1-8. 1930-37 – 4r – 1 – us Ross [320]

REVOLIUTSIIA I NATSIONALNOSTI – Moscow. May 1930-Dec 1937. Incomplete – 1 – us NY Public [321]

REVOLIUTSIIA I VKP – (The revolution and the Communist party). 7 v. 1924-1928 – 3 – us Readex [947]

REVOLIUTSIIA I VNIESHNIAIA POLITIKA ROSSII : SOBRANIE MATERIALOV / Gubskii, N P – Moskva: "Nar. pravo", 1917 – 1 – CSUX89-B4546 – us Hoover Inst Photo [947]

REVOLIUTSIIA PRAVA – Sbornik.Moscow, 1925. 182p. Issued by the Section of Law and Construction of the Communist Academy.1 vol. issued.BR-9289/1 – 9 – ne IDC [947]

REVOLIUTSIONNA ROMANTIKA V BALGARSKOTO VAZRAZHDANE / Konstantinov, G – Sofiia. 1944. BR-3883 2 – 8 – ne IDC [460]

REVOLIUTSIONNAIA ROL' PRAVA I GOSUDARSTAVA / Stuchka, Petr Ivanovich – Ed. 2. M., 1923 – 2mf – 9 – ne IDC [320]

REVOLIUTSIONNAIA ROL' PRAVA I GOSUDARSTVA – M., 1921 – 2mf – 9 – 21.00 – ne IDC [340]

REVOLIUTSIONNAIA ROL' PRAVA I GOSUDARSTVA / Stuchka, Petr Ivanovich – Moskva 1932. 153 1 p. LL-4055 – 1 – us L of C Photodup [340]

REVOLIUTSIONNAIA ROL' SOVETSKOGO PRAVA / Stuchka, Petr Ivanovich – Ed. 3. M., 1934 – 2mf – 9 – ne IDC [340]

REVOLIUTSIONNAIA ROSSIIA – n1-77. 1900-05 – 1 – us Ross [947]

REVOLIUTSIONNAIA ZAKONNOST' I NASHA KARATEL'NAIA POLITIKA / Sol'ts, A & Fainblit, S – Moscow, 1925. 127p. BR-9443/1 – 9 – ne IDC [340]

REVOLIUTSIONNOE DVIZHENIE V IRKUTSKOI GUBERNII V PERIOD PERVOI RUSSKOI REVOLIUTSII / Irkutsk. (Province). Gosudarstvennyi arkhiv – sbornik documental'nykh materialov. Irkutsk, 1955 – 1 – 35.00r – us Hoover Inst Photo [947]

REVOLIUTSIONNOE DVIZHENIE V OMSKE V GODY PERVOI RUSSKOI REVOLIUTSII 1905-1907 / Omsk. Siberia. (Province). Upravlenie vnutrennikh Arkhivnyi otdel'. del' – Sbornik dokumental'nykh materialov. Omsk, 1957 – 1 – 35.00r – us Hoover Inst Photo [947]

REVOLIUTSIONNOE DVIZHENIE V SIBIRI I NA DAL'NEM VOSTOKE / ed by Flerov, V S – Tomsk, 1965-1970. v. 3-5 – 1 – 35.00r – us Hoover Inst Photo [335]

Revoliutsionnogo Kommunizma Partii. Tsentral'nogo komiteta *see* VOLIA TRUDA

REVOLIUTSIONNYE SOBYTIIA NA ALTAE V 1905-1907 GG / ed by Borodkin, P A – Sbornik dokumentov. Barnaul, 1967 – 1 – 35.00r – us Hoover Inst Photo [947]

REVOLIUTSIONNYI VOSTOK – Moscow. 1927-1937 – 1 – 35.00r – us Hoover Inst Photo [335]

REVOLIUTSIONNYI VOSTOK – Moscow. v. 1, no. 1-v. 11, no. 1. 1927-1937 – 1 – us NY Public [335]

REVOLIUTSIONNYI VOSTOK / Nauchno-Issle Dovatel'skaia Assotsiatsiia Poizucheniiu Natsional'nykh i Kolonial'nykh Problem – Moscow. v1-11. 1927-37 – 3r – 1 – us Ross [335]

REVOLIUTSIONNYI VOSTOK / Nauchno-issledo-vatel'skoi assotsiatsii po izucheniiu natsional'nykh i kolonial'nykh problem – v. 1-41. M. 1927-37. Lacking: v. 1, 1927; v. 9-10, 1929; v. 13-14, 1929; v. 29-33, 1934; v. 35-40, 1934. BR-5655 2 – 8 – ne IDC [073]

REVOLJUCIONNAJA ROSSIJA / Partija socialistov-revoljucionerov – Prague, 1920-21, 1922 (incompl)-1931 – 1 – us Hoover Inst Photo [072]

REVOLT : THE VOICE OF THE MILITANT WORKER – v1-3. no. 8 (all publ). 1911-1912 – 1 reel – 1 – $65.00 – us UPA [335]

THE REVOLT IN INDIA 1857-1858: ANNOTATED BIBLIOGRAPHY OF ENGLISH LANGUAGE MATERIALS / Ladendorf, J M – I-1056 1. 1966 – ne IDC [950]

REVOLT IN PARADISE / K'tut Tantri [pseud] – In Indonesian. SE-4808 1. 1964 – 9 – ne IDC [950]

THE REVOLT OF ISLAM : A POEM, IN TWELVE CANTOS / Shelley, Percy Bysshe – London: Printed for C. and J. Ollier, 1818 – 1 roll – 1 – 1-55879-282-1 – uk Libr Preservation [810]

THE REVOLT OF THE FIELD: A SKETCH OF THE RISE AND PROGRESS OF THE MOVEMENT AMONG THE AGRICULTURAL LABOURERS, KNOWN AS THE "NATIONAL AGRICULTURAL LABOURERS' UNION" : WITH A REPRINT OF THE CORRESPONDENCE TO THE DAILY NEWS DURING A TOUR THROUGH CANADA WITH MR. ARCH / Clayden, Arthur – London: Hodder and Stroughton, 1874. 006078. (Pre-1900 Canadiana) – 9 – cn C.I.H.M. [331]

LE REVOLTE – 9oct 1910-28 sept 1913. mq 18 aout, 27 oct 1912. devient: L' Avant-garde. 5 oct 1913-5 juil 1914. MQ 5 mai 1913. Lens – 1 – fr A.C.R.P.P. [073]

LE REVOLTE – fevr 1879-10 sept 1887. devenu: La Revolte. 17 sept 1887-mars 1894 contient le Suppl. litteraire. devenu: Les Temps nouveaux. puis Ex-journal La Revolte; Revue internationale des idees communistes. mai 1895-aout 1914, mai 1916-juin juil 1921. mq mai 1916-avr 1919. Geneve puis Paris. Pour le suppl. litteraire voir a: Les Temps nouveaux – 1 – fr A.C.R.P.P. [073]

A REVOLUCAO – Campanha, 5 Jan-15 Dec 1889 – 1,5,6 – bl Biblioteca [072]

REVOLUCIJA – avr 1918. devenu: Vsemirnaja revolucija. juin-dec 1918.devenu: Svjetska revolucija. janv-mars 1919. Moscou. UDC. G.F.P. 232 – 1 – fr A.C.R.P.P. [073]

REVOLUCION CONSTRUCTIVA DEL PUEBLO : PLAN ARGENTINO DE MOVILIZACION INDUSTRIAL / Catalano, Luciano R – [Buenos Aires]: Editorial Catedra Lisandro de la Torre, 1959 – 1 – CSUXADN0108-B – us Hoover Inst Photo [338]

LA REVOLUCION DEL 4 DE JUNIO Y LOS PARTIDOS POLITICOS / Benitez, Juan J – La Plata [Argentina]: Fanetty y Gasperini, 1943 – 1 – CSUXADQ4899-B – us Hoover Inst Photo [320]

LA REVOLUCION DEL 43 / Casal, Horacio Nestor – [Buenos Aires: Centro Editor de America Latina, 1971] – 1 – CSUXADQ6619-B – us Hoover Inst Photo [320]

LA REVOLUCION ESPANOLA / Maranon, Gregorio – n.p. 1938. Fiche W 1022. (Blodgett Collection of Spanish Civil War Pamphlets) – 9 – us H.U. College Libr [946]

LA REVOLUCION ESPANOLA ANTE EL MUNDO – Barcelona, 1937. Fiche W1137. (Blodgett Collection of Spanish Civil War Pamphlets) – 9 – us H.U. College Libr [946]

LA REVOLUCION NACIONAL-SINDICALISTA Y LOS TRABAJADORES / Montero Diaz, Santiago – Reimpresion. Zaragoza, 1939. Fiche W 1057. (Blodgett Collection of Spanish Civil War Pamphlets) – 9 – us H.U. College Libr [946]

LA REVOLUCION PERONISTA / Camparo, Hector, Jose – Buenos Aires: Editorial Universitaria, [1973] – 1 – CSUXADH4109-B – us Hoover Inst Photo [320]

LA REVOLUCION PERONISTA / Galimberti, Rodolfo – [Buenos Aires]: Fondo Editorial de la Revolucion Peronista, [1983] – 1 – CSUXAJB7919-B – us Hoover Inst Photo [320]

LA REVOLUCION SOCIAL ARGENTINA / Aloe, Carlos – Buenos Aires: Gobernacion de Buenos Aires, [1953] – 1 – CSUXADN3479-B – us Hoover Inst Photo [320]

LA REVOLUCION Y EL PERONISMO / Cooke, John William – [Buenos Aires?]: Ediciones A.R.P., 1968 – 1 – CSUXADL6502-B – us Hoover Inst Photo [320]

LA REVOLUCION Y LAS REVOLUCIONES / Gonzalez Paz, Amancio – [Buenos Aires]: Ediciones "La Cruz y la Espada", [1944] – 1 – CSUXADJ2741-B – us Hoover Inst Photo [320]

REVOLUSI AGAMA / Amrullah, Abdul Malik Karim – SE-4587 1. 1949 – 9 – ne IDC [950]

REVOLUSI OKTOBER DAN KEBANGUNAN RAKJAT ASIA / Sukarno, Pres. Indonesia – SE 2093 1. 1957 – 9 – ne IDC [335]

REVOLUSI SOSIALIS, 7 NOV 1917 / Communist Party. Indonesia – 1947. SE-5251-1 – 9 – ne IDC [335]

REVOLUSIONER – (Lacking: 1945/1946, V.1(1-3, 6-18, 20-23, 25, 30)) – Jogjakarta, 1946-1947 – 8mf – 9 – SE-406/1 – ne IDC [073]

LA REVOLUTION – no. 4-6, 13-56. Paris. fevr-mars 1909 – 1 – fr A.C.R.P.P. [073]

LA REVOLUTION – no. spec., no. 1-59. Paris. 17 sept-2 dec 1851 – 1 – fr A.C.R.P.P. [073]

REVOLUTION – (Also available on CD-ROM) – France. 1980-1995 – 2r per y – 5,6 – Sfr722.00 – sz Infoprint [944]

REVOLUTION – Organe des jeunesses socialistes de la region parisienne. Dir. David Rousset. Paris. dec 1934-avr 1939 – 1 – fr A.C.R.P.P. [073]

REVOLUTION : UNABHANGIGES SOCIALDEMOKRATISCHES JAHRBUCH FUER POLITIK UND PROLETARISCHE KULTUR – Berlin, 1920 – 1r – 1 – us Ross [335]

THE REVOLUTION – v1-8, no. 5 (weekly: all publ). 1868-1871 – 2r – 1 – $195.00 – us UPA [360]

THE REVOLUTION AND CULTURAL PROBLEMS IN CUBA / Castro, Fidel – In Indonesian. SE-10,454 1. 1963 – 9 – ne IDC [335]

REVOLUTION AND INDEPENDENCE, 1775-1815 – 1 – us Ross [975]

REVOLUTION AND QUIT INDIA / Tagore, Saumyendranath – 1946. 40p – 1 – us U.W. Library [950]

REVOLUTION BEFORE BREAKFAST : ARGENTINA, 1941-1946 / Greenup, Ruth Robinson & Greenup, Leonard – Chapel Hill: Univ. of North Carolina Press, 1947 – 1 – CSUXADQ4422-B – us Hoover Inst Photo [320]

LA REVOLUTION CHIMIQUE : LAVOISIER... / Berthelot, Marcelin – Paris: Alcan, 1890 – 1 – F183.12 – fr Armell [540]

LA REVOLUTION DE 1848 – puis et les revolutions du XIXe siecle: 1830, 1848, 1870. Bulletin de la Societe d'histoire de la revolution de 1848. Paris. mars 1904-51 – 1 – fr A.C.R.P.P. [073]

REVOLUTION ET CONTRE-REVOLUTION EN ESPAGNE. LUEURS SUR L'ESPAGNE REPUBLICAINE / Lapeyre, Paul – Paris, 1938. Fiche W990. (Blodgett Collection of Spanish Civil War Pamphlets) – 9 – us H.U. College Libr [946]

REVOLUTION FLUGSCHRIFTEN : GENERALSEKRETARIAT ZUM STUDIUM DES BOLSCHEWISMUS – Berlin. n2 1919; ns: n3 – 1r – 1 – us Ross [073]

LA REVOLUTION FRANCAISE – Paris. 13 janv-14 juin 1879 – 1 – fr A.C.R.P.P. [073]

LA REVOLUTION FRANCAISE... / Basdevant, J – Paris, 1901 – 3mf – 9 – ILM-1139/1 – ne IDC [340]

LA REVOLUTION FRANCAISE. ESTAMPES ET DESSINS / Reunion des musees nationaux. Paris – 1939. 1 fiche – 9 – fr Réunion [760]

THE REVOLUTION IN CONSTANTINOPLE AND TURKEY : A DIARY / Ramsay, William Mitchell – London: Hodder and Stoughton, 1909 – 1mf – us A.T.L.A. [956]

THE REVOLUTION IN TANNER'S LANE. EDITED BY [THE AUTHOR'S] FRIEND, REUBEN SHAPCOTT / White, William Hale – London: Trbner, 1887 – 1 roll – 1 – 1-55879-453-0 – uk Libr Preservation [880]

LA REVOLUTION NATIONALE – Hebdomadaire politique et litteraire. Paris. 12 oct 1941-17 aout 1944 – 1 – fr A.C.R.P.P. [073]

LA REVOLUTION PROLETARIENNE – no. 1-301. Paris. 1925-aout 1939 – 1 – fr A.C.R.P.P. [073]

REVOLUTION QUEBECOISE – Montreal. v1 no 1-8. 1964-65. SEM16P241 – 1r – 5 – Can$12.00 – cn Bibl Nat [440]

LA REVOLUTION SOCIALE – I, no. 1-16; II, no. 1-40. Saint-Cloud. 12 sept 1880-18 sept 1881 – 1 – fr A.C.R.P.P. [073]

Revolution Socialiste Francais *see* LE FRANCISTE

LA REVOLUTION SURREALISTE – no. 1-12. dec 1924-29. remplace par: Le Surrealisme au service de la revolution. no. 1-6. juin 1930-mai 1933. Paris – 1 – fr A.C.R.P.P. [073]

LA REVOLUTION SURREALISTE – Paris, 1924-29 – 1r – 1 – £60.00 – uk Chadwyck [760]

Revolution Vendee *see* MEMOIRE ADRESSE A L'ASSEMBLEE NATIONALE PAR PLUSIEURS CURES DU DEPARTEMENT DE LA VENDEE

DER REVOLUTIONAER – Mannheim. Feb. 19, 1919-Oct. 1920; nos. 1-25 – 1 – 35.00r – us Hoover Inst Photo [335]

DER REVOLUTIONAER – Mannheim, Germany. 1919-23 – 1 – gw Mikrofilm [072]

REVOLUTIONAERE GEDICHTE / Barthel, Max – Stuttgart: Internationaler sozialistischer Jugendverlag, [1919?] – 1r – 1 – us U.W. Library [810]

REVOLUTIONARY AGE / Communist Labor Party – 1-2, no. 7 (all publ). 1918-19 – 1 reel – 1 – $115.00 – us UPA [335]

REVOLUTIONARY AGE / Communist Party. U.S.A – 1-3 2+5 (all publ). 1929-1932 – 2r – 1 – $115.00 – us UPA [335]

THE REVOLUTIONARY ALMANAC – 19??-. New York: Rabelais Press – 1 – us U.W. Library [335]

REVOLUTIONARY CONSTRUCTIVISM / Kaznelson, B – New York, 1937. BJ-28-12/1 – 9 – ne IDC [750]

THE REVOLUTIONARY FLAME OF BANDUNG / Asian-African Conference. First Executive Command, 10th Anniversary – SE-5424 1. 1965 – 9 – ne IDC [335]

REVOLUTIONARY JUSTICE IN SPAIN / Berryer – London, 1937. Fiche W 753. (Blodgett Collection of Spanish Civil War Pamphlets) – 9 – us H.U. College Libr [946]

THE REVOLUTIONARY MOVEMENT IN SPAIN / Dashar, M – NY, 1935? Fiche W 823. (Blodgett Collection of Spanish Civil War Pamphlets) – 9 – us H.U. College Libr [946]

REVOLUTIONARY PENSIONERS – Item C. A transcript of the pension list of the U.S. for 1813. Listed alphabetically by states. 47p.SW16-0065 – 5 – us A.G.L.L. [975]

THE REVOLUTIONARY RECORDS OF THE STATE OF GEORGIA / Georgia – v1-3. Comp. by Allen D. Candler. Indexed. F-0133/F-0135 – 9 – us A.G.L.L. [920]

REVOLUTIONARY REVIEW – London, UK. 1889. -irr. 9 feet – 1 – uk British Libr Newspaper [072]

REVOLUTIONARY SOLDIERS BURIED IN ILLINOIS / Illinois. Military Records – By Harriet J. Walker, 1917. Includes index, 178p. SW16-0093 – 5 – us A.G.L.L. [920]
REVOLUTIONARY SOLDIERS IN ALABAMA – Comp. by Thomas M. Owen, 1967. Listed alphabetically. Orig. publ., 1911. 3 fiches. F-0002 – 9 – us A.G.L.L. [978]
REVOLUTIONARY SOLDIERS IN KENTUCKY, ALSO A ROSTER OF THE VIRGINIA NAVY – Comp. by Anderson Chenault Quisenberry, 1968. Orig. publ. 1896 in Year Book, Kentucky Society, Sons of the American Revolution. Indexed. 4 fiches. F-0854 – 9 – us A.G.L.L. [920]
REVOLUTIONARY WAR PENSION AND BOUNTY-LAND WARRANT APPLICATION FILES, 1800-1900 / U. S. Veterans Administration – 2670 rolls. M804 – 1 – us Nat'l Archives [324]
REVOLUTIONARY WAR PRIZE CASES: RECORDS OF THE COURT OF APPEAL IN CASES OF CAPTURE, 1776-87 / U.S. Court of Appeals – 15 rolls. Printed guide – 1 – M162 – us Nat'l Archives [324]
REVOLUTIONARY WAR ROLLS, 1775-83 / U.S. War Department. Collection of Revolutionary War Records – 138 rolls. M246 – 1 – us Nat'l Archives [324]
REVOLUTIONARY WAR SOLDIERS BURIED IN GEAUGA CO., OHIO / Sherman, E H – (Typescript compilation; filmed by Genealogical Society of Utah, 1974) – 1r – 1 – us Western Res [920]
REVOLUTIONARY WORLD – v1-50 1973-82 1; v16-50 5,6,9 – us UMI [900]
LES REVOLUTIONNAIRES DE L'A.B.C / Erdant, Alexandre – Paris: Coulon-Pineau, 1854. 281p. 3 fiches. (Political Science Collection). (Historical Studies Series) – 9 – 8.00 – fr Bibl Nationale [320]
REVOLUTIONS DE FRANCE ET DE BRABANT – Par Camille Desmoulins. no. 1-86. 28 nov 1789-juil 1791.; no. 87-104. juil a dec 1791. Paris – 1 – fr A.C.R.P.P. [073]
REVOLUTIONS DE LA LANGUE FRANCAISE DEPUIS CHARLEMAGNE JUSQU'A SAINT LOUIS. LEBER, [J.M.] C. COLLECTION DES MEILLEURES DISSERTATIONS, NOTICES ET TRAITES PARTICULIERS RELATIFS A L'HISTORE DE FRANCE / Levesque de la Ravaliere, P-A – Paris. v14(p161-244). 1838 – 2mf – 9 – ne IDC [440]
REVOLUTIONS DE PARIS, DEDIEES A LA NATION ET AU DISTRICT DES PETITS-AUGUSTINS – Paris. juil 1789-fevr 1794 – 1 – fr A.C.R.P.P. [073]
REVOLUTIONS IN ENGLISH HISTORY / Vaughan, Robert – London: J.W. Parker, 1859-1863 – 5mf – us A.T.L.A. [941]
THE REVOLUTIONS OF CIVILISATION / Petrie, William Matthew Flinders – London, New York: Harper and Brothers, 1912 – 1mf – us A.T.L.A. [900]
DIE REVOLUTIONSKIRCHEN ENGLANDS : EIN BEITRAG ZUR INNEREN GESCHICHTE DER ENGLISCHEN KIRCHE UND DER REFORMATION / Weingarten, Hermann – Leipzig: Breitkopf und Haertel, 1868 – 2mf – us A.T.L.A. [240]
REVOLVING LOAN FUNDS AND CREDIT PROGRAMMES FOR FISHING COMMUNITIES : MANAGEMENT GUIDELINES – 1989 – 172p – it F.A.O. [332]
REVONTULET – Lulea, Sweden. 1919-21 – 2r – 1 – sw Kungliga [072]
LA REVUE – Paris. 1948-67 – 1 – fr A.C.R.P.P. [073]
LA REVUE – Paris. avr 1855-janv 1858 (I-IX) – 1 – fr A.C.R.P.P. [073]
REVUE : UNABHAENGIGE GERICHTSZEITUNG – Bremen, 1928-mar 23 1933 – 2r – 1 – Inquire at Mikrofilmarchiv for details – gw Misc Inst [360]
REVUE ADMINISTRATIVE – Paris. v1-21. 1948-68 – 5,9 – Dfl2,100.00; Dfl100.00v – ne Swets [323]
REVUE AFRICAINE – Algiers. 1856-1957; 1959-62 – 1 – 35.00r – us Hoover Inst Photo [073]
LA REVUE AGRICOLE – St-Hyacinthe, Canada. 1/16 mai 1875-v1 n8. avr 1876 – 1r – 1 – Can$30.00 – cn Can Microfilming [630]
REVUE AGRICOLE, MANUFACTURIERE, COMMERCIALE ET DE COLONISATION – (A absorbe: Agriculteur. L'autre ed de lang: Lower Canada Agriculturist, Manufacturing, Commercial, and Colonization Intelligencer) – Montreal: Bureau au depot agricole provincial, [1861-1868] – 9 – cn C.I.H.M. [630]
REVUE ALBANAISE / Albania – v. 1-12. 1897-1909 – 1 – 38.00 – us L of C Photodup [949]
REVUE ANECDOTIQUE DES DEUX MONDES – Dir. A.B. de Liptay. no. 1-12. Paris. juin-dec 1894 – 1 – fr A.C.R.P.P. [073]
REVUE ARTISTIQUE – London, UK. 17 Jun-30 Sept 1882 – 1 – uk British Libr Newspaper [072]
REVUE AUGUSTINIENNE – 1(1902)-17(1910) – 223mf – 9 – Dfl760.00 – ne Slangenburg [073]
REVUE BANQUES – 1989-1995 – 2r per y – 5,6 – Sfr481.00 – sz Infoprint [332]
REVUE BENEDICTINE – Province de Namur. v1-9. 1884-92 – 101mf – 9 – H-229/2 – ne IDC [240]
REVUE BIBLIQUE – 1(1892)-53(1946) – 612mf – 9 – Dfl2,142.00 – ne Slangenburg [073]
REVUE BIBLIQUE – (Published as Vivre et Penser in 1941) – Paris. 1892-1941. v1-50 – 597mf – 8 – ne IDC [220]
REVUE BIOLOGIQUE DU NORD DE LA FRANCE – Lille. v1-7. 1888/1889-1894/1895 – 65mf – 9 – 1186/2 – ne IDC [574]
LA REVUE BLANCHE – Paris. oct 1891-avr 1903 (n.s., I-XXX) – 1 – fr A.C.R.P.P. [073]
LA REVUE BLEUE – Montreal: G W Parent [1895] – 9 – cn C.I.H.M. [840]
REVUE BLEUE, POLITIQUE ET LITTERAIRE – Dec 1863-Sept 1939 – 1 – 1886.00 – us L of C Photodup [073]
REVUE BOSSUET – Oeuvres inedites, documents et bibliographie. Paris. 1900-11 – 5 – fr A.C.R.P.P. [073]
REVUE BOTANIQUE / ed by Duchartre, P E S – Paris, 1845-47 – 18mf – 9 – 5547/2 – ne IDC [580]
REVUE BOURDALOUE – Sermons inedits, lettres, documents, bibliographie. Dir. Eugene Griselle. Paris. 1902-04 – 5 – fr A.C.R.P.P. [073]
REVUE BRESILIENNE, OU RECUEIL DE MORCEAUX ORIGINAUX SUR LES AFFAIRES INTERIEURES DE L'EMPIRE, LA POLITIQUE, ET SUR LA STATISTIQUE LOCALE – Rio de Janeiro, Sep 1830 – 1,5,6 – bl Biblioteca [073]
REVUE BRITANNIQUE – ou Choix d'articles traduits des meilleurs ecrits periodiques de la Grande-Bretagne. Par MM. Saulnier fils, Dondey-Dupre fils, etc. Paris. juin 1825-fevr 1831 – 1 – fr A.C.R.P.P. [073]
REVUE BRITANNIQUE, OU CHOIX D'ARTICLES TRADUITS DES MEILLEURS ECRITS PERIODIQUES DE LA GRANDE-BRETAGNE – Paris, 1825-71 – 2289mf – 9 – H-1393/2 – ne IDC [941]
REVUE BRITANNIQUE, OU CHOIX D'ARTICLES TRADUITS DES MEILLEURS ECRITS PERIODIQUES DE LA GRANDE-BRETAGNE. – Paris. (Ser. 1 – Ser. 9). 1825-1873; annee 74-77. 1898-1901 and tables 1825-1835 – 1 – us NY Public [420]
REVUE BRYOLOGIQUE ET LICHENOLOGIQUE – (v42-46 1915-19; v54 1927 have not been publ) – Paris. v1-66. 1874-1941 – 163mf – 9 – 2230c/2 – ne IDC [580]
LA REVUE CANADIENNE : PERIODIQUE LITTERAIRE IMPORTANT – Montreal, Canada. 14 dec 1844-3 oct 1848 – 1r – 1 – Can$50.00 – cn Can Microfilming [073]
REVUE CANADIENNE – v1-52. 1864-1907. NS. 1909-1922 – 1 – cn Precision [971]
REVUE CANADIENNE D'ECONOMIE PUBLIQUE ET COOPERATIVE = CANADIAN JOURNAL OF PUBLIC AND COOPERATIVE ECONOMY – Montreal. v1- 1968- – 5 – cn Micromedia [330]
LA REVUE CATHOLIQUE – Tarbes. 1872-81 – 1 – fr A.C.R.P.P. [240]
LA REVUE CATHOLIQUE DE TROYES – Troyes. 1873-80 – 1 – fr A.C.R.P.P. [073]
REVUE CATHOLIQUE DES INSTITUTIONS ET DU DROIT, PAR UNE SOCIETE DE JURISCONSULTES & DE PUBLICISTES. – Grenoble. On film: v1-30, 1-77 n.s.; 1872-1939 – 1 – 529.00 – us L of C Photodup [340]
REVUE CHRETIENNE – (Includes index 1854-1903) – v1-72. 1854-avr 1926 (complete) – 28r – 1 – ATLA S0270 – us A.T.L.A. [073]
LA REVUE CLAIRE – no. 1. Paris. fevr 1898 – 1 – fr A.C.R.P.P. [073]
REVUE COLEOPTEROLOGIQUE / ed by Branden, C van den – Bruxelles, Berlin. v1(1-4). 1882 – 2mf – 9 – Z-999/2 – ne IDC [580]
LA REVUE COMIQUE A L'USAGE DES GENS SERIEUX – no. 1-38. nov 1848-49. devenu: Musee comique. Toutes sortes de choses en images. no. 1-20. 1850. Paris – 1 – fr A.C.R.P.P. [073]
LA REVUE COMMERCIALE – Quebec: N Le Vasseur, E LaSalle, [1894] – 9 – cn C.I.H.M. [380]
LA REVUE COMMUNISTE – no. 1-17. Paris. mars 1920-juil 1921 – 1 – fr A.C.R.P.P. [073]
LA REVUE CONTEMPORAINE – Litterature, politique et philosophique. Paris. 1885-aout sept 1886 – 1 – fr A.C.R.P.P. [073]
REVUE CONTEMPORAINE ET ATHENAEUM FRANCAIS – Paris. 1854-60 – 1 – fr A.C.R.P.P. [073]
LA REVUE CRITIQUE – Journal litteraire hebdomadaire. no. 1-130. Paris. 1882-juil 1884 – 1 – fr A.C.R.P.P. [073]
REVUE CRITIQUE – no. 1-4. Paris. janv-mars 1840 – 5 – fr A.C.R.P.P. [073]
REVUE CRITIQUE DE DROIT INTERNATIONAL PRIVE – Paris. 1905-59 – 1 – fr A.C.R.P.P. [340]
LA REVUE CRITIQUE DE LEGISLATION ET DE JURISPRUDENCE DU CANADA – Montreal: Dawson, [1871-1875] – 9 – cn C.I.H.M. [340]
REVUE CRITIQUE D'HISTOIRE ET DE LITTERATURE – Paris. v1-102. 1866-1920 – 991mf – 9 – H-1394/2 – ne IDC [944]
LA REVUE D'ART – Revue hebdomadaire. Paris. nov 1899-janv 1900 – 1 – fr A.C.R.P.P. [073]
REVUE D'ART DRAMATIQUE ET MUSICAL – Paris, 1886-1909 – 10r – 1 – us Ross [790]
REVUE D'ART DRAMATIQUE ET MUSICAL – Paris. v. 1-40. 1886-1896; n.s. v. 1-9. 1897-1900; annea1e 16-24 1901-Jan 1909 – 1 – us NY Public [780]
REVUE D'ASSYRIOLOGIE ET D'ARCHEOLOGIE ORIENTALE – (Missing: v3(p33-65) 1893; v4(p1-37) 1897; v6(p1-33) 1904; v16(p1-49) 1919) – Paris. v1-38. 1884-1941 – 124mf – 9 – NE-477c/1 – ne IDC [930]
REVUE D'AUJOURD'HUI – no. 1-15. Paris. janv-sept 1890 – 1 – fr A.C.R.P.P. [073]
REVUE DE BELGIQUE – Bruxelles. v. 1-133. 1869-1914 – 1 – 488.00 – us L of C Photodup [073]
REVUE DE CYTOLOGIE ET DE BIOLOGIE VEGETALE – v1-40. 1934-77 – 1,5,6 – us Princeton Micro [580]
REVUE DE CYTOLOGIE ET DE BIOLOGIE VEGETALE: LE BOTANISTE – v1-2. 1978-79 – 1,5,6 – us Princeton Micro [580]
REVUE DE DEFENSE NATIONALE – Red. en chef Edmond Delage. Nancy. mai 1939-mai 1940, juil 1945-66 – 1 – fr A.C.R.P.P. [073]
REVUE DE DROIT CANONIQUE – Strasbourg. mars 1951-72 (t. I-XXII) – 5 – fr A.C.R.P.P. [073]
REVUE DE DROIT INTERNATIONAL – Paris. v1-25. 1927-1940 – 212mf – 9 – IL-9/1 – ne IDC [340]
REVUE DE DROIT INTERNATIONAL DE SCIENCES DIPLOMATIQUES, POLITIQUES ET SOCIALES – Geneva. v1-18. 1923-1940 – 82mf – 9 – IL-13/1 – ne IDC [300]
REVUE DE DROIT INTERNATIONAL ET DE LEGISLATION COMPAREE – Bruxelles, 1869-1939. S1: v1-30. 1869-98; S2: v1-16. 1899-1914; S3: v1-20. 1920-39 – 548mf – 9 – IL-7/1 – ne IDC [320]
REVUE DE DROIT JUDICIARE *see* RAPPORTS DE PRATIQUE DE QUEBEC
LA REVUE DE GATINEAU – Gatineau, Canada. 3 sep 1959-v15 n43. 4 fev 1976 – 1r – 1 – Can$25.00 – cn Can Microfilming [073]
LA REVUE DE GATINEAU – Gatineau. v7-15. 1966- 1977). SEM35P281 – 15r – 1 – Can$818.00 – cn Bibl Nat [971]
LA REVUE DE GATINEAU : SECTEUR GATINEAU-TEMPLETON – Gatineau. v15-18. 1977-81. SEM35P287 – 6r – 1 – Can$432.00 – cn Bibl Nat [971]
LA REVUE DE GATINEAU : SECTEUR POINTE-GATINEAU-TOURAINE – Gatineau. v15-18. 1977-1981. SEM35P288 – 5r – 1 – Can$237.00 – cn Bibl Nat [072]
LA REVUE DE GATINEAU (1981) – Gatineau, v18- 1981-. SEM35P289 – 39r – 1 – cn Bibl Nat [073]
LA REVUE DE GATINEAU (BUCKINGHAM, QUEBEC) – Buckingham. v1- 1959-. SEM105P1357 – 1mf – 9 – Can$2.25 – cn Bibl Nat [073]
REVUE DE GEOMORPHOLOGIE DYNAMIQUE – (v1-13. Dfl35.00v; v14-29. Dfl75.00v) – Paris. v1-29. 1950-80 – 5,9 – Dfl1,655.00 – ne Swets [550]
LA REVUE DE GRANBY – (Cont by: La Nouvelle Revue 5 oct 1961-27 dec 1978) – Granby, Canada. v1 n1. 25 jan 1930-28 sep 1961 – 28r – 1 – Can$65.00r – cn Can Microfilming [073]
REVUE DE HONGRIE : ORGANE DE LA SOCIETE LITTERAIRE FRANCAISE DE BUDAPEST – (Missing: v1-2(1-8) 1908; 1914(1) de la serie entierement consacree a la guerre) – Budapest. v1-23. 1908-20 – 184mf – 9 – R-5245/2 – ne IDC [440]
LA REVUE DE JURISPRUDENCE / Canada. Quebec – v1-48. 1890-1942 (all publ) – 314mf – 9 – $471.00 – LLMC 81-064 – us L.L.M.C. [340]
REVUE DE LA DOCUMENTATION – The Hague. v1-34. 1934-65 – 5,9 – Dfl1,190.00; Dfl35.00v – ne Swets [070]
REVUE DE LA JEUNESSE – oct 1909-14. devenu: La Revue des jeunes. 1915-janv 1929. Paris – 1 – fr A.C.R.P.P. [073]
REVUE DE LA LITTERATURE MODERNE – Paris. nov 1889-mars 1892 – 1 – fr A.C.R.P.P. [073]
REVUE DE LA MUSIQUE RELIGIEUSE, POPULAIRE ET CLASSIQUE – v. 1-4. 1845-1854 – 1 – us Schnase [780]
REVUE DE LA PAPETERIE FRANCAISE ET ETRANGERE – Paris. -f 1 Jan 1900-1 Aug 1914. 9 reels – 1 – uk British Libr Newspaper [073]
LA REVUE DE LA PETITE-NATION – Saint Andre Avellin. v24- 1985-. SEM35P243 – 15r – 1 – cn Bibl Nat [073]
REVUE DE LA RENAISSANCE / Amis du XVIe siecle et de la Pleiade – Organe international mensuel. Paris. 1901-13 – 5 – fr A.C.R.P.P. [073]
LA REVUE DE LA SEMAINE – Sherbrooke, Canada. 12 jul-25 oct 1900 – 1r – 1 – Can$40.00 – cn Can Microfilming [073]
REVUE DE L'ACTION POPULAIRE – devenu: Travaux de l'action populaire. no. 1-9; n.s., no. 1-193. Paris. oct 1945-65 – 1 – fr A.C.R.P.P. [073]
REVUE DE L'AMERIQUE LATINE – Paris. 1922-32 – 1 – fr A.C.R.P.P. [073]
REVUE DE L'ARMORIQUE ET DE L'OUEST – Saint-Brieuc puis Quimper. sept 1844-sept 1846 – 1 – fr A.C.R.P.P. [073]
REVUE DE L'ART – Montreal: [s.n., 1895-189-?] – 9 – cn C.I.H.M. [700]
REVUE DE LEGISLATION ET DE JURISPRUDENCE – [Montreal?: s.n., 1845-1848] (Montreal: Lovell et Gibson) – 9 – cn C.I.H.M. [340]
REVUE DE LEGISLATION ET DE LA JURISPRUDENCE / Canada. Quebec – v1-3. 1845-48 (all publ) – 18mf – 9 – $27.00 – LLMC 81-085 – us L.L.M.C. [340]
REVUE DE L'ENSEIGNEMENT DES LANGUES VIVANTES – Paris. mars 1884-mai 1940 – 1 – fr A.C.R.P.P. [073]
REVUE DE L'ENSEIGNEMENT PRIMAIRE ET PRIMAIRE SUPERIEUR – Paris. sept 1893-juil 1929 – 1 – fr A.C.R.P.P. [073]
LA REVUE DE L'EPOQUE – no. 1-32. Paris. oct 1919-mai 1923 – 1 – fr A.C.R.P.P. [073]
REVUE DE L'EVOLUTION SOCIALE, SCIENTIFIQUE ET LITTERAIRE – no. 1-36. Paris. fevr 1891-sept 1892 – 1 – fr A.C.R.P.P. [073]
REVUE DE L'HISTOIRE DE L'EGLISE DE FRANCE – 1(1910)-26(1940) – 284mf – 9 – Dfl868.00 – ne Slangenburg [073]
REVUE DE L'HISTOIRE DES COLONIES FRANCAISES – Paris. 1913-1927 – 286mf – 8 – ne IDC [944]
REVUE DE L'HISTOIRE DES RELIGIONS – 1(1880)-110(1934) – 757mf – 9 – Dfl2,650.00 – ne Slangenburg [073]
REVUE DE L'HISTOIRE DES RELIGIONS – Paris. v1-110. 1880-1934 – 757mf – 9 – ne IDC [200]
REVUE DE L'HORTICULTURE BELGE ET ETRANGERE – Ghent. v1-40. 1875-1914 – 323mf – 9 – 7367/2 – ne IDC [630]
REVUE DE LINGUISTIQUE ROMANE – Paris. v1-15. 1925-39 – 63mf – 9 – H-10030/1 – ne IDC [440]
REVUE DE LITTERATURE COMPAREE – Paris. 1935-40 1946 (XV-XX) – 1 – fr A.C.R.P.P. [073]
REVUE DE L'ORIENT CHRETIEN – 1(1896)-30(1936) – 267mf – 9 – Dfl935.00 – ne Slangenburg [073]

REVUE DE L'ORIENT CHRETIEN – Paris. v1-25. 1896-1935/1936 – 234mf – 9 – H-2509/1 – ne IDC [240]

REVUE DE L'ORIENT ET DE L'ALGERIE – Paris. 18v. 1847-55 – 94mf – 9 – AR-1769/1 – ne IDC [073]

REVUE DE L'ORIENT LATIN – Paris. v1-12. 1893-1911 – 117mf – 9 – H-2510/1 – ne IDC [073]

REVUE DE L'YONNE – Avallon. 1920-32 – 1 – fr A.C.R.P.P. [073]

REVUE DE MADAGASCAR – Antananarivo: Impr officielle. n1-27 1933-jul 1939; 3rd ser: n7-13 4th qtr 1949-52, n18-33 1854-57; 4th ser: n1-4,7-8,12,14-19,21-47/48 1958-69 – us Res Libr [073]

REVUE DE METALLURGIE – v1-59. 1904-1962 – 1 – us Princeton Micro [660]

REVUE DE METAPHYSIQUE ET DE MORALE – Paris. 1893-1941. v1-48 – 702mf – 8 – ne IDC [110]

REVUE DE METAPHYSIQUE ET DE MORALE – Paris. Dir., Jean Wahl.1893-nov 1914, 1916-oct 1941, 1944-1971 – 5 – fr A.C.R.P.P. [073]

LA REVUE DE MONTE-CARLO – Nice and Beausoleil. -w 24 Dec 1905-5 Nov 1939. 13 reels – 1 – uk British Libr Newspaper [072]

LA REVUE DE MONTREAL – Montreal, Canada. 1 oct 1893 – 1r – 1 – Can$25.00 – cn Can Microfilming [073]

REVUE DE MONTREAL – [Montreal?: s.n.], 1877-1881 – 9 – cn C.I.H.M. [910]

REVUE DE MORALE SOCIALE – Geneva, 1899-1903 – 24mf – 9 – W-28/1 – ne IDC [301]

LA REVUE DE MUSIQUE ET DE BRODERIE VENNAT *see* MONTREAL-MODE

REVUE DE MUSIQUE RELIGIEUSE ET DE CHANT GREGORIEN – no. 1-25. Marseille. juil 1895-97 – 1 – fr A.C.R.P.P. [073]

REVUE DE MUSIQUE RELIGIEUSE ET DE CHANT GREGORIEN – v. 1-6. 1895-1900 – 1 – us Schnase [780]

LA REVUE DE PAPINEAU = PAPINEAU REVUE – Buckingham: (s.n.), (ca 1975)-1985. SEM35P262 – 8r – 1 – Can$288.00 – cn Bibl Nat [072]

LA REVUE DE PAPINEAU PLUS – Saint Andre Avellin: Hebdos de l'Outaouais. v12 nos 14-45. 1985. SEM35P247 – 1r – 1 – Can$37.00 – cn Bibl Nat [971]

LA REVUE DE PARIS – Politique, litteraire, artistique et mondaine. Dir. Leo D'Orter. Paris. mars 1887 (n.s., I) – 1 – fr A.C.R.P.P. [073]

REVUE DE PARIS – 1894-1970 – 1 – us UMI [073]

REVUE DE PARIS – avr 1829-33 (I-LVII), 1834-38 (2e s., I-LX), 1839-41 (n.s., I-XXXVI), 1842-avr 1844 (n.s., I-XXVIII), mai 1844-juin 1845 (n.s., I-IV, no. 1-175). Paris. Absorbe par: L'ARTISTE. Voir a ce titre – 1 – fr A.C.R.P.P. [073]

REVUE DE PARIS – Litterature, sciences, politique, arts, economie sociale. Red. en chef Th. Gautier. Paris. oct 1851-janv 1858 – 1 – fr A.C.R.P.P. [073]

REVUE DE PARIS ET DE SAINT-PETERSBOURG – nov 1887-juin 1888. devenu: La Grande revue. Paris et Saint-Petersbourg. juil 1888-avr 1893. Paris – 1 – fr A.C.R.P.P. [073]

REVUE DE PHILOLOGIE, DE LITTERATURE ET D'HISTOIRE ANCIENNE – Paris. ns: v1-50; series 3: v1-7. 1877-1933 – 9r – 1 – us Ross [450]

REVUE DE PHILOLOGIE, DE LITTERATURE ET D'HISTOIRE ANCIENNES – Paris. 1845-47. v1-2. N.S., 1877-1926, v1-50. S. 3. 1927-1941, v1-15 – 657mf – 9 – ne IDC [930]

REVUE DE PHONETIQUE – Paris. v1-6. 1911-29 – 42mf – 9 – H-1398/2 – ne IDC [440]

REVUE DE PHONETIQUE APPLIQUEE – 1965-1; 1976- 5,6,9 – us UMI [400]

LA REVUE DE POCHE LITTERAIRE ET ANECDOTIQUE – no. 1-18. Paris. dec 1866-sept 1867 – 1 – fr A.C.R.P.P. [073]

REVUE DE PSYCHOLOGIE DES PEUPLES *see* ETHNOPSYCHOLOGIE

LA REVUE DE QUEBEC : JOURNAL HEBDOMADAIRE – Quebec, Canada. 10 oct-14 dec 1889 – 1r – 1 – Can$30.00 – cn Can Microfilming [073]

LA REVUE DE SHAWINIGAN FALLS – Shawinigan, Canada. v1 n13. 28 fev 1921-v20 n15. 19 dec 1939; v24 n15. 19 dec 1944; v36 n13. 4 jun 1956 – 2r – 1 – Can$50.00r – cn Can Microfilming [073]

LA REVUE DE TERREBONNE – Terrebonne, Canada. v8 n5. 17 jun 1966-15 jun 1972 – 163r – 1 – cn Can Microfilming [072]

LA REVUE DE TERREBONNE – Terrebonne. v1-18. 1959-1977. SEM35P37 – 13r – 1 – Can$713.00 – cn Bibl Nat [073]

REVUE DE THEOLOGIE ET D'ACTION EVANGELIQUES – 2(1942)-8(1948) – 57mf – 9 – Dfl300.00 – ne Slangenburg [073]

REVUE DE THEOLOGIE ET D'ACTION EVANGELIQUES – (Missing: v1 1941) – Aix. v1-8. 1941-1948 – 57mf – 9 – ne IDC [240]

REVUE DES BIBLIOPHILES – Sauveterre-de-Guyenne. 1881 – 1 – fr A.C.R.P.P. [073]

REVUE DES COLONIES – Paris. juil 1834-juin 1837, juil 1838, dec 1838-fevr 1839, juil-oct 1840, mars 1841-juin 1842 – 1 – fr A.C.R.P.P. [073]

REVUE DES COURS ET CONFERENCES – Paris. 1892-1939/40. v1-41(2) – 1,151mf – 8 – ne IDC [720]

REVUE DES COURS ET CONFERENCES – Paris. dec 1892-juil 1914, dec 1921-mai 1940 – 1 – fr A.C.R.P.P. [073]

REVUE DES COURS LITTERAIRES DE LA FRANCE ET DE L'ETRANGER – Paris. Dec 1863-nov 1870. Devenu: La Revue politique et litteraire. Revue des Cours litteraires. Puis Revue bleue. dec 1863-avr/sept 1939 – 1 – fr A.C.R.P.P. [073]

LA REVUE DES DEUX FRANCES – Quebec: [s.n., 1897-1899] – 9 – cn C.I.H.M. [800]

REVUE DES DEUX MONDES – (Missing: 1830(4)) – Paris, 1829-57(8) – 1950mf – 9 – H-527/2 – ne IDC [073]

REVUE DES DEUX MONDES – Paris. France. 1879-1964 – 1 – us UMI [072]

REVUE DES DEUX MONDES – Paris. juil 1829-sept 1944 – 1 – fr A.C.R.P.P. [073]

REVUE DES ECLAIRAGES – Paris, France. -m. Jan 1905-Dec 1909. 2 reels – 1 – uk British Libr Newspaper [073]

REVUE DES ETATS DU NORD ET PRINCIPALEMENT DES PAYS GERMANIQUES – Paris. mars-aout, nov 1835, 1836-juin 1838 – 1 – fr A.C.R.P.P. [073]

REVUE DES ETUDES ARMENIENNES – Paris. S1: 11v. 1920-33 – 45mf – 9 – R-14548/1 – ne IDC [470]

REVUE DES ETUDES ETHNOGRAPHIQUES SOCIOLOGIQUES – Paris. -bim. Apr 1908-09. -m. Jan-Mar 1908. 1 reel – 1 – us I.U. Libraries [301]

REVUE DES ETUDES ISLAMIQUES – Paris. v1-15. 1927-40 – 146mf – 9 – I-493c/2 – ne IDC [260]

REVUE DES ETUDES JUIVES – (Index included) – Paris. v1-77. 1880-1923 – 351mf – 9 – NE-354/1 – ne IDC [270]

REVUE DES ETUDES LATINES – Paris. v24-36. 1946-58. 287/2 – 8 – ne IDC [073]

REVUE DES ETUDES LATINES / La Societe des Etudes Latines – Paris. oct 1923-65 – 1 – fr A.C.R.P.P. [073]

REVUE DES ETUDES NAPOLEONIENNES – Paris. 1912-26, 1929-36, 1939-40 – 1 – fr A.C.R.P.P. [073]

REVUE DES ETUDES NAPOLEONIENNES – Paris. 1912-40. v1-46 – 304mf – 8 – ne IDC [900]

REVUE DES ETUDES RABELAISIENNES – Paris. 1903-12 (I-X). suivi de: Revue du seizieme siecle voir a ce titre – 1 – fr A.C.R.P.P. [073]

REVUE DES ETUDES SLAVES – Paris. 1921-64. v1-43 – 271mf – 8 – ne IDC [073]

REVUE DES FEUILLETONS – Journal litteraire illustre compose de romans, voyages, legendes, anecdotes, contes, nouvelles historiques, etc. Paris. 1880 – 1 – fr A.C.R.P.P. [073]

REVUE DES JEUNES POETES – Paris. avr 1872-fevr 1881. Fuisonne avec: Le Parnasse – 1 – fr A.C.R.P.P. [073]

REVUE DES JEUX SCOLAIRES – Bordeaux. No.1-48. dec 1890-94 – 1 – fr A.C.R.P.P. [073]

LA REVUE DES JOURNAUX POLITIQUES ET LITTERAIRES – Paris. nov 1829-juin 1830. Suppl. de: L' Echo francais – 1 – fr A.C.R.P.P. [073]

REVUE DES LANGUES VIVANTES – (v1-15. Dfl45.00v; v16-35. Dfl65.00v) – Brussels. v1-35. 1935-69 – 5,9 – Dfl1,975.00 – ne Swets [400]

REVUE DES LETTRES ET DES ARTS – Paris. oct 1867-mars 1868 – 1 – fr A.C.R.P.P. [073]

REVUE DES MARCHES MINIERS – London, UK. 8 Feb-5 Apr 1902 – 1 – uk British Libr Newspaper [072]

REVUE DES MISSIONS – v17. 1940 (complete) – Inquire – 1 – ATLA 1993-S503 – us A.T.L.A. [073]

REVUE DES OEUVRES NOUVELLES DE LITTERATURE ET DE THEATRE – Paris. oct 1913-mai juin 1918, 1921-fevr 1922 – 1 – fr A.C.R.P.P. [073]

REVUE DES PATOIS GALLO-ROMANS : RECUEIL TRIMESTRIEL – (Suppl included) – Paris, Neuchatel. 5v. 1887-92 – 46mf – 9 – H-1397/2 – ne IDC [440]

LA REVUE DES PRODUITS CHIMIQUES – Paris, France. -f. May 1898-Dec 1909. 5 reels – 1 – uk British Libr Newspaper [073]

REVUE DES QUESTIONS HISTORIQUES – Fondee en 1866 par le Marquis de Beaucourt. Paris. 1894-1914, juil 1922-juil 1939 – 1 – fr A.C.R.P.P. [073]

REVUE DES QUESTIONS HISTORIQUES – v1-54. 1866-92 – 27r – 1 – $1,800.00 – us OmniSys [073]

LA REVUE DES REVUES – Paris. 1890-juin 1900. Devenu: La Revue. Ancienne Revue des Revues juil 1900. 1890-10 fevr 1936 – 1 – fr A.C.R.P.P. [073]

LA REVUE DES REVUES *see* LA REVUE MONDIALE

REVUE DES SCIENCES PHILOSOPHIQUES ET THEOLOGIQUES – 1(1907)-30(1942) – 291mf – 9 – Dfl1,019.00 – ne Slangenburg [073]

REVUE DES SCIENCES PHILOSOPHIQUES ET THEOLOGIQUES – Kain, Paris. v1-30. 1907-1941/1942 – 291mf – 9 – ne IDC [500]

REVUE DES SCIENCES RELIGIEUSES – 1(1921) – 11(1931) – 124mf – 8 – Dfl3.50ea – ne Slangenburg [240]

REVUE DES SCIENCES RELIGIEUSES – Strasbourg. v1-11. 1921-1931 – 124mf – 9 – ne IDC [210]

REVUE DES SCIENCES RELIGIEUSES – Strasbourg. v1-54. 1921-80 – 5,9 – Dfl3,780.00; Dfl70.00v – ne Swets [200]

REVUE DES TRADITIONS POPULAIRES : RECUEIL MENSUEL DE MYTHOLOGIE, LITTERATURE ORALE, ETHNOGRAPHIE TRADITIONNELLE ET ART POPULAIRE – Paris. v1-34. 1886-1919 – 346mf – 9 – H-1399/2 – ne IDC [390]

REVUE DES TROUPES COLONIALES – juil 1902-juil 1914, juil 1920-juin 1940, oct 1945-47. devenu: Tropiques. 1948-53. Paris – 1 – fr A.C.R.P.P. [073]

REVUE D'ESTHETIQUE – Paris. 1948-51 – 1 – fr A.C.R.P.P. [073]

REVUE D'ETHNOGRAPHIE ET DE SOCIOLOGIE – Paris. 1910-13. French, Eng. and German. Institut ethnographique international de Paris – 1 – us I.U. Libraries [301]

LA REVUE D'HISTOIRE : JOURNAL – Trois-Rivieres, Canada. v1 n6. nov 1940 – 1r – 1 – Can$25.00 – cn Can Microfilming [073]

REVUE D'HISTOIRE DE LA DEUXIEME GUERRE MONDIALE – Paris. v1-36. 1950-59.H-187/2 – 8 – ne IDC [073]

REVUE D'HISTOIRE DE LA GASPESIE – Gaspe. v1 n1. jan-mar 1963 – automne 1991 – 3r – 1 – cn Can Microfilming [072]

REVUE D'HISTOIRE DE L'AMERIQUE FRANCAISE – (v.33-. 1979$ 5,6,9) – v.1-. 1947- – 1 – us UMI [073]

REVUE D'HISTOIRE DE L'AMERIQUE-FRANCAISE – Montreal, Canada. jun 1947-v45 n4. printemps 1992 – 14r – 1 – cn Can Microfilming [073]

REVUE D'HISTOIRE DES DOCTRINES ECONOMIQUES ET SOCIALES – puis d'histoire economique et sociale. Paris. 1913-14, 1920-33 (VI-XXI) – 1 – fr A.C.R.P.P. [073]

REVUE D'HISTOIRE DES MISSIONS – v1-16. 1924-39 (complete) – Inquire – 1 – ATLA 1993-S502 – us A.T.L.A. [073]

REVUE D'HISTOIRE DIPLOMATIQUE – Paris. v53-78. 1939-64. H-188/2 – 8 – ne IDC [944]

REVUE D'HISTOIRE DU BAS-SAINT-LAURENT – Rimouski. v1 n1. oct 1973-v12 n3,4. sep 1987 – 1r – 1 – cn Can Microfilming [072]

REVUE D'HISTOIRE DU THEATRE – Paris. 1948 49-1965 – 1 – fr A.C.R.P.P. [073]

REVUE D'HISTOIRE ECCLESIASTIQUE – (Includes bibliography) – 1(1900)-15(1914) – 267mf – 9 – Dfl935.00 – ne Slangenburg [073]

REVUE D'HISTOIRE ECCLESIASTIQUE / Universite de Louvain – Louvain. v1-37(2). 1900-1941 – 916mf – 9 – 305c/2 – ne IDC [240]

REVUE D'HISTOIRE ET DE LITTERATURE RELIGIEUSE – Paris. v1-12. 1896-1907; ns: v1-8. 1910-22 – 215mf – 9 – H-218/2 – ne IDC [200]

REVUE D'HISTOIRE ET DE PHILOSOPHIE RELIGIEUSES – Strasburg. v1-54 1921-74 – 8r – 1 – us Ross [200]

REVUE D'HISTOIRE LITTERAIRE DE LA FRANCE – Paris. 1894-1939, 1947-67 – 1 – fr A.C.R.P.P. [073]

REVUE D'IMMUNOLOGIE ET DE THERAPIE ANTIMICROBIENNE – v. 1-36. 1935-1972 – 1,5,6 – us Princeton Micro [616]

REVUE DOMINICAINE – v21-67. 1894-1961. SEM16P223 – 17r – 5 – Can$621.00 – cn Bibl Nat [240]

REVUE D'OPTIQUE THEORIQUE ET INSTRUMENTALE – v. 1-47. 1922-1968. All pub – 1,5,6 – us Princeton Micro [530]

LA REVUE DOREE – no. 1-37. Paris. mars 1900-mars 1903 – 1 – fr A.C.R.P.P. [073]

REVUE D'OTO-NEURO-OPHTALMOLOGIE – v2-1924- 1; v49- 5,6,9 – us UMI [617]

REVUE D'OTTAWA – Ottawa, Ontario. v1 n2. jun 1926 – 1r – 1 – Can$25.00 – cn Can Microfilming [073]

REVUE DU 19E SIECLE – Les lettres, les arts, la philosophie, romans et voyages. S. de Rouville, dir.Paris.avr 1866-avr/juin 1867 (1-5) – 1 – fr A.C.R.P.P. [073]

LA REVUE DU CANADA ET DES INTERETS FRANCAIS – Paris, France. oct 1910 – 1r – 1 – Can$25.00 – cn Can Microfilming [073]

REVUE DU CHANT GREGORIEN – 1(1892)-44(1940) – 230mf – 9 – Dfl805.00 – ne Slangenburg [073]

REVUE DU CHANT GREGORIEN – (1914-1919 have not been publ) – Grenoble. v1-44. 1892-1940 – 230mf – 9 – ne IDC [780]

REVUE DU CHANT GREGORIEN – v. 1-44, no. 2. 1892-1940 – 1 – 87.00 – us L of C Photodup [780]

REVUE DU CHANT GREGORIEN – v. 1-44. no. II. 1892-1940 – 1 – us Schnase [780]

REVUE DU COMMERCE FRANCO BRITANNIQUE *see* COMMUNIQUE DE LA CHAMBRE DE COMMERCE FRANCAISE DE LONDRES

REVUE DU MONDE MUSULMAN – Paris. v1-64. 1906-1926 – 458mf – 8 – ne IDC [950]

REVUE DU MONDE MUSULMAN – v1-66. 1906-26 (complete) – Inquire – 1 – ATLA 1994-S511 – us A.T.L.A. [073]

REVUE DU NORD / l'Universite de Lille – no. 1-195. Lille, Bruxelles. fevr 1910-1944 – 1 – fr A.C.R.P.P. [073]

LA REVUE DU NOTARIAT – Levis, Quebec: s.n., 1898-19– – 9 – cn C.I.H.M. [340]

LA REVUE DU PATRIOTE – devenu: Le Creole patriote. 30 no. Paris. juin 1792-fevr 1794 – 1 – fr A.C.R.P.P. [073]

LA REVUE DU PRATICIEN – Journal d'enseignement post-universitaire. Paris. 1963-1993 – 5 – fr A.C.R.P.P. [073]

REVUE DU PROGRES MORAL, LITTERAIRE, SCIENTIFIQUE ET ARTISTIQUE – I-II, no. 1-12. Paris. mars 1863-mars 1864 – 1 – fr A.C.R.P.P. [073]

REVUE DU SEIZIEME SIECLE – Paris. 1913-26 (I-XIII). suite de: Revue des etudes rabelaisiennes voire a ce titre – 1 – fr A.C.R.P.P. [073]

LA REVUE DU SIECLE – no. 2; N.S., no. 1-3, 5. Paris. mai 1933-mars avr 1935. suite de: Reaction et de Les Cahiers d'Occident voir a ces titres – 1 – fr A.C.R.P.P. [073]

REVUE DU TIERS-ORDRE ET DE LA TERRE SAINTE – Montreal: Franciscain de l'Observance de Montreal, [1891-1916] – 9 – cn C.I.H.M. [240]

REVUE DU TIERS-ORDRE ET DE LA TERRE SAINTE *see* PETITE REVUE DU TIERS-ORDRE ET DES INTERETS DU COEUR DE JESUS

LA REVUE DU TRAVAIL – Revue syndicaliste bimensuelle. Dir. Pierre Dumas. Paris. oct 1919-avr 1921 – 1 – fr A.C.R.P.P. [073]

LA REVUE DU TRAVAILLEUR – Journal bimensuel. Dir. Girard-Hugot. Noumea. aout 1924-sept 1937 – 1 – fr A.C.R.P.P. [073]

REVUE ECCLESIASTIQUE – (Fait suite a: Recueil de documents pour le clerge du Diocese de Valleyfield – Valleyfield [Quebec: s.n., 1896-1905] (Montreal: Arbour & LaPerle) – 9 – cn C.I.H.M. [240]

REVUE ECCLESIASTIQUE *see* RECUEIL DE DOCUMENTS POUR LE CLERGE DU DIOCESE DE VALLEYFIELD

REVUE EGYPTOLOGIQUE – Paris. v1-14. 1880-1912; ns: v1-2. 1919-21 – 83mf – 9 – NE-356-1 – ne IDC [930]

LA REVUE ENCYCLOPEDIQUE – ou Analyse raisonnee des productions les plus remarquables dans la litterature, les sciences et les arts. Paris. 1819-33, janv-mars 1835 (I-LXI) – 1 – fr A.C.R.P.P. [073]

REVUE ENCYCLOPEDIQUE : ANALYSE RAISONNEE DES PRODUCTIONS LES PLUS REMARQUABLES DANS LA LITTERATURE, LES SCIENCES ET LES ARTS – (Missing: v59. Includes index. Called: Magasin encyclopedique 1975-1816. Annales encyclopediques 1817-1818) – Paris. v1-60. 1819-1833 – 820mf – 9 – H-1395/2 – ne IDC [030]

REVUE ENTOMOLOGIQUE / ed by Silbermann, G – Strasbourg, Paris. v1-5. 1833-1837[-1840] – 33mf – 9 – Z-1001/2 – ne IDC [590]

REVUE ET GAZETTE DES THEATRES – Journal des auteurs, des artistes et des gens du monde. Paris. 1862-64, 1868, janv-aout 1870, 1872-75 – 1 – fr A.C.R.P.P. [073]

REVUE ET GAZETTE MUSICAL DE PARIS – Paris. 1834-1880. v1-47. Lacking: 1845,v12(p73-80) – 987mf – 8 – ne IDC [790]

REVUE ET GAZETTE MUSICALE DE PARIS – Paris. 1834-80. Lacking: v.2. 1835. 16 reels – 1 – 325.00 – us L of C Photodup [780]

REVUE ET GAZETTE MUSICALE DE PARIS – Paris. v1-15. 1827-35 – 3r – 1 – us Ross [780]

REVUE ET GAZETTE MUSICALE DE PARIS – v. 1-47. 1834-1880. v. 1-2 have title: Gazette Musicale de Paris. v. 3 and thereafter have title: Revue et Gazette Musicale de Paris. v. 6 (1839), Nos. 1-26 of Revue Musicale were published laterally with the Revue et Gazette Musicale de Paris. Suspended from September 1870 to September 1871 – 1 – us Sibley [780]

LA REVUE EUROPEA1ENNE – Paris. v. 1-8; n.s. v. 1-8, no. 7. Mar 1923-Dec 1926; Jan 1927-July 1931 – 1 – us NY Public [073]

LA REVUE EUROPEENNE – puis et coloniale. puis Litteraire, politique, financiere et sportive. Paris. 1910-juin 1914 – 1 – fr A.C.R.P.P. [073]

REVUE EUROPEENNE – Lettres, sciences, arts, voyages, politique. t. 13-18. Paris. 1861 – 1 – fr A.C.R.P.P. [073]

REVUE EUROPEENNE – no. 1-39; N.S., no. 1-17. Paris. 1831-nov 1834, avr-oct 1835. Remplace: Le Correspondant – 1 – fr A.C.R.P.P. [073]

REVUE FANTAISISTE – no. 1-19. Paris. fevr-nov 1861 – 1 – fr A.C.R.P.P. [073]

LA REVUE FELIBREENNE – Paris. 1885-1900 02, janv sept 1903, janv-avr 1909 – 1 – fr A.C.R.P.P. [073]

REVUE FINANCIERE DE LONDRES – London, UK. 13 Jan, 9 Jun 1906 – 1 – uk British Libr Newspaper [072]

LA REVUE FRANCAISE – no. 1. Paris. aout 1880 – 1 – fr A.C.R.P.P. [073]

REVUE FRANCAISE : LITTERATURE, SCIENCE, BEAUX, ARTS, POLITIQUE E COMMERCE – Rio de Janeiro, 1 May 1839-1 Apr 1840 – 1,5,6 – bl Biblioteca [073]

REVUE FRANCAISE – no. 1-16. Paris. 1828-juil 1830 – 1 – fr A.C.R.P.P. [073]

REVUE FRANCAISE – Paris. Fevr 1855-juil 1859. (t.1-17) – 1 – fr A.C.R.P.P. [073]

REVUE FRANCAISE D'ADMINISTRATION PUBL. – 1992-1995 – 10 times per yr – 9 – F1,600.00 – sz Infoprint [350]

REVUE FRANCAISE D'HISTOIRE D'OUTRE-MER – Revue de l'Histoire des Colonies Francaises. 1913-1938 – 1 – 35.00r – us Hoover Inst Photo [073]

REVUE FRANCAISE D'HISTOIRE D'OUTRE-MER – v. 1-53. 1913-66. 1962 And 1965 Wanting – 1 – 209.00 – us L of C Photodup [944]

REVUE FRANCAISE D'INFORMATIQUE ET DE RECHERCHE OPERATIONNELLE – Paris. Toutes series. 1967-72 – 5 – fr A.C.R.P.P. [073]

REVUE FRANCAISE D'OUTRE-MER – 1938-JUIL 1939 (XLII-XLIII). suite de: Bulletin de l'Union coloniale francaise. 1894 95-1896 (I-II), 1923-aout 1924 (XXII-XXIII). La Quinzaine coloniale. 1897-JUIL 1914 (I-XVIII), 1928-37. Contient un suppl. Bulletin bibliographique colonial. juil 1900-1901, fevr-dec 1908. Bulletin mensuel de l'Union coloniale. sept 1924-27 (XXIV-XXVI). Paris. 1894 95-juil 1914, 1923-juil 1939, suppl – 1 – fr A.C.R.P.P. [073]

REVUE FRANCAISE DU TRAVAIL – Paris. 1946-47. (La Condition Ouvriere. Part Two.) – 9 – 52.50 – fr Bibl Nationale [360]

REVUE FRANCO-PERSANE – Paris. juin 1900-sept oct 1902 – 1 – fr A.C.R.P.P. [073]

LA REVUE GENERALE : JOURNAL HISTORIQUE ET LITTERAIRE – Bruxelles. v1-143. Jan 1865-May 1940 – 1 – $1,127.00 – us L of C Photodup [073]

REVUE GENERALE – Bruxelles: Comptoir universel d'impr et de librairie. v1-73 n5. 1965-may 1940; index to v-140 – 64r – 1 – us Res Libr [073]

REVUE GENERALE DE BOTANIQUE – (1929-1946. v41-53. Sfr490.00) – Paris. 1889-1940. v1-52 – 616mf – 8 – ne IDC [580]

REVUE GENERALE DE DROIT – (v1-15 1970-84 on reel $165.00. v16-25 1985-94 on mf $264.00) – University of Ottawa. v1-25. 1970-94 – 9 – $429.00 set – us Hein [340]

REVUE GENERALE DE LA COLONIE BELGE – Brussels. Nov. 1920-Mar. 1940 – 1 – 35.00r – us Hoover Inst Photo [073]

REVUE GENERALE DE L'ACETYLENE – Paris, France. -f. July 1903-Dec 1908. 3 reels – 1 – uk British Libr Newspaper [072]

REVUE GENERALE DE MEDECINE, DE PHARMACIE ET D'HYGIENE *see* REVUE GENERALE DE PHARMACIE ET D'HYGIENE PRATIQUES

REVUE GENERALE DE MEDECINE, DE PHARMACIE ET D'HYGIENE PRATIQUES – (Fait suite a: Revue generale de pharmacie et d'hygiene pratiques) – Montreal?: s.n., 1898-1900? – 9 – cn C.I.H.M. [610]

REVUE GENERALE DE PHARMACIE ET D'HYGIENE PRATIQUES – (Suivi de: Revue generale de medecine, de pharmacie et d'hygiene pratiques) – Montreal?: s.n., 1898 – 9 – cn C.I.H.M. [615]

REVUE GENERALE DE PHARMACIE ET D'HYGIENE PRATIQUES *see* REVUE GENERALE DE MEDECINE, DE PHARMACIE ET D'HYGIENE PRATIQUES

REVUE GENERALE DES CHEMINS DE FER – Paris. juil 1878-72 – 1 – fr A.C.R.P.P. [073]

REVUE GENERALE DES MATIERES PLASTIQUES – v3-8. 1927-32 – 1,5,6 – us Princeton Micro [073]

REVUE GERMANIQUE – Paris, 1905-1921. v1-12 – 8 – ne IDC [430]

REVUE GERMANIQUE – Paris. v. 1-10, no. 4. 1905-Aug 1914 – 1 – us NY Public [073]

REVUE GREGORIENNE – Paris. 1911-mai juin 1914, 1920-31, 1946-55 – 1 – fr A.C.R.P.P. [073]

REVUE GREGORIENNE – v. 1-24. 1911-1939 – 1 – us Schnase [780]

LA REVUE HEBDOMADAIRE – Paris. mai 1892-93, mars-aout 1912, 1923, 1925 – 1 – fr A.C.R.P.P. [073]

REVUE HISTORIQUE DE LA NOBLESSE / Borel d'Hauterive – Paris, 1841-1846. 4v – 6mf – 9 – F180.00 – fr F.F.G. [920]

REVUE HISTORIQUE DE L'ARMEE – Paris. 1968 – 1 – fr A.C.R.P.P. [073]

REVUE HISTORIQUE DU SUD-EST EUROPEA1EN – Bucharest. v. 1-17. 1924-Mar 1940 – 1 – us NY Public [949]

REVUE HISTORIQUE DU SUD-EST EUROPEEN – Bucharest. v1-17. 1924-40 – 2r – 1 – us Ross [940]

REVUE HORTICOLE – (S2, v1-3 have not been publ) – Paris. S1: v1-6. 1829-45; S2: v4-5. 1845-46; S3: v1-5. 1847-51; S4: v1-5. 1852-56; v29-92. 1857-1921 – 704mf – 9 – 7366/1 – ne IDC [630]

REVUE ICARIENNE – Corning, IA. v1-10. 1878-88 – 1r – 1 – us Ross [073]

LA REVUE IMMORALISTE – no. 1. Paris. avr 1905 – 1 – fr A.C.R.P.P. [073]

LA REVUE IMMORALISTE – Reprod. du no.1, avril 1905. 40p. 1 fiche. (Selected Periodicals) – 9 – 6.00 – fr Bibl Nationale [073]

LA REVUE INDEPENDANTE – puis avec un bulletin bibliographique. Paris. nov 1841-fevr 1848 (I-XXIII; 2e s., I-XIII) – 1 – fr A.C.R.P.P. [073]

REVUE INDEPENDANTE – puis de litterature et d'art. I-II; n.s., I-XXVI, no. 1-78. Paris. mai 1884-aout 1895 – 1 – fr A.C.R.P.P. [073]

LA REVUE INDEPENDANTISTE – Montreal, Printemps 1977-Printemps 1989 – 1r – 1 – Can$40.00 – cn Can Microfilming [072]

LA REVUE INDIGENE – Paris. No.1-278. 1906-avr 1932 – 1 – fr A.C.R.P.P. [073]

LA REVUE INDOCHINOISE – Hanoi. aout 1893-oct 1894, aout 1899-1925. Absorbe par: Extreme-Asie voir a ce titre – 1 – fr A.C.R.P.P. [073]

REVUE INDO-CHINOISE – (Missing: v1-2(305) 1893; v2(7-13, 15). 1894; v1(p494-578). 1904; v6(p1151-1166). 1906; 1918; 1919(1-2)) – Hanoi. v1-6. 1893-1903; NS: v1-44. 1904-25 – 524mf – 9 – SE-34/1 – ne IDC [950]

REVUE INDOCHINOISE JURIDIQUE ET ECONOMIQUE – Hanoi, 1937-1939. v1-3 – 35mf – 9 – ne IDC [950]

REVUE INDUSTRIELLE DE L'EST – Nancy, France. -w. Jan 1897-Dec 1900. 2 reels – 1 – uk British Libr Newspaper [072]

LA REVUE INTERNATIONALE – no. 1-24. Paris. dec 1945-51 – 1 – fr A.C.R.P.P. [073]

REVUE INTERNATIONALE DE L'ENSEIGNEMENT / La Societe de l'Enseignement Superieur – Paris. 1881-1940 – 1 – fr A.C.R.P.P. [370]

REVUE INTERNATIONALE DE MUSIQUE – Dir. Comte de Chalot. no. 1-18. Paris. mars-dec 1898 – 1 – fr A.C.R.P.P. [073]

REVUE INTERNATIONALE DE MUSIQUE – Paris. v. 1-2. Mar 1898-Feb 1899. Incomplete – 1 – us NY Public [780]

REVUE INTERNATIONALE DE MUSIQUE – Paris. v1-2. 1898-99 – 2r – 1 – us Ross [780]

REVUE INTERNATIONALE DE PHILOSOPHIE – Brussels. 1938-39. v1-2 – 18mf – 8 – ne IDC [100]

REVUE INTERNATIONALE DE THEOLOGIE – Berne: v1-18. 1893-1910 – 268mf – 9 – H-228/2 – ne IDC [200]

REVUE INTERNATIONALE DE THEOLOGIE = INTERNATIONALE THEOLOGISCHE ZEITSCHRIFT – 1(1893)-18(1910) – 258mf – 9 – Dfl903.00 – ne Slangenburg [073]

REVUE INTERNATIONALE DE THEOLOGIE *see* INTERNATIONALE KIRCHLICHE ZEITSCHRIFT

REVUE INTERNATIONALE DU TRAVAIL 1921-1977 / International Labour Organisation – 9 – Sfr5,000.00 – 92-2-207129-8 – sz I.L.O. [331]

LA REVUE IRAN – (Shumarah-i 7-17. Sal-i 3, shumarah-i 7-10 (Day, Bahman, Isfand 1344-Mihr, Aban, Azar 1305[January to April, 1926-September to December 1926]). Sali 4, shumarah-i 11-14 (Day, Bahman, Isfand 1305-Mihr, Aban, Azar 1306[January to April 1927-October to December 1927]). Sal-i 5, shumarah-i 15-17 (Day to Farvardin 1307-Mihr 1307[January to April 1928-October 1928])) – Tehran – 1 reel – 1 – $45.00 – us MEDOC [950]

REVUE JURIDIQUE THEMIS DE L'UNIVERSITE DE MONTREAL – (os: v1-15 1966-65. ns: v1-18 1966-84 on reel $308.00. ns: v19-29 1985-95 on mf $23208.00) – os: v1-15. 1951-65; ns: v1-29. 1951-95 – 5,6,9 – $540.00 set – us Hein [340]

REVUE LATINE : JOURNAL DE LITTERATURE COMPAREE – Paris. 7v. 1902-08 – 98mf – 9 – H-1396/2 – ne IDC [450]

LA REVUE, LE BULLETIN (HEBDOS DE L'OUTAOUAIS 1984 INC.) – Buckingham: Hebdos de l'Outaouais. v1-5. 1983-86. SEM35P274 – 5r – 1 – Can$207.00 – cn Bibl Nat [073]

LA REVUE LEGALE / Canada. Quebec – v1-21. 1868-91 + index digest; ns: v1-48. 1895-1942 + 1943-82 – 763mf – 9 – $1,144.00 – LLMC 81-065 – us L.L.M.C. [340]

LA REVUE LEGALE – Sorel, Quebec?: s.n., 1869? – 9 – cn C.I.H.M. [340]

LA REVUE LIBERTAIRE – Reprod. des nos.1 a 5, 1893-94. Paris. 72p. 1 fiche. (Selected Periodicals) – 9 – 6.00 – fr Bibl Nationale [073]

LA REVUE LIBRE – Dir. Jean d'Estray. Paris. nov 1901-fevr 1905 – 1 – fr A.C.R.P.P. [073]

LA REVUE LIBRE – Politique, litteraire, theatrale et artistique. Dir. Gabriel Martin. no. 2-3. Paris. 28 avr-13 mai 1892; n.s., no. 1-3. 1er dec 1896-1er janv 1897; n.s., no. 1-6. 23 juin 13 oct 1917 – 1 – fr A.C.R.P.P. [073]

LA REVUE LITTERAIRE – Romans, nouvelles, poemes, theatre, etudes, critiques, etc. Dir.-red. en chef Etienne Renaud. no. 1-5. Paris. juil-nov 1904 – 1 – fr A.C.R.P.P. [073]

REVUE LITTERAIRE DE L'UNIVERSITE D'OTTAWA – Ottawa?: Juniorat du Sacre-Coeur, 1900?-1906? – 9 – cn C.I.H.M. [370]

REVUE MABILLON – (1914-1918 have not been publ) – Paris. v1-54. 1905/1906-1964 – 308mf – 9 – ne IDC [240]

REVUE MABILLON : ARCHIVES DE LA FRANCE MONASTIQUE – 1(1905)-54(1964) – 308mf – 9 – Dfl1,092.00 – ne Slangenburg [073]

REVUE MAME – Journal hebdomadaire de la famille. Paris. oct 1894-sept 1909 (I-XV) – 1 – fr A.C.R.P.P. [073]

LA REVUE MARXISTE – no. 1-7. Paris. fevr-aout sept 1929 – 1 – fr A.C.R.P.P. [073]

REVUE MENSUELLE DE CULTURE ET DE SYNTHESE FRANCO-ASIATIQUE – (Missing: v1(1, 6-10) 1946; v2(16-18) 1947) – Saigon. v1-21. 1946-67 – 371mf – 9 – I-474/2 – ne IDC [950]

REVUE MENSUELLE DES QUESTIONS SOCIALES, OUVRIERES ET FISCALES / Union des Industries Metallurgiques et Minieres – no. 1 2-47. Paris. mars avr 1920-janv 1924. mq no. 13, 21, 23-24, 28 – 1 – fr A.C.R.P.P. [336]

LA REVUE MERIDIONALE – Journal litteraire. no. 1-246. Toulouse. nov 1822-juil 1827 – 1 – fr A.C.R.P.P. [073]

REVUE MERIDIONALE – Revue de l'Aude. Carcassonne. 1890-96 – 1 – fr A.C.R.P.P. [073]

REVUE MINIERE ILLUSTREE – London, UK. 30 Sept 1899-7 Jul 1901 – 1 – uk British Libr Newspaper [072]

LA REVUE MODERNE – Montreal, Canada. nov 1919-jun 1960 – 16r – 1 – Can$60.00r – cn Can Microfilming [073]

LA REVUE MODERNISTE – Litteraire, artistique et philosophique. no. 1-11 13. Marseille. dec 1884-fevr 1886 – 1 – fr A.C.R.P.P. [073]

REVUE MONCHANIN JOURNAL – 1968-88.Continued annually – 1 – uk World [073]

LA REVUE MONDIALE – (Lacking: annee 1 n2-annee 11 n6-annee 47 n4-5) – Paris. v(1)-47. 1890-1936 – 1 – $962.00 – us L of C Photodup [073]

LA REVUE MUSICALE – Including La Revue d'Histoire et de Critique Musical. Paris. v. 1-12. no. 1. 1901-Jan 1 1912 – 1 – us NY Public [780]

REVUE MUSICALE – Paris. v. 1-15. Feb 1827-Dec 1835. Incomplete – 1 – us NY Public [780]

REVUE MUSICALE – Paris. v1-12. 1901-12 – 3r – 1 – us Ross [780]

REVUE MUSICALE – v. 1-9, no. 1-15. 1827-35. Merged with "La Gazette Musicale de Paris"ON 1 Nov 1835: superseded by "Revue et Gazette Musicale de Paris" – 9 – us Sibley [780]

REVUE MYCOLOGIQUE – Toulouse. v1-28. 1878-1906 – 127mf – 9 – 477/2 – ne IDC [580]

LA REVUE NATIONALE – Montreal: E Senegal, [1895-1896] – 9 – cn C.I.H.M. [073]

REVUE NATIONALE – Fondee par MM. Buchez et Bastide. Paris. mai 1847-29 juin 1848 – 1 – fr A.C.R.P.P. [073]

REVUE NATIONALE ET ETRANGERE, POLITIQUE, SCIENTIFIQUE ET LITTERAIRE – Paris. No.1-27, 10 nov 1860-27 juil 1867. 2e serie, aout 1867-avr 1868 – 1 – fr A.C.R.P.P. [073]

REVUE NEO-SCOLASTIQUE DE PHILOSOPHIE, VOL 17 – v.17-. 1910- – 1 – us UMI [140]

REVUE NEO-SCOLASTIQUE, VOL 1 – v.1-. 1894- – 1 – us UMI [140]

LA REVUE NOUVELLE – Par Eugene Forcade. 1845-47 (I-XVI) – 1 – fr A.C.R.P.P. [073]

REVUE NOUVELLE – Dir. Albert Collignon. Paris. dec 1863-15 mai 1864 – 1 – fr A.C.R.P.P. [073]

REVUE NOUVELLE – Revue mensuelle. Dir. Y. Manuel-Lelis. no. 1-43. Paris. dec 1924-nov 1928 – 1 – fr A.C.R.P.P. [073]

REVUE PARISIENNE – Dir. M. de Balzac. no. 1-3. Paris. 25 juil-25 sept 1840 – 5 – fr A.C.R.P.P. [073]

LA REVUE PHILANTHROPIQUE – v. 1-54. 1897-1934. (no. 31-32 wanting) – 1 – 388.00 – us L of C Photodup [360]

REVUE PHILOSOPHIQUE DE LOUVAIN – (v78-1980- 5,6,9) – v44- 1946- – 1 – us UMI [100]

LA REVUE PHILOSOPHIQUE, LITTERAIRE ET POLITIQUE – Paris. 1794-sept 1807. A paru sous le titre de: La Decade philosophique, litteraire et politique. 1794-1804 – 1 – fr A.C.R.P.P. [073]

REVUE PHOTOGRAPHIQUE – Paris. nov 1855-65 – 1 – fr A.C.R.P.P. [073]

LA REVUE POLITIQUE – Montreal, Canada. 15 jul 1936-v1 n7. 12 aut 1936 – 1r – 1 – Can$35.00 – cn Can Microfilming [073]

LA REVUE POLITIQUE – puis et litteraire. Paris. juin 1868-fevr 1869 – 1 – fr A.C.R.P.P. [073]

UNE REVUE POLITIQUE – Montreal, Canada. 15 avr 1896 – 1r – 1 – Can$25.00 – cn Can Microfilming [073]

REVUE POLITIQUE ET PARLEMENTAIRE – puis ECONOMIQUE, FINANCIERE. Paris. 1903-juil 1914, juin 1945-63 – 1 – fr A.C.R.P.P. [073]

LA REVUE POPULAIRE : HEBDOMADAIRE ILLUSTRE – Montreal, dec 1907-nov 1963f – 31r – 1 – Can$75.00 – cn Can Microfilming [072]

LA REVUE POPULAIRE (1907) – Montreal: Poirier, Bessette & Cie. v1- 1907-. SEM35P294 – 1r – 1 – Can$37.00 – cn Bibl Nat [073]

REVUE RETROSPECTIVE – juil 1884-juin 1894. devenu: Nouvelle revue retrospective. JUIL 1894-JUIN 1904. Paris – 1 – fr A.C.R.P.P. [073]

LA REVUE RHENANE-RHEINISCHE BLAETTER – Mainz. Oct. 1920-Aug. Sept. 1930 – 1 – 35.00r – us Hoover Inst Photo [073]

LA REVUE ROUGE – 1er janv 1890. devenu: L' Idee nouvelle. 5 janv-5 juin 1890. Paris – 1 – fr A.C.R.P.P. [073]

REVUE SCIENTIFIQUE – Paris. v1-78. 1863-1940 – 58r – 1 – us Ross [500]

REVUE SOCIALE – ou Solution pacifique du probleme du proletariat. Dir. Pierre Leroux. Paris. oct 1845-aout 1850 – 1 – fr A.C.R.P.P. [073]

LA REVUE SOCIALISTE – puis socialiste, syndicaliste et cooperative. no. 1-354. Paris. 1885-juin 1914 – 1 – fr A.C.R.P.P. [073]

LA REVUE SOCIALISTE – Revue de culture politique et sociale. n.s., no. 1-227. Paris. mai 1946-juin 1971 – 1 – fr A.C.R.P.P. [073]

LA REVUE SOCIALISTE / ed by Roy, Raoul – Montreal, Canada. printemps 1959-printemps 1965 – 1r – 1 – Can$35.00 – cn Can Microfilming [073]

LA REVUE SOCIALISTE, SYNDICALISTE ET COOPERATIVE – v. 1-59. 1885-1914 – 1 – 364.00 – us L of C Photodup [335]

REVUE STATISTIQUE DE LA NAVIGATION, DU COMMERCE ET DE L'INDUSTRIE – La Havre. 1930-34, 1937-38 – 1 – fr A.C.R.P.P. [073]

REVUE STATISTIQUE DU CANADA – (Cont: Canadian Statistical Review/Revue statistique du Canada. Cont by: Canadian Economic Observer/L'Observateur economique canadien, 1988) – Ottawa. v56-62. 1981-87 – 9 – Can$55.00y – cn Micromedia [310]

REVUE STATISTIQUE DU CANADA *see*
- CANADIAN ECONOMIC OBSERVER
- CANADIAN STATISTICAL REVIEW

REVUE SUISSE DE ZOOLOGIE ET ANNALES DU MUSEE D'HISTOIRE NATURELLE DE GENEVE – Geneve. v1-48. 1893-1941 – 611mf – 9 – 2257c/2 – ne IDC [590]

REVUE SYNDICALE, ECONOMIQUE ET SOCIALE – no. 1-5. Paris. mai 1937-janv 1938 – 1 – fr A.C.R.P.P. [073]

LA REVUE TECHNIQUE – Paris, France. - f. Jan 1894-Jan 1906. 5 reels – 1 – uk British Libr Newspaper [073]

REVUE THOMISTE – 1(1893)-45(1939) – 422mf – 9 – Dfl1,477.00 – ne Slangenburg [073]

REVUE THOMISTE – Paris. v1-45. 1893-1939 – 422mf – 9 – ne IDC [240]

REVUE THOMISTE – Revue doctrinale de theologie et de philosophie. Paris. 1950-72 – 5 – fr A.C.R.P.P. [073]

LA REVUE TRIMESTRIELLE CANADIENNE – Montreal: Assoc des anciens eleves...v1-40. 1915-54. SEM16P357 – 8r – 5 – Can$258.00 – cn Bibl Nat [370]

REVUE TRIMESTRIELLE DE DROIT CIVIL – Paris. 1902-29, 1931-39 – 1 – fr A.C.R.P.P. [073]

REVUE UNIVERSEL – Quebec: L Feval, [1895-189- ou 19–] – 9 – cn C.I.H.M. [073]

LA REVUE UNIVERSELLE – Dir. Jean Bainville. Paris. avr 1920-aout 1944 – 1 – fr A.C.R.P.P. [073]

REVUE UNIVERSELLE; RECUEIL DOCUMENTAIRE UNIVERSEL ET ILLUSTRE – Paris. 15v. 1891-1905 – 1 – 368.00 – us L of C Photodup [073]

LA REVUE VOIR – Montreal: Communications Voir ltee. v1-3. 1986-1989. SEM35P361 – 3r – 1 – Can$162.00 – cn Bibl Nat [073]

REVUE WAGNERIENNE – 1-3, Feb 1885-July 1888 – 1 – 23.00 – us L of C Photodup [780]

REVUE WAGNERIENNE – Paris. fevr 1885-juil 1888 – 1 – fr A.C.R.P.P. [073]

REWARD AND PUNISHMENT / Etievant, George – 9p – 9 – 1.00f – at Libertarian Micro [335]

THE REWARDS OF THE PROFESSION OF THE LAW / Cady, Philander Kinney – New York: The Trustees, 1868. 26p. LL-876 – 1 – us L of C Photodup [340]

REX : GESCHICHTE EINES HUNDES UND ZWEIER MENSCHEN / Strobl, Karl Hans – 4. Aufl. Reichenberg: Stiepel, 1942 – 1r – 1 – us U.W. Library [430]

Rex, Benjamin F *see* THE NOTARIES' MANUAL

REX CHRISTUS : AN OUTLINE STUDY OF CHINA / Smith, Arthur Henderson – (Includes index) – New York: Publ for the Central Committee on the United Study of Missions [by] Macmillan, 1903 – 1mf – 9 – 0-8370-6615-8 – 1986-0615 – us A.T.L.A. [950]

Rex, John *see* APARTHEID AND SOCIAL RESEARCH

REXUE RIBAO – (Warm Blood Daily). China. 4 Jun-27 Jun 1925. F B3 – 2mf – 9 – $9.00 – cc Microforms [072]

EL REY D. PEDRO DEFENDIDO / Vera y Figueroa, Juan Antonio – 1648 – 9 – $1.50f – sp Bibl Santa Ana [946]

REY DE NUESTROS ESCRITURARIOS / Arias Montano, Benito – Madrid: Biblioteca Nueva, 1943 – sp Bibl Santa Ana [240]

Rey Fajardo, J del S J *see* BIO-BIBLIOGRAFIA DE LOS JESUITAS EN LA VENEZUELA COLONIAL

Rey, J *see* TRIO POUR UN VIOLON, ALTO, ET BASSE

EL REY JOSE NAPOLEON. LA MISION DEL BARON DE AGRA. ALGUNOS CUADROS DEL MUSEO DEL PRADO. EL PAPA DE VELAZQUEZ. MADRID, 1929 / Villaurrutia, W R – Madrid: Razon y Fe, 1930 – 1 – sp Bibl Santa Ana [946]

Rey Trujillo, G del *see* LA MONEDA EMERITENSE

Reybaud, Louis *see*
- LE COTON, SON REGIME, SES PROBLEMES, SON INFLUENCE EN EUROPE
- ETUDES SUR LE REGIME DES MANUFACTURES. CONDITIONS DES OUVRIERS EN SOIE
- LE FER ET LA HOUILLE, SUIVI DU CANON KRUPP ET DU FAMILISTERE DE GUISE. DERNIERE SERIE DES ETUDES SUR LE REGIME DES MANUFACTURES
- LA LAINE. NOUVELLE SERIE DES ETUDES SUR LE REGIME DES MANUFACTURES

Reyburn, Hugh Y *see* JOHN CALVIN

DIE REYEN IN DEN TRAUERSPIELEN DES ANDREAS GRYPHIUS / Steinberg, Johannes – (Includes bibliographical references) – Goettingen: E A Huth, 1914 – 1r – 1 – us U.W. Library [430]

Reyes, Fr. Antonio de los *see* VIDA...FRANCISCO VALERO Y LOSA

Reyes Franco, G *see* ELYSIUS JUCUNDARUM QUAESTIONUM CAMPUS, OMNIUM LITERARUM AMOENNISSIMA VARIETATE...

Reyes Huertas, Antonio *see*
- BLASON DE ALMAS
- LA CIENAGA
- LA COLORINA. BADAJOZ, ARQUEROS, 1928
- MIRTA
- LA NOSTALGIA DE LOS DOS
- NOSTALGIAS
- LO QUE ESTA EN EL CORAZON

Reyes, R *see* TRATADO DE LAS INFLAMACIONES INTERNAS EXPLICADO POR LAS LEYES MECANICAS

Reyes, Rafael de los *see* VIDA DEL JOVEN DON FRANCISCO ROMERO Y FERNANDEZ DE CORDOBA

Reyes, Rodolfo *see* DE MI VIDA; MEMORIAL POLITICAS

Reyes y Florentino, Isabelo de los *see*
- (CLIPPINGS AND HANDBILLS BY OR ABOUT ISABELO DE LOS REYES FROM HIS PERSONAL NOTEBOOK...UNIVERSITY OF THE PHILIPPINES LIBRARY....)
- LA RELIGION ANTIGUA DE LOS FILIPINOS

Reyes-Lagunes, Isabel *see* IMPACT OF EDUCATIONAL TELEVISION ON YOUNG CHILDREN

Reyger, G *see* TENTAMEN FLORA GEDANENSIS METHODO SEXUALI ACCOMODATAE

Rey-Lescure, P *see* CORRESPONDANCE

Reymann, Mathaeus *see* NOCTES MUSICAE, STUDIO ET INDUSTRA MATTAEI REYMANI TORONENSIS BORUSSI CONCINNATAE

Reymondez del Campo, Jesus *see* CORRESPONDENCIA EPISTOLAR DEL P. ANDRES MARCOS BURRIEL, EXISTENTE EN LA BIBLIOTECA REAL DE BRUSELAS

Reyna, Francisco de la *see*
- LIBRO DE ALBEYTERIA...
- LIBRO DE ALBEYTERIA...FERNANDO CALVO

Reyna y Reyna, Tomas de la *see* DESCUBRIMIENTO Y CONQUISTA DEL PERU

Reynaud, Francois Leonce *see* TRAITE D'ARCHITECTURE

Reynaud, Jean *see*
- DE LA NECESSITE D'UNE REPRESENTATION SPECIALE POUR LES PROLETAIRES
- DE LA SOCIETE SAINT-SIMONIENNE ET DES CAUSES QUI ONT AMENE SA DISSOLUTION

Reynaud, Louis *see* FRANCAIS ET ALLEMANDS, HISTOIRE DE LEURS RELATIONS INTELLECTUELLES ET SENTIMENTALES

Reynerus, Cl. OSB *see* DE ANTIQUITATE BENEDICTINORUM IN REGNO ANGLIAE

Reynier, J B *see*
- CORRECTIONS RAISONNEES DES FAUTES DE LANGAGE ET DE PRONONCIATION
- LES PROVENCALISMES CORRIGES

Reynolds, Cuyler *see* GENEALOGICAL AND FAMILY HISTORY OF SOUTHERN NEW YORK AND HUDSON RIVER VALLEY

Reynolds, Elon G *see* COMPENDIUM OF HISTORY AND BIOGAPHY OF HILLSDALE COUNTY

Reynolds, George Greenwood *see* THE DISTRIBUTION OF POWER TO REGULATE INTERSTATE CARRIERS BETWEEN THE NATION AND THE STATES

Reynolds, H *see* INFLUENCE OF POST-EXERCISE GLUCOSE INGESTION ON PLASMA POTASSIUM LEVELS AND ECG MEASUREMENTS

Reynolds, Henry Robert *see* ATHANASIUS

Reynolds, J *see* DRAPER MANUSCRIPT, 24 NOV. 1842-27 OCT. 1869

Reynolds, John *see*
- THE PIONEER HISTORY OF ILLINOIS
- THE RELIGION OF JESUS DELINEATED

Reynolds, Joseph William *see* THE MYSTERY OF MIRACLES

REYNOLDS NEWS AND SUNDAY CITIZEN – (Issues for jan-sep 16 1962 filmed with: Sunday Citizen and Reynolds News, sep 23-dec 1962) – London: Cooperative Press Ltd, 1953-55 (3r); 1956-sep 16 1962 (7r) – 1 – us Res Libr [072]

REYNOLDS' POLITICAL INSTRUCTOR – 1-27 (all publ). 1849-50 – 2r – 1 – $65.00 – us UPA [335]

Reynolds, Quentin James *see* COURTROOM

Reynolds, Richard *see*
- DIARY
- THE FOUNDACION OF RHETORIKE

Reynolds, Thomas C *see* PAPERS

Reynolds, Thomas H *see*
- CANON LAW
- CIVIL LAW 1
- CIVIL LAW 2
- CIVIL LAW 3

Reynolds, Winton A *see* HERNAN CORTES EN EXTREMADURA

REYNOLDS'S POLITICAL INSTRUCTOR – London, England. -w. 5 Jan-11 May 1850. 15 ft – 1 – uk British Libr Newspaper [072]

REYNOLDS'S WEEKLY NEWSPAPER – (Reynolds's Newspaper Reynolds News). London. -w. 1850-1962. 148 reels – 1 – uk British Libr Newspaper [072]

Rey-Pailhade, C de *see* LES FOUGERES DE FRANCE

DE REYSENDE SIELE TOT D'EEUWIGHEYDT VOOR EEN NIEUW-JAER GHESCHONCKEN AEN ALLE LIEF-HEBBERS VAN HAERE SALIGHEYDT : DOOR EENEN PRIESTER DER SOCIET. IESU / Smidt, A de – Den tweeden druck. Antwerpen, 1669 – 1mf – 9 – O-3168/1 – ne IDC [760]

Rez, Heinrich *see* BIBLIOGRAPHIE ZUR VOLKSKUNDE DER DONAUSCHWABEN

Rezanov, V I *see*
- IZ ISTORII RUSSKOI DRAMY
- IZ RAZYSKANII O SOCHINENIIAKH V.A. ZHUKOVSKAGO

Rezek, Antonin *see* DEJINY CECH A MORAVY NOVE DOBY

REZENSIONEN : WIENER THEATER 1901 BIS 1903 / Bahr, Hermann – (Includes index) – Berlin: S Fischer, 1903 – 1r – 1 – us U.W. Library [790]

REZHIM EKONOMII I KOOPERATSIIA / Vorob'ev-Nabatov, N A – M., 1926 – 1mf – 9 – COR-194/1 – ne IDC [334]

REZIPROKE FORSCHUNG, IM PSYCHOSOZIALEN PRAXISFELD, EINER KREBSSTATION – UNTER DER BERUECKSICHTIGUNG DES, HERRSCHENDEN, BIOMEDIZINISCHEN PARADIGMAS / Weidkuhn, Wilmar – 1992 – 17p – 9 – DM28.00 – 3-89349-462-6 – gw Hänsel [616]

REZOLIUTSII...VSEROSSIISKAGO SIEZDA SOVIETOV NARODNAGO KHOZIA ISTVA – (Includes c.1: 1918: May/June 1-1921 (4)) – Moskva: Red. zhurnala "Narodnogo khozia istva", 1918- – 1 – CSUXAKZ3919-S – us Hoover Inst Photo [380]

REZOLIUTSII...VSEROSSIISKOGO SEZDA SOVETOV NARODNOGO KHOZIAISTVA *see* REZOLIUTSII...VSEROSSIISKAGO SIEZDA SOVIETOV NARODNAGO KHOZIA ISTVA

RF DESIGN – (Radio Frequency). v.1-. 1978- – 1,5,6,9 – us UMI [073]

RFD – -q. Aug. 1974-. Wolf Creek Oregon: s.n., 1974- – 1 – us U.W. Library [073]

RFD NEWS – PORTAGE RIVER EDITION – Genoa, Ohio, 1979-1989 – 4r – 1 – $32.50r – us Archival [978]

RGANUM DIALECTICUM ET RHETORICUM / Sanchez de las Brozas, Francisco – 1579 – 9 – 1.50f – sp Bibl Santa Ana [410]

THE RHAPSODIST / Brown, Charles Brockden – (The Man at Home.1798. A series of original letters. 1798. Other uncollected writings) – 1789 – 9 – us Scholars' Facs [880]

Rhau, Georg *see*
- ENCHIRIDION MUSICAE MENSURALIS
- ENCHIRIDION MVSICAE MENSVRALIS, A GEORGIO RHAV CONGESTUM
- ENCHIRIDION UTRIUSQUE MUSICAE PRACTICAE
- ENCHIRIDION VTRIVSQVE MVSICAE PRACTICAE A GEORGIO RHAW EX UARIJS MUSICORUM LIBRIS

Rhazes *see* DE VARIOLIS ET MORBILIS...CUM NONNULIS EUISDEM ARGUMENTI

RHEA : ZEITSCHRIFT FUER DIE GESAMMTE ORNITHOLOGIE – Leipzig. v1-2. 1846-49 – 8mf – 9 – Z-2038/2 – ne IDC [590]

Rhea, Sarah J *see* LIFE OF HENRY MARTYN

Rheede Tot Drakestein, H A van *see* HORTUS INDICUS MALABARICUS

Rhees, Rush *see* THE LIFE OF JESUS OF NAZARETH

Rhegius, Urbanus *see*
- AIN KURTZER EINFELTIGER BERICHT, VOM HAILIGEN SACRAMENT DESZ LEIBS VND BLUTS JESU CHRISTI. ITEM ZEHEN HAUPTARTICUL CHRISTLICHER LEERE
- REG, URB. WIDDERLEGUNG DER MUENSTERISCHEN NEWEN VALENTINIANER VND DONATISTEN BEKENTNUS, AN DIE CHRISTEN ZU OSNABRUCK, JNN WESTFALEN. MIT EINER VORRHEDE M. LUTHERS
- EIN SENDBRIEFF HANS HUTHEN ETWA AINS FURNEMEN VORSTEERS IM WIDERTAUFFERORDENN, VERANTWORT
- WIDER DEN NEWEN TAUFFORDEN, NOTWENDIGE WARNUNG AN ALLE CHRISTGLEUBIGEN
- WIE MAN DIE FALSCHEN PROPHETEN ERKENNEN IA GREIFFEN MAG

Rheims *see* MONITEUR OFFICIEL DU GOUVERNEMENT GENERAL DE REIMS

RHEIN ECHO – Duesseldorf, Germany. -d. 9 Mar 1946-12 Nov 1951. (Imperfect). (17 reels) – 1 – uk British Libr Newspaper [072]

Rhein, Monika *see* GESCHICHTE UND GESCHICHTSWISSENSCHAFT IN DER METHODOLOGISCHEN DISKUSSION DER GEGENWART

RHEIN NECKAR ZEITUNG – Heidelberg, Germany. Sept 1945-1968 – 94r – 1 – us L of C Photodup [072]

RHEIN- UND MOSELZEITUNG – Koblenz, Germany. 1847-Juni 1848; 1849-Jun 1850 – 4r – 1 – gw Mikrofilm [072]

RHEIN ZEITUNG – Ahrweiler, Koblenz, Germany. 1 Jun 1983- – 8r per yr – 1 – gw Mikrofilm [072]

Rheinallt Jones, J D *see* BANTU STUDIES AND GENERAL SOUTH AFRICAN ANTHROPOLOGY

DER RHEINBOTE *see* DER VOLKSFREUND

RHEIN-EMS-ZEITUNG – Emden, Germany. 1969- – ca 7r per yr – 1 – gw Mikrofilm [072]

RHEINHART-BRIEFE – (Title change: Neue Politische Briefe) – Paris. Summer 1933-Sept 1939 – 1r – 1 – gw Mikrofilm [072]

RHEINISCH-BERGISCHE ZEITUNG *see* VOLKSBLATT FUER BERGISCH GLADBACH UND UMGEBUNG

RHEINISCHE ALLGEMEINE ZEITUNG – Bonn, dec 1 1869-sep 30 1870 – 1 – Inquire at Mikrofilmarchiv for details – gw Misc Inst [943]

RHEINISCHE BEAMTENZEITUNG – Berlin, Koeln. apr 15 1926-may 18 1932 – 1r – 1 – Inquire at Mikrofilmarchiv for details – gw Misc Inst [331]

RHEINISCHE BLAETTER FUER ERZIEHUNG UND UNTERRICHT – Schwelm/Essen, 1827-29, 1831-49 – 8r – 1 – gw Mikrofilm [370]

RHEINISCHE FILM-KUNST-BUEHNE – Koeln, nov 1919-apr 1920 (incomplete) – 1 – gw Mikrofilm [790]

RHEINISCHE POST – Duesseldorf, Germany. 1992- – 12r per yr – 1 – gw Mikrofilm [072]

RHEINISCHE POST – Duesseldorf, Germany. -d. March 1946-Dec 1951; Jan 1953-Aug 1957. 87 reels – 1 – uk British Libr Newspaper [072]

RHEINISCHE POST – Dusseldorf, 1953-80 – us Res Libr [072]

RHEINISCHE POST – Kleve, Germany. 1992- – 9r per yr – 1 – gw Mikrofilm [072]

RHEINISCHE POST – Moenchengladbach, Germany. Mar 1992- – 10r per yr – 1 – gw Mikrofilm [072]

RHEINISCHE REPUBLIK : ORGAN DES RHEINLANDBUNDES – Koeln, Bonn. Apr 1919-Oct 1923 – 1r – 1 – DM80.00 – gw Mikro Press [072]

RHEINISCHE REPUBLIK : ORGAN DES RHEINLANDBUNDES – Koeln, Germany. 11 Apr 1919-13 Oct 1923 – 1r – 1 – gw Mikrofilm [072]

RHEINISCHE URBARE, BD 2 : DIE URBARE DER ABTEI WERDEN A. D. RUHR – A. DIE URBARE VOM 9-13. JAHRH. / ed by Koetzschke, R – Bonn, 1906 – Dfl49.00 – ne Slangenburg [240]

RHEINISCHE URBARE, BD 3 : DIE URBARE DER ABTEI WERDEN A. D. RUHR – LAGERBUECHER, HEBE- UND ZINSREGISTER VOM 14. BIS INS 17. JAHRHUNDERT / ed by Koetzschke, R – Bonn, 1917 – Dfl56.00 – ne Slangenburg [240]

RHEINISCHE VIERTELJAHRESBLAETTER : MITTEILUNGEN DES INSTITUTS FUER GESCHICHTLICHE LANDESKUNDE DER RHEINLANDE AN DER UNIVERSITAET BONN – 1931-34 – 1r – 1 – DM80.00 – gw Mikro Press [073]

RHEINISCHE VOLKSHALLE – (Title change: Deutsche Volkshalle, 2 Oct 1849) – Koeln, Germany. Oct 1848-10 Jul 1855 – 9r – 1 – gw Mikrofilm [072]

RHEINISCHE VOLKSHALLE/DEUTSCHE VOLKSHALLE – Koeln, Oct 1848-Jul 1855 – 9r – 1 – DM900.00 – gw Mikro Press [072]

RHEINISCHE ZEITUNG – Bonn, 1980 – 1 – Inquire at Mikrofilmarchiv for details – gw Misc Inst [072]

RHEINISCHE ZEITUNG – Koeln, 1842-1843 – 2r – 1 – DM240.00 – gw Mikro Press [072]

RHEINISCHE ZEITUNG – Koeln, 1842/43 – 9 – gw Olms [320]

RHEINISCHE ZEITUNG – Koeln, 1892-1933 – 82r – 1 – DM6,150.00 – gw Mikro Press [072]

RHEINISCHE ZEITUNG – Koeln, Germany. 2 Apr 1892-27 Feb 1933 – 82r – 1 – gw Mikrofilm [072]

RHEINISCHE ZEITUNG : NIEDERRHEINISCHE VOLKSZEITUNG – Duesseldorf, 1860-68 – 13r – 1 – DM1,040.00 – gw Mikro Press [943]

RHEINISCHE ZEITUNG *see* DUESSELDORFER KREISBLATT UND TAEGLICHER ANZEIGER

RHEINISCHE ZEITUNG FUER POLITIK, HANDEL UND GEWERBE – Koeln, Germany. 1842-Mar 1843 – 5r – 1 – gw Mikrofilm [072]

RHEINISCHER BEOBACHTER – Koeln, Germany. 4 Mar 1845-Mar 1848 – 6r – 1 – gw Mikrofilm [072]

RHEINISCHER MERKUR – Cologne, Germany. Mar 1946-1957; 1960-78; 1980-81 – 50r – 1 – us L of C Photodup [072]

RHEINISCHER MERKUR – Koblenz, 1814-16 – 9 – gw Olms [320]

RHEINISCHER MERKUR : WOCHENZEITUNG FUER POLITIK, WIRTSCHAFT UND KULTUR – (Cont by: Rheinischer Merkur – Christ und Welt, jan 1 1980) – Koblenz, Bonn, Wiesbaden. apr 24 1946-dec 18 1990 – 1 – gw Mikrofilm [072]

RHEINISCHER MERKUR *see* DEUTSCHE ZEITUNG/CHRIST UND WELT

RHEINISCHER MERKUR – CHRIST UND WELT *see* RHEINISCHER MERKUR

RHEINISCHER MERKUR / CHRIST UND WELT – 1979- – 9 – inquire – us Ross [072]

RHEINISCHER-WESTFAELISCHER ANZEIGER *see* WESTPHAELISCHER ANZEIGER

RHEINISCHES CONVERSATIONS-LEXICON ODER ENCYCLOPAEDISCHES HANDWOERTERBUCH FUER GEBILDETE STAENDE (AEL, ABT 1;20) / ed by Gesellschaft rheinlaendischer Gelehrter – 4. Aufl. Koeln. 12 bde. 1837-1845 (mf ed 1994) – 76mf – 9 – DM1,540.00 – 3-89131-168-0 – gw Fischer [030]

RHEINISCHES MUSEUM FUER PHILOLOGIE, GESCHICHTE UND GRIECHISCHE PHILOSOPHIE – (1929-1957. v78-100. Sfr436.00) – Bonn, Frankfurt am Main, 1827-1829. v1-3; 1833-1839. v1-6; 1842-1941. v1-90 – 1,084mf – 8 – ne IDC [400]

RHEINISCHES VOLK – Bonn, feb 1921-aug 10 1923 – 5r – 1 – Inquire at Mikrofilmarchiv for details – gw Misc Inst [943]

RHEINISCHES VOLK – Bonn, Feb 1921-Aug 1923 – 5r – 1 – DM400.00 – gw Mikro Press [072]

RHEINISCHES VOLK – Bonn, Germany. Feb 1921-10 Aug 1923 – 5r – 1 – gw Mikrofilm [072]

RHEINISCHE-WESTFAELISCHE ARBEITER-ZEITUNG *see* WESTFAELISCHE ARBEITER ZEITUNG

RHEINISCH-WESTFAELISCHE ARBEITER-ZEITUNG *see*
- VOLKSBLATT FUER DEN WAHLKREIS BOCHUM UND UMGEBUNG

RHEINISCH-WESTFAELISCHE FILMZEITUNG – Duesseldorf. 1934-37 – 2r – 1 – gw Mikrofilm [790]

DAS RHEINISCH-WESTFAELISCHE KOHLENSYNDIKAT UND SEIN EINFLUSS AUF DIE KOHLENPREISE UND DIE LAGE DER BERGARBEITER / Liefering, Max – Tuebingen 1910 – 1 – DM30.00 – gw Mikro Press [338]

RHEINISCH-WESTFAELISCHE ZEITUNG – Essen, Germany. 16 Mai 1883-Aug 1944 – 186r – 1 – gw Mikrofilm [072]

RHEINLANDS WUNDERHORN: SAGEN, GESCHICHTEN UND LEGENDEN, AUCH RAENKE UND SCHWAENKE, AUS DEN ALTEN RITTERBURGEN KLOESTERN UND STAEDTEN DER RHEINUFER UND DES RHEINGEBIETES, VON DEN QUELLEN BIS ZUR MUENDUNG DES STROMES / Trog, Carl – Dem deutschen Volk gewidmet von C. Trog. Essen & Leipzig, Verlag von A. Silbermann, 1882-84. 15 v. Film Mas C 370 – 1 – us H.U. Library [080]

RHEINLAND-WESTFALER ANZEIGER *see* WESTPHAELISCHER ANZEIGER

RHEIN-MAINISCHE VOLKSZEITUNG – Frankfurt, Germany. 1926-2 Mai 1933 – 8r – 1 – gw Mikrofilm [072]

RHEIN-MAINISCHE VOLKSZEITUNG *see* RHEIN-MAINISCHE VOLKSZEITUNG UND HANDELSBLATT

RHEIN-MAINISCHE VOLKSZEITUNG UND HANDELSBLATT – (Cont as: Rhein-Mainische Volkszeitung 1930-33) – Frankfurt M., 1926-30 – 8r – 1 – DM640.00 – gw Mikro Press [072]

RHEIN-NECKAR-ZEITUNG – Heidelberg, Germany. 1968- – ca 9r per yr – 1 – gw Mikrofilm [072]

DIE RHEINPFALZ : LUDWIGSHAFENER RUNDSCHAU – Ludwigshafen, Germany. 1969-1990 – 179r – 1 – gw Mikrofilm [072]

DIE RHEINPFALZ – Neustadt-Ludwigshafen, Germany. 1945-1948 (incomplete) – 1 – gw Mikrofilm [072]

RHEIN-SIEG-ANZEIGER : BA DES KOELNER STADT-ANZEIGERS – Siegburg, Germany. 1992- – 15r per yr – 1 – gw Mikrofilm [072]

RHEIN-SIEG-RUNDSCHAU *see* KOELNISCHE RUNDSCHAU

Rheinwald, F H *see* EPITOME THEOLOGIAE CHRISTIANAE

RHEIN-ZEITUNG – (Also Bereichsausgaben available: ALTENKIRCHEN, 1977-apr 14 1995, 138r; BIRKENFELD, Nahe-Zeitung, 1981- ; COCHEM, 1977- ; BAD NEUENAHR-AHRWEILER, jun 1 1983- ; NEUWIED, jan 3 1972-) – Koblenz, 1950- – 1 – Inquire at Mikrofilmarchiv for details – gw Misc Inst [072]

RHEIN-ZEITUNG – Cochem-Koblenz, Germany. 1977- – ca 8r per yr – 1 – gw Mikrofilm [072]

RHEIN-ZEITUNG – Koblenz, Germany. 1969- – ca 10r per yr – 1 – gw Mikrofilm [072]

RHEIN-ZEITUNG – Neuwied-Koblenz, Germany. 1 Sept 1978-1989 – 79r – 1 – gw Mikrofilm [072]

Rhenanus, Johann *see* SOLIS E PVTEO EMERGENTIS, SIVE, DISSERTATIONIS CHYMIATECHNICAE LIBRI TRES

RHEOLOGY ABSTRACTS – v1- 1958- – 5,6,9 – us UMI [530]

RHERORS LATINI MINORES / ed by Halm, Carolus – Lipsiae, 1863 – 12mf – 8 – ne Slangenburg [450]

THE RHETORIC AND REALITY OF INCOME DISTRIBUTION / Tullock, Gordon – 2fiches (29x) – 9 – 1.00f – at Libertarian Micro [320]

RHETORIC, OR A VIEW OF ITS PRINCIPAL TROPES AND FIGURES / Gibbons, Thomas – 1767. 503p. (English Linguistics Series 1500-1800) – 9 – us UMI [400]

RHETORICA – (1985- . 5,6,9) – v1- . 1983- – 1 – us UMI [410]

RHETORICA AD HERENNIUM, ETC / Cicero, Marcus Tullius – 14th cent. Holkham mss. 144, 360, 373. Holkham Hall, Norfolk, England – 1 – uk Microform Academic [760]

RHETORICA CASTELLANA...HABLAR BIEN... ORACION / Pabon Guerrero, Alonso – 1764 – 9 – 1.50f – sp Bibl Santa Ana [410]

RHETORICA ELEMENTA QUESTIONIBUS ET RESPONSIONIBUS EXPLICATA / Dugard, William – 1648. 144p. (English Linguistics Series 1500-1800) – 9 – us UMI [450]

A RHETORICAL GRAMMAR / Walker, John – 1785. 364p. (English Linguistics Series 1500-1800) – 9 – us UMI [400]

A RHETORICAL GRAMMAR OF THE ENGLISH LANGUAGE / Kenrick, William – 1784. 140p. (English Linguistics Series 1500-1800) – 9 – us UMI [420]

A RHETORICAL GRAMMAR OF THE ENGLISH LANGUAGE / Sheridan, Thomas – 1781. 270p. (English Linguistics Series 1500-1800) – 9 – us UMI [420]

RHETORICORUM LIBRI 4 / Arias Montano, Benito – 1775 – 9 – $1.50f – sp Bibl Santa Ana [160]

RHETORIK DER FRANZOESISCHEN REVOLUTION : UNTERSUCHUNGEN AUF DER BASIS EINES ERWEITERTEN VERSTAENDNISSES VON RHETORIK / Lohe, Elisabeth – 1994 – 3mf – 9 – DM98.00 – 3-89349-860-5 – gw Hänsel [440]

LA RHETORIQUE / Lamy, B – 3e ed. 1688 – 9 – fr I.C.S. [440]

RHETORIQUE / Courcelles, P de – 1557 – 9 – fr I.C.S. [440]

LA RHETORIQUE FRANCOISE / Bary, R – 1665 – 9 – fr I.C.S. [440]

LA RHETORIQUE FRANCOISE / Foclin, A – 1555 – 9 – fr I.C.S. [440]

RHETORIQUE FRANCOISE / Crevier, Jean-Baptiste-Louis – 1765 – 9 – fr I.C.S. [440]

LA RHETORIQUE (SIC) FRANCOISE / Le Gras – 1671 – 9 – fr I.C.S. [440]

RHEUMATIC DISEASES *see* ANNALS OF THE RHEUMATIC DISEASES

RHEUMATOLOGY INTERNATIONAL CLINICAL AND EXPERIMENTAL INVESTIGATIONS – v.1, 1981. ISSN:0172-8172 – 1,5,6,9,13 – 76.00v – us UMI [616]

Rhind, William Graeme *see* THE TABERNACLE IN THE WILDERNESS

RHIPIPHORIDUM COLEOPTERORUM FAMILIAE DISPOSITIO SYSTEMATICA / Gerstaecker, C E A – Berolini, 1855. 36p,1pl. Z/1280/2 – 8 – ne IDC [590]

RHODE ILAND SUPERIOR COURT RESCRIPTS / Rhode Island. Supreme Court – v1-2. 1917-1919 (all publ) – 4mf – 9 – $6.00 – LLMC 90-306 – us L.L.M.C. [340]

RHODE ISLAND : GENERAL LAWS OF RHODE ISLAND – Charlottesville: Michie Company, 1956-Nov 1994 update – 9 – $1,384.50 set – us Hein [340]

RHODE ISLAND : SESSION LAWS OF AMERICAN STATES AND TERRITORIES – 1776-1994 – 9 – $2,697.00 set – us Hein [340]

Rhode Island *see*
- REPORTS, POST-NRS
- REPORTS, PRE-NRS
- STATE REPORTS, POST-NRS

RHODE ISLAND 1782 CENSUS – (Lists alphabetically all persons within each community and the first 1782 listing for the towns of Barrington, Johnston, Richmond and New Shoreham. An introductory demographic essay explores population characteristics from 1774 to 1790 and includes data on household size, wealth, fertility, and age and sex structures for each community) – (mf ed 1979) – 1mf – 9 – 0-931248-00-0 – us Holbrook [978]

RHODE ISLAND ADVOCATE – Kingston. R.I. 1831-1832 – 1 – us UMI [071]

Rhode Island. Agricultural Experiment Station *see*
- ANNUAL FEED CIRCULAR
- ANNUAL FERTILIZER CIRCULAR
- ANNUAL REPORT
- BULLETIN
- MISCELLANEOUS PUBLICATION
- RHODE ISLAND AGRICULTURE
- RHODE ISLAND RESEARCH

Rhode Island. Agricultural Extension Service *see*
- BETTER RURAL LIFE
- BULLETIN
- CIRCULAR
- EXTENSION REVIEW
- GARDENERS' NOTEBOOK
- NATURE GUARD

RHODE ISLAND AGRICULTURE / Rhode Island. Agricultural Experiment Station – v. 1-15. 1954-69 – 1,5,6 – us Spaulding [630]

RHODE ISLAND ATTORNEY GENERAL REPORTS AND OPINIONS – (Earlier vols unavailable. Subject: State Law) – 1985-1994 – 9 – $37.50 set – us Hein [340]

RHODE ISLAND BAPTIST – v1-54. 1917-70 (complete) – 4r – 1 – ATLA R0113 – us A.T.L.A. [073]

Rhode Island Bar Association *see* JOHN MARSHALL DAY, CELEBRATION BY THE RHODE ISLAND BAR ASSOCIATION AND BROWN UNIVERSITY, FEBRUARY 4, 1901: ADDRESS BY HON. LE BARON BRADFORD COLT.

RHODE ISLAND BAR ASSOCIATION REPORTS – (Lacking: v1-3,6,8-9,18-28) – 1901-29 (all publ) – 15mf – 9 – $22.50 – LLMC 84-670 – us L.L.M.C. [073]

RHODE ISLAND BAR JOURNAL – v1-43. 1952-94 – 9 – $366.00 set – us Hein [340]

Rhode Island. Bureau of Industrial Statistics *see* STATE LABOR REPORTS

RHODE ISLAND COUNTY JOURNAL – Providence. R.I. 1879-1896 – 1 – us UMI [071]

RHODE ISLAND DEMOCRAT – Providence. R.I. 1879-1894 – 1 – us UMI [071]

RHODE ISLAND HERALD – Providence. R.I. -w. 1959- – 1 – us UMI [071]

RHODE ISLAND HISTORY – v1- 1942- 1; v36- 5,6,9 – us UMI [978]

RHODE ISLAND JEWISH REVIEW – Providence. R.I. 1920-1929 – 1 – us UMI [071]

RHODE ISLAND PENDULUM – East Greenwich. R.I. -w. 1857- – 1 – us UMI [071]

RHODE ISLAND PILOT – West Warwick. R.I. 1945-1950 – 1 – us UMI [071]

RHODE ISLAND PRESS – Providence. R.I. 1863-1886 – 1 – us UMI [071]

RHODE ISLAND RELIGIOUS MESSENGER – 1826-28 (complete) – 1r – 1 – ATLA R0122 – us A.T.L.A. [073]

RHODE ISLAND REPUBLICAN – Newport. R.I. 1809-1820 – 1,3 – us Readex [071]

RHODE ISLAND REPUBLICAN – Newport. R.I. 1831-1833 – 1 – us UMI [071]
RHODE ISLAND REPUBLICAN – Providence. R.I. 1802-1830; 1834-1840 – 1 – us UMI [071]
RHODE ISLAND RESEARCH / Rhode Island. Agricultural Experiment Station – v. 1-4. 1950-54 – 1,5,6 – us Spaulding [630]
Rhode Island. State Bar Association *see* PROCEEDINGS
Rhode Island. Supreme Court *see*
- RHODE ILAND SUPERIOR COURT RESCRIPTS
- RHODE ISLAND SUPREME COURT REPORTS

RHODE ISLAND SUPREME COURT REPORTS / Rhode Island. Supreme Court – (Pre-NRS: v1-14 1828-86 34mf $153.00. Updates planned) – v1-42. 1828-1920 – 92mf (1:42) 48mf (1:24) – 9 – $486.00 – LLMC 84-207 – us L.L.M.C. [340]
RHODE ISLAND TELEGRAPH – Warren. R.I. 1855-1860 – 1 – us UMI [071]
Rhode Island. Warren Baptist Association *see* PRINTED MINUTES
RHODE ISLANDER – East Providence. R.I. 1896-1916 – 1 – us UMI [071]
RHODE ISLANDER – Newport. R.I. 1842- – 1 – us UMI [071]
RHODE ISLANDER – Olneyville. R.I. 1891-1893 – 1 – us UMI [071]
RHODE ISLANDER – Providence. R.I. 1896-1916; 1927-1933 – 1 – us UMI [071]
THE RHODE-ISLAND GAZETTE – Newport, RI. 1732-33. Also: Gazette Francoise, 1780-81; The Newport Herald, 1787-91. Sold as one unit – 1,3 – us Readex [071]
Rhodes, Albert John *see* DARTMOOR PRISON.
Rhodes, E C *see*
- COMPARISON OF THE LACTATE AND VENTILATORY THRESHOLDS DURING PROLONGED WORK
- PREDICTION OF TRIATHLON PERFORMANCE FROM VENTILATORY THRESHOLD MEASUREMENTS

Rhodes House *see* ANTI-SLAVERY PAPERS
Rhodes House Library. Oxford *see* ANTI-SLAVERY COLLECTION
RHODES' JOURNAL OF BANKING AND THE BANKERS' MAGAZINE CONSOLIDATED *see* BANKERS MAGAZINE
Rhodes, Robert E et al *see* SANCTIONS IMPOSABLE FOR VIOLATIONS OF THE FEDERAL RULES OF CIVIL PROCEDURE
Rhodes, Ronald L *see* THE EFFECTS OF A WEIGHT TRAINING COURSE ON STRESS LEVELS AND LOCUS OF CONTROL IN COLLEGE FEMALES
Rhodesia *see*
- PUBLIC SECTOR INVESTMENT PROGRAMME, 1969-1972
- PUBLIC SECTOR INVESTMENT PROGRAMME, 1970-1973

RHODESIA ADVERTISER – Umtali. Zimbabwe. -w. Jan 1903-Dec 1918. (9 reels) – 1 – uk British Libr Newspaper [072]
RHODESIA HERALD – Salisbury. Zimbabwe. -w. Jan 1903-Dec 26. (41 reels) – 1 – uk British Libr Newspaper [072]
THE RHODESIA HERALD – Salisbury, Mashuanaland: Argus Printing & Pub Co, [1892-] 1956-aug 14 1978 – us Res Libr [072]
RHODESIA JOURNAL – Bulawayo. Zimbabwe. -w. 13 Dec 1907-15 Jun 1911, 9 Nov 1911-17 Apr 1913. (Imperfect). (8 reels) – 1 – uk British Libr Newspaper [072]
Rhodesia. Ministry of Education. Division of African Education *see* ANNUAL REPORT OF THE SECRETARY FOR AFRICAN EDUCATION 1967-1977
Rhodesia. Ministry of Education. European, Asian and Coloured Division of Education *see* REPORT ON EDUCATION FOR THE YEAR 1964-1977
Rhodesia. National Archives *see* MICROFILM ACCESSIONS REGISTER, NOS 1-299 [-435]
Rhodesia. Northern *see*
- GOVERNMENT PUBLICATIONS
- REVISION OF THE NORTHERN RHODESIA TEN-YEAR DEVELOPMENT PLAN, NOV 1953
- TEN YEAR DEVELOPMENT PLAN (1947-1956)

Rhodesia. Northern. Commission Appointed to Enquire into the Disturbances in the Copperbelt *see* EVIDENCE TAKEN BY THE COMMISSION...
Rhodesia. Northern. Development Authority *see*
- REPORT FOR THE YEAR 1952
- REPORT FOR THE YEAR 1953
- REPORT FOR THE YEAR 1954
- REPORT FOR THE YEAR 1955

Rhodesia. (Northern). Legislative Council *see* DEBATES
Rhodesia. (Southern) *see* SECOND FOUR YEAR PLAN CAPITAL EXPENDITURE FROM LOAN FUNDS, APRIL 1951 TO MARCH 1955
Rhodesia. Southern *see*
- ANNUAL DEPARTMENTAL REPORTS
- GOVERNMENT PUBLICATIONS

Rhodesia. Southern. Department of Native Affairs *see* NADA
Rhodesia. Southern. Division of African Education *see* ANNUAL REPORT OF THE SECRETARY..
Rhodesia. Southern. Legislative Council (later Legislative Assembly) *see*
- DEBATES
- MINUTES OF PROCEEDINGS AND VOTES AND PROCEEDINGS

THE RHODESIAN – Special evening war edition. Salisbury. Zimbabwe. -d. 28 Sep-31 Oct 1914. (16 ft) – 1 – uk British Libr Newspaper [072]
THE RHODESIAN HERALD *see* HERALD
Rhodes-Livingstone Institute *see*
- JOURNAL
- PAPERS

Rhodes-Livingstone Museum *see* OCCASIONAL PAPERS
THE RHODIAN SEA-LAW / ed by Ashburner, W – Oxford, 1909 – 5mf – 9 – ILM-861/1 – ne IDC [340]
RHODIORVM OPPVGNATIO & DEDITIO EPISTOLA EXPLICATA – N.p., [1522] – 1mf – 9 – H-8138/1 – ne IDC [956]
THE RHODODENDRONS OF SIKKIM-HIMALAYA / Hooker, JD – 3v. London. 1849-51. B-7152 2 – 8 – ne IDC [580]
DIE RHODOMELACEEN DES GOLFES VON NEAPEL / Falkenberg, P – 670 2. 1901 – 8 – ne IDC [580]
DIE RHODOMELACEEN DES GOLFES VON NEAPEL / Falkenberg, P – Berlin, 1901. xvi/754p, 24pls. Flora und Fauna des Golfes von Neapel, 26 – 8 – ne IDC [580]
RHODORA : JOURNAL OF THE NEW ENGLAND BOTANICAL CLUB – Boston, Providence, Lancaster. v1-34. 1899-1932 – 116mf – 9 – 8574/1 – ne IDC [580]
RHOEN- UND SAALEPOST – Bad Neustadt a.d. Saale, Germany. 1978- – ca 6r per yr – 1 – gw Mikrofilm [072]
RHONDDA SOCIALIST NEWSPAPER – Pontypridd & Merthyr Tydfil, Wales. South Wales Worker. -w. 19 Aug 1911-25 July 1914. 49 ft – 1 – uk British Libr Newspaper [072]
RHOS HERALD – Wales. 1894-1903. -w. 9 reels – 1 – uk British Libr Newspaper [072]
RHYL JOURNAL AND ADVERTISER – England.1980. -w. 3 reels – 1 – uk British Libr Newspaper [072]
RHYL RECORD *see* RHYL RECORD AND ADVERTISER
RHYL RECORD AND ADVERTISER – Wales, 5 Jul 1855-31 Dec 1869; 9 Oct 1874-28 Aug 1886 – 21r – 1 – uk British Libr Newspaper [072]
RHYL RECORD AND ADVERTISER – Wales. Record & Advertiser. -w. 1887-1911. 21 reels – 1 – uk British Libr Newspaper [072]
RHYL RECORD AND VISITOR *see* RHYL RECORD AND ADVERTISER
Rhys, Lloyd *see* HIGH LIGHTS AND FLIGHTS IN NEW GUINEA...ACCOUNT OF THE DISCOVERY AND DEVELOPMENT OF THE MOROBE GOLDFIELDS
RHYTHMUS, METRIK UND STROPHIK IN DER BIBLISCH-HEBRAEISCHEN POESIE / Doeller, Johannes – Paderborn: F. Schoeningh, 1899. 1 fiche – 9 – us A.T.L.A. [220]
Riabinina L *see* DESIAT LET SOVETSKOGO STROITELSTVA
LA RIADA / Trigueros, Candido Maria – 1784 – 1mf – 9 – Pta1,000.00 – 84-7848-337-3 – sp Pentalfa [440]
RIAI TECHNICAL INFORMATION MICROFILE – 1992 – 9 – uk Tech [624]
RIALTO RECORD – Rialto, CA. 1973- – 53+ r – 1 – $2,650.00 ($125.00y) – R02688 – us Library Micro [071]
RIAM KANAN PROJECT: SPECIFICATION FOR PURCHASE, TRANSPORTATION AND ERECTION OF PENSTOCK AND ACCESSORIES / Indonesia. Kementerian Pekerdjaan Umum dan Tenaga – SE-5538 1. 1963 – 9 – ne IDC [620]
Rianzuela, Marques de *see*
- OPUSCULO FUNEBRE
- LA SOMBRA DE HERNAN CORTES...NUEVA ESPANA

RIAQUISTO DELLA CITTADINANZA ITALIANA PERDUTA COLO SCOPO DI OTTENERE IL DIVORZIO / Esperson, P – Milano, [1913] – 1mf – 1 – ILM-3669/1 – ne IDC [327]
Riazanov, N (pseud.) *see* OBUKHOVSKOE DELO. S PRILOZHENIEM SUDEBNAGO PRIGOVORA
THE RIBA DRAWINGS COLLECTION : MICROFILMS FROM THE GENERAL CATALOGUES / Royal Institute of British Architects – (Phase E: 1590-1780 A-Z complete £1250.00 12r. Phase F: 1780-1840 A-D £1995.00 21r. Phase G: 1780-1840 E-P £1050.00 11r. Phase H: 1780-1840 R-Z £595.00 6r. Phase I: 1840-1914 A-B £495.00 5r. Phase J: 1840-1914 Bentley to Burges £1250.00 13r. Phase K: 1840-1914 B-F £1500.00 14r. Phase M: 1840-1914 G-L £2195.00 21r. Phase N: 1840-1914 L-M £1595.00 12r. Phase O: 1840-1914 M-P £695.00 6r. Phase P: 1840-1914 P-S £1295.00 11r. Phase Q: 1840-1914 Salvin-Simpson £975.00 8r. Phase R: 1840-1914 15r £1750.00) – 14 – uk World [720]
THE RIBA DRAWINGS COLLECTION: EARLIER PHASES : MICROFILMS FROM THE SPECIALIST CATALOGUES / Royal Institute of British Architects – (Phase A: Colen Campbell, Jacques Gentilhatre, Inigo Jones and John Webb, Alfred Stevens, Antonio Visentini, C.F.A. Voysey £1250.00 14r 1,14. Phase B: The Pugin Family, the Wyatt Family and J.B. Papworth £1300.00 16r 1,14. Phase C: the Drawings of Sir Edwin Lutyens and the Scott Family Drawings £2950.00 1. Available separately: Lutyens drawings £780.00 12r Scott drawings £2400.00 38r. Phase D: the Palladio drawings, the Adam drawings and the Smythson collection £395.00 4r 14. Phase L: the Charles Holden collection £1350.00 13r 14) – 1,14 – uk World [720]
RIBA JOURNAL – v1- 1893- 1; v78- 5,6; v83- 9 – us UMI [720]
RIBA NOMINATION PAPERS 1834-1900 / British Architectural Library – (With printed index) – 1993 – 119mf – 9 – $606.00 – 1-869934-50-4 – uk Emmett [720]
RIBA. TI OCCUPATIONAL HEALTH AND SAFETY MICROFILE – 1991 – 9 – uk Tech [360]
RIBA. TI PLANNING FILE – 1988 – 9 – uk Tech [307]
RIBA TI TECHNICAL INFORMATION MICROFILE – (Engineering Supplement and Building Supplement available) – 1985 – 9 – uk Tech [624]
Ribadineira, P *see* GENERALE LEGENDE DER HEYLIGHEN MET HET LEVEN IESU CHRISTI ENDE MARIE
Ribas, L M de *see* BIBLIOGRAFICHESKIE MATERIALY PO ISTORII NOVOROSSII. UKAZATEL'
LES RIBAUD: UNE IDYLLE DE 37 / Choquette, Ernest – Montreal: E. Senecal, 1898. 02270. (Pre-1900 Canadiana) – 9 – cn C.I.H.M. [971]
Ribbentrop, Joachim von *see* THE RIBBENTROP MEMOIRS
THE RIBBENTROP MEMOIRS / Ribbentrop, Joachim von – Trans. by Oliver Watson. Introd. by Alan Bullock. London: Weidenfeld and Nicolson, 1954. 216p – 1 – us U.W. Library [943]
Ribbert, Hugo *see* "ZWECKMAESSIGKEIT" IN DER PATHOLOGIE
Ribbing, Sigurd *see* CHR. JAC. BOSTROEMS FOERELAESNINGAR I RELIGIONSFILOSOFI
Ribe, CF *see* CHIRURGISKE FOERSOEK OCH ANMAERKNINGAR VID OEGONSJUKDOMAR
RIBE STIFTS-TIDENDE – Ribe, Denmark. 10 July 1916-2 Aug 1919 – 7r – 1 – uk British Libr Newspaper [072]
Ribeiro, Joao *see* O ELEMENTO NEGRO: HISTORIA, FOLKLORE, LINGUISTICA
Ribera, F *see*
- DE TEMPLO, ET DE IIS QUAE AD TEMPLUM PERTINENT, LIBRI QUINQUE
- IN LIBRUM DUODECIM PROPHETARUM COMMENTARII
- IN SACRAM BEATI JOHANNIS APOSTOLI APOCALIPSIN COMMENTARII

Ribero, Vera Masagao *see* O CAMINHO DA ESCOLA
Ribes, Bruno *see* BIOLOGY AND ETHICS
Ribes, Bruno et al *see* DOMINATION OR SHARING
Ribeyrol, M *see* LES FORMES ANIMALES DANS L'ORNEMENTATION POPULAIRE EN BULGARIE AU 19E ET AU DEBUT DU 20E SIECLE
Ribie *see* LE PIED DE MOUTON
Ribot, Theodule Armand *see*
- ENGLISH PSYCHOLOGY
- GERMAN PSYCHOLOGY OF TODAY, THE EMPIRICAL SCHOOL

Riboutte *see*
- L'ASSEMBLEE DE FAMILLE
- LE MINISTRE ANGLAIS

RIBS OF THE LAW. / Mayes, Edward – Jackson, Tenn.: M'Cowat-Mercer, 1909. 180p. L.C. copy imperfect: p. 133-142 wanting. LL-267 – 1 – us L of C Photodup [340]
Ribton-Turner, Charles James *see* A HISTORY OF VAGRANTS AND VAGRANCY, AND BEGGARS AND BEGGING
RICAN – (v. 5- 1975- 5,6,9) – v. 1-. 1971- – 1 – us UMI [073]
Ricard, Robert *see* LA CONQUETE SPIRITUELLE...DU MEXIQUE...NOUVELLE ESPAGNE 1523-1524 A 1572
RICARDA HUCH / Baeumer, Gertrud – Tuebingen: R Wunderlich Verlag H Leins, 1949 – 1r – 1 – us U.W. Library [920]
RICARDI DE CIRENCESTRIA SPECULUM HISTORIALE DE GESTIS REGUM ANGLIAE (RS30) / Richard of Circencester; ed by Mayor, J E B – (v1 1863 Dfl28.00. v2 1869 Dfl35.00) – ne Slangenburg [941]
RICARDO WAGNER, EL HOMBRE I EL ARTISTA / Guerrero – Chile: Imp. Universitaria, 1913 – 1 – us U.W. Library [790]
RICARDO WAGNER, EL HOMBRE I EL ARTISTA / Guerrero, Eduardo Garcia – Chile: Imp. Universitaria, 1913 – 1 – us U.W. Library [780]
Riccati, Giordano *see* SAGGIO SOPRA LE LEGGI DEL CONTRAPPUNTO..
Ricci, Clemente *see* ENSAYO SOBRE VIRGILIO
Ricci, P *see* TRIOS, SEI, 2 VIOLINS ET VIOLONCELLO, OP.3
Ricci, Umberto *see* DAL PROTEZIONISMO AL SINDACALISMO
Riccoldo, Montecroce de *see* CONTENTA. RICOLDI ORDINIS PRAEDICATORUM CONTRA SECTAM MA-HUMETICAM...
RICE : SELECTED ASPECTS OF PRODUCTION, TRADE AND PRICE POLICIES – 1985 – 87p – it F.A.O. [338]
Rice, A L *see* DEEP-SEA CHALLENGE
Rice, B L *see* EPIGRAPHIA CARNATICA
Rice, Clinton *see* MANUAL OF THE U.S. BANKRUPTCY ACT, 1867.
RICE DEVELOPMENT AND RAINFED RICE PRODUCTION – 1982 – 109p – it F.A.O. [338]
RICE DURING AND AFTER THE WAR. BIBLIOGRAPHY OF THE LITERATURE, 1940-47. 1949. WARTIME DEVELOPMENTS IN RICE / Kuilman, L W – SE-11,973 1. 1948 – 9 – ne IDC [338]
Rice, Edwin Wilbur *see*
- COMMENTARY ON THE GOSPEL ACCORDING TO LUKE
- COMMENTARY ON THE GOSPEL ACCORDING TO MATTHEW
- A HISTORY OF THE AMERICAN SUNDAY-SCHOOL UNION
- PEOPLE'S COMMENTARY ON THE GOSPEL ACCORDING TO MATTHEW
- A PICTORIAL COMMENTARY ON THE GOSPEL ACCORDING TO MARK
- A SHORT HISTORY OF THE INTERNATIONAL LESSON SYSTEM

Rice, Elwood E *see* STANDARDS OF BUSINESS
Rice, James M *see* PEORIA CITY AND COUNTY
Rice, John *see* AN INTRODUCTION TO THE ART OF READING WITH ENERGY AND PROPRIETY
Rice, Luther *see*
- JOURNALS AND LETTERS
- JOURNALS, LEDGERS, MEMO BOOK
- LETTERS AND OTHER MANUSCRIPTS

RICE MARKETING – 1972 – 189p – it F.A.O. [650]
RICE MARKETING IN THE REPUBLIC OF INDONESIA / Mears, Leon A – SE-2212 1. 1957 – 9 – ne IDC [380]
RICE MARKETING IN THE REPUBLIC OF INDONESIA / Mears, Leon A – SE-2213 1. 1961 – 9 – ne IDC [380]
Rice, Mary Berenice *see* DIAGNOSIS OF THE MENTAL HYGIENE PROBLEMS OF COLLEGE WOMEN BY MEANS OF PERSONALITY RATINGS
RICE MILLING EQUIPMENT OPERATION AND MAINTENANCE – 1981 – 101p – it F.A.O. [660]

RICE PARBOILING – 1984 – 97p – it F.A.O. [660]

RICE TESTING METHODS AND EQUIPMENT – 1979 – 55p – it F.A.O. [631]

Rice Township. Sandusky County.Ohio. Trinity Evangelical Lutheran Church *see* RECORDS

RICE TRIALS IN TAURGA / Libya. Agricultural Information and Publicity Committee. Administration of Agriculture – Bulletin nr. 32. Mar 1963. Province of Tripolitania. Sgaier, K. BNE-1028 1 – 9 – ne IDC [630]

Rice, Walter Ayscoughe *see* CRUSADERS OF THE TWENTIETH CENTURY

Rice, William North *see* CHRISTIAN FAITH IN AN AGE OF SCIENCE

RICE-HUSK CONVERSION TO ENERGY – 1981 – 175p – it F.A.O. [333]

RICERCA IN CLINICA E IN LABORATORIO – 1971- 1; 1977- 5,6,9 – us UMI [610]

RICERCHE ECONOMICHE – 1947- 1; 1974- 5,6; 1975- 4 x 6 in. 9 – us UMI [330]

RICERCHE ENTOMOLOGICHE SOPRA I MONTI PARTENII NEL PRINCIPATO ULTERIORE / Costa, A – Napoli, 1858. 29p. 1 pl. Z-1149/2 – 8 – ne IDC [590]

RICE'S CASES IN EQUITY / South Carolina. Supreme Court – (A Pre-NRS title) – 1v. 1838-1839 (all publ) – 5mf – 9 – $7.50 – LLMC 94-032 – us L.L.M.C. [340]

RICE'S CREEK BAPTIST CHURCH. LIBERTY ASSOCIATION. PICKENS COUNTY. SOUTH CAROLINA : CHURCH RECORDS – 1940-1977 – 1 – 20.16 – us Baptist [240]

RICE'S DIGEST OF U.S. PATENT OFFICE LAW AND PRACTICE – (Bk 1 by D.G. & L.C. Rice, 1869-1880. bk 2 by L.H. Rice) – Boston: Geo B Reed. 2bks. 1890-1900 (all publ) – 11mf – 9 – $16.50 – LLMC 84-331 – us L.L.M.C. [340]

RICE'S LAW REPORTS / South Carolina. Supreme Court – (A Pre-NRS title) – 1v. 1838-1839 (all publ) – 6mf – 9 – $9.00 – LLMC 94-020 – us L.L.M.C. [340]

RICH AND POOR – London, UK. 1867-68 – 3ft – 1 – uk British Libr Newspaper [072]

Rich, Barnaby *see* FAULTES FAULTS, AND NOTHING ELSE BUT FAULTES

Rich, Burdett A *see* RULING CASELAW

Rich et al *see* REGISTER OF CURRENT AUSTRALIAN ORNITHOLOGICAL RESEARCH

Rich, Giles S *see* A BRIEF HISTORY OF THE COURT OF CUSTOMS AND PATENT APPEALS

THE RICH MAN AND LAZARUS / MacArthur, Arthur – London: James Nisbet, 1885. 1 fiche – 9 – us A.T.L.A. [240]

Richa, G *see* NOTIZIE ISTORICHE DELLE CHIESE FIORENTINE DIVISE NE' SUOI QUARTIERI

Richard, A *see* VOYAGES DE LA CORVETTE "L'ASTROLABE"

Richard, Achille *see*
- BOTAANIQUE MEDICALE,...
- HISTOIRE NATURELLE ET MEDICALE D'IPECACUANHA...
- MEMOIRE SUR LA FAMILLE DES RUBIACEES
- PLANTES VASCULAIRES
- SERTUM ASTROLABIANUM
- TENTAMEN FLORAE ABYSINICAE; SEU ENUMERATIO PLANTARUM.
- VOYAGE EN ABYSSINIE, EXECUTE PENDANT LES ANNEES

Richard, Anne B *see* THE EFFECTS OF FREEDOM OF CHOICE ON THE PARTICIPANTS IN A LEISURE EDUCATION PROGRAM

RICHARD CAMERON / Herkless, John – Edinburgh: Oliphant Anderson & Ferrier, [1896?] – 1mf – us A.T.L.A. [240]

Richard, Charles Louis Florentin *see*
- DU GOUVERNEMENT ARABE ET DE L'INSTITUTION QUI DOIT L'EXERCER
- ETUDE SUR L'INSURRECTION DU DHARA (1845-1846)

RICHARD COBDEN, 1887 / Cowing, Richard – With The Tariff Idea by W. M. Curtiss, 1953. 2 fiches (24x) – 9 – $1.00f – at Libertarian Micro [320]

RICHARD COBDEN AND THE FREE TRADERS / Apjohn, Lewis – 1fiche (29x) – 9 – $1.00f – at Libertarian Micro [320]

RICHARD COBDEN PAPERS : CORRESPONDENCE AND OTHER PAPERS IN W. SUSSEX RECORD OFFICE / Cobden, Richard – (With guide and printed catalogue) – 1988 – 663mf – 9 – $4,300.00 – 0-907716-48-2 – uk Mindata [920]

RICHARD COBDEN – THE INTERNATIONAL MAN / Hobson, J A – 1918. 1 fiche (29x) – 9 – $1.00f – at Libertarian Micro [320]

Richard de la Vergne, Pierre *see* LA PROVIDENCE, POEME

RICHARD DE MIDDLETON / Hocedez, E S J – Louvain: Paris, 1925 – 10mf – 8 – ne Slangenburg [290]

Richard, Dorothy E *see* UNITED STATES NAVAL ADMINISTRATION OF THE TTPI

THE RICHARD H. FIELD PAPERS / Field, Richard H – (Guide only $100.00) – 28r – 1 – $3,080.00 – 0-89093-805-9 – us UPA [340]

THE RICHARD HODGES RESEARCH COLLECTION ON SPELLING / Svobodny, Dolly – 1884-1976. 9326 titles on 750mf. Printed card indexes and CD/ROM index – 9 – us A.T.B.I. [400]

Richard, [J M] C *see* CATALOGUE DU JARDIN DE LA REUNION

Richard, J W *see* CHRISTIAN WORSHIP

Richard, James William *see* PHILIP MELANCHTON

Richard, Jean *see* CARTULAIRE DE MARCIGNY-SUR-LOIRE, 1045-1144

Richard, Jerome *see* LA THEORIE DES SONGES

Richard, Juliana J *see* PERCEPTIONS OF "UTILITY" AND "LIKEABILITY" DIMENSIONS OF A PHYSICAL EDUCATION FITNESS CURRICULUM

Richard, L C M *see*
- COMMENTATIO BOTANICA DE CONIFEREIS ET CYCADEIS
- DE ORCHIDEIS EUROPAEIS ANNOTATIONES

Richard, Marie-France *see* BIO-BIBLIOGRAPHIE ANALYTIQUE DU POETE ADOLPHE POISSON

Richard, Nicolas Louis Antoine *see* TRADITIONS POPULAIRES, CROYANCES, SUPERSTITIEUSES..

Richard of Circencester *see* RICARDI DE CIRENCESTRIA SPECULUM HISTORIALE DE GESTIS REGUM ANGLIAE (RS30)

RICHARD PARRISH PAPERS, 1950-1975 : FROM THE HOLDINGS OF THE SCHOMBURG CENTER FOR RESEARCH IN BLACK CULTURE, MANUSCRIPTS, ARCHIVES AND RARE BOOKS DIVISION: THE NEW YORK PUBLIC LIBRARY, ASTOR, LENOX AND TILDEN FOUNDATIONS – (Guide which covers all coll under "Civil Rights Advocates" sold separately for $20.00 D3305.G3) – 1995 – 10r – 1 – $850.00 – D3305P10 – Dist. us Scholarly Res – us L of C Photodup [320]

RICHARD ROTHE : GEDAECHTNISREDE / Troeltsch, Ernst – Freiburg i.B.: J.C.B. Mohr, 1899 – 1mf – us A.T.L.A. [240]

Richard, Simon *see* HISTOIRE CRITIQUE DU VIEUX TESTAMENT

RICHARD SIMON ET LA CRITIQUE BIBLIQUE / Trochon, Charles – Rouen: Cagniard, 1868. 1 fiche – 9 – us A.T.L.A. [220]

RICHARD SIMON ET SON HISTOIRE CRITIQUE DU VIEUX TESTAMENT : LA CRITIQUE BIBLIQUE AU SIECLE DE LOUIS 14 / Bernus, Auguste – Lausanne: Georges Bridel, 1869 – 1mf – 9 – 0-8370-2298-3 – 1985-0298 – us A.T.L.A. [220]

Richard, Timothy, Mrs *see* CHRISTIAN BIOGRAPHIES (CCC270)

RICHARD VON ST VICTOR UND JOHANNES RUSBROEK / Engelhardt, D J – Erlangen, 1838 – 7mf – 8 – ne Slangenburg [240]

RICHARD VOSS : EIN LITTERARISCHES CHARAKTERBILD / Goldmann, Karl – Berlin: R Eckstein, [1890?] – 1r – 1 – us U.W. Library [430]

RICHARD WAGNER / Wolzogen, Hans von – Berlin; Leipzig: Schuster & Loeffler, [1905] – 1 – us U.W. Library [780]

RICHARD WAGNER ALS DICHTER / Schrenck, Erich von – (Includes bibliographical references) – Muenchen: C H Beck, 1913 – 1r – 1 – us U.W. Library [430]

RICHARD WAGNER ET LE ROI DE BAVIERE – Lettres de Wagner a Eliza Wille traduites par Jacques Saint-Cere (pseud. d'Armand Rosenthal). Paris: A. Dupret, 1887. 53p. 1 fiche. (Music Collection) – 9 – 6.00 – fr Bibl Nationale [920]

RICHARD WAGNER IN SEINER ZEIT UND NACH SEINER ZEIT : EINE JAHRHUNDERTBETRACHTUNG / Walzel, Oskar Franz – Muenchen: G Mueller und E Rentsch, 1913 – 1r – 1 – us U.W. Library [780]

RICHARD WAGNER JAHRBUCH / Wagner, Richard – Leipzig. 1906-1913. v1-5 – 29mf – 9 – ne IDC [920]

RICHARD WAGNER UND DIE ENGLISCHE LITERATUR / Reichelt, Kurt – (Includes bibliographical references) – Leipzig: Xenien-Verlag, 1912 – 1r – 1 – us U.W. Library [780]

RICHARD WAGNER UND DIE SCHWEIZ / Gysi, Fritz – (Includes bibliographical references) – Frauenfeld: Huber, c1929 – 1r – 1 – us U.W. Library [790]

RICHARD WAGNERS DICHTUNG DER RING DES NIBELUNGEN AUS DER SAGE NEU ERLAEUTERT / Meinck, Ernst – (Includes bibliographical references) – Liegnitz: J H Burmeister, 1920 – 1r – 1 – us U.W. Library [790]

RICHARD WAGNERS DRAMATISCHER ENTWURF JESUS VON NAZARETH : ENTSTEHUNGSGESCHICHTE UND VERSUCH EINER KURZEN WUERDIGUNG / Graap, Paul-Gerhard – (Includes bibliographical references) – Leipzig: Breitkopf & Haertel, 1921 – 1 – us U.W. Library [790]

RICHARD WAGNERS "PARSIFAL" : AUFBAU UND GEDANKENWELT DES BUEHNENWEIHFESTSPIELS UNTER BERUECKSICHTIGUNG DER QUELLEN / Hemmes, E – (Includes bibliographical references) – 3. Aufl. Mainz: Kirchheim, 1914 – 1 – us U.W. Library [780]

RICHARD WAGNERS PARSIFAL : AUFBAU UND GEDANKENWELT DES BUEHNENWEIHFESTSPIELS UNTER BERUECKSICHTIGUNG DER QUELLEN / Hemmes, E – (Includes bibliographical references) – 3. Aufl. Mainz: Kirchheim, 1914 – 1r – 1 – us U.W. Library [790]

RICHARD WAGNER'S TONDRAMA : DER RING DES NIBELUNGEN / Koestlin, Karl Reinhold von – Tuebingen: H Laupp, 1877 – 1 – us U.W. Library [790]

RICHARD WAGNERS TONDRAMEN = OPERAS. LIBRETTOS / Wagner, Richard; ed by Kruse, Georg Richard – Leipzig: P Reclam, [1890?] – 1 – us U.W. Library [790]

RICHARD WAGNERS TRISTAN UND ISOLDE ALS DICHTUNG : NEBST EINIGEN ALLGEMEINEN BEMERKUNGEN UEBER WAGNERS KUNST / Weltrich, Richard – Berlin: G Reimer, 1904 – 1r – 1 – us U.W. Library [430]

Richards *see* HISTORY OF SUSQUEHANNA AND JUNIATA VALLEYS

Richards, A *see* BEMBA MARRIAGE AND PRESENT ECONOMIC CONDITIONS

Richards, Anna Matlock *see* A NEW ALICE IN THE OLD WONDERLAND

Richards & Company. New York *see* UNITED STATES PATENTS, TRADE MARKS, DESIGNS AND COPYRIGHTS

Richards, Ellen Henrietta *see* PLAIN WORDS ABOUT FOOD: THE RUMFORD KITCHEN LEAFLETS

Richards, G W *see* LIFE PICTURES OF JOHN CALVIN

Richards, George W *see* THE HEIDELBERG CATECHISM

Richards, Grant *see* ARCHIVES OF GRANT RICHARDS, 1897-1948

Richards, Harry Edward *see* THE MYSTERY OF LIFE

Richards, James C *see* DIARY

Richards, Randolph A *see* HISTORY OF MONROE COUNTY PAST AND PRESENT

Richards, Thomas Cole *see* SAMUEL J. MILLS

Richards, Walter Buck *see* GENESIS OF THE FEDERAL JUDICIARY SYSTEM; ADDRESS BEFORE VIRGINIA STATE BAR ASSOCIATION, AUGUST 2, 1904

Richards, William Carey *see* THE APOSTLE OF BURMA

Richards, William Joseph *see* THE INDIAN CHRISTIANS OF ST THOMAS: OTHERWISE CALLED THE SYRIAN CHRISTIANS OF MALABAR..

Richardson, B W *see* ON CHLOROFORM AND OTHER ANAESTHETICS: THEIR ACTION AND ADMINISTRATION

Richardson, Charles Herbert *see* MANUAL OF THE LAWS OF MARYLAND, DISTRICT OF COLUMBIA, VIRGINIA AND WEST VIRGINIA RELATIVE TO RELIGIOUS CORPORATIONS, CHARITABLE USES.

RICHARDSON COUNTY RECORD – Falls City, NE. -w. Dec. 1877-May 1878 – 1 – us NE Hist [071]

(Richardson, Dorothy) *see* THE LONG DAY; THE STORY OF A NEW YORK WORKING GIRL, AS TOLD BY HERSELF

Richardson, E C *see* HIERONYMUS LIBER DE VIRIS INLUSTRIBUS

RICHARDSON ECHO – Richardson. Tex. 1920-1966 – 1 – us UMI [071]

Richardson, Ernest Cushing *see*
- THE BEGINNINGS OF LIBRARIES
- SOME OLD EGYPTIAN LIBRARIANS

Richardson, J *see*
- ARCTIC SEARCHING EXPEDITION
- BOTANICAL APPENDIX
- NARRATIVE OF A MISSION TO CENTRAL AFRICA
- TRAVELS IN THE GREAT DESERT OF SAHARA
- VOYAGE OF H.M.S. HERALD DURING 1848-1851. ZOOLOGY. VERTEBRATES INCLUDING FOSSIL MAMMALS
- THE ZOOLOGY OF THE VOYAGE OF H.M.S. EREBUS AND TERROR, 1839-1843

Richardson, Jacques *see*
- INTEGRATED TECHNOLOGY TRANSFER
- MANAGING THE OCEAN: RESOURCES, RESEARCH, LAW
- MODELS OF REALITY: SHAPING THOUGHT AND ACTION
- WINDOWS ON CREATIVITY AND INVENTION

Richardson, James D *see*
- MESSAGES AND PAPERS OF THE PRESIDENTS, 1789-1897
- MESSAGES AND PAPERS OF THE PRESIDENTS, 1789-1914

Richardson, Jane Marion Wakefield *see* SIX GENERATIONS OF FRIENDS IN IRELAND (1655 TO 1890)

Richardson, John *see*
- ARCTIC SEARCHING EXPEDITION: A JOURNAL OF A BOAT-VOYAGE THROUGH RUPERT'S LAND AND THE ARCTIC SEA, IN SEARCH OF THE DISCOVERY SHIPS UNDER THE COMMAND OF SIR JOHN FRANKLIN
- A GRAMMAR OF THE ARABICK LANGUAGE
- HARDSCRABBLE, OR, THE FALL OF CHICAGO.
- HARDSCRABBLE OR THE FALL OF CHICAGO
- SELECTED WORKS BY CANADA'S FIRST NOVELIST
- WAR OF 1812

Richardson, Nathaniel Smith *see* THE CHURCHMAN'S REASONS FOR HIS FAITH AND PRACTICE

Richardson, R *see* THE PRINCIPLES AND OBJECTS OF THE RELIGIOUS REFORMATION URGED BY A. CAMPBELL AND OTHERS

Richardson, Samuel *see*
- CORRESPONDENCE
- PAMELA; OR, VIRTUE REWARDED.

Richardson, William *see* A MARINER OF ENGLAND: AN ACCOUNT OF THE CAREER OF WILLIAM RICHARDSON... 1780-1819, AS TOLD BY HIMSELF

Richardson, William Adams *see* HISTORY, JURISDICTION, AND PRACTICE OF THE COURT OF CLAIMS OF THE UNITED STATES

Richardson, William Payson *see*
- OUTLINES OF EVIDENCE, PREPARED FOR THE STUDENTS OF THE BROOKLYN LAW SCHOOL
- OUTLINES OF THE LAW OF CONTRACTS, PREPARED FOR THE USE OF STUDENTS IN THE BROOKLYN LAW SCHOOL OF ST LAWRENCE UNIVERSITY

RICHARDSON, WM. W., DIARIES, MS 2136 – 1862-1865 – 1 reel – 1 – us Western Res [976]

RICHARDSON'S CASES IN EQUITY / South Carolina. Supreme Court – (A Pre-NRS title) – 1v. 1831-1832 (all publ) – 6mf – 9 – $9.00 – LLMC 94-038 – us L.L.M.C. [340]

RICHARDSON'S CASES IN EQUITY / South Carolina. Supreme Court – (A Pre-NRS title) – v1-2. 1844-1846 (all publ) – 12mf – 9 – $18.00 – LLMC 94-036A – us L.L.M.C. [340]

RICHARDSON'S CASES IN EQUITY / South Carolina. Supreme Court – (A Pre-NRS title) – v3-14. 1850-1868 (all publ) – 70mf – 9 – $105.00 – LLMC 94-036B – us L.L.M.C. [340]

RICHARDSON'S COVE BAPTIST CHURCH. SEVIERVILLE, TENNESSEE : CHURCH RECORDS – (1,156p) – April 1914-1978, lacking Dec 1941-June 1943 – 1 reel – 1 – $52.02 – us Baptist [240]

RICHARDSONS ERSTER ROMAN : ENTSTEHUNGSGESCHICHTE / Danielowski, Emma – Tuebingen, 1917 – 2mf – DM62.00 – 3-8267-3071-2 – gw Hänsel [420]

RICHARDSON'S LAW REPORTS / South Carolina. Supreme Court – (A Pre-NRS title) – v1-2. 1844-1846 (all publ) – 15mf – 9 – $22.50 – LLMC 94-024A – us L.L.M.C. [340]
RICHARDSON'S LAW REPORTS, N.S. / South Carolina. Supreme Court – (A Pre-NRS title) – v3-15. 1850-1868 (all publ) – 84mf – 9 – $126.00 – LLMC 94-024B – us L.L.M.C. [340]
RICHARDUS SANCTI VICTORIS : OPERA OMNIA – Lyon, 1534 – 18mf – 8 – ne Slangenburg [290]
RICHARDUS SANCTI VICTORIS : OPERA OMNIA – Lyon, 1534 – 18mf – 8 – ne Slangenburg [290]
Richart, WP *see* ST. ALDEMAR COMMANDERY NO. 18 – KNIGHTS TEMPLAR STATIONED AT ST LOUIS
Richaud, Leon *see* NOTRE COLONIE DE LA COTE D'IVOIRE
Richelet, Cesar-Pierre *see* DICTIONNAIRE FRANCOIS CONTENANT LES MOTS ET LES CHOSES, VERSCH. AUSGABEN (AEL, ABT 2;16)
Richelet, P *see*
- DICTIONNAIRE DE LA LANGUE FRANCOISE
- DICTIONNAIRE DES RIMES
- DICTIONNAIRE FRANCOIS CONTENANT LES MOTS ET LES CHOSES, PLUSIEURS NOUVELLES REMARQUES SUR LA LANGUE FRANCOISE
- LA VERSIFICATION FRANCOISE

LE RICHELIEU – (Becomes: Le Richelieu Agricole 5 mai 1878-13 jan 1987. Becomes: Le Richelieu Dimanche 18 jan 1987-28 jun 1992) – St-Jean, Canada. ns: v44 n1. 29 mar 1977-25 avr 1978 – 15r – 1 – Can$75.00r – cn Can Microfilming [072]
LE RICHELIEU / ed by L'Ecuyer, Paul – St-Jean, Canada. 26 sep 1935-31 dec 1969 – 36r – 1 – Can$60.00r – cn Can Microfilming [072]
LE RICHELIEU – Sorel, Canada. 18 dec 1872-v2 n12. 11 fev 1874 – 1r – 1 – Can$75.00 – cn Can Microfilming [072]
Richelieu, (A J Du Plessis) *see* TRAITTE QUI CONTIENT LA METHODE LA PLUS FACILE...
LE RICHELIEU AGRICOLE *see* LE RICHELIEU
LE RICHELIEU DIMANCHE *see* LE RICHELIEU
Richelmann, G *see* MAINE ERLEBNISSE IN DER WISSMANN-TRUPP
Richeome, L *see*
- L'IDOLATRIE HUGUENOTE FIGUREE AU PATRON DE LA VIEILLE PAYENNE...
- LE PANTHEON HUGUENOT DECOUVERT ET RUINE...
- TROIS DISCOURS POUR LA RELIGION CATHOLIQUE

Richer, Adrien *see* VIE DE BARBEROUSSE, GENERAL DES ARMEES NAVALES DE SOLIMAN 2...
Richer, Julia *see* NOTRE-TEMPS
Richer, Leopold *see* NOTRE-TEMPS
RICHER VISION : THE DEVELOPMENT OF ETHNIC MINORITY MEDIA IN WESTERN DEMOCRACIES / ed by Husband, Charles – 1994 – 149p – 9 – 92-3-102941-X – fr UNESCO [302]
RICHERCHE SULL' AUTONOMIA DEI LICHENI CROSTOSI / Massalongo, A B – Verona, 1852. 207 pp. 64 pls. B-584 2 – 8 – ne IDC [580]
RICHERI HISTORIARUM LIBRI 3 (MGH 7: 51.BD) – Ed 2a. 1877 – Dfl13.00 – ne Slangenburg [240]
Richer-Louveteau, H *see* L'ACTION DES JEUNES
THE RICHES OF GRACE, OR, THE BLESSING OF PERFECT LOVE: AS EXPERIENCED, ENJOYED AND RECORDED BY SIXTY-TWO LIVING WITNESSES – 1857 – 9 – us A.T.L.A. [240]
LA RICHESSE DE LA FRANCE: FORTUNE ET REVENUES PRIVES / Lavaissiere de Lavergne, Alexandre de – Paris: Marcel Riviere, 1908. xiv,216p. ill., map. (Systemes et Faits sociaux). Bibliog. ref. and index – 1 – us U.W. Library [336]
RICHESSE OU PAUVRETE. EXPOSITION DES CAUSES ET DES EFFETS DE LA DISTRIBUTION ACTUELLE DES RICHESSES SOCIALES / Cherbuliez, A E – (Condition of 19th C. French working class series). 1841 – 9 – fr Hachette [360]
LES RICHESSES DU CANADA / Buron, Edmond Joseph Pierre – Preface de Gabriel Hanotaux. 2eme ed., rev. Paris: E. Guilmoto, 18??. 03825. (Pre-1900 Canadiana) – 9 – cn C.I.H.M. [971]
RICHESSES ET RESSOURCES DE LA FRANCE. / Bonvallet des Brosses – Lille: J. Jacquez, 1789.4 fiches. (Economics Collection) – 9 – 10.00 – fr Bibl Nationale [339]
RICHESSES ORNITHOLOGIQUES DU MIDI DE LA FRANCE / Jaubert, J B & Barthelemy-Lapommeraye, C J – Z 1814. 1859 – 9 – ne IDC [590]
Richey, Charles R *see* MANUAL ON EMPLOYMENT DISCRIMINATION LAW AND CIVIL RIGHTS ACTIONS
Richey, Homer *see* CONSTITUTIONAL LAW; FROM THE ARTICLE ON THIS SUBJECT IN THE ENCYCLOPEDIA OF UNITED STATES SUPREME COURT REPORTS.
Richey, Thomas *see* TRUTH AND COUNTER TRUTH
RICHFIELD, OHIO, TAXES, MS V.F. O – (List of land in the Township) – 1805 – 1r – 1 – us Western Res [978]
RICHFIELD, OHIO, TAXES, MS V.F. O – (List of polls and taxable property in the township on May 1 1802) – 1802 – 1r – 1 – us Western Res [978]
RICHFIELD, OHIO, TAXES, MS V.F. O – (True copy of individual lists of all the lands holden in the District, Aug 22 1801) – 1801 – 1r – 1 – us Western Res [978]
RICHFIELD, OHIO, TAXES, MS V.F.O. – (List of all property subject to taxation by the act entitled: An Act to Regulate County Levies, Aug 20 1801) – 1801 – 1r – 1 – us Western Res [978]
Richier, C *see* DE REBUS TURCARU...
Rich-Jones, W *see* VETUS REGISTRUM SARISBERIENSE
RICHLAND SHIELD AND BANNER – Mansfield. Ohio. -w. 1850-61, 1865-88, 1896-1913 – 1 – us UMI [071]
RICHLAND SPRINGS BAPTIST CHURCH (FORMERLY: EDGEFIELD DISTRICT). SALUDA COUNTY. SOUTH CAROLINA : CHURCH RECORDS – 1859-1949 – 1 – 18.72 – us Baptist [240]
Richman, George J *see* HISTORY OF HANCOCK COUNTY
Richman, Irving B *see* HISTORY OF MUSCATINE COUNTY
THE RICHMOND *see* RICHMOND HERALD
RICHMOND 1791-1901 – (Mf 1: Town Reocrds 1791-95. Mf 2: Town Records 1795-1800. Mf 3: Town Records 1800-04. Mf 4: Town Records 1804-08. Mf 5: Town Records 1808-11. Mf 6: Town Records 1811-14. Mf 7: Town Records 1814-17. Mf 8: 1817-23. Mf 9: Town Records 1823. Mf 10: Births, Marriages 1812-48. Mf 11: Intentions & Earmarks 1812-48. Mf 12: Deaths 1844-94. Mf 13: Deaths 1895-1919. Mf 14: Marriages 1844-1919. Mf 15: Births 1844-75. Mf 16: Births 1876-1901) – (mf ed 1988) – 16mf – 9 – 0-87623-073-7 – us Holbrook [920]
RICHMOND AND MARTINEZ CITY DIRECTORIES – Contra Costa Co, CA. 1921-1950 – 22r – 1 – $1,100.00 – D013 – us Library Micro [910]
RICHMOND AND TWICKENHAM HERALD *see* RICHMOND HERALD
RICHMOND AND TWICKENHAM INFORMER – 1986-Jun 1997 – 36r – 1 – uk British Libr Newspaper [072]
RICHMOND AND TWICKENHAM TIMES – England.1985-Jun 1987.-w. 5 reels – 1 – uk British Libr Newspaper [072]
RICHMOND AND TWICKENHAM TIMES – (Lacking: Oct 1882) – London, 31 May 1873- – 207+ r – 1 – uk British Libr Newspaper [072]
RICHMOND BANNER – San Francisco, CA. 1894-1976 – 20r – 1 – $1,000.00 – C03492 – us Library Micro [071]
RICHMOND CHRISTIAN ADVOCATE – (Lacking: v1-34 1832-65. Includes indexes. Title varies) – v1-38; v1-47. 1867-1965 – 48r – 1 – ATLA S0331 – us A.T.L.A. [073]
Richmond County. Georgia *see* INVENTORY OF THE COUNTY ARCHIVES.
RICHMOND EXAMINER – Richmond, VA. 1861-67 – 4r – 1 – us Ross [071]
THE RICHMOND GUARDIAN – Richmond, Canada. ns: v4 n1864. 26 nov 1864-v51 n2486. 26 jul 1908 – 1r – 1 – Can$40.00 – cn Can Microfilming [072]
RICHMOND HERALD – London, 4 Jul 1885-Dec 1981 – 143r – 1 – uk British Libr Newspaper [072]
Richmond, I A *see* THE FIRST YEARS OF EMERITA AUGUSTA. (LOS PRIMEROS ANOS DE EMERITA AUGUSTA)
RICHMOND INDEPENDENT *see* NORTH EAST BAY INDEPENDENT AND GAZETTE
THE RICHMOND INDEX TO THE GENERA AND SPECIES OF BIRDS / National Museum of Natural History, Smithsonian Institution – 1992. 72,000 cards on 92mf – $495.00 export $550.00 – 0-8161-1795-0 – uk Hall [590]
RICHMOND LANCET – Petersburg. Va. 1882-85 – 1 – us UMI [071]
Richmond, Mabel E *see* CENTENNIAL HISTORY OF DECATUR AND MACON COUNTY
Richmond, Maine.Baptist Church in Richmond Village *see* RECORDS
Richmond, Maine.Bowdoinham Ridge Free Baptist Society *see* RECORDS
Richmond, Maine.Bowdoinham Ridge Free Will Baptist Church/Third Free Will Baptist Church *see* RECORDS
Richmond, Maine.Free Will Baptist Church of Bowdoinham Ridge *see* RECORDS
Richmond, Maine.Ridge Meetinghouse Company *see* RECORDS
Richmond, New Hampshire.Richmond Baptist Church *see* RECORDS
THE RICHMOND NEWS – Richmond, Canada. v1 n16. 30 avr 1897-v67 n2. 18 dec 1914 – 1r – 1 – Can$25.00 – cn Can Microfilming [072]
RICHMOND NEWS LEADER – Richmond. Va. 1903- – 1 – us UMI [071]
THE RICHMOND POST – Richmond, CA. 1979-81 (incomplete); 1988- – 15+ r – 1 – $750.00 ($120.00y) – B02697 – us Library Micro [071]
RICHMOND RECORD – (Cont by: San Francisco Municipal Journal and Richmond Record) – San Francisco, CA. 1913-1936 – 6r – 1 – $300.00 – C03493 – us Library Micro [071]
RICHMOND RIVER EXPRESS (CASINO) – Jan 2 1919-Dec 24 1944 – 9 – at Pascoe [072]
RICHMOND RIVER HERALD – Coraki, Jan 2 1892-Dec 29 1914 – 1 – at Pascoe [072]
RICHMOND SENTINEL – Richmond, VA -d. 1863-65. 2 reels – 1 – us Western Res [071]
RICHMOND STAR – Richmond. Va. 1893-1896 – 1 – us UMI [071]
RICHMOND TIMES – Richmond, VA. v1-5. 1865-67 – 3r – 1 – us Ross [071]
RICHMOND TIMES-DISPATCH – Richmond, VA. 1903- – 1 – us UMI [071]
THE RICHMOND TIMES-GUARDIAN – Richmond, Canada. v54 n32. 15 avr 1910-v64. 6 avr 1928 – 1r – 1 – Can$40.00 – cn Can Microfilming [072]
Richstaetter, C *see*
- CHRISTUSFORMMIGKEIT IN IHRER HISTORISCHEN ENTFALTUNG
- CHRISTUSFROMMIGKEIT IN IHRER HISTORISCHEN ENTFALTUNG

Richter, Ae.L *see* DIE EVANGELISCHEN KIRCHENORDNUNGEN DES 16. JAHRHUNDERTS
Richter, Albert *see* DEUTSCHE SAGEN
Richter, Eugen *see* DAS PREUSSISCHE STAATSSCHULDENWESEN UND DIE PREUSSISCHEN STAATSPAPIERE
Richter, F *see* DAS CHRISTLICHE GLAUBENSBEKENNTNIS
Richter, Fritz *see* HERMANN STEHR, SCHLESIER, DEUTSCHER, EUROPAEER
Richter, Heinrich Moriz *see* DIE PICCOLOMINI
Richter, Jean Paul *see* QUELLEN DER BYZANTINISCHEN KUNSTGESCHICHTE
Richter, Johann Paul Friedrich *see* THE CAMPANER THAL, AND OTHER WRITINGS
Richter, Julius *see*
- A HISTORY OF MISSIONS IN INDIA
- INDISCHE MISSIONSGESCHICHTE
- MISSION UND EVANGELISATION IM ORIENT
- WELTMISSION UND THEOLOGISCHE ARBEIT

Richter, K *see* PLANTAE EUROPEAE
Richter, Ludwig *see* GESCHICHTE DER EVANGELISCHEN KIRCHENVERFASSUNG IN DEUTSCHLAND
Richter, P E *see* LITTERATUR DER LANDES- UND VOLKSKUNDE DES DEUTSCHEN REICHS
DER RICHTER UND DIE RECHTSPFLEGE IN DER DEUTSCHEN VERGANGENHEIT / Heinemann, Franz – 1995 – 2mf – 9 – DM62.00 – 3-8267-3153-0 – gw Hänsel [943]
Richter, W *see* THE POLITICS OF CONSCIENCE
Richter, W M *see* ISTORIJA MEDICINY V ROSSII
Richter, Werner *see* DER LANZELET DES ULRICH VON ZAZIKHOVEN
DIE RICHTERIN / Meyer, Conrad Ferdinand – Hellerau/Wien: Avalun-Verlag, c1923 – 1 – us U.W. Library [830]
Richthofen, F P W von *see* CHINA. ERGEBNISSE EIGENER REISEN UND DARAUF GEGRUENDETEN STUDIEN
RICHTLINIEN FUER DIE LEIBERSERZIEHUNG IN JUNGENSCHULEN / Germany. Reichsministerium fuer Wissenschaft, Erziehung und Volksbildung – Berlin, 1937. 84p – 1 – us U.W. Library [943]
RICINOVO OLJE – Buenos Aires, Argentina, 1930 – 1mf or 1 reel – 9,1 – us I.H.R.C. [972]
Rickaby, Joseph *see*
- DEVELOPMENT
- MORAL PHILOSOPHY
- OXFORD AND CAMBRIDGE CONFERENCES, 1897-1899

Rickards, George Kettilby *see* REMARKS ON THE LAWS RELATING TO ATTEMPTS AGAINST THE PERSON OF THE SOVEREIGN, INCLUDING THE NEW STATUTE FOR THE BETTER SECURITY OF HER MAJESTY'S PERSON
Rickert, Horace *see* PENNSYLVANIA NEGLIGENCE CASES, STREET AND STEAM RAILWAYS &C., INDEXED
Ricketts, Alfred Herbert *see* A MANUAL OF AMERICAN MINING LAW
Ricketts, Palmer Chamberlain *see* HISTORY OF THE RENSSELAER POLYTECHNIC INSTITUTE, 1824-1894
Rickly-Kunkle Family *see* REUNION RECORDS
Ricoeur, P *see* GABRIEL MARCEL ET KARL JASPERS
Ricol, D *see* LES ANIMAUX VERTICAUX ET RENVERSES DANS LES REPRESENTATIONS PARIETALES PALEOLITHIQUES
IL RICONOSCIMENTO DELLE SENTENZE STRANIERE DI DIVORZIO... / Anzilotti, D – Bologna, 1908 – 2mf – 9 – ILM-3639/1 – ne IDC [340]
Ricord, F W *see* HISTORY OF UNION COUNTY
Ricord, P *see* TRAITE PRATIQUE DES MALADIES VENERIENNES
RICOSTRUZIONE – Rome. Italy. -d. 6 Jun 1944-13 Jun 1946. (Imperfect). (4 reels) – 1 – uk British Libr Newspaper [072]
RIDALA ARKAMISE AJALUGU-THE HISTORY OF THE REVIVAL IN RIDALA / Busch, M – Keilas, Estonia: Kulwaja, 1928. 132p – 1 – 5.28 – us Baptist [240]
Riddel, Alexander *see* A GRAMMAR OF THE CHINYANJA LANGUAGE AS SPOKEN AT LAKE NYASSA
Riddell, Janet M *see* A QUALITATIVE EVALUATION OF CHILDBIRTH EDUCATION BOOKLETS
Ridder, N de et al *see* MODELLING OF EXTENSIVE LIVESTOCK PRODUCTION SYSTEMS
Riddle, Daniel S *see* THE LAW AND PRACTICE IN PROCEEDINGS SUPPLEMENTARY TO EXECUTION. UNDER THE NEW YORK CODE
Riddle, L H *see* DIARIES
Riddle, Matthew Brown *see*
- THE GOSPEL ACCORDING TO LUKE
- THE GOSPEL ACCORDING TO MARK
- THE STORY OF THE REVISED NEW TESTAMENT

RIDDLE NEWS – Riddle, OR. -w. 6 May 1955-30 Dec 1955. 1 roll – 1 – us U.O. Library [071]
THE RIDDLE OF EXISTENCE SOLVED : OR, AN ANTIDOTE TO INFIDELITY: BEING AN ANSWER TO PROFESSOR GOLDWIN SMITH'S 'GUESSES AT THE RIDDLE OF EXISTENCE' / Fenton, W J – Toronto: Henderson, 1898. 03083. (Pre-1900 Canadiana) – 9 – cn C.I.H.M. [240]
THE RIDDLE OF THE RHINE, CHEMICAL STRATEGY IN PEACE AND WAR.. / Lefebure, Victor – Preface by Marshal Foch and introd. by Field-Marshall Sir Henry Wilson. New York: E.P. Dutton & Company, (1923). 282p. front., plates – 1 – us U.W. Library [660]
RIDDLE TRIBUNE – Riddle, OR. -w. 24 Oct 1912-8 Aug 1918. 1 roll – 1 – us U.O. Library [071]
RIDDLETON BAPTIST CHURCH. TENNESSEE : CHURCH RECORDS – 1888-1963 – 1 – 29.25 – us Baptist [240]
A RIDE IN MOROCCO, AND OTHER SKETCHES / Campbell, Arthur – Toronto: W. Briggs; Montreal: C. Coates; Halifax: S. Huestis, 1897. 00400. (Pre-1900 Canadiana) – 9 – cn C.I.H.M. [910]

Ridenour, Marcella *see* THE MOTOR DEVELOPMENT OF INFANTS AND CHILDREN EXPOSED TO COCAINE WHILE IN UTERO
RIDENTE AMORE, THE FAVORITE RONDO IN THE OPERA 2 MARCHESE TULIPANO (BY PAISIELLO) / Toniolo, A – London: John Preston, 1786 – 1 – us Sibley [780]
RIDER – Ashford, Kent, England. 1974. -w. 2 reels – 1 – uk British Libr Newspaper [072]
Rider *see* MISSOURI BAPTIST BIOGRAPHY
Rider, George T *see* LYRA AMERICANA, OR, VERSES OF PRAISE AND FAITH FROM AMERICAN POETS
Rider, John *see* BIBLIOTHECA SCHOLASTICA
Rider, Sidney S *see* AN HISTORICAL ENQUIRY CONCERNING THE ATTEMPT TO RAISE A REGIMENT OF SLAVES BY RHODE ISLAND DURING THE WAR OF THE REVOLUTION
RIDES IN THE MISSION FIELD OF SOUTH AFRICA : BETWEEN THE KEI AND BASHEE RIVERS, KAFFRARIA: ALSO, A VISIT TO THE MISSIONARY COLLEGES OF LOVEDALE AND HEALD TOWN, IN BRITISH KAFFRARIA / Malan, C H – London: Morgan and Scott, [1872?] – 1mf – us A.T.L.A. [240]
Ridet, J M *see* ANALYSE QUANTITATIVE DE L'ENCEPHALE DES TELEOSTEENS: CARACTERES EVOLUTIFS ET ADAPTATIFS DE L'ENCEPHALISATION
Ridge, Lola *see* SUN-UP AND OTHER POEMS
RIDGE SPRINGS, SOUTH CAROLINA : CHURCH RECORDS – 1856-1902 – 1 – 36.72 – us Baptist [240]
RIDGECREST BAPTIST CHURCH. JACKSON, MISSISSIPPI : CHURCH RECORDS – Nov 1952-59 – 1 – 17.73 – us Baptist [240]
Ridgecrest. North Carolina. Ridgecrest Baptist Assembly *see*
- FINANCIAL RECORDS AND JOURNALS
- HOTEL GUEST REGISTERS, 1922-38; 1965-66
- MATERIALS-BOOKS, CLIPPINGS, PAMPHLETS, PROGRAMS, 1909-45
- MINUTES AND RECORDS
- PRESS RELEASES
- SCRAPBOOKS...OF SUMMER ACTIVITIES, 1931-33, 1938, 1940, 1942-44, 1948, 1949-50

RIDGEDALE BAPTIST CHURCH. CHATTANOOGA, TENNESSEE : CHURCH RECORDS – Oct 1946-56 – 1 – 24.93 – us Baptist [240]
RIDGELAND BAPTIST CHURCH. JASPER COUNTY. SOUTH CAROLINA : CHURCH RECORDS – 1892-97, 1906-48, 1960-84 – 1 – $41.67 – us Baptist [240]
Ridgely, L B *see* AN INTRODUCTION TO CHURCH HISTORY (CCC271)
Ridgeway, William *see* THE DRAMAS AND DRAMATIC DANCES OF NON-EUROPEAN RACES IN SPECIAL REFERENCE TO THE ORIGIN OF GREEK TRAGEDY..
Ridgway, E *see* TRUTH DEFENDED
Ridgway, R *see*
- THE BIRDS OF NORTH AND MIDDLE AMERICA
- A HISTORY OF THE NORTH AMERICAN BIRDS
- A MANUAL OF NORTH AMERICAN BIRDS

Ridgway, Ronald S *see* LA PROPAGANDE PHILOSOPHIQUE DANS LES TRAGEDIES DE VOLTAIRE
Ridha, Muhammad *see* JACQUELINE KENNEDY
Ridings, Daniel *see* A CONCORDANCE TO GREGORY OF NYSSA
Ridley College *see* ACTA RIDDLEIANA
Ridley, H *see* THE ANATOMY OF THE BRAIN
Ridley, H N *see*
- THE FLORA OF SINGAPORE
- A LIST OF THE FERNS OF THE MALAY PENINSULA

Ridolfi, C *see*
- LE MERAVIGLIE DELL'ARTE...
- VITA DI GIACOPE ROBUSTI DETTO IL TINTERETTO...
- VITA DI GIACOPO ROBUSTI DETTO IL TINTORETTO

Ridout, Thomas *see* TEN YEARS OF UPPER CANADA IN PEACE AND WAR, 1805-1815: BEING THE RIDOUT LETTERS
RIECH OBERA, PROIZNESENNAIA V ZASHCHITU POLUNINA PERED SUDOM PRISIAZHNYKH V LOZANNI E PO DIELU OB UBIISTVI E VOROVSKAGO / Aubert, Theodore William – Bielgrad: Izd-vo M.A. Suvorina "Novoe vremi a", 1924 – 1 – CSUX89-B4170 – us Hoover Inst Photo [947]
Riechert, Traugott *see* DIE PROGNOSE DER RAUSCHGIFTSUCHTEN
RIECHI OKTIABRISTA 1905-1907 GG. / Chistiakov, P S – S-Peterburg: T-vo R. Golike i A. Vilborg, 1907 – 1 – CSUX89-B4320 – us Hoover Inst Photo [947]
RIECHO RUSSKO I REVOLIUTSII / Reclus, Elisee – Niu-Iork: Izd. Federatsii soiuzov russkikh rabochikh Soed. Shtatov i Kanady, 1919 – 1 – CSUX88-B1247 – us Hoover Inst Photo [947]
RIE/CIJE COMBINED CUMULATED SUBJECT AND FICHE INDEX – (1981-82. $112.00 in North America, $115.00 elsewhere. 1983. $112.00y in North America, $115.00y elsewhere) – 1966-80 – 9 – $1,099.00 in North America, $1,114.00 elsewhere – us Oryx [370]
Riedel, Adolf Friedrich *see* CODEX DIPLOMATICUS BRANDENBURGENSIS
Riedel, F J *see* UEBER DIE MUSIK DES RITTERS CHRISTOPH VON GLUCK; VERSCHEIDENE SCHRIFTEN GESAMMELT UND HERAUSGEGEBEN
Riedel, Hella *see* DAS SCHOENE LAND ITALIA
Riedel, K *see* TAFSIRAN-TAFSIRAN ALKITAB INDJIL MATIUS
Riedel, Wilhelm *see*
- ALTTESTAMENTLICHE UNTERSUCHUNGEN, ERSTES HEFT
- DIE AUSLEGUNG DES HOHENLIEDES IN DER JUEDISCHEN GEMEINDE UND DER GRIECHISCHEN KIRCHE
- THE CANONS OF ATHANASIUS OF ALEXANDRIA
- DIE KIRCHENRECHTSQUELLEN DES PARTRIARCHATS ALEXANDRIEN

Riederer, Frank *see* LUDWIG TIECKS BEZIEHUNGEN ZUR DEUTSCHEN LITERATUR DES 17. JAHRHUNDERTS
Riedt, Friedrich W *see* VERSUCH UEBER DIE MUSIKALISCHE INTERVALLEN..
Riege, Matthias *see* REALISIERUNG DIGITALER SCHALTUNGEN MIT AND-EXOR-STRUKTUR
Riegel, E C *see*
- DOLLAR DOOMSDAY
- FLIGHT FROM INFLATION – THE MONETARY ALTERNATIVE
- FREE ENTERPRISE MONEY
- THE NEW APPROACH TO FREEDOM

Rieger, Paul *see* VERSUCH EINER TECHNOLOGIE UND TERMINOLOGIE DER HANDWERKE IN DER MISNAH
Rieger, Wilhelm *see* DIE UNTERNEHMUNG IM MARKT. FESTSCHRIFT FUER WILHELM RIEGER, ZU SEINEM 75 GEBURTSTAG
Riehl, Wilhelm Heinrich *see*
- AUS DER ECKE
- BURG NEIDECK
- DER FLUCH DER SCHOENHEIT
- GESAMMELTE GESCHICHTEN UND NOVELLEN
- GESCHICHTEN UND NOVELLEN: GESAMTAUSGABE
- LEBENSRAETHSEL
- DAS SPIELMANNSKIND – DER STUMME RATSHERR

Riehle, Gerhard *see* DIE RECHTSSTAATLICHE BEDEUTUNG DER STAATSANWALTSCHAFT UNTER BESONDERER BERUECKSICHTIGUNG IHRER ROLLE IN DER NATIONALSOZIALISTISCHEN ZEIT
Riehm, Eduard *see*
- ALTTESTAMENTLICHE THEOLOGIE
- MESSIANIC PROPHECY
- ZUR REVISION DER LUTHERBIBEL

Rieker, Karl *see*
- GRUNDSAETZE REFORMIERTER KIRCHENVERFASSUNG
- DIE RECHTLICHE STELLUNG DER EVANGELISCHEN KIRCHE DEUTSCHLAND

RIEL : REPONSE A MONSIEUR J.A. CHAPLEAU / Tremblay, Ernest – St-Hyacinthe: des presse a vapeur de "L'Union", 1885. SEM35P86 – 1r – 1 – Can$15.00 – cn Bibl Nat [971]
Riel, Louis *see* POLEMIQUES ET DOCUMENTS TOUCHANT LE NORD-OUEST ET L'EXECUTION DE LOUIS RIEL
THE RIEL QUESTION / Chapleau, Joseph Adolphe – 1885? 02856. (Pre-1900 Canadiana) – 9 – cn C.I.H.M. [971]
THE RIEL QUESTION / Chapleau, Joseph Adolphe – s.l, s.n, 1885. SEM105P37 – 1mf – 9 – Can$2.25 – cn Bibl Nat [971]
Riemann, H *see*
- KATECHISMUS DER KOMPOSITIONSLEHRE
- KATECHISMUS DES GENERALBASS-SPIELS
- MUSIKALISCHE DYNAMIK UND AGOGIK
- MUSIKALISCHE SYNTAXIS
- SYSTEMATISCHE MODULATIONSLEHRE ALS GRUNDLAGE DER MUSIKALISCHE FORMENLEHRE

Riemanns, Carl Friedrich *see* VERSUCH EINER BESCHREIBUNG DER RECKANSCHEN SCHULEINRICHTUNG
Riemer, Harold A *see* DEVELOPMENT OF THE ATHLETE SATISFACTION QUESTIONNAIRE
Riepe, Christian *see* EICHENDORFFS MENSCHENGESTALTUNG
Ries, H de *see*
- CORT ENDE CLAER BEWIJS, DAT DIE TWAELF JONGHEREN DAER D'EUANGELIST LUCAS VAN MELDET
- LIETBOECK INHOUDENDE SCHRIFTUERLIJCKE VERMAEN LIEDEREN, CLAECH LIEDEREN, GEBEDEN, DANCK LIEDEREN, LOFSANGHEN, PSALMEN

Riesebrodt, Martin *see* ZUR THEORIEDISKUSSION IN DER WIRTSCHAFTSETHNOLOGIE
Riesenberg, Saul H *see* THE NATIVE POLITY OF PONAPE
DAS RIESENRAD : ROMAN / Muehlen, Hermynia zur – Stuttgart: J Engelhorns, 1932 – 1r – 1 – us U.W. Library [830]
Riesenthal, O von *see* DIE RAUBVOEGEL DEUTSCHLANDS UND DES ANGRENZENDEN MITTELEUROPAS
Riesman, David *see* AN AMERICAN TEXT-BOOK OF PATHOLOGY
Riess, Gertrud *see* DIE BEIDEN FASSUNGEN VON GOETHES DIE LEIDEN DES JUNGEN WERTHERS
Riess, Richard *see* HUMORBUCH
Riesser, G *see* GESAMMELTE SCHRIFTEN VON G. RIESSER
Riessler, Paul *see* DAS BUCH DANIEL
Rietschel, Georg *see* OFFENER BRIEF AN DEN VERFASSER DER SCHRIFT "ERNSTE GEDANKEN"
Rievallensis, Aelredus *see*
- OPERA ASCETICA
- SERMONES 1-46

LE RIF AGRICOLE / Morocco. Ministere de l'Agriculture – 1960. BNE-3066 1 – 9 – ne IDC [630]
Rifai, Ali *see* MUSIM BERAHI
Rifat, Ilaveli *see* ILAVELI NUEZHET UEL-MUENSEAT
Rifaux, Marcel *see* LES CONDITIONS DU RETOUR AU CATHOLICISME
THE RIFLE, AXE, AND SADDLE-BAGS, AND OTHER LECTURES / Milburn, William Henry – New York: Derby & Jackson; Cincinnati: H.W. Derby, 1857, c1856 – 1mf – us A.T.L.A. [240]
RIFLESSIONI FATTE DE EUCHERO PASTORE ARCADE SOPRA ALLA MAGGIOR FACILITA CHE TROVASI NELL' APPRENDERE IL CANTO / Chigi, Zondadari, 1 – Venezia. C. Pecora. 1746. BP-211 1 – 9 – ne IDC [780]
RIFMA MAIAKOVSKOGO / Shtomkmar, M P – M. 1958. BR-2146 2 – 8 – ne IDC [460]
LA RIFORMA – Rome, Italy. -w. 26 Oct 1888; 1 Jan 1891-31 July 1896. 12 reels – 1 – uk British Libr Newspaper [072]
RIGA AM SONNTAG – (Cont by: Rigasche Post) – Riga, U.S.S.R. 25 Dec 1927-Dec 1934 – 3r – 1 – gw Mikrofilm [947]
RIGA AM SONNTAG *see* RIGASCHE POST
RIGAER JUEDISCHE RUNDSCHAU – Riga, Latvia (U.S.S.R.). 12-21 Oct 1929; Jan-1 Feb 1930; 16 Sept-15 Dec 1931 – 1r – 1 – gw Mikrofilm [072]
RIGAER TAGEBLATT – Riga, 1898-1907 – 19 – 1 – gw Mikrofilm [947]
RIGAER TAGESBLATT *see* NEUE ZEITUNG FUR STADT UND LAND
RIGAER TAGESZEITUNG – Riga, U.S.S.R. 24 Feb-16 Mai 1934 – 1r – 1 – gw Mikrofilm [947]
Rigal, J L *see* CARTULAIRE DE L'ABBAYE DE BONNEVAL EN ROUERGUE
RIGAS MATEUS BAPTISTU DRAUDSES GADA PAHRSKATAS PAR 1911. GADU = ANNUAL REPORT FOR 1911 OF THE MATEUS BAPTIST CHURCH OF RIGA – Riga, 1911. Publ. No. 6346,no. 2. One of six items on reel. Total Pages 152 – 1 – us Baptist [240]
RIGAS PESTISCHANAS TEMPLA ATWEHRSCHANAS SWEHTKI = DEDUCATION SERVICES OF THE RIGA SALVATION TEMPLE – Riga, 1927. Publ. No. 6346,no. 4. One of six items on reel. Total pages, 152 – 1 – us Baptist [240]
RIGASCHE NACHRICHTEN – Riga, U.S.S.R. 22 Okt 1924-9 Jan 1925 – 1r – 1 – gw Mikrofilm [947]
RIGASCHE POST – Riga, U.S.S.R. 1935-26 Nov 1939 – 3r – 1 – gw Mikrofilm [947]
RIGASCHE POST *see* RIGA AM SONNTAG
RIGASCHE RUNDSCHAU – Riga, U.S.S.R. 3 Aug 1920-13 Dec 1939 – 45r – 1 – gw Mikrofilm [947]
RIGASCHE RUNDSCHAU – Riga, U.S.S.R. -d. 3 Jan 1938-13 Dec 1939. 10 reels – 1 – uk British Libr Newspaper [947]
RIGASCHE ZEITUNG – Riga, U.S.S.R. 17 Jul-Dec 1918 – 1r – 1 – gw Mikrofilm [947]
RIGASCHER ALMANACH – (Missing: v50 1907) – Riga. v1-51. 1858-1908 – 258mf – 9 – R-1786/2 – ne IDC [947]
Rigaux, B *see* ST. PAUL
Rigel, H J *see*
- SECOND OEUVRE DE SIMPHONIES POUR LE CLAVECIN OU PIANOFORTE AVEC ACCOMPAGNEMENT DE DEUX VIOLONS, DEUX CORS, ET VIOLONCELLE. OP.17
- TROIS SONATES POUR FORTEPIANO AVEC ACCOMPAGNEMENT DE VIOLON AD LIB

Rigg, J M *see* ST. ANSELM OF CANTERBURY
Rigg, James H *see*
- THE CHURCHMANSHIP OF JOHN WESLEY AND THE RELATIONS OF WESLEYAN METHODISM TO THE CHURCH OF ENGLAND
- OXFORD HIGH ANGLICANISM AND ITS CHIEF LEADERS
- THE RELATIONS OF JOHN WESLEY AND OF WESLEYAN METHODISM TO THE CHURCH OF ENGLAND

Rigg, James Harrison *see* JABEZ BUNTING
Riggen, Katherine J *see* SPORT PROGRAM EFFECTS ON PARTICIPANTS WITH MENTAL RETARDATION
Riggenbach, Christoph Johannes *see*
- DIE MOSAISCHE STUFTSHUETTE
- DIE ZEUGNISSE FUER DAS EVANGELIUM JOHANNIS

Riggenbach, Eduard *see*
- DIE LEHRE VON DER RECHTFERTIGUNG AUS DEM GLAUBEN IM KAMPFE DER GEGENWART
- THE RESURRECTION OF JESUS

Riggs, CW *see* HOW WE FIND RELICS
Riggs, Donna M *see* THE BODY COMPOSITION OF MASTERS WOMEN ENDURANCE ATHLETES FROM 35 TO 74 YEARS OF AGE
Riggs, Elias *see*
- NOTES ON DIFFICULT PASSAGES OF THE NEW TESTAMENT
- SUGGESTED EMENDATIONS OF THE AUTHORIZED ENGLISH VERSION OF THE OLD TESTAMENT

Riggs, Fred W *see*
- HELP FOR SOCIAL SCIENTISTS
- INTERCOCTA MANUAL

Riggs, James Stevenson *see* THE MESSAGES OF JESUS ACCORDING TO THE GOSPEL OF JOHN
Riggs, Stephen R *see*
- CORRESPONDENCE CONCERNING LAC QUI PARLE MISSION, DAKOTA AND SIOUX INDIANS
- MARY AND I

Righini, V *see*
- AUS DER FERNE. ARIE FUR SINGSTIMME UND PIANOFORTE
- DANCES AND MARCHES, TWELVE, IN CHARACTER, FOR THE QUADRILLE, AT THE CLOSE OF THE BERLIN CARNIVAL, 1799

THE RIGHT AND WRONG USES OF THE BIBLE / Newton, Richard Heber – New York: John W Lovell, c1883 – 1mf – 9 – 0-8370-4581-9 – 1985-2581 – us A.T.L.A. [220]
RIGHT AT LAST : AND OTHER TALES / Gaskell, Elizabeth Cleghorn – London: Sampson Low, 1860 – 1 roll – 1 – 1-55879-370-4 – uk Libr Preservation [830]
THE RIGHT HONOURABLE BENJAMIN DISRAELI, M.P. A LITERARY AND POLITICAL BIOGRAPHY / Macknight, Thomas – London: R. Bentley, 1854. 646p – 1 – us U.W. Library [941]
THE RIGHT OF SYSTEMATIC THEOLOGY / Warfield, Benjamin Breckinridge – Edinburgh: T.& T. Clark, 1897. 1 fiche – 9 – us A.T.L.A. [240]
THE RIGHT OF THE NATIONAL LIFE INSURANCE CO. TO ESTABLISH AGENCIES IN THE STATE OF NEW YORK / Cushing, Caleb – Washington, D.C., McGill & Witherow, 1868. 20 p. LL-256 – 1 – us L of C Photodup [340]
THE RIGHT TO BELIEVE / Wembridge, Eleanor Rowland – Boston: Houghton Mifflin, 1909. 1 fiche – 9 – us A.T.L.A. [240]

RIGHT TO COMMUNICATE : A STATUS REPORT / Fischer, Desmond – 1982 – 55p – 9 – 92-3-101991-0 – fr UNESCO [380]
RIGHT TO EDUCATION : WHAT KIND OF MANAGEMENT / Haag, Daniel – 1982 – 175p – 9 – 92-3-101930-9 – fr UNESCO [370]
RIGHT TO FOOD : A SELECTION FROM SPEECHES – 1976 – 177p – it F.A.O. [340]
THE RIGHT TO LOVE = DAS RECHT ZU LIEBEN / Nordau, Max Simon – New York: F T Neely, c1895 – 1r – 1 – us U.W. Library [820]
THE RIGHT TO SELF-DETERMINATION / Cohen, Joseph J – 1951. 4p – 9 – 1.00f – at Libertarian Micro [335]
THE RIGHT WING COLLECTION OF UNIVERSITY OF IOWA LIBRARIES – 177r – 1 – $12,750.00 – us UMI [977]
RIGHTEOUSNESS OF GOD A REDEMPTIVE QUALITY: A STUDY IN BIBLICAL THEOLOGY / Humphrey, George C – 1939 – 1 – 9.24 – us Baptist [240]
RIGHTS : A PAMPHLET FOR PLAIN PEOPLE: GOD'S RIGHTS, SATAN'S RIGHTS – New York: Henry W Turner, 1882 – 1mf – 9 – 0-8370-3967-3 – 1985-1967 – us A.T.L.A. [210]
THE RIGHTS AND DUTIES OF NEUTRALS / Hall, W E – London, 1874 – 3mf – 1 – ILM-1002/1 – ne IDC [327]
RIGHTS AND DUTIES OF SPANIARDS – n.p., n.d. Fiche W1139. (Blodgett Collection of Spanish Civil War Pamphlets) – 9 – us H.U. College Libr [946]
RIGHTS AND FREEDOMS – (Nos 1-32 1972-1978 Can$115.00. Ceased 1990/91) – Maniwaki. nos 1-70. 1972-1990/91 – 1,9 – Can$20.00y – cn Micromedia [320]
THE RIGHTS AND OBLIGATIONS OF MARRIAGE / Maxwell Brothers – New York: Strouse, 1886. 114p. LL-855 – 1 – us L of C Photodup [306]
RIGHTS COME NOT FROM NATURE BUT FROM REASON / Cord, Steven – Georgist, 1982. 5p – 9 – 1.00f – at Libertarian Micro [335]
THE RIGHTS, DUTIES, REMEDIES AND INCIDENTS BELONGING TO AND GROWING OUT OF THE RELATION OF LANDLORD AND TENANT. / McAdam, David – (Supplement. New York, 1892. 320p) – 2nd ed. New York, Diossy, 1882. 878 p. LL-612 – 1 – us L of C Photodup [340]
THE RIGHTS OF JURORS IN CRIMINAL CASES. OPINION BY HON. B. F. THOMAS. / Massachusetts. Supreme Judicial Court – Boston: Lee and Shepard, 1874. 68p. LL-315 – 1 – us L of C Photodup [340]
THE RIGHTS OF MAN : A STUDY IN TWENTIETH CENTURY PROBLEMS / Abbott, Lyman – Boston: Houghton, Mifflin, 1901 – 1mf – us A.T.L.A. [323]
THE RIGHTS OF MAN : A STUDY IN TWENTIETH CENTURY PROBLEMS / Abbott, Lyman – Boston, New York: Houghton, Mifflin, 1901 – 4mf – 9 – $6.00 – LLMC 92-110 – us L.L.M.C. [340]
RIGHTS OF THE MINORITY STOCKHOLDER / Harvey, Richard S – New York: Baker, Voorhis, 1909. 164p. LL-1265 – 1 – us L of C Photodup [340]
RIGHTS OF THE MINORITY STOCKHOLDER AND OF THE RAILWAY SECURITY HOLDER / Harvey, Richard S – New York: Baker, Voorhis, 1929. 452p. LL-1257 – 1 – us L of C Photodup [340]
THE RIGHTS OF WAR AND PEACE : INCLUDING THE LAW OF NATURE AND OF NATIONS / Grotius, Hugo de – Washington, London: M Walter Dunne, 1901 – 5mf – 9 – $7.50 – LLMC 92-126 – us L.L.M.C. [327]
THE RIGHTS OF WOMEN IN THE CHURCH / Kellison, Barbara – 1862 – 9 – us A.T.L.A. [240]
RIGISCHE ANZEIGEN VON ALLERHAND SACHEN – Riga, Russia. 1763-65; 1778-79 – 1 – gw Mikrofilm [947]
Rigula y Ochotorena, Jose de *see*
– EL ADELANTADO HERNANDO DE SOTO
– LOS ALVARADOS EN EL – NUEVO MUNDO
Rih, Sjeh *see*
– IDROES AND SITY NOERMA
– NASIB, PUTOS HARA AN
RIIGI TEATAJA – Tallinn, Estonia. 1918-40 – 17r – 1 – sw Kungliga [073]
Riis, Hans Nicolaus *see* GRAMMATICAL OUTLINE AND VOCABULARY OF THE OJI LANGUAGE
Rijcen, Chr *see* TGETUYGENISSE ENDE DE NAEGHELAETEN SCHRIFTEN VAN CHRISTIAEN RIJCEN GHEDRUCKT T' HAERLEM, BY MY GILLIS ROOMAN
HET RIJCK GODTS INDER ZIELEN OFT BINNEN U-LIEDEN / Hertogenbosch, Ioannes Evangelista van 'S – Antwerpen, 1639 – 6mf – 8 – ne Slangenburg [240]
Rijn, C P van *see* PROJECT REPORT ON A MANPOWER INFORMATION PROGRAMME IN LIBYA
Rijn, J van *see* OUDHEDEN EN GESTICHTEN
Rijnhart, Susie Carson *see* WITH THE TIBETANS IN TENT AND TEMPLE
Rijoatmodjo, Suharto *see* PENGANTAR ANTHROPOLOGI BUDAJA DAN SOSIALSE-5427/1. 1964
Rike, Charles Jesse *see* FIRST BAPTIST CHURCH, FARMERSVILLE, TEXAS CENTENNIAL STORY
Rikhter, V *see* ISTORIIA MEDITSINY V ROSSII
Rikker, K L *see* UKAZATEL' RUSSKOI MEDITSINSKOI LITERATURY
RIKUGU ZASSHI – Japan, 1880-1921 – 25r – 1 – inquire – us Ross [950]
RIKUGUN. OSAMU BUTAI. EISEIHO DAN KYUKYUHO / Japan. Ministry of War – Djakarta ? 260?. 83, 83p – 54-55mf – 9 – ne IDC [350]
Riley, B F *see*
– DIARY
– HISTORY OF SOUTHERN BAPTISTS, 1684-1918
– A HISTORY OF THE BAPTISTS IN THE SOUTHERN STATES EAST OF THE MISSISSIPPI
– THE WHITE MAN'S BURDEN
Riley, G Michael *see* HERNANDO CORTES AND THE MARQUESADO IN MORELOS, 1522-1547
Riley, H T *see*
– CHRONIA MONASTEREII S ALBANI (RS28)
– MEMORIALS OF LONDON AND LONDON LIFE IN THE 13TH, 14TH, AND 15TH CENTURIES
Riley, H Th *see* MUNIMENTA GILDHALLAE LONDONIENSIS (RS12)
Riley, I Woodbridge *see* THE FOUNDER OF MORMONISM
Riley, Isaac *see*
– SYRIAN HOME LIFE
– SYRIAN HOME-LIFE
– THE WOMEN OF THE ARABS
Riley, J *see* CATALOGUE OF FERNS
Riley, James *see* NAUFRAGE DU BRIGANTINE AMERICAIN "LE COMMERCE"
Riley, James D *see* LETTERS
Riley, Robert G *see* AN EXPLORATORY STUDY OF QUALITY ASSURANCE METHODOLOGY IN THERAPEUTIC RECREATION USING THE DELPHI TECHNIQUE
RILEY'S CASES IN EQUITY / South Carolina. Supreme Court – (A Pre-NRS title) – 1v. 1836-1837 (all publ) – 4mf – 9 – $6.00 – LLMC 94-039 – us L.L.M.C. [340]
RILEY'S CREEK BAPTIST CHURCH. WELMINTON ASSOCIATION. NORTH CAROLINA : CHURCH RECORDS – 1850-1931 – 1 – 13.32 – us Baptist [240]
RILEY'S LAW REPORTS / South Carolina. Supreme Court – (A Pre-NRS title) – 1v. 1836-1837 (all publ) – 4mf – 9 – $6.00 – LLMC 94-018 – us L.L.M.C. [340]
RILINDJA – Pristina, Yugoslavia. Mar 1945-1949; 1950-62; Sept 1963-Jul 1990 (incomplete) – 127r – us L of C Photodup [949]
Rilke, Clara *see* THREE LETTERS TO ELLEN KEY
Rilke, Rainer Maria *see* UNPUBLISHED LETTERS TO ELLEN KEY
RIMAS DE JUVENTUD. POESIAS / Morillo-Velarde, D – Villanueva de la Serena: Imp. Nicolas Diestro, 1931 – 1 – sp Bibl Santa Ana [810]
RIMAS VARIAS DE LUIS DE CAMOENS... COMMENTADAS PRO MANUEL DE FARIA Y SOUSA / Camoes, Luiz de – Lisboa, 1685-89 – 1 – us U.W. Library [810]
RIMAS Y ESTROFAS / Salcedo, Antonio – Zafra: Imp.Lib.y Pap.La Moderna, 1912 – 1 – sp Bibl Santa Ana [946]
Rimbault, E F *see* THE BOOK OF COMMON PRAYER WITH MUSICAL NOTES
RIME DIVISE IN SETTE LIBRI, NELLE QUALI AD IMITATIONE DEI GROTTESCHI USATI DA' PITTORI, HA CANTATO LE LODI DI DIO / Lomazzo, G P – O-1001. 1587 – 9 – ne IDC [810]
RIME Y TRIONFI / Petrarca – SL, (S. XV) – 9 – sp Cultura [440]
Rimmer, R *see* SHELLS OF THE BRITISH ISLES
RIMON – A Magazine of Art and Letters. Ed. by M. Vishnitzer and B. Krupnik. Berlin. 1922-24. BJ-291-33 1 – 9 – ne IDC [073]
RIMOUSKI STAR – Rimouski, Canada. 20 dec 1876-10 fev 1877 – 1r – 1 – Can$30.00 – cn Can Microfilming [072]
LE RIMOUSKOIS – Rimouski, Canada. 6 dec 1967-31 dec 1991 – 50r – 1 – Can$60.00r – cn Can Microfilming [072]
RIMUR AF SIGURDI SNARFARA OG AETTMONNUM HANS: KVEDNAR ARIN 1879-81 / Natansson, Hans – Akureyri: B. Jonsson, 1883. vii,115p – 1 – us U.W. Library [430]
RIN CHEN GTER MDZOD CHEN MO – 1,133mf – $600.00 – us I.A.S.W.R. [090]
RIN CHEN GTER MDZOD CHEN MO – 111 vol – 1,133mf – 9 – $600.00 – us I.A.S.W.R. [280]
Rinaldi, Nancy E *see* EVALUATION OF THE WASHINGTON STATE UNIVERSITY INTRAMURAL SPORTS PROGRAM
LA RINASCENZA – Stamford, CT. 1922 – us I.H.R.C. [073]
RINASCITA – 1991 – 1r per year – 5,6 – F1,600.00 – sz Infoprint [072]
RINASCITA – -m. (June 1944-Apr. 1962), -w. (May 5, 1962-Dec. 22, 1972). Anno 1-Giugno 1944-. Roma, etc.: s.n – 1 – us U.W. Library [073]
RINASCITA – Milano, IT. 1969-1976 – 16r – $800.00 – R3616 – us Library Micro [072]
RINASCITA SOCIALISTA / Partito Socialisto Unitario dei Lavoratori Italiani – Paris, 1928-1930 – 1 – fr A.C.R.P.P. [335]
Rincon del Obispo *see* FIESTAS EN RINCON DEL OBISPO EN HONOR DE SAN JOSE OBRERO. MAYO 1973
Rincon del Obispo-Coria. Ayuntamiento *see* FIESTAS EN HONOR DE SAN JOSE OBRERO 1971
Rincon Jimenez, Jesus *see*
– MEMORIAL OLIVENTINO
– PERIODICOS Y PERIODISTAS EXTREMENOS
Rincon Martin, Jose Maria *see* NORMAS DE TRABAJO VIGENTES EN LAS INDUSTRIAS DE LA CONSTRUCCION YUNOBRAS PUBLICAS Y TABLAS DE LIQUIDACION DE SALARIOS
Rinfret, Fernand *see* LE LIBERALISME DE LAURIER
Rinfret, Raoul *see*
– DICTIONNAIRE DE NOS FAUTES CONTRE LA LANGUE FRANCAISE
DER RING – Berlin, 1928-oct 26 1934 – 1 – Inquire at Mikrofilmarchiv for details – gw Misc Inst [072]
DER RING DES NIBELUNGEN : EINE STUDIE ZUR EINFUEHRUNG IN DIE GLEICHNAMIGE DICHTUNG RICHARD WAGNERS / Mueller, Franz Karl Friedrich – (Includes bibliographical references) – Leipzig: C F Peters, 1876 – 1r – 1 – us U.W. Library [790]
Ringgren, H *see* STUDIES IN ARABIAN FATALISM
Ringi, Daniel *see* DIARIES
RINGING WORLD – Guildford, UK. 1982-1987 – 6r – $300.00 – R63601 – us Library Micro [072]
RINGKASAN KETETAPAN, NO. 1 DAN 2/MPRS/1960 / Indonesia. Madjelis Permusjawaratan Rakjat Sementara – Bandung. 1961. BD-207 1 – 9 – ne IDC [330]
Ringrose, Hyacinthe *see* THE INNS OF COURT
Ringwalt, Ralph Curtis *see* BRIEF DRAWING
Rini, K W *see* PELADJARAN MERANGKAI BUNGA
Rinieri, Ilario *see* S. PIETRO IN ROMA ED I PRIMI PAPI
Rink, H J *see*
– EETBLADSTRYK DATERET GODTHAAB DEN 23 APRIL 1861. FOLGESKRIVELSE TIL ET PROVENUMMER AF "ATUAGAGDLIUTIT" HVIS UDGIVELSE JUST VAR PABEGYNDT
– THE ESKIMO TRIBES 1-2
– ESKIMOISKE EVENTRY OG SAGN OVERSATTE EFTER DE INDODTE FORTAELLERES OPSKR. OG MEDDELELSER EVENTYR OG SAGN
– GRONLAND GEOGRAPHISK OG STATISTISK BESKREVET
– OM ESKIMOERNES HERKOM AARBOG FOR NORDISK OLDKYNDIGHED
– TALES AND TRADITIONS OF THE ESKIMOES
Rinkes, J *see* EENIGE OORZAKEN VAN DEN FINANTIEELEN NOOD DER NEDERLANDSCH-INDISCHE REGEERING, ENKELE BEZUINIGING- SUGGESTIES EN IETS OVER DE VERHOUDING INDIE-HOLLAND
Rinne, Karl-Friedrich *see* INNERE GESCHICHTE DER ENTWICKLUNG DER DEUTSCHEN NATIONAL-LITTERATUR
IL RINNOVAMENTO *see* THE RENEWAL
Rintala, P *see* VALIDATION OF A CARDIORESPIRATORY FITNESS TEST FOR MEN WITH MENTAL RETARDATION
Rintelen, Fritz-Joachim von *see*
– PHILOSOPHIA PERENNIS
Rinuccini, Giovani B *see* DE HAERESIS ANGLICANAE INTRUSIONE ET PROGRESSU
Rinuccini, Ottavio *see*
– L'ARIANNA TRAGEDIA
– L'EURIDICE D'OTTAVIO RINUCCINI
O RIO ACRE – Rio Branco, Acre. 15 Nov-Dez 1908; Fev-3 Jul 1909 – 1,5,6 – bl Biblioteca [072]
RIO ACRE – Pennapolis, Acre. 17 Out 1909 – 1,5,6 – bl Biblioteca [072]
O RIO BRANCO : ORGAM HEBDOMADARIO, LITTERARIO, NOTICIOSO E COMMERCIAL – Boa Vista, Amazonas. 7 Jul 1918 – 1,5,6 – bl Biblioteca [072]
O RIO BRANCO – Rio Branco, Acre. 20 Abr 1969; 12 Abr 1985 – 1,5,6 – bl Biblioteca [072]
RIO BRANCO : JORNAL INDENPENDENTE – Boa Vista, Amazonas. 15 Mar 1914 – 1,5,6 – bl Biblioteca [072]
RIO BRANCO : ORGAO DO PARTIDO CONSERVADOR – Manaos, Amazonas. 14 Ago 1887 – 1,5,6 – bl Biblioteca [072]
O RIO CASCA – Rio Casca, Brazil. Jan 1916 – 1 – bl Biblioteca [072]
RIO DE JANEIRO DE ANTANHO / Taunay, Alfonso de E – Sao Paulo, 1942 – 7mf – 8 – ne Slangenburg [910]
Rio de Janeiro. Federal District. Camara Legislativa *see* DIARIO MUNICIPAL
Rio de Janeiro. Federal District. Prefeitura *see* DIARIO MUNICIPAL AND SUPPLEMENTS
Rio de Janeiro. (State). Brazil *see* DIARIO OFICIAL DO ESTADO DO RIO DE JANEIRO
THE RIO HERALD – Rio de Janeiro, 8 Mar-5 Jul 1828 – 1,5,6 – bl Biblioteca [072]
Rio, I de *see* GUIA DEL ARCHIVO FRANCISCANO DE LA BIBLIOTECA NACIONAL DE MEXICO
O RIO JAMARY : ORGAM LITTERARIO E NOTICIOSO – Manaos, Amazonas. 15 Abr, 15 Nov 1908 – 1,5,6 – bl Biblioteca [072]
RIO LINDA NEWS – Rio Linda, CA. 1983-1990 – 3r – 1 – $150.00 – B05049 – us Library Micro [071]
O RIO MADEIRA : ORGAM DO COMMERCIO – Manicore, Amazonas. 15-26 Nov 1905; 1 Fev 1906 – 1,5,6 – bl Biblioteca [072]
O RIO MADEIRA : ORGAM LITTERARIO, NOTICIOSO E COMMERCIAL – Manicore, Amazonas. 1 Mar-Dez 1917; Jan-Jun, Set, 10-29 Dez 1918 – 1,5,6 – bl Biblioteca [072]
RIO MADEIRA : FOLHA CRITICA E NOTICIOSA – Manicore, Amazonas. 18 Dez 1881; Jun, 30 Jul 1882 – 1,5,6 – bl Biblioteca [072]
O RIO NEGRO – Manaos, Amazonas. 24 Jul-Ago, Nov-Dez 1897; Jan-Abr, 6-15 Jun 1898 – 1,5,6 – bl Biblioteca [072]
O RIO NEGRO : ORGAO DOS INTERESSES POPULARES – Sao Jaoquim, Amazonas. 10 Maio 1906 – 1,5,6 – bl Biblioteca [072]
RIO NOVO – Rio Novo, Brazil. Mar 1916 – 1 – bl Biblioteca [072]
RIO NU *see* BICHINHO
O RIO PURUS : ORGAO IMPARCIAL – Labrea-Amazonas. 7 Fev 1892; 15 Set 1893 – 1,5,6 – bl Biblioteca [072]
RIOJA / Lopez de Ayala, Adelardo – 1854 – 9 – 1.50f – sp Bibl Santa Ana [820]
Riol, Eladio *see* EL PADRE JOSE MHA RUIZ, MARTIR EN SIGUENZA
Riolan, Jean *see*
– ANTHROPOGRAPHIA EX PROPIIS ET NOVIS OBSERVATIONIBUS COLLECTA
– OPUSCULA ANATOMICA NOVA
O RIO-MAR : ORGAO DEMOCRATICO – Manaos, Amazonas. 26 Maio 1877 – 1,5,6 – bl Biblioteca [072]
Rionegro, Friolan *see*
– CARTAS Y DOCUMENTOS DE LAS MISIONES DE LOS P.P. CAPUCHINOS EN VENEZUELA 1781-1788
– MISIONES DE LOS PADRES CAPUCHINOS DE VENEZUELA

RIONOVENSE – Rio Novo, Brazil. Apr 1916 – 1 – bl Biblioteca [072]
O RIO-NU – Rio de Janeiro, 21 May, Oct-Dec 1898; Jan-May, Aug-Nov 1899; Jan 1903-Dec 1912; Mar-May 1913; Jan 1914-30 Dec 1916 – 1,5,6 – bl Biblioteca [072]
Rios, Fernando de los *see*
- COMPLETE TEXT OF THE ADDRESS DELIVERED BY THE SPANISH AMBASSADOR...NOVEMBER 5, 1936
- WHAT IS HAPPENING IN SPAIN?
RIOS INTERNACIONALES SU LIBRE NAVEGACION / Florez, L A – Bogota, 1921 – 1mf – 1 – ILM-1822/1 – ne IDC [327]
Rios, Roman *see*
- MISIONES AUSTRALIANAS DE LOS BENDICTINOS ESPANOLES
- LOS MONUMENTA HUMANAE SALUTIS
RIOT DATA REVIEW – n1-3. 1968-69 – 4mf – 9 – $5.00f – us Ross [303]
Ripa, Cesare *see*
- ICONOLOGIA DEL CAVALIERE
- ICONOLOGIA, OF BEELDESPRAECK
- ICONOLOGIA, OF UYTBEELDINGHE DES VERSTANTS. UYT HET ITALIAENS VERTAELT DOOR D. P. PERS
- ICONOLOGIE, OU, EXPLICATION NOUVELLE DE PLUSIEURS IMAGES
EL RIPIO – Canaveral, 1907 – 5 – sp Bibl Santa Ana [073]
RIPIOS. POESIAS / Garcia Jimeno, Fernando – 1899 – 9 – 1.50f – sp Bibl Santa Ana [810]
Ripley, George *see* REVIEW OF THE RATIONALE OF RELIGIOUS ENQUIRY
Ripley, Mississippi *see* MISCELLANEOUS EARLY NEWSPAPERS
RIPLEY NEWS – Apr 5 1889-Dec 28 1890; 1891-92; Jan 6-Dec 8 1893; Jan 5 1894-Dec 21 1895; 1896-97; 1899-1957; 1966-Dec 22 1978; 1979; 1986-Jun 1988; 1989-91; 1993; Jan 7-Mar 25, Apr-Jun 24, Jul 1994-96 – 85 1/2r – 1 – uk British Libr Newspaper [072]
RIPLEY REVIV'D: OR, AN EXPOSITION UPON SIR GEORGE RIPLEY'S HERMETICO-POETICAL WORKS / Philalethes, Eirenaeus, pseud – London, 1678. 539p – 1 – us U.W. Library [540]
RIPM *see* REPERTOIRE INTERNATIONAL DE LA PRESSE MUSICALE (RIPM)
THE RIPON FORUM – Cambridge. Mass. 1968-1969 – 1 – us UMI [071]
RIPON RECORD – Ripon, CA. 1912-81; 1983- – 41+ r – 1 – $2,050.00 ($50.00y) – B02710 – us Library Micro [071]
RIPONSHIRE ADVOCATE – 1874-1901. RA1-10 – 10r – 1 – at Corangamite [072]
RIPONSHIRE ADVOCATE – 1921-1941 – 6r – 1 – at Corangamite [072]
IL RIPOSO / Borghini, R – O-971 1. 1730 – 9 – ne IDC [440]
LA RIPOSTE / ed by Fortin, J-A – Montreal, Canada. 11 mai 1927-23 mai 1936 – 1r – 1 – Can$35.00 – cn Can Microfilming [072]
Rippel, Gregorius *see* DIE SCHOENHEIT DER KATHOLISCHEN KIRCHE
Rippin, Markus *see* ALLEY-CROPPING AND MULCHING WITH ERYTHRINA POEPPIGIANA (WALP.) O.F. COOK AND GLIRICIDIA SEPIUM (JACQ.) WALP
Rippon, John *see*
- BAPTIST ANNUAL REGISTER
- PSALMS AND HYMN TUNES OF DR. WATTS
- THE SELECTION OF TUNES IN MINIATURE
Rippon, R H F *see* ICONES ORNITHOPTERORUM
Riquelme Salar, Jose *see* SEMBLANZA DE EMERITA AUGUSTA
Riquer, Martin de *see* MANUAL DE HERALDICA ESPANOLA
LE RIRE – Paris. nov 1894-19 juin 1940; 1946-1959 – 1 – fr A.C.R.P.P. [073]
RIRE : JOURNAL HUMORISTIQUE – Paris, 1894-1970 – 20r – 1 – us Ross [073]
RIS ET CROQUIS / Ducharme, Charles Marie – Montreal: C. Beauchemin, 1889. 02783. (Pre-1900 Canadiana) – 9 – cn C.I.H.M. [971]
RISALAH PERTEMUAN EX P.A.I. DENGAN ORGANISASI MASA(PRESS RELEASE P.A.I.). SE 4834/1 – 9 – ne IDC [025]
RISALAH STENOGRAFIS – Djakarta. Indonesia. 1967- – 1 – us UMI [072]
RISALAT – Shumarah-'i 353-1115 (1985-15 Nov 1989) – 4r – 1 – $80.00 – us MEDOC [950]
IL RISCATTO – Chicago, IL, 1914 – 3r – 1 – us I.H.R.C. [978]
Risch, Gabriela *see* VERBPRAEFIGIERUNG DES DEUTSCHEN
Risco, A *see* LAS CORTES DE CADIZ Y EL OBISPO DE ORENSE (EPISODIO CURIOSO DE LAS CORTES CONSTITUYENTES
Risco, Alberto *see* DON FRANCISCO DE PAULA ROMERO Y PALOMEQUE
Risco, Manuel *see*
- LA CASTILLA Y EL MAS FAMOSO CASTELLANO
- ESPANA SAGRADA. TOMO 30
- ESPANA SAGRADA. TOMO 31
- ESPANA SAGRADA. TOMO 32
- ESPANA SAGRADA. TOMO 33
- ESPANA SAGRADA. TOMO 34
- ESPANA SAGRADA. TOMO 35
- ESPANA SAGRADA. TOMO 36
- ESPANA SAGRADA. TOMO 37
- ESPANA SAGRADA. TOMO 38
- ESPANA SAGRADA. TOMO 39
- ESPANA SAGRADA. TOMO 40
- ESPANA SAGRADA. TOMO 41
- ESPANA SAGRADA. TOMO 42
- HISTORIA DE LA CIUDAD Y CORTE DE LEON Y DE SUS REYES
- IGLESIA DE LEON Y MONASTERIOS ANTIGUOS Y MODERNOS
LA RISCOSSA – Brooklyn, NY, 1916-1917 – 11mf or 1r – 1,9 – us I.H.R.C. [978]
LA RISCOSSA – no. 1-119. Paris. 19 juil 1924-23 oct 1926 – 1 – fr A.C.R.P.P. [073]
THE RISE AND DEVELOPMENT OF CHRISTIAN ARCHITECTURE / Ayer, Joseph Cullen – Milwaukee: Young Churchman, 1902 – 1mf – us A.T.L.A. [720]
THE RISE AND FALL OF PAPACY / Fleming, Robert; ed by Thomson, Thomas – London: John Johnstone: Hamilton, Adams, 1849 – 1mf – 9 – 0-8370-8339-7 – 1986-2339 – us A.T.L.A. [230]
THE RISE AND GROWTH OF AMERICAN POLITICS : SKETCH OF CONSTITUTIONAL DEVELOPMENT / Ford, Henry Jones – New York: Macmillan, 1911 – 5mf – 9 – $7.50 – LLMC 95-072 – us L.L.M.C. [323]
RISE AND PROGRESS OF THE SEVENTH-DAY ADVENTISTS : WITH TOKENS OF GOD'S HAND IN THE MOVEMENT AND A BRIEF SKETCH OF THE ADVENT CAUSE FROM 1831 TO 1844 / Loughborough, J N – Battle Creek, Mich.: General Conference Association of the Seventh-Day Adventists, 1892 – 1mf – us A.T.L.A. [240]
THE RISE AND THE FALL : OR, THE ORIGIN OF MORAL EVIL: IN THREE PARTS – New York: Hurd and Houghton, 1866 – 1mf – 9 – 0-8370-6363-9 – 1986-0363 – us A.T.L.A. [230]
THE RISE OF FERNANDO CORTES / Wagner, Henry R – (Documents and Narratives Concerning the Discovery and conquest of Latin America) – Los Angeles: The Cortes Society, 1944 – sp Bibl Santa Ana [350]
THE RISE OF MODERN RELIGIOUS IDEAS / McGiffert, Arthur Cushman – New York: Macmillan, 1915 – 1mf – us A.T.L.A. [200]
THE RISE OF OUR EAST AFRICAN EMPIRE : EARLY EFFORTS IN NYASALAND AND UGANDA / Lugard, Frederick John Dealtry – 2v. 1893 – 1r – 1 – us Ross [960]
THE RISE OF OUR EAST AFRICAN EMPIRE: EARLY EFFORTS IN NYASALAND AND UGANDA / Lugard, Frederick John Dealtry – 2v. Edinburgh. 1893. BA-338 2 – 8 – ne IDC [960]
THE RISE OF RELIGIOUS LIBERTY IN AMERICA / Cobb, Sanford H – 1902 – 1 – 19.95 – us Baptist [240]
THE RISE OF RELIGIOUS LIBERTY IN AMERICA : A HISTORY / Cobb, Sanford H – New York: Macmillan, 1902 – 2mf – us A.T.L.A. [240]
THE RISE OF THE AMERICAN PEOPLE : A PHILOSOPHICAL INTERPRETATION OF AMERICAN HISTORY / Usher, Roland G – New York: Century, 1914 – 1mf – us A.T.L.A. [975]
THE RISE OF THE MEDIAEVAL CHURCH : AND ITS INFLUENCE ON THE CIVILISATION OF WESTERN EUROPE FROM THE FIRST TO THE THIRTEENTH CENTURY / Flick, Alexander Clarence – (Includes index) – New York: G P Putnam, 1909 – 2mf – 9 – 0-8370-8815-1 – 1986-2815 – us A.T.L.A. [240]
THE RISE OF THE NEW TESTAMENT / Muzzey, David Saville – New York: Macmillan, 1900. 1 fiche – 9 – us A.T.L.A. [240]
Risebergius, L *see* COMPENDIARIA PRAECIPVARVM RERVM TVRCICARVM
THE RISEN REDEEMER : THE GOSPEL HISTORY FROM THE RESURRECTION TO THE DAY OF PENTECOST / Krummacher, Friedrich Wilhelm – NY: Robert Carter, 1863 – 1mf – 9 – 0-8370-4008-6 – 1985-2008 – us A.T.L.A. [240]
THE RISEN SUN / Suyematsu, Kencho – New York, 1905 – 1r – 1 – us Ross [950]
Rishell, Charles Wesley *see* THE OFFICIAL RECOGNITION OF WOMAN IN THE CHURCH: AN HISTORICAL STUDY
Rishiraj, Neetu *see* THE ROLE OF FUNCTIONAL KNEE BRACING IN A DYNAMIC SETTING
RISHTON NEWS AND DISTRICT HERALD – England.Jan-Jul 1900. -w. 1/2 reel – 1 – uk British Libr Newspaper [072]
RISING CHURCHES IN NON-CHRISTIAN LANDS : LECTURES DELIVERED ON THE COLLEGE OF MISSIONS LECTURESHIP, INDIANAPOLIS, THE SEVERANCE LECTURESHIP, WESTERN THEOLOGICAL SEMINARY, PITTSBURGH / Brown, Arthur Judson – New York: Missionary Education Movement of the United States and Canada, 1915 – 1mf – us A.T.L.A. [240]
RISING CITY INDEPENDENT – Rising City, NE. -w. Jul 1892; Jun 1894; Oct 1895-Jun 1896; Aug 1896-May 1898; Jul 1898; Nov 1898-Jun 1930 – 1 – us NE Hist [071]
THE RISING FAITH / Bartol, Cyrus Augustus – Boston: Roberts Bros., 1874. 1 fiche – 9 – us A.T.L.A. [240]
RISING FROM THE ASHES : DEVELOPMENT STRATEGIES IN TIMES OF DISASTER / Anderson, Mary B & Woodrow, Peter J – 1989 – 9 – 92-3-102618-6 – Co-published with the Westview Press, Boulder and San Francisco – fr UNESCO [360]
RISING OF THE LAND AROUND HUDSON BAY / Bell, Robert – Washington: GPO, 1898. 02326. (Pre-1900 Canadiana) – 9 – cn C.I.H.M. [550]
RISING STAR RECORD – Palestine. TX. 1924-51 – 1 – us UMI [071]
THE RISINGS OF THE LUDDITES, CHARTISTS AND PLUGDRAWERS / Peel, Frank – 2nd ed. Heckmondwike, England: Senior, 1888. 354p. illus – 1 – us U.W. Library [941]
RISK ANALYSIS – (v8-12 1988-92 $100.00v. v13-14 1993-94 $125.00v) – v1-7. 1981-87 – 1,5 – $80.00v – us UMI [000]
RISK ANALYSIS IN DRYLAND FARMING SYSTEMS – 1992 – 119p – it F.A.O. [650]
RISK MANAGEMENT BEHAVIORS OF NCAA DIVISION 3 HEAD FOOTBALL COACHES / McKinstrey, Jay P – Iowa State University, 1993 – 2mf – 9 – $8.00 – PE3612 – us Microform Publ [790]
RISK MANAGEMENT REPORTS – (v.8-. 1981-. 5,6,9) – v.1-. 1974- – 1 – us UMI [332]
Risley, H H *see* THE TRIBES AND CASTES OF BENGAL; NORTH WESTERN PROVINCES, AND PUNJAB
Rismunandar *see* BERTANAM ANGGUR DAN PASSIFLORA
O RISO : PERIODICO JOCO-SERIO-LITTERO-NOTICIOSO-ORGAO DO HUMORISIMO, DA IRONIA E DA ALACRIDADE – Patria dos Bares, Amazonas. 18 Nov 1912-4 Jan 1913 – 1,5,6 – bl Biblioteca [072]
RISORGIMENTO – Brooklyn, NY. 1919-? – us I.H.R.C. [073]
THE RISORGIMENTO COLLECTION – (Distribution rights for German-speaking Europe and Eastern Europe) – 1992 – 770 fiches (1:24) – 9 – silver DM18,400.00 – 0-86291-791-3 – gw Saur [945]
DAS RISORGIMENTO IM ROMAN BEI GEORGE MEREDITH UND ANTONIO FOGAZZARO / Friebe, Freimut – Frankfurt a.M., 1970 – 2mf – DM62.00 – 3-89349-843-5 – gw Hänsel [400]
RISP, REVUE INTERNATIONALE DE SCIENCE POLITIQUE = INTERNATIONAL POLITICAL SCIENCE REVIEW – (1983-. 1,5,6,9) – v1-. 1980- – 1 – us UMI [073]
Risse, Wilhelm *see* THESAURUS LOGICUS
Risso, J A *see* HISTOIRE NATURELLE DES PRINCIPALES PRODUCTIONS DE L'EUROPE MERIDIONALE ET PARTICULIEREMENT DE CELLES DES ENVIRONS DE NICE ET DES ALPES MARITIMES
Ristelhuber P *see* DICTIONNAIRE TOPOGRAPHIQUE, HISTORIQUE ET STATISTIQUE DU HAUT ET DU BAS RHIN
Ristelhuber, Paul *see* UNE FABLE DE FLORIAN
IL RISVEGLIO – Des Moines, IA. -w. 7 Dec 1923-3 Jul 1925. 1 reel, 50 feet – 1 – us I.H.R.C. [071]
IL RISVEGLIO – Dunkirk, Fredonia, New York. -w. 7 Sept-30 Nov 1935; 5 Sept 1936-8 Jan 1938. 1 reel, 75 feet – 1 – us I.H.R.C. [071]
Ritchie, Andrew Jackson *see* SKETCHES OF RABUN COUNTY (GEORGIA) HISTORY
Ritchie, Anne Thackeray *see*
- CHAPTERS FROM SOME MEMOIRS
- THE STORY OF ELIZABETH
Ritchie, Arthur *see* WHAT CATHOLICS BELIEVE AND DO
RITCHIE GAZETTE – Harrisville. West Virginia. 1936-1968 – 1 – us UMI [071]
Ritchie, J F *see* THE AFRICAN AS SUCKLING AND AS ADULT
Ritchie, Leitch *see* WANDERINGS BY THE LOIRE...WITH TWENTY-ONE ENGRAVINGS BY J.M.W. TURNER...
Ritchie, W B *see* REVELATION AND RELIGIOUS CERTITUDE
Ritchie, William *see*
- LIFE FOR GOD EXEMPLIFIED IN THE CHARACTER AND WORK OF NEHEMIAH
- THE PRODIGAL'S RETURN
RITCHIE'S EQUITY REPORTS : NOVA SCOTIA / Nova Scotia. Canada; ed by Russell, Benjamin – 1v. 1873-82 (all publ) – 6mf – 9 – $9.00 – LLMC 81-035 – us L.L.M.C. [340]
LES RITES DE MARIAGE TURC A CHYPRE ET EN ANATOLIE / Birerdinc, E – 9 – F30.00 – fr Ethnologie [390]
LES RITES DE NAISSANCE CHEZ LES INDIENS MAYA DES CUCHUMATANES-GUATEMALA ET LE PROFESSIONALISME DES SAGES-FEMMES / Bataille, M-C – 9 – F50.00 – fr Ethnologie [306]
RITES MORTUAIRES ET REPRESENTATION COLLECTIVE DE LA MORT A LA MARTINIQUE / Montreuil, Fr – 9 – F30.00 – fr Ethnologie [306]
RITM KAK DEALEKTIKA I "MEDNYI VSADNIK" / Belyi, A – (Issledovanie). M. 1929. BR-589 2 – 8 – ne IDC [460]
RITRATTI DI ALCUNI CELEBRI PITTORI DEL SECOLO 17. CON LE VITE DE'MEDESIMI / Lioni, O & Bellori, Giovanni Pietro – O 976. 1731 – 9 – ne IDC [920]
Ritschl, Albertus *see* EXPOSITIO DOCTRINAE AUGUSTINI DE CREATIONE MUNDI, PECCATO, GRATIA
Ritschl, Albrecht Benjamin *see*
- DIE ENTSTEHUNG DER ALTKATHOLISCHEN KIRCHE
- GESCHICHTE DES PIETISMUS IN DER LUTHERISCHEN KIRCHE DES 17. UND 18. JAHRHUNDERTS
- GESCHICHTE DES PIETISMUS IN DER REFORMIERTEN KIRCHE
- THEOLOGIE UND METAPHYSIK
Ritschl, Otto *see*
- DIE CAUSALBETRACHTUNG IN DEN GEISTESWISSENSCHAFTEN
- CYPRIAN VON KARTHAGO UND DIE VERFASSUNG DER KIRCHE
- DOGMENGESCHICHTE DES PROTESTANTISMUS
- NIETZSCHES WELT- UND LEBENSANSCHAUUNG IN IHRER ENTSTEHUNG UND ENTWICKLUNG
- SCHLEIERMACHERS STELLUNG ZUM CHRISTENTUM IN SEINEN REDEN UEBER DIE RELIGION
Ritson, Joseph *see*
- LETTERS FROM JOSEPH RITSON, ESQ. TO MR. GEORGE PATON
- THE ROMANCE OF NONCONFORMITY
- THE ROMANCE OF PRIMITIVE METHODISM
RITT GEN MITTERNACHT : ROMAN AUS DEUTSCH-SUEDWEST-AFRIKA / Kaempffer, Adolf – Braunschweig: G Westermann, c1939 – 1r – 1 – us U.W. Library [830]
Ritter, Bernhard *see* PHILO UND DIE HALACHA
Ritter, Eli Foster *see* MORAL LAW AND CIVIL LAW
Ritter, Ernst *see* LAGEBERICHTE (1920-1929) UND MELDUNGEN (1930-1933)
Ritter, H *see* DREISSIG JAHRE PROTESTANTISCHER MISSION IN JAPAN
Ritter, Immanuel Heinrich *see* MENDELSSOHN UND LESSING
Ritter, J *see* DREY SONATEN DEN LIEBHABERN DES KLAVIERS VERFERTIGET VON JOHANN CHRISTOPH RITTER..ERSTER THEIL [OP.1]

Ritter, Joerg Eberhard *see* UEBEREXPRESSION UND ANWENDUNG DER PHOSPHOMANNOMUTASE UND GDP-ALPHA-D-MANNOSE-PYROPHOSPHORYLASE AUS SALMONELLA ENTERICA, GRUPPE B ZUR PRAEPARATIVEN SYNTHESE VON GDP-ALPHA-D-MANNOSE

Ritter, John R *see* SEDIMENT TRANSPORT AND TURBIDITY IN THE EEL RIVER BASIN

Ritter, P *see*
- CONCERT POUR LE VIOLONCELL

Ritterling, E *see* DAS FRUEHROEMISCHE LAGER BEI HOFHEIM IM TAUNUS

Rittershausen, Beckerath, Zander et al *see* FOUR LAW DRAFTS TO FIGHT DEFLATION, PREVENT INFLATION AND LOWER THE INTEREST RATE

Rittershausen, Heinrich *see*
- DAS ANDERE SYSTEM
- BANKNOTEN, GELDUMLAUF UND DEVISENFRAGE
- DER NEUBAU DES DEUTSCHEN KREDITSYSTEMS
- DIE ZUKUNFT DER NOTENDECKUNG DURCH HANDELSWECHSEL

DER RITTMEISTER / Naso, Eckart von – Hamburg: W Krueger, 1943, c1942 – 1r – 1 – us U.W. Library [830]

RITUAL AND BELIEF: STUDIES IN THE HISTORY OF RELIGION / Hartland, Edwin Sidney – London: Williams and Norgate, 1914. xv,352p. Bibliography and index – 1 – us U.W. Library [200]

RITUAL AND SERVICE FOR LODGE OF SORROW, COMPILED, ARRANGED AND ADAPTED FOR USE IN LODGES OF A.F. AND A.M.,.. – Ottawa, 1888. 03249. (Pre-1900 Canadiana) – 9 – cn C.I.H.M. [360]

RITUAL DEL MAESTRO FRANCMASON E HISTORIA DE LA MASONERIA / Caballero De Puga, Eduardo – 1888. Libros en Microficha no. 08 – 1mf – 9 – Pta1,000.00 – 84-85422-33-3 – sp Pentalfa [360]

RITUAL NACH DEM GEISTE UND DEN ANORDNUNGEN DER KATHOLISCHEN KIRCHE / Wessenberg, I – Stuttgart-Tuebingen, 1831 – 6mf – 8 – Dfl25.00 – ne Slangenburg [240]

RITUALE ARMENORUM / Conybeare, Frederick C – Oxford, 1905 – 15mf – 8 – Dfl53.00 – ne Slangenburg [240]

RITUALE GRAECORUM / ed by Goar, J – Venetiis, 1730 – 33mf – 8 – Dfl116.00 – ne Slangenburg [240]

RITUALE MELCHITARUM : A CHRISTIAN PALESTINIAN EUCHOLOGION / Black, M – Stuttgart, 1938 – 2mf – 8 – Dfl9.00 – ne Slangenburg [240]

RITUALE ROMANUM BENEDICTI PAPAE 14, JUSSU EDITUM ET AUCTUM PERPETUIS COMMENTARIIS EXORNATUM. T. 1 / Catalanus, J – Romae, 1757 – 20mf – 8 – ne Slangenburg [240]

RITUALE ROMANUM BENEDICTI PAPE 14, JUSSU EDITUM ET AUCTUM PERPETUIS COMMENTARIIS EXORNATUM. T. 2 / Catalanus, J – Romae, 1757 – 18mf – 8 – ne Slangenburg [240]

DAS RITUALE VON ST FLORIAN AUS DEM 12 JHT / Franz, Albert – Freiburg i/Br., 1904 – 6mf – 8 – Dfl25.00 – ne Slangenburg [240]

THE RITUALISTS : THEIR ROMANISING OBJECTS AND WORK: A BOOK FOR THE PEOPLE / Walsh, Walter – London: J. Nisbet, 1900 – 1mf – us A.T.L.A. [240]

DER RITUALMORD VOR DEN GERICHTSHOEFEN DER WAHRHEIT UND DER GERECHTIGKEIT / Frank, Friedrich – (Includes index) – 2. Aufl. Regensburg:G.J. Manz, 1901 – 1mf – 9 – 0-8370-3178-8 – 1985-1178 – us A.T.L.A. [230]

DER RITUALMORD VOR DEN GERICHTSHOEFEN DER WAHRHEIT UND DER GERECHTIGKEIT / Frank, Friedrich – Regensburg: G.J. Manz, 1901. 1 fiche – 9 – us A.T.L.A. [240]

RITUEL DU DIOCESE DE QUEBEC – 2e ed. Paris: S Langlois, 1703. SEM16P35 – 1r – 5 – Can$12.00 – cn Bibl Nat [240]

RITUEL DU DIOCESE DE QUEBEC – Paris: S Langlois, 1703. SEM16P34 – 1r – 5 – Can$12.00 – cn Bibl Nat [240]

LE RITUEL POPULAIRE DANS LES REGIONS ANDINES DE BOLIVIE / Girault, L – 9 – F180.00 – fr Ethnologie [306]

LES RITUELS DE CONSTRUCTION DES PAYSANS ROUMAINS / Stahl, A – 9 – F60.00 – fr Ethnologie [306]

LES RITUELS LIEGEOIS / Malherbe, G – 1951 – 1mf – 8 – Dfl6.00 – ne Slangenburg [240]

RITUS DANDI PRESBYTERIUM PAPAE, CARDINALIBUS ET CLERICIS NONNULLARUM ECCLESIARUM URBIS / Moretti, Pietro – Romae, 1741 – 9mf – 8 – Dfl32.00 – ne Slangenburg [240]

DIE RITUS DES SYNAGOGALEN GOTTESDIENSTES / Zunz, L – Berlin: J. Springer, 1859 – 1mf – us A.T.L.A. [270]

Ritzer, Christine L *see* STABILITY OF EXPERIENCED FEMALE LIFTERS' HEART RATES ACROSS DAYS DURING AND AFTER PYRAMID EXERCISES OF BENCH PRESS AND PARALLEL SQUAT

Riva, Juan Antonio de la *see* BAUTISMO DE LOS FETOS ABORTIVOS...CESAREA

Riva Palacio, Vicente *see* ESTABLECIMIENTO...NUEVA ESPANA

Rivadeneira, Pedro de *see* VIDA DE SAN PEDRO DE ALCANTARA

Rivain, V *see* CONTRIBUTION A L'ETUDE DYNAMIQUE ET FONCTIONNELLE DES PEUPLEMENTS DE SABLES FINS DU GOLFE NORMANO-BRETON

Rivard, Dominique-Francois *see* RECUEIL DE MEMOIRES TOUCHANT L'EDUCATION DE LA JEUNESSE, SURTOUT PAR RAPPORT AUX ETUDES

RIVAROL – Paris. Dir., Rene Malliavin. No.1-1850. 18 janv 1951-1993 – 1 – fr A.C.R.P.P. [073]

RIVAROL – Paris: Rivarol. -w. Began in 1951 – 1 – us U.W. Library [073]

Rivarol, Antoine *see*
- DISCOURS SUR L'UNIVERSALITE DE LA LANGUE FRANCAISE
- MEMOIRES DE RIVAROL

Rivas Mateos, Marcelo *see*
- DISCURSO LEIDO EN LA SOLEMNE INAUGURACION DEL CURSO ACADEMICO 1912 A 1913
- ESTUDIOS PRELIMINARES PARALA HORA DE LA PROVINCIA DE CACERES

Rivaux, Jean Joseph, Abbe *see* HISTORY OF THE REVEREND MOTHER SACRED HEART OF JESUS

LA RIVE GAUCHE – puis Journal international de la jeune Republique. Red. en chef Robert Luzarche. Paris puis Bruxelles, Londres, Geneve. nov 1864-aout 1866 – 1 – fr A.C.R.P.P. [073]

LA RIVE NORD – Joliette, Canada. 20 oct 1880-4 jan 1881; Berthier, 27 mai 1881-v1 n53. 11 oct 1881 – 1r – 1 – Can$50.00 – cn Can Microfilming [072]

RIVER BASIN SURVEYS PAPERS / Stephenson, Robert L – 1967 – 9 – $5.00f – us Ross [550]

THE RIVER COLUMN : A NARRATIVE OF THE ADVANCE OF THE RIVER COLUMN OF THE NILE EXPEDITIONARY FORCE, AND ITS RETURN DOWN THE RAPIDS / Brackenbury, Henry – Edinburgh: W Blackwood, 1885 – us Res Libr [910]

RIVER CURRENTS – (Jan 1975-Dec 1980-Jan 1981. 9) – v28-. 1974-Dec 1980-Jan 1981 – 1,5,6 – us UMI [073]

RIVER CURRENTS – v1-. Apr-May 1981-. Vol. numbering started again – 1,5,6,9 – us UMI [073]

RIVER DESERT INDIANS OF QUEBEC / Speck, F G – BN 396 2. 1927 – 8 – ne IDC [971]

THE RIVER DUDDON : A SERIES OF SONNETS; VAUDRACOUR AND JULIA: AND OTHER POEMS... / Wordsworth, William – London: Printed for Longman, Hurst, Rees, Orme, and Brown, 1820 – 1 roll – 1 – 1-55879-437-9 – uk Libr Preservation [810]

RIVER FISHERIES – 1985 – 339p – it F.A.O. [338]

RIVER NEWS – Rio Vista. Calif. 1943-57 – 1 – us UMI [071]

RIVER NEWS – Sacramento, CA. 1890-1893 – 2r – 1 – $100.00 – BC02740 – us Library Micro [071]

RIVER NEWS – (See Rio Vista) – River News, CA. 1890-93 – 2r – 1 BC02740 – $100.00 – us Library Micro [071]

THE RIVER NEWS – Rio Vista, CA. 1902-08; 1915-17; 1919; 1920-29; 1931-54 – 26r – 1 BC02705 – $1,300.00 – us Library Micro [071]

RIVER NEWS HERALD AND ISLETON JOURNAL – Rio Vista, CA. 1959- – 33+ r – 1 BC02707 – $1,650.00 ($90.00y) – us Library Micro [071]

RIVER NEWS-HERALD – (1965 special anniversary issue) – Rio Vista, CA. 1959-62 – 5r – 1 – $250.00 – B02706 – us Library Micro [071]

RIVER NEWS-HERALD – Rio Vista. Calif. 1957-58 – 1 – us UMI [071]

RIVER PLATE OBSERVER – Buenos Aires. Argentina. -w. 4 May 1917-25 May 1923. (15 reels) – 1 – uk British Libr Newspaper [072]

RIVER PRESS – Fort Benton. Mont. 1902-1954; 1956-1957; 1966- – 1 – us UMI [071]

RIVER SIDE – Independence OR. May 2 30 1878, Nov 19 1880 – 1 – us U.O. Library [071]

Rivera Cambas, Manuel *see* LOS GOBERNANTES DE MEXICO

Rivera Casas, Francisco Mioses *see* CUADERNO DE MATEMATICAS NO 1

Rivera Casas, Francisco Moises *see* CUADERNO DE MATEMATICAS. CURSO 1ST

Rivera, Luis *see* LOS HIJOS DE LA FORTUNA. NOVELA ORIGINAL DE COSTUMBRES ESPANOLAS

Rivera Reno, Juan Francisco *see* LA IGLESIA EN TOLEDO...

RIVERBANK NEWS – Riverbank, CA. 1913-58; 1987- – 35+ r – 1 BC02711 – $1,750.00 ($135.00y) – us Library Micro [071]

RIVERINA DAILY NEWS – Griffith – at Pascoe [980]

RIVERINA EXPRESS – Wagga Wagga, Apr 2 1958-Sep 30 1963 – 1 – at Pascoe [072]

RIVERINA RECORDER – Balranald, Oct 31 1885-Dec 24 1938; Jan 8 1944 – 1 – at Pascoe [072]

RIVERINE GRAZIER (HAY) – Oct 29 1873-Dec 31 1895 – 9 – at Pascoe [072]

RIVERINE HERALD – Echuca, Jan 1 1885-Dec 30 1950 – 1 – at Pascoe [072]

RIVERLON BAPTIST CHURCH. ORANGEBURG COUNTY. SOUTH CAROLINA : CHURCH RECORDS – 1960-72 – 1 – 10.31 – us Baptist [240]

Rivero, Marciano *see* MI VOZ PARA TU RECUERDO

Rivero Sanchez, Manuel *see* ODISEA Y GESTA DE OVEIDO; EPOPEYA DE UNA CIUDAD MARTIR Y HEROICA, 18 JULIO 1936-21 OCTUBRE 1937

Riverola, Rofolfo *see* ENSAYOS HISTORICOS. PUBLICACION DE HOMENAJE

Rivers, Debra A *see* THE INFLUENCE OF CRYOTHERAPY AND AIRCAST BRACING ON TOTAL BODY BALANCE AND PROPRIOCEPTION

Rivers, Elias *see* FAMILY PAPERS

Rivers, Elias L *see* FRANCISCO DE ALDANA. EL DIVINO CAPITAN

Rivers, W H R *see* THE TODAS

Rivers, William Halse R *see* THE INFLUENCE OF ALCOHOL AND OTHER DRUGS ON FATIGUE

RIVERSIDE – 1909-33; 1992- – 29+ r – 1 – $1,450.00 – P00090 – us Library Micro [910]

RIVERSIDE BAPTIST CHURCH. WASHINGTON, D.C. : CHURCH RECORDS – (Formerly Fifth B.C.) – Membership Records, 1856-1943. 1856-1898 – 1 reel – 1 – $58.16 – us Baptist [240]

RIVERSIDE CITY AND COUNTY HISTORY / Gabbert, John R – Riverside: Record Publ. Co., 1935. California Reel 23. (The Cox Library Collection) – 5 – us Americana [978]

RIVERSIDE COUNTY – 1909-33 – 25r – 1 – $1,250.00 – P00091 – us Library Micro [910]

RIVERSIDE COUNTY RECORD NEWS – Riverside, CA. 1963-1993 – 28r – 1 – $1,400.00 – R03417 – us Library Micro [071]

THE RIVERSIDE PREACHERS: MODELS FOR PREACHING PEACE / Hull, David William – 1982 – 1 – 5.76 – us Baptist [240]

RIVERSIDE QUARTERLY – Richardson. v1-5. 1964/65-1971/73 – 5 – Can$100.00 – cn Micromedia [073]

RIVERSIDE REFLEX – Riverside, CA. 1983 – 1r – 1 – $50.00 – R04096 – us Library Micro [071]

RIVERSIDE WEEKLY NEWS – Riverside, CA. 1875-1876 – 1r – 1 – $50.00 – R04097 – us Library Micro [071]

RIVERSIDE WEEKLY READER – Riverside, CA. 1980-1981 – 1r – 1 – $50.00 – R04098 – us Library Micro [071]

RIVERTON REVIEW – Riverton, NE. -w. Jul 1881; Dec 1892; Nov 1895-Jan 1899; Sept 1901-Sept 1906; Jan-Aug 1908; May 1909; Aug 1911-Dec 1917; Feb 1918-May 1922; Oct 1922-Jun 1940 – 1 – us NE Hist [071]

RIVERTON TIMES – New Zealand. -w. 30 Jan-16 April 1964. Imperfect. 8 ft – 1 – uk British Libr Newspaper [072]

RIVES CHAPEL BAPTIST CHURCH. SANDY CREEK ASSOCIATION. NORTH CAROLINA : CHURCH RECORDS – 1832-Sep 1964 – 1 – 37.84 – us Baptist [240]

Rives, George Lockhart *see* SELECTIONS FROM THE CORRESPONDENCE OF THOMAS BARCLAY, FORMERLY BRITISH CONSUL-GENERAL AT NEW YORK

Rivet, A *see*
- LE CATHOLIQUE ORTHODOXE OPPOSE AU CATHOLIQUE PAPISTE,...
- ESCHANTILLON DES PRINCIPAUX PARADOXES DE LA PAPAUTE

Rivet, D *see* REFUTATION DU SYSTEME DE LA RAVALIERE SUR LES ORIGINES DE LA LANGUE FRANCAISE. LEBER, [J.M.]C. COLLECTIONS DES MEILLEURES DISSERTATIONS, NOTICES ET TRAITES PARTICULIERS RELATIFS A L'HISTOIRE DE FRANCE

Rivet, Paul *see* EXPOSITION EN HOMMAGE A PAUL RIVET

Rivetus, Andr. *see*
- APOLOGIA PRO SANCTISSIMA VIRGINE MARIA, MATRE DOMINI
- CRITICI SACRI LIBRI 4

LE RIVIERA – (Cont by: Le Courrier Riviera 10 jul 1963-21 dec 1966. Cont by: Le Nouveau Courrier Riviera 28 dec 1966-3 aut 1971. Cont by: Le Courrier Riviera 10 aut 1971-3 jun 1981) – Sorel, Canada. 17 nov 1960-2 jul 1963 – 25r – 1 – Can$75.00r – cn Can Microfilming [072]

Riviere, Emile *see* EXPEDITION SCIENTIFIQUE DU CAP HORN

Riviere, G *see* LES CULTES POPULAIRES EN VENDEE

Riviere, Jacques *see* JACQUES RIVIERE ET ALAIN FOURNIER: CORRESPONDANCE, 1905-14

Riviere, Jean *see* LE DOGME DE LA REDEMPTION

Riviere, Louis *see* MENDIANTS ET VAGABONDS

RIVIERES DU SUD – Cercle de Dubreka et Konakry. Bordeaux. 1890 – 9 – 5.00 – fr Orientalistes [910]

LES RIVIERES DU SUD DE LA SENEGAMBIE / Vigne, Paul – Bordeaux. 1889 – 9 – 5.00 – fr Orientalistes [910]

LES RIVIERES DU SUD ET LE FOUTA DIALLON (GUINEE FRANCAISE) : ESSAI DE SYNTHESE DES DOCUMENTS IMPRIMES CONCERNANT LA GEOGRAPHIE PHYSIQUE ET LES CIVILISATIONS INDIGENES DE CES PAYS / Machat, J – Paris: A Challamel, 1905 – us Res Libr [980]

Rivilla y Bonet y Pueyo, J *see* DESVIOS DE LA NATURALEZA O TRATADO DEL ORIGEN DE LOS MONSTRUOS A QUEVA ANADIDO SU COMPENDIO DE CURACIONES CHYRURGICAS...

Rivington, Luke *see*
- AUTHORITY
- DEPENDENCE, OR, THE INSECURITY OF THE ANGLICAN POSITION
- THE ROMAN PRIMACY, A.D. 430-451

RIVINGTONS NEW YORK GAZETEER – New York. Mar 18 1773-Dec 17 1783 – 1 – us NY Public [071]

RIVINGTON'S NEW YORK GAZETTE AND UNIVERSAL ADVERTISER – New York. n1-754. 1773-83 – 4r – 1 – us Ross [071]

RIVINGTON'S NEW YORK GAZETTEER – New York, NY. 1773-75. Also: Rivington's New York Gazette, 1777; Rivington's New York Loyal Gazette, 1777; Royal Gazette, 1777-83; Rivington's New York Gazette, 1783. Sold as one unit – 1,3 – us Readex [071]

Rivinus, A Q *see* INTRODUCTIO GENERALIS IN REM HERBARIAM

RIVISTA COLONIALE / Instituto Coloniale Italiano – 1906-1927 and Index complete – 1 – $35.00r – us Hoover Inst Photo [945]

RIVISTA D'ARTE – (Index, 1903-1942. Sfr108.00) – Firenze, 1903-1934. v1-16 – 93mf – 9 – ne IDC [700]

RIVISTA DEGLI STUDI ORIENTALI – Roma. 1907-41. v1-19 – 241mf – 8 – ne IDC [073]

ROBERT MORRIS / Tucker, Marcia – New York, Published for the Whitney Museum of American Art, by Praeger Publishers, 1970 – 1 – us U.W. Library [920]
ROBERT MORRIS – Washington, D.C., Corcoran Gallery of Art, c1969 – 1 – us U.W. Library [700]
THE ROBERT MORRIS COLLECTION – 12r – 1 – $420.00 – Dist. us Scholarly Res – us L of C Photodup [332]
ROBERT MORRISON : A MASTER-BUILDER / Broomhall, M – (In Chinese) – 1st ed. Hong Kong: Council on Christian Literature for Overseas Chinese, 1956 – 1r – 1 – 1984-6590 – us A.T.L.A. [920]
ROBERT MORRISON : THE PIONEER OF CHINESE MISSIONS / Townsend, William John – London: S.W. Partridge, [1888?] – 1mf – us A.T.L.A. [240]
ROBERT MORRISON, 1782-1934 (CCC250) : THE FIRST PROTESTANT MISSIONARY TO THE CHINESE / Green, Katharine R – (In Chinese) – Hong Kong: Bible Book and Tract Depot for Council on Christian Literature for Overseas Chinese, 1953 – 1r – 1 – 1984-6589 – us A.T.L.A. [920]
Robert O. Law Co *see*
- HISTORY OF FORT WAYNE AND TOWNSHIPS OF ALLEN COUNTY
- MEMOIRS OF THE MIAMI VALLEY
Robert Of Gloucester *see* METRICAL CHRONICLE OF ROBERT OF GLOUCESTER (RS86)
Robert of Torigni *see* CHRONICLE (CHRONICLES..4)
ROBERT OWEN'S JOURNAL – London, UK. 1850, 1852.-irr. 1/2 reel – 1 – uk British Libr Newspaper [072]
ROBERT OWEN'S MILLENIAL GAZETTE – London, UK. 1856-57. -irr. 22 feet – 1 – uk British Libr Newspaper [072]
ROBERT QUEN I OSNOVY POTREBITEL'SKOI KOOPERATSII / Kil'chevskii, V A – M., 1915 – 1mf – 9 – COR-48/1 – ne IDC [334]
ROBERT RAIKES : HIS SUNDAY SCHOOLS AND HIS FRIENDS : INCLUDING HISTORICAL SKETCHES OF THE SUNDAY SCHOOL CAUSE IN EUROPE AND AMERICA / Belcher, Joseph – Philadelphia: American Baptist Publication Society; [1859?] – 1mf – us A.T.L.A. [240]
ROBERT RAIKES : THE MAN AND HIS WORK / ed by Harris, J Henry – Bristol: J.W. Arrowsmith; London: Simpkin, Marshall, Hamilton, Kent, [1899?] – 1mf – us A.T.L.A. [240]
ROBERT RAIKES: FOUNDER OF SUNDAY SCHOOLS / Walters, Thomas – 132p – 1 – $5.00 – us Baptist [240]
ROBERT RAIKES, JOURNALIST AND PHILANTHROPIST : A HISTORY OF THE ORIGIN OF SUNDAY SCHOOLS / Gregory, Alfred – London: Hodder and Stoughton, 1880 – 1mf – us A.T.L.A. [240]
Robert, Ricard *see* ETUDES ET DOCUMENTS POUR L'HISTOIRE MISSIONAIRE DE L'ESPAGNE ET DU PORTUGAL
Robert Robertsz *see*
- ONDER VERBETERINGE. KORTE INLEYDINGE DER FEESTEN ISRAELS, TWELCK RECHTE TIJTKAARTEN ZIJN
- ONDER VERBETERINGHE. DE RECHTER VLUEGEL
- ONDER VERBETERINGHE. DE SLINCKER VLUEGEL
- ONDER VERBETERINGHE. EEN TUCHT ROEDE GHEMAECKT WT LIEFDE VAN JACOB JANSZ. KIST, OMDAT HY DIE WAERHEYT IN ZIJN GHEDRUCKTEN BRIEF AEN L.G. HEEFT GHEMIST
Robert, Roger *see* INDICATEURS DE FRANCISATION DES ENTREPRISES
ROBERT SMALLS – 1 – us Ross [920]
ROBERT SMITHSON: DRAWINGS. APRIL 19-JUNE 16, 1974 / Smith, Robert – The New York Cultural Center in association with Fairleigh Dickinson University...New York. New York, New York Cultural Center, 1974 – 1 – us U.W. Library [740]
ROBERT TODD LINCOLN COLLECTION OF PAPERS OF A. LINCOLN / Lincoln, Abraham – 1 – 2208.00 – us L of C Photodup [920]
ROBERT VON MOHL / Schultze, H – Heidelberg; 1886 – 2mf – 9 – ILM-1890/1 – ne IDC [920]
ROBERT WANDELT : ROMAN / Wilhelm, Hans Hermann – Berlin: Brunnen-Verlag, W Bischoff, c1944 – 1r – 1 – us U.W. Library [830]
ROBERT WHITAKER MCALL : FOUNDER OF THE MCALL MISSION, PARIS / McAll, Mrs. Robert Whitaker – London: Religious Tract Society, 1896 – 1mf – us A.T.L.A. [240]
ROBERTI GROSSETESTE EPISCOPI QUONDAM LINCOLNIENSI EPISTOLAE (RS25) / Grosseteste, Robert; ed by Luard, H R – 1861 – Dfl39.00 – ne Slangenburg [240]
Roberti, J M *see* SAN FRANCISCO DE PAULA
Roberts *see* HISTORICAL REVIEW OF SOUTHEAST TEXAS
Roberts, Albert R *see* CRISIS INTERVENTION AND TIME-LIMITED TREATMENT
Roberts, Alexander *see*
- COMPANION TO THE REVISED VERSION OF THE NEW TESTAMENT
- THE LIFE AND WORK OF ST. PAUL PRACTICALLY CONSIDERED AND APPLIED
- OLD TESTAMENT REVISION
Roberts, Archibald E *see* BULLETIN
Roberts, Benjamin Titus *see* ORDAINING WOMEN
Roberts, C V *see* EARLY FRIENDS OF UPPER BUCKS WITH SOME ACCOUNT OF THEIR DESCENDANTS
Roberts, Charles R *see* HISTORY OF LEHIGH COUNTY
Roberts, E *see* NOTES OF AN OVERLAND JOURNEY THROUGH FRANCE AND EGYPT TO BOMBAY...: WITH A MEMOIR
Roberts, E L *see* TEACHERS' BELIEFS ABOUT PURPOSES AS REFLECTED IN TEACHING PRACTICES
Roberts, Edmund *see* PAPERS
Roberts, Ellwood *see* BIOGRAPHICAL ANNALS OF MONTGOMERY COUNTY
Roberts, H *see* SONGS OF THE COPPER ESKIMOS
Roberts, Helene E *see* VISUAL RESOURCES
Roberts, Isaac N *see* ACCOUNT BOOK
Roberts, John A *see*
- APPLICATION OF THE TRANSTHEORETICAL MODEL TO EXERCISE ADHERENCE
- THE EFFECTS OF VARIOUS EXERCISE MODALITIES ON SERUM CHOLESTEROL AND TRIGLYCERIDE CONCENTRATIONS
Roberts, John H *see* THE AXE
Roberts, John Stuart *see* CASES ON BAILMENTS AND CARRIERS
Roberts, Julian *see* RENAISSANCE MAN: THE RECONSTRUCTED LIBRARIES OF EUROPEAN SCHOLARS, 1450-1700
Roberts, M *see* A POPULAR HISTORY OF THE MOLLUSCA
Roberts, Michael *see* SOUND PRODUCTION
Roberts, Morley *see*
- THE PRIVATE LIFE OF HENRY MAITLAND
- THE WESTERN AVERNUS
Roberts, N A *see* THE INFLUENCE OF SITUATION CRITICALITY ON THE PERFORMANCE OF MALE COLLEGIATE BASKETBALL PLAYERS
Roberts, Oran Milo *see* THE ELEMENTS OF TEXAS PLEADING
Roberts, Peter *see* THE NEW IMMIGRATION
Roberts, R *see* THE SOCIAL LAWS OF THE QURAN
Roberts, Scott O *see* SYSTOLIC BLOOD PRESSURE VERSUS HEART RATE TO PREDICT STEADY-STATE OXYGEN UPTAKE IN MALE CYCLISTS
Roberts, Vasco Harold *see* A SELECTION OF CASES ON THE LAW OF EXTRAORDINARY LEGAL REMEDIES, INCLUDING MANDAMUS, QUO WARRANTO, PROHIBITION.
Roberts, W Henry *see* ADDRESSES AT THE CELEBRATION OF THE TWO HUNDRED AND FIFTIETH ANNIVERSARY OF THE WESTMINSTER ASSEMBLY BY THE GENERAL ASSEMBLY OF THE PRESBYTERIAN CHURCH IN THE U.S.A.
Robertson, A T *see*
- EPOCHS IN THE LIFE OF PAUL
- A HARMONY OF THE GOSPELS
- THE PHARISEES AND JESUS
- A SHORT GRAMMAR OF THE GREEK NEW TESTAMENT
- SYLLABUS OF THIRTY-ONE LESSONS ON NEW TESTAMENT GREEK SYNTAX
- A TRANSLATION OF LUKE'S GOSPEL
Robertson, Alexander *see*
- THE BIBLE OF ST. MARK
- FRA PAOLO SARPI
Robertson, Andrew *see* PAPERS IN THE TAMIL LANGUAGE ON MATTERS OF PUBLIC BUSINESS
Robertson, Archibald *see* REGNUM DEI
Robertson, Charles *see* HISTORY OF MORGAN COUNTY
Robertson, Diana Forbes *see* SEND FOOD TO SPAIN
Robertson, Frederick William *see*
- EXPOSITORY LECTURES ON ST. PAUL'S EPISTLES TO THE CORINTHIANS
- NOTES ON GENESIS
- SERMONS ON ST. PAUL'S EPISTLES TO THE CORINTHIANS
Robertson, G A *see* NOTES ON AFRICA
Robertson, H A *see* ERROMANGA
Robertson, Henrietta *see* MISSION LIFE AMONG THE ZULU-KAFIRS..
Robertson, J C *see*
- THE GORGIANIC FIGURES IN EARLY GREEK PROSE
- MATERIALS FOR THE HISTORY OF THOMAS BECKET (RS67)
Robertson, James B *see* A COMPARISON OF DIRECT INSTRUCTION AND COMPUTER-ASSISTED INSTRUCTION ON LEARNING A MOTOR SKILL BY FOURTH GRADE STUDENTS
Robertson, James Craigie *see*
- BECKET, ARCHBISHOP OF CANTERBURY
- HOW SHALL WE CONFORM TO THE LITURGY OF THE CHURCH OF ENGLAND?
- OUR LORD'S TEACHING
- PLAIN LECTURES ON THE GROWTH OF THE PAPAL POWER
- THE POETRY AND THE RELIGION OF THE PSALMS
Robertson, James Errol *see* AN APPLICATION OF BOWEN FAMILY SYSTEM THEORY TO THE PASTORAL MINISTRY OF THE SHARON BAPTIST CHURCH
Robertson, John George *see*
- GOETHE AND THE TWENTIETH CENTURY
- A HISTORY OF GERMAN LITERATURE
- OUTLINES OF THE HISTORY OF GERMAN LITERATURE
Robertson, John M *see* A SHORT HISTORY OF CHRISTIANITY
Robertson, Joseph *see* AN ESSAY ON PUNCTUATION
Robertson, Norvell *see* CHURCH-MEMBERS' HANDBOOK OF THEOLOGY
Robertson, Reynolds *see* APPELLATE PRACTICE AND PROCEDURE IN THE SUPREME COURT OF THE UNITED STATES
Robertson, Robert *see* THE HISTORY AND PRESENT CONSTITUTION OF THE SHERIFF COURTS OF SCOTLAND; A LETTER TO WILLIAM STIRLING
Robertson, Stuart A *see* AN EVALUATION OF THE CHARACTERISTICS OF SUCCESSFUL STUDENTS AT THE BRINKMAN-FROEMMING UMPIRE SCHOOL
Robertson, Tolaver *see* ACCOUNT OF MARRIAGES SOLEMNIZED BY TOLAVER ROBERTSON SINCE OCTOBER 1842, AN
Robertson, William *see*
- A GATE OR DOOR TO THE HOLY TONGUE, OPENED IN ENGLISH
- STUDIES IN THE ACTS OF THE APOSTLES
ROBERTSON'S CANADIAN RAILWAY AND STEAM NAVIGATION GUIDE – Toronto: J R Robertson, [18–18– or 19–] – 9 – cn C.I.H.M. [380]
ROBERTSONS'S CREEK BAPTIST CHURCH. BULL'S GAP, TENNESSEE : CHURCH RECORDS – (398p) – 1850-1928 – 1 reel – 1 – $17.91 – us Baptist [240]
ROBERTSVILLE BAPTIST CHURCH. OAK RIDGE, TENNESSEE : CHURCH RECORDS – Mar 1946-1980. 844p. Lacks Oct 1953-Jan 1956 – 1 – 37.98 – us Baptist [240]
Robert-Tournay-Feuillet *see* LE CANTIQUE DES CANTIQUES
Robertus Gaguinus *see* DE ORIGINE ET GESTIS FRANCORUM COMPENDIUM
Robertus Holkot *see* PRAELECTIONES IN LIBRUM SAPIENTIAE
Roberval, Gilles de *see*
- ARISTARCHI SAMII DE MUNDI SYSTEMATE, PARTIBUS ET MOTIBUS EJUSDEM LIBELLUS. ADJECTAE SUNT AE DE ROBERVAL
- DIVERS OUVRAGES DE MATHEMATIQUE ET DE PHYSIQUE PAR MESSIEURS DE L'ACADEMIE ROYALE DES SCIENCES
- TRAITE DE MECANIQUE DES POIDS SOUTENUS PAR DES PUISSASNCES SUR LES PLANS INCLINES
ROBESONIAN – Lumberton. N.C. 1900- – 1 – us UMI [071]
EL ROBESPIERRE ESPANOL – Ano 1811 – 9 – sp Cultura [946]
ROBESPIERRE ET LES FEMMES / Noiset, L – Paris: Nilsson, 1932. 123p. (Les Femmes Collection) – 2mf – 9 – $6.00 – fr Bibl Nationale [944]
Robespierre, Maximilien de *see*
- A LA NATION ARTESIENNE, SUR LA NECESSITE DE REFORMER LES ETATS D'ARTOIS
- ADRESSE AU PEUPLE BELGIQUE
- ADRESSE DES REPRESENTANS DE LA COMMUNE DE PARIS A LEURS CONCITOYENS
- AUX FEDERES, PAR DES CITOYENS AMIS DE LA CONSTITUTION
- AVIS AU PEUPLE ARTESIAN
- PETITION DES FEDERES A L'ASSEMBLEE NATIONALE
- PROJET DE LA CONSTITUTION FRANCAISE DE 1791
- RAPPORT SUR LES PRINCIPES DE MORALE POLITIQUE QUI DOIVENT GUIDER LA CONVENTION NATIONALE
- SECTION DES CITOYENS ARMES DE LA PLACE VENDOME
ROBESPIERRES KIRCHENPOLITIK / Kerl, Georg – Leipzig, 1912 – 9 – DM48.00 – 3-89349-249-6 – gw Hänsel [320]
Robillard, Charles *see* LA GRANDE GUERRE ET L'EFFORT BRITANNIQUE
Robillard, L-G *see* LE COURRIER CANADIEN
Robillard, M *see* LE BON SECOURS
Robin, Leon *see* GREEK THOUGHT AND THE ORIGINS OF THE SCIENTIFIC SPIRIT
Robineau-Desvoidy, J B *see* ESSAI SUR LES MYODAIRES
Robins, Edward *see* TWELVE GREAT ACTORS
ROBINSON – Paris. avr 1936-42, janv-juil 1944 – 1 – fr A.C.R.P.P. [073]
Robinson, Addie M *see* COURT REPORTING; A MANUAL OF LEGAL DICTATION AND FORMS FOR TEACHERS, STENOGRAPHERS AND TYPEWRITERS
Robinson, Alvan *see*
- MASSACHUSETTS COLLECTION OF MARTIAL MUSICK.
- MASSACHUSETTS COLLECTION OF MARTIAL MUSICK, CONTAINING A PLAIN, EASY AND CONCISE INTRODUCTION TO THE GROUNDS OF MARTIAL MUSICK.
Robinson, Arthur W *see* THE MISSION OF HELP TO THE CHURCH IN SOUTH AFRICA
Robinson, Benjamin Coulson *see* THE LAW OF WARRANTS OF ATTORNEY, COGNOVITS, AND CONSENTS OF JUDGES' ORDERS FOR JUDGMENT, WITH FORMS
Robinson, Benjamin Willard *see*
- THE LARGENESS OF THE IMAGERY IN THE DEUTERO-ISAIAH
- SOME ELEMENTS OF FORCEFULNESS IN THE COMPARISONS OF JESUS
Robinson, C S *see* THE WOMEN OF THE ARABS
Robinson, Charles *see*
- LETTERS TO ELIZABETH CADY STANTON
- ROBINSON'S PRIVATE PAPERS
Robinson, Charles H *see* THE MISSIONARY PROSPECT
Robinson, Charles Seymour *see*
- THE GOSPEL IN ISAIAH:...EXPOSITIONS... UPON THE SIXTH CHAPTER
- SIMON PETER, HIS EARLY LIFE AND TIMES
- STUDIES IN LUKE'S GOSPEL. FIRST SERIES
- STUDIES IN MARK'S GOSPEL
Robinson, D *see* TEXTS AND STUDIES
Robinson, Doane *see*
- ENCYCLOPEDIA OF SOUTH DAKOTA
- HISTORY OF SOUTH DAKOTA
- SIOUX INDIAN COURTS; AN ADDRESS DELIVERED BY DOANE ROBINSON...BEFORE THE SOUTH DAKOTA BAR ASSOCIATION AT PIERRE, SOUTH DAKOTA, JANUARY 21, 1909
Robinson, Edward *see*
- THE BIBLE AND ITS LITERATURE
- BIBLICAL RESEARCHES IN PALESTINE
- PHILOLOGY AND LEXICOGRAPHY OF THE NEW TESTAMENT
Robinson, Edward Kay *see* THE RELIGION OF NATURE
Robinson, Emmett *see* PLAYS
Robinson, Ezekiel Gilman *see*
- CHRISTIAN EVIDENCES
- CHRISTIAN THEOLOGY
Robinson, F *see* COPTIC AOPCRYPHAL GOSPELS
Robinson, George F *see* HISTORY OF GREENE COUNTY
Robinson, George Livingstone *see* THE PROPHECIES OF ZECHARIAH
Robinson, H Wheeler *see*
- THE CROSS IN THE OLD TESTAMENT
- REDEMPTION AND REVELATION
- THE VEIL OF GOD
Robinson, Hercules *see* SEA DRIFT
Robinson, Ira Ellsworth *see* THREE GREAT PROTESTS AGAINST TRIAL OF CIVILIANS BY MILITARY COMMISSIONS

Robinson, J *see* THE FLORA OF ESSEX COUNTY, MASSACHUSETTS

Robinson, J A *see*
- CONTRIBUTIONS TO BIBLICAL AND PATRISTIC LITERATURE
- EUTHANALIA
- THE PASSION OF S. PERPETUA

Robinson, J Armitage *see* SOME THOUGHTS ON THE ATHANASIAN CREED

Robinson, James Harvey *see* THE NEW HISTORY

Robinson, Jane Marie Bancroft *see* DEACONESSES IN EUROPE: AND THEIR LESSONS FOR AMERICA

Robinson, John *see* ORGANIZING EDUCATIONAL BROADCASTING

Robinson, Joseph Armitage *see*
- THE HISTORICAL CHARACTER OF ST. JOHN'S GOSPEL
- ST. PAUL'S EPISTLE TO THE EPHESIANS

Robinson, Luther E *see* HISTORICAL AND BIOGRAPHICAL RECORD OF MONMOUTH AND WARREN COUNTIES

Robinson, Paschal *see* THE RERAL ST FRANCIS OF ASSISI

Robinson, R L *see* HISTORY OF THE GEORGIA BAPTIST ASSOCIATION

Robinson, Robert *see*
- THE ART OF PRONUNCIATION
- ECCLESIASTICAL RESEARCHES
- THE HISTORY OF BAPTISM

Robinson, Sara T D *see* ROBINSON'S PRIVATE PAPERS

Robinson, Sarah M *see* AN INTERPRETIVE INQUIRY OF THE PROFESSIONAL LIFE HISTORIES OF SELECTED WOMEN DANCE/ PHYSICAL EDUCATORS

Robinson, Stephen B *see*
- THE CIVIL CODE OF GUAM, 1933
- THE PENAL CODE OF GUAM, 1933

Robinson, T H *see* AN INTRODUCTION TO THE BOOKS OF THE OLD TESTAMENT

Robinson, Thomas H *see* OLD HANOVER CHURCH, PA

Robinson, Tracey L *see* BONE MINERAL AND MENSTRUAL CYCLE STATUS IN COMPETITIVE FEMALE ATHLETES

Robinson, W J *see* EXPOSITORY AND PRACTICAL LECTURES ON HAGGAI AND ZECHARIAH

Robinson, William *see*
- NAUTICAL ECONOMY
- RAPPORT DU MAJOR WILLIAM ROBINSON, CAPITAINE DES INGENIEURS ROYAUX,...
- RAPPORT...SUR LA LIGNE PROJETEE DU CHEMIN DE FER INTERCOLONIAL

Robinson, William C *see* THE LAW OF PATENTS FOR USEFUL INVENTIONS

Robinson, William Callyhan *see* ELEMENTARY LAW

Robinson, William F *see* RADIO FREE EUROPE / RADIO LIBERTY

LES ROBINSONS DU SPITZBERG / Sverdrup, Jacobo – Paris, Madrid: Razon y Fe, 1933 – 1 – sp Bibl Santa Ana [920]

ROBINSON'S PRIVATE PAPERS / Robinson, Charles & Robinson, Sara T D – 1834-1911. In Kansas State Historical Society. Guide – 1 – us KS Hist [920]

Robison, David *see* INTERVIEWS WITH US GOVERNMENT OFFICIALS CONCERNING THE NIGERIA-BIAFRA WAR, 1971-72

EL ROBLEDAL DE RUIDIAZ / Sanchez Ocana y Acedo Rico, Pedro – Plasencia: Tip. de Generoso Montero Santos, 1903 – 1 – sp Bibl Santa Ana [946]

Robledo, D *see* COMPENDIO QUIRURGICO...

Robles Vives, Antonio *see* REPRESENTACION CONTRA EL VOTO DE SANTIAGO

ROBOTICS AGE – (v6-. 1984-. 5,6,9) – v1-. 1979- – 1 – us UMI [073]

ROBOTICS AND COMPUTER-INTEGRATED MANUFACTURING – v1- 1984- – 5,6,9 – us UMI [629]

ROBOTICS INDUSTRY DIRECTORY – 1985- – 1 – us UMI [073]

ROBOTICS TODAY – (1982-. 1,5,6,9) – v1-. 1979- – 1 – us UMI [073]

ROBOTICS WORLD – v1-. 1983- – 1,5,6,9 – us UMI [073]

ROBOTNIK : CZASOPISMO POLITYCZNE SPOLECZNE / Polska Partia Socjalistyczna – Lwow/Warszawa, 1912, 1915-20, 1931-38, 1944-46 (incompl) – 1 – us Hoover Inst Photo [335]

ROBOTNIK – Lodz, Poland. Feb-Dec 1945 – 2r – 1 – us L of C Photodup [947]

ROBOTNIK – London, UK. Centralny organ P.P.S. 1950- – 1 – uk British Libr Newspaper [072]

ROBOTNIK – Lublin, Poland. Dec 1944-Jan 1945 – 2r – 1 – us L of C Photodup [947]

ROBOTNIK : OFFICIAL PAPER OF THE POLISH SOCIALIST PARTY – London, 1950-71, 1981 (incompl) – 1 – us Hoover Inst Photo [335]

ROBOTNIK – Warsaw. Poland. -d. Jul-Dec 1945, Apr 1946-Dec 1948. (12 reels) – 1 – uk British Libr Newspaper [947]

ROBOTNIK POLSKI : OFFICIAL ORGAN OF THE POLISH SOCIALIST ALLIANCE OF AMERICA – New York, 1941 (compl), 1944-47, 1950, 1967 (all incompl) – 1 – us Hoover Inst Photo [335]

ROBOTNIK POLSKI W WIELKIEJ BRYTANJI – London, UK. Pismo socjalistow polskich, czlonkow P.P.S.25 Aug 1940-1949 – 1 – uk British Libr Newspaper [072]

ROBOTS IN MANUFACTURING: KEY TO INTERNATIONAL COMPETITIVENESS / Baranson, Jack – 1983. 168p. ISBN:0-912338-40-7 – 9 – 16.50 – us Lomond [380]

Robson, John *see* THE BIBLE: ITS REVELATION, INSPIRATION AND EVIDENCE

Roca, Alfredo M *see* LOS MUCHACHOS PERONISTAS

Roca Puig, P *see* A LA FUTURA MADRE. BARCELONA, 1930

Rocafuerte, Vicente *see* CONTESTACION DE ROCAFUERTE AL ARTICULO...EN LA CONCORDIA 5 DE FEBRERO DE 1844

LA ROCAMBOLE DES JOURNAUX – ou Histoire aristo-capucino-comique de la Revolution. Paris. juin 1791-aout 1792 (I-IV) – 1 – fr A.C.R.P.P. [073]

ROCH AUBRY, B.A., B.P., COMMANDEUR DE L'ORDRE DU MERITE SCOLAIRE DE LA PROVINCE DE QUEBEC, 1895-1949 : BIO-BIBLIOGRAPHIE ANALYTIQUE / Aubry, Roch – 1959. SEM105P4 – 2mf – 9 – Can$4.50 – cn Bibl Nat [370]

ROCHA, COMMUNAUTE NOIRE DE LA COTE CARAIBE COLOMBIENNE / Reichel-Dolmatoff, I – 9 – F50.00 – fr Ethnologie [306]

Rocha, Hugo *see* BAYETE

Rocha, Manuel de la *see*
- DISCURSO PRONUNCIADO EN LA SOCIEDAD PATRIOTICA CONSTITUCIONAL DE BADAJOZ EL DIA 9 DE JULIO DE 1820
- DISCURSO...6 NOVIEMBRE DE 1822...APERTURA DE LA UNIVERSIDAD...BADAJOZ
- DISCURSO...SOCIEDAD...BADAJOZ
- DISCURSO...UNIVERSIDAD..
- EGLOGAS DEL PASTOR DE EXTREMADURA
- SERMON...CATEDRAL DE BADAJOZ
- SERMON...REGIMIENTO DE PLASENCIA

Rocha Silva, G *see*
- L'ABRI TOCA DA BOA VISTA I, UN SITE DE L'AIRE DE SAO RAIMUNDO NONATO, SUD-EST DU PIAUI, BRESIL
- L'ABRI TOCA DO BAIXAO DO CAPIM, SITE DES SOUS-TRADITIONS VARZEA GRANDE ET SERRA DO TAPIUO

Rocha y Figueroa, Gomez *see* FILOSOFIA MORAL

ROCHAMBEAU PAPERS – Haiti – 1 – us UMI [972]

ROCHDALE CANAL PAPERS – 1792-4 – 1 – uk Microform Academic [941]

Rochdale Equitable Pioneers *see* PAPERS

ROCHDALE LABOUR NEWS – England. -m. Jan 1899-Apr 1900. (11 ft) – 1 – uk British Libr Newspaper [331]

ROCHDALE OBSERVER. (OBSERVER AND STANDARD) – England. 16 Feb 1856-Dec 1899 (missing 1897).-w. 38 reels – 1 – uk British Libr Newspaper [072]

ROCHDALE TIMES – England. -w. 9 Dec 1871-1 Nov 1924. Lacking 1895, Jan-June 1913. 63 reels – 1 – uk British Libr Newspaper [072]

Roche, G *see* LA SOCIETE DES MISSIONS EVANGELIQUES DE PARIS AU SENEGAL DE 1863 A 1914

Roche, Harriet A *see* ON TREK IN THE TRANSVAAL; OR, OVER BERG AND VELDT IN SOUTH AFRICA

Roche, J *see*
- MORAVIAN HERESY, WHEREIN THE PRINCIPAL ERRORS OF THAT DOCTRINE, AS TAUGHT THROUGHOUT SEVERAL PARTS OF EUROPE AND AMERICA BY COUNT ZINZENDORF, MR. CENNICK AND OTHER MORAVIAN TEACHERS,...
- NUEVAS Y RARAS OBSERVACIONES PARA DIAGNOSTICAR CRISIS POR EL PULSO...

Roche, James Jeffrey *see* THE STORY OF THE FILIBUSTERS, TO WHICH IS ADDED THE LIFE OF COLONEL DAVID CROCKETT

Roche, Josephine *see* PAPERS 1913-1923

Roche, William Lundy *see* COLLECTION

Rochechouart, Louis Victor Leon *see* MEMOIRS OF THE COUNT DE ROCHECHOUART, 1788-1822, IN FRANCE, SOUTHERN RUSSIA, IN THE NAPOLEONIC WARS, AND AS COMMANDANT OF PARIS

Rochefort, C de *see* DICTIONNAIRE GENERAL ET CURIEUX

ROCHELLE INDEPENDENT – Rochelle, IL. sep 11 1872-jul 3 1873 – us Res Libr [071]

ROCHELLE TELEPHONE – Rochelle, IL: J M King, jul 12 1879-jul 23 1881 – us Res Libr [071]

Rochemonteix, C de *see* JOSEPH AMIOT ET LES DERNIERS SURVIVANTS DE LA MISSION FRANCAISE A PEKIN (1780-1795)

ROCHESTER 1646-1900 – (Mf 1-3: Vital Records 1646-1755. Mf 4-7: Proprietors 1679-1795. Mf 8-19: Town & Vitals 1708-1826. Mf 20: Marriages 1810-52. Mf 21-40: Town & Vitals 1744-1848. Mf 41-46: Parish Records 1770-1869. Mf 47-57: Town Records 1818-83. Mf 58-62: Vital Record 1760-1857. Mf 63-64: Town Records 1800-23. Mf 65-73: Town & Vitals 1708-1847. Mf 74: Marriages 1695-1799. Mf 75-78: Vital Records 1790-1861. Mf 79: Militia 1824-32. Mf 80-85: Town Records 1835-53. Mf 86-90: Deeds 1839-56. Mf 91-94: Births 1844-72. Mf 94-96: Marriages & Deaths 1842-54. Mf 97-98: Births 1872-1900. Mf 98-100: Marriages 1855-1900. Mf 100-103: Deaths 1855-1900. Mf 104-106: Intentions 1857-1910. Mf 106-108: Oaths 1861-1922. Mf 109-111: Intentions Index 1732-1910. Mf 112-116: Birth Index 1646-1989. Mf 117-120: Marriage Index 1687-1989. Mf 121-123: Death Index 1697-1989) – (mf ed 1992) – 123mf – 9 – 0-87623-148-2 – us Holbrook [920]

Rochester Cemetery, Topeka, KS *see* LOT RECORD CARDS

Rochester Codex *see* CODEX SAECULI XI, CONTINENS TRATATUS VARIOS AD HISTORIAM MUSICAE MEDIIAEVI PERTINENTES

ROCHESTER GAZETTE – England. -w. 1830-59. Lacking 1837. 10 reels – 1 – uk British Libr Newspaper [072]

ROCHESTER MUSICAL TIMES – Rochester, 1869-72 – 1 – £60.00 – uk Chadwyck [780]

Rochester, New York *see* MISCELLANEOUS EARLY NEWSPAPERS

Rochester, New York. Andrews Street Baptist Church *see* RECORDS

Rochester, New York. First Baptist Church *see* RECORDS

Rochester, New York. Rochester Church Women United *see* SCRAPBOOKS

ROCHESTER-A STORY HISTORICAL / Parker, Jenny M – Rochester: Scranton, Wetmore and Co., 1884. New York Reel 22. (The Cox Library Collection) – 5 – us Americana [978]

Rochet d'Hericourt, C E X *see*
- SECOND VOYAGE SUR LES DEUX RIVES DE LA MER ROUGE, DANS LE PAYS DES ADELS ET LE ROYAUME DE CHOA
- VOYAGE SUR LA COTE ORIENTALE DE LA MER ROUGE, DANS LE PAYS D'ADEL ET LE ROYAUME DE CHOA

Rochlitz, Johann Friedrich *see* FUER FREUNDE DER TONKUNST

Rocholl, Rudolf *see* DER CHRISTLICHE GOTTESBEGRIFF

ROCK – 1958-64 (complete) – 1r – 1 – ATLA S0710B – us A.T.L.A. [073]

ROCK COUNTY LEADER – Bassett, NE. -w. Dec. 1897-Jan. 1901; Apr. 1901- – 1 – us NE Hist [071]

ROCK COUNTY LEADER – Bassett. Neb. 1897-1963 – 1 – us UMI [071]

Rock, David *see* ARGENTINA IN THE TWENTIETH CENTURY

Rock James A *see* MEASUREMENT OF STROKE VOLUME DURING EXERCISE, RECOVERY FROM EXERCISE, AND CALCIUM CHANNEL BLOCKADE USING ELECTROCARDIOGRAPHY

ROCK MECHANICS/FELSMECHANIK/MECANIQUE DES ROCHES – v1-14 1969-81. ISSN: 0035-7448 – 1,5,6,9,13 – $64.00v – us UMI [550]

ROCK MERCURY – Lockhart, Nov 26 1910-Apr 30 1920 – 1 – at Pascoe [072]

THE ROCK OF AGES / Bickersteth, Edward Henry – New York: E.P. Dutton, 1871. 1 fiche – 9 – us A.T.L.A. [240]

THE ROCK OF AGES; OR, A SCRIPTURE TESTIMONY TO THE ONE ETERNAL GODHEAD OF THE FATHER / Bickersteth, Edward Henry – Introd. by Rt. Rev. F.D. Huntington. Boston: E.P. Dutton and Co., 1860. vi/214p – 1 – us U.W. Library [240]

ROCK PICTURES AND ARCHEAEOLOGY IN THE LIBYAN DESERT / Newbold, D – (Antiquity). 1928. BA-633 2 – 8 – ne IDC [930]

ROCK PRODUCTS – v1- 1902- 1; v73- 5,6; v79- 9 – us UMI [670]

THE ROCK RIVER VALLEY – Covering Jefferson, Dodge, Dane and Rock Counties, Wisconsin and Winnebago, Stephenson, Boone, Ogle, Lee, Whiteside, Henry and Rock Island Counties, Illinois. Chicago, 1926. v1-2. Wisconsin Reel 9. The Cox Library Collection – 5 – us Americana [978]

ROCK SPECIMENS COLLECTED ON OCEANIC ISLANDS VOYAGE OF H.M.S. CHALLENGER, 1873-1876 / Renard, A – B2819 2 – 8 – ne IDC [550]

Rockaway. Presbytery (Pres. Ch. in the U.S.A. New School) *see* MINUTES, 1839-1870

THE ROCKEFELLER FOUNDATION ARCHIVES, SERIES 1.1 (PROJECTS) : SERIES 600 (ASIA)/AND SERIES 601 (CHINA) – (Comes with printed guide) – 1993 – 43r – 1 – $3,655.00 – S3299 – us Scholarly Res [610]

Rockefeller University. Archives *see* BUREAU OF SOCIAL HYGIENE PROJECT AND RESEARCH FILES, 1913-1940

Rockel, William Mahlon *see*
- 20TH CENTURY HISTORY OF SPRINGFIELD AND CLARK COUNTY
- INTRODUCTION TO THE STUDY OF THE DECISIONS OF THE SUPREME COURT OF OHIO.

Rockenbach, M *see* DEUTSCHE LITERATURGESCHICHTE

Rocker, Rudolf *see*
- PIONEERS OF AMERICAN FREEDOM
- DIE PRINZIPIENERKLAERUNG DES SYNDIKALISMUS
- THE TRAGEDY OF SPAIN
- THE TRUTH ABOUT SPAIN

ROCKETEER – China Lake. Calif. 1954-1967 – 1 – us UMI [071]

Rockey, J L *see* HISTORY OF NEW HAVEN COUNTY

ROCKFORD TODAY – Rockford, 1903. (Illinois Reel 63). (The Cox Library Collection) – 5 – us Americana [978]

ROCKHAMPTON BULLETIN (MORNING BULLETIN) – Rockhampton, Australia. 1864-88 – 58r – 1 – uk British Libr Newspaper [980]

Rockhill, Bryan H *see* EFFECT OF THE AIRCAST ON FUNCTIONAL MOVEMENTS USING THE BIOTRAN

ROCKINGHAM REGISTER – Harrisonburg. Va. 1905-1907 – 1 – us UMI [071]

ROCKPORT 1840-1900 – (Mf 1-2: Birth Index 1840-67. Mf 2-3: Marriage Index 1840-67. Mf 3-4: Death Index. Mf 5: Births 1840-53. Mf 6: Births 1853-64. Mf 7: Births 1865-67; Marriages 1840-50. Mf 8: Marriages 1851-60. Mf 9: Marriages 1860-67; Deaths 1840-43. Mf 10: Deaths 1844-66. Mf 11: Deaths 1866-67. Mf 12-14: Birth Index 1868-1900. Mf 14-15: Marriage Index 1868-1900. Mf 15-17: Death Index 1868-1900. Mf 18: Births 1868-77. Mf 19: Births 1877-92. Mf 20: Births 1892-1900. Mf 21: Marriages 1869-77. Mf 22: Marriages 1877-89. Mf 23: Marriages 1889-98. Mf 24: 1899-1900; Deaths 1868-77. Mf 25: Deaths 1877-93. Mf 26: Deaths 1893-1900) – (mf ed 1989) – 26mf – 9 – 0-87623-096-6 – us Holbrook [920]

ROCKS AND MINERALS – v1-57 1926-82 1; v50-57 5,6,9 – us UMI [550]

Rockstroh, Manfred *see* BEITRAG ZUR BESTIMMUNG DER PARAMETER UND ZUR DETEKTION DER STRUKTUR VON ZWEIPHASENSTROEMUNGEN MITTELS ULTRASCHALL

Rockwell et al *see* THE GENESIS OF CALIFORNIA'S FIRST CONSTITUTION, 1846-1849

Rockwell, William Locke *see* THE TENEMENT-HOUSE ACT OF NEW JERSEY, 1904, WITH INDEX

Rockwood, Albert S *see* PRACTICAL QUESTIONS AND ANSWERS ON WILLS; HOW TO MAKE YOUR WILL

THE ROCKWOOD REVIEW – Kingston [Ont.]: Miss Goldie and Miss M Clarke, [1895?-19–] – 9 – cn C.I.H.M. [073]

ROCKY CREEK BAPTIST CHURCH. GREENVILLE COUNTY. SOUTH CAROLINA : CHURCH RECORDS – (846p) – 1929-1972 – 1 reel – 1 – $38.07 – us Baptist [240]

ROCKY GROVE BAPTIST CHURCH. ALKEN COUNTY. SOUTH CAROLINA : CHURCH RECORDS – (1,687p) – 1868-1950 – 1 reel – 1 – $75.92 – us Baptist [240]

ROCKY MOUNTAIN BAPTIST – Englewood, CO. 1986-1991. 458p – 1 – $33.68 – us Baptist [071]

ROCKY MOUNTAIN DIRECTORY AND COLORADO GAZETTEER / S.S. Wallihan and Co – Denver, 1870. Colorado Reel 3. The Cox Library Collection – 5 – us Americana [978]

ROCKY MOUNTAIN HOUSE PAPERS – Alberta, CN. 1911-1970 – 18r – 1 – cn Commonwealth Micro [072]

ROCKY MOUNTAIN HUSBANDMAN – Great Falls. Mont. 1906-1911 – 1 – us UMI [071]

ROCKY MOUNTAIN HUSBANDMAN – White Sulphur Springs. Mont. 1890; 1893-1905 – 1 – us UMI [071]

ROCKY MOUNTAIN MINERAL LAW INSTITUTE : PROCEEDINGS – v1-37. 1955-91 – 1,5,6 – $810.00 – us Hein [340]

ROCKY MOUNTAIN NEWS – Denver. Col. 1947- – 1 – us UMI [071]

ROCKY MOUNTAIN PILLAR OF FIRE – v6-9 no 32. 1905-July 1908 (complete) – Inquire – 1 – ATLA S0934 – us A.T.L.A. [073]

ROCKY MOUNTAIN PRESBYTERIAN *see* PRESBYTERIAN HOME MISSIONARY

ROCKY MOUNTAIN RESOURCES FOR AEROSPACE SCIENCE AND TECHNOLOGY – 1969 – 22mf – 9 – $30.00 – 0-87703-230-0 – us Univelt [629]

ROCKY POINT BAPTIST CHURCH. RUSSELLVILLE, HAMBLEN COUNTY, TENNESSEE : CHURCH RECORDS – (Formerly: Union Grove BC) – 1868-1946, 1956-1969 – 1r – 1 – $45.81 – us Baptist [240]

ROCKY RIVER BAPTIST CHURCH. SANDY CREEK ASSOCIATION. NORTH CAROLINA : CHURCH RECORDS – 1825-71 – 1 – 5.94 – us Baptist [240]

ROCZNIK SLAWISTYCZNY; WYD. PRZEZ J. LOS; REVUE SLAVISTIQUE – v. 1-15. Krakow. 1908-39. B-1168 2 – 8 – ne IDC [073]

ROCZNIKI HUMANISTYCZNE – Poland, 1949-72 – 11r – 1 – $1,375.00 – us Ross [072]

ROD AND CANOE, RIFLE AND SNOWSHOE IN QUEBEC'S ADIRONDACKS / Fairchild, George Moore – s.l.: s.n., 1896 (Quebec: F. Carrel). 05482. (Pre-1900 Canadiana) – 9 – cn C.I.H.M. [971]

ROD AND GUN AND MOTOR SPORTS IN CANADA *see* ROD AND GUN IN CANADA

ROD AND GUN IN CANADA – (Cont by: Rod and Gun and Motor Sports in Canada) – Montreal: Rod and Gun Pub. Co., [1899-1906] – 9 – cn C.I.H.M. [790]

THE ROD, THE ROOT, AND THE FLOWER / Patmore, Coventry Kersey Dighton – London: G. Bell, 1895 – 1 roll – 1 – 1-55879-175-2 – uk Libr Preservation [810]

RODA ROSTER – Borlange, Sweden. 1920-30 – 1 reel – 1 – sw Kungliga [073]

RODALE'S ENVIRONMENT ACTION BULLETIN – v9. 1971 – 5mf – 9 – $5.00f – us Ross [360]

RODALE'S NEW SHELTER – v.1-. 1980- – 1,5,6,9 – us UMI [574]

Rodbertus, Karl *see* ZUR BELEUCHTUNG DER SOCIALEN FRAGE

Rodenbach, Georges *see* LA JEUNESSE BLANCHE: POESIES

Rodenberg, Julius *see*
- DEUTSCHE RUNDSCHAU 1874-1942
- HERRN SCHELLBOGEN'S ABENTEUER
- KLOSTERMANN'S GRUNDSTUECK

Rodenburg, Th *see* EGLENTIERS POETENS BORS

RODENT PEST BIOLOGY AND CONTROL : BIBLIOGRAPHY 1970-1974 – 1977 – 836p – it F.A.O. [590]

RODENT PESTS AND THEIR CONTROL IN THE NEAR EAST – 1989 – 115p – it F.A.O. [590]

RODENT PESTS. BIOLOGY AND CONTROL : BIBLIOGRAPHY 1970-1974 – 1977 – 836p – it F.A.O. [630]

RODENTICIDES : ANALYSES, SPECIFICATIONS, FORMULATION FOR USE IN PUBLIC HEALTH AND AGRICULTURE – 1979 – 81p – it F.A.O. [660]

RODERIC ET CUNEGONDE OU L'HERMITE DE MONTMARTRE OU LA FORTERESSE DE MOULINOS OU LE REVENANT DE LA GALERIE DE L'OUEST / Martainville – (French Theatre Series). Paris. Barba, an XIV. 1805 – 9 – fr Hachette [820]

RODERICK, THE LAST OF THE GOTHS / Southey, Robert – London: Printed for Longman, Hurst, Rees, Orme, and Brown..., 3rd ed 1815 – 1 roll – 1 – 1-55879-243-0 – uk Libr Preservation [810]

Rodero del Brio, Juan *see* OPUSCULO... GOBIERNO...ESPANOLES

Rodes, R G *see* EDUCATION AND TRAINING OF USERS OF SCIENTIFIC AND TECHNICAL INFORMATION

Rodger, James George *see*
- A SCIENCE OF THE ULTIMATE
- SYLLABUS OF TWO COURSES OF LECTURES

Rodgers, John *see* SERMONS, 1747-1801

Rodgers, William Champ *see* A TREATISE ON THE LAW OF DOMESTIC RELATIONS

Rodier, J A *see* HYDROLOGICAL ASPECTS OF DROUGHT

Rodin, H *see* LAS PLANTES MEDICINALES ET USUELLES...

RODINA – Illiustrirovannyi zhurnal dlia semeinogo chteniia. Spb. 1879-1917. Lacking: (12) 1881; (8-12) 1883; 1884-1912; 1915; 1917. B-1843 2 – 8 – ne IDC [073]

Rodionov, Stanislav N *see* SCIENCE AND GLOBAL SECURITY

Rodkey, Fred S *see* RUSSIAN HISTORICAL SOURCES

RODNAI A ZEMLI A (PARIS, FRANCE) = LE PAYS NATAL – (Includes c.1: 1925:Feb.16-Apr.13, May 4-Oct.5; 1927:Aug.1-Dec.15) – Paris: G.A. Aleksinksi i, 1925- – 1 – CSUXANS1130-S – us Hoover Inst Photo [947]

RODNEY MERCURY – Ontario Prov., Canada. Oct 1887- – 1 – cn Commonwealth Micro [072]

Rodney, Mississippi *see* MISCELLANEOUS EARLY NEWSPAPERS

RODNOE I VSELENSKOE / Ivanov, V – Stat'i. Izd. Leman i Sakharov. M. 1918. BR-743 2 – 8 – ne IDC [460]

Rodnykii, A A *see* SISTEMATICHESKII I KHRONOLOGICHESKII KATALOG BIBLIOTEKI BIBLIOFILA I BIBLIOGRAFA IA.F. BEREZINA-SHCHIRIAEVA. 1. RUSSKIIA KNIGI

THE RODODENDRONS OF SIKKIM-HIMALAYA / Hooker, JD – Ed. 2. 3 v. London. 1849-51. B-5956 2 – 8 – ne IDC [580]

Rodolphe, J J *see* SOLFEGES OU NOUVELLE METHODE DE MUSIQUE PAR DEMANDES ET PAR REPONCES, DIVISEES EN DEUX PARTIES

Rodon y Bell, M *see* RELACION DE LAS EPIDEMIAS...DE CARTAGENA...Y LA EXPOSIXION DEL NUEVO METODO DE JOSE MASDEVALL

RODOPSKA BORBA – Khaskovo, Bulgaria. 1951-Sept 1958 – 3r – 1 – us L of C Photodup [949]

RODOSLOVNAIA KNIGA KNIAZEI I DVORIAN ROSSIISKIKH / Novikov, N I – v. 1-2. M. 1787. BR-5780 2 – 8 – ne IDC [070]

RODOSLOVNAIA TURKMEN / Kononov, A N – Sochinenie Abu-l-Gazi khana khivinskogo. M., L. 1958. BU-367 2 – 8 – ne IDC [947]

Rodosskii, Aleksei S *see* OPISANIE 432-KH RUKOPISEI, PRINADLEZHASHCHIKH S. PETERSBURGSKOI DUKHOVNOI AKADEMII

O RODOVIARIO : ORGAO AO SERVICO DO RODOVIARIO – Manaus, Amazonas. 27 Jan 1926 – 1,5,6 – bl Biblioteca [072]

Rodrigo, A S *see* NOCIONES Y TABLAS DE ARITMETICA...

Rodrigo de la Cerda, Jose *see* COMPENDIO...CRISTIANA

Rodrigo, Sanchez *see* HISTORIA DE SANTA MARIA DE LA VICTORIA

Rodrigo, Valerio *see* LUZ Y CONSUELO DEL ALMA. TAGALOG

Rodrigues, Eugene *see* LETTRES SUR LA RELIGION ET LA POLITIQUE, 1829, SUIVI DE L'EDUCATION DU GENRE HUMAIN, TRADUIT DE L'ALLEMAND, DE LESSING

Rodrigues, Hippolyte *see* LES ORIGINES DU SERMON DE LA MONTAGNE

Rodrigues, Jose C *see*
- BIBLIOTECA BRASILIENSE. CATALOGO ANNOTADO DOS LIVROS SOBRE O BRASIL
- CATALOGO ANNOTADO DOS LIBROS SOBRE O BRASIL...PERTENCENTES A J.C. RODRIGUES..., PARTE 1...

Rodrigues, O *see*
- OLINDE RODIGUES AUX SAINT-SIMONIENS
- SAINT-SIMON. SON PREMIER ECRIT

Rodrigues, Olinde *see* OPINIONS LITERAIRES, PHILOSOPHIQUES ET INDUSTRIELLES

Rodriguez *see* ELEMENTS DE LA GRAMMAIRE JAPONAISE

Rodriguez Alvarez, Angel *see*
- METODO DE ENSENANZA DE LA LECTURA Y LA ESCULTURA
- RAYAS. CARTILLA 1ST
- RAYAS METODO DE ENSENANZA PARA LA LECTURA

Rodriguez Amaya, Esteban *see*
- A PROPOSITO DE UN DOCUMENTO. NOTICIAS SOBRE LOS SANCHEZ DE BADAJOZ
- DEL SIGLO 17 EXTREMENO. CONTIENDA ENTRE TORRE DE MIGUEL SESMERO Y ALMENDRAL
- DOCUMENTOS HISTORICOS. TESTAMENTO DE DON BARTOLOME MARTINEZ, OBISPO DE PANAMA Y ARZOBISPO DE SANTA FE
- FELIPE 5 Y PORTUGAL. MATRIMONIOS REALES EN CAYA (1729)
- INSTRUCCION SOBRE CUMPLIMIENTO PASCUAL Y VIDA RELIGIOSA EN LAS HERMANDADES SINDICALES DE LABRADORES
- UNA RELACION DESCONOCIDA DE LA EXPEDICION A AFRICA DEL REY DON SEBASTIAN
- VIAJE DE CAMPOMANES A EXTREMADURA

Rodriguez Bautista, Ambrosio *see* EL ACCIDENTE DE TRABAJO EN LA HISTORIA Y EN LA REALIDAD ESPANOLA

Rodriguez Campomanes, Pedro *see*
- APENDICE A LA EDUCACION POPULAR. TOMO 1
- APENDICE A LA EDUCACION POPULAR. TOMO 2
- APENDICE A LA EDUCACION POPULAR. TOMO 3
- APENDICE A LA EDUCACION POPULAR. TOMO 4
- DISCURSO SOBRE EL FOMENTO DE LA INDUSTRIA POPULAR
- DISCURSO SOBRE LA EDUCACION POPULAR DE LOS ARTESANOS
- DISERTACIONES HISTORICAS SOBRE LOS TEMPLARIOS

Rodriguez de Castro, Jose *see*
- BIBLIOTECA ESPANOLA. TOMO 1
- BIBLIOTECA ESPANOLA. TOMO 2

Rodriguez Diaz, Felix *see* MONOGRAFIA... VILLA DE AZUAGA

Rodriguez Guerrero, D *see* DISPUTATIO DE NATURA FEBRIS

Rodriguez Leal, Joaquin *see* RESULTADO... LIBERTAD...MAURICIO CERESOLES

Rodriguez Marcos, Antonio *see* BELLEZAS DEL ALMA: LA CARIDAD

Rodriguez Marin, Francisco *see* DISCURSOS LEIDOS ANTE LA REAL ACADEMIA SEVILLANA DE BUENAS LETRAS EL 3 DE ENERO DE 1897

Rodriguez Mohedano, P *see*
- APOLOGIA DEL TOMO 5 DE LA HISTORIA LITERARIA DE ESPANA
- HISTORIA LITERARIA DE ESPANA. TOMO 1
- HISTORIA LITERARIA DE ESPANA. TOMO 2 PARTE 1
- HISTORIA LITERARIA DE ESPANA. TOMO 2 PARTE 2
- HISTORIA LITERARIA DE ESPANA. TOMO 3
- HISTORIA LITERARIA DE ESPANA. TOMO 4
- HISTORIA LITERARIA DE ESPANA. TOMO 5
- HISTORIA LITERARIA DE ESPANA. TOMO 6
- HISTORIA LITERARIA DE ESPANA. TOMO 7
- HISTORIA LITERARIA DE ESPANA. TOMO 8
- HISTORIA LITERARIA DE ESPANA. TOMO 9

Rodriguez Mohedano R *see*
- APOLOGIA DEL TOMO 5 DE LA HISTORIA LITERARIA DE ESPANA
- HISTORIA LITERARIA DE ESPANA. TOMO 1
- HISTORIA LITERARIA DE ESPANA. TOMO 2 PARTE 1
- HISTORIA LITERARIA DE ESPANA. TOMO 2 PARTE 2
- HISTORIA LITERARIA DE ESPANA. TOMO 3
- HISTORIA LITERARIA DE ESPANA. TOMO 4
- HISTORIA LITERARIA DE ESPANA. TOMO 5
- HISTORIA LITERARIA DE ESPANA. TOMO 6
- HISTORIA LITERARIA DE ESPANA. TOMO 7
- HISTORIA LITERARIA DE ESPANA. TOMO 8
- HISTORIA LITERARIA DE ESPANA. TOMO 9

Rodriguez Monino, Antonio *see*
- BIBLIOGRAFIA DE D. VICENTE BARRANTES. (1829-1898)
- EPISTOLARIO DE MENENDEZ PELAYO CON JOSE LOPEZ PRUDENCIO (1902-1910)
- LA ERUDICION EXTREMENA Y LA ACADEMIA DE LA HISTORIA
- RELATO DE LA CAIDA DE GODOY POR UN TESTIGO PRESENCIAL

Rodriguez Monino, Rafael *see* MEMORIA...1916 DEL AYUNTAMIENTO DE DOS HERMANAS (SEVILLA)...

Rodriguez Obregon, Francisco Xavier *see* EL OBISPO DE BADAJOZ...CATOLICOS

Rodriguez Ordonez, Joaquin *see* LA VETTONIA

Rodriguez Pedreira, Jose *see* EDUQUEMOS A LAS MADRES

Rodriguez Perera, Francisco *see* APORTACION AL VOCABULARIO

Rodriguez Pineres, Eduardo *see* DIEZ ANOS DE POLITICA LIBERAL, 1892-1902

Rodriguez Rosillo, Abilio *see*
- PRACTICAS ELEMENTALES DE FISIOLOGIA E HIGIENE
- ULTIMA LECCION DEL..."ABEJAS Y FLORES"

Rodriguez Rubio, Inocencia *see* BATIENDO LA ESPERANZA

Rodriguez Solis, Enrique *see* ESPRONCEDA... OBRAS

Rodriguez Soriano y Alvarez, Rafael *see* POESIA...INMACULADA

Rodriguez, Teodoro *see* NUEVA RECONQUISTA DE ESPANA. VALLADOLID, 1938

Rodriguez Valdes, Manuel M *see* ESCRITO EN VISTA DE PRUEBAS

Rodriguez Vega, Jose *see* IMPRESSIONS OF FRANCO'S SPAIN

Rodriguez Victoria, Armando *see* TRUJILLO Y EL PRINCIPIO DE UNIDAD NACIONAL

Rodriguez Villa, Antonio *see*
- D. FRANCISCO DE ROJAS, EMBAJADOR DE LOS REYES CATOLICOS
- DUQUE DE T'SERCLAES TOMA POSESION ACADEMICO NUMERO REAL DE LA HISTORIA. NOTICIAS
- DURANTE EL SEMESTRE PASADO FALLECIERON...TAMBIEN D. PEDRO MARIA PLANO, EN MERIDA...
- EPIGRAFIA ROMANA DE MERIDA
- LAPIDA ROMANA INEDITA DE ALMENDRALEJO
- NECROLOGIA DEL MARQUES DE MONSALUD
- NOTICIAS DE...
- PRESENTO...NUEVAS INSCRIPCIONES ROMANAS QUE ACABAN DE HACER EN PLASENICA...EXTENSION DE LA PENINSULA

Rodriguez y Hernandez, Juan Antonio *see* LECCIONES DE MORAL

Rodriguez y Rivero, Cecilio *see* NOCIONES DE GEOGRAFIA DESCRIPTIVO-FISICO-POLITICA DE ESPANA

Rodriguez y Rivero, Jose *see* DE LA VIDA, SENTIRES Y SABERES DE D. JOSE MORENO NIETO

RODRIGUEZ-MONINO Y LA REAL ACADEMIA DE LA HISTORIA / Valgoma y Diaz-Varela, Dalmiro de la – Caceres: Revista Alcantara, 1970. No 161 – 1 – sp Bibl Santa Ana [946]

Rodulfus Glaber *see* RAOUL GLABER. LES CINQ LIVRES DE SES HISTOIRES (900-1044)

Rodway, James *see*
- CHRONOLOGICAL HISTORY OF THE DISCOVERY AND SETTLEMENT OF GUIANA, 1493-1668
- STORY OF GEORGETOWN

Rodwell, George *see* NEW TESTAMENT GREEK

Roe, Alfred *see* ROSE NEIGHBORHOOD SKETCHES OF WAYNE COUNTY

Roe, E T *see* BUSINESS AND LAW, OR THE CAREFUL MAN'S GUIDE

Roe, Edward Thomas *see* CRIMINAL PROCEDURE OF UNITED STATES COURTS

Roe, Gilbert Ernstein *see* SELECTED OPINIONS OF LUTHER S. DIXON AND EDWARD G. RYAN, LATE CHIEF JUSTICES OF THE SUPREME COURT OF WISCONSIN

Roe, S *see* ENTHUSIASM DETECTED, DEFEATED, WITH PREVIOUS CONSIDERATIONS CONCERNING REGENERATION, THE OMNIPRESENCE OF GOD, AND DIVINE GRACE

Roeckerath, Peter Joseph *see* BIBLISCHE CHRONOLOGIE BIS AUF DAS JAHR DER GEBURT JESU

Roedder, Edwin Carl *see* DIE STEINKLOPFER

Roeder, F *see* DER ALTENGLISCHE REGIUS-PSALTER

Roehl *see* INSCRIPTIONES GRAECAE ANTIQVISSIMAE

Roehl, Hans *see*
- GESCHICHTE DER DEUTSCHEN DICHTUNG
- WOERTERBUCH ZUR DEUTSCHEN LITERATUR

Roehling, J C *see*
- DEUTSCHLANDS FLORA
- DEUTSCHLANDS FLORA. NACH EINEM VERAENDERTEN UND ERWEITERTEN PLANE BEARBEITET VON F. C. MERTENS UND W. D. J. KOCH

Roehm, Johann Baptist *see* AUFGABEN DER PROTESTANTISCHEN THEOLOGIE

Roehr, Julius *see* WILDENBRUCH ALS DRAMATIKER

Roehrenbeck, Carol A *see* PEOPLE VS. GOETZ

Roehrich, T W *see* GESCHICHTE DER REFORMATION IM ELSASS UND BESONDERS IN STRASBURG, NACH GLEICHZEITIGEN QUELLEN

Roehricht, R *see* BIBLIOTHECA GEOGRAPHICA PALAESTINAE, CHRONOLOGISCHES VERZEICHNIS DER AUF DIE GEOGRAPHIE DES HEILIGEN LANDES BEZUEGLICHEN LITERATUR VON 333 BIS 1878 UND VERSUCH EINER CARTOGRAPHIE

Roel del Rio, Antonio V *see* INSTITUCION HARMONICA, O DOCTRINA MUSICAL, THEORICA, Y PRACTICA..

Roelker, Bernard *see* A MANUAL FOR THE USE OF NOTARIES PUBLIC AND BANKERS.

Roemer, J J *see*
- ARCHIV FUER DIE BOTANIK
- CATALOGUES HORTI BOTANICI SOCIETATIS PHYSICAE TURICENSIS
- COLLECTANEA AD OMNEM REM BOTANICAM SPECTANTIA
- ENCYCLOPAEDIE FUER GAERTNER UND LIEBHABER DER GAERTNEREI
- FAMILIARUM NATURALIUM REGNI VEGETABILIS SYNOPSES MONOGRAPHICAE
- FLORA EUROPAEA INCHOATA
- GENERA INSECTORUM LINNAEI ET FABRICII ICONIBUS ILLUSTRATA
- MAGAZIN FUER DIE BOTANIK
- VERSUCH EINES MOEGICHST VOLLSTAENDIGEN WOERTERBUCHS DER BOTANISCHEN TERMINOLOGIE

Roemer, Karl *see* DER CODEX ARABICUS MONACENSIS AUMER 238: EINE SPANISCH-ARABISCHE EVANGELIENHANDSCHRIFT

Roemer, Olaf *see* BERECHNUNG UND DIMENSIONIERUNG PERMANENTERREGTER GLEICHSTROMLINEARANTRIEBE DER FEINWERKTECHNIK

DER ROEMERBRIEF / Barth, Karl – First ed., 1919 – 1 – us A.T.L.A. [240]

DER ROEMERBRIEF / Zimmer, Friedrich – Quedlinburg: Chr Friedr Vieweg, 1887 – 1mf – 9 – 0-8370-9678-2 – 1986-3678 – us A.T.L.A. [220]

DER ROEMERBRIEF AUSGELEGT FUER BIBELLESER / Schlatter, Adolf von – 3. Aufl. Calw:Verlag der Vereinsbuchh., 1895 – 1mf – 9 – 0-8370-5092-8 – 1985-3092 – us A.T.L.A. [220]

DER ROEMERBRIEF: EINE EXEGETISCHE STUDIE / Feine, Paul – Goettingen: Vandenhoeck & Rup., 1903. 1 fiche – 9 – us A.T.L.A. [240]

DER ROEMERBRIEF UND SEINE GESCHICHTLICHEN VORAUSSETZUNGEN / Mangold, Wilhelm – Marburg: N.G. Elwert, 1884. 1 fiche – 9 – us A.T.L.A. [240]

DER ROEMERBRIEFTEXT DES ORIGENES (T.U.U. 3-44/3) / Bauernfeind, O – Leipzig, 1923 – 2mf – 9 – ne Slangenburg [240]

DIE ROEMERFAHRT DES EPIGONEN : HISTORISCHER ROMAN / Samarow, Gregor – Berlin: Globus-Verlag, [1912?] – 1r – 1 – us U.W. Library [830]

DIE ROEMERZEIT / Friedrich, Johann – Bamberg: O. Reindl, 1867. (Kirchengeschichte Deutschlands / von J. Friedrich; 1. T.) – 2mf – us A.T.L.A. [240]

DIE ROEMISCH-BAROCKE STILKOMPONENTE IM WERK PETER ANTON VON VERSCHAFFELTS / Kraemer, Gerhard – Heidelberg, 1973 – 4mf – 9 – DM90.00 – 3-89349-701-3 – gw Hänsel [750]

ROEMISCHE ASCHE : NEUE XENIEN / Barth, Hans – Bern: Ferdinand Wyss, 1919 – 1r – 1 – us U.W. Library [430]

DAS ROEMISCHE CONCIL : VIER VORTRAEGE IM EVANGELISCHEN VEREIN ZU HANNOVER / Uhlhorn, Gerhard – Hannover: Carl Meyer, 1870 – 1mf – 9 – 0-8370-8558-6 – 1986-2558 – us A.T.L.A. [240]

DAS ROEMISCHE CONCLAVE ODER GENAUE BESCHREIBUNG DER PAPSTWAHL – Leipzig, 1823.-64p – DM50.00 – 3-89349-214-3 – gw Hänsel [240]

ROEMISCHE GESCHICHTE / Ihne, Wilhelm – Leipzig. W. Engelmann, 1868-90. 8 v. Film Mas C 671 – 1 – us H.U. Library [930]

DIE ROEMISCHE KAPELLE SANCTA SANCTORUM UND IHR SCHATZ . REINE ENTDECKUNGEN UND STUDIEN IN DER PALASTKAPELLE DER MITTELALTERLICHEN PAEPSTE / Grisar, Hartmann – Freiburg i.B., St. Louis, Mo.: Herder, 1908 – 1mf – us A.T.L.A. [240]

DIE ROEMISCHE PAPSTMYTHE – Zuerich, 1873 – Dfl6.00 – ne Slangenburg [240]

ROEMISCHE PRAELATEN AM DEUTSCHEN RHEIN 1761-1764 / Weech, Friedrich von – Heidelberg, 1898 – 80p – 9 – DM48.00 – 3-89349-062-0 – gw Hänsel [943]

ROEMISCHE QUARTALSCHRIFT : FUER CHRISTLICHE ALTERTHUMSKUNDE UND FUER KIRCHENGESCHICHTE – 1(1887)-54(1959) – 581mf – 9 – Dfl2,034.00 – ne Slangenburg [073]

ROEMISCHE QUARTALSCHRIFT FUER CHRISTLICHE ALTERTHUMSKUNDE UND FUER KIRCHENGESCHICHTE – Rome. v1-54. 1887-1959 – 581mf – 9 – ne IDC [240]

DER ROEMISCHE STAAT UND DIE ALLGEMEINE KIRCHE BIS AUF DIOCLETIAN / Neumann, Karl Johannes – Leipzig: Veit, 1890 – 1mf – us A.T.L.A. [240]

ROEMISCHE TRAUERSPIELE : AGRIPPINA, EPICHARIS / Lohenstein, Daniel Casper von; ed by Just, Klaus Guenther – (Includes bibliographical references and index) – Stuttgart: Hiersemann, 1955 – 1 – us U.W. Library [820]

ROEMISCHEN FESTE UND FEIERTAGE NACH DEN TRAKTATEN UEBER FREMDEN DIENST (ABODAH ZARAH) IN MISCHNA, TOSEFTA, JERUSALEMER UND BABYLONISCHEN TALMUD / Blaufuss, H – Nuernberg. 1909. BJ-32-58 1 – 9 – ne IDC [250]

ROEMISCHES IDYLL / Ponten, Josef – Berlin-Grunewald: Horen-Verlag, 1927 – 1r – 1 – us U.W. Library [810]

Roenne, L *see* DIE FRUEHEREN UND GEGENWAERTIGEN VERHAELTNISSE DER JUDEN IN DE SAEMMTLICHEN LANDESTHEILEN DES PREUSSISCHEN STAATES

Roenning, F *see* TIL KARAKTERISTIK AF N.F.S. GRUNDTVIG

Roensch, Hermann *see*
- ITALA UND VULGATA

ROENTGEN- UDN PHOTOELEKTRONEN-SPEKTROSKOPISCHE UNTERSUCHUNGEN VON VERBINDUNGEN DER 3D-UEBERGANGSMETALLE UND DEM 5D-UEBERGANGSMETALL PLATIN / Baumannn, Frank – 1994 – 1mf – DM60.00 – 3-8267-2038-5 – gw Hänsel [540]

ROENTGENOGRAPHISCHE UDN SPEKTROSKOPISCHE UNTERSUCHUNGEN AN ALKALI-MANGAN(3)-VERBINDUNGEN VOM KRYOLITH-TYP, SOWIE AN CR(H20)6MNF6 / Englich, Ulrich – 1994 – 1mf – DM60.00 – 3-89349-911-3 – gw Hänsel [540]

Roentsch, Johannes *see* JESUS-MESSIAS: DER HERR UND SEIN VOLK

Roeper, J A C *see* ENUMERATIO EUPHORBIARUM QUAE IN GERMANIA ET PANNONIA GIGUNTUR

ROEPER REVIEW – v1- 1978- – 1,5,6,9 – us UMI [370]

Roer, Hans Henning *see* SCHILDKROETE, FROSCH UND EIDECHSE IN DER GRIECHISCHEN UND ROEMISCHEN ANTIKE

Roesch, Friedrich *see* BRUCHSTUECKE DES ERSTEN CLEMENSBRIEFES

Roesch, Herbert *see* GRUNDLAGEN, STILE, GESTALTEN DER DEUTSCHEN LITERATUR

Roeschlaub, Andreas *see* MAGAZIN ZUR VERVOLLKOMMNUNG DER THEORETISCHEN UND PRAKTISCHEN HEILKUNDE, 10 BAENDE 1799-1807

Roeschlein, Debra L *see* GENDER DIFFERENCES REGARDING KNOWLEDGE OF CHILD HEALTH AND DEVELOPMENT AMONG HIGH SCHOOL STUDENTS

Roesdi, Imam *see* SOME PROBLEMS OF STATE BUDGETING

Roesel, Ludwig Karl *see* DIE LITTERARISCHEN UND PERSOENLICHEN BEZIEHUNGEN SIR WALTER SCOTT'S ZU GOETHE

Roesel von Rosenhof, A J *see* HISTORIA NATURALIS RANARUM NOSTRATIUM

Roesicke, Helmut *see* PHYLOGENETISCHE UNTERSUCHUNGEN DER GATTUNG KALANCHOE MITTELS FINGERPRINT-VERFAHREN

Roesiger, Ferdinand *see* UEBER KLOPSTOCKS NATURBETRACHTUNG

Roesler, J *see* TROIS QUATUORS OP.6

Roesner, Werner *see* INNERE RECHTSKRAFT IM ERBHOFRECHT

Roesslin, E *see*
- THE BYRTH OF MANKYNDE, OTHERWYS NAMED THE WOMANS BOOKE
- THE BYRTH OF MANKYNDE, OTHERWYSE NAMED THE WOMANS BOOKE
- DER SWANGERN FRAWEN

Roest, M *see*
- CATALOG... HEBRAEISCHER UND JUEDISCHER BUECHER, HANDSCHRIFTEN, KUPFERSTICHE, PORTRAITS ETC. NACHGELASSEN VON G. ALMANZI, J. EMDEN, M.J. LEBENSTEIN U.A.
- KIRIAT SEFER, AUSFUEHRLICHER BIBIOGRAPHISCHER CATALOG... HEBRAEISCHER UND JUEDISCHER BUECHER UND HANDSCHRIFTEN, NACHGELASSEN VOM J. EMDEN, M.J. LEWENSTEIN U.A. ERSTE LIEFERUNG

ROETE DICH JUNGER TAG : GEDICHTE / Preczang, Ernst – Berlin: Arbeiterjugend-Verlag, 1927 – 1r – 1 – us U.W. Library [810]

Roeykens, Auguste *see* LES DEBUTS DE L'OEUVRE AFRICAINE DE LEOPOLD 2 1875-1879

ROFE U-VEIT MIRKAHAT – (Luah Yerushalayim). v. 2. 1887. BJ-27-237 1 – 9 – ne IDC [360]

ROGER DE FLOR / Justiniano Arribas, Juan – 1892 – 9 – $1.50f – sp Bibl Santa Ana [830]

ROGER DE SICILE / Berton, H – Paris: Benoist, 1817 – 1 – us Sibley [780]

Roger, Jacques F *see*
- FABLES SENEGALAISES RECUEILLIES DE L'OUOLOF ET MISES EN VERS FRANCAIS AVEC DES NOTES
- KELEDOR, HISTOIRE AFRICAINE
- RECHERCHES LANGUE OUOLOFE, SUIVIES D'UN VOCABULAIRE ABREGE FRANCAIS-OUOLOF

Roger, Jean-Francois *see* L'AVOCAT

Roger, Maurice *see* L'ENSEIGNEMENT DES LETTRES CLASSIQUES D'AUSONE A ALCUIN

Roger Of Hoveden *see* CHRONICA MAGISTRI ROGERI DE HOUEDENE (RS51)

Roger Of Wendover *see* LIBER QUI DICITUR FLORES HISTORIARUM AB A. D. 1154 ANNOQUE HENRICI ANGLORUM REGIS SECUNDI PRIMO (RS84)

ROGER WILLIAMS : THE PIONEER OF RELIGIOUS LIBERTY / Straus, Oscar S – New York: Century, 1894 – 1mf – us A.T.L.A. [240]

ROGER WILLIAMS, THE FOUNDER OF PROVIDENCE THE PIONEER OF RELIGIOUS LIBERTY / Eaton, Amasa M – 1908 – 1 – 5.00 – us Baptist [240]

Roger Williams University *see*
- CATALOGUES
- THE ROGERANA

Roger Williams University. Nashville, Tenn *see* CATALOGS AND COLLEGE RECORDS

THE ROGERANA / Roger Williams University – 1901-04 – 1 – 20.16 – us Baptist [073]

ROGERI BACON OPERA QUAEDAM HACTENUS INEDITA (RS15) : 1: OPUS TERTIUM 2: OPUS MINUS 3: COMPENDIUM PHILOSOPHIAE / Bacon, Roger; ed by Brewer, J S – 1859 – Dfl42.00 – ne Slangenburg [941]

Rogers, Arthur Kenyon *see*
- THE LIFE AND TEACHINGS OF JESUS
- PROPHECY AND POETRY: STUDIES IN ISAIAH AND BROWNING
- THE RELIGIOUS CONCEPTION OF THE WORLD

Rogers, C *see* TRANSACTIONS OF THE ROYAL HISTORICAL SOCIETY

Rogers, Earl M *see* MEMOIRS OF VERNON COUNTY

Rogers, Ebenezer Platt *see*
- THE OBLIGATIONS AND DUTIES OF THE FEMALE SEX TO CHRISTIANITY
- THE PRECIOUS THINGS OF ST PETER

Rogers, H A *see* SHORT ACCOUNT AND JOURNAL, 1775-1789

Rogers, Henry Wade *see* THE LAW OF EXPERT TESTIMONY

Rogers, Howard S *see* HISTORY OF CASS COUNTY FROM 1825 TO 1875

Rogers, J *see* DIARY, 1794-1805

Rogers, J E T *see* A HISTORY OF AGRICULTURE AND PRICES IN ENGLAND

Rogers, Justus H *see* COLUSA COUNTY

Rogers, Mary Eliza *see* DOMESTIC LIFE IN PALESTINE

Rogers, Mary Jane L *see* THE EFFECTS OF MENSTRUAL CYCLE PHASE ON COMPETITIVE SWIMMING PERFORMANCE

Rogers, Nancy B *see* THE MEANING OF LEISURE FROM THE PERSPECTIVE OF WIFE CAREGIVERS OF OLDER HUSBANDS

Rogers, Robert *see* JOURNAL OF MAJOR ROBERT ROGERS

Rogers, Samuel *see*
- HUMAN LIFE
- ITALY

ROGER'S SOUVENIR HISTORY OF MERCER COUNTY / W.B. Rogers Printing Co – Trenton, n.d. Missouri Reel 25. The Cox Library Collection – 5 – us Americana [978]

Rogerson, Cuthbert Harry *see* PLAY THERAPY IN CHILDHOOD

Rogge, Christian *see* LUTHER UND DIE KIRCHENBILDER SEINER ZEIT

Rogge, Friedrich Wilhelm *see* MNEMOSYNE

Rogge, Hendrik Cornelis *see*
- EEN BAND MET TRACTATEN VAN DAVID JORIS
- BESCHRIJVENDE CATALOGUS DER PAMFLETTEN-VERZAMELING VAN DE BOEKERIJ DER REMONSTRANTSCHE KERK TE AMSTERDAM
- JOHANNES WTENBOGAERT EN ZIJN TIJD

Roginson, G B *see* HISTORY OF PETERBOROUGH COUNTY, ONTARIO

Rogniat, Joseph *see* CONSIDERATIONS SUR L'ART DE LA GUERRE

Rogov, A I *see* SVEDENIIA O NEBOL'SHIKH SOBRANIIAKH SLAVIANO-RUSSKIKH RUKOPISEI V SSSR

Rogozhin, N *see* LITERATURNO-KHUDOZHESTVENNYE AL'-MANAKHI I SBORNIKI. TOM VTOROI 1912-1917. VSESOIUZNAIA KNIZHNAIA PALATA

Rogozhin, V N *see* UKAZATEL' K OPYTU ROSSIISKOI BIBLIOGRAFII V.S. SOPIKOVA

ROGUE REVIEW – Grants Pass OR. June 22 1978-Jan 5 1981 – 1 – us U.O. Library [071]

ROGUE RIVER ARGUS – Rogue River, OR. -w. 11 Feb 1915-26 Oct 1916. 1 roll – 1 – us U.O. Library [071]

ROGUE RIVER COURIER – Grants Pass, OR. And Rogue River Courier and Oregon Observer. -w. 1917-29 – 1 – 113.00 – us Oregon Hist [071]

ROGUE RIVER COURIER – Grants Pass OR. May 9 1913-Dec 31 1918,-d – 1 – us U.O. Library [071]

ROGUE RIVER COURIER – Grants Pass. Or. -w. 1917-29 – 1 – us UMI [071]

ROGUE RIVER COURIER – Grants Pass, OR. -w. 4 June 1886-13 Oct 1919 Set incl. Grants Pass Courier – 5r – 1 – us U.O. Library [071]

ROGUE RIVER COURIER AND OREGON OBSERVER – Grants Pass OR. Jan 8 1928-Dec 13 1929 – 1 – us U.O. Library [071]

Rohan, Henry I *see* LE PARFAIT CAPITAINE, AUTREMENT L'ABREGE DES GUERRES DE GAULE, DES COMMENTAIRES DE CESAR

Rohde, Erwin *see* PSYCHE

Rohm, Eva Maria *see* BEZIEHUNGEN ZWISCHEN DEN SYMBIOSEPARTNERN IN DER ORCHIDEEN-MYCORRHIZA

THE ROHNERT PARK NEWS – Rohnert Park, CA. 1972-1975 – 1r – 1 – $50.00 – B05054 – us Library Micro [071]

ROHNERT PARK PRESS AND CENTRAL SONOMA NEWS – Rohnert Park, CA. 1963-1964 – 1r – 1 – $50.00 – B03418a – us Library Micro [071]

ROHNERT PARK/COTATI TIMES – Rohnert Park, CA. 1977-1982 – 4r – 1 – $200.00 – B03643 – us Library Micro [071]

Rohnert, Wilhelm *see* DIE INSPIRATION DER HEILIGEN SCHRIFT UND IHRE BESTREITER

Rohr, Jean-Geoffroy *see* UN MISSIONNAIRE REPUBLICAN EN RUSSIE

Rohrbach, Paul *see* DER SCHLUSS DES MARKUSEVANGELIUMS, DER...KANON UND DIE KLEINASIATISCHEN PRESBYTER

Rohrscheidt, Joachim von *see*
DAS VERSTEIGERERGEWERBE IN GEWERBEPOLITISCH-RECHTLICHER ENTWICKLUNGSBETRACHTUNG

Rohwaldt, Karl *see* BERTOLDO

LE ROI DE COCAGNE, COMEDIE / Legrand, Marc-Antoine – (Utopias in the Enlightment series). 1719 – 9 – fr Hachette [830]

LE ROI DES ETUDIANTS / Dick, Wenceslas E – St-Henri: Decarie, Hebert & cie, (1903). SEM35P63 – 1r – 1 – Can$15.00 – cn Bibl Nat [830]

LE ROI ET SES MINISTRES / Thiery, Avocat – Dialogues. 3 pt. en 1 v – 9 – fr Hachette [190]
Roig y Mesa, J T *see* DICCIONARIO BOTANICO...
LES ROIS ROUMAINES ET LEUR CONNEXITE AVEC LE DROIT BYZANTIN ET SLAV / Pic, Josef Ladislav – Bucarest: Gobl, 1887. 60p. LL-4048 – 1 – us L of C Photodup [340]
Rojas, Aristides *see* ESTUDIOS HISTORICOS. CARACAS, 1927
Rojas, C *see* COMPENDIO...DE FORTIFICACION...
Rojas-Beltran, R *see* BIOLOGIE, ECOLOGIE ET DYNAMIQUE DES CREVETTES DE LA MANGROVE GUADELOUPEENNE (ANTILLES FRANCAISES): PHASE LAGUNAIRE DES PENAEIDES
Rojo Cerezo, Virgilio *see* CUADERNO DE UNIDADES DIDACTICAS 1-3
Rojo, Vincente *see* POURQUOI SE BAT L'ARMEE ESPAGNOLE; UN DISCOURS DU GENERAL ROJO
ROK 1830 W POLSKICH ARCHIWACH PANSTWOWYCH – v. 8. Archeion. 1930. BR-9830 1 – 9 – ne IDC [947]
Rokach, nE *see* RE'AMIM U-RE'ASHIM
ROKEBY : A POEM / Scott, Walter – Edinburgh: John Ballantyne; London: Longman, Hurst, Rees, Orme, and Brown, 1813 – 1 roll – 1 – 1-55879-862-5 – uk Libr Preservation [810]
ROL EVREEV V RUSSKOM REVOLIUTSIONNOM DVIZHENII / Deutsch, Lev Grigorevich – Berlin: "Grani", 1923- – 1 – CSUX89-B5271 – us Hoover Inst Photo [947]
Rol Press Agency. France *see* LA VIE EN AEROPLANE DE LOUIS BLERIOT
DE ROL VAN DEN MOEDERLIJKEN OOM IN DE INLANDSCHE FAMILIE / Reeth, P van – Brussels. 1935 – 1 – us Res Libr [306]
ROLA BOZA = GOD'S FIELD – Scranton, PA: Polski Narodowy Katolicki Kosciol, dec 25 1923-dec 13 1975 – 26r – 1 – us Res Libr [073]
ROLA-MOCA : ROMANCE / Alphonsus, Joao – Rio de Janeiro: Livraria J Olympio, 1938 – us Res Libr [830]
ROLAND / Lully, Jean-Baptiste – Paris: Academie Royale de musique, 1709 – 1 – us Sibley [780]
Roland, C-G *see*
- RECEUIL DES CHARTES DE L'ABBAYE DE GEMBLOUX
- RECEUIL DES CHARTES DE L'ABBAYE DE STAVELOT-MALMEDY

Roland Holst(van der Schalk), Henriette *see* PERALIHAN KE SOSIALISME. TERDJEMAHAN KAMARUZZAMAN
Roland, Jacqueline *see* BIBLIOGRAPHIE ANALYTIQUE DE PAUL LEGENDRE, REALISATEUR A RADIO-CANADA, MEMBRE DE LA "SOCIETE DES ECRIVAINS CANADIENS"
ROLAND YORKE / Wood, Ellen – British Fiction Archive: Unit 1 – 9 – uk Bell [830]
Roldan, Federico *see* FISONOMIA MORAL DE A. MONTANO
THE ROLE AND FUNCTIONS OF THE COOPERATIVE ORGANIZATIONS IN MARKETING OF RICE IN CALIFORNIA / Halim, Barli – SE-3694 1. 1959 – 9 – ne IDC [380]
ROLE DE L'ICONOSTASE DANS LE CULTE DIVIN / Dwirnyk, J – Montreal, 1960 – 3mf – 8 – Dfl13.00 – ne Slangenburg [200]
ROLE DES INSECTES DANS LA FECONDATION DES VEGETAUX / Barrois, T – Paris, 1886. 124p. Z-1047/2 – 8 – ne IDC [580]
ROLE DES LIGNEUX FOURRAGERS DANS LA NUTRITION DES RUMINANTS EN AFRIQUE SUBSAHARIENNE : ETUDE BIBLIOGRAPHIQUE / Miranda, Rui – 1989 – 9 – $14.00 – 92-9053-196-7 – et ILRI [631]
LE ROLE DES MISSIONNAIRES DANS L'ACCULTURATION EN AMERIQUE DU SUD / Pelligra, D – Un cas precis: les Indiens Bari du Venezuela et les missionnaires Capucins et protestants – 9 – F30.00 – fr Ethnologie [240]
LE ROLE DU DESSIN DANS L'OEUVRE DE DELACROIX / Reunion des musees nationaux. Paris – 1963. 12 illus. 1 fiche – 9 – fr Réunion [700]
ROLE ECONOMIQUE DE L'APPRENTISSAGE / Retail, Leon – Paris. 1925. (La Condition Ouvriere. Part Two.) – 9 – 7.50 – fr Bibl Nationale [360]
THE ROLE OF AEROBIC FITNESS AND SOCIAL SUPPORT IN REACTIVITY TO PSYCHOLOGICAL STRESS / Helgans, R M – 1991 – 3mf – 9 – $12.00 – us Microform Publ [150]
ROLE OF AFRICAN STUDENT MOVEMENTS IN THE POLITICAL AND SOCIAL EVOLUTION OF AFRICA FROM 1900 TO 1975 – 1994 – 210p – 9 – 92-3-102804-9 – fr UNESCO [320]
THE ROLE OF COGNITIVE APPRAISAL AND FRIENDSHIP PROVISIONS IN CHILDREN'S EXPERIENCE OF AFFECT IN PHYSICAL ACTIVITY / Duncan, Susan C & Weiss, Maureen R – 1992 – 2mf – 9 – $8.00 – us Microform Publ [150]
THE ROLE OF DIET AND EXERCISE IN WEIGHT CONTROL IN OBESE WOMEN : A META-ANALYSIS / Gustafson, R P – 1991 – 3mf – 9 – $12.00 – us Microform Publ [613]
ROLE OF EDUCATION PROJECTIONS IN EDUCATIONAL PLANNING IN BANGLADESH : NATIONAL CONTRIBUTION / Bangladesh. National Foundation for Research on Human Resource Development – Dacca, 1980 – 2mf – 9 – DE-533/1 – ne IDC [370]
ROLE OF ENERGETIC FACTORS IN THE EVOLUTION OF THE BREEDING BIOLOGY OF THE SHORT-TAILED SHEARWATER (PUFFINUS TENUIROSTRIS TEMMENIK) / Fitzherbert, K – (PhD Thesis) – 1985 – microfiche – A$15.00 – at R.A.O.U. [590]
THE ROLE OF EXTERNAL NON-RIGID ANKLE BRACING IN THE PREVENTION OF INVERSION INJURIES / Anderson, Daphne L & Sanderson, David – 1992 – 1mf – 9 – $4.00 – us Microform Publ [617]
ROLE OF FISHERY TECHNOLOGY IN THE MANAGEMENT AND DEVELOPMENT OF FRESHWATER FISHERIES IN AFRICA – 1979 – 71p – it F.A.O. [639]
ROLE OF FORESTRY IN COMBATING DESERTIFICATION – 1989 – 344p – it F.A.O. [634]
THE ROLE OF FUNCTIONAL KNEE BRACING IN A DYNAMIC SETTING / Rishiraj, Neetu – University of British Columbia, 1995 – 2mf – 9 – $8.00 – PE3619 – us Microform Publ [611]
THE ROLE OF LAND POLICY IN AGRICULTURAL PRODUCTION AND INCOME DISTRIBUTION IN THE NEAR EAST / United Nations. Food and Agriculture Organization. Development Center on Land Policy and Settlement for the Near East – FAO Headquarters, Rome. Tripoli, Libya. 16-28 Oct 1965. Ghonemy, R. E. (Land Tenure Specialist). BNE-1012 1 – 9 – ne IDC [333]
THE ROLE OF LANGUAGE IN BLACK EDUCATION : PAPERS PRESENTED AT THE CONFERENCE ON THE ROLE OF LANGUAGE IN BLACK EDUCATION, PRETORIA, 17-18 FEBRUARY 1986 / South Africa. Human Sciences Research Council. Institute for Educational Research – Pretoria, 1986 – 4mf – 9 – DE-648/1 – ne IDC [370]
THE ROLE OF LAW AND ECONOMIC DEVELOPMENT / Nyhart, J Daniel – Cambridge: School of Industrial Management, Massachusetts Institute of Technology, 1964?. LL-4196 – 1 – us L of C Photodup [340]
ROLE OF LEGISLATION IN LAND USE PLANNING FOR DEVELOPING COUNTRIES – 1985 – 165p – it F.A.O. [350]
THE ROLE OF MAGISTRATES : NINE CASE STUDIES / Seron, Carroll – Washington: GPO, 1985 – 2mf – 9 – $3.00 – LLMC 95-326 – us L.L.M.C. [340]
THE ROLE OF MAGISTRATES IN FEDERAL DISTRICT COURTS / Seron, Carroll – Washington: FJC, 1984 – 2mf – 9 – $3.00 – LLMC 95-315 – us L.L.M.C. [340]
THE ROLE OF MUSCULOSKELETAL FORCES IN THE HUMAN WALK-RUN TRANSITION / Fewster, Jonathan B – Oregon State University, 1996 – 2mf – 9 – $8.00 – PE 3637 – us Microform Publ [612]
THE ROLE OF PHYSICAL EXPERIENCE IN EDUCATION / Snell, Christopher R et al – 1993 – 2mf – 9 – $8.00 – us Microform Publ [370]
ROLE OF PUBLIC AND PRIVATE AGENTS IN THE FOOD AND AGRICULTURAL SECTORS OF DEVELOPING COUNTRIES – 1991 – 130p – it F.A.O. [338]
THE ROLE OF STAFF ATTORNEYS AND FACE-TO-FACE CONFERENCING IN NON-ARGUMENT DECISIONMAKING : A VIEW FROM THE TENTH CIRCUIT COURT OF APPEALS / Steinstra, Donna & Cecil, Joe S – Washington: FJC, 1989 – 1mf – 9 – $1.50 – LLMC 95-381 – us L.L.M.C. [340]
THE ROLE OF THE AMERICAN SLOVAKS / Stolarik, Mark – 1967 – 1 reel – 1 – us I.H.R.C. [975]
THE ROLE OF THE ARMY IN THE OXFORD, MISSISSIPPI, INCIDENT, 1962-1963 / Scheips, Paul J – Histories Div, Off. of the Chief of Military History, Dept of the Army, 1965 – 4mf – 9 – $6.00 – LLMC 97-009 – us L.L.M.C. [355]
THE ROLE OF THE COURT EXPERT IN PATENT LITIGATION / Whinery, Leo H – Washington, Govt. Print. Off., 1958. 96 p. LL-2302 – 1 – us L of C Photodup [340]
THE ROLE OF THE JUDGE IN THE SETTLEMENT PROCESS / Will, Hubert L et al – Washington: GPO, 1983 – 1mf – 9 – $1.50 – LLMC 95-392 – us L.L.M.C. [340]
THE ROLE OF THE MEMBER STATES IN THE UNIFICATION WORK OF THE INTERNATIONAL LABOUR ORGANIZATION / Suviranta, Antti – Helsinki, Institutum Jurisprudentiae Comparativae Universitatis Helsingiensis, 1966. 79 p. LL-4209 – 1 – us L of C Photodup [340]
THE ROLE OF THE MISSIONARIES IN CONQUEST / Majeke, Nosipho – [Johannesburg: Society of Young Africa, 1952] – us Res Libr [240]
ROLE OF WATER IN SOCIOECONOMIC DEVELOPMENT : REPORT 1 OF IHP-2 PROJECT C1 ON HEIGHTENING AWARENESS OF THE SOCIOECONOMIC ROLE OF WATER / ed by Cox, W E – 1988 – xii/91p – 9 – 92-3-102534-1 – fr UNESCO [333]
ROLE STRESS AND SECONDARY TEACHER/COACHES IN THE STATE OF WASHINGTON / Wu, Y – 1991 – 1mf – 9 – $4.00 – us Microform Publ [150]
ROLES OF VISUALS IN SCIENTIFIC PRESENTATIONS = ROLE DES SUPPORTS VISUELS DANS LA COMMUNICATION SCIENTIFIQUE / Tripathi, Bansh R – 1991 – 9 – $6.00 – 92-9053-216-5 – et ILRI [000]
Rolf, A *see* DAS PAPSTTUM UND SEINE UNFEHLBAREN
Rolffs, Ernst *see*
- DAS INDULGENZ-EDICT DES ROEMISCHEN BISCHOFS KALLIST (T.U.U. 1-11/3)
- URKUNDEN AUS DEM ANTIMONTANISTISCHEN KAMPFE DES ABENDLANDES
- URKUNDEN AUS DEM ANTIMONTANISTISCHEN KAMPFE DES ABENDLANDES (T.U.U. 1-12/4A)

Rolfus, Hermann *see*
- EXPLANATION OF THE HOLY SACRAMENTS
- ILLUSTRATED EXPLANATION OF THE COMMANDMENTS...OF GOD AND OF THE CHURCH

ROLIG TEKNIK – Jaervsoe, 1983-89 – 1r – 1 – sw Kungliga [073]
ROLL AND GO – 1924 – 1 – us I.U. Libraries [390]
THE ROLL OF ARMS, OF THE PRINCES, BARONS, AND KNIGHTS WHO ATTENDED KING EDWARD I TO THE SIEGE OF CAERLAVEROCK, IN 1300;...FROM MS. IN THE BRITISH MUSEUM – Trans. and notes by Thomas Wright. London: J.C. Hotten, 1864. viii,39p. 5 col. pl – 1 – us U.W. Library [941]
ROLL OF ATTORNEYS OF THE STATE OF KANSAS / Kansas. Supreme Court – Topeka: Smith, 1917. 65p. LL-312 – 1 – us L of C Photodup [340]
ROLL OF OFFICERS AND ENLISTED MEN. / U.S. Army. Third, Fourth, Eighteenth & Nineteenth Kansas Volunteers – 1861. Item I. Reprint of Appendix 4 to the Adjutant General's Thirteenth Biennial Report, Topeka, KS 1920. 154p. SW16-0028 – 5 – us A.G.L.L. [920]
ROLL OF THE 4TH QUEENSLAND IMPERIAL BUSHMEN FROM NEWCASTLE TO STORMBERG, 1901-1901 / Chief Secretary's Office, Queensland – 6r – 1 – CRS B5181 – at Archives [920]
ROLL OF THE INDIAN MEDICAL SERVICE, 1615-1930 / Crawford, D G – London, Calcutta, Simla. 1930. BI-335 2 – 8 – ne IDC [610]
ROLL OF THE PROCEEDINGS OF THE KING'S COUNCIL IN IRELAND (RS69) : FOR A PORTION OF THE 16TH YEAR OF THE REIGN OF RICHARD 2, 1392-1393 / Ireland. King's Council; ed by Graves, J – 1877 – Dfl30.00 – ne Slangenburg [941]
Rolla, A *see*
- GRANDES QUATUORS, TROIS, 2E LIVRE
- QUATUORS, DEUX, POUR FLUTE, VIOLON, ALTO, ET VIOLONCELLE

Rolland d'Erceville, Barthelemy Gabriel *see* RECUEIL DE PLUSIEURS DES OUVRAGES DE MONSIEUR LE PRESIDENT ROLLAND
Rolland, Eugene *see* ALMANACH DES TRADITIONS POPULAIRES
Rolland, Henri *see* PLANCHES DE L'ARMORIAL GENERAL DE J.-B. RIETSTAP, 6 [TA A ZY]
Rolland, J B *see* HUIT MOIS A MADAGASCAR
DIE ROLLE DES AUTORS : ANALYSEN UND GESPRAECHE / ed by Schneider, Irmela – (Includes bibliographical references) – Stuttgart: Klett, 1981 – 1 – us U.W. Library [430]
DIE ROLLE ITALIENS BEI DER ENTSTEHUNG DER EUROPAEISCHEN WIRTSCHAFTSGEMEINSCHAFT BIS 1958 / Bendig, Helmut – 1995 – 3mf – 9 – DM98.00 – 3-8267-2138-1 – gw Hänsel [945]
Rolle, Richard *see*
- THE PRICK OF CONSCIENCE
- RELIGIOUS WRITINGS

Rollenhagen, G *see* NUCLEUS EMBLEMATUM SELECTISSIMORUM
Rollett, Hermann *see* DIE GOETHE-BILDNISSE
ROLLING FORK BAPTIST CHURCH. LOUISVILLE, KENTUCKY : CHURCH RECORDS – Jul 1878 – Nov 1950 – 1 – 20.25 – us Baptist [240]
ROLLING HILLS HERALD *see* PALOS VERDES NEWS AND ROLLING HILLS HERALD
ROLLING STONE – (1983-.) – 1967- – 1,9 – us UMI [073]
ROLLING STONES – Boulder, CO. 1970-79 – 14r – 1 – $700.00 – R04000 – us Library Micro [071]
Rollings, Anne T *see* PREDICTORS OF UPHILL RIDING PERFORMANCE IN TRAINED CYCLISTS
THE ROLLS SERIES *see*
- ALEXANDRI NECKAM DE NATURIS RERUM, LIBRI DUO (RS34)
- ANGLO-LATIN SATIRICAL POETS AND EPIGRAMMATISTS OF THE TWELFTH CENTURY (RS59)
- ANGLO-SAXON CHRONICLE (RS23)
- ANNALES CAMBRIAE (A.D. 444-1288) (RS20)
- ANNALES MONASTICI (RS36)
- ANNALS OF LOCH CE (RS54)
- BLACK BOOK OF THE ADMIRALITY (RS55)
- BRUT Y TYWYSOGION (RS17)
- THE BUIK OF THE CHRONICLES OF SCOTLAND (RS6)
- CARTULARIUM MONASTERII DE RAMESEIA (RS79)
- CHARTERS AND DOCUMENTS ILLUSTRATING THE HISTORY OF THE CATHEDRAL, CITY AND DIOCESE OF SALISBURY, IN THE TWELFTH AND THIRTEENTH CENTURIES (RS97)
- CHARTULARIES OF ST MARY'S ABBEY, DUBLIN (RS80)
- CHRONIA MONASTEREII S ALBANI (RS28)
- CHRONICA MAGISTRI ROGERI DE HOUEDENE (RS51)
- CHRONICA MAJORA (RS57)
- CHRONICA MONASTERII DE MELSA, A FUNDATIONE USQUE AD ANNUM 1396 (RS43)
- CHRONICA (RS13)
- CHRONICLE OF ENGLAND (RS1)
- CHRONICLE OF PIERRE DE LANGTOFT (RS47)
- THE CHRONICLE OF THE REIGNS OF HENRY 2 AND RICHARD 1, 1169-1192 (RS49)
- CHRONICLES AND MEMORIALS OF THE REIGN OF RICHARD 1 (RS38)
- CHRONICLES OF THE REIGNS OF EDWARD 1 AND EDWARD 2 (RS76)
- CHRONICLES OF THE REIGNS OF STEPHEN, HENRY 2 AND RICHARD 1 (RS82)
- CHRONICON ABBATIAE DE EVESHAM AD ANNUM 1418 (RS29)
- CHRONICON ABBATIAE RAMESIENSIS (RS83)
- CHRONICON ANGLIAE (RS64)
- CHRONICON ANGLICANUM (RS66)
- CHRONICON HENRICI KNIGHTON, VEL CNITTHON, MONACHI LEYCESTRENSIS (RS92)
- CHRONICON MONASTERII DE ABINGTON (RS2)

- CHRONICON SCOTORUM (RS46)
- A COLLECTION OF CHRONICLES AND ANCIENT HISTORIES OF GREAT BRITAIN (RS40)
- CONTINUATIO CHRONICARUM (RS93)
- DE GESTIS PONTIFICUM ANGLORUM LIBRI QUINQUE (RS52)
- DE GESTIS REGUM ANGLORUM LIBRI QUINQUE
- DESCRIPTIVE CATALOGUE OF MATERIALS RELATING TO THE HISTORY OF GREAT BRITAIN AND IRELAND TO THE END OF THE REIGN OF HENRY 7 (RS26)
- EADMERI HISTORIA NOVORUM IN ANGLIA (RS81)
- EULOGIUM (HISTORIARUM SIVE TEMPORIS) (RS9)
- FASCICULI ZIZANIORUM MAGISTRI WYCLIF CUM TRITICO (RS5)
- FLORES HISTORIARUM (RS95)
- GIRALDI CAMBRENSIS OPERA, VOLS 8 (RS21)
- GIRALDI CAMBRENSIS OPERA, VOLS 1-4 (RS21)
- GIRALDI CAMBRENSIS OPERA, VOLS 5-7 (RS21)
- HENRICI DE BRACTON DE LEGIBUS ET CONSUETUDINES ANGLIAE LIBRI QUINQUE IN VARIOS TRACTATUS DISTINCTI (RS70)
- HENRICI HUNTENDUNIENSIS HISTORIA ANGLORUM (RS74)
- HISTORIA ANGLICANA (A.D. 449-1298) (RS16)
- HISTORIA ANGLORUM, SIVE, UT VULGO DICITUR, HISTORIA MINOR (RS44)
- HISTORIA ET CARTULARIUM MONSTERII S. PETRI CLOUCESTRIAE (RS33)
- HISTORIA MONASTERII S. AUGUSTINI CANTUARIENSIS BY THOMAS OF ELMHAM, FORMERLY MONK AND TREASURER OF THAT FOUNDATION (RS8)
- THE HISTORIANS OF THE CHURCH OF YORK AND ITS ARCHBISHOPS (RS71)
- HISTORIC AND MUNICIPAL DOCUMENTS, IRELAND, A.D. 1172-1320 (RS53)
- HISTORICAL PAPERS AND LETTERS FROM THE NORTHERN REGISTERS (RS61)
- THE HISTORICAL WORK OF MASTER RALPH DE DICETO, DEAN OF LONDON (RS68)
- HISTORICAL WORKS, THE CHRONICLE OF THE REIGNS OF STEPHEN, HENRY 2 AND RICHARD 1 (RS73)
- ICELANDIC SAGAS AND OTHER HISTORICAL DOCUMENTS RELATING TO THE SETTLEMENTS AND DESCENTS OF THE NORTHMEN ON THE BRITISH ISLES (RS88)
- LEECHDOMS, WORTCUNNING AND STARCRAFT OF EARLY ENGLAND (RS35)
- LESTORIE DES ENGLES SOLUM LA TRANSLACION MAISTRE GEFFREI GAIMAR (RS91)
- LETTERS AND PAPERS ILLUSTRATIVE OF THE REIGN OF RICHARD 3 AND HENRY 7 (RS24)
- LETTERS AND PAPERS ILLUSTRATIVE OF THE WARS OF THE ENGLISH IN FRANCE DURING THE REIGN OF HENRY 6 (RS22)
- LIBER DE ILLUSTRIBUS HENRICIS (RS7)
- LIBER MONASTERII DE HYDA (RS45)
- LIBER QUI DICITUR FLORES HISTORIARUM AB A. D. 1154 ANNOQUE HENRICI ANGLORUM REGIS SECUNDI PRIMO (RS84)
- LITERAE CANTUARIENSES (RS85)
- LE LIVERE DE REIS DE BRITTANIE E LE LIVERE DE REIS DE ENGLETERRE (RS42)
- LIVES OF EDWARD THE CONFESSOR (RS3)
- MAGNA VITA S. HUGONIS, EPISCOPI LINCOLNIENSIS (RS37)
- MATERIALS FOR A HISTORY OF THE REIGN OF HENRY 7 (RS60)
- MATERIALS FOR THE HISTORY OF THOMAS BECKET (RS67)
- MEMORIALE FRATRIS WALTERI DE COVENTRIA (RS58)
- MEMORIALS OF HENRY 7 (RS10)
- MEMORIALS OF HENRY THE FIFTH (RS11)
- MEMORIALS OF ST DUNSTAN, ARCHBISHOP OF CANTERBURY (RS63)
- MEMORIALS OF ST EDMUNDS ABBEY (RS96)
- MEMORIALS OF THE REIGN OF KING HENRY 6 (RS56)
- METRICAL CHRONICLE OF ROBERT OF GLOUCESTER (RS86)
- MONUMENTA FRANCISCANA (RS4)
- MUNIMENTA ACADEMICA
- MUNIMENTA GILDHALLAE LONDONIENSIS (RS12)
- NARRATIVES OF THE EXPULSION OF THE ENGLISH FROM NORMANDY, 1449-1450 (RS32)
- OPERA OMNIA (RS75)
- POLITICAL POEMS AND SONGS RELATING TO ENGLISH HISTORY
- POLYCHRONICON RANULPHI HIGDEN MONACHI CESTRENSIS (RS41)
- RECORDS OF THE PARLIAMENT HOLDEN AT WESTMINSTER, 28 FEBRUARY IN THE 33RD YEAR OF THE REIGN OF EDWARD 1 (1305) (RS98)
- RECUEIL DES CRONIQUES ET ANCHIENNES ISTORIES DE LA GRANT BRETAGNE (RS39)
- RED BOOK OF THE EXCHEQUER (RS99)
- REGISTER OF THE ABBEY OF ST THOMAS THE MARTYR, DUBLIN (RS94)
- REGISTRUM EPISTOLARUM FRATRIS JOHANNIS PECKHAM (RS77)
- REGISTRUM MALMESBURIENSE (RS72)
- REGISTRUM PALATINUM DUNELMENSE (RS62)
- THE REPRESSOR OF OVERMUCH BLAMING OF THE CLERGY (RS19)
- RICARDI DE CIRENCESTRIA SPECULUM HISTORIALE DE GESTIS REGUM ANGLIAE (RS30)
- ROBERTI GROSSETESTE EPISCOPI QUONDAM LINCOLNIENSI EPISTOLAE (RS25)
- ROGERI BACON OPERA QUAEDAM HACTENUS INEDITA (RS15)
- ROLL OF THE PROCEEDINGS OF THE KING'S COUNCIL IN IRELAND (RS69)
- ROYAL AND HISTORICAL LETTERS DURING THE REIGN OF HENRY THE FOURTH, KING OF ENGLAND AND OF FRANCE, AND LORD OF IRELAND (RS18)
- ROYAL AND OTHER HISTORICAL LETTERS LLUSTR. OF THE REIGN OF HENRY 2 (RS27)
- THE STORY OF ENGLAND BY ROBERT MANNING OF BRUNNE (RS87)
- THOMAS BECKET (RS65)
- TRIPARTITE LIFE OF PATRICK (RS89)
- VETUS REGISTRUM SARISBERIENSE
- WAR OF THE GAEDHIL WITH THE GAIL (RS48)
- YEAR BOOKS OF THE REIGN OF KING EDWARD 1 (RS31A)
- YEAR BOOKS OF THE REIGN OF KING EDWARD 3 (RS31B)

THE ROLLS SERIES (RS) - RERUM BRITTANNICARUM MEDIIAEVI SCRIPTORES : OR CHRONICLES AND MEMORIALS OF GREAT BRITAIN AND IRELAND, DURING THE MIDDLE AGES – Dfl8,750.00 set – ne Slangenburg [941]

ROL'NICKA NEDEL'A – Bratislava, Czechoslovakia. 24,31 Aug; 5 Oct 1952 – 1r – 1 – us L of C Photodup [072]

ROL'NICKE NOVINY – Bratislava, Czechoslovakia. Apr 1953-Dec 1961; Jan 1983-Dec 1992 – 25r – 1 – us L of C Photodup [072]

ROLNIK POLSKI – Warsaw, Poland. Jun 1948-May 1952 (scattered issues) – 5r – 1 – us L of C Photodup [943]

Roloff, C L *see* INDEX PLANTARUM IN HORTO KRAUSIANO...

ROM UND JERUSALEM DIE LETZTE NATIONALITAETENFRAGE / Hess, M – Leipzig. 1862. BJ-28-57 1 – 9 – ne IDC [956]

ROMA – 1988-1995 – 6r per y – 5,6 – Sfr1,203.00 – sz Infoprint [945]

ROMA NOBILITATA NELLE SUE FABBRICHE DALLA SANTITA DI NOSTRO SIGNORE CLEMENTE XII / Gaddi, G B – Roma. 1736. BO-956 1 – 9 – ne IDC [240]

ROMA POPOLARESCA / Veo, Ettore – 1929 – 1 – us I.U. Libraries [390]

ROMA SOTTERANEA : OPERA POSTUMA COMPITA.DAL GIOV. SEVERANO / Bosio, A – Roma, 1632 – Dfl105.00 – ne Slangenburg [240]

ROMA SOTTERRANEA : OPERA POSTUMA COMPITA...DAL GIOV. SEVERANO... / od by Bosio, A – Roma, 1632 – 30mf – 8 – ne Slangenburg [240]

ROMA SOTTERRANEA CRISTIANA / Rossi, G B de – Roma. v1-3. 1864-77 – 90mf – 8 – Dfl315.00 – ne Slangenburg [240]

ROMA SOTTERRANEA, OR, SOME ACCOUNT OF THE ROMAN CATACOMBS, ESPECIALLY OF THE CEMETERY OF SAN CALLISTO / Northcote, J Spencer & Brownlow, W R – London: Longmans, Green, Reader and Dyer, 1869 – 2mf – us A.T.L.A. [240]

Romack, Jennifer L *see* OBSERVATIONAL LEARNING AND ACQUISITION OF COMPLEX MOTOR PATTERNS BY CHILDREN

Romain, Georges *see* L'EGLISE CATHOLIQUE ET LES PROTESTANTS

Romain, J Ch. *see*
- LES CHARTES DE L'ORDRE DE CHALAIS (1101-1400)

LE ROMAN AU CANADA-FRANCAIS, 1925-1949 / Bourassa, Lucette – 1949. SEM105P4 – 1mf – 9 – cn Bibl Nat [440]

ROMAN BEZ VRAN'IA / Mariengof, A – Ed. 2. Berlin. 1928. BR-1080 2 – 8 – ne IDC [460]

ROMAN BIBLIOTEK = ROMAN LIBRARY – (In Yiddish) – Moscow, RU. no1 1929; no3 1929 – 1r – 1 – $25.00 – cn Can Microfilming [072]

LE ROMAN CANADIEN-FRANCAIS, DES DEBUTS A NOS JOURS / Montreuil, Denise – 1949. SEM105P4 – 1mf – 9 – cn Bibl Nat [440]

ROMAN CANON LAW IN THE CHURCH OF ENGLAND / Maitland, Frederick William – London, 1898 – 4mf – 9 – H-1185/2 – ne IDC [240]

ROMAN CANON LAW IN THE CHURCH OF ENGLAND : SIX ESSAYS / Maitland, Frederick William – London: Methuen, 1898 – 1mf – us A.T.L.A. [240]

ROMAN CATHOLIC AND PROTESTANT BIBLES COMPARED: THE GOULD PRIZE ESSAYS / Jacobus, Melancthon Williams – New York: Charles Scribner, 1908. 1 fiche – 9 – us A.T.L.A. [240]

ROMAN CATHOLIC OPPOSITION TO PAPAL INFALLIBILITY / Sparrow-Simpson, William John – (Includes index) – London: John Murray, 1909 – 1mf – 9 – 0-8370-8869-0 – 1986-2869 – us A.T.L.A. [240]

ROMAN CATHOLIC PRIESTS' ATTITUDES AND BEHAVIORS REGARDING SELECTED SEXUALITY ISSUES / Lukiewski, Mary A – 1982 – 1mf – 9 – $4.00 – us Microform Publ [240]

ROMAN CATHOLICISM AS A FACTOR IN EUROPEAN POLITICS / Conybeare, Frederick C – London: Skeffington, 1901 – 1mf – us A.T.L.A. [240]

ROMAN CATHOLICISM, OLD AND NEW : FROM THE STANDPOINT OF THE INFALLIBILITY DOCTRINE / Schulte, Johann Friedrich von – New York: R Worthington, 1877 – 1mf – 9 – 0-8370-8712-0 – 1986-2712 – us A.T.L.A. [240]

ROMAN CITIZEN – Rome. N.Y. 1840-1863 – 1 – us UMI [071]

THE ROMAN COURT : OR, A TREATISE ON THE CARDINALS, ROMAN CONGREGATIONS AND TRIBUNALS, LEGATES, APOSTOLIC VICARS, PROTONOTARIES, AND OTHER PRELATES OF THE HOLY ROMAN CHURCH / Baart, Peter A – New York: Fr Pustet, c1895 – 1mf – 9 – 0-8370-7121-6 – 1986-1121 – us A.T.L.A. [240]

ROMAN D'AMOUR / Champagne, Louis – no 1(5 mars 1948?)-no 478(24 avr 1957). SEM16P328 – 4r – 5 – Can$212.00 – cn Bibl Nat [830]

ROMAN D'AMOUR MENSUEL – no 1(22 juin 1955)-. SEM16P334 – 1r – 5 – Can$27.00 – cn Bibl Nat [830]

ROMAN D'AMOUR POPULAIRE – no P-1(dec 1958)-no P-33(juin 1961); no 84(aout 1961)-. SEM16P335 – 1r – 5 – Can$24.00 – cn Bibl Nat [830]

ROMAN D'AMOUR SPECIAL – no S-1(dec 1958)-no S-34(juil 1961); no 83(aout 1961)-. SEM16P336 – 1r – 5 – Can$11.00 – cn Bibl Nat [830]

LE ROMAN DE LA FEMME CHRETIENNE / Giraud, Leon – Paris: Ghio, 1880. 322p. (Les Femmes Collection) – 4mf – 9 – $10.00 – fr Bibl Nationale [240]

ROMAN DE TROIE / Sainte-Maure, Benoit de – Oesterreichische Nationalbib Wien, Cod 2571 – 44p + 7 color mf – DM650.00 – 3-89219-010-0 – gw Lengenfelder [440]

A ROMAN DIARY AND OTHER DOCUMENTS RELATING TO THE PAPAL INQUIRY INTO ENGLISH ORDINATIONS, MDCCCXCVI / Lacey, T A – London; New York: Longmans, Green, 1910 – 1mf – us A.T.L.A. [240]

ROMAN EDUCATION / Wilkins, A S – Cambridge: University Press; New York: Putnam [Distributor], 1914 – 1mf – us A.T.L.A.

ROMAN EMPEROR WORSHIP / Sweet, Louis Matthews – Boston: R.G. Badger, (c1919). 153p – 1 – us U.W. Library [250]

ROMAN EMPIRE – 1993 – 36p – 9 – 92-3-102679-8 – fr UNESCO [930]

LE ROMAN EN PROSE DE TRISTAN, LE ROMAN DE PALAMEDE, ET LA COMPILATION DE RUSTICIEN DE PISE; ANALYSE CRITIQUE.. / Loseth, Eilert – D'apres les manuscrits de Paris. Paris: E. Bouillon, 1890. 4,1 leaf, xxvi,542p. (Bibliotheque de l'Ecole des Hautes Etudes...Sciences philologiques et historiques...) – 1 – us U.W. Library [830]

THE ROMAN FESTIVALS OF THE PERIOD OF THE REPUBLIC : AN INTRODUCTION TO THE STUDY OF THE RELIGION OF THE ROMANS / Fowler, William Warde – London; New York: Macmillan, 1899 (Handbooks of archaeology and antiquities) – 1mf – us A.T.L.A. [250]

A ROMAN FRONTIER POST AND ITS PEOPLE. THE FORT OF NEWSTEAD / Curle, J – 1911 – 1 – uk Microform Academic [941]

THE ROMAN FRONTIER SETTLEMENT AT GHIZA: AN INTERIM REPORT / Brogan, O & Smith, D – (Journal of Roman Studies, v. 47). London. 1957. BA-643 2 – 8 – ne IDC [930]

ROMAN IDEAS OF DEITY IN THE LAST CENTURY BEFORE THE CHRISTIAN ERA : LECTURES DELIVERED IN OXFORD FOR THE COMMON UNIVERSITY FUND / Fowler, William Warde – London; New York: Macmillan, 1914 – 1mf – us A.T.L.A. [240]

THE ROMAN JOURNALS OF FERDINAND GREGOROVIUS 1852-1874 / Gregorovius, Ferdinand; ed by Althaus, Friedrich – London: G. Bell, 1907 – 2mf – us A.T.L.A. [240]

ROMAN LAW IN MEDIAEVAL EUROPE / Vinogradoff, Paul – London, New York: Harper, 1909 – 1mf – us A.T.L.A. [240]

THE ROMAN LAW OF SALE WITH MODERN ILLUSTRATIONS – (Justinian's Digest. Titles 18.1 + 19.1, treating of the Contract of Sale. Translated with notes and references to Cases and the Sale of Goods Act) – 2nd enl ed. Edinburgh: T & T Clark, 1907 – 4mf – 9 – $6.00 – LLMC 95-172 – us L.L.M.C. [340]

ROMAN LIFE AND MANNERS UNDER THE EARLY EMPIRE / Friedlaender, Ludwig – Authorized translation of the 7th enl. and rev. ed. of the Sittengeschichte Roms. 4 v. 1908-13 – 1 – us A.T.L.A. [930]

Roman, M J *see* DICTIONNAIRE TOPOGRAPHIQUE DU DEPARTEMENT DES HAUTS-ALPES

ROMAN MOEI ZHIZNI / Iasinskii, I I – Kniga vospominanii. M., L. 1926. BR-9212 1 – 9 – ne IDC [460]

ROMAN PORTRAITS AND MEMPHIS (4) / Petrie, William Matthew Flinders – BSA, 1911 – 9 – $10.00 – us I.R.C. [930]

THE ROMAN PRIMACY, A.D. 430-451 / Rivington, Luke – London, New York: Longmans, Green, 1899 – 1mf – us A.T.L.A. [240]

ROMAN REVOLUSI: PERAHU LAJAR "MAPPASIKUWAE."SE-4512/1. 1963 / Bahar Mattaliu – 9 – ne IDC [950]

THE ROMAN SEE IN THE EARLY CHURCH : AND OTHER STUDIES IN CHURCH HISTORY / Bright, William – London; New York: Longmans, Green, 1896 – 2mf – us A.T.L.A. [240]

ROMAN SOCIETY FROM NERO TO MARCUS AURELIUS / Dill, Samuel – London; New York: Macmillan, 1905 – 2mf – us A.T.L.A. [930]

ROMAN SOCIETY IN THE LAST CENTURY OF THE WESTERN EMPIRE / Dill, Samuel – London: Macmillan, 1899 – 2mf – us A.T.L.A. [930]

ROMAN STOICISM : BEING LECTURES ON THE HISTORY OF THE STOIC PHILOSOPHY WITH SPECIAL REFERENCE TO ITS DEVELOPMENT WITHIN THE ROMAN EMPIRE / Arnold, E Vernon – Cambridge: University Press; New York: Putnam [distributor], 1911 – 2mf – us A.T.L.A. [180]

ROMAN TRIPOLITANIA: RECONNAISANCE IN THE DESERT FRONTIER ZONE / Goodchild, R G – (Geographical Journal, v. 115). London. 1950. BA-649 2 – 8 – ne IDC [930]

ROMAN TSAREVICH / Gippius, Z N – Istoriia odnogo nachinaniia. M. 1913. BR-720 2 – 8 – ne IDC [947]

Roman y Zamora, Jeronimo *see* REPUBLICAS DE INDIAS; IDOLATRIAS Y GOBIERNO EN MEXICO Y PERU ANTES DE LA CONQUISTA.

ROMANA LIBERA – 1976- – 1 – us Ross [072]

LA ROMANCE / Berton, H – Paris: Berton & Loraux, 1804 – 1 – us Sibley [780]

ROMANCE LINGUISTIC AND DIALECTOLOGY – 9 – ne IDC [440]

ROMANCE NOTES – (1963-. 1,5,6,9) – v1-. 1959- – 1 – us UMI [440]

THE ROMANCE OF ALEXANDER – 12th Century. (From Trinity College, Cambridge) – 1 reel – 14 – uk Microform Academic [830]

THE ROMANCE OF ALEXANDER: A COLLOTYPE FACSIMILE OF MS. BODLEY 264.. / Lambert le Tort – Introd. by M.R. James. Oxford: Clarendon Press, 1933. 50p. Reproduces only the French metrical Roman d'Alexandre. Interpolations included – 1 – us U.W. Library [810]

ROMANCE OF AN ALTER EGO / Bryce, Lloyd – Toronto: Rose, 1889. 00309. (Pre-1900 Canadiana) – 9 – cn C.I.H.M. [830]

THE ROMANCE OF DOLLARD / Catherwood, Mary Hartwell – New York: Century Co., 1899. c1888. 00511. (Pre-1900 Canadiana) – 9 – cn C.I.H.M. [830]

THE ROMANCE OF LIFE / Cholmondeley, Mary – British Fiction Archive: Unit 3 – 9 – uk Bell [830]

THE ROMANCE OF M. RENAN AND THE CHRIST OF THE GOSPELS : THREE ESSAYS / Schaff, Philip & Roussel, Napoleon – New York: Carlton & Lanahan; Cincinnati: Hitchcock & Walden, 1868 – 1mf – 9 – 0-8370-5068-5 – 1985-3068 – us A.T.L.A. [240]

THE ROMANCE OF NONCONFORMITY / Ritson, Joseph – London: W.A. Hammond, 1910 – 1mf – us A.T.L.A. [240]

THE ROMANCE OF OLD NEW ENGLAND CHURCHES / Crawford, Mary C – Boston: L.C. Page, c1903 – 1mf – us A.T.L.A. [720]

THE ROMANCE OF PRIMITIVE METHODISM / Ritson, Joseph – London, 1909. vii/312p – 4mf – 9 – ne IDC [240]

THE ROMANCE OF PRIMITIVE METHODISM / Ritson, Joseph – London: E. Dalton, 1910 – 1mf – us A.T.L.A. [240]

THE ROMANCE OF PROTESTANTISM / Alcock, Deborah – Cincinnati: Jennings & Graham; New York: Eaton & Mains, 1908 – 1mf – 9 – 0-8370-6081-8 – 1986-0081 – us A.T.L.A. [240]

THE ROMANCE OF THE FLORIDAS. THE FINDING OF THE FOUNDING. NEW YORK, 1934 / Kenny, Michael – Madrid: Razon y Fe, 1936 – 1 – sp Bibl Santa Ana [975]

A ROMANCE OF TWO WORLDS / Corelli, Marie – British Fiction Archive: Unit 1 – 9 – uk Bell [830]

ROMANCE PHILOLOGY – v1- 1947- 1; v23-5,6; v30- 9 – us UMI [440]

EL ROMANCERO DE LA PRINCESA / Hurtado, Antonio – 1852 – 9 – 1.50f – sp Bibl Santa Ana [830]

ROMANCERO DEL CORONEL VILLALBA / Delgado Fernandez, Manuel – Caceres: Imp. El Noticiero, 1949 – sp Bibl Santa Ana [946]

EL ROMANCERO ESPANOL / Espinosa, Aurelio Macedonio – 1931 – 1 – us I.U. Libraries [390]

ROMANCES / Sanchez-Arjona, Vicente – Sevilla: Imp. Alvarez, Tomo 1-4. 1958 – 1 – sp Bibl Santa Ana [810]

ROMANCES AL ATARDECER / Sanchez-Arjona, Vicente – Sevila: Imp. Carlos Acuna, 1953 – 1 – sp Bibl Santa Ana [810]

ROMANCES CABALLERESCOS / Cobos de Villalobos, Amantina – Sevilla: Casa Velazquez, 1924 – sp Bibl Santa Ana [946]

ROMANCES CORTOS / Sanchez-Arjona, Vicente – Sevilla: Imp. Alvarez, Tomo 1-3. 1959 – 1 – sp Bibl Santa Ana [810]

ROMANCES DE ULTIMA HORA / Sanchez-Arjona, Vicente – Sevilla: Imp. Zambrano, 1956 – 1 – sp Bibl Santa Ana [810]

ROMANE : BIS ZUM TODE GETREU – WELTUNTERGANG / Dahn, Felix – Leipzig: Breitkopf & Haertel, 1899 – 1 – us U.W. Library [830]

ROMANE : BISSULA – ATTILA / Dahn, Felix – Leipzig: Breitkopf & Haertel, 1898 – 1 – us U.W. Library [830]

ROMANE : FELICITAS – CHLODOVECH / Dahn, Felix – Leipzig: Breitkopf & Haertel, 1898 – 1 – us U.W. Library [830]

ROMANE : GELIMER – DIE SCHLIMMEN NONNEN VON POITIERS / Dahn, Felix – Leipzig: Breitkopf & Haertel, 1898 – 1 – us U.W. Library [830]

ROMANE : DIE KREUZFAHRER – KAEMPFENDE HERZEN [VIER ERZAEHLUNGEN] / Dahn, Felix – Leipzig: Breitkopf & Haertel, 1899 – 1 – us U.W. Library [830]

ROMANE : SIND GOETTER? – ODHINS TROST / Dahn, Felix – Leipzig: Breitkopf & Haertel, 1899 – 1 – us U.W. Library [830]

ROMANE : VOM CHIEMGAU – EBROIN / Dahn, Felix – Leipzig: Breitkopf & Haertel, 1899 – 1 – us U.W. Library [830]

ROMANE UND NOVELLEN / John, Eugenie – (1. Das Geheimnis der alten Mamsell. 2. Das Heideprinzesschen. 3. Reichsgraefin Gisela. 4. Im Schillingshof. 5. Im Hause des Kommerzienrates.. 6. Die Frau mit den Karfunkelsteinen. 7. Die zweite Frau. 8. Goldelse. 9. Das Eulenhaus. 10. Thueringer Erzaehlungen) – Von E. Marlitt (pseud.). Stuttgart, etc., Union deutsche Verlagsgesellschaft, 1919. 10v. Film Mas C 376 – 1 – us H.U. Library [830]

DIE ROMANE VON FRIEDRICH VON UECHTRITZ / Meyer, Curt – (Includes bibliographical references) – Breslau: F Hirt, 1911 – 1 – us U.W. Library [430]

DIE ROMANE VON JOHANN TIMOTHEUS HERMES : EIN BEITRAG ZUR KULTUR- UND LITERATUR-GESCHICHTE DES ACHTZEHNTEN JAHRHUNDERTS / Muskalla, Konstantin – (Includes bibliographical references) – Breslau: F Hirt, 1912 – 1 – us U.W. Library [430]

Romanes, Ethel *see* CHARLOTTE MARY YONGE

Romanes, George John *see*
– A CANDID EXAMINATION OF THEISM
– THOUGHTS ON RELIGION

ROMANESQUE ART AND ARCHITECTURE – 1993 – 36p – 9 – 92-3-102685-2 – fr UNESCO [700]

ROMANIA : ANUARUL STATISTIC AL ROMANIEI 1904-1939/40 / Romania. Institut Central de Statistica – (Irregular. 1905-08, 1910-11 not publ. 1930 not available. Coll title: European Official Statistical Serials, 1841-1984) – 93mf – 9 – £6.00f (set £1,375.00 218mf) – uk Chadwyck [949]

ROMANIA : ANUARUL STATISTIC AL RPR 1957-1970 / Romania. Directiunea Centrala de Statistica – (Coll title: European Official Statistical Serials, 1841-1984) – 125mf – 9 – £5.00f (set £1,375.00 218mf) – uk Chadwyck [949]

ROMANIA – Paris. avr 1887-1888 – 1 – fr A.C.R.P.P. [949]

ROMANIA : RECUEIL TRIMESTRIEL CONSACRE A L'ETUDE DES LANGUES ET DES LITTERATURES ROMANES – Paris. v1-66. 1872-1940 – 452mf – 9 – H-10031/1 – ne IDC [470]

Romania *see*
– BULETINUL OFICIAL
– DRAFT DIRECTIVES OF THE NINTH CONGRESS OF THE RUMANIAN COMMUNIST PARTY ON THE DEVELOPMENT OF THE NATIONAL ECONOMY ON THE 1966-1970 PERIOD
– MONITORUL OFICIAL
– MONITORUL OFICIAL AL ROMANIA

Romania. Directiunea Centrala de Statistica *see* ROMANIA

Romania. Institut Central de Statistica *see* ROMANIA

ROMANIA LIBERA – Bucharest, Romania. Aug 1944-1976 – 57r – 1 – us L of C Photodup [949]

ROMANIA LIBERA – Bucuresti, 1976-1992ff – 34r – 1 – DM2,550.00 – gw Mikro Press [949]

ROMANIA LIBERA – no. 1, 3, 5, 36, 42, 45-49, 58. Paris. oct 1943-sept 1948 – 1 – fr A.C.R.P.P. [949]

ROMANIA LITERARA – Bucuresti, 1976-1992ff – 17r – 1 – DM1,275.00 – gw Mikro Press [949]

Romania. Marea Adunare Nationala *see* BULETINUL OFICIAL

Romania. Monitorul Oficial *see* LEGEA NR. 1 PENTRU PLANUL GENERAL ECONOMIC AL REPUBLICII POPULARE ROMANE PE ANUL 1949

ROMANIA MUNCITOARE *see* MUNCA

Romania.Ministerul Finantelor *see* EXPUNEREA SITUATIUNEI FINANCIARE A TESAURULUI PUBLIC

ROMANIAN PRESS REVIEW – Bucharest. Jan 27, 1946-May 12, 1967 – 1 – $644.00 – us L of C Photodup [949]

ROMANISCHE STUDIEN / ed by Boehmer, E – Strassburg, Bonn. v1-6. 1871-95 – 69mf – 9 – H-1400/2 – ne IDC [470]

DIE ROMANISCHEN WALDENSER : IHRE VORREFORMATORISCHEN ZUSTAENDE UND LEHREN, IHRE REFORMATION IM 16. JAHRHUNDERT UND DIE RUECKWIRKUNGEN DERSELBEN, HAUPTSAECHLICH NACH IHREN EIGENEN SCHRIFTEN / Herzog, Johann J – Halle: E. Anton, 1853 – 2mf – us A.T.L.A. [240]

ROMANISM : THE DANGER AHEAD: THE REASON WHY A GOOD ROMAN CATHOLIC CANNOT BE A GOOD CITIZEN OF THIS REPUBLIC / Grover, Alonzo J – Chicago: Craig & Barlow, 1887 – 1mf – 9 – 0-8370-8429-6 – 1986-2429 – us A.T.L.A. [240]

ROMANISM / Mattison, Hiram – 1871 – 9 – us A.T.L.A. [240]

ROMANISM AS IT IS : AN EXPOSITION OF THE ROMAN CATHOLIC SYSTEM, FOR THE USE OF THE AMERICAN PEOPLE / Barnum, Samuel Weed – (Includes index) – Hartford, CT: Connecticut Pub Co, 1877 – 2mf – 9 – 0-8370-8883-6 – 1986-2883 – us A.T.L.A. [240]

ROMANISM AS IT IS: AN EXPOSITION OF THE ROMAN CATHOLIC SYSTEM.. / Barnum, Samuel Weed – Hartford, CT; Conn. Publishing Co., 1872. xviii,753p.illus – 1 – us U.W. Library [240]

ROMANISM IN AMERICA / Clark, Rufus W – Boston: S.K. Whipple, 1855, c1854 – 1mf – us A.T.L.A. [240]

ROMANISM IN ITS HOME / Eager, John Howard – (Includes bibliographical references and index) – Philadelphia: American Baptist Publication Society, c1899 – 1mf – 9 – 0-8370-8505-5 – 1986-2505 – us A.T.L.A. [240]

ROMANISM IN THE LIGHT OF PROPHECY AND HISTORY : ITS FINAL DOWNFALL: AND THE TRIUMPH OF THE CHURCH OF CHRIST / Brownlee, William Craig – (Includes bibliographical references) – New York: American and Foreign Christian Union, 1854 – 1mf – 9 – 0-8370-8322-2 – 1986-2322 – us A.T.L.A. [240]

ROMANISM VERSUS THE PUBLIC SCHOOL SYSTEM / Dorchester, Daniel – New York: Phillips & Hunt; Cincinnati: Cranston & Stowe, 1888 – 1mf – us A.T.L.A. [240]

ROMANISTS DISQUALIFIED FOR CIVIL POWER : PROVED FROM THE DECREES OF THE COUNCIL OF TRENT, AND OTHER AUTHENTIC DOCUMENTS OF THE ROMISH CHURCH: A TRACT FOR THE TIMES / Taylor, W F – Birkenhead: R Pinkney, 1851 – 1mf – 9 – 0-8370-8475-X – 1986-2475 – us A.T.L.A. [240]

ROMANO LAVO-LIL / Borrow, George Henry – London: John Murray, 1874 – 1 – uk Libr Preservation [800]

ROMANO LAVO-LIL, WORD-BOOK OF THE ROMANY; OR, ENGLISH GYPSY LANGUAGE / Borrow, George Henry – New York: G.P. Putnam's Sons, 1905. 274p – 1 – us U.W. Library [490]

Romano, R *see* CANZONETTE MUSICALI

Romanov, I N *see* ATEISTICHESKAIA RABOTA B KLUBE

ROMANS : INTRODUCTION, AUTHORIZED VERSION, REVISED VERSION WITH NOTES, INDEX, AND MAP / ed by Garvie, Alfred Ernest – (Includes an index) – Edinburgh: T C & E C Jack, [c1900] – 1mf – 9 – 0-8370-3233-4 – 1985-1233 – us A.T.L.A. [220]

Romanski, S *see* BIBLIOGRAFISKI PREGLED NA SLAVIANSKITE KIRILSKI IZTOCHNISTSI ZA ZHIVOTA I DEINOSTTA NA KIRILA I METODIIA

DIE ROMANTECHNIK BEI FRIEDRICH GERSTAECKER / Jacobstroer, Bernhard – Greifswald, 1914 – 1mf – DM48.00 – 3-8267-3100-X – gw Hänsel [400]

A ROMANTIC ROMANCE / Harris, Carrie Jenkins – Windsor: J. Anslow, 1893. 05378. (Pre-1900 Canadiana) – 9 – cn C.I.H.M. [830]

THE ROMANTIC STORY OF THE PURITAN FATHERS, & THEIR FOUNDING OF NEW BOSTON & THE MASSACHUSETTS BAY COLONY – By Albert C. Addison, 1912. Item O. Indexed, 243p. SW16-0095 – 5 – us A.G.L.L. [978]

ROMANTICHESKIE TSVETY / Gumilev, Nikolai Sepanovich – Stikhi 1903-07 g. Ed. 3. "Kn-vo Prometei". Petrograd. 1918. BR-1152 2 – 8 – ne IDC [460]

ROMANTIKI / Merezhkovskii, Dimitrii – P'esa v 4-kh deistviiakh. Petrograd. 1917. BR-785 2 – 8 – ne IDC [460]

ROMANTISCHE ELEMENTE BEI THEODOR STORM / Dreesen, Willrath – Dortmund: F W Ruhfus, 1905 – 1r – 1 – us U.W. Library [430]

ROMANTISCHER "KATHOLIZISMUS" UND KATHOLISCHE "ROMANTIK" : DAS WESEN DER ROMANTISCHEN RELIGIOSITAET / Martin, Alfred Wilhelm von – (Die zwei 1924/1925 erschienenen Aufsaetze) – 9 – DM48.00 – 3-89349-103-1 – gw Hänsel [240]

ROMANTISCHES / Walzel, Oskar Franz – Bonn a. Rh.: L Roehrscheid, 1934 – 1r – 1 – us U.W. Library [430]

ROMAN-TSAITUNG – Warsaw. v. 1-2 no. 37. 1907-1908 – 1 – us NY Public [072]

ROMANUL – Cleveland: Epaminonda Lucaciu, [1906-apr 15 1928] – 19r – 1 – us Res Libr [071]

ROMANULU – Bucharest, Romania. Romanul. -d. 1 Jan 1870-13 Dec 1904; March, April 1905. 45 reels – 1 – uk British Libr Newspaper [949]

Romaskevich, A A *see* SPISOK PERSIDSKIKH, TURETSKO-TATARSKIKH I ARABSKIKH RUKOPISEI BIBLIOTEKI PETROGRADSKOGO UNIVERSITETA

Romberg, B *see*
– QUARTET, STRINGS, NO. 11, OP. 60
– QUARTETS, STRINGS, NO. 10, OP. 59

Rombouts, Ph *see* DE LIGGEREN EN ANDERE HISTORISCHE ARCHIEVEN DER ANTWERPSCHE SINT LUCAS GILDE

ROME AND ITALY AT THE OPENING OF THE OECUMENICAL COUNCIL / Pressense, Edmond Dehault de – 1870 – 9 – us A.T.L.A. [240]

ROME AND THE NEWEST FASHIONS IN RELIGION : THREE TRACTS, THE VATICAN DECREES, VATICANISM, SPEECHES OF THE POPE / Gladstone, William Ewart – (Includes bibliographical references) – Coll ed. London: John Murray, 1875 – 1mf – 9 – 0-8370-8510-1 – 1986-2510 – us A.T.L.A. [240]

ROME ET L'EGLISE SYRIENNE-MARONITE D'ANTIOCHE (517-1531) : THESES, DOCUMENTS, LETTRES / Al-Ghaziri, Bernard Ghobaeira – (In French, Latin, Syriac, and Arabic) – Beyrouth: Khalil Sarkis, 1906 – 1mf – 9 – 0-8370-9760-6 – 1986-3760 – us A.T.L.A. [240]

ROME FIRST BAPTIST CHURCH. ROME, GEORGIA : CHURCH RECORDS – 1835-96 – 1 – 34.83 – us Baptist [240]

ROME FROM THE INSIDE, OR, THE PRIESTS' REVOLT / ed by Brierley, Jonathan – 1st ed. London: James Clarke, 1899 – 1mf – 9 – 0-8370-8652-3 – 1986-2652 – us A.T.L.A. [240]

ROME IN CANADA : THE ULTRAMONTANE STRUGGLE FOR SUPREMACY OVER THE CIVIL AUTHORITY / Lindsey, Charles – Toronto: Williamson, 1889 – 1mf – us A.T.L.A. [971]

ROME, REFORM AND REACTION / Forsyth, Peter Taylor – Four lectures on religious situations. 1879 – 1 – 9.10 – us Baptist [240]

ROME, REFORM AND REACTION : FOUR LECTURES ON THE RELIGIOUS SITUATION / Forsyth, Peter Taylor – London: Hodder & Stoughton, 1899 – 1mf – 9 – 0-8370-2880-9 – 1985-0880 – us A.T.L.A. [240]

THE ROME WEEKLY COURIER – Rome, GA: M Dwinell, jan 6 1860-dec 1865 – 1r – 1 – us Res Libr [071]

Romein, J M *see* APPARAAT VOOR DE STUDIE DER GESCHIEDENIS

Romejko, Lynn C *see* A SOMATOGRAPHIC ANALYSIS OF YOUNG AND OLDER WOMEN BASED ON THE REFERENCE WOMAN

ROMEO ET JULIETTE, OVERTURE-FANTASIE / Tschaikovsky, Pl & LeMare, E – (Arranged for organ) – New York: Schirmer, 1909 – 1 – us Sibley [780]

ROMEO UND JULIA AUF DEM DORFE : ERZAEHLUNG / Keller, Gottfried – Stuttgart: J G Cotta, 1912 – 1r – 1 – us U.W. Library [830]

ROMEO UND JULIA AUF DEM DORFE / Keller, Gottfried; ed by Adams, W A – (German text with an introduction and notes in English) – Boston: D C Heath, c1900 – 1 – us U.W. Library [830]

O ROMEOS – Athens, Greece. -m. April 1883-Nov 1918. 6 reels – 1 – uk British Libr Newspaper [949]

Romera de la Torre, Francisco *see* IDEA DE UN PERFECTO PRELADO DISCURRIDA A LA ELECCION DE MINISTRO PROVINCIAL...

LA ROMERIA DE LA LUZ / Cordero, Juan Luis – Caceres: Imp. Moderna, 1944 – 1 – sp Bibl Santa Ana [810]
ROMERIA DE SAN ISIDRO. EN VENTA E CULEBRIN / Hermandad Sindical de Labradores y Ganaderos – Zafra: Imp. Segedana, 1970 – sp Bibl Santa Ana [946]
ROMERIA DE SAN ISIDRO EN VENTAS DE CULEBRIN. 1971 / Monesterio – Zafra: Imp. Segedana, 1971 – 1 – sp Bibl Santa Ana [240]
LA ROMERIA ESPANOLA AL VATICANO EN EL ANO DE 1876 / Aguilar Gallegos, Manuel – 9 – 1.50f – sp Bibl Santa Ana [946]
Romero Cabot, R *see*
– PALENCIA. ARCHIVO HISTORICO PROVINCIAL INVENTARIO DE LA SECCION 1. PROTOCOLOS
– PALENCIA. ARCHIVO HISTORICO PROVINCIAL INVENTARIO DE LA SECCION 2. CONTADURIA DE HIPOTECAS
– PALENCIA. ARCHIVO HISTORICO PROVINCIAL INVENTARIO DE LA SECCION 4. DESAMORTIZACION
– PALENCIA. ARCHIVO HISTORICO PROVINCIAL INVENTARIO DE LA SECCION 7. HACIENDAS LOCALES
– PALENCIA. ARCHIVO HISTORICO PROVINCIAL INVENTARIO DE LA SECCION 9. SINDICATOS
Romero, Carlos A *see* FUNDACION ESPANOLA...POR EL VIRREY DEL PERU, DON FRANCISCO DE TOLEDO. LIMA, 1926
Romero Carvajal, Jose Ignacio *see*
– INFORME PRONUNCIADO POR DON...ACTUANDO COMO DEFENSOR EN LA VISTA SEGUIDA CONTRA URBANO CALVO SANCHEZ
– VERDAD DEL MOVIMIENTO (CONFERENCIA... DISCURSO DE LA FUNDACION
Romero de Castilla, Pedro *see*
– CUADERNO DE CONCORDANCIAS Y ORACIONES GRAMATICALES LATINAS PARA USO PARTICULAR DE LOS ESTUDIANTES DE DICHA LENGUA
– CUADERNOS...GRAMATICALES...ESTUDIANTES
Romero de Castilla, Tomas *see*
– ELEMENTOS DE LOGICA
– ELEMENTOS DE PSICOLOGIA
– INVENTARIO DE...MUSEO...BADAJAZ
– NI INCREDULO NI INTOLERANTE
– NUESTRO CONCEPTO DE LA RAZON...SANTO TOMAS DE AQUINO
Romero de Castillay Perosso, Francisco *see*
– APUNTES...ARCHIVO GENERAL DE SIMANCAS
– LA DOCTRINA QUE...INFALIBIDAD DE LA RAZON..
– ELEMENTOS DE FILOSOFIA MORAL..
Romero Galvan, J R *see* LA CRONICA MEXICANA DE HERNANDO ALVARADO TEZOZOMOC
Romero, L *see* DESENGANO DEL ABUSO DE LA SANGRIA...
Romero, Luis *see*
– APUNTES DE LA SUBLEVACION FASCISTA; IMPRESIONES DE UN MILITAR REPUBLICANO
– EXPEDICION CORTESIANA A LAS MOLUCAS 1527
Romero Mendoza, Pedro *see*
– CAMINOS DE SERVIDUMBRE
– MEDITACIONES DE UN LECTOR CON MOTIVO DE LA FIESTA DEL LIBRO
Romero Morera, Joaquin *see*
– BREVES DEFINICIONES DE HISTORIA GENERAL Y DE ESPANA...SUCESOS...BADAJOZ
– HISTORIA...ESPANA...BADAJOZ
– NOCIONES DE AGRIMENSURA
Romero Munoz, Manuel *see* LA PROPIA HONRA. BOCETO DRAMATICO EN UN ACTO ORIGINAL DE...
Romero Rizo, Jose Maria *see* MUNOZ TORRERO, APUNTES HISTORICOS-BIOGRAFICOS
Romero, Sylvio *see* HISTORIA DA LITTERATURA BRAZILEIRA
Romero y Delgado, Antonio *see* SERMON... ALMENDRALEJO
Romeyn, John B *see* A COLLECTION OF FACTS AND OBSERVATIONS MADE RELATIVE TO THE STATE OF MORALS AND RELIGION IN HOLLAND IN 1814
Romier, L *see*
– LES ORIGINES POLITIQUES DES GUERRES DE RELIGION (1547-1559)
– LE ROYAUME DE CATHERINE DE MEDICIS
THE ROMISH CHURCH OPPOSED TO THE LIBERTIES.. / Carroll, Anna E – 1856 – 1 – $50.00 – us Presbyterian [240]
THE ROMISH DOCTRINE OF THE IMMACULATE CONCEPTION TRACED FROM ITS SOURCE / Preuss, Edward – (Includes bibliographical references) – Edinburgh: T & T Clark, 1867 – 1mf – 9 – 0-8370-8781-3 – 1986-2781 – us A.T.L.A. [230]
Rommeiskichen, Giovanni *see* BIBLIOGRAFIA MISSIONARIA ANNO 30, 1966. ROMA, 1967
Rommel, Erwin *see* SELECTED DOCUMENTS ON THE LIFE AND CAMPAIGNS OF FIELD MARSHAL ROMMEL
Rommerskichen, Giovanni *see*
– BIBLIOGRAFIA MISSIONARIA ANNO 39, 1965. ROMA, 1966
– BIBLIOGRAFIA...ANNO 28, 1964
ROMOLA / Eliot, George – London: Smith, Elder, 1863 – 1 roll – 1 – 1-55879-214-7 – uk Libr Preservation [830]
Romoli, Cathleen *see* VASCO NUNEZ DE BALBOA. DESCUBRIDOR DEL PACIFICO
ROMPIMIENTO DEL ISTMO DE SUEZ / Montesino, Cipriano S – 1857 – 9 – 1.50f – sp Bibl Santa Ana [910]
ROMS KAMPF UM DIE WELTHERRSCHAFT : EINE KIRCHENGESCHICHTLICHE STUDIE / Schubert, Hans von – Halle: Verein fuer Reformationsgeschichte, 1888. ([Schriften des Vereins fuer Reformationsgeschichte; Bd. 23]) – 1mf – us A.T.L.A. [240]
ROMSEY EXAMINER – 1884-1920. RE1-15 – 15r – 1 – at Corangamite [072]
Roncesvalles, Maria N C *see* THE DEVELOPMENT OF WEIGHTBEARING SKILLS
Ronco Tovar, O F M *see* UN VIAJE FASCINANTE POR LA AMERICA HISPANA DEL SIGLO 16. MADRID, 1969
RONDALLAS V PRUEBA MUSICAL DE UNIVERSIDADES LABORALES / Universidad Laboral Hispanoamericana – Caceres: Imp. La Minerva, 1977 – 1 – sp Bibl Santa Ana [780]
RONDE TAFEL – (Lacking: 1947, V.2(25)) – Batavia, 1946-1949 – 32mf – 9 – SE-958/1 – ne IDC [073]
Rondeau, C *see* LA SOCIETE SENUFO DU SUD MALI (1870-1950)
Rondelet, G *see*
– LIBRI DE PISCIBUS MARINIS, IN QUIBUS VERAE PISCIUM EFFIGIES EXPR. SUNT...
– UNIVERSAE AQUATILIUM HISTORIAE PARS ALTERA
Rondelet, Jean Baptiste *see* TRAITE THEORIQUE ET PRATIQUE DE L'ART DE BATIR
Rondet-Saint, Maurice *see* DANS NOTRE EMPIRE NOIR
LA RONDINE / Puccini, G – (Piano-vocal score, Ms, copyist hand) – Milano: Sonzogro, 1917 – 1 – us Sibley [780]
RONDO FOR THE FORTE PIANO / Taylor, Raynor – Philadelphia: Printed for the Author 179?. MUSIC 123, Item 9 – 1 – us L of C Photodup [780]
RONDO PER CLAVICEMBALO O FORTE-PIANO / Mozart, Wolfgang Amadeus – (Andante fuer eine Walze in eine kleine Orgel,K. 616). 1791 – 9 – us Sibley [780]
RONDO POUR LE VIOLON AVEC ACCOMPAGNEMENT DE GRAND ORCHESTRA COMPOSE PAR MOZART. OUEVRE 85ME. [K. 373] / Mozart, Wolfgang Amadeus – (Edition faite d'apres la partition en manuscript, lst edition) – S/M.J. Andre, [1800] – 1 – us Sibley [780]
RONDOM HET WOORD – v9-33. 1967-91 (complete) – 6r – 1 – ATLA S0817 – us A.T.L.A. [073]
LE ROND-POINT – Quebec, Canada. 24 aut 1966-v8 n30. 10 jul 1974 – 1r – 1 – Can$25.00 – cn Can Microfilming [072]
Ronge, Bertha *see* A PRACTICAL GUIDE TO THE ENGLISH KINDERGARTEN
Ronge, Johann *see* A PRACTICAL GUIDE TO THE ENGLISH KINDERGARTEN
RONGJIA QIYE SHILIAO – Historical materials on enterprises owned by the Rong family. Comp. by the Institute of Economics, Shanghai Academy of Social Sciences. 1 reel. M-H175 – 5 – $40.00 – cc Microforms [950]
Rood, John Romain *see* AN AGRICULTURAL CONCILIATION COMMISSIONER'S GUIDE.
Roode, C L de *see* LE COURRIER FRANCAIS DU CANADA
ROOIYARD SOCIOLOGICAL SURVEY OF AN URBAN NATIVE SLUM YARD / Hellmann, E – 5mf – 7 – uk Microform Academic [960]
Rooke, Ian *see* SOCIAL BEHAVIOUR OF THE NEW HOLLAND HONEYEATER
Rooke, Thomas George *see* INSPIRATION AND OTHER LECTURES
ROOM OF ONE'S OWN – Vancouver. v1-17. 1975/76-1994 – 9 – Can$20.00y – cn Micromedia [073]
Roon, Albrecht, Graf von *see* PAPERS
ROOPA-LEKHA : AN ILLUSTRATED QUARTERLY ART JOURNAL – (Includes Index v20-39) – v20-40. New Delhi. 1948-70. Lacking: v39(2) – 75mf – 8 – ne IDC [073]
Roorda, Taco *see* COMMENTARIUS IN VATICINIUM MICHAE
Roos, Carl *see* KLEINE DEUTSCHE LITERATURGESCHICHTE
Roos, Friedrich *see*
– DIE BRIEFE DES APOSTELS PAULUS UND DIE REDEN DES HERRN JESU
– DIE GESCHICHTLICHKEIT DES PENTATEUCHS...PRUEFUNG DER WELLHAUSEN'SCHEN HYPOTHESE
Roos, J F *see* DEUTSCHE ENCYCLOPAEDIE ODER ALLGEMEINES REALWOERTERBUCH ALLER KUENSTE UND WISSENSCHAFTEN, (AEL, ABT 1;2)
Roosevelt, Eleanor *see*
– IT'S UP TO THE WOMEN
– THE PAPERS OF ELEANOR ROOSEVELT, 1933-45
Roosevelt, Franklin D *see*
– MAP ROOM MESSAGES OF PRESIDENT ROOSEVELT (1939-45)
– THE MESSAGES BETWEEN FRANKLIN D. ROOSEVELT AND WINSTON S. CHURCHILL
Roosevelt, Theodore *see*
– ATRAVES DO SERTAO DO BRASIL
– THE NAVAL OPERATIONS OF THE WAR BETWEEN GREAT BRITAIN AND THE UNITED STATES, 1812-1815
– PAPERS
ROOT AND TUBER CROPS, PLANTAINS AND BANANAS IN DEVELOPING COUNTRIES : CHALLENGES AND OPPORTUNITIES – 1988 – 90p – it F.A.O. [634]
Root, Elihu *see* EXPERIMENTS IN GOVERNMENT AND THE ESSENTIALS OF THE CONSTITUTION
Root, James P *see* THE LAW OF CORPORATIONS, CONTAINING THE GENERAL STATUTES OF THE STATE OF ILLINOIS ON THE SUBJECT.
Root, Jean C *see* EDWARD IRVING
ROOT'S REPORTS / Connecticut. Supreme Court – (A Pre-NRS title) – v1-2. 1798-1802 (all publ) – 13mf – 9 – $19.50 – LLMC 90-005 – us L.L.M.C. [340]
ROOTS, TUBERS AND PLANTAINS IN FOOD SECURITY : IN SUB-SAHARAN AFRICA, IN LATIN AMERICA AND THE CARIBBEAN, IN THE PACIFIC – 1989 – 59p – it F.A.O. [630]
ROOTS, TUBERS, PLANTAINS AND BANANAS IN ANIMAL FEEDING – 1992 – 299p – it F.A.O. [636]
ROOTS, TUBERS, PLANTAINS AND BANANAS IN HUMAN NUTRITION – 1990 – 198p – it F.A.O. [640]
Rooy, K van *see* OUDHEIDKUNDIGE INLICHTINGEN IN KERKELIJK OPZICHT
Roper, E M *see* TU BEDAWIE
Ropes, J -H *see* DIE SPRUECHE JESU DIE IN DEN KANONISCHEN EVANGELIEN NICHT UEBERLIEFERT SIND (T.U.U. 1-14/2)
Ropes, James Hardy *see* THE APOSTOLIC AGE IN THE LIGHT OF MODERN CRITICISM
Ropp, Goswin von der *see* HANSERECESSE
Roquebrune, Robert de *see* LE NIGOG
Roques, J *see*
– HISTOIRE DES CHAMPIGNONS COMESTIBLES ET VENENEUX
– PHYTOGRAPHIE MEDICALE,...
Roques, M *see* ETUDES DE GEOGRAPHIE LINGUISTIQUE D'APRES L'ATLAS LINGUISTIQUE DE LA FRANCE
LE ROQUET – no. 1-28. Paris. mars-nov 1890 – 1 – fr A.C.R.P.P. [073]
Roquette, Otto *see*
– EIN BAUM IM ODENWALD
– GESCHICHTE DER DEUTSCHEN DICHTUNG VON DEN AELTESTEN DENKMAELERN BIS AUF DIE NEUZEIT
Rordam, H F *see* FORTAELLINGER AF DANMARKS KIRKEHISTORIE FRA 1517 TIL 1848
Rordam, Holger Frederik *see* DANSKE KIRKELOVE SAMT UDVALG AF ANDRE BESTEMMELSER VEDRORENDE KIRKEN, SKOLEN OG DE FATTIGES FORSORGELSE FRA REFORMATIONEN INDTIL CHRISTIAN V'S DANSKE LOV, 1536-1683
Ros Biosca, Godofredo *see* DEFENSA...DIOCESIS DE PLASENCIA...VICARIO CAPITULAR
Ros, D *see* L'ABRI TOCA DO SALITRE, SITE TYPIQUE DE LA SOUS-TRADITION SALITRE
A ROSA – Codajas, Amazonas. 18 Dez 1897 – 1,5,6 – bl Biblioteca [072]
ROSA CANDOLLEANA, SEU DESCRIPTIO NOVAE SPECIEI GENERIS ROSAE / Thory, C A – Paris. 1819. B-5763 2 – 8 – ne IDC [580]
LA ROSA DE PALERMO, ANTIDOTO DE LA PESTE Y DE TODO MAL CONTAGIOSO / Calasibeta, M – Madrid, 1668 – 5mf – 9 – sp Cultura [616]
LA ROSA DEL GUAYAS : BIOGRAFIA DE LA R.M. MERCEDES DE JESUS MOLINA / Fajardo, Eliecer L – Madrid: Razon y Fe, 1927 – 1 – sp Bibl Santa Ana [240]
Rosa, Enrico *see* LOS JESUITAS DESDE SUS ORIGENES HASTA NUESTROS DIAS; APUNTES HISTORICOS
ROSA, LA DE VILLAMBRO / Gonzalez Gonzalez, Valeriano – Madrid: Biblioteca Patria, S.A. – 1 – sp Bibl Santa Ana [946]
Rosa, Narcisse *see* LA CONSTRUCTION DES NAVIRES A QUEBEC ET SES ENVIRONS
ROSA REDUTEA, SEU DESCRIPTIO NOVAE SPECIEI GENERIS ROSAE / Thory, C A – Paris. 1817. B-5762 2 – 8 – ne IDC [580]
Rosa Roque, Julio *see* GUIA DE CACERES Y SU PROVINCIA
Rosa, Salvatore *see* SATIRE, LIRICHE, LETTERE, CON NOTE DI ANTON MARIA SALVINI E DI ALTRI
Rosaccio, G *see* VIAGGIO DA VENETIA, A COSTANTINOPOLI PER MARE, E PER TERRA, ET INSIEME QUELLO DI TERRA SANTA
ROSACEARUM MONOGRAPHIA / Trattinick, L – 4v. Vindobonae. 1823-24. B-7381 1 – 8 – ne IDC [580]
Rosadi, Giovanni *see* THE TRIAL OF JESUS
Rosado H de Sotomayor, Jose *see* ALBUM (POESIAS)
Rosado, Joaquin *see*
– BOSQUEJO HISTORICO DE LA VILLA DE CECLAVIN
– GUIA DE LA CIUDAD DE PLASENCIA (CACERES) POR...ANO 1906
LE ROSAIRE *see* LA ROSAIRE POUR TOUS
LE ROSAIRE ET LES AUTRES DEVOTIONS DOMINICAINES *see* REVUE DOMINICAINE
LA ROSAIRE POUR TOUS – (Suivi de: Le Rosaire) – St-Hyacinthe [Quebec]: Peres dominicains du couvent de St-Hyacinthe, [1897?-1931?] – 9 – cn C.I.H.M. [240]
ROSAL : DEDICADO A MULHER ALAGOANA – Maceio, Alagoas. 31 Ago 1903 – 1,5,6 – bl Biblioteca [072]
ROSALIE RIP-SAW – Rosalie, NE. -w. Oct 1911-May 1916; Apr 1918-Apr 1926; Sept 1926-Apr 1945 – 1 – us NE Hist [071]
ROSALIND AND HELEN : A MODERN ECLOGUE, WITH OTHER POEMS / Shelley, Percy Bysshe – London: Printed for C. and J. Ollier, 1819 – 1 roll – 1 – 1-55879-738-6 – uk Libr Preservation [810]
Rosambert, Andre *see* LA VEUVE EN DROIT CANONIQUE
Rosanoff, S *see* RECHERCHES ANATOMIQUES SUR LES MELOBESIEES
Rosario, D. do *see* THEATRO ECCLESIASTICO EM QUE SE ACHAO MUITOS DOCUMENTOS DE CANTOCHAO
Rosario, Ruben del *see* LA LENGUA DE PUERTO RICO. ENSAYOS
ROSAS Y ESPIGAS / Spinola de Gironza, Araceli – Madrid: Graficas Nebrija, 1950 – 1 – sp Bibl Santa Ana [946]
ROSAS Y LIRIOS / Neria Serranos, Vicente – Zafra: Imp. La Moderna de Emilio Hernandez, 1915 – 1 – sp Bibl Santa Ana [630]
Rosaura la de Trujillo *see* RELACION DE UN CASO LASTIMOSO QUE SUCEDIO A UNA...DONCELLA...NATURAL DE LA CIUDAD DE TRUJILLO
Rosbrook, Alden Ivan *see*
– 1924 SUPPLEMENT TO ROSBROOK ON NEW YORK CORPORATIONS (2D ED.) AND BENDER'S CORPORATION MANUAL.
– BENDER'S CORPORATION MANUAL, STATE OF NEW YORK.
– A TREATISE ON THE LAW OF CORPORATIONS IN NEW YORK, INCLUDING THE BUSINESS COPORATIONS LAW.
Roscher, Wilhelm Heinrich *see* UEBER SELENO UND VERWYANDTES
Roscius, L *see* DOUBLE FORTRESSE SACRAMENTALE DE FOY
Roscoe, Henry *see* A DIGEST OF THE LAW OF EVIDENCE IN CRIMINAL CASES

Roscoe, J *see*
- THE BAGESU AND OTHER TRIBES OF THE UGANDA PROTECTORATE
- THE BANYANKOLE
- NORTHERN BANTU. AN ACCOUNT OF SOME CENTRAL AFRICAN TRIBES OF THE UGANDA PROTECTORATE

THE ROSCOE PAPERS – (BRRAM). Liverpool Central Library. 1792-1831 – 2r – 1 – uk Microform Academic [025]
THE ROSCOE POUND PAPERS / Pound, Roscoe – (Pt 1: Correspondence 1907-64 $14,300. Pt 2: Writings, Lectures, Addresses, Teaching Notes and Miscellaneous Manuscripts. Pt 3: Personal, Biographical, Bibliographical, Miscellany and Activities $8,520. Guides only $230.00 ea) – 1 – us UPA [340]
Roscoe, Thomas *see* WANDERINGS AND EXCURSIONS IN SOUTH WALES, WITH THE SCENERY OF THE RIVER WYE
Roscoe, W *see* MONANDRIAN PLANTS OF ORDER SCITAMINEAE, CHIEFLY DRAWN FROM LIVING SPECIMENS IN THE BOTANIC GARDEN AT LIVERPOOL
Roscoe, William *see* LETTERS TO THOMAS WILIAM COKE
Roscoe, William E *see* HISTORY OF SCHOHARIE COUNTY
ROSCOMMON AND LEITRIM GAZETTE – Boyle, Ireland. 1851-62; 1864-74; 1876-17 Jun 1882. -w. 11 reels – 1 – uk British Libr Newspaper [072]
ROSCOMMON CONSTITUTIONALIST – Boyle, Ireland. -w. 19 Jan, 16 March, 20 April 1889-7 Nov 1891. 1 reel – 1 – uk British Libr Newspaper [072]
ROSCOMMON HERALD – 1882-1980 – ca 94r – 1 – ie Microforms [941]
ROSCOMMON HERALD – Roscommon, Ireland. -d.1882-1986. 120 reels – 1 – PS27.50r – ie European Micro [072]
ROSCOMMON JOURNAL – Ireland. -w. 12 July 1828-7 Oct 1848; 13 Jan-10 March, 25 Aug 1849-28 Dec 1918; 25 Jan, 15 March 1919-26 Dec 1925; 1 Jan-31 Dec 1927. 43 reels – 1 – uk British Libr Newspaper [072]
ROSCOMMON WEEKLY MESSENGER – Ireland. Roscommon Messenger. -w. 10 May 1848-21 28 Dec 1935. Lacking 1887. 45 1 2 reels – 1 – uk British Libr Newspaper [072]
THE ROSE AND THE RING : OR, THE HISTORY OF PRINCE GIGLIO AND PRINCE BULBO, A FIRE-SIDE PANTOMIME FOR GREAT AND SMALL CHILDREN BY MR. M.A. TITMARSH / Thackeray, William Makepeace – London: Smith, Elder, and Co., 1855 – 1 roll – 1 – 1-55879-275-9 – uk Libr Preservation [820]
Rose, Arthur P *see*
- AN ILLUSTRATED HISTORY OF LYON COUNTY
- AN ILLUSTRATED HISTORY OF YELLOW MEDICINE COUNTY

Rose, E A *see* METHODIST NEW CONNEXION CIRCUITS AND MINISTERS, 1797-1907
ROSE EL-YOUSSEF – 1925- – 52mf per y – 9 – $300.00y – us Ross [072]
ROSE ET COLAS : COMDEDIE EN UN ACTE / Monsigny, P-A – Paris: Bailleux, 176- – 1 – us Sibley [780]
Rose, Felicitas *see* PROVINZMAEDEL
Rose, George Maclean *see* A CYCLOPAEDIA OF CANADIAN BIOGRAPHY BEING CHIEFLY MEN OF THE TIME
Rose, H A *see* A GLOSSARY OF THE TRIBES AND CASTES OF THE PUNJAB AND THE NORTH-WEST FRONTIER PROVINCE
Rose, J *see* INTERNATIONAL JOURNAL OF ENVIRONMENTAL STUDIES
Rose, James H *see* THE STORY OF AMERICAN PRESSED GLASS OF THE LACY PERIOD 1825-1850
Rose, Moritz *see* DIE WALLFAHRT NACH LOURDES
ROSE NEIGHBORHOOD SKETCHES OF WAYNE COUNTY / Roe, Alfred – Also Butler, Wolcott, Huron, Sodus, Lyons, and Savannah. Worchester, 1893. New York Reel 37. (The Cox Library Collection) – 5 – us Americana [978]
THE ROSE OF LIFE / Braddon, Mary Elizabeth – British Fiction Archive: Unit 5 – 9 – uk Bell [830]
THE ROSE OF SHARON MONTHLY – (Cont by: The Monthly Rose) – Bridgewater, NS: D F Hutchinson, 1868 – 9 – cn C.I.H.M. [240]
THE ROSE OF SHARON MONTHLY *see* THE MONTHLY ROSE
Rose, Shannon *see* THE RATE OF TEMPERATURE REDUCTION IN DEEP HUMAN MUSCLE FOLLOWING THERMAL ULTRASOUND
Rose, Walter M *see* ROSE'S NOTES ON THE TEXAS REPORTS, 1910 ED.
Rose, William *see* MEN, MYTHS, AND MOVEMENTS IN GERMAN LITERATURE
ROSE WOOD, OR, THE OCTOROON'S BRIDE / Fairweather, Jean – Montreal?: s.n., 1889 (Montreal: J. Robinson). 02942. (Pre-1900 Canadiana) – 9 – cn C.I.H.M. [830]
ROSE-BELFORD'S CANADIAN MONTHLY AND NATIONAL REVIEW – (Cont: The Canadian Monthly and National Review) – Toronto: Rose-Belford Pub Co, [187-?-18– or 19–] – 9 – cn C.I.H.M. [971]
ROSE-BELFORD'S CANADIAN MONTHLY AND NATIONAL REVIEW – v1-8. Jul 1878-Jun 1882 – 1 – cn Precision [971]
ROSE-BELFORD'S CANADIAN MONTHLY AND NATIONAL REVIEW *see* THE CANADIAN MONTHLY AND NATIONAL REVIEW
ROSEBUD : REPORT ON THE TRANSITIONAL HOUSING EXPERIMENT, ROSEBUD INDIAN RESERVATION / U.S. Department of Housing and Urban Development – 1969 – 1mf – 9 – $5.00f – us Ross [360]
ROSEBUD COUNTY NEWS – Forsyth. Mont. 1902-1905 – 1 – us UMI [071]
ROSEBUD COUNTY RECORD – Forsyth. Mont. 1924-1926 – 1 – us UMI [071]
ROSEBUD SIOUX HERALD – 1963-69.(American Indian Periodicals in the Princeton University Library). 14 fiches – 9 – $70.00 – us UPA [073]
ROSEBUD TEPEE TALK – 1959-68. (American Indian Periodicals in the Princeton University Library) – 17mf – 9 – $75.00 – us UPA [305]
ROSEBURG CHIEFTAIN – Roseburg, OR. -w. 4 Sept 1931-6 Aug 1943. 3 rolls – 1 – us U.O. Library [071]
ROSEBURG ENSIGN – Roseburg OR. Apr 30 1867-June 10 1871 – 1 – us U.O. Library [071]
ROSEBURG EXPRESS – Roseburg OR. Nov 17 1859 – 1 – us U.O. Library [071]
ROSEBURG REVIEW – Roseburg, OR. -d. 18 Oct 1906-31 Mar 1920. – 1 – us U.O. Library [071]
ROSEBURG REVIEW – Roseburg, OR. -w. – 1 – us U.O. Library [071]
ROSEBURG TWICE A WEEK REVIEW – Roseburg OR. July 31 1893-Dec 31 1903 – 1 – us U.O. Library [071]
ROSEDALE FIRST BAPTIST CHURCH. ROSEDALE, OKLAHOMA : CHURCH RECORDS – Feb 1930-Feb 1977. 536p – 1 – 24.12 – us Baptist [240]
ROSEDALE TOPICS – Toronto. 1921-23 – 1 – 75.00 – cn McLaren [971]
Rosegger, Peter *see*
- ALS ICH JUNG NOCH WAR
- AUSGEWAEHLT WERKE
- BERGPREDIGTEN
- GESAMMELTE WERKE
- DER LEX VON GUTENHAG
- MEINE FERIEN
- NEUE WALDGESCHICHTEN
- DIE SCHRIFTEN DES WALDSCHULMEISTERS
- DIE WALDBAUERN
- WALDHEIMAT
- ZITHER UND HACKBRET

THE ROSEHARP – Toronto: Roseharp Patriotic Academy, 1834?-18– – 9 – cn C.I.H.M. [420]
Rose-Innes, R W *see* REV JOHN BROWNLEE
ROSELAND GAZETTE – Roseland, NE. -w. Dec 1894-Nov 1905, scattered issues missing – 1 – us NE Hist [071]
Rosell, J F *see* EL VERDADERO CONOCIMIENTO DE LA PESTE, SUS CAUSAS, SENALES Y PRESERVACION...
Rosell y Lopez, Cayetano *see* CRONICAS DE LOS REYES DE CASTILLA, DESDE DON ALFONSO DE SABIO, HASTA LOS CATOLICOS DON FERNANDO Y DONA ISABEL
ROSEMEAD REVIEW – Rosemead, CA. 1970-1971 – 4r – 1 – $200.00 – H04037 – us Library Micro [071]
THE ROSEMERE JOURNAL – Rosemere, Canada. 1 nov 1956; v1 n9. 21 fev 1957 – 1r – 1 – Can$25.00 – cn Can Microfilming [073]
Rosemont, Louis Reutter de *see* DE L'EMBAUMEMENT AVANT ET APRES JESUS CHRIST
Rosen, Julius *see* DER MANN IN DER FLASCHE
Rosen, Sven *see* SKRIFTER OCH BREF, SAMLADE OCH UTGIFNA AF EMANUEL LINDERHOLM
Rosenau, William *see*
- A BRIEF HISTORY OF CONGREGATION OHEB SHALOM, BALTIMORE, MD
- SOME ANCIENT ORIENTAL ACADEMIES

Rosenbach, A SW *see* AN AMERICAN JEWISH BIBLIOGRAPHY, BEING A LIST OF BOOKS AND PAMPHLETS BY JEWS OR RELATING TO THEM; PRINTED... UNTIL 1850
Rosenberg, Alfred *see* FRIEDRICH WILHELME
Rosenberg, Curt *see* BILDER AUS EINEM LEBEN
Rosenberg, Gary *see* SOCIAL WORK IN HEALTH CARE
Rosenberg, Isaak *see* LEHRBUCH DER SAMARITANISCHEN SPRACHE UND LITERATUR
Rosenberg, Walter *see* DER KAISER UND DIE PROTESTANTEN IN DEN JAHREN 1537-1539
Rosenbloom, Bert *see* JOURNAL OF MARKETING CHANNELS
Rosenbuch, C H F *see*
- ELEMENTE DER GESTEINSLEHRE
- MIKROSKOPISCHE PHYSIOGRAPHIE DER MINERALIEN UND GESTEINE

Rosenfeld, Anatol *see* DOZE ESTUDOS
Rosenfeld, W *see* GOTTFRIED KELLER
Rosengart, Cecel *see* LE CRIME COMME PRODUIT SOCIAL
Rosenheim, J *see* SEFER HA-YOVEL LE-YA'AKOV ROSENHEIM
Rosenmann, M *see* STUDIEN ZUM BUCHE TOBIT
Rosenmueller, Max Clemens *see* JOHANN ULRICH VON KOENIG
Rosenmund, R *see* DIE AELTESTEN BIOGRAPHIEN DES HEILIGEN NORBERT
Rosenstock-Huessy, Eugen *see* DAS GEHEIMNIS DER UNIVERSITAET
ROSENSTOCK'S BUSINESS DIRECTORY OF THE CITY OF MANILLA – 1-45. 1903-39 40 – 1 – us Res Libr [380]
ROSENSTOCK'S MANILA CITY DIRECTORY – v21. (1915). Manila: Rosenstock, Elser. Continued as: Rosenstock's Directory of China and Manila.1281 – 1 – us U.W. Library [950]
Rosenthal, A *see* THE TALMUD EDITIONS OF DANIEL BOMBERG
Rosenthal, D A *see* SYNOPSIS PLANTARUM DIAPHORICARUM
Rosenthal, Gisela *see* BUERGERLICHES NATURGEFUEHL UND OFFIZIELLE LANDSCHAFTSMALEREI IN FRANKREICH 1753-1824
Rosenthal, Hermann *see* WORTE DES SAMMLERS (KOHELITH)...IN DEUTSCHE REIME GEBRACHT
Rosenthal, J L *see* TOLEDOT HEVRAT MARBEI HA-HASKALAH BE-YISRA'EL
Rosenzweig, F *see*
- BRIEFE
- JEHUDA HALEVI
- JEHUDA HALEVI, SECHZIG HYMNEN UND GEDICHTE
- JEHUDA HALEVI. ZWEIUNDNEUNZIG HYMNEN UND GEDICHTE
- KLEINERE SCHRIFTEN
- DER STERN DER ERLOESUNG. 1-2-3

Roser, Andreas *see*
- SCHELLING UND HEGEL. ODER DIE NEUESTE PHILOSOPHIE IM VERNICHTUNGSKRIEGE MIT SICH SELBST BEGRIFFEN
- UEBER DEN ZUFALL

LES ROSES D'EUROPE DE L'HERBIER CREPIN / Boulenger, G A – 2v. (Bull. Jard. Bot. Etat Bruxelles, 1924-1925, v10, p1-417; 1931-32, v12, p1-542). B-8125/1 – 9 – ne IDC [580]
ROSE'S HAND-BOOK OF DOMINION POLITICS, ETC., ETC., ETC – Comp. and ed. by A.C. Campbell. Toronto: Rose, 1886. 00980. (Pre-1900 Canadiana) – 9 – cn C.I.H.M. [971]
ROSE'S NOTES ON THE TEXAS REPORTS, 1910 ED. / Texas. Supreme Court; ed by Rose, Walter M – (Includes 1913 suppl vol) – San Francisco: Bancroft-Whitney. Bks 1-6. 1910 – 105mf – 9 – $157.50 – LLMC 92-410 – us L.L.M.C. [340]
ROSES: OR A MONOGRAPH OF THE GENUS ROSA / Andrews, H C – 2V. 8033 1. 1805-1828 – 9 – ne IDC [580]
ROSETEAGUE / Bray, Anna Eliza – British Fiction Archive: Unit 2 – 9 – uk Bell [830]
THE ROSETTA STONE : THE DECREES OF MEMPHIS AND CANOPUS / Budge, E A W – 3v. London, 1904. BNE20,018 1 – 9 – ne IDC [410]
ROSETUM EXERCITIORUM SPIRITUALIUM – Impr. Jacobus de Pfortzen. Basel, 1504 – 23mf – 8 – ne Slangenburg [290]
ROSEVILLE TRIBUNE – Auburn. Calif. 1916-1944 – 1 – us UMI [071]
Rosicky, Rose *see* HISTORY OF CZECHS (BOHEMIANS) IN NEBRASKA
Rosin, B F *see* PARA SAKSI
Rosin, David *see*
- DIE ETHIK DES MAIMONIDES
- REIME UND GEDICHTE DES ABRAHAM IBN ESRA

ROSINA [BY] SHIELD [SIC]. OVERTURE / Shield, W – (Arranged for pianoforte) – Philadelphia: B Carr & Co, 179-? – 1 – us Sibley [780]
Rosinis, C de *see* LYCEUM LATERANENSE
Roskoff, Gustav *see* DIE SIMONSSAGE: NACH IHRER ENTSTEHUNG, FORM UND BEDEUTUNG UND DER HERACLESMYTHUS
ROSLAGEN – Norrtalje, Sweden. 1911-16 – 2r – 1 – sw Kungliga [072]
ROSLAGENS NYHETER – Norrtalje, Sweden. 1909-23 – 14r – 1 – sw Kungliga [072]
ROSLAGENS TIDNING – Norrtalje, Sweden. 1902-04 – 2r – 1 – sw Kungliga [072]
ROSLAGSBLADET – Norrtalje, Sweden. 1907-08 – 1 reel – 1 – sw Kungliga [072]
ROSLAGSBLADET – OEsthammar, Enkoeping. 1879-94 – 9 – sw Kungliga [072]
ROSLAGSPOSTEN – Stockholm, Sweden. 1946-52 – 3r – 1 – sw Kungliga [072]
Rosmini, Antonio *see* DELLE CINQUE PIAGHE DELLA SANTA CHIESA
ROSMINI. DOCTRINAS ETICO-JURIDICAS (SINTESIS) / Perez Bueno, Fernando – Madrid: Imp. Blass y Cia, 1919 – sp Bibl Santa Ana [340]
Rosner, Ferdinand *see* BITTERES LEIDEN
Rosner, L *see* ERINNERUNGEN AN ANZENGRUBER
Rosny *see* ADONIS OU LE BON NEGRE
Rosny, J H *see* LA GUERRE ANGLO-BOER
Rosny, Leon de *see*
- ANTHOLOGIE JAPONAISE. POESIES ANCIENNES ET MODERNES DES INSULAIRES DU NIPPON
- ETUDES ASIATIQUES DE GEOGRAPHIE ET D'HISTOIRE
- INTRODUCTION A L'ETUDE DE LA LITERATURE JAPONAISE
- KAMI YO NO MAKI
- LES PEUPLES ORIENTAUX CONNUS DES ANCIENS CHINOIS
- SUR LES AINO
- VARIETES ORIENTALES HISTORIQUES, GEOGRAPHIQUES, SCIENTIFIQUES, BIBLIOGRAPHIQUES ET LITTERAIRES

Roso de Luna, Mario *see*
- ATLANTES EXTREMENOS?
- AVANCES ARQUEOLOGICOS EN SANTA AMALIA
- BEETHOVEN, TEOSOFO, UN CAPITULO DE LA OBRA EL...DRAMA LIRICO DE...
- EL BIERZO. NUEVAS LAPIDAS ROMANAS
- CONFERENCIAS TEOSOFICAS EN AMERICA DEL SUR
- COSAS DEL TAPETE VERDE
- DE GENTES DEL OTRO MUNDO
- DEL ARBOL DE LAS HESPERIDES
- EN EL UMBRAL DEL MISTERIO
- LA ESCRITURA OGNEICA EN EXTREMADURA
- EVOLUCION SOLAIRE ET SERIES ASTRO-CHIMIQUES PAR...
- EXCAVACIONES EN LA SIERRA DE SANTA CRUZ
- HACIA LA GNOSIS
- INSCRIPCION ROMANA DE TITULCIA
- LAPIDA VISIGOTICA DE HERGUIJUELA
- LOSA SEPULCRAL DE SOLANA DE CABANAS EN EL PARTIDO DE LOGROSAN (CACERES)
- UNA MARTIR DEL SIGLO 19TH. HELENA PETROUNA BLAVATSKY
- NOTAS ARQUEOLOGICAS
- NOTAS EPIGRAFICAS
- NUEVA INSCRIPCION ROMANA DE VILLAMESIAS...
- NUEVA INSCRIPCION ROMANA DEL ESCURIAL (TRUJILLO)
- NUEVAS INSCRIPCIONES DE IBAHERNANDO, CUMBRE Y SANTA ANA
- NUEVAS INSCRIPCIONES ROMANAS DE LA REGION NORBENSE
- PROTOHISTORIA EXTREMENA
- RUINAS PROTOHISTORICAS DE LOGROSAN
- EL SIMBOLISMO DE LAS RELIGIONES DEL MUNDO Y EL PROBLEMA DE LA FIDELIDAD. COMENTARIOS A LA DOCTRINA SECRETA
- SIMBOLOGIA ARCAICA
- SOBRE LAS CITAMAS EXTREMENAS
- LAS VIAS ROMANAS DEL NORDESTE DE MERIDA

- EL VUELO DE ISIS A LASMIL Y UNA NOCHES OCULTISTAS
- WAGNER, MITOLOGO Y OCULTISTA (EL DRAMA MUSICAL DE WAGNER Y LOS MISTERIOS DE LA ANTIGUEDAD), PROLOGO DE ADOLFO BONILLA Y SAN MARTIN

ROSPIS' OTDEL'NYKH KNIG PO SEL'SKOMU KHOZIAISTVU NAPECHATANNYKH S 1730 PO 1884 GOD / Pede, I, N N -v – M. 1889. BR-7205 2 – 8 – ne IDC [070]

ROSPIS' ROSSIISKIM KNIGAM DLIA CHTENIIA, IZ BIBLIOTEKI ALEKSANDRA SMIRDINA, SISTEMATICHESKIM PORIADKOM RASPOLOZHENNAIA / AF. Smirdin Biblioteka – Spb. 1828. BR-4376 2 – 8 – ne IDC [010]

Ross, A Hastings *see* THE CHURCH-KINGDOM

Ross, A M *see* THE FLORA OF CANADA

ROSS AND CROMARTY, 1837 : BRITISH ISLES CENSUS DIRECTORIES PROJECT, SCOTLAND. VOL 52 – 1mf – 9 – A$9.00 – at Vine [941]

ROSS AND CROMARTY, 1852 : BRITISH ISLES CENSUS DIRECTORIES PROJECT, SCOTLAND. VOL 18 – 1mf – 9 – A$9.00 – at Vine [941]

Ross, Carolyn K *see* PREDISPOSING, REINFORCING, AND ENABLING FACTORS IDENTIFIED BY DIVISION 1 COACHES OF WOMEN'S CROSS-COUNTRY TEAMS AND THE RELATIONSHIP TO THE PERCEIVED ONSET OF EATING DISORDERS

Ross, D H *see* EDUCATING HANDICAPPED YOUNG PEOPLE IN EASTERN AND SOUTHERN AFRICA

Ross, Frederick Augustus *see* THE DOCTRINE OF REPROBATION

ROSS GAZETTE – Ross on Wyne, England. 1867-96; 1898-1983. -w.82 1- – 1 – uk British Libr Newspaper [072]

Ross, George W *see* THE HON. ALEXANDER MACKENZIE: HIS LIFE AND TIMES

ROSS GROVE BAPTIST CHURCH. SHELBY, NORTH CAROLINA : CHURCH RECORDS – 1881-1963 – 1 – 20.61 – us Baptist [240]

Ross, James *see* A HISTORY OF CONGREGATIONAL INDEPENDENCY IN SCOTLAND

Ross, James Campbell *see* PAPERS RELATING TO PAPUA NEW GUINEA, C. 1941-1945

Ross, James Clark *see*
- NARRATIVE OF A SECOND VOYAGE IN SEARCH OF A NORTHWEST PASSAGE. INCL THE REP. OF J. C. ROSS, AND THE DISCOVERY OF THE NORTHERN MAGNETIC POLE
- A VOYAGE OF DISCOVERY AND RESEARCH IN THE SOUTHERN AND ANTARCTIC REGIONS, DURING THE YEARS 1839-43
- A VOYAGE OF DISCOVERY. FOR THE PURPOSE OF EXPLORING BAFFIN'S BAY

Ross, James R *see* A COMPARISON OF DIRECT INSTRUCTION AND COMPUTER-ASSISTED INSTRUCTION ON LEARNING A MOTOR SKILL BY FOURTH GRADE STUDENTS

Ross, John *see*
- MEMOIRS AND CORRESPONDENCE OF ADMIRAL LORD DE SAUMAREZ, FROM ORIGINAL PAPERS
- MISSION METHODS IN MANCHURIA
- OLD WANG
- A TREATISE ON NAVIGATION BY STEAM: COMPRISING A HISTORY OF THE STEAM ENGINE
- A VOYAGE OF DISCOVERY, MADE UNDER THE ORDERS OF THE ADMIRALTY, IN HIS MAJESTY'S SHIPS ISABELLA AND ALEXANDER FOR THE PURPOSE OF EXPLORING BAFFIN'S BAY, AND ENQUIRING INTO THE POSSIBILITY OF A NORTH-WEST PASSAGE

Ross, Mary Jane *see* TYPED TRAVEL DIARY

Ross, Peter *see*
- HISTORY OF LONG ISLAND
- SAINT ANDREW: THE DISCIPLE, THE MISSIONARY, THE PATRON SAINT

Ross, Peter V *see* INHERITANCE TAXATION; A TREATISE ON LEGACY SUCCESSION AND INHERITANCE TAXES UNDER THE LAWS OF ARKANSAS, CALIFORNIA, COLORADO.

Ross, William Stewart *see* THE BOOK OF VIRGINS AND LAYS AND LEGENDS OF THE CHURCH AND THE WORLD

ROSSBACH UND ZORNDORF / Naso, Eckart von – Bielefeld: Velhagen & Klasing, [1943] – 1r – 1 – us U.W. Library [830]

ROSSBACHER ZEITUNG – Rossbach (Hranice), Czechoslovakia. 3 Nov 1928-1938 – 5r – 1 – gw Mikrofilm [072]

LA ROSSE-QUI-DETELLE : GENESE, CEREMONIE D'INITIATION, STATUTS EQUESTRES, CANTATE / Morin, Victor – Montreal, 1956. SEM105P828 – 1mf – 9 – Can$2.25 – cn Bibl Nat [780]

Rossetti, Christina *see*
- THE FACE OF THE DEEP
- NEW POEMS BY CHRISTINA ROSSETTI
- A PAGEANT
- SING-SONG
- TIME FLIES

Rossetti, Dante Gabriel *see*
- BALLADS AND SONNETS
- THE COMPLETE POETICAL WORKS OF DANTE GABRIEL ROSSETTI
- LETTERS OF DANTE GABRIEL ROSSETTI TO WILLIAM ALLINGHAM, 1854-1870
- PAINTINGS AND DRAWINGS

Rossetti, William Michael *see*
- THE DIARIES OF WILLIAM MICHAEL ROSSETTI
- THE DIARY OF DR. JOHN WILLIAM POLIDORI, 1816
- LIFE OF JOHN KEATS
- NEW POEMS BY CHRISTINA ROSSETTI
- THE POETICAL WORKS OF MRS. FELICIA HEMANS...

THE ROSSETTIS : DANTE GABRIEL AND CHRISTINA / Cary, Elisabeth Luther – New York, London: G.P. Putnam's Sons, Knickerbocker Press, [1903, c1900] – 1 roll – 1 – 1-55879-462-X – uk Libr Preservation [420]

ROSSFORD RECORD – Rossford, Ohio. 1965-72 – 2r – 1 – $32.50r – us Archival [071]

ROSSFORD RECORD JOURNAL – Rossford, Ohio. 1981- – 2r – 1 – $32.50r – us Archival [071]

Rossi, Cav. Battista, Giovanni de *see* BULLETINO DI ARCHEOLOGIA

Rossi, D de *see* RACCOLTA DI STATUE ANTICHE E MODERNE DATA IN LUCE SOTTO I GLORIOSI AUSPICJ, DELLA SANTITA DI N.S. PAPA CLEMENTE 11...

Rossi, F *see* PAPYRUS DE TURIN. FACSIMILES

Rossi, G B de *see* ROMA SOTTERRANEA CRISTIANA

Rossi, Giovanni Battista de *see* PIANTE ICONOGRAFICHE E PRO PETTICHE DI ROMA ANTERIORI AL SEC. 16

ROSSI ISKAI A SOTSIALISTICHESKAI A ARMII A : 1. RAZVAL IMPERIALISTSKO I ARMII. 2. SOTSIALISTICHESKAI A KRASNAI A ARMII A. 3. V CHEM SILA KRASNO I ARMII / Bergman, Genrikh – Moskva: Izd-vo Vseros. t sentr. ispolnitelnogo kom-ta Sovetov r., s., k. i k. deputatov, 1919 – 1 – CSUX89-B691 – us Hoover Inst Photo [947]

ROSSI ISKAIA REVOLIUTSIIA I GOSUDARSTVENNAIA DUMA / Bickerman, Joseph – S-Peterburg: Kn-vo "Novoe t-vo", 1906 – 1 – CSUX89-B3567 – us Hoover Inst Photo [947]

Rossi, J B de *see*
- BIBLIOTHECA JUDAICA ANTICHRISTIANA...
- MSS CODICES HEBRAICI BIBLIOTH... ACCEDIT APPENDIX QUA CONTINENTUR MSS CODICES RELIQUI AL. LINGUARUM

Rossi, Michelangelo *see* MADRIGALI DEL S. MICHEL'ANGELO ROSSI

ROSSICA ET SOVIETICA / Victoroff-Toporoff, V – Saint-Cloud, 1931 – 3mf – 9 – ne IDC [947]

Rossignol, Claude *see* LE BAILLIAGE DE DIJON APRES LA BATAILLE DE ROCROY

ROSSII A : EZHENEDEI ELNAI A GAZETA – (Library has: no. 1-37 (Aug. 28, 1927-May 26, 1928); some issues slightly mutilated) – Paris: Rossii a, 1927-1928. 1v – 1 – CSUX86-S548 – us Hoover Inst Photo [947]

ROSSII A I KITA I / Badmaev, Petr Aleksandrovich – S-Peterburg: G.P. Pozharov, 1900 – 1 – CSUX91-B4184 – us Hoover Inst Photo [327]

ROSSII A (NEW YORK, N.Y.: 1932) – (Library has: Jan. 1, 1946-Dec. 29, 1962; Jan. 7, 1966-Jun. 20, 1973[some issues wanting]) – New York: Rossiya Pub. Co., 1932- – 1 – CSUX87-S278 – us Hoover Inst Photo [947]

ROSSII A (PARIS, FRANCE: 1927) *see* ROSSII A

ROSSIIA – (Backfile through 1998 $85r) – 1999- – 2r per y – 1 – $160.00 standing order – us Ross [072]

ROSSIIA – (Backfile through 1998 $85r) – Russia, 1999- – 2r per y standing order – 1 – us Ross [072]

ROSSIIA I BOLSHEVIZM = RUSSIA AND BOLSHEWISM : MATERIALY PO ISTORII REVOLIUTSII I BORBY S BOLSHEVIZMOM / Gutman, Anatolii – V Shankhaie: Pechatano v tip. Russkago t-va pechatnago i izdatelskago diela, 1921- – 1 – CSUX88-B6892 – us Hoover Inst Photo [320]

ROSSIIA I EIA NARODY / Gredeskul', N A – Pg, 1916 – 1mf – 1 – ILM-2505/1 – ne IDC [327]

ROSSIIA I REVOLIUTSIIA / Parvus – Spb., 1906. 264p – 3mf – 9 – ne IDC [320]

ROSSIIA V MIROVOI VOINIE 1914-1915 G / Danilov, I Uri i Nikiforovich – Berlin: "Slovo", 1924 – 1 – CSUX89-B3814 – us Hoover Inst Photo [355]

ROSSIIA V PIS'MENNAKH / Remizov, A – Moscow, Berlin, 1922. v1. 220p. BR-844 2 – 8 – ne IDC [460]

ROSSIISKAIA BIBLIOGRAFIIA – Vestnik russkoi pechati. v. 1-4. Spb. 1879-82. B-1848 2 – 8 – ne IDC [010]

ROSSIISKAIA GAZETA – (1994 11r $935. 1995-98 12r per y $1,020. Backfile through 1993 $85r) – 1999- – 12r per y – 1 – $960.00 standing order – us Ross [072]

ROSSIISKAIA RODOSLOVNAIA KNIGA / Dolgorukov, P V – 4pts. Spb. 1854-57. BR-6018 2 – 8 – ne IDC [947]

Rossiiskaia Sotsial' Demokraticheskaia Rabochaia Partiia *see*
- BOL'SHEVIKI ZAPADNOI SIBIRI V PERIOD PERVOI RUSSKOI REVOLIUTSII 1905-1907 GG
- PROTOKOLY

ROSSIISKIE VESTI – Moscow: Rossiiskie vesti, 1991- – 2mf – 9 – $199.95y – us East View [320]

ROSSIISKII GOSUDARSTVENNYI ISTORICHESKII ARKHIV-RGIA = RUSSIAN STATE HISTORICAL ARCHIVES : MATERIALY DLIA ISTORII RUSSKOGO FLOTA 4. 1-17 (1865-1904) / MATERIALS FOR HISTORY OF RUSSIAN NAVY – 228mf – 9 – $1,140.00 – us Ross [355]

ROSSIISKII GOSUDARSTVENNYI ISTORICHESKII ARKHIV-RGIA = RUSSIAN STATE HISTORICAL ARCHIVES : POLNOE SOBRANIE POSTANOVLENII I RASPORIAZHENII PO VEDOMSTVU PRAVOSLAVNOGO ISPOVEDANIIA ROSSIISKOI IMPERII 1721-1835 – (Complete coll of decrees and instructions of the Orthodox Faith of Russian Empire) – 207mf – 9 – $1,000.00 – us Ross [240]

ROSSIISKII GOSUDARSTVENNYI ISTORICHESKII ARKHIV-RGIA = RUSSIAN STATE HISTORICAL ARCHIVES : PRAVOSLAVNYI PALESTINSKII SBORNIK [ZHURNAL] / ORTHODOX PALESTINE HANDBOOK [JOURNAL] – 183mf – 9 – $900.00 – us Ross [956]

ROSSIISKII GOSUDARSTVENNYI ISTORICHESKII ARKHIV-RGIA = RUSSIAN STATE HISTORICAL ARCHIVES : SBORNIK POSTANOVLENII PO MINISTERSTVU NARODNOGO PROSVESHCHENIIA (1875-1904) / HANDBOOK OF DECREES BY THE MINISTRY OF PUBLIC EDUCATION – 322mf – 9 – $1,600.00 – us Ross [350]

ROSSIISKII TEATR – Ili polnoe sobranie vsekh Rossiiskikh teatral'nykh sochinenii. v. 1-43. Spb. 1786-94. Lacking: (5) 1786-87. B-1849 2 – 8 – ne IDC [790]

ROSSIISKII TEATR ILI POLNOE SOBRANIE ROSSIISKIKH IEATRAL'NYKH SOCHINENII – St Petersburg. v. 1-43. 1786-1794 – 1 – us NY Public [460]

ROSSIISKII TEATR ILI POLNOE SOBRANIE VSIEKH ROSSIISKIKH TEATRAL'NYKH SOCHINENII – v1-43. 1768-94 – 4r – 1 – us Ross [790]

Rossiiskoi Sotsialdemokraticheskoi rabochei partii *see* ISKRA

Rossijskaja Social-Demokraticeskaja Rabocaja Partija *see* SOCIALISTICESKIJ VESTNIK

ROSSING NEWS – Swakopmund, South West Africa. 1977- – 9 – sa State Libr [072]

Rossini, Carlo Conti *see* STORIA D'ETIOPIA

Rossini, G *see*
- LA DONNA DEL LAGO
- MAOMETTO II
- SIGISMONDO. MELODRAMA IN DUE ATTI DI GUISEPPE FOPPA
- TANCREDI. OPERA SERIE IN DUE ATTI. ACT 1, GERMAN

ROSSISKII MAGAZIN – 3pts. Spb. 1792-94. Available: 1792. B-1850 2 – 8 – ne IDC [073]

Rossiter, Stealy Bales *see* THE RED CORD: FROM CREATION TO CHRIST: THE BIBLE... MADE PLAIN TO YOUNG READERS

ROSSIYA *see* ROSSII A (NEW YORK, N.Y.: 1932)

ROSSLAND MINER – Canada. -w. Oct 1896-April 1904. 7 reels – 1 – uk British Libr Newspaper [072]

THE ROSSLYN MISSAL / Lawler, H J – 1899 – 5mf – 8 – Dfl22.00 – ne Slangenburg [240]

Rossman, B B Robbie *see* JOURNAL OF EMOTIONAL ABUSE

ROSS'S WEEKLY – Charlottetown, Canada. 1861-64 – 2r – 1 – $136.00 – cn Library Assoc [971]

ROSS-SHIRE JOURNAL – 1 – £42.00r – uk Scot News [072]

Rost, P *see* DIE SPRACHRESTE DER DRAVAENOV-POLABEN IM HANNOEVERSCHEN

Rost, Pierre Adolphe *see* EULOGY UPON LIFE AND CHARACTER OF GEORGE EUSTIS, FORMERLY CHIEF JUSTICE OF THE SUPREME COURT OF LA....AT LYCEUM HALL, ON THE 31ST MAR., 1859, BY HON. PIERRE A. ROST, AT THE REQUEST OF NEW ORLEANS LAW ASSOC

Rostaing de Rivas, Eugene P de *see* NOTICE SUR EUGEN BONAMY

Rostand, Edmond *see* CYRANO DE BERGERAC; A PLAY IN FIVE ACTS

ROSTEM UND SUHRAB = RUSTAM VA SUHRAB : EINE HELDENGESCHICHTE IN ZWOELF BUECHERN / Firdawsi – 2. Aufl. Stuttgart: [S G Liesching]; Guetersloh: C Bertelsmann, 1846 – 1 – us U.W. Library [830]

ROSTER AND HISTORY OF CO. K / U.S. Army. Cavalry, Kansas. 11th Regiment. Company K – 11 Sept 1862-24 May 1865 – 1 – us KS Hist [324]

ROSTER OF NEBRASKA VOLUNTERES / Adjutant General of the State – Hastings, Nebraska: Wigton & Evans, State Printers, 1888 – 1 reel – 1 – us Western Res [978]

ROSTER OF PUBLIC OFFICIALS OF CALIFORNIA / Jordan, Frank C – Sacramento: Bureau of Documents, 1937. California Reel 38. (Cox Library Collection) – 5 – us Americana [920]

ROSTER OF REVOLUTIONARY SOLDIERS IN GEORGIA – Comp. by Mrs. Howard K. McCall, 1968. Orig. publ., 1941. From pension papers, Bible & tombstone records, land grants, lottery lists, wills, estates, official records of military service. Indexed. 5 fiches. F-0856 – 9 – us A.G.L.L. [920]

ROSTER OF SOLDIERS AND PATRIOTS OF THE AMERICAN REVOLUTION, BURIED IN INDIANA – Comp. and ed. by Mrs. Roscoe C. O'Byrne. 1968. Orig. publ. 1938. Arranged by counties. 7 fiches. F-0995 – 9 – us A.G.L.L. [920]

ROSTER OF THE FOURTH IOWA CAVALRY 1861-1865 / Scott, William Forse – (New York: J. J. Little & Co., 1902). Iowa Reel 4. (The Cox Library Collection) – 5 – us Americana [978]

ROSTERS OF STATION HOSPITAL, FORT LEAVENWORTH, KANSAS. SEPT 1918-DEC 1919. ALSO, MONTHLY STRENGTH RETURNS OF STATION HOSPITAL...JUL 1918-JUL 1919 / U.S. Army. A.E.F., 1917-1920. Fort Leavenworth, Kansas – 1 – us KS Hist [324]

O ROSTLINSTVU VRSTEV BREZENSKYCH / Bayer, E – (The Flora of the Brezensky district). Sitzungsberichte Koeniglich-Boehmische Gesellschaft der Wissenschaften. 1893. B-5362 2 – 8 – ne IDC [940]

Rostoker, J *see* MONOGRAPHIE D'UN ARTISAN PARISIEN

Rostotskii, B *see* MAIAKOVSKII I TEATR

Rostovcev, M *see* SKYTHIEN UND DER BOSPORUS: I, KRITISCHE UBERSICHT DER SCHRIFTLICHEN UND ARCHAEOLOGISCHEN QUELLEN

ROSTOVSKAIA KOOPERATIVNAIA ZHIZN' – (Missing: 1918 n1-6) – Rostov-Iaroslavskii, 1918-19 n4 – 1mf – 9 – COR-674/1 – ne IDC [334]

Rostovtsev, A *see* TSERKOVNIKI I SEKTANTI NA SLUZHBE U KULAKI

Rostovtzeff, M *see* IRANIANS AND GREEKS IN SOUTH RUSSIA

Rosweydus, H *see* GENERALE LEGENDE DER HEYLIGHEN MET HET LEVEN IESU CHRISTI ENDE MARIE

ROTATED TITLE PHRASE LIST – v78-81. 1973. Includes manual – 6,9 – $40.00 – us Chemical [540]

DAS ROTE BLATT DER KATHOLISCHEN SOZIALISTEN – Koeln, Mannheim. 1929-30 – 1r – 1 – DM75.00 – gw Mikro Press [072]

DAS ROTE BLATT DER KATHOLISCHEN SOZIALISTEN – Koeln-Mannheim, Germany. 1929-1930 – 1r – 1 – gw Mikrofilm [072]
ROTE ERDE – (Later: Westfaelische Landeszeitung, Ausgabe B) – Bochum, feb 2 1931-mar 10 1945 – 1 – Inquire at Mikrofilmarchiv for details – gw Misc Inst [943]
DIE ROTE FAHNE – 1918-38 – 28r – 1 – us Ross [335]
DIE ROTE FAHNE – Berlin, 1918-1933 – 36r – 1 – DM2,880.00 – gw Mikro Press [072]
DIE ROTE FAHNE – Berlin etc. Nov 9 1918-1938. Incomplete – 1 – us NY Public [335]
DIE ROTE FAHNE – Berlin. Germany. v. 1-16. Nov. 1918-Feb. 1933 – 1 – 35.00r – us Hoover Inst Photo [072]
DIE ROTE FAHNE – Prague, Czechoslovakia. Aug 1934-Sept 1938 – 4r – 1 – us L of C Photodup [072]
DIE ROTE FAHNE / Zentralkomitees der Kommunistischen Partei Lettlands – Riga. no. 1-108. Jan 5-May 15 1919 – 1 – us NY Public [335]
DIE ROTE FAHNE : ZENTRALORGAN DER KPD – (Cont as an underground newspaper until 1941) – Berlin, nov 9 1918-feb 27 1933, 1935-38 (incomplete) – 1 – Inquire at Mikrofilmarchiv for details – gw Misc Inst [335]
DIE ROTE FAHNE : ZENTRALORGAN DER KPD – (Continued illegally until 1941) – Berlin, Germany. 9 Nov 1918-27 Feb 1933 – 36r – 1 – gw Mikrofilm [072]
ROTE FAHNE – (Berlin: 1970-). ill. -w – 1 – us U.W. Library [335]
ROTE FAHNE *see*
– DER KOMMUNIST
DIE ROTE FRONT : ORGAN DES FRONTKAEMPFERBUNDES – Berlin, Germany. 15 Okt 1924-Apr 1929 – 1r – 1 – gw Mikrofilm [072]
DIE ROTE FRONT : ORGAN DES FRONTKAEMPFERBUNDES – Berlin, oct 15 1924-apr 1929 – 1 – Inquire at Mikrofilmarchiv for details – gw Misc Inst [943]
DIE ROTE GEWERKSCHAFTS-INTERNATIONALE – Berlin, 1930 – 1 – Inquire at Mikrofilmarchiv for details – gw Misc Inst [331]
DIE ROTE GEWERKSCHAFTS-INTERNATIONALE – Berlin, Germany.1930 – 1 – gw Mikrofilm [072]
DIE ROTE GEWERKSCHAFTS-INTERNATIONALE : ORGAN DES VOLLZUGSBUEROS DER ROTEN GEWERKSCHAFTS-INTERNATIONALEN – Berlin, 1921-33. Hildesheim, 1980 – 110mf – 9 – DM690.00 – gw Olms [335]
DER ROTE HAHN – Berlin, 1917-1925. v. 2, 4-25, 27-36, 38-43, 45-48, 50-60 – 1 – us NY Public [073]
ROTE HAND – Munich. Dec. 1918-Oct. 1920 (complete) – 1 – 35.00r – us Hoover Inst Photo [073]
DER ROTE HELFER – Berlin, 1925-28 – 1r – 1 – Inquire at Mikrofilmarchiv for details – gw Misc Inst [360]
DER ROTE HELFER – Berlin, Germany. 1925-1928 – 1r – 1 – gw Mikrofilm [072]
DIE ROTE KERZE : ROMAN / Landesen, Wera von – Nuernberg: J L Schrag, 1942 – 1r – 1 – us U.W. Library [830]
DER ROTE LEUTNANT : SCHAUSPIEL IN DREI AKTEN / Goldbeck, Eduard – Berlin-Charlottenburg: Vita Deutsches Verlagshaus, 1907 – 1r – 1 – us U.W. Library [820]
DIE ROTE PFLUGSCHAR – Hannover, Germany. 1924-1926 – 1 – gw Mikrofilm [072]
DER ROTE SAND – Bremen, aug 1919-mar 1923 – 1r – 1 – Inquire at Mikrofilmarchiv for details – gw Misc Inst [072]
DER ROTE SAND – Bremen, Germany. 1919-1923 – 1r – 1 – gw Mikrofilm [072]
DIE ROTE SPINDEL – Bremen, 1928 n7 – 1 – Inquire at Mikrofilmarchiv for details – gw Misc Inst [072]
DIE ROTE STANDARTE – Berlin, Mai 1935 – 1 – Inquire at Mikrofilmarchiv for details – gw Misc Inst [335]
DER ROTE STERN – Berlin, 1924-29, 1930-33 (incomplete) – 2r – 1 – Inquire at Mikrofilmarchiv for details – gw Misc Inst [335]
DER ROTE STERN – Berlin, Germany. 1924-1933 (incomplete) – 2r – 1 – gw Mikrofilm [072]
ROTEIRO DA UNIFICACAO – Nanuque, Brazil. Mar-Dec 1968; Jan 1969 – 1 – bl Biblioteca [072]
DIE ROTEN STREIFEN : ROMAN EINES GENERALSTABSOFFIZIERS / Volkmann, Erich Otto – Hamburg: Hanseatische Verlagsanstalt, c1942 – 1r – 1 – us U.W. Library [830]
ROTENBURGER ANZEIGER – (Title changes: Amtliches Verordnungs- und Anzeigenblatt fuer den Kreis Rotenburg in Hannover; Kreiszeitung fuer den Kreis Rotenburg in Hannover; Rotenburger Kreiszeitung) – Rotenburg a.d. Wuemme, Germany. 1977- – ca 6r per yr – 1 – gw Mikrofilm [072]
ROTENBURGER KREISZEITUNG *see* ROTENBURGER ANZEIGER
ROTER ADLER : TAGESZEITUNG DER MARK BRANDENBURG – Berlin, jan-jul 1931 – 2r – 1 – Inquire at Mikrofilmarchiv for details – gw Misc Inst [943]
ROTER PFEFFER – (Cont by: Der Eulenspiegel, 1932) – Berlin, 1928-33 n4 – 1 – Inquire at Mikrofilmarchiv for details – gw Misc Inst [870]
ROTER PFEFFER : SATIRISCHE ZEITSCHRIFT – (Title change: Der Eulenspiegel, 1932) – Berlin, Germany. 1928-1933 – 1 – gw Mikrofilm [073]
ROTER VORWAERTS – Aussig, apr 5 1930-aug 30 1931 – 1r – 1 – Dist. gw Mikrofilm – gw Misc Inst [072]
Rotermund, Heinrich Wilhelm *see* DAS GELEHRTE HANNOVER
ROTES HERZ DER ERDE : AUSGEWAEHLTE BALLADEN, GEDICHTE, GESAENGE / Zech, Paul – Berlin: Arbeiterjugendverlag, 1929 – 1r – 1 – us U.W. Library [810]
ROTES SCHUPO-SPRACHROHR – Berlin, may 1935 – 1 – Inquire at Mikrofilmarchiv for details – gw Misc Inst [072]
Roth, A W *see*
– BEITRAEGE ZUR BOTANIK
– BEMERKUNGEN UEBER DAS STUDIUM DER CRYPTOGAMISCHEN WASSERGEWAECHSE
– BOTANISCHE ABHANDLUNGEN UND BEOBACHTUNGEN
– BOTANISCHE BEMERKUNGEN UND BERICHTUNGEN
– CATALECTA BOTANICA
– ENUMERATIO PLANTARUM PHAENOGAMARUM
– NEUE BEYTRAEGE ZUR BOTANIK
– NOVAE PLANTARUM SPECIES PRAESERTIM INDIAE ORIENTALIS, EX COLLECTIONE HEYNII
– TENTAMEN FLORAE GERMANICAE
– VERZEICHNISS DERJENIGEN PFLANZEN, WELCHE NACH DER ANZAHL UND DER BESCHAFFENHEIT
Roth, Alberto G *see* CATALECTA BOTANICA
Roth, F *see* LEONHARD KAISER
Roth, Friedrich *see*
– DER EINFLUSS DES HUMANISMUS UND DER REFORMATION AUF DAS GLEICHZEITIGE ERZIEHUNGS- UND SCHULWESEN
– WILIBALD PIRKHEIMER
Roth, G *see* DIE AUSSEREUROPAEISCHEN LAUBMOOSE
Roth, J D *see* HAND-BOOK OF LUTHERANISM
Roth, J L A *see* ALLGEMEINE UND CHEMISCHE GEOLOGIE
Roth, J R *see* MOLLUSCORUM SPECIES QUAS IN ITINERE PER ORIENTEM FACTO COMITES
Roth, Julius *see* RELIGION UND PRIESTERTHUM
Roth, K *see* ARMENIACA
Roth, L *see* SPINOZA, DESCARTES AND MAIMONIDES
Roth, Lottie R *see* HISTORY OF WHATCOM COUNTY
Roth, Robert R *see* RECONTEXTUALIZING EDUCATION THROUGH THE PHYSICAL
Rothacker, Gottfried *see* BLEIB STET!
Rothbard, Murray N *see*
– DEPRESSIONS: THEIR CAUSE AND CURE
– EGALITERIANISM AS A REVOLT AGAINST NATURE AND OTHER ESSAYS
– WAR, PEACE AND THE STATE
Rothblum, Esther D *see*
– JOURNAL OF LESBIAN STUDIES
– WOMEN AND THERAPY
Rothe, B *see* ERLAEUTERUNGEN ZU GOETHES WERKEN FUER SCHULGEBRAUCH UND SELBSTSTUDIUM ALS LITTERATURKUNDLICHES REPETITORIUM
ROTHE LIEDER UND ZWANGLOSE REIME / Ohly, Karl – Zuerich: C Koehler, 1849 – 1r – 1 – us U.W. Library [780]
Rothe, Richard *see*
– STILL HOURS
– THEOLOGISCHE ENCYCLOPAEDIE
Rothenburg, Adelheid von *see* IM UMKREIS VON VIER MEILEN
DIE ROTHENBURGER : ROMAN / Wilbrandt, Adolf von – 6. Aufl. Stuttgart: J G Cotta, 1901 – 1r – 1 – us U.W. Library [830]
Rother-Carlowitz, Alfred *see* SAENGER, SOLDAT UND HELD
ROTHERHAM ADVERTISER – Yorkshire. 1858-90 and 1899-1908 – 1858-1890 31r, 1899-1908 14r – uk Microform Academic [072]
ROTHERHAM AND MASBORO' GUARDIAN – England. -w. 24 March-13 Oct 1877. 35 ft – 1 – uk British Libr Newspaper [072]
ROTHERHAM EVENING ECHO – Yorkshire. 1906-08 – 1 – uk Microform Academic [072]
ROTHERHAM FREE PRESS – England. -w. 6 Jan-24 March 1894. 15 ft – 1 – uk British Libr Newspaper [072]
ROTHERHAM JOURNAL – Yorkshire. 1857-61 – 2r – 1 – uk Microform Academic [072]
ROTHERHAM WEEKLY NEWS – England. -w. 15 April 1899-24 Feb 1900. 1 reel – 1 – uk British Libr Newspaper [072]
Rothert, Otto A *see* A HISTORY OF MUHLENBERG COUNTY
Rothery, Agnes Edwards *see* NORWAY, CHANGING AND CHANGELESS
Rothfuss, Joerg *see*
– VERAENDERUNG STRUKTURELLER UND SOZIALETHISCHER GRUNDLAGEN DES DEUTSCHEN GESUNDHEITSWESENS DURCH DAS GESUNDHEITSREFORMGESETZ UND DAS GESUNDHEITSSTRUKTURGESETZ
– DIE WIRKUNG VON DEHYDRATION UND REHYDRATION AUF DIE HERZFUNKTION GESUNDER PROBANDEN
Rothman, Ellen K *see* NEW ENGLAND WOMEN AND THEIR FAMILIES IN THE 18TH AND 19TH CENTURIES: PERSONAL PAPERS, LETTERS, AND DIARIES
Rothmann, B *see* VAN VERBORGENHEIT DER SCHRIFFT DES RYKES CHRISTI, VNDE VAN DEM DAGHE DES HEREN, DURCH DE GEMEINTE CHRISTI THO MUENSTER
Rothmann, B. et al *see* BEKENTNISSE VAN BEYDEN SACRAMENTEN. DOPE VNDE NACHTMAELE DER PREDICANTEN THO MUNSTER
Rothrock, Thomas *see* ELM SPRINGS METHODIST CHURCH: A PARTIAL HISTORY
Rothschild, Jay Leo *see* OUTLINES OF THE NEW YORK LAW OF EVIDENCE AND PRACTICE, WITH PRACTICE TIME TABLE AND FORMS
Rothschild, L W *see*
– THE AVIFAUNA OF LAYSAN
– EXTINCT BIRDS
ROTHSCHILD SIEGT BEI WATERLOO : EIN SCHAUSPIEL / Moeller, Eberhard Wolfgang – 5. Aufl. Berlin: A Langen, G Mueller, 1941, c1937 – 1r – 1 – us U.W. Library [820]
Rothstein, Johann Wilhelm *see* GRUNDZUEGE DES HEBRAEISCHEN RHYTHMUS UND SEINER FORMENBILDUNG
ROTHUGGAREN – Litchfield, MN. 1881-82, 1885-86. Scattered issues available – 1 reel – 1 – sw Kungliga [071]
Rothwell, Annie *see* LOVED I NOT HONOUR MORE
THE ROTIFERA; OR WHEELANIMALCULES / Hudson, C T – Z-220 2. 2 v. 1886 – 8 – ne IDC [590]
ROTKAEPPCHEN : UND ZWOELF ANDERE MAERCHEN / Grimm, Jacob – Reichenberg: P Sollor, [19–?] – 1r – 1 – us U.W. Library [390]
Rotmann, Bernhard *see* RESTITUTION
Rots, B D *see* AALTEN EN BREDEVOORT IN VERVLOGEN TIJDEN
Rottboll, C F *see*
– DESCRIPTIONES PLANTARUM QUARANDAM SURINAMENSIUM
– DESCRIPTIONES PLANTARUM RARIORUM ICONIBUS ILLUSTRANDAS
– DESCRIPTIONUM ET ICONUM RAIORES
– HERBARIUM
Rotteck, K von *see* DAS STAATS-LEXIKON
ROTTENBURGER POST : BA DER SUEDWESTPRESSE – Rottenburg, Germany. 1980- – 1 – gw Mikrofilm [072]
Rottermund, E S, Comte de *see*
– RAPPORT DE E.S. DE ROTTERMUND, ECUYER, CHIMISTE DE L'EXPLORATION GEOLOGIQUE DE LA PROVINCE
– REPONSE A UNE ADRESSE DE L'ASSEMBLEE LEGISLATIVE POUR COPIE DU RAPPORT DU COMTE [SIC] DE ROTTERMUND SUR SON EXPLORATION DES LACS SUPERIEUR ET HURON
– REPORT..
– REPORT ON THE QUEBEC COAL, TO HIS WORSHIP THE MAYOR OF QUEBEC
– SECOND RAPOORT SUR L'EXPLORATION DES LACS SUPERIEUR ET HURON
Rottermund, W D de *see* RAPPORT SUR L'EXPLORATION DES LACS SUPERIEUR ET HURON
Rottier, Ch. J M *see* A NEW COURSE OF ENGLISH FOR SCHOOLS IN INDONESIA
ROTTWEILER BOTE (R2) : BA DES SCHWARZWAELDER BOTEN – Rottweil-Oberndorf, Germany. 2 Aug 1947-9 Sep 1950; 30 Sep 1950-30 Dec 1960; 2 Jul 1973-31 Dec 1979 – 68r – 1 – gw Mikrofilm [072]
ROTULORUM ORIGINALIUM IN CURIA SCACCARIO ABBREVIATIO – (v1: Temporibus Regum Henrici 3, Edwardi 1, And Edwardi 2 London, 1805 Dfl67.00. v2: Tempore Regis Edwardi 3 London, 1810 Dfl74.00) – ne Slangenburg [240]
ROTUNDA – Toronto. v1-26. 1968-1993/94 – 9 – Can$20.00y – cn Micromedia [073]
Rotundis, P *see* CATHARRI SUFFOCATIVI EJESQUE CURATIONES HISTORIA
Rotwein, Abraham *see* LABOR LAW
Rotwein, Noah *see* OUTLINE OF CONSTITUTIONAL LAW
ROUBAIX-TOURCOING – Tourcoing (Nord), May – Dec. 1891 – 1r – fr Armell [320]
Roubo, Andre J *see* L'ART DU MENUISIER
Roucel, F A *see* FLORE DU NORD DE LA FRANCE
Rouche, Max *see* HERDER PRECURSEUR DE DARWIN?
Rouchon, Ulysse *see* LA VIE BRUYANTE DE JULES VALLES
Roue, M *see* LES RELATIONS SOCIALES CHEZ LES LAPONS DE KAUTOKEINO
Rouech, August Eugene *see* ROUECH'S MANUAL OF THE RIGHTS, DUTIES AND LIABILITIES OF NOTARIES PUBLIC UNDER THE COMMON LAW AS MODIFIED BY THE STATUTES OF MICHIGAN
ROUECH'S MANUAL OF THE RIGHTS, DUTIES AND LIABILITIES OF NOTARIES PUBLIC UNDER THE COMMON LAW AS MODIFIED BY THE STATUTES OF MICHIGAN / Rouech, August Eugene – Detroit: Richmond & Backus Co., 1900. 184, 13p. LL-1610 – 1 – us L of C Photodup [340]
Roue-Delaporte, M *see* LE VETEMENT DES LAPONS DE KAUTOKEINO
Rouen, Marie-de *see* TRAVAUX SCIENTIFIQUES DES MEDECINS DE L'HOPITAL SAINT-MICHEL-ARCHANGE ET DE LA CLINIQUE ROY-ROUSSEAU, 1930-1950
ROUGE – (Also available on CD-ROM) – 1989-1995 – 2r per y – 5,6 – Sfr454.00 – sz Infoprint [072]
ROUGE ET LA NOIR – Paris. n1-9. 1927-31 – 1r – 1 – us Ross [800]
LE ROUGE ET LE NOIR – Paris. Apr 1927-June 1928 and Supplements – 1 – us NY Public [073]
ROUGE ET NOIR – (Cont by: Trinity University Review) – Toronto: Students of Trinity College, [1880?-1887] – 9 – cn C.I.H.M. [370]
ROUGE ET NOIR – no. 1-3. Bruxelles puis Londres. oct-nov 1874 – 1 – fr A.C.R.P.P. [073]
ROUGE ET NOIR *see* TRINTIY UNIVERSITY REVIEW
ROUGE HEBDOMADAIRE D'ACTION COMMUNISTE – Paris, France. -w. 22 Dec 1969-Dec 1976. 7 reels – 1 – uk British Libr Newspaper [072]
ROUGE (PARIS, FRANCE: 1968) – Paris: [s.n.], 1968 – 1 – CSUXAMJ4560-S – us Hoover Inst Photo [944]
ROUGE QUOTIDIN MAR. 15, 1976- *see* ROUGE (PARIS, FRANCE: 1968)
ROUGE-MIDI – Marseille. 1934-aout 1939 – 1 – fr A.C.R.P.P. [073]
Rougemont, Frederic *see* LA REVELATION... : EXPLIQUEE PAR LES ECRITURES ET EXPLIQUANT L'HISTOIRE
LES ROUGES ET LEURS OEUVRES: DEPLORABLES RESULTATS DES DIX-HUIT MOIS DE POUVOIR DES LIBERAUX: LA PROVINCE DE QUEBEC ABAISSEE, ASSERVIE, MEPRISEE – 1875?. 03188. (Pre-1900 Canadiana) – 9 – cn C.I.H.M. [971]
Rouget, Fernand *see* LA GUINEE
ROUGH JUSTICE / Braddon, Mary Elizabeth – British Fiction Archive: Unit 5 – 9 – uk Bell [830]
ROUGH JUSTICE / Braddon, Mary Elizabeth – London: Simpkin, Marshall, Hamilton, Kent, 1898.392p – 1 – us U.W. Library [830]

ROUGH NOTES BY AN OLD SOLDIER, DURING FIFTY YEARS' SERVICE, FROM ENSIGN G.B. TO MAJOR-GENERAL G.B / Bell, George – 2v. London: Day, 1867. 03610, 03611. (Pre-1900 Canadiana) – 9 – cn C.I.H.M. [920]
ROUGH NOTES OF CITY LIFE – Hamilton, C.W. [Ont.: s.n., 1861-18–?] – 9 – cn C.I.H.M. [073]
ROUGH TIMES – (See now: R T: A Journal of Radical Therapy; State and Mind) – v1-4. 1970-74 – 1 – us UMI [150]
Rougier, J C Paul *see* LES ASSOCIATIONS OUVRIERES. ETUDES SUR LEUR PASSE, LEUR PRESENT, LEURS CONDITIONS DE PROGRES
Rouillard, Eugene *see*
- LE MATIN
- NOMS GEOGRAPHIQUES DE LA PROVINCE DE QUEBEC ET DES PROVINCES MARITIMES EMPRUNTES AUX LANGUES SAUVAGES
- LE PROTECTIONNISTE

Rouillard, J B *see* L'IMPARTIAL
Rouillard, Jean-Baptiste *see* LE SUD
Rouillard, Joseph *see* BIO-BIBLIOGRAPHIE D'EUGENE ROUILLARD, NOTAIRE, MEMBRE DE LA SOCIETE ROYALE DU CANADA, MEMBRE FONDATEUR DE LA SOCIETE DU PARLER FRANCAIS...
Rouilliard, Jean-Baptiste *see* ANNEXION: CONFERENCE: L'UNION CONTINENTALE
Rouleau, C E *see* L'OUVRIER
Roullaud, Henri *see* RECTIFICATION DU VOCABULAIRE
Roullier, H *see* ORAISON FUNEBRE DE LOUIS 16TH(...)PRONONCEE LE 30 JUIN 1814(...)
Roulliet, Antony *see* LES HABITATIONS OUVRIERES
LA ROUMANIE – no. 1-74. Paris. 1918-juin 1919. mq no. 21, 42 – 1 – fr A.C.R.P.P. [073]
LA ROUMANIE INDEPENDANTE – Paris and Detroit. -m. Jan 1946-Dec 1947. (2 reels) – 1 – uk British Libr Newspaper [949]
Roumeguere, C *see* FLORE MYCOLOGIQUE DU DEPARTEMENT DE TARN-ET-GARONNE
Round, J H *see*
- THE COMMUNE OF LONDON
- FEUDAL ENGLAND. HISTORICAL STUDIES ON THE 11TH AND 12TH CENTURIES
- GEOFFREY DE MANDEVILLE
- PEERAGE AND PEDIGREE
- STUDIES IN PEERAGE AND FAMILY HISTORY

THE ROUND TABLE – 82v – 9 – £156.50 – 0035-8533 – uk Carfax [650]
THE ROUND TABLE – (v. 1-31 and 38. 15.00v; 9. v. 32-37, 39-62. 249.00v; WDS; 9) – A quarterly Journal of British Commonwealth Affairs. v. 1-62. London. 1910 11-1972 – 9 – 24750.00 – uk Dawson [941]
THE ROUND TABLE – (v.1-31, plus 38. 2415.00v; 9. v.32-37, 39-62. 249.00v; WDS; 9) – A quarterly journal of British Commonwealth affairs. v.1-62. 1910 11-1972 – 9 – 24750.00 – uk Dawson [073]
THE ROUND TABLE. A QUARTERLY REVIEW OF THE POLITICS OF THE BRITISH COMMONWEALTH – v.1-, no.1-, Nov. 1910-. London, Macmillan – 1 – us U.W. Library [073]
ROUND THE WORLD / Kingsley, Calvin – 2v. 1870 – 9 – us A.T.L.A. [240]
ROUND THE WORLD WITH ENGLISH / Bongers, Herman – In Indonesian. SE-10,305 1. 1955? – 9 – ne IDC [420]
ROUND THE YULE LOG / Asbjornsen, Peter Christen – 193? – 1 – us I.U. Libraries [390]
ROUND VALLEY NEWS – Covelo, CA. 1972-1993 – 16r – 1 – $800.00 – B06018 – us Library Micro [071]
ROUNDABOUT PAPERS / Thackeray, William Makepeace – London: Smith, Elder, 1863 – 1 roll – 1 – 1-55879-660-6 – uk Libr Preservation [830]
ROUNDEL – Nov 1948-63 – 1 – 127.00 – us L of C Photodup [355]
Rounds, H J *see* A CHINESE BOY'S PERSONAL PROBLEM (CCC210)
Roundy, Elmo S *see*
- CARDIOVASCULAR AND BODY COMPOSITION RESPONSES TO AEROBIC DANCE TRAINING OF VARYING FREQUENCIES AND TOTAL PROGRAM LENGTHS
- EFFECTS OF HIGH SCHOOL CONCEPTS-BASED PHYSICAL EDUCATION ON STUDENT BEHAVIOR, KNOWLEDGE, AND MOTIVATION

Rouquie, Alain *see* ARGENTINA, HOY
Roure-Torent, J *see* THE ORGANIZATION OF THE SPANISH ARMY
Rous, H J *see* ON THE LAWS AND PRACTICE OF HORSE RACING
Rouse, George Henry *see* OLD TESTAMENT CRITICISM IN NEW TESTAMENT LIGHT
Rousse, Joseph *see* OEUVRES COMPLETES
Rousseau, Abbe *see* NOTICES SUR LES 70 SERVITEURS DE DIEU
Rousseau, Andre Michel *see* VOLTAIRE'S BRITISH VISITORS
Rousseau, Edmond *see*
- ALCOOL ET ALCOOLISME (CAUSERIES SUR L'INTEMPERANCE)
- PETIT MANUEL DU CULTIVATEUR A L'USAGE DES ECOLES PRIMAIRES

Rousseau, F *see* ACTES DES COMTES DE NAMUR DE LA PREMIERE RACE (946-1196)
Rousseau, Jean-Baptist *see* LE DIABLE A BRUXELLES
Rousseau, Jean-Jacques *see*
- DICTIONNAIRE DE MUSIQUE
- DISSERTATION SUR LA MUSIQUE MODERNE
- EXTRAIT DU PROJET DE PAIX PERPETUELLE DE M. L'ABBE DE SAINT PIERRE
- HERBARIUM
- LETTRE SUR LA MUSIQUE FRANCOISE
- METHODE CLAIRE, CERTAINE ET FACILE, POUR APPRENDRE A CHANTER LA MUSIQUE
- PETITS CHEFS-D'OEUVRE
- LA POSTE
- PROJET CONCERNANT DE NOUVEAUX SIGNES POUR LA MUSIQUE
- TRAITE DE LA VIOLE..
- TRAITE DE LA VIOLE
- TRAITES SUR LA MUSIQUE

Rousseau, Thomas *see* A BAS LA CALOTTE OU LES DEPRETRISES
ROUSSEAUISM: 1788-1797 / ed by Barny, Roger – 9 – fr Hachette [190]
Roussel, Gilles *see* TOPOGRAPHIE RURALE ET MEDICALE DE LA PARTIE MERIDIONALE DES DEPARTEMENTS DE LA MANCHE ET DU CALVADOS
Roussel, H F A *see* FLORE DU CALVADOS ET DES TERREINS ADJACENS, COMPOSEE SUIVANT LA METHODE DE M. JUSSIEU COMPAREE AVEC CELLE DE TOURNEFORT ET DE LINNE
Roussel, Napoleon *see*
- CATHOLIC AND PROTESTANT NATIONS COMPARED IN THEIR THREEFOLD RELATIONS TO WEALTH, KNOWLEDGE, AND MORALITY
- THE ROMANCE OF M. RENAN AND THE CHRIST OF THE GOSPELS

Roussel-Despierres, Fr *see* L'IDEAL ESTHETIQUE
Rousselet, L *see* INDIA AND ITS NATIVE PRINCES
Rousselot, P *see* POUR L'HISTOIRE DU PROBLEME DE L'AMOUR AU MOYEN-AGE
Rousselot, Paul *see*
- LOS MISTICOS ESPANOLES: MALON DE CHAIDE, JUAN DE AVILA, LUIS DE GRANADA, LUIS DE LEON, SANTA TERESA, SAN JUAN DE LA CRUZ Y SU GROUPO
- LA PEDAGOGIE FEMININE

Roussey, Charles *see* CONTES POPULAIRES
Roussier, Pierre-Joseph *see*
- L'HARMONIE PRATIQUE..
- MEMOIRE SUR LA MUSIQUE DES ANCIENS..
- OBSERVATIONS SUR DIFFERENS POINTS D'HARMONIE
- TRAITE DES ACCORDS..

Roussin, Alb *see* MEMOIRE SUR LA NAVIGATION AUX COTES OCCIDENTALES D'AFRIQUE DEPUIS LE CAP BOJADOR JUSQU'AU MONT SOUZOS
Roussin, Alfred *see* UNE CAMPAGNE SUR LES COTES DU JAPON
Roussy, Jean de *see* AURELIA OU ORLEANS DELIVRE: POEME TRADUIT EN FRANCAIS
LA ROUTE BANGUI-KAGA BANDERO, REPUBLIQUE CENTRAFRICAINE.STRUCTURES HERITEES ET MUTATIONS CONTEMPORAINES DANS UNE REGION DE LA SAVANE CENTRAFRICAINE / Piermay, J L – 9 – F100.00 – fr Ethnologie [306]
ROUTE BOOK OF THE GOLD COAST COLONY, ASHANTI AND THE NORTHERN TERRITORIES / Great Britain. War Office. General Staff – (Filmed with: Great Britain. War Office: Precis of information concerning the colony of the Gold Coast and Ashanti) – [London: s.n.], 1906 – us Res Libr [960]
ROUTE BOOKS, MILITARY REPORTS AND INFORMATION PRECIS FOR BRITISH AFRICA / Great Britain. War Office – (Part 2: 1906-33. 280.00. – 70 fiche) – Part 1: 1867-1912. – 136 fiche – 9 – uk Microform Academic [960]
LA ROUTE DE LA GUERRE TOTALE : ESSAI SUR LES RELATIONS ENTRE LA GUERRE ET LE PROGRES HUMAIN / Nef, J U – 1949 – F50.00 – fr Ethnologie [320]
ROUTENOPTIMIERUNG MIT GREEDY-ALGORITHMEN / Hillert, Freimut – 1992 – 130p – 9 – DM98.00 – 3-89349-584-3 – gw Hänsel [510]
THE ROUTES AND MINERAL RESOURCES OF NORTH WESTERN CANADA / Dyer, E Jerome – London: Published under the auspices of the incorporated London Chamber of Mines, 1898. 05206. (Pre-1900 Canadiana) – 9 – cn C.I.H.M. [971]
ROUTES MALGACHES : LE SUD DE MADAGASCAR / Harry, Myriam – Paris: Plon, 1943 – us Res Libr [910]
Routh, M J *see* RELIQUIAE SACRAE
Routhier, Adolphe-Basile *see* QUEBEC ET LEVIS A L'AURORE DU 20E SIECLE
Routier, Simone *see*
- ADIEU PARIS
- LES TENTATIONS

Routley, Erik *see* MUSIC IN CHRISTIAN HYMNODY
Rouvellat de Cussas *see* SITUATION DES ESCLAVES DANS LES COLONIES FRANCAISES
Rouvrais, A *see* LE DESTIN SOCIAL D'UNE FAMILLE PAYSANNE BRETONNE (FIN DU XIXE SIECLE-1985)
Roux, Edward *see* SP BUNTIG
Roux, Emile *see* MANUEL A L'USAGE DES ADMINISTRATEURS ET DU PERSONNEL DES AFFAIRES INDIGENES DE LA COLONIE DU SENEGAL ET DES COLONIES RELEVANT DU GOUVERNEMENT GENERAL DE L'AFRIQUE OCCIDENTALE FRANCAISE
Roux, Prosper C *see* SCIENCE NOUVELLE. LETTRE D'UN DISCIPLE DE LA SCIENCE NOUVELLE AUX RELIGIONNAIRES PRETENDUS SAINT-SIMONIENS
O ROUXINOL : ORGAM LITTERARIO E RECREATIVO – Penedo, Alagoas. 14 Mar-18 Jul 1909 – 1,5,6 – bl Biblioteca [072]
ROUX'S ARCHIVES OF DEVELOPMENTAL BIOLOGY – v. 121-189. 1930-80 – 1,5,9 – 14,904.00 – us UMI [574]
ROUYN-NORANDA PRESS – Rouyn, Canada. v2 n12. 21 jun 1934; 5 jan 1949-29 dec 1950; v35 n35. 31 aut 1967 – 2r – 1 – Can$50.00r – cn Can Microfilming [072]
Rouzier, S *see* DICTIONNAIRE GEOGRAPHIQUE ET ADMINISTRATIF UNIVERSEL D'HAITI
Rovegno, Inez C *see* THE SUBSTANCE AND DEVELOPMENT OF PRESERVICE TEACHERS' KNOWLEDGE DURING A FIELD-BASED ELEMENTARY PHYSICAL EDUCATION METHODS COURSE
ROVER – (Weekly newspaper publ in Mexico by Americans during the Mexican War) – nov 15, 1847 – 1 – us Western Res [071]
Rovini, Robert *see* HOELDERLIN
ROVNOST – Brno, Czechoslovakia. 1950; Feb 1953-Oct 1966 – 20r – 1 – us L of C Photodup [072]
Row, Charles Adolphus *see*
- CHRISTIAN THEISM:...THE EVIDENCE...AND THE OBJECTIONS URGED AGAINST IT
- THE JESUS OF THE EVANGELISTS, HIS HISTORICAL CHARACTER VINDICATED
- A MANUAL OF CHRISTIAN EVIDENCES
- THE NATURE AND EXTENT OF DIVINE INSPIRATION...DEDUCED FROM...THE N.T
- REASONS FOR BELIEVING IN CHRISTIANITY: ADDRESSED TO BUSY PEOPLE

Row, T Venkaswami *see* A MANUAL OF THE DISTRICT OF TANJORE
Rowan, W H *see* TWO YEARS IN HELL OR TWENTY MONTHS IN THE PRISON PENS OF THE NORTH, 24 JUN 1865
ROWE 1774-1848 – (Mf 1: Births & Deaths by Family 1774-97; Intentions 1795-1820. Mf 2: Marriages & Intentions 1798-1805; Index to Vital Records 1780-1836. Mf 4-7: Births & Deaths by Family 1780-1836. Mf 7: Marriages 1790-98. Mf 8: Index, Marriages & Intentions 1820-42. Mf 9: Marriages & Intentions 1842-49; Marriages 1788-1832 p74-100) – (mf ed 1983) – 9mf – 9 – 0-931248-32-9 – us Holbrook [920]
Rowe, Alan *see*
- "THE 1927 EXCAVATIONS AT BEISAN"
- "THE EXPEDITION AT BEISAN"
- "THE PALESTINIAN EXPEDITION"

Rowe, Daivd A *see* HEALTH-RELATED FITNESS LEVELS IN BAHAMIAN ELEMENTARY SCHOOL AGE CHILDREN
Rowe, H M *see* BUSINESS BOOKKEEPING AND PRACTICE
Rowe, Henry Kalloch *see* LANDMARKS IN CHRISTIAN HISTORY
Rowe, J A *see* ABAKAMA BA BUNYORO KITARA
Rowe, John Allen *see* SELECTED ARTICLES ON THE BATAKA CONTROVERSY APPEARING IN MUNNO, 1922-1923
Rowell, Chester H *see* ROWELL'S HISTORICAL AND LEGAL DIGEST OF ALL CONTESTED ELECTION CASES IN THE HOUSE OF REPRESENTATIVES OF THE U.S.
Rowell, T *see* NATAL AND THE BOERS
ROWELL'S HISTORICAL AND LEGAL DIGEST OF ALL CONTESTED ELECTION CASES IN THE HOUSE OF REPRESENTATIVES OF THE U.S. : 1ST TO THE 56TH CONGRESS, 1789-1901 / Rowell, Chester H – Washington: GPO. 1v. 1901 (all publ) – 9 – LLMC 95-125 – us L.L.M.C. [340]
Rowen, W H *see* THE STANDARD
Rowland, Adoniram Judson *see* THE PENTATEUCH
Rowland, David *see* A COMFORTABLE AYDE FOR SCHOLERS
Rowland, Dunbar *see*
- COURTS, JUDGES, AND LAWYERS OF MISSISSIPPI 1798-1935
- HISTORY OF MISSISSIPPI: THE HEART OF THE SOUTH

ROWLEY 1639-1900 – (Mf 1-9: Vital Records 1639-1752. Mf 10-22: Vital Records 1737-1844. Mf 23: Marriage Intentions 1844-1891. Mf 24-30: Vital Records 1665-1838. Mf 31-37: Freeholders & Fences 1634-1830. Mf 38-44: Freeholders & Mortgages 1713-86. Mf 45-51: Proprietors Records 1674-1852. Mf 52-56: Abridged Town Records 1643-1883. Mf 57-73: Town Records 1648-1807. Mf 74: Rebellion Records 1861-65. Mf 75-78: Index Births, Marriages, Deaths 1843-1909. Mf 79-89: Births, Marriages, Deaths 1843-1900) – (mf ed 1990) – 89mf – 9 – 0-87623-108-3 – us Holbrook [920]
Rowley, G D *see* ORNITHOLOGICAL MISCELLANY
Rowley, H H *see*
- FROM JOSEPH TO JOSHUA
- THE SERVANT OF THE LORD AND OTHER ESSAYS
- STUDIES IN OLD TESTAMENT PROPHECY

Rowson, A H *see* DIARY AND FINANCIAL ACCOUNTS
ROXANE / Lacerte, E A Bourgeois – Montreal: Ed. E Garand, c1924. SEM105P69 – 2mf – 9 – Can$4.50 – cn Bibl Nat [830]
Roxburgh, W *see*
- FLORA INDICA
- HORTUS BENGALENSIS
- PLANTS OF THE COAST OF COROMANDEL

ROXBURGHSHIRE, 1837 : BRITISH ISLES CENSUS DIRECTORIES PROJECT, SCOTLAND. VOL 53 – 1mf – 9 – A$9.00 – at Vine [941]
ROXBURGHSHIRE, 1866 : BRITISH ISLES CENSUS DIRECTORIES PROJECT, SCOTLAND. VOL 8 – 4mf – 9 – A$27.00 – at Vine [941]
ROXBURY 1630-1867 – (Mf 1-3: Vital Records 1633-1735. Mf 4-7: Index, Vitals Transcript 1630-1785. Mf 8-12: Births & Deaths 1785-1844. Mf 13-19: Vital Records 1630-1844. Mf 20-24: Vital Records 1843-49. Mf 25-27: Vital Records Index 1843-49. Mf 28-30: Birth Index 1642-1844. Mf 31.50: Births 1843-67. Mf 51-53: Births 1864-67. Mf 54-58: Birth Index 1843-60. Mf 59-62: Birth Index 1860-67. Mf 63-65: Marriage Index 1632-1860. Mf 66-67: Out-of-Town Marriages 1671-1799. Mf 68: Publishments & Marriages 1785-93. Mf 69-75: Marriages & Publishments 1785-1846. Mf 76-87: Marriages 1841-67. Mf 88-95: Marriages 1849-65. Mf 96-97: Marriages 1865-68. Mf 98-103: Marriage Intentions 1846-68. Mf 104-105: Marriage Index 1860-67. Mf 106-110: Death Index 1633-1860. Mf 111-123: Deaths 1843-60. Mf 124-139: Deaths 1850-67. Mf 140-142: Death Index 1860-67. Mf 143-146: Church Records 1771-1861. Mf 147-148: First Baptist Church 1821-84) – (mf ed 1985) – 148mf – 9 – 0-931248-83-3 – us Holbrook [920]
Roxo de Flores, Felipe *see* ELOQUENCIA FORENSE
Roy, Antoine *see* INDEX DU BULLETIN DES RECHERCHES HISTORIQUES

Roy, Camille *see*
- L'AVENIR DES MINORITES FRANCAISES AU CANADA
- L'UNIVERSITE LAVAL ET LES FETES DU CINQUANTENAIRE

LE ROY ET LE FERMIER. COMEDIE EN TROIS ACTES / Monsigny, P & Sedaine (Libretto) – Paris: Herissant, 1762 – 1 – us Sibley [780]

Roy, Jean *see* BIBLIOGRAPHIE ANALYTIQUE DE L'OEUVRE DU REVEREND PERE EUGENE LEFEBVRE...

Roy, Jean-Luc *see* BIBLIOGRAPHIE SUR LE CINEMA

ROY L. ELSON, SENATE SERVICE 1955-1969 : ADMINISTRATIVE ASSISTANT TO SENATOR CAROL HAYDEN AND CANDIDATE FOR THE U.S. SENATE – 4mf – 9 – $20.00 – us Scholarly Res [320]

Roy, Louis *see* MONTREAL GAZETTE

Roy, Marguerite *see* BIBLIOGRAPHIE ANALYTIQUE DU SUJET PEDAGOGIQUE

Roy, P-G *see* LE QUOTIDIEN

Roy, Pierre Georges *see* SAINTE ANNE DE LA POCATIERE, 1672-1900

Roy, Raoul *see*
- LES CAHIERS DE LA DECOLONISATION DU FRANC-CANADA
- L'INDEPENDANTISTE
- LA REVUE SOCIALISTE

Roy, Reina L *see* BIBLIOGRAPHIE ANALYTIQUE DE L'OEUVRE DE LEOPOLD LAMONTAGNE DE LA SOCIETE ROYALE DU CANADA, DOYEN DE LA FACULTE DES LETTRES A L'UNIVERSITE LAVAL

Roy, Sarat Chandra *see* THE MUNDAS AND THEIR COUNTRY

ROY STRYKER PAPERS, 1912-72 / Stryker, Roy – (Includes guide) – University of Louisville. – 15r – 1 – £860.00 – uk Chadwyck [920]

Roy, W *see* MILITARY ANTIQUITIES OF THE ROMANS IN BRITAIN

ROYAL ACADEMY EXTRA ILLUSTRATED CATALOGS – 28r – 1 – $1,800.00 – us UMI [700]

ROYAL ACADEMY OF ARTS ARCHIVES – (Pt 1 Council and General Assembly Minute Books, 20 reels $1360.00; Pt 2 Royal Academy Extra-Illustrated Catalogues, 1769-1940 25 reels $1700.00) – 48r – 1 – $3240.00 complete collection – us UMI [700]

ROYAL ACADEMY OF ARTS CATALOGUE – (Individual titles not listed separately) – London, 1852-1976 – 150 catalogues on 219mf – 9 – £1,380.00 – uk Chadwyck [700]

Royal Academy of Arts. London *see* REGISTER OF STUDENTS. 1769-1922

Royal Agricultural Society of England *see*
- JOURNAL

The Royal Agriculture and Commercial Society of British Guiana *see* TIMEHRI

ROYAL AIR FORCE FINAL REPORTS ON OPERATIONS : NIGHT RAIDS, 1941-45 / Great Britain. Royal Air Force – 1977 – 5r – 1 – $425.00 – S1292 – us Scholarly Res [941]

ROYAL AND HISTORICAL LETTERS DURING THE REIGN OF HENRY THE FOURTH, KING OF ENGLAND AND OF FRANCE, AND LORD OF IRELAND (RS18) / ed by Hingeston, F C – (v1: A.D. 1399-1404 1860 Dfl35.00. v2: A.D. 1405-1413 1864 (1965) Dfl32.00) – ne Slangenburg [941]

ROYAL AND OTHER HISTORICAL LETTERS LLUSTR. OF THE REIGN OF HENRY 2 (RS27) : FROM THE ORIGINALS IN THE PUBLIC HOUSE RECORD OFFICE / ed by Shirley, W W – (v1 1862 Dfl42.00. v2 1866 Dfl32.00) – 2v – ne Slangenburg [941]

Royal Anthropological Institute. Library *see* ANTHROPOLOGICAL INDEX TO CURRENT PERIODICALS

ROYAL ANTHROPOLOGICAL INSTITUTE NEWS *see* ANTHROPOLOGY TODAY

Royal Anthropological Institute of Great Britain and Ireland *see*
- JOURNAL
- PROCEEDINGS

ROYAL ARCHAEOLOGICAL INSTITUTE OF GREAT BRITAIN AND IRELAND *see* ARCHAEOLOGICAL JOURNAL

Royal Architectural Institute of Canada *see* PUBLICATIONS

ROYAL ARCHIVES AT WINDSOR CASTLE : CHANGES OF GOVERNMENT CABINET RECONSTRUCTION AND POLITICAL CRISES IN BRITAIN, 1837-1901 / Great Britain – 1 – us Primary [941]

Royal Army Veterinary Corps *see* JOURNAL

Royal Asiatic Society *see*
- JOURNAL
- PUBLICATIONS
- TRANSACTIONS

Royal Asiatic Society. Bombay Branch *see*
- JOURNAL OF THE ROYAL ASIATIC SOCIETY, BOMBAY BRANCH

Royal Asiatic Society. Malayan Branch *see* JOURNAL OF THE MALAYAN BRANCH OF THE ROYAL ASIATIC SOCIETY

Royal Asiatic Society of Bengal *see*
- AMAL-I-SALIH
- JOURNAL OF THE ROYAL ASIATIC SOCIETY OF BENGAL

Royal Asiatic Society of Great Britain and Ireland *see*
- ASIATIC SOCIETY MONOGRAPHS OF THE ROYAL ASIATIC SOCIETY OF GREAT BRITAIN AND IRELAND
- TRANSACTIONS OF THE ROYAL ASIATIC SOCIETY OF GREAT BRITAIN AND IRELAND

Royal Asiatic Society of Great Britain and Ireland. Korea Branch, Seoul *see* TRANSACTIONS

Royal Asiatic Society of Great Britain. Ceylon Branch *see* JOURNAL OF THE CEYLON BRANCH OF THE ROYAL ASIATIC SOCIETY

Royal Asiatic Society of Great Britain. Straits Branch *see* JOURNAL OF THE STRAITS BRANCH OF THE ROYAL ASIATIC SOCIETY

ROYAL ASTRONOMICAL SOCIETY – v.61-173. 1900-75 – 1,5,6 – 22966.00 – us Princeton Micro [520]

Royal Astronomical Society *see* MEMOIRS

ROYAL AUSTRALIAN HISTORICAL SOCIETY : CONSOLIDATED INDEX – (Apply to publ for details) – v1-70. 1901-85 – 9 – at Pascoe [020]

Royal Bank of Scotland. Archives *see* DARIEN RECORDS

Royal Botanic Gardens Library. Kew *see*
- AUTHOR AND CLASSIFIED CATALOGUES OF THE ROYAL BOTANIC GARDENS LIBRARY

Royal Botanical Garden, Madrid *see*
- ANTONIO JOSE CAVANILLES, 1745-1804
- HIPOLITO RUIZ LOPEZ, 1754-1815 AND JOSE ANTONIO PAVON Y JIMENEZ, 1754-1844
- MARTIN DE SESSE Y LACASTA, 1751-1808 AND JOSE MARIANO MOCINO, 1757-1820

Royal Botanical Gardens. Kew *see*
- THE CUMULATED INDEX KEWENSIS
- RARE BOOKS

ROYAL CANADIAN INSTITUTE *see* TRANSACTIONS OF THE CANADIAN INSTITUTE

Royal Canadian Military Institute *see* SELECTED PAPERS

THE ROYAL COLLECTION OF DRAWINGS AND WATERCOLOURS / Royal Library. Windsor Castle – (Bolognese ISBN: 0-907006-06-X $190.00. Canaletto ISBN: 0-907006-11-6 $95.00. Carracci ISBN: 0-907006-16-7 $95.00. Castiglione & Stefano ISBN: 0-907006-21-3 $95.00. Domenichino ISBN: 0-907006-26-4 $380.00. Early Italian, 15th and 16th C. ISBN: 0-907006-31-0 $285.00. English ISBN: 0-907006-36-1 $475.00. Fontana ISBN: 0-907006-41-8 $190.00. French ISBN: 0-907006-46-9 $190.00. German and Supplements ISBN: 0-907006-51-5 $190.00. Holbein ISBN: 0-907006-56-6 $95.00. Leonardo ISBN: 0-907006-61-2 $95.00. Roman ISBN: 0-907006-66-3 $190.00. Sandby ISBN: 0-907006-71-X $95.00. Venetian ISBN: 0-907006-76-0 $190.00. Guercino ISBN: 0-907006-81-7 $190.00. Dutch & Flemish ISBN: 0-907006-86-8 $95.00) – The complete collection of illustrations to all the catalogues. Available separately – 32r – 1 – $2,600.00 coll – 0-907006-91-4 – uk Mindata [740]

The Royal College of Obstetricians and Gynaecologists The Markland Library *see* ROYAL MATERNITY CHARITY MINUTES 1761-1949

Royal College of Physicians *see*
- INDEX TO PORTRAITS IN BOOKS
- PHARMACOPOEIA

Royal College of Surgeons of England *see* ANNALS

Royal Colonial Institute *see* PROCEEDINGS OF THE ROYAL COLONIAL INSTITUTE

THE ROYAL COMMISSION AND THE ORNAMENTS RUBRIC / MacColl, Malcolm – London; New York: Longmans, Green, 1906 – 2mf – us A.T.L.A. [240]

ROYAL COMMISSION ON BILINGUALISM: RESEARCH STUDIES / Canada – 16r – 1 – $1,040.00 – cn Library Assoc [971]

Royal Commonwealth Society *see*
- AFRICAN CLASSICS
- THE SLAVE TRADE BOOK AND PAMPHLET COLLECTION

THE ROYAL COMMONWEALTH SOCIETY, LONDON / ed by Falconer, John – (Includes finding aids on microfiche and in printed form) – 774mf – 9 – ne IDC [306]

ROYAL CORNWALL GAZETTE. (CORNWALL ROYAL GAZETT) – Truro, England. 1825-60.-w. 20 reels – 1 – uk British Libr Newspaper [072]

ROYAL COURT THEATRE : UPDATE 1990 – (Contains production records, publicity and stage plans of 27 plays presentations in 1990) – 38 b/w 1 colour mf – 9,15 – $302.00 – ISSN 0963-8903 – uk Emmett [790]

THE ROYAL DICTIONARY ABRIDGED / Boyer, Abel – 1700. 1061p. (English Linguistics Series 1500-1800) – 9 – us UMI [420]

THE ROYAL DOMINION NEWS BOY – Teeswater, Ont.: [s.n., 1867-18–?] – 9 – cn C.I.H.M. [073]

Royal Economic Society *see* ECONOMIC JOURNAL

Royal Empire Society *see* CATALOGUE 1930-32

THE ROYAL ENGINEER / Head, Francis Bond – London: J. Murray, 1869. 05527. (Pre-1900 Canadiana) – 9 – cn C.I.H.M. [620]

Royal Gardens Kew *see* BULLETIN OF MISCELLANEOUS INFORMATION

ROYAL GAZETTE / Bermuda – Hamilton. 1950-64 – 1 – us UMI [324]

ROYAL GAZETTE – Bermuda. 1950-1961 – 1 – us UMI [072]

ROYAL GAZETTE / British Guiana – 1803-1889 – 1 – us UMI [324]

ROYAL GAZETTE – Charlottetown, 1830-1831 – 1r – 1 – cn Preston [971]

ROYAL GAZETTE – Charlottetown, Prince Edward Island. v13 n663. 25 avr 1843 – 1r – 1 – Can$25.00 – cn Can Microfilming [072]

ROYAL GAZETTE – Charlottetown, Prince Edward Island. v83-94. 1957-68 – 3r – 1 – us Ross [324]

ROYAL GAZETTE – Fredericton, New Brunswick, 1957-68 – 4r – 1 – us Ross [971]

ROYAL GAZETTE – Guiana. 1803-1889 – 1 – us UMI [072]

ROYAL GAZETTE – Halifax, Nova Scotia. v158-178. 1949-68 – 22r – 1 – us Ross [324]

ROYAL GAZETTE – Hamilton, Bermuda. Mar 1941-Dec 1975.-d. 176 reels – 1 – uk British Libr Newspaper [072]

ROYAL GAZETTE – Kingston, Jamaica. -w. 28 Dec 1816-27 Dec 1817. 1 reel – 1 – uk British Libr Newspaper [072]

ROYAL GAZETTE – Nassau. Bahamas. 1804-1837 – 1 – us UMI [072]

ROYAL GAZETTE / New Brunswick – Saint John and Fredericton. 1785-1841 – 16r – 1 – $1,040.00 – cn Library Assoc [971]

ROYAL GAZETTE / New Brunswick. Canada – v. 115-126. 1957-1968 – 1 – us UMI [324]

ROYAL GAZETTE / Nova Scotia – 1801-24 – 6r – 1 – $390.00 – cn Library Assoc [971]

ROYAL GAZETTE / Nova Scotia – (1969-82 5. 1983- 9) – 1949-68 – 1,5,9 – cn Micromedia [971]

ROYAL GAZETTE / Prince Edward Island – 1832-53 – 9r – 1 – $585.00 – cn Library Assoc [971]

ROYAL GAZETTE AND BAHAMA ADVERTISER – Bahamas. -sw. 1804-1837 – 1 – us UMI [072]

ROYAL GAZETTE AND MISCELLANY OF THE ISLAND OF SAINT JOHN / Prince Edward Island – 1791-94 – 1r – 1 – $68.00 – cn Library Assoc [971]

ROYAL GAZETTE AND NEWFOUNDLAND ADVERTISER / Newfoundland – 1810-1900 – 17r – 1 – $1,105.00 – cn Library Assoc [971]

ROYAL GAZETTE; AND SIERRA LEONE ADVERTISER – Freetown. Sierra Leone. -w. Jan 1821-Jul 1825. (1 reel) – 1 – uk British Libr Newspaper [072]

ROYAL GAZETTE WEEKLY – Hamilton, Bermuda. -w. 1961. 1 reel – 1 – uk British Libr Newspaper [072]

Royal Geographic Society *see* PROCEEDINGS

THE ROYAL GOLD COAST GAZETTE – Ghana. 1822-23 – 1 – uk Microform Academic [072]

ROYAL HISTORICAL SOCIETY – v1-10. 1872-82.New Series v1-20, 1883-1906; Series 3 v1-11, 1907-17; Series 4 v1-32, 1918-50; Series 5 v1, 1951 – 1 – us Princeton Micro [900]

Royal Historical Society *see* TRANSACTIONS

ROYAL HISTORICAL SOCIETY OF VICTORIA JOURNAL – 1911-1967 – 95mf – 9 – A$185.00 – at State Libr Vic [920]

Royal Horticultural Society *see* JOURNAL

THE ROYAL HOSPITAL OF ST BARHOLOMEW, LONDON. MINUTE BOOKS, ACCOUNTS AND OTHER RECORDS – 1547-1801. 19 reels with printed guide – £775.00 – uk World [610]

Royal Institute of British Architects *see*
- COMPLETE MICROFICHE CATALOGUE OF BOOKS HELD BY THE BRITISH ARCHITECTURAL LIBRARY
- THE GREY BOOKS INDEX
- NOMINATION PAPERS
- THE RIBA DRAWINGS COLLECTION
- THE RIBA DRAWINGS COLLECTION: EARLIER PHASES
- TRANSACTIONS OF THE ROYAL INSTITUTE OF BRITISH ARCHITECTS

ROYAL INSTITUTE OF BRITISH ARCHITECTS CARD CATALOGNE : AUTHOR/TITLE AND SUBJECT CATALOGUE OF BOOKS – 1132mf – 9 – £3,500.00 – uk World [720]

Royal Institute of International Affairs *see* INDEX TO PERIODICAL ARTICLES, 1979-1989, IN THE LIBRARY OF THE ROYAL INSTITUTE OF INTERNATIONAL AFFAIRS

Royal Institute of International Affairs. London *see* A BRIEF POLITICAL AND ECONOMIC SURVEY

Royal Institute of Philosophy *see* JOURNAL

Royal Institution *see* QUARTERLY JOURNAL OF SCIENCE AND ARTS

Royal Institution of Chartered Surveyors *see*
- ABSTRACTS AND REVIEWS
- WEEKLY BRIEFINGS

Royal Institution of Great Britian *see* PROCEEDINGS

Royal Irish Academy *see*
- THE IRISH MANUSCRIPT COLLECTION
- NOTEBOOKS OF JOHN WINDELE
- ORDNANCE SURVEY MEMOIRS
- PROCEEDINGS
- PROCEEDINGS. SERIES A: MATHEMATICAL, ASTRONOMICAL AND PHYSICAL SCIENCE
- PROCEEDINGS. SERIES B: BIOLOGICAL, GEOLOGICAL, AND CHEMICAL SCIENCE
- PROCEEDINGS. SERIES C: ARCHEOLOGY, CELTIC STUDIES, HISTORY, LINGUISTICS AND LITERATURE

Royal, Joseph *see* HISTOIRE DU CANADA, 1841 A 1867

ROYAL LEAMINGTON SPA COURIER *see* LEAMINGTON SPA COURIER

ROYAL LEAMINGTON SPA OBSERVER – (Also known as: Leamington Spa Observer) – Sep 29-Dec 29 1988; 1989; Jan-Jul 5 1990; Oct-Dec 1991; 1992; Jan-Dec 21 1995; 1996 – 19r – 1 – uk British Libr Newspaper [072]

Royal Library. Windsor Castle *see*
- ANATOMICAL DRAWINGS
- THE CUMBERLAND MAPS
- HORSES AND OTHER ANIMALS
- LEONARDO DRAWINGS
- NATURE STUDIES
- THE ROYAL COLLECTION OF DRAWINGS AND WATERCOLOURS
- TITLES ON COLOUR MICROFICHE

Royal Literary Fund *see* ARCHIVES

ROYAL MATERNITY CHARITY MINUTES 1761-1949 / The Royal College of Obstetricians and Gynaecologists The Markland Library – (Minutes, 1761-1791. v1-5; Minutes, 1791-1816. v6-9; Minutes, 1816-1830. v10-13; Minutes, 1832-1846. v14-17; Minutes, 1846-1863. v18-20; Minutes, 1863-1886. v21-24; Minutes, 1887-1915. v25-28; Minutes, 1916-1949. v29-30; Robert Barnes Case-book, 1857-1868; Account of the Royal Maternity Charity, 1829) – 8r – 1 – £350.00 set – uk Academic [618]

[THE ROYAL MELODY COMPLEAT] / Tan'sur, W – (2 vols) – Newbury-Port, 1773 – 1 – us Sibley [780]

Royal Meteorological Society *see* PROCEEDINGS

Royal Microscopical Society, London *see* TRANSACTIONS

ROYAL MILITIA AND YEOMANRY CAVALRY: THE ARMY LIST, 1850 / Great Britain. Royal Army – 6mf – 7 – uk Microform Academic [324]

Royal Miscroscopical Society *see* JOURNAL

ROYAL NAVAL BIOGRAPHY / Marshall, John – 10v. plus 4 suppls – 9 – $520.00 – uk Libr Preservation [920]

THE ROYAL NAVY: A HISTORY FROM THE EARLIEST TIMES TO THE PRESENT / Clowes, William Laird – 7v. 1897-1903 – 9 – $280.00 – uk Libr Preservation [355]

Royal Netherlands Academy of Science *see* PROCEEDINGS

The Royal Numismatic Society *see* NUMISMATIC CHRONICLE AND JOURNAL

Royal Philosophical Society of Glasgow *see* PROCEEDINGS

THE ROYAL POLITICIAN REPRESENTED IN ONE HUNDRED EMBLEMS / Saavedra, Faxardo D de – O 741 1. 1700 – 9 – ne IDC [320]

THE ROYAL PROVINCE OF NEW SCOTLAND AND HER BARONETS / Duncan, Francis – London: W. Clowes, 1878. 05196. (Pre-1900 Canadiana) – 9 – cn C.I.H.M. [971]

ROYAL SHAKESPEARE THEATRE PROMPT BOOKS 1976-85 – (Prompt bks for all 82 productions of 36 Shakespeare plays staged by the RSC between 1976-85, giving full performance details. With printed index) – 1991 – 195mf – 9 – $1,094.00 – 1-869934-45-8 – uk Emmett [790]

Royal Society *see*
- BOOK CATALOGUE OF THE LIBRARY OF THE ROYAL SOCIETY
- COLLECTIONS FROM THE ROYAL SOCIETY
- COUNCIL MINUTES, 1660-1800
- THE EARLY LETTERS AND CLASSIFIED PAPERS, 1660-1740
- JOURNAL BOOKS OF SCIENTIFIC MEETINGS, 1660-1800
- LETTERS AND PAPERS OF ROBERT BOYLE
- LETTERS AND PAPERS OF SIR JOHN HERSCHEL
- MISCELLANEOUS MANUSCRIPTS

Royal Society of Arts *see*
- THE AMERICAN CORRESPONDENCE
- ARCHIVES: SERIES A

ROYAL SOCIETY OF ARTS: JOURNAL – v1-104. 1852-1955 – 1,5,6 – us Princeton Micro [073]

Royal Society of Canada *see*
- PROCEEDINGS AND TRANSACTIONS
- TRANSACTIONS AND PROCEEDINGS

Royal Society of Edinburgh *see*
- PROCEEDINGS
- PROCEEDINGS. SECTION A. MATHEMATICAL AND PHYSICAL SCIENCES
- PROCEEDINGS. SECTION B. BIOLOGY
- TRANSACTIONS

Royal Society of Health *see* JOURNAL

ROYAL SOCIETY OF HEALTH JOURNAL – (v96-102, no.6. 5,6,9) – v1-102, no.6. 1879-1982 – 1 – us UMI [073]

Royal Society of London *see*
- CATALOGUE OF SCIENTIFIC PAPERS
- PHILOSOPHICAL TRANSACTIONS
- PROCEEDINGS

Royal Society of Medicine *see* PROCEEDINGS

Royal Society of New South Wales *see* JOURNAL AND PROCEEDINGS

THE ROYAL STANDARD / ed by Campbell, Rollo – Montreal, Canada. v1 n3. 21 mai 1842 – 1r – 1 – Can$25.00 – cn Can Microfilming [072]

THE ROYAL STANDARD – Toronto. 1836-37 – 1 – 45.00 – cn McLaren [971]

ROYAL STATISTICAL SOCIETY *see* HISTORY OF ECONOMICS SERIES

Royal Statistical Society. Great Britain *see* JUBILEE VOLUME...JUNE 22-24, 1885

Royal Television Society *see* TELEVISION.

ROYAL THAI GOVERNMENT GAZETTE – Bangkok, 1946-67 – 10r – 1 – us Ross [324]

THE ROYAL TOMBS OF THE EARLIEST DYNASTIES (MEES VOL 21) : PART 2 / Flinders Petrie, W M – London, 1901 – 9mf – 8 – Dfl32.00 – ne Slangenburg [930]

THE ROYAL TOMBS OF THE FIRST DYNASTIES / Petrie, William Matthew Flinders – 2v. 1901 – 9 – $18.00 – us I.R.C. [930]

THE ROYAL TOMBS OF THE FIRST DYNASTY (MEES VOL 18) : PART 1 / Flinders Petrie, W M – London, 1900 – 8mf – 8 – Dfl30.00 – ne Slangenburg [930]

Royal United Service Institute for Defence Studies *see* RUSI

THE "ROYAL WILLIAM", THE PIONEER OF STEAM NAVIGATION: A PAPER READ BEFORE THE LITERARY AND HISTORICAL SOCIETY OF QUEBEC, ON THE 31ST DAY OF MARCH, 1891 / Campbell, Archibald – Quebec: Morning Chronicle, 1891. 02822. (Pre-1900 Canadiana) – 9 – cn C.I.H.M. [380]

THE ROYAL WOMAN / Mann, Heinrich – Trans. by Arthur J. Ashton. New York: Macaulay, (c1930). 320p.1 reel. 1297 – 1 – us U.W. Library [830]

LE ROYALISTE – (5 missing numbers) – Angers, March – July 1830 – 1r – fr Armell [320]

ROYALSTON 1772-1895 – (Mf 1-3: Births & Deaths 1756-1845. Mf 3: Marriages 1840-41; Intentions & Marriages 1797-1813. Mf 4: Marriages & Intentions 1813-28. Mf 5: Intentions & Marriages 1828-41. Mf 6: Births & Marriages 1843-52. Mf 6-7: Deaths 1843-52. Mf 8: Birth Index 1852-1905; Births 1852-55. Mf 9: Births 1855-72. Mf 10: Births 1873-95. Mf 10-11: Marriage Index 1852-1905. Mf 11: Marriages 1852-60. Mf 12: Marriages 1861-87. Mf 13: Marriages 1888-95. Mf 13-14: Death Index 1852-1905. Mf 14: Deaths 1852-66. Mf 15: Deaths 1867-84. Mf 16: Deaths 1885-95. Mf 17: Vital Records Index 1843-52. Mf18-21: Index [not available]. Mf 22: Births & Marriages 1896-1905. Mf 22-23: Deaths 1896-1905) – (mf ed 1987) – 21mf – 9 – 0-87623-031-1 – us Holbrook [920]

LE ROYANNAIS – Royan. 28 juil 1867-26 juin 1870, 2 sept, 9 sept 1871 – 1 – fr A.C.R.P.P. [073]

LE ROYAUME DE BENIN / Nadaillac – Paris, de Soye et fils imprimeurs. 1898 – 9 – 5.00 – fr Orientalistes [960]

LE ROYAUME DE CATHERINE DE MEDICIS / Romier, L – H 382 2. v. 1-2. 1922 – 8 – ne IDC [944]

LE ROYAUME DE FRANCE ET LES ETATS DE LORRAINE : DICTIONNAIRE DES PROVINCES, VILLES, BOURGS, NOMBRE DE FEUX, DIOCESES, BAILLIAGES, ETC / Doisy, M – Paris, 1753 – 3mf – 9 – F90.00 – fr F.F.G. [944]

LE ROYAUME DE NAUDELIT, OU LA FRANCE RESSUSCITEE PAR LES ETATS-GENERAUX, PAR UN SOLITAIRE – (Utopias in the Enlightenment series). 1789 – 9 – fr Hachette [830]

UN ROYAUME HAMITE AU CENTRE DE L'AFRIQUE / Pages, Pere – Brussels, 1933 – 1 – us Res Libr [960]

Royce, Josiah *see*
- THE CONCEPTION OF IMMORTALITY
- STUDIES OF GOOD AND EVIL
- THE WORLD AND THE INDIVIDUAL. FIRST SERIES, THE FOUR HISTORICAL CONCEPTIONS OF BEING

Royce, Josiah et al *see* THE CONCEPTION OF GOD

Roychoudhury, Makhanlal, Sastri *see* THE DIN-I-ILAHI: OR, THE RELIGION OF AKBAR

ROYCROFT QUARTERLY – 1-3. May-November 1896 – 1 – us UMI [073]

Royen, A van *see* FLORAE LEYDENSIS PRODOMUS

Royen, J van *see*
- S' MENSCHEN LEVEN VAN DE WIEG TOT HET GRAF
- 'S MENSCHEN LEVEN VAN DE WIEG TOT HET GRAF

Royle, J F *see*
- THE FIBROUS PLANTS OF INDIA
- ILLUSTRATIONS OF THE BOTANY AND OTHER BRANCHES OF NATURAL HISTORY OF THE HIMALAYAN MOUNTAINS AND OF THE FLORA OF CASHMERE

Roys y Mendoza, Francisco *see* CONSTITUCIONES SYNODALES

Royston. Yorkshire. St. John the Baptist *see* PARISH REGISTERS

DER ROYTER FALK = THE RED HAWK – (In Yiddish. Mimeographed) – 1947-1949 – 1r – 1 – $25.00 – cn Can Microfilming [072]

DER ROYTER SHTERN = THE RED STAR – Vitiebsk, RU. v2 no355 28 Oct 1921; v2 no356 29 Oct 1921 – 1r – 1 – $25.00 – cn Can Microfilming [072]

Roy-Tessier, Antoinette *see* ESSAI DE BIO-BIBLIOGRAPHIE SUR CECILE ROULEAU, EDUCATRICE

ROZANA AKALI PATTRAKA – (In Punjabi language) – Jullundur, India. May-22 Sep 1948; 8 Mar 1950-1959; 1962-93 – 115r – 1 – us L of C Photodup [072]

ROZANA HIND – Calcutta, India. Oct 1942-1947; Mar 1948-1953 – 21r – 1 – us L of C Photodup [072]

Rozanov, I *see* RUSSKIE LIRIKI

Rozanov, I N *see* PUTEVODITEL PO SOVREMENNOJ RUSSKOJ LITERATURE

ROZARYER LEBN = ROSARIO LIFE – (In Yiddish. Weekly) – Rosario, AG. v23 no1080. Sep 1946 – 1r – 1 – $25.00 – cn Can Microfilming [072]

Rozaven, R P *see* L'EGLISE RUSSE ET L'EGLISE CATHOLIQUE

ROZBUDOVA DERZHAVY – Biulleten' Zareva. (21). Montreal. 1949-57. Lacking: 1949-50. BR-5750 2 – 8 – ne IDC [073]

Roze, Louis *see* LIVRE DE FAMILLE

Rozenberg, V A *see* RUSSKAIA PECHAT' I TSENZURA V PROSHLOM I NASTOIASHCHEM

Rozenfel'd, B A *see* ARABSKIE I PERSIDSKIE FIZIKO-MATEMATICHESKIE RUKOPISI V BIBLIOTEKAKH SOVETSKOGO SOIUZA

Rozenkampf, G A *see* OBOZRENIE KORMCHEI KNIGI V ISTORICHESKOM VIDE

Rozhdeistvenskii, N F *see* NALOGOVYI SPRAVOCHNIK DLIA KUSTAREI I REMESLENNIKOV I IKH PERVICHNIKH OB"EDINENII

ROZHDENIE BOGOV / Merezhkovskii, Dimitrii – Tutankamon na Krite. Prague. 1925. BR-786 2 – 8 – ne IDC [460]

Rozhdestvenskii, I *see* KNIGA ESFIR'. V TEKSTAKH: EVREISKOM-MASORETSKOM, GRECHESKOM, DREVNEM LATINSKOM I SLAVIANSKOM

Rozhkov, N *see* AGRARNYI VOPROS V ROSSII I EGO RESHENIE V PROGRAMMAKH RAZLICHNYKH PARTII

ROZHLEDY – Chrudim, Czechoslovakia. v1-8, 10-17. 1892-1899, 1901-1907 – 1 – us I.U. Libraries [073]

ROZHLEDY (IOWA ROZHLEDY) – Cedar Rapids, IA. -w. 1 Jul 1909-20 Jul 1910 – 1 – us NE Hist [071]

ROZVIDKY MYKHAILA DRAHOMANOVA PRO UKRAINS KU NARODNIU SLOVESNIST I PIS MENSTVO / Drahomaniv, Mykhailo Petrovych – L'vovi: Nakl. Naukovoho tovarystva im. Shevchenka, 1899-1907. 4v. ill – 1 – us U.W. Library [390]

RQ – v1- 1960- 1; v11- 5,6; v15- 9 – us UMI [073]

RS / Kentucky. Agricultural Extension Service – v. 1-31. 1951-68 – 1,5,6 – us Spaulding [630]

RS / University of Kentucky. Department of Rural Sociology – No.32-72. 1971-83. 1 reel – 1,5 – us Spaulding [630]

RS MEANS COST DATA PUBLICATIONS – 1943-87. Backfiles of annual cost manuals published by R.S. Means Co., Inc – 500mf – 9 – $2,050.00 – us UPA [380]

RSF MITTEILUNGEN - RADIKAL-SOZIALE FREIHEITSPARTEI – Bremen, aug 1 1948-53 – 2r – 1 – Inquire at Mikrofilmarchiv for details – gw Misc Inst [072]

R.S.F.S.R. Gosplan *see* EKONOMICHESKOE RA IONIROVANII ROSSII PRI GOSUDARSTVENNO I OBSHCHEPLANOVO I KOMISSII S.T.O.

R.S.F.S.R., Narodny i komissariat zemledelii a *see*
- BORBA S ZASUKHOI

R.S.F.S.R. T Sentralnoe statisticheskoe upravlenie, Leningradski i gubernski i otdel statistiki *see* BI UDZHETY LENINGRADSKIKH RABOCHIKH I SLUZHASHCHIKH V 1922-1926 G.G.

RSFSR V T SIFRAKH : T SENTRALNOE STATISTICHESKOE UPRAVLENIE PRI SOVETE MINISTROV RSFSR – (Includes c.1: 1965) – Moksva: "Statistika", 1966- – 1 – CSUXALJ7425-S – us Hoover Inst Photo [947]

RSFSR V T SIFRAKH : T SENTRALNOE STATISTICHESKOE UPRAVLENIE PRI SOVETE MINISTROV RSFSR – (Includes c.1: 1965) – Moskva: "Statistika", 1966- – 1 – CSUXALJ7433-S – us Hoover Inst Photo [947]

RSFSR V...GODU : T SENTRALNOE STATISTICHESKOE UPRAVLENIE PRI SOVETE MINISTROV RSFSR – (Includes c.1: 1959, 1962-1964.//) – Moskva: Gosstatizdat T SSU SSSR, 1960-1965. 6v – 1 – CSUXAKZ6083-S – us Hoover Inst Photo [947]

RSI ROOFING/SIDING/INSULATION – May 1948- – 1,5,6,9 – us UMI [690]

RSSI-RESEARCHES SEMIOTIQUES = SEMIOTIC INQUIRY – (Cont: Canadian Journal of Research in Semiotics, 1981) – Montreal. v1-14. 1981-94 – 9 – Can$20.00y – cn Micromedia [400]

RSSI-RESEARCHES SEMIOTIQUES/SEMIOTIC INQUIRY *see* CANADIAN JOURNAL OF RESEARCH IN SEMIOTICS

RT : A JOURNAL OF RADICAL THERAPY – (See now: State and Mind. See also: Rough Times) – v-5. 1974-76 – 1 – us UMI [150]

THE RT. HON. SIR ERNEST SATOW / Allen, B M – London, 1933 – 2mf – 9 – ILM-1186/1 – ne IDC [340]

RTA RECORDS, LR-RA 0001, 1848-1958 – (Records of several plank toll road and street car companies, predecessors to the Cleveland Railway Co., of the CRC, of the Shaker Heights Rapid Transit, and copies of the Taylor Grant negotiations and settlement) – Cuyahoga County – 25r – 1 – us Western Res [338]

RTA-NACHRICHTEN – Berlin, 1934-jun 26 1935, 1936-37 – 3r – 1 – Inquire at Mikrofilmarchiv for details – gw Misc Inst [072]

RTCA (RADIO TECHNICAL COMMISSION FOR AERONAUTICS) – Standards. Printed index. Updated every 60 days – 6,9 – us Info Handling [621]

RTSD NEWSLETTER – (v.4-. 1977- 5,6,9) – (Resources and Technical Services Division). v.1-. 1976- – 1 – us UMI [073]

A RUA : JORNAL INDEPENDENTE, POLITICO, LITERARIO E NOTICIOSO – Maceio, Alagoas. 19, 20, 22 Jan 1920 – 1,5,6 – bl Biblioteca [072]

A RUA – Lisbon. No.1-90. 8 Apr 1976-30 Jan 1980. Incomplete. (Portuguese Revolution of 1974. Newspapers from Portugal publ. from 21 Feb 1971 to 15 Feb 1980, collected and filmed by University of Wisconsin-Madison libraries.) – 1 – us U.W. Library [072]

RUAM PRAKAT KHONG KHANA PATIWAT CHABAP THI-L THUNG CHABAP SUTTHAI.. / Sathian Wichailak – Krungthep: Nitiwet, 1961. 86p. Thailand proclamations, executive orders. In Thai – 1 – us U.W. Library [340]

Ruan, Nianyu *see* SPORT ACHIEVEMENT ORIENTATION OF MALE AND FEMALE INTERCOLLEGIATE ATHLETES, INTRAMURAL ATHLETES, AND NONATHLETES

RUANDA : KLEINE ANFAENGE-GROSSE AUFGABEN DER EVANGELISCHEN MISSION IM ZWISCHENSEENGEBIET DEUTSCHE-OSTAFRIKAS / Johansen, Ernst – 2. Aufl. Bielefeld: Verlagshandlung der Anstalt Bethel, 1915 – us Res Libr [240]

Ruanda-Urundi *see* PLAN DECENNAL ETUDE SUR L'EVOLUTION ECONOMIQUE DU RUANDA-URUNDI DE 1949 A 1955

Ruanda-Urundi. Belgium. Ministere des Colonies *see* PLAN DECENNAL POUR LE DEVELOPPEMENT ECONOMIQUE ET SOCIAL

RUANG PHRA PATHOMCHEDI / Thipphakonrawong (Kham), Chao Phraya – 1926. 32p. ill. In Thai – 1 – us U.W. Library [290]

Ruano, Jesus Maria *see*
- LAS DOS ROMAS
- RESUMEN HISTORICO-CRITICO DE LITERATURA COLOMBIANA

Ruant, F *see* LA TRIBUNE CANADIENNE

Ruault, Nicolas *see* ELOGE DE MARIE-FRANCOIS DE VOLTAIRE

Rubakin, N A *see* SREDI KNIG. OPYT OBZORA RUSSKIKH KNIZHNYKH BOGATSTV V SVIAZI S ISTORIEI NAUCHNOFILOSOFSKIKH I LITERATURNO-OBSHCHESTVENNYKH IDEI

Rubanyi, Gabor M *see* ENDOTHELIUM

RUBBER AGE – (Continued as: Elastomerics) – v1-108 1917-76 1; v98-108 5,6; v108 1976 9 – us UMI [670]

RUBBER AND PLASTICS NEWS – (1983-. 1,5,6,9) – v1-. 1979- – 1 – us UMI [073]

RUBBER: AREA, PRODUCTION, TRADE AND CONSUMPTION / Indonesia. Biro Pusat Statistik – SE-154 1. 1958 – 9 – ne IDC [310]

RUBBER CHEMISTRY AND TECHNOLOGY – v1- 1928- 1; v39- 5,6; v50- 9 – us UMI [660]

RUBBER DEVELOPMENTS – v16- 1963- 1; v30- 5,6,9 – us UMI [600]

RUBBER JOURNAL – v1-155 1884-1973 1; v153-155 5,6 – us UMI [600]

RUBBER JOURNAL AND INTERNATIONAL PLASTICS – v. 63-127. 1922-1954 – 1,5,6 – us Princeton Micro [600]

RUBBER WORLD – v1- 1889- 1; v163- 5,6; v175- 9 – us UMI [600]

RUBBER WORLD – v1-120. 1889-1949. Continues: India Rubber World and Electrical Review – 1,5,6 – us Princeton Micro [600]

Rube, Wolrad see DER FUENFFUESSIGE JAMBUS BEI HEBBEL
Rubeis, Il de see
- PARERGA ATQUE ORNAMENTA...
- PARERGA ATQUE ORNAMENTA. QUAE EXTABANT IN RUINIS DOMUS IMPERAT
RUBENS ET SON TEMPS / Reunion des musees nationaux. Paris – 1936. 40 illus. 3 fiches – 9 – fr Réunion [750]
Rubens, Pieter-Paul see PALAZZI ANTICHI DI GENOVA RACCOLTI E DESIGNATI DA PIETRO PAOLO RUBENS
Ruberti, A see SYSTEMS, SCIENCES AND MODELLING
Rubin, Alvin B see LAW CLERK HANDBOOK
Rubin, Cynthia see THE SHAKER COLLECTION
Rubin, Jerome see THE SHAKER COLLECTION
Rubinkam, Nathaniel Irwin see THE SECOND PART OF THE BOOK OF ZECHARIAH
Rubino, J A see LEXICON BONAVENTURIANUM
Rubinstein, S M see DIVREI SOFERIM
Rubinstein, Susanna see SCHILLER-PROBLEME
Rubio, A see
- COMMENTARII IN LIBROS ARISTOTELIS STAGIRITAE PHILOSOPHORUM PRINCIPIS DE ANIMA...
- COMMENTARII IN LIBROS ARISTOTELIS STAGYRITAE PHILOSOPHORUM PRINCIPIS, DE ANIMA...
- COMMENTARII IN OCTO LIBROS ARISTOTELIS DE PHYSICO AUDITU, SEU AUSCULTATIONE CONTINENTUR
Rubio, Angel see LA EMIGRACION EXTREMENA A INDIAS. SIGLO 16. FICHERO DOCUMENTAL
Rubio Cercas, Manuel see ESTANCIA DE ISABEL LA CATOLICA EN TRUJILLO
Rubio Diaz, Felix see POBRES CANTOS
Rubio Garcia, Jose see INFORME ESTADISTICO GANADERO
Rubio German, Francisco see HISTORIA DE NUESTRA SENORA DE GUADALUPE...
Rubio, Julio see COLEGIO OFICIAL DE SECRETARIOS, INTERVENTORES Y DEPORTIVOS DE ADMINISTRACION LOCAL DE LA PROVINCIA DE CACERES. MEMORIA QUE FORMULA EL SECRETARIO...DEL EJERCICIO 1941...
Rubio Merino, Pedro see
- CATALOGO DEL ARCHIVO DE LA CASA DEL SOL
- DON DIEGO CAMACHO Y AVILA...
- SAN JUAN DE RIBERA. OBISPO DE BADAJOZ
Rubio Moreno, Luis see
- INVENTARIO GENERAL DE RAGISTROS CEDULARIOS DEL ARCHIVO GENERAL DE INDIAS DE SEVILLA...
- PASAJEROS A INDIAS
Rubio Recio, Jose Manuel see BADAJOZ APUNTE ESTRUCTURAL Y GENETICO
Rubio y Lluch, A see LOS CATALANES EN GRECIA...
Rubio y munoz-Bocanegra, A see EXTREMADURA Y AMERICA. SEVILLA, 1929
RUBY BAPTIST CHURCH. CHESTERFIELD COUNTY. SOUTH CAROLINA : CHURCH RECORDS – (90p) – 1975-June 1976. History, 1903-1975 – 1 reel – 1 – $5.00 – us Baptist [240]
RUBY HILL MINING REPORT – Eureka, NV. 14 Aug 1879 – 1r – 1 – $50.00 – U04515 – us Library Micro [071]
Ruchat, Abraham see HISTORY OF THE REFORMATION IN SWITZERLAND
LA RUCHE ARTISTIQUE ET LITTERAIRE – devenu: Les Ecrivains contemporains et la Ruche. no. 1-122. Paris. nov 1880-juil 1883. mq no. 27, 29-30, 33, 43-50, 55-99 – 1 – fr A.C.R.P.P. [073]
LA RUCHE LITTERAIRE – Montreal, Canada. jul 1853-fev 1855; mar-jun 1859 – 1r – 1 – Can$40.00 – cn Can Microfilming [073]
LA RUCHE POPULAIRE – Paris. dec 1839-1842, oct 1843-mars 1845, 1847-49 – 1 – fr A.C.R.P.P. [073]
Rucinski, Terri J see THE EFFECTS OF INTERMITTENT COMPRESSION ON EDEMA IN POST-ACUTE ANKLE SPRAINS
EIN RUCKBLICK AUF MEIN LEBEN: INBESONDERE ANF DIE ENTWICKLUNG DES HANDELS IN DEN LETZTEN FUNFZIG JAHREN / Pilet, Otto – Magdeburg: Faber, 1900 – 1 – us U.W. Library [943]
Rudakov, V E see POSLEDNIE DNI TSENZURY V MINISTERSTVE NARODNAGO PROSVESHCHENIIA
Rudan, P see ETUDE ANTHROPOLOGIQUE DE L'ILE DE SILBA
Rudas, L see ABENTEURER- UND LUIQUIDATORENTUM
Rudbeck, O see THESAURUS LINGUARUM ASIAE ET EUROPAE HARMONICUS...
Rudberg, SY see EUSTATHIUS
Rudd, George R see THE BIBLE IN OUR PUBLIC SCHOOLS
Rudd, Sayer see PRODROMOS: OR, OBSERVATIONS ON ENGLISH LETTERS
Ruddiman, Thomas see THE RUDIMENTS OF THE LATIN TONGUE
RUDDIMAN'S WEEKLY MERCURY – Edinburgh, Scotland. Dec 1781-June 1783 – 1 – us Res Libr [072]
RUDE PRAVO – 1991-1994 – 4r – 1 – Sfr480.00 – sz Infoprint [947]
RUDE PRAVO – Prague, Czechoslovakia. -d. 17 July 1945-Dec 1952. 1945-49 imperfect. 22 reels – 1 – uk British Libr Newspaper [072]
RUDE PRAVO – Prague, Czechoslovakia. Jan-May 1938; May 1945-1966 – 25r – 1 – us L of C Photodup [072]
RUDE PRAVO : USTREDNI ORGAN KOMUNISTICKE STRANY CESKOSLOVENSKA – Praha: Ustredni vybor KSC, feb 20-dec 1952; 1953-55; 1956-88; 1989-90; apr-dec 1991 – us Res Libr [072]
Rudenko, M B see OPISANIE KURDSKIKH RUKOPISEI LENINGRADSKIKH SOBRANII
Rudge, E see PLANTARUM GUIANAE RARIORUM ICONES ET DESCRIPTIONES HACTENUS INEDITAE
RUDHOLM'S SHORT HISTORY AND SURVEY OF PIXLEY UNION SCHOOL DISTRICT – 1r – 1 – $50.00 – B40282 – us Library Micro [978]
Rudhyar, Dane see THE ASTROLOGY OF PERSONALITY
RUDIMENTA GRAMMATICES / Linacre, Thomas – 1423?. 101p. (English Linguistics Series 1500-1800) – 9 – us UMI [400]
RUDIMENTA MUSICAE IN GRATIAM STUDIOSAE IUVENTUTIS DILIGENTER COMPORTATA / Listenius, Nicolaus – P-373. 1533 – 9 – ne IDC [780]
RUDIMENTA MUSICES.. / Agricola, Martin – 1539 – 9 – us Sibley [780]
THE RUDIMENTES OF P. RAMUS HIS LATINE GRAMMAR: ENGLISHED AND NEWLY CORRECTED / La Ramee, Pierre de – 1585. 69p. (English Linguistics Series 1500-1800) – 9 – us UMI [450]
THE RUDIMENTS OF ENGLISH GRAMMAR / Priestley, Joseph – 1761. 109p. (English Linguistics Series 1500-1800) – 9 – us UMI [420]
THE RUDIMENTS OF GRAMMAR FOR THE ENGLISH-SAXON TONGUE / Elstob, Elizabeth – 1715. 121p. (English Linguistics Series 1500-1800) – 9 – us UMI [420]
THE RUDIMENTS OF THE LATIN TONGUE / Ruddiman, Thomas – 1714. 117p. (English Linguistics Series 1500-1800) – 9 – us UMI [450]
RUDIMENTS OF THEOLOGY: A FIRST BOOK FOR STUDENTS / Norris, John Pilkington – London: Longmans, Green, 1894. 1 fiche – 9 – us A.T.L.A. [240]
RUDJAK MANIS / Jajasan, Bakti – SE-5380 1. 1949 – 9 – ne IDC [950]
Rudkovskogo, V I see GOD RABOTY PO SNABZHENIIU ZHELEZNYKH DOROG TOPLIVOM
RUDNICHAR – Sofia, Bulgaria. 1951-73; 1982-83; Jan 1984-87 – 13r – 1 – us L of C Photodup [949]
RUDOLF PECHEL UND DIE "DEUTSCHE RUNDSCHAU" 1946-1961 : ZEITGESCHEHEN UND ZEITGESCHICHTE IM SPIEGEL EINER KONSERVATIVEN POLITISCHEN ZEITSCHRIFT / Knesebeck, Rosemarie von dem – 1995 – 5mf – 9 – DM118.00 – 3-8267-2250-7 – gw Hänsel [943]
RUDOL'F STEINER I GETE / Belyi, A – Izd. Dukhovnoe Znanie. M. 1917. BR-590 2 – 8 – ne IDC [460]
Rudolf Virchow Medical Society in the City of New York see PROCEEDINGS
RUDOLF VIRCHOW MEDICAL SOCIETY IN THE CITY OF NEW YORK. PROCEEDINGS see VIRCHOW-PIRQUET MEDICAL SOCIETY
RUDOLF VON GOTTSCHALL : EIN LITERARISCHES PORTRAIT / Brasch, Moritz – Leipzig: O Gottwald, 1893 – 1r – 1 – us U.W. Library [920]
Rudolph, L see ATLAS DER PFLANZENGEOGRAPHIE...
Rudometov, N M see DELOVOI SPRAVOCHNIK "MOSKVA"
RUDRA / Arbman, Ernst – 1922 – 1 – us I.U. Libraries [390]
Rudzkii, A see
- LITERATURA RUSSKAGO LESOVODSTVA
- POLNAIA ENTSIKLOPEDIIA RUSSKAGO SEL'SKAGO KHOZIAISTVA
Rudzutak, Ia.E, et al see TRI RECHI O PROMYSLOVOI KOOPERATSII NA 6 SOBRANII UPOLNOMOCHENNYKH VSEKOMPOMSOIUZA, IIUN' 1928 G.
LA RUE – no. 1-34. Paris. juin 1867-janv 1868. mq no. 21, 34; n.s., no. 1-27. 17 mars-13 avr 1870. mq no. 17-18, 25 – 1 – fr A.C.R.P.P. [073]
Rue, Charles de la see IDYLLIA
RUE DE LA FRIPONNE – Montreal. jun 1982; v1 n2. aut 1982 – 1r – 1 – Can$25.00 – cn Can Microfilming [072]
UNE RUE DE TOMBEAUX A SAQQARAH / Copart, J – 9 – ne IDC [930]
RUEBAB – Nos. 1-115 (26 Kanunisani 1328-8 Mayis 1330) – 25mf – 9 – $52.50 – us MEDOC [949]
RUEBEZAHL: DER SCHLESISCHEN PROVINCIALBLAETTER – Breslau. N.F. Bd. 4-14. 1865-Juni 1875. Title varies: 1785-1867, Schleisische Provincialblaetter. Ceased with June 1875 issue. Film Mas C 320 – 1 – us H.U. Library [073]
RUECKBLICKE AUF DIE LETZTEN SECHS JAHRE SEINER LOGENTHAETIGKEIT / Fessler, I A – Dresden, 1804 – 4mf – ne IDC [360]
RUECKBLICKE AUF MEIN LEBEN / Gutzkow, Karl – Berlin: A Hofmann, 1875 – 1r – 1 – us U.W. Library [920]
RUECKENSCHULE FUER ANGEHOERIGE IM PFLEGEDIENST : EFFEKTIVITAETS- UND EFFIZIENZKONTROLLE EINER AUF DEN ARBEITSPLATZ BEZOGENEN RUECKENSCHULE FUER KRANKENPFLEGEPERSONAL / Winkler, Joerg – 1995 – 2mf – 9 – DM80.00 – 3-8267-2251-5 – gw Hänsel [360]
Rueckert, Friedrich see LIEBESFRUEHLING
DIE RUECKWIRKUNG DES OSTASIATISCHEN KRIEGES... / Fitger, E – Berlin, 1904 – 1mf – 1 – ILM-1043/1 – ne IDC [327]
DER RUECKZUG DER DREIHUNDERT : ROMAN / Watzlik, Hans – Karlsbad: A Kraft, 1943 – 1r – 1 – us U.W. Library [830]
RUEDA DE LA DESGRACIA. MANUSCRITO DE UN CONDE / Coronado, Carolina – 1873 – 9 – $1.50f – sp Bibl Santa Ana [830]
Rueda Sanchez Malo, Jose Miguel see APUNTES DE HERALDICA CACERENA
Ruedin, Charles see VIE DE LA VENEREE ANNE-ELISABETH GOTTRAU, ABBESE DES BERNARDINES DE LA MAIGRAUGE
Rueff, Hans see ZUR ENTSTEHUNGS-GESCHICHTE VON GOETHE "TORQUATO TASSO"
Rueff, J see
- DE CONCEPTU ET GENERATIONE HOMINIS
- THE EXPERT MIDWIFE
Ruelf, I see ARUCHAS BAS-AMMI: ISRAELS HEILUNG
Rueling, J P see ORDINES NATURALES PLANTARUM
Rueling, Joseph see CHRISTUS FUER UNS
Ruelius, Hermann see KARL CHRISTIAN PLANCK UND DIE DEUTSCHE ERNEUERUNGSBEWEGUNG NACH 1870
Ruelle, Charles see DE LA VERITE DANS L'HISTOIRE DU CHRISTIANISME: LETTRES D'UN LAIQUE SUR JESUS
DER RUEPP : ROMAN / Thoma, Ludwig – Muenchen: A Langen, 1922 – 1r – 1 – us U.W. Library [830]
Rueppell, E see SYSTEMATISCHE UEBERSICHT DER VOEGEL NORDOSTAFRIKAS
RUERO DEL BAYLIO / Borrallo Salgado, Teofilo – Badajoz: Imp. Vicente Rodriguez, 1915 – 1 – sp Bibl Santa Ana [946]
Ruesdi, Mehmed see MUEKEMMEL VE MUFASSAL TUERKIYE CUMHURIYETI ATLASI
Ruest, Anselm see MAX STIRNER, LEBEN-WELTANSCHAUUNG, VERMAECHTNIS
Ruete, Edmund see PAUL HEYSE
Ruete, Hermann see LUDWIG HEINRICH CHRISTOPH HOELTY
Rueter, H see
- SYMPHONIE
Ruettel, F C see TI AAR BLANDT OASTGROANLANDS HEDNINGER
Ruettenauer, Benno see ZEITIGES AND STREITIGES
Ruetz, Caspar see WIDERLEGTE VORURTHEILE VOM URSPRUNGE DER KIRCHEN MUSIC
Ruexner, G see THURNIER BUCH...
DER RUF – New York. [n1-26 mar 1945-apr 1 1946] suppl jun 1? 1945 – us Res Libr [071]
DER RUF DES SCHICKSALS : ERZAEHLUNGEN AUS DEM ALTEN MECKLENBURG / Griese, Friedrich – Hamburg: O Meissner, [19–?] – 1r – 1 – us U.W. Library [830]
DER "RUF NACH SYNODE" ALS KIRCHENPOLITISCHE ERSCHEINUNG IM JUNGEN ERZBISTUM FREIBURG (1827-1860) / Bechtold, O – Freiburg I. Br., 1958 – Dfl56.00 – ne Slangenburg [240]
RUFE IN DIE ZEIT : SPRUECHE UND GEDICHTE / Vesper, Will – Muenchen: A Langen/G Mueller, 1937 – 1r – 1 – us U.W. Library [830]
Ruffin, Edmund see DIARY
RUFFINO / Ouida – British Fiction Archive: Unit 3 – 9 – uk Bell [830]
Ruffner, Henry see THE FATHERS OF THE DESERT; OR, AN ACCOUNT OF THE ORIGIN AND PRACTICE OF MONKERY AMONG HEATHEN NATIONS; ITS PASSAGE INTO THE CHURCH...AND STORIES.
Ruffolo, Robert R Jr see PHARMACOLOGY COMMUNICATIONS
RUFTGAR – (Sal-i 1: shumarah-'i 1-19 (5 Mihr 1359-4 Isfand 1359[27 Sep 1981-23 Feb 1982]). Missing issue 14) – Tehran – 1 reel – 1 – $25.00 – us MEDOC [950]
RUFUS PUTNAM PAPERS AND MEMOIRS / Putnam, Rufus – 2r – 1 – $150.00 – us UMI [920]
RUG AND TEXTILE ARTS: A PERIODICAL INDEX, 1890-1982 / Textile Museum. Washington, DC.Arthur D. Jenkins Library – 1983.-9870 entries 1 reel.-ISBN: 0-8161-1441-2; or 14mf.-ISBN: 0-8161-1734-9 – 1,9 – $280.00 – uk Hall [740]
RUGBY ADVERTISER – (1897 imperfect) – England, Feb 1850- – 224+ r – 1 – uk British Libr Newspaper [072]
RUGBY ADVERTISER : RUGBY AND KINETON EDITION – England, 1913-14 – 1r – 1 – uk British Libr Newspaper [072]
RUGBY RECORDER AND WEEKLY LOCAL ADVERTISER – England, 31 Jul 1857-19 Mar 1858 – 12ft – 1 – uk British Libr Newspaper [072]
RUGBY REVIEW – England, Jan-Dec 1896 – 12ft – 1 – uk British Libr Newspaper [072]
Ruge, Eva see SINNDIMENSIONEN AESTHETISCHER ERFAHRUNG
Rugheimer, John see MEASURE BOOK
Rugula, Jose de see LOS VALDIVIA
RUH see AR-RUH
Ruhl, Gustav see KARL ODEBREKT, UHE BAPTISTI ELU- JA UMBERPOORAMISE LUGU
Ruhlen, Merritt see
- MANUAL FOR ADMINISTRATIVE LAW JUDGES
DAS RUHRGEBIET UND OSTPREUSSEN / Franke, Eberhard – Essen, 1936 – 1 – DM30.00 – gw Mikro Press [943]
RUHR-NACHRICHTEN – (Also Bereichsausgaben available: RUHR-NACHRICHTEN IM MUENSTERLAND – Ahauser Kreiszeitung/ Gronauer Zeitung/Steinfurter Zeitung, oct 1 1957-jun 27 1959; BOCHUM, jan-mar 1953, 1954, apr 1 1955-nov 25 1960, jun 17 1961-jun 30 1967; BOCHUM, AUSGABE WATTENSCHEID, oct 1 1957-60 (incomplete); BOTTROP, oct 2-dec 13 1957, 1958-nov 14 1960; CASTROP-RAUXEL, 1950, apr 2 1951-56, oct 1 1957-jan 1958, apr 1 1958-jun 9 1961, oct 28 1961-66; ESSEN, 1958-aug 31 1960; GELSENKIRCHEN, oct 1-dec 30 1957, apr 5 1958-66; GELSENKIRCHEN-BUER, oct 1 1957-nov 30 1958 (incomplete); GLADBECK, oct 2-dec 30 1957, apr 1 1958-60; HALTERN, oct 1 1957-jun 29 1959; HATTINGEN, apr 1 1958-60; HERNE, AUSGABE WANNE-EICKEL; oct 1-dec 31 1957, apr 1 1958-59; LUEDINGHAUSEN, apr 1 1958-60; LUENEN, apr 1-dec 31 1958, jul 22 1959-66; RECKLINGHAUSEN, oct 1 1957-60; WITTEN, apr 1 1958-66) – Dortmund, mar 1 1949- – 1 – Inquire at Mikrofilmarchiv for details – gw Misc Inst [072]
RUHR-NACHRICHTEN – (Bereichsausgabe der Ruhr-Nachrichten, Dortmund) – Witten, apr 1 1958-66, 1996 – 6r – 1 – gw Mikrofilm [072]
RUHR-NACHRICHTEN – Dortmund, Germany. 1992- – 10r per yr – 1 – gw Mikrofilm [072]

RUHR-NACHRICHTEN IM MUENSTERLAND see RUHR-NACHRICHTEN

RUI, O ESTADISTA DA REPUBLICA / Mangabeira, Joao – Rio de Janeiro. 1943 – 1 – us Res Libr [920]

THE RUIN OF METHODISM – [London], 1776 – 2mf – 9 – MP-516/1 – ne IDC [240]

Ruinart, Thierry see ACTA SANCTORUM ORDINIS ST BENEDICTI

LAS RUINAS DE EMERITA Y DE ITALICA A TRAVES DE NEBRIJA Y RODRIGO CARO / Alvarez Saenz de Buruaga, Jose – Badajoz: Imp. Prov, 1950 – 1 – sp Bibl Santa Ana [930]

RUINAS PROTOHISTORICAS DE LOGROSAN / Roso de Luna, Mario – Caceres: Tip. Enc. y Lib. de Jimenez, 1901 – 1 – sp Bibl Santa Ana [930]

THE RUINED CITIES OF CEYLON / Cave, H W – London, 1897, 4, 126 pp., ills. BI-1049 2 – 8 – ne IDC [930]

LES RUINES DE BABYLONE OU GIAGGAR ET ZAIDA / Guilbert de Pixerecourt – (French Theatre Series). Paris. Barba. 1810 – 9 – fr Hachette [820]

LES RUINES LIBERALES: QUELQUES PAGES DE POLITIQUE / Dansereau, Clement Arthur – Montreal?: s.n., 1878. 02266. (Pre-1900 Canadiana) – 9 – cn C.I.H.M. [971]

Ruisbroeck, Jan van see
- DIE ZIERDE DER GEISTLICHEN HOCHZEIT, UN DIE KLEINEREN SCHRIFTEN
- DIE ZIERDE DER GEISTLICHEN HOCHZEIT, UND DIE KLEINEREN SCHRIFTEN

Ruiz Campos, Manuel see TRATADO DE LA CAZA DEL PERDIGON

Ruiz de la Serna, Manuel see DISCURSO PRONUNCIADO POR EL EXCMO. SR. GOBERNADOR CIVIL-PRESIDENTE...EN LA REUNION...25 DE FEBRERO DE 1950

Ruiz de Montoya, Antonio see ARTE DE LA LENGUA GUARANI, O' MAS BIEN TUPI

Ruiz de Ribayaz, Lucas see LVS, Y NORTE MVSICAL PARA CAMINAR POR LAS CIFRAS DE LA GUITARRA ESPANOLA, Y ARPA TANER, Y CANTAR A COMPAS POR CANTO DE ORGANO; Y BREVE EXPLICACION DEL ARTE, CON PRECEPTOS FACILES, INDUBITABLES, Y EXPLICADOS CON CLARAS REGLAS POR TEORICA, Y PRACTICA

Ruiz de Silva, Enrique see DOLOR BOHEMIO

Ruiz de Vergara Alava, Francisco see REGLA Y ESTABLECIMIENTO DE LA ORDEN...DE SANTIAGO

Ruiz Garcia, Felix see EJERCITO DE EXTREMADURA EN 1644. COMPETENCIAS DE JURISDICCION

Ruiz Ginenez, Joaquin y Jose Maria Perez Lozano see FE Y COMPROMISO HUMANO

Ruiz Gomez, Juan Eugenio see LA SALVACION, EL ENGRANDECIMIENTO MORAL Y LA FELICIDAD DE ESPANA, O SEAN LOS MEDIOS SEGUROS DE CONSEGUIRLOS

Ruiz Gonzalez Valero, Manuel see MUSA ENTRE HIERROS (POESIAS VARIAS)

Ruiz Lopez, Hipolito see
- FLORA PERUANA..., 1778-1783
- FLORA PERUVIANA ET CHILENSIS...
- FLORAE PERUVIANAE ET CHILENSIS PRODROMUS......
- MEMORIA DE LAS VIRTUDES Y USOS DE LA RAIZ DE LA PLANTA ILAMADA EN EL PERU BEJUCO E LA ESTRELLA
- MEMORIA DE LAS VIRTUDES Y USOS DE LA RAIZ DE LA PLANTA ILAMADA YALLHOY EN EL PERU
- MEMORIA SOBRE LA LEGITIMA CALAGUALA Y OTRAS DOS RAICES QUE CON EL MISMO NOMBRE NOS VIENEN DE LA AMERICA MERIDIONAL
- QUINOLOGIA, O TRATADO DEL ARBOL DE LA QUINA O CASCARILLA, CON SU DESCRIPCION Y LA DE OTROS ESPECIES...
- RELACION DEL VIAJE HECHO A LOS REYNOS DEL PERU Y CHILE POR LOS BOTANICOS DE S.M.
- RESPUESTA PARA DESENGANO DEL PUBLICO A LA IMPUGNACION QUE HA DIVULGADO PREMATURAMENTE EL PRESBITERO...
- SUPLEMENTO A LA QUINOLOGIA, EN EL QUAL SE AUMENTAN LAS ESPECIES DE QUINA NUEVAMENTE DESCUBIERTAS EN EL PERU...
- SYSTEMA VEGETABILIUM FLORAE PERUVIANAE ET CHILENSIS

Ruiz-Contreras, Jose see MATERNIDAD, GENERACION, CRIANZA...

Ruiz-Gonzalez Valero, Manuel see RESCATADO

Rujula, Jose de see JUAN MARTIN ROCO. SENOR DE CAMPOFRIO

Rujula, Solar y Manzano see DON PEDRO DE VALDIVIA...BADAJOZ, 1928

Rukapan, W see ETUDE SYNTAXIQUE ET SEMANTIQUE DU COUPLE QUESTION-REPONSE EN FRANCAIS ORAL

Rukhmanova, E D see ISTOCHNIKI PO ISTORII RUSSKO-SKANDINAVSKIKH OTNOSHENII V RUKOPISNYKH SOBRANIIAKH G. LENINGRADA

RUKHOVOD'STVO PO OBLICHENII RATINALISTICHESKIKH SEKT SHTUNDOBAPTIZMA I ADVENTIZMA / Peretrukhin, IK – Warsaw, 1924. A Handbook on the Exposure of the Rationalistic Sects of Stundo-Baptism and Adventism – 1 – 16.00 – us Baptist [240]

Rukiah Kertapati, S see DJAKA TINGKIR, DITJERITAKAN KEMBALI

RUKOPISI / Akademiia Nauk. SSSR Opisanie Rukopisnogo otdeleniia Biblioteki Akademii nauk SSSR – v. 3, PT. 1. Istoriia. L. 1930. BR-10,955 1 – 9 – ne IDC [010]

RUKOPISI / Moscow. Biblioteka Moskovskoi Sinodal'noi tipografii – section 1. 6 v. m. 1896-1912; Pechatnye knigi. section 2. 2 v. 1903-12. BR-11,161 1 – 9 – ne IDC [070]

RUKOPISI / Russia. Opisanie Rukopisnogo otdeleniia Biblioteki Imperatorskoi Akademii nauk – v. 1-2. Spb. 1910-15. BR-10,953 1 – 9 – ne IDC [500]

Rukopisi A P Chekhova see OPISANIE

RUKOPISI A.N. OSTROVSKOGO : KATALOG – Moscow, 1939. 51p. BR-11,017/1 – 9 – ne IDC [010]

RUKOPISI A.N. OSTROVSKOGO : OPISANIE – Leningrad, 1956. 32p. BR-10,907/1 – 9 – ne IDC [010]

RUKOPISI I PEREPISKA V.G. BELINSKOGO : KATALOG – Moscow, 1948. 42p. BR-11,009/1 – 9 – ne IDC [010]

Rukopisi IS Turgeneva see OPISANIE

Rukopisi M I Glinki see KATALOG

Rukopisi M Iu. Lermontova see OPISANIE

RUKOPISI M.E. SALTYKOVA-SHCHEDRINA / Saltykov-Shchedrin Library – Opisanie. Comp. by E. E. Naidich. L. 1954. PKG-F-84 BR-10,911 1 – 9 – ne IDC [020]

RUKOPISI MOSKOVSKOI SINODALNOI PATRIARSHEI BIBLIOTEKI / Popov, AN – 2v. Moscow, 1905, 1910.BR-7319/2 – 8 – ne IDC [240]

Rukopisi N A Nekrasova see KATALOG

RUKOPISI N.A. NEKRASOVA / Saltykov-Shchedrin Library – Katalog. Comp. by A. N. Mikhailova. L. 1940. GPB PKG-F-79 BR-11,117 1 – 9 – ne IDC [020]

RUKOPISI N.G. CHERNYSHEVSKOGO V SOBRANII INSTITUTA LITERATURY (PUSHKINSKOGO DOMA) AKADEMII NAUK SSSR – Nauchnoe opisanie. Moscow, Leningrad, 1939. 56p. BR-10,964/1 – 9 – ne IDC [460]

RUKOPISI N.V. GOGOLIA / Saltykov-Shchedrin Library – Opisanie. Comp. by R. B. Zaborova. L. 1952. GPB PKG-F-75 BR-10,903 1 – 9 – ne IDC [460]

RUKOPISI, PEREPISKA I DOKUMENTY / Turgenev, Ivan Sergeevich – Moscow, 1935. 182p. BR-10,700/1 – 9 – ne IDC [025]

RUKOPISI, PIS'MA, BIOGRAFICHESKIE DOKUMENTY, VOSPOMINANIIA, TEATRAL'NYE POSTANOVKI, RISUNKI, FOTOGRAFII.. / Chekhov, A P – Moscow, 1960. 272p. Description of Chekov papers in TsGALI. BR-10,686/1 – 9 – ne IDC [460]

RUKOPISI PRINADLEZHASHCHIIA BIBLIOTEKE IMP. ODESSKAGO OBSHCHESTVA ISTORII I DREVNOSTEI / Rystenko, A V – Odessa, 1910. 88p. BR-7323/2 – 8 – ne IDC [947]

RUKOPISI PUSHKINA, KHRANIASHCHIESIA V PUSHKINSKOM DOME – Nauchnoe opisanie. Moscow, 1937. 395p.BR-10,965/1 – 9 – ne IDC [460]

RUKOPISI PUSHKINA, POSTUPIVSHIE V PUSHKINSKII DOM POSLE 1937 GODA – Kratkoe opisanie. Leningrad, 1964. 112p. BR-10,966- – 9 – ne IDC [460]

Rukopisi S A Esenina see KATALOG

RUKOPISI SHAKH-NAME V LENINGRADSKIKH SOBRANIIAKH / Giuzal'ian, LT & D'Iakonov, M M – Leningrad, 1934. 124p. BR-10,779/1 – 9 – ne IDC [956]

RUKOPISI SLAVIANSKIE I ROSSIISKIE, PRINADLEZHASHCHIE...IVANU NIKITICHU TSARSKOMU / Stroev, P M – Moscow, 1848. 918p. BR-7338/2 – 8 – ne IDC [947]

RUKOPISI SLAVIANSKIE I RUSSKIE, PRINADLEZHASHCHIE...I.A. VAKHRAMEEVU / Titov, A A – 6v. Moscow, 1888-1907. BR-7290/2 – 8 – ne IDC [947]

RUKOPISI S.N. GLINKI / Saltykov-Shchedrin Library – Katalog. Comp. by E. P. Fedoseeva. L. 1963. GPB PKG-F-74 BR-10,902 1 – 9 – ne IDC [780]

RUKOPISI T.F. BOL'SHAKOVA, KHRANIASHCHIESIA V IMP. MOSKOVSKOM I RUMIANTSEVSKO MUZEE / Georgievskii, G P – Petrograd, 1915.viii,455p. Describes MSS in the Bol'shakov Collection now in the Lenin Library. BR/7291/2 – 8 – ne IDC [947]

RUKOPISI TSERKOVNO-ARKHEOLOGICHESKAGO MUZEIA IMP. KIEVSKOI DUKHOVNOI AKADEMII / Lebedev, A A – Saratov, 1916. 472p. BR/7293/2 – 8 – ne IDC [930]

O RUKOPISIAKH PO GEOLOGII I GEOMORFOLOGII, KHRANIASHCHIKHSIA V ARKHIVE GOSUDARSTVENNOGO GEOGRAFICHESKOGO OBSHCHESTVA / Vereiskii, N G – BR-10,991/1 – 9 – ne IDC [910]

RUKOPISNAIA KNIZHNOST' DREVNERUSSKIKH BIBLIOTEK (XI-XVII) MATERIALY DLIA SLOVARIA VLADELTSEV RUKOPISEI PISTSOV, PEREVODCHIKOV. / Nikolskii, N K – v1, A-B.Petrograd, 1914, xliv,163p. BR/7306-2 – 8 – ne IDC [025]

RUKOPISNOE OTDELENIE VILENSKOI PUBLICHNOI BIBLIOTEKI / Gil'Terbrandt, P – Vilna, 1871. v1-2. 245p. BR-5932/2 – 8 – ne IDC [947]

RUKOPISNYE FONDY LENINGRADSKIKH KHRANILISHCH / ed by Myl'nikov, A S – Brief directory of ms. holdings in libraries, museums and other institutions in Leningrad. 1970. 92p. BR-10,654/1 – 9 – ne IDC [090]

RUKOPISNYE FONDY PUBLICHNOI BIBLIOTEKI. PECHATNYE KATALOGI I OBZORY / Zubkova, N A; ed by Myl'nikov, A S – L. 1971. PKG-F-1 BR-11,099 1 – 9 – ne IDC [025]

RUKOPISNYE MATERIALY, KHRANIASHCHIESIA V GTSTM / Fridenberg, A – Trudy Gosudarstvennogo tsentral'nogo teatral'nogo muzeia im A.A. Bakhrushina. Moscow, Leningrad, 1941, p175-307. BR-10,839/1 – 9 – ne IDC [410]

RUKOPISNYE MATERIALY OTNOSIASHCHIESIA K L. N. TOLSTOMU / Saltykov-Shchedrin Library – Katalog. Comp. by R. B. Zaborova. L. 1966. GPB PKG-F-89 BR-10,915 1 – 9 – ne IDC [460]

RUKOPISNYI FOND VOSTOCHNOGO FAKUL'TETA LGU I EGO IZUCHENIE / Tagirdzhanov, A T – Surveys oriental MS holdings in Leningrad University Library. BR-10,919/1 – 9 – ne IDC [025]

RUKOVODSTVO DLYA BESED S ADVENTISTAMI, BAPTISTAMI, PASHKOVSTAMI, I DRUG / Vladykov, D I – A Guide for Discussions with Adventists, Baptists, Pashkovites and Others. Akhytrka, 1924. 3rd installment. 1 of 13 titles on reel – 1 – 86.44 – us Baptist [240]

RUKOVODSTVO PO OBLOZHENIIU PODOKHODNYM I PROMYSLOVYM NALOGAMI GOSUDARSTVENNYKH I KOOPERATIVNYKH PREDPRIIATII I SMESHANNYKH OBSHCHESTV – M., 1924 – 2mf – 9 – COR-738/1 – ne IDC [310]

RUKOVODSTVO PO SEL'SKOI KOOPERATSII / Kancher, E S – Spb., 1913 – 4mf – 9 – COR-43/1 – ne IDC [334]

RUKOVODSTVO PO VSEM OTRASLIAM KOOPERATSII : TEORIIA, PRAKTIKA I ISTORIIA POTREB. KREDIT., PROIZV. I S.-KH KOOP / Shapiro, I A – Spb., 1914 – 2mf – 9 – COR-142/1 – ne IDC [334]

RUL – Berlin, 1920-31 (incomplete) – 20r – 1 – gw Mikrofilm [072]

RUL – Berlin, 1920-31 (incomplete) – 20r – 1 – Inquire at Mikrofilmarchiv for details – gw Misc Inst [072]

Ruland, Ilse see WILHELM WAIBLINGER IN SEINEN PROSAWERKEN

Ruland, Wilhelm see KLEIST'S AMPHITRYON

THE RULE 11 SANCTIONING PROCESS : HIGHLIGHTS AND SUMMARY / Willging, Thomas E – Washington: FJC, 1988 – 1mf – 9 – $1.50 – LLMC 95-359 – us L.L.M.C. [340]

THE RULE 11 SANCTIONING PROCESS / Willging, Thomas E – Washington: FJC, 1988 – 3mf – 9 – $4.50 – LLMC 95-343 – us L.L.M.C. [340]

THE RULE FOR NUNS OF ST CAESARIUS OF ARLES : A TRANSLATION WITH A CRITICAL INTRODUCTION / McCarthy, M C – Washington, 1960 – 4mf – 8 – Dfl19.00 – ne Slangenburg [240]

Rule, M see EADMERI HISTORIA NOVORUM IN ANGLIA (RS81)

THE RULE OF FAITH AND THE DOCTRINE OF INSPIRATION / Watts, Robert – London: Hodder & Stoughton, 1885. 1 fiche – 9 – us A.T.L.A. [240]

Rule, William Harris see
- COUNCILS, ANCIENT AND MODERN
- AN HISTORICAL EXPOSITION OF THE BOOK OF DANIEL THE PROPHET
- HISTORY OF THE INQUISITION: FROM ITS ESTABLISHMENT IN THE TWELFTH CENTURY TO ITS EXTINCTION IN THE NINETEENTH
- HISTORY OF THE KARAITE JEWS
- MEMOIR OF A MISSION TO GIBRALTAR AND SPAIN
- RECOLLECTIONS OF MY LIFE AND WORK AT HOME AND ABROAD
- THE RELIGIOUS ASPECT OF THE CIVIL WAR IN CHINA
- WESLEYAN METHODISM REGARDED AS THE SYSTEM OF A CHRISTIAN CHURCH

RULES...: ALSO THE COMPANY'S ACT OF 1886 / Canada Permanent Loan and Savings Company – Toronto?, 1887. 03832. (Pre-1900 Canadiana) – 9 – cn C.I.H.M. [336]

RULES AND ORDERS : HOUSE OF REPRESENTATIVES / Massachusetts. Supreme Court – 1v. 1840 – 2mf – 9 – $3.00 – LLMC 92-164 – us L.L.M.C. [340]

RULES AND ORDERS OF PRACTICE, FOR THE COURT OF KING'S BENCH, DISTRICT OF MONTREAL : FEBRUARY TERM, 1811 / Canada. Bas-Canada. Cour du Banc du Roi – Montreal: Printed by T A Turner, 1823. SEM105P131 – 2mf – 9 – Can$4.50 – cn Bibl Nat [340]

RULES AND ORDERS OF PRACTICE OF THE SUPERIOR COURT, LOWER CANADA; RULES AND ORDERS OF PRACTICE OF THE CIRCUIT COURT, LOWER CANADA / Canada. Supreme Court – Quebec: Printed by J T Brousseau, 1858. SEM105P349 – 2mf – 9 – Can$4.50 – cn Bibl Nat [340]

RULES AND ORDERS OF THE SUPERIOR COURT OF CUMBERLAND COUNTY, IN THE STATE OF MAINE / Maine. Superior Court. Cumberland County – Portland: Thurston, 1871. 471p. LL-725 – 1 – us L of C Photodup [340]

RULES AND REGULATIONS FOR ADMINISTRATION AND OPERATION OF CONSTABULARY / Trust Territory of the Pacific Islands. (U.S.) – Saipan: Office of the High Commissioner, 30 Jan 1952 – 1mf – 9 – $1.50 – LLMC 82-100F Title 14 – us L.L.M.C. [324]

RULES AND REGULATIONS OF THE SOUTH AFRICAN INSTITUTE – (Filmed with: The South African quarterly journal) – Cape Town: Printed by W Bridekirk, 1830 – us Res Libr [060]

RULES AND STATUTES REGULATING THE PRACTICE OF THE COURT OF CHANCERY IN THIS PROVINCE / New Brunswick. Canada. Court of Chancery – Fredericton: Fenety, 1865. 177p. LL-2382 – 1 – us L of C Photodup [340]

RULES FOR DRAWING CARICATURES: WITH AN ESSAY ON COMIC PAINTING / Grose, F – O-1153 1. 1788 – 9 – ne IDC [740]

RULES FOR PLAYING IN A TRUE TASTE ON THE VIOLIN, GERMAN FLUTE, VIOLONCELLO, AND HARPSICHORD, PARTICULARLY THE THOROUGH-BASS. OPERA 8 / Geminiani, Francesco – CA.1746 – 9 – us Sibley [780]

RULES FOR PLAYING IN A TRUE TASTE ON THE VIOLIN, GERMAN FLUTE, VIOLONCELLO AND HARPSICORD PARTICULARLY THE THOROUGH BASS EXEMPLIFY'D IN A VARIETY OF COMPOSITIONS / Geminiani, Francesco – 1738. BP-683 – 9 – ne IDC [780]

RULES FOR THE CARE AND USE OF THE COMMINGLER STEAM HEATING SYSTEM AND THE BAKER HEATER / Canadian Pacific Railway Company – Montreal: 1897. 05706. (Pre-1900 Canadiana) – 9 – cn C.I.H.M. [380]

RULES FOR THE DISCOVERY OF FALSE PROPHETS : OR, THE DANGEROUS IMPOSITIONS OF THE PEOPLE CALLED METHODISTS DETECTED AT THE BAR OF SCRIPTURE AND REASON:... / Free, J –

London, 3rd ed 1759 – 1mf – 9 – MP-378/1 – ne IDC [240]
RULES OF ALL THE COURTS OF RECORD OF NEW YORK / New York. (State) – New York. 1v. 1888 – 5mf – 9 – $7.50 – LLMC 80-050 – us L.L.M.C. [340]
RULES OF APPELLATE PROCEDURE, 1983 / Lanham, John C – 27 Apr 1983 – 1mf – 9 – $1.50 – LLMC 82-100I Title 3 – us L.L.M.C. [324]
RULES OF BUSINESS / India. Laws, Statutes, etc – (Filmed with: India. Legislative Council: The Imperial Legislative Council Manual 1916) – [s.l: s.n], 1946 – us Res Libr [340]
THE RULES OF PLEADING AS ADAPTED TO COURTS OF LAW IN TENNESSEE. / Morison, James Henderson Stuart – St. Louis: Thomas Law Book Co., 1907. 554p. LL-1343 – 1 – us L of C Photodup [340]
RULES OF PRACTICE IN THE COURTS OF COMMON PLEAS, OYER AND TERMINER, QUARTER SESSIONS OF THE PEACE AND GENERAL JAIL DELIVERY OF SCHUYLKILL COUNTY / Pennsylvania. Court of Common Pleas (Schuykill County) – Pottsville: Republican, 1944. 166p. LL-1346 – 1 – us L of C Photodup [340]
THE RULES OF PRIVATE INTERNATIONAL LAW... / Cheng, F T – London, 1916 – 2mf – 1 – ILM-2983/1 – ne IDC [327]
RULES OF PROBATE COURTS / Massachusetts. Supreme Court – 1v. 1934 – 1mf – 9 – $1.50 – LLMC 92-158 – us L.L.M.C. [340]
THE RULES OF THE COURTS OF QUEEN'S BENCH AND COMMON PLEAS, THE MUNICIPAL COUNCIL RULES, THE COUNTY COURTS' EQUITY EXTENSION AND THE NEW DIVISION COURT RULES. / Draper, William George – Toronto, Maclear, 1855. 525 1 xlix p. LL-2383 – 1 – us L of C Photodup [340]
RULES OF THE NEW JERSEY COURTS. / New Jersey. Courts – 2nd ed. Newark: Soney & Sage, 1898. 308p. LL-964 – 1 – us L of C Photodup [340]
RULES OF THE SUPERIOR COURT, COURT OF CHANCERY, ORPHANS' COURT, COURT OF GENERAL SESSIONS, AND SUPREME COURT OF THE STATE OF DELAWARE / Delaware. Courts – Wilmington, Mercantile, 1917. 231 p. LL-1620 – 1 – us L of C Photodup [340]
RULES OF THE SUPREME COURT OF THE UNITED STATES, 1790-1984 / U.S. Supreme Court – (A compilation of every separately publ pamphlet of the above rules in the Library of the Supreme Court. Printed bibliography. To be supplemented) – 1v – 9 – $103.00 set – 0-89941-432-X – us Hein [340]
RULES OF THE UNITED STATES CIRCUIT COURT OF APPEALS FOR THE FOURTH CIRCUIT; 1930 / U.S. Court of Appeals for the Fourth Circuit – Washington, Govt. Print. Off., 1930. 48 p. LL-1229 – 1 – us L of C Photodup [340]
THE RULES OF TYCONIUS / ed by Burkitt, F C – 1894 – 5mf – 9 – ne Slangenburg [240]
RULES, ORDERS AND FORMS OF PROCEEDING.... / Canada. Parliament. Legislative Council – Quebec: Printed by Hunter, Rose & Lemieux, 1862. SEM105P166 – 1mf – 9 – Can$2.25 – cn Bibl Nat [324]
RULES, ORDERS, AND FORMS OF PROCEEDING OF THE UPPER HOUSE OF THE PARLIAMENT OF CANADA / Canada. Parliament. Legislative Council – Toronto: Printed by Lovell and Gibson, 1858. SEM105P168 – 2mf – 9 – Can$4.50 – cn Bibl Nat [324]
Ruley, A N *see* HISTORY OF BROWN COUNTY
RULING CASELAW / ed by McKinney, William M & Rich, Burdett A – (Suppl entitled: Ruling Caselaw, Permanent Annotations offered in 1929-30) – Northport,NY, San Francisco: Rochester, Thompson Co; Bancroft-Whitney; Lawyers' Co-op. v1-28. 1914-21 (all publ) – 399mf – 9 – $598.00 – LLMC 90-417 – us L.L.M.C. [340]
RULING IDEAS IN EARLY AGES AND THEIR RELATION TO OLD TESTAMENT FAITH / Mozley, James Bowling – New York: E.P. Dutton, 1880. 1 fiche – 9 – us A.T.L.A. [240]
RULING IDEAS OF OUR LORD / D'Arcy, Charles Frederick – New York: A.C. Armstrong, 1901. 1mf – 9 – us A.T.L.A. [240]
RULING IDEAS OF THE PRESENT AGE / Gladden, Washington – Boston: Houghton, Mifflin, 1895 – 1mf – 9 – 0-8370-4937-7 – 1985-2937 – us A.T.L.A. [240]
RULO REGISTER – Rulo, NE. -w. Dec 1903-Jul 1904; Oct 1907-May 1908, scattered issues missing; Aug 1909-Jul 1916 – 1 – us NE Hist [071]
RULO REPORTER – Rulo, NE. -w. Apr 1896-Dec 1900, scattered issues missing – 1 – us NE Hist [071]
RUMAENISCHE MAERCHEN – 1882 – 1 – us I.U. Libraries [390]
RUMAENISCHER LLOYD – Bukarest, Rumaenien. 3 Sept 1889-4 Aug 1896 – 12r – 1 – gw Mikrofilm [949]
RUMAENISCHER LLOYD – Bukarest, sep 3 1889-aug 4 1896 – 12r – 1 – Inquire at Mikrofilmarchiv for details – gw Misc Inst [072]
Rumball, Edwin Alfred *see* JESUS AND MODERN RELIGION
Rumberg, E *see* PARTES FRUCTIFICATIONIS, SEU PRINCIPIA BOTANICES ILLUSTRATA
Rumble, Greville *see* MANAGEMENT OF DISTANCE LEARNING SYSTEMS
Rumble, L *see* THE BAPTISTS
RUMBURGER ZEITUNG – Rumburg (Rumburk), Germany. 21 Jul 1928-6 Feb 1937 – 14r – 1 – gw Mikrofilm [072]
RUMELI – Selanik. Cikaran: Mustafa; Sahib ve Imtiyaz Vekili: Hamdi, 1872-1881 – 9 – $25.00 – us MEDOC [956]
RUMELI – Selanik. Mueduer-i Mes'ul: Ali Nihad; Umur-i Tahririyye: Yunus Nadi [Abalioglu], 1909-1911) – 9 – $25.00 – us MEDOC [956]
Rumen de Armas, Antonio *see* LOS VIAJES DE JOHN HAWKINS A AMERICA (1562-1595)
Rumeu de Armas, Antonio *see* COLON EN BARCELONA. SEVILLA, 1944
LA RUMEUR DU PORTAGE / ed by Hamel, Marcel – L'Assomption, Canada. 2 mai 1973-22 jan 1975 – 1r – 1 – Can$60.00 – cn Can Microfilming [072]
Rumford, Benjamin T *see*
– MEMOIRES SUR LA CHALEUR
– RECHERCHES SUR LA CHALEUR DEVELOPPEE DANS LA COMBUSTION, ET DANS LA CONDENSATION DES VAPEURS
Rumiantsev, N E *see* OBZOR LITERATURY PO PSIKHOLOGII DETSTVA
RUMINANT NUTRITION : SELECTED ARTICLES FROM THE WORLD ANIMAL REVIEW – 1978 – 165p – it F.A.O. [636]
RUMMELSBURGER KREISBLATT – Rummelsburg (Miastko), Germany. 1884-1887 – 2r – 1 – gw Mikrofilm [072]
RUMPHIA, SIVE COMMENTATIONES BOTANICAE IMPRIMIS DE PLANTIS INDIAE ORIENTALIS / Blume, C L – Lugduni-Batavorum, 1835-48/49. 4v. B-5851/2 – 50mf – 8 – ne IDC [580]
Rumphius, G E *see* HERBARIUM AMBOINENSE,...
RUN – Dansk. 1984- – 1,5,6,9 – us UMI [073]
RUN – Germany.1984- – 1,5,6,9 – us UMI [073]
RUN – v1-. 1984- – 1,5,6,9 – us UMI [073]
RUN TO EARTH / Braddon, Mary Elizabeth – British Fiction Archive: Unit 5 – 9 – uk Bell [830]
Runa, Hermannus de *see* SERMONES FESTIVALES
Runchock, Rita *see*
– LIBRARY OF CONGRESS CLASSIFICATION SCHEDULES
– LIBRARY OF CONGRESS CLASSIFICATION SCHEDULES, COMBINED WITH ADDITIONS AND CHANGES THROUGH 1989
Runchock-Droste, Rita *see*
– LIBRARY OF CONGRESS CLASSIFICATION SCHEDULES THROUGH 1993
Runciman, S *see* A HISTORY OF THE FIRST BULGARIAN EMPIRE
Runciman, St *see* A HISTORY OF THE CRUSADES
RUNCORN WEEKLY NEWS – England, 1913-33; 1936-63 – 49r – 1 – uk British Libr Newspaper [072]
RUND UM DEN GEISINGBERG *see* DER BOTE VOM GEISING UND MUEGLITZTHAL-ZEITUNG
Rundall, Thomas *see* VOYAGES TOWARDS THE NORTH WEST
DER RUNDFUNK : AUSGABE LEIPZIG – Berlin, 1949-52 – 4r – 1 – gw Mikrofilm [790]
DER RUNDFUNK – (Cont by: Unser Rundfunk, mar 1953. FF Funk und Fernsehen der DDR, dec 27, 1959. FF-Dabei, dec 29, 1969) – Berlin. feb 3, 1946-jan 4, 1991 – 46r – 1 – gw Mikrofilm [073]
RUNDFUNK PRESSESPIEGEL – Bielefeld-Bethel, oct 1 1951-dec 20 1954 – 1r – 1 – Inquire at Mikrofilmarchiv for details – gw Misc Inst [790]
RUNDFUNK PRESSESPIEGEL – Bielefeld-Bethel. oct 1, 1951-dec 20, 1954 – 1r – 1 – gw Mikrofilm [072]
DER RUNDFUNK-HOERER – (Filmed with: Der Rundfunkhoerer, Muenchen) – Hamburg. 1929-dec 22, 1933 – 9r – 1 – gw Mikrofilm [790]
DER RUNDFUNKHOERER – (Filmed with: Der Rundfunk-Hoerer, Hamburg) – Muenchen, may 23 1926-28 – 1 – gw Mikrofilm [790]
DIE RUNDSCHAU – Brusque, dec 23 1922-may 26 1928, jun 5 1928-dec 23 1933, jan 6 1934-sep 24 1937 – 3r – 1 – Inquire at Mikrofilmarchiv for details – gw Misc Inst [072]
RUNDSCHAU UEBER DIE LEISTUNGEN – Leipzig, DE. Feb 1887-Dec 1890 – 2r – 1 – uk British Libr Newspaper [072]
RUNDSCHAU UEBER POLITIK, WIRTSCHAFT UND ARBEITERBEWEGUNG – Basel. v1,no1-v8,no52. Jul 1932-Oct 1939. 169 fiches – 9 – $450.00 – us UPA [335]
RUNDSCHAU UEBER POLITIK, WIRTSCHAFT UND ARBEITERBEWEGUNG – (Cont by: Die Welt, Stockholm) – Basel, jul 1 1932-jan 27 1940 – 16r – 1 – Dist. gw Mikrofilm – gw Misc Inst [072]
RUNDSCHAU VOM BERGE KARMEL – Niagara Falls, Ont.: Mount Carmel College, 1897-1899 – 9 – cn C.I.H.M. [370]
RUNDTISCHGESPRACHES *see* ERGEBNISSE DER RUNDTISCHGESPRACHES
Runeberg, Johan Ludvig *see* SAMLADE SKRIFTER
Runge, Dieter *see* MECHANISMUS DER PERMISSIVEN WIRKUNG DES GLUCOCORTICOIDS DEXAMETHASEN AUF DIE GLUCAGON-ABHAENGIGE AKTIVIERUNG DES PHOSPHOENOLPYRUVAT CARBOXYKINASE GENS IM KULTIVIERTEN RATTENHEPATOCYTEN
Runge, Dorothee Monika *see* UNTERSUCHUNGEN ZUM AUFBAU VON HISTON-GEN-GRUPPEN DES MENSCHEN
RUNHUA YU MIFENG – Lubrication Engineering. 1977, 1979, 1981. F/P 278 – 9 – $4.50f – cc Microforms [620]
THE RUNIC ROODS OF RUTHWELL AND BEWCASTLE : WITH A SHORT HISTORY OF THE CROSS AND CRUCIFIX IN SCOTLAND / Hewison, James King – Glasgow: John Smith, 1914 – 1mf – us A.T.L.A. [240]
RUNNER – Edmonton. v26-32. 1988-94 – 9 – Can$20.00y – cn Micromedia [790]
RUNNER – v.1-. 1978- – 1,5,6,9 – us UMI [073]
RUNNING ECONOMY AND KINEMATIC DIFFERENCES AMONG RUNNING WITH THE FOOT SHOD, WITH THE FOOT BARE, AND WITH THE BARE FOOT EQUATED FOR WEIGHT / Flaherty, Robert F & Scheuchenzuber, H Joseph – 1993 – 2mf – $8.00 – us Microform Publ [612]
RUNNING ECONOMY FOLLOWING AN INTENSE CYCLING BOUT IN TRAINED FEMALE DUATHLETES AND TRIATHLETES / Danner, Tracy – 1993 – 1mf – $4.00 – us Microform Publ [612]
THE RUNNYMEDE TRUST – London. 106 docs. 1980-1990 – 70mf – 9 – ne IDC [360]
RUNORNA – 1933 – 1 – us I.U. Libraries [390]
Runturambi, F *see* ARAH PERKEMBANGAN EKONOMI-KEUANGAN INDONESIA
Runze, Georg *see*
– DER ONTOLOGISCHE GOTTESBEWEIS
– DAS ZEICHEN DES MENSCHENSOHNES UND DER DOPPELSINN DES JONAZEICHENS
Ruoff, Henry W *see* BIOGRAPHICAL AND PORTRAIT CYCLOPEDIA OF SCHUYLKILL COUNTY
RUOTGERI VITA BRUNONIS ARCHIEPISCOPI COLONIENSIS (MGH 6: 10.BD) / ed by Ott, I – 1951 – Dfl9.00 – ne Slangenburg [240]
RUOTGERI VITA BRUNONIS ARCHIEPISCOPI COLONIENSIS (MGH 7: 52.BD) – 1841 – Dfl9.00 – ne Slangenburg [240]
RUOTSIN SUOMALAINEN – Stockholm, Sweden. 1979- – 1 – sw Kungliga [072]
RUPAM : AN ILLUSTRATED QUATERLY JOURNAL OF ORIENTAL ART. CHIEFLY INDIAN. / ed by Gangoly, Ordhendra C – 34 v. Calcutta. 1920-30. BI-1078 1 – 45mf – 9 – ne IDC [073]
RUPANYUP SPECTATOR – 1896-1903. RS1-8 – 8r – 1 – at Corangamite [072]
RUPERT GODWIN / Braddon, Mary Elizabeth – British Fiction Archive: Unit 5 – 9 – uk Bell [830]
Rupert, Greenberry G *see* THE THEOCRACY OF ISRAEL
RUPERT VON DEUTZ (MGH QUELLEN..: 5.BD) : DE VICTORIA VERBI DEI – 1970 – Dfl32.00 – ne Slangenburg [240]
RUPOR – (Includes c.1: 1927:Aug.1-1932:Dec.6; 1933:Jan.1-Apr.25, May 3-Dec.25; 1934:Apr.30-1935:May 25; Library lacks many issues) – Kharbin: E.S. Kaufman, 19uu – 1 – CSUXAKB0098-S – us Hoover Inst Photo [947]
Rupp, Israel *see* HISTORY OF LANCASTER CO., PA
Ruppli, M *see* LA COORDINATION EN FRANCAIS MODERNE
Rupprecht, Eduard *see* DAS RAETSEL DES FUENFBUCHES MOSE UND SEINE FALSCHE LOESUNG
Ruprecht, Erich *see* WANDERUNG UND HEIMKUNFT
Ruprecht, F J *see*
– FLORA INGRICA SIVE HISTORIA PLANTARUM GUBERNII PETROPOLITANI
– ILLUSTRATIONES ALGARUM
Ruprich-Robert, V *see* REFLEXIONS SUR L'ENSEIGNEMENT DE L'ARCHITECTURE EN 1881
RURAL AMERICAN INDIANS IN POVERTY / U.S. Department of Agriculture. Economic Research Council – 1969 – 1mf – 9 – $5.00f – us Ross [339]
RURAL AND REGIONAL DEVELOPMENT / ed by Auerbach, Devoira – (Development plans, programmes and projects for countries in Africa, Middle East/North Africa, East Asia, South Asia, South-East Asia, Pacific and Latin America. Individual titles available, minimum order Dfl75.00) – 1990-. updated yearly – 775mf – 9 – ne IDC [338]
THE RURAL CANADIAN – (Absorbed: Farm Journal. Absorbed: Canadian Farmer and Grange Record) – Toronto: C B Robinson, [1882-1898] – 9 – cn C.I.H.M. [630]
RURAL DAIRY TECHNOLOGY : EXPERIENCES IN ETHIOPIA / O'Mahony, Frank – 1988 – 9 – $13.00 – 92-9053-148-7 – et ILRI [636]
RURAL DEVELOPMENT AND HUMAN RIGHTS IN SOUTH-EAST ASIA – 1982 – sz I.C.J. [320]
RURAL EDUCATION – v.1-. 1980- – 1,5,6,9 – us UMI [370]
RURAL ENERGY PLANNING IN CHINA AND OTHER DEVELOPING COUNTRIES OF ASIA – 1985 – 160p – it F.A.O. [350]
RURAL ENTERPRISE – Halsey OR. Dec 24 1924-Nov 3 1927 – 1 – us U.O. Library [071]
THE RURAL HOME – Kentville, NS: A J Pineo, [1885?-18– or 19–] – 9 – cn C.I.H.M. [630]
RURAL HOME TECHNIQUES – it F.A.O. [640]
RURAL JOURNALISM IN AFRICA / Ansah, Paul et al – 1981 – 9 – 92-3-101752-7 – fr UNESCO [070]
RURAL LIFE IN LITCHFIELD COUNTY / Litchfield County. Connecticut – By Charles Shepherd Phelps, 1917. Hist. and biog. sketches. 3 fiches. F-0085 – 9 – us A.G.L.L. [978]
RURAL NORTHWEST – Eugene. Or. 1891-96 – 1 – us UMI [073]
RURAL NORTHWEST – Portland. Or. 1891-96 – 1 – us UMI [073]
RURAL NORTHWEST – Portland, OR. 1891-96 – 1 – 24.00 – us Oregon Hist [071]
THE RURAL PRESS – Arthabaska, Canada. v1 n33. 25 jun 1870 – 1r – 1 – Can$25.00 – cn Can Microfilming [072]
RURAL PROGRAM SERVICE / South Dakota. Agricultural Extension Service. State College of Agriculture and Mechanic Arts – May 1924-Aug. 1939 – 1,5,6 – us Spaulding [307]
RURAL RADIO : PROGRAMME FORMATS / Dikshit, Kiranmani A et al – 1979 – 94p – 9 – 92-3-101616-4 – fr UNESCO [380]
RURAL RESEARCH SERIES: MONOGRAPHS / Tennessee. University. Agricultural Experiment Station – n.1-275 – 1,5 – us Spaulding [307]

RURAL REVIEW – Georgetown, CA. 1963-65 – 1r – 1 – $50.00 – C02270 – us Library Micro [071]
RURAL RIDES IN THE COUNTIES OF SURREY, KENT, SUSSEX, HAMPSHIRE, WILTSHIRE... : WITH ECONOMICAL AND POLITICAL OBSERVATIONS... / Cobbett, William – London: Cobbett, 1830 – 1 roll – 1 – 1-55879-867-6 – uk Libr Preservation [910]
RURAL SCHOOL AGRICULTURAL BULLETIN / Minnesota. College of Agriculture – nos.1-3 – apply; – us Spaulding [630]
RURAL SCHOOL AGRICULTURE / Minnesota. Agricultural Extension Service – v.1-4. Sep 1911-Apr 1915 – 1,5,6 – us Spaulding [630]
RURAL SOCIOLOGY – (v.34- 1969- 5,6,. v.40- 1975- 9) – v.1- 1936- – 1 – us UMI [300]
RURAL SOCIOLOGY IN ACTION / Constandse, AK & Hofstee, E W – 1978 – 64p – it F.A.O. [307]
RURAL SOCIOLOGY PAMPHLET / South Dakota. State University. Agricultural Experiment Station – nos.1-124.1940-71 – 1,5,6 – us Spaulding [307]
RURAL SOCIOLOGY REPORT / Virginia. Agricultural Experiment Station. Blacksburg – v.1-82. Mar 1933-Sep 1955 – 1,5 – us Spaulding [630]
RURAL SOCIOLOGY SERIES / Auburn University. Agricultural Experiment Station – No.1-5. 1974-81. 1 reel – 1, 5 – us Spaulding [300]
RURAL TALES, BALLADS, AND SONGS / Bloomfield, Robert – London: Printed for Vernor and Hood [etc.], 2nd ed 1802 – 1 roll – 1 – 1-55879-276-7 – uk Libr Preservation [810]
RURAL USE OF LIGNOCELLULOSIC RESIDUES – 1989 – 98p – it F.A.O. [660]
RURAL VIRGINIA – Richmond. Va. 1947- – 1 – us UMI [071]
RURAL WORKER : 1935-1937 / Agricultural and Rural Workers – (Coll title: Labor Union Periodicals, Pt 3) – 1996 – 1r – 1 – $135.00 – 1-55655-611-X – us UPA [331]
RURAL WORLD : EDUCATION AND DEVELOPMENT / Malassis, Louis – 1976 – 127p – 9 – 92-3-101238-X – fr UNESCO [370]
RURAL WORLD – London. -w and m. Dec 1888-Dec 1915. (Wanting 1893). (15 reels) – 1 – uk British Libr Newspaper [072]
RURAL WORSHIP SERVICES (CCC110) / Chu, Ching-i & Chang, Pei-ying – (In Chinese) – Shanghai: Christian Literature Society, 1940 – 1r – 1 – 1984-B500 – us A.T.L.A. [240]
RUS' – M. 1880-86. B-1852 2 – 8 – ne IDC [999]
RUS (BUENOS AIRES, ARGENTINA) – (Includes c.1: 1937:Jan.7, Mar.6) – Buenos Aires: Don Jorge Bashkirow, 1936 – 1 – CSUXANS1532-S – us Hoover Inst Photo [947]
RUS'. PESNI I DUMY / Gorodetskii, S – Moscow, 1910. BR-1130-2 – 8 – ne IDC [460]
RUS (SOFIA, BULGARIA) – (Includes c.1: 1922:Nov.15, 1923:Apr.4, June 6, 12, 22; 1924:Nov.11) – Sofia: Izd-vo "Rus", 192u – 1 – CSUXADP4385-S – us Hoover Inst Photo [947]
RUS (SOFIA, BULGARIA: 1934) – (Includes c.1: 1934:Apr.8-Dec.9; 1935:Jan.20-June 16, July 7-Nov.17; 1936:May 17-July 19, Aug.2, 30-Nov.22) – Sofia: I.P. Butov, 1934- – 1 – CSUXANS1871-S – us Hoover Inst Photo [947]
Ruscelli, Girolamo *see* DE' SECRETI DEL R. D. ALESSIO PIEMONTESE
Ruscelli, I *see* LE IMPRESSE ILLUSTRI
Ruscelli, Jeronimo *see* LE IMPRESE ILLUSTRI CON ESPOSITIONI, ET DISCORSI
Rusconi, G A *see*
- DELLA ARCHITETTURA CON CENTOSESSANTA FIGURE DISSEGNATE DAL MEDESIMO, SECONDO I PRECETTI DI VITRUVIO

Rush, B *see*
- AN ACCOUNT OF THE BILIOUS REMITTING YELLOW FEVER
- MEDICAL INQUIRIES AND OBSERVATIONS UPON THE DISEASES OF THE MIND

Rush, Richard *see* THE LETTERS AND PAPERS OF RICHARD RUSH
Rushbrooke, WG *see* COMMON TRADITION OF THE SYNOPTIC GOSPELS
RUSHCLIFFE ADVERTISER *see* HUCKNALL MORNING STAR AND ADVERTISER
Rushe, James P *see* CARMEL IN IRELAND
RUSHINGS CREEK BAPTIST CHURCH. STEWART COUNTY. TENNESSEE : CHURCH RECORDS – 1894-1929 – 1 – 15.21 – us Baptist [240]
RUSHVILLE STANDARD – Rushville. Sheridan County, Nebraska. -w. (-sw 1892). Jul 30, 1885-Jul 10, 1891; Jul 1892; Aug 1895-Dec 1901; Aug 1904-Jul 1912; Aug 1918-Mar 1933 – 1 – us NE Hist [071]
RUSI / Royal United Service Institute for Defence Studies – v1- 1857- 1; v120- 5,6; v121- 9 – us UMI [355]
RUSIA EN ESPANA / Krivitsky, Walter G – n.p. 1937? Fiche W 980. (Blodgett Collection of Spanish Civil War Pamphlets) – 9 – us H.U. College Libr [946]
Rusillon, Henri *see* AU PAYS TSIMIHETY
Rusillon, Henry *see* UN CULTE DYNASTIQUE AVEC EVOCATION DES MORTS CHEZ LES SAKALAVES DE MADAGASCAR, LE "TROMBA"
RUSIN : RUTHENIAN – New York: Rada svobodnoj Podkarpatskoi Rusy v ekzylie. v1 n1/2-v9 n10/12. oct/nov 1952-1960 – us Res Libr [073]
RUSIN = THE RUTHENIAN – Philadelphia: [s.n.]; Allegheny, PA: Rev Joseph Hanulya, jun 10 1910-dec 1916 – us Res Libr [073]
RUS-IRAN TEVASSUTI – (Numrah-'i 2, 4-6, 10-16 (29 Jan 1911-17 Mar 1911)) – Baku – 1 reel – 1 – $10.00 – us MEDOC [950]
Rusjan, Tbg *see* SEDJARAH BANTEN
RUSKE SLOVO – (Also under: Novi Sad, 1967-78) – Ruski Kerestur, Yugoslavia. 1950-52; 1955-62; 1967-78 (incomplete) – 15r – 1 – us L of C Photodup [949]
Ruskin, John *see*
- ARROWS OF THE CHACE
- THE CROWN OF WILD OLIVE
- DEUCALION
- THE ETHICS OF THE DUST
- FORS CLAVIGERA
- HORTUS INCLUSUS
- THE LAWS OF FAESOLE
- LOVE'S MEINIE
- MODERN PAINTERS
- MORNINGS IN FLORENCE
- THE NATURE OF GOTHIC
- THE POLITICAL ECONOMY OF ART
- PROSERPINA
- THE QUEEN OF THE AIR
- ST. MARK'S REST
- THE SEVEN LAMPS OF ARCHITECTURE
- TIME AND TIDE BY WEARE AND TYNE
- "UNTO THIS LAST"

RUSKIN LEADER – Ruskin, NE. -w. Jan-Aug 1903; Dec 1903-Jun 1905; Jan 1908- Sept 1911 – 1 – us NE Hist [071]
RUSKIN LEADER – Ruskin, NE. -w. May 1914-Feb 1916; Feb 1925 to date – 1 – us NE Hist [071]
RUSKIN RELICS / Collingwood, WG – London: T.Y. Crowell, 1904 – 1 roll – 1 – 1-55879-765-3 – uk Libr Preservation [110]
RUSKIN – ROSSETTI – PRERAPHAELITISM : PAPERS 1854 TO 1862 – London: G Allen, 1899 – 1r – 1 – 1-55879-693-2 – uk Libr Preservation [700]
Ruslan, Abdulgani *see*
- BANDUNG MAKES HISTORY AGAIN; FOURTH ANNIVERSARY OF A.A. CONFERENCE
- BANDUNG SPIRIT; MOVING ON THE TIDE OF HISTORY
- HEROES DAY AND THE INDONESIAN REVOLUTION
- IN SEARCH OF AN INDONESIAN IDENTITY
- NASIONALISME ASIA
- PANTJA SILA IDEOLOGI PEMERSATU
- PANTJASILA DOKTRIN REVOLUSI NASIONAL KITA
- PANTJASILA, THE PRIME MOVER OF THE INDONESIAN REVOLUTION
- PEDOMAN-KERDJA PENERANGAN DALAM ALAM MANIPOL
- RESAPKAN DAN AMALKAM PANTJASILA
- SOSIALISME INDONESIA; PERKEMBANGAN TJITA2-NJA DAN KETEGASANNJA
- SOSIALISME INDONESIA; PERKEMBANGAN TJITA2NJA, KETEGASANNJA, SOSIALISME UTOPIA, SOSIALISME ILMIJAH

Rusler, William *see* A STANDARD HISTORY OF ALLEN COUNTY
Russel, W *see*
- A CALM REPLY TO THE FALLACIOUS ARGUMENTS AND VIRULENT INVECTIVES CONTAINED IN MR. JOSEPH BENSON'S 'FARTHER DEFENCE OF THE METHODISTS'
- A FEW HINTS FOR THE CONSIDERATION OF THE METHODISTS AND OTHER DISSENTERS,...

RUSSELL 1776-1896 – (Mf 1: Vital Records 1776-1814; Church Records 1800-33, 1845. Mf 2-5: Vital Records 1844-59. Mf 6-8: Birth Index 1860-1965. Mf 9-11: Marriage Index 1860-1971. Mf 12-13: Death Index 1860-1971. Mf 14-15: Births 1860-91. Mf 16-17: Marriages 1860-91. Mf 18-19: Deaths 1860-90. Mf 19: Vital Records 1891-96) – (mf ed 1990) – 19mf – 9 – 0-87623-113-X – us Holbrook [920]
Russell, Adolph *see* GESAMMT-VERLAGS-KATALOG DES DEUTSCHEN BUCHHANDELS UND DES MIT IHM IM DIREKTEN VERKEHR STEHENDEN AUSLANDES
Russell, Alfred *see* THE POLICE POWER OF THE STATE AND DECISIONS THEREON AS ILLUSTRATING THE DEVELOPMENT AND VALUE OF CASE LAW
Russell, Anna B *see* WRITINGS, LETTERS AND HYMNS AND SPIRITUAL SONGS
Russell, Benjamin *see* RITCHIE'S EQUITY REPORTS
Russell, Bertrand *see* MARRIAGE AND MORALS
Russell, Charles Edward *see* DIARIES, 1914-1919
Russell, Cora *see* WRITINGS, LETTERS AND HYMNS AND SPIRITUAL SONGS
RUSSELL COUNTY RECORD – Russell. Kan. 1874-77 – 1 – us UMI [071]
Russell, Diane *see* THE EFFECTS OF PROTOTYPIC EXAMPLES AND VIDEO REPLAY ON ADOLESCENT GIRLS' ACQUISITION OF BASIC FIELD HOCKEY SKILLS
RUSSELL DIARIES 1731-1801 – BRRAM – 1 – uk Microform Academic [920]
Russell, Edward Francis *see* ALEXANDER HERIOT MACKONOCHIE
Russell, Elbert *see* JESUS OF NAZARETH IN THE LIGHT OF TODAY
Russell, Frank *see* WHAT JESUS SAYS
Russell, George W E *see*
- DR. LIDDON
- LETTERS OF MATTHEW ARNOLD, 1848-1888
- A SHORT HISTORY OF THE EVANGELICAL MOVEMENT

RUSSELL H. CONWELL : FOUNDER OF THE INSTITUTIONAL CHURCH IN AMERICA: THE WORK AND THE MAN / Burr, Agnes Rush – Philadelphia: J.C. Winston, c1908 – 1mf – us A.T.L.A. [240]
Russell, Howard Hyde *see*
- A LAWYER'S EXAMINATION OF THE BIBLE
- PAPERS

Russell, I Jon *see* JOURNAL OF MUSCULOSKELETAL PAIN
Russell, James *see* FIRST ANNUAL REVIEW OF THE COPPER MINING INDUSTRY OF LAKE SUPERIOR: CONTAINING A CAREFULLY AND CONCISELY WRITTEN ACCOUNT OF EARLY EXPLORATIONS AND DISCOVERIES IN THE LAKE SUPERIOR COPPER REGION
Russell, John Scott *see* THE FLEET OF THE FUTURE: IRON OR WOOD? CONTAINING A REPLY TO SOME CONCLUSIONS OF GENERAL SIR HOWARD DOUGLAS IN FAVOUR OF WOODEN WALLS
Russell. Kansas. First Congregational Church *see* RECORDS
Russell. Kansas. Free Public Library. Board of Directors *see* MINUTES OF MEETINGS
Russell, Linda M *see* DENTAL HEALTH ATTITUDES AND KNOWLEDGE LEVELS OF RURAL AND SUBURBAN TEXAS
Russell, Matthew *see* AT HOME WITH GOD
Russell, Norman *see* VILLAGE WORK IN INDIA
Russell, P *see*
- AN ACCOUNT OF INDIAN SERPENTS
- DESCRIPTIONS AND FIGURES OF TWO HUNDRED FISHES; COLLECTED AT VIZAGAPATAM ON THE COAST OF COROMANDEL

Russell, R V *see* THE TRIBES AND CASTES OF THE CENTRAL PROVINCES OF INDIA
Russell, Richard Joel *see* REPORT ON SCIENTIFIC RESEARCH IN INDONESIA
THE RUSSELL SAGE FOUNDATION : SOCIAL RESEARCH AND SOCIAL ACTION IN AMERICA, 1907-1947 – 9 – $2,085.00 – us UPA [300]
RUSSELL TOWNSHIP, OHIO, RECORDS, MS 3106 – (Copies of election poll books, indentures and financial receipts, and minutes of trustee meetings) – 1827-50 – 1r – 1 – us Western Res [978]
Russell Townsite Company. Kansas *see* SECRETARY'S BOOK
Russell, W *see* A PHYSICAL TREATISE
Russell, William *see* SOME BRIEF ANIMADVERSIONS UPON MR. ALLEN'S ESSAY, TO PROVE THE COMMON PRACTICE OF SINGING IN RHIME. TO BE A CHRISTIAN DUTY
Russell, William Oldnall *see* A TREATISE ON CRIMES AND MISDEMEANORS
RUSSELL'S ELECTION CASES / Massachusetts. Supreme Court – v1-4. 1853-1902 (all publ) – 12mf – 9 – $18.00 – LLMC 84-156 – us L.L.M.C. [340]
RUSSELL'S ELECTION CASES : NOVA SCOTIA / Nova Scotia. Canada – 1v. 1874 (all publ) – 1mf – 9 – $1.50 – LLMC 81-036 – us L.L.M.C. [340]
RUSSELLVILLE BAPTIST CHURCH. FORSYTH, GEORGIA : CHURCH RECORDS – 1849-1924 – 1 – 9.60 – us Baptist [240]
RUSSIA = ANNUAIRE DE LA RUSSE 1904-1911 : EZHEGODNIK ROSSII 1904-1911 / Russia. Tsentral'nyi Statisticheski Komitet Ministerstva Vnutrennykh Del – (Coll title: European Official Statistical Serials, 1841-1984) – 59mf – 9 – £435.00 – uk Chadwyck [947]
RUSSIA : FROM CZAR TO COMMISSARS, 1914-1918 / U.S. Department of State – Series: Confidential U.S. Diplomatic Post Records: Russia and the Soviet Union, Part 1. 1983 – 1 – $1,105.00 – us UPA [947]
Russia *see*
- CENSUS OF RUSSIA, 1897
- CENSUS REPORTS 1926
- GAZETA RABOCHEGO I KREST'IANSKOGO
- GUBERNSKIIA VIEDOMOSTI
- IRKUTSKIIA GUBERNSKIIA VIEDOMOSR
- KATALOG MASONSKIKH RUKOPISEI MOSKOVSKOGO PUBLICHNOGO I RUMIANTSEVSKOGO MUZEEV
- KATALOG VOENNO-UCHENOGO ARKHIVA GLAVNOGO SHTABA
- KOSTROMSKIIA GUBERNSKIIA VIEDOMOSTI
- NIZHEGORODSKIIA GUBERNSKIIA VIEDOMOSTI
- OBSCHCHESTVA ISTORII I DREVNOSTEI ROSSIIKIKH
- OBSHCHESTRIO ISTORII I DREVNOSTEI ROSSIISKIKH PRI MOSKOVSKOM UNIVERSITETE: VREMENNIKH
- OPIS' KAZACH'IKH DEL MOSKOVSKOGO OTDELENIIA OBSHCHEGO ARKHIVA GLAVNOGO SHTABA
- OPISANIE DOKUMENTOV I DEL, KHRANIASHCHIKHSIA V ARKHIVE SVIATEISHEGO PRAVITEL'STVUIUSHCHEGO SINODA
- OPISANIE RUKOPISEI A.I. GERTSENA
- OPISANIE RUKOPISEI SINODAL'NOGO SOBRANIIA (NE VOSHEDSHIKH V OPISANIE A.V. GORSKOGO I K.I. NEVOSTRUEVA)
- OSOBYI ZHURNAL SOVETA MINISTROV
- POLNOE SOBRANIE RUSSKIKH LETOPISEI
- PRAVITEL'STVENNYI VIESTNIK
- RECH
- RUSSKII ARKHIV
- RUSSKII BIOGRAFICHESII SLOVAR
- SBORNIK IMPERATORSKOGO RUSSKOGO ISTORICHESKOGO OBSHEHESTVA
- SOBRANIE GOSUDARSTVENNYKH GRAMOT I DOGOVOROV, KHRANIASHCHIKHSIA V GOSUDARSTVENNOI KOLLEGII INOSTRANNYKH DEL
- STENOGRAPHIC RECORDS OF THE DEBATES IN THE IMPERIAL DUMA
- ZHURNAL MINISTERSTVA NARODNAGO PROSVESHCHENIIA

Russia. (1917-Provisional Government) *see* VIESTNIK VREMENNAGO PRAVITEL'STVA
Russia. (1917-Provisional Government). Chrezvychainaia Sledstvennaia Komissiia *see* PADENIE TSARSKOGO REZHIMA
Russia. (1917-Provisional Government). Glavnyi Zemel'nyi Komitet *see* TRUDY KOMISSII PO PODGOTOVKE ZEMEL'NOI REFORMY
Russia. (1917-Provisional Government). Laws, Statutes, etc *see* SBORNIK UKAZOV I POSTANOVLENII VREMENNAGO PRAVITEL'STVA
Russia. (1917-R.S.F.S.R.). Constitution *see* NASH "OSNOVNOI ZAKON"
Russia. (1917-R.S.F.S.R.). Laws, Statutes, etc *see*
- THE FIRST CODE OF LAWS..
- THE PENAL CODE OF THE RUSSIAN SOCIALIST FEDERAL SOVIET REPUBLIC; TEXT OF 1926 (WITH AMENDMENTS UP TO DECEMBER 1, 1932) WITH THREE APPENDICES.

- SOBRANIE UZAKONEII I RASPORIAZHENII RABOCHEKREST'IANSKOGO PRAVITEL 'STRA R.S.F.S.R
- TSERKOV' I GOSUDARSTVO PO ZAKONODATEL' STVU R.S.F.S.R. SBORNIK UZAKONENII I RASPORAZHENII A RAZ'IASNENIIAMI V OTDELA NKIU, POD REDAKTSEI P. A. KRASIKOVA

Russia. (1917-R.S.F.S.R). Narodnyi Komissariat Zemledeliia *see* BIULLETEN' UZAKONENII I RASPORIAZHENII PO SEL'SKOMU I LESNOMU KHOZIAISTVU

Russia. (1917-R.S.F.S.R.). S'ezd Sovetov *see* STENOGRAFICHESKII OTCHET

Russia. (1917-R.S.F.S.R.). Tsentral'ania komissiia pomoshchi golodaiushchim *see* ITOGI POSLEDGOL

Russia. (1917-R.S.F.S.R.). Tsentral'noe arkhivnoe upravlenie *see* RAZLOZHENIE ARMII V 1917 GODU

Russia. (1917-R.S.F.S.R.). Tsentral'nyi Irmii vspolnitel'nyi Komitet *see* ITET. 7-37

Russia. (1919-). Tsentral'noe Statisticheskoe Upravlenie *see* VESTNIK STATISTIKI

Russia. (1920- RSFSR). Laws, Statutes, etc *see* SOBRANIE UZAKONENII I RASPORIAZHENII

Russia. (1923- U.S.S.R.). Laws, Statutes, etc *see* SOBRANIE ZAKONOV I RASPORIAZHENII

Russia. (1923-U.S.S.R.). Gidrograficheskoe Upravlenie *see* ZAPISKI PO GIDROGRAFII

Russia. (1923-U.S.S.R.). Glavnaia Palata Mer i Vesov *see* VREMENNIK

Russia. (1923-U.S.S.R.). Gosudarstvennaia Planovaia Komissiia.State Planning Commission *see* PLANOVOE KHOZIAISTVO

Russia. (1923-U.S.S.R.). Laws, Statutes, etc *see*
- DIREKTIVY KPSS I SOVETSKOGO PRAVITEL'STVA PO KHOZIAISTVENNYM VOPROSAM, 1917-1957 GODY
- FUNDAMENTALS OF CIVIL LEGISLATION OF THE U.S.S.R. AND THE UNION REPUBLICS. FUNDAMENTALS OF CIVIL PROCEDURE OF THE U.S.S.R. AND THE UNION REPUBLICS
- THE MERCHANT SHIPPING CODE OF THE USSR (1968)
- NALOGOVOE OBLOZHENIE CHASTNOGO SEKTORA
- SOBRANIE ZAKONOV I RASPORIAZHENII RABOCHEKREST'IANSKOGO PRAVITAL'STVA SSR
- SOVIET MARRIAGE CODE
- VEDOMOSTI VERKHOVNOGO SOVETA SSSR

Russia. (1923-U.S.S.R.). Tsentral'noe Statisticheskoe Upravlenie *see*
- STATISTICHESKOE OBOZRENIE
- TRUDY

Russia. (1923-U.S.S.R.). Tsentral'noe statisticheskoe upravlenie. Otdel perepisi *see* VSESOIUZNAIA PEREPIS' NASELENIIA 1926 GODA

Russia. (1923-U.S.S.R.). Tsentral'nyi ispolnitel'nyi Komitet *see* SOVETSKOE STROITEL'STVO

Russia. (1923-U.S.S.R.). Verkhovnyi Sud. Plenum *see* SBORNIK DEISTVUIUSHCHIKH POSTANOVLENII PLENUMA I DIREKTIVNYKH PISEM VERKHOVHOGO SUDA SSR, 1924-1944 GG

RUSSIA AND REUNION : A TRANSLATION OF WILBOIS' L'AVENIR DE L'EGLISE RUSSE / Biggs, C R Davey – London: Published for the Eastern Church Association by A.R. Howbray, 1908 – 1mf – us A.T.L.A. [240]

RUSSIA AND THE ENGLISH CHURCH DURING THE LAST FIFTY YEARS : CONTAINING A CORRESPONDENCE BETWEEN MR. WILLIAM PALMER, FELLOW OF MAGDALEN COLLEGE, OXFORD, AND M. KHOMIAKOFF, IN THE YEARS 1844-1854 / Palmer, William P; ed by Birkbeck, W J – London: Published for the Eastern Church Association [by] Rivington, Percival, 1895 – 1mf – us A.T.L.A. [240]

RUSSIA AND THE SOVIET UNION, 1914-1941 : CONFIDENTIAL DIPLOMATIC POST RECORDS / U.S. Department of State – (Pt 1. Russia: From Czars to Commissars, 1914-18. $1,105.00; Pt 2. The Soviet Union, 1919-33. $8,255.00; Pt 3. The Soviet Union, 1934-41. $6,600.00. With printed guides) – 1983. Nearly 200,000 pages of reports and documents on Russia and the Soviet Union from 1914 through 1941 – 1 – $15,150.00 set – us UPA [947]

Russia. Arkheograficheskaia Kommissiia *see*
- AKTY IURIDICHESKIE ILI SOBRANIE FORM STARINAGO DIELOPROIZVODSTA
- AKTY, OTNOSYASHCHIESYA DO YURIDICHESKAGO BYTA DREVNEI ROSSII
- AKTY YURIDICHESKIYE
- DOPOLNENIIA K AKTAM ISTORICHESKIM
- RUSSKAIA ISTORICHESKAIA BIBLIOTEKA

RUSSIA BY A MANCHESTER MANUFACTURER / Cobden, Richard – In French. (Russia – 19th C.). 1836 – 9 – fr Hachette [947]

Russia. Central Library *see* NOTNYI KATALOG TSENTRAL'NOI BIBLIOTEKI

RUSSIA, CHINA AND THE CHINESE EASTERN RAILWAY / Chang, Tao-hsing – 1972 – 1 – 35.00r – us Hoover Inst Photo [380]

RUSSIA, CHINA AND THE CHINESE EASTERN RAILWAY / Tao-shing, Chang – Manuscript in Microfilm Series. 1972 – 1 – 35.00r – us Hoover Inst Photo [380]

The Russia Company *see* MINUTES AND TREASURER'S ACCOUNTS

RUSSIA CORRESPONDENCE, 1883-1948 / British Foreign Office – (1883-85 51r $4,335 S1183-85. 1886-88 49r $4,165 S1186-88. 1889-92 47r $3,995 S1189-92. 1893-96 50r $4,350 S1193-96. 1897-1900 46r $3,910 S1197-00. 1901-03 33r $2,805 S1201-03. 1904-05 40r $3,400 S1204-05. 1906-13 45r $3,825 S1206-13. 1914-17 44r $3740 S1214-17. 1918 72r $6,120 S1218. 1919 81r $6,885 S1219. 1920-21 38r $3,230 S1220-21. 1922-23 38r $3,230 S1222-23. 1924-27 44r $3,740 S1224-27. 1928-31 45r $3,825 S1228-31. 1932-35 46r $3,910 S1232-35. 1936-40 40r $3,200 S1236-40. 1941-45 94r $7,990 S1241-45. 1946-48 63r $5,355 S1246-48. Index 1883-1919 20r $1,700 S0983-1019. With printed guide) – 1 – us Scholarly Res [327]

Russia. Crown *see* SVOD VYSOCHAISHIKH OTMETOK PO VSEPODDANEISHIM OTCHETAM GENERAL-GUBERNATOROV

RUSSIA FROM A TO Z : REVOLUTION, STATE AND PARTY, FOREIGN RELATIONS, ECONOMIC SYSTEM, SOCIAL PRINCIPLES, GENERAL KNOWLEDGE / Freund, H A – Sydney, 1945 – 8mf – 9 – ILM-382/1 – ne IDC [320]

Russia. Glavnoe Upravlenie Neukladnykh Sborov i Kazennoi Prodazhi pitei *see* STATISTIKA PROIZVODSTV, OBLAGAEMYKH AKTSIZOM

Russia. Gosudarstvennaia duma, I-II *see* STENOGRAFICHESKII OTCHETY

Russia. Gosudarstvennaia duma, III *see* STENOGRAFICHESKII OTCHETY

Russia. Gosudarstvennaia Duma. I-IV *see* STENOGRAFICHESKOE OTCHETY

Russia. Gosudarstvennaia duma, IV *see* STENOGRAFICHESKII OTCHETY

Russia. Gosudarstvennyi sovet *see*
- ARKHIV GOSUDARSTVENNAGO SOVETA
- VSEPODDANNEISHII OTCHET PREDSEDATELIA

Russia. Gosudarstvennyi sovet. Arkhiv gosudarstvennago soveta *see* ZHURNALY SEKRETNAGO I GLAVNAGO KOMITETOV PO KREST'IANSKOMU DELU

Russia. Gosudarstvennyi Sovet. Upper House of the Imperial Russian Government Council *see* STENOGRAPHIC RECORDS

Russia. Gosudarstvennyi Sovyet *see*
- OPIS' DYEL ARKHIVA
- STENOGRAFICHESKIE OTCHETY

Russia. Imperial Foreign Ministry *see*
- SBORNIK DEISTVUIUSHCHIKH TRAKTATOV, KONVENTSII I SOGLASHENII, ZAKLIUCHENNYKH ROSSIEI S DRUGIMI GOSUDARSTVAMI I KASAIUSHCHIKHSIA RAZLICHNYKH VOPROSOV CHASTNAGO MEZHDUNARODNOGO PRAVA
- SBORNIK MOSKOVSKOGO GLAVNOGO ARKHIVA MINISTERSTVA INOSTRANNYKH DEL

RUSSIA IN TRANSITION : THE DIPLOMATIC PAPERS OF DAVID ROWLAND FRANCIS, U.S. AMBASSADOR TO RUSSIA, 1916-18 – 11 reels with printed guide – 1 – $1,060.00 – 0-89093-749-4 – us UPA [977]

Russia. Kavkazskaya Arkheograficheskaya Kommissiya. Tiflis *see* AKTY

Russia. Laws, statutes, etc *see* ZAKONY O PECHATI

Russia. Ministarstvo Narodnovo Prosveshcheniya *see* ZHURNAL

Russia. Ministerstva Finansov. Library *see* SISTEMATICHESKII KATALOG BIBLIOTEKI UCHENAGO KOMITETA MINISTERSTVA FINANSOV

Russia. Ministerstva gosudarstvennykh imuzhchestv *see* SEL'SKOE KHOZIAISTVO I LESOVODSTVO

Russia. Ministerstva Narodnago Prosveshcheniia *see* ZHURNAL

Russia. Ministerstvo Finansov *see*
- VESTNIK FINANSOV PROMYSHLENNOSTI I TORGOVLI
- VIESTNIK FINANSOV, PROMYSHLENNOSTI I TORGOVLI

Russia. Ministerstvo torgovli i promyshiennosti. Otdiel promyshiennosti *see* SVOD OTCHESTOV FABRICHNYKH INSPEKTOROV ZA 1900-1914

Russia. Ministerstvo Vnutrennikh Del'. Tsentral'nyi statisticheskii komitet *see* STATISTIKA ROSSIISKOI IMPERII

Russia. Ministerstvo vnutrennykh del'. Tsentral'nyi statisticheskii komitet *see* STATISTIKA ROSSIISKOI IMPERII

Russia. Morskoe Ministerstvo *see*
- MATERIALY DLYA ISTORII RUSSKAGO FLOTA
- OPIS' DELAM ARTILLERIISKOGO DEPARTAMENTA MORSKOGO MINISTERSTVA
- OPIS' DELAM DEPARTAMENTA KORABEL'NYKH LESOV MORSKOGO MINISTERSTVA, KHRANIASHCHIMSIA V GLAVNOM MORSKOM ARKHIVE, 1799-1853 G
- OPIS' DELAM GLAVNOGO MEDITSINSKOGO UPRAVLENIIA MORSKOGO MINISTERSTVA, KHRANIASHCHIMSIA V ARKHIVE MINISTERSTVA
- OPIS' DELAM I ZHURNALAM BUMAG VOENNO-POKHODNOI E.I.V. KANTSELIARII PO MORSKOI CHASTI I DELAM KANTSELIARII MORSKOGO MINISTERSTVA
- OPIS' DELAM KANTSELIARII FLOTA GENERAL-INTENDANTA KHRANIASHCHIMSIA V OBSHCHEM ARKHIVE...1827-55
- OPIS' DELAM KORABLESTROITEL'NOGO DEPARTAMENTA MORSKOGO MINISTERSTVA KHRANIASHCHIMSIA V GLAVNOM MORSKOM ARKHIVE
- OPIS' DELAM UPRAVLENIIA GENERAL-GIDROGRAFA I GIDROGRAFICHESKOGO DEPARTAMENTA MORSKOGO MINISTERSTVA, 1827-1852 GG
- OPISI DELAM DOKUMENTAM KOMISSII DLIA SOSTAVLENIIA SMETNYKH ISCHISLENII NA POSTROENNIE KORABLEI I DRUGIKH SUDOV, 1824-1827 GG. I DELAM I ZHURNALAM KORABLESTROITEL'NOGO I UCHETNOGO KOMITETA, 1827-1852 GG

Russia. Narodnyi Komissariat Snabzheniia *see* SOVETSKAIA TORGOVLIA

Russia. Opisanie Rukopisnogo otdeleniia Biblioteki Imperatorskoi Akademii nauk *see* RUKOPISI

Russia. Osoboe soveshchanie o nuzhdakh sel'skokhoziaistvennoi promsyshlennosti *see* TRUDY MIESTNYKH KOMITETOV O NUZHDAKH SEL'SKOKOZIAISTVENNOI PROMYSHLENNOSTI

Russia. Osoboe Soveshohanie o Nuzhdakh Sel'Skokhoziaistvennai Promyshlennosti *see* SVOD TRUDOV MIESTNYKH KOMITETOV PO 49 GUBERNIIAM EVROPEISKOI ROSSII

RUSSIA, POLAND AND THE WEST / Lednicki, W – London. 1954. BR-1360 2 – 8 – ne IDC [947]

Russia. Russian-American Company *see* RECORDS, 1802-67

RUSSIA: THE OLD AND THE NEW / Charnock, Joan Thomson – 1st ed.. London: J. Murray, 1948. vii,195p. plates, maps – 1 – us U.W. Library [947]

Russia. Tsentral'noe Statisticheskoe Upravlenie *see*
- ONE: VSESOIUZNAIA PEREPIS' NASELENIIA 17 DEKABRIA 1926 A. GODA. PREDVARITEL'NYE ITOGI
- TRUDY

Russia. Tsentral'noe statisticheskoe upravlenie *see* ONE: VSESOIUZNAIA PEREPIS' NASELENIIA. KRATKIE SVODKI, V. 4-7

Russia. Tsentral'nyi Komitet Tsenzury Inostrannoi *see* ALFAVITNYI SPISOK

Russia. Tsentral'nyi Statisticheski Komitet *see*
- STATISTICHESKI EZHEGODNIK ROSSII
- STATISTICHESKI YEZHEGODNIK ROSSII

Russia. Tsentral'nyi Statisticheski Komitet Ministerstva Vnutrennykh Del *see* RUSSIA

Russia. Tsentralnyi Statisticheskii Komitet *see*
- PERVAIA VSEOBSHCHAIA PEREPIS' NASELENIIA ROSSIISKOI IMPERII, 1897
- RESULTATS GENERAUX DE LA RECOLTE EN RUSSIE
- STATISTICHESKII VREMENNIK ROSSIISKOI
- STATISTIKA ROSSIISKOI IMPERII

RUSSIA, USSR, EASTERN EUROPE GENERAL CATALOGUE : BOOKS AND SERIALS ON MICROFISCHE. – (circa 8,000 monographs & 1,700 periodicals.) – 9 – ne IDC [947]

RUSSIA, VELIKITE SILI I BALGARSKIIAT VAPROS SLED IZBORA NA KNIAZ FERDINANDA (1888-1896 / Panaiotov, I – Sofia. 1941. BR-3899 2 – 8 – ne IDC [947]

Russia. Voennoe Ministerstvo *see*
- STOLIETIE VOENNOGO MINISTERSTVA, 1802-1902
- VSEPODDANNEISHII OTCHET O DEISTVIAKH VOENNAGO MINISTERSTVA

RUSSIAN ACADEMY OF SCIENCES LIBRARY, ST PETERSBURG (BAN) : CATALOGUE OF FOREIGN LANGUAGE BOOKS AND PERIODICALS TO 1930 – 992mf – 9 – £3,420.00 – uk Chadwyck [020]

RUSSIAN AND EAST EUROPEAN RESOURCE MATERIAL COLLECTION – (Coll is divided into 7 units numbered 4-10 and contains guides, library studies, historical and documentary studies and unique Communist Party histories. Each unit has a general description and individual items within each unit are annotated. Coll can be purchased as a whole or as individual units. Enquire for details) – units 4-10 – $3,940.00 set – B70000 – us Library Micro [947]

RUSSIAN AND SOVIET STATISTICS / ed by Pries, Anne – 145 titles. 2,455mf – 9 – ne IDC [304]

THE RUSSIAN BALLET OF SERGE DIAGHILEV / Victoria and Albert Museum. London. Theatre Museum – (Records the life and times of 20th C ballet's leading lights, combining biographical details with photographs, designs and ephemera. With printed index) – 28 colour mf – 15 – $448.00 – 0-907696-22-8 – uk Emmett [790]

RUSSIAN BAPTIST MATERIALS – (Sovremennoe shtundo-baptistskoe dvizhenie v" Severo-Zapadnom" krae. Vilna, 1910. (The Contemporary Stundo-Baptist Movement in the North-West Region). 5.00; 1. Zapis' zasedanii 13-go Kavkazskogo s"ezda baptistov Pyatigorsk. 1925. (Transactions of the meetings of the 13th Caucasus Congress of Baptists). 5.00; SBC; 1. Protokoly i materialy pervogo s"ezda Volgo-Kamskogo soyuza baptistov v Samare Samara. 1928. (Minutes and Materials of the First Congress of the Volga-Kama Union of Baptists in Samara.) 5.00; SBC; 1. Khristianin. February-December, 1906. 38.67; SBC; 1. Molodoi Vinogradnik. 1909-1910, 1912, 1917. 41.42; SBC; 1. Raspredelenie Staroobryadtesev" i Sektantov" potolkam" i sektam." St. Petersburg, 1901. (Distribution of the Old Believers and Sectarians according to doctrines and sects.)) – 1 – 5.00 – us Baptist [240]

RUSSIAN BIBLIOGRAPHIES: BIBLIOGRAPHIES AND BOOKS ON LIBRARIANSHIP PRINTED IN RUSSIAN CHARACTERS IN THE HELSINKI LIBRARY / Aav, Yrjo – Zug, IDC, 1970. 171p. BR-8368 1 – 9 – ne IDC [020]

THE RUSSIAN BIOGRAPHICAL DICTIONARY = RUSSKII BIOGRAFICHESKII SLOVAR' / ed by Polovtsov, A A et al – (Comes in two binders with index. Vols V & T available in book form only $400) – St Petersburg: Imperial Russian Historical Society. v1-25. 1896-1918 – 276mf – $600.00 – us Ross [947]

RUSSIAN BOOKS BEFORE 1701 – (Based on MME Zernova's bibliography) – 315r – 1 – $20,500.00 – us OmniSys [460]

RUSSIAN CENTRE FOR THE PRESERVATION AND STUDY OF DOCUMENTS OF MOST RECENT HISTORY (RTSKHIDNI), FOND 17 CENTRAL COMMITTEE OF THE COMMUNIST PARTY OF THE USSR : OPIS 1: CENTRAL COMMITTEE OF THE COMMUNIST PARTY [RSDRP(B)] 1918-1941 – Dela 1-321 – 5r – 1 – Reel nos 2.56-2-60 – uk Chadwyck [324]

RUSSIAN CENTRE FOR THE PRESERVATION AND STUDY OF DOCUMENTS OF MOST RECENT HISTORY (RTSKHIDNI), FOND 17 CENTRAL COMMITTEE OF THE COMMUNIST PARTY OF THE USSR : OPIS 109: RTSKHIDNI COLLECTION OF DOCUMENTS ON DEFENCE 1917-1924 – Dela 1-248 – 24r – 1 – Reel nos 2.1515-2.1538 – uk Chadwyck [324]

RUSSIAN CENTRE FOR THE PRESERVATION AND STUDY OF DOCUMENTS OF MOST RECENT HISTORY (RTSKHIDNI), FOND 17 CENTRAL COMMITTEE OF THE COMMUNIST PARTY OF THE USSR : OPIS 139: ORGANISATION AND PARTY WORK DEPARTMENT: INFORMATION SECTOR 1971 – Dela 1-1499 – 210r – 1 – Reel

nos 2.900-2.940; 2.1213-2.1381 – uk Chadwyck [324]
RUSSIAN CENTRE FOR THE PRESERVATION AND STUDY OF DOCUMENTS OF MOST RECENT HISTORY (RTSKHIDNI), FOND 17 CENTRAL COMMITTEE OF THE COMMUNIST PARTY OF THE USSR : OPIS 2: PLENUMS OF THE CENTRAL COMMITTEE OF THE RKP(B) 1918-1941 – Dela 1-266 – 23r – 1 – Reel nos 2.2435-2.2457 – uk Chadwyck [324]
RUSSIAN CENTRE FOR THE PRESERVATION AND STUDY OF DOCUMENTS OF MOST RECENT HISTORY (RTSKHIDNI), FOND 17 CENTRAL COMMITTEE OF THE COMMUNIST PARTY OF THE USSR : OPIS 7: STATISTICS DEPARTMENT 1920-1941 – Dela 1-587 – 79r – 1 – Reel nos 2.61-2.108; 2.583-2.607; 2.759-2.764 – uk Chadwyck [324]
RUSSIAN CENTRE FOR THE PRESERVATION AND STUDY OF DOCUMENTS OF MOST RECENT HISTORY (RTSKHIDNI), FOND 17 CENTRAL COMMITTEE OF THE COMMUNIST PARTY OF THE USSR : OPIS 75: FINANCE AND BUDGET DEPARTMENT: ADMINISTRATION OF CC AFFAIRS 1939-1965 – Dela 1-24 – 10r – 1 – Reel nos 2.318-2.327 – uk Chadwyck [324]
RUSSIAN CENTRE FOR THE PRESERVATION AND STUDY OF DOCUMENTS OF MOST RECENT HISTORY (RTSKHIDNI), FOND 17 CENTRAL COMMITTEE OF THE COMMUNIST PARTY OF THE USSR : OPIS 76: FINANCE AND BUDGET DEPARTMENT: ADMINISTRATION OF CC AFFAIRS 1939-1955 – Dela 1-2722 – 262r – 1 – uk Chadwyck [324]
RUSSIAN CENTRE FOR THE PRESERVATION AND STUDY OF DOCUMENTS OF MOST RECENT HISTORY (RTSKHIDNI), FOND 17 CENTRAL COMMITTEE OF THE COMMUNIST PARTY OF THE USSR : OPIS 77: FINANCE AND BUDGET DEPARTMENT: ADMINISTRATION OF CC AFFAIRS 1939-1963 – Dela 1-259 – 56r – 1 – Reel nos 2.407-2.462 – uk Chadwyck [324]
RUSSIAN CENTRE FOR THE PRESERVATION AND STUDY OF DOCUMENTS OF MOST RECENT HISTORY (RTSKHIDNI), FOND 17 CENTRAL COMMITTEE OF THE COMMUNIST PARTY OF THE USSR : OPIS 79: ADMINISTRATION OF CC AFFAIRS: ORDERS AND INSTRUCTIONS 1935-1956 – Dela 19-94 – 5r – 1 – Reel nos 2.463-2.467 – uk Chadwyck [324]
RUSSIAN CENTRE FOR THE PRESERVATION AND STUDY OF DOCUMENTS OF MOST RECENT HISTORY (RTSKHIDNI), FOND 17 CENTRAL COMMITTEE OF THE COMMUNIST PARTY OF THE USSR : OPIS 8: ALL-RUSSIAN CENSUS OF PARTY MEMBERS 1922-1924 – Dela 1-794 – 282r – 1 – uk Chadwyck [324]
RUSSIAN CENTRE FOR THE PRESERVATION AND STUDY OF DOCUMENTS OF MOST RECENT HISTORY (RTSKHIDNI), FOND 17 CENTRAL COMMITTEE OF THE COMMUNIST PARTY OF THE USSR : OPIS 86: BUREAU OF THE SECRETARIAT 1918-1934 – Dela 1-255 – 17r – 1 – Reel nos 2.1498-2.1514 – uk Chadwyck [324]
RUSSIAN CENTRE FOR THE PRESERVATION AND STUDY OF DOCUMENTS OF MOST RECENT HISTORY (RTSKHIDNI), FOND 17 CENTRAL COMMITTEE OF THE COMMUNIST PARTY OF THE USSR : OPIS 9: ALL-RUSSIAN CENSUS OF PARTY MEMBERS 1926-1927 – (Dela 1-3113 1180r. Dela 3127-3489 134r) – 1 – uk Chadwyck [324]
RUSSIAN CENTRE FOR THE PRESERVATION AND STUDY OF DOCUMENTS OF MOST RECENT HISTORY (RTSKHIDNI), FOND 17 CENTRAL COMMITTEE OF THE COMMUNIST PARTY OF THE USSR : OPIS SERIES – 55r – 1 – 2.1-2.55 – uk Chadwyck [324]
RUSSIAN CENTRE FOR THE PRESERVATION AND STUDY OF DOCUMENTS OF MOST RECENT HISTORY (RTSKHIDNI), FOND 37 : 6TH (PRAGUE) CONFERENCE OF THE RSDRP 1912 – Dela 1-13 – 1r – 1 – Reel no 2.468 – uk Chadwyck [324]
RUSSIAN CENTRE FOR THE PRESERVATION AND STUDY OF DOCUMENTS OF MOST RECENT HISTORY (RTSKHIDNI), FOND 54 : 14TH CONGRESS OF THE VKP(B) 1925 – Dela 1-164 – 20r – 1 – Reel nos 2.469-2.488 – uk Chadwyck [324]
RUSSIAN CENTRE FOR THE PRESERVATION AND STUDY OF DOCUMENTS OF MOST RECENT HISTORY (RTSKHIDNI), FOND 58 : 16TH CONGRESS OF THE VKP(B) 1930 – Dela 1-52 – 13r – 1 – Reel nos 2.489-2.501 – uk Chadwyck [324]
RUSSIAN CENTRE FOR THE PRESERVATION AND STUDY OF DOCUMENTS OF MOST RECENT HISTORY (RTSKHIDNI), FOND 337 : 5TH CONGRESS OF THE RSDRP 1907 – Dela 1-48 – 3r – 1 – Reel nos 2.502-2.504 – uk Chadwyck [324]
RUSSIAN CENTRE FOR THE PRESERVATION AND STUDY OF DOCUMENTS OF MOST RECENT HISTORY (RTSKHIDNI), FOND 447 : 4TH (UNIFYING) CONGRESS OF THE RSDRP 1906 – Dela 1-18 – 2r – 1 – Reel nos 2.505-2.506 – uk Chadwyck [324]
RUSSIAN CENTRE FOR THE PRESERVATION AND STUDY OF DOCUMENTS OF MOST RECENT HISTORY (RTSKHIDNI), FOND 477 : 18TH CONGRESS OF THE VKP(B) 1941V – Dela 1-126 – 26r – 1 – 2.507-2.532 – uk Chadwyck [324]
RUSSIAN CENTRE FOR THE PRESERVATION AND STUDY OF DOCUMENTS OF MOST RECENT HISTORY (RTSKHIDNI), FOND 572 : CENTRAL REVISION COMMISSION OF RKP(B)-KPSS 1921-1925; 1944-1950 – (Dela 1-9 1r. Dela 1-23 3r) – 1 – Reel nos 2.533; 2.534-2.536 – uk Chadwyck [324]
RUSSIAN CENTRE FOR THE PRESERVATION AND STUDY OF DOCUMENTS OF MOST RECENT HISTORY (RTSKHIDNI), FOND 582 : 24TH CONGRESS OF THE VKP(B) 1971 – Dela 1-26 – 2r – 1 – Reel nos 5.537-2.538 – uk Chadwyck [324]
RUSSIAN CENTRE FOR THE PRESERVATION AND STUDY OF DOCUMENTS OF MOST RECENT HISTORY (RTSKHIDNI), FOND 586 : PREPARATORY MATERIALS FOR 3RD PROGRAMME OF THE CPSU 1958-1961 – Dela 1-324 – 33r – 1 – Reel nos 2.539-2.571 – uk Chadwyck [324]
RUSSIAN CENTRE FOR THE PRESERVATION AND STUDY OF DOCUMENTS OF MOST RECENT HISTORY (RTSKHIDNI), FOND 593 : 23RD CONGRESS OF THE CPSU 1966 – Dela 1-16 – 1r – 1 – Reel no 2.572 – uk Chadwyck [324]
RUSSIAN CENTRE FOR THE PRESERVATION AND STUDY OF DOCUMENTS OF MOST RECENT HISTORY (RTSKHIDNI), FOND 604 : 25TH CONGRESS OF THE CPSU 1976 – Dela 1-31 – 4r – 1 – Reel no 2.573-2.576 – uk Chadwyck [324]
RUSSIAN CENTRE FOR THE PRESERVATION AND STUDY OF DOCUMENTS OF MOST RECENT HISTORY (RTSKHIDNI), FOND 620 : 26TH CONGRESS OF THE CPSU 1981 – Dela 1-36 – 3r – 1 – Reel nos 2.577-2.579 – uk Chadwyck [324]
RUSSIAN CENTRE FOR THE PRESERVATION AND STUDY OF DOCUMENTS OF MOST RECENT HISTORY (RTSKHIDNI), FOND 628 : 27TH CONGRESS OF THE CPSU 1986 – Dela 1-13 – 1r – 1 – Reel no 2.580 – uk Chadwyck [324]
RUSSIAN CENTRE FOR THE PRESERVATION AND STUDY OF DOCUMENTS OF MOST RECENT HISTORY (RTSKHIDNI), FOND 646 : 28TH CONGRESS OF THE CPSU 1990 – Dela 1-22 – 2r – 1 – Reel nos 2.581-2.582 – uk Chadwyck [324]
RUSSIAN CHEMICAL BULLETIN – (Continues: Bulletin. Russian Academy of Sciences) – v1-43. 1952-94 – 1,5 – $200.00v – us UMI [540]
THE RUSSIAN CHURCH AND RUSSIAN DISSENT : COMPRISING ORTHODOXY, DISSENT, AND ERRATIC SECTS / Heard, Albert F – New York: Harper, 1887 – 1mf – us A.T.L.A. [240]
RUSSIAN CORRESPONDENCE – Issued by the sympathisers with the Russian struggle for freedom. London. -w. 7 Oct 1905-17 Feb 1906. (6 ft) – 1 – uk British Libr Newspaper [947]
RUSSIAN CULTURE SERIES : 1800-1917 – 56r – 1 – $3,700.00 – us OmniSys [947]
RUSSIAN DICTIONARIES / Aav, Yrjo – Dictionaries and Glossaries printed in Russia 1627-1917. (Bibliotheca Slavica No. 10). Zug. 1977. BR-15001 1 – 9 – ne IDC [460]
RUSSIAN EMIGRE JOURNALS 1855-1917 / International Institute of Social History. Amsterdam – 168 titles – ne IDC [947]
THE RUSSIAN EMPIRE – (Napoleonic Wars 1806-19. 4 fiches. Turkish Affairs/Crimean War 1828-80. 97 fiches. Polish Affairs 1831-98. 6 fiches. Affairs of Central Asia 1873-95. 20 fiches. The Hague Conference 1899. 4 fiches. Misc. Papers 1835-99. 12 fiches. Commercial Reports 1825-99.84 fiches) – Russian economic development and the growth of Anglo-Russian trade – 227mf – 9 – Ir£228.00 – ie Microforms [941]
RUSSIAN FAIRY TALES FROM THE SKAZKI OF POLEVOI / Polevoi, Petr – 1901 – 1 – us I.U. Libraries [390]
RUSSIAN FUTURIST MANIFESTOS – 1910-14.19 color and 58 monochrome fiches – 9 – $593.00 – uk Chadwyck [750]
RUSSIAN GAZETTE – (In Russian) – Montreal, Canada. v1 n3. 23 aut 1925 – 1r – 1 – Can$25.00 – cn Can Microfilming [072]
RUSSIAN GLASS OF THE 17TH-20TH CENTURIES / Asharina, Nina et al – Corning, N.Y.: The Corning Museum of Glass, 1990. 191p. Fiche No. 11,540 – 4mf – 9 – $7.50 plus $0.65 postage and handling plus N.Y. State tax where applicable – 0-87290-123-8 – us Corning Mus [740]
THE RUSSIAN GOVERNMENT IN POLAND / Day, W A – London, 1867 – 4mf – 1 – ILM-685/1 – ne IDC [327]
RUSSIAN GREEK CATHOLIC CHURCH OF AMERICA : YEARBOOK AND CHURCH DIRECTORY – (Lacking some pgs) – 1950-70 – 4r – 1 – ATLA S0654 – us A.T.L.A. [240]
RUSSIAN HISTORICAL SOCIETY *see* SBORNIK MATERIALOV, OTNOSIASCHIKHSIA DO ARKHIVNOI CHASTI V ROSSII
RUSSIAN HISTORICAL SOURCES – 2nd Series. Approx. 900,000 pages – 3 – us Readex [947]
RUSSIAN HISTORICAL SOURCES / ed by Rodkey, Fred S – 1st Series. Approx. 500,000 pages – 3 – us Readex [947]
RUSSIAN HISTORY AND CULTURE – (Titles selected by Slavic and East European Dept. of University of Illinois at Urbana-Champaign. Cataloging available) – 8409mf – 9 – $28,665.00 Units 1-21 – us UMI [947]
RUSSIAN IMPERIAL GOVERNMENT PUBLICATIONS – 880 monograph and serial titles. 207 reels. Governmental and nongovernmental publs – 1 – 23.00r – us L of C Photodup [947]
RUSSIAN IMPERIAL GOVERNMENT PUBLICATIONS: COLLECTION.. / U.S. Library of Congress. European Division – 1984 – 1 – 4700.00 – us L of C Photodup [947]
RUSSIAN JOURNAL OF APPLIED CHEMISTRY – (Cont: Journal of Applied Chemistry of the USSR) – v23-66. 1950-93 – 1,5 – $240.00v – us UMI [540]
RUSSIAN JOURNAL OF BIOORGANIC CHEMISTRY – (Continues: Soviet Journal of Bioorganic Chemistry) – v1-20. 1975-94 – 1,5 – $100.00v – us UMI [540]
RUSSIAN JOURNAL OF COORDINATION CHEMISTRY – (Cont: Soviet Journal of Coordination Chemistry) – v1-19. 1975-93 – 1,5 – $100.00v – us UMI [540]
RUSSIAN JOURNAL OF DEVELOPMENTAL BIOLOGY – v1-25. 1970-94 – 1,5 – $65.00 – us UMI [574]
RUSSIAN JOURNAL OF ECOLOGY – (Cont: Soviet Journal of Ecology) – v1-24. 1970-93 – 1,5 – $70.00v – us UMI [574]
RUSSIAN JOURNAL OF ELECTROCHEMISTRY – (Cont: Soviet Electrochemistry) – v1-29. 1965-93 – 1,5 – $180.00v – us UMI [540]
RUSSIAN JOURNAL OF GENERAL CHEMISTRY – (Cont: Journal of General Chemistry of the USSR) – v19-64. 1949-94 – 1,5 – $240.00v – us UMI [540]
RUSSIAN JOURNAL OF GENETICS – (Cont: Soviet Genetics) – v2-29. 1966-93 – 1,5 – $180.00v – us UMI [575]
RUSSIAN JOURNAL OF INORGANIC CHEMISTRY – v. 1-17. 1956-1972 – 1,5,6 – us Princeton Micro [540]
RUSSIAN JOURNAL OF MARINE BIOLOGY – v1-20. 1975-94 – 1,5 – $65.00v – us UMI [574]
RUSSIAN JOURNAL OF NONDESTRUCTIVE TESTING – (v14-29. 1978-93. $90.00v) – v1-13.1965-77 – 1,5 – $60.00v – us UMI [620]
RUSSIAN JOURNAL OF ORGANIC CHEMISTRY – (Cont: Journal of Organic Chemistry of the USSR) – v1-29. 1965-93 – 1,5 – $240.00v – us UMI [540]
RUSSIAN JOURNAL OF PHYSICAL CHEMISTRY – v. 33-46. 1959-1972 – 1,5,6 – us Princeton Micro [540]
RUSSIAN JOURNAL OF PLANT PHYSIOLOGY – (Cont: Soviet Plant Physiology) – v4-40. 1957-93 – 1,5 – $100.00v – us UMI [580]
RUSSIAN LAWS (MOSCOW) – 1649-1825 – 1 – sz Infoprint [072]
RUSSIAN LINGUISTICS – (v8-. 1984-. 5,6,9) – v1-. Jul 1974- – 1 – us UMI [460]
RUSSIAN LITERATURE – 1972-1995 – 6,1 – sz Infoprint [072]
RUSSIAN LITERATURE – v1-15. 1972-84 – 1,5,6,13 – sz Elsevier [460]
RUSSIAN MATHEMATICAL SURVEYS – (v. 15-20. 2415.00v; 9. v. 21-27. 2420.00v; WDS; 9) – (English translation). v. 15-27. London. 1960-72 – 9 – 24230.00 – uk Dawson [510]
RUSSIAN MICROELECTRONICS – v3-23. 1974-94 – 1,5 – $65.00v – us UMI [621]
RUSSIAN MILLIONS – (Filmed with other titles. Cont by: The Friends of Russians) – nos1-11. 1941-42 – 1r – 1 – us A.T.L.A. [073]
RUSSIAN MILLIONS *see* THE FRIEND OF RUSSIANS
RUSSIAN MUSIC PERIODICALS OF THE 1920'S – 1922-29 – 2r – 1 – us Ross [780]
Russian National Library *see*
– CARD CATALOG OF THE DEPARTMENT OF THE LITERATURE OF THE NATIONALITIES OF THE FORMER SOVIET UNION
– CARD CATALOG OF THE SLAVIC COLLECTION OF THE LIBRARY OF THE ACADEMY OF SCIENCES, ST PETERSBURG, 16TH CENTURY TO 1930
RUSSIAN NECROPOLIS / ed by Danilenko, Boris – 17 titles – 9 – ne IDC [947]
RUSSIAN NEWSPAPERS 1828-1917 – 737r – 1 – fi H.U. Libr [072]
RUSSIAN NOBILITY, HISTORY OF...(BOOKS AND PERIODICALS ON MICROFICHE) : FROM THE NATIONAL LIBRARY OF RUSSIA, ST PETERSBURG – 213mf – 9 – $990.00 coll – us Ross [947]
RUSSIAN OLD (SIC) CATALOG / Helsinki University. Slavic Department – 1 – 414.00 – us L of C Photodup [460]
RUSSIAN PHYSICS JOURNAL – (Cont: Soviet Physics Journal) – v8-37. 1965-94 – 1,5 – $90.00v – us UMI [530]
THE RUSSIAN PLOT TO SEIZE GALICIA (AUSTRIAN RUTHENIA) / Stepankowsky, Vladimir – 2nd ed. enl. by extracts from the American Press. Jersey City: Ukrainian National Council, 1915. 55p. maps. 2 fold. maps – 1 – us U.W. Library [947]
RUSSIAN POLITICAL PARTIES : A MICROFICHE COLLECTION OF BOOKS ILLUSTRATING THE BROAD ARRAY OF POLITICAL PARTIES IN THE FORMER RUSSIAN EMPIRE. / ed by Pries, Anne – 240 titles – 9 – ne IDC [320]
RUSSIAN POLITICS AND LAW – (6 v1-23. 1962-1985 $375.00. 9 v24-33. 1985-1995 $480.00. Title varies: v1-31 n3, 1962-1992, as Soviet Law and Government) – v1-33. 1962-1995 – 6,9 – $855.00 set – us Hein [340]
RUSSIAN REVIEW : A QUARTERLY REVIEW OF RUSSIAN HISTORY, POLITICS, ECONOMICS AND LITERATURE – London. v1-3. 1912-14 – 1r – 1 – us Ross [947]
RUSSIAN REVIEW – (v30- 1971- 5,6; v34-1975- 9) – v1- 1941- – 1 – us UMI [947]
THE RUSSIAN REVIEW – London. v. 1-3. no. 2. 1912-May 1914 – 1 – us NY Public [330]
RUSSIAN REVOLUTIONARY LITERATURE COLLECTION – Filmed from the holdings of the Houghton Library at Harvard University – 1 – us Primary [947]
RUSSIAN REVOLUTIONARY PAMPHLETS, 1860-1923 – From Slavonic collections, British Library of Political and Economic Science, London. Printed guide. In Russian – 243 pamphlets on 330 fiches – 9 – £1,100.00 – uk Altair [335]
RUSSIAN RIVER ADVERTISER – Santa Rosa. Calif. 1901-1909 – 1 – us UMI [071]
RUSSIAN RIVER FLAG – Healdsburg, CA. 1880-86 – 1r – 1 – $50.00 – C02293 – us Library Micro [071]
RUSSIAN RIVER FLAG – Healdsburg. Calif. 1880-1886 – 1 – us UMI [071]
THE RUSSIAN RIVER NEWS – Guerneville, CA. 1970-1993 – 16r – 1 – $800.00 – B06031 – us Library Micro [071]
Russian S.F.S.R. *see*
– DE ISTVUI USHCHEE ZAKONODATELSTVO O TRUDE
– LAWS, ETC.
– SANITARNAIA OKHRANA ZHILISHCH
– SBORNIK DEKRETOV I RASPORIAZHENII PO FINANSAM
Russian S.F.S.R. Narodny i komissariat i ustit sii *see* MATERIALY NARODNOGO KOMISSARIATA I USTIT SII

Russian S.F.S.R. Narodnyi komissariat vnutrennikh del *see* TSIRKULI ARY NARODNOGO KOMISSARIATA VNUTRENNIKH DEL

Russian S.F.S.R. Narodnyi komissariat zemledeliia *see*
- OTCHET NARODNOGO KOMISSARIATA ZEMLEDELIIA R.S.F.S.R....VSEROSSI ISKOMU S"EZDU SOVETOV ZA...
- OTCHET NARODNOGO KOMISSARIATA ZEMLEDELIIA...VSEROSSIISKOMU S"EZDU SOVETOV ZA...

Russian S.F.S.R. Narodnyi komissariati ustitsii *see* TSIRKULIARNYE RASPORIAZHENIIA NARODNOGO KOMISSARIATA I USTITSII

Russian S.F.S.R. Strakhovoi sovet *see* VESTNIK STRAKHOVOGO SOVETA

Russian S.F.S.R. Ugolovnaia kassatsionnaia kollegiia *see* OPREDELENIIA UGOLOVNOI KASSATSIONNOI KOLLEGII VERKHSUDA R.S.F.S.R. ZA...

Russian S.F.S.R. Voenno-khoziaistvennyi sovet *see* IZVIESTIIA VOENNO-KHOZIAISTVENNAGO SOVIETA NARODNAGO KOMISSARIATA PO VOENNYM DIELAM

Russian S.F.S.R. Vysshii sovet narodnogo khoziaistva *see* SBORNIK PRIKAZOV POVSNKH I EGO GLAVNYM I FUNKTSIONALNYM UPRAVLENII AM

RUSSIAN, SOVIET, AND MONGOLIAN LAW / ed by Butler, W E – 1,509 titles – 9 – ne IDC [340]

Russian Soviet Government Bureau *see*
- WEEKLY BULLETIN

THE RUSSIAN STATE BANK / Gosudarstvenny i bank RSFSR – Moscow: The Bank, [192-] – 1 – CSUX90-B5983 – us Hoover Inst Photo [332]

Russian State Military Archive *see* THE 1941 SOVIET WAR GAME

RUSSIAN SYMBOLISM / ed by Pries, Anne – 1,055 titles – 9 – ne IDC [460]

RUSSIAN VERSIFICATION / Unbegaun, B O – Oxford. 1956. BR-2183 2 – 8 – ne IDC [460]

RUSSIAN WOMEN'S SERIALS : FROM THE NATIONAL LIBRARY OF ST PETERSBURG ON MICROFICHE – (Individual titles also listed separately) – 3327mf coll – 9 – $16,600.00 coll – us Ross [305]

RUSSIAN WOMEN'S SERIALS *see*
- AVRORA
- BIULLETEN' OTDELA TSK PO RABOTE SREDI ZHENSHCHIN
- DAMSKII MIR
- DELEGATKA
- KOMMUNARKA UKRAINY
- MIR ZHENSHCHINY
- MODNYI KUR'ER
- MODNYI SVET
- NOVYI RUSSKII BAZAR
- RABOTNITSA
- RABOTNITSA I KREST'IANKA
- TRUZHENITSA SEVERNOGO KAVKAZA
- UDARNITSA URALA
- VAZA
- ZHENSKAIA ZHIZN'
- ZHENSKIE RABOTY
- ZHENSKII VESTNIK
- ZHENSKII ZHURNAL
- ZHENSKOE OBRAZOVANIE
- ZHURNAL DLIA KHOZIAEK
- ZHURNAL DLIA ZHENSHCHIN

RUSSIAN/EASTERN EUROPEAN MATERIALS, BOOKS/BOOKLETS – Orthodox authors. 1905-15. Stundists, Stundo-Baptists, Baptists, Baptism, Prayer, Sectarianism.711p – 1 – us Baptist [240]

RUSSIAN-ENGLISH SCIENTIFIC AND TECHNICAL DICTIONARY OF USEFUL COMBINATIONS AND EXPRESSIONS / Zimmerman, M G – Moscow. n.d. BR-11,129/1 – 4mf – 9 – ne IDC [500]

RUSSIAN-ENGLISH SCIENTIFIC AND TECHNICAL DICTIONARY OF USEFUL COMBINATIONS AND EXPRESSIONS / Zimmerman, M G – n.d. – 4mf – 9 – ne IDC [056]

RUSSIAN/SOVIET LAW CARD CATALOGUE / ed by Pries, Anne – (Includes printed guide) – 87mf – 9 – ne IDC [340]

RUSSIA'S DECLINE AND FALL, THE SECRET HISTORY OF THE GREAT DEBACLE / Radziwill, Ekaterina Rzewuska Kniagina – London, New York: Cassell and Co., 1918.viii,256p – 1 – us U.W. Library [940]

RUSSIA'S WORK IN SPAIN / Dingle, Reginald James – London, 1939. Fiche W 841. (Blodgett Collection of Spanish Civil War Pamphlets) – 9 – us H.U. College Libr [946]

LA RUSSIE / Custine, Astolphe de – (Russia – 19th C. series). 1855 – 9 – fr Hachette [947]

RUSSIE D'AUJOURD'HUI – Paris. 1933-aout 1939 – 1 – fr A.C.R.P.P. [073]

LA RUSSIE EN 1844. SYSTEME DE LEGISLATION, D'ADMINISTRATION ET POLITIQUE, PAR UN HOMME D'ETAT RUSSE / Peltchinski, VS – (Russia – 19th C. series). 1845 – 9 – fr Hachette [321]

LA RUSSIE ET LES RUSSES / Tourgueniev, Nicolas Ivanovitch – (Russia – 19th C. series). 1847 – 9 – fr Hachette [947]

LA RUSSIE ET L'EUROPE / Martin, Henri – (Russia 19th C. series). 1866 – 9 – fr Hachette [947]

LA RUSSIE ET L'OPINION FRANCAISE AU 19E SIECLE (SERIES) – (See also the following authors from this Series listed separately in this Directory:. Ancelot, Francois. Bakounine, M.A. Barante, Baron Guillaume-Prosper de. Cobden, Richard. Coeurderoy, Ernest. Courriere, C. Custine, Astolphe de. Dolgoroukov. Gallet de Kulture, Achille. Gennadi, G.N. Golovine, Ivan Gavrilovitch. Haxthausen, August von. Henningsen, Charles-Frederick. Herzen, A.I. Jourdier, Auguste. Laverdant, Gabriel-Desire. Lesur. Levy, Armand. Marmier, Xavier. Martin, Henri. Masson, C.F. Ph. Mickiewicz, Adam. Ogarev, N.P. Peltchinski, V.S. Piotrowski, Rufin. Pradt, D.G.F. de. Rohr, Jean-Geoffroy. Sazonov, Nicolas Ivanovitch. Schnitzler, Jean-Henri. Tchadaief, Pierre. Thoerner, Th. de. Tourgueniev, Nicolas Ivanovitch) – Rare 19th C. works covering serfdom, the Czars, literature, socialism and the crusades. In French. Titles also available individually – 9 – fr Hachette [947]

LA RUSSIE SUR LE DANUBE, AVEC LA PROTESTATION DES ROUMAINS CONTRE L'INVASION DE LEUR PATRIE / Levy, Armand – (Russia – 19th C. series). 1853 – 9 – fr Hachette [947]

RUSSISCH – (v10-. 1976-. 5,6,9) – v. 1-. 1967- – 1 – us UMI [460]

RUSSISCHE FACHWORTSCHAETZE UND IHRE SEMANTIK / Wenzel, Natalja – 1992 – 171p – 9 – DM98.00 – 3-89349-560-6 – gw Hänsel [460]

RUSSISCHE REVUE – St. Petersburg etc. Bd. 1-31; 1872-1891. Vol 1-31 also numbered Jahrg. 1-20. Vol. 31 includes Generalregister, Bd. 1-31. Film Mas C 341 – 1 – us H.U. Library [073]

RUSSISCHE REVUE : ZEITSCHRIFT ZUR KUNDE DES GEISTIGEN LEBENS IN RUSLAND – Leipzig. 3v. 1863-64 – 26mf – 9 – H-670/2 – ne IDC [947]

DIE RUSSISCHEN SEKTEN / Grass, Karl Konrad – Leipzig: J.C. Hinrichs, 1907-1914 – 4mf – us A.T.L.A. [240]

RUSSISCHES CHRISTENTHUM / Frank, Viktor – 2. Ausg. Paderborn: Ferdinand Schoeningh, 1894 – 1mf – 9 – 0-8370-9232-9 – 1986-3232 – us A.T.L.A. [240]

RUSSKAI A REVOLIUTSII A: EI A NACHALO, AREST TSARI A, PERSPEKTIVY : VPECHATLI ENII A I MYSLI OCHEVIDT SA I UCHASTNIKA / Bublikov, Aleksandr Aleksandrovich – Niulork: [s.n.], 1918 – 1 – CSUX88-B746 – us Hoover Inst Photo [320]

RUSSKAI A ZHIZN *see* NOVAI A RUSSKAI A ZHIZN

RUSSKAIA ARMIIA – Omsk, USSR. Dec 29 1918-Nov 2 1919 – 1r – 1 – us L of C Photodup [072]

RUSSKAIA ARMIIA I FLOT V 18. VEKE (OCHERKI) / Akademiia Nauk. SSSR Institut Istorii – Beskrovnyi, L.T. 1958. BR-10,517 1 – 9 – ne IDC [947]

RUSSKAIA ARMIIA NA CHUZHBINIE / Davatts, Vladimir Khristianovich – Belgrad: Russkoe izd-vo, 1923 – 1 – CSUX88-B3624 – us Hoover Inst Photo [355]

RUSSKAIA BASNIA 18 I NACHALA 19 VEKA / ed by Stepanov, N L – L. 1949. BR-7895 2 – 8 – ne IDC [390]

RUSSKAIA BESEDA – Ezhemesiachnoe literaturno-politicheskoe izdanie. Spb. 1895-96. B-1854 2 – 8 – ne IDC [460]

RUSSKAIA BESEDA – M. 1856-60. B-1853 2 – 8 – ne IDC [460]

RUSSKAIA BESEDA – Sobranie sochinenii russkikh literatorov. v. 1-3. Spb. 1841-42. BR-1608 2 – 8 – ne IDC [460]

RUSSKAIA BESIEDA – Leningrad. v1-2. 1895-96 – 2r – 1 – us Ross [947]

RUSSKAIA BESIEDA – St Petersburg, 1895-1896 – 1 – us NY Public [073]

RUSSKAIA BIBLIOGRAFIIA, GOD PERVYI (1878) / Golubev, A & Sodko, N P – Sost. A. G. i N. S. v. 1. Sistematicheskii katalog knig, napechatannykh v Rossii v 1878 god s ukazaniem gazetnykh i zhurnal' nykh retsenzii. v. 2. Sistematicheskii ukazatel' zhurnal' nykh statei za 1878 god. v. 3. Ocherk knigopechatnago dela v Rossii. Spb. 1879. BR-4716 2 – 8 – ne IDC [010]

RUSSKAIA BIBLIOGRAFIIA PO ESTESTVOZNANIIU I MATEMATIKE – 1(1901 g)-9 (1912-1913 g.). 1904-18. BR-7237 2 – 8 – ne IDC [510]

RUSSKAIA BIBLIOGRAFIIA PO ISTORII DREVNEI FILOSOFII / Iashchenko, A – Iur'ev. 1915. BR-5907 2 – 8 – ne IDC [100]

RUSSKAIA BOGOSLOVSKAIA LITERATURA 1888-1892 GG / Lebedev, A A – Bibliograficheskii ukazatel' knig otdel'nykh ottiskov i broshiur. Saratov. 1908. BR-7128 2 – 8 – ne IDC [460]

RUSSKAIA BUDUSHNOST' – Natsional'no-progressivnyi, obshchestvenno-politicheskii ezhenedel'nik. Petrograd. 1915-17. Lacking: (10) 1915; (46) 1916; (5-end) 1917. BR-2273 2 – 8 – ne IDC [320]

RUSSKAIA BURZHUAZIIA V STAROE I NOVOE VREMIA / Berlin, Pavel Abramovich – 2-e dop. izd. Moskvo: Kniga, 1925 – 1 – CSUX89-B5391 – us Hoover Inst Photo [947]

RUSSKAIA I INOSTRANNAIA KNIGA 15-19 VEKA / Vereshchagin, V A – Spb. 1914. BR-4562 2 – 8 – ne IDC [010]

RUSSKAIA ILLIUSTRATSIIA – Ezhenedel'nyi illiustrirovannyi zhurnal. nr. 1-31. M. 1915. BR-3740 2 – 8 – ne IDC [073]

RUSSKAIA ISTORICHESKAIA BIBIOGRAFIIA ZA 1865-1876 VKLIUCHITEL'NO – (Russian historical bibliography). 8 v. 1882-90 – 3 – us Readex [010]

RUSSKAIA ISTORICHESKAIA BIBLIOGRAFIIA / Mezhov, VI – St. Petersburg. (Russian bibliography, 1882-1890). 8 v – 3 – us Readex [010]

RUSSKAIA ISTORICHESKAIA BIBLIOGRAFIIA. 1855-1864 – v. 1-10. Spb. 1861-84. BR-7242 2 – 8 – ne IDC [947]

RUSSKAIA ISTORICHESKAIA BIBLIOTEKA / Russia. Arkheograficheskaia Kommissiia – (The Russian Archaeographic Commission's "Historical Library"). 39 v. 1872-1927 – 3 – us Readex [947]

RUSSKAIA ISTORICHESKAIA BIBLIOTEKA IZDAVAEMAIA ARKHEOGRAFICHESKOIU KOMMISSIEIU – St. Petersburg, 1872-1927. v1-39. B-1162 2 – 8 – ne IDC [930]

RUSSKAIA KAMENA / Sadovskoi, B – Stat'i. Izd. Musaget, 1910 – 8 – BR-2106 2 – ne IDC [947]

RUSSKAIA LETOPIS' – v. 1-7. Paris. 1921-25. BR-3792 2 – 8 – ne IDC [520]

RUSSKAIA LIRIKA – Antologiia. Mirskii, D., sostavitel'. Paris. 1925. BR-3544 2 – 8 – ne IDC [460]

RUSSKAIA LIRIKA / Sipovskii, V V – Vyp. 1. XVIII vek. Petrograd. 1914. BR-7863 2 – 8 – ne IDC [460]

RUSSKAIA LITERATURA – (Akad. Nauk. SSSR. Inst. Russkoi literatury). Leningrad, 1958-72. BR-5751 1 – 9 – ne IDC [460]

RUSSKAIA LITERATURA 18 VEKA / Arkhangel'skii, A S – I. Kazan'. 1911. BR-5977 2 – 8 – ne IDC [460]

RUSSKAIA LITERATURA 19 I PERVOI CHETVERTI 20 V / Bagrii, A V – Baku. 1926. BR-3549 2 – 8 – ne IDC [460]

RUSSKAIA LITERATURA 20 VEKA – 1890-1910. Pod. red. S.A. Vengerova. v. 1-3. M. 1914-16. BR-2098 2 – 8 – ne IDC [460]

RUSSKAIA LITERATURA 20 VEKA / Vengerov, S A – v1-3. M. 1914-16 (1918). BR-3304 2 – 8 – ne IDC [460]

RUSSKAIA LITERATURA O SLAVIANSTVE / Voznesenskh, S – Opyt bibliograficheskago ukazatelia. Petrograd. 1915. BR-5923 2 – 8 – ne IDC [460]

RUSSKAIA LITERATURA OT SEMIDESIATYKH GODOV DO NASHIKH DNEI / Ivanov-Razumnik, R I – Berlin. 1923. BR-1313 2 – 8 – ne IDC [460]

RUSSKAIA LITERATURA OT SIMVOLIZMA DO NASHIKH DNEI / Nikitina, E – Literaturno-sotsiologicheskii seminarii. S. predisloviem N.K. Piksanova (Bibliografiia do 1925 g.). M. 1926. BR-154 2 – 8 – ne IDC [460]

RUSSKAIA LITERATURA POD RED. BELCHIKOVA / Lunacharskii, A V – 1800-1917. M., Ogiz. 1947. BR-1381 2 – 8 – ne IDC [460]

RUSSKAIA MORSKAIA BIBLIOTEKA 1701-1851. ISCHISLENIE I OPISANIE KNIG, RUKOPISEI I STATEI PO MORSKOMU DELU ZA 150 LET. 2-OE IZD / Sokolov, A P – Spb. 1883. BR-4540 2 – 8 – ne IDC [020]

RUSSKAIA MUZYKAL'NAIA KUL'TURA XVIII VEKA V EE SVIAZIAKH S LITERATURNOI, TEATROM I BYTOM / Livanova, T – v. 1-2. M. 1952-53. BR-7655 2 – 8 – ne IDC [780]

RUSSKAIA MYSL – (Includes c.1: 1920:Nov.25) – Bielgrad: Knizhn. magazin "Russkaia mysl", 1920- – 1 reel – 1 – CSUXANS1454-S – us Hoover Inst Photo [073]

RUSSKAIA MYSL = PENSEE RUSSE – (Library has holdings (incomplete) from between July 1, 1976 and Dec. 20, 1985) – Paris: "La Pensee russe", 1947- – 1 – CSUX87-S250 – us Hoover Inst Photo [073]

RUSSKAIA MYSL' – Moscow. After 1921: Sofia-Prague-Berlin. 1880-1927 (suspended 1918-1920, 1925-1926). Complete – 1 – 35.00r – us Hoover Inst Photo [072]

RUSSKAIA MYSL' – Paris. mai 1947-1993 – 1 – fr A.C.R.P.P. [073]

RUSSKAIA MYSL' – v. 1-43. 1880-1924 – 1 – 1,848.00 – us L of C Photodup [460]

RUSSKAIA MYSL' I RECH. SVOE I CHUZHOE. OPYT ROSSKOI FRAZEOLOGII / Mikhel'son, M I – Spb., 1903-1904. v1-2 – 43mf – 9 – R-8397/2 – ne IDC [460]

RUSSKAIA NARODNAIA DRAMA 17-20 VEKOV / Berkov, P N – M. 1953. BR-6104 2 – 8 – ne IDC [460]

RUSSKAIA OKHOTNICH'IA BIBLIOTEKA / Anofriev, N I – Polnyi spisok knig i broshiur s kratkimi o kazhdoi iz nikh otzyvami. Brest-Litovsk, 1905. 160p. BR-7055 2 – 8 – ne IDC [020]

RUSSKAIA PALEOGRAFIA / Tikhonravov, N S – Moscow, 1889. BR-10,363/1 – 9 – ne IDC [090]

RUSSKAIA PALEOGRAFIIA / Chaev, N S & Cherepnin, LV – Moscow, 1946. BR-10,317/1 – 9 – ne IDC [930]

RUSSKAIA PALEOGRAFIIA / Cherepnin, LV – Moscow, 1956. B-1588/2 – 8 – ne IDC [930]

RUSSKAIA PECHAT' I TSENZURA V PROSHLOM I NASTOIASHCHEM / Rozenberg, V A & Iakushkin, V E – Stat'i VI. Rozenberga i V. Iakushkina. 1905. BR-9793 1 – 9 – ne IDC [380]

RUSSKAIA PERIODICHESKAIA PECHAT' – 1. Bibliografiia russkoi periodicheskoi pechat'. 2. Graficheskiia tablitsy russkoi periodicheskoi pechati. (In: Bibliograf, 1896-1900). Spb. 1896-1900. Lacking: (4-6) 1897; (1-2) 1899. BR-4415 2 – 8 – ne IDC [073]

RUSSKAIA PERIODICHESKAIA PECHAT' 1703-1900 / Lisovskii, N M – (Bibliografiia i graficheskie tablitsy). Petrograd. 1915. Pages missing in the original: I-XIV, 1-96. BR-7992 2 – 8 – ne IDC [760]

RUSSKAIA POEZIIA / ed by Vengerov, S A – Vyp. 1-VII. Spb. 1893-1901. BR-7942 2 – 8 – ne IDC [460]

RUSSKAIA POEZIIA 20 VEKA / Ezhov, I S & Shamurin, E I – Antologiia. M. 1925. BR-1253 2 – 8 – ne IDC [460]

RUSSKAIA POEZIIA 1918-1923 G / Gruzdev, I – "Kniga i revoliutsiia". nr. 3. 1923. BR-3267 2 – 8 – ne IDC [335]

RUSSKAIA PRAVDA PO STAREISHEMU SPISKU. VVEDENIE, TEKST, SNIMKI, PEREVOD, UKAZATELI AVTOROV I SLOVARNOGO SOSTAVA / Karskii, E F – Leningrad, 1926-30. BR-10,337/1 – 9 – ne IDC [460]

RUSSKAIA PROZA 18 VEKA / Zapadov, A V & Makogonenko, E P – 2v. M., L. 1950. BR-7978 2 – 8 – ne IDC [460]

RUSSKAIA RECH' – Obozrenie literatury, istorii, iskusstva i obshchestvennoi zhizni na Zapade i Rossii. v. 1-104. M. 1861. BR-3742 2 – 8 – ne IDC [460]

RUSSKAIA RECH' – Zhurnal literatury, politiki i nauki. (5) Spb. 1879-82. Lacking: (6-12) 1882. B-1858 2 – 8 – ne IDC [460]

RUSSKAIA REVOLIUTSIIA V SUDEBNYKH PROTSESSAKH I MEMUARAKH / Kovalenskii, Mikhail N – Moskva, Mir, 1923-1925. 4 v. LL-4023 – 1 – 23.00 – us L of C Photodup [340]

RUSSKAIA SATIRA PERVOI REVOLIUTSII 1905-1906 / Botsianovskii, Vladimir & Gollerbakh, E – Leningrad: Gos. izd-vo, 1925 – 1 – CSUX88-B580 – us Hoover Inst Photo [947]

RUSSKAIA SKAZKA. IZBRANNYE MASSHERA / Azadovskii, M K – v. 1-2. 1932. B-1515 2 – 8 – ne IDC [460]
RUSSKAIA SLOVESNOST' / Mez'er, A V – St. Petersburg. (Russian literature of the 11th to the 19th century). 1899-1902 – 3 – us Readex [460]
RUSSKAIA SLOVESNOST'S 11 PO 19 STOLIETIIA VKLIUCHITEL'NO – (Russian literature of the 11th to the 19th century). 2 v. 1899-1902 – 3 – us Readex [460]
RUSSKAIA SOVETSKAIA LITERATURA / Dement'ev, A & Naumov, E & Plotkin, L – 1951. BR-2047 2 – 8 – ne IDC [460]
RUSSKAIA STARINA – Ezhemesiachnoe istoricheskoe izdanie. v. 1-176. Spb. 1870-1918. Lacking: v. 174-176, 1918. B-1283 2 – 8 – ne IDC [073]
RUSSKAIA STARINA – Petrograd. 1870-Feb. 1918 – 1 – 35.00r – us Hoover Inst Photo [072]
RUSSKAIA STARINA – (Russian antiquity). 176 v. 1870-1918 – 3 – us Readex [947]
RUSSKAIA STARINA – St Petersburg. 1887-Sept 1918. (Incomplete) and Index – 1 – us NY Public [930]
RUSSKAIA STSENA – Teatral'nyi zhurnal. Spb. 1864-65. Lacking: (8-12) 1965. B-1859 2 – 8 – ne IDC [410]
RUSSKAJA LITERATURA 20 VEKA (1890-1915 GG.) / Ivanov-Razumnik, R I – R-1312 2. 1920 – 8 – ne IDC [460]
RUSSKAYA ZHIZN – Helsinki, Finland. Novaya russkaya zhizn. -d. 13 Feb 1919-31 May 1922. Very imperfect. 6 reels – 1 – uk British Libr Newspaper [947]
RUSSKI I ANARKHIZM V VELIKO I RUSSKO I REVOLIUTSII / Akovlev, Akov Arkadevich – Moskva: Gos. izdvo, 1921 – 1 – CSUX89-B2556 – us Hoover Inst Photo [320]
RUSSKI I ANARKHIZM V VELIKO I RUSSKO I REVOLIUTSII / Akovlev, Akov Arkadevich – Niulork: Kn-vo "Iskry", 1922 – 1 – CSUX88-B9102 – us Hoover Inst Photo [320]
RUSSKI I PATRIOT = PATRIOTE RUSSE – (Library has holdings (incomplete) from between Dec. 1943 and Mar. 17, 1945) – Parizh: "Russki i patriot", 1943-1945. 1v – 1 – CSUX87-S202 – us Hoover Inst Photo [947]
RUSSKIE ARKHIVNYE DOKUMENTY PO SNOSHENIIAM S OIRATAMI V 17 I 18 VV. IAN / Kotvich, V L – Petrograd. 1919. BU-727 2 – 8 – ne IDC [947]
RUSSKIE ARKHIVY I TSARSKII KONTROL' PRIKAZNOI SLUZHBY V 17 VEKE / Samokvasov, D Ia – M. 1902. PKG-A-88.1 BR-11,068 1 – 9 – ne IDC [025]
RUSSKIE BIOGRAFICHESKIE I BIBLIOGRAFICHESKIE SLOVARI / Kaufman, IM – Ed.2. M., 1955 – 16mf – 9 – R-3532/2 – ne IDC [580]
RUSSKIE DIPLOMATICHESKIE AGENTY V LONDONE V 18 V. / Aleksandrenko, V N – Warsaw, 1897. 2v. BR-9466 1 – 9 – ne IDC [947]
RUSSKIE DOSTOPAMIATNOSTI – Moscow: A Martynov Publ, 1862-1863 – 11mf – 9 – $110.00 – us Ross [947]
RUSSKIE DOSTOPAMIATNOSTI, TOMA 1-4 – Moscow: A. Martynov Publ, 1877-1883 – 15mf – 9 – $150.00 – us Ross [947]
RUSSKIE ENTSIKLOPEDII : V.1: OBSHCHIE ENTSIKLOPEDII – BIBLIOGRAFIIA I KRATKIE OCHERKI / Kaufman, IM – M., 1960 – 2mf – 9 – R-18496/1 – ne IDC [947]
RUSSKIE FEODAL'NYE ARKHIVY XIV-XV VEKOV / Cherepnin, LV – Moscow, Leningrad, 1948-51. 2v. 472p,428p. BR-11,065/1 – 9 – ne IDC [947]
RUSSKIE LIRIKI / Rozanov, I – M. 1929. BR-2094 2 – 8 – ne IDC [460]
RUSSKIE NOVOSTI = NOUVELLES RUSSES – (Library has: no. 1-500 (May 18, 1945-Dec. 31, 1945[3 issues missing]) – Paris: "Russkie novosti", 1945- – 1 – CSUX86-S550 – us Hoover Inst Photo [460]
RUSSKIE NOVOSTI – Paris. France. -w. 2 Jan 1948-5 May 1967. (1948, 49 imperfect). (7 reels) – 1 – uk British Libr Newspaper [947]
RUSSKIE PISATELI / Vladislavlev, I V – Opyt bibliograficheskogo posobija po russkoi literature XIX-XX st. Ed. 4. GIZ. M. L. 1924. B-1166 2 – 8 – ne IDC [460]
RUSSKIE PISATELI O LITERATURNOM TRUDE – "Sovetskii Pisatel'". v. 1-4. L. 1954-56. BR-3335 2 – 8 – ne IDC [460]
RUSSKIE PISATELI POSLE GOGOLIA V OTZYVAKH KRITIKI / Kozlov, K – Opyt bibliograficheskago spravochnika. Tiflis. 1908. BR-5955 2 – 8 – ne IDC [460]
RUSSKIE PROSVETITELI 1790-1800-KH GODOV / Orlov, V N – Ed. 2. M. 1953. BR-7741 2 – 8 – ne IDC [947]
RUSSKIE SATIRICHESKIE ZHURNALY 1769-1774 GG / Semennikov, V P – Razyskaniia ob izdateliakh i ikh sotrudnikakh. Spb. 1914. BR-4418 2 – 8 – ne IDC [073]
RUSSKIE SATIRO-IUMORISTICHESKIE ZHURNALY / Masanov, I F – (Bibliograficheskoe opisanie: I Vesel'chak, 1858-1859 gg.). II Iskra, 1859-1873 gg. Vladimir. 1911. BR-4403 2 – 8 – ne IDC [460]
RUSSKIE SIMVOLISTY / Ellis – K. Bal'mont, V. Briusov, A. Belyi. M. 1910. B-2186 2 – 8 – ne IDC [460]
RUSSKIE SIMVOLISTY – Sborniki pod. red. pt. 1-3. Briusova. 1894-95; Izd. Maslova, M. 1894. Lacking: pt. 3. BR-2101 2 – 8 – ne IDC [750]
RUSSKIE VRACHI PISATELI / Zmeev, L F – v. 1-5. Spb. 1886-89. BR-7020 2 – 8 – ne IDC [460]
RUSSKII ANTROPOLOGICHESKII ZHURNAL – v. 1-38. M. 1900-16. B-1492 2 – 8 – ne IDC [301]
RUSSKII ARKHIV – Moscow. 1863-1915. Missing: 1872 (entire year; no. 5, 1919) – 1 – 35.00r – us Hoover Inst Photo [073]
RUSSKII ARKHIV / Russia – (Russian archives). 55 v. 1863-1917 – 3 – us Readex [025]
RUSSKII BIBLIOFIL – Illiustrirovannyi vestnik dlia sobiratelei knig i graviur. Spb. 1911-16. B-1861 2 – 8 – ne IDC [760]
RUSSKII BIBLIOGRAFICHESKII UKAZATEL' ZA 1855 GOD / Lambin, P P – (Izvestiia Imp. Akad. nauk po otdniiu russkago izazyka i slovesnosti. Pribavleniia. v. 5. 1856). Spb. 1856. BR-4357 2 – 8 – ne IDC [010]
RUSSKII BIOGRAFICHESII SLOVAR / Russia – St. Petersburg. 1896-1918 – 1 – us UMI [920]
RUSSKII BIOGRAFICHESKII SLOVAR – (Russian biographical dictionary). 25 v. 1896-1918 – 3 – us Readex [920]
RUSSKII BIOGRAFICHESKII SLOVAR' / St. Petersburg. Imperatorskago Russkago istoricheskago obshchestva – Spb. 1896-1913. B-1572 2 – 8 – ne IDC [920]
RUSSKII BYLEVOI EPOS / Zhdanov, I – Izsledovaniia i materialy. Spb. 1895. B-2197 2 – 8 – ne IDC [947]
RUSSKII DEMOKRATICHESKII TEATR 18 VEKA / Kuz'mina, V D – M. 1958. BR-6228 2 – 8 – ne IDC [460]
RUSSKII DRAMATICHESKII TEATR 17-18 VEKOV / Aseev, N – M. 1958. BR-6078 2 – 8 – ne IDC [460]
RUSSKII EKONOMICHESKII SBORNIK – v. 1-12. Prague. 1925-28. BR-3790 2 – 8 – ne IDC [330]
RUSSKII EMIGRANT – Berlin. nos. 1-7. Sep 1920-15 Feb 1921 – 1 – us NY Public [073]
RUSSKII EVREI – Leningrad. v1-6. 1879-84 – 2r – 1 – us Ross [270]
RUSSKII EVREI – St Petersburg. v. 1-6. Aug 31 1879-Dec 31 1884 – 1 – us NY Public [073]
RUSSKII EVREI – v. 1-4. M. 1915. BR-3782 2 – 8 – ne IDC [270]
RUSSKII EZHENEDI ELNIK V BELGII = L'HEBDOMADAIRE RUSSE EN BELGIQUE – (Library has holdings (incomplete) from between Dec. 22, 1932 and Apr. 19, 1940) – Bruxelles: Russki i ezhenedi elnik v belgii, 1927- – 1 – CSUX86-S597 – us Hoover Inst Photo [072]
RUSSKII FILOLGICHESKII VESTNIK – Warsaw. v1-78. 1879-1918 – 651mf – 9 – ne IDC [460]
RUSSKII FOL'KLOR / Akademiia Nauk. SSR Institut russkoi literatury. Pushkinskii dom – Stat'i i issledovaniia. v. 1-10. M. 1956-66. BR-5754 2 – 8 – ne IDC [390]
RUSSKII FOLKLOR / Mel'ts, M Ia; ed by Astrakhova, A M & Luppov, S P – Bibliograficheskii ukazatel'. 3v. Bibliog. of Soviet publications relating to folklore, includes descriptions of archival holdings. BR-10,749/1 – 19mf – 9 – ne IDC [010]
RUSSKII FOTOGRAFICHESKII VESTNIK – Populiarno-nauchnyi i khudozhestvennyi zhurnal. Odessa. 1915-16. BR-3777 2 – 8 – ne IDC [073]
RUSSKII FUTURIZM POSLE REVOLIUTSII / Malakhov, S – v. 10. Molodaia Gvardiia. 1926. BR-3569 2 – 8 – ne IDC [700]
RUSSKII GERAL'DICHESKII SLOVAR / Belinksii, VE – Spb., 1912-1913. v1-2 (unfinished). viii, 56 pp., 5 tabs; p. 57-96 – 4mf – 9 – R-8382/2 – ne IDC [460]
RUSSKII GOLOS – Belgrade, Yugoslavia. May 1936-Mar 1941 (incomplete) – 2r – 1 – us L of C Photodup [949]
RUSSKII GOLOS – (Library has: no. 612-895 (June 11, 1933-Jan. 18, 1939) – L'vov: "Russkii golos", [1922?]- – 1 – CSUX87-S188 – us Hoover Inst Photo [072]
RUSSKII GOLOS : NATSIONALNAIA, OBSHCHESTVENNAIA I VOENNAIA EZHENEDIELNAIA GAZETA – (Library has: no. 1-465 (April 12, 1931-March 3, 1940)[missing twelve issues; some issues slightly mutilated]) – Bielgrad: Russki i golos, 1931- – 1 – CSUX86-S588 – us Hoover Inst Photo [072]
RUSSKII GOMILET NACHALA 18 VEKA IOAKIM BOGOMOLEVSKII / Sovitskii, D – Kiev, 1902 – 8 – BR-7891 2 – ne IDC [947]
RUSSKII INVALID – Ezhenedel'noe prilozhenie. Spb. 1874-75. BR-3778 2 – 8 – ne IDC [073]
RUSSKII INVALID – St Petersburg, 1848-1912 – 10r – 1 – us Ross [355]
RUSSKII INVALID – St Petersburg. 1848-1912 – 1 – us NY Public [073]
RUSSKII ISTORICHESKII AL'BOM / ed by Pogodin, M P – M. 1853. BR-10,046 1 – 9 – ne IDC [947]
RUSSKII ISTORICHESKII SBORNIK – v. 1-7. M. 1837-44. Obshchestvo istorii i drevnostei rossiiskikh pri Moskovskom universitete. B-1863 2 – 8 – ne IDC [947]
RUSSKII KNIZHNYI ZNAK / Vereshchagin, V A – Spb, 1902 – 8 – BR-4598 2 – ne IDC [947]
RUSSKII LITSEVOI APOKALIPSIS / Buslaev, Fedor Ivanovich – Moscow, 1884. BR-10,011/2 – 8 – ne IDC [010]
RUSSKII MUZYKAL'NYI VESTNIK – St Petersburg, 1880-82 (weekly 78 issues publ) – 12mf – 9 – us Ross [780]
RUSSKII NACHAL'NYI UCHITEL' – Ezhemesiachnyi zhurnal. Spb. 1880-1911. Lacking: (12) 1881; (2) 1883; (10) 1892; (10) 1893; (1-12) 1898. BR-3745 2 – 8 – ne IDC [073]
RUSSKII NARODNYI VESTNIK – Belgrade, Yugoslavia. Sept 1940-Mar 1941 – 1r – 1 – us L of C Photodup [949]
RUSSKII OB IASNITEL'NYI SLOVAR' ZAKLIUCHAIUSHCHII V SEBE ODNI NEPONIATNYIA SLOVA RUSSKOGO KNIZHNOGO IAZYKA / Starchevskii, A V – Spb., 1891. v1 – 44mf – 9 – R-8406/2 – ne IDC [460]
RUSSKII PARNAS – Antologiia pod. red. A. i D. Eliasberg. (Bibliotheca Mundi): Leipzig, 1921. 330p. Index. BR-3336 2 – 8 – ne IDC [460]
RUSSKII PEDAGOGICHESKII VESTNIK – Spb. 1857-60. BR-3788 – 8 – ne IDC [073]
RUSSKII PUT' – Organ Rossisskago otechestvennago soiuza. Oct-Nov 1948. Fevr. 1952. Paris. 1948, 1952. BR-5762 2 – 8 – ne IDC [073]
RUSSKII SOTSIALIZM I KOOPERATSIIA : VZAIMOOT NOSHE NIIA SOTS. I KOOP. DVIZHENIIA V ROSSII V IKH IST. RAZVITII / Frommett, B R – Pg., 1919 – 2mf – 9 – COR-226/1 – ne IDC [334]
RUSSKII STIAG – 1906-17 – 11r – 1 – $850.00 – us Ross [355]
RUSSKII UCHITEL' – Ezhemesiachnyi professional'-nyi organ uchitel'stva nachal'noi i srednei shkoly. Spb. 1912-13. BR-3779 2 – 8 – ne IDC [073]
RUSSKII V ARGENTINIE – (Library has: no. 129-739 (Jan. 1, 1933-Sept. 30, 1944)[missing three issues; some issues slightly mutilated]) – Buenos Aires: "El Ruso en la Argentina", [1929?] – 1 – CSUX86-S148 – us Hoover Inst Photo [072]
RUSSKII VESTNIK – Moscow. 1857-1906 – 1 – 35.00r – us Hoover Inst Photo [072]
RUSSKII VESTNIK – Spb. 1841-44. Lacking: (5-7, 10-12) 1841; (1-12) 1843. B-1865 2 – 8 – ne IDC [073]
RUSSKII VIESTNIK – (Library has holdings (incomplete) from between Dec. 4, 1915 and Nov. 16, 1918) – Berlin: "Russkii viestnik", 1915- – 1 – CSUX87-S261 – us Hoover Inst Photo [073]
RUSSKII VOENYI VIESTNIK – Belgrade, 1925-27 – us Res Libr [072]
RUSSKII ZAGRANICHNYI ISTORICHESKII ARKHIV PRI MINISTERSTVE INOSTRANNYKH DEL CHEKHOSLOVATSKOI RESPUBLIKI V 1929 GODU; V 1930 GODU; V 1931 GODU – 3v. Prague. 1930-32. BR-11.233 1 – 9 – ne IDC [025]
RUSSKII ZAGRANICHNYI ISTORICHESKII ARKHIV (RZIA), CARD CATALOGUE – 267mf – 9 – $1,500.00 – us Ross [010]
RUSSKII ZRITEL' – Zhurnal istorii, arkheologii, slovesnosti i sravnitel'nykh kostiumov. M. 1828-30. B-1866 2 – 8 – ne IDC [930]
RUSSKIIA EPARKHII V 16-19 VV, IKH OTKRYTIE, SOSTAV I PREDIELY : OPYT TSERKOVNO-ISTORICHESKAGO, STATISTICHESKAGO I GEOGRAFICHESKAGO IZSLIEDOVANIIA / Pokrovskii, Ivan Mikhailovich – (MF-7699: v2 1913 1r) – Kazan: Tipo-litografiia Imp Universiteta, 1897- – 1 – us Res Libr [947]
RUSSKIIA ILLIUSTRIROVANNYIA IZDANIIA 18 I 19 STOLETII (1720-1870) / Vereshchagin, V A – Bibliograficheskii opyt. Spb. 1898. BR-4708 2 – 8 – ne IDC [760]
RUSSKIIA KNIGI. S BIOGRAFICHESKIMI DANNYMI OB AVTORAKH I PEREVODCHIKAKH, (1708-1893) / Vengerov, S A – v. 1-3. Spb. 1897-99. Lacking: 1897 (1). BR-5697 2 – 8 – ne IDC [920]
RUSSKIIA VEDOMOSTI – (Missing: 1890-91; 1896 and several nos of subsequent yrs) – 1863, 1890-1918 – 67r – 1 – RF-5/3 – ne IDC [072]
RUSSKIIA VEDOMOSTI – Moscow. Jan.-Dec. 1890; Jan. 1892-Mar. 1918. Missing: 19 issues – 1 – 35.00r – us Hoover Inst Photo [072]
RUSSKIIA ZAPISKI – Ezhemesiachnyi literaturnyi, nauchnyi i politicheskii zhurnal. Petrograd. 1914-17. BR-3775 2 – 8 – ne IDC [460]
RUSSKIIA ZAPISKI – Ezhemesiachnyi zhurnal. v. 1-21. Paris. 1937-39. BR-3746 2 – 8 – ne IDC [073]
Russko Istoricheskoe Obshchestvago. Leningrad *see*
– SBORNIK
– SBORNIK IMPERATORSKAGO RUSSKAGO ISTORICHESKOVO OBSHCHESTVA
RUSSKO-AMERIKANSKII PRAVOSLAVNYI VIESTNIK – Sept 1896-Dec 1973 – 1 – 345.00 – us L of C Photodup [073]
RUSSKO-AMERIKANSKIJI PRAVOSLAVNIJI KALENDAR – Bridgeport, CT, Wilkes-Barre, PA: Russian Orthodox Catholic Mutual Aid Society of the USA, 1904 – us Res Libr [520]
RUSSKO-ANGLIISKIE OTNOSHENIIA I PROBLEMY SREDIZEMNOMOR'IA (1798-1807) / Stanislavskaia, A M – Akademiia nauk SSSR. Institut istorii. M. 1962. BR-10,534 1 – 9 – ne IDC [941]
RUSSKO-AVSTRIISKII SOIUZ VO VREMIA SEMILETNEI VOINY, 1746-1758 GG / Shchepkin, E N – Spb. 1902. BR-7838 2 – 8 – ne IDC [947]
Russkoe Arkheologicheskoe Obshchestvo. Leningrad *see* VOSTOCHNOE OTDIELENIE
Russkoe Arkheologicheskoe Obshchestvo. Leningrad. Klassicheskoe Otdelenie *see* ZAPISKI
Russkoe Arkheologicheskoe Obshchestvo. Leningrad. Vostochnoe Otdelenie *see* ZAPISKI
RUSSKOE BIBLIOLOGICHESKOE OBSHCHESTVO. DOKLADY I OTCHETY. (NOVAIA SERIIA) – pt. 1-2. Spb. 1908, 1913. BR-4332 2 – 8 – ne IDC [010]
RUSSKOE DIELO – (Includes c.1: 1919:Apr.2-Dec.30; 1920:Jan.1-July 30, Aug.5, 12, 19, 24-28; 1920: Sept.2-7, 14, 25-28, Oct.2, 7, 14, 21-23) – Praga: [s.n.], 1919- – 1 – CSUXADP4352-S – us Hoover Inst Photo [073]
RUSSKOE DIELO – (Library has: no.138, 173, 180, 183, 189, 194, 233, 240-241, 244, 248, 251, 271 (1922-1923)) – Bielgrad: "Natsionalnoe vozrodzhdenie", 1921- – 1 – CSUX89-S128 – us Hoover Inst Photo [073]
RUSSKOE DIELO – (Library has: no.2 (Apr. 1936)) – Beograd: M.F. Kozmin, 1936- – 1 – CSUX89-S130 – us Hoover Inst Photo [073]
RUSSKOE DIELO : ODNODNEVNAIA GAZETA KHARBINSKAGO KOMITETA POMOSHCHI RUSSKIM BIEZHENTSAM – (Includes c.1: no.1(1932:Jan.1) – no.6(1933:Aug.20)) – [Kharbin]: Pravlenie komta, 1932- – 1 reel – 1 – CSUXANS2006-S – us Hoover Inst Photo [073]

RUSSKOE DIELO, SOFIA, BULGARIA – (Includes c.1: 1921: Dec.4-14, 23; 1922: Feb.19-22, Mar.10-Apr.26, 28-May 17) – Sofiia: Izdvo "Natsionalnoe vozrozhdenie, 1921-22 – 1 reel – 1 – CSUXANS3283-S – us Hoover Inst Photo [320]

RUSSKOE EKONOMICHESKOE OBOZRENIE – Ezhemesiachnyi ekonomicheskii zhurnal. Spb. 1897-1905. not published: v. 9-12, 1897. BR-3770 2 – 402mf – 8 – R-3770/2 – ne IDC [073]

RUSSKOE GRAZHDANSKOE PRAVO / Meier, D I – Ed. 4. Spb. 1868. BR-9803 1 – 9 – ne IDC [460]

RUSSKOE ISTORICHESKOE OBSHCHESTO SBORNIK – v. 1-148. 1867-1916 – 1 – us UMI [500]

RUSSKOE ISTORICHESKOE OBSHCHESTVO – Imperatorskoe Russkoe Istoricheskoe Obshchestvo, 1866-1916. Petrograd. 1916. BR-4091 2 – 8 – ne IDC [947]

RUSSKOE KOOPERATIVNOE ZAKONODATEL'STVO / Povolotskii, Ll – Ed 2. M., 1924. (S. Kooperativnaia shkola no. 13) – 2mf – 9 – COR-734/1 – ne IDC [334]

RUSSKOE KOOPERATIVNOE ZAKONODATEL'STVO : S PRILOZHENIEM DEKRETOV O VSEKH VIDAKH KOOPERATSII / Povolotskii, Ll – Ed 2. M., 1924 – 2mf – 9 – COR-303/1 – ne IDC [334]

RUSSKOE L'NOVODSTVO, L'NIANOI RYNOK I L'NIANAIA KOOPERATSIIA / Chaianov, A V – M., 1918 – 2mf – 9 – COR-239/1 – ne IDC [334]

RUSSKOE MASONSTVO. (28 I PERVAIA CHETVERT' 19 V.) / Pypin, AN – Petrograd. 1916. BR-7797 2 – 8 – ne IDC [947]

RUSSKOE MOLOCHNOE KHOZIAISTVO I KOOPERATSIIA / Stepanovskii, I K – Spb., 1913 – 1mf – 9 – COR-109/1 – ne IDC [334]

RUSSKOE OBOZRENIE – (Library has: v.3, no.9-v.21, no.45 (Sept. 7, 1929-Dec. 20, 1947)[missing 38 issues; some issues slightly mutilated]) – Chicago: Russian Review Pub. Co., 1929-1947 – 1 – CSUX86-S151 – us Hoover Inst Photo [072]

Russkoe Obshchestvo Dieiatelei Pechatnago Diela *see* PECHATNOE ISKUSSTVO

RUSSKOE OBSHCHESTVO I FRANTSUZSKAIA REVOLIUTSIIA 1789-1794 GG / Shtrange, M M – M. 1956. BR-7896 2 – 8 – ne IDC [944]

RUSSKOE OBSHCHESTVO I REVOLIUTSIIA / Izgoev, A S – M., 1910. 273p – 3mf – 9 – ne IDC [320]

RUSSKOE PROSHLOE – Istoricheskie sborniki. v. 1-5. Petrograd. 1923. BR-3774 2 – 8 – ne IDC [947]

RUSSKOE SADOVODSTVOI OGORODNICHESTVO – (Library has: no. 4/5, 1919) – Moskva: izd. Narodnogo komissariata zemledeliia, 1919-1921. 3v – 1 – CSUX89-S638 – us Hoover Inst Photo [631]

RUSSKOE SEL'SKOE KHOZIAISTVO – Zhurnal Imp. Moskovskago sel'skago obshchestva. v. 1-27. M. 1869-76. BR-2291 2 – 8 – ne IDC [073]

RUSSKOE SLOVO – Moscow. 1907, 1909, Jan 1915-Mar 1917. Incomplete – 1 – us NY Public [073]

RUSSKOE SLOVO – Moscow, 1907-17 – 12r – 1 – us Ross [073]

RUSSKOE SLOVO = RUSSIAN WORD – RUSSIAN NEWSPAPER IN AMERICA : RUSSKAIA PROGRESSIVNAIA GAZETA – (Issues at MF-5060 filmed by: New York Public Library. MF-11303 [sep 1917-aug 19 1920] (8r); lacking: all Sunday issues for 1918 and 1920. jan 7 1918; mar 12,26, apr 17 1920; issues for 1919 not collated. MF-5060: [dec 23-31 1918; jan-jun 1920]. MF-4863: 1919) – New York: [s.n.] – 1 – us Res Libr [071]

RUSSKOE TSARSTVO – Ezhenedel'naia politicheskaia gazeta. v. 1-8. M. 1907. Lacking: (2, 4, 6-7) 1907. BR-2250 2 – 8 – ne IDC [947]

RUSSKOE UGOLOVNOE SUDOPROIZVODSTVO PO SUDEBNYM USTAVAM 20 NOIABRIA 1864 G / Chebyshev-Dmitriev, A P – St. Petersburg, 1875. 765p. BR-9778/1 – 9 – ne IDC [360]

RUSSKOE VOSKRESENE – Paris. France. -w. 15 Jun 1955-15 Nov 1956, 6 Nov 1957-6 May 1961. (2 reels) – 1 – uk British Libr Newspaper [947]

RUSSKOE VREMIA = LE TEMPS RUSSE – Paris: [s.n.], 192u – 1 – CSUXADM8087-S – us Hoover Inst Photo [073]

RUSSKOE ZEMLE USTROITEL'NOE ZAKONODATEL'STVO / Khauke, OA – M. pt 1. 1910 – 2mf – 9 – COR-132/1 – ne IDC [334]

RUSSKO-SHVEDSKIE OTNOSHENIIA I POLITIKA VELIKIKH DERZHAV V 1721-1726 GG / Nekrasov, G A – Akademiia nauk SSSR, institut istorii. M. 1964. BR-10,527 1 – 9 – ne IDC [320]

RUSSKY GOLOS – (In Russian). Warsaw. Poland. -w. Jan 1957-Dec 1965. (3 reels) – 1 – uk British Libr Newspaper [947]

RUSSLAND; EINE EINFUEHRUNG AUF GRUND SEINER GESCHICHTE VOM JAPANISCHEN BIS ZUM WELTKRIEG / Hoetzsch, Otto – Berlin: G. Reimer, 1917.xx,439p. 2 fold. maps – 1 – us U.W. Library [947]

RUSSLAND UND ASIEN / ed by Cleinow, G – Erfurt. v2. 1925 – 2mf – 1 – ILM-3795/1 – ne IDC [327]

RUSSLANDS MUSIK-ZEITUNG – v. 1-4. Spb. 1895-98. BP-620 1 – 30mf – 9 – ne IDC [073]

THE RUSSO JAPANESE WAR : A PHOTOGRAPHIC AND DESCRIPTIVE REVIEW OF THE GREAT CONFLICT IN THE FAR EAST – 1r – 1 – $50.00 – B40146 – us Library Micro [950]

Russo, Nicolaus *see* DE PHILOSOPHIA MORALI

Russwurm, Lorne H *see* ESSAYS ON CANADIAN URBAN PROCESS AND FORM 2

Russwurm, Lorne H et al *see* ESSAYS ON CANADIAN URBAN PROCESS AND FORM

Rust, Johann Nepomuk *see* THEORETISCH-PRAKTISCHES HANDBUCH DER CHIRURGIE

RUST, SMUT, MILDEW, AND MOULD / Cooke, M C – An introduction to the study of microscopic fungi. With nearly 300 figures by J. E. Sowerby. London. 1865. B-6253 2 – 8 – ne IDC [580]

Rust, William *see* SPAIN FIGHTS FOR VICTORY

Rustaing de Saint-Jory, Louis *see* LES FEMMES MILITAIRES, RELATION HISTORIQUE D'UNE ILE NOUVELLEMENT DECOUVERTE PAR LE C. D

Rustam, Didong *see* KUMPULAN SEMINAR EKONOMI INDUSTRI

RUSTENBURG HEROUT-HERALD – Rustenburg, SA. 1925-1979 – 1 – sa State Libr [960]

RUSTICATING IN REALITY: A PIERIAN PARAPHRASE / Albyn – Halifax: J. Bowes, 1873.06134.(Pre-1900 Canadiana) – 9 – cn C.I.H.M. [810]

RUSTLER – Nauvoo. Ill. 1890-1893 – 1 – us UMI [071]

RUSTLER – Rawhide, NV. 1907-09 – 1r – 1 – $50.00 – U04656 – us Library Micro [071]

RUSTLER – Yerington, NV. 1895-1900 – 1r – 1 – $50.00 – U04828 – us Library Micro [071]

THE RUSTLER – (Also known as: Rustler-Herald) – King City, CA. May 1901- – 65+ r – 1 – $3,250.00 – B02326 – us Library Micro [071]

RUSTLER-HERALD *see* THE RUSTLER

Rusula, Jose de *see* PEDRO DE VALDIVIA CONQUITADOR DE CHILE

LA RUTA DE HERNANDO CORTES / Segarra, Jose y Joaquin Julia – Madrid: Imprenta Alemana, 1910 – 1 – sp Bibl Santa Ana [910]

RUTA DE LA ALTA EXTREMADURA, CUNA DE LOS CONQUISTADORES / Junta Provincial de Informacion, Turismo y Educacion Popular – Caceres, Vitoria: Huecograbado Fournier, 1961 – 1 – sp Bibl Santa Ana [946]

LA RUTA DE LO DESCONOCIDO... / Comas Roca, Jose M; ed by Bayle, Constantino – Madrid: Razon y Fe, 1928 – 9 – sp Bibl Santa Ana [910]

RUTAS VENEZOLANAS... / Patrizi, J A – Madrid: Razon y Fe, 1940 – 1 – sp Bibl Santa Ana [972]

Rutenberg, G *see* DIE BALTISCHEN STAATEN UND DAS VOELKERRECHT

RUTGERS COMPUTER AND TECHNOLOGY LAW JOURNAL – (Title varies: v1-6 1970-78 as Rutgers Journal of Computers and the Law. v7-8 no 1 1979-80 as Rutgers Journal of Computer Technology and the Law) – v1-21. 1970-95 – 9 – $312.00 set – us Hein [340]

Rutgers, F *see* ACTA VAN DE NEDERL. SYNODE DER ZESTIENDE EEUW

Rutgers, F L *see* ACTA VAN DE NEDERLANDSCHE SYNODEN DER ZESTIENDE EEUW (DE WERKEN..2,3)

RUTGERS JOURNAL OF COMPUTER TECHNOLOGY AND THE LAW *see* RUTGERS COMPUTER AND TECHNOLOGY LAW JOURNAL

RUTGERS JOURNAL OF COMPUTERS AND THE LAW *see* RUTGERS COMPUTER AND TECHNOLOGY LAW JOURNAL

RUTGERS LAW JOURNAL – v1-25. 1969-94 – 1,5,6 – $585.00 – us Hein [073]

RUTGERS LAW REVIEW – (Title varies: v1-2 1947-1948 as Rutgers University Law Review. Supersedes New Jersey Law Review, Mercer Beasley Law Review, and the University of Newark Law Review) – v1-47. 1947-1995 – 9 – $974.00 set – us Hein [340]

Rutgers, S J *see* INDONESIE

Rutgers University. Center of Alcoholic Studies *see* RAYMOND G MCCARTHY MEMORIAL COLLECTION OF ALCOHOL LITERATURE

RUTGERS UNIVERSITY LAW REVIEW *see* RUTGERS LAW REVIEW

RUTH : ERZAEHLUNG / Andreas-Salome, Lou – Stuttgart: J G Cotta, 1911 – 1r – 1 – us U.W. Library [830]

Ruth, Paul Hermann *see* ERNST MORITZ ARNDT

RUTH, THE FAITHFUL BRIDE / Southworth, Emma Dorothy Eliza Nevitte – Sequel to Woman's Fate. London: Milner, 189?. 255p – 1 – us U.W. Library [830]

RUTH THE GLEANER; AND ESTHER THE QUEEN / Taylor, William MacKergo – New York: Harper, 1891. 269p. 1 fiche – 9 – us A.T.L.A. [240]

RUTH YOUNG WATT, SENATE SERVICE 1949-1979 : CHIEF CLERK, SENATE PERMANENT SUBCOMMITTEE ON INVESTIGATIONS – 4mf – 9 – $20.00 – us Scholarly Res [320]

Ruthenberg, Charles E *see* PAPERS

Rutherford, T *see* FOUR CHARGES TO THE CLERGY OF THE ARCHDEACONRY OF ESSEX:...

Rutherglen, George *see*
- MAJOR ISSUES IN THE FEDERAL LAW OF EMPLOYMENT DISCRIMINATION

RUTH'S RECOMPENCE : OR, A COMMENTARY UPON THE BOOK OF RUTH DELIVERED IN SEVERAL SERMONS... / Bernard, Richard – Edinburgh:James Nichol, 1865 – 1mf – 9 – 0-8370-2651-2 – 1985-0651 – us A.T.L.A. [220]

RUTLAND, 1822 : BRITISH ISLES CENSUS DIRECTORIES PROJECT, ENGLAND – (In prep) – at Vine [941]

RUTLAND, 1828 : BRITISH ISLES CENSUS DIRECTORIES PROJECT, ENGLAND. VOL 105 – 1mf – 9 – A$9.00 – at Vine [941]

RUTLAND, 1835 : BRITISH ISLES CENSUS DIRECTORIES PROJECT, ENGLAND – at Vine [941]

RUTLAND, 1841 : BRITISH ISLES CENSUS DIRECTORIES PROJECT, ENGLAND. VOL 234 – 1mf – 9 – A$9.00 – at Vine [941]

RUTLAND, 1848 : BRITISH ISLES CENSUS DIRECTORIES PROJECT, ENGLAND – at Vine [941]

RUTLAND, 1850 : BRITISH ISLES CENSUS DIRECTORIES PROJECT, ENGLAND – at Vine [941]

RUTLAND, 1862 : BRITISH ISLES CENSUS DIRECTORIES PROJECT, ENGLAND. VOL 59 – 1mf – 9 – A$9.00 – at Vine [941]

RUTLAND, 1877 : BRITISH ISLES CENSUS DIRECTORIES PROJECT, ENGLAND. VOL 37 – 4mf – 9 – A$27.00 – at Vine [941]

RUTLAND, 1888 : BRITISH ISLES CENSUS DIRECTORIES PROJECT, ENGLAND – at Vine [941]

RUTLAND, 1896 : BRITISH ISLES CENSUS DIRECTORIES PROJECT, ENGLAND – at Vine [941]

RUTLAND, 1916 : BRITISH ISLES CENSUS DIRECTORIES PROJECT, ENGLAND – at Vine [941]

RUTLAND, 1928 : BRITISH ISLES CENSUS DIRECTORIES PROJECT, ENGLAND – at Vine [941]

RUTLAND 1719-1894 – (Mf 1-3: Births 1719-1815. Mf 3,6,8: Church Certificates 1810-13. Mf 3,6,8: Deaths 1729-1813. Mf 3-5: Marriages & Intentions 1723-1817. Mf 7: Birth Index 1719-1815; Marriage/Intention Index 1723-1816. Mf 7-8: Death Index 1729-181. Mf 9-10: Births 1759-1851. Mf 10-11: Deaths 1802-44. Mf 11-13: Intentions/ Marriages 1817-50. Mf 14: Birth Index 1759-1851; Death Index 1802-44; Marriage/ Intention Index 1817-50. Mf 15: Births 1844-55. Mf 15-16: Marriages 1844-55. Mf 16: Deaths 1844-55. Mf 17-18: Births 1856-94. Mf 18-20: Marriages 1856-1903. Mf 20-21: Deaths 1856-95. Mf 22-24: Birth Index 1844-94. Mf 25-27: Marriage Index 1844-1901. Mf 28-32: Death Index 1844-95) – (mf ed 1987) – 32mf – 9 – 0-931248-23-X – us Holbrook [920]

RUTLAND AND STAMFORD MERCURY *see* STAMFORD MERCURY

RUTLAND MERCURY – 1990-92; 1996-Jun 1997 – 12r – 1 – uk British Libr Newspaper [072]

RUTLEDGE AVENUE BAPTIST CHURCH. CHARLESTON, SOUTH CAROLINA : CHURCH RECORDS – 1892-1966 – 1 – 130.14 – us Baptist [240]

Rutledge, John *see*
- JOHN RUTLEDGE PAPERS
- LETTERS

Rutsch, E *see* FOUNDING FATHERS

Rutt, Chris L *see* HISTORY OF BUCHANAN COUNTY AND THE CITY OF ST JOSEPH

Rutten, Adolphe *see* LA POPULATION BELGE DEPUIS 1830: TOME I, ETAT DE LA POPULATION

Ruttenbur, Edward M *see* HISTORY OF THE COUNTY OF ORANGE

Rutty, John *see* AN ESSAY TOWARDS A CONTRAST BETWEEN QUAKERISM AND METHODISM,...

Rutz, Kathy *see* JOURNAL OF HEALTH CARE CHAPLAINCY

LE RUY-BLAS – Paris. 22 dec 1903-5 avr 1905, 30 oct-4 dec 1913, 15 sept-1er dec 1923, 11 sept-2 oct 1926, 15 fevr-15 dec 1927 – 1 – fr A.C.R.P.P. [073]

RUYSBROECK / Underhill, Evelyn – London: G. Bell, 1915 – 1mf – us A.T.L.A. [240]

Ruysch, W A *see* ANTIQUITY AND SURVIVAL. VOL. 2; THE HOLY LAND: NEW LIGHT ON THE PREHISTORY AND EARLY HISTORY OF ISRAEL

Ruzek, Sheryl *see*
- CHOOSING WHETHER OR NOT TO USE HORMONE REPLACEMENT THERAPY DURING THE MENOPAUSAL TRANSITION
- TAMPON LABELING AND ITS EFFECT ON FEMALE ADOLESCENTS' KNOWLEDGE OF TAMPON ABSORBENCY, KNOWLEDGE OF TOXIC SHOCK SYNDROME AND TAMPON USAGE PATTERNS

RUZNAMAH-'I RASMI-I JUMHURI-I ISLAMI – (Missing issues: 11471, 11540, 11558, 11590, 12182, 12619, 12634, 12658, 12663, 12679, 12984-13138) – Tehran: Vizarat-i Dadgustari. No. 10642-13400 (Shahrivar 1360-14 Isfand 1369 [Aug 1981-5 Mar 1991]) – 22r – 1 – $400.00 – us MEDOC [950]

RUZNAMAH-'I RASMI-I JUMHURI-I ISLAMI – (Shumarah-i 10642-14000 (Shahrivar 1360-15 Farvardin 1372[Aug 1981-4 Apr 1993]. Missing issues: 11471, 11540, 11558, 11590, 12182, 12619, 12634, 12658, 12663, 12679, 12984-13138, 13713-13742. For new run only: $900.00. Shumarah-'i 14001-14295 (16 Farvardin 1372–16 Farvardin 1373[5 Mar 1993-5 Apr 1994])) – Tehran: Vizarat-i Dadgustari – $3300.00 – us MEDOC [956]

RUZNAMAH-'I RASMI-I JUMHURI-I ISLAMI – (Some issues missing) – Tehran: Vizarat-i Dadgustari. Shumarah-i 10642-14000 (Shahrivar 1360-15 Farvardin 1372 [Aug 1981-4 Apr 1993]) – 9 – $2,400.00 – us MEDOC [956]

RUZNAMAH-I RASMI-I JUMHURI-I ISLAMI – (Some issues missing) – Tehran: Vizarat-i Dadgustari. Shumarah-'i 10642-14295 (Shahrivar 1360-16 Farvardin 1373 [Aug 1981-5 March 1994] – 9 – $3,300.00 – us MEDOC [260]

RUZNAMAH-'I RASMI-I KISHVAR-I SHAHANSHAHI-I IRAN / Iran – (1979- . ca $80.00y) – 1970-78 – 23r – 1 – $460.00; outside North America add $1.25r – us L of C Photodup [324]

RUZNAMAH-'I SHAMS – (Shumarah-'i 1-48 22 Aghustus 1324-23 Tammuz 1325 (8 Sha'ban 1326-19 Rajab 1327[6 September 1908-7 August 1909])) – Istanbul: Hilal Matba'asi – 1 reel – 1 – $50.00 – us MEDOC [950]

RUZNAMAH-I VAQAYI'-I ITTIFAQIYAH – Tehran: Shumarah-i 1-558. (Rabi II 1267-21 Zu'l Qadah 1280 [7 February 1851-28 April 1864]; Issues 472-588 titled Ruznamah-i Dawlat-i Aliyyah-i Iran – 2r – 1 – $650.00 – us MEDOC [950]

Rwanda *see*
- ECONOMIE ET PLAN DE DEVELOPPEMENT
- ETUDE DE DEVELOPMENT. PLAN INTERIMAIRE D'URGENCE
- ETUDE DE DEVELOPPEMENT. PLAN INTERIMAIRE D'URGENCE
- JOURNAL OFFICIEL

Rwanda. Direction Generale des Etudes et Recherches Pedagogiques *see* CARTE SCOLAIRE DE L'ENSEIGNEMENT PRIMAIRE, ANNEE SCOLAIRE 1984-1985

Rwanda. Ministere de l'Enseignement Superieur et de la Recherche Scientifique *see* DES DISPARITES REGIONALES ET ETHNIQUES DANS L'ENSEIGNEMENT SUPERIEUR RWANDAIS

Rwanda. Ministere du Plan. Ministere de la Jeunesse *see* L'INTEGRATION ECONOMIQUE DES JEUNES NON SCOLARISES ET DESCOLARISES (AVANT PROJET)

Ryan, Alonzo *see* FREE LANCE POLITICAL CARICATURE IN CANADA

Ryan, D D Edwin *see* THE CHURCH IN THE SOUTH AMERICAN REPUBLICS 2ND EDIC. WESTMENSTER, 1943

Ryan, Dessins d'Alonzo *see* THE IDEAL MAGAZINE

Ryan, John *see*
- IRISH MONASTICISM, ORIGINS AND EARLY DEVELOPMENT
- IRISH MONASTICISM. ORIGINS AND EARLY DEVELOPMENT

Ryan, Mike *see* SPACE COMMERCE

Ryan, Patrick John *see* SOME OF THE CAUSES OF MODERN RELIGIOUS SKEPTICISM

Ryan, Patrick T *see* A COMPARISON OF PHYSIOLOGIC RESPONSES TO FORWARD AND RETROGRADE SIMULATED STAIR STEPPING ON THE STAIRMASTER

Ryang, J S *see* SOUTHERN METHODISM IN KOREA..

RYBAK MORSKI – Warsaw and Gdynia. Poland. -w. Mar 1955-Jun 1958. (1 reel) – 1 – uk British Libr Newspaper [947]

Rybinski, J *see* DER MAL'AKH JAHWE

Rybnikov, A A *see* MELKAIA PROMYSHLENNOST'I EE ROL'V VOSSTANOVLENII RUSSKOGO NARODNOGO KHOZIAISTVA

RYCCARDI DE SANCTO GERMANO NOTARII CHRONICA (MGH 7: 53.BD) – 1864 – Dfl13.00 – ne Slangenburg [240]

Rydberg, Viktor *see* THE MAGIC OF THE MIDDLE AGES

RYDE LEADER – Oct 28 1958-Dec 18 1963 – 1 – at Pascoe [072]

Ryder, Arthur Gore *see* THE SCRIPTURAL DOCTRINE OF ACCEPTANCE WITH GOD

Ryder, Henry Ignatius Dudley *see* ESSAYS

Ryder, M L *see* ANIMAL BONES IN ARCHAEOLOGY

Ryding, S-O *see* CONTROL OF EUTROPHICATION OF LAKES AND RESERVOIRS

Rye, W B *see* FLORIDA, DISCOVERY AND CONQUEST

Rye, Walter *see*
- A HISTORY OF NORFOLK
- NORFOLK FAMILIES

Ryerson, Adolphus Egerton *see*
- CASE AND CORRESPONDENCE RESPECTING THE PRICES OF BOOKS FOR SCHOOL LIBRARIES AND PRIZES
- RAPPORT SUR UN SYSTEME D'INSTRUCTION ELEMENTAIRE PUBLIQUE POUR LE HAUT CANADA
- REPORT ON A SYSTEM OF PUBLIC ELEMENTARY INSTRUCTION FOR UPPER CANADA
- UNIVERSITY QUESTION

Ryff, Walther Hermann *see* NEW GROSS DISTILLIER-BUCH..

Rykunov, L N *see* VOLCANOLOGY AND SEISMOLOGY

Ryland, Arthur *see* THE ASSAY OF GOLD AND SILVER WARES

Ryland, Charles H *see* THE DISTRICT ASSOCIATION A REVIEW AND A PLEA

Rylands, Louis Gordon *see* THE BEGINNINGS OF GNOSTIC CHRISTIANITY

Ryle, Herbert Edward *see*
- THE EARLY NARRATIVES OF GENESIS: A BRIEF INTRODUCTION TO...GENESIS I-XI
- ON HOLY SCRIPTURE AND CRITICISM: ADDRESSES AND SERMONS
- PHILO AND HOLY SCRIPTURE, OR, THE QUOTATIONS OF PHILO FROM...THE OLD TESTAMENT
- PSALMS OF THE PHARISEES, COMMONLY CALLED THE PSALMS OF SOLOMON

Ryle, John Charles *see* EXPOSITORY THOUGHTS ON THE GOSPELS

Ryley, John Horton *see* RALPH FITCH, ENGLAND'S PIONEER TO INDIA AND BURMA; HIS COMPANIONS AND CONTEMPORARIES..

Rymchronyk van Klaas Kolyn *see* BENEDIKTINER MONNIK DER ABTDYE TE EGMONT, MET TAAL- EN HISTORIKUNDIGE AANTEEKENINGEN OPGEHELDERD DOOR MR. GERARD VAN LOON

Rymer, Thomas *see*
- FOEDERA, CONVENTIONES, LITERAE, ET CUJUSCUNQUE GENERIS ACTA PUBLICA, INTER REGES ANGLIAE, ET ALIOS QUOSVIS IMPERATORES, REGES, PONTIFICES, PRINCIPES, VEL COMMUNITATES
- FOEDERA, CONVENTIONES, LITERAE ET CUJUSCUNQUE GENERIS ACTA PUBLICA, INTER REGES ANGLIAE, ET ALIOS QUOSVIS IMPERATORES, REGES PONTIFICES, PRINCIPES, VEL COMMUNITATES

RYNOK KHLEBOV I EGO REGULIROVANIE VO VREMIA VOINY I REVOLIUTSII / Kondrat'ev, N D – M., 1922 – 4mf – 9 – COR-201/1 – ne IDC [334]

RYOJI HOKOKU SHIRYO = JAPANESE CONSULAR REPORTS 1881-1913 – 74r and index 1 reel – 1 – Y700,000.00 – ja Yushodo [950]

RYOSEN'EKI KAIKO DAN / Shigeta, Fujii – Tokyo, Kaikosha, 1936. 300p. On the Chinese-Japanese War (1894-95) and the Russo-Japanese War (1904-5) – 1 – $35.00r – us Hoover Inst Photo [950]

Ryser, Frieder *see* REVERSE PAINTINGS ON GLASS

Ryssel, Victor *see*
- DIE BUECHER EXODUS UND LEVITICUS
- DE ELOHISTAE PENTATEUCHICI SERMONE
- DIE SYNONYMA DES WAHREN UND GUTEN IN DEN SEMITISCHEN SPRACHEN
- UNTERSUCHUNGEN UEBER DIE TEXTGESTALT UND DIE ECHTHEIT DES BUCHES MICHA

Rystenko, A V *see* RUKOPISI PRINADLEZHASHCHIIA BIBLIOTEKE IMP. ODESSKAGO OBSHCHESTVA ISTORII I DREVNOSTEI

RYUEI HINAMI-KI = THE CALENDAR OF THE TOKUGAWA FEUDAL GOVERNMENT / Japan. (Tokugawa Feudal Government) – 1656-1856. Government personnel, laws, ordinances, ceremonial events and the hereditary line of the Tokugawa Shogunate – 130r – 1 – Y1,380,000.00 – ja Yushodo [950]

Ryukyu Islands. (United States). Office of Plans and Programs, and Department of Plans and Statistics *see* JOINT ECONOMIC PLAN FOR RYUKYU ISLANDS, FY 1962-1966

Ryzhov, N N et al *see* TSENTRAL'NYI GOSUDARSTVENNYI ISTORICHESKII ARKHIV LATVIISKOI SSR. KRATKII SPRAVOCHNIK

RZECZPOSPOLITA – 1983 – 1 – sz Infoprint [947]

RZECZPOSPOLITA – (1993 6r $510. 1994 8r $680. 1995-98 12r per y $1,020y) – Poland, 1999- – 12r per y – 1 – $960.00 standing order – us Ross [072]

RZECZPOSPOLITA – Warsaw, Poland. Jul 1944-Jan 1945; 1983-92 – 39r – 1 – us L of C Photodup [947]

RZECZPOSPOLITA – Warsaw. Poland. -w. 16 Jun 1946-31 Dec 1950. (22 reels) – 1 – uk British Libr Newspaper [947]

RZEZPOSPOLITA POLSKA – London, UK. 17 May 1957- – 1 – uk British Libr Newspaper [072]

RZHEVSKAIA PRAVDA : ORGAN RZHEVSKOGO UISPOLKOMA I UEZDKOMA R.K.P. (B) – (Includes c.1: 1922: Mar.12; 1928: Apr.11) – Rzhev: Uispolkom i Uezdkom, 19uu – 1r – 1 – CSUXANQ9836-S – us Hoover Inst Photo [073]

S A M ADVANCED MANAGEMENT JOURNAL *see* ADVANCED MANAGEMENT JOURNAL

S. BENEDICTUS ILLUSTRATUS SIVE DISQUISITIONUM MONASTICARUM LIBRI 12 / Haeften, Benedictus van – Antverp, Tom. 2. 1644 – 25mf – 8 – ne Slangenburg [240]

S CORPORATIONS : THE JOURNAL OF TAX, LEGAL AND BUSINESS STRATEGIES – v1-4. 1988-91 (all publ) – 9 – $80.00 set – us Hein [330]

S. EPHRAEMI SYRI, RABULAE EPISCOPI EDESSENI, BALAEI ALIORUMQUE OPERA SELECTA = SELECTIONS : E CODICIBUS SYRIACIS MANUSCRIPTIS IN MUSEO BRITANNICO ET BIBLIOTHECA BODLEIANA ASSERVATIS PRIMUS / Ephraem Syrus, Saint; ed by Overbeck, J Josephus – (Text in Syriac. Introduction and table of contents in Latin) – Oxonii [Oxford]: Clarendoniano, 1865 – 2mf – 9 – 0-8370-7059-7 – 1986-1059 – us A.T.L.A. [240]

S. FRANCIS DE SALES : BISHOP AND PRINCE OF GENEVA / Lear, H L Sidney – London: Rivingtons, 1877 (Christian biographies) – 1mf – us A.T.L.A. [240]

S. FRANCISCO : MENSAGEIRO PAROCHIAL DE PIRAPORA – Pirapora, 15 Jan-Dec 1933; Jan-Mar, May-Dec 1934; Jan-Feb, May-Oct 1935; 19 Jan 1936 – 1,5,6 – bl Biblioteca [072]

S Granny, Tito *see* EL PADRE PABLO DE GRAYMOOR...

'S GUELTETRUEKLI : NUE VAERS / Lienert, Otto Hellmut – Einsiedeln: Benziger, 1937 – 1r – 1 – us U.W. Library [810]

A S H A – (American Speech and Hearing Association). v1-21 1959-79. Continues as: Asha – 1 – us UMI [073]

'S JURAMAREILI : GEDICHT IN AARGAUER MUNDART / Haller, Paul – Aarau: H R Sauerlaender, [1937?] – 1r – 1 – us U.W. Library [810]

S. KIERKEGAARD'S BLADARTIKLER : MED BILAG SAMLEDE EFTER FORFATTERENS DOD / Kierkegaard, Soren – Kjobenhavn: C.A. Reitzel, 1857 – 1mf – us A.T.L.A. [190]

S KINOAPPARATOM PO SSSR = WITH A MOVIE CAMERA IN THE SOVIET UNION / Terskoi, An – Moscow, Leningrad, 1931 – 1 – 7.20 – us Baptist [240]

S KRESTOM I EVANGELIEM PROTIV KOLKHOZOV = WITH CROSS AND GOSPEL AGAINST THE KOLKHOZES / Eliashevich, I Ya – Leningrad, 1930. One of 13 titles by Soviet authors on reel – 1 – 74.32 – us Baptist [240]

S. LIVINGSTON MATHER PAPERS *see* MATHER, S. LIVINGSTON, PAPERS, MS 4613

S. MATTHEW'S GOSPEL / Maldonado, Juan de – London: John Hodges. 2v. 1888 – 4mf – 9 – 0-8370-9079-2 – 1986-3079 – us A.T.L.A. [220]

'S MENSCHEN LEVEN VAN DE WIEG TOT HET GRAF / Royen, J van – Amsterdam, [c.1690] – 1mf – 9 – ne IDC [700]

'S MENSCHEN LEVEN VAN DE WIEG TOT HET GRAF / Royen, J van – Amsterdam, [c.1690] – 2mf – 9 – ne IDC [700]

S' MENSCHEN LEVEN VAN DE WIEG TOT HET GRAF / Royen, J van – Amsterdam, [c.1695] – 2mf – 9 – ne IDC [700]

'S NULLERL : VOLKSSTUECK MIT GESANG IN FUENF AKTEN / Morre, Karl – 6. Aufl. Graz: M Pock, 1909 – 1r – 1 – us U.W. Library [820]

IL S. OFFICIO E LA RIFORMA RELIGIOSA IN FRIULI : APPUNTI STORICI DOCUMENTATI / Battistella, Antonio – Udine: P. Gambierasi, 1895 – 1mf – us A.T.L.A. [240]

S P W L A Annual Logging Symposium *see* TRANSACTIONS

S. PIETRO IN ROMA ED I PRIMI PAPI : SECONDO I PI U VETUSTI CATALOGHI DELLA CHIESA ROMANA / Rinieri, Ilario – (Includes bibliographical references and index) – Torino: G B Berruti, 1909 – 2mf – 9 – 0-8370-7258-1 – 1986-1258 – us A.T.L.A. [240]

LA S SOCIEDADES DE CREDITO Y LOS FERROCARRILES EXTREMENOS / Gonzalez Hernandez, Juan – Plasencia: Imp. y Lib. de Pinto Sanchez, 1864 – 1 – sp Bibl Santa Ana [946]

S UND T : SPORT UND TECHNIK – Berlin, 1984. ill – 1 – us U.W. Library [073]

Sa, E *see*
- APHORISMI CONFESSARIORUM
- NOTATIONES IN TOTAM SCRIPTURAM SACRAM
- NOTATIONES IN TOTAM SRIPTURAM SACRAM
- SCHOLIA IN QUATUOR EVANGELIA EX SELECTIS DOCTORUM SACRORUM SENTENTIIS COLLECTA
- SCHOLIAE IN QUATUOR EVANGELIA

S.A. JEWISH CHRONICLE *see* SOUTH AFRICAN JEWISH CHRONICLE

SAA BULLETIN *see* AMERICAN ANTIQUITY

Saa Maldonado, Manuel *see*
- ENSENANZA...BADAJOZ
- INTERPRETACION...HORACIO FLACO
- MEMORIA ACERCA DEL ESTADO DEL INSTITUTO DE SEGUNDA ENSENANZA DE LA PROVINCIA DE BADAJOZ DURANTE EL CURSO DE 1872 A 1873 LEIDA...POR EL DIRECTOR DON...

SAA NEWSLETTER / Society of American Archivists – Mar 1973-Jul 1990 – 9 – $16.00 + shipping ($4.00 domestic; $5.50 outside US) – us S.A.A. [025]

SAA NEWSLETTER INDEX / Society of American Archivists – Jul 1974-Nov 1988 – 9 – $9.00 + shipping ($4.00 domestic; $5.50 outside US) – us S.A.A. [025]

SAA (STANDARDS ASSOCIATION OF AUSTRALIA) – Printed index. Updated every 30 days – 9 – us Info Handling [380]

Saabye, H E *see* BRUCHSTUECKE EINES TAGEBUCHES GEHALTEN IN GROENLAND

SAAD / Israel. Ministry of Social Welfare – v. 11-20. 1967-76. BJ-81-15 1 – 9 – ne IDC [360]

Saad, Ahmed Zaki *see* LE "WAKF" DE FAMILLE; ETUDE CRITIQUE

Saadiah, Rabbi *see* COMMENTARY ON EZRA AND NEHEMIAH

SAADYA STUDIES / Gaon, S – Ed. by E. I. J. Rosenthal. Manchester. 1943. BJ-100-68 1 – 9 – ne IDC [270]

Saalfeld, Guenther Alexander *see* DE BIBLIORUM SACRORUM VULGATAE EDITIONIS GRAECITATE

SAAMSTAAN – Oudtshoorn, South Africa. 1984-88. -irr. 1 reel – 1, 16 diazo available at reduced price – sa SA Libr [072]

Saar, Ferdinand von *see*
- KAISER HEINRICH 4
- OESTERREICHISCHE FESTDICHTUNGEN
- DIE PINCELLIADE
- DIE STEINKLOPFER
- TEMPESTA
- THASSILO
- WIENER ELEGIEN
- EINE WOHLTHAT

SA'AR U-DEMAMAH / Shimonovitz, D (Shimoni) – Warsaw. 1912. BJ-422-83 1 – 9 – ne IDC [470]

SAAR VOLKSSTIMME – Saarbruecken. Germany. -d. 28 Nov 1951-31 Dec 1954. (14 reels) – 1 – uk British Libr Newspaper [072]

SAARBRUECKER ZEITUNG : BA DER SAARBRUECKER ZEITUNG – Saarlouis, France. 1978- – ca 8r per yr – 1 – gw Mikrofilm [072]

SAARBRUECKER ZEITUNG – Saarbruecken, Germany. 21 Sept 1968- – ca 9r per yr – 1 – gw Mikrofilm [072]

SAARBRUECKER ZEITUNG – Saarbruecken, sep 3 1946-jan 9 1947 – us Res Libr [072]

SAARBRUECKER ZEITUNG – St. Wendel-Saarbruecken, Germany. 1978- – ca 8r peryr – 1 – gw Mikrofilm [072]

DIE SAAR-ENTE / ed by Schutzverband Deutscher Schriftsteller – Saarbruecken, Germany. 6 Jan 1935 – 1r – 1 – gw Mikrofilm [072]

SAAR-FREUND – Berlin. Feb. 1920-Mar. 1935 gaps – 1 – 35.00r – us Hoover Inst Photo [073]

SAAR-FREUND : NACHRICHTEN AUS DEM ABGETRENNTEN SAAR- UND PFALZ-GEBIET – (Available: no13 1921; no13/14, 17 1922) – N.p. – 5mf – 9 – H-654/2 – ne IDC [943]

Saarland *see* AMTSBLATT DES SAARLANDES

SAAR-VOLKSSTIMME – Saarbruecken, Germany. 28 Nov 1951-Dec 1954 – 14r – 1 – gw Mikrofilm [072]

SAAT AUF HOFFNUNG – Leipzig, etc. 1-63; 1863-1926. Incomplete. Imprint varies. Organ der Evangelisch-Lutherischen Missionsvereine fuer Israel in Sachsen und Bayern. Film Mas C 426 – 1 – us H.U. Library [270]

Saavedra, Eduardo *see* EL SEPULCRO DE ALMANZOR 1 DE BADAJOZ

Saavedra, Emiliana Lopez *see* APELACION A LA DEMOCRACIA

Saavedra, Faxardo D de *see*
- CHRISTELYKE STAETS-VORST IN HONDERT SIN-SPREUKEN...
- IDEA DE UN PRINCIPE POLITICO CHRISTIANO, REPRESENTADA EN CIEN EMPRESAS
- IDEA DE UN PRINCIPE POLITICO CHRISTIANO REPRESENTADA EN CIEN EMPRESAS
- THE ROYAL POLITICIAN REPRESENTED IN ONE HUNDRED EMBLEMS

Saavedra, J *see*
- ADICION AL DISCURSO...PROVANDO QUE NO SE DEVE SANGRAR EN EL SARAMPION...
- EL DOCTOR...MEDICO DE SEVILLA
- PARECER QUE DIERON LOS DOCTORES...EN UN ACCIDENTE RECOGIDO POR...
- PRUEBA QUE NO SE DEVE SANGRAR EN EL SARAMPION

SAAZER ANZEIGEN – Saaz (Zatec), Czechoslovakia. 1 Jan-15 Feb 1938 – 1r – 1 – gw Mikrofilm [072]
SAB, SOUTH ATLANTIC BULLETIN – (v.44-45. 1979-80. 5,6,9) – v.1-45. 1935-80. Continued by, South Atlantic Review – 1 – us UMI [073]
SABADO SECRETO – Mexico. 1889 – 1 – us A.J.P.C. [072]
Sabah *see* TRADE MARKS SUPPLEMENT TO THE GOVERNMENT GAZETTE
Sabah. Department of Education *see* LAPORAN TAHUNAN JABATAN PELAJARAN SABAH
SABAH DEVELOPMENT PLAN 1965-1970 – (To be absorbed into First Malaysia Development Plan, 1966-1970 with revisions as desirable). D 1466 1. 1964 – 9 – ne IDC [338]
SABAH EL-KHEIR – 1956- – 52mf per y – 9 – $300.00y – us Ross [072]
Sabaneev, L P *see* UKAZATEL' KNIG I STATEI OKHOTNICH'-IAGO I ZOOLOGICHESKAGO SODERZHANIIA
SABARA-GAZETA – Sabara, 1 Sep 1918-27 Jul 1919 – 1,5,6 – bl Biblioteca [072]
Sabaruddin, Ahmad *see*
- GAJA BAHASA INDONESIA
- INTISARI ROMAN INDONESIA, MASA BALAI PUSTAKA S/D MASA ANGK. 45

Sabatie, Alexandre Camille *see* LA SENEGAL, SA CONQUETE & SON ORGANISATION (1364-1925)
Sabatier, A *see* ETUDES SUR LA REVOCATION DE L'EDIT DE NANTES
Sabatier, Auguste *see*
- THE APOSTLE PAUL: A SKETCH OF THE DEVELOPMENT OF HIS DOCTRINE
- L'APOTRE PAUL
- DOCTRINE DE L'EXPIATION ET SON EVOLUTION HISTORIQUE
- ESQUISSE D'UNE PHILOSOPHIE DE LA RELIGION D'APR ES LA PSYCHOLOGIE ET L'HISTOIRE
- ESQUISSE D'UNE PHILOSOPHIE DE LA RELIGION D'APRES LA PSYCHOLOGIE ET L'HISTOIRE
- OUTLINES OF A PHILOSOPHY OF RELIGION BASED ON PSYCHOLOGY AND HISTORY
- RELIGIONS D'AUTHORITE ET LA RELIGION DE L'ESPRIT

Sabatier, Paul *see*
- DISESTABLISHMENT IN FRANCE
- DOM PETRUS, BIBLIORUM SACRORUM LATINAE VERSIONES ANTIQUAE, SEU VETUS ITALICA
- FRANCE TO-DAY
- LIFE OF ST FRANCIS OF ASSISI
- AN OPEN LETTER TO HIS EMINENCE CARDINAL GIBBONS

SABATINA FAMILIAR DE AMIGOS DO BEM-COMMUM – Rio de Janeiro, 8 Dec 1821-5 Jan 1822 – 1,5,6 – bl Biblioteca [072]
Sabatini, Rafael *see* TORQUEMADA AND THE SPANISH INQUISITION
SABATO – 1991-1995 – 3r per y – 5,6 – Sfr642.00 – sz Infoprint [073]
LES SABATS JACOBITES – no. 1-75. Paris. 1791-92 – 1 – fr A.C.R.P.P. [073]
SABBAT GRUNDEN = SABBATH HOURS – (In German. Weekly) – Berlin, DE. no1 Jan 1906-1909 – 1r – 1 – $45.00 – cn Can Microfilming [072]
SABBAT STUNDEN = SABBATH HOURS – (In German. Weekly) – Berlin, DE. no1 1886-no52 1890 – 1r – 1 – $50.00 – cn Can Microfilming [072]
DER SABBATH – Monatsblatt zur Foerderung der Sabbathheiligung im socialen und wirtschaftlichen Leben der Gegenwart. Frankfurt a.M. v1-14. 1901-1914. Lacking: 1901-1905; 1913-1914. B343 (Leo Baeck Institute. German-Jewish Periodicals, Pt 1) – 1r – 1 – $75.00 – us UPA [270]
SABBATH ESSAYS : PAPERS AND ADDRESSES PRESENTED AT THE MASSACHUSETTS SABBATH CONVENTIONS AT BOSTON AND SPRINGFIELD, OCTOBER, 1879 / McKenzie, Alexander; ed by Wood, Will C – Boston: Congregational Pub. Society, c1880 – 2mf – us A.T.L.A. [240]
THE SABBATH FOR MAN, A STUDY OF THE ORIGIN, OBLIGATION, HISTORY, ADVANTAGES AND PRESENT STATE OF SABBATH OBSERVANCE.. / Crafts, Wilbur Fisk – New York: Funk & Wagnalls, 1885.638p. illus. map – 1 – us U.W. Library [240]
SABBATH HOURS / Phelps, Austin – Boston: Congregational Publ Society, 1875, c1874 – 1mf – 9 – 0-8370-5971-2 – 1985-3971 – us A.T.L.A. [230]
THE SABBATH IN DARTMOUTH / Albyn – Halifax: J. Bowes, 1870.06135.(Pre-1900 Canadiana) – 9 – cn C.I.H.M. [240]
THE SABBATH IN PURITAN NEW ENGLAND / Earle, Alice Morse – New York: Scribner, 1892, c1891 – 1mf – us A.T.L.A. [240]
SABBATH JOURNAL – (New York). 1905-09 – 1 – us A.J.P.C. [240]
SABBATH OBSERVANCE: SPEECH OF JOHN CHARLTON, M.P. ON BILL TO PROVIDE FOR BETTER OBSERVANCE OF THE LORD'S DAY, HOUSE OF COMMONS, 26TH FEBRUARY, 1885 / Charlton, John – Ottawa: MacLean, Roger, 1885. 02961. (Pre-1900 Canadiana) – 9 – cn C.I.H.M. [240]
THE SABBATH OBSERVER – Halifax, NS: Printed for the Committee of the Nova Scotia Sabbath Alliance by J Barnes, [1853?-1854?] – 9 – cn C.I.H.M. [240]
THE SABBATH QUESTION / Bacon, Leonard – New York: G.P. Putnam, 1882 – 1mf – us A.T.L.A. [240]
SABBATH RECORDER : A SEVENTH DAY BAPTIST WEEKLY – (Lacking: some issues) – v1-193. 13 Jun 1844-1972 – 76r – 1 – ATLA S0231 – us A.T.L.A. [240]
SABBATH RECORDER – Westerly. R.I. 1863-1872 – 1 – us UMI [071]
Sabbath School and Colportage Union *see* PAPERS
THE SABBATH SCHOOL COMPANION – (Charleston). 1895-96 – 1 – us A.J.P.C. [240]
THE SABBATH VISITOR – Cincinnati. Ohio. 1874-93 – 1 – us A.J.P.C. [071]
SABBATH-DAY JOURNEYS : A STUDY OF THE THIRTY-THIRD CHAPTER OF NUMBERS / Harsha, William Justin – New York: Fleming H Revell, 1896 – 1mf – 9 – 0-8370-3502-3 – 1985-1502 – us A.T.L.A. [220]
Sabbatini, L A *see* TRATTATO SOPRA LE FUGHE MUSICALI. CORREDATO DA. FRANCESCO ANTONIO VALLOTI
SABBAT-STUNDEN – Berlin, 1887 n14-1888 n51, 1894 n44, 1895 n23-27 – 1 – Inquire at Mikrofilmarchiv for details – gw Misc Inst [072]
SABER CLUB WORLD – Portland OR. Aug 5 1932, Aug 16 1934, Jan 30 Mar 19 1936, Jan 21 1937 – 1 – us U.O. Library [071]
Sabido y Martinez, Antonio *see*
- DESCUBRIMIENTO...MINAS
- LLERENA, SU PASADO Y SU PRESENTE

Sabin, Joseph *see* DICTIONARY OF BOOKS RELATING TO AMERICA
SABINA ZEMBRA: A NOVEL / Black, William – British Fiction Archive: Unit 4 – 9 – uk Bell [830]
O SABINOPOLIS – S. Sebastiao dos Conventos, 22 Jul 1921 – 1,5,6 – bl Biblioteca [072]
EL SABIO INSTRUIDO DE LA GRACIA... / Garau, F – Barcelona, 1703 – 10mf – 9 – sp Cultura [240]
EL SABIO. LAS SIETE PARTIDAS (ANNO 1587) / Alfonso 10 el Sabio, Rey de Castilla – Caceres – 1r – 5,6 – sp Cultura [946]
Sablier, C *see* ESSAI SUR LES LANGUES EN GENERAL; SUR LA LANGUE FRANCOISE EN PARTICULIER...
LES SABLONS (L'ILE DU SABLE) ET L'ILE SAINT-BARNABE / Tache, Joseph C – Montreal: Librarie Saint-Joseph, 1885. SEM16P86 – 1r – 5 – Can$9.00 – cn Bibl Nat [830]
Sabo, James M *see* AN ANALYSIS OF NATIONAL ATHLETIC TRAINING ASSOCIATION ACCREDITED EDUCATION PROGRAM FACILITIES FOR THE ATHLETIC TRAINER
Sabran, Francoise Eleonore *see* CORRESPONDENCE INEDITE DE LA COMTESSE DE SABRAN ET DU CHEVALIER DE BOUFFLERS, 1778-88
Sabri, Eyueb *see* TARIH-I VAHHABIYUN
Sabuco, M *see* NUEVA FILOSOFIA DE LA NATURALEZA DEL HOMBRE
Sabur, Moch *see* BUNG KARNO DAN INDONESIA
SAC SUN – Sac City. Iowa. -w. 1951- – 1 – us UMI [071]
Saccardo, P A *see*
- LA BOTANICA IN ITALIA
- FUNGI ITALICI AUTOGRAPHICE DELINEATI
- ICONES FUNGORUM JAVANICORUM
- MICHELIA
- SYLLOGE FUNGORUM OMNIUM HUCUSQUE COGNITORUM

Sacchi, B G *see*
- DELLA DIVISIONE DEL TEMPO NELLA MUSICA
- DELLE QUINTE SUCCESSIVE NEL CONTRAPPUNTO E DELLE REGOLE DEGLI ACCOMPAGNAMENTI

Sacchi, BG *see*
- DELLA NATURA E PERFEZIONE DELLA ANTICA MUSICA DE' GRECI
- DELLA NATURA E PERFEZIONE DELLA ANTICA MUSICA DE' GRECI. DISSERTAZIONI 3

Sacchi, F *see* I TIPOGRAFI EBREI DI SONCINO, STUDII BIBLIOGRAFICI
Sacchi, Giovenale *see* DON PLACIDO...DOVE CERCASI..
Sacchini, A M *see*
- [DIDONE ABBANDONATA] SON REGINA E SONO AMANTE
- EVELINA. A FAVOURITE MARCH...
- LUCIO VERO. [OPERA IN TRE ATTI DI APOSTOLO ZENO. MUSICA]

Sacco, F *see* I MOLLUSCHI DEI TERRENI TERZIARI DEL PIEMONTE E DELLA LIGURIA
THE SACCO-VANZETTI CASE PAPERS – (Guide only $100.00) – Legal mss. from Harvard Law School Library. 23 reels. Printed guide – 1 – $2,530.00 – 0-89093-800-8 – us UPA [340]
SACERDOTALISM IN THE NINETEENTH CENTURY : A CRITICAL HISTORY / Sheldon, Henry Clay – New York: Eaton & Mains; Cincinnati: Jennings & Graham, c1909 – 2mf – us A.T.L.A. [240]
UN SACERDOTE CAUTIVO DE LOS ARAUCANOS / Bayle, Constantino – Madrid: Missionalia Hispanica, 1945 – 1 – sp Bibl Santa Ana [946]
Sachar, Abram L *see* THE PUBLIC PAPERS OF LOUIS DEMBITZ BRANDEIS IN THE JACOB AND BERTHA GOLDFARB LIBRARY OF BRANDEIS UNIVERSITY
Sacher-Masoch *see* REALISTISCHE CABINETSTUCKE
Sacher-Masoch, Leopold, Ritter von *see*
- GUTE MENSCHEN UND IHRE GESCHICHTEN
- UNSERE SCLAVEN
- ZUR EHRE GOTTES

SACHGEHALT UND WAHRHEITSGEHALT IN SHAKESPEARES "THE TEMPEST" / Auerbach, Guenter – Frankfurt a.M., 1973 – 247p – 9 – DM48.00 – 3-89349-054-X – gw Hänsel [420]
SACHINENIIA / Drinov, M S – 3v. Sofiia. 1909-15. BR-3859 2 – 8 – ne IDC [940]
SACHINENIIA / Rakovski, G S – Sofiia. 1922. BR-3909 2 – 8 – ne IDC [999]
SACHKATALOG DER DEUTSCHEN BUECHEREI LEIPZIG 1913 – (MAI) 1945 : KARTEN – (Suppl: (Juni) 1945-73; 1974- 27mf silver DM540.00 ISBN: 3-598-33698-5. Diazo DM440.00 ISBN: 3-598-33686-1) – 1913-(Mai) 1945; (Juni) 1945-73; 1974- (mf ed 1994) – 38mf (1:42) – diazo DM880.00 silver DM 1,080.00 – 3-598-33689-6 – silver ISBN: 3-598-33701-9 – gw Saur [070]
SACHKATALOG DER DEUTSCHEN BUECHEREI LEIPZIG 1913 – MAI (1945) : ZEITSCHRIFTEN – (Suppl: (Juni) 1945-73, 1974- 108mf silver DM2,100.00 ISBN: 3-598-33697-7. Diazo DM1,800 ISBN: 3-598-33685-3) – 1913-(Mai) 1945; (Juni) 1945-1973; 1974- (mf ed 1994) – 169mf (1:42) – 9 – diazo DM3,600.00 silver DM4,200.00 – 3-598-33688-8 – silver ISBN: 3-598-33700-0 – gw Saur [070]
SACHKATALOG DER DEUTSCHEN BUECHEREI LEIPZIG 1913 – (MAI)1945 : MONOGRAPHIEN – ZEITSCHRIFTEN – KARTEN – (Segments also listed separately) – 1994 – 603mf (1:24) in 5 installments – 9 – diazo set DM9,860.00 silver set DM10,980.00 – 3-598-33678-0 – silver ISBN: 3-598-33679-9 – gw Saur [070]
Sachlan, M *see* NOTES ON PARASITES OF FRESHWATER FISHES IN INDONESIA
DIE SACHMAENGELHAFTUNG BEIM KAUF BEWEGLICHER SACHEN... / Fischer, H – Charlottenburg, 1936 – 1mf – 1 – ILM-3019/1 – ne IDC [327]
Sachs, E S *see* GARMENT WORKERS IN ACTION
Sachs, Ignacy *see* FOOD AND ENERGY
Sachs, M *see*
- MIKHTAV MI-YERUSHALAYIM
- DIE RELIGIOESE POESIE DER JUDEN IN SPANIEN, BERLIN, 1845

Sachs, Michael L *see*
- THE EFFECTIVENESS OF THE STAGES OF CHANGE MODEL AND EXPERIMENTAL EXERCISE PRESCRIPTIONS IN INCREASING FEMALE ADULTS' PHYSICAL ACTIVITY AND EXERCISE BEHAVIOR
- EXPLORING THE KARATE WAY OF LIFE
- PSYCHOLOGICAL FACTORS THAT PREDISPOSE ATHLETES TO INJURY

Sachs, W *see* DIE URSRPUNG DES MYTHOSBEGRIFFES IN DER MODERNEN BIBELWISSENSCHAFT
Sachse, Julius Friedrich *see*
- THE GERMAN PIETISTS OF PROVINCIAL PENNSYLVANIA, 1694-1708
- THE GERMAN SECTARIANS OF PENNSYLVANIA, 1708-1800
- JUSTUS FALCKNER

SACHSEN-LANDESVERSAMMLUNG / Sozialdemokratische Partei Deutschlands – 12-14 Jul 1914 – 1 – DM80.00 – gw Mikro Press [335]
SACHSEN-LANDESVERSAMMLUNGEN / Sozialdemokratische Partei Deutschlands – 1899-1909 – 1 – DM80.00 – gw Mikro Press [335]
SACHSEN-PARTEITAG / Sozialdemokratische Partei Deutschlands – Dresden, 18-20 Aug 1912 – 1 – DM80.00 – gw Mikro Press [335]
SACHSEN'S VOLKSSAGEN : BALLADEN, ROMANZEN UND LEGENDEN / Ziehnert, Widar – Annaberg: Rudolph & Dieterici, 1838-1839 – 1r – 1 – us U.W. Library [390]
SACHSENSPIEGEL LAND- UND LEHNRECHT (QUEDLINBURGER HANDSCHRIFT) (MGH LEGES 4: 8.BD) – Dfl13.00 – ne Slangenburg [240]
SACHSENSPIEGEL (MGH LEGES 3: 1.BD) : LAND- UND LEHNRECHT – 1933 – Dfl19.00 – ne Slangenburg [240]
SACHSISCHE ZEITUNG – Dresden, Germany. May 1947-1953; Jul 1965-Sept 1967 – 14r – 1 – us L of C Photodup [072]
Sack, Karl Heinrich *see* THEOLOGISCHE AUFSAETZE
THE SACKBUT: A MUSICAL REVIEW – v. 1-14, no.7. May 1920-February 1934 – 1 – 60.00 – us L of C Photodup [780]
Sackville Gallery. London *see* EXHIBITION BY THE ITALIAN FUTURIST PAINTERS
Sackville West, Vita *see* VITA SACKVILLE WEST AND HAROLD NICOLSON
DIE SACRA PARALLELA DES JOHANNES DAMASCENUS (T.U.U. 2-16/1) / Holl, Karl – Leipzig, 1897 – 6mf – 9 – ne Slangenburg [240]
SACRAE ANTIQUITATIS MONUMENTA / Hugo, Lud. – Etival. Tomus 1. 1725; Saint-Die. Tomus 2. 1731 – v1 16mf; v2 15mf – 8 – Dfl109.00 – ne Slangenburg [240]
SACRAE MELODIAE UNICA / Lappi, Pietro – 1621. Cantus only – 5,15 – us Sibley [780]
THE SACRAMENT OF REGENERATION: THE DOCTRINE OF HOLY BAPTISM / Forest, Charles – s.l.: Published under the auspices of the St. Lawrence Clerical Union, 18??. 03148. (Pre-1900 Canadiana) – 9 – cn C.I.H.M. [971]
SACRAMENTAIRE GELASIEN D'ANGOULEME' / Gagin, Dom. P – Angouleme, s.d. – 8mf – 8 – Dfl30.00 – ne Slangenburg [240]
LE SACRAMENTAIRE GREGORIEN : SES PRINCIPALES FORMES D'APRES LES PLUS ANCIENS MANUSCRITS / Deshusses, J – Fribourg, 1971 – 13mf – 8 – Dfl46.00 – ne Slangenburg [240]
SACRAMENTALE (SIECLE 14) / Monte-Lauduno, Guillermo de – Barcelona – 2r – 5,6 – sp Cultura [220]
SACRAMENTARIUM BERGOMENSE / ed by Paredi, A – Bergamo, 1962 – 13mf – 8 – Dfl46.00 – ne Slangenburg [240]
SACRAMENTARIUM GELASIANUM / ed by Chavasse, A – Strassbourg, 1958 – 18mf – 8 – Dfl63.00 – ne Slangenburg [240]
SACRAMENTARIUM GELASIANUM / ed by Mohlberg, C – Roma, 1960 – 6mf – 8 – Dfl25.00 – ne Slangenburg [240]
SACRAMENTARIUM VERONENSE (LEONIANUM) / ed by Mohlberg, C – Roma, 1956 – 12mf – 8 – Dfl42.00 – ne Slangenburg [240]
SACRAMENTO – 1992- – 7+ r – 1 – $350.00 – P00092 – us Library Micro [910]
SACRAMENTO AGE – Sacramento, CA. -d. 1856. Incomplete – 1 – 17.00 – us Oregon Hist [071]

THE SACRAMENTO AGE – Sacramento, CA. 1856-1858 – 1r – 1 – $50.00 – BC03439 – us Library Micro [071]

SACRAMENTO BEE – Sacramento, CA. 1857 – 2300+ r – 1 – $115,100.00 ($1,540.00y) – R02728 – us Library Micro [071]

SACRAMENTO BEE INDEX – (Also available on mf $2,200.00 set B06005) – Sacramento, CA. 1900-37 – 30r – 5 – $1,500.00 – us Library Micro [071]

SACRAMENTO BEE WEEKLY – Sacramento, CA. 1877-1900 – 11r – 1 – $550.00 – B02729 – us Library Micro [071]

SACRAMENTO BUSINESS JOURNAL – Sacramento, CA. 1985-1990 – 10r – 1 – $500.00 – B05053 – us Library Micro [073]

SACRAMENTO COUNTY / Davis, William J – Chicago: Lewis Publ. Co., 1890. California Reel 23. (The Cox Library Collection) – 5 – us Americana [978]

SACRAMENTO COUNTY, 1860; 1870-1901; 1936-1949 – 38r – 1 – $1,900.00 – D078 – us Library Micro [978]

SACRAMENTO COUNTY LEDGER *see* OAK PARK LEDGER

SACRAMENTO LEGAL PRESS – Sacramento, CA. 1945-72 – 24r – 1 – $1,200.00 – C02736 – us Library Micro [071]

SACRAMENTO NEWS AND REVIEW – Sacramento, CA. 1994 – 1+ r – 1 – $50.00 ($50.00y) – B03646 – us Library Micro [071]

SACRAMENTO OBSERVER – Sacramento, CA. 1963- – 81+ r – 1 – $4,050.00 ($180.00) – B02737 – us Library Micro [071]

SACRAMENTO REPORTER – Sacramento, CA. 1870-1872 – 5r – 1 – $250.00 – BC03432 – us Library Micro [071]

SACRAMENTO RIVER NEWS – Rio Vista, CA. 1890-95 – 3r – 1 BC02708 – $150.00 – us Library Micro [071]

SACRAMENTO SHOPPING NEWS – Sacramento, CA. 1946-1948; 1950-1955 – 8r – 1 – $400.00 – B03433 – us Library Micro [071]

SACRAMENTO SOCIETY FOR MEDICAL IMPROVEMENT : CONSTITUTION AND MINUTES – Sacramento Co, CA. 1868-1924 – 5r – 1 – $250.00 – D079 – us Library Micro [978]

SACRAMENTO STAR – Sacramento, CA. 1904-1925 – 70r – 1 – $3,500.00 – B03434 – us Library Micro [071]

SACRAMENTO SUNDAY LEADER – Sacramento, CA. 1905-1922 – 6r – 1 – $300.00 – C03435 – us Library Micro [071]

SACRAMENTO TRIBUNE-PROGRESS – (Also known as: Independent-Leader) – Sacramento, CA. 1928-1943 – 8r – 1 – $400.00 – B03437 – us Library Micro [071]

THE SACRAMENTO UNION – Sacramento, CA. 1851-54; 1856-64; 1872-74; 1880; 1881-82; 1906-94 – 1460r – 1 BC02746 – $73,000.00 – us Library Micro [071]

SACRAMENTO WEEKLY UNION – Sacramento, CA. Jan-May 1880 – 1r – 1 – $50.00 – B03438 – us Library Micro [071]

SACRARIUM BENEDICTINUM / Bucelini, Gabr. – Feldkirch, 1656 – 2mf – 8 – Dfl9.00 – ne Slangenburg [240]

Sacre-Coeur, Florence-du *see* BIBLIOGRAPHIE ANALYTIQUE SUR LE FORUM CATHOLIQUE DE MONTREAL (CATHOLIC INQUIRY FORUM) 1952-1962

THE SACRED BOOKS OF CHINA : PART 1: THE SHU KING, THE RELIGIOUS PORTIONS OF THE SHIH KING, AND THE HSIAO KING / ed by Mueller, Friedrich Max – (Translated by James Legge) – 1879 – 9mf – 8 – ne Slangenburg [290]

THE SACRED BOOKS OF CHINA. THE TEXTS OF CONFUCIANISM : PART 2: THE YI KING / ed by Mueller, Friedrich Max – (Translated by James Legge) – 1882 – 9mf – 8 – ne Slangenburg [290]

THE SACRED BOOKS OF CHINA. THE TEXTS OF CONFUCIANISM : PART 3: THE LI KI, OR COLLECTION OF TREATISES ON THE RULES OF PROPRIETY, OR CEREMONIAL USAGES 1-10 / ed by Mueller, Friedrich Max – (Translated by James Legge) – 1885 – 9mf – 8 – ne Slangenburg [290]

THE SACRED BOOKS OF CHINA. THE TEXTS OF CONFUCIANISM : PART 4: THE LI KI, OR COLLECTION OF TREATISES ON THE RULES OF PROPRIETY, OR CEREMONIAL USAGES 1, 11-46 / ed by Mueller, Friedrich Max – (Translated by James Legge) – 1885 – 9mf – 8 – ne Slangenburg [290]

THE SACRED BOOKS OF CHINA. THE TEXTS OF TAOISM : PART 1 / ed by Mueller, Friedrich Max – (Translated by James Legge) – 1891 – 7mf – 8 – ne Slangenburg [290]

THE SACRED BOOKS OF CHINA. THE TEXTS OF TAOISM : PART 2 / ed by Mueller, Friedrich Max – (Translated by James Legge) – 1891 – 6mf – 8 – ne Slangenburg [290]

THE SACRED BOOKS OF THE EAST / ed by Mueller, Friedrich Max – Oxford. v1-51. 1879-1910 – 422mf – 9 – Dfl1,477.00 – ne Slangenburg [200]

SACRED DIRGES, HYMNS, AND ANTHEMS, COMMEMORATIVE OF THE DEATH OF GENERAL GEORGE WASHINGTON, THE GUARDIAN OF HIS COUNTRY AND THE FRIEND OF MAN / Holden, Oliver – An original composition by a citizen of Massachusetts. Boston: Thomas and Andrews 1800. MUSIC 123, Item 2 – 1 – us L of C Photodup [780]

SACRED DRAMAS : CHIEFLY INTENDED FOR YOUNG PERSONS, THE SUBJECTS TAKEN FROM THE BIBLE... / More, Hannah – London: T. Cadell, 1782 – 1 roll – 1 – 1-55879-312-7 – uk Libr Preservation [820]

THE SACRED HARP / Cates, J M D – 1880 ED – 1 – 18.97 – us Baptist [240]

THE SACRED HARP / White, B F & King, E J – 1847 – 1 – 12.84 – us Baptist [240]

SACRED HARP HYMN BOOK – 4th ed – 1 – $15.96 – us Baptist [780]

SACRED HYMNES OF 3, 4, 5, AND 6 PARTS FOR VOICES AND VIOLS / Amner, J – 1615 – 9 – us Sibley [780]

THE SACRED LAWS OF THE ARYAS, AS TAUGHT IN THE SCHOOLS OF APASTAMBA, GAUTAMA, VASISHTHA AND BAUDHYANA : PART 1: APASTAMBA AN GAUTAMA / ed by Mueller, Friedrich Max – (Translated by Georg Buehler) – 1879 – 7mf – 8 – ne Slangenburg [280]

THE SACRED LAWS OF THE ARYAS, AS THAUGHT IN THE SCHOOLS OF APASTAMBA, GAUTAMA, VASISHTA AND BAUDHAYANA : PART 2: VASIHTA AND BAUDHAYANA / ed by Mueller, Friedrich Max – (Translated by Georg Buehler) – 1882 – 7mf – 8 – ne Slangenburg [280]

SACRED MELODIES – 3rd ed. Dover. 1839 – 1 – 6.93 – us Baptist [240]

THE SACRED TENTH / Lansdell, Henry – v. 1-2. 1906 – 1 – 26.88 – us Baptist [240]

SACRI CONCENTUS BINIS, TERNIS, QUATERISQUE VOCIBUS / Cherubini, N – (Cantus book only) – Venetiis: Magni, 1640 – 1 – us Sibley [780]

SACRI ET CANONICI ORDINIS PRAEMONSTRATENSIS ANNALES / Hugo, Lud. – Nancy. v 1-2. 1734-1736 – v1 41mf; v2 45mf – 8 – Dfl301.00 – ne Slangenburg [240]

SACRIFICE AS SET FORTH IN SCRIPTURE / Murphy, James Gracey – 1889 – 1 – us A.T.L.A. [240]

SACRIFICE IN THE OLD TESTAMENT / Gray, George Buchanan – 1925 – 9 – $18.00 – us I.R.C. [220]

SACRIFICE IN THE OLD TESTAMENT / Kidner, FD – London, 1952 – 1mf – 8 – ne Slangenburg [220]

THE SACRIFICE OF CHRIST : ITS VITAL REALITY AND EFFICACY / Wace, Henry – New York: Macmillan, 1898 – 1mf – 9 – 0-8370-2912-0 – 1985-0912 – us A.T.L.A. [240]

EL SACRIFICIO GLADATORIO / Mendoza y Gonzalez, Luis de – Barcelona: Piferrer, 1834 – 1 – sp Bibl Santa Ana [946]

SACRIFICIO VESPERTINO / Secretariado Diocesano de Catequesis – Plasencia: Imp. La Victoria, 1972 – 1 – sp Bibl Santa Ana [240]

SACRIFICIO Y RECOMPENSA: NOVELA / Cabello de Carbonera, Mercedes – Lima: Imp. de Torres Aguirre, 1886. 369p – 1 – us U.W. Library [830]

SACRIS BIBLIIS / Jimenez Arias, Diego – 1618 – 9 – 1.50f – sp Bibl Santa Ana [240]

SACRIS ERUDIRI / Callewaert, C – Steenbrugge, 1940 – 19mf – 8 – ne Slangenburg [240]

SACRORUM CONCENTUUM OCTONIS VOCIBUS MODULANDORUM...LIBER PRIMUS-SECUNDUS / Gumpelzhaimer, Adam – 1601-1614 – 9 – us Sibley [780]

SACRORUM CONCILIORUM NOVA ET AMPLISSIMA COLLECTIO / ed by Mansi, J D – Florence, etc. v1-53. 1759-1927 – 912mf – 9 – 203/2 – ne IDC [240]

SACRORUM EVANGELIORUM VERSIO SYRIACA PHILOXENIANA... / White, Joseph – (Tomos 1, Oxford, 1778. 10mf; Tomos 2, Oxford, 1778. 13mf) – 8 – ne Slangenburg [240]

Sacy, I Silvestre de *see* PRINCIPES DE GRAMMAIRE GENERALE MIS A LA PORTEE DES ENFANTS, AN 7

Sacy, I Sylvestre de *see* PRINCIPES DE GRAMMAIRE GENERALE MIS A LA PORTEE DES ENFANTS, ET PROPRES A SERVIR D'INTRODUCTION A L'ETUDE DE TOUTES LES LANGUES

SAD NEWS – Sacramento, CA. Apr-Jun 1943 (broken file) – 1r – 1 – $50.00 – C02741 – us Library Micro [071]

SADA – Izmir. Hak ve hakikati muedafaa eder muestakillue'l-efkar gazetedir. Mesul Mueduerue: Huesnue Osman. No. 3 (30 Tesriniewel 1918) – 9 – $20.00 – us MEDOC [956]

SADA AS-SAHRA' – Alger. 1926, 1934 – 1 – fr A.C.R.P.P. [073]

Sadarjun, Siswomartojo *see* HUMAN RESOURCES AND THE APPLICATION OF SCIENCE AND TECHNOLOGY IN THE DEVELOPING AREAS

THE SADDHARMA-PUNDARIKA; OR THE LOTUS OF THE TRUE LAW / ed by Mueller, Friedrich Max – (Translated by H. Kern) – 1884 – 9mf – 8 – ne Slangenburg [280]

SADDLEBACK VALLEY NEWS – Laguna Niguel, CA. 1969-1976 – 14r – 1 – $700.00 – R03260 – us Library Micro [071]

SADDLEBACK VALLEY NEWS – South Co, CA. 1969 – 18+ r – 1 – $900.00 ($50.00y) – R04122 – us Library Micro [071]

Saddleworth. Yorkshire. St. Chad's *see* PARISH REGISTERS

Sadeddin *see* TAC UET-TEVARIH

SADHANA – Poona, India. 1962-64 – 1r – 1 – us L of C Photodup [072]

Sa'di *see* DIVAN-I GUELZAR

Sadiq, Fawziyah Mahmud *see* IMKANIYAT AL-TANMIYAH AL-ZIRAIYAH FI SINA

Sadler, B S *see* COMMUNICATION STRATEGIES FOR HEIGHTENING AWARENESS OF WATER

Sadler, Gilbert T *see* THE RELATION OF CUSTOM TO LAW

Sadler, J *see*
- DE FILICIBUS VERIS HUNGARIAE, TRANSSYLVANIAE, CROATIAE ET LITORALIS HUNGARICI
- FLORAE COMITATUS PESTIENSIS

Sadler, Michael Ferrebee *see*
- THE EPISTLE TO THE ROMANS
- THE EPISTLES OF ST. PAUL TO THE COLOSSIANS, THESSALONIANS, AND TIMOTHY
- THE EPISTLES OF ST PAUL TO THE GALATIANS, EPHESIANS, AND PHILIPPIANS
- THE EPISTLES OF ST PAUL TO TITUS, PHILEMON, AND THE HEBREWS
- THE GENERAL EPISTLES OF SS. JAMES, PETER, JOHN, AND JUDE

Sadler, W H *see* BUSINESS BOOKKEEPING AND PRACTICE

SADLER'S REPORTS : UNREPORTED / Pennsylvania. Superior Court – (A Pre-NRS title) – v1-10. 1885-88 (all publ) – 24mf – 9 – $108.00 – LLMC 84-206 – us L.L.M.C. [340]

Sadli, Mohammad *see*
- ASPECTS OF INTER-REGIONAL INDUSTRIAL DEVELOPMENT, WITH SPECIAL REFERENCE TO INDONESIA
- ECONOMIC STABILIZATION AS AN ESSENTIAL CONDITION FOR EFFECTIVE ECONOMIC DEVELOPMENT
- INDUSTRIAL ECONOMICS
- STRUCTURAL AND OPERATIONAL ASPECTS OF PUBLIC (ESPECIALLY INDUSTRIAL) ENTERPRISES

SADLIER AND CO *see* CATALOGUE OF SCHOOL BOOKS, STATIONERY, ETC

SADLIER'S CATHOLIC ALMANAC AND ORDO FOR THE YEAR OF OUR LORD... – New York: D and J Sadlier and Co, 1864-66 – 1r – 1 – $40.00r – us U.N.D. Archives [240]

SADLIER'S CATHOLIC DIRECTORY, ALMANAC, AND ORDO FOR THE YEAR OF OUR LORD... – New York: D & J Sadlier & Co, 1867-79; 1881-91 – 9r – 1 – $40.00r – us U.N.D. Archives [240]

Sadoleti, Iac. *see*
- EPISCOPI CARPENTORACTI S.R.E.CARD. EPISTOLARUM LIBRI SEXDECIM
- OPERA QUAE EXSTNT OMNIA

Sadoleto, J *see* DE BELLO TURCIS INFERENDO, ORATIO

Sadovnikov, Dmitrii Nikolaevich *see*
- PEVETS VOLGI D.N. SADOVNIKOV
- SKAZKI I PREDANIIA SAMARSKAGO KRAIA

Sadovskoi, B *see* RUSSKAIA KAMENA

SADRACH A.B. DNEGO : EIN BABYLONISCHER KEILSCHRIFTLEHRER: 120 INSCHRIFTEN ENTZIFFERT UND UMGEDICHTET / Treugold, Fritz – 6. Aufl. Stuttgart: R. Lutz, 1889 – 1r – 1 – us U.W. Library [810]

SADUCISMUS TRIUMPHATUS; OR, FULL AND PLAIN EVIDENCE CONCERNING WITCHES AND APPARITIONS / Glanvill, Joseph – London, 1689. Reprint Gainesville, 1966. Introd. by Coleman O. Parsons – 9 – 35.00 – us Scholars' Facs [390]

SADY / Ivanov, G – Ed. 2. Berlin. 1923. BR-1185 2 – 8 – ne IDC [460]

SADY / Ivanov, G – Spb. 1921. BR-1184 2 – 8 – ne IDC [460]

SAE IN AEROSPACE ENGINEERING *see* AEROSPACE ENGINEERING

SAE JOURNAL / Society of Automotive Engineers – v1-72. 1917-1964 – 1,5,6 – us Princeton Micro [629]

SAE QUARTERLY TRANSACTIONS / Society of Automotive Engineers – v1-6. 1947-1952 – 1 – us Princeton Micro [629]

SAE (SOCIETY OF AUTOMOTIVE ENGINEERS) – Standards. Printed index. Updated every 60 days – 6,9 – us Info Handling [629]

SAE TECHNICAL PAPERS ON MICROFICHE : ANNUAL EDITION / Society of Automotive Engineers – (Appears in February) – 9 – $1,950.00 – 1-56091-381-9 – us S.A.E. [629]

SAE TECHNICAL PAPERS ON MICROFICHE : QUARTERLY SUBSCRIPTION / Society of Automotive Engineers – (Appears in May, August, November and February) – 9 – $3,500.00 – 1-56091-517-X – us S.A.E. [629]

SAECHISCHE ARBEITER-ZEITUNG – Leipzig. Nov 3 1926-Dec 31 1932. Incomplete – 1 – us NY Public [072]

SAECHSISCHE ARBEITER-ZEITUNG – (Title change: Dresdner Volkszeitung, 8 May 1908) – Dresden, Germany. 1890-Apr 1915; Sept 1915-2 Mar 1933 – 152r – 1 – gw Mikrofilm [072]

SAECHSISCHE INDUSTRIE – Dresden. jan 10, 1909-1925. 1931-sep 25, 1936 (incomplete) – 12r – 1 – gw Mikrofilm [670]

SAECHSISCHE KRIEGSNOT IN DEN JAHREN 1806 BIS 1815 / Krebs, Kurt – Leipzig: Teutonia-Verlag, 19–. 243p. illus – 1 – us U.W. Library [943]

SAECHSISCHE NEUESTE NACHRICHTEN – Dresden, East Germany. Aug 1954-30 Jun 1969; 1 Apr 1970-31 Aug 1990 – 63r – 1 – gw Mikrofilm [072]

SAECHSISCHE VATERLANDSBLAETTER – Leipzig, 1843-44 – 3r – 1 – gw Mikrofilm [072]

SAECHSISCHE WELTCHRONIK – 23p + 4 color mf – DM520.00 – 3-89219-014-3 – gw Lengenfelder [900]

SAECHSISCHE WELTCHRONIK. – EBERHARDS REIMCHRONIK VON GANDERSHEIM. – BRAUNSCHWEIGISHE REIMCHRONIK. – CHRONIK DES STIFTES S. SIMON UND JUDAS IN GOSLAR. – HOLSTEINISCHE REIMCHRONIK (MGH 8: 2.BD) – 1877 – Dfl67.00 – ne Slangenburg [240]

SAECHSISCHE ZEITUNG – (Also Bereichsausgaben available (nur Kreisseiten): BAUTZEN, apr 5 1958-oct 31 1960, apr 16 1962-dec 20 1968 (incomplete); BAUTZEN-LAND, apr 1 1958-oct 30 1960; BISCHOFSWERDA, apr 4 1958-oct 30 1961; DIPPOLDISWALDE, 1958-dec 12 1962 (incomplete); FREITAL, apr 1 1958-feb 28 1969 (incomplete); GOERLITZ, apr 1 1958-mar 28 1970 (incomplete); GOERLITZ-LAND, apr 3 1958-oct 30 1961, apr 16 1962-dec 20 1968 (incomplete); GROSSENHAIN, apr 3 1958-oct 31 1961; KAMENZ, apr 1 1958-nov 30 1964, apr 4 1967-jul 23 1969 (all incomplete); LOEBAU, jun 1 1964-dec 20 1969 (incomplete); MEISSEN, apr 18 1958-apr 4 1960, may 23 1962-dec 24 1966 (incomplete); MEISSEN-LAND, apr 3 1958-65, mar 23 1967-jul 26 1969 (incomplete); MEISSEN UND COSWIG, 1967, 1969 (incomplete); NIESKY, apr 1

1958-nov 13 1963 (incomplete), jul 13-nov 4 1966; PIRNA, apr 1 1958-66 (incomplete); RIESA, apr 1 1958-65 (incomplete), feb 16 1967-oct 8 1969 (incomplete), jul 9 1983-dec 23 1990; SEBNITZ, apr 1 1958-oct 31 1961, 1963, 1965 (incomplete)) – Dresden, apr 13 1946-47, apr 1952- – 1 – Inquire at Mikrofilmarchiv for details – gw Misc Inst [072]

SAECHSISCHE ZEITUNG – Dresden, Apr 1946-1947 – 2r – 1 – DM150.00 – gw Mikro Press [072]

SAECHSISCHE ZEITUNG – Dresden, Germany. 1992- – 8r per yr – 1 – gw Mikrofilm [072]

Saechsischer Berg- und Huettenarbeiter Deligiertentag. Bergmanns Fluch *see* BERICHT..

Saechsischer Berg- und Huettenarbeiter-Verband *see* PROTOKOLL DES KONGRESSES SAECHSISCHER BERG..

SAECHSISCHES SCHRIFTSTELLER-LEXICON / Haan, Wilhelm – Leipzig, 1875. Hildesheim, 1983 – 5mf – 9 – DM40.00 diazo DM50.00 silver – gw Olms [430]

SAECHSISCHES TAGEBLATT – Dresden, East Germany. 16 Feb-5 Oct 1946; Aug 1954-1990 – 58r – 1 – gw Mikrofilm [072]

SAECHSISCHES TAGEBLATT – Dresden, Feb-Oct 1946 – 1r – 1 – DM80.00 – gw Mikro Press [072]

SAECHSISCHES VOLKSBLATT – Hermannstadt (Sibiu), Rumaenien. 1 Jan 1925-31 Dec 1930 – 1r – 1 – gw Mikrofilm [949]

Saedler, Heinrich *see* DIE ENTSTEHUNGSGESCHICHTE VON HEBBELS MOLOCH

Saeed, A M et al *see* CHARACTERISATION OF KENANA CATTLE AT UM BANEIN, SUDAN

Saeed, O H *see* THE INDUSTRIAL BANK OF SUDAN, 1962-1968: AN EXPERIMENT IN DEVELOPMENT BANKING

DIE SAEGE VON MARIELS / Zahn, Ernst – Wiesbaden: E Behrend, [n.d.] – 1r – 1 – us U.W. Library [830]

Saelan, A T *see* FINLANDS BOTANISKA LITERATUR TILL OCH MED AR 1900

DER SAEMANN – Hillsboro, KN. v1. 1897-98 (complete) – 1r – 1 – ATLA 1994-S026 – us A.T.L.A. [073]

SAEMANN – Leigh, KN. v12 nos12-16. 1908-12 (incomplete) – 1r – 1 – ATLA 1994-S028 – us A.T.L.A. [073]

SAEMMTLICHE GEDICHTE / Buerger, Gottfried August – Berlin: G Hempel, [1879] – 1 – us U.W. Library [810]

SAEMMTLICHE LIEDER, BALLADEN, UND ROMANZEN.. / Zelter, C – 1810-13 – 9 – us Sibley [780]

SAEMMTLICHE NOVELLEN / Zschokke, Heinrich – Wien, Leipzig: M Stern, [1888?] – 2r – 1 – us U.W. Library [830]

SAEMMTLICHE POETISCHE WERKE / Voss, Johann Heinrich; ed by Voss, Abraham – Leipzig: I Mueller, 1835 – 1r – 1 – us U.W. Library [810]

SAEMMTLICHE REDEN DES HL. LEO DES GROSSEN, PAPSTES UND KIRCHENLEHRERS = SERMONS / Leo 1, Pope – (In German. Includes bibliographical references) – Kempten: Jos Koesel, 1876 – 2mf – 9 – 0-8370-8529-2 – 1986-2529 – us A.T.L.A. [240]

SAEMMTLICHE ROMANE / Paalzow, Henriette Wach von – (v. 1. Godwie-Castle. v. 2. Ste. Roche. v.3. Jakob van der Nees. v. 4. Thomas Thyrnau) – Neue Ausg. Stuttgart, A. Heitz, 1874-75. 4v. Film Mas 8590 – 1 – us H.U. Library [830]

SAEMMTLICHE SCHRIFTEN UEBER FREYMAUREREY / Fessler, I A – Dresden. v2. 1804 – 5mf – ne IDC [360]

SAEMMTLICHE SCHRIFTEN UEBER FREYMAUREREY / Fessler, I A – Freiburg. v1. 1805 – 5mf – ne IDC [360]

SAEMMTLICHE SCHRIFTEN UEBER GENERALBASZ, HARMONIE-LEHRE UND TONSETZKUNST; ZUM SELBSUNTERRICHTE / Albrechtsberger, Johann G – Wien. BP-123 1 – 9 – ne IDC [780]

SAEMMTLICHE SCHWARZWAELDER DORFGESCHICHTEN : VOLKSAUSGABE IN ACHT BAENDEN / Auerbach, Berthold – Stuttgart: J G Cotta, 1871 – 1r – 1 – us U.W. Library [830]

SAEMMTLICHE WERKE / Dingelstedt, Franz von – Iue Gesamtausg. Berlin, Gebrueder Paetel, 1877. 12 v. Film Mas C 573 – 1 – us H.U. Library [080]

SAEMMTLICHE WERKE UND HANDSCHRIFTLICHER NACHLASS : ERSTE KRITISCHE GESAMMT-AUSGABE / Buechner, Georg; ed by Franzos, Karl Emil – (Includes bibliographical references) – Frankfurt am Main: J D Sauerlaender, 1879 – 1 – us U.W. Library [800]

SAEMTLICHE AUFSAETZE UND MISZELLEN / Bastgen, Hubert; ed by Haensel-Hohenhausen, Markus – (Nur lieferbar mit der Hauptsammlung) – Egelsbach, Koeln, New York, 1993 – 9 – 3-89349-203-8 – gw Hänsel [240]

SAEMTLICHE BRIEFE / Gregorius des Grossen, H; ed by Feyerabend, M – Kempten, Band 1-6, 1807-1808 – 45mf – 8 – ne Slangenburg [240]

SAEMTLICHE POETISCHE WERKE, NEBST EINER AUSWAHL SEINER BRIEFE / Buechner, Georg; ed by Zweig, Arnold – Muenchen: Roesl, 1923 – 1 – us U.W. Library [800]

SAEMTLICHE WERKE : DIE ALLERWAERTS GESAMMELTEN BRIEFE NACH DER ZEITORDNUNG, FRAGMENTE, ABBILDUNGEN UND VIERFACHER INDEX / Winckelmann, Johann Joachim; ed by Eiselein, Joseph – (Includes bibliographical references) – Donauoeschingen: Im Verlage Deutscher Classiker. 12v. 1825-29 – 1 – us U.W. Library [800]

SAEMTLICHE WERKE / Droste-Huelshoff, Annette von; ed by Schulte Kemminghausen, Karl – Muenchen: G Mueller. 3v in 5. 1925 – 1 – us U.W. Library [800]

SAEMTLICHE WERKE : HISTORISCH-KRITISCHE GESAMTAUSGABE / Guenther, Johann Christian; ed by Kraemer, Wilhelm – Leipzig: K W Hiersemann. 6v. 1930-36 – 1 – us U.W. Library [810]

SAEMTLICHE WERKE IN 24 BAENDEN / Gotthelf, Jeremias; ed by Hunziker, Rudolf & Bloesch, Hans – (Includes bibliographical references) – Erlenbach, Zuerich: E Rentsch. 24v. 1911-32 – 1 – us U.W. Library [800]

SAEMTLICHE WERKE IN ZWOELF BAENDEN = WORKS / Heine, Heinrich – (Mit Bildnis und einer Biographie Heines von Gustav Karpeles) – Leipzig: Hesse & Becker, [18–?] – 1 – us U.W. Library [800]

SAEMTLICHE WERKE MIT BIOGRAPHIE, EINLEITUNGEN UND ILLUSTRATIONEN, DARUNTER ORIGINALZEICHNUNGEN SCHAUMBERGERS / Schaumberger, Heinrich – Herausgegeben von Hermine Sobius. Ausgabe in neuester Rechtschreibung. Leipzig, C. Grumbach, 1905. 4 v. Film Mas 8545 – 1 – us H.U. Library [800]

SAENGE VON LIEBEN UND STERBEN : NOVELLEN / Wittmer, Felix – Augsburg: Dom-Verlag, [1929?] – 1r – 1 – us U.W. Library [780]

Saenger, Fritz *see* POLITIK FUER DEUTSCHLAND

SAENGER, SOLDAT UND HELD : LEBEN UND STERBEN THEODOR KOERNERS / Rother-Carlowitz, Alfred – Burg b.M.: Schildhorn Verlag, c1942 – 1 – us U.W. Library [430]

Saengerbund des Nordwestens Saengerfest. 18th. Davenport, Iowa, 1898 *see* FEST-ZEITUNG

Saengerbund des Nordwestens Saengerfest. 24th. Omaha. 1910 *see* FEST-ZEITUNG

Saenz de Santa Maria, C *see* BAYLE, CONSTANTINO. EL PROTECTOR DE INDIOS. SEVILLA, 1944

Saenz, Vicente *see* ESPANA EN SUS GLORIOSAS JORNADAS DE JULIO Y AGOSTO DE 1936; REPRODUCCION DE 18 ARTICULOS Y DE 2 DISCURSOS DEL AUTOR

Saerozi, A M *see* ACHMAD. TIGA ORANG ANAK PETUALWNG

DIE SAEUGETHIERE IN ABBILDUNG NACH DER NATUR... / ed by Schreber, J C D von – (Suppl. v1-5) – Erlangen, Leipzig. v1-7. 1775-1855 – 239mf – ne IDC [590]

SAEUGETIERKUNDLICHE MITTEILUNGEN – Stuttgart, 1963-1968. v1-16 – 8 – ne IDC [590]

Saeve-Soederbergh, T *see* STUDIES IN THE COPTIC (MANICHAEAN) PSALMBOOK. PROSODY AND MANDAEAN PARALLELS

Saeve-Soederbergh, Torgny *see* TEMPLES AND TOMBS OF ANCIENT NUBIA

Safa, Ismail *see* HUZMA SAFA

SAFAK – Nos. 1-7 (1301) – 4mf – 9 – $36.75 – us MEDOC [949]

SAFARI ZA WASUAHELI / Velten, Carl – Gottingen: Vandenhoeck & Ruprecht, 1901 – us Res Libr [960]

SAFE CONTAINERS CONVENTION ACT AND REGULATIONS / Canada. Laws, Statutes, etc – (Amendment service. YX76-S1EM. Standing order) – Basic set. YX76-S1-1-EM – 9 – Can$5.00 – cn Communication [380]

SAFETY BELT KNOWLEDGE, ATTITUDES, AND BEHAVIORS AMONG MINORITY ADOLESCENTS / Paczolt, T M – 1991 – 1mf – 9 – $4.00 – us Microform Publ [360]

SAFETY PRODUCTS NEWS – v.1-11. 1967-77. Continued by yindustrial safety products news – 1 – us UMI [600]

SAFETY STANDARDS *see* OCCUPATIONAL SAFETY AND HEALTH ADMINISTRATION REPORTS

Saffell, WT R *see* RECORDS OF THE REVOLUTIONARY WAR: CONTAINING THE MILITARY AND FINANCIAL CORRESPONDENCE OF DISTINGUISHED OFFICERS

SAFFLETIDNINGEN – Saffle, Sweden. 1979- – 1 – sw Kungliga [072]

SAFFLETIDNINGEN *see* SAFFLETIDNINGEN VASTRA VARMLAND

SAFFLETIDNINGEN VASTRA VARMLAND – (Saffletidningen, 1894-1924; Saffletidningen Vastra Varmland, 1925-30; Saffletidningen 1968-78) – Saffle, Sweden – 61r – 1 – sw Kungliga [072]

SAFFORD EXPRESS – Palisade, NV. 1883 – 1r – 1 – $50.00 – U04637 – us Library Micro [071]

Safford, Mary Augusta *see* WOMAN AS A MINISTER OF RELIGION

SAFFRON WALDEN AND DISTRICT OBSERVER – (Also known as: Herts and Essex Observer (Saffron Walden Edn)) – Oct 6-Dec 29 1961; 1962; Jan 4-Apr 5 1963; Jun 19 1964; 1965-71; Jan 14-Jun 30, Jul 7-Dec 15 1972; Jan 12-Dec 28 1973; 1974-75; Oct 10-Dec 1991; 1992-96 – 49r – 1 – uk British Libr Newspaper [072]

SAFFRON WALDEN WEEKLY NEWS – Jun 1889-90; 1892-Dec 7 1978; Jan 25 1979-Mar, May 16 1980-86; Jan 8-Jun 25, Jul 1987-Jun 1992; Jul 1993-96 – 164 1/2r – 1 – uk British Libr Newspaper [072]

Safronova, G F *see* FONDY I DEIATEL'NOST' OTDELA RUKOPISEI GOSUDARSTVENNOI BIBLIOTEKI SSSR IMENI V.I. LENINA

LA SAGA DEL PERONISMO : [UNA CRONICA POETICA] / Canton, Dario – Buenos Aires: Editorial Ancora, [1964] – 1 – CSUXADP7361-B – us Hoover Inst Photo [320]

SAGA JATVARDAR KONUNGS HINS HELGA / ed by Sigurdsson, Jon – 1852. Icelandic saga about Edward, King of England, 1003-1066 – 1 – us I.U. Libraries [390]

SAGA OM THORVALD VIDFORLE ELLER DEN VIDTBEREISTE / Hauch, Johannes Carsten – Kjobenhavn: Reitzel, 1849. 2v – 1 – us U.W. Library [830]

LES SAGAIES DECOREES DU PALEOLITHIQUE SUPERIEUR DANS LA ZONE FRANCO-CANTABRIQUE / Baulois, A – 9 – F350.00 – fr Ethnologie [306]

SAGANER WOCHEN-BLATT – Sagan (Zagan), Poland. 1847-1848 – 1r – 1 – gw Mikrofilm [943]

Sagard, G *see* LE GRAND VOYAGE AU PAYS DES HURONS

DIE SAGE VOM HEILIGEN GRAL UND PARCEVAL : VORTRAG IM POLYTECHNISCHEN VEREIN ZU BAYREUTH AM 30. JANUAR 1878 / Kraussold, Lorenz – Erlangen: A Deichert, 1878 – 1r – 1 – us U.W. Library [390]

SAGEBRUSH – Reno, CA. University of Nevada: 1893-1908; 1909-1985 – 25r – 1 – $1,250.00 – U04714 – us Library Micro [370]

SAGEBRUSH LEGIONNAIRE – Reno, NV. Feb-Aug 1922 (scats) – 1r – 1 – $50.00 – U04715 – us Library Micro [071]

SAGEN UND MAERCHEN AUS DER OBERLAUSITZ / Willkomm, Ernst – 1843 – 1 – us I.U. Libraries [390]

DIE SAGENGESCHICHTLICHEN GRUNDLAGEN DER RINGDICHTUNG RICHARD WAGNERS / Golther, Wolfgang – Charlottenburg (-Berlin): Verlag der Allgem. Musik-Zeitung, 1902 – 1r – 1 – us U.W. Library [790]

Sager, JC *see* TERMINOLOGICAL PROBLEMS INVOLVED IN THE PROCESS OF EXCHANGE OF NEW TECHNOLOGY BETWEEN DEVELOPING AND DEVELOPED COUNTRIES

LA SAGESSE D'ANI. TEXTE, TRADUCTION ET COMMENTAIRE / Suys, E – (Analecta Orientalia. v. 11). Roma. 1935. BNE-459 1 – 9 – ne IDC [470]

LA SAGESSE DE SHAKESPEARE ET DE GOETHE / Berthelot, Rene – 4eme ed.Paris: Gallimard, (1930). 239p. With: Shakespeare Criticism by C.N. Menon.1 reel. 1186 – 1 – us U.W. Library [420]

SAGGI CRITICI / Amoretti, Giovanni Vittorio – (In Italian or German. Includes bibliographical references and index) – Torino: Bottega d'Erasmo, 1962 – 1 – us U.W. Library [400]

SAGGI DI LETTERATURA TEDESCA / Vincenti, Leonello – (Includes bibliographical references) – Milano: R Ricciardi, 1953 – 1 – us U.W. Library [430]

SAGGI SCIENTIFICI E LETTERARI DELL' ACCADEMIA DI PADOVA / Accademia Patavina di Scienze, Lettere ed Arti – Padova, 1786-1794 – 3 – us Readex [500]

SAGGIO CRITICO DI DIRITTO INTERNAZIONALE "CICLO D'EVOLUZIONE" / Constanza, M – Roma, Torino, 1925 – 2mf – 1 – ILM-3655/1 – ne IDC [327]

SAGGIO PER BEN SONARE IL FLAUTO TRAVERSO / Lorenzoni, A – 1779 – 9 – us Sibley [780]

SAGGIO PITTORICO ED ANALISI DELLE PITTURE PIU FAMOSE ESISTENTI IN ROMA... / Prunetti, M A – Roma, 1818 – 3mf – ne IDC [700]

SAGGIO SOPRA LE LEGGI DEL CONTRAPPUNTO.. / Riccati, Giordano – 1762 – 2 – us Sibley [780]

SAGGIO SUL CATTOLICESIMO, IL LIBERALISMO E IL SOCIALISMO / Donoso Cortes, Juan Francisco – Milan: Rusconi Editore, 1972 – 1 – sp Bibl Santa Ana [320]

SAGGIO SUL PROTETTORATO / Fedozzi, P – Venezia, 1897 – 2mf – 1 – ILM-1964/1 – ne IDC [327]

Saggione, G *see* SONGS IN THE NEW OPERA CALL'D THE TEMPLE OF LOVE

Sagiv, Michael *see* LEFT VENTRICULAR FUNCTION DURING ISOMETRIC EXERCISE

SAGN OG FORTAELLINGER FRA ANGMAGSALIK / Holm, G – BN 254 2. 1888 – 8 – ne IDC [999]

SAGNER – v1-3. 1924-31 – 1 – us I.U. Libraries [390]

SAGO PALM – 1983 – 91p – it F.A.O. [634]

SAGOR I URVAL – v1-2. 1917-20 – 1 – us I.U. Libraries [390]

SAGOR, REFERATSAMLING / Hackmann, Oskar – v1-2. 1917-20 – 1 – us I.U. Libraries [390]

Sagoskin, L *see* UEBER DIE REISE UND ENTDECKUNGEN DES LIEUTENANT. IM RUSSISCHEN AMERIKA

Sagra, R de la *see*
– HISTOIRE PHYSIQUE ET POLITIQUE DE L'ILE DE CUBA
– HISTOIRE PHYSIQUE, POLITIQUE ET NATURELLE DE L'ILE DE CUBA

SAGRADA BIBLIA : VERSION CASTELLANA DEL ILMO. SR. FELIX TORRES AMAT... / ed by Bayle, Constantino – Madrid: Razon y Fe, 1926 – 1 – sp Bibl Santa Ana [240]

SAGRADAS DECLAMACIONES FUNEBRES PANEQYRICAS, EN LAS SOLEMNES EXEQUIAS...A LOS GLORIOSAS E INMORTALES... / Luna, Juan & Luna, Francisco – 1 – sp Bibl Santa Ana [946]

Sagredo, D *see* MEDIDAS DEL ROMANO, NECESARIAS A LOS OFICIALES QUE QUIEREN SEGUIR LAS FORMACIONES...

SAGSET JOURNAL / ed by Society for Academic Gaming and Stimulation in Education and Training – v.5-8. 1975-78 – 1 – us UMI [370]

LE SAGUENAY / Boucher de la Bruere, Pierre – St. Hyacinthe: Des presses du Courrier de St. Hyacinthe, 1880. 03712. (Pre-1900 Canadiana) – 9 – cn C.I.H.M. [971]

LE SAGUENAY – Chicoutimi, Canada. 19 jun 1963-v1 n7. 21 jul 1963 – 1r – 1 – Can$25.00 – cn Can Microfilming [072]

LE SAGUENAY – Chicoutimi, Canada. 5 sep 1882-14 aut 1883 – 1r – 1 – Can$25.00 – cn Can Microfilming [072]

LE SAGUENAY ET LA VALLEE DU LAC SAINT-JEAN: ETUDE HISTORIQUE, GEOGRAPHIQUE, INDUSTRIELLE ET AGRICOLE / Buies, Arthur – Quebec: A. Cote, 1880. 00360. (Pre-1900 Canadiana) – 9 – cn C.I.H.M. [971]

THE SAGUENAY POST – Jonquiere. 22 oct 1948-v1 n9. 30 dec 1948 – 1r – 1 – Can$40.00 – cn Can Microfilming [072]
SAGUENAYENSIA : REVUE DE LA STE HISTORIQUE DU SAGUENAY – Chicoutimi, jan/fev 1959-avr/jun 1990 – 3r – 1 – Can$70.00 – cn Can Microfilming [072]
SAHAFA – Khartoum, Sudan. 1972- – 1 – us Res Libr [072]
SAHAGUN / Chavero, Alfredo – 1877 – 9 – 1.50f – sp Bibl Santa Ana [830]
SAHAJIYA SAHITYA / Bose, Manindra Mohan – Calcutta: Calcutta University Press, 1932 – us Res Libr [950]
EN SAHARA A TRAVERS LE PAYS DES MAURES NOMADES / Donnet, Gaston – Paris: H May, [1901] – 1 – us Res Libr [910]
SAHARA AND SUDAN / Nachtigal, Gustave – Berlin. 1879. BA-170 2 – 8 – ne IDC [910]
EL SAHARA ESPANOL : ESTUDIO GEOLOGICO, GEOGRAFICO Y BOTANICO POR EDUARDO HERNANDEZ PACHECO, FRANCISCO HERNANDEZ PACHECO, MANUEL ALIA MEDINA, CARLOS VIDAL BOX Y EMILIO GRINEA LOPEZ / Hernandez Pacheco, E et al – Madrid: Instituto de Estudios Africanos, 1949 – 1 – sp Bibl Santa Ana [946]
SAHARA ET SOUDAN / Nachtigal, Gustave – Paris. 1881 – 9 – 15.00 – fr Orientalistes [960]
LE SAHARA; SES OASIS / Lehuraux, Leon Joseph – Alger. 1934 – 1 – us Res Libr [960]
Sahara, Tamotsu *see* LAND CLASSIFICATION PROGRAM PROPOSAL FOR THE TTPI
SAHARAN PEOPLES SUPPORT COMMITTEE (SPSC) – Ada. 38 docs. 1980-1990 – 7mf – 9 – ne IDC [320]
SAHAYAK PATRIKA – (Lacking: 7 May 1924) – 28 Mar 1923-25 Jun 1924 – 1r – 1 – ATLA S0714B – us A.T.L.A. [073]
SAHEL : DOCUMENTS AND DISSERTATIONS / ed by Lauer, Joseph – (1000 documents from Michigan University's Sahel Documentation Center and UMI's dissertation database) – 2134mf – 9 – $5940.00 – us UMI [960]
SAHEL : ECOLOGICAL APPROACHES TO LAND USE – 1975 – 99p – 9 – 92-3-101237-1 – fr UNESCO [333]
SAHIWAL CATTLE = LE BETAIL SAHIWAL. UNE EVALUATION DE SA CONTRIBUTION POTENTIELLE A LA PRODUCTION DE LAIT ET DE VIANDE BOVINE EN AFRIQUE : AN EVALUATION OF THEIR POTENTIAL CONTRIBUTION TO MILK AND BEEF PRODUCTION IN AFRICA / Trail, J C M & Gregory, KE – 1981 – 128p – 9 – $8.00 – 92-9053-127-4 – et ILRI [636]
Sahlu, Marcos *see*
– ILCA IN PRINT
– PRODUCTION AND PROCESSING OF MILK FROM CATTLE IN SUB-SAHARAN AFRICA
Sahn, David E et al *see* METHODS FOR THE EVALUATION OF THE IMPACT OF FOOD AND NUTRITION PROGRAMMES
Sai, F A *see* FRUITS AND VEGETABLES IN WEST AFRICA
Saianov, V *see* ZAMETKI O RUSSKOM FUTURIZME
Said, M *see*
– 101 ONE HUNDRED ONE
– EMPATBELAS BOELAN PENDOEDOEKAN INGGERIS DI INDONESIA
– HUKUM NIKAH, THALAK RUDJU' (N.T.R.) KU M. SA'ID
Said, M. *see* 4 (I.E EMPAT)
Said, Nawir *see* PEMBERONTAKAN SILUNGKANG 1927, SUMATRA BARAT
Said, Titie *see* PERDJUANGAN DAN HATI PEREMPUAN. SE 3830/1. 1962
SAIDISCHE AUSZUEGE AUS DEM 8. BUCHE DER APOSTOLISCHEN KONSTITUTIONEN (T.U.U. 2-26/1B) / Leipoldt, Johannes – Leipzig, 1904 – 1mf – 9 – ne Slangenburg [240]
Saifuddin, Zuhri *see* ULAMA'S CONTRIBUTION TO THE STATE
Saige, Joseph *see*
– CODE NATIONAL, OU MANUEL FRANCAIS A L'USAGE DES 3 ORDRES, ET PRINCIPALEMENT DES DEPUTES AUX PROCHAINS ETATS GENERAUX
– VOYAGE A LA NOUVELLE PHILADELPHIE
SAIGON DAILY NEWS – Saigon, Vietnam. Nov 22 1963-June 14 1969 – 12r – 1 – us L of C Photodup [072]
SAIGON GIAI PHONG – [Saigon]: s.n. jul 1975-jun 1986 (13r); jul-deec 1986 (1r) – 1 – us Res Libr [072]
THE SAIGON POST – Saigon, dec 23 1963-apr 24 1975 – 34r – 1 – us Res Libr [072]
SAIGON-SONG – South Vietnam. 1964-1967 – 1 – us UMI [072]
SAIKO SHIKIKAN. KETERANGAN SAIKOO SIKIKAN. TENTANG HAL TOEROET MENGAMBIL BAHAGIAN DALAM PEMERINTAHAN NEGERI DAN PENDJELASAN PEMERINTAH / Java – Djakarta, Djawa-Gunseikanbu (2603). 14p – 86mf – 9 – ne IDC [950]
SAIL – v1- 1970- 1; v6- 5,6; v7- 9 – us UMI [790]
SAILING ON THE GREAT LAKES AND RIVERS OF AMERICA: EMBRACING A DESCRIPTION OF LAKES ERIE, HURON, MICHIGAN & SUPERIOR, AND RIVERS ST MARY, ST CLAIR, DETROIT, NIAGARA & ST LAWRENCE; ALSO, THE COPPER AND SILVER REGION OF LAKE SUPERIOR / Disturnell, John – Philadelphia: J. Disturnell, 1874. 02720. (Pre-1900 Canadiana) – 9 – cn C.I.H.M. [910]
A SAILOR'S LIFE UNDER FOUR SOVEREIGNS / Keppel, Henry – 3v. 1899 – 9 – 60.00 – uk Libr Preservation [920]
SAILOR'S MAGAZINE – v1-105. 1828-1933 (complete) – 17r – 1 – ATLA S0864 – us A.T.L.A. [073]
SAILOR'S MAGAZINE AND NAVAL JOURNAL – New York. 1832-33, 1835 – 1 – 30.75 – us A.B.H.S. [073]
THE SAILOR'S WORD-BOOK : AN ALPHABETICAL DIGEST OF NAUTICAL TERMS AS WELL AS ARCHAISMS OF EARLY VOYAGERS / Smyth, William Henry; ed by Belcher, E – 1867 – 9 – uk Libr Preservation [623]
SAILS, STEAM AND OARS : PLANS AND DRAWINGS OF DUTCH SHIPS AND VESSELS, C. 1650-1960 – 1994. Subsets avail – ca 9,600mf – 9 – Dfl10,500.00 – ne MMF Publ [623]
LA SAINCTE LIBERTE DES ENFANS DE DIEU / Meynier, B – Rouen, 1656 – 2mf – 9 – CA-141/1 – ne IDC [240]
Sainliens, Cl. de *see* DE PRONUNTIATIONE LINGUAE GALLICAE LIBRI DUO
Sainson, Camille *see* HISTOIRE PARTICULIERE DU NAN-TCHAO
THE SAINT = (IL SANTO) / Fogazzaro, Antonio – New York: G.P. Putnam, 1906 – 2mf – us A.T.L.A. [240]
SAINT AGOBARD, ARCHEVEQUE DE LYON : SA VIE ET SES ECRITS / Chevallard, P – Lyon: P N Josserand, 1869 – 2mf – 9 – 0-8370-6893-2 – 1986-0893 – us A.T.L.A. [920]
St Albans Abbey *see*
– CHRONIA MONASTEREII S ALBANI (RS28)
– REGISTRA QUORUNDAM ABBATUM MONASTERII S. ALBANI QUI SAEC. 15 FLORUERE (JOH. WETHAMSTEDE, WILL. ALBON, ETC.) (CHRONIA..6)
ST. ALBANS ADVISER – St. Albans, Vt. 1808$1809; yChamplain Reporter, St. Albans, 1809-10; Franklin County Advertiser, St. Albans, 1810; Bennington News-Letter, Bennington, Vt., 1811-15. Sold as one unit – 3 – us Readex [071]
ST. ALBANS AND HARPENDEN REVIEW *see* REVIEW (ST. ST ALBANS)
ST ALBANS TIMES *see* HERTS ADVERTISER
SAINT ALBERT LE GRAND / Garreau, Albert – Paris, 1932; Madrid: Razon y Fe, 1933 – 1 – sp Bibl Santa Ana [240]
ST. ALDEMAR COMMANDERY NO. 18 – KNIGHTS TEMPLAR STATIONED AT ST LOUIS / Richart, WP – 1 Jan 1894-31 Dec 1903. 1903. Missouri Reel 28. (The Cox Library Collection) – 5 – us Americana [978]
ST. ALDHELM : HIS LIFE AND TIMES : LECTURES DELIVERED IN THE CATHEDRAL CHURCH OF BRISTOL, LENT, 1902 / Browne, G F – London: S.P.C.K., 1903 – 1mf – us A.T.L.A. [240]
Saint Alphonsus Catholic Church (Peru, Ohio) *see* RECORDS
SAINT ALPHONSUS CATHOLIC CHURCH RECORDS – Peru. Ohio. 1834-1984 – 1 reel – 1 – us Archival [240]
Saint Amand, Adele de *see*
– PROCLAMATION AUX FEMMES SUR LA NECESSITE DE FONDER UNE SOCIETE DES DROITS DE LA FEMME
– PROCLAMATIONS AUX FEMMES SUR LA NECESSITE DES DROITS DE LA FEMME
Saint Amand, Jean F B de *see*
– DESCRIPTION ABREGEE DU DEPARTEMENT DE LOT ET GARONNE
– FLORE AGENAISE
St. Amant, C. Penrose *see* A SHORT HISTORY OF LOUISIANA BAPTISTS
SAINT AMBROISE / ed by Labriolle, Pierre de – Paris: Bloud, 1908 – 1mf – us A.T.L.A. [240]
ST. AMBROSE / Broglie, Albert, Duc de – London: Duckworth; New York: Bezinger, 1899 – 1mf – us A.T.L.A. [240]
THE SAINT AND HIS SAVIOUR : THE PROGRESS OF THE SOUL IN THE KNOWLEDGE OF JESUS / Spurgeon, Charles Haddon – New York: Sheldon, Blakeman, 1857 – 1mf – 9 – 0-8370-9827-0 – 1986-3827 – us A.T.L.A. [240]
SAINT ANDREW: THE DISCIPLE, THE MISSIONARY, THE PATRON SAINT / Ross, Peter – New York: Scottish American, 1886. 1 fiche – 9 – us A.T.L.A. [240]
ST. ANDREWS BEACON – Canada. The Beacon. -w. Aug 1914-Aug 1919. Imperfect. 2 reels – 1 – uk British Libr Newspaper [072]
SAINT ANDREWS EAST NEWS – St-Andrews East (Argenteuil), Canada. v1 n3. jan 1957-v1 n8. jun 1957 (incomplete) – 1r – 1 – Can$40.00 – cn Can Microfilming [072]
ST. ANDREW'S GAZETTE – Anstruther, Scotland, UK. 24 Jul 1914-19 Feb 1915. -w – 1 – uk British Libr Newspaper [072]
ST. ANDREW'S GAZETTE – Cupar, Scotland, UK. 17 Jul 1869-30 Dec 1871; 1872-24 Feb 1883.-w. 5 reels – 1 – uk British Libr Newspaper [072]
ST. ANDREWS TIMES – Scotland, UK. 15 Dec 1937-1938; 1939-6 Mar 1940. -w. 5 reels – 1 – uk British Libr Newspaper [072]
ST. ANSELM OF CANTERBURY : A CHAPTER IN THE HISTORY OF RELIGION / Rigg, J M – London: Methuen, 1896 – 1mf – us A.T.L.A. [240]
ST. ANSELME DE CANTORBERY : TABLEAU DE LA VIE MONASTIQUE ET DE LA LUTTE DU POUVOIR SPIRITUEL AVEC LE POUVOIR TEMPOREL AU ONZIEME SIECLE / Remusat, Charles de – Paris: Didier, 1868 – 2mf – us A.T.L.A. [240]
SAINT ANTHONY OF PADUA ROMAN CATHOLIC CHURCH : MARRIAGE RECORD BOOK – Cleveland, OH, 1887-1912 – 1r – 1 – us I.H.R.C. [920]
ST. ANTHONY'S CANADIAN MESSENGER – (Other lang. ed: Le Messager de Saint-Antoine) – Chicoutimi [Quebec]: Published under the patronage of His Grace The Bishop of Chicoutimi, [1894?-189- or 19–] – 9 – cn C.I.H.M. [240]
ST. ANTHONY'S CANADIAN MESSENGERS *see* LE MESSAGER DE SAINT-ANTOINE
St. Anthony's Church (Milan, Ohio) *see* RECORDS
ST. ANTHONY'S HIGH SCHOOL YEARBOOK – Anthonian, Long Beach, CA. 1942-93 – 18r – 1 – $900.00 – R60015 – us Library Micro [370]
ST. ARNAUD BOUROUGH RATES – 1863-1950 – 5r – 1 – at Corangamite [910]
ST. ARNAUD MERCURY – 1864. SAM AA – 1r – 1 – at Corangamite [072]
ST. ARNAUD MERCURY – 1871-1876. SAM A-C – 3r – 1 – at Corangamite [072]
ST. ARNAUD MERCURY – 1877-1957 – 76r – 1 – at Corangamite [072]
ST. ARNAUD TOWN RATES – 1950-1993 – 6r – 1,5 – at Corangamite [910]
SAINT ASELLUS: TRANSLATION DE SES RELIQUES DAN LA CHAPELIE DU COLLEGE JOLIETTE, LE 3 NOVEMBRE 1892: SERMON PRONONCE A CETTE OCCASION / Corcoran, A – par le R. P. A. Corcoran. Joliette Quebec: Impr. de l'Etudiant et du Couvent, 1892. 00235. (Pre-1900 Canadiana) – 9 – cn C.I.H.M. [971]
St Aubin, Emmanuel Blain de *see* QUELQUES MOTS SUR LA LITTERATURE CANADIENNE-FRANCAISE
ST. AUGUSTIN / Bertrand, Louis Jacques – London: Constable, 1914 – 1mf – us A.T.L.A. [240]
SAINT AUGUSTIN / Bertrand, Louis Jacques – Trans. by Vincent O'Sullivan. London: Constable and Co., Ltd., 1914. viii,396p – 1 – us U.W. Library [920]
SAINT AUGUSTIN ET LA FIN DE LA CULTURE ANTIQUE / Marrou, H -I – Paris, 1958 – 15mf – 8 – ne Slangenburg [240]
SAINT AUGUSTIN ET LE NEO-PLATONISME / Grandgeorge, L – Paris, 1896 – 3mf – 8 – ne Slangenburg [240]
SAINT AUGUSTIN, MELANCHTHON, NEANDER : THREE BIOGRAPHIES / Schaff, Philip – (Includes bibliographical references) – New York: Funk & Wagnalls, 1886, c1885 – 1mf – 9 – 0-8370-9818-1 – 1986-3818 – us A.T.L.A. [920]
ST. AUGUSTINE : ASPECTS OF HIS LIFE AND THOUGHT / Montgomery W – London; New York: Hodder and Stoughton, 1914 – 1mf – us A.T.L.A. [240]
SAINT AUGUSTINE / Cutts, Edward L – London: S.P.C.K., [1909?] (The Fathers for English readers) – 1mf – us A.T.L.A. [920]
ST. AUGUSTINE EXAMINER – St. Augustine. Fl. Oct. 1859-June 1861; Sept. 1866-May 1874 – 1 – us P.K. Yonge [071]
SAINT AUGUSTINE OF CANTERBURY / Howorth, Henry H – New York: E.P. Dutton, 1913 – 2mf – us A.T.L.A. [240]
ST. AUGUSTINE, THE DIVINATION OF DEMONS AND CARE FOR THE DEAD / Antwerp, E I Van – Washington D.C., 1955 Nr. 86 – 2mf – 8 – ne Slangenburg [240]
ST. AUSTELL ADVERTISER – Camborne, England. 19 Oct 1973-22 Nov 1974. -w. 1/2 reel – 1 – uk British Libr Newspaper [072]
ST. AUSTELL SHOPPER – Falmouth, England. 1985-86. -w. 2 reels – 1 – uk British Libr Newspaper [072]
ST. BASIL AND HIS RULE : A STUDY IN EARLY MONASTICISM / Morison & E F – London; New York: Oxford University Press, 1912 (The S. Deiniol's series; 3) – 1mf – us A.T.L.A. [240]
ST. BASIL THE GREAT / Smith, Richard Travers – 1879 – 1 – us A.T.L.A. [240]
SAINT BERIN, THE APOSTLE OF WESSEX: THE HISTORY, LEGENDS AND TRADITIONS OF THE BEGINNING OF THE WEST-SAXON CHURCH / Field, John Edward – London: Society for Promoting Christian Knowledge; New York; E. & J.B. Young and Company, 1902. xxx,248p – 1 – us U.W. Library [240]
ST. BIRGITTA / Hammerich, Frederik – 1872 – 1 – us A.T.L.A. [240]
ST. BONIFACE LA LIBERTE – St Boniface, Manitoba, CN. 1981- – 2r per yr – 1 – Can$57.00r – cn Commonwealth Micro [072]
ST. CATHARINES CONSTITUTIONAL – St Catharines, Canada. 1855-60; 1862-71 – 5r – 1 – $325.00 – cn Library Assoc [971]
ST. CATHARINES EVENING JOURNAL – St Catharines, Canada. 1862-73 – 10r – 1 – $650.00 – cn Library Assoc [971]
ST. CATHARINES JOURNAL – St Catharines, Canada. 1835-61 – 9r – 1 – $585.00 – cn Library Assoc [971]
SAINT CATHERINE OF SIENNA AS SEEN IN HER LETTERS / Catherine of Sienna – Trans. and ed. with introd. by Vida D. Scudder. 2nd ed.London: J.M. Dent; New York: E.P. Dutton, 1906. x/352p – 1 – us U.W. Library [920]
THE ST CHARLES – Camden. N.J. 1935 – 1 – us UMI [071]
St. Christopher's Mission to the Navajo *see* NEWSLETTER
ST. CLAIR – East St. Louis. IL. 1889-1964.Also, Madison County Evening and Sunday Journal – 1 – us UMI [071]
St Clair *see* BIOGRAPHICAL SKETCHES OF THE LEADING MEN OF CHICAGO
St Clair, Arthur *see* PAPERS
St Clair Drake *see* [COLLECTION OF AFRICANA]
ST CLAIR DRAKE COLLECTION OF AFRICANA *see*
– BANTU MIRROR
– BARAZA
St Clair, George *see* MYTHS OF GREECE EXPLAINED AND DATED
ST. CLARENS REVIEW – Toronto?: Publ by the E.L. of C.E. of St. Clarens Avenue Methodist Church, [188-?-189- or 19– – 9 – cn C.I.H.M. [240]
ST. CROIX COURIER – St Stephen, Canada. 1865-73 – 3r – 1 – $204.00 – cn Library Assoc [971]
St Croix, F W de *see*
– THE FULANI OF NORTHERN NIGERIA
SAINT CROIX REVIEW – (See also: Religion and Society) – v7- 1974- 1,5,6; v9- 9 – us UMI [240]
SAINT DOMINIC / Guiraud, Jean – London: Duckworth; New York: Benziger Bros., 1901 (The Saints) – 1mf – us A.T.L.A. [240]

LE SAINT DU PEUPLE ANTONIE DE PADOUE / Fachenetti, Cesar – Paris, 1931; Madrid: Razon y Fe, 1933 – 1 – sp Bibl Santa Ana [240]

SAINT EDMUND, KING AND MARTYR : A HISTORY OF HIS LIFE AND TIMES, WITH AN ACCOUNT OF THE TRANSLATIONS OF HIS INCORRUPT BODY, ETC. / Mackinlay, J B – London: Art and Book Co.; New York: Benziger Bros., 1893 – 2mf – us A.T.L.A. [240]

ST. EDWARD ADVANCE – St. Edward, NE. -w. Jan 1908-Dec 1915; Jan 1918 to date – 1 – us NE Hist [071]

ST. EDWARD SUN – St. Edward, NE. -w. Oct-Dec 1895; Feb 1896; Apr 1896; May 1896-Mar 1898; Jul-Oct 1899; May 1900-Dec 1916 – 1 – us NE Hist [071]

ST. ETIENNE ET SON SANCTUAIRE A JERUSALEM / Lagrange, Marie Joseph – Paris, 1894 – 4mf – 8 – ne Slangenburg [240]

ST EUSTATIUS GAZETTE – St Eustatius. -w. 19 June 1790; 17 Aug 1792; 5 July 1793; 17 Oct 1794. 3 ft – 1 – uk British Libr Newspaper [072]

Saint Felix Mauremont, A J M *see* ARCHITECTURE RURALE THEORIQUE ET PRATIQUE.

ST. FFRANCIS COURIER *see* SHERBROOKE GAZETTE

St Francis' Boys Home. Kansas *see* DIRECTORS' MINUTES OF MEETINGS

St. Francis College. Richmond, Canada *see* THE ECHO

SAINT FRANCIS COURIER AND SHERBROOKE GAZETTE – Stanstead, Canada. v2 n16. 18 dec 1832-v3 n45. 4 jun 1835 – 1r – 1 – Can$25.00 – cn Can Microfilming [072]

THE SAINT FRANCIS TELEGRAPH AND COMMERCIAL ADVERTISER – Sherbrooke, Canada. v1 n44. 12 nov 1851 – 1r – 1 – Can$25.00 – cn Can Microfilming [072]

ST. FRANCOIS COUNTY JOURNAL – Flat River. Mo. 1935-1940; 1961- – 1 – us UMI [071]

SAINT FRANCOIS D'ASSISE / Ghyvelde, Frederic de – Montreal, 1913. SEM105P535 – 6mf – 9 – Can$13.50 – cn Bibl Nat [240]

SAINT FRANCOIS D'ASSISE / Ghyvelde, Frederic de – Montreal, 1946. SEM105P537 – 3mf – 9 – Can$6.75 – cn Bibl Nat [240]

SAINT GABRIEL JOURNAL – St-Gabriel-de-Brandon, Canada. v1 n29. 4 sep 1954-v2 n12. 18 mai 1955 (incomplete) – 1r – 1 – Can$25.00 – cn Can Microfilming [073]

ST. GEORGE AND SUTHERLAND LEADER (HURSTVILLE) – 1962-1995 – 110r – 1 – at Pascoe [072]

ST. GEORGE LEADER (SUTHERLAND) – 1960-1995 – 122r – 1 – at Pascoe [072]

ST. GEORGE'S CHURCH PARISH MAGAZINE *see* ST. GEORGE'S PARISH MAGAZINE

ST. GEORGE'S HOSPITAL, HYDE PARK CORNER. MINUTES OF THE BOARD OF GOVERNORS – 1733-1888. 40 reels with printed guide – £1,800.00 – uk World [610]

ST. GEORGE'S PARISH JOURNAL – (Cont: St. George's Parish Magazine. Cont by: St. George's Parish Magazine) – Toronto?: s.n., 1884?-188- or 189- – 9 – cn C.I.H.M. [240]

ST. GEORGE'S PARISH JOURNAL *see*
– ST. GEORGE'S PARISH MAGAZINE

ST. GEORGE'S PARISH MAGAZINE – (Cont: Parish Church Work. Cont by: St. George's Parish Journal) – Toronto?: s.n., 1883 – 9 – cn C.I.H.M. [240]

ST. GEORGE'S PARISH MAGAZINE – (Cont: St. George's Parish Journal. Cont by: St. George's Church Parish Magazine) – Toronto?: s.n., 188- or 189-19– – 9 – cn C.I.H.M. [240]

ST. GEORGE'S PARISH MAGAZINE *see*
– PARISH CHURCH WORK
– ST. GEORGE'S PARISH JOURNAL

ST. GILBERT OF SEMPRINGHAM AND THE GILBERTINES. A HISTORY OF THE ONLY ENGLISH MONASTIC ORDER / Graham, Rose – H-1233 1901 – 8 – ne IDC [240]

SAINT GREGOIRE DE NAZIANZE : ARCHEVEQUE DE CONSTANTINOPLE ET DOCTEUR DE L'EGLISE : SA VIE, SES OEUVRES ET SON EPOQUE / Benoit, Alphonse – Paris: Poussielgue, 1884 – 2mf – us A.T.L.A. [240]

SAINT GREGOIRE LE GRAND : METHODE SPIRITUELLE TIREE DE SES ECRITS / Bouchage, F – Paris, 1930 – 8mf – 8 – ne Slangenburg [240]

SAINT GREGORY THE GREAT / Howorth, Henry H – London: J. Murray, 1912 – 1mf – us A.T.L.A. [240]

ST. HELENA : A GUIDE TO THE MANUSCRIPT SOURCES FOR THE HISTORY OF... / Smith, Brian S – 1mf – 9 – uk Microform Academic [960]

ST. HELENA CHRONICLE – Jamestown, St Helena. -w. 27 March 1852-19 March 1853. 24 ft – 1 – uk British Libr Newspaper [072]

SAINT HELENA GOVERNMENT GAZETTE – 1948-68 – 4r – 1 – us Ross [324]

ST. HELENA GUARDIAN – Jamestown, St. Helena. 2 May 1861-24 Oct 1866; 4 Jan-20 Dec 1883; 1 Jan 1885-30 Dec 1886; 24 Mar 1887-25 Dec 1912 (1887-1912 imperfect).-w. 9mqn reels – 1 – uk British Libr Newspaper [072]

ST. HELENA HERALD – St Helena. -w. 17 Feb 1853-5 Feb 1857; 11 Feb 1858-2 Feb 1860. 1 1 2 reels – 1 – uk British Libr Newspaper [072]

ST. HELENA STAR – St Helena, CA. 1874-1911, 1913- – 59+ r – 1 BC02748 – $2,950.00 ($50.00y) – us Library Micro [071]

ST. HELENS CHRONICLE – St. Helens, OR. -sw,-w. 5 Aug 1936-27 Jul 1968. 16 rolls – 1 – us U.O. Library [071]

ST. HELENS MIST – St. Helens, OR. -w. 1913-33 – 1 – 257.00 – us Oregon Hist [071]

ST. HELENS MIST – St. Helens, OR. -w. 2 Jan 1913-6 Dec 1929. 9 rolls. Set incl. Oregon Mist (St. Helens) – 1 – us U.O. Library [071]

ST. HELEN'S NEWSPAPER AND ADVERTISER – England.1875. -w. 1 reel – 1 – uk British Libr Newspaper [072]

ST. HELENS SENTINEL – St. Helens, OR. -w. 4 Mar 1926-30 Mar 1933. 2 rolls – 1 – us U.O. Library [071]

ST. HELENS SENTINEL MIST – St. Helens, OR. -sw. 2 Jan 1953-27 Jun 1968. 14 rolls – 1 – us U.O. Library [071]

St Hilaire, Michel *see* REPONSE A UN SOPHISTE AU SUJET DE LA QUESTION UNIVERSITAIRE A MONTREAL

ST. HIPPOLYTUS AND THE CHURCH OF ROME IN THE EARLIER PART OF THE THIRD CENTURY : FROM THE NEWLY DISCOVERED "REFUTATION OF ALL HERESIES" / Wordsworth, Christopher – London: Rivingtons, 1880 – 1mf – us A.T.L.A. [240]

SAINT HUBERT SOCIAL NEWS AND LOCAL NEWS = BULLETIN DE NOUVELLES LOCALES ET SOCIALES DE SAINT HUBERT – St-Hubert, Canada. v2 n8. 2 avr 1956-v2 n11. 2 jun 1956 – 1r – 1 – Can$25.00 – cn Can Microfilming [072]

ST. HUGH OF LINCOLN, A BIOGRAPHY.. / Clayton, Joseph – London: Burns, Oates & Washbourne Ltd, 1931. xxi,237,(1) p – 1 – us U.W. Library [240]

SAINT HYACINTHE ILLUSTRE – St-Hyacinthe, Canada. 20 dec 1886 – 1r – 1 – Can$25.00 – cn Can Microfilming [072]

Saint Hyacinthe Quebec *see* CHARTE ET REGLEMENTS DE LA CITE.

ST. IRVYNE, OR THE ROSICRUCIAN / Shelley, Percy Bysshe – London: Printed for J.J. Stockdale, 1811 – 1 roll – 1 – 1-55879-675-4 – uk Libr Preservation [830]

SAINT ISIDORE DE SEVILLE : SON ROLE DANS L'HISTOIRE DU DROIT CANONIQUE / Sejourne, P – Paris, 1929 – 9mf – 9 – ne Slangenburg [240]

ST. IVES : BEING THE ADVENTURES OF A FRENCH PRISONER IN ENGLAND / Stevenson, Robert Louis – New York: Charles Scribner's Sons, 1897 – 1 roll – 1 – 1-55879-812-9 – uk Libr Preservation [830]

ST IVES AND HUNTINGDON TOWN CRIER – (Also known as: Huntingdon Tonn Crier) – Jan 10 1987-Jun 1991; Jul-Dec 1991 (and c/p of St Neots To); 1992; Jan 2-Mar 27, Apr 3-Jun 26 1993; Jul 1993-96 – 42 1/2r – 9 – uk British Libr Newspaper [072]

ST. JAGO DE LA VEGA GAZETTE – Spanish Town. Jamaica. -w. 30 Mar, 13 Jul, 5 Oct 1839-18 Apr 1840. (22 ft) – 1 – uk British Libr Newspaper [072]

SAINT JAMES IN SPAIN / Kendrick, T D – London, 1960 – Dfl19.00 – ne Slangenburg [240]

ST. JAMES'S CHRONICLE – London. -tw. Jan 1801-Jul 1866. 70 reels. Wanting Jan-Jun 1816 – 1 – uk British Libr Newspaper [072]

ST. JAMES'S EVENING POST – Dublin, Ireland. -d. 3 July 1719; 5 Jan 1723; 3 June, 15, 22 July 1724; 21 May, 6 Oct 1725. 10 ft – 1 – uk British Libr Newspaper [072]

ST. JAMES'S GAZETTE – London. 31 May 1880-13 March 1905.-d. 107 reels – 1 – uk British Libr Newspaper [072]

SAINT JEROME / Cutts, Edward L – London: S.P.C.K.; New York: Pott, Young, [1878?] (The Fathers for English readers) – 1mf – us A.T.L.A. [240]

SAINT JEROME / Largent, Augustin – London: Duckworth; New York: Benziger, 1900. (The Saints) – 1mf – us A.T.L.A. [240]

SAINT JEROME / ed by Turmel – Paris: Librairie Bloud, [1906?] – 1mf – us A.T.L.A. [240]

SAINT JOAN: A CHRONICLE PLAY IN SIX SCENES AND AN EPILOGUE / Shaw, Bernard – New York: Brentano's, 1924. lxxxviii,163p – 1 – us U.W. Library [820]

ST. JOHN : THE AUTHOR OF THE FOURTH GOSPEL / Evans, Howard Heber – (Includes an appendix) – London:James Nisbet, 1888 – 1mf – 9 – 0-8370-3079-X – 1985-1079 – us A.T.L.A. [220]

ST. JOHN CANTIUS R.C. CHURCH *see* RECORDS

SAINT JOHN CHRYSOSTOM, HIS LIFE AND TIMES : A SKETCH OF THE CHURCH AND THE EMPIRE IN THE FOURTH CENTURY / Stephens, William Richard Wood – London: J. Murray, 1883 – 1mf – us A.T.L.A. [240]

SAINT JOHN DAILY NEWS – Saint John, Canada. 1839-84 – 57r – 1 – $3,705.00 – cn Library Assoc [971]

ST. JOHN DAILY TELEGRAPH AND MORNING JOURNAL – St. John's, Canada. Daily Telegraph. -d. Feb 1871-March 1913. Lacking Dec 1886-May 1894. 140 1 2 reels – 1 – uk British Libr Newspaper [072]

ST. JOHN DAMASCENE ON HOLY IMAGES (PROS TOUS DIABALLONTAS TAS HAGIAS EIKONAS) : FOLLOWED BY THREE SERMONS ON THE ASSUMPTION (KOIMESIS) / John, of Damascus, Saint – London: Thomas Baker, 1898 – 1mf – us A.T.L.A. [240]

SAINT JOHN GAZETTE – Saint John, Canada. 1784-1807 – 4r – 1 – $260.00 – cn Library Assoc [971]

SAINT JOHN GLOBE – Saint John, Canada. 1862-73 – 11r – 1 – $715.00 – cn Library Assoc [971]

ST John Hope, W H *see* INVENTORIES OF CHRIST CHURCH CANTERBURY

St John, James Augustive *see* FOUR CONQUEST OF ENGLAND

St John, Katherine *see* A CULTURAL AND HISTORICAL STUDY OF SELECTED WOMEN'S DANCE FROM HERAT, AFGANISTAN

THE SAINT JOHN MONTHLY MAGAZINE – Saint John, NB?: s.n., 1836?-188-? – 9 – cn C.I.H.M. [910]

SAINT JOHN MORNING JOURNAL – Saint John, Canada. 1865-69 – 4r – 1 – $260.00 – cn Library Assoc [971]

SAINT JOHN PRICES CURRENT – Saint John, NB: [s.n., 18–?-1968?] ([Saint John, N.B.]: Barnes) – 9 – cn C.I.H.M. [380]

THE ST JOHN RIVER IN MAINE, QUEBEC, AND NEW BRUNSWICK / Bailey, Joseph Whitman – Cambridge, Mass?: 1894. 00811. (Pre-1900 Canadiana) – 9 – cn C.I.H.M. [910]

ST. JOHN TELEGRAPH – St John, Canada. 1862-73 – 14r – 1 – $910.00 – cn Library Assoc [971]

ST. JOHN WEEKLY FREEMAN – Canada. -w. 26 Aug 1864-25 May 1866; 16 Nov 1878-2 Aug 1884. 3 reels – 1 – uk British Libr Newspaper [072]

St. John's Berkeley Parish. South Carolina *see* RECORDS

ST. JOHNS BESTIARY – 13th century. Ms. 61. St. Johns College, Oxford – 14 – uk Microform Academic [025]

SAINT JOHN'S CHRONICLE – (Lacking: 1942. 1944) – v3-9. 1937-49 – 1r – 1 – ATLA S0661 – us A.T.L.A. [073]

ST. JOHN'S CHURCH RECORD AND PARISH NOTES – (Cont: Parish Notes) – [Saint John, N.B.?]: G A Knodell, [1892-1893?] – 9 – cn C.I.H.M. [240]

ST. JOHN'S CHURCH RECORD AND PARISH NOTES *see* PARISH NOTES

ST. JOHN'S COUNTY HERALD – St. Augustine. FL. 1915-16 – 1 – us UMI [071]

ST. JOHN'S COURIER – St John's, Canada. 1862-73 – 5r – 1 – $325.00 – cn Library Assoc [971]

ST. JOHN'S DAILY NEWS – St John's, Canada. 1862-70 – 7r – 1 – $455.00 – cn Library Assoc [971]

ST. JOHN'S DAILY STAR – Canada. -d. Jan 1916-May 1921. 23 reels – 1 – uk British Libr Newspaper [072]

SAINT JOHN'S EDMONTON REPORT – (Cont by: Alberta Report at v7 1979/80. v6 nos 33-34 not available for filming) – Edmonton. v1-6. 1973/74-1978/79 – 9 – Can$73.00y – cn Micromedia [073]

SAINT JOHN'S EDMONTON REPORT *see* ALBERTA REPORT

St. John's Episcopal Church (Napoleon, Ohio) *see* RECORDS

St. John's Evangelical Lutheran Church (Sulphur Springs, Ohio) *see* RECORDS

ST. JOHN'S JOURNAL OF LEGAL COMMENTARY – v1-9. 1985-94 – 9 – $111.00 set – us Hein [340]

ST. JOHN'S LAW REVIEW – (v1-59 1926-85 on reel/mf $535.00. v60-69 1985-95 on mf $180.00) – v1-69. 1926-95 – 5,6,9 – $715.00 set – us Hein [340]

St. John's Lutheran Church, Herington, KS *see* RECORDS

St. John's Lutheran Church, Russell, KS *see* RECORDS

ST. JOHN'S MESSENGER – Toronto: [s.n., 1892?-19–] – 9 – cn C.I.H.M. [240]

THE ST. JOHN'S PARISH RECORD – Port Medway, NS: [s.n., 1873-18–?] (Halifax [N.S.]: T. Chamberlain) – 9 – cn C.I.H.M. [240]

ST. JOHN'S REVIEW – Portland, OR. -w. 11 Nov 1904-7 Oct 1976+. 24 rolls – 1 – us U.O. Library [071]

ST. JOHN'S (SOUTH AFRICA) DIOCESAN RECORDS / United Society for the Propagation of the Gospel. Archives – 19th Century – 1 – uk Microform Academic [025]

ST. JOHN'S TEST OF KNOWING CHRIST, AND BEING BORN OF HIM : A SERMON PREACHED AT ST. PAUL'S CATHEDRAL IN LONDON, OCTOBER 14, 1739... / Wheatly, C – London, 1739 – 1mf – 9 – MP-257/1 – ne IDC [240]

St. John's United Church of Christ (Holgate, Ohio) *see* RECORDS

St. John's United Church of Christ (Milan, Ohio) *see* RECORDS

ST. JOSEPH COUNTY, INDIANA / Howard, T E – Chicago: Lewis Publishing Company, 1907.2v. Indiana Reel 26. (The Cox Library Collection) – 5 – us Americana [978]

ST. JOSEPH IN HOMESPUN / Silliman, Sue I – Three Rivers: Three Rivers Publ. Co., 1931. Michigan Reel 21. (The Cox Library Collection) – 5 – us Americana [978]

St. Joseph Publishing Co *see* THE DAILY NEWS HISTORY OF BUCHANAN COUNTY AND ST JOSEPH

ST. JOSEPH'S BLATT – 1980-91 (complete) – 1r – 1 – ATLA S0920 – us A.T.L.A. [073]

ST. JOSEPHS BLATT – Mount Angel OR. Jan 1 1901-Sep 11 1914 – 1 – us U.O. Library [071]

ST. JOSEPHS BLATT – St. Benedict, OR. -w. 3 Jan 1896-Nov 1974+. 28 rolls. Set incl. St. Josephs Blatt (Mt. Angel) – 1 – us U.O. Library [071]

St Joseph's College *see* STUFF

ST. JOSEPH'S MAGAZINE – v33-69. 1932-68 (complete) – 16r – 1 – ATLA S0911 – us A.T.L.A. [073]

Saint Just, Antoine Louis Leon de *see* EXPRIT DE LA REVOLUTION ET DE LA CONSTITUTION DE FRANCE

SAINT KAVIN: A BALLAD / Carman, Bliss – Cambridge, Mass.: J. Wilson, 1894. 00492. (Pre-1900 Canadiana) – 9 – cn C.I.H.M. [810]

ST. KITTS DAILY EXPRESS – Basseterre, St. Kitts. -d. 23 Jan-2 Nov 1906; 8 June 1909-31 July, 29 Aug, 5-11 Sept 1914; 4 Feb-17 March 1915. Imperfect. 4 reels – 1 – uk British Libr Newspaper [072]

ST. KITTS-NEVIS DAILY BULLETIN – Basseterre, St Kitts-Nevis. 3 Jan 1930-30 Jul 1938; 3 Jan 1939-30 Sep 1940; 30 Dec 1940-28 Nov 1951; 2 Jan 1957-23 Dec 1967 – 57r – 1 – uk British Libr Newspaper [073]

SAINT LAURENT NEWS AND CARTIERVILLE COURIER – Ville de St-Laurent, Canada. v4 n13. 29 mar 1956 – 1r – 1 – Can$25.00 – cn Can Microfilming [072]
ST. LAWRENCE BRIDGE AND MANUFACTURING SCHEME: ENGINEER'S REPORT, 18TH JANUARY 1882 / Bateman, F Foster – Montreal. Dawson Bros., 1882. 02969. (Pre-1900 Canadiana) – 9 – cn C.I.H.M. [971]
ST. LAWRENCE CHURCH – Cleveland, OH, 1902-1959 – 1 reel – 1 – us I.H.R.C. [240]
ST. LAWRENCE: OUR COUNTY AND ITS PEOPLE / Curtis, Gates – Syracuse, D. Mason and Co., 1894. New York Reel 33. (The Cox Library Collection) – 5 – us Americana [978]
ST. LAWRENCE PLAIN DEALER – Canton. N.Y. -w. 1864- – 1 – us UMI [071]
ST. LAWRENCE SEAWAY AUTHORITY ACT, REGULATIONS & ST LAWRENCE SEAWAY AUTHORITY HANDBOOK / Canada. Laws, Statutes, etc – (Amendment service. YX76-S2EM. Standing order) – YX76-S2-1-EM – 9 – Can$7.50 – cn Communication [340]
THE SAINT LAWRENCE SUN – (Cont by: The Saint Lawrence Sun/Le Soleil du Saint Laurent 5 avr 1962- 19 dec 1963. Cont by: The Saint Lawrence Sun/Le Soleil 9 jan 1964-28 dec 1977) – Beauharnois, Canada. 11 mai 1955-22 mar 1962 – 19r – 1 – Can$70.00r – cn Can Microfilming [072]
THE SAINT LAWRENCE SUN *see* THE SAINT LAWRENCE SUN
ST. LEON : A TALE OF THE SIXTEENTH CENTURY / Godwin, William – London: Printed for G.G. and J. Robinson, ... R. Noble, printer, ..., 1799 – 2 rolls – 1 – 1-55879-027-6 – uk Libr Preservation [830]
ST. LIN ET SA JOURNEE DU 9 OCTOBRE 1872 / Dion, J O – Montreal: s.n., 1872?. 02181. (Pre-1900 Canadiana) – 9 – cn C.I.H.M. [971]
Saint Lo, Alexis de *see*
– RELATION DU VOYAGE DU CAP VERT
– RELATION DU VOYAGE DU CAP-VERD
SAINT LOUIS – (See also: Saint Louisan) – v9 n8- 1977- – 1,5,6,9 – us UMI [073]
SAINT LOUIS AND THE THIRTEENTH CENTURY / Guizot, Francois – Ed. from Guizot's History of France, with notes, geneal., historical and other Tables by Gustav Masson.Boston: Estes & Lauriat; London: S. Low, Marston, Searle & Rivington, 1881. 123p. Fold. map – 1 – us U.W. Library [940]
ST. LOUIS ARGUS – St. Louis. Mo. june 7, 14; Dec. 13, 1940; July 30, 1948 – 1 – us NY Public [071]
ST. LOUIS BAR JOURNAL – (Updates planned) – v1-32. 1950-87 – 111mf – 9 – $166.00 – LLMC 84-671 – us L.L.M.C. [073]
ST. LOUIS BAR JOURNAL – v1-41. 1950-94 – 9 – $315.00 set – us Hein [340]
ST. LOUIS ES VIDEKE – St. Louis, Mo. 1918-1919, 940, 1950-1956 – 1 – us Res Libr [071]
ST. LOUIS GLOBE-DEMOCRAT – St. Louis. 1 Jan 1888-21 Mar 1898.-d. 123 reels – 1 – uk British Libr Newspaper [071]
ST. LOUIS LAW REVIEW *see* WASHINGTON UNIVERSITY LAW QUARTERLY
St. Louis, Missouri *see* MISCELLANEOUS EARLY NEWSPAPERS
ST. LOUIS POST-DISPATCH – St. Louis. MO. 1874- – 1 – us UMI [071]
ST. LOUIS POST-DISPATCH INDEX – St. Louis. MO. 1979- – 1 – us UMI [071]
ST. LOUIS PRESBYTERIAN – (Presbyterian of Our Union 1860-61. Missouri Presbyterian 1866-70. Old School Presbyterian 1870-74. St Louis Presbyterian and the Memphis Presbyterian 1874-79. St Louis Presbyterian 1879-89, 1894-96. Incomplete file) – 1854-60 – 1 – $600.00 – us Presbyterian [240]
SAINT LOUIS QUARTERLY – Baguio, Philippines. v1-7. 1963-69 – 76mf – 9 – $5.00f – us Ross [370]
ST. LOUIS: THE FOURTH CITY 1764-1909 / Stevens, Walter B – St. Louis: S.J. Clarke Publ. Co., 1909. 3v. Missouri Reel 31. (The Cox Library Collection) – 5 – us Americana [978]
SAINT LOUIS UNIVERSITY LAW JOURNAL – (v1-29 1949-85 on reel $390.00. v30-39 1985-95 on mf $216.00. Title varies: v1 no 1-3 1941-51 as Intramural Law Review) – v1-39. 1949-95 – 5,6,9 – $606.00 set – us Hein [340]
SAINT LOUIS UNIVERSITY PUBLIC LAW REVIEW – (Title varies: v1-5 no 1 1981-85 as Public Law Forum) – v1-14. 1981-95 – 9 – $194.00 set – us Hein [340]
SAINT LOUIS UNIVERSITY RESEARCH JOURNAL – Baguio City, Philippines. v1-4. 1970-73 – 38mf – 9 – $5.00f – us Ross [370]
SAINT LOUISAN – v. 9. 1977 – 1,5,6"9 – us UMI [073]
SAINT LOUISAN *see* SAINT LOUIS
SAINT LUC / Lagrange, Marie Joseph – 1941 – 14mf – 8 – ne Slangenburg [220]
ST LUCIA : ANNUAL STATISTICAL DIGEST 1966-1974 / St Lucia. Development, Planning and Statistics Division – (1972-73 not available. Coll title: Latin American and Caribbean Official Statistical Serials, 1821-1982) – 9mf – 9 – £75.00 – uk Chadwyck [972]
St Lucia. Development, Planning and Statistics Division *see* ST LUCIA
SAINT LUCIA GAZETTE – v125-139. 1956-70 – 13r – 1 – us Ross [324]
ST. LUCIA OBSERVER – (The Observer). Castries. St. Lucia. -w. 11 Jul 1874-25 Dec 1875, 11 Mar-13 May, 7 Oct-16 Dec 1876. (Imperfect). (2 reels) – 1 – uk British Libr Newspaper [072]
St. Lucia. Premier's Office *see* FIVE YEAR DEVELOPMENT, 1966-1970
THE ST LUCIAN – Castries. St. Lucia. -w. 5 Dec 1863-29 Oct 1864, 8 Jul 1865-27 Jan 1866. (Imperfect). (1 reel) – 1 – uk British Libr Newspaper [072]
St. Luke's Episcopal Church (Milan, Ohio) *see* RECORDS
ST. LUKE'S PARISH POST – Halifax [N.S.]: St. Luke's Church Association, [18–1873] – 9 – cn C.I.H.M. [240]
SAINT MAIXENT: SOUVENIRS D'ECOLE MILITAIRE / Des Ecorres, Charles – Preface de Theo-Critt. Paris: Charles Lavauzelie, 1888?. 03019. (Pre-1900 Canadiana) – 9 – cn C.I.H.M. [920]
SAINT MARC / Lagrange, Marie Joseph – 1942 – 12mf – 8 – ne Slangenburg [220]
St. Marcel-les-Chalon, France. (Benedictine priory) *see* CARTULAIRE DU PRIEURE DE SAINT MARCEL-LES-CHALON, PUBLIS D'APRES LES MANUSCRITS DE MARCEL CANAT DE CHIZY PAR PAUL CANAT DE CHIZY
ST. MARK'S CHURCH: AN EXPLANATION AND APPEAL / Garrett, John C – s.l.: s.n., 1896?. 00995. (Pre-1900 Canadiana) – 9 – cn C.I.H.M. [971]
St. Mark's Episcopal Church, Medicine Lodge, KS *see* CHURCH REGISTER
ST. MARK'S EPISCOPAL CHURCH RECORDS – Toledo, Ohio. 1899-1988 – 2r – 1 – us Archival [240]
St. Mark's Episcopal Church (Toledo, Ohio) *see* RECORDS
ST. MARK'S REST : THE HISTORY OF VENICE, WRITTEN WITH THE HELP OF THE FEW TRAVELLERS WHO STILL CARE FOR HER MONUMENTS / Ruskin, John – Orpington, Kent: G. Allen, 1884-89 – 1 roll – 1 – 1-55879-608-8 – uk Libr Preservation [945]
ST. MARTIN DE TOURS / Babut, E C – Paris: H. Champion, [1912?] – 1mf – us A.T.L.A. [240]
SAINT MARTIN DE TOURS / Babut, E C – Paris, 1913 – Dfl25.00 – ne Slangenburg [240]
Saint Martin, Louis Claude de *see*
– LA CROCODILE OU LA GUERRE DU BIEN ET DU MAL ARRIVEE SOUS LE REGNE DE LOUIS XV
– LE CROCODILE OU LA GUERRE DU BIEN ET DU MAL, ARRIVEE SOUS LE REGNE DE LOUIS XV
– ECCE HOMO
– ECLAIR SUR L'ASSOCIATION HUMAINE
– LE NOUVEL HOMME
ST. MARTIN'S EVE / Wood, Ellen – British Fiction Archive: Unit 1 – 9 – uk Bell [830]
ST. MARYLEBONE AND PADDINGTON RECORD – London. -w. 1914-71. (49 reels) – 1 – uk British Libr Newspaper [072]
ST. MARY'S BEACON – Leonardtown. Md. -w. 1936-54 – 1 – us UMI [071]
St. Mary's Cemetery, Geary County, KS *see* CEMETERY CARDS
ST. MARY'S CHURCH BAPTISTS (COBDEN) – 1867-1994 – 4mf – 9 – at Corangamite [240]
St. Mary's College. St. Mary's, Kansas *see* DIARIES AND RECORDS, 1838-1967
ST. MARY'S JOURNAL – (Some issues missing) – Argus, Ontario, CN. 1931-83 – 46r – 1 – cn Commonwealth Micro [072]
ST. MARY'S LAW JOURNAL – v1-25. 1969-94 – 1,5,6 – $630.00 – us Hein [073]
ST. MATHEWS BAPTIST CHURCH. DORCHESTER COUNTY. SOUTH CAROLINA : CHURCH RECORDS – 1961 72 – 1 – 5.00 – us Baptist [240]
ST. MATTHEW: INTRODUCTION, AV, RV, WITH NOTES, INDEX AND MAP / Slater, William Fletcher – New York: Henry Frowde, 1901?.1 fiche – 9 – us A.T.L.A. [240]
ST. MATTHEW'S MESSAGE – London, Ont.: Young People's Society of Christian Endeavor, [1889-19–] – 9 – cn C.I.H.M. [240]
SAINT MATTHEW'S WITNESS TO WORDS AND WORKS OF THE LORD : OR, OUR SAVIOUR'S LIFE AS REVEALED IN THE GOSPEL OF HIS EARLIEST EVANGELIST / Upham, Francis William – NY: Hunt & Eaton; Cincinnati: Cranston & Stowe, 1891 – 1mf – 9 – 0-8370-5601-2 – 1985-3601 – us A.T.L.A. [220]
SAINT MATTHIEU / Lagrange, Marie Joseph – Paris, 1941 – 13mf – 8 – ne Slangenburg [220]
THE SAINT MAURICE VALLEY CHRONICLE – Trois-Rivieres, Canada. v2 n71. 13 fev 1920-v52 n4. 14 mai 1970 – 17r – 1 – Can$70.00r – cn Can Microfilming [072]
ST. NEOTS ADVERTISER – Cambridgeshire. 1966-74 – 19r – 1 – uk Microform Academic [072]
ST. NEOTS ADVERTISER – England.1911. -w. 1/2 reel – 1 – uk British Libr Newspaper [072]
ST. NICHOLAS CHRONICLE – Korea. 1928-1934 – 1 – us UMI [072]
ST. PATRICK APOSTLE OF IRELAND : A MEMOIR OF HIS LIFE AND MISSION / Todd, James Henthorn – Dublin: Hodges, Smith, 1864 – 2mf – us A.T.L.A. [240]
SAINT PATRICK IN HISTORY / Shahan, Thomas Joseph – New York: Longmans, Green, 1905, c1904 – 1mf – 9 – 0-8370-6948-3 – 1986-0948 – us A.T.L.A. [240]
ST. PAUL : EPITRE AUX ROMAINS / Lagrange, Marie Joseph – 1950 – 9mf – 8 – ne Slangenburg [220]
ST. PAUL : LES EPITRES AUX THESSALONICIENS / Rigaux, B – 1956 – 14mf – 8 – ne Slangenburg [240]
ST. PAUL : LES EPITRES PASTORALES / Spicq, C – 1947 – 11mf – 8 – ne Slangenburg [220]
ST. PAUL / Hageman, Samuel Miller – New York: Authors' Publ Co, 1880, c1879 – 1mf – 9 – 0-8370-3447-7 – 1985-1447 – us A.T.L.A. [920]
ST. PAUL : HIS LIFE AND TIMES / Iverach, James – (Includes bibliographical references) – London: James Nisbet, [1890] – 1mf – 9 – 0-8370-3736-0 – 1985-1736 – us A.T.L.A. [920]
ST. PAUL : PREMIERE EPITRE AUX CORINTHIENS (ETB) / Allo, E B – Paris,1956 – Dfl30.00 – ne Slangenburg [220]
ST. PAUL : SECONDE EPITRE AUX CORINTHIENS (ETB) / Allo, E B – Paris, 1937 – Dfl30.00 – ne Slangenburg [220]
SAINT PAUL : EPITRE AUX GALATES / Lagrange, Marie Joseph – 1942 – 5mf – 8 – ne Slangenburg [220]
SAINT PAUL : HIS LIFE, LABOURS, AND EPISTLES / Bungener, Felix – London: Religious Tract Society, 1870 – 1mf – 9 – us A.T.L.A. [240]
SAINT PAUL / Renan, Ernest – (In English) – New York: G W Carleton, 1869 – 1mf – 9 – 0-8370-6314-0 – 1985-0314 – us A.T.L.A. [920]
SAINT PAUL AND HIS MISSIONS / Fouard, Constant – New York: Longmans, Green, 1894 – 9 – us A.T.L.A. [240]
ST PAUL AND PROTESTANTISM : WITH AN ESSAY ON PURITANISM AND THE CHURCH OF ENGLAND; AND LAST ESSAYS ON CHURCH AND RELIGION / Arnold, Matthew – New York: Macmillan, 1883 – 1mf – 9 – 0-8370-9761-4 – 1986-3761 – us A.T.L.A. [240]
SAINT PAUL AND THE ANTE-NICENE CHURCH / Means, Stewart – London: A. & C. Black, 1903. 1 fiche – 9 – us A.T.L.A. [240]
ST. PAUL AND THE ROMAN LAW : AND OTHER STUDIES ON THE ORIGIN OF THE FORM OF DOCTRINE / Ball, William Edmund – Edinburgh: T & T Clark, 1901 – 1mf – 9 – 0-8370-2171-5 – 1985-0171 – us A.T.L.A. [220]
ST. PAUL AND WOMAN / Love, William Deloss – 1894 – 9 – us A.T.L.A. [240]
ST. PAUL AND WOMEN / Schmauk, Theodore Emanuel – (The Lutheran Church Review, v. 18, 1899, p. 505-524) – 9 – us A.T.L.A. [240]
ST. PAUL AT ATHENS / Alexander, William – Edinburgh: Adam and Charles Black, 1865 – 1mf – 9 – 0-8370-2068-9 – 1985-0068 – us A.T.L.A. [220]
ST. PAUL AT ATHENS: SPIRITUAL CHRISTIANITY IN RELATION TO...MODERN THOUGHT / Shakspeare, Charles – New York: Charles Scribner, 1878. 1 fiche – 9 – us A.T.L.A. [240]
ST. PAUL AT ROME / Merivale, Charles – London: S.P.C.K., 1877. 1 fiche – 9 – us A.T.L.A. [240]
ST. PAUL ECHO – St. Paul. Minn. May 8, Nov. 20, Dec. 11, 25, 1926; Jan. 1, 8, 22, 1927 – 1 – us NY Public [071]
SAINT PAUL: FIVE DISCOURSES / Monod, Adolphe – Andover: Warren F. Draper, 1876.1 fiche – 9 – us A.T.L.A. [240]
ST. PAUL: HIS LIFE, HIS WORK AND HIS WRITINGS / Adams, William H Davenport – London: T. Nelson, 1875.1 fiche – 9 – us A.T.L.A. [240]
ST. PAUL IN GREECE / Davies, Gerald Stanley – (Includes index) – London: SPCK, [1876?] – 1mf – 9 – 0-8370-2840-X – 1985-0840 – us A.T.L.A. [910]
ST. PAUL IN ROME: LECTURES / Butler, Clement Moore – Philadelphia: J.B. Lippincott, 1865. 1 fiche – 9 – us A.T.L.A. [240]
St. Paul, Kansas. Osage Mission *see* RECORDS OF BAPTISMS, MARRIAGES, BURIALS
ST. PAUL PAST AND PRESENT / Bliss, Frank C – Historical, financial and commercial. St. Paul: F.C. Bliss Publ. Co., 1888. Minnesota Reel 11. (The Cox Library Collection) – 5 – us Americana [978]
St. Paul Pioneer Press *see* ILLUSTRATED HISTORY OF KANDIYOHI COUNTY
St. Paul. Presbytery (Pres. Ch. in the U.S.A.) *see* MINUTES
ST. PAUL PRESS – St. Paul, NE. -w. May 1888-Jan 1892; Sep 1895; Nov 1895-Aug 1898; Oct-Dec 1898; Feb 1899-Jan 1902 – 1 – us NE Hist [071]
SAINT PAUL, SES MISSIONS = SAINT PAUL AND HIS MISSIONS / Fouard, Constant – (In English) – New York:Longmans, Green, 1894 – 2mf – 9 – 0-8370-3172-9 – 1985-1172 – us A.T.L.A. [240]
St. Paul. Synod. (Pres. Ch. in the U.S.A.) *see* MINUTES
ST. PAUL THE APOSTLE: A BIBLICAL PORTRAIT / Besser, Wilhelm Friedrich – New York: Robert Carter, 1864. 1 fiche – 9 – us A.T.L.A. [240]
ST. PAUL: THE MAN AND HIS WORK / Weinel, Heinrich – New York: G.P. Putnam, 1906. 1 fiche – 9 – us A.T.L.A. [240]
ST. PAUL, THE TRAVELLER AND THE ROMAN CITIZEN / Ramsay, William Mitchell – (Includes indexes) – [2nd ed.] New York: G P Putnam; London: Hodder & Stoughton, 1896 – 1mf – 9 – 0-8370-4837-0 – 1985-2837 – us A.T.L.A. [920]
St. Paul's American Lutheran Church, Galatia, KS *see* RECORDS
St. Paul's Church, Geary County, KS *see* CHURCH RECORDS
ST. PAUL'S CHURCH MONTHLY MAGAZINE – St. John, NB: The Church, [1895?-189- or 19–] – 9 – cn C.I.H.M. [240]
ST. PAUL'S CONCEPTION OF CHRIST, OR, THE DOCTRINE OF THE SECOND ADAM / Somerville, David – Edinburgh: T. & T. Clark, 1897. 1 fiche – 9 – us A.T.L.A. [240]
ST. PAUL'S CONCEPTION OF CHRISTIANITY / Bruce, Alexander Balmain – New York: Scribner's, 1894 – 1mf – 9 – 0-8370-2486-2 – 1985-0486 – us A.T.L.A. [220]
ST. PAUL'S CONCEPTIONS OF THE LAST THINGS / Kennedy, H A A – London: Hodder & Stoughton, 1904. 1 fiche – 9 – us A.T.L.A. [240]

SAINT PAUL'S DOCTRINE OF JUSTIFICATION BY FAITH EXPLAINED IN THREE DISCOURSES PREACHED BEFORE THE UNIVERSITY OF CAMBRIDGE IN THE YEAR 1760 / Hallifax, S – (Missing: Title-page) – Cambridge, 1760 – 1mf – 9 – MP-391/1 – ne IDC [240]

Saint Paul's Episcopal Church (Maumee, Ohio) *see* RECORDS

SAINT PAUL'S EPISCOPAL CHURCH RECORDS – Maumee. Ohio. 1837-1989 – 1 reel – 1 – us Archival [978]

ST. PAUL'S EPISTLE TO THE EPHESIANS : A REVISED TEXT AND TRANSLATION: WITH EXPOSITION AND NOTES / Robinson, Joseph Armitage – (Includes bibliographical references and indexes) – 2nd ed. London; New York: Macmillan, 1904 – 1mf – 9 – 0-8370-6354-X – 1986-0354 – us A.T.L.A. [220]

SAINT PAUL'S EPISTLE TO THE EPHESIANS: THE GREEK TEXT WITH NOTES AND ADDENDA / Westcott, Brooke Foss – London: Macmillan, 1906.1 fiche – 9 – us A.T.L.A. [240]

SAINT PAUL'S EPISTLE TO THE GALATIANS : A REVISED TEXT WITH INTRODUCTION, NOTES, AND DISSERTATIONS / Lightfoot, Joseph Barber – (Includes bibliographical references and index) – 10th ed. London; New York: Macmillan, 1890 – 1mf – 9 – 0-8370-9802-5 – 1986-3802 – us A.T.L.A. [220]

ST. PAUL'S EPISTLE TO THE GALATIANS: A CRITICAL AND GRAMMATICAL COMMENTARY / Ellicott, Charles J – London: Longman, Green 1863. 1 fiche – 9 – us A.T.L.A. [240]

ST. PAUL'S EPISTLE TO THE PHILIPPIANS / Lightfoot, Joseph B – London, 1903 – 7mf – 8 – ne Slangenburg [220]

SAINT PAUL'S EPISTLE TO THE PHILIPPIANS: A REVISED TEXT / Lightfoot, Joseph B – London: Macmillan, 1869 – 1mf – 9 – us A.T.L.A. [240]

ST. PAUL'S EPISTLE TO THE PHILLIPIANS, COLOSSIANS, AND PHILEMON / Ellicott, Charles J – London: Longman, Green, 1865. 1 fiche – 9 – us A.T.L.A. [240]

ST. PAUL'S EPISTLE TO THE ROMANS : ...FROM A MISSIONARY POINT OF VIEW / Colenso, John William – (Includes a sermon on the Eucharist) – New York: D Appleton, 1863 – 1mf – 9 – 0-8370-2709-8 – 1985-0709 – us A.T.L.A. [220]

ST. PAUL'S EPISTLES TO THE COLOSSIANS AND TO PHILEMON – J. B. Lightfoot. 1875, 1904 – 9 – us A.T.L.A. [240]

SAINT PAUL'S EPISTLES TO THE COLOSSIANS AND TO PHILEMON / Lightfoot, Joseph B – London: Macmillan, 1879.1 fiche – 9 – us A.T.L.A. [240]

ST. PAUL'S EPISTLES TO THE THESSALONIANS : THE GREEK TEXT WITH INTRODUCTION AND NOTES / Milligan, George – (Includes indexes) – London: Macmillan, 1908 – 1mf – 9 – 0-8370-4436-7 – 1985-2436 – us A.T.L.A. [220]

ST. PAUL'S EPISTLES TO THE THESSALONIANS: CRITICAL AND GRAMMATICAL COMMENTARY / Ellicott, Charles J – London: Longman, Green, 1866. 1 fiche – 9 – us A.T.L.A. [240]

St. Paul's Evangelical Lutheran Church (Jenera, Ohio) *see* RECORDS

St. Paul's Lutheran Church, Paradise Twp., Russell County, KS *see* RECORDS

ST. PAUL'S MAGAZINE – London. v. 1-14. Oct 1867-Mar 1874 – 1 – 142.00 – us L of C Photodup [073]

ST. PAUL'S PARISH MAGAZINE – London, Ont.: Southam & Brierley, [1887-18– or 19–] – 9 – cn C.I.H.M. [240]

ST. PAUL'S TEACHING ON SANCTIFICATION: A PRACTICAL EXPOSITION OF ROMANS 6 / Morison, James C – London: Hodder & Stoughton, 1886. 1 fiche. 8370-4493-6 – 9 – us A.T.L.A. [240]

ST. PAUL'S VOCABULARY: ST PAUL AS A FORMER OF WORDS / Adams, Myron Winslow – Hartford: Hartford Seminary Press, 1895.1 fiche – 9 – us A.T.L.A. [240]

ST. PAULUS, DER APOSTEL: EINE APOLOGETISCHE STUDIE / Stosch, Georg – Leipzig: Akademischen Buchh., 1894. 1 fiche – 9 – us A.T.L.A. [240]

ST. PETER: AN ORATORIO / Paine, John Knowles – Boston: Oliver Ditson, 1872. Piano-vocal score. music 296 – 1 – us L of C Photodup [780]

ST. PETER IN ROME AND HIS TOMB ON VATICAN HILL / Barnes, Arthur Stapylton – London: Swan Sonnenschein, 1900 – 1mf – 9 – us A.T.L.A. [240]

St. Peter's Church (Norwalk, Ohio) *see* RECORDS

ST. PETER'S CHURCH PARISH MAGAZINE – Toronto: [s.n., 1891?-18– or 19–] – 9 – cn C.I.H.M. [240]

St. Peter's Lutheran Church (Lyme Township, Huron County, Ohio) *see* RECORDS

St. Petersburg. Imp. Arkheograficheskoi Kommissii *see* PSKOVSKAIA SUDNAIA GRAMOTA

St. Petersburg. Imperatorskago Russkago istoricheskago obshchestva *see* RUSSKII BIOGRAFICHESKII SLOVAR'

St. Petersburg. University. Faculty of Historical Philology *see* ZAPISKI ISTORIKO-FILOLOGICHESKOGO FAKUL' TETA IMPERATORSKOGO S.-PETERBURGSKOGO UNIVERSITETA

St. Petersburg. University. Imperial Library *see* SPISOK GLAVNEISHIKH PERIODICHESKIKH IZDANII, IMEIUSHCHIKHSIA

St. Petersburg. University. Law Society *see* ZHURNAL IURIDICHESKAGO OBSHCHESTVA PRI IMP. S-PETERBURGSKOM UNIVERSITETE

ST. PETERSBURGER ZEITUNG – (Inkl hardcopy-filmregister) – St. Petersburg, 1883-1913 – 57r – 1 – DM4,560.00 – gw Mikro Press [947]

ST. PETERSBURGISCHE ZEITSCHRIFT – St. Petersburg, Russia. 1822-1825 – 1 – us Res Libr [072]

SAINT ROCH. HISTOIRE ET LEGENDES / Bessodes, Maurice – Torino, 1931; Madrid: Razon y Fe, 1932 – 1 – sp Bibl Santa Ana [946]

ST SEGMENT CHANGES DUE TO HANDRAIL SUPPORT DURING GRADED EXERCISE TREADMILL TESTING / Cunningham, K M – 1992 – 1mf – 9 – $4.00 – us Microform Publ [612]

Saint Simon, Claude Henri de *see* NOUVEAU CHRISTIANISME

ST. STEPHEN'S ROMAN CATHOLIC CHURCH : MARRIAGE, BAPTISM, DEATH RECORDS – Streator, IL, 1884-1908 – 1 reel – 1 – us I.H.R.C. [240]

Saint Thomas and Principe *see* BOLETIM OFICIAL

ST. THOMAS JOURNAL – Ontario Prov., Canada. Mar 1859-May 1880 – 1 – cn Commonwealth Micro [072]

ST. THOMAS LIBERAL – St. Thomas, Canada. 1832-33 – 1 reel – 1 – $68.00 – cn Library Assoc [971]

ST. THOMAS OF CANTERBURY : HIS DEATH AND MIRACLES / Abbott, Edwin Abbott – London: A.& C. Black, 1898 – 2mf – us A.T.L.A. [240]

ST. THOMAS STANDARD – Ontario Prov., Canada. May 1844-May 1846 – 1 – cn Commonwealth Micro [072]

ST THOMAS VAN AQUINO : DRIE VOORLEZINGEN / Shaepman, Herman Johan Aloysius Maria – (Includes bibliographical references) – Utrecht: Wed J R van Rossum, 1898 – 1mf – 9 – 0-8370-7104-6 – 1986-1104 – us A.T.L.A. [240]

ST. VINCENT : DIGEST OF STATISTICS 1959-1974 / St Vincent. Statistical Office – (1959-61 entitle: Quarterly Digest Of Statistics. 1959, 1961, 1964, 1966, 1974 not available. Coll title: Latin American and Caribbean Official Statistical Serials, 1821-1982) – 13mf – 9 – £110.00 – uk Chadwyck [972]

ST. VINCENT 1828-1938 – September 1991, M.A.P. West Yorkshire – 14r – 1 – uk Microform Academic [972]

St. Vincent. Development Committee *see* A PLAN OF DEVELOPMENT FOR THE COLONY OF ST VINCENT

Saint Vincent, Philippe de *see* RECHERCHES SUR LE PAUPERISME ET SUR LES MOYENS D'Y REMEDIER

St Vincent. Statistical Office *see* ST. VINCENT

ST. WENDELIN'S PARISH : CHANCERY RECORDS – Cleveland, OH, 1911-1926 – 1 reel – 1 – us I.H.R.C. [240]

Saint-Achillas, Soeur *see* BIBLIOGRAPHIE ANALYTIQUE SUR L'ARTISANAT CANADIEN

Saint-Alphonse-de-Jesus *see* BIBLIOGRAPHIE ANALYTIQUE DE L'OEUVRE DE MONSIEUR LE CHANOINE GEORGES PANNETON, TROIS-RIVIERES

Saint-Alphonse-de-Liguori, Marie de *see* BIBLIOGRAPHIE ANALYTIQUE DE L'OEUVRE DU DOCTEUR LOUIS-EDMOND HAMELIN, PROFESSEUR TITULAIRE DE GEOGRAPHIE A L'UNIVERSITE LAVAL...

Saint-Amour, L G de *see* JOURNAL DE CE QUI S'EST FAIT A ROME DANS L'AFFAIRE DES CINQ PROPOSITIONS

Saint-Antoine-de-Padoue, Soeur *see* BIBLIOGRAPHIE ANALYTIQUE, PRECEDEE D'UNE BIOGRAPHIE, DU R.P. HENRI-MARIE GUINDON, S.M.M., DOCTEUR EN THEOLOGIE DE LA SOCIETE CANADIENNE D'ETUDES MARIALES

Saint-Augustin, Catherine-de *see* BIBLIOGRAPHIE DES BIOGRAPHIES DES RELIGIEUSES DECEDEES A L'HOTEL-DIEU DU SACRE-COEUR DE JESUS DE QUEBEC

Saint-Augustin, Soeur *see* BIO-BIBLIOGRAPHIE DE ALCIDE FLEURY, HISTORIEN ET JOURNALISTE

Saint-Aulaire, Yrieix Beaupoil de *see* HISTOIRE D'UNE DETENTION DE TRENTE-NEUF ANS...

Saint-Camille-de-Jesus, Marie-de *see* BIO-BIBLIOGRAPHIE ANALYTIQUE, 1918 A 1961 INCLUSIVEMENT, DE L'ABBE ERNEST ARSENAULT, MISSIONNAIRE-COLONISATEUR

Saint-Clement, Soeur *see* LES FETES DU TROISIEME CENTENAIRE DE L'HOTEL-DIEU DE QUEBEC, 1639-1939

Saint-Cyr, Reveroni *see*
– LE DELIRE OU LES SUITE D'UNE ERREUR
– ELISA OU LE VOYAGE AU MONT BERNARD
– HELENA OU LES MIQUELETS

Saint-Cyran, abbe de et al *see* PORT-ROYAL EDUCATION

Saint-Damase-Marie, Soeur *see* BIBLIOGRAPHIE ANALYTIQUE DE L'OEUVRE DU R.P. J.-HERMANN POISSON

Saint-Denis, Soeur *see* GASPESIANA

Saint-Denys-Garneau, Hector de *see* REGARDS ET JEUX DANS L'ESPACE

Saint-Donat-Joseph, Soeur *see* BIBLIOGRAPHIE ANALYTIQUE, PRECEDEE D'UNE BIOGRAPHIE, DU REVEREND PERE FRANCIS GOYER, CONGREGATION DES PERES DU TRES SAINT-SACREMENT, QUEBEC, 1948-1962

SAINTE ANNE / CELESTINO PACE... : BIBLIOTHEQUE NATIONALE DU QUEBEC, SECTEUR DE LA PHOTOGRAPHIE ET DE LA MICROGRAPHIE, 1993 / Pace, Celestino – Sherbrooke: Apostolat de la presse, [1951 ?]. SEM105P1956 – 1mf – 9 – Can$2.25 – cn Bibl Nat [240]

SAINTE ANNE DE LA POCATIERE, 1672-1900 / Dionne, Narcisse Eutrope; ed by Roy, Pierre Georges – 1900. SEM105P501 – 1mf – 9 – Can$2.25 – cn Bibl Nat [971]

SAINTE CHRISTINE L'ADMIRABLE DE SAINT-TROND : TRADUIT DU FLAMAND PAR A. GIRON / Henckens, R P – Saint-Trond, 1892 – Dfl13.00 – ne Slangenburg [240]

LA SAINTE ECRITURE ET LA REGLE DE FOI / Begin, Louis Nazaire – Quebec: A. Cote, 1874. 02332. (Pre-1900 Canadiana) – 9 – cn C.I.H.M. [240]

Sainte Marie-Madeleine, Soeur *see* BIBLIOGRAPHIE DES BIOGRAPHIES DES RELIGIEUSES DECEDEES A L'HOTEL-DIEU SAINT-VALLIER DE CHICOUTIMI (1884-1959)

Sainte Therese-de-l'Enfant-Jesus, Mere *see* BIBLIOGRAPHIE ANALYTIQUE DE L'OEUVRE DE DOM ALBERT JAMET DE L'ABBAYE BENEDICTINE DE SOLESMES

LA SAINTE TRINITE / Regnon, T de – (Serie 1: Expose du Dogme. Paris, 1892. 9mf; Serie 2: Theories Scolastiques, id.id. 10mf; Serie 3a: Theories Grecques des Processions Divines. Paris, 1898. 10mf; Serie 3b: Theories Grecques des Processions Divines. Paris, 1898. 10mf) – 8 – ne Slangenburg [240]

LA SAINTE VIERGE DANS L'HISTOIRE / Turmel, Joseph – Paris: Emile Nourry, 1908 – 1mf – 9 – 0-8370-8393-1 – 1986-2393 – us A.T.L.A. [420]

THE SAINTE-AGATHE WEEKLY TRIBUNE = LE JOURNAL HEBDOMADAIRE DE SAINTE-AGATHE – Ste-Agathe, Canada. 14 dec 1935-8 aut 1936 – 1r – 1 – Can$50.00 – cn Can Microfilming [072]

Sainte-Agilberte, Soeur *see* BIBLIOGRAPHIE ANALYTIQUE, PRECEDEE D'UNE BIOGRAPHIE, DU REV. PERE FLORIAN LARIVIERE, S.J., RECTEUR DU COLLEGE DES JESUITES, QUEBEC, 1943-1962

Sainte-Angele, Soeur *see* BIBLIOGRAPHIE DE L'OEUVRE DE L'ABBE ANSELME LONGPRE, LICENCIE EN PHILOSOPHIE, LICENCIE EN THEOLOGIE, BACHELIER EN DROIT CANON, 1947-1964

Sainte-Anne-de-Marie, Soeur *see* BIBLIOGRAPHIE ANALYTIQUE DE L'OEUVRE DE ODILON ARTEAU, REDACTEUR A L'ACTION CATHOLIQUE

Sainte-Anne-du-Sauveur, Soeur *see* BIBLIOGRAPHIE CANADIENNE DE L'ACCREDITATION DES HOPITAUX, 1955-1962

Sainte-Apollonie, Soeur *see* BIBLIOGRAPHIE ANALYTIQUE DE L'OEUVRE DE REVERENDE SOEUR SAINTE-CLAIRE-DE-RIMINI (1887-), SOEUR DE LA CHARITE DE QUEBEC

Sainte-Beuve, Charles Augustin *see* PORT-ROYAL

Sainte-Candide, Soeur *see* BIBLIOGRAPHIE ANALYTIQUE DE MONSIEUR L'ABBE ROLAND DUFOUR, DIRECTEUR DE LA REVUE TEMOIGNAGES, AUMONIER A L'INSTITUT FAMILIAL N.-D. DU BON-CONSEIL, CHICOUTIMI

LA SAINTE-CATHERINE ET SES SOUVENIRS, 25 NOVEMBRE – Montreal: Librairie Saint-Joseph, Cadieux & Derome, [1887]. SEM105P530 – 2mf – 9 – Can$4.50 – cn Bibl Nat [971]

Sainte-Catherine-de-Sienne, Mere *see* BIO-BIBLIOGRAPHIE DE MERE MARGUERITE-MARIE LASALLE, O.S.U., URSULINE DES TROIS-RIVIERES

Sainte-Cecile, Soeur *see* BIO-BIBLIOGRAPHIE ANALYTIQUE DE L'OEUVRE DU REVEREND PERE OVILA MELANCON

Sainte-Claire-de-la-Trinite, Soeur *see* REVERENDE SOEUR SAINTE-BLANCHE DES SOEURS DE LA CHARITE DE QUEBEC

Sainte-Daniella, Soeur *see* BIBLIOGRAPHIE ANALYTIQUE DE L'OEUVRE DE M. EUGENE L'HEUREUX, JOURNALISTE, MEMBRE DE LA SOCIETE ROYALE DU CANADA, 1918-1929

Sainte-Enfance, Marie-de-la *see* BIBLIOGRAPHIE DE MONSIEUR L'ABBE EMILE BEGIN, PROFESSEUR A L'UNIVERSITE LAVAL

Sainte-Fernande, Soeur *see* BIBLIOGRAPHIE 1950-1958 DE LA BIENHEUREUSE MARGUERITE D'YOUVILLE, FONDATRICE DES SOEURS DE LA CHARITE (SOEURS GRISES) DE MONTREAL

Sainte-Foy, Charles *see* VIE DU VENERABLE JOSEPH ANCHIETA

Sainte-Heliene-de-Marie, Soeur *see* BIBLIOGRAPHIE ANALYTIQUE DES NOTICES BIOGRAPHIQUES ET DES ECRITS DES SOEURS DE LA CHARITE DE QUEBEC DECEDEES, 1851-1917

Sainte-Hildegarde, Mere *see* BIBLIOGRAPHIE ANALYTIQUE DE L'OEUVRE DE BERAUD DE SAINT MAURICE (MERE CLOTILDE-ANGELE DE JESUS, O.S.U., URSULINE DE TROIS-RIVIERES)

Sainte-Janviere, Soeur *see* BIBLIOGRAPHIE ANALYTIQUE DE L'HONORABLE JUGE SIR ADOLPHE-BASILE ROUTHIER, HOMME DE LETTRES

Sainte-Jeanne-d'Annecy, Soeur *see* BIO-BIBLIOGRAPHIE ANALYTIQUE DE SOEUR SAINT-FRANCOIS-DE-L'ALVERNE, C.N.D., PREFETE PROVINCIALE DES ETUDES

Sainte-Jeanne-de-Domremy, Marie de *see* BIBLIOGRAPHIE ANALYTIQUE DES ECRITS PUBLIES AU CANADA FRANCAIS DE 1930 A 1960 SUR LA PEINTURE RELIGIEUSE

Sainte-Jeanne-de-Jesus, Soeur *see* BIO-BIBLIOGRAPHIE ANALYTIQUE D'UNE RELIGIEUSE EDUCATRICE, SOEUR SAINTE-MADELEINE-DES-ANGES DE LA CONGREGATION DE NOTRE-DAME

Sainte-Leonie, Soeur *see* L'HOTEL-DIEU DE QUEBEC, 1639-1900

Sainte-Madeleine, Soeur *see* BIBLIOGRAPHIE ANALYTIQUE DE L'OEUVRE DE SOEUR MARIE-EMMANUEL, RELIGIEUSE URSULINE, PROFESSEUR DE LITTERATURE FRANCAISE AU COLLEGE DES URSULINES DE QUEBEC

Sainte-Madeleine-du-Calvaire, Soeur *see* BIBLIOGRAPHIE ANALYTIQUE DE L'OEUVRE DE JEAN-PAUL LEGARE, JOURNALISTE DE RIMOUSKI, PRESIDENT DU JOURNAL L'ECHO DU BAS ST-LAURENT, 1945-1961

Sainte-Marie, Jean de *see* LES ETRANGES EVENEMENTS DU VOYAGE DE SON ALTESSE LE PRINCE ZAGA-CHRIST D'ETHIOPIE DU GRAND EMPIRE DES ABYSSINE

Sainte-Marie-Antonin, Soeur *see* BIO-BIBLIOGRAPHIE ANALYTIQUE DE SOEUR SAINT-IGNACE-DE-LOYOLA, C.N.D.

Sainte-Marie-Cleophas, Soeur *see* BIBLIOGRAPHIE ANALYTIQUE DE L'OEUVRE DE LOUIS-PHILIPPE ROY, M.D., COMMANDEUR DE L'ORDRE DE SAINT-GREGOIRE LE GRAND...
Sainte-Marie-de-l'Ange-Gardien, Soeur *see* ESSAI DE BIO-BIBLIOGRAPHIE DE MONSIEUR LOUIS-GERARD "GERRY" GOSSELIN, AVOCAT, ECRIVAIN, JOURNALISTE
Sainte-Marie-de-Pontmain, Soeur *see* BIO-BIBLIOGRAPHIE ANALYTIQUE DES IMPRIMES DES SOEURS DE LA CONGREGATION DE NOTRE-DAME DE MONTREAL
Sainte-Marie-Gedeon, Soeur *see* BIO-BIBLIOGRAPHIE ANALYTIQUE DE SOEUR SAINT-DAMASE-DE-ROME, C.N.D., DIRECTRICE DU CENTRE MARGUERITE BOURGEOYS
Sainte-Marie-Rita, Soeur *see* BIO-BIBLIOGRAPHIE ANALYTIQUE DU REVEREND FRERE MARIE-MAXIMIN, E.C., DIRECTEUR-ADJOINT DE LA LEGION DE MARIE, MAISON PROVINCIALE, QUEBEC
Sainte-Mariette, Soeur *see* BIBLIOGRAPHIE ANALYTIQUE DES NOTICES BIOGRAPHIQUES ET DES ECRITS DES SOEURS DE LA CHARITE DE QUEBEC DECEDEES, 1918-1938
Sainte-Marthe, Denys de *see* GALLIA CHRISTIANA IN PROVINCIAS ECCLESIASTICAS DISTRIBUTA
Sainte-Maure, Benoit de *see* ROMAN DE TROIE
Saint-Emile, Soeur *see* BIO-BIBLIOGRAPHIE ANALYTIQUE DE ME JEAN-CHARLES BONENFANT, MEMBRE DE LA SOCIETE ROYALE DU CANADA, CONSERVATEUR DE LA BIBLIOTHEQUE DE LA LEGISLATURE PROVINCIALE DE QUEBEC ET PROFESSEUR A L'UNIVERSITE LAVAL
Sainte-Monique, Soeur *see* BIBLIOGRAPHIE DES BIOGRAPHIES DES RELIGIEUSES DECEDEES A L'HOTEL-DIEU DU SACRE-COEUR DE JESUS DE QUEBEC, 1879-1925
Sainte-Pauline, Soeur *see* BIO-BIBLIOGRAPHIE DE M. L'ABBE ANDRE LALIBERTE, PTRE, JOURNALISTE ET EDUCATEUR, 1926-32
Sainte-Rachel-Therese, Soeur *see* BIBLIOGRAPHIE ANALYTIQUE, PRECEDEE D'UNE BIOGRAPHIE, DE MONSIEUR L'ABBE ALEXANDRE PARADIS, P.M.E., AUMONIER AU FOYER VILLA-MARIA, SAINT-ALEXANDRE, KAMOURASKA
Sainte-Rollande-de-l'Immaculee, Soeur *see* BIO-BIBLIOGRAPHIE ANALYTIQUE DU REVEREND PER PAUL-HENRI BARABE, O.M.I., SUPERIEUR DE LA PROVINCE OBLATE NOTRE-DAME-DU-TRES-SAINT-ROSAIRE, QUEBEC
Sainte-Thecle, Soeur *see* BIBLIOGRAPHIE ANALYTIQUE DE L'ABBE HENRI-RAYMOND CASGRAIN
Sainte-Therese-d'Alencon, Soeur *see* REVEREND PERE HILAIRE DE LA PERADE, O.F.M., CAP.
Sainte-Therese-de-l'Enfant-Jesus, Soeur *see* BIBLIOGRAPHIE ANALYTIQUE DES NOTICES BIOGRAPHIQUES ET DES ECRITS DES SOEURS DE LA CHARITE DE QUEBEC DECEDEES, 1939-1959
Sainte-Theresita, Marie-de *see* VIE SPIRITUELLE
Sainte-Veronique, Soeur *see* BIBLIOGRAPHIE ANALYTIQUE DE L'OEUVRE DU DOCTEUR ROLAND DESMEULES, M.D.
Sainte-Zelia, Soeur *see* ECRITS SUR LA BIENHEUREUSE MARGUERITE BOURGEOIS, 1945-1962
Saint-Fidele, Soeur *see* BIBLIOGRAPHIE ANALYTIQUE DE L'OEUVRE DE M. LOUIS-PHILIPPE ROBIDOUX DE LA SOCIETE ROYALE DU CANADA, REDACTEUR EN CHEF DE LA TRIBUNE DE SHERBROOKE
Saint-Gaudens, Augustus *see* PAPERS OF AUGUSTUS SAINT-GAUDENS, 1848-1907
Saint-Gerard, Soeur *see* BIO-BIBLIOGRAPHIE ANALYTIQUE DE MONSIEUR L'ABBE PASCAL POTVIN, L.PH., L.L., PRINCIPAL DE L'ECOLE NORMALE DE LEVIS
Saint-Gilbert-de-la-Croix, Soeur *see* NOTES BIO-BIBLIOGRAPHIQUES SUR "TANTE CHANTAL", MADAME CECILE LACHAINE-BROSSEAU
LE SAINT-HENRI – Montreal, Canada. v1 n3. 15 dec 1917 – 1r – 1 – Can$25.00 – cn Can Microfilming [072]
Saint-Hilaire, A F C P de *see*
- FLORA BRASILIAE MERIDIONALIS
- HISTOIRE DES PLANTES LES PLUS REMARQUABLES DU BRESIL
- PLANTES USUELLES DES BRASILIENS
- TABLEAU GEOGRAPHIQUE DE LA VEGETATION PRIMITIVE DANS LA PROVINCE DE MINAS GERAES

Saint-Hilaire, Alphonse *see* BIBLIOGRAPHIE DE NOS GRANDS PRIX DE LA PROVINCE, 1944-1954
Saint-Hyacinthe, Soeur *see* BIENHEUREUSE MARGUERITE D'YOUVILLE, FONDATRICE DES SOEURS DE LA CHARITE (SOEURS GRISES) DE MONTREAL
Saint-Jean, J-M *see* L'AMI DU PEUPLE
Saint-Jean-de-Brebeuf-Hudon, Mere *see* BIBLIOGRAPHIE ANALYTIQUE DE L'OEUVRE DU REVEREND PERE EDMOND GAUDRON, O.F.M., D.PH. (LOUVAIN), PROFESSEUR D'HISTOIRE DE LA PHILOSOPHIE ANCIENNE A LA FACULTE DE PHILOSOPHIE DE L'UNIVERSITE LAVAL DE QUEBEC
Saint-Jean-Eudes, Marie *see* BIBLIOGRAPHIE DE L'OEUVRE DE LA VENERABLE ANNE-MARIE RIVIER, UNE FEMME-APOTRE, 1768-1838
Saint-Jean-Marie, Soeur *see* BIBLIOGRAPHIE ANALYTIQUE DE FRANCOISE L.-ROY, JOURNALISTE, VICE-PRESIDENTE DU CERCLE DES FEMMES JOURNALISTES DE MONTREAL, MEMBRE DE LA SOCIETE DES ECRIVAINS CANADIENS
ST-JOE HERALD – St-Joseph's Island, Canada. v1 n21. 17 may 1900 – 1r – 1 – Can$25.00 – cn Can Microfilming [072]
Saint-Joseph-de-la-Charite, Soeur *see* BIO-BIBLIOGRAPHIE ANALYTIQUE DE MONSEIGNEUR JOSEPH FERLAND, P.D., V.U., CURE DE SAINT-ROCH DE QUEBEC
Saint-Joseph-du-Redempteur, Marie de *see* BIBLIOGRAPHIE DE SOEUR MARIE DE SAINT-PAUL-DE-LA-CROIX, S.C.I.M. (GEORGIANNA JUNEAU) (1873-1940)
Saint-Joseph-Jean, Marie de *see* BIBLIOGRAPHIE ANALYTIQUE DE LA VALLEE DE LA MATAPEDIA
Saint-Jure, J -B *see* LA VIE DE M. DE RENTY OU L'IDEE D'UN CHRETIEN PARFAIT
LE SAINT-LAURENT : JOURNAL BI-HEBDOMADAIRE – (Becomes: Saint-Laurent, Echo du Grand-Portage 18 oct 1977-6 mar 1985. Becomes: Le Saint-Laurent/L'Echo 12 mar 1985-20 jul 1985) – Riviere-du-Loup, Canada. 19 nov 1895-12 oct 1977 – 60r – 1 – Can$75.00r – cn Can Microfilming [072]
SAINT-LAURENT, ECHO DU GRAND-PORTAGE *see* LE SAINT-LAURENT
THE SAINT-LAURENT NEWS – (Becomes: The News 2 dec 1965-30 mar 1967. Becomes: The News/Les Nouvelles 6 avr 1967-3 aut 1983. Becomes: Les Nouvelles/St-Laurent News 10 aut 1983-25 fev 1992) – Ville St-Laurent, Canada. v9 n25. 25 jun 1959-25 nov 1965 – 3r – 1 – Can$70.00r – cn Can Microfilming [072]
LE SAINT-LAURENT/L'ECHO *see* LE SAINT-LAURENT
ST-LAWRENCE NEWS *see* THE ENSIGN
Saint-Leonce, Soeur *see* BIBLIOGRAPHIE DE L'OEUVRE DU DOCTEUR MARCEL LAPOINTE (PSEUDONYME: MARCEL PORTAL
ST-LOUIS ELECTOR = DER IDISHER VEYLER – (In Yiddish and English) – Montreal, CN, 1948 – 1r – 1 – Can$25.00 – cn Can Microfilming [072]
Saint-Louis-Daniel, Soeur *see* BIBLIOGRAPHIE ANALYTIQUE DE L'OEUVRE DE ME EUGENE L'HEUREUX, JOURNALISTE, MEMBRE DE LA SOCIETE ROYALE DU CANADA ET DE L'ACADEMIE CANADIENNE, 1940-1949
Saint-Majella, Soeur *see* BIBLIOGRAPHIE ANALYTIQUE DE L'OEUVRE DE LOUIS-PHILIPPE ROY, M.D., DIRECTEUR DE L'ACTION, 1920-1948
Saint-Marc, Mere *see* BIBLIOGRAPHIE ANALYTIQUE DE L'OEUVRE DU R. PERE PHILIAS F. BOURGEOIS DE LA CONGREGATION DE SAINTE-CROIX, PROFESSEUR DE LITTERATURE ET D'HISTOIRE A L'UNIVERSITE SAINT-JOSEPH
Saint-Maurice, Alcide de *see* REMARQUES SUR LES PRINCIPES DIFFICULTEZ QUE LES ESTRANGERS ONT EN LA LANGUE FRANCOISE
Saintoyant, J F *see*
- LA COLONISATION FRANCAISE SOUS L'ANCIEN REGIME

Saint-Palais D'aussac, Fr de *see* LA RECONCILIATION DES HERETIQUES DANS L'EGLISE LATIN
Saint-Philippe-Andre, Soeur *see* LES ACTES DE SA SAINTETE LE PAPE JEAN 23 (OCTOBRE 1958-JANVIER 1962)
Saint-Pierre, Antoine de *see* LA JOURNEE RELIGIEUSE OU INSTRUCTIONS PRATIQUES
Saint-Pierre, Charles Irenee Castel *see* REFLEXIONS SUR L'ANTIMACHIAVEL DE 1740

Saint-Pierre, Dde *see* SYNOPSIS ANALYTIQUE DE LA FLORE DES ENVIRONS DE PARIS
Saint-Pierre, Jacques Henri de *see* VOYAGE A L'ILE D'UTOPIE
Saint-Pierre, Jeanne-M *see* BIBLIOGRAPHIE CANADIENNE DES ARCHIVES MEDICALES D'UN HOPITAL, 1951-1956
Saint Priest, *coo* MEMOIRES SUR L'AMBASSADE DE FRANCE PRES LA PORTE OTTOMANE
Saint-Raymond-du-Sauveur, Soeur *see* BIBLIOGRAPHIE ANALYTIQUE DE L'OEUVRE DE MONSIEUR PIERRE-H. RUEL, DOYEN, FACULTE DES SCIENCES DE L'EDUCATION, UNIVERSITE DE SHERBROOKE
Saint-Remi, Tranquille de *see* VERITABLE RELATION DES IUSTES PROCEDURES OBSERVEES AU FAICT DE LA POSSESSION DES URSULINES DE LOUDUN
LES SAINTS : I. LE BIENHEREUX PIERRE JULIEN EYMARD (1811-1868) / Jambert – Madrid: Razon y Fe, 1926 – 1 – sp Bibl Santa Ana [240]
THE SAINTS : A SATIRE / Combe, W – London, 1778 – 1mf – 9 – MP-530/1 – ne IDC [870]
SAINTS AND THEIR SYMBOLS: A COMPANION IN THE CHURCHES AND PICTURE GALLERIES OF EUROPE / Greene, E A – 6th ed. London: Sampson Low, Marston, Searle, Rivington, 1891. iv,150p., front. illus – 1 – us U.W. Library [240]
Saints Peter and Paul Catholic Church (Ottawa, Ohio) *see* RECORDS
THE SAINTS' SACRIFICE, OR, A COMMENTARY ON PSALM 116 : WHICH IS A GRATULATORY PSALM FOR DELIVERANCE FROM DEADLY DISTRESS / Gouge, William – (Includes bibliographical references) – Edinburgh: James Nichol, 1868 – 1mf – 9 – 0-8370-2162-6 – 1985-0162 – us A.T.L.A. [220]
Saint-Sacrement, Beatrice-du *see* BIO-BIBLIOGRAPHIE ANALYTIQUE 1917-1941 DE MONSIEUR L'ABBE PIERRE GRAVEL CURE DE BOISCHATEL
Saint-Saens, Camille *see*
- 1ER MAZURKA POUR LE PIANO, OP. 21
- CAPRICE BRILLIANT POUR PIANO ET VIOLON
- DANSE MACABRE
- DUO POUR DEUX PIANOS. D'APRES LES DUOS POUR PIANO ET ORGUE
- SIX BAGATELLES POUR PIANO, OP. 3

Saintsbury, George *see*
- CORRECTED IMPRESSIONS
- MISCELLANEOUS ESSAYS

LE SAINT-SIEGE EN DROIT INTERNATIONAL / Autremont, P d' – Paris, 1910 – 2mf – 9 – ILM-1097/1 – ne IDC [340]
Saint-Simon, Leon H *see* OPINIONS LITERAIRES, PHILOSOPHIQUES ET INDUSTRIELLES
Saint-Simon, M H de *see* DES JACINTHES, DE LEUR ANATOMIE, REPRODUCTION ET CULTURE
SAINT-SIMON. SON PREMIER ECRIT / ed by Rodrigues, O – LETTRE D'UN HABITANT DE GENEVE A SES CONTEMPORAINS, 1802. SA PARABOLE POLITIQUE, 1819. LE NOUVEAU CHRISTIANISME, 1825. CATECHISME POLITIQUE DES INDUSTRIELS, 1824. VUES SUR LA PROPRIETE ET LA LEGISLATION, 1818. Paris, librairie Saint-Simonienne, (puis) Ad. Naquet librairie, 1832. 2 v. Propectus, 201 a 364 p. Les Saint-Simoniens, 1825-1834. 6961 – 9 – fr Hachette [335]
LA SAINT-SIMONIENNE / Lebassu d'Helf, Josephine – Paris, 1833 – 1 – us U.W. Library [944]
LA SAINT-SIMONIENNE / Lebassu d'Helt, Josephine – Paris, L. Tenre, 1833, viii-487 p. Les Saint-Simoniens, 1825-1834. 7002 – 9 – fr Hachette [305]
LES SAINT-SIMONIENS / Boissieu, Alphonse de – Lyon, impr. de S. Rossary, 1831, 16 p. Les Saint-Simoniens, 1825-1834. 6978 – 9 – fr Hachette [335]
LES SAINT-SIMONIENS: 1825-1834 / ed by Agulhon, Maurice – 159 titles. Available individually – 9 – fr Hachette [360]
DES SAINT-SIMONIENS. ENFANTIN RETRIBUE SUIVANT SA CAPACITE ET SELON SES OEUVRES – Paris, 1832, 8 p. Les Saint-Simoniens, 1825-1834. 7000 – 9 – fr Hachette [335]
DES SAINT-SIMONIENS ET DE L'IMPUISSANCE DU GOVERNEMENT A REPRIMER LEURS DOCTRINES – Paris, 1832, 45 p. Les Saint-Simoniens, 1825-1834. 7001 – 9 – fr Hachette [335]

LES SAINTS-SIMONIENS, COMEDIE BURLESQUE EN TROIS ACTES ET EN PROSE / Cornede-Miramont, A C – Cahors, impr. de M.-C. Cornede, 1835, iv-80 p. Les Saint-Simoniens, 1825-1834. 7006 – 9 – fr Hachette [820]
ST. LOUIS PRESBYTERIAN AND THE MEMPHIS PRESBYTERIAN 1874-79. MISSOURI PRESBYTERIAN *see* ST. LOUIS PRESBYTERIAN
Saint-Vallier, Jean B de la *see* ESTAT PRESENT DE L'EGLISE ET DE LA COLONIE FRANCOISE DANS LA NOUVELLE FRANCE
Saintyves, Pierre *see*
- LES CONTES DE PERRAULT ET LES RECITS PARALLELES
- EN MARGE DE LA LEGENDE DOREE
- LE REFORME INTELLECTUELLE DU CLERGE ET LA LIBERTE D'ENSEIGNEMENT
- LES RELIQUES ET LES IMAGES LEGENDAIRES
- LES VIERGES MERES ET LES NAISSANCES MIRACULEUSES

Sainz y Gomez, Manuel *see* EL AMOR FAMILIAR...POESIAS
Sainz y Rodriguez, Pedro *see* DON BARTOLOME JOSE GALLARDO Y LA CRITICA LITERARIA DE SU TIEMPO
Saionji, Kinmochi *see* THE SAIONJI-HARADA MEMOIRS, 1931-40
THE SAIONJI-HARADA MEMOIRS, 1931-40 / Saionji, Kinmochi – 1978. Compl. translation into English – 1 – $295.00 – 0-89093-274-3 – us UPA [950]
LA SAISIAZ : THE TWO POETS OF CROISIC / Browning, Robert – London: Smith, Elder, 1878 – 1 roll – 1 – 1-55879-586-3 – uk Libr Preservation [440]
LA SAISIE ET LA VENTE JUDICIAIRE DES FONDS DE COMMERCE. / Bayle, Pierre Georges – Paris, Librairie generale de droit de jurisprudence, 1939. 244 p. LL-4089 – 1 – us L of C Photodup [340]
Saitschick, Robert *see*
- GOETHES CHARAKTER
- MEISTER DER SCHWEIZERISCHEN DICHTUNG DES NEUNZEHNTEN JAHRHUNDERTS

Saive, A *see* OUVRIER CHAPELIER. L'AVENIR DE L'OUVRIER DEDIE A LA CLASSE OUVRIERE ET PLACE SOUS SA PROTECTION
Saiz Otero, Concepcion y Urbano Gonzales Serrano *see* CARTAS PEDAGOGICAS
SAJ REVIEW – New York. N.Y. 1926-28 – 1 – us A.J.P.C. [071]
Sajanello, J -B *see* HISTORICA MONUMENTA ORDINIS S. HIERONYMI CONGREGATIONIS B. PETRI DE PISIS
Sajnovics, J *see* DEMONSTRATIO, IDIOMA UNGARORUM ET LAPPONUM INDEM ESSE
Sajudi *see* LALAKI DI TEGAL PATI; SADJAK-SADJAK SUNDA
Sajus, B *see* ESSAI SUR LES VICES DU LANGAGE
SAKACI – Istanbul: A. Asaduryan Matbaasi. Sahibi ve Muharriri: Tepedelenlizade Kamil; Mueduerue: Salih Zeki. Nos. 1-9 (24 Eyluel 1324-19 Tesrinisani 1324 [1 Oct 1908-26 Dec 1908]) – 9 – $30.00 – us MEDOC [956]
SAKAL – Poona, India. Jul-Sept 1961 – 1r – 1 – us L of C Photodup [072]
SAKASSO, EXPLOITATION MANUELLE DE L'ENQUETE DEMOGRAPHIQUE. RESULTATS PARTIELS / Ancey, G – 1967 – 9 – fr Hachette [960]
Sakazov, I *see* BULGARISCHE WIRTSCHAFTGESCHICHTE
Sakharov, F K *see*
- LITERATURA ISTORII I OBLICHENIYA RUSSKAGO
- LITERATURA ISTORII I OBLITSENIIA RUSSKAGO RASKOLA. SISTEMATICHESKII UKAZATEL' KNIG, BROSHIUR I STATEI O RASKOLE. 1-3

Sakharov, I P *see*
- OPISANIE SLAVIANO-RUSSKIKH RUKOPISEI, NAKHODIASHCHIKHSIA V BIBLIOTEKE VOSKRESENSKOGO NOVO-IERUSALIMSKOGO MONASTYRIA
- SLAVIANO-RUSSKIE RUKOPISI. OTDELENI PERVOE

SAKRAMENTE UND SAKRAMENTALIEN IN DEN DREI ERSTEN CHRISTLICHEN JAHRHUNDERTEN / Probst, Ferdinand – Tuebingen: H. Laupp, 1872 – 2mf – us A.T.L.A. [240]
Saks, Michael J *see* SMALL-GROUP DECISION MAKING, COMPLEX INFORMATION TASKS
Sakti, Slamet S *see* MATA PELADJARAN KEWARGAAN NEGARA (CIVICS)

Sakura *see* TOEDJOEAN NIPPON KE INDONESIA
Sakurai, T *see* NIKU-DAN KOERBAN MANOESIA
SAL TERRAE – (Lacking some issues and pgs. Includes index) – Spain, 1923-91 – 30r – 1 – ATLA S0566 – us A.T.L.A. [073]
Sala, A *see* MEMORIA SOBRE LA ARNICA DE LOS MONTES LEIDA EN LA REAL ACADEMIA DE CIENCIAS NATURALES Y ARTES DE BARCELONA
SALA ALLEHANDA – Sala, Sweden. 1879-1978 – 257r – 1 – sw Kungliga [072]
SALA ALLEHANDA – Sala, Sweden. 1979- – 1 – sw Kungliga [072]
Sala, George Augustus *see* THINGS I HAVE SEEN AND PEOPLE I HAVE KNOWN
LE SALABERRY / ed by Boyer, J A N – Valleyfield, Canada. 2 nov 1899-24 oct 1902 – 1r – 1 – Can$45.00 – cn Can Microfilming [072]
LE SALABERRY – Valleyfield, Canada. 2 aut 1943-27 jul 1961 – 11r – 1 – Can$60.00r – cn Can Microfilming [072]
Saladin *see* GOD AND HIS BOOK
Saladin d'Anglure, B *see* L'ORGANISATION SOCIALE TRADITIONELLE DES ESQUIMAUX DE KANGIRSUJUAK. (NOUVEAU-QUEBEC)
Salado Garces de Leon, D *see* APOLOGETICO DISCURSO...EN QUE SE PRUEBA QUE LOS POLVOS DE QUARANGO SE DEBEN USAR...
Salado Garces y Ribera, F *see* VARIAS MATERIAS DE DIVERSAS FACULTADES Y CIENCIAS
SALAH ABDEL SABOUR – The Princess Waits. A poetic drama transl. by Shafik Megally. Zug, 1974. BNE-384/1 – 9 – ne IDC [820]
LES SALAIRES AU XIXE SIECLE / Chevallier, Emile – Preface de E. Levasseur.(Condition of 19th C. French Working Class Series). 1887 – 9 – fr Hachette [331]
SALAIRES ET DUREE DU TRAVAIL DANS L'INDUSTRIE FRANCAISE / France. Ministere du Commerce, de l'Industrie, des Postes et Telegraphes. Office du Travail – (Condition of 19th C. French working class series). 1894-97 – 9 – fr Hachette [331]
SALAM IFRIKYA – Culture nord-africaine et actualite musulmane. Dir. Hamza Boubekeur. Alger. sept 1946-47, mars-juil 1948, fevr-mai 1950 – 1 – fr A.C.R.P.P. [073]
Salaman *see* AN ALLEGORY. TRANSLATED FROM THE PERSIAN OF JAMI
DER SALAMANDER : EIN TAGEBUCH IN TERZINEN / Heyse, Paul – 2. Aufl. Berlin: W Hertz, [1879?] – 1 – us U.W. Library [810]
Salame, Abraham *see* A NARRATIVE OF THE EXPEDITION TO ALGIERS IN THE YEAR 1816, UNDER THE COMMAND OF ADMIRAL LORD VISCOUNT EXMOUTH
Sala-Molins, L *see* LA PHILOSOPHIE DE L'AMOUR CHEZ RAYMOND LULLE
SALAPOSTEN – Sala, 1906-60 – 9 – sw Kungliga [072]
SALARIES/CONTRACTS/LABOR REC. / Hancock County. Ohio. Biglick Township. Township Clerk – 1968-1988 gaps in holdings – 1r – 1 – $32.50r – us Archival [324]
Salas, Francisco Gregorio de *see*
- LA CASTREIDA
- COLECCION DE EPIGRAMES
- COLECCION DE LOS EPIGRAMAS Y OTRAS POESIAS CRITICAS, SATIRICAS Y JOCOSAS
- CONTINUACION DE LAS NUEVAS POESIAS DE...
- CONTINUACION DEL JUICIO CRITICO DEL ANO DE 1788
- CONTINUACION...POESIAS
- COPIA POETICA DEL CUADRO DE LA ANUNCIACION...
- COPIA...ANUNCIACION...ANTONIO R. MENGS
- DALMIRO Y SILVANO
- ELOGIO POETICO...A...PERSONAS...DE EXTREMADURA
- ELOGIOS POETICOS
- LAS LAMENTACIONES, HIMNOS
- NUEVAS POESIAS SERIAS
- LAS NUEVE LAMENTACIONES...SEMANA SANTA
- OBSERVATORIO RUSTICO
- OBSERVATORIO RUSTICO: SEGUNDA PARTE
- PARAFRASIS DE...DELORES
- POESIAS
- POESIAS. TOMOS 1 Y 2
- EL PSALMO
- EL PSALMO: MISERERE MEI DEUS
- SEGUNDA PARTE DEL OBSERVATORIO RUSTICO, DONDE SE HACE UNA DESCRIPCION POETICA DE LA VIDA PACIFICA Y SUS VENTAJAS
- VERSION PARAFRASEADA DE LA ORACION ANGELICA, QUE CANTA LA IGLESIA EN EL SABADO SANTO DEL CIRIO PASCUAL
- VERSION...LAMENTACIONES DE JEREMIAS
- VERSION...ORACION ANGELICAL...PASCUAL
- VERSION...TE DEUM LAUDAMUS...MAGNIFICAT ANIMA MEA

Salaverria, Jose Maria *see* LAS SOMBRAS DE LOYOLA
Salaville, Jean-Baptiste *see* DE L'ORGANISATION D'UN ETAT MONARCHIQUE
Salazar Alonso, Rafael *see*
- CARTA SIN SOBRE ESCRITO AL SR. OSSORIO Y GALLARDO
- LA JUSTICIA BAJO LA DICTADURA

Salazar, Antonio *see* GARCIA LASO DE LA VEGA
Salazar, D *see* TRATADO DE RE MILITARI...
Salazar Fernandez, Antinio *see* EL CASTILLO DE CASTELLAR
Salazar, Petrus *see* DE VOV ET CONSVETVDINE ET DE STILO CVRIAE REGALIS
Salazar, T *see* TRATADO DEL USO DE LA QUINA
Salcedo, Antonio *see* RIMAS Y ESTROFAS
Salcedo, Coronel Garcia *see*
- INSCRIPCION...SATURNINO PENITENTE
- INSCRIPCION...SATURNINO...MERIDA

Saldern, Axel von *see*
- GERMAN ENAMELLED GLASS: THE EDWIN J. BEINECKE COLLECTION AND RELATED PIECES
- GLASS AND GLASSMAKING IN ANCIENT MESOPOTAMIA

Salditt, Barbara *see* DAS WERDEN DES GRIMMELSHAUSENBILDES IM 19. UND 20. JAHRHUNDERT
SALE AND EXHIBITION CATALOGUES RELATING TO JOHN RUSKIN / ed by Dearden, James S – (Includes Allen and Goodspeed catalogs) – 22mf – 9 – $75.00 – us UMI [700]
Sale, G *see* THE KORAN; COMMONLY CALLED THE ALCORAN OF MOHAMMED
Saleh, Ruslan *see* KEPUTUSAN-KEPUTUSAN TENTANG PERKARA PIDANA
SALEM, AN INDIAN COLLECTORATE / Dykes, J W B – I-150-3 2. 1853 – 8 – ne IDC [306]
SALEM BAPTIST CHURCH. ANDERSON COUNTY. SOUTH CAROLINA : CHURCH RECORDS – 1805-1902, 1908-81. Sunday School Records, 1915-33. 665p – 1 – $29.88 – us Baptist [240]
SALEM BAPTIST CHURCH. EDGEFIELD COUNTY. SOUTH CAROLINA : CHURCH RECORDS – (274p) – 1837-1942 – 1 reel – 1 – $12.33 – us Baptist [240]
SALEM BAPTIST CHURCH. JEFFERSON COUNTY. MISSISSIPPI : CHURCH RECORDS – 1815-34 – 1 – 15.66 – us Baptist [240]
SALEM BAPTIST CHURCH. JONES COUNTY. GEORGIA : CHURCH RECORDS – (168p) – 1839-Apr 1870 – 1 reel – 1 – $7.56 – us Baptist [240]
SALEM BAPTIST CHURCH. LEXINGTON, GEORGIA : CHURCH RECORDS – (480p) – 1951-January 1990 – 1 reel – 1 – $21.60 – us Baptist [240]
SALEM BAPTIST CHURCH. MARLBORO COUNTY. SOUTH CAROLINA : CHURCH RECORDS – 1797-1930 – 1 – 32.49 – us Baptist [240]
SALEM BAPTIST CHURCH. ORANGEBURG COUNTY. SOUTH CAROLINA : CHURCH RECORDS – (829p) – Nov 1892-1946, 1948-1985 – 1 reel – 1 – $37.31 – us Baptist [240]
SALEM CHAPEL / Oliphant, Margaret – Edinburgh, London: W. Blackwood and Sons, 1863 – 1 roll – 1 – 1-55879-797-1 – uk Libr Preservation [830]
SALEM DAILY PRESS – Salem OR. Apr 15-June 9 1870 – 1 – us U.O. Library [071]
SALEM (DAILY) RECORD – Salem, OR. 10 Jun 1867-15 Jul 1868; 14 May 1877; 14 Aug 1874; 30 Apr, 14 Aug, 15 Oct 1878 – 1 – us U.O. Library [071]
SALEM DAILY TALK – Salem OR. May 24 25 1880, Oct 19 24 Dec 1 1882, July 19 1884 – 1 – us U.O. Library [071]
SALEM EVENING POST – Salem OR. Mar 25 1896 – 1 – us U.O. Library [071]
THE SALEM GAZETTE – Salem. Mass. 1781-1785. The Massachusetts Gazette. 1785-1788. Sold as one unit – 1,3 – us Readex [071]
SALEM GAZETTE AND PUBLIC ADVERTISER – (Weekly newspaper) – Salem, OH. May 3 1825-Jun 24 1826 – 1r – 1 – us Western Res [071]
SALEM INDEX – Salem, NE. -w. Jul 1892; Oct 1895-May 1898; Feb 1899-Jun 1900; Jun 1903; May 1910 – 1 – us NE Hist [071]
SALEM LABOR REVIEW – Salem OR. Oct 10-Dec 17 1913 – 1 – us U.O. Library [071]
THE SALEM MERCURY – Salem. Mass. 1786-1789. Salem Gazette. 1790-1820. Sold as one unit – 1,3 – us Readex [071]
SALEM, OHIO, TAXES, MS V.F.O. – (List of the residents land in Salem Township, Ashtabula Co.) – 180? – 1r – 1 – us Western Res [978]
SALEM ON RENNIX CREEK / Kentucky – 1867-1946 – 1 – 24.64 – us Baptist [240]
Salem. Presbytery *see* MINUTES
SALEM REPUBLICAN – (Weekly Republican newspaper) – Salem, OH. Jun 24 1857-May 17 1877 – 2r – 1 – us Western Res [071]
SALEM SENTINEL – Salem OR. Dec 18 25 1897, Jan 1 Aug 6 1898, Aug 22 1902, Nov 27 Dec 4 1903, Apr 27 1901-Jan 31 1902, Feb 7-June 27 1902 – 1 – us U.O. Library [071]
SALEM STANDARD – Salem, NE. -w. Oct 1911-Feb 1916 – 1 – us NE Hist [071]
SALEM WAGE EARNER – Salem OR. Aug 12-Dec 30 1927, Jan 6-Aug 3 1928, Aug 10 1928 – 1 – us U.O. Library [071]
SALEM WEEKLY DEMOCRAT – (Weekly Democratic newspaper) – Salem, OH. Sep 23 1854-10 Feb 1855 – 1r – 1 – us Western Res [071]
SALEM WITCHCRAFT – (Ca 60 works, 7000p of information from Salem Village Witchcraft Collection at Danvers, MA Archival Center) – 3r – 1 – $225.00 – us UMI [978]
SALEM WORLD – Salem, OR. -d. 2 Oct 1927-30 Jul 1928. – 2r – 1 – us U.O. Library [071]
Salen-Picard, C *see* CONTRIBUTION A L'ETUDE DYNAMIQUE DE PEUPLEMENTS MARINS DE SUBSTRATS MEUBLES: LES PEUPLEMENTS MACROBENTHIQUES CIRCALITTORAUX SOUMIS A L'ENVASEMENT DANS LA REGION PROVENCALE
Salerno *see*
- REGIMEN
- REGIMEN SANITATIS SALERNI
- REGIMENT OF HEALTH

SALES AND MARKETING MANAGEMENT – (See also: Sales Management) – v115-1975- – 1,5,6,9 – us UMI [380]
SALES MANAGEMENT – (102-115. 1969-75. 5,6. 104-115. 1970-75. 9. See now: Sales and Marketing Management) – v1-115. 1918-75 – 1 – us UMI [650]
Salesbury, Henry *see* GRAMMATICA BRITANNICA
Salesbury, William *see*
- A BRIEFE AND A PLAYNE INTRODUCTION, TEACHYNG HOW TO PRONOUNCE THE LETTERS IN THE BRITISH TONGUE (NOW COMMENLY CALLED WALSH)
- A DICTIONARY IN ENGLYSHE AND WELSHE

Saleski, Maria Agnes *see* GOETHE ALS ERZIEHER NIETZSCHES
Salette, Marie-de-la *see* BIBLIOGRAPHIE ANALYTIQUE DE L'OEUVRE DE MAITRE EUGENE L'HEUREUX, JOURNALISTE, 1950-1960, BIBLIOTHECAIRE-ADJOINT AU PARLEMENT
Salfeld, Siegmund *see*
- DAS HOHELIED SALOMO'S BEI DEN JUEDISCHEN ERKLAERERN DES MITTELALTERS
- DAS MARTYROLOGIUM DES NUERNBERGER MEMORBUCHES

SALFORD LABOUR PARTY RECORDS, 1920-1986 – 7r – 1 – uk Microform Academic [320]
SALFORD WEEKLY NEWS – 1889-1961 – 1 – uk Manchester Libr [072]
Salgues, Jacques B *see* DES ERREURS ET DES PREJUGES
SALICES BOREALI-AMERICANAE / Andersson, N J – 7498 2. 1860 – 8 – ne IDC [580]
Salicis, Gustave A *see* ENSEIGNEMENT PRIMAIRE ET APPRENTISSAGE
Salieri, A *see*
- LA GROTTA DI TROFONIO. OPERA COMICA...
- PARTIRO DEL CARO SPOSO. A FAVORITE SONG

SALIH IBN YAHYA. HISTOIRE DE BEYROUTH... / ed by Cheikho, L – Beyrouth, 1902 – 4mf – NE-20168/1 – ne IDC [956]
Salih Kambo, M *see* AMAL-I-SALIH
Salim, A *see* DE PERHIMPOENAN INDONESIA EN DE INDONESISCHE NATIONALISTISCHE BEWEGING
Salim, Agus *see* CURSUSSEN OVER DE ISLAM
Salim, Emil *see* SISTIM EKONOMI DAN EKONOMI INDONESIA
SALIMBENE UND SEINE CHRONIK : EINE STUDIE ZUR GESCHICHTSSCHREIBUNG DES DREIZEHNTEN JAHRHUNDERTS / Michael, Emil – Innsbruck: Wagner, 1889 – 1mf – us A.T.L.A. [900]
SALINAS DAILY JOURNAL – Salinas, CA. Apr 1889-Dec 1897 – 4r – 1 – $200.00 – C02751 – us Library Micro [071]
SALINAS DAILY POST – Salinas, CA. 1934-1935 – 6r – 1 – $300.00 – C03446 – us Library Micro [071]
SALINAS DEMOCRAT – (Also known as: Weekly Journal) – Salinas, CA. 1890-1915 – 9r – 1 – $450.00 – C03444 – us Library Micro [073]
Salinas, F *see* FRANCISCI SALINAE. DE MUSICA LIBRI SEPTEM, IN QUIBUS EIUS DOCTRINAE VERITAS TAM QUAE AD HARMONIAM, QUAM QUAE AD RHYTHMUM PERTINET
SALINAS FIRST SOUTHERN BAPTIST CHURCH (FORMERLY: CALVARY). SALINAS, CALIFORNIA : CHURCH RECORDS – 21 Jan 1938-2 May 1973 – 1 – 31.01 – us Baptist [240]
SALINAS MORNING POST – Salinas, CA. 1936-1942 – 36r – 1 – $1,800.00 – C03447 – us Library Micro [071]
SALINE COUNTY DEMOCRAT – Wilber, NE. -w. Nov 1888-Apr 1892; Jul 1892-Jun 1894, scattered issues missing; Sep 1894-Jan 1942 – 1 – us NE Hist [071]
SALINE COUNTY EXPRESS – Friend, NE. -w. Dec. 1892-Dec. 1893. Incomplete – 1 – us NE Hist [071]
SALINE COUNTY GAZETTE – Friend, NE. -w. Feb. 1886-Sep. 1887 – 1 – us NE Hist [071]
SALINE COUNTY JOURNAL – Tobias, NE. -w. Jun-Dec 1905 – 1 – us NE Hist [071]
SALINE COUNTY NEWS – Crete, NE. -w. Jan. 1876-May 1877 – 1 – us NE Hist [071]
SALINE COUNTY REGISTER – Harrisburg. Ill. 1898-1906 – 1 – us UMI [071]
SALINE COUNTY STANDARD – Crete, NE. -w. Dec. 1878-Dec. 1881; J? 1883-Dec. 1883 – 1 – us NE Hist [071]
SALINE COUNTY UNION – Crete, NE. -w. May 1871-Jan. 1873; Mar. 1873-Nov. 1876. Incomplete; Feb. 1877-Dec. 1883 – 1 – us NE Hist [071]
SALINE DEMOCRAT – Crete, NE. -w. Oct. 1877-Jul. 1878; Oct. 1878-Nov. 1878 – 1 – us NE Hist [071]
SALINE RECORD – Friend, NE. -w. Jul. 1885-Feb. 1886 – 1 – us NE Hist [071]
O SALINENSE – Salinas, 25 Feb 1929 – 1,5,6 – bl Biblioteca [072]
Salinero, Fernando G *see* ACTUALIDAD LINGUISTICA DE FRANCISCO SANCHEZ DE LAS BROZAS
SALISBURY AND WINCHESTER JOURNAL *see* SALISBURY JOURNAL
Salisbury (Diocese) *see*
- CHARTERS AND DOCUMENTS ILLUSTRATING THE HISTORY OF THE CATHEDRAL, CITY AND DIOCESE OF SALISBURY, IN THE TWELFTH AND THIRTEENTH CENTURIES (RS97)
- VETUS REGISTRUM SARISBERIENSE

SALISBURY JOURNAL – (Salisbury & Winchester Journal 1775-1817) – Salisbury, England. 21 Jan 1765; 1769; 13 Apr 1772-12 Apr 1773; 10 Jan 1780-9 Dec 1782; 5 Jan-20 Dec 1784; 1786-89. (imperfect) – 3r – 1 – uk British Libr Newspaper [072]
Salisbury, New Hampshire. Salisbury Heights Baptist Church *see* RECORDS
Salisbury, New Hampshire. Second Baptist Church *see* RECORDS
Salisbury, R A *see*
- THE GENERA OF PLANTS
- THE PARADISUS LONDINENSIS
- PRODROMUS STIRPIUM IN HORTO AD CHAPEL ALLERTON VIGENTIUM

SALISBURY TIMES – England.14 Mar 1868-25 Sept 1869; 16 May 1874-1895; 1898-1911; 5 Jan-19 Jul, 30 Aug-Dec 1912; 1913-58; 1960-62. -w. 89 reels – 1 – uk British Libr Newspaper [072]
SALITA AL PARNASSO....GRADUS AD PARNASSUM / Fux, J J – 1761 – 2 – us Sibley [780]
SALIX / Host, N T – v. 1. Vindobonae. 1828. B-5969 2 – 8 – ne IDC [580]
Sallaberry, Juan Faustino *see*
- APOLOGIA CATOLICA...
- EL FUNDADOR DE MONTEVIDEO. MONTEVIDEO, 1928
- LA IGLESIA EN LA INDEPENDENCIA DEL URUGUAY
Salleh, Salmah *see* NUTRITION IN MALAYSIA
Saller, Robert Michael *see* DESIGN VON LOCUS- UND GEWEBESPEZIFISCHEN RETROVIRALEN VEKTOREN FUER EINE IN VIVO GENTHERAPIE
Saller, Sylvester J *see* THE MEMORIAL OF MOSES ON MOUNT NEBO
Sallet, Friedrich von *see* GESAMMELTE GEDICHTE
Salley, A S *see* HISTORY OF ORANGEBURG COUNTY
Sallows, J F *see* THE BLACKSMITHS GUIDE
Sallust *see*
- CATILINA ET JUGURTHA AND OFFICIUM B. V. MARIAE
- CATILINA ET JUGURTHA, ETC
- GAI SALLUSTI CRISPI BELLUM CATILINAE
Sallustius *see* ORATIONES
Sallwuerk, Edmund von *see* OBERON
Salm, C L *see* THE PROBLEM OF POSITIVE THEOLOGY
Salm, Peter *see* FAUST, FIRST PART
Salmelainen, Eero *see* SUOMEN KANSAN SATUJA JA TARINOITA
Salmen, Walter *see* DAS ERBE DES OSTDEUTSCHEN VOLKSGESANGES
Salmeron, A *see* COMMENTARII IN EVANGELICAM HISTORIAM, ET IN ACTA APOSTOLORUM...
Salmon, E S A *see*
- THE ERYSIPHACEA-A MONOGRAPH
- A MONOGRAPH OF THE ERYSIPHACEAE
Salmon, George *see* SOME THOUGHTS ON THE TEXTUAL CRITICISM OF THE NEW TESTAMENT
SALMON P. CHASE PAPERS / Chase, Salmon Portland – 1825-71. Ohio Governor Series. Includes official (1856-60) and personal (1825-) papers, letterbooks (1853-60) – 1 – us Ohio Hist [920]
THE SALMON P. CHASE PAPERS – 1 – $4,735.00 – 0-89093-519-X – us UPA [320]
SALMON PORTLAND CHASE / Hart, Albert Bushnell – Boston & NY: Houghton, Mifflin & Co, 1899 – 6mf – 9 – $9.00 – LLMC 96-035 – us L.L.M.C. [975]
Salmon, W *see* ARS CHIRURGICA
Salmond, John W *see* ESSAYS IN JURISPRUDENCE AND LEGAL HISTORY
Salmond, Stewart Dingwall Fordyce *see* THE THEOLOGY OF THE OLD TESTAMENT
Salm-Reifferscheid-Dyck, J *see* MONOGRAPHIA GENERUM ALOES ET MESEMBRYANTHEMI
SALNAMAH [FROM THE PERIOD OF NASIR AL-DIN SHAH] – 1290 [1874?] – 1r – 1 – $150.00 – us MEDOC [949]
SALNAMAH VA AMAR – Majmu'ah-i Qavanin va Muqarrarat-i Farhangi. Vizarat-i Farhang-i Idarah-'i Nigarish–Da'irah-'i Amar. 1315-1316 va 1316-1317 [1936-1937 and 1937-1938] – 2r – 1 – $375.00 – us MEDOC [949]
SALNAMAH VA AMAR – Majmu'ah-'i Qavanin va Muqarrarat-i Farhangi. Vizarat-i Farhang-i Idarah-'i Nigarish–Da'irah-'i Amar. 1317-1318 va 1318-1319 [1938-1939 and 1939-1940] – 1r – 1 – $225.00 – us MEDOC [949]
SALNAMAH VA AMAR – Majmu'ah-'i Qavanin va Muqarrarat-i Farhangi. Vizarat-i Farhang-i Idarah-'i Nigarish–Da'irah-'i Amar. 1319-1320 va 1320-1321 va 1321-1322 [1940-1941 and 1941-1942 and 1942-1943] – 1r – 1 – $200.00 – us MEDOC [949]
SALNAMAH VA AMAR – Majmu'ah-i Qavanin va Muqarrarat-i Farhangi. Vizarat-i Farhang-i Idarah-'i Nigarish–Da'irah-'i Amar. 1322-1323 va 1323-1324 va 1324-1325 va 1325-1326 va 1326-1327 [1943-1944 and 1944-1945 and 1945-1946 and 1946-1947 and 1947-1948] – 1r – 1 – $200.00 – us MEDOC [949]
SALNAMAH-'I DANISHSARA-YI ALI – Tehran: Sal-i tahlsili, 1315-1316 va 1316-1317 [1936-1937 and 1937-1938] – 1r – 1 – $100.00 – us MEDOC [949]
SALNAMAH-'I MA'ARIF-I ISFAHAN – Tehran: Sal-i talsili, 1313-1314 [1934-1935] – 1r – 1 – $120.00 – us MEDOC [949]
Salomon, C *see*
- VERZEICHNISS DER BOTANISCHEN AUTOREN... ERLANGEN, 1870
- WOERTERBUCH DER DEUTSCHEN PLANZEN-NAMEN,...
Salomon, Ludwig *see* ALLGEMEINE GESCHICHTE DES ZEITUNGSWESENS
Salomon, Th *see* DEN GHEESTELIJCKEN NACHTEGAEL
DIE SALOMO-SAGE IN DER SEMITISCHEN LITERATUR / Salzberger, Georg – Berlin-Nikolassee: Max Harrwitz, 1907. 1 fiche – 9 – us A.T.L.A. [270]
DER SALON FUER LITERATUR, KUNST UND GESELLSCHAFT – Leipzig, 1868-72; 1888-89 – 14r – 1 – gw Mikrofilm [072]
Salonius, A H *see* VITAE PATRUM
THE SALOON PROBLEM AND SOCIAL REFORM / Barker, John Marshall – Boston, Mass.: Everett Press, 1905 – 1mf – us A.T.L.A. [360]
SALT – Edmonton. v11-15. 1989/90-1993/94 – 9 – Can$20.00y – cn Micromedia [073]
Salt, Henry *see* VOYAGE EN ABYSSINIE
Salt, Henry Stephens *see* PERCY BYSSHE SHELLEY, POET AND PIONEER
Salt Lake Art Center. Salt Lake, Utah *see* THE COMPLETE PHOTOGRAPHIC WORK OF JACOB A. RIIS
Salt Lake Tribune *see* SKETCHES OF THE INTER-MOUNTAIN STATES OF UTAH, IDAHO, AND NEVADA
SALT RIVER HERALD – Phoenix. Ariz. -w. and s-w. 1878-97 – 1 – us UMI [071]
SALT SPRING ISLAND CHURCH MONTHLY *see* SALT SPRING ISLAND PARISH AND HOME
SALT SPRING ISLAND PARISH AND HOME – (Cont by: Salt Spring Island Church Monthly) – S.l.: s.n., 1895-1901 – 9 – cn C.I.H.M. [910]
Salt, W *see* A MEMORIAL OF THE WESLEYAN METHODIST NEW CONNEXION; CONTAINING A SHORT ACCOUNT OF THE CIRCUIT PREACHERS WHO HAVE DIED...
SALT-AFFECTED SOILS AND THEIR MANAGEMENT – 1988 – 143p – it F.A.O. [631]
SALTBURN AND CLEVELAND ADVERTISER – England. -m. July 1927-Sept 1932. 30 ft – 1 – uk British Libr Newspaper [072]
SALTBURN OBSERVER – England. -m. Oct 1938-Oct 1939. 7 ft – 1 – uk British Libr Newspaper [072]
SALTBURN TIMES. (SALTBURN & GUISBRO' TIMES) – England. 17 Jun-16 Dec 1887; 27 Jun 1891-26 Jun 1896; 2 Jun 1900-29 Sep 1916; 28 Jun 1924-3 Jan 1925.-w. 8 reels – 1 – uk British Libr Newspaper [072]
SALTERIO – Caceres: Tip. La Minerva, 1962 – 1 – sp Bibl Santa Ana [946]
SALTERIO DE MIS HORAS (MECANOGRAFIADO) / Belloso Rodriguez, Pedro – 1975 – 1 – sp Bibl Santa Ana [810]
Saltet, Louis *see* LES REORDINATIONS
Saltiternik, C *see* REPORT
SALTO DE CEDILLO. SERVICIO DE MEDICINA Y SEGURIDAD DE H.E. 122ND CURSO DE FORMACION DE MONITORES DE SEGURIDAD / Hidroelectrica Espanola, S.A. – Caceres: Imp. La Minerva, 1972 – 1 – sp Bibl Santa Ana [350]
Saltus, Edgar *see* THE ANATOMY OF NEGATION
Saltykov-Shchedrin Library *see*
- A.A. TITOV COLLECTION. OKHRANNYI KATALOG SLAVIANO-RUSSKIKH RUKOPISEI A.A. TITOVA. V G. ROSTOVE IAROSLAVSKOI GUBERNII
- RUKOPISI M.E. SALTYKOVA-SHCHEDRINA
- RUKOPISI N.A. NEKRASOVA
- RUKOPISI N.V. GOGOLIA
- RUKOPISI S.N. GLINKI
- RUKOPISNYE FONDY PUBLICHNOI BIBLIOTEKI. PECHATNYE KATALOGI I OBZORY
- RUKOPISNYE MATERIALY OTNOSIASHCHIESIA K L. N. TOLSTOMU
- SREDNEVEKOV'E V RUKOPISIAKH PUBLICHNOI BIBLIOTEKI
- TUKOPISI V.G. BELINSKOGO
- TVORCHESKOE NASLEDIE M.A. BALAKIREVA
The Saltykov-Shchedrin State Public Library, St. Petersburg. (Russian National Library) *see* ZEMSTVO LIBRARY CARD CATALOGUE
Saltzer, Walter Gabriel *see* PARMENIDES, LEUKIPPOS UND DIE GRUNDLAGE DER EPIKURISCHEN PHYSIK UND ETHIK BEI LUKREZ
LA SALUD DE LA AMERICA ESPANOLA. PARIS, 1926 / Teran, Juan B; ed by Bayle, Constantino – Madrid: Razon y Fe, 1929 – 9 – sp Bibl Santa Ana [972]
SALUDA BAPTIST CHURCH. PICKENS COUNTY. CLEVELAND, SOUTH CAROLINA : CHURCH RECORDS – 1878-1977 – 1 – 18.99 – us Baptist [240]
SALUDA BAPTIST CHURCH. SALUDA COUNTY. SOUTH CAROLINA : CHURCH RECORDS – 1968-72 – 1 – 6.75 – us Baptist [240]
SALUT AU NOVEAU MONDE / Duguet, Ch – Paris, impr. Duverger avril 1833, 4 p. ADIEUX A L'ANCIEN MONDE. Ibid., mai 1833, 4 p. Les Saint-Simoniens, 1825-1834. 6966 – 9 – fr Hachette [335]
LE SALUT PUBLIC – Journal de Lyon. Dir.-red. en chef Max Grassis. Lyon. 1858 – 1 – fr A.C.R.P.P. [073]
LE SALUT PUBLIC – Journal quotidien, politique, scientifique et litteraire. Red. en chef l'abbe Orsini. no. 1-58. Paris. mars-mai 1848 – 1 – fr A.C.R.P.P. [073]
LA SALVACION, EL ENGRANDECIMIENTO MORAL Y LA FELICIDAD DE ESPANA, O SEAN LOS MEDIOS SEGUROS DE CONSEGUIRLOS / Ruiz Gomez, Juan Eugenio – Madrid, 1898. Fiche W1151. (Blodgett Collection of Spanish Civil War Pamphlets) – 9 – us H.U. College Libr [946]
EL SALVADOR : PLAN DE DESARRLLO ECONOMICO Y SOCIAL 1989-1994 / Ministerio de Planificacion y Coordinacion... – San Salvador, [1990] – 3mf – 9 – ne IDC [338]
El Salvador *see*
- DIARIO OFICIAL
EL SALVADOR, 1930-45 / U.S. Department of State – (See also series listing) – 28 reels with printed guide. Series: Confidential U.S. Diplomatic Post Records: Central America and the Caribbean – 1 – $3,080.00 – us UPA [972]
EL SALVADOR AND GUATEMALA COMMITTEES FOR HUMAN RIGHTS (ESCHR) – London. 62 docs. 1982-1991 – 18mf – 9 – ne IDC [320]
El Salvador. Consejo Nacional de Planificacion *see* PRIMER PLAN DE LA NACION PARA EL DESARROLLO ECONOMICO Y SOCIAL, 1965-1969
El Salvador. Consejo Nacional de Planificacion y Coordinacion Economica *see*
- PLAN DE DESARROLLO ECONOMICO Y SOCIAL 1968-1972
- PLAN DE DESARROLLO ECONOMICO Y SOCIAL 1973-1977
- PRIMER PLAN DE DESARROLLO ECONOMICO Y SOCIAL, 1965-1969
El Salvador. Courts *see* CORTE DE CUENTAS
El Salvador. Direccion General de Educacion Superior *see* EDUCACION SUPERIOR EN CIFRAS 1987-1988
El Salvador. Instituto Salvadoreno de Fomento de la Produccion *see* PROGRAMA QUINQUENAL, 1961-1965
Salvador, T A *see* ORNITHOLOGIA DELLA PAPUASIA E DELLE MOLUCCHE
Salvador, T.A *see* AGGIUNTE ALLA ORNITOLOGIA DELLA PAPUASIA E DELLE MOLUCCHE
Salvador y Conde, Jose *see*
- FV. PEDRO DE FERIA Y SU DOCTRINA ZAPOTECA. ESTUDIO BIBLIOGRAFICO
- EL PADRE DOMINGO DE LA ANUNCIACION Y SU PERSONALIDAD MISIONERA
Salvadore, Carlos F *see* REVIEW OF REAL PROPERTY
SALVATION : THE WAY MADE PLAIN / Brookes, James Hall – London: Pickering & Inglis, [188-?] – 1mf – 9 – 0-8370-6245-4 – 1986-0245 – us A.T.L.A. [240]
SALVATION / Wilder, Robert Parmelee – Calcutta: Christian Tract and Book Society, 1901 – 1mf – 9 – 0-8370-5758-2 – 1985-3758 – us A.T.L.A. [210]
Salvation Army *see*
- DARKEST ENGLAND GAZETTE
- WAR CRY
- WAR CRY, 1881-1981
THE SALVATION ARMY IN RELATION TO THE CHURCH AND STATE : AND OTHER ADDRESSES / Booth, Catherine Mumford – London: S.W. Partridge, 1883 – 1mf – us A.T.L.A. [360]
SALVATION BY CHRIST : A SERIES OF DISCOURSES ON SOME OF THE MOST IMPORTANT DOCTRINES OF THE GOSPEL / Wayland, Francis – [rev enl ed]. Boston: Gould and Lincoln, 1859, c1858 – 1mf – 9 – 0-8370-7515-7 – 1986-1515 – us A.T.L.A. [240]
SALVATION IN A TWO-FOLD ASPECT : THE GOSPEL: IS IT MERELY AN ADDITION TO THE "LAW," OR IS IT IN TRUTH THE "GLAD TIDINGS" OF AN INFINITE LOVE? / Scull, David – Philadelphia: John C Winston, 1897, c1896 – 1mf – 9 – 0-8370-5322-6 – 1985-3322 – us A.T.L.A. [240]
THE SALVATIONIST – 1879 – 1 – uk Microform Academic [073]
SALVE – 1987-1995 – 3r per y – 5,6 – Sfr642.00 – sz Infoprint [073]
SALVIANI PRESBYTERI MASSILIENSIS LIBRI QUI SUPERSUNT (MGH1: 1.BD. 1.TEIL) / ed by Halm, C – 1877 – ne Slangenburg [240]
Salvin, O *see*
- EXOTIC ORNITHOLOGY
- NOMENCLATOR AVIUM NEOTROPICALIUM
SALVS EX JNIMICIS. GOLIATHS SCHWERDT. AUGENSCHEINLICHE ERWEYSUNG, WAS WIR CATHOLISCHE VNND ALTE CHRISTEN FUER KLARE VND KRAEFFTIGE ARGUMENTA VNND ZEUGNUSSEN HABEN / Erhard, Chr – Ingolstatt, W. Eder. 1586. BME-139 1 – 9 – ne IDC [240]
Salvy, S F A *see* BIBLIOGRAPHIE DES OEUVRES DU TRES REVEREND PERE FREDERIC JANSSOONE DE GHYVELDE, APOTRE DE PALESTINE ET DE NOTRE-DAME DU CAP, FONDATEUR DU COMMISSARIAT DE TERRE SAINTE AU CANADA, 1838-1916
Salzberger, Georg *see* DIE SALOMO-SAGE IN DER SEMITISCHEN LITERATUR
Salzburg. Landtag *see* VERHANDLUNGEN
SALZBURGER NACHRICHTEN – Salzburg. Jan 1979-Jun 82 – 9 – 22310.00y – gw Alpha Com [072]
THE SALZBURGERS AND THEIR DESCENDANTS : BEING THE HISTORY OF A COLONY OF GERMAN (LUTHERAN) PROTESTANTS WHO EMIGRATED TO GEORGIA IN 1734, AND SETTLED AT EBENEZER, TWENTY-FIVE MILES ABOVE THE CITY OF SAVANNAH / Strobel, P A – Baltimore: T. Newton Kurtz, 1855 – 1mf – us A.T.L.A. [978]
Salzer, Anselm *see*
- ILLUSTRIERTE GESCHICHTE DER DEUTSCHEN LITERATUR VON DEN AELTESTEN ZEITEN BIS ZUR GEGENWART
- ILLUSTRIERTE GESCHICHTE DER DEUTSCHER LITERATUR VON DEN AELTESTEN ZEITEN BIS ZUR GEGENWART
Salzer, E *see* BRIEFE VON UND AN FRIEDRICH VON GENTZ
SALZGITTER-ZEITUNG : BA DER BRAUNSCHWEIGER ZEITUNG – Salzgitter, Germany. 1977- – ca 9r per yr – 1 – gw Mikrofilm [072]
Salzmann, Auguste *see* JERUSALEM
SAM ADVANCED MANAGEMENT JOURNAL – v49, no.2-. Spring 1984- – 1,5,6,9 – us UMI [650]
SAM HAYYIM – Prague. 1590. BJ-43-77 1 – 9 – ne IDC [470]
SAM SLY'S AFRICAN JOURNAL – Cape Town, South Africa.1 Jun 1843-25 Sept 1851. Title varies: African Journal, 1849-51 – 3r – 1, 16 diazo available at reduced price – sa SA Libr [072]
Sama, J *see* INDICACIONES DE FILOSOFIA Y PEDAGOGIA
THE SAMACHAR – Zanzibar, Tanzania. -w. Jan 1941-June 1944; Jan 1945-Dec 1951; Jan 1958-April 1962. 15 reels – 1 – uk British Libr Newspaper [072]
SAMAJ – (Oriya language) – Cuttack, India. 18 Apr 1944-1993 – 137r – 1 – us L of C Photodup [072]
SAMANTHA AMONG THE BRETHREN / Holley, Marietta – 1892 – 9 – us A.T.L.A. [240]
SAMARIA IN AHAB'S TIME, HARVARD EXCAVATIONS AND THEIR RESULTS / Jack, J W – T. and T. Clark, 1929 – 9 – $10.00 – us I.R.C. [930]
SAMARIA, THE CAPITAL OF THE KINGDOM OF ISRAEL / Parrot, Andre – S.C.M. Press, 1958 – 9 – $10.00 – us I.R.C. [930]
SAMARIA UND SEINE PROPHETEN: EIN RELIGIONSGESCHICHTLICHER VERSUCH / Lincke, Karl F A – Tuebingen: J.C.B. Mohr, 1903. 1 fiche – 9 – us A.T.L.A. [240]

SAMARITAN WORD-BOOK : OR, THE PRINCIPAL WORDS IN THE SAMARITAN VERSION OF THE PENTATEUCH: IN ALPHABETICAL ORDER, WITH ENGLISH EXPLANATIONS / Young, Robert – Edinburgh: Robert Young, [186-?] – 1mf – 9 – 0-8370-7117-8 – 1986-1117 – us A.T.L.A. [470]

SAMARITANA / Clavier, Irene – Montevideo: Editorial America Latina, 1948 – 1 – CSUXAJA7516-B – us Hoover Inst Photo [972]

THE SAMARITANS, THE EARLIEST JEWISH SECT; THEIR HISTORY, THEOLOGY, AND LITERATURE / Montgomery, James A – 1907 – 1 – us A.T.L.A. [270]

Samarow, Gregor *see*
- DIE GROSSFUERSTIN
- IM BANN DER IRREDENTA
- DES KRONPRINZEN REGIMENT
- PLEWNA
- DIE ROEMERFAHRT DES EPIGONEN
- UM SZEPTER UND KRONEN
- UM ZEPTER UND KRONEN

Samarskii, Aleksandr Andreevich *see* VVEDENIE V TEORIIU RAZNOSTNYKH SKHEM

SAMARSKOE GUBERNSKOE STATISTICHESKOE BIURO *see* SOSTOIANIE OZIMYKH I IAROVYKH POSEVOV V SAMARSKOI GUBERNII K...

Samarskoe gubernskoe statisticheskoe biuro *see*
- CHISLENNOST SELSKOGO NASELENIIA V SAMARSKOI GUBERNII
- UROZHAI TRAV V SAMARSKOI GUBERNII V...GODU
- VESTNIK SAMARSKOGO GUBERNSKOGO STATISTICHESKOGO BIURO
- ZAPASY ZERNOVYKH KHLEBOV I KORMOV V SAMARSKOI GUBERNII NA...

THE SAMAS RELIGIOUS TEXTS : CLASSIFIED IN THE BRITISH MUSEUM CATALOGUE AS HYMNS, PRAYERS, AND INCANTATIONS / Gray, Clifton Daggett – (In English and Akkadian) – Chicago: University of Chicago Press, 1901 – 1mf – 9 – 0-8370-7046-5 – 1986-1046 – us A.T.L.A. [470]

SAMBATION – (In Yiddish) – Warsaw, PL. no1 Passover 1922-no6 6 Sep 1922 – 1r – 1 – $25.00 – cn Can Microfilming [072]

Sambeeck, J *see* HET GEESTELYCK JUBILEE VAN HET JAER O.H. M.D.C.L....

Samber, Johann B *see*
- ELUCIDATIO MUSICAE CHORALIS..
- MANUDUCTIO AD ORGANUM..

LA SAMBUCA LINCEO, OVERO DELL'INSTROMENTO MUSICO PERFETTO LIB 3, DI FABIO COLONNA LINCEO NE'QUALIOLTRE LA DESCRITTIONE / Colonna, F – P 666 – 9 – ne IDC [780]

Sambucus, Joannes *see*
- EMBLEMATA, CUM ALIQUOT NUMMIS ANTIQUI OPERIS
- EMBLEMATA, ET ALIQUOT NUMMI ANTIQUI OPERIS
- EMBLEMATA I. SAMBUCI

Sambuga, Joseph Anton *see* REDEN UND AUFSAETZE

Sambuscus, Joannes *see* EMBLEMATA: CUM ALIQUOT NUMMIS ANTIQUI OPERIS

SAME-DAY SURGERY – (v.3-. 1979- 5,6,9) – v.1-. 1977- – 1 – us UMI [617]

LE SAMEDI : REVUE, HEBDOMADAIRE ILLUSTREE – (3 jan 1942-mai 1963 22r Can$60.00) – Montreal, Canada. 15 jun 1889-2 jun 1917 – 19r – 1 – Can$60.00r – cn Can Microfilming [072]

SAMEDI-DIMANCHE / ed by Poulin, Henri – Verdun. v1 n7. 21 jun 1952-v1 n52. 2 mai 1953; 2 oct 1954-v5 n1. 1 dec 1954 – 1r – 1 – Can$45.00 – cn Can Microfilming [072]

SAMEDI-SOIR – Paris. 16 juin 1945-46 – 1 – fr A.C.R.P.P. [073]

SAMEN, FRUECHTE UND KEIMLINGE / Tubeuf, C von – Berlin. 1891. B-7372 1 – 9 – ne IDC [580]

SAMFUNDET TIL UDGIVELSE AF GAMMEL NORDISK LITTERATUR – Kobenhavn. v1-60. 1880-1943 – 391mf – 9 – H-398/2 – ne IDC [430]

SAMHAIN : EDITED FOR THE IRISH LITERARY THEATRE – Dublin. v1-7. 1901-08 – 1r – 1 – us Ross [790]

SAMHALLSGEMENSKAP – Stockholm, Sweden. 1979-88 – 1 – sw Kungliga [072]

Sami, Ebuesuereyya *see* ABDUELHAMID'IN KAYGULARI

Sami, Mustafa et al *see* TARIH-I SAMI VE SAKIR VE SUBHI

Samidi, A *see*
- KOMPAS BAHASA; BUKU LATIRAN BAHASA INDONESIA BAGI SEKOLAH LANDJUTAN ATAS
- SIMPAI SASTRA; DIHIDANGKAN KEPADA PELADJAR SEKOLAH LANDJUTAN

Samillan, L *see* DISCURSO...DEL SARAMPION Y VIRUELAS...

THE SAMIZDAT BULLETIN – San Mateo. 101 docs. 1980-88 – 25mf – 9 – HRD-1238/1 – ne IDC [073]

THE SAMIZDAT BULLETIN – San Mateo. 109 docs. 1980-1990 – 29mf – 9 – ne IDC [320]

THE SAMKHYA SYSTEM / Keith, Arthur Berriedale – A history of the Samkhya Philosophy. Ed. 2. London. 1924. BI-1074 1 – 9 – ne IDC [180]

SAMLA MICROFORM SERIES – 1018mf – 9 – $2,465.00 – us OmniSys [440]

SAMLADE SKRIFTER / Runeberg, Johan Ludvig – Stockholm, 1870.6v in 5 – 1 – us U.W. Library [948]

SAMLUNG VERSCHIEDENER UND AUSERLESENER...1. THEIL / Graefe, J F – Halle: s.n., 1737 – 7mf – 9 – us Sibley [780]

Sammartini, Giuseppe *see* 7 SONATAS A OBOE SOLO CON IL BASSO; 18 SONATAS A FLUTA TRAVERSIER CON IL BASSO; 1 SONATA A? SOLO CON IL BASSO

SAMMELBAENDE DER INTERNATIONALEN MUSIK-GESELLSCHAFT – Leipzig. v. 1-15. 1899 1900-1914 – 127mf – 9 – ne IDC [780]

DIE SAMMLUNG : LITERARISCHE MONATSSCHRIFT – Amsterdam, sep 1933-aug 1935 – 1r – 1 – Dist. gw Mikrofilm – gw Misc Inst [800]

SAMMLUNG ABENDSMAHLSORDNUNGEN : A COLLECTION OF 306 ORDERS FOR THE ADMINISTRATION OF THE LORD'S SUPPER IN THE CHURCHES OF THE REFORMATION ALL OVER THE WORLD FROM 1523 / Pfahl, I – Slangenburg, 1973 – 9 – Dfl1,208.00 – ne Slangenburg [240]

SAMMLUNG AUSERLESNER GEISTLICHER LIEDER / Bimeler, Joseph Michael – Zoar, Tuscarawas, OH. 1855 – 1r – 1 – us Western Res [780]

SAMMLUNG AUSERLESNER GEISTLICHER LIEDER / Bimeler, Joseph Michael – Zoar, Tuscarawas, OH. 1867 – 1r – 1 – us Western Res [780]

SAMMLUNG BERNISCHER BIOGRAPHIEN – Bern, 1884-1906. Schmid and Francke, 1884-1902. Francke. 5v. 1906 – 38mf – 9 – ne IDC [240]

SAMMLUNG BERUEHMTER SONATEN, REVIDIRT UND MIT FINGERSATZ VERSEHEN VON LOUIS KOEHLER UND F.A. ROITZSCH / Clementi, Muzio – Leipzig: C F Peters, [187-] – 1 – us Sibley [780]

SAMMLUNG DER DEUTSCHEN ABHANDLUNGEN / Akademie der Wissenschaften. Berlin – 6V. 1788-1803 – 1 – us Schnase [500]

SAMMLUNG DER DEUTSCHEN ABHANDLUNGEN WELCHE IN DER KOENIGLICHEN AKADEMIE DER WISSENSCHAFTEN ZU BERLIN VORGELESEN WORDEN, 1788/1789-1803 – Berlin, 1793-1806 – 51mf – 9 – H-640/2 – ne IDC [943]

SAMMLUNG DER DRUCKSACHEN / Prussia. Landtag. Haus der Abgeordneten – 1901-16 18. 15v – 1 – 1127.00 – us L of C Photodup [324]

SAMMLUNG EUROPAEISCHER SCHMETTERLINGE / Huebner, J – 2154 2. (1793- 1796-1830(-41) – 8 – ne IDC [590]

SAMMLUNG MUSIKALISCHER SCHRIFTEN, GROESSTENTHEILS AUS DEM WERKEN DER ITALIAENER UND FRANZOSEN UEBERSETZT / Hertel, J W – Leipzig. Breitkopf. 1757; 1758. BP-695 1 – 9 – ne IDC [780]

SAMMLUNG MUSIKALISCHER SCHRIFTEN, GROESSTENTHEILS AUS DEN WERKEN DER ITALIAENER UND FRANZOSEN UEBERSETZT,... / Hertel, J W – Leipzig: Breitkopf, 1757-1758 – 2mf – ne IDC [780]

SAMMLUNG NEUER, ODER WENIG BEKANNTER, AUSSEREUROPAEISCHER SCHMETTERLINGEN / Herrich-Schaeffer, G A W – Regensburg, 1850-58. Z/1346/2 – 8 – ne IDC [590]

SAMMLUNG SAMMTLICHER DRUCKSACHEN / Prussia. Landtag. Haus der Abgeordneten – 1855 56-1866. (1849, 1850 51 and scattered issues of 1866 wanting) – 1 – 875.00 – us L of C Photodup [943]

SAMMLUNG VERMISCHTER SCHRIFTEN UEBER KIRCHENGESCHICHTE UND KIRCHENRECHT / Fessler, Joseph – Freiburg im Breisgau: Herder, 1869 – 1mf – us A.T.L.A. [240]

SAMMLUNG VERTRAEGE DER SCHWEIZ MIT... / Eichman, A – Zuerich, 1885 – 4mf – 1 – ILM-1763/1 – ne IDC [327]

SAMMLUNG VON KLAVIER UND SING-STUCKEN VERSCHIEDENER VERFERTIGER ZUSAMMENGETRAGEN VON J.C. BAUMBACH / Baumbach, J C – Ms – 1 – us Sibley [780]

SAMMLUNG VON KRITISCHEN AUFSAETZEN UND KURZBIOGRAPHIEN ZUR GESCHICHTE DER DEUTSCHEN LITERATUR – Bukarest: Verlag "Das Buch", 1956 – 1r – 1 – us U.W. Library [430]

SAMMLUNG VON NATUR- UND MEDICIN-[...] GESCHICHTEN – Breslau, jul 1717-jun 1718, jul 1721-jun 1722 – 1 – Inquire at Mikrofilmarchiv for details – gw Misc Inst [600]

SAMMLUNG VON VORTRAEGEN FUER DAS DEUTSCHE VOLK, ERSTER BAND / ed by Frommel, Wilhelm & Pfaff, Friedrich – Heidelberg: Carl Winter, 1879 – 1mf – 9 – 0-8370-5030-8 – 1985-3030 – us A.T.L.A. [240]

SAMMLUNGEN HISTORISCHER NACHRICHTEN UEBER DIE MONGOLISCHEN VOELKERSCHAFTEN... / Pallas, Peter Simon – Spb. 2v. 1776-1801 – 26mf – 9 – ne IDC [950]

DIE SAMMLUNGEN INLAENDISCHER ALTERTUEMER UND ANDERER AUF DIE BALTISCHEN PROVINZEN BEZUEGLICHEN GEGENSTAENDE DES ESTLAENDISCHEN PROVINZIAL-MUSEUMS / Hansen, G von – Reval, 1875 – 2mf – 9 – ne IDC [947]

Sammut, C *see* L'IMPERIALISME DU CAPITALISME FRANCAIS EN TUNISIE ET LE NATIONALISME TUNISIEN (1891-1914)

Samoa *see* CONSTITUTION OF AMERICAN SAMOA, 1960

SAMOA AND ITS STORY / Cowan, James – Christchurch, Wellington, Dunedin, Melbourne, London: Whitcombe & Tombs, 1914 – 1mf – 9 – $1.50 – LLMC 82-100C Title 30 – us L.L.M.C. [980]

SAMOA BULLETIN – 9 jan 1953-5 mar 1954 – 1r – 1 – PMB Doc407 – at Pacific Mss [073]

SAMOA BULLETIN – (In English and Samoan) – Apia, Western Samoa: William Tarr, 3 nov 1950-31 dec 1952 – 1r – 1 – PMB Doc406 – at Pacific Mss [073]

SAMOA COMES OF AGE : A CASE STUDY / Bishop, James K – US State dept Senior Seminar in Foreign Policy, 19th sess. Washington: State Dept?, apr 1977 – 1mf – 9 – $1.50 – LLMC 82-100C Title 47 – us L.L.M.C. [327]

Samoa. Western. Economic Development Board *see* WESTERN SAMOAS ECONOMIC DEVELOPMENT PROGRAMME, 1966-1970

SAMOAN AFFAIRS : MESSAGE FROM THE PRESIDENT OF THE U.S. TO THE CONGRESS / Cleveland, President – 53rd Congress 3rd sess. Senate Exec Doc No 97 26 Feb 1895. Washington: GPO?, n.d. – 5mf – 9 – $7.50 – LLMC 82-100C Title 31 – us L.L.M.C. [327]

THE SAMOAN CRISES AND ITS CAUSES / Leigh, John G – NS: v389. may 1899 – 1mf – 9 – $1.50 – LLMC 82-100C Title 28 – us L.L.M.C. [980]

SAMOAN LAND TITLES : NOTES ON THE PRACTICE OF THE COURT AND THE PRINCIPLES ADOPTED IN THE HEARING OF CASES AFFECTING MATAI TITLES AND LANDS HELD ACCORDING TO THE CUSTOMS AND USAGES OF WESTERN SAMOA / Marsack, C C – Apia, Western Samoa: Land & Titles Court, jul 1958 – 1mf – 9 – $1.50 – LLMC 82-100C Title 21 – us L.L.M.C. [340]

THE SAMOAN PACIFIC LAW JOURNAL / American Samoa. Bar Association – (Irregular publ schedule. Became an annual in 1980) – Pago Pago: American Samoa Bar Assoc. v1-7. 1973-81 – 23mf – 9 – $34.50 – LLMC 82-100C Title 18 – us L.L.M.C. [340]

THE SAMOAN SETTLEMENT OF 1899 : BETRAYAL OF NEW ZEALAND INTERESTS? / Andrew, A L – sep 25 1966 – 1mf – 9 – $1.50 – LLMC 82-100C Title 38 – us L.L.M.C. [980]

SAMOANISCHE ZEITUNG – Apia, apr 9 1901-dec 26 1914 – 1 – Dist. gw Mikrofilm – gw Misc Inst [980]

SAMODEIATEL'NOST' POTREBITELIA – (Missing: 1915 n7-9; 1916 n7; 1917 n1-2) – Krasnoiarsk, 1915-17 n4 – 5mf – 9 – COR-675/1 – ne IDC [334]

SAMODERZHAVIE I LIBERALY V REVOLIUTSIIU 1905-1907 GODOV / Alekseev, S A – M., L., 1925. 168p – 2mf – 9 – ne IDC [320]

SAMODERZHAVIE I PECHAT' V ROSSII – (Biblioteka Svetocha no. 4, pod. red. S. A. Vengerova): St. Petersburg, 1906. 80p. BR-10,091 1 – 9 – ne IDC [460]

SAMOEDERA – (Lacking: 1946-1947, V.1-2(1-2)) – Tandjoeng Balai, Penerangan Pangkalan Besar Tandjoeng Balai, 1946-1947.-v1-2(1-5) – 1mf – 9 – SE-104/1 – ne IDC [950]

Samoff, Joel *see* COPING WITH CRISIS

SAMOKOVSKA TRIBUNA – Samokov, Bulgaria. Apr-May 1958 – 1r – 1 – us L of C Photodup [949]

Samokvasov, D Ia *see*
- ARKHIVNOE DELO V ROSSII
- PROEKT ARKHIVNOI REFORMY I SOVREMENNOE SOSTOIANIE OKONCHATEL'NYKH ARKHIVOV V ROSSII
- RUSSKIE ARKHIVY I TSARSKII KONTROL' PRIKAZNOI SLUZHBY V 17 VEKE

SAMOPOMOSHCH' – (Missing: 1915 n2) – Iaroslavl', 1915-17 n12 – 13mf – 9 – COR-677/1 – ne IDC [334]

SAMOPOMOSHCH' *see* IZVESTIJA SAMARSKOGO OBSHCHESTVA POTREBITELEI "SAMOPOMOSHCH"

SAMOPOZNANIE / Berdiaev, N A – Paris. 1949. BR-1996 2 – 8 – ne IDC [190]

Samorukova, N A *see* SPRAVOCHNIK SOKRASHCHENII, PRINIATYKH V ISTORICHESKOI LITERATURE

SAMOSOZHZHENIE V RUSSKOM RASKOLE. (SO VTOROI POLOVINY 17 VEKA DO KONTSA 18 V.) / Sapozhnikov, D I – M. 1891. BR-7831 2 – 8 – ne IDC [947]

O SAMOUBIISTVIE / Berdiaev, N A – Paris. 1931 – 1 – us Res Libr [150]

SAMOUCHITEL CHTENIIA RUKOPISEI 17 STOLETIIA – Moscow, 1872. BR-10,051/2 – 8 – ne IDC [947]

SAMOUCHITEL' CHTENIIA RUKOPISEI 17 STOLETIIA / Esipov, G V – Moscow, 1892. BR/10,322/1 – 9 – ne IDC [947]

Samouelle, G *see*
- THE ENTOMOLOGICAL CABINET: BEING A NATURAL HISTORY OF BRITISH INSECTS
- THE ENTOMOLOGIST'S USEFUL COMPENDIUM: OR, AN INTRODUCTION TO THE KNOWLEDGE OF BRITISH INSECTS

SAMOUPRAVA – Belgrade, Yugoslavia. -w. 19 Oct 1938-22 March 1941. Imperfect. 1 reel – 1 – uk British Libr Newspaper [949]

Sampaio, G *see* ELEVEN SELECTED PAPERS

Sampey, John R *see*
- THE PROPER ATTITUDE OF YOUNG MINISTERS TOWARD ISSUES OF THE DAY
- SOUTHERN BAPTIST THEOLOGICAL SEMINARY, 1859-89

SAMPLE SURVEYS OF CURRENT INTEREST / United Nations – E.45 – 9 (ST/STAT/Ser.C/1-13; ST/ESA/STAT/Ser.C/14-15) – us U.N. Pubs [310]

SAMPLES, DEMONSTRATIONS AND PACKAGING, THEIR USE IN ADVERTISING / Lewis, Norman – New York: The Ronald Press Company, (c1928). vii,250p. Plates.1 reel. 1290 – 1 – us U.W. Library [380]

SAMPLING METHODS FOR AGRICULTURAL SURVEYS – 1989 – 269p – it F.A.O. [630]

Samsel, N Ancilla *see* POLISH-CATHOLIC BOOK PUBLISHING IN THE U.S. AND ITS DISTRIBUTION DURING THE PERIOD 1871-1900

SAMSON, AN ORATORIO, THE WORDS TAKEN FROM MILTON / Handel, George Frederic – London: I Walsh, ca 1763 – 1 – us Sibley [780]

Samson, George Whitefield *see*
- THE ATONEMENT
- THE CLASSIC TEST OF AUTHORSHIP, AUTHENTICITY AND AUTHORITY
- THE ENGLISH REVISERS' GREEK TEXT
- GUIDE TO BIBLE INTERPRETATION

SAMSON OCCOM AND THE CHRISTIAN INDIANS OF NEW ENGLAND / Love, William Deloss – Boston: Pilgrim Press, c1899 – 1mf – us A.T.L.A. [240]

SAMSUN – Samsun, Cikaran: Samsun Vilayeti, 1925-?. No. 150 (20 Eyluel 1927) – 1mf – 9 – $10.00 – us MEDOC [949]

SAMTLICHE WERKE / Brahms, Johannes – v. 1-26. 1926-27 – 1 – 74.00 – us L of C Photodup [780]

THE SAMUEL ADAMS DIARIES – (Includes printed guide) – Rare Books and Manuscript Division: The New York Public Library, Astor, Lenox and Tilden Foundations 1995 – ca 7r – 1 – ca $595.00 – D3335 – us Scholarly Res [320]
SAMUEL AND HIS AGE: A STUDY IN THE CONSTITUTIONAL HISTORY OF ISRAEL / Douglas, George C M – London: Eyre & Spottiswoode, 1901. 1 fiche – 9 – us A.T.L.A. [240]
SAMUEL AND SAUL; THEIR LIVES AND TIMES / Deane, William John – London, 1888 – 1 – us U.W. Library [920]
Samuel Bowles and Co *see* SPRINGFIELD COUNTY DIRECTORY 1867/68
Samuel, E *see* AN HISTORICAL ACCOUNT OF THE BRITISH ARMY AND OF THE LAW MILITARY...
THE SAMUEL FRANCIS DU PONT PAPERS / Du Pont, Samuel Francis; ed by Nash, Michael – (With printed guide) – 48r – 1 – $4,080.00 – S3161 – us Scholarly Res [976]
SAMUEL GOBAT : BISHOP OF JERUSALEM : HIS LIFE AND WORK : A BIOGRAPHICAL SKETCH / Gobat, Samuel – London: J. Nisbet, 1884 – 1mf – us A.T.L.A. [240]
SAMUEL GOMPERS AND THE AMERICAN FEDERATION OF LABOR – (Coll 1: American Federation of Labor Records: The Samuel Gompers Era 144r £6,825 Guide £48. Coll 2: American Federation of Labor and the Unions: National and International Union Records from the Samuel Gompers Era 5r £310 Guide £36) – 2 coll – 1 – uk Chadwyck [331]
SAMUEL HEBICH OF INDIA : THE MASTER FISHER OF MEN / Thomssen, George Nicholas – Cuttack, India: Orissa Mission Press, 1905 – 1mf – 9 – 0-8370-6626-3 – 1986-0626 – us A.T.L.A. [920]
SAMUEL HOLDEN PARSONS PAPERS, MS 3204 / Parsons, Samuel Holden – 1760-1830 (1770-1790). 1 reel. Includes 4 page guide – 1 – us Western Res [920]
SAMUEL J. MILLS : MISSIONARY, PATHFINDER, PIONEER AND PROMOTER / Richards, Thomas Cole – (Includes appendixes) – Boston: Pilgrim Press, 1906 – 1mf – 9 – 0-8370-6606-9 – 1986-0606 – us A.T.L.A. [920]
SAMUEL NESHKIN SCRAPBOOKS *see* NESHKIN, SAMUEL, SCRAPBOOKS, MS 3804
Samuel, P *see* JOURNAL, 1841-1851, 1853-1859
Samuel, Peter *see* THE WESLEYAN-METHODIST MISSIONS IN JAMAICA AND HONDURAS DELINEATED
Samuel, Richard H *see* DIE POETISCHE STAATS- UND GESCHICHTSAUFFASSUNG FRIEDRICH VON HARDENBERGS (NOVALIS)
SAMUEL THE PROPHET / Meyer, Frederick Brotherton – New York: Fleming H Revell, [ca 1902] – 1mf – 9 – 0-8370-9720-7 – 1986-3720 – us A.T.L.A. [920]
SAMUEL THORNTON SEA ATLAS / Thornton, Samuel – New York, 1991 – 22mf – 15 – $295.00 – Co-published with the New York Public Library – us Comics [900]
SAMUEL UND SAUL : 1551 / Schmeltzl, Wolfgang; ed by Spengler, Franz – (Original t.p. of 1551 ed. added) – Wien: C Konegen, 1883 – 1r – 1 – us U.W. Library [943]
SAMUEL'S AYLESBURY SHOPPING GUIDE – England.Apr 1926-1927.-w. 1 reel – 1 – uk British Libr Newspaper [074]
Samuelson, James *see* BULGARIA, PAST AND PRESENT; HISTORICAL, POLITICAL, AND DESCRIPTIVE
Samuelson, Paul A *see* ECONOMICS
Samuelsson, A *see* DIE ARTEN DER GATTUNG ALISMA
Samuely, N *see* LYRISCHE KLAENGE
SAMYUKTA KARNATAKA – Hubli, India. 11 May-31 Dec 1953; Mar 1966-Jul 1987 – 83r – 1 – us L of C Photodup [072]
S.A.N. *see* THE ABC OF WALL STREET
SAN AGUSTIN DE JOVEN / Fabo de Maria – Madrid, 1931; Madrid: Razon y Fe, 1933 – 1 – sp Bibl Santa Ana [240]
SAN ANDREAS INDEPENDENT – San Andreas, CA. 1858-1860 – 1r – 1 – $50.00 – C03448 – us Library Micro [071]
SAN ANDRES ISLAND FIRST BAPTIST CHURCH. SAN ANDRES ISLAND, COLOMBIA : CHURCH RECORDS – 1852-1959 – 1 – 56.24 – us Baptist [240]
San Antonio Baptist Association *see* A BAPTIST CENTURY AROUND THE ALAMO
San Antonio Capilla, Fr. Fernando *see* VIDA...MARIA DE CRISTO
SAN ANTONIO EXPRESS – San Antonio, Texas. 1868- – 1 – us UMI [071]
San Antonio, Gabriel de *see* RELACION DE LOS SUCESOS DEL REINO DE LA CAMBODJA. MADRID, 1929
SAN BENITO ADVANCE – Hollister, CA. 1894-1920 – 7r – 1 – $350.00 – C03604 – us Library Micro [071]
SAN BENITO/MONTEREY COUNTIES – 1909-34; 1992- – 22+ r – 1 – $1,100.00 – P00066 – us Library Micro [910]
SAN BERNARDINO AMERICAN – San Bernardino, CA. 1979-92 – 14r – 1 – $700.00 – R02768 – us Library Micro [071]
SAN BERNARDINO COUNTY : SAN BERNARDINO, LAKE ARROWHEAD, CRESTLINE, COLTON, ETIWANDA, FONTANA, HIGHLAND, LOMA LINDA, RIALTO AND BIG BEAR LAKE – 1900-34; 1942-61 – 46r – 1 – $2,300.00 – P00093 – us Library Micro [910]
SAN BERNARDINO COUNTY, 1817-1949 – 32r – 1 – $1,600.00 – D080 – us Library Micro [978]
SAN BERNARDINO COUNTY EVENING TRANSCRIPT – San Bernardino, CA. 1902 – 2r – 1 – $100.00 – R03457 – us Library Micro [071]
SAN BERNARDINO INDEPENDENT NEWS ADVERTISER – San Bernardino, CA. 1941-1947 – 1r – 1 – $50.00 – R03458 – us Library Micro [071]
SAN BERNARDINO NEWS – San Bernardino, CA. 1912-1918 – 14r – 1 – $700.00 – R03459 – us Library Micro [071]
SAN BERNARDINO TRI-COUNTY BULLETIN – San Bernardino, CA. 1945-1946 – 1r – 1 – $50.00 – R03460 – us Library Micro [071]
SAN BERNARDINO WEEKLY TIMES INDEX – San Bernardino, CA. 1891-1906 – 5r – 1 – $250.00 – R03461 – us Library Micro [071]
San Bernardo, Alonso de *see* VIDA...SAN PEDRO DE ALCANTARA
SAN BRUNO HERALD – (San Bruno Herald 1920-71 31r $1,550.00. Peninsula News and San Bruno Progress 1971-74 22r $1,100.00. San Bruno Herald and Recorder Progress 1974-75 1 1r $550.00. San Bruno Herald 1980. Incl area pages for: South San Francisco Enterprise; Brisbane Bee Democrat; Coastwise Chronicle x(Pacifica); Recorder Progress x(Burlingame-Millbrae); and San Francisco Today) – San Bruno, CA. Title varies – 247+ r – 1 – $12,350.00 ($100.00y) – B02773 – us Library Micro [071]
SAN BRUNO HERALD – San Mateo, CA. 1976-1977 – 11r – 1 – $550.00 – R04106 – us Library Micro [071]
SAN BRUNO HERALD *see*
– BEE-DEMOCRAT
– ENTERPRISE-JOURNAL
– SAN BRUNO HERALD
– TODAY
SAN BRUNO HERALD AND RECORDER PROGRESS *see* SAN BRUNO HERALD
SAN CARLOS BULLETIN – San Carlos, CA. 1936-1940; 1944 – 2r – 1 – $100.00 – C03466 – us Library Micro [071]
SAN CARLOS ENQUIRER BULLETIN *see* CARLMONT-ENQUIRER BULLETIN
SAN CLEMENTE NEWS – South Co, CA. 1993 – 2+ r – 1 – $100.00 ($100.00y) – R04123 – us Library Micro [071]
SAN DIEGO BEE – San Diego, CA. 1887 – 1r – 1 – $50.00 – C03658 – us Library Micro [071]
SAN DIEGO BLADE TRIBUNE – San Diego, CA. 1972-1986 – 157r – 1 – $7,850.00 – H04038 – us Library Micro [071]
SAN DIEGO BULLETIN – San Diego, CA. 1872 – 1r – 1 – $50.00 – C03659 – us Library Micro [071]
SAN DIEGO COUNTY, 1807; 1875; 1886-1902; 1937-1950 – 32r – 1 – $1,600.00 – D083 – us Library Micro [978]
SAN DIEGO COUNTY: EAST – 1987 – 8+ r – 1 – $400.00 – P00095 – us Library Micro [910]
SAN DIEGO COUNTY: INLAND – 1986; 1988- – 11+ r – 1 – $550.00 – P00101 – us Library Micro [910]
SAN DIEGO COUNTY: NORTH – 1976-79; 1981-85; 1989-91; 1993- – 22+ r – 1 – $1,100.00 – P00099 – us Library Micro [910]
SAN DIEGO COUNTY: NORTH COAST – 1986; 1988-91; 1993- – 11+ r – 1 – $550.00 – P00100 – us Library Micro [910]
SAN DIEGO COUNTY: SOUTH – 1987- – 8+ r – 1 – $400.00 – P00097 – us Library Micro [910]
SAN DIEGO COUNTY: SOUTHEAST – 1991 – 1r – 1 – $50.00 – P00096 – us Library Micro [910]
SAN DIEGO COUNTY: SOUTHWEST – 1991 – 1r – 1 – $50.00 – P00098 – us Library Micro [910]
SAN DIEGO COUNTY: SPANISH – 1992- – 3+ r – 1 – $150.00 – P00102 – us Library Micro [910]
SAN DIEGO COUNTY: SUBURBAN AND GREATER – 1887; 1905-07; 1911-13; 1943; 1976-79; 1981- – 68+ r – 1 – $3,400.00 – P00094 – us Library Micro [910]
SAN DIEGO DAILY TRANSCRIPT – San Diego, CA. 1965- – 182+ r – 1 BC02779 – $9,100.00 ($450.00y) – us Library Micro [071]
SAN DIEGO JUSTICE JOURNAL – (Supersedes Criminal Justice Journal) – Western State University. v1-3. 1993-95 – 9 – $43.00 set – us Hein [340]
SAN DIEGO JUSTICE JOURNAL *see* CRIMINAL JUSTICE JOURNAL
SAN DIEGO LAW REVIEW – v1-31. 1964-94 – 9 – $501.00 set – us Hein [340]
SAN DIEGO PLAIN TRUTH – San Diego, CA. 1885-1891 – 1r – 1 – $50.00 – C03661 – us Library Micro [071]
SAN DIEGO TRIBUNE – 1895- – 1 – us UMI [071]
SAN DIEGO UNION – San Diego, CA. 1871-73; 1874-76 (broken series) – 1r – 1 – $50.00 – C02783 – us Library Micro [071]
SAN DIEGO UNION CARD INDEX – 1976-81.Over 120,000 local news entries as comp. by the San Diego Public Library Newspaper Room staff. 300 fiches. Individual fiches available – 9 – 555.00 – uk Libr Preservation [071]
SAN DIEGO WEEKLY BULLETIN – San Diego, CA. 1970-1872 – 1r – 1 – $50.00 – C03660 – us Library Micro [071]
SAN EPITACIO...TUY...MARTIR DE PLASENCIA / Tamayo de Salazar, Juan – 1646 – 9 – 1.50f – sp Bibl Santa Ana [240]
San Estanislao, German de *see* CARTAS Y EXTASIS DE GEMA GALGANI. BARCELONA, 1933
SAN EULOGIO DE CORDOBA / Bayle, Constantino & Perez de Urbel, Justo – Madrid: Razon y Fe, 2nd ed 1944 – 1 – sp Bibl Santa Ana [240]
SAN EULOGIO DE CORDOBA. MADRID, 1928 / Perez de Urbel, Justo; ed by Bayle, Constantino – Madrid: Razon y Fe, 1929 – 9 – sp Bibl Santa Ana [240]
SAN FERNANDO – 1931-50 – 10r – 1 – $500.00 – P00103 – us Library Micro [910]
SAN FERNANDO GAZETTE – Trinidad. 1850-1853; 1865; 1867-1872; 1874-1896 – 1 – us UMI [072]
SAN FERNANDO SUN – California. 25 Jan 1951-2 Jul 1953; 5 Jul 1953-25 Oct 195?. 2 rolls – 1 – 60.00 – uk Libr Preservation [071]
SAN FERNANDO VALLEY-EAST – 1987- – 14+ r – 1 – $700.00 – P00104 – us Library Micro [910]
SAN FERNANDO VALLEY-SPANISH – 1992- – 3+ r – 1 – $150.00 – P00106 – us Library Micro [910]
SAN FERNANDO VALLEY-WEST – 1989-90; 1993- – 10+ r – 1 – $500.00 – P00105 – us Library Micro [910]
SAN FRANCESCO DI ASSISI – Assisi, Italy. -m. Oct 1920-Dec 1930. 4 reels – 1 – uk British Libr Newspaper [073]
SAN FRANCISCO – 1878; 1893; 1902-26; 1928-30; 1932; 1948-50; 1976- – 139+ r – 1 – $6,950.00 – P00107 – us Library Micro [910]
SAN FRANCISCO AIRPORT HISTORY AND DEVELOPMENT OF SFO – San Francisco, CA. – 1r – 1 – $50.00 – B40310 – us Library Micro [380]
SAN FRANCISCO AND THEREABOUTS / Keeler, Charles – San Francisco: The California Promotion Committee, 1903.California reel 38. (Cox Library Collection) – 5 – us Americana [978]
SAN FRANCISCO BAR – v1-6 no 2. 1937-42 + special ed Dec 1943 (all publ) – 11mf – 9 – $16.50 – LLMC 84-672 – us L.L.M.C. [073]
SAN FRANCISCO BAY AREA JEWISH GENEALOGICAL SOCIETY NEWSLETTER – (June 1984-Febr. 1990; Continued by: Zichron note) – San Francisco, California – 1 – us A.J.P.C. [920]
SAN FRANCISCO BAY BRIDGE : NEWSPAPER CLIPPINGS – 1r – 1 – $50.00 – B40311 – us Library Micro [978]
THE SAN FRANCISCO BAY REGION / Millard, Bailey – San Francisco: American Historical Society, 1924. 3v. California Reel 28. (The Cox Library Collection) – 5 – us Americana [978]
SAN FRANCISCO BEFORE THE EARTHQUAKE – 1899-1900. 730 maps. 6 vol. of Sanborn Company Fire Insurance Maps on a single reel – 1 – $80.00r – us Shkurkin [910]
THE SAN FRANCISCO BLOCK BOOK / Hicks-Judd Co – San Francisco, 1906. California Reel 29. (The Cox Library Collection) – 5 – us Americana [978]
SAN FRANCISCO BLUE BOOK AND PACIFIC COAST ELITE DIRECTORY / Bancroft Co – San Francisco, 1890. Calif. reel 37. (Cox Library Collection) – 5 – us Americana [978]
San Francisco. Board of Supervisors *see* REAL ESTATE OWNED BY THE CITY AND COUNTY OF SAN FRANCISCO 1909
THE SAN FRANCISCO BUSINESS DIRECTORY / Dalton & Co – Includes Oakland and Alameda. San Francisco, 1880. Calif. reel 37. (Cox Library Collection) – 5 – us Americana [380]
SAN FRANCISCO CALL INDEX : AZ: 1894-1894; AK: 1899-1902 – 3r – 1 – $150.00 – C06008 – us Library Micro [071]
THE SAN FRANCISCO CATHOLIC – San Francisco, CA. 1987-1990 – 1r – 1 – $50.00 – B05069 – us Library Micro [240]
SAN FRANCISCO CHRONICLE – San Francisco. California. 1865- – 1 – us UMI [071]
THE SAN FRANCISCO CHRONICLE INDEX – San Francisco. CA. 1976- – 1 – us UMI [071]
SAN FRANCISCO CITY DIRECTORIES – San Francisco, CA. 1852-1953: 1960; 1968; 1872; 1877; 1887-1888; 1911-1912; 1936-1982 – 91r – 1 – $4,550.00 – D084 – us Library Micro [910]
SAN FRANCISCO DAILY NEWS – San Francisco, Oct-Dec 1906 – 1r – 1 – $50.00 – B40312 – us Library Micro [071]
SAN FRANCISCO DE ASIS / Cooperativa de viviendas de proteccion oficial – Caceres: Estatutos. Caceres. Imp. Marosa, 1977 – sp Bibl Santa Ana [946]
SAN FRANCISCO DE PAULA / Roberti, J M – Barcelona, 1931; Madrid: Razon y Fe, 1931 – 1 – sp Bibl Santa Ana [240]
SAN FRANCISCO DISTRICTS – (Apply for detailed listing) – 503mf – 9 – $630.00 – B03724 – us Library Micro [978]
SAN FRANCISCO EXAMINER – San Francisco, 1906 – 2r – 1 – us Ross [071]
SAN FRANCISCO FEDERAL WRITERS PROJECT – 1r – 1 – $50.00 – B40313 – us Library Micro [420]
SAN FRANCISCO FERRY BUILDING : NEWSPAPER CLIPPINGS – San Francisco, 1896-98 – 1r – 1 – $50.00 – B40314 – us Library Micro [978]
SAN FRANCISCO JAVIER. EL HOMBRE Y EL SANTO / Bayle, Constantino – Madrid: Missionalia Hispanica, 1952 – 1 – sp Bibl Santa Ana [240]
SAN FRANCISCO JOURNAL : CHINESE EDITION – San Francisco, CA. Feb 1972-Nov 1986 – 21r – 1 – $1,050.00 – B02827 – us Library Micro [073]
SAN FRANCISCO JOURNAL : ENGLISH EDITION – San Francisco, CA. Jun 1976-Jul 1980 – 5r – 1 – $250.00 – B02828 – us Library Micro [073]
SAN FRANCISCO JOURNAL – San Francisco, CA. 1921-1924 – 14r – 1 – $700.00 – C03497 – us Library Micro [071]
SAN FRANCISCO JOURNAL *see* JOURNAL OF COMMERCE
SAN FRANCISCO LAW REVIEW – (Title varies: v1-3. 1990-1993, as Res Ipsa Loquitur) – v1-5. 1990-1995 – 9 – $52.00 set – us Hein [340]
San Francisco Membrio, Andres *see* CHRONICA...SAN GABRIEL DE FRANCISCO DESCALZOS
SAN FRANCISCO MUNICIPAL JOURNAL AND RICHMOND RECORD – (Cont: Richmond Record) – San Francisco, CA. 1936-1942 – 2r – 1 – $100.00 – C03498 – us Library Micro [071]
SAN FRANCISCO MUNICIPAL JOURNAL AND RICHMOND RECORD *see* RICHMOND RECORD
SAN FRANCISCO MUSIC TREASURES – San Francisco Public Lib. 1917-49 – 1r – 1 – $50.00 – B40316 – us Library Micro [780]

SAN FRANCISCO NEWSPAPER CLIPPINGS – San Francisco, Nov 25 1934-Aug 4 1965 – 1r – 1 – $50.00 – B40315 – us Library Micro [978]
SAN FRANCISCO, PORTLAND, SEATTLE, TACOMA, VICTORIA, VANCOUVER TO ATLIN LAKE AND DAWSON CITY (VIA SKAGWAY AND LAKE BENNETT): AND ALL INTERMEDIATE POINTS ON THE LEWIS AND YUKON RIVERS / Canadian Development Company – Victoria, The Company 1898?. 00436. (Pre-1900 Canadiana) – 9 – cn C.I.H.M. [971]
THE SAN FRANCISCO POST – San Francisco, CA. 1979-Apr 1982; Sept-Dec 1982; 1987; 1991- – 19+ r – 1 – $950.00 ($120.00) – B02853 – us Library Micro [071]
SAN FRANCISCO RAIL STRIKE : CLIPPINGS – San Francisco Public Lib, 1906 – 1r – 1 – $50.00 – B40317 – us Library Micro [978]
SAN FRANCISCO REVIEW OF BOOKS – (v.6-. 1980-. 5,6,9) – v.1-. 1975- – 1 – us UMI [410]
SAN FRANCISCO SHIPPING LIST AND PRICES CURRENT – San Francisco, 1852-1858 – 3r – 1 – inquire – us Ross [380]
SAN FRANCISCO STATE UNIVERSITY STRIKE SCRAPBOOKS – San Francisco, 1967-70 – 1r – 1 – $50.00 – B03725 – us Library Micro [978]
SAN FRANCISCO TRADES GUIDE – San Francisco Co, CA. 1874 – 1r – 1 – $50.00 – D085 – us Library Micro [380]
SAN FRANCISCO WATER – San Francisco: Spring Water Valley Water Co, 1922-30 – 1r – 1 – $35.00 – B40320 – us Library Micro [360]
SAN FRANCISCO WATER DEPARTMENT TAP RECORDS : SERVICE PIPE RECORDS – San Francisco. v1-10 – 10r – 1 – $500.00 – B03726 – us Library Micro [360]
SAN FRANCISCO-CHINESE – 1917-44; 1946-47; 1949-50 – 46r – 1 – $2,300.00 – P00108 – us Library Micro [910]
SAN GABRIEL VALLEY – 1991- – 5+ r – 1 – $250.00 – P00109 – us Library Micro [910]
SAN GABRIEL VALLEY TRIBUNE – San Gabriel, CA. 1955- – 833+ r – 1 – $41,650.00 ($975.00y) – R02869 – us Library Micro [071]
SAN GABRIEL-SPANISH – 1993- – 2+ r – 1 – $100.00 – P00110 – us Library Micro [910]
San Jacinto. Presbytery (Cum. Pres. Ch.) *see* MINUTES, 1885-1906
SAN JACINTO VALLEY REGISTER – San Jacinto, CA. Mar 1886-1894 (broken series) – 46+ r – 1 RC02871 – $2,300.00 ($100.00y) – us Library Micro [071]
SAN JACINTO WEEK – San Jacinto, CA. 1990-1992 – 1r – 1 – $50.00 – R04105 – us Library Micro [071]
SAN JOAQUIN COUNTY INCLUDING LODI – San Joaquin Co, CA. 1878; 1883-1900 – 6r – 1 – $300.00 – D087 – us Library Micro [978]
SAN JOAQUIN VALLEY ARGUS – Merced, CA. 1873-90 – 5r – 1 – $250.00 – B02450 – us Library Micro [071]
SAN JOAQUIN VALLEY ARGUS – Snelling, CA. 1869-73 – 1r – 1 – $50.00 – B02997 – us Library Micro [071]
SAN JONAS / Solano de Figueroa y Altamirano, Juan – 1665 – 9 – 1.50f – sp Bibl Santa Ana [240]
SAN JOSE – 1911-14; 1919-22; 1924-29; 1949; 1976-92 – 83r – 1 – $4,150.00 – P00111 – us Library Micro [910]
SAN JOSE COMMUNITY NEWS *see* SEDITION
San Jose, Francisco de *see*
– HISTORIA DE PIEDRA ESCRITA
– HISTORIA UNIVERSAL...GUADALUPE
– MILAGROS...GUADALUPE
– NOVENA...PIEDRAESCRITA...CAMPANARIO
SAN JOSE REPORTER – San Jose, CA. 1959 – 1r – 1 – $50.00 – B05063 – us Library Micro [071]
San Jose State College *see* SPARTAN DAILY
SAN JOSE STUDIES – (v.6-. 1980- 5,6,9) – v.1-. 1975- – 1 – us UMI [073]
SAN JOSE/SANTA CLARA – 1892; 1909; 1911-50; 1976-92 – 56r – 1 – $2,800.00 – P00112 – us Library Micro [910]
SAN JOSE/SANTA CLARA/SANTA CRUZ, CENSUS ROLL OF THE INDIANS OF CALIFORNIA – Santa Clara Co, CA. 1890-1891 – 1r – 1 – $50.00 – D095 – us Library Micro [978]
SAN JUAN DE RIBERA. OBISPO DE BADAJOZ / Rubio Merino, Pedro – Badajoz: Imprenta de la Diputacion Provincial, 1961 – sp Bibl Santa Ana [240]
SAN JUAN ISLANDER – Friday Harbor. Wash. -w. 1894-1914 – 1 – us UMI [071]
SAN JUAN MISSION NEWS – San Juan Bautista, CA. 1918-56 – 18r – 1 – $900.00 – C02896 – us Library Micro [240]
SAN JUAN RECORD – Fair Oaks, CA. 1933-35 (broken series); 1935-65 – 23r – 1 BC02232 – $1,150.00 – us Library Micro [071]
SAN LEANDRO REPORTER – San Leandro, CA. 1913-51 – 13r – 1 – $650.00 – C02898 – us Library Micro [071]
SAN LORENZO VALLEY SUN *see* INDEPENDENT
SAN LUIS OBISPO – 1909-34; 1992- – 15+ r – 1 – $750.00 – P00113 – us Library Micro [910]
SAN LUIS OBISPO BREEZE – San Luis Obispo, CA. 1895-1909 – 15r – 1 BC02906 – $750.00 – us Library Micro [071]
SAN LUIS OBISPO COUNTY, 1912; 1931-1932; 1942; 1950 – 4r – 1 – $200.00 – D090 – us Library Micro [978]
SAN LUIS OBISPO COUNTY AND ENVIRONS / Historic Record Co – Los Angeles, 1917. California Reel 31. (The Cox Library Collection) – 5 – us Americana [978]
SAN LUIS OBISPO DAILY TELEGRAM – San Luis Obispo, CA. 1925-1936 – 3r – 1 – $150.00 – C03508 – us Library Micro [071]
SAN LUIS OBISPO MIRROR – San Luis Obispo, CA. 1894-95 – 1r – 1 – $50.00 – B02908 – us Library Micro [071]
SAN LUIS OBISPO PIONEER – San Luis Obispo, CA. Jan-Dec 1868 – 1r – 1 – $50.00 – B02910 – us Library Micro [071]
SAN LUIS OBISPO TRIBUNE – San Luis Obispo, CA. 1883-88; 1890-1926 – 30r – 1 BC02912 – $1,500.00 – us Library Micro [071]
San Luis Potosi. Mexico (State) *see* PERIODICO OFICIAL
SAN LUIS SEMI-WEEKLY BREEZE – San Luis Obispo, CA. 1896-1901 – 4r – 1 – $200.00 – B02907 – us Library Micro [071]
SAN MARCOS DEFENDIDO EN EL MILAGRO QUE OBRA DIOS / Antonio de Trujillo – 1690 – 9 – 1.50f – sp Bibl Santa Ana [240]
San Martin, Julio *see* YO TENGO UN ABRAZO PARA TI MIAJA
SAN MASONA. ARZOBISPO DE MERIDA / Lopez Prudencio, Jose – Badajoz: Imp.Provincial, 1945 – 1 – sp Bibl Santa Ana [946]
SAN MATEO COUNTY – 1929-34 – 5r – 1 – $250.00 – P00114 – us Library Micro [910]
SAN MATEO COUNTY GAZETTE – (Also known as: Times and Gazette) – Redwood City, CA. 1859-1931 – 16r – 1 – $800.00 – B02682 – us Library Micro [071]
SAN MATEO COUNTY INCLUDING BURLINGAME AND HILSBOROUGH – San Mateo Co, CA. 1884-1885; 1909-1910; 1918-1948 – 13r – 1 – $650.00 – D091 – us Library Micro [978]
SAN MATEO COUNTY-CENTRAL : ATHERTON, BELMONT, BURLINGAME, DALY CITY, HILLSBOROUGH, PALO ALTO, ETC. – 1992- – 5+ r – 1 – $250.00 – P00116 – us Library Micro [910]
SAN MATEO COUNTY-NORTH : ATHERTON, BELMONT, E. PALO ALTO, FOSTER CITY, HALF MOON BAY, PACIFICA, ETC. – 1992- – 4+ r – 1 – $200.00 – P00115 – us Library Micro [910]
SAN MATEO JOURNAL – San Mateo, CA. 1880-842 – 1r – 1 – $50.00 – C03509 – us Library Micro [073]
SAN MATEO POST (NORTH COUNTY ED.) – Daly City, CA. 1963- – 65r – 1 – $3,250.00 – B02159 – us Library Micro [071]
San Miguel FCP. Facultades de Filosofia y Teologia *see* CIENCIA Y FE
SAN MIN CH'EN PAO = SAN MIN MORNING PAPER – Chicago, IL: San Min Che'n Pao, [sep 30 1930-jan 9 1968] – us Res Libr [071]
San Nicolo, Mariano *see* NEUBABYLONISCHE RECHTS- UND VERWALTUNGSURKUNDEN.
SAN PABLO NEWS – San Pablo, CA. 1947-Sept 1948; Dec 1949-Dec 1950; 1958-82 – 26r – 1 – $3,100.00 – B02925 – us Library Micro [071]
San Pedro de Alcantara, Domingo de *see*
– CAMINO ESPIRITUAL
– CURSUS FHILOSOPHIU TOMUS SECUNDUS PARTIS SECUNDAE
– CURSUS PHILOSOPHICI
– MURO INVENCIBLE...CONTRA LOS..
– ORATORIOS REGULARES...RELIGIOSOS
– PALMA...CIUDAD DE DIOS CONTRA SATANAS
SAN PEDRO DE ALCANTARA...MADRID, 1965 / Garcia Oro, J – Madrid: Graf. Celleja, 1966 – 1 – sp Bibl Santa Ana [240]
San Pedro, Diego de *see* THE CASTLE OF LOVE 1549?, A TRANSLATION BY JOHN BOURCHIER
San Roman de Ribadeneyra, A *see* HISTORIA GENERAL DE LA YNDIA ORIENTAL
San Roman, M de *see* EXPEDITIONUM SPIRITUALIUM SOCIETATIS IESU, LIBRI QUINQUE
SAN SEBASTIAN DE LOS REYES. CARACAS, 1929 / Bolet, Julio C – Madrid: Razon y Fe, 1930 – 1 – sp Bibl Santa Ana [946]
San Vicente de Alcantara *see* FERIA Y FIESTAS 1945
SAN VICENTE PAUL, DIRECTOR DE CONCIENCIA / D'Angel, Arnaldo – Madrid: Razon y Fe, 1927 – 1 – sp Bibl Santa Ana [240]
San Victor, Hugo de *see* POSTILLA SUPER ECCLESIASTICUM (SIECLE 15)
SANA BUDAJA – Jogjakarta, Djawatan P.P.K. SE 786 1. 1955-1964 – 9 – ne IDC [073]
Sana Catalan, Jose et al *see* 1ST CONGRESO SINDICAL AGRARIO DE EXTREMADURA. PONENCIA 7, SOLUCIONES URGENTES A LOS PROBLEMAS FUNDAMENTALES DEL CAMPO EXTREMENOS
Sanahuja, Pedro de *see* HISTORIA DE LA SERAFICA PROVINCIA DE CATALUNA POR EL R.P...
SANAT – Konya, 1928-19? – 9 – $10.00 – us MEDOC [956]
SANATORIUM – Denver. Col. 1907-08 – 1 – us A.J.P.C. [610]
Sanborn, Charlotte F *see*
– ACCURACY OF A TREADMILL SCORING SYSTEM FOR PREDICTION OF CORONARY ARTERY DISEASE IN FEMALE SUBJECTS
– THE EFFECTS OF ATHLETIC TRAINING ON BONE MINERAL DENSITY IN FEMALE COLLEGIATE GYMNASTS
SANBORN FIRE INSURANCE MAPS 1867-1970 – (Contains more than 660,000 maps of 10,000 American towns and cities. Individual states and cities available) – 2pts. pt1 1867-1950 pt 2 1950-70 – 1099r – 1 – enquire for price details – uk Chadwyck [910]
Sanborn, Frank B *see* SCRAPBOOK
Sanborn Map Company *see* INSURANCE MAPS
Sanborn Map Company, Topeka, KS *see* MAPS
Sanbornton, New Hampshire. First Free Will Baptist Church *see* RECORDS
Sanbornton, New Hampshire. Sanbornton Baptist Church *see* RECORDS
Sanchamau, J B *see* L'ECOLE DES PEUPLES ET DES ROIS. OU ESSAI PHILOSOPHIQUE SUR LA LIBERTE LE POUVOIR ARBITRAIRE, LES JUIFS ET LES NOIRS
Sanches Loro, Domingo *see* LUGARES DE EXTREMADURA
Sanchez Aliseda, C *see* POESIA CRISTIANA. ANTOLOGIA DE POESIA ROMANO-CRISTIANA Y LATINO MEDIEVAL (SIGLOS 4-15) TOLEDO, 1946
Sanchez Aliseda, Casimiro *see*
– CUARESMA Y SEMANA SANTA
– LA MUERTE, TRANSITO PASCUAL
– LAS ORDENES RELIGIOSAS
– PASTORAL DE URGENCIA
– LOS SEMINARIOS TRIDENTINOS
Sanchez Alonso, B *see* HISTORIA DE LA HISTORIOGRAFIA ESPANOLA. TOMO 1. HASTA LA PUBLICACION DE LA CRONICA DE OCAMPO. TOMO 2 DE OCAMPO A SOLIS. MADRID, 1941, 1944
Sanchez Arjona, Vicente *see*
– AL PASAR ANTE LAS HORAS
– EL ALCAZAR DE TOLEDO
– AMOR Y FLORES
– ANALES DEL PARAISO
– ANTOLOGIA DE MIS ANTOLOGIAS DE MIS DOCE MIL SONETOS
– ANTOLOGIA DE MIS CANTARES
– ANTOLOGIA DE MIS PENAS CORTAS, PENSAMIENTOS Y MADRIGALES
– ANTOLOGIA DE MIS SONETOS
– ANTOLOGIA DE MIS ULTIMOS SONETOS
– ANTOLOGIO DE MIS -HASTA AHORA-SEISCIENTOS SONETOS
– CAJON DE SASTRE
– CANTARES DE JUVENTUD
– CANTARES VIEJOS
– CARMINA
– CHISPAZOS (AQUI-DULCES DE TIEMPOS PASADOS)
– CIEN LETRILLAS
– LOS CON RAZON OLVIDADOS
– CUATROCIENTAS ESPINELAS
– DE EL...!SIGLO PASADO!
– DE MI ALBUM DE FIRMA. SEMBLANZAS DE ILUTRES VARONES
– DE MIS CANTARES INEDITOS
– DE MIS OCHO MIL CONETOS
– DE MIS POESIAS INEDITAS
– DE PUERTAS ADENTRO
– DE PUERTAS ADENTRO. POESIAS INTIMAS
– DE PUERTAS ADENTRO (TODO EN BROMA)
– DE VARIOS COLORES
– DEDICATORIAS DE MIS LIBROS
– DEDICATORIAS EN MIS LIBROS
– DEL PASADO Y DEL PRESENTE
– DEL PERIODO MARXISTA
– DEL TIEMPO EN QUE FUISTEIS ANGELES
– DEUDA SAGRADA
– EL DIA FAMILIAR
– DIARIO DE UN INGENIERO
– DIVAGAR...
– DIVAGAR...(DE MIS ARCHIVOS)
– DOSCIENTAS OBRAS...!EN UNA!
Sanchez Arjona y Sanchez Arjona, Francisco *see*
– FABULAS DE SALON Y POESIAS
– GUIA GENERAL...BADAJOZ
– POESIAS LIRICAS
Sanchez Arjona y Sanchez Arjona, Jose *see*
– CANTOS Y CUENTOS
– LA CIENCIA DE LAS MUGERES
– ENSAYOS POETICOS
– NOTICIAS REFERENTES...TEATRO EN SEVILLA
– PADRES ANTE TODO
– POESIAS LIRICAS Y LA VIRGEN DE LA SERVILLETA
– VENGANZA CUMPLIDA
Sanchez Asensio, Nicolas *see* MEMORIA LEIDA POR EL SECRETARIO DON NICOLAS SANCHEZ ASENSIO EN LA JUNTA GENERAL (16 DE) FEBRERO 1949
Sanchez Belda, L *see* GUIA DEL ARCHIVO HISTORICO NACIONAL
Sanchez Bella, Ismael *see* GENESIS DE ESTADO MODERNO EN ESPANA
Sanchez Bendito, Maria Jose *see* ULTIMATUM
Sanchez Calvo, Estanislao *see* FILOSOFIA DE LO MARAVILLOSO POSITIVO
Sanchez Canton, Francisco Javier *see*
– LA LIBRERIA DE JUAN DE HERRERA
– LA SENSIBILIDAD DE ZURBARAN
Sanchez Castanar, Eduardo *see* PRECEPTIVA LITERARIA
Sanchez Cid, Antonio *see* EPITOME HISTORICO...FREGENAL
Sanchez de Badajoz, Diego *see*
– RECOPILACION EN METRO
– RECOPILACION EN METRO DEL BACHILLER...CON UN ESTUDIO DE JOSE LOPEZ PRUDENCIO
– RECOPILLACION EN METRO DEL BACHILLER DIEGO SANCHEZ CON UN ESTUDIO DE DON JOSE LOPEZ PRUDENCIO
Sanchez de las Brozas, Francisco *see*
– ANGEL POLICIANO-SILVAE NUTRITIA
– AULIO PERSIO FLACO-SATURNAE...ET SCHOLIIS (SIC)
– DE NONNULLI PORPHYRII...SCHOLAE
– DE NONULLIS PORPLIYRY, ALRIORUMQ; IN DIALECTICA ER RORIBUS SCHOLA DIALECTTICA
– DOCTRINA DEL ESTOICO...EPICTETO... ENCHIRIDION
– FRANCISCI...ALCIATI...ILUSTRATA
– FRANCISCII SANCTII BROCENSIS...COMENT. IN AND. ALCIATI EMBLEMATA...FIGURIS ILUSTRATA
– GRAMATICA GRAECA
– GRAMATICES...FALLACES E PROLIXAE
– GRAMATICUS LATINAE INSTITUTIONES
– GRAMMATICAE LATINAE INSTITUTIONES
– IN ARTEM POETICAM HORATII
– IN IBIN OCIDI IN TERNARIUM... ANNOTATIONES
– MINERVA
– MINERVA: PARTE SEGUNDA
– MINERVA, SIVE DE CAUSIS LINGUAE LATINAE
– LAS OBRAS DEL...JUAN DE MENA
– OPERA OMNIA
– ORGANUM DIALECTICUM ET RETORICORUM
– PARADOXA
– PRINCIPIOS DE RETORICA Y POETICA

- RGANUM DIALECTICUM ET RHETORICUM
- SELECTA QUAE...POETARUM
- SELECTA...VETERUM POETARUM
- SPHAERA MUNDI
- TRATADO DE LOS ERRORES DE PAFIVIO Y DE LAS OTRAS DE LA ESCUELA DIALECTICA

Sanchez de Leon Perez, Enrique *see* PREGON PRONUNCIADO...EN LA 6 FIESTA DE LA VENDIMIA LOS SANTOS DE MAIMONA

Sanchez de Oropesa, F *see* DICURSO...MAL DE URINA SEA EL QUE PADECE DIEGO ENRIQUEZ LEON...

Sanchez, F *see*
- PROPOSICION DEL DOCTOR...SOBRE LA ENFERMEDAD QUE ANDA EN SEVILLA...
- SEGUNDA PROPOSICION DEL DOCTOR SOBRE LA ENFERMEDAD QUE ANDA EN SEVILLA

Sanchez Felipe, Juan A *see* CARTAS BOCA ARRIBA

Sanchez, Francisco *see*
- LAS OBRAS DEL FAMOSO POETA JUAN DE MENA
- QUOD NIHIL SCITUR

Sanchez Galindo, Benito *see* PRIMERA Y...DE LA CHRISTI VICTORIA

Sanchez Garrido, Eduardo *see* PLASENCIA EN LA...EJECUCION

Sanchez, James Joseph *see* PACKET SWITCHING NETWORKS: AN INTRODUCTION WITH SOME ATTENTION TO SELECTED VENDORS

Sanchez, Juan *see* PRINCIPIOS DE LA GRAMMATICA LATINA

Sanchez Juarez, Francisco *see*
- PANEGIRICO DE SANTA BARBARA...BADAJOZ
- SERMONES...VILLAFRANCA DE LOS BARROS
- SERMON...SOBERANIA PONTIFICIA

(Sanchez) Larragoiti, Antonio de *see* VASCO NUNEZ DE BALBOA

Sanchez Loro, Domingo *see*
- ALCONETAR
- BIBLIOGRAFIA DE EXTREMADURA
- EN EL PORTAL DE BELEN
- LUGARES DE EXTREMADURA, EMERITA AUGUSTA. 1ST PARTE
- MISA COMUNITARIA DE SAN PEDRO DE ALCANTARA PATRON DE EXTREMADURA
- EL PUENTE DE ALCANTARA
- SANTA EULALIA DE MERIDA
- TORRE DE BUJACO. PASACALLE PARA RONDALLA SOBRE MOTIVOS EXTREMENOS
- VIRIATO

Sanchez, Lozano *see* TAQUIMETRO

Sanchez Marin, Venancio *see* UMBRAL DE ARMONIA, DE ALFONSO ALBALA

Sanchez Mateos, Dorita *see* HERALDICA DE EXTREMADURA

Sanchez Montes, Juan *see*
- LA GENERACION ESPANOLA QUE VIVIO LA DERROTA
- UNA REVISION ACTUAL DE LAS IDEAS SOBRE LA DECADENCIA ESPANOLA

Sanchez Morales, Narciso *see*
- CRISIS ESPIRITUAL DE UNAMUNO Y SU EVASION A EXTREMADURA
- LA GRAN EXTREMADURA, UNA UTOPIA
- DIE LEBENSSCHAU DES YUSTIMUS
- UNAMUNO EN ALEMANIA
- VISION DEL MUNDO DESDE YUSTE

Sanchez Ocana *see* UN RECUERDO HISTORICO

Sanchez Ocana, Pedro *see* LO QUE SE VA. MADRID, 1928

Sanchez Ocana y Acedo Rico, Pedro *see* EL ROBLEDAL DE RUIDIAZ

Sanchez Paredes, Antonio *see* REBATE ARQUEOLOGICO EN TORNO A UN BERRACO PROTOHISTORICO

Sanchez Parejo, Bartolome *see* VIDA...FRAY SEBASTIAN DE APARICIO. MEXICO. 1965

Sanchez Perez, Andres *see* LOS MORISCOS DE HORNACHOS, CORSARIOS DE SALE

Sanchez Rodrigo, A *see* NOCICONES Y TABLAS DE ARITMETICA

Sanchez Rodrigo, Agustin *see*
- UN ANO DE VIDA SERRADILLANA POR UN AMANTE DE SERRADILLA
- APUNTES PARA LA HISTORIA DE SERRADILLA (CACERES)

Sanchez Rodrigo, Angel *see* NUEVA FIGURACION DEL RAYO LUMINOSO PARA MEJOR EXPLICAR LA POLIZACION ROTATORIA POR...

Sanchez Ruiz, Valentin *see* NUEVO SALTERIO LATINO-ESPANOL. VERSION LATINA PROMULGADA POR S.S. PIO 12...

Sanchez Ruiz, Valentin M *see*
- CATECISMO SOCIAL
- CATECISMO SOCIAL...
- MARTIROLOGIO DE LA COMPANIA DE JESUS
- MARTIROLOGIO ROMANO
- NUEVO SALTERIO LATINO-ESPANOL
- NUEVO SALTERIO LATINO-ESPANOL. 2ND EDICION
- SEMANA SANTA DE PASCUA EN LATIN Y EN CASTELLANO

Sanchez, S *see* EXTRACTO PUNTUAL DE TODAS LAS PRAGMATICAS, CEDULAS, PROVISIONES PUBLICADAS EN EL REINADO DE CARLOS III. 2 VOL

Sanchez, Tomas Antonio *see*
- COLECCION POESIAS CASTELLANAS ANTERIORES AL SIGLO 15. TOMO 1
- COLECCION POESIAS CASTELLANAS ANTERIORES AL SIGLO 15. TOMO 2
- COLECCION POESIAS CASTELLANAS ANTERIORES AL SIGLO 15. TOMO 3
- COLECCION POESIAS CASTELLANAS ANTERIORES AL SIGLO 15. TOMO 4
- DE SANCTO MATRIMONII SACRAMENTO DISPVTATIONVM; TOMI TRES..
- DEFENSA...FERNANDO PEREZ...PARACUELLOS
- DISPUTATIONUM DE SANCTO MATRIMONII SACRAMENTUM
- OPUS MORALE IN PRAECEPTA DECALOGI
- R. PATRIS THOMAE SANCHEZ...DE SANCTO MATRIMONII SACRAMENTO DISPVTATIONVM

Sanchez Torres, Clemente *see* LA INDUSTRIALIZACION DE LOS REGADIOS DE LA PROVINCIA DE CACERES

Sanchez Torres, Eloy *see* MI CRUCERO A SPITZBURG. CACERES, 1935

Sanchez Yusta, Urbano *see* PRACTICAS PEDAGOGICAS. TERCER CURSO

Sanchez-Arjona, Vicente *see*
- DE MIS POESIAS INEDITAS
- DE MIS SOLEDADES VENGO
- DE MIS VEINTE MIL CANTARES
- ECOS DEL PARAISO
- EQUILIBRIOS POETICOS, DE UN...! DESEQUILIBRADO!
- EQUILIBRIOS POETICOS DE UN !DESEQUILIBRADO!
- EQUILIBRIOS POETICOS DE UN !DESEQULIBRADO!
- ESPIGANDO EN !MI HEREDA!
- ESPIGANDO EN !MI HEREDAD!
- EN FAMILIA
- LA FANTASIA EN !SONETOS!
- LA FANTASIA EN...!SONETOS!
- FLORES SIN AROMA
- GLOSAS
- GRANOS DE ARENA
- GRANOS DE ARENAS
- HOMENAJE. POESIAS DEDICADAS A LA EXIMIA POETISA EVA CERVANTES EN OCASION DE SUS ONOMASTICAS Y OTROS VARIOS MOTIVOS
- HUMORADAS
- IDEALIDAD
- INTIMAS (POESIAS DE LOS TIEMPOS IDOS)
- IRONIAS
- IRONIAS Y SUTILEZAS CON HONORES
- JUVENTUD Y...DESENCANTO
- UN LIBRO MAS DE CANTARES
- LLUVIA MENUDA
- LLUVIA MENUDA (PENSAMIENTOS INTRASCENDENTES)
- MAGDALENA
- MARAVILLAS
- MARINA
- MAS SONETOS...TODAVIA?
- MIL Y CUATRO SONETOS
- MIL Y TRES SONETOS
- MIL Y UN SONETOS
- MISTICAS
- LOS MOMENTOS DE LA RAZA
- MUJER...!COQUETA!
- NADA DE TODO
- LA OCIOSIDAD EN SONETOS
- LA OCIOSIDAD EN...!SONETOS!
- PARA TI
- PARAFRASIS A VARIAS COMPOSICIONES DEL BELLISIMO LIBRO "EN VUELO HERIDO" DE LA EGREGIA POETISA EVA CERVANTES
- PARAFRASIS PEQUENAS A LA GRAN OBRA MISTICA "ESTRELLAS MINIMAS" DE LA EGREGIA POETISA EVA CERVANTES
- PARA...!QUEMARLOS!
- PENSAMIENTOS
- PENSAMIENTOS Y SENTIRES
- PENSAMIENTOS...MALOS!
- LOS PIES DE CARLOS
- POESIAS
- POR MIS SOLEDADES VOY...
- LO QUE SE PIENSA,...SONANDO!
- RAMOS DE...!ORTIGAS!
- ROMANCES
- ROMANCES AL ATARDECER
- ROMANCES CORTOS
- ROMANCES DE ULTIMA HORA
- SEGUIDILLAS
- SEGUN LOS ANOS...!SE PIENSA!
- SEISCIENTOS SONETOS
- SELECCIONES
- SELECCIONES.IRONIAS.RELAMPAGOS
- SEVILLA!
- SIMPLEZAS DE AMOR
- SIMPLEZAS DE AMOR (DE TIEMPOS PASADOS)
- SIMPLEZASDE AMOR (DE TIEMPOS PASADOS)
- SIN PIES NI CABEZA
- SOMBRAS QUE SE HICIERON. !LUZ!
- SONETOS AL CUARTO DE HORA
- SONETOS INTRANSCENDENTES
- SONETOS INTRANSCENDENTES QUE MIS TORPEZAS DAN !POR EVIDENTES!
- SONETOS VULGARES
- SONTETOS AL CUARTO DE HORA
- TREINTA SONETOS
- TU, EN PRESENCIA
- LOS ULTIMOS...!HASTA AHORA!
- VERSOS DE JUVENTUDY...VEJEZ
- LA VIDA EN SONETOS. SONETOS DE JUVENTED
- LA VIDA EN SONETOS. SONETOS DE JUVENTUD
- LA VIRGEN DE LOS REMEDIOS
- YA, CON EL PIE EN EL ESTRIBO

Sanchez-Ocana y Acedo-Rico, Pedro *see* LO QUE SE VA

Sanchis Alventosa, Joaquin *see* DOCE NOS...

Sanchis Lopez, Manuel *see* SELECCIONES CONTINUAS

SANCHO SALDANA / Espronceda, Jose de – v1. 1870 – 9 – $1.50f – sp Bibl Santa Ana [830]

SANCHO SALDANA O EL CASTELLANO DE CUELLAR / Espronceda, Jose de – Madrid: J. de Castro y Compania, Tomo 2. 1869 – 1 – sp Bibl Santa Ana [946]

Sancho y Gonzalez, Javier *see* DE COSAS EXTREMENAS Y DE ALGO MAS

SANCHONIATHO'S PHOENICIAN HISTORY / Cumberland, Richard – 1720 – 1 – $50.00 – us Presbyterian [930]

UNA SANCTA – 1(1946)-4(1949) – 2mf – 9 – Dfl9.00 – ne Slangenburg [073]

Sancta Birgitta *see* REVELACIONES EXTRAVAGANTES

Sancta Clara, Abraham a *see* NEUE PREDIGTEN

SANCTAE SEDIS – 1(1865)-41(1908/09) – 386mf – 9 – Dfl1,351.00 – ne Slangenburg [073]

SANCTI BENEDICTI REGULA MONASTERIORUM / Linderbauer, BS – (Flor. Patr., 17) Muenster Wf., 1928 – 2mf – 8 – Dfl9.00 – ne Slangenburg [240]

SANCTI BENEDICTI REGULA MONASTERIORUM, PHILOLOGISCH ERKLAERT / Linderbauer, BS – Freiburg i. Br., 1922 – Dfl30.00 – ne Slangenburg [240]

SANCTI EPHRAEM SYRI OPERA – v. 1-6. 1732 – 1 – us Princeton Micro [780]

SANCTI THOMAE AQUINATIS OPERA OMNIA : LEONINA EDITION / Aquinas, Thomas – Romae: Ex Typographia Polyglotta S.C. De Propaganda Fide, 1888. v4-8 – 102mf – 8 – ne Slangenburg [240]

THE SANCTIFIED LIFE / Carradine, B – Cincinnati, O[hio]: Office of the Revivalist, c1897 – 1mf – us A.T.L.A. [240]

LES SANCTIONS COUTUMIERE CONTRE L'ADULTERE CHEZ LES NKUNDO / Hulstaert, G – Brussels. 1938 – 1 – us Res Libr [306]

LES SANCTIONS DE L'ARBITRAGE... / Dumas, J – Paris, 1905 – 5mf – 1 – ILM-825/1 – ne IDC [327]

SANCTIONS IMPOSABLE FOR VIOLATIONS OF THE FEDERAL RULES OF CIVIL PROCEDURE / Rhodes, Robert E et al – Washington: FJC, Jul 1981 – 2mf – 9 – $3.00 – LLMC 95-312 – us L.L.M.C. [340]

SANCTISSIMI MAXIMIGNE... / Jeronimo de Guadalupe – Toledo – 1 – sp Bibl Santa Ana [240]

A SANCTO AUGSTINO : LEVEN VAN DE WEERDICHE MOEDER MARIA STA TERESIA (ALIAS) PETYT / Michael, P – Gendt, 1683 – 11mf – 8 – ne Slangenburg [240]

SANCTO SEVERINATIS MEDICA AC PHILOSOPHI OPUSCULA ANATOMICA / Eustacchi, B – Venetiis, 1564 – 7mf – 9 – ne IDC [611]

LE SANCTUAIRE DE KIRJATH-JEARIM : ETUDE SUR LE LIEU DU CULTE CHEZ LES ISRAELITES AU TEMPS DE SAMUEL / Poels, Henricus Andreas – (Includes bibliographical references) – Louvain: JB. Istas; Gand: H. Engelcke, 1894 – 1mf – 9 – 0-8370-4774-9 – 1985-2774 – us A.T.L.A. [956]

LE SANCTUAIRE DE L'EMAM REZA, MASHAD, IRAN / Battesti, T – 9 – F50.00 – fr Ethnologie [260]

THE SANCTUARIES AND SANCTUARY SEEKERS OF MEDIAEVAL ENGLAND / Cox, John Charles – London: George Allen, 1911 – 1mf – us A.T.L.A. [240]

O SANCTUARIO : ORGAO CATHOLICO E OFICIAL DA PAROCHIA – Cidade de Uba, 6 May 1917 – 1,5,6 – bl Biblioteca [072]

SAND DUNE STABILIZATION, SHELTERBELTS AND AFFORESTATION IN DRY ZONES – 1985 – 247p – it F.A.O. [634]

SAND IN THEIR CRAWS / Kelly, Mary E H – 1 – us KS Hist [830]

Sand, M *see* CATALOGUE RAISONNE DES LEPIDOPTERES DU BERRY ET DE L'AUVERGNE

SAND RUN BAPTIST CHURCH. HEBRON, KENTUCKY : CHURCH RECORDS – 1810-1972 – 1 – 88.74 – us Baptist [240]

Sandaeus, M *see* PRO THEOLOGICA MYSTICA CLAVIS

Sandal Magna. Yorkshire *see* PARISH REGISTERS

Sandars, Mary Frances *see* HONORE DE BALZAC, HIS LIFE AND WRITINGS

Sanday, John *see* KATHMANDU VALLEY

Sanday, W., et al *see* CRITICISM OF THE NEW TESTAMENT

Sanday, William *see*
- APPENDICES AD NOVUM TESTAMENTUM STEPHANICUM
- THE AUTHORSHIP AND HISTORICAL CHARACTER OF THE FOURTH GOSPEL
- THE CRITICISM OF THE FOURTH GOSPEL: EIGHT LECTURES
- DIFFERENT CONCEPTIONS OF PRIESTHOOD AND SACRIFICE
- THE GOSPELS IN THE SECOND CENTURY: AN EXAMINATION OF...SUPERNATURAL RELIGION
- INSPIRATION
- THE LIFE OF CHRIST IN RECENT RESEARCH
- THE ORACLES OF GOD: NINE LECTURES ON THE NATURE AND EXTENT OF BIBLICAL INSPIRATION
- OUTLINES OF THE LIFE OF CHRIST

Sandberg, Graham *see* TIBET AND THE TIBETANS

Sande Lacoste, C M v.d. *see* SYNOPSIS HEPATICARUM JAVANICARUM...

SANDEBUDET : TIDING FOR ALTARE OCH HAERD – (Lacking some issues) – 1862-1969 – 50r – 1 – ATLA S0293 – us A.T.L.A. [240]

Sandels, Friedrich *see* DIE STELLUNG DER KAISERLICHEN FRAUEN AUS DEM JULISCH-CLAUDISCHEN HAUSE

Sandeman, Robert *see* LETTERS ON THERON AND ASPASIO: ADDRESSED TO THE AUTHOR OF THAT WORK: WITH TWO PREFACES, AND TWO APPENDIXES,.

Sanden, J C van *see* THE CHIEFTAINS OF CEYLON

SANDERS COUNTY LEDGER – Thompson Falls. Mont. 1951-1954; 1956- – 1 – us UMI [071]

SANDERS COUNTY SIGNAL – Camas. Mont. 1906-1920; 1922-1924 – 1 – us UMI [071]

Sanders, Daniel *see*
- DEUTSCHER SPRACHSCHATZ GEORDNET NACH BEGRIFFEN ZUR LEICHTEN AUFFINDUNG UND AUSWAHL DES PASSENDEN AUSDRUCKS
- WOERTERBUCH DER DEUTSCHEN SPRACHE

Sanders, Francis Williams *see* AN ESSAY ON USES AND TRUSTS, AND ON THE NATURE AND OPERATION CONVEYANCES AT COMMON LAW.

Sanders, Frank Knight *see*
- THE MESSAGES OF THE EARLIER PROPHETS
- OUTLINES FOR THE STUDY OF BIBLICAL HISTORY AND LITERATURE

Sanders, Helen F *see* HISTORY OF MONTANA

Sanders, James U *see* SOCIETY OF MONTANA PIONEERS

Sanders, John L *see* AMENDMENTS TO THE CONSTITUTION OF NORTH CAROLINA, 1776-1974

Sanders, P B *see* THE BASUTOLAND GENERAL ELECTION 1965

Sanders, Ralph *see* SCIENCE AND TECHNOLOGY: VITAL NATIONAL RESOURCES

Sanderson, David *see*
- THE EFFECT OF CADENCE ON AEROBIC AND ANAEROBIC CONTRIBUTIONS TO THE TOTAL ENERGY REQUIREMENTS OF CYCLING AT CONSTANT POWER OUTPUT
- THE EFFECT OF MASS ON THE KINEMATICS OF STEADY STATE WHEELCHAIR PROPULSION IN ADULTS AND CHILDREN WITH SPINAL CORD INJURY
- EVIDENCE OF BIOMECHANICAL FUNCTIONAL SYMMETRY IN THE PRESENCE OF LOWER EXTREMITY STRUCTURAL ASYMMETRY DURING RUNNING
- THE ROLE OF EXTERNAL NON-RIGID ANKLE BRACING IN THE PREVENTION OF INVERSION INJURIES

Sanderson, Joseph *see* JESUS ON THE HOLY MOUNT

Sanderson, M *see* UNESCO SOURCEBOOK IN CLIMATOLOGY FOR HYDROLOGISTS AND WATER RESOURCE ENGINEERS

Sanderson, Meredith *see* A YAO GRAMMAR

Sanderson, Natalie *see* FINANCIAL AND PRODUCT SPONSORSHIP WITHIN ATHLETIC TRAINING PROGRAMS

Sanderson, Thomas W *see* 20TH CENTURY HISTORY AND BIOGRAPHY OF YOUNGSTOWN AND MAHONING COUNTY

Sanderus, A *see* FLANDRIA ILLUSTRATA

Sanderus, Antoine *see* ANTONII SANDERI PRESBYTERI GANDAVUM SIVE GANDAVENSIUM RERUM LIBRI SEX

Sanderus, Nic. *see* DE VISIBILI MONARCHIA ECCLESIAE LIBRI OCTO

Sanderval, Aime Olivier *see*
- CONQUETE DU FOUTAH-DJALON
- DE L'ATLANTIQUE AU NIGER PAR LE FOUTAH-DJALON
- KAHEL

SANDESA – Ahmedabad, India. Jan-Aug 1966 – 1r – 1 – us L of C Photodup [072]

Sandford, K S *see*
- PREHISTORIC SURVEY OF EGYPT AND WESTERN ASIA
- PREHISTORIC SURVEY OF EGYPT AND WESTERN ASIA, VOL 2
- PREHISTORIC SURVEY OF EGYPT AND WESTERN ASIA, VOL 3
- PREHISTORIC SURVEY OF EGYPT AND WESTERN ASIA, VOL 4

Sandford, S *see* ORGANISATION AND MANAGEMENT OF WATER SUPPLIES IN TROPICAL AFRICA

SANDFORD'S CHANCERY APPEALS REPORTS / New York. (State) – (A Pre-NRS title) – v1-4. 1843-47 (all publ) – 33mf – 9 – $49.50 – LLMC 80-301 – us L.L.M.C. [340]

SANDHILL NEWS – Mullen, NE. -w. Sept 1952-Mar 1956 – 1 – us NE Hist [071]

SANDHILLER – Ainsworth, NE. -w. Feb. 1960-Sep. 1960 – 1 – us NE Hist [071]

SANDIACRE AND STAPLEFORD WEEKLY NEWS – Oct 3 1919-Oct 20 1920; Mar 25 1921-Jun, Jul 13-Dec 21 1973; Jan-Jun, Jul 5-Dec 20 1974; 1975-Dec 23 1976; Jan-Jun, Jul 7-Dec 22 1977; 1978-85; Jan 3-Dec 19 1986; 1988-92; Jan 15 1993-Jun 1996 – 93r – 1 – uk British Libr Newspaper [072]

SANDIK – Istanbul, nos. 1-3 (1290-1291 [1874-1875]) – 1mf – 9 – $20.00 – us MEDOC [949]

Sandinista National Liberation Front *see* BARRICADA INTERNACIONAL

SANDISFIELD 1762-1894 – (Mf 1-3: Rhodes' Index to B,M,D 1746-1850. Mf 4-10: Shepherd's Index to B,M,D 1746-1850. Mf 11-17: Town & Vital Records 1762-1804. Mf 18-22: Town & Vital Records 1806-92. Mf 23-27: Proprietors Records 1735-61. Mf 28: Births 1843-60. Mf 29: Births 1860-64; Marriages 1841-54. Mf 30: Deaths 1843-57. Mf 31: Marriages 1855-90. Mf 32: Marriages 1890-93; Deaths 1858-90. Mf 33: Deaths 1890-94; Births 1865-93. Mf 34: Index to Births 1894-1987. Mf 35-36: Index to Marriages 1894-1987. Mf 37-38: Index to Deaths 1894-1987) – (mf ed 1988) – 38mf – 9 – 0-87623-067-2 – us Holbrook [920]

SANDISFIELD FIRST BAPTIST CHURCH. SANDISFIELD, MASSACHUSETTS : CHURCH RECORDS – 1779-1798 – 1 – 5.00 – us Baptist [240]

Sandius, C *see* BIBLIOTHECA ANTI-TRINITARIORUM

SANDIWARA CHUSINGURA. PEMANDANGAN OLEH SAKAE SHIOYA : DITERDJEMAHKAN OLEH H.B. JASSIN AND KARIM HALIM – Djakarta, Gunseikanbu Kokumin Toshokyoku, 2605. 219p – 28-30mf – 9 – ne IDC [950]

Sandklef, Albert *see* ALDRE BISKOTSEL I SVERIGE OCH DANMAR

DER SANDMANN : EIN NACHTSTUECK / Hoffmann, Ernst Theordor Amadeus – Leipzig: P Reclam jun, [18–?] – 1 – us U.W. Library [830]

Sandner, Wolfgang *see* DIE KLARINETTE BEI CARL MARIA VON WEBER

Sandoval, Adolfo de *see* LO QUE QUIEREN LOS ESPANOLES DE BUENA VOLUNTAD...

Sandoval, B *see* TRATADO DEL CUYDADO QUE SE DEVE TENER DE LOS PRESOS PROBRES

Sandoval, M de *see*
- GLORIAS DE ESPANA. HERNANDO CORTES
- GLORIAS...HERNANDO CORTES
- HERNANDO CORTES

SANDOW'S MAGAZINE OF PHYSICAL CULTURE – (Issues for apr-dec 1899 filmed with: Physical Culture (London jul 1898), jul 1898-mar 1899; for jan-jul 1907 filmed with Physical Culture (London, apr 1898), apr-may 1898) – London: H R Francis Game. v2 n4-v19 n30. apr 1899-jul 1907 – us Res Libr [790]

THE SANDPIPER – Eureka, CA. 1969-1990 – 2r – 1 – $100.00 – B05032 – us Library Micro [071]

SANDPOINT DAILY BEE – Sandpoint, ID. 1977-80 – 16r – 1 – $800.00 – B04200 – us Library Micro [071]

Sandra *see* KEKOEATAN PROLETAR

Sandrart, J von *see*
- L'ACADEMIA TODESCA...
- ICONOLOGIA DEORU, ODER ABBILDUNG DER GOETTER...

Sands, Alexander Hamilton *see* HISTORY OF A SUIT IN EQUITY, AS PROSECUTED AND DEFENDED IN THE VIRGINIA STATE COURTS.

SANDS AND KENNY MELBOURNE DIRECTORIES 1857-1861 – 5v – 23mf and hard copy contents list – 9 – A$25.00 – at State Libr Vic [980]

SANDS AND MCDOUGALL MELBOURNE AND VICTORIAN DIRECTORIES 1862-1910 – 49v – 814mf – 9 – A$700.00 – at State Libr Vic [980]

SANDS AND MCDOUGALL MELBOURNE DIRECTORIES 1862-72 – 11v – 103mf and hard copy contents list – 9 – A$100.00 – at State Libr Vic [980]

SANDS AND MCDOUGALL MELBOURNE DIRECTORIES 1873-1883 – 11v – 143mf and hard copy contents list – 9 – A$150.00 – at State Libr Vic [980]

SANDS AND MCDOUGALL MELBOURNE DIRECTORIES 1884-1900 – 17v – 308mf and hard copy suburbs listing – 9 – A$320.00 – at State Libr Vic [980]

SANDS AND MCDOUGALL VICTORIAN DIRECTORIES – 1911-1920 – 386mf – 9 – A$400.00 – at State Libr Vic [920]

SANDS AND MCDOUGALL VICTORIAN DIRECTORIES – 1921-1930 – 379mf – 9 – A$400.00 – at State Libr Vic [920]

SANDS AND MCDOUGALL VICTORIAN DIRECTORIES 1901-1910 – 10v – 260mf – 9 – A$275.00 – at State Libr Vic [980]

Sands, P C *see* THE CLIENT PRINCES OF THE ROMAN EMPIRE UNDER THE REPUBLIC

SANDS SYDNEY DIRECTORY – (Apply to publ for details) – 1858-1932/33 – 9 – at Pascoe [910]

Sandt, G W *see* A BRIEF STUDY OF CHRISTIAN SCIENCE

Sandusky County. Ohio. Board of County Commissioners *see*
- COMMISSIONERS' JOURNALS
- COUNTY HOME RECORDS

Sandusky County. Ohio. County Home *see*
- CERTIFICATES OF ADMISSION
- STATEMENTS OF FACT

Sandusky County. Ohio. Fremont Township. Board of Education *see* CLASS REGISTER

Sandusky County. Ohio. Probate Court *see* NATURALIZATIONS. DECLARATIONS

Sandusky County. Ohio. Woodville Township. Board of Education *see*
- ENUMERATION: SCHOOL, AGE, YOUTH
- ENUMERATION SCHOOL AGE YOUTH

Sandusky County. Ohio. Woodville Township. Board of Trustees *see*
- BURIAL REGISTER
- MINUTES

Sandusky County. Ohio. Woodville Township. Cemetery Association *see* MINUTES AND LOT OWNERS

Sandusky County. Ohio. Woodville Township. Village Clerk *see* PHYSICIANS' BIRTH RECORDS

Sandusky. Ohio. First Congregational United Church of Christ *see* RECORDS

Sandusky. Ohio. First Presbyterian Church *see* RECORDS

Sandusky. Ohio.Grace Episcopal Church *see* RECORDS

Sandusky. Ohio.St. John Lutheran Church *see* RECORDS

Sandusky. Ohio.St. Stephen's United Church of Christ *see* RECORDS

SANDVIKENS TIDNING – Gavle, Sandviken, Sweden. 1911-78 – 89r – 1 – sw Kungliga [072]

SANDVIKENS TIDNING – Sandviken, Sweden. 1979 – 1 – sw Kungliga [072]

Sandwell, Bernard K *see* THE MUSICAL RED BOOK OF MONTREAL

SANDWICH 1651-1900 – (Mf 1-3: Town Records 1650-1700. Mf 2: Births 1643-92. Mf 3: Vital Records: 1634-87, 1754. Mf 4-6: Births & Deaths ca 1641-1809. Mf 4: Marriages ca 1695-1724. Mf 5: Marriages ca 1725-67; Deaths ca 1737-48. Mf 6: Marriages ca 1767-1812; Ear Marks & Miscellaneous ca 1752-1811. Mf 7: Marriages 1807-12. Mf 8: Vital Records Index 1671-1815. Mf 9-14: Index; Vitals 1803-42. Mf 15: Birth & Death Index 1803-42. Mf 16-17: Births & Deaths 1836-42. Mf 17: Out-of-Town Marriages 1670-1799. Mf 18: Vital Records Index 1836-42. Mf 19: Marriage Intentions 1783-1813; Earmarks ca 1813-31. Mf 20-21: Marriage Intentions 1838-86. Mf 21: Marriages 1834-44. Mf 22-30: Vital Records 1843-1900. Mf 31: Birth Index 1843-1900. Mf 32-33: Marriage Index 1844-1900. Mf 34: Death Index 1845-1900. Mf 35: Marriage Intentions 1887-93. Mf 36: Births, Marriages, Deaths 1891-1900) – (mf ed 1986) – 36mf – 9 – 0-931248-97-3 – us Holbrook [920]

SANDY BOULEVARD BULLETIN – Portland OR. Aug 15 1930 – 1 – us U.O. Library [071]

SANDY CREEK BAPTIST CHURCH (PRIMITIVE). BUTTS COUNTY. GEORGIA : CHURCH RECORDS – 1824-75 – 1 – 24.62 – us Baptist [240]

SANDY CREEK BAPTIST CHURCH. RANDOLPH ASSOCIATION. NORTH CAROLINA : CHURCH RECORDS – 1773-1845 – 1 – $8.28 – us Baptist [240]

SANDY CREEK BAPTIST CHURCH. TAMMS, ILLINOIS : CHURCH RECORDS – 1840-1979 – 1 – 60.30 – us Baptist [240]

SANDY CREEK CHURCH. GASPER RIVER ASSOCIATION. KENTUCKY : CHURCH RECORDS – 1805-1929 – 1 – 56.07 – us Baptist [240]

SANDY NEWS – Sandy, OR. -w. 18 Feb 1915-14 Sept 1917. 1 roll – 1 – us U.O. Library [071]

SANDY PLAINS BAPTIST CHURCH. SHELBY, NORTH CAROLINA : CHURCH RECORDS – 1854-1963 – 1 – 57.96 – us Baptist [240]

SANDY POST – Sandy, OR. -w. 6 Jan 1938-. – 1 – us U.O. Library [071]

SANDY ROAD NEWS – Portland, OR. -w. 3 Dec 1926-30 Dec 1927. 1 roll – 1 – us U.O. Library [071]

SANDY RUN BAPTIST CHURCH. WEST CHOWAN ASSOCIATION. NORTH CAROLINA : CHURCH RECORDS – 1773-1804 – 1 – 5.00 – us Baptist [240]

SANDY SHOPPER – Portland OR. Mar 20-June 20 1947 – 1 – us U.O. Library [071]

SANDY SOILS – 1979 – 251p – it F.A.O. [631]

Sandys, Edwin *see* HARVARD LECTURES ON THE REVIVAL OF LEARNING

Sandys, John Lewis *see* A COMPANION TO LATIN STUDIES

SANE EVANGELISM / ed by Hamilton, William Wistar – Philadelphia: Judson Press, c1909 – 1mf – 9 – 0-8370-6064-8 – 1986-0064 – us A.T.L.A. [240]

SANEFREEZE NEWS *see* PEACE ACTION

Saney, P *see* READINGS ON POPULATION FOR LAW STUDENTS

Sanford, Carlton E *see* EARLY HISTORY OF THE TOWN OF HOPKINTON

Sanford, Elias B *see* CHURCH FEDERATION

Sanford, John *see*
- AN ENTRANCE TO THE SPANISH TONGUE
- A GRAMMER OR INTRODUCTION TO THE ITALIAN TONGUE

Sanford, Maine. Sanford Baptist Church *see* RECORDS

SANG KURIANG; OPERA DUA BABAK / Utuy Tatang Sontani – In Sundanese. SE 3962 1. 1962 – 9 – ne IDC [950]

SANGAMO JOURNAL – Springfield. Ill. -w., sw. 1832-49 – 1 – us UMI [071]

SANGAR – (Missing issues: 8, 52, 61-77, 79-82, 87, 263-266, 268-273) – Toronto: Shumarah-'i 1-303 (10 Bahman 1358-14 Murdad 1365 [30 Jan 1980-5 Aug 1986]) – 2r – 1 – $135.00 – us MEDOC [950]

SANGEET KALA VIHAR *see* JOURNAL OF THE INDIAN MUSICOLOGICAL SOCIETY

THE SANGER HERALD – Sanger, CA. 1957-63; 1965- – 31+ r – 1 – $1,550.00 ($50.00y) – B02870 – us Library Micro [071]

Sangermano, V *see*
- THE BURMESE EMPIRE A HUNDRED YEARS AGO
- DESCRIPTION OF THE BURMESE EMPIRE

Sangh, Bharatiya Jana *see* ELECTION MANIFESTO, 1967

Sangidanzan, D *see* BNAMU-UIN SHUA5UA5KH

SANGONCALENSE – Sao Goncalo do Para, 5 Apr 1953 – 1,5,6 – bl Biblioteca [072]

SANGRE EN LOS TAPEHUANES / Bayle, Constantino & Cardoso, Joaquin – Madrid: Missionalia Hispanica, 1949 – 1 – sp Bibl Santa Ana [240]

Sangree, Walter H *see* A STUDY OF THE PEOPLE OF MIDDLETOWN OF SICILIAN EXTRACTION

Sangroniz, Jose Antonio de *see* LA EXPANSION CULTURAL DE ESPANA EN EL EXTRANJERO...

LA SANGSUE – Quebec, Canada. 14,21 sep 1867 – 1r – 1 – Can$25.00 – cn Can Microfilming [072]

Sanguino y Michel, Juan *see*
- ANTIGUEDADES DE TORRECILLAS (ALCUESCAR)
- ANTIGUEDADES ROMANAS DEL CORTIJO DE LAS VIRGENES, CERCA DE BAENA
- FALLECIMIENTO
- HUEBNER
- INSCRIPCION ROMANA INSIGNE DE CACERES
- INSTRUCCIONES SOBRE LAPIDAS
- MEMORIA DEL MUSEO DE BELLAS ARTES DE CACERES
- NOTICIA INEDITA
- LA NUEVA LAPIDA ROMANA DE IBAHERNANDO
- NUEVA LAPIDA ROMANA DE IBAHERNANDO
- NUEVOS HALLAZGOS EN TURMULES
- OBJETOS INGRESADOS EN EL MUSEO PROVINCIAL (DE CACERES)
- PIEDRA DE SACRIFICIOS Y ANTIGUEDADES DE MAYORALGUILLO DE VARGAS
- TURMOLUS?. ANTIGUEDADES DESCUBIERTAS Y OTRAS YA CONOCIDAS

SANGUIS NATURAE: OR, A MANIFEST DE LARATION OF THE SANGUINE AND SOLAR CONGEALED LIQUOR OF NATURE – By Anonimus. London: Printed for A. R. and sold by T. Soule, 1696 – 1 – us U.W. Library [540]

Sani Poblete, Margot *see* BOSQUEJO SOBRE EL TRABAJO Y LA SEGURIDAD SOCIAL EN EL DOMINIO DEL CANADA

Sanidad Militar Divisionaria de la 74 Division *see* PROGRAMA Y TEXTO PARA UN CURSILLO DE AUXILIARES DE PRACTICANTES

Sanif, Sutan *see*
- DJAGOENG. SING NDJAWAKAKE WASIR REKSAWARDAJA. TJAP2AN KAPINDO
- ILMU TUMBUH-TUMBUHAN

SANITARNAIA OKHRANA ZHILISHCH : DEKRETY I RASPORIAZHENIIA SOVETA NARODNYKH KOMISSAROV I NARODNOGO KOMISSARIATA ZDRAVOOKHRANENIIA... / Russian S.F.S.R. – (Includes c.1: v.1 1919) – Moskva: Komissariat, 1919-1920 – 1 – CSUXAKY9971-S – us Hoover Inst Photo [613]

SANITARY CODE OF THE PENTATEUCH / Gillespie, Charles George Knox – New York: Fleming H. Revell, (1894). 1 fiche – 9 – us A.T.L.A. [220]

SANITATION DI INDONESIA / Mertonegoro, KR T – SE-1154 1. 1955? – 9 – ne IDC [628]

SANITY – Toronto. v1 n1. jan 1963-v4 n9. nov 1967 – 1r – 1 – Can$50.00 – cn Can Microfilming [072]

Sanizade, Mehmed Ataullah *see* TARIH-I SANIZADE

SANJAK-SANJAK INDONESIA / Liao, Chien-yue – In Indonesian and Chinese on opposite pages. SE-14,711 1. 1959 – 9 – ne IDC [950]
Sanjana, D D P *see* PAHLAVI TEXT SERIES
Sankalia, Hasmukhlal Dhirajlal *see* THE UNIVERSITY OF NALANDA
Sankaran Nair, Chettur *see* GANDHI AND ANARCHY
Sankawulo, Wilton *see* TWO NOVELS AND A COLLECTION OF KPELLE TALES
SANKEI SHIMBUN – Japan, 1950-81 – 1 – inquire – us Ross [072]
SANKEI SHIMBUN – March 1950-December 1994 – 592r – 1 – Y5,920,000 – ja Japan Micro [950]
Sankey, Ira D *see*
- GOSPEL HYMNS AND SACRED SONGS
- THE SANKEY SCRAPBOOK, 1840-1908

THE SANKEY SCRAPBOOK, 1840-1908 / Sankey, Ira D – 1 – 55.16 – us Baptist [240]
SANKHAYANA S'RAUTA SUTRA – 4v. Calcutta. 1888-99. BI-502 2 – 8 – ne IDC [280]
SANKHUA5UA5-ZEELIN TALAARKHI KHULL'CHILSAN ARTUUDIN SISTEMCHILSEN EMKHTGEL / Mongolia. U.S.S.R – Ulan Bator, 1966. 2 vols. BR-15.018 1 – 9 – ne IDC [324]
SANKHYA KARIKA WITH THE BHASHYA OF ISVARA KRSNA GAURAPADA – 1837 – 1 – uk Microform Academic [280]
Sankoku, Tsuran Dzusetsu *see* APERCU GENERAL DES TROIS ROYAUMES
SANKT BLEHK : ODER DIE GROSSE VERAENDERUNG / Tuegel, Ludwig – Hamburg: Hanseatische Verlagsanstalt, c1934 – 1r – 1 – us U.W. Library [830]
SANKT MICHAEL / Werner, E – 10. Aufl. Stuttgart: Union Deutsche Verlagsgesellschaft, 1890 – 1 – us U.W. Library [830]
SANKT PETERBURGSKII VESTNIK, IZDAVAEMYI OBSHCHESTVOM LIUBITELEI SLOVESNOSTI, NAUK I KHUDOZHESTV – St. Petersburg, 1812. v.1-3. B-1872 2 – 8 – ne IDC [460]
SANKT PETERBURGSKOE EKHO – (Backfile through 1998 $85r) – 1999- – 3r per y – 1 – $240.00 standing order – us Ross [072]
SANKT PETERSBURGISCHE ZEITUNG – (Missing: 1728-1731 (several nos); 1753; 1755-1806; 1807(2); 1808-1827; 1828(2, 35, 36, 38); 1830-1917) – Spb., 1728-1917 – 98mf – 9 – R-18363/1 – ne IDC [072]
SANKT PETERSBURGSKII VESTNIK – Zhurnal slovesnosti, teatra, novostei, i muzyki. St. Petersburg, 1831. v.1-48. BR-3747 2 – 8 – ne IDC [460]
SANKT-PETERBURGSKII MERKURII – 4v. Spb. 1793-94. B-1454 2 – 8 – ne IDC [073]
SANKT-PETERBURGSKII VESTNIK – v. 1-7. 1778-81. B-1871 2 – 8 – ne IDC [073]
SANKT-PETERBURGSKIIA VEDOMOSTI – (Missing: Several numbers) – 1743-1913 (scattered issues) – 169r – 1 – RF-1/3 – ne IDC [072]
SANMARGA – Banaras, India. Aug 1950-Nov 1952; 1953-78; 1980-Jul 1987 – 67r – 1 – us L of C Photodup [072]
Sannazaro, Jacopo *see* ARCADIA
SANS FAMILLE / Malot, Hector Henri – In Indonesian. SE-11,673 1. 1949 – 9 – ne IDC [306]
SANSIBAR : EIN OSTAFRIKANISCHES CULTURBILD / Schmidt, Karl Wilhelm – Leipzig: F A Brockhaus, 1888 – us Res Libr [960]
Sansinena Araguete, Enrique *see*
- DER VALLE A LA SIERA (EXTREMAURA)
- DER VALLE A LA SIERRA

THE SANSKRIT BUDDHIST LITERATURE OF NEPAL / Mitra, Rajendralala, Raja – Calcutta: Asiatic Society of Bengal, 1882. xlvii,340p – 1 – us U.W. Library [280]
SANSKRIT-ENGLISH DICTIONARY / Monier-Williams, Monier, Sir – 23 fiches – 9 – $25.00 – us I.A.S.W.R. [490]
SANSKRIT-ENGLISH DICTIONARY, ETYMOLOGICALLY AND PHILOLOGICALLY ARRANGED / Monier-Williams, Monier, Sir – 23mf – $25.00 – us I.A.S.W.R. [420]
Sanson, Guillaume *see* ATLAS DE SANSON
Sanson, Henry *see* DENKWUERDIGKEITEN DER SCHARFRICHTERFAMILIE SANSON
Sansovino, F *see*
- GL' ANNALI AVERO LE VITE DE' PRINCIPI ET SIGNORI DELLA CASA OTHOMANA
- L'HISTORIA DI CASA ORSINA...
- L'HISTORIA DI CASA ORSINA
- HISTORIA VNIVERSALE DELL' ORIGINE, ET IMPERIO DE' TVRCHI, ...

Sansum, Oliver B *see* SANSUM'S DIGEST OF THE LAW OF INSURANCE
SANSUM'S DIGEST OF INSURANCE CASES *see* BERRYMAN'S DIGEST OF THE LAW OF INSURANCE
SANSUM'S DIGEST OF THE LAW OF INSURANCE : BEING AN ANALYSIS OF FIRE, MARINE; LIFE AND ACCIDENT INSURANCE CASES / Sansum, Oliver B – (Cont by: Berryman's Digest of Insurance Cases) – Chicago: Callaghan. 1v. 1881 (all publ) – 9 – LLMC 95-128 – us L.L.M.C. [340]
SANTA ANA – 1906-08; 1910-13; 1916-17 – 13r – 1 – $650.00 – P00117 – us Library Micro [910]
SANTA ANA – Caceres, 1975 – 5 – sp Bibl Santa Ana [073]
SANTA ANA CITY DIRECTORIES INCLUDING TUSTIN AND GARDEN GROVE – Orange Co, CA. 1905; 1908-1923; 1936; 1949-1950 – 15r – 1 – $750.00 – D067 – us Library Micro [910]
SANTA ANA HERALD – Santa Ana, CA. 1886-1889 – 1r – 1 – $50.00 – R04109 – us Library Micro [071]
SANTA ANA JOURNAL – Santa Ana, CA. 1935-1938 – 18r – 1 – $900.00 – C03511 – us Library Micro [071]
Santa Ana, Juan de *see* EXEMPLAR...ANTONIO DE LA VISITACION
SANTA ANITA PACEMAKER *see* NEWSPAPERS PUBLISHED IN INTERNMENT CAMPS
Santa Anna, Antonio Lopez de *see* MI HISTORIA MILITAR Y POLITICA, 1810-1874; MEMORIAS INEDITAS
SANTA BARBARA – 1909-39 – 15r – 1 – $750.00 – P00118 – us Library Micro [910]
SANTA BARBARA / Ouida – British Fiction Archive: Unit 3 – 9 – uk Bell [830]
Santa Barbara. Arts Library at the University of California *see* ART EXHIBITION CATALOGS SUBJECT INDEX, 1977-1990
SANTA BARBARA COUNTY INCLUDING MONTECITO AND SANTA MARIA – Santa Barbara Co, CA. 1904-1912; 1923-1949 – 23r – 1 – $1,150.00 – D093 – us Library Micro [978]
SANTA BARBARA DAILY INDEPENDENT – Santa Barbara, CA. 1883-1913 – 39r – 1 – $1,950.00 – R02938 – us Library Micro [071]
SANTA BARBARA DAILY NEWS – Santa Barbara, CA. 1895-1927 – 37r – 1 – $1,850.00 – R02940 – us Library Micro [071]
SANTA BARBARA INDEX – Santa Barbara, CA. Sept 1872-Aug 1876 – 1r – 1 – $50.00 – R02939 – us Library Micro [071]
SANTA BARBARA NEWS – Santa Barbara, CA. 1983 – 11+ r – 1 – $550.00 ($50.00y) – H04064 – us Library Micro [071]
SANTA BARBARA NEWS PRESS – (Also known as: Daily Press; Morning Press) – Santa Barbara, CA. 1872- – 1318+ r – 1 RC02941 – $65,900.00 ($1,080.00y) – us Library Micro [071]
SANTA BARBARA POST – Santa Barbara, CA. Nov 1963-Jan 1965 – 1r – 1 – $50.00 – R02942 – us Library Micro [071]
SANTA BARBARA PRESS HOME EDITION – Santa Barbara, CA. 1953 – 1r – 1 – $50.00 – R04110 – us Library Micro [071]
SANTA BARBARA STAR – Santa Barbara, CA. 1950-62 – 10r – 1 – $500.00 – R02943 – us Library Micro [071]
SANTA BARBARA WEEKLY PRESS – Santa Barbara, CA. 1869-1880 – 4r – 1 – $200.00 – R03513 – us Library Micro [071]
THE SANTA CLARA – Santa Clara. CA. (Univ. of Santa Clara). -w. 1944-58 – 1 – us UMI [370]
THE SANTA CLARA – Santa Clara, CA: University of Santa Clara, 1922-82 – 10r – 1 BC02945 – $500.00 – us Library Micro [370]
SANTA CLARA ARGUS – (Also known as: The Daily Argus) – San Jose, CA. 1870-72; 1876-77 – 2r – 1 – $100.00 – B02887 – us Library Micro [071]
SANTA CLARA COUNTY – 1892; 1909; 1914-18; 1928-50 – 42r – 1 – $2,100.00 – P00119 – us Library Micro [910]
SANTA CLARA COUNTY AND SAN JOSE CITY DIRECTORIES – Santa Clara Co, CA. 1870-1950 – 65r – 1 – $3,250.00 – D094 – us Library Micro [910]

SANTA CLARA COUNTY PATRIOT – San Jose, CA. 1866 – 3r – 1 – $150.00 – C03678 – us Library Micro [071]
SANTA CLARA DE ASIS. ANTOLOGIA POETICA / Corredor Garcia, Antonio – Caceres: Edic. Cruzada Mariana, 1959 – 1 – sp Bibl Santa Ana [240]
SANTA CLARA JOURNAL INDEX – Santa Clara, CA. 1965-70 – 5,9 B06009 – $50.00 set – us Library Micro [073]
SANTA CLARA LAW REVIEW – (v1-24 1961-84 on reel $410.00. v25-35 1985-96 on mf $294.00. Title varies: v1-15 1961-75 as Santa Clara Lawyer) – v1-35. 1961-96 – 1,5,6,9,13 – $704.00 set – us Hein [340]
SANTA CLARA LAWYER *see* SANTA CLARA LAW REVIEW
SANTA CLARA NEWS – San Jose, CA. 1944-56 – 5r – 1 – $250.00 – C02888 – us Library Micro [071]
SANTA CLARA REGISTER – San Jose, CA. Jan-Oct 1853 – 1r – 1 – $50.00 – B02889 – us Library Micro [071]
SANTA CLARITA VALLEY – 1992 – 3+ r – 1 – $150.00 – P00120 – us Library Micro [910]
Santa Criz, Fr. Jose *see* CHRONICA...SAN MIGUEL
SANTA CRUZ CITY AND COUNTY DIRECTORIES – Santa Cruz Co, CA. 1904-1950 – 31r – 1 – $1,550.00 – D096 – us Library Micro [978]
SANTA CRUZ COUNTY – 1904-33; 1992- – 27+ r – 1 – $1,350.00 – P00121 – us Library Micro [910]
SANTA CRUZ COUNTY / H.S. Crocker Co – San Francisco, 1896. California Reel 33. The Cox Library Collection – 5 – us Americana [978]
SANTA CRUZ COUNTY SENTINEL – Santa Cruz, CA. 1866-1906; 1907- – 760+ r – 1 BC02961 – $38,000.00 ($720.00y) – us Library Micro [071]
SANTA CRUZ DE LA SIERRA. FIESTAS COMARCALES A SANTA RITA. 1977 / Pastor Serrano, Juan Jose – Trujillo: Imp. Gexme, 1977 – 1 – sp Bibl Santa Ana [390]
Santa Cruz de Paniagua. Ayuntamiento *see* LA VILLA DE SANTA CRUZ DE PANIAGUA Y SAN PEDRO DE ALCANTARA
SANTA CRUZ EXPRESS – (Index available) – Santa Cruz, CA. Mar 1981-Feb 1985 – 4r – 1 – $200.00 – B02953 – us Library Micro [071]
SANTA CRUZ EXPRESS – Santa Cruz, Washington, DC. 1981-1985 – 1r – 1 – $50.00 – B02953 – us Library Micro [071]
Santa Cruz Mission. Calif *see* ORIGINAL RECORDS OF BAPTISMS AND CORRESPONDENCE
SANTA CRUZ MISSION RECORDS OF BAPTISMS AND CORRESPONDENCE – (In Spanish) – Santa Cruz, 1791-1814 (incomplete) – 1r – 1 – $50.00 – B40267 – us Library Micro [920]
SANTA CRUZ NEWS – Santa Cruz, CA. 1859-1860 – 1r – 1 – $50.00 – B03514 – us Library Micro [071]
SANTA CRUZ TIMES : APTOS VOICE: INDEX – Santa Cruz, CA – 1 – 1 – $50.00 – B03683 – us Library Micro [071]
SANTA CRUZ TIMES – Santa Cruz, CA. 1867 – 5r – 1 – $250.00 – C03684 – us Library Micro [071]
Santa Cruz y Mallen, Francisco Xavier de *see* HISTORIA DE FAMILIAS CUBANAS
SANTA EULALIA DE ABAMIA (INFORME) / Monsalud, Marques de – Madrid: Est. Tip. Fortanet, 1906. B.R.A.H. t. 48, 1906, pp. 40-42 – 1 – sp Bibl Santa Ana [946]
SANTA EULALIA DE MERIDA / Melida, Jose Ramon – Madrid: Fortanet, 1919. B.R.A.H. 74. pp. 529-530 – 1 – sp Bibl Santa Ana [240]
SANTA EULALIA DE MERIDA / Sanchez Loro, Domingo – Caceres, 1947 – 1 – sp Bibl Santa Ana [946]
SANTA EULALIA DE MERIDA, SU VIDA, MARTIRIO Y CULTO A TRAVES DE LA MODERNA CRITICA HISTORICA Y DE LOS RECIENTES DESCUBRIMIENTOS ARQUEOLOGICOS / Navarro del Castilio, Vicente – Badajoz: Imprenta dela Diputacion Provincial, 1971 – 1 – sp Bibl Santa Ana [240]
Santa Fe and Los Angeles Harbor Railway Company *see* MINUTES OF MEETINGS
SANTA FE BAPTIST CHURCH. SANTA FE, TENNESSEE : CHURCH RECORDS – 1882-1946 – 1 – 12.33 – us Baptist [240]

SANTA FE RATE SCHEDULES / Atchison, Topeka and Santa Fe Railroad Company – 1870-79 – 1 – us KS Hist [380]
SANTA FE WEEKLY GAZETTE – Santa Fe, New Mexico, -w 1853-1956 – 13 – $25.00r – us I.M.R. [071]
Santa Infancia *see* MEMORIA ANUAL DE LA SANTA INFANCIA. EJERCICIO 1966-67
SANTA ISABEL BAPTIST CHURCH. PROVIDENCE ISLAND, COLOMBIA : CHURCH RECORDS – 1Nov 1927-2 Apr 1940. Church minutes. Feb 1936-1 Jul 1949 – 1 – 23.76 – us Baptist [240]
Santa Isabel Misioneros Hijos del Immaculado *see* LA GUINEA ESPANOLA
Santa Lucia y Amaya, Jose *see* COLECCION DE POESIAS LATINAS Y CASTELLANAS
SANTA MARIA EN INDIAS / Bayle, Constantino; ed by Valle, A – Madrid: Razon y Fe, 1928 – 9 – sp Bibl Santa Ana [972]
SANTA MARIA TIMES – Santa Maria, CA. 1882- – 399+ r – 1 RC02966 – $19,950.00 ($600.00y) – us Library Micro [071]
Santa Maria, Tomas de *see* LIBRO LLAMADO, ARTE DE TANER FANTASIA. Y APROVADO POR EL EMINENTE MUSICO DE SU MAGESTAD ANTONIO DE CABECON, Y POR JUAN DE CABECON, SU HERMANO
SANTA MONICA NORTHSIDE ADVERTISER – Santa Monica, CA. 1977-81 – 5r – 1 – $250.00 – R02969 – us Library Micro [071]
SANTA MONICA SOUTHSIDE ADVERTISER – Santa Monica, CA. Jul 1977-1980 – 6r – 1 – $300.00 – R02971 – us Library Micro [071]
SANTA PAULA NEWS – Santa Paula, CA. 1946-56 – 5r – 1 – $250.00 – C02973 – us Library Micro [071]
SANTA PAULA WEEKLY REVIEW – Santa Paula, CA. 1928 – 1r – 1 – $50.00 – R02974 – us Library Micro [071]
SANTA ROSA – 1922-28 – 6r – 1 – $300.00 – P00122 – us Library Micro [910]
SANTA ROSA EVENING PRESS AND SANTA ROSA REPUBLICAN – Santa Rosa, CA. 1948-49 – 10r – 1 – $500.00 – B02977 – us Library Micro [071]
Santa Rosa o Alcala, Marcos de *see* CHRONICA DE A SANTA PROVINCIA DE SAN JOSEPH...
SANTA ROSA REPUBLICAN *see* THE REPUBLICAN
SANTA ROSA, SONOMA COUNTY AND SANTA ROSA JR. COLLEGE HISTORY : NEWSPAPER ACCOUNTS – 1r – 1 – $50.00 – B40277 – us Library Micro [370]
SANTA TERESA : BEING SOME ACCOUNT OF HER LIFE AND TIMES: TOGETHER WITH SOME PAGES FROM THE HISTORY OF THE LAST GREAT REFORM IN THE RELIGIOUS ORDERS / Graham, Gabriela Cunninghame – (Includes index) – New ed. London: Eveleigh Nash, 1907 – 2mf – 9 – 0-8370-6815-0 – 1986-0815 – us A.T.L.A. [920]
SANTA TERESA DE JESUS. MADRID 1934 / Dominguez Berrueta, Juan – Madrid: Razon y Fe, 1935 – 1 – sp Bibl Santa Ana [240]
SANTA YNEZ VALLEY NEWS – Solvang. Calif. -w. 1956-67 – 1 – us UMI [071]
Santalov, A I *see* KOMMENTARII K UGOLOVNO-PROTSESSUAL'NOMU KODEKSU MOLDAVSKOI SSR
Santamaria, Francisco *see* DICCIONARIO GENERAL DE AMERICANISMO. 3 VOL. MEXICO, 1943
Santana, Jose Epigmeno *see* NUNO BELTRAN DE GUZMAN Y SU OBRA EN LA NUEVA ESPANA
Santanello, T *see* GENDER RELATED DIFFERENCES IN PERFORMANCE LEVELS OF TRIATHLETES
Santano de Membrio, Juan *see*
- CEREMONIAL DEL ALTAR...SAN GABRIEL
- ECLESIASTICO...SANTA...SAN GABRIEL
- MANUAL ECLESIASTICO Y REGULAR PARA LOS RELIGIOSES DE LA SANTA PROVINCIA DE SAN GABRIEL...

Santarem *see* RECHERCHES SUR LA PRIORITE DE LA DECOUVERTE DES PAYS SITUES SUR LA COTE OCCIDENTALE D'AFRIQUE
LA SANTE / ed by Chaput, Marcel – Montreal, mai 1969-v1 n8. mai 1970 (numero special) – 1r – 1 – Can$45.00 – cn Can Microfilming [610]

O SANTELMO : ORGAM OFFICIAL DA CAMARA DO FRUCTAL – Cidade do Frutal, 22 Mar, Sep 1896; Jun-4 Jul 1897 – 1,5,6 – bl Biblioteca [072]

O SANTELMO : ORGAO DE ESTUDANTES – Curitiba, 1 Mar-2 Jul 1888 – 1,5,6 – bl Biblioteca [072]

SANTELMO : PERIODICO POLITICO, LITTERARIO E NOTICIOSO – Maceio, Alagoas. 14 Set-1 Out 1873 – 1,5,6 – bl Biblioteca [072]

Santerre, Alec *see* LE POTAGER, JARDIN DU CULTIVATEUR

Santiago de Alcantara. Ayuntamiento *see* FERIAS Y FIESTAS...1972

Santiago de Chile, Biblioteca del Congreso *see* BIBLIOGRAFIA CHILENA DE FILOSOFIA DESDE FINES DEL SIGLO 16 HASTA EL PRESENTE

Santiago de Chile, Biblioteca Nacional *see* CATALOGO DE LOS MANUSCRITOS RELATIVOS A LOS ANTIGUOS JESUITAS DE CHILE QUE SE CUSTODIAN EN LA BIBLIOTECA NACIONAL

SANTIAGO EN AMERICA. MEXICO, 1946 / Valle, Rafael Heliodoro – Madrid: Razon y Fe, 1947 – 1 – sp Bibl Santa Ana [972]

Santiago Rodriguez, Miguel *see* NOTICIAS GENERALES Y UN DATO INEDITO PARA LA BIOGRAFIA DE VASCO DIAZ TANCO, DE FREGENAL, EN RELACION CON CANARIAS

SANTIAM NEWS – Scio, OR. -w. 5 Aug 1898-2 Feb 1906. 1 roll – 1 – us U.O. Library [071]

Santibanez, Leandro *see* RETRATO...ALCANTARA

Santkin, Paul *see* LUDWIG BOERNES EINFLUSS AUF HEINRICH HEINE

IL SANTO OFFICIO DELLA INQUISIZIONE IN NAPOLI : NARRAZIONE CON MOLTI DOCUMENTI INEDITI / Amabile, Luigi – Citta di Castello: S. Lapi, 1892 – 2mf – us A.T.L.A. [240]

SANTOA4 NO ICHI SHUA4SHICHIN NO SHAKAITEKI KOA4ZOA4 / National Peking University. Chinese Agricultural Economics Research Institute – Peking. 1942 50 p. Rural conditions in one village of Shantung Province. (J 612.221 P35s) – 1 – 35.00r – us Hoover Inst Photo [305]

SANTOA4-SHOA4 KEIMIN-KEN NOA4SON CHOA4SA HOA4KOKU / National Peking University. Chinese Agricultural Economics Research Institute – Peking. 1939 72 p. Rural conditions in Shantung Province (Shan-tung sheng Hui-min hsien). (J 612.221 P35) – 1 – 35.00r – us Hoover Inst Photo [360]

Santoli, Vittorio *see* WACKENRODER E IL MISTICISMO ESTETICO

Santonja Gomez, M *see* INDUSTRIAS PALEOLITICAS EN EL TRAMO EXTREMENO DEL TAJO

SANTORAL SERAPHICO / Duran de Montijo, Juan – 1718 – 9 – 1.50f – sp Bibl Santa Ana [240]

Santos Alvarez, Miguel de los *see* MARIA

Santos Calderon de la Barca, Bernardo *see* INFORME...GUADALUPE...FISCAL...A ABADIA ALVANEZA

Santos Coco, Francisco *see*
- GRAMATICA LATINA
- LA PRONUNCIACION DEL LATIN

SANTOS COCO, FRANCISCO. LA PRONUNCIACION DEL LATIN. BADAJOZ, 1929 / Errandonea, Ignacio – Madrid: Razon y Fe, 1930 – 1 – sp Bibl Santa Ana [450]

Santos Cuenda, Juan y Consortes *see*
- ALEGACION AL DERECHO...DUQUE DE MEDINACELI
- OBSERVACIONES...CONTRA LA SENTENCIA... DUQUE DE MEDINACELI

Los Santos de Maimona *see* EL CARRO DE LA ALEGRIA, 1967

Santos de Maimona, Los. Ayuntamiento *see* FIESTAS PATRONALES DE NTRA. SRA. DE LA ESTRELLA. 1975

Santos, Jean Dos *see* HISTOIRE DE L'ETHIOPIE ORIENTALE COMPOSEE EN PORTUGAIS

Santos Joao dos *see* HISTOIRE DE L'ETHIOPIE ORIENTALE...TRADUIT EN FRANCOIS PAR...GAETAN CHARPY

Santos, Jose *see* INDICE GENERAL ALFABETICO DE LAS OBRAS DE FEIJOO Y SARMIENTO

Santos Neila, Francisco *see*
- LA ETICA O ESTETICA POLITICA DE MAQUIAVELO
- LA MORAL ISLAMICA Y TIRSO GONZALEZ DE SANTALLA

Santos Olivera, Balbino *see* BENITO ARIAS MONTANO, PADRE DE LA ARQUEOLOGIA BIBLICA

Santos Redondo, Ignacio *see*
- ARITMETICA
- MEMORIA DE LA ESCUELA MUNICIPAL DE ARTES Y OFICIOS DE BADAJOZ. LEIDA EN EL ACTO DE LA APERTURA DEL CURSO 1896-97

EL SANTUARIO DE LA MONTANA – Caceres, 1952 – 5 – sp Bibl Santa Ana [073]

Sanuto, L *see* GEOGRAFIA...DISTINTA IN 12 LIBRI

Sanvisenti, Bernardo *see* I PRIMI INFLUSSI DI DANTE, DEL PETRARCA, E DEL BOCCACCIO SULLA LETTERATURA SPAGNUOLA, CON APPENDICE DI DOCUMENTI INEDITI..

Sanyal, B C et al *see* GRADUATE EMPLOYMENT AND HIGHER EDUCATION IN WEST BENGAL

Sanz, Angel B *see* MENSAJE DE ARTESANIA, LO QUE TE DECIAN OBRERO

Sanz Catalan, Jose *see*
- 1ST CONGRESO SINDICAL AGRARIO DE EXTREMADURA. PONENCIA 4 SERVICIOS ECONOMICOS DE LAS HERMANDADES
- ORDEN DE DELEGACION NO 43. NUMERO 18 DE FOMENTO FUNCIONAL Y DIRECCION DE ENTIDADES LOCALES. FUNCIONES Y ATRIBUCIONES DE LAS JUNTAS SINDICALES AGROPECUARIAS DE LAS HERMANDADES
- ORDEN DE DELEGACION NUM. 45, NO 19 DE FOMENTO FUNCIONAL Y DIRECCION DE ENTIDADES LOCALES. NORMAS PARA REDACCION POR LAS HERMANDADES DE SUS PRESUPUESTOS ORDINARIOS, ESPECIALES Y EXTRAORDINARIOS
- ORDEN DE DELEGACION NUM. 50. NO 4 DE ELECCIONES SINDICALES Y VARIOS. CONCENTRACION DE MANDOS...
- ORDEN DE DELEGACION NUM. 51 NUM. 5 DE ELECCIONES SINDICALES. REALIZACION PRACTICA DE LAS ELECCIONES SINDICALES EN LOS GREMIOS Y HERMANDADES SINDICALES LOCALES
- ORDEN DE DELEGACION NUM. 52. NUM. 6 DE ELECCIONES SINDICALES. PLAN DE DESARROLLO DE LAS ELECCIONES SINDICALES DE 2ND GRADO O PROVINCIALES
- ORDEN DE DELEGACION NUM. 53 NUM. 7 DE ELECCIONES SINDICALES. NORMAS PARA LA ELECCION DE JEFES EN LAS ENTIDADES MENORES
- ORDEN DE DELEGACION NUM. 57 NUM. 22 DE FOMENTO FUNCIONAL Y DIRECCION ENTIDADES. NORMAS PARA EL TRASPASO DE LAS FUNCIONES DE LAS ANTIGUAS JUNTAS LOCALES A JUNTAS SINDICALES AGROPECUARIAS A LOS CABILDOS DE LAS HERMANDADES
- ORDEN DE DELEGACION NUMERO 40 NUMERO 16 DE FOMENTO FUNCIONAL Y DIRECCION DE ENTIDADES LOCALES PLAN E INSTRUCCIONES PARA UNA ACTUACION EFICAZ Y DECISIVA DELAS HERMANDADES
- ORDEN DE DELEGACION NUMERO 46. NUMERO 20 DE FOMENTO FUNCIONAL Y DIRECCION DE ENTIDADES LOCALES. CREACION DEL SERVICIO DEEXPLOTACION ECONOMICA Y SUMINISTROS AGRICOLAS EN LAS HERMANDADES SINDICALES DEL CAMPO

Sanz de Dios y Guadalupe, Francisco *see* MEDICINA...GUADALUPE

Sanz de Moreta, Emilio *see* LAVISION Y LA VIDA

Sanz, Gasper *see*
- INSTRUCCION DE MUSICA SOBRE LA GUITARRA ESPANOLA..
- INSTRUCCION DE MUSICA SOBRE LA GUITARRA ESPANOLA, Y METODO DE SVS PRIMEROS RUDIMENTOS, HASTA TANERLA CON DESTREZA
- LIBRO SEGUNDO DE CIFRAS SOBRE LA GUITARRA ESPANOLA, CON ARTE NUEVO PARA APRENDER A TANERLA SIN MAESTRO, CON GRAN FACILIDAD
- LIBRO TERCERO DE MUSICA

Sanzio, Raffaelle *see* AN ALBUM OF 35 DRAWINGS, MAINLY OF BUILDINGS, ANTIQUE STATUES, ETC

SAO DANG BAO – China. 1935-37 – 9 – 1310.00 – cc Globe [072]

SAO FRANCISCO DAS CHAGAS... / Willeke, Venencio – Madrid: Arch. Ibero Americano, 1963 – 1 – sp Bibl Santa Ana [240]

Sao Paulo. Brazil. Camara Municipal *see* REGISTO GERAL DA CAMARA DA CIDADE DE SAO PAULO

Sao Paulo. Divisao do Arquivo Historico do Departamento de Cultura *see* ATLAS DA CAMARA DA CIDADE DE SAO PAULO

Sao Paulo. (State). Brazil *see* DIARIO OFICIAL DO ESTADO DE SAO PAULO

Sao Tome and Principe Islands. Ministerio da Educacao e Cultura. Seccao de Estatistica *see* ANUARIO ESTATISTICO, ANO LECTIVO 1986/87

Sao Tome and Principe Islands. (Portugal) *see*
- FINANCE PLANS:
- PLANO DE FOMENTO (LEI NO. 2058) REVISAO DE 1955 (LEI NO. 2077)

AN SAOGHAL GAEDHEALACH – Dublin, Ireland.7 Sept 1918-20 Sept 1919 – 1 – ie Microforms [072]

LA SAPE: DRAME SOCIAL EN TROIS ACTES / Leneveu, Georges – Paris: P. Ollendorff, 1899. 169p. With: Poesies choisies xClovis Hugues – 1 – us U.W. Library [820]

Sapeto, Giuseppe *see* VIAGGIO E MISSIONE CATTOLICA FRA I MENSA I BOGOS E GLI HABAB

Saphir, Adolph *see*
- THE DIVINE UNITY OF SCRIPTURE
- THE SINNER AND THE SAVIOUR

Saphir, Moritz Gottlieb *see*
- AUSGEWAEHLTE SCHRIFTEN
- SCHRIFTEN

SAPHO ET PHAON, THE GRAND BALLET, AS PERFORMED AT THE KING'S THEATRE HAYMARKET, COMPOSED BY MONR. DIDELOT / Mazzinghi, J – (The music arranged for the piano or harp by Joseph Mazzinghi, Op. 26) – London: G Goulding, [1797?] – 1 – us Sibley [780]

O SAPO : SEMANARIO LITTERARIO E HUMORISTICO – Curitiba, 6 Mar, Nov-Dec 1898; Feb-Apr, Nov-Dec 1899; Mar-Jun, Aug 1900; Mar 1901; 10 Aug 1902 – 1,5,6 – bl Biblioteca [072]

Sapora, Allen V *see* A RECREATION SURVEY OF THE ROCKFORD PARK DISTRICT, ROCKFORD, ILL

Saporte, C *see* L'OEUVRE ISOPODOLOGIQUE D'ALBERT VANDEL

Sapozhnikov, D I *see* SAMOSOZHZHENIE V RUSSKOM RASKOLE. (SO VTOROI POLOVINY 17 VEKA DO KONTSA 18 V.)

Sapp, Stephen *see* JOURNAL OF RELIGIOUS GERONTOLOGY

SAPPHO : TRAUERSPIEL IN FUENF AUFZUEGEN / Grillparzer, Franz – Stuttgart, Berlin: J G Cotta, 1906 – 1r – 1 – us U.W. Library [820]

SAPTA AKSI / Suhardiman – SE 5642 1. 1964 – 9 – ne IDC [950]

SAPTA DHARMA / Yamin, Muhammad – (Patriotism Indonesia). SE 809 1 – 9 – ne IDC [320]

SAPTA DHARMA, DENING PUDJANGGA RANGGAWARSITA / Ranggawarsita, Raden Ngabehi – SE-4048 1. 1958 – 9 – ne IDC [950]

SAPTAHIK BHARATA – Prayag, India. Sept 1946-Aug 1948 – 1r – 1 – us L of C Photodup [072]

SAPU TANGAN PANGAPUS ILU / Simanare, Sinuan Tunas – SE 5443 1 – 9 – ne IDC [950]

SAQUEO E INCENDIO DE VALENCIA DE MOMBUEY EN 1641 Y UN CURIOSO DOCUMENTO DE 1693 SOBRE ESTE PUEBLO / Barajas Salas, Eduardo – Badajoz: Dip. Provincial, 1973. Sep. REE – sp Bibl Santa Ana [946]

Saquet, D *see* DOCTEUR D. SAQUET

SAR AND QSAR IN ENVIRONMENTAL RESEARCH / ed by Devillers, James – 9,5,1 – us Gordon [540]

SAR SHALOM SHARABI / Bension, A – Jerusalem. 1930. BJ-27-29 1 – 9 – ne IDC [290]

SARA / Atabeyoglu, Salahattin Enis – [Istanbul]: Orhaniye Matbaasi, 1339 [1924] – $15.00 – us MEDOC [470]

SARABANDE AND ALLEGRO / Corelli, Arcangelo & Kreisler, F – Mainz: B Schotts Sohne, ca 1913 – 1 – us Sibley [780]

SARABIA, REDENTORISTA. RAMON. SACERDOTES, NINOS Y CATEQUISTAS. TOMO 1. MADRID, 1942 / Marquez, Gabino – Madrid: Razon y Fe, 1944 – 1 – sp Bibl Santa Ana [240]

Sarab'ianov, V N *see* KOOPERATSIIA V SISTEME SOVETSKOGO KHOZIAISTVA

Saracco, Maria *see* AUGUST VON PLATEN IN ITALIA E GIOSUE CARDUCCI

SARACENIA, SIUE MOAMETHICA : IN QVIBVS ISMAELITICAE SEU MOAMETHICAE SECTAE... / Sylburgius, F – [Heidelburg], 1595 – 2mf – 9 – H-8428/1 – ne IDC [956]

Saragossa. Spain (City). Ayuntamiento *see* BOLETIN MUNICIPAL DE ZARAGOZA

SARAH B. JUDSON: A MEMORIAL / Judson, Sarah B – By Walter Newton Wyeth. 1889 – 9 – us A.T.L.A. [920]

SARAJEVSKI DNEVNIK – Sarajevo, Yugoslavia. Jul 1945-1946 – 3r – 1 – us L of C Photodup [949]

SARAN / O'Malley, Lewis Sydney Steward – Calcutta: Bengal Secretariat Book Depot, 1908. xiv,177p. fold. map – 1 – us U.W. Library [950]

Saran, Franz *see* MELODIK UND RHYTHMIK DER 'ZUEIGNUNG' GOETHES

Sarasa, Alphonso Antonio de *see* COMPENDIUM OF THE ART OF ALWAYS REJOICING

SARA-SAMUCCAYA : A CLASSICAL INDONESIAN COMPENDIUM OF HIGH IDEALS / Vararuci, Bhagavan – SE 5948 1. 1962 – 9 – ne IDC [280]

Sarasate, P *see* PABLO SARASATE CORRESPONDANCE. 30 LETTERS [1 TO 6P. EACH] WRITTES BETWEEN FEB 9 1869 AND SEPT 27 1871

Sarasin, C F *see* DIE LAND-MOLUSKEN VON CELEBES

Sarasin, P B *see* DIE LAND-MOLUSKEN VON CELEBES

SARASOTA FIRST BAPTIST CHURCH. SARASOTA, FLORIDA : CHURCH RECORDS – 1902-60 – 1 – 76.05 – us Baptist [240]

SARATOGA CHANCERY SENTINEL / Saratoga. New York – v1-6. 1841-47 (all publ) – 7mf – 9 – $10.50 – LLMC 80-045 – us L.L.M.C. [340]

SARATOGA CITIZEN – Saratoga, CA. 1958-1959; 1962 – 2r – 1 – $100.00 – B03649 – us Library Micro [071]

SARATOGA COUNTY: OUR COUNTY AND ITS PEOPLE / Boston History Publishers – Boston, 1899. New York Reel 32. (The Cox Library Collection) – 5 – us Americana [978]

SARATOGA ITEM – Saratoga, CA. 1898-1899 – 1r – 1 – $50.00 – B05060 – us Library Micro [071]

Saratoga. New York *see* SARATOGA CHANCERY SENTINEL

SARATOGA NEWS – Saratoga, CA. 1955-92 – 78r – 1 – $3,900.00 – B02982 – us Library Micro [071]

SARATOGA OBSERVER *see* MISCELLANEOUS SARATOGA NEWSPAPERS

SARATOGA RECORD *see* MISCELLANEOUS SARATOGA NEWSPAPERS

SARATOGA SENTINAL *see* MISCELLANEOUS SARATOGA NEWSPAPERS

SARATOGA STANDARD *see* MISCELLANEOUS SARATOGA NEWSPAPERS

SARATOGA STAR – Saratoga, CA. 1917-1922; 1923 – 2r – 1 – $100.00 – B05062 – us Library Micro [071]

SARATOGIAN – Saratoga Springs. N.Y. -sw. 1902-05 – 1 – us UMI [071]

THE SARATOGIAN – Saratoga Springs. N.Y. 1872-1874; 1901-1904; 1905- – 1 – us UMI [071]

Saratov Iuridicheskii Institut *see* UCHENYE ZAPISKI

SARATOVSKII SBORNIK : MATERIALY DLIA IZUCHENIIA SARATOVSKOI GUBERNII. IZDANIE SARATOVSKOGO STATISTICHESKOGO KOMITETA – Saratov. 2v. 1881-1882 – 11mf – 9 – ne IDC [947]

Sarawak *see* DEVELOPMENT PLANS

Sarawak. Education Department *see* PENYATA TAHUNAN

SARAWAK GAZETTE – Kuching. Malaysia. -m. 1874-1932. (11 reels) – 1 – uk British Libr Newspaper [072]

SARAWAK GAZETTE – Sarawak, Malaysia. v83-96. 1957-70 – 5r – 1 – us Ross [324]

SARAWAK TRIBUNE – Kuching. Federation of Malaysia. 1958- – 1 – us UMI [072]

Sarbah, John Mensah *see* FANTI LAW REPORT OF DECIDED CASES ON FANTI CUSTOMARY LAWS

SARBAZ VA INQILAB – (Shumarah-'i 10-11 (10 Murdad 1358-29 Murdad 1358[1 Aug 1979-23 Aug 1979])) – Tehran: Pirsunil-i Inqilabi-i Niruha-yi Musallah – 1 reel – 1 – $25.00 – us MEDOC [950]

Sarchet, Cyrus P B *see* HISTORY OF GUERNSEY COUNTY

UN SARCOFAGO ROMANO DE MERIDA / Fita, Fidel – Madrid: Fortanet, 1913. B.R.A.H. 62. pp. 85-87 – 1 – sp Bibl Santa Ana [946]

Sardaa y Salvany, Felix *see* LIBERALISMO ES PECADO

Sardagna, C *see* THEOLOGIA DOGMATICO-POLEMICA...

SARDANAPALUS : A TRAGEDY. THE TWO FOSCARI, TRAGEDY. CAIN, A MYSTERY / Byron, George Gordon Byron – London: John Murray, 1821 – 1 roll – 1 – 1-55879-649-5 – uk Libr Preservation [820]

Sardesai, D R *see* THESES AND DISSERTATIONS ON SOUTHEAST ASIA. INTERNATIONAL BIBLIOGRAPHY IN SOCIAL SCIENCES, EDUCATION, AND FINE ARTS

Sardi, Vincenzo *see* VITA DELLA B. GIOVANNA DI LESTONNAC

SARDIS BAPTIST CHURCH. BURKE COUNTY. GEORGIA : CHURCH RECORDS – 1803-52 – 1 – $10.53 – us Baptist [240]

SARDIS BAPTIST CHURCH. HENRY COUNTY. GEORGIA : CHURCH RECORDS – (252p) – 1847-1880 – 1 reel – 1 – $11.34 – us Baptist [240]

SARDIS BAPTIST CHURCH. TIMMONSVILLE, SOUTH CAROLINA : CHURCH RECORDS – 1835-73; History, 1840-1963 – 1 – 19.17 – us Baptist [240]

SARDIS BAPTIST CHURCH. WILKES COUNTY. GEORGIA : CHURCH RECORDS – 1805-1951 – 1 – 76.95 – us Baptist [240]

SARDIS, SOUTH CAROLINA : CHURCH RECORDS – 1835-80 – 1 – 9.60 – us Baptist [240]

Sardjito, K *see*
- THE DEVELOPMENT OF MEDICAL SCIENCE IN INDONESIA
- DJALWN RINGKAS KE BAHASA INGGERIS
- INAUGURAL SPEECH ON STUDIUM GENERALE
- "QUO VADIS."IN ENGLISH. SE 3460/1. 3E ED. 1958

SARDOU, IBSEN, UND DIE ZUKUNFT DES DEUTSCHEN DRAMAS / Wolff, Eugen – Kiel: Lipsius und Tischer, 1891 – 1r – 1 – us U.W. Library [430]

Saresberiensis, Ioannes *see* METALOGICON

SARGENT ECHO – Sargent, NE. -w. Apr-Aug 1897 – 1 – us NE Hist [071]

Sargent, John *see* MEMOIR OF THE REV. HENRY MARTYN, B.D.

Sargent, John Osborne *see*
- COMMON SENSE VERSUS JUDICIAL LEGISLATION.
- JOHN OSBORNE SARGENT PAPERS, 1831-1912
- A THIRD CHAPTER ON THE RULE IN MINOT'S CASE

Sargent, Mrs. John T *see* SKETCHES AND REMINISCENCES OF THE RADICAL CLUB OF CHESTNUT STREET, BOSTON

SARGENT LEADER – Sargent, NE. -w. May 1900-Jul 1903; Mar 1904-Dec 1905, scattered issues missing; Jun 1910; Dec 1911 to date – 1 – us NE Hist [071]

Sargent, Moses H *see* TRADITIONS OF PALESTINE, OR, SCENES IN THE HOLY LAND IN THE DAYS OF CHRIST

Sargent, Winthrop *see*
- PAPERS, 1776-1865
- WINTHROP SARGENT PAPERS, 1771-1948

DIE SARGONSSTELE DES BERLINER MUSEUMS / Schrader, Eberhard – (Text in German and Akkadian. Introduction and notes in German) – Berlin: Verlag der Koeniglichen Akademie der Wissenschaften, 1882 – 1mf – 9 – 0-8370-7585-8 – 1986-1585 – us A.T.L.A. [470]

SARI – Bandung. Incomplete. SE 960 1. 1962-1969 – 9 – ne IDC [073]

SARIBU SATU SOAL-SOAL HIDUP *see* 1001 SOAL-SOAL HIDUP

Sarikat Buruh Technik dan Perindustrian *see* ANGGARAN DASAR ("S.B.T.P.")

SARINAH IAN SARINO / Hudaya, M A M – SE-4702 1. 1951 – 9 – ne IDC [950]

SARK KADINI – Baku: Azerbaycan Komunist Firkasinin Merkezi Kadinlar Suebesi Nesriyati. No. 8 (10) (Agustos 1923) – 1mf – 9 – $12.00 – us MEDOC [949]

SARK ORDUSIDA AZIZ PASA FIRKASI / Niyazi, Mehmet – Istanbul: Kadir Matbaasi, 1331 [1915] – $25.00 – us MEDOC [956]

SARMATIAE EUROPEAE DESCRIPTIO/ QUAE REGNUM POLONIAE, LITVANIAM SAMOGITIAM, RUSSIAM, MASSOVIAM, PRUSSIAM, POMERANIAM, LIVONIAM ET MOSCHOVIAE TARTARIAEQUE PARTEM COMPLECTITUR / Guagnino, A – Spirae. 1581. Index. BU-767 2 – 8 – ne IDC [947]

SARMATIAE EUROPEAE DISCRIPTIO... / Guagnino, A – Spirae, 1581 – 11mf – 9 – ne IDC [947]

Sarmiento, Domingo F *see* OBRAS

Sarmiento, Martin *see*
- DEMOSTRACION CRITICO-APOLOGETICA. TOMO 1
- DEMOSTRACION CRITICO-APOLOGETICA. TOMO 2

SARNIA OBSERVER – Sarnia, Canada. 1853-1900 – 21r – 1 – $1,365.00 – cn Library Assoc [971]

SARON BAPTIST CHURCH. PEE DEE ASSOCIATION. NORTH CAROLINA : CHURCH RECORDS – 1828-59 – 1 – 12.78 – us Baptist [240]

Saron, Gilbert *see* MADAGASCAR ET LES COMORES

SARONI'S MUSICAL TIMES – New York City. v1-5. 1849-52 – 2r – 1 – £115.00 – uk Chadwyck [780]

SARPY COUNTY AGRICULTURALIST – Bellevue, NE. -w. Jan. 1927-Jan. 1928; Nov. 1929-Nov. 1934 – 1 – us NE Hist [071]

SARPY COUNTY GAZETTE – Bellevue, NE. -w. Jun. 1959-Oct. 1961 – 1 – us NE Hist [071]

SARPY COUNTY HERALD – Papillion, NE. -w. Apr-Nov 1898; Nov 1899-Nov 1900 – 1 – us NE Hist [071]

SARPY COUNTY REPUBLICAN – Papillion, NE. -w. Mar-Dec 1905; Aug-Dec 1906; Jan 1908-Feb 1910 – 1 – us NE Hist [071]

SARPY COUNTY SUN – Omaha, NE. -w. Dec 1971 to date – 1 – us NE Hist [071]

Sars, G O *see* AN ACCOUNT OF THE CRUSTACAE OF NORWAY

Sarsowsky, Abraham *see* DIE ETHISCH-RELIGIOESE BEDEUTUNG DER ALTTESTAMENTLICHEN NAMEN: NACH TALMUD

Sartain, James Alfred *see* HISTORY OF WALKER COUNTY, GEORGIA

SARTEL : ORGAO DE GREMIO DE LETRAS "EULALIO CHAVES" – Manaus, Amazonas. Dez 1966 – 1,5,6 – bl Biblioteca [072]

Sarti, G *see*
- GIULIO SABINO. CARI FIGLI UN'ALTRO AMPLESSO
- REUIL D'AIR (6) AVEC ACCOMPAGNEMENT DE VIOLIN, VIOLE, FLUTE ET CORNI

Sartono, S *see* NOTES ON A NEW KIND OF A PITHECANTHROPUS MANDIBLE

SARTOR RESARTUS / Carlyle, Thomas; ed by MacMechan, Archibald – Boston, London: Ginn and Co., Athenaeum press, 1896 – 1 roll – 1 – 1-55879-361-5 – uk Libr Preservation [890]

THE SARUM MISSAL – 2D ED. Rev. and enl. 1884 – 1 – us A.T.L.A. [240]

THE SARUM MISSAL / Legg, J Wickham – Oxford, 1916 – 11mf – 8 – Dfl39.00 – ne Slangenburg [240]

THE SARVODAYA MOVEMENT IN INDIA IN THE 1950S : TEXTS IN HINDI AND ENGLISH / International Institute of Social History (IISH), Amsterdam – (With guide) – 1996 – 252mf – 9 – Dfl2,995.00 – ne MMF Publ [950]

Sarwoto Kertopiduro *see* KAHARINGAN, RELIGI DAN PENGHIDUPAN DI PEHULUAN KALIMANTAN

Sarytchew, G *see* ACCOUNT OF A VOYAGE OF DISCOVERY OF THE NORTHEAST OF SIBERIA

Saskatchewan *see* CURRENT PUBLICATIONS

SASKATCHEWAN BAR REVIEW *see* SASKATCHEWAN LAW REVIEW

SASKATCHEWAN BULLETIN – Saskatoon. v53-60. 1986/87-1993/94 – 1 – Can$60.00y – cn Micromedia [370]

SASKATCHEWAN BUSINESS – Saskatoon. v1-15. 1979-94 – 9 – Can$20.00y – cn Micromedia [338]

Saskatchewan. Canada *see*
- LAW SOCIETY'S GAZETTE
- SASKATCHEWAN LAW REPORTS
- SASKATCHEWAN STATUTES, SESSION LAWS AND REVISIONS

SASKATCHEWAN GAZETTE – Regina, Saskatchewan. v54-64. 1958-68 – 7r – 1 – us Ross [324]

SASKATCHEWAN GAZETTE – (v54-64 1958-68 $475.00 1. v65-78 1969-82 Can$105.00y 5. v79- 1983- 9) – Regina. v54- 1958- – 1,5,9 – Price varies – cn Micromedia [971]

SASKATCHEWAN HERALD – Battleford, Canada. 1878-1900 – 5r – 1 – $325.00 – cn Library Assoc [971]

SASKATCHEWAN INDIAN – (v1-3a 1970-73, 4-5 1974-75 Can$115.00. 6-8 1976-78, 9-10 1979-80 Can$100.00 . v11-14 1981-84, nos 1-2 1985 Can$50.00y. 1988-90 Can$60.00y) – Saskatoon. v1-14. 1970-84; nos 1-2. 1985; 1988-90 – 1,5 – Price varies – cn Micromedia [971]

THE SASKATCHEWAN INDIAN / Federation of Saskatchewan Indians – 1971-82.(American Indian Periodicals in the Princeton University Library). 68 fiches – 9 – $265.00 – us UPA [073]

SASKATCHEWAN JOURNAL OF EDUCATION – (Cont: Saskatchewan Journal of Educational Research and Development at v8 1977/78) – Saskatoon, v8-18. 1977/78-1987/88 – 5 – Can$50.00y – cn Micromedia [370]

SASKATCHEWAN JOURNAL OF EDUCATION *see* SASKATCHEWAN JOURNAL OF EDUCATIONAL RESEARCH AND DEVELOPMENT

SASKATCHEWAN JOURNAL OF EDUCATIONAL RESEARCH AND DEVELOPMENT – (Cont by: Saskatchewan Journal of Education at v8 1977/78) – Saskatoon. v1-7. 1970/71-1976/77 – 5 – Price varies – cn Micromedia [370]

SASKATCHEWAN JOURNAL OF EDUCATIONAL RESEARCH AND DEVELOPMENT *see* SASKATCHEWAN JOURNAL OF EDUCATION

SASKATCHEWAN LAW REPORTS / Saskatchewan. Canada – v1-25. 1908-31 (all publ) – 167mf – 9 – $250.00 – LLMC 81-090 – us L.L.M.C. [340]

SASKATCHEWAN LAW REVIEW – (v1-49 1936-85 on reel $390.00. v50-59 1985-94 on mf $170.00. Title varies: v1-31 1936-66 as Saskatchewan Bar Review) – v1-59. 1936-94 – 1,5,6,9,13 – $560.00 set – us Hein [340]

Saskatchewan. Legislative Assembly *see* JOURNALS

SASKATCHEWAN LIBRARY ASSOCIATION BULLETIN – 1945-56 – 1r – 1 – $68.00 – cn Library Assoc [020]

SASKATCHEWAN STATUTES, SESSION LAWS AND REVISIONS / Saskatchewan. Canada – (Updates planned) – 1906-1945 – 392mf – 9 – $588.00 – LLMC 90-200 – us L.L.M.C. [324]

SASKATCHEWAN TEACHER'S BULLETIN – 1921-80 – 11r – 1 – cn Commonwealth Micro [073]

SASKATOON DAILY STAR – Canada. -d. 13 Aug 1912-13 May 1914. Imperfect. 18 1 2 reels – 1 – uk British Libr Newspaper [072]

SASKATOON DAILY STAR – Saskatoon, Saskatchewan, CN. Mar 1912-May 1913; 1921-Jun 1928 – 53r – 1 – cn Commonwealth Micro [072]

SASO (SAUDI ARABIAN STANDARDS ORGANIZATION) – Printed index. Updated every 120 days – 6,9 – us Info Handling [380]

Sass, Edward George *see* RECORDS OF COFFIN PLATES

Sasson, Albert *see*
- BIOTECHNOLOGIES AND DEVELOPMENT
- BIOTECHNOLOGIES IN DEVELOPING COUNTRIES
- BIOTECHNOLOGIES IN PERSPECTIVE
- NEW TECHNOLOGIES AND DEVELOPMENT

Sassone, Felipe *see*
- A FUGITIVE FROM SPAIN
- EL TEATRO, ESPECTACULO LITERARIO

Sassong, Albert *see* FEEDING TOMORROW'S WORLD

SASTA JOURNAL – (1982-. 1,5,6,9) – South Australian Science Teachers Association. v1-. 1900- – 1 – us UMI [073]

Sastradiwirya, Umar *see* EDJAAN BAHASA INDONESIA DENGAN HURUF ARAB

Sastranegara, Rd. M *see* KAMUS DJEPANG-INDONESIA

Sastrasuwignja, S *see* PAK SURA, KALIJAN PETIKAN SANES-SANESIPUN KANGGE SMA BG. A

Sastrawinata, Saleh *see* KEMBANG PANTJAWARNA (BATJAAN ANAK2 UMUR 10-12 TAHUN) DITJERITAKAN KEMBALI

Sastri, T Anjaneya *see* A MANUAL OF TELUGU GRAMMAR

Sastroamidjojo, Achmad Seno *see*
- ATLAS GAMBAR-GAMBAR TERMASUK BILANGAN BUKU FUNGSI MAKANAN
- HAKEKAT HIDUP; SUATU TAFSIRAN
- SEKELUMIT UNSUR FILOSOFIK ARDJUNA WIWAHA (TJIPTAAN MPU KANWA) DIBUBUHI BEBERAPA TJATATAN PINGGIR

Sastroamidjojo, Ali *see*
- ADDRESS BY AUTHOR, PRESIDENT OF ASIAN-AFRICAN-CONFERENCE
- BANGSA DAN KEBANGSAAN
- DR. ALI SASTROAMIDJOJO OF INDONESIA; A PICTURE STORY OF THE INDONESIAN PRIME MINISTER
- INDONESIA FACES ITS ECONOMIC PROBLEMS
- INDONESIA IN THE UNITED NATIONS

Sastrowardojo, Samud *see* MERTJU; BUNGARAMPAI UNTUK SEKOLAH LANDJUTAN

SATAKE MONJO = DOCUMENTS OF THE SATAKES, FEUDAL LORDS OF THE AKITA DOMAIN (AKITA PREF., NORTHEAST JAPAN) IN THE MODERN AGE / ed by Akita Prefectural Library – By Feudal lord "Satake" in Akita prefecture. Handwriting in India ink. 652v – 52r – 1 – Y605,000.00 – ja Yushodo [025]

SATAN – Paris. fevr 1843-sept 1844 – 1 – fr A.C.R.P.P. [073]

SATAN : A POEM / Montgomery, Robert – London: Printed for Samuel Maunder, 1830 – 1 roll – 1 – 1-55879-844-7 – uk Libr Preservation [810]

Satanow, I *see* DIVREI RIVOT

THE SATAPATHA-BRAHMANA : PART 2: BOOKS 3 AND 4 / ed by Mueller, Friedrich Max – (Translated by Julius Eggeling) – 1885 – 9mf – 8 – ne Slangenburg [280]

THE SATAPATHA-BRAHMANA : PART 3 / ed by Mueller, Friedrich Max – (Translated by Julius Eggeling) – 1894 – 8mf – 8 – ne Slangenburg [280]

THE SATAPATHA-BRAHMANA : PART 4: BOOKS 8, 9 AND 10 / ed by Mueller, Friedrich Max – (Translated by Julius Eggeling) – 1897 – 8mf – 8 – ne Slangenburg [280]

THE SATAPATHA-BRAHMANA : PART 5: BOOKS 11, 12, 13 AND 14 / ed by Mueller, Friedrich Max – (Translated by J. Eggeling) – 1900 – 11mf – 8 – ne Slangenburg [280]

THE SATAPATHA-BRAHMANA, ACCORDING TO THE TEXT OF THE MADHYANDINA SCHOOL / ed by Mueller, Friedrich Max – (Trans by Julius Eggeling Pt 1 Bks 1 & 2) – 1882 – 9mf – 8 – ne Slangenburg [280]

SATELLITE COMMUNICATIONS – v. 1-. 1977- – 1,5,6,9 – us UMI [380]

SATELLITE NEWS – (v.3-. 1980- 5,6,9) – v.1-. 1978- – 1 – us UMI [380]

Sater, Henry *see* SATERS BAPTIST CHURCH, MARYLAND, 1742-1917; SATER GENEALOGY

SATER OCH AVESTA ELLER SODRA DARLENES VECKOBLAD *see* SODRA DALARNES TIDNING

SATERS BAPTIST CHURCH, MARYLAND, 1742-1917; SATER GENEALOGY / Sater, Henry – 1 – 8.26 – us Baptist [240]

SATERS TIDNING *see* SODRA DALARNES TIDNING

Sathas *see* BIBLIOTHECA MEDIEVALIS GRAECA

Sathian Wichailak *see* RUAM PRAKAT KHONG KHANA PATIWAT CHABAP THI-L THUNG CHABAP SUTTHAI..

SATICOY JOURNAL – Saticoy, CA. 1948-1949 – 1r – 1 – $50.00 – B03650 – us Library Micro [073]

SATIRA V.V. MAIAKOVSKOGO / Zubov, Iu. S – Rekomendatel'nyi ukazatel' literatury. M. 1955. BR-2243 2 – 8 – ne IDC [460]

SATIRAE / Persius – With Horatius. Opera. 15th cent. Holkham ms. 318. Holkham Hall, Norfolk, England – 1. ; 14 – uk Microform Academic [760]

DIE SATIRE IN DER JUEDISCHEN LITERATUR / Gross, H – (Monatsschrift fuer Geschichte und Wissenschaft des Judentums v. 52). Augsburg. 1908. BJ-421-17 1 – 9 – ne IDC [470]

SATIRE, LIRICHE, LETTERE, CON NOTE DI ANTON MARIA SALVINI E DI ALTRI / Rosa, Salvatore – Milano: E. Sonzogno, 1892. 306p. (Biblioteca classica economica, no. 97) – 1 – us U.W. Library [920]

SATIRES OF CIRCUMSTANCE : LYRICS AND REVERIES WITH MISCELLANEOUS PIECES / Hardy, Thomas – London: Macmillan, 1914 – 1 roll – 1 – 1-55879-474-3 – uk Libr Preservation [870]

SATIRICHESKIE ZHURNALY / Novikov, N I – Ed. by P. N. Berkov. 1951. BR-6097 2 – 8 – ne IDC [460]

SATIRICHESKIE ZHURNALY N.I. NOVIKOVA – M., L. 1951. BR-7832 2 – 8 – ne IDC [460]

SATIRIKON – v. 1-7. Spb. 1908-14. BR-5830 2 – 8 – ne IDC [073]

THE SATIRIST – Montreal, Canada. v1 n2. 9 jun 1847 – 1r – 1 – Can$25.00 – cn Can Microfilming [072]

THE SATIRIST – Montreal: [s.n., 1847-184-] ([Montreal]: Satirist) – 9 – cn C.I.H.M. [073]

THE SATIRIST OR, THE CENSOR OF THE TIMES – London, England. 10 April 1831-15 Dec. 1849. 6 1 2 reels – 1 – uk British Libr Newspaper [072]

SATISFACCION AL PUBLICO CONTRA LA ADICION APOLOGETICA QUE A SU DISSERTACION MEDICO-MORAL DEL PRIMER TOMO DE LA PALESTRA CRITICA. MEDICA : ESCRIVIO EN EL SEGUNDO EL DR. ANTONIO JOSEPH RODRIGUEZ / Gomez, P – Madrid, 1747 – 2mf – 9 – sp Cultura [610]

SATISFACCION APOLOGETICA QUE DA A LA MUY ILUSTRE JUNTA DE SANIDAD DE VALENCIA...SOBRE EL ACERTADO CONOCIMIENTO DE UNA LARGA ENFERMEDAD CONTRA EL DICTAMEN DEL DR. ANDRES PIQUER – Valencia, 1746 – 1mf – 9 – sp Cultura [610]

SATISFACCION PUBLICA DE UNA...CALUMNIA SOBRE LA CONSTITUCION PLEURISTICO CATHARRAL...DE AIG / Herrera Carrasco, F – Valladolid, 1716 – 2mf – 9 – sp Cultura [610]

SATISFACION HISTORICO-JURIDICA...ORDEN DE ALCANTARA / Zancudo y Barrado, Antonio – 1806 – 9 – 1.50f – sp Bibl Santa Ana [340]

SATISFACION RELIGIOSA...SAN FRANCISCO / Trujillo, Antonio de – 1675 – 9 – 1.50f – sp Bibl Santa Ana [240]

Satjadibrata, R *see*
- KAMOES LEUTIK SOENDA-INDONESIA
- KAMOES SOENDA-MELAJOE

Satler, Michiel *see* VEREENINGE (BROEDERLICKE) VAN SOMMIGHE KINDEREN GODS

Sato, T *see* NICHI-DJO NIPPONGO RADJIO KOZA

SATOW PAPERS – Japan. PRO 30-33, 15-17. 1861-1926 – 11r – 1 – us Ross [950]

A SATRICAL INTERPRETATION OF THE HISTORY OF SELECTED PERSONS, EVENTS AND ORGANIZATIONS IN AMERICAN PHYSICAL EDUCATION / Kent, M Chris – 1981 – 3mf – 9 – $12.00 – us Microform Publ [790]

SATROOBRIADCHESKII POMORSKII ZHURNAL – v. 1-2. M. 1908-09. BR-3998 2 – 8 – ne IDC [073]

Satthianadhan, Samuel *see* STORIES OF INDIAN CHRISTIAN LIFE

Sattler, M *see*
- CONCORDANTIE ENDE AENWYSINGHE DER VERNAEMSTER SPROKEN ALLER BYBELSCHER BOECKEN...
- WIE DIE GSCHRIFFT VERSTENDIGKLICH SOLL VNTERSCHIDEN UNDE ERKLAERT WERDEN

SATURARUM LIBRI 5; MIT ERKLARENDEN ANMERKUNGEN VON L. FRIEDLAENDER / Juvenal – Leipzig, 1895. 612, 108p. Latin text – 1 – us U.W. Library [450]

SATURDAY AMERICAN – Portland OR. Nov 14 21 1914 – 1 – us U.O. Library [071]

THE SATURDAY BUDGET *see* THE BUDGET

THE SATURDAY DISPATCH – Hull, Canada. v19. 4,18 nov 1899 – 1r – 1 – Can$25.00 – cn Can Microfilming [072]

SATURDAY DOLLAR CHRONICLE – Pittsburgh. Pa. 1859-1861 – 1 – us UMI [071]

SATURDAY EVENING JOURNAL – Crawfordsville. Ind. 1875-1885; 1889 – 1 – us UMI [071]

SATURDAY EVENING MAGAZINE – Montreal: Leclere, Jones, [1833-18–?] – 9 – cn C.I.H.M. [073]

THE SATURDAY EVENING NEWS – Kimberley, South Africa.16 Jan 1937-28 Jan 1939. 4 reels – 1, 16 diazo available at reduced price – sa SA Libr [072]

SATURDAY EVENING POST – v170-242 1897-1969 1; v240-242 5,6 – us UMI [073]

SATURDAY EVENING POST – Burlington. Iowa. 1882-1933 – 1 – us UMI [071]

SATURDAY EVENING POST – Grand Rapids. Mich. -w. 1873-82 – 1 – us UMI [071]

SATURDAY EVENING POST – v. 243- 1971- – 1,5,6,9 – us UMI [073]

THE SATURDAY EVENING VISITOR – (Cont by: The Monthly Visitor) – Halifax [N.S.]: R Nugent, [1842] – 9 – cn C.I.H.M. [240]

THE SATURDAY EVENING VISITOR *see* THE MONTHLY VISITOR

SATURDAY EYE – Portland, OR. 7 Jun 1900-8 Dec 1900. 1 roll – 1 – us U.O. Library [071]

SATURDAY GLOBE – Oskaloosa. Iowa. 1885-1891 – 1 – us UMI [071]

SATURDAY GLOBE – Utica. N.Y. 1895-1924 – 1 – us UMI [071]

SATURDAY HERALD – Decatur. Ill. -w. 1880-90 – 1 – us UMI [071]

SATURDAY HERALD – St. Joseph. MI.-w. 1889-1916 – 1 – us UMI [071]

SATURDAY LEDGER – Toronto: [s.n., 1889?-189-] – 9 – cn C.I.H.M. [073]

SATURDAY MORNING POST – Cobourg, 1989-1990 – 2r – 1 – cn Preston [971]

SATURDAY NEWS – Collingwood, 1906-1930 – 8r – 1 – cn Preston [971]

SATURDAY NIGHT – Halifax, NS: Saturday Night Co, [194-19–] – 9 – cn C.I.H.M. [073]

SATURDAY NIGHT – (Individual vols available) – Toronto. v1-110. 1887-1995/96 – 1,9 – Price varies – cn Micromedia [073]

SATURDAY NIGHT REVIEW – Ulysses, NE. -w. Mar 1911-Mar 1914; May 1914-Aug 1917 – 1 – us NE Hist [071]

SATURDAY OR SUNDAY : WHICH SHOULD WE OBSERVE? / Rauschenbusch, August – New York: American Tract Society, [1908?] – 1mf – us A.T.L.A. [240]

SATURDAY POST – London, UK. 25 Aug 1979-6 Feb 1982. -w. 1 reel – 1 – uk British Libr Newspaper [072]

SATURDAY POST-DEMOCRAT – Lincoln, NE. -w. Aug 1904-Jan 1905 – 1 – us NE Hist [071]

SATURDAY PRESS – Saskatoon, Canada. -w. Dec 1912-May 1917. 3 1 4 reels – 1 – uk British Libr Newspaper [072]

SATURDAY READER *see* ILLUSTRATED SATURDAY READER

THE SATURDAY READER – (Cont by: Illustrated Saturday Reader) – Montreal: W B Cordier, 1865-[1866] – 9 – cn C.I.H.M. [971]

THE SATURDAY READER – (Cont: Illustrated Saturday Reader) – Montreal: R Worthington, 1867 – 9 – cn C.I.H.M. [971]

SATURDAY REPORTER – Sparks, NV. 20 Nov 1915 – 1r – 1 – $50.00 – U04755 – us Library Micro [071]

SATURDAY REVIEW – London. -w. 1855-70. (27 reels) – 1 – uk British Libr Newspaper [072]

SATURDAY REVIEW – Medford OR. Aug 23 1913 – 1 – us U.O. Library [071]

SATURDAY REVIEW – Medford OR. June 11-Nov 26 1910 – 1 – us U.O. Library [071]

SATURDAY REVIEW – San Bernardino, CA. 1896 – 1r – 1 – $50.00 – R03462 – us Library Micro [071]

SATURDAY REVIEW – v. 3-9. 1975-82 – 1,5,6,9 – us UMI [800]

SATURDAY REVIEW – (v. 50-55. 1967-72. 5,6,9) – 1-55. 1924-72 – 1 – us UMI [073]

SATURDAY REVIEW OF EDUCATION – v. 1 Feb-May 1973 – 1,5,6,9 – us UMI [370]

SATURDAY REVIEW OF THE ARTS – v. 1 Jan-Apr 1973 – 1,5,6,9 – us UMI [700]

SATURDAY REVIEW OF THE SCIENCES – v. 1 Feb-May 1973 – 1,5,6,9 – us UMI [500]

SATURDAY REVIEW OF THE SOCIETY – v. 1 Feb-May 1973 – 1,5,6,9 – us UMI [360]

SATURDAY REVIEW/WORLD – (See now: Saturday Review) – v1-2. 1973-75 – 1,5,6,9 – us UMI [073]

SATURDAY STANDARD – North Tonawanda. N.Y. 1885-1886 – 1 – us UMI [071]

THE SATURDAY TIMES – Montreal, Canada. 12 mai 1894 – 1r – 1 – Can$25.00 – cn Can Microfilming [072]

SATURDAY VISITOR – Pittsburgh. Pa. 1848-1853 – 1 – us UMI [071]

SATURDAY WESTMINSTER GAZETTE – London. 1916-21.-w. 6 reels – 1 – uk British Libr Newspaper [072]

SATURDAY WORLD – Toledo, Ohio. 1904-07 – 3r – 1 – $32.50r – us Archival [071]

SATURN 5/APOLLO AND BEYOND – 1968 – 62mf – 9 – $65.00 – 0-87703-225-4 – us Univelt [629]

THE SATURNIAN – Cleveland. v. 1, no. 1-3. June July 1921-Mar 1922 – 1 – us NY Public [073]

DER SATURNISCHE VERS / Leo, F – Berlin, 1905 – 3mf – 8 – ne Slangenburg [943]

SATVET-I MILLIYE – Elazig, 1922-19? – 9 – $10.00 – us MEDOC [956]

SATYAYUGA – Calcutta, India. 1952-Aug 1953 – 4r – 1 – us L of C Photodup [072]

SATYODAYA CENTRE FOR SOCIAL RESEARCH AND ENCOUNTER – Kandy. 45 docs. 1980-1990 – 9mf – 9 – ne IDC [320]

SATYRARUM HECATOSTICHON / Philelphus, Franciscus – 15th cent. Holkham ms. 431. Holkham Hall, Norfolk, England – 1 – uk Microform Academic [760]

SATZ UND GEGENSATZ : SECHS ESSAYS / Szondi, Peter – (Includes bibliographical references) – Frankfurt am Main: Insel-Verlag, 1964 – 1r – 1 – us U.W. Library [430]

SATZLEHRE DER ARAMAEISCHEN SPRACHE DES BABYLONISCHEN TALMUDS / Schlesinger, Max – (Veroeffentlichungen der Alexander Kohut-Stiftung. v. 1. Leipzig. 1928). BJ-32-53 1 – 9 – ne IDC [470]

SAU KAU-TOO – Thesaurus of Karen Knowledge. 4v. Tavoy, Burma, 1847-1850 – 1 – us Res Libr [480]

SAU SUIHSTE IUT! : SCHWAENKE UND GESCHICHTEN / Henze, Wilhelm – Hannover: F Gersbach, 1921 – 1r – 1 – us U.W. Library [830]

Saubinet, E *see* VOCABULAIRE DU BAS LANGAGE REMOIS

Saucerotte, Louis Sebastien *see* EXAMEN DE PLUSIEURS PREJUGES ET USAGES ABUSIFS CONCERNANT LES FEMMES ENCEINTES

Saude, E de *see* DE MISSIONE LEGATORVM IAPONENSIUM AD ROMANAM CURIAM

Saudi Arabia *see*
- THE IMPACT OF TECHNICAL COOPERATION BETWEEN SAUDI ARABIA AND THE UNITED NATIONS AND ITS SPECIALIZED AGENCIES
- LAND AND WATER SURVEYS FROM THE WADI JIZAN, KINGDOM OF SAUDI ARABIA: FINAL REPORT 1966
- UMM AL-QURA

Saudi Arabia. Central Department of Statistics *see*
- FOREIGN TRADE STATISTICS, 1969, 1972
- STATISTICAL YEAR BOOK
- SUMMARY OF FOREIGN TRADE STATISTICS 1963-1966

Saudi Arabia. Central Planning Organization *see* DEVELOPMENT PLAN A.H. 1390 (1970-1974?)

Saudi Arabia. Directorate General for the Development of Higher Education. Data Centre *see* STATISTICS OF HIGHER EDUCATION IN THE KINGDOM OF SAUDI ARABIA 1983/84

Saudi Arabia. Directorate General of Mineral Resources *see* MINERAL RESOURCES ACTIVITIES 1967-1970

Saudi Arabia. General Petroleum and Mineral Organization *see*
- THE ESTABLISHMENT OF PETROMIN
- FOREIGN INVESTMENT ATMOSPHERE IN SAUDI ARABIA
- PETROMIN AND ITS ROLE IN THE INTERNATIONAL OIL INDUSTRY

Saudi Arabia. Industrial Studies and Development Centre *see* GUIDE FOR INDUSTRIAL INVESTMENTS IN SAUDI ARABIA, 1392 A.H. (1972 A.D.)

Saudi Arabia. Islamic Development Bank *see* THE FIRST ANNUAL REPORT 1395/1396 H

Saudi Arabia. Ministry of Agriculture and Water *see* MINISTRY OF AGRICULTURE AND WATER DURING ONE YEAR

Saudi Arabia. Ministry of Education. Educational Development *see* DEVELOPMENT OF EDUCATION IN THE KINGDOM OF SAUDI ARABIA 1403-1406 A.H./1983-1986 A.D.

Saudi Arabia. Ministry of Information. The Kingdom of Saudi Arabia *see* FACTS AND FIGURES

Saudi Arabia. Ministry of Planning *see* AL NADWA AL'ILMIYA LI AL TA'LIM

Saudi Arabia. Monetary Agency *see*
- ANNUAL REPORTS
- STATISTICAL SUMMARY, 1974/1975

Saudi Arabia. National Commercial Bank *see* ANNUAL REPORTS

SAUDI ARABIA NEWSLETTER – 1979- – 1,5,6,9 – us UMI [073]

Saudi Arabia. Saudi Arabia Monetary Agency *see* SAUDI ARABIAN BUDGET FOR THE YEAR 1385-1386 A.H.

SAUDI ARABIA, SUPPLY AND DEMAND PROJECTIONS FOR FARM PRODUCTS TO 1975 / U.S. Department of Agriculture – Moe, L. E. 1966. BNE-6609 1 – 9 – ne IDC [338]

SAUDI ARABIAN BUDGET FOR THE YEAR 1385-1386 A.H. / Saudi Arabia. Saudi Arabia Monetary Agency – November 9, 1965 – 9 – ne IDC [339]

SAUDI ARABIAN STANDARDS ORGANIZATION (SASO) – 1982 – 9 – uk Tech [380]

SAUDI GAZETTE – (1983-84. 400.00y; 1. 1985-86. 450.00y; SAU; 1. 1987-88. 500.00y; SAU; 1. 1989- . 1) – Saudi Arabia. 1983- . National English Daily Newspaper. Yearly: 360 issues and weekly Suppl – su Okaz [072]

SAUDI GAZETTE – (In English. Yrly reel count varies) – 1970- – 1 – inquire – us Ross [072]

SAUDI GAZETTE – Jeddah, SU. 1979-1985 – 25r – $1,250.00 – R63579 – us Library Micro [072]

SAUDI GAZETTE INDEX – (1983-84. 50.00y; 5. 1985-86. 75.00y; SAU; 5. 1987-88. 100.00y; SAU; 5. 1989- . 5) – 1983- . Annual cumulation – su Okaz [072]

Sauer, August *see* AKADEMISCHE FESTREDE ZU GRILLPARZERS HUNDERTSTEM GEBURTSTAGE

Sauer, Egbert *see* INTERVALLING-EFFEKT DER BETAFAKTOREN AM DEUTSCHEN AKTIENMARKT

Sauer, Jutta *see* TUERKISCHES BIOGRAPHISCHES ARCHIV

Sauer, Oskar *see* DIE QUELLEN DER CHEVY CHASEBALLADE

Sauerbeck, F *see* GENERA ET SPECIES MUSCORUM SYSTEMATICE DISPOSITA SEU ADUMBRATIO FLORAE MUSCORUM

SAUERLAENDISCHER ANZEIGER – Brilon, Bueren. 1868-69, 1873, 1877-78 – 1r – 1 – Inquire at Mikrofilmarchiv for details – gw Misc Inst [943]

SAUERLAENDISCHES VOLKSBLATT – (Further titles: Olper Kreis-Blatt. Olper Intelligenz-Blatt. Neuer Westfaelischer Kurier) – Olpe, feb 19-jun 25 1842; jan 14 1843-46; may 15 1847; nov 11 1848; jul 11 1849-jul 22 1854; 1855-jul 24 1858; mar 12 1859-60; mar 30 1861-sep 6 1862; 1863-dec 24 1868; feb 20-sep 11 1869; 1870-71; 1873-78; feb 19 1879-1903; 1905-jun 1 1941; aug 11 1945-mar 29 1947; sep 3 1949-sep 29 1979 – 145r – 1 – gw Mikrofilm [943]

Sauerwein, Helga *see* DIE BEDEUTUNG DER SOMATOTROPEN ACHSE FUER MUSKELWACHSTUM UND REPRODUKTION BEI LANDWIRTSCHAFTLICHEN NUTZTIEREN

Sauger-Preneuf, F *see*
- DICTIONNAIRE DES LOCUTIONS VICIEUSES LES PLUS REPANDUES DANS LA SOCIETE
- DICTIONNAIRE DES LOCUTIONS VICIEUSES USITEES DANS LE MIDI DE LA FRANCE

Saugnier *see* RELATIONS DE PLUSIEURS VOYAGES A LA COTE D'AFRIQUE, AU MAROC, AU SENEGAL EN GOREE, GALAM, ETC. AVEC DES DETAILS INTERSSANTS POUR CEUX QUI SE DESTINENT A LA TRAITE DES NEGRES, L'OR, ET DE L'IVOIRE, ETC

SAUGUS ENTERPRISE *see* NEWHALL SIGNAL

SAUL / More de Chedeville & Deschamps & Despres – (French Theatre Series). Paris. Ballard et Defrelle. 1803 – 9 – fr Hachette [820]

Saul, D *see* SCHILLER IM DICHTERMUND

SAUL SOLOMAN'S PAPERS – 1 reel – 1 – sa Microfile [960]

SAULDAM BAPTIST CHURCH. COLLETON COUNTY. SOUTH CAROLINA : CHURCH RECORDS – 1856-1945, 1966-1983 – 1 – $36.27 – us Baptist [240]

Saulnier, P *see*
- LE MEURTRE DU VODUN DAN
- NOMS DE NAISSANCE: CONCEPTION DU MONDE ET SYSTEME DE VALEURS CHEZ LES GUN AU SUD BENIN

Sault Sainte Marie, Michigan *see* MISCELLANEOUS EARLY NEWSPAPERS

SAULT STAR – Ontario, CN. 1851- – 12r per yr – 1 – Can$53.00r – cn Commonwealth Micro [072]

LE SAULT-AU-RECOLLET: SES RAPPORTS AVEC LES PREMIERS TEMPS DE LA COLONIE: MISSION-PAROISSE / Beaubien, Charles Philippe – Montreal: C. Beauchemin, 1898. 02994. (Pre-1900 Canadiana) – 9 – cn C.I.H.M. [971]

SAUMAREZ PAPERS : MATERIAL RELATING TO SOUTH CAROLINA DERIVING FROM THE MIDDLETON FAMILY – 1725-1860 – 1 – uk Microform Academic [978]
Saunders *see* EARLY SETTLERS OF ALABAMA
Saunders, Cornelius Thomas *see* THE AMALGAMATION OF THE TWO BRANCHES OF THE LEGAL PROFESSION.
SAUNDERS COUNTY NEW ERA – Wahoo. Neb. 1899-1906 – 1 – us UMI [071]
Saunders, Denis *see* BIOLOGY OF THE SHORT-BILLED FORM OF THE WHITE-TAILED BLACK COCKATOO
Saunders, E *see*
– THE HEMIPTERA HETEROPTERA OF THE BRITISH ISLANDS
– THE HYMENOPTERA ACULEATA OF THE BRITISH ISLANDS
Saunders, James E *see* EARLY SETTLERS OF ALABAMA
Saunders, John *see*
– DRUG DESIGN AND DISCOVERY
– TASK ACCOUNT ABILITY IN SCHOOL PHYSICAL EDUCATION AND SPORTS SETTINGS
Saunders, Kenneth James *see* BUDDHIST IDEALS (A STUDY IN COMPARATIVE RELIGION)
Saunders, Mildred L *see* GENEALOGICAL RECORDS OF HANOVER, NEW HAMPSHIRE
SAUNDERS NEWSLETTER – Ireland.35 reels – 1 – ie Microforms [072]
Saunders, Thomas Bailey *see*
– THE APOSTLES' CREED
– THE QUEST OF FAITH: BEING NOTES ON THE CURRENT PHILOSOPHY OF RELIGION
SAUNDERS'S NEWS-LETTER – Dublin. Ireland. -d. 10 Mar 1773-31 Dec 1787, 26 Feb-17 Nov 1794, Jan-Dec 1795; 1798. (33 reels) – 1 – uk British Libr Newspaper [072]
Saunois, Victor *see*
– CONSTITUTION MEDICALE ET MORTALITE DE LA VILLE DE METZ PENDANT L'ANNEE 1851: RAPPORT STATISTIQUE
– RAPPORT SUR LA CONSTITUTION MEDICALE ET LA MORTALITE DE LA VILLE DE METZ PENDANT L'ANNEE 1865
Sauppe, H *see* EUGIPPII VITA SANCTI SEVERINI (MGH1: 1.BD. 2.TEIL)
Sauret, E *see* FARFALLA. POUR VIOLIN ET PIANO [PAR] MILE AURET
SAUSALITO BOOSTER – Mill Valley, CA. Mar 1914-Nov 1915 – 1r – 1 – $50.00 – B02462 – us Library Micro [071]
SAUSALITO NEWS – (Cont by: Marin News) – Sausalito, CA. 1885-1960 – 29r – 1 – $1,450.00 – B02987 – us Library Micro [071]
Saussaye, Chantepie de la *see* LA CRISE RELIGIEUSE EN HOLLANDE
Saussure, H de *see* SPICILEGIA ENTOMOLOGICA GENAVENSIA
Sautebin, G *see* THOMAS CORNEILLE GRAMMAIRIEN
LE SAUVAGE – (Fait suite a: L'Avenir) – Montreal: [s.n., 1847] (Quebec: J Roch-Lettore) – 9 – cn C.I.H.M. [073]
LE SAUVAGE – Montreal, Canada. 24 jun-3 jul 1847 – 1r – 1 – Can$25.00 – cn Can Microfilming [072]
LE SAUVAGE DE TAITI AUX FRANCAIS AVEC UN ENVOI AU PHILOSOPHE AMI DES SAUVAGES / La Dixmerie, Nicolas Bricaire de – (Utopias in the Enlightment series). 1770 – 9 – fr Hachette [190]
Sauvageau, C *see*
– REMARQUES SUR LES SPHACELARIACEES
– SUR QUELQUES MYRIONEMACOOS
Sauvages, F B *see* METHODUS FOLIORUM, SEU PLANTAE MONSPELIENSES JUXTA FOLIORUM ORDINEM DIGESTAE
Sauvalle, F A *see* FLORA CUBANA
Sauvalle, Marc *see*
– LA BATAILLE
– LE COURRIER FRANCAIS DU CANADA
– LA LOI DE CONCILIATION
Sauve, Arthur *see*
– LE CANADIEN
– LA MINERVE
Sauveur, Joseph *see* LE NEPTUNE FRANCOIS OU ATLAS NOUVEAU DES CARTES MARINES
Sauveur, Maria-du *see* BIO-BIBLIOGRAPHIE DE MONSIEUR GERARD FILTEAU, CONSEILLER TECHNIQUE EN PEDAGOGIE AU DEPARTEMENT DE L'INSTRUCTION PUBLIQUE
Sauzay, Antoine de *see* STATISTIQUE DU DEPARTEMENT DU MONT-BLANC
Sauzet, Marc *see* DE LA RESPONSABILITE DES PATRONS VIS-A-VIS DES OUVRIERS DANS LES ACCIDENTS INDUSTRIELS
Savage *see* HISTORY OF THE CITY OF OMAHA AND SOUTH OMAHA
Savage, Carlton *see* POLICY OF THE U.S. TOWARD MARITIME COMMERCE IN WAR
Savage, Howard J *see* AMERICAN COLLEGE ATHLETICS
Savage, I O *see* HISTORY OF REPUBLIC COUNTY
Savage, Minot Judson *see*
– BELIEF IN GOD: AN EXAMINATION OF SOME FUNDAMENTAL THEISTIC PROBLEMS
– BELIEFS ABOUT THE BIBLE
– DR. ABBOTT AND CHRISTIAN EVOLUTION: I...CONFLICT BETWEEN TWO WORLD-THEORIES
– EVOLUTION AND RELIGION: FROM THE STANDPOINT OF ONE WHO BELIEVES IN BOTH
– THE RELIGION OF EVOLUTION
Savage, S *see* INDEX TO THE SMITH HERBARIUM
Savall, Domingo *see* MESA REVUELTA...
SAVANNA AFFORESTATION IN AFRICA : LECTURE NOTES FROM THE F.A.O./ D.A.N.I.D.A. TRAINING COURSE ON FOREST NURSERY AND ESTABLISHMENT TECHNIQUES FOR AFRICAN SAVANNAS AND PAPERS FROM THE SYMPOSIUM ON SAVANNA AFFORESTATION, KADUNA, NIGERIA, 1976 – 1979 – 318p – it F.A.O. [634]
Savannah & Charleston Railroad. Board of Directors, etc *see* MINUTES
SAVANNAH FIRST BAPTIST CHURCH. SAVANNAH, GEORGIA : CHURCH RECORDS – (2,619p) – 1805-1822, 1831-1836, 1852-1922, 1925-1953, 1966-1986 – 2r – 1 – $117.86 – us Baptist [240]
SAVANNAH JEWISH NEWS – Savannah. Ga. 1961-66 – 1 – us A.J.P.C. [071]
Savard, Leo *see* BIBLIOGRAPHIE DU REV. F. ELOI-GERARD, MARISTE, GENEALOGISTE, HISTORIEN, PEDAGOGUE
Savard, Marcelle *see* BIO-BIBLIOGRAPHIE DE L'ABBE FELIX-ANTOINE SAVARD, PROFESSEUR A LA FACULTE DES LETTRES DE L'UNIVERSITE LAVAL, QUEBEC
Savarkar, Vinayak Damodar *see* VEER SAVARKAR'S "WHIRL-WIND PROPAGANDA": STATEMENTS, MESSAGES & EXTRACTS FROM THE PRESIDENT'S DIARY OF HIS PROPAGANDISTIC TOURS.
Savary, Claude *see* LETTRES SUR LA GRECE: POUR SERVIR DE SUITE A CELLES SUR L'EGYPTE
Savathier, P A L *see* ENUMERATIO PLANTARUM IN JAPONICA SPONTE CRESCENTIUM
Savatier, Rene *see* LE DROIT DE L'ART ET DES LETTRES
SAVE SPAIN FROM FASCISM / Pollitt, Harry – London, 1936? Fiche W1113. (Blodgett Collection of Spanish Civil War Pamphlets) – 9 – us H.U. College Libr [946]
Savelov, L M *see*
– BIBLIOGRAFICHESKII UKAZATEL PO ISTORII, GERALDIKE I RODOSLOVIIU ROSSIISKAGO DVORIANSTVA
– IZBRANNAIA BIBLIOTEKA RUSSKAGO GENEALOGA. (BIBLIOGRAFICHESKII OPYT). 1
– OPYT BIBLIOGRAFICHESKAGO UKAZATELIA PO ISTORII I GENEALOGII ROSSIISKAGO DVORIANSTVA
Savi, G *see* FLORA PISANA
Savi, P *see*
– ORNITHOLOGIA
– ORNITHOLOGIA ITALIANA
Savile, Bourchier Wrey *see* THE TRUTH OF THE BIBLE
SAVILE CHARTERS – XVIth Century – 1 – uk Microform Academic [930]
SAVINGS AND LOAN ASSOCIATION OF SAN DIEGO – San Diego Co, CA. 1947-1948 – 1r – 1 – $50.00 – D083 – us Library Micro [360]
SAVINGS BANK OF CASTLEMAINE : INDEX TO REGISTER – 1860-1889 – 1mf – 9 – at Corangamite [332]
SAVINGS BANK OF CASTLEMAINE : REGISTER – 1855-1888 – 1mf – 9 – at Corangamite [332]
Savio, Fedele *see*
– NUOVI STUDI SULLA QUESTIONE DI PAPA LIBERIO
– LA QUESTIONE DI PAPA LIBERIO
Savitskaia, R M *see*
– BIBLIOGRAFIIA OBSHCHESTVENNOI-POLITICHESKOI LITERATURY
– IZDANIIA PROIZVEDENIIA KLASSIKOV MARKSIZMA-LENINIZMA V SSSR
Savitskii, M I *see* SOVETSKOE VOENNO-UGOLOVNOE PRAVO
SAVONAROLA, ERASMUS AND OTHER ESSAYS / Milman, Henry Hart – London: J. Murray, 1870.xviii,500p – 1 – us U.W. Library [190]
SAVONAROLA, ERASMUS, AND OTHER ESSAYS / Milman, Henry Hart – London: J. Murray, 1870 – 2mf – us A.T.L.A. [190]
SAVONAROLA IM STREITE MIT SEINEM ORDEN UND SEINEM KLOSTER / Schnitzer, Joseph – Muenchen: J.F. Lehmanns, 1914 – 1mf – us A.T.L.A. [240]
SAVONAROLA IN DER DEUTSCHEN DICHTUNG / Teichmann, Alfred – (Includes bibliographical references and index) – Berlin: W de Gruyter & Co, 1937 – 2r – 1 – us U.W. Library [430]
Savorgnan de Brazza, Pierre Paul Francois Camille *see* CONFERENCES ET LETTRES SUR L'OUEST AFRICAIN
Savot, Louis *see* L'ARCHITECTURE FRANCAISE DES BASTIMENS PARTICULIERS
SAVOY 1736-1854 – (Mf 1: Index, Births & Deaths 1736-1839. Mf 2-3: Births & Deaths 1781-1859. Mf 4: Marriage Intentions 1797-1854. Mf 5: Marriage Intentions 1854-67. Mf 6: Marriage Intentions 1867-86. Mf 7: Marriage Intentions 1886-1905. Mf 8: Marriages 1799-1870. Mf 8: Index of Births & Marriages. Mf 9: Births 1844-54, Marriages 1845-63, Deaths 1843-54) – (mf ed 1983) – 9mf – 9 – 0-931248-28-0 – us Holbrook [920]
Savva, Arkhimandrit *see* UKAZATEL DLIA OBOZRENIIA MOSKOVSKOI PATRIARSHEI RIZNITSY: BIBLIOTEKI
Savvas, Pasha *see*
– LE DROIT MUSULMAN EXPLIQUE
– ETUDE SUR LA THEORIE DU DROIT MUSULMAN
– LE TRIBUNAL MUSULMAN
SAVVY – v.1-. 1980- – 1,5,6,9 – us UMI [073]
THE SAW = LA SCIE : CARICATURES DE J.-B. COTE – Quebec, Canada. 29 oct 1863-11 mar 1865 – 1r – 1 – Can$35.00 – cn Can Microfilming [072]
Sawadogo, Mahamadou *see* STATUT DE L'ERREUR ET VARIATION LINGUISTIQUE
SAWDOCTORING MANUAL – 1985 – 229p – it F.A.O. [621]
Sawer, Simon *see* SAWERS' DIGEST OF THE KANDYAN LAW
SAWERS' DIGEST OF THE KANDYAN LAW / Sawer, Simon; ed by Ondaatje, Aelian – 3rd ed. Colombo: Clifton Printing Works, 1900 – us Res Libr [340]
SAWGAND – (Continued by: Ittihad-i Mardum. Dawrah-'i 2: shumarah-'i 1-21 (27 Isfand 1357-16 Mihr 1358[18 Mar 1979-7 Oct 1979]). Issues 20-22 are microfilmed with: Ittihad-i mardum) – Tehran, 1979- – 1 reel – 1 – $25.00 – us MEDOC [950]
SAWGAND – (Sal-i 1: shumarah-'i 2, 8-10; sal-i 2: 1-3, 5, 8-11; sal-i 3: 2, 4-5, 7-8) – Muenchen: Javanan-i Susyalist-i Milli-i Nahzat-i Milli-i Iran – 1 reel – 1 – $25.00 – us MEDOC [950]
SAWGAND *see* ITTIHAD-I MARDUM
SAWTELLE TRIBUNE – Sawtelle, CA. 1916-1917 – 1r – 1 – $50.00 – R03529 – us Library Micro [071]
SAWYER – Hoquiam. Wash. -w. 1903-05, 1906-07 – 1 – us UMI [071]
Sawyer, Alvah L *see* A HISTORY OF NORTHERN PENINSULA OF MICHIGAN AND ITS PEOPLE
Sawyer, Andrew J *see* LINCOLN THE CAPITOL CITY AND LANCASTER COUNTY
Sawyer, Arthur Robert *see* THE GOLDFIELDS OF MASHONALAND
Sawyer, Eugene T *see* HISTORY OF SANTA CLARA COUNTY
Sawyer, LSB *see* SAWYER'S REPORTS OF CASES IN THE NINTH CIRCUIT, 1870-1891
SAWYER'S BOOKSELLING, PRINTING, AND STATIONERY TRADE CIRCULAR – Freetown. Sierra Leone. -bm. Sep 1885-Apr 1886. (14 ft) – 1 – uk British Libr Newspaper [073]
SAWYER'S GAS TURBINE INTERNATIONAL – v. 17$18. 1976-77 – 1,5,6,9 – us UMI [621]
SAWYER'S REPORTS OF CASES IN THE NINTH CIRCUIT, 1870-1891 / Sawyer, LSB – San Francisco: Bancroft. v1-14. 1873-91 (all publ) – 110mf – 9 – $165.00 – LLMC 81-468 – us L.L.M.C. [340]
Saxe, Hermann Maurice de *see* MES REVERIES
SAXIFRAGEARUM ENUMERATIO. ACCEDUNT REVISIONES PLANTARUM SUCCULENTARUM / Haworth, A H – Londini. 1821. B-5950 2 – 8 – ne IDC [580]
SAXON BAPTIST CHURCH. SPARTANBURG COUNTY. SOUTH CAROLINA : CHURCH RECORDS – 1909-Mar 1973 – 1 – 21.74 – us Baptist [240]
THE SAXON CHURCH AND THE NORMAN CONQUEST / Cruttwell, CT – London: Methuen, 1909. (Handbooks of English church history; 2) – 1mf – us A.T.L.A. [240]
SAXON NEWS VOLKSBLATT – Cleveland, OH May 6, 1954-Dec. 29, 1980 – 10r – 1 – us I.H.R.C. [978]
SAXON OBSEQUIES / Neville, R C – H-1143 2. 1852 – 8 – ne IDC [941]
Saxon, Samuel *see* THE ENGLISH SCHOLLAR'S ASSISTANT: OR, THE RUDIMENTS OF THE ENGLISH TONGUE
SAY IT IN: BAHASA INDONESIA, ENGLISH, NIPPONGO / Algamar, B – SE-4238 1. 1962 – 9 – ne IDC [400]
Say, Jean Baptiste *see* OLBIE OU ESSAI SUR LES MOYENS DE REFORMER LES MOEURS D'UNE NATION
SAYAM NIKON – Bangkok.Thailand. 1963- – 1 – us UMI [072]
SAYAM RAT SAPDA WICHAN : THAI-LANGUAGE WEEKLY NEWS MAGAZINE – (Jan 1975-Dec 1978 $50.00v; Jan 1979-Dec 1982 $75.00v; Jan 1983-Dec 1985 $85.00v; Jan 1986-Dec 1988 $90.00v; Jan 1989-Dec 1992 $100.00v) – Bangkok, Thailand. Tabloid format – 1 – us Asia Libr [072]
SAYAMRAT – Bangkok. Thailand. 1963- – 1 – us UMI [072]
SAYAMRAT SAPPADA WICHAN – Bangkok.Thailand. 1962-66 – 1 – us UMI [072]
Sayans Castanos, Marcelo *see*
– CONTACTO LIPOCRATICO Y ENTRADA DE NUEVOS CONCEPTOS EN EL SABER MEDICO DE DOS EPOCAS MUY LIGADAS
– PETROGLIFOS EN LA ALTA EXTREMADURA
Sayce, A H *see* HISTORY OF EGYPT, CHALDEA, SYRIA, BABYLONIA, AND ASSYRIA
Sayce, Archibald Henry *see*
– BABYLONIAN LITERATURE
– EARLY ISRAEL AND THE SURROUNDING NATIONS
– AN ELEMENTARY GRAMMAR
– THE HIGHER CRITICISM...VERDICT OF THE MONUMENTS
– AN INTRODUCTION TO THE BOOKS OF EZRA, NEHEMIAH, AND ESTHER
– MONUMENT FACTS AND HIGHER CRITICAL FANCIES
– A PRIMER OF ASSYRIOLOGY
– THE RACES OF THE OLD TESTAMENT
Sayers, Dorothy Leigh *see* OP. 1
SAYINGS OF THE JEWISH FATHERS / Taylor, C – 2v. (v. 1 both in Hebrew and English). Cambridge. 1877-1900. Appendix. BJ-32-9 1 – 9 – ne IDC [270]
Sayler, John Riner *see* SAYLER'S AMERICAN FORM BOOK.
SAYLER'S AMERICAN FORM BOOK. / Sayler, John Riner – 3rd ed. by Milton Sayler...4th ed. by W. S. Walker...Chicago: Illinois Correspondence School of Law, 1915. 523p. LL-1090 – 1 – us L of C Photodup [340]
Sayles, John *see* A TREATISE ON THE CIVIL JURISDICTION OF JUSTICE OF THE PEACE, IN THE STATE OF TEXAS, INCLUDING FORMS OF PROCESS
Sayous, E *see*
– JESUS CHRIST D'APRES MAHOMET OU LES NOTIONS ET LES DOCTRINES MUSULMANES SUR LE CHRISTIANISME
– JESUS-CHRIST D'APRES MAHOMET OU LES NOTIONS ET LES DOCTRINES MUSULMANES SUR LE CHRSTIANISME
SAYRE EVENING TIMES – Sayre, PA., 1960-1963 – 13 – $25.00r – us I.M.R. [071]
Sayre, Francis Bowes *see* A SELECTION OF CASES AND OTHER AUTHORITIES ON LABOR LAW.
Sazonov, Nicolas Ivanovitch *see* LA VERITE SUR L'EMPEREUR NICOLAS. HISTORIE INTIME DE SA VIE ET DE SON REGNE, PAR UN RUSSE
S.B. Nelson and Company *see*
– HISTORY OF CINCINNATI AND HAMILTON COUNTY
– HISTORY OF VIGO COUNTY WITH A BIOGRAPHICAL SELECTION
SBAC (SOCIETY OF BRITISH AEROSPACE COMPANIES) – Printed index. Updated every 60 days – 6,9 – us Info Handling [629]

Sbath, P see TRAITES RELIGIEUX, PHILOSOPHIQUES ET MORAUX, EXTRAITS DES OEUVRES D'ISAAC DE NINIVE (7 SIECLE) PAR IBN AS-SALT (9 SIECLE)

SBIRKA ZAKONU A ZARIZENI STATU REPUBLIKY CESKOSLOVENSKEHO / Czechoslovakia – (Suppl.: 1990-92. 106mf. Dfl645.00) – Praze, 1918-92. Missing parts of Index 1988; 1989; 1991. BR-6918/1 – 1448mf – 9 – ne IDC [340]

SBORNIK / Akademiia Nauk. Otdelyeniye Russakavo Yazyka i Slovesnosti. St Petersburg – v. 11-12, 14-16, 19-82, 89-99. 1875-1923 – 1 – us NY Public [500]

SBORNIK / Filippov, T – Spb. 1896. BR-10.573 2 – 8 – ne IDC [460]

SBORNIK / Gruppa "Osvobozhdenie Truda. Moscow – n1-6.1923-28 – 1r – 1 – us Ross [947]

SBORNIK / Russko Istoricheskoe Obshchestvago. Leningrad – v. 1-148. 1867-1916. W Index on final reel – 1 – 855.00 – us L of C Photodup [947]

SBORNIK / U.S.S.R. Gosudarstvennaia Publichnaia biblioteka im. M.E. Saltykova-Shchedrina – v. 1-13. L. 1953-55. BR-10,848 1 – 9 – ne IDC [025]

SBORNIK" 17-TI GLAVNEISHIKH" PROTOVOSEKTANTSKIKH" = A COLLECTION OF SEVENTEEN OF THE MOST IMPORTANT ANTI-SECTARIAN DISCUSSIONS / Kal'nev, Mikhail A – Odessa, 1913 – 1r – 1 – $15.24 – us Baptist [240]

SBORNIK AKTOV SOBRANYKH V ARKHIVAKH I BIBLIOTEKAKH / ed by Likhachev, N P – Spb. 1895. Index. BR-4273 2 – 8 – ne IDC [025]

SBORNIK ARKHEOLOGICHESKOGO INSTITUTA – v. 1-6. Spb. 1878-86. B-1873 2 – 8 – ne IDC [930]

SBORNIK BOEVYKH DOKUMENTOV'VELIKOI OTECHESTVENNOI VOINY [1947] : DOKUMENTY PO NASTUPATEL'NOMU BOIU / General'nyi shtab Vooruzhennykh Sil SSSR, Upravlenie izucheniia opyta voiny – (Part 1 of 43 parts) – 1947 – 2mf – 9 – $89.95 – us East View [355]

SBORNIK DE ISTVUI USHCHIKH POSTANOVLENI I, INSTRUKT SI I I TELEGRAFNYKH RASPORI AZHENI I PO PROVEDENII U TRUDOVYKH I GUZHEVYKH POVINNOSTE I 1921, NO.21/22 see BIULLETEN TRUDOVOGO FRONTA

SBORNIK DEISTVUIUSHCHIKH DEKRETOV I POSTANOVLENII PO VNESHNE I TORGOVLE / Soviet Union; ed by Sostavlen Iuridichesko i chasti u NKVT – (Includes c.1: v.1 1918:Apr./1924:Mar.-; v.4 1925:July/1926:Apr) – Moskva: RIO N.K.V.T., 1924- – 1 – CSUXAKZ6221-S – us Hoover Inst Photo [355]

SBORNIK DEISTVUIUSHCHIKH POSTANOVLENII PLENUMA I DIREKTIVNYKH PISEM VERKHOVHOGO SUDA SSR, 1924-1944 GG / Russia. (1923-U.S.S.R.). Verkhovnyi Sud. Plenum – Moscow, 1946 – 1 – 35.00r – us Hoover Inst Photo [324]

SBORNIK DEISTVUIUSHCHIKH POSTANOVLENII [SIC] PO VNESHNE I TORGOVLE [V.1] see SBORNIK DEISTVUIUSHCHIKH DEKRETOV I POSTANOVLENII PO VNESHNE I TORGOVLE

SBORNIK DEISTVUIUSHCHIKH TRAKTATOV, KONVENTSII I SOGLASHENII, ZAKLIUCHENNYKH ROSSIEI S DRUGIMI GOSUDARSTVAMI I KASAIUSHCHIKHSIA RAZLICHNYKH VOPROSOV CHASTNAGO MEZHDUNARODNOGO PRAVA / Russia. Imperial Foreign Ministry – 4v. Spb. 1889-96 – 9 – BR-9047 1 – ne IDC [947]

SBORNIK DEISTVUIUSHCHIKH ZAKONOPOLOZHENII, POSTANOVLENII, INSTRUKTSII I TSIRKULIAROV PO POTREBITEL'SKOI KOOPERATSII / Bat', A G & Baranov, A A – M., 1928 – 8mf – 9 – COR-307/1 – ne IDC [334]

SBORNIK DEKRETOV I POSTANOVLENII PO KOOPERATSII (NACHINAIA S ZAKONA 20 MARTA 1918 GODA – Pg., v1. 1919 – 3mf – 9 – COR-740/1 – ne IDC [334]

SBORNIK DEKRETOV I POSTANOVLENII PO SOIUZU KOMMUN SEVERNOI OBLASTI – Pg. v1(1-2). 1919 (Sost. komissariatom Iustitsii Soiuza kommun Severnoi oblasti) – 15mf – 9 – COR-741/1 – ne IDC [334]

SBORNIK DEKRETOV I RASPORIAZHENII PO FINANSAM / Russian S.F.S.R. – (Includes c.1: v.3 1920/1921-v.5 (1921/1922)) – Petrograd: [Institut, 1919- – 1 – CSUXAKZ0510-S – us Hoover Inst Photo [336]

SBORNIK DOGOVOROV ROSSII S DRUGIMI GOSUDARSTVAMI : 1856-1917 / ed by Adamov, E A – Moscow, 1952. 464p. BR-8543 1 – 9 – ne IDC [947]

SBORNIK DOKUMENTOV KASAIUSHCHIKHSIA ADMINISTRATIVNOGO USTROISTVA SEVERO-ZAPADNOGO KRAIA PRI IMPERATRITSE EKATERINE 2 (1792-1796) – Vilnius, 1903 – 9mf – 9 – ne IDC [947]

SBORNIK GEOGR. TOPOGR. I STAT. MATERIALOV PO AZLI – v. 59. St Petersburg. 1895 – 1 – us NY Public [910]

SBORNIK GOSUDARSTVENNOGO PEDAGOGICHESKOGO INSTITUTA (1925-1937) – Kharbin. n.d. BR-8063 2 – 8 – ne IDC [370]

SBORNIK GRAMOT I DOGOVOROV O PRISOEDINENII TSARSTVE I OBLASTEI K GOSUDARSTVU ROSSIISKOMU V 17-19 VEKAKH / ed by Pazukhin, A A – v. 1 only publ. Petrograd. 1921. BR-9495 1 – 9 – ne IDC [947]

SBORNIK I. POD / Maiakovskii, Vladimir – red. A. L. Dymshitsia i O. V. Tsekhovitsera. M., L. 1940. BR-2199 2 – 8 – ne IDC [460]

SBORNIK I UKAZATEL' DOKUMENTOV I RUKOPISEI, OTNOSIASHCHIKHSIA K KAZANSKOI GUBERNII I KHRANIASHCHIKHSIA V MOSKOVSKOM GLAVNOM ARKHIVE MINISTERSTVA INOSTRANNYKH DEL I EGO BIBLIOTEKE / Tokmakov, I F – (Trudy Chetvertogo Arkheologicheskogo s"ezda v Rossii, byvshego v Kazani, 1877 gg.) v. 2. Kazan. 1891. PKG-B-75.75 BR-11,173 1 – 9 – ne IDC [025]

SBORNIK IMPERATORSKAGO RUSSKAGO ISTORICHESKOVO OBSHCHESTVA / Russko Istoricheskoe Obshchestvago. Leningrad – (Collection of the Imperial Russian History Society). 148 v. 1867-1916 – 3 – us Readex [947]

SBORNIK IMPERATORSKOGO RUSSKOGO ISTORICHESKOGO OBSHEHESTVA / Russia – St. Petersburg. 1867-1916 – 1 – us UMI [947]

SBORNIK ISTORICHESKIKH MATERIALOV I DOKUMENTOV, OTNOSIASHCHIKHSIA K NOVOI RUSSKOI ISTORIIA XVIII I XIX VEKA / ed by Mikhailov, M – Spb. 1873. BR-10,526 1 – 9 – ne IDC [947]

SBORNIK ISTORIKO-FILOLOGICHESKOGO OBSHCHESTVA PRI INSTITUTE KN. BEZBORODKO V NEZHINE – v. 1-7. Nezhin. 1896-1911. B-1874 2 – 8 – ne IDC [400]

SBORNIK MATERIALOV / Moscow. Arkhivnoe delo Moskovskoi oblasti – v1. M. 1931; v 2/3. M. 1932. BR-10,937 1 – 9 – ne IDC [947]

SBORNIK MATERIALOV DLIA ISTORII IMP. AKADEMII NAUK V 18 VEKE / Kunik, A A – 2pts. Spb. 1865. BR-6063 2 – 8 – ne IDC [500]

SBORNIK MATERIALOV DLIA OPISANIIA MESTNOSTI I PLEMEN KAVKAZA – (Missing: 1881, v1(pv-viii, 1-12); 1886, v5(p205-208); 1889, v8(p195-196, 271-272)) – Tiflis. v1-46. 1881-1916 – 326mf – 9 – RET-16/1 – ne IDC [947]

SBORNIK MATERIALOV I STATEI PO KOOPERATSII : POSOBIE DLIA AGITATSIONNO-POLITICHESKIKH KOOPERATIVNYKH KURSOV – M., 1921 – 3mf – 9 – COR-273/1 – ne IDC [334]

SBORNIK MATERIALOV OB ARTELIAKH V ROSSII – Spb. 3v. 1873-1875 – 12mf – 9 – COR-102/1 – ne IDC [334]

SBORNIK MATERIALOV, OTNOSIASCHIKHSIA DO ARKHIVNOI CHASTI V ROSSII / Imperial Russian Historical Society – 2v. Petrograd. 1916-17 – 9 – PKG-A-87 BR-10,768 1 – ne IDC [340]

SBORNIK MATERIALOV PO EVENSKIISKOMU (TUNGUSSKOMU) FOL'KLORU / Vasilevich, G M – (INS). L. 1936. BU-446 2 – 8 – ne IDC [390]

SBORNIK MATERIALOV PO IZUCHENIIU OPYTA VOINY : DEISTVIIA PO UNICHTOZHENIIUI OKRUZHNYKH KRUPNYKH GRUPPIROVOK PROTIVNIKA / General'nyi shtab Vooruzhennykh Sil SSSR, Otdel Upravlenie izucheniia opyta – (Part 1 of 26 parts) – Minneapolis: East View Publications, 1993 – 2mf – 9 – $89.95 – us East View [947]

SBORNIK MATERIALOV PO OPYTU BOEVOI DEIATEL'NOSTI VOENNO-MORSKOGO FLOTA SSSR : OPERATSIIA PO RAZGROMU DESANTA PROTIVNIKA U O. SUKHO LADOZHSKAIA VOENNAIA FLOTILIIA, 22.10.42 / Glavnyi Morskoi shtab NKBMF SSSR – (Part 1 of 41 parts) – 1943 – 2mf – 9 – $95.00 – us East View [355]

SBORNIK MOSKOVSKOGO GLAVNOGO ARKHIVA MINISTERSTVA INOSTRANNYKH DEL / Russia. Imperial Foreign Ministry – 7v in 6. M. 1880-1900. PKG-B-75.2 BR-11,148 1 – 9 – ne IDC [324]

SBORNIK NA BALGARSKATA AKADEMIIA NA NAUKITE – Sofia, 1913, v.1; 1914, v.3. BR-181 2 – 8 – ne IDC [500]

SBORNIK NARODNOGO KOMISSARIATA IUSTITSII PO STATISTICHESKOMU OTDELU ZA... – (Includes c.1: v.1 1921) – [Kharkov]: Komissariat, 1922- – 1 – CSUXAKZ2177-S – us Hoover Inst Photo [340]

SBORNIK NARODNYKH IURIDICHESKIKH OBYCHAEV ARKHANGEL'SKOI GUBERNII / Efimenko, R S – Arkhangel'sk. 336p. 1869 – 4mf – 9 – R-9005/1 – ne IDC [947]

SBORNIK NORMATIVNYKH AKTOV I INSTRUKTIVNYKH MATERIALOV / Reigas, A – Riga. 1969 – 3mf – 9 – ne IDC [340]

SBORNIK OTDELENIIA RUSSKOGO IAZYKA I SLOVESNOSTI IMPERATORSKOI AKADEMII NAUK – Spb. v1-101. 1867-1928 – 1508mf – 9 – ne IDC [947]

SBORNIK PALEOGRAFICHESKIKH SNIMKOV S DREVNIKH GRAMOT I AKTOV, KHRANIASHCHIKHSIA V VILENSKOM TSENTRAL'NOM ARKHIVE I VILENSKOI PUBLICHNOI KOMISSII, VYP. 1 (1432-1548 GG.) – Vil'na, 1884 – 2mf – 9 – ne IDC [947]

SBORNIK PALEOGRAFICHESKIKH SNIMKOV S POCHERKOV DREVNEGO I NOVAGO PIS'MA RAZNYKH PERIODOV VREMENI, IZDANNYI DLIA VOSPITANNIKOV MEZHEVAGO VEDOMSTVA / Ivanov, PI – M. 1844. BR-10,026 1 – 9 – ne IDC [410]

SBORNIK PARTIINYKH I PRAVITEL'STVENNYKH POSTANOVLENII PO SEL'SKOKHOZIAISTVENNOI KOOPERATSII (ZA VREMIA S AVGUSTA 1926 G. – 20 DEKABRIA 1927 G.) –' Ed 4. M., 1928 – 3mf – 9 – COR-311/1 – ne IDC [334]

SBORNIK PEDAGOGICHESKAGO ZHURNALA "VOSPITANIE I OBUCHENIE" – Dlia starshago vosrasta. 1. Spb. 1877. BR-3772 2 – 8 – ne IDC [370]

SBORNIK PO MELKOMU KREDITU / Borodaevskii, S V – Ed 6. Pg., 1915 – 7mf – 9 – COR-105/1 – ne IDC [334]

SBORNIK PO RUSSKOMU YAZYKU I SLOVESNOSTI / Akademiia Nauk. SSSR – Leningrad. v. 1-2, no. 1. 1928-1930 – 1 – us NY Public [460]

SBORNIK PO TEKUSHCHEMU ZAKONODATEL'STVU I SUDEBNOI PRAKTIKE (V POMOSCH' ADVOKATU) – 6issues. 1946-47 – 9 – ne IDC [460]

SBORNIK PO TEORII POETICHESKAGO IAZYKA – v. 1-2. Petrograd. 1916-17. BR-1807 2 – 8 – ne IDC [410]

SBORNIK PO VOPROSAM EKONOMIKI I KOOPERATSII – M., 1915 – 3mf – 9 – COR-104/1 – ne IDC [334]

SBORNIK PO VOPROSAM KOOPERATSII – M., 1917 – 3mf – 9 – COR-103/1 – ne IDC [334]

SBORNIK POLOZHENII I INSTRUKTSII PO BUKHGALTERSKOMU UCHETU I OTCHETNOSTI SOIUZOV KUSTARNO-PROMYSLOVOI I LESNOI KOOPERATSII / Lapshov, II; ed by Bolotov, P A – M., 1929 – 2mf – 9 – COR-444/1 – ne IDC [334]

SBORNIK POSTANOVLENI I I RASPORI AZHENI I OBSHCHIKH I MI ESTNYKH, REGULIRUI USHCHIKH PRODOVOLSTVENNOE DI ELO V MOSKVI E / ed by Moskovski i gorodsko i prodovolstvenny i komitet S.R.D., Redaktsionnoizdatelski i otdi el – (Includes c.1: v.1 1918: Jan.-v.3 (1918:June)) – Moskva: [Otdi el], 1918- – 1 – CSUXAKZ1251-S – us Hoover Inst Photo [640]

SBORNIK POSTANOVLENI I PRIKAZOV INSTRUKTSI I PO FINANSOVOKHOZI A ISTVENNYM VOPROSAM – (Library has: no.13/14-17/18, 1940; no.3, no.10/11, 1945) – Moskva: Gosfinizdat, 1940- – 1 – CSUX89-S834 – us Hoover Inst Photo [336]

SBORNIK POSTANOVLENII I DEKRETOV PO KOOPERATSII : SO VVEDENIEM, SOST. IURIDICHESKIM OTDELOM SOVETA VSEROSSIISKIKH KOOPERATIVNIKH S"EZDOV – M., 1919 – 2mf – 9 – COR-743/1 – ne IDC [334]

SBORNIK POSTANOVLENII I PRIKAZOV PO PROMYSHLENNOSTI / Soviet Union, Vysshii sovet narodnogo khoziaistva – (Includes c.1: 1926/1927:no.2-no.14) – Moskva: Promizdat, 192u – 1 – CSUXALJ7446-S – us Hoover Inst Photo [338]

SBORNIK POSTANOVLENII I PRIKAZOV PO PROMYSHLENNOSTI / Soviet Union, Vysshii sovet narodnogo khoziaistva – (Includes c.1: 1926/1927:no.2-no.14) – Moskva: Promizdat, 192u – 1 – CSUXALJ7453-S – us Hoover Inst Photo [330]

SBORNIK POSTANOVLENII O PROMYSLOVOI KOOPERATSII I KUSTARNOI PROMYSHLENNOSTI / Selitskii, I A et al; ed by Genkin, D M – M., 1930 – 7mf – 9 – COR-315/1 – ne IDC [334]

SBORNIK POSTANOVLENII PLENUMA VERKHOVNOGO SUDA LITOVSKOI SSR, 1961-1973 GG. – (In Russian and Lithuanian) – Vilnius, 1974 – 4mf – 9 – ne IDC [947]

SBORNIK PRIKAZOV POVSNKH I EGO GLAVNYM I FUNKTSIONALNYM UPRAVLENII AM / Russian S.F.S.R. Vysshii sovet narodnogo khoziaistva – (Includes: c.1: no.1 1922:June) – Moskva: Redaktsionno-izdatelskii otdel, 1922- – 1 – CSUXAKZ0175-S – us Hoover Inst Photo [330]

SBORNIK RASPORIAZHENII PO RECHNOMU TRANSPORTU – Moscow, 1922. 197p. BR-9357/1 – 9 – ne IDC [340]

SBORNIK RUKOVODIASHCHIKH MATERIALOV DLIA KOOPERATIVOV – Iakutsk, 1924 – 2mf – 9 – COR-312/1 – ne IDC [334]

SBORNIK RUKOVODIASHCHIKH MATERIALOV PO KOLKHOZNOMU STROITEL'STVU – Moscow, 1948. 351p. BR-9072/1 – 9 – ne IDC [947]

SBORNIK RUKOVODIASHCHIKH POSTANOVLENII I MATERIALOV PO SEL'SKOKHOZIAISTVENNOI KREDITNOI KOOPERATSII (1924-1929 GG.) – M., 1929 – 4mf – 9 – COR-313/1 – ne IDC [334]

SBORNIK RUSSKAGO INSTITUTA V PRAGUE – v. 1-2. Prague. 1929-31. BR-3771 2 – 8 – ne IDC [947]

SBORNIK RUSSKOGO ISTORICHESKOGO OBSHCHESTVA – 148 v. Spb. 1867-1916. B-1876 2 – 8 – ne IDC [947]

SBORNIK SIBIRSKOGO STATISTICHESKOGO UPRAVLENIIA – (Includes c.1: v.2 1922) – Novonikolaevsk: [Upravlenie], 19uu – 1 – CSUXAKY5537-S – us Hoover Inst Photo [310]

SBORNIK SNIMKOV S SLAVIANORUSSKIKH STAROPECHATNYKH IZDANII / Ptashitskii, S L – St. Petersburg, 1895. 30p. BR-4587/2 – 8 – ne IDC [947]

SBORNIK STATEI / ed by Sipovskii, V V – M.V. Lomonosov. Spb. 1911. BR-7862 2 – 8 – ne IDC [460]

SBORNIK STATEI 1912-1922 / Chulkov, G I – Izd. Vasil'eva. M. 1922. BR-2039 2 – 8 – ne IDC [460]

SBORNIK STATEI DUKHOVNAGO SODERZHANIYA see PASHKOVITES

SBORNIK STATEI I MATERIALOV PO SEL'SKOKHOZIAISTVENNOI KOOPERATSII : K 9 VSEROSSIISKOMU S"EZDU SOVETOV – M., 1921 – 1mf – 9 – COR-503/1 – ne IDC [334]

SBORNIK STATEI I MATERIALOV PO VRACHNOMU I SEMEINOMU PRAVU / Kurskii, D I – Moscow, 1926. 224p. Collection of articles and materials, including expert testimony, of the draft family code of the RSFSR. BR-8654/1 – 9 – ne IDC [340]

SBORNIK STATEI PO ARKHEOLOGII I VIZANTINOVEDENIIU, IZDAVAEMYI SEMINARIEM IMENI N.P. KONDAKOVA – v. 1-8. Prague. 1927-36. BR-5826 2 – 8 – ne IDC [930]

SBORNIK STATEI PO KLASSICHESKOI FILOLOGII – Spb. 1874-1916. Lacking: (1-4) 1877-84; (2) 1886; (4) 1887; (4) 1888; (2) 1899; (1, 3) 1909. B-1878 2 – 8 – ne IDC [400]

SBORNIK STATEI PO PROLETARSKOI REVOLIUTSII I PRAVU – Petrograd, 1918.186p. BR-9290/1 – 9 – ne IDC [335]

SBORNIK STATEI PO PROLETARSKOI REVOLIUTSII I PRAVU – Petrograd: izd. Nar. komissariata i ustitsii, 1918. 1v – 1 – CSUX89-S864 – us Hoover Inst Photo [335]

SBORNIK STATEI V OBLICHENIE SHTUNDIZMA I V UTVERZHDENIE NEOPYTNYKH V ISTINAKH PROVOSLAVNOI VERY / Raznogorskii, Mikhail – Orel, 1891. One of 13 titles on reel – 1 – 86.44 – us Baptist [240]

SBORNIK STATEI...POSVIASHCHENNYKH PAMIATI...V.M. GORDONA – Kharkov, 1927. 322p. Articles by the Kharkov law faculty dedicated to V.M. Gordon, with biography and bibliography of his writings. BR-8620/1 – 9 – ne IDC [340]

SBORNIK STATISTICHESKIKH SVEDENII O ROSSII – v. 1-3. Spb. 1851-58. B-1879 2 – 8 – ne IDC [947]

SBORNIK SVEDENII O CHASTNYKH POVREMENNYKH IZDANIIAKH, VYKHODIASHCHIKH V S-PETERBURGE I MOSKVE – Bokrama. 1865. BR-9241 1 – 9 – ne IDC [380]

SBORNIK SVEDENII O KAVKAZSKIKH GORTSAKH, IZDAVAEMYI ... ARMIEIU PRI KAVKAZSKOM GORSKOM UPRAVLENII – Tiflis. v1-10. 1868-1881 – 54mf – 9 – RET-17/1 – ne IDC [947]

SBORNIK SVEDENII O POVREMENNYKH IZDANIIAKH – (po 1 noiabria 1870 g.). Spb, 1870 – 8 – BR-4417 2 – ne IDC [947]

SBORNIK SVEDENIIA PO KNIZHNOLITERATURNOMU DELU – 1-2. M. 1867. BR-7252 2 – 8 – ne IDC [460]

SBORNIK TARIFOV ZHEL.-DOR. I VODNOGO TRANSPORTA R.S.F.S.R. – (Library has: no. 57-101, 1922-1923; missing many issues) – Moskva: Finansovo- ekonomicheskoe upravlenie Narodnogo komissariata pute i soobshchenii a, 1922-1923 – 1 – CSUX89-S539 – us Hoover Inst Photo [332]

SBORNIK TARIFOV ZHEL.-DOR. I VODNOGO TRANSPORTA S.S.S.R. – (Library has: no. 103-390, 1923-1926; missing many issues) – Moskva: "Tramnspechati" N.K.P.S., 1923-1930 – 1 – CSUX89-S598 – us Hoover Inst Photo [380]

SBORNIK TARIFOV ZHELEZNODOR-OZHNOGO I VODNOGO TRANSPORTA R.S.F.S.R. *see* SBORNIK TARIFOV ZHEL.-DOR. I VODNOGO TRANSPORTA R.S.F.S.R.

SBORNIK TARIFOV ZHELEZNODOR-OZHNOGO I VODNOGO TRANSPORTA SSSR *see* SBORNIK TARIFOV ZHEL.-DOR. I VODNOGO TRANSPORTA S.S.S.R.

SBORNIK TOVARISHCHESTVA "ZNANIE" ZA 1903-1906 GG – v. 1-12. Spb. 1904-06. BR-8070 2 – 8 – ne IDC [460]

SBORNIK TSIRKULIAROV I RAPORIAZHENII PO DELAM PECHATI.. / Karamyshev, IP – Saint Petersburg, 1882. 60p. Collection of secret circulars issued to circumvent Article 140 of 1873 censorship statutes.BR-9251/1 – 9 – ne IDC [380]

SBORNIK TSIRKULIAROV I RAZ"IASNENII NARODNOGO KOMISSARIATA IUSTITSII RSFSR – Moscow, 1934. 312p. BR-8735/1 – 9 – ne IDC [080]

SBORNIK TSIRKULIAROV I RAZ"IASNENII PROKURATURY SOIUZA SSR DEIST – Moscow, 1936. 168p. BR-9601/1 – 9 – ne IDC [340]

SBORNIK TSIRKULIAROV N.K. IU. POLIKVIDATSIONNOMU OTDELU I OTCHETOV LIKV. OTDELA POOTDELENIIU TSERKVI OT GOSUDARSTVA / Ukraine, Narodnyi komisariat iustytsii – (Includes c.1: v.2 1921-v.3 (1921)) – Kharkov: Komisariat, 19uu – 1 – CSUXAKY5342-S – us Hoover Inst Photo [320]

SBORNIK UCHENO-LITERATURNOGO OBSHCHESTVA PRI IUR'EVSKOM UNIVERSITETE – Iur'ev. v1-22. 1898-1916 – 119mf – 9 – ne IDC [947]

SBORNIK UKAZOV I POSTANOVLENII VREMENNAGO PRAVITEL'STVA / Russia. (1917-Provisional Government). Laws, Statutes, etc – Petrograd, 1917-1918. 2 vols – 1 – 35.00r – us Hoover Inst Photo [324]

SBORNIK UZAKONENII, RASPORIAZHENII, TSIRKULIAROV, RAZ"IASNENII I USTAVOV PO POTREBKOOPERATSII – M., 1925 – 5mf – 9 – COR-314/1 – ne IDC [334]

SBORNIK VAZHNEISHIKH DEISTVUIUSHCHIKH DEKERETOV I RASPORIAZHENII PRAVITEL'STVA OB ORGANIZATSII I DEIATEL'NOSTI RAZNOGO RODA OBSHCHESTV, SOIUZOV, ARTELEI, TOVARISHCHESTV,... – M., 1922 – 2mf – 9 – COR-739/1 – ne IDC [334]

SBORNIK VAZHNEISHIKH POSTANOVLENII PO TRUDU / Kiselev, Ia. L & Malkins, S E – 10th and last ed. of standard collection of labor Law in the 1930s; status juris: 1 Sept 1938. BR-9367/1 – 9 – ne IDC [340]

SBORNIK VAZHNEISHIKH POSTANOVLENII PO TRUDU / Kiselev, Ia. L & Malkins, S E – 4th ed., rev. Moscow, 1932. 296p. Decrees on labor laws as of July 1932. BR-8480-1 – 9 – ne IDC [340]

SBORNIK VIZANTIISKIKH I DREVNERUSSKIKH ORNAMENTOV / Gagarin, G G – St. Petersburg, 1887. BR/10,019/2 – 8 – ne IDC [947]

SBORNIK VOENNO-ISTORICHESKIKH MATERIALOV VELIKOI OTECHESTVENNOI VOINY : TALLIN OFFENSIVE OPERATION (1944); MOBILE ARMY GROUPS / General'nyi shtab Vooruzhennykh Sil SSSR, Glavnoe voenno-nauchnoe upravlenie – (Part 4 of 19 parts) – 1949 – 2mf – 9 – $89.95 – us East View [355]

SBORNIK ZAKONODATEL'NYKH AKTOV PO SEL'SKOMU KHOZIAISTVU TADZHIKSKOI SSR – Dushanbe, 1962. 411p. BR-8739/1 – 9 – ne IDC [630]

SBORNIK ZAKONODATEL'NYKH I INSTRUKTIVNYKH MATERIALOV O PROMYSLOVOI-KOOPERATIVNYKH ORGANIZATSIIAKH I TRUDIVYKH ARTELIAKH – Saratov, 1928 – 2mf – 9 – COR-309/1 – ne IDC [334]

SBORNIK ZAKONODATEL'NYKH MATERIALOV, INSTRUKTSII I RAZ"IASNENII PO KOOPERATSII INVALIDOV / Timrot, L & Zubarovskii, N; ed by Aleksandrov, M – M., 1928 – 4mf – 9 – COR-310/1 – ne IDC [334]

SBORNIK ZAKONODATEL'STVA PO VNUTRENNEMU VODNOMU TRANSPORTU – Moscow, 1964. 175p. BR-8492/1 – 9 – ne IDC [340]

SBORNIK ZAKONOV AZERBA IDZHANSKO I SSR I UKAZOV PREZIDIUMA VERKHOVNOGO SOVETA AZERBA IDZHANSKO I SSR, 1938-1966 GG = LAWS, ETC. : V DVUKH TOMAKH / Azerbaijan S.S.R. – Baku: Verkhovny i Sovet, 1966-1967. 2v – 1 – CSUX91-B1493 – us Hoover Inst Photo [340]

SBORNIK ZAKONOV AZERBAIDZHANSKOI SSR I UKAZOV PREZIDIUMA VERKHOVNOGO SOVETA AZERBAIDZHANSKOGO SSR: 1938-1966 – Baku, 1966-67. 2v. BR-8799/1 – 9 – ne IDC [340]

SBORNIK ZAKONOV BELORUSSKO I SSR I UKAZOV PREZIDIUMA VERKHOVNOGO SOVETA BELORUSSKO I SSR, 1938-1955 GG : LAWS, ETC / Byelorussian S.S.R. – Minsk: Izd. Prezidiuma Verkhovnogo Soveta Belorussko i SSR, 1956 – 1 – CSUX91-B1736 – us Hoover Inst Photo [340]

SBORNIK ZAKONOV BELORUSSKOI SSR I UKAZOV PREZIDIUMA VERKHOVNOGO SOVETA BELORUSSKOI SSR ZA 1956-1958 GG – Minsk, 1959. 433p. BR-8493/1 – 9 – ne IDC [340]

SBORNIK ZAKONOV BERLORUSSKOI SSR I UKAZOV PREZIDIUMA VERKHOVNOGO SOVETA BELORUSSKOI SSR: 1938-1955 GG – Minsk, 1956. 347p. BR-8763/1 – 9 – ne IDC [340]

SBORNIK ZAKONOV I RASPORIAZHENII OTNOSIASHCHIKHSIA K VODNOMU TRANSPORTU / Andreev, N N – Moscow, 1936. 581p. BR-9358 1 – 9 – ne IDC [340]

SBORNIK ZAKONOV KAZAKHSKOI SSR I UKAZOV PREZIDIUMA VERKHOVNOGO SOVETA KAZAKHSKOI SSR 1938-1957 – Alma-Ata, 1958. 671p. BR-8762/1 – 9 – ne IDC [947]

SBORNIK ZAKONOV KIRGIZSKOI SSR I UKAZOV PREZIDIUMA VERKHOVNOGO SOVETA KIRGISKOI SSR; 1938-1956 GG – Frunze, 1957. 272p. BR-9073/1 – 9 – ne IDC [947]

SBORNIK ZAKONOV TADZHIKSKOI SSR, UKAZOV I POSTANOVLENII PREZIDIUMA VERKHOVNOGO SOVETA TADZHIKSKOI SSR 1938-1958 GG – Stalinabad, 1959. 402p.BR-9084/1 – 9 – ne IDC [947]

SBORNIK ZAKONOV UZBEKSKOI SSR I UKAZOV PREZIDIUMA VERKHOVNOGO SOVETA UZBEKSKOI SSR, 1938-1964 GG – Tashkent, 1964. 527p. BR-8764/1 – 9 – ne IDC [947]

SBORNIKI ZHURNALA "NARODNOE KHOZIAISTVO" – (Library has: vol. 1, 1918) – Moskva: Red. izdatelski i otdel VSNKh, 1918- – 1 – CSUX89-S661 – us Hoover Inst Photo [330]

LA S.C. DE PROPAGANDA FIDE E LE MISSIONI DEL GINPPANE (1622-1838) / Bayle, Constantino & Pedot, Lino M – Vicenza, 1946; Madrid: Missionalia Hispanica, 1948 – 1 – sp Bibl Santa Ana [240]

THE S.C. STATE CENSUS OF 1869 – 6r – 1 M-17 – $30.00r – us SC Archives [978]

LO SCACCIAPENSIERI – Omaha, Nebraska 1932-1933 – us I.H.R.C. [073]

SCALA DI MUSICA...CON L'AGGIONTA D'UN DUO IN FUGA.. / Scaletta, Orazio – 1634 – 9 – us Sibley [780]

SCALA PARADISI : EINE STUDIE ZU JOHANNES CLIMACUS UND ZUGLEICH EINE VORSTUDIE ZU SYMEON DEN NEUEN THEOLOGEN / Voelker, W – 1968 – 7mf – 9 – ne Slangenburg [240]

SCALABRINI ORTIZ : EL HOMBRE QUE ESTUVO SOLO / Bares, Enrique – [Buenos Aires]: A. Pena Lillo, [1962, c1961] – 1 – CSUXADJ0125-B – us Hoover Inst Photo [920]

Scaletta, Orazio *see* SCALA DI MUSICA...CON L'AGGIONTA D'UN DUO IN FUGA..

Scaliger, Julius Caesar *see* POETICES

Scaliger, Julius Caesar, *see* IULII CAESARIS SCALIGERI EXOTICARUM EXERCITATIONUM, LIBER QUINTUS: DE SUBTILITATE, AD HIERONYMUM CARDANUM; IN EXTREMO DUO SUNT INDICES; PRIOR BREUIUSCULUS, CONTINENS SENTENTIAS NOBILIORES; ALTER OPULENTISSIMUS, PENE OMNIA COMPLECTENS

Scaliger, Julius Cesar *see* DE CAUSIS LINGUAE LATINAE

THE SCALIGER PATERIKON / Veder, W R – v1. A palaeographic, linguistic and structural description. (Diss.). Zug. 1976. BR-11,331 1 – 9 – ne IDC [450]

Scammon, C M *see* THE MARINE MAMMALS OF THE NORTH-WESTERN COAST OF NORTH AMERICA

Scamozzi, V *see*
- DISCORSI SOPRA L'ANTICHITA DI ROMA
- L'IDEA DELLI UNIVERSAE ARCHITECTURE DIVISA IN 10. LIBRI
- THE MIRROR OF ARCHITECTURE: OR THE GROUND-RULES OF THE ART OF BUILDING

Scamozzi, Vincenzo *see* LES CINQ ORDRES D'ARCHITECTURE.

SCANDINAVIAN BOOKS BEFORE 1701 – 477r – 1 – $30,000.00 $1,200.00y – us OmniSys [948]

Scandinavian Institute of Asian Studies *see* SCANDINAVIAN UNION CATALOGUE OF EAST ASIAN MATERIALS

SCANDINAVIAN JOURNAL OF DENTAL RESEARCH – Copenhagen. v78-94. 1970-86 – 5,9 – Dfl2,210.00; Dfl130.00v – ne Swets [617]

SCANDINAVIAN JOURNAL OF EDUCATIONAL RESEARCH – (1981-. 1,5,6,9) – v15-. 1971- – 1 – us UMI [073]

THE SCANDINAVIAN JOURNAL OF EDUCATIONAL RESEARCH – 1957- 37v – 9 – £124.50 – 0031-3831 – uk Carfax [370]

SCANDINAVIAN JOURNAL OF GASTROENTEROLOGY – (1981-. 1,5,6,9) – v1-. 1966- – 1 – us UMI [073]

SCANDINAVIAN JOURNAL OF GASTROENTEROLOGY.SUPPLEMENT – (1981-. 1,5,6,9) – 1968- – 1 – us UMI [073]

SCANDINAVIAN JOURNAL OF MANAGEMENT – 1,5,69 – us UMI [650]

SCANDINAVIAN POLITICAL STUDIES – (1981-. 1,5,6,9) – v1-. 1978- – 1 – us UMI [073]

SCANDINAVIAN REVIEW – (See also: American and Scandinavian Review) – v63- 1975- 1,5,6; v65- 9 – us UMI [073]

SCANDINAVIAN UNION CATALOGUE OF EAST ASIAN MATERIALS : PRELIMINARY CHINESE AND JAPANESE TITLE CATALOGUE / Wagner, Donald Blackmore – (This preliminary catalogue lists material written in Chinese and Japanese languages collected from 23 Scandinavian libraries) – Zug, 1981 – 97mf – 9 – CH-1216-CH-1217/1 – ne IDC [020]

Scandura, J M *see* JOURNAL OF STRUCTURAL LEARNING

Scanlan, Charles Martin *see* LAW OF HOTELS, BOARDING HOUSES AND LODGING HOUSES, PARTICULARLY ADAPTED TO THE STATE OF WISCONSIN

Scannell, Thomas Bartholomew *see* THE PRIEST'S STUDIES

THE SCANSION OF MEDIAEVAL HEBREW POETRY / Halper, B – (Jewish Quarterly Review). v. 4. 1913 14. BJ-421-25 1 – 9 – ne IDC [470]

SCANTEIA – Bucharest, Romania. -d. 14 Nov 1944-11 Dec 1951; 16 Oct 1952-Dec 1970. 68 reels – 1 – uk British Libr Newspaper [949]

SCANTEIA TINERETULUI – Bucharest, Romania. Scinteia tineretului. -d. Nov 1950-Dec 1966. 28 reels – 1 – uk British Libr Newspaper [949]

SCAP DIRECTIVES TO THE IMPERIAL JAPANESE GOVERNMENT / Supreme Commander for the Allied Powers – 7V. 1945-46 – 1 – 27.00 – us L of C Photodup [950]

LE SCAPIN – Paris. dec 1885-86 – 1 – fr A.C.R.P.P. [073]

SCAPPOOSE REGISTER – Scappoose, OR. -w. 17 Feb 1928-25 Oct 1929. 1 roll – 1 – us U.O. Library [071]

SCAPPOOSE SPOTLIGHT – Scappoose, OR. -w. 23 Mar 1961-19 Sept 1974; 5 Oct 1978-. – 6r – 1 – us U.O. Library [071]

SCARABS AND CYLINDERS / Petrie, William Matthew Flinders – 1917 – 9 – $10.00 – us I.R.C. [930]

Scaramella, B *see* [MADRIGALS, 5 VOICES, BOOK 1]

Scarboro, J A *see* THE BIBLE, THE BAPTIST AND THE BOARD SYSTEM

SCARBOROUGH CONSUMER – Toronto, 1977-1983 – 10r – 1 – cn Preston [971]

Scarborough, Jewel Davis *see* THE GEORGIA BATTALION IN THE TEXAS REVOLUTION: A CRITICAL STUDY

SCARBOROUGH MIRROR – (1962-1992.-101r) – Toronto, 1993 – 4r – 1 – cn Preston [971]

SCARBOROUGH NEWS – Toronto, 1953-1988 – 32r – 1 – cn Preston [971]

Scarborough. Yorkshire *see* PARISH REGISTERS

Scarfe, N V *see* A HANDBOOK OF SUGGESTIONS ON THE TEACHING OF GEOGRAPHY

Scarlatti, Alessandro *see*
- [31 CANTATA, FOR ONE VOICE WITH A THOROUGH BASS]
- 31 CANTATAS
- PETITES CANTANDES A SEULE VOIX DE CHANT

Scarth, A M E *see* THE STORY OF THE OLD CATHOLIC AND KINDRED MOVEMENTS

Scasta, David L *see* JOURNAL OF GAY AND LESBIAN PSYCHOTHERAPY

SCELTA DI CANZONI POPOLARI IN DIALETTO NAPOLITANO – 1875 – 1 – us I.U. Libraries [390]

DIE SCENE – Berlin, Vereinigung Kuenstlerischer Buehnenvorstaende. Jahrg. 1-23, Heft 6; 1911-June 1933. "Blaetter fuer Buehnenkunst." Film Mas C 423 – 1 – us H.U. Library [410]

SCENE MUSICALE – (See also: Music Scene. Ceased 1990) – nos 237-371. 1967-90 – 9 – Can$20.00y – cn Micromedia [780]

SCENES AND CHARACTERS OF THE MIDDLE AGES / Cutts, Edward L – London: Virtue, 1886 – 2mf – us A.T.L.A. [900]

SCENES AND INCIDENTS IN IRISH LIFE / Clayton, F H – By an Irishman. Montreal: J. Lovell, 1884. 00679. (Pre-1900 Canadiana) – 9 – cn C.I.H.M. [941]

SCENES DE LA NATURE DANS LES ETATS UNIS ET LE NORD DE L'AMERIQUE / Audubon, John James – Tome deuxieme, ouvrage traduit par Eugene Bazin, avec preface et notes du traducteur. Paris, A. Sauton, 1868. 04053. (Pre-1900 Canadiana) – 9 – cn C.I.H.M. [574]

SCENES DE LA NATURE DANS LES ETATS UNIS ET LE NORD DE L'AMERIQUE / Audubon, John James – Tome premier, ouvrage traduit d'Audubon par Eugene Bazin avec preface et notes du traducteur. Paris: A. Sauton, 1868. 04053. (Pre-1900 Canadiana) – 9 – cn C.I.H.M. [574]

SCENES DE LA NATURE DANS LES ETATS-UNIS... : T. 1 AND 2, TRAD., PREF. ET NOTES PAR EUGENE BAZIN / Audubon, Jean-Jacques – Paris: Sauton, 1868 – 1 – F476.30 – fr Armell [500]

SCENES DE LA VIE DE CAMPAGNE. LES PAYSANS. / Balzac, Honore de – Paris, 1855. (La Condition Ouvriere. Part Two.) – 9 – 6.00 – fr Bibl Nationale [360]

SCENES DE MOEURS ELECTORALES : SUIVI DES ANECDOTES POLITIQUES ET ELECTORALES / DeCelles, Alfred Duclos – (Contes canadiens; no 1553). SEM16P20 – 1r – 5 – Can$9.00 – cn Bibl Nat [320]

SCENES ET CROQUIS DE LA VIE OUVRIERE / Maignen, Maurice – Lille: Desclee, de Brouwer, s.d.183p. illus. 2 fiches. (Political Science Collection) – 9 – 6.00 – fr Bibl Nationale [331]
SCENES IN ETHIOPIA : DESIGNED FROM NATURE, WITH DESCRIPTION OF THE PLATES AND EXTRACTS FROM A JOURNAL OF TRAVEL IN THAT COUNTRY / Bernatz, Johann Martin – London: F G Moon, 1852 – us Res Libr [910]
SCENES IN HAWAII, OR, LIFE IN THE SANDWICH ISLANDS / Forsyth Grant, Minnie – Toronto: Hart, 1888. 03168. (Pre-1900 Canadiana) – 9 – cn C.I.H.M. [910]
SCENES IN THE CARIBBEAN SEA : BEING SKETCHES FROM A MISSIONARY'S NOTE-BOOK / Bleby, Henry – London, 1868 – 1r – 1 – us Ross [972]
Scepin, C *see* DE ACIDO VEGETABILI
THE SCEPTICAL CHYMIST / Boyle, R – Ed. 2. M-311. 1680 – 9 – ne IDC [540]
SCEPTICISM: A RETROGRESSIVE MOVEMENT IN THEOLOGY AND PHILOSOPHY / Lindsay, Alexander Wm. C, Earl – London: John Murray, 1861. 1 fiche – 9 – us A.T.L.A. [240]
THE SCEPTIC'S CREED : CAN IT BE REASONABLY HELD? IS IT WORTH THE HOLDING? A REVIEW OF THE POPULAR ASPECTS OF MODERN UNBELIEF / Loraine, Nevison – (Includes bibliographical references) – New York:James Pott, [1884?] – 1mf – 9 – 0-8370-4177-5 – 1985-2177 – us A.T.L.A. [210]
Scerbo, Francesco *see* NUOVO SAGGIO DI CRITICA BIBLICA
Schaack, Henry Cruger Van *see* THE LIFE OF PETER VAN SCHAACK.
Schaaf, Cornelia *see* DIE IDENTIFIZIERUNG UND CHARAKTERISIERUNG CHOLINERGER UND NITREGER ENTERISCHER SCHALTKREISE IM MYENTERISCHEN PLEXUS DES MEERSCHWEINCHENMAGENS
Schaar, E *see* STUDIEN ZU NICOLAES BERCHEM
Schab, M *see* LES INCUNABLES ORIENTAUX... AU COMMENCEMENT DU 16 SIECLE
SCHABBATH: DER MISCHNATRAKTAT SABBATH / Strack, Hermann Leberecht – Leipzig: J.C. Hinrichs, 1890. 1 fiche – 9 – us A.T.L.A. [270]
SCHACH DEM KOENIG : HISTORISCHES LUSTSPIEL IN FUENF AUFZUEGEN / Schaufert, Hippolyt August – Wien: Wallishausser (J. Klemm), 1869 – 1r – 1 – us U.W. Library [820]
Schacht, Hjalvar *see* GENERAL ECONOMIC CONDITIONS IN INDONESIA
Schack, Adolf Friedrich von *see*
– GEDICHTE
– EIN HALBES JAHRHUNDERT
Schackmann, Archi V *see* REDUKTION AROMATISCHER NITROVERBINDUNGEN DURCH VERSCHIEDENE PSEUDOMONAS-SPECIES
Schadaeus, O *see*
– SUMMUM ARGENTORATENSIUM TEMPLUM
– SUMMUM ARGENTORATENSIUM TEMPLUM...
Schade, A *see* THE PHILOSOPHY OF HISTORY
Schade, Heidemarie *see* DAS PROMPTUARIUM EXEMPLORUM DES ANDREAS HONDORFF
Schaeder, Erich *see* DIE BEDEUTUNG DES LEBENDIGEN CHRISTUS FUER DIE RECHTFERTIGUNG NACH PAULUS
Schaefer, Aloys *see*
– DIE BIBLISCHE CHRONOLOGIE
– ERKLAERUNG DER ZWEI BRIEFE AN DIE THESSALONICHER UND DES BRIEFES AN DIE GALATER
Schaefer, Dietrich *see* HANSERECESSE
Schaefer, Ernst *see*
– EL CONSEJO REAL Y SUPREMO DE LAS INDIAS; SU HISTORIA, ORGANIZACION Y LABOR ADMINISTRATIVA HASTA LA TERMINACION DE LA CASA DE AUSTRIA
– LUTHER ALS KIRCHENHISTORIKER
– SEVILLA UND VALLADOLID
Schaefer, Johann Wilhelm *see* LITERATURBILDER
Schaefer, Mary Tonne *see*
– TECHNOLOGY AND COPYRIGHT: SOURCES AND SELECTED MATERIALS
– TECHNOLOGY & COPYRIGHT: RESOURCES ON LAW, PRACTICE, OPINION
Schaefer, Theodor *see* LEITFADEN DER INNEREN MISSION
Schaefer, Thomas *see* AUSGEWAEHLTE WERKE
Schaefer, Wilhelm *see*
– DAS HAUS MIT DEN DREI TUEREN
– EIN MANN NAMENS SCHMITZ
– SPAETLESE ALTER UND NEUER ANEKDOTEN
– WIE ENTSTANDEN MEINE ANEKDOTEN
Schaeffer, Carl *see* DIE BEDEUTUNG DES MUSIKALISCHEN UND AKUSTISCHEN IN E.T.A. HOFFMANNS LITERARISCHEM SCHAFFEN
Schaeffer, F-A, Cl. *see*
– UGARITICA
– UGARITICA 2
– UGARITICA 3
Schaeffer, J C *see*
– ABHANDLUNG VON INSECTEN
– ELEMENTA ENTOMOLOGICA
– FUNGI QUI IN BAVARIA ET PALATINATU
– DER GICHTSCHWAMM MIT GRUENSCHLEIMIGEM HUTE
– ICONES ET DESCRIPTIO FUNGORUM QUORUNDAM SINGULARIUM
– VORLAEUFIGE BEOBACHTUNGEN DER SCHWAEMME UM REGENSBURG
Schaeffer, Kelly R *see* OUTDOOR RECREATION PARTICIPATION OF MARYLAND RESIDENTS IN MARYLAND STATE FORESTS AND PARKS
Schaeffner, Georg *see* DICHTERTUM UND FUEHRERSCHAFT
Schaep, J C *see*
– BLOEM-TUYNTJE
– BLOEM-TUYNTJE, BESTAANDE IN TWEE DEELEN
– BLOEM-TUYNTJE, BESTAENDE IN INDERLIJCKE BEDENCKINGEN, GELIJCKENISSEN, OFTE EXEMPELEN
– BLOEM-TUYNTJE, BESTAENDE IN TWEE DEELEN
Schaepman, Herman Johan Aloysius Maria *see* BOLLAND EN PETRUS
Schaerer, L E *see*
– ENUMERATIO CRITICA LICHENUM EUROPAEORUM
– LICHENUM HELVETICORUM SPICILEGIUM
Schaerf, Theodor *see* DAS GOTTESDIENSTLICHE JAHR DER JUDEN
Schaezler, Constantin, Freiherr von *see* NATUR UND UEBERNATUR
Schaf, Philipp *see*
– DIE SUENDE WIDER DEN HEILIGEN GEIST
– DAS VERHAELTNISS DES JAKOBUS, BRUDER DES HERRN, ZU JAKOBUS ALPHAEI
Schafer, Joseph *see* FOUR WISCONSIN COUNTIES
Schafer, Paul D *see* ASPECTS OF CANADIAN CULTURAL POLICY
Schaff, David Schley *see*
– JOHN HUSS
– PRESBYTERIANISM AND EDUCATION
Schaff, Philip *see*
– CHRIST AND CHRISTIANITY
– CHRIST IN SONG
– CHURCH AND STATE IN THE UNITED STATES
– GERMANY
– THE GOSPEL ACCORDING TO MATTHEW
– THE HARMONY OF THE REFORMED CONFESSIONS AS RELATED TO THE PRESENT STATE OF EVANGELICAL THEOLOGY
– LITERATURE AND POETRY
– THE MORAL CHARACTER OF CHRIST, OR, THE PERFECTION OF CHRIST'S HUMANITY, A PROOF OF HIS DIVINITY
– THE PERSON OF CHRIST
– THE RENAISSANCE; THE REVIVAL OF LEARNING AND ART IN THE FOURTEENTH AND FIFTEENTH CENTURIES
– THE ROMANCE OF M. RENAN AND THE CHRIST OF THE GOSPELS
– SAINT AUGUSTIN, MELANCHTHON, NEANDER
– SYSTEMATIC BENEVOLENCE
– THE TEACHING OF THE TWELVE APOSTLES; DIDACHE TON DODEKA APOSTOLON, OR, THE OLDEST CHURCH MANUAL
– THEOLOGICAL PROPAEDEUTIC
– THE TOLERATION ACT OF 1689
– WHAT IS CHURCH HISTORY?
Schaff, Philip et al *see* EVENING POST ESSAYS IN REVIEW OF "THE BIBLE FOR LEARNERS"
Schaff, Philipp *see* AMERIKA
Schaffarik, P J *see* GESCHICHTE DES SLAWISCHEN SPRACHE UND LITERATUR NACH ALLEN MUNDARTEN
DIE SCHAFFENDEN *see*
– GEWERKSCHAFTS-ZEITUNG
– GEWERKSCHAFTS-ZEITUNG FUER DAS GEBIET SUEDWUERTTEMBERG UND HOHENZOLLERN
Schaffer, Aaron *see* GEORG RUDOLF WECKHERLIN
Schaffer, Bernhard *see* CAN EQUITY BE ORGANIZED?
Schaffhausen. (Canton). Obergericht *see*
– BERICHT DES OBERGERICHTS VON SCHAFFHAUSEN AN DEN GROSSEN RATH DES KANTONS SCHAFFHAUSEN UEBER DIE GESCHAFTSFUHRUNG SAMMTLICHER GERICHTSSTELLEN UND DEN ZUSTAND DES GERICHTSWESENS IN DEM AMTSJAHRE VOM 1. JUNI 1871 BIS UND MIT DEM 31. MAI 1872
– BERICHT DES OBERGERICHTS VON SCHAFFHAUSEN AN DEN GROSSEN RATH DES KANTONS SCHAFFHAUSEN UEBER DIE GESCHAFTSFUHRUNG SAMMTLICHER GERICHTSSTELLEN UND DEN ZUSTAND DES GERICHTSWESENS VOM 1. JUNI 1873 BIS UND MIT DEM 31. MAI 1874
Schaffner, Jakob *see* DIE KLARINETTE
Schaffnit, K *see* EIN BEITRAG ZUR CHRISTOLOGIE DES ALTEN TESTAMENTES
Schalck *see* HISTORY OF SCHUYLKILL COUNTY
Schalkhausser, Georg *see*
– ZU DEN SCHRIFTEN DES MAKARIOS VON MAGNESIA
– ZU DEN SCHRIFTEN DES MAKARIOS VON MAGNESIA (T.U.U. 3-31/4)
Schall, Eduard *see* MOSAISCHES RECHT
Schantz, Richard *see* DER SINNLICHE GEHALT DER WAHRNEHMUNG
Schanz, Paul *see* DIE COMPOSITION DES MATTHAEUS-EVANGELIUMS VON PAUL SCHANZ
Schanze, Wolfgang *see* DIE RELIGION GOETHES UND DAS EVANGELIUM
Schanzenbach, Otto *see* FRANZOESISCHE EINFLUESSE BEI SCHILLER
Schapera, I *see* WESTERN CIVILIZATION AND THE NATIVES OF SOUTH AFRICA
Schapiro, L B *see* LENIN: THE MAN, THE THEORIST, THE LEADER
Scharf, George *see*
– DESCRIPTION OF THE WILTON HOUSE DIPTYCH, CONTAINING A CONTEMPORARY PORTRAIT OF KING RICHARD THE SECOND
– NOTEBOOKS
Scharf, Thomas J *see*
– HISTORY OF BALTIMORE CITY AND COUNTY
– HISTORY OF DELAWARE 1609-1888
– HISTORY OF ST LOUIS CITY AND COUNTY
Scharfe, Ernst *see* DIE PETRINISCHE STROEMUNG DER NEUTESTAMENTLICHEN LITERATUR
Scharl, E *see* RECAPITULATIO MUNDI
Scharnagl, Anton *see* DAS FEIERLICHE GELUEBDE ALS EHEHINDERNIS
Scharnhorst, Gerhard Johann David von *see*
– MILITAERISCHE SCHRIFTEN
– PAPERS
Scharnhorst, R L *see* THE EFFECTS OF HIGH AND LOW INTENSITY ECCENTRIC EXERCISE ON MUSCLE SORENESS AND STRENGTH
Scharrer, Eduard *see* ADOLF WILBRANDT ALS DRAMATIKER
Scharwenka, X *see* WALZER FUR DAS PIANOFORTE ZU VIER HAENDEN...OP. 44
SCHASTLIVYI DOMIK / Khodasevich, V – Vtoraia kniga stichov. M. 1914. BR-699 – 8 – ne IDC [460]
Schaten, N S J *see*
– ANNALES PADERBORNENSES
– HISTORIA WESTFALIA
Schatt, P *see* DEVELOPPEMENT ET CROISSANCE EMBRYONNAIRE DE L'OURSIN INCUBANT ABATUS CORDATUS (ECHINOIDEA: SPATANGOIDA)
SCHATZ (ALBERT) COLLECTION OF MANUSCRIPT MATERIALS – 1 – $2599.00 – us L of C Photodup [780]
SCHATZ (ALBERT) COLLECTION OF OPERA LIBRETTOS – 1 – $5612.00 – us L of C Photodup [780]
DER SCHATZ AUF GOTLAND : EINE STOERTEBEKER-ERZAEHLUNG / Uhlenbusch, Hugo Paul – Bayreuth: Der Gauverlag, 1943 – 1r – 1 – us U.W. Library [430]
Schatz, E *see* EXOTISCHE SCHMTTERLINGE
Schatz H *see* CATALOGUE OF KNOWN SPECIES OF ACARI FROM THE GALAPAGOS ISLANDS. (ECUADOR, PACIFIC OCEAN)
Schatz, Michael *see* INVARIANTE KLASSIFIZIERUNG ELEKTRONENMIKROSKOPISCHER AUFNAHMEN VON EISEINGEBETTETEN BIOLOGISCHEN MAKROMOLEKUELEN
DER SCHATZ VON ALISEDA / Melida, Jose Ramon – Berlin, 1928 – 1 – sp Bibl Santa Ana [946]
DIE SCHATZHOEHLE "ME'ARATH GAZZE" / ed by Bezold, C – Lz., 1883-1888 – 7mf – 8 – ne Slangenburg [200]
SCHAUBUEHNE – Berlin. v. 1, no. 1-v. 29, no. 10. Sept 7 1905-Mar 7 1933. Incomplete – 1 – us NY Public [790]
SCHAUBUEHNE / Dahn, Felix – Leipzig: Breitkopf & Haertel. 2v. 1898-99 – 1 – us U.W. Library [820]
Schauenburg, L *see* DIE TAEUFERBEWEGUNG IN DER GRAFSCHAFT OLDENBURG-DELMENHORST UND DER HERRSCHAFT JEVER ZUR ZEIT DER REFORMATION
Schauer, J C *see* MONOGRAPHIA MYRTACEARUM XEROCARPICARUM. SECTIO I. CHAMAELAUCIERUM HUCUSQUE COGNITARUM GENERA ET SPECIES ILLUSTRANS
Schaufert, Hippolyt August *see*
– SCHACH DEM KOENIG
– VATER BRAHM
Schauffler, Theodor *see* GOETHE'S LEBEN, LEISTEN UND LEIDEN
Schaufuss, C *see* ENTOMOLOGISCHE MITTEILUNGEN
Schaukal, Richard von *see*
– DIONYS-BACSI
– E.T.A. HOFFMANN
– KRIEGSLIEDER AUS OESTERREICH
SCHAUM : DICHTUNGEN / Jordan, Wilhelm – Leipzig: E Keil, 1846 – 1r – 1 – us U.W. Library [810]
Schaum, H R *see*
– ANALECTA ENTOMOLOGICA
– CATALOGUS COLEOPTERORUM EUROPAE
Schaumann, Ruth *see*
– DER BLUEHENDE STAB
– DER KRIPPENWEG
– LORENZ UND ELISABETH
Schaumann, Ursula *see* ZUR GESCHICHTE DER ERZAEHLENDEN SCHAEFERDICHTUNG IN DEUTSCHLAND
Schaumberger, Heinrich *see*
– IM HIRTENHAUS
– SAEMTLICHE WERKE MIT BIOGRAPHIE, EINLEITUNGEN UND ILLUSTRATIONEN, DARUNTER ORIGINALZEICHNUNGEN SCHAUMBERGERS
SCHAUMBURG-LIPPISCHE LANDESZEITUNG – Bueckeburg, 1958-60 – 1 – Inquire at Mikrofilmarchiv for details – gw Misc Inst [072]
Schaus, W *see* ON A COLLECTION OF SIERRA LEONE LEPIDOPTERA
SCHAUSPIELE : DICHTUNGEN AUS DEM NACHLASS / Wolff, Julius – Leipzig: P List, c1913 – 1 – us U.W. Library [810]
SCHAUSPIELE; DICHTUNGEN AUS DEM NACHLASS / Wolff, Julius – Leipzig: P List, c1913 – 1 – us U.W. Library [820]
Schechter, Solomon *see*
– SOME ASPECTS OF RABBINIC THEOLOGY
– STUDIES IN JUDAISM: SECOND SERIES
– ZIONISM: A STATEMENT
Schedel, H *see* LIBER CRONICARUM CUM FIGURIS ET YMAGINIBUS AB INICIO MUNDI
SCHEDULAE CRITICAE DE LICHENIBUS EXSICCATIS SUECIAE / Fries, E M – Londini Gothorum, etc. 1824-33. B-482 2 – 8 – ne IDC [580]
SCHEDULE OF ACCOUNTS RESPECTING THE PUBLIC INCOME AND EXPENDITURE OF THE PROVINCE OF LOWER-CANADA,... – [Quebec ?: s.n., 1828 ?]. SEM105P1404 – 3mf – 9 – Can$6.75 – cn Bibl Nat [336]
SCHEDULES ENUMERATING UNION VETERANS AND WIDOWS OF UNION VETERANS OF THE CIVIL WAR, 1890 / U. S. Veterans Administration – 118 rolls. M123 – 1 – us Nat'l Archives [324]
SCHEDULES OF THE COLORADO STATE CENSUS OF 1885 / U.S. Bureau of the Census – 8 rolls.M158. Printed guide – 1 – us Nat'l Archives [310]
SCHEDULES OF THE FLORIDA STATE CENSUS OF 1885 / U.S. Bureau of the Census – 13 rolls. M845 – 1 – us Nat'l Archives [310]
SCHEDULES OF THE NEBRASKA STATE CENSUS OF 1885 / U.S. Bureau of the Census – 56 rolls. M352. Printed guide – 1 – us Nat'l Archives [310]
SCHEDULES OF THE NEW MEXICO TERRITORY CENSUS OF 1885 / U.S. Bureau of the Census – 6 rolls.M846 – 1 – us Nat'l Archives [310]
Scheeben, Matthias Joseph *see* SCHULTE UND DOELLINGER GEGEN DAS CONCIL
Scheel, Otto *see*
– DIE ANSCHAUUNG AUGUSTINS UEBER CHRISTI PERSON UND WERK
– DAENEMARK UND WIR
Scheer, Brigitte *see* UNTERSUCHUNGEN ZU EINER TYPIK DES SELBST IN DER ERFAHRUNG
Scheerbart, Paul *see* KOMETENTANZ

Schefer, C *see*
- CHRESTOMATHIE PERSANE
- RECUEIL D'ITINERAIRES ET DE VOYAGES DANS L'ASIE CENTRALE ET L'EXTREME-ORIENT
- RELATION DE L'AMBASSADE AU KHAREZM DE RIZA QOULY KHAN
- SEFER NAMEH, RELATION DU VOYAGE EN SYRIE

Schefer, Leopold *see* LAIENBREVIER

SCHEFFEL : EIN DICHTERLEBEN / Proelss, Johannes Moritz – Stuttgart: A Bonz, 1902 – 1r – 1 – us U.W. Library [430]

SCHEFFEL IN ITALIEN : BRIEFE INS ELTERNHAUS, 1852-1853 / Scheffel, Joseph Viktor von; ed by Zentner, Wilhelm – (Includes index) – Karlsruhe: [s.n.], 1929 – 1r – 1 – us U.W. Library [920]

Scheffel, Joseph Viktor von *see*
- BERGPSALMEN
- BRIEFWECHSEL ZWISCHEN JOSEPH VICTOR VON SCHEFFEL UND PAUL HEYSE
- EKKEHARD
- FRAU AVENTIURE
- GAUDEAMUS!
- HUGIDEO
- J.V. VON SCHEFFELS GESAMMELTE WERKE...MIT EINER BIOGRAPHISCHEN EINLEITUNG VON JOHANNES PROELSS
- SCHEFFEL IN ITALIEN
- DER TROMPETER VON SAEKKINGEN
- THE TRUMPETER
- WERKE

Scheffer, Thassilo von *see* DIE KYPRIEN

Scheffer-Boichorst, Paul *see* AUS DANTES VERBANNUNG

Scheibe, J A *see* DER CRITISCHE MUSICUS

Scheibe, Johann Adolph *see*
- EINE ABHANDLUNG VON DEN MUSICALISCHEN INTERVALLEN UND GESCHLECHTEN..
- DER CRITISCHE MUSICUS
- DER CRITISCHE MUSICUS, HERAUSGEGEBEN VON JOHANN ADOLPH SCHEIBE
- CRITISCHER MUSIKUS
- CRITISCHER MUSIKUS: NEUE, VERMEHRTE UND VERBESSERTE AUFLAGE
- JOHANN ADOLPH SCHEIBENS, CRITISCHER MUSIKUS. NEUE, VERMEHRTE UND VERBESSERTE AUFLAGE
- UEBER DIE MUSIKALISCHE COMPOSITION

Scheibe, Max *see*
- DIE BEDEUTUNG DER WERTURTEILE FUER DAS RELIGIOESE ERKENNEN
- CALVINS PRAEDESTINATIONSLEHRE

Scheiding, Oliver *see* DER AMERIKANISCHE ROMAN IM SPANISCHEN BUERGERKRIEG

Schein, J H *see* CANTIONAL, ODER GESANGBUCH AUGSPURGISCHER CONFESSION. IN WELCHEM DES HERRN D. MARTINI LUTHERI UND ANDERER FROMMEN CHRISTAN...

Scheindlin, A E *see* THERMAL PHYSICS REVIEWS

SCHEINWERFER – Bremen, 1928 n1 – 1 – Inquire at Mikrofilmarchiv for details – gw Misc Inst [072]

Scheips, Paul J *see* THE ROLE OF THE ARMY IN THE OXFORD, MISSISSIPPI, INCIDENT, 1962-1963

Scheips, Paul Joseph *see* ALBERT JAMES MYER, FOUNDER OF THE ARMY SIGNAL CORPS: A BIOGRAPHICAL STUDY

DAS SCHEITERN DES SUBJEKTS BEI SAMUEL BECKETT / Renschler, Ulrich – 1993 – 1mf – 9 – DM60.00 – 3-89349-770-6 – gw Hänsel [420]

Schekel, Daniel *see* LUTHER UND SEINE KAMPFGENOSSEN

Scheler, Elke Verena Ulrike *see* KOMMUNIKATIONSSTOERUNGEN BEI KINDERN MIT SYNDROMEN

Schell, Herman *see*
- CHRISTUS
- DIE NEUE ZEIT UND DER ALTE GLAUBE

Schellberg, Wilhelm *see*
- JOSEF VON GOERRES

Schellenberg, J R *see* GENRES DES MOUCHES DIPTERES REPRESENTES EN 42 PLANCHES, PROJETTEES ET DESSINEES

Schellenberg, Theodore R *see*
- ABRAHAM SCHELLENBERG PAPERS
- PAPERS

SCHELLENS COLLECTION. SAN MATEO COUNTY HISTORICAL COLLECTION : HISTORICAL CALIFORNIA CLIPPING COLLECTION FOR REDWOOD CITY SAN MATEO COUNTY COMMUNITIES / Shellens, Richard – 34r – 1 – $1,700.00 – B40097 – us Library Micro [978]

Schelling, Friedrich Wilhelm Joseph *see* JAHRBUECHER DER MEDIZIN ALS WISSENSCHAFT

Schelling, Karoline Michaelis *see* CAROLINE UND DOROTHEA SCHLEGEL IN BRIEFEN

SCHELLING UND HEGEL. ODER DIE NEUESTE PHILOSOPHIE IM VERNICHTUNGSKRIEGE MIT SICH SELBST BEGRIFFEN : UEBER DAS VERHAELTNISS DER PHILOSOPHIE ZUM GESUNDEN MENSCHENVERSTANDE... / Krug, Wilhelm Traugott; ed by Roser, Andreas – 1835 repr 1994 – 1mf – 9 – DM60.00 – 3-89349-858-3 – gw Hänsel [190]

Schem, Alexander J *see* DEUTSCH-AMERIKANISCHES CONVERSATIONS-LEXICON

THE SCHEME OF CHRISTIAN AND PHILOSOPHICAL NECESSITY ASSERTED, IN OPPOSITION TO MR. JOHN WESLEY'S TRACT ON THAT SUBJECT;... / Toplady, Augustus Montague – London, 1775 – 3mf – 9 – MP-498/1 – ne IDC [240]

Schenck, Ferdinand Schureman *see* THE TEN COMMANDMENTS AND THE LORD'S PRAYER

Schenck, John L *see* HISTORY OF IONIA AND MONTCALM COUNTIES

Schenck, Leland H *see* SCRAPBOOK

Schenck, William E *see* NEW YORK LIQUOR TAX LAW REPORTS

Schenck, William Edward *see* NEARING HOME

Schenckendorff, E von *see* ZUR VERSOEHNUNG DES BESITZES UND DER ARBEIT

Schenk, A *see* FOSSILE FLORA DER GRENZSCHICHTEN DES KEUPERS UND LIAS FRANKENS

Schenk, H *see* BEITRAEGE ZUR BIOLOGIE UND ANATOMIE DER LIANEN, IM BESONDEREN DER IN BRASILIEN EINHEIMISCHEN ARTEN

Schenk, J A von *see* PLANTARUM SPECIES, QUAS IN INTENERE PER AEGYPTYM, ARABIAM ET SYRIAM

Schenk, L *see* "WENN DEIN ICH DENK". LISD FUER EINE SINGSTIMME MIT BEGLEITUNG DES PIANO

Schenk von Stauffenberg, Alexander, Graf *see* DER TOD DES MEISTERS

Schenk, Walter *see* KAMPFJUGEND

Schenke, H M *see* DIE BERLINER HANDSCHRIFT DER SAHIDISCHEN APOSTELGESCHICHTE (T.U.U. 5-109)

Schenkel, Daniel *see*
- DIE BILDUNG DER EVANG. THEOLOGEN FUER DEN PRAKTISCHEN KIRCHENDIENST
- DIE BRIEFE AN DIE EPHESER, PHILIPPER, KOLOSSER
- CHARAKTERBILD JESU
- DAS CHRISTUSBILD DER APOSTEL UND DER NACHAPOSTOLISCHEN ZEIT
- DER DEUTSCHE PROTESTANTENVEREIN
- FRIEDRICH SCHLEIERMACHER
- DIE KIRCHLICHE FRAGE UND IHRE PROTESTANTISCHE LOESUNG
- DIE PROTESTANTISCHE FREIHEIT IN IHREM GEGENWAERTIGEN KAMPFE MIT DER KIRCHLICHEN REAKTION
- DIE REFORMATOREN UND DIE REFORMATION
- A SKETCH OF THE CHARACTER OF JESUS: A BIBLICAL ESSAY
- DER UNIONSBERUF DES EVANGELISCHEN PROTESTANTISMUS
- DAS WESEN DES PROTESTANTISMUS

SCHENKER, HEINRICH (DIARY) – Riverside, CA. 1896-1929 – 3r – 1 – $150.00 – R04099 – us Library Micro [920]

Schenkl, C *see* D. MAGNI AUSONII OPUSCULA (MGH 1: 5.BD. 2.TEIL)

Schenkling *see* CATALOGUS COLEOPTERORUM

Schenkling, S *see*
- COLEOPTERORUM CATALOGUS
- ENTOMOLOGISCHE MITTEILUNGEN

SCHENUTE VON ATRIPE UND DIE ENTSTEHUNG DES NATIONAL AEGYPTISCHEN CHRISTENTUMS / Leipoldt, Johannes – Leipzig: J.C. Hinrichs, 1903. (Texte und Unterschungen zur Geschichte der altchristlichen Literatur; der ganzen Reihe 25. Bd., Heft 4. n.F., 10. Bd., Heft 1) – 1mf – us A.T.L.A. [240]

SCHENUTE VON ATRIPE UND DIE ENTSTEHUNG DES NATIONAL AEGYPTISCHEN CHRISTENTUMS (T.U.U. 2-25/1) / Leipoldt, Johannes – Leipzig, 1903 – 4mf – 9 – ne Slangenburg [240]

Schenzinger, Karl Aloys *see* DER HITLERJUNGE QUEX

Scherer, Edmond Henri Adolphe *see* MELANGES DE CRITIQUE RELIGIEUSE

Scherer, F E *see* PUXBAUM

Scherer, Jean *see*
- LE COMMENTAIRE D'ORIGENE SUR ROM. 3, 5-V, 7 D'APRES LES EXTRAITS DU PAPYRUS NO 88748 DU MUSEE DU CAIRE
- ENTRETIEN D'ORIGENE AVEC HERACLIDE ET LES EVEQUES SES COLLEGUES SUR LE PERE, LE FILS ET L'AME

Scherer, Wilhelm *see*
- DEUTSCHE STUDIEN
- GESCHICHTE DER DEUTSCHEN LITERATUR
- GESCHICHTE DER DEUTSCHEN LITTERATUR
- A HISTORY OF GERMAN LITERATURE
- KLEINE SCHRIFTEN
- KLEMENS VON ALEXANDRIEN UND SEINE ERKENNTNISPRINZIPIEN

Scherff, W von *see* ETUDES SUR LA NOUVELLE TACTIQUE DE L'INFANTERIE

Scherg, Theodor Joseph *see* DAS SCHULWESEN UNTER KARL THEODOR VON DALBERG BESONDERS IM FUERSTENTUM ASCHAFFENBURG 1803-1813 UND IM GROSSHERZOGTUM FRANKFURT 1810-1813

Schermann, Theodor *see*
- DIE GESCHICHTE DER DOGMATISCHEN FLORILEGIEN VOM 5.-8. JAHRHUNDERT (T.U.U. 2-28/1)
- GRIECHISCHE ZAUBERPAPYRI UND DAS GEMEINDE- UND DANKGEBET IM 1. KLEMENSBRIEFE (T.U.U. 3-34/2B)
- DER LITURGISCHE PAPYRUS VON DER-BALYZEH
- PROPHETEN- UND APOSTELLEGENDEN
- PROPHETEN- UND APOSTELLEGENDEN (T.U.U.3-31-/3)

Schermerhorn, Holden Bovee *see* ESSENTIALS TO THE PRINCIPAL ACTIONS IN TORT AT COMMON LAW

Scherpe, Klaus Ruediger *see* POESIE DER DEMOKRATIE

Scherr, Johannes *see* MISCHMASCH

Scherzer, F *see* RECUEIL D'ITINERAIRES ET DE VOYAGES DANS L'ASIE CENTRALE ET L'EXTREME-ORIENT

SCHERZGEDICHTE / Blumenthal, Oskar – Leipzig: P Reclam, c1914 – 1 – us U.W. Library [870]

Scheschet ben Isaac, Gerundi *see* KOMMENTAR ZU DEN PROVERBIEN. THEIL I

SCHETOVODSTVO PROIZVODITEL'NO-TRUDOVYKH ARTELEI V SVIAZI S OSNOVAMI OBSHCHEGO SCHETOVODSTVA / Bolotov, P A – Ed.2. L., 1925 – 2mf – 9 – COR-413/1 – ne IDC [334]

Scheuchenzeuber, H Joseph *see* MECHANICAL AND PHYSIOLOGICAL DIFFERENCES BETWEEN RUNNING AND WALKING AT VARIOUS VELOCITIES

Scheuchenzuber, H Joseph *see*
- THE RELATIONSHIP BETWEEN THE TIMING OF ARM MOVEMENT AND THE FORCE OF LANDING
- RUNNING ECONOMY AND KINEMATIC DIFFERENCES AMONG RUNNING WITH THE FOOT SHOD, WITH THE FOOT BARE, AND WITH THE BARE FOOT EQUATED FOR WEIGHT

Scheuer, Oskar Franz *see* HEINRICH HEINE ALS STUDENT

Scheulh, Heinrich *see* PAPERS

Scheve, Donald *see* FRANKLIN D. ROOSEVELT AND FOREIGN AFFAIRS

Scheven, Katharina *see* DER ABOLITIONIST, 1. 1902 – 32. 1933 (HQ 28)

Schewe, Guenter *see* STUDIEN ZUM IRRTUM UEBER DIE UNRECHTMASSIGKEIT DES VERHALTENS

Scheyb, F C de *see* PEUTINGERIANA TABULA ITINERARIA 1753

Schian, Martin *see*
- DIE MODERNE GEMEINSCHAFTSBEWEGUNG
- ORTHODOXIE UND PIETISMUS IM KAMPF UM DIE PREDIGT

Schiaparelli, Giovani Virginio *see*
- ASTRONOMY IN THE OLD TESTAMENT
- DIE HOMOCENTRISCHEN SPHAEREN DES EXODUS DES KALLIPPUS UND DES ARISTOTELES

SCHICHT UND SCHACHT : EINE HALDENSINFONIE / Gottschalk, Hanns – Muenchen: Zentralverlag der NSDAP, Eher, 1937 – 1r – 1 – us U.W. Library [810]

Schickele, Rene *see*
- HIMMLISCHE LANDSCHAFT
- MEIN HERZ, MEIN LAND

Schickhard, Johann Christian *see* 6 SONATES A UNE FLUTE TRAVERSIERE, UN HAUTBOIS OU VIOLON ET BASSE CONTINUE...20ME OUVRAGE, LIVRE SECOND

Schickhelm, Franz *see* DIE METHODE DES ANSCHAUUNGS-UNTERRICHTS AUF PSYCHOLOGISCHER GRUNDLAGE DURCHGEFUHRT AN DER BOTANIK

SCHICKSAL : DREI ERZAEHLUNGEN / Leutelt, Gustav – Karlsbad: A Kraft, 1944 – 1r – 1 – us U.W. Library [830]

DAS SCHICKSAL DER WESTFAELISCHEN DOMAENENKAEUFER IN KURHESSEN / Kuhring, Otto – Kassel, 1913 – xi/145p – 9 – DM48.00 – 3-89349-042-6 – gw Hänsel [943]

DAS SCHICKSAL EINER FRAU : IN GEDICHTEN – Berlin: E Fleischel, 1913 – 1r – 1 – us U.W. Library [810]

SCHICKSAL EINER GOETHESCHRIFT : DRUCKGESCHICHTLICHE FUNDE ZUR FARBENLEHRE / Schmid, Guenther – Burg Giebichenstein: Werkstaetten der Stadt Halle, 1937 – 1r – 1 – us U.W. Library [430]

SCHICKSAL UND LIEBE DES NIKLAS VON CUES : ROMAN / Kuenkel, Hans – Leipzig: P Reclam, 1936 – 1r – 1 – us U.W. Library [830]

SCHICKSALSJAHRE DER UNGARNDEUTSCHEN : DIE UNGARISCHE WENDUNG / Weidlein, Johann – (Includes bibliographical references) – Wuerzburg: Holzner-Verlag, 1957 – 10r – 1 – us U.W. Library [947]

Schicler, Fernand de, Baron *see* LES EGLISES DU REFUGE EN ANGLETERRE

Schiefelbein, Ernesto *see* REDEFINING BASIC EDUCATION FOR LATIN AMERICA

Schieffelin, Samuel Bradhurst *see*
- CHILDREN OF GOD AND UNION WITH CHRIST
- THE FOUNDATIONS OF HISTORY

Schiefferens, Matthias *see* QUELLENMAESSIGE DARLEGUNG DER LEHRE VON DER WILLENSFREIHEIT BEI THOMAS VON AQUIN

Schiefner, A *see*
- BARON GERHARD VON MAYDELL'S TUNGUSISCHE SPRACHPROBEN
- GRUNDZUEGE EINER TUNGUSISCHEN SPRACHLEHRE NEBST KURZEM WOERTERVERZEICHNISS
- REISEBERICHTE UND BRIEFE AUS DEN JAHREN 1845-1849
- VERSUCH EINER BURJAETISCHEN SPRACHLEHRE NEBST KURZEM WOERTERVERZEICHNISS

Schieker-Ebe, Sofie *see* WAS TUN, SIBYLLE

Schier, Alfred *see* DIE LIEBE IN DER FRUEHROMANTIK MIT BESONDERER BERUECKSICHTIGUNG DES ROMANS

Schiern, Frederik Eginhard Amadeus *see* LIFE OF JAMES HEPBURN, EARL OF BOTHWELL

DIE SCHIFFAHRT – Berlin, may 1935 – 1 – Inquire at Mikrofilmarchiv for details – gw Misc Inst [072]

SCHIFFE UND STERNE / Schnabel, Ernst – (Autobiographical narratives) – Hamburg: H Govert, c1943 – 1r – 1 – us U.W. Library [430]

Schiffer, Sinai *see* DAS BUCH KOHELET...TALMUD UND MIDRASCH UND DER JUEDISCHEN ERKLAERER DES MITTELALTERS

Schiffner, K *see* WILHELM JORDAN

Schiffner, V *see*
- CONSPECTUS HEPATICARUM ARCHIPELAGI INDICI
- DIE HEPATICAE DER FLORA VON BUITENZORG...
- KRITISCHE BEMERKUNGEN UEBER DIE EUROPAEISCHEN LEBERMOOSE MIT BEZUG AUF DIE EXEMPLARE DES EXSICCATENWERKES HEPATICAE EUROPAE EXSICCATAE
- MUSCI BORNMULLERIANA; BRYOPHTEN AUS IRAN

DER SCHILD : ZEITSCHRIFT DES REICHSBUNDES JUEDISCHER FRONTSOLDATEN – Berlin, oct 1922-23 (incomplete), 1925-nov 4 1938 (incomplete) – 2r – 1 – Inquire at Mikrofilmarchiv for details – gw Misc Inst [943]

DER SCHILD – Zeitschrift des Reichsbundes juedischer Frontsoldaten. Berlin. v1-17. 1921-38. Lacking misc. issues. B345 (Leo Baeck Institute. German-Jewish Periodicals, Pt 1) – 2r – 9 – $135.00 – us UPA [270]

HET SCHILDER-BOECK / Mander, Carel van – O 358. 1618 – 9 – ne IDC [920]

DAS SCHILDERHAUS VON FROZZELBORN : ERGOETZLICHE GESCHICHTEN / Schworm, Karl – 4. Aufl. Muenchen: F Eher, 1944 – 1r – 1 – us U.W. Library [430]

SCHILDKROETE, FROSCH UND EIDECHSE IN DER GRIECHISCHEN UND ROEMISCHEN ANTIKE / Roer, Hans Henning – 1995 – 4mf – 9 – DM112.00 – 3-8267-2215-9 – gw Hänsel [930]
Schill, Andreas *see* DIE CONSTITUTION UNIGENITUS
Schill, Jeremias J A *see* OVER DE DRUKPRS IN NEDERLANDSCH-INDIE
SCHILLER : ANEKDOTEN ERZAEHLT VON SEINEN ZEITGENOSSEN / Goetz, Wolfgang – Berlin, Wien: Frundsberg-Verlag, c1943 – 1r – 1 – us U.W. Library [430]
SCHILLER : EINE EINFUEHRUNG IN LEBEN UND WERK / Wiese, Benno von – Stuttgart: Reclam, c1955 – 1r – 1 – us U.W. Library [920]
SCHILLER : EIN LEBENSBILD FUER DEUTSCHE ARBEITER / Mehring, Franz – Berlin: Gebrueder Weiss, [1948?] – 1r – 1 – us U.W. Library [920]
SCHILLER : SEIN LEBEN UND SEINE WERKE / Berger, Karl – (Includes bibliographical references and index) – 13. Aufl. Muenchen: C H Beck, 1921 – 1r – 1 – us U.W. Library [920]
SCHILLER / Sime, James – Philadelphia: J B Lippincott, [1882?] – 1r – 1 – us U.W. Library [920]
SCHILLER ALS DRAMATISCHER DICHTER : IM URTEIL VON OTTO LUDWIG / Sevenig, N – Diekirch: J Schroell, 1905 – 1r – 1 – us U.W. Library [430]
SCHILLER ALS HERAUSGEBER DER RHEINISCHEN THALIA, THALIA, UND NEUEN THALIA, UND SEIN MITARBEITER / Ferresheim, Fritz – (Includes bibliographical references) – Stuttgart: Metzler, 1914 – 1 – us U.W. Library [430]
SCHILLER ALS HISTORIKER / Janssen, Johannes – (Includes bibliographical references) – Freiburg im Breisgau: Herder'sche Verlagshandlung, 1863 – 1r – 1 – us U.W. Library [943]
SCHILLER ALS KRITIKER / Pietsch, Otto – Koenigsberg i.Pr.: E Rautenberg, 1898 – 1 – us U.W. Library [430]
SCHILLER ALS POLITISCHER DICHTER. SHAKESPEARE UND DAS DEUTSCHE DRAMA : ZWEI AUFSAETZE ZUR DEUTSCHEN LITERATURGESCHICHTE / Nussberger, Max – (Includes bibliographical references) – Zuerich: Rascher, 1917 – 1r – 1 – us U.W. Library [410]
SCHILLER – ANEKDOTEN ERZAEHLT VON SEINEN ZEITGENOSSEN / Goetz, Wolfgang – Berlin, Wien, 1943 – 2mf – DM62.00 – 3-8267-3013-5 – gw Hänsel [430]
Schiller, Charlotte *see* CHARLOTTE VON SCHILLER UND IHRE FREUNDE
SCHILLER DEM DEUTSCHEN VOLKE DARGESTELLT / Wychgram, Jakob – 3. durchges. und verm. Aufl. Bielefeld: Velhagen & Klasing, 1898 – 1 – us U.W. Library [920]
SCHILLER DER DICHTER DER GESCHICHTE : EINE AUSLEGUNG DES WALLENSTEIN / Vowinckel, Hans August – Berlin: Junker und Duennhaupt, 1938 – 1 – us U.W. Library [430]
SCHILLER, EINE BIOGRAPHIE IN BILDERN : FESTSCHRIFT ZUR ERINNERUNG AN DIE 100. WIEDERKEHR SEINES TODESTAGES AM 9. MAI 1905: MIT 208 ABBILDUNGEN UND EINEM TITELBILDE / Koennecke, Gustav – 2., unveraend. Aufl. Marburg: N G Elwertsche, 1905 – 1 – us U.W. Library [430]
Schiller, Friedrich von *see*
- DEMETRIUS
- DON CARLOS
- ESSAYS AESTHETICAL AND PHILOSOPHICAL
- DAS FRAGMENT DES DEMETRIUS
- DER GEISTERSEHER
- HISTORY OF THE THIRTY YEARS' WAR, COMPLETE: HISTORY OF THE REVOLT OF THE NETHERLANDS, TO THE CONFEDERACY OF THE GUEUX
- DIE HOREN
- ICH HABE MICH RASIEREN LASSEN
- DAS LIED VON DER GLOCKE
- THE MAID OF ORLEANS, TRANSLATED FROM THE GERMAN BY ANNA SWANWICK
- MARIA STUART
- NEUE THALIA
- THE POEMS AND BALLADS OF SCHILLER
- THE POEMS OF SCHILLER
- DIE RAEUBER
- SCHILLERS BALLADEN
- SCHILLERS LIED VON DER GLOCKE
- SCHILLERS SAEMMTLICHE WERKE
- SCHILLERS SAEMTLICHE WERKE
- SCHILLERS WERKE
- SCHILLER'S WORKS
- THALIA
- VERNUNFT UND SCHOENHEIT
- WALLENSTEIN

SCHILLER IM DICHTERMUND / Saul, D – Stuttgart: F Frommann, 1896 – 1r – 1 – us U.W. Library [430]
Schiller, Nina Glick *see* IDENTITIES
SCHILLER UND BEETHOVEN : ZUR WESENSGESTALT DEUTSCHER KLASSIK: EIN VORTRAG / Buchwald, Reinhard – Waibstadt, Heidelberg: Kemper, c1946 – 1r – 1 – us U.W. Library [410]
SCHILLER UND DIE BIBEL / Schlurick, Johannes – (Includes bibliographical references) – Leipzig: A Edelmann, 1895 – 1r – 1 – us U.W. Library [430]
SCHILLER UND GOETHE IN DEN XENIEN / Thiemann, Georg – [S.l.: s.n.] Born-Leipzig: Buchdruckerei R Noske, 1909 – 1r – 1 – us U.W. Library [430]
SCHILLER-BIBLIOTHEK : VERZEICHNISS DERJENIGEN DRUCKE, WELCHE DIE GRUNDLAGE DES TEXTES DER SCHILLER'SCHEN WERKE BILDEN / Troemel, Paul Friedrich – Leipzig: F A Brockhaus, 1865 – 1 – us U.W. Library [430]
SCHILLER-PROBLEME / Rubinstein, Susanna – Leipzig: A Edelmann, 1908 – 1r – 1 – us U.W. Library [430]
SCHILLERS BALLADEN / Schiller, Friedrich von; ed by Ey, Adolf – Leipzig: P Reclam, [18–?] – 1 – us U.W. Library [810]
SCHILLERS BEZIEHUNGEN ZUR MEDIZIN / Neuburger, Max – (Includes bibliographical references) – Wien, Leipzig: W Braumueller, 1905 – 1r – 1 – us U.W. Library [430]
SCHILLERS BRIEFE / ed by Jonas, Fritz – (Includes bibliographical references and indexes) – Stuttgart: Deutsche Verlags-Anstalt, [1892-1896?] – 2r – 1 – us U.W. Library [920]
SCHILLER'S BRIEFWECHSEL MIT SEINER SCHWESTER CHRISTOPHINE UND SEINEM SCHWAGER REINWALD / ed by Maltzahn, Wendelin von – (Includes bibliographical references and index) – Leipzig: Veit, 1875 – 1 – us U.W. Library [920]
SCHILLERS DEMETRIUS : DAS FRAGMENT: DAZU EIN NACHSPIEL MIT PROLOG UND RHAPSODISCHEM, VON VIER LEBENDEN BILDERN BEGLEITETEN EPILOG / Greif, Martin – Leipzig: C F Amelang, 1902 – 1r – 1 – us U.W. Library [430]
SCHILLERS DEMETRIUS : NACH SEINEM SZENISCHEN AUFBAU UND SEINEM TRAGISCHEN GEHALT / Mielke, Adolf – (Includes bibliographical references) – Dortmund: F W Ruhfus, 1906 – 1r – 1 – us U.W. Library [430]
SCHILLER'S DRAMAS AND POEMS IN ENGLAND / Rea, Thomas – (Includes bibliographical references and index) – London: T Fisher Unwin, 1906 – 1r – 1 – us U.W. Library [430]
SCHILLERS EINFLUSS AUF DIE JUGENDDRAMEN HEBBELS : DIE JUNGFRAU VON ORLEANS UND HEBBELS JUDITH; EINE STUDIE UEBER DAS DRAMA / Eckelmann, Ernst Otto – (Includes bibliographical references) – Heidelberg: [s.n.], 1906 – 1r – 1 – us U.W. Library [430]
SCHILLERS EINFLUSS AUF THEODOR KOERNER : EIN BEITRAG ZUR LITTERATURGESCHICHTE / Reinhard, Gustav Edgar – Strassburg: K J Truebner, 1899 – 1r – 1 – us U.W. Library [430]
SCHILLERS FLUCHT / Streicher, Andreas – (Includes bibliographical references) – Berlin: Pan-Verlag, [1905?] – 1 – us U.W. Library [920]
SCHILLERS FLUCHT AUS STUTTGART : SPIEL IN EINEM AKT UND DREI BILDERN ZUR SCHILLERFEIER 1905 / Vetter, Ferdinand – Zuerich: E Rascher, Meyer & Zeller, 1905 – 1r – 1 – us U.W. Library [820]
SCHILLERS FRAGMENT : "DIE POLIZEY" / Stettenheim, Ludwig – (Includes bibliographical references) – Berlin: F Fontane, 1893 – 1r – 1 – us U.W. Library [430]
SCHILLER'S HEIMATHJAHRE / Kurz, Hermann – Stuttgart: J G Cotta, 1879-1880 – 1r – 1 – us U.W. Library [830]
SCHILLERS HEIMATJAHRE : HISTORISCHER ROMAN / Kurz, Hermann – 3. Aufl. Stuttgart: Franckh, [1878?] – 1r – 1 – us U.W. Library [830]
SCHILLERS JOURNALISTISCHE TAETIGKEIT AN DEN "NACHRICHTEN ZUM NUZEN UND VERGNUEGEN" IM JAHRE 1781 / Mueller, Hermann – (Includes bibliographical references) – Stuttgart: W Kohlhammer, 1915 – 1r – 1 – us U.W. Library [430]
SCHILLER'S JUGENDDRAMEN / Eckardt, Ludwig – (Includes bibliographical references) – 2. Ausg. Jena: C Hochhausen (W. Lutze), 1862 – 1r – 1 – us U.W. Library [430]
SCHILLERS LIED VON DER GLOCKE : UEBERSICHTLICH GEORDNETER TEXT MIT NEBENSTEHENDER EINGEHENDER GLIEDERUNG UND EINER BILDLICHEN VERANSCHAULICHUNG DES GLOCKENGUSSES / Schiller, Friedrich von; ed by Teetz, Ferdinand – (Includes bibliographical references) – 2. verb. Aufl. Leipzig: W Engelmann, 1905 – 1r – 1 – us U.W. Library [430]
SCHILLERS LYRISCHE GEDANKENDICHTUNG IN IHREM IDEELLEN ZUSAMMENHANGE BELEUCHTET / Philippi, E – (Includes bibliographical references) – Augsburg: A Votsch, 1888 – 1r – 1 – us U.W. Library [430]
SCHILLERS LYRISCHE GEDICHTE / Duentzer, Heinrich – (Includes bibliographical references) – Leipzig: E Wartig, 1874-1875 – 1r – 1 – us U.W. Library [810]
SCHILLERS MUTTER : EIN LEBENSBILD / Mueller, Ernst – (Includes bibliographical references) – Leipzig: Artur Seemann, 1894 – 1r – 1 – us U.W. Library [920]
SCHILLERS SAEMMTLICHE SCHRIFTEN : HISTORISCH-KRITISCHE AUSGABE / Goedeke, Karl – Stuttgart: J G Cotta, 1867-76 – 1r – 1 – us U.W. Library [430]
SCHILLERS SAEMMTLICHE WERKE / Schiller, Friedrich von – Stuttgart: J G Cotta, 1869 – 1r – 1 – us U.W. Library [430]
SCHILLERS SAEMMTLICHE WERKE IN ZWOELF BAENDEN / ed by Hoffmeister, Karl – Stuttgart, Tuebingen: J G Cotta, 1853-57 – 1r – 1 – us U.W. Library [430]
SCHILLERS SAEMTLICHE WERKE : SAEKULAR-AUSGABE / Schiller, Friedrich von; ed by Hellen, Eduard von der – (Includes bibliographical references) – Stuttgart: J G Cotta, [1904?] – 1 – us U.W. Library [800]
SCHILLER'S UND GOETHE'S XENIEN-MANUSCRIPT : ZUM ERSTENMAL BEKANNT GEMACHT VON EDUARD BOAS / Boas, Eduard; ed by Maltzahn, Wendelin von – Berlin: L Hirsch, 1856 – 1r – 1 – us U.W. Library [430]
SCHILLERS VERHAELTNIS ZUR GESPROCHENEN SPRACHE / Stock, Eberhard – (Includes bibliographical references) – Halle Saale: Max Niemeyer, 1966 – 1r – 1 – us U.W. Library [430]
SCHILLERS VERHAELTNIS ZUR IDYLLE / Knippel, Richard – (Includes bibliographical references) – Leipzig: Quelle & Meyer, 1909 – 1 – us U.W. Library [430]
SCHILLERS WERKE / ed by Fischer, J G – Stuttgart: Deutsche Verlags-Anstalt, [189-?] – 1r – 1 – us U.W. Library [430]
SCHILLERS WERKE : WORKS. 1895 / Schiller, Friedrich von; ed by Bellermann, Ludwig – Leipzig; Wien: Bibliographisches Institut, [1895] – 1 – us U.W. Library [430]
SCHILLER'S WORKS / Schiller, Friedrich von; ed by Fischer, J G – Philadelphia: G Barrie, c1883 – 2r – 1 – us U.W. Library [430]
SCHILLERS "XENIEN" UND "TABULAE VOTIVAE" IM MUSENALMANACH FUER 1797 : BEITRAEGE ZUM VERSTAENDNIS DER BEDEUTSAMSTEN TEILE SCHILLERSCHER EPIGRAMMENDICHTUNG / Deppe, Oskar – [S.l.: s.n.] Duderstadt: Druck von F Wagner, 1907 – 1r – 1 – us U.W. Library [430]
Schilling, Helmut *see* DER FRANZOSE IM DEUTSCHEN DRAMA
Schilling, Kerstin *see* DIFFERENZIERTE BETRACHTUNGEN DES EINSATZES VON LYRIK UND KARIKATUREN BEI DER BILDUNG VON UMWELTRELEVANTEN EINSTELLUNGEN IM UNTERRICHT DER KLASSENSTUFEN 7 BIS 10
Schilling, O *see* REICHTUM UND EIGENTUM IN DER ALTKIRCHLICHEN LITERATUR
Schils, G H *see* GRAMMAIRE COMPLETE DE LA LANGUE DES NAMAS
DEN SCHILT TEGHEN DIE WEDERDOOPERS / Browershaven, P C van – Louen, R. Velpius. 1568. BME-232 1 – 9 – ne IDC [240]
Schim, H *see* BYBEL-EN ZEDEDICHTEN, BESTAENDE IN ZINNEBEELDEN; HET ZALIGE LANTLEVEN
Schimmel, Kimberly S *see* FROM NAPTOWN TO SPORTSTOWN
DER SCHIMMELREITER / Storm, Theodor; ed by Brandl, Leopold – (Includes bibliographical references) – Leipzig: G Freytag, 1920 – 1r – 1 – us U.W. Library [830]
Schimper, W P *see*
- BRYOLOGIA EUROPAEA
- MUSCI EUROPAEI NOVI, VEL BYROLOGIAE EUROPAEAE SUPPLEMENTUM
- RECHERCHES ANATOMIQUES ET MORPHOLOGIQUES SUR LES MOUSSES
- SYNOPSIS MUSCORUM EUROPAEORUM

Schindel, Carl Wilhelm Otto August von *see* DIE DEUTSCHEN SCHRIFTSTELLERINNEN DES 19. JAHRHUNDERTS
DER SCHINDELMACHER : NOVELLE / Stehr, Hermann – 2. Aufl. Leipzig: P Reclam, 1944 – 1r – 1 – us U.W. Library [830]
DER SCHINDERHANNES ZIEHT UEBERS GEBIRGE / Perkonig, Josef Friedrich – Muenchen: A Langen, G Mueller, 1943, c1934 – 1r – 1 – us U.W. Library [430]
SCHINDERHANNES : SCHAUSPIEL IN VIER AKTEN / Zuckmayer, Carl – Berlin: Im Propylaen Verlag, c1927 – 1r – 1 – us U.W. Library [820]
Schindler, Solomon *see* MESSIANIC EXPECTATIONS AND MODERN JUDAISM LECTURES
Schiner, Hildebrand *see* DESCRIPTION DU DEPARTEMENT DU SIMPLON OU DE LA CI-DEVANT REPUBLIQUE DU VALAIS
Schiner, J R *see*
- CATALOGUS SYSTEMATICUS DIPTERORUM EUROPAE
- FAUNA AUSTRIACA. DIE FLIEGEN (DIPTERA)

Schippel, Max *see* SOZIALDEMOKRATISCHES REICHSTAGSHANDBUCH
Schippers, T K *see* DOSSIER D'ETHNOLOGIE PROVENCALE, NO. 4. "LES QUATRE SAISONS"
SCHIR HA-SCHIRIM = SHIR HA-SHIRIM : ODER, DAS SALOMONISCHE HOHELIED / Graetz, Heinrich – (Text in German and Hebrew. Commentary in German) – Wien: Wilhelm Braumueller, 1871 – 1mf – 9 – 0-8370-3358-6 – 1985-1358 – us A.T.L.A. [220]
Schirley, W W *see* FASCICULI ZIZANIORUM MAGISTRI WYCLIF CUM TRITICO (RS5)
Schirlitz, Samuel Christoph *see* GRUNDZUEGE DER NEUTESTAMENTLICHEN GRAECITAET
Schirmer, Jo *see* BREVIER DER LEBENSKUNST
Schischa, A *see* TAKKANOT YESHIVAT "HAVERIM MAKSHIVIM" BI-YERUSHALAYIM
LE SCHISME D'ANTIOCHE (4E-5E SIECLE) / Cavallera, F – Paris, 1905 – Dfl35.00 – ne Slangenburg [240]
LE SCHISME ORIENTAL DU 11E SIECLE / Brehier, Louis – Paris: E. Leroux, 1899 – 1mf – us A.T.L.A. [240]
Schiwietz, St *see* DAS MORGENLAENDISCHE MOENCHTUM
SCHIZOPHRENIA BULLETIN – (v.5-. 1979- 5,6,9) – v.1-. 1969- – 1 – us UMI [616]
Schkuhr, C *see*
- BESCHREIBUNG UND ABBILDUNG. RIEDGRAESERN
- BOTANISCHES HANDBUCH DER MEHRESTEN THEILS IN DEUTSCHLAND WILD WACHSENDEN. GEWAECHSE
- DEUTSCHLANDS KRYPTOGAMISCHE GEWAECHSE

Schlabach, G A *see* THE EFFECTS OF TRAINING AND DETRAINING ON CORTICOSTERONE RHYTHMS AND DIETARY FAT SELECTION IN THE OSBORNE-MENDEL RAT
DIE SCHLACHT VOR PAVIA LA BATTAGLIA TALIANA A QUATRO VOCI, COMPOSTA DA M. MATHIAS FIAMENGO, MAESTRO DI CAPELLA DEL DOMO DI MILANO, CON ALCUNE VILLOTTE PIACEVOLE NOVAMENTE CON OGNI DILIGENTIA STAMPATE, E CORRETTE / Werrekoren, H M – 1550 – 5,15 – us Sibley [780]
Schlaf, Johannes *see* NOVALIS UND SOPHIE VON KUEHN
Schlagintweit, E *see* INDIEN IN WORT UND BILD
SCHLAGWORTKATALOG DER UNIVERSITAETSBIBLIOTHEK KIEL BIS 1988 – Hildesheim, 1991 – 186mf – 9 – DM1,200.00 diazo DM1,300.00 silver – gw Olms [020]

Schlatter, Adolf von *see*
- DER CHRONOGRAPH AUS DEM ZEHNTEN JAHRE ANTONINS
- DER CHRONOGRAPH AUS DEM ZEHNTEN JAHRE ANTONINS (T.U.U. 1-12/1A)
- DER ROEMERBRIEF AUSGELEGT FUER BIBELLESER

Schlechte, Horst *see* ERZBISCHOF BRUNO VON TRIER. EIN BEITRAG ZUR GESCHICHTE DER GEISTIGEN STROEMUNGEN IM INVESTITURSTREIT

Schlechtendal, D F L *see* BOTANISCHE ZEITUNG

Schlechtendal, D F L von *see* LINNAEA

Schlechter, R *see*
- FIGUREN-ATLAS ZU DEN ORCHIDACEEN VON DEUTSCH-NEU-GUINEA
- FIGUREN-ATLAS ZU DEN ORCHIDEEN FLOREN DER SUEDAMERIKANISCHEN KORDILLERENSTAATEN

Schlegel, August Wilhelm *see* ATHENAEUM

Schlegel, Frederick von *see* THE PHILOSOPHY OF LIFE, AND PHILOSOPHY OF LANGUAGE IN A COURSE OF LECTURES

Schlegel, Friedrich *see* ATHENAEUM

Schlegel, Friedrich von *see* LUCINDE

Schlegel, H *see*
- ESSAI SUR LA PHYSIONOMIE DES SERPENS
- KRITISCHE UEBERSICHT DER EUROPAEISCHEN VOEGEL
- DE VOGELS VAN NEDERLANDSCH-INDIE...

Schlegel, Ursula *see* KENNEN UND SAMMELN

SCHLEGELS AESTHETISCHER INTELLEKTUALISMUS : STUDIEN UEBER DIE PARADOXE EINHEIT VON PHILOSOPHIE UND KUNST IN DEN JAHREN VOR 1800 / Peter, Klaus – Frankfurt a.M., 1966 – 2mf – DM62.00 – 3-89349-845-1 – gw Hänsel [140]

Schleicher, J C *see*
- CATALOGUS PLANTARUM IN HELVETIA CIS-ET TRANSALPINA SPONTE NASCENTIUM

Schleicher, K *see* UEBER DAS VERHALTNIS DER GRIECHISCHEN ZUR MODERN MUSIK

Schleiden, M J *see* HANDBUCH DER MEDICINISCH-PHARMACEUTISCHEN BOTANIK...

Schleiden, Matthias Jacob *see* THE IMPORTANCE OF THE JEWS FOR THE PRESERVATION AND REVIVAL OF LEARNING DURING THE MIDDLE AGES

Schleiermacher, Friedrich *see*
- A CRITICAL ESSAY ON THE GOSPEL OF ST LUKE
- FRIEDRICH SCHLEIERMACHER'S REDEN UEBER DIE RELIGION

SCHLEIERMACHER UND DIE UNION : FESTREDE AM 21. NOVEMBER 1868 IN DER AULA ZU MARBURG / Henke, E LT – Marburg: N.G. Elwert, 1868 – 1mf – us A.T.L.A. [240]

SCHLEIERMACHER'S LITURGIK / Albrecht, Chr. – Goettingen, 1963 – 4mf – 8 – Dfl19.00 – ne Slangenburg [240]

SCHLEIERMACHERS RELIGIONSPHILOSOPHIE / Thilo, C A – O.O., 1906 – 2mf – DM62.00 – 3-8267-3079-8 – gw Hänsel [240]

SCHLEIERMACHERS STELLUNG ZUM CHRISTENTUM IN SEINEN REDEN UEBER DIE RELIGION : EIN BEITRAG ZUR EHRENRETTUNG SCHLEIERMACHERS / Ritschl, Otto – Gotha: F.A. Perthes, 1888 – 1mf – us A.T.L.A. [240]

SCHLEIERMACHERS WIRKSAMKEIT ALS PREDIGER / Schweitzer, Alexander – Halle: C.A. Kuemmel, 1834 – 1mf – us A.T.L.A. [240]

Schleinitz, GE G von *see* DIE FORSCHUNGSREISE S.M.S. "GAZELLE" 1874 BIS 1876

Schleiter, Frederick *see* RELIGION AND CULTURE: A CRITICAL SURVEY OF METHODS OF APPROACH TO RELIGIOUS PHENOMENA

Schleiter, Ingrid M *see*
- ERFASSUNG UND BEURTEILUNG GEOBOTANISCHER DATEN
- PFLANZENSOZIOLOGISCH-OEKOLOGISCHE UNTERSUCHUNGEN IN AUSGEWAEHLTEN FEUCHTGEBIETEN IM NATURPARK SCHWALM-NETTE (NORDRHEIN-WESTFALEN)

SCHLEMIEL : ILLUSTRIERTES JUEDISCHES WITZBLATT – Berlin, 1903-05 (incomplete), 1919-20 (incomplete) – 1 – Inquire at Mikrofilmarchiv for details – gw Misc Inst [870]

SCHLESIEN LEBT : ZEITUNGEN, ZEITSCHRIFTEN UND RUNDBRIEFE DER SCHLESISCHEN HEIMATVERTRIEBENEN / Bunzel, Ulrich – Wuerzburg: Holzner Verlag, 1963 – 1r – 1 – us U.W. Library [943]

Schlesier, G *see* BRIEFE UND VERTRAUTE BLAETTER VON FRIEDRICH VON GENTZ

Schlesinger, A J *see* KOL NEHI MI-ZIYYON

Schlesinger, Arthur Meier *see* ORESTES A. BROWNSON: A PILGRIM'S PROGRESS

SCHLESINGER LIBRARY VERTICAL FILE FOR WOMEN'S STUDIES – (Biography 749mf £0,020. Organizations ca 1100mf £4,515 Subjects ca 1100mf £4,100. With printed index) – Schlesinger Library, Radcliffe College – ca 3,000mf – 9 – enquire – uk Chadwyck [305]

Schlesinger, Max *see*
- DAS ARAMAEISCHE VERBUM IM JERUSCHALEMISCHEN TALMUD
- THE HISTORICAL JESUS OF NAZARETH
- SATZLEHRE DER ARAMAEISCHEN SPRACHE DES BABYLONISCHEN TALMUDS

SCHLESISCHE ARBEITER ZEITUNG – (Title change: Arbeiter Zeitung, 1 May 1926) – Breslau (Wroclaw), Poland. 31 Mar 1919-1926; 1928-1933 – 19r – 1 – gw Mikrofilm [943]

SCHLESISCHE ARBEITER-ZEITUNG – Breslau, 1919-20 – 1r – 1 – DM80.00 – gw Mikro Press [072]

SCHLESISCHE ARBEITER-ZEITUNG – (Cont by: Arbeiter-Zeitung, may 1 1926) – Breslau, mar 31 1919-22, 1923-24 (incomplete), 1925-26, 1928-feb 19 1933 – 19r – 1 – Inquire at Mikrofilmarchiv for details – gw Misc Inst [943]

SCHLESISCHE FUNKSTUNDE – Breslau, 1928-33 – 1 – Inquire at Mikrofilmarchiv for details – gw Misc Inst [790]

SCHLESISCHE FUNKSTUNDE – Breslau. oct 17, 1924-33. 1936. 1938-41 – 15r – 1 – gw Mikrofilm [073]

SCHLESISCHE GEDICHTE / Holtei, Karl von – Breslau: E Trewendt, 1861 – 1r – 1 – us U.W. Library [810]

SCHLESISCHE NOUVELLEN-COURIER – Breslau (Wroclaw), Poland. 1712 (incomplete); 1714-20; 1722-24; 1726; 1728; 1730-39; 1741 (incomplete) – 15r – 1 – gw Mikrofilm [943]

SCHLESISCHE PRIVILEGIRTE STAATS-KRIEGS- UND FRIEDENS-ZEITUNG *see* SCHLESISCHE ZEITUNG

SCHLESISCHE PRIVILEGIRTE STAATS-, KRIEGS- UND FRIEDENS-ZEITUNGEN *see* SCHLESISCHE ZEITUNG

SCHLESISCHE PRIVILEGIRTE STAATS-, KRIEGS- UND FRIEDENS-ZEITUNG/ PRIVILEGIRTE SCHLESISCHE ZEITUNG *see* SCHLESISCHE ZEITUNG

SCHLESISCHE PRIVILEGIRTE ZEITUNG – Breslau, 1742, 1797-1847 – 9 – gw Olms [320]

SCHLESISCHE PRIVILEGIRTE ZEITUNG *see* SCHLESISCHE ZEITUNG

SCHLESISCHE PRIVILEGIRTE ZEITUNGEN *see* SCHLESISCHE ZEITUNG

SCHLESISCHE PROVINZIAL-BLAETTER – (Also known as: Streits Schlesische Provinzialblaetter) – Breslau, 1785-1806, 1807 (incomplete), 1808-35, 1836 (incomplete), 1837-49 – 1 – Inquire at Mikrofilmarchiv for details – gw Misc Inst [943]

SCHLESISCHE PROVINZIAL-BLAETTER – Breslau (Wroclaw), Poland. 1785-1849; 1862; 1867 – 138r – 1 – gw Mikrofilm [943]

DIE SCHLESISCHE ROMANTIK / Lubos, Arno – (Includes bibliographical references) – Wuerzburg: Holzner-Verlag, 1956 – 10r – 1 – us U.W. Library [943]

SCHLESISCHE TAGESZEITUNG – Breslau, sep 8-22 1935, oct 1 1939-44, jan-may 6 1945 (incomplete) – 1 – Inquire at Mikrofilmarchiv for details – gw Misc Inst [943]

SCHLESISCHE TAGESZEITUNG – Breslau (Wroclaw), Poland. 1939 (incomplete); 1940-1944; 1945 (incomplete) – 11r – 1 – gw Mikrofilm [943]

SCHLESISCHE TAGESZEITUNG – Wroclaw, Poland. Aug 1935-Jan 1937 – 4r – 1 – us L of C Photodup [943]

SCHLESISCHE VOLKSZEITUNG – Breslau (Wroclaw), Poland. 1789-1806; 1943 (incomplete); 1944 – 5r – 1 – gw Mikrofilm [943]

SCHLESISCHE VOLKSZEITUNG – (Cont: Breslauer Hausblaetter, 1863-jun 30 1871) – Breslau, jan 3 1863-feb 29 1944 – 1 – Inquire at Mikrofilmarchiv for details – gw Misc Inst [943]

SCHLESISCHE WARTE MIT ANZEIGER FUER DEN KREIS PLESS *see* DER DEUTSCHE IN POLEN

SCHLESISCHE ZEITUNG – Bielitz-Biala, aug 26 1925-mar 27 1938 – 1 – Inquire at Mikrofilmarchiv for details – gw Misc Inst [943]

SCHLESISCHE ZEITUNG – Bielitz-Biala (Bielsko-Biala), Poland. 26 Aug 1925-27 Mar 1938 – 1 – gw Mikrofilm [943]

SCHLESISCHE ZEITUNG – (Cont: Schlesische Privilegirte Staats- Kriegs- und Friedens-Zeitung, 1742; Schlesische Privilegirte Staats, Kriegs- und Friedens-Zeitungen, 1743-aug 1766; Schlesische privilegirte Zeitungen, -aug 1790; Schlesische privilegirte Zeitung, -1819; Privilegirte Schlesische Zeitung, 1820-dec 31 1847) – Breslau, 1742, jul 29 1743, mar 18 1744-45, 1756-70, 1771 (many issues missing), 1773 (many issues missing), 1776-86, 1788-98, 1799 (incomplete), 1800-1944 – 1 – Inquire at Mikrofilmarchiv for details – gw Misc Inst [943]

SCHLESISCHE ZEITUNG – (Preceded by: Schlesische Privilegirte Staats-, Kriegs- und Friedens-Zeitung/Privilegirte Schlesische Zeitung, 1848) – Breslau (Wroclaw), Poland. 1742; 1743 (incomplete); 1744-45; 1756-71; 1773; 1776-86; 1788-1944 – 1 – gw Mikrofilm [943]

SCHLESISCHE ZEITUNG – Wroclaw, Poland. 14 Jul 1938; Feb, Mar 1941; Mar-Oct 1944 (scattered issues) – 1r – 1 – us L of C Photodup [943]

SCHLESISCHE ZEITUNG – Wroclaw, Poland. -d. 15 Aug 1916-10 Aug 1919. Imperfect. 16 reels – 1 – uk British Libr Newspaper [943]

DIE SCHLESISCHEN MUSENALMANACHE VON 1773-1823 / Herzog, Rudolph – (Includes bibliographical references) – Breslau: F Hirt, 1912 – 1 – us U.W. Library [430]

SCHLESISCHER GOTTESFREUND – v16-41. 1965-90 (complete) – 3r – 1 – ATLA S0782 – us A.T.L.A. [073]

SCHLESISCHER NOUVELLEN-COURIER – Breslau, 1710 (many issues missing), 1712 (many issues missing), 1714, 1715 (incomplete), 1716-17, 1718 (incomplete), 1719-26, 1728 (incomplete), 1730-33 (incomplete), 1734, 1735-36 (incomplete), 1737-39, 1741 (incomplete) – 15r – 1 – Inquire at Mikrofilmarchiv for details – gw Misc Inst [943]

Schleswig. Regierungsbezirk *see* AMTSBLATT DER REGIERUNG ZU SCHLESWIG

SCHLESWIGER NACHRICHTEN – Schleswig, Germany. 1 Sept 1978- – ca 7r per yr – 1 – gw Mikrofilm [072]

SCHLESWIG-HOLSTEINISCHE LANDESZEITUNG – Rendsburg, West Germany. 1976- – ca 7r per yr – 1 – gw Mikrofilm [072]

SCHLESWIG-HOLSTEINISCHE VOLKSZEITUNG – Kiel, 1946-49 – 3r – 1 – DM210.00 – gw Mikro Press [072]

SCHLESWIG-HOLSTEINISCHE VOLKSZEITUNG – Kiel, Germany. 3 Apr 1946-1949 – 3r – 1 – gw Mikrofilm [072]

SCHLETTSSTAEDTER TAGEBLATT – Selestat, France. 1896-1918 – 1 – fr A.C.R.P.P. [072]

Schleusner, J F *see*
- LEXICON IN 70 ET RELIQUOS INTERPRETES.. VET. TESTAMENTI
- NOVUS THESAURUS PHILOLOGICO-CRITICUS SIVE LEXICON IN 70 ET RELIQUOS INTERPRETES GRAECOS AC SCRIPTORES APOCRYPHOS VETERIS TESTAMENTI

Schlichtegroll, Friedrich *see* NEKROLOG

Schlichting *see* MOLTKES VERMAECHTISS

DAS SCHLICHTUNGSWESEN IM RUHRBERGBAU SEIT DER STABILISIERUNG DER WAEHRUNG BIS ZUR MITTE DES JAHRES 1929 / Siebke, Friedrich – (Teildruck). Berlin 1931 – 1 – DM30.00 – gw Mikro Press [331]

Schlieffen, Alfred, Graf von *see*
- GESAMMELTE SCHRIFTEN
- PAPERS

Schlimbach, Alice *see* LICHTENBERG IM SPIEGEL SEINER KRITISCHEN AEUSSERUNGEN UEBER KLOPSTOCK

DIE SCHLIMMEN NONNEN VON POITIERS : HISTORISCHER ROMAN AUS DER VOELKERWANDERUNG / Dahn, Felix – Leipzig: Breitkopf und Haertel, 1885 – 1 – us U.W. Library [830]

Schlitter, H *see*
- CORRESPONDANCE SECRETE CENTRE LE COMTE A.W. KAUNITZ-RIETBERG...
- GEHEIME CORRESPONDENZ JOSEFS 2. MIT SEINEM MINISTER IN DEN OESTERREICHISCHEN NIEDERLANDEN...1787-1789

Schlobies, H *see* DER AKKADISCHE WETTERGOTT IN MESOPOTAMIEN

Schloegl, Nivardus *see*
- DE RE METRICA VETERUM HEBRAEORUM: DISPUTATIO IN UNIVERSITATE VINDOBONENSI
- ECCLESIASTICUS 39, 12-49, 16...IN FORMAM ORIGINALEM REDACTUS
- LIBRI SAMUELIS

Schloemilch, O et al *see* ZEITSCHRIFT FUER MATHEMATIK UND PHYSIK, 1. 1856 – 64. 1917

Schloemilch, Oskar *see* ZEITSCHRIFT FUER MATHEMATIK UND PHYSIK MIT LITERATURZEITUNG DER ZEITSCHRIFT FUER MATHEMATIK UND PHYSIK

Schloesser, Rudolf *see*
- DIE QUELLEN ZU HEINRICH VON KLEISTS MICHAEL KOHLHAAS
- ZUR GESCHICHTE UND KRITIK VON FRIEDRICH WILHELM GOTTER'S MEROPE

Schloessinger, Max *see* RASHI

Schloezer, A L von *see* NESTOR

Schlomer, Harm Henry *see* GOTTFRIED KELLERS POLITISCHE ANSCHAUUNGEN

SCHLOSS UND FABRIK : ROMAN / Otto-Peters, Louise – Leipzig: Adolph Wienbrack, 1846 – 1r – 1 – us U.W. Library [830]

Schlossar, Anton *see*
- NIKOLAUS LENAUS BRIEFE AN EMILIE VON REINBECK UND DEREN GATTEN GEORG VON REINBECK
- PETER ROSEGGER

Schlosser, Gustav *see* DAS ALTE TESTAMENT IN PREDIGTEN UND BIBELSTUNDEN

Schlosser, Heinrich *see* DIE PISCATORBIBEL: EIN BEITRAG ZUR GESCHICHTE DER DEUTSCHEN BIBELUEBERSETZUNG

Schlosser, J C *see* ANLEITUNG DIE IM MAEHRISCHEN GOUVERNEMENT WILD WACHSENDEN UND AM HAEUFIGSTEN CULTIVIRTEN PHANEROGAMEN PFLANZEN

Schlosser, Julius von *see*
- QUELLENBUCH ZUR KUNSTGESCHICHTE DES ABENDLAENDISCHEN MITTELALTERS
- SCHRIFTQUELLEN ZUR GESCHICHTE DER KAROLINGISCHEN KUNST
- VASARISTUDIEN VON WOLFGANG KALLAB

DIE SCHLOSSKIRCHE ZU WITTENBERG : UEBERSICHT IHRER GESCHICHTE BIS AUF DIE GEGENWART / ed by Stier, G – Wittenberg: Zimmermann Buchh., 1860 – 1mf – us A.T.L.A. [943]

Schlotter, Herbert *see* FOLGEN DER TECHNIK – VERANTWORTUNG DER INGENIEURE

Schlottmann, Konstantin *see*
- DIE INSCHRIFT ESCHMUNAZARS, KOENIGS DER SIDONIER
- KOMPENDIUM DER BIBLISCHEN THEOLOGIE DES ALTEN UND NEUEN TESTAMENTS VON KONSTANTIN SCHLOTTMANN
- DIE SIEGESSAEULE MESA'S KOENIGS DER MOABITER
- WIDER KLIEFOTH UND LUTHARDT

Schluchter, Wolfgang *see* BESTIMMUNGSGRUENDE UND PROBLEME STAATLICHER UND INSTITUTIONELLER FAMILIENPOLITIK AM BEISPIEL DER BUNDESREPUBLIK DEUTSCHLAND

SCHLUESSEL DER CHIMISTISCHEN PHILOSOPHIE : DURCH EIN LIEBHABER DER DELEN PHILOSOPHIE IN TUETSCHSPRACH GEBRACHT / Dorn, Gerhard – Strassburg, 1602 – 1 – us U.W. Library [190]

SCHLUESSEL ZUM HORTUS INDICUS MALABARICUS / Dennstedt, A W – Weimar. 1818. B-976 1 – 9 – ne IDC [580]

Schluesselburg, C *see* HAERETICORUM CATALOGUS

DIE SCHLUESSELGEWALT DER EHEFRAU INSBESONDERE BEI GETRENNT LEBENDEN EHEGATTEN / Nolde, Clara – 1995 – 1mf – 9 – DM48.00 – 3-8267-3180-8 – gw Hänsel [340]

Schlueter, Gerda *see* STRUKTURWANDEL ALS HERAUSFORDERUNG

Schlueter, Otto *see* DIE ZIELE DER GEOGRAPHIE DES MENSCHEN

DER SCHLUNGSBRIEF – Berlin. Jahrg. 1-11, Folge 5 6; Mar 1934-1944. Lacks Jahrg. 11, Folge 1-2. Film Mas C 649 – 1 – us H.U. Library [073]

Schlupmann, Klaus *see* DOCUMENTS ICONOGRAPHIQUES SUR SAN ANDRES SAJCABAJA

Schlurick, Johannes *see* SCHILLER UND DIE BIBEL

DER SCHLUSS DES MARKUSEVANGELIUMS, DER...KANON UND DIE KLEINASIATISCHEN PRESBYTER / Rohrbach, Paul – Berlin: Georg Nauck, 1894. 1 fiche – 9 – us A.T.L.A. [240]
Schmahl, Ludwig *see* DIE AUSUBUNG DES VERORDNUNGSRECHTS IM FREISTAATE HESSEN SEIT DER REVOLUTION
DER SCHMALKALDISCHE BUND, 1530-1532, UND DER NUERNBERGER RELIGIONSFRIEDE / Winckelmann, Otto – Strassburg: J.H.Ed. Heitz, 1892 – 1mf – us A.T.L.A. [240]
Schmauk, Theodore Emanuel *see*
- THE EPISTLE TO TIMOTHY AND THE WOMAN QUESTION
- THE NEGATIVE CRITICISM AND THE OLD TESTAMENT
- ST. PAUL AND WOMEN

Schmeding, G *see* JACOB THOMSON
Schmeidler, B *see* THOLOMEI LUCENSIS ANNALES (MGH 6: 8.BD)
Schmeing, Karl *see* FLUCHT- UND WERBUNGSSAGEN IN DER LEGENDE
Schmeltzl, Wolfgang *see* SAMUEL UND SAUL
Schmelz, S *see* FUNDAMENTA MUSICA CANTUS ARTIFIALIS
Schmemann, Karl *see* GEDENKBUCH, ERINNERUNG AN KARL HEINZEN UND AN DIE ENTHUELLUNGSFEIER DES HEINZEN-DENKMALS AM 12. JUNI 1886 IN BOSTON, MASS.
DIE SCHMERZZEICHNUNG ("PATIENT PAIN DRAWING") ALS SCREENING-METHODE FUER LUMBAGO-ISCHIALGIE-SYNDROM-PATIENTEN : EINE PROSPEKTIVE STUDIE / Hofstadt, Ulrich H E – 1995 – 1mf – 9 – DM60.00 – 3-8267-2181-0 – gw Hänsel [616]
Schmid, C *see*
- EIN CHRISTL. ERMANUNG ZU WARER HOFFNUNG IN GOTT
- DIE PREDIGEN SO VONN DEN FROEMBDEN PREDICANTEN

Schmid, Carlo *see* DAS PROGRAMM DER OPPOSITION
Schmid, Erasmus *see* NOVI TESTAMENTI GRAECI JESU CHRISTI TAMEION
Schmid, Guenther *see*
- SCHICKSAL EINER GOETHESCHRIFT
- DIE WALLENSTEIN-LITERATUR, 1626-1878

Schmid, Heinrich *see*
- DIE GESCHICHTE DES PIETISMUS
- DER KAMPF DER LUTHERISCHEN KIRCHE UM LUTHERS LEHRE VOM ABENDMAHL IM REFORMATIONSZEITALTER

Schmid, Herman *see* SUEDEN UND NORDEN
Schmid, Hermann von *see* GESAMMELTE SCHRIFTEN: VOLKS- UND FAMILIEN-AUSGABE
Schmid, John Henry *see* CASES ON THE LAW OF WILLS
Schmid, Otto *see* UEBER VERSCHIEDENE EINTHEILUNGEN DER HEILIGEN SCHRIFT
Schmid, Rudolf *see*
- DIE DARWINISCHEN THEORIEN UND IHRE STELLUNG ZUR PHILOSOPHIE, RELIGION UND MORAL
- DARWINISCHEN THEORIEN UND IHRE STELLUNG ZUR PHILOSOPHIE, RELIGION UND MORAL
- THE SCIENTIFIC CREED OF A THEOLOGIAN
- THE THEORIES OF DARWIN AND THEIR RELATION TO PHILOSOPHY, RELIGION, AND MORALITY

Schmidgall Tellings, Aluzius Eduard *see*
- INDONESIAN FOR TODAY; A PRACTICAL COURSE FOR ENGLISH-SPEAKING PEOPLE
- INDONESIAN-ENGLISH SUPPLEMENTAL WORD-LIST TO EXISTING DICTIONARIES

Schmidkunz, Walter *see* BILD DES FUEHRERS
Schmidlin, Johann Josef *see* CATHOLICON, OU DICTIONNAIRE UNIVERSEL DE LA LANGUE FRANCOISE, CATHOLICON ODER FRANZOESISCH-DEUTSCHES UNIVERSALWOERTERBUCH DER FRANZOESISCHEN SPRACHE (AEL, ABT 2;12)
Schmidt, A W F *see* ATLAS DER DIATOMACEEN-KUNDE
Schmidt, Ambrosius *see* VERGLEICHENDE ANALYTISCHE STUDIE ZWISCHEN DER NATUERLICHEN UND DER EINGESTELLTEN KOPFHALTUNG NACH AESTHETISCH-METRISCHEN FAKTOREN ZUR BESTIMMUNG EINES HARMONISCHEN PROFILS
Schmidt, Arno *see* DAS ESSAYISTISCHE WERK ZUR DEUTSCHEN LITERATUR IN 4 BAENDEN
Schmidt, August *see* DIE RELIGION DES ZWEIFLERS
Schmidt, C F *see* ATLAS DER OFFICINELLEN PFLANZEN...
Schmidt, Carl *see*
- DIE ALTEN PETRUSAKTEN IM ZUSAMMENHANG MIT DER APOKRYPHEN APOSTELLITTERATUR (T.U.U. 2-24/1)
- DER BENANBRIEF
- DER ERSTE CLEMENSBRIEF IN ALTKOPTISCHER UEBERSETZUNG (T.U.U. 3-32/1)
- FRAGMENT EINER SCHRIFT DES MAERTYRER-BISCHOFS PETRUS VON ALEXANDRIEN (T.U.U. 2-20/4B)
- GESPRAECHE JESU MIT SEINEN JUENGERN NACH DER AUFERSTEHUNG
- GNOSTISCHE SCHRIFTEN IN KOPTISCHER SPRACHE AUS DEM CODEX BRUCIANUS (T.U.U. 1-8/1.2.)
- PLOTINS STELLUNG ZUM GNOSTICISMUS UND KIRCHLICHEN CHRISTENTUM
- PLOTIN'S STELLUNG ZUM GNOSTICISMUS UND KIRCHLICHEN CHRISTENTUM (T.U.U. 2-20/4A)
- STUDIEN ZU DEN PSEUDO-CLEMENTINEN NEBST EINEM ANHANGE

Schmidt, Charles *see*
- LE GRAND-DUCHE DE BERG (1806-1813)
- THE SOCIAL RESULTS OF EARLY CHRISTIANITY

Schmidt, Eric F *see* ANATOLIA THROUGH THE AGES
Schmidt, Erich *see*
- G. E. LESSINGS UEBERSETZUNGEN AUS DEM FRANZOESISCHEN FRIEDRICHS DES GROSSEN UND VOLTAIRES
- HEINRICH VON KLEIST
- H.V. KLEISTS WERKE
- LENZ UND KLINGER
- LESSING
- VERTHEIDIGUNG DES HERRN WIELAND GEGEN DIE WOLKEN

Schmidt, F A *see* NEUER NEKROLOG DER DEUTSCHEN
Schmidt, F W *see*
- FLORA BOEEMICA INCHOATA
- NEUE UND SELTENE PFLANZEN, NEBST EINIGEN ANDERN BOTANISCHEN BEOBACHTUNGEN

Schmidt, Ferdinand *see* DER CISTERZIENSER
Schmidt, G L *see* GEORG WITZEL, EIN ALTKATHOLIK DES 16. JAHRHUNDERTS
Schmidt, Gordon J *see* AEROBIC EXERCISE RELATED TO FUNCTIONAL AEROBIC CAPACITY, REPETITIVE/INTERFERING BEHAVIOR, AND PLATELET SEROTONIN CONCENTRATION OF INDIVIDUALS WITH AUTISM
Schmidt, H *see* GLAUCOM, ESSENTIELLE PHTHISIS BULBI. HB. GES. AUGENHK
Schmidt, H C *see* THE VEDAS, OR THE RELIGIOUS BOOKS OF THE HINDOOS; A LECTURE DELIVERED IN CENTRAL HALL, BROOKLYN, NEW YORK, NOV. 11TH, 1884
Schmidt, Hans *see* DER STEIGERNDE STIL IN DER TRAGOEDIE FRIEDRICH HEBBELS
Schmidt, Hermann *see*
- ERZBISCHOF ALBRECHT 2. VON MAGDEBURG
- DAS VERHAELTNIS DER CHRISTLICHEN GLAUBENSLEHRE ZU...AKADEMISCHER WISSENSCHAFT

Schmidt, I J *see* TIBETSKO-RUSSKY SLOVAR'...
Schmidt, J *see* WOERTERBUCH BIBLISCHER EIGENNAMEN DES ALTEN UND NEUEN TESTAMENTES
Schmidt, Johann *see* DIE HOSEN DES DOKTORS IM NONNENKLOSTER
Schmidt, Karl *see* VERKAUFSORGANISATIONEN VON UNTERNEHMUNGEN DER WESTDEUTSCHEN MASCHINENINDUSTRIE
Schmidt, Karl Ludwig *see*
- DIE POLIS IN KIRCHE UND WELT

Schmidt, Karl Wilhelm *see* SANSIBAR
Schmidt, Kathryn *see* THE EFFECTS OF AGE AND ENDURANCE TRAINING ON RAT ADRENAL TISSUE
Schmidt, Leopold *see* ZUR GESCHICHTE DER MAERCHENOPER
Schmidt, M G *see* HISTORIA DEL COMERCIO MUNDIAL...
Schmidt, Martin H *see*
- JOHANN GOTTFRIED SCHADOW
- JOHANN GOTTFRIED SCHADOWS AUSEINANDERSETZUNG MIT JOHANN WOLFGANG V. GOETHE – BEZOGEN AUF DIE JAHRE 1800 BIS 1823

Schmidt, Mary Emilia Schwandt *see* PAPERS
Schmidt, Maximilian *see*
- AM GOLDENEN STEIG UND ANDERE ERZAEHLUNGEN AUS DEM BAYER- UND BOEHMERWALD
- DER HERRGOTTSMANTEL
- DER ZUGGEIST

Schmidt, Michael *see* AN ATTEMPT TO DISENTANGLE SPACE- AND MOMENTUM COORDINATES
Schmidt, Nathaniel *see* THE PROPHET OF NAZARETH
Schmidt, Nicole D *see*
- PHILOSOPHIE UND PSYCHOLOGIE
- ZUM ZUSAMMENHANG VON SELBSTVERWIRKLICHUNG UND MORALITAET

Schmidt, Oscar *see* GOETHE'S VERHAELTNIS ZU DEN ORGANISCHEN NATURWISSENSCHAFTEN
Schmidt, P J *see* SIX SONATAS; TROIS POUR DEUX VIOLONS ET VIOLONCELLE ET TROIS POUR UN VIOLON, TENOR ET VIOLONCELLS, OEUVRE 11
Schmidt, Richard *see* DIE PAULINISCHE CHRISTOLOGIE
Schmidt, Traugott *see* DER LEIB CHRISTI....EINE UNTERSUCHUNG ZUM URCHRISTLICHEN GEMEINDEGEDANKEN
Schmidt, Walter *see* GEOGRAFIA ECONOMICA
Schmidt, Werner *see* "PENTHESILEA" IN DER KLEISTLITERATUR
Schmidt, Wilhelm *see* DIE KIRCHEN- UND SCHULVISITATION IM SAECHSISCHEN KURKREISE VOM JAHRE 1555
Schmidt, Wolfgang *see* BEITRAEGE ZUR STILISTIK VON HOELDERLIN "TOD DES EMPEDOKLES"
Schmidtborn, Otto *see* CHRISTOPH ERNST FRHR. V. HOUWALD ALS DRAMATIKER
Schmidt-Goebel, H M *see* FAUNULA COLEOPTERORUM BIRMANIAE
Schmidtke, Alfred *see*
- DAS KLOSTERLAND DES ATHOS
- NEUE FRAGMENTE UND UNTERSUCHUNGEN ZU DEN JUDENCHRISTLICHEN EVANGELIEN (T.U.U. 3-37/1)

Schmidt-Oberloessnitz, Wilhelm *see* DIE MAKKABAEER
Schmidt-Rimpler, H *see* GLAUKOM UND OPHTHALMOMALACIE. HB. GES. AUGENHK
SCHMIDT'S LAW JOURNAL *see* THE LOUISIANA LAW JOURNAL
DER SCHMIED VON HASSBERG : ROMAN / Tremel-Eggert, Kuni – Muenchen: F Eher, 1937 – 1r – 1 – us U.W. Library [830]
Schmiedeknecht, H L O *see* DIE HYMENOPTEREN MITTELEUROPAS
Schmiedel, Otto *see* DIE HAUPTPROBLEME DER LEBEN-JESU-FORSCHUNG
Schmiedel, Paul Wilhelm *see*
- JESUS IN MODERN CRITICISM: A LECTURE
- PERSON JESU IM STREITE DER MEINUNGEN DER GEGENWART
- RELIGIONSPHILOSOPHIE IM UMRISS

Schmieden, Alfred *see* DIE BUEHNENGERECHTEN EINRICHTUNGEN DER SCHILLERSCHEN DRAMEN FUER DAS KOENIGLICHE NATIONAL-THEATER ZU BERLIN
Schmieder, Ulrike *see* PREUSSEN UND DER KONGRESS VON VERONA
Schmitt, Bernhard *see* AMBROSIUS VON MAILAND UND DER TOD KAISER VALENTINIANS 2
Schmitt, Carl *see*
- DONOSO CORTES
- SU POSICION EN LA HISTORIA DE LA FILOSOFIA DEL ESTADO EUROPEA

Schmitt, Fritz *see*
- ABRISS DER DEUTSCHEN LITERATURGESCHICHTE IN TABELLEN
- DEUTSCHE LITERATURGESCHICHTE IN TABELLEN
- TABELLEN ZUR DEUTSCHEN LITERATURGESCHICHTE

Schmitt, Jacob *see* SONATINEN FUER PIANOFORTE ZU VIER HAENDEN..
Schmitter-Hug, Johann Baptist *see* REDEN UND AUFSAETZE
Schmitz, Elisabeth *see* EDWIN VON MANTEUFFEL ALS QUELLE ZUR GESCHICHTE FRIEDRICH WILHELMS 4TH
Schmitz, Hermann Joseph *see* DIE BUSSBUECHER UND DIE BUSSDISCIPLIN DER KIRCHE
Schmitz, Reta *see* DAS PROBLEM "VOLKSTUM UND DICHTUNG" BEI HERDER
Schmitz, Robert *see* LES BAHOLOHOLO (CONGO BELGE)
Schmitz-Kallenberg, L *see* BRIEFE UEBER DIE MORALITAET DER LEIDEN DES JUNGEN WERTHERS
Schmoller, Otto *see*
- THE BOOK OF AMOS
- THE BOOK OF HOSEA
- THE BOOK OF JOEL
- DER BRIEF PAULI AN DIE GALATER
- THE EPISTLE OF PAUL TO THE GALATIANS
- DIE LEHRE VOM REICHE GOTTES IN DEN SCHRIFTEN DES NEUEN TESTAMENTS

Schmuck, Hilmar *see*
- GESAMTVERZEICHNIS DES DEUTSCHSPRACHIGEN SCHRIFTTUMS 1700-1910
- JEWISH BIOGRAPHICAL ARCHIVE SUPPLEMENT

Schmuelling, Michael *see* UNTERSUCHUNG DER REAKTIVITAET-MECHANISMUS-BEZIEHUNG BEI SUBSTITUTIONSREAKTIONEN VON PLATIN(II)-KOMPLEXEN
Schnabel, Ernst *see* SCHIFFE UND STERNE
Schnabel, Franz *see* DER ZUSAMMENSCHLUSS DES POLITISCHEN KATHOLIZISMUS IN DEUTSCHLAND IM JAHRE 1848
Schnass, Franz *see* HEBBELS LYRIK UND EPIK IM RAHMEN SEINES LEBENS
Schneckenburger, Matthias *see* VORLESUNGEN UEBER NEUTESTAMENTLICHE ZEITGESCHICHTE
Schneegass, Cyriacus *see* ISAGOGES MUSICAE LIBRI DUO..
Schneeweiß, Burkhard *see* PEDIATRICS AND RELATED TOPICS
Schneideberg,O *see* ARCHIV FUER EXPERIMENTELLE PATHOLOGIE UND PHARMAKOLOGIE
Schneider, A *see*
- BEITRAEGE ZUR PSYCHOLOGIE ALBERTS DES GROSSEN
- ENCYKLOPEDYA DO KRAJOZNAWSTWA GALICYI POD WZGLEDEM HISTORYCZNYM, STATYSTYCZYM, TOPOGRAFICZNYM, OROGRAFICZNYM, HYDROGRAFICZNYM, GEOGNOSTYCZNYM, ETNOGRAFICZNYM, HANDLOWYM, PRZEMYSLOWYM, SFRAGISTYCZNYM,...

Schneider, A F *see* MONOGRAPHIE DER NEMATODEN
Schneider, Allison K *see* DIET COMPOSITIONAL CHANGES DURING MOUNTAINEERING AT HIGH ALTITUDE IN COLD WEATHER
Schneider, Carl Edward *see* THE GERMAN CHURCH ON THE AMERICAN FRONTIER
Schneider, Doris *see* DIE AUSWIRKUNGEN DES INTRAFAMILIALEN SEXUELLEN MISSBRAUCHS VON MAEDCHEN AUF DIE PERSOENLICHKEITSENTWICKLUNG DER OPFER
Schneider, Ferdinand Josef *see* GOETHES WELTWENDE-SCHICKSAL
Schneider, Ferdinand Joseph *see* FESTGABE PHILIPP STRAUCH ZUM 80. GEBURTSTAGE AM 23. SEPTEMBER 1932 DARGEBRACHT VON FACHKOLLEGEN UND SCHUELERN
Schneider, Friedrich *see* HANDBUCH DES ORGANISTEN
Schneider, Georg A *see* TROIS QUATUORS POUR FLUTE, VIOLON, VIOLE ET VIOLONCELLE..
Schneider, Hermann *see*
- GERMANISCHE HELDENSAGE
- GESCHICHTE DER DEUTSCHEN DICHTUNG NACH IHREN EPOCHEN DARGESTELLT
- HELDENDICHTUNG, GEISTLICHENDICHTUNG, RITTERDICHTUNG
- "DAS MAEHRCHEN"
- STUDIEN ZU HEINRICH VON KLEIST
- WORKING AND WAITING FOR TIBET

Schneider, Hermann G *see*
- IHRER VIER
- MISSIONSARBEIT DER BRUEDERGEMEINDE IN AUSTRALIEN
- ZWEI AUFSATZE ZUR RELIGIONSGESCHICHTE VORDERASIENS

Schneider, Irmela *see* DIE ROLLE DES AUTORS
Schneider, J *see*
- DIE LEHRE VOM DREIEINIGEN GOTT IN DER SCHULE DES PETRUS LOMBARDUS

Schneider, Lucien *see*
- GRAMMAIRE ESQUIMAUDE DU SOUS-DIALECTE DE L'UNGAVA
- INUKTITUORUTIT
- INUKTITUORUTIT: GRAMMAIRE PUREMENT ESQUIMAUDE

Schneider, Manfred *see* WERKE
Schneider, Reinhold *see*
- AAR MIT GEBROCHENER SCHWINGE
- DER DICHTER VOR DER GESCHICHTE
- IM ANFANG LIEGT DAS ENDE

Schneider, Sznejder, Mordecai Bezalel *see* TORAT HA-LASHON BE-HITPATTEHUTAH

Schneider, Ursula *see* PERSEPOLIS AND ANCIENT IRAN
Schneider, Werner *see* DIE VERMEIDBARKEIT DES VERBOTSIRRTUMS
Schnell, H *see* HEINRICH V, DER FRIEDFERTIGE
SCHNELLER FUSS UND PFEILMAEDCHEN : EINE ERZAEHLUNG AUS DER ZEIT, ALS TECUMSEH ZWOELF JAHRE ALT WAR / Wittek, Erhard – Stuttgart: Franckh, c1935 – 1r – 1 – us U.W. Library [830]
Schnellmann *see* INVESTIGATION OF MINERAL DEPOSITS IN THE HASHEMITE KINGDOM OF JORDAN
Schneweis, E *see* ANGELS AND DEMONS ACCORDING TO LACTANTIUS
Schnitzer, Joseph *see*
- HAT JESUS DAS PAPSTTUM GESTIFTET?
- DER KATHOLISCHE MODERNISMUS
- SAVONAROLA IM STREITE MIT SEINEM ORDEN UND SEINEM KLOSTER

Schnitzler, Jean Henri *see* ETUDES SUR L'EMPIRE DES TSARS. HISTOIRE INTIME DE LA RUSSIE SOUS LES EMPEREURS ALEXANDRE ET NICOLAS ET PARTICULIEREMENT PENDANT LA CRISE DE 1825
Schnoering, Wilhelm *see* JOHANNES BLANKENFELD
Schnorr von Carolsfeld, Franz *see* ARCHIV FUER LITERATURGESCHICHTE
Schnuetgen, Alexander *see* DAS ELSASS UND DIE ERNEUERUNG DES KATHOLISCHEN LEBENS IN DEUTSCHLAND VON 1814 BIS 1848
SCHNURREN UDN SPAESSE / Queri, Georg – Leipzig: L Staackmann, 1935 – 1r – 1 – us U.W. Library [430]
Schocher, Christian G *see* SOLL DIE REDE AUF IMMER EIN DUNKLER GESANG BLEIBEN
Schodde, George *see* THE ERROR OF MODERN MISSOURI
Schodde, George H *see*
- THE BOOK OF ENOCH: TRANSLATED FROM THE ETHIOPIC, WITH INTRODUCTION AND NOTES
- THE PROTESTANT CHURCH IN GERMANY

Schodde, Georghe Henry *see* HERMA NABI
Schoder, Detlef *see* WISSENSBASIERTES INFORMATIONSSYSTEM ZU PROBLEMSTELLUNGEN AUS EMPIRISCHEN LOGISTIK-UNTERSUCHUNGEN
Schoebel, Charles *see*
- DE L'UNIVERSALITE DU DELUGE
- LE MOISE HISTORIQUE ET LA REDACTION MOSAIQUE DU PENTATEUQUE CHARLES SCHOEBEL

Schoeberlein, Ludwig *see* DIE GEHEIMNISSE DES GLAUBENS
Schoech, Dick *see* COMPUTERS IN HUMAN SERVICES
Schoelcher, Victor *see*
- DES COLONIES FRANCAISES. ABOLITION IMMEDIATE DE L'ESCLAVAGE
- DE L'ESCLAVAGE DES NOIRS ET DE LA LEGISLATION COLONIALE
- L'ESCLAVAGE AU SENEGAL EN 1880
- HISTOIRE DE L'ESCLAVAGE PENDANT LES DEUX DERNIERES ANNEES

Schoell, Adolf *see* GOETHES BRIEFE AN FRAU VON STEIN
Schoemann, Milian *see* NAPOLEON IN DER DEUTSCHEN LITERATUR
Schoen, Christopher H *see* COMPETITIVE ORIENTATION OF BASKETBALL STARTERS AND NONSTARTERS ACROSS DIFFERENT PLAYING LEVELS
Schoen, E *see* UNDERWEYSUNG DER PROPORTION UND STELLUNG DER POSSEN
Schoen, James Frederick *see* DICTIONARY OF THE HAUSA LANGUAGE.
SCHOEN, LIEBER JOSEPH! : SCHWANK IN 1 AKT / Barriere, Theodore – Berlin: A W Hayn's Erben, 1873 – 1 – us U.W. Library [820]
Schoenbaum, S *see* SHAKESPEARE IN CONTEXT
Schoenberg-Cotta, Family *see* MARTYRS AND SAINTS OF THE FIRST TWELVE CENTURIES
EYNE SCHOENE ARTZNEY, DADURCH DER LEIDENDEN CHRISTEN SORGE UND TRUBNUS GELINDERT...WERDEN / Magdeburg, J – [Luebeck, 1555] – 4mf – ne IDC [240]
EIN SCHOENE CRONICA, ODER HYSTORIBUCH VON DEN FUER NAMLICHSTEN WEYBERN / Boccaccio, G – Augspurg, 1541. BO-1011 1 – 9 – ne IDC [830]
DAS SCHOENE LAND ITALIA : TEXTE UND KONTEXTE DER ITALIENREISEN FONTANES / Riedel, Hella – 1992 – 9 – DM125.00 – 3-89349-528-2 – gw Hänsel [910]
SCHOENE LITERATUR *see* LITERARISCHES ZENTRALBLATT FUER DEUTSCHLAND 1850-1945
Schoeneberk, CS *see* DUOS CONCERTANS, TROIS, POUR VIOLIN ET VIOLONCELLE. OEUVRE 8
Schoener, Juergen Josef *see* PHAENOTYPISIERUNG ZYTOMEGALIEVIRUS-INFIZIERTER ZELLEN
Schoenfelder, A *see*
- DIE AGENDA DER DIOZESE NAUMBURG VON 1502
- DIE AGENDE DER DIOZESE SCHWERIN VON 1521
- DAS BENEDICTIONALE DES DIOZESE MEISSEN VON 1512

Schoenfelder, Josef M *see* DIE KLAGELIEDER DES JEREMIAS NACH RABBINISCHER AUSLEGUNG
Schoengen, Utif M *see* NARRATIO DE INCHOATIONE DOMUS CLERICORUM IN ZWOLLIS
DIE SCHOENHEIT DER KATHOLISCHEN KIRCHE / Rippel, Gregorius; ed by Himioben, Heinrich – (Includes index) – Mainz: Kirchheim, 1906 – 2mf – 9 – 0-8370-6835-5 – 1986-0835 – us A.T.L.A. [240]
Schoenherr, C J *see* SYNONYMIA INSECTORUM
Schoenholz, F A von *see* TRADITIONEN ZUR CHARAKTERISTIK OESTERREICHS
Schoenthan, Paul von *see* KINDERMUND
Schoepf, Ignaz *see* DIE KIRCHLICHEN ZUSTAENDE IN OESTERREICH UND DAS ALLGEMEINE KONZIL IN ROM
Schoepf, J D *see* MATERIA MEDICA AMERICANA...
DER SCHOEPFER : EIN SCHAUSPIEL IN VIER AUFZUEGEN / Mueller, Hans von – 1.-7. Aufl. Stuttgart: J G Cotta, 1918 1550 1r – 1 – us U.W. Library [820]
Schoepfer, Aemilian *see* BIBEL UND WISSENSCHAFT
DIE SCHOEPFUNG – Duesseldorf, Germany. Jul 1921-1923 (incomplete) – 1 – gw Mikrofilm [072]
Schoepp, F *see* SUIKER
Schoeps, Hans-Joachim *see* BEITRAEGE ZUR ENTWICKLUNG RELIGIONSSYSTEMATISCHEN DENKENS IM JUDENTUM DES 19. JAHRHUNDERTS
Schoeps, Richard *see* ZU GOETHES WILHELM MEISTER
Schoettle, Holger Hans *see* INTEGRIERTE MODELLKONZEPTE
Schoettler, Wilhelm *see* DIE INNERE MOTIVIERUNG IN GRABBES DRAMEN
Schoewerling, Rainer *see* ANTI-NAPOLEONISCHE PAMPHLETE
Schoewerling, Rainer et al *see* CORVEY
Schofield, A T *see* MEMORIALS OF R. HAROLD A. SCHOFIELD, FIRST MEDICAL MISSIONARY TO SHAN-SI, CHINA; CHIEFLY COMP. FROM HIS LETTERS AND DIARIES...
Schola Cantorum *see*
- TRIBUNE DE SAINT-GERVAIS: REVUE DE LA SCHOLA CANTORUM
- TRIBUNE DE ST. GERVAIS

SCHOLA CORDIS SIVE AVERSI A DEO CORDIS AD EUMDEM REDUCTIO, ET INSTRUCTIO / Haeften, Benedictus van – Antwerpen, 1663 – 8mf – 9 – O-3223/1 – ne IDC [760]
SCHOLARLY PUBLISHING – (1982-. 1,5,6,9) – v1-. 1969- – 1 – us UMI [073]
SCHOLARLY PUBLISHING – Downsview. v1- 1969/70- – 9 – Can$20.00y – cn Micromedia [070]
SCHOLARS' FACSIMILES AND REPRINTS SERIES – 191 v. 1936-71 – 9 – us Scholars' Facs [080]
THE SCHOLARS GUIDE FROM THE ACCIDENCE TO THE UNIVERSITY / Johnson, Ralph – 1665. 53p. (English Linguistics Series 1500-1800) – 9 – us UMI [450]
THE SCHOLARS' MONTHLY – (Cont by: High School Monthly (New Glasgow, N.S.)) – New Glasgow, NS: New Glasgow High School, [1886-1890?] – 9 – cn C.I.H.M. [370]
SCHOLASTIC ACTION – (v.4-. 1980- 5,6,9) – v.1-. 1977- – 1 – us UMI [073]
SCHOLASTIC COACH – (v. 38- 1968- 5,6. v. 45- 1975- 9) – v. 1- 1931- – 1 – us UMI [790]
SCHOLASTIC DYNAMATH – (1985-. 1,5,6) – v1-. 1982- – 9 – us UMI [370]
SCHOLASTIC EDITORS' TRENDS IN PUBLICATIONS – v62-. 1982- – 1,5,6,9 – us UMI [073]
SCHOLASTIC LET'S FIND OUT – (v.15-. 1980- 5,6,9) – v.1-. 1966- – 1 – us UMI [073]
SCHOLASTIC MATH MAGAZINE. 1980- – 1,5,6,9 – us UMI [370]
SCHOLASTIC NEWS – 2. Ranger. v39-. 1982- – 1,5,6,9 – us UMI [073]
SCHOLASTIC NEWS – 3. Trails. v39-. 1982- – 1,5,6,9 – us UMI [073]
SCHOLASTIC NEWS – 4. Explorer. v45-. 1982- – 1,5,6,9 – us UMI [073]
SCHOLASTIC NEWS – 5. Citizen. v51-. 1982- – 1,5,6,9 – us UMI [073]
SCHOLASTIC NEWS – 6. Newstime. v55-. 1982- – 1,5,6,9 – us UMI [073]
SCHOLASTIC NEWS – v39-. 1982- – 1,5,6,9 – us UMI [073]
SCHOLASTIC NEWS CITIZEN – (v48- Sep 1979- 5,6,9) – v38- Feb. 1973- – 1 – us UMI [073]
SCHOLASTIC NEWS EXPLORER – (v.43-. 1980- 5,6,9) – v.1-. 1957- – 1 – us UMI [073]
SCHOLASTIC NEWS PILOT – (v.37-38. 1980-82. 5,6,9) – v.1-38. 1960-82 – 1 – us UMI [073]
SCHOLASTIC NEWS RANGER – (v.36-. Sep 1979- 5,6,9) – v.1-. Sep 1960- – 1 – us UMI [073]
SCHOLASTIC NEWS TRAILS – (1980- 5,6,9) – 1960- – 1 – us UMI [073]
THE SCHOLASTIC PHILOSOPHY CONSIDERED IN ITS RELATION TO CHRISTIAN THEOLOGY : IN A COURSE OF LECTURES DELIVERED BEFORE THE UNIVERSITY OF OXFORD, IN THE YEAR MDCCCXXXII, AT THE LECTURE FOUNDED BY JOHN BAMPTON, M.A., CANON OF SALISBURY / Hampden, R D – London: B. Fellowes, 1837 – 2mf – us A.T.L.A. [180]
SCHOLASTIC SPRINT – (v5-. 1979- 5,6,9) – v1-. 1975- – 1 – us UMI [073]
SCHOLASTIC UPDATE – v115-. 1983- – 1,5,6,9 – us UMI [073]
SCHOLASTICA COMMENTARIA IN PRIMAM PARTEM ANGELICI DOCTORIS S. THOMAE / Banes, Dom – Duaci, 1614 – 54mf – 8 – ne Slangenburg [240]
SCHOLASTICA COMMENTARIA IN PRIMAM PARTEM ANGELICI DOCTORIS S. THOMAE USQUE AD 63 QUAESTIONEM COMPLECTENTIA / Banes, Dom – Romae, 1584 – 14mf – 8 – ne Slangenburg [240]
SCHOLASTICA COMMENTARIA IN PRIMAM PARTEM, SUMMAE THEOLOGICAE S. THOMAE AQUINATIS / Banes, Dom – Madrid, Valencia, 1935 – 7mf – 9 – CA-64/1 – ne IDC [240]
SCHOLASTICA COMMENTARIA IN PRIMAM PARTEM SUMMAE THEOLOGICAE S. THOMAE AQUINATIS. Q1-Q26 / ed by Urbano, L – Madrid-Valencia, 1934 – 12mf – 8 – ne Slangenburg [240]
SCHOLASTICA COMMENTARIA IN SECUNDAM SECUNDAE ANGELICI DOCTORIS S. THOMAE / Banes, Dom – Duaci, 1614 – 42mf – 8 – ne Slangenburg [240]
Scholastici, Agathiae *see* DE IMPERIO ET REBUS GESTIS IUSTINIANI (CBH 4)
SCHOLASTIK – 1(1926)-19(1944) – 142mf – 9 – Dfl497.00 – ne Slangenburg [073]
SCHOLASTIK – Freiburg i.B. v1-19. 1926-1944 – 142mf – 9 – ne IDC [240]
DIE SCHOLASTIK DES 13 / Guttmann, J – Jahrhundrets in ihren Beziehungen zum Judenthum und zur juedischen Literatur. Breslau. 1902. BJ-33-37 1 – 9 – ne IDC [270]
DIE SCHOLASTIK DES SPAETEREN MITTELALTERS : BAND 3: DER AUGUSTINISMUS IN DER SCHOLASTIK DES SPAETEREN MITTELALTERS / Werner, K – Wien, 1883 – 6mf – 8 – ne Slangenburg [100]
DIE SCHOLASTIK DES SPAETEREN MITTELALTERS : BAND 3: DER AUGUSTINISMUS IN DER SCHOLASTIK DES SPAETEREN MITTELALTERS / Werner, K – Wien, 1883 – 6mf – 8 – ne Slangenburg [180]
Scholberg, Henry *see*
- THE DISTRICT GAZETTEERS OF BRITISH INDIA
- INDIA GAZETTEERS

Scholefield, E OS *see* BRITISH COLUMBIA
Scholefield, James *see* HINTS FOR SOME IMPROVEMENTS IN THE AUTHORIZED VERSION OF THE NEW TESTAMENT
Scholem, G *see* BIBLIOGRAPHIA KABBALISTICA, VERZEICHNIS DER GEDRUCKTEN; DIE JUEDISCHE MYSTIK (GNOSIS, KABBALA...) VON REUCHLIN BIS ZUR GEGENWART
Scholes, Theophilus E Samuel *see* GLIMPSES OF THE AGES
SCHOLIA IN QUATUOR EVANGELIA EX SELECTIS DOCTORUM SACRORUM SENTENTIIS COLLECTA / Sa, E – Antverpiae, 1595 – 11mf – 8 – ne Slangenburg [220]
SCHOLIAE IN QUATUOR EVANGELIA / Sa, E – Antverpiae, 1596 – 6mf – 9 – CA-01/1 – ne IDC [240]
DER SCHOLIEN-KOMMENTAR DAS ORIGENES ZUR APOKALYPSE JOHANNIS (T.U.U. 3-38/3) / Diobounioits, C & Harnack, Adolf von – Leipzig, 1911 – 2mf – 9 – ne Slangenburg [240]
Scholl, Bernadette *see* BUCHGEMEINSCHAFTEN IN DEUTSCHLAND 1918-1933
Scholl, Warren *see* HISTORY AND BELIEFS OF THE MAJOR RELIGIONS
SCHOLLE – Braunau, 1938 – 1 – Inquire at Mikrofilmarchiv for details – gw Misc Inst [943]
Schollenheber, Wilhelm Heinrich *see* E.T.A. HOFFMANNS PERSOENLICHKEIT
Schols, France V *see* DON DIEGO QUIJADA...
Scholte Nollen, John *see* PRINZ FRIEDRICH VON HOMBURG
Scholten, Johannes Henricus *see*
- HISTORISCH-CRITISCHE BIJDRAGEN
- LEER DER HERVORMDE KERK...UIT DE BRONNEN VOORGESTELD
- DAS PAULINISCHE EVANGELIUM

Scholtze, Christian Achmed *see* PHILANDER VON SITTEWALD
Scholz, Anton *see*
- DIE ALEXANDRINISCHE UEBERSETZUNG DES BUCHES JESAIAS: EINE RECTORSREDE
- COMMENTAR UEBER DAS BUCH JUDITH UND UEBER BEL UND DRACHE
- COMMENTAR ZUM BUCHE DES PROPHETEN HOSEAS
- COMMENTAR ZUM BUCHE DES PROPHETEN JOEL

Scholz, Harry *see* AERZTE IN OST- UND WESTPREUSSEN
Scholz, Hermann *see* DIE CHRISTLICHE ERFAHRUNG...LUTHERS KATECHISMUS ARTIKEL 3: SECHS VORLESUNGEN
Scholz, R *see* WILHELM VON OCKHAM ALS POLITISCHER DENKER UND SEIN BREVILOQUIUM DE PRINCIPATU TYRANNICO (MGH SCHRIFTEN..: 8.BD)
Scholz, Wilhelm *see* FRIEDRICH SCHILLER
Scholz, Wilhelm von *see*
- ANNETTE VON DROSTE-HUELSHOFF ALS WESTFAELISCHE DICHTERIN
- HEBBEL
- DER TOD DES EMPEDOKLES

Scholze, Werner *see* DIE AESTHETISCHEN KONZEPTIONEN VON JOHN KEATS UND G.W.F. HEGELS VORLESUNGEN UEBER DIE AESTHETIK
Schomberg, Isaac *see* NAVAL CHRONOLOGY: OR, AN HISTORICAL SUMMARY OF NAVAL AND MARITIME EVENTS, FROM THE TIME OF THE ROMANS TO THE TREATY OF PEACE, 1802
Schomburg Center for Research in Black Culture *see*
- DU BOIS NEWSPAPER CLIPPING BOOKS
- A SELECTION OF TITLES. SERIES 1
- A SELECTION OF TITLES. SERIES 2

SCHOMBURG CLIPPING FILE / New York Public Library – (Pt 1 1924-75 9,673mf £19,425.00. Africa 1,362mf £3,895.00. Pt 2 1975-88 3,861mf £12,900. Pt 1 and Africa with printed names and subject index £58) – 9 – £29,215.00 – uk Chadwyck [080]
Schomburgk, R H *see* THE NATURAL HISTORY OF THE FISHES OF GUIANA
Schomer, Abraham Shaikewitz *see* THE PRIMARY CAUSE OF ANTISEMITISM: AN ANSWER TO THE JEWISH QUESTION
SCHONGAUER NACHRICHTEN – Schongau, Germany. 1 Sept 1978- – ca 13r per yr – 1 – gw Mikrofilm [072]
Schonsleder, W *see* ARCHITECTIONICE MUSICES UNIVERSALIS
SCHOOL AND COMMUNITY – v1- 1915- 1; v57- 5,6; v62- 9 – us UMI [370]
SCHOOL AND HOME – Toronto: Educational Pub Co, [1895?-19–] – 9 – cn C.I.H.M. [370]
SCHOOL AND HOME – Toronto: Educational Pub Co, [1895?-19–] – 9 – cn C.I.H.M. [370]
SCHOOL AND HOME – Toronto: Educational Pub. Co., [1895?-19–] – 9 – cn C.I.H.M. [370]

SCHOOL AND HOME – Toronto: Educational Pub Co, [1895?-19–] – 9 – cn C.I.H.M. [370]
SCHOOL AND SOCIETY – v. 1-58. 1915-1943 – 1 – us Princeton Micro [370]
SCHOOL ARTS – (v. 68- 1968- 5,6. v. 69-1969- 9) – v. 1- 1901- – 1 – us UMI [700]
SCHOOL ATTENDANCE REPORTS / Fulton County. Ohio. Board of Education – 1923-1933 – 1r – 1 – $32.50r – us Archival [324]
THE SCHOOL BOOK QUESTION – Montreal: John Lovell, 1866. SEM105P366 – 1mf – 9 – Can$2.25 – cn Bibl Nat [370]
SCHOOL BUILDINGS AND NATURAL DISASTERS / Vickery, D J – 1982 – 9 – 92-3-102031-5 – fr UNESCO [360]
SCHOOL BUSINESS AFFAIRS – v1- 1936- 1; v42- 5,6,9 – us UMI [370]
SCHOOL BUSINESS MANAGEMENT – Piedmont, CA: Public School Business Assoc. v19-20. jul 1953-jan 1955 – us Res Libr [370]
SCHOOL CERTIFICATE EXAMINATION: REPORT OF THE PANEL OF INVESTIGATORS / Great Britain – 1932 – 2mf – 9 – uk Microform Academic [324]
SCHOOL COUNSELOR – (v.19- 1971- 5,6. v.23- 1975- 9) – v.1- 1953- – 1 – us UMI [073]
A SCHOOL DICTIONARY : ENGLISH AND CANARESE / Ziegler, F – 3rd rev enl ed. Mangalore: Basel Mission & Tract Depository, 1896 – us Res Libr [040]
SCHOOL DISTRICT RECORD / Monroe County. Mich, Bedford Township. Board of Education – 1864-1912 – 1r – 1 – $32.50r – us Archival [324]
SCHOOL EXAMINERS' REPORTS / Fulton County. Ohio. Board of Education – 1927-1935 – 1r – 1 – $32.50r – us Archival [324]
THE SCHOOL FOR RAKES, A COMEDY : AS IT IS PERFORMED AT THE THEATRE-ROYAL IN DRURY-LANE / Griffiths, E – London, 1769 – 2mf – 9 – ne IDC [820]
SCHOOL FUND ACCOUNT BOOK / Ottawa County. Ohio. Carroll Township. Township Clerk – 1887-1890 – 1r – 1 – $32.50r – us Archival [324]
SCHOOL FUND ACCOUNT RECORDS / Hancock County. Ohio. Biglick Township. Board of Education – 1866-1903 – 1r – 1 – $32.50r – us Archival [324]
SCHOOL FUND ACCOUNT RECORDS / Wyandot County. Ohio. Auditor – 1845-1859 – 1r – 1 – $32.50r – us Archival [324]
SCHOOL FUND RECORD / Ottawa County. Ohio. Carroll Township. Township Clerk – 1866-1885 – 1r – 1 – $32.50r – us Archival [324]
SCHOOL FUND RECORD / Paulding County, Ohio. Crane Township. Township Clerk – 1915-1926 – 1r – 1 – us Archival [324]
SCHOOL FUND RECORD / Paulding County. Ohio. Crane Township. Township Clerk – 1915-1926 – 1r – 1 – $32.50r – us Archival [324]
SCHOOL FUND SETTLEMENTS / Fulton County. Ohio. Auditor – 1850-1859 – 2r – 1 – $32.50r – us Archival [324]
A SCHOOL GRAMMAR OF ATTIC GREEK / Goodell, Thomas Dwight – (Includes indexes) – New York: D Appleton, 1907, c1902 – 1mf – 9 – 0-8370-9234-5 – 1986-3234 – us A.T.L.A. [480]
SCHOOL GUIDANCE WORKER – v1- 1944- 1; v36- 1980- 5,6,9 – us UMI [370]
SCHOOL IDEALS : SERMONS / James, Herbert A – London; New York: Macmillan, 1887 – 1mf – 9 – 0-8370-7393-6 – 1986-1393 – us A.T.L.A. [240]
SCHOOL JOURNAL – Marshfield OR. Nov 1883 – 1 – us U.O. Library [071]
SCHOOL LAND RECORD / Van Wert County. Ohio. Auditor – 1844 – 1r – 1 – $32.50r – us Archival [324]
SCHOOL LAND RECORDS / Allen County. Ohio. Auditor – 1850-1881 – 1r – 1 – $32.50r – us Archival [324]
SCHOOL LAND RECORDS / Fulton County. Ohio. Auditor – 1847-1883 – 1r – 1 – $32.50r – us Archival [324]
SCHOOL LAND RECORDS / Huron County. Ohio. Auditor – 1819-1900 – 1r – 1 – $32.50r – us Archival [324]
SCHOOL LAND RECORDS / Ottawa County. Ohio. Auditor – 1820-1887 – 2r – 1 – $32.50r – us Archival [324]
SCHOOL LAW BULLETIN – v1- 1970- 1; v8- 5,6,9 – us UMI [340]
SCHOOL LIBRARIES IN CANADA – 1980-1990 – 4r – 1 – cn Library Assoc [020]
SCHOOL LIBRARIES IN CANADA – Ottawa. v1-15. 1980/81-1995 – 9 – Can$20.00y – cn Micromedia [020]
SCHOOL LIBRARY JOURNAL – v. 21-. 1975- – 1,5,6,9 – us UMI [370]
SCHOOL LIBRARY SERVICE CATALOGUE ON MICROFICHE – 1994. Four issues/y – NZ$144.00 – nz Nat'l Libr [020]
SCHOOL LIFE *see* AMERICAN EDUCATION
SCHOOL MAGAZINE *see*
- THE CANADA EDUCATIONAL MONTHLY AND SCHOOL CHRONICLE
- THE QUARTERLY

THE SCHOOL MAGAZINE – (Cont: The Quarterly. Is absorbed by: The Canada Educational Monthly and School Chronicle) – Hamilton, Ont.?: s.n., 1880?-1881 – 9 – cn C.I.H.M. [370]
SCHOOL MANAGEMENT – (v. 13-18. 1969-74. 5,6. v. 15-18. 1971-74. 9) – 1-18. 1957-74 – 1 – us UMI [370]
SCHOOL MANUAL OF THE LAW OF MOSES / Pirie, James – London: Edward Stanford, 1880. 1 fiche – 9 – us A.T.L.A. [240]
SCHOOL MUSIC NEWS – v1- 1936- 1; v38- 5,6; v39- 9 – us UMI [370]
SCHOOL MUSIC REVIEW; A MONTHLY PERIODICAL, DEVOTED TO THE INTERESTS OF MUSIC SCHOOLS – 1-38. 1892-May 1930 – 1 – us UMI [780]
School of Administration, Hoover Institute, Stanford University *see* TRUST TERRITORY OF THE PACIFIC ISLANDS NAVAL ADMINISTRATION
THE SCHOOL OF LIFE / Alger, William Rounseville – Boston: Roberts, 1881 – 1mf – 9 – 0-8370-6082-6 – 1986-0082 – us A.T.L.A. [240]
SCHOOL OF LIVING – Some papers on its anarchism and monetary freedom views. 1 fiche – 9 – 1.00f – at Libertarian Micro [320]
School of Living *see* HOW TO ECONOMIZE ON CANNED FOODS, A MANUAL ON HOME CANNING AND PRESERVING
School of Oriental and African Studies *see* CONFERENCE OF BRITISH MISSIONARY SOCIETIES ARCHIVES
SCHOOL OF ORIENTAL AND AFRICAN STUDIES, LONDON – ca 650.000 cards on 695mf – 9 – ne IDC [950]
School of Oriental and African Studies, London *see*
- ARABIC MANUSCRIPTS IN THE SOAS, LONDON
- COUNCIL FOR WORLD MISSION ARCHIVES 1775-1940
- EARLY WESTERN BOOKS 1500-1599
- JAPANESE MANUSCRIPTS
- THE JOINT IMC/CBMS MISSIONARY ARCHIVES
- LIBRARY CATALOGUE, 5TH SUPPLEMENT 1978-1989
- METHODIST MISSIONARY SOCIETY ARCHIVES 1791-1948
- PRESBYTERIAN CHURCH OF ENGLAND 1847-1950
- UNITED SOCIETY FOR CHRISTIAN LITERATURE ARCHIVES 1799-1960

THE SCHOOL OF PLATO : ITS ORIGIN, DEVELOPMENT, AND REVIVAL UNDER THE ROMAN EMPIRE / Bussell, FW – London: Methuen, 1896 – 1mf – us A.T.L.A. [180]
THE SCHOOL OF ST MATTHEW AND ITS USE OF THE OLD TESTAMENT / Stendahl, K – Uppsala, 1954 – 5mf – 8 – ne Slangenburg [220]
THE SCHOOL OF THE PROPHETS, OR, FATHER MCROREY'S CLASS, AND SQUIRE FIRSTMAN'S KITCHEN FIRE: A FICTION FOUNDED ON FACTS, A BOOK FOR THE METHODISTS / Carroll, John – Toronto: Burrage and Magurn, 1876. 00489. (Pre-1900 Canadiana) – 9 – cn C.I.H.M. [240]
SCHOOL ORGANISATION – 1981- 13v – 9 – £135.50 – 0260-1362 – uk Carfax [370]
SCHOOL ORGANISATION AND MANAGEMENT ABSTRACTS – 1982- 12v – 9 – £197.00 – 0261-2755 – uk Carfax [370]
SCHOOL PROGRAM IN PHYSICAL EDUCATION / Hetherington, Clark W – 1922 – 3mf – 9 – $9.00 – us Microform Publ [790]
SCHOOL PSYCHOLOGY DIGEST – v.1-8. 1972-79 – 1 – us UMI [150]
SCHOOL PSYCHOLOGY REVIEW – v.9-. 1980- – 1,5,6,9 – us UMI [150]
SCHOOL RECORD / Crawford. County, Ohio. Liberty Township. Board of Education – 1857-1896 – 1r – 1 – $32.50r – us Archival [324]
SCHOOL REGISTERS / Hancock County. Ohio. Marion Township. Board of Education – 1893-1907 – 1r – 1 – $32.50r – us Archival [324]
SCHOOL REGISTERS, DISTRICT NO. 2 / Hancock County. Ohio. Biglick Township. Board of Education – 1900-1907 – 1r – 1 – $32.50r – us Archival [324]
SCHOOL REVIEW – v. 1-53. 1893-1945 – 1 – us Princeton Micro [370]
SCHOOL REVIEW – (v. 77-87. 1969-79. 5,6. v. 86-87. 1977-79. 9) – v. 1-87. 1893-1979 – 1 – us UMI [370]
SCHOOL REVIEW *see* AMERICAN JOURNAL OF EDUCATION
SCHOOL SCIENCE AND MATHEMATICS – v. 1-40. 1902-1940 – 1 – us Princeton Micro [370]
SCHOOL SCIENCE REVIEW – v1- 1919- 1; v68- 1968- 5,6; v75- 1975- 9 – us UMI [370]
SCHOOL SOCIAL WORK JOURNAL – v.1-. 1976- – 1 – us UMI [370]
THE SCHOOL SUPPLEMENT – Toronto, Mar 1884 Extra – 1r – 1 – Can$25.00 – cn Can Microfilming [072]
THE SCHOOL TIMES – Winnipeg: School Times Co, [1888-18– or 19–] – 9 – cn C.I.H.M. [370]
SCHOOL TREASURER'S REPORTS / Wyandot County. Ohio. Auditor – 1846-1859 – 1r – 1 – $32.50r – us Archival [324]
SCHOOL VAN NEDERLANDS-INDIE : NEDERLANDSCH-INDISCH ONDERWIJZERS GENOOTSCHAP – (Lacking: 1921, V.11(p.1-31); 1929/1930, V.20(p.1-95)) – Batavia, 1910-1954 – 568mf – 9 – SE-20,003/1 – ne IDC [950]
Schoolcraft, Henry Rowe *see* PAPERS
DE SCHOOLE DER WERELD, GEOPENT IN 140. VLIEGENDE BEDENKINGEN OP VEERLERHANDE VOORVALLENDE GEZICHTEN EN ZAEKEN : IN'T LATYN OPGESTELT DOOR JOSEF HALL, EN IN NEDERDUITS DIGT GEVOLGD DOOR FRANCOIS VAN HOOGSTRATEN / Hoogstraten, Francois van – Amsterdam, n.d. – 5mf – 9 – O-3086/1 – ne IDC [760]
SCHOOLFLORA VOOR JAVA (RANUNCULACEAS – MYRTACEAE) / Backer, C A – Weltevreden, 1911 – 10mf – 9 – ne IDC [580]
THE SCHOOLHOUSE / Earl, Edward Curtis – Washington, DC, 1919. 20p – 1 – us U.W. Library [370]
SCHOOLHOUSE BLUEPRINTS / Hancock County. Ohio. Biglick Township. Board of Education – 1911-1912 – 1r – 1 – $32.50r – us Archival [324]
SCHOOLMASTER AND EDINBURGH WEEKLY MAGAZINE – London, UK. 1832-33. -irr. 1/2 reel – 1 – uk British Libr Newspaper [073]
THE SCHOOLMASTER, OR PLAINE AND PERFITE WAY OF TEACHING CHILDREN THE LATIN TONG / Ascham, Roger – 1570. 151p. (English Linguistics Series 1500-1800) – 9 – us UMI [450]
THE SCHOOLMASTER'S STORIES, FOR BOYS AND GIRLS / Eggleston, Edward – Boston: H.L. Shepard..., 1874. 279p. illus. plates – 1 – us U.W. Library [830]
THE SCHOOLMISTRESS – London, England. -w. Dec 1881-Dec 1914. 40 reels – 1 – uk British Libr Newspaper [072]
SCHOOLS AND KINDERGARTENS 1973/1974 / Israel. Prime Minister's Office. Ministry of Education and Culture – Jerusam, 1975. 21, 104, 24 p. (Special Series no. 491). Text also in Hebrew – 9 – 3.00 – is I.T.T.I. [324]
SCHOOLS AND MASTERS OF FENCE, FROM THE MIDDLE AGES TO THE EIGHTEENTH CENTURY / Castle, Egerton – With complete bibliography. Illus. New and rev. ed. London and New York: G. Bell & Sons, 1893. lxxviii,355p – 1 – us U.W. Library [790]
SCHOOLS AND UNIVERSITIES ON THE CONTINENT / Arnold, Matthew – London: Macmillan, 1868 – 1 roll – 1 – 1-55879-192-2 – uk Libr Preservation [370]
THE SCHOOLS OF CHARLES THE GREAT AND THE RESTORATION OF EDUCATION IN THE NINTH CENTURY / Mullinger, James Bass – (Includes bibliographical references) – London: Longmans, Green, 1877 – 1mf – 9 – 0-8370-7652-8 – 1986-1652 – us A.T.L.A. [370]
THE SCHOOLS OF MEDIEVAL ENGLAND / Leach, A F – H-1201 2. 1915 – 8 – ne IDC [941]
EEN SCHOONE ENDE PROFITELIJCK LEERINGHE WT GODS WOORDT ALLEN MENSCHEN VERMANENDE TOT DIE HEMELSCHE WEDERGEBOORTE ENDENIEUWE CREATURE / Simons, Menno – BME-275 1 – 9 – ne IDC [240]
EEN SCHOONE ENDE PROFITELIJCKE VERMANENDE ENDE BESTRAFFENDE REDENE AEN DIE OUERHEYT, GHELEERDE ENDE GHEMEYN VOLCK / Simons, Menno – BME-274 1 – 9 – ne IDC [240]
EEN SCHOONE VERMANINGHE ENDE CORTTE ONDERWYSINGHE VANDER WARACHTIGHER KENNISSEN GODTS / Philips, Dirk – 1558. BME-305 1 – 9 – ne IDC [240]
Schoop, Michael *see* AUSGEWAEHLTE ASPEKTE RECHNERGESTUETZTER INFORMATIONS- UND KOMMUNIKATIONSTECHNOLOGIEN
Schopenhauer, Arthur *see*
- ERISTISCHE DIALEKTIK
- ESSAI SUR LE LIBRE ARBITRE
- THE WORLD AS WILL AND IDEA

SCHOPENHAUER BIBLIOGRAPHIE / Aul, Joachim – 1995 – 2mf – 9 – DM80.00 – 3-8267-2266-3 – gw Hänsel [120]
Schopenhauer, Johanna *see* DAMALS IN WEIMAR
SCHOPENHAUERS BEGRUENDUNGSTHEORIE IM LICHTE DER ERGEBNISSE DER MODERNEN WISSENSCHAFTSTHEORIE / Aul, Joachim – 1994 – 2mf – DM80.00 – 3-8267-2008-3 – gw Hänsel [190]
Schopeni, Lud. *see*
- BYZANTINA HISTORIA (CSHB 6-8)
- IOANNIS CANTACUZENI EXIMPERATORIS HISTORIARUM LIBRI 4 (CSHB 2-4)

DIE SCHOPFUNG. CREATION, AN ORATORIO, ARRANGED AS A QUARTET / Haydn, Joseph – (4 parts) – London: Preston, 181- – 1 – us Sibley [780]
DIE SCHOPFUNG. ORATORIUM, TEXT VON HOFBAUM. PARTITUR / Krause, B – Contemporary Ms copy, 1790 – 1 – us Sibley [780]
Schopperus, H *see* DE OMNIBUS ILLIBERALIBUS SIVE MECHANICIS ARTIBUS
Schor, J *see* MISHNAT R. YA'AKOV. MAVO AL HA-TOSEFTA
Schorr, M *see*
- KOVEZ MADDA'I LE-ZEKHER MOSHEH SCHORR
- URKUNDEN DES ALTBABYLONISCHEN ZIVIL- UND PROZESSRECHTS

Schotel, G D J *see*
- ANNA MARIA VAN SCHURMAN
- GESCHIEDENIS VAN DEN OORSPRONG, DE INVOERING EN DE LOTGEVALLEN VAN DEN HEIDELBERGSCHEN CATECHISMUS

Schott, H W *see*
- ANALECTA BOTANICA
- DRAWINGS OF ARACEAE
- ENUMERATIO PLANTARUM QUAS IN NOVAE HOLLANDIAE
- GENERA AROIDEARUM EXPOSITA
- GENERA FILICUM
- ICONES AROIDEARUM
- MELETEMATA BOTANICA
- PRODROMUS SYSTEMATIS AROIDEARUM
- SYNOPSIS AROIDEARUM

Schott, Theodor *see*
- DIE AUFHEBUNG DES EDIKTES VON NANTES IM OKTOBER 1685
- DIE KIRCHE DER WUESTE 1715 BIS 1787

Schott, W *see* VERZEICHNIS DER CHINESISCHEN UND MANDSCHU-TUNGUSISCHEN BUECHER UND HANDSCHRIFTEN DER KOENIGLICHEN BIBLIOTHEK ZU BERLIN
Schotte, Heinrich *see* HANS HEINER ROSELIEB'S EWIGER SONNTAG
Schottelius-Winter, Lotti *see* DER FUNKTIONALE ASPEKT DER TRAEUME IM WERK WILHELM RAABES
Schottman, W *see* LA PAROLE DANS LA VIE SOCIALE DES BAATOMBU
Schouler, James *see*
- A TREATISE ON THE LAW OF BAILMENTS, INCLUDING CARRIERS, INNKEEPERS, AND PLEDGE
- A TREATISE ON THE LAW OF THE DOMESTIC RELATIONS

Schouppe, Francois Xavier *see* EVANGELIA DE COMMUNI SANCTORUM
Schouten, Joost *see* A TRUE DESCRIPTION OF THE MIGHTY KINGDOMS OF JAPAN AND SIAM

SCHOUWTOONEEL DER MARTELAREN / Luiken, J – O 346. 1738 – 9 – ne IDC [240]

HET SCHOUWTOONEEL VAN DEUGDEN EN GEBREEKEN... – Amsterdam, 1781 – 2mf – 9 – ne IDC [700]

Schrader, Eberhard *see*
- DIE ASSYRISCH-BABYLONISCHEN KEILINSCHRIFTEN
- ASSYRISCHES SYLLABAR
- DIE KEILINSCHRIFTEN AM EINGANGE DER QUELLGROTTE DES SEBENEH-SU
- KEILINSCHRIFTLICH BIBLIOTHEK
- DIE NAMEN DER MEERE IN DEN ASSYRISCHEN INSCHRIFTEN
- DIE SARGONSSTELE DES BERLINER MUSEUMS
- STUDIEN ZUR KRITIK UND ERKLAERUNG DER BIBLISCHEN URGESCHICHTE, GEN. CAP. 1-11
- UEBER EINEN ALTBABYLONISCHEN KOENIGSCYLINDER DES KOENIGL. MUSEUMS UND EINIGE ANDERE CYLINDER UND GEMMEN

Schrader, Fr. Ch *see* A RECONNAISSANCE IN NORTHERN ALASKA ACROSS THE ROCKY MOUNTAINS, ALONG KOYUKUK, JOHN, ANAKTUVUK, AND COLVILLE RIVERS, AND THE ARCTIC COAST TO CAPE LISBURNE IN 1901

Schrader, H A *see*
- ANALECTA AD FLORAM CAPENSEM
- HORTUS GOTTINGENSIS SEU PLANTAE NOVAE ET RARIORES HORTI REGII BOTANICI GOTTINGENSIS DESCRIPTAE ET ICONIBUS ILLUSTRATAE
- JOURNAL FUER DIE BOTANIK
- NOVA GENERA PLANTARUM
- SERTUM HANNOVERANUM
- SPICILEGIUM FLORAE GERMANICAE

Schrader, Hans *see* HOELDERLINS DEUTUNG DES "OEDIPUS" UND DER "ANTIGONE"

Schrader, Hermann *see* DAS GEHEIMNIS UND DIE INNERE EINHEIT DER DREY GOETHE'SCHEN BALLADEN

Schrader, Marianne *see* POLYDAKTYLIEN DER HAENDE

Schrader, Otto *see* VICTOR HEHN

Schramm, Edmund *see* DER JUNGE DONOSCO CORTES (1809-1836)

Schramm, George *see* CHU JIH YUAN LIU (CCC272)

Schramm, Heinz-Eugen *see* MICHEL BUCK ALS MUNDARTDICHTER

Schramm, P E *see* HERRSCHAFTSZEICHEN UND STAATSYMBOLIK (MGH SCHRIFTEN..: 13.BD)

Schrank, F von *see*
- BAIERSCHE FLORA
- NATURHISTORISCHE BRIEFE UEBER OESTREICH, SALZBURG, PASSAU UND BERCHTESGADEN
- PLANTAE RARIORES HORTI ACADEMICI MONACENSIS
- PRIMITIAE FLORAE SALISBURGENSIS

Schrank, W *see* BABYLONISCHE SUEHNRITEN BESONDERS MIT RUECKSICHT AUF PRIESTER UND BUESSER

Schrauf, Torsten *see* QUANTITATIVE UND QUALITATIVE PROGNOSE DES ZUKUENFTIG ANFALLENDEN AUFKOMMENS AN ELEKTRONIKSCHROTT

Schreber, J C D von *see*
- BESCHREIBUNG DER GRAESER
- ICONES ET DESCRIPTIONES PLANTARUM MINUS COGNITARUM
- PLANTAE VERTICILLATAE UNILABIATAE
- DIE SAEUGETHIERE IN ABBILDUNG NACH DER NATUR...
- SPICILEGIUM FLORAE LIPSICAE

SCHREIBEN UEBER DIE BERLINISCHE MUSIK.. / Reichardt, Johann F – 1775 – 2 – us Sibley [780]

Schreiber, Albert *see* NEUE BAUSTEINE ZU EINER LEBENSGESCHICHTE WOLFRAMS VON ESCHENBACH

Schreiber, Emanuel *see* REFORMED JUDAISM AND ITS PIONEERS

Schreiber, F *see* VERGISSMEINNICHT

Schreiber, Hans Ulrich *see* JOSEPH HILLEBRAND

Schreiber, Heinrich *see*
- JOHANN ALBRECHT 1, HERZOG VON MECKLENBURG
- DIE REFORMATION LUEBECKS

Schreiner, M *see*
- DER KALAM IN DER JUEDISCHEN LITERATUR
- LE KITAB AL-MOUHADARA WA-L-MOUDHAKARA DE MOISE IBN EZRA ET SES SOURCES
- STUDIEN UEBER JESCHU'A BEN JEHUDA

Schreiner, Wilhelm *see* INSEL IM SEEWIND

Schrempf, Christof *see* LESSING ALS PHILOSOPH

Schrenck, Erich von *see*
- DIE JOHANNEISCHE ANSCHAUUNG VOM LEBEN
- RICHARD WAGNER ALS DICHTER

Schrenk, L von *see* REISEN UND FORSCHUNGEN IM AMUR-LANDE IN DEN JAHREN 1854-1895

SCHRIFTEN / Bund der technischen Angestellten und Bund der technischen Angestellten und Beamten – no.1, 3, 24. 1920-24. (Serial publications of German trade unions in the Memorial Library, University of Wisconsin-Madison.) – 1 – us U.W. Library [330]

SCHRIFTEN / Maehrische Gesellschaft zur Befoerderung der Landwirtschaft, der Natur- und Landeskunde. Historisch-Statistische Section – Bruenn. Bd. 17-30; 1886-95. Film Mas C 638 – 1 – us H.U. Library [630]

SCHRIFTEN / Saphir, Moritz Gottlieb – Bruenn, etc., Karafiat & Sohn, 1887-89. 26 v. (On cover: Gesamt-Ausgabe. Title-pages of vols. 5, 9, 25, and 26 read: M. G. Saphir's Schriften: Volks-Ausgabe.) Film Mas C 500 – 1 – us H.U. Library [800]

SCHRIFTEN DER LDPD – Berlin, Der Morgen – 1 – us U.W. Library [320]

DIE SCHRIFTEN DER MAINZER JAKOBINER UND IHRER GEGNER (1792-1802) : REVOLUTIONAERE UND GEGENREVOLUTIONAERE PROKLAMATIONEN...UND DER LINKSRHEINISCHEN REVOLUTIONSBEWEGUNG BIS ZUR FRUEHEN FRANZOSENZEIT IN RHEINHESSEN UND DER PFALZ (1797-1802) / ed by Stadtbibliothek Mainz – (Reden, Pamphlete, Proklamationen, Schauspiele u.a. aus der Zeit der Mainzer Republik) – 1993 – 357mf (1:24) – 9 – diazo DM3,600.00 (silver DM4,400.00 ISBN: 3-598-33033-2) – 3-598-33034-0 – gw Saur [943]

SCHRIFTEN DER PHYSIKALISCH-OEKONOMISCHEN GESELLSCHAFT ZU KOENIGSBERG I PR – Koenigsberg. v26-68. 1886-1933 – 137mf – 9 – 8619/1 – ne IDC [943]

DIE SCHRIFTEN DES ALEXANDER VON ROES (MGH DEUTSCHES..: 4.BD) – 1949 – Dfl13.00 – ne Slangenburg [240]

DIE SCHRIFTEN DES ALEXANDER VON ROES UND DES ENGELBERT VON ADMONT (MGH 10: 1.BD) : 1. STUECK: ALEXANDER VON ROES – 1958 – Dfl30.00 – ne Slangenburg [240]

SCHRIFTEN DES DHV / Deutsche Angestelltenschaft – v23,29,37,40-41,43,56-61,65-67,70. 1905-13. Each vol. also has distinctive title. (Serial publications of German trade unions in the Memorial Library, University of Wisconsin-Madison.) – 1 – us U.W. Library [331]

SCHRIFTEN DES NATURWISSENSCHAFTLICHEN VEREINS FUER SCHLESWIG-HOLSTEIN – v1-3. 1873-78 – 1 – us U.W. Library [500]

DIE SCHRIFTEN DES URIEL DA COSTA / Gebhardt, C – Amsterdam. 1922. BJ-262-22 1 – 9 – ne IDC [920]

SCHRIFTEN DES VEREINS FUER MEININGISCHE GESCHICHTE UND LANDESKUNDE – Meiningen: Commissionsverlag von Bruedner & Renner, 1888- – 1 – us U.W. Library [073]

SCHRIFTEN DES VEREINS FUER SACHSEN MEININGISCHE GESCHICHTE UND LANDESKUNDE – Hildburghausen: Gadow, 1925-. illus – 1 – us U.W. Library [073]

SCHRIFTEN DES VEREINS FUER SACHSEN MEININGISCHE GESCHICHTE UND LANDESKUNDE – Hildburghausen: Kesselring, 1924 – 1 – us U.W. Library [073]

DIE SCHRIFTEN DES WALDSCHULMEISTERS / Rosegger, Peter – (German text with introd & notes in English) – New York: H Holt, 1899 – 1r – 1 – us U.W. Library [430]

DIE SCHRIFTEN TERTULLIANS NACH DER ZEIT IHRER ABFASSUNG / Bonwetsch, Nathanael – Bonn: A. Marcus, 1878 – 1mf – us A.T.L.A. [240]

SCHRIFTEN UND BRIEFE / Hamann, Johann Georg – Zu leichterem Verstaendniss im Zusammenhange seines Lebens erlaeutert und hrsg. von M. Petri. Hannover, C. Mener, 1872-74. 4 v. Film Mas 8594 – 1 – us H.U. Library [920]

SCHRIFTEN ZUR DEUTSCHEN LITERATUR / Boerne, Ludwig; ed by Dietze, Walter – (Includes bibliographical references) – 1. Aufl. Leipzig: P Reclam, [1960?] – 1 – us U.W. Library [430]

SCHRIFTLEHRE UND NATURWISSENSCHAFT: NEUN VORLESUNGEN, IM WINTER 1868 / Stueler, A – Berlin: Nicolai, 1869. 1 fiche – 9 – us A.T.L.A. [240]

DAS SCHRIFTPRINZIP DER LUTHERISCHEN KIRCHE : 1. BAND, DIE VORGESCHICHTE, DAS ERBE DES MITTELALTERS: GESCHICHTLICHE UND DOGMATISCHE UNTERSUCHUNGEN / Kropatscheck, Friedrich – (Includes bibliographical references) – Leipzig: A Deichert, 1904 – 2mf – 9 – 0-8370-8756-2 – 1986-2756 – us A.T.L.A. [220]

SCHRIFTQUELLEN ZUR GESCHICHTE DER KAROLINGISCHEN KUNST / Schlosser, Julius von – (Quellenschriften fuer Kunstgeschichte...Wien, 1892. N.S. v4) – 9 – ne IDC [700]

SCHRIFTSTELLER IM EXIL; ZWEI JAHRE DEUTSCHE LITERARISCHE SENDUNG AM RUNDFUNK IN NEW YORK / Lindt, Peter M – Forward by George N. Shuster. New York: Willard Publishing Co., (1944). 5p,1 leaf,13-192p – 1 – us U.W. Library [430]

DIE SCHRIFTSTELLER- UND GELEHRTENLEXIKA DES 17., 18. UND 19. JAHRHUNDERTS *see* LEXIKON VERSTORBENER BAIERISCHER SCHRIFTSTELLER DES 18. UND 19. JAHRHUNDERTS

DIE SCHRIFTSTELLER- UND GELEHRTENLEXIKA DES 17., 18., UND 19. JAHRHUNDERTS – (See individual titles: Lexikon der schleswig-holstein-lauenburgischen und eutinischen Schriftsteller. Lexikon verstorbener baierischer Schriftsteller. Gelehrtes Fuerstenthum Baireut. Biographisches Lexikon fuer das Gebiet zwischen Inn und Salzach. Das gelehrte Schwaben. Saechsisches Schriftsteller-Lexicon. Allgemeines Gelehrten-Lexicon. Biographisch-literarisches Lexikon der katholischen deutschen Dichter. Lexicon der seit dem 15. Jahrhundert verstorbenen... Lexikon deutscher Frauen der Feder. Das gelehrte Hannover. Die deutschen Schriftstellerinnen des 19. Jahrhunderts. Lexikon der hamburgischen Schriftsteller bis zur Gegenwart. Grundlage zu einer Hessischen Gelehrten- und Schriftsteller-Geschichte. Nuernbergisches Gelehrten-Lexicon.) – Hildesheim, 1983-84 – 538mf – 9 – DM3,600 diazo DM4,300.00 silver – gw Olms [430]

DIE SCHRIFTSTELLER- UND GELEHRTENLEXIKA DES 17., 18., UND 19. JAHRHUNDERTS *see*
- ALLGEMEINES GELEHRTEN-LEXICON
- BIOGRAPHISCHES LEXIKON FUER DAS GEBIET ZWISCHEN INN UND SALZACH
- BIOGRAPHISCH-LITERARISCHES LEXIKON DER KATHOLISCHEN DEUTSCHEN DICHTER, VOLKS-UND JUNGENDSCHRIFTSTELLER IM 19. JAHRHUNDERT
- DIE DEUTSCHEN SCHRIFTSTELLERINNEN DES 19. JAHRHUNDERTS
- DAS GELEHRTE HANNOVER
- DAS GELEHRTE SCHWABEN
- GELEHRTES FUERSTENTHUM BAIREUT
- GRUNDLAGE ZU EINER HESSISCHEN GELEHRTEN- UND SCHRIFTSTELLER-GESCHICHTE
- LEXICON DER SCHLESWIG-HOLSTEIN-LAUENBURGISCHEN UND EUTINISCHEN SCHRIFTSTELLER VON 1796 BIS 1828
- LEXICON DER SEIT DEM 15. JAHRHUNDERT VERSTORBENEN UND JETZT LEBENDEN OBERLAUSITZISCHEN SCHRIFTSTELLER UND KUENSTLER
- LEXIKON DER HAMBURGISCHEN SCHRIFTSTELLER BIS ZUR GEGENWART
- LEXIKON DER SCHLESWIG-HOLSTEIN-LAUENBURGISCHEN UND EUTINISCHEN SCHRIFTSTELLER VON 1829-1882
- LEXIKON DEUTSCHER FRAUEN DER FEDER
- NUERNBERGISCHES GELEHRTEN-LEXICON
- SAECHSISCHES SCHRIFTSTELLER-LEXICON

DAS SCHRIFTTUM ALS GEISTIGER RAUM DER NATION / Hofmannsthal, Hugo von – Muenchen: Bremer Presse, 1927 – 1r – 1 – us U.W. Library [840]

DAS SCHRIFTWESEN IM MITTELALTER / Wattenbach, W – 2406 2. Ed. 3. 1896 – 8 – ne IDC [940]

Schrijnen, J *see* STUDIEN ZUR SYNTAX DER BRIEFE DES HL. CYPRIAN

Schrodt, P Barbara *see* A HISTORICAL-ETHNOGRAPHIC ACCOUNT OF A CANADIAN WOMAN IN SPORT, 1920-1938

Schroeckius, Lucas Luc. *see* HISTORIA MOSCHI, AD NORMAM ACADEMIAE NATURAE CURIOSORUM CONSCRIPTA

Schroedel, Karl *see* PASSAVIA SACRA

Schroeder, August *see* OVERBERG UND FUERSTENBERG IN IHRER BEDEUTUNG FUER DIE GEISTIGE UND KULTURELLE HEBUNG DER LAENDLICHEN BEVOELKERUNG

Schroeder, Christine *see* THE EFFECT OF COLD WATER BATHS ON POST TREATMENT LEG ELECTRICAL ACTIVITY AND ISOMETRIC STRENGTH

Schroeder, Edward *see* PAUL DE LAGARDE

Schroeder, Friedrich Wilhelm *see* WIELANDS "AGATHON" UND DIE ANFAENGE DES MODERNEN BILDUNGSROMANS

Schroeder, Friedrich Wilhelm Julius *see* DEUTERONOMY

Schroeder, Gustavus W *see* HISTORY OF THE SWEDISH BAPTISTS IN SWEDEN AND AMERICA

Schroeder, Hans *see* LEXICON DER SCHLESWIG-HOLSTEIN-LAUENBURGISCHEN UND EUTINISCHEN SCHRIFTSTELLER VON 1796 BIS 1828

Schroeder, Hans et al *see* LEXIKON DER HAMBURGISCHEN SCHRIFTSTELLER BIS ZUR GEGENWART

Schroeder, Helmuth *see* UT MINEN LUETTEN GORDEN

Schroeder, J J *see* THESAURUS LINGUAE ARMENICAE, ANTIQUAE ET HODIERNAE,...

Schroeder, Kerstin *see* PROBLEME DER BEGRIFFSBILDUNG IN DER HANDLUNGSKONTROLL-THEORIE VON J. KUHL

Schroeder, Leopold von *see* DIE VOLLENDUNG DES ARISCHEN MYSTERIUMS IN BAYREUTH

Schroeder, Lisa M *see* A COMPARISON OF RATING OF PERCEIVED EXERTION IN TREADMILL VS TRACK WALKING AND RUNNING

Schroeder, Paul *see* AERZTE IN OST- UND WESTPREUSSEN

Schroeder, Severin *see* UEBER NAMENSPHILOSOPHISCHE INTUITIONEN UND EIN GEFUEHL SCHLECHTHINNIGER NOTWENDIGKEIT

Schroeder, W *see* AUFGABEN AUS "DIE JUNGFRAU VON ORLEANS"

Schroers, H *see* ZUR TEXTGESCHICHTE UND ERKLAERUNG VON TERTULLIANS APOLOGETIKUM (T.U.U. 3-40/4)

Schroers, Heinrich *see*
- DIE KOELNER WIRREN (1837)
- KONSTANTINS DES GROSSEN KREUZERSCHEINUNG
- EIN VERGESSENER FUEHRER AUS DER RHEINISCHEN GEISTESGESCHICHTE DES NEUNZEHNTEN JAHRHUNDERTS, JOHANN WILHELM JOSEPH BRAUN (1801-1863)

Schroeter, Astrid *see* VERAENDERUNGEN VON PLASMAFAKTOREN WAEHREND DER LAGERUNG VON THROMBOZYTEN UND IHR EINFLUSS AUF DEREN FUNTKIONSFAEHIGKEIT

Schroeter, C *see* GESAENGE MIT BEGLEITUNG DER FORTEPIANO

Schroeter, J S *see* EINLEITUNG IN DIE CONCHYLIENKENNTNISS NACH LINNE

Schrumpf, Ernst *see* GOETHE UND WEIMAR

DER SCHTAERN VO BUEBEBAERG : DES "SCHTAERN VO BUEBEBAERG" ERSTER TEIL: E GSCHICHT US DE TRUEEBSCHTE TAGE VOM ALTE BAERN / Tavel, Rudolf von – Bern: A Francke, 1919 – 1r – 1 – us U.W. Library [430]

Schuback, Jacob *see* VON DER MUSICALISCHEN DECLAMATION

Schubart, Herta *see* ARIAS MONTANO Y EL MONUMENTO AL DUQUE DE ALBA

Schubart, W *see*
- ALTCHRISTLICHE TEXTE
- DAS BUCH BEI DEN GRIECHEN UND ROMERN

Schubert *see* DEUTUNGEN UND BEKENNTNISSE

Schubert, Ernst *see* AUGUSTUS BOHSE GENANNT TALANDER

Schubert, Franz *see*
- ABENDLIED, SCHLUMMERLIED AND DIE BLUMENSPRACHE
- FREUDE DER KINDERJAHRE. GRABLIED AUF EINEN SOLDATEN
- MESSE IN ES
- MESSE [IN F]

- VARIATIONEN UEBER EIN FRANZOESISCHES LIED IN E FUER KLAVIER ZU 4 HAENDEN, OP.10

Schubert, Hans von *see*
- DAS AELTESTE GERMANISCHE CHRISTENTUM, ODER, DER SOGEN. "ARIANISMUS" DER GERMANEN
- BUENDNIS UND BEKENNTNIS 1529/1530
- GOETHES RELIGIOESE JUGENDENTWICKLUNG
- OUTLINES OF CHURCH HISTORY
- REICH UND REFORMATION
- ROMS KAMPF UM DIE WELTHERRSCHAFT
- DER SOGENANNTE PRAEDESTINATUS
- STAAT UND KIRCHE IN DEN ARIANISCHEN KOENIGREICHEN UND IM REICHE CHLODWIGS

Schubert, Johann *see* DIE TROUVEREHANDSCHRIFT R. DIE HANDSCHRIFT PARIS, BIBL. NAT. FR. 1591

Schubert, Johannes *see* DIE PHILOSOPHISCHEN GRUNDGEDANKEN IN GOETHES WILHELM MEISTER

Schubert, Kurt *see* CLEMENS BRENTANOS WELTLICHE LYRIK

Schubert, Paul *see* DAS NATURGEFUEHL BEI F.L. ZACHARIAS WERNER

Schubiger, Scott, P *see* PERCEIVED AND PREFERRED COACH LEADER BEHAVIORS OF HIGH SCHOOL AND COLLEGE FOOTBALL PLAYERS

Schubin, Ossip *see*
- DIE GESCHICHTE EINES GENIES
- GRAEFIN ERIKA LEHR- UND WANDERJAHRE
- SLAWISCHE LIEBE

Schuchert, C *see* HISTORICAL GEOLOGY OF THE ANTILLEAN CARIBBEAN REGION

Schuchhardt, Karl *see* AUS LEBEN UND ARBEIT

Schuder, Kurt *see* FRIEDRICH HEBBEL

Schuecking, Levin *see*
- DER BAUERNFUERST
- DER KAMPF IM SPESSART
- EINES KRIEGSKNECHTS ABENTEUER

Schuecking, W *see* DIE GESCHICHTE DER PAN-AMERIKANISCHEN BEWEGUNG

Schueler, Herbert *see* HEBBEL AND THE DREAM

Schuerer, Emil *see* DAS MESSIANISCHE SELBSTBEWUSSTSEIN JESU CHRISTI

Schuermeyer, Manfred *see*
- DAS DEUTSCHE TABU
- DER KORNGARTEN CODE

Schuett, Bodo *see* GESTIRN DES KRIEGES

Schuette, Ulrich *see* ORDNUNG UND VERZIERUNG

Schuetz *see* STICHTAGSAMMLUNG

Schuetz, A von *see* VORLAEUFIGER PROSPEKT EINER SCHULBIBEL

Schuetz, C G *see* ALLGEMEINE LITERATUR-ZEITUNG

Schuetz, Christian Gottfried *see* ALLGEMEINE LITERATUR-ZEITUNG

Schuetze, J *see* WOERTERBUCH BIBLISCHER EIGENNAMEN DES ALTEN UND NEUEN TESTAMENTES

Schuetze, Paul *see* THEODOR STORM

Schuez, Alfred *see* PHILOSOPHIE UND CHRISTENTUM:...HARTMANN'SCHEN WELTANSCHAUUNG FUER JEDEN GEBILDETEN

Schuh, Joerg *see* SENSORISCHE UNTERSUCHUNGEN AN OBERFLAECHENMODIFIZIERTEN PHTHALOCYANINEN

Schuhmacher, Wilhelm *see* LEBEN UND SEELE UNSERES SOLDATENLIEDS IM WELTKRIEG

Schukart, Hanns *see* GESTALTUNGEN DES FRAUEN-BILDES IN DEUTSCHER LYRIK

Schulbaum, Moses *see* ALLGEMEINES, VOLLSTAENDIGES NEUHEBRAEISCH-DEUTSCHES WOERTERBUCH

SCHULCHAN ARUCH ODER ENCYCLOPAEDISCHE DARSTELLUNG DES MOSAISCHEN GESETZES... : VIERTER THEIL / Creizenach, M C – 1996 – 4mf – 9 – DM90.00 – 3-8267-3194-8 – gw Hänsel [270]

SCHULCHAN-URUCH UND DIE RABBINEN UEBER DAS VERHAELTNISS DER JUDEN ZU ANDERSGLAEUBIGEN / Hoffmann, David – Berlin: Juedischen Presse, 1885.1 fiche – 9 – us A.T.L.A. [270]

SCHULD UND UEBERWINDUNG DER SCHULD IN DEN DRAMEN ERNST BARACHS / Deppert, Fritz – Frankfurt a.M., 1966 – 2mf – 9 – DM62.00 – 3-89349-643-2 – gw Hänsel [430]

DIE SCHULE FUER DAS VIOLONCELLO / Valder, Barbara – 1994 – 1mf – DM60.00 – 3-8267-2044-X – gw Hänsel [780]

Schuleit, H H *see* EINE EINFACHE ELEKTRONENROEHRENANORDNUNG

Schulenburg, Wilibald von *see* WENDISCHES VOLKSTHUM IN SAGE, BRAUCH UND SITTE

DER SCHULFUNK – Berlin. jun 1, 1927-mar 16, 1941 – 7r – 1 – gw Mikrofilm [370]

Schulhof, John Maurice *see* THE LAW OF FORGIVENESS AS PRESENTED IN THE NEW TESTAMENT

Schulien, C M *see* THE RELATIONSHIP BETWEEN LACTATE THRESHOLD, VENTILATORY THRESHOLD, AND HEART RATE THRESHOLD IN CHILDREN

Schulken, Adolf *see*
- MERIDA DAS SPANISCHE ROM
- MERIDA, LA ROMA ESPANOLA
- VIRIATO

SCHULLENGRIEPER UND TUNGENKNIEPER : FINKENWAERDER FISCHER- UND SEEGESCHICHTEN / Fock, Gorch – (Includes glossary) – Hamburg: M Glogau, 1918 – 1r – 1 – us U.W. Library [830]

Schuller, Gustav *see* MEISTER LUKAS

Schullze, Erich *see* GESETZ ZUR BEFREIUNG VON NATIONALSOZIALISMUS UND MILITARISMUS MIT DEN AUSFUEHRUNGSVORSCHRIFTEN UND FORMULAREN

Schulman, K *see* MISTEREI PARIS

Schulmann, E *see* ZIKHRONOT IR MOLADETI

Schulmann, Robert J *see* THE PAPERS OF GENERAL FRIEDRICH WILHELM VON STEUBEN, 1777-1794

DER SCHULMEISTER VON HANDEWITT : EINE NOVELLE / Kroeger, Timm – Hamburg: A Janssen, 1905 – 1r – 1 – us U.W. Library [830]

Schulte, Adalbert *see*
- DIE KOPTISCHE UEBERSETZUNG DER VIER GROSSEN PROPHETEN
- DIE MESSIANISCHEN WEISSAGUNGEN DES ALTEN TESTAMENTS NEBST DESSEN TYPEN

Schulte, Johann Friedrich von *see*
- DENKSCHRIFT UEBER DAS VERHAELTNISS DES STAATES ZU DEN SAETZEN DER PAEPSTLICHEN CONSTITUTION VOM 18. JULI 1870: GEWIDMET DEN REGIERUNGEN DEUTSCHLANDS UND OESTERREICHS
- DIE GESCHICHTE DER QUELLEN UND LITERATUR DES CANONISCHEN RECHTS
- DIE NEUEREN KATHOLISCHEN ORDEN UND CONGREGATIONEN BESONDERS IN DEUTSCHLAND
- ROMAN CATHOLICISM, OLD AND NEW
- DIE STELLUNG DER CONCILIEN, PAEPSTE UND BISCHOEFE
- UEBER KIRCHENSTRAFEN

Schulte Kemminghausen, Karl *see* SAEMTLICHE WERKE

SCHULTE UND DOELLINGER GEGEN DAS CONCIL : KRITISCHE BELEUCHTUNG DER SCHULTE'SCHEN BROSCHUERE UEBER DIE MACHT DER PAEPSTE UND DER JUENGSTEN ERKLAERUNG DOELLINGERS / Scheeben, Matthias Joseph – (Includes bibliographical references) – Regensburg; New York: Friedrich Pustet, 1871 – 1mf – 9 – 0-8370-8863-1 – 1986-2863 – us A.T.L.A. [240]

Schulte vom Bruehl, Walther *see* DIE OHNEHOSEN

SCHULTE WITTE : ERZAEHLUNG IN MUENSTERLAENDER MUNDART / Wibbelt, Augustin – 3. Aufl. Essen (Ruhr): Fredebeul und Koenen, 1919 – 1r – 1 – us U.W. Library [390]

Schulten, Aolf *see* NUMANTIA, EINE TOPOGRAPHISCH-HISTORISCHE UNTERSUCHUNG

Schultes, J A *see*
- OBSERVATIONES BOTANICAE IN LINNEI SPECIES PLANTARUM EX EDITIONE C.L. WILLDENOW
- OESTREICHS FLORA

Schulthess, Friedrich *see*
- CHRISTLICH-PALAESTINISCHE FRAGMENTE AUS DER OMAJJADEN-MOSCHEE ZU DAMASKUS
- HOMONYME WURZELN IM SYRISCHEN
- DIE SYRISCHEN KANONES DER SYNODEN VON NICAEA BIS CHALCEDON

Schulthess-Rechberg, Gustav von *see* HEINRICH BULLINGER, DER NACHFOLGER ZWINGLIS

Schultz, F W *see*
- ARCHIVES DE FLORE; JOURNAL BOTANIQUE
- ARCHIVES DE LA FLORE DE FRANCE ET D'ALLEMAGNE

Schultz, Franz *see*
- CHARAKTERISTIKEN UND KRITIKEN VON JOSEPH GOERRES
- CHARAKTERISTIKEN UND KRITIKEN VON JOSEPH GOERRES AUS DEN JAHREN 1804 UND 1805

Schultz, G O *see* UEBER DEN EINFLUSS IONISIERENDER STRAHLEN AUF DIE ERBSTRUKTUR

Schultz, Hermann *see*
- GRUNDRISS DER CHRISTLICHEN APOLOGETIK
- GRUNDRISS DER EVANGELISCHEN DOGMATIK
- GRUNDRISS DER EVANGELISCHEN ETHIK
- OUTLINES OF CHRISTIAN APOLOGETICS: FOR USE IN LECTURES

Schultz, Jon S *see* DISABILITY LAW IN THE UNITED STATES

Schultz, K F *see*
- PRODROMI FLORAE STARGARDIENSIS SUPPLEMENTUM PRIMUM
- PRODROMUS FLORAE STARGARDIENSIS, CONTINENS PLANTAS IN DUCATU MEGAPOLITANO-STARGARDIENSI SEU STRELITZENSI SPONTE PROVENIENTES

Schultze, Augustus *see* THE THEOLOGY OF THE APOSTLES PETER AND PAUL IN THEIR OWN WORDS

Schultze, H *see* ROBERT VON MOHL

Schultze, K *see* DAS MARTYRIUM DES HEILIGEN ABO VON TIFLIS (T.U.U. 2-28/4B)

Schultze, Martin *see*
- GRAMMATIK DER ARAMAEISCHEN MUTTERSPRACHE JESU
- HANDBUCH DER EBRAEISCHEN MYTHOLOGIE

Schultze, V *see* ALTCHRISTLICHE STAEDTE UND LANDSCHAFTEN 1, KONSTANTINOPEL (324-450)

Schultze-Gaevernitz, G von *see* CARLYLES STELLUNG ZU CHRISTENTUM UND REVOLUTION

Schultze-Gallera, Siegmar Baron von *see* FALK UND GOETHE

DIE SCHULTZEN-KATHRIN : KRIEGSERLEBNISSE EINES SAARBRUECKER MAEDCHENS / Kath, Lydia – Berlin: Junge Generation Verlag, [1944] – 1r – 1 – us U.W. Library [830]

Schultz-Lorentzen, C W *see*
- ESKIMOERNES INDVANDRING I GRONLAND
- DEN GRØNLANDSKE ORDBOG. GRØNLANDSK-DANSK
- DET VESTGRONLANDSKE SPROG

Schultz-Venrath, Ulrich *see* ERNST SIMMELS PSYCHOANALYTISCHE KLINIK "SANATORIUM SCHLOß TEGEL GMBH" (1927-1983)

DER SCHULUNGSBRIEF : (DAS ZENTRALE MONATSBLATT DER NSDAP) – Berlin, 1934-44 (incomplete) – 1 – Inquire at Mikrofilmarchiv for details – gw Misc Inst [335]

SCHULUNGSPROGRAMME ZU AKZEPTANZPROBLEMEN BEIM EINSATZ INNOVATIVER INFORMATIONSTECHNOLOGIE IM BUERO- UND VERWALTUNGSBEREICH ANALYSIERT AM BEISPIEL EINES INDUSTRIEBETRIEBES / Wagner, Albert – Nuernberg, 1980 – 3mf – DM48.00 – 3-89349-905-9 – gw Hänsel [650]

DAS SCHULWESEN DES MITTELALTERS UND DESSEN REFORM IM SECHSZEHNTEN JAHRHUNDERT : MIT EINEM ABDRUCK VON BUGENHAGENS SCHULORDNUNG DER STADT LUEBECK / Heppe, H – Marburg: N.G. Elwert, 1860 – 1mf – us A.T.L.A. [370]

DAS SCHULWESEN UNTER KARL THEODOR VON DALBERG BESONDERS IM FUERSTENTUM ASCHAFFENBURG 1803-1813 UND IM GROSSHERZOGTUM FRANKFURT 1810-1813 / Scherg, Theodor Joseph – Muenchen, 1939 – 6mf – DM148.00 – 3-89349-185-6 – gw Hänsel [370]

Schulz, Thomas *see* INDIVIDUELLE UND GESELLSCHAFTLICHE REPRAESENTATIONEN VON AIDS

Schulze, Bernhard *see* DAS RELIGIOESE BEI H.W. LONGFELLOW UND DESSEN STELLUNG ZUR BIBEL

Schulze, Berthold *see*
- KLEISTS "PENTHESILEA"
- NEUE STUDIEN UEBER HEINRICH VON KLEIST

Schulze, Erich *see* DIE DEUTSCHE LITERATUR

Schulze, Franz *see*
- BALTHAZAR SPRINGERS INDIENFAHRT 1505/06
- DIE POLNISCHE ZUWANDERUNG IM RUHRREVIER UND IHRE WIRKUNGEN

Schulze, Georg *see* VOELKERWOHLSTAND UND WELTWIRTSCHAFT

Schulze, Martin *see* ZUR FRAGE NACH DER BEDEUTUNG DER HEILIGEN SCHRIFT

Schulze, Wilhelm *see* GRAECA LATINA

Schulzen, B *see* ORIENTALISCH- UND OCCIDENTALISCHES A.B.C.-BUCH WELCHES HUNDERT ALPHABETE NEBST IHRER AUSSPRACHE SO BEY DENEN MEISTEN EUROPAEISCH-ASIATISCH-AFRICANISCH- UND AMERICANISCHEN VOELKERN UND NATIONEN GEBRAEUCHLICH SIND,...

Schulze-Smidt, Bernhardine *see* DIE TAT

Schumacher, Alois *see* FRANKREICHS SICHERHEITS- UND DEUTSCHLANDPOLITIK 1931-1935 IM WIDERSTREIT DER FRANZOESISCHEN OEFFENTLICHEN DISKUSSION

Schumacher, Eva-Maria *see* KLIENTENZENTRIERTE PSYCHOTHERAPIE/ BERATUNG UND WEIBLICHES SELBSTKONZEPT

Schumacher, H C F *see* BESKRIVELSE AV GUINEISKA PLANTER

Schumacher, Joachim *see* JOHANN WILHELM SIMLER

Schumacher, Kurt *see*
- EUROPA ODER EUROPA AG?
- DAS PROGRAMM DER OPPOSITION

Schumacher, Pedro *see* CARTAS PASTORALES. BAHIA, 1928

Schumacher, Stefan *see* DASEINSANGST ALS URSPRUNG MENSCHLICHEN FEHLVERHALTENS

Schumann, Gerhard *see*
- GUDRUNS TOD
- DIE LIEDER VOM KRIEG
- WIR ABER SIND DAS KORN

Schumann, Gustav *see* PARTIKULARIST BLIEMCHEN AUS DRESDEN IN BAYREUTH

Schumann, Harry *see* ERNST HARDT UND DIE NEUROMANTIK

Schumann, K *see* DIE FLORA DER DEUTSCHEN SCHUTZGEBIETE IN DER SUEDSEE

Schumann, Robert *see*
- [LIEDERKREIS VON EICHENDORFF] OP. 39, 1842
- OPUS 39, LIEDERKREIS VON EICHENDORF.
- OPUS 39, NO. 12, FRUEHLINGSNACHT

Schumann, Stanley H *see* JOURNAL OF AGROMEDICINE

Schumann, Wolfgang *see* DAS EIGENE VERSCHULDEN EIN VERSCHULDEN GEGEN SICH SELBST ODER GEGEN DRITTE

Schumm, Felix *see* JEAN MARIE GUYAUS RELIGIONSPHILOSOPHIE (L'IRRELIGON DE L'AVENIR)

Schupp, Harald Thomas *see* PSYCHOPHYSIOLOGIE VON EMOTIONEN

Schupp, J *see* DIE GNADENLEHRE DES PETRUS LOMBARDUS

Schupp, Johannes Martin *see*
- EBBE UND FLUT
- DER VERLORENE KLANG

Schur, Ernst *see* HEINRICH VON KLEIST IN SEINEN BRIEFEN

Schure, Edouard *see* JESUS: THE LAST GREAT INITIATE

Schurig, Arthur *see* DER JUNGE HEINSE

Schurman, Jacob Gould *see* BELIEF IN GOD

Schurr, V *see* DIE TRINITAETSLEHRE DES BOETHIUS

Schurz, Anton Xaver *see* LENAUS LEBEN

Schurz, Carl *see*
- HENRY CLAY
- LEBENSERINNERUNGEN, BAND 3
- PAPERS

Schuster, Carl Fr. Th *see* DAS STUDIUM DER THEOLOGIE IN DER GEGENWART: ANLEITUNG FUER ANFAENGER

Schuster, J *see* [DIDONE ABBANDONATA] OMBRA CARA, OMBRA TRADITA

Schuster, Ludwig *see* NEUERE TRISTANDICHTUNGEN (TANTRIS DER NARR)

Schuster, W H *see* GUIDE FOR THE DETERMINATION OF FISHES

DER SCHUTZ DES KREDITVERKEHRS VOR DEN GEFAHREN AUS ZU UMFANGREICHEN SICHERUNGSUEBEREIGNUNGEN / Krotoschiner, Hermann Alfred – 1994 – 2mf – 9 – DM62.00 – 3-8267-3002-X – gw Hänsel [340]

Schutz, R W *see* RANDOM AND DETERMINISTIC (NONRANDOM) ASPECTS OF ATHLETIC BEHAVIOR WITH SPECIAL REFERENCE TO THE NATIONAL HOCKEY LEAGUE

Schutz, Robert *see* TEAM-BASED ATTITUDE

Schutz, Robert W *see* COMPUTER-AIDED RECORDING AND MATHEMATICAL ANALYSIS OF TEAM PERFORMANCE IN VOLLEYBALL
DER SCHUTZBUND : MONATSSCHRIFT DES REPUBLIKANISCHEN SCHUTZBUNDES – Wien, Jun 1924-1931 – 1r – 1 – DM120.00 – gw Mikro Press [073]
DER SCHUTZENGEL – Donauwoerth, Germany. 1875-77, 1880-81, 1907-10 – 1 – gw Mikrofilm [072]
Schutzverband Deutscher Schriftsteller *see* DIE SAAR-ENTE
Schuurmans Stekhoven, J Z *see* DE ALEXANDRIJNSCHE VERTALING VAN HET DODEKAPROPHETON
Schuyler, Eugene *see* TURKISTAN: NOTES OF A JOURNEY IN RUSSIAN TURKISTAN, KHOKAND, BUKHARA, AND KULDJA
SCHUYLER HERALD – Schuyler, NE. -w. Nov 1882; Aug 1895-Jun 1898 – 1 – us NE Hist [071]
SCHUYLER MESSENGER – Schuyler, NE. -w. Nov 1909-Sep 1920 – 1 – us NE Hist [071]
SCHUYLER SUN – Schuyler, NE. -w. Sep 1881; Jul 1883-Jan 1888; Mar 1888-Jun 1890; Oct 1892; Aug 1895-Oct 1905; Dec 1905-Dec 1908; Oct 1911-Dec 1915; Jan-Sep 1918; Jan 1919 to date – 1 – us NE Hist [071]
SCHUYLKILL HAVEN CALL – Schuykill Haven, PA. -w 1892-1977 – 13 – $25.00r – us I.M.R. [071]
SCHUYLKILL REPUBLICAN – Pottsville, PA. -w 1889-1910 – 13 – $25.00r – us I.M.R. [071]
SCHUYLKILL TELEGRAM – Schuylkill Haven, PA., 1893 – 13 – $25.00r – us I.M.R. [071]
Schwab, Christoph Theodor *see*
– AUSGEWAEHLTE WERKE
– GUSTAV SCHWAB'S LEBEN
Schwab, George *see* BASA FIELD NOTES
Schwab, Guenther *see* KAMERAD MIT DEM HAARIGEN GESICHT
Schwab, Gustav Benjamin *see* KLEINE PROSAISCHE SCHRIFTEN
Schwab, Kai Michael *see* ZWANGSVOLLSTRECKUNG WEGEN BAGATELLFORDERUNGEN
Schwab, Laurence Henry *see* THE KINGDOM OF GOD
Schwabe, Johann Joachim *see* BELUSTIGUNGEN DES VERSTANDES UND DES WITZES
SCHWABENECHO – Oberndorf, West Germany. 1947-49 – 1 – gw Mikrofilm [072]
DIE SCHWABENMARGRET : ROMAN AUS DEN KARAWANKEN / Widmann, Ines – Stuttgart: J G Cotta, 1936 – 1r – 1 – us U.W. Library [830]
SCHWABENSPIEGEL, KURZFORM (MGH LEGES 3: 4.BD. 1.TEIL) : LANDRECHTSTEIL – 1960 – Dfl28.00 – ne Slangenburg [240]
SCHWABENSPIEGEL, KURZFORM, MITTELDEUTSCH-NIEDERDEUTSCHE HANDSCHRIFTEN (MGH LEGES 3: 5.BD) – 1964 – Dfl30.00 – ne Slangenburg [240]
SCHWABISCHER BEOBACHTER – Zrenjanin, Yugoslavia. Jul 1934-May 1935 – 1r – 1 – us L of C Photodup [949]
SCHWABISCHER KRONIK *see* SCHWABISCHER MERKUR
SCHWABISCHER MERKUR – (Library has: Jan. 2, 1914-Dec. 31, 1927; few issues missing) – Stuttgart: [Schwabischer Merkur], 1914- – 1 – CSUX90-S513 – us Hoover Inst Photo [943]
SCHWABISCHER VOLKSBOTE – Pancevo, Yugoslavia. Mar-Oct 1935 – 1r – 1 – us L of C Photodup [949]
SCHWAEBISCHE DONAU-ZEITUNG – Aalen, nov 23 1946-feb 21 1948 – 1r – 1 – Dist. gw Mikrofilm – gw Misc Inst [943]
SCHWAEBISCHE DONAU-ZEITUNG – (Title change: Suedwest-Presse, 2 Jan 1968) – Ulm, Germany. 1968-1990 – 163r – 1 – gw Mikrofilm [072]
SCHWAEBISCHE DONAUZEITUNG : BA DER SUEDWEST-PRESSE – Heidenheim a.d. Brenz-Ulm, Germany. 1977- – ca 7r per yr – 1 – gw Mikrofilm [072]
SCHWAEBISCHE DONAUZEITUNG – Blaubeuren-Ulm, Germany. 16 Aug 1948-31 Dec 1958 – 23r – 1 – gw Mikrofilm [072]
SCHWAEBISCHE LANDESZEITUNG *see* AUGSBURGER ALLGEMEINE
SCHWAEBISCHE RUNDSCHAU *see* GEMEINNUETZIGES WOCHENBLATT
SCHWAEBISCHE TAGWACHT : ORGAN DER SOZIALDEMOKRATEN WUERTTEMBERGS – Stuttgart, Germany. Sep-Dec 1890; Jul 1891-1916; Nov 1918-1921; Jul-Dec 1923; 1926-Sep 1928; 1929-Mar 1931; Jul-Sep 1931; Apr-Jun 1932 – 77r – 1 – gw Mikrofilm [072]
SCHWAEBISCHE TAGWACHT – Stuttgart, Sept-Dec 1890; Jul 1891-1916; Nov 1918-21; Jul-Dec 1923; 1926-27; Jan-Sept 1928; 1929; Jan-Mar, Jul-Sept 1931; Apr-Jun 1932 – 77r – 1 – DM5,775.00 – gw Mikro Press [072]
SCHWAEBISCHE VOLKSZEITUNG – (Cont: Volkszeitung, -1895; Muenchener Post und Augsburger Volkszeitung, 1899; Augsburger Volkszeitung, mar 31 1905) – Augsburg, 1892-jun 30 1898, apr 3 1900-mar 10 1933 – 1 – Dist. gw Mikrofilm – gw Misc Inst [943]
SCHWAEBISCHE ZEITUNG – Ehingen-Leutkirch, Germany. 2 Jan 1975- – 98r (1975-1990) – 1 – gw Mikrofilm [072]
SCHWAEBISCHE ZEITUNG – Laichingen-Leutkirch, Germany. 1991- – 1 – gw Mikrofilm [072]
SCHWAEBISCHE ZEITUNG – Laupheim-Leutkirch, Germany. 2 Jan 1975- – 97r (1975-1990) – 1 – gw Mikrofilm [072]
SCHWAEBISCHE ZEITUNG – Leutkirch, Germany. 1969- – ca 7r per yr – 1 – gw Mikrofilm [072]
SCHWAEBISCHE ZEITUNG – Ravensburg-Leutkirch, Germany. 1977- – ca 8r per yr – 1 – gw Mikrofilm [072]
SCHWAEBISCHE ZEITUNG – Tettnang-Leutkirch, Germany. 2 Jan 1975- – 97r (1975-1990) – 1 – gw Mikrofilm [072]
SCHWAEBISCHE ZEITUNG – (Title change: Lindauer Zeitung, 2 Jul 1950) – Lindau-Leutkirch, Germany. 1 Jun 1983- – ca 7r per yr – 1 – gw Mikrofilm [072]
SCHWAEBISCHE ZEITUNG – (Title change: Lindauer Zeitung, 2 Jun 1950) – Lindau-Leutkirch, Germany. 1 Jun 1983- – ca 7r per yr – 1 – gw Mikrofilm [072]
SCHWAEBISCHE ZEITUNG – Ulm-Leutkirch, Germany. 2 Jan 1975- – 122r (1975-1990) – 1 – gw Mikrofilm [072]
SCHWAEBISCHE ZEITUNG – Waldsee-Leutkirch, Germany. 2 Jan 1975- – 95r (1975-1990) – 1 – gw Mikrofilm [072]
SCHWAEBISCHE ZEITUNG – Wangen-Leutkirch, Germany. 2 Jan 1975- – 100r (1975-1990) – 1 – gw Mikrofilm [072]
SCHWAEBISCHE ZEITUNG *see*
– ANZEIGER VOM OBERLAND
– DONAU-BODENSEE-ZEITUNG
– WUERTTEMBERGISCHES SEEBLATT
SCHWAEBISCHER HAUSFREUND *see* HALLISCHES WOCHENBLATT
SCHWAEBISCHER MERKUR – Stuttgart, 1897-98 – 4r – 1 – DM320.00 – gw Mikro Press [072]
SCHWAEBISCHER MERKUR – Stuttgart, 1925-may 31 1941 – 1 – gw Mikrofilm [943]
SCHWAEBISCHER MERKUR – Stuttgart, Germany. -d. 31 March-31 Dec 1915; 1 April 1916-9 Aug 1919. Imperfect. 14 reels – 1 – uk British Libr Newspaper [072]
SCHWAEBISCHES TAGBLATT – (Title change: Graenzbote, 17 Dec 1949) – Tuttlingen, Germany. 1983- – 8r per yr – 1 – gw Mikrofilm [072]
SCHWAEBISCHES TAGBLATT *see* DER VOLKSFREUND
SCHWAEBISCHES TAGBLATT/RUND UM DEN URSPRUNG : BA DER SUED-WEST PRESSE – Tuebingen-Ulm, Germany. 1978- – ca 8r per yr – 1 – gw Mikrofilm [072]
Schwaegrichen, C F *see* HISTORIAE MUSCORUM HEPATICORUM PRODROMUS
DIE SCHWAEMME DES WALDES ALS NAHRUNGSMITTEL / Trogg, J G – Bern. 1848. B-6331 2 – 8 – ne IDC [590]
SCHWAENKE UND SCHNURREN AUS BAUERN MUND / Jahn, Ulrich – 1889 – 1 – us I.U. Libraries [390]
DIE SCHWAENKE UND SCHNURREN DES PFARRERS ARLOTTO / Mainardi, Arlotto – 1910 – 1 – us I.U. Libraries [390]
Schwager, Frederick *see* THE MOST VITAL MISSION PROBLEM OF THE DAY
Schwager, Lothar Helmut *see* GERHART HAUPTMANNS "TILL EULENSPIEGEL"
Schwalb, Moritz *see* KRITIK DER REVIDIERTEN LUTHERBIBEL
Schwalbenberg, Henry M *see* THE COMPACT OF FREE ASSOCIATION
Schwally, Friedrich *see*
– DER HEILIGE KRIEG IM ALTEN ISRAEL
– DAS LEBEN NACH DEM TODE
Schwan, Christian Friedrich *see* NOUVEAU DICTIONNAIRE DE LA LANGUE ALLEMANDE ET FRANCOISE, FRANCOISE ET ALLEMANDE (AEL, ABT 2;13)
SCHWANDORFER TAGBLATT : BA DER MITTELBAYERISCHEN ZEITUNG – Schwandorf-Regensburg, Germany. Jul 1952-Jul 1973 – 249r – 1 – gw Mikrofilm [072]
Schwartz, A *see* FESTSCHRIFT
Schwartz, Diana L *see* GENDER DIFFERENCES IN SPORT PARTICIPATION AND INCENTIVE MOTIVATION OF FORMER COLLEGE BASKETBALL PLAYERS AND SWIMMERS
Schwartz, E *see*
– KONZILSTUDIEN
– PUBLIZISTISCHE SAMMLUNGEN ZUM ACACIANISCHEN SCHISMA
Schwartz, Eduard *see*
– ACTA CONCILIORUM OECUMENICORUM
– ATHENAGORAE LIBELLUS PRO CHRISTIANIS; ORATIO DE RESURRECTIONE CADAVERUM
– ATHENAGORAE LIBELLUS PRO CHRISTIANIS RECENSUIT E. SCHWARTZ (T.U.U.-1-4/2)
– BUSSTUFEN UND KATECHUMEN-TATSKLASSEN
– CHRISTLICHE UND JUEDISCHE OSTERTAFELN
– KAISER CONSTANTIN UND DIE CHRISTLICHE KIRCHE
– KYRILLOS VON SKYTHOPOLIS (T.U.U. 4-49/2)
– TATIANI ORATIO AD GRAECOS
– UEBER DEN TOD DER SOEHNE ZEBEDAEI: EIN BEITRAG ZUR GESCHICHTE DES JOHANNESEVANGELIUMS
Schwartz, Emanuel *see* DIE SYRISCHE UEBERSETZUNG DES ERSTEN BUCHES SAMUELIS UND...MT., 70 UND TRG
Schwartz, Herbert F *see* PATENT LAW AND PRACTICE
Schwartz, O *see* LICHENES AMERICANI QUOS PARTIM IN FLORA INDIAE OCCIDENTALIS DESCRIPSIT
Schwartzkopff, Paul *see*
– DIE GOTTESOFFENBARUNG IN JESU CHRISTO
– DIE IRRTUMSLOSIGKEIT JESU CHRISTI UND DER CHRISTLICHE GLAUBE
– PROPHECIES OF JESUS CHRIST RELATING TO HIS DEATH, RESURRECTION... SECOND COMING
– DIE PROPHETISCHE OFFENBARUNG
– DIE WEISSAGUNGEN JESU CHRISTI
– WEISSAGUNGEN JESU VON SEINEM TODE, SEINER AUFERSTEHUNG UND WIEDERKUNFT UND IHRE ERFUELLUNG
Schwarz, A *see* SEFER HA-ZIKKARON LE-VEIT HA-MIDRASH LE-RABBANIM BE-VINAH, YOZE LA-OR LI-MELOT ME'AH SHANIM LE-HULEDET R. ARYEH SCHWARZ
Schwarz, Adolf *see*
– DIE ERLEICHTERUNGEN DER SCHAMMAITEN UND DIE ERSCHWERUNGEN DER HILLELITEN
– UNTER MARIA THERESIA
Schwarz, Carl *see* ZUR GESCHICHTE DER NEUESTEN THEOLOGIE
Schwarz, Conrad Herman Alfred *see* AUTOBIOGRAPHY
Schwarz, Hans *see* DU UND DEUTSCHLAND
Schwarz, J A T *see*
– TONTEMBOANSCHE TEKSTEN
– TONTEMBOANSCH-NEDERLANDSCH WOORDENBOEK MET NEDERLANDSCH-TONTEMBOANSCH REGISTER
Schwarz, Petra *see* QUALIFIZIERUNG STUDENTISCHER TUTOREN FUER DAS "PRAKTIKUM ZUR EINFUEHRUNG IN DIE KLINISCHE MEDIZIN" (EKM)
Schwarz, Werner *see* FLURNAMENSTUDIEN ANHAND EINER SAMMLUNG DER ALTEN NAMEN VON OFFENBACH/M.-BIEBER
Schwarz, Y *see* TEVU'OT HA-AREZ. JERUSALEM
DER SCHWARZE ADLER – Kattowitz (Katowice), Poland. Mar-Jun 1919; 1920-1921 – 1 – gw Mikrofilm [943]
Schwarze, Alexis *see* UNTERSUCHUNGEN UEBER DIE AEUSSERE ENTWICKLUNG DER AFRIKANISCHEN KIRCHE
DIE SCHWARZE ELSTER – Bad Liebenwerda, Germany. 1905-1940 – 1 – gw Mikrofilm [072]
DIE SCHWARZE FRONT – Buenos Aires, feb 15 1936 – 1 – Inquire at Mikrofilmarchiv for details – gw Misc Inst [943]
Schwarze, Hulbert *see* DAVID ZEISBERGER'S HISTORY OF THE NORTHERN AMERICAN INDIANS
DAS SCHWARZE KORPS : ZEITUNG DER SCHUTZSTAFFELN DER NSDAP – Berlin, Germany. 6 Mar 1935-29 Mar 1945 – 8r – 1 – gw Mikrofilm [072]
DAS SCHWARZE KORPS : ZEITUNG DER SCHUTZSTAFFELN DER NSDAP – Berlin, Mar 1935-1945 – 9r – 1 – DM720.00 – gw Mikro Press [072]
DAS SCHWARZE KORPS : ZEITUNG DER SCHUTZSTAFFELN DER NSDAP – Berlin, mar 6 1935-mar 29 1945 – 8r – 1 – Inquire at Mikrofilmarchiv for details – gw Misc Inst [335]
Schwarze, Michael *see* PROLETARISCHE PARTEI UND BUERGERLICHES ERBE
DER SCHWARZE NIKOLAUS : EIN BUCH VOLL SONNE, WEIN UND GLOCKENKLANG: ROMAN / Schwarzkopf, Nikolaus – Karlsbad; Leipzig: A Kraft, 1944 – 1r – 1 – us U.W. Library [830]
Schwarze, William Nathaniel *see* DAVID ZEISBERGER'S HISTORY OF THE NORTHERN AMERICAN INDIANS
SCHWARZENAU / Alexander Mack Historical Society – (Some pgs missing) – v1-3. Jul 1939-Jan 1942 – 1r – 1 – ATLA S0446 – us A.T.L.A. [240]
Schwarzer, Ralf *see* ANXIETY, STRESS, AND COPING
Schwarzer, William *see* THE ELEMENTS OF CASE MANAGEMENT
Schwarzer, William W et al *see* THE ANALYSIS AND DECISION OF SUMMARY JUDGEMENT MOTIONS
Schwarzkopf, Nikolaus *see*
– DER SCHWARZE NIKOLAUS
– DER STORCH
Schwarzlose, Carl *see* DIE PATRIMONIEN DER ROEMISCHEN KIRCHE BIS ZUR GRUENDUNG DES KIRCHENSTAATES
SCHWARZWAELDER BOTE – (Title changes: Oberndorfer Nachrichten, 30 Aug 1945-29 Sep 1945; Schwarzwaelder Post, 1950; Schwarzwaelder Bote) – Oberndorf, Germany. 1969- – 9r – 1 – gw Mikrofilm [072]
SCHWARZWAELDER BOTE *see* SCHWARZWAELDER BOTE
SCHWARZWAELDER BOTE (B5) : BA DES SCHWARZWAELDER BOTEN – Donaueschingen-Oberndorf, Germany. 2 Jul 1973-1979 – 45r – 1 – gw Mikrofilm [072]
SCHWARZWAELDER BOTE/C *see* NAGOLD-ENZ-BOTE
SCHWARZWAELDER BOTE/H : BA DES SCHWARZWAELDER BOTEN – Horb-Oberndorf, Germany. 2 Jul 1973-31 Dec 1979 – 44r – 1 – gw Mikrofilm [072]
SCHWARZWAELDER BUERGER-ZEITUNG – Rottweil, Germany. 1922-1923 – 2r – 1 – gw Mikrofilm [072]
SCHWARZWAELDER BUERGERZEITUNG – Rottweil, 1922-23 – 2r – 1 – DM160.00 – gw Mikro Press [072]
SCHWARZWAELDER POST *see* SCHWARZWAELDER BOTE
SCHWARZWAELDER VOLKSFREUND : BA DER SCHWAEBISCHEN ZEITUNG – Rottweil-Leutkirch, Germany. 2 Jan 1975- – 107r (1975-1990) – 1 – gw Mikrofilm [072]
DER SCHWARZ-WEISS-ROTE KONTINENT : LATEINAMERIKA, REFORMER UND REBELLEN / Wendt, Herbert – Oldenburg: G. Stalling, [1964] – 1 – CSUXAGP9725-B – us Hoover Inst Photo [320]
SCHWEDISCHEN ZOOLOGISCHEN EXPEDITION NACH DEM KILIMANDJARO,... 1905-1906 – Stockholm, [1907]-1910 – 3 vols – 8 – ne IDC [590]
Schwegler, A *see* GESCHICHTE DER PHILOSOPHIE
Schwegler, Johann S *see* DIE RESORPTION VON AMINOSAEUREN UND PROTEINEN AUS DEM PROXIMALEN TUBULUS DER NIERE
Schweiger-Lerchenfeld, Amand *see* AFRIKA, DER DUNKLE ERDTHEIL IM LICHTE UNSERER ZEIT
Schweigger, A F *see* ENUMERATIO PLANTARUM HORTI BOTANICI REGIOMONTANI
SCHWEINFURTER TAGBLATT : BA DER MAIN-POST – Schweinfurt-Wuerzburg, Germany. 1977- – ca 10r per yr – 1 – gw Mikrofilm [072]

Schweinfurth, Georg A *see*
- AU COEUR DE L'AFRIQUE, 1868-1871
- AU COEUR DE L'AFRIQUE, 1868-1871. VOYAGES ET DECOUVERTES DANS LES REGIONS INEXPLOREES DE L'AFRIQUE CENTRALE
- BEITRAG ZUR FLORA AETHIOPIENS
- THE HEART OF AFRICA
- THE HEART OF AFRICA: THREE YEARS TRAVELS AND ADVENTURES

Schweinitz, L D von *see*
- MONOGRAPH OF THE NORTH-AMERICAN SPECIES OF THE GENUS CAREX
- SYNOPSIS FUNGORUM CAROLINAE SUPERIORIS SECUNDUM OBSERVATIONES

DAS SCHWEISSTUCH DER VERONIKA : ROMAN / Le Fort, Gertrud – 6. Aufl. Muenchen: M Beckstein, 1946, c1928 – 1r – 1 – us U.W. Library [830]

Schweitzer, Albert *see*
- GOETHE
- DIE MONATSFEIER
- THE MYSTICISM OF ST PAUL
- THE QUEST FOR THE HISTORICAL JESUS
- VON REIMARUS ZU WREDE

Schweitzer, Alexander *see*
- DIE PROTESTANTISCHEN CENTRALDOGMEN
- SCHLEIERMACHERS WIRKSAMKEIT ALS PREDIGER
- ZWINGLIS BEDEUTUNG NEBEN LUTHER

Schweitzer, Jean Baptist von *see* DER ZEITGEIST UND DAS CHRISTENTHUM

Schweizer, Abraham *see* UNTERSUCHUNGEN UEBER DIE RESTE EINES HEBRAEISCHEN TEXTES VOM ERSTEN MAKKABAEERBUCH

SCHWEIZER AUSGABE *see* DIES BLATT GEHOERT DER HAUSFRAU

SCHWEIZER JOURNAL – (In Swiss) – San Francisco, CA. 1942-1950 – 3r – 1 – $150.00 – C03674 – us Library Micro [073]

SCHWEIZER MONATSHEFTE – 1921- 1; 1975- 5,6,9 – us UMI [073]

Schweizer, V *see* PLATENS WERKE

SCHWEIZER VOLKSKUNDE – v1-15. 1911-25 – 1 – us I.U. Libraries [390]

SCHWEIZERISCHE BAUZEITUNG – Zurich, Switzerland. -w. 1890-94. 3 reels – 1 – uk British Libr Newspaper [949]

SCHWEIZERISCHE ELEKTROTECHNISCHE ZEITSCHRIFT – Zurich, Switzerland. -w. 1904-09. 3 reels – 1 – uk British Libr Newspaper [073]

SCHWEIZERISCHE EVANGELISCHE PRESSEDIENST – (Lacking some pgs) – 1939-86 – Inquire – 1 – ATLA S0350 – us A.T.L.A. [240]

SCHWEIZERISCHE KIRCHENZEITUNG – (Lacking: 1838-1957) – 1832-1992 – Inquire – 1 – ATLA S0562 – us A.T.L.A. [073]

SCHWEIZERISCHE MASCHINENBAU-ZEITUNG – Aarau, oct 1907-10 – 1 – Dist. gw Mikrofilm – uk British Libr Newspaper [620]

SCHWEIZERISCHE MEDIZINISCHE WOCHENSCHRIFT – v85-105.1955-75 – 1,5,6 – us Princeton Micro [616]

SCHWEIZERISCHE MUSIKZEITUNG – v. 1-68. 1861-1928 – 1 – us Schnase [780]

DIE SCHWEIZERISCHEN GOLDHYPOTHEKEN IN DEUTSCHLAND... / ed by Geiler, K & Pfefferle, W – Mannheim, 1924 – 5mf – 1 – ILM-3705/1 – ne IDC [327]

SCHWEIZERISCHES ARCHIV FUER VOLKSKUNDE – v1-10. 1897-1906 – 1 – us I.U. Libraries [390]

SCHWEIZERISCHES JAHRBUCH FUER MUSIKWISSENSCHAFT – Basel. v1-7. 1924-38. All published – 5,9 – Dfl280.00; Dfl40.00v – ne Swets [780]

SCHWEIZ-INDEX : BILDDOKUMENTATION ZUR KUNST IN DER SCHWEIZ / ed by Bildarchiv Foto Marburg – Deutsches Dokumentationszentrum fuer Kunstgeschichte Philipps-Universitaet Marburg – (DM1,680 to subsc of the Marburger Index) – 1995 – 148 silver mf (1:24) – 9 – DM2,400.00 – 3-598-33219-X – gw Saur [700]

Schwendel, P J *see* TRADITIONAL BASEBALL WEIGHT TRAINING VERSUS POWER WEIGHT TRAINING

Schwendener, S *see* UNTERSUCHUNGEN UEBER DEN FLECHTENTHALLUS

SCHWENKFELDER HYMNOLOGY AND THE SOURCES OF THE FIRST SCHWENKFELDER HYMN-BOOK PRINTED IN AMERICA / Seipt, Allen Anders – Philadelphia: Americana Germanica Press, 1909 – 1mf – us A.T.L.A. [240]

THE SCHWENKFELDERS IN PENNSYLVANIA : A HISTORICAL SKETCH / Kriebel, Howard Wiegner – Lancaster, Pa.: [s.n.] 1904 (Lancaster, Pa.: New Era) – 1mf – us A.T.L.A. [240]

SCHWENKFELDIAN – (Lacking: Dec 1953) – Dec 1903-1986 – 13r – 1 – ATLA S0829 – us A.T.L.A. [073]

Schwennicke, Tobias *see* SEDIMENTTEXTUREN DER SOHLBANKFLAECHE IM NATURDENKMAL "SAURIERFAEHRTEN MUENCHEHAGEN" (BERRIAS), REHBURGER BERGE

SCHWERBEHINDERTE IM BETRIEB : EINE EMPIRISCHE UNTERSUCHUNG ZUR SITUATION UND SELBST-WAHRNEHMUNG BEHINDERTER ARBEITNEHMERINNEN / Matheis, Juergen – 1994 – 2mf – DM80.00 – 3-8267-2028-8 – gw Hänsel [360]

DER SCHWERE GANG : EINE ERZAEHLUNG / Lux, Hanns Maria – 4. Aufl. Muenchen: F Eher [1944] – 1r – 1 – us U.W. Library [830]

SCHWERINER VOLKSZEITUNG – (Cont: Landeszeitung, -aug 13 1952. Also available: Ausgabe SCHWERIN-LAND (nur Kreisseiten), apr 1 1958-oct 31 1961 (incomplete), mar 14 1963-jul 7 1982 (incomplete), may 19 1988-dec 14 1990; Ausgabe RUEGEN (nur Kreisseiten), oct 1 1949-jun 30 1950, 1951-jun 28 1952, mf. Also Bereichsausgaben available (nur Kreisseiten): BUETZOW, apr 1 1958-66, oct 6 1972-84 (all incomplete); GADEBUSCH, apr 3 1958-oct 25 1961 (incomplete), feb 11-nov 18 1967, nov 14 1972-mar 7 1976 (incomplete), 1980-90 (incomplete); GUESTROW, apr 1-may 15 1949, jan 2-mar 31 1950, oct 2 1950-mar 31 1951 (all mf), apr 2 1958-aug 5 1984 (incomplete); HAGENOW, sep 1-30, nov 1-dec 31 1948, apr 1-21 1949 (all mf), apr 2 1958-90 (incomplete); LUDWIGSLUST, apr 21 1958-nov 3 1981 (incomplete), 1984-sep 29 1990; LUEBZ, apr 2 1958-oct 28 1981 (incomplete); PARCHIM, oct 1-dec 31 1948 (mf), apr 2 1958-83 (incomplete), sep 20 1985-90; PERLEBERG, apr 1 1958-oct 31 1961 (incomplete), mar 9-dec 31 1965, 1984-sep 28 1990; STERNBERG, aug 2 1960-oct 2 1962 (incomplete), nov 15 1964-aug 26 1984 (incomplete)) – Schwerin, apr 10 1946- – 1 – Inquire at Mikrofilmarchiv for details – gw Misc Inst [072]

SCHWERINER VOLKSZEITUNG – Schwerin, Germany. Jul 1966-Jun 1975 – 16r – 1 – us L of C Photodup [072]

SCHWERINER VOLKSZEITUNG *see* LANDESZEITUNG

SCHWERTLILIEN / Lueddecke, Theodor – Leipzig: P List, c1943 – 1r – 1 – us U.W. Library [810]

Schwertner, Heiko *see*
- ENTWICKLUNG EINES HPLC-SYSTEMS ZUR ANALYSE VON BENZO(A)PYREN-(DNA)-ADDUKTEN SOWIE UNTERSUCHUNGEN ZUR SYNTHESE VON BENZO(A)PYREN-DNA-ADDUKTEN
- ISOLIERUNG UND SEQUENZIERUNG EINER MITOCHONDRIALEN FORM DER KATALYTISCHEN UNTEREINHEIT DER CYCLO-ADENOSIN-3',5'-MONOPHOSPHAT-ABHAENGIGEN PROTEINKINASE AUS RINDERLEBER

Schwicker, J H *see* GESCHICHTE DER UNGARISCHEN LITTERATUR

Schwickerath, Robert *see* JESUIT EDUCATION

Schwietering, Julius *see* SINGEN UND SGEN

Schwind, Moritz von *see* MOERIKE-ALBUM

Schwindl, F *see* 24 MENUETTOS FOR TWO VIOLINS AND A BASS

Schwizerbart, E *see* BRYOLOGIA EUROPA

Schwob, Marcel *see*
- VIES IMAGINAIRES
- VOYAGE A SAMOA

Schworck, Andreas *see* GRUNDIDEEN, ERSCHEINUNGSFORMEN UND URSACHEN POLITISCHEN HINDU-FUNDAMENTALISMUS IN INDIEN VON 1875 BIS HEUTE AUS MODERNISIERUNGSTHEORETISCHER SICHT

Schworm, Karl *see*
- DIE FEUER SIND ENTGLOMMEN
- DER LETZTE CHRISTOFFELSTRUNK
- DAS SCHILDERHAUS VON FROZZELBORN

SCHYNVOETS MUNTKABINET DER ROOMSCHE KEIZERS EN KEIZERINNEN / Bogaert, A S – Amsteldam. 1695. BO-162 1 – 9 – ne IDC [700]

SCICAT : SCIENCE REFERENCE AND INFORMATION SERVICE / British Library – (Author/Title Catalogue, 1997, four issues. £245.00 in UK. Classified Catalogue, four issues. £151.00 in UK. Author/Title and Classified, four issues. £326.00 in UK) – Contains additions to stock from 1974 plus many items published earlier, including all serials held by SRIS. Quarterly cumulations – 9 – uk British Libr Humanities [010]

Scidmore, Eliza Ruhamah *see* ALASKA, ITS SOUTHERN COAST AND THE SITKAN ARCHIPELAGO

LA SCIE : JOURNAL HEBDOMADAIRE ILLUSTRE – Montreal, Canada. v1 n1. 25 jul 1878 – 1r – 1 – Can$25.00 – cn Can Microfilming [072]

LA SCIE ILLUSTREE : CARICATURES – Quebec, Canada. 17 fev 1865-12 mai 1866 – 1r – 1 – Can$35.00 – cn Can Microfilming [072]

SCIENCE : THE ANCIENT HEBREW SIGNIFICANCE OF THE BOOK OF GENESIS / Haviland, Frank Wood – New York: Frank Wood Haviland, c1897 – 1mf – 9 – 0-8370-3538-4 – 1985-1538 – us A.T.L.A. [220]

SCIENCE : PROGRES DECOUVERTE (LA NATURE) – Paris. v77-97. 1949-69 – 5r – 5 – inquire – us Ross [500]

SCIENCE – v. 1- 1883- – 1. ; 5,6. ; 9 – apply; v.139-; v.167- – us UMI [500]

SCIENCE – v1-22. 1883-93.New series v1-130. 1895-1959 – 1,5,6 – us Princeton Micro [500]

SCIENCE 79 – Title carries year's designation. v.1-. 1979- – 1,5,6,9 – us UMI [500]

SCIENCE ABSTRACTS OF CHINA – 1 reel – 5 – uk Microform Academic [950]

SCIENCE AFRIQUE / CCTA CSA Joint Secretariat. African Headquarters. London – 23 nos. 1958- Available: nos. 10, 11, 13, 15, 17, 20, 23. BA-746 1 – 9 – ne IDC [324]

SCIENCE AND CHILDREN – v1- 1963- 1; v8- 5,6; v13- 9 – us UMI [370]

SCIENCE AND CHRISTIAN TRADITION: ESSAYS / Huxley, Thomas Henry – New York: D. Appleton and Company, 1898.34+419p – 1 – us U.W. Library [240]

SCIENCE AND CHRISTIANITY / Bettex, Frederic – Cincinnati: Jennings & Pye, 1901. 1 fiche – 9 – us A.T.L.A. [240]

SCIENCE AND GLOBAL SECURITY : THE TECHNICAL BASIS FOR ARMS CONTROL AND ENVIRONMENTAL POLICY INITIATIVES / ed by Feiveson, Harold A & Rodionov, Stanislav N – 9,5,1 – us Gordon [320]

SCIENCE AND HEBREW TRADITION : ESSAYS / Huxley, Thomas Henry – New York: D Appleton, 1894 – 1mf – 9 – 0-8370-3711-5 – 1985-1711 – us A.T.L.A. [210]

SCIENCE AND IMMORTALITY / Lodge, Oliver – New York: Moffat, Yard, 1908 – 1mf – 9 – us A.T.L.A. [240]

SCIENCE AND RELIGION IN CONTEMPORARY PHILOSOPHY / Boutroux, Emile – London: Duckworth, 1909 – 1mf – us A.T.L.A. [190]

SCIENCE AND REVELATION : A SERIES OF LECTURES IN REPLY TO THE THEORIES OF TYNDALL, HUXLEY, DARWIN, SPENCER, ETC – (Includes bibliographical references) – Belfast:William Mullan; New York:Scribner, Welford & Armstrong, 1875 – 1mf – 9 – 0-8370-5187-8 – 1985-3187 – us A.T.L.A. [210]

SCIENCE AND REVELATION:...IN REPLY TO... TYNDALL, HUXLEY, DARWIN, SPENCER / Porter, Josias Leslie – Belfast: William Mullan, 1875. 1 fiche – 9 – us A.T.L.A. [240]

SCIENCE AND SCIENTIFIC RESEARCHERS IN MODERN SOCIETY / Dickinson, John P – 2nd ed 1986 – 260p – 9 – 92-3-102427-2 – fr UNESCO [306]

SCIENCE AND SOCIETY – (v.34- 1970- 5,6. v.39- 1975- 9) – v.1- 1936- – 1 – us UMI [303]

SCIENCE AND TECHNOLOGY COMMITTEE / UN Economic Commission for Europe (ECE) – 1947-1989 – E.240 F.193 R.162 – 9 – us U.N. Pubs [340]

SCIENCE AND TECHNOLOGY EDUCATION AND NATIONAL DEVELOPMENT – 1983 – 197p – 9 – 92-3-102144-3 – fr UNESCO [338]

SCIENCE AND TECHNOLOGY IN COUNTRIES OF ASIA AND THE PACIFIC : POLICIES, ORGANIZATION AND RESOURCES – 1985 – 701p – 9 – 92-3-002078-8 – fr UNESCO [350]

SCIENCE AND TECHNOLOGY IN DEVELOPING COUNTRIES : STRATEGIES FOR THE 1990S – 1992 – 9 – 92-3-102739-5 – fr UNESCO [600]

SCIENCE AND TECHNOLOGY IN DEVELOPMENT : A UNESCO APPROACH / Behrman, Daniel – 1979 – 9 – 92-3-101726-8 – fr UNESCO [500]

SCIENCE AND TECHNOLOGY IN THE PRIMARY SCHOOL OF TOMORROW / Orpwood, Graham & Werdelin, Ingvar – 1988 – 9 – 92-3-102502-3 – fr UNESCO [370]

SCIENCE AND TECHNOLOGY LIBRARIES / ed by Seidman, Ruth K – v1- 1980- – 1, 9 ($160.00 in US $224.00 outside hardcopy subsc) – us Haworth [020]

SCIENCE AND TECHNOLOGY POLICIES INFORMATION EXCHANGE SYSTEM (SPINES) : FEASIBILITY STUDY / Coblans, H et al – 1974 – 115p – 9 – 92-3-101185-5 – fr UNESCO [000]

SCIENCE AND TECHNOLOGY POLICY AND THE ORGANIZATION OF RESEARCH IN THE GERMAN DEMOCRATIC REPUBLIC – 1986 – 9 – 92-3-102301-2 – fr UNESCO [350]

SCIENCE AND TECHNOLOGY: VITAL NATIONAL RESOURCES / Sanders, Ralph – 1975. 146p. ISBN: 0-912338-12-1 – 9 – 9.50 – us Lomond [500]

SCIENCE AND THE BIBLE: A LECTURE / Perry, Charles – London: S.P.C.K., 1869. 1 fiche. 8370-4711-0 – 9 – us A.T.L.A. [240]

SCIENCE AND THE FACTORS OF INEQUALITY : LESSONS OF THE PAST AND HOPES FOR THE FUTURE / Moraze, Charles et al – 1979 – 273p – 9 – 92-3-101732-2 – fr UNESCO [306]

SCIENCE AND THE SUPERNATURAL / Carlson, A J – 1963 – 9 – $1.00f – at Libertarian Micro [130]

SCIENCE BOOKS *see* AAAS SCIENCE BOOKS

SCIENCE BOOKS AND FILMS *see* AAAS SCIENCE BOOKS

SCIENCE BULLETIN / South Africa. Agriculture and Forestry Dept – Pretoria. 1911-1955 no. 1-362. Incomplete – 1 – us NY Public [630]

SCIENCE COLLECTION / Bibliotheque Nationale – 27 titles relating to science and mathematics authors include Agrippa, de Condorcet, Scopoli, P.S. Pallas, J. Swammerdam. Studies dealing with alchemy, thermodynamics, geometry, chemistry, meteorology and probabilities. In French, but several in Latin, English or German. Titles available separately. 122 fiches – 9 – 302.00 – fr Bibl Nationale [500]

LA SCIENCE DE LA RECLAME / Grenier, WA – Montreal: Railway and Commercial Printing Co., 1896. 04387. (Pre-1900 Canadiana) – 9 – cn C.I.H.M. [971]

LA SCIENCE DES HIEROGLYPHES, OU L'ART D'EXPRIMER PAR DES FIGURES SYMBOLIQUES, LES VERTUS, LES VICES... / La Feuille, D de – Den Haag, 1736 – 3mf – 9 – ne IDC [700]

SCIENCE DIGEST – (v. 63- 1968- 5,6. v. 67- 1970- 9) – v. 1- 1937- – 1 – us UMI [500]

SCIENCE DIMENSION – 1969- 1; 1978- 5,6,9 – us UMI [500]

SCIENCE DIMENSION – (Ceased v18 no 1 1986) – Ottawa. v1-18. 1969-86 – 9 – Can$20.00y – cn Micromedia [500]

LA SCIENCE DU BLASON : SES PRINCIPES, SES REGLES ET LEUR APPLICATION / Morin, Victor – Montreal, 1958. SEM105P756 – 1mf – 9 – Can$2.25 – cn Bibl Nat [920]

SCIENCE EDUCATION – v. 1-. 1916- – 1,5,6,9 – us UMI [370]

SCIENCE EDUCATION – v1-70. 1916-86 – 1,5,6 – us Princeton Micro [370]

SCIENCE EDUCATION ABROAD: A LECTURE, BEING THE ANNUAL UNIVERSITY LECTURE OF THE SESSION 1870-71, DELIVERED IN THE WILLIAM MOLSON HALL, NOV. 18, 1870 / Dawson, John William – Montreal: Gazette Steam Printing House, 1870. 02607. (Pre-1900 Canadiana) – 9 – cn C.I.H.M. [971]

LA SCIENCE ET LA PRATIQUE DU PLAIN-CHANT / Jumilhac, P B de – 1673 – 9 – us Sibley [780]

LA SCIENCE ET L'ENSEIGNEMENT DE L'ADMINISTRATION PUBLIQUE AUX ETATS-UNIS / Langrod, G – F30.00 – fr Ethnologie [350]

SCIENCE FICTION – v1-3 (all publ). 1939-43 – 1 reel – 1 – $90.00 – us UPA [830]

SCIENCE FICTION CHRONICLE – v.1-. 1979- – 1,5,6,9 – us UMI [830]

SCIENCE FICTION PERIODICALS, SERIES 1 – 1926-45. Amazing Stories; Amazing Stories Annual; Amazing Stories Quarterly; Comet; Cosmic Stories; Dynamic Science Stories; Extrapolation; Fantastic Adventures; Miracle Stories; Planet Stories; Science Fiction; Science Fiction Quarterly; Science Wonder Stories; Wonder Stories; Science Wonder Quarterly; Wonder Stories Quarterly; Stirring Science Stories. Titles available separately; see under title for price – 54r – 1 – $3,545.00 – us UPA [830]
SCIENCE FICTION PERIODICALS, SERIES 2 – 1936-78. Amazing Science Fiction; Astonishing Stories; Fantastic Stories; Startling Stories; Thrilling Wonder Stories; Extrapolation. Titles available separately; see under title for price – 78r – 1 – $4,285.00 – us UPA [830]
SCIENCE FICTION QUARTERLY – Nos. 1-10 (all publ). 1940-43 – 1 reel – 1 – $85.00 – us UPA [830]
SCIENCE FICTION REVIEW *see* ALIEN CRITIC
SCIENCE FICTION SOURCES – 137mf – 9 – us UMI [830]
SCIENCE FOR DEVELOPMENT : AN ESSAY ON THE ORIGIN AND ORGANIZATION OF NATIONAL SCIENCE POLICIES / Spaey, Jacques et al – 1971 – 9 – 92-3-100893-5 – fr UNESCO [500]
SCIENCE FORUM – Ottawa. v1-12. 1968-79 – 9 – Can$20.00y – cn Micromedia [500]
LA SCIENCE HEROIQVE, TRAITANT DE LA NOBLESSE, DE L'ORIGINE DES ARMES, DE LEURS BLASONS, & SYMBOLES / Vulson, Marc de, Sieur de la Colombiere – Paris: Sebastien Cramoisy, Imp. Ordinaire du Roy, et Gabriel Cramoisy, 1644. SEM35P323 – 1r – 1 – $23.00 – cn Bibl Nat [920]
SCIENCE IN ARCADY / Allen, Grant – London: Lawrence & Bullen, 1892.05069.(Pre-1900 Canadiana) – 9 – cn C.I.H.M. [971]
SCIENCE IN CHINA (SCIENTIA SINICA) SERIES A – 1,5,69 – us UMI [500]
SCIENCE IN CHINA (SCIENTIA SINICA) SERIES B – 1,5,69 – us UMI [500]
SCIENCE IN LITERATURE; A COLLECTION OF LITERARY SCIENTIFIC ESSAYS.. / Law, Frederick Houk – First ed. New York and London: Harper and Brothers, 1929. xvii, 364p. Books for further reading at end of each essay. With: Veld Trails xC.S. Stokes – 1 – us U.W. Library [410]
SCIENCE IN THEOLOGY : SERMONS / Farrar, Adam Storey – London: J. Murray, 1859 – 1mf – us A.T.L.A. [200]
SCIENCE IN WORLD WAR 2 – 1983 – 51mf – 9 – $255.00 – S1665 – us Scholarly Res [940]
LA SCIENCE INGENIEURS DANS LA CONDUITE DES TRAVAUX DE FORTIFICATION ET D'ARCHITECTURE CIVILE / Belidor, Bernard Forest de – Paris, Cl. Jombert, 1729. 4 fol., il (Architecture Series) – 9 – fr Hachette [720]
SCIENCE NEWS – v1- 1922- 1; v93- 5,6; v97- 9 – us UMI [500]
SCIENCE NOUVELLE. LETTRE D'UN DISCIPLE DE LA SCIENCE NOUVELLE AUX RELIGIONNAIRES PRETENDUS SAINT-SIMONIENS / Roux, Prosper C – Paris, 1831, 124 p. Les Saint-Simoniens, 1825-1834. 6986 – 9 – fr Hachette [335]
SCIENCE OF COMPUTER PROGRAMMING – v1-4. 1981-84 – 1,5,6,13 – sz Elsevier [073]
THE SCIENCE OF ECONOMICS AND ITS RELATION TO FREE EXCHANGE AND SOCIALISM / Dunning, McLeod, Henry – 1894. 1 fiche (29x) – 9 – 1.00f – at Libertarian Micro [320]
THE SCIENCE OF EDUCATION AND ART OF TEACHING / Ogden, John – 1868. 478p – 1 – us U.W. Library [370]
THE SCIENCE OF ETHICS / Stephen, Leslie – London: Smith, Elder, 1882 – 2mf – 9 – 0-8370-6395-7 – 1986-0395 – us A.T.L.A. [170]
THE SCIENCE OF ETHICS / Stephen, Leslie – London: Smith, Elder, & Co., 1882 – 1 roll – 1 – 1-55879-611-8 – uk Libr Preservation [170]
THE SCIENCE OF GOVERNMENT AS EXHIBITED IN THE INSTITUTIONS OF THE U.S. / Goodrich, Charles B – Boston: Little, Brown, 1853 – 4mf – 9 – $6.00 – LLMC 95-060 – us L.L.M.C. [323]
THE SCIENCE OF LAW / Amos, Sheldon – New York: D Appleton & Co, 1875 – 5mf – 9 – $7.50 – LLMC 95-204 – us L.L.M.C. [340]
THE SCIENCE OF LAW AND LAWMAKING : BEING AN INTRODUCTION TO LAW, A GENERAL VIEW OF ITS FORMS AND SUBSTANCE, AND A DISCUSSION OF THE QUESTION OF CODIFICATION / Clarke, R Floyd – N.Y.: The Macmillan Co, 1898 – 5mf – 9 – $7.50 – LLMC 95-199 – us L.L.M.C. [340]
SCIENCE OF LEGAL METHOD : SELECT ESSAYS BY VARIOUS AUTHORS / AALS – N.Y.: The Macmillan Co., 1917(1921) – 8mf – 9 – $12.00 – LLMC 95-189 – us L.L.M.C. [340]
THE SCIENCE OF LEGAL METHOD : SELECT ESSAYS BY VARIOUS AUTHORS – N.Y.: The Maxmillan Co, 1921 – 8mf – 9 – $12.00 – LLMC 95-189 – us L.L.M.C. [340]
THE SCIENCE OF MARKETING BY MAIL / Buckley, Homer John – New York: B.C. Forbes Publishing Co., c1924. xix,323p. illus – 1 – us U.W. Library [380]
THE SCIENCE OF MOTHERHOOD / Smith, Hannah Whitall – c1894 – 9 – us A.T.L.A. [240]
THE SCIENCE OF NATURAL THEOLOGY : OR, GOD THE UNCONDITIONED CAUSE, AND GOD THE INFINITE AND PERFECT AS REVEALED IN CREATION / Mahan, Asa – Boston:Henry Hoyt, 1867 – 1mf – 9 – 0-8370-4256-9 – 1985-2256 – us A.T.L.A. [210]
SCIENCE OF PSYCHIC PHENOMENA / Abhedananda, Swami – Calcutta: Ramarkrishna Vedanta Math, 1946. xv,100p. plates – 1 – us U.W. Library [150]
THE SCIENCE OF RELIGION AND ITS BEARING UPON CHRISTIAN CLAIMS / Major, Henry Dewsbury Alves – London: Francis Griffiths, 1909.1 fiche. 8370-4264-X – 9 – us A.T.L.A. [240]
THE SCIENCE OF RELIGIONS / Burnouf, Emile & Rapson, E J – London: S. Sonnenschein, Lowrey, 1888 – 1mf – us A.T.L.A. [200]
SCIENCE OF REVEALED TRUTH IMPREGNABLE / Gordon, William R – New York: Board of Publications Reformed Church in America, 1878 – 9 – us A.T.L.A. [240]
THE SCIENCE OF REVEALED TRUTH IMPREGNABLE : AS SHOWN BY THE ARGUMENTATIVE FAILURES OF INFIDELITY AND THEORETICAL GEOLOGY... / Gordon, William Robert – New York: Board of Publ of the Reformed Church in America, 1878 – 1mf – 9 – 0-8370-3346-2 – 1985-1346 – us A.T.L.A. [230]
THE SCIENCE OF SOCIETY / Andrews, Stephen Pearl – 1848. 211p. 1 fiche (24x) – 9 – 1.00f – at Libertarian Micro [320]
SCIENCE OF SPIRITUAL LIFE / Cooper, John – London: Sampson Low, Marston, 1877. 1 fiche – 9 – us A.T.L.A. [240]
SCIENCE OF THE TOTAL ENVIRONMENT – v1-37. 1972-84 – 1,5,6,13 – sz Elsevier [574]
A SCIENCE OF THE ULTIMATE / Rodger, James George – Los Angeles: Calif. Univ. Union, 1908. 1 fiche.8370-4942-3 – 9 – us A.T.L.A. [240]
SCIENCE, PHILOSOPHY AND RELIGION : LECTURES DELIVERED BEFORE THE LOWELL INSTITUTE, BOSTON / Bascom, John – New York:G P Putnam, 1871 – 1mf – 9 – 0-8370-2572-9 – 1985-0572 – us A.T.L.A. [210]
SCIENCE POLICY AND ORGANIZATION OF RESEARCH IN THE REPUBLIC OF KOREA – 1985 – 9 – 92-3-102237-7 – fr UNESCO [350]
LA SCIENCE POPULAIRE ILLUSTREE – Montreal, Canada. 1 aut 1886-v1 n10. 1 dec 1887 – 1r – 1 – Can$30.00 – cn Can Microfilming [073]
SCIENCE PROGRESS – 1906-60 – 854mf – 7 – uk Microform Academic [500]
SCIENCE PROGRESS – v. 54-61. 1966-1974 – 1,5,6 – us Princeton Micro [500]
SCIENCE REFERENCE AND INFORMATION SERVICE CATALOGUE *see* SCICAT
SCIENCE REPORTS OF THE RESEARCH INSTITUTE / Tohoku University – v. 1-6. 1949-54 – 1 – us Princeton Micro [500]
SCIENCE SCOPE-NATIONAL SCIENCE TEACHERS ASSOCIATION – (1985-. 5,6,9) – v6-. 1982- – 1 – us UMI [370]
SCIENCE TEACHER – v1- 1934- 1; v38- 5,6; v42- 9 – us UMI [370]
SCIENCE, TECHNOLOGY AND ENDOGENOUS DEVELOPMENT IN AFRICA : CASTAFRICA 2 – 1988 – 9 – 92-3-102563-5 – fr UNESCO [500]
SCIENCE, TECHNOLOGY AND GOVERNMENTAL POLICY : A MINISTERIAL CONFERENCE FOR EUROPE AND NORTH AMERICA (MINESPOL 2) – 1979 – 183p – 9 – 92-3-101718-7 – fr UNESCO [500]
SCIENCE, TECHNOLOGY AND HUMAN VALUES – (v.29-. 1979- 5,6,9) – v.25-. 1978$ – 1 – us UMI [500]
SCIENCE WONDER QUARTERLY-WONDER STORIES QUARTERLY – v1-4 (all publ). 1929-33 – 2r – 1 – $120.00 – us UPA [830]
SCIENCE WONDER STORIES-WONDER STORIES – v1-7 (all publ). 1929-36 – 9r – 1 – $625.00 – us UPA [830]
SCIENCE-GOSSIP: AN ILLUSTRATED MONTHLY RECORD OF NATURE AND COUNTRY-LORE – London, 1895-1902 – 3 – us Readex [500]
LES "SCIENCES DE LA POLITIQUE" AUX ETATS-UNIS : DOMAINES ET TECHNIQUES / Lasswell, DH & Lerner, D – F60.00 – fr Ethnologie [320]
SCIENCES ET AVENIR ET SUPPLEMENT – (Also available on CD-ROM) – 1988-1995 – 2r per y – 5,6 – Sfr642.00 – sz Infoprint [500]
SCIENCES ET TECHNIQUES / La Societe des Ingenieurs Civils de France – Nos 1-17, Paris. Apr 1966-69; n.s. nos 1-4, 15 Feb-15 May 1973 – 1 – fr A.C.R.P.P. [624]
SCIENCES ET VIE FRANCE ET SUPPLEMENT – 1989-1995 – 2r per y – 5,6 – Sfr642.00 – sz Infoprint [500]
SCIENCES ET VIE MICRO – 1991-1995 – 2r per y – 5,6 – Sfr855.00 – sz Infoprint [500]
THE SCIENCES OF NATURE VERSUS THE SCIENCE OF MAN / Porter, Noah – New York: Dodd & Mead, 1871 – 98p – 1 – us U.W. Library [190]
A SCIENCIA : ORGAM DE PROPAGANDA SPIRITA – Maceio, Alagoas. 25 Abr, 15 Jul 1901 – 1,5,6 – bl Biblioteca [072]
SCIENTIA HORTICULTURAE – v1-23. 1973-84 – 1,5,6,13 – sz Elsevier [580]
SCIENTIA SINICA (A) – F p74. In Chinese – 9 – $4.50f – cc Microforms [073]
SCIENTIA SINICA (B) – In Chinese. F p75 – 9 – $4.50f – cc Microforms [073]
SCIENTIA TINERETULUI – Bucharest, Romania. Apr 1949-1976 – 48r – 1 – us L of C Photodup [949]
SCIENTIFIC ACTIVITIES / Israel. Ministry of Agriculture – 1971-74. Bet-Dagan. 91p – 9 – $2.00 – is I.T.T.I. [324]
SCIENTIFIC ACTIVITIES / Israel. Ministry of Agriculture. Institute for Technology and Storage of Agricultural Products – 1971-74. Bet Dagan. 1975. 190 p – 9 – 3.00 – is I.T.T.I. [630]
SCIENTIFIC ACTIVITIES / Israel. Ministry of Agriculture. Institute of Plant Protection – 1971-74. Bet-Dagan. 157 p – 9 – 3.00 – is I.T.T.I. [324]
SCIENTIFIC ACTIVITIES / Israel. Ministry of Agriculture. Institute of Soils and Water – 1971-74. Bet-Dagan. Jan 1975. 191 p – 9 – 3.00 – is I.T.T.I. [630]
SCIENTIFIC AMERICAN – Color Edition. v.242-. 1980- – 1 – us UMI [500]
SCIENTIFIC AMERICAN – New York City, NY. v1 n9. 13 nov 1845 – 1r – 1 – Can$25.00 – cn Can Microfilming [071]
SCIENTIFIC AMERICAN – (v. 216- 1967- 5,6. v. 222- 1970- 9) – v. 1- 1845- – 1 – us UMI [500]
SCIENTIFIC AMERICAN – v1-141. 1859-1929 – 1,5,6 – us Princeton Micro [500]
SCIENTIFIC AND APPLIED PHARMACOGNOSY, INTENDED FOR THE USE OF STUDENTS IN PHARMACY,...PHARMACISTS,...FOOD AND DRUG ANALYSTS...PHARMACOLOGISTS / Kraemer, Henry – Illus. Philadelphia: the author, c1915. viii,857p – 1 – us U.W. Library [615]
SCIENTIFIC AND APPLIED PHOTOGRAPHY / ed by Alfimov, M V – 9,5,1 – us Gordon [540]
SCIENTIFIC AND TECHNICAL AEROSPACE REPORTS (STAR) – v1-21. 1963-83 – 1,5,6,; 35 – apply; Annual subscription 70.00 per year (y); mm. Reel Mi – us Princeton Micro [629]
SCIENTIFIC AND TECHNICAL AEROSPACE REPORTS (STAR): INDEXES – 1915-81 – 1,5,6. ; 1,5,6 – apply; Annual subscription. 69.00y – us Princeton Micro [629]
SCIENTIFIC AND TECHNICAL PERIODICALS – 1 – us Primary [500]
SCIENTIFIC ASPECTS OF CHRISTIAN EVIDENCES / Wright, George Frederick – New York: D. Appleton, 1898. 1 fiche – 9 – us A.T.L.A. [240]
SCIENTIFIC CANADIAN MECHANICS' MAGAZINE AND PATENT OFFICE RECORD – (Cont: Canadian Mechanic's Magazine and Patent Office Record. Cont by: Canadian Magazine of Science and the Industrial Arts, Patent Office Record) – Montreal: Burland-Desbarats Lith. Co, [1879-1882] – 9 – cn C.I.H.M. [600]
SCIENTIFIC CANADIAN MECHANICS' MAGAZINE AND PATENT OFFICE RECORD *see*
– THE CANADIAN MAGAZINE OF SCIENCE AND THE INDUSTRIAL ARTS, PATENT OFFICE RECORD
– CANADIAN MECHANICS MAGAZINE AND PATENT OFFICE RECORD
SCIENTIFIC CONFIRMATIONS OF OLD TESTAMENT HISTORY / Wright, George Frederick – (Includes index) – 2nd ed. Oberlin, OH: Bibliotheca Sacra Co, 1907, c1906 – 2mf – 9 – 0-8370-9673-1 – 1986-3673 – us A.T.L.A. [210]
SCIENTIFIC CONTRIBUTIONS / New Hampshire. Agricultural Experiment Station – 1908-69 – 1,5,6 – us Spaulding [630]
THE SCIENTIFIC CREED OF A THEOLOGIAN / Schmid, Rudolf – London: Hodder & Stoughton, 1906. 1 fiche – 9 – us A.T.L.A. [240]
SCIENTIFIC DICTIONARY, ENGLISH-INDONESIAN (KAMUS ISTILAH PENGETAHUAN ALAM, INGGERIS INDONESIA) – BY Ratna Wilis Dahar et al. SE 11,196 1. 1964 – 9 – ne IDC [490]
SCIENTIFIC DIVING : A GENERAL CODE OF PRACTICE / ed by Flemming, N C & Max, M D – 1990 – 254p – 9 – 92-3-102641-0 – Co-published with the Florida Sea Grant Program – fr UNESCO [627]
SCIENTIFIC ENTERPRISE, TODAY AND TOMORROW / Buzzati-Traverso, Adriano A – 1978 – 9 – 92-3-101268-1 – fr UNESCO [500]
THE SCIENTIFIC EVIDENCES OF REVEALED RELIGION : THE BISHOP PADDOCK LECTURES FOR THE YEAR 1900 / Shields, Charles Woodruff – New York: Charles Scribner, 1900 – 1mf – 9 – 0-8370-5249-1 – 1985-3249 – us A.T.L.A. [230]
SCIENTIFIC FORECASTING AND HUMAN NEEDS : TRENDS, METHODS, MESSAGE / ed by Forti, Augusto – 1984 – 204p – 9 – 92-3-102134-6 – fr UNESCO [350]
SCIENTIFIC HONEYWELLER – v.1-. 1980- – 1 – us UMI [500]
SCIENTIFIC INVESTIGATIONS OF ANCIENT GLASSES AND LEAD-ISOTOPE STUDIES : THE COLLECTED PAPERS OF ROBERT H. BRILL AND COAUTHORS, 1960-87 / Brill, Robert H – $285.00 – us UPA [660]
SCIENTIFIC JOURNAL SERIES / Colorado. Agricultural Experiment Station. Fort Collins – nos. 1-275. 1936-48 – 1,5,6 – us Spaulding [630]
SCIENTIFIC MANPOWER: REPORT OF A COMMITTEE APPOINTED BY THE LORD PRESIDENT OF COUNCIL / Great Britain. Committee Appointed by the Lord President of Council – Cmd. 6824. 1946. Barlow Report – 1mf – 9 – uk Microform Academic [324]
SCIENTIFIC, MEDICAL AND TECHNOLOGICAL PUBLICATIONS OF THE EIGHTEENTH CENTURY – Scientific, medical and technological titles selected from The Eighteenth Century collection – 1 – us Primary [600]
SCIENTIFIC MONTHLY – (See now: Science) – v1-85. 1915-57 – 1 – us UMI [500]
SCIENTIFIC MONTHLY – v. 1-64. 1915-1946 – 1,5,6 – us Princeton Micro [500]
SCIENTIFIC MONTHLY – Washington, DC. 1915-41 – 13r – 1 – us Ross [500]
THE SCIENTIFIC OBSTACLES TO CHRISTIAN BELIEF / Curteis, George Herbert – London: Macmillan, 1885 – 1mf – 9 – 0-8370-7378-2 – 1986-1378 – us A.T.L.A. [230]
SCIENTIFIC OPINION; A WEEKLY REPORT OF SCIENTIFIC PROGRESS. – London, 1869-70 – 3 – us Readex [500]
SCIENTIFIC PAPERS / U.S. National Bureau of Standards – v1-22. 1904-28 – 1,5,6 – us Princeton Micro [500]

SCIENTIFIC PAPERS / U.S. National Bureau of Standards – (v.1-22. 1904-28. $22236.00) – v.17-18. 1922-23 – 1,5,6 – $2229.00 – us Princeton Micro [500]

SCIENTIFIC PRESS – San Francisco. Calif. 1904-1918; 1920-1921 – 1 – us UMI [071]

SCIENTIFIC PROCEEDINGS OF THE AMERICAN VETERINARY MEDICAL ASSOCIATION *see* JOURNAL OF THE AMERICAN VETERINARY MEDICAL ASSOCIATION

SCIENTIFIC PRODUCTIVITY : THE EFFECTIVENESS OF RESEARCH GROUPS IN SIX COUNTRIES / ed by Andrews, Frank M – 1979 – iv/469p – 9 – 92-3-101599-0 – fr UNESCO [500]

SCIENTIFIC PUBLICATIONS PUBLISHED IN INDONESIA / Madjelis Ilmu Pengetahuan Indonesia – SE-10,822 1. 1958? – 9 – ne IDC [500]

SCIENTIFIC REPORT OF THE INTERCALIBRATION EXERCICE : THE I.O.C./W.M.O./U.N.E.P. PILOT PROJECT ON MONITORING BACKGROUND LEVELS OF SELECTED POLLUTANTS IN OPEN OCEAN WATERS – 1982 – 91p – 9 – 92-3-102077-3 – fr UNESCO [550]

SCIENTIFIC RESEARCH IN EARLY CHINESE GLASS : PROCEEDINGS OF THE ARCHAEOMETRY OF GLASS SESSIONS, 1984, BEIJING / ed by Brill, Robert H & Martin, John H – Corning, NY: Corning Museum of Glass, 1991 – 9 – 0-87290-126-2 – us Corning Mus [740]

SCIENTIFIC RESEARCH IN ISRAEL / Israel. Prime Minister's Office – 1976. 264 p. illus – 9 – 5.00 – is I.T.T.I. [500]

SCIENTIFIC RESULTS OF A JOURNEY IN BRAZIL/BY LOUIS AGASSIZ AND HIS TRAVELLING COMPANIONS. GEOLOGY AND PHYSICAL GEOGRAPHY OF BRAZIL / Agassiz, Louis et al – By Ch. Fred. Hartt. Boston: Fields, Osgood, 1870. 03016. (Pre-1900 Canadiana) – 9 – cn C.I.H.M. [550]

SCIENTIFIC RESULTS OF EXPLORATIONS BY THE U.S. FISH COMM. STEAMER ALBATROSS / Dall, W H – No. VII.Preliminary Report on the collection of Mollusca and Brachiopoda obtained in 1887-88. (Proc. U.S. Nat. Mus., 1889, v12, p219-362, pls. 5-14). Z-2232/1 – 9 – ne IDC [590]

SCIENTIFIC RESULTS OF THE VOYAGE OF H.M.S. CHALLENGER DURING THE YEARS 1873-1876. BOTANY – v. 1, PT. 3: Hemsley, W. B. Botany of Juan Fernandez, the south-eastern Moluccas and the Admiralty Islands. London. 1885. B-110 2 – 8 – ne IDC [910]

THE SCIENTIFIC REVIEW, AND JOURNAL OF THE INVENTORS' INSTITUTE – London. v1-7. 1866-72 – 3 – us Readex [500]

SCIENTIFIC SOFTWARE DIRECTORY – 1985- – 1 – us UMI [073]

Scientific Temperance Federation *see* PAPERS

SCIENTIFIC THEISM / Abbot, Francis Ellingwood – (Includes bibliographical references) – Boston: Little, Brown, 1888 – 1mf – 9 – 0-8370-2009-3 – 1985-0009 – us A.T.L.A. [210]

SCIENTIFIC THEOLOGY : ESSAYS TOWARDS THE DEVELOPMENT OF RELIGIOUS TRUTH ON THE BASIS OF MODERN SCIENCE / Barber, Thomas Walter – London: Elliot Stock, 1884 – 1mf – 9 – 0-8370-2175-8 – 1985-0175 – us A.T.L.A. [210]

SCIENTIFIC VALUE OF TRADITION: A CORRESPONDENCE / Arundell, John Francis – London: Pickering, 1879.1 fiche – 9 – us A.T.L.A. [240]

SCIENTOMETRICS – v1-6. 1979-84 – 1,5,6,13 – sz Elsevier [500]

LA SCIENZA DE' SUONI E DELL'ARMONIA / Pizzati, G – 1782 – 9 – us Sibley [780]

THE SCIMITAR – Kettle Falls. Wash. 1910-1912 – 1 – us UMI [071]

SCINTEIA – Bucharest, Romania. Sept 1944-1977 – 61r – 1 – us L of C Photodup [949]

SCINTEIA – (Cont as: Adevarul 1989) – Bucuresti, 1976-1992ff – 33r – 1 – DM2,475.00 – gw Mikro Press [949]

SCINTEIA *see* ADEVARUL

SCINTEIA TINERETULUI – (Cont as: Tineretul Liber 1989) – Rumaenien, 1976-1992 – 31r – 1 – DM2,325.00 – gw Mikro Press [949]

SCINTILLAE JURIS / Darling, Charles John Darling – 3d ed. London, Davis, 1879. 111 p. LL-1673 – 1 – us L of C Photodup [340]

SCINTILLAE JURIS / Darling, Hon. Mr. Justice – London: Stevens & Haynes, 1903 – 3mf – 9 – $4.50 – LLMC 95-169 – us L.L.M.C. [340]

SCINTILLE DI MUSICA / Lanfranco, G M – 1533 – 9 – us Sibley [780]

Scio de San Miguel, Felipe *see* LOS SEIS LIBROS DE JUAN CRISOSTOMO

SCIO TRIBUNE – Scio, OR. -w. 12 Nov 1925-22 Oct 1970; 2-26 Jan 1975 – 12r – 1 – us U.O. Library [071]

SCIOTO GAZETTE – (Daily edition of this Whig newspaper) – Chillicothe, OH. nov 14, 1849-feb 16, 1850 – 2r – 1 – us Western Res [071]

SCIOTO GAZETTE – (Weekly edition of this Republican newspaper) – Chillicothe, OH. oct 23, 1860-dec 25, 1866 – 1 – us Western Res [071]

SCIOTO GAZETTE – (Weekly edition of this Whig, later Republican, newspaper) – Chillicothe, OH. apr 22, 1835-mar 27, 1850 – 5r – 1 – us Western Res [071]

SCIOTO GAZETTE : WEEKLY NATIONAL REPUBLICAN NEWSPAPER – Chillicothe, OH. Jan 1 1801-Aug 3 1815 – 3r – 1 – us Western Res [071]

SCIOTO GAZETTE – (Weekly Whig newspaper) – Chillicothe, OH. mar 1, 1827-apr 16, 1834 – 3r – 1 – us Western Res [071]

SCIOTO GAZETTE AND CHILLICOTHE ADVERTISER – (Weekly, National Republican newspaper) – Chillicothe, OH. [oct 9]-dec 25, 1800 – 1r – 1 – us Western Res [071]

SCIOTO GAZETTE AND FREDONIAN CHRONICLE – (Weekly, National Republican newspaper) – Chillicothe, OH. aug 10, 1815-feb 15, 1821 – 2r – 1 – us Western Res [071]

SCIOTO GAZETTE AND INDEPENDENT WHIG – (Weekly Whig newspaper) – Chillicothe, OH. apr 23, 1834-apr 15, 1835 – 2r – 1 – us Western Res [071]

SCIQUEST – v36-55. 1962-82. Continues: Chemistry – 1,5,6,9 – us A.C.S. [073]

SCIROCCO : PARTITUR NR. 5 – Berlin: Drei Masken-Verlag GMBH, ca 1920 – 1 – us Sibley [780]

SCISSORS AND PASTE – Dublin, Ireland.12 Dec 1914-27 Feb 1915 – 1 – ie Microforms [072]

SCITUATE 1633-1900 – (Mf 1-5: Vital Records 1639-1805. Mf 6-13: Land Records 1633-1735. Mf 14-19: Land Records 1633-99. Mf 20-28: Town and Vitals 1665-1884. Mf 29-32: Marriages & Earmarks 1659-1802. Mf 33-34: Town Accounts 1665-1779. Mf 35-42: Land Records 1699-1788. Mf 43-50: Proprietors 1723-53. Mf 51-55: Town Records 1665-1743. Mf 56-64: Town Meetings 1743-96. Mf 65-71: Town Meetings 1795-1821. Mf 72-77: Vital Records 1753-1850. Mf 78-81: Militia Records 1841-81. Mf 82-87: Voter Registers 1884-1916. Mf 88-90: Intentions 1849-1901. Mf 91-95: Index Births 1843-1972. Mf 96-100: Index Marriages 1843-1972. Mf 101-104: Index Deaths 1844-1972. Mf 105-107: Vital Records 1844-62. Mf 108-111: Deaths 1862-97. Mf 112-113: Marriages 1862-97. Mf 114-115: Births 1861-98) – (mf ed 1991) – 115mf – 9 – 0-87623-119-9 – us Holbrook [920]

Sclater, P L *see*
- ARGENTINE ORNITHOLOGY
- THE BOOK OF ANTELOPES
- CATALOGUE OF A COLLECTION OF AMERICAN BIRDS
- EXOTIC ORNITHOLOGY
- A MONOGRAPH OF THE JACAMARS AND PUFF-BIRDS
- NOMENCLATOR AVIUM NEOTROPICALIUM
- SYNOPSIS AVIUM TANAGRINARUM

Sclater, P L et al *see* IBIS

Sclater, W L *see* THE BIRDS OF AFRICA

SCLERO-CORNEAL TREPHINING IN THE OPERATIVE TREATMENT OF GLAUCOMA / Elliot, R H – London, 1913 – 3mf – 9 – ne IDC [617]

Scobel, A *see* ANDREES WORLD ATLAS 1912

Scobey *see* BIOGRAPHICAL ANNALS OF OHIO – A HANDBOOK OF THE GOVERNMENT AND INSTITUTIONS OF THE STATE OF OHIO

Scofield, William Campbell *see* THE HOLY SPIRIT IN THE NEW TESTAMENT SCRIPTURES

Scollay, Roland *see* DEVELOPMENTAL IMMUNOLOGY

Sconce, Robert Clement *see* LIFE AND LETTERS OF R.C. SCONCE, FORMERLY SECRETARY TO ADMIRAL SIR JOHN THOMAS DUCKWORTH

SCONE ADVOCATE – Oct 7 1887-Dec 29 1896; Jan 4 1927-Dec 24 1931 – 9 – at Pascoe [072]

LA SCOPA – Paterson, NJ, 1926-1928 – 3r – 1 – us I.H.R.C. [978]

SCOPERTA DELL'AMERICA CATTOLICA / D'Amico, Silvio – (Note al Congresso eucaristico di Chicago). 1927 – 1 – us A.T.L.A. [240]

THE SCOPES CASE – (Orig. published by Michael Glazier Inc.) – 1r – 1 – $85.00 – D3260 – us Scholarly Res [340]

Scopoli, Giovanni Antonio *see*
- ANNUS 1-5, HISTORICO-NATURALIS
- FLORA CARNIOLICA
- INTRODUCTIO AD HISTORIAM NATURALEM

THE SCORE – Boston, 1877-82 – 1 – £60.00 – uk Chadwyck [780]

SCORE: STERILIZATION CENTRAL SERVICE OPERATING ROOM EPIDEMIOLOGY – (1983-. 1,5,6,9) – v1-. 1970- – 1 – us UMI [617]

Scoresby, W *see* JOURNAL OF A VOYAGE TO THE NORTHERN WHALE-FISHERY

LE SCORPION : PREMIER JOURNAL ILLUSTRE AU CANADA – Montreal, Canada. 5 aut-26 aut 1854 – 1r – 1 – Can$25.00 – cn Can Microfilming [072]

Scot, Reginald *see* THE DISCOVERIE OF WITCHCRAFT...BEING A REPRINT OF THE FIRST EDITION PUBLISHED IN 1584

SCOTCH AND IRISH SEEDS IN AMERICAN SOIL : THE EARLY HISTORY OF THE SCOTCH AND IRISH CHURCHES, AND THEIR RELATIONS TO THE PRESBYTERIAN CHURCH OF AMERICA / Craighead, J G – Philadelphia: Presbyterian Board of Publication, c1878 – 1mf – us A.T.L.A. [240]

THE SCOTCH GHOST, OR, LITTLE FANNY'S LOVE / Capeletti, G – London: Longman & Broderip, [1797?] – 1 – us Sibley [780]

SCOTCH IRISH PIONEERS IN ULSTER AND AMERICA / Bolton, Charles Knowles – Boston: Bacon and Brown, 1910 – 1mf – us A.T.L.A. [305]

SCOTCH PLAINS BAPTIST CHURCH. SCOTCH PLAINS, NEW JERSEY : CHURCH RECORDS – 1747-1941. 1780p – 1 – 80.10 – us Baptist [240]

Scotch Ridge. Ohio. United Presbyterian Church *see* RECORDS

THE SCOTCH-IRISH IN AMERICA / Ford, Henry Jones – Princeton, N.J.: Princeton University Press, 1915 – 2mf – us A.T.L.A. [305]

THE SCOTCH-IRISH, OR, THE SCOT IN NORTH BRITAIN, NORTH IRELAND, AND NORTH AMERICA / Hanna, Charles Augustus – New York: G.P. Putnam, 1902 – 3mf – us A.T.L.A. [305]

Scotch-Irish Society of the U.S.A *see* PROCEEDINGS, 1890-1974

SCOTIA REGISTER – Scotia, NE. -w. Oct 1895-Feb 1896; Apr 1896-May 1898; Oct-Nov 1898; Jan 1899-Jan 1901; Apr 1901-Sep 1902; Aug 1908-Jul 1918; Jan 1919 to date – 1 – us NE Hist [071]

Scotland *see* THE ACTS OF THE PARLIAMENTS OF SCOTLAND, 1124-1707

SCOTLAND (ALL COUNTIES), 1868 : BRITISH ISLES CENSUS DIRECTORIES PROJECT, SCOTLAND – at Vine [941]

SCOTLAND (ALL COUNTIES), 1872 : BRITISH ISLES CENSUS DIRECTORIES PROJECT, SCOTLAND. VOL 62 – 10mf – 9 – A$63.00 – at Vine [941]

SCOTLAND (ALL COUNTIES), 1882 : BRITISH ISLES CENSUS DIRECTORIES PROJECT, SCOTLAND – at Vine [941]

SCOTLAND (ALL COUNTIES), 1912 : BRITISH ISLES CENSUS DIRECTORIES PROJECT, SCOTLAND – at Vine [941]

SCOTLAND AND THE UNION : A HISTORY OF SCOTLAND FROM 1695 TO 1747 / Mathieson, William Law – Glasgow: J. Maclehose, 1905 – 1mf – us A.T.L.A. [240]

Scotland. Court of Session *see*
- CASES
- THE DECISIONS OF THE COURT OF SESSION OF SCOTLAND

Scotland. Courts *see* LAW REPORTS

Scotland. Home Department *see* A PROGRAMME OF HIGHLAND DEVELOPMENT

Scotland. North of Scotland Hydro-Electric Board *see* ANNUAL REPORT AND STATEMENT OF ACCOUNTS

Scotland. Parliament *see* ACTS OF PARLIAMENT

Scotland. Scottish Development Department *see* CENTRAL SCOTLAND A PROGRAMME FOR DEVELOPMENT AND GROWTH

Scotland. Scottish Office *see* THE SCOTTISH ECONOMY, 1965-1970. A PLAN FOR EXPANSION

Scotland. South of Scotland Electricity Board *see* ANNUAL REPORT AND STATEMENT OF ACCOUNTS

SCOTLAND'S BATTLES FOR SPIRITUAL INDEPENDENCE / Macpherson, Hector Carswell – London: Hodder and Stoughton, 1905 – 1mf – us A.T.L.A. [240]

SCOTLAND'S DEBT TO PROTESTANTISM / Macpherson, Hector Carswell – Edinburgh: W. Blackwood, 1912. (Knox Club publications; no. 32) – 1mf – us A.T.L.A. [240]

SCOTLAND'S INFLUENCE ON CIVILIZATION / Halsey, Leroy J – Philadelphia: Presbyterian Board of Publication, c1885 – 1mf – us A.T.L.A. [240]

SCOTS OBSERVER – (National Observer National Observer and British Review British Review and National Observer). Edinburgh and London. -w. 24 Nov 1888-16 Oct 1897. (17 reels) – 1 – uk British Libr Newspaper [073]

SCOTS TIMES – Glasgow. Scotland. -sw. Jun 1832-May 1833. (1 reel) – 1 – uk British Libr Newspaper [072]

THE SCOTS WORTHIES / Howie, John – Rev...by the Rev. W.H. Carslow. Edinburgh: Johnstone, Hunter, 1870. xxxii,627p. illus. First ed., 1775 under title: Biographia Scoticana – 1 – us U.W. Library [920]

THE SCOTSMAN – 1965-1994 – 1 – F4,889.00 – sz Infoprint [072]

THE SCOTSMAN – Edinburgh: J Ritchie, 1860-1956-58 – 18r – 1 – us Res Libr [072]

THE SCOTSMAN – Edinburgh. Scotland. -d. 1817-1927. (370 reels) – 1 – uk British Libr Newspaper [072]

THE SCOTSMAN – (From April 1994 onwards includes Scotland On Sunday) – Edinburgh. 1965- – 1 – us Primary [072]

THE SCOTSMAN – Subscription – 1 – F4,278.00 – sz Infoprint [072]

Scott *see* HISTORY OF ALLEN AND WOODSON COUNTIES

Scott, A W *see* AUSTRALIAN LEPIDOPTERA, AND THEIR TRANSFORMATIONS

Scott, Adolphus G *see* A DIGEST OF THE MECHANICS' LIEN LAW OF ILLINOIS

Scott, Andrew *see* THE BRITISH PARASITIC COPEPODA

Scott, Anna Miller *see* DAY DAWN IN AFRICA

Scott, Anne Firor *see*
- SOUTHERN WOMEN AND THEIR FAMILIES IN THE 19TH CENTURY: PAPERS AND DIARIES
- WOMAN'S SUFFRAGE

Scott, Anony *see* WORLD WIDE FUND FOR NATURE

Scott, Archibald Black *see* THE PICTISH NATION, ITS PEOPLE & ITS CHURCH

Scott, Charles A Anderson *see* ULFILAS, APOSTLE OF THE GOTHS

SCOTT COUNTY DEMOCRAT – Benton. MO. 1908-14; 1916-21; 1923-61; 1963-70 – 1 – us UMI [071]

SCOTT COUNTY TIMES – Forest. Miss. 1939-1966 – 1 – us UMI [071]

Scott, Cyrus McNeely *see* DIARY

Scott, D F S *see* SOME ENGLISH CORRESPONDENTS OF GOETHE

Scott, David *see* THE EFFECTS OF SUCCESS AND FAILURE ON CASUAL ATTRIBUTIONS AMONG SCHOLASTIC WRESTLERS

Scott, E H *see* THE FEDERALIST AND OTHER CONSTITUTIONAL PAPERS

Scott, Ernest Findlay *see*
- THE APOLOGETIC OF THE NEW TESTAMENT
- THE HISTORICAL AND RELIGIOUS VALUE OF THE FOURTH GOSPEL

Scott Family *see* THE SCOTT STORY

Scott, G R et al *see* MANUAL ON THE DIAGNOSIS OF RINDERPEST

Scott, George W *see* INDEX-ANALYSIS OF THE FEDERAL STATUTES, 1789-1907

Scott, H W *see* HISTORY OF PORTLAND

Scott, Harvey *see* COMPLETE HISTORY OF FAIRFIELD COUNTY

Scott, Hattie Marshall *see* SCOTT'S PAPERS: KENTUCKY COURT & OTHER RECORDS,

Scott, Henry W *see* THE EVOLUTION OF LAW

Scott, Hugh M *see* THE IMPORTANCE OF HISTORIC RESEARCH FOR THE THEOLOGICAL STUDENT OF TO-DAY

SCOTT I. PEEK, SENATE SERVICE 1952-1963 : ADMINISTRATIVE ASSISTANT TO SEN. GEORGE A. SMATHERS – 2mf – 9 – $10.00 – us Scholarly Res [320]

Scott, J *see*
- THE BRITISH HEMIPTERA
- A CATALOGUE OF BRITISH HEMIPTERA

Scott, James *see* PRINCIPLES OF NEW TESTAMENT QUOTATION

Scott, James B *see* THE DEBATES IN THE FEDERAL CONVENTION OF 1789

Scott, James Brown *see*
- CLASSICS OF INTERNATIONAL LAW. CARNEGIE INSTITUTION. MICRO-MINI-PRINTS EDITION...
- JAMES MADISON'S NOTES OF DEBATES IN THE FEDERAL CONVENTION OF 1789
- THE UNITED STATES OF AMERICA

Scott, John *see*
- MOORE AND SCOTT'S REPORTS
- SCOTT'S NEW REPORTS
- SCOTT'S REPORTS

Scott, Kate M *see* HISTORY OF JEFFERSON COUNTY

Scott, Lisa A *see* ARE HEALTH EDUCATORS SOCIALIZED TO PERCEIVE ROLE MODELING AS A PROFESSIONAL RESPONSIBILITY

Scott, Minnie *see*
- ILLUSTRATED JOURNAL

Scott, Morgan *see* HISTORY OF THE SEPARATE BAPTIST CHURCH, WITH A NARRATIVE OF OTHER DENOMINATIONS

Scott, Oral E *see* THE STARS IN MYTH AND FACT

Scott, Pamela *see* THE PAPERS OF ROBERT MILLS, 1781-1855

Scott, Robert *see*
- THE CHURCH, THE PEOPLE, AND THE AGE
- THE MILITARY LAW OF ENGLAND
- THE PAULINE EPISTLES

Scott, S P *see* THE VISIGOTHIC CODE

THE SCOTT STORY / Scott Family – undated, History of the Scott Family in the eastern United States and Burlington, KS – 1 – us KS Hist [920]

Scott, Thomas *see* ENGLISH LIFE OF JESUS, PT 2

Scott, Thomas Lucas *see*
- THE BRITISH PARASITIC COPEPODA
- CREDIBILITY OF THE GOSPEL NARRATIVES OF THE BIRTH AND INFANCY OF CHRIST
- THE VISIONS OF THE APOCALYPSE AND THEIR LESSONS

SCOTT VALLEY ADVANCE – Etna Mills, CA. 1897-1912; 1913-17 – 10r – 1 – $500.00 – B02206 – us Library Micro [071]

SCOTT VALLEY ADVANCE – (See Etna) – Fort Jones, CA. 1897-1908; 1911; 1912; 1913-1916 – 9r – 1 – $450.00 – B02241 – us Library Micro [071]

SCOTT VALLEY NEWS – Fort Jones, CA. 1878-95 – 3r – 1 – $150.00 – B02242 – us Library Micro [071]

Scott, W *see* BIBLE OUTLINES

Scott, Walter *see*
- BALLADS AND LYRICAL PIECES
- HAROLD THE DAUNTLESS
- THE LADY OF THE LAKE
- THE LAY OF THE LAST MINSTREL
- THE LIVES OF THE NOVELISTS
- THE LORD OF THE ISLES
- THE MISCELLANEOUS PROSE WORKS OF SIR WALTER SCOTT, BART
- THE POETICAL WORKS OF SIR WALTER SCOTT
- ROKEBY
- TALES OF A GRANDFATHER

Scott, William Bell *see*
- AUTOBIOGRAPHICAL NOTES ON THE LIFE OF WILLIAM BELL SCOTT
- POEMS

Scott, William Forse *see* ROSTER OF THE FOURTH IOWA CAVALRY 1861-1865

Scott, William L *see* A TREATISE UPON THE LAW OF TELEGRAPHS; WITH AN APPENDIX, CONTAINING THE GENERAL STATUTORY PROVISIONS OF ENGLAND, CANADA, THE UNITED STATES.

Scott, William Robert *see* AN INTRODUCTION TO CUDWORTH'S TREATISE CONCERNING ETERNAL AND IMMUTABLE MORALITY

Scotti, Anita *see* OTTO LUDWIG IN SEINER STELLUNG ZUR ITALIENISCHEN RENAISSANCE

SCOTTISH AMERICAN JOURNAL WEEKLY – New York. Jan 7 1865-1916; 1918-1919; Dec 1923-May 13 1925. Incomplete. Not collated – 1 – us NY Public [071]

Scottish Anthropological and Folklore Society *see*
- PROCEEDINGS

THE SCOTTISH BANNER – (In English) – Canada, 1978-89 – 6r – 1 – cn Commonwealth Micro [072]

SCOTTISH CHARTIST BIOGRAPHIES / Wilson, A – 1 reel 16mf – 7,9 – uk Microform Academic [320]

THE SCOTTISH CHURCH CRISIS / Macpherson, Hector Carswell – London: Hodder and Stoughton, 1904 – 1mf – us A.T.L.A. [240]

SCOTTISH CHURCH HISTORY / Walker, Norman Lockhart – 1882 – 1 – us A.T.L.A. [240]

SCOTTISH CRYPTOGAMIC FLORA / Greville, R K – 6v. Edinburgh. 1822-, 1823-28. B-5403 2 – 8 – ne IDC [580]

THE SCOTTISH ECONOMY, 1965-1970. A PLAN FOR EXPANSION / Scotland. Scottish Office – Edinburgh. 1966. BD-563 1 – 9 – ne IDC [338]

SCOTTISH HEALTH STATISTICS 1958-1977 – (Coll title: British Government Publications... 1801-1977, Health and Public Welfare) – 77mf – 9 (£1,080.00 health and public welfare set of 171mf) – uk Chadwyck [613]

SCOTTISH HIGHLANDER AND NORTH OF SCOTLAND ADVERTISER – 1885-1893 – 1. 305-313 – £42.00r – uk Scot News [072]

SCOTTISH HISTORICAL REVIEW – (Index included) – Glasgow. v1-25. 1904-28 – 215mf – 9 – H-794c/2 – ne IDC [941]

Scottish Institute of Missionary Studies *see* BULLETIN

SCOTTISH JOURNAL OF POLITICAL ECONOMY – (1985- . 5,6,9) – v1- . 1954- – 1 – us UMI [330]

SCOTTISH JOURNAL OF THEOLOGY – 1(1948)-13(1960) – 101mf – 9 – Dfl354.00 – ne Slangenburg [073]

SCOTTISH JOURNAL OF THEOLOGY – Edinburgh. v1-13. 1948-1960 – 101mf – 9 – ne IDC [240]

A SCOTTISH KNIGHT-ERRANT : A SKETCH OF THE LIFE AND TIMES OF JOHN OGILVIE, JESUIT / Forbes, Frances Alice & Cahill, M – (Includes bibliographical references) – London: Burns Oates & Washbourne, [19–] – 1mf – 9 – 0-8370-6901-7 – 1986-0901 – us A.T.L.A. [920]

SCOTTISH LAW REVIEW AND SHERIFF COURT RECORD – (More vols planned) – Glasgow. v1-28. 1885-1912 – 84mf – 9 – $378.00 – LLMC 84-673 – us L.L.M.C. [073]

SCOTTISH MEDICAL JOURNAL – v. 1-14. 1956-1969 – 1,5,6 – us Princeton Micro [610]

SCOTTISH MONUMENTAL INSCRIPTIONS FROM EDINBURGH AND GLASGOW, ETC / Cramer, Sydney – 1 – uk Microform Academic [410]

SCOTTISH NATION – Montrose, Scotland, UK. 8 May-25 Dec 1923. -w.1/2 reel – 1 – uk British Libr Newspaper [072]

THE SCOTTISH NATION / Anderson, W – v. 1-9 – 2r – 1 – uk Microform Academic [920]

SCOTTISH NATIONAL ANTARCTIC EXPEDITION, 1902-1904. DEEP SEA DEPOSITS / Harvey Pirie, J H – 2816 2. 1912-1913 – 8 – ne IDC [910]

SCOTTISH NATIONAL ANTARCTIC EXPEDITION REPORTS. (BOTANY, PHYSICS AND ZOOLOGY) ON SCIENTIFIC RESULTS OF VOYAGE OF S.Y. "SCOTTIA" DURING 1902-1904 – (Physics: v. 2. 1907. SF 33.00; 9. Botany: v. 3. 1912. SF 21.00; IDC; 9. Zoology: v. 4-6. 1908-09, 1912. SF 154.00; IDC; 9. Lacking: v. 1. 1907) – 2825. 1907-1912 – ne IDC [530]

SCOTTISH NATIONALISM PAMPHLETS – 1844-1975. Based on K. C. Fraser's Bibliography of the Scottish National Movement – 147mf – 9 – uk Microform Academic [941]

THE SCOTTISH NATURALIST – (Cont as: The Annals of Scottish Natural History. Edinburgh v1-20 1892-1911. Cont as: The Scottish Naturalist. Edinburg 1912-1939. Missing: v1 1872; v8(p289-336) 1885/86) – Perth. v1-11. 1872-90 – 192mf – 9 – 8603/1 – ne IDC [500]

THE SCOTTISH NATURALIST *see* THE SCOTTISH NATURALIST

SCOTTISH PHILOSOPHY : A COMPARISON OF THE SCOTTISH AND GERMAN ANSWERS TO HUME / Seth Pringle-Pattison, Andrew – Edinburgh: W. Blackwood, 1885 – xii/218p – 1 – us U.W. Library [190]

THE SCOTTISH REFORMATION : A HISTORICAL SKETCH / Lorimer, Peter – New York: R. Carter, 1861 – 1mf – us A.T.L.A. [240]

THE SCOTTISH REFORMATION : ITS EPOCHS, EPISODES, LEADERS, AND DISTINCTIVE CHARACTERISTICS (BEING THE BAIRD LECTURE FOR 1899) / Mitchell, Alexander F; ed by Fleming, David Hay – Edinburgh: W. Blackwood, 1900. (Baird lectures; 1899) – 1mf – us A.T.L.A. [240]

SCOTTISH STUDIES – Edinburgh. v1-11. 1957-67 – 5,9 – Dfl440.00; Dfl40.00v – ne Swets [941]

Scottish Trades Union Congress *see*
- ANNUAL REPORTS
- MINUTES, ETC

Scottish Womens' Suffrage Movement *see* MINUTES AND CORRESPONDENCE, ETC

SCOTTISH-AMERICAN – New York. 1865-1925 – 16r – 1 – us Ross [071]

Scott-Moncrieff, GK *see* EASTERN MISSIONS FROM A SOLDIER'S STANDPOINT

SCOTTS CREEK CEMETERY REGISTER – 1889-1993 – 1mf – 9 – at Corangamite [920]

SCOTT'S NEW REPORTS : IN THE COURT OF COMMON PLEAS AND EXCHEQUER CHAMBER / Scott, John – v1-8. 1841-45. London: S Sweet/H Butterworth, 1841-45 (all publ) – 85mf – 9 – $127.00 – LLMC 84-787 – us L.L.M.C. [324]

SCOTT'S PAPERS: KENTUCKY COURT & OTHER RECORDS, / Scott, Hattie Marshall; ed by Hardin, Bayless E – 1953. Court records, wills, deeds, marriage bonds, tombstone inscriptions, newspaper clippings of various KY counties. Indexed. 5 fiches. F-1304 – 9 – us A.G.L.L. [920]

SCOTT'S REPORTS : CASES IN THE COURT OF COMMON PLEAS AND EXCHEQUER CHAMBER / Scott, John – v1-8. 1834-40. London: S Sweet, 1835-41 (all publ) – 75mf – 9 – $112.00 – LLMC 84-786 – us L.L.M.C. [324]

SCOTTS VALLEY BANNER – Scotts Valley, 1981-1994 – 13r – 1 – $650.00 – B06056 – us Library Micro [071]

SCOTTSBLUFF FARM JOURNAL – Scottsbluff, NE. -w. Sep 1930-Nov 1939; Jan 1940-Oct 1942 – 1 – us NE Hist [071]

SCOTTSBLUFF REPUBLICAN – Scottsbluff, NE. -w. (-sw 1916-36). Jul 1900-Jul 1904, scattered issues missing; Jan 1908-Jun 1945; Dec 1945-Nov 1964 – 1 – us NE Hist [071]

SCOTTSBLUFF STAR – Scottsbluff, NE. -w. Jul 1907; Oct 1908-Sep 1912 – 1 – us NE Hist [071]

SCOTTSBLUFF STAR-HERALD – Scottsbluff, NE. -w. (-d 1924 to date). Oct 1912 to date – 1 – us NE Hist [071]

SCOTTSVILLE FIRST BAPTIST CHURCH. SCOTTSVILLE, KENTUCKY : CHURCH RECORDS – 1841-1947 – 1 – 49.41 – us Baptist [240]

Scottus, Iohannes *see* DE DIVINA PRAEDESTINATIONE

Scottus, Sedulius *see* COLLECTANEUM MISCELLANEUM

SCOUT – Battle Mountain. Nev. -w. 1957- – 1 – us UMI [071]

SCOUT – Battle Mountain, NV. 1913-57 (incomplete) – 14r – 1 – $700.00 – U04412 – us Library Micro [071]

SCOUT – La Mesa.CA. -w. 1944-58 – 1 – us UMI [071]

THE SCOUT – Oceanside, CA. 1982 – 28+ r – 1 – $1,400.00 ($100.00y) – H04055 – us Library Micro [071]

SCOUT, BATTLE MOUNTAIN *see* STAR

A SCOUTING MAGAZINE FOR THE AMERICAN GIRL *see* AMERICAN GIRL

Scoville, C H *see* HISTORY OF THE ELKHORN VALLEY

SCP NEWSLETTER – (1985-. 5,6,9) – 1980- – 1 – us UMI [073]

SCRAGGS GENERAL ADVERTISER – (City & County Cork General Advertiser. 1862-64) – Cork, Ireland. 1859-14 May 1864. -w – 2r – 1 – uk British Libr Newspaper [072]

SCRAMBLES AMONGST THE ALPS : IN THE YEARS 1860-69 / Whymper, Edward – London: J. Murray, 1871 – 1 roll – 1 – 1-55879-802-1 – uk Libr Preservation [910]

Scranton, Erastus *see* GENEALOGICAL REGISTER OF THE DESCENDANTS

SCRANTON REPUBLICAN – Scranton, PA., 1889-1936 – 13 – $25.00r – us I.M.R. [071]

Scranton, S S *see* HISTORY OF MERCER COUNTY AND REPRESENTATIVE CITIZENS

SCRANTON TRUTH – Scranton, PA. -d 1904-1909; 1910-1912; 1912-1915 – 13 – $25.00r – us I.M.R. [071]

SCRANTONIAN TRIBUNE – Scranton. Pa. 1954- – 1 – us UMI [071]

A SCRAP OF PAPER : THE INNER HISTORY OF GERMAN DIPLOMACY AND HER SCHEME OF WORLD-WIDE CONQUEST / Dillon, Emile Joseph – London, New York: Hodder & Stoughton, 1914. xxvii,220p – 1 – us U.W. Library [943]

SCRAPBOOK / Baptist State Conventions (American Baptist). Maine – 1903-20 – 1 – 15.50 – us A.B.H.S. [240]

SCRAPBOOK / Butler, J M – Trenton, Kentucky. 624p – 1 – 21.84 – us Baptist [920]

SCRAPBOOK / Converse, John Melvin – 1863-1864 – 1 – us KS Hist [920]

SCRAPBOOK / Independence. Missouri. Calvary Baptist Church – 1953-1978 – 1 – 5.00 – us Baptist [240]

SCRAPBOOK / Lewellen, Emerson Calvin – 1 – us KS Hist [920]

SCRAPBOOK / Lewellen, Emerson Calvin – undated – 1 – us KS Hist [920]

SCRAPBOOK / Maverick Family – 1879-80. 1 fiche – 9 – us South Carolina Historical [920]

SCRAPBOOK / Mendenhall, J K – 1871-91 – 1 – 7.56 – us Baptist [240]

SCRAPBOOK / Sanborn, Frank B – undated, Scrapbooks kept by Frank B. Sanborn, abolitionist, about the slavery issue in Kansas and the United States – 1 – us KS Hist [920]

SCRAPBOOK / Schenck, Leland H – 1 – us KS Hist [978]

SCRAPBOOK / Southern Baptist Convention. Hospitals – Lewis J. Bristow – 1 – 5.00 – us Baptist [240]

SCRAPBOOK / Wabaunsee. Kansas – 1 – us KS Hist [978]

SCRAPBOOK COLLECTION / McKinley, William – 1901. 2 reels – 1 – us Ohio Hist [920]

SCRAPBOOK OF NEWSPAPER CLIPPINGS AND OTHER ARTICLES ON MORMONISM – n.p. 1891 – 1 – us NY Public [240]

SCRAPBOOK OF PICTURES ILLUSTRATING VARIOUS HOLIDAYS – 1927 – 1r – 1 – us Ross [920]

SCRAPBOOK OF YOUNG COUNTY / Young County Federation of Women's Clubs. (Texas) – A pictorial history. Texas Reel 12. (The Cox Library Collection) – 5 – us Americana [978]

SCRAPBOOK, SOUTHERN BAPTIST HOSPITALS / Bristow, Lewis J – 98p – 1 – 5.00 – us Baptist [240]

SCRAPBOOKS / Canclini, Santiago – 1-10. Originals in Seminario International Theologico Bautista, Argentino. 2682p – 1 – 93.87 – us Baptist [240]

SCRAPBOOKS / Chenowith, Edith – 1890-1963 – 1 – us KS Hist [978]

SCRAPBOOKS / Daly's Fifth Avenue Theatre. New York – v. 1-43. 1863-1899 – 1 – us NY Public [790]

SCRAPBOOKS / Houdini, Harry – 1 – 378.00 – us L of C Photodup [920]

SCRAPBOOKS / Jackson, Sheldon – 65 v – 65v – 1 – $550.00 – us Presbyterian [080]

SCRAPBOOKS / Metcalf, Wilder S – undated, Relating to his military career and the Spanish-American War – 1 – us KS Hist [920]

SCRAPBOOKS / Rochester, New York. Rochester Church Women United – 1922-67; 1978-82 – 1 – us A.B.H.S. [240]

SCRAPBOOKS / Seeburger, Mattie (Riga, Michigan) – 1913-1981 – 3r – 1 – $32.50r – us Archival [978]

SCRAPBOOKS / Toledo Museum of Art (Toledo, Ohio) – 1903-1969 – 16r – 1 – $32.50r – us Archival [700]

SCRAPBOOKS / Wheeler, John H – Relating to Nicaragua 1855-1857 and manuscript volume on Nicaragua – 1 – 54.00 – us L of C Photodup [920]

SCRAPBOOKS / Wright, Orville & Wright, Wilbur – 1876-1970. Related Guide Book not available. 2 rolls 35mm set – 1 – us Ohio Hist [025]

SCRAPBOOKS, 1910-30 / World Conference on Faith and Order – Newspaper and Magazine Chippings from American, Canadian, British and continental sources on Christian Union. 42v – 1 – us A.T.L.A. [240]

SCRAPBOOKS AND PHOTOS / Sirmans, M Eugene, Jr – ca1934. 29 fiches – 9 – us South Carolina Historical [025]

SCRAPBOOKS, LETTERS, AND CLIPPINGS / Washburn, Pat – undated, Relating to noted Ottawa, KS, architect George P. Washburn – 1 – us KS Hist [920]
SCRAPBOOKS OF CITY AFFAIRS / Erie County. Ohio. Huron, City City Council – 1934-1970 – 2r – 1 – $32.50r – us Archival [324]
SCRAPBOOKS OF ERSKINE CALDWELL / Caldwell, Erskine – 5r – 1 – $365.00 – us UMI [830]
THE SCRAPBOOKS OF ERSKINE CALDWELL – 5r – 1 – $80.00 set – us Dartmouth [420]
SCRAPBOOKS OF NEWSPAPER CLIPPINGS RELATING TO THE GREAT WAR – v1-21. 1914-18 – 3r – 1 – us Ross [940]
SCRAPBOOKS OF THE EUROPEAN WAR – v2-37. 1915-18 – 6r – 1 – us Ross [940]
SCRAPBOOKS OF WINSTON CHURCHILL / Churchill, Winston S – (The American novelist and Progressive politician, author of Coniston (1906)) – 5r – 1 – us UMI [420]
THE SCRAPBOOKS OF WINSTON CHURCHILL, AMERICAN NOVELIST AND POLITICIAN / Churchill, Winston S – 5r – 1 – $85.00 set – us Dartmouth [420]
SCRAPBOOKS...OF SUMMER ACTIVITIES, 1931-33, 1938, 1940, 1942-44, 1948, 1949-50 / Ridgecrest. North Carolina. Ridgecrest Baptist Assembly – 1584p – 1 – 55.44 – us Baptist [240]
SCREEN: INCORPORATING SCREEN EDUCATION – v23-. 1982- – 1,5,6,9 – us UMI [073]
SCREEN INTERNATIONAL – 1 – uk World [790]
SCREVEN BAPTIST CHURCH. GEORGETOWN COUNTY. SOUTH CAROLINA : CHURCH RECORDS – 1949-1972. Scattered – 1 – $9.54 – us Baptist [240]
Screven, William *see* HISTORICAL WORK
Scriba, Carl *see* GEDICHTE
Scriba, L G *see* JOURNAL FUER DIE LIEBHABER DER ENTOMOLOGIE
Scriba, Otto *see* DAS ALTE TESTAMENT IN PREDIGTEN UND BIBELSTUNDEN
THE SCRIBBLER – Burlington & Montreal, VT. v2 n53. 28 jun 1822-v2 n78. 26 jul 1827 – 1r – 1 – Can$50.00 – cn Can Microfilming [071]
THE SCRIBBLER / ed by MacCulloch, Lewis Luke & Wilcocke, Samuel Hill – Montreal, Canada. v1 n1. 28 jun 1821-n192. 26 jul 1827 – 1r – 1 – Can$50.00 – cn Can Microfilming [072]
SCRIBE – Portland. Or. 1919-42 – 1 – us A.J.P.C. [071]
SCRIBE – Portland, OR. 22 Feb 1972-5 Oct 1974. 2 rolls – 1 – us U.O. Library [071]
SCRIBE – Sunnyvale, CA. 1972-76 – 12r – 1 – $600.00 – B03022 – us Library Micro [071]
THE SCRIBE – Los Angeles, CA.1931 – 1 – us A.J.P.C. [071]
THE SCRIBE – Minneapolis. Minn. 1907-08 – 1 – us A.J.P.C. [071]
Scribner, Harvey *see* MEMOIRS OF LUCAS COUNTY AND CITY OF TOLEDO
SCRIBNER NEWS – Scribner, NE. -w. Aug 1886-Dec 1888, scattered issues missing; Mar 1889-Mar 1890; May 1892; Oct 1895-Aug 1898; Oct 1898-Nov 1909; Jan 1911-Oct 1912 – 1 – us NE Hist [071]
SCRIBNER RUSTLER – Scribner, NE. -w. Oct-Nov 1895; Feb 1896; May 1896-May 1898; Feb 1899 to date – 1 – us NE Hist [071]
Scribner, William *see* LOVE FOR SOULS
SCRIBNER'S MAGAZINE – 1887-1900 – 1 – us UMI [073]
SCRIBNER'S MAGAZINE – New York. v1-38. 1887-1905 + index for v1-10 – 11r – 1 – us Ross [073]
SCRIBNER'S MAGAZINE – v. 1-105. 1887-1939 – 1 – us Princeton Micro [073]
SCRIBNER'S MAGAZINE – v. 1-105. 1887-1939 – 1 – us UMI [000]
SCRIPT – Toledo. Ohio. 1947-1948 – 1 – us UMI [071]
SCRIPT AND PHOTOS / Wallace, David Duncan – 1945. South Carolina historian.3 fiches – 9 – us South Carolina Historical [978]
SCRIPT WRITER NEWS – v.1-. 1980- – 1 – us UMI [410]
SCRIPTA MATHEMATICA – v1-24. 1932-59 – 1,5,6 – us Princeton Micro [073]
SCRIPTA METALLURGICA ET MATERIALIA – v1- 1967- – 5,6,9 – us UMI [660]
SCRIPTA SUPER 4 LIBROS SENTENTIARUM / Argentina, Thomas d' – 1490 – 37mf – 8 – ne Slangenburg [290]
SCRIPTORES ECCLESIASTICI DE MUSICA SACRA POTISSIMUM / Gerbert, Martin – 3v. 1784 – 9 – us Sibley [780]
SCRIPTORES ORDINIS PRAEDICATORUM : TOMUS 1 AB INITIO AD 1499... / Quetif, J & Echard, J – Parisiis, 1719 – 42mf – 8 – Dfl147.00 – ne Slangenburg [240]
SCRIPTORES ORDINIS PRAEDICATORUM : TOMUS 2 AB 1500 AD 1700.. / Quetif, J & Echard, J – Parisiis, 1723 – 44mf – 8 – Dfl154.00 – ne Slangenburg [240]
SCRIPTORES ORDINIS PRAEDICATORUM : TOMUS 3 AB ANNO 1701 AD 1750 PERDUCTI / Coulon, R & Papillon, A – Romae/Parisiis, 1909-1934 – 38mf – 8 – Dfl133.00 – ne Slangenburg [240]
SCRIPTORES ORDINIS S. BENEDICTI QUI 1750-1880 FUERUNT IN IMPERIO AUSTRIACO-HUNGARICO – Vindobonae, 1881 – 19mf – 8 – Dfl63.00 – ne Slangenburg [240]
SCRIPTORES POST THEOPHANEM (CBH 7) / ed by Combefis, FR – Parisiis, 1685 – Dfl91.00 – ne Slangenburg [220]
SCRIPTORES RERUM GERMANICARUM SEPTENTRIONALIUM / Lindenbrogius, E – Hamburgi, 1706 – Dfl46.00 – ne Slangenburg [240]
SCRIPTORES RERUM MYTHICARUM LATINI TRES ROMAE NUPER REPERTI / ed by Bode, G H – Cellis, 1834 – 9mf – 8 – ne Slangenburg [220]
SCRIPTORES RERUM MYTHICARUM TRES ROMAE NUPER REPERTI / Bode, G H – 1834 – 7 – uk Microform Academic [450]
SCRIPTORES RERUM SANGALLIENSIUM (MGH 5: 2.BD) : ANNALIUM ET CHRONICORUM AEVI CAROLINI – (Continuatio: Historiae Aevi Carolini) – 1829 – Dfl77.00 – ne Slangenburg [240]
SCRIPTORUM ILLUSTRIUM MAIORIS BRYTANNIAE / Bale, J – H-1309 2. 1559 – 8 – ne IDC [941]
SCRIPTORUM VETERUM NOVA COLLECTIO E VATICANIS CODICIBUS / ed by Maio, Angelo – Romae. Tom 1-10. 1825-1838 – 234mf – 9 – Dfl819.00 – ne Slangenburg [220]
A SCRIPTURAL ACCOUNT OF THE DOCTRINE OF PERFECTION, HUMBLY OFFERED TO THE CONSIDERATION OF ALL WHO ARE DESIROUS OF CONTENDING EARNESTLY FOR THE FAITH AS ONCE DELIVERED TO THE SAINTS – London, 1763 – 1mf – 9 – MP-426/1 – ne IDC [240]
A SCRIPTURAL COMMENT UPON THE THIRTY-NINE ARTICLES OF THE CHURCH OF ENGLAND, WITH AN OCCASIONAL PREFACE AND APPENDIX / Madan, M – London, 1772 – 2mf – 9 – MP-482/1 – ne IDC [240]
THE SCRIPTURAL DOCTRINE OF ACCEPTANCE WITH GOD : CONSIDERED IN REFERENCE TO THE NEOLOGIAN HERMENEUTICS: IN SIX LECTURES / Ryder, Arthur Gore – (Includes appendix on Hamiltonian theodicy and Hegel) – Dublin: Hodges, Smith, 1865 – 1mf – 9 – 0-8370-5004-9 – 1985-3004 – us A.T.L.A. [210]
THE SCRIPTURAL IDEA OF MAN / Hopkins, Mark – Six lectures given before the theological students at Princeton. 1883 – 1 – us A.T.L.A. [240]
SCRIPTURAL REMEDIES FOR HEALING THE UNHAPPY DIVISIONS IN THE CHURCH OF ENGLAND, PARTICULARLY OF THOSE PEOPLE CALLED METHODISTS / Goldney, E – London, 1760 – 1mf – 9 – MP-395/1 – ne IDC [240]
THE SCRIPTURAL WAY OF SUPPORTING SERVICES OF RELIGION : A CHARGE DELIVERED AT VISITATIONS OF THE CLERGY AND CHURCH WARDENS...AT NEWMARKET ON THE 13TH, AND AT ST. CATHARINES ON THE 30TH SEPTEMBER, AT PETERBORO ON THE 5TH, COBOURG THE 6TH, AND WHITBY THE 7TH OF NOVEMBER, 1869 / Fuller, Thomas Brock – Toronto: s.n., 1869? (Toronto: Bell, Barker). 03268. (Pre-1900 Canadiana) – 9 – cn C.I.H.M. [971]
SCRIPTURE – v1-20. 1946-68 (complete) – Inquire – 1 – ATLA 1993-S501 – us A.T.L.A. [073]
SCRIPTURE CATECHISM (CCC266) = HSIN CHIU YUEH WEN TA / Price, P F & Chen, Ta-san – (In Chinese) – Hankow: Religious Tract Society, 1932 – 1r – 1 – 1984-6605 – us A.T.L.A. [220]
SCRIPTURE CHARACTERS / Candlish, Robert Smith – London: T. Nelson, 1866.1 fiche – 9 – us A.T.L.A. [240]
THE SCRIPTURE DOCTRINE OF CHRISTIAN PERFECTION / Peck, George – 1842 – 9 – us A.T.L.A. [240]
THE SCRIPTURE DOCTRINE OF CREATION : WITH REFERENCE TO RELIGIOUS NIHILISM AND MODERN THEORIES OF DEVELOPMENT / Birks, Thomas Rawson – London: SPCK, 1873 – 1mf – 9 – 0-8370-2347-5 – 1985-0347 – us A.T.L.A. [210]
THE SCRIPTURE GROUND OF JUSTIFICATION : OR, AN INQUIRY INTO THE DOCTRINE OF SCRIPTURE CONCERNING THE ACTIVE AND PASSIVE OBEDIENCE OF CHRIST / Hoare, Edward Hatch – (Includes bibliographical references) – London: William Macintosh, 1867 – 1mf – 9 – 0-8370-4868-0 – 1985-2868 – us A.T.L.A. [220]
SCRIPTURE HISTORY OF OUR BLESSED LORD AND SAVIOUR / Clark, M B Sterling – New York: H.B. Durand, 1861. 1 fiche – 9 – us A.T.L.A. [240]
SCRIPTURE NATURAL HISTORY: I: THE TREES AND PLANTS MENTIONED IN THE BIBLE / Groser, William H – Religious Tract Society, 1888. 1 fiche – 9 – us A.T.L.A. [240]
SCRIPTURE PROOF FOR SINGING OF SCRIPTURE PSALMS, HYMNS, AND SPIRITUAL / H, E – London. 1696 – 1 – 5.00 – us Baptist [240]
SCRIPTURE READINGS FOR USE IN THE PUBLIC AND HIGH SCHOOLS OF ONTARIO – rev ed. Toronto: William Briggs, 1888 – 2mf – 9 – 0-8370-8710-4 – 1986-2710 – us A.T.L.A. [220]
SCRIPTURE READINGS: FOR USE IN THE PUBLIC AND HIGH SCHOOLS OF ONTARIO – Toronto: Printed for the Education Dept., 1885. 00838. (Pre-1900 Canadiana) – 9 – cn C.I.H.M. [240]
SCRIPTURE STUDIES ON THE ORIGIN AND DESTINY OF MAN / Morgan, Anne Eugenia – (In English) – Bosoton: Leach, Shewell & Sanborn, c1887 – 1mf – 9 – 0-8370-4046-9 – 1985-2046 – us A.T.L.A. [220]
THE SCRIPTURE TYPES : A COURSE OF LECTURES / Frey, Joseph Samuel Christian Frederick – (Includes index) – Philadelphia: American Baptist Publ Society, c1841 – 2mf – 9 – 0-8370-6046-X – 1986-0046 – us A.T.L.A. [220]
THE SCRIPTURE-DOCTRINE OF IMPUTED RIGHTEOUSNESS ASSERTED AND MAINTAINED BY THE REV. MR. JOHN WESLEY, M.A., LATE FELLOW OF LINCOLN COLLEGE, OXFORD... / Mason, William – London, 2nd ed 1763 – 1mf – 9 – MP-422/1 – ne IDC [240]
SCRIPTWRITING FOR SHORT FILMS / Beveridge, James A – 2nd ed 1972 – 9 – 92-3-100744-0 – fr UNESCO [790]
SCRITTI ECONOMICI / Cattano, Carlo – Firenze: F. LeMonier, 1956 – 1 – us U.W. Library [330]
Scrivener, Frederick Henry Ambrose *see*
– ADVERSARIA CRITICA SACRA
– THE AUTHORIZED EDITION OF THE ENGLISH BIBLE (1611)
– A PLAIN INTRODUCTION TO THE CRITICISM OF THE NEW TESTAMENT FOR THE USE OF BIBLICAL STUDENTS
Scrofani, Saverio *see*
– TUTTI HAN TORTO
– VOYAGE EN GRECE DE XAVIER SCROFANI, SICILIEN: FAIT EN 1794 ET 1795; TRAD. DE L'ITALIEN PAR J. F. C. BLANVILLE
THE SCROLL – Montreal: J Macaulay, [1900-19–] – 9 – cn C.I.H.M. [073]
Scrub, T *see* A LETTER TO ROBERT SEAGRAVE, M.A., OCCASIONED BY HIS TWO LATE PERFORMANCES,...
Scrugham, James G *see* A NARRATIVE OF THE CONQUEST OF A FRONTIER LAND
SCRUTINIUM RELIGIONUM ET LINGUARUM / Brerewood, E – Francofurti, 1679 – 3mf – 9 – ne IDC [400]
SCRUTINY – v1-20. 1932-63 – 4r – 1 – us Ross [073]
Scrutton, Thomas Edward *see* THE INFLUENCE OF THE ROMAN LAW ON THE LAW OF ENGLAND
Scrymgeour, William *see* LESSONS ON THE LIFE OF JESUS
Scudder, S H *see*
– THE FOSSIL INSECTS OF NORTH AMERICA, WITH NOTES ON SOME EUROPEAN SPECIES
– NOMENCLATOR ZOOLOGICUS
Scudder, Vida Dutton *see*
– THE CHURCH AND THE HOUR
– THE LIFE OF SPIRIT IN THE MODERN ENGLISH POETS
– SOCIAL IDEALS IN ENGLISH LETTERS
– SOCIALISM AND CHARACTER
– THE WITNESS OF DENIAL
Scudder, William W (Mrs) *see* NINETEEN CENTURIES OF MISSIONS
Scudery, Madeleine de *see* CONVERSATIONS NOUVELLES SUR DIVERS SUJETS, DEDIEES AU ROY
Scull, David *see*
– SALVATION IN A TWO-FOLD ASPECT
– UNION WITH GOD IN THOUGHT AND FAITH
Scullard, Herbert Hayes *see* EARLY CHRISTIAN ETHICS IN THE WEST
SCULPTURE / Caisse Nationale des Monuments Historiques et des Sites. Paris – (Including the Musee Rodin and important collections of ivories and bronzes in the Louvre, together with stained glass. 6000 reproductions) – 100mf – 9 – $490.00 – 0-907006-80-9 – uk Mindata [730]
SCULPTURE : SUBJECT COLLECTIONS – (Individual titles not listed separately) – 296 catalogues on 329mf – 9 – £1,730.00 – uk Chadwyck [730]
THE SCULPTURES AND INSCRIPTIONS OF DARIUS 1, KING OF PERSIA, 548-485 BC / King, L W & Thompson, R C – London: British Museum, 1907. Prefatory note by E.A. Wallis Budge – 1r – 1 – us U.W. Library [730]
Scultet, J *see* L'ARCENAL DE CHIRURGIE...
Scultetus, Abraham *see* MEDULLAE THEOLOGIAE PATRUM SYNTAGMA..
SCULTORI PEREGRINI A EMERITA : DEMETRIOS / Ferri – 1937 – 1 – sp Bibl Santa Ana [946]
Scupham, John *see* OPEN LEARNING
SCYLLA OR CHARYBDIS? A NOVEL / Broughton, Rhoda – British Fiction Archive: Unit 4 – 9 – uk Bell [830]
SDE-DGE BKA'-'GYUR – Delhi Karmapae Chodhey Gyalwae Sungrab Partun Khang, 1976-1979 – 1,730mf – $1,000.00 – us I.A.S.W.R. [280]
SDE-DGE BSTAN-'GYUR – Delhi Karmapae Chodhey, Gyalwae Sungrab Partun Khang, Delhi, 1982 – 3,235mf – $2,100.00 – us I.A.S.W.R. [280]
SDP NEWS : A MONTHLY JOURNAL OF INTERNAL AFFAIRS FOR MEMBERS OF THE SOCIAL DEMOCRATIC PARTY / Social Democratic Party – v1-2, 1-13 (all publ.). 1910-1911 – 1 reel – 1 – $65.00 – us UPA [335]
SDS-INFO – Biweekly – 1 – us U.W. Library [073]
SDVIGOLOGIIA RUSSKOGO STIKHA / Kruchenykh, A – Izd. "MAF". M. 1923. BR-959 2 – 8 – ne IDC [460]
SDYNEY MORNING HERALD INDEX / State Library of New South Wales – (Apply to publ for details) – 1979-87 – 9 – at Pascoe [020]
SE – Stockholm, 1938-81 – 71r – 1 – sw Kungliga [073]
S.E. ASSEMANUS : ACTA SANCTORUM MARTYRUM ORIENTALIUM ET OCCIDENTALIUM – Romae. v1-2. 1748 – 36mf – 98 – Dfl126.00 – ne Slangenburg [200]
...SE DIRIGE A LOS CURAS.. / Blazquez Prieto, Gabriel R – 1810 – 9 – 1.50f – sp Bibl Santa Ana [240]
SE IL CIEL MI DIVIDE FROM "DIDONE ABBANDONATE" / Piccinni, N – (Full score) – London: Longman & Broderip, 1787 – 1 – us Sibley [780]
SE IL GIUDIZIO DI DELIBAZIONE... / Fiore, P – Napoli, 1904 – 1mf – 1 – ILM-2585/1 – ne IDC [327]
SE INICIA LA ERA DE LA POLITICA SOCIAL ARGENTINA / Peron, Juan Domingo – Buenos Aires: Secretaria de Trabajo y Prevision, Direccion de difusion y Propaganda, 1943 – 1 – CSUXADH9083-B – us Hoover Inst Photo [320]
SE POSSA CONCEDERSI "L'EXEQUATUR"... / Astuni, D – Milano, 1901 – 1mf – 9 – ILM-2245/1 – ne IDC [340]
SE UN R. AGENTE DIPLOMATICO POSSA ESERCITARE LE FUNZIONI DI UFFICIALE DI STATO CIVILE... / Fiore, P – Roma, 1902 – 1mf – 1 – ILM-3664/1 – ne IDC [327]
SEA COAST ECHO – Bay St. Louis. Miss. 1898-1957 – 1 – us UMI [071]
SEA DRIFT / Robinson, Hercules – 1858 – 9 – $20.00 – uk Libr Preservation [623]
SEA FRONTIERS – (v. 13- 1967- 5,6. v. 16- 1970- 9) – v. 1- 1954- – 1 – us UMI [550]
SEA FRONTIERS – (v.13- 1967- 5,6. v.16- 1970- 9) – v.1- 1954- – 1 – us UMI [550]

SEA GRANT REPORT / University of Florida. Florida Cooperative Extension Service. Florida Sea Grant – No.1-25.1974-78. 63 fiches – 9 – us Spaulding [639]

SEA HORSE – Gold Beach OR. Feb 23 1935 – 1 – us U.O. Library [071]

THE SEA LADY : A TISSUE OF MOONSHINE / Wells, H G – London: Methuen, 1902 – 1 roll – 1 – 1-55879-926-5 – uk Libr Preservation [830]

SEA LAW... / Bowles, T G – London, 1910 – 4mf – 1 – ILM 344/1 – ne IDC [327]

SEA LAW AND SEA POWER, AS THEY WOULD BE AFFECTED BY RECENT PROPOSALS; WITH REASONS AGAINST THOSE PROPOSALS / Bowles, Thomas Gibson – 1910 – 9 – $20.00 – uk Libr Preservation [340]

SEA MAGAZINE – Northwest ed. 1975- – 9 – us UMI [073]

SEA MAGAZINE – Southern ed. 1977- – 9 – us UMI [073]

SEA MAGAZINE – Western ed. 1977- – 9 – us UMI [073]

SEA POWER – (1984- 5,6,9) – 1971- – 1 – us UMI [355]

SEA POWER *see* ALMANAC OF SEAPOWER

SEA POWER IN ITS RELATIONS TO THE WAR OF 1812 / Mahan, Alfred Thayer – 2v 1905 – 9 – uk Libr Preservation [941]

SEA SONGS AND BALLADS – 1906 – 1 – us I.U. Libraries [390]

Seabury, Joseph Bartlett *see* THE VISION OF A SHORT LIFE

Seabury, Samuel *see*
- AMERICAN SLAVERY DISTINGUISHED FROM SLAVERY OF ENGLISH THEORISTS, AND JUSTIFIED BY THE LAW OF NATURE
- AMERICAN SLAVERY DISTINGUISHED FROM THE SLAVERY OF ENGLISH THEORISTS
- ANSWERS TO THE QUESTIONS SUGGESTED BY THE REGENTS OF THE UNIVERSITY OF THE STATE OF NEW YORK, FOR THE EXAMINATION OF CANDIDATES FOR THE DEGREE OF BACHELOR OF LAWS.
- MANUSCRIPTS
- MARY THE VIRGIN

SEAFARER – v34- 1985- – 1,5,6,9 – us UMI [623]

Seafarers' International Union of North America *see* SEAFARERS' LOG

SEAFARERS' LOG / Seafarers' International Union of North America – New York, 1939-71 – 13r – 1 – us Ross [380]

Seafield, Frank *see* THE LITERATURE AND CURIOSITIES OF DREAMS; A COMMONPLACE BOOK OF SPECULATIONS CONCERNING THE MYSTERY OF DREAMS AND VISIONS

THE SEA-FISHES OF INDIA AND BURMA / Day, F – Report on the Sea-Fish and Fisheries, 1873. Calcutta. 1873. BZ-266 2 – 8 – ne IDC [590]

SEAGRASS RESEARCH METHODS / ed by Phillips, Ronald C et al – 1990 – 9 – 92-3-102660-7 – fr UNESCO [550]

SEAHORSE, 1971-1993 – 147mf – 9 – uk Microform Academic [073]

Seal, J B *see* HIGH-LEVEL MANPOWER REQUIREMENTS AND RESOURCES, 1968-1972

SEAL OF HEAVEN, OR, THE IMPRESSION OF DIVINE TRUTH ON A CANDID MIND / Jeter, J B – New York: American Tract Society, 1871. 1 fiche – 9 – us A.T.L.A. [240]

Seale, A *see* THE FISHES OF SAMOA

THE SEALS OPENED, OR, THE APOCALYPSE EXPLAINED / Pond, Enoch – Portland: Hoyt, Fogg, & Breed, 1871. 1 fiche – 9 – us A.T.L.A. [240]

Sealsfield, Charles *see*
- DIE GRABESSCHULD
- HEITERE GESCHICHTEN
- NATHAN LE SQUATTER, OU, LE PREMIER AMERICAIN AU TEXAS
- DIE PRAERIE AM JACINTO

SEALSFIELD-POSTL : BISHER UNVEROEFFENTLICHTE BRIEFE UND MITTHEILUNGEN ZU SEINER BIOGRAPHIE / ed by Hamburger, Victor – (Includes bibliographical references) – Wien: L Rosner, 1879 – 1r – 1 – us U.W. Library [920]

SEAMAN – London, UK. 1915. -m. 22 feet – 1 – uk British Libr Newspaper [072]

THE SEA-MANS DICTIONARY / Manwayring, Henry – 1644. 142p. (English Linguistics Series 1500-1800) – 9 – us UMI [623]

A SEAMARK: A THRENODY FOR ROBERT LOUIS STEVENSON / Carman, Bliss – Boston: Copeland and Day, 1895. 00492. (Pre-1900 Canadiana) – 9 – cn C.I.H.M. [810]

SEANCES / Congres National du Parti Ouvrier Francais, Guesdiste (10e), 24 au 28 septembre 1892, Marseille – (Un Registre Manuscrit de 46 Fueillets. Au Musee social. 5660. 9; $5.00) – Imp. Ouvriere, G. Delory, Lille. s.d. 40p 5663 – 9 – fr Hachette [335]

SEANCES / Congres National du Parti Ouvrier Francais, Guesdiste (11e), 7-8 octobre, 1893, Paris – Imp. ouvriere, G. Delory, Lille. 1893. 23p 5664 – 9 – fr Hachette [335]

SEANCES / Congres National du Parti Ouvrier Francais, Guesdiste (12e), 14 au 16 septembre 1894, Nantes – (Extrait, Revue socialiste. 5851; 9) – Imp. ouvriere, G. Delory, Lille. 1894. 30p 5665 – 9 – fr Hachette [335]

SEANCES / Congres National du Parti Ouvrier Francais, Guesdiste (15e), 10 au 13 juillet 1897, Paris – Suivi des principales resolutions des 14 et 13 congres nationaux. Imp. ouvriere, P. Lagrange, Lille. 1897. 48p 5674 – 9 – fr Hachette [335]

SEANCES / Congres National du Parti Ouvrier Francais, Guesdiste (16e), 17 au 20 septembre 1898, Montlucon – Imp. speciale du Parti Ouvrier, Paris. 1898. 40p et no. 9-SOCIALISTE, 18-25 septembre 1898. 5676 7 – 9 – fr Hachette [335]

SEANCES / Congres National du Parti Ouvrier Francais, Guesdiste (19e), 15 au 18 septembre 1901, Roubaix – Suivi des Principales Resolutions des 17 et 18 congres. Imp. du "Socialiste." Paris. 1901. 51p 5686 – 9 – fr Hachette [335]

SEANCES / Congres National du Parti Ouvrier Francais, Guesdiste (6e), 26 sept au 1 oct 1882, Roanne – Imp. du Centre, Paris. 1882. 36p 5827 – 9 – fr Hachette [335]

SEANCES / Congres National du Parti Ouvrier Francais, Guesdiste (7e), 29 mars au 7 avril 1884, Roubaix – H. Oriol, Paris. s.d. 24p 5651 – 9 – fr Hachette [335]

SEANCES / Congres National du Parti Ouvrier Francais, Guesdiste (8e), 11 et 12 oct 1890, Lille – Imp. du Parti Ouvrier, Lille. 1890. 32p 5656 – 9 – fr Hachette [335]

SEANCES / Congres National du Parti Ouvrier Francais, Guesdiste (9e), 26 au 28 nov 1891, Lyon – Imp. du Parti Ouvrier, Lille. s.d. 24p 5657 – 9 – fr Hachette [335]

SEANCES / Congres Ouvrier de France (1e), 2-10 oct 1876, Paris – Sandoz, Paris. 1877. 534p 5947 – 9 – fr Hachette [335]

SEANCES / Congres Ouvrier de France (2), 28 jan-8 fev 1878, Lyon – J. Trichot: Lyon, 1878. 650p 5640 – 9 – fr Hachette [335]

SEANCES / Congres Ouvrier Socialiste de France (3e), 20-31 oct 1879, Marseille – J. Doucet: Marseilles, 1879. 831p 5641 – 9 – fr Hachette [335]

SEANCES / Les Congres Socialistes moderes. Congres National Ouvrier Socialiste (5e) – 27 nov-5 dec 1881, Paris. Manuscrit au Musee social. 5645 – 9 – fr Hachette [335]

SEANCES / Les Congres Socialistes Moderes. Congres Socialiste National Ouvrier de Bordeaux (6e) – Sept 1882, Bordeaux. Manuscrit au Musee social. 5648 – 9 – fr Hachette [335]

SEANCES DU CONGRES OUVRIER SOCIALISTE DE FRANCE.20-31 OCTOBRE 1879 / Congres Ouvrier de France (3rd: 1879: Marseille) – Marseille: J. Doucet, 1879. xviii,831p – 1 – us U.W. Library [335]

SEA-POWER, AND OTHER STUDIES / Bridge, Cyprian Arthur George – 1910 – 9 – $20.00 – uk Libr Preservation [355]

THE SEARCH AND SEIZURE EXCLUSIONARY RULE, 26 FEB 1986 – Washington: GPO, 1988 – 1mf – 9 – $1.50 – LLMC 94-361 – us L.L.M.C. [340]

SEARCH FOR EXTRATERRESTRIAL LIFE – (Suppl to v22, Advances) – 1968 – 4mf – 9 – $12.00 – 0-87703-132-0 – us Univelt [570]

THE SEARCH FOR EXTRATERRESTRIAL LIFE – (v22 1967, Advances) – 1967 – 9 – $30.00 – us Univelt [629]

SEARCH LIGHT – Valentine. Neb. 1913-1918 – 1 – us UMI [071]

SEARCHING TOGETHER – (1985-. 5,6,9) – v11-. 1982- – 1 – us UMI [073]

SEARCHINGS IN THE SILENCE : A SERIES OF DEVOTIONAL MEDITATIONS / Matheson, George – New York: Anson D F Randolph, [189-?] – 1mf – 9 – 0-8370-6331-0 – 1986-0331 – us A.T.L.A. [240]

SEARCHLIGHT – 1917-27 – 1 – us Baptist [240]

SEARCHLIGHT – Bremerton. Wash. 1904-12; 1919-20 – 1 – us UMI [071]

SEARCHLIGHT – Cleveland, OH, 21 July 1917-6 Apr 1918 – 1 reel – 1 – us Western Res [240]

SEARCHLIGHT – Culbertson. Mont. 1902-1924; 1929-1946; 1956-1959; 1966-1967 – 1 – us UMI [071]

SEARCHLIGHT – Patna, India. 1962-Aug 1986 – 81r – 1 – us L of C Photodup [072]

SEARCHLIGHT – Portland OR. Apr July Oct-Nov Dec 1922, Jan 1923 – 1 – us U.O. Library [071]

SEARCHLIGHT – Redding. Calif. 1898-1941 – 1 – us UMI [071]

SEARCHLIGHT – Redding. Calif. -sw. 1899-1916, 1918-21 – 1 – us UMI [071]

SEARCHLIGHT – Redding. Calif. -w. 1895-98, 1917-33, 1934-41 – 1 – us UMI [071]

SEARCHLIGHT – Searchlight, Clark County, NV. v8 n20. 15 oct 1909 – 1r – 1 – Can$25.00 – cn Can Microfilming [071]

SEARCHLIGHT – Valentine, NE. -w. Sept 1913-Nov 1918 – 1 – us NE Hist [071]

THE SEARCHLIGHT – NV. 1903-08; 1910-15 – 5r – 1 – $250.00 – U04737 – us Library Micro [071]

THE SEARCHLIGHT – South Africa. 13 Sept-20 Dec 1946. 1 reel – 1, 16 diazo available at reduced price – sa SA Libr [072]

THE SEARCHLIGHT – Toronto: Searchligth Pub Co, [1896-189- or 19–] – 9 – cn C.I.H.M. [073]

SEARCHLIGHT ON INDONESIA / Djojohadikusumo, Sumitro – SE-2230 1. 1959 – 9 – ne IDC [950]

SEARCHLIGHT ON THE DUCHESS OF ATHOLL / Maitland, Frank – Edinburgh, 1937? Fiche W1016. (Blodgett Collection of Spanish Civil War Pamphlets) – 9 – us H.U. College Libr [946]

Searchlight Publishing Co *see* WHO'S WHO IN RELIGIOUS, FRATERNAL, SOCIAL, CIVIC AND COMMERCIAL LIFE ON THE PACIFIC COAST, STATE OF WASHINGTON

THE SEARCHLITE – Menlo Park, CA. 1929-32 – 1r – 1 – $50.00 – B02445 – us Library Micro [071]

Searl, Albert *see* LEGISLATIVE SOUVENIR MANUAL 1895-1896

Searle, George Mary *see* PLAIN FACTS FOR FAIR MINDS

Searle, W G *see* ANGLO-SAXON BISHOPS, KINGS AND NOBLES

Searles Family (Rachel Stanton Papers) *see* CIVIL WAR LETTERS

SEARMG NEWSLETTER – (Apply to publ for details) – 1972- – 9 – at Pascoe [980]

Sears, Charles Hatch *see* THE REDEMPTION OF THE CITY

Sears, Clara Endicott *see* BRONSON ALCOTT'S FRUITLANDS

Sears, Edmund Hamilton *see* REGENERATION

Sears, M Earl *see* A THACKERAY DICTIONARY

Sears, Mary *see* OCEANOGRAPHIC INDEX

THE SEASIDE NEWS – Cape Town, South Africa.29 Nov 1902-31 Oct 1903. 2 reels – 1, 16 diazo available at reduced price – sa SA Libr [072]

SEASIDE POST NEWS SENTINEL – Seaside, CA. 1987 – 1r – 1 – $50.00 – B03651 – us Library Micro [071]

SEASIDE SIGNAL – Seaside, OR. -w. 1905-63 – 1 – 528.00 – us Oregon Hist [071]

SEASIDE SIGNAL – Seaside, OR. -w. 2 Jan 1964-. – 1 – us U.O. Library [071]

SEA-SIDE STUDIES AT ILFRACOMBE, TENBY, THE SCILLY ISLES, AND JERSEY / Lewes, George Henry – Edinburgh: Blackwood, 1858 – 1 roll – 1 – 1-55879-568-5 – uk Libr Preservation [420]

SEASIDE TOPICS – Providence. R.I. 1913-1951 – 1 – us UMI [071]

SEASIDE TOPICS – Watch Hill. R.I. -w. 1913- – 1 – us UMI [071]

SEASIDE TOPICS. PIER ED – Narragansett. R.I. 1915-1917 – 1 – us UMI [071]

A SEASONABLE ANTIDOTE AGAINST RELIGIOUS DELUSION;... / Mason, William – London, 1763 – 1mf – 9 – MP-421/1 – ne IDC [240]

SEASONAL CHANGES IN SELECTED PHYSIOLOGICAL VARIABLES OF FEMALE BASKETBALL PLAYERS / Earnest, Edward K & Durrant, Earlene – 1992 – 1mf – $4.00 – us Microform Publ [612]

SEASONS – (Cont: Ontario Naturalist at v20 1980) – Don Mills. v20-34. 1980-94 – 9 – Can$20.00y – cn Micromedia [550]

SEASONS *see* ONTARIO NATURALIST

THE SEAT OF EMPIRE / Coffin, Charles Carleton – Boston: Fields, Osgood, 1870. 00694. (Pre-1900 Canadiana) – 9 – cn C.I.H.M. [971]

Seaton, A A *see* THE THEORY OF TOLERATION UNDER THE LATER STUARTS

SEATONIAN POEMS / Neale, John Mason – Cambridge: Deighton, Bell; London: Bell and Daldy, 1864 – 1mf – us A.T.L.A. [240]

SEATTLE *see* PACIFIC NORTHWEST

SEATTLE ET AL : URBAN KING COUNTY, WASHINGTON – 1888-1908. 550 maps, mostly Seattle. Sanborn Company Fire Insurance Maps – 1 – $69.00r – us Shkurkin [910]

Seaver, Fredrick J *see* HISTORICAL SKETCHES OF FRANKLIN COUNTY

Seaver, Jay W *see* ANTHROPOMETRY AND PHYSICAL EXAMINATION

Seay, Warren Mosby *see* BIOGRAPHY OF BARON DEKALB GRAY

Seay, William A *see* KENTUCKY AT BOGOR; A REVIEW AFTER SIX YEARS

Seba, A *see* LOCUPLETISSIMI RERUM NATURALIUM THESAURI ACCURATA DESCRIPTIO ET ICONIBUS

SEBASTAPOL TIMES AND NEWS – Sebastapol, CA. 1895-1933; 1950-57; 1962- – 53+ r – 1 – $2,650.00 ($90.00y) – B02988 – us Library Micro [071]

Sebastian, Astrid *see* AUF DEM SCHNITTPUNKT ZWEIER GATTUNGEN

SEBASTIAN CASTELLIO : EIN BIOGRAPHISCHER VERSUCH NACH DEN QUELLEN / Maehly, Jakob – Basel: Bahnmaier, 1862 – 1mf – us A.T.L.A. [240]

SEBASTIAN FRANCK VON WOERD, DER SCHWARMGEIST : EIN BEITRAG ZUR REFORMATIONSGESCHICHTE / Hase, Karl Alfred von – Leipzig: Breitkopf und Haertel, 1869 – 1mf – us A.T.L.A. [240]

SEBASTIAN FRANCKS LATEINISCHE PARAPHRASE DER DEUTSCHEN THEOLOGIE : UND SEINE HOLLAENDISCH ERHALTENEN TRAKTATE / Hegler, Alfred – Tuebingen: G. Schnuerlen, 1901 – 1mf – us A.T.L.A. [240]

Sebastian Latre, Tomas *see* ENSAYO SOBRE EL TEATRO ESPANOL

Sebastiani, A *see* FLORAE ROMANAE PRODROMUS

Sebastiani, Claudio *see* BELLUM MUSICALE..

SEBASTIAN'S DIGEST OF TRADEMARK CASES *see* COX'S MANUAL OF TRADEMARK CASES

SEBAT – Istanbul: Sirket-i Muerettibiyye Matbaasi, 1886 – 9 – $45.00 – us MEDOC [956]

SEBIL UER-RESAD / ed by Edip, Esref & Akif, Mehmed – Istanbul, second series, cilt 1-15 (1948-1964) – 89mf – 9 – $445.00 – us MEDOC [949]

SEBIL UER-RESAD – Istanbul, first series, cilt 1-25 (1324-1341 [1908-1924]) – 197mf – 9 – $985.00 – us MEDOC [949]

Sebillet, Th *see* ART POETIQUE FRANCOIS

Sebillot, Paul *see*
- LA BRETAGNE PITTORESQUE ET LEGENDAIRE
- LE FOLK-LORE

Seboek, Mark *see*
- DIE SYRISCHE UEBERSETZUNG DER ZWOELF KLEINEN PROPHETEN

Seboni, Michael Ontefetse Martinus *see* DEVELOPMENT OF EDUCATION IN THE BECHUANALAND PROTECTORATE (1824-1944)

SEBRANE SPISY / Herites, Frantisek – 1908-13. 12v – 1 – 46.00 – us L of C Photodup [460]

Sebren, Mary A *see* AN INTERPRETIVE INQUIRY OF PRESERVICE TEACHERS' REFLECTIONS AND DEVELOPMENT DURING A FIELD-BASED ELEMENTARY PHYSICAL EDUCATION METHODS COURSE

SEC DOCKET / U.S. Securities and Exchange Commission – v. 1-. 1973- – 9 – us UMI [336]

THE SEC DOCKET / U.S. Securities and Exchange Commission – (Cont: The SEC Release Series Preceding the SEC Docket. Includes other matter relative SEC. LLMC offers only yrs between 1873-71 after which title is only available from GPO on mf) – v1-23 no 17. 1973-81 – 9 – us L.L.M.C. [332]

THE SEC DOCKET *see* THE SEC RELEASE SERIES PRECEDING THE SEC DOCKET

THE SEC RELEASE SERIES PRECEDING THE SEC DOCKET / U. S. Securities and Exchange Commission – (Cont by: The S.E.C. Docket. Individual titles also listed separately) – 2062mf – 9 – $3,313.00 set – us L.L.M.C. [340]

THE SEC RELEASE SERIES PRECEDING THE SEC DOCKET *see*
- ACCOUNTING SERIES RELEASES
- ASIAN DEVELOPMENT BANK RELEASE
- BRETTON WOODS AGREEMENT RELEASES
- CORPORATE REORGANIZATION RELEASES
- HOLDING COMPANIES ACT OF 1935 RELEASES
- INTER-AMERICAN DEVELOPMENT BANK RELEASE
- INVESTMENT ADVISERS ACT OF 1940 RELEASES
- INVESTMENT COMPANY ACT OF 1940 RELEASES
- LITIGATION RELEASES
- MONOPOLY STUDY RELEASES
- THE SEC DOCKET
- SECURITIES ACT OF 1933 RELEASES
- SECURITIES EXCHANGE ACT OF 1934 RELEASES
- SECURITY INVESTOR PROTECTION ACT OF 1970 RELEASES
- SOLICITOR OF THE POST OFFICE OPINIONS
- SPECIAL MARKET STUDY RELEASES
- SURVEY SERIES RELEASES
- TRUST INDENTURE ACT OF 1939 RELEASES
- U SERIES RELEASES

Seccion Femenina de Falange Espanola... Caceres *see* PROGRAMA DEL PRIMER CONSEJO PROVINCIAL DE LA...

SECERA SI CIOCANUL – Pitesti, Romania. 1962-Oct 1981 – 21r – 1 – us L of C Photodup [949]

SECESSION – Vienna etc. no. 1-8. Spring 1922-April 1924 – 1 – us NY Public [073]

SECHELT PENINSULA TIMES – British Columbia, CN. Dec 1963-Jun 1980 – 16r – 1 – cn Commonwealth Micro [072]

SECHS CHRISTLICHER PREDIG UEBER DEN EIN VNND FUENFFZIGSTEN PSALMEN DAUIDS... / Andreae d.A E, J – Tuebingen, 1561 – 2mf – 9 – ne IDC [240]

SECHS CHRISTLICHER PREDIG VON DEN SPALTUNGEN... / Andreae d.A E, J – Tuebingen, 1573 – 2mf – 9 – ne IDC [240]

SECHS FUGEN FUER PIANOFORTE ODER ORGEL...11TES : ZWEYTE AUGLAGE / Albrechtsberger, Johann G – Wien: Johann Cappi, [1802?] – 1 – us Sibley [780]

SECHS HAAGER ABKOMMEN UEBER INTERNATIONALES PRIVATRECHT / Dungs, H – Berlin, 1910 – 2mf – 1 – ILM-4095/1 – ne IDC [327]

SECHS LEICHTE CLAVIER SONATEN / Bach, C P E – Leipzig: Berhard Christoph Breitkopf & Sohn, 1766 – 1 – us Sibley [780]

SECHS SONATEN FUER CLAVIER MIT VERAENDERTEN REPRISEN / Bach, C P E – (Contains also: Zweyte Fortsetzung von sechs Sonaten. 1763.) 1785 – 9 – us Sibley [780]

SECHS SONATEN: VERSUCH UEBER DIE WAHRE ART DAS KLAVIER ZU SPIELEN...THEIL 1 / Bach, C P E – Leipzig: Schwickert, 1787 – 1 – us Sibley [780]

Secker, William *see* THE NONSUCH PROFESSOR IN HIS MERIDIAN SPLENDOR

Seckler-Hudson, Catheryn *see* ORGANIZATION AND MANAGEMENT: THEORY AND PRACTICE

SECOLI AGOSTINIANI, OVERO HISTORIA GENERALE DEL SACRO ORDINE EREMITANO DEL GRAN DOTTORE DI SANTA CHIESE S. AVRELIO AGOSTINO / ed by Torelli, L – Bologna. 8v. 1659-86 – 219mf – 9 – 302/2 – ne IDC [240]

IL SECOLO – Milan, Italy. -d. 1 Feb 1888-20 Jan 1889; 15 Sept 1914-9 Aug 1919. Imperfect. 16 reels – 1 – uk British Libr Newspaper [072]

IL SECOLO *see* JOURNAUX DIVERS

SECOLO 19 – 1924-1995 – 3r per y – 5,6 – Sfr1,016.00 – sz Infoprint [073]

SECOLO D'ITALIA – 1992-1995 – 2r per y – 5,6 – Sfr936.00 – sz Infoprint [072]

SECOLO NUOVO – San Francisco, CA, 1903 – 3mf or 1r – 1,9 – us I.H.R.C. [978]

SECOND ADVENT OF CHRIST – Cleveland, OH, 18 Jan-26 July, 1843 – 1 reel – 1 – us Western Res [240]

SECOND ADVENT OF CHRIST / Lynd, SW – Cincinnati, Ohio: J.B. Wilson, 1843 – 1 reel – 1 – us Western Res [240]

SECOND ADVENT WATCHMAN – v. 1-8. 1850-1854 – 1 – us UMI [240]

THE SECOND AEON – (1972-74. 5,6. Ceased publication) – v1-19-21. 1967-74 – 1 – us UMI [550]

SECOND AND THIRD EPISTLES OF ST PAUL TO THE CORINTHIANS / Kennedy, James Houghton – London: Methuen, 1900. 1 fiche – 9 – us A.T.L.A. [240]

SECOND ANNUAL ACTIVITY REPORT / Israel. Ministry of the Interior. Environmental Protection Service – Apr 1974-Mar 1975. Jerusalem, 1975. 35p – 9 – $2.00 – is I.T.T.I. [360]

SECOND ANNUAL REPORT ON THE ECONOMIC AND SOCIAL DEVELOPMENT PLAN OF SYRIA, 1961-1962 / Syria. Ministry of Planning – Damascus. 1963. BD-651 1 – 9 – ne IDC [338]

A SECOND ANSWER TO MR. JOHN WESLEY, BEING A SUPPLEMENT TO THE LETTER OF AMERICANUS,... / Denham, W – London, 1775 – 1mf – 9 – MP-509/1 – ne IDC [240]

SECOND BIANNUAL REVIEW OF THE CAPITAL EXPENDITURE PROGRAMME, 1957-62 / Mauritius – (Sessional Paper No. 3 of 1959). Port Louis. 1959. BD-666 1 – 9 – ne IDC [338]

THE SECOND BOOK OF KINGS / Farrar, Frederic William – New York:A.C. Armstrong, 1894 – 2mf – 9 – 0-8370-2409-9 – 1985-0409 – us A.T.L.A. [220]

SECOND BOOK OF SAMUEL / Kirkpatrick, Alexander F – Cambridge: University Press, 1886. 1 fiche – 9 – us A.T.L.A. [220]

THE SECOND BOOK OF SAMUEL / Blaikie, William Garden – New York: A C Armstrong, [1888?] – 1mf – 9 – 0-8370-2363-7 – 1985-0363 – us A.T.L.A. [220]

THE SECOND BOOK OF SAMUEL : WITH MAPS, NOTES AND INTRODUCTION / Kirkpatrick, Alexander Francis – (Includes appendix on special events and interpretations of 2nd Samuel. Includes index) – Cambridge: University Press, 1886 – 1mf – 9 – 0-8370-3908-8 – 1985-1908 – us A.T.L.A. [220]

THE SECOND BOOK OF THE KINGS: WITH INTRODUCTION AND NOTES / Lumby, Joseph Rawson – Cambridge: University Press, 1887 – 1mf – 9 – us A.T.L.A. [240]

SECOND CENSUS OF KENTUCKY, 1800 / Kentucky. Census – Comp. by G. Glenn Clift, 1954. Is not state or Federal schedule of inhabitants. Privately comp. list of tax payers in the 42 counties of the Kentucky of 1800. 6 fiches. F-0159 – 9 – us A.G.L.L. [920]

SECOND CENSUS OF THE UNITED STATES / U.S. Bureau of the Census – 1800. 52 rolls. M32 – 1 – us Nat'l Archives [324]

SECOND CENTURY – (1986- . 5,6,9) – v1- . 1981- – 1 – us UMI [073]

A SECOND CENTURY OF FERNS / Hooker, W J – London. 1861. B-7198 2 – 8 – ne IDC [580]

THE SECOND CIRCUIT SENTENCING STUDY : A REPORT TO THE JUDGES OF THE 2ND CIRCUIT / Partridge, Anthony & Eldridge, William B – Washington: FJC, Aug 1974 – 2mf – 9 – $3.00 – LLMC 95-829 – us L.L.M.C. [340]

THE SECOND COMEDIE OF PUB. TERENTIUS, CALLED EUNUCHUS / Webbe, Joseph – 1629. 247p. (English Linguistics Series 1500-1800) – 9 – us UMI [820]

SECOND COMPTROLLER, DEPARTMENT OF THE TREASURY, DIGEST OF DECISIONS : 1817-1894 – (The Office of the 2nd Comptroller dealt with the War & Navy departments and the Indian & Pension Bureaus. The office was abolished in 1894 and coverage of the successor office begins with the next title. This title is also offered as part of LLMC's Military Law Collection, Section 13 of the LLMC Sourcebook) – Washington: GPO. v1-4. 1855-99 – 17mf – 9 – $25.50 – LLMC 90-418 – us L.L.M.C. [340]

THE SECOND DEATH AND THE RESTITUTION OF ALL THINGS : WITH SOME PRELIMINARY REMARKS ON THE NATURE AND INSPIRATION OF HOLY SCRIPTURE: A LETTER TO A FRIEND / Jukes, Andrew John – 14th ed. New York: Thomas Whittaker, 1891 – 1mf – 9 – 0-8370-8753-8 – 1986-2753 – us A.T.L.A. [230]

SECOND DEVELOPMENT PLAN, 1959-64 / Ghana – Accra. 1959 – 9 – ne IDC [338]

SECOND DEVELOPMENT WEEK SHA'ABAN 1376 / Iraq. Board of Development and Ministry of Development – March 1957. BD-1790 1 – 9 – ne IDC [956]

SECOND EDITION OF THE DICTIONARY CATALOG / New York Public Library. Research Libraries. Music Collection – 1982-83.-700,000 cards 45 reels.-ISBN: 0-8161-1387-4 – 1 – $6865.00 – uk Hall [017]

SECOND EDITION OF THE DICTIONARY CATALOG OF THE MUSIC COLLECTION / New York Public Library. Research Libraries – 1983. 677,824 cards on 45 reels – 1 – $6,240.00 export $7,488.00 – 0-8161-1387-4 – uk Hall [780]

THE SECOND EPISTLE OF PAUL TO THE CORINTHIANS / Kling, Christian Friedrich – New York: Charles Scribner, 1886. vii,220p. 1 fiche – 9 – us A.T.L.A. [240]

THE SECOND EPISTLE TO THE CORINTHIANS / Denney, James – New York: A C Armstrong, 1899 – 1mf – 9 – 0-8370-2891-4 – 1985-0891 – us A.T.L.A. [220]

THE SECOND EPISTLE TO THE CORINTHIANS : WITH COMMENTARY / Plumptre, Edward Hayes; ed by Ellicott, Charles John – (Includes indexes) – London, New York: Cassell, 1883 – 1mf – 9 – 0-8370-3858-8 – 1985-1858 – us A.T.L.A. [220]

THE SECOND EPISTLE TO THE CORINTHIANS: WITH NOTES, MAP AND INTRODUCTION / Lias, John James – Cambridge: University Press, 1890. 1 fiche – 9 – us A.T.L.A. [240]

A SECOND EXPEDITION THROUGH THE BARREN LANDS OF NORTHERN CANADA / Tyrrell, J B – BN 430 2. 1895 – 8 – ne IDC [910]

SECOND EXPERT CONSULTATION ON ENVIRONMENTAL CRITERIA FOR REGISTRATION OF PESTICIDES. ROME, 1981 – 1981 – 64p – it F.A.O. [660]

SECOND FIVE YEAR DEVELOPMENT PLAN, 1955-1959 / Ethiopia – D-1041 1 – 9 – ne IDC [338]

SECOND FIVE YEAR DEVELOPMENT PLAN, 1963-1967 / Ethiopia – Addis Ababa. 1962. BD-216 1 – 9 – ne IDC [338]

SECOND FIVE YEAR DEVELOPMENT PLAN 1971-1975 / Western Samoa. Department of Economic Development – D 1235 1. 1970 – 9 – ne IDC [338]

SECOND FIVE YEAR DEVELOPMENT PLAN OF ETHIOPIA, 1955-1959 E.C. 1963-1967 G.C. OUTLINE / Ethiopia – Addis Ababa. 1963 – 9 – ne IDC [338]

SECOND FIVE YEAR INDUSTRIAL PLAN / Egypt. Ministry of Industry – 1960. BNE-4668 1 – 9 – ne IDC [338]

SECOND FIVE YEAR PLAN / Rajasthan. India (State). Planning and Development Department – Jaipur. 1956 – 9 – ne IDC [338]

SECOND FIVE YEAR PLAN, 1341-45. MAR 1962-MAR 1967 / Afghanistan. Ministry of Planning – Kabul. 1963. BD-365 1 – 9 – ne IDC [338]

THE SECOND FIVE YEAR PLAN (1960-65) / Pakistan. Planning Commission – Karachi. 1960 – 9 – ne IDC [338]

SECOND FIVE YEAR PLAN 1966-1970 (BASIC ELEMENTS) / Syria. Ministry of Planning – Damas, Office Arabe de Presse et de Documentation. 1966. BD-283 1 – 9 – ne IDC [338]

SECOND FIVE YEAR PLAN 1970-75 / Jamaica. Central Planning Unit – 5v. Kingston. BD-1678 1 – 9 – ne IDC [338]

SECOND FIVE YEAR PLAN FOR ECONOMIC AND SOCIAL DEVELOPMENT, 1966-1970 / Syria. Government Planning Agency – 1967. BNE-9703 1 – 9 – ne IDC [338]

SECOND FIVE YEAR PLAN OF WEST BENGAL ANNUAL PLAN, 1958-59 / West Bengal. India. Development Department – Alipore. 1958. BD-421 1 – 9 – ne IDC [338]

SECOND FIVE YEAR PLAN PROGRESS REPORT, 1958-59 / India. Planning Commission – Delhi. 1960. BD-529 1 – 9 – ne IDC [338]

SECOND FIVE YEAR PLAN PROGRESS REPORT, 1958-59 / Rajasthan. India (State). Directorate of Economics and Statistics – Jaipur. 1959. BD-498 1 – 9 – ne IDC [338]

SECOND FIVE YEAR PLAN PROGRESS REPORT, 1959-60 / Rajasthan. India (State). Directorate of Economics and Statistics – Jaipur. 1960 – 9 – ne IDC [338]

SECOND FIVE YEAR PLAN PROGRESS REPORT FOR 1956-57 / Rajasthan. India (State). Directorate of Economics and Statistics – Jaipur. 1957. BD-496 1 – 9 – ne IDC [338]

SECOND FIVE YEAR PLAN PROGRESS REPORT FOR 1957-58 / Rajasthan. India (State). Directorate of Economics and Statistics – Jaipur. 1958 – 9 – ne IDC [338]

THE SECOND FIVE YEAR PLAN (REVISED ESTIMATES) / Pakistan – Karachi. 1961. BD-388 1 – 9 – ne IDC [338]

THE SECOND FIVE-YEAR ECONOMIC DEVELOPMENT PLAN, 1967-1971 / Korea. South – Seoul. 1966. BD-114 1 – 9 – ne IDC [338]

SECOND FIVE-YEAR PLAN / India. Planning Commission – New Delhi. 1956 – 9 – ne IDC [338]

SECOND FIVE-YEAR PLAN (1956-57 TO 1960-61) / Bombay. India. Political and Services Department – Bombay. 1956. BD-485 1 – 9 – ne IDC [324]

SECOND FIVE-YEAR PLAN, 1961-1965 / Malaya – Kuala Lumpur. 1961 – 9 – ne IDC [338]

SECOND FIVE-YEAR PLAN 1964-1968, MODIFICATIONS TO DRAFT PLAN AS APPROVED BY PARLIAMENT, NOV 1963 / Trinidad and Tobago – Trinidad. 1965. BD-1757 1 – 9 – ne IDC [338]

THE SECOND FIVE-YEAR PLAN, 1966-1971 / Uganda – Entebbe. 1966. BD-167 1 – 9 – ne IDC [338]

THE SECOND FIVE-YEAR PLAN (1967-1971) / Cyprus. Planning Bureau – Nicosia. 1967 – 9 – ne IDC [338]

SECOND FIVE-YEAR PLAN, 1971-1975 / Malaysia – D-1120 1. 1971 – 9 – ne IDC [338]

SECOND FIVE-YEAR PLAN A DRAFT OUTLINE / India. Planning Commission – New Delhi. 1956. BD-723 1 – 9 – ne IDC [338]

THE SECOND FIVE-YEAR PLAN FOR DEVELOPMENT OF SCIENCE AND TECHNOLOGY, 1967-1971 / Korea. South – Seoul. 1966. BD-708 1 – 9 – ne IDC [338]

SECOND FIVE-YEAR PLAN FOR ECONOMIC AND SOCIAL DEVELOPMENT 1ST / Tanzania – July 1969-30th June 1974. 4v. Dar-es-Salaam. BD-1569 1 – 9 – ne IDC [338]

THE SECOND FIVE-YEAR PLAN FOR THE DEVELOPMENT OF THE NATIONAL ECONOMY OF THE USSR (1933-1937) / U.S.S.R. Gosudarstvennaia Planovaia Komissiia – M. 1936. BD-536 1 – 9 – ne IDC [338]

SECOND FIVE-YEAR PLAN OF WEST BENGAL PROGRAMME FOR 1956-57 / West Bengal. India. Development Department – Alipore. 1956 – 9 – ne IDC [338]

SECOND FIVE-YEAR PLAN PROGRAMME FOR 1959-60 / Mysore. India – Bangalore. 1959 – 9 – ne IDC [338]

SECOND FOUR YEAR PLAN CAPITAL EXPENDITURE FROM LOAN FUNDS, APRIL 1951 TO MARCH 1955 / Rhodesia. (Southern) – D 1476 1. 1951 – 9 – ne IDC [336]

SECOND FOUR-YEAR PLAN FOR THE UNION OF BURMA / Burma. Ministry of National Planning – (1961-62 to 1964-65). Rangoon. 1961. BD-236 1 – 9 – ne IDC [338]

SECOND FRUTES / Florio, John – 1591 – 9 – 15.00 – us Scholars' Facs [440]

SECOND GENERAL ASSEMBLY, 1ST SESSION, 1814 / Illinois. General Assembly – V148-0008 – 1 – us A.G.L.L. [978]

SECOND GRAND CONCERTO IN F.. / Dussek, J L – Opus 27. 1795? – 9 – us Sibley [780]

SECOND INTERIM REPORT 1968 / Hong Kong. Special Committee on Higher Education – Hong Kong, 1968 – 2mf – 9 – DE-181/1 – ne IDC [370]

THE SECOND JUNGLE BOOK / Kipling, Rudyard – London, New York: Macmillan, 1895 – 1 roll – 1 – 1-55879-913-3 – uk Libr Preservation [830]

A SECOND LETTER TO THE MEMBERS OF THE HONOURABLE HOUSE OF COMMONS RELATING TO THE SUBSCRIPTION REQUIRED OF GRADUATES IN THE UNIVERSITIES – London, 1772 – 1mf – 9 – MP-478/1 – ne IDC [240]

A SECOND LETTER TO THE REV. MR. WHITEFIELD UPON THE FORMER SUBJECT OF REGENERATION OR THE NEW BIRTH,... / Land, T – London, [1741] – 1mf – 9 – MP-291/1 – ne IDC [240]
A SECOND LETTER TO THE REVEREND MR. GEORGE WHITEFIELD, OCCASIONED BY HIS REMARKS UPON A PAMPHLET ENTITLED 'THE ENTHUSIASM OF METHODISTS AND PAPISTS COMPARED' – London, 1751 – 2mf – 9 – MP-342/1 – ne IDC [240]
THE SECOND LINE / New Orleans Jazz Club – v1-28. Apr 1950-Fall 1976. (Jazz Periodicals) – 2r – 1 – $245.00 – us UPA [073]
SECOND LIST OF RESIDENT AND NON-RESIDENT MEMBERS AND ASSOCIATES: WEDNESDAY, 6 P.M., AUGUST 18, 1897 / British Association for the Advancement of Science. Canada – Toronto: Murray Print., 1897. 02503. (Pre-1900 Canadiana) – 9 – cn C.I.H.M. [971]
SECOND LIVRE D'ARCHITECTURE / Androuet du Cerceau, Jacques – Paris: Andre Wechel, 1561. 4p., 68 pl. (Architecture Series) – 9 – fr Hachette [720]
SECOND MALAYSIAN PLAN, 1971-1975 / Malaysia – D-1527 1. 1971 – 9 – ne IDC [338]
SECOND MEMOIRE SUR LA STATISTIQUE DU DEPARTEMENT DES DEUX-SEVRES / Dupin, Claude FE – an X – 9 – fr Hachette [944]
SECOND MEMOIRE SUR LE PAIS DES CAFRES ET LA TERRE DE NUYTS / Purry, Jean-Pierre – Amsterdam, Pierre Humbert. 1718 – 9 – 5.00 – fr Orientalistes [960]
SECOND MORTGAGES AND LAND CONTRACTS IN REAL ESTATE FINANCING / Reep, Samuel N – New York, Prentice-Hall, 1928. 255 p. LL-1022 – 1 – us L of C Photodup [340]
THE SECOND MRS. TANQUERAY : A PLAY IN FOUR ACTS / Pinero, Arthur Wing – London: W. Heinemann, 1895 – 1 roll – 1 – 1-55879-468-9 – uk Libr Preservation [820]
SECOND NATIONAL DEVELOPMENT PLAN 1972-1976 / Zambia. Ministry of Development. Planning and National Guidance – D 1531 1. 1971 – 9 – ne IDC [338]
SECOND NATIONAL DEVELOPMENT PLAN, 1973-1977 / Swaziland – Mbabane. 1973. BD-2021 1 – 9 – ne IDC [338]
THE SECOND NATIONAL ECONOMIC AND SOCIAL DEVELOPMENT PLAN, 1967-1971 / Thailand. National Economic Development Board – Bangkok. 1967 – 9 – ne IDC [338]
THE SECOND NATIONAL ECONOMIC AND SOCIAL DEVELOPMENT PLAN, 1967-1971 / Thailand. National Economic Development Board – Bangkok. 1968. BD-1832 1 – 9 – ne IDC [338]
SECOND OEUVRE DE SIMPHONIES POUR LE CLAVECIN OU PIANOFORTE AVEC ACCOMPAGNEMENT DE DEUX VIOLONS, DEUX CORS, ET VIOLONCELLE. OP.17 / Rigel, H J – (Hpschd, vln I, vc parts only) – Paris: Landie, 1783 – 1 – us Sibley [780]
THE SECOND PART OF THE BOOK OF ZECHARIAH : WITH SPECIAL REFERENCE TO THE TIME OF ITS ORIGIN / Rubinkam, Nathaniel Irwin – Basel: R Reich, 1892 – 1mf – 9 – 0-8370-4992-X – 1985-2992 – us A.T.L.A. [220]
THE SECOND PARTITION OF POLAND / Lord, R H – Cambridge. 1915. BR-5479 2 – 8 – ne IDC [940]
SECOND PLAN GENERAL DE DEVELOPPEMENT ECONOMIQUE ET SOCIAL, 1953-1957 / French Cameroons – D-1052 1. 1952 – 9 – ne IDC [338]
A SECOND PRACTICAL GUIDE TO THOROUGHBASS / Kollman, A – London: Author, 1807 – 1 – us Sibley [780]
SECOND PROGRAMME FOR ECONOMIC EXPANSION / Ireland – 2v. Dublin. 1963-64 – 9 – ne IDC [338]
SECOND PROGRAMME FOR ECONOMIC EXPANSION PROGRESS REPORT FOR 1964 / Ireland – Dublin. 1965. BD-575 1 – 9 – ne IDC [338]
SECOND PROGRAMME FOR ECONOMIC EXPANSION PROGRESS REPORT FOR 1965 / Ireland – Dublin. 1966 – 9 – ne IDC [330]
SECOND PROGRESS REPORT ON THE ECONOMIC PROGRAMME, 1955-60 / Nigeria – (Sessional Paper no. 1 of 1958). Lagos. 1958 – 9 – ne IDC [338]
SECOND PROGRESS REPORT ON THE RECONSTRUCTION AND DEVELOPMENT PROGRAMME 1960-65 FOR THE PERIOD 1961-62 / Mauritius – (Sessional Paper no. 9 of 1962). Port Louis. 1962 – 9 – ne IDC [338]
SECOND RAPOORT SUR L'EXPLORATION DES LACS SUPERIEUR ET HURON / Rottermund, E S, Comte de – Toronto: imprime par John Lovell, 1857. SEM105P1786 – 1mf – 9 – Can$2.25 – cn Bibl Nat [910]
SECOND RAPPORT DU COMITE PERMANENT DE GRIEFS : SECOND... / Bas-Canada. Chambre d'Assemblee. Comite Permanent des Griefs – [s.l.]: [s.n.], [1831?] – 1mf – 9 – Can$2.25 – cn Bibl Nat [971]
SECOND RAPPORT DU COMITE SPECIAL SUR DIVERSES COMMUNICATIONS DE SON EXCELLENCE LE GOUVERNEUR EN CHEF LORD AYLMER, SUR LE SUJET DES FINANCES DE LA PROVINCE DU BAS-CANADA / Bas-Canada. Parlement. Chambre d'Assemblee. Comite Special sur Diverses Communications... – Quebec: Imprime par Frechette & Cie, 1834. SEM105P1148 – 1mf – 9 – Can$2.25 – cn Bibl Nat [336]
THE SECOND RECENSION OF THE QUIGNON BREVIARY, VOL. 1 / Wickham Legg, J – 1908 – 7mf – 8 – ne Slangenburg [240]
THE SECOND RECENSION OF THE QUIGNON BREVIARY, VOL. 2 : LITURGICAL INTRODUCTION / Wickham Legg, J – 1912 – 6mf – 8 – ne Slangenburg [240]
SECOND REPORT / Great Britain. Committee on Modern Languages Research and Development – 1970 – 1mf – 9 – uk Microform Academic [324]
SECOND REPORT / Great Britain. Public Schools Commission – 1970 – 8mf – 9 – uk Microform Academic [324]
THE SECOND REPORT... : ORAL AND WRITTEN COMMUNICATION BETWEEN GOVERNMENT AND THE PUBLIC APRIL 1971 / Hong Kong. Chinese Language Committee – Hong Kong, 1971 – 1mf – 9 – DE-160/1 – ne IDC [370]
SECOND REPORT FROM THE SPECIAL COMMITTEE ON VARIOUS COMMUNICATIONS FROM HIS EXCELLENCY... / Bas-Canada. Parlement. Chambre d'Assemblee. Comite Special sur Diverses Communications... – Quebec: Printed by Frechette & Co, 1834 – 1mf – 9 – Can$2.25 – cn Bibl Nat [971]
SECOND REPORT OF PROGRESS OF EXPLORATION IN THE COUNTRY BETWEEN LAKE ST JOHN AND JAMES BAY INCLUDING THE REGION OF LAKE MISTASSINI AND THE BASINS OF THE GREAT NOTTAWAY AND RUPERT RIVERS.. / O'Sullivan, Henry – Quebec: Charles Pageau..., 1901. SEM105P478 – 2mf – 9 – Can$4.50 – cn Bibl Nat [910]
SECOND REPORT OF THE COMMISSION CHARGED WITH THE REVISION AND AMENDMENT OF THE CODE OF CIVIL PROCEDURE OF LOWER CANADA / Quebec Province – Quebec: Morning Chronicle Steam Print, 1894. SEM105P1517 – 3mf – 9 – Can$6.75 – cn Bibl Nat [340]
SECOND REPORT OF THE CONNECTICUT SOCIETY, AUXILIARY TO THE BAPTIST BOARD OF FOREIGN MISSIONS / Baptist Association. Connecticut – Convened in Hartford, on 6 Nov 1816 – 1 – 5.00 – us Baptist [240]
A SECOND SERIES OF FLEET STREET ECLOGUES / Davidson, John – London: J. Lane; New York: Dood, Mead, 1896 – 1 roll – 1 – 1-55879-408-5 – uk Libr Preservation [810]
A SECOND SET OF SIX CONCERTOS FOR THE HARPSICHORD OR ORGAN [ARRANGEMENT VON 6 CONCERTI GROSSI AUS OP. 6] / Handel, George Frederic – London: Walsh, [1740?] – 1 – us Sibley [780]
A SECOND SET OF SIX GRAND QUARTETTOS, OP. 16 / Haydn, Joseph – (Parts) – London: Blundell, 178- – 1 – us Sibley [780]
A SECOND SET OF SIX QUARTETTOS.. / Lidel, A – Opus VII. 1785 – 9 – us Sibley [780]
SECOND SIX-YEAR PLAN, 1941-1946 / Mexico. Mexico Revolution Party – D-1378 1. 1939 – 9 – ne IDC [335]
SECOND THOUGHTS / Broughton, Rhoda – British Fiction Archive: Unit 4 – 9 – uk Bell [830]
SECOND THOUGHTS ON DEMOCRACY IN SPAIN / Dingle, Reginald James – London, 1938? Fiche W 842. (Blodgett Collection of Spanish Civil War Pamphlets) – 9 – us H.U. College Libr [946]
SECOND VOYAGE DANS L'INTERIEUR DE L'AFRIQUE, DEPUIS DE GOLFE DE BENIN JUSQUA SACKATOU. PENDANT LES ANNEES 1825, 1826, ET 1827 / Clapperton, Hugh – (African Library). Paris. A. Bertrand. 1829 – 9 – fr Hachette [960]
SECOND VOYAGE SUR LES DEUX RIVES DE LA MER ROUGE, DANS LE PAYS DES ADELS ET LE ROYAUME DE CHOA / Rochet d'Hericourt, C E X – Paris, Arthus Bertrand. 1846 – 9 – 12.50 – fr Orientalistes [910]
SECONDARY EDUCATION IN HONG KONG DURING THE NEXT DECADE : TABLED IN THE LEGISLATIVE COUNCIL, 16TH OCTOBER 1974 / Hong Kong – Hong Kong, 1974 – 1mf – 9 – DE-149/1 – ne IDC [370]
SECONDARY EDUCATION IN SINGAPORE / Singapore. Ministry of Education – Singapore, c. 1979 – 1mf – 9 – DE-267/1 – ne IDC [370]
SECONDARY EDUCATION, MANPOWER AND EDUCATIONAL PLANNING IN THAILAND / Thailand. National Economic Development Board – (In Thai and English) – Bangkok, c. 1966 – 2mf – 9 – DE-280/1 – ne IDC [370]
SECONDARY EDUCATION WITH SPECIAL REFERENCE TO GRAMMAR SCHOOLS AND TECHNICAL HIGH SCHOOLS / Great Britain. Ministry of Education – 1938. Spens Report – 8mf – 9 – uk Microform Academic [324]
SECONDARY PUNISHMENT. THE MARK SYSTEM / Maconochie, Alexander – London. 1848 – 1 – us Res Libr [360]
SECONDARY SCHOOL THEATRE JOURNAL – (v17- . 5,6,9) – v. 1- 1961- – 1 – us UMI [370]
SECONDARY SCHOOLS AND PREPARATORY SCHOOLS IN ENGLAND RECOGNIZED BY THE BOARD AS EFFICIENT – List 60/Board of Education. London: H.M. Stat. Office. ill. annual. 1923/24- . Title varies – 1 – us U.W. Library [370]
UNE SECONDE ACADIE / Casgrain, Henri-Raymond – Quebec: L. Demers, 1894. 02147. (Pre-1900 Canadiana) – 9 – cn C.I.H.M. [971]
SECONDE LETTRE...A MESSIEURS DE L'ACADEMIE DES SCIENCES : LETTRES EDIFIANTES ET CURIEUSES... / Parennin, D – Paris, 1780-1783 – 1mf – 9 – ne IDC [610]
IL SECONDRO LIBRO DELLI CONCERTI A DUE, TRE, & QUATTRO VOCI...OPERA SECONDA / Cima, A – 1627 – 9 – us Sibley [780]
Secrest, William *see* MISCELLANEOUS MATERIALS RELATING TO THE LIFE AND CAREER OF BENJAMIN FRANKLIN DAN
SECRET AND CONFIDENTIAL CORRESPONDENCE..., 1919-27 / U.S. Navy. Chief of Naval OperationsOffice of the Secretary – RG 80. M1140. 117 rolls – 1 – us Nat'l Archives [977]
LE SECRET D'ARCHITECTURE. / Jousse, Mathurin – La Fleche, 1642.227p. pl. (Architecture Series) – 9 – fr Hachette [720]
SECRET DEBATES OF THE CONVENTION : SECRET PROCEEDINGS AND DEBATES...IN 1787 FOR THE PURPOSE OF FORMING THE CONSTITUTION OF THE UNITED STATES OF AMERICA / U. S. Constitutional Convention – Albany: Websters & Skinner, 1821 – 1mf – 9 – $4.50 – LLMC 84-246 – us L.L.M.C. [323]
[LE SECRET DES MUSES, LIV. 1] PARADISUS MUSICUS TESTUDINIS, IN QUO, MULTAE INSIGNES ET ANTE HUNC DIEM INAUDITE, GALLICAE, GERMANICAE, ANGLICAE, HYSPANICAE... / Vallet – Amstelodami: Apud Joannem Janssonium Bibliopolam. A., 1618 – 1 – us Sibley [780]
THE SECRET DISCLOSED : OR, THE ITINERANT FIELD ORATOR'S METHODIST GIBBERISH,... – (Reprinted in The Gentleman's Magazine, 58 (1788)) – [Lichfield, 1788] – 1mf – 9 – MP-557/1 – ne IDC [240]
LE SECRET DU MENAGE / Creuze de Lesser – (French Theatre Series) – 9 – fr Hachette [820]
LE SECRET DU PEUPLE DE PARIS / Carbon, Anthime – (Condition of 19th C. French working class series). 1863 – 9 – fr Hachette [360]
SECRET ENEMIES OF TRUE REPUBLICANISM / Smolnikar, Andrew B – Donnally's Mill, Perry Co., PA: Robert D. Eldridge, 1859 – 1r – 1 – us Western Res [240]
THE SECRET HISTORY OF THE OXFORD MOVEMENT / Walsh, Walter – London: S. Sonnenschein, 1898 – 1mf – us A.T.L.A. [240]
SECRET JOURNAL OF THE CONTINENTAL CONGRESS, 1775-1788 – Washington: T B Wait. v1-4. 1821 (all publ) v.1-4. 82-102 – 23mf – 9 – $34.50 – us L.L.M.C. [073]
SECRET MEMOIRS...BEING HER JOURNALS, LETTERS AND CONVERSATIONS DURING HER CONFIDENTIAL RELATIONS WITH MARIE ANTOINETTE / Lamballe, Marie Therese Louise – Ed. and annot. by Catherine Hyde...introd. by Oliver H.G. Leigh. Washington: M. Walter Dunne, c1901. xx,356p. illus – 1 – us U.W. Library [944]
THE SECRET OF A GOOD MEMORY / Granville, Joseph Mortimer – (Pittsfield?, MA): Printed for author by Eagle Printing and Binding Co., c1906. 114p – 1 – us U.W. Library [150]
SECRET OF CHRISTIANITY / Hebberd, Stephen Southric – Boston: Lee & Shepard, 1874. 1 fiche – 9 – us A.T.L.A. [240]
THE SECRET OF POWER : AND OTHER SERMONS / Maclaren, Alexander – London: Macmillan, 1882 – 1mf – 9 – 0-8370-7406-1 – 1986-1406 – us A.T.L.A. [240]
THE SECRET OF SWEDENBORG : BEING AN ELUCIDATION OF HIS DOCTRINE OF THE DIVINE NATURAL HUMANITY / James, Henry – Boston: Fields, Osgood & Co., 1869. xv,243p – 1 – us U.W. Library [190]
THE SECRET OF THE ANDES: A ROMANCE / Hassaurek, Friedrich – Cincinnati: Robert Clarke & Co., 1879. 466p. 1 reel. 1294 – 1 – us U.W. Library [830]
THE SECRET OF THE LORD / Shipton, Anna – 4th ed. London:Morgan and Scott, [1870?] – 1mf – 9 – 0-8370-2545-1 – 1985-0545 – us A.T.L.A. [240]
THE SECRET POWER / Corelli, Marie – British Fiction Archive: Unit 1 – 9 – uk Bell [830]
SECRET PROCEEDINGS AND DEBATES OF THE CONVENTION : ASSEMBLED AT PHILADEPHIA IN THE YEAR 1789 FOR THE PURPOSE OF FORMING THE CONSTITUTION OF THE UNITED STATES OF AMERICA – Albany: Websters & Skinner. 1v. 1821 – 1mf – 9 – $1.50 – LLMC 84-246 – us L.L.M.C. [323]
Secretan, G A S J L *see* MYCOGRAPHIE SUISSE, OU DESCRIPTION DES CHAMPIGNONS QUI CROISSENT EN SUISSE
Secretaria Gestora del Plan Badajoz *see* EL PLAN BADAJOZ, 1966
Secretariado Catequistico *see* MISA DIALOGADA
Secretariado Catequistico de la Diocesis de Plasencia *see* LITURGIA ELEMENTAL 4TH EDICION
Secretariado de Asuntos Economicos de Badajoz *see* APROXIMACION A LA EVOLUCION SOCIO-ECONOMICA DE LA PROVINCIA DE BADAJOZ EN 1972
Secretariado Diocesano de Catequesis *see*
- ORDINARIODE LA MISA, PARA FIELES
- SACRIFICIO VESPERTINO

Secretariado Diocesano de Misiones de Badajoz *see* MEMORIAS ANUALES, 1968. DOMUND JUSTICIA Y PAZ
SECRETARIADO EXTREMENO – Badajoz.1897, solo no. 5 – 9 – 1.50f – sp Bibl Santa Ana [072]
SECRETARIAT FOR PROMOTING CHRISTIAN UNITY – 1967-85 (complete) – 2r – 1 – ATLA S0828 – us A.T.L.A. [073]
Le Secretariat general de l'UAM *see*
- COMPTE-RENDU DES TRAVAUX DE LA CONFERENCE DE LIBREVILLE 10-13 SEP 1962
- COMPTE-RENDU DES TRAVAUX DE LA CONFERENCE DE OUAGADOUGOU 10-14 MARS 1963

SECRETARIAT INTERNATIONAL DES JURISTES POUR L'AMNISTIE EN URUGUAY (SIJAU) = INTERNATIONAL SECRETARIAT OF JURISTS FOR AMNESTY IN URUGUAY – Paris. 36 docs. 1980-1985 – 13mf – 9 – ne IDC [320]
SECRETARY – (v38- . 5,6,9) – v. 1-. 1942- – 1 – us UMI [650]

SECRETARY'S BOOK / Mount Nebo Sunday School, Mount Nebo, KS – 1902-1903 – 1 – us KS Hist [240]
SECRETARY'S BOOK / Russell Townsite Company. Kansas – 1871 – 1 – us KS Hist [978]
SECRETARY'S NOTES ON THE NINTH MEETING HELD AT ST JAMES PLACE / Great Britain. Colonial Office.Conferences on Palestine. U.K.-Jewish Agency Delegation – London. 1939. BJ-28-86 1 – 9 – ne IDC [324]
SECRETARY'S ORDERS : INTERIOR DEPARTMENT / U.S. Department of the Interior Law Library – nos 1-3104 29 Jan 1925-28 Sept 1984 – 109mf – 9 – $163.00 – LLMC 85-300 – us L.L.M.C. [324]
EL SECRETO A VOCES, ARCANIDADES DE LOS POLVOS DE AIX / Perez, V – Madrid, 1753 – 2mf – 9 – sp Cultura [615]
SECRETOS RAROS DE ARTES Y OFICIOS – 1807 – 9 – 1.50f – sp Bibl Santa Ana [946]
LES SECRETS DE NOSTRE LANGUE / Bary, R – 1673 – 9 – fr I.C.S. [440]
SECRETS POUR TEINDRE LA SOYE, LE FIL, LA LENNE, LE BOIS, L'OR ET L'YVOIRE... / Houdmon, A – 18th cent – 1 – F76.85 – fr Armell [944]
SECRETS REVEAL'D: OR, AN OPEN ENTRANCE TO THE SHUT-PALACE OF THE KING; CONTAINING THE GREATEST TREASURE IN CHYMISTRY.. / Philalethus, Eirenaeus – Composed by a most famous Englishman, styling himself Anonymus, or Eyrenaeus Philaletha Cosmopolita... London, 1669. Profusely annotated in the hand of Sir Isaac Newton – 1 – us U.W. Library [540]
SECRETUM SECRETORUM: THE GOVERNAUNCE OF KYNGES AND PRYNCES – 1511 – 9 – 10.00 – us Scholars' Facs [321]
DE SECTE DER LOISTEN, OF, ANTWERPSCHE LIBERTIJNEN (1525-1545) : ELIGIUS PRNYSTINCK (LOY DE SCHALIEDECKER) EN ZIJNE AANHANGERS / Frederichs, Julius – Gent: J. Vuylsteke, 1891. (Werken van den practischen leergang van vaderlandsche geschiedenis; 2) – 1mf – us A.T.L.A. [240]
LE SECTEUR ALGERIEN DES INDUSTRIES AGRICOLES ET ALIMENTAIRES / Algeria. Institut pour l'Etude et le Developpement de l'Industrie en Algerie – 3v. 1959-60. BNE-8652 1 – 9 – ne IDC [338]
SECTION DES CITOYENS ARMES DE LA PLACE VENDOME / Robespierre, Maximilien de – Paris, s.d. 1 fiche. (Political Science Collection) – 9 – 6.00 – fr Bibl Nationale [323]
SECULAR CHRONICLE – Birmingham, then London. 1872-79 – 1 – uk Microform Academic [073]
SECULAR REVIEW – London. 1876-77 – 1 – uk Microform Academic [073]
SECULAR REVIEW – London. 1878-88 – 1 – uk Microform Academic [073]
SECULAR REVIEW – London. -w. 9 Jun 1877-18 Oct 1879, 2 Aug 1884-29 Dec 1888. (6 reels) – 1 – uk British Libr Newspaper [073]
SECULAR REVIEW AND SECULARIST – London. 1877-78 – 1 – uk Microform Academic [073]
SECULAR THOUGHT – Toronto: C M Ellis, [1885-1911?] – 9 – cn C.I.H.M. [210]
SECULAR VIEW OF THE BIBLE / Grethenbach, Constantine – New York: Peter Eckler, 1902 – 9 – us A.T.L.A. [240]
SECULAR WORK – London. 1896-97 – 1 – uk Microform Academic [073]
SECULAR WORLD – London. 1862-64 – 1 – uk Microform Academic [073]
SECULARISM: ITS PROGRESS AND ITS MORALS / Bonham, John Milton – New York: G.P. Putnam, 1894. 1 fiche – 9 – us A.T.L.A. [240]
SECULARIST – London. 1876-77 – 1 – uk Microform Academic [073]
SECULARIST (INCORPORATING TRUTHSEEKER) – Bradford. 1902 – 1 – uk Microform Academic [073]
THE SECULARIZATION OF AMERICAN EDUCATION AS SHOWN BY STATE LEGISLATION, STATE CONSTITUTIONAL PROVISIONS AND STATE SUPREME COURT DECISIONS / Brown, Samuel Windsor – 1912 – 1 – us A.T.L.A. [370]
O SECULO – Bom-Successo, 8 Apr 1900 – 1,5,6 – bl Biblioteca [072]
O SECULO – Lisboa, 1956-oct 1975; 1976-feb 12 1977 – us Res Libr [072]
O SECULO – Lisbon, Portugal. 1940-55; Arp 1986-Jul 1989 – 78r – 1 – us L of C Photodup [072]
O SECULO – Lisbon, Portugal. -d. 18 March 1941-30 April 1945. Imperfect. 18 reels – 1 – uk British Libr Newspaper [072]
O SECULO : ORGAO DO COMMERCIO, DA LAVOURA E DA INDUSTRIA – Maceio, Alagoas. 10-14 Set 1877; Jan, Mar 5 Set 1878 – 1,5,6 – bl Biblioteca [072]
O SECULO : ORGAO POPULAR – Manaos, Amazonas. 11 Jan 1890 – 1,5,6 – bl Biblioteca [072]
O SECULO : POLITICO, LITTERARIO E COMMERCIAL – '(s.l.')-Bahia, Brazil. 5 Dec 1848; Jun, Aug, Oct-Dec 1849; Jan-Dec 1850; 26-31 Jul 1851 – 1,5,6 – bl Biblioteca [072]
O SECULO – Sao Luiz, 2 Dec 1858-4 Mar 1861 – 1,5,6 – bl Biblioteca [072]
O SECULO 19 : ORGAO DA ASSOCIACAO TYPOGRAPHICA ALAGOANA – Maceio, Alagoas. 12, 20 Ago 1870; 9, 23 Fev 1871 – 1,5,6 – bl Biblioteca [072]
SECURITIES ACT OF 1933. RELEASE NUMBER 1-5359, MAY 27, 1933-JAN. 26, 1973 / U.S. Securities and Exchange Commission – Release nos. 1-220 in this series were issued by the Federal Trade Commission. The SEC continued FTC numbering, and all are included here. The series will continue in the SEC Docket – 9 – us UMI [336]
SECURITIES ACT OF 1933 RELEASES / U.S. Securities and Excahnge Commission – Federal Trade Comm. nos 1-220. 27 May 1933-4 Sept 1934; SEC. nos 221-5359. 10 Aug 1934-26 Jan 1973 (all publ) – 232mf – 9 – $348.00 – LLMC 85-353; 85-354 – us L.L.M.C. [340]
SECURITIES AND EXCHANGE COMMISSION ANNUAL REPORTS / U.S. Securities and Exchange Commission – (Updates planned) – 1st-46th. 1935-80 – 128mf – 9 – $192.00 – LLMC 80-516 – us L.L.M.C. [332]
SECURITIES AND EXCHANGE COMMISSION DECISIONS AND REPORTS / U.S. Securities and Exchange Commission – (Add vols planned) – v1-48. 1934-88 – 524mf – 9 – $786.00 – LLMC 78-224B – us L.L.M.C. [332]
SECURITIES AND EXCHANGE COMMISSION DECISIONS AND REPORTS *see* PROTECTIVE AND REORGANIZATION COMMITTEES REPORTS
SECURITIES EXCHANGE ACT OF 1934. RELEASE NUMBER 1-9984, AUG. 13, 1934-FEB. 2, 1973 / U.S. Securities and Exchange Commission – Release nos. 9965, 9969, and 9972-9983 are in the SEC Docket, vol 1, no. 1. The series will continue in subsequent issues – 9 – us UMI [336]
SECURITIES EXCHANGE ACT OF 1934 RELEASES / U.S. Securities and Exchange Commission – nos 1-9971. 13 Aug 1934-26 Jan 1973 (all publ) – 450mf – 9 – $675.00 – LLMC 84-355 – us L.L.M.C. [340]
SECURITIES INVESTOR PROTECTION ACT OF 1970. RELEASE NUMBER 1-2, DEC. 22, 1971-JUN. 24, 1973 / U.S. Securities and Exchange Commission – Release no. 2 appeared in two parts on December 21, 1972 and January 24, 1973, respectively – 9 – us UMI [336]
SECURITY AFFAIRS – Washington, DC. Nov/Dec 1984-Oct 1985. Continues: Newsletter (Jewish Institute for National Security Affairs, Washington, DC) – 1 – us A.J.P.C. [071]
SECURITY AND EXCHANGE COMMISSION JUDICIAL DECISIONS : A COMPILATION OF ALL COURT DECISIONS, REPORTED AND UNREPORTED, IN CIVIL AND CRIMINAL CASES, INVOLVING STATUTES ADMINISTERED BY THE SECURITY AND EXCHANGE COMMISSION / U.S. Securities and Exchange Commission. Office of the General Counsel – GPO: v1-5. 1934-48 (all publ) – 58mf – 9 – $87.00 – LLMC 80-518 – us L.L.M.C. [340]
SECURITY COUNCIL OFFICIAL RECORDS : RESOLUTIONS AND DECISIONS / United Nations – (1st Year – 22nd Year: S/RES/-; S/INF/ 1946-1967. E/F.22 S.22; 23rd Year – 44th Year: S/RES/-; S/INF/ 1968-1989. E.22 F.22 S.22) – 9 – us U.N. Pubs [324]
SECURITY COUNCIL OFFICIAL RECORDS : SUPPLEMENTS AND SPECIAL SUPPLEMENTS / United Nations – (1st Year – 22nd Year: S/ 1946-1967. E/F.365 S.216; 23rd Year: S/1968. E/F.25 E.2 F.2 S.17; 24th Year – 40th Year: S/ 1969-1985. E.339 F.353 S.315) – 9 – us U.N. Pubs [324]
SECURITY COUNCIL OFFICIAL RECORDS : VERBATIM RECORDS OF MEETINGS / United Nations – (1st Year – 21st Year: S/PV. 1946-1966. E/F.769 S.730; 22nd Year – 37th Year: S/PV. 1967-1982. E.451 F.390 S.370; 36th and 37th Years in French and Spanish are not yet available) – 9 – us U.N. Pubs [324]
SECURITY COUNCIL. OFFICIAL RECORDS / United Nations – 2500mf – 9 – $4600.00; $1.90f – uk UNIMICRO [900]
SECURITY INVESTOR PROTECTION ACT OF 1970 RELEASES – nos1-3. 22 Dec 1971-24 Jan 1973 (all publ) – 1mf – 9 – $1.50 – LLMC 89-008 – us L.L.M.C. [340]
SECURITY LETTER – (v5- . 5,6,9) – v.1- 1970- – 1 – us UMI [073]
SECURITY MANAGEMENT – (v20- . 5,6,9) – v. 1-. 1957- – 1 – us UMI [380]
SECURITY SYSTEMS DIGEST – (v7- . 5,6,9) – v. 1-. 1970- – 1 – us UMI [360]
SECURITY SYSTEMS DIGEST *see* WASHINGTON CRIME NEWS SERVICES' CORPORATE SECURITY DIGEST
LA SED DE AMAR / Trigo, Felipe – Madrid: Renacimiento, 9th ed s.a. – sp Bibl Santa Ana [946]
Sedah, Mpu *see*
– APA SEBAB TERDJADI BHARATAYUDHA
– DAMAYANTI; TJARITANE RESHI BHRIGADDHASWA MARANG JUDISTHIRA NALIKANE PANDAWA NEMAHI PAPA SANGSARA ING SATENGAHING WANAWASA
SEDAIA STARINA MOSKVY : ISTORICHESKII OBZOR I POLNYI UKAZATEL' EE DOSTOPRIMECHATEL'NOSTEI / ed by Kondrateyv, I – Moscow: I Morozov Publ, 1893 – 6mf – 9 – $60.00 – us Ross [947]
Sedaine, Jean Michel *see* LES FEMMES VENGEES
Sedaine (Libretto) *see* LE ROY ET LE FERMIER. COMEDIE EN TROIS ACTES
SEDELYCK VERMAECK TONNEEL VERTHOONENDE DOOR SINNE-BEELDEN DEN LEERSAMEN HANDEL VAN DE ONREDELIJCKE DIEREN AEN DE VERKEERDE, EN BEEST-AERDIGHE WERELT OP-GHERECHT VAN VERSCHEYDEN SOO GRIECKSCHE, ALS LATYNSCHE SCHRIJVERS VERCIERT MET AERDIGHE PRINTEN,... / Moons, J – (Engraved titlepage missing) – 1st ed. Antwerpen, 1675 – 6mf – 9 – O-3126/1 – ne IDC [760]
SEDELYCK VREUGHDE-PERCK OFT DERDEN DEEL VAN HET ZEDELYCK VERMAECK-TONNEEL.... / Moons, J – Antwerpen, 1685 – 9mf – 9 – O-3127/1 – ne IDC [760]
SEDELYCKEN VERMAECK-SPIEGEL OFT LESTE DEEL VAN HET SEDELYCK VERMAECK-TONNEEL VERTHOONENDE DEN LEERSAMEN HANDEL VAN DE ONREDELYCKE DIEREN AEN DE VERKEERDE, EN BEESTAERDIGHE WERELDT OP-GHEHANGHEN VAN VERSCHEYDEN SOO GRIECKSCHE, ALS LATYNSCHE SCHRYVERS,... / Moons, J – Antwerpen, 1689 – 7mf – 9 – O-3128/1 – ne IDC [760]
SEDELYCKEN VERMAECK-TROOST IN ALLE LYDEN SOO WEL IN PEYS, ALS IN OORLOGHS-TYDEN... / Moons, J – Antwerpen, 1702 – 6mf – 9 – O-3129/1 – ne IDC [760]
SEDELYCKEN VREUGHDEN-BERGH VERTHOONENDE DOOR SINNE BEELDEN DEN LEERSAEMEN HANDEL VAN DE ONREDELYCKE DIEREN AEN DE VERKEERDE, EN BEEST-AERDIGHE WERELDT OP-GHEMAECKT VAN VERSCHEYDE SOO GRIECKSCHE, ALS LATYNSCHE SCHRYVERS / Moons, J – Antwerpen, 1682 – 7mf – 9 – O-3130/1 – ne IDC [760]
SEDELYK VERMAEK-TROOST IN ALLE LYDEN SOO WEL IN PEYS ALS IN OORLOGS TYDEN, VOOR ALLE STATEN VAN MENSCHEN, OM NIET DOOR DROEFHEYD TE VERFLENSCHEN, GESOGT, EN GEVONDEN IN DE SCHOLE VAN VERDULDIGHEYD,... / Moons, J – Antwerpen, [c1764] – 5mf – 9 – O-3131/1 – ne IDC [760]
SEDELYK VREUGDE-PERK VERTOONENDE DOOR ZINNE-BELDEN DEN LEERSAMEN HANDEL VAN DE ONREDELIJKE DIEREN AEN DE VERKEERDE, EN BEEST AERDIGE WERELD OPGEREGT VAN VERSCHEYDE SOO GRIEKSCHE, ALS LATYNSCHE SCHRYVERS, VERCIERT MET AERDIGE PRINTEN,... / Moons, J – Antwerpen, 1772 – 7mf – 9 – O-3125/1 – ne IDC [760]
SEDELYKEN VERMAEK-SPIEGEL VERTOONENDE DOOR ZINNE-BELDEN DEN LEERZAMEN HANDEL VAN DE ONREDELIJKE DIEREN AEN DE VERKEERDE, EN BEESTAERDIGE WERELD OPGEREGT VAN VERSCHEYDE SOO GRIEKSCHE, ALS LATYNSCHE SCHRYVERS,... / Moons, J – Antwerpen, [c1764] – 5mf – 9 – O-3132/1 – ne IDC [760]
SEDELYKEN VREUGDEN-BERG VERTHOONENDE DOOR ZINNE-BELDEN DEN LEERZAMEN HANDEL... / Moons, J – Den tweeden druk. Antwerpen, [c1764] – 5mf – 9 – O-3124/1 – ne IDC [760]
Sedeno de Meca, A *see* TRADUCCION DE LOS AFORISMOS DE HIPOCRATES
SEDER NASHIM – Prague. 1629. BJ-43-78 1 – 9 – ne IDC [270]
Sedgefield, Walter John *see* KING ALFRED'S VERSION OF THE CONSOLATIONS OF BOETHIUS
Sedger, John *see* THE STRUCTURE OF THE ENGLISH LANGUAGE
Sedgwick, A *see* A SYNOPSIS OF THE CLASSIFICATION OF THE BRITISH PALAEOZOIC ROCKS... WITH A SYSTEMATIC DESCRIPTION OF THE BRITISH PALAEOZOIC FOSSILS IN THE GEOLOGICAL MUSEUM OF THE UNIVERSITY OF CAMBRIDGE
Sedgwick, Arthur George *see*
– ELEMENTS OF THE LAW OF DAMAGES.
– A TREATISE ON THE PRINCIPLES AND PRACTICE GOVERNING THE TRIAL OF TITLE TO LAND.
Sedgwick, Catharine Maria *see* CATHARINE MARIA SEDGWICK PAPERS, 1798-1867
Sedgwick County. Kansas. District Court *see* RECORDS
Sedgwick County. Kansas. Sheriff *see* JAIL CALENDAR
Sedgwick County. Kansas. Wichita Township *see* JUSTICE OF THE PEACE DOCKETS
Sedgwick, Dwight *see* ITALY IN THE THIRTEENTH CENTURY
Sedgwick, T E *see* HISTORY OF YORK COUNTY AND ITS PEOPLE
Sedgwick, Theodore *see*
– A TREATISE ON THE MEASURE OF DAMAGES
SEDIGHE ONDERWIISEN DER CREATUREN : IN RHIJM GHESTELT – Antwerpen, 1649 – 2mf – 9 – ne IDC [700]
DEN SEDIGHEN TOET-STEEN VAN DE ONVERDRAEGHELYCKE WELDE / Bie, C de – O 148. 1689 – 9 – ne IDC [700]
SEDIKIT DARI HAL HOMILETIK ATAU ILMU BERI WAJAT / Pouw, Peng Hong – SE-5189 1. 2 v. in 1. 1960 – 9 – ne IDC [950]
SEDIKIT TENTANG ADMINISTRASI KEUANGAN DAN STATISTIK GEREDJA / Baas, H – SE-5037 1. 1963 – 9 – ne IDC [310]
SEDIKIT TENTANG SEDJARAH ASIA TIMOER RAJA DAN SEDJARAH TANAH DJAWA / Prijono, R – (Microfiche No 132) – Djakarta: Balai Poestaka, 2605 – 1mf – 9 – SE-2002/1 – ne IDC [950]
SEDIMENT TRANSPORT AND TURBIDITY IN THE EEL RIVER BASIN / Brown, Wm. M, 3rd & Ritter, John R – Humboldt Co, 1970 – 1r – 1 – $50.00 – B40222 – us Library Micro [550]
SEDIMENTARY GEOLOGY – v1-40. 1967-84 – 1,5,6,13 – sz Elsevier [550]
DIE SEDIMENTE DES SUEDATLANTISCHEN OZEANS *see* WISSENSCHAFTLICHE ERGEBNISSE DER DEUTSCHEN ATLANTISCHEN EXPEDITION AUF DEM FORSCHUNGS-UND VERMESSUNGSSCHIFF "METEOR", 1925-1927
SEDIMENTTEXTUREN DER SOHLBANKFLAECHE IM NATURDENKMAL "SAURIERFAEHRTEN MUENCHEHAGEN" (BERRIAS), REHBURGER BERGE : RIPPELMARKEN UND ICHNOFOSSILIEN ALS GRUNDLAGE EINER DEUTUNG DES ABLAGERUNGSRAUMES / Schwennicke, Tobias – 1993 – 2mf – 9 – DM98.00 – 3-89349-722-6 – gw Hänsel [560]

SEDITION – (Also known as: San Jose Community News) – San Jose, CA. 1971-1977 – 1r – 1 – $50.00 – B03505 – us Library Micro [071]
SEDJARAH BANTEN / Rusjan, Tbg – SE 4890 1. 1954 – 9 – ne IDC [950]
SEDJARAH EKONOMIS SOSIOLOGIS INDONESIA / Burger, Dionijs H – SE-2010 1. 1960 – 9 – ne IDC [330]
SEDJARAH GEREDJA DI INDONESIA / Mueller-Krueger, Th – 1959 – 9 – SE-10 177 1 – ne IDC [331]
SEDJARAH INDONESIA UNTUK SEKOLAH MENENGAH / Rangkuti, A D – SE-5421 1. 1949 – 9 – ne IDC [950]
Sedjarah Militer Angkatan Darat, Semdam 2, Burit Barisan *see* BERKELA "SEDJARAH MILITER"
SEDJARAH MUSIK DI EROPAH / Kau Besin, AF – Djakarta, Soeroengan, 1958. 67p. ports. SEM-7257- – 9 – ne IDC [780]
SEDJARAH MUSIK DI EROPAH / Kau Besin, AF – SE-4883 1. 1958 – 9 – ne IDC [950]
SEDJARAH NABI IBRAHIM / Amin, M – SE-5708 1. 1967 – 9 – ne IDC [950]
SEDJARAH NIPPON. DITERDJEMAHKAN OLEH HABIBANA-ALWIE / Nakamura, K – Palembang, Barisan Propaganda Dai Nippon, 2602. 97p – 114-115mf – 9 – ne IDC [950]
SEDJARAH PEMBANGUNAN JAJASAN BADAN WAKAF SEMARANG / Sulchan, M – SE 4850 1. 1964 – 9 – ne IDC [950]
SEDJARAH PERGARAKAN NASIONAL INDONESIA; RINGKASAN DARI SERI TJEREMAH DIMUKA "KURSUS PENJEGARAN" DARI DEPARTEMEN LUAR NEGERI DALAM BULAN2 MEI / Susanto Tirtoprodjo – SE 4570 1. 1962 – 9 – ne IDC [950]
SEDJARAH REVOLUSI INDONESIA; PERIODE REVOLUSI PHYSIK 1945-1950 / Indonesia – SE-6118 1. v. 1 only. 1966- – 9 – ne IDC [950]
SEDJARAH SASTERA INDONESIA MODERN / Siregar, Bakri – SE 4648 1. v. 1 only. 1964 – 9 – ne IDC [950]
Sedulius, fifth century *see* THE EASTER SONG; BEING THE FIRST EPIC OF CHRISTENDOM.
Seebach, M R *see* WOMEN: SHALL THEY PREACH?
Seeberg, P *see* DAS GESETZ DES HERRN
Seeberg, Reinhold *see*
- BRAUCHEN WIR EIN NEUES DOGMA?
- THE FUNDAMENTAL TRUTHS OF THE CHRISTIAN RELIGION
- DIE GRUNDWAHRHEITEN DER CHRISTLICHEN RELIGION
- OFFENBARUNG UND INSPIRATION
- REVELATION AND INSPIRATION
- DIE THEOLOGIE DES JOHANNES DUNS SCOTUS

SEEBLATT *see* WUERTTEMBERGISCHES SEEBLATT
SEEBLATT FUER KREIS UND STADT FRIEDRICHSHAFEN *see* WUERTTEMBERGISCHES SEEBLATT
SEEBLATT FUER STADT UND LAND *see* WUERTTEMBERGISCHES SEEBLATT
Seebohm, Frederic *see* THE OXFORD REFORMERS JOHN COLET, ERASMUS, AND THOMAS MORE
Seebohm, H *see*
- CLASSIFICATION OF BIRDS
- A HISTORY OF BRITISH BIRDS

Seeburger, Mattie (Riga, Michigan) *see* SCRAPBOOKS
Seeck, O *see*
- NOTITIA DIGNITATUM
- NOTITIA DIGNITATUM, ACCEDUNT NOTITIA CONSTANTINOPOLITANAE ET LATERCULI PROVINCIARUM
- Q. AURELII SYMMACHI QUAE SUPERSUNT (MGH 1: 6.BD. 1.TEIL)

Seeck, Otto *see*
- DIE BRIEFE DES LIBANIUS (T.U.U. 2-30/1.2)
- GESCHICHTE DES UNTERGANGS DER ANTIKEN WELT

Seeckt, Hans von *see* PAPERS, 1866-1936
SEED – Irvine, CA. 1981-1983 – 1r – 1 – $50.00 – R04038 – us Library Micro [071]
SEED BED AND THE ARC NEWSLETTER – 1971-76 (complete) – 1r – 1 – ATLA S0594 – us A.T.L.A. [073]
SEED CALENDAR BULLETIN / North Dakota. University. Agricultural Experiment Station – no.1. 1913 – 1,5,6 – us Spaulding [631]
SEED CAMPAIGNS – 1984 – 46p – it F.A.O. [631]
SEED CATALOGUE / Houtte, L van – (Etablissement Horticole). Gand. 1839-96. Lacking: v. 2, 5, 7, 31, 51, 69, 73, 83, 101, 107. B-7479 1 – 9 – ne IDC [631]
SEED CIRCULAR / North Dakota. University. Agricultural Experiment Station – nos.1-10. 1909-20 – 1,5,6 – us Spaulding [631]
SEED LEGISLATION – 1980 – 121p – it F.A.O. [340]
SEED WORLD – (v.118-. 1980- 5,6,9) – v.1-. 1915- – 1 – us UMI [073]
SEEDS : PROCEEDINGS FAO/SIDA TECHNICAL CONFERENCE ON IMPROVED SEED PRODUCTION. NAIROBI, 1981 – 1982 – 583p – it F.A.O. [631]
SEEDS FOR THE PARISH – v1-5. 1988-12 (complete) – 1r – 1 – ATLA S0896 – us A.T.L.A. [073]
SEEDS OF PROGRESS / Read, Leonard E – 1980. Together with: Outlook for Freedom. 1951; Essays from "Essays on Liberty". v.I-III. 270p. 1 fiche (24x) – 9 – 1.00f – at Libertarian Micro [320]
SEEDTIME IN KASHMIR:...WILLIAM JACKSON ELMSLIE...MEDICAL MISSIONARY / Elmslie, William Jackson – London: James Nisbet, 1876. 294p. 1 fiche – 9 – us A.T.L.A. [240]
SEED-TRUTHS : OR, BIBLE VIEWS OF MIND, MORALS, AND RELIGION / Church, Pharcellus – New York: Sheldon, 1871 – 1mf – 9 – 0-8370-2661-X – 1985-0661 – us A.T.L.A. [220]
DER SEEFRACHTVERTRAG IM INTERNATIONALEN PRIVATRECHT / Donner, E O – Goettingen, 1910 – 1mf – 1 – ILM-3245/1 – ne IDC [327]
SEEING OF URINES = SEYNGE OF URYNES – London, [1555] – 2mf – 9 – ne IDC [612]
SEEKING LIFE AND OTHER SERMONS / Brooks, Phillips – New York: E.P. Dutton, 1904 – 1mf – us A.T.L.A. [240]
SEEKONK 1760-1900 – (Mf 1-3: Vital Records 1779-1843. Mf 4-5: Town Records 1811-39. Mf 6-7: Intentions 1812-54. Mf 8-13: Town Records 1812-27. Mf 14-19: Town Records 1827-47. Mf 20-23: Tax Records 1812-27. Mf 24-25: Death Index 1850-1954. Mf 26-29: Marriage Index 1850-1944. Mf 30-32: Birth Index 1850-1954. Mf 33: Deaths 1843-69. Mf 33: Births & Deaths 1768-1859. Mf 34: Births 1843-83; Marriages 1843-53. Mf 35: Deaths 1843-65. Mf 36: Births 1884-1900. Mf 37: Marriages 1840-47, 1853-83. Mf 38: Marriages 1883-99. Mf 39: Deaths 1866-98) – (mf ed 1991) – 39mf – 9 – 0-87623-143-1 – us Holbrook [920]
Seel, Otto *see* TROGUS POMPEIUS
Seele, Keith *see* THE COREGENCY OF RAMSES 2
SEELEN ARSTEDYE VOR DE GESUNDEN VND KRANCKEN... / Huberinus, Caspar – Magdeburg: Hans Walther, [1559]. [G.F.: 4.14] – 2mf – 9 – HUB-17/1 – ne IDC [240]
DER SEELENCULT IN SEINEN BEZIEHUNGEN ZUR ALTHEBRAEISCHEN RELIGION / Lippert, Julius – Berlin: Theodor Hofmann, 1881. 1 fiche – 9 – us A.T.L.A. [270]
SEELENGLAUBE UND UNSTERBLICHKEIT-SHOFFNUNG IM ALTEN TESTAMENT / Torge, Paul – Leipzig: J.C. Hinrichs, 1909. 1 fiche – 9 – us A.T.L.A. [240]
Seeley, H G *see* THE FRESH-WATER FISHES OF EUROPE
Seeley, John Robert *see*
- ECCE HOMO
- ECCE HOMO: A SURVEY OF THE LIFE AND WORK OF JESUS CHRIST
- NATURAL RELIGION BY THE AUTHOR OF "ECCE HOMO"

Seeley, Robert Benton *see*
- ESSAYS ON THE BIBLE BY THE AUTHOR OF "ESSAYS ON THE CHURCH" ETC
- HAVE WE ANY "WORD OF GOD"?
- THE LIFE AND REIGN OF EDWARD 1 BY THE AUTHOR OF "THE GREATEST OF THE PLANTAGENETS"

Seelig, Gottfried *see* DER JUDE
Seeliger, Ewald Gerhard *see* DER GELBE SEEDIEB
Seeligmann, S *see*
- BIBLIOGRAPHIE EN HISTORIE
- DIE JUDEN IN HOLLAND

Seely, Amos W *see* DOCTRINAL THOUGHTS
Seelye, Julius Hawley *see*
- CHRISTIAN MISSIONS
- THE WAY, THE TRUTH, AND THE LIFE

Seemann, B *see* BONPLANDIA...
Seemann, Berthold Carl *see*
- FLORA VITIENSIS: A DESCRIPTION OF THE PLANTS OF THE VITI OR FIJI ISLANDS
- NARRATIVE OF THE VOYAGE OF H.M.S. HERALD DURING THE YEARS 1845-51, UNDER THE COMMAND OF CAPTAIN H. KELLETT...CIRCUMNAVIGATION OF THE GLOBE, AND THREE CRUISES TO THE ARCTIC REGIONS IN SEARCH OF SIR J. FRANKLIN

Seemann, Berthold Carl et al *see* JOURNAL OF BOTANY, BRITISH AND FOREIGN
Seemann, Otmar *see*
- BILDNISSE DER BERUEHMTESTEN MENSCHEN ALLER VOELKER UND ZEITEN (AEL, ABT 1;25)
- ENZYKLOPAEDISCHE INFORMATION IM 19. JAHRHUNDERT: DIE ERGAENZUNSWERKE ZUM BROCKHAUS KONSERVATIONSLEXIKON

Seemann, Otto *see* THE MYTHOLOGY OF GREECE AND ROME: WITH SPECIAL REFERENCE TO ITS USE IN ART
Seemann, W E G *see* BONPLANDIA...
SEEN AND HEARD – Philadelphia. v1-4. 1903 – 1r – 1 – us Ross [975]
SEER GRONDIGHE ENDE WT GODES WOORDT WEL GHEFONDEERDE ONDERRICHTINGE, TEGHENS DE LASTERINGHE ENDE HET GESCHREY, DAT DE WEDERDOOPEREN / Acronivs, R – Franeker, G. V.d. Rade. 1599. BME-229 1 – 9 – ne IDC [240]
EEN SEER GRONTLIJCKE ANTWOORT, VOL MET ALDERLEY ONDERWIJSINGE ENDE GOEDER VERMANINGHE, OP ZYLIS ENDE LEMMEKES ONVERDIENDE LASTERLIJCKE FAEM ROUEN, ACHTERCLAPPEN ENDE ONGESOLTENE ENDE BITTERE SCHELTWOORDEN / Simons, Menno – Van my Menno Symons. Anno. 1559. Den 23, Januarij. Harlingen, Gherit Andrieszoon. 1587. BME-292 1 – 9 – ne IDC [240]
EYNE SEER LIEFLIJCKE MEDITATION VND GODTSALIGE OEFFENINGE, MIT VELE CHRISTELIJCKE LEERINGEN / Simons, Menno – BME-277 1 – 9 – ne IDC [240]
EEN SEER SCHOON ENDE WAERACHTIGE VERCLARINGE ENDE WTLEGGHINGE DES TABERNAKELS OFT DER HUTTEN MOSI / Philips, Dirk – 1556. BME-300 – 9 – ne IDC [240]
SEER SCHOONE AENWYSINGEN VNDE GRONDIGE ONTDECKINGEN VAN DIE VERBORGHEN WYSHEYDT GODES / Joris, David – 1550. BME-366 1 – 9 – ne IDC [240]
EEN SEER SCHOONE, ENDE GRONT-LIJCKE LERINGE WT DES HEEREN WOORDT, ALLEN MENSCHEN / Simons, Menno – Anno M. CCCCC.LVI. 1556. BME-279 1 – 9 – ne IDC [240]
EENEN SEER SCHOONEN TROOSTELIJCKEN ENDE CHRISTELIJCKEN SENDTBRIEF / Philips, Dirk – 1579. BME-314 1 – 9 – ne IDC [240]
THE SEERESS OF PREVOST; BEING REVELATIONS CONCERNING THE INNER-LIFE OF MAN, AND THE INTER-DIFFUSION OF A WORLD OF SPIRITS IN THE ONE WE INHABIT / Kerner, Justinus Andreas Christian – From the German by Mrs. Crowe. New York: C. Partridge, 1859. xii,119p – 1 – us U.W. Library [150]
SEESCHLACHT : TRAGOEDIE / Goering, Reinhard – Berlin: S Fischer Verlag, 1931 – 1r – 1 – us U.W. Library [820]
Seesemann, Otto *see*
- ISRAEL UND JUDA BEI AMOS UND HOSEA
- ISRAEL UND JUDA BEI AMOS UND HOSEA NEBST EINEM EXKURS UEBER HOS. 1-3

SEETA / Taylor, Philip Meadows – British Fiction Archive: Unit 5 – 9 – uk Bell [830]
SEFAT EMET / Hagiz, M – Amsterdam. 1847. BJ-27-13 1 – 9 – ne IDC [900]
SEFATEJNOE – 's-Gravenhage, 1939-40 – 2mf – 9 – J-261-108/1 – ne IDC [949]
SEFER BIALIK / Bialik, H N – Tel Aviv. 1934. BJ-100-46 1 – 9 – ne IDC [956]
SEFER DANIEL DOS DONIEL BUKH – Cracow. 1588. Cowley. BJ-43-80 1 – 9 – ne IDC [220]
SEFER DIBBER TOV – Cracow. 1590. BJ-43-81 1 – 9 – ne IDC [270]
SEFER DINABURG / Dinur, B – Jerusalem. 1949. BJ-100-47 1 – 9 – ne IDC [956]
SEFER HA-GAN – Cracow. 1579? BJ-43-82 1 – 9 – ne IDC [270]
SEFER HA-GAN – Hanau. c.1620. BJ-43-83 1 – 9 – ne IDC [270]
SEFER HA-HUGGIM SHEL MEMSHELET HA-MANDAT / Israel. Ministry of Justice – (Laws of the Mandat Government). 7 v. BJ-81-30 1 – 9 – ne IDC [320]
SEFER HA-SHANAH / ed by Sokolow, N – v. 1-5. Warsaw. 1900-06. BJ-100-110 1 – 9 – ne IDC [270]
SEFER HA-SHANAH – Warsaw. v. 1-5. 1900-1906 – 1 – us NY Public [072]
SEFER HA-SHANAH – Warsaw. v1-5. 1900-06 – 1r – 1 – us Ross [270]
SEFER HA-SHANAH LI-YHUDEI AMERIKAH – 11 v. in 9. New York. 1931-49. BJ-91-73 1 – 9 – ne IDC [270]
SEFER HA-SHANAH SHEL EREZ YISRA'EL – 2v. Tel Aviv. 1934, 1935. BJ-91-93 1 – 9 – ne IDC [270]
SEFER HA-SHANAH SHEL EREZ YISRA'EL – v. 1-2. Tel Aviv. 1923-26. BJ-91-74 1 – 9 – ne IDC [270]
SEFER HA-SHANAH SHEL HA-ITTONA'IM – v. 1-33. Tel Aviv. 1942-74. BJ-91-75 1 – 9 – ne IDC [270]
SEFER HA-SHORASHIM = HEBREW BIBLICAL LEXICON / David ben Joseph Kimhi – (In Hebrew) – Venice, 1546 – 5mf – H-8442/1 – ne IDC [220]
SEFER HA-TAKKANOT VE-HA-HASKAMOT – Jerusalem. 1842. BJ-27-2 1 – 9 – ne IDC [956]
SEFER HA-YOVEL LE B. M. LEWIN / Lewin, B M – Jerusalem. 1940. BJ-100-53 1 – 9 – ne IDC [470]
SEFER HA-YOVEL LE-AHARON KAMINKA / Kaminka, A I – Vienna. 1937. BJ-100-58 1 – 9 – ne IDC [900]
SEFER HA-YOVEL LE-LEVI GINZBERG / Ginzberg, L – v. 1-2. New York. 1945. BJ-100-52 1 – 9 – ne IDC [900]
SEFER HA-YOVEL LE-MORDEKHAY ZE'EV BRAUDE / Braude, M – Warsaw. 1931. BJ-100-51 1 – 9 – ne IDC [900]
SEFER HA-YOVEL LE-NAHUM SOKOLOW / Sokolow, N – Warsaw. 1904. BJ-100-56 1 – 9 – ne IDC [956]
SEFER HA-YOVEL LE-YA'AKOV ROSENHEIM / Rosenheim, J – Frankfurt a.M. 1931. BJ-100-60 1 – 9 – ne IDC [270]
SEFER HA-YOVEL LI-KHEVOD ALEXANDER MARX / Marx, Alexander – New York. 1943. BJ-100-54 1 – 9 – ne IDC [900]
SEFER HA-YOVEL LIKHVOD NAHUM SOKOLOW – Warsaw. 1904. BJ-422-76 1 – 9 – ne IDC [470]
SEFER HA-YOVEL LI-SHEMU'EL KRAUSS / Krauss, S – Jerusalem. 1936. BJ-100-59 1 – 9 – ne IDC [900]
SEFER HA-YOVEL LI-YEHUDAH LEIB HA-KOHEN FISHMAN / Maimon. (Fishman, J L) – Jerusalem. 1926. BJ-100-57 1 – 9 – ne IDC [999]
SEFER HA-YOVEL. MOSHEH ARYEH BLOCH / Bloch, Moses – Budapest. 1905. BJ-100-50 1 – 9 – ne IDC [900]
SEFER HA-ZIKHRONOT / Friedberg, A S – Warsaw. 1899. BJ-422-17 1 – 9 – ne IDC [470]
SEFER HA-ZIKKARON LE-VEIT HA-MIDRASH LE-RABBANIM BE-VINAH, YOZE LA-OR LI-MELOT ME'AH SHANIM LE-HULEDET R. ARYEH SCHWARZ / Schwarz, A – Jerusalem. 1946. BJ-100-78 1 – 9 – ne IDC [956]
SEFER HE-'ARUKH = A TALMUDICAL DICTIONARY, WITH AN INDEX OF PASSAGES BY SAMUEL ARCHIVOLTI / Nathan ben Jehiel, of Rome – (In Hebrew and Aramaic) – Venice, 5413 A.M. c. 1553 A.D. – 6mf – 9 – H-8439/1 – ne IDC [470]
SEFER IYYOV – Prague. 1597. Cowley. BJ-43-84 1 – 9 – ne IDC [220]
SEFER JAWITZ / Jawitz, Z – Tel-Aviv. 1934. BJ-100-83 1 – 9 – ne IDC [900]
SEFER KLAUSNER / Klausner, J G – Tel Aviv. 1937. BJ-100-62 1 – 9 – ne IDC [900]
SEFER MAGNES / Magnes, J L – Jerusalem. 1938. BJ-100-61 1 – 9 – ne IDC [270]
SEFER MELAKHIM DOS MLOKHIM BUKH – Cracow. 1582. Cowley. BJ-43-85 1 – 9 – ne IDC [220]
SEFER METURGEMAN. LEXICON CHALDAICVM / Levita, E – Isny. 1541 [1542] – 7mf – ne IDC [470]
SEFER MIDDOT – Isny. 1542. BJ-43-87 1 – 9 – ne IDC [270]
SEFER MISHLE – Cracow. 1582. Cowley. BJ-43-88 1 – 9 – ne IDC [270]
SEFER NAMEH, RELATION DU VOYAGE EN SYRIE / Khosrau, Nassiri & Schefer, C – 1881 – 9 – fr Orientalistes [910]
SEFER PESHER DAVAR / Reifmann, J – Warsaw, 1845 – 9 – BJ-100-15 1 – ne IDC [270]

SEFER PINSKER / Pinsker, L – Jerusalem. 1921. BJ-100-63 1 – 9 – ne IDC [920]
SEFER RASHI, KOVEZ TORANI-MADDA'I / Rashi – Jerusalem. 1941. BJ-100-84 1 – 9 – ne IDC [270]
SEFER SHEL RABBI ANSHEL VE-HU MIRKEVET HA-MISHNEH – Cracow. 1584. BJ-43-90 1 – 9 – ne IDC [270]
SEFER SHEMUEL – (Shmuel Bukh). Basle. 1612. Cowley. BJ-43-92 1 – 9 – ne IDC [220]
SEFER SHIR HA-SHIRIM – Cracow. 1579. Cowley. BJ-43-93 1 – 9 – ne IDC [270]
SEFER TEHILLIM – Venice. 1545. Cowley. BJ-43-94 1 – 9 – ne IDC [270]
SEFER TEHILLIM – Zurich. 1558. Cowley. BJ-43-95 1 – 9 – ne IDC [270]
SEFER TOLDOT YESHU: BOOK OF THE GENERATION OF JESUS – New York: D.M. Bennett, 1879. 1 fiche – 9 – us A.T.L.A. [240]
SEFER TUROV / Touroff, N – Boston. 1938. BJ-100-49 1 – 9 – ne IDC [956]
SEFER USSISHKIN / Ussishkin, A M M – Jerusalem. 1934. BJ-100-45 1 – 9 – ne IDC [956]
SEFER YEHEZKEL IN TAYTSHN – Prague. 1602. Cowley. BJ-43-96 1 – 9 – ne IDC [220]
SEFER YEHOSHUA – (Yehoyshue Bukh). Cracow. 1594. Cowley. BJ-43-97 1 – 9 – ne IDC [220]
SEFER YETSIRAH = DAS BUCH DER SCHOEPFUNG / Goldschmidt, Lazarus – Frankfurt a.M.: J. Kauffmann, 1894. 1 fiche – 9 – us A.T.L.A. [270]
SEFER YETSIRAH...A BOOK ON CREATION, OR, THE JEWISH METAPHYSICS OF REMOTE ANTIQUITY / Kalisch, Isador – New York: L.H. Frank, 1877. 1 fiche – 9 – us A.T.L.A. [270]
SEFER YOHANAN LEWY / Lewy, Y – Jerusalem. 1949. BJ-100-82 1 – 9 – ne IDC [270]
SEFER ZIKKARON / Rabinovitz, AZ – Tel-Aviv. 1924. BJ-100-48 1 – 9 – ne IDC [470]
SEFER ZIKKARON : STUDIES IN JEWISH THEOLOGY – London, 1950 – 9 – ne IDC [270]
SEFER ZIKKARON LE-ASHER GULAK VELI-SHEMU'EL KLEIN / Gulak, A & Klein, S – Jerusalem. 1942. BJ-100-79 1 – 9 – ne IDC [956]
SEFER ZIKKARON LE-YIZHAK YEHUDAH GOLDZIHER / Goldziher, I – v. 1. Budapest. 1948; v. 2. Jerusalem. 1958. Lacking: 1955. BJ-100-88 1 – 9 – ne IDC [900]
SEFER ZIKKARON. LIVRE D'HOMMAGE A. S. POZNANSKI / Poznanski, S A – Warsaw. 1927. BJ-100-81 1 – 9 – ne IDC [956]
SEFFLEPOSTEN – Karlstad, Sweden. 1894-95 – 1 reel – 1 – sw Kungliga [072]
SEFFLETIDNINGEN – Saeffle, 1894-1924 – 9 – sw Kungliga [072]
Seffrin, John R *see* INTERRELATIONSHIPS AMONG STRESS, SOCIAL SUPPORT, HEALTH BEHAVIORS AND SELF-ASSESSED HEALTH STATUS
SEG: SUPPLEMENTUM EPIGRAPHICUM GRAECUM – Alphen aan den Rijn (etc.): Sijthoff & Noordhoff. v1- 1923-. Annual. Suspended 1972-75 – 1 – us U.W. Library [410]
Segal, Bernard *see* DRUGS AND SOCIETY
Segarra, Jose y Joaquin Julia *see* LA RUTA DE HERNANDO CORTES
SEGEBERGER ZEITUNG – Bad Segeberg, Germany. May 1976- – ca 6r per yr – 1 – gw Mikrofilm [072]
SEGELSURFEN IM SCHULSPORT / Boll, Stefan – 1994 – 2mf – DM80.00 – 3-8267-2050-4 – gw Hänsel [790]
SEGERING KEMBANG ALUM / Purwono, P H – In Javanese. SE-5602 1. 1965 – 9 – ne IDC [950]
Segesser, H *see* KOMOEDIE DER IRRUNGEN
Seghers, Anna *see* AUFSTAND DER FISCHER VON ST BARBARA
Segneri, Paolo *see*
- IL QUARESIMALE
- QUARESIMALE

SEGODNIA – (Many missing nos) – Riga. 1923-25, 1927-35, 1937-40 – 65r – 1 – RF-763/3 – ne IDC [072]
SEGODNIA / ed by Ostal'skii, D V – Moscow: Segodnia, 1993- – 2mf – 9 – $199.95y – us East View [320]
SEGODNYA – Moscow. U.S.S.R. no. 1-154. 22 Aug, 4 Sep 1906-21 Feb, 6 Mar 1907 – 1 – us NY Public [072]
SEGODNYA – Riga, U.S.S.R. -d. 1 Dec 1929-31 Dec 1935; 4 Sept 1939-21 June 1940. 1940 imperfect. 16 reels – 1 – uk British Libr Newspaper [947]
Segoing, Charles *see* MERCURE ARMORIAL, ENSEIGNANT LES PRINCIPES ET ELEMENS DU BLAZON DES ARMOIRIES
Segond, Frederique *see* GRAMMAIRE CATEGORIELLE DU FRANCAIS. ETUDE THEORIQUE ET IMPLANTATION. LE SYSTEME GRACE (GRAMMAIRE CATEGORIELLE ETENDUE)
Segonzac, M R de *see* DANS L'OUEST AFRICAIN
Segovia, A *see* FIGURAS Y FIGURONES, BIOGRAFIAS DE LOS HOMBRES QUE MAS FIGURAN ACTUALMENTE EN ESPANA. 2 VOL
LE SEGREEN – L'hebdomadaire de l'arrondissement de Segre. Segre. mai 1945-61 – 1 – fr A.C.R.P.P. [073]
SEGUALAZION ORIZZONTALI IN SPAGUE / Agundez Fernandez, Antonio – Roma: Tip. Luigi Morara, 1958 – 1 – sp Bibl Santa Ana [945]
Seguer, Mariano *see* CARTA DEL DOCTOR MARIANO SEGUER...A UN ERUDITO Y SABIO...
SEGUIDILLAS / Sanchez-Arjona, Vicente – Sevilla: Imp. Cuadrado, 1957 – 1 – sp Bibl Santa Ana [810]
Seguier, J F *see* BIBLIOTHECA BOTANICA, SIVE CATALOGUS AUCTORUM...
Seguin, Charles *see* MANUEL D'ARCHITECTURE OU PRINCIPES DES OPERATIONS PRIMITIVES DE CET ART
Seguin de Pazzis, Maxime *see* MEMOIRE STATISTIQUE SUR LE DEPARTEMENT DU VAUCLUSE
Seguin, J-O *see* LE JOURNAL DE WATERLOO
Seguin, M *see* LA CHASSE AU FILET DANS LA REGION DU POOL
SEGUN LOS ANOS...!SE PIENSA! / Sanchez-Arjona, Vicente – Sevilla: Imp. Zambrano, Libros 1-3. 1957 – 1 – sp Bibl Santa Ana [810]
LA SEGUNDA IMPRENTA DE CORDOBA / Cabrera, Pablo – Cordoba...1930; Madrid: Razon y Fe, 1932 – 1 – sp Bibl Santa Ana [972]
SEGUNDA PARTE DA MEMORIA ESTATISTICA SOBRE OS DOMINIOS PORTUQUEZES NA AFRICA ORIENTAL / Botelho, S X. – Lisboa. 1837. BA-282 2 – 8 – ne IDC [910]
SEGUNDA PARTE DE LA CRONICA...INCAS YUPANQUIS.. / Cieza Leon, Pedro de – 1880 – 9 – 1.50f – sp Bibl Santa Ana [972]
SEGUNDA PARTE DEL OBSERVATORIO RUSTICO, DONDE SE HACE UNA DESCRIPCION POETICA DE LA VIDA PACIFICA Y SUS VENTAJAS / Salas, Francisco Gregorio de – Madrid: Libreria Josef Ferrer, 1774 – 1 – sp Bibl Santa Ana [440]
SEGUNDA PARTE DEL USO DE LA ARCHITECTURA...CON LAS ORDENANZAS DE LA IMPERIAL CIUDAD DE TOLEDO / Lorenzo de San Nicolas, Fray – SL, SA – 8mf – 9 – sp Cultura [720]
SEGUNDA PARTE...MONOLOGOS DE LA INFANCIA / Redondo y Poblacion, Pedro – 1893 – 9 – 1.50f – sp Bibl Santa Ana [370]
EL SEGUNDA PLAN QUINQUENAL EN LA ENSENANZA MEDIA : DESARROLLO DE LOS PROGRAMAS DEL CIBLO BASICO EN LOS PUNTOS QUE HACEN REFERENCIA AL 2 PLAN QUINQUENA / Garcia, Oscar J & Zelicman, Cecilio – [Buenos Aires]: Hemisferio, [1953] – 1 – CSUXAGN1675-B – us Hoover Inst Photo [972]
SEGUNDA PROPOSICION DEL DOCTOR SOBRE LA ENFERMEDAD QUE ANDA EN SEVILLA / Sanchez, F – Sevilla, 1599 – 1mf – 9 – sp Cultura [610]
SEGUNDO CENSO DE LA REPUBLICA VENEZOLANA. ANO 1881 – Caracas, 1881 – 9mf – 9 – sp Cultura [304]
Segundo, Llorente *see* EN EL PAIS DE LOS ETERNOS HIELOS
SEGUNDO MANIFIESTO...CONTRA EL DOCTOR IVAN BERNES / Mayorga y Guzman, D – Zaragoza, 1675 – 3mf – 9 – sp Cultura [610]
EL SEGUNDO PLAN QUINQUENAL Y EL PODER JUDICIAL : CONFERENCIA PRONUNCIADA EL 23 DE JUNIO DE 1953 / Coronas, Juan Enrique – Buenos Aires: [s.n.], 1953 – 1 – CSUXAGQ4367-B – us Hoover Inst Photo [320]
SEGUNDO PLAN SEXENAL, 1941-1946 / Mexico – 1939 – 9 – ne IDC [338]
SEGUNDO PLANO DE FOMENTO, 1959-64 / Cape Verde Islands – D-998-1 – 9 – ne IDC [338]
SEGUNDO PLANO DIRECTOR DE DESENVOLVIMENTO ECONOMICA E SOCIAL DO NORDESTE, 1963-65 / Brazil. Superintendencia do Desenvolvimento do Nordeste – Recife. 1966. BD-1834 1 – 9 – ne IDC [338]
EL SEGUNDO TRIBUNE – El Segundo, CA. 1965-1972 – 5r – 1 – $250.00 – H04010 – us Library Micro [071]
Segur, Louis Gaston *see*
- CAUSERIES SUR LE PROTESTANTISME D'AUJOURD'HUI. ENGLISH
- DER GLAUBE DER MODERNEN WISSENSCHAFT GEGENUEBER

Segur, Sophie, Comtesse de *see*
- HISTOIRE DE BLONDINE, DE BONNE-BICHE ET DE BEAU-MINON
- HISTOIRE DE LA PRINCESSE ROSETTE
- LA PETITE SOURIS GRISE

Segura Covarsi, Enrique *see*
- APORTACIONES AL LENGUAJE DE TORRES NAHARRO
- INDICE DE LA REVISTA DE OCCIDENTE
- EL PLATERESCO EN LA LITERATURA EXTREMENA

Segura de la Garmilla, Ramon *see* EJEMPLOS DE ORTOGRAFIA ESPANOLA...
Segura, Enrique *see* GUY DE MAUPASSANT A TRAVES DE LA CORRESPONDENCIA DE GUSTAVO FLAUBERT
Segura Otano, Enrique *see*
- CARTAS DE ARTURO GAZUL A FERNANDO VILLALBA
- EL ESCULTOR EXTREMENO JUAN DE AVALOS
- UN MONTERO GENIAL
- NOTAS BIOGRAFICAS DE ANTONIO RODRIGUEZ MONINO
- PERSONAJES DEL SIGLO 18

Segura Saenz, Pedro *see* EN LA CATEDRAL DE TOLEDO
SEGURIDAD SOCIAL EN LA ARGENTINA / Arce, Jose – Buenos Aires, Editorial Losada, s.a. [1945] – 1 – CSUXADJ0165-B – us Hoover Inst Photo [360]
EL SEGURO DE ENFERMEDAD EN EL MUNDO Y EN NUESTRA PATRIA / Marcos Calleja, Leopoldo – Caceres: Tip. El Noticiero, 1950 – sp Bibl Santa Ana [360]
SEGYE ILBO – (Formerly: Segye Sinbo) – New York, NY. 1988-1990 – 21r – 1 – us L of C Photodup [071]
SEGYE SINBO *see* SEGYE ILBO
SEHBAL – Istanbul: 1909-1914 – 9 – $300.00 – us MEDOC [956]
Seheult, Francois-L *see* RECUEIL D'ARCHITECTURE, DESSINE ET MESURE EN ITALIE...
Sehling, Emil *see*
- DIE EVANGELISCHEN KIRCHENORDNUNGEN DES 16. JAHRHUNDERTS
- GESCHICHTE DER PROTESTANTISCHEN KIRCHENVERFASSUNG

SEHNSUCHT / Hart, Julius – Berlin: S Fischer, 1893 – 1r – 1 – us U.W. Library [830]
Sehring, Wilhelm *see* DIE CENSORIADE
SEI DUETTI NOTTURNI PER DUE FLAUTI...3 OEUVRE / Dothel, Nicholas – c.1750 – 9 – us Sibley [780]
SEI QUARTETTI CON FUGHE PER DIVERSI STROMENTI... / Albrechtsberger, Johann G – Vienne: Artaria, [179-?] – 1 – us Sibley [780]
SEI QUARTETTI, OP. 9 / Demachi, G – (Parts) – Lyon: Guera, 1775? – 1 – us Sibley [780]
SEI QUARTETTI...OP. 26. [G. 183-188] / Boccherini, Luigi – (Parts) – Paris: M de la Chevardiere, 1775? – 1 – us Sibley [780]
SEI QUARTETTI...OP. 33. G. 201-206 / Boccherini, Luigi – Vienna: Artaria Co, 1781? – 1 – us Sibley [780]
SEI QUARTETTI...OP.26, G. 183-188 / Boccherini, Luigi – (Parts) – Paris: Le Duc, 178- – 1 – us Sibley [780]
SEI QUINTETTI PER DUE VIOLINI, ALTOS E DUE VIOLONCELLO CONCERTANTI...OPERA 23 / Boccherini, Luigi – (pts) – Paris: Chez M Venier – 1 – us Sibley [780]
SEI SEXTOUR PER DUE VIOLINI, VIOLA, DUE VIOLONCELLE E FLAUTO. OP. 15, G. 461-466 / Boccherini, Luigi – (Parts) – 1 – us Sibley [780]
SEI SINFONIE O SIA QUARTETTI...PER DUE VIOLINI, ALTO E VIOLONCELLO OBBLIGATI / Boccherini, Luigi – 1767 – 9 – us Sibley [780]
SEI SONATE A TRE, OP. 3. G. 119-124 / Boccherini, Luigi – (Parts) – ca 1770 – 1 – us Sibley [780]
SEI SRIE WITH CHAMBER MUSIC ACCONPANIMENT, OP. 4 / Giardini, F de – Author, 175- – 1 – us Sibley [780]
SEI TRII PER 2 VIOLONCELLO / Gasparini, F – (3 pts in 3 vols) – London: Johnson, 176- – 1 – us Sibley [780]
SEI TRIJ PER VIOLINO, VIOLA, E VIOLONCELLO CONCERTANTI, OP. 18 / Cirri, G B – (Parts) – Venezia: A Zatta e Figli, 1791 – 1 – us Sibley [780]
SEI TRIO E UNA SERENATA PER DUE VIOLINI E VIOLONCELLO OBBLIGATO, CON UNA PARTE DI PIU DA ESEGUIRSI CON LA VIOLA IN VOCE DEL VIOLONCELLO / Marescalchi, L – (4 pts) – [Naples, 179-?] – 1 – us Sibley [780]
SEI TRIO PER DUE VIOLINI... / Boccherini, Luigi – (2nd violin part only) – 1 – us Sibley [780]
SEI TRIO PER DUS VIOLINI E VIOLONCELLO OBBLIGATO... / Boccherini, Luigi – (Parts) – Venezia: Luigi Marescalchi, ca 1775 – 1 – us Sibley [780]
SEI TRITETTI PER DUE VIOLINI ET BASSO, OP.2. G. 77-82 / Boccherini, Luigi – Paris: Bailleux, 177- – 1 – us Sibley [780]
SEIATEL' PRAVDY – (Missing: 1925 n71) – Samara, 1924-27 n58 – 72mf – 9 – COR-686/1 – ne IDC [334]
Seibert, Grant *see* "HISTORY OF SEIBERT AND BOESE FAMILIES."
Seid, Bradford S *see* THE PERCEPTIONS OF RESIDENTS OF MONROE COUNTY ON THE IMPACT OF TOURISM IN MONROE COUNTY, PA.
Seidel, E *see* MECHITHAR'S DES MEISTERARTZES AUS HER "TROST BEI FIEBERN"
Seidel, Heinrich *see*
- GESAMMELTE SCHRIFTEN
- KINDERLIEDER UND GESCHICHTEN
- LEBERECHT HUEHNCHEN
- REINHARD FLEMMINGS ABENTEUER ZU WASSER UND ZU LANDE
- VORSTADTGESCHICHTEN

Seidel, Ina *see*
- ACHIM VON ARNIM
- BETTINA
- HOCHWASSER
- THE LABYRINTH
- WELTINNIGKEIT

Seidel, Kerstin *see* ABRUF VERBALER ODER VISUELLER INOFRMATIONEN BEIM ENTSTEHEN EINER KINDERZEICHNUNG
Seidel, Martin *see* ZUR ZEIT JESU
Seidel, Matthias Frank *see* METHODOLOGISCHE UNTERSUCHUNGEN ZUR ISOLIERUNG VON HIRNRINDENARTERIOLEN DES MEERSCHWEINCHENS UND KULTUR VON GEFAESSWANDZELLEN
Seidel, Robert *see* AUS KAMPFGEWUEHL UND EINSAMKEIT
Seidel, Siegfried *see* GOTTHOLD EPHRAIM LESSING
Seidel, Wolfgang *see* THEODOR STORMS BRIEFE AN FRIEDRICH EGGERS
SEIDELS REKLAME – Berlin. 1914. 1920-21. apr 1922-23 n1. jan-may 1925. feb, oct-nov 1926. 1927-sep 1928. oct-dec 1929. 1932-34. mar 1943 – 9r – 1 – gw Mikrofilm [380]
Seidensticker, Johann Anton Ludwig *see* EINLEITUNG IN DEN CODEX NAPOLEON
Seidl, Arthur *see* HAT RICHARD WAGNER EINE SCHULE HINTERLASSEN?
Seidl, Florian *see* DER BAU
Seidl, Johann Gabriel *see* JOHANN GABRIEL SEIDL, SEINE SAGEN UND GESCHICHTEN..
Seidlitz, G C M von *see* DIE BILBUNGSGESETZE DER VOGELZIER
Seidman, Ruth K *see* SCIENCE AND TECHNOLOGY LIBRARIES
SEIFENSIEDER-ZEITUNG – Augsburg, 1901-09. – 10,5r – 1 – uk British Libr Newspaper [680]
Seiffert, Hans Werner *see* FESTGABE FUER EDUARD BEREND, ZUM 75. GEBURTSTAG, AM 5. DEZEMBER 1958
Seifriz, J J *see* THE RELATIONSHIP OF PERCEIVED MOTIVATIONAL CLIMATE TO ACHIEVEMENT-RELATED AFFECT AND COGNITIONS IN A SPORT SETTING

SEIGNEURIES DE MONTREAL, DES DEUX-MONTAGNES ET DE SAINT SULPICE (1640-1931) / Seminaire Saint Sulmipe de Montreal. Archives – Montreal, Canada – 16r – 1 – cn Can Microfilming [971]
SEIGNEURS ET CENSITAIRES, CASTES DISPARUES / Morin, Victor – Montreal, 1941. SEM105P761 – 2mf – 9 – Can$4.50 – cn Bibl Nat [305]
THE SEIGNIORIAL ACTS: VIZ: THE SEIGNIORIAL ACT OF 1854, 16 VICT. CAP. 3 / Canada. Laws, Statutes, etc – Toronto: Derbishire and Desbarats, 1856. 63p LL-2372 – 1 – us L of C Photodup [340]
THE SEIGNIORIAL ACTS: VIZ: THE SEIGNIORIAL ACT OF 1854...THE SEIGNIORIAL AMENDMENT ACT OF 1855...THE SEIGNIORIAL AMENDMENT ACT OF 1856.. – Toronto: S Derbishire and G Desbarats, 1856. SEM105P268 – 1mf – 9 – Can$2.25 – cn Bibl Nat [971]
Seignobos, C *see* INTRODUCTION TO THE STUDY OF HISTORY
Seignobos, Charles *see*
- HISTOIRE DE LA CIVILISATION CONTEMPORAINE
- A POLITICAL HISTORY OF EUROPE SINCE 1814
- TARIKH AL-TAMADDUN AL-HADITH

SEIGNORIAL QUESTIONS: A COMPILATION CONTAINING THE SEIGNORIAL ACT OF 1854, THE AMENDMENT TO THE SEIGNORIAL ACT OF 1854 – Partly at Quebec by A Cote; partly at Montreal by Duvernay Bros., 1856. SEM105P245 – 13mf – 9 – Can$29.25 – cn Bibl Nat [971]
Seikado Library. Tokyo *see* KAGAKU SHIRYO SHUSEI
Seiler, Friedrich *see*
- DIE BEHANDLUNG DES SITTLICHEN PROBLEMS IN SCHILLERS "KAMPF MIT DEM DRACHEN", DER ERZAEHLUNG BEI LIVIUS 8, 7, KLEISTS "PRINZ VON HOMBURG" UND SOPHOKLES' "ANTIGONE"
- DER ENTWICKLUNG DER DEUTSCHEN KULTUR IM SPIEGEL DES DEUTSCHEN LEHNWORTS

Seilhac, Leon de *see* LES CONGRES OUVRIERS EN FRANCE DE 1876 A 1897
Seiling, Max *see* GOETHE UND DER OKKULTISMUS
SEIN BAUERNMAEDCHEN : LEBENSBILD DER EHEGEFAEHRTIN VON MATTHIAS CLAUDIUS / Fleischhack, Marianne – (Includes bibliographical references) – Berlin: Evangelische Verlagsanstalt, 1966 – 1 – us U.W. Library [920]
SEIN LEBEN, SEIN WERKEN UND SEINE MITTHEILUNGEN UBER DIE FREYMAUREREY / Ramsay, M A – 4mf – ne IDC [360]
SEIN UND SOLLEN DES MENSCHEN BEI IMMANUEL HERMANN FICHTE : VON SPAETIDEALISTISCHER SPEKULATION ZUR EXISTENZ / Ebert, Johannes – Wuerzburg, 1938 – 151p – 9 – DM48.00 – 3-89349-008-6 – gw Hänsel [190]
SEIN ZWILLINGSBRUDER : LUSTSPIEL IN FUENF AUFZUEGEN / Jordan, Wilhelm – Frankfurt a.M.: W Jordan, 1883 – 1r – 1 – us U.W. Library [820]
SEINE MAJESTAET, DER REKRUT : DAS LUSTIGSTE AUS MEINEM SOLDATENLEBEN / Paust, Otto – 5. Aufl. Muenchen: F Eher, 1944 – 1r – 1 – us U.W. Library [920]
Seiner, F *see* ERGEBNISSE EINER BEREISUNG DES GEBIETS ZWISCHEN OKAWANGO
DER SEINSBEGRIFF BEI BOETHIUS / Brosch, Hermann Josef – Innsbruck, 1931 – 3mf – 8 – ne Slangenburg [140]
DER SEINSBEGRIFF BEI BOETHIUS : MIT BESONDERER BERUECKSICHTIGUNG DER BEZIEHUNG VON SOSEIN UND DASEIN / Brosch, Hermann Josef – Innsbruck, 1931 – 2mf – 9 – DM62.00 – 3-89349-309-3 – gw Hänsel [110]
Seipel, I *see*
- NATION UND STAAT
- DIE WIRTSCHAFTSETHISCHEN LEHREN DER KIRCHENVAETER

Seipt, Allen Anders *see* SCHWENKFELDER HYMNOLOGY AND THE SOURCES OF THE FIRST SCHWENKFELDER HYMN-BOOK PRINTED IN AMERICA
SEIS FORMULAS DE CEBO CONTRA LA LANGOSTA / Moreno Marquez, Victor – Madrid: Estacion de Fitopatologia Agricola, 1940. Publicacion no 6 – 1 – sp Bibl Santa Ana [630]
SEIS INSCRIPCIONES ROMANAS EN TIERRAS CACERENAS / Ramon Fernandez Oxea, Jose – Madrid: Maestre, 1962 – 1 – sp Bibl Santa Ana [946]
LOS SEIS LIBROS DE JUAN CRISOSTOMO / Scio de San Miguel, Felipe – 1773 – 1mf – 9 – Pta1,000.00 – 84-7848-351-9 – sp Pentalfa [440]
SEIS MESES DE ANARQUIA EN EXTREMADURA / Diaz de Entresotos, Baldomero – Caceres: Editorial Extremadura, 1937 – 1 – sp Bibl Santa Ana [946]
SEIS MESES DE SOLIDARIDAD ANTIFASCISTA / International Red Aid. Spain. (Socorro Rojo de Espana) – np, 1937 – 9 – fiche W1157il War Pamphlets) – us H.U. College Libr [946]
SEIS ROMANCES DE LA GUERRA CIVIL. JOSE MORENO VILLA, RAFAEL ALBERTI, MIGUEL HERNANDEZ, MANUEL ALTOLAGUIRRE, ERNESTO LOPEZ PARRS – n.p., 1937? Fiche W1158. (Blodgett Collection of Spanish Civil War Pamphlets) – 9 – us H.U. College Libr [946]
SEISCIENTOS SONETOS / Sanchez-Arjona, Vicente – Sevilla: Imp. Carlos Acuna, 1949 – 1 – sp Bibl Santa Ana [810]
SEISMIC ZONES IN INDONESIA / Soetadi, R – 1962. 10p, fold., maps. (Indonesia. Djawatan Meteorologi dan Geofisik. Geophysical notes, no.2) – 9 – ne IDC [550]
SEISMIC ZONES IN INDONESIA / Sutadi, R – Also bound in: Hubungan Antara Intensity Dan Djarak Epicenter, by Supomo. SE 6605 1. 1962 – 9 – ne IDC [550]
Seiss, Joseph Augustus *see*
- THE GOSPEL IN LEVITICUS
- VOICES FROM BABYLON

SEIT WANN GIEBT ES EINE PREDIGT IN DEUTSCHER SPRACHE? : BEANTWORTET DURCH DIE GESCHICHTE DER PREDIGT IN DEUTSCHLAND VON 814-1100 / Albert, F R – Guetersloh: C. Bertelsmann, 1893. (Die Geschichte der Predigt in Deutschland bis Luther / von F.R. Albert; 2. T.) – 1mf – us A.T.L.A. [240]
SEIT WANN KANNTEN DIE CHINESEN DIE TOCHARER ODER INDOGERMANEN UEBERHAUPT / Haloun, G – v. 1. Leipzig. 1926. (Unfinished publication). BU-562 2 – 8 – ne IDC [900]
Seiterich, Eugen *see* DIE GOTTESBEWEISE BEI FRANZ BRENTANO
LE SEJOUR DES ISRAELITES AU DESERT ET LE SINAI DANS LA RELATION PRIMITIVE : L'EVOLUTION DU TEXTE BIBLIQUE ET LA TRADITION CHRISTIANO-MODERNE / Weill, Raymond – (Includes bibliographical references) – Paris: Paul Geuthner, 1909 – 1mf – 9 – 0-8370-5741-8 – 1985-3741 – us A.T.L.A. [220]
Sejourne, P *see* SAINT ISIDORE DE SEVILLE
SEKAI BUNKA = WORLD CULTURE – Japan, 1935-37 – 3r – 1 – inquire – us Ross [073]
SEKEDAR TENTANG BIBLIOGRAFI NASIONAL, DENGAN TAMBAHAN TEKS BAHASA INGGERIS: SOME NOTES ON CURRENT NATIONAL BIBLIOGRAPHICAL AND OTHER DOCUMENTAL ACTIVITIES IN INDONESIA / Gunung Agung, n.v. Djakarta – SE 2852 1. 1960 – 9 – ne IDC [010]
SEKELUMIT UNSUR FILOSOFIK ARDJUNA WIWAHA (TJIPTAAN MPU KANWA) DIBUBUHI BEBERAPA TJATATAN PINGGIR / Sastroamidjojo, Achmad Seno – SE 4844 1. 1963 – 9 – ne IDC [950]
SEKITAR PERATURAN PEMERINTAH PENGGANTI UNDANG UNDANG TAHUN 1960 NO. 19 TENTANG PERUSAHAAN NEGARA / Tirtodiningrat, D – SE 4495 1. 1960 – 9 – ne IDC [950]
SEKITAR WALP SANGA / Solichin Salam – SE 4482 1. 1963 – 9 – ne IDC [950]
SEKITER PROKLAMASI 17 AGUSTUS 1945 / Sidik Kertapati – SE 2089 1. 1957 – 9 – ne IDC [950]
SEKOLAH LANDJUTAN UMUM – Incomplete. SE 504 1. 1952-1971 – 9 – ne IDC [950]
SEKOLAH TINGGI RAKJAT. FOLK HIGH SCHOOL / Sumodiwirjo, Teko – SE 4385 1. 1954 – 9 – ne IDC [370]
Sekretariat der Internationalen Arbeiter-Assoziation *see* DIE INTERNATIONALE
SEKTA PASHKOVTSEV" I RAZGOVOR" PRAVOSLAVNAGO S" PASHKOVTSEM" = THE SECT OF THE PASHKOVITES AND A CONVERSATION OF AN ORTHODOX WITH A PASHKOVITE – St. Petersburg, 1895 – 1r – 1 – $5.00 – us Baptist [240]
SEKTANTSTVO I MIROVAYA VOINA = SECTARIANISM AND THE WORLD WAR / Kandidov, Boris Pavlovich – Moscow, 1930. One of 13 titles by Soviet authors on reel – 1 – 74.32 – us Baptist [240]
SEKTANTSTVO PREZHDE I TEPER' = SECTARIANISM PAST AND PRESENT / Lukachevdkii, Aleksandr Timofeevich (Emelyan Yaroslavdkii) – Moscow, 1925. One of 13 titles by Soviet authors on reel – 1 – 74.32 – us Baptist [240]
Sektor narodno-khozi a istvennogo ucheta Zapsibkra iplana *see* BI UDZHETY GORODSKOGO NASELENII A SIBIRI ZA 1928-29 I 1929-30 G.G.
SEKTZIYA STATISTIKI SOTZIAL'NOVE SOSTAVA I DVIZHENIYA NASELENIYA. YESTESTVENNOE DVIZHENIE NACELENIYA SSSR / U.S.S.R. Tzentral'noye Statisticheskoye Upravleniye – Moskow. T 1. 1923-1926 – 1 – us NY Public [310]
SELAMET – Selanik. Mueduer: A. Kemaleddin; Muharriri: M. Salahaddin, 1921-19? – 9 – $25.00 – us MEDOC [956]
Selangor *see* GOVERNMENT GAZETTE
Selassie, Besear Kifle *see* CONSENSUS AND PEACE
SELBER TAGBLATT : BA DER FRANKENPOST – Selb-Hof, Germany. 2 Okt 1978- – ca 8r per yr – 1 – gw Mikrofilm [072]
Selbie, W B *see*
- THE LIFE OF ANDREW MARTIN FAIRBAIRN
- NON-CONFORMITY

Selbmann, Eugen *see* POLITIK FUER DEUTSCHLAND
Selborne, Roundell Palmer *see* LETTERS TO HIS SON ON RELIGION
Selborne, Roundell Palmer, Earl of *see*
- ANCIENT FACTS AND FICTIONS CONCERNING CHURCHES AND TITHES
- HYMNS

Selbst, Joseph *see* JOSEPH LUDWIG COLMAR. BISCHOF VON MAINZ 1802-1818
DIE SELBSTBEHAUPTUNG DER DEUTSCHEN UNIVERSITAET / Heidegger, M – 1933 – 1mf – 8 – ne Slangenburg [370]
SELBSTBETRACHTUNGEN / Wassermann, Jakob – 1.-3. Aufl. Berlin: S Fischer, 1933 – 1r – 1 – us U.W. Library [430]
SELBSTBEWUSSTSEIN ALS BILDKATEGORIE : DAS SELBSTBILDNIS BEI REMBRANDT / Marzluf, Arnulf – Frankfurt a.M., 1978 – 1mf – 9 – DM48.00 – 3-89349-392-1 – gw Hänsel [750]
DAS SELBSTBEWUSSTSEIN JESU IM LICHTE DER MESSIANISCHEN HOFFNUNG SEINER ZEIT / Baldensberger, Wilhelm – Strassburg: J.H. Heitz, 1903. 1 fiche – 9 – us A.T.L.A. [240]
EINE SELBSTSCHAU / Zschokke, Heinrich – (Includes bibliographical references) – Aarau: H R Sauerlaender. 2v in 1. 1842 – 1 – us U.W. Library [920]
SELBSTTAETIGE IDENTIFIKATION UND ADAPTION VON PARAMETERN EINER FELDORIENTIERT GEREGELTEN ASYNCHRONMASCHINE / Weidauer, Jens – 1994 – 2mf – 9 – DM80.00 – 3-89349-853-2 – gw Hänsel [621]
SELBSTWEHR – Prague. 1917; Nov 10 1923-1938 – 1 – us NY Public [072]
SELBSTWEHR = SELF DEFENCE – (German weekly) – Prague, CS. v17 no29 20 Jul 1923-v17 no40 2 Oct 1923 – 1r – 1 – $25.00 – cn Can Microfilming [072]
SELBSTWEHR – Unabhaengige Juedische Wochenschrift. Prague. v1-32. 1907-1938. Lacking misc. issues. B350 (Leo Baeck Institute. German-Jewish Periodicals, Pt 1) – 5r – 1 – $340.00 – us UPA [270]
Selby *see* THE WHITE CITY
Selby P *see* HISTORICAL ENCYCLOPEDIA OF ILLINOIS AND HISTORY OF WARREN COUNTY
Selby, P *see* HISTORICAL ENCYCLOPEDIA OF ILLINOIS AND HISTORY OF ROCK ISLAND COUNTY
Selby, P J *see*
- A CATALOGUE OF THE GENERIC AND SUB-GENERIC TYPES OF THE CLASS AVES, BIRDS
- ILLUSTRATIONS OF BRITISH ORNITHOLOGY
- ILLUSTRATIONS OF ORNITHOLOGY

Selby, Thomas Gunn *see* THE MINISTRY OF THE LORD JESUS
Selden, Camilla *see* HEINRICH HEINE'S LETZTE TAGE
Selden, Elizabeth S *see* THE DANCER'S QUEST; ESSAYS ON THE AESTHETIC OF THE CONTEMPORARY DANCE
Selden, J *see* THE HISTORY OF TYTHES
SELDEN'S NOTES OF CASES / New York. (State) – 1v. 1852-54 (all publ) – 4mf – 9 – $6.00 – LLMC 80-046 – us L.L.M.C. [340]
Seldner, K *see* LESSINGS VERHAELTNIS ZUR ALTROEMISCHEN KOMOEDIE
SELECCION DE ANTONIO TOVAR / Donoso Cortes – Ediciones Fe, 2nd ed S.I. 1938 – 1 – sp Bibl Santa Ana [946]
SELECCION DE SUS ESCRITOS, CONFERENCIAS Y DISCURSOS / Peron, Juan Domingo – Buenos Aires: Ediciones Sintesis, [1973] – 1 – CSUXADQ7443-B – us Hoover Inst Photo [320]
SELECCIONES / Sanchez-Arjona, Vicente – Sevilla: Graficas Sevillanas, Tomo 1. 1960 – 1 – sp Bibl Santa Ana [810]
SELECCIONES CONTINUAS / Sanchis Lopez, Manuel – 1mf – 9 – Pta1,000.00 – 84-85422-47-3 – sp Pentalfa [999]
SELECCIONES DEL READER'S DIGEST – (1986-. 1,5,6) – Latin American ed. 1976- – 9 – us UMI [073]
SELECCIONES.IRONIAS.RELAMPAGOS / Sanchez-Arjona, Vicente – Sevilla: Imp. Zambrano, Tomo 1-3. 1959 – 1 – sp Bibl Santa Ana [810]
O SELECIONADO : ORGAO ESTUDANTIL ACREANO – Rio Branco, Acre. 13 Mar 1958 – 1,5,6 – bl Biblioteca [072]
SELECT ANTI-PELAGIAN TREATISES OF ST AUGUSTINE : AND THE ACTS OF THE SECOND COUNCIL OF ORANGE / Bright, William & Augustine, Saint, Bishop of Hippo – Oxford: Clarendon, 1880 – 2mf – us A.T.L.A. [240]
SELECT BIBLIOGRAPHY OF MAURITIUS / Toussaint, A – (Societe de l'histoire de l'ile Maurice). Port Louis. 1951. BA-405 2 – 8 – ne IDC [960]
SELECT CASES AND OTHER AUTHORITIES ON THE LAW OF PRIVATE CORPORATIONS / Warren, Edward Henry – 2d ed. Cambridge Mass. 1919. 1040 p. LL-1318 – 1 – us L of C Photodup [340]
SELECT CASES ON THE LAW OF REAL PROPERTY / Walsh, William Francis – New York, Tompkins 1906 1102 p. LL-1630 – 1 – us L of C Photodup [340]
SELECT COLLECTION OF...SONGS, ETC / Corri, D – London, Edinburgh: Corri, Dussek & Co, 1795? – 1 – us Sibley [780]
THE SELECT COMMITTEE APPOINTED ON THE 21ST DAY OF SEPTEMBER LAST FOR ..INQUIRING INTO THE ACCUSATIONS MADE AGAINST THE MEMBERS OF THE LATE ADMINISTRATION / Canada. (Province). Parlement. Assemblee legislative. Comite... sur les accusations contre la derniere administration – Quebec, 1855. SEM105P645 – 1mf – 9 – Can$2.25 – cn Bibl Nat [971]
Select Committee of the Legislative Assembly *see* REPORT OF THE SELECT COMMITTEE OF THE LEGISLATIVE ASSEMBLY INTO THE CAUSES AND IMPORTANCE OF THE EMIGRATION...
SELECT DIALOGUES / Plato – New and literal version by Henry Cary. New York: Harper & Brothers, 1879. 551p. (Harper's New Classical Library) – 1 – us U.W. Library [450]
SELECT DISCOURSES / Monod, Adolphe et al – New York: Sheldon, Blakeman, 1858 – 1mf – us A.T.L.A. [240]
SELECT DOCUMENTS FROM THE IMMANUEL WALLERSTEIN COLLECTION OF POLITICAL EPHEMERA OF THE LIBERATION MOVEMENTS OF ANGLOPHONE SOUTHERN AFRICA, 1958-1975 – [New Haven, CT]: Yale University Library Photographic Services, 1976 – us Res Libr [960]
SELECT DOCUMENTS FROM THE IMMANUEL WALLERSTEIN COLLECTION OF POLITICAL EPHEMERA OF THE LIBERATION MOVEMENTS OF LUSOPHONE AFRICA, 1954-1974 – New Haven, CT: Yale University Library Photographic Services, 1976 – us Res Libr [960]
SELECT ESSAYS IN ANGLO-AMERICAN LEGAL HISTORY / Association of American Law Schools – Washington Association of American Law Schools. 3v. 1907-09 – 27mf – 9 – $40.50 – LLMC 81-401 – us L.L.M.C. [340]
SELECT FERNS AND LYCOPODS: BRITISH AND EXOTIC / Williams, B S – 7279. 1868 – 9 – ne IDC [580]
SELECT HOMES – (Cont by: Select Homes and Food at v16 no 7 1989) – Vancouver, 1948-89 – 9 – Can$28.00y – cn Micromedia [640]

SELECT HOMES *see* SELECT HOMES AND FOOD

SELECT HOMES AND FOOD – (Cont: Select Homes at v16 no 7 1989. Cont by: Canadian Select Homes at v21 no 7 1994) – Vancouver. v17-20. 1990-93 – 9 – Can$28.00y – cn Micromedia [640]

SELECT HOMES AND FOOD *see*
- CANADIAN SELECT HOMES
- SELECT HOMES

Select Knights of Canada *see* JOURNAL AND ADVOCATE

SELECT LETTERS AND OTHER ORIGINAL DOCUMENTS RELATING TO THE NEW WORLD / Columbus, Christopher – Ed. by R. H. Major. Hakluyt Society – 8mf – 7 – uk Microform Academic [970]

A SELECT LIBRARY OF NICENE AND POST-NICENE FATHERS OF THE CHRISTIAN CHURCH. SECOND SERIES – Trans. into English with prolegomena and notes under ed. super. of Philip Schaff and Henry Wace. New York: Christian Lit. Co., 1890-1900. 14v – 1 – us U.W. Library [240]

SELECT MEDIAEVAL DOCUMENTS : AND OTHER MATERIAL ILLUSTRATING THE HISTORY OF CHURCH AND EMPIRE 754 A.D.-1254 A.D. / ed by Mathews, Shailer – New York; Boston: Silver, Burdett, c1900 – 1mf – us A.T.L.A. [240]

SELECT PAPYRI IN THE HIERATIC CHARACTER FROM THE COLLECTIONS OF THE BRITISH MUSEUM – London, 1841-44. BNE-368 1 – 9 – ne IDC [470]

SELECT PASSAGES ILLUSTRATING MITHRAISM...WITH AN INTRODUCTION / ed by Geden, Alfred Shenington – New York, Toronto: The Macmillan co., 1925. vi,87p – 1 – us U.W. Library [290]

SELECT PLANTS READILY ELIGIBLE FOR INDUSTRIAL CULTURE OR NATURALISATION IN VICTORIA, WITH INDICATIONS OF THEIR NATIVE COUNTRIES AND SOME OF THEIR USES / Mueller, Ferdinand Jakob Heinrich von – Melbourne. 1876; suppl. 3. Melbourne. 1878. B-8088 1 – 9 – ne IDC [631]

SELECT PLEAS IN THE COURT OF ADMIRALITY / ed by Marsden, R G – London, 1894. 2v – 19mf – 9 – H-1299/2 – ne IDC [340]

SELECT POEMS OF WILLIAM BARNES / Barnes, William; ed by Hardy, Thomas – London: H. Frowde, 1908 – 1 roll – 1 – 1-55879-200-7 – uk Libr Preservation [810]

SELECT POEMS...EDITED, WITH INTRODUCTIONS, NOTES, AND APPENDICES, BY FRANCIS P. SIMPSON / Catullus, Gaius Valerius – London: Macmillan and Co. Ltd., 1915. xlv,1 leaf, 207p.(Macmillan's School Class Books) – 1 – us U.W. Library [450]

SELECT REPORTS OF THE AMERICAN COMMISSION TO NEGOTIATE PEACE : 1914-19 / U.S. Commission to Negotiate Peace – An original microform collection which includes over 100 archival reports written by prominent scholars for the use of American negotiators at the Versailles Peace Conference of 1919 – 1 – $770.00 – 0-89093-013-9 – us UPA [943]

SELECT SERMONS / Philaret, Metropolitan of Mosow – London: J. Masters, 1873 – 1mf – us A.T.L.A. [240]

SELECT SPECIMENS OF NATURAL HISTORY, COLLECTED IN TRAVELS TO DISCOVER THE SOURCE OF THE NILE, IN EGYPT, ARABIA, ABYSSINIA, AND NUBIA / Bruce, James – 5501 2. 1790 – 8 – ne IDC [500]

SELECT TEXAS STATUTES, ANNOTATIONS AND FORMS AND NOTARIES' MANUAL, EMBRACING CONSTITUTIONAL AND STATUTORY PROVISIONS AFFECTING INTEREST, PROPERTY RIGHTS UNDER MARITAL CONTRACTS, AND EXEMPTIONS. / Jackson, Nathaniel P – Austin, Gammel Book Co. 1897 327 p. LL-328 – 1 – us L of C Photodup [340]

SELECTA FUNGORUM CARPOLOGIA / Tulasne, LR & Tulasne, C – 3v. Parisiis. 1861-65. B-6181 1 – 9 – ne IDC [580]

SELECTA QUAE...POETARUM / Sanchez de las Brozas, Francisco – 1513 – 9 – 1.50f – sp Bibl Santa Ana [440]

SELECTARUM STIRPIUM AMERICANARUM HISTORIA / Jacquin, N J von – Vindobonae. 1763. B-934 2 – 8 – ne IDC [580]

SELECTA...VETERUM POETARUM / Sanchez de las Brozas, Francisco – 1613 – 9 – 1.50f – sp Bibl Santa Ana [450]

SELECTED AMERICANA FROM SABIN'S DICTIONARY OF BOOKS RELATING TO AMERICA FROM ITS DISCOVERY TO THE PRESENT TIME – (Over 12,000 full-text selections from Joseph Sabin's Bibliotheca Americana. Subject breakouts available) – 9 – us Primary [975]

SELECTED ARCHIVES OF THE JAPANESE ARMY, NAVY, AND OTHER GOVERNMENT AGENCIES, 1868-1945 – (In Japanese) – 163r – 9 – $5,705.00 in US $40.00r outside – L9400011 – Dist. us Scholarly Res – us L of C Photodup [350]

SELECTED ARTICLES ON MINIMUM WAGES AND MAXIMUM HOURS / ed by Nichols, Egbert Ray & Baccus, Joseph H – New York: The H.W. Wilson Co., 1937. 461p. Bibliography – 1 – us U.W. Library [331]

SELECTED ARTICLES ON THE BATAKA CONTROVERSY APPEARING IN MUNNO, 1922-1923 / Rowe, John Allen – (Filmed with: Kagwa, Apolo: The Clans of the Baganda, Mengo, 1949. Gray, J M: Mutesa of Buganda 1934. Katake, A G: Abagabe B'Ankole, Kampapa 1955) – Bukalasa, Uganda, 1922-23 – us Res Libr [960]

SELECTED ARTICLES ON THE OPEN VERSUS CLOSED SHOP / Robbins, Edwin Clyde – Minneapolis: H.W. Wilson, 1911. xx,194p – 1 – us U.W. Library [338]

SELECTED ASPECTS OF BIOMECHANICAL AND NEUROMUSCULAR RESPONSES TO LANDING PERFORMANCE / Zhang, Songning – University of Oregon, 1996 – 2mf – 9 – $8.00 – PE 3681 – us Microform Publ [612]

A SELECTED BIBLIOGRAPHY OF HISPANIC BAPTIST HISTORY / Atkinson, Ernest Edwin – 1981. 104p – 1 – 5.00 – us Baptist [240]

A SELECTED BIBLIOGRAPHY OF MISSIONARY LITERATURE / Murray, J Lovell – New York City: Student Volunteer Movement, c1912 – 1mf – us A.T.L.A. [240]

A SELECTED BIBLIOGRAPHY OF THE RELIGIOUS DENOMINATIONS OF THE UNITED STATES / Bowerman, George Franklin – New York: Cathedral Library Association, 1896 – 1mf – us A.T.L.A. [240]

SELECTED BIBLIOGRAPHY ON MAJOR AFRICAN RESERVOIRS – 1983 – 58p – it F.A.O. [333]

SELECTED CASE RECORDS / Ford County. Kansas. District Court – 1876-80 – 1 – us KS Hist [978]

SELECTED CASES ON CONTRACTS / Pierson, Ward W & Callender, Clarence N – 7th ed. Philadelphia: The Budenz Co, 1925 – 4mf – 9 – $6.00 – LLMC 96-041 – us L.L.M.C. [340]

SELECTED CASES ON GOVERNMENT AND ADMINISTRATION / Goodnow, Frank Johnson – Chicago: Callaghan, 1906. 250p. LL-1260 – 1 – us L of C Photodup [340]

SELECTED CHARACTERISTICS OF U.S. WHEELCHAIR BASKETBALL PLAYERS, THEIR SPORT PARTICIPATION AND THEIR ATTITUDES TOWARDS THEIR COACHES / Gambetta, C – 1991 – 1mf – 9 – $4.00 – us Microform Publ [150]

SELECTED CHRISTIAN ESSAYS (CCC230) = LUN TAO WEN HSUAN / Lo, Yun-yen – (In Chinese) – Shanghai: Christian Literature Society, 1931 – 1r – 1 – 1984-B500 – us A.T.L.A. [240]

SELECTED CLASSES OF LETTERS RECEIVED BY THE INDIAN DIVISION OF THE OFFICE OF THE SECRETARY OF THE INTERIOR / U.S. Bureau of Indian Affairs – 1849-80. 32 rolls. M825 – 1 – us Nat'l Archives [324]

SELECTED COMPUTER PROGRAMS IN FORTRAN FOR FISH STOCK ASSESSMENT – 1985 – 188p – it F.A.O. [639]

SELECTED CONTEMPORARY CHINESE NEWSPAPERS – (Comes in Chinese. Chung-Kuo Ch'ing-Nien Pao: Peking: Jun 1952-Aug 1966, 1979-86, 1989 24r L9300081. Jen-Min Jih-Pao: Peking: 1950-91 98r L9300082. Kuang-Ming Jih-Pao: Peking: Mar 1950-91 79r L9300083. Kung-Jen Jih-Pao: Peking: Dec 1949-66, May 1979-83, 1987-88 37r L9300084. Ta Kung Pao: Tientsin: Nov 1929-Jul 1937, Dec 1945-48, Feb 1949-52 (under the title Chin pu jih-pao), 1952-1956 55r L9300085. Shanghai: Aug-Dec 1937, Nov 1945-May 1949, Aug 1949-52 20r L9300086; Hong Kong: 1939-41, 1948-69 79r L9300087; Chungking: Aug 1941, Jun 1942-Dec 1946 11 reels L9300088. Peking: 1957-66 22r L9300089) – 425r – 1 – $40.00r – Dist. us Scholarly Res – us L of C Photodup [072]

SELECTED DECISIONS AND DIGESTS OF DECISIONS *see* RULES OF APPELLATE PROCEDURE, 1983

SELECTED DOCUMENTS / Nassau, Robert Hamill – 1 – $100.00 – us Presbyterian [240]

SELECTED DOCUMENTS / West Africa Mission. (Pres. Ch. in the U.S.A.) – 1 – $50.00 – us Presbyterian [240]

SELECTED DOCUMENTS FROM THE ARCHIVES AND MANUSCRIPTS DEPTS., KSHS, TOPEKA / Realf, Richard – 1850-1905, Documents are about Realf, not by him – 1 – us KS Hist [920]

SELECTED DOCUMENTS OF THE INTERNATIONAL PETROLEUM INDUSTRY / Organization of Petroleum Exporting Countries – 1967-71 – 1 – 18.00 – us L of C Photodup [330]

SELECTED DOCUMENTS ON THE LIFE AND CAMPAIGNS OF FIELD MARSHAL ROMMEL / Rommel, Erwin – Comp. by David Irving. Index – 11r – 1 – uk Microform Academic [943]

SELECTED DOCUMENTS RELATING TO BLACKS NOMINATED FOR APPOINTMENT TO THE U.S. MILITARY ACADEMY DURING THE 19TH CENTURY / U.S. Military Academy – 1870-87. RG 94, 107, 153. 21 rolls. M1002 – 1 – us Nat'l Archives [355]

SELECTED DOCUMENTS; SOME ASPECTS CONCERNING PROGRESS; 7 PRINCIPLES OF THE INDONESIAN REVOLUTION / Indonesia – SE-10,922 1. v. 1 only – 9 – ne IDC [335]

SELECTED EAST AFRICAN CASES ON COMMERCIAL LAW / Brownwood, David O – Lower Kabete, Kenya Institute of Administration 1968. 134 p. LL-12045 – 1 – us L of C Photodup [340]

SELECTED ENACTMENTS IN VIETNAMESE... – 2mf – 9 SEL-108/1 – ne IDC [340]

SELECTED ESSAYS / Sumner, William Graham – 1924. From the 4 vol. ed. of 1918. 369p. 1 fiche (24x) – 9 – 1.00f – at Libertarian Micro [320]

SELECTED FACTORS REALTED TO HELP-SEEKING BEHAVIOR IN COLLEGE WOMEN VICTIMS OF SEXUAL COERCION / Ogletree, R J – 1991 – 2mf – 9 – $8.00 – us Microform Publ [150]

SELECTED ILLUMINATIONS FROM MANUSCRIPTS / Fitzwilliam Museum. Cambridge – Ms 12, 44, 330 – 1 colour reel – 14 – uk Microform Academic [240]

SELECTED INDEXES TO NATURALIZATION RECORDS / U.S. Circuit and District Courts. California. Northern District – 1852-1928. 3 rolls – 1 – T1220 – us Nat'l Archives [340]

SELECTED LETTERS OF WILLIAM BRIGHT : REGIUS PROFESSOR OF ECCLESIASTICAL HISTORY IN THE UNIVERSITY OF OXFORD, CANON OF CHRIST CHURCH / Bright, William; ed by Kidd, J B – London: Wells Gardner, Darton,1903 – 1mf – us A.T.L.A. [240]

SELECTED LETTERS RECEIVED BY THE OFFICE OF INDIAN AFFAIRS RELATING TO THE CHEROKEE OF NORTH CAROLINA / U.S. Bureau of Indian Affairs – 1851-1905. 7 rolls. M1059 – 1 – us Nat'l Archives [324]

A SELECTED LIST OF PROBATE ATTORNEYS WITH GENERAL PRACTICE, AS COMPILED FOR FISHER'S PROBATE LAW DIRECTORY... 1935-36 / Fisher, Jacob Carney – St. Louis: Smith 1935. 128p. LL-377 – 1 – us L of C Photodup [340]

SELECTED LIST OF RESEARCH PROJECTS / Indonesia. Department of National Research – SE-6204 1. 1945-1965 – 9 – ne IDC [500]

SELECTED MANUSCRIPT MATERIALS FROM THE DUTCH STATE ARCHIVES AND THE R.I.L.A. ON PEASANT MOVEMENT / Indonesian Nationalist Movement – BSD-100-BSD-113 1 – 9 – ne IDC [950]

SELECTED MATERIALS ON FEDERAL-STATE COOPERATION IN THE ATOMIC ENERGY FIELD / U.S. Congress. Joint Committee on Atomic Energy – Washington: GPO. 1v. 1959 – 6mf – 9 – $9.00 – LLMC 81-103 – us L.L.M.C. [324]

SELECTED MEDICINAL PLANTS – 1984 – 99p – it F.A.O. [580]

SELECTED MUSIC PERIODICALS PUBLISHED IN LONDON – 1770-1851 – 1r – 1 – us Ross [780]

SELECTED NAVAL ATTACHE REPORTS RELATING TO THE WORLD CRISIS / U.S. Navy – 1937-43. M975 – 3r – 1 – us Nat'l Archives [355]

SELECTED OPINIONS OF LUTHER S. DIXON AND EDWARD G. RYAN, LATE CHIEF JUSTICES OF THE SUPREME COURT OF WISCONSIN / Roe, Gilbert Ernstein – Chicago: Callaghan, 1907. 615p. LL-1083 – 1 – us L of C Photodup [340]

SELECTED PAMPHLETS, HANDBOOKS, CONGRESS AND OTHER REPORTS RELATING TO SOUTH AFRICA / South Africa – 1 – uk Microform Academic [080]

SELECTED PAPERS / Carlson, Frank – 1952-1966, Relating to the International Council for Christian Leadership and the annual prayer breakfasts – 1 – us KS Hist [920]

SELECTED PAPERS / Howell, George – From the Bishopsgate Institute, London – 25r – 1 – uk Microform Academic [920]

SELECTED PAPERS / Montgomery, James & Williams, John Monroe – 1859-1907, Relate to southeast Kansas and South Carolina – 1 – us KS Hist [920]

SELECTED PAPERS / Royal Canadian Military Institute – v1-41 1890-1946 – 1 – cn Precision [355]

SELECTED PAPERS AND PUBLICATIONS OF ARTHUR T. PIERSON / Pierson, Arthur Tappan – 1879-1908 – 1 – $50.00 – us Presbyterian [240]

SELECTED PAPERS FROM THE KSHS COLLECTION / Brown, John – 1849-1919 – 1 – us KS Hist [920]

SELECTED PAPERS ON THE ENVIRONMENT IN ISRAEL / Israel. Ministry of the Interior – no. 1-5. Jerusalem, 1974-77 – 9 – 15.00 – is I.T.T.I. [360]

SELECTED PENSION APPLICATION FILES RELATING TO THE MORMON BATTALION, MEXICAN WAR – 1846-48 – 1 – us Nat'l Archives [975]

SELECTED PERIODICALS / Bibliotheque Nationale – 4titles on 158 fiches. Available separately – 9 – 391.00 – fr Bibl Nationale [073]

SELECTED PERSIAN TITLES FROM PERSIAN COLLECTION / Hoover Library. Stanford University – 20 items: Aprim, What Must Be Done, Tehran, 1946; Tabari, "Chand mas'alayi ijtima'i," 1948, Tehran; "Jang-i dakhili," Tehran, 1946; "Farmanrava'iyi proletaria."; Kiyanuri, "Mubarezat-i tabaqati," Tehran, 1948; Alatur, "Hizb-i Tudayi Iran sar-i do rah," Tehran, 1947; Alavi, "Panjah va seh nafer," Tehran, 1947"; Mubariz, P. S., Aya Hizb-i tudeh shikast khordeh ast?, Tehran, 1947; Maliki, Khalil; Shahid (newspaper). "What did the Tudeh Party claim and what did it achieve? What has the National Front done and what must it do?," Tehran, 1951-1952; Tamaddun, "Dar barayi Jebhayi matbuati Zidd-i Diktaturi," Tehran, 1948; Radmanish, "On the violation of law by the government...," Tehran, 1948; Mubariz, P. S., "Dar piramuni Hizb-i demokrat-i Iran," Tehran, 1946; Qasimi, Ahmad, "Several subjects from economics," Tehran, 1948; Ravandi, "A commentary on the Iranian Constitution." Maliki, "The Third Force shall win," Tehran, 1951; Maliki, "What is the Third Force?," Tehran, 1951-1952; Maliki, "The historical development of socialism," Tehran, 1951-1952; Qasimi, Ahmad, "Law" – 1 – $35.00r – us Hoover Inst Photo [320]

SELECTED PHOTOGRAPHS OF CALVIN COOLIDGE, 1917-1943 / U.S. National Archives and Records Service – 1r – 1 – M867 – us Nat'l Archives [977]

SELECTED PHOTOGRAPHS OF DWIGHT D. EISENHOWER, 1943-1961 / U.S. National Archives and Records Service – 1 – M868 – us Nat'l Archives [977]

SELECTED PHOTOGRAPHS OF FRANKLIN D. ROOSEVELT, 1913-45 / U.S. National Archives and Records Service – 1r – 1 – M865. Printed guide – us Nat'l Archives [025]

SELECTED PHOTOGRAPHS OF HARRY S. TRUMAN, 1885-1953 / U.S. National Archives and Records Service – 2r – 1 – M835. Printed guide – us Nat'l Archives [025]

SELECTED PHYSIOLOGICAL VARIABLES AND DISTANCE RUNNING PERFORMANCE AMONG NON-ELITE, HETEROGENEOUS GROUPS OF MALE AND FEMALE RUNNERS / Chen, J A – 1991 – 1mf – 9 – $4.00 – us Microform Publ [612]

SELECTED PLANS OF STREETS AND BUILDINGS / Westminster. London – From the Public Record Office – 1 – uk Microform Academic [941]

SELECTED POEMS / Watkins, Vernon Phillips – (Norfolk, CT): New Directions, (1943). 92p – 1 – us U.W. Library [810]

SELECTED POEMS OF CARL SPITTELER / Spitteler, Carl – New York: Macmillan, 1928 – 1r – 1 – us U.W. Library [810]

SELECTED PRINTED MATERIALS / Indonesian Nationalist Movement – From the R.I.L.A. on Modern Nationalism. Complete collection. BSE-1279 FF 1 – 9 – ne IDC [950]

SELECTED PROSE WORKS / Lessing, Gotthold Ephraim; ed by Bell, Edward – London: G Bell, 1889 – 1 – us U.W. Library [800]

SELECTED PUBLICATIONS / Nassau, Robert Hamill – 1 – $100.00 – us Presbyterian [960]

SELECTED QUESTIONS FOR NEW JERSEY LAW STUDENTS. / Loughran, Frank E – Jersey City, Linn, 1896. 312 p. LL-1666 – 1 – us L of C Photodup [340]

SELECTED QUOTATIONS ON PEACE AND WAR : WITH ESPECIAL REFERENCE TO A COURSE OF LESSONS ON INTERNATIONAL PEACE, A STUDY IN CHRISTIAN FRATERNITY INCLUDED IN THIS VOLUME / Federal Council of the Churches of Christ in America. Commission on Christian Education – New York City: Federal Council, c1915 – 2mf – us A.T.L.A. [240]

SELECTED RECORDS FROM REVOLUTIONARY WAR PENSION AND BOUNTY-LAND WARRANT APPLICATION FILES, 1800-1900 / U. S. Veterans Administration – 898 rolls. M805 – 1 – us Nat'l Archives [324]

SELECTED RECORDS OF THE GENERAL ACCOUNTING OFFICE RELATING TO THE FREMONT EXPEDITIONS AND THE CALIFORNIA BATTALION, 1818-90 / U.S. General Accounting Office – 3rolls – 1 – T135 – us Nat'l Archives [910]

SELECTED RECORDS OF THE TENNESSEE FIELD OFFICE OF THE BUREAU. / U.S. Bureau of Refugees, Freedmen, and Abandoned Lands – 73 rolls. T142 – 1 – us Nat'l Archives [324]

SELECTED RECORDS...RELATING TO CONFEDERATE PRISONERS OF WAR, 1861-65 / U.S. War Department. Confederate Records – 145 rolls. M598. Printed guide – 1 – us Nat'l Archives [324]

SELECTED REPORTS OF CASES / U.S. Veteran's Education Appeals Board – 1950-57, 2 vols. 80-523 – 9 – 16.00 – us L.L.M.C. [324]

SELECTED RESEARCH IN MICROFICHE (SRIM) – Selected government technical reports as issued. More than 350 subject selections – 9 – $1.45 – us N.T.I.S. [600]

SELECTED SERIES OF RECORDS ISSUED BY THE COMMISSIONER..., 1865-72 / U.S. Bureau of Refugees, Freedmen, and Abandoned Lands – 7 rolls.M742. Printed guide – 1 – us Nat'l Archives [324]

SELECTED STUDIES ON THE DYNAMICS, PATTERNS AND CONSEQUENCES OF MIGRATION – 9 – fr UNESCO [304]

SELECTED TEMPLE DOCUMENTS / Keiser, C E – New Haven, 1919.BNE-437/1 – 9 – ne IDC [930]

SELECTED TERMS IN FISH CULTURE – 1981 – 158p – it F.A.O. [639]

SELECTED TERMS OF IRRIGATION – 1980 – 115p – it F.A.O. [631]

SELECTED TERMS ON BANANAS – 1979 – 81p – it F.A.O. [634]

SELECTED TIDE-STAFF READINGS AND HYDROGRAPHIC SURVEY SOUNDINGS / Peary, Robert E – 1908-09. North Polar Expedition. 1 roll. T296 – 1 – us Nat'l Archives [550]

A SELECTED TOPICAL INDEX TO NEWSPAPERS – 2mf – $14.95 – 0-9632139-0-3 – us Stemmons [071]

SELECTED TOPICS IN EMBRYOLOGY / Ignat'eva, G M et al – 542p – 1,5,9 – 0-677-30710-1 – us Gordon [590]

SELECTED TRANSLATIONS FROM VOYENNAYA MYSL' – 1959-73 – 1 – 230.00 – us L of C Photodup [355]

SELECTED WORKS / Bomberger, John H A – (A Funeral Discourse...Samuel Helfenstein.... 1866. The Faithful Pastor's Monument.... 1852. Our Position....1856. The Revisited Liturgy.... 1867. Spiritual Libertinism.... 1846) – 1 – $50.00 – us Presbyterian [240]

SELECTED WORKS / Cleyre, Voltairine de – 1914. 480p.1 fiche (29x) – 9 – 1.00f – at Libertarian Micro [320]

SELECTED WORKS / Goodell, William – 1845-53 – 1r – 1 – us Ross [975]

SELECTED WORKS / Harper, Frances Ellen Watkins – Philadelphia, 1869-1900 – 1r – 1 – us Ross [975]

SELECTED WORKS / Higginson, Thomas Wentworth – 1855-1905 – 1r – 1 – us Ross [420]

SELECTED WORKS / Olmsted, Frederick Law – 1857-1904 – 1r – 1 – us Ross [976]

SELECTED WORKS / Straker, David Augustus et al – 1647-1906 – 1r – 1 – us Ross [975]

SELECTED WORKS BY AMERICAN INDIAN AUTHORS – 1860-1939 – 2r – 1 – us Ross [970]

SELECTED WORKS BY AND ABOUT PHILLIS WHEATLEY / Wheatley, Phillis – 1753-94 – 1r – 1 – us Ross [975]

SELECTED WORKS BY AND ABOUT WENDELL PHILLIPS / Phillips, Wendell – 1847-91 – 1r – 1 – us Ross [975]

SELECTED WORKS BY CANADA'S FIRST NOVELIST / Richardson, John – 1829-1902 – 1r – 1 – us Ross [420]

SELECTED WORKS, MANUSCRIPT AND PUBLISHED / Davies, Samuel – 1 – $50.00 – us Presbyterian [920]

SELECTED WORKS OF HULDREICH ZWINGLI, 1484-1531 : THE REFORMER OF GERMAN SWITZERLAND / Zwingli, Ulrich – Philadelphia: University of Pennsylvania, 1901 – 1mf – us A.T.L.A. [240]

SELECTED WRITINGS OF ISAAC M. WISE / Wise, Isaac Mayer; ed by Philipson, David & Grossmann, Louis – (With a Biography by the Editors) – Cincinnati: R. Clarke, 1900 – 1mf – us A.T.L.A. [240]

SELECTING INTERVENTIONS FOR NUTRITIONAL IMPROVEMENT : A MANUAL – 1983 – 85p – it F.A.O. [640]

SELECTION AND TRAINING OF INDIAN CANDIDATES FOR THE CIVIL SERVICE / India – (Papers included). Report of a Commission of 1854. v. 55. London. 1876. BI-510 2 – 8 – ne IDC [324]

THE SELECTION AND USE OF TEAM CAPTAINS IN COLLEGE FOOTBALL / Holmoe, Thomas A – Brigham Young University, 1995 – 1mf – 9 – PE 3653 – us Microform Publ [790]

SELECTION DE JOURNAUX DE LA PERIODE DE LA COMMUNE MARS A MAI 1871 : BOBINE 1 / France – (SOCIALE (LA). Journal politique quotidien du soir. – Paris. 31 mars-17 mai 1871 (no. 1-48); mq no. 11, 32. COMMUNE (LA). Par les redacteurs du Combat et du Vengeur. – Paris. 20 mars-18 mai 1871 (no. 1-59). PATRIE (LA). – Paris. 18 mars-19 mai 1871; mq 13-14 mai) – 1 – fr A.C.R.P.P. [072]

SELECTION DE JOURNAUX DE LA PERIODE DE LA COMMUNE MARS A MAI 1871 : BOBINE 2 / France – (MOT (LE) D'ORDRE. Red. en chef H. de Rochefort. – Paris. 3 fevr-20 mai 1871 (no. 1-86). NATIONAL (LE) DE 1869. Dir. I. Rousset. – Paris. 19 mars-15 mai 1871 (no. 782-839); fragm. CRI (LE) DU PEUPLE. Red. en chef J. Valles. – Paris. 22 fevr-23 mai 1871 (no. 1-83). VENGEUR (LE). Dir. politique Felix Pyat. – Paris. 30 mars-24 mai 1871 (2e s. no. 1-56). MONITEUR (LE) DU PEUPLE. Ancien Moniteur de la guerre. – Paris. Ed. du matin de: Avant-garde (L'). 18 mars-19 avr 1871 (no. 383-447); mq 28 mars) – 1 – fr A.C.R.P.P. [072]

SELECTION DE JOURNAUX DE LA PERIODE DE LA COMMUNE MARS A MAI 1871 : BOBINE 3 / France – (BIEN (LE) PUBLIC. Journal politique quotidien. Red. en chef H. Vrignault. – Paris. 5 mars-31 mai 1871 (no. 1-63). VERITE (LA). Journal politique et quotidien. Red. en chef Ed. Portalis. – Paris. 18 mars-23 mai 1871 (no. 163-229); mq. no. 179-181. NATION (LA) SOUVERAINE. Red. Al. Rey. – Paris. 15 avr-19 mai 1871 (no. 1-23); mq no. 20-21. PARIS-LIBRE. Journal du soir. Gerant P. Minetti. – Paris. 12 avr-24 mai 1871 (no. 1-43)) – 1 – fr A.C.R.P.P. [072]

SELECTION DE JOURNAUX DE LA PERIODE DE LA COMMUNE MARS A MAI 1871 : BOBINE 4 / France – (AVENIR (L') NATIONAL. – Paris. 18 mars-31 mai 1871 (no. 2244-2307). FRANCE (LA) POLITIQUE, SCIENTIFIQUE ET LITTERAIRE. – Paris. 18 mars-6 mai 1871 (no. 77-126); mq no. 91, 93. REVEIL (LE) DU PEUPLE. Dir. O. Advenant. – Paris. 18 avr-22 mai 1871 (no. 1-34). SALUT (LE) PUBLIC. Dir. politique Gustave Maroteau. – Paris. 16-23 mai 1871 (no. 1-7). TRIBUM (LE) DU PEUPLE. Red. en chef Lissagaray. – Paris. 17-24 mai 1871 (no. 1-8); mq no. 7. ECHO (L') DU SOIR. – Paris. 26 avr-1er mai 1871 (no. 1-6)) – 1 – fr A.C.R.P.P. [072]

SELECTION DE JOURNAUX DE LA PERIODE DE LA COMMUNE MARS A MAI 1871 : BOBINE 5 / France – (UNION (L') FRANCAISE. Journal de la republique federale. Fond. E. de Girardin. – Paris. 5-16 mai 1871 (no. 1-12). FEDERALISTE (LE). Red. en chef Odysse-Barot. % Paris. 21-22 mai 1871 (no. 1-2). OPINION (L') NATIONALE. Journal politique quotidien. Red. en chef Ad. Gueroult. – Paris. 18 mars-30 mai 1871 (no. 75-110). AMI (L') DU PEUPLE. Journal politique quotidien. Dir. A. Vermorel. – Paris. 23-29 avr 1871 (no. 1-4). JUSTICE (LA). Journal politique quotidien. Red. Charles Delescluze. – Paris. 10-19 mai 1871 (no. 1-10). MONITEUR (LE) UNIVERSEL. – Paris. 18 mars-31 mai 1871 (no. 77-147)) – 1 – fr A.C.R.P.P. [072]

SELECTION DE JOURNAUX DE LA PERIODE DE LA COMMUNE MARS A MAI 1871 : BOBINES 1-5 / France – 1 – fr A.C.R.P.P. [072]

SELECTION DE JOURNAUX EPHEMERES 1848-1849 : BOBINE 1 / France – (CROQUE-MORT (LE) DE LA PRESSE. Necrologie politique, litteraire, typographique et bibliographique de tous le journaux. par un bibliophile bien informe H. Delombardy. – Paris. dec 1848-janv 1849 (no.1-6). COURRIER (LE) DU SOIR. Nouvelles de la journee. devenu: Depeche (LA). Courrier du soir. Red. L. Chambelland. – Paris. mars 1848 (no.1-5). JOURNAL DES SANS-CULOTTES. Par le citoyen Constant Hilbey. – Paris. 28 mai 1848-mars 1849 (no.1-7). AMI (L') DU PEUPLE EN 1848. An premier de la republique reconquise, par F.-V. Raspail. – Paris. 27 fevr-14 mai 1848 (no.1-21). JOURNAL DES TRAVAILLEURS. Fonde par les ouvriers delegues au Luxembourg. – Paris. 4-22; 25 juin 1848 (no.1-6). PILIER (LE) DES TRIBUNAUX. Compte rendu des cours d'Assises, Police correctionnelle, Justice de Paix, Conseils de discipline. chronique, nouvelles, varietes. – Paris. juil-oct 1848 (no.1-4). UNITE (L') NATIONALE. puis Journal democratique quotidien. Organe des departements algeriens. – Paris. 16 mai-14 juin 1848 (no.1-27). TOCSIN (LE) DES TRAVAILLEURS. Comite de redaction E. Barrault, F. Delente, ouvrier. – Paris. 1er-24 juin 1848 (no. 1-24)) – 1 – fr A.C.R.P.P. [072]

SELECTION DE JOURNAUX EPHEMERES 1848-1849 : BOBINE 10 / France – (CLUB INDEPENDANT, JOURNAL DE MARSEILLE. – Marseille. avr 1848 (no. 5-6, 8-11). ERE (L') NOUVELLE. Journal des principes et des interets democratiques. – Aix-Marseille. avr-dec 1848 (no. 8-70); mq no. 11-13, 15-18, 20, 22-23, 25-26, 35-36, 42. GARDE (LE) NATIONAL. – Marseille. Bihbed. 3 mars-14 mai 1848, inc. LIBERTE (LA) ELECTORALE. Journal des Bouches-du-Rhone. – Marseille. Quot. avr-sept 1848, inc.; mq no. 1-8, 10-25, 29, 31, 36-37, 39, 41, 43-44) – 1 – fr A.C.R.P.P. [072]

SELECTION DE JOURNAUX EPHEMERES 1848-1849 : BOBINE 11 / France – (NATIONAL (LE) DU MIDI. Marseille. 1er mars-16 avr 1848 (no. 1-39); mq no. 2-12, 15-19, 21, 23, 25, 27, 33, 38. ORGANISATION (L') DU TRAVAIL. Journal du soir. – Marseille. 26 mars-23 avr 1848 (no. 1-25). PROGRES (LE) SOCIAL. Publication du comite democratique de Marseille. – Marseille. Quot. janv-juin 1848 (no. 30-34, 36-99, 101-102, 105-109, 111-149)) – 1 – fr A.C.R.P.P. [072]

SELECTION DE JOURNAUX EPHEMERES 1848-1849 : BOBINE 12 / France – (SPECTATEUR DU MIDI. Journal des libertes religieuses, des interets populaires et des droits de tous. – Marseille. sept-dec 1848 (no. 103-200), inc.; mq 22 no. VOIX (LA) DU PEUPLE. – Marseille. Quot. 13 oct-dec 1848, inc.; mq no. spec., no. 10) – 1 – fr A.C.R.P.P. [072]

SELECTION DE JOURNAUX EPHEMERES 1848-1849 : BOBINE 2 / France – (CANARD (LE). Journal drolatique fantastique, anecdotique, politique et critique de l'an 1er de la Republique. Red. en chef Xavier de Montepin. – Paris. 9; 17 avr-18; 25 juin 1848 (no. 1-11). COLERE (LA) D'UN VIEUX REPUBLICAIN CONTRE TOUT LE MONDE. – Paris. 1er-22 juin 1848 (no. 1-7). MONTAGNE (LA). Tribune du peuple. Red. Gally, Ch. d'Amyot, Etude, Dugaillon, etc. – Paris. dec 1848-mars 1849 (no. 1-4; spec. du 19 nov 1848). REPUBLICAIN (LE) ROUGE. Drapeau de la democratie. Red. Galley et J. Danin. – Paris. janv-mai 1849 (no. 1-5). TRAVAIL (LE). Journal du travailleur electeur et eligible puis Au travailleur electeur et eligible. Fonde par E. Houel. – Paris. 30 mars-2 avr 1848 (no. 1-3). COMMUNISTE (LE). Journal mensuel. Red.-gerant J. Gay. – Paris. mars 1849 (no. 1). OMNIBUS (L'). Journal du dimanche. – Paris. 1848 (no. 1). OPINION (L') DES FEMMES. Liberte egalite, fraternite pour tous et pour toutes. Publication de la Societe d'education mutuelle des femmes puis Revue mensuelle. Red. en chef Jeanne Deroin. – Paris. prosp., 21 aout 1848 (no. 1), 28 janv-aout 1849 (no. 1-6). COLERE (LA) ET LE DESESPOIR D'UN VIEUX REPUBLICAIN. An 1er de la Republique nouvelle. – Paris. aout 1848 (no. 1-2). DEMOCRATE (LE) egalitaire. Semaine sociale et republicaine. Red. en chef Frederic Gerard. – Paris. 20 avr 1848 (no. 1). PEUPLE (LE). Red. Alphonse Esquiros. – Paris. 1er mars 1848 (no. 1). COLPORTEUR (LE) PARISIEN. – PARIS. 2 juil 1848 (no. 1). SCORPION (LE) POLITIQUE. Satire sur les evenements du jour, par le citoyen Bouche de Cluny. – Paris. juin 1848 (no. 1-2). SALTIMBANQUES (LES). Pochades politiques. – Paris. juin 1848 (no. 1-2). MAYEUX. Journal politique, critique et litteraire. – Paris. 17; 19 juin-8; 10 juil 1848 (no. 1-6)) – 1 – fr A.C.R.P.P. [072]

SELECTION DE JOURNAUX EPHEMERES 1848-1849 : BOBINE 4 / France – (ORGANISATION (L') DU TRAVAIL. Journal des ouvriers. Red. en chef H. Lacolonge. – Paris. 3-24 juin 1848 (no. 1-22). TRAVAIL (LE). Veritable organe des interets populaires puis Journal du Club de la Revolution. Red. en chef E.A. Dambel. – Paris. mai-juin 1848 (no. 1-11). VOYANT-POURVOYEUR (LE) DE TRAVAIL, D'EMPLOIS ET DE CREDIT AUX TRAVAILLEURS ABONNES. – Paris. nov 1849 (spec., no. 2). VERITE (LA). Feuille mensuelle illustree de la religion socialiste. Philosophique historique, critique et litteraire, par Pinto. – Paris. 1849 (no. 1). MONTAGNARD (LE) SATIRIQUE. Journal politico-litteraire, charivarique. – Paris. janv 1849 (no. 1). PETIT (LE) MESSAGER DU VILLAGE. Dir.-gerant Sugier du Grand-Prat. – Paris. 1er mai-1er juin 1849 (no. 1-3). LABOUREUR (LE). Journal politique et agricole des habitants des campagnes. Red. en chef Louis-Napoleon Grollet. – Paris. nov 1848-juil 1849 (no. 1-15). TRAVAIL (LE) AFFRANCHI. Journal des associations ouvrieres, par F. Vidal, redacteur. – Paris. 7 janv-17 juin 1849 (no. 1-24 avec spec. de 1848). COMMUNE (LA) SOCIALE. Journal mensuel des travailleurs. Red. E. Fomberteaux. – Paris et Lyon. dec 1848-mai 1849 (no. 1-5). SOLIDARITE (LA). Red. en chef E. Fomberteaux. – Paris. 25 oct-25 dec 1849 (no. 1-3). SOCIALISTE (LE). Journal de l'egal-echange. – Paris. juil-oct 1849 (no. 1-4 avec prosp.). POSITIF (LE). Journal des travailleurs. Red. Charles Fauvety. – Paris. juil-nov 1849 (no. 1-4)) – 1 – fr A.C.R.P.P. [072]

SELECTION DE JOURNAUX EPHEMERES 1848-1849 : BOBINE 5 / France – (SALUT (LE) PUBLIC. Journal quotidien, politique, scientifique et litteraire. Red. en chef l'abbe Orsini. – Paris. 16 mars-14 mai 1848 (no. 1-58). JOURNAL (LE) puis Messager du matin. Red. Alph. Karr. – Paris. 28 juil-31 oct 1848 (no. 1-96)) – 1 – fr A.C.R.P.P. [072]

SELECTION DE JOURNAUX EPHEMERES 1848-1849 : BOBINE 6 / France – (COMMUNE (LA) DE PARIS. Moniteur des clubs. – Paris. 9 mars-7 juin 1848 (no. 1-86). fevr-mars 1849 (no. 1-2)) – 1 – fr A.C.R.P.P. [072]

SELECTION DE JOURNAUX EPHEMERES 1848-1849 : BOBINE 7 / France – (PEUPLE (LE) CONSTITUANT. Journal quotidien. Red. en chef Lamennais. – Paris. 27 fevr-11 juil 1848 (no. 1-134). PERE (LE) DUCHENE. Gazette de la revolution. Red. Colfavru. –

Paris. 10 avr-24 aout 1848 (no. 1-35)) - 1 - fr A.C.R.P.P. [072]

SELECTION DE JOURNAUX EPHEMERES 1848-1849 : BOBINE 8 / France - (MONDE (LE) REPUBLICAIN. - Paris. 1er avr-25 juin 1848 (no. 1-86); mq no. 72, 85 Les no. 1-4 ont paru sous le titre de: Monde (Le) de 1848. REVOLUTION (LA) DE 1848. - Paris. 23 mai-27 juin 1848 (no. 1-36); mq no. 34-36. BIEN (LE) PUBLIC. Red. en chef Eugene Pelletan. - Paris. Quot. 24 mai-juin 1848. voir suite sur bobine no. 9) - 1 - fr A.C.R.P.P. [072]

SELECTION DE JOURNAUX EPHEMERES 1848-1849 : BOBINE 9 / France - (BIEN (LE) PUBLIC. Red. en chef Eugene Pelletan. - Paris. Quot. juil-12 dec 1848) - 1 - fr A.C.R.P.P. [072]

SELECTION DE JOURNAUX EPHEMERES 1848-1849 : BOBINES 1-12 / France - 1 - fr A.C.R.P.P. [072]

SELECTION DE JOURNAUX EPHEMERES 1848-1849, 1 : BOBINE 3 / France - (CONSTITUTION (LA) COMME JE LA VOUDRAIS, AVEC DES DEBATS IMAGINAIRES. Par L. Emar.- Paris. oct 1848 (no spec.). PERSIFLEUR (LE). Journal mensuel de la republique democratique et sociale. Red. en chef Laroche. - Paris. 14 dec 1848 (no.1). FRANCE (LA) LIBRE. Politique et philosophique. Par Maximilien Marie.- Paris. avr-oct 1848 (no.1-5). REPUBLICAIN (LE) LYRIQUE. Journal des chanteurs, politique, comique et satirique, redige par nos meilleurs chansonniers.- Paris. juil 1848-juil 1849 (no.1-13). ORDRE (L') SOCIAL. Journal du peuple francais. Moniteur des villes et des campagnes.- Paris. 6 mai 1849 (no.1). ORDRE (L'). Revue universelle et quotidienne. Red. en chef Nouguier pere. - Paris. 14 aout, 6 sept 1848 avec no.spec. et prosp. ORDRE (L') PUBLIC. Journal des barricades. Red. Eugene Blanc.- Paris. 2 mars 1848 (no.1). ORGANISATEUR (L') DU TRAVAIL. Journal de la Societe universelle, sous la direction du citoyen Letellier.- Paris. avr 1848 (no.1-2). ORGANISATION (L') DU TRAVAIL. La verite aux ouvriers. Red. en chef Amedee Sellier. - Paris. 20-27 avr 1848 (no.1-3). BULLETIN DE LA REPUBLIQUE. Ministere de l'Interieur. 13 mars-20 avr 1848 (no.1-18) et Reimpression: Bulletins de la republique emanes du Ministere de l'Interieur. Avec une preface par un haut fonctionnaire en activite.- Paris. 13 mars-6 mai 1848 (no.1-25).) - 1 - fr A.C.R.P.P. [072]

SELECTION DE JOURNAUX EPHEMERES 1848-1849, 2 : BOBINE 3 CONT'D - (REFORMATEUR (LE). Journal de la ligue viticole et de tous les interets de l'agriculture et de l'industrie nationale.- Paris. (no spec. de 1848). TRIBUNE (LA) POPULAIRE. Dir. M.L. Menier.- Paris. (no du 27 avr 1848). DEFENSEUR (LE) DU PEUPLE. Journal mensuel.- Paris. nov 1848-avr 1849 (no.1-6). PERE (LE) ANDRE.- Paris. 1848 (no.1-2). GUIDE (LE) DES ELECTEURS. Journal politique mensuel.- Paris. 7 sept 1848. MICROMEGAS, OU LE MIROIR DE PARIS CIVIL ET POLITIQUE EN EPIGRAMMES HISTORIQUES. Par Reynaud.- Paris. aout 1848. CAUCHEMAR (LE) DES INTRIGANTS POLITIQUES. Revue mensuelle, critique et philosophique. Red. par J.-B.H. Munier. - Paris. 9 oct 1848 (no.1). ORIENT (L') EUROPEEN. Revue des interets politiques, religieux et litteraires des peuples de l'EUROPE, orientale. Publication de la Societe slave de Paris. Red. en chef Cyprien Robert. - Paris. juin-juil 1849 (no.1-2)) - 1 - fr A.C.R.P.P. [072]

SELECTION DE JOURNAUX EPHEMERES 1869-1871 : BOBINE 1 / France - (ACTION (L'). Journal politique quotidien. - Paris. 4-9 avr 1871 (no. 1-6). AFFRANCHI (L'). Journal des hommes libres. Red. en chef P. Grousset. - Paris. 2-25 avr 1871 (no. 1-24). ANONYME (L'). Journal politique. - Paris. 11-12 mai 1871 (no. 1-2). BONNET (LE) ROUGE. Red. en chef Secondigne. - Paris. 10-22 avr 1871 (no. 1-13); mq no. 5. BULLETIN COMMUNAL. Organe des clubs. - Paris. 6 mai 1871 (no. 1). BULLETIN (LE) DU JOUR. - Paris. 16-22 mai 1871 (no. 1-7). CAIN ET ABEL. Red. en chef A. Le Bealle. - Paris. 15 avr 1871 (no. 1). CANDIDAT (LE) HUMAIN. Journal social, philosophique, humanitaire. Dir. A. Berton. - Paris. janv-avr 1871 (no. 1-5). CANDIDE. Oragne anti-religieux. Gerant G. Metenier. - Paris. 13-16 avr 1870 (no. 1-2). CARICATURE (LA) POLITIQUE. - Paris. 8 fevr-23 mars 1871 (no. 1-6). CARMAGNOLE (LA). - Paris. 10 fevr-2 avr 1871 (2 no. spec., no. 1-5). CHATIMENT (LE). Journal politique quotidien. Red. en chef Alfred Sirven. - Paris. Ed. de Paris. 5 mars-13 avr 1871 (no. 1-2, 18-30, 33-39). Ed. hors Paris. 25 fevr-13 mars 1871 (no. 1-2, 5, 8, 17). CHEFS (LES) REVOLUTIONNAIRES. Gustave Flourens par le citoyen Vindex. - Paris. 19 mai 1871 (no. 1). COMEDIE (LA) PATRIOTIQUE JOUEE PAR DES HOMMES ET RACONTEE PAR LES FEMMES. - Paris. 18 fevr-11 mars 1871 (no. 1-3). Commune (LA) DEVOILEE PAR UN AMI DES TRAVAILLEURS. Auguste Petit. - Paris. 1871 (1 no.). CONSTITUTION (LA) POLITIQUE ET SOCIALE. Red. en chef A. Beau de Rochas, C. Morel. - Paris. 18 mai-5 juil 1871 (no. 1-37); mq no. 12, 16-17. A partir du 14 juin 1871, fusionne avec la redaction du Tricolore et devient Constitution (La) tricolore. CORSAIRE (LE). Journal quotidien. - Paris. 8-16 mai 1871 (no. 1-9)) - 1 - fr A.C.R.P.P. [072]

SELECTION DE JOURNAUX EPHEMERES 1869-1871 : BOBINE 2 / France - (COURRIER (LE) DU DIMANCHE. Dr. Et. Vatier. - Paris. 19 mars-23 avr 1871 II, no. 1-6 (16-21). COURRIER (LE) FRANCAIS. Red. Vermorel. - Paris. 9-22 sept 1870 (no. 1-13). DEFENSE (LA). BUlletin du Comite civil des moyens de defense. - Paris. oct 1870 (no. 1). DEFENSE (LA) NATIONALE. Journal des interets de la patrie. Dir. Ch. Henry. - Paris. 24 oct-8 dec 1870 (no. 6-39); mq no. 7, 9-10, 24-38. DEFENSE (LA) NATIONALE. Journal quotidien. Gerant J. Trousset. - Paris. 8 sept 1870 (no. 1). DEPECHE-BALLON. Journal des evenements du Siege. - Paris. 28 oct 1870-8 janv 1871 (no. 1-28). DIOGENE, SATIRE POPULAIRE. - Paris. 5 mars 1871 (no. 1). DISCUSSION (LA). Red. en chef A. Gaulier. - Paris. 12-16 mai 1871 (no. 1-5). 18 Dix-huit (LE) MARS. Journal hebdomadaire par Jules Bergeret ex-membre du Comite central et de la Commune de Paris. - Londres, Bruxelles. aout-sept 1871 (no. 1-3). DRAPEAU (LE) ROUGE. Red. en chef G. Maroteau. - Paris. 2-4 nov 1870 (no. 1-2). DRAPEAU (LE) ROUGE. Revue hebdomadarie politique, critique et humoristique. - Paris. 11 mai 1871 (no. 1). ECOLE DE L'HOMME ET DU CITOYEN. Journal hebdomadaire, paraissant le samedi. Red. en chef M. Gracieux-Faure. - Paris. 29 oct-26 nov 1870 (no. 1-2). ESTAFETTE (L'). Red. en chef Secondigne. - Paris. 23 avr-23 mai 1871 (no. 1-30) suite de: Bonnet (Le) rouge voir a ce titre. ETOILE (L'). Journal des dernieres nouvelles. Gerant A. Dubois. - Paris. 5-12 mai 1871 (no. 1-8). EUROPE (L') LIBRE. Journal des Etats-unis d'Europe. Red. L. Tabary. - Paris. 7 sept 1870 (no. 1). FAUBOURG (LE). Journal puis politique quotidien. Red. en chef G. Maroteau. - Paris. 26 fevr 1870-26 mars 1871 (no spec., no. 1-2, n.s. no. 1). FAUBOURIEN (LE). Journal quotidien. Politique, nouvelles, feuilletons, varietes. - Paris. 20-28 nov 1870 (no. 1-9)) - 1 - fr A.C.R.P.P. [072]

SELECTION DE JOURNAUX EPHEMERES 1869-1871 : BOBINE 4 / France - (INCENDIAIRE (L'). Red. en chef Henri Bara. - Paris. 1871 (no spec.). INDEMNITE (L'). Journal hebdomadaire. Dir. Charles de Villedeuil. - Paris. 12 mars 1871 (no. 1). INDEPENDANCE (L') COMMUNALE. - Paris. mars 1870 (no. spec., no. suppl.). INDEPENDANCE (L') FRANCAISE. Journal politique quotidien. Dir. Ed. Sternheim. - Paris. 13 mai-1er juin 1871 (no. 1-12). INDEPENDANT (L') NATIONAL. Journal des interets du peuple. Red. en chef Ch. de Bussy. - Paris. 4 sept 1869 (no. 5). INTERNATIONAL (L'). Londres. 3-28; 29 mai 1871 (no. 2941-2963); mq no. 2959, 2961-2962. JACQUES BONHOMME. La grande colere de Jacques Bonhomme. - Paris. 1871 (no. 1-8). Titre different pour les no. 4, 6-8. JE SUIS LE VERITABLE PERE DUCHESNE, FOUTRE. Les memoires du Pere Duchesne. - Paris. 30 floreal an 79 avr 1871. JOURNAL DE LA REVOLUTION. (Eouvres illustrees des condamnes. - Paris. 1870 (no. 1). JOURNAL DU Xe ARRONDISSEMENT. - Paris. 4-22 dec 1870 (no. 1-3). 1er janv 1871 (no. 1). JOURNAL DU SOIR. - Paris. 5-7 mai 1871 (no. 1-3). JOURNAL (LE) POPULAIRE. Dir. Ch. Francais. - Paris. 17-24 mai 1871 (no. 1-7). LAMENTATIONS (LES) DE LA MERE DUCHENE. - Paris. 1er mai 1871 (no. 1). LETTRES PARISIENNES.- Paris. 11 fevr 1871 (no. 1). LIBRE (LA) PENSEE. Science, philosophie, histoire. Secretaire de la redaction Henri Verlet. - Paris. 24 janv-juil 1870 (no. 1-28); mq no. 27. LIGUE (LA) DU BIEN PUBLIC. Pour la defense la pratique et la propagation des principes: liberte, egalite, fraternite. - Paris. 15 avr 1871 (no. 1)) - 1 - fr A.C.R.P.P. [072]

SELECTION DE JOURNAUX EPHEMERES 1869-1871 : BOBINE 6 / France - (PATRIE (LA) EN DANGER. Journal quotidien. Red. en chef Auguste Blanqui. - Paris. 7 sept-8 dec 1870 (no. 1-89). PATRIE (LA) EN DEUIL. Nouvel appel aux electeurs. Chapitre des revelations. - Paris. 4-8 mars 1871 (no. 2-6). PATRIOTE (LE). Organe de la republique francaise et universelle. Red. en chef Armand Levy. - Paris. Quot. 6-29 sept 1870. 19-23 mars 1871, inc. PATRIOTE (LE) FRANCAIS. Gerant L.X. de Ricard. - Paris. 7-25 juil 1870 (no. 1-3). PERE (LE) DUCHENE. Journal quotidien. Red. en chef G. Maroteau. - Paris. 3-9 dec 1869 (no. 1-7). PERE (LE) DUCHENE ENFIN EXPLIQUE PAR LE PERE DUBOIS, LE DUCHENE REACTIONNAIRE. - Paris. avr 1871 (no. 1). PETITE (LA) GAZETTE. Journal de la guerre. - Paris. 30-31 janv 1871 (no. 1-2). PETITE (LA) MARSEILLAISE. Red. Henri Rochefort. - Paris. 30 juil-8 aout 1870 (no. 1-10). PEUPLE (LE). Red. en chef Jules Valles. - Paris. 4-18 fevr 1869 (no. 1-15). POLITIQUE (LA). Red. en chef A. Gaulier. Paris. 17 mai-1er juin 1871 (no. 1-11)) - 1 - fr A.C.R.P.P. [072]

SELECTION DE JOURNAUX EPHEMERES 1869-1871 : BOBINE 7 / France - (POPULACE (LA). Journal quotidien. Red. en chef A. Pages.- Paris. 30 nov-5 dec 1870 (no.1-6); mq no.3. POPULACE (LA). Journal radical quotidien. Gerant L. Saunier.- Paris. 7-8 oct 1870 (no.1-2). PROLETAIRE (LE). Organe des revendications sociales. (11e arrondissement). - Paris. 10-24 mai 1871 (no.1-4). PUCE (LA) EN COLERE. Feuille satirique.- Paris. 1871 (no.1-4). QUESTION DU JOUR. Journal-livre. Red. Charles Laurent.- Paris. 5 nov 1870 (no.1). REACTION (LA). - Paris. 1871 ? (no.1). REGENERATEUR (LE). Organe de la solidarite et de la fraternite des peuples. Par A. Javel (d'Arbois).- Paris. dec 1870 (no.1). REGENERATION (LA) SOCIALE. Par la prophylactique. OEuvre nationale et patriotique.- Paris. avr 1871 (no.1). REGIME (LE) CONSTITUTIONNEL, POLITIQUE ET SOCIAL. Red. en chef A. Beau de Rochas. - Paris. 14-17 mai 1871 (no.1-4). REPARATEUR (LE).- Paris. fevr-avr 1871 (no.1-11). REPROUVE (LE). Organe de la libre pensee. Gerant. A. Michel.- Paris. aout 1870 (no.spec.). REPUBLICAIN (LE). Echo du coeur de Jesus.- Paris. 5 janv 1871 (no.1). REPUBLICAIN (LE). Journal politique quotidien.- Paris. 14-19 mai 1871 (no.1-5). REPUBLICAIN (LE). Journal quotidien. Red. E. Mabry.- Paris. 15-16 sept 1870 (no.1-2). REPUBLICAIN (LE). Journal quotidien. Red. E. Lambry.- Paris. sept 1870 %no.1). REPUBLIQUE (LA). Journal de la constituante.- Paris. 4-16 fevr 1871. REPUBLIQUE (LA). Journal quotidien. Moniteur de la Garde nationale et de la Garde mobile. Gerant J. Lemer.- Paris. 4 sept-18 oct 1870 (no. 1-45). REPUBLIQUE (LA) A OUTRANCE. Dir. F. Regamey.- Paris. 8-18 fevr 1871 (no.1-2). REPUBLIQUE (LA) DES TRAVAILLEURS. Organe de l'Association internationale (Section des Batignolles et des Ternes).- Paris. janv-fevr 1871 (no.1-6). REPUBLIQUE (LA) SAUVEE.- Paris. 19 fevr 1871 (no.1). RESISTANCE (LA). Organe democratique et social du XIVe arrondissement. - Paris. 10 nov 1870-2 janv 1871 (no.1-17). REVENDICATION (LA). Journal des amis de la constitution de 1793. Red. en chef J.A. Mancel.- Paris. 10 sept 1870 (1 no.)) - 1 - fr A.C.R.P.P. [072]

SELECTION DE JOURNAUX EPHEMERES 1869-1871 : BOBINE 8 / France - (REVOLUTION (LA). Journal quotidien. Red. en chef Alexandre Marin. - Paris. 5 dec 1870-11 avr 1871 (no. 1-2). REVOLUTION (LA) PACIFIQUE, MORALE, POLITIQUE, ECONOMIQUE, SOCIALE. Red. en chef Alfred Sirven. - Paris. 1871 ? (Programme). REVOLUTION (LA) POLITIQUE ET SOCIALE. Red. en chef J.-J. Danduran. - Paris. 16 mai 1871 (no. spec.). REVOLUTION (LA) POLITIQUE ET SOCIALE. Association internationale des travailleurs. - Paris. 2 avr-15 mai 1871 (no. 1-7). SALUT (LE). puis Journal des conciliateurs republicians. Dir. M.-A. Gromier. - Paris. 12-13 mars 1871 (no. 12-13). SANS-CULOTTE (LE). Red. en chef Olivier Pain. - Paris. 19-26 mars 1870 (no. 1-2). SOUVERAINETE (LA) DU PEUPLE. Journal des idees sociales. Red. en chef Auguste Petit. - Paris. 1871 (no. 1). SPECTATEUR (LE). Politique, scientifique et litteraire. Gerant Pasquier. - Paris. 10-12 mai 1871 (no. 1-3). TOCSIN (LE). Journal quotidien. Paris. 16-17 sept 1870 (no. 1-2). TRAC (LE). Journal des peureux. - Paris. 22-29 nov 1870 (no. 1-2). TRICOLORE (LE). Journal politique et quotidien. Red. en chef C. Morel. - Paris. 31 mai-1er juin 1871 (no. 1-2). TRIOMPHE (LE) DE LA REPUBLIQUE puis Journal politique quotidien. Red. en chef J.P. Bertrand. - Paris. mars 1871 (no. 1-6; mq no. 4-5. UNION (L') REPUBLICAINE. Journal politique quotidien. - Paris. nov 1870 (no. spec.). VOLONTE (LA) NATIONALE. Manifeste des patriotes de Paris et de la province. - Paris. nov 1870 (2 no.). VRAI (LE) PERE DUCHENE. Red. en chef G. Maroteau. - Paris. 13 mars 1871 (no. 1). VRAI (LE) REPUBLICAIN. Journal politique quotidien. - Paris. 13 oct 1870 (no. spec.)) - 1 - fr A.C.R.P.P. [072]

SELECTION DE JOURNAUX EPHEMERES 1869-1871 : BOBINES 1-8 / France - 1 - fr A.C.R.P.P. [072]

SELECTION DE JOURNAUX EPHEMERES 1869-1871, 1 : BOBINE 3 / France - (FEDERATION.- BORDEAUX. 16 Avr-4 mai 1871 (no.1-5). FEDERATION (LA) COMMUNALE. (Etude).- Paris. 1871 (1 fascicule). FEDERATION (LA) REPUBLICAINE DE LA GARDE NATIONALE.- Paris. fevr-15 avr 1871 (no.1-4). FEDERE (LE) DES BATIGNOLLES.- Paris. 25 avr 1871 (no.1). FEU (LE) GREGEOIS. Pamphlet-journal intermittent. Gerant A. Leon.- Paris. oct 1870 (no.61). FILS (LE) DUCHENE. Feuille publique par les citoyens Hugene, Gugusse et Dodorre.- Bruxelles. (no.1-10). FLAMBEAU (LE) REPUBLICAIN. Etudes politiques et sociales. Par A. Jamet.- Paris. 26 fevr-13 mai, juil 1871 (no.1-10). FLECHE (LA). Journal politique, satirique, illustre. Red. en chef Pierre Deschamps.- Paris. 1; 7-8; 14 avr 1871 (no.1-2). FRANCE (LA) NOUVELLE. Journal politique quotidien. Red. en chef Victor Dictys.- Paris. 3 oct 1870 (no.1). FRANCE (LA) REPUBLICAINE. Journal politique quotidien. Red. Victor Dictys.- Paris. 27 sept 1870 (no.1). GARDE (LE) NATIONAL. Journal politique. Organe special de la juin-juil 1870 (no.1-4). IMPARTIAL (L'). Par le troupier Biyot, ami de Boquillon.- Paris. oct 1870 (no.1-2). Garde nationale. Red. en chef Mignien.- Paris. 2-4 nov 1870 (no.1-3). GARIBALDI. Defenseur des peuples opprimes. Journal bihebdomadaire. Red. J. Morel. - Paris. 23 nov-4 dec 1870 (no.1-4). GAVROCHE. Paraissant tous le samedis. Red. en chef-gerant Lucien Rabuel.- Paris. 4 juin-9 juil 1870 (no.1-6). Gnafron (LE). Journal de la revolution. Red. en chef Stanislas Charnal.- Lyon. 11 sept-15 dec 1870 (no.1-15)) - 1 - fr A.C.R.P.P. [072]

SELECTION DE JOURNAUX EPHEMERES 1869-1871, 2 : BOBINE 3 CONT'D - (GRAND'GARDE (LA) REPUBLICAINE. Journal du soir. Gerant L. Lhoir.- Paris. 7 nov 1870 (no.1). GRANDE (LA) JOIE DE LA MERE DUCHENE.- Paris. 1871. GUEUX (LES). Ils s'aiment entre eux, vivent les gueux Red. Victor Cosse.- Paris. 28 fevr 1870 (no.1). HOMME (L') puis L'Homme libre. Organe politique et quotidien de la Federation universelle. Red. en chef L. Baretheux. - Paris. 9 mars-7 avr 1871 (no.1-12); mq no.4, 11. HORIZON (L'). Journal-revue.- Paris. 8 fevr 1871 (no.1). IMPARTIAL (L'). Organe universel de la jeunesse. Journal litteraire hebdomadaire. Red. en chef Marc de Rossieny.- Paris) - 1 - fr A.C.R.P.P. [072]

SELECTION DE JOURNAUX EPHEMERES 1869-1871, 3 : BOBINE 5 / France - (LUTTE (LA). Journal satirique illustre. Red. en chef Victor Dictys. - Paris. 1870 (no spec.). LUTTE (LA) A OUTRANCE. Journal du club de l'ecole de medecine.- Paris. 6-28 nivose an 79 dec 1870-janv 1871 (no. 1-

4). MARSEILLAISE (LA) EN VACANCES.- Paris. juin 1870 (no.1). MEPHISTOFELES. Journal politique hebdomadaire.- Paris. mars 1871 (no. 1-2). MERE (LA) DUCHENE.- Paris. 26 dec 1869-20 fevr 1870 (no.1-8, no spec.) suivi de: Tante (La Duchene. 26 fevr-12 mars 1870 (no.1-3). MERE (LA) DUCHENE.- Paris. 3-5 avr 1871 (no.1-3) Le no.3 a paru sous le titre: Avis (Les) de la Mere Duchene. MERE (LA) MICHEL. Gerant Marchal de Bussy.- Paris. 19 mars 1870 (no.1). MISERABLE (LE). Journal quotidien. Red. et Administrateur A. Passedouet.- Paris. 28 fevr-6 mars 1870 (no. 1-6). MISERE (LA). Journal quotidien. Red. et Administrateur A. Passedouet.- Paris. 6-12 fevr 1870 (no.1-7). MOBLOT (LE). Revue de la semaine. Journal politique et litteraire Red. en chef Leon Halevy. – Paris. 25 dec 1870-1er janv 1871 (no.1-2). MONITEUR (LE) DE LA PAIX. – Paris. 1871 (no.1-3). MONITEUR DE LA REPUBLIQUE. Dir. William Reymond.- Paris. 14 sept-3 oct 1870 (no.1-8). MONITEUR (LE) DES CITOYENNES. Journal du droit et de l'interet des femmes. Dir. Barse. – Paris. 6 nov 1870 (no.1). MONITEUR (LE) PARISIEN.- Paris. 10 mars 1871 (no.1). MONT-AVENTIN (LE). Echo des Buttes Montmartre. Red. en chef A. Secondigne.- Paris. 26-30 mars 1871 (no.1-2)) – 1 – fr A.C.R.P.P. [072]

SELECTION DE JOURNAUX EPHEMERES 1869-1871, 4 : BOBINE 5 CONT'D – (MONTAGNE (LA). Journal de la revolution sociale. Red. en chef Gustave Maroteau.- Paris. 2-25 avr 1871 (no.1-22). MOUCHES (LES) ET LES ARAIGNEES. Par Mme Paule Mink.- Paris. 17-24 dec 1869 (no.1-2). OEIL (L') DE MARAT. Moniteur des XIXe, et XXe arrondissements adherent a la ligue republicaine. Dir. Ch. Dumont.- Paris. 29 nov-2 dec 1870 (no.1-2). ORDRE (L'). Journal politique quotidien. Red. en chef A. Vermorel.- Paris. 20-23 mars 1871 (no.1-4). OUVRIER (L') DE L'AVENIR. Journal politique et social. Organe des Chambres syndicales et des associations ouvrieres.- Paris. 12-19 mars 1871 (no.1-3). Paix (La). Journal politique quotidien.- Paris. 28 avr-1er mai 1871 (no.1-4). PANTHEON (LE). Journal du Ve arrondissement. Dir.-gerant Auguste Arbois.- Paris. nov 1870 (no.1-2, n.s. no.2). Paris-Belleville. Journal quotidien, politique et litteraire.- Paris. 22-28 avr 1871 (no.1-7)) – 1 – fr A.C.R.P.P. [072]

SELECTION DE JOURNAUX EPHEMERES DE LA PERIODE DE LA REVOLUTION : BOBINE 1 / France – (SENTINELLE (LA) DU PEUPLE. Rennes. 10 nov-25 dec 1788 (no. 1-5). PREMIERE (LA) puis deuxieme; troisieme AUX GRANDS. Pour servir a l'histoire de la Revolution. Paris. 1789 (no. 1-3). BULLETIN SUR LES AFFAIRES DU TEMPS. – s.l. 17 avr 1789 (no. 1). OBSERVATEUR (L') FRANCAIS, AMI DE LA PATRIE, A LA NATION ASSEMBLEE. – Paris. 1789 (no. 1-4). TRIBUN (LE) DU PEUPLE, OU recueil de lettres. Paris. 2e ed. (Lettres 1-4); 3e ed. (Lettres 1-17); 4e ed. augmentee (Lettres 1-30). NOUVELLES DE VERSAILLES. De Moreau de Mersan le jeune. – Paris. 25 juin, 28-29 juil 1789) – 1 – fr A.C.R.P.P. [072]

SELECTION DE JOURNAUX EPHEMERES DE LA PERIODE DE LA REVOLUTION : BOBINE 2 / France – (SUITE DES NOUVELLES DE VERSAILLES devenu: Assemblee nationale. Seance et suite des Nouvelles de Versailles. Par M. de Beaulieu. – Paris. 20 juin-15 oct 1789. 5 juil-15 oct 1789, ed. differente, inc. VERITES BONNES A DIRE. Supplement a tous les journaux. – Paris. 1789 (1 no. s.d.). DECLIN (LE) DU JOUR, OU RESOLUTIONS DE L'ASSEMBLEE NATIONALE. – Paris. 7 juil-21 aout 1789 (no. 1-6, 8-9, 18). JOURNAL POLITIQUE NATIONAL. Par l'abbe Sabatier de Castres et Rivarol. – Versailles. juil-aout 1789 (no. 1-23). CODE DE LA PATRIE ET DE L'HUMANITE. Ouvrage periodique, par M. Baumier. – Paris. 30 juil-6 aout 1789 (no. 1-2). JOURNAL DU VRAI HONNETE HOMME. – Paris. 1789 (no. 1). SUITE DU COURRIER DE PARIS A VERSAILLES. – Paris. 3-22 aout 1789. ANNALES PARISIENNES, POLITIQUES ET CRITIQUES, MAIS VERITABLES. – Paris. juil; aout 1789 (no. 1). DENONCIATEUR (LE) NATIONAL. – s.l. 1789 (no. 1-7). JOURNAL DE LA VILLE. – Paris. juil 1789 (no. 1, 8)) – 1 – fr A.C.R.P.P. [072]

SELECTION DE JOURNAUX EPHEMERES DE LA PERIODE DE LA REVOLUTION : BOBINE 3 / France – (SPECTATEUR (LE) A L'ASSEMBLEE NATIONALE. 1789 (no. 1-17). DEBATS A L'ASSEMBLEE NATIONALE. Par Gauthier de Briozat. aout 1789 (1 no.). NOUVELLES EPHEMERIDES DE L'ASSEMBLEE NATIONALE, OU correspondance d'UN DEPUTE A L'ASSEMBLEE NATIONALE AVEC UN MEMBRE DU PARLEMENT D'ANGLETERRE. – Paris. 7-31 aout 1789 (no. 1-25) devenu: Ephemerides de l'Assemblee nationale. 31 aout-3 oct 1789 (no. 26-60). SOLITAIRE (LE). – Paris. 1789 (no. 1). VOYAGES (LES) DE L'OPINION DANS LES QUATRE PARTIES DU MONDE. – PARIS. aout 1789 (no. 1-5). dec 1789 (no. 6). MAGASIN HISTORIQUE, OU JOURNAL GENERAL. – PARIS. sept. 1789 (no. 1-2)) – 1 – fr A.C.R.P.P. [072]

SELECTION DE JOURNAUX EPHEMERES DE LA PERIODE DE LA REVOLUTION : BOBINE 4 / France – (PETIT JOURNAL DU PALAIS-ROYAL EN AFFICHES, ANNONCES ET AVIS DIVERS. – Paris. sept-nov 1789 (no. 1-6). FURET (LE) PARISIEN. – Paris. dec 1789-1790 (no. 1-10). VOIX (LA) DU PEUPLE, OU LES ANECDOTES POLITIQUES DU BONHOMME RICHARD SUR LES AFFAIRES DU TEMPS. – Paris. 3 sept-9 oct 1789 (no. 1-2). ECOUTEUR (L') AUX PORTES. – Paris. oct 1789 (no. 1-2). COLPORTEUR (LE) NATIONAL, DEDIE AUX FRANCAIS PATRIOTES. – Paris. oct-nov 1789 (no. 1-2). HISTOIRE DE LA REVOLUTION PRESENTE, OU MEMOIRES PERIODIQUES IMPARTIAUX ET FIDELES POUR SERVIR A L'HISTOIRE DE FRANCE. – Paris. nov 1789 (prosp., no. 1). ANNALES POLITIQUES ET NATIONALES. – Paris. 20 oct 1789 l. AMI (L') DES HONNETES GENS, OU L'OPTIMISTE. – Paris. 25 oct-2 nov 1789 (no. 1-5). COURRIER DE L'ASSEMBLEE NATIONALE. – Paris. 29 oct-1er nov 1789 (no. 1-4). DISCIPLE (LE) DES APOTRES. – Paris. 1789 (prosp., no. 1-6). PATRIOTE (LE) INCORRUPTIBLE, OU L'HOMME DE PROVINCE. – Paris. nov. 1789 (no. 1, 4, avec prosp.). FASTES DE LA LIBERTE. Par M. de Belair. – Paris. nov 1789-janv 1790 (no. 1-9 avec prosp.)) – 1 – fr A.C.R.P.P. [072]

SELECTION DE JOURNAUX EPHEMERES DE LA PERIODE DE LA REVOLUTION : BOBINE 5 / France – (COURIER (LE) DE BORDEAUX, OU NOUVELLE CORRESPONDANCE. – Paris. 17 nov-23 dec 1789 (no. 1-11). ESPION (L') DES CAMPAGNES, OU LES VEILLEES VILLAGEOISES DE LA PLAINE D'IVRY. Journal dedie aux hommes utiles. – Paris. 19 nov-8 dec 1789 (no. 1-8 avec prosp.). PERE (LE) DES PAUVRES, OU LES VEILLEES D'UN HERMITE. Ouvrage periodique. – Paris. 1789 (no. 1). JUGEMENT DU PEUPLE AUX GALERIES DE L'ASSEMBLEE NATIONALE. – Paris. 1789 (2 no., avec prosp.). JOURNAL NATIONAL M. du Morier. – Paris. 1789 (no. 1). SOLITAIRE (LE) DES TUILERIES. s.d. (no. 1-4). CE QUE VOUS NE SAVEZ PAS ET CE QUE VOUS NE VOYEZ PAS. – Paris. s.d. (no. 1). SENTINELLE (LA) DE LA NOBLESSE. 1788 (no. 1-2). FOUS (LES) POLITIQUES. Par Publius. – Paris. 1789 (no. 1). JOURNAL DES PROVINCES. – Paris. 6 juin 1789 (no. 6). DENONCIATEUR (LE). – s.l. 1789 (no. 1). OPINION (L') PUBLIQUE A L'ASSEMBLEE DES COMMUNES. – Paris. 1789 (no. 1). PETITE POSTE DE L'ASSEMBLEE NATIONALE, OU PRECIS DE SES SEANCES. – Paris. 29 juil-8 aout 1789 (no. 1-2, 9-10). VEILLEES D'UN FRANCAIS. 14 aout-15 nov 1789 (no. 1-48)) – 1 – fr A.C.R.P.P. [072]

SELECTION DE JOURNAUX EPHEMERES DE LA PERIODE DE LA REVOLUTION, 1 : BOBINE 7 / France – (SECRETAIRE DE L'ASSEMBLEE NATIONALE.- Paris. 1er-19 sept 1789 (no.1-17). VOYAGE A L'ASSEMBLEE NATIONALE.- s.l. 1790 ? (no.1). SPECTATEUR (LE) PATRIOTIQUE, OU OBSERVATIONS IMPARTIALES.- Paris. 29-30 sept 1789 (no.1-2). OBJET DU JOUR. Questions, reflexions, motions faites par un politique de la rue Popincourt.- Paris. Oct 1789 (no. 1-4). REVOLUTIONS DE VERSAILLES ET DE PARIS, DEDIEES AUX DAMES FRANCAISES. – Paris. 3-29 oct 1789 (no.1-5). RECUEIL PERIODIQUE DE BONS MOTS, CONTES, LETTRES ET CHANSONS SUR LES ARISTOCRATES.- Paris. 1789 (no.1). ETRENNES NATIONALES DES DAMES. Par M. de Pussy et une societe de gens de lettres. 3 nov 1789 (no.1). HOCQUET ARISTOCRATE, OU LE JOURNALISTE DE PARIS A L'A.B.C.- Paris. nov 1789 (no.1). MON REVE, OU LA FEMME SANS TETE. – Paris. 1789 ? (no.1). NOUVEAUTES POLITIQUES, CRITIQUES ET AMUSANTES. – Paris. 1789 (no.1-2). CLUB DES OBSERVATEURS. L'an premier de la liberte francaise.- Paris. 1789 (no.1-7). ESPION (L') DE PARIS ET DES PROVINCES, OU NOUVELLES LES PLUS SECRETES DU JOUR.- Paris. Juil 1789 (no. 2). FEUILLE DU SOIR. Par une Societe de femmes de lettres. 1791? (prosp. s.d.). SPECTACLE DE LA NATION.- Paris. 1789 (no.1). GRAND (LE) INQUISITEUR, OU LE JOURNAL GENERAL DES ABUS.- Paris. 1789 (no.1).) – 1 – fr A.C.R.P.P. [072]

SELECTION DE JOURNAUX EPHEMERES DE LA PERIODE DE LA REVOLUTION, 2 : BOBINE 7 CONT'D – (MONITEUR (LE) PATRIOTE. Marat.- Paris. aout 1789 (no.1). APOCALYPSE (L')MONACLE, OU LES MOINES TELS QU'ILS ONT ETE ET TELS QU'ILS NE PEUVENT PLUS L'ETRE.- Paris. 1789 (no.1-3). JOURNAL DE L'EUROPE. Dedie a l'Assemblee nationale.- Londres. 31 juil 1789 (no.1). FEUILLE POLITIQUE ET NATIONALE. 20 oct 1789 (no.1). BULLETIN. Etats generaux.- Paris. 14-24 mai 1789 (no.1-3). COURRIER PATRIOTIQUE.- Paris. juil-sept 1789 (no.55, 58-59, 66, 74). JOURNAL DE LA PREMIERE LEGISLATURE.- Paris. 1er-10 janv 1792. CENSEUR (LE) NATIONAL.- Paris. 27 sept-4 oct 1789 (no. 1-2). PHARE POLITIQUE ET LITTERAIRE.- Londres, Paris. 30 oct 1789 (no. 40), 16-20 fevr 1790 (no.41-42, avec prosp.). ANGLAIS (L') PARIS, OU LETTRES SUR L'ETAT ACTUEL DE LA FRANCE.- Paris. avr-mai 1789 (no.1-3). C'EST INCROYABLE, La confession amphigouri-TRAGICOMIQUE.- Paris. 1er-5 aout 1789 (no.1-5). IDEES PATRIOTIQUES. Par M.C.N. Roland. oct-nov 1789 (no.1-10). NOUVEAUX ESSAIS SUR PARIS. 10 oct 1789. COURRIER (LE) NOCTURNE.- Paris. 22 juil 1789 (no.1-2)) – 1 – fr A.C.R.P.P. [072]

SELECTION DE JOURNAUX EPHEMERES DE LA PERIODE DE LA REVOLUTION, BOBINE 6 / France – (NOUVELLES ET ANECDOTES DU PALAIS-ROYAL. – Paris. 7-8 juil 1789 (no. 1-2). JOURNAL (LE) DES COMMUNES, OU LES HORREURS DE LA PROSCRIPTION. – S.l. 23 juil 1789 (no. 11). NOUVEAU (LE) NOSTRADAMUS. 12-31 juil 1789 (no. 1-2). SOURD (LE) DU PALAIS-ROYAL, OU ANECDOTE SINGULIERE ARRIVEE DANS LES DERNIERS TROUBLES DE PARIS. – s.l. 1789 (no. 1). COURRIER (LE) DE PARIS, OU ANECDOTES INTERESSANTES. – s.l. 23 juil-20 aout 1789 (no. 1-19). SUPPLEMENT AUX JOURNAUX. – Paris. 29 juil 1789 (no. 1). SPECTATEUR (LE). – Paris. juil 1789 (no. 1-2). CENSEUR (LE) PATRIOTE, OU L'ESPRIT DES FEUILLES POLITIQUES ET NATIONALES. – Paris. 31 juil 1789 (no. 1). JE NE SAURAIS RIRE TANT JE SUIS FACHE, OU LE JOURNALISTE DEVALISE. s.d. (no.1). CORRESPONDANCE DE JEAN ET DE PIERRE SUR LES AFFAIRES DU TEMPS. – Paris. s.d. (no. 1). CORRESPONDANCE DU PALAIS ROYAL. Par M. le Chevalier de Morgan. – Paris. 4-19 aout 1789 (no. 1-16). COURRIER DES PROVINCES, OU L'AVANT-COUREUR DES JOURNAUX. – Paris. aout 1789 (no. 1). ENTRETIENS D'UN PATRIOTE ET D'UN DEPUTE SUR LES BASES DU BONHEUR PUBLIC. s.d. (no. 1-2, 4). CAUSE (LA) DU PEUPLE SOUMISE AU TRIBUNAL DE LA RAISON. Par M.J.D.L. – Paris. 1789 (no. 1-2). NOUVELLISTE (LE) UNIVERSEL, OU ANALYSE RAISONNEE DE TOUTES LES FEUILLES PERIODIQUES, VOLANTES ET EPHEMERES RELATIVES AUX AFFAIRES DU TEMPS. – Paris. aout-8 oct 1789 (no. 1-24). GAZETTE (LA) DES HALLES. Dialogue mele de chansons pour ceux qui les aiment. – Paris. 1789 (no. 1-2). JOURNAL DU PALAIS-ROYAL. – Paris. 1er-4 sept 1789 (no. 1-4)) – 1 – fr A.C.R.P.P. [072]

SELECTION DE JOURNAUX EPHEMERES DE LA PERIODE DE LA REVOLUTION, BOBINES 1-7 / France – 1 – fr A.C.R.P.P. [072]

A SELECTION FROM THE CORRESPONDENCE. / Chalmers, Thomas – Ed. by William Hanna. Edinburgh: Constable, 1853. xi,538p – 1 – us U.W. Library [920]

A SELECTION FROM THE PSALMS OF DAVID / Miller, Edward – 1821. Arr. by G. Jenkins – 9 – us Sibley [780]

A SELECTION FROM THE PUBLIC AND PRIVATE CORRESPONDENCE OF VICE-ADMIRAL LORD COLLINGWOOD: INTERSPERSED WITH MEMOIRS OF HIS LIFE / Collingwood, Cuthbert – 1829 – 9 – $20.00 – uk Libr Preservation [920]

A SELECTION FROM THE WORKS OF ALFRED TENNYSON, D.C.L., POET LAUREATE / Tennyson, Alfred, Lord – London: Edward Moxon, 1865 – 1 roll – 1 – uk Libr Preservation [810]

LA SELECTION NATURELLE, ESSAIS / Wallace, Alfred Russel – Paris, Reinwald, 1872, 435 p. Histoire des Sciences XVIIe-XIXe Siecles. 7945 – 9 – fr Hachette [575]

A SELECTION OF ADJUDICATED CRIMINAL FORMS AND PRECEDENTS OF INDICTMENTS AND INFORMATIONS. / Kerr, James Manford – San Francisco, Bender-Moss Co., 1918. 1628 p. LL-1279 – 1 – us L of C Photodup [340]

A SELECTION OF CASES AND OTHER AUTHORITIES ON LABOR LAW. / Sayre, Francis Bowes – Cambridge: Harvard, 1922. 1017, 1p. LL-1109 – 1 – us L of C Photodup [340]

A SELECTION OF CASES ILLUSTRATING EQUITY PLEADING AND PRACTICE. / Shipp, Eli Richard – Washington, D.C.: Byrne, 1901. 409p. LL-1693 – 1 – us L of C Photodup [340]

A SELECTION OF CASES IN EQUITY JURISDICTION. / Ames, James Barr – Cambridge, Harvard, 1901-04. 2 v. LL-909 – 1 – us L of C Photodup [340]

A SELECTION OF CASES ON AGENCY / Wambaugh, Eugene – Cambridge, Harvard, 1896. 1061 p. LL-1311 – 1 – us L of C Photodup [340]

A SELECTION OF CASES ON INSURANCE / Wambaugh, Eugene – Cambridge, Harvard, 1902. 1197 p. LL-1316 – 1 – us L of C Photodup [340]

A SELECTION OF CASES ON PLEADING, WITH REFERENCES AND CITATIONS / Ames, James Barr – 2d ed.. Cambridge, Harvard, 1905. 349 p. LL-661 – 1 – us L of C Photodup [340]

A SELECTION OF CASES ON PRIVATE CORPORATIONS / Smith, Jeremiah – 2d ed. Cambridge Mass.: Harvard, 1902. 2v. LL-1145 – 1 – us L of C Photodup [340]

A SELECTION OF CASES ON PRIVATE CORPORATIONS / Smith, Jeremiah – (Ibid. Cambridge Mass.: Harvard, 1897. 2v. LL-1147. 2d ed. Part I. Cambridge Mass.: Harvard, 1901-1902. 3v. in 1. LL-1473) – Cambridge Mass.: Harvard, 1896-97. 4v. LL-1138 – 1 – us L of C Photodup [340]

A SELECTION OF CASES ON THE LAW OF CARRIERS / Beale, Joseph H, Jr. – Pt. I. Cambridge, Harvard, 1898. 283 p. LL-302 – 1 – us L of C Photodup [340]

A SELECTION OF CASES ON THE LAW OF CARRIERS OF GOODS AND PASSENGERS / McClain, Emlin – 2nd ed. Boston, Little, Boston, 1896. 744 p. LL-449 – 1 – us L of C Photodup [340]

A SELECTION OF CASES ON THE LAW OF CONTRACTS, WITH A SUMMARY OF THE TOPICS COVERED BY THE CASES / Langdell, Christopher Columbus – 2nd ed. Boston, Little, Brown, 1879. 1 v. in 2 pt. LL-305 – 1 – us L of C Photodup [340]

A SELECTION OF CASES ON THE LAW OF EXTRAORDINARY LEGAL REMEDIES, INCLUDING MANDAMUS, QUO WARRANTO, PROHIBITION. / Roberts, Vasco Harold – Indianapolis: Bobbs-Merrill, 1905. 878p. LL-1164 – 1 – us L of C Photodup [340]

A SELECTION OF CASES ON THE LAW OF PRIVATE CORPORATIONS / Keener, William Albert – New York, Baker, Voorhis, 1899. 2 v. LL-1273 – 1 – us L of C Photodup [340]

A SELECTION OF CASES ON THE LAW OF TORTS / Ames, James Barr – Cambridge, Harvard, 1909-10. 2 v. in 3. LL-523 – 1 – us L of C Photodup [340]

A SELECTION OF CASES UNDER THE INTERSTATE COMMERCE ACT / Frankfurter, Felix – 2d ed. Cambridge: Harvard, 1922. 789p. LL-233 – 1 – us L of C Photodup [340]

SELECTION OF FINNISH NATIONAL LIBRARY COLLECTION OF MICROFILMED MAPS BEFORE 1810 – Helsinki: Yliopistopaino, 1994 – 1,9 – fi H.U. Libr [910]

SELECTION OF FINNISH NATIONAL LIBRARY COLLECTION OF RUSSIAN LITERATURE ON MICROFICHE. 1810-1944 – Helsinki: Helsinki University Library, 1992 – ca 600mf – 9 – fi H.U. Libr [460]

A SELECTION OF FORMS TO ACCOMPANY THE VOLUME ON WISCONSIN CODE PRACTICE. / Bryant, Edwin Eustace – Madison, Democrat, 1900. 1017 p. LL-687 – 1 – us L of C Photodup [340]

A SELECTION OF HYMNS AND SPIRITUAL SONGS / Purify, John – 269p – 1 – us Baptist [240]

A SELECTION OF ITEMS BY AND ABOUT THE NACGN / National Association of Colored Graduate Nurses – 1908-51 – 1r – 1 – us Ross [610]

A SELECTION OF LEADING CASES IN CRIMINAL LAW / Bennett, Edmund Hatch – 2d ed. Boston, Little, Brown, 1869. 2 v. LL-1404 – 1 – us L of C Photodup [340]

A SELECTION OF LEADING CASES IN EQUITY, WITH NOTES / White, Frederick Thomas – 3d Amer. from the 2d London ed. Philadelphia, Johnson, 1859. 3 v. LL-908 – 1 – us L of C Photodup [340]

SELECTION OF LITERATURE FROM TURCICA COLLECTION IN HELSINKI UNIVERSITY LIBRARY ON MICROFICHE – Helsinki: Helsinki University Library, 1992 – ca 100mf – 9 – fi H.U. Libr [490]

A SELECTION OF NEGRO MELODIES, MINSTRELS AND SONGSTERS – 1850-1902 – 1r – 1 – us Ross [780]

A SELECTION OF NEGRO SONGS / ed by Wood, Clement – 1924 – 1 – us Ross [780]

SELECTION OF PAPERS FROM THE RECORDS AT THE EAST-INDIA HOUSE RELATING TO THE REVENUE, POLICE, AND CIVIL AND CRIMINAL JUSTICE UNDER THE COMPANY'S GOVERNMENTS IN INDIA / East India Company – London, 1820-26 – us Res Libr [950]

SELECTION OF PAPERS REGARDING THE HILL TRACTS BETWEEN ASSAM AND BURMAH / India – Bengal Secretariat Press. 1873. BSE-64 2 – 8 – ne IDC [950]

A SELECTION OF RARE AND CURIOUS FISHES FOUND UPON THE COAST OF CEYLON / Bennett, J W – (3rd edition. London. 1851. B-2599-2) – London. 1828-30. B-2610 2 – 8 – ne IDC [590]

A SELECTION OF THE MOST ADMIRED BALLADS, TAKEN FROM THE NEWEST COMIC OPERAS AND VAUXHALL ENTERTAINMENTS – Composed by the ablest masters and set to the harpsichord and piano forte. 1801 – 9 – us Sibley [780]

A SELECTION OF TITLES. SERIES 1 / Schomburg Center for Research in Black Culture – 610r – 1 – $40,500.00 complete coll – us Ross [305]

A SELECTION OF TITLES. SERIES 2 / Schomburg Center for Research in Black Culture – 1534-1955 – 50r – 1 – $3,200.00 complete coll – us Ross [305]

THE SELECTION OF TUNES IN MINIATURE / Rippon, John – 1806 – 1 – 5.67 – us Baptist [240]

A SELECTION OF WORKS / Brown, William Wells – 1847-1880 – 1r – 1 – us Ross [976]

A SELECTION OF WORKS / Chesnutt, Charles W – 7v. 1899-1905 – 1r – 1 – us Ross [975]

A SELECTION OF WORKS / Child, Lydia Maria – 1833-81 – 1r – 1 – us Ross [830]

A SELECTION OF WORKS / Crummell, Alexander – 1856-98 – 12r – 1 – us Ross [975]

A SELECTION OF WORKS / Douglass, Frederick – 1845-94 – 1r – 1 – us Ross [975]

A SELECTION OF WORKS / Whitman, Albery A – 1877-1901 – 1r – 1 – us Ross [975]

A SELECTION OF WORKS BY AND ABOUT BENJAMIN BANNEKER / Banneker, Benjamin – 1793-1854 – 1r – 1 – us Ross [920]

A SELECTION OF WORKS BY AND ABOUT EDWARD W. BLYDEN / Blyden, Edward Wilmot – 1857-1908 – 1r – 1 – us Ross [830]

A SELECTION OF WORKS BY AND ABOUT H.R. HELPER / Helper, Hinton Rowan – 1857-68 – 1r – 1 – us Ross [975]

A SELECTION OF WORKS BY AND ABOUT JOHN BROWN / Brown, John – 1860-1906. 18 titles – 2r – 1 – us Ross [920]

A SELECTION OF WORKS BY AND ABOUT JOHN MARRANT / Marrant, John – 1785-89 – 1r – 1 – us Ross [975]

A SELECTION OF WORKS BY AND ABOUT PAUL L. DUNBAR / Dunbar, Paul Laurence – 1893-1927 – 9r – 1 – us Ross [830]

A SELECTION OF WORKS BY JOHN GREENLEAF WHITTIER / Whittier, John Greenleaf – 1830-54 – 1r – 1 – us Ross [810]

SELECTION OF...COUNTRY DANCES AND REELS ETC., WITH THEIR PROPER FIGURES FOR THE HARP, HARPSICHORD AND VIOLIN / Dale, J – London: J Dale, 1800? – 1 – us Sibley [780]

SELECTIONS / Augustine, St, Bishop of Hippo – Edinburgh: T & T Clark, 1872 – 2mf – 9 – 0-8370-2533-8 – 1985-0533 – us A.T.L.A. [240]

SELECTIONS / Augustine, Saint, Bishop of Hippo – (Includes indexes) – Edinburgh: T & T Clark, 1872 – 2mf – 9 – 0-8370-2529-X – 1985-0529 – us A.T.L.A. [290]

SELECTIONS / Ovid – Introd., notes, vocabulary by Francis W. Kelsey.3rd ed. Boston: Allyn and Bacon, 1895, c1890. vii,298, 142p. ill – 1 – us U.W. Library [450]

SELECTIONS = THESAURUS THEOLOGIAE THOMISTICAE / Thomas Aquinas, Saint – Nannetis [Nantes]: Lanoe Mazeau. 2v. 1900 – 4mf – 9 – 0-8370-7269-7 – 1986-1269 – us A.T.L.A. [240]

SELECTIONS *see* EL GOBIERNO, EL ESTADO Y LAS ORGANIZACIONES LIBRES DEL PUEBLO, LA COMUNIDAD ORGANIZADA

SELECTIONS, CHIEFLY LYRICAL, FROM THE POETICAL WORKS. / Hugo, Victor – Tr. by various authors. Collected by Henry Llewellyn Williams. London: G. Bell, 1885.xix,319p – 1 – us U.W. Library [810]

SELECTIONS: ED. BY MAY WRIGHT SEWALL. 1894 – Selections. Ed. by May Wright Sewall. 1894 – 9 – us A.T.L.A. [240]

SELECTIONS FOR THE SERVICE OF PRAISE – Alliance of the Reformed Churches Holding the Presbyterian System. 1892?.05683.(Pre-1900 Canadiana) – 9 – cn C.I.H.M. [240]

SELECTIONS FROM A TREATISE ON THE CONFLICT OF LAWS / Beale, Joseph H, Jr. – New York, Baker, Voorhis, 1935. 1663 p. LL-862 – 1 – us L of C Photodup [340]

SELECTIONS FROM CHINA MAINLAND MAGAZINES / U.S. Consulate General. Hong Kong – 15 Aug 1955-74; 1975- – 1 – $503.00 – us L of C Photodup [950]

SELECTIONS FROM DESPATCHES, ADDRESSED TO THE GOVERNMENT OF INDIA BY THE SECRETARY OF STATE IN COUNCIL, 1858-1936 / India. Secretary of State – 112 v. Lacking: 1892, v. 35. BI-472 2 – 3,394mf – 8 – ne IDC [950]

SELECTIONS FROM HEINE'S POEMS / Heine, Heinrich; ed by Stevens White, Horatio – (Includes bibliographical references) – Boston: D C Heath, 1900 – 1 – us U.W. Library [810]

SELECTIONS FROM HIS WORKS / Mann, Thomas – (Includes bibliographical references) – Muenchen: E Reinhardt, 1931 – 1r – 1 – us U.W. Library [800]

SELECTIONS FROM LUCIAN / Lucian of Samosato – Trans. by Emily James Smith. New York: Harper & Bros., 1892. xiv,(3), 287p – 1 – us U.W. Library [450]

SELECTIONS FROM THE CORRESPONDENCE OF THOMAS BARCLAY, FORMERLY BRITISH CONSUL-GENERAL AT NEW YORK / Barclay, Thomas; ed by Rives, George Lockhart – New York: Harper & Bros., 1894. 03365. (Pre-1900 Canadiana) – 9 – cn C.I.H.M. [975]

SELECTIONS FROM THE HOME DEPARTMENT ESTABLISHMENTS, JUDICIAL AND PUBLIC FILES, 1908, 1918-1926, 1931-1932 / Spangenberg, Bradford – New Delhi: National Archives of India, 1972 – reels 6-15 – 1 – us Res Libr [324]

SELECTIONS FROM THE HOME POLITICAL FILES, 1915-1919 OF THE NATIONAL ARCHIVES OF INDIA / Ellinwood, DeWitt – New Delhi: National Archives of India, 1970 – us Res Libr [324]

SELECTIONS FROM THE HOME POLITICAL FILES JULY 1914-1916, 1918, AND THE ARMY DEPARTMENT FILES 1914-MAY 1919 / Ellinwood, DeWitt – (Filmed with: Khaparde, G S: Papers 1914-19. Jayakar, M R: Papers 1916-25. Baksh, Ahmad: Correspondence 1914-18) – New Delhi: National Archives of India, 1969 – us Res Libr [324]

SELECTIONS FROM THE PESHWA DAFTAR – v.1-45 – 1 – us Res Libr [950]

SELECTIONS FROM THE RECORDS OF INDIA 1849-1937 / ed by Sims, John – (This series includes a printed bibliography by John Sim) – 3,167mf – 9 – ne IDC [950]

SELECTIONS FROM THE RECORDS OF THE GOVERNMENT OF INDIA / India – Account of the Valley of Munnipore and of the Hill Tribes by W. McCullock. v. 27. Calcutta. 1859. BSE-65 2 – 8 – ne IDC [950]

SELECTIONS ON THE VIETNAM WAR / Echols Collection. Cornell University – 9 – us UMI [977]

SELECTIVE INVENTORY OF SOCIAL SCIENCE INFORMATION AND DOCUMENTATION SERVICES – (Trilingual: English/French/Spanish) – 3rd ed 1989 – xviii/680p – 9 – 92-3-002583-6 – Co-published with Berg – fr UNESCO [301]

SELECTORUM SYMBOLORUM HEROICORUM CENTURIA GEMINA ENOTATA ATQUE ENODATA / Neugebauer, S – O-1253 1. 1619 – 9 – ne IDC [760]

Seletskii, A K *see* OSTROZHSKAIA TIPOGRAFIIA I EIA IZDANIIA

SELF – v. 1- 1979- – 1,5,6,9 – us UMI [610]

Self, Donald R *see* JOURNAL OF NONPROFIT AND PUBLIC SECTOR MARKETING

THE SELF-COMMISSIONED APOSTLE AN IMPOSTOR : OR, THE METHODIST MISSIONARIES PROVED DESTITUTE OF A LAWFUL MINISTRY,... – Chippenham, 1765 – 1mf – 9 – MP-434/1 – ne IDC [240]

SELF-CONCEPT AS A PREDICTOR OF LEISURE BEHAVIOR / Miller, Carol J – 1981 – 2mf – 9 – $8.00 – us Microform Publ [790]

SELF-CONSECRATION / Ware, John Fothergill Waterhouse – Boston: American Unitarian Association, 187?. 11p. (Fourth series: no.8) – 1 – us U.W. Library [240]

SELF-EDITED CHRONICLE OF LING-HUNG-HSUN / Ling-hung-hsun – (Ling-hung-hsun tzu-ting nien-pu). 1973. 341p. 1 reel – 1 – 17.50 – ch Transmission [920]

SELF-EFFICACY OF MALE AND FEMALE GOLFERS AT DIFFERING ABILITY LEVELS / Johnson, Dave R & Murray, Mimi – 1992 – 2mf – $8.00 – us Microform Publ [150]

SELF-ESTEEM AND ADOLESCENT PREGNANCY / Franks, Dorothy W & Cramer, Barbara J – 1991 – 1mf – 9 – $4.00 – us Microform Publ [613]

SELF-ESTEEM AND HEALTH RELATED PHYSICAL FITNESS OF MALE COLLEGE STUDENTS IN HONG KONG / Chung, Pak K – 1993 – 2mf – $8.00 – us Microform Publ [150]

SELF-HELP / Smiles, Samuel – 1859. 510p. 1 fiche (29x) – 9 – 1.00f – at Libertarian Micro [320]

SELF-HELP AND MUTUAL-AID HOUSING / Indonesia. Departemen Kesedjahteraan Sosial – In Indonesian and English. SE-10,921 1. 1961? – 9 – ne IDC [360]

SELF-HELP GROUPS AND HEALTH INFORMATION IN BRITAIN : THE ANNUAL "GREY LITERATURE" MEDICAL REFERENCE COLLECTION – (Pt 1: The Basic Set to 1988. Pt 2: 1989 Update) – 9 – us Primary [610]

SELF-HELP WELLS – 1977 – 86p – it F.A.O. [631]

SELF-MANAGEMENT IN EDUCATIONAL SYSTEMS – 1981 – 48p – 9 – 92-3-101759-4 – fr UNESCO [370]

SELF-PERCEPTION AND MOTOR PROFICIENCY OF HEARING-IMPAIRED CHILDREN / Jonson, Linnea M & Sherrill, Claudine – 1992 – 2mf – 9 – $8.00 – us Microform Publ [150]

SELF-PERCEPTIONS OF FEMALE DANCERS, ATHLETES, EXERCISERS, AND NON-EXERCISERS / Li, Gladys S – Springfield College, 1994 – 3mf – 9 – $12.00 – PSY1851 – us Microform Publ [150]

SELF-SACRIFICE, OR, THE PIONEERS OF FUEGIA / Myers, Sarah Ann – Philadelphia: Presbyterian Board of Publ., 1861.300p. 1 fiche – 9 – us A.T.L.A. [240]

Selifontov, N N *see*
- PODROBNAIA OPIS' 142 RUKOPISIAM 17 DO NACHALA 19 STOLETII TRET'IAGO (LOSEVSKAGO) SOBRANIIA LINEVSKAGO ARKHIVA
- PODROBNAIA OPIS' 272 RUKOPISIAM KONSTA 16 DO NACHALA 19 STOLETII VTORAGO (SHEVLIAGINSKAGO) SOBRANIIA LINEVSKAGO ARKHIVA
- PODROBNAIA OPIS' 440 RUKOPISIAM 17, 18 I NACHALA 19 STOLETII PERVAGO SOBRANIIA LINEVSKAGO ARKHIVA

DER SELIGE JOHANNES VON TRIORA, EIN MAERTYRER CHINAS ZU ANFANG DES NEUNZEHNTEN JAHRHUNDERTS.. / Maria Paula, Sister – 1912 – 1 – us A.T.L.A. [240]

Seligman, Edwin R A *see* THE INCOME TAX

Seligmann, Caesar *see* DAS BUCH DER WEISHEIT DES JESUS SIRACH (JOSUA BEN SIRA) IN SEINEM VERHAELTNISS ZU DEN SALOMONISCHEN SPRUECHEN UND SEINER HISTORISCHEN BEDEUTUNG

SELIHOT – Cracow. 1594. BJ-43-99 1 – 9 – ne IDC [270]

Selinov, I P *see* IZOTOPY

SELINSGROVE TIMES – Selinsgrove, PA. -w 1862-1955 – 13 – $25.00r – us I.M.R. [071]

SELINSGROVE TRIBUNE – Selinsgrove, PA. -w 1943-1970 – 13 – $25.00r – us I.M.R. [071]

Selitskii, I A et al *see* SBORNIK POSTANOVLENII O PROMYSLOVOI KOOPERATSII I KUSTARNOI PROMYSHLENNOSTI

Selivanovskii, A *see* OCHERKI PO ISTORII RUSSKOI SOVETSKOI POEZII

SELJACKA BORBA – Belgrade, Yugoslavia. Sept 1945-Feb 1949 – 1r – 1 – us L of C Photodup [949]

Seljevold, Peter J *see* PREDICTION OF RUNNING PERFORMANCE FROM SELECTED VARIABLES MEASURED DURING BICYCLE ERGOMETRY

Selke, Erich *see* AN ANALYSIS AND EVALUATION OF THE COURSES IN ELEMENTARY SCHOOL SUPERVISION OFFERED IN COLLLEGES, NORMAL SCHOOLS AND UNIVERSITIES

THE SELKIRK JOURNAL – Selkirk, Manitoba. v3 n10. 22 jun 1899 – 1r – 1 – Can$25.00 – cn Can Microfilming [072]

Selkirk, Thomas D *see* ESQUISSE DU COMMERCE DE PELLETERIES DES ANGLOIS, DANS L'AMERIQUE SEPTENTRIONALE

SELKIRKSHIRE, 1837 : BRITISH ISLES CENSUS DIRECTORIES PROJECT, SCOTLAND. VOL 54 – 1mf – 9 – A$9.00 – at Vine [941]

SELKIRKSHIRE, 1866 : BRITISH ISLES CENSUS DIRECTORIES PROJECT, SCOTLAND. VOL 9 – 2mf – 9 – A$15.00 – at Vine [941]

SELKIRKSHIRE ADVERTISER – 1854-1858 – 1. 132 – £42.00r – uk Scot News [072]

Sell, Edward *see*
- THE 'AYYUB AND MAMLUK SULTANS
- THE FAITH OF ISLAM

Sell, Jesse C *see* 20TH CENTURY HISTORY OF ALTOONA AND BLAIR COUNTIES

Sell, Karl *see*
- THE CHURCH IN THE MIRROR OF HISTORY
- PHILIPP MELANCHTHON UND DIE DEUTSCHE REFORMATION BIS 1531
- DIE RELIGION UNSERER KLASSIKER LESSING, HERDER, SCHILLER, GOETHE

Sellar, W Y *see* VIRGIL

Sellers, John R *see* A PEOPLE AT WAR

Sellers, Robert Victor *see* TWO ANCIENT CHRISTOLOGIES

Sellers, W W *see* HISTORY OF MARION COUNTY

Sellew, Walter Ashbel *see* WHY NOT?: A PLEA FOR THE ORDINATION OF THOSE WOMEN WHOM GOD HAS CALLED TO PREACH THE GOSPEL

Sellier, Walter *see* KOTZEBUE IN ENGLAND

Selliers von Moranville, L *see* DIE VOEGEL EUROPAS

Sellin, Ernst *see*
- EINLEITUNG IN DAS ALTE TESTAMENT
- DAS RAETSEL DES DEUTEROJESAJANISCHEN BUCHES

- SERUBBABEL:...GESCHICHTE DER MESSIANISCHEN ERWARTUNG UND DER ENTSTEHUNG DES JUDENTUMS

SELLING DIRECT – v72, no.3-. Mar 1983- – 1,5,6,9 – us UMI [650]

SELLO LEGIONARIO (DE AZUAGA) / Fita, Fidel – Madrid: Tip. Fortanet, 1900 – sp Bibl Santa Ana [946]

Sells, Arthur Lytton *see* LES SOURCES FRANCAISES DE GOLDSMITH

Sellschopp, Herta *see* EIN MAIDENSOMMER

SELLWOOD BEE – Portland. Or. -w. 1910-49 – 1 – us UMI [071]

SELLWOOD BEE – Portland, OR. -w. 1910-49 – 1 – 240.00 – us Oregon Hist [071]

SELLWOOD MORELAND BEE – Portland OR. Feb 21 1952-Dec 25 1952, Oct 4 1956, Jan 2 1964-Jan 22 1970 – 1 – us U.O. Library [071]

SELLWOOD-MORELAND BEE – Portland, OR. 1949-51, 1953-63. Incomplete – 1 – 120.00 – us Oregon Hist [071]

SELLWOOD-MORELAND BEE – Portland. Or. -w. 1949-63 – 1 – us UMI [071]

Selm, B van *see* DUTCH SONG-BOOKS

SELMA ENTERPRISE – (Cont by: Selma Enterprise and Irrigator) – Selma, CA. 1912-29 – 9r – 1 – $450.00 – B02990 – us Library Micro [071]

SELMA ENTERPRISE *see* FRESNO COUNTY ENTERPRISE

SELMA ENTERPRISE AND IRRIGATOR – Selma, CA. 1929- – 66+ r – 1 – $3,300.00 ($90.00y) – B02991 – us Library Micro [071]

SELMA ENTERPRISE AND IRRIGATOR *see* SELMA ENTERPRISE

SELMA EVENING DISPATCH – (Daily Confederate newspaper) – Selma, AL. May 12 1864 – 1r – 1 – us Western Res [071]

SELMA, KINGSBURG AND FOWLER CITY DIRECTORIES – Fresno Co, CA. 1962-1991 – 13r – 1 – $650.00 – D028 – us Library Micro [910]

SELO – Belgrade, Yugoslavia. Apr 1945-Mar 1952 – 2r – 1 – us L of C Photodup [949]

SELO I GOROD V ROSSIISKOI KOOPERATSII / Evdokimov, Andrei Aandreevich – M., 1914 – 1mf – 9 – COR-25/1 – ne IDC [334]

SEL'SHII KHOZIAIN – Zhurnal prakticheskago sel'skago khoziaistva i domovodstva. Spb. 1887-1917. Lacking: (3, 51) 1888; (4) 1889; 1896-1906; (1-9) 1907; 1910; (15) 1911; (12) 1912; (7, 10) 1914; (3, 6, 24, 35) 1915; (13, 16, 49) 1916; (32-52) 1917. BR-2252 2 – 8 – ne IDC [073]

SEL'SKAIA KOOPERATSIIA – (Missing: 1930 n5) – Novonikolaevsk, (Novosibirsk), 1925-30 n17/18 – 118mf – 9 – COR-681/1 – ne IDC [334]

SEL'SKAIA KOOPERATSIIA *see* KOOPERATIVNAIA SIBIR'

SELSKAIA NOV – (Library has: 1966-1971) – [Moskva]: s.n., 1966- – 1 – CSUX89-S828 – us Hoover Inst Photo [630]

SELSKAIA ZHIZN – Moscow. U.S.S.R. 1953- – 1 – us UMI [072]

SELSKAYA ZHIZN – Moscow. 17 Apr 1960-Dec 1968.-d. 20 reels – 1 – uk British Libr Newspaper [072]

SEL'SKIE SSUDNYE TOVARICHESTVA : IKH USTROISTVO I NAZNACHENIE / Luginin, V F & Iakovlev, A V – Spb., 1870 – 2mf – 9 – COR-64/1 – ne IDC [334]

SEL'SKII BYT I SEL'SKOE KHOZIAISTVO V ROSSII / Vasil'chikov, A I – Spb., 1881 – 2mf – 9 – COR-13/1 – ne IDC [334]

SEL'SKII KHOZIAIN : ZHURNAL PRAKTICHESKOGO SEL'SKOGO KHOZIAISTVA I DOMOVODSTVA – (Missing: 1888 n3, 51; 1889 n4; 1895-1906; 1907 n1-9; 1910; 1911 n15; 1912 n12; 1914 n7, 10; 1915 n3, 6, 14, 24, 35; 1916 n13, 16, 49; 1917 n32-52) – Spb., 1887-1917 – 729mf – 9 – R-2252/2 – ne IDC [334]

SELSKII KOOPERATIVNYI KALENDARNA... – (Includes c.1: 1924) – Moskva: Soiuz, 19uu – 1 – CSUXAKZ3631-S – us Hoover Inst Photo [630]

SEL'SKII KOOPERATOR – Rybinsk, 1922 n1-8 – 3mf – 9 – COR-682/1 – ne IDC [334]

SEL'SKOE KHOZIAISTVO – (Cont as: Sel'skoe Khoziaistvo I Kooperatsiia. Viatka, 1924 n1-38. Missing: 1924 n17-20) – Viatka, 1923 – 16mf – 9 – COR-683/1 – ne IDC [334]

SEL'SKOE KHOZIAISTVO I KOOPERATSIIA : SBORNIK STATEI. (KOOPERATIVNAIA BIBLIOTEKA. VYP. 1) – M., 1918 – 1mf – 9 – COR-504/1 – ne IDC [334]

SEL'SKOE KHOZIAISTVO I KOOPERATSIIA *see* SEL'SKOE KHOZIAISTVO

SEL'SKOE KHOZIAISTVO I LESOVODSTVO : ZHURNAL MINISTERSTVA GOSUDARSTVENNYKH IMUSHCHESTOV / Russia. Ministerstva gosudarstvennykh imuzhchestv – (Lacking: n4 1865. n4 1866. n8,11-12 1867. n12 1868. n1-3 1882. n10-12 1884. n1-10 1908. n12 1909. n3-4,10,12 1910. n1-3,7-8,12 1911. n7 1915. n4,6-12 1916. n1-4 1917. v9 1889: Pp 56-57 missing in the original) – Spb, 1865-1917 – 2176mf – 8 – R-8162/2 – ne IDC [073]

SEL'SKOE KHOZIAISTVO NA PUTIAKH VOSSTANOVLENIIA – M., 1925 – 10mf – 9 – COR-505/1 – ne IDC [334]

SELSKOE KHOZIAISTVO SSSR / ed by Narkomzem SSSR i Narkomsovkhozov – (Includes c.1: 1935) – Moskva: Gosudarstvennoe izdatelstvo kolkhoznoi i sovkhozno i literatury "Selkhozgiz", 1936 – 1 – CSUXAKZ6142-S – us Hoover Inst Photo [630]

SELSKOE KHOZIAISTVO UZBEKISTANA : ORGAN MINISTERSTVA SELSKOGO KHOZI A ISTVA UZBEKSKO I SSR – (Library has: Jan. 1967) – Tashkent: T SK Kompartii Uzbekistana, 1965- – 1 – CSUX89-S653 – us Hoover Inst Photo [630]

SELSKOE KHOZYAIESTVO – Moscow, U.S.S.R. -d. 3 April 1953-16 April; 19 May-31 Dec 1959. 15 reels – 1 – uk British Libr Newspaper [947]

SEL'SKOKHOZIAISTVENNAIA KOOPERATSIIA : SODOKLAD NA XIV PARTKONFERENTSII K DOKLADU O KOOPERATSII / Kaminskii, GN – M., 1925 – 1mf – 9 – COR-478/1 – ne IDC [334]

SEL'SKOKHOZIAISTVENNAIA KOOPERATSIIA – Krasnodar, 1923-24 n24 – 32mf – 9 – COR-684/1 – ne IDC [334]

SEL'SKOKHOZIAISTVENNAIA KOOPERATSIIA : SBORNIK DEKRETOV, POSTANOVLENII, TSIRULIAROV, INSTRUKTSII I RAZ"IASNENII PO VOPROSAM. SEL'SKOKHOZIAISTVENNYKH KOOPERATSII S PRIL. PRIMERNYKH... – M., 1924 – 3mf – 9 – COR-316/1 – ne IDC [334]

SEL'SKOKHOZIAISTVENNAIA KOOPERATSIIA – (Title varies. Missing: 1921 n2-1922 n8, 10, 16-17) – M., 1921-29 n7 – 131mf – 9 – COR-685/1 – ne IDC [334]

SEL'SKOKHOZIAISTVENNAIA KOOPERATSIIA / Totomiants, V F – Ed 4. M., 1919 – 4mf – 9 – COR-122/1 – ne IDC [334]

SEL'SKOKHOZIAISTVENNAIA KOOPERATSIIA, EE FORMY, ZNACHENIE I ZADACHI / Maslov, S L – Ed.2. M., 1922 – 1mf – 9 – COR-486/1 – ne IDC [334]

SEL'SKOKHOZIAISTVENNAIA KOOPERATSIIA I BIUDZHET KREST'IANSKOGO KHOZIAISTVA / Prokopovich, SN – M., L., 1922 – 1mf – 9 – COR-501/1 – ne IDC [334]

SEL'SKOKHOZIAISTVENNAIA KOOPERATSIIA I GOSPROMYSHLENNOST' / Zhirmunskii, M M; ed by Seredy, S P & Karatygina, E S – Moscow, Leningrad, 1927 – 1mf – 9 – COR-475/1 – ne IDC [334]

SEL'SKOKHOZIAISTVENNAIA KOOPERATSIIA I STANDARTIZATSIIA SEL'SKOKHOZIAISTVENNOI PRODUKTSII / ed by Papernov, Z A – M., 1927 – 2mf – 9 – COR-510/1 – ne IDC [334]

SEL'SKOKHOZIAISTVENNAIA KOOPERATSIIA I ZNACHENIE EE V SOVREMENNYKH USLOVIIAKH / Lozovyi, A – M., 1923 – 3mf – 9 – COR-481/1 – ne IDC [334]

SEL'SKOKHOZIAISTVENNAIA KOOPERATSIIA SSSR / Minin, A A – M., L., 1925 – 2mf – 9 – COR-493/1 – ne IDC [334]

SEL'SKOKHOZIAISTVENNAIA KOOPERATSIIA V TSIFRAKH : (STATISTICHESKII SPRAVOCHNIK) – M., 1927 – 2mf – 9 – COR-508/1 – ne IDC [310]

SEL'SKOKHOZIAISTVENNAIA KOOPERATSIIA V USLOVIIAKH NOVOI EKONOMICHESKOI POLITIKI – M., 1923 – 2mf – 9 – COR-507/1 – ne IDC [334]

SEL'SKOKHOZIAISTVENNOE KREDITNOE TOVARISHCHESTVO – ORGANIZATOR RAIONA : VZAIMOOTNOSHENIIA SO SPETSIAL'NYMI VIDAMI KOOPERATIVOV / Kil'chevskii, V A – M., 1928 – 1mf – 9 – COR-386/1 – ne IDC [334]

SELSKO-KHOZIAISTVENNOE PROIZVODSTVO / Bogdanov, N – [Moskva]: Gos. izd-vo, 1921 – 1 – CSUX91-B3099 – us Hoover Inst Photo [630]

SEL'SKOKHOZIAISTVENNYE KREDITNYE TOVARISHCHESTVA PO IKH OTCHETAM : 1924-1927 OPERATSIONNYE GODY – M., 1929 – 3mf – 9 – COR-401/1 – ne IDC [334]

SEL'SKOKHOZIASTVENNYE TOVARISHCHESTVA, KAK IKH USTRAIVAT'I VESTI / Evdokimov, Andrei Aandreevich – Khar'kov, 1914 – 1mf – 9 – COR-26/1 – ne IDC [334]

SELTENE URSACHEN DER GASTROINTESTINALEN BLUTUNG INNERHALB DER CHIRURGIE AM BEISPIEL EIGENER FAELLE UND NEUERER LITERATUR / Patas, Janus Robert – 1995 – 2mf – 9 – DM80.00 – 3-8267-2242-6 – gw Hänsel [617]

Seltmann, C *see* ANGELUS SILESIUS UND SEINE MYSTIK

DER SELTSAME SPRINGINSFELD / Grimmelshausen, Hans Jakob Christoph von; ed by Vesper, Will – Muenchen: Zinnen-Verlag, c1944 – 1r – 1 – us U.W. Library [830]

A SELVA : ACTUALIDADES, POLITICA, LETRAS, PROBLEMAS SOCIAES – Manaus, Amazonas. Set-Out 1937; Jun, 31 Out 1938 – 1,5,6 – bl Biblioteca [072]

O SELVAGEM / Magelhaes, Couto de – Sao Paulo, 3.a ed 1935 – 11mf – 8 – ne Slangenburg [972]

IL SELVAGGIO – 1987-1943 – Cumul – 1 – L100,000 – sz Infoprint [072]

IL SELVAGGIO – Italy, 1924-43 – inquire – us Ross [072]

LE SELVE / Ouida – British Fiction Archive: Unit 3 – 9 – uk Bell [830]

Selwyn, E G *see* THE FIRST EPISTLE OF ST PETER

Selwyn, Edward Carus *see* THE CHRISTIAN PROPHETS AND THE PROPHETIC APOCALYPSE

LA SEMAINE – Brazzaville, Congo: Impr Saint-Paul, 1966- – us Res Libr [072]

LA SEMAINE – Grand-Mere, Canada. v3 n16. 1 jun 1911-v8 n28. 3 aut 1917 – 1r – 1 – Can$40.00 – cn Can Microfilming [072]

LA SEMAINE – Montreal, Canada. 8 jun 1899; v1 n4. 29 jun 1899 – 1r – 1 – Can$25.00 – cn Can Microfilming [072]

LA SEMAINE : POLITIQUE, LITTERAIRE / ed by Comte, Gustave – Montreal, Canada. 3 jul-24 jul 1909 – 1r – 1 – Can$25.00 – cn Can Microfilming [072]

LA SEMAINE – Quebec: C Darveau, [1864] – 9 – cn C.I.H.M. [073]

LA SEMAINE – Quebec: L Brousseau, [1895] – 9 – cn C.I.H.M. [073]

LA SEMAINE : REVUE DE LA PRESSE – Quebec, Canada. 16 fev 1895-v1 n3. 30 mar 1895 – 1r – 1 – Can$25.00 – cn Can Microfilming [073]

LA SEMAINE A RADIO-CANADA : REVUE – (Cont by: Ici Radio-Canada. Includes: Culture – Information – Madame – Jeunesse – Divertissements avr 1966-avr 1967) – Montreal, Canada. 15 oct 1950-1 avr 1966 – 6r – 1 – Can$60.00r – cn Can Microfilming [073]

LA SEMAINE A RADIO-CANADA *see* ICI RADIO-CANADA

LA SEMAINE AGRICOLE : EDITION HEBDOMADAIRE DE LA MINERVE – (24 mai 1872-v46 n16. 27 dec 1879 2r Can$70.00) – Montreal, Canada. 12 oct 1869-26 avr 1872 – 1r – 1 – Can$50.00 – cn Can Microfilming [072]

LA SEMAINE AGRICOLE – Ottawa, Ontario. vA n1. 14 aut 1900 – 1r – 1 – Can$25.00 – cn Can Microfilming [630]

LA SEMAINE AGRICOLE ILLUSTREE – Montreal: Duvernay, Freres, [1869-1872] – 9 – cn C.I.H.M. [630]

LA SEMAINE COMMERCIALE – Quebec: L E Thompson, [1894] – 9 – cn C.I.H.M. [380]

LA SEMAINE DES FAMILLES – Levis, Canada. 18 nov 1869-17 mar 1870 – 1r – 1 – Can$25.00 – cn Can Microfilming [640]

LA SEMAINE EN GUYANE ET DANS LE MONDE – French Guiana. 1944-1948 – 1 – us UMI [072]

SEMAINE FRANCAISE ET LE COURRIER DE L'EUROPE *see* COURRIER DE L'EUROPE

LA SEMAINE INTERNATIONALE – Montreal, 19 au 25 sep 1981 – 1r – 1 – Can$25.00 – cn Can Microfilming [072]

SEMAINE JURIDIQUE : ED. ENTREP. – 1989-1995 – 2r per y – 5,6 – Sfr642.00 – sz Infoprint [340]

SEMAINE JURIDIQUE : ED. GENER. – 1988-1995 – 2r per y – 5,6 – Sfr642.00 – sz Infoprint [340]

SEMAINE JURIDIQUE : ED. NOTAR – (Also available on CD-ROM) – France. 1989-1995 – 2r per y – 5,6 – Sfr642.00 – sz Infoprint [340]

SEMAINE LITTERAIRE – Revue de la litterature, des sciences, des arts, des theatres, etc. Supplement a La Quotidienne. Paris. 11 nov 1840-6 mai 1843 – 1 – fr A.C.R.P.P. [073]

LA SEMAINE POLITIQUE : CONSERVATEUR – Quebec, 17 mar 1894-9 aut 1894f – 1r – 1 – Can$35.00 – cn Can Microfilming [072]

LA SEMAINE RELIGIEUSE DE MONTREAL – (Suivi de: Eglise de Montreal) – [Montreal]: Publiee avec l'approbation de Sa Grandeur Mgr l'Eveque de Montreal, [1883-1964] – 9 – cn C.I.H.M. [240]

LA SEMAINE RELIGIEUSE DE QUEBEC – (Suivi de: L'Eglise de Quebec) – Quebec: [s.n., 1888-1965] (Quebec: A Cote) – 9 – cn C.I.H.M. [240]

A SEMANA : FOLHA INDEPENDENTE – Penedo, Alagoas. 19-26 Set 1909 – 1,5,6 – bl Biblioteca [072]

A SEMANA : JORNAL HEBDOMADARIO – Maceio, Alagoas. 4 Maio-3 Ago 1884 – 1,5,6 – bl Biblioteca [072]

A SEMANA : LETRAS, SCIENCIAS, ARTES – Curityba, 1 Jan-12 Mar 1893 – 1,5,6 – bl Biblioteca [072]

A SEMANA : ORGAM IMPARCIAL – CRITICO, HUMORISTICO E NOTICIOSO – Cidade do Rio Preto, 25 Aug-Sep, 21 Nov 1912 – 1,5,6 – bl Biblioteca [072]

A SEMANA : ORGAO OFICIAL DAS PAROQUIAS DE DIVINOPOLIS, CIRCULO OPERARIO E EDUCANDARIOS – Divinopolis, 9 Jul 1950 – 1,5,6 – bl Biblioteca [072]

A SEMANA – Rio de Janeiro, 3 Jan 1885-Apr 1888; Aug 1893-29 Jun 1895 – 1,5,6 – bl Biblioteca [072]

LA SEMANA – Badajoz, 1917 – 5 – sp Bibl Santa Ana [073]

LA SEMANA – Don Benito, 1881 y 1882 – 5 – sp Bibl Santa Ana [073]

LA SEMANA – Riverside, CA. 1976-77 – 2r – 1 – $100.00 – R02720 – us Library Micro [071]

SEMANA – [Managua, Nicaragua]: La Prensa, [jul 1970-dec 24 1972] – us Res Libr [072]

LA SEMANA CATOLICA – Badajoz, 1912 – 5 – sp Bibl Santa Ana [073]

SEMANA DE LA JUVENTUD. MADRONERA, 20 AL 27 MAYO 1972 / Delegacion Local de la Juventud – Trujillo: Imp. Gexme, 1946 – 1 – sp Bibl Santa Ana [946]

LA SEMANA LLERENENSE – Llerena, 1897 – 5 – sp Bibl Santa Ana [073]

SEMANA PEDAGOGICA. DON BENITO. 10-16 DE JUNIO DE 1934 – Badajoz, 1934. Imp.La Min.Ex. – 1 – sp Bibl Santa Ana [370]

SEMANA RELIGIOSA : ORGAO OFFICIAL DA DIOCESE DE POUSO ALEGRE – Pouso Alegre, 22 Jan-Apr 1927; Jul-Dec 1933; Jul-Dec 1935; Apr-Aug, Oct-Dec 1936; Jan, Mar-Jun, Sep 1938; Apr 1939; Feb 1940; Mar-Apr, Sep, Nov-Dec 1941; Jan, May-Jul 1942; Jan 1943-Aug 1944; Sep 1963-19 Jul 1964 – 1,5,6 – bl Biblioteca [072]

SEMANA SANTA. BADAJOZ, 1968 / Junta de Cofradias de Penitencia y C.I.T.E. – Badajoz: Imp. Provincial, 1968 – sp Bibl Santa Ana [946]

SEMANA SANTA. BADAJOZ, 1969, 70 / Junta de Cofradias de Penitencia y C.I.T.E. – Badajoz: Imprenta Provincial, 1969 y 1970 – sp Bibl Santa Ana [946]

SEMANA SANTA BADAJOZ. 1971. PROGRAMA OFICIAL / Badajoz. Junta de Cofradias de Penitencia – Badajoz: Graf. Nemesio Jimenez, 1971 – 1 – sp Bibl Santa Ana [946]

SEMANA SANTA CACERENA, 1958 / Comision Semana Santa. Caceres – Caceres: Edit. Extremadura, 1958 – 1 – sp Bibl Santa Ana [350]

SEMANA SANTA CACERENA, 1959 / Comision Semana Santa. Caceres – Caceres: Editorial Extremadura, S.A., 1959 – 1 – sp Bibl Santa Ana [350]

SEMANA SANTA CACERENA 1960 / Comision de Semana Santa – Caceres: Edit. Extremadura, 1960 – 1 – sp Bibl Santa Ana [946]

SEMANA SANTA CACERENA 1961 / Comision Semana Santa. Caceres – Caceres: Editorial Extrememadura, s.a., 1961 – 1 – sp Bibl Santa Ana [350]

SEMANA SANTA CACERENA 1976 / Comision Semana Santa. Caceres – Caceres: Imp. Sergio Dorado, 1976 – 1 – sp Bibl Santa Ana [946]

SEMANA SANTA CACERENA 1978 / Comision Semana Santa. Caceres – Caceres: Imp. M. Sergio Dorado, 1978 – sp Bibl Santa Ana [946]

SEMANA SANTA. CACERES, 1963 / Comision Semana Santa. Caceres – Caceres: El Noticiero, S.L., 1963 – 1 – sp Bibl Santa Ana [350]

SEMANA SANTA. CACERES 1974 / Comision de Semana Santa – Caceres: Imp. Sergio Dorado, 1974 – 1 – sp Bibl Santa Ana [350]

SEMANA SANTA CACERES 1977 / Comision Semana Santa. Caceres – Caceres: Imp. Sergio Dorado, 1977 – 1 – sp Bibl Santa Ana [946]

SEMANA SANTA DE PASCUA EN LATIN Y EN CASTELLANO / Sanchez Ruiz, Valentin M – Madrid: Apostolado de la Prensa, 1943 – 1 – sp Bibl Santa Ana [240]

SEMANA SANTA DE PLASENCIA. MARZO 1959 / Comision Semana Santa. Caceres – S.L.s.i. 1959 – 1 – sp Bibl Santa Ana [946]

SEMANA SANTA EN CACERES, 1957 / Caceres. Comision Semana Santa – Caceres: Tip. El. Noticiero, 1957 – 1 – sp Bibl Santa Ana [946]

SEMANA SANTA EN GUARENA Y ORACION A LA VIRGEN / Chamizo, Luis – Badajoz: Imprenta de la Excma. Diputacion Provincial, 1963 – 1 – sp Bibl Santa Ana [810]

SEMANA SANTA EN GUARENA Y ORACION DE LA VIRGEN / Chamizo, Luis – Don Benito: Tip. de Trejo, S.A. – 1 – sp Bibl Santa Ana [240]

O SEMANARIO – Rio de Janeiro, 5 Apr 1956-1 Apr 1964 – 1,5,6 – bl Biblioteca [072]

SEMANARIO – Rio de Janeiro, BL. 1956-1964 – 8r – $400.00 – R04182 – us Library Micro [072]

O SEMANARIO CIVICO – Bahia, Brazil. 12 Sep-3 Oct 1822 – 1 – bl Biblioteca [072]

SEMANARIO DE SAUDE PUBLICA : PELA SOCIEDADE DE MEDICINA DO RIO DE JANEIRO – (Cont as: Revista Medica Fluminense) – Rio de Janeiro, 3 Jan 1831-15 Jun 1833 – 1,5,6 – bl Biblioteca [073]

SEMANARIO ECONOMICO. TOMO 2 / Araus, Pedro – 1766 – 1mf – 9 – Pta1,000.00 – 84-7848-130-3 – sp Pentalfa [330]

SEMANARIO ECONOMICO. TOMO 3 / Araus, Pedro – 1767 – 2mf – 9 – Pta1,500.00 – 84-7848-131-1 – sp Pentalfa [330]

SEMANARIO ERUDITO. TOMOS 1 Y 2 / Valladares Sotomayor, Antonio – 1787 – 2mf – 9 – Pta1,500.00 – 84-7848-317-9 – sp Pentalfa [946]

SEMANARIO ERUDITO. TOMOS 3 Y 4 / Valladares Sotomayor, Antonio – 1787 – 2mf – 9 – Pta1,500.00 – 84-7848-318-7 – sp Pentalfa [946]

SEMANARIO ERUDITO. TOMOS 5 Y 6 / Valladares Sotomayor, Antonio – 1787 – 2mf – 9 – Pta1,500.00 – 84-7848-319-5 – sp Pentalfa [946]

SEMANARIO ERUDITO. TOMOS 7 Y 8 / Valladares Sotomayor, Antonio – 1788 – 2mf – 9 – Pta1,500.00 – 84-7848-320-9 – sp Pentalfa [946]

SEMANARIO ERUDITO. TOMOS 9 Y 10 / Valladares Sotomayor, Antonio – 1788 – 2mf – 9 – Pta1,500.00 – 84-7848-321-7 – sp Pentalfa [946]

SEMANARIO ERUDITO. TOMOS 11 Y 12 / Valladares Sotomayor, Antonio – 1788 – 2mf – 9 – Pta1,500.00 – 84-7848-322-5 – sp Pentalfa [946]

SEMANARIO ERUDITO. TOMOS 13 Y 14 / Valladares Sotomayor, Antonio – 1788 – 2mf – 9 – Pta1,500.00 – 84-7848-323-3 – sp Pentalfa [946]

SEMANARIO ERUDITO. TOMOS 15 Y 16 / Valladares Sotomayor, Antonio – 1788-89 – 2mf – 9 – Pta1,500.00 – 84-7848-324-1 – sp Pentalfa [946]

SEMANARIO ERUDITO. TOMOS 17 Y 18 / Valladares Sotomayor, Antonio – 1789 – 2mf – 9 – Pta1,500.00 – 84-7848-325-X – sp Pentalfa [946]

SEMANARIO ERUDITO. TOMOS 19 Y 20 / Valladares Sotomayor, Antonio – 1789 – 2mf – 9 – Pta1,500.00 – 84-7848-326-8 – sp Pentalfa [946]

SEMANARIO ERUDITO. TOMOS 21 Y 22 / Valladares Sotomayor, Antonio – 1789 – 2mf – 9 – Pta1,500.00 – 84-7848-327-6 – sp Pentalfa [946]

SEMANARIO ERUDITO. TOMOS 23 Y 24 / Valladares Sotomayor, Antonio – 1789 – 2mf – 9 – Pta1,500.00 – 84-7848-328-4 – sp Pentalfa [946]

SEMANARIO ERUDITO. TOMOS 25 Y 26 / Valladares Sotomayor, Antonio – 1790 – 2mf – 9 – Pta1,500.00 – 84-7848-329-2 – sp Pentalfa [946]

SEMANARIO ERUDITO. TOMOS 27 Y 28 / Valladares Sotomayor, Antonio – 1790 – 2mf – 9 – Pta1,500.00 – 84-7848-330-6 – sp Pentalfa [946]

SEMANARIO ERUDITO. TOMOS 29 Y 30 / Valladares Sotomayor, Antonio – 1790 – 2mf – 9 – Pta1,500.00 – 84-7848-331-4 – sp Pentalfa [946]

SEMANARIO ERUDITO. TOMOS 31 Y 32 / Valladares Sotomayor, Antonio – 1790 – 2mf – 9 – Pta1,500.00 – 84-7848-332-2 – sp Pentalfa [946]

SEMANARIO ERUDITO. TOMOS 33 Y 34 / Valladares Sotomayor, Antonio – 1790-91 – 2mf – 9 – Pta1,500.00 – 84-7848-333-0 – sp Pentalfa [946]

SEMANARIO JUDICIAL DE LA FEDERACION. – Mexico. Susp. 1877-80. On film: ser. 1-6, v138; 1871-1968. Lacking: Ser.4, v36 and ser.6, v127-129. LL-0286 – 1 – us L of C Photodup [340]

SEMANARIO MARANHENSE – San'Luiz, 1 Sep 1867-8 Sep 1868 – 1,5,6 – bl Biblioteca [072]

SEMANARIO MERCANTIL – Rio de Janeiro, 4 Jun 1823-28 May 1824 – 1,5,6 – bl Biblioteca [072]

O SEMANARIO OFFICIAL – '(s.l.')-Sao Luis, Brazil. 22 Dec 1830. Jan, Mar-20 Apr 1831 – 1,5,6 – bl Biblioteca [072]

"SEMANARIO PATRIOTICO" – 1808-1811 – 20mf – 9 – sp Cultura [946]

THE SEMAPHORE – Yarmouth, NS: Semaphore Pub Co, [1889-189- or 19–] – 9 – cn C.I.H.M. [360]

LE SEMAPHORE DE MARSEILLE – Marseille. dec 1827-19 aout 1944 – 1 – fr A.C.R.P.P. [073]

Semaun *see* SKETS SEDJARAH PAK MATOSIN

Sembene, Ousmane *see* LE DOCKER NOIR

SEMBLANZA DE DON ANDRES MANJON / Marquez, Gabino – Madrid: Razon y Fe, 1941 – sp Bibl Santa Ana [946]

SEMBLANZA DE EMERITA AUGUSTA / Riquelme Salar, Jose – Alicante – 1 – sp Bibl Santa Ana [946]

SEMBLANZA DE SANTA TERESA DE JESUS / Bayle, Constantino – Madrid: Administracion Razon y Fe, 1922 – 1 – sp Bibl Santa Ana [240]

LA SEMBRA DE ARTEAGA / Queretaro. Mexico (State) – Queretaro. On film: 1880-1913, 1916-24. LL-02032 – 1 – us L of C Photodup [340]

SEM'DNEI MKT = 7 DAYS OF MKT – Moscow. n1-20. oct 1923-apr 1924 – 2mf – 9 – $50.00 – us Ross [790]

O SEMEADOR : DIARIO CATHOLICO VESPERTINO – Maceio, Alagoas. 1 Jul-22 Dez 1916 – 1,5,6 – bl Biblioteca [072]

O SEMEADOR : ORGAO ESPIRITA – Parintins, Amazonas. Jul 1907-Jul 1908 – 1,5,6 – bl Biblioteca [072]

SEMEINOE PRAVO / Asadov, A – Baku, 1959. 224p. BR-8419 1 – 9 – ne IDC [640]

SEMEINYI KRUG – Ezhenedel'nyi zhurnal literatury. iskusstv i sovremennykh novostei. v. 1-52. Spb. 1860. B-1882 2 – 8 – ne IDC [073]

SEMEINYI KRUG – Zhurnal literatury, iskusstv, nauk, technologii, promyshlennosti, khoziaistva, domovodstva, okhoty i mod. v. 1-2. Spb. 1858-59. B-1881 2 – 8 – ne IDC [073]

SEMEIOTICA URANICA OR AN ASTROLOGICAL JUDGMENT OF DISEASES... / Culpeper, N – London, 1651 – 4mf – 9 – ne IDC [130]

Semennikov, V P *see*
- MATERIALY DLIA ISTORII RUSSKOI LITERATURY I DLIA SLOVARIA PISATELEI EPOKHI EKATERINY 2
- RUSSKIE SATIRICHESKIE ZHURNALY 1769-1774 GG
- SOBRANIE STARAIUSHCHEESIA O PEREVODE INOSTRANNYKH KNIG, UCHREZDENNOE EKATERINOI 2 1768-1783 GG

Semenov, P P *see* GEOGRAFICHESKO-STATISTICHESKII SLOVAR' ROSSIISKOI IMPERII

SEMENOVSKIE ZASTENKI : ZAPISKI OCHEVIDT SA / Daurets, N P – Kharbin: "Mai ak", 1921 – 1 – CSUX88-B7494 – us Hoover Inst Photo [830]

Semenov-Tianshanskii, P *see* ZHIVOPISNAIA ROSSIIA

LE SEMEUR – Audincourt, Belfort, Besancon, Troyes. mars 1923-mai 1924, oct 1924-aout 1930. Devient: Le Semeur ouvrier voir a ce titre – 1 – fr A.C.R.P.P. [073]

LE SEMEUR – Belfort. avr-juin 1932 – 1 – fr A.C.R.P.P. [073]

LE SEMEUR – Journal religieux, politique, philosophique et litteraire. Paris. sept 1831-aout 1850 – 1 – fr A.C.R.P.P. [073]

LE SEMEUR – Revue litteraire et artistique. no. 1-7. Paris. oct 1887-mars 1888 – 1 – fr A.C.R.P.P. [073]

LE SEMEUR CANADIEN : PROTESTANT – Napierville, Montreal, Canada. 27 fev -25 dec 1851; 13 jun 1856-24 mai 1861 – 1r – 1 – Can$40.00 – cn Can Microfilming [072]

LE SEMEUR OUVRIER – Besancon, Lons-le-Saunier puis Vieux-Charmont par Sochaux. oct 1930-avr 1932. Devient: Le Semeur ouvrier et paysan voir a ce titre – 1 – fr A.C.R.P.P. [073]

LE SEMEUR OUVRIER ET PAYSAN – Besancon puis Dole. juin 1932-sept 1935 – 1 – fr A.C.R.P.P. [073]

LA SEMEUSE – Port-au-Prince. 1938, 1940, 1941. Scattered issues – 1 – us NY Public [073]

Semevskii, M I *see*
- OCHERKI I RAZSKAZY IZ RUSSKOI ISTORIIA XVIII VEKA. TSARITSA PRASKOV'IA 1664-1723
- SLOVO I DELO. 1700-1725

SEMI (SEMICONDUCTOR EQUIPMENT AND MATERIALS INSTITUTE, INC) – Printed index. Updated every 60 days – 6,9 – us Info Handling [621]

SEM'IA, OPEKA, BRAK: SBORNIK MATERIALOV K PROEKTAM SEMEINOGO KODEKSA UKSSR I RSFSR – Kharkov, 1926. 242p. BR-9400/1 – 9 – ne IDC [947]

SEMI-ANNUAL CIRCULAR – (Cont by: The Education Circular) – Fredericton, NB: Education Office, [1875] – 9 – cn C.I.H.M. [370]

SEMIANNUAL REPORT OF THE DIRECTOR OF THE SELECTIVE SERVICE SYSTEM / U.S. Selective Service System – (No issues between Oct 1979-Mar 1980. Prior to 1968 an annual publ) – 1940-86 (all publ) – 103mf – 9 – $154.00 – LLMC 80-520 – us L.L.M.C. [324]

SEMI-ANNUAL REPORTS / Fulton County. Ohio. County Home – 1891-1916 – 1r – 1 – $32.50r – us Archival [324]

SEMI-ANNUAL REPORTS / Putnam County. Ohio. County Home – 1923-1925 – 1r – 1 – $32.50r – us Archival [324]

SEMI-ANNUAL REPORTS / Van Wert County. Ohio. County Home – 1876-1904 – 1r – 1 – $32.50r – us Archival [324]

SEMI-CENTENNIAL / Brooklyn. New York. Siloam Presbyterian Church – 1899 – 1 – $50.00 – us Presbyterian [240]

THE SEMI-CENTENNIAL HISTORY OF NEBRASKA / Sheldon, Addison E – Lincoln: Lemon Publ. Co., 1904. Nebraska Reel 1. (The Cox Library Collection) – 5 – us Americana [978]

SEMICONDUCTOR INTERNATIONAL – v.1-. 1978- – 1,5,6,9 – us UMI [073]

SEMICONDUCTOR PRODUCTS – v.1-5. 1958-62 – 1 – us UMI [621]

SEMICONDUCTOR PRODUCTS AND SOLID STATE TECHNOLOGY – v.5-10. 1962-67 – 1 – us UMI [621]

SEMICONDUCTOR SCIENCE AND TECHNOLOGY – v1-. 1986- – 1,5,6,9 – £535.00 – uk I.O.P. [530]

SEMICONDUCTORS – v1- 1967- – 1,5,6 – us A.I.P. [530]

SEMICONDUCTORS AND INSULATORS – 1,5,9 – us Gordon [540]

SEMIGROUP FORUM – v. 1-21. 1970-80 – 1,5,9 – 977.00 – us UMI [073]

Semikhatov, M A *see* GEOLOGY REVIEWS

SEMINA IN HORTO BOTANICO ACAD. LUDOVIC / Giessen – Giessensis. 1843-1900. B-7664 1 – 9 – ne IDC [580]

Seminaire de Nicolet. Odanak (Canada). Archives *see* DICTIONNAIRES ABENAQUIS (AUBERY), GRAMMAIRE MIC-MAC (MAILLARD) ET "RADICUM..." (NUDENAS)

Seminaire de Quebec. Archives *see*
- DICTIONNAIRES, GRAMMAIRES, LEXIQUES ALGONQUINS, ABENAQUIS, HURONS, IROQUOIS
- FONDS CONTRECOEUR ET PARTIE DU FONDS VERREAU

Seminaire des Trois Rivieres (Canada). Archives *see*
- FONDS BOUCHER
- FONDS HART

SEMINAIRE NATIONAL POPULATION ET DEVELOPPEMENT : RAPPORT GENERAL, TUNIS 1989 / Tunisia. Ministere, du Plan et du Developpement Regional – Tunis, 1991 – 2mf – 9 – ne IDC [338]

Seminaire Saint Sulmipe de Montreal. Archives *see* SEIGNEURIES DE MONTREAL, DES DEUX-MONTAGNES ET DE SAINT SULPICE (1640-1931)

Seminaire Saint Sulpice de Montreal. Archives *see*
- DICTIONNAIRES, GRAMMAIRES, LEXIQUES, ETC (CUOQ, GUICHART, MATHEVET, MARCOUX, ETC)
- FONDS FAILLON
- REPONSE A UNE ADDRESSE DE L'ASSEMBLEE LEGISLATIVE...DEMANDANT UN ETAT COMPLET, CLAIR ET DETAILLE DES BIENS...DES "ECCLESIASTIQUES"..
- RETURN TO AN ADDRESS TO THE GOVERNOR-GENERAL FOR A STATEMENT OF ALL THE PECUNIARY AND TEMPORAL AFFAIRS OF THE CORPORATION OF THE ECCLESIASTICS OF THE SEMINARY OF ST SULPICE..

SEMINAR – (1983-. 1,5,6,9) – v1-. 1965- – 1 – us UMI [400]

SEMINAR – Downsview. v1-30. 1965-94 – 9 – Can$20.00y – cn Micromedia [073]

SEMINAR. (INDIA) – v. 1-48, Sept 1959-Aug 1963 – 1 – us Res Libr [073]

SEMINAR KARET SE-INDONESIA, MEDAN, INDONESIA, 1962 – Indonesian or English. SE 5562 1. 3 v. 26-29 November 1962 – 9 – ne IDC [950]

SEMINAR KEBATHINAN INDONESIA, 1ST,DJAKARTA, 1959 – Hasil Seminar Kebathinan Indonesia ke-I, Djakarta. SE 4192 1. 1959 – 9 – ne IDC [950]

SEMINAR PENDIDIKAN MENGABDI MANIPOL – SE 4472 1. 1963 – 9 – ne IDC [950]

SEMINAR PROCEEDINGS / Sudan. National Agricultural Extension Seminar for Sudan – v. 1. 1964. BNE-7680 1 – 9 – ne IDC [630]

SEMINAR SEDJARAH, UNIVERSITAS GADJAH MADA, JOGJAKARTA, 1957 – SE 4646 1. Seminar Sedjarah, 14-18 Desember 1957 – 9 – ne IDC [370]

SEMINAR TENAGA ATOM INSTITUTE TECHNOLOGI BANDUNG 27/31 MARET 1962 / Indonesia. Seminar Tenaga Atom, 1st – SE-5622 1. 1963 – 9 – ne IDC [530]

SEMINAR TRANSMIGRASI, DJAKARTA, 1963 – SE 4473 1. Laporan Seminar Transmigrasi, tanggal 17 dan 18 September, 1963 – 9 – ne IDC [950]

SEMINARIO CONCILIAR DE SAN ATON. GABINETE NUMISMATICO. CATALOGO / Gomez Villafranca, Ramon – Badajoz: Tip. Lit. y Enc. de Uceda Hermanos, 1910 – sp Bibl Santa Ana [240]

SEMINARIO DE BADAJOZ. LAS MONEDAS ARABES DE SU MONETARIO / Perez Hernandez, Justo – Madrid, 1916 – 1 – sp Bibl Santa Ana [332]

SEMINARIO DE PLASENCIA, EL. APUNTES HISTORICOS / Garcia Vidal, Ceferino – Plasencia: Talleres Tip. La Victoria, 1946 – sp Bibl Santa Ana [390]

Seminario Diocesano de San Anton *see*
- CALENDARIO ESCOLAR 1968/69
- CALENDARIO ESCOLAR 1969/70

SEMINARIO SOBRE "BASES PARA UN PLAN PROVINCIAL DE ASITENCIA HOSPITALARIA" – Badajoz: Imp. Provincial, 1970 – 1 – sp Bibl Santa Ana [946]

LOS SEMINARIOS TRIDENTINOS / Sanchez Aliseda, Casimiro – Madrid: Razon y Fe, 1945 – 1 – sp Bibl Santa Ana [946]

EL SEMINARISTA / Fernandez, Placido Jose – Caracas, 1930; Madrid: Razon y Fe, 1931 – 1 – sp Bibl Santa Ana [999]

SEMINARIUM KONDAKOVIANUM : RECUEIL D'ETUDES ARCHEOLOGIE, HISTOIRE DE L'ART, ETUDES BYZANTINES – Prague. 11v. 1927-40 – 46mf – 9 – OA-247/1 – ne IDC [930]

SEMINARS IN ADOLESCENT MEDICINE – 1985- – 1,5,6,9 – us UMI [610]

SEMINARS IN DERMATOLOGY – v1-. 1982- – 1,5,6,9 – us UMI [616]

SEMINARS IN HEARING – v4-. 1983- – 1,5,6,9 – us UMI [616]

SEMINARS IN HEMATOLOGY – New York. v1-11. 1964-74 – 5,9 – Dfl770.00; Dfl70.00v – ne Swets [610]

SEMINARS IN INTERVENTIONAL RADIOLOGY – 1984- – 1,5,6,9 – us UMI [616]
SEMINARS IN LIVER DISEASE – v1-. 1981- – 1,5,6,9 – us UMI [616]
SEMINARS IN NEUROLOGY – v1-. 1981- – 1,5,6,9 – us UMI [616]
SEMINARS IN OCCUPATIONAL MEDICINE – v1-. 1986- – 1,5,6,9 – us UMI [615]
SEMINARS IN REPRODUCTIVE ENDOCRINOLOGY – v1-. 1983- – 1,5,6,9 – us UMI [618]
SEMINARS IN RESPIRATORY MEDICINE – v2-. 1980- – 1,5,6,9 – us UMI [616]
SEMINARS IN SPEECH AND LANGUAGE – v4-. 1983- – 1,5,6,9 – us UMI [400]
SEMINARS IN THROMBOSIS AND HEMOSTASIS – (1979-. 1,5,6,9) – v1-. 1974- – 1 – us UMI [616]
THE SEMINARY BEMA – (Cont by: The Bema) – St Martins, NB: Union Baptist Seminary, 1889-[1893?] – 9 – cn C.I.H.M. [370]
SEMINARY MAGAZINE / Southern Baptist Seminary – Feb 1888-Feb 1904 – 1 – 280.21 – us Baptist [240]
THE SEMINARY METHOD OF ORIGINAL STUDY IN THE HISTORICAL SCIENCES : ILLUSTRATED FROM CHURCH HISTORY / Foster, Frank Hugh – New York: Scribner, 1888 – 1mf – us A.T.L.A. [240]
SEMINARY NEWS / Southern Baptist Seminary – May 1929-43. (Formerly: Seminary Newspaper. 1929-31) – 1 – 19.67 – us Baptist [240]
IL SEMINATORE – Rome, Italy. May 1876-1882 – 1 – 50.00 – us A.B.H.S. [073]
SEMINOLE BILINGUAL EDUCATION PROJECT NEWSLETTER – 1972-78.(American Indian Periodicals in the Princeton University Library). 6 fiches – 9 – $45.00 – us UPA [073]
(SEMIRAMIS). PREMIERE SUITE D'HARMONIE A HUIT PARTIES...TIREE DE L'OPERA DE SEMIRAMIS. / Catel, Charles-Simon – Parts. 180-? – 9 – us Sibley [780]
SEMITEN UND INDOGERMANEN IN IHRER BEZIEHUNG ZU RELIGION UND WISSENSCHAFT : EINE APOLOGIE DES CHRISTENTHUMS VOM STANDPUNKTE DER VOELKERPSYCHOLOGIE / Grau, Rudolf Friedrich – (Includes bibliographical references) – Stuttgart: S G Liesching, 1864 – 1mf – 9 – 0-8370-8818-6 – 1986-2818 – us A.T.L.A. [930]
SEMITIC STUDIES IN MEMORY OF REV. DR. ALEXANDER KOHUT / ed by Kohut, G A – Berlin. 1897. BJ-100-69 1 – 9 – ne IDC [470]
THE SEMITIC THEORY OF CREATION: A STUDY IN LANGUAGE / Peck, Harry Thurston – Chicago: Barclay, White, 1886. 1 fiche – 9 – us A.T.L.A. [240]
SEMITIC WRITING / Driver, G R – 1944 – 9 – $12.00 – us I.R.C. [470]
DER SEMITISCHE INFINITIV : EINE SPRACHWISSENSCHAFTLICHE UNTERSUCHUNG / Koch, Adolf – (Includes bibliographical references) – Stuttgart: E Schweizerbart (E Koch), 1874 – 1mf – 9 – 0-8370-7227-1 – 1986-1227 – us A.T.L.A. [470]
SEMITISCHE MISZELLEN / Vollers, Karl – (Includes bibliographical references) – Strassburg: Karl J Truebner, 1903 – 1mf – 9 – 0-8370-7350-2 – 1986-1350 – us A.T.L.A. [470]
SEMITISCHE SPRACHWISSENSCHAFT / Brockelmann, C – Ed 2. Leipzig. 1916. BNE-20,051-1 – 9 – ne IDC [470]
DIE SEMITISCHEN EIGENNAMEN IM ALTEN TESTAMENT. 1. TEIL : AUF IHRE ENTSTEHUNG UND ELEMENTE HIN / Ulmer, Friedrich – (Includes bibliographical references) – Leipzig: W Drugulin, 1901 – 1mf – 9 – 0-8370-7273-5 – 1986-1273 – us A.T.L.A. [470]
DIE SEMITISCHEN FREMDWOERTER IM GRIECHISCHEN / Lewy, Heinrich – (Includes bibliographical references and index) – Berlin: R Gaertner, 1895 – 1mf – 9 – 0-8370-9291-4 – 1986-3291 – us A.T.L.A. [450]
DIE SEMITISCHEN SPRACHEN : EINE SKIZZE / Noeldeke, Theodor – (Includes bibliographical references) – 2. verb Aufl. Leipzig: Chr Herm Tauchnitz, 1899 – 1mf – 9 – 0-8370-8775-9 – 1986-2775 – us A.T.L.A. [470]
SEMI-WEEKLY AGE – Clinton. Iowa. 1897, 1899; 1901 – 1 – us UMI [071]
SEMI-WEEKLY AMERICAN – Waterbury. Conn. 1899-1921 – 1 – us UMI [071]
SEMI-WEEKLY CITIZEN – Ottawa, Canada. -sw. 29 Jan 1885-29 May 1890. 2 reels – 1 – uk British Libr Newspaper [072]
SEMI-WEEKLY COURIER AND NEW YORK ENQUIRER – New York, 1829-56 – 7r – 1 – us Ross [071]
SEMI-WEEKLY EXPRESS – San Antonio. Tex. 1886-1909 – 1 – us UMI [071]
SEMI-WEEKLY GAZETTE – Meadville, PA., 1889-1891 – 13 – $25.00r – us I.M.R. [071]
SEMI-WEEKLY HERALD – Mansfield. Ohio. 1861-1862 – 1 – us UMI [071]
SEMI-WEEKLY INDEPENDENT – Red Bluff, CA. 1860-1861 – 1r – 1 – $50.00 – C03641 – us Library Micro [071]
SEMI-WEEKLY IOWEGIAN – Centerville. Iowa. 1896-1899; 1910; 1916-1919 – 1 – us UMI [071]
THE SEMI-WEEKLY ITEM – Mount Carmel, PA. -w 1896-1902 – 13 – $25.00r – us I.M.R. [071]
SEMI-WEEKLY JOURNAL *see* JOURNAL
SEMI-WEEKLY KEARNEY HUB – Kearney.NE. 1873-1906. Includes Central Nebraska Press – 1 – us UMI [071]
SEMI-WEEKLY KEARNEY HUB AND CENTRAL NEBRASKA PRESS – Kearney, NE. (-d 1873). Mar 1873-Mar 1881, scattered issues missing; Nov 1889-Feb 1891, scattered issues missing; Jun 1891-Feb 1906; Apr-Jun 1906, scattered issues missing – 1 – us NE Hist [071]
SEMI-WEEKLY MISSOULIAN – Missoula. Mont. 1899-1904 – 1 – us UMI [071]
SEMI-WEEKLY NEWS – Frederick. Md. 1952-53 – 1 – us UMI [071]
SEMI-WEEKLY NEWS – Huntingdon, PA. -w 1878-1927 – 13 – $25.00r – us I.M.R. [071]
SEMI-WEEKLY NEWS – Mansfield. Ohio. 1899-1900 – 1 – us UMI [071]
SEMI-WEEKLY NEWS – San Antonio. Tex. 1862-1969 – 1 – us UMI [071]
SEMI-WEEKLY PALLADIUM – Benton Harbor. Mich. 1894-1897 – 1 – us UMI [071]
SEMI-WEEKLY POST *see* ORANGE POST
SEMI-WEEKLY RECORD – Chico. Calif. 1898-1906 – 1 – us UMI [071]
SEMI-WEEKLY REPUBLICAN – Lansing.MI. 1875-78 – 1 – us UMI [071]
SEMI-WEEKLY SENTINEL – Parkersburg. West Virginia. 1895-1912 – 1 – us UMI [071]
SEMI-WEEKLY SENTINEL – Santa Cruz, CA. 1862-67 – 2r – 1 – $100.00 – B02960 – us Library Micro [071]
SEMI-WEEKLY SENTINEL – Yazoo City. Miss. 1916-1919; 1934-1937 – 1 – us UMI [071]
SEMI-WEEKLY SIGNAL – Goderich, Canada. 1862-73 – 6r – 1 – $390.00 – cn Library Assoc [971]
SEMI-WEEKLY TELEGRAPH – St. John, Canada. Semi-Weekly Telegraph & the News. -sw. 4 Aug 1906; March 1910-Nov 1916. 12 1 2 reels – 1 – uk British Libr Newspaper [072]
SEMI-WEEKLY TIMES – Alliance. NE. 1922-25.Includes Alliance-Herald – 1 – us UMI [071]
SEMI-WEEKLY TIMES – Falls City, NE. Oct. 1895-Aug. 1896; Oct. 1897-Nov. 1898 – 1 – us NE Hist [071]
SEMI-WEEKLY UNION – Yreka, CA. 1862-65 – 1r – 1 – $50.00 – B03119 – us Library Micro [071]
Semkovskii, S M *see* KOOPERATIVY I SOTSIALIZM
Semmedo, Alvaro *see* RELATIONE DELLA GRANDE MONARCHIA DELLA CINA
Semmelweis, I P *see* DIE AETIOLOGIE, DER BEGRIFF UND DIE PROPHYLAXIS DES KINDBETTFIEBERS
SEMNADTSAT' PERVYKH LET V ZHIZNI IMPERATORA PETRA VELIKAGO, 1672-1689 / Pogodin, M P – M. 1875. BR-8330 2 – 8 – ne IDC [947]
Semon, R *see* ZOOLOGISCHE FORSCHUNGSREISEN IN AUSTRALIEN UND DEM MALAYISCHEN ARCHIPEL, 1891-1893
Sempebwa, Joshua Wantate *see* THE ONTOLOGICAL AND NORMATIVE STRUCTURE IN THE SOCIAL REALITY OF A BANTU SOCIETY
Semper, C G *see* REISEN IM ARCHIPEL DER PHILIPPINEN, THEIL 2, WISSENSCHAFTLICHE RESULTATE
Semper, Hans *see*
– DONATELLO, SEINE ZEIT UND SCHULE
Sempere y Guarinos, Juan *see* SUPLEMENTO AL ARTICULO DE TRIGUEROS
SEMPEX 93 – 1992. Microfiches A: Specialites Pharmaceutiques, Produits Veterinaires et de Chimiophytotherapie – 9 – FF817.00 – fr S.E.M.P. [610]
SEMPEX-PARAPHARMEX 93 – 1992. Microfiches A: Specialites Pharmaceutiques, Produits Veterinaires et de Chimiophytotherapie. Microfiches B: Produits Dietetiques et de Parapharmacie. Microfiches D: Denominations Communes Internationales et Equivalences de Certaines Specialites Etrangeres – 18mf – 9 – FF1,157.00y – fr S.E.M.P. [610]
SEMPEX-PARAPHARMEX-ACCESSOIREX – (Microfiches A: Specialites Pharmaceutiques, Produits Veterinaires et de Chimiophytotherapie. Microfiches B: Produits Dietetiques et de Parapharmacie. Microfiches C: Accessoires et Divers Vendus en Officine. Microfiches D: Denominations Communes Internationales et Equivalences de Certaines Specialites Etrangeres. Microsempex: Most of SEMPEX and all of PARAPHARMEX on a single fiche. 11 fiches per year. FF85.00) – 24 fiches par an – 9 – FF1,560.00y – fr S.E.M.P. [610]
Semple, James H *see* ON WINGS OF EAGLES. A HISTORY OF THE FIRST BAPTIST CHURCH OF WHITE SETTLEMENT, TEXAS
Semple, R B *see* HISTORY OF THE RISE AND PROGRESS OF THE BAPTISTS IN VIRGINIA
A SEMPRE VIVA – Curitiba, 15 May-Jun, Aug-Dec 1924; Jan-15 Dec 1925 – 1,5,6 – bl Biblioteca [072]
Semprini, Giovanni *see* I PLATONICI ITALIANI
Semprun Gurrea, Jose Maria *see* A CATHOLIC LOOKS AT SPAIN
Semrau, Eberhard *see* DIDO IN DER DEUTSCHEN DICHTUNG
SEMS – Istanbul, Nos. 3-4, 6, 18, 24 (1876). Mehmed 'Arif – 1mf – 9 – $36.75 – us MEDOC [949]
Sen, Asit Kumar *see* DIE STELLUNG DES EUROPAEISCHEN PARLAMENTS IN DER EUROPAEISCHEN WIRTSCHAFTSGEMEINSCHAFT BIS ZUR FUSION DER EXEKUTIVEN
Sen, Dinesh Chandra, rai banadur *see* CHAITANYA AND HIS AGE
Sena, I Gusti Ktut *see* PROSEDURE PRAKTIS DALAM BALIK NAMA
SENADOR FIRMINO – Senador Firmino, 10 Nov-Dec 1958; Jan, Mar-Oct 1959; Jan-3 Apr 1960 – 1,5,6 – bl Biblioteca [072]
Senaille, J B *see* SONATAS, VIOLIN ET CONTINUO, LER LIVRE
SENALES...DE DIA Y...JOSE SOLANO Y BOTE – 1781 – 9 – 1.50f – sp Bibl Santa Ana [920]
SENALES...NOCHE...ARMADA DEL REY / Solano Bote, Jose – 1794 – 9 – $1.50f – sp Bibl Santa Ana [946]
SENATE AND HOUSE BILLS / U.S. Congress – 1957-65 – 3 – us Readex [324]
THE SENATE AND TREATIES 1789-1817 / Hayden, R – New York, 1920 – 3mf – 1 – ILM-700/1 – ne IDC [327]
SENATE CLOTURE RULE – Washington: GPO, 1975. 89p. LL-2394 – 1 – us L of C Photodup [340]
SENATE JOURNALS / Hawaii Legislature – (Add vols after 1994 planned) – 1902-94 – 1087mf – 9 – $1,630.00 – LLMC 77-106 – us L.L.M.C. [323]
SENATE JOURNALS / Michigan Legislature – (Updates planned) – 1835-1979 – 1814mf – 9 – $2,721.00 – LLMC 79-438S – us L.L.M.C. [340]
SENATE JOURNALS 1966-79 : 2ND REG SESS OF THE CONGRESS OF MICRONESIA TO SESS OF THE INTERIM CONGRESS OF THE FEDERATED STATES OF MICRONESIA (1978-79) / Congress of Micronesia – n.p, n.d. – 117mf – 9 – $175.00 – LLMC 82-100F, Title 32 – us L.L.M.C. [323]
SENATE REPORT APPROVING THE COMPACT OF FREE ASSOCIATION : SENATE REPORT N98-626, 98TH CONG, 2ND SESS, SEP 20, 1984 / U.S. Congress. Commission on Energy and Natural Resources – n.p, n.d. – 4mf – 9 – $6.00 – LLMC 82-100F, Title 18 – us L.L.M.C. [980]
SENATE REPORT APPROVING THE COMPACT OF FREE ASSOCIATION : SENATE REPORT N99-16, 99TH CONG, 1ST SESS, MAR 22, 1985 / U.S. Congress. Commission on Energy and Natural Resources – n.p, n.d. – 5mf – 9 – $7.50 – LLMC 82-100F, Title 20 – us L.L.M.C. [980]
THE SENATOR – Ottawa: Senator Pub Co, [1900-19–] – 9 – cn C.I.H.M. [070]
SENCILLOS...GEOGRAFIA / Garcia Rubio, Manuel – 1849 – 9 – 1.50f – sp Bibl Santa Ana [910]
SENCKENBERGISCHE BIBLIOTHEK, FRANKFURT AM MAIN : SCHLAGWORTKATALOG DER MONOGRAPHIEN UND PERIODIKA BIS ERWERBUNGSJAHR 1964 / ed by Burkhard,H – (Alphabetischer Katalog der Zeitschriften und Serien. Stand 8 Jan 1985. 73 fiches. diazo DM2,100.00 ISBN 3-598-30322-X) – 1983 – 161mf (1:42) – 9 – diazo DM2,800.00 (silver DM3,100.00 ISBN: 3-598-30321-1) – 3-598-30320-3 – gw Saur [610]
SEND FOOD TO SPAIN / Robertson, Diana Forbes – London, 1938. Fiche W1144. (Blodgett Collection of Spanish Civil War Pamphlets) – 9 – us H.U. College Libr [946]
DER SENDBOTE – 1930-71. 29,466p – 1 – 1031.31 – us Baptist [240]
DER SENDBOTE : ORGAN DER DEUTSCHEN BAPTISTEN NORD-AMERIKAS – (Lacking: no7 Jan 1862. no50 Dec 1870. no21 May 1881) – 1853-1929 – 59r – 1 – ATLA S0134 – us A.T.L.A. [073]
DER SENDBOTE – v78-119. 1930-71 (complete) – 19r – 1 – ATLA R0131 – us A.T.L.A. [073]
SENDBRIEFF AN DIE...BURGERMEISTER VND RHAT DER LOEBLICHEN STATT ZUERICH. DARJNNEN SIE ERJNNERT...WERDEN WAS JRE KICHENDIENER VNTER DEM SCHEIN EINER ANTWORT AUFF D. PHILIPPI NICOLAI BUCH FUER SEIN WERCK WIDER JESUM CHRISTUM... / Huber, S – Yrsel, 1598 – 1mf – ne IDC [240]
EIN SENDBRIEFF HANS HUTHEN ETWA AINS FURNEMEN VORSTEERS IM WIDERTAUFFERORDENN, VERANTWORT / Rhegius, Urbanus – Augspurg, A. Weyssenhorn. 1528. BME-109 1 – 9 – ne IDC [240]
EIN SENDBRIEFF WIDER ETLICHER ROTTENGEISTER / Luther, Martin – Wittemberg, N. Schirlentz. 1532. BME-94 1 – 9 – ne IDC [240]
EYN SENDEBRIEFF... / Bugenhagen, J – [Wittenberg, 1525] – 1mf – 9 – ne IDC [240]
Sender, Ramon Jose *see* LA ESFERA
DIE SENDING DER FRAU IN DER DEUTSCHEN GESCHICHTE : MIT 16 BILDNISSEN / Koehler, Ruth – Leipzig: Hase & Koehler, (c1940). 248p. Ports. 1272 – 1 reel – 1 – us U.W. Library [305]
Sendivogius, Michael *see*
– COSMOPOLITE OV NOVVELLE LVMIERE DE LA PHISIQUE NATURELLE
– A PHILOSOPHICAL ACCOUNT OF NATURE IN GENERAL, AND OF THE GENERATION OF THE THREE PRINCIPLES OF NATURE, VIZ. MERCURY, SULPHUR, AND SALT, OUT OF THE FOUR ELEMENTS
SENDJINKOEN DAN TENTERA SOEKARELA. (TERKOEMPOEL OLEH K. HIRATO, A.O.) / ed by Hirato, K – Medan, Badan Penjiaran Bunka Ka (2603). 138p – 41-42mf – 9 – ne IDC [355]
SENDJINKOEN. PENOENTOEN BAGI BALATENTARA DAI NIPPON. DITERDJEMAHKAN OLEH M. JOELI. DIPERIKSA SERTA DIPERBAIKI OLEH. T. ITJIKI / Japan. Ministry of War – Djakarta, Pertjetakan Asia-Raya, 2602. 19, 18p – 53mf – 9 – ne IDC [350]
EENEN SENDTBRIEF AEN DIERCK VOLKERTZ CORNHERT: OP SYN BOECK GHENAEMPT: KLEYN MUNSTER, WTGEGHAEN TEGHENS DIE SCHRIFTEN VAN DAVID JORIS / Theophilus, J – BME-270 1 – 9 – ne IDC [240]
SENDTBRIEF (EEN CHRISTELIJCKE), GESCHREUEN AAN ALLEN GHEMEYNTEN, DIE OP HET GHELOOUE IN GODT. DOOPEN – 1580. BME-224 1 – 9 – ne IDC [240]
DIE SENDUNG – Berlin. apr 1924-may 25, 1941 – 18r – 1 – gw Mikrofilm [072]
DIE SENDUNG SEMAELS : JUEDISCHE TRAGOEDIE IN FUENF AUFZUEGEN / Zweig, Arnold – Muenchen: K Wolff, 1920 – 1r – 1 – us U.W. Library [820]
Seneca *see* OPERA PHILOSOPHICA ET TRAGAEDIAE
SENECA ADLER – Tiffin, Ohio. 1848 – 1r – 1 – $32.50r – us Archival [071]
SENECA ADVERTISER – Tiffin, Ohio. 1842-1919 – 25r – 1 – $32.50r – us Archival [071]

SENECA BAPTIST CHURCH. OCONEE COUNTY. SOUTH CAROLINA : CHURCH RECORDS – (Deacons' Minutes, 1953-72. 38.84; 1) – 1956-72 – 1 – 7.34 – us Baptist [240]
Seneca County. Ohio. Bloom Township. Board of Trustees *see*
- BOOK OF MISCELLANEOUS RECORDS
- MINUTES

Seneca County. Ohio. Board of County Commissioners *see*
- BLIND RELIEF RECORDS
- COMMISSIONERS' JOURNAL

Seneca County. Ohio. Common Pleas. Criminal Division *see* CORONERS' INQUESTS
Seneca County. Ohio. Fostoria, City. City Council *see*
- MINUTES
- ORDINANCES AND RESOLUTIONS

Seneca County. Ohio. Liberty Township. Board of Education *see* MINUTES
Seneca County. Ohio. Liberty Township. Board of Trustees *see*
- DITCH JOURNALS
- MINUTES

Seneca County. Ohio. Liberty Township. Justice of the Peace *see*
- CIVIL DOCKETS
- CRIMINAL DOCKETS

Seneca County. Ohio. Presbyterian Church of Melmore *see* RECORDS
Seneca County, Ohio. Tiffin, City. City Council *see*
- INDEX TO RECORDS AND MINUTES
- MINUTES
- ORDINANCES
- RESOLUTION RECORD

Seneca County. Ohio. Zion Lutheran Church *see* RECORDS
SENECA PATRIOT – Tiffin. Ohio. 1832-1841 – 1 – us UMI [071]
SENECA SENTINEL – Tiffin, Ohio. 1975-76 – 1r – 1 – $32.50r – us Archival [071]
Seneca Township.Seneca County. Ohio. Evangelical Jerusalem Church *see* RECORDS
SENECA WHIG – Tiffin, Ohio. 1848-50 – 1r – 1 – $32.50r – us Archival [071]
Senechal, J *see* ESPACE ET MOBILITE RURALE EN MILIEU SOUDANOSAHELIEN: LE CHANGEMENT DANS L'ISOLEMENT, GOURMA DU NORD, HAUTE-VOLTA
SENEGAL : SITUATION ECONOMIQUE DU SENEGAL 1962-1976 / Senegal. Direction de la Statistique – (1969, 1973 not available. Coll title: African Official Statistical Serials, 1867-1982) – 33mf – 9 – £275.00 – uk Chadwyck [960]
Senegal *see*
- LE 4EME PLAN QUADRIENNAL 1973-1977
- BULLETIN ADMINISTRATIF
- DEUXIEME PLAN QUADRIENNAL DE DEVELOPPEMENT ECONOMIQUE ET SOCIAL, 1965-1969
- DEVELOPMENT PLANS: DEUXIEME PLAN QUADRIENNAL DE DEVELOPPEMENT ECONOMIQUE ET SOCIAL 1965-1969
- ECONOMIE ET PLAN DE DEVELOPPEMENT
- JOURNAL OFFICIEL
- RAPPORT GENERAL SUR LES PERSPECTIVES DE DEVELOPPEMENT DU SENEGAL
- TRADITION, DIVERSIFICATION, AND ECONOMIC DEVELOPMENT

SENEGAL D'AUJOURD'HUI – Dakar. sept 1963-67 – 1 – fr A.C.R.P.P. [073]
Senegal. Direction de la Statistique *see* SENEGAL
LE SENEGAL DROLATIQUE / Picrochole – Paris, 1896 – 1 – us Res Libr [960]
LE SENEGAL EN 1925 / Oxoby, Jean Daramy d' – Paris, 1925 – 1 – us Res Libr [960]
SENEGAL ET NIGER : LA FRANCE DANS L'AFRIQUE OCCIDENTALE, 1879-1883 / France. Ministere de la Marine et des Colonies – Paris: Challamel, 1884 – us Res Libr [960]
Senegal. Ministere du Plan, du Developpement *see* PLAN QUADRIENNAL DE DEVELOPPEMENT, 1961-1964
Senegal. Ministere du Plan et de la Cooperation *see*
- ETUDE PROSPECTIVE "SENEGAL 2015"
- PLAN D'ORIENTATION POUR LE DEVELOPPEMENT ECONOMIQUE ET SOCIAL 1989-1995 (HUITIEME PLAN)

Senegal. Parliament *see* JOURNAL OFFICIEL
LA SENEGAL, SA CONQUETE & SON ORGANISATION (1364-1925) / Sabatie, Alexandre Camille – St.Louis. Senegal. 1925 – 1 – us Res Libr [960]
SENEGAMBIE ET GUINEE / Tardieu, Amedee-Eugene – Paris, Firmin Didot Freres. 1847 – 9 – 12.50 – fr Orientalistes [960]
SENEGOR *see* HA-SENEGOR
SENELIK IHSAIYAT-I MALIYE – (1325[1909/1910], 1. sene.-10mf. $75.00; 1326[1910/1911], 2. sene.-8mf. $75.00; 1327[1911/1912], 3. sene.-7mf. $75.00) – us MEDOC [650]
SENGA HANDBOOK : A SHORT INTRODUCTION TO THE SENGA DIALECT AS SPOKEN ON THE LOWER LUANGWA NORTH-EASTERN RHODESIA / Madan, Arthur Cornwallis – Oxford: Clarendon Press, 1905 – us Res Libr [470]
Sengle, Friedrich *see* WIELAND
Sengupta, Rahul *see* CHIRURGISCHE BEHANDLUNGSERGEBNISSE GUTARTIGER SCHILDDRUESENERKRANKUNGEN
SENHORA ANNINHA : BRASILIANISCHER ROMAN / Tanera, Karl – Berlin: Carl Duncker, [19–?] – 1r – 1 – us U.W. Library [830]
THE SENHOUSE PAPERS – 1762-1831. Relating to the West Indies. BRRAM – 2r – 1 – uk Microform Academic [972]
SENIOR CITIZEN NEWSREEL – Cincinnati, OH. 1962-86 – 1 – us A.J.P.C. [071]
SENIOR ECONOMIC ADVISERS TO ECE GOVERNMENTS COMMITTEE / UN Economic Commission for Europe (ECE) – 1973-88 – E/F.39 E.279 F.184 R.182 – 9 – us U.N. Pubs [340]
SENIOR EDUCATIONAL PERSONNEL: NEW FUNCTIONS AND TRAINING – 9 – fr UNESCO [370]
Senior, Nassau William *see* ESSAYS ON FICTION
THE SENIOR NEWS – Eureka, CA. 1981-1990 – 2r – 1 – $100.00 – B05033 – us Library Micro [071]
SENIOR SCHOLASTIC – (v. 95- 1969- 5,6. v. 97- 1970- 9) – Teacher's edition. v. 8-. 1926- – 1 – us UMI [073]
SENIOR TEACHER AND PUPIL BOOK, YEAR 1-4 – 1 – 108.99 – us Baptist [240]
SENIOR WORLD – San Diego, CA. 1983 – 21+ r – 1 – $1,050.00 ($100.00y) – R04102 – us Library Micro [071]
Senkovskii *see* SOBRANIE SOCHINENII
Senning, A *see*
- SULFUR LETTERS
- SULFUR REPORTS

SENORES DE PASARON / Velo Nieto, Gervasio – Madrid: Accasor, 1956 – 1 – sp Bibl Santa Ana [946]
EL SENORIO DE CASTELLANOS / Munoz de San Pedro, Miguel – Badajoz: (Imp. Diput. Provinc.), 1964. Sep. Revista Estudios Extremenos – 1 – sp Bibl Santa Ana [946]
LA SENORITA MALCRIADA / Iriarte, Tomas – s.a. – 1mf – 9 – Pta1,000.00 – 84-7848-234-2 – sp Pentalfa [440]
SENRYO-GUN KEN-ETSU ZASSI – Copyright reserved and edited by The Gordon W. Prange Collection, East Asia Collection, McKeldin Library of Maryland at College Park – 260r – 1 – Y3,200,000.00 – ja Yushodo [950]
SENSE OF RHYTHM AND MOTOR RHYTHM ABILITY IN EDUCABLE MENTALLY RETARDED AND INTELLECTUALLY NORMAL CHILDREN / Leahy, Teresa – 1981 – 1mf – 9 – $4.00 – us Microform Publ [790]
Sensenich, Ila Jeanne *see* COMPENDIUM OF THE LAW ON PRISONERS' RIGHTS
THE SENSES AND THE INTELLECT / Bain, Alexander – London: Longmans, Green, 3rd ed 1868 – 1 roll – 1 – 1-55879-712-2 – uk Libr Preservation [150]
LA SENSIBILIDAD DE ZURBARAN / Sanchez Canton, Francisco Javier – Granada: Imprenta Francisco Guzman, 1944 – 1 – sp Bibl Santa Ana [946]
SENSORISCHE UNTERSUCHUNGEN AN OBERFLAECHENMODIFIZIERTEN PHTHALOCYANINEN / Schuh, Joerg – 1994 – 2mf – DM 80.00 – 3-89349-895-8 – gw Hänsel [540]
SENSORS AND ACTUATORS – v1-6. 1981-84 – 1,5,6,13 – sz Elsevier [621]
SENSORY SYSTEMS – v1-8. 1987-94 – 1,5 – $65.00v – us UMI [574]
SENTENCES DE MONSIEUR L'OFFICIAL DE L'EVECHE DE TOULON – Toulon. 1732 – 9 – fr Hachette [360]
SENTENCES ET ARRESTS, SERVANS A LA JUSTIFICATION DE LA CALOMNIEUSE ACCUSATION FAITE CONTRE SOEUR FRANCOISE DE LA CROIX – Paris. 1654 – 9 – fr Hachette [360]
SENTENCIA DADA POR...NUNCIO...EN EL PLEYTO QUE HA TRATADO EL...PADRE GENERAL DE LA ORDEN DE SAN GERONIMO Y OTROS RELIGIOSOS DEL MONASTERIO DE YUSTE CON EL PRIOR DE... / Fachenetti, Cesar – S.l., s.i., s.a. 1641 – 1 – sp Bibl Santa Ana [240]
SENTENCIA DE LA SUPREMA CORTE DE JUSTICIA DE LA NACION SOBRE LOS BIENES MAL HABIDOS DEL DICTADOR / Argentina. Suprema Corte – Buenos Aires: [s.n.], 1957 – 1 – CSUXAJA7095-B – us Hoover Inst Photo [340]
SENTENCIA DEL PLEITO / Spain. Consejo de Hacienda – 1721 – 9 – 1.50f – sp Bibl Santa Ana [340]
SENTENCIA QUE N.R.P.M.F., GENERAL DE LA ORDEN DE N.P.S. GERONIMO, DIO Y PRONUNCIO EN EL MONASTERIO DE SAN BARTOLOME...EN 15 DIAS DEL MESDE OCTUBRE : EN 15 DIAS DEL MESDE OCTUBRE DE 1641 ANOS CONTRA LOS PADRES FR. JUAN DE LA SERENA, FR. DIEGO DE SAN ILDEFONSOY FR. ANTONIO DE SAN JUAN SOBRE DIVERSOS Y GRAVES DELITOS QUE SE LES IMPUTA AVER COMETIDO... / Caceres, Diego de – s.l., s.i., s.a. – 1 – sp Bibl Santa Ana [240]
SENTENCIA TRADUCIDO DEL LATIN EN ROMANCE QUE DIO EL NUNCIO EN LAS CONTROVERSIAS QUE HAN PASADO ENTRE EL CAPITULO DIFINITORIO DE LA ORDEN DE SAN GERONIMO Y EL PADRE GENERAL CACERES DELLA / Fachenetti, Cesar – S.l., s.i., s.a. 1642 – 1 – sp Bibl Santa Ana [240]
SENTENCIA...PLEITO...MONTIJO...MERIDA / Portal y Canton, Salustiano – 1894 – 9 – 1.50f – sp Bibl Santa Ana [340]
SENTENCIAS SOBRE PASOS Y CAMINOS (ANNO 1326) – Albarracin – 1r – 5,6 – sp Cultura [946]
SENTENCIA...VARIOS VECINOS DE VALDEOBISPO...SOBRE LAS DEHESAS... – Plasencia: Imp. Y Enc. M. Ramos, 1911 – 1 – sp Bibl Santa Ana [946]
SENTENCING FEDERAL OFFENDERS FOR CRIMES COMMITTED BEFORE NOVEMBER 1, 1987 / Eaglin, James B – Washington: FJC, Sep 1991 – 1mf – 9 – $7.50 – LLMC 95-358 – us L.L.M.C. [340]
THE SENTENCING OPTIONS OF FEDERAL DISTRICT JUDGES : FEBRUAR 1981 REVISION / Partridge, Anthony et al – Washington: FJC, 1981 – 1mf – 9 – $1.50 – LLMC 95-828 – us L.L.M.C. [340]
THE SENTENCING OPTIONS OF FEDERAL DISTRICT JUDGES : JUNE 1983 REVISION / Partridge, Anthony et al – Washington: FJC, 1983 – 1mf – 9 – $1.50 – LLMC 95-373 – us L.L.M.C. [340]
THE SENTENCING OPTIONS OF FEDERAL DISTRICT JUDGES : JUNE 1985 REVISION / Partridge, Anthony – Washington: FJC, 1985 – 1mf – 9 – $1.50 – LLMC 95-374 – us L.L.M.C. [340]
SENTENTIA...NUNTII APSTOLICI... / Fachenetti, Cesar – S.l., s.i., s.a., 1642 – 1 – sp Bibl Santa Ana [946]
LE SENTENZE ESTERE DI DIVORZIO E IL GIUDIZIO DI DELIBAZIONE / Cassuto, D – Torino, 1901 – 1mf – 1 – ILM-3105/1 – ne IDC [327]
DIE SENTENZEN DES KARDINALS HUMBERT (MGH SCHRIFTEN..: 7.BD) : DAS ERSTE RECHTSBUCH DER PAEPSTLICHE REFORM / Michel, A – 1943 – Dfl25.00 – ne Slangenburg [240]
DIE SENTENZEN DES PETRUS LOMBARDUS : IHRE QUELLEN UND IHRE DOGMENGESCHICHTLICHE BEDEUTUNG / Baltzer, Otto – Leipzig: Dieterich, 1902. (Studien zur Geschichte der Theologie und der Kirche; 8. Bd., Heft 3) – 1mf – us A.T.L.A. [240]
DER SENTENZENKOMMENTAR PETERS VON CANDIA / Ehrle, Franz – Muenster, 1925 – 7mf – 8 – ne Slangenburg [290]
DER SENTENZENKOMMENTAR PETERS VON CANDIA / Ehrle, Franz – Muenster in Westfalen: Aschendorffsche Verlagsbuchhandlung, 1925. (Franziskanische Studien. Beiheft 9) – xii/363p – 1 – us U.W. Library [450]
SENTIDO Y FORMA DE LA LEALTAD / Franco, Alberto – Buenos Aires: Subsecretaria de Informaciones, 1953 – 1 – CSUXAJB7815-B – us Hoover Inst Photo [320]
SENTIMENS DES PLUS HABILES PEINTRES DU TEMPS, SUR LA PRATIQUE DE LA PEINTURE / Testelin, H – O 439. 1680 – 9 – ne IDC [760]
SENTIMENS SUR LA DISTINCTION DES DIVERSES MANIERES DE PEINTURE, DESSEIN ET GRAVUEURE / Bosse, A – Paris. 1649. BO-171 1 – 9 – ne IDC [760]
SENTIMENTAL AND LITERARY MAGAZINE – v. 1-3. 1 Jul 1795-23 Aug 1797 – 1 – us UMI [073]
SENTIMENTAL TOMMY : THE STORY OF HIS BOYHOOD / Barrie, James Matthew – London: Cassell, 1896 – 1 roll – 1 – uk Libr Preservation [830]
O SENTIMENTO DA NATUREZA NO FAUSTO DE GOETHE : A EXPRESSAO ESTETICA / Almeida, Ferrand Pimentel d' – (Includes bibliographical references) – Coimbra: Imprensa da Universidade, 1918 – 1r – 1 – us U.W. Library [430]
SENTIMENTS DE CLEANTE SUR LES ENTRETIENS D'ARISTE ET D'EUGENE / Barbier d'Aucour, J – 4th ed. 1776 – 9 – fr I.C.S. [440]
SENTIMIENTOS...VIRTUDES DE FRANCISCO DE SAN MIGUEL / Plazuelos, Fr. Gabriel – 1699 – 9 – 1.50f – sp Bibl Santa Ana [240]
SENTINEL – Ashtabula. Ohio. 1890-1900 – 1 – us UMI [071]
SENTINEL – Butler. Pa. 1824-30 – 1 – us UMI [071]
SENTINEL – Carlisle, PA., 1981-1982 – 13 – $25.00r – us I.M.R. [071]
SENTINEL – Centralia. Ill. 1884- – 1 – us UMI [071]
SENTINEL – Centralia. Ill. -w. 1863-76, 1884-1916 – 1 – us UMI [071]
SENTINEL – Cheney. Kan. -w. 1894-1958 – 1 – us UMI [071]
SENTINEL – (Daily Confederate newspaper) – Richmond, VA. mar 12, 1863-apr 1, 1865 – 2r – 1 – us Western Res [071]
SENTINEL – Darby. Mont. 1895-1897 – 1 – us UMI [071]
SENTINEL – Dublin, London. 1854-Jul 1856. -d. 3 1/2 reels – 1 – uk British Libr Newspaper [072]
SENTINEL – Dutton. MT. 1922-41 – 1 – us UMI [071]
SENTINEL – Eureka. Nev. -w. 1949- – 1 – us UMI [071]
SENTINEL – Fairfield. Iowa. 1847-49 – 1 – us UMI [071]
SENTINEL – Fort Dodge. Iowa. 1856-1860 – 1 – us UMI [071]
SENTINEL – Fort Lauderdale. Fl. -w. 1913-23 – 1 – us UMI [071]
SENTINEL – Grafton. West Virginia. 1907-1916; 1917-1966; 1967-1969 – 1 – us UMI [071]
SENTINEL – Grafton. West Virginia. -w. 1895-1929 – 1 – us UMI [071]
SENTINEL – Grand Junction. Col. 1893- – 1 – us UMI [071]
SENTINEL – Grenada. Miss. 1902-1936 – 1 – us UMI [071]
SENTINEL – Hanford. Calif. 1943-47; 1955- – 1 – us UMI [071]
SENTINEL – Harper. Kansas. 1882-1917 – 1 – us UMI [071]
SENTINEL – Hays. Kan. 1876-81; 1887-95 – 1 – us UMI [071]
SENTINEL – Hempstead. N.Y. -w. 1900-49 – 1 – us UMI [071]
SENTINEL – Hot Springs. Mont. 1952-1957 – 1 – us UMI [071]
SENTINEL – Jacksonville. Ill. -w. 1868-71 – 1 – us UMI [071]
SENTINEL – Julian, CA. 1887-89; 1890-92 – 2r – 1 – $100.00 – B02321 – us Library Micro [071]
SENTINEL – Kalida, Ohio. 1855-65 – 1r – 1 – $32.50r – us Archival [071]
SENTINEL – L'Abette. Kan. 1870-1871 – 1 – us UMI [071]
SENTINEL – L'Anse. Mich. 1893-1896 – 1 – us UMI [071]
SENTINEL – Largo. Fl. -w. 1922-41, 1945- – 1 – us P.K. Yonge [071]
SENTINEL – Lewistown. Pa. and pred. 1871-1956, 1958- – 1 – us UMI [071]
SENTINEL – Lewistown, PA. -d 1956-1990 – 13 – $25.00r – us I.M.R. [071]
SENTINEL – Los Angeles. Calif. -w. 1946- – 1 – us UMI [071]
SENTINEL – McPherson. Kan. 1970- – 1 – us UMI [071]
SENTINEL – Milwaukee. Wis. 1910- – 1 – us UMI [071]

SENTINEL – Mitchell. Or. 1915-1925 – 1 – us UMI [071]
SENTINEL – Orlando. Fl. 1924-1941; 1951- – 1 – us UMI [071]
SENTINEL – Parkersburg. West Virginia. 1889-1948; 1955- – 1 – us UMI [071]
SENTINEL – Pomeroy. Ohio. 1971- – 1 – us UMI [071]
SENTINEL – Pontiac. Ill. 1897-1900 – 1 – us UMI [071]
SENTINEL – Pontotoc. Miss. 1902-1908; 1909-1928 – 1 – us UMI [071]
SENTINEL – Ramona. Calif. -w. 1944-58 – 1 – us UMI [071]
SENTINEL – Red Bluff, CA. 1870-1882; 1883; 1887-1888; 1891-1892; 1904-1905; 1912-1915; 1921-1927; 1931 – 21r – 1 – $1,050.00 – B02664 – us Library Micro [071]
SENTINEL – Richmond. Va. 1863-65 – 1 – us UMI [071]
SENTINEL – Rochester. Ind. 1862-1865; 1870-71; 1873- – 1 – us UMI [071]
SENTINEL – Rome. N.Y. -w. 1842-47, 1849-55, 1863-83 – 1 – us UMI [071]
SENTINEL – Santa Cruz. Calif. 1884-1945; 1950- – 1 – us UMI [071]
SENTINEL – Sedalia. Mo. -w. 1898-1906 – 1 – us UMI [071]
SENTINEL – Shelton. Wash. 1890-1893 – 1 – us UMI [071]
SENTINEL – South Haven. Mich. 1867-1904 – 1 – us UMI [071]
SENTINEL – St. Louis. MO. -w. 1968- – 1 – us UMI [071]
SENTINEL – Summit. Miss. 1902-1905; 1906-1910; 1936-1941 – 1 – us UMI [071]
SENTINEL – Sumner. Miss. 1936-1951 – 1 – us UMI [071]
SENTINEL – Sydney, 1845-48 – 1r – 1 – A$35.00 silver A$30.00 vesicular – at Pascoe [072]
SENTINEL – Utica. Mich. 1876-1971 – 1 – us UMI [071]
SENTINEL – Vicksburg. Miss. and Expositor. 1837-46 – 1 – us UMI [071]
SENTINEL – Waterville. Maine. 1904- – 1 – us UMI [071]
SENTINEL – (Weekly newspaper oh the 14th Michigan Mounted Infantry, U.S. Army) – Columbia, TN. feb 20 & 29, 1864 – 1r – 1 – us Western Res [071]
SENTINEL – White Sulphur Springs. West Virginia. 1911-1968 – 1 – us UMI [071]
SENTINEL – Woodsdale. Kan. -w. 1889-94 – 1 – us UMI [071]
SENTINEL – Woodstock. Ill. 1960- – 1 – us UMI [071]
SENTINEL – Woonsocket. R.I. 1842-1843 – 1 – us UMI [071]
SENTINEL – Yazoo City. Miss. 1902-1911; 1922-1933 – 1 – us UMI [071]
THE SENTINEL – Boulder. Mont. 1901-1904 – 1 – us UMI [071]
THE SENTINEL – (Chicago). 1911-28 – 1 – us A.J.P.C. [073]
THE SENTINEL : A MONTHLY JOURNAL DEVOTED TO THE EXPOSITION AND ADVANCEMENT OF PUBLIC MORALITY AND TO THE SUPPRESSION OF VICE – London, 1882-1899 – 46mf – 9 – W-29/1 – ne IDC [360]
THE SENTINEL / The National Congress of American Indians – 1963-72.(American Indian Periodicals in the Princeton University Library). 9 fiches – 9 – $50.00 – us UPA [073]
THE SENTINEL – Seaside, CA. 1993 – 2+ r – 1 – $100.00 ($50.00y) – B06057 – us Library Micro [071]
THE SENTINEL – Winston-Salem. N.C. 1906- – 1 – us UMI [071]
SENTINEL AND GAZETTE – Utica. N.Y. 1825-1834 – 1 – us UMI [071]
LE SENTINEL DE PRESCOTT – Hawkesbury, Ontario. 17 fev 1911 – 1r – 1 – Can$25.00 – cn Can Microfilming [072]
SENTINEL FOR JUNIORS – 1932-58 – 1 – 285.11 – us Baptist [240]
SENTINEL MIST CHRONICLE – St. Helens OR. July 1 1968-Dec 30 1971 – 1 – us U.O. Library [071]
THE SENTINEL OF THE BLESSED SACRAMENT – (Other language ed.: Le Petit messager du Tres Saint Sacrement) – Montreal: Fathers of the Blessed Sacrament, 1898-1917 – 9 – cn C.I.H.M. [240]
THE SENTINEL OF THE BLESSED SACRAMENT *see* LE PETIT MESSAGER DU TRES SAINT SACREMENT
SENTINEL (SHOPPER) – Pittsburg. Calif. -w. 1945-54 – 1 – us UMI [071]
SENTINEL STAR – Grenada. Miss. 1950- – 1 – us UMI [071]
A SENTINELA – Itambacuri, 1 Mar-Apr 1951 – 1,5,6 – bl Biblioteca [072]
A SENTINELA : ORGAM REPUBLICANO – Cidade do Serro, 21 Apr-25 May 1893 – 1,5,6 – bl Biblioteca [072]
A SENTINELA : ORGAO LIBERAL CONSAGRADO AOS INTERESSES DA COMARCA DE SAO FIDELIS – S. Fidelis, 14 Jun 1883-Dec 1884; Jan-Feb, Jun-12 Nov 1885 – 1,5,6 – bl Biblioteca [072]
SENTINELA DA LIBERDADE : HOJENA GUARITA DO QUARTEL GENERAL DE PIRAJA, HOJE BAHIA DE TODOS OS SANTOS – '(s.l.')-Bahia, Brazil. 12 Jan-9 Mar 1831 – 1,5,6 – bl Biblioteca [072]
A SENTINELLA – Alto Rio Doce, Brazil. Oct 1934 – 1 – bl Biblioteca [072]
A SENTINELLA – Muriae, Brazil. Feb 1902 – 1 – bl Biblioteca [072]
A SENTINELLA – Queluz, 1 Mar-27 Jul 1908 – 1,5,6 – bl Biblioteca [072]
A SENTINELLA – Sao Luiz, 30 Jun-Dec 1855; Jan-May, 7 Jul 1856 – 1,5,6 – bl Biblioteca [072]
LA SENTINELLA – Hoboken, NJ, 1907 – 2mf or 1r – 1,9 – us I.H.R.C. [978]
LA SENTINELLA – Utica, NY, 1915 – 39mf or 1r – 1,9 – us I.H.R.C. [978]
SENTINELLA DA LIBERDADE A BEIRA MAR DA PRAIA GRANDE – Rio de Janeiro, 5 Aug-25 Oct 1823 – 1,5,6 – bl Biblioteca [072]
SENTINELLA DO SERRO – Cidade do Serro, 1 Jun, 1 Dec 1927 – 1,5,6 – bl Biblioteca [072]
LA SENTINELLE : CARICATURES – Quebec, Canada. 21 mar 1885 – 1r – 1 – Can$25.00 – cn Can Microfilming [072]
LA SENTINELLE / ed by Choquette, Ph-Aug – Montmagny, Canada. 7 mai-14 dec 1883; ns: 9 jul 1891-v3 n30. 2 fev 1894 – 1r – 1 – Can$40.00 – cn Can Microfilming [072]
LA SENTINELLE – (Cont by: Le Lingot 5 fev 1943) – Arvida, Canada. 4 dec 1936-22 jan 1943 – 1r – 1 – cn Can Microfilming [072]
LA SENTINELLE – (Cont by: Paix (Trois-Rivieres, Quebec)) – Trois-Rivieres [Quebec: s.n., 1884-1887] – 9 – cn C.I.H.M. [971]
LA SENTINELLE – Lachute, Canada. 7 fev-22 aut 1936 – 1r – 1 – Can$50.00 – cn Can Microfilming [072]
LA SENTINELLE / ed by Lemaitre, Francois – Quebec, Canada. 11 mai 1826 – 1r – 1 – Can$25.00 – cn Can Microfilming [072]
LA SENTINELLE / ed by Marquis, Gerard & Marquis, Maurice – (Cont by and filmed with: Le Courrier-Sentinelle 14 aut 1925-14 avr 1933-28 sep 1935) – Montmagny, Canada. 22 avr 1922-23 mai 1925 – 3r – 1 – Can$55.00r – cn Can Microfilming [072]
LA SENTINELLE – Mattawa, Ontario. v1 n10. 1 mar 1895-v1 n52. 27 dec 1895 – 1r – 1 – Can$30.00 – cn Can Microfilming [072]
LA SENTINELLE – Nosbonsing, Ontario. v1 n7. 18 aut 1894 – 1r – 1 – Can$25.00 – cn Can Microfilming [072]
LA SENTINELLE : ORGANE DU MOUVEMENT SENTINELLISTE – Woonsocket, RI. 4 avr 1924-24 mar 1927 – 2r – 1 – Can$60.00r – cn Can Microfilming [071]
LA SENTINELLE – Par J.-B. Louvet. Paris. mars-nov 1792, sept 1795-sept 1796 – 1 – fr A.C.R.P.P. [073]
LA SENTINELLE – Providence. R.I. 1924-1926; 1928 – 1 – us UMI [071]
LA SENTINELLE – Trois-Rivieres, Canada. v1 n1. 2 aut 1884-v1 n5. 30 aut 1884 – 1r – 1 – Can$25.00 – cn Can Microfilming [072]
LA SENTINELLE DE CHIBOUGAMAU-CHAPAIS – Chibougamau, Canada. v2 n24. 2 mai 1958-28 dec 1960 – 2r – 1 – Can$50.00r – cn Can Microfilming [072]
LA SENTINELLE DU PEUPLE – no. 1-5. 10 nov-25 dec 1788. suivi par les imitations et reponses de: La Sentinelle de la noblesse. no. 1-2. 1788. Le Caporal. no. 1-2. 1788 89. La Confession de la sentinelle. 1 no. 1788. Rennes – 1 – fr A.C.R.P.P. [073]
LA SENTINELLE DU PEUPLE – no. 1-98. oct 1830-sept 1832. fusionne avec: Le Ruban tricolore dont il reprend la numerotation d'annee. NO. 402-501. pour former: Le Telegraphe. Journal de Paris. nov 1832-37. Paris. oct 1830-oct 1833 – 1 – fr A.C.R.P.P. [073]
LA SENTINELLE DU PEUPLE – Quebec, Canada. v1 n2. 9 mar 1850-v2 n22. 12 jul 1850 – 1r – 1 – Can$35.00 – cn Can Microfilming [072]
SENTINEL-MIST – St. Helens, OR. -w. 1933-52 – 1 – 384.00 – us Oregon Hist [071]
SENTINEL-MIST – St. Helens. OR.1933-52 – 1 – us UMI [071]
SENTINEL-NEWS – Santa Cruz. Calif. 1946-56 – 1 – us UMI [071]
SENTINEL-STANDARD – Ionia. Mich. 1880-1883; 1929; 1939; 1956- – 1 – us UMI [071]
SENTINEL-STANDARD – Ionia. Mich. -w. 1866-1900 – 1 – us UMI [071]
SENTINEL-TRIBUNE – Bowling Green. Ohio. 1910-1920; 1931-1935; 1964- – 1 – us UMI [071]
Sentral Organisasi Buruh Seluruh Indonesia *see*
- AKSI AMBILALIH TONGGAK BERSEDJARAH MENGGANJANG "MALAYSIA." SE 4723/1. 1964
- KONSTITUSI SOBSI
- PERANAN DAN TUGAS DEWAN PERUSAHAAN

Sentral Organisasi Buruh Seluruh Indonesia. Kongres Nasional. 3d Solo, 1960 *see* RESOLUSI2
Sentral Organisasi Buruh Seluruh Indonesia. Kongres Nasional. 3d Solo Surakarta, 1960 *see* PROGRAM TUNTUTAN SOBSI UNTUK SANDANG PANGAN DAN DEMOKRASI
THE SENTRY – Kingstown, Jamaica. -w. 5 Feb 1897-23 May 1902; 3 Jan 1930-30 Dec 1932. Imperfect. 3 reels – 1 – uk British Libr Newspaper [072]
Sentzer, Bonifaz *see* PIUS 10TH
Seo, Chungjin *see* EFFECTS OF ETHANOL ON THERMOREGULATORY RESPONSES DURING COLD AIR EXPOSURE IN MALE AND FEMALE SUBJECTS
SEOUL ECONOMIE DAILY – 1960-1995 – 12 times per yr – 1 – F2,770.00 – sz Infoprint [072]
A SEPARACAO – Uberaba, 17 Jul, Sept 1921; Jan, Mar, 21-28 May 1922 – 1,5,6 – bl Biblioteca [072]
SEPARACI ON DE LA IGLESIA DEL ESTADO / Justo, Juan Bautista – Buenos Aires: Editorial "La Vanguardia", 1946 – 9 – us Hoover Inst Photo [972]
SEPARACION DE LAS CATEDRALES DE ALBARRACIN Y SEGORBE (ANNO 1580-1581) – Albarracin – 1r – 5,6 – sp Cultura [240]
THE SEPARATED LIFE: A BIBLICAL DEFENCE OF THE DIVINITY OF CHRIST / Whitteker, John Edwin – Philadelphia: Gen. Coun. Pub. H., 1909. 1 fiche. 8370-5832-5 – 9 – us A.T.L.A. [240]
THE SEPARATES, OR, STRICT CONGREGATIONALISTS OF NEW ENGLAND / Blake, S Leroy – Boston: Pilgrim Press, c1902 – 1mf – us A.T.L.A. [240]
SEPARATION AND PURIFICATION METHODS – (v13-. 1984-. 5,6,9) – v1-. 1972- – 1 – us UMI [073]
SEPARATION AND SERVICE, OR, THOUGHTS ON NUMBERS VI,VII / Taylor, James Hudson – London: Morgan & Scott, 1896. 1 fiche – 9 – us A.T.L.A. [240]
LA SEPARATION DES EGLISES ET DE L'ETAT : PRECIS HISTORIQUE, DISCOURS ET DOCUMENTS / Reveillaud, Eugene – Paris: Fischbacher, 1907 – 2mf – us A.T.L.A. [320]
SEPARATION SCIENCE – v1-12. 1966-77 – 1 – us UMI [073]
THE SEPARATIST – Ireland.18 Feb-9 Sept 1922 – 1 – ie Microforms [072]
SEPHARDIC VOICE – (Missing: Mar 1986-Feb 1987; May 1987-Oct 1987) – Brooklyn, NY. Jan 1986-Feb 1986; Mar 1987-Apr 1987; Nov 1987 – us A.J.P.C. [073]
SEPHARDIM / Kayserling, M – Romanische Poesien der Juden in Spanien. Leipzig. 1859. BJ-421-4 1 – 9 – ne IDC [470]
Sepher, Pierre Jacques *see* CATALOGUE DES LIVRES RARES ET SINGULIERS DE LA BIBLIOTHEOUE DE M. L'ABBE SEPHER. DONT DA VENTE SE FERA LE LUNDI 6 MARS 1786
SEPIA – v15- 1966- 1; v24- 5,6 – us UMI [305]
SEPIA CITY PRESS – Toledo. Ohio. 1948-1950 – 1 – us UMI [071]
THE SEPIA SOCIALITE – New Orleans. Aug. 10, 17, 1940 – 1 – us NY Public [073]
Sepp, C *see* NEDERLANDSCHE VOGELEN; VOLGENS HUNNE HUISHOUDING, AERT EN EIGENSCHAPPEN BESCHREEVEN
Sepp, Christiaan *see* KERKHISTORISCHE STUDIEN
Sepp, Johann Nepomuk *see* GOERRES
Sepstrup, Preben *see* TV TRANSNATIONALIZATION – EUROPE AND ASIA
SEPT – no. 1-183. Paris. 3 mars 1934-27 aout 1937 – 1 – fr A.C.R.P.P. [073]
SEPT ANS EN AFRIQUE OCCIDENTALE. / Bouche, Pierre Bertrand – Paris, 1885 – 1 – us Res Libr [910]
SEPT CONTES SANGU DANS LEUR CONTEXTE CULTUREL ET LINGUISTIQUE, TANZANIE / Bilodeau, J – Paris. 1979 – 7mf – 9 – F100.00 – fr Ethnologie [390]
Sept-Douleurs, Marie-des *see* BIBLIOGRAPHIE DE L'HOTEL-DIEU D'ALMA
SEPTEMBRE 1792. HISTOIRE POLITIQUE DES MASSACRES... / Gautherot, Gustave; ed by Bayle, Constantino – Madrid: Razon y Fe, 1928 – 9 – sp Bibl Santa Ana [320]
SEPTEMVRI – Mesechno spisanie za khudozhestvena literatura, kritika i obshchestvenni vaprosi. Organ na Saiuza na balgarskite pisatelei. Sofia. 1948-57, 1962-68. Lacking: (11-12) 1949. BR-5755 2 – 8 – ne IDC [073]
SEPTEMVRI – Stara Zagora, Bulgaria. 1955-1959 – 2r – 1 – us L of C Photodup [949]
SEPTEMVRI – v1-25. 1948-1972 – 1 – us I.U. Libraries [073]
SEPTEMVRIISKA POBEDA – Pleven, Bulgaria. May-Dec 1945; 1952-82 – 27r – 1 – us L of C Photodup [949]
SEPTEMVRIISKO ZNAME – Pazardzhik, Bulgaria. Dec 1954-1969 – 8r – 1 – us L of C Photodup [949]
SEPT-ILES JOURNAL – (Cont by: L'Avenir et Sept-Iles Journal 13 mar 1954-6 oct 1973. Cont by: L'A L'Avenir 9 oct 1973-23 jun 1977) – Sept-Isles, Canada. 5 jul 1952-27 fev 1954 – 27r – 1 – Can$70.00r – cn Can Microfilming [072]
SEPTIMA CONFERENCIA DE MINISTROS DE HACIENDA : IMPUESTOS DE COPARTICIPACION: CUADROS ESTADISTICOS / Conferencias de Ministros de Hacienda, Secretar ia Permanente – [Buenos Aires]: Ministerio de Hacienda de la Nacion, Direccion General de Impuestos y Contribuciones, 1953 – 1 – CSUXAGN1099-B – us Hoover Inst Photo [360]
Septimus Severus *see* EMPEROR OF ROME. ...IN QVO VIDETVR FINIS TVRCARUM IN PRAESENTI EORUM IMPERATORE
SEPT-JOURS : REVUE HEBDOMADAIRE D'INFORMATION – Montreal. 17 sep 1966-v1 n52. 9 sept 1967 – 1r – 1 – cn Can Microfilming [073]
SEPTUAGINT – 5th ed. Vetus Testamentum graece iuxta LXX interpretes... Leipzig, 1875. 2v – 1 – us U.W. Library [240]
THE SEPTUAGINT AND MODERN STUDY / Jellicoe, S – 1968 – 9 – $15.00 – us I.R.C. [220]
SEPTUAGINTA / Rahlfs, Alfred – 1932 – 9 – $66.00 – us I.R.C. [220]
SEPTUAGINTA / Wevers, John W – (Gottingen). 16v – 9 – $300.00 – us I.R.C. [220]
SEPTUOR POUR 2 CORS, ALRINETTE IN B, 2 VIOLONS, ALTO, ET BASSE, OP. 10 / Winter, Peter van – (Parts) – Leipzig: Breitkopf & Hartel, 178- – 1 – us Sibley [780]
THE SEPULCHRE IN THE GARDEN: A SERMON PREACHED ON THE 13TH OCTOBER, 1867, IN ST ANDREW'S CHURCH, TORONTO, AFTER THE FUNERAL OF THE LATE JOHN CAMERON, ESQ.. / Barclay, John – Toronto: J. Lovell, 1868. 05681. (Pre-1900 Canadiana) – 9 – cn C.I.H.M. [920]
EL SEPULCRO DE ALMANZOR 1 DE BADAJOZ / Saavedra, Eduardo – Madrid: Tip. Fortanet, 1889 – 1 – sp Bibl Santa Ana [946]
Sepulvada, Ion. Gen. *see* OPERA OMNIA
THE SEQUEL OF THE ABSTRACT OF THOSE PARTS OF THE CUSTOM OF THE VISCOUNTY AND PROVOSTSHIP OF PARIS, WHICH WERE RECEIVED AND PRACTIFIED IN THE PROVINCE OF QUEBEC IN THE TIME OF THE FRENCH GOVERNMENT – London: Charles Eyre and William Strahan, 1773. SEM105P369 – 2mf – 9 – Can$4.50 – cn Bibl Nat [971]

THE SEQUEL TO CATHOLIC EMANCIPATION : THE STORY OF THE ENGLISH CATHOLICS CONTINUED DOWN TO THE RE-ESTABLISHMENT OF THEIR HIERARCHY IN 1850 / Ward, Bernard – London, New York: Longmans, Green, 1915 – 2mf – us A.T.L.A. [240]
SEQUENCE – 1946-52 – 5 – uk World [073]
SEQUENCES / Centre Catholique du Cinema de Montreal. Commission des Cine-Clubs – Montreal: la Commission. no 1 1955-. SEM16P298 – 5r – 5 – Can$167.00 – cn Bibl Nat [790]
SEQUENTIAL ANALYSIS – v3-. 1984- – 1,5,6,9 – us UMI [073]
Serafimovich, Aleksandr Serafimovich *see* OPIS DOKUMENTAL'NYKH MATERIALOV LICHNOGO FONDA NO. 457
SERAMPORE LETTERS : BEING THE UNPUBLISHED CORRESPONDENCE OF WILLIAM CAREY AND OTHERS WITH JOHN WILLIAMS, 1800-16 / ed by Williams, Leighton & Williams, Mornay – New York: Fleming H Revell, c1892 – 1mf – 9 – 0-8370-6632-8 – 1986-0632 – us A.T.L.A. [920]
Serane, Philippe *see*
- L'HEUREUX NAUFRAGE OU L'ON TROUVE UNE IDEE DE LEGISLATION CONFORME A L'HUMANITE, A LA NATURE, AU BIEN PUBLIC
- NEWTONIANISME DE VOLTAIRE
- THEORIE D'UNE EDUCATION REPUBLICAINE

SERAT NITISASTRA / Surja Anjakrakusuma, Prabu – SE 4851 1 – 9 – ne IDC [950]
SERAT TUNTUNAN TJAKING PAKELIRAN PADALANGAN RINGGIT PURWA LAMPAHAN: DONORODJO, DENING R.M. SOEMANTRI SOEMOSAPOETRO / Sumosaputro, Sumantri – In Javanese, with music in number notation. SE 5458 1. 1964 – 9 – ne IDC [780]
SERAT: WEDARAN WIRID. ISI: WEDARANWEDARAN KANTI BARESKURES ADADASAR; AKAL IAN BUDI SAHA KALAWAN BLAK-BLAKAN, MIJAK WEWADOSING GESANG KASUNJATAN / Partojuwono, R S Yudi – In Javanese. SE-5586 1. 2 v. 1962-64 – 9 – ne IDC [950]
SERBANEKA STANVAC / Standard-Vacuum Oil Company – SE 3467 1. 1958? – 9 – ne IDC [660]
SERBA-SERBI DOKUMEN PARTAI 1961 / Communist Party. Indonesia – SE-4045 1. 1962 – 9 – ne IDC [335]
Serbia *see* SRPSKE NOVINE
SERBIA; HER PEOPLE, HISTORY AND ASPIRATIONS / Petrovic, Vojislav M – New York: Frederick A. Stokes, 1915. 280p. illus – 1 – us U.W. Library [949]
Serbia. Uprava Drzavne Statistike *see* STATISTICKI GODISNJAK KREALJEVINE SRBIJE
SERBIAN HERALD – (In Serbian) – Canada, 1946-48 – 3r – 1 – cn Commonwealth Micro [072]
SERBIAN ORTHODOX CHURCH (IN AMERICA) – 1898-1925 – 1 reel – 1 – us I.H.R.C. [240]
SERBO-CROATIAN FOLK SONGS / Bartok, Bela – 1951 – 1 – us I.U. Libraries [390]
SERBSKE NOWINY – Bautzen, 1848-1937 – 52r – 1 – Dist. gw Mikrofilm – gw Misc Inst [943]
SERBSKI PESME, OR, NATIONAL SONGS OF SERBIA / Lytton, Edward Robert Bulwer Lytton – London: Chapman and Hall, 1861 – 1 roll – 1 – 1-55879-887-0 – uk Libr Preservation [780]
SERDALO – Groznyi, USSR. Apr 20 1991-Dec 5 1992 – 1r – 1 – us L of C Photodup [072]
SERDTSE DUMKA. PRIKLIUCHENIE / Veltman, A F – Moscow, 1838. B-1466/2 – 8 – ne IDC [460]
Serebrennikov, V *see* KIEVSKAIA AKADEMIIA S POLOVINY 18 V. DO PREOBRAZOVANIIA V 1819 G
Serebriakov, F S *see*
- KAK KOOPERATSIIA SOZDAET KREST'IANSKOE BOGATSTVO
- KAK USTROIT' I VESTI KREDITNOE TOVARISHCHESTVO

SEREBRIANNYI GOLUB' / Belyi, A – Roman. v. 1-2. Berlin. 1922. BR-592 2 – 8 – ne IDC [460]
SEREBRIANNYI GOLUB' BELOGO. RETSENZIIA / Berdiaev, N A – Russkaia Mysl'. 1910. BR-3251 2 – 8 – ne IDC [190]
SEREBRIANNYI GOLUB'. POVEST V SEMI GLAVAKH / Belyi, A – M. 1910. BR-591 2 – 8 – ne IDC [460]
Seredy, S P *see* SEL'SKOKHOZIAISTVENNAIA KOOPERATSIIA I GOSPROMYSHLENNOST'
A SEREIA : SEMANARIO, CRITICO, MUNDANO E NOTICIOSO – Manaos, Amazonas. 11 Set 1934 – 1,5,6 – bl Biblioteca [072]
Serena, Juan de la, et al *see* MEMORIAL...P. CACERES
SERENADE, D MAJOR, G. 501 / Boccherini, Luigi – (8 pts) – Lyon: Guerra, 1777 – 1 – us Sibley [780]
LES SERENADES ET LES JOUERS...BALLET / Campra, A – Paris: Ballard, 1710 – 1 – us Sibley [780]
Serenius, J *see* AN ENGLISH AND SWEDISH DICTIONARY...
EL SERENO STAR – Los Angeles. Calif. -w. 1953-64 – 1 – us UMI [071]
Seret, C *see* TAXONOMIE, BIOLOGIE ET BIOGEOGRAPHIE DES COPEPODES PELAGIQUES RECOLTES AU COURS DE LA CAMPAGNE MD 03 DU "MARION DUFRESNE" (ILES CROZET, KERGUELEN ET HEARD)
SERGE PROKOFIEV ET LES COURANTS ESTHETIQUES DE SON TEMPS / Moisson-Franckhauser, Suzanne – 1975 – 9 – fr Orientalistes [780]
SERGEANT AND RAWLE'S REPORTS / Pennsylvania. Superior Court – (A Pre-NRS title) – v1-14. 1814-28 (all publ) – 101mf – 9 – $151.00 – LLMC 84-197 – us L.L.M.C. [340]
DER SERGEANT WEBER : ERZAEHLUNG / Klaehn, Friedrich Joachim – 11. Aufl. Muenchen: F Eher, 1944 – 1r – 1 – us U.W. Library [830]
Sergeev, V N *see* BANKROTSTVO MELKOBURZHUAZNYKH PARTII NA DONU
SERGEI ESENIN / Esenin, Sergei – Comp. by A. A. Esenina and E. A. Esenina. M. 1958. BR-2125 1 – 9 – ne IDC [920]
SERGEI ESENIN / Kulinich, A V – Kritiko-biograficheskii ocherk. Kiev. 1959. BR-1354 2 – 8 – ne IDC [920]
SERGEI ESENIN / Naumov, E – Zhizn' i tvorchestvo. L. 1960. BR-1455 2 – 8 – ne IDC [460]
SERGEI ESENIN / Prokushev, I – M. 1958. BR-2082 2 – 8 – ne IDC [920]
Sergent, E *see* DETERMINATION DES INSECTES PIQUEURS ET SUCEURS DE SANG
Sergent, Evelyn H *see* THE EFFECTS OF EXERCISE ON STRESS AND FUNCTIONAL ABILITIES IN COMMUNITY DWELLING ELDERLY
Sergi, Giuseppe *see* AFRICA
Sergio Sanchez, Luis *see* DISCURSO... SEGUNDA ENSENANZA DE CACERES
O SERGIPANO – Capela, Brazil. 1 Dec 1901 – 1 – bl Biblioteca [072]
SERGIPE : JORNAL DEDICADO AOS INTERESSES DA LAVOURA, COMMERCIO E MELHORAMENTOS GERAES DA PROVINCIA – Aracaju, 16 Sep 1881-7 Dec 1882 – 1,5,6 – bl Biblioteca [072]
SERGIPE AGRADECIDO : HOMENAGEM AO CAPITAO JOAQUIM ALONSO MOREIRA DE ALMEIDA – Aracaju, 17 Jan 1886 – 1,5,6 – bl Biblioteca [072]
Sergl, Hans Georg *see*
- STATISTISCHE UNTERSUCHUNGEN ZUM ALTERS- UND GESCHLECHTSUNTERSCHIED IM KARIESBEFALL DER EINZELNEN ZAEHNE
- TIEREXPERIMENTELLE UNTERSUCHUNGEN ZUR FRAGE DER FUNKTIONELLEN ANPASSUNG IM KAUSYSTEM

SERIAL PUBLICATIONS OF GERMAN TRADE UNIONS IN THE MEMORIAL LIBRARY, UNIVERSITY OF WISCONSIN-MADISON – A microfilm collection of publs. of trade unions and related organizations from German-speaking countries from the start of the trade union movement until 1933 and from 1949 to 1970 – 1 – us U.W. Library [331]
SERIALS IN THE BRITISH LIBRARY / British Library – Cumulation on fiche 1981-86 – 9 – £29.00; £37.00 overseas – uk British Libr Humanities [073]
SERIALS IN THE BRITISH LIBRARY / British Library. National Bibliographic Service – All subject areas. Bibliographic records of new serial titles acquired throughout the British Library and 17 other libraries in the U.K. 1976-86 – 17 – £240.00 + VAT, £285.00 overseas – uk British Libr [073]
SERIALS IN THE BRITISH LIBRARY 1976-86 / British Library. Humanities and Social Sciences – 57,000 titles worldwide acquired for the London-based reference collections of the British Library. Alphabetically by catalogue heading in author/title sequence. Keyword subject index – 57mf in ring-bound folder – 9 – £240.00 (+ VAT UK); £285.00 overseas – uk British Libr Humanities [073]
SERIALS IN WESTERN LANGUAGES – 1,903 titles – 9 – ne IDC [073]
THE SERIALS LIBRARIAN : THE INTERNATIONAL JOURNAL OF SERIALS MANAGEMENT / ed by Cole, Jim – v1-1976- – 1, 9 ($125.00 in US $175.00 outside hardcopy subsc) – us Haworth [020]
SERICULTURE MANUAL – it F.A.O. [631]
SERICULTURE TRAINING MANUAL – 1990 – 125p – it F.A.O. [634]
SERIE DE CONFERENCIAS EXPLICADAS EN DICHA CORPORACION DURANTE EL CURSO DE 1908-1909 (FEDERACION TAQUIGRAFA ESPANOLA) / Garcia Bote, Eduardo – Madrid: Imp. Juan Pueyo, 1912 – 1 – sp Bibl Santa Ana [946]
SERIE DE SEIS ARTICULOS SOBRE PROBLEMAS POLITICOS, SOCIALES Y ECONOMICOS / Peron, Juan Domingo – Buenos Aires, 1948. 6v – 1 – CSUXADL6484-B – us Hoover Inst Photo [320]
SERIE D'ETUDES SUR LE JAPON / Congres International des Orientalistes – Ed. by Maisonneuve et Cie. Paris. 1874 – 9 – 10.00 – fr Orientalistes [950]
SERIE LEGISLATIVE 1920-1965 / International Labour Organisation – 9 – Sfr2,500.00 – 92-2-208482-9 – sz I.L.O. [340]
SERIE POLICE MYSTERE – Montreal: Ed. Police journal. no 1-. SEM16P337 – 1r – 5 – Can$9.00 – cn Bibl Nat [350]
SERIES A / Westminster Cathedral. Archives – 1509-1793 – 46r – 1 – uk Microform Academic [240]
SERIES A: INDICES TO THE ARCHIVES / Westminster Cathedral. Archives – 1501-1793 – 2r – 1 – uk Microform Academic [941]
SERIES A (INSECT CIRCULARS) – nos.1-63. 1942-47 – 1,5,6 – us Spaulding [630]
SERIES A: JUDGEMENTS. NOS. 1-24. 1922-30 / Permanent Court of International Justice. Hague – (Series B: Advisory Opinions nos 1-18 1922-1930. Series A, B: Judgements, orders and advisory opinions nos 40-80 1931-1940. Series C: Pleadings, oral statements and documents v1-88 1922-1940. Series D: Acts and documents concerning the Organization of the Court 12v. Series E: Annual reports 1st-16th 1922-1945. Series F: General Indexes v1 1922-1926; v2 1927-1930; v3 1931-1935; v4 Statutes and rules of court) – 1 – us Primary [340]
SERIES B (PLANT DISEASE CIRCULAR) / Montana. Agricultural Extension Service – nos.1-16. 1947 – 1,5,6 – us Spaulding [630]
SERIES CONCHYLIOLOGIQUES / Morelet, P M A – Z-677 2. 1858-1875 – 8 – ne IDC [590]
SERIES DE LOS MAS IMPORTANTES DOCUMENTOS DEL ARCHIVO Y BIBLIOTECA DEL EXCMO. SR. DUQUE DE MEDINACELI, ELEGIDOS POR SU ENCARGO Y PUBLICADOS A SUS EXPENSAS... / Ahagon, Marques de Laurencin – Madrid: Fortanet, 1916. B.R.A.H. 68, pp. 270-282 – sp Bibl Santa Ana [946]
A SERIES OF LETTERS ON THE EVIDENCES OF CHRISTIANITY : AS THEY FIRST APPEARED IN THE OCCIDENT / Fernandes, Benjamin Dias – Philadelphia: [s.n., 1853?] – 1mf – 9 – 0-8370-9285-X – 1986-3285 – us A.T.L.A. [270]
SERIES: OSS/STATE DEPT. INTELLIGENCE AND RESEARCH REPORTS / U.S. Office of Strategic Services – Available by parts. See individual titles under U.S. Office of Strategic Services – 1 – us UPA [080]
SERIES PRICE: UNIT 1-3 – Cumul – 1 – F33,440.00 – sz Infoprint [072]
Serif, Ahmet *see* ANADOLU'DA TANIN
SERIIA BIOLOGICHESKIKH I SEL'SKOKHOZIAISTVENNYKH NAUK / Akademiia Nauk Azerbaidzhanskoi SSRAzaerbajgan S S R Elmlaer Akademiiasynyn Chaebaerlaeri – Baku. 1958-69 (4). Lacking: 1959, v. 5-6. BR-1591 2 – 8 – ne IDC [370]
SERIIA GEOLOGO-GEOGRAFICHESKIKH NAUK / Akademiia Nauk Azerbaidzhanskoi SSRAzaerbajgan. S S R Elmaer Akademiiasynyn Chaebaerlaeri – Baku. 1958-59 (5). Lacking: 1959, v. 5-6. BR-1593 2 – 8 – ne IDC [550]
SERIKATBURUH SOVJET / Verbin, Andrei – SE 10,556 1. 1962 – 9 – ne IDC [950]
Serin, Paul *see* LA PETITE FEUILLE
Serino, Gustave *see* ITALIAN IN THE POLITICAL LIFE OF BOSTON
A SERIOUS ADDRESS TO LAY METHODISTS TO BEWARE OF THE FALSE PRETENCES OF THEIR TEACHERS;... / Grey, Zachary – London, 1745 – 1mf – 9 – MP-319/1 – ne IDC [240]
A SERIOUS AND EXPOSTULATORY LETTER TO THE REV. MR. GEORGE WHITEFIELD ON OCCASION OF HIS LATE LETTER TO THE BISHOP OF LONDON AND OTHER BISHOPS,... / Church, T – London, 1744 – 1mf – 9 – MP-310/1 – ne IDC [240]
A SERIOUS AND FRIENDLY ADDRESS TO THE REVEREND MR. JOHN WESLEY IN RELATION TO A PRINCIPAL DOCTRINE ADVANCED AND MAINTAINED BY HIM AND HIS ASSISTANTS / Parkhurst, J – London, 1753 – 1mf – 9 – MP-364/1 – ne IDC [240]
A SERIOUS ANSWER TO MR. WESLEY'S 'CALM ADDRESS TO OUR AMERICAN COLONIES' – Bristol, 1775 – 1mf – 9 – MP-508/1 – ne IDC [240]
A SERIOUS QUESTION : WHAT IS TRUE REPENTANCE / Kinsey, Robert Baldwin – Reading, PA:Wm. H. Miller, c1908 – 1mf – 9 – 0-8370-4471-5 – 1985-2471 – us A.T.L.A. [240]
A SERIOUS REPLY TO THE REV. MR. JOHN WESLEY IN PARTICULAR AND TO THE PEOPLE CALLED METHODISTS IN GENERAL,... / Boyce, G – Boston [Lincolnshire], 1770 – 3mf – 9 – MP-467/1 – ne IDC [240]
Serlio, Sebastian *see* CINCO LIBROS DE ARQUITECTURA
LE SERMENT DU ROI ET LES CATHOLIQUES / Chapais, Thomas – Quebec: Imprimerie de L J Demers & Frere..., 1901. SEM105P475 – 1mf – 9 – Can$2.25 – cn Bibl Nat [971]
Sermet, Jean *see* L'ESPAGNE DU SUD
SERMO GRAECUS QUO SENATUS POPULUSQUE ROMANUS MAGISTRATUSQUE POPULI ROMANI USQUE AD TIBERII CAESARIS AETATEM IN SCRIPTIS PUBLICIS USI SUNT EXAMINATUR / Viereck, Paulus – (Includes bibliographical references) – Gottingae: Officina Academica Dieterichiana, 1888 – 1mf – 9 – 0-8370-9194-2 – 1986-3194 – us A.T.L.A. [450]
SERMON / Buckminster, Joseph Stevens – With a memoir of his life and character by S. C. Thacher. 1814 – 9 – us A.T.L.A. [240]
THE SERMON – Toronto: Sermon Pub Co, [1889?-19–] – 9 – cn C.I.H.M. [130]
A SERMON AGAINST THE METHODISTS, PREACH'D AT COLNE AND MARSDEN IN THE COUNTY OF LANCASTER TO A VERY NUMEROUS AUDIENCE, AT COLNE, JULY 24 AND AT MARSDEN, AUGUST 7, 1748 / White, George – Preston, [1748] – 1mf – 9 – MP-333/1 – ne IDC [240]
SERMON AND LECTURE: DELIVERED IN THE ST JAMES STREET CHURCH, AND THE JAMES FARRIER HALL, THEOLOGICAL COLLEGE, DURING THE SESSION OF THE BRITISH ASSOCIATION AT MONTREAL, AUGUST, 1884 / Dallinger, William Henry – Montreal: s.n., 1884 (Montreal: Gazette). 02257. (Pre-1900 Canadiana) – 9 – cn C.I.H.M. [971]
SERMON DE DEDICACION DE UN RETABLO / Martinez la Rios, Jose – 1 – sp Bibl Santa Ana [240]
SERMON DE SAN ROQUE / Solano de Figueroa y Altamirano, Juan – 1 – sp Bibl Santa Ana [240]
SERMON DEL DOCTOR SERAPHICO S. BUENAVENTURA... / Gomez, Antonio – Salamanca: Melchor Estevez – 1 – sp Bibl Santa Ana [240]
SERMON DELIVERED AT THE FUNERAL OF MISS SARAH POTTER WILLIAMS: SABBATH, 25 JUL 1824 / Perry, Gideon B – 1 – 5.00 – us Baptist [240]
A SERMON DELIVERED AT THE FUNERAL OF MR. HENRY G. PALMER, PRECEPTER OF WESTFIELD ACADEMY, N. J., SABBATH, 25 JUL 1824 / Perry, Gideon B – 1 – 5.00 – us Baptist [240]

SERMON DELIVERED BEFORE ST ANDREW'S SOCIETY IN KNOX CHURCH, OTTAWA, ON SUNDAY EVENING, NOVEMBER 25TH, 1888 / Farries, Francis Wallace – Ottawa?: The Society, 1888 (Ottawa: A. Woodburn). 03038. (Pre-1900 Canadiana) – 9 – cn C.I.H.M. [971]

A SERMON DELIVERED IN THE CHAPEL OF THE BAPTIST LITERARY AND THEOLOGICAL SEMINARY, HAMILTON, NEW YORK, 19 MAR 1824 / Kendrick, Nathaniel – Occasioned by the recent deaths of Rev. Obed Warren, of Covert, N. Y., and Rev. Clark Kendrick, of Poultney, Vermont – 1 – 5.00 – us Baptist [240]

SERMON DES 50 SAGES DE GENEVE... – 18th c. – fr Armell [240]

SERMON ON CHANNING / Clarke, James Freeman – Boston: Geo. H. Ellis, 1883 – 1mf – us A.T.L.A. [240]

A SERMON ON SCRIPTURAL DIVORCE / McCall, E A – 1892 – 1 – $5.00 – us Baptist [240]

SERMON ON THE MOUNT: ITS LITERARY STRUCTURE / Bacon, Benjamin Wisner – New York: Macmillan, 1902. 1 fiche – 9 – us A.T.L.A. [220]

SERMON OUTLINES / Landrum, John W – 1580p – 1 – 55.30 – us Baptist [240]

SERMON PANEGYRICO / Soto y Marne, Francisco de – 1743 – 9 – 1.50f – sp Bibl Santa Ana [240]

SERMON PANEGYRICO DEL SR. S. PEDRO DE ARBUES, MARTYR DE JESUCHRISTO... / Sevilla, Luis Antonio de – Ecija (Sevilla): Imp. Benito Daza, 1774 – 1 – sp Bibl Santa Ana [240]

A SERMON PREACH'D AT ST PAUL'S CATHEDRAL.. / Sherlock, William – 1699 – 2 – us Sibley [780]

SERMON PREACHED AT WAREHAM (MASSACHUSETTS), 31 MAR 1695 / Brown, Clark – 1 – 5.00 – us Baptist [240]

A SERMON, PREACHED AT YORK, UPPER CANADA ON THE THIRD OF JUNE, BEING THE DAY APPOINTED FOR A GENERAL THANKSGIVING / Strachan, John – Montreal: W Gray. 1814. SEM16P85 – 1r – 5 – Can$9.00 – cn Bibl Nat [240]

A SERMON PREACHED IN ST ANDREW'S CHURCH, OTTAWA, TO STRATHCONA'S HORSE PREVIOUS TO THEIR DEPARTURE FOR SERVICE IN SOUTH AFRICA, ON SUNDAY, THE 11TH MARCH, 1900 / Herridge, William Thomas – Ottawa: Taylor & Clarke, 1900?. 05559. (Pre-1900 Canadiana) – 9 – cn C.I.H.M. [971]

A SERMON PREACHED IN THE CHURCH OF ST GEORGE THE MARTYR, TORONTO, ON SUNDAY, NOVEMBER 19, 1876, ON THE OCCASION OF THE DEATH OF THE HONORABLE JOHN HILLYARD CAMERON, Q. C., LATE CHANCELLOR OF THE DIOCESE OF TORONTO / Bethune, Alexander Neil – Toronto: Roswell and Hutchison, 1876. 00097. (Pre-1900 Canadiana) – 9 – cn C.I.H.M. [240]

A SERMON PREACHED IN THE PRESBYTERIAN CHURCH IN STAMFORD, UPPER CANADA, ON THE 3RD DAY OF JUNE, 1814: BEING THE DAY APPOINTED BY HIS HONOR THE PRESIDENT OF UPPER CANADA FOR A PROVINCIAL THANKSGIVING / Burns, John – Chippewa, Ont?: Lundy's Lane Historical Society, 1892; Welland, Ont.: W. Saule. 00345. (Pre-1900 Canadiana) – 9 – cn C.I.H.M. [240]

SERMON PREDICADO EN LA MISA NUEVA DEL PRESBITERO DON CONSTANTINO LANCHO SOLANA CELEBRADA EN LA IGLESIA PARROQUIAL DE SANTA MARINA, EN CANAVERAL (CACERES) POR EL FR / Gabriel de Jesus, C D – Madrid: Imp. Juan Perez Tores, s.a. – sp Bibl Santa Ana [240]

SERMON PRONONCE A L'OCCASION DE LA BENEDICTION DES CLOCHES DE LA BASILIQUE NOTRE DAME DE QUEBEC, 4 OCTOBRE, 1891 / Cote, Georges-Pierre – Quebec?: s.n., 1891 (Quebec: L. Erousseau). 00476. (Pre-1900 Canadiana) – 9 – cn C.I.H.M. [971]

SERMON REGISTERS, 1774-1803 / Cricket, J – (Coll title: The People Called Methodists, Phase 2: Primary Sources 1738-1800) – 6mf – 9 – MP-625/1 – ne IDC [240]

A SERMON SUITABLE TO THE TIMES, PREACHED AT ST MARY'S OXFORD ON SUNDAY THE 18TH OF NOVEMBER,... / Tatham, E – London, 2nd ed 1792 – 1mf – 9 – MP-581/1 – ne IDC [240]

SERMON SUR L'ACCORD DE LA RELIGION ET DE LA LIBERTE / Fauchet, Claude – 1791. Paris. Impr. du Cercle Social – 9 – fr Hachette [321]

SERMON SUR L'AUTORITE DES EVEQUES: DONNE LE LER MAI 1894 DANS LA CATHEDRALE DE MONTREAL A L'OCCASION DU 21E ANNIVERSAIRE DE LA CONSECRATION EPISCOPALE DE MGR. EDOUARD-CHARLES FABRE. / Archambault, Alfred – Montreal: Arbour & Laperle, 1894. 02207. (Pre-1900 Canadiana) – 9 – cn C.I.H.M. [240]

A SERMON UPON THE TURF...PREACHED AT THE LAST NEWMARKET MEETING – (A second edition was published in 1776) – London, 1774 – 1mf – 9 – MP-497/1 – ne IDC [240]

EYN SERMON VON DER EYGENSCHAFFT VND WEYSE DES SACRAMENTS DER TAUFF... / Bugenhagen, J – [Hagenau], 1529 – 1mf – 9 – ne IDC [240]

EYN SERMON VONN MENSCHLICHER SACHWACHEIT / Langen, Joachim – Erffordt. 1523. BME-18 1 – 9 – ne IDC [240]

SERMON...A MARIA SANTISMA...EL BENEFICIO DE LA LLUVIA / Cobo Sampedro, Ramon – 1874 – 9 – 1.50f – sp Bibl Santa Ana [240]

SERMON...ALMENDRALEJO / Romero y Delgado, Antonio – 1832 – 9 – 1.50f – sp Bibl Santa Ana [240]

SERMON...ALMENDRALEJO...MARIA MARTIN LLANOS / Palacios, Juan Jose – 1861 – 9 – 1.50f – sp Bibl Santa Ana [240]

SERMON...CATEDRAL DE BADAJOZ / Flores, Antonio – 1813 – 9 – 1.50f – sp Bibl Santa Ana [240]

SERMON...CATEDRAL DE BADAJOZ / Rocha, Manuel de la – 1813 – 9 – 1.50f – sp Bibl Santa Ana [240]

SERMONES / Chobham, Thomas de – 1993 – 8mf – 9 – Bf1,950.00 – 2-503-63824-4 – be Brepols [450]

SERMONES : DE COMMENDATIONE FIDEI / Forda, Balduinus de – 1991 – 11mf – 9 – Bf2,250.00 – 2-503-63992-5 – be Brepols [240]

SERMONES / Petrus Damiani – 1983 – 12mf – 9 – Bf1,550.00 – 2-503-63572-5 – be Brepols [240]

SERMONES 1-46 / Rievallensis, Aelredus – 1989 – 11mf – 9 – Bf1,950.00 – 2-503-63024-3 – be Brepols [240]

SERMONES. ADVERSVS ANABAPTISTAS / Faber, J & Fabri, J – Lipsiae, M. Lotterus. 1528. BME-114 1 – 9 – ne IDC [240]

SERMONES CAPITULARES / Hacki, Michael O Cist. – Olivia. Tomus 4. 1700 – 30mf – 8 – Dfl105.00 – ne Slangenburg [240]

SERMONES (CCCM 57) / Petrus Damiani – 1990 – 8mf – 9 – Bf1,995.00 – 2-503-73572-X – be Brepols [240]

SERMONES DE ADVENTU / Maillard, O – (Missing: Title page) – [Paris, 1506] – 8mf – 9 – CA-93/1 – ne IDC [240]

SERMONES DE CUARESMA...SIETE SABIOS DE GRECIA / Duran de Montijo, Juan – 1708 – 9 – 1.50f – sp Bibl Santa Ana [240]

SERMONES DOMINICALES DE TEMPORE... / Biel, G – Haguenau, [1515] – 5mf – 9 – CA-88/1 – ne IDC [240]

SERMONES FESTIVALES / Runa, Hermannus de – 1986 – 14mf – 9 – Bf1,900.00 – 2-503-63642-X – be Brepols [240]

SERMONES PANEGIRICOS DE SANTOS / Duran de Montijo, Juan – 1714. 3v – 9 – 1.50f – sp Bibl Santa Ana [240]

SERMONES VARIOS DE DIVERSOS ASUNTOS PANEGIRICOS / Caceres, Antonio de – 1713 – 9 – 1.50f – sp Bibl Santa Ana [850]

SERMONES Y DISCURSOS DE TIEMPO... PREDICADOS POR.. / Caceres y Sotomayor, Antonio – 1612 – 9 – 1.50f – sp Bibl Santa Ana [240]

SERMONES...VILLAFRANCA DE LOS BARROS / Sanchez Juarez, Francisco – 1874 – 9 – 1.50f – sp Bibl Santa Ana [240]

SERMON...LA LIMPIEZA DE LA VIRGEN EN SU INMACULADA / Jimenez de Zalamea, Fr. Juan – 1653 – 9 – 1.50f – sp Bibl Santa Ana [240]

EYN SERMONN VOM NEWEN JARE / Voyt, J – Zwickaw, Joerg Gastel. n.d. BME-74 1 – 9 – ne IDC [240]

SERMON...ORDEN SERAPHICA / Pedro de Almendralejo – 1677 – 9 – 1.50f – sp Bibl Santa Ana [240]

SERMON...REGIMIENTO DE PLASENCIA / Rocha, Manuel de la – 1820 – 9 – 1.50f – sp Bibl Santa Ana [240]

SERMONS : 6TH SERIES / Brooks, Phillips – New York: E.P. Dutton, 1893 – 1mf – us A.T.L.A. [240]

SERMONS / Alison, Francis – 1752-1777 – 1 – $50.00 – us Presbyterian [240]

SERMONS / Bachman, John – 1867-68. 2 fiches – 9 – us South Carolina Historical [240]

SERMONS / Brooks, Phillips – New York: Dutton, 1883 – 1mf – us A.T.L.A. [240]

SERMONS / Browne, John – Containing the Bampton Lecture of 1806. 1809 – 9 – us A.T.L.A. [240]

SERMONS / Clements, Rex S – 1932-1969 – 1 – $50.00 – us Presbyterian [240]

SERMONS – Delivered by: George B. Eager, SBC, Washington, D.C., 10 May 1895; Justin D. Fulton, First Baptist Church, Summerville, Mass., 22 Sep 1895; J. B. Moody, Baccalaureate sermon, Ouachita College, Hot Springs, Ark., 14p – 1 – 5.00 – us Baptist [240]

SERMONS : DELIVERED ON VARIOUS OCCASIONS / Beecher, Lyman – Boston: J.P. Jewett; Cleveland, Ohio: Jwett, Proctor & Worthington, 1852, c1851. (Beecher's works; v2) – 1mf – us A.T.L.A. [240]

SERMONS : DOCTRINAL AND PRACTICAL / Grant, David – 1793 – 1 – $50.00 – us Presbyterian [240]

SERMONS / Edwards, Jonathan – 1766-1800 – 1 – us A.T.L.A. [240]

SERMONS / Grosseteste, Robert – 15th century. From York Minster Library – 1 – uk Microform Academic [240]

SERMONS / Haweis, Hugh Reginald – 1872 – 1 – us A.T.L.A. [240]

SERMONS / King, John – 1 – $50.00 – us Presbyterian [240]

SERMONS / La Badie, Jean de – Montaban, 17e Siecle – 1 – us U.W. Library [240]

SERMONS : LECTURES AND NOTES, 1840-1864 / Giger, George Musgrave – 1r – 1 – $50.00 – us Presbyterian [240]

SERMONS / Moore, Martha Jordan – 1908-1915 – 1r – 1 – $32.50r – us Archival [240]

SERMONS / Murlin, J – (Coll title: The People Called Methodists, Phase 2: Primary Sources 1738-1800) – 5mf – 9 – MP-633/1 – ne IDC [240]

SERMONS / Pattison, Mark – London: Macmillan, 1885 – 1mf – us A.T.L.A. [240]

SERMONS : PREACHED BEFORE THE CONGREGATION OF THE PRESBYTERIAN CHURCH, CORNER OF FIFTH AVENUE AND NINETEENTH STREET AT THE "MEMORIAL SERVICES", OCT 9, 1859 / Hodge, Charles & Hall, John – New York: Anson D F Randolph, 1859 – 1mf – 9 – 0-8370-7389-8 – 1986-1389 – us A.T.L.A. [240]

SERMONS / Steel, John – 1 – $50.00 – us Presbyterian [240]

THE SERMONS.. / Taylor, Jeremy – Complete in one volume. Philadelphia: H. Hooker, 1845. 565p – 1 – us U.W. Library [240]

SERMONS, 1742-1763 / Tennent, Gilbert – 1 – $100.00 – us Presbyterian [240]

SERMONS, 1747-1801 / Rodgers, John – 1 – $50.00 – us Presbyterian [240]

SERMONS, 1755-1801 / Ewing, John – 1 – $50.00 – us Presbyterian [240]

SERMONS, 1798-1821 / Freeman, Jonathan – 1 reel – 1 – $50.00 – us Presbyterian [240]

SERMONS, 1842-66 / MacMaster, Erasmus D – 1 – $50.00 – us Presbyterian [240]

SERMONS, ACADEMICAL AND OCCASIONAL / Keble, John – (Includes bibliographical references) – Oxford: John Henry Parker; London: F and J Rivington, 1847 – 2mf – 9 – 0-8370-9799-1 – 1986-3799 – us A.T.L.A. [240]

SERMONS AND ADDRESSES / Bascom, John – New York: G.P. Putnam, 1913 – 1mf – us A.T.L.A. [240]

SERMONS AND ADDRESSES / Flint, Robert – New York: Scribner, 1899 – 1mf – us A.T.L.A. [240]

THE SERMONS AND CONFERENCES OF JOHN TAULER. / Tauler, Johannes – First complete Eng. trans. Introd. and index by Walter Elliott. Brookland Station, Washington DC: Apostolic Mission House, 1910. 780p – 1 – us U.W. Library [240]

SERMONS AND CONTROVERSIAL WRITINGS / Kobner, Johann – Material from the Oncken Archives, Hamburg, Germany – 1 – 27.30 – us Baptist [240]

SERMONS AND DISCOURSES / MacHale, John; ed by MacHale, Thomas – Dublin: M H Gill, 1883 – 2mf – 9 – 0-8370-7084-8 – 1986-1084 – us A.T.L.A. [240]

SERMONS AND ESSAYS : BY THE TENNENTS AND THEIR CONTEMPORARIES / Tennent, Gilbert et al – 1856 – 1 – $50.00 – us Presbyterian [240]

SERMONS AND ESSAYS IN THE APOSTOLIC AGE / Stanley, Arthur Penrhyn – 3rd ed. 1874 – 9 – us A.T.L.A. [240]

SERMONS AND LECTURES / McCombie, William – Edinburgh: T & T Clark, 1871 – 1mf – 9 – 0-8370-7001-5 – 1986-1001 – us A.T.L.A. [240]

SERMONS AND MISCELLANEOUS PAMPHLETS / Furman, Hart, Botsford et al – 2,160p – 1 – 75.60 – us Baptist [240]

SERMONS AND MORAL DISCOURSES FOR ALL THE SUNDAYS AND PRINCIPLE FESTIVALS OF THE YEAR : ON THE MOST IMPORTANT TRUTHS AND MAXIMS OF THE GOSPEL / Gahan, William – 5th rev corr ed. Dublin: Richard Grace, 1846 – 2mf – 9 – 0-8370-6904-1 – 1986-0904 – us A.T.L.A. [240]

SERMONS AND SAYINGS, FIRST SERIES / Jones, Samuel Porter – 1885 – 9 – us A.T.L.A. [240]

SERMONS BEARING ON SUBJECTS OF THE DAY / Newman, John Henry – New ed. London: Longmans, Green & Co., 1891. xxi,424p – 1 – us U.W. Library [240]

SERMONS BY SAM JONES AND SAM SMALL / Jones, Samuel Porter – 1887? – 9 – us A.T.L.A. [240]

SERMONS BY THE REV. THOMAS FRASER: FORMERLY OF LANARK AND OTHER PLACES, AND LEFT BY HIM AS A MEMENTO OF HIS PRESENCE AND LABOURS AMONG THEM / Fraser, Thomas – Montreal?: s.n., 1867 (Montreal: J. Lavell). 03161. (Pre-1900 Canadiana) – 9 – cn C.I.H.M. [971]

SERMONS COLLECTED... *see* THEOLOGICAL MISCELLANY 1

SERMONS DE JEAN DAILLE SUR L'EPITRE DE L'APOTRE S. PAUL AUX COLOSSIANS = AN EXPOSITION OF THE EPISTLE OF SAINT PAUL TO THE COLOSSIANS / Daille, Jean – (In English. Includes index) – Edinburgh: James Nichol, 1863 – 1mf – 9 – 0-8370-5994-1 – 1985-3994 – us A.T.L.A. [220]

SERMONS FOR CHURCH WORKERS (CCC115) / Chu, Wei-yu – (In Chinese) – Shanghai: Christian Literature Society, 1932 – 1r – 1 – 1984-B500 – us A.T.L.A. [240]

SERMONS FOR THE PEOPLE / Huntington, Frederic Dan – 1879 – 9 – us A.T.L.A. [240]

SERMONS FOR THE YEAR (CCC303) = CHOU NIEN CHIANG TAN / Walter, E – (In Chinese) – 1st ed. Shanghai: Christian Literature Society, 1931 – 1r – 1 – 1984-6642 – us A.T.L.A. [240]

SERMONS FROM PERSONAL FILES OF DR. PORTER ROUTH, EXECUTIVE SECRETARY-TREASURER OF THE SBC, 1951-79 / Southern Baptist Convention. Annual Convention – Period covers 1846-1978 with some years missing.1596p – 1 – 55.86 – us Baptist [240]

SERMONS IN STONES, OR, SCRIPTURE CONFIRMED BY GEOLOGY / M'Causland, Dominick – London: Richard Bentley, 1862. 1 fiche – 9 – us A.T.L.A. [240]

SERMONS, INCLUDING AN ESSAY ON THE RIGHT INTERPRETATION AND UNDERSTANDING OF THE SCRIPTURES, AND TWO SERMONS ON THE RIGHT INTERPRETATION OF PROPHECY / Arnold, Thomas – 3v. 1874 – 9 – us A.T.L.A. [240]

SERMONS, NOW FIRST PUBLISHED FROM THE AUTHOR'S MANUSCRIPTS / Buckminster, Joseph Stevens – 1829 – 9 – us A.T.L.A. [240]

SERMONS OF COURAGE AND CHEER / Herford, Brooke – 1894 – 9 – us A.T.L.A. [240]

THE SERMONS OF MR. YORICK / Sterne, L – (Missing: 1768, V.1(p. 108-124)) – London, 9th ed 1768.-2v – 6mf – 9 – MP-402/1 – ne IDC [240]

SERMONS ON IMPORTANT SUBJECTS / Finney, Charles G – New York: John S. Taylor, c1836 – 1mf – us A.T.L.A. [240]

SERMONS ON ST. PAUL'S EPISTLES TO THE CORINTHIANS / Robertson, Frederick William – (Later ed publ under title:Expository Lectures on St. Paul's Epistles to the Corinthians) – Boston:Ticknor and Fields, 1866 – 1mf – 9 – 0-8370-4923-7 – 1985-2923 – us A.T.L.A. [220]
SERMONS ON SUBJECTS CONNECTED WITH THE OLD TESTAMENT / Driver, Samuel Rolles – New York: Charles Scribner, 1893 – 1mf – 9 – 0-8370-2973-2 – 1985-0973 – us A.T.L.A. [220]
SERMONS ON THE EIGHTH CHAPTER OF THE EPISTLE TO THE ROMANS / Jacombe, Thomas – Verses 1-4. Edinburgh: James Nichol, 1868. 1 fiche – 9 – us A.T.L.A. [240]
SERMONS ON THE HIGHER LIFE / Dunn, Lewis R – Cincinnati: Walden and Stowe; New York: Phillips & Hunt, 1882 – 1mf – us A.T.L.A. [240]
SERMONS ON THE SONG OF SONGS: PREACHED IN...S. MARGARET'S, EAST GRINSTED / Neale, John Mason – London: J.T. Hayes, 1867. 1 fiche – 9 – us A.T.L.A. [240]
SERMONS ON THE WAY OF SALVATION : FINNEY, CHARLES G. – Oberlin, Ohio: E.J. Goodrich, c1891 – 2mf – us A.T.L.A. [240]
SERMONS ON VARIOUS AND IMPORTANT SUBJECTS.. / Jarrett, Devereux – 3v. 1793-94 – 1 – us A.T.L.A. [240]
SERMONS ON VARIOUS SUBJECTS / Finney, Charles G – 1835 – 9 – us A.T.L.A. [240]
SERMONS, PRAYERS, AND PULPIT ADDRESSES / Henderson, Alexander – 1867 – 1 – $50.00 – us Presbyterian [240]
SERMONS PREACHED IN ANTEBELLUM SOUTH CAROLINA : FROM HOLDINGS OF BAPTIST HISTORICAL COLLECTION, FURMAN UNIVERSITY, GREENVILLE, SOUTH CAROLINA – 1791-1860 – 1r – 1 – 53.88 – us Baptist [240]
SERMONS PREACHED IN ST ANDREW'S CHURCH, QUEBEC / Cook, John – Montreal: Dawson, 1888. 00319. (Pre-1900 Canadiana) – 9 – cn C.I.H.M. [971]
SERMONS PREACHED ON VARIOUS OCCASIONS / Newman, John Henry – London: Burns, Oates, 4th ed 1874 – 1 roll – 1 – 1-55879-385-2 – uk Libr Preservation [240]
SERMONS TO ASSES / Murray, J – (A second edition was published in 1768, a third and fourth in 1769, and a fifth in 1770. The work was further reprinted in 1800, 1817 and, with other sermons, in 1819) – London, 1768 – 3mf – 9 – MP-456/1 – ne IDC [240]
SERMONS TO THE NATURAL MAN / Shedd, William Greenough Thayer – New York: Charles Scribner, 1871 – 1mf – 9 – 0-8370-9822-X – 1986-3822 – us A.T.L.A. [240]
SERMONS TO YOUNG WOMEN / Fordyce, James – 1796 – 9 – us A.T.L.A. [240]
SERMONS, WITH A HISTORY OF HIS LIFE BY THEODORE M. SMITH / Jones, Samuel Porter – 1887 – 9 – us A.T.L.A. [240]
SERMON...SAN IGNACIO DE LOYOLA / Solano de Figueroa y Altamirano, Juan – 1681 – 9 – 1.50f – sp Bibl Santa Ana [240]
A SERMON...SEPTEMBER 19, 1722 / Dickinson, Jonathan – 1723 – 1 – $50.00 – us Presbyterian [240]
SERMON...SOBERANIA PONTIFICIA / Sanchez Juarez, Francisco – 1877 – 9 – 1.50f – sp Bibl Santa Ana [240]
SERMON...VIRGEN DE LA PIEDAD / Solano de Figueroa y Altamirano, Juan – 1643 – 9 – 1.50f – sp Bibl Santa Ana [240]
SERMON...ZAFRA...LIBERTAD DE...SENOR / Martinez del Rio, Manual A – 1824 – 9 – 1.50f – sp Bibl Santa Ana [850]
Seron, Carroll *see*
– ATTORNEYS' VIEWS OF LOCAL RULES LIMITING INTERROGATORIES
– CERTIFYING QUESTIONS OF STATE LAW
– THE ROLE OF MAGISTRATES
– THE ROLE OF MAGISTRATES IN FEDERAL DISTRICT COURTS
– USE OF STANDARD PRETRIAL PROCEDURES
Seroux D'Agincourt, J B L G *see* RECUEIL DE FRAGMENTS DE SCULPTURE ANTIQUE EN TERRE CUITS
SERP. DVENADTSATAIA KNIGA STIKHOV / Gorodetskii, S – St. Petersburg, 1921. BR-1131-2 – 8 – ne IDC [460]
Serpe, C T *see* ANALYSES ET CRITIQUES DES OUVRAGES DE M. DE VOLTAIRE
SERPENT AND SIVA WORSHIP AND MYTHOLOGY, IN CENTRAL AMERICA, AFRICA, AND ASIA / Clarke, Hyde – New York: J.W. Bouton, 1877. xviii, 19-48p. Reprinted from the Journal of the Anthropological Institute. Contains vocabularies – 1 – us U.W. Library [280]
THE SERPENT POWER: BEING THE SHATCHAKRA-NIRUPANA AND PADUKA-PANCHAKA / Avalon, A – London. 1919. BI-1073 1 – 9 – ne IDC [290]
Serpillon, Francois *see* CODE CRIMINEL, OU COMMENTAIRE SUR L'ORDONNANCE DE 1670
Serra Boldu, Valerio *see*
– LEVENDAS TAUMATINGICAS REFERIDAS A LOS PEQUENOS. BARCELONA, 1933
– VERDAGUER
Serrablo Aguareles, Eugenio *see* DON ALVARO DE SANDE Y LA ORDEN DE MALTA
Serradilla Calvo, Martin *see*
– CUADERNO DE MATEMATICAS NO 4. 1
– CUADERNO DE MATEMATICAS NO 4 B
Serradillo Calvo, Martin *see* CUADERNO DE MATEMATICAS 4TH 2
Serrag, M *see* ARAB TRADITIONAL FARMING AND THE NEED FOR REFORM
SERRANA – Serro, 6 Apr, 31 Jul 1930 – 1,5,6 – bl Biblioteca [072]
Serrano, A *see*
– CUADERNO DE MATEMATICAS 4TH 2
– CUADERNO DE MATEMATICAS NO 4. 1
– CUADERNO DE MATEMATICAS NO 4 B
Serrano Poncela, Segundo *see* LA CONFERENCIA NACIONAL DE JUVENTUDES
Serrano, Rosalio *see*
– DICCIONARIO DE TERMINOS COMUNES TAGALO-CASTELLANO
– DICCIONARIO MANUAL DE TERMINOS COMUNES ESPANOL-TAGALO
Serrano Sanz, Manuel *see*
– LA EXPEDICION DE HERNANDO DE SOTO A LA FLORIDA
– PEDRO DE VALENCIA. ESTUDIO BIOGRAFICO Y CRITICO
Serrano Serrano, Ildefonso *see*
– CONFERENCIAS PRONUNCIADAS EN LA LIGA CONTRA LA BLASFEMIA DE OLIVA DE JEREZ
– CUADROS SINOPTICOS DE TEOLOGIA MORAL
– LA EUROPEADA
– TEOFANIA O MANISFETACION DE DIOS EN LAS CRIATURAS
DIE SERRA-POST : DEUTSCHSPRACHIGE WOCHENBEILAGE ZUM "CORREIO SERRANO" – Ijui, Brasilien. 1972-1975 – 1 – gw Mikrofilm [072]
Serrarius, P *see* GODDELYCKE AANDACHTEN OFTE VLAMMENDE BEGEERTEN EENS BOETVAERDIGE GEHEIJLIGD EN LIEF-RIJCKE ZIELE
Serre, J A *see*
– ESSAIS SUR LES PRINCIPES DE L'HARMONIE
– OBSERVATIONS SUR LES PRINCIPES DE L'HARMONIE OCCASIONNEES PAR QUELQUES ECRITS MODERNES SUR CE SUJET
Serrero, Andre *see* PROTECTION DES OEUVRES LITTERAIRES ET ARTISTIQUES ETRANGERES AUX ETATS-UNIS, LES FORMALITES
O SERRO : ORGAM DO PARTIDO REPUBLICANO MUNICIPAL – Serro, 15 Oct 1922-3 Jan 1923 – 1,5,6 – bl Biblioteca [072]
O SERRO : ORGAO DEMOCRATA – Cidade do Serro, 5 Oct 1890-Sep 1891; Oct 1892-Oct 1893; Apr-27 May 1894 – 1,5,6 – bl Biblioteca [072]
O SERRO – Serro, 15 Jan 1922 – 1,5,6 – bl Biblioteca [072]
O SERRO AZUL – Ponte Nova, 14 Aug 1897 – 1,5,6 – bl Biblioteca [072]
SERRURES DOGON. ANALYSE ETHNO-MORPHOLOGIQUE / Calame-Griaule, G. et al – 9 – F150.00 – fr Ethnologie [306]
O SERTANEJO – Corumba, Brazil. 9 Dec 1897 – 1 – bl Biblioteca [072]
O SERTANEJO – Pao d'Assucar, Alagoas. 17-24 Fev, Maio 1895; Dez 1896; 39 Maio 1897 – 1,5,6 – bl Biblioteca [072]
SERTULUM ORIENTALE SEU RECENSIO PLANTARUM IN OLYMPO BITHYNICO / Clementi, G – v. 16 (Mem. della Reale Acc. Sc. S.2). 1857 – 8 – ne IDC [580]
SERTUM ANGLICUM, SEU PLANTAE RARIORES / L'Heritier de Brutelle, C L Cornus – Parisiis, 1788; 1789-92 – 8 – B-5532 2 – ne IDC [580]
SERTUM ANGOLENSE / Welwitsch, F M J – (Transact. Linn. Soc. London, v. 27, 1871). B-5507 2 – 8 – ne IDC [580]
SERTUM ASTROLABIANUM / Richard, Achille – Paris. 1832-34. B-5214 2 – 8 – ne IDC [580]
SERTUM AUSTROCALEDONICUM / Labillardiere, J J H de – Parisiis. 1824-25. B-2301 2 – 8 – ne IDC [580]
SERTUM BENGUELENSE / Wawra, H & Peyritsch, J J – (Sitzungsber. Akad. Wissensch. Wien, 1860, v. 38). Wien. 1860. B-5801 2 – 8 – ne IDC [580]
SERTUM CABULICUM / Endlicher, S L & Fenzl, E – Vindobonae. 1836. B-725 2 – 8 – ne IDC [580]
SERTUM EXOTICUM / Miquel, F A W – Rotterdam, 1842. 8 pp., 5 pls. B-6072 2 – 8 – ne IDC [580]
SERTUM HANNOVERANUM / Schrader, H A & Wendland, J C – Goettingae. 1795-98. B-5724 2 – 8 – ne IDC [580]
SERTUM LICHENAEAE TROPICAE E LABUAN ET SINGAPORE ACCEDENT OBSERV / Nylander, W – Parisiis. 1891. B-563 2 – 8 – ne IDC [580]
SERTUM LIPSICUM SEU STIRPES OMNES. CIRCA URBEM. PLANTATAS / Baumgarten, J C G – Lipsiae. 1790. B-5841 2 – 8 – ne IDC [580]
SERTUM ORCHIDACEUM / Lindley, J – London. 1837-38-41. B-6028 2 – 8 – ne IDC [580]
SERTUM PETROPOLITANUM SEU ICONES ET DESCRIPTIONES PLANTARUM QUAE IN HORTO BOTANICO / Fischer, FE L von & Meyer, C A von – 4v. Petropoli. 1846-69. B-1009 2 – 8 – ne IDC [580]
SERUBABEL – Berlin. 1886-89. Available: 1886; (Sep-Dec); 1887; (Jan-Sep); 1888; (Jan-May). BJ-23-55 1 – 9 – ne IDC [270]
SERUBBABEL:...GESCHICHTE DER MESSIANISCHEN ERWARTUNG UND DER ENTSTEHUNG DES JUDENTUMS / Sellin, Ernst – Leipzig: A. Deichert, 1898. 1 fiche – 9 – us A.T.L.A. [240]
SERULING DEWATA DAN NAGA SAKTI (SIAN TIE SIN LIONG) / Yung, Tse – SE 5140/1. 2v. 1964? – 9 – ne IDC [950]
Servaes, Franz *see*
– HEINRICH VON KLEISTS TRAGISCHER UNTERGANG
– PRAELUDIEN
Servain, G *see* HISTOIRE MALACOLOGIQUE DU LAC BALATON EN HONGRIE
Servais, W *see* TEACHING SCHOOL MATHEMATICS
Servan de Gerbey, Joseph *see* LE SOLDAT CITOYEN, OU VUES PATRIOTIQUES SUR LA MANIERE LA PLUS AVANTAGEUSE DE POURVOIR A LA DEFENSE DU ROYAUME
Servan, Juan *see* ELEMENTOS DE GRAMATICA
THE SERVANT OF JEHOVAH = 'EVED YEHOVAH : A COMMENTARY, GRAMMATICAL AND CRITICAL UPON ISAIAH 52. 13-53. 12... / Urwick, William – Edinburgh: T & T Clark, 1877 – 1mf – 1 – 0-8370-6437-6 – 1986-0437 – us A.T.L.A. [220]
THE SERVANT OF JEHOVAH, OR, THE PASSION-PROPHECY OF SCRIPTURE / Workman, George Coulson – London: Longmans, Green, 1907. 1 fiche – 9 – us A.T.L.A. [240]
THE SERVANT OF THE LORD AND OTHER ESSAYS / Rowley, H H – Blackwell. 1965 – 9 – $12.00 – us I.R.C. [240]
THE SERVANT OF THE LORD IN ISAIAH 40-66 : RECLAIMED TO ISAIAH AS THE AUTHOR FROM ARGUMENT, STRUCTURE, AND DATE / Forbes, John – (Includes indexes of topics) – Edinburgh:T & T Clark, 1890 – 1mf – 9 – 0-8370-3162-1 – 1985-1162 – us A.T.L.A. [220]
SERVANT OF THE LORD IN ISAIAH 40-66 RECLAIMED TO ISAIAH AS THE AUTHOR / Forbes, John – Edinburgh: T.& T. Clark, 1890 – 9 – us A.T.L.A. [220]
SERVANTS OF THE KING / Speer, Robert Elliott – (Includes index) – New York: Educational Dept, Board of Foreign Missions of the Presbyterian Church in the USA, 1909 – 1mf – 9 – 0-8370-6524-0 – 1986-0524 – us A.T.L.A. [920]
SERVE ONE ANOTHER (CCC290) / Surdam, T Janet – (In Chinese) – 1st ed. Hong Kong: Council on Christian Literature for Overseas Chinese, 1958 – 1r – 1 – 1984-6629 – us A.T.L.A. [240]
SERVETUS AND CALVIN / Willis, Robert – 1877 – 1 – us A.T.L.A. [240]
SERVICE – v1-18, no. 12 (all publ). 1936-54 – 8r – 1 – $480.00 – us UPA [976]
SERVICE ABROAD : LECTURES / Montgomery, H H – London, New York: Longmans, Green, 1910 – 1mf – us A.T.L.A. [240]
SERVICE BULLETIN / Georgia. University. Agricultural Extension Service – 1922-29 – 1,5 – us Spaulding [630]
SERVICE BUREAU NEWS BULLETIN OF THE INTERNATIONAL PRINTING PRESSMEN AND ASSISTANTS' UNION OF NORTH AMERICA, 1937-1952 *see* AMERICAN PRESSMAN, 1890-1955 : SERVICE BUREAU NEWS BULLETIN OF THE INTERNATIONAL PRINTING PRESSMEN AND ASSISTANTS' UNION OF NORTH AMERICA, 1937- 1952
LE SERVICE DE CINE-PHOTOGRAPHIE (O.F.Q.) VU A TRAVERS SES COMMUNIQUES DE PRESSE, 1940-1960 – Montreal: Bibliotheque Nationale du Quebec, 1974. SEM35P91 – 1r – 1 – Can$15.00 – cn Bibl Nat [380]
Service d'Information *see* LE SOUDAN FRANCAIS
THE SERVICE FOR THE CONSECRATION OF A CHURCH AND ALTAR ACCORDING TO THE COPTIC RITE / ed by Horner, G – London, 1902 – 11mf – 8 – Dfl39.00 – ne Slangenburg [240]
THE SERVICE OF BLOOD TRANSFUSION AT THE FRONT / Duran i Jorda, Frederic – Barcelona, 193? Fiche W 847. (Blodgett Collection of Spanish Civil War Pamphlets) – 9 – us H.U. College Libr [946]
THE SERVICE OF MAN : AN ESSAY TOWARDS THE RELIGION OF THE FUTURE / Morison, James Cotter – 2nd ed. London: Kegan Paul, Trench, 1887 – 1mf – 9 – 0-8370-4494-4 – 1985-2494 – us A.T.L.A. [210]
SERVICE ROLLS OF CONTINGENTS OF THE QUEENSLAND DEFENCE FORCE WHO SERVED IN THE BOER WAR, 1899-1901 / Chief Secretary's Office, Queensland – 7r – 1 – CRS B5199 – at Archives [920]
SERVICE SOCIAL – v1- 1951- 1; v25- 5,6,9 – us UMI [360]
SERVICE SOCIAL / Ecole de service social affiliee a la Faculte des sciences sociales – Montreal: Presses universitaires. v1- 1951-. SEM16P312 – 4r – 5 – Can$173.00 – cn Bibl Nat [360]
SERVICE WORLD INTERNATIONAL-SWI – v1-15. 1966-81 – 1 – us UMI [073]
THE SERVICE-HYMNAL: WITH AN INTRODUCTORY SERVICE / Krauskopf, J & Miller, Russell King – Philadelphia: Keneseth Israel, 1904. 1 fiche – 9 – us A.T.L.A. [270]
LES SERVICES JURIDIQUES EN MILIEU RURAL – 1987 – sz I.C.J. [340]
LES SERVICES JURIDIQUES EN MILIEU RURAL : LIBREVILLE SEMINAR – 1989 – sz I.C.J. [340]
SERVICES OFFERED BY ATHLETIC TRAINERS AT PRIVATE SPORTS MEDICINE CLINICS IN THE UNITED STATES / Papez, David M – Iowa State University, 1993 – 2mf – 9 – $8.00 – PE3615 – us Microform Publ [617]
Servicio Internacional Radiofonico Argentino *see* EVA PERON, INMORTAL
Servicio Nacional de Sindicatos *see* CIRCULAR N° 11 DE ORGANIZACION ENCUADRAMIENTO DE PROFESIONES POR SINDICATOS Y SECCIONES
SERVICIO PAZ Y JUSTICIA (SERPAJ-CHILE) = PEACE AND JUSTICE SERVICE-CHILE – Santiago. 127 docs. 1980-1990 – 37mf – 9 – ne IDC [320]
SERVICIO PAZ Y JUSTICIA (SERPAJ-URUGUAY) = JUSTICE AND PEACE SERVICE-URUGUAY – Montevideo. 122 docs. 1982-1991 – 61mf – 9 – ne IDC [320]
SERVIDUMBRE NATURAL Y LIBERTAD CRISTIANA SEGUN LOS TRATADISTAS ESPANOLES DE LOS SIGLOS 16 Y 17. BUENOS AIRES, 1944 / Zavala, Silvio – Madrid: Razon y Fe, 1947 – 1 – sp Bibl Santa Ana [972]
SERVIDUMBRES PERSONALES DE INDIOS / Agia, Miguel – Madrid: Missionalia Hispanica, 1949 – 1 – sp Bibl Santa Ana [240]
Serviere *see* MONSIEUR BOTTE OU LE NEGOCIANT ANGLAIS
Servieres *see* MEMOIRES POUR SERVIR A L'HISTOIRE DE M. DE VOLTAIRE
Serviez, Emmanuel G R de *see* STATISTIQUE DU DEPARTEMENT DES BASSES-PYRENEES

SERVING GEORGIA THROUGH RESEARCH: BIENNIAL REPORT / University of Georgia. Agricultural Experiment Station – 1969-82.8 fiches – 9 – us Spaulding [630]
SERVITEURS ET SERVANTES DE DIEU EN CANADA; QUARANTE BIOGRAPHIES / Dionne, Narcisse Eutrope – Quebec: les Jesuites, 1904. SEM105P498 – 4mf – 9 – Can$9.00 – cn Bibl Nat [240]
LA SERVITUDE AMOUREUSE DE JULIETTE DROUET A VICTOR HUGO / Souchon, Paul – Paris: Albin Michel, 1943. 318p. (Les Femmes Collection) – 4mf – 9 – $10.00 – fr Bibl Nationale [360]
Serzhputovskii, I *see* SPRAVOCHNIK O RUSSKIKH KNIGAKH GRAZHDANSKOI PECHATI, IZD. V SVET S 1708 PO 1855 GOD. VYP. 1. A-ALLER
SESAME AND SAFFLOWER : STATUS AND POTENTIALS – 1985 – 228p – it F.A.O. [631]
SESAME, STATUS AND IMPROVEMENT : PROCEEDINGS OF EXPERT CONSULTATION, ROME, 1980 – 1981 – 203p – it F.A.O. [630]
DIE SESENHEIMER LIEDER : EINE KRITISCHE STUDIE / Maurer, Theodor – (Anhang: H. Kruses Abschrift der Sesenheimer Lieder) – Strassburg: J H E Heitz, 1907 – 1r – 1 – us U.W. Library [430]
SESII A 1938-45 *see* STENOHRAFICHNY IZVIT ZASIDANNIA VERKHOVNOI RADI SRSR
A SESQUI-CENTENNIAL HISTORY OF KENTUCKY – v2,3,4. By Frederick A. Wallis and Hambleton Tapp, 1945. v2-3 contain complete indexes covering hist. and biog. sections of v4. F-1063, F-1064, and F-1065 – 9 – us A.G.L.L. [920]
Sesse y Lacasta, Martin de *see*
- FLORA MEXICANA
- PLANTAE NOVAE HISPANIAE...

SESSION (DAWRAH) 8 : MEETINGS (JALASAH) 1-129 (25 AZAR 1309-24 DAY 1311 [15 DECEMBER 1930-13 JANUARY 1933]) – $150.00 – us MEDOC [470]
SESSION (DAWRAH) 9 : MEETINGS (JALASAH) 1-137 (24 ISFAND 1311-21 FARVARDIN 1314 [14 MARCH 1933-10 APRIL 1935] – $150.00 – us MEDOC [470]
SESSION (DAWRAH) 10 : MEETINGS (JALASAH) 1-108 (15 KHURDAD 1314-22 KHURDAD 1316 [5 JUNE 1935-11 JUNE 1937]) – $300.00 – us MEDOC [470]
SESSION (DAWRAH) 12 : MEETINGS (JALASAH) 1-133 (3 ABAN 1318-9 ABAN 1320 [25 OCTOBER 1939-30 OCTOBER 1941]) – $300.00 – us MEDOC [470]
SESSION (DAWRAH) 20 : MEETINGS (JALASAH) 1-20 (2 ISFAND, 1339-14 URDIBISHISHT 1340 [20 FEBRURY 1961-3 MAY 1961]) – $150.00 – us MEDOC [470]
SESSION GENERALE DU 23 FEVRIER AU 2 MARS 1959: ANNEXE 2: AVANT-PROJECT, DEUXIEME PLAN DECENNAL, NOTES DOCUMENTAIRES (1960-1969) / Congo. (Belgian). Conseil – (General Session, 23 Feb 1958 to 2 Mar 1959; Annex 2: Preliminary Draft of the Second Ten-Year Plan, Documentary Notes). Leopoldville. 1959? BD-1617 1 – 9 – ne IDC [338]
SESSION LAWS : FROM THE KINGDOM TO DATE / Hawaii Legislature – (Updates planned) – 1843-1993 – 597mf – 9 – $895.00 – LLMC 77-102 – us L.L.M.C. [340]
SESSION LAWS / Michigan Legislature – (Add vols planned) – 1821-1993 – 1373mf – 9 – $2,059.00 – LLMC 77-002 – us L.L.M.C. [340]
SESSION LAWS / Minnesota – 1849- – 9 – us UMI [340]
SESSION LAWS / New Mexico Territory – 1846- – 9 – us UMI [340]
SESSION LAWS / New York – 1777- – 9 – us UMI [340]
SESSION LAWS / North Dakota – 1889- – 9 – us UMI [340]
SESSION LAWS / Ohio – 1803- – 9 – us UMI [340]
SESSION LAWS / Oklahoma. Territory – 1890- – 9 – us UMI [978]
SESSION LAWS / Oregon – 1844- – 9 – us UMI [340]
SESSION LAWS / Pennsylvania – 1776- – 9 – us UMI [978]
SESSION LAWS, 1776- / New Jersey – 9 – us UMI [340]
SESSION LAWS, 1777- / North Carolina – 9 – us UMI [340]
SESSION LAWS, 1783- / New Hampshire – 9 – us UMI [340]
SESSION LAWS, 1799- / Mississippi – 9 – us UMI [340]
SESSION LAWS, 1813- / Missouri – 9 – us UMI [340]
SESSION LAWS, 1855- / Nebraska – 1 – us UMI [340]
SESSION LAWS, 1861- / Nevada – 9 – us UMI [340]
SESSION LAWS, 1864- / Montana – 9 – us UMI [340]
SESSION LAWS, 1788-1801 / Northwest Territory – 9 – us UMI [340]
SESSION LAWS, 1821-99 / Michigan – 9 – us UMI [340]
SESSION LAWS OF GUAM, 1975/76-1991/92 / Guam Legislature – (Includes general legislation and executive orders and resolutions. Pre-1975 legislation not located) – 13th-21st Legislatures – 84mf – 9 – $126.00 – LLMC 82-100B Title 17 – us L.L.M.C. [324]
SESSION MINUTES OF THE SALEM CONGREGATION OF THE CUMBERLAND PRESBYTERIAN CHURCH 1865-1905, BOONSBORO, WASHINGTON CO., AR – Also: Session Minutes of the Cane Hill Congregation of the Cumberland Presbyterian Church, Cane Hill, Washington Co., AR. 4 fiches.F-0053 – 9 – us A.G.L.L. [978]
SESSION PROGRAMME FOR THE PRIMARY DEPARTMENT – (Cont by: Primary Quarterly) – S.l.: s.n., 1896?-1898 – 9 – cn C.I.H.M. [240]
SESSION PROGRAMME FOR THE PRIMARY DEPARTMENT *see* THE PRIMARY QUARTERLY
SESSIONAL PAPERS / British Columbia. Legislative Assembly – Victoria, BC: British Columbia Legislative Assembly, 1872-1982 – 122r – 1 – Can$70.00r – cn U.B.C. Preserve [971]
SESSIONAL PAPERS / Canada. Parliament – (Annual reports only) – 14th-29th Parliaments. 1924-75 – 9 – cn Micromedia [323]
SESSIONAL PAPERS / Great Britain. Parliament. House of Commons – 1731-1800 – 1 – $582.00 – us L of C Photodup [941]
SESSIONAL PAPERS / Great Britain. Parliament. House of Commons – 1731-1900. Available in separate chronological groups – 3,9 – us Readex [324]
SESSIONAL PAPERS / Great Britain. Parliament. House of Commons – Indexes. 1696-1900 – 3,9 – us Readex [324]
SESSIONAL PAPERS / Great Britain. Parliament. House of Lords – 1788-1835 – 1 – $3,696.00 – us L of C Photodup [941]
SESSIONAL PAPERS / Great Britain. Parliament. House of Lords – 1806-59.560 reels – 1 – $14,950.00 – us Trans-Media [323]
SESSIONAL PAPERS / Great Britain. Parliament. House of Lords – 1940/41-1969/70 – 3 – us Readex [941]
Sestini, Valerio *see* SHERPA ARCHITECTURE
SET' SEL'SKOKHOZIAISTVENNOI KOOPERATSII SSSR : SBORNIK STATISTICHESKIKH MATERIALOV / Brenner, Vl; ed by Ratner, G M – M., 1929 – 2mf – 9 – COR-512/1 – ne IDC [334]
SETANTI I PEREVYBORY SOVETOV = SECTARIANS AND THE ELECTION OF SOVIETS / Putintsev, Fedor Maksimovich – Moscow, 1930. One of 13 titles by Soviet authors on reel – 1 – 74.32 – us Baptist [240]
SETE DE ABRIL : JORNAL POLITICO E NOTICIOSO – Campanha, 8 Feb 1877 – 1,5,6 – bl Biblioteca [072]
O SETE DE NOVEMBRO : DIARIO POLITICO E COMMERCIAL – '(s.l.')-Bahia, Brazil. 21 Nov-22 Dec 1837 – 1,5,6 – bl Biblioteca [072]
SETE DE SETEMBRO : JORNAL POLITICO, COMMERCIAL E NOTICIOSO – Pilar, Alagoas. 16 Jun-12 Ago 1876 – 1,5,6 – bl Biblioteca [072]
SETE DE SETEMBRO : ORGAO DO PARTIDO CONSERVADOR – Diamantina, 2 Apr, Sept 1887; Apr 1888-28 Mar 1889 – 1,5,6 – bl Biblioteca [072]
SETENA PARTIDA, COM. DE GREGORIO LOPEZ / Alfonso 10 el Sabio, Rey de Castilla Rey de Castilla – 1610 – 9 – 1.50f – sp Bibl Santa Ana [946]
SETENGAH LOESIN PERTJAKAPAN ERASMUS / Erasmus, Desiderius – SE-10,656 1. 1946? – 9 – ne IDC [450]
Seth, James *see* A STUDY OF ETHICAL PRINCIPLES
SETH PEASE PAPERS *see* PEASE, SETH, PAPERS, MS 3234
Seth Pringle-Pattison, Andrew *see*
- SCOTTISH PHILOSOPHY
- TWO LECTURES ON THEISM

Sethe, K *see*
- AEGYPTISCHE LESESTUECKE
- DAS AEGYPTISCHE VERBUM IM ALTAEGYPTISCHEN, NEUAEGYPTISCHEN UND KOPTISCHEN
- EGYPTIAN LETTERS TO THE DEAD. MAINLY FROM THE OLD AND MIDDLE KINGDOMS
- HISTORISCH-BIOGRAPHISCHE URKUNDEN DES MITTLEREN REICHES
- URKUNDEN DER 18. DYNASTIE
- URKUNDEN DES ALTEN REICHS

SETHOS: HISTOIRE OU VIE TIREE DES MONUMENS ANECDOTES DE L'ANCIENNE EGYPTE: TRADUITE D'UN MANUSCRIT GREC / Terrasson, Jean – Paris, 1731. (Historical Studies Series) – 9 – 48.00 – fr Bibl Nationale [900]
SETI / Kuzmin, M – Pervaia kniga stikhov. M. 1908. BR-3622 2 – 8 – ne IDC [460]
SETI / Kuzmin, M – Stikhi. (Sobranie sochinenii V.I). Ed. 2. Petrograd. 1916. BR-1199 2 – 8 – ne IDC [460]
SETJARIK PELANGI DI RICHTINGWIJZER / Basari, Moh – SE-3986 1. 1955 – 9 – ne IDC [950]
Seton, BG *see* THE PRISONERS OF THE FORTY-FIVE
SETON HALL JOURNAL OF SPORT LAW – v1-3. 1991-93 – 9 – $38.00 set – us Hein [340]
SETON HALL LAW REVIEW – (v1-15 1970-85 on reel $245.00. v16-25 1986-95 on mf $219.00) – v1-25. 1970-95 – 5,6,9 – $464.00 set – us Hein [340]
SETON HALL LEGISLATIVE JOURNAL – v1-18. 1975-94 – 9 – $193.00 set – us Hein [320]
Seton, Walter Warren *see* CHRISTIAN APOLOGETICS
Seton-Watson, Robert William *see* MAXIMILIAN I, HOLY ROMAN EMPEROR. (STANHOPE HISTORICAL ESSAY 1901)
Setsinskii, E *see* OPIS' STAROPECHATNYKH KNIG
Sette, Mario *see* SOMBRAS DE BARAUNAS
SETTI GIORNI *see* 7 GIORNI (SUPPL. CORRIERE DELLA SERA)
IL SETTIMANALE DI MONTREAL – (In Italian) – Montreal, Canada. v1 n8. 20 avr 1976-v3 n15. 11 avr 1978 – 1r – 1 – Can$25.00 – cn Can Microfilming [072]
SETTIMO LIBRO DE MADRGALI, A CINQUE VOCI DI GIO. DOMENICO MONTELLA NAPOLITANO / Montella, G D – (Imperfect copy, quinto and tenor parts only) – Napoli: Gio. Battista Scottile, 1605 – 1 – us Sibley [780]
THE SETTING OF THE CRESCENT AND THE RISING OF THE CROSS : OR, KAMIL ABDUL MESSIAH: A SYRIAN CONVERT FROM ISLAM TO CHRISTIANITY / Jessup, Henry Harris – Philadelphia: Westminster Press, 1898 – 1mf – 9 – 0-8370-7160-7 – 1986-1160 – us A.T.L.A. [920]
SETTING UP A PARENT-TEACHER ASSOCIATION / Botswana. Ministry of Education – Gaborone, [1981] – 1mf – 9 – DE-421/1 – ne IDC [370]
THE SETTLEMENT OF ESTATES OF DECEASED PERSONS, INCLUDING THE SUBJECTS OF WILLS, EXECUTORS, ADMINISTRATORS, TESTAMENTARY TRUSTEES...WITH SUCH ESTATES IN OHIO / Giauque, Florien – 6th ed. Cincinnati: Clarke, 1902. 866p. LL-834 – 1 – us L of C Photodup [340]
SETTLEMENT OF OTAGO / Hocken, T M – (Contributions to Early History. Lists early European settlers) – 1898 – 3mf – NZ$13.00 – 0-908797-38-9 – NZNB H1004 – nz BAB [980]
SETTLEMENT SHEETS / Ottawa County. Ohio. Carroll Township. Township Clerk – 1900-1903 – 1r – 1 – $32.50r – us Archival [324]
SETTLEMENT STRATEGIES FOR FEDERAL DISTRICT JUDGES / Provine, D Marie – Washington: FJC, 1986 – 2mf – 9 – $3.00 – LLMC 95-362 – us L.L.M.C. [340]
THE SETTLER / ed by Thom, Adam – Montreal, Canada. 1 jan 1833-v1 n53. 31 dec 1833 – 1r – 1 – Can$35.00 – cn Can Microfilming [072]
SETTLER'S GUIDE, PROVINCE OF QUEBEC / Province of Quebec Crown Lands Department – Quebec: Commissioner of Lands, Forest and Fisheries..., 1880?-. SEM105P619 – 10mf – 9 – Can$22.50 – cn Bibl Nat [971]
SETTLERS, MINERS AND TOURISTS GUIDE FROM OCEAN TO OCEAN BY THE C. P. R., THE GREAT TRANS-CONTINENTAL SHORT LINE THROUGH A REGION OF UNSURPASSED ATTRACTION FOR SETTLER, MINER AND TOURIST / Chittenden, Newton H – Ottawa: J. Hope, 1885? 03051. (Pre-1900 Canadiana) – 9 – cn C.I.H.M. [971]
SEU 2 FESTIVAL VERANO. CACERES 58 – Caceres, s.i. 1958 – 1 – sp Bibl Santa Ana [390]
SEU CODICUM MANUSCRIPTORUM QUI IN TABULARIO CASINENSI ASSERVANTUR / Bibliotheca Casinensis – Abb. Montis Casini Tomus 1-5 1873-1894 – 143mf – 8 – ne Slangenburg [090]
SEU LEXICON AMHARICO-LATINUM... / Ludolf, Hiob – Francofurti ad Moenum. 1698 – 2mf – ne IDC [470]
LA SEUDRE – no. 27-261. Marennes. 29 juin 1872-76 – 1 – fr A.C.R.P.P. [073]
SEUENTICH SLUYTREDENEN VAN DER RECHTER HANT GODS EN DER MACHT CHRISTI / Huberinus, Caspar – [Antwerpen oder Vianen], 1566. [G.F.: 10.7] – 1mf – 9 – HUB-29/1 – ne IDC [240]
Seuffert, Bernhard *see*
- DER DICHTER DES OBERON
- GOETHES THEATER-ROMAN
- WIELANDS ABDERITEN

Seuhl, Antonin *see* LA GREVE DES MACHINES
Seume, Johann Gottfried *see*
- FREIHEIT UND RECHT
- PROSAISCHE UND POETISCHE WERKE

Seurin, J L *see* LA STRUCTURE INTERNE DES PARTIS POLITIQUES AMERICAINS
Seuse, Heinrich *see* DEUTSCHE SCHRIFTEN
...SEV TVRCARVM EXPEDITIO IN SICULUM FRETUM / Colossa, N A – Messanae, 1595 – 1mf – 9 – H-8382/1 – ne IDC
THE SEVEN ARTS – New York. v. 1-2. Nov 1916-Oct 1917 – 1 – us NY Public [400]
THE SEVEN CHURCHES OF ASIA : OR, WORLDLINESS IN THE CHURCH / Crosby, Howard – New York:Funk & Wagnalls, 1890 – 1mf – 9 – 0-8370-2782-9 – 1985-0782 – us A.T.L.A. [220]
SEVEN CHURCHES OF ASIA, OR, WORLDLINESS IN THE CHURCH / Crosby, Howard – New York: Funk & Wagnalls, 1890.1 fiche – 9 – us A.T.L.A. [240]
THE SEVEN CHURCHES OF ASIA: SEVEN DISCOURSES / Tophel, Gustave – Chicago: Chicago Foundlings', 1883. 1 fiche – 9 – us A.T.L.A. [240]
THE SEVEN CITIES OF DELHI / Hearn, G – Calcutta, 1928. BI-1042 2 – 8 – ne IDC [950]
SEVEN DAYS – v. 1- 1975- – 1 – us UMI [073]
SEVEN GREAT STATESMEN IN THE WARFARE OF HUMANITY WITH UNREASON / White, Andrew Dickson – New York: Century Co., 1910 – 2mf – us A.T.L.A. [320]
THE SEVEN LAMPS OF ARCHITECTURE / Ruskin, John – London: Smith, Elder, 1849 – 1 roll – 1 – 1-55879-922-2 – uk Libr Preservation [720]
SEVEN LECTURES ON ECONOMICS / Pearce, H G – 1fiche (29x) – 9 – 1.00f – at Libertarian Micro [320]
SEVEN LECTURES ON SHAKESPEARE AND MILTON / Coleridge, Samuel Taylor – London: Chapman and Hall, 1856 – 1 roll – 1 – 1-55879-630-4 – uk Libr Preservation [420]
SEVEN LECTURES ON THE CREDIBILITY OF THE GOSPEL HISTORIES / Barrows, John Henry – Boston: D. Lothrop, 1891. 1 fiche – 9 – us A.T.L.A. [240]
SEVEN MINOR EPICS OF THE ENGLISH RENAISSANCE / ed by Miller, Paul W – 1596-1624 – 9 – 20.00 – us Scholars' Facs [810]
SEVEN PUZZLING BIBLE BOOKS : A SUPPLEMENT TO "WHO WROTE THE BIBLE" / Gladden, Washington – Boston: Houghton, Mifflin, 1897 – 1mf – 9 – 0-8370-3303-9 – 1985-1303 – us A.T.L.A. [220]
(SEVEN SAGES OF ROME): THE HISTORY OF THE SEVEN WISE MASTERS OF ROME – 1885 – 1 – us I.U. Libraries [390]

SEVEN SISTERS AND FINSBURY PARK JOURNAL – (Hornsey and Finsbury Park Journal Hornsey Journal). London. -w. 1879-1981. (126 reels) – 1 – uk British Libr Newspaper [072]

SEVEN SOUNDS; A MUSICAL MAGAZINE DEVOTED TO THE YOUTH – V.3, no. 1-3 (March-Oct) 1865 – 9 – us Sibley [073]

SEVEN TROUGH DISTRICT NEWS – Vernon, NV. 1908-09 – 1r – 1 – $50.00 – U04780 – us Library Micro [071]

SEVEN TROUGH MINER – Vernon, NV. 1907-10 – 1r – 1 – $50.00 – U04781 – us Library Micro [071]

SEVEN TROUGHS DISTRICT NEWS – Mazuma, NV. 1908-09 – 1r – 1 – $50.00 – U04634 – us Library Micro [071]

SEVEN VALLEY'S FARMER – Callaway, NE. -w. Mar. 1908-Oct. 1917; May 1937-Aug. 1965; Oct. 1965-Sep. 1967 – 1 – us NE Hist [071]

SEVEN YEAR PLAN FOR ECONOMIC DEVELOPMENT OF JORDAN, 1964-1970 / Jordan. Development Board – 1966? BNE-9786 1 – 9 – ne IDC [338]

SEVEN YEAR PROGRAM FOR ECONOMIC DEVELOPMENT, 1964-70 / Jordan. Development Board – Amman. 1966 – 9 – ne IDC [338]

SEVEN YEARS IN SIERRA LEONE...THE WORK OF WILLIAM A.B. JOHNSON...FROM 1816 TO 1823 / Pierson, Arthur Tappan – New York: Fleming H. Revell, 1897. 252p. 1 fiche – 9 – us A.T.L.A. [240]

SEVEN YEARS MILITARY LIFE IN SOUTHERN INDIA / Bridgewater, Thomas – Toronto: W. Chewett, 1867. 00268. (Pre-1900 Canadiana) – 9 – cn C.I.H.M. [920]

SEVEN YEARS OF TRANSPORT AND COMMUNICATIONS IN THE EGYPTIAN REGION OF THE UAR / Egypt. Ministry of Communications – 1960. BNE-4658 1 – 9 – ne IDC [380]

SEVEN YEARS' SERVICE ON THE SAVLE COAST OF WESTERN AFRICA / Huntley, Henry Veel – London, 1850 – 1 – us Res Libr [960]

Sevenig, N *see* SCHILLER ALS DRAMATISCHER DICHTER

SEVENOAKS CHRONICLE – England. 18 Feb 1881-Dec 1977 (missing May 1893-May 1896; Jan-Dec 1897; Jan-Dec 1907).-w. 136mqn reels – 1 – uk British Libr Newspaper [072]

Sevensma, Tietse Pieter *see*
- DE ARK GODS: HET OUD-ISRAELITISCHE HEILIGDOM
- DE ARK GODS

SEVENTEEN PROBLEMS OF MAN AND SOCIETY / Borsodi, Ralph – 1968. 595p – 9 – 1.00f – at Libertarian Micro [335]

SEVENTEEN YEARS IN PARIS : A CHAPLAIN'S STORY / Noyes, H E – London: Baines and Scarsbrook, 1910 – 1mf – us A.T.L.A. [240]

SEVENTEEN YEARS IN THE YORUBA COUNTRY. MEMORIALS OF ANNA HINDERER / Hinderer, Anna Martin – Gathered from her journals and letters. Introd. by Richard E. Bone. 3rd ed. London: Seeley, Jackson, and Halliday, 1873. 343p. illus – 1 – us U.W. Library [240]

SEVENTEENTH AND EIGHTEENTH CENTURY PERIODICALS AND ACADEMY PUBLICATIONS – (Academy publications. Scientific, medical and related periodicals. Learned, literary and bibliographical periodicals. Historical and political periodicals. Theological and ecclesiastical periodicals) – 1 – us Primary [073]

SEVENTEENTH- AND EIGHTEENTH-CENTURY BOOK PROSPECTUSES – (Gough Collection $80; Johnson Collection $145) – 38mf – 9 – $225.00 complete – us UMI [070]

SEVENTEENTH CENTURY DOCUMENTS RELATED TO BAPTISTS / Mennonite Seminary Library. Amsterdam – 136p – 1 – us Baptist [240]

SEVENTEENTH CENTURY PAMPHLETS / Lincoln Cathedral. Library – 2nd ed. With printed index – 1 – £2,850.00 – uk World [941]

THE SEVENTH AND JAMES STREET BAPTIST CHURCH OF WACO, TEXAS / Browne, P D – 1948 – 1 – 6.65 – us Baptist [240]

SEVENTH BRIGADE JOURNAL – (Weekly newspaper for the Seventh Brigade, Army of the Ohio, U.S. Army) – Columbia, TN. apr 15, 1862 – 1r – 1 – us Western Res [071]

SEVENTH CENSUS OF THE UNITED STATES / U.S. Bureau of the Census – 1850. 1009 rolls. M432 – 1 – us Nat'l Archives [324]

SEVENTH CENSUS OF THE U.S. – 1850 – 1r – 1 – $50.00 – B50003 – us Library Micro [975]

THE SEVENTH CIRCUIT PREAPPEAL PROGRAM : AN EVALUATION / Goldman, Jerry – Washington: FJC, May 1982 – 1mf – 9 – $1.50 – LLMC 95-801 – us L.L.M.C. [340]

Seventh Day Baptist General Conference *see* PROCEEDINGS

SEVENTH DAY BAPTIST HANDBOOK, 1948 – Also incl.: The Sabbath Recorder, 1962-64; Seventh Day Baptist in Arkansas Historical Calendar, 1963. 122p – 1 – 5.00 – us Baptist [240]

SEVENTH DAY BAPTISTS : CHURCH RECORDS, MANUSCRIPTS, LETTERS, ETC – 4 reels. 3974p – 1 – us Baptist [240]

SEVENTH DAY BAPTISTS IN EUROPE AND AMERICA, 1910 – v. 1 and 2 – 1 – 68.46 – us Baptist [240]

SEVENTH FIVE YEAR PLAN (1992/93-1996/97) : V1: MAIN DOCUMENT / Bhutan. Planning Commission – Bhutan, 1992 – 4mf – 9 – ne IDC [338]

SEVENTH MEETING OF THE EAST AND SOUTHERN AFRICAN SUB-COMMITTEE FOR SOIL CORRELATION AND EVALUATION, GABORONE, BOTSWANA, MARCH-APRIL 1987 – 1988 – 164p – it F.A.O. [631]

SEVENTH NATIONAL ECONOMIC AND SOCIAL DEVELOPMENT PLAN (1992-1996) / Thailand. National Economic and Social Development Board – Bangkok, 1992 – 5mf – 9 – ne IDC [338]

SEVENTH U.S. ARMY REPORT OF OPERATIONS-FRANCE AND GERMANY, 1944-45 / U.S. Army. Seventh Army – 1r – 1 – $85.00 – S1681 – us Scholarly Res [355]

SEVENTIES – (1971-72. 1,5,6) – 1958-72 – 1 – us UMI [073]

SEVENTIETH ANNUAL REPORT OF THE ASSOCIATION OF GRADUATES OF THE UNITED STATES MILITARY ACADEMY AT WEST POINT, NEW YORK, JUNE 10, 1939 / Moore Printing Co., Inc – Newburgh, 1939. Military Books, reel 2. Cox Library Collection – 5 – us Americana [920]

SEVENTY YEARS IN NORTON COUNTY, KANSAS. 1872-1942 / Bowers, D N – Norton: The Norton County Champion, 1942. Kansas Reel 10 – 5 – us Americana [978]

SEVENTY YEARS OF NEW BRUNSWICK LIFE: AUTO-BIOGRAPHICAL SKETCHES / Baird, William Thomas – St. John, N.B.: G. E. Day, 1890. 02502. (Pre-1900 Canadiana) – 9 – cn C.I.H.M. [971]

SEVENTY-FIFTH JUBILEE MEMORIALS, 1860-1935 / Moratuwa. Ceylon. Holy Emmanuel Church – Moratuwa: Jubilee Memorials Committee, 1935 – us Res Libr [240]

SEVEN-YEAR DEVELOPMENT PLAN A BRIEF OUTLINE / Ghana. Planning Commission – Accra. 1963. BD-719 1 – 9 – ne IDC [338]

SEVEN-YEAR PLAN, 1961-1967 / Korea. North – Pyongyang. 1962. BD-312 1 – 9 – ne IDC [338]

SEVER – Ezhenedel'nyi literaturno-khudozhestvennyi zhurnal. v. 1-7. Spb. 1888-94. Lacking: v. 1, 1888; v. 2 (1-23), 1889; v. 3 (1), 1890; v. 7 (1), 1894. B-1883 2 – 8 – ne IDC [073]

SEVERAL CHIRURGICALL TREATISES / Wiseman, R – London. 1676. BM-145 1 2 – 8,9 – ne IDC [617]

Severance, H O *see* PALMER HARTSOUGH, MICHIGAN SONG WRITER AND MINISTER, 1880-1932

Severianin, I *see*
- ANANASY V SHAMPANSKOM. POEZY
- FEIA EIOLE. POEZY 1920-1921 GG
- GROMOKIPIASHCHII KUBOK. POEZY
- KLASSICHESKIIA RECHI. STIKHI 1922-1930 GG
- MEDAL'ONY. SONETY
- MENESTREL'. NOVEISIIA POEZY
- MIRRELIIA. NOVYIA POEZY
- OSTROVA OCHAROVANII
- PADUCHAIA STREMNINA
- POEZOANTRAKT. PIATAIA KNIGA POEZ
- PUEHAJOGI. ESTLIANDSKIIA POEZY
- SOBRANIE POEZ
- VERVENA. POEZY 1918-1919 GG
- WICTORIA REGIA. CHETVERTAIA KNIGA POEZ
- ZLATOLIRA

Severien, Frere *see* BIO-BIBLIOGRAPHIE ANALYTIQUE DE RODOLPHE LAPLANTE, REGISSEUR ET SECRETAIRE-GENERAL DE L'OFFICE DU CREDIT AGRICOLE DU QUEBEC

Severn, M D *see* GRAY'S INN LIBRARY

SEVERNAGO KRAIA / Arkhangel'skago obshchestva izucheniia Russkago Severa – v. 1-9. Arkhangel'sk. 1909-17. BR-3220 2 – 8 – ne IDC [073]

SEVERNAIA AZIIA – Obshchestvenno-nauchnyi zhurnal. M. 1925-30. BR-1616 2 – 8 – ne IDC [500]

SEVERNAIA KOOPERATSIIA – Arkhangel'sk, 1919 n7/8 – 3mf – 9 – COR-678/1 – ne IDC [334]

SEVERNAIA MINERVA – Zhurnal literaturnyi. Spb. 1832-33. B-1884 2 – 8 – ne IDC [073]

SEVERNAIA PAL'MIRA – Dvukhnedel'noe izdanie. Literaturno- i obshchestvenno-politicheskii zhurnal. v. 1-2. Spb. 1906. BR-3761 2 – 8 – ne IDC [321]

SEVERNAIA SISTEMA / Aleksandrov, P A – M., 1914 – 3mf – 9 – ILM-2518/1 – ne IDC [340]

SEVERNAYA PCHELA – Gazeta politicheskaia i literaturnaia. Spb., 1825-1863. Lacking: 1836(43); 1849(91); 1861(41-43, 49, 250, 281, 298 298-299); 1862(292); 1863(169-171). BR-4240 2 – 8 – ne IDC [320]

SEVERNAYA PCHELA – Leningrad. USSR. -w. 1825-62. (57 reels) – 1 – uk British Libr Newspaper [947]

SEVERNOE KHOZIAISTVO : ZHURNAL ARKHANGELSKOGO GUBISPOLKOMA – (Library has: Jan./Feb. 1928) – Arkhangelsk: Arkhangelski i Gubispolkom, 1923-1929. 7v – 1 – CSUX89-S944 – us Hoover Inst Photo [330]

SEVERNOE OBOZRENIE – Ucheno-literaturnyi zhurnal. Spb. 1848-50. Lacking: (3) 1849; (1-2) 1850. B-1886 2 – 8 – ne IDC [073]

SEVERNOE PRICHERNOMOR'E V 1775-1800 GG / Druzhinina, E I – Akademiia nauk SSSR, institut istorii. M. 1959. BR-10,521 1 – 9 – ne IDC [947]

SEVERNOE SIIANIE – Russkii khudozhestvennyi al'bom. v. 1-4. Spb. 1862-65. B-1887 2 – 8 – ne IDC [073]

SEVERNOE SIIANIE. STIKHI O LITVE I RUSI / Bal'mont, K D – Paris. 1931. BR-533 2 – 8 – ne IDC [460]

SEVERNS VALLEY BAPTIST CHURCH. ELIZABETHTOWN, KENTUCKY : CHURCH RECORDS – v. 1-3. 1788-1884 – 1 – 52.02 – us Baptist [240]

SEVERNYE TSVETY – Sborniki. Izd. "Skorpion". v. 1-5. M. 1901-11. BR-1909 2 – 8 – ne IDC [073]

SEVERNYE ZAPISKI – Literaturno-politicheskii ezhemesiachnik. Spb. 1913-17. B-1408 2 – 8 – ne IDC [320]

SEVERNYI ARKHIV – Zhurnal istorii, statistiki i puteshestvii. Spb. 1822-28. B-1888 2 – 8 – ne IDC [073]

SEVERNYI DNI – v. 1-2. M. 1922. Lacking: v. 1. BR-1910 2 – 8 – ne IDC [073]

SEVERNYI KHOZIAIN *see* IZVESTIIA VOLOGDSKOGO OBSHCHESTVA SEL'SKOGO KHOZIAISTVA

SEVERNYI KOOPERATOR – Arkhangel'sk, 1925-27 n25 – 29mf – 9 – COR-679/1 – ne IDC [334]

SEVERNYI KRAI – Iaroslavl, Russia. 1905 – 1 – us Res Libr [072]

SEVERNYI MURAVEI – Gazeta promyshlennosti. Spb. 1830-33. BR-3769 2 – 8 – ne IDC [380]

SEVERNYI VESTNIK – v. 1-8. Spb. 1804-05. B-1422 2 – 8 – ne IDC [073]

SEVERNYIA ZAPISKI – St. Petersburg. Jan. 1913-Jan. 1917. Missing May, June 1913 – 1 – 35.00r – us Hoover Inst Photo [910]

SEVERO-KAVKAZSKI IKRAI : ORGAN SEVEROKAVKAZSKO I PLANOVOI KOMISSII – (Includes c.1: v.12:no.1/2 1933-v.12:no.4/6 (1933)) – Rostov na Donu: Severny i Kavkaz, 1924 – 1 – CSUXAKZ2923-S – us Hoover Inst Photo [639]

SEVIER COUNTY REPUBLICAN – Sevierville. Tenn. and Record. 1909-52 – 1 – us UMI [071]

SEVILLA! / Sanchez-Arjona, Vicente – Sevilla: Imp. Cuadrado, 1957 – 1 – sp Bibl Santa Ana [810]

Sevilla Andres, Diego *see* DONOSO CORTES Y LA DICTADURA

SEVILLA. ARCHIVO GENERAL DE INDIAS GUIA DEL VISITANTE / Pena y Camara, J M – Madrid, 1958 – 9 – sp Cultura [025]

SEVILLA. ARCHIVO GENERAL DE INDIAS. SECCION DE CONTRATACION. CATALOGO DE PASAJEROS DE INDIAS...(1509-1599) / Bermudez Plata, C – Sevilla, 1946 – 9 – sp Cultura [972]

SEVILLA INTELECTUAL, SUS ECRITORES Y ARTISTAS CONTEMPORANEOS / Cascales Munoz, Jose – 1896 – 9 – 1.50f – sp Bibl Santa Ana [440]

SEVILLA INTELECTUAL. SUS ESCRITORES Y ARTISTAS CONTEMPORANEOS POR D. JOSE CASCALES Y MUNOZ (INFORME) / Uhagon, Francisco R de – Madrid: Fortanet, 1899, pp. 513-515. B.R.A.H. 34, 1899 – 1 – sp Bibl Santa Ana [700]

Sevilla, Luis Antonio de *see* SERMON PANEGYRICO DEL SR. S. PEDRO DE ARBUES, MARTYR DE JESUCHRISTO...

SEVILLA UND VALLADOLID : DIE EVANGELISCHEN GEMEINDEN SPANIENS IM REFORMATIONSZEITALTER / Schaefer, Ernst – Halle: Verein fuer Reformationsgeschichte, 1903 (Schriften des Vereins fuer Reformationsgeschichte; 21. Jahrg., Schrift 78) – 1mf – us A.T.L.A. [240]

Sevillano, Casimiro *see* DESCRIPCION... CORRIDAS DE TOROS...CACERES

SEVIMLI AY – (Continued as Resimli Ay) – Istanbul: Matbaa-i Ebuezziya, 1926-1927 – 9 – $125.00 – us MEDOC [956]

Sevin, Hermann *see*
- CHRONOLOGIE DES LEBENS JESU VON HERMANN SEVIN
- SYNOPTISCHE ERKLAERUNG DER DREI ERSTEN EVANGELIEN
- ZUR CHRONOLOGIE DES LEBENS JESU NACH DEN SYNOPTIKERN

Sevruk, P N *see* KOOPERATSIIA V SOIUZE SSR

Sewall, Frank *see* REASON IN BELIEF, OR, FAITH FOR AN AGE OF SCIENCE

Sewan Susanto, K *see* BUKU PENUNTUN BATIK

SEWANEE REVIEW – v. 1-48. 1892-1940 – 1 – us Princeton Micro [073]

SEWANEE REVIEW – v1- 1892- – 1 – inquire – us Ross [420]

Seward, A C *see* THE JURASSIC FLORA

SEWARD CITIZEN – Milford, NE. -w. Feb 1962-Apr 1963 – 1 – us NE Hist [071]

SEWARD COUNTY INDEPENDENT – Seward, NE. -w. Jun 1892; Jun 1893; Aug 1895-Oct 1896; Mar 1897 to date – 1 – us NE Hist [071]

SEWARD COUNTY TRIBUNE – Seward, NE. -w. Sep 1915-Jan 1920 – 1 – us NE Hist [071]

SEWARD INDEPENDENT – Seward, NE. -w. Jan 1894-Oct 1895 – 1 – us NE Hist [071]

SEWARD INDEPENDENT – Seward, NE. -w. Jan 1895; Oct-Dec 1895; Mar 1896-Jun 1897 – 1 – us NE Hist [071]

SEWARD JOURNAL – Seward, NE. -w. Jan 1908-Mar 1912; Jun 1912; Dec 1913-Dec 1931 – 1 – us NE Hist [071]

SEWARD WEEKLY REPORTER – Seward, NE. Jan-Feb 1874; May 1874-Dec 1878; Apr 1879; Apr 1881; Jan 1883-Dec 1884; Jan 1887-Dec 1889; Jan 1891-Nov 1892; May 1896-Sep 1900 – 1 – us NE Hist [071]

Seward, William *see* BIOGRAPHIANA. BY THE COMPILER OF ANECDOTES OF DISTINGUISHED PERSONS

Seward, William F *see* HISTORY OF BINGHAMPTON AND BROOME COUNTIES

Sewel, W *see* THE HISTORY OF THE RISE, INCREASE, AND PROGRESS OF THE CHRISTIAN PEOPLE CALLED QUAKERS

Sewell, Elizabeth Missing *see* PRINCIPLES OF EDUCATION, DRAWN FROM NATURE AND REVELATION, AND APPLIED TO FEMALE EDUCATION IN THE UPPER CLASSES

Sewell, J F *see* JOURNALS, 1875-97; ESTATE, 1897-99

Sewell, Jonathan *see* AN ESSAY ON THE JURIDICAL HISTORY OF FRANCE, SO FAR AS IT RELATES TO THE LAW OF THE PROVINCE OF LOWER-CANADA

Sewell, R *see*
- THE HISTORICAL INSCRIPTIONS OF SOUTHERN INDIA
- LISTS OF INSCRIPTIONS AND A SKETCH OF THE DYNASTIES OF SOUTHERN INDIA

Sewell, Richard Clarke *see* CASE AND OPINION ON THE WILL OF THE REVEREND GEORGE POWELL, DECEASED, EX-PARTE THE PRESIDENT AND GOVERNORS OF THE RADCLIFFE INFIRMARY, OXFORD

Sewell, William *see* THE MICROSCOPE OF THE NEW TESTAMENT

SEWINDU PEMBANGUNAN DESA. CIVIL ADMINISTRATION AND EIGHT YEARS OF VILLAGE ADMINISTRATION / Sunarto Hadiwidjojo, R – SE 2612 1. 1959 – 9 – ne IDC [950]

Sewrin *see* JULIA OU LES SOUTERRAINS DU CHATEAU DE MAZZINI

SEX MELEA, S. ARIAE CUM VARIATIONIBUS / Neufville, J J – 1708 – 9 – us Sibley [780]

SEX RESEARCH: EARLY LITERATURE, FROM STATISTICS TO EROTICA – 1 – us Primary [613]

SEX ROLE PERCEPTIONS AND DEFENSE MECHANISMS OF FEMALE ATHLETES / Workman, Gayle J & Braden, Roberta L – 1991 – 2mf – 9 – $8.00 – us Microform Publ [150]

SEX ROLES – v1-31. 1975-94 – 1,5 – $85.00v – us UMI [306]

LOS SEXOS, EL AMOR Y LA HISTORIA / Caba, Pedro – Barcelona: Ediciones S.L.C. v2. 1950 – sp Bibl Santa Ana [946]

SEXTA PARTIDA, COM. DE GREGORIO LOPEZ / Alfonso 10 el Sabio, Rey de Castilla Rey de Castilla – 1610 – 9 – 1.50f – sp Bibl Santa Ana [946]

SEXTI EMPIRICI : OPERA GRAECE ET LATINE... / ed by Fabricius, J A – Leipzig, 1718 – 33mf – 8 – ne Slangenburg [180]

SEXTI EMPIRICI OPERA GRAECE ET LATINE... / ed by Fabricius, J A – Leipzig, 1718 – 33mf – 8 – ne Slangenburg [100]

Sexton, Lydia *see* AUTOBIOGRAPHY OF LYDIA SEXTON

SEXTUS AMARCIUS, SERMONES (MGH QUELLEN..: 6.BD) – 1969 – Dfl22.00 – ne Slangenburg [240]

SEXTUS EMPIRICUS AND GREEK SCEPTICISM / Patrick, Mary Mills – Cambridge: Deighton Bell & Co; London: George Bell & Sons, 1899 – vii/1/163p – 1 – us U.W. Library [180]

SEXUAL ABUSE – v1-6. 1988-93 – $60.00v – us UMI [360]

SEXUAL AND MARITAL THERAPY – 1986- 8v – 9 – £137.50 – 0267-4653 – uk Carfax [306]

SEXUAL EXPLOITATION OF CHILDREN SLIM / U.S. National Institute of Justice NCJRS – 1987. 70 selected documents, indexed – 9 – $58.00 – us N.C.J.R.S. [360]

THE SEXUAL LIFE OF SAVAGES IN NORTHWESTERN MELANESIA; AN ETHNOGRAPHIC ACCOUNT OF COURTSHIP, MARRIAGE, AND FAMILY LIFE AMOUNG THE NATIVES OF THE TROBRIAND ISLANDS, BRITISH NEW GUINEA / Malinowski, Bronislaw – 3rd ed. London: G. Routledge & Sons, 1932. i,505p – 1 – us U.W. Library [306]

SEXUAL POLITICS IN BRITAIN – (1979-82. 9) – Supplement. Gay News. 1977-78 and 1979-1982 – 9 – us Primary [305]

SEXUAL POLITICS IN BRITAIN – (Updates for 1975, 1976, 1977-78 available separately) – Basic Set. 1967-74. Pubs. and docs of Banshee; Big Flame Women's Group; Campaign for Homosexual Equality; Enough; Gay International News; Gay Left; Gay News; Journal of Irish Women United; Lunch; Outcome; Red Rag; Sappho; Scottish Minorities Group; Socialist Women; Spare Rib; Union for Sexual Freedoms in Ireland; Union of Women for Liberation; Women's Report; Women's Struggle; Women's Voice. Series: Harvester Primary Social Sources. Includes bibliographic guide – 1 – us Primary [306]

SEXUALITY AND DISABILITY – v1- 1978- – 1,5,6,9 – us UMI [613]

SEXUALITY EDUCATION : A DESCRIPTIVE STUDY OF ADOLESCENT INTERESTS AND PERCEIVED NEEDS AS REPORTED BY MIDDLE SCHOOL STUDENTS / Sims, Gigi-Terese & Smith, Margaret M – 1992 – 2mf – 9 – $8.00 – us Microform Publ [613]

SEXUALITY, SEX EDUCATION, AND REPRODUCTIVE RIGHTS – (Pt A: Schlesinger Library Family Planning Oral History Project 3r ISBN 1-55655-502-4 $355.00. Pt B: The Papers of Mary Ware Dennett and the Voluntary Parenthood League 36r ISBN 1-55655-503-2 $4,290.00) – Series 3: Women's Studies Manuscript Collections from the Schlesinger Library, Radcliffe College – 1 – $4,645.00 set – us UPA [305]

SEXUALITY TODAY – v1- 1977- – 1,5,6,9 – us UMI [613]

SEXUALLY TRANSMITTED DISEASES – (See also: American Venereal Disease Association. Journal) – v4- 1977- – 1,5,6,9 – us UMI [616]

SEXUALLY TRANSMITTED DISEASES *see* JOURNAL OF THE AMERICAN VENEREAL DISEASE ASSOCIATION

SEXUAL-PROBLEME (HQ 7) / ed by Marcuse, Max – Frankfurt/M., 4(1908)-10 (1914) (mf ed 1992) – 68mf – 9 – DM560.00 – 3-89131-061-7 – gw Fischer [150]

SEXUALREFORM (HQ 4) : BEIBLATT ZU GESCHLECHT UND GESELLSCHAFT / Vanselow, Karl et al – v1-12. 1906-1924/25. Berlin, Leipzig, Wien, spaeter: Dresden, Leipzig (mf ed 1991) – 37mf – 9 – DM290.00 – 3-89131-045-5 – gw Fischer [305]

SEYATEL' ISTINY = THE SOWER OF TRUTH – March 1916-1926, lacking April-May 1919. Seyatel' through March 1919. Organ of the Russian-Ukranian Evangelical Baptist Union. Hartford, CT. Russian Baptist Periodical in the U.S.A. – 1 – $78.72 – us Baptist [240]

Seychelles *see*
- DEVELOPMENT PLAN, 1966-1969
- A PLAN FOR SEYCHELLES

SEYCHELLES CLARION – Victoria, Seychelles. -w. Jan 1941-3 March 1951. Imperfect. 3 reels – 1 – uk British Libr Newspaper [072]

SEYCHELLES GOVERNMENT BULLETIN – Seychelles. Seychelles Bulletin. 7 Nov 1959-31, Dec 1969 – 57r – 1 – uk British Libr Newspaper [960]

SEYCHELLES GOVERNMENT GAZETTE – Seychelles. v70-92. 1946-68 – 9r – 1 – us Ross [324]

Seychelles. Ministere de l'Education et de l'Information *see* LE PLAN SECTORIEL ET LA REFORME DE L'EDUCATION AUX SEYCHELLES 1982-1986

Seychelles. Ministry of Education and Information *see*
- ADULT LITERACY
- THE REPUBLIC OF SEYCHELLES NATIONAL REPORT ON EDUCATION

Seychelles. Ministry of Education and Social Development *see* EDUCATION WHITE PAPER

Seydel, Rudolf *see* RELIGIONSPHILOSOPHIE IM UMRISS

Seyer, N *see* DOSSIER D'ETHNOLOGIE PROVENCALE, NO. 3. LES JARDINS OUVRIERS CODER, 1941-79, MARSEILLE ST MARCEL

Seyfried, Joseph von *see* (WIENER) ALLGEMEINE MUSIKALISCHE ZEITUNG

Seymour, Edward Hobart *see* MY NAVAL CAREER AND TRAVELS

Seymour, George Franklin *see* WHAT IS MODERN ROMANISM?

Seymour, Mabel *see* A LAWYER OF KENT: BARZILLAI SLOSSON AND HIS ACCOUNT BOOKS, 1794-1812

SEYMOUR PAPERS. BOXES 1-18, VOLS. 1-23, PLUS INDEX / Bath. Archives (Marquess). Longleat – 20r – 1 – uk Microform Academic [025]

Seymour, Raymond B *see* THE LAWS OF NEW YORK FAVOR AND PROTECT WOMAN

SEYNDT-BRIEF, WAERIN BEGREPEN IS EEN CORTE BEKENTENISSE BEUESTICHT MET DE H. SCHRIFT – 1581. BME-219 1 – 9 – ne IDC [240]

Seyoum, Senait *see* DAIRY MARKETING IN SUB-SAHARAN AFRICA

S'ezd narodov Vostoka. 1st, Baku *see* STENOGRAFICHESKIE OTCHETY

S'EZD SOVETOV SOIUZA SOVETSHIKH SOTSIALISTICHESKIKH RESPUBLIK: STENOGRAFICHESKII OTCHET / U.S.S.R. – Moscow. 1922-35 – 1 – us UMI [324]

S'EZD ZASEDANIIA VERKHNOVNOVO SOVETA SSSR: STENOGRAFICHESKII OTCHET / U.S.S.R. – Moscow. 1938-61 – 1 – us UMI [324]

SEZNAM ROSTLIN KVETENY CESKE / Opiz, P M – Praze. 1852. B-535 2 – 8 – ne IDC [580]

SEZONNOST RUSSKOGO EKSPORTA DO VO INY I V NSTOI ASHCHEE VREMI A / Geller, G M & Sovalov, A A – Moskva: RIO NKVT, 1925 – 1 – CSUX89-B1614 – us Hoover Inst Photo [380]

SF STATE UNIVERSITY STRIKE NOTEBOOKS – San Francisco, CA. SF State University: 1967-1970 – 1r – 1 – $50.00 – B03719 – us Library Micro [370]

SGA JOURNAL *see* GASTROENTEROLOGY NURSING

S.H. HADLEY OF WATER STREET : A MIRACLE OF GRACE / Chapman, John Wilbur – New York: Fleming H Revell, c1906 – 1mf – 9 – 0-8370-6657-3 – 1986-0657 – us A.T.L.A. [920]

SHA' ALU SHELOM YERUSHALAVIM / Gedalia of Siemiatycze – v. 2. Reshummot. 1927. BJ-27-19 1 – 9 – ne IDC [956]

SHA'ALAT HA-NESHAMAH – Prague. 1598. BJ-43-100 1 – 9 – ne IDC [270]

SHAAN-GAN-NING BIANGU CANYIHUI WENXIAN HUIJI – A collection of documents of the Councils of the Shaanxi-Gansu-Ningxia border region.Comp. by the Institute of History, Chinese Academy of Social Sciences. 5 fiches. F-H136 – 9 – $22.50 – cc Microforms [950]

SHAAN-GAN-NING GEMING GENJUDI SHILIAO XUANJI, 1 – Historical documents of the revolutionary bases of the Shaanxi-Gansu-Ningxia border region, v1. Comp. by Li Guang. 6 fiches. F-H137 – 9 – $27.00 – cc Microforms [950]

SHAANXI RIBAO – Shaanxi Daily. China. In Chinese. Current subscription. Annual delivery. 1981- , 1 reel/y. M D23 – 1 – $55.00r – cc Microforms [072]

SHAANXI SHI DA XUEBAO – (Shanghai Teacher's Univ. Journal). In Chinese but Table of Contents in English in each issue. F p220 – 9 – $4.50f – cc Microforms [073]

SHA'AR HA-SHIR / Brody, H & Albrecht, K – The New Hebrew School of Poets of the Spanish-Arabian Epoch. Leipzig. 1905. BJ-421-37 1 – 9 – ne IDC [470]

SHA'AREI TORAT EREZ YISRA'EL / Rabinowitz, Z W – Jerusalem. 1940. BJ-32-22 1 – 9 – ne IDC [900]

SHA'AREI YERUSHALAYIM / Reischer, M – Lvov. Lemberg. 1866. BJ-27-48 1 – 9 – ne IDC [270]

SHAAREI ZIYON – Jerusalem. v. 1-7. May 1876-Aug 12 1881 – 1 – us NY Public [073]

SHAAREI ZIYON – Jerusalem. v1-7. 1876-81 – 1r – 1 – us Ross [270]

Shabeeny, H A S *see* AN ACCOUNT OF TIMBUCTOO

SHABOS ZHURNAL – New York. v. 1-3 no. 4. Apr 1905-Apr 1909 – 1 – us NY Public [290]

SHACHIKU CHIKUREI CHIJU COLLECTION OF RENGA (LINKED VERSE) AND HAIKAI-SHO (17 SYLLABLED VERSE) / Tokyo University. General Library – 1872-1913. 3674 mss. and printed books. Printed chronologically-classified catalog. Index in Japanese character order: a-i-u-e-o – 11,143mf – 9 – Y5,348,640.00 – ja Yushodo [480]

Shackleton, E H *see* BRITISH ANTARCTIC EXPEDITION 1907-1909 UNDER THE COMMAND OF SIR E. H. SHACKLETON. GEOLOGY

Shaddock, Daniel Kenneth *see* INVOLVING THE LAITY OF THE NORTH DUNEDIN BAPTIST CHURCH IN A PROGRAM OF PARTICIPATION IN THE PREACHING EVENT

THE SHADE OF THE BALKANS: A COLLECTION OF BULGARIAN FOLKSONGS AND PROVERBS / Bernard, H & Dillon, E J & Slaveikoff, P – London. 1904. BR-3949 2 – 8 – ne IDC [390]

SHADES VALLEY SUN – Homewood. Ala. 1945-1963 – 1 – us UMI [071]

Shadily, Hassan *see* FRANKLIN'S ROLE IN THE DEVELOPMENT OF BOOK-PUBLISHING IN INDONESIA

THE SHADOW CHRIST : AN INTRODUCTION TO CHRIST HIMSELF / Lee, Gerald Stanley – NY: Century, 1916, c1896 – 1mf – 9 – 0-8370-4079-5 – 1985-2079 – us A.T.L.A. [240]

THE SHADOW MAGAZINE – New York. v.3-55. 1932-49 – 1 – 414.00 – us L of C Photodup [073]

THE SHADOW OF ASHLYDYAT / Wood, Ellen – British Fiction Archive: Unit 1 – 9 – uk Bell [830]

SHADOWS OF THE ROOD : OR, TYPES OF OUR SUFFERING REDEEMER JESUS CHRIST OCCURRING IN THE BOOK OF GENESIS / Bonus, John – London: [s.n.], 1856 (Cox & Wyman) – 1mf – 9 – 0-8370-6803-7 – 1986-0803 – us A.T.L.A. [240]

SHADY GROVE BAPTIST CHURCH. PICKENS COUNTY. SUNSET, SOUTH CAROLINA : CHURCH RECORDS – 1902-1977 – 1 – 25.43 – us Baptist [240]

SHADY GROVE BAPTIST CHURCH. RALEIGH ASSOCIATION. NORTH CAROLINA : CHURCH RECORDS – 1825-54 – 1 – 6.66 – us Baptist [240]

Shaeffer, Kristen L *see* THE EFFECT OF CALCIUM SUPPLEMENTATION ON BLOOD PRESSURE AND HEMODYNAMIC VARIABLES IN HYPERTENSIVE MALES

Shaen, Margaret J *see* MEMORIALS OF TWO SISTERS

Shaepman, Herman Johan Aloysius Maria *see* ST THOMAS VAN AQUINO

Shafer, J A *see* NORTH-AMERICAN TREES

Shaffer, Ellen K *see* NUREMBERG CHRONICLE

Shaffer, Laurence Frederic *see* EXPERIMENTS AND DEMONSTRATIONS IN PSYCHOLOGY

SHAFIR BERACHIA – (Yiddish book) – Krakow, PL. 1886 – 1r – 1 – $35.00 – cn Can Microfilming [470]

Shafter, William R *see* PAPERS

Shaftesbury, Anthony Ashley Cooper *see* CHARACTERISTICS OF MEN, MANNERS, OPINIONS, TIMES, ETC

SHAFTESBURY HALL – Toronto: Toronto Young Men's Christian Association, [1880-18–?] – 9 – cn C.I.H.M. [240]

Shaftesbury Society. Great Britain. Archives *see* VICTORIAN PHILANTHROPY AND SOCIAL PROBLEMS. SERIES ONE: ARCHIVES OF THE RAGGED SCHOOL UNION AND THE SHAFTESBURY SOCIETY

SHAFTESBURY (THE FIRST EARL) / Traill, Henry Duff – New York: D. Appleton and Co., 1886. (v)-xii,218p – 1 – us U.W. Library [920]

SHAFTESBURYS EINFLUSS AUF CHR. M. WIELAND : MIT EINER EINLEITUNG UEBER DEN EINFLUSS SHAFTESBURYS AUF DIE DEUTSCHE LITERATUR BIS 1760 / Grudzinski, Herbert – (Includes bibliographical references) – Stuttgart: J B Metzler, 1913 – 1 – us U.W. Library [410]

SHAFTSBURY FIRST (WEST) BAPTIST CHURCH. SHAFTSBURY, VERMONT : CHURCH RECORDS. 1768-1843. EXTRACTS FROM ORIGINAL MANUSCRIPT RECORDS OF FIRST BAPTIST CHURCH. 1768-1779. MINUTES – 1768-1805; 1817-1844 – 1 – $9.00 – us Baptist [240]

Shaginian, M *see* LITERATURNYI DNEVNIK. STAT'I 1921-1923 G

SHAH NAMEH / Firdausi – 1832. Royal Asiatic Society – 1 – uk Microform Academic [950]

Shah, V P *see* THE EDUCATIONAL PROBLEMS OF SCHEDULED CASTE AND SCHEDULED TRIBE SCHOOL AND COLLEGE STUDENTS IN INDIA

Shahan, Thomas Joseph *see* SAINT PATRICK IN HISTORY

Shahani, Dayaran Gidumal *see* THE STATUS OF WOMEN IN INDIA

SHAHAR *see* HA-SHAHAR

SHAHARIT – Odessa. Warsaw. 1913. BJ-291-29 1 – 9 – ne IDC [947]

SHAHID – (Missing issues: 307, 309, 343, 442, 443, 508, 581) – Iran: Shumarah-i 194-585 (21 Shahrivar 1329-5 Bahman 1330 [2 Sep. 1950-26 Jan. 1952]) – 1 reel – 1 – $100.00 – us MEDOC [950]

Shaikevich, N M *see*
- CAIN
- HA-NIDDAHAT

Shairp, John Campbell *see*
- CULTURE AND RELIGION IN SOME OF THEIR RELATIONS
- SKETCHES IN HISTORY AND POETRY
- STUDIES IN POETRY AND PHILOSOPHY

SHAJI TORISHIRABE RUISAN = A COMPILATION OF DOCUMENTS OF THE RELIGIOUS REFORM IN THE MEIJI PERIOD / ed by Fujii, Sadafumi & Tamamuro, Fumio – Shaji Torishirabe Ruisan. National Diet Library. 195 mss. 144p – 68r – 1 – Y600,000.00 – ja Yushodo [280]

SHAKAI-SHISO = SOCIALISTIC IDEOLOGY – Japan, 1922-29 – 8r – 1 – inquire – us Ross [320]

THE SHAKER *see* THE MANIFESTO

SHAKER AND SHAKERESS MONTHLY *see* THE MANIFESTO

THE SHAKER COLLECTION / Rubin, Cynthia & Rubin, Jerome – v1. Contains monographs and The Shaker. 1871-99 – 314mf – 9 – $950.00 – us OmniSys [240]

SHAKER COLLECTION, 1723-1952 / ed by Stefani, Marie T – (From holdings of Western Reserve Historical Society) – 123r + 1187mf – 1 + 9 – $9875.00 – us UMI [240]

SHAKER COLLECTION ON MICROFILM – 9r – 1 – $650.00 – us OmniSys [240]

SHAKER COMMUNITY PAPERS – 1792-1937 – 32r – 1 – $1,120.00 – Dist. us Scholarly Res – us L of C Photodup [290]

SHAKER HEIGHTS NEIGHBORHOOD ASSOCIATION – (Articles of incorporation, constitutions, minutes, correspondence, newsletters, clippings and financial documents of this association, which promoted opening housing policies in this Cleveland suburb) – Shaker Heights, Cuyahoga, OH. 1959-88 – 3r – 1 – us Western Res [360]

THE SHAKER MANIFESTO *see* THE MANIFESTO

SHAKER MUSIC : INSPIRATIONAL HYMNS AND MELODIES ILLUSTRATIVE OF THE RESURRECTION LIFE AND TESTIMONY OF THE SHAKERS / Evans, F W – Albany, N.Y.: Weed, Parsons, 1875 – 2mf – us A.T.L.A. [780]

SHAKERISM IN KENTUCKY, FOUNDED IN AMERICA BY ANN LEE – By Mary Webb Gibson, 1942. Indexed. 3 fiches. F-1302 – 9 – us A.G.L.L. [240]

SHAKERS : COMPENDIUM OF THE ORIGIN, HISTORY, PRINCIPLES, RULES AND REGULATIONS, GOVERNMENT, AND DOCTRINES OF THE UNITED SOCIETY OF BELIEVERS IN CHRIST'S SECOND APPEARING / Evans, F W – New Lebanon, N.Y.: [s.n.], 1867, c1858 – 1mf – us A.T.L.A. [240]

SHAKESPEARE – (Lists 31 productions) – 38mf – 9 – £210.00 – uk Chadwyck [790]

SHAKESPEARE AND CHAUCER EXAMINATIONS / Thom, William Taylor – Examination papers by pupils of Hollins Institute, VA. 2nd enl. ed. 346p. Boston: Ginn & Company, 1889. 1 reel. 1295 – 1 – us U.W. Library [370]

SHAKESPEARE AND HIS PREDECESSORS / Boas, Franz – London, 1910 – 19mf – ne IDC [420]

SHAKESPEARE AND THE STAGE : BASIC DOCUMENTARY SOURCES CONCERNING TEXT AND PERFORMANCE, SERIES 2 – Prompt Books from the Harvard Theater Collection – 1 – us Primary [790]

SHAKESPEARE AND THE STAGE: BASIC DOCUMENTARY SOURCES CONCERNING TEXT AND PERFORMANCE, SERIES 1 – (Pt 1: All's Well that Ends Well; Julius Caesar. Pt 2: King Henry IV Pt 1; Macbeth. Pt 3: Measure for Measure; Pericles. Pt 4: Romeo and Juliet; The Winter's Tale; Misc. Vols) – Prompt books from the Folger Shakespeare Library, Washington, DC – 1 – us Primary [790]

SHAKESPEARE AND THE STAGE: BASIC DOCUMENTARY SOURCES CONCERNING TEXT AND PERFORMANCE, SERIES 3 – (Pt 1: Birmingham Theatre Royal; Frank Benson and other prompt books; and the Gordon Crosse Theatrical Diary, 1890-1953) – Prompt Books and Related Material from the Shakespeare Library, Birmingham Public Library – 1 – us Primary [790]

SHAKESPEARE AND THE STAGE: BASIC DOCUMENTARY SOURCES CONCERNING TEXT AND PERFORMANCE, SERIES 4 – (Pt 1: All's Well that Ends Well-Henry IV Pt 2. Pt 2: Henry V-Measure for Measure. Pt 3: The Merchant of Venice-Richard III. Pt 4: Romeo and Juliet-The Winter's Tale) – Prompt Books from the Shakespeare Centre Library, Stratford-upon-Avon – 1 – us Primary [790]

SHAKESPEARE AND TYPOGRAPHY; BEING AN ATTEMPT TO SHOW SHAKESPEARE'S PERSONAL CONNECTION WITH, AND TECHNICAL KNOWLEDGE OF, THE ART OF PRINTING.. / Blades, William – London: Truebner & Co., 1872. viii,78p.A mock argument – 1 – us U.W. Library [420]

SHAKESPEARE AT STRATFORD-UPON-AVON / Libraries of the Royal Shakespeare Theatre and the Shakespeare Birthplace Trust – (Pt 1: Costume and set design 1919-74 $512. Pt 2: Theatre records (press cuttings) 1879-1974 $5,700. Pt 3: Posters, programmes, playbills, photographs and pictures $1,748. Pt 4: Pamphlet collection $2,850. Production record 1947-74 $1,140. Pt 5: Printed books to 1700 $5,700. Pt 6: Shakespeare Centre Library Catalogue $ 1,140. Printed catalog and indexes included) – 27 color, 5017 b/w mf – 9,15 – $15,032.00 set – 1-869934-20-2 – uk Emmett [790]

SHAKESPEARE AT STRATFORD-UPON-AVON / Libraries of the Royal Shakespeare Theatre and the Shakespeare Birthplace Trust – (Sections available separately; Costume and Set Design., 1989.-19mf.$595.00.- ISBN 0-8161-1763-2; Theatre Records., 1989.-1079mf.$6,565.00.-ISBN 0-8161-1763-2; Posters, Programs, Playbills, Photographs and Pictures., 1990.-470mf.$2,025.00.-ISBN 0-8161-1766-7; Pamphlet Collection., 1990.-160mf.$3,285.00.-ISBN 0-8161-1767-5; Production Records., 1946-1960.-1990.-311mf.$1,325.00.-ISBN 0-8161-1769-1; Printed Books to 1700., 1990.-2,847mf.$6,565.00.-ISBN 0-8161-1765-9; Shakespeare Centre Library, Catalogue., 1989.-110mf.$1,325.00.-ISBN 0-8161-1769-1) – 32 color and 4964 black and white microfiche – 9,15 – $17,500.00 set – 0-8161-1759-4 – uk Hall [790]

SHAKESPEARE CENTRE LIBRARY, CATALOGUE *see* SHAKESPEARE AT STRATFORD-UPON-AVON

SHAKESPEARE CRITICISM: AN ESSAY IN SYNTHESIS / Menon, C Narayana – (London, New York, etc.). H. Milford, Oxford University Press, 1938. vi,276p. 1 reel. 1186 – 1 – us U.W. Library [420]

SHAKESPEARE: HIS TRAGIC WORLD : PSYCHOLOGICAL EXPLANATIONS / Dias, Walter Patrick – New Delhi: S. Chand (1973). xxii,532p – 1 – us U.W. Library [420]

SHAKESPEARE IN CONTEXT / ed by Schoenbaum, S – 1 – £395.00 – uk World [420]

SHAKESPEARE IN DEUTSCHEN UEBERSETZUNGEN / Heun, Hans Georg – (Accompanied by supplement) – Berlin: Akademie-Verlag, 1957 – 1r – 1 – us U.W. Library [420]

SHAKESPEARE IN FRANCE UNDER THE ANCIEN REGIME / Jusserand, Jean Adrien Antoine Jules – London: T.F. Unwin, 1899. xxviii,496p. illus., ports – 1 – us U.W. Library [420]

SHAKESPEARE IN ITALIA / Nulli, Siro Attilio – Milano: Hoepli, 1918. 245p. 1 reel. 1296 – 1 – us U.W. Library [420]

SHAKESPEARE QUARTERLY – v1- 1950- 1; v29- 5,6 – us UMI [410]

Shakespeare, William *see*
- AMLETO-HAMLET
- MALCOLM LOWRY'S SHAKESPEARE
- SOGNO D'UNA NOTTE D'ESTATE-A MIDSUMMER NIGHT'S DREAM

SHAKESPEAREAN – v1-4. 1895-98 – 1r – 1 – us Ross [073]

THE SHAKESPEAREAN – London. v. 1-4; no. 1-33. 1895-1898 – 1 – us NY Public [420]

SHAKESPEARE-CHARACTERS : CHIEFLY THOSE SUBORDINATE / Clarke, Charles Cowden – London: Smith, Elder; Edinburgh: James Nichol, 1863 – 1 roll – 1 – 1-55879-896-X – uk Libr Preservation [420]

EINE SHAKESPEAREFEIER AN DER ILM / Gutzkow, Karl – Leipzig: F A Brockhaus, 1864 – 1r – 1 – us U.W. Library [410]

SHAKESPEARE'S INFLUENCE UPON GRABBE / Hoch, Horace Lind – Philadelphia: s.n., 1910 – 1r – 1 – us U.W. Library [410]

SHAKESPEARES NATURSCHILDERUNGEN / Voigt, Edmund – Heidelberg, 1909 – 2mf – DM62.00 – 3-8267-3022-4 – gw Hänsel [420]

SHAKESPEARES UND TIECKS MAERCHENDRAMEN / Pfeiffer, Emilie – (Inclues bibliographical references) – Bonn a. Rh.: L Roehrscheid, 1933 – 1r – 1 – us U.W. Library [410]

SHAKESPEARIANA / ed by Brockbank, J P & Brock, Susan – (Ca 3000 titles, 1 million pages. 30 subject units covering: Shakespeare's life and society; Shakespeare's texts; his reading; his predecessors and contemporaries; visual arts in Shakespeare's England; Shakespeare in performance; Shakespearian criticism and scholarship; historical context. Adaptations and Acting Versions, 1660-1980 $1210; Folklore, Superstition, and Witchcraft $950; Prose Fiction in Shakespeare's Time $1575; Shakespeare's Editors Since Rowe $2500) – 9 – $35,000.00 complete collection (pre-publication) – us UMI [820]

Shakhmatov, A A *see* SOBRANIE GOSUDARSTVENNYKH GRAMOTI DOGOVOROV

Shakhovskaia, L *see* SLOVAR' RIFM RUSSKOGO IAZYKA

Shakspeare, Charles *see* ST. PAUL AT ATHENS: SPIRITUAL CHRISTIANITY IN RELATION TO...MODERN THOUGHT

SHAKSPEARE PAPERS / Maginn, William – London: R. Bentley, 1860 – 1 roll – 1 – 1-55879-425-5 – uk Libr Preservation [420]

SHAKSPER NOT SHAKESPEARE / Edwards, William Henry – Cincinnati: The Robert Clarke Company, 1900. xi,507p. Illus. 1 reel. 1295 – 1 – us U.W. Library [420]

Shalaby, Ahmad *see* HISTORY OF MUSLIM EDUCATION

SHALL OUR COMMON SCHOOLS BE DESTROYED? : AN ARGUMENT AGAINST PERVERTING THE SCHOOL-FUND TO SECTARIAN USES / Thompson, Joseph Parrish – New York. Edward O Jenkins, 1870 – 1mf – 9 – 0-8370-7592-0 – 1986-1592 – us A.T.L.A. [370]

SHALL ROME RECONQUER ENGLAND? / Horton, Robert Forman & Hocking, Joseph – (Includes bibliographical references) – London: National Council of Evangelical Free Churches, 1910 – 1mf – 9 – 0-8370-8437-7 – 1986-2437 – us A.T.L.A. [240]

SHALL THE NEGRO BE ENCOURAGED TO SEEK CULTURAL EQUALITY? / Du Bois, W E B – Chicago, 1929 – 1r – 1 – us Ross [305]

SHALL WE BELIEVE IN A DIVINE PROVIDENCE? / Faunce, Daniel Worcester – (Includes bibliographical references) – New York: Funk & Wagnalls, 1900 – 1mf – 9 – 0-8370-3746-8 – 1985-1746 – us A.T.L.A. [210]

SHALL WE CONTINUE IN SIN? : A VITAL QUESTION FOR BELIEVERS ANSWERED IN THE WORD OF GOD: THE SUBSTANCE OF ADDRESSES DELIVERED IN GREAT BRITAIN AND IRELAND IN 1896 / Pierson, Arthur Tappan – NY: Baker & Taylor, c1897 – 1mf – 9 – 0-8370-5468-0 – 1985-3468 – us A.T.L.A. [210]

SHALL WOMAN PREACH? / Harvey, William Patrick – 1905 – 9 – us A.T.L.A. [240]

SHALL WOMAN PREACH? / Harvey, William Patrick – 1906. 40p – 1 – $5.00 – us Baptist [240]

SHALL WOMAN PREACH? / Woosley, Louisa M – 1891 – 1 – $50.00 – us Presbyterian [240]

SHALL WOMAN PREACH? OR, THE QUESTION ANSWERED / Woosley, Louisa M – 1891 – 9 – us A.T.L.A. [240]

SHALL WOMEN VOTE IN THE CHURCH? / Mayser, Frederick Peter – (The Lutheran Church Review, v. 18, July 1899, p. 479-486) – 9 – us A.T.L.A. [240]

SHALLEKHET / ed by Shofman, G – Lemberg. 1911. BJ-422-77 1 – 9 – ne IDC [470]

Shallenberger, E H *see* STARK COUNTY AND ITS PIONEERS

SHALOM – Istanbul, Turkey. 1990-Dec 9 1992 – 1r – 1 – us L of C Photodup [072]

Shalov, I S *see*
- MATERIALY DLIA VEDENIA PRAKTICHESKIKH ZANIATII NA KURSAKH PO SCHETOVODSTVU POTREBITEL'NYKH OBSHCHESTV
- OBSHCHII KURS SCHETOVODSTVA POTREBITEL'SKIKH OBSHCHESTV

SHAMA'A : A MAGAZINE OF ART, LITERATURE AND PHILOSOPHY – Madras. v 1-8 1920-31. Lacking: v3. BI-142 2 – 46mf – 8 – ne IDC [100]

Shamasira'j'afif *see* TARIKH-I-FIROZ SHAHI

Shambaugh, Benjamin Franklin *see* HISTORY OF THE CONSTITUTIONS OF IOWA

Shambaugh, Bertha, MH *see* AMANA, THE COMMUNITY OF TRUE INSPIRATION

Shamel, Charles Harmonas *see* MINING, MINERAL AND GEOLOGICAL LAW

Shami, S et al *see* WOMEN IN ARAB SOCIETY

SHAMOKIN CANALBOAT – Shamokin, PA. -w 1827-33. 1 roll – 13 – $25.00r – us I.M.R. [071]

SHAMOKIN DAILY NEWS – Shamokin, PA. -d 1931-1933 – 13 – $25.00r – us I.M.R. [071]

THE SHAMOKIN DISPATCH – Shamokin, PA., 1923-1933 – 13 – $25.00r – us I.M.R. [071]

SHAMOKIN HERALD – Shamokin, PA. -w 1862-93. 9 rolls – 13 – $25.00r – us I.M.R. [071]

SHAMOKIN NEWS DISPATCH – Shamokin, PA. -d 1934-1968 – 13 – $25.00r – us I.M.R. [071]

SHAMOKIN NEWS ITEM – Shamokin, PA. -d 1971-1975 – 13 – $25.00r – us I.M.R. [071]

SHAMOKIN REGISTER – Shamokin, PA. -w 1860-62. 1 roll – 13 – $25.00r – us I.M.R. [071]

THE SHAMOKIN TIMES WEEKLY – Shamokin, PA. -w 1878-87. 3 rolls – 13 – $25.00r – us I.M.R. [071]

THE SHAMROCK – New York, NY. 1810-17. Also: Observer, 1809-11; New York Weekly Observer, 1811. Sold as one unit – 1,3 – us Readex [073]

Shamurin, E I *see* RUSSKAIA POEZIIA 20 VEKA

SHAN VAN VOCHT – Dublin, Ireland.15 Jan 1896-6 Mar 1899 – 1 – ie Microforms [072]

Shanafelt, T M *see* THE BAPTIST HISTORY OF SOUTH DAKOTA

SHANDON BELLS: A NOVEL / Black, William – British Fiction Archive: Unit 4 – 9 – uk Bell [830]

SHANDONG DAXUE XUEBAO (ZIRAN KEXUE BAN) – Journal of Shandong University, Natural Science Edition.1982-83, 1985. F/P 293 – 9 – $4.50f – cc Microforms [073]

SHANDONG HAIYANG XUEYUAN XUEBAO – Bulletin of the Shandong College of Oceanography. 1983.F/P 201 – 9 – $4.50f – cc Microforms [073]

SHANDONG HAIYANG XUEYUAN XUEBAO – Bulletin of the Shandong College of Oceanography. In Chinese but English abstracts to the main articles. F p201 – 9 – $4.50f – cc Microforms [073]

Shandong Province. China *see*
- JIAJING LAIWU XIAN ZHI, 1548
- JIAJING LINQU XIAN ZHI, 1552
- JIAJING QINGZHOU FU ZHI, 1565
- JIAJING WUCHENG XIAN ZHI, 1525
- JIAJING WUDING ZHOU ZHI, 1548
- JIAJING XIAJIN XIAN ZHI, 1540
- JIAJING ZICHUAN XIAN ZHI, 1546
- ZHENGDE XIN XIAN ZHI, 1515

SHANDONG YIXUEYUAN XUEBAO – Acta Academiae Medicinae Shandong. In Chinese but English abstracts to the main articles. F p164 – 9 – 4.00f – cc Microforms [073]

SHANDONG ZHONGYI XUEYUAN XUEBAO – Journal of Shandong College of Traditional Chinese Medicine. In Chinese but Table of Contents in Chinese in each issue. F p170 – 9 – 4.00f – cc Microforms [616]

Shane, Martha P *see* THE PAPERS OF EMILY GREENE BALCH, 1875-1961

SHANG BAO – China. 1929 – 9 – 700.00 – cc Globe [072]

SHANGHAI BEIKE ZILIAO XUANJI – Selection of historical materials inscribed on tablets in Shanghai. Comp. by the Shanghai Museum. 6 fiches. F-H196 – 9 – $45.50f – cc Microforms [950]

Shanghai. Bureau of Social Affairs *see* WAGE RATES IN SHANGHAI

SHANG-HAI CHIH-NAN – (Guide to Shanghai A Chinese directory of the port. ed. 2. Shanghai. 1920. BCH-984 2 – 8 – ne IDC [950]

SHANGHAI DIYI YIXUEYUAN XUEBAO – Acta Academiae Medicinae Primae Shanghai. In Chinese but English abstracts to the main articles. F p163 – 9 – 4.00f – cc Microforms [073]

SHANGHAI EVENING COURIER – Shanghai. China. -d. 3 Jan-31 Dec 1874. (2 reels) – 1 – uk British Libr Newspaper [072]

SHANGHAI FOR YOUR INFORMATION: YENON BROADCAST / U.S. Information Service – 1946-47 – 1 – 23.00r – us L of C Photodup [000]

SHANGHAI GAZETTE – Shanghai, 1919-21 – 2r – 1 – us Ross [072]

THE SHANGHAI GAZETTE – Shanghai, China. Nov 1 1919-Mar 24 1921. Incomplete – 1 – us NY Public [072]

SHANGHAI GONGYUN BAO *see* LAODONG BAO

Shanghai. Historical Bureau *see* SHANG-HAI T'UNG-CHIK-KUAN CH'I-K'AN

SHANGHAI HUOYOU – Shanghai Companion. Oct 1920-Jan 1921. F C19. In Chinese – 9 – $10.00 – cc Microforms [073]

SHANGHAI. ITS MIXED COURT AND COUNCIL : CHINESE MODERN LAW AND SHANGHAI MUNICIPAL LAND REGULATIONS... / Kotenev, A L – Shanghai, 1925 – 11mf – 9 – CH-987/2 – ne IDC [340]

SHANGHAI. ITS MUNICIPALITY AND THE CHINESE / Kotenev, A L – Shanghai. 1927. BCH-988 2 – 8 – ne IDC [950]

Shanghai Japanese Trade Association *see* SHANHAI NIHON SHOGYO KAIGISHO NEMPO

SHANGHAI JIATONG DAXUE XUEBAO – Journal of Shanghai Jiatong University. In Chinese but English abstracts to the main articles. F p173 – 9 – 4.00f – cc Microforms [073]

Shanghai. Kuang-ts'ang Society *see* KUANG-TS'ANG HSUEH-HUI YEN-SHUO PAO

Shanghai. Municipal Government of Shanghai *see* SHE-HUI PAN-YUEH-K'AN
SHANGHAI MUNICIPAL POLICE FILES, 1929-1944 – (With printed guide) – 1990 – 67r – 1 – $5,695.00 – S3193 – us Scholarly Res [950]
THE SHANGHAI NEWSLETTER – v28-31. 1947-49 (incomplete) – 1r – 1 – ATLA S0703H – us A.T.L.A. [073]
SHANGHAI QIANZHUANG SHILIAO – Historical materials on the old-type private banks in Shanghai. Comp. by the Shanghai branch of the Chinese People's Bank. 1 reel. M-H176 – 5 – $40.00 – cc Microforms [950]
SHANGHAI SHIFAN XUEYUAN XUEBAO – (Shehui Kexue Ban). Journal of Shanghai Teacher's College, Social Science. In Chinese but Table of Contents in English in each issue. F p223 – 9 – $4.50f – cc Microforms [073]
SHANGHAI TIMES – Shanghai, 1914-21 – 20r – 1 – us Ross [072]
SHANGHAI TIMES – Shanghai, China. Feb 11 1914-Mar 31 1921. Incomplete – 1 – us NY Public [072]
SHANG-HAI T'UNG CHIH-KUAN – 4v. 1936-37 – 8 – BCH-983 2 – ne IDC [920]
SHANG-HAI T'UNG-CHIK-KUAN CH'I-K'AN / Shanghai. Historical Bureau – 2v. Shanghai. 1933-35. (Reprint: Lung-men). BCH-328 1 – 9 – ne IDC [073]
SHANG-HAI WAN PAO – Shanghai, China. Aug 23 1966-Feb 6 1967 – 1r – 1 – us L of C Photodup [072]
SHANGHAI XIAODAO HUI QIYI SHILIAO HUIBIAN – A collection of source materials on the Shanghai Little Sword Society. Comp. by the Shanghai Institute of History. 11 fiches. F-H81 – 9 – $67.50 – cc Microforms [950]
SHANGHAI ZARIA *see* SHANKHAISKAIA ZARIA
SHANGHAI ZHONGYI-YAO ZAZHI – Shanghai Journal of Traditional Chinese Medicine. In Chinese but English abstracts to the main articles. F p55 – 9 – 4.00f – cc Microforms [616]
SHANG-SSU CHOU-CHIH – 1684. 4. BCH-656 2 – 8 – ne IDC [950]
SHANHAI KAIKAN JUNENHO = CHINA IMPERIAL MARITIME CUSTOMS, DECENIAL REPORTS – 1st report to 5th report (1882-1931) all published – 9r – 1 – Y83,000 – ja Yushodo [380]
SHANHAI NIHON SHOGYO KAIGISHO NEMPO / Shanghai Japanese Trade Association – Shanghai, 1918-29. n.1-12. In Japanese. Yearbook; 1930-43. n.13-26. Lacking: n.20,22,23. 5 reels – 1 – 95.70 – us Chinese Res [380]
SHAN-HSI HSIANG-SHIH LU – List of successful candidates in the imperial examination in Shansi province: 1726, 1798, 1873, 1900, 1901, 1903. 1 reel – 1 – 15.00 – us Chinese Res [950]
SHAN-HSI JIH-PAO = SHANSI DAILY – Taiyuan, Shansi, China. Apr-Jun 1950; Aug 1950-1960; Jun-Jul 1961; Jan-Jun 1962 – 16r – 1 – $445.00 – us Chinese Res [072]
SHANIKO LEADER – Shaniko OR. Aug 28 1902 – 1 – us U.O. Library [071]
SHANIM KADMONIYYOT / Goldmann, I – Warsaw. 1879. BJ-422-19 1 – 9 – ne IDC [470]
SHANKHAISKAIA ZARIA – (Library has holdings (incomplete) for: May 13-15, 1929; Apr. 1, 1932-Jan. 7, 1933) – Shankhai: "Shanghaiskaia zaria, 1925- – 1 – CSUX87-S272 – us Hoover Inst Photo [072]
Shanks, T J *see* A COLLEGE OF COLLEGES
Shanly, Walter *see* REPORT...ON THE OTTAWA SURVEY
Shannon Patrick *see* REVIEW OF EDUCATION/PEDAGOGY/CULTURAL STUDIES
SHANNON'S UNREPORTED CASES / Tennessee. Supreme Court – (A Pre-NRS title) – v1-3. 1847-1870 (all publ) – 26mf – 9 – $39.00 – LLMC 91-042 – us L.L.M.C. [340]
SHANSI DAILY *see* SHAN-HSI JIH-PAO
Shanta *see* HANDBOOK OF HINDU NAMES
SHANTOU RIBAO = SHANTOU DAILY – China. 1983-. M-D55 – 1 reel/y – 1 – $55.00r – cc Microforms [072]
SHAN-TUNG HSIANG-SHIH LU – List of successful candidates in the imperial examination in Shantung province. Scattered years 1672-1903. 1 reel – 1 – 28.00 – us Chinese Res [950]
Shantung. Provincial Library *see* SHAN-TUNG SHENG-LI T'U-SHU-KUAN CHI-K'AN
SHAN-TUNG SHENG-LI T'U-SHU-KUAN CHI-K'AN / Shantung. Provincial Library – Quarterly journal. v. 1 (1-2). Tsinan. 1931-36. Available: v. 1 (1). BCH-327 2 – 8 – ne IDC [073]
SHANXI RIBAO = SHANXI DAILY – China. 1982-. M-D28 – 1 reel/y – 1 – $55.00r – cc Microforms [072]
SHANXI RIBAO – Shanxi Daily. 1981- . M/D 23 – 1 – $55.00r – cc Microforms [072]
Shanxi, Shaanxi and Ganso Provinces. China *see*
– JIAJING LUEYANG XIAN ZHI, 1552
– JIAJING NINGXIA XINZHI, 1540
– JIAJING TAIYUAN XIAN ZHI, 1551
SHANZDAH-I AZAR – (Sal-i 1, shumarah-'i 1-12, 13, 15-18; sal-i 3: shumarah-'i 3, 5-6 (29 Aban 1340-Tir/Shahrivar 1345[7 Dec 1961-Jun/Aug 1966])) – [S.l.]: Kunfidirasyun-i Jahani-i Muhassilin va Danishjuyan-i Irani – 1 reel – 1 – $25.00 – us MEDOC [950]
SHAO NIAN ZHONG GUO – Jul 1919-May 1924. 60 ill. DL70f – 9 – 280.00 – cc Globe [073]
SHAOAR HA-SHIR : THE NEW-HEBREW SCHOOL OF POETS OF THE SPANISH-ARABIAN EPOCH / ed by Brody, Heinrich & Albrecht, Karl – (Text in Hebrew; notes in English. Includes a dictionary and an alphabetic list of the poems) – London: Williams and Norgate; New York: Lemcke & Beuchner, 1906 – 1mf – 9 – 0-8370-5892-9 – 1985-3892 – us A.T.L.A. [470]
SHAONIAN – Les Jeunes. 1922. 1 reel. M/C 87 – 1 – $45.00 – cc Microforms [073]
SHAONIAN SHIJIE – Young World. 1920. M C13. In Chinese – 1 – $45.00 – cc Microforms [073]
SHAONIAN ZHONGGUO – Journal of the Young China Association. 1919-1924. M C14. In Chinese – 1 – $180.00 – cc Microforms [073]
SHAO-NIEN CHUNG-KUO – (Young China). v. 1-2. 1920-21. Available: v. 1 (9), 1920; v. 2 (8), 1921. BCH-960 2 – 8 – ne IDC [073]
Shapard, J E *see* INFLUENCE OF RULES FOR RECOVERY OF ATTORNEYS' FEES ON SETTLEMENT OF CIVIL CASES
Shapard, John *see*
– ATTORNEYS' VIEWS OF LOCAL RULES LIMITING INTERROGATORIES
– THE VOIR DIRE EXAMINATION, JUROR CHALLENGES, AND ADVERSARY ADVOCACY
Shapard, John E *see*
– EVALUATION OF COURT-ANNEXED ARBITRATION IN THREE FEDERAL DISTRICT COURTS
"SHAPING AND RESHAPING" INDONESIA; MANGGALANG MASSAAKSI REVOLUSIONER MENUDJU MASJARAKAT ADIL DAN MAKMUR / Sukarno – SE 2208 1. 1957 – 9 – ne IDC [335]
Shapira, K A *see* SHIRIM NIVHARIM
Shapiro, Harry L *see* RACE MIXTURE
Shapiro, I A *see* RUKOVODSTVO PO VSEM OTRASLIAM KOOPERATSII
Shapleigh, Maine. Second Free Will Baptist Church *see* RECORDS
Shapleigh, Maine. Shapleigh Baptist Church *see* RECORDS
Shapley, Rufus E *see* THE LIBRARY OF WIT AND HUMOR, PROSE AND POETRY
SHARAF-AL-ZAMAN TAHIR MARVAZI ON CHINA, THE TURKS AND INDIA / Minorsky, V – 1942 – 1 – uk Microform Academic [910]
Sharar, Brian D *see* AN ANALYSIS OF SWIMMING ECONOMY AS ASSESSED BY A COMPARISON BETWEEN VO2 VALUES AND ARM STROKE INDEX
SHARE – (Scattered issues lacking) – Toronto, v1-12, no 36, Apr 8, 1978-Dec 27, 1989 – 14r – 1 – Can$1,285.50 – cn McLaren [305]
SHARECROPPER'S VOICE, 1935-1937 : SOUTHERN FARM LEADER, 1936 : STFU NEWS, 1938-1939 : TENANT FARMER, 1941-1942 : FARM WORKER, 1943-1944 : FARM LABOR NEWS, 1946-1951 : THE UNION FARMER, 1952-1953 : AGRICULTURAL UNIONIST, 1952-1954 / Southern Tenant Farmers Union – (Coll title: Labor Union Periodicals, Pt 3) – 1996 – 1r – 1 – $135.00 – 1-55655-612-8 – us UPA [331]
THE SHAREHOLDER – Montreal, Canada. v1 n23. 3 oct 1879-v32 n9. 1 mar 1912 – 1r – 1 – Can$35.00 – cn Can Microfilming [072]
Sharevskaia, B I *see* STARYE I NOVYE RELIGII TROPICHESKOI I IUZHNOI AFRIKI
SHARING THE PRACTICE – (1985-. 5,6,9) – v1-. 1978- – 1 – us UMI [073]
SHARING THE PRACTICE – (Lacks some pgs. Cont: Academy of Parish Clergy) – 1978-92 – Inquire – 1 – ATLA S0465 – us A.T.L.A. [240]
SHARING THE PRACTICE *see* ACADEMY OF PARISH CHURCH
SHARK UTILIZATION AND MARKETING – 1982 – 187p – it F.A.O. [636]
Sharma, R *see* A BIBLIOGRAPHY OF MUGHAL INDIA, 1526-1707
Sharman, Henry Burton *see* THE TEACHING OF JESUS ABOUT THE FUTURE: ACCORDING TO THE SYNOPTIC GOSPELS
SHARMANKA PIESY, STIKHI, PROZA / Guro, E – Spb. 1909. BR-932 2 – 8 – ne IDC [460]
SHARON 1727-1900 – (Mf 1: Births 1745-1843. Mf 2-3: Marriages 1765-1844. Mf 3: Deaths 1746-1844. Mf 4: Births & Deaths 1727-1843. Mf 5: Births 1759-1815; Marriages 1765-1844. Mf 6: Deaths 1746-1844. Mf 7-9: Precinct Records 1740-1821. Mf 10-25: Town Records 1753-1836. Mf 26-30: Town Accounts 1810-26. Mf 31: Index Intentions 1816-1900. Mf 32-38: Intentions 1816-1907. Mf 39-40: Index Births 1844-1900. Mf 41: Index Marriages 1844-1900. Mf 42: Index Deaths 1844-1900. Mf 43-44: Vital Records 1843-57. Mf 45-47: Births 1858-1900. Mf 47-48: Marriages 1857-1900. Mf 48-51: Deaths 1857-1900. Mf 52-54: Deaths 1844-1901. Mf 55-56: Marriages 1843-1901. Mf 57-59: Births 1844-1900) – (mf ed 1992) – 59mf – 9 – 0-87623-124-5 – us Holbrook [920]
SHARON BAPTIST CHURCH. GALLATIN COUNTY. KENTUCKY : CHURCH RECORDS – 1825-56. Dissolved about 1856. 208p – 1 – 9.36 – us Baptist [240]
SHARON BAPTIST CHURCH. KNOXVILLE, TENNESSEE : CHURCH RECORDS – Apr 1871-Jan 1987. Lacking Aug 1914-Sept 1924. 2260p – 1 – 101.70 – us Baptist [978]
SHARON, CONNECTICUT BIRTHS, MARRIAGES AND DEATHS FROM 1721-1870 / Litchfield County. Connecticut – By Lawrence VanAlstyne, 1897. Item C. Listed alphabetically. 143p. SW16-0154 – 5 – us A.G.L.L. [920]
THE SHARON EAGLE – Sharon Hill, PA. -w 1889-1910 – 13 – $25.00r – us I.M.R. [071]
Sharp, Bartholomew *see* DIARY OF A BUCCANEER
Sharp, Cecil James *see* FOLK SONGS FROM SOMERSET
Sharp, James A *see* MEMOIRS OF THE LIFE AND SERVICES OF REAR-ADMIRAL SIR WILLIAM SYMONDS, SURVEYER OF THE NAVY, FROM 1832 TO 1847
SHARP PARK BREAKERS – Pacifica, CA. 1938-57 – 6r – 1 – $300.00 – B02584 – us Library Micro [071]
Sharp, T *see* REMARKS ON A BOOK INTITLED 'AN EARNEST APPEAL TO MEN OF REASON AND RELIGION', IN A LETTER TO THE REV. MR. JOHN WESLEY
Sharp, William *see*
– FROM THE HILLS OF DREAM
– LIFE OF ROBERT BROWNING
Sharpe, Alfred B *see* THE PRINCIPLES OF CHRISTIANITY
Sharpe, D *see* DESCRIPTION OF THE FOSSIL REMAINS OF MOLLUSCA FOUND IN THE CHALK OF ENGLAND, (CEPHALOPODA)
Sharpe, E M B *see* A MONOGRAPH OF THE GENUS TERACOLUS
Sharpe, John *see* TRUE POLITICAL ECONOMY
Sharpe, R B *see*
– CATALOGUE OF THE BIRDS IN THE BRITISH MUSEUM
– A HANDBOOK TO THE BIRDS OF GREAT BRITAIN
Sharpe, R R *see* CALENDAR OF CORONERS ROLLS OF THE CITY OF LONDON, 1300-1378
Sharpe, S *see* EGYPTIAN INSCRIPTIONS FROM THE BRITISH MUSEUM AND OTHER SOURCES
Sharpe, Samuel *see*
– THE CHRONOLOGY OF THE BIBLE
– HEBREW INSCRIPTIONS, FROM THE VALLEYS BETWEEN EGYPT AND MOUNT SINAI
SHARPEVILLE ENQUIRY – ((Case history)) – 6r – 1 – sa Microfile [960]
Sharpless, Isaac *see* THE AMERICAN COLLEGE
Sharrock, J A *see* SOUTH INDIAN MISSIONS
Sharswood, George *see*
– LEADING CASES IN THE AMERICAN LAW OF REAL PROPERTY
– A TABLE OF CASES IN THE REPORTS OF THE STATE OF CONNECTICUT 1785-1876, WHICH HAVE BEEN CITED, EXPLAINED, LIMITED, DOUBTED, OR OVERRULED IN SUBSEQUENT DECISIONS
SHASTA COLLEGE LANCE – Redding, CA. 1965-91 – 8r – 1 – $300.00 – B02675 – us Library Micro [370]
SHASTA COUNTY, 1881 – 1r – 1 – $50.00 – D097 – us Library Micro [978]
SHASTA COURIER – Redding. Calif. -w. 1909-36, 1944-52 – 1 – us UMI [071]
SHASTA DIAL – Redding, CA. 1936-42 – 5r – 1 – $250.00 – B02676 – us Library Micro [071]
SHASTA/SISKIYOU/TRINITY – 1909-33; 1992- – 27+ r – 1 – $1,350.00 – P00123 – us Library Micro [910]
SHASTA/TEHAMA/TRINITY – 1909-19 – 10r – 1 – $500.00 – P00146 – us Library Micro [910]
SHATER / Gumilev, Nikolai Sepanovich – Stikhi 1918 g. Reval. 1921. BR-1153 – 8 – ne IDC [460]
Shatsillos, S A *see* AVTORSKOE PRAVO NA LITERATURNYE PROIZVEDENIIA: SBORNIK OFITSIAL'NYKH MATERIALOV
Shattuck, Abel *see* A. SHATTUCKS BOOK
Shattuck, Harriette R *see* THE WOMAN'S MANUAL OF PARLIAMENTARY LAW
Shaver, B M *see* KRIMINALISTIKA
THE SHAVER SHAVED : A MACARONIC DIALOGUE BETWEEN B. AND S. – London, 1769 – 1mf – 9 – MP-457/1 – ne IDC [240]
THE SHAVING OF SHAGPA : AN ARABIAN ENTERTAINMENT / Meredith, George – London: Chapman and Hall, 1856 – 1 roll – 1 – 1-55879-506-5 – uk Libr Preservation [830]
Shavrov, I E *see* UKAZATEL' STATEI PO PTSELOVODSTVU S 1741 PO 1890 GOD
Shavrov, M *see* O TRET'EI KNIGE EZDRY. OPYT IZSLEDOVANIIA O KNIGAKH APOKRIFICHESKIKH
SHAVU ON – (Many missing) – (Cambridge, Mass.) Feb. 18, 1964-Febr. 1975 – us A.J.P.C. [270]
Shaw, Albert *see* ICARIA
Shaw, Anna Howard *see* WOMEN IN THE MINISTRY
Shaw, Bernard *see*
– SAINT JOAN: A CHRONICLE PLAY IN SIX SCENES AND AN EPILOGUE
– WIDOWERS' HOUSES
Shaw, Charles Gray *see*
– CHRISTIANITY AND MODERN CULTURE: AN ESSAY IN PHILOSOPHY OF RELIGION
– THE PRECINCT OF RELIGION IN THE CULTURE OF HUMANITY
Shaw, D J *see* THE MANAGIL SOUTH-WESTERN EXTENSION; AN EXTENSION TO THE GESIRA SCHEME; AN EXAMPLE OF AN IRRIGATION DEVELOPMENT PROJECT IN THE REPUBLIC OF THE SUDAN
Shaw, Daniel W *see* SHOULD THE NEGROES OF THE METHODIST EPISCOPAL CHURCH BE SET APART IN A CHURCH BY THEMSELVES?
Shaw, Elizabeth A *see* CHARLES WRIGHT ON THE BOUNDARY, 1849-1852
Shaw, G *see*
– THE NATURALIST'S MISCELLANY, OR COLORED FIGURES OF NATURAL OBJECTS, DRAWN AND DESCRIBED FROM NATURE
– ZOOLOGY OF NEW HOLLAND
Shaw, George A *see* MADAGASCAR OF TO-DAY
Shaw, J *see* BASHAQRA AREA SETTLEMENTS 1963; A CASE STUDY IN VILLAGE DEVELOPMENT IN THE GEZIRA SCHEME
Shaw, Janet M *see* THE EFFECTS OF RESISTANCE TRAINING ON FRACTURE RISK AND PSYCHOLOGICAL VARIABLES IN POSTMENOPAUSAL WOMEN
Shaw, Knowles *see* THE GOLDEN GATE; SPARKLING JEWELS; GOSPEL TRUMPET; SHINING PEARLS
Shaw, Lemuel *see* LEMUEL SHAW PAPERS, 1648-1923
Shaw, R *see* THE GENTLEMENS AMUSEMENT
Shaw, Robert *see* AN EXPOSITION OF THE CONFESSION OF FAITH OF THE WESTMINSTER ASSEMBLY OF DIVINES
Shaw, Samuel *see*
– GRAMMATICA ANGLO-ROMANA: OR,A SYNCRITICAL GRAMMAR, TEACHING ENGLISH YOUTH THE LATIN TONGUE
– WORDS MADE VISIBLE

Shaw, T M *see* THE FOREIGN POLICY OF TANZANIA, 1961-68

Shaw, William *see*
- AN ANALYSIS OF THE GALIC LANGUAGE
- MEMOIR OF THE REV. WILLIAM SHAW, LATE GENERAL SUPERINTENDENT OF THE WESLEYAN MISSIONS IN SOUTH-EASTERN AFRICA

Shaw, William Arthur *see* A HISTORY OF THE ENGLISH CHURCH DURING THE CIVIL WARS AND UNDER THE COMMONWEALTH, 1640-1660

Shaw, William H *see* HISTORY OF ESSEX AND HUDSON COUNTIES

SHAWINIGAN FALLS AND ITS INDUSTRIES / Shawinigan Water and Power Company – s.l: The Company, 1901. SEM105P396 – 1mf – 9 – Can$2.25 – cn Bibl Nat [338]

THE SHAWINIGAN STANDARD – Shawinigan, Canada. v3 n35. 4 jan 1933-22 dec 1970 – 22r – 1 – Can$50.00r – cn Can Microfilming [072]

Shawinigan Water and Power Company *see* SHAWINIGAN FALLS AND ITS INDUSTRIES

SHAWNEE – Topeka. Kan. 1913-1921 – 1 – us UMI [071]

Shawnee Center Cemetery, Shawnee County, KS *see* DEATH LISTS AND LOT REGISTERS

Shawnee County. Kansas. Board of Commissioners *see* JOURNAL

Shawnee County. Kansas. Pleasant Hill United Methodist Church *see*
- RECORDS

Shawnee County. Kansas. Register of Deeds *see* RECORDS

Shawnee County. Kansas. School District 26 *see* CLERK'S RECORD

Shawnee County. Kansas. School District 35 *see* OFFICIAL SCHOOL DISTRICT TREASURER'S RECORD BOOK

Shawnee County. Kansas. School District 38 *see* RECORDS

Shawnee County. Kansas. Sheriff *see* JAIL RECORDS OF SHAWNEE COUNTY, KANSAS

Shawnee County. Kansas. Surveyor *see* FIELD NOTES

Shawnee Mission *see* STEWARD'S BOOK AND SELECTED ARTICLES FROM THE TRANSACTIONS

SHAY LE-MOREH. JUBELSCHRIFT. ISRAEL HILDESHEIMER / Hildesheimer, I – Berlin. 1890. BJ-100-40 1 – 9 – ne IDC [900]

SHAYKHI MANUSCRIPT COLLECTION – 7 sections 24r – 1 – $90.00r $1,944.00 collection – us MEDOC [956]

Shchebal'skii, P K *see* POLITICHESKAIA SISTEMA PETRA 3

Shchegoleva, P E *see*
- BATKO MAKHNO
- FRANTSUZY V ODESSE

Shchepkin, E N *see* RUSSKO-AVSTRIISKII SOIUZ VO VREMIA SEMILETNEI VOINY, 1746-1758 GG

Shchepkina, E *see* STARINNYE POMESHCHIKI NA SLUZHBE I DOMA. IZ SEMEINOI KHRONIKI (1578-1762)

Shchepkina, M V *see* OPISANIE RUKOPISEI SINODAL'NOGO SOBRANIIA (NE VOSHEDSHIKH V OPISANIE A.V. GORSKOGO I K.I. NEVOSTRUEVA)

Shchepkina, M V et al *see* OPISANIE PERGAMENTNYKH RUKOPISEI GOSUDARSTVENNOGO ISTORICHESKOGO MUZEIA

Shcherbatsky, T *see* THE CENTRAL CONCEPTION OF BUDDHISM AND THE MEANING OF THE WORD DHARMA

Shchipanov, I I *see*
- IZ ISTORII RUSSKOI FILOSOFII 18 I 19 VEKOV
- IZBRANNYE PROIZVEDENIIA RUSSKIKH MYSLITELEI VTOROI POLOVINY 18 VEKA

SHCHIT I MECH – (Backfile through 1998 $85r) – 1999- – 1r per y – 1 – $80.00 standing order – us Ross [072]

Shea, John Dawson Gilmary *see*
- DISCOVERY AND EXPLORATION OF THE MISSISSIPPI VALLEY
- THE HIERARCHY OF THE CATHOLIC CHURCH IN THE U.S
- HISTORY OF THE CATHOLIC MISSIONS AMONG THE INDIAN TRIBES OF THE UNITED STATES, 1529-1854
- LIFE OF POPE PIUS IX, AND THE GREAT EVENTS IN THE HISTORY OF THE CHURCH DURING HIS PONTIFICATE

Shea, Kyla *see* GENDER DIFFERENCES IN SUBSTRATE METABOLISM AND THERMOREGULATION DURING REST AND EXERCISE IN COLD AND WARM WATER

A SHEAF OF WHEAT GATHERED FROM THE FIELD OF DIVINE REVELATION : A SERIES OF BRIEF EXPOSITORY STUDIES ON THE EPISTLE OF JAMES / Lee, E Trumbull – Cincinnati, OH: Western Tract Society, [1899?] – 1mf – 9 – 0-8370-4078-7 – 1985-2078 – us A.T.L.A. [220]

SHEAR YASHUV / Goldmann, J – v. 1. Ha-Asif. 1885. BJ-27-241 1 – 9 – ne IDC [360]

Sheard, Terence *see* THE ADMINISTRATION OF ESTATES

SHE'ARIM – Tel Aviv. 1934-76. BJ-91-102 3 – 1 – ne IDC [270]

Shearman, Thomas Gaskell *see* A TREATISE ON THE LAW OF NEGLIGENCE

SHEARS – v1-67 1892-1959. Continued as: Boxboard Containers – 1 – us UMI [670]

Shebbeare, John *see* LE PEUPLE INSTRUIT, OU LES ALLIANCES DANS LESQUELLES LES MINISTRES DE LA GRAND BRETAGNE ONT ENGAGE LA NATION...

SHEDD MONITOR – Shedd OR. July 27 1917 – 1 – us U.O. Library [071]

Shedd, William Ambrose *see* ISLAM AND THE ORIENTAL CHURCHES

Shedd, William Greenough Thayer *see*
- CALVINISM, PURE AND MIXED
- A CRITICAL AND DOCTRINAL COMMENTARY UPON... PAUL TO THE ROMANS
- DISCOURSES AND ESSAYS
- THE DOCTRINE OF ENDLESS PUNISHMENT
- A HISTORY OF CHRISTIAN DOCTRINE
- LECTURES UPON THE PHILOSOPHY OF HISTORY
- ORTHODOXY AND HETERODOXY
- THE PROPOSED REVISION OF THE WESTMINSTER STANDARDS
- SERMONS TO THE NATURAL MAN
- THEOLOGICAL ESSAYS

SHEDLETSER VOKHENBLAT – (Yiddish weekly) – Siedlce, PL. v5 no11 12 Mar 1926-v5 no28 9 Aug 1926 – 1r – 1 – $25.00 – cn Can Microfilming [072]

Sheehan, Laurieanne *see* ACCURACY OF A TREADMILL SCORING SYSTEM FOR PREDICTION OF CORONARY ARTERY DISEASE IN FEMALE SUBJECTS

Sheehey, Diane *see* GUIDELINE SENTENCING

Sheel, Andrew W *see* THE TIME COURSE OF PULMONARY DIFFUSION CAPACITY CHANGES FOLLOWING MAXIMAL EXERCISE

SHE'ELAH NIKHBADAH / Ben-Yehuda, E – v. 9. Ha-Shahar. 1877-79. BJ-27-232 1 – 9 – ne IDC [072]

SHE'ELAT EREZ-YISRA'EL BI-SHENOTH 1840-1842 / Gelber, N M – v4. Ziyyon. Me'assef. 1930. BJ-27-41 1 – 9 – ne IDC [956]

SHEEP AND GOAT BREEDS OF INDIA – 1982 – 197p – it F.A.O. [636]

SHEEP AND GOAT MEAT PRODUCTION IN THE HUMID TROPICS OF WEST AFRICA – 1989 – 269p – it F.A.O. [338]

SHEEP AND GOATS IN HUMID WEST AFRICA : PROCEEDINGS OF THE WORKSHOP ON SMALL RUMINANT PRODUCTION SYSTEMS IN THE HUMID ZONE OF WEST AFRICA, HELD IN IBADAN, NIGERIA, 23-26 JANUARY 1984 / ed by Sumberg, J E & Cassaday, K – 1985 – 9 – $12.00 – 92-9053-137-1 – et ILRI [636]

SHEEP AND GOATS IN PAKISTAN – 1985 – 145p – it F.A.O. [636]

SHEEP AND GOATS IN TURKEY – 1986 – 181p – it F.A.O. [636]

THE SHEEP AND ITS COUSINS / Lydekker, R – 1912 – 9mf – 7 – uk Microform Academic [636]

SHEEP, THEIR BREEDS, MANAGEMENT AND DISEASES / Youatt, W – 10mf – uk Microform Academic [636]

SHE-ERIT YISRA'EL / Amelander, M M – Amsterdam. 1743. BJ-262-4 1 – 9 – ne IDC [956]

SHEERNESS GUARDIAN – England. Sheerness Times & Guardian Sheerness Times Guardian. -w. 1920-79. 60 1 2 reels – 1 – uk British Libr Newspaper [072]

SHEET METAL INDUSTRIES – The only Journal solely devoted to the manufacture. of ferrous and non-ferrous metals. London. 1927. Available: 1940-60, v. 14-37. B-733 2 – 8 – ne IDC [600]

Sheet Metal Workers' International Association *see* SHEET METAL WORKERS' JOURNAL

SHEET METAL WORKERS' JOURNAL : 1897-1955 / Sheet Metal Workers' International Association – (Coll title: Labor Union Periodicals, Pt 1) – 10r – 1 – $1,350.00 – 1-55655-247-5 – us UPA [331]

SHEFFIELD 1726-1897 – (Mf 1-3: Vital Records 1730-1860. Mf 4-10: Town & Vital Records 1726-89. Mf 11-15: Town & Vital Records 1763-1809. Mf 16-24: Town & Vital Records 1794-1821. Mf 25-27: Town & Vital Records 1769-1827. Mf 28: Marriages 1797-1850. Mf 29-31: Marriages & Intentions 1813-55. Mf 32-33: Index to Births 1843-97. Mf 34-36: Index Marriages & Intentions 1797-1897. Mf 37-38: Index to Deaths 1843-97. Mf 39-41: Births, Marriages, Deaths 1843-55. Mf 42-49: Births, Marriages, Deaths 1856-97) – (mf ed 1988) – 49mf – 9 – 0-87623-074-5 – us Holbrook [920]

Sheffield, Alfred Dwight *see* THE OLD TESTAMENT NARRATIVE

Sheffield. Central Library *see* VASSAL LETTER BOOKS, 1769-1800

Sheffield. City Library *see* WHARNCLIFFE MANUSCRIPTS RELATING TO AMERICAN CIVIL WAR

SHEFFIELD DAILY TELEGRAPH – England. 1897-1900; Jan-Jun 1910; Jan-Mar 1911.-d. 17 reels – 1 – uk British Libr Newspaper [072]

SHEFFIELD FORWARD – England. The organ of the Sheffield Federated Traders & Labour Council. -m. May 1921-Dec 1927. 31 ft – 1 – uk British Libr Newspaper [072]

SHEFFIELD FREE PRESS – England. -w. Jan 1851-Dec 1857. (12 reels) – 1 – uk British Libr Newspaper [072]

SHEFFIELD GUARDIAN – England. -w. 20 Jan 1906-3 March 1916. 5 reels – 1 – uk British Libr Newspaper [072]

SHEFFIELD, HENRY E., ACCOUNT BOOK – (Accounts of income, 1899-1939 and expenses, 1899-1911, along with a genealogy chart and biographical article on Joseph E. Sheffield, the father of this Bratenahl lawyer, businessman, and politician) – 1899-1939 – 1r – 1 – us Western Res [920]

SHEFFIELD INDEPENDENT – England. Sheffield & Rotherham Independent Sheffield Daily Independent Daily Independent. -w, -d. 11 Dec 1819; 17, 24 Nov 1821; 29 Nov, 27 Dec 1823; 3 Jan-6 March, 3 April, 11 Dec 1824; 17 Dec 1825; 7 Jan, 11, 25 Feb, 18 March, 2-30 Dec 1826; 2 Aug 1828-Oct 1938. Lacking May-Aug 1897; Jan-March 1911. 381 reels – 1 – uk British Libr Newspaper [072]

SHEFFIELD PLAYBILLS / York Minster Library – 1781-83 – 1 – uk Microform Academic [790]

Sheffield. -Ranmoor College *see* METHODIST NEW CONNEXION COLLEGE, RANMOOR, SHEFFIELD

SHEFFIELD WEEKLY TELEGRAPH – (Weekly Telegraph, 1887-1951) – England, 1884-98; 1950 – 23r – 1 – uk British Libr Newspaper [072]

LE SHEFFORD – Waterloo, Canada. v3 n37. 24/31 mai 1961-v10 n19. 27 dec 1967 – 1r – 1 – Can$65.00 – cn Can Microfilming [072]

Shefler, M E *see*
- KAK USTROIT' I VESTI KREDITNOE TOVARISHCHESTVO
- OSNOVY SEL'SKOI KREDITNOI KOOPERATSII

Shehadeh, Kuttab *see* THE WEST BANK AND THE RULE OF LAW

SHEHITOT – Prague. c.1640? BJ-43-101 1 – 9 – ne IDC [470]

SHEHRI KAZAN – Kazan, USSR. Jan-Sept 15 1992 – 1r – 1 – us L of C Photodup [072]

SHE-HUI HSIN-WEN – (The Social Mercury). Oct. 4, 1932-Sep. 1935. Missing: 5 scattered issues. (9200 3807) – 1 – 35.00r – us Hoover Inst Photo [072]

SHE-HUI PAN-YUEH-K'AN / Shanghai. Municipal Government of Shanghai – (Social affairs fortnightly). 21 v. 1934-35. BCH-335 1 – 9 – ne IDC [073]

SHE-HUI-HSUEH CHIEH. "SOCIOLOGICAL WORLD" – v. 1-2. Peiping. 1927-28. BCH-330 1 – 9 – ne IDC [300]

SHE-HUI-K' O-HSUEH TSA-CHIH / Peiping. Institute of Social Research. Academia Sinica – "Quarterly Review of Social Sciences." 10 v. Peiping. 1930-48. Index. Available: v. 1-8 (3), 1930-37; index, 1930-48. BCH-333 1 – 9 – ne IDC [073]

SHE-HUI-K' O-HSUEH TS'UNG-K'AN – Journal of Social Sciences. v. 1-2. Nanking. 1934-36. Available: v. 1-2 (1). BCH-334 2 – 9 – ne IDC [300]

SHE'IFOTEINU – Jerusalem. 1927-33. BJ-91-78 1 – 9 – ne IDC [470]

Sheikovskii, K *see* OPYT IUZHNO-RUSSKOGO SLOVARIA

SHEILA! MY DARLING COLLEEN : THE MARRIAGE REVISED AND INSCRIBED TO THE HONORABLE MRS. FOLSON, GROVENOR [SIC] CLEVELAND, WASHINGTON D.C... / Crouch, FN – Holograph, signed and dated by composer, 11/25/1887 – 5 – us Sibley [780]

Sheinin, Lev Romanovich *see* PEOPLE'S COURTS IN THE U.S.S.R

Sheinman, M *see* RELIGIONZNOST' I PRESTUPNOST'

SHEKEL HAKODESH / Gollancz, H – (The Holy Shekel). The metrical Work of Joseph Kimchi. London. 1919. BJ-421-63 1 – 9 – ne IDC [470]

SHEKPENDEH – Freetown, Sierra Leone. -w. 1 Jan 1959-13 April 1961. 2 reels – 1 – uk British Libr Newspaper [072]

SHELBURNE 1756-1895 – (mf ed 1987) – 26mf – 9 – 0-87623-050-8 – us Holbrook [920]

SHELBY DEMOCRAT – Shelbyville. Ind. -w. 1929-34 – 1 – us UMI [071]

SHELBY FIRST BAPTIST CHURCH. SHELBY, NORTH CAROLINA : CHURCH RECORDS – 1871-1954 – 1 – 71.69 – us Baptist [240]

SHELBY SECOND BAPTIST CHURCH. SHELBY, NORTH CAROLINA : CHURCH RECORDS – 1943-62 – 1 – 83.61 – us Baptist [240]

THE SHELBY SENTINEL – Shelbyville, KY. 30 Nov 1967. 129p – 1 – us Baptist [071]

SHELBY SUN – Shelby, NE. -w. Jun 1892; Aug 1895; Oct 1895-May 1898; Nov-Dec 1898; Feb-Nov 1899; Feb 1900-Jun 1904; Jan 1905 to date – 1 – us NE Hist [071]

Sheldon, Addison E *see*
- NEBRASKA BLUE BOOK AND HISTORICAL REGISTER 1918
- NEBRASKA: THE LAND AND THE PEOPLE
- THE SEMI-CENTENNIAL HISTORY OF NEBRASKA

Sheldon, Charles Monroe *see* LETTERS

THE SHELDON GLUECK PAPERS / Glueck, Sheldon – (Guide only $100.00) – 126r – 1 – $13,620.00 – 0-89093-804-0 – us UPA [920]

Sheldon, Henry Clay *see*
- CHRISTIAN SCIENCE SO-CALLED
- SACERDOTALISM IN THE NINETEENTH CENTURY
- STUDIES IN RECENT ADVENTISM
- UNBELIEF IN THE NINETEENTH CENTURY: A CRITICAL HISTORY

Sheldon, Henry Olcott *see*
- JOURNALS

SHELDON JACKSON : PATHFINDER AND PROSPECTOR OF THE MISSIONARY VANGUARD IN THE ROCKY MOUNTAINS AND ALASKA / Stewart, Robert Laird – (Includes index) – 2nd ed. New York: Fleming H Revell, c1908 – 2mf – 9 – 0-8370-6416-3 – 1986-0416 – us A.T.L.A. [920]

THE SHELDON JACKSON COLLECTION, 1835-1909 – (Includes printed guide) – 41r – 1 – $3,485.00 – D3332 – Co-publ with the Presbyterian Historical Society, Dept of History, Presbyterian Church (U.S.A.) 1995 – us Scholarly Res [200]

Sheldon, W L *see* AN ETHICAL MOVEMENT

SHELDON'S SUPERIOR COURT REPORTS / Buffalo. New York. Superior Court – 1v. 1854-75 (all publ) – 7mf – 9 – $10.50 – LLMC 80-042 – us L.L.M.C. [340]

SHELF LIST OF RARE AND VALUABLE MATERIALS IN DARGAN-CARVER LIBRARY – 1 – 16.82 – us Baptist [240]

THE SHELF LIST OF THE LIBRARY / Union Theological Seminary Library – 1960.- 203,000 cards 20 reels.-ISBN: 0-8161-1306-8 – 1 – $975.00 – uk Hall [290]

THE SHELF LIST OF THE UNION THEOLOGICAL SEMINARY LIBRARY / Union Theological Seminary Library – 1960. 203,000 cards on 20 reels – 1 – $885.00 export $1,070.00 – 0-8161-1306-8 – uk Hall [290]

SHELFLIST / U.S. Library of Congress – 3221 fiches – 9 – us UMI [020]

SHELFLIST OF SELECTED CLASSES OF PJ AND PL (AFRICAN LINGUISTICS AND LITERATURE) AS OF 2/82 / U.S. Library of Congress – 1 – us Res Libr [020]

Shelkunov, I *see* PIS'MA IMPERATRITSY EKATERINY 2 K DATSKOI KOROLEVE IULIANE MARII

Shell Oil Company. Marketing Organization in Indonesia *see* OIL FOR INDONESIA'S FUTURE; AN OUTLINE OF TASKS AHEAD FOR THE OIL INDUSTRY

THE SHELL-COLLECTOR'S HANDBOOK FOR THE FIELD / Williams, J W – Z 873 2. 1888 – 8 – ne IDC [590]
Shellens, Richard *see* SCHELLENS COLLECTION. SAN MATEO COUNTY HISTORICAL COLLECTION
SHELLEY : A POEM, WITH OTHER WRITINGS RELATING TO SHELLEY / Thomson, James – [London]: Printed for the private circulation by C. Whittingham at the Chiswick Press, 1884 – 1 roll – 1 – 1-55879-521-9 – uk Libr Preservation [810]
Shelley, G E *see* THE BIRDS OF AFRICA
Shelley, Jane Gibson *see*
– SHELLEY MEMORIALS
– SHELLEY MEMORIALS: FROM AUTHENTIC SOURCES
Shelley, Mary Wollstonecraft *see* HISTORY OF A SIX WEEKS' TOUR THROUGH A PART OF FRANCE, SWITZERLAND, GERMANY AND HOLLAND...
SHELLEY MEMORIALS / Shelley, Jane Gibson – London: Smith, Elder and Co, 1859 – 1r – 1 – 1-55879-634-7 – uk Libr Preservation [420]
SHELLEY MEMORIALS: FROM AUTHENTIC SOURCES / ed by Shelley, Jane Gibson – Ed. by Lady Shelley. Includes: An Essay on Christianity by Percy Bysshe Shelley. Boston: Ticknor & Fields, 1859. vi,308p – 1 – us U.W. Library [920]
Shelley, Percy Bysshe *see*
– ALASTOR
– A DEFENSE OF POETRY
– EPIPSYCHIDION
– HELLAS
– THE MASK OF ANARCHY
– A PHILOSOPHICAL VIEW OF REFORM
– THE POETICAL WORKS OF PERCY BYSSHE SHELLEY
– POSTHUMOUS POEMS OF PERCY BYSSHE SHELLEY
– QUEEN MAB
– THE REVOLT OF ISLAM
– ROSALIND AND HELEN
– ST. IRVYNE, OR THE ROSICRUCIAN
– THE WORKS OF PERCY BYSSHE SHELLEY
– ZASTROZZI
SHELLS OF NEW ENGLAND / Stimpson, W – Z 818 2. 1851 – 8 – ne IDC [590]
SHELLS OF THE BRITISH ISLES / Rimmer, R – Z 748 2. 1907 – 8 – ne IDC [590]
SHELOM YERUSHALAYIM / Frumkin, I D – (Havazzelet, Jerusalem, 5633). 1873. BJ-27-206 1 – 9 – ne IDC [900]
SHELOMOH DA PIERRA / Brody, H – Devarim Ahadim Odotav ve-Odot Sefarav. Berlin. 1893. BJ-421-83 1 – 9 – ne IDC [890]
SHELOSHAH MIKHTAYIM ME-RASHEI KEHAL ASHKENAZIM BI-YERUSHALAYIM – Ed. by Luncz. v. 2. Yerushalayim. 1887. BJ-27-71 1 – 9 – ne IDC [956]
SHELTON CLIPPER – Shelton, NE. -w. Oct 1895-Feb 1896; Apr 1896 to date – 1 – us NE Hist [071]
Shelton, Don Odell *see* HEROES OF THE CROSS IN AMERICA
SHELTON STAR – Shelton, NE. -w. Mar 1899-Jun 1900 – 1 – us NE Hist [071]
SHELTON-MASON COUNTY JOURNAL – Shelton. Wash. 1896-1898; 1908-1950 – 1 – us UMI [071]
SHELUHEI EREZ-YISRA'EL / Yaari, A – Jerusalem. 1951. BJ-27-1 1 – 9 – ne IDC [956]
Shemshurin, A *see*
– FUTURIZM V STIKHAKH BRIUSOVA
– STIKHI V. BRIUSOVA I RUSSKII IAZYK
SHEN CHAO *see* CALL FROM GOD
Shen, Chuen *see* HISTORY OF THE DUTCH EAST INDIES
Shen, J Wesley *see* A NEW HISTORY OF SOCIALISM (CCC277)
SHEN PAO – Shanghai. China. 1872-1912, 1923-49 – 1 – 1790.00 – us Chinese Res [072]
Shen, T'i-lan *see* CHRISTIANS AND THE NATIONAL SALVATION MOVEMENT (CCC278)
Shen, Ts'ing-lai *see* WHAT IS CHRISTIANITY (CCC279)
Shen, Tzu-kao *see* LIFE AND WORK OF THE MINISTER (CCC280)
SHENANDOAH COUNTY RECORD – Woodstock. Va. 1891-1892 – 1 – us UMI [071]
SHENANDOAH HERALD – Shenandoah, PA. -w 1889-1907; 1971 – 13 – $25.00r – us I.M.R. [071]
SHENANDOAH VALLEY – New Market. Va. 1869-1883; 1886-1924; 1935-46; 1950- – 1 – us UMI [071]
SHENANDOAH VALLEY PIONEERS AND THEIR DECENDANTS / Cartnell, T K – Winchester, Eddy Press, 1909. Virginia Reel 3. (The Cox Library Collection) – 5 – us Americana [978]
Shenango. Presbytery *see*
– MINUTES, 1838-1859
– MINUTES, 1870-72
SHENATON STATISTI LE-ISRAEL / Israel. Central Bureau of Statistics – (Israel statistical yearbook). 1949-75. Lacking: v. 24, 1973. BJ-81-43 1 – 9 – ne IDC [310]
SHENBAO – Shanghai. Shanghai Daily. Apr 1872-Dec 1903; 29 Jul 1912-Dec 1937. M/B 27 – 220r – 1 – $15,400.00 – cc Microforms [072]
SHEN-CHOU KUO-KUANG CHI – (Collection of Chinese Art). v. 1-21. Shanghai. 1908-11. BCH-807 2 – 8 – ne IDC [700]
SHEN-CHOU TA-KUAN – (Survey of Chinese Art). v. 1-12. Shanghai. 1912-17. BCH-808 2 – 8 – ne IDC [700]
Shengeli, G *see* TEKHNIKA STIKHA
SHENG-HO – Life. Shanghai, 1925-33. 8v. -w. Lacking: 1932, v7 (31,40,41,49-52). BCH-336/1 – 9 – ne IDC [073]
SHENGHUO JIAOYU = EDUCATION AND LIFE – v1-3. Feb 1934-Aug 1938. 1 reel. M-C74 – 5 – $40.00 – cc Microforms [073]
SHENGHUO ZHOUKAN – Life Weekly. Oct 1925-Dec 1933. M C67 In Chinese – 1 – $160.00 – cc Microforms [073]
SHENGLI XUEBAO – Acta Physiologica Sinica. In Chinese but English abstracts to the main articles. F p34 – 9 – $4.50f – cc Microforms [073]
SHENGTAI XUEBAO – Acta Ecologica Sinica. In Chinese but English abstracts to the main articles. F p100 – 9 – 4.00f – cc Microforms [073]
SHENGWU HUAXUE YU SHENGWU WULI XUEBAO – (1984 $3.50f; 1983, 1986 $4.50f) – Acta Biochimica et Biophysica Sinica. In Chinese but English abstracts to the main articles. F p64 – 9 – cc Microforms [073]
SHENGWU HUAXUE ZAZHI – Chinese Biochemical Journal. 1985. F/P 283 – 9 – $4.50f – cc Microforms [073]
SHENGXUE XUEBAO – Acta Acoustica. In Chinese but English abstracts to the main articles. F p73 – 9 – 4.00f – cc Microforms [073]
SHENGZHI YU BIYUN – Reproduction and Contraception. In Chinese but English abstracts to the main articles. F p158 – 9 – 4.00f – cc Microforms [073]
SHEN-HSI HSIANG-SHIH LU – List of successful candidates in the imperial examination in Shensi province. Scattered years 1690-1901. 1 reel – 1 – 20.00 – us Chinese Res [950]
SHEN-HSI JIH-PAO – Sian, China. Shensi Daily. Oct 1954-62. 16 reels. Original title was Ch'un-chung Daily – 1 – 415.00 – us Chinese Res [072]
Shenk *see* A HISTORY OF BLAIR COUNTY
Shenoy, Sudha *see*
– FROM WALRAS TO MENGER: GENERAL EQUILIBRIUM AND ITS MICRO FOUNDATIONS.
– WAGE AND PRICE CONTROL
SHEN-PAO YUEH-K'AN – Sheng-pao Monthly. v. 1-4 (12). Shanghai. 1932-35. BCH-337 2 – 8 – ne IDC [073]
SHENYANG RIBAO = SHENYANG DAILY – China. 1984-. M-D63 – 1 reel/y – 1 – $55.00r – cc Microforms [072]
SHENZHEN TEQU BAO = SHENZHEN SPECIAL ZONE DAILY – (1983-88, 1r/y; 1989- , 2r/y) – China. 1983-. M-D49 – 1 – $55.00r – cc Microforms [072]
Shepard, Elliott Fitch *see* THE COURT OF ARBITRATION: ITS ADVANTAGES AND IMPORTANCE TO BUSINESS MEN
SHEPARD'S FEDERAL AND STATE CITATORS – 5,6 – Inquire – us Hein [340]
Shepelev, L E *see*
– ARKHIVNYE RAZYSKANIIA I ISSLEDOVANIIA
– ARKHIVOVEDENIE UCHEBNOE POSOBIE
Shepheard, H *see* THE TREE OF LIFE
SHEPHERD : A LONDON WEEKLY PERIODICAL ILLUSTRATING THE PRINCIPLES OF UNIVERSAL SCIENCE – London. v1-3. 1834-38 – 1r – 1 – us Ross [500]
THE SHEPHERD – (Lacks some issues and pgs) – v39-61. 1963-85 – 6r – 1 – ATLA S0378 – us A.T.L.A. [073]
Shepherd, Edward John *see* THE HISTORY OF THE CHURCH OF ROME
THE SHEPHERD KINGS OF EGYPT / Campbell, John – 18?? 00385. (Pre-1900 Canadiana) – 9 – cn C.I.H.M. [930]
Shepherd, Philippa *see* JOHN TYNDALL, NATURAL PHILOSOPHER, 1820-1893: CATALOGUE OF CORRESPONDENCE, JOURNALS AND COLLECTED PAPERS
THE SHEPHERD PSALM / Meyer, Frederick Brotherton – New York:Fleming H. Revell, c1889 – 1mf – 9 – 0-8370-4413-8 – 1985-2413 – us A.T.L.A. [220]
Shepherd, Richard Herne *see* STUDIES OF SENSATION AND EVENT
Shepherd, Robert Henry Wishart *see* LOVEDALE, SOUTH AFRICA, 1824-1955
THE SHEPHERD SONG ON THE HILLS OF LEBANON : THE TWENTY-THIRD PSALM / Moghabghab, Faddoul – New York:E P Dutton, c1907 – 1mf – 9 – 0-8370-4458-8 – 1985-2458 – us A.T.L.A. [220]
Shepherd, William Ashton *see* FROM BOMBAY TO BUSHIRE, AND BUSSORA; INCLUDING AN ACCOUNT OF THE PRESENT STATE OF PERSIA, AND NOTES ON THE PERSIAN WAR
SHEPHERDS BUSH GAZETTE ETC – (Also known as: Hammersmith Fulham and Shepherd's Bush Gazette) – Aug 20 1909-10; Jan 6-Dec 29 1911; Jan 5-May 31, Jul 12-Dec 1912; Jan 3-Dec 5 1913; May 20 1955-Jun 1973; Jul 5-Nov 8 1973; Jan 24-Jun 27, Jul-Dec 1973; Jan-Jun, Jul 10-Dec 25 1975; 1976-78; Feb 15-Jun 28, Jul-Dec 1979; Jan 10-Jun 26, Jul 3-Dec 29 1980; 1981-83; Jan 5-Jun 28, Jul 5-Dec 28 1984; 1985-Jun 1989; Jul 7-Sep 29, Oct 9-Dec 29 1989; Jul 1990-92; Jan 8-Dec 1993; Jan 7-Jun 24, Jul 8-Dec 30 1994; 1995-Jun 1997 – 110r – 1 – uk British Libr Newspaper [072]
SHEPHERDS BUSH-HAMMERSMITH GAZETTE – London, UK. 1985-Jun 1987. -w.9 1/2 reels – 1 – uk British Libr Newspaper [072]
THE SHEPHERD'S CALENDAR : WITH VILLAGE STORIES AND OTHER POEMS / Clare, John – London: J. Taylor, 1827 – 1 roll – 1 – 1-55879-320-8 – uk Libr Preservation [810]
A SHEPHERD'S LIFE : IMPRESSIONS OF THE SOUTH WILTSHIRE DOWNS / Hudson, William Henry – London: Methuen, 1910 – 1 roll – 1 – 1-55879-564-2 – uk Libr Preservation [830]
Sheppard *see* HISTORICAL ENCYCLOPEDIA OF ILLINOIS AND HISTORY OF EVANSTON
Sheppard, J B *see* LITERAE CANTUARIENSES (RS85)
Sheppard, Wheeler *see* MISTAKES OF DR W.E.B. DUBOIS
Sheppart, J P *see* MATERIALS FOR THE HISTORY OF THOMAS BECKET (RS67)
SHEPPARTON WATERWORKS TRUST – 1882-1900. NSCWW A – 1r – 1 – at Corangamite [910]
SHEPPARTON WATERWORKS TRUST – 1900-1983. NSCWW1-3 – 3r – 1 – at Corangamite [910]
Sherborn *see* INDEX ANIMALIUM
THE SHERBRO AND ITS HINTERLAND / Alldridge, Thomas Joshua – New York: Macmillan and Co., 1901. xvi,356p. Plates, maps – 1 – us U.W. Library [960]
SHERBROOKE DAILY RECORD – Sherbrooke, Canada. 1897-1910 – 35r – 1 – $2,275.00 – cn Library Assoc [971]
THE SHERBROOKE DAILY RECORD – Sherbrooke, Canada. Special issues: Eastern Townships Agriculture, annuals, etc. 9 fev 1897; 3 jan 1911-22 jul 1969 – 3r – 1 – Can$75.00r – cn Can Microfilming [072]
THE SHERBROOKE EXAMINER *see* THE WEEKLY EXAMINER
THE SHERBROOKE FREEMAN – Sherbrooke, Canada. v1 n36. 24 nov 1864-v2 n49. 1 mar 1866 – 1r – 1 – Can$30.00 – cn Can Microfilming [072]
SHERBROOKE GAZETTE – (Includes: St. Francis Courier, 1832-34) – Sherbrooke, Canada. 1837-96 – 6r – 1 – $390.00 – cn Library Assoc [971]
SHERBROOKE GAZETTE AND EASTERN TOWNSHIPS ADVERTISER – Sherbrooke, Canada. 23 sep 1837-v55 n23. 9 jun 1893 – 1r – 1 – Can$70.00 – cn Can Microfilming [072]
THE SHERBROOKE ILLUSTRATED – Sherbrooke, Canada. sep 1886 – 1r – 1 – Can$25.00 – cn Can Microfilming [072]
SHERBROOKE NEWS – Sherbrooke, Canada. v2 n103. 11 dec 1873-v7 n331. 25 avr 1878 – 1r – 1 – Can$45.00 – cn Can Microfilming [072]
THE SHERBROOKE NEWS-LETTER – Sherbrooke, Canada. 16 nov 1895 – 1r – 1 – Can$25.00 – cn Can Microfilming [072]
THE SHERBROOKE RECORD – (Cont by: The Record 5 nov 1979-31 dec 1992) – 23 jul 1969-2 nov 1979 – 241r – 1 – Can$70.00 – cn Can Microfilming [072]
SHERBROOKE TELEGRAM – Sherbrooke, Canada. v1 n1. 19 mai 1932-v28 n41. 10 mar 1960 – 7r – 1 – Can$75.00r – cn Can Microfilming [072]
LE SHERBROOKOIS *see* LE JOURNAL DE SHERBROOKE
SHERIDAN COUNTY STAR – Rushville, NE. -w. Oct-Dec 1895; Feb 1896-Dec 1900; Jul 1904-Jul 1918; Jul 1919-Jul 1920; Jul 1922-Jun 1927; Jul 1928-Jun 1932; May 1933 to date – 1 – us NE Hist [071]
Sheridan, F *see* THE DISCOVERY
Sheridan, Philip H *see* PAPERS
Sheridan, Sol. N *see* HISTORY OF VENTURA COUNTY
SHERIDAN SUN – Sheridan, OR. -w. 1901-04, 1908-62 – 1 – 456.00 – us Oregon Hist [071]
SHERIDAN SUN – Sheridan, OR. -w. 3 Jan 1963-.; 26 Oct 1900 – 5r – 1 – us U.O. Library [071]
Sheridan, Thomas *see*
– A COURSE OF LECTURES ON ELOCUTION
– A DISSERTATION ON THE CAUSES OF THE DIFFICULTIES WHICH OCCUR IN LEARNING THE ENGLISH TONGUE
– ELEMENTS OF ENGLISH
– A GENERAL DICTIONARY OF THE ENGLISH LANGUAGE
– A RHETORICAL GRAMMAR OF THE ENGLISH LANGUAGE
SHERIT JACOB ISRAEL SYNAGOGUE – Cleveland, OH, 1919-1938 – 1r – 1 – us I.H.R.C. [270]
Sherlock, James (Thomas?) *see* THE TRIAL OF THE WITNESSES OF THE RESURRECTION OF JESUS
Sherlock, William *see* A SERMON PREACH'D AT ST PAUL'S CATHEDRAL..
Sherman *see* REGISTER OF OHIO SOCIETY OF SONS OF THE AMERICAN REVOLUTION 1917-18-19-20-21
SHERMAN COUNTY DARK HORSE – Eustis. Kan. 1886-1894 – 1 – us UMI [071]
SHERMAN COUNTY JOURNAL – Moro. Or. 1931-1963 – 1 – us UMI [071]
SHERMAN COUNTY JOURNAL – Moro, OR. -w. 1931-62 – 1 – 144.00 – us Oregon Hist [071]
SHERMAN COUNTY JOURNAL – Moro, OR. -w. 4 Jan 1952-. – 6r – 1 – us U.O. Library [071]
Sherman County. Kansas. Homesteaders Union Association. Lodge No. 3 *see* MINUTES
SHERMAN COUNTY NEWS – (Set incl. News Enterprise (Wasco)) – Wasco, OR. -w. 19 Aug 1927-29 Aug 1930. – 2r – 1 – us U.O. Library [071]
SHERMAN COUNTY NEWS – Voltaire. KS. 1886-88 – 1 – us UMI [071]
SHERMAN COUNTY OBSERVER – Moro. Or. -w. 1900-31 – 1 – us UMI [071]
SHERMAN COUNTY OBSERVER – Moro, OR. -w. Moro, OR. -w. 1900-31 – 1 – 137.00 – us Oregon Hist [071]
SHERMAN COUNTY OBSERVER – (Set incl. Moro Observer) – Moro, OR. -w. 1 Sep 1897-17 Nov 1899. – 1r – 1 – us U.O. Library [071]
SHERMAN COUNTY TIMES – Loup City, NE. -w. Aug 1876; Oct 1878; Jul 1879; Jan-May 1887; Jul 1887-Oct 1888; Dec 1888-Nov 1901; Jan 1902 to date – 1 – us NE Hist [071]
Sherman, David *see* HISTORY OF THE REVISIONS OF THE DISCIPLINE OF THE METHODIST EPISCOPAL CHURCH
Sherman, E H *see* REVOLUTIONARY WAR SOLDIERS BURIED IN GEAUGA CO., OHIO
Sherman, Edwin A *see* FIFTY YEARS OF MASONRY IN CALIFORNIA
SHERMAN INDIAN INSTITUTE HIGH SCHOOL ANNUALS – Riverside Co, CA. 1892-1973 – 21r – 1 – $1,050.00 – D077 – us Library Micro [370]
Sherman, William M *see* IN VIVO INSULIN ACTION ON WHOLE BODY AND INDIVIDUAL TISSUES IN OBESE SHHF/MCC-CP RATS WITH OR WITHOUT ACUTE EXERCISE

Sherman, William T *see* PAPERS
Sherman, William Tecumseh *see*
- MEMOIRS
- PAPERS

SHERPA ARCHITECTURE / Sestini, Valerio & Somigli, Enzo – 1978 – 78p – 9 – 92-3-101612-1 – fr UNESCO [720]
Sherrill, Claudine *see* SELF-PERCEPTION AND MOTOR PROFICIENCY OF HEARING-IMPAIRED CHILDREN
Sherrin *see* EARLY NEW ZEALAND
Sherring, Matthew Atmore *see*
- THE HISTORY OF PROTESTANT MISSIONS IN INDIA
- THE HISTORY OF PROTESTANT MISSIONS IN INDIA FROM THEIR COMMENCEMENT IN 1706 TO 1881

Sherry, L F *see* THESAURUS PSEUDO-NONNI QUONDAM PANOPOLITANI, PARAPHRASIS EVANGELII S. IOANNIS
Sherry, Richard *see* A TREATISE OF SCHEMES AND TROPES 1550 BY RICHARD SHERRY AND HIS TRANSLATION OF
Shershenevich, V *see*
- 2 X 2 EQUALS 5. LISTY IMAZHINISTA
- CARMINA. LIRIKA (1911-1912)
- ITAK ITOG
- LOSHAD' KAK LOSHAD'. TER'IA KNIGA LIRIKI
- ZELENAIA ULITSA

Sherwani, Haroon Khan *see* STUDIES IN MUSLIM POLITICAL THOUGHT AND ADMINISTRATION
Sherwood, Adiel *see* NOTES ON THE NEW TESTAMENT
SHERWOOD JOURNAL – Sherwood, OR. 2 Jan 1914-16 Jan 1915. – 1r – 1 – us U.O. Library [071]
Sherwood, Julia L *see* MEMOIRS OF ADIEL SHERWOOD
SHERWOOD NEWS SHEET – Sherwood OR. Oct 4 1911-Oct 1 1913 – 1 – us U.O. Library [071]
Sherwood, Robert *see* THE FRENCH TUTOUR
SHERWOOD VALLEY NEWS – (Set incl. Sherwood News-Sheet; Tualatin Valley News (Sherwood)) – Sherwood, OR. -w. 6 Jan 1927-4 Oct 1951. – 8r – 1 – us U.O. Library [071]
Shestakoza, M *see* TSERKOVNIKI I SEKTANSKIE VOZHAKI NA SLUZHBE FASHISTSKIKH RAZVEDOK
Shestov, L *see*
- VIACHESLAV IVANOV. RUSSKAIA MYSL'
- VLADIMIR SLOV'EV. SOVREMENNYE ZAPISKI

SHETEI IGGAROT AL ZEFAT ME-ET RABBI TEHUDAH ARYEH MI-MODENA / Tamar, D – Sefer Y. Baer. 1961. BJ-27-61 1 – 9 – ne IDC [956]
SHETLAND ADVERTISER – 1862-1863 – 1. 126 – £42.00r – uk Scot News [072]
SHETLAND FISHING NEWS – 1985-1993 – 1. 128-131 – £42.00r – uk Scot News [630]
SHETLAND ISLES, 1837 : BRITISH ISLES CENSUS DIRECTORIES PROJECT, SCOTLAND. VOL 48 – 1mf – 9 – A$9.00 – at Vine [941]
SHETLAND ISLES, 1915 : BRITISH ISLES CENSUS DIRECTORIES PROJECT, SCOTLAND. VOL 14 – 1mf – 9 – A$9.00 – at Vine [941]
SHETLAND JOURNAL – 1836-1839 – 1. 127 – £42.00r – uk Scot News [072]
SHETLAND JOURNAL – Lerwick. Scotland. -w. Sep 1836-Nov 1837. (1 reel) – 1 – uk British Libr Newspaper [072]
SHETLAND NEWS – 1893-1963 – 1. 8-78 – £42.00r – uk Scot News [072]
SHETLAND OIL NEWS – 1976-1992 – 1. 120 – £42.00r – uk Scot News [338]
SHETLAND TIMES – 1980-1992 – 1. 79-117 – £42.00r – uk Scot News [072]
SHEVCHENKO V LITERATURE I ISKUSSTVE / Komarov, M – Bibliograficheskii ukazatel' materialov dlia izucheniia zhizni i proizvedenii T. Shevchenka. Odessa. 1903. BR-5954 2 – 8 – ne IDC [460]
Shevelev, A *see* SISTEMATICHESKII KATALOG BIBLIOTEKI NIKOLAEVSKOI AKADEMII GENERAL'NAGO SHTABA; V. 2 (1866-1887)
SHEVET YEHUDAH – Amsterdam. 1648. BJ-43-103 1 – 9 – ne IDC [470]
SHEVET YEHUDAH – Cracow. 1591. BJ-43-102 1 – 9 – ne IDC [470]
Shevtsov, A *see* DESIAT'LET NA KOOPERATIVNOI RABOTE
Shevyrev, S *see* ISTORIIA IMP. MOSKOVSKOGO UNIVERSITETA, NAPISANNAIA K STOLETNEMU EGO IUBILEIU
SHI HUA – Oct 1930-Mar 1931. 1 ill. DL16f – 9 – 30.00 – cc Globe [073]
Shi, Shaoping *see* TOURIST TRAVEL MOTIVATIONS AND SATISFACTION STUDY OF CHINA/YANGZTE RIVER ADVENTURE TOURS
Shi, Xiaocai *see* EFFECT OF SODIUM AND WATER INTAKE ON PLASMA ALDOSTERONE DURING PROLONGED EXERCISE IN WARM ENVIRONMENT
SHIBALIM = SHEAVES – (In Hebrew) – Warsaw, PL. no7. 29 Jun 1922 – 1r – 1 – $25.00 – cn Can Microfilming [072]
Shibikah, Makki *see* BRITISH POLICY IN THE SUDAN 1882-1902
SHIBOLIM – (New York). 1909 – 1 – us A.J.P.C. [071]
SHICHANG BAO = MARKET NEWS – China. In Chinese. Current subscription. Annual delivery. 1980- . 1 reel per yr. As Shichang (Market Journal) until 1989. M D11 – 1 – $34.00r – cc Microforms [072]
SHICI QUYUCI HUISHI – Explanations of vocabulary in classical verses. Comp. by Zhang Xiang. 1 reel. M-J34 – 5 – 35.00 – cc Microforms [480]
SHIELD : THE ANTI-CONTAGIOUS DISEASES ACTS ASSOCIATION'S WEEKLY CIRCULAR / ed by Butler, Josephine E – (Cont as: Shield. The Official Organ of the British Committee of the Federation for the Abolition of State Regulation of Vice. NS: London 1897-1916(Mar). Cont as: Shield. A Review of Moral and Social Hygiene. London 1916(Apr)-1970(Nov). Missing: 1905-1908(79-103); 1909-1910(107, 111-113); 1915-1916(151, p17-24)) – London, 1870-86 – 153mf – 9 – W-30/1 – ne IDC [360]
THE SHIELD – Waco. Texas. 1947-50 – 1 – Dfl856.00 – us Baptist [240]
Shield, W *see*
- ROSINA [BY] SHIELD [SIC]. OVERTURE
- THE STREAMLET. A FAVORITE SONG

SHIELDS ADVOCATE – South Shields, England. Shields Advertiser & Tyneside Advocate. -w. Jan 1855-May 1858. 3 reels – 1 – uk British Libr Newspaper [072]
SHIELDS AND TYNEMOUTH ARGUS – South Shields, England. -w. Sept 1881-March 1882. 1 reel – 1 – uk British Libr Newspaper [072]
Shields, Charles Woodruff *see*
- THE HISTORIC EPISCOPATE
- RELIGION AND SCIENCE IN THEIR RELATION TO PHILOSOPHY
- THE SCIENTIFIC EVIDENCES OF REVEALED RELIGION
- THE UNITED CHURCH OF THE UNITED STATES

SHIELDS DAILY NEWS – Tynemouth, England. -d. Aug 1864-Dec 1868; 1873-74. 12 reels – 1 – uk British Libr Newspaper [072]
SHIELDS DAILY STANDARD – South Shields, England. -d. Jan-March 1881. 1 2 reel – 1 – uk British Libr Newspaper [072]
Shields, John A *see* FEDERAL COURTS AND PRACTICE: ALL SHERMAN LAW TRUST PROSECUTIONS AND SYLLABUS OF EQUITY, JURISDICTION, PLEADING AND PRACTICE
Shields, Joseph J *see* SOCIAL THOUGHT
Shields, Lionell *see* A COMPARISON BETWEEN THE NUMBER OF EUROPEAN AMERICANS, AFRICAN AMERICANS, AND OTHER MINORITY RACES WHO ENTER PHASE 1 AND PHASE 2 CARDIAC REHABILITATION PROGRAMS
SHIELDS MORNING MAIL – South Shields, England. -d. Aug 1899-Feb 1901. 6 1 2 reels – 1 – uk British Libr Newspaper [072]
SHIELD'S TAMORA LYRE – Tamora, NE. -w. May 1901-Aug 1913; Mar 1918 – 1 – us NE Hist [071]
THE SHIELDSMAN – South Shields, England. -w. May 1932-Sept 1939. 8 1 2 reels – 1 – uk British Libr Newspaper [072]
Shier, Nathan W *see* EFFECTS OF NUTRITIONAL INTERVENTION ON BLOOD GLUCOSE LEVELS IN WOMEN (AGE 73-85)
SHIFTING AGRICULTURE AND SUSTAINABLE DEVELOPMENT : AN INTERDISCIPLINARY STUDY FROM NORTH-EASTERN INDIA / Ramakrishnan, P S – 1992 – 424p – 9 – 92-3-102749-2 – Co-published with Parthenon Publishing, UK – fr UNESCO [630]
SHIFTING CULTIVATION AND SOIL CONSERVATION IN AFRICA – 1978 – 254p – it F.A.O. [631]
SHIGAKU ZASSHI – "Journal of Historical Science." v. 1-38. Kyoto. 1889-1927. BCH-475 2 – 8 – ne IDC [500]
Shigeta, Fujii *see* RYOSEN'EKI KAIKO DAN
SHIH CHIEH CHIH SHIH CH'U PAN SHE, PEKING – (Documents of Communist Parties in Indonesia, India and Japan). In Chinese. SE 6239 1. 1957 – 9 – ne IDC [335]
SHIH CHING – The book of Chinese poetry...collection of ballads, sagas, hymns, and other pieces..; or, Classic of Poetry. Metrically trans. by Clement F.R. Allen.London: K. Paul, Trench, Truebner, 1891. 528p – 1 – us U.W. Library [800]
Shih ch'uan, San szu lang *see* CHINESE CHRISTIAN MONOGRAPH (CCC281)
SHIH NIEN LAI CHIH CHUNG-KUO CHING-CHI – (Chinese Economy in the Past Ten Years). Compiled by Tan Hsi-hung. Shanghai, 1948. 3v. 1 reel – 1 – 23.50 – us Chinese Res [950]
SHIH PAO = THE EASTERN TIMES: SHANG-HAI (IN CHINESE NEWSPAPER) – (This microfilm edition does not contain the films of November and December, 1911; January, 1921 to June, 1923, January and February, 1827 because the originals are not locatable) – Daily newspaper, Shang-hai, 1909-1937 – 299r – 1 – Y2,100,000.00 – ja Yushodo [950]
SHIH PAO – Peking. China. 1928-44 – 1 – 287.10 – us Chinese Res [072]
Shih, Tao-hung *see* THE SUCCESS AND FAILURE OF THE CHURCH (CCC282)
SHIH YEH PU YUEH K'AN. MONTHLY BULLETIN / China. Ministry of Industries – 2v. Nanking. 1936-37. Lacking: v. 2 (8-9) 1937. BCH-1079 1 – 9 – ne IDC [380]
SHIH-CH'ENG HSIEN-CHIH – 1892, 9, 2. BCH-632 2 – 8 – ne IDC [950]
SHIH-CHIEH CHIH-SHIH – (World Affairs). Peking. 1950-54. Available: v. 22 (24) 1950; v. 23 (4, 5, 7-12, 14-19, 23-24) 1951; v. 24 (14, 15, 17-19, 23, 25); (1-4, 6, 8-10, 12-14, 15-18, 22, 23, 27, 29-31, 33, 34, 37, 38, 42, 44-50) 1952; 1953; (1-8, 10-24) 1954; 1955. BCH-928 2 – 8 – ne IDC [320]
SHIH-HSUEH CHUAN-K'AN – Journal of Historical Research. v. 1 (1-4). Canton. 1935-38. BCH-339 2 – 8 – ne IDC [073]
SHIH-HSUEH HSIAO-HSI – Historical Newsletters. v. 1 (1-8). Peiping. 1936-37. Lacking: v. 1 (6). BCH-340 2 – 8 – ne IDC [900]
SHIH-HSUEH LUN TS'UNG – Historical Review. v. 1-2. Peking. 1934-35. BCH-809 2 – 8 – ne IDC [900]
SHIH-MSUEH YU TI-HSUEH – (History and Geography). v. 1-4. Shanghai. 1926-28. quarterly. BCH-341 1 – 9 – ne IDC [950]
SHIH-P'ING CHOU-CHIH – 1759; 1780, 8. BCH-669 2 – 8 – ne IDC [950]
SHIH-TI HSUEH-PAO – (Journal of Historico-Geography). 4 v. Nanking. 1921-26. Lacking: v. 1 (2, 4) 1921. BCH-342 1 – 9 – ne IDC [950]
SHIH-TSUNG CHOU-CHIH – 1717, 2. BCH-680 2 – 8 – ne IDC [950]
SHIHUA – The Truth. Oct 1930-Mar 1931. F C5. In Chinese – 9 – $4.50f – cc Microforms [073]
SHIH-YEH T'UNG-CHI – Industrial Statistics. Nanking: Ministry of Industries, 1933-36. 4v. bimonthly. BCH-343/1 – 9 – ne IDC [310]
SHIJIE JINGJI DAOBAO – Wourld Economic Herald. China. In Chinese. Current subscription. Annual delivery. 1980-89. 1 reel per yr. M D9 – 1 – $34.00r – cc Microforms [072]
SHIJIE RIBAO – (May 1926-Jun 1937. 62r. $2,790.00; Nov 1945-Feb 1949. 6r. $270.00) – China. The World Daily. M/B5 – 1 – cc Microforms [072]
SHILLING BOOK...NEW TESTAMENT HISTORY FOR NATIONAL AND ELEMENTARY SCHOOLS / Maclear, George Frederick – London: Macmillan, 1875 – 1mf – 9 – us A.T.L.A. [240]
Shillock, Anna Felicia *see* SHILLOCK PAPERS
Shillock, Matilda *see* SHILLOCK PAPERS
SHILLOCK PAPERS / Shillock, Matilda & Shillock, Anna Felicia – 1854-1905. 2 rolls including filmed inventory – 1 – $30.00r – us M.H.S. [920]
Shilo, N A *see* GEOLOGY OF THE PACIFIC OCEAN
SHILOH BAPTIST CHURCH. BERNICE, LOUISIANA : CHURCH RECORDS – Aug 1865-2 Aug 1919 – 1 – 30.42 – us Baptist [240]
SHILOH BAPTIST CHURCH. CARSON, VIRGINIA : CHURCH RECORDS – 1845-1960 – 1 – 35.73 – us Baptist [240]
SHILOH BAPTIST CHURCH. JASPER COUNTY. GEORGIA : CHURCH RECORDS – 1839-59 – 1 – 9.63 – us Baptist [240]
Shimakawa, Tsuguyo *see* EFFECTS OF VISUAL TRAINING ON VISUAL PURSUIT, CATCHING, AND ATTENTIVENESS
Shimidzu, Linda K *see* THE EFFECT OF SEVEN WEEKS OF TRAINING ON THE DIETARY INTAKE AND SKINFOLDS OF A WOMAN 82 YEARS OF AGE
SHIMOFUSA SAKURA-HAN HOTTA-KE MONJO = DOCUMENTS OF THE HOTTAS, FEUDAL LORD OF THE SAKURA DOMAIN (CHIBA PREF.), IN TOKUGAWA / ed by Ohtani, S – 1172 items – 238r – 1 – Y2,380,000.00 – ja Yushodo [950]
Shimonovitz, D (Shimoni) *see* SA'AR U-DEMAMAH
Shimura, Kenichi *see* THE EFFECTS OF LEISURE EDUCATION ON LIFE SATISFACTION AND LEISURE SATISFACTION AMONG JAPANESE AMERICAN OLDER ADULTS
SHIN AICHI – July 1888-August 1942 – 336r – 1 – Y3,242,400 – ja Japan Micro [950]
SHIN JAVA – (Lacking: 1944, V.1,(1-3). Microfiche Nos 408-422) – Djakarta: Jawa Shinbunsha, 2604-2605.-1944-1945. 2v – 15mf – 9 – SE-2002/1 – ne IDC [950]
SHINA KAKUSHO KEIZAI JIJO – Tokyo, Feb. 1936. v.1-3. Economic data on the Chinese provinces. In Japanese. 1 reel – 1 – 16.50 – us Chinese Res [330]
SHINA KENKYU = REPORTS OF THE STUDY OF CHINA / ed by Shoin, Toa Dobun – In Japanese. v1-70, 1920-1944 – 20r – 1 – Y231,000.00 – ja Yushodo [950]
SHINA SAIKIN DAIJI NEMPYO / Shotaro, Kojima – Tokyo, 1942. 980 p. Chronology of major historical events in China, 1840-1941. (J 222.0032 Ko39) – 1 – 35.00r – us Hoover Inst Photo [520]
SHINA SYO-BETSU ZENSHI = COMPLETE GEOGRAPHICAL DESCRIPTIONS BY PROVINCES IN ALL CHINA / ed by Toadobunkai, Tokyo – (In Japanese) – 18v. 1917-20 – 9r – 1 – Y102,000.00 – ja Yushodo [910]
SHINAGAKU. "SINOLOGY."KYOTO. CH 479. LACKING: V. 4; 1927-28, PT. 4. 1920-1942 – 9 – ne IDC [950]
SHINAICHI – Japan, 1888-1942 – 336r – 1 – inquire – us Ross [072]
SHINANO MAINICHI SHIMBUN – Japan, 1873-1984 – 1027r – 1 – inquire – us Ross [072]
SHINANO MAINICHI SHIMBUN – July 1873-Dec 1994 – 1100r – 1 – Y11,119,500 – ja Japan Micro [950]
SHINGLE *see* PHILADELPHIA LAWYER
Shining Light Staff *see* CHARACTERS OF MODERN TIMES (CCC283)
Shinn, Benjamin *see* BLACKFORD AND GRANT COUNTIES
Shinn, George Wolfe *see* SOME MODERN SUBSTITUTES FOR CHRISTIANITY
Shinn, Josiah H *see*
- PIONEERS AND MAKERS OF ARKANSAS

Shinn, William H *see* THE COUNTY OF WILLIAMS
SHIN-SHAKAI = NEW SOCIETY – Japan, 1915-20 – 4r – 1 – inquire – us Ross [072]
SHIP DRAWING COLLECTION / Smith, Walter. (Marine City, Michigan) – 1900-20 – 1r – 1 – $32.50r – us Archival [740]
THE SHIP OF THE LINE IN BATTLE : WITH SPECIAL REFERENCE TO THE RUSSO-JAPANESE WAR, 1904-5 / Custance, Reginald Neville – 1912 – 9 – $20.00 – uk Libr Preservation [355]
SHIP REGISTERS AND ENROLLMENTS / U.S. Work Projects Administration. Connecticut – 1762-1867 – 9 – $575.00 – us Opus [380]
SHIPBUILDER – v6. 1911 – 1r – 1 – us Ross [623]
THE SHIPBUILDER : 1936-1955 / Industrial Union of Marine and Shipbuilding Workers – (Coll title: Labor Union Periodicals, Pt 1) – 5r – 1 – $675.00 – 1-55655-248-3 – us UPA [331]
THE SHIPBUILDER'S ASSISTANT, OR MARINE ARCHITECTURE / Sutherland, William – Rev. and improved. 1794 – 9 – uk Libr Preservation [623]
SHIPBUILDING AND SHIPREPAIRING INDUSTRY IN INDONESIA / Moeller, A – SE-5573 1. 1960 – 9 – ne IDC [623]
SHIPIN KEXUE = FOOD SCIENCE – (1983 $3.50f; 1984 $4.50f) – 1982-. F-P246 – 9 – cc Microforms [660]

SHIPIN YU FAXIAO GONGYE – Food and Fermentation Industries. 1983-84. F/P 284 – 9 – $4.50f – cc Microforms [660]

SHIPIN ZHOUBAO = THE FOOD WEEKLY – 1984. M-D61 – 1 reel – 1 – $23.00r – cc Microforms [660]

Shipler, Guy Emery *see* A LETTER

Shipley, Maynard *see* NEW LIGHT ON THE TEN COMMANDMENTS

SHIPOVNIK : LITERATURNO-KHUDOZHESTVENNYIE AL'MANAKH – Leningrad. v1-26. 1907-17 – 3r – 1 – us Ross [460]

SHIPOVNIK – Literaturno-Khudozhestvennyye Al'Manakhi. St Petersburg. v. 1-26. 1907-1917 – 1 – us NY Public [700]

SHIPOVNIK – v1. 1922 – 1r – 1 – us Ross [073]

Shipp, Barnard *see* THE HISTORY...HERNANDO DE SOTO

Shipp, Eli Richard *see*
- QUESTIONS AND ANSWERS ON CRIMINAL LAW AND PROCEDURE.
- QUESTIONS AND ANSWERS ON PARTNERSHIP.
- A SELECTION OF CASES ILLUSTRATING EQUITY PLEADING AND PRACTICE.

SHIPPENSBURG NEWS – Shippensburg, PA., 1849-1899 – 13 – $25.00r – us I.M.R. [071]

SHIPPING AND COMMERCIAL LIST AND NEW YORK PRICE CURRENT – New York. v. 1-80. 1815 1816-June 30 1894 – 1 – us NY Public [071]

SHIPPING AND MERCANTILE GAZETTE – London, England. -d. 12 March 1838-Dec 1914. 218 reels – 1 – uk British Libr Newspaper [072]

SHIPPING GAZETTE – Sydney, Australia. -w. July 1846-March 1848; Jan 1850-Dec 1851; 1883. 2 reels – 1 – uk British Libr Newspaper [072]

SHIPPING GUIDE – (Also known as: Th e Guide) – San Francisco, CA. 1906-66; 1970-71; May-Aug 1972 – 72r – 1 – $3,600.00 – B02859 – us Library Micro [071]

SHIPPING GUIDE – Sydney, Juli 5 1887-Dec 31 1890 – 1 – at Pascoe [072]

SHIPPING GUIDE *see* THE GUIDE

SHIPPING LISTS FOR EAST FLORIDA / Great Britain. Naval Office – 1764-69.BRRAM – 1 – uk Microform Academic [975]

SHIPPING LISTS FOR GEORGIA / Great Britain. Naval Office – 1752-67.BRRAM – 1 – uk Microform Academic [975]

SHIPPING LISTS FOR HALIFAX, NOVA SCOTIA / Great Britain. Naval Office – 1730-1820 – 3r – 1 – uk Microform Academic [971]

SHIPPING LISTS FOR JAMAICA / Great Britain. Naval Office – 1683-1818. BRRAM – 7r – 1 – uk Microform Academic [972]

SHIPPING LISTS FOR MARYLAND / Great Britain. Naval Office – 1689-1754. BRRAM – 1 – uk Microform Academic [975]

SHIPPING LISTS FOR MASSACHUSETTS / Great Britain. Naval Office – 1686-1765. BRRAM – 2r – 1 – uk Microform Academic [975]

SHIPPING LISTS FOR NEW HAMPSHIRE / Great Britain. Naval Office – 1723-69.BRRAM – 1 – uk Microform Academic [975]

SHIPPING LISTS FOR NEW JERSEY / Great Britain. Naval Office – 1722-64.BRRAM – 1 – uk Microform Academic [975]

SHIPPING LISTS FOR NEW YORK, 1713-65 / Great Britain. Naval Office – 3r – 1 – uk Microform Academic [975]

SHIPPING LISTS FOR SOUTH CAROLINA / Great Britain. Naval Office – 1716-67.BRRAM – 2r – 1 – uk Microform Academic [975]

SHIPPING LISTS FOR VIRGINIA / Great Britain. Naval Office – 1698-1769. BRRAM – 4r – 1 – uk Microform Academic [975]

SHIPPING LISTS FOR WEST INDIES (EXCLUDING JAMAICA) / Great Britain. Naval Office – BRRAM – 15r – 1 – uk Microform Academic [324]

SHIPPING NEWS – Portland, OR. -d. 1956-63 – 1 – 264.00 – us Oregon Hist [071]

SHIPPING NEWS *see* HERALD ENTERPRISE

SHIPPING WORLD – London, England. -m, -w. May 1883-Dec 1918. 57 1 2 reels – 1 – uk British Libr Newspaper [072]

SHIPPING WORLD AND SHIPBUILDER – 1898-1; v168- 5,6,9 – us UMI [623]

SHIPS OF FOOLS / Brant, Sebastian; ed by Dongen, Wim van – 15 titles – 9 – ne IDC [430]

SHIPS PICTURES INDEX 1491-1991 : AN INDEX TO SHIPS PICTURES IN PRINT / Hall, Nick Vine – 3mf – 9 – A$21.00 – 1-86404-222-2 – at Vine [380]

Shipton, Anna *see* THE SECRET OF THE LORD

Shipton, Clifford K *see*
- EARLY AMERICAN IMPRINTS, 1639-1800
- EARLY AMERICAN IMPRINTS, 1801-1819

Shipton, Geoffrey M *see* NOTES ON THE MEGGIDO POTTERY

THE SHIPWRECK : A COMIC OPERA IN TWO ACTS OP. 40 / Arnold, Samuel – London: Longman, Clementi & Co, 180- – 1 – us Sibley [780]

SHIPWRECKS – MAHOGANY SHIP – 1890-1989. Reports etc – 7mf – 9 – at Corangamite [360]

SHIR HA-YIHUD – Cracow. 1609. BJ-43-105 1 – 9 – ne IDC [470]

SHIR HA-YIHUD – Isny. 1540-42? BJ-43-104 1 – 9 – ne IDC [470]

SHIR VE-ZEMER NA'EH AL OREKH HA-GALUT – Lublin. 1624. BJ-43-106 1 – 9 – ne IDC [470]

Shiras, Oliver Perry *see* EQUITY PRACTICE IN THE UNITED STATES CIRCUIT COURTS

SHIRAT HA-ZAMIR / Buki Ben Yogli (Katzenelson, J L B) – Tel-Aviv. 1944. BJ-422-10 1 – 9 – ne IDC [470]

SHIREI / Kaminer, I – Odessa. 1905. BJ-422-34 1 – 9 – ne IDC [470]

SHIREI ANACREON / Tchernichowsky, S – Warsaw. 1920. BJ-422-93 1 – 9 – ne IDC [470]

SHIREI SEFAT EVER / Mandelkern, S – 2v. Leipzig. 1882-89. BJ-422-58 1 – 9 – ne IDC [470]

SHIREI SEFAT KODESH / L EBENSOHN, A D – Ed. 2. Vilna. 3v. 1861-1869 – 9mf – 9 – ne IDC [810]

SHIREI SEFAT KODESH / Lebensohn, A D – ed. 2. 3 v. Vilna. 1861-69. BJ-422-42 1 – 9 – ne IDC [470]

SHIREI TIFERET / Wessely, N H – pts. 1-5. Berlin. 1789-92; pt. 6. Prague. 1829. BJ-422-98 1 – 9 – ne IDC [470]

SHIRIM / Piera, M da; ed by Brody, H – (Yediot ha-Makhon Le-Heker ha-Shirah ha-Ivrit). v. 4. 1938. BJ-421-73 1 – 9 – ne IDC [470]

SHIRIM NIVHARIM / Shapira, K A – Warsaw. 1911. BJ-422-80 1 – 9 – ne IDC [470]

SHIRLEY 1729-1892 – (Mf 1-4,8: Town Records 1753-91. Mf 4-11: Intentions 1769-1804. Mf 4-5: Marriages 1762-1811. Mf 5-7: Births 1729-1821. Mf 8,25: Deaths 1752-1813. Mf 9-10: Births, Deaths 1729-1822. Mf 11,13: Marriages 1762-1811. Mf 11-13: Town Records 1753-86. Mf 14-15: Births, Deaths 1788-1843. Mf 16: Marriages 1825-43; Out-of-Town Marriages 1750-99. Mf 17-20: Intentions 1805-1905. Mf 18: Marriages 1806-25. Mf 21-22: Intentions Index 1848-1905. Mf 23-51: Town Records 1774-1896. Mf 52: Births 1800-42. Mf 53-54: Marriages & Intentions 1800-42. Mf 54: Deaths 1800-42. Mf 55: Births 1843-55. Mf 56: Marriages & Deaths 1843-56. Mf 57-61: Vital Records 1856-92. Mf 62-66: Birth Index 1848-1900) – (mf ed 1994) – 66mf – 9 – 0-87623-182-2 – us Holbrook [920]

Shirley, Evelyn Philip *see* THE NOBLE AND GENTLE MEN OF ENGLAND; OR, NOTES TOUCHING THE ARMS AND DESCENTS OF THE ANCIENT KNIGHTLY AND GENTLE HOUSES OF ENGLAND

Shirley, J *see* THE TRIUMPH OF PEACE

Shirley, James *see*
- AN ESSAY TOWARDS AN UNIVERSAL AND RATIONAL GRAMMAR
- GRAMMATICA ANGLO-LATINA

Shirley, John L *see* EVERYBODY'S LAW BOOK

Shirley, W *see* A NARRATIVE OF THE PRINCIPAL CIRCUMSTANCES RELATIVE TO THE REV. MR. WESLEY'S LATE CONFERENCE HELD IN BRISTOL, AUGUST THE 6TH, 1771,...

Shirley, W W *see* ROYAL AND OTHER HISTORICAL LETTERS LLUSTR. OF THE REIGN OF HENRY 2 (RS27)

Shirokogoroff, S M *see* SOCIAL ORGANIZATION OF THE NORTHERN TUNGUS WITH INTRODUCTORY CHAPTERS CONCERNING GEOGRAPHICAL DISTRIBUTION AND HISTORY OF THESE GROUPS

Shirton, J *see* ON NEW LICHENS FROM AUSTRALIA AND NEW ZEALAND

Shishkin, Ivan Ivanovich *see* OPIS' DOKUMENTAL'NYKH MATERIALOV LICHNOGO FONDA NO. 917

Shishkov, A *see* MORSKOI SLOVAR' NA ANGLIISKOM, FRANTSUSKOM I ROSSIISKOM IAZYKAKH

Shishkov, A S *see* SOBRANIE SOCHINENII I PEREVODOV

Shishmarev, V F *see* FRANTSUZSKIE RUKOPISI GOSUDARSTVENNOI PUBLICHNOI BIBLIOTEKI

SHISOKYOKU YOKO / Japan. Shisokyoku. Thought Control Bureau. Japanese Ministry of Education – Tokyo. A study of Japanese socialism and nationalism. 389 p. 1934 – 1 – 35.00r – us Hoover Inst Photo [072]

SHIVBE ELOHIM: ZEH SEFER HADAR HU – Oran: Impr. Ad. Perrier, 1855.288p. Includes some Arabic text in Hebrew characters. Jewish religious poetry – 1 – us U.W. Library [800]

SHIYAN SHENGWU XUEBAO – Acta Biologiae Experimentalis Sinica. In Chinese but English abstracts to the main articles. F p38 – 9 – 4.00f – cc Microforms [073]

SHIYOU DIQIU WULI KANTAN – Oil Geophysical Prospecting. In Chinese, with English abstracts to the main articles – 9 – $4.00f – cc Microforms [550]

SHIYOU WU TAN – Geophysical Prospecting for Petroleum. In Chinese, with English abstracts to the main articles – 9 – $4.00f – cc Microforms [550]

SHIYOU XUEBAO – Acta Petrolei Sinica. In Chinese, with English abstracts to the main articles – 9 – $4.00f – cc Microforms [660]

SHIYOU YU TIANRANQI DIZHI – Oil and Gas Geology. In Chinese but English abstracts to the main articles. F p127 – 9 – 4.00f – cc Microforms [073]

Shklovskii, V *see*
- CHULKOV I LEVSHIN
- O MAIAKOVSKOM
- "ZAUMNYI IAZYK" I POEZIIA. SBORNIKI PO TEORII POETICHESKOGO IAZYKA

SHKOL'NOE ZAKONODATEL'STVO V RSFSR / Charnoluskii, V – Moscow, 1927. 127p. BR-9438/1 – 9 – ne IDC [370]

Shliapnikov, D D *see* KOOPERATSIIA I REVOLIUTSIIA

SH'MA – (v.11-. 1980- 5,6,9) – v.1-. 1970- – 1 – us UMI [073]

Shmidt, G R *see*
- KAK UCHREDIT' I OTKRYT' KRDITNOE TOVARISHCHESTVO
- KOOPERATIVNYI KREDIT

Shmidt, Sigurd Ottovich *see* OPISI TSARSKOGO ARKHIVA XVIVEKA I ARKHIVA POSOL'SKOGO PRIKAZA 1614 GODA

DOS SHMUEL BUKH – Cracow. 1578. BJ-43-107 1 – 9 – ne IDC [220]

SHMUEL BUKH – Cracow. 1593. BJ-43-108 1 – 9 – ne IDC [220]

Shmurlo, E F *see*
- BIBLIOGRAFICHESKII SPISOK LITERATURNYKH TRUDOV KIEVSKAGO MITROPOLITA EVGENIIA BOLKHOVITINOVA. 1
- MITROPOLIT EVGENII KAK UCHENII. RANNIE GODY ZHIZNI 1767-1804
- PETR VELIKII V OTSENKE SOVREMENNIKOV I POTOMSTVA
- PETR VELIKII V RUSSKOI LITERATURE

Shmurlo, E G *see* VOL'TER I EGO KNIGA O PETRE VELIKOM

Shmygin, I P *see* BOL'SHEVISTSKIE ORGANIZATSII SREDNEGO POVOLZH'IA V BOR'BE ZA KREST'IANSKIE MASSY V REVOLIUTSII 1905-1907 GG

DER SHNAYDER-ARBAYTER – Lwow, PL. v2 no2. 1 Feb 1913 – 1r – 1 – $25.00 – cn Can Microfilming [072]

SHO KAI-SEKI TO GENDAI SHINA / Bunroku, Yoshioka – Tokyo, 1936. 250 p. Chiang Kai-Shek's China and its relations with Japan. (J 312.22 Y93) – 1 – 35.00r – us Hoover Inst Photo [950]

SHOAL CREEK BAPTIST CHURCH. OCONEE COUNTY. SOUTH CAROLINA : CHURCH RECORDS – 1796-1853 – 1 – 12.80 – us Baptist [240]

SHOAL CREEK BAPTIST CHURCH. OCONEE COUNTY. SOUTH CAROLINA : CHURCH RECORDS – 1796-1853 – 1 – 14.40 – us Baptist [240]

SHOALHAVEN NEWS (NOWRA) – May 11 1867-Dec 25 1873. Jan 2 1875-Dec 28 1895. Jan 7 1899-Dec 20 1890 – 9 – at Pascoe [072]

SHOALHAVEN TELEGRAPH- – 1879-1937 – 19r – 1 – at Pascoe [072]

Shochat, A *see* HA-YEHUDIM BI-YERUSHALAYIM BA-ME'AH HA-18

SHOE AND LEATHER JOURNAL *see* CANADIAN FOOTWEAR JOURNAL

Shoemaker, Floyd C *see*
- A HISTORY OF MISSOURI AND MISSOURIANS
- MISSOURI'S HALL OF FAME

Shoemaker, William David *see* TRADE-MARKS

Shofman, G *see* SHALLEKHET

Shoin, Toa Dobun *see* SHINA KENKYU

SHOKEN KEIZAI SHIRYO = HISTORICAL TREND OF THE JAPAN STOCK EXCHANGE, 1878-1945 – (Tokyo Stock Exchange Monthly Report, 1886-1924. T.S.E. Monthly Statistical Report, 1930-43. Japan Securities Exchange Monthly Statistical Report, 1943-44. T.S.E. Bulletins, 1926-43. Japan Securities Exchange Survey Monthly Report, 1943-44. T.S.E., Its History and Statistics, 1878-1907. A History of Tokyo Stock Exchange, 1878-1915. A 50-Year History of Tokyo Stock Exchange, 1878-1927. A History of Tokyo Stock Exchange, 1828-1937. Annual Reports of Tokyo Stock Exchange, 1878-1943) – (Shoken Keizai Shiryo) – 38r – 1 – Y370,000.00 – ja Yushodo [332]

SHOKI NIHON EIGAKU SHIRYO SHUSEI = COLLECTION OF HISTORICAL MATERIALS PERTAINING TO THE DEVELOPMENT OF ENGLISH LANGUAGE STUDY IN JAPAN (1840-84) – 230 items in 295v – 34r – 1 – Y357,000.00 – ja Yushodo [420]

SHOKI NIHON RAN, FUTSU, DOKU, RO GO BUNKEN-SHU = COLLECTION OF EARLY JAPANESE MANUALS OF DUTCH, FRENCH, GERMAN AND RUSSIAN LANGUAGE – 1793-1904. 154 items in 227v – 34r – 1 – Y357,000.00 – ja Yushodo [400]

Shola, J J *see* THE RELATIONSHIP BETWEEN TRAIT AND STATE ANXIETY AND TRAIT AND STATE SELF-CONFIDENCE IN HIGH SCHOOL BASEBALL PLAYERS

SHOMER ZIYYON HA-NE'EMAN – Ed. by J. Ettlinger and S. J. Enoch. 222 nrs. 1846-56. BJ-100-185 1 – 9 – ne IDC [270]

SHONAN SHIMBUN – Singapore. Feb-Sept 1945 – 1r – 1 – us L of C Photodup [072]

Shontz, Howard B *see* A SURVEY OF SOME PHASES OF ADMINISTRATION FACULTY OF ECONOMICS, UNIV. OF INDONESIA

Shoolbred, James *see* LETTERBOOKS AND JOURNALS

SHOOTING INDUSTRY – 1986- – 1,5,6,9 – us UMI [790]

SHOOTING TIMES – Peoria. Ill. 1966- – 1 – us UMI [071]

SHOP REVIEW – Detroit, Mich. v. 2-26. 1905-1929 – 1 – us NY Public [073]

SHOP STEWARDS' MOVEMENT JOURNALS OF THE 1930'S – London – 1 – uk World [331]

SHOP TALK ON SPAIN. THE TRADE UNIONS AND THE WAR IN SPAIN / Joseph, Don – N.Y., 193? Fiche W975. (Blodgett Collection of Spanish Civil War Pamphlets) – 9 – us H.U. College Libr [946]

SHOPPER – Poplar. Mont. 1970- – 1 – us UMI [071]

SHOPPERS EXTRA : FRESNO BEE – Fresno, CA. 1983 – 1r – 1 – $50.00 – R04028 – us Library Micro [071]

SHOPPING GUIDE – Lincoln, NE. -w. Mar 1933-Feb 1942; Jan 1943-Aug 1951 – 1 – us NE Hist [071]

SHOPPING GUIDE – Lincoln, NE. -w. Sep 1951-Nov 1953 – 1 – us NE Hist [071]

SHOPPING NEWS – (Bi-weekly advertising newspaper) – Cleveland, Cuyahoga, OH. 1 Jul 1929-20 Dec 1945 – 30r – 1 – us Western Res [071]

SHOPPING NEWS – Daly City, CA. 1939-44 – 2r – 1 – $100.00 – B02160 – us Library Micro [071]

SHOPPING NEWS – San Francisco, CA. 1945-50 – 25r – 1 – $1,250.00 – C02860 – us Library Micro [071]

SHOPPING NEWS – San Francisco. Calif. -w. 1945-50 – 1 – us UMI [071]

SHOPPING NEWS REMINDER – Reno, NV. 1947; Jun, Sep 1949 – 1r – 1 – $50.00 – U04716 – us Library Micro [071]

SHORE NEWS – St. Clair. MI. 1926-31 – 1 – us UMI [071]

SHORE PRESS – Asbury Park. N.J. 1905-1919 – 1 – us UMI [071]

Shore, Thomas Teignmouth *see* THE FIRST EPISTLE TO THE CORINTHIANS

SHOREHAM BAPTIST CHURCH. SHOREHAM, VERMONT : CHURCH RECORDS – 1794-1837 – 1 – 9.90 – us Baptist [240]

SHORT ACCOUNT, 1772-1792 / Hodgson, S – (Coll title: The People Called Methodists, Phase 2: Primary Sources 1738-1800) – 4mf – 9 – MP-631-1 – ne IDC [240]

SHORT ACCOUNT AND JOURNAL, 1775-1789 / Rogers, H A – (Coll title: The People Called Methodists, Phase 2: Primary Sources 1738-1800) – 10mf – 9 – MP-634/1 – ne IDC [240]

A SHORT ACCOUNT OF GOD'S DEALINGS WITH MRS. ELIZABETH MAXFIELD,... : FROM THE TIME OF HER BEING AWAKENED AT THE BEGINNING OF MR. WHITEFIELD'S PREACHING TILL HER DEATH,... / Maxfield, T – London, 1778 – 1mf – 9 – MP-526/1 – ne IDC [240]

A SHORT ACCOUNT OF THE LAND REVENUE AND ITS ADMINISTRATION IN INDIA: WITH A SKETCH OF THE LAND TENURES / Baden-Powell, Baden Henry – 2nd ed., 1907 rev. by Sir Thomas Holderness with an appendix (Dec 1912). Oxford: Clarendon Press, 1913. vi,(2),268p. fold. map – 1 – us U.W. Library [336]

SHORT AND FUNDAMENTAL INSTRUCTIONS FOR LEARNING THOROUGH BASS / Heck, J C – 1760 – 9 – us Sibley [780]

SHORT AND MEDIUM-TERM PROSPECTS FOR EXPORTS OF MANUFACTURES FROM SELECTED DEVELOPING COUNTRIES / United Nations. Conference on Trade and Development (UNCTAD) – Algeria. 1970. BNE-8670 1 – 9 – ne IDC [338]

Short, C W *see* SURVEY OF THE ARCHITECTURE OF COMPLETED PROJECTS OF THE PUBLIC WORKS ADMINISTRATION

A SHORT CATALOGUE / India House Library – London, 1933 – 12mf – 9 – ne IDC [950]

A SHORT COMMENTARY ON THE BOOK OF DANIEL FOR THE USE OF STUDENTS / Bevan, Anthony Ashley – (Includes index of Hebrew & Aramaic words used) – Cambridge, [England]: University Press, 1892 – 1mf – 9 – 0-8370-2322-X – 1985-0322 – us A.T.L.A. [220]

A SHORT COMPARATIVE GRAMMAR OF ENGLISH AND GERMAN AS TRACED BACK TO THEIR COMMON ORIGIN AND CONTRASTED WITH THE CLASSICAL LANGUAGES / Henry, Victor – Transl. by the author. London: Swan Sonnenschein, New York: Macmillan, 1894. xxviii,394p – 1 – us U.W. Library [420]

SHORT COURSE FOR SEEDMEN; PROCEEDINGS / Mississippi State University. Agricultural Experiment Station. Agricultural and Forestry Experiment Station – 1970-82.No.13-24 – 1,5 – us Spaulding [631]

SHORT COURSE FOR SEEDSMEN. PROCEEDINGS / Mississippi. Agricultural Experiment Station. State College – 1960-69 – 1,5,6 – us Spaulding [631]

SHORT CREEK REPUBLICAN – Galena. Kan. 1883-1893 – 1 – us UMI [071]

SHORT CUTS BY BIRDS TO NECTARIES / Swynnerton, C F M – 617 2. 1915 – 8 – ne IDC [590]

A SHORT DECLARATION OF THE MYSTERY OF INIQUITY / Helwys, Thomas – 1612 – 1 – 14.70 – us Baptist [240]

A SHORT DESCRIPTION OF THE ATMOSPHERIC ENGINE, 1734 / Triewald, M – 3mf – 7 – uk Microform Academic [600]

A SHORT DISCOURS...UPON CHIRURGERIE / Fioravanti, L – M 347. 1580 – 9 – ne IDC [617]

A SHORT EXPOSITION OF THE EPISTLE TO THE GALATIANS...AS A TEXT-BOOK / Stevens, George Barker – Hartford: Student Pub., 1890. 1 fiche – 9 – us A.T.L.A. [240]

A SHORT GRAMMAR OF THE GREEK NEW TESTAMENT : FOR STUDENTS FAMILIAR WITH THE ELEMENTS OF GREEK / Robertson, A T – (Includes indexes) – New York: A C Armstrong, 1908 – 1mf – 9 – 0-8370-9266-3 – 1986-3266 – us A.T.L.A. [450]

A SHORT GUIDE TO JOGJAKARTA / Indonesia. Jogjakarta – SE-11,544 1. 1958 – 9 – ne IDC [950]

A SHORT GUIDE TO THE EXHIBITION OF THE PALESTINE ARCHAEOLOGICAL MUSEUM, ILLUSTRATING THE STONE AND BRONZE AGES IN PALESTINE / Iliffe, J H – Govt. of Palestine, 1949 – 9 – $10.00 – us I.R.C. [930]

A SHORT GUIDE TO THE LARA DJONGGRANG TEMPLE GROUP / Kaelan. Indonesia – Trans. by Mardijo, rev. by M. Juska. 1963. 40p. SEM-9694/1 – 9 – ne IDC [280]

A SHORT GUIDE TO THE PRAMBANAN COMPLEX / Suharsono – SE 11,691 1. 1964 – 9 – ne IDC [950]

A SHORT GUIDE TO THE SANCTUARY OF BARABUDUR / Suharsono – SE 6531 1. 1964 – 9 – ne IDC [950]

A SHORT HANDBOOK OF MISSIONS / Stock, Eugene – (Includes appendix) – 2nd ed. London; New York: Longmans, Green, 1905 – 1mf – 9 – 0-8370-6397-3 – 1986-0397 – us A.T.L.A. [240]

A SHORT HISTORICAL REVIEW OF THE LIFE OF THE EGBAS FROM 1829 TO 1930 / Folarin, Abedesin – Abeokuta, Nigerai: [s.n., 1931] – us Res Libr [305]

A SHORT HISTORY OF BAPTIST MISSIONARY WORK IN BRITISH HONDURAS, 1822-1939 / Cleghorn, Robert – 80 p. 4566 – 1 – 5.00 – us Baptist [240]

A SHORT HISTORY OF BRITISH COLONIAL POLICY / Egerton, Hugh Edward – London: Methuen, 1897. 02890. (Pre-1900 Canadiana) – 9 – cn C.I.H.M. [971]

A SHORT HISTORY OF BUGANDA, BUNYORO, BUSOGA, TORO AND ANKOLE... / Miti, James Kibuka – Kampala, Uganda: Makerere University College Library, Photographic Dept, [19–] – us Res Libr [960]

A SHORT HISTORY OF CHEMISTRY / Venable, Francis Preston – 3rd ed. Boston: D.C. Heath, 1909, c1894. vii,163p – 1 – us U.W. Library [540]

SHORT HISTORY OF CHRISTIAN MISSIONS : FROM ABRAHAM AND PAUL TO CAREY, LIVINGSTONE, AND DUFF / Smith, George Adam – (Includes index) – 2nd ed. Edinburgh: T & T Clark, [1886?] – 1mf – 9 – 0-8370-6382-5 – 1986-0382 – us A.T.L.A. [240]

A SHORT HISTORY OF CHRISTIANITY / Robertson, John M – London: Watts, 1902 – 1mf – us A.T.L.A. [240]

A SHORT HISTORY OF CHRISTIANITY IN THE APOSTOLIC AGE / Gilbert, George Holley – (Includes bibliographies and index) – Chicago, IL: University of Chicago Press, 1906 – 1mf – 9 – 0-8370-9385-6 – 1986-3385 – us A.T.L.A. [220]

A SHORT HISTORY OF CHRISTIANITY...APOSTOLIC AGE / Gilbert, George Holley – Chicago: University of Chicago Press, 1906. 1 fiche – 9 – us A.T.L.A. [240]

A SHORT HISTORY OF ENGLISH COMMERCE AND INDUSTRY / Price, Langford Lovell – London: E. Arnold, 1900.xi,252p – 1 – us U.W. Library [941]

A SHORT HISTORY OF ENGLISH. WITH A BIBLIOGRAPHY OF RECENT BOOKS ON THE SUBJECT, AND LISTS OF TEXTS AND EDITIONS / Wyld, Henry Cecil Kennedy – London: J. Murray, 1914 – 1 roll – 1 – 1-55879-484-0 – uk Libr Preservation [420]

A SHORT HISTORY OF GERMAN LITERATURE / Hosmer, James Kendall – (Includes bibliographical references) – St. Louis: G L Jones and Company, 1879 – 1r – 1 – us U.W. Library [430]

A SHORT HISTORY OF GERMAN LITERATURE / Waterhouse, Gilbert – (Includes bibliographical references and index) – London: Methuen and Co, [1942] – 1r – 1 – us U.W. Library [430]

A SHORT HISTORY OF GLASS / Zerwick, Chloe – 1980. 96p., 94 illus: 29 color, 65 b w. 2 fiches Fiche no. 6172 – 9 – $5.00 – us Corning Mus [740]

A SHORT HISTORY OF GLASS / Zerwick, Chloe – (Fiche No. 11,642) – New York: H.N. Abrams in association with Corning, NY: The Corning Museum of Glass, 1990. 112p – 9 – $5.00 – us Corning Mus [740]

A SHORT HISTORY OF INDEPENDENT METHODISM : A SOUVENIR OF THE HUNDREDTH ANNUAL MEETING OF THE INDEPENDENT METHODIST CHURCHES, 1905 / ed by Mounfield, A – Wigan, [1905]. viii/203p – 3mf – 9 – ne IDC [240]

A SHORT HISTORY OF KELOWNA AND ITS SURROUNDINGS IN THE PROVINCE OF BRITISH COLUMBIA, DOMINION OF CANADA / Agricultural and Trades Association of Okanagan Mission Valley – Victoria B.C.: Province Pub. Co., 1898. 00018. (Pre-1900 Canadiana) – 9 – cn C.I.H.M. [971]

A SHORT HISTORY OF LOUISIANA BAPTISTS / St. Amant, C. Penrose – (166p) – Nashville: Broadman, 1948 – 1 reel – 1 – $6.64 – us Baptist [240]

A SHORT HISTORY OF MORAL THEOLOGY / Slater, Thomas – New York: Benziger, 1909 – 1mf – 9 – 0-8370-7019-8 – 1986-1019 – us A.T.L.A. [230]

A SHORT HISTORY OF PURITANISM : A HANDBOOK FOR GUILDS AND BIBLE CLASSES / Heron, James – Edinburgh: T.& T. Clark; New York: Scribner [distributor], 1908 – 1mf – us A.T.L.A. [240]

A SHORT HISTORY OF ST ANDREW'S CATHEDRAL, SINGAPORE / Swindell, Frank G – Reel 4001. 1929 – 1 – ja CEACS [240]

A SHORT HISTORY OF SYRIAC LITERATURE / Wright, W – 9 – $12.00 – us I.R.C. [470]

A SHORT HISTORY OF THE BIBLE : BEING A POPULAR ACCOUNT OF THE FORMATION AND DEVELOPMENT OF THE CANON / Keeler, Bronson C – (Includes bibliographical references and index) – NY: C P Farrell, c1881 – 1mf – 9 – 0-8370-3860-X – 1985-1860 – us A.T.L.A. [220]

A SHORT HISTORY OF THE CANADIAN PEOPLE / Bryce, George – London: Low, Marston, Searle & Rivington; Toronto: Gage, 1887. 02849. (Pre-1900 Canadiana) – 9 – cn C.I.H.M. [971]

A SHORT HISTORY OF THE DONATISTS;... / Trevor, J – London, 1741 – 1mf – 9 – MP-285/1 – ne IDC [240]

SHORT HISTORY OF THE EARLY CHURCH / Hurst, John F – New York: Chautauqua, 1886 – 1mf – us A.T.L.A. [240]

SHORT HISTORY OF THE ENGLISH BIBLE: WITH BRIEF NOTICES OF THE TRANSLATORS / Freeman, James M – New York: Phillips & Hunt, 1879.1 fiche – 9 – us A.T.L.A. [240]

A SHORT HISTORY OF THE EVANGELICAL MOVEMENT / Russell, George W E – London: Mowbray; Milwaukee, U.S.A.: Young Churchman, 1915 – 1mf – us A.T.L.A. [240]

SHORT HISTORY OF THE FRENCH REVOLUTION, 1789-1795 / Bradby, Eliza Dorothy – Oxford: Clarendon Press, 1932. ix/375p. front, plates, ports – 1 – us U.W. Library [944]

A SHORT HISTORY OF THE HEBREW TEXT OF THE OLD TESTAMENT / Weir, Thomas Hunter – (Includes bibliographical references and index) – London: Williams and Norgate, 1899 – 1mf – 9 – 0-8370-9343-0 – 1986-3343 – us A.T.L.A. [220]

A SHORT HISTORY OF THE INTERNATIONAL LESSON SYSTEM / Rice, Edwin Wilbur – Philadelphia: American Sunday-School Union, c1902 – 1mf – us A.T.L.A. [240]

SHORT HISTORY OF THE MEDIAEVAL CHURCH / Hurst, John F – New York: Chautauqua, 1887 – 1mf – us A.T.L.A. [240]

A SHORT HISTORY OF THE METHODISTS IN THE U.S. OF AMERICA, BEGINNING IN 1766 AND CONTINUED TILL 1809 : TO WHICH IS PREFIXED A BRIEF ACCOUNT OF THEIR RISE IN ENGLAND IN THE YEAR 1729, AND C / Lee, Jesse – [S.l.]: Cokesbury, [19–?] – 1mf – us A.T.L.A. [240]

SHORT HISTORY OF THE NATIVE TRIBES OF THE TRANSVAAL / Transvaal. (Colony). Native Affairs Department – Pretoria: Govt Printer & Stationery Office, 1905 – us Res Libr [960]

A SHORT HISTORY OF THE OXFORD MOVEMENT / Ollard, Sidney Leslie – London: A.R. Mowbray; Milwaukee, U.S.A.: Young Churchman, 1915 – 1mf – us A.T.L.A. [240]

A SHORT HISTORY OF 'THE PEOPLE CALLED METHODISTS', FROM THE DAYS OF THE WESLEYS TO THE METHODIST OECUMENICAL CONFERENCE HELD AT... / Daniels, W H – London, 1882 – 5mf – 9 – ne IDC [240]

A SHORT HISTORY OF THE PRESBYTERIAN CHURCH IN THE PARISH OF CHIPMAN: CONTAINING ALSO BRIEF REFERENCES TO THE GROWTH OF THE PARISH / Baird, Frank – Fredericton, N.B.: Reporter Steam Publ. Office, 1895. 06054. (Pre-1900 Canadiana) – 9 – cn C.I.H.M. [240]

A SHORT HISTORY OF THE UNITARIANISM SINCE THE REFORMATION / Mott, Frederick Blount – (Includes index) – Boston: Unitarian Sunday-School Society, 1893 – 1mf – 9 – 0-8370-8843-7 – 1986-2843 – us A.T.L.A. [240]

A SHORT INSTITUTION OF GRAMMAR / Busby, Richard – 1647. 99p. (English Linguistics Series 1500-1800) – 9 – App – us UMI [400]

A SHORT INTRODUCTION TO ENGLISH GRAMMAR / Lowth, Robert – 1762. 215p. (English Linguistics Series 1500-1800) – 9 – us UMI [420]

A SHORT INTRODUCTION TO GRAMMAR / Wedderburn, David – 1632. 63p. (English Linguistics Series 1500-1800) – 9 – us UMI [420]

A SHORT INTRODUCTION TO THE ART OF PLAYING THE HARPSICHORD. / Broderip, Robert – op. 6. c.1790 – 9 – us Sibley [780]

SHORT INTRODUCTION TO THE GOSPELS / Burton, Ernest De Witt – Chicago: University of Chicago, 1904. 1 fiche – 9 – us A.T.L.A. [240]

A SHORT INTRODUCTION TO THE LATIN TONGUE – Anon. 1709. 70p. (English Linguistics Series 1500-1800) – 9 – us UMI [450]

A SHORT INTRODUCTION TO THE LITERATURE OF THE BIBLE / Moulton, Richard Green – (Includes indexes) – Boston: D C Heath, 1907, c1901 – 1mf – 9 – 0-8370-9808-4 – 1986-3808 – us A.T.L.A. [220]

A SHORT INTRODUCTION TO THE LITERATURE OF THE OLD TESTAMENT / Box, George Herbert – (Includes bibliographies & index) – London: Rivingtons, 1909 – 1mf – 9 – 0-8370-2431-5 – 1985-0431 – us A.T.L.A. [220]

A SHORT INTRODUCTORY DICTIONARY OF THE KAONDE LANGUAGE : WITH ENGLISH-KAONDE APPENDIX / Woods, R E Broughall – London: Religious Tract Society, 1924 – us Res Libr [470]

Short, Ken *see* WORLD WAR II THROUGH THE AMERICAN NEWSREELS, 1942-1945

Short, Kenneth et al *see* THE HISTORY OF THE CINEMA, 1895-1940

Short, Kevin R *see* THE EFFECTS OF TWO AEROBIC FITNESS LEVELS ON EXCESS POST-EXERCISE OXYGEN CONSUMPTION IN YOUNG ADULTS

A SHORT LIFE OF CARDINAL NEWMAN / Fletcher, J S – London: Ward and Downey, 1890 – 1mf – us A.T.L.A. [240]

A SHORT LIFE OF D L MOODY (CCC184) / Hsieh, Sung-kao – (In Chinese) – Hong Kong: Bible Book and Tract Depot, 1952 – 1r – 1 – 1984-B500 – us A.T.L.A. [920]

A SHORT LIFE OF SPURGEON (CCC185) / Hsieh, Sung-kao – (In Chinese) – [s.l: s.n, 1952] – 1r – 1 – 1984-B500 – us A.T.L.A. [920]

SHORT NOTES ON THE ACTS OF THE APOSTLES / Menet, John – London: S P C K; New York: E & J B Young, [1874?] – 1mf – 9 – 0-8370-4387-5 – 1985-2387 – us A.T.L.A. [220]

A SHORT PRESERVATIVE AGAINST THE DOCTRINES REVIV'D BY MR. WHITEFIELD AND HIS ADHERENTS;... – London, 1739 – 1mf – 9 – MP-266/1 – ne IDC [240]

SHORT SERMONS / Brooke, Stopford Augustus – London, New York: Macmillan, 1892 – 1mf – us A.T.L.A. [240]

SHORT SHORT STEPS (CCC267) = TSUI CH'IEN YU CH'IEN JU SHEN / Price, P F – (In Chinese) – Hankow: Religious Tract Society, 1941 – 1r – 1 – 1984-6606 – us A.T.L.A. [240]

A SHORT STATEMENT OF THE ADVANTAGES OF UNIVERSITY CONSOLIDATION:.. / Association for Promoting University Consolidation – (Halifax: Nova Scotia Print. Co.), 1881.06155.(Pre-1900 Canadiana) – 9 – cn C.I.H.M. [370]

SHORT STEPS TO GREAT TRUTHS (CCC268) / Price, P F – (In Chinese) – Hankow: Religious Tract Society, 1935-1947 – 1r – 1984-6607 – us A.T.L.A. [240]

SHORT STORIES – Portland OR. vol 25 nr 1 (no date) – 1 – us U.O. Library [071]

SHORT STORIES – Reno, NV. (undated) – 1r – 1 – $50.00 – U04718 – us Library Micro [071]

SHORT STORIES FOR YOUNG PEOPLE, VOL 1 (CCC328) / ed by Woman's Messenger Staff – (In Chinese) – Hong Kong: Bible Book and Tract Depot for Council on Christian Literature for Overseas Chinese, 1953 – 1r – 1 – 1984-6667 – us A.T.L.A. [830]

SHORT STORIES IN SPANISH – 1979- – 1,5,6,9 – us UMI [830]

SHORT STUDIES IN ECCLESIASTICAL HISTORY AND BIOGRAPHY / Oxenham, H N – London: Chapman and Hall, 1884 – 1mf – us A.T.L.A. [240]

SHORT STUDIES IN EVIDENCE / Browne, Irving – New York, Banks, 1897. 242 p. LL-752 – 1 – us L of C Photodup [340]

SHORT STUDIES IN THE SCIENCE OF COMPARATIVE RELIGIONS, EMBRACING ALL THE RELIGIONS OF ASIA / Forlong, James George Roche – London: B. Quaritch, 1897. xxviii,662p.Illus.Maps. With: Shakespeare Criticism by C.N. Menon. 1 reel. 1186 – 1 – us U.W. Library [230]

SHORT STUDIES OF GREAT LAWYERS / Browne, Irving – Albany, N.Y., Albany Law Journal, 1878. 382 p. LL-428 – 1 – us L of C Photodup [340]

A SHORT STUDY OF EDUCATION IN THE CHRISTIAN HOME = CHIA T'ING CHIAO YU TI YEN CHIU / Hsieh, Sung-kao – (In Chinese) – 2nd ed. Shanghai: Christian Literature Society, 1930 – 1r – 1 – 1984-B500 – us A.T.L.A. [640]

A SHORT STUDY OF ETHICS / D'Arcy, Charles Frederick – (Includes bibliographical references & index) – 2nd ed. London: Macmillan, 1901 – 1mf – 9 – 0-8370-6101-6 – 1986-0101 – us A.T.L.A. [170]

A SHORT STUDY OF RELIGIONS (CCC183) = CHU CHIAO TI YEN CHIU / ed by Hsieh, Sung-kao & Yu, mu-jen – (In Chinese) – 13th ed. Shanghai: Christian Literature Society, 1946 – 1r – 1 – 1984-B500 – us A.T.L.A. [240]

A SHORT SURVEY OF THE MAIN FACTORS AND PRINCIPLES BEARING UPON THE DEVELOPMENT OF EFFICIENT NATIONAL SHIPPING SERVICES / Etherington, A G – SE-5514 1. 1959 – 9 – ne IDC [380]

SHORT TERM DEVELOPMENT PROGRAMME, 1968-1970 / Somali Republic. Planning Commission – D 867 1. 1968 – 9 – ne IDC [338]

SHORT TERM READERS FOR ILLITERATE CHURCH MEMBERS (CCC186) / Hsieh, Sung-kao – (In Chinese) – Hong Kong: Bible Book and Tract Depot. 6v. 1953 – 1r – 1 – 1984-B500 – us A.T.L.A. [240]

SHORT TITLES OF FAMILIAR BIBLE TEXTS, MISTRANSLATED, MISINTERPRETED, AND MISQUOTED / Condit, Blackford – (Includes indexes of subjects and texts discussed) – Chicago: Fleming H Revell, 1898 – 1mf – 9 – 0-8370-2721-7 – 1985-0721 – us A.T.L.A. [220]

A SHORT TOPOGRAPHICAL DESCRIPTION OF HIS MAJESTY'S PROVINCE OF UPPER CANADA, IN NORTH AMERICA / Faden, W – London: Printed by W Bulmer and Co. Russell-court, 1799. SEM105P130 – 2mf – 9 – Can$4.50 – cn Bibl Nat [971]

Short, William *see* PAPERS

A SHORTE INTRODUCTION OF GRAMMAR / Lily, William – 1567 – 9 – 15.00 – us Scholars' Facs [450]

A SHORTE INTRODUCTION OF GRAMMAR / Lily, William & Colet, John – 1549. 92p. (English Linguistics Series 1500-1800) – 9 – us UMI [400]

SHORTER CATECHISM / Luther, Martin – 1805 – 1 – $50.00 – us Presbyterian [240]

Shorter, Clement King *see*
- VICTORIAN LITERATURE
- THE WORKS OF GEORGE BORROW

A SHORTER MANUAL OF THEOLOGY / Beet, Joseph Agar – 1908 – 9 – us A.T.L.A. [240]

THE SHORTEST WAY TO END DISPUTES ABOUT RELIGION : IN TWO PARTS / Manning, Robert – 5th American stereotype ed. Boston: Patrick Donahoe, 1853 – 1mf – 9 – 0-8370-6821-5 – 1986-0821 – us A.T.L.A. [230]

Shorthouse, Joseph Henry *see*
- BLANCHE, LADY FALAISE
- THE COUNTESS EVE
- JOHN INGLESANT
- THE LITTLE SCHOOLMASTER
- SIR PERCIVAL
- A TEACHER OF THE VIOLIN

Shortridge, Charles *see* SUNSHINE, FRUIT AND FLOWERS, SAN JOSE, CALIFORNIA

Shortt, John *see*
- INFORMATIONS (CRIMINAL AND QUO WARRANTO) MANDAMUS AND PROHIBITION
- THE LAW RELATING TO WORKS OF LITERATURE AND ART: EMBRACING THE LAW OF COPYRIGHT.

THE SHORT-TERM IMPLEMENTATION PROGRAMME / Ceylon. Department of National Planning – Colombo. 1962 – 9 – ne IDC [338]

Shostakovich, S *see* POLITICHESKII STROI I MEZHDUNARODNO-PRAVOVYE POLOZHENIE TANNUTUVY V PROSHLOM I NASTOIASHCHEM

Shotaro, Kojima *see* SHINA SAIKIN DAIJI NEMPYO

SHOU TU JIH PAO (HARIAN IBUKOTA) – Indonesia. Djakarta. 1963-1965 – 1 – us UMI [072]

SHOULD AUSTRALIA HAVE FOREIGN AFFAIRS? / Forbes, Viv – 1fiche (29x) – 9 – $.00f – at Libertarian Micro [980]

SHOULD JURIES IN CRIMINAL CASES BE JUDGES OF THE LAW AND FACT? / Lehmayer, Martin – Baltimore, Cushings & Bailey, 1886. 80 p. LL-569 – 1 – us L of C Photodup [340]

SHOULD THE NEGROES OF THE METHODIST EPISCOPAL CHURCH BE SET APART IN A CHURCH BY THEMSELVES? / Shaw, Daniel W – New York: Eaton & Mains; Cincinnati: Jennings & Graham, c 1912 – 1mf – us A.T.L.A. [240]

SHOULD THERE BE A FEDERAL INCORPORATION LAW FOR COMMERCIAL CORPORATIONS? / Wilgus, Horace La Fayette – Ann Arbor, Mich., Wahr, 1905. 57 p. LL-2277 – 1 – us L of C Photodup [340]

SHOULEI XUEBAO – (Acta Theriological Sinica). In Chinese but English abstracts to the main articles. F p143 – 9 – 4.00f – cc Microforms [073]

SHOUTING, GENUINE AND SPURIOUS / Henry, G W – Oneida, Madison County, N.Y.: G.W. Henry, 1859 – 1mf – us A.T.L.A. [240]

Show, Arley Barthlow *see* THE MOVEMENT FOR REFORM IN THE TEACHING OF RELIGION IN THE PUBLIC SCHOOLS OF SAXONY

SHOW BUSINESS – New York, NY. 1977-78 – 2r – 1 – $100.00 – R04916 – us Library Micro [790]

SHOW BUSINESS – New York. v24-27. 1964-68 – 4r – 1 – us Ross [790]

Show, SB *see* FOREST FIRE CONTROL

SHOWA ZAISEI-SHI SHIRYO : HISTORY OF FINANCE IN SHOWA ERA – 312r – 1 – inquire – us Ross [336]

SHOWMAN : AN ILLUSTRATED JOURNAL FOR SHOWMEN AND ALL ENTERTAINERS – London. v1-4. 1900-02 – 1r – 1 – us Ross [790]

THE SHOWMAN – London. v. 1-4. Sept 1900-Mar 28 1902 – 1 – us NY Public [790]

SHPROTSUNGEN = SPROUTS – (In Yiddish) – Warsaw, PL. no6. Dec 1925 – 1r – 1 – $25.00 – cn Can Microfilming [072]

A SHRED OF EVIDENCE ON PUBLIC ACCEPTANCE OF PRIVATELY ISSUED CURRENCY / Eichenbaum, Martin S & Wallace, Neil – 1985, 1p – 9 – 1.00f – at Libertarian Micro [332]

Shreter, Viktor Nikolaevich *see* VNUTRENNIAIA TORGOVLIA

SHREWSBURY 1717-1890 – (Mf 1-5: Births 1701-98. Mf 5-6: Deaths 1731-1829. Mf 6-8: Marriages 1764-1808. Mf 9-10: Births 1769-1829. Mf 10-11: Fences 1828-1919. Mf 12-13: Marriages 1723-1836. Mf 13-16: Births 1713-1845. Mf 16-17: Deaths 1717-1844. Mf 17-19: Marriages 1720-1891. Mf 20-21: Births 1716-1848. Mf 21-22: Deaths 1721-1844. Mf 22-24: Marriages 1720-1843. Mf 25: Marriages 1808-29. Mf 26: Births 1843-52. Mf 26-27: Marriages 1843-52. Mf 27: Deaths 1843-52. Mf 28-29: Births 1853-65. Mf 29-30: Marriages 1853-66. Mf 30-32: Deaths 1853-65. Mf 33-36: Births 1843-91. Mf 36-38: Marriages 1843-90. Mf 38-41: Deaths 1843-91. Mf 42-49: Birth Index 1843-1977. Mf 50-57: Marriage Index 1843-1976. Mf 58-63: Death Index 1843-1977. Mf 64: Vital Records 1890-92) – (mf ed 1985) – 64mf – 9 – 0-931248-89-2 – us Holbrook [920]

SHREWSBURY CHRONICLE – England. -w. 1772-1891. (79 reels) – 1 – uk British Libr Newspaper [072]

SHREWSBURY PAPERS / Broughton House. Northamptonshire – 1696-1708. BRRAM – 3r – 1 – uk Microform Academic [970]

THE SHREWSBURY PAPERS / Lambeth Palace Library – 15th-early 17th centuries – 1 – £350.00 – uk World [025]

SHRIFTN = WRITINGS – (Yiddish monthly) – Warsaw, PL. v1 no1 Jun 1936-v3 no10-11 Nov/Dec 1938 – 1r – 1 – $30.00 – cn Can Microfilming [072]

THE SHRINES AND SEPULCHRES OF THE OLD AND NEW WORLD; RECORDS OF PILGRIMAGES IN MANY LANDS. / Madden, Richard Robert – London: T.C. Newby, 1851. 2v. plates – 1 – us U.W. Library [390]

THE SHRINES, OR, CHIEF PLACES OF PILGRIMAGE OF THE ADHERENTS OF THE CHURCH OF ROME / Cust, Robert Needham – London: E. Stock, 1892 – 1mf – us A.T.L.A. [240]

Shriver, Timothy C *see* EFFECTS OF EXERCISE INTENSITY ON GLUCOSE TOLERANCE AND INSULIN SENSITIVITY

SHROPSHIRE, 1822 : BRITISH ISLES CENSUS DIRECTORIES PROJECT, ENGLAND – (In prep) – at Vine [941]

SHROPSHIRE, 1828 : BRITISH ISLES CENSUS DIRECTORIES PROJECT, ENGLAND – at Vine [941]

SHROPSHIRE, 1835 : BRITISH ISLES CENSUS DIRECTORIES PROJECT, ENGLAND – at Vine [941]

SHROPSHIRE, 1842 : BRITISH ISLES CENSUS DIRECTORIES PROJECT, ENGLAND – (In prep) – at Vine [941]

SHROPSHIRE, 1850 : BRITISH ISLES CENSUS DIRECTORIES PROJECT, ENGLAND – at Vine [941]

SHROPSHIRE, 1851 : BRITISH ISLES CENSUS DIRECTORIES PROJECT, ENGLAND. VOL 5 – 5mf – 9 – A$33.00 – at Vine [941]

SHROPSHIRE, 1871 : BRITISH ISLES CENSUS DIRECTORIES PROJECT, ENGLAND – at Vine [941]

SHROPSHIRE, 1888 : BRITISH ISLES CENSUS DIRECTORIES PROJECT, ENGLAND. VOL 41 – 4mf – 9 – A$27.00 – at Vine [941]

SHROPSHIRE, 1909 : BRITISH ISLES CENSUS DIRECTORIES PROJECT, ENGLAND – at Vine [941]

SHROPSHIRE, 1917 : BRITISH ISLES CENSUS DIRECTORIES PROJECT, ENGLAND – at Vine [941]

SHROPSHIRE, 1926 : BRITISH ISLES CENSUS DIRECTORIES PROJECT, ENGLAND – at Vine [941]

Shropshire County Library *see* ASTRONOMICAL BOOKS FROM SHROPSHIRE COUNTY LIBRARY, 17TH AND EARLY 18TH CENTURIES

SHROPSHIRE EXAMINER AND ALL ROUND THE WREKIN ADVERTISER – Wenlock. England. -w. 2 May 1874-5 Oct 1877. (3 reels) – 1 – uk British Libr Newspaper [072]

A SHROPSHIRE LAD / Housman, Alfred Edward – London: Kegan Paul, Trench, Trbner, and Co. Ltd, 1896 – 1 roll – 1 – 1-55879-781-5 – uk Libr Preservation [830]

Shteina, B E *see* BREST-LITOVSKAI A KONFERENTSIIA

DER SHTERN – (Missing. Many numbers) – Kiev. v1-17. 1925-1941 – 5r – 1 – J-92-38/3 – ne IDC [072]

DI SHTIME = VOICE OF ISRAEL – Mexico, MX. v39 no 3624,3627. 1976 – 1r – 1 – Can$30.00 – cn Can Microfilming [072]

SHTIMME – New York, NY. 1910 – 1 – us A.J.P.C. [071]

Shtomkmar, M P *see* RIFMA MAIAKOVSKOGO

SHTOTISHE KOOPERATSYE = CITY COOPERATION – Kiev, UA. v1 no2-3 Feb-Mar 1920-no6 Jun 1920 – 1r – 1 – $30.00 – cn Can Microfilming [072]

SHTRAF LID – Prague. c.1620? BJ-43-110 1 – 9 – ne IDC [956]

Shtrange, M M *see* RUSSKOE OBSHCHESTVO I FRANTSUZSKAIA REVOLIUTSIIA 1789-1794 GG

O SHTUNCIZME I MERAKH BOR'BY S SEKTOYU / Skvortsov, Vasilii M – On Stundism and on the Means of Struggle with the Sect. Chernigov, 1894. One of 13 titles on reel – 1 – 86.44 – us Baptist [240]

O SHTUNDE I PROTESTANTSVE V IKH VEROUCHENII – On the Stunda and Protestantism in Their Belief.Odessa, 1892. One of 13 titles on reel – 1 – 86.44 – us Baptist [240]

SHTUNDIZM. OCHERK RELIGIOZNOGO-BYTOVOI ZHIZNI V MALOROSSII / Voronov, A D – A study of every-day religious life in Little Russia. Russkii Vestnik. 1884, no.3, p7-45 – 1 – 5.00 – us Baptist [240]

SHU HSIN-CH'ENG. CHUNG-KUO CHIN-TAI CHIAO-YU SHIH TZU-LIAO – (Sources for Modern Chinese Education). v. 1-3. 1962. BCH-847 2 – 8 – ne IDC [370]

SHU XUN BAO – China. Book Information. -w. 1985-. M-D93 – 1 – $23.00r – cc Microforms [072]

SHUANG-LIU HSIEN-CHIH – 1894, 2. BCH-695 2 – 8 – ne IDC [950]

Shuart, Kathy L *see* THE WAYNE COUNTY MEDIATION PROGRAM IN THE EASTERN DISTRICT OF MICHIGAN

SHUBERT CITIZEN – Shubert, NE. -w. Mar 1897-Jul 1902, scattered issues missing; Mar 1908-Sep 1917, scattered issues missing; Feb 1920-Sep 1925; Nov 1925-Nov 1926, scattered issues missing; Nov 1936-Sep 1942 – 1 – us NE Hist [071]

SHUBH CHINTAK – Jubbulpore, India. Oct 1942-1950 – 4r – 1 – us L of C Photodup [072]

Shubinskii, S N *see* ISTORICHESKIE OCHERKI I RASSKAZY

Shuck, Oscar T *see* HISTORY OF THE BENCH AND BAR OF CALIFORNIA

Shuckard, W E *see*
- THE BRITISH COLEOPTERA DELINEATED: CONSISTING OF FIGURES OF ALL THE GENERA OF BRITISH BEETLES
- ELEMENTS OF BRITISH ENTOMOLOGY
- ESSAY ON THE INDIGENOUS FOSSORIAL HYMENOPTERA

SHUFA BAO – China. Journal of Calligraphy. -w. 1986-. M-D111 – 1 – $28.00r – cc Microforms [073]

Shufani, Ilyas *see* ISRAIL WA-"MASHRU KARTIR"

SHUICHAN XUEBAO – Journal of Fisheries of China. In Chinese but English abstracts to the main articles. F p72 – 9 – $4.50f – cc Microforms [073]

SHUIHU QUANZHUAN – By Shi Nai'an. Outlaws of the marsh. 100v. A block-printed ed. of the reign of Emperor Wanli, 1573-1619, of Ming. Rev. by the Shiqu Studio in the 5th year (1666) of Emperor Kangxi of Qing. 2 reels. M-G1 – 1 – $200.00 – cc Microforms [950]

SHUILI FADIAN – Water Power. 1986. F/P 274 – 9 – $4.50f – cc Microforms [073]

SHUILI XUEBAO – Journal of Hydraulic Engineering. In Chinese, with English abstracts to the main articles. 60p – 9 – $4.00f – cc Microforms [627]

SHUISHENG SHENGWU XUEBAO – Acta Hydrobiologica Sinica. In prep. F/P 309 – 9 – 4.00f – cc Microforms [073]

SHUIWEN DIZHI GONGCHENG DIZHI = HYDROLOGY AND ENGINEERING GEDOGY SIC – 1981-. F-P248 – 9 – $4.50f – cc Microforms [073]

SHUKONG JISHU TONGXUN – Communication on NC Technique. 1983. F/P 288 – 9 – $4.50f – cc Microforms [073]

SHUKYO KENKYU. "JOURNAL OF RELIGIOUS STUDIES."TOKYO. 1916-1969. LACKING: 1960-1863. PTS. 164-174, NOS. 443-475 – 9 – ne IDC [200]

SHULAMITH – New York. 1-2 (42 nos) May 31 1889-Apr 4 1890 – 1 – us NY Public [071]

SHULBLAT = SCHOOL LEAVES – (Yiddish monthly) – New York City, NY. v1 no1 Sep 1937-Feb 1938 – 1r – 1 – $25.00 – cn Can Microfilming [071]

Shuleva, K M *see* EXERCISE OXYGEN UPTAKE IN 3- THROUGH 6-YEAR-OLD CHILDREN

Shumaker, Elmer Ellsworth *see* GOD AND AMN

Shumaker, Walter Adams *see* A TREATISE ON THE LAW OF PARTNERSHIP

Shumakov, S A *see* OBZOR "GRAMOT KOLLEGII EKONOMII"

Shuman, Bruce A *see* LIBRARY AND ARCHIVAL SECURITY

Shumigorskii, E S *see*
- EKATERINA IVANOVA NELIDOVA, 1758-1839
- IMPERATOR PAVEL I. ZIZN' I TSARSTVOVANIE
- IMPERATRITSA MARIIA FEDOROVNA (1759-1828)

Shumway, Grant L *see* HISTORY OF WESTERN NEBRASKA AND ITS PEOPLE

SHUMY GORODA / Remizov, A – Revel', (1913). 176p. BR-849 2 – 8 – ne IDC [460]

SHUN-CH'ING FU-CHIH – 1868; 1807, 10, 1. BCH-721 2 – 8 – ne IDC [950]

SHUN-NING FU-CHIH – 1761, 3-10. BCH-679 2 – 8 – ne IDC [950]

Shuster, Donald R *see*
- MORE CONSTITUTIONS FOR PALAU
- PALAU'S CONSTITUTIONAL TANGLE

Shuster, Robert *see* THE BILLY SUNDAY PAPERS, 1882-1974

Shustorovich, E M *see* SLAVIANO-RUSSKIE RUKOPISI BIBLIOTEKI IMENI A.M. GOR'KOGO LENINGRADSKOGO GOSUDARSTVENNOGO UNIVERSITETA
SHUTESBURY 1746-1890 – 19mf – 9 – us Holbrook [920]
DOS SHUTSLOZE KIND = THE UNPROTECTED CHILD – (In Yiddish) – Warsaw, PL. v2 no12 Dec 1929-Jan 1930 – 1r – 1 – $25.00 – cn Can Microfilming [072]
Shutter, Marion Daniel *see*
– HISTORY OF MINNEAPOLIS THE GATEWAY TO THE NORTHWEST
– WIT AND HUMOR OF THE BIBLE: A LITERARY STUDY
Shuvalov, S *see* POETICHESKOE ISKUSSTVO BLOKA
SHUXUE WULI XUEBAO – Acta Mathematica Scientia. In Chinese but English abstracts to the main articles. F p116 – 9 – 4.00f – cc Microforms [073]
SHUXUE XUEBAO – Acta Mathematica Sinica. In Chinese but Table of Contents in English in each issue. F p41 – 9 – $4.50f – cc Microforms [073]
SHUZHI JISUAN YU JISUANJI YINGYONG – Journal on Numerical Methods and Computer Applications. In Chinese but English abstracts to the main articles. F p117 – 9 – $4.50f – cc Microforms [073]
Shvetsov, A I *see* SOVETSKAIA KOOPERATSIIA
SHVEYSDISH LID – Prague. 1649. BJ-43-111 1 – 9 – ne IDC [470]
Shyamaladasa, Kaviraja *see* VIRAVINODA, MEWARAKA ITIHASA
SHYLOCK UND NATHAN : VORTRAG GEHALTEN IM VEREIN FUER JUEDISCHE GESCHICHTE UND LITERATUR ZU FRANKFURT A.M.: AM 20. JANUAR 1886 / Heinemann, H – Frankfurt a.M.: J Kauffmann, 1886 – 1r – 1 – us U.W. Library [850]
SI BUSINESS – (v2-4 1991-93 Can$28.00y) – Willowdale. v1-5. 1990-94 – 9 – Can$20.00y – cn Micromedia [380]
EL SI DE LAS NINAS / Fernandez de Moratin, Leandro – 1806 – 1mf – 9 – Pta1,000.00 – 84-7848-190-7 – sp Pentalfa [946]
SI KABAIAN. RASSKAZ-STSENKA V DVUK CHASTIAKH / Utuy Tatang Sontani – SE 5210 1. 1960 – 9 – ne IDC [950]
SI KAMPENG / Utuy Tatang Sontani – SE 5283 1964 – 9 – ne IDC [950]
SI LA TORTURE EST UN MOYEN SEUR A VERIFIER LES CRIMES SECRETS / Nicolas, Augustin – Amsterdam. 1682 – 9 – fr Hachette [360]
SI LES FEMMES SAVAIENT / Lantenay, Jeanne de – Paris: France Edition, 1923. 63p. (Les Femmes Collection) – 1mf – 9 – $6.00 – fr Bibl Nationale [305]
SI, MUJER / Aradillas Agudo, Antonio – Madrid: Studium, 1964 – 1 – sp Bibl Santa Ana [946]
SI PAHIT LIDAH – SE 5011 1 – 9 – ne IDC [950]
SI UNITS AND NOMENCLATURE IN SOIL SCIENCE – 1975 – 25p – it F.A.O. [631]
SI WONG GEH – 1971-76.(American Indian Periodicals in the Princeton University Library). 23 fiches – 9 – $90.00 – us UPA [073]
Siagian, Abu Arab *see* MAGODANG AEK, MARALI TAPIAN
Siagian, Gajus *see* HAVE A GOOD TIME; POCKET MANUAL FOR PRACTICAL INDONESIAN
Siahaan, A M S *see* PENDIDIKAN OLAHRAGA DAN PEMBANGUNAN MASJARAKAT BARU INDONESIA
Siahaan, L *see* ICHTISAR SEDJARAH INDONESIA, OENTOEK SEKOLAH MENENGAH
Sialkot, India. Associate Church *see* RECORDS, 1856-1882
SIAM AND LAOS AS SEEN BY OUR AMERICAN MISSIONARIES – Philadelphia: Presbyterian Board of Publ, c1884 – 2mf – 9 – 0-8370-6783-9 – 1986-0783 – us A.T.L.A. [950]
SIAM CHRONICLE – Bangkok, Thailand. Jan-Jul 1939 – 4r – 1 – us L of C Photodup [072]
SIAM JOURNAL OF MATHEMATICAL ANALYSIS – v1- . 1970- – 1,5,6,13 – us S.I.A.M. [510]
SIAM JOURNAL ON ALGEBRAIC AND DISCRETE METHODS – v1- . 1980- . Continued as: SIAM Journal on Matrix Analysis and Applications – 1,5,6,13 – us S.I.A.M. [510]
SIAM JOURNAL ON APPLIED MATHEMATICS – v1- . 1953- – 1,5,6,13 – us S.I.A.M. [510]
SIAM JOURNAL ON COMPUTING – v1- . 1972- – 1,5,6,13 – us S.I.A.M. [510]
SIAM JOURNAL ON CONTROL AND OPTIMIZATION – v1- . 1963- – 1,5,6,13 – us S.I.A.M. [510]
SIAM JOURNAL ON DISCRETE MATHEMATICS – v1- . 1988- – 1,5,6,13 – us S.I.A.M. [510]
SIAM JOURNAL ON NUMERICAL ANALYSIS – v1- . 1964- – 1,5,6,13 – us S.I.A.M. [510]
SIAM JOURNAL ON OPTIMIZATION – v1-. 1991-. Quarterly – us S.I.A.M. [000]
SIAM JOURNAL ON SCIENTIFIC COMPUTING – v1- . 1980- – 1,5,6,13 – us S.I.A.M. [510]
SIAM NEWS – Published ten times per year – us S.I.A.M. [510]
SIAM NIKORN – Bangkok, Thailand. 1947-62 – 44r – 1 – us L of C Photodup [072]
THE SIAM OUTLOOK – (Some issues lacking. Title varies) – v1-17 no 3. Jul 1921-Jul 1941 – 3r – 1 – ATLA S0141 – us A.T.L.A. [073]
SIAM RATH – Bangkok, Thailand. 1955-62 – 18r – 1 – us L of C Photodup [072]
SIAM RATH WEEKLY REVIEW – Bangkok. Thailand. 1954-1964 – 1 – us UMI [072]
SIAM REVIEW – v1- . 1959- – 1,5,6,13 – us S.I.A.M. [510]
SIAM WEEKLY ADVERTISER – Bangkok, Thailand. Aug 26, 1869-Aug 7, 1886 – 1 – us Res Libr [072]
The, Sian Kie *see* PERSOALAN-PERSOALAN ORGANISASI EKONOMIS DAN POLITIK EKONOMIS
SIANG PASASON : LAO-LANGUAGE DAILY NEWSPAPER – (Jul 1975-Dec 1975 $50.00v; Jan 1976-Dec 1982 $100.00v; Jan 1983-Jun 1983 $50.00v. Continued as Pasason) – Vientiane, Laos – 1 – us Asia Libr [072]
Siara, Norbert *see* SZENISCHE BAUWEISE DES ERZAEHLERS EICHENDORFF NACH DEM OPERNVORBILD GLUCKS UND MOZARTS
SIARAN ASIAN GAMES, AGUSTUS 1962 / Indonesia. Departemen Penerangan – SE-3898 1 – 9 – ne IDC [790]
SIASSET NAMEH – Texte persan et traduction francaise par Ch. Schefer. 1891, 1893 – 9 – fr Orientalistes [490]
[SIBARIS] FRAGMENTS DE SIBARIS; BALLET AJOUTE AUX SUPRISES DE L'AMOUR / Rameau, Jean-Philippe – Paris: Sieurs, 1757 – 1 – us Sibley [780]
SIBBET'S WESTERN REVIEW AND COUNTERFEIT DETECTOR – Pittsburgh, PA. 1839-1850. 4 issues – 1 – us Western Res [071]
DAS SIBEND CAPITTEL DANIELIS VON DES TUERCKEN GOTTES LESTERUNG VND SCHRECKLICHER MOERDEREY MIT VNTERRICHT JUSTI JONE / Jonas, J – Wittemberg, 1530 – 1mf – ne IDC [240]
SIBENDTZIG SCHLUSSRED DAS BEIDE TEIL DES SACRAMENTS ALLEN GLEUEBIGE CHRISTEN GEREICHET SOLL WERDEN / Huberinus, Caspar – [Augsburg: Philipp Ulhart], 1545. [G.F.: 18.1] – 1mf – 9 – HUB-43/1 – ne IDC [240]
SIBENTZIG SCHLUSSREDE DAS BEYDE THEYL DES SACRAMENTES ALLEN GLAUBIGEN CHRISTEN GEREYCHET SOLL WERDEN / Huberinus, Caspar – Nuernberg: Johann Daubmann, 1550. [G.F.: 18.2] – 1mf – 9 – HUB-78/1 – ne IDC [240]
SIBENZIG SCHLUSRED ODDER PUNCTEN VON DER RECHTEN HANDT GOTTES VND DER GEWALT CHRISTI / Huberinus, Caspar – Wittenberg: [Joseph Klug], 1529. [G.F.: 10.1] – 1mf – 9 – HUB-28/1 – ne IDC [240]
SIBENZIG SCHLUSREDE ODDER PUNCTE VON DER RECHTEN HANDT GOTTES VND DER GEWALT CHRISTJ. ZU TROSTE DENEN DIE SICH IN DER ZWINGELISCHEN SACHE NICHT BERICHTEN KOENEN RC / Huberinus, Caspar – Magdeburg: H[ans] W[alther], 1530. [G.F.: 10.2] – 1mf – 9 – HUB-76/1 – ne IDC [240]
SIBERIA AND THE EXILE SYSTEM / Kennan, George – New York: Century Co., 1891. 2v. illus. maps – 1 – us U.W. Library [947]
SIBERIAN MATHEMATICAL JOURNAL – v7-35. 1966-94 – 1,5 – $100.00v – us UMI [510]
SIBERIAN PICTURES / Niemojowski, Ludwik – ed. from the Polish by Major Szulczewski. London: Hurst and Blackett, 1883. 2v – 1 – us U.W. Library [910]
SIBERT SCORPION *see* THE DESERT SCORPION
SIBIR, SOIUZNIKII KOLCHAK : POVOROTNYI MOMENT RUSSKOI ISTORIII, 1918-1920 G.G.: VPECHATLIENIIA I MYSLI CHLENA OMSKAGO PRAVITELSTVA / Guins, George Constantine – V g. Kharbinie: Izd. Ob-va vozrozhdeniia Rossii, 1921 (Pekin: Tipo-lit. Russko i dukhovno i missii). 2v – 1 – CSUX88-B7171 – us Hoover Inst Photo [947]
SIBIRISCHE GESCHICHTE VON DER ENTDECKUNG SIBIRIENS BIS AUF DIE EROBERUNG DIESES LANDES DURCH DIE RUSSISCHE WAFFEN / Fischer, J E – v. 1-2. Spb. BU-786 2 – 8 – ne IDC [947]
SIBIRSKAIA BIBLIOGRAFIIA – (Bibliography of Siberia). 4 v. 1891-92 – 3 – us Readex [010]
SIBIRSKAIA BIBLIOGRAFIIA / Mezhov, VI – St. Petersburg. (Bibliography of Siberia). 4 v. 1891-1892 – 3 – us Readex [010]
SIBIRSKAIA BIBLIOGRAFIIA / Mezhov, VI – Ukazatel' knig i statei o Sibiri na russkom iazyke i odnekh tol'ko knig na inostrannykh iazykakh za ves' period knigopechataniia. v. 1-3. Spb. 1891-92. BR-5620 2 – 8 – ne IDC [010]
SIBIRSKAIA DEREVNIA *see* SPRAVOCHNIK VOSTOCHNO-SIBIRSKOGO OBSHCHESTVA SELSKOGO KHOZIASTVA, PROMYSHLENNOSTI I TORGOVLI V ENISEISKOI GUBERNII
SIBIRSKAIA GAZETA – (Only backfile through 1997 available $85r) – Russia, until 1997 – 1 – us Ross [072]
SIBIRSKAIA KOOPERATSIIA I MOSKOVSKII NARODNYI BANK / Ilimskii, D I – Ed.2. M., 1919 – 2mf – 9 – COR-381/1 – ne IDC [334]
SIBIRSKAIA NOV' – Ezhenedel'nyi literaturnokriticheskii zhurnal. v. 1-7. Tomsk. 1910. BR-3760 2 – 8 – ne IDC [073]
SIBIRSKAIA SEL'SKOKHOZIAISTVENNAIA KOOPERATSIIA *see* VESTNIK SIBIRSKOI SEL'SKOKHOZIAISTVENNOI KOOPERATSII
SIBIRSKAIA SOVETSKAIA ENTSIKLOPEDIIA – 1929-1930. v1(A-ZH); v2(ZH-K); v3(L-N) – 41mf – 9 – $165.00 – U-295/2 – ne IDC [947]
SIBIRSKIE VOPROSY – St. Petersburg. 1905, no. 1 – 1 – 35.00r – us Hoover Inst Photo [073]
SIBIRSKII ARKHIV – Prague. Supplement to Vol'naia Sibir'. 1929-1935, nos. 1-5 – 1 – 35.00r – us Hoover Inst Photo [073]
SIBIRSKII ARKHIV – Zhurnal arkheologii, istorii i etnografii Sibiri. Cont. as: Sibriskaia letopis'. Minusinsk. 1911-16. Lacking: 1911-13; (2, 6, 9) 1914; 1915; (1-5) 1916. BR-8163 2 – 8 – ne IDC [930]
SIBIRSKII VESTNIK – Spb. 1818-24. Lacking: (5-10, 13-20) 1823; (1) 1824. B-1893 2 – 8 – ne IDC [073]
SIBIRSKII VESTNIK POLITIKI, LITERATURY I OBSHCHESTVENNOI ZHIZNI – v. 1-255, 1905 – 1 – us Res Libr [073]
SIBIRSKII VIESTNIK – St Petersburg, 1818-24 – 2r – 1 – us Ross [073]
SIBIRSKII VIESTNIK – Tomsk, 1885 – 1r – 1 – us Ross [073]
SIBIRSKII VIESTNIK – Tomsk. v. 1. May 15-Dec 24 1885 – 1 – us NY Public [072]
SIBIRSKOE KRAEVOE STATISTICHESKOE BI URO *see* BI UDZHETY KRESTI AN SIBIRSKOGO KRAI A V...GODU
Sibirskoe kraevoe statisticheskoe biuro *see* STATISTICHESKI I BIULLETEN
SIBIRSKOE OBOZRIENIE – (Includes c.1: v.1:no.108 1906:June 15) – Irkutsk: [s.n.], 1906 – 1 – CSUXADM8169-S – us Hoover Inst Photo [073]
Sibley, Henry H *see* PAPERS
Sibrava, Frank *see* "THE FIGHTING CUSTERS"
Sibree, J *see* A REGISTER OF MISSIONARIES, DEPUTATIONS, ETC. FROM 1796 TO 1923
Sibree, James *see* A MADAGASCAR BIBLIOGRAPHY
Sibscota, George *see* THE DEAF AND DUMB MAN'S DISCOURSE
Sibthorp, J *see*
– FLORA GRAECA, SIVE PLANTARUM RARIORUM HISTORIA, QUAS IN PROVINCIIS AUT INSULIS GRAECIAE
– FLORA OXONIENSIS
– FLORAE GRAECAE PRODROMUS
Sibthorpe, W M *see* THE WAYS OF GOD WITH MAN
LA SIBYLE GAULOISE OU LA FRANCE TELLE QU'ELLE FUT, TELLE QU'ELLE EST, TELLE, A PEU PRES, QU'ELLE POURRA ETRE / Bricaire de la Dixmarie, Nicolas – Reprod. de l'ed. de Londres et Paris: Volleyre et Lacombe, 1775. xxvi,276p. 4 fiches. (Political Science Collection) – 9 – 10.00 – fr Bibl Nationale [944]
SIBYLLINE LEAVES : A COLLECTION OF POEMS / Coleridge, Samuel Taylor – London: Rest Fenner, 1817 – 1 roll – 1 – 1-55879-670-3 – uk Libr Preservation [810]
SIBYLLINISCHE BLAETTER / Diels, Hermann – Berlin: Georg Reimer, 1890. 1 fiche – 9 – us A.T.L.A. [240]
SIBYLLINISCHE BLAETTER DES MAGUS / Hamann, Johann Georg; ed by Unger, Rudolf – (Includes bibliographical references) – Jena: E Diederichs, 1905 – 1 – us U.W. Library [110]
SIC LE MAGAZINE DES AFFAIRES – (Filmed together with: Affaires Sic mar 1980-nov 1980. Affaires dec 1980. Le Magazine Affaires jan/fev 1981-aut 1981. Le Magazine des Affaires sep 1981. Le Magazine Affaires oct 1981-sep 1987. Le Magazine Affaires Plus oct 1987-dec 1992) – Montreal, oct/nov 1978-dec 1979 – 5r – 1 – Can$75.00r – cn Can Microfilming [073]
Sicard, Roch A C *see* ELEMENTS DE GRAMMAIRE GENERALE APPLIQUES A LA LANGUE FRANCAISE
DER SICH SELBST INFORMIRENDE CLAVIERSPIELER... / Wiedeburg, Michael Johann Friedrich – Halle, Leipzig: Verlag der Buchhandlung des Waisenhauses, 1765-75 – 1 – us Sibley [780]
SICHEL UND HAMMER *see*
– SOWJETRUSSLAND IM BILD
Sichel, Walter Sydney *see* EMMA LADY HAMILTON
SICHERHEIT IN CHEMIE UND UMWELT – v.1, 1981. ISSN:0720-1370 – 1,5,6,9,13 – 65.00v – us UMI [540]
Sicherl, M *see* DIE HANDSCHRIFTEN, AUSGABEN UND UEBERSETZUNGEN VON IAMBLICHOS DE MYSTERIIS
DIE SICHERSTELLUNG DES MONOTHEISMUS DURCH DIE GESETZGEBUNG IM VOREXILISCHEN JUDA / Erbt, Wilhelm – Goettingen: Vandenhoeck & Rup., 1903. 1 fiche – 9 – us A.T.L.A. [270]
DIE SICHERUNG DER GOLDWAEHRUNG; DIE AUFHEBUNG DER GELDENTWERTUNGSKLAUSEL; AUFRECHNUNG UNTER FRIEDRICH DEM GROSSEN / Beckerath, Ulrich von – 9 – 1.00f – at Libertarian Micro [335]
Sichuan Province. China *see*
– JIAJING HONGYA XIAN ZHI, 1562
– JIAJING MAHU FU ZHI, 1555
– JIAJING YUNYANG XIAN ZHI, 1541
– ZHENGDE KUIZHOU FU ZHI, 1513
SICHUAN RIBAO – Sichuan Daily. China. In Chinese. Current subscription. Annual delivery 1980- , 1 reel/y. M D20 – 1 – $55.00r – cc Microforms [072]
SICHUAN XINHAI GEMING SHILIAO (SHANG-XIA CE) – Historical materials on the Revolution of 1911 in Sichuan, v1-2.Comp. by Kui Yintao, Zhao Qing. 14 fiches. F-H113 – 9 – $67.50 – cc Microforms [950]
SICHUAN YIXUEYUAN XUEBAO – Acta Academiae Medicinae Sichuan. In Chinese but English abstracts to the main articles. F p166 – 9 – 4.00f – cc Microforms [073]
SICILL-I OSMANI YAHUT TEZKERE-I MESAHIR I OSMANIVE ISTANBUL / Mehmet Sureyya – 4v. Matbaa-i Amire. 1308-11. BA-412 2 – 8 – ne IDC [956]
Sicily *see*
– GAZETA UFFICIALE
– PLANO QUINQUENNALE PER LO SVILUPPO ECONOMICO E SOCIALE DELLA SICILIA
Sicioff, A A *see* EL CASO DEL JUDAIZANTE JERONIMO FRAY DIEGO DE MARCHENA
SICK CALLS : FROM THE DIARY OF A MISSIONARY PRIEST / Price, Edward – new ed. London: R Washbourne, 1892 – 1mf – 9 – 0-8370-6694-8 – 1986-0694 – us A.T.L.A. [920]
SICK ROOM ALTER MANUAL: WITH PRAYERS, FORMULAS, INSTRUCTIONS IN ADMINISTERING THE SACRAMENTS: AND A COMPLETE COURSE OF INSTRUCTIONS TO NURSES IN ATTENDING THE SICK / Eummelen, H – Vancouver, B.C.: H. Eummelen, 1895. 02921. (Pre-1900 Canadiana) – 9 – cn C.I.H.M. [971]
Sickel, Th *see* ZUR GESCHICHTE DES CONCILS VON TRIENT (1559-63)

Sickenberger, J *see*
- FRAGMENTE DER HOMILIEN DES CYRILL VON ALEXANDRIEN ZUM LUKASEVANGELIUM (T.U.U. 3-34/1B)
- DIE LUKASKATENE DES NIKETAS VON HERAKLEIA (T.U.U. 2-22/4)
- TITUS VON BOSTRA STUDIEN ZU DESSEN LUKASHOMILIEN (T.U.U. 2-21/1)

SICKINGEN UND KARL 5 / Jelusich, Mirko – Stuttgart: Deutsche Volksbuecher, 1943 – 1r – 1 – us U.W. Library [830]
SICKINGEN UND LANDSCHAD / Kueck, Eduard – (Includes bibliographical references) – Rostock: Adler, 1899 – 1r – 1 – us U.W. Library [943]
SICKINGENS RING : NOVELLE / Noelle, Fritz – Muenchen: Deutscher Volksverlag, 1943 – 1r – 1 – us U.W. Library [830]
SICKLE AND SHEAF – Oskaloosa. Kan. 1873-1886 – 1 – us UMI [071]
Sickles, Daniel E *see* PAPERS
Sicotte, Louis W *see*
- CADASTRAL PLANS
- PLANS OFFICIELS DE LA PAROISSE DE MONTREAL
- PLANS OFFICIELS DES COMTES D'HOCHELAGA ET DE JACQUES-CARTIER

SICULAE PRODROMUS / Gussone, G – 2v. Neapoli. 1827-28.; Suppl. 1832-43. B-98 2 – 8 – ne IDC [580]
Siculus, Calpurnius *see* BUCOLICA, ETC
SIDANG DESRAA / Asia-African Peoples' Solidarity Council – Bandung. SE-10,252 1. 10-15 April, 1961 – 9 – ne IDC [950]
SIDANG MAHKAMAH TENTERA AGUNG DALAM PEMERIKSAAN PROCES SUDARSONO CS; STENOGRAFISCH VERSLAG / Sudarsono, R P – SE 5267/1. 1949 – 9 – ne IDC [950]
SIDCUP AND BEXLEY MERCURY – (Also known as: Mercury Bexley Borough) – 1989-Mar, Apr 6-Jun 29, Jul 1995-Mar 1997 – 23 1/2r – 1 – uk British Libr Newspaper [072]
SIDE LIGHTS ON THE CONFLICTS OF METHODISM DURING THE SECOND QUARTER OF THE NINETEENTH CENTURY, 1827-1852,...CHIEFLY FROM THE NOTES OF JOSEPH FOWLER... / Gregory, B – London, 1898. viii/584p – 7mf – 9 – ne IDC [240]
SIDE LIGHTS UPON SUPERSTITION / Macvicar, Neil – [s.l]: Lovedale Press, 1939 – us Res Libr [290]
SIDELIGHTS FROM PATMOS BY GEORGE MATHESON / Matheson, George – London, New York: Hodder & Stoughton, [1897] – 1mf – 9 – 0-8370-4316-6 – 1985-2316 – us A.T.L.A. [220]
SIDELIGHTS ON RELIGION / Jonathan Brierley – New York: Thomas Whittaker, 1908. 1 fiche – 9 – us A.T.L.A. [240]
Sidersky, D *see* LES ORIGINES DES LEGENDES MUSULMANES DANS LE CORAN ET DANS LES VIES DU PROPHETE
Sidgwick, Henry *see*
- LECTURES ON THE PHILOSOPHY OF KANT AND OTHER PHILOSOPHICAL LECTURES & ESSAYS
- THE METHODS OF ETHICS
- MISCELLANEOUS ESSAYS AND ADDRESSES
- OUTLINES OF THE HISTORY OF ETHICS FOR ENGLISH READERS
- PRACTICAL ETHICS

SIDI HENNINI – 2no. Alger. aout 1937 – 1 – fr A.C.R.P.P. [073]
Sidibe, Fode Moussa Balla *see* DEUX RECITS DE CHASSE
SIDIC : ENGLISH EDITION – v1-18. 1967-85 (complete) – 2r – 1 – ATLA S0866 – us A.T.L.A. [073]
Sidik Gondowarsito *see* BRIEF NOTES ON JAVANESE CUSTOMS AND MANNERS AND WEDDING CEREMONIES
Sidik Kertapati *see* SEKITER PROKLAMASI 17 AGUSTUS 1945
Sidis, Boris *see* THE PSYCHOLOGY OF LAUGHTER
Sidjabat, Walter Bonar *see* RELIGIOUS TOLERANCE AND THE CHRISTIAN FAITH; A STUDY CONCERNING THE CONCEPT OF DIVINE OMNIPOTENCE IN THE INDONESIAN CONSTITUTION IN THE LIGHT OF ISLAM AND CHRISTIANITY
SIDNEY AND ISLANDS REVIEW – Canada. -w. 25 April 1913-29 Dec 1921. 3 reels – 1 – uk British Libr Newspaper [072]
SIDNEY JANIS GALLERY CATALOGUE – (Individual titles not listed separately) – New York, 1950-1976 – 110 catalogues on 113mf – 9 – £710.00 – uk Chadwyck [700]
SIDNEY MORNING HERALD – 1 – F5,935.00 – sz Infoprint [072]
SIDNEY NEWS – Sidney, NE. -w. Oct 1926-Jan 1930 – 1 – us NE Hist [071]
Sidney, Philip *see* DEFENSA DE LA POESIA (SIECLE 17)
SIDNEY PLAINDEALER – Sidney, NE. -w. Oct 1878-Oct 1879 – 1 – us NE Hist [071]
Sidney. Presbytery (Pres. Ch. in the U.S.A. Old School) *see* MINUTES, 1837-1870
SIDNEY REPUBLICAN – Sidney, NE. -w. Oct 1901-Apr 1902 – 1 – us NE Hist [071]
SIDNEY TELEGRAPH – Sidney, NE. -w. (-sw 1945-54; -tw 1926-43; 1945 to date). Jul 1876; Jan 1877; Jan 1878-Aug 1879; May 1880-Jan 1881; Sep 1881 to date – 1 – us NE Hist [071]
Sidorenko, A V *see* GIDROGEOLOGIIA SSSR
Sidorov, N P *see* MASONSTVO V EGO PROSHLOM I NASTOIASHCHEM
DEN SIDSTE FRANKLIN-EXPEDITION / Petersen, C – 266 p., illus., maps. BN 340 2. 1860 – 8 – ne IDC [910]
SIDWAYA – Ouagadougou, Burkina Faso. Mar 23-Oct 3 1986; June 1987-May 5 1988 – 3r – 1 – us L of C Photodup [072]
SIE : WOCHENZEITUNG FUER FRAUENRECHT UND MENSCHENRECHT – Berlin, dec 1945-sep 28 1952 – 4r – 1 – Inquire at Mikrofilmarchiv for details – gw Misc Inst [320]
SIE DJIN KWIE TJENG TANG – SE 4568 1 – 9 – ne IDC [950]
SIE WERDEN AUFERSTEHEN! / Goote, Thor – Berlin: E S Mittler, 1931 – 1r – 1 – us U.W. Library [830]
SIEBEN JAHRE IN SUED-AFRIKA / Holum, E – 2v. Wien. 1881. BA-172 2 – 8 – ne IDC [960]
SIEBEN NEUE BRUCHSTUECKE DER SYLLOGISMEN DES APELLES (T.U.U. 1-6/3B) / Harnack, Adolf von – Leipzig, 1890 – 1mf – 9 – ne Slangenburg [240]
SIEBEN REDEN / Burte, Hermann – Strassburg: Huenenburg-Verlag, 1943 – 1r – 1 – us U.W. Library [430]
SIEBEN VOR VERDUN : EIN KRIEGSROMAN / Wehner, Josef Magnus – Muenchen: G Mueller, 1930 – 1r – 1 – us U.W. Library [830]
DIE SIEBEN WORTE DES ERLOSERS AM KREUTZ... STRING QUARTET VERSION. H. 20:1B, OP. 31 / Haydn, Joseph – (4 parts) – Berlin: Hummel, 1788 – 1 – us Sibley [780]
SIEBENBUERGISCH-DEUTSCHE ZEITUNG *see* BISTRITZER DEUTSCHE ZEITUNG
SIEBENBUERGISCH-DEUTSCHES TAGEBLATT – Hermannstadt (Sibiu), Rumaenien. 1 Jan 1874-31 Mar 1944 (incomplete) – 1 – gw Mikrofilm [949]
SIEBENBUERGISCHER VOLKSBOTE – Kronstadt (Brasov), Rumaenien. 4 Jul-30 Sept 1931 – 1r – 1 – gw Mikrofilm [949]
SIEBENBURISCH-AMERIKANISCHES VOLKSBLATT – Cleveland, Ohio. -w. 1907-54. Inc. predecessor titles: Die Neue Heimat; Deutsch Ungarisches Volksblatt; Nationale Gazette – 1 – us Western Res [071]
SIEBENZAHL UND SABBAT BEI DEN BABYLONIERN UND IM ALTEN TESTAMENT / Hehn, Johannes – Leipzig: J.C. Hinrichs, 1907. 1 fiche – 9 – us A.T.L.A. [240]
SIEBENZAHL UND SABBAT BEI DEN BABYLONIERN UND IM ALTEN TESTAMENT / Hehn, Johannes – (Leipziger semitistische studien. v. 2, pt. 5. Leipzig. 1908). Leipzig. 1907. BNE-20,111 1 – 9 – ne IDC [290]
Sieber, F W *see*
- HERBARIUM FLORAE AEGYPTIACAE
- REISE NACH DER INSEL KRETA IM GRIECHISCHEN ARCHIPELAGUS IM JAHRE 1817

Siebert, Johannes *see* METRIK UND RHYTHMIK IN TANNHAEUSERS GEDICHTEN
Siebert, Otto *see* DIE RELIGIONSPHILOSOPHIE IN DEUTSCHLAND...RUDOLF EUCKEN ALS FESTGABE
Siebert, Wilhelm *see* HEINRICH HEINES BEZIEHUNGEN ZU E.T.A. HOFFMANN
Siebert, Wolfgang *see* VOLKSGESETZBUCH. GRUNDREGEL UND BUCH I
Siebke, Friedrich *see* DAS SCHLICHTUNGSWESEN IM RUHRBERGBAU SEIT DER STABILISIERUNG DER WAEHRUNG BIS ZUR MITTE DES JAHRES 1929
Siebke, J H S *see* ENUMERATIO INSECTORUM NORVEGICORUM
SIEBMACHER ARMORIAL COLLECTION / ed by Siebmacher, Johann – 18r – 1 – $1330.00 – us UMI [920]
Siebmacher, Johann *see* SIEBMACHER ARMORIAL COLLECTION
Siebold, P F von *see*
- FAUNA JAPONICA, SIVE DESCRIPTIO ANIMALIUM, QUAE IN ITINERE PER JAPONIAM
- FLORA JAPONICA
- LUI HO, SIVE VOCABULARIUM SINENSE IN KORAIANUM CONVERSUM...
- MAMMALIA FAUNA JAPONICAE

SIEBOLDIA – Leiden, 1875-1883. v1-9 – 135mf – 8 – ne IDC [580]
DIE SIEBTE AM SONNTAG – Goettingen. oct 11, 1987-feb 3, 1991 – 2r – 1 – gw Mikrofilm [072]
Sieburg, Erich *see* DIE VORGESCHICHTE DER ERBFOERSTER-
Siecke, Ernst *see* DIE LIEBESGESCHICHTE DES HIMMELS
LE SIECLE – Paris. 23 juin 1836-1927 – 1 – fr A.C.R.P.P. [073]
LE SIECLE – t. 1-2. Paris. janv-juin 1833 – 1 – fr A.C.R.P.P. [073]
LE SIECLE DE REMBRANDT. TABLEAUX HOLLANDAIS DES COLLECTIONS PUBLIQUES FRANCAISES / Reunion des musees nationaux. Paris – 1970. 241 illus. 4 fiches – 9 – fr Réunion [700]
LE SIECLE LITTERAIRE – no. 1-14. Paris. oct 1875-avr 1876 – 1 – fr A.C.R.P.P. [073]
SIECUS REPORT OF THE SEX INFORMATION AND EDUCATION COUNCIL OF THE UNITED STATES – v1- 1972- 1,5,6; v4- 9 – us UMI [370]
SIEDM SIEDMIOLICI, CZYLI POT WIEKU ZYCIA:...HISTORJI POLSKIEJ W AMERYCE / Kruszka, Waclaw – Milwaukee, 1924.2v – 1 – us U.W. Library [305]
Sieffert, Friedrich *see* DER BRIEF AN DIE GALATER
Sieg, Paul Eugen *see* DETATOM
LA SIEGA / Coronado, Carolina – 1854 – 9 – $1.50f – sp Bibl Santa Ana [830]
SIEGE DE NANTES (1793) : 6 DOCUMENTS MICROFILMES ENSEMBLE/MICROFILMED TOGETHER – (Velasque, A. – Le Siege de Nantes et ses prodromes : 29 juin 1793. -[Nantes]:[s.n.],[1922]; – Chassin, Charles-L. – Centenaire national du 29 juin 1793 : recit authentique de la defense de Nantes. – Nantes: Schwob, 1893;- Centenaire de la defense de Nantes, 29 juin 1793: catalogue du Musee artistique et historique. – Nantes: Schwob, 1893; – Comptes-rendus a la Convention nationale et au Ministre de la Guerre de l'attaque de Nantes par l'armee des rebelles. – Nantes: Malassis,[1793]; – Jean-Michel Beysser(...)commandant temporaire de la ville et chateau de Nantes, aux representants du peuple Gillet, Merlin et Coustard(...). – Nantes: Herault, 1793; – Seance du Comite central des corps administratifs du departement de la Loire-Inferieure du 29 juin 1793(...). – Nantes: Malassis, 1793) – fr Armell [910]
THE SIEGE OF BELGRADE: AN OPERA IN THREE ACTS. / Storace, Stephen – (Vocal score). 1791 – 9 – us Sibley [780]
THE SIEGE OF CORINTH : A POEM; PARISINA: A POEM / Byron, George Gordon Byron – London: Printed for John Murray, 1816 – 1 roll – 1 – 1-55879-340-2 – uk Libr Preservation [810]
THE SIEGE OF FORT ERIE: AN EPISODE IN THE WAR OF 1812 / Babcock, Louis L – Buffalo: Peter Paul Book Co., 1899. 00931. (Pre-1900 Canadiana) – 9 – cn C.I.H.M. [971]
THE SIEGE OF QUEBEC AND THE BATTLE OF THE PLAINS OF ABRAHAM / Dionne, Narcisse Eutrope – Quebec: Dussault & Proulx..., 1903. SEM105P500 – 1mf – 9 – Can$2.25 – cn Bibl Nat [355]
THE SIEGE OF SAVANNAH IN 1779 AS DESCRIBED IN TWO CONTEMPORANEOUS JOURNALS OF FRENCH OFFICERS IN THE FLEET OF COUNT D'ESTAING / Estaing, Charles Henri – Albany, N.Y.: J. Munsell, 1874. 05491. (Pre-1900 Canadiana) – 9 – cn C.I.H.M. [971]
Siegel, F R *see* REVIEW OF RESEARCH ON MODERN PROBLEMS IN GEOCHEMISTRY
Siegelberg, W *see* KOPTISCHES HANDWOERTERBUCH
SIEGEL'S NEWSLETTER – Bronx, NY. 1975 – 1 – us A.J.P.C. [071]
SIEGENER ZEITUNG – Siegen, Germany. 1992- – 7r per yr – 1 – gw Mikrofilm [072]
SIEGESSAEULE – Berlin. -m. illus. 1987- . Gay liberation movement-periodical – 1 – us U.W. Library [073]
DIE SIEGESSAEULE MESA'S KOENIGS DER MOABITER : EIN BEITRAG ZUR HEBRAEISCHEN ALTERTHUMSKUNDE / Schlottmann, Konstantin – (Includes Hebrew text and German translation of the inscription) – Halle: Buchhandlung des Waisenhauses, 1870 – 1mf – 9 – 0-8370-7105-4 – 1986-1105 – us A.T.L.A. [470]
Siegfried, A *see* LES FORCES RELIGIEUSES ET LA VIE POLITIQUE
Siegfried, Carl *see*
- ESRA, NEHEMIA UND ESTHER
- GRAMMATIK DER NEUHEBRAEISCHEN SPRACHE
- PREDIGER UND HOHESLIED

DIE SIEGFRIED-TRAGOEDIE IM NIBELUNGENRING : EINE AUFKLAERUNG UEBER WAGNERS LEBENSANSCHAUUNG / Friedrich, Erich – Breslau: W Markgraf, 1913 – 1r – 1 – us U.W. Library [790]
SIEGKREIS RUNDSCHAU *see* KOELNISCHE RUNDSCHAU
Siegl, Dora *see* OESTERREICHS DICHTERFUERSTIN MARIE VON EBNER-ESCHENBACH
Siegmund, A *see* DIE UEBERLIEFERUNG DER GRIECHISCHEN CHRISTL. LIT.
SIEGWART / Werner, E – Stuttgart: Union Deutsche Verlagsgesellschaft, c1909 – 1 – us U.W. Library [830]
SIEMENS FORSCHUNGS- UND ENTWICKLUNGSBERICHTE – v. 1-9. 1971-80 – 1,5,9 – 594.00 – us UMI [073]
SIEMENS ZEITSCHRIFT – v. 1-21. 1921-1940 – 1,5,6 – us Princeton Micro [500]
Siemering, A *see* EIN VERFEHLTES LEBEN
Siemers, Beverly J *see* BONE DENSITY PATTERNS IN ADULT FEMALES WITH A HISTORY OF ANOREXIA NERVOSA
SIEMPRE – (Has suppl: Cultura en Mexico 1962) – Mexico: Editorial Siempre! v1-1228 jun 23 1953-sep 1977 (81r); n1280-1801 jan 1978-dec 1987 (32r) – 1 – us Res Libr [073]
SIEMPRE – Vallarta, MX. 1973- – 84+ r – $4,200.00 ($200.00y) – R04226 – us Library Micro [072]
Sienkiewicz, Henryk *see* THE KNIGHTS OF THE CROSS
SIERRA ADVOCATE – Downieville, CA. 1866-1867 – 1r – 1 – $50.00 – C03200 – us Library Micro [071]
SIERRA AGE – Downieville, CA. 1871 – 1r – 1 – $50.00 – C03591 – us Library Micro [071]
SIERRA BOOSTER – Loyalton, CA. 1949-72 – 12r – 1 – $600.00 – B02412 – us Library Micro [071]
SIERRA CLUB BOOKS OUT OF PRINT – (Individual titles listed separately) – 1 – $50.00r – us Library Micro [333]
SIERRA CLUB BOOKS OUT OF PRINT *see*
- CLEAR CUT
- ENERGY
- MERCURY
- OIL ON ICE
- OILSPILL WESLEY MARX
- PERSONAL PAPERS OF "THE FATHER OF SEQUOIA NATIONAL PARK, 1890-1930"
- THE SILVER RUSH AT MINERAL KING, CALIFORNIA 1873-1882
- STRIPPING
- THE WATERHUSTLERS
- WILDERNESS
- WILDERNESS IN A CHANGING WORLD ANTHOLOGY

Sierra, Francisco et al *see* 1ST CONGRESO SINDICAL AGRARIO DE EXTREMADURA 3 PONENCIA. PLAN NACIONAL DE TRANSFORMACION EN EL CAMPO
SIERRA LEONE : ANNUAL STATISTICAL DIGEST 1968-1976 / Sierra Leone. Central Statistics Office – (1972-75 not publ. Coll title: African Official Statistical Serials, 1867- 1982) – 10mf – 9 – £84.00 – uk Chadwyck [960]
Sierra Leone *see*
- ANNUAL DEPARTMENTAL REPORTS
- DRAFT FIVE YEAR PLAN OF ECONOMIC AND SOCIAL DEVELOPMENT, 1 JUL 1966-30 JUN 1971
- GOVERNMENT PUBLICATIONS
- MISCELLANEOUS DOCUMENTS AND PAPERS
- A PLAN OF ECONOMIC DEVELOPMENT FOR SIERRA LEONE
- A PROGRESS REPORT ON ECONOMIC AND SOCIAL DEVELOPMENT, 27 APR 1961-31 MAR 1965
- PROGRESS REPORT ON THE DEVELOPMENT PROGRAMME FOR 1947
- PROGRESS REPORT ON THE DEVELOPMENT PROGRAMME FOR 1948

- PROGRESS REPORT ON THE DEVELOPMENT PROGRAMME FOR 1949
- PROGRESS REPORT ON THE DEVELOPMENT PROGRAMME FOR 1951
- TEN-YEAR PLAN OF ECONOMIC AND SOCIAL DEVELOPMENT FOR SIERRA LEONE, 1962/63-1971/72

Sierra Leone. Central Statistics Office *see* SIERRA LEONE

SIERRA LEONE CHURCH TIMES – Freetown. Sierra Leone. -m. May 1884-Apr 1886. (Imperfect). (29 ft) – 1 – uk British Libr Newspaper [072]

Sierra Leone. Court of Appeals *see* TREASON TRIAL 1970: DAVID LANDSANA AND ELEVEN OTHERS

SIERRA LEONE DEMOGRAPHIC DATA – Population Census, 1963, and Household Surveys, 1966-69 – 2r – 1 – $79.00 – us African Imprint [960]

SIERRA LEONE FARM AND TRADE REPORT – Freetown. Sierra Leone. -m. Oct 1886-Mar 1887. (5 ft) – 1 – uk British Libr Newspaper [073]

SIERRA LEONE GAZETTE – 1808-10 and 1817-27 – 1 – uk Microform Academic [960]

SIERRA LEONE GUARDIAN – Freetown, Sierra Leone. -w. 10 April 1908-Dec 1919; Jan 1930-Dec 1932. 11 reels – 1 – uk British Libr Newspaper [072]

Sierra Leone. Laws, Statutes, etc *see*
- THE ORDINANCES OF THE COLONY OF SIERRA LEONE, NOW IN FORCE, COMMENCING 12TH OCTOBER 1811, AND ENDING 5TH OCTOBER 1857
- ORDINANCES OF THE SETTLEMENT OF SIERRA LEONE, PASSED IN THE YEARS 1875, 1876, 1877, 1878, 1879, TO JUNE 1880; ROYAL CHARTERS; TREATIES OF THE GOVERNMENT OF SIERRA LEONE WITH THE NATIVE CHIEFS.

Sierra Leone. Legislative Council *see* DEBATES

Sierra Leone. Office of the Resident Representative *see* DEVELOPMENT CO-OPERATION SIERRA LEONE

SIERRA LEONE QUARTERLY STATISTICAL BULLETIN – 1963-71 – 1 – $39.50 – us African Imprint [960]

SIERRA LEONE ROYAL GAZETTE – Sierra Leone. v87-101. 1956-70 – 16r – 1 – us Ross [324]

SIERRA LEONE STATISTICAL DATA – (Annual Statistical Digest 1968-71, National Accounts 1966-1963/64-1968/69) – 1 – $39.50 – us African Imprint [960]

SIERRA LEONE STUDIES – Freetown, Sierra Leone: Institute of African Studies, Fourah Bay College. ns: n13. jun 1960 – us Res Libr [960]

Sierra Leone. Supreme Court *see* JUDGMENTS

Sierra Leone. UNESCO Educational Planning Mission *see* THE DEVELOPMENT PROGRAMME IN EDUCATION FOR SIERRA LEONE, 1964-1970

SIERRA LEONE WEEKLY NEWS – Freetown. Sierra Leone. -w. 6 Sep 1884-30 Dec 1939, 7 Sept 1940-22 Dec 1951. 93 reels – 1 – uk British Libr Newspaper [072]

THE SIERRA LEONE WEEKLY NEWS – Freetown. Sierra Leone. mar. 3, 1906; Jan. 23, 1915 – 1 – us NY Public [072]

SIERRA LIFE – Nevada City, CA. Dec 1978-81 – 4r – 1 – $200.00 – B02523 – us Library Micro [071]

SIERRA MADRE NEWS – Sierra Madre, CA. 1984-1993 – 10r – 1 – $500.00 – R03532 – us Library Micro [071]

SIERRA MAGAZINE – Lake Tahoe, NV. 1959-1961 – 1r – 1 – $50.00 – B06061 – us Library Micro [071]

Sierra, Nelson *see* DETERMINING THE VALIDITY AND RELIABILITY OF THE NICHOLAS MANUAL MUSCLE TESTER AS A MEASURE OF ISOMETRIC STRENGTH IN WOMEN WITH ARTHRITIS

SIERRA STAR – Oakhurst, CA. Jul-Dec 1977 (incomplete); 1978-83 – 7r – 1 – $350.00 – B02537 – us Library Micro [071]

SIERRA SUN – Truckee, CA. Apr 1971- – 59+ r – 1 – $2,950.00 ($270.00y) – N03040 – us Library Micro [071]

SIERRA SUN – Truckee, CA, NV. 1971 – 65+ r – 1 – $3,250.00 ($270.00y) – N03040 – us Library Micro [071]

SIERRA VALLEY NEWS – Loyalton, CA. 1926-37; 1940-42 – 7r – 1 – $350.00 – B02413 – us Library Micro [071]

Sierra, Vicente D *see* LOS JESUITAS GERMANOS EN LA CONQUISTA ESPIRITUAL DE HISPANO AMERICA. SIGLOS 16-17

SIETE CARTAS INEDITAS DEL REY D. FELIPE 2 / Perez de Guzman, Juan – Madrid: Est. Tip. Fortanet, 1912 – 1 – sp Bibl Santa Ana [910]

LAS SIETE CENTURIAS DE LA CIUDAD DE PLASENCIA. INFORME DE ALEJANDRO MATIAS GIL / Barrantes Moreno, Vicente – Madrid: Fortanet, 2nd ed 1909. B.R.A.H. i. 1877. reimp. 1909. pp222-225 – 1 – sp Bibl Santa Ana [946]

LAS SIETE CENTURIAS...ALFONSO 8 / Matias Gil, Alejandro – 1877 – 9 – $1.50f – sp Bibl Santa Ana [946]

LAS SIETE CENTURIAS...DE PLASENCIA... (PROSPECTO) / Matias Gil, Alejandro – Plasencia: Tip. de E. Pinto Sanchez, 1876 – 1 – sp Bibl Santa Ana [946]

LOS SIETE DIAS DE LA PASION O LECCIONES PRACTICAS DE VIRTUD / Amado, Manuel – 1831 – 9 – 1.50f – sp Bibl Santa Ana [170]

SIETE EDITORIALES DE ARRIBA Y SU COMENTARIO / Arriba. Madrid – Destinados a los espanoles que pelean en los frentes, y a los que trabajan en la retaguardia, para esclarecer su conciencia nacional-sindicalista. Madrid? 1936? Fiche W 729. (Blodgett Collection of Spanish Civil War Pamphlets) – 9 – us H.U. College Libr [946]

Siete Iglesias, Antonio de *see*
- LAS DOS PARTIDAS DE BAUTISMO DE DON LUIS DE SALAZAR Y CASTRO
- NUEVAS NOTAS SOBRE EL CONDADO DE LA GOMERA
- LA SUBLEVACION DE CATALUNA. ANTECEDENTES DE UNOS TITULOS DEL REINO
- TITULOS Y GRANDEZAS DEL REINO, SEGUNDA PARTE. TITULOS DE LA CORONA DE ARAGON HASTA LA MUERTE DE FERNANDO EL, CATOLICO
- TITULOS Y GRANDEZAS DEL REYNO. TITULOS DE LA CORONA DE CASTILLA, CONCEDIDOS POR LOS REYES DE CASTILLA, HASTA LA MUERTE DE FERNANDO 5 EL CATOLICO. 1516

Siete Iglesias, Marques de *see* CONDADO DE LA GOMERA

LOS SIETE LIBROS...DE LA GUERRA QUE TUVIERON LOS JUDIOS CON LOS ROMANOS... / Flavio Josefo – Sevilla, 1532 – 5mf – 9 – sp Cultura [956]

LAS SIETE PARTIDAS DE ALFONSO 10 / Lopez de Tovar, Gregorio – (Partida 1a. 1587. Partida 1-7. 1758. Tomo II. Partidas 3-5. 1789. Tomo II. Partidas 1-4. 1610. Tomo III. Partidas 1-7. 1767. Tomo III. Partidas 6-7. 1789) – Tomo I, 1a y 2a partidas. 1789 – 9 – $1.50f – sp Bibl Santa Ana [946]

SIETE PARTIDAS. LAS...NUEVAMENTE GLOSADAS POR EL LICENCIADO / Lopez de Tovar, Gregorio et al – Madrid: Maguncia Balthasar Lipsius, 1611 (Al fin 1610). Contiene Partidas 1 y 2 – sp Bibl Santa Ana [946]

Sieveking, I Giberne *see* MEMOIR AND LETTERS OF FRANCIS W. NEWMAN

SIEVERNNYE TSVIETY : AL'MANAKH – 1901-05 – 1r – 1 – us Ross [947]

SIEVERNOE UTRO – Arkhangel'sk, USSR. Aug 1918-Dec 1919 – 3r – 1 – us L of C Photodup [072]

SIEVERNYI VIESTNIK – 1885-98. Incomplete – 1 – 736.00 – us L of C Photodup [073]

Sievers, E *see* DIE ALTHOCHDEUTSCHEN GLOSSEN

Sievers, Wilhelm *see* GEOGRAFIA DE BOLIVIA Y PERU

LE SIFFLEUX : CARICATURES – Montreal, Canada. v1 n3. 13 fev 1937-v1 n11. 10 avr 1937 – 1r – 1 – Can$30.00 – cn Can Microfilming [072]

SIFREI AGORAH / Ben-Avigdor – new ed. 3v. Warsaw. 1922. BJ-422-5 1 – 9 – ne IDC [890]

SIFRUT / ed by Frischmann, D – 4v. Warsaw. 1909-10. BJ-422-84 1 – 9 – ne IDC [470]

SIFTINGS – Jetmore. Kan. 1886-1895 – 1 – us UMI [071]

Sigart, J D *see* GLOSSAIRE ETYMOLOGIQUE MONTOIS

SIGER DE BRABANT D'APRES SES OEUVRES INEDITES, VOL 1 : LES OEUVRES INEDITES / Steenbergen, F van – 1931 – 12mf – 8 – ne Slangenburg [180]

SIGER DE BRABANT D'APRES SES OEUVRES INEDITES, VOL 2 : SIGER DANS L'HISTOIRE DE L'ARISTOTELISME / Steenbergen, F van – Louvain 1942 – 11mf – 8 – ne Slangenburg [180]

SIGER DE BRABANT ET L'AVERROISME LATIN AU 13E SIECLE. ETUDE CRITIQUE / Mandonnet, P – Louvain, 1911 – 9mf – 8 – ne Slangenburg [100]

SIGER DE BRABANT ET L'AVERROISME LATIN AU 13E SIECLE. TEXTES INEDITS / Mandonnet, P – Louvain, 1908 – 6mf – 8 – ne Slangenburg [100]

SIGER DE BRABANT, QUESTIONS SUR LA PHISIQUE D'ARISTOTE / Delhaye, P – 1949 – 8mf – 8 – ne Slangenburg [110]

Sigerist, Henry Ernest *see* MAN AND MEDICINE; AN INTRODUCTION TO MEDICAL KNOWLEDGE

SIGHT: AN EXPOSITION OF THE PRINCIPLES OF MONOCULAR AND BINOCULAR VISION / LeConte, Joseph – (2nd ed. rev. and enl. New York: D. Appleton, 1897. xvi,318p. illus. 1) – New York: D. Appleton, 1881. 275p. illus. diagrs – 1 – us U.W. Library [530]

SIGHT AND SOUND – 1932- – 1-2r per y – 1 – inquire – us Ross [790]

SIGHT AND SOUND – (Incorporates Monthly Film Bulletin after 1991) – 1932-93 – 1 – £950.00 – uk World [790]

SIGHT SAVING REVIEW – v1-50 1931-80 1; v40-50 5,6; v47-50 9 – us UMI [617]

SIGHTSAVING – v51-. 1982- – 1,5,6,9 – us UMI [617]

SIGISMONDO. MELODRAMA IN DUE ATTI DI GUISEPPE FOPPA / Rossini, G – (Vocal score) – Milano: Ricordi, [185-?] – 1 – us Sibley [780]

SIGLA CODICUM MANUSCRIPTORUM QUI OLIM IN BIBLIOTHECA PUBLICA LENINOPOLITANA EXSTANTES NUNC IN BIBLIOTHECA UNIVERSITAS VARSOVIENSIS ASSERVANTUR – Prepared by W. Suchodolski. Krakow. 1928. Supplementum ad sigla codicum manuscriptorum. Krakow. 1937. PKG-F-18.52 BR-11,205 1 – 9 – ne IDC [010]

Sigleur, Johannes *see* DAS STAEHLERNE ABENTEUER

SIGLO *see* EL-SIGLO

EL SIGLO JEROGLIFICO AZTECA...1897 / Sotomayor, Damaso; ed by Bayle, Constantino – Madrid: Razon y Fe, 1928 – 9 – sp Bibl Santa Ana [972]

THE SIGN OF FOUR / Doyle, Arthur Conan – London: Spencer Blackett, 1890 – 1 roll – 1 – 1-55879-784-X – uk Libr Preservation [830]

THE SIGN OF THE CROSS IN MADAGASCAR : OR, FROM DARKNESS TO LIGHT / Fletcher, John Joseph Kilpin – Boston: United Society Christian Endeavor, c1900 – 1mf – 9 – 0-8370-6572-0 – 1986-0572 – us A.T.L.A. [240]

SIGNA / Ouida – British Fiction Archive: Unit 3 – 9 – uk Bell [830]

LE SIGNAL / ed by Buies, Arthur – Montreal, Canada. 1885 – 1r – 1 – Can$25.00 – cn Can Microfilming [072]

LE SIGNAL – Montreal, Canada. 14 nov 1896-18 jun 1898 – 1r – 1 – Can$35.00 – cn Can Microfilming [072]

LE SIGNAL – Quebec, 11 dec 1915 – 1r – 1 – Can$25.00 – cn Can Microfilming [072]

SIGNAL / Armed Forces Communications Association – Journal of the Armed Forces Communications Association. v. 1-17. Sep Oct 1946-Aug 1963 – 1 – 243.00 – us L of C Photodup [355]

SIGNAL – Berlin. 1940-45 n5 – 4r – 1 – gw Mikrofilm [072]

SIGNAL – Berlin, Germany. Ed. in Swedish. 1941:7-1945:4 – 1 – sw Kungliga [073]

SIGNAL – Chester.MT. 1905-15 – 1 – us UMI [071]

SIGNAL – Guide Rock. Neb. 1883-1957 – 1 – us UMI [071]

SIGNAL – Holton. Kan. 1878-1886 – 1 – us UMI [071]

SIGNAL – Huntingburg. Ind. 1915-1925; 1935-1937; 1953-1955; 1956-1958; 1959-1963 – 1 – us UMI [071]

SIGNAL – Huntington Park. Calif. 1925- – 1 – us UMI [071]

SIGNAL – Joliet. Ill. -w. 1846-48, 1861-64 – 1 – us UMI [071]

SIGNAL – Kalida, Ohio. 1899-1900 – 1r – 1 – $32.50r – us Archival [071]

SIGNAL – Lyndon. Kan. 1870-71 – 1 – us UMI [071]

SIGNAL – Middletown. Ohio. -w. 1881-84, 1891-93, 1896-1900 – 1 – us UMI [071]

SIGNAL – New York. (Yiddish Monthly). v. 1, 3-4 no. 11. Mar 1933-Nov 1936 – 1 – us NY Public [073]

SIGNAL – Seaside. Or. 1905-1963 – 1 – us UMI [071]

SIGNAL – Zanesville. Ohio. 1864-1959 – 1 – us UMI [071]

SIGNAL *see* ALARM SIGNAL

THE SIGNAL – Atwater, CA. 1911-Aug 1918; Jan 1927-Dec 1931; 1933- – 42+ r – 1 – $2,100.00 ($50.00y) – B02025 – us Library Micro [071]

SIGNAL PROCESSING – v1-7. 1979-84 – 1,5,6,13 – sz Elsevier [621]

SIGNALE FUER DIE MUSIKALISCHE WELT – Berlin. v1-41. 1843-83; v86-88. 1928-30 – 634mf – 9 – P-846/2 – ne IDC [780]

SIGNALE FUER DIE MUSIKALISCHE WELT – v. 42-43, 54, 59-62, 64-66, 73, 77-78, 80, 85-86, 94. 1884-1936 – 1 – us Schnase [780]

SIGNALE FUER DIE MUSIKALISCHE WELT... 1843-1941 – 1993 – 315mf (1:42) – 9 – diazo DM5,980.00 (silver 7,480.00 ISBN: 3-598-33193-2) – 3-598-33192-4 – gw Saur [780]

SIGNATURE – London, 1946-54 – 2r + 32 col slides – 1 – £200.00 – uk Chadwyck [760]

Signer, Paul *see* ERNST TOLLER

EL SIGNIFICADO DEL "GIRO A LA IZQUIERDA" DEL PERONISMO / Codovilla, Victorio – Buenos Aires: Editorial Anteo, 1962 – 1 – CSUXAJA7588-B – us Hoover Inst Photo [320]

THE SIGNIFICANCE OF THE PERSONALITY OF CHRIST FOR THE MINISTER OF TODAY / Guthrie, Ernst Graham – Boston: Pilgrim Press, 1907. 1 fiche – 9 – us A.T.L.A. [240]

SIGNIFICANT FEATURES OF STATE AND LOCAL TAXES / U.S. Advisory Committee on Intergovernmental Relations – Washington: GPO, 1968 – 3mf – 9 – $4.50 – LLMC 82-700 – us L.L.M.C. [336]

Signoriello, Nuntio *see*
- ETHICA GENERALIS
- ETHICA SPECIALIS

SIGNPOSTS TO PEACE – AN INDEPENDENT SURVEY OF THE VIOLENCE IN NATAL, SOUTH AFRICA – 1990 – sz I.C.J. [320]

SIGNS – v. 1-. 1975- – 1,5,6,9 – us UMI [073]

SIGNS OF THE TIMES – Boston, MA. v1 n16. 15 nov 1840-v5 n11. 17 may 1843 – 1r – 1 – Can$35.00 – cn Can Microfilming [071]

SIGNS OF THE TIMES : DEVOTED TO THE OLD SCHOOL BAPTIST CAUSE – 1832-70 – 4r – 1 – us Ross [240]

SIGNS OF THE TIMES – Devoted to the Old School Baptist Cause. New-Vernon, N.Y. etc. v. 1-38. Nov 28 1832-Dec 1870. Incomplete – 1 – us NY Public [240]

SIGNS OF THE TIMES : LETTERS TO ERNST MORITZ ARNDT ON THE DANGERS TO RELIGIOUS LIBERTY IN THE PRESENT STATE OF THE WORLD / Bunsen, Christian Charles Josias – London: Smith, Elder, 1856 – 2mf – us A.T.L.A. [240]

SIGTUNA MARSTA POSTEN *see* NORRORT

SIGTUNA NYA TIDNING – Sigtuna, Sweden.1907-27 – 1 – sw Kungliga [072]

SIGTUNA TIDNING – Sigtuna, Sweden.1883-86 – 1 – sw Kungliga [072]

SIGTUNA TIDNING – Sigtuna, Sweden.1887-1906 – 1 – sw Kungliga [072]

SIGTUNA VECKOTIDNING – Sigtuna, Sweden.1882 – 1 – sw Kungliga [072]

SIGTUNABYGDEN – Uppsala, Sweden.1984- – 1 – sw Kungliga [072]

Siguan, Miguel *see* EDUCATION AND BILINGUALISM

Siguenza, Jose de et al *see* EL MONASTERIO DE YUSTE Y LA RETIRADA DEL EMPERADOR CARLOS 5. JARAIZ DE LA VERA

Siguenza y Gongora, Carlos *see*
- ALBOROTO Y MOTIN DE MEXICO DEL 8 DE JUNIO DE 1692. MEXICO, 1932
- PIEDAD HEROYCA DE DON' HERNANDO CORTES
- POEMAS RECOPILADOS Y ORDENADOS POR EL PROF. IRVING A. LEONARD

Sigurdsson, Jon *see* SAGA JATVARDAR KONUNGS HINS HELGA

SIHAM-I ILHAM – [Istanbul]: Mahmud Bey Matbaasi, 1921 – $60.00 – us MEDOC [470]

SIHOBU. GUNSEI KEIZIREI KAISETU / Java – Djakarta, Djawa Gunseikanbu Sihobu, 2604. 63p – 87mf – 9 – ne IDC [950]

Sihombing gelar Sutan Mulia Parlinggoman, T M *see* DAPOTNA PABIDANGKON DOHOT PABAGASHON; BUKU PARSIADJARAN HATA BATAK IU ANGKA SEKOLAH LANDJUTAN
SIIANIE – Illiustrirovannyi literaturno-politicheskii zhurnal. (38) Spb. 1872-73. Lacking: (1, 14-15, 22-40) 1872; (25-26) 1873. B-1894 2 – 8 – ne IDC [321]
SIIANIIA / Gippius, Z N – Stikhi. Paris. 1938. BR-721 2 – 8 – ne IDC [460]
LA SIIDA LAPONE / Delaporte, Y – 9 – F30.00 – fr Ethnologie [306]
SIKAP; MIMBAR POLITIK – Djakarta. Incomplete. SE 409 1. 1948-1959 – 9 – ne IDC [320]
SIKESTON FIRST BAPTIST CHURCH. SIKESTON, MISSOURI : CHURCH RECORDS – 1906, 1968 – 1 – 83.07 – us Baptist [240]
SIKKIM EDUCATION NEWSLETTER : EDUCATIONAL CHANGE IN SIKKIM / India. Sikkim. Directorate of Education – Gangtok, 1977 – 3mf – 9 – DE-556/1 – ne IDC [370]
Sikorskii, Vilen Vladimirovich *see* INDONEZIISKAIA LITERATURA; KRATKII OCHERK
SILAH – Selanik: Asir Matbaasi. Sahib ve Mueduerue: Muelazim Tahsin, 1908-1921 – 9 – $25.00 – us MEDOC [956]
SILAHDAR TARIHI / Aga, Silahdar Findiklili Mehmet – Istanbul: Devlet Matbaasi, [1928] – 18mf – 9 – $36.75 – us MEDOC [949]
Silahi, Inan *see* TJARA MERAWAT DAN MEMADJUKAN: 1 WARUNG DAN 2 TOKO
SILAS MARNER : THE WEAVER OF RAVELOE / Eliot, George – Edinburgh: William Blackwood, 1861 – 1 roll – 1 – uk Libr Preservation [830]
SILBER AND FLEMING CATALOGUES – (Sections are fully indexed) – 4r – 1 – $350.00 – 0-907006-73-6 – uk Mindata [730]
Silberbush, D I *see* HADASHIM GAM YESHANIM
DIE SILBERDISTELKLAUSE / Juenger, Friedrich Georg – Hamburg: H Dulk, [1947] – 1r – 1 – us U.W. Library [830]
Silberer, Victor *see* WIENER LUFTSCHIFFER-ZEITUNG 1. 1902-13. 1914
Silbergleit, H *see* DIE BEVOELKERUNGS-UND BERUFSVERHAELTNISSE DER JUDEN IM DEUTSCHEN REICH
Silberman, Leo *see* THE HORN OF AFRICA
Silbermann, G *see* REVUE ENTOMOLOGIQUE
Silbermann, Josef *see* DIE SPRACHE DER PRESSE UND DES PARLAMENTS
SILBERNE SAITEN : GEDICHTE / Zweig, Stefan – Berlin: Schuster & Loeffler, 1901 – 1r – 1 – us U.W. Library [810]
DER SILBERNE WAGEN : SIEBEN NOVELLEN / Wiechert, Ernst Emil – Berlin: G Grote, 1940, c1938 – 1r – 1 – us U.W. Library [830]
Silberstein, August *see* DORFSCHWALBEN AUS OESTERREICH
SILCOTES OF SILCOTE / Kingsley, Henry – British Fiction Archive: Unit 2 – 9 – uk Bell [830]
LE SILENCE DE LA MER / Bruller, Jean – In Indonesian. SE-6365 1949 – 9 – ne IDC [950]
THE SILENCE OF GOD / Anderson, Robert – (Includes index) – New York: Dodd Mead, 1897 – 1mf – 9 – 0-8370-2231-2 – 1985-0231 – us A.T.L.A. [240]
THE SILENCE OF SCRIPTURE / Wharton, Francis – (Includes bibliographical references) – Boston: E P Dutton, 1867 – 1mf – 9 – 0-8370-5764-7 – 1985-3764 – us A.T.L.A. [220]
SILENT ECHO – Winnipeg: Institution for the Deaf and Dumb, [1892-189- or 19–] – 9 – cn C.I.H.M. [360]
THE SILENT ERA – 1907-28. (From Kine Weekly) – 1 – uk World [790]
Silentiarii, Pauli *see*
- DESCRIPTIO MAGNAE ECCLESIAE SEU SANCTAE SOPHIAE (CBH 11,2)
- DESCRIPTIO TEMPLI SANCTAE SOPHIAE (CSHB 32)

SILENUS ALCIBIADIS, SIVE PROTEUS : HUMANAE VITAE IDEAM, EMBLEMATE TRIFARIAM VARIATO, OCULIS SUBJICIENS / Cats, J – Amsterdam, [c.1630] – 3mf – 9 – ne IDC [700]
SILENUS ALCIBIADIS SIVE PROTEUS, HUMANAE VITAE IDEAM, EMBLEMATE TRIFARIAM VARIATO, OCULIS SUBJICIENS / Cats, J – Amsterdam, 1620, 1619 – 5mf – 9 – ne IDC [700]
SILENUS ALCIBIADIS SIVE PROTEUS, HUMANAE VITAE IDEAM, EMBLEMATE TRIFARIAM VARIATO, OCULIS SUBJICIENS / Cats, J – Amsterdam, 1622 – 4mf – 9 – ne IDC [700]
SILENUS ALCIBIADIS, SIVE PROTEUS, VITAE HUMANAE IDEAM, EMBLEMATE TRIFARIÀM VARIATO, OCULIS SUBIJCIENS / Cats, J – 1st ed. Middelburg, 1618 – 5mf – 9 – ne IDC [700]
SILENUS ALCIBIADIS SIVE PROTEUS, VOORGHESTELT IN MINN'-EN-ZINNE-BEELDEN... / Cats, J – Dordrecht, [1645] – 3mf – 9 – ne IDC [700]
Silesia. Upper *see* JOURNAL OFFICIEL
LA SILHOUETTE – Paris. dec 1844-sept 1850 – 1 – fr A.C.R.P.P. [073]
SILHOUETTEN AUS DER WERTHERZEIT : AUS DEM NACHLASS VON JOHANN HEINRICH VOSS UND CARL SCHUBERTS SILHOUETTENBUCH / ed by Braeuning-Oktavio, Hermann – Darmstadt: L C Wittich, 1926 – 1r – 1 – us U.W. Library [430]
SILHOUETTES CANADIENNES / Conan, Laure – Quebec, 1917. SEM105P924 – 3mf – 9 – Can$6.75 – cn Bibl Nat [971]
Silio, Francisco Javier *see* DONOSO CORTES, EN SU TIEMPO Y EN EL NUESTRO
THE SILK AND DYE WORKER – (Library has: v.1, no. 1 (June 15, 1934)) – Paterson, N.J.: Paterson Silk Workers Union, 1934- – 1 – CSUX89-S105 – us Hoover Inst Photo [331]
SILK AND SPICE ROUTES : EXPLORATION BY LAND / Strathern, Paul – 1993 – 48p – 9 – 92-3-102761-1 – Co-published with Belitha Press, which has exclusive sales rights in the UK. exclusive sales rights in North America: Macmillan – fr UNESCO [910]
SILK AND SPICE ROUTES : EXPLORATION BY SEA / Reid, Struan – 1993 – 48p – 9 – 92-3-102762-X – Co-published with Belitha Press, which has exclusive sales rights in the UK. Exclusive eales rights in North America: Macmillan – fr UNESCO [910]
Silk, Dana *see* FOOD AND ENERGY
Silkstone. Yorkshire *see* PARISH REGISTERS
SILKWORM DISEASES – 1991 – 86p – it F.A.O. [636]
SILKWORM EGG PRODUCTION – 1990 – 71p – it F.A.O. [636]
SILLABARIO... / Olgiati, Francesco – Madrid: Razon y Fe, 1927 – 1 – sp Bibl Santa Ana [999]
SILLAGINID FISHES OF THE WORLD : AN ANNOTATED AND ILLUSTRATED CATALOGUE OF THE SILAGO, SMELT OR INDO-PACIFIC WHITING SPECIES KNOWN TO DATE – 1993 – 93p – it F.A.O. [590]
Sillans, R *see* MOTOMBI MYTHES ET ENIGMES INITIATIQUES DES MITSOGHO DU GABON CENTRAL
Sillem, C H W *see* DIE EINFUEHRUNG DER REFORMATION IN HAMBURG
Siller, Vilem *see* PAMATNIK CESKYCH EVANJELICKYCH CIRKVI
Silliman, Benjamin *see* REMARKS MADE ON A SHORT TOUR BETWEEN HARTFORD AND QUEBEC, IN THE AUTUMN OF 1819
Silliman, Sue I *see* ST. JOSEPH IN HOMESPUN
SILLIMAN TRUTH – (Also: The Sillimanian v1-20 1920-65 (incomplete)) – v3-19. 1905-20 (incomplete) – 1 – $200.00 – us Presbyterian [240]
THE SILLIMANIAN *see* SILLIMAN TRUTH
SILLOGISMO E PROPORZIONE : CONTRIBUTO ALLA TEORIA E ALLA STORIA DELLA LOGICA PURA / Pastore, Annibale – Torino: Fratelli Bocca, 1910 – us Res Libr [510]
LE SILLON – Paris. 1894-1910 – 1 – fr A.C.R.P.P. [073]
SILLUS LESONOT. DICTIONARIVM TRILINGVE,... / Muenster, S – Basileae, 1530 – 5mf – ne IDC [400]
Silman, James B *see* THE GEORGIA FORM BOOK.
LE SILO ET LE PATURAGE: CONFERENCE DE L'HONORABLE LOUIS BEAUBIEN...A ST HYACINTHE, LE 13 JANVIER 1886 / Beaubien, Louis – 1886?. 00912. (Pre-1900 Canadiana) – 9 – cn C.I.H.M. [630]
SILOAM BAPTIST CHURCH. ABBEVILLE ASSOCIATION. SOUTH CAROLINA : CHURCH RECORDS – 1834-76 – 1 – 18.81 – us Baptist [240]
SILSKO-HOSPODARSKY I NAUKOVY I KOMITET UKRA INY *see* BI ULETEN BOROTBY Z SHKIDNYKAMY SILSKO-HOSPODARSKYKH ROSLYN
SILUETA BIOGRAFICA DEDICADA AL EXCMO. SR. D. RAFAEL DURAN Y MARTINEZ. (MANUSCRITO) / Monteleon, C de – 1 – sp Bibl Santa Ana [946]
SILUETY RUSSKIKH PISATELEI / Aikhenvald, Iu – Vyp. 1. ed. 4. M. 1914. BR-1961 2 – 8 – ne IDC [460]
SILUMAN DJALUGIGIS / Widjajanto, M R – SE 5285 1 – 9 – ne IDC [950]
Silva, Alejandro de *see* GUERRA DE EXTREMADURA Y SITIOS DE BADAJOZ (1706)
SILVA CAPENSIS / Pappe, CW L – Ed. 2. London. 1862. B-5146 2 – 8 – ne IDC [580]
SILVA CAPENSIS, OR A DESCRIPTION OF SOUTH AFRICAN FOREST TREES AND ARBORESCENT SHRUBS / Pappe, CW L – Cape Town. 1854. B-428 2 – 8 – ne IDC [580]
SILVA DRAMATICA... / Gomez Bravo, Vicente – Madrid: Razon y Fe, 4th ed 1957 – 1 – sp Bibl Santa Ana [440]
SILVA DRAMATICA. ASUNTOS DEL TEATRO ESPANOL DISPUESTOS PARA ESTUDIO LITERARIO / Gomez Bravo, Vicente – Madrid: Razon y Fe, 1943 – 1 – sp Bibl Santa Ana [440]
Silva, J Francisco *see* VIAJE DE UN MONJE JERONIMO AL VIRREINATO DEL PERU EN EL SIGLO 17
Silva Leite, A da *see* ESTUDIO DE GUITARRA, EM QUE SE EXPOEM O MEIO MAIS FACIL PARA APRENDER A TOCAR ESTE INSTRUMENTO: DIVIDIDO EM DUAS PARTES
Silva Rego, Antonio da *see*
- AS MISSOES...
- HISTORIA DAS MISSIOES DO PADROADO PORTUGUES DE ORIENTE

Silva Rosa, J S da *see*
- CATALOGUS DER TENTOONSTELLING IN HET PORTUGEESCH ISREALIETISCH SEMINARIUM "ETS HAIM" TE AMSTERDAM...
- GESCHIEDENIS DER PORTUGEESCHE JODEN TE AMSTERDAM, 1593-1925
- OVER DE OUDSTE PORTUGESE SYNAGOGES TE AMSTERDAM

SILVA Y FIGUEROA, GARCIA DE. COMENTARIOS A LA EMBAJADA DE PERSIA / Fita, Fidel – Madrid: Fortanet, 1904. B.R.A.H. 44, 1904, p. 196 – sp Bibl Santa Ana [946]
SILVER – (7,500 reproductions of Objects of Virtu£2, Faberge£1 and jewellery) – 127mf – 9 – $690.00 – 0-907006-27-2 – uk Mindata [740]
SILVER AGE – Carson City, NV. Jul-Oct 1861 (scats) – 1r – 1 – $50.00 – U04473 – us Library Micro [071]
SILVER AGE – Silverton, Australia. -w. June 1886-Nov 1888; June-Oct 1893. 2 reels – 1 – uk British Libr Newspaper [072]
SILVER BEND REPORTER – Belmont, NV. 1867-68 – 1r – 1 – $50.00 – U04417 – us Library Micro [071]
SILVER BEND WEEKLY REPORTER – Belmont, NV. 1867 – 1r – 1 – $50.00 – U04418 – us Library Micro [071]
THE SILVER CHRIST AND A LEMON TREE / Ouida – British Fiction Archive: Unit 3 – 9 – uk Bell [830]
SILVER, COPPER, PEWTER AND TOLEWARE (TIAM, PT 9) – (With printed catalogue ISBN: 0-914146-78-5 £30) – 11mf – 15 – £300.00 – uk Chadwyck [730]
SILVER CREEK SAND – Silver Creek, NE. -w. Nov 1907; Jan 1908; Mar 1908-Dec 1964 – 1 – us NE Hist [071]
SILVER CREEK TIMES – Silver Creek, NE. -w. Nov 1891-Dec 1896; Jul 1897-Dec 1900; Apr 1901-May 1902; Jul-Oct 1902 – 1 – us NE Hist [071]
THE SILVER DOMINO / Corelli, Marie – British Fiction Archive: Unit 1 – 9 – uk Bell [830]
SILVER IN ITS RELATION TO INDUSTRY AND TRADE: THE DANGER OF DEMONETIZING IT: THE UNITED STATES MONETARY COMMISSION IN 1876: REVIEW OF PROF. FRANCIS BOWEN'S MINORITY REPORT / Brown, William – Montreal: J. Lovell, 1880. 00281. (Pre-1900 Canadiana) – 9 – cn C.I.H.M. [336]
SILVER JUBILEE OF THE UNIVERSITY OF NOTRE DAME, JUNE 23RD, 1869 / ed by Lyons, Joseph A – 2nd rev enl ed. Chicago: E B Myers, 1869 [i.e. 1870?] – 1mf – 9 – 0-8370-7307-3 – 1986-1307 – us A.T.L.A. [370]
SILVER LAKE HERALD – Joseph OR. Jan 19-Mar 6 1896, Apr 24 May 29 1896, Feb 5 May 7 Dec 10 1897, Dec 29 1899 + – 1 – us U.O. Library [071]
SILVER LAKE HERALD – Joseph OR. June 7 Aug 2 Nov 8 29 1895, Dec 6 27 1895, Jan 17-Mar 6 Apr 24 May 29 1896, June 7 1901-Dec 27 1901 + – 1 – us U.O. Library [071]
SILVER LAKE LEADER – Silver Lake OR. June 11 1909-Dec 12 1919 – 1 – us U.O. Library [071]
SILVER LAKE LEADER AND LAKE COUNTY TRIBUNE – Silver Lake OR. Feb 5 1920-Apr 5 1928 – 1 – us U.O. Library [071]
Silver Lake Methodist Church *see* RECORDS
SILVER LAKE, OR, LOST IN THE SNOW / Ballantyne, Robert Michael – London: Jackson, Walford and Hodder, 1867. 07478. (Pre-1900 Canadiana) – 9 – cn C.I.H.M. [830]
THE SILVER RUSH AT MINERAL KING, CALIFORNIA 1873-1882 / Porter, Samuel Thomas – 1r – 5,9 – $50.00 – B70016 – us Library Micro [622]
SILVER STATE – Deer Lodge. Mont. 1893-1926 – 1 – us UMI [071]
SILVER STATE – (Title varies: Daily Silver State, Silver State News, Winnemucca Republican) – Winnemucca, NV. 1875-1925 – 42r – 1 – $2,100.00 – U04821 – us Library Micro [071]
SILVER STATE *see* STAR
SILVER STATE NEWS *see* SILVER STATE
SILVER STATE POST – Deer Lodge. Mont. 1927-1950; 1956-1959; 1966- – 1 – us UMI [071]
THE SILVERADO SQUATTERS / Stevenson, Robert Louis – London: Chatto and Windus, 1883 – 1 roll – 1 – 1-55879-602-9 – uk Libr Preservation [830]
Silvernail, WM H *see* FEDERAL AND STATE CRIMINAL REPORTER
SILVERNAIL'S APPEALS CASES : UNREPORTED / New York. (State). Court of Appeals – (A Pre-NRS title) – v1-4. 1886-92 (all publ) – 30mf – 9 – $45.00 – LLMC 80-048 – us L.L.M.C. [340]
SILVERNAIL'S SUPREME COURT REPORTS / New York. (State). Supreme Court – v1-5. 1889-90 (all publ) – 37mf – 9 – $55.00 – LLMC 80-213 – us L.L.M.C. [340]
SILVERTON APPEAL – (Set incl. Silvertonian Appeal (Silverton)) – Silverton, OR. -w. 30 Sept. 1893-1 Aug 1930. – 9r – 1 – us U.O. Library [071]
SILVERTON APPEAL TRIBUNE – Silverton OR. Aug 8 1930-Sep 30 1976 – 1 – us U.O. Library [071]
SILVERTON APPEAL-TRIBUNE AND MT. ANGEL NEWS – Silverton, OR. -w. 8 Aug 1930-19 Oct 1978+. 26 rolls – 1 – us U.O. Library [071]
SILVERTON JOURNAL – Silverton, OR. -w. 13 Jun 1913-2 Jul 1915. 1 roll – 1 – us U.O. Library [071]
SILVERTON SEMAPHORE – Silverton OR. Nov 28 1908, Jan 16 1909 – 1 – us U.O. Library [071]
SILVERTON TRIBUNE – Silverton, OR. -w. 14 Mar 1924-1 Aug 1930. 2 rolls – 1 – us U.O. Library [071]
SILVERTONIAN – Silverton OR. June 1902 – 1 – us U.O. Library [071]
SILVERTONIAN APPEAL – Silverton OR. Oct 23 1903-July 22 1910 – 1 – us U.O. Library [071]
SILVERWOOD GAZETTE. (FARMERS' GAZETTE) – Brisbane, Australia. May 1908-Dec 1921 (1908-10 imperfect).-w. 11 reels – 1 – uk British Libr Newspaper [072]
SIL'VESTR MEDVEDEV / Kozlovskii, I – (Ocherk iz istorii ruskogo prosveshcheniia i obshchestvennoi zhizni v kontse XVII veka.). Kiev. 1895. BR-6222 2 – 8 – ne IDC [947]
Silvestre, Gregorio *see* OBRAS...POETA
Silvestre, V *see* MASAKA AU RWANDA. CONTRIBUTION A L'ETUDE DE LA COLONISATION DES TERRES NEUVES EN AFRIQUE
SILVESTRI 2 PAPAE OPERA MATHEMATICA / Gerberti; ed by Bubnov, N – Berlin, 1899 – 13mf – 8 – ne Slangenburg [510]
Silvey, C M *see* INFLUENCE OF MENSTRUAL CYCLE PHASE AND ORAL CONTRACEPTIVE USE ON CARDIOVASCULAR REACTIVITY IN WOMEN WITH A PARENTAL HISTORY OF HYPERTENSION

SILVICULTURE – (Incorporated within: Logging and Sawmilling Journal, 1993) – Toronto. v4-7. 1989-92 – 9 – Can$20.00y – cn Micromedia [634]
SIM – v. 1-10. 1905-14 – 1 – 105.00 – us L of C Photodup [780]
Sim, James D *see* ALTERATIONS IN 72 KILODALTON STRESS PROTEIN LEVELS FOLLOWING ECCENTRICALLY BIASED EXERCISE
SIM NOW – (1985-. 5,6,9) – v1-. 1982- – 1 – us UMI [073]
Sim, T R *see*
- THE BRYOPHYTA OF SOUTH AFRICA
- THE FERNS OF SOUTH AFRICA
- HANDBOOK OF THE FERNS OF KAFFRARIA
- SIM'S DESCRIPTION CATALOGUE OF BRITISH AND EXOTIC FERNS

Simacek, Matej Anastasia *see* LACNA SRDCE: ROMAN
Simakov, V *see* CHTO TAKOE PROMYSLOVAIA ARTEL' I KAK EE USTROIT'
SIMAL OCKUNLARI – Kemi, Finland. Seyren Surak Caga Turgan Dini Milli Edebi ve Ictimai Mecmuadir. Muharriri: Hasan Hamidulla. No. 1 (Eyluel 1945) – 9 – $20.00 – us MEDOC [956]
Simanare, Sinuan Tunas *see* SAPU TANGAN PANGAPUS ILU
Simandjuntak, L *see* FITNAH SEBAGAI SUATU SISTIM "PEREBUTAN KEKUASAAN."SE 5914/1. 1966?
Simar, Hubert Theophil *see* DAS GEWISSEN UND DIE GEWISSENSFREIHEIT
Simard, G-A *see* LE PETIT JOURNAL
Simard, Henri *see* TRAITE ELEMENTAIRE DE PHYSIQUE
Simatupang, Tahi Bonar *see* PEMERINTAH – MASJARAKAT – ANGKATAN PERANG; PIDATO-PIDATO DAN KARANGAN-KARANGAN, 1955-1958
SIMBIRSKII SBORNIK : CHAST' ISTORICHESKAIA / ed by Valuev, D A et al – M., [1844] – 8mf – 9 – ne IDC [947]
SIMBIRSKII SBORNIK : CHAST' ISTORICHESKAIA / ed by Valuev, D A et al – M., [1844] – 8mf – 9 – RET-19/1 – ne IDC [947]
EL SIMBOLISMO DE LAS RELIGIONES DEL MUNDO Y EL PROBLEMA DE LA FIDELIDAD. COMENTARIOS A LA DOCTRINA SECRETA / Roso de Luna, Mario – Madrid: Editorial Eyras, 1977 – 1 – sp Bibl Santa Ana [240]
EL SIMBOLISMO MEDICO INDIGENA / Farias Galindo, Jose – Mexico, D.F., Editor V. Rea, 1956. 58p.(Biblioteca deHistoriadores mexicanos) – 1 – us U.W. Library [306]
SIMBOLOGIA ARCAICA / Roso de Luna, Mario – Madrid: Editorial Pueyo, 1921 – 1 – sp Bibl Santa Ana [240]
Simchoni, J N H *see* RABBI SHELOMOH BEN GABIROL
SIMCOE REFORMER – (1840-1992.-222r) – Simcoe, 1993 – 6r – 1 – cn Preston [971]
Simcox, William Henry *see*
- THE REVELATION OF S. JOHN THE DIVINE
- THE WRITERS OF THE NEW TESTAMENT: THEIR STYLE AND CHARACTERISTICS

Sime, James *see*
- DEUTERONOMY: THE PEOPLE'S BOOK: ITS ORIGIN AND NATURE: A DEFENCE
- SCHILLER

Simensky, Steven G *see* THE EFFECTS OF AN EVALUATIVE AUDIENCE UPON COLLEGE MALES' SELF-EFFICACY, PERCEIVED ABILITY, ANXIETY, AND LEARNING OF A NOVEL MOTOR TASK
Simeon Of Durham *see* OPERA OMNIA (RS75)
Simeon Polotskii *see* ZHEZL PRAVLENIIA
Simeone, Laurentius *see* NEGOTIA A SUPERIORIBUS FRANCISCALIBUS...
Simeoni, G *see*
- HEROICA M. CLAUDI PARADINI, BELLIIOCENSIS CANONICI, ET D. GABRIELIS SYMEONIS, SYMBOLAT
- PRINCELIICKE DEVIISEN VAN CLAUDE PARADIN, GABRIEL SIMEON, ENDE MEER ANDER
- SYMBOLA HEROICA M. CLAUDII PARADINI, BELLIIOCENSIS CANONICI

Simerwell, Ann *see* PAPERS
Simerwell Elizabeth *see* JOURNAL AND ACCOUNT BOOK
Simerwell, Robert *see* PAPERS
Simhah, ben Joshua of Zalozhstsy *see* AHAVAT ZIYYON
Simharaja *see* PRAKRITARUPAVATARA
SIMI VALLEY/MOORPARK – 1992- – 5+ r – 1 – $250.00 – P00124 – us Library Micro [910]
SIMILAR FATES: TOWNS OF ENGLAND, TOWNS OF FRANCE YOU WILL ALSO BE RAIDED / Falcon, Cesar – Valencia, 1936? Fiche W 875. (Blodgett Collection of Spanish Civil War Pamphlets) – 9 – us H.U. College Libr [946]
Simkins, William Stewart *see* EQUITY AS APPLIED IN THE STATE AND FEDERAL COURTS IN TEXAS AND OTHER STATES
Simler, J *see*
- BIBLIOTHECA INSTITUTA ET COLLECTA PRIMUM A CONRADO GESNERO
- EPITOME BIBLIOTHECAE CONRADI GESNERI

SIMLER MANUSCRIPT COLLECTION : SOURCES TO THE HISTORY OF REFORMATION AND CHURCH HISTORY / ed by Buesser, F – (Includes indexes which are also available separately 370mf Dfl2,229.00) – 1,909mf – 9 – ne IDC [090]
SIMLERSCHEN SAMMLUNG : REGISTER- UND REGESTENBAENDE – (Index alphab. and chron. manuscript. seculi 16(17). 6v 1501-1620. Index rerum et personarum 9v 1541-1573. Indices ceu commentarii mscr. de rebus sec. 16. 39v 1501-1600; sec. 17. 8v 1601-1660. Index chronologicus alphabeticus collectionis Simleranae... 4v 1501-1620) – 370 mf – 9 – H-3001/1 – ne IDC [943]
SIMLERSCHEN SAMMLUNG : REGISTER- UND REGESTENBAENDE – N.p., n.d. – 370mf – 9 – ne IDC [240]
THE SIMMENDINGER REGISTER – By Ulrich Simmendinger 1934. Item I. Trans. from German by Herman F. Vesper. Register of German immigrants to America in 1709. Listed alphabetically. 20p. SW16-0078 – 5 – us A.G.L.L. [978]
Simmler, J *see* VITA...CONRADI GESNERI TIGURINI, CONSCRIPTA A IOSIA SIMLERO TIGURINO
SIMMOND'S COLONIAL MAGAZINE AND FOREIGN MISCELLANY – (Continued as COLONIAL MAGAZINE AND EAST INDIA REVIEW. 1849-1852, v.16-19, 21-23. (V.20-22 are wrongly numbered V.21-23)) – 1844-48. v.1-15. Lacking 1849. v17(5,p.385-480) – 220mf – 8 – ne IDC [073]
SIMMONDS'S COLONIAL MAGAZINE – S.l.: s.n., 18- – 9 – cn C.I.H.M. [073]
Simmons, C Thomas *see* HOCHAUFLOESENDE PHOTOELEKTRONEN-SPEKTROSKOPISCHE UNTERSUCHUNGEN DES SUPRALEITENDEN ZUSTANDS VON BI2SR2CACU08+D(DELTA)
Simmons, Thomas Frederick *see* IDEAS AS TO THE EFFECT OF HEAVY ORDNANCE DIRECTED AGAINST AND APPLIED BY SHIPS OF WAR
Simmons, W J *see* THE ABC OF THE KNIGHTS OF THE KU KLUX KLAN
Simmons, W June *see* HOME HEALTH CARE SERVICES QUARTERLY
Simmons, William J *see* MEN OF MARK
Simmons, William Joseph *see* AMERICA'S MENACE, OR, THE ENEMY WITHIN
Simms, William Gilmore *see* THE LIFE OF THE CHEVALIER BAYARD; THE GOOD KNIGHT, SAN PEUR ET SANS REPROCHE
Simocattae, Theophylacti *see*
- HISTORIARUM LIBRI 8 (CBH 2,1)
- HISTORIARUM LIBRI 8 (CSHB 22)

SIMOLACHRI, HISTORIE, E FIGVRE DE LA MORTE / Huberinus, Caspar – [Venedig]: Vincent Vaugris, 1545. [G.F.: 5.17] – 3mf – 9 – HUB-22/1 – ne IDC [240]
SIMON BOLIVAR. THE HOPE OF THE UNIVERSE / Bolivar, Simon – 1983 – 308p – 9 – 92-3-102103-6 – fr UNESCO [900]
SIMON CAMERON PAPERS / Cameron, Simon – 1824-92. In Dauphin County, Pa., Historical Society. 10 reels. Guide – 1 – us Penn Hist [920]
SIMON CAMERON PAPERS – Harrisburg, PA., 1824-1892 – 13 – $25.00r – us I.M.R. [071]
SIMON CAMERON PAPERS 1824-1892 / Pennsylvania Historical and Museum Commission – (With guide) – 10r – 1 – $850.00 – D3291 – Dist. us Scholarly Res – us Scholarly Res [978]
Simon, David Worthington *see*
- THE BIBLE: AN OUTGROWTH OF THEOCRATIC LIFE
- RECONCILIATION BY INCARNATION

SIMON DUBNOV, L'HOMME ET SON OUEVRE : PUBL. A L'OCCASION DU CENTENAIRE DE SA NAISSANCE (1860-1960) / Dubnov, S; ed by Steinberg, A – Paris, 1963 – 1mf – ne IDC [270]
Simon, E *see*
- LES ARACHNIDES DE FRANCE
- HISTOIRE NATURELLE DES ARAIGNEES (ARANEIDES)
- LA VRAYE ET ANCIENNE ORTHOGRAPHE FRANCOISE

SIMON EICHELKATZ, THE PATRIARCH : TWO STORIES OF JEWISH LIFE / Frank, Ulrich – Philadelphia: Jewish Publication Society of America, 1907 – 1 – us U.W. Library [830]
Simon, Frank *see*
- CHARAKTERISIERUNG VON UNMODIFIZIERTEN UND OLIGOMERMODIFIZIERTEN ANORGANISCHEN METALLOXIDOBERFLAECHEN DURCH ELEKTROKINETISCHE MESSMETHODEN
- ELEKTROKINETISCHE UNTERSUCHUNGEN VON AEROSILOBERFLAECHEN UND AEROSIL-TRIARYLMETYLHALOGENID-ADSORBATEN IN ORGANISCHEN MEDIEN

Simon, G *see* ISLAM UND CHRISTENTUM IM KAMPF UM DIE EROBERUNG DER ANIMISTISCHEN HEIDENWELT
SIMON GRYNAEUS VON BASEL, 1725-1799 : DER ERSTE DEUTSCHE UEBERSETZER VON SHAKESPEARES ROMEO UND JULIA / Kuery, Hans – (Includes bibliographical references) – Zuerich, Leipzig: M Niehans, 1935 – 1 – us U.W. Library [430]
Simon, H *see*
- DIE FRUEHEREN UND GEGENWAERTIGEN VERHAELTNISSE DER JUDEN IN DE SAEMMTLICHEN LANDESTHEILEN DES PREUSSISCHEN STAATES
- DAS WELTBILD GABIROLS

Simon, J M *see* LES ORIGINES DE LA CROIX-ROUGE
Simon, J S *see* A SUMMARY OF METHODIST LAW AND DISCIPLINE; BEING A NEW EDITION OF 'THE LARGE MINUTES'
Simon, Jules *see* VICTOR COUSIN
Simon, Karl-Theodor *see* DAS VERHAELTNIS VON RELIGION UND SITTLICHKEIT IN DER AUFFASSUNG DES JUENGEREN SCHLEIERMACHER
Simon, P H *see*
- L'ESPRIT ET L'HISTOIRE
- TEMOINS DE L'HOMME
- THEATRE ET DESTIN

SIMON PETER : HIS LIFE, TIMES, AND FRIENDS / Hodder, Edwin – London, New York: Cassell, 1884 – 1mf – 9 – 0-8370-3603-8 – 1985-1603 – us A.T.L.A. [920]
SIMON PETER, FISHERMAN / Upham, Francis Bourne – NY: Eaton & Mains ; Cincinnati: Jennings & Pye, c1904 – 1mf – 9 – 0-8370-5600-4 – 1985-3600 – us A.T.L.A. [830]
SIMON PETER, HIS EARLY LIFE AND TIMES / Robinson, Charles Seymour – New York: American Tract Society, 1889. 1 fiche – 9 – us A.T.L.A. [240]
SIMON PETER: HIS LIFE, TIMES AND FRIENDS / Hodder, Edwin – London: Cassell, 1884. 1 fiche – 9 – us A.T.L.A. [240]
Simon, R *see* HISTOIRE CRITIQUE DU VIEUX TESTAMENT
Simon, Renee *see* NICOLAS FRERET, ACADEMICIEN, 1688-1749
Simon, Richard *see* CRITICAL ENQUIRIES INTO THE VARIOUS EDITIONS OF THE BIBLE
Simon, Theodor *see* DIE PSYCHOLOGIE DES APOSTELS PAULUS
Simon, V *see* ASSIMILATION-REGENERATION DES SELS NUTRITIFS DANS L'OCEAN AUSTRAL: CARACTERISATION ET RELATION AVEC LA STRUCTURE HYDROLOGIQUE DANS LE BASSIN DE WEDDELL-ENDERBY
Simonde de Sismondi, Jean Charles Leonar *see* DE LA LITTERATURE DU NIDI (SIC) DE L'EUROPE
Simonds D'Ewes *see* JOURNALS OF ALL THE PARLIAMENTS DURING REIGN OF ELISABETH, BOTH LORDS AND COMMONS
SIMONDS' DIGEST OF PATENT DECISIONS : FEDERAL AND STATE, 1789-1888 / Simonds, William Edgar – NY: Strouse & Co. 1888 (all publ) – 3mf – 9 – $13.50 – LLMC 84-336 – us L.L.M.C. [340]
Simonds, William Edgar *see*
- A DIGEST OF PATENT CASES
- MANUAL OF PATENT LAW
- SIMONDS' DIGEST OF PATENT DECISIONS

Simoni, P K *see*
- K 40-LETIIU UCHENO-LITERATURNOI DEIATEL'NOSTI PROFESSORA I AKADEMIKA A.N. VESELOVSKAGO. 1859-1902
- KHRONOLOGICHESKII SPISOK UCHENYKH I LITERATURNYKH TRUDOV I IZDANII L.N. MEIKOVA

Simonne, Jean-Claude *see* MOYEN DE RENDRE LES PEUPLES LIBRES ET HEUREUX, OU, IDEES SUR LEUR EDUCATION
Simonovich, Ia.A *see* ANALIZ OTCHETNOSTI PROMYSLOVYKH I PROMYSLOVO-KREDITNYKH KOOPERATIVOV
Simonovskii, V *see* UKAZATEL' LUCHSHIKH, PO OTZYVAM PECHATI, UCHEBNIKOV, NAGLIADNYKH UCHEBNYKH POSOBII I METODICHESKIKH RUKOVODSTV NA RUSSKOM I UKRAINSKOM IAZYKAKH
SIMONS AND STUART'S REPORTS : REPORTS OF CASES DECIDED IN THE HIGH COURT OF CHANCERY / Simons, Nicholas & Stuart, John – v1-2. 1822-26. London: J & W T Clarke, 1824-27 (all publ) – 4mf – 9 – $18.00 – LLMC 84-788 – us L.L.M.C. [324]
Simons, C J *see* MEMOIR OF CORNELIS JEAN SIMONS, GOVERNOR AND DIRECTOR OF CEYLON, FOR HIS SUCCESSOR HENDRICK BECKER, 1707
Simons, Eduard *see* HAT DER DRITTE EVANGELIST DEN KANONISCHEN MATTHAEUS BENUTZT?
Simons, J *see* HANDBOOK FOR THE STUDY OF EGYPTIAN TOPOGRAPHICAL LISTS
Simons, Menno *see*
- EEN CHRISTELIJCKE ENDE LIEFLIJCKE VERMANINGE AEN ALLEN OUERHEYDEN, GHELEERDEN. GHEMENEN VOLCKE, SECTEN, ENDE BRUYDT CHRISTI, DIE VAN DIE HETTE DER SONNEN NIET WEYNICH OP ALLE PLAETSEN VERBRANT WORT
- EEN CLAER ONDERWYSINGHE WT DES HEEREN WOORT VAN DIE GHEESTELICKE VERRYSENISSE, ENDE NIEUWE GEBOORTE
- EEN CORTE ENDE CLARE BELIJDINGHE ENDE SCHRIFTELIJCKE AENWIJSINGE. GESCHREUEN AEN. JOHAN A LASCO, MET T'SAMEN ZIJNEN MEDEHULPEREN BINNEN EMDEN
- EEN CORTE VERMANINGHE VTH GODES WOORT VAN DIE WEDERGEBOORTE, VNDE WIE DIE GHENE SYN, DIE BELOFTE HEBBEN
- FONDAMENTUM. EEN FONDAMENT
- EEN FUNDAMENT
- DAT FUNDAMENT DES CHRISTELYCKEN LEERS OP DAT ALDER CORSTE GESCHREUEN. ANNO 1939
- EIN FUNDAMENT VND KLARE ANWISINGE, VAN DE HEYLSAME VND GODTSELLYGHE LEERE JESU CHRISTI
- FVNDAMENTVM. EEN FONDAMENT
- FVNDAMENTVM. EIN FUNDAMENT VND KLARE ANWEISUNG VON DER SELIGMACHENDEN LEHRE VNSERS HERREN JESU CHRISTI. AUSZ NIDERL. SPRACH IN HOCHTEUTSCH GEBRACHT
- EEN GANS DUYTLIJCKE, ENDE BESCHEYDEN ANTWOORDT. AN". 1556. WT WAERHEYT ENDE CRACHT DER HEYLIGHEN GODLICKEN SCHRIFT GRONDLYCKEN VERUAETET, OP MARTINI MIKRONS ANTICHRISTISSCHE LEERE ENDE ONWAERACHTIGHE VALSCHE VERHAEL VAN DEN HANDEL OFTE BISPRECK
- EEN GANS GRONTLIJCKE ONDERWIJS OFT BERICHT, VAN DE EXCOMMUNICATIE, BAN-WTSLUYTINGE, OFTE AFSONDERINGE DER KERCKEN CHRISTI, WAT SY INDER CRACHT ZY
- EEN GANTS DUYTLIJCK ENDE BESCHEYDEN ANTWOORT AN. 1566. WT WAERHEYT ENDE CRACHT DER H. GODLICKER SCHRIFT
- EYNE KLARE VNWEDERSPREKELIKE BEKENTENISSE VNDE ANWIJSINGE VTH DEN GRONT VNDE KRAFT DER HEYLIGER SCRIFT VORUATED, DAT DIE GHEHEELE CHRISTUS JESUS GODT VNDE MENSCE, MENSCHE VNDE GODT, GODES EINGEBORENE VNDE EERSTGEBORENE EYGEN SONE IS
- EEN LIEFFELIJCKE VERMANINGE OFTE ONDERWIJSINGE WT GODS WOORT
- EEN SCHOONE ENDE PROFITELIJCK LEERINGHE WT GODS WOORDT ALLEN MENSCHEN VERMANENDE TOT DIE HEMELSCHE WEDERGEBOORTE ENDENIEUWE CREATURE
- EEN SCHOONE ENDE PROFITELIJCKE VERMANENDE ENDE BESTRAFFENDE REDENE AEN DIE OUERHEYT, GHELEERDE ENDE GHEMEYN VOLCK

- EEN SEER GRONTLIJCKE ANTWOORT, VOL MET ALDERLEY ONDERWIJSINGE ENDE GOEDER VERMANINGHE, OP ZYLIS ENDE LEMMEKES ONVERDIENDE LASTERLIJCKE FAEM ROUEN, ACHTERCLAPPEN ENDE ONGESOLTENE ENDE BITTERE SCHELTWOORDEN
- EYNE SEER LIEFLIJCKE MEDITATION VND GODTSALIGE OEFFENINGE, MIT VELE CHRISTELIJCKE LEERINGEN
- EEN SEER SCHOONE, ENDE GRONT-LIJCKE LERINGE WT DES HEEREN WOORDT, ALLEN MENSCHEN
- SOMMARIE OFTE BY EEN VERGADERINGE VAN SOMMIGE SCHRIFTELIJCKE BEKENTENISSEN DES GHELOOFS, MITSGADERS EENIGHE WAERACHTIGE VERANTWOORDINGEN OP SOMMIGE SCHRIFTEN, VAN GELLIO FABRO ENDE JOANNE A LASCO VOORGESTELT
- EYNE TROESTELIJKE VERMANINGE VAN DAT LIJDEN, CRUYZE, VND VERUOLGINGE DER HEYLIGEN
- VAN HET RECHT CHRISTEN GHELOOUE, DAT DES MENSCHEN HARTE OMKEERT, VERANDERT. ENDE SALICH MAECKET
- VOELE GOEDE VND CHRISTELYCKE LERINGHEN OP DEN 25. PSALM IN EEN MANIERE VAN BIDDEN GESCREUEN. ANNO 1539

Simons, Nicholas *see*
- SIMONS AND STUART'S REPORTS
- SIMON'S REPORTS, OLD SERIES
- SIMONS'S REPORTS, NEW SERIES

SIMON'S REPORTS, OLD SERIES : REPORTS OF CASES DECIDED IN THE HIGH COURT OF CHANCERY / Simons, Nicholas – v1-17. 1826-52. London: J & W T Clarke/Stevens & Norton, 1829-54 (all publ) – 127mf – 9 – $190.00 – LLMC 95-272 – us L.L.M.C. [324]

Simons, Robert Bentham *see* AUTOBIOGRAPHY

Simons, Royal D. *see* PAPERS AND CORRESPONDENCE OF ROYAL D. SIMONS

SIMON'S TOWN AND DISTRICT CHRONICLE – Simon's Town, South Africa. 11 Aug 1899-15 Sept 1900. 1 reel – 1, 16 diazo available at reduced price – sa SA Libr [072]

Simonsens, D *see* FESTSCHRIFT

SIMONS'S REPORTS, NEW SERIES : REPORTS OF CASES DECIDED IN THE HIGH COURT OF CHANCERY / Simons, Nicholas – (Cases after p191 of v2 reported by C. Stewart Drewry) – v1-2. 1850-52. London: Stevens & Norton, 1851-52 (all publ) – 11mf – 9 – $16.50 – LLMC 95-273 – us L.L.M.C. [340]

DIE SIMONSSAGE: NACH IHRER ENTSTEHUNG, FORM UND BEDEUTUNG UND DER HERACLESMYTHUS / Roskoff, Gustav – Leipzig: Ernst Bredt, 1860. 1 fiche – 9 – us A.T.L.A. [240]

Simonton, Charles Henry *see* THE FEDERAL COURTS

Simonyi, S *see* DIE UNGARISCHE SPRACHE

Simorangkir, J C T *see* PELADJARAN HUKUM INDONESIA

SIMOUN – Revue litteraire et artistique. Dir. Jean-Michel Guirao. no. 1-31. Oran. 1952-60 – 1 – fr A.C.R.P.P. [073]

SIMPAI SASTRA; DIHIDANGKAN KEPADA PELADJAR SEKOLAH LANDJUTAN / ed by Samidi, A – SE 4687 1. 1962 – 9 – ne IDC [950]

DER SIMPL – Munich. DE. Jan 1947-50 – 1r – 1 – uk British Libr Newspaper [072]

THE SIMPLE ADVENTURES OF A MEMSAHIB / Duncan, Sara Jeannette – With illustrations by F. H. Townsend. New York: D. Appleton, 1893. 05295. (Pre-1900 Canadiana) – 9 – cn C.I.H.M. [830]

SIMPLE AND RELIGIOUS CONSULTATION.. / Herman von Wied, Abp. of Cologne – 2v. 1548 – 1 – us A.T.L.A. [240]

SIMPLE BIO-ECONOMIC ANALYTICAL SIMULATION MODELS FOR SEQUENTIAL FISHERIES ON TROPICAL SHRIMP : SOFTWARE FOR BIO-ECONOMIC ANALYSIS OF FISHERIES – 1992 – 68p – it F.A.O. [639]

THE SIMPLE COBBLER OF AGGAWAM IN AMERICA / Ward, Nathaniel – 1647 – 9 – 5.00 – us Scholars' Facs [830]

SIMPLE ECONOMICS AND BOOKKEEPING FOR FISH FARMERS – 1992 – 100p – it F.A.O. [650]

SIMPLE METHODS FOR AQUACULTURE – it F.A.O. [639]

SIMPLE REVUE – Bulletin mensuel, litteraire, artistique et mondain. Paris. avr. 1892-1906 – 1 – fr A.C.R.P.P. [073]

SIMPLE STAKES A CLAIM / Hughes, Langston – New York: Rinehart, c1957. 191p – 1 – us U.W. Library [830]

SIMPLE SUGGESTION ON CLUBS AND OTHER WORK WITH BOYS (CCC138) / Hall, K L – (In Chinese) – 1st ed. Shanghai: Association Press of China, 1922 – 1r – 1 – 1984-B500 – us A.T.L.A. [360]

SIMPLE TECHNOLOGIES FOR CHARCOAL MAKING – 1983 2nd print 1987 – 160p – it F.A.O. [660]

SIMPLE TRUTH FOR EARNEST MINDS / Macleod, Norman – London; New York: Alexander Strahan, 1866 – 1mf – 9 – 0-8370-7239-5 – 1986-1239 – us A.T.L.A. [240]

SIMPLE TRUTH VINDICATED, IN SUNDRY IMPORTANT THEOLOGICAL QUERIES WHICH ARE EXAMINED AND RESOLVED BY THE SCRIPTURES ONLY, UNDER FOUR HEADS,... / Pike, S – London, 1760 – 2mf – 9 – MP-390/1 – ne IDC [240]

A SIMPLETON / Reade, Charles L – British Fiction Archive: Unit 2 – 9 – uk Bell [830]

SIMPLEZAS DE AMOR / Sanchez-Arjona, Vicente – Sevilla: Graficas Tirvia, Tomo 3. 1956 – 1 – sp Bibl Santa Ana [810]

SIMPLEZAS DE AMOR (DE TIEMPOS PASADOS) / Sanchez-Arjona, Vicente – Sevilla: Imp. Carlos Acuna, Tomo 1. 1955 – 1 – sp Bibl Santa Ana [810]

SIMPLEZAS DE AMOR (DE TIEMPOS PASADOS) / Sanchez-Arjona, Vicente – Sevilla: Imp. Carlos Acuna, Tomo 2. 1955 – 1 – sp Bibl Santa Ana [810]

SIMPLEZASDE AMOR (DE TIEMPOS PASADOS) / Sanchez-Arjona, Vicente – Sevilla: Graficas Tirvia, Tomo 4. 1956 – 1 – sp Bibl Santa Ana [810]

SIMPLICISSIMUS : POLITISCH-SATIRISCHE WOCHENSCHRIFT – (1954-1967 8r DM600.00) – Muenchen, 1896-1944 – 27r – 1 – DM2,025.00 – gw Mikro Press [072]

SIMPLICISSIMUS : POLITISCH-SATIRISCHE WOCHENSCHRIFT – Muenchen, DE. 1896-1944; 1954-67 – 1 – gw Mikrofilm [072]

DER SIMPLICUS : SATIRISCHE WOCHENSCHRIFT – (Title change: Der Simpl/Prager Satirische Wochenschrift, 25 Sep 1935) – Prag, Czechoslovakia. 25 Jan-13 Sept 1934; 25 Sept 1934-26 Jun 1935 – 2r – 1 – gw Mikrofilm [072]

SIMPLIFIED ENGLISH GRAMMAR FOR INDONESIAN STUDENTS / Nasution, A Diapari – SE-5312 1. 1949 – 9 – ne IDC [420]

A SIMPLIFIED GUIDE TO THE HOLDINGS.. / Detroit. Public Library. Automotive History Collection – 1966.-22,900 cards 2 reels.- ISBN: 0-8161-1446-3 – 1 – $220.00 – uk Hall [629]

DER SIMPL/PRAGER SATIRISCHE WOCHENSCHRIFT *see* DER SIMPLICUS

Simpson, Albert B *see* THE FOUR-FOLD GOSPEL

Simpson, Archibald *see* JOURNALS AND SERMONS

Simpson, C L *see* THE SYMBOL OF LIBERIA

Simpson, Christopher *see*
- CHELYS, MINURITIONUM ARTIFICIO EXORNATA...THE DIVISION-VIOL..
- A COMPENDIUM OF PRACTICAL MUSICK IN FIVE PARTS..
- A COMPENDIUM OF PRACTICAL MUSICK IN FIVE PARTS. TOGETHER WITH LESSONS FOR VIOLS
- A COMPENDIUM: OR INTRODUCTION TO PRACTICAL MUSIC
- A COMPENDIUM OR INTRODUCTION TO PRACTICAL MUSIC, IN FIVE PARTS
- THE DIVISION-VIOLIST OR AN INTRODUCTION TO THE PLAYING UPON A GROUND: DIVIDED INTO TWO PARTS

SIMPSON COUNTY NEWS – Mendenhall. Miss. 1938-1943; 1949-1954 – 1 – us UMI [071]

Simpson, CT *see* THE MOLLUSCA OF PORTO RICO

Simpson, Frank Leslie *see* MASSACHUSETTS LAW

Simpson, Georgiana Rose *see* HERDER'S CONCEPTION OF "DAS VOLK"

Simpson, J *see* OBSERVATIONS ON THE WESTERN ESQUIMAUX

Simpson, Michael et al *see* BRITISH PLANNING HISTORY, 1900-1952

Simpson, Nellie *see* CORRESPONDENCE AND OTHER PAPERS RELATED TO THEIR SERVICE WITH THE METHODIST OVERSEAS MISSION

Simpson, Patrick Carnegie *see* THE FACT OF CHRIST

Simpson, Richard *see* THE RELIGION OF SHAKESPEARE

Simpson, Samuel *see* LIFE OF ULRICH ZWINGLI

Simpson, Th *see* NARRATIVE ON THE DISCOVERIES OF THE NORTH COAST OF AMERICA

Simpson, Thomas Nevison *see* CORRESPONDENCE AND OTHER PAPERS RELATED TO THEIR SERVICE WITH THE METHODIST OVERSEAS MISSION

Simpson, William *see*
- THE JONAH LEGEND
- A PRIVATE JOURNAL KEPT DURING THE NIGER EXPEDITION

SIMPSONS AND SIMPSONS-SEARS CATALOGUES – 1896-1979 – 54r – 1 – cn Library Assoc [380]

SIMPSONS DAILY LEADER – Kittanning. Pa. 1909-1920 – 1 – us UMI [071]

Simrock, Karl Joseph *see*
- GEDICHTE
- KARL SIMROCKS AUSGEWAEHLTE WERKE IN ZWOELF BAENDEN

SIM'S DESCRIPTION CATALOGUE OF BRITISH AND EXOTIC FERNS / Sim, T R – 7259A. Pt. 1, 1863. Lacking: Pt. 2, 1863 – 9 – ne IDC [580]

Sims, Gigi-Terese *see* SEXUALITY EDUCATION

Sims, J *see* ANNALS OF BOTANY

Sims, John *see* SELECTIONS FROM THE RECORDS OF INDIA 1849-1937

Simson, John *see* THE GREAT JOY OF SAINTS

SIMULATING/ GAMING – (See also: Simulation/ Gaming/News) – v3-. 1976- – 1,5,6,9 – us UMI [000]

A SIMULATION APPROACH TO CROWDING IN OUTDOOR RECREATION : A STUDY OF THE YANGMINGSHAN NATIONAL PARK / Chang, Chun-Yen & Graefe, Alan R – 1993 – 3mf – 9 – $12.00 – us Microform Publ [790]

SIMULATION METHODS IN WATER DEVELOPMENT – 1974 repr 1984 – 62p – it F.A.O. [333]

SIMULATION/GAMES FOR LEARNING – (v.11-. 1981-. 5,6,9) – v.9-. 1979- – 1 – us UMI [370]

SIMULATION/GAMING/NEWS – v. 1-3. 1972-1976 – 1 – us UMI [000]

SIMVOLISTY O SIMVOLIZME – "Zavety". nr. 2. 1914. BR-3338 2 – 8 – ne IDC [073]

SIMVOLIZM – Literaturnoe nasledstvo. Tom 27-28. M. 1937. B-1174 2 – 8 – ne IDC [460]

SIMVOLIZM. KNIGA STATEI / Belyi, A – Izd. Musaget. M. 1910. BR-598 2 – 8 – ne IDC [460]

SIMVOLY / Merezhkovskii, Dimitrii – (Pesni i poemy). Spb. 1892. BR-787 2 – 8 – ne IDC [460]

SIN / Foster, Randolph Sinks – New York: Eaton & Mains; Cincinnati: Curts & Jennings, 1899 – 1mf – 9 – us A.T.L.A. [240]

SIN AND HOLINESS OR WHAT IT IS TO BE HOLY / Huntington, DeWitt C – 1898 – 9 – us A.T.L.A. [240]

SIN AND ITS PENALTY : PRESENT AND FUTURE / Hawkins, Joshua – London: Elliot Stock, 1880 – 1mf – 9 – 0-8370-8906-9 – 1986-2906 – us A.T.L.A. [210]

SIN AND SALVATION (CCC160) / Hollister, G W – (In Chinese) – 1st ed. Hong Kong: Council on Christian Literature for Overseas Chinese, 1955 – 1r – 1 – 1984-B500 – us A.T.L.A. [240]

SIN CHE KI – Titre francais: Le Siecle nouveau. no. 1-41. Paris. 1909-10. mq no. 3 – 1 – fr A.C.R.P.P. [073]

SIN CHUNG JIT POH – Singapore. In Chinese. -d. Jan 1937-Dec 1938. 24 reels – 1 – uk British Libr Newspaper [072]

SIN HIJOS Y CON BIENES / Moreno Torrado, Luis – 1893 – 9 – 1.50f – sp Bibl Santa Ana [810]

SIN I BAO : LUTHERAN WEEKLY – (Lacking: 1918-19. 1922) – v5-20. 1917-32 – 4R – 1 – ATLA S0233 – us A.T.L.A. [073]

THE SIN OF THE ANGELS : THE CATHOLIC UNIVERSITY OF AMERICA STUDIES IN SACRAD THEOLOGY / Montang, E J – Washington, D.C., 1955 – 10mf – 8 – ne Slangenburg [240]

SIN PIES NI CABEZA : POESIAS / Sanchez-Arjona, Vicente – Portada de Hohenleiter. Sevilla: Imp. y Pap. Casa de la Vega, 1934 – 1 – sp Bibl Santa Ana [810]

SIN PO – Djakarta. Indonesia. -d. 1 Mar 1948-6 Oct 1949, 3, 8, 9 May 1951. (4 reels) – 1 – uk British Libr Newspaper [072]

SIN PO – Indonesia. Djakarta. 1954-1959 – 1 – us UMI [072]

Sin, Po *see* JUBILEUM-NUMMER, 1910-1935

SIN TIAUW HIAP LU, ATAU SI RADJAWALI SAKTI DAN PASANGAN PENDEKAR / Chin, Yung – SE-4598 1. 2 v. 1963 – 9 – ne IDC [950]

LA SINAGOGA DE ZARAGOZA / Monsalud, Marques de – Madrid: Est. Tip. Fortanet, 1898. B.R.A.H. 32, 1898, pp. 89-90 – 1 – sp Bibl Santa Ana [270]

SINAI – (Baltimore). 1856-63 – 1 – us A.J.P.C. [071]

SINAI AND PALESTINE IN CONNECTION WITH THEIR HISTORY / Stanley, Arthur Penrhyn – (Includes index) – new ed. New York: W J Widdleton, 1875 – 2mf – 9 – 0-8370-9830-0 – 1986-3830 – us A.T.L.A. [956]

Sinaiskii, V *see* OSNOVY GRAZHDANSKOGO PRAVA V SVIAZI S CHAST'IU 3 SVODA UZAKONENII DEISTVUIUSHCHIKH V LATVII I ESTONII

Sinaloa. Mexico *see*
- EL ESTADO DE SINALOA
- PERIODICO OFICIAL

Sinan, Shaikh *see* MUSAHABAH RUHANIYA BAIN AL-ALIMAIN

Sinar, Baroe *see*
- NOMER PERINGATAN SETAHOEN PEMBANGOENAN DJAWA BAROE
- NOMER SETAHOEN PERINGATAN

SINAR HARAPAN – Djakarta, Indonesia. 1964-Oct 1986 – 79r – 1 – us L of C Photodup [072]

SINAR MATAHARI (JOGJAKARTA) : NJANJIAN NIPPON OENTOEK OEMOEM – (Microfiche Nos 168-169) – Djokjakarta (2602).-1v – 2mf – 9 – SE-2002/1 – ne IDC [950]

SINAR ROHANI – v1-5. Jun 1935-Mar 1940 (complete) – 1r – 1 – ATLA B0242 – us A.T.L.A. [073]

Sinaver *see* DIVANCE

Sinay, Pierre G *see* CARBOHYDRATE LETTERS

SINCERIDAD – Badajoz.1888. no.15 – 1.50f – sp Bibl Santa Ana [073]

SINCERITY AND SUBSCRIPTION : A PLEA FOR TOLERATION IN THE CHURCH OF ENGLAND / Henson, H Hensley – London, New York: Macmillan, 1903 – 1mf – us A.T.L.A. [240]

Sinclair, Addie M *see* AUTOBIOGRAPHY

Sinclair, Francis Isabella *see* INDIGENUS FLOWERS OF THE HAWAIIAN ISLANDS

Sinclair, Gary D *see*
- CHARACTERISTICS OF THOUGHT PROCESSES AND KNOWLEDGE STRUCTURES OF NOVICE TENNIS PLAYERS
- THE EFFECTS OF PROTOTYPIC EXAMPLES AND VIDEO REPLAY ON ADOLESCENT GIRLS' ACQUISITION OF BASIC FIELD HOCKEY SKILLS
- EFFECTS OF SUPERVISORY PROFILING ON TARGETED FEEDBACK BEHAVIORS OF PRESERVICE PHYSICAL EDUCATORS
- A TEST OF THE VARIABILITY OF PRACTICE HYPOTHESIS

Sinclair, H M *see* WORLD NUTRITION AND NUTRITION EDUCATION

Sinclair, Isabella *see* INDIGENOUS FLOWERS OF THE HAWAIIAN ISLANDS

Sinclair, J *see* ADDRESS TO THE SOCIETY FOR THE IMPROVEMENT OF BRITISH WOOL

SINCLAIR'S JOURNAL OF B.N.A – Quebec, Canada. v1 n7. 26 mai 1849-v1 n13. 1 aut 1849 – 1r – 1 – Can$35.00 – cn Can Microfilming [073]

SINCLAIR'S MONTHLY CIRCULAR AND LITERARY GAZETTE – Montreal, Canada. v1 n3. mar 1855 – 1r – 1 – Can$25.00 – cn Can Microfilming [073]

SINCLAIR'S WEEKLY ADVERTISER – Quebec, Canada. v1 n40. 30 nov 1860; v1 n41. 14 dec 1860 – 1r – 1 – Can$25.00 – cn Can Microfilming [072]

SINCRETISMO RELIGIOSO AFRO-BRASILEIRO / Valente, Waldemar – Sao Paulo, 1955 – 4mf – 8 – ne Slangenburg [210]

SIND DIE REICHSDEUTSCHEN BERECHTIGT UND VERPFLICHTET, DAS DEUTSCHTHUM IM AUSLANDE ZU STUETZEN? / Proell, Karl – Kiel: Lipsius und Tischer, 1891 – 1 – us U.W. Library [943]

SIND FRAUEN ESSBAR? : ZUR SYMPTOMATIK DES WEIBLICHEN KOERPERS IM WERK MARGRET ATWOODS / Poole, Ralph J – 1992 – 145p – DM98.00 – 3-89349-464-2 – gw Hänsel [420]

Sind Historical Society *see* THE JOURNAL OF THE SIND HISTORICAL SOCIETY

SINDBAD = SINDBAD THE SAILOR : ODER, DIE SIEBEN WEISEN MEISTER – (In German and Syriac. Includes bibliographical references) – Leipzig: J C Hinrichs, 1879 – 1mf – 9 – 0-8370-7681-1 – 1986-1681 – us A.T.L.A. [390]

Sindhupramana, S *see* MEMBANGUN DESA, TJEPAT, SERENTAK, PRAKTIS; PEDOMAN BAGI SETIAP WARGA-NEGARA

O SINDICALISMO : ORGAO DO SINDICATO DOS JORNALISTAS PROFISSIONALS DO AMAZONAS – Manaus, Amazonas. Jun-Jul 1966 – 1,5,6 – bl Biblioteca [072]

EL SINDICALISMO JUSTICIALISTA A TRAVES DEL PENSAMIENTO DE PERON / Argentina. Presidencia. Subsecretaria de Informaciones – Buenos Aires, 1951 – 1 – CSUXAHZ5331-B – us Hoover Inst Photo [320]

SINDICALISMO Y JUSTICIA SOCIAL / Banegas, Fortunato – Buenos Aires: [s.n.], 1968 – 1 – CSUXAHZ3411-B – us Hoover Inst Photo [360]

SINDICALISMO Y PERONISMO : LOS COMIENZOS DE UN VINCULO PERDURABLE / Campo, Hugo del – Buenos Aires, Argentina: Consejo Latinoamericano de Ciencias Sociales, 1983 – 1 – CSUXADH7652-B – us Hoover Inst Photo [320]

SINDICALISMO Y POLITICA : PERON HABLA A LOS TRABAJADORES, 2 DE NOVIEMBRE DE 1973 / Peron, Juan Domingo – [Buenos Aires]: Presidencia de la Nacion, Secretaria de Prensa y Difusion, [1974?] – 1 – CSUXADJ2883-B – us Hoover Inst Photo [320]

Sindicato Amanecer, Hoyos *see* ESTATUTO DEL SINDICATO DE OBRAS AGRICOLAS Y OFICIOS VARIOS

Sindicato Independiente de trabajadores del Credito (S.I. T.C.). Caceres *see* ESTATUTOS

EL SINDICATO OBRERO EN FUNCION DE PATRIA / Cardillo, Francisco Ramon – [Buenos Aires?], 1953 – 1 – CSUXAHZ2952-B – us Hoover Inst Photo [306]

Sindicato Prov. de la Alimentacion y Productos Coloniales, Badajoz *see* CONVENIO COLECTIVO SINDICAL DE TRABAJO, DE AMBITO PROVINCIAL PARA EL COMERCIO DE LA ALIMENTACION (MAYOR Y MENOR) APROBADO POR EL ILMO. SR. DELEGADO PROV. DE TRABAJO

Sindicato Provincial del Metal *see*
- CONVENIO COLECTIVO SINDICAL DE SIDERMETALURGIA (N° 188 DE 18.8.76)
- CONVENIO COLECTIVO SINDICAL DE SIDEROMETALURGICA. NUMERO 159 DE 13-7-74

SINDICATOS Y POLITICA EN ARGENTINA / Cavarozzi, Marcelo – Buenos Aires, Argentina: Centro de Estudios de Estado y Sociedad, [1984] – 1 – CSUXADJ0052-B – us Hoover Inst Photo [320]

Sinding, C *see* SONATE [C DUR], OP. 12

LOS SIN-DIOS. LA CAMPANA DE NUESTROS DIAS / Bayle, Constantino – Madrid: Razon y Fe, 1934 – 1 – sp Bibl Santa Ana [946]

SINDITSIROVANNAIA KOZHEVENNAIA PROMYSHLENNOST ZA... / ed by Vsesoiuzny i kozhevennyi sindikat – (Includes c.1: 1927/1928) – Moskva: Sindikat, 1922 – 1 – CSUXAKZ1339-S – us Hoover Inst Photo [338]

Sine, Barbara *see* NON-FORMAL EDUCATION AND EDUCATION POLICY IN GHANA AND SENEGAL

SINENSIA – (In English) – v. 1-9 (5-6). Nanking. 1929-38. Lacking: v. 6 (2) 1935; v. 7 (6) 1936. B-8149 1 – 52mf – 9 – ne IDC [073]

SINFONIA CON VIOLINI, OBOE, CORNI, VIOLA, FAGOTTO, E BASSO, NO. 29 / Brunetti, Gaetano – (Score) – Original MS, [1783?] – 1 – us Sibley [780]

SINFONIA CON VIOLINI, OBOE, CORNI, VIOLA, FAGOTTO E BASSO. NO.25 / Brunetti, Gaetano – Manusript – 9 – us Sibley [780]

SINFONIA CONCERTANTE NO. 1, G. 76; ARRANGED FOR PIANOFORTE BY D. STEIBEL / Viotti, Giovanni B – Ms, 1786 – 1 – us Sibley [780]

SINFONIE, [ES DUR]...OP. 28 / Bruch, M – Leipzig: C F W Siegel, [187-] – 1 – us Sibley [780]

SINFONIE NO. 6, D MINOR, FUR GROSSES ORCHESTER, OP. 18 / Raff, J – Berlin: Bote & Book, 1874 – 1 – us Sibley [780]

DIE SINFONIEN ERNST EICHNERS (1740-1777) / Reissinger, Marianne – Frankfurt a.M., 1970 – 3mf – 9 – DM76.00 – 3-89349-709-9 – gw Hänsel [780]

SING TAO – 1791-1995 – 1 – F3,166.00 – sz Infoprint [072]

SING TAO JIH PAO = SING TAO DAILY – (Yrly reel count varies) – 1938- – 1 – inquire – us Ross [072]

SING TAO WAN PAO = SING TAO EVENING POST – (Yrly reel count varies) – 1946- – 1 – inquire – us Ross [072]

Singapore *see* MASTER PLAN REPORT OF SURVEY

Singapore. Adult Education Board *see*
- ANNUAL REPORT OF THE LEMBAGA GERAKAN PELAJARAN DEWASA 1970-1977/78
- PROCEEDINGS OF THE NATIONAL CONFERENCE ON ADULT EDUCATION 23-25 SEPTEMBER 1971 SINGAPORE

SINGAPORE CHRONICLE – 1827-35 – 3r – 1 – uk Microform Academic [072]

Singapore. Commission of Inquiry into Education *see*
- FINAL REPORT
- INTERIM REPORT ON THE SIX-DAY WEEK

Singapore. Commission of Inquiry into Vocational and Technical Education in Singapore *see* REPORT

SINGAPORE DAILY TIMES – Singapore. -d. 1881-82. (4 reels) – 1 – uk British Libr Newspaper [072]

SINGAPORE DIOCESAN QUARTERLY LEAFLET – v1-2. 1939-41 (complete) – 1r – 1 – ATLA S0725F – us A.T.L.A. [073]

Singapore. Education Study Team *see* REPORT ON THE MINISTRY OF EDUCATION 1978

SINGAPORE FREE PRESS – Singapore. May 1946-56; Feb-May 1959; Nov 1959-1960 – 36r – 1 – us L of C Photodup [072]

SINGAPORE HERALD – Singapore. -d. 11 Apr 1939-30 Sep 1941. (10 reels) – 1 – uk British Libr Newspaper [072]

SINGAPORE. HISTORICAL DOCUMENTS AND MANSUCRIPTS *see* HISTORICAL DOCUMENTS AND MANUSCRIPTS

Singapore. Ministry of Education *see*
- EDUCATION AND TRAINING OF ENGINEERS, TECHNICIANS CRAFTSMEN AND OPERATIVES IN SINGAPORE
- KEY EDUCATION STATISTICS 1981-1986
- NEW EDUCATION SYSTEM (PRIMARY LEVEL)
- NEW EDUCATION SYSTEM (SECONDARY LEVEL)
- PRIMARY EDUCATION IN SINGAPORE
- PUPIL STATISTICAL BULLETIN
- SECONDARY EDUCATION IN SINGAPORE

Singapore. Ministry of Education. Planning and Review Division *see* ANTHROPOMETRIC DATA OF PUPILS AND STUDENTS IN SINGAPORE

Singapore. Ministry of Education. Research and Statistics Unit *see* A PROJECTION OF SCHOOL ENROLMENTS AND TEACHER REQUIREMENTS FOR SINGAPORE 1971 TO 1980

Singapore. Ministry of Finance *see* STATE OF SINGAPORE DEVELOPMENT PLAN, 1961-1964

SINGAPORE NIPPO – Singapore. -w. 23 May 1938-26 Mar 1939. (28 ft) – 1 – uk British Libr Newspaper [072]

Singapore. Prime Ministers Office. Economic Planning Unit *see* FIRST DEVELOPMENT PLAN, 1961-1964 REVIEW OF PROGRESS FOR THE THREE YEARS ENDING 31 DEC 1963

Singapore. Public Relations Office *see* WEEKLY DIGEST OF NON-ENGLISH PRESS

Singapore. Singapore Teachers' Union *see* THE TEACHER AND THE DYNAMICS OF NATION BUILDING

Singapore. Vocational and Industrial Training Board *see* KEY STATISTICS ON VOCATIONAL TRAINING 1983-1989

SINGAPOREAN EDUCATION IN PERSPECTIVE : A SELECT BIBLIOGRAPHY / Lee, Mui Sin – 1987 – 9 – A$10.00 – 0-86758-234-0 – at BISA [370]

SINGAPORE-MALAYSIA CONFERENCES ON HEALTH AND RELATED SCIENCES / ed by Yap, Sylvia – 1981 – A$10.00 – 0-86758-061-5 – at BISA [610]

Singarimbun, Masri *see*
- THE POPULATION OF INDONESIA, 1930-1968; A BIBLIOGRAPHY
- THE POPULATION OF INDONESIA, 1930-1968: A BIBLIOGRAPHY

SINGEN UND SAGEN / Thurau, Gustav – 1912 – 1 – us I.U. Libraries [390]

SINGEN UND SGEN / Schwietering, Julius – Goettingen, 1908 – 1mf – 9 – DM48.00 – 3-89349-319-0 – gw Hänsel [410]

Singer, A *see* BELI TEKUMAH

Singer, Ch *see* STUDIES IN THE HISTORY AND METHOD OF SCIENCE

Singer, I *see* DICTATOR-DEMOCRAT

Singer, Ignatius *see* DICTATOR – DEMOCRAT

Singer, S W *see* THE TABLE-TALK OF JOHN SELDEN

Singer-Kerel, J *see* LE COUT DE LA VIE A PARIS DE 1840 A 1954

SINGERS AND SONGS OF THE LIBERAL FAITH : BEING SELECTIONS OF HYMNS AND OTHER SACRED POEMS OF THE LIEBERAL CHURCH IN AMERICA / Putnam, Alfred P – Boston: Roberts, 1875, c1874 – 2mf – us A.T.L.A. [780]

SINGET UND SPIELET DEM HERRN IN EUREN HERZEN,... – Ms, 175- – 1 – us Sibley [780]

Singh, H *see* FARM PLAN FOR A 4-HECTARE FARM IN GWARSHA PROJECT AREA (BENGHAZI)

THE SINGING MASTER'S ASSISTANT, OR A KEY TO PRACTICAL MUSIC / Billings, William – Boston: Draper and Folsom, 1778. MUSIC 123, Item 11 – 1 – us L of C Photodup [780]

THE SINGING MINISTER OF NIGERIA : THE LIFE OF THE REV CANON J J RANSOME-KUTI / Delano, Isaac O – London: United Society for Christian Literature, 1942 – us Res Libr [920]

SINGLE COURT OF PATENT OF PATENT APPEALS: A LEGISLATIVE HISTORY / U.S. Library of Congress. Legislative Reference Service – Washington, Govt. Print. Off., 1959. 55 p. LL-2304 – 1 – us L of C Photodup [340]

A SINGLE STAGE SUBMAXIMAL TREADMILL JOG TEST TO ESTIMATE VO2 MAX IN SUBJECTS AGES 30 TO 39 YEARS / Babcock, Garth J & Myrer, William – 1992 – 1mf – $4.00 – us Microform Publ [612]

THE SINGLE TAX – (Land Values). Glasgow. Scotland. -m. Jun 1894-Dec 1914. (6 reels) – 1 – uk British Libr Newspaper [336]

SINGLE TAX BROACHER – Portland OR. Sep 1912 – 1 – us U.O. Library [071]

SINGLE TAX, FREE TRADE & LAND VALUES TAXATION: HENRY GEORGE IN THE SYDNEY SINGLE TAX LEAGUE / Clark, DL – 24p – 9 – 1.00f – at Libertarian Micro [380]

SINGLEHEART AND DOUBLE FACE / Reade, Charles L – British Fiction Archive: Unit 2 – 9 – uk Bell [830]

SINGLETON ARGUS – 1874-1968 – 7r – 9 – at Pascoe [072]

Singleton, William R *see* THE HISTORY OF FREEMASONRY

SING-SONG : A NURSERY RHYME BOOK / Rossetti, Christina – London: Macmillan, 1915 – 1 roll – 1 – 1-55879-420-4 – uk Libr Preservation [390]

SINGULARITES HISTORIQUES ET LITTERAIRES / Haureau, B – Paris, 1861 – Dfl25.00 – ne Slangenburg [240]

SINGULARITES HISTORIQUES ET LITTERAIRES / Haureau, B – Paris: M. Levy, 1861 – 1mf – us A.T.L.A. [240]

Sinha, Radha *see* LANDLESSNESS

SINHALESE DIARY, 1893 / Goonewardene, T W & Fernando, Henry – Colombo, 1892 – us Res Libr [950]

SINHALESE MATERIAL / United Society for the Propagation of the Gospel – "C" series. Ceylon. 1827-56; "D" series, Colombo. 1857-59; "E" series, Ceylon 1845-1928 – 1 – uk Microform Academic [240]

SINIAIA KNIGA. PETERBURGSKII DNEVNIK 1914-1918 / Gippius, Z N – Belgrad. 1929. BR-722 2 – 8 – ne IDC [800]

Siniavskii, A *see* POEZIIA PERVYKH LET REVOLIUTSII 1917-1920

Siniavskii, N *see* 1814-4 IIULIA 1914. PUSHKIN V PECHATI. 1814-1837. KHRONOLOGICHESKII UKAZATEL' PROIZVEDENII PUSHKINA, NAPCCHATANNYKH PRI EGO ZHIZNI

SINICA : ZEITSCHRIFT FUER CHINAKUNDE UND CHINAFORSCHUNG – Frankfurt am Main, 1925-1927. v1-17. Irregular. CH-874/2 – 210mf – 8 – ne IDC [950]

Sinker, Robert *see*
- MEMORIALS OF THE HON. ION KEITH-FALCONER
- TESTAMENTA XII PATRIARCHARUM: AD FIDEM CODICIS CANTABRIGIENSIS EDITA

Sinkewicz, Robert E *see*
- MANUSCRIPT LISTINGS FOR THE AUTHORED WORKS OF THE PALAEOLOGAN PERIOD
- MANUSCRIPT LISTINGS FOR THE AUTHORS OF CLASSICAL AND LATE ANTIQUITY
- MANUSCRIPT LISTINGS FOR THE AUTHORS OF THE PATRISTIC AND BYZANTINE PERIODS
- THE ONE HUNDRED AND FIFTY CHAPTERS

SINKING CREEK BAPTIST CHURCH. CARTER COUNTY. JOHNSON CITY, TENNESSEE : CHURCH RECORDS – 1773-1893 – 1 – 62.37 – us Baptist [240]

SINKING SPRING BAPTIST CHURCH. MURRAY, KENTUCKY : CHURCH RECORDS – 1831-1958, 1963-80 – 1 – 65.00 – us Baptist [240]

Sinko, T *see* KLASYCZNE PRZYSLOWIA W POLSZCZYZNIE

THE SINLESSNESS OF JESUS: AN EVIDENCE FOR CHRISTIANITY / Ullmann, Karl – Edinburgh: T.& T. Clark, 1882. 1 fiche – 9 – us A.T.L.A. [240]

THE SINLESSNESS OF JESUS; AN EVIDENCE FOR CHRISTIANITY / Ullmann, Karl – 1858 – 1 – us A.T.L.A. [240]

THE SINLESSNESS OF JESUS; AN EVIDENCE FOR CHRISTIANITY / Ullmann, Karl – 1870 – 1 – us A.T.L.A. [240]

SINN FEIN – Dublin, 1906-25 – 3r – 1 – us Ross [072]

SINN FEIN – Dublin. Weekly. May 12 1906-Nov 28 1914; Aug 7 1923-June 13 1925. Incomplete – 1 – us NY Public [941]

SINN FEIN – Ireland.7 Aug 1923-13 Jun 1925 – 1 – ie Microforms [072]

SINN FEIN (DAILY) – Ireland.-d. 23 Aug 1909-21 Jan 1910 – 1 – ie Microforms [072]

SINN FEIN REBELLION HANDBOOK – A contemporary account of Easter Rising.4 fiches – 9 – PS150.00 – ie Irish Times [941]

SINN FEIN REBELLION HANDBOOK / Weekly Irish Times – 1917 – 4 silver mf – Ir£150.00 – ie Irish Times [940]

SINN FEIN (WEEKLY) – Dublin, Ireland.-w. 25 May 1906-28 Nov 1914 – 1 – ie Microforms [072]

THE SINN FEINER – Ireland.12 Jun 1920-10 Dec 1921 – 1 – ie Microforms [072]

SINN UND UMSETZUNG EINES VERTRIEBSWIRTSCHAFTLICHEN MARKETING-KONZEPTES IM PRODUKTIONSBETRIEB IM ALLGEMEINEN UND SPEZIELL AM BEISPIEL DER KFZ-ZULIEFERINDUSTRIE / Kessler, Franz Josef – 1992 – 216p – 9 – DM98.00 – 3-89349-516-9 – gw Hänsel [650]

SINNDIMENSIONEN AESTHETISCHER ERFAHRUNG : BILDUNGSRELEVANTE ASPEKTE DER AESTHETIK WALTER BENJAMINS / Ruge, Eva – 1995 – 3mf – 9 – DM98.00 – 3-8267-2240-X – gw Hänsel [370]

DIE SINNE / Kaufmann, David – Beitraege zur Geschichte der Physiologie und der Psychologie im Mittelalter. Budapest. 1884. BJ-33-5 1 – 9 – ne IDC [180]

SINNE-BEELDEN DER DEUGHDEN VOOR EEN NIEUW-JAER GHESCHONCKEN AEN ALLE GODT-VRUCHTIGHE SIELEN : VERMEERDERT EN VERBETERT / Smidt, A de – Derden druck. Antwerpen, 1667 – 1mf – 9 – O-3260/1 – ne IDC [760]

SINNEPOPPEN / Visscher, R – O 797. 1614 – 9 – ne IDC [760]

SINNEPOPPEN VAN ROEMER VISSCHER / Visscher, R – Amsterdam. n.d. – 4mf – 9 – ne IDC [700]

THE SINNER AND THE SAVIOUR / Saphir, Adolph – New York: Gospel Pub House, [18–] – 1mf – 9 – 0-8370-6366-3 – 1986-0366 – us A.T.L.A. [240]

DER SINNLICHE GEHALT DER WAHRNEHMUNG / Schantz, Richard – Heidelberg, 1983 – 4mf – 9 – DM90.00 – 3-89349-368-9 – gw Hänsel [120]

O SINO : ORGAO CRITICO E NOTICIOSO – Humaytha, Amazonas. 20 Out 1901 – 1,5,6 – bl Biblioteca [072]

SINO DA BASILICA : ORGAO DA BASILICA DE NOSSA SENHORA DA SAUDE DE POCOS DE CALDAS – Pocos de Caldas, 27 Nov 1949 – 1,5,6 – bl Biblioteca [072]

SINO-BRITISH TRADE / Sino-British Trade Council – Nos. 1-40. 1964-68 – 10mf – 7 – uk Microform Academic [380]

Sino-British Trade Council *see* SINO-BRITISH TRADE

SINODO DIOCESANO DE CORIA / Peris Mencheta, Ramon – 1897 – 9 – 1.50f – sp Bibl Santa Ana [240]

SINODO PLACENTINO DEL OBISPO NORONA (1582) / Perez Coca y Sanchez Matas, Carmen – Caceres: Facultad de Derecho, Universidad de Extremadura, 1978 – 1 – sp Bibl Santa Ana [946]
SINO-PORTUGUESE TRADE FROM 1514 TO 1644 : A SYNTHESIS OF PORTUGUESE AND CHINESE SOURCES / Chang, T T – Leiden, 1933 – 2mf – 1 – ILM-1131/1 – ne IDC [327]
SINOPSIS DE FAMILIAS Y GENEROS DE PLANTAS LENOSAS DE FILIPINAS / Vidal y Soler, S – Manila. 1883. B-682 2 – 8 – ne IDC [580]
Sinor, D *see* THE OUTLINES OF HUNGARIAN PREHISTORY
Sintenis, Franz *see* GOETHE'S EINFLUSS AUF UHLAND
SINTESIS BIOGRAFICA DE CACERES / Agundez Ferrandez, Antonio – Badajoz: Dip. Provincial, 1958 – sp Bibl Santa Ana [920]
SINTESIS DE HISTORIA DE LA IGLESIA / Philips, Hughes – Madrid: Arch. Ibero Americano, 1959 – 1 – sp Bibl Santa Ana [240]
SINTESIS DE LA ESTRATEGIA PARA EL DESARROLLO DE LA REGION DE MAGALLANES / Chile. Oficina de Planificacion Nacional – Santiago. 1969. BD-1837 1 – 9 – ne IDC [338]
SINTESIS HISTORICA DE LA POLITICA ARGENTINA / Argentine Republic. Servicio International Publicaciones Argentinas – [Buenos Aires, 1952] – 1 – CSUXADQ5372-B – us Hoover Inst Photo [320]
DIE SINTFLUT : ROMAN / Andres, Stefan Paul – Muenchen: R Piper, 1949-59 – 1r – 1 – us U.W. Library [830]
SINTONIA – Manaus, Amazonas. Mar-Abr 1944 – 1,5,6 – bl Biblioteca [072]
Sioc'han de Kersabiec, Edouard *see* ETUDES ARCHEOLOGIQUES
SION – Athens, Greece. -w. 7 Jan 1881-26 July 1889. 2 reels – 1 – uk British Libr Newspaper [949]
SION – Organ russkikh evreev. v. 1-43. Odessa. 1861-62. BR-3759 2 – 8 – ne IDC [270]
Sion, Marie-de *see* BIBLIOGRAPHIE ANALYTIQUE PRECEDEE D'UNE BIOGRAPHIE DU REV. PERE JEAN-PAUL DALLAIRE, S.J. COLLEGE DES JESUITES, QUEBEC
SIONA – Monatschrift fuer Liturgie und Kirchenmusik. Guetersloh. v. 1-45, no. 6. 1876-1920. Incomplete – 1 – us NY Public [240]
SIONISTSKOE OBOZRENIE – Elizavetgrad. 1902-03. BR-3758 2 – 8 – ne IDC [270]
SIOUX COUNTY HERALD – Harrison, NE. -w. Apr 1887; Nov 1887; Jul 1889-Aug 1892 – 1 – us NE Hist [071]
SIOUX COUNTY NEWS – Harrison, NE. -w. Aug 1959-May 1961 – 1 – us NE Hist [071]
SIOUX INDIAN COURTS; AN ADDRESS DELIVERED BY DOANE ROBINSON...BEFORE THE SOUTH DAKOTA BAR ASSOCIATION AT PIERRE, SOUTH DAKOTA, JANUARY 21, 1909 / Robinson, Doane – Sioux Falls: Sessions 1909?. 14p. LL-1708 – 1 – us L of C Photodup [340]
SIOUX SAN SUN – 1967-73.(American Indian Periodicals in the Princeton University Library). 11 fiches – 9 – $65.00 – us UPA [073]
S.I.P.A., International Service Argentine Publications *see* EVA PERON
SIPAHI MECMUASI – (Mueduer-i Mes'ul: H. Bedreddin, Mueduer ve Sermuharriri: Kececizade Izzet Fuad. Nos. 1, 4-12 (15 Agustos 1333-15 Temmuz 1334[1917-1918])) – Istanbul: Tanin Matbaasi, 1917-? – 4mf – 9 – $75.00 – us MEDOC [949]
Siple, V A *see* AGRICULTURAL MARKETING, SEED PRODUCTION FARM, AGRICULTURAL CREDIT, PUBLIC LAW, 480 CEREALS
Sipovskii, V V *see*
– KARAMZIN, AVTOR
– RUSSKAIA LIRIKA
– SBORNIK STATEI
Sipovskij, V V *see* POESIJA NARODNA
Sipp, T L *see* EFFECT OF CHRONIC ETHANOL CONSUMPTION AND MODERATE INTENSITY ENDURANCE TRAINING ON MURINE PLASMA CORTICOSTERONE CONCENTRATION
SIPPURIM / Tchernichowsky, S – Berlin. 1922. BJ-422-90 1 – 9 – ne IDC [470]
Siqueira, A de et al *see* L'ART RUPESTRE DE LA PEDRA PINTADA DE COCAIS, MINAS GERAIS, BRESIL
THE SIR BENJAMIN STONE COLLECTION OF PHOTOGRAPHS – c1860-1910. 600 fiches or film – 1,9 – £1,850.00 – uk World [770]
SIR CHARLES DANVERS / Cholmondeley, Mary – British Fiction Archive: Unit 3 – 9 – uk Bell [830]
SIR EDWIN LANDSEER / Stephens, Frederic George – London: S. Low, Marston, Searle & Rivington, 3rd ed 1880 – 1 roll – 1 – 1-55879-574-X – uk Libr Preservation [750]
SIR F.B. HEAD: COPY OF A DESPATCH FROM SIR F.B. HEAD, IN ANSWER TO CHARGES PREFERRED AGAINST HIM BY DR. C. DUNCOMBE.. / Canada – s.l: House of Commons, 1837. SEM105P411 – 2mf – 9 – Can$4.50 – cn Bibl Nat [971]
SIR FRANCIS DRAKE, HIS VOYAGE, 1595 / Maynarde, Thomas – Ed. by W. D. Cooley. Hakluyt Society – 2mf – 7 – uk Microform Academic [910]
SIR FRANCIS HINCKS' BUDGET SPEECH, FRIDAY, MARCH 10, 1871 / Hincks, Sir Francis – 1871?. 05622. (Pre-1900 Canadiana) – 9 – cn C.I.H.M. [971]
SIR GEORGE TRESSADY / Ward, Mary Augusta – British Fiction Archive: Unit 2 – 9 – uk Bell [830]
SIR GUY CARLETON PAPERS / Carleton, Guy – (10,434 items in 10?v 1747-83. Last British Commander-in-Chief in America) – 30r – 1 – $2220.00 – us UMI [920]
SIR HARRY HOTSPUR OF HUMBLETHWAITE / Trollope, Anthony – London: Hurst and Blackett, 1871 – 1 roll – 1 – 1-55879-815-3 – uk Libr Preservation [830]
SIR ISAAC NEWTON : MANUSCRIPTS AND PAPERS – (With printed guide £58.00) – 43r – 1 – £2,865.00 – uk Chadwyck [510]
SIR JASPER'S TENANT / Braddon, Mary Elizabeth – British Fiction Archive: Unit 5 – 9 – uk Bell [830]
SIR JOHN FRANKLIN / Beesly, Augustus Henry – London: M. Ward, 1881. 03998. (Pre-1900 Canadiana) – 9 – cn C.I.H.M. [971]
THE SIR JOHN GIELGUD ARCHIVE – (With printed guide) – 72mf – 9 – $266.00 – 1-869934-33-4 – uk Emmett [790]
SIR JOHN JERVIS ON THE OFFICE AND DUTIES OF CORONERS WITH FORMS AND PRECEDENTS / Jervis, John B – 3d ed. London, Sweet, Maxwell, 1866. 455 1 p. LL-1660 – 1 – us L of C Photodup [340]
SIR JOHN JOHNSON, THE FIRST AMERICAN BORN BARONET: AN ADDRESS DELIVERED BEFORE THE NEW YORK HISTORICAL SOCIETY, AT ITS ANNUAL MEETING, TUESDAY, JANUARY 6TH, 1880 / De Peyster, John Watts – s.l.: s.n., 1880?. 04225. (Pre-1900 Canadiana) – 9 – cn C.I.H.M. [971]
SIR JOHN THOMPSON / Belding, Albert Martin – 1895?. 05870. (Pre-1900 Canadiana) – 9 – cn C.I.H.M. [920]
SIR JOHN WILLIAM DAWSON: A BRIEF BIOGRAPHICAL SKETCH / Ami, Henry Marc – 1900? 02192. (Pre-1900 Canadiana) – 9 – cn C.I.H.M. [910]
SIR LOMER GOUIN OU LE PREMIERMINISTRE DES "CONTRACTEURS" / Fournier, Jules – [Quebec (Province): s.n., 1912 ?]. SEM105P1504 – 1mf – 9 – Can$2.25 – cn Bibl Nat [971]
SIR NIGEL / Doyle, Arthur Conan – London: Smith, Elder, 1906 – 1 roll – 1 – 1-55879-683-5 – uk Libr Preservation [830]
SIR PERCIVAL / Shorthouse, Joseph Henry – British Fiction Archive: Unit 1 – 9 – uk Bell [830]
SIR RICHARD CARTWRIGHT AT MASSEY MUSIC HALL, TORONTO, AUGUST 24TH 1899 / Cartwright, Richard – Toronto?: A. Smith?, 1899? 00503. (Pre-1900 Canadiana) – 9 – cn C.I.H.M. [971]
SIR RICHARD HAWKINS: OBSERVATIONS IN HIS VOYAGE INTO THE SOUTH SEAS, 1593 / ed by Drinkwater-Bethune, C R – Hakluyt Society – 6mf – 7 – uk Microform Academic [910]
SIR THOMAS FOWELL BUXTON, BART. : A STUDY FOR YOUNG MEN; THE WIFE, OR, A MIRROR FOR MAIDENHOOD: A SKETCH / Binney, Thomas – 2nd ed. London: James Nisbet: Hamilton, Adams, 1853 – 1mf – 9 – 0-8370-7285-9 – 1986-1285 – us A.T.L.A. [920]
SIR THOMAS MORE / Hutton, William Holden – London: Methuen, 1895 – 1mf – us A.T.L.A. [240]
SIR THOMAS MORE (THE BLESSED THOMAS MORE) / Bremond, Henri – London: Duckworth; New York: Benziger, 1904. (The Saints) – 1mf – us A.T.L.A. [240]
SIR THOMAS OVERBURY'S VISION (1616) BY RICHARD NICCOLS AND OTHER ENGLISH SOURCES OF NATHANIEL HAWTHORNE'S 'THE SCARLET LETTER' / Niccols, Richard – 9 – $15.00 – us Scholars' Facs [420]
SIR WILLIAM BLACKSTONE AND THE FOUNDATION OF ENGLISH LAW : THE BLACKSTONE LECTURE NOTEBOOKS FROM ALL SOUL'S COLLEGE, OXFORD – 5 – 1 – us Primary [340]
SIRAEJ. HALLAH : MAIMONIDES' COMMENTAR ZUM TRACTAT CHALLAH / Maimonides, Moses; ed by Bamberger, Selig – (In German & Hebrew) – Frankfurt a. M.: J Kauffmann, 1895 – 1mf – 9 – 0-8370-4259-3 – 1985-2259 – us A.T.L.A. [270]
Sire, J Y *see* DEVELOPPEMENT, CROISSANCE ET REGENERATION DES ECAILLES D'HEMICHROMIS BIMACULATUS (GILL, 1862) (PERCIFORMES CICHLIDES)
Sire, JY *see* STRUCTURE, FORMATION ET REGENERATION DES ECAILLES D'UN POISSON TELEOSTEEN, HEMICHROMIS BIMACULATUS (PERCIFORME, CICHLIDE)
Siregar, Bakri *see*
– GADIS TERATAI, SEBUAH DONGENG RAKJAT KOREA; DRAMA TIGA BABAK
– SEDJARAH SASTERA INDONESIA MODERN
Sirelius, U T *see*
– UEBER DIE ART UND ZEIT DER ZAEHMUNG DES RENNTIERS
Sirey, J -B *see* RECUEIL GENERAL DES LOIS ET DES ARRETS EN MATIERE CIVILE, CRIMINELLE, COMMERCIALE ET DE DROIT PUBLIC
SIRIN – Al'manakhi. 1-3. Izd. "Tereshchenko". Spb. 1913-14. BR-1912 2 – 8 – ne IDC [030]
SIRIN UCHENOGO VARVARSTVA / Belyi, A – Spb. 1922. BR-599 2 – 8 – ne IDC [460]
SIRKET-I HAYRIYE'NIN...VARIDAT VE MASARIFAT VAKIYESIYLE MUVAZINE-YI UMUMIYESINE MUEBIN-I CEDVELDIR (1334-1335, 1335-1336, 1336-1337) – Matbaa-yi Bahriye, 1334-1337 [1918-1921] – 9 – $20.00 – us MEDOC [380]
Sirkis, I *see* ESTHER
Sirmans, M Eugene, Jr *see* SCRAPBOOKS AND PHOTOS
Sirmondi, J *see* CONCILIA ANTIQUA GALLIAE
...SIROE, OPERA DI...[DRAMMA PER MUSICA DA RAPPRESENTARSI NEL NUOVE TEATRO DI CORTE...NEL CARNOVALE 1767. LA POESIA E DEL SIGNOR ABBATE PIETRO METASTASIO... / Traetta, T – (Library has act 1 and 2 only. (out of 3 acts)) – n.p., 177- – 1 – us Sibley [780]
Sirr, H C *see* CHINA AND THE CHINESE
SIRVEN : ETUDE HISTORIQUE SUR L'AVENEMENT DE LA TOLERANCE / Rabaud, Camille – Paris: Fischbacher, 1891 – 1mf – us A.T.L.A. [900]
Sisakyan, N M *see* PROBLEMS IN SPACE BIOLOGY
SISALAHETYS – 1970-80 (complete) – 2r – 1 – ATLA S0736 – us A.T.L.A. [073]
SISERA / Fischmann, N I – Lemberg. 1841. BJ-422-16 1 – 9 – ne IDC [290]
SISKIYOU COUNTY MESSENGER – Montague, CA. 1933-35 – 1r – 1 – $50.00 – B02475 – us Library Micro [071]
SISKIYOU DAILY NEWS – (Cont: Siskiyou News) – Yreka, CA. 1941-83; 1984- – 119+ r – 1 – $5,950.00 ($140.00) – C03116 – us Library Micro [071]
SISKIYOU DAILY NEWS – Yreka. Calif. 1960- – 1 – us UMI [071]
SISKIYOU DAILY NEWS *see* SISKIYOU NEWS
SISKIYOU NEWS – (Cont by: Siskiyou Daily News) – Yreka, CA. 1895-1917; 1919-41 – 24r – 1 – $1,200.00 – B03120 – us Library Micro [071]
SISKIYOU NEWS *see* SISKIYOU DAILY NEWS
SISKIYOU STANDARD – Fort Jones, CA. 1917-22 – 2r – 1 – $100.00 – B02243 – us Library Micro [071]
SISKIYOU TELEGRAM – Yreka, CA. 1890-92 – 1r – 1 – $50.00 – B03121 – us Library Micro [071]
SISKIYOU TIMES – Yreka, CA. 1927-30 – 2r – 1 – $100.00 – B03122 – us Library Micro [071]
Sismondi, Jean Charles Leonard Simonde de *see* A HISTORY OF THE FALL OF THE ROMAN EMPIRE...A VIEW OF THE INVASION & SETTLEMENT OF THE BARBARIANS
Sismondi, Leonard Simonde de *see* DE L'INTERET DE LA FRANCE A L'EGARD DE LA TRAITE DES NEGRES
SISSON HEADLIGHT – Mt Shasta, CA. 1904-17; 1919-22 – 9r – 1 – $450.00 – B02496 – us Library Micro [071]
SISSON HEADLIGHT – Sisson, CA. 1904-22 – 9r – 1 – $450.00 – B02994 – us Library Micro [071]
SISSON MASCOT – Mt Shasta, CA. 1891-95 – 1r – 1 – $50.00 – B02497 – us Library Micro [071]
SISSON MIRROR – Mt Shasta, CA. 1896-1904 – 2r – 1 – $100.00 – B02498 – us Library Micro [071]
THE SISSON MIRROR – Sisson, CA. 1896-1904 – 2r – 1 – $100.00 – B02996 – us Library Micro [071]
SISTEMA I ORGANIZATSIIA – (Library has: 1927, no. 1-4) – Moskva: izd. Akts. O-va "Promizdat", 1923-1929. 7v – 1 – CSUX89-S634 – us Hoover Inst Photo [330]
SISTEMA KOOPERATSII / Gibner, N P – M., 1911 – 2mf – 9 – COR-19/1 – ne IDC [334]
SISTEMA RACIONALIZADO DE LIQUIDACION Y RECAUDACIOM EN LAS HACIENDAS LOCALES / Lorenzo Fraguas, Francisco & Mahilla Santos, Juan – Caceres: Tip. El Noticiero, 1959 – 1 – sp Bibl Santa Ana [336]
SISTEMATI POLITICHESKOGO RAVNOVESIIA I LEGITIMIZMA I NACHALO NATSIONAL'NOSTI V IKH VZAIMNOI SVIAZI / Danevskii, V P – Spb. 1882. BR-10,003 1 – 9 – ne IDC [080]
SISTEMATICHESKAIA ROSPIS' KNIGAM PRODAIUSHCHIMSIA V KNIZHNOM MAGAZINE I. I. GLAZUNOVA / Efremov, P A – Pervoe Piatoe pribavlenie. 1-5. Spb. 1869-89. BR-5872 2 – 8 – ne IDC [070]
SISTEMATICHESKAIA ROSPIS' KNIGAM PRODAIUSHCHIMSIA V KNIZHNOM MAGAZINE I. I. GLAZUNOVA / Efremov, P A – Sostavlena za poslednee desiatiletie (1855-1866). Spb. 1867. BR-5871 2 – 8 – ne IDC [073]
SISTEMATICHESKAIA ROSPIS' KNIGAM, VYSHEDSHIM V ROSSII NA RUSSKOM I INYKH IAZYKAKH ZA 1899 G – I(1-2), II(1). Spb. 1901-05. BR-7265 2 – 8 – ne IDC [010]
SISTEMATICHESKII BIBLIOGRAFICHESKII UKAZATEL' KNIG, BROSHIUR I ZHURNALOV PO VSEM OTRASLIAM TECHNIKI. VYSHEDSHIKH / Zverintsev, L N – v1884 g i v pervom pologodii 1885 g. v Rossii i za granitsei. God 2-i i 3-ii. Spb. 1886. BR-7047 2 – 8 – ne IDC [460]
SISTEMATICHESKII I ALFAVITNYIA UKAZATEL' STATEI, POMESHCHENYKH V PERIODICHESKIKH IZDANIIAKH I SBORNIKAKH IMP. AKADEMII NAUK, A TAKZHE SOCHINENII, IZDANNYKH AKADEMIEIU OTDEL'NO / Akademiia Nauk – pt. 2. Sochineniia na russkom iazyke. Spb. 1875. Pribavlenie 1-2. Spb. 1882, 1885. BR-4818 2 – 8 – ne IDC [500]
SISTEMATICHESKII I KHRONOLOGICHESKII KATALOG BIBLIOTEKI BIBLIOFILA I BIBLIOGRAFA IA.F. BEREZINA-SHCHIRIAEVA. 1. RUSSKIIA KNIGI / Gusev, A M & Rodnykii, A A – Spb. 1900. BR-5903 2 – 8 – ne IDC [010]
SISTEMATICHESKII KATALOG BIBLIOTEK IMP. MEDIKOKHIRURGICHESKOI AKADEMII / Imp. Mediko-Khirurgicheskoi Akademii. Saint Petersburg – I(1,2), II(1,2,3). Spb. 1871-78. BR-7258 2 – 8 – ne IDC [617]
SISTEMATICHESKII KATALOG BIBLIOTEKI GLAVNAGO SHTABA. 1-2 / Glavnago Shtaba Library. Saint Petersburg – Spb. 1879-80. BR-4515 2 – 8 – ne IDC [020]
SISTEMATICHESKII KATALOG BIBLIOTEKI IMP. S.-PETERBURGSKAGO BOTANICHESKAGO SADA / Gerder, FE fon – Petropolis. 1886. BR-4541 2 – 8 – ne IDC [580]
SISTEMATICHESKII KATALOG BIBLIOTEKI MIKHAILOVSKOI ARTILLERIISKOI AKADEMII I UCHILISHCHA / Mikhailovskoi Artilleriiskoi Akademii – Spb. 1895. BR-4527 2 – 8 – ne IDC [355]
SISTEMATICHESKII KATALOG BIBLIOTEKI NIKOLAEVSKOI AKADEMII GENERAL'NAGO SHTABA; V. 2 (1866-1887) / Shevelev, A – Spb. 1887. BR-7254 2 – 8 – ne IDC [020]
SISTEMATICHESKII KATALOG BIBLIOTEKI NIKOLAEVSKOI INZHENERNOI AKADEMII I UCHILISHCHA / Naidenov, V F & Kalinin, V A – v. 2-3. Spb. 1904. BR-7175 2 – 8 – ne IDC [010]

SISTEMATICHESKII KATALOG BIBLIOTEKI UCHENAGO KOMITETA MINISTERSTVA FINANSOV / Russia. Ministerstva Finansov. Library – 1-2. Spb. 1901-04. BR-7261 2 – 8 – ne IDC [336]

SISTEMATICHESKII KATALOG DELAM DEPARTAMENTA TAMOZHENNYKH SBOROV / Kaidanov, N I – Saint Petersburg, 1886. 227p. Covers customs and trade documents (1825-83) now located in TsGIA SSSR. BR-10,821/1 – 9 – ne IDC [380]

SISTEMATICHESKII KATALOG DELAM DEPARTAMENTA VNESHNEI TORGOVLI.. / Kaidanov, N I – St. Petersburg, 1877. 643p. Index: Dopolneniia, 1888. BR-10,733/1 – 9 – ne IDC [380]

SISTEMATICHESKII KATALOG DELAM GOSUDARSTVENNOI KOMMERTS-KOLLEGII / Kaidanov, N I – 1718-1810. St. Petersburg, 1884. 408p.BR-10,716/1 – 9 – ne IDC [380]

SISTEMATICHESKII KATALOG DELAM KOMMISSII O KOMMERTSII I O POSHLINAKH, KHRANIASHCHIMSIA V ARKHIVE DEPARTAMENTA TAMOZHENNYKH SBOROV / Kaidanov, N I – Saint Petersburg, 1887. 91p. Describes commercial records now in TsGADA. BR-10,814/1 – 9 – ne IDC [380]

SISTEMATICHESKII KATALOG DELAM SIBIRSKOGO PRIKAZA, MOSKOVSKOGO KOMMISSARSTVA I DRUGIKH BYVSHIKH UCHREZHDENII PO CHASTI PROMYSHLENNOSTI I TORGOVLI, KHRANIASHCHIMSIA V ARKHIVE / Kaidanov, N I – Departamenta tamozhennykh sborov. Saint Petersburg, 1888. 204p. BR-10,717/1 – 9 – ne IDC [010]

SISTEMATICHESKII KATALOG KNIG BIBLIOTEKI KIEVO-PECHERSKOI LAVRY / Kiev. Pecherskoi Library – 1-2. Kiev. 1908, 1912. BR-4494 2 – 8 – ne IDC [020]

SISTEMATICHESKII KATALOG KNIG BIBLIOTEKI KIEVSKOI DUKHOVNOI AKADEMII / Kiev. Dukhovnoi Akademii. Library – I(3), II(5), IV(12). (sost. A.S. Krylovskii). Kiev. 1893, 1901, 1913. BR-4493 – 8 – ne IDC [020]

SISTEMATICHESKII KATALOG KNIG BIBLIOTEKI MOSKOVSKOI DUCHOVNOI AKADEMII / Moscow. Duchovnoi Akademii. Library – I(1). Sost. I. Korsunskii. M. 1881; II(3) Sost. I. Korsunskii. M. 1885; III(5) Sost. I. Korsunskii. M. 1889; IV(7:2) Sost. I. Korsunskii. M. 1897; V(8) i pervoe prod. Sost. K.M. Popov. M. 1910. BR-4745 2 – 8 – ne IDC [020]

SISTEMATICHESKII KATALOG KNIG BIBLIOTEKI MOSKOVSKOI DUKHOVNOI AKADEMII / Popov, K – Biblioteka. Savvy, arkhiepiskopa Tverskago i Kashinskago. M. 1900. BR-7220 2 – 8 – ne IDC [010]

SISTEMATICHESKII KATALOG KNIG BIBLIOTEKI VYSOKOPREOSVIASHCHENNAGO FLAVIANA, MITROPOLITA KIEVSKAGO I GALITSKAGO / Flaviana, Metropolitan of Kiev – Kiev. 1910. BR-7260 2 – 8 – ne IDC [020]

SISTEMATICHESKII KATALOG KNIG FUNDAMENTAL'NOI BIBLIOTEKI KAZANSKOI DUKHOVNOI AKADEMII / Kazan. Academy – 2v. Kazan'. 1874-39. Alfavitnyi ukazatel'. Kazan'. 1883. Prodolzhenie. II (3-4). Kazan'. 1896-1904. Dopolnenie. Kazan'. 1913. BR-7259 2 – 8 – ne IDC [020]

SISTEMATICHESKII KATALOG KNIG VYSHEDSHIKH V 1910 GODU, S PRILOZHENIEM UKAZATELIA RETSENZII – M. 1911. BR-7262 2 – 8 – ne IDC [010]

SISTEMATICHESKII KATALOG KNIZHNYKH MAGAZINOV T-VA M.O. VOL'F / Vol'f, M O – Spb. 1902-03. BR-5667 2 – 8 – ne IDC [020]

SISTEMATICHESKII KATALOG NOVEISHIKH KNIG IZD. M.O. VOL'F / Vol'f, M O – Spb., M. 1913, 1916. BR-5673 2 – 8 – ne IDC [020]

SISTEMATICHESKII KATALOG (NOVYI) RUSSKAGO OTDELENIIA KNIZHNAGO MAGAZINA M. O. VOL'FA. 1830-1880 / Vol'f, M O – v. 1-2. Spb., M. 1881-82. BR-7194 2 – 8 – ne IDC [010]

SISTEMATICHESKII KATALOG RUSSKAGO OTDELENIIA VILENSKOI PUBLICHNOI BIBLIOTEKI / Vil'na. Public Library – v. 1-2; Suppl. v. 2-3. Vil'na. 1879-1902. BR-7263 2 – 8 – ne IDC [020]

SISTEMATICHESKII KATALOG RUSSKIKH KNIG ZA 1875 I 1876 GODY PRODALUSHCHIKHSIA V KNIZHNOM MAGAZINE IA. A. ISAKOVA / Mezhov, VI – Spb. 1877. BR-7165 2 – 8 – ne IDC [010]

SISTEMATICHESKII KATALOG RUSSKIKH KNIG ZA 1877 I 1878 GODY / Mezhov, VI – Spb. 1880. BR-7166 2 – 8 – ne IDC [010]

SISTEMATICHESKII KATALOG RUSSKIM KNIGAM, PRODAIUSHCHIMSIA V KNIZHNOM MAGAZINE A. F. BAZUNOVA / Mezhov, VI – Spb. 1869. Pervoeshoestoe pribavlenie. Spb. 1870-75. BR-7164 2 – 8 – ne IDC [010]

SISTEMATICHESKII KATALOG RUSSKOGO OTDELENIIA VILENSKOI PUBLICHNOI BIBLIOTHEKI – Vil'na. 2v. 1879-1902. Suppl. v2-3 – 44mf – 9 – ne IDC [947]

SISTEMATICHESKII KNIZHNYI KATALOG BIBLIOTEKI IMP. VOENNO-MEDITSINSKOI AKADEMII / Imp. Voenno-Meditsinsko Akademii. Library – 1-2, 4. Spb, 1901-03 – 8 – BR-7264 2 – ne IDC [610]

SISTEMATICHESKII REESTR RUSSKIM KNIGAM S 1831 PO 1846 GOD – Izd. M. D. Ol'khina. Spb. 1846. BR-5867 2 – 8 – ne IDC [010]

SISTEMATICHESKII SPISOK KOOPERATIVNOI LITERATURY, BYVSHEI NA VYSTAVKE PRI KURSAKH PO ORGANIZATSII MESTNYKH KOOPERATIVNYKH KURSOV S 27 MARTA PO 5 APRELIA 1915 GODA – Moscow, 1915 – 1mf – 9 – COR-540/1 – ne IDC [334]

SISTEMATICHESKII UKAZATEL' KNIG (1832-1910) BIBLIOTEKI IMP. NIKOLAEVSKOI VOENNOI AKADEMII / Maslovskii, S D – Spb. 1910. BR-7147 2 – 8 – ne IDC [460]

SISTEMATICHESKII UKAZATEL' KNIG I STATEI PO GRECHESKOI FILOLOGII. NAPECHATANNYKH V ROSSI S 17 STOLETIIA PO 1892 GOD NA RUSSKOM I INOSTRANNYKH IAZYKAKH, S PRIBAVLENIEM ZA 1893-1895 GODY / Prozorov, P – Spb. 1898. BR-7226 2 – 8 – ne IDC [014]

SISTEMATICHESKII UKAZATEL' KNIG I STATEI PO VNESHKOL'NOMU OBRAZOVANIIU / Medynskii, E & Lapsov, I – M. 1916. BR-7150 2 – 8 – ne IDC [460]

SISTEMATICHESKII UKAZATEL' LITERATURY O EVREIAKH NA RUSSKOM IAZYKE SOVREMENI GRAZHDANSKAGO SHRIFTA (1708 G.) PO DEKABR' 1889 G – Spb. 1892. Missing in the original: pages 10-11. BR-7266 2 – 8 – ne IDC [460]

SISTEMATICHESKII UKAZATEL' RUSSKAGO INVALIDA ZA 1869-1890 GG – Spb. 1891. BR-7267 2 – 8 – ne IDC [947]

SISTEMATICHESKII UKAZATEL' RUSSKOI LITERATURY PO GRAZHDANSKOMU PRAVU / Povorinskii, A F – Spb. 1886. BR-5637 2 – 8 – ne IDC [460]

SISTEMATICHESKII UKAZATEL' RUSSKOI LITERATURY PO KOOPERATSII 1856-1924 GG / Gritsenko, I F & Merkulov, A V – Moscow, 1925 – 4mf – 9 – COR-531/1 – ne IDC [334]

SISTEMATICHESKII UKAZATEL'K SOCHINENIIAM BELINSKAGO S PRISOEDINENIEM SOOTVETSTVUIUSHCHIKH UKAZANII NA SOCHINENIIA DOBROLIUBOVA / Petrov, K – Spb. 1879. BR-7209 2 – 8 – ne IDC [947]

SISTEMATICHESKOE OPISANIE RUKOPISEI MOSKOVSKOI SINODAL'NOI (PATRIARSHEI) BIBLIOTEKI / Vladimir, Arkhimandrit – 1. Rukopisi grecheskiia. M. 1894. BR-7043 2 – 8 – ne IDC [947]

SISTEMATICHESKOE OPISANIE SLAVIANO-RUSSKIKH RUKOPISEI SOBRANIIA GRAFA A.S.UVAROVA / Leonid, Arkhimandrit – Moscow, 1893-94.BR/7296/2 – 8 – ne IDC [460]

SISTER TERESA / Moore, George – London: T. Fisher Unwin, 1901 – 1 roll – 1 – 1-55879-942-7 – uk Libr Preservation [830]

SISTERHOOD – (Cont by and filmed with: Affirmations) – v1-2. 1971-73 (complete) – 1r – 1 – ATLA S0343A – us A.T.L.A. [073]

SISTERHOOD *see* AFFIRMATIONS

SISTIM EKONOMI DAN EKONOMI INDONESIA / Salim, Emil – SE 5906 1. 1965 – 9 – ne IDC [338]

SITARAH-'I SUBH – (Sal 1, shumarah 1-7 (12 Tir 1304-3 Murdad 1304[3 Jul 1925-25 Jul 1925]). Continued by: Nahid) – Tehran – 1 reel – 1 – $60.00 – us MEDOC [950]

SITARAH-'I SUBH *see* AFLAK

LE SITE DE LA TOCA DO ARAPOA DO GONGO, UN ABRI PEINT DE L'AIRE DE SAO RAIMUNDO NONATO, SUD-EST DU PIAUI, BRESIL / Monzon, S – 9 – F40.00 – fr Ethnologie [306]

SITE EXPERIENCE – 1983 – 58p – 9 – 92-3-101796-9 – fr UNESCO [380]

LE SITE TOCA DO BAIXAO DAS MULHERES 2, UN ABRI PEINT DE L'AIRE DE SAO RAIMUNDO NONATO, SUD-EST DU PIAUI, BRESIL / Pessis, A M – 7mf – 9 – Fr90.00 – fr Ethnologie [306]

SITE-SPECIFIC CHANGES IN BONE MASS AND ALTERATIONS IN CALCIOTROPIC HORMONES WITH ELECTRICAL STIMULATION EXERCISE IN INDIVIDUALS WITH CHRONIC SPINAL CORD INJURY / Bloomfield, Susan A et al – 1992 – 3mf – 9 – $12.00 – us Microform Publ [612]

SITI KALASUN / Sjamsuddin, Sutan – SE 4730 1. 1961 – 9 – ne IDC [950]

SITI NURLELA; MENGANDUNG BEBERAPA PELADJARAN SEDIH, GEMBIRA, LUTJU, DIHIASI BEBERAPA PANTUN DAN PEPATAH / Sjamsuddin, Sutan – SE 4480 1. 1961 – 9 – ne IDC [950]

Siti Zakiah, Aman *see* TRADE AND INDUSTRY IN MALAYSIA

SITIO DE AMBERES 1584-85 / Barado, Francisco – 1895 – 9 – 1.50f – sp Bibl Santa Ana [946]

EL SITIO DE BALER, DE SATURNINO MARTIN CEREZO / Barado, Francisco – Madrid: Tip. Fortanet, 1908. B.R.A.H. LII, pp. 540-542 – sp Bibl Santa Ana [946]

SITIO, NATURALEZA Y PROPIEDADES DE LA CIUDAD DE MEJICO, AGUAS Y VIENTOS. A QUE ESTA SUJETA Y SI TIEMPOS DEL ANO. NECESIDAD DE SU CONO CIMIENTO PARA EL EXERCICIO DE LA MEDICINA... / Cisneros, D – Mejico, 1618 – 6mf – 9 – sp Cultura [610]

SITIZ – London, no. 1 (Bahar 1355 [Spring 1976]) – 1 reel – 1 – $50.00 – us MEDOC [950]

Sitler, Michael R *see* THE EFFECTS OF HIP POSITION AND ANGULAR VELOCITY ON QUADRICEPS AND HAMSTRING ECCENTRIC PEAK TORQUE

Sitor Situmorang *see* PANGERAN; KUMPULAN TJERITA-PENDEK

SITOR SITUMORANG SEBAGAI PENJAIR DAN PENGARANG TJERITA PENDEK / Nasution, Jahja Udin – SE-3454 1. 1963 – 9 – ne IDC [950]

DIE SITTE / Toennies, Ferdinand – Frankfurt (Main): Ruetten & Loening, 1909, c1905 – 1mf – 9 – 0-8370-6425-2 – 1986-0425 – us A.T.L.A. [170]

Sitterly, Charles Fremont *see* PRAXIS IN MANUSCRIPTS OF THE GREEK TESTAMENT

SITTINGBOURNE AND SHEERNESS GAZETTE – England. East Kent Gazette Sittingbourne & East Kent Gazette. -w. 11 April 1857-Dec 1964. Lacking Jan-March 1896. 101 reels – 1 – uk British Libr Newspaper [072]

A SITUACAO – Cuiaba, 15 Aug-Nov 1869; Mar 1871; Jul-Aug, Nov 1872; Jan-Apr, Aug 1873; Jan, Nov 1874; Jan-Mar, May-Dec 1875; Jan-Feb, May, Oct, Dec 1876; Jun-Sep 1877; Feb 1878; Dec 1880; Oct, Dec 1881; Mar-Apr, Jun 1882; Jul, Oct 1884; Jun, Oct 1885; May 1886; Feb, 26 Jun 1887 – 1,5,6 – bl Biblioteca [072]

A SITUACAO : JORNAL POLITICO – Sao Luis, 18 Jun 1863-Nov 1866; Mar-Oct 1868; Feb 1869; Apr, 3 Sept 1870 – 1,5,6 – bl Biblioteca [072]

SITUACION DE LA ANTIGUA NORBA / Huebner, Emilio – Madrid: Fortanet, 2nd ed 1909. B.R.A.H. i. 1877. reimp. 1909. pp. 88-97 – 1 – sp Bibl Santa Ana [946]

LA SITUACION ECONOMICA / Ghioldi, Americo – Buenos Aires: Partido Socialista, [1948] – 1 – CSUXADP7771-B – us Hoover Inst Photo [330]

SITUACION ECONOMICA DEL AYUNTAMIENTO DE MERIDA EN 30-6-1934 – Merida: Rodriguez, 1939 – 1 – sp Bibl Santa Ana [330]

LA SITUATION – Journal politique quotidien du soir. Dir. politique E. Hollander puis Red. en chef A. Grenier. Paris. 9 juin 1867-9 avr 1868. Bibliotheque Lovenjoul, Chantilly – 1 – fr A.C.R.P.P. [073]

LA SITUATION – Journal quotidien. Politique, litteraire et commercial. Londres. sept 1870-aout 1871 – 1 – fr A.C.R.P.P. [073]

SITUATION ACTUELLE ET PREVISIONS D'EVOLUTION POUR 1970 DES INDUSTRIES DE TRANSFORMATION / Morocco. Direction de l'Industrie – 1966. BNE-3034 1 – 9 – ne IDC [338]

SITUATION ACTUELLE ET PREVISIONS D'EVOLUTION POUR 1970 DES INDUSTRIES DE TRANSFORMATION / Morocco. Direction de l'Industrie – 1967. BNE-3032 1 – 9 – ne IDC [338]

LA SITUATION DE L'INDUSTRIE. ET PERSPECTIVES. 1962-1971 / Morocco. Secretariat d'Etat charge du Plan – (lacking 1967-68). BNE-3092 1 – 9 – ne IDC [338]

SITUATION DES CLASSES OUVRIERES. EXTRAIT DU JOURNAL DES ECONOMISTES, CAHIER DE DECEMBRE 1844 / Fix, Theodore – Paris. 1844. (La Condition Ouvriere. Part Two.) – 9 – 2.50 – fr Bibl Nationale [360]

SITUATION DES ESCLAVES DANS LES COLONIES FRANCAISES / Houvellat de Cussas – (Slave Trade and Abolitionism in France series). 1845 – 9 – fr Hachette [305]

LA SITUATION DES OUVRIERS DE L'INDUSTRIE TEXTILE DANS LA REGION LILLOISE / Lasserre, Andre – Lausanne. 1952. (La Condition Ouvriere. Part Two.) – 9 – 7.50 – fr Bibl Nationale [360]

SITUATION DES PRETS EXTERIEURS / Algeria. Caisse Algerienne de Developpement – 2v. in 2. 1968-69. BNE-8611 1 – 9 – ne IDC [336]

LA SITUATION ECONOMIQUE DE L'ALGERIE / Detours, J & Nectoux, G – Paris. 1967. BNE-8720 1 – 9 – ne IDC [338]

SITUATION ECONOMIQUE DE L'ALGERIE / Algeria. Chambre de Commerce et d'Industrie d'Alger – 3v. 1964-67. (lacking 1966-68). BNE-8622 1 – 9 – ne IDC [339]

LA SITUATION ECONOMIQUE DE L'ALGERIE, AU LER JANVIER / Algeria. Direction Generale du Plan et des Etudes Economiques – 1963. 1964. BNE-8632 1 – 9 – ne IDC [339]

LA SITUATION ECONOMIQUE DE L'ESPAGNE / Delamarre, C – 634 2. 1869 – 8 – ne IDC [338]

SITUATION ECONOMIQUE EN 1963 / Algeria. Direction Generale du Plan et des Etudes Economiques – 1964. BNE-8635 1 – 9 – ne IDC [339]

SITUATION "EMPLOIS-RESSOURCES ETAT" / Algeria. Caisse Algerienne de Developpement – 4v. in 2. 1966-69. BNE-8612 1 – 9 – ne IDC [331]

LA SITUATION HOSPITALIERE A MONTREAL / Dube, J -E – Montreal: [s.n.], 1928. SEM105P1428 – 1mf – 9 – Can$2.25 – cn Bibl Nat [360]

SITUATION INTERNATIONALE DE L'EGYPTE ET DU SOUDAN / Cocheris, J – Paris, 1903 – 7mf – 1 – ILM-1950/1 – ne IDC [327]

LA SITUATION PROVINCIALE: POURQUOI LES ELECTEURS DOIVENT VOTER CONTRE LE GOUVERNEMENT MERCIER: DISCOURS DE L'HON. M. FLYNN, PRONONCE A MONTREAL LE 30 OCTOBRE 1889 / Flynn, Edmund James – Montreal: Association conservatrice due district de Montreal, 1889. 03120. (Pre-1900 Canadiana) – 9 – cn C.I.H.M. [971]

THE SITUATION: 'READ MARK LEARN AND INWARDLY DIGEST' / Blake, Edward – Speech of the Hon. Edward Blake before the Young Men's Liberal Club of Toronto on...January 13th, 1884. 1885. 00176. (Pre-1900 Canadiana) – 9 – cn C.I.H.M. [971]

LA SITUATION RELIGIEUSE DE L'AFRIQUE ROMAINE DEPUIS LA FIN DU IVE SIECLE JUSQU'A L'INVASION DES VANDALES (429) / Ferrere, F – 1897 – 1 – us A.T.L.A. [240]

SITUATION REPORT / Palau Political Status Commission – Koror: Palau Political Status Commission, oct 1976 – 2mf – 9 – $3.00 – LLMC 82-100G, Title 12 – us L.L.M.C. [323]

SITUATIONAL AND CONTEXTUAL INFLUENCES ON GOAL ORIENTATIONS / Williams, Lavon – University of North Carolina at Greensboro, 1996 – 2mf – 9 – $8.00 – PSY1874 – us Microform Publ [150]

Situmorang, F *see* KAMUS BAHASA DJERMAN; DJERMAN-INDONESIA DAN INDONESIA-DJERMAN

DIE SITZE DER MUSICALISCHEN HAUPT-SAETZE IN EINER HARTEN UND WEICHEN TONART. IN ZWO TABELLEN ENTWORFFEN, ERKLAERT UND MIT EXEMPELN ERLAEUTERT VON GEORGE FRIEDRICH LINGKEN / Lingken, G Fr – Leipzig. 1766. BP-370 1 – 9 – ne IDC [780]

SITZUNGEN DES ARBEITER- UND SOLDATENRATS IN BREMEN – Bremen, 1918-19 – 1r – 1 – DM80.00 – gw Mikro Press [072]

SITZUNGSBERICHTE / Akademie der Wissenschaften. Berlin – 1882-1921 – 1 – us Schnase [500]

SITZUNGSBERICHTE / Gesellschaft Naturforschender Freunde. Berlin – 1839-1927. Minutes of meetings and scholarly articles – 7r – 1 – $150.00; outside North America add $1.25r – us L of C Photodup [574]

SITZUNGSBERICHTE. / Bayerische Akademie der Wissenschaften – Munich, 1860-70 – 3 – us Readex [500]

SITZUNGSBERICHTE DER KAISERLICHEN AKADEMIE DER WISSENSCHAFTEN – (Band 97 1880(1) Dfl63.00) – Wien: Philosophish-Historische Klasse. Band 82 1876(3) – 9 – Dfl35.00 – ne Slangenburg [073]

SITZUNGSBERICHTE DER KAISERLICHEN AKADEMIE DER WISSENSCHAFTEN : PHILOSOPHISCH-HISTORISCHE KLASSE – (Indices included) – Wien. v1-220. 1848-1942 – 2694mf – 9 – H-1097c/2 – ne IDC [370]

SITZUNGSBERICHTE DER KOENIGLICHEN BAYERISCHEN AKADEMIE DER WISSENSCHAFTEN ZU MUENCHEN – (Cont as: Sitzungsberichte der mathematisch-physikalischen Classe der k.b. Akademie der Wissenschaften zu Muenchen. Muenchen, 1871-1923. Register. Cont as: Sitzungsberichte der mathematisch-naturwissenschaftlichen Abteilung der Bayerischen Akademie der Wissenschaften zu Muenchen. Muenchen, 1924-1944. Register. Missing: 1915(1)) – Muenchen, 1860-1870. Register – 529mf – 9 – H-3012/1 – ne IDC [370]

SITZUNGSBERICHTE DER MATHEMATISCH-NATURWISSENSCHAFTLICHEN ABTEILUNG DER BAYERISCHEN AKADEMIE DER WISSENSCHAFTEN ZU MUENCHEN *see* SITZUNGSBERICHTE DER KOENIGLICHEN BAYERISCHEN AKADEMIE DER WISSENSCHAFTEN ZU MUENCHEN

SITZUNGSBERICHTE DER MATHEMATISCH-PHYSIKALISCHEN CLASSE DER K.B. AKADEMIE DER WISSENSCHAFTEN ZU MUENCHEN *see* SITZUNGSBERICHTE DER KOENIGLICHEN BAYERISCHEN AKADEMIE DER WISSENSCHAFTEN ZU MUENCHEN

SITZUNGSBERICHTE PHYSIKALISCH-MATHEMATISCHE KLASSE / Akademie der Wissenschaften. Berlin – Years: 1927-1933 – 1 – us Princeton Micro [500]

SITZUNGS-PROTOKOLLE / Prussia. Landtag. Herrenhaus – 1849 50-66 67. v.1-3 – 1 – 46.00 – us L of C Photodup [324]

SITZUNGSPROTOKOLLE DES ARBEITER-UND SOLDATENRATS IN BREMEN – Bremen, 1918-19 – 1r – 1 – Inquire at Mikrofilmarchiv for details – gw Misc Inst [943]

SIUSLAW NEWS – Florence, OR. -w. 15 May 1924-21 May 1925. 1 roll – 1 – us U.O. Library [071]

SIUSLAW NEWS – Florence, OR. -w. 29 Dec 1960-. – 1 – us U.O. Library [071]

SIUSLAW OAR – Florence, OR. -w. 8 Jun 1928-22 Dec 1960. 8 rolls – 1 – us U.O. Library [071]

SIUSLAW PILOT – Florence, OR. -w. 12 Mar 1913-29 Dec 1915. 1 roll – 1 – us U.O. Library [071]

Siuts, Hans *see* JENSEITSMOTIVE IM DEUTSCHEN VOLKSMAERCHEN

SIVAS – Sivas: Vilayet Matbaasi, 1879-1927 – 9 – $10.00 – us MEDOC [956]

SIVASAMHITA – English and Sanskrit. Trans. by Rai Bahadur Srisa Chandra Vidyarnava. 2nd ed., rev. Allahabad: The Panini Office, 1923. 87p – 1 – us U.W. Library [280]

SIVASAMHITA. ENGLISH AND SANSKRIT – Trans. by Rai Bahadur Srisa Chandra Vidyarnava. 2nd ed., rev. Allahabad: The Panini Office, 1923. 87p – 1 – us U.W. Library [280]

Sivkov, K V *see* PUTESHESTVIIA RUSSKIKH LIUDEI ZA GRANITSU V 18 V

SIX AIR CONNUS, MIS EN VARIATIONS POUR LE VIOLON AVEC ACCOMPAGNEMENT DE BASS...OP. V / Avolio, J – Paris: Durieu, 177- – 1 – us Sibley [780]

SIX ANTHEMS AND TEN CHANTS / Battihill, J; ed by Page, John – London, 1804 – 1 – us Sibley [780]

SIX BAGATELLES POUR PIANO, OP. 3 / Saint-Saens, Camille – Paris: Durand & Fils, [188-] – 1 – us Sibley [780]

SIX CONCERTOS FOR THE HARPSICHORD OR ORGAN...OP. 4 / Handel, George Frederic – London: J. Walsh, [ca. 1745] – 1 – us Sibley [780]

SIX CONCERTOS...OPERA 2 / Hebden, John – London: Printed for the Author in Lancaster Court, Charing Cross, [1745] – 1 – us Sibley [780]

SIX CONCERTS POUR LE CLAVECIN / Bach, Johann Christian – Opus 1, nos. 1-6. 1763 – 9 – us Sibley [780]

SIX CORNET PIECES, WITH AN INTRODUCTION FOR THE DIAPSONS AND A FUGUE / Burney, Charles – 1751 – 9 – us Sibley [780]

SIX DUETTE POUR DEUX VIOLONS...OP. 3 / Chapelle, P – Paris: Frere, 178- – 1 – us Sibley [780]

SIX DUETTI POUR DEUX VIOLONS...OP. 6 / Chapelle, P – (Parts) – Paris: Frere, 178- – 1 – us Sibley [780]

SIX DUETTOS FOR THE VIOLIN AND VIOLONCELLO / Barbella, E – London: G Gardon, 178- – 1 – us Sibley [780]

SIX DUETTOS FOR TWO VIOLINS, OP. 18 / Stumpf, J C – (2 pts) – London: John Kerpen, [ca 1810] – 1 – us Sibley [780]

SIX DUOS A DEUX VIOLONES, OP. 4 / Cambini, G – (Parts) – Paris: Sr. Sieber, 177- – 1 – us Sibley [780]

SIX DUOS POUR DEUX FLUTES / Devienne, Francois – Paris: Pleyel; London: Goulding & Phipps, D'Almaire & Co, 179- – 1 – us Sibley [780]

SIX FUGES POUR LE FORTEPIANO [W. 119] / Bach, C P E – Bonn et Cologne: N Simrock, 1822 or 1823 – 1 – us Sibley [780]

SIX FUGUES FOR THE ORGAN OR HARPSICHORD / Kellner, Johann C – A La Haye: Chez B Hummel, [ca 1770] – 1mf – 9 – us Sibley [780]

SIX FUGUES POUR LE PIANOFORTE...OP. 17 / Albrechtsberger, Johann G – Wien: S A Steiner et Comp., [1824?] – 1 – us Sibley [780]

SIX GENERATIONS OF FRIENDS IN IRELAND (1655 TO 1890) / Richardson, Jane Marion Wakefield – London: E. Hicks, 1893. 239p – 1 – us U.W. Library [920]

SIX IMITATIONS OF ENGLISH, SCOTCH, IRISH, WELCH, SPANISH & GERMAN AIRS / Carr, Benjamin – (No. 20 of the Musical Journal for the Piano-forte). Baltimore: J. Carr 1800. MUSIC 123, Item 8 – 1 – us L of C Photodup [780]

THE SIX LAMBETH CONFERENCES (1867-1920) – London, 1920 – 10mf – 8 – ne Slangenburg [240]

SIX LECONS SUR LES EVANGILES / Batiffol, Pierre – Paris: Victor Lecoffre, 1897. 1 fiche – 9 – us A.T.L.A. [240]

SIX LECTURES ON HARMONY / MacFarren, G – London: Longman, Green, Reader, and Ryer, 1867 – 1 – us Sibley [780]

SIX LECTURES ON THE INNS OF COURT AND CHANCERY / Odgers, William B – (Delivered in Middle Temple Hall during Easter and Trinity terms, 1912) – London: Macmillan, 1912 – 3mf – 9 – $4.50 – LLMC 84-310 – us L.L.M.C. [340]

SIX LECTURES ON THE OXFORD MOVEMENT : AND ITS RESULTS ON THE CHURCH OF ENGLAND / Cruttwell, CT – London: Skeffington, 1899 – 1mf – us A.T.L.A. [240]

SIX MAITRES DE L'ESTAMPE JAPONAISE AU 18E SIECLE / Reunion des musees nationaux. Paris – 1971, Haronobu, Shunsho, Kiyonaga, Shunman, Utamaro, Sharaku. 1 fiche – 9 – fr Réunion [700]

SIX MOIS CHEZ LES TOUAREGS DU AHAGGAR / Benhazera, Maurice – Alger: Jourdan, 1908 – 1 – F131.88 – fr Armell [960]

SIX MOIS DANS LES MONTAGNES-ROCHEUSES: COLORADO, UTAH, NOUVEAU-MEXIQUE / Beaugrand, Honore – Montreal: Granger, 1890.03525.(Pre-1900 Canadiana) – 9 – cn C.I.H.M. [910]

SIX MOIS EN RUSSIE. LETTRES ECRITES A M.X.B. SAINTINE EN 1826 A L'EPOQUE DU COURONNEMENT DE S.M. L'EMPEREUR / Ancelot, Francois – (Russia – 19th C. series). 1827 – 9 – fr Hachette [947]

SIX MORCEAUX POUR PIANO, OP. 19 / Tschaikovsky, PI – (From binder's collection made up by previous owner) – Hamburg: D Rahtwe, [18–] – 1 – us Sibley [780]

SIX MORCEAUX POUR PIANO, OP. 21 / Tschaikovsky, PI – (From binder's collection made up by previous owner) – St. Petersbourg: W Bessel & Co, [18–] – 1 – us Sibley [780]

THE SIX NATIONS – 1926-30.(American Indian Periodicals in the Princeton University Library). 2 fiches – 9 – $45.00 – us UPA [073]

SIX NOTTURNOS FOR TWO VIOLINS AND A VIOLONCELLO OBLIGATTO / Agus, G – London: Welcker, 176-? – 1 – us Sibley [780]

SIX NOUVEAUX QUATUORS, VOL 1 / Cambini, G – (Pts) – Paris: l'auteur, ca 1780 – 1 – us Sibley [780]

SIX NOUVEAUX QUATUORS, VOL. 2 / Cambini, G – (Parts) – Paris: l'auteur, ca 1780 – 1 – us Sibley [780]

SIX OXFORD THINKERS : EDWARD GIBBON, JOHN HENRY NEWMAN, R.W. CHURCH, JAMES ANTHONY FROUDE, WALTER PATER, LORD MORLEY OF BLACKBURN / Cecil, Algernon – London: John Murray, 1909 – 1 roll – 1 – 1-55879-497-2 – uk Libr Preservation [420]

SIX PRELUDES A L'USAGE DES COMMENCANTS POUR LE CLAVECIN = KLEINE PRAELUDIEN, S. 933-938 / Bach, Johann Sebastian – 1st ed. Leipsic: Hoffmeister et Kuhnel, 1802 – 1 – us Sibley [780]

SIX PRELUDES FACILES POUR L'ORGUE OU LE PIANO-FORTE... / Wanhal, J B – (Vault in process) – Offenbach: Chez Jean Andre, [1810] – 1 – us Sibley [780]

SIX PRINCIPLE BAPTISTS / Baptist Association. Rhode Island – Ms. materials. 1743-1818 – 1 – 6.00 – us Baptist [240]

SIX QUARTETTI, OP. 32. G. 195-200 / Boccherini, Luigi – (Parts) – Paris: LeDuc, 178- – 1 – us Sibley [780]

SIX QUARTETTOS / Latilla, G – (Parts) – London: A Hummel, 177- – 1 – us Sibley [780]

SIX QUARTETTOS FOR A GERMAN FLUTE, VIOLIN, VIOLA AND VIOLONCELLO, WITH AN OCCASIONAL ACCOMPANYMENT FOR TWO FRENCH HORNS.. / Kroll, Adam – Parts. ca.1780 – 9 – us Sibley [780]

SIX QUARTETTOS IN THE COMIC STILE, OP. 2 / Navoigille, H – (Parts) – London: Bremner, 1780? – 1 – us Sibley [780]

SIX QUARTETTOS, OP. 4 / Stamitz, K – (In binder's collection. 4 pts) – London: Napier, [178-?] – 1 – us Sibley [780]

SIX QUATUORS CONCERTANS / Bruni, A – (Parts) – Paris: Sieber, 1785 – 1 – us Sibley [780]

SIX QUATUORS CONCERTANS, OP. 11. G. 191, 194, 192, 190, 189, 193 / Boccherini, Luigi – (Parts) – Berlin: J J Hummel, 1775 – 1 – us Sibley [780]

SIX QUATUORS CONCERTANS POUR DEUX VIOLONS, ALTO ET BASSE / Fodor, J – Paris: Imbault (ecrit par Ribiere) ca 1790 – 1 – us Sibley [780]

SIX QUATUORS CONCERTANTES A UN VIOLON, DEUX ALTO ET VIOLONCELLE. OP. 2DA... / Stamitz, K – (4 pts) – Lomdrea: Betz, [177-?] – 1 – us Sibley [780]

SIX QUATUORS CONCERTANTS POUR DEUX VIOLONS, ALTO ET BASSE...4E LIVRE DU QUATUORS, OUEVRE 17 1ER PARTIE / Gyrowetz, Adalbert – Paris: Janet et Cotelle, [179-?] – 1 – us Sibley [780]

SIX QUATUORS CONCERTANTS POUR FLUTE, VIOLON, ALTO ET BASSE / Fiorillo, F – Oeuvre 4. 179-? – 5,15 – us Sibley [780]

SIX QUATUORS CONCERTANTS POUR FLUTE, VIOLON, ALTO ET BASSE...OEUVRE 4 / Fiorillo, F – Paris: Sieber, [179-?] – 2mf – 9 – us Sibley [780]

SIX QUATUORS D'AIR CONNUS / Cambini, G – (Pts) – Paris: LeMenu et Boyer, 1785? – 1 – us Sibley [780]

SIX QUATUORS EN FUGUES, A DEUX VIOLONS, TAILLE ET BASSE...OEUVRE SECOND / Albrechtsberger, Johann G – Berlin; J J Hummel, [178-?] – 1 – us Sibley [780]

SIX QUATUORS, OP. 2. G. 166, 165, 167-170 / Boccherini, K – (Parts) – Amsterdam: J J Hummel, 176- – 1 – us Sibley [780]

SIX QUATUORS, OP. 7. G. 171-176 / Boccherini, Luigi – (Pts) – Amsterdam: J J Hummel, 176- – 1 – us Sibley [780]

SIX QUATUORS, OP. 10 / Cambini, G – (Pts) – Offenbach: Andre, ca 1775 – 1 – us Sibley [780]

SIX QUATUORS, OP. 90, LIV. 1 / Reicha, A – (Parts) – Berlin et Cologne: N Simrock, 180- – 1 – us Sibley [780]

SIX QUATUORS, OR DIVERTISSEMENT...OP. 8. G. 177-182 / Boccherini, Luigi – Amsterdam: J J Hummel, 176- – 1 – us Sibley [780]

SIX QUATUORS POUR DEUX VIOLONS, ALTO ET VIOLONCELLE, OEUVRE 21 / Albrechtsberger, Johann G – Bureau des arts et industrie, No 174 – 1 – us Sibley [780]

SIX QUATUORS POUR UNE FLUTE, VIOLON, ALTO ET BASSE....OEUVRE 4 / Eichner, Ernst – Parts. 1773 – 9 – us Sibley [780]

SIX QUATUORS-CONCERTANS / Bruni, A – (Parts) – Paris: Boyer, ca 1785 – 1 – us Sibley [780]

SIX QUATUORS...OP. 6, LIV. 2 / Distler, J – (Parts) – Paris: Gunther, 179- – 1 – us Sibley [780]

SIX QUINTETS, OP. 13, G. 271-276 / Boccherini, Luigi – (Parts) – London: Preston & Son – 1 – us Sibley [780]

SIX SAINTS OF THE CONVENANT : PEDEN, SEMPLE, WELWOOD, CAMERON, CARGILL, SMITH / Walker, Patrick; ed by Fleming, Hay – London: Hodder and Stoughton, 1901 – 2mf – us A.T.L.A. [240]

SIX SERMONS ON IMPORTANT SUBJECTS / Tucker, J – Bristol, 1772 – 2mf – 9 – MP-483/1 – ne IDC [240]

SIX SOLOS FOR A FLUTE AND A BASS... BEING THE SECOND PART OF HIS FIFTH OPERA. / Corelli, Arcangelo – Sonatas, violin and basso continuo, op. 5. Arranged. Includes nos. 7-12. Parts. ca. 1730 – 9 – us Sibley [780]

SIX SOLOS FOR A VIOLIN WITH A THOROUGH BASS FOR THE HARPSICHORD / Tartini, G – London: Longman & Broderip, [178-] – 1 – us Sibley [780]

SIX SOLOS FOR THE VIOLONCELLO / Taylor, Raynor – Contemporary manuscript, not dated. Bound and filmed with: Schekty, J.G.C. Six solos for a violoncello & bass. London: J. Bland 1785?. MUSIC 3017 – 1 – us L of C Photodup [780]

SIX SONATAS / Aqus, G – London: Longman & Broderip, 178-? – 1 – us Sibley [780]

SIX SONATAS FOR 2 VIOLINS AND A BASS, OP. 6 / Barsanti, F – (Parts) – London: Welcker, 1865? – 1 – us Sibley [780]

SIX SONATAS FOR 2 VIOLINS AND A VIOLONCELLO, WITH A THOROUGH-BASS FOR HARPSICHORD / Deller, F J – (3 parts) – London: Welcker, 1776 – 1 – us Sibley [780]

SIX SONATAS FOR 2 VIOLINS AND CONTINUO / Alessandri, F – London: Welcker, 176- – 1 – us Sibley [780]

SIX SONATAS FOR 2 VIOLINS AND VIOLONCELLO, OP. 12 / Wanhal, J B – (3 pts) – London: Betz, 1780? – 1 – us Sibley [780]

SIX SONATAS FOR A VIOLIN, TENOR AND VIOLONCELLE / Nussen, F – London: Longman & Broderip, 178- – 1 – us Sibley [780]

SIX SONATAS FOR HARPSICHORD OR PIANOFORTE WITH AN ACCOMPANYMENT FOR VIOLIN / Barthelmon, M – 1785 – 9 – us Sibley [780]

SIX SONATAS FOR PIANO FORTE OR HARPSICHORD WITH AN ACCOMPANIMENT FOR A VIOLIN AND VIOLONCELLO / Barber, R of N – (There is a 7th sonata added to this collection) – London: Author-Longman, Lukey & Co., 1775? – 1 – us Sibley [780]

SIX SONATAS FOR THE HARPSICHORD WITH AN ACCOMPANIMENT FOR A VIOLIN OR GERMAN FLUTE / Vento, M – (Autographed) – London: Author, Carusos, 1765? – 1 – us Sibley [780]

SIX SONATAS FOR TWO GERMAN FLUTES AND VIOLONCELLO WITH A THORO'BASS FOR HARPSICHORD OR ORGAN / Cambini, G – (Pts) – London: Longman & Broderip, 178- – 1 – us Sibley [780]

SIX SONATAS FOR TWO VIOLINS AND A THOROUGH-BASS / Tortoriti, G – (3 pts) – London: John Simpson, ca 1745 – 1 – us Sibley [780]

SIX SONATAS FOR TWO VIOLINS AND VIOLONCELLO WITH A THOROUGH BASS FOR THE HARPSICHORD...OPERA 2 / Franceschini, Gaetano – 1776? – 9 – us Sibley [780]

SIX SONATAS POUR LE CLAVECIN AVEC ACCOMP. D'UN VIOLON AD LIB., OP. 1 / Edelmann, J F – Paris: M Boyer, 179- – 1 – us Sibley [780]

SIX SONATAS POUR LE CLAVECIN AVEC UN VIOLON OBLIGE...OEUVRE 5 / Breuning, C – Paris: Mr. Cornouaille aux adresses ordinaire – 1 – us Sibley [780]

SIX SONATAS (SECOND SET) FOR TWO VIOLINS WITH A TENOR AND THOROUGH BASS FOR THE HARPSICHORD OR VIOLONCELLO / Pasquali, N – 1750? – 9 – us Sibley [780]
SIX SONATAS; TROIS POUR DEUX VIOLONS ET VIOLONCELLE ET TROIS POUR UN VIOLON, TENOR ET VIOLONCELLS, OEUVRE 11 / Schmidt, P J – (3 parts) – Bruxelles: Van Ypen et Mechtler, [ca. 1785] – 1 – us Sibley [780]
SIX SONATES A VIOLON SEUL...ET BASSE / Boccherini, Luigi – Paris: M. de la Cherardiere de musique du Roi, rue du Roule a la Croix d'or, [177-?] – 2mf – 9 – us Sibley [780]
SIX SONATES A VIOLON, VIOLA, ET BASSE, OP. 1 / Erdman, C B – (Parts) – Offenbach: Andre, 178- – 1 – us Sibley [780]
SIX SONATES POUR LE CLAVECIN / Boccherini, Luigi – Oeuvre XII. ca. 1786 – 9 – us Sibley [780]
SIX SYMPHONIES A DEUX VIOLINS, DEUX HAUTBOIS, DEUX CORS DE CHASSE, ALTO VIOLA E BASSE. / Abel, K F – Oeuvre VII. 1780 – 9 – us Sibley [780]
SIX TO SIXTEEN / Ewing, Juliana Horatia – British Fiction Archive: Unit 1 – 9 – uk Bell [830]
SIX TRIOS A UN VIOLON, TAILE ET VIOLONCELLO CONCERTANS, OP. 1 / Baldenecker, U – Francfort sur le Mein: W N Hauseisen, 1784 – 1 – us Sibley [780]
SIX TRIOS CONCERTANS POUR VIOLON, VIOLA ET VIOLONCELLE, OEUVRE 9EME / Albrechtsberger, Johann G – Offenbach sur le Main: J Andre, [1795?] – 1 – us Sibley [780]
SIX TRIOS CONCERTANTS...OP. 34 / Bruni, A – (Parts) – 1 – us Sibley [780]
SIX TRIOS FOR TWO GERMAN FLUTES OR 2 VIOLINS WITH A VIOLONCELLO OBLIGATO, OP. 4 / Figlio, D – London: Thompson, 1766? – 1 – us Sibley [780]
SIX TRIOS, OP. 9, G. 95-100 / Boccherini, Luigi – (Parts) – Berlin: J J Hummel, ca 1784 – 1 – us Sibley [780]
SIX TRIOS POUR 2 VIOLONS ET ALTO ET VIOLONCELLE / Bruni, A – Paris: Janet et cotelle, 179- – 1 – us Sibley [780]
SIX TRIOS POUR DEUX VIOLONS ET VIOLONCELLE: 3E OEUVRE E TRIOS... / Pleyel, Ignaz J – 1 – us Sibley [780]
SIX VEILLEES DE CONTES EN PAYS AGNI / Quaireau, A – 3mf – 9 – F50.00 – fr Ethnologie [390]
LES SIX VOYAGES EN TURQUIE, EN PERSE, ET AUX INDES, PENDANT L'ESPACE DE QUARANTE ANS, ET PAR TOUTES LES ROUTES QUE L'ON PEUT TENIR : ACCOMPAGNEZ D'OBSERVATIONS PARTICULIERES SUR LA QUALITE, LA RELIGION, LE GOUVERNMENT, LES COUTUMES ET LE COMMERCE DE CHAQUE PAIS / Tavernier, Jean-Baptiste – Paris, G. Clouzier et C. Barbin, 1676, 2 v., 30-698-8 plus 8-525 p. French Voyagers in the Mediterranean 16th to 18th Centuries. 5972-73 – 9 – fr Hachette [950]
SIX YEAR DEVELOPMENT PROGRAMME JULY 1951 TO JUNE 1957. D-1408/1 / Pakistan. Ministry of Economic Affairs – (Planning Commission. Fourth five year plan 1970-75. D-1149; 1. July, 1970. SF 25.00; 9. Planning Commission. Mid-plan review of the third five year plan 1965-70. D-900; 1. 1968. SF 14.00; IDC; 9. Planning Commission. Revised list of schemes included in second five year plan (1960-65). D-1146; 1. 1961. SF 12.00; IDC; 9) – 9 – ne IDC [338]
SIX YEAR PRIMARY CURRICULUM / Papua New Guinea. Department of Education – Konedobu, 1972 – 1mf – 9 – DE-250/1 – ne IDC [370]
SIX YEARS IN SEYCHELLES / Estridge, H W – [s.l: s.n.], 1885 – us Res Libr [920]
SIX YEARS OF A TRAVELLER'S LIFE IN WESTERN AFRICA / Travassos Valdez, Francisco – London: Hurst & Blackett. 2v. 1861 – us Res Libr [910]
SIX YEARS WITH WILLIAM TAYLOR IN SOUTH AMERICA / Barchwitz-Krauser, O von – Boston, Mass.: McDonald & Gill, c1885 – 1mf – us A.T.L.A. [240]
SIXANG ZHANXIAN – Ideological Front – Journal of Yunan University. In Chinese but Table of Contents in English in each issue. F p212 – 9 – $3.50f – cc Microforms [073]
SIXIEME RAPPORT ANNUEL SUR LES TRAVAUX DE LA SOCIETE D'HISTOIRE NATURELLE DE L'ILE MAURICE / Desjardins, J F – Port Louis. 1835. B-5502 2 – 8 – ne IDC [574]
SIXTEEN OLD MAPS OF OXFORDSHIRE / Mowatt – 1888 – 1 – uk Microform Academic [910]
SIXTEEN SERMONS, ALL (EXCEPT ONE) PREACH'D BEFORE THE UNIVERSITY OF OXFORD, AT ST MARY'S UPON SEVERAL OCCASIONS LONDON / Tilly, William – 1712 – 1 – us A.T.L.A. [240]
SIXTEEN YEARS IN SIBERIA / Deutsch, Lev Grigorevich – Trans. by Helen Chisholm, with notes and brief summary of the revolutionary movement in Russia. Cheap ed. London: J. Murray, 1905. xxii,376p. illus., plates, ports – 1 – us U.W. Library [950]
SIXTEENTH AND SEVENTEENTH CENTURY MANUSCRIPTS FROM THE RAWLINSON COLLECTION, BODLEIAN LIBRARY, OXFORD UNIVERSITY – (Seven Parts covering the most important volumes from both the Rawlinson A and Rawlinson B and C Collections) – 1 – us Primary [090]
SIXTEENTH AVENUE BAPTIST CHURCH. MORGAN COUNTY. DECATUR, ALABAMA : CHURCH RECORDS – 1896-1960 – 1 – 39.60 – us Baptist [240]
SIXTEENTH CENTURY PAMPHLETS IN GERMAN AND LATIN / ed by Koehler, Hans-Joachim – (Part 1: 1501-1530. 1,956mf. Dfl19,300.00; Part 2: 1531-1600, 1993. 570mf. Includes printed guides) – 9 – ne IDC [430]
SIXTH ANNIVERSARY OF THE SPANISH REPUBLIC IN BARCELONA; EYEWITNESS ACCOUNT BY EDWARD H. OLIVER / Oehler, Hugo – Chicago, 19? Fiche W 1085. (Blodgett Collection of Spanish Civil War Pamphlets) – 9 – us H.U. College Libr [946]
SIXTH CENSUS OF THE UNITED STATES / U.S. Bureau of the Census – 1840. 580 rolls. M704 – 1 – us Nat'l Archives [324]
SIXTH DEVELOPMENT PLAN 1971-1973 / Solomon Islands. British. Protectorate – D 1523 1. 1971 – 9 – ne IDC [338]
SIXTH, DJAKARTA, 1959. (TENTANG PROGRAM PKI) / Communist Party. Indonesia. Kongres Nasional – SE-6825 1. 1959 – 9 – ne IDC [950]
SIXTH FOUR-YEAR PLAN FOR ECONOMIC DEVELOPMENT OF TAIWAN / China. Republic. Council for International Economic Cooperation and Development – Taipei, 1973. 299p. BD-1635/1 – 9 – ne IDC [338]
SIXTH FOUR-YEAR PLAN FOR ECONOMIC DEVELOPMENT OF TAIWAN 1973-1976 / China. Republic. Council for Economic Planning – Taipei. 1974. BD-2005 1 – 9 – ne IDC [338]
SIXTH MEETING OF THE EASTERN AFRICAN SUB-COMMITTEE FOR SOIL CORRELATION AND LAND EVALUATION : MASERU, 1985 – 1986 – 209p – it F.A.O. [631]
SIXTH PLENUM OF THE CENTRAL COMMITTEE OF THE COMMUNIST PARTY OF INDONESIA, MARCH 31-APRIL 3, 1958: DOCUMENTS / Communist Party. Indonesia. Comite Central – SE-1250 1. 1958 – 9 – ne IDC [950]
SIXTH PROGRESS REPORT ON THE RECONSTRUCTION AND DEVELOPMENT PROGRAMME 1960-66, FOR THE YEAR 1965-66 / Mauritius – (Sessional Paper no. 5 of 1967). Port Louis. 1967 – 9 – ne IDC [338]
SIXTH WARD NEWS – Grand Rapids. Mich. -w. 1909-18 – 1 – us UMI [071]
Sixtus of Siena *see* BIBLIOTHECA SANCTA
Sixtus, V *see* BULLARIUM SIVE COLLECTIO CONSTITUTIONUM
SIXTY CURIOUS AND AUTHENTIC NARRATIVES AND ANECDOTES RESPECTING EXTRAORDINARY CHARACTERS / Hone, William – 1822 – 1 – us I.U. Libraries [390]
SIXTY REASONS WHY THE CAMBELLITE CHURCH IS NOT AND CAN NOT BE THE CHURCH OF CHRIST / Whitlock, J H – 1897 – 1 – 5.00 – us Baptist [240]
SIXTY SEVENTH ANNUAL MEETING...: TORONTO MEETING: AUGUST 18-25, 1897: PROGRAMME OF LOCAL ARRANGEMENTS WITH MAP OF CITY, SHOWING STREET RAILWAY, PLAN OF UNIVERSITY GROUNDS AND QUEEN'S PARK. / British Association for the Advancement of Science. Canada – Toronto: Published by the Local Committee, 1897? 02831. (Pre-1900 Canadiana) – 9 – cn C.I.H.M. [971]
SIXTY YEARS IN TEXAS / Jackson, George – Dallas: Wilkinson Printing Co., 1908. Texas Reel 12. (The Cox Library Collection) – 5 – us Americana [978]
SIXTY YEARS OF THE LIFE OF A COUNTRY VILLAGE BAPTIST CHURCH, DAHLONEGA, GEORGIA / Price, W P – 1897 – 1 – 5.00 – us Baptist [240]
SIXTY-SEVEN SPECIAL REPORTS AND BIBLIOGRAPHIES *see* 67 SPECIAL REPORTS AND BIBLIOGRAPHIES
SIX-YEAR DEVELOPMENT PLAN OF THE UNION OF INDIA, 1951-57 / India – D-1327 1. 1950 – 9 – ne IDC [338]
SIX-YEAR PROGRAMME OF INVESTMENT, 1954/55 TO 1959/60 / Ceylon. Planning Secretariat – Colombo. 1955 – 9 – ne IDC [330]
SIYAR AL-MUT'AKHKHIRIN / Ghulam Husain Khan Tuba Tubee – Calcutta. 1836. BI-771 2 – 8 – ne IDC [490]
SIYASAT – Kanpur, India. 5 Sept-4 Dec 1950; 24 Jan 1952-1954; Jul-Sept 1966 – 6r – 1 – us L of C Photodup [072]
Siyasifar, Farzanah *see* JAHAN-I ZANAN
SIYER-I ENBIYA-I 'AZAM VE AHVAL-I HULEFA-I KIRAM / Pasa, Nisanci Mehmed – Istanbul: Matba'a-i 'Amire, 1279 [1862] – 4mf – 9 – $75.00 – us MEDOC [949]
SIYER-I VEYSI – Istanbul, 1286 – 5mf – 9 – $30.00 – us MEDOC [949]
SI-YU-KI / Hsuan-Tsang – Buddhist records of the Western World. Trans. from the Chinese by Samuel Beal. London: Truebner & Co., 1906. 2v. map – 1 – us U.W. Library [290]
DE SIZILISCHE GROSSHOF UNTER KAISER FRIEDRICH 2 (MGH SCHRIFTEN..: 4.BD) : EINE VERWALTUNGS- GESCHICHTLICHE STUDIE / Heupel, WE – 1940 – Dfl22.00 – ne Slangenburg [240]
Sjaf'at *see*
– DEMOKRASI DAN ADJARAN ISLAM
– PENGANTAR STUDI ISLAM, MENGANTARKAN PEMBATJA MENGGALI API ISLAM
Sjahrul Sjarif *see* TERAS BAHASA; PELADJARAN BAHASA INDONESIA UNTUK SEKOLAH LANDJUTAN PERTAMA DAN JANG SEDERADJAT DENGAN ITU
Sjaiful Nawas *see* IRAMA MINANG MODERN AND INDONESIA POPULER
Sjamsuddin, Sutan *see*
– KABA SI GADIH RANTI DENGAN SI BUDHANG SAMAN
– KABA TJURITO SITI SJAMSIAH
– SITI KALASUN
– SITI NURLELA; MENGANDUNG BEBEBERAPA PELADJARAN SEDIH, GEMBIRA, LUTJU, DIHIASI BEBERAPA PANTUN DAN PEPATAH
– STATISTICAL DATA PERTAINING TO THE COLONIAL PERIOD
SJI (STEEL JOIST INSTITUTE) – Printed index. Updated every 60 days – 6,9 – us Info Handling [620]
SJOLOUM WEREINGOES – v. 1-7. Amsterdam. 1934-40. Lacking: v. 2 (11-12) 1936; v. 3, 1936 37; v. 5 (9-10) 1938 39. BJ-261-109 1 – 8mf – 9 – ne IDC [073]
SJUHARADSBYGDENS TIDNING – Boras, 1930- – 1 – sw Kungliga [072]
Skabichevskii, A M *see* OCHERKI ISTORII RUSSKOI TSENZURY (1700-1863)
SKAFFAREN – St. Paul & Red Wing, MN. 1878-95 – 6r – 1 – sw Kungliga [071]
SKAL DEN LUTHERSKE REFORMATION VIRKELIG FORTSOETTES? / Grundtvig, N F S – Kobenhavn: K. Schonberg, 1863 – 1mf – us A.T.L.A. [240]
Skal'kovskii, K A *see*
– MALEN'KAIA KHRESTOMATIIA DLIA VZROSLYKH. MNENIIA RUSSKIKH O SAMIKH SEBE. ED. 3
– NASHI GOSUDARSTVENNYE I OBSHCHESTVENNYE DEIATELI
– OCHERKI I FANTAZII
Skalon, V Iu *see* PO ZEMSKIM VOPROSAM
SKAMAKOWA EAGLE – Cathlamet. Wash. 1899-1914; 1915-1934 – 1 – us UMI [071]
SKANDINAVEN – Chicago.IL. 1866-1910 – 1 – us UMI [071]
SKANDINAVIENS HYMENOPTERA / Thomson, C G – Z 1678 2.m 5 v. 1871-1878 – 9 – ne IDC [590]
SKANDINAVIENS RATVINGADE INSEKTERS NATURAL HISTORIA / Borck, J B von – Lund, 1848. xvi,144p. 4 pls. Z-1087/2 – 8 – ne IDC [590]
SKANDINAVISKA FOGLAR / Koerner, M – 2095 2. 1839-1846 – 8 – ne IDC [948]
SKANDINAVSKII LISTOK *see* SKANDINAWSKIJ LISTOK
SKANDINAWSKIJ LISTOK – (Includes c.1: no.248 1917:Jan.13, no.259 (1917:Feb.21); no.297 1917:July 4-no.347/348 (1917:Dec.29); no.391/392 1918:June 1; no.427/428 1918:Oct.5-no.431/432 (19)) – Stockholm: "Skandinawskij listok", 1915 – 1 – CSUXADM8836-S – us Hoover Inst Photo [073]
SKANES ANNONSBLAD – Helsingborg, Sweden. 1953 – 1 – sw Kungliga [072]
SKÅNETIDNINGEN – Malmoe, 1897-98 – 9 – sw Kungliga [072]
SKANNER – Portland, OR. 9 Oct 1975-. – 1 – us U.O. Library [071]
SKANSKA AFTONBLADET – Malmo, Helsingborg, Sweden. 1880-1949 – 1 – sw Kungliga [072]
SKANSKA AFTONBLADET POSTUPPLAGAN – Malmoe, Helsingborg, Sweden. 1907-20 – 1 – sw Kungliga [072]
SKANSKA DAGBLADET – Malmo, Sweden. 1888-1978 – 630r – 1 – sw Kungliga [072]
SKANSKA DAGBLADET – Malmo, Sweden. 1979- – 1 – sw Kungliga [072]
SKANSKA RESA / Linnaeus, Carl – Stockholm. 1751. B-7110 2 – 8 – ne IDC [580]
SKANSKA SOCIALDEMOKRATEN – (Skanska Socialdemokraten 1907-54; Nyheterna 1954-58) – Helsingborg, Sweden – 238r – 1 – sw Kungliga [072]
SKARA NYA TIDNING – Skara, Sweden. 1855-63 – 1 – sw Kungliga [072]
SKARA TIDNING – Skara, Sweden. 1863-1944 – 1 – sw Kungliga [072]
SKARA TIDNING *see* SKARABORGS LANS TIDNING
SKARABORGAREN OST – Boras, Sweden. 1983-85 – 1 – sw Kungliga [072]
SKARABORGAREN VAST – Boras, Sweden. 1983-85 – 1 – sw Kungliga [072]
SKARABORGS LANS ALLEHANDA – Skovde, Sweden. 1981- – 1 – sw Kungliga [072]
SKARABORGS LANS ANNONSBLAD – Skovde, Sweden. 1884-1920; 27 reels. 01 03-03 30 1968. 2 reels – 1 – sw Kungliga [072]
SKARABORGS LANS ANNONSBLAD – Skovde, Sweden. 1979-81 – 1 – sw Kungliga [072]
SKARABORGS LANS TIDNING – (Skaraborgs Lans Tidning, Veckouppl., 1887; Skara Tidning, 1979-82) – Skara, Sweden. 1884- – 1 – sw Kungliga [072]
SKARABORGSBYGDEN – Skara, Sweden. 1979- – 1 – sw Kungliga [072]
SKARGARDEN – Uddevalla, Sweden. 1896-1994 – 8r – 1 – sw Kungliga [072]
Skaryszewski, Tomasz *see* NAROD POLSKI
SKATTEGRAVEREN – v1-12. 1884-89 – 1 – us I.U. Libraries [390]
SKAZANIIA O SVIATYKH BORISE I GLEBE / Sreznevskii, 2 – Sil'vestrovskii spisok XIV veka. Spb. 1860. BR-10,312 1 – 9 – ne IDC [947]
SKAZANIIA OB ANTIKHRISTE V SLAVIANSKIKH PEREVODAKH, S ZAMECHANIIAMI O SLAVIANSKIKH PEREVODAKH TVORENII SV. IPPOLITA / Sreznevskii, 1 – Spb. 1874. BR-4073 2 – 8 – ne IDC [947]
O SKAZENIU JEZYKA POLSKIEGO. WYD. 3 / Skobel, F K – Krakow, 1872 – 8 – BR-8015 2 – ne IDC [943]
SKAZKA O BOLSHEVIKI E I IVANI E DURAKI E : KAK BOLSHEVIK IVANA DURAKA OBMANUL / ILICHEVSKAGO / Ilichevskii – Omsk: "Nasha zaria", 1919 – 1 – CSUX88-B8412 – us Hoover Inst Photo [320]
SKAZKI I PESNI BELOZERSKOGO KRAIA / ed by Sokolov, Boris Matveevich – 1915. Russian folklore – 1 – us I.U. Libraries [390]
SKAZKI I PREDANIIA SAMARSKAGO KRAIA / ed by Sadovnikov, Dmitrii Nikolaevich – 1884. Russian folk literature – 1 – us I.U. Libraries [390]
SKAZKI RUSSKAGO NARODNA. DOKUKA I BALAGUR'E. RUSSKIIA ZHENSHCHINY. RUSSKAIA VERA / Remizov, A – Berlin, 1923. 346, (5)p. BR-845 2 – 8 – ne IDC [460]
Skeat, W W *see*
– 12 FACSIMILES OF OLD ENGLISH MANUSCRIPTS
– MALAY MAGIC
Skeels, William O *see* FRAZIER-LEMKE FARM DEBT MORATORIUM ACT.
SKEERA HODSHIT / Israel. Zahal. Israel Defence Forces – Monthly survey of world politics for Zahal officers. Tel Aviv. 1954-. Text in Hebrew – 9 – $170.00; $12.00y – is I.T.T.I. [956]

SKEGNESS STANDARD *see* LINCOLNSHIRE STANDARD (SKEGNESS ED)

SKEIREINS AIVAGGELJONS PAIRH IOHANNEN / Cromhout, Emile Henri Antoine – Delft: E.H.A. Cromhout, 1900. 1 fiche – 9 – us A.T.L.A. [240]

SKELETAL RADIOLOGY – Including Computed Tomography. xJournal of the International Skeletal Society. v.1-6, 1976-81. ISSN:0364-2348 – 1,5,6,9,13 – 60.00v – us UMI [616]

SKELLEFTEA NYA TIDNING – Skelleftea, 1860-1919 – 1r – 1 – sw Kungliga [072]

SKELLEFTEÅ TIDNING – Skellefteå, 1849-60 – 9 – sw Kungliga [072]

SKELLEFTEBLADET – Skelleftea, Sweden. 1887-91 – 2r – 1 – sw Kungliga [072]

Skelton, John *see*
– ESSAYS IN HISTORY AND BIOGRAPHY
– THE TABLE-TALK OF SHIRLEY

SKEPTICAL INQUIRER *see* ZETETIC

SKEPTICISM ASSAILED / Tabor, Britton H – New York:S S Wood, 1895 – 1mf – 9 – 0-8370-5476-1 – 1985-3476 – us A.T.L.A. [230]

THE SKEPTICS OF THE FRENCH RENAISSANCE / Owen, John – London: S. Sonnenschein; New York: Macmillan, 1893 – 1mf – us A.T.L.A. [180]

THE SKEPTICS OF THE ITALIAN RENAISSANCE / Owen, John – London: S. Sonnenschein; New York: Macmillan, 1908 – 2mf – us A.T.L.A. [180]

Skepto *see* L'HYPNOTISME ET LES RELIGIONS, OU, LA FIN DU MERVEILLEUX

SKETCH BOOK OF NAPA, SONOMA, LAKE AND MENDOCINO COUNTIES, 1873 / Menefee, C A – Sonoma Co, CA. – 1r – 1 – $50.00 – B40276 – us Library Micro [978]

SKETCH OF AN ACT TO ESTABLISH A UNIFORM SYSTEM OF BANKRUPTCY THROUGHOUT THE UNITED STATES / Lowell, John – n.p. 1880. 45 p. LL-940 – 1 – us L of C Photodup [340]

SKETCH OF ASSAM, WITH SOME ACCOUNT OF THE HILL TRIBES / Butler, J – London. 1847. BSE-68 2 – 8 – ne IDC [306]

SKETCH OF ELDER DANIEL PARKER AND THE PILGRIM BAPTIST CHURCH / Walston, Ben B, Jr – 1935 – 1 – 5.00 – us Baptist [240]

A SKETCH OF ENGLISH LEGAL HISTORY / Maitland, Frederick William – New York: Putnam's, 1915. 229p. LL-2262 – 1 – us L of C Photodup [340]

A SKETCH OF HERDER AND HIS TIMES / Nevinson, Henry Woodd – (Includes index) – London: Chapman and Hall, 1884 – 1r – 1 – us U.W. Library [920]

A SKETCH OF HOW "THE DIAMOND ANTHEM" WAS SUNG AROUND THE WORLD THROUGH THE COLONIES OF THE EMPIRE ON THE 20TH JUNE, 1897: THE 60TH ANNIVERSARY OF THE ACCESSION DAY OF HER MAJESTY QUEEN VICTORIA / Cumberland, Barlow – being an extract from the annual report of the supreme grand president of the Sons of England, given at St. Catherines, Canada, 8th March, 1898. Toronto: Robinson-Arbuthno, 1898. 02235. (Pre-1900 Canadiana) – 9 – cn C.I.H.M. [971]

SKETCH OF J. C. LOHNES AND HIS SETTLING ON PAWNEE CREEK / Lohnes, J C – 1 – us KS Hist [920]

A SKETCH OF THE BOTANY OF SOUTH-CAROLINA AND GEORGIA / Elliott, S – 2v. Charleston. -1821-24. B-881 2 – 8 – ne IDC [580]

A SKETCH OF THE CHARACTER OF JESUS: A BIBLICAL ESSAY / Schenkel, Daniel – London: Longmans, Green, 1869. 1 fiche – 9 – us A.T.L.A. [240]

A SKETCH OF THE GEOGRAPHY AND GEOLOGY OF THE HIMALAYA MOUNTAINS AND TIBET / Burrard, SC & Hayden, H H – G-157 2. 1907-1908 – 8 – ne IDC [910]

SKETCH OF THE GEOLOGY OF THE PUNJAB / Medlicott, H B – Calcutta. 1888. BG-160 2 – 8 – ne IDC [550]

SKETCH OF THE HISTORY OF EDUCATION IN THE SOCIETY OF FRIENDS : WITH A REVIEW OF THE PROCEEDINGS OF THE FRIENDS' EDUCATIONAL SOCIETY AND OTHER PAPERS – 2nd ed. York: William Sessions, 1871 – 1mf – 9 – 0-8370-8573-X – 1986-2573 – us A.T.L.A. [240]

SKETCH OF THE HISTORY OF PROTESTANT MISSIONS IN CHINA / Lyon, David Willard – (Includes bibliographical references) – New York: Fleming H. Revell, c1895 – 1mf – 9 – 0-8370-6210-1 – 1986-0210 – us A.T.L.A. [240]

SKETCH OF THE HISTORY OF ST ANDREW'S LODGE OF ANCIENT, FREE AND ACCEPTED MASONS, NO. 16, G.R.C., TORONTO / Bain, James – 1868. 06709. (Pre-1900 Canadiana) – 9 – cn C.I.H.M. [360]

A SKETCH OF THE HISTORY OF THE APOSTOLIC CHURCH / Thatcher, Oliver Joseph – (Includes bibliographical references, appendix & index) – Boston: Houghton, Mifflin, 1893 – 1mf – 9 – 0-8370-5503-2 – 1985-3503 – us A.T.L.A. [240]

SKETCH OF THE LIFE AND MINISTRY OF THE REV. C.H. SPURGEON: FROM ORIGINAL DOCUMENTS, INCLUDING ANECDOTES AND INCIDENTS OF TRAVEL. / Spurgeon, Charles Haddon – New York: Sheldon, Blakeman & Co., 1858.141p – 1 – us U.W. Library [920]

A SKETCH OF THE LIFE AND PAINTINGS OF THOMAS GAINSBORGOUGH / Thicknesse, P – London, 1788 – 1mf – ne IDC [750]

SKETCH OF THE LIFE OF ELDER HUMPHREY POSEY / Fleming, Robert – 1851 – 1 – $5.00 – us Baptist [240]

A SKETCH OF THE MODERN LANGUAGES OF AFRICA / Cust, Robert Needham – 2v. London. 1883. BA-360 2 – 8 – ne IDC [470]

SKETCH OF THE PARISH OF ST MARY, ALMONTE, ONTARIO, 1823 TO 1885 / Foley, Deodatus Francis – by a priest of the diocese of Ottawa. s.l.: s.n., 1885? (Almonte Ont: Gazette). 03121. (Pre-1900 Canadiana) – 9 – cn C.I.H.M. [971]

A SKETCH OF THE PROFESSIONAL AND JUDICIAL CHARACTER OF THE LATE GEORGE SHARSWOOD / Biddle, George Washington – Philadelphia, Law Association, 1883. 53p LL-471 – 1 – us L of C Photodup [340]

A SKETCH OF THE TALMUD : THE WORLD RENOWNED COLLECTION OF JEWISH TRADITIONS / Kalisch, Isidor – NY: L H Frank, 1877 – 1mf – 9 – 0-8370-3835-9 – 1985-1835 – us A.T.L.A. [270]

SKETCH OF THE TALMUD : THE WORLD-RENOWNED COLLECTION OF JEWISH TRADITIONS / Kalisch, Isador – New York: L.H. Frank, 1877 – 1mf – 9 – us A.T.L.A. [270]

A SKETCH OF THE TIMES : A SATIRE / Combe, W – London, 1780 – 1mf – 9 – MP-542/1 – ne IDC [870]

THE SKETCHBOOKS OF ALFRED WATERHOUSE 1853-1899 – (Includes extensive, detailed contents list and index to all places included) – 1996 – 3r – 1 – £150.00 – uk World [720]

SKETCHES AND INCIDENTS, OR, A BUDGET FROM THE SADDLEBAGS OF A SUPERANNUATED ITINERANT / ed by Peck, George – New York: G. Lane & C.B. Tippett for the Methodist Episcopal Church, 1845, c1843-1845 – 1mf – us A.T.L.A. [240]

SKETCHES AND NOTICES OF THE CHICAGO BAR. / Wilkie, Franc Bangs – 3d ed. Chicago, Sumner, 1871. 90 p. LL-1363 – 1 – us L of C Photodup [340]

SKETCHES AND REMINISCENCES OF THE RADICAL CLUB OF CHESTNUT STREET, BOSTON / Sargent, Mrs. John T – Boston: J.R. Osgood, 1880. 1 fiche – 9 – us A.T.L.A. [240]

SKETCHES FOR TABERNACLE-FRAMES : A POEM / Combe, William – London, 1778 – 1mf – 9 – MP-534/1 – ne IDC [810]

SKETCHES FROM THE KAREN HILLS / Bunker, Alonzo – New York: Fleming H Revell, c1910 – 1mf – 9 – 0-8370-6029-X – 1986-0029 – us A.T.L.A. [240]

SKETCHES, HISTORICAL AND BIOGRAPHICAL OF THE BROAD RIVER AND KINGS MOUNTAIN BAPTIST ASSOCIATION / Logan, John R – 1800-82 – 1 – 21.21 – us Baptist [240]

SKETCHES IN HISTORY AND POETRY / Shairp, John Campbell; ed by Veitch, John – Edinburgh: D. Douglas, 1887 – 1 roll – 1 – 1-55879-921-4 – uk Libr Preservation [810]

SKETCHES IN THE CANADAS / Smyth, Coke – London: Thos. McLean, 183? SEM35P293 – 1r – 1 – Can$15.00 – cn Bibl Nat [971]

SKETCHES OF AMERICAN POLICY / Webster, Noah – 1785 – 9 – 5.00 – us Scholars' Facs [323]

SKETCHES OF ARMY LIFE IN RUSSIA / Greene, Francis Vinton – New York: C. Scribner's sons, 1885, c1880. v,326p – 1 – us U.W. Library [947]

SKETCHES OF CAESAREA (PALESTINAE): BIBLICAL, MEDIAEVAL, MODERN : FROM EARLIEST CA SAR TO LATEST SULTAN / Dowling, Theodore Edward – London: S.P.C.K., 1912 – 1mf – us A.T.L.A. [930]

SKETCHES OF CHURCH HISTORY IN SCOTLAND / Lloyd, Julius – London: S.P.C.K.; New York: Pott, Young, [189-?] – 1mf – us A.T.L.A. [240]

SKETCHES OF CIVIL WAR SCENES – undated, Presented to Charles W. Reed from Major Bigelow, 9th Massachusetts Battery, Christmas, 1864 – 1 – us KS Hist [976]

SKETCHES OF GEORGIAN CHURCH HISTORY / Dowling, Theodore Edward – London: S.P.C.K.; New York: E.S. Gorham, 1912 – 1mf – us A.T.L.A. [240]

SKETCHES OF HINDOO LIFE / Das, Devandra Nath – London: Chapman and Hall, 1887. viii,271p – 1 – us U.W. Library [950]

SKETCHES OF HISTORY : IN SIX SERMONS / Godwin, William – London: Printed for T. Cadell..., 1784 – 1 roll – 1 – 1-55879-294-5 – uk Libr Preservation [240]

SKETCHES OF HISTORY OF THE BAPTIST CHURCHES WITHIN THE LIMITS OF THE RAPPAHANNOCK ASSOCIATIONS IN VIRGINIA / Baptist Association – 1850 – 1 – 5.00 – us Baptist [240]

SKETCHES OF ILLUSTRIOUS DOMINICANS = HISTOIRE DES HOMMES ILLUSTRES DE L'ORDRE DE SAINT DOMINIQUE : ST. LOUIS BERTRAND, JULIAN GARCES, JEROME DE LOAYSA / Touron, Antoine – Boston: T B Noonan, 1884 – 1mf – 9 – 0-8370-6844-4 – 1986-0844 – us A.T.L.A. [920]

SKETCHES OF INDIAN CHRISTIANS : COLLECTED FROM DIFFERENT SOURCES / Murdoch, John – (Includes bibliographical references) – 1st ed. London: Christian Literature Society for India, 1896 – 1mf – 9 – 0-8370-6512-7 – 1986-0512 – us A.T.L.A. [920]

SKETCHES OF JEWISH SOCIAL LIFE IN THE DAYS OF CHRIST / Edersheim, Alfred – Boston: Ira Bradley, 1876. 1 fiche – 9 – 12.50f – us A.T.L.A. [240]

SKETCHES OF LIFE AND SPORT IN SOUTH-EASTERN AFRICA / Hamilton, Charles – Ed. by F.G.H. Price. London: Chapman and Hall, 1870. xii,268p. illus – 1 – us U.W. Library [306]

SKETCHES OF LIFE IN THE GOLDEN STATE / Evans, Albert S – San Francisco: A.L. Bancroft & Co., 1873. California Reel 1. (The Cox Library Collection) – 5 – us Americana [978]

SKETCHES OF LONGER WORKS IN ENGLISH VERSE AND PROSE / ed by Morley, Henry – London: Cassell, Petter, Galpin & Co., n.d. viii,448p. illus – 1 – us U.W. Library [420]

SKETCHES OF PITT COUNTY 1704-1910 / King, Henry T – Raleigh: Edwards and Broughton Printing Co., 1911. North Carolina Reel 2. (The Cox Library Collection) – 5 – us Americana [978]

SKETCHES OF RABUN COUNTY (GEORGIA) HISTORY / Ritchie, Andrew Jackson – 1948. Biog. and hist. sketches.8 fiches. F-0730 – 9 – us A.G.L.L. [920]

SKETCHES OF SOME OF THE FIRST SETTLERS OF UPPER GEORGIA, OF THE CHEROKEES, AND THE AUTHOR / Gilmer, George R – 1926. Biog. sketches and hist. notes. 7 fiches. F-0088 – 9 – us A.G.L.L. [920]

SKETCHES OF SUCCESSFUL NEW HAMPSHIRE MEN / Clarke, John B – Manchester, NH, 1882. New Hampshire Reel 1. (The Cox Library Collection) – 5 – us Americana [978]

SKETCHES OF THE EAST AFRICA CAMPAIGN / Dolbey, Robert Valentine – London: J. Murray, 1918.xxiv,219p. plates, fold. map – 1 – us U.W. Library [960]

SKETCHES OF THE FAMILIES OF THOMAS EWING / Ewing, Joseph L – 1910 – 1 – $50.00 – us Presbyterian [920]

SKETCHES OF THE HUNGARIAN EMIGRATION INTO TURKEY / Honved, A – 1 – uk Microform Academic [360]

SKETCHES OF THE INTER-MOUNTAIN STATES OF UTAH, IDAHO, AND NEVADA / Salt Lake Tribune – Salt Lake City, 1909. Utah reel 3. (Cox Library Collection) – 5 – us Americana [978]

SKETCHES OF THE LIFE, TIMES, AND CHARACTER OF THE RT. REV. BENEDICT JOSEPH FLAGET, FIRST BISHOP OF LOUISVILLE / Spalding, Martin John – Louisville, KY: Webb & Levering, 1852 – 1mf – 9 – 0-8370-6702-2 – 1986-0702 – us A.T.L.A. [920]

SKETCHES OF THE MISSIONS OF THE AMERICAN BOARD / Barlett, S C – Boston: The Board, 1872 – 1mf – us A.T.L.A. [240]

SKETCHES OF THE NATURAL HISTORY OF CEYLON / Tennent, J E – Including a monograph of the elephant and a description of the modes of capturing and training it. London. 1861. BZ-292 2 – 8 – ne IDC [574]

SKETCHES OF THE ORIGIN, PROGRESS AND EFFECTS OF MUSIC, WITH AN ACCOUNT OF THE ANCIENT BARDS AND MINSTRELS / Eastcott, R – London. 1793. BP-673 1 – 9 – ne IDC [780]

SKETCHES OF THE PRESBYTERY OF THE WESTERN DISTRICT OF TENNESSEE *see* AMERICAN PRESBYTERIANA 1

SKETCHES OF THE THEOLOGICAL HISTORY OF NEW ENGLAND / Pond, Enoch – Boston: Congregational Publishing Society, c1880 – 1mf – us A.T.L.A. [240]

SKETCHES OF VIRGINIA / Foote, William H – Historical and biographical. Philadelphia, William S. Martin, 1850. Virginia Reel 1. (The Cox Library Collection) – 5 – us Americana [978]

SKETCHES OF VOCAL AND INSTRUMENTAL MUSIC / Hook, James – Dated 1816-1817. music 1873 – 1 – us L of C Photodup [780]

SKETCHES OF WESLEYAN PREACHERS / West, R A – London, 1849 – 5mf – 9 – ne IDC [240]

SKETCHES OF WESTERN METHODISM : BIOGRAPHICAL, HISTORICAL, AND MISCELLANEOUS, ILLUSTRATIVE OF PIONEER LIFE / Finley, James B; ed by Strickland, W P – Cincinnati: Methodist Book Concern, 1854 – 2mf – us A.T.L.A. [975]

SKETCHES REPRESENTING THE NATIVE TRIBES, ANIMALS AND SCENERY OF SOUTHERN AFRICA / Daniell, Samuel (drawings) – Pretoria, State Library, 1978. Origin. publ, London: W. Daniell, 1820. Engraved by William Daniell. 48 engravings with descriptive notes. (Microfiche Reprint Series, State Library, no.1). Printed booklet – 4mf – 9 – sa State Libr [960]

SKETCHES TOWARDS A HORTUS BOTANICUS AMERICANUS / Titford, W J – 7629 2. 1811-1812 – 8 – ne IDC [580]

SKETS SEDJARAH PAK MATOSIN : PELUKIS SUKARDI / Semaun – 1962? – 9 – SE-4055 1 – ne IDC [700]

SKETSMASA – Surabaja. Incomplete. SE 965 1. 1957-1971 – 9 – ne IDC [073]

SKEWARKEY BAPTIST CHURCH. KEHUKEE ASSOCIATION. NORTH CAROLINA : CHURCH RECORDS – 1786-1861 – 1 – 27.45 – us Baptist [240]

Skewes, J H *see* A COMPLETE AND POPULAR DIGEST OF THE POLITY OF METHODISM, EACH SUBJECT ALPHABETICALLY ARRANGED

SKI CANADA – (v15-17 1986/87-1988/89 Can$28.00y) – Toronto. v15-22. 1986/87-1993/94 – 9 – Can$37.00y – cn Micromedia [790]

SKIER'S WORLD – v.8-. 1980- – 1,5,6,9 – us UMI [073]

SKIFY – Sbornik. St Petersburg. v. 1-2. 1917-1918 – 1 – us NY Public [073]

SKIFY – Sborniki. M. 1917-18. B-184 2 – 8 – ne IDC [073]

SKIING TRADE MONTHLY NEWS – 1976-83 – 1 – us UMI [073]

SKIING TRADE NEWS – 1985-. -a – 1 – us UMI [073]

SKIING TRADE NEWS – (v8-. 1984-. 5,6,9) – v7-. 1983- – 1 – us UMI [073]

SKILL DEVELOPMENT FOR SELF RELIANCE : REGIONAL PROJECT IN EASTERN AND SOUTHERN AFRICA; REPORT OF AN EVALUATION MISSION ... ILO/SIDA / Hultin, M – Stockholm, 1985 (Education division documents no. 25) – 2mf – 9 – DE-313/1 – ne IDC [370]

SKILL IN TRIALS: CONTAINING A VARIETY OF CIVIL AND CRIMINAL CASES WON BY THE ART OF ADVOCATES. / Donovan, Joseph Wesley – Rochester, N.Y., Williamson, 1891. 173 p. LL-482 – 1 – us L of C Photodup [340]
Skillman, Isaac *see* PAPERS
SKIN PHARMACOLOGY – v1-. 1988- – 1,5,9 – us UMI [615]
Skinner, A *see*
– NOTES ON THE EASTERN CREE AND NORTHERN SAULTEAUX
– NOTES ON THE PLAINS CREE
– POLITICAL ORGANIZATION, CULTS AND CEREMONIES OF THE PLAINS-CREE
Skinner, John *see*
– THE BOOK OF EZEKIEL
– THE BOOK OF THE PROPHET ISAIAH, CHAPTERS 1-39
– THE BOOK OF THE PROPHET ISAIAH, CHAPTERS 40-66
Skinner, Joseph Osmun *see*
– A BOOK OF THE LAWS OF WASHINGTON RELATING TO NOTARIES PUBLIC
– A HANDBOOK FOR NOTARIES PUBLIC AND COMMISSIONERS OF DEEDS OF NEW YORK.
Skinner, Robert Peet *see* ABYSSINIAN SCRAPBOOKS
Skinner, S *see* ETYMOLOGICON LINGUA ANGLICANAE...
SKINNER'S RECORD OF THE MAN-MADE FIBRES INDUSTRY – v.41. Jan-Jun 1967 – 1 – us UMI [680]
SKIPPER GEORGE NETMAN: A STORY OF OUT-PORT METHODISM IN NEWFOUNDLAND / Bond, George John – London: C. Kelly, 18??. 00177. (Pre-1900 Canadiana) – 9 – cn C.I.H.M. [240]
SKIPTON COMMUNITY NEWS – 1977-1986. SCN1-3 – 3r – 1 – at Corangamite [072]
SKIZZEN UND ENTWUERFE ZUR RING-DICHTUNG : MIT DER DICHTUNG DER JUNGE SIEGFRIED / Wagner, Richard; ed by Strobel, Otto – (Includes bibliographical references) – Muenchen: F Bruckmann, 1930 – 1r – 1 – us U.W. Library [790]
SKIZZEN ZUR GESCHICHTLICHEN VOELKERKUNDE VON MITTELASIEN UND SIBIRIEN / Marquart, J – (Hirth Festschrift 1920). BU-663 2 – 8 – ne IDC [301]
SKIZZEN-BUCH FUER INGENIEURE UND MASCHINENBAUER – Leipzig, DE. Jan 1890-Sept 1896 – 3r – 1 – uk British Libr Newspaper [073]
Skobel, F K *see* O SKAZENIU JEZYKA POLSKIEGO. WYD. 3
SKOFDEPOSTEN – Skovde, Sweden. 1882-84 – 1 reel – 1 – sw Kungliga [072]
SKOMOROKHI NA RUSI / Famintsyn, A S – Spb. 1889. BR-6030 2 – 8 – ne IDC [947]
SKONCENI PRIPRAVNEHO RIZENI PODLE TRESTNIHO RADI CSSR / Stepan, J – Praha. 1968. BR-8769 1 – 9 – ne IDC [943]
SKOOKUM TIMES – Skookum, NV. 1908 – 2r – 1 – $100.00 – U03713 – us Library Micro [071]
Skordilis, Emmanouil K *see* COMPARISON OF SPORT ACHIEVEMENT ORIENTATION BETWEEN WHEELCHAIR BASKETBALL ATHLETES AND ABLE-BODY BASKETBALL ATHLETES
SKOROPORTIASHCHIESIA PRODUKTY I KHOLODILNOE DELO / ed by Narkomtorga R.S.F.S.R. – (Library has: March-May 1929) – Moskva: Izdvo Narkomtorga SSSR i RSFSR, 1928-1929. 2v – 1 – CSUX89-S651 – us Hoover Inst Photo [660]
SKOTLANDS RIMUR / Gutmundsson, Einar – 1908 – 1 – us I.U. Libraries [390]
SKOVDE NYHETER – Skovde, Sweden. 1979- – 1 – sw Kungliga [072]
SKRAELINGERNE I VINLAND OG ESKIMOERNES SYDOSTGRAENSE / Birket-Smith, K – BN 128 2. 1918 – 8 – ne IDC [306]
SKRIFTER OCH BREF, SAMLADE OCH UTGIFNA AF EMANUEL LINDERHOLM / Rosen, Sven – Uppsala & Stockholm: Almquist & Wilsells, 1910. 304p – 1 – us U.W. Library [948]
SKRIFTER OF NATURHISTORIE-SELSKABET – Kjobenhavn. v1-2. 1790-92 – 16mf – 9 – 5497/2 – ne IDC [500]
SKRIFTER, SOM UDI DET KIOBENHAVNSKE SELSKAB AF LAERDOMS OG RIDENSKABERS ELSKERE, ERE FREMLAGTE OG OPLAESTE / Danske Videnskabernes selskab. Copenhagen – 1743-1779 – 3 – us Readex [500]
SKRIFTER UTGIFNA AF K. HUMANISTISKA VETENSKAPSSAMFUNDET I UPSALA, V9 *see* OM BEVISEN FOER GUDS VERKLIGHET
Skrine, John Huntley *see* WHAT IS FAITH?
SKRIP – Athens, Greece. -d. 14 March 1917-10 May 1918. Imperfect. 2 reels – 1 – uk British Libr Newspaper [949]
SKROMNYI NABLIUDATEL' / Lukin, A P – Otgoloski zhizni Nabliudeniia i zametki. v. 1-2. M. 1901. BR-10.600 2 – 8 – ne IDC [460]
SKRZYDLAA – London. v. 1, no. 20-v. 20, no. 80. Apr 6 1940-Jan Aug 1959. Incomplete – 1 – us NY Public [073]
Skuja, H L *see* DIE ALGENFLORA DER INSEL MORTIZHOLM...
Skulachev, V P *see* PHYSICOCHEMICAL BIOLOGY REVIEWS
Skvortsov, Vasilii M *see*
– BOGUSLAVSKOE OBSHCHESTVO TREZVOSTI I BOR'BA SO SHTUNDOYU
– MISSIONERSKII SPUTNIK
– O SHTUNCIZME I MERAKH BOR'BY S SEKTOYU
– VTOROI MISSIONERSKII SVEZD V MOSKVE
SKVOZ' GROZY LET / Zenkevich, M – M. 1962. BR-1240 2 – 8 – ne IDC [460]
SKY AND TELESCOPE – (v. 35- 1968- 5,6. v. 37- 1970- 9) – v. 1- 1941- – 1 – us UMI [520]
SKYLAB RESULTS – (Suppl to v31, Advances) – 1975 – 8mf – 9 – $15.00 – 0-87703-143-6 – us Univelt [629]
THE SKYLAB RESULTS – (v31 pt 1 + 2, 1975, Advances) – 9 – $45.00 – us Univelt [629]
SKYLAB SCIENCE EXPERIMENTS – (v38 1975, Science and Technology) – 1975 – 9 – $20.00 – us Univelt [629]
SKYLARK – Sherbrooke, Canada. v1 n5. 3 aut 1837 – 1r – 1 – Can$25.00 – cn Can Microfilming [072]
SKYTHIEN UND DER BOSPORUS: I, KRITISCHE UBERSICHT DER SCHRIFTLICHEN UND ARCHAEOLOGISCHEN QUELLEN / Rostovcev, M – Berlin, 1931. 651p. BU-544/2 – 8 – ne IDC [930]
Slaart, Pieter van der *see* DE BOEKZAAL VAN EUROPA
Slabber, Martinus *see* NATUURKUNDIGE VERLUSTIGINGEN.
Slade, Ruth M *see* ENGLISH-SPEAKING MISSIONS IN THE CONGO INDEPENDENT STATE (1878-1908)
Sladen, WP *see* TERTIARY AND UPPER CRETACEOUS FAUNA OF WESTERN INDIA
Slamet, Ina E *see* KEHIDUPAN SUKU-SUKU IRIAN BARAT
Slamet, Mas *see*
– THE AFTERGLOW OF THE JAPANESE SUNSET
– JAPANESE MACHINATIONS
Slamet Wijadi Atmosudarmo *see* ADMINISTRASI NEGARA, SEBUAH PEDOMAN KERDJA
Slametmuljana, R B *see*
– DRAMA CHANG FU TANG
– KAIDAH BAHASA INDONESIA
– POLITIK BAHASA NASIONAL
Slane, B William MacGuckin de *see* CATALOGUE DES MANUSCRITS ARABES DE LA BIBLIOTHEQUE NATIONALE
Slas, Mariano Picon *see* IMAGENES DE CHILE VIDA Y COSTUMBRES CHILENAS EN LOS SIGLOS 18 Y 19 A TRAVES DE...
SLASKI KURJER PORANNY – Chorzow, Poland. 1936-Apr 1939 – 7r – 1 – us L of C Photodup [943]
SLATE – New York. v. 1, nos. 1-5. (Jan.-May 1917) – 1 – us NY Public [073]
Slaten, Arthur Wakefield *see* QUALITATIVE NOUNS IN THE PAULINE EPISTLES AND THEIR TRANSLATION IN THE REVISED VERSION
Slater, D A *see* TOWARDS A TEXT OF THE METAMORPHOSIS OF OVID. PROLEGOMENA; APPARATUS CRITICUS; LACTANTIUS
Slater, Gilbert *see* THE DRAVIDIAN ELEMENT IN INDIAN CULTURE
Slater, Thomas *see* A SHORT HISTORY OF MORAL THEOLOGY
Slater, Thomas Ebenezer *see* MISSIONS AND SOCIOLOGY
Slater, William Fletcher *see* ST. MATTHEW: INTRODUCTION, AV, RV, WITH NOTES, INDEX AND MAP
SLATEY POINT BAPTIST CHURCH. MOREHEAD, KENTUCKY : CHURCH RECORDS – Jul 1946-Apr 1973 – 1 – 15.21 – us Baptist [240]
Slattery, Charles Lewis *see* THE MINISTRY (CCC284)
SLAUGHTER BAPTIST CHURCH. SLAUGHTER, LOUISIANA : CHURCH RECORDS – 1874-1922 – 1 – 10.08 – us Baptist [240]
Slaughter, Philip *see* MAN AND WOMAN: OR THE LAW OF HONOR APPLIED TO THE SOLUTION OF THE PROBLEM, WHY ARE SO MANY MORE WOMEN THAN MEN CHRISTIANS?
SLAUGHTERHOUSE AND SLAUGHTERSLAB DESIGN AND CONSTRUCTION – 1978 – 97p – it F.A.O. [660]
SLAUGHTERHOUSE CLEANING AND SANITATION – 1985 – 52p – it F.A.O. [360]
SLAVE NARRATIVES / U.S. Federal Writers' Project and Library of Congress – Typescripts of interviews gathered from over 2,000 former slaves in 17 southern states between 1936 and 1938 by Federal Writers Project – 1 – 198.00 – us L of C Photodup [976]
SLAVE NARRATIVES: APPRAISAL SHEETS / U.S. Federal Writers' Project and Library of Congress – Typescript evaluation of interviews of former slaves prepared by Library of Congress Project 1939-41 – 1 – 66.00 – us L of C Photodup [976]
SLAVE NARRATIVES, OHIO 1937 (INTERVIEWS) / ed by Levstik, Frank R – 1 – us Ohio Hist [976]
SLAVE TRADE : A SELECTION OF WORKS – 1791-1904 – 1 – us Ross [976]
THE SLAVE TRADE, 1858-1892 : BRITISH FOREIGN OFFICE, COLLECTION 541, CONFIDENTIAL PRINT SERIES – (With printed guide) – 1977 – 10r – 1 – $850.00 – D3255 – us Scholarly Res [941]
THE SLAVE TRADE AND ABOLITIONISM IN FRANCE: 1744-1848 / ed by Deschamps, Hubert – 44 titles in French. Printed guide – 9 – fr Hachette [944]
THE SLAVE TRADE AND ABOLITIONISM IN FRANCE AND ITS COLONIES, 1744-1848 – 18th and 19th century works, economic and social reports and French abolitionist writings. In French. Titles available individually. Printed guide – 9 – fr Hachette [944]
THE SLAVE TRADE BOOK AND PAMPHLET COLLECTION / Royal Commonwealth Society – 1680-1865. With printed index – 1 – £875.00 – uk World [080]
THE SLAVE TRADE, DOMESTIC AND FOREIGN: WHY IT EXISTS AND HOW IT MAY BE EXTINGUISHED / Carey, Henry Charles – Philadelphia, 1853 – 1 – us Res Libr [305]
SLAVE TRADE PAPERS – (The papers of Sir Thomas Fowell Buxton, 1786-1845, Abolitionist and Reformer) – Oxford: Rhodes House Library – 1 – us Primary [941]
Slaveikoff, P *see* THE SHADE OF THE BALKANS: A COLLECTION OF BULGARIAN FOLKSONGS AND PROVERBS
SLAVENHALERS IN SLAVENHANDEL / Vrijman, L C – Amsterdam: P N van Kampen, 1937 – us Res Libr [960]
SLAVERY : CATALYST FOR CONFLICT – 6708mf – 9 – $18,385.00 – us UMI [976]
SLAVERY : CATALYST FOR CONFLICT – 6715mf – 9 – us UMI [976]
SLAVERY : SOME EARLY WORKS – 1835-63 – 1r – 1 – us Ross [976]
SLAVERY AND ABOLITION, 1831-1841 / Hart, Albert Bushnell – New York: Harper, 1907, c1906 – 1mf – us A.T.L.A. [976]
THE SLAVERY AND ABOLITION COLLECTIONS : FROM THE HOLDINGS OF THE SCHOMBURG CENTER FOR RESEARCH IN BLACK CULTURE, MANUSCRIPTS, ARCHIVES AND RARE BOOKS DIVISION: THE NEW YORK PUBLIC LIBRARY, ASTOR, LENOX AND TILDEN FOUNDATIONS – (Guide sold separately for $20.00 which covers other Schomburg Center collections) – 1r – 1 – $85.00 – D3305P07 – us Scholarly Res [320]
SLAVERY AND ANTI-SLAVERY PAMPHLETS FROM THE LIBRARIES OF SALMON P. CHASE AND JOHN P. HALE – 5r – 1 – $370.00 – us UMI [976]
SLAVERY AND ANTISLAVERY PAMPHLETS FROM THE LIBRARIES OF SALMON PORTLAND. CHASE AND JOHN P. HALE – 5r – 1 – $80.00 set – us Dartmouth [976]
SLAVERY AND FOUR YEARS OF WAR / Keifer, Joseph Warren – 2v. 1900 – 1r – 1 – us Ross [976]
SLAVERY AND FREEDOM / Berdiaev, N A – London: G. Bles, the Centenary Press, 1943. 268p. Transl. by R.M. French – 1 – us U.W. Library [190]
SLAVERY AND THE CHURCH / Hosmer, William – Auburn: W.J. Moses, 1853 – 1mf – us A.T.L.A. [240]
SLAVERY AND THE EPISCOPACY / Peck, George – 1845 – 9 – us A.T.L.A. [240]
SLAVERY AND THE SLAVE TRADE IN AFRICA / Stanley, Henry Morton – New York, 1893 – 1r – 1 – us Ross [306]
SLAVERY AND THE SLAVE TRADE IN AFRICA / Stanley, Henry Morton – New York, 1893 – 1 – us Res Libr [960]
SLAVERY DISCUSSED IN OCCASIONAL ESSAYS : FROM 1833 TO 1846 / Bacon, Leonard – New York: Baker and Scribner, 1846 – 1mf – us A.T.L.A. [320]
SLAVERY IN AMERICA : WITH NOTICES OF THE PRESENT STATE OF SLAVERY AND THE SLAVE TRADE THROUGHOUT THE WORLD – Nos. 1-14 (all publ). 1836-1837 – 4mf – 9 – $55.00 – us UPA [976]
SLAVERY IN ANTE-BELLUM SOUTHERN INDUSTRIES – (Series A: Selections from the Duke University Library 28r $3,500.00 ISBN 1-55655-282-3. Series B: Selections from the Southern Historical Collection, University of North Carolina, Chapel Hill 38r $4,750.00 ISBN 1-55655-464-8. Series C: Selections from the Virginia Historical Society, Pt 1 Mining and Smelting Industries ca 26r $3,250.00 ISBN 1-55655-547-4. All with printed guides) – 1993 – 1 – us UPA [976]
SLAVERY IN ANTE-BELLUM SOUTHERN INDUSTRIES, SERIES C : PART 2: RAILROAD AND CANAL CONSTRUCTION INDUSTRIES AND OTHER TRADE AND INDUSTRIES – (With printed guide. Coll: Black Studies Research Sources series) – 1996 – 42r – 1 – ca $5,250.00 – 1-55655-548-2 – us UPA [976]
SLAVERY, SOURCE MATERIAL AND CRITICAL LITERATURE – Includes titles from Dwight L. Drummond's Bibliography of Anti-Slavery Literature in America and Sabin's Bibliotheca Americana – 9 – us Primary [976]
SLAVERY SOURCE MATERIALS – (Complete collection) – 1 – $2,450.00 – us UPA [305]
SLAVERY TRACTS AND PAMPHLETS / West India Committee – 1 – £1,300.00 – uk World [080]
LES SLAVES, BYZANCE ET ROME AU 9 S / Dvornik, F – Paris, 1926 – Dfl30.00 – ne Slangenburg [240]
LES SLAVES, HISTOIRE ET LITTERATURE DES NATIONS POLONAISE, BOHEME, SERBE ET RUSSE / Mickiewicz, Adam – (Russia – 19th C. series). 1849 – 9 – fr Hachette [947]
SLAVIA, CASOPIS PRO SLOVANSKOU FILOLOGII – Rocnik 1. Praha. 1922. (Quarterly). BR-1808 2 – 8 – ne IDC [460]
SLAVIANE – Ezhemesiachnyi zhurnal literatury, politiki i nauki. v. 1-5. Petrograd. 1915. BR-3757 2 – 8 – ne IDC [321]
SLAVIANE – Moscow. June 1942-Dec. 1958. Missing no. 10, 1945, and no. 10, 1957 – 1 – 35.00r – us Hoover Inst Photo [947]
SLAVIANE V DREVNOSTI; KUL'TURNO-ISTORICHESKII OCHERK / Derzhavin, N S – M. 1946. BR-4967 2 – 8 – ne IDC [940]
SLAVIANIN – Voenno-literaturnyi zhurnal. v. 1-16. Spb. 1827-30. Lacking: v. 1, 1827. BR-8032 2 – 8 – ne IDC [073]
SLAVIANO-BALTIISKIE ETIUDY / Endzelin, I – Khar'kov, 1911 – 4mf – 9 – ne IDC [947]
SLAVIANOFIL'STVO I NATSIONALIZM / Kireev, A A – Otvet g. Solov'evy. Spb. 1890. BR-10.585 2 – 8 – ne IDC [947]
SLAVIANO-RUKOPISI V.M. UNDOLSHOGO. / Undolskii, V M – Moscow, 1870. iv,469,65p. BR-7039/2 – 8 – ne IDC [947]
SLAVIANO-RUSSKIE RUKOPISI 13-17 VV. V FONDAKH NAUCHNOI BIBLIOTEKI IMENI A.M. GOR'KOGO MOSKOVSKOGO GOSUDARSTVENNOGO UNIVERSITETA – Opisanie. Moscow, 1964.102p. Description of early Slavic mss. in Moscow University Library. BR-11,019/1 – 9 – ne IDC [947]
SLAVIANO-RUSSKIE RUKOPISI BIBLIOTEKI IMENI A.M. GOR'KOGO LENINGRADSKOGO GOSUDARSTVENNOGO UNIVERSITETA / Shustorovich, E M – 1963. Surveys medieval mss. in Leningrad University Library. BR-10,918/1 – 9 – ne IDC [947]

SLAVIANO-RUSSKIE RUKOPISI. OTDELENI PERVOE / Sakharov, I P – Spb. 1839; variant ed. Spb. 1842. BR-11,150 1 – 9 – ne IDC [947]
SLAVIANO-RUSSKIIA STAROPECHATNYIA KNIGI DREVNEKHRANIKISHCH G. ZHITOMIRA / Trebin, A A – St. Petersburg, 1913. BR-4693/2 – 8 – ne IDC [025]
SLAVIANOVEDENIE V 1901 GODU – Spb, 1903 – 8 – BR-7268 2 – ne IDC [947]
SLAVIANSKAIA PALEOGRAFIIA. LEKTSII...ARKHEOLOGICHESKOM INSTITUTE / Karinskii, N M – Petrograd, 1915.BR-10,333/1 – 9 – ne IDC [930]
SLAVIANSKAIA PISMENNOST DO KIRILLA I MEFODIIA / Georgiev, E – izd. Bolgarskoi akademii nauk). Sofiia, 1952 – 9 – BR-10 020 1 – ne IDC [460]
SLAVIANSKAIA ZARIA – (Includes c.1: v.1:no.58 1920:Feb.2) – Praga: "Politika", 1919 – 1 – CSUXADM8058-S – us Hoover Inst Photo [320]
SLAVIANSKIA SKAZANIIA O SOLOMONE I KITOVRASE I ZAPADNYIA LEGENDY O MOROLFE I MERLINE / Veselovskii, A – St. Petersburg. 1872. BR-4070/2 – 7mf – 9 – ne IDC [460]
SLAVIANSKIE KNIGI KIRILLOVSKOI PECHATI 15-18 VV / Briuk, D I & Zolotar, T P & Petrov, SO – Opisanie knig, khraniashchikhsia v Gosudarstvennoi publichnoi biblioteke SSSR. Kiev, 1958. 266p. BR-6101/2 – 8 – ne IDC [020]
SLAVIANSKIE RUKOPISI, KHRANISHCHIESIA RIZNITSE SVIATO-TROITSKOI SERGIE- VOI LAVRY / Leonid, Arkhimandrit – Moscow, 1881. 490. BR/7297/2 – 8 – ne IDC [460]
SLAVIANSKIE RUKOPISI SOBRANIIA GRAFA F.A. TOLSTOGO. MATERIALY K ISTORII SOBRANIIA I UKAZATELI STARYKH I NOVYKH SHIFROV / Waugh, D C – BR-9898 1 – 9 – ne IDC [460]
SLAVIANSKIE SKAZANIIA O SOLOMONE I KITOVRASE I ZAPADNYE LEGENDY O MOROL'FE I MERLINE / Veselovskii, A – Spb., 1872 – 7mf – 9 – ne IDC [947]
SLAVIANSKII MIR – v. 1-2. Spb. 1877-78. B-1895 2 – 8 – ne IDC [073]
SLAVIANSKIIA I RUSSKIIA RUKOPISI RUMYNSKIKH BIBLIOTEK / Iatsmirskii, A I – St. Petersburg, 1905. 1005p, 21 tabs. BR-7286/2 – 8 – ne IDC [460]
SLAVIANSKIIA IZVESTIIA – Spb. 1890-91. Lacking: (1-7, 22) 1890; (40-42) 1891. BR-3765 2 – 8 – ne IDC [073]
SLAVIANSKOE OBOZRENIE – Istoriko-literaturnii i politicheskii zhurnal. v. 1-3. Spb. 1892. B-1896 2 – 8 – ne IDC [947]
SLAVIANSKOE OBOZRENIE – Sbornik statei po slavianovedeniiu. Spb. 1894. B-1897 2 – 8 – ne IDC [073]
SLAVIANSTVO – Bespartiinyi, nezavisimyi zhurnal. v. 1-6. Spb. 1911. BR-3764 2 – 8 – ne IDC [073]
SLAVIANSTVO V RUSSKOI ZHURNALISTIKE 1896-1914 GG / Voznesenskii, S – Ukazatel' statei. Petrograd. 1915. BR-5924 2 – 8 – ne IDC [947]
SLAVIC AND BALTIC CHRONICLE *see* MANY NATIONS
THE SLAVIC AND BALTIC CHRONICLE – (Cont by and filmed with: Many Nations) – v1-45. 1951-62 (complete) – 1r – 1 – ATLA S0723 – us A.T.L.A. [073]
SLAVIC AND EAST EUROPEAN JOURNAL – NSv1- 1957- 1; v15- 5,6; v21- 9 – us UMI [947]
SLAVIC CATALOG OF THE LIBRARY OF THE NATIONAL MUSEUM OF CZECHOSLOVAKIA – 1992 – 117mf – 9 – $990.00 – us Ross [010]
SLAVIC EUROPE / Kerner, R J – (Index) – Cambridge, 1918 – 8mf – 9 – ne IDC [460]
SLAVIC EUROPE: A SELECTED BIBLIOGRAPHY IN THE WESTERN EUROPEAN LANGUAGES, COMPRISING HISTORY, LANGUAGES AND LITERATURES / Kerner, R J – Cambridge. 1918. Index. BR-4876 2 – 8 – ne IDC [947]
THE SLAVIC EVANGEL – Chicago. nos 45-109. 1948-49 (complete) – 1r – 1 – ATLA S0713D – us A.T.L.A. [073]
THE SLAVIC EVANGEL – London. nos 180-223. 1948-51 (incomplete) – 1r – 1 – ATLA S0702C – us A.T.L.A. [073]
SLAVIC PALAEOGRAPHY / ed by Baar, A H van den & Meijer, Hilda – 9 – ne IDC [460]
SLAVISCHE PHONETIK / Broch, O – (Sammlung slavischer Lehr- und Handbuecher, Reihe: Grammatiken) Heidelberg, 1911. Nr. 2. 347p – 8 – ne IDC [460]
DAS SLAVISCHE UND BALTISCHE VERBUM / Stang, C S – Oslo, 1942 – 5mf – 9 – ne IDC [460]
SLAVISCHES ETYMOLOGISCHES WOERTERBUCH / Berneker, E – Heidelberg. 1913. B-1473 2 – 8 – ne IDC [460]
SLAVISCH-GERMANISCHE LEHNWORTKUNDE / Stender-Petersen, A – Goeteburg. 1927. B-1139 2 – 8 – ne IDC [460]
SLAVONIC AND EAST EUROPEAN REVIEW – v. 1-20. 1922-41 – 1 – 129.00 – us L of C Photodup [460]
THE SLAVONIC AND EAST EUROPEAN REVIEW – v. 1-43. London. 1922-1964 65. BR-4237 1 – 490mf – 9 – ne IDC [947]
SLAVONIC BULLETIN – NY City, NY. 1941-1942 – 1r – 1 – $50.00 – R04929 – us Library Micro [460]
SLAVONIC DICTIONARIES AND ENCYCLOPEDIAS – 88 titles – 9 – ne IDC [030]
SLAVONIC NEWSPAPERS ON MICROFILM – Helsinki: Yliopistopaino, 1995 – 9 – fi H.U. Libr [072]
THE SLAVS / Maclear, George Frederick – London: S.P.C.K.; New York: Pott, Young, 1879. (Conversion of the West) – 1mf – us A.T.L.A. [240]
SLAWISCHE LIEBE : DREI ERZAEHLUNGEN / Schubin, Ossip – Braunschweig: G Westermann, c1921 – 1 – us U.W. Library [830]
SLAWONISCHER VOLKSBOTE – Osijek, Yugoslavia. Sept 1936-39 – 1r – 1 – us L of C Photodup [949]
SLEAFORD STANDARD – (Also known as: Lincolnshire Standard (Sleaford Ed)) – 1961-82; Jan 6-Dec 1983; 1986-Jun, Jul 4-Dec 26 1991; 1992-96 – 114 1/2r – 1 – uk British Libr Newspaper [072]
SLEEPING BEAUTY AND OTHER PROSE FANCIES / Le Gallienne, Richard – London, New York: John Lane, The Bodley head, 1900 – 1 roll – 1 – 1-55879-895-1 – uk Libr Preservation [810]
SLEEPING FIRES / Gissing, George Robert – London: T. Fisher Unwin, 1895 – 1 roll – 1 – 1-55879-471-9 – uk Libr Preservation [890]
THE SLEEPY LAGOON MYSTERY / Endore, S Guy – Los Angeles, 1944 – 1r – 1 – $50.00 – C63012 – us Library Micro [978]
Sleeth, Asa *see* THE INFLUENCE OF THE HOLY SPIRIT IN CONVERSION
Sleidanus, Johannes *see* DOS INFORMAZIONES: UNA DIRIJIDA AL EMPERADOR CARLOS 5
Slesser, Henry Herman *see* ORDER AND DISORDER (A STUDY OF MEDIAEVAL PRINCIPLES)
Slevogt, B *see* DIE GROSSFALTER (MACROLEPIDOPTERA) KURLANDS, LIVLANDS, ESTLANDS UND OSTPREUSSENS...
Slicer, Thomas Roberts *see* THE FOUNDATIONS OF RELIGION: A STUDY OF FIRST PRINCIPLES
Slicher van Bath, B H *see* MENSCH EN LAND IN DE MIDDELEEUWEN
Slight, Joseph *see* PAPERS
SLIGO CHAMPION – Ireland. 1867-70, 1885, 1926.-w. 3 reels – 1 – uk British Libr Newspaper [072]
SLIGO CHAMPION – Sligo, Ireland. -d. 1879-1950.62 reels – 1 – PS27.50r – ie European Micro [072]
SLIGO CHRONICLE – Ireland. 1856; 1881, 1883, Jan 1891-Apr 1893. -w. 3 reels – 1 – uk British Libr Newspaper [072]
SLIGO GUARDIAN – or Western Advertiser. Ireland. -w. 26 Jan 1849-31 May 1850. (44 ft) – 1 – uk British Libr Newspaper [072]
SLIGO INDEPENDENT – Ireland. 1856; 1860-70, 1885, 1901; 1920-23. -w. 8 reels – 1 – uk British Libr Newspaper [072]
SLIGO JOURNAL – Ireland. 1 Jan 1828-16 Mar 1866.-w. 13mqn reels – 1 – uk British Libr Newspaper [072]
SLIGO OBSERVER – Ireland. -w. 9 Oct 1828-10 Feb 1831. (1 reel) – 1 – uk British Libr Newspaper [072]
SLIGO STAR – Ireland. -w. 14 Sept 1899-Nov 1902. 2 reels – 1 – uk British Libr Newspaper [072]
SLIGO TIMES – Ireland. 20 Feb 1909-24 Jan 1914.-w. 5 reels – 1 – uk British Libr Newspaper [072]
SLIGO-LEITRIM LIBERATOR – Ireland.30 Apr-11 Jun 1927 – 1 – ie Microforms [072]
SLIKE IZ SLAVENSKE POVJESTI / Klaic, Vjekoslav – Zagreb: Matica Hrvataka, 1903. 177p – 1 – us U.W. Library [460]
SLIKHES IN TAYTSHN – Prague. 1602. BJ-43-112 1 – 9 – ne IDC [470]
SLIKHES IN TAYTSHN – Prague. 1620-57. BJ-43-113 1 – 9 – ne IDC [470]
Sliupas, Jonas *see* KUNINGAS VLADISLAVAS DEMBSKIS
Sliusarenko, O V *see* UKAZATEL' TEKUSHCHEI PEDAGOGICHESKOI LITERATURY ZA 1897 GOD
SLIVENSKO DELO – Sliven, Bulgaria. 1956-69 – 12r – 1 – us L of C Photodup [949]
SLJUCHT EN RJUCHT – Leeuwarden, Netherlands. -w. 6 Feb 1897-27 Dec 1941. Lacking Feb 1899-Jan 1900. 37 reels – 1 – uk British Libr Newspaper [949]
SL-KONTAKT – Stockholm, Sweden. 1943-66 – 3r – 1 – sw Kungliga [330]
Sloan & Adams *see* HISTORY OF ARIZONA
Sloan, Edward L *see* GAZETTEER OF UTAH AND SALT LAKE CITY DIRECTORY 1874
SLOAN MANAGEMENT REVIEW – v1- 1960- 1; v13- 5,6; v17- 9 – us UMI [650]
Sloan, Robert W *see* UTAH GAZETTEER AND DIRECTORY OF LOGAN, OGDEN, PROVO, AND SALT LAKE CITY FOR 1884
Sloane, H *see*
- CATALOGUS PLANTARUM QUAE IN INSULA JAMAICA SPONTE PROVENIUNT
- A VOYAGE TO THE ISLANDS MADERA, BARBADOS, NIEVES, ST CHRISTOPHERS AND JAMAICA

Sloane, Hans *see* CORRESPONDENCE
Sloane, William Milligan *see* THE FRENCH REVOLUTION AND RELIGIOUS REFORM
SLOBODA – Bratislava, Czechoslovakia. 1960-1964 – 3r – 1 – us L of C Photodup [072]
SLOBODNA DALMACIJA – (Also see: Croatia) – Split, Yugoslavia. Mar 1944-1993 (incomplete) – 142r – 1 – us L of C Photodup [949]
SLOBODNA REC – Pittsburgh, PA, 1934-1948 – 5r – 1 – us I.H.R.C. [978]
SLOBODNA TRIBUNA – Zagreb, Yugoslavia. -tw. 1 Dec 1921-31 Dec 1924. 3 reels – 1 – uk British Libr Newspaper [949]
SLOBODNA VOJVODINA – Novi Sad, Yugoslavia. 1945-Jul 1948; Mar 1949-1952 – 8r – 1 – us L of C Photodup [949]
Slobozhanin, M *see*
- NOVYE POSTROENIIA V IDEOLOGII I TEORII KOOPERATIZMA-ARTEL'NOSTI
- SMOTR KOOPERATIVNYM SILAM

Slocum, Bowen & Co *see* HISTORY OF NAPA AND LAKE COUNTIES
Slocum, Charles Elihu *see* HISTORY OF THE MAUMEE RIVER BASIN
Sloet, L *see* OORKONDENBOEK DER GRAAFSCHAPPEN GELRE EN ZUTPHEN
SLOGA – Cleveland, OH, 1915, 1919 – 3mf or 1 reel – 9,1 – us I.H.R.C. [975]
SLOGANS AND THOUGHTS FOR LIBERTY / Zube, John, et al – 1fiche. (24X) – 9 – 1.00f – at Libertarian Micro [320]
Slomkowski, A *see* L'ETAT PRIMITIF DE L'HOMME DANS LA TRADITION DE L'EGLISE AVANT SAINT AUGUSTIN
SLONCE – St. Paul, MN, 1898-1900 – 1r – 1 – us I.H.R.C. [978]
Slooten, T R van *see* DUTCH INTERNATIONAL LAW...
SLOUGH AND LANGLEY EXPRESS *see* SLOUGH EXPRESS
SLOUGH AND LANGLEY OBSERVER *see* SLOUGH ETON AND WINDSOR OBSERVER
SLOUGH ETON AND WINDSOR OBSERVER – (Also known as: Slough Observer; Slough and Langley Observer) – 1889; 1940-41; 1943-Dec 23 1959; 1960-Dec 24 1963; Jan-Dec 23 1964; 1965-76; Jan-Oct, Nov 7-Dec 19 1986; 1987-Jun 1990; Jan-Jun 28 1991-92; 1995-Jun 1997 – 144 1/2r – 1 – uk British Libr Newspaper [072]
SLOUGH EXPRESS – (Also known as: Slough and Langley Express) – 1985-Jun 1997 – 55r – 1 – uk British Libr Newspaper [072]
SLOUGH OBSERVER *see* SLOUGH ETON AND WINDSOR OBSERVER
Slouschz, Nahum *see*
- LA LANGUE ET LA LITTERATURE HEBRAIQUES DEPUIS LA BIBLE JUSQU'A NOS JOURS
- THE RENASCENCE OF HEBREW LITERATURE (1743-1885)

SLOVAK – Munich. DE. Mar 1955-Sep 1964 – 1 – uk British Libr Newspaper [072]
SLOVAK – (Some issues lacking) – Bratislava, Czechoslovakia. 14 Mar 1939-23 Mar 1945 – 7r – 1 – us L of C Photodup [072]
SLOVAK EVANGELICAL CHURCH OF THE AUGSBURG CONFESSION – We imenu Pana Jezisse Poradak swate Passie (In the Name of the Lord Jesus Order of Passion Service, annually conducted by the Slovak Churches in Presspurk, on Palm Sunday and on Good Friday.) 1905 – 1 – us A.T.L.A. [240]
Slovak, John P *see* THE UTILIZATION OF THE 225-TEST T PREDICT ONE REPETITION MAXIMUM BENCH PRESS WITH COLLEGE FOOTBALL PLAYERS
SLOVAK TYZDENNIK – Bratislava, Czechoslovakia. May 1942; Oct 1944 (scattered issues) – 6r – 1 – us L of C Photodup [072]
SLOVAK V AMERIKE – Middletown, PA, 1884-1904, 1905-1938 – 2r – 1 – us I.H.R.C. [978]
SLOVAK V AMERIKE = SLOVAK AMERICAN – New York: John Spevak, 1905-38 – us Res Libr [071]
SLOVAN – Pueblo, CO. 1915 – 1mf or 1r – 9,1 – us I.H.R.C. [975]
SLOVAN AMERIKANSKY – Iowa City, IA. -w. 5 Nov 1869-30 Oct 1889. In Czech. Title varies – 1 – us NE Hist [071]
SLOVANSKA KNIHOVNA, PRAGUE – 368mf – 9 – $5,000.00 – us Ross [010]
SLOVAR' AKADEMII ROSSIISKOI – 6v. Spb. 1789-94. BR-8403/2 – 85mf – 8 – ne IDC [947]
SLOVAR' BELORUSSKOGO NARECHIIA / Nosovich, II – Spb., 1870 – 24mf – 9 – R-8399/2 – ne IDC [460]
SLOVAR' BIBLIOFILA / Arkad'ev, E I – Moscow, 1903. 122p. BR-4654/2 – 4mf – 8 – ne IDC [020]
SLOVAR' BIBLIOFILA T.E. SLOV KASAIUSHCHIKHSIA KNIZHNAGO I PECHATNAGO DELA / Arkad'ev, E I – Moscow, 1890. 88p. BR-5853/2 – 2mf – 8 – ne IDC [020]
SLOVAR' DREVNEGO AKTOVOGO IAZYKA SEVERO-ZAPADNOGO KRAIA I TSARSTVA POL'SKOGO / Gorbachevskii, N – Vil'na, 1874 – 8mf – 9 – R-8390/2 – ne IDC [460]
SLOVAR' DREVNE-RUSSKIKH LICHNYKH SOBSTVENNYKH IMEN / Tupikov, N M – Spb., 1903 – 15mf – 9 – 764/2 – ne IDC [460]
SLOVAR' IAKUTSKOGO IAZYKA / Pekarskii, E K – L., 1958-1959. v1-3 – 66mf – 9 – U-336/2 – ne IDC [460]
SLOVAR' ISTORICHESKII – v1-14. Moscow. 1790-98. B-1898/2 – 137mf – 8 – ne IDC [947]
SLOVAR' ISTORICHESKII O BYVSHIKH V ROSSII PISATELIAKH, DUKHOVNAGO CHINA, GREKOROSSIISKIIA TSERKVI / Evgenii, Mitropolit – v. 1-2. Spb. 1818. BR-5893 2 – 8 – ne IDC [947]
SLOVAR' ISTORICHESKII O BYVSHIKH V ROSSII PISATELIAKH DUKHOVNOGO CHINA GREKOROSSIISKIIA TSERKVI / Evgenii, Mitropolit – Ed. 2. 2 pts. Spb. 1827. BR-6028 2 – 8 – ne IDC [460]
SLOVAR' IURIDICHESKII, ILI SVOD ROSSIISKIKH UZAKONENII, PO AZBUCHNOMU PORIADKU DLIA PRAKTICHESKOGO UPOTREBLENIIA IMP. MOSKOVSKOGO UNIVERSITETA V IURIDICHESKOM FAKUL'TETE / Langans, F – M., 1788 – 4mf – 9 – R-9314/1 – ne IDC [340]
SLOVAR' K SOCHINENIIAM I PEREVODAM D.I. FONVIZINA / Petrov, K – Spb., 1904 – 9mf – 9 – 924/2 – ne IDC [460]
SLOVAR' KRATKOI ENTSIKLOPEDII MEZHDUNARODNOGO PRAVA / Gorovtsev', A M – Spb., 1909 – 5mf – 9 – R-8559/1 – ne IDC [340]
SLOVAR' PISATELEI DREVNEGO PERIODA RUSSKOI LITERATURY 9-17 VEKA / Arsenev, A V – Spb. 1882. B-1081 2 – 8 – ne IDC [460]
SLOVAR' PISATELEI SREDNIAGO I NOVAGO PERIODA RUSSKOI LITERATURY S KARTOI DLIA NAGLIADNAGO OBOZRENIIA / Arsenev, A V – Spb. 1887. BR-5694 2 – 8 – ne IDC [460]
SLOVAR' RIFM RUSSKOGO IAZYKA / Shakhovskaia, L – M., 1890 – 5mf – 9 – 1158/2 – ne IDC [460]

SLOVAR' RUSSKIKH SVETSKIKH PISATELEI, SOOTECHESTVENNIKOV I CHUZHESTRANTSEV, PISAVSHIKH V ROSSII / Evgenii, Mitropolit – 1. M. 1838. BR-5894 2 – 8 – ne IDC [947]

SLOVAR' RUSSKIKH SVETSKIKH PISATELEI, SOOTECHESTVENNIKOV I CHUZHESTRANTSEV, PISAVSHIKH V ROSSII / Evgenii, Mitropolit – v. 1-2. M. 1845. BR-5961 2 – 8 – ne IDC [460]

SLOVAR' RUSSKO-SUAKHILI GAZETNOI LEKSIKI / Kutuzov, A I – Moskow. 1963. BR-2464/2 – 3mf – 8 – ne IDC [460]

SLOVAR' TSERKOVNO-SLAVIANSKOGO IAZYKA / Vostokov, A K – N.p., 1858-1861. 2 vols – 15mf – 9 – R-10372/1 – ne IDC [290]

SLOVAR' UKRAINSKOGO IAZYKA / Hrynchenko, BD – Kiev, 1907-1909. v1-4 – 60mf – 9 – R-8392/2 – ne IDC [460]

SLOVARNYI UKAZATEL' PO KNIGOVEDENIIU / Mez'er, A V – Ed. 2. 3v. Leningrad, 1931-34.1198 cols.; 700 cols.; 814 cols. BR-11,220/1 – 9 – ne IDC [010]

SLOVAR'RUSSKIKH SINONIMOV I SKHODNYKH PO SMYSLU SLOV / Abramov, N – Spb., 1900 – 4mf – 9 – R-8381/2 – ne IDC [460]

SLOVENEC – Ljubljana, Yugoslavia. Oct 1936-Jun 1943 (scattered issues) – 8r – 1 – us L of C Photodup [949]

SLOVENIJA – Cleveland, OH. 1915, 1916, 1919, 1921 – 6mf or 1r – 9,1 – us I.H.R.C. [975]

SLOVENSKA NARODNA PODPORNA JEDNOTA, LODGE NO 5 "NAPREJ" – Cleveland, OH. 1904-1923 – 1r – 1 – us I.H.R.C. [975]

SLOVENSKA OZVENA V AMERIKE – Cleveland: Slovenska Ozvena Pub Co, jan 12 1928-dec 1 1931 – 5r – 1 – us Res Libr [071]

SLOVENSKA POLITIKA – Zilina, Czechoslovakia. Apr 1942-Oct 1944 (scattered issues) – 1r – 1 – us L of C Photodup [072]

SLOVENSKA PRAVDA – Bratislava, Czechoslovakia. Jun 1944-Mar 1945; 3 Jan-21 Mar 1945 – 2r.00r – 1 – us L of C Photodup [072]

SLOVENSKE LUDOVE NOVINY – Pressburg (Bratislava), Slovakia. 1910-1918 – 9r – 1 – us I.H.R.C. [947]

SLOVENSKE NOVICE – Calumet, MI, 1916, 1919 – 3mf or 1 reel – 9,1 – us I.H.R.C. [975]

SLOVENSKE NOVINY : WEEKLY CATHOLIC SLOVAK NEWSPAPER – Cleveland, OH, 23 Dec 1949-24 Dec 1959 – 4r – 1 – us Western Res [071]

SLOVENSKI BRATSTVO – (In English and Slovakian) – Montreal, Canada. v11 n51. 22 dec 1939-v14 n32. 7 aut 1942 – 1r – 1 – Can$35.00 – cn Can Microfilming [072]

SLOVENSKI DOM – Buenos Aires, Argentina, 1932 – 1mf or 1 reel – 9,1 – us I.H.R.C. [972]

SLOVENSKI GLADIATOR – Milwaukee, WI, 1927-1928 – 5mf or 1 reel – 1,9 – us I.H.R.C. [975]

SLOVENSKI GLAS – Buenos Aires, Argentina, 1946 – 4mf or 1 reel – 9,1 – us I.H.R.C. [972]

SLOVENSKI ILUSTROVANI LIST – New York, NY, 1913 – 6mf or 1 reel – 1,9 – us I.H.R.C. [975]

SLOVENSKI LIST – Buenos Aires, Argentina, 1937 – 4mf or 1 reel – 9,1 – us I.H.R.C. [972]

SLOVENSKI NAROD – New York, NY, 1915-1917 – 1 reel – 1 – us I.H.R.C. [975]

SLOVENSKI NAROD – New York, NY, 1916 – 1mf or 1 reel – 9,1 – us I.H.R.C. [975]

SLOVENSKI NAROD – Pueblo, CO, 1908, 1909, 1912, 1915 – 3mf or 1 reel – 9,1 – us I.H.R.C. [975]

SLOVENSKI POROCEVALEC – Ljubljana, Yugoslavia. May 1945-Apr 1959 – 26r – 1 – us L of C Photodup [949]

SLOVENSKI SVET – Washington, DC, 1917 – 2mf or 1 reel – 9,1 – us I.H.R.C. [975]

SLOVENSKI TEDNIK – Buenos Aires, Argentina, 1930 – 1mf or 1 reel – 9,1 – us I.H.R.C. [972]

SLOVENSKO BRATSTVO – v1-. 1947-. Organ of Slovenski Komitet Jugoslavije. -m – 1 – us U.W. Library [947]

SLOVENSKO-HRVATSKE NOVINE – Calumet, MI, 1930 – 1mf or 1 reel – 9,1 – us I.H.R.C. [975]

SLOVENSKY HLASNIK = SLOVAK HERALD : URADNY ORGAN SLOV. EVANJ. JEDNOTY A SLOV. ZENSKEJ JEDNOTY – Allegheny, PA: Slavonic Evang. Union of America, [1908-may 1962] – us Res Libr [240]

SLOVENSKY OBCAN = SLOVAK CITIZEN – (In Slovak) – Hazletonske ed. Hazleton, PA. 1936; 1941-46 – 2r – 1 – $170.00 – D3371 – us Scholarly Res [071]

SLOVI I ZHIZN' = WORD AND LIFE – v1,no.1, 11-12; v2,no.3-4, 5-6. Jun 1921, May-Jun 1921, Sept-Oct 1922. 192p – 1 – 7.68 – us Baptist [073]

SLOVNYTSIA UKRAINS'KOI (ABO IUGOVOI-RUSS'KOI) MOVY. (SLOVAR' UKRAINSKOGO IAZYKA) / Piskunov, F M – Odessa, 1873 – 3mf – 9 – R-8400/2 – ne IDC [460]

SLOVO – Nauchnyi, literaturnyi i politicheskii zhurnal. Spb. (4). 1878-81. Lacking: (3) 1880. B-1899 2 – 8 – ne IDC [321]

SLOVO – Sofia. Bulgaria. -d. 4 Sep 1939-25 Apr 1944. (Imperfect). (6 reels) – 1 – uk British Libr Newspaper [949]

SLOVO – Warsaw, Poland. In Russian. -w. 13 Sept 1936-25 July 1937. Imperfect. 1 reel – 1 – uk British Libr Newspaper [947]

SLOVO A SLOVESNOST – Rost. 1, 1935- .-q. Suspended 1944-46. In Czech. Summaries in English, German and Russian. Issued by Ceskoslovenska Akademie vei. Slovo a Slovesnost – 1 – us U.W. Library [460]

SLOVO I DELO. 1700-1725 / Semevskii, M I – ed. 3. Spb. 1885. BR-7849 2 – 8 – ne IDC [947]

SLOVO I MYSL' / Kalitin, N – O poeticheskom masterstve V1. Maiakovskogo. M. 1959. BR-1321 2 – 8 – ne IDC [460]

SLOVO K NARODU = A WORD TO THE PEOPLE – Pittsburgh, PA, 1943-1944 – 1r – 1 – us I.H.R.C. [975]

SLOVO KAK TAKOVOE / Kruchenykh, A & Khlebnikov, V – Spb. 1913. BR-3602 2 – 8 – ne IDC [460]

SLOVO O MUZYKE / Bal'mont, K D – M. 1917. BR-534 2 – 8 – ne IDC [460]

Slowacki, J *see*
– LISTY
– POEZYE

SLOWNIK GEOGRAFICZNY KROLESTWA POSLKIEGO I INNYCH KRAJOW SLOWIANSKICH – Warszawa. 1880-1902. v1-15(2).B-1234/2 – 399mf – 8 – ne IDC [910]

SLOWNIK GEOGRAFIEZNY – Krolestwa Polskiego. v1-15. 1880-1904 – 6r – 1 – us Ross [910]

SLOWNIK GWAR POLSKICH / Karlowicz, J – 6v. Krakow. 1900-11. BR-5518 2 – 8 – ne IDC [943]

SLOWO LUDU – Kielce, Poland. -d. April 1954-Dec 1958. 13 reels – 1 – uk British Libr Newspaper [072]

SLOWO LUDU – Kielce, Poland. Jul 1952-1992 – 84r – 1 – us L of C Photodup [943]

SLOWO POLSKI – (In Polish) – Montreal, Canada. v3 n43. 22 oct 1932; v3 n44. 29 oct 1932 – 1r – 1 – Can$25.00 – cn Can Microfilming [072]

SLOWO POLSKIE – Utica. N.Y. 1912-1940 – 1 – us UMI [071]

SLOWO POLSKIE – Wroclaw, Poland. 1953-92 – 82r – 1 – us L of C Photodup [943]

SLOWO POWSZECHNE – Warsaw, Poland. Aug 1947-1975; 1977-Jan 1993 – 90r – 1 – us L of C Photodup [943]

SLOWO PRAWDY – (Lacking: n4-6 1966; n1-5 1973; n1-3, 5-6 1975) – 1966-85 – 4r – 1 – ATLA S0765 – us A.T.L.A. [073]

Sluchevskii, K *see* STIKHI I POEMY

Sluimers, B *see* ADAM MALIK; A SKETCH

Slukhovskii, M I *see* BIBLIOTECHNOE DELO V ROSSII DO 18 VEKA

Sluys, D E *see* HANDBOEK VOOR DE GESCHIEDENIS DER JODEN

Sluys, D M *see* DE AMBTSDATA VAN DE OUDSTE OPPERRABBIJNEN BIJ DE HOOGDUITSCHE JOODSCHE GEMEENTE TE AMSTERDAM

SLUYTER'S MONTHLY – (Inter-Ocean). Indonesia. -m. May 1920-Dec 1926. (7 reels) – 1 – uk British Libr Newspaper [073]

SLUZBA ZDROWIA – Warsaw. Poland. -w. Jan 1952-Dec 1958. (4 reels) – 1 – uk British Libr Newspaper [947]

SLUZBENE NOVINE / Yugoslavia – Beograd. On film: Jan 1919-Apr 1941 – 1 – 1035.00 – us L of C Photodup [340]

SLUZBENE NOVINE / Yugoslavia – Kraljevine Jugoslavije. London. v1-20, 10 Aug 1941-25 Oct 1944. LL-0116 – 1 – us L of C Photodup [340]

SLUZBENE NOVINE KRALJEVINE JUGOSLAVIJE – -irr. Broj 1 (19 aug. 1941) – broj 22 (3 marta 1945). London, Eng.: s.n., 1941-1945 – 1 – us U.W. Library [940]

SLUZBENI LIST – Belgrade, 1947-70 – 20r – 1 – us Ross [324]

SLUZBENI LIST / Montenegro – Sarajevo. Jan. 1, 1947-Dec. 20, 1950 – 1 – us NY Public [949]

SLUZBENI LIST / Vojvodina. Yugoslavia – Novi Sad. June 27, 1946-Dec. 1965 – 1 – us NY Public [949]

SLUZBENI LIST SOCIJALISTICKE FEDERATIVNE REPUBLIKE JUGOSLAVIJE / Yugoslavia – (Suppl: 1985(1)-87(4) 202mf Dfl1,221.00. Cont as: Medunarodni Ugovori i Drugi Sporazumi 1954-87) – 1973-87 – 1,814mf – 9 – BH-1112/1 – ne IDC [949]

SLUZHBA BYTA : EZHEMESIACHNYI PROIZVODSTVENNO-MASSOVYI ZHURNAL GLAVNOGO UPRAVLENII A BYTOVOGO OBSLUZHIVANIIA NASELENIIA PRI SOVETE MINISTROV RSFSR I T SK PROFSOIUZA RABOCHIKH MESTNO I PROMYSHLENNOSTII KOMMUNALNOGO KHOZI A ISTVA – (Library has: June 1963-Dec. 1971; missing Nov. 1970) – [Moskva]: Upr., 1963- – 1 – CSUX90-S540 – us Hoover Inst Photo [331]

SM22, EIN ENIGMATISCHES PROTEIN DER GLATTEN MUSKULATUR / Wickel, Marc – 1995 – 1mf – 9 – DM60.00 – 3-8267-2217-5 – gw Hänsel [574]

SMACNA (SHEET METAL AND AIR CONDITIONING CONTRACTORS' ASSOCIATION, INC) – Printed index. Updated every 60 days – 6,9 – us Info Handling [670]

SMALANDS ALLEHANDA – (Editorial pages, 1962-67. 3 reels) – Jonkoping, Sweden. 1879-1950. 203 reels – 1 – sw Kungliga [072]

SMALANDS DAGBLAD *see* SMALANDSTIDNINGEN

SMALANDS FOLKBLAD – Jonkoping, 1957-91 – 1 – sw Kungliga [072]

SMALANDS FOLKBLAD – Jonkoping, Sweden. 1901-56; 1977-78 – 212r – 1 – sw Kungliga [072]

SMALANDSBYGDENS TIDNING – Jonkoping, Sweden. 1979- – 1 – sw Kungliga [072]

SMALANDSPOSTEN – Vaxjo, Sweden. 1866-1978 – 403r – 1 – sw Kungliga [072]

SMALANDSPOSTEN – Vaxjo, Sweden. 1979- – 1 – sw Kungliga [072]

SMALANDSTIDNINGEN – Eksjo, Sweden. 1899-1908 – 8r – 1 – sw Kungliga [072]

SMALANDSTIDNINGEN – Eksjo, Sweden. Vetlandaposten. 1960-62 – 1 – sw Kungliga [072]

SMALANDSTIDNINGEN – (Smalands Dagblad, 1980-87. Tranas Tidning, 1980- . Vetlandaposten, 1980-) – Eksjo, Sweden. 1979- – 1 – sw Kungliga [072]

SMALANNINGEN – Ljungby, Sweden. 1981- – 1 – sw Kungliga [072]

Smalbroke, R *see* A CHARGE DELIVER'D TO THE REVEREND THE CLERGY IN SEVERAL PARTS OF THE DIOCESE OF LICHFIELD AND COVENTRY...IN 1741

SMALL AND MEDIUM SAWMILLS IN DEVELOPING COUNTRIES : A GUIDE FOR THEIR PLANNING AND ESTABLISHMENT – 1981 – 160p – it F.A.O. [670]

Small, Annie H *see* LETTERS TO MISSIONARY FRIENDS

SMALL BUSINESS – (Previous title: Magazine About Small Business. Cont by: Profit: the Magazine for Canadian Entrepreneurs at v9 1990) – Toronto, 1985-86; v6-8. 1987-89 – 9 – Can$37.00y – cn Micromedia [338]

SMALL BUSINESS *see* PROFIT

SMALL BUSINESS REPORT – (1985-. 5,6,9) – v1-. 1976- – 1 – us UMI [380]

Small, Charles H *see* CORNER-STONES OF FAITH, OR THE ORIGIN AND CHARACTERISTICS OF THE CHRISTIAN DENOMINATIONS OF THE UNITED STATES

A SMALL COLLECTION OF VALUABLE TRACTS...HERRING FISHERY... – London, 1751 – 2mf – 9 – ILM-894/1 – ne IDC [327]

SMALL COMPUTERS IN LIBRARIES – (1984-. 5,6,9) – v1-. 1981- – 1 – us UMI [020]

Small, Edwin S *see* A CENTENNIAL REVIEW OF THE BOWDOINHAM ASSOCIATION OF BAPTIST CHURCHES IN MAINE

THE SMALL END OF GREAT PROBLEMS / Herford, Brooke – 1902 – 9 – us A.T.L.A. [240]

A SMALL ENGLISH-TELUGU DICTIONARY : FOR THE TELUGU AND ENGLISH LOWER SECONDARY CLASSES / Holler, P – (Filmed with: Holler, P: Vocabulary to the Telugu Bible) – Rajahmundry: A E L Mission School of Industry Press, 1900 – us Res Libr [040]

SMALL FARM IMPLEMENTS / Hopfen, H J & Biesalski, E – 1978 – 79p – it F.A.O. [332]

SMALL FARMER DEVELOPMENT IN ASIA AND THE PACIFIC : SOME LESSONS FOR STRATEGY FORMULATION AND PLANNING – 1990 – 105p – it F.A.O. [630]

SMALL GRAIN VARIETY REPORT / Alabama. Agricultural Experiment Station – 1955-63 – 1,5,6 – us Spaulding [630]

SMALL GRAIN VARIETY TESTS / Mississippi. Agricultural Experiment Station. State College – 1956-60 – 1,5,6 – us Spaulding [631]

SMALL HYDRAULIC STRUCTURES – 1975 – 2V – it F.A.O. [624]

SMALL INDUSTRY BULLETIN FOR ASIA AND THE FAR EAST / United Nations – Nos. 1-11 – E/F.9 E.37 – 9 (ST/ECAFE/Ser.M/19-29) – us U.N. Pubs [338]

SMALL INDUSTRY BULLETIN FOR ASIA AND THE PACIFIC / United Nations – 74 fiches – 9 – 140.00; 1.90f – uk UNIMICRO [380]

SMALL INDUSTRY BULLETIN FOR ASIA AND THE PACIFIC / United Nations – Nos. 12-22; 24 – E/F.22 E.13 – 9 (ST/ESCAP/Ser.M/30-40; 42) – us U.N. Pubs [338]

SMALL LIFT-IRRIGATION PROJECTS FOR UPLAND CROPS IN MONSOON REGIONS / Israel. Ministry of Agriculture – Submitted to the 31st session of cESCAPn, New Delhi. Feb-Mar 1975. Rehovot. Feb 1975. 11 p – 9 – 2.00 – is I.T.T.I. [631]

SMALL-, MEDIUM- AND LARGESCALE STARCH PROCESSING – 1992 – 339p – it F.A.O. [660]

SMALL PELAGIC FISHES AND FISHERIES IN AFRICAN INLAND WATERS – 1984 – 30p – it F.A.O. [338]

SMALL PRESS – v1-. 1983- – 1,5,6,9 – us UMI [073]

SMALL PRESS REVIEW – Paradise, CA. 1981-82 – 1r – 1 – $50.00 – R02610 – us Library Micro [071]

SMALL PRINTING HOUSES AND MODERN TECHNOLOGY – 1981 – 80p – 9 – 92-3-101637-7 – fr UNESCO [338]

SMALL RUMINANT BREED PRODUCTIVITY IN AFRICA : PROCEEDINGS OF A SEMINAR HELD AT ILCA, ADDIS ABABA, IN OCTOBER 1982 / ed by Gatenby, R M & Trail, J C M – 1982 – 96p – 9 – $7.00 – 92-9053-133-9 – et ILRI [636]

SMALL RUMINANT PRODUCTION AND THE SMALL RUMINANT GENETIC RESOURCES IN TROPICAL AFRICA – 1991 – 250p – it F.A.O. [636]

SMALL RUMINANT PRODUCTION IN THE DEVELOPING COUNTRIES – 1986 – 240p – it F.A.O. [338]

SMALL RUMINANT PRODUCTION IN THE HUMID TROPICS = L'ELEVAGE DES PETITS RUMINANTS DANS LES REGIONS TROPICALES HUMIDES – 1979 – 9 – $9.00 – 92-9053-123-1 – et ILRI [636]

SMALL RUMINANTS IN AFRICAN AGRICULTURE : PROCEEDINGS OF A CONFERENCE HELD AT ILCA, ADDIS ABABA, ETHIOPIA, 30TH SEPTEMBER-4TH OCTOBER 1985 / ed by Wilson, R T & Bourzat, D – 1985 – 9 – $30.00 – 92-9053-138-X – et ILRI [630]

SMALL RUMINANTS IN THE NEAR EAST – it F.A.O. [636]

SMALL SCHOOL FORUM – v.1-. 1980- – 1,5,6,9 – us UMI [370]

SMALL STOCK MAGAZINE – v9-55. 1925-71 – 1 – us UMI [073]

Small, Walter Herbert *see* EARLY NEW ENGLAND SCHOOLS

SMALL-GROUP DECISION MAKING, COMPLEX INFORMATION TASKS / Saks, Michael J – (A jury-focused study) – Washington: FJC, Feb 1981 – 1mf – 9 – $1.50 – LLMC 95-819 – us L.L.M.C. [340]

SMALLHOLDER RUBBER IN INDONESIA / Beery, Lawrence A – SE-10,564 1. 1956 – 9 – ne IDC [380]

SMALL-SCALE CANE SUGAR PROCESSING AND RESIDUE UTILIZATION – 1980 – 61p – it F.A.O. [660]

SMALL-SCALE CASH CROP FARMING IN SOUTH ASIA – 1981 – 93p – it F.A.O. [630]
SMALL-SCALE FISH LANDING AND MARKETING FACILITIES – 1988 – 75p – it F.A.O. [639]
SMALL-SCALE FISHING WITH DRIFTNETS – 1987 – 70p – it F.A.O. [639]
SMALL-SCALE FOREST-BASED PROCESSING ENTERPRISES – 1987 – 254p – it F.A.O. [670]
SMALL-SCALE HARVESTING OPERATIONS OF WOOD AND NON-WOOD FOREST PRODUCTS INVOLVING RURAL PEOPLE – 1988 – 88p – it F.A.O. [634]
SMALL-SCALE POULTRY PROCESSING – 1992 – 117p – it F.A.O. [660]
SMALL-SCALE PROCESSING OF MICROBIAL PESTICIDES – 1992 – 100p – it F.A.O. [660]
SMALL-SCALE SAUSAGE PRODUCTION – 1985 – 136p – it F.A.O. [338]
Smaragdus *see* LIBER IN PARTIBUS DONATI
SMARAGDUS. LIBER HOMILIARUM (SIECLE 10) – Cordoba – 1r – 5,6 – sp Cultura [946]
Smaridge, Norah *see* THE LIGHT WITHIN; THE STORY OF MARIA MONTESSORI
Smart, Benjamin Humphrey *see* A MANUAL OF LOGIC
Smart, James S *see* AMERICAN METHODIST LADIES' ASSOCIATION-ITS CONNECTIONAL CHARACTER
Smart, John Semple *see* JAMES MACPHERSON
SMART MATERIALS AND STRUCTURES – v1. 1992 – 1,5,6,9 – £146.00 – uk I.O.P. [530]
SMART SET – New York. N.Y. 1900-29 – 1 – us UMI [073]
Smart, Thomas *see* GENERAL WOLFE
SME – 1996- – 6r per y – 1 – inquire – us Ross [072]
SME – (Backfile through 1998 $85r) – Slovakia, 1999- – 4r per y – 1 – $320.00y standing order – us Ross [072]
Smeathman, H *see* MEMOIRE POUR SERVIR A L'HISTOIRE DE QUELQUES INSECTES
Smeathman, Henry *see* PLAN OF A SETTLEMENT TO BE MADE NEAR SIERRA LEONE ON THE GRAIN COAST OF AFRICA
Smeaton, John *see*
- CATALOGUE OF CIVIL AND MECHANICAL ENGINEERING DESIGNS
- CIVIL AND MECHANICAL ENGINEERING DESIGNS
- DIARY OF HIS JOURNEY TO THE LOW COUNTRIES

Smeaton, Oliphant *see* THOMAS GUTHRIE
SMEDES AND MARSHALL'S CHANCERY CASES / Mississippi. Supreme Court – (Not a Pre-NRS title) – 1v. 1840-1843 (all publ) – 24mf – 9 – $6.00 – LLMC 95-099 – us L.L.M.C. [340]
Smedt, C de *see* CULTO ANTIGUO DE SAN MASONA METROPOLITANO DE MERIDA
Smellie, Kingsley B *see* THE AMERICAN FEDERAL SYSTEM
SMELTER – Pittsburg. Kan. 1881-1891 – 1 – us UMI [071]
SMENA – (Backfile through 1998 $85r) – Slovakia, 1999- – 2r per y – 1 – $160.00 standing order – us Ross [072]
SMENA – Bratislava, Czechoslovakia. Jul 1953-1966; 1969-71; 1973-Jun 1980 – 34r – 1 – us L of C Photodup [072]
SMENA : DENNIK SUV SZM – (Coll title: Czech/Slovakian Periodicals. Cont. as: Smena. Dennik Mladych. Praha, 1989(Dec 29-30). In Slovak) – Praha, 1971-1989 – 1398mf – 9 – R-15379/1 – ne IDC [320]
SMENA – (Includes c.1: no.1 1919:Dec.18) – Petrograd: Izdvo Peterburgskogo gubernskogo komiteta rossi iskogo kommunisticheskogo soiuza molodezhi, 1919- – 1 – CSUXADM8041-S – us Hoover Inst Photo [360]
SMENA. (GENERATION) – Moscow. U.S.S.R. 1961- – 1 – us UMI [072]
SMENA VEKH – Ezhendel'nyi zhurnal pod red. Iu.V. Kliuchnikova. nrs. 1-20. Paris. 1921-22. BR-8276 2 – 8 – ne IDC [073]
Smend, Rudolf *see*
- KRIEG UND KULTUR
- LEHRBUCH DER ALTTESTAMENT. RELIGIONSGESCHICHTE
- DER PROPHET EZECHIEL
- DIE WEISHEIT DES JESUS SIRACH

Smentsovskii, M N *see* BRAT'IA LIKHUDY. (OPYT ISSLEDOVANIIA IZ ISTORII TSERKOVNOGO PROSVESHCHENIIA I TSERKOVNOI ZHIZNI KONTSA 17 I NACHALA 18 VEKOV)
SMER – Banska Bystrica, Czechoslovakia. May 1955-1964 – 5r (incomplete) – 1 – us L of C Photodup [072]
SMERT' BOGOV / Merezhkovskii, Dimitrii – Iulian Otstupnik. Berlin. 1922. BR-788 2 – 8 – ne IDC [460]
Smet, A J *see* INITIA COMMENTARIORUM QUAESTIONUM ET TRACTATUUM LATINORUM IN ARISTOTELIS LIBROS DE ANIMA. SAECULIS XIII, XIV, XV EDITORUM
Smet, J J de *see* CARTULAIRE DE L'ABBAYE DE CAMBRON
Smetanka, Emil *see* TSCHECHISCH-DEUTSCHES GESPRAECHSBUCH
SMETHWICK TELEPHONE. (WARLEY COURIER.-WARLEY NEWS TELEPHONE) – England. 1941-81. -w. 62mqn reels – 1 – uk British Libr Newspaper [072]
Smets, Wilhelm *see* CANONES ET DECRETA: DES HOCHHEILIGEN, OEKUMENISCHEN UND ALLGEMEINEN CONCILS VON TRIENT CANONES UND BESCHLUESSE
SMHI : SYNOPTISKA TABELLER – Stockholm, Sweden. 1881-1966 – 13r – 1 – sw Kungliga [530]
SMI ETA NA PERIOD... : M.S.R.D., MOSKOVSKII I GORODSKO I PRODOVOLSTVENNY I KOMITET / Moskovski i gorodsko i prodovolstvenny i komitet – (Includes c.1: 1918:May/July) – Moskva: [Komitet], 1918- – 1 – CSUXAKZ2091-S – us Hoover Inst Photo [947]
Smids, L *see* EMBLEMATA HEROICA, OF DE MEDALISCHE SINNEBEELDEN...
Smidt, A de *see*
- DE MINNENDE SIELE GHESCHONCKEN AEN ALLE LIEF-HEBBERS GODTS VOOR EEN NIEUW-IAER
- DE LYDENDE SIELE GHESCHONCKEN VOOR EEN NIEUW-IAER TOT TROOST VAN ALLE BEDRUCKTE
- ONFEYLBARE GHEPEYSEN TER SALIGHEYDT, VOOR EEN NIEUW-IAER TOE-GHE-EYGHENT AEN ALLE VYERIGHE BE-YVERAERS DER SALIGHEYDT, VAN HAERE SIELE
- DE REYSENDE SIELE TOT D'EEUWIGHEYDT VOOR EEN NIEUW-JAER GHESCHONCKEN AEN ALLE LIEF-HEBBERS VAN HAERE SALIGHEYDT
- SINNE-BEELDEN DER DEUGHDEN VOOR EEN NIEUW-JAER GHESCHONCKEN AEN ALLE GODT-VRUCHTIGHE SIELEN

Smidt, Gary L *see* THE COMPARISON OF ACTIVE PLANTARFLEXOR MUSCLE STIFFNESS BETWEEN YOUNG AND ELDERLY HUMAN FEMALES
Smidt, Heinrich *see* HAMBURG UND DIE ANTILLEN
SMILES AND TEARS, OR, SKETCHES FROM REAL LIFE / Barrass, Edward – With introd. by W. H. Withrow. Toronto: Hunter, Rose, 1879. 03380. (Pre-1900 Canadiana) – 9 – cn C.I.H.M. [971]
Smiles, Samuel *see*
- THE LIFE OF GEORGE STEPHENSON, RAILWAY ENGINEER
- A PUBLISHER AND HIS FRIENDS
- SELF-HELP
- THRIFT

Smiley, Francis Edward *see* THE EVANGELIZATION OF A GREAT CITY
Smiley, Sarah Frances *see*
- THE FULNESS OF BLESSING
- WHO IS HE?: AN APPEAL TO THOSE WHO REGARD WITH ANY DOUBT THE NAME OF JESUS

Smiley, Thomas *see* HISTORY OF THE CHEMUNG BAPTIST ASSOCIATION
Smirnov, A *see*
- DEISTVUIUSHCHIE RASPORIAZHENIIA PO KOMMUNALNOMU KHOZIAISTVU
- KAK PROSHLI VYBORY VO 2-IU GOSUDARSTVENNUIU DUMU

Smirnov, N A *see* ZAPADNOE VLIIANIE NA RUSSKII IAZYK V PETROVSKUIU EKOPHU
Smirnov, P *see* ARGENTERIE ORIENTALE
Smirnov, P S *see*
- IZ ISTORII RASKOLA PERVOI POLOVINY 18 VEKA. (PO NEIZDANNYM PAMIATNIKAM)
- SPORY I RAZDELENIIA V RUSSKOM RASKOLE V PERVOI CHETVERTI 18 VEKA

Smising, T *see* DISPUTATIONUM THEOLOGICARUM... TOMUS PRIMUS
Smissen, Betty van der *see* PARTICIPATION IN WHITE WATER RAFTING INSTRUCTION BY ADULTS WITH DEVELOPMENTAL DISABILITIES
Smit, Phillipus *see* DIE BETEKENIS VAN WALVISBAAI AS HAWE VIR SUIDWES-AFRICA
Smith *see* LAND MARKS OF WAYNE COUNTY
Smith, A H *see*
- CATALOGUE OF BANTU, KHOISAN AND MALAGASY IN THE STRANGE COLLECTION OF AFRICANA
- VILLAGE LIFE IN CHINA

Smith, A L *see* A MONOGRAPH OF THE BRITISH LICHENS
Smith, Adam *see*
- ESSAI SUR LA PREMIERE FROMATION DES LANGUES ET SUR LA DIFFERENCE DU GENIE
- INVESTIGACION DE LA NATURALEZA Y CAUSAS DE LA RIQUEZA DE LAS NACIONES

Smith, Alan L *see* EFFECT OF AN ACTIVE ATTENTIONAL STRATEGY ON RUNNING ECONOMY OF LOW ECONOMICAL RUNNERS
Smith, Alexander *see*
- CITY POEMS
- POEMS

Smith, Allen Hart *see* THE NEGRO CHURCH
Smith, Amanda Berry *see* AN AUTOBIOGRAPHY: THE STORY OF THE LORD'S DEALINGS WITH MRS. AMANDA SMITH, THE COLORED EVANGELIST
SMITH AND BATES' AMERICAN RAILWAY CASES – v1-2 – 9 – LLMC 95-118 – us L.L.M.C. [340]
Smith and Elliott *see* ILLUSTRATIONS OF NAPA COUNTY WITH HISTORICAL SKETCH
Smith, Arthur Henderson *see*
- REX CHRISTUS
- THE UPLIFT OF CHINA

Smith, Borden Dodge *see* THE POWERS, DUTIES AND LIABILITIES OF CORONERS AND CONSTABLES.
Smith, Brian A *see* USE OF RATING OF PERCEIVED EXERTION FOR PHYSICAL CONDITIONING
Smith, Brian S *see* ST. HELENA
Smith, C G *see* THE DISPUTED WATERS OF THE JORDAN
Smith, C S *see* HISTORY OF THE AFRICAN METHODIST EPISCOPAL CHURCH
Smith, Campbell *see* GEORGE BUCHANAN
Smith, Charles Edward *see* THE WORLD LIGHTED: A STUDY OF THE APOCALYPSE
Smith, Charles Ernest *see* IN THE HOUSEHOLD OF FAITH
Smith, Charlotte Turner *see* ELEGIAC SONNETS AND OTHER POEMS
Smith, Clinton *see* BOONE COUNTY, MISSOURI DIRECTORY 1921
Smith, Clyde *see* MANDALA AND THE MEN'S MOVEMENT(S) IN THE LIGHT OF FEMINISM
SMITH, CORREL, DIARY, MS 3285 – 1861-1862 – 1 reel – 1 – us Western Res [976]
SMITH COUNTY REFORMER – Raleigh. Miss. 1902-1904; 1919-1953 – 1 – us UMI [071]
Smith, CS *see* GLIMPSES OF AFRICA, WEST AND SOUTHWEST COAST
Smith, C.W., Mortuary, Douglas County, KS *see* UNDERTAKER'S RECORDS
Smith, D *see* THE ROMAN FRONTIER SETTLEMENT AT GHIZA: AN INTERIM REPORT
Smith, D A *see* PERCEPTUAL ESTIMATION AND PRODUCTION OF EXERCISE INTENSITY USING THE BORG CATEGORY-RATIO SCALE
Smith, D H *see* THE BUREAU OF NATURALIZATION...
Smith, Datus C *see* ECONOMICS OF BOOK PUBLISHING IN DEVELOPING COUNTRIES
Smith, Dix W *see* CHATTEL MORTGAGES AND CONDITIONAL SALES IN THE STATE OF NEW YORK
Smith, E W *see* THE ILA-SPEAKING PEOPLES OF NORTHERN RHODESIA
Smith, Edwin William *see* ILA MADE EASY
Smith, Eli *see*
- AN ADDRESS ON THE MISSIONARY CHARACTER
- BRIEF DOCUMENTARY HISTORY OF THE TRANSLATION OF THE SCRIPTURES INTO THE ARABIC LANGUAGE

Smith, Elizabeth Thomasina Meade (1854-1914) *see* A MASTER OF MYSTERIES
Smith, Elizur Yale *see* VITAL RECORDS OF SANDISFIELD MASSACHUSETTS TO 1850
SMITH FALLS RECORD NEWS – Smith Falls, Canada. 1887-1978 – 116r – 1 – $7,540.00 – cn Library Assoc [072]
SMITH FORK BAPTIST CHURCH. WATERTOWN, TENNESSEE : CHURCH RECORDS – Jun 1873-Apr 1974. 1148p – 1 – 51.66 – us Baptist [240]
Smith, Frank Charles *see* COURT TO COURT PROCEDURE, WITH FORMS.
Smith, Frank Hart *see* THE DEVELOPMENT OF A MANUAL FOR RECREATION LEADERS IN SOUTHERN BAPTIST ASSOCIATIONS
Smith, G *see*
- HISTORY OF WESLEYAN METHODISM
- A NARRATIVE OF AN EXPLORATORY VISIT TO EACH OF THE CONSULAR CITIES OF CHINA
- THE NOTIONS OF THE METHODISTS FARTHER DISPROV'D, IN ANSWER TO THEIR 'EARNEST APPEAL',...
- THE NOTIONS OF THE METHODISTS FULLY DISPROV'D, BY SETTING THE DOCTRINE OF THE CHURCH OF ENGLAND CONCERNING JUSTIFICATION AND REGENERATION IN A TRUE LIGHT;...

Smith, G M *see* HISTORY OF DAKOTA TERRITORY, SOUTH DAKOTA, ITS HISTORY AND ITS PEOPLE
Smith, Geoffrey C *see* VALUE ORIENTATIONS OF PRESERVICE PHYSICAL EDUCATION TEACHERS
Smith, George *see*
- THE LIFE OF ALEXANDER DUFF, D.D, LL.D
- THE LIFE OF JOHN WILSON, D.D. F.R.S.

Smith, George Adam *see*
- BISHOP HEBER
- THE BOOK OF ISAIAH
- THE BOOK OF THE TWELVE PROPHETS
- THE CONVERSION OF INDIA
- THE DOCTRINE OF THE PASTORATE, OR, THE DIVINE INSTITUTION, RELIGIOUS RESPONSIBILITIES, AND SCRIPTURAL CLAIMS OF THE CHRISTIAN MINISTRY
- THE FORGIVENESS OF SINS AND OTHER SERMONS
- HENRY MARTYN
- A HISTORICAL GEOGRAPHY OF THE HOLY LANDS
- HISTORY OF DELAWARE COUNTY
- THE LIFE OF HENRY DRUMMOND
- MODERN CRITICISM AND THE PREACHING OF THE OLD TESTAMENT
- SHORT HISTORY OF CHRISTIAN MISSIONS
- THE TWELVE MINOR PROPHETS
- TWELVE PIONEER MISSIONARIES

Smith, George Barnett *see* POETS AND NOVELISTS
Smith, George G *see*
- LIFE AND LABORS OF FRANCIS ASBURY
- THE STORY OF GEORGIA AND THE GEORGIA PEOPLE, 1732 TO 1860

Smith, George H *see* ELEMENTS OF RIGHT AND OF THE LAW
Smith, George J P *see* BEST AND SMITH'S REPORTS
Smith, George Putnam *see* THE LAW OF FIELD-SPORTS
Smith, George W *see* HISTORY OF ILLINOIS AND HER PEOPLE
Smith, Gerrit *see* PETER SMITH PAPERS, 1763-1850; THE GERRIT SMITH PAPERS, 1775-1924
Smith, Goldwin *see*
- THE EMPIRE
- THE FOUNDER OF CHRISTENDOM
- GOLDWIN SMITH PAPERS, 1823-1910
- GUESSES AT THE RIDDLE OF EXISTENCE AND OTHER ESSAYS ON KINDRED SUBJECTS
- IN QUEST OF LIGHT
- NO REFUGE BUT IN TRUTH
- RATIONAL RELIGION AND THE RATIONALISTIC OBJECTIONS OF THE BAMPTON LECTURES FOR 1858

Smith, Goldwin Albert *see* ENGLAND; A SHORT HISTORY
Smith, Gregory *see*
- BONIFACE
- CHRISTIAN MONASTICISM

Smith, Gregory K P *see* AN INVESTIGATION OF THE QUALIFICATIONS OF CONTRACT ADVISORS FOR PROFESSIONAL ATHLETES
SMITH GROVE BAPTIST CHURCH. PICKENS COUNTY. SOUTH CAROLINA : CHURCH RECORDS – (Also, Membership Rolls, 1926-1982. 175p) – 1965-1972 – 1 reel – 1 – $7.88 – us Baptist [240]
Smith, Guillaume *see* NOUVEAU VOYAGE DE GUINEE, DESCRIPTION DES COUTUMES, MANIERES, TERRAIN, CLIMAT, ETC. HABILLEMENTS, BATIMENTS, EDUCATION, ARTS MANUELS, AGRICULTURE, COMMERCE, EMPLOIS, LANGAGES, RANGS DE DISTINCTION, HABITATIONS, DIVERTISSEMENTS
Smith, Gustave *see* LES BEAUX-ARTS
Smith, H *see*
- METHODISTICAL DECEIT
- THE TREATMENT OF CATARACT

Smith, H et al *see* THE STORY OF THE UNITED METHODIST CHURCH

SMITHFIELD BAPTIST CHURCH. JOHNSTON ASSOCIATION. NORTH CAROLINA : CHURCH RECORDS – 1904-19 – 1 – 9.09 – us Baptist [240]
SMITHFIELD BAPTIST CHURCH. KENTUCKY : CHURCH RECORDS – 1802-1978. Lacks Jun 1828-Jan 1888, Feb 1926-Dec 1930. 1244p – 1 – 55.98 – us Baptist [240]
SMITHFIELD ENTERPRISE – Smithfield, NE. -w. May-Jul 1908; Oct 1908-Oct 1911; Jan-Jul 1913 – 1 – us NE Hist [071]
SMITH-KLINE FORUM FOR A HEALTHIER AMERICAN SOCIETY – "Issues for Action". Leaflets for Free Enterprise. 1979 80. 98p. 1 fiche (24x) – 9 – 1.00f – at Libertarian Micro [320]
SMITH'S DIGEST OF CONTESTED ELECTION CASES IN THE HOUSE OF REPRESENTATIVES OF THE UNITED STATES : 1871-1876, 42ND-44TH CONGRESSES / Smith, J M – Washington: GPO. 1v. 1878 – 9 – LLMC 95-126 – us L.L.M.C. [340]
SMITH'S DIGEST OF NATIONAL BANK DECISIONS / Smith, Hal Horace – Chicago: Flood & Co, 1864-98 (all publ) – 4mf – 9 – $6.00 – LLMC 84-393 – us L.L.M.C. [336]
SMITH'S LEADING CASES : EIGHTH EDITION, WITH NOTES AND REFERENCES TO AMERICAN DECISIONS / Smith, John Wilson et al; ed by Hare, J I C & Wallace, H B – Philadelphia: T & J W Johnson. 2v 4pts. 1885 (all publ) – 32mf – 9 – $48.00 – LLMC 95-045 – us L.L.M.C. [340]
SMITH'S LEADING CASES : NINTH AMERICAN EDITION FROM THE NINTH ENGLISH EDITION WITH AMERICAN NOTES TO DATE / Smith, John Wilson et al – Boston: Chas H Edson & Co. 3v. 1888-89 (all publ) – 25mf – 9 – $37.50 – LLMC 95-046 – us L.L.M.C. [340]
SMITH'S REPORTS / Indiana. Supreme Court – (Not a Pre-NRS title) – 1v. 1848-1849 (all publ) – 5mf – 9 – $7.50 – LLMC 95-098 – us L.L.M.C. [340]
SMITH'S REPORTS / New Hampshire. Superior and Supreme Courts – 1v. 1796-1816 (all publ) – 7mf – 9 – $10.50 – LLMC 84-164 – us L.L.M.C. [340]
SMITH'S WEEKLY – Tallahassee. Fl. -w. 1925-1928 – 1 – us P.K. Yonge [071]
SMITHS WEEKLY – 1919-50 – 32r – 1 – A$1,702.00 silver A$1,446.00 vesicular – at Pascoe [072]
SMITHSONIAN – (v6- 1975- 9) – v1- 1970- – 1,5,6 – us UMI [500]
Smithsonian Institution *see*
– INDIAN IMAGES
– NORTH AMERICAN INDIANS
– PUBLICATIONS
– THE THOMAS EAKINS COLLECTION IN THE HIRSHHORN MUSEUM AND SCULPTURE GARDEN
– UNITED STATES NATIONAL HERBARIUM, SMITHSONIAN INSTITUTION VASCULAR PLANT TYPES
Smithsonian Institution. Bureau of American Ethnology *see* SMITHSONIAN INSTITUTION BUREAU OF AMERICAN ETHNOLOGY BULLETINS AND ANNUAL REPORTS
SMITHSONIAN INSTITUTION BUREAU OF AMERICAN ETHNOLOGY BULLETINS AND ANNUAL REPORTS / Smithsonian Institution. Bureau of American Ethnology – 42r – 1 – $3105.00 – us UMI [306]
Smithsonian Institution.Washington, DC. Library of the Freer Gallery of Art *see* DICTIONARY CATALOG OF THE LIBRARY
Smithsonian Science Information Exchange, Inc. *see* INFORMATION SERVICES ON RESEARCH IN PROGRESS
SMITHSONIAN STUDIES IN AMERICAN ART *see* AMERICAN ART
SMITH-TOWNSEND FAMILY PAPERS, 1670-1892 – Massachusetts Historical Society – 1r – 1 – $85.00 – us UMI [920]
SMOKE BELLEW / London, Jack – Illus. by P.J. Monahan. New York: The Century Co., 1912. 1 reel. 1296 – 1 – us U.W. Library [830]
SMOKE GENERATOR OPERATIONS IN THE MEDITERRANEAN AND EUROPEAN THEATERS OF OPERATIONS / U.S. Army. Chemical Corps – 1948 – 1 – 18.00 – us L of C Photodup [600]
SMOKE SIGNALS – 1951-68.U.S. Indian Arts & Crafts Board. Dept of Interior (American Indian Periodicals in the Princeton University Library). 11 fiches – 9 – $50.00 – us UPA [073]
SMOKE SIGNALS – 1956-79.Colorado River Indian Tribes. (American Indian Periodicals in the Princeton University Library). 35 fiches – 9 – $125.00 – us UPA [073]
SMOKE SIGNALS – 1970-74.United American Indians. (American Indian Periodicals in the Princeton University Library).8 fiches – 9 – $45.00 – us UPA [073]
SMOKE SIGNS, FIRE FLAMES – 1969-70.(American Indian Periodicals in the Princeton University Library). 5 fiches – 9 – $45.00 – us UPA [073]
SMOKELESS TOBACCO USE AMONG BIG TEN WRESTLERS AND FACTORS ASSOCIATED WITH USE / Hannam, Susan E & Crowe, James W – 1992 – 2mf – 9 – $8.00 – us Microform Publ [613]
THE SMOKERS COMPANION – New York. v. 1. nos. 1-2,4. v. 2. no. 1. Mar.-Apr., June-Sept. 1927 – 1 – us NY Public [073]
THE SMOKY VALLEY MEMO – Round Mountain, NV. 1982-1983 – 1r – 1 – $50.00 – U04896 – us Library Micro [071]
Smolenskin, M (Smilansky) *see* TOLEDOT AHAVA AHAT
Smolenskin, P *see*
– HA-SHAHAR
– KOL SIFREI
– MA'AMARIM
Smolin, Ioann *see* MECH' DUKHOVNYI V" OGRAZHDENIE OT" SEKTANTSKIKH"
Smolnikar, Andrew B *see*
– EITHER GREAT DESTRUCTION OF HUMAN LIFE AND FINAL MONARCHY...
– LECTURE ON THE DREADFUL ABUSE OF HUMAN MAGNETISM...
– REDEMPTION OF OPPRESSED HUMANITY!
– RESOLUTIONS OF THE CONVENTION OF CHRIST'S MESSENGERS...
– SECRET ENEMIES OF TRUE REPUBLICANISM
– TO THE REFORMERS OF THE UNITED STATES AND ELSEWHERE...
SMOLOSKYP ORGANIZATION FOR THE DEFENSE OF HUMAN RIGHTS IN THE UKRAINE – Ellicott. 39 docs. 1980-1989 – 24mf – 9 – ne IDC [320]
SMOOTH WATER BAY BAPTIST CHURCH. PROVIDENCE ISLAND, COLOMBIA : CHURCH RECORDS – 26 Dec 1934-29 Nov 1954 – 1 – 9.36 – us Baptist [240]
SMOTR KOOPERATIVNYM SILAM / Slobozhanin, M – Spb., 1909 – 2mf – 9 – COR-107/1 – ne IDC [334]
SMOTR RABOCHEI KOOPERATSII NA KONKURSE "PRAVDY" – M., 1928 – 3mf – 9 – COR-361/1 – ne IDC [334]
SMU LAW REVIEW – (v1-38 1947-85 on reel or mf $950.00. v39-49 1985-95 on mf $305.00. Title varies: v1 no 1-2 1947 as Texas Law and Legislation. v2-45 1975-92 as Southwestern Law Journal) – Southern Methodist University. v1-49. 1947-95 – 5,6,9 – $1,219.00 set – us Hein [340]
Smucker, Donovan E *see* SOCIOLOGY OF CANADIAN MENNONITES, HUTTENITES AND AMISH
Smulders, P *see* DE TRINITATE
Smuts, Jan C *see* FREEDOM
SMYCHKA : EZHEDNEVNAIA GAZETA VERKHNE-KAMSKOGO OKRUZHNOGO KOMITETA VKP (B), OKRUZHNOGO ISPOLN. K-TA SOVETOV I OKRUZHNOGO BIURO PROF. SOI UZOV – (Includes c.1: 1928:Apr.8, 27) – Usole: Tip. Okrispolkoma, 192u – 1 – CSUXADM8154-S – us Hoover Inst Photo [331]
SMYCHKA : ORGAN ORENBURGSKOGO GUBKOMA VKP (B), GUBISPOLKOMA I GUBPROFSOVETA – (Includes c.1: 1928:Apr.27) – [Orenburg]: Gubispolkom, 192u – 1 – CSUXADM8122-S – us Hoover Inst Photo [331]
SMYCHKA : RABOCHE-KREST'IANSKII KOOPERATIVNYI ZHURNAL / ed by Gubel'man, M I – (Missing: s2, 1928, No 2 n7-24) – M., 1925 n1-24-1929 n1-24. s2 Smychka. M., 1928 No1 n1-6-1929 n1-24 – 98mf – 9 – COR-689/1 – ne IDC [334]
SMYCHKA GORODA S DEREVNEI : EZHENEDELNYI ORGAN KRASNOSLOBODSKOGO UKOMA V.K.P. (B), UISPOLKOMA I PROFSOI UZOV. SMYCHKA – (Includes c.1: 1928:Feb.29, Mar.9, 17, May 31) – Krasnoslobodsk: "Smychka", 19uu – 1 – CSUXADM8767-S – us Hoover Inst Photo [331]
SMYRNA FIRST BAPTIST CHURCH. SMYRNA, GEORGIA : CHURCH RECORDS – 1884-1974 – 1 – 157.73 – us Baptist [240]
SMYRNA MAIL – Turkey. -f. 23 Sep 1862-21 May 1864. (36 ft) – 1 – uk British Libr Newspaper [949]
O SMYSLE ZHIZNI / Ivanov-Razumnik, R I – (Sologub, Andreev, Shestov). Spb. 1908. BR-1310 2 – 8 – ne IDC [100]
Smysliaev, D *see* ISTOCHNIKI I POSOBIIA DLIA IZUCHENIIA PERMSKAGO KRAIA
Smyth, Charles P *see* OUR INHERITANCE IN THE GREAT PYRAMID
Smyth, Coke *see* SKETCHES IN THE CANADAS
Smyth, E T *see* LETTER TO WILLIAM JOHNSTON FROM E.T. SMYTH, BENTON COUNTY, ALABAMA, 1854
Smyth, Edward Coffin *see* AN ACCOUNT OF THE TRIAL OF EDWARD SMYTH, LATE CURATE OF BALLYCULTER IN THE DIOCESE OF DOWN
Smyth, Egbert Coffin *see*
– THE ANDOVER HERESY
– VALUE OF THE STUDY OF CHURCH HISTORY IN MINISTERIAL EDUCATION
Smyth, Herbert Warington *see* FIVE YEARS IN SIAM, FROM 1891 TO 1896
Smyth, John *see*
– PROPOSITIONS AND CONCLUSIONS CONCERNING TRUE CHRISTIAN RELIGION
– TRUTH AND REALITY WITH SPECIAL REFERENCE TO RELIGION
– WORKS
Smyth, John Paterson *see*
– THE DIVINE LIBRARY: SUGGESTIONS HOW TO READ THE BIBLE
– HOW GOD INSPIRED THE BIBLE: THOUGHTS FOR THE PRESENT DISQUIET
– THE OLD DOCUMENTS AND THE NEW BIBLE
Smyth, Newman *see*
– THE MORALITY OF THE OLD TESTAMENT
– THE ORTHODOX THEOLOGY OF TO-DAY
– THROUGH SCIENCE TO FAITH
Smyth, William Henry *see*
– THE LIFE AND SERVICES OF CAPTAIN PHILIP BEAVER
– THE SAILOR'S WORD-BOOK
Smyth, William Woods *see* EVOLUTION EXPLAINED AND COMPARED WITH THE BIBLE
Smythe, Augustus T *see* LIBRARY CATALOG
Smythe, Sarah Annie *see* LETTERS
Smythe, W Herbert *see* THE INVITATION ANSWERED
Smythe, William E *see* HISTORY OF SAN DIEGO 1542-1908
SMYTHESDALE BOROUGH MINUTE BOOKS – 1861-1904. Book 4 lost. SB1-3 – 3r – 1 – at Corangamite [910]
Smythies, Harriet Maria Gordon *see* IDOLS OF CLAY, A NOVEL
SNABZHENIE DEREVNI SREDSTVAMI PROIZVODSTVA I SEL'SKOKHOZIAISTVENNAIA KOOPERATSIIA / Anisimov, M – M., 1928 – 1mf – 9 – COR-460/1 – ne IDC [334]
SNABZHENIE MOLOKOM KRUPNYKH GORODOV I MOLOCHNAIA KOOPERATSIIA / Litoshenko, LN – Spb., [1910] – 1mf – 9 – COR-62/1 – ne IDC [334]
SNABZHENIE MOSKVY I DRUGIKH BOL'SHIKH GORODOV MOLOKOM / Litoshenko, LN – M., 1910 – 5mf – 9 – COR-63/1 – ne IDC [334]
Snaith. Yorkshire *see* PARISH REGISTERS
SNALLPOSTEN *see* SYDSVENSKA DAGBLADET SNALLPOSTEN
SNAP NEWS – San Antonio. Tex. 1968- – 1 – us UMI [071]
Snape, A *see* THE ANATOMY OF A HORSE
Snape, Anne *see* PROCLAMATIONS, BROADSIDES, BALLADS AND POEMS
Snapp, William L *see* EARLY DAYS IN GREENBUSH
SNAPPY STORIES – v93-105. 1925-27 – 2r – 1 – us Ross [073]
THE SNARLER – St Catherines, Ont.: [s.n., 1870-18–] – 9 – cn C.I.H.M. [073]
SNAR-THAN BKA'-'GYUR – 1980 – 2,404mf – $1,200.00 – us I.A.S.W.R. [280]
SNAR-THANG BKA'-'GYUR – 100v. 2,404 fiches – 9 – $1,200.00 – us I.A.S.W.R. [280]
SNCC *see* THE STUDENT NONVIOLENT COORDINATING COMMITTEE PAPERS, 1959-1972 (SNCC)
SNEAK PREVIEW – v1-4. 1971-74. Continued by: Media Digest – 1 – us UMI [370]
Sneed, S G *see* TEXAS LAND TITLES; AN ESSAY ON DEFECTS IN TEXAS TITLES, AND REMEDIES THEREFOR
SNEEDVILLE FIRST BAPTIST CHURCH. SNEEDVILLE, TENNESSEE : CHURCH RECORDS, 1866-1986 – Also Minutes, 1884-1986. Formerly Greasy Rock Baptist Church and Sneedville Baptist Church. 1930p – 1 – $86.85 – us Baptist [978]
Sneevliet, H *see* HET PROCES SNEEVLIET. DE SOCIAAL-DEMOCRATIE IN NEDERLANDSCH-INDIE
Snegirev, I *see* MOSKVA
Snell, Bernard Joseph *see* GAIN OR LOSS?: AN APPRECIATION OF THE RESULTS OF RECENT BIBLICAL CRITICISM
Snell, Christopher R et al *see* THE ROLE OF PHYSICAL EXPERIENCE IN EDUCATION
Snell, Edmund Henry Turner *see* THE PRINCIPLES OF EQUITY, INTENDED FOR THE USE OF STUDENTS AND THE PROFESSION
Snell, Jessie Kennedy *see* "WRITINGS OF JESSIE KENNEDY SNELL"
Snellen, P C T *see*
– DE VLINDERS VAN NEDERLAND. MACROLEPIDOPTERA, SYSTEMATISCH BESCHREVEN
– DE VLINDERS VAN NEDERLAND. MICROLEPIDOPTERA, SYSTEMATISCH BESCHREVEN
Snethen, Nicholas *see* A REPLY TO AN APOLOGY FOR PROTESTING AGAINST THE METHODIST EPISCOPAL GOVERNMENT
Snethen, Worthington Garrettson *see* THE BLACK CODE OF THE DISTRICT OF COLUMBIA, IN FORCE SEPTEMBER 1ST, 1848
Snider, Cecil A *see*
– THE ATTITUDES TOWARD MORMONISM IN ILLINOIS AS RECORDED BY THE PRESS
– THE ATTITUDES TOWARD MORMONISM IN ILLINOIS AS RECORDED BY THE PRESS FOR THE PERIOD OF 1831 THROUGH 1849
Snigireva, I A *see* ODNODNEVNYE GAZETY SSSR 1917-1983
Snively, William Andrew *see* GENEALOGICAL MEMORANDA
Snodgrass, Gabriel *see* LETTER TO H. DUNDAS AND TO THE COURT OF DIRECTORS OF THE EAST INDIA COMPANY, ON THE MODE OF IMPROVING THE NAVY OF GREAT BRITAIN
Snodgrass, Marjorie P *see* ECONOMIC DEVELOPMENT OF AMERICAN INDIANS AND ESKIMOS, 1930-1967
SNOP – (Lacking: 1973 and some issues) – 1971-92 – Inquire – 1 – ATLA S0589 – us A.T.L.A. [073]
O SNOSHENIIAKH ROSSII S FRANTSIEI / Bezobrazov, P V – Moscow, 1892. 465p. BR-5989 2 – 8 – ne IDC [944]
THE SNOW DROP OR JUVENILE MAGAZINE – Montreal: Lovell and Gibson: John M'Coy; Toronto: Scobie and Balfour. v1-3. 1847-50. ns: v1-5. 1850-53. SEM16P294 – 1r – 5 – Can$29.00 – cn Bibl Nat [073]
SNOW HILL BAPTIST CHURCH. NEUSE ASSOCIATION. NORTH CAROLINA : CHURCH RECORDS – 1850-1927 – 1 – 13.32 – us Baptist [240]
Snow, J *see* ON CHLOROFORM AND OTHER ANAESTHETICS: THEIR ACTION AND ADMINISTRATION
Snow, J F *see* SNOW'S HISTORY OF ADAMS COUNTY
Snow, Susan Eliza *see* LETTERS..
Snowden, Gilbert T *see*
– HISTORY OF SOUTH CAROLINA
– JOURNAL
Snowden, Steven R *see* THE EFFECT OF THE LEAD LEG PLANT ON FACTORS AFFECTING DISTANCE ON KICKOFFS IN FOOTBALL
SNOWDON POST – Montreal, Canada. v1 n18. 2 jul 1958 – 1r – 1 – Can$25.00 – cn Can Microfilming [072]
THE SNOWFLAKE – Miramichi [N.B.: Snowflake Club, 1878-1879] – 9 – cn C.I.H.M. [073]
SNOW'S HISTORY OF ADAMS COUNTY / Snow, J F – Historical and biographical sketches. Indianapolis: B. F. Bowen and Co., 1907. Indiana Reel 3. (The Cox Library Collection) – 5 – us Americana [978]
THE SNOWS OF KILIMANJARO / Hemingway, Ernest – In Indonesian. SE-3444 1. 1951 – 9 – ne IDC [830]
SNYDER BANNER – Snyder, NE. -w. Jan 1908-Oct 1910; Jan 1914-Nov 1925; Nov-Dec 1927; Feb 1928-Jun 1932; Oct 1938-Nov 1942; Jan 1947-Apr 1954 – 1 – us NE Hist [071]

SNYDER COUNTY ANNALS / Wagenseller & Winey – Middleburgh, Middleburgh Post, 1919. Vols. 1-2. Pennsylvania Reel 38. (The Cox Library Collection) – 5 – us Americana [978]

SNYDER COUNTY MARRIAGES 1835-1899 / Wagenseller, George W – Middleburgh, Wagenseller Publishing Co., 1899. Pennsylvania Reel 38. (The Cox Library Collection) – 5 – us Americana [978]

SNYDER COUNTY TRIBUNE – Selinsgrove, PA. -w 1877-1942 – 13 – $25.00r – us I.M.R. [071]

Snyder, Edward Douglas *see* THE CELTIC REVIVAL IN ENGLISH LITERATURE 1760-1800

Snyder, Edwin *see* DIARY

Snyder, Emil William *see*
- KENT'S COMMENTARIES.
- QUIZZER NO. 2...BEING QUESTIONS AND ANSWERS ON CRIMINAL LAW.

Snyder, Gail A *see* DENTAL HYGIENISTS' KNOWLEDGE, ATTITUDES AND INFECTION CONTROL PRACTICES IN RELATION TO AIDS AND AIDS PATIENTS

Snyder, Louis Leo *see* ABAD PEMIKIRAN

Snyder, S J H *see* DIARY

Snyder, William Lamartine *see*
- GREAT OPINIONS BY GREAT JUDGES
- GREAT SPEECHES BY GREAT LAWYERS
- THE INTERSTATE COMMERCE ACT AND FEDERAL ANTI-TRUST LAWS, INCLUDING THE SHERMAN ACT; THE ACT CREATING THE BUREAU OF CORPORATIONS.
- LAWS AUTHORIZING THE INCORPORATON OF CLUBS, SOCIETIES AND ASSOCIATIONS, FOR LITERARY, LIBRARY, SOCIAL RECREATIVE AND SPORTING PURPOSES
- LAWS RELATING TO MECHANICS' LIENS, APPLICABLE TO NEW YORK CITY AND THE COUNTIES OF KINGS AND QUEENS, AND THE CITIES OF THE STATE OF NEW YORK.
- LIEN LAW OF THE STATE OF NEW YORK
- THE NOTARIES' AND COMMISSIONERS' MANUAL, CONTAINING FULL INSTRUCTIONS AS TO THEIR APPOINTMENT, POWERS, RIGHTS, AND DUTIES, UNDER FEDERAL AND NEW YORK LAWS.

SNYMAN COMMISSION – ((Case history)) – 1 reel – 1 – sa Microfile [960]

SO IST DAS LEBEN *see* KOENIG NICOLO, ODER, SO IST DAS LEBEN

SO TAY NQUOI THAM PHAN = THE JUDGE'S HANDBOOK / The People's Supreme Court – v1. 1969 – 2mf – 9 SEL-117/1 – ne IDC [340]

SOAL DEWASA / Mahadi – SE-5397 1 – 9 – ne IDC [999]

SOAL HIDUP ATAU MATI / Sukarno, Pres. Indonesia – SE 1221 1. 1958 – 9 – ne IDC [025]

SOAL INDONESIA. TERDJEMAHAN DAJAT HARDJAKOESOEMAH / Court, Jesaias Frederik H. A. de la – SE-10,307 1. 1948? – 9 – ne IDC [950]

Soaloon, A Sutan *see* PEDAS BELUH. KITAB OGEN MAN DANAK-DANAK SI MBARU ERLADJAR NGOGE HURUP LATIN, IBAS SEKOLAH-SEKOLAH SI MAKE TJAKAP KARO

Soames, Henry *see* THE ANGLO-SAXON CHURCH

SOANE DRAWINGS IN THE VICTORIA AND ALBERT MUSEUM – 2r – 1 – $190.00 – 1-900853-40-X – uk Mindata [720]

SOAP COSMETICS CHEMICAL SPECIALITIES – v1-31. 1925-55.Continues: Soap and Sanitary Chemicals – 1,5,6 – us Princeton Micro [660]

Soar, C D *see* THE BRITISH HYDRACARINA

O SOARES – Maceio, Alagoas. 12 Maio 1898 – 1,5,6 – bl Biblioteca [072]

Soares, J C de Macedo *see* FONTES DA HISTORIA DA IGREJA NO BRASIL

Soares, Theodore Gerald *see* HEROES OF ISRAEL

SOBERANIA – (Includes c.1: v.1:no.2 1946:Nov) – 1 – CSUXADN3421-S – us Hoover Inst Photo [073]

SOBERANIA ARGENTINA EN LA ANTARTIDA : NOTA PRELIMINAR DEL PRESIDENTE DE LA NACION, JUAN PERON / Argentine Republic. Comision Nacional del Antartico – Buenos Aires: Ministerio de Relaciones Exteriores y Culto, Departamento de Cultura, 2nd ed 1948 – 1 – CSUXADH3639-B – us Hoover Inst Photo [320]

SOBESEDNIK LIUBITELEI ROSSIISKOGO SLOVA – v. 1-14. Spb. 1783-84; v. 15-16. 1809. B-1423 2 – 8 – ne IDC [073]

Sobieszek, Robert A *see* BRITISH MASTERS OF THE ALBUMEN PRINT

SOBIRATEL' – Khudozhestvenno-bibliograficheskii zhurnal. (Izd. A.E. Burtsev). Spb. 1910. BR-4334 2 – 8 – ne IDC [010]

Sobolev, A *see* PROTIV RELIGII ZA SOTSIALIZM VO VTORI PYATILETKE

Soboleva, M N *see* EKONOMIKA I POLITIKA VNESHNE I TORGOVLI

SOBORNOST – (Series 3-7 (1947-1978) Dfl266.00) – NS: (1935)-1938) – 17mf – 9 – Dfl60.00 – ne Slangenburg [073]

SOBORNOST INCORPORATING EASTERN CHURCHES REVIEW – v.1-. 1979- – 1,5,6,9 – us UMI [073]

SOBORNYI BLAGOVEST / Sologub, F – "Epokha". Spb. 1921. BR-872 2 – 8 – ne IDC [460]

Sobota, E *see* DAS TSCHECHOSLOVAKISCHE NATIONALITAETENRECHT. (TSCHECHOSL. QUELLEN UND DOKUMENTE. NO. 7)

Soboul, Albert *see* UTOPIAS OF THE ENLIGHTENMENT

Sobral, Maria da Luz *see* FLORECILLAS DE SAN FRANCISCO DE SAN FRANCISCO CONTADAS A LOS NINOS

SOBRANIE DEISTVUIUSHCHIKH DOGOVOROV, ZAKLIUCHENNYKH ROSSIEIU S INOSTRANNYMI DERZHAVAMI – Odessa, 1889-90.3v. BR-9187/1 – 9 – ne IDC [947]

SOBRANIE DOKUMENTOV PO DELU CAREVICA ALEKSEJA / Pogodin, M P – R 8331 2. 1861 – 8 – ne IDC [947]

SOBRANIE DOKUMENTOV SAMIZDATA / ed by Boiter, Albert – (Cont as: Materialy Samizdata Doc nos 3001-6314 Muenchen, 23 September 1977 – 22 November 1988. Register of Documents (Russian version), listing documents 3001-6314 comes as a guide with the microfiches 238mf) – Radio Liberty. Munich. 30 vols – 653mf – 9 – ne IDC [947]

SOBRANIE EPICHESKIKH POEM / Belyi, A – I. Severnaia simfoniia (1-aia geroicheskaia). II. Simfoniia (2-aia, dramaticheskaia). 1917. BR-600 2 – 8 – ne IDC [460]

SOBRANIE GOSUDARSTVENNYKH GRAMOT I DOGOVOROV, KHRANIASHCHIKHSIA V GOSUDARSTVENNOI KOLLEGII INOSTRANNYKH DEL / Russia – 5v. M. 1813-28, 1894. BR-9046 1 – 9 – ne IDC [947]

SOBRANIE GOSUDARSTVENNYKH GRAMOTI DOGOVOROV / Shakhmatov, A A – Entsiklopediia Slavianskoi filologii. Moscow, 1915. v2 (1). BR-10,376/1 – 9 – ne IDC [460]

SOBRANIE I.IA. LUKASHEVICHA I N.A. MARKEVICHA – Opisanie. Moscow, 1959. 144p. Describes collections in the MS division of the Lenin Library. BR-11,005/1 – 9 – ne IDC [090]

SOBRANIE KNIG, IZDANNYKH V TSARSTVOVANIE PETRA VELIKAGO / Petrov, A – Ed. 2. Spb. 1913. BR-4684 2 – 8 – ne IDC [947]

SOBRANIE LIRIKI / Bal'mont, K D – v. 6. M. 1917. BR-537 2 – 8 – ne IDC [460]

SOBRANIE MALOROSSIJSKIH NARODNYH PESEN... – Saint-Petersbourg: Bernarda, [1860] – 1 – F50.00 – fr Armell [306]

SOBRANIE PEREDOVYKH STATEI "MOSKOVSKIKH VEDOMOSTEI" 1863-1887 / Katkov, MN – (A coll of leading articles. See also: Moskovskie vedomosti) – Moscow. v1-25. 1897-98 – 281mf – 9 – R-10584/1 – ne IDC [072]

SOBRANIE POEZ / Severianin, I – 1. Gromokipiashchii kubok. 2. Zlatolira. v. 1-2. M., Petrograd. 1918. BR-1039 2 – 8 – ne IDC [460]

SOBRANIE POEZ / Severianin, I – v. 1-4. M. 1915-16. BR-1038 2 – 8 – ne IDC [460]

SOBRANIE PROIZVEDENII / Khlebnikov, V – v. 1-5. L. 1928-33. BR-928 2 – 8 – ne IDC [460]

SOBRANIE RECHI GG. DEPUTATOV GOSUDARSTVENNOI DUMY 1-GO I 2-GO SOZYVA – Spb., 1908. 576p – 7mf – 9 – ne IDC [320]

SOBRANIE RUKOPISEI I.D. BELIAEVA / Viktorov, A E – Moscow, 1881. 127p. BR-7038/2 – 8 – ne IDC [947]

SOBRANIE RUKOPISEI P.I. SEVAST'IANOVA / Viktorov, A E – Moscow, 1881. 120p. BR-7036/2 – 8 – ne IDC [947]

SOBRANIE RUKOPISEI V.I. GROGOROVICHA / Viktorov, A E – Moscow, 1879. iv/60p BR-7037/2 – 8 – ne IDC [025]

SOBRANIE SLAVIANSKIKH PAMIATNIKOV / Keppen, P & Vostokov, AKh. – St. Petersburg, 1827. BR/10,031/2 – 8 – ne IDC [947]

SOBRANIE SOCHINENII / Fonvizin, D I – 2v. M., L. 1959. BR-6162 2 – 8 – ne IDC [460]

SOBRANIE SOCHINENII / Kapnist, V V – 2v. M., L. 1960. BR-6198 2 – 8 – ne IDC [460]

SOBRANIE SOCHINENII / Senkovskii – v. 1-9. Spb. 1858-59. Lacking: v. 5. BR-10.614 2 – 8 – ne IDC [460]

SOBRANIE SOCHINENII / Solov'ev, Vsevolod S – v6. Izd. Obshchestvennaia pol'za". Spb. 1912. BR-3295 2 – 8 – ne IDC [190]

SOBRANIE SOCHINENII. 1-20 / Sologub, F – Toma 1-12, Izd. "Shipovnik". 1909-12; Toma 13-20, Izd. Sirin-Spb. 1913-14. BR-876 2 – 8 – ne IDC [460]

SOBRANIE SOCHINENII I PEREVODOV / Shishkov, A S – 17 v. Spb. 1818-39. Available: v. 2, 1824. BR-7867 2 – 8 – ne IDC [460]

SOBRANIE SOCHINENII POD. RED. G. P. STRUVE. IZD. IMENI CHEKHOVA / Mandelstam, Osip E – New York. 1955. BR-1164 2 – 8 – ne IDC [460]

SOBRANIE SOCHINENII TOM 7 / Solov'ev, Vsevolod S – ed. 2. Spb. n.d. BR-2141 2 – 8 – ne IDC [190]

SOBRANIE SOCHINENII V 4-KH TOMAKH / Maiakovskii, Vladimir – v. 1-4. M. 1936. Lacking: v. 1, 3. BR-994 2 – 8 – ne IDC [460]

SOBRANIE SOCHINENII V 5 TOMAKH, TOM I / Aseev, N – Izd. Khudozhestvennoi literatury. M. 1963. BR-909 2 – 8 – ne IDC [460]

SOBRANIE SOCHINENII V CHETYREKH TOMAKH / Gumilev, Nikolai Sepanovich – Stikhotvoreniia. v. 1-2, 4. Regensburg. 1947. BR-1154 2 – 8 – ne IDC [460]

SOBRANIE SOCHINENII V ODNOM TOME / Maiakovskii, Vladimir – M. 1936. BR-995 2 – 8 – ne IDC [460]

SOBRANIE SOCHINENII V PIATI TOMAKH / Esenin, Sergei – 5v. M. 1961-62. BR-1058 2 – 8 – ne IDC [460]

SOBRANIE SOCHINENII VNUTRENNIIA OBOZRENIIA, KHRONIKA I DR. STAT'I IZ "OTECHESTVENNYKH ZAPISOK" (1873-1884) / Krivenko, S N – v. 1-2. Spb. 1911. BR-10.595 2 – 8 – ne IDC [460]

SOBRANIE SOCHINENII, VYBRANNYKH IZ MESIATSOSLOVOV NA RAZNYE GODY – v. 1-10. Spb. 1785-93. B-1900 2 – 8 – ne IDC [073]

SOBRANIE STARAIUSHCHEESIA O PEREVODE INOSTRANNYKH KNIG, UCHREZDENNOE EKATERINOI 2 1768-1783 GG / Semennikov, V P – Istoriko-literaturnoe izsledovanie. Spb. 1913. BR-4689 2 – 8 – ne IDC [947]

SOBRANIE STATEI / Gringmut, V A – 4v. M. 1908-10. BR-10.583 2 – 8 – ne IDC [460]

SOBRANIE STATEI, PISEM I RECHEI PO POVODU SLAVIANSKAGO VOPROSA / Pogodin, M P – M. 1878. BR-8332 2 – 8 – ne IDC [947]

SOBRANIE STIKHOTVORENII / Aseev, N – v. 2, 4. M. 1928-30. BR-910 2 – 8 – ne IDC [460]

SOBRANIE STIKHOTVORENII / Esenin, Sergei – 3v. M. 1926. BR-1059 2 – 8 – ne IDC [460]

SOBRANIE STIKHOTVORENII V DVUKH TOMAKH / Maiakovskii, Vladimir – 2v. L. 1950. BR-996 2 – 8 – ne IDC [460]

SOBRANIE STIKHOV / Bal'mont, K D – 2v. M. 1904-05. BR-538 2 – 8 – ne IDC [460]

SOBRANIE STIKHOV / Gippius, Z N – Kniga 1. "Skorpion". M. 1904. BR-724 2 – 8 – ne IDC [460]

SOBRANIE STIKHOV / Gippius, Z N – Kniga 2. "Musaget". M. 1910. BR-725 2 – 8 – ne IDC [460]

SOBRANIE STIKHOV / Gorodetskii, S – 1. Iar'. 2. Dikaia volia. Ed. 2. Spb. 1910. BR-1132 2 – 8 – ne IDC [460]

SOBRANIE STIKHOV / Khodasevich, V – Paris. 1927. BR-700 2 – 8 – ne IDC [460]

SOBRANIE STIKHOV (1883-1903) / Merezhkovskii, Dimitrii – M. 1904. BR-789 2 – 8 – ne IDC [460]

SOBRANIE STIKHOV. (1897-1903) / Sologub, F – M. 1904. BR-877 2 – 8 – ne IDC [460]

SOBRANIE STIKHOV I POEM / Esenin, Sergei – Berlin. 1922. BR-1060 2 – 8 – ne IDC [460]

SOBRANIE UZAKONEII I RASPORIAZHENII RABOCHEKREST'IANSKOGO PRAVITEL 'STRA R.S.F.S.R / Russia. (1917-R.S.F.S.R.). Laws, Statutes, etc – Moscow. 1917-Aug 1938; 1944-45 – 1 – $690.00 – us L of C Photodup [947]

SOBRANIE UZAKONENII I RASPORIAZHENII / Russia. (1920- RSFSR). Laws, Statutes, etc – (RSFSR, Department of Justice, Code of Laws). 1920-1949 – 3 – us Readex [340]

SOBRANIE VAZHNEISHIKH PAMIATNIKOV PO ISTORII DREVNIAGO RUSSKAGO PRAVA / Lazarevskii, I & Utin, Ia. – St. Petersburg, 1859. 428p. BR-11,140/2 – 8 – ne IDC [340]

SOBRANIE VAZHNEISHIKH TRAKTATOV I KONVENTSII ZAKLIUCHENNYKH ROSSIEI S INOSTRANNYMI DERZHAVAMI (1774-1906) / ed by Aleksandrenko, V N – Warsaw, 1906. vii, 585, vi pp. BR-9130 1 – 9 – ne IDC [947]

SOBRANIE ZAKONOV I RASPORIAZHENII / Russia. (1923- U.S.S.R.). Laws, Statutes, etc – (USSR Code of Laws). 1924-1949 – 3 – us Readex [340]

SOBRANIE ZAKONOV I RASPORIAZHENII RABOCHEKREST'IANSKOGO PRAVITAL'STVA SSR / Russia. (1923-U.S.S.R.). Laws, Statutes, etc – 28 v. 1924-37 – 1 – $160.00 – us L of C Photodup [947]

SOBRANIIA D.V. RAZUMOVSKOGO I V.F. ODOEVSKOGO – Arkhiv D.V. Razumovskogo. Opisaniia. Moscow, 1960. 261p. Describes collections in the MS division of the Lenin Library. BR-11,004/1 – 9 – ne IDC [090]

SOBRE EL DERRIBO DE UNA CAMPANA HISTORICA EN BADAJOZ / Barrantes Moreno, Vicente – Madrid: Tip. Fortanet, 2nd ed 1909. B.R.A.H. i. 1877. reimp. 1909. pp. 361-366 – 1 – sp Bibl Santa Ana [946]

SOBRE EL PERONISMO Y LA SITUACION POLITICA ARGENTINA / Codovilla, Victorio – Buenos Aires: Editorial Anteo, 1945 – 1 – CSUXADP3551-B – us Hoover Inst Photo [320]

SOBRE INTERPRETACION / Cheavens, J S – 1911. 296p – 1 – 10.36 – us Baptist [240]

SOBRE INVENTARIO...DEL MUSEO DE BADAJOZ / Informe – Madrid: Tip. de Fortanet, 1898 – sp Bibl Santa Ana [946]

SOBRE LA "ESCUELA NUEVA" / Bayle, Constantino – Madrid: Razon y Fe, 1928 – 9 – sp Bibl Santa Ana [999]

SOBRE LA VIDA Y LA MUERTE / Caba, Pedro – Melilla: Taller Rodriguez Impresor, 1953. vol 3 de la coleccion "Mirto y Laurel" – sp Bibl Santa Ana [830]

SOBRE LAS CITAMAS EXTREMENAS / Roso de Luna, Mario – Madrid: Fortanet, 1904. B.R.A.H. 45, 1904, pp. 507-510 – sp Bibl Santa Ana [946]

SOBRE LAS MUERTES CAUSADAS EN LA POBLACION CIVIL POR LA REVOLUCION COMUNISTA ESPANOLA / Muntadas, V – Sevilla, 1938. Fiche W 1066. (Blodgett Collection of Spanish Civil War Pamphlets) – 9 – us H.U. College Libr [946]

Sobrevida, M *see* HISTORIA DE LAS MISIONES

Sobrino, Francisco *see* EL CICLO DEL CERDO EN ESPANA. INVESTIGACIONES SOBRE LAS FLUCTUACIONES DE LA PRODUCCION Y DE LOS PRECIOS DESDE 1939 A 1956 POR...Y..., BAJO LA DIRECCION DE GASPAR GONZALEZ

Sobukwe, Robert Mangaliso *see* MATERIALS RELATING TO THE APPEALS OF ROBERT M SOBUKWE AND SHANTAVOTHIE NAIDOO, AND THE MINISTER OF JUSTICE (RESPONDENT) TO THE END OF OBTAINING EXIT PERMITS FROM THE REPUBLIC OF SOUTH AFRICA

THE SO-CALLED EGYPTIAN CHURCH ORDER AND DERIVED DOCUMENTS / Connolly, R H – Cambridge, 1916 – 4mf – 9 – Dfl13.00 – ne Slangenburg [240]

Socard, Emile *see* DICTIONNAIRE TOPOGRAPHIQUE DU DEPARTEMENT DE L'AUBE

SOCCER CORNER – (v.3-. 1979- 5,6,9) – 1974- – 1 – us UMI [073]

SOCCER DIGEST – v. 1- 1978- – 1,5,6,9 – us UMI [790]

Socha, M L *see* COMPARISON OF TOTAL PERIPHERAL RESISTANCE AND BLOOD VELOCITY AS OBTAINED FROM DOPPLER ULTRASOUND WAVEFORMS DURING REST, EXERCISE AND RECOVERY

SOCHINENIIA / Ablesimov, A O – St Petersburg, 1849. 164p – 8 – BR-5975 2 – ne IDC [890]

SOCHINENIIA / Chulkov, M D – v. 1. Spb. 1913. BR-6012 2 – 8 – ne IDC [460]

SOCHINENIIA / Dmitriev, I I – 2v. Spb. 1893. BR-6014 2 – 8 – ne IDC [947]

SOCHINENIIA / Ekaterina 2 – Proizvedeniia literaturnyia. Izd. A. F. Marksa. Spb. 1893. BR-6024 – 8 – ne IDC [460]
SOCHINENIIA / Eshevskii, S V – v. 1-3. M. 1870. BR-6026 2 – 8 – ne IDC [460]
SOCHINENIIA / Gorchakov, D P – Moscow, 1890. BR-6035-2 – 8 – ne IDC [460]
SOCHINENIIA / Karamzin, N M – 3v. Spb. 1848. BR-6045 2 – 8 – ne IDC [460]
SOCHINENIIA / Karamzin, N M – Stikhotvorenia. v. 1. Petrograd. 1917. BR-6049 2 – 8 – ne IDC [947]
SOCHINENIIA / Karamzin, Nikolai M – Ed. 3. 9 v. M. 1820. BR-6044 2 – 8 – ne IDC [460]
SOCHINENIIA / Kireev, A A – Spb. 1912. BR-10.586 2 – 8 – ne IDC [460]
SOCHINENIIA / Kniazhnin, Ia. B – Spb. 2v. 1847 – 8 – BR-6057 2 – ne IDC [890]
SOCHINENIIA / Longinov, M N – v. 1. 1915. BR-7662 2 – 8 – ne IDC [460]
SOCHINENIIA / Murav'ev, M N – Spb. 2v. 1847 – 8 – BR-7717-2 – ne IDC [890]
SOCHINENIIA / Plekhanov, Georgi Valentinovich – Moscow. 24v. 1923-27 – 1 – 69.00 – us L of C Photodup [335]
SOCHINENIIA / Pogodin, M P – v. 4. M. 1874. BR-8333 2 – 8 – ne IDC [947]
SOCHINENIIA / Remizov, A – Izd. Shipovnik i Sirin: St. Petersburg, 1910-12. v1-8. Lacking v1. BR-846 2 – 8 – ne IDC [460]
SOCHINENIIA / Spasovich, V D – Ed 2. Spb. v1-10. 1913 – 9 – BR-10 629 1 – ne IDC [890]
SOCHINENIIA GOSIZDAT / Trotskii, L – Moscow. 1925-27 – 1 – us UMI [335]
SOCHINENIIA I PEREVODY / Lukin, Vl & El'chaninov, BE – Spb. 1868. BR-7666 2 – 8 – ne IDC [460]
SOCHINENIIA I' PEREVODY / Barkov, I S – St. Petersburg, 1872. v, 308p. BR-5983 2 – 8 – ne IDC [460]
SOCHINENIIA I PEREVODY, IZDAVAEMYE ROSSIISKOI AKADEMIEIU – v1-7. Spb. 1805-23. B-1901 2. Lacking: v7 1823 – 8 – ne IDC [947]
SOCHINENIIA I PEREVODY K POL'ZE I UVESELENIIU SLUZHASHCHIIA – v. 7-16. Spb. 1758-62. BR-3803 2 – 8 – ne IDC [073]
SOCHINENIIA I PIS'MA / Chaadaev, Pla – Moscow, 1913-14.v1-2. BR-10,562/1 – 9 – ne IDC [947]
SOCHINENIIA I PIS'MA / Khemnitser, II – Spb. 1873. BR-6004 2 – 8 – ne IDC [460]
SOCHINENIIA IMPERATRITSY EKATERINY 2. NA OSNOVANII PODLINNYKH RUKOPISEI / ed by Pypin, A N – v1-12. Spb. 1901-7. Lacking: v6, v11-12. BR-10,533 2 – 8 – ne IDC [947]
SOCHINENIIA IMPERATRITSY EKATERINY 2 NA OSNOVANII PODLINNYKH RUSKOPISEI S OB"IASNITEL'NIMI PRIMECHANIIAMI A. N. PYPINA / Ekaterina 2 – v. 1-12 (v. 6 never pub.). Spb. 1901-07. BR-6025 2 – 8 – ne IDC [947]
SOCHINENIIA, PIS'MA I IZBRANNYE PEREVODY / Kantemir, A D – 2v. Spb. 1867-68. BR-6042 2 – 8 – ne IDC [460]
SOCHINENIIA POD. RED. G.P. STRUVE / Pasternak, B – v. 1-3. Ann Arbor. 1961. BR-1018 2 – 8 – ne IDC [460]
SOCHINENIIA V 2 TOMAKH / Esenin, Sergei – 2v. M. 1955. BR-1061 2 – 8 – ne IDC [460]
SOCHINENIIA V ODNOM TOME / Maiakovskii, Vladimir – M. 1940. BR-997 2 – 8 – ne IDC [460]
SOCHTENNYE DNI / Sologub, F – Revel'. 1921. BR-878 2 – 8 – ne IDC [460]
SOCIAAL KOMPAS – 's-Gravenhage. 1954-55. BH-1799 1 – 9 – ne IDC [310]
SOCIAAL SPECTRUM VAN INDONESIE – (Formerly published as: Sociaal Spectrum van de Archipel) – Batavia, 1948-49. v2(3-12)-3(1-6). Lacking: 1948(9) – 15mf – 9 – SE-567/1 – ne IDC [306]
Sociaal-Democratische Arbeiderspartij *see* HET VOLK
SOCIAL ACTION – v1-22. 1935-Jun 1956 (complete) – 4r – 1 – ATLA S0002 – us A.T.L.A. [073]
SOCIAL ACTION NEWSLETTER – 1937-84 (complete) – 4r – 1 – ATLA S0142 – us A.T.L.A. [073]
THE SOCIAL AND CIVIL STATUS OF WOMAN / Cox, William M – The Presbyterian Quarterly, v9, Oct 1895, p584-606 – 9 – us A.T.L.A. [240]
SOCIAL AND ECONOMIC ADMINISTRATION – v4-12. 1970-78 – 1 – us UMI [650]
SOCIAL AND ECONOMIC CONDITIONS OF THE BRITISH PROVINCES AFTER THE CANADIAN REBELLIONS 1838-40 / Bourinot, John George – 1900? 03813. (Pre-1900 Canadiana) – 9 – cn C.I.H.M. [971]
THE SOCIAL AND ECONOMIC STRUCTURE OF BRITAIN: NATIONAL AND LOCAL DIRECTORIES, 1781-1914 – (Part 1: The Bailey, Tunnicliff, Universal British, and Holden and Underhill Directories) – Series 1: The National and General Directories from the Guildhall Library, London – 9 – us Primary [300]
SOCIAL AND ETHICAL INTERPRETATIONS IN MENTAL DEVELOPMENT : A STUDY IN SOCIAL PSYCHOLOGY / Baldwin, James Mark – New York: Macmillan, 1902 – 2mf – us A.T.L.A. [302]
SOCIAL AND LABOUR BULLETIN / International Labour Organisation – (Includes a printed index for 1974-80) – 1974-1992 – 17 – Sfr1,000.00 – 92-2-108928-2 – sz I.L.O. [331]
SOCIAL AND POLITICAL AFFAIRS IN THE AGE OF THE TUDORS – The Talbot Papers from Lambeth Palace Library, London – 1 – us Primary [941]
THE SOCIAL AND POLITICAL STATUS OF WOMEN, SERIES 1 – (Part 1: 1870-1928. Part 2: 1858-1936. Part 3: Women Workers' Quarterly Magazine, 1891-1923; Anti-Suffrage Review, 1908-19; The Freewoman, 1911-12; and four other titles, 1870-1930) – Rare political, reforming and professional journals for and by women – 1 – us Primary [305]
THE SOCIAL AND POLITICAL STATUS OF WOMEN, SERIES 2 – (Part 2: The English Woman's Review and Drawing Room Journal, 1857-59; Myra's Journal of Dress and Fashion, 1875-1912. Part 3: The Ladies' Pocket Magazine, 1826-39; The Ladies' Treasury, 1858-95, and others. Part 4: La Belle Assemblee and continuations, 1806-47; The Lady's Monthly Museum, 1798-1811; The Ladies' Museum, 1829-32) – Popular women's magazines. Part 1: Woman, 1890-1912 – 1 – us Primary [305]
SOCIAL ASPECTS OF CHRISTIAN MORALITY / Bruce, Wiliam S – London: Hodder and Stoughton, 1905 – 1mf – us A.T.L.A. [240]
SOCIAL ASPECTS OF CHRISTIANITY : AND OTHER ESSAYS / Ely, Richard Theodore – New York: T.Y. Crowell, c1889 – 1mf – us A.T.L.A. [240]
SOCIAL ASPECTS OF CHRISTIANITY, AND OTHER ESSAYS / Ely, Richard Theodore – New York: T.Y. Crowell & Co., (c1889). x,1 leaf, 132p. Reprinted in part from various periodicals – 1 – us U.W. Library [240]
THE SOCIAL ASPECTS OF FOREIGN MISSIONS / Faunce, William Herbert Perry – New York: Methodist Book Concern, c1914 – 1mf – us A.T.L.A. [240]
SOCIAL ASPECTS OF SPORT PARTICIPATION OF SWEDISH ATHLETES WITH DISABILITIES : A PILOT STUDY / Johannson, J-O – 1991 – 2mf – 9 – $8.00 – us Microform Publ [150]
SOCIAL ASPECTS OF THE QUAKER FAITH / Grubb, Edward – (Includes bibliographical references) – London: Headley, 1899 – 1mf – 9 – 0-8370-8820-8 – 1986-2820 – us A.T.L.A. [240]
SOCIAL BEHAVIOR AND PERSONALITY – v1- 1973- 1; v3- 5,6,9 – us UMI [300]
SOCIAL BEHAVIOUR AND VOCALISATIONS OF AUSTRALIAN MAGPIE LARKS IN SOUTH-WESTERN AUSTRALIA / Tingay, Susan – (PhD Thesis) – 1981 – 9 – A$15.00 – at R.A.O.U. [590]
SOCIAL BEHAVIOUR OF THE NEW HOLLAND HONEYEATER / Rooke, Ian – (PhD Thesis) – 1979 – microfiche – A$15.00 – at R.A.O.U. [590]
SOCIAL CASEWORK – v1- 1920- 1; v49- 5,6,9 – us UMI [300]
SOCIAL CASEWORK *see* FAMILIES IN SOCIETY
SOCIAL CHANGE: IDEAS AND APPLICATION – v1- 1971- 1; v8- 5,6,9 – us UMI [300]
SOCIAL CHRISTIANITY IN THE ORIENT : THE STORY OF A MAN, A MISSION AND A MOVEMENT / Clough, John Everett – New York: Macmillan, 1914 – 1mf – us A.T.L.A. [240]
SOCIAL COGNITION – v1-. 1982- – 1,5,6,9 – us UMI [073]
SOCIAL COLLECTIONS IN THE TAMIMENT LIBRARY – 1872-1956. An inside view of American Socialist Organizations. 68 reels – 1 – us UMI [080]
SOCIAL CONDITION, BELIEFS, AND LINGUSTIC RELATIONSHIP OF THE TLINGIT INDIANS / Swanton, J R – BN 410 2. 1908 – 8 – ne IDC [306]
THE SOCIAL CONSTRUCTION OF LEISURE FOR WOMEN IN ACADEME : A GROUNDED THEORY OF MEANING / Gruver, BM – 1991 – 2mf – 9 – $8.00 – us Microform Publ [790]
SOCIAL CREDIT – The official organ of the Social Credit Secretariat. London. -w. 17 Aug 1934-21 Apr 1939. (4 reels) – 1 – uk British Libr Newspaper [073]
SOCIAL DEMOCRACY, DOES IT MEAN DARKNESS OR LIGHT? : A SUMMARY OF THE WORKS OF HERMANN KUTTER / Heath, Richard – Letchworth: Garden City Press, 1910 – 1mf – us A.T.L.A. [320]
SOCIAL DEMOCRAT – Haverhill. Mass. 1900-1901 – 1 – us UMI [071]
THE SOCIAL DEMOCRAT – A Monthly Socialist Review. v. 1-15. 1897-1911 – 1 – 81.00 – us L of C Photodup [335]
SOCIAL DEMOCRAT, 1897-1911 : A MONTHLY SOCIALIST REVIEW – v1-15 (all publ) – 4r – 1 – $255.00 – us UPA [335]
SOCIAL DEMOCRAT, 1944-1955 – v1-5 (all publ) – 1r – 1 – $65.00 – us UPA [335]
SOCIAL DEMOCRATIC FEDERATION / Social Democratic Federation and British Socialist Party. Great Britain – Pamphlets and Leaflets from 1883-1931 – 1 – us Primary [360]
Social Democratic Federation and British Socialist Party. Great Britain *see* SOCIAL DEMOCRATIC FEDERATION
SOCIAL DEMOCRATIC HERALD / Social Democratic Party – v1-16, no. 21 (all publ). 1898-1913 – 5r – 1 – $580.00 – us UPA [335]
Social Democratic Labor Party. Russia *see* VPERED
Social Democratic Party *see*
– SDP NEWS
– SOCIAL DEMOCRATIC HERALD
SOCIAL DEMOKRATS – Riga, 1918-34 – 21r – 1 – inquire – us Ross [072]
SOCIAL DEMOKRATS – Riga, De 1918 a 1934 – 9r – 1 – Sfr1,080.00 – sz Infoprint [320]
A SOCIAL DEPARTURE: HOW ORTHODOCIA AND I WENT AROUND THE WORLD BY OURSELVES / Duncan, Sara Jeannette – With 111 illustrations by F. H. Townsend. London: Chatto & Windus, 1890. 05296. (Pre-1900 Canadiana) – 9 – cn C.I.H.M. [910]
SOCIAL DEVELOPMENT IN THE GEZIRA, 1950-1960 / Sudan. Gezira Board – 1961? – 9 – ne IDC [338]
SOCIAL DEVELOPMENT OVERVIEW – (Publ irregularly from 1991/92 on) – Ottawa. v1-8. 1983/84-1990/91; 1991/92 – 9 – Can$20.00y – cn Micromedia [303]
SOCIAL DUTIES FROM THE CHRISTIAN POINT OF VIEW : A TEXTBOOK FOR THE STUDY OF SOCIAL PROBLEMS / Henderson, Charles Richmond – Chicago: University of Chicago Press, 1909 – 1mf – us A.T.L.A. [240]
SOCIAL ECONOMIST : INDUSTRIAL PARTNERSHIPS' RECORD AND COOPERATIVE REVIEW – v1-3. 1-31 (all publ). 1867-1869 – 1 reel – 1 – $65.00 – us UPA [335]
SOCIAL EDUCATION – v1- 1937- 1; v35- 5,6; v39- 9 – us UMI [370]
SOCIAL ELEMENTS : INSTITUTIONS, CHARACTER, PROGRESS / Henderson, Charles Richmond – New York: Scribner, 1898 – 1mf – us A.T.L.A. [306]
SOCIAL ENGINEERING: A RECORD OF THINGS DONE BY AMERICAN INDUSTRIALISTS EMPLOYING UPWARDS OF ONE AND ONE-HALF MILLION OF PEOPLE / Tolman, William Howe – Introd. by Andrew Carnegie. New York: McGraw Pub. Co., 1909. viii,384p. Plates – 1 – us U.W. Library [331]
SOCIAL ENGLAND IN THE FIFTEENTH CENTURY : A STUDY OF THE EFFECTS OF ECONOMIC CONDITIONS / Abram, A – London: G.Routledge; New York: E.P. Dutton, 1909. (The Research library) – 1mf – us A.T.L.A. [941]
SOCIAL ETIQUETTE, OR, MANNERS AND CUSTOMS OF POLITE SOCIETY: CONTAINING RULES OF ETIQUETTE FOR ALL OCCASIONS.. / Cooke, Maud C – London: McDermid & Logan, 1896. 00092. (Pre-1900 Canadiana) – 9 – cn C.I.H.M. [971]
SOCIAL EVILS OF THE NON-CHRISTIAN WORLD / Dennis, James Shepard – New York: Student Volunteer Movement for Foreign Missions, c 1898 – 1mf – us A.T.L.A. [240]
SOCIAL FACTS AND FORCES : THE FACTORY, THE LABOR UNION, THE CORPORATION, THE RAILWAY, THE CITY, THE CHURCH / Gladden, Washington – New York: G.P. Putnam, 1897 – 1mf – us A.T.L.A. [303]
SOCIAL FORCES – 1975- – 9 – us UMI [073]
SOCIAL FORCES – v. 1-23. 1922-1944 – 1 – us Princeton Micro [360]
SOCIAL FORCES – (v. 47- 1968- 5,6. v. 54- 1975- 9) – v. 1- 1922- – 1 – us UMI [300]
SOCIAL FRANCE AT THE TIME OF PHILIP AUGUSTUS / Luchaire, Achille – New York: H. Holt, 1912 – 2mf – us A.T.L.A. [240]
SOCIAL FUNCTION OF RELIGIOUS BELIEF / Elwang, William Wilson – Columbia: University of Missouri, 1908. 1 fiche – 9 – us A.T.L.A. [240]
THE SOCIAL FUNCTION OF RELIGIOUS BELIEF / Elwang, William Wilson – Columbia, MO:Uni of Missouri, 1908 – 1mf – 9 – 0-8370-3060-9 – 1985-1060 – us A.T.L.A. [230]
THE SOCIAL GOSPEL (CCC341) = SHE-HRI FU-YIN / Wu, Yao-tsung – (In Chinese) – [s.l: s.n, 1934] – 1r – 1 – 1984-6680 – us A.T.L.A. [220]
SOCIAL HELP FOR WAR EMIGRANTS – n.p., 193? Fiche W1162. (Blodgett Collection of Spanish Civil War Pamphlets) – 9 – us H.U. College Libr [946]
SOCIAL HINTS FOR YOUNG CHRISTIANS : IN THREE SERMONS / Crosby, Howard – New York: Broughton & Wyman, 1866 – 1mf – 9 – 0-8370-7376-6 – 1986-1376 – us A.T.L.A. [240]
SOCIAL HISTORY OF PROPERTY AND POSSESSIONS – Part 1: Inventories and wills, including Renaissance Library Catalogues, from the Bodleian Library, Oxford, 1436-1813 – 1 – us Primary [360]
SOCIAL HISTORY OF THE UNITED STATES : HOW THE COMIC ARTISTS SAW US / Weitenkampf, Frank – 1953 – 1r – 1 – us Ross [975]
SOCIAL HISTORY OF THE UNITED STATES: HOW THE COMIC ARTISTS SAW US / Weitenkampf, Frank – 1 – us NY Public [970]
SOCIAL IDEALS IN ENGLISH LETTERS / Scudder, Vida Dutton – Boston: Houghton Mifflin, c1898 – 1mf – us A.T.L.A. [321]
SOCIAL IDENTITIES – 1995, Vol 1 – £75.00 – uk Carfax [301]
SOCIAL IMPACT FOUNDATION – Manila. 123 docs. 1980-1991 – 75mf – 9 – ne IDC [320]
SOCIAL IMPACT FOUNDATION (IMPACT) – Manila. 87 docs. 1980-88 – 47mf – 9 – HRD-526/1 – ne IDC [360]
SOCIAL IMPLICATIONS OF THE SCIENTIFIC AND TECHNOLOGICAL REVOLUTION : A UNESCO SYMPOSIUM – 1981 – 408p – 9 – 92-3-101664-4 – fr UNESCO [306]
SOCIAL INDICATORS RESEARCH – (v14-. 1984-. 5,6,9) – v1-. May 1974- – 1 – us UMI [073]
SOCIAL INSURANCE IN THE KINGDOM OF LIBYA / International Labour Office. International Social Security Association – (International Social Security Review). v. 20. Geneva. 1967. Wasfy, M. BNE-1405 1 – 9 – ne IDC [310]
SOCIAL ISSUES OF BAPTISTS – 1914-30. Misc. reel of articles from books, periodicals and annuals. 350p – 1 – 12.25 – us Baptist [240]
SOCIAL JUSTICE RESEARCH – v1-7. 1987-94 – 1,5 – $80.00v – us UMI [340]
SOCIAL JUSTICE REVIEW – v33- . 1940- – 1 – us UMI [073]
THE SOCIAL LAW OF SERVICE / Ely, Richard Theodore – 1896 – 1 – us A.T.L.A. [300]
THE SOCIAL LAWS OF THE QURAN / Roberts, R – 1925 – 3mf – 8 – ne Slangenburg [260]
SOCIAL LEGISLATION INFORMATION SERVICE, BULLETIN *see* WASHINGTON BULLETIN
SOCIAL LIFE AT ROME IN THE AGE OF CICERO / Fowler, William Warde – New York: Macmillan, 1909 – 1mf – us A.T.L.A. [306]
SOCIAL LIFE OF THE ESKIMO OF ST LAWRENCE ISLAND / Moore, R D – BN 318 2. 1923 – 8 – ne IDC [306]

SOCIAL LOAFING AND CREW : THE EFFECTS OF ATHLETE IDENTIFIABILITY ON GROUP PERFORMANCE / Stroope, Sandra L & Gould, Daniel R – 1992 – 1mf – 9 – $4.00 – us Microform Publ [150]
THE SOCIAL MEANING OF MODERN RELIGIOUS MOVEMENTS IN ENGLAND / Hall, Thomas Cuming – 1900 – 1 – us A.T.L.A. [300]
THE SOCIAL MISSION OF THE CHURCH / Wishart, Alfred Wesley – Philadelphia: Published for the Social Service Commission of the Northern Baptist Convention [by] American Baptist Publ. Society, c1909, 1910 – 1mf – us A.T.L.A. [240]
SOCIAL MORALITY / Maurice, John Frederick Denison – London: Macmillan & Co., 1886 – xv/414p – 1 – us U.W. Library [170]
SOCIAL ORGANIZATION OF THE NORTHERN TUNGUS WITH INTRODUCTORY CHAPTERS CONCERNING GEOGRAPHICAL DISTRIBUTION AND HISTORY OF THESE GROUPS / Shirokogoroff, S M – Shanghai. 1929. BU-470 2 – 8 – ne IDC [306]
SOCIAL PATHOLOGY AND CHILD HEALTH IN JOGJAKARTA / Pandam, Guritno Siswoharsojo – SE-2908 1 – 9 – ne IDC [360]
THE SOCIAL PHILOSOPHY AND RELIGION OF COMTE / Caird, Edward – Glasgow: J. MacLehose, 1885 – 1mf – us A.T.L.A. [240]
THE SOCIAL PHILOSOPHY OF WILLIAM MORRIS / Phelan, Anna Augusta – Durham: N.C., Duke University Press, 1927 – 1 – us U.W. Library [920]
SOCIAL PHILOSOPHY & POLICY – v1-. 1983- – 1,5,6,9 – us UMI [073]
SOCIAL POLICY – 1976- – 9 – us UMI [073]
SOCIAL POLICY AND ADMINISTRATION – (1985-. 5,6,9) – v13-. 1979- – 1 – us UMI [300]
THE SOCIAL PROBLEM / Stuckenberg, John Henry Wilburn – York, Pa.: Social Problem Publishing, 1897 – 1mf – us A.T.L.A. [240]
SOCIAL PROBLEMS – v1- 1953- 1; v17- 5,6; v23- 9 – us UMI [360]
SOCIAL PROBLEMS AND THE CHURCHES – Based on the Harlan Paul Douglass collection – 1 – us Primary [240]
SOCIAL PROGRAMMES IN THE WEST : LECTURES / Henderson, Charles Richmond – Chicago: University of Chicago Press, 1913 – 1mf – us A.T.L.A. [360]
SOCIAL PROGRESS – 1-3. 1904-1906 – 1 – us UMI [300]
SOCIAL PROGRESS – (Title varies) – New York. v1-14. 1908-22 (complete) – 2r – 1 – ATLA S0026 – us A.T.L.A. [073]
SOCIAL PROGRESS *see* CHURCH AND SOCIETY
SOCIAL PSYCHIATRY – v. 1-15. 1966-80 – 1,5,9 – 1103.00 – us UMI [073]
SOCIAL PSYCHOLOGY – (See also: Sociometry and Social Psychology Quarterly) – v41. 1978 – 1,5,6,9 – us UMI [300]
SOCIAL PSYCHOLOGY QUARTERLY – v. 42-. 1979- – 1,5,6,9 – us UMI [300]
SOCIAL REFORM AND THE CONSTITUTION / Goodnow, Frank Johnson – New York: Macmillan, 1911 – 5mf – 9 – $7.50 – LLMC 95-084 – us L.L.M.C. [323]
SOCIAL REFORM PAPERS / McCook, John James – 14 reels. Guide to collection included – 1 – 322.00 – us Antiquarian [978]
SOCIAL REFORM PAPERS OF JOHN JAMES MCCOOK / McCook, John James – 14r – 1 – $1035.00 – us UMI [360]
SOCIAL REFORMER – London, UK. 1839. -w. 7 feet – 1 – uk British Libr Newspaper [072]
THE SOCIAL REFORMER – Toronto: Toronto Single Tax Association, [1889-189- or 19–] – 9 – cn C.I.H.M. [336]
SOCIAL RELATIONSHIPS IN THE LIGHT OF CHRISTIANITY : THE HULSEAN LECTURES FOR 1909-1910 / Chadwick, William Edward – London; New York: Longmans, Green, 1910 – 1mf – us A.T.L.A. [302]
SOCIAL, RELIGIOUS, AND LEISURE PURSUITS OF NORTHERN CALIFORNIA'S AFRICAN AMERICAN POPULATION : THE DISCOVERY OF GOLD THROUGH WORLD WAR 2 / Captain, Gwendolyn – University of California at Berkeley, 1995 – 4mf – 9 – $16.00 – RC 497 – us Microform Publ [306]
SOCIAL RESEARCH – v1- 1934- 1; v36- 5,6; v42- 9 – us UMI [300]
SOCIAL RESEARCH – v. 1-10. 1934-1943 – 1 – us Princeton Micro [300]
SOCIAL RESPONSIBILITY : BUSINESS, JOURNALISM, LAW, MEDICINE – (v1-10 1975-84 on reel $57.00. v11-21 1985-95 on mf $81.00. Title varies: v1-9 1975-83 as Social Responsibility: Journalism, Law, Medicine) – Washington and Lee University. v1-21. 1975-96 – 5,6,9 – $138.00 set – us Hein [300]
SOCIAL RESPONSIBILITY: JOURNALISM, LAW, MEDICINE *see* SOCIAL RESPONSIBILITY
THE SOCIAL RESULTS OF EARLY CHRISTIANITY / Schmidt, Charles – Trans. by Mrs. Thorpe with preliminary essay by R.W. Dale. London: Wm. Isbister, 1885. xxxii,480p – 1 – us U.W. Library [240]
SOCIAL SCIENCE AND MATHEMATICS – (v.68-1968- 5,6. v.75- 1975- 9) – v.1- 1901- – 1 – us UMI [300]
SOCIAL SCIENCE AND MEDICINE – (Back issues of journal available from UMI) – 24 issues/y. v36-37. 1993 – 9 – £872.00y – uk Elsevier Sci [300]
SOCIAL SCIENCE AND MEDICINE – v1- 1967- – 5,6,9 – us UMI [300]
SOCIAL SCIENCE AND MEDICINE. PART A: MEDICAL PSYCHOLOGY AND SOCIOLOGY – (SOCIAL SCIENCE AND MEDICINE. PART B: MEDICAL ANTHROPOLOGY. v12- 1978-. SOCIAL SCIENCE AND MEDICINE. PART C: MEDICAL ECONOMICS. v12- 1978-. SOCIAL SCIENCE AND MEDICINE. PART D: MEDICAL GEOGRAPHY. v12- 1978-) – v12- 1978- – 5,6,9 – us UMI [300]
SOCIAL SCIENCE BIBLIOGRAPHY OF INDONESIA : WITH SPECIAL EMPHASIS ON DEMOGRAPHIC AND GEOGRAPHIC MATERIALS / Bhatta, Jitandra Nath – SE-5965/1 – 9 – ne IDC [300]
SOCIAL SCIENCE HISTORY – (1985- . 5,6,9) – v1- . 1976- – 1 – us UMI [073]
SOCIAL SCIENCE METHODS, DECISION-MAKING AND DEVELOPMENT PLANNING – 1984 – 104p – 9 – 92-3-102207-5 – fr UNESCO [300]
SOCIAL SCIENCE MICRO REVIEW – v2-2. Fall 1983-Summer 1984 – 1 – us UMI [073]
SOCIAL SCIENCE MICROCOMPUTER REVIEW – v3- . Spring 1985- – 1,5,6,9 – us UMI [073]
SOCIAL SCIENCE QUARTERLY – v1- 1920- 1; v49- 5,6; v57- 9 – us UMI [300]
SOCIAL SCIENCE QUARTERLY – 1976- – 9 – us UMI [073]
Social Science Research Council *see* ITEMS
SOCIAL SCIENCE SERIES *see* SOCIOLOGICAL MICROJOURNAL
SOCIAL SCIENCES IN ASIA – 9 – fr UNESCO [300]
SOCIAL SCIENCES IN ASIA AND THE PACIFIC – 1984 – 612p – 9 – 92-3-102148-6 – fr UNESCO [300]
SOCIAL SCIENCES IN CHINA – 1980-81. -bim. in Chinese, -qtr. in English. Journal of the Chinese Academy of Social Sciences. Annual delivery. F E4 – 9 – $4.50f – cc Microforms [073]
SOCIAL SCIENCES IN LATIN AMERICA AND THE CARIBBEAN, 1 : SOCIAL SCIENCE NEEDS AND PRIORITIES – 1982 – 54p – 9 – 92-3-101962-7 – fr UNESCO [300]
SOCIAL SCIENCES INFORMATION – v. 1-3. Den haag, Parijs. 1962-64. BH-1800 1 – 9 – ne IDC [300]
SOCIAL SECURITY ADMINISTRATION, FEDERAL SECURITY AGENCY ANNUAL REPORTS / U.S. Dept of Health and Human Services – 1940-52 (all publ) – 57mf – 9 – $85.00 – LLMC 80-508 – us L.L.M.C. [360]
SOCIAL SECURITY BOARD ANNUAL REPORTS / U.S. Dept of Health and Human Services – (The SSB became the Social Security Administration in 1946, and that agency became a part of HEW in 1953) – 1935/36-1940/4 (all publ) – 18mf – 9 – $27.00 – LLMC 81-241 – us L.L.M.C. [360]
SOCIAL SECURITY BULLETIN – v1- 1938- 1; v33- 5,6; v38- 9 – us UMI [360]
SOCIAL SECURITY BULLETIN / U. S. Dept of Health and Human Services – (Includes v54 suppl. Add vols planned) – Social Security Board/Administration. v1-54. 1938-91 – 669mf – 9 – $1,004.00 – LLMC 80-501 – us L.L.M.C. [360]
SOCIAL SERVICE NEWS – 1939-49 – 1 – uk World [360]
SOCIAL SERVICE REVIEW – v1- 1927- 1; v45- 5,6; v51- 1977- 9 – us UMI [360]
THE SOCIAL SERVICES COUNCIL: SURVEY OF ITS ACTIVITIES SINCE ITS ESTABLISHMENT / Egypt. Permanent Council for Social Services – 1955. BNE-4676 1 – 9 – ne IDC [360]
SOCIAL SERVICES DIRECTORY OF PASADENA – Los Angeles Co, July 1932 – 1r – 1 – $50.00 – B06099 – us Library Micro [360]
SOCIAL SETTLEMENTS / Henderson, Charles Richmond – New York: Lentilhon, c1899. (Handbooks for practical workers in church and philanthropy) – 1mf – us A.T.L.A. [240]
SOCIAL STATICS / Spencer, Herbert – 1850. 449p. 1 fiche (36x) – 9 – 1.00f – at Libertarian Micro [320]
SOCIAL STATICS, ABRIDGED AND REVISED / Spencer, Herbert – London: Watts & Co., 1910. 142p – 1 – us U.W. Library [300]
SOCIAL STATISTICS, 1870 / Illinois. Census – Alphabetical by county. V123-0014 – 1 – us A.G.L.L. [310]
SOCIAL STATISTICS, 1870 / Kansas.Census – T1130-0005 – 1 – us A.G.L.L. [310]
SOCIAL STATISTICS, AGRICULTURAL & INDUSTRIAL SCHEDULES, 1860 / Kansas.Census – T1130-0001 – 1 – us A.G.L.L. [310]
SOCIAL STRATIFICATION AND SOCIAL MOBILITY IN INDONESIA; TREND REPORT AND ANNOTATED BIBLIOGRAPHY / Jaspan, M A – SE-3009 1. 2nd enl. ed. 1961 – 9 – ne IDC [305]
SOCIAL STUDIES – (v. 60-73. 1969-82. 5,6. v. 62-73. 1971-82. 9) – v. 1-73. 1909-82 – 1 – us UMI [300]
SOCIAL STUDIES JOURNAL – (1981-. 5,6,9) – 1971- – 1 – us UMI [300]
SOCIAL STUDIES PROFESSIONAL – 1969- 1; 1977- 5,6,9 – us UMI [370]
SOCIAL STUDIES REVIEW – v1- 1962- 1; v15- 1975- 5,6,9 – us UMI [300]
A SOCIAL SURVEY OF THE AFRICAN POPULATION OF LIVINGSTONE / McCulloch, M – 3mf – 7 – uk Microform Academic [960]
SOCIAL THEORY : A GROUPING OF SOCIAL FACTS AND PRINCIPLES / Bascom, John – New York: T.Y. Crowell, c1895 – 2mf – us A.T.L.A. [300]
SOCIAL THEORY AND PRACTICE – v1- 1970- 1; v4- 5,6,9 – us UMI [300]
SOCIAL THOUGHT : JOURNAL OF RELIGION IN THE SOCIAL SERVICES / ed by Shields, Joseph J – v19 n1. 1996- – 1,9 – $105.00 in US $147.00 outside hardcopy subsc – us Haworth [360]
SOCIAL TRENDS 1970-1977 – (Coll title: British Government Publications...1801-1977, Health and Public Welfare) – 23mf – 9 (£1,080.00 health and public welfare set of 171mf) – uk Chadwyck [300]
SOCIAL WELFARE – Toronto. v1-18. 1918/19-1938/39 – 9 – Can$20.00y – cn Micromedia [360]
SOCIAL WELFARE FORUM – v.101- 1974- – 1,5,6,9 – us UMI [073]
Social Welfare Forum *see* NATIONAL CONFERENCE ON SOCIAL WELFARE
SOCIAL WELFARE PERIODICALS – Sources for the history of social welfare in America. National Conference on Social Welfare. Social Welfare Forum. Official Proceedings; American Child; Lend a Hand; Charities Review; Survey (Charities; Charities and the Commons; Survey Graphic; Survey Midmonthly; Commons). Titles available seperately; see under title for price – 9 – $4,545.00 – us UPA [360]
SOCIAL WORK – v1- 1956- 1; v15- 5,6; v20- 9 – us UMI [360]
SOCIAL WORK IN EDUCATION – v. 1- 1978- – 1,5,6,9 – us UMI [370]
SOCIAL WORK IN HEALTH CARE : A QUARTERLY JOURNAL / ed by Rosenberg, Gary – v1- 1975- – 1, 9 ($150.00 in US $210.00 outside hardcopy subsc) – us Haworth [360]
SOCIAL WORK IN THE NEW SPAIN – London, 1938. Fiche W1163. (Blodgett Collection of Spanish Civil War Pamphlets) – 9 – us H.U. College Libr [946]
SOCIAL WORK RESEARCH AND ABSTRACTS *see* ABSTRACTS FOR SOCIAL WORKERS
SOCIAL WORK WITH GROUPS : A JOURNAL OF COMMUNITY AND CLINICAL PRACTICE / ed by Kurland, Roselle & Malekoff, Andrew – v1- 1978- – 1, 9 ($260.00 in US $364.00 outside hardcopy subsc) – us Haworth [360]
SOCIAL WORKER = LE TRAVAILLEUR SOCIAL – (v1-37 1932-69 Can$250.00. 38-41 1970-73, 42-45 1974-77 Can$100.00. v46-63 1) – Ottawa. v1-63. 1932-1994/95 – 5,9 – Can$20.00y – cn Micromedia [360]
SOCIALARISTOKRATEN / Holz, Arno – Rudolstadt, Leipzig: Maenicke & Jahn, 1896 – 1r – 1 – us U.W. Library [840]
SOCIAL-DEMOCRATEN – Stockholm, jul 1938-sep 1942 – 46r – 1 – us Res Libr [072]
DER SOCIAL-DEMOKRAT – Berlin, 1864-1868; 1869; 1870 – 6r – 1 – DM600.00 – gw Mikro Press [335]
DER SOCIAL-DEMOKRAT – Berlin, Germany. 15 Dec 1864-16 Oct 1868; 1869; 11 Feb-30 Dec 1870 – 6r – 1 – gw Mikrofilm [335]
DER SOCIAL-DEMOKRAT – (Cont by: Social-Demokrat, jul 1 1865) – Berlin, dec 15 1864-sep 27 1876, 1883-90 – 1 – Inquire at Mikrofilmarchiv for details – gw Misc Inst [335]
SOCIAL'-DEMOKRAT : CENTRAL'NYJ-ORGAN ROSSIJSKOJ SOCIAL'-DEMOKRATICESKOJ RABOCEJ PARTII – St Petersburg, Vilna, Paris, Geneve, 1909-16 – 1 – us Hoover Inst Photo [335]
SOCIAL-DEMOKRAT *see* DER SOCIAL-DEMOKRAT
SOCIAL-DEMOKRATEN / Sveriges Socialdemokratiska Arbetareparti – Stockholm, 1885-1942 – 1 – sw Kungliga [335]
SOCIAL-DEMOKRATEN / Sveriges Socialdemokratiska Arbetareparti – Stockholm, 1914-18, 1933-38, 1939-50 – 1 – us Hoover Inst Photo [335]
SOCIALDEMOKRATEN : ORGAN FOR SVERGES SOCIAL-DEMOKRATISKA ARBETAREPARTI – Stockholm, 1933-38 – 1 – us Hoover Inst Photo [335]
SOCIALDEMOKRATEN *see* MORGONTIDNINGEN
SOCIAL-DEMOKRATEN; AKTUELT; DET FRI AKTUELT / Socialdemokratisk Forbund – Copenhagen, 1916, 1919, 1920, 1939, 1940-54 (all incompl) – 1 – us Hoover Inst Photo [335]
SOCIALDEMOKRATEN VECKOUPPLAGA – Stockholm, Sweden. 1890-92 – 1 – sw Kungliga [072]
Socialdemokratisk Forbund *see* SOCIAL-DEMOKRATEN; AKTUELT; DET FRI AKTUELT
LA SOCIALE – Paris. mai 1895-oct 1896. Remplace: Le Pere peinard voir a ce titre – 1 – fr A.C.R.P.P. [073]
SOCIALISM / Mill, John Stuart – Chicago: Belfords, Clarke & Co., 1879. Reprinted from the Fortnightly Review – 1 – us U.W. Library [335]
SOCIALISM = SOZIALISMUS : ITS THEORETICAL BASIS AND PRACTICAL APPLICATION / Cathrein, Victor – (In English. Includes bibliographical references) – [3rd ed]. New York: Benziger, c1904 – 1mf – 9 – 0-8370-7371-5 – 1986-1371 – us A.T.L.A. [320]
SOCIALISM AND CHARACTER / Scudder, Vida Dutton – Boston: Houghton Mifflin, 1912 – us A.T.L.A. [335]
SOCIALISM AND CHRISTIANITY / Behrends, Adolphus Julius Frederick – 1886 – 1 – us A.T.L.A. [335]
SOCIALISM AND CHRISTIANITY / Grant, Percy Stickney – New York: Brentano, 1910 – 1mf – us A.T.L.A. [240]
SOCIALISM AND INDIVIDUALISM / Belfort Bax, Ernest & Levy, J H – 9 – 1.00f – at Libertarian Micro [335]
SOCIALISM AND LABOR : AND OTHER ARGUMENTS, SOCIAL, POLITICAL, AND PATRIOTIC / Spalding, J L – Chicago: A.C. McClurg, 1902 – 1mf – us A.T.L.A. [320]
SOCIALISM EXPOSED AND REFUTED = SOZIALISMUS : A CHAPTER FROM THE AUTHOR'S MORAL PHILOSOPHY WITH APPENDIX CONTAINING THE ENCYCLICALS OF POPE LEO 13 ON THE CONDITION OF LABOR AND CHRISTIAN DEMOCRACY / Cathrein, Victor – (Includes bibliographical references) – 2nd ed. New York: Benziger, 1902 – 1mf – 9 – 0-8370-7372-3 – 1986-1372 – us A.T.L.A. [335]
SOCIALISM FOR SOUTH AFRICA / Miles-Casman, Cecil Frank – Johannesburg: South African Labour Party, [1942] – us Res Libr [320]
SOCIALISM IN CHURCH HISTORY / Noel, Conrad – London: F. Palmer, 1910 – 1mf – us A.T.L.A. [240]
SOCIALISM VERSUS CHRISTIANITY / Hartman, Edward R – New York: Cochrane, 1909 – 1mf – us A.T.L.A. [335]

LE SOCIALISME – Dir. Jules Guesde. Paris. nov 1907-sept 1912 – 1 – fr A.C.R.P.P. [335]
SOCIALISME *see* SOCIALISME QUEBECOIS
LE SOCIALISME AU JOUR LE JOUR / Guesde, Jules – Paris. 1899. (La Condition Ouvriere. Part Two.) – 9 – 15.00 – fr Bibl Nationale [360]
LE SOCIALISME AU JOUR LE JOUR / Guesde, Jules – Paris: V. Giard & E. Briere. 1899. vii,488p – 1 – us U.W. Library [335]
SOCIALISME CATHOLIQUE. LA DEROUTE DES CESARS. LA GAULE TRES CHRETIENNE ET LE CZAR ORTHODOXE / Laverdant, Gabriel-Desire – (Russia – 19C. series). 1851 – 9 – fr Hachette [240]
LE SOCIALISME EN BELGIQUE / Destree, Jules – Avec un appendice sur la bibliographie du Socialisme belge par Deutscher. Paris, 1898. 515p. (Bibliotheque socialiste internationale; 4) – 1 – us U.W. Library [335]
SOCIALISME ET LUTTE DE CLASSE – Revue marxiste de langue francaise. Dir. Jules Guesde. Red. en chef Bracke. no. 1-14. Paris. janv-juil 1914. MS. 21850 – 1 – fr A.C.R.P.P. [335]
SOCIALISME ET SEXUALISME: PROGRAMME DU PARTI SOCIALISTE FEMININ – Paris: Beaudelot, 1893. 92p. (Les Femmes Collection) – 1mf – 9 – $6.00 – fr Bibl Nationale [305]
SOCIALISME, HARIINI AND HARISOK BANGSA2 – SE 4303 1. 1963 – 9 – ne IDC [335]
LE SOCIALISME INTEGRAL / Malon, Benoit – Paris: F. Alcan, 1890.2v. 16 fiches. (Political Science Collection) – 9 – 40.00 – fr Bibl Nationale [335]
SOCIALISME OU BARBARIE – Organe de critique et d'orientation revolutionnaire. Red. en chef Ph. Guillaume. no. 1-40. Paris. mars avr 1949-juin aout 1965 – 1 – fr A.C.R.P.P. [335]
SOCIALISME QUEBECOIS – Montreal: [Saint-Lambert: Payette & Simms]. no 20-24. 1964-74. SEM16P243 – 1r – 5 – Can$39.00 – cn Bibl Nat [335]
SOCIALISMO / Justo, Juan Bautista – Buenos Aires, 1928 – 1 – us Res Libr [972]
SOCIALISMO INDIVIDUALISTA (INDICE PARA SU ESTUDIO ANTROPOLOGICO) / Trigo, Felipe – Madrid: Renacimiento, 1920 – sp Bibl Santa Ana [335]
SOCIALISMO NACIONAL : LA MARCHA DEL PODER PERONISTA / Fernandez, Pardo & Carlos, Alberto – [Buenos Aires]: Editorial Relevo, [1973] – 1 – CSUXAJA7597-B – us Hoover Inst Photo [320]
EL SOCIALISMO Y EL ESTADO : CONFERENCIA DICTADA EN LA CASA DEL PUEBLO DE BUENOS AIRES, EN LA CATEDRA JUAN B. JUSTO, DE LA COMISION DE CULTURA DEL PARTIDO SOCIALISTA, EL 2 DE JUNIO DE 1948 / Repetto, Nicolas – Buenos Aires: Casa del Pueblo, 1948 – 1 – CSUXADP7801-B – us Hoover Inst Photo [335]
EL SOCIALISMO Y LA ACTUAL CRISIS ARGENTINA / Ghioldi, Americo – Buenos Aires: P[artido] S[ocialista], 1948 – 1 – CSUXADQ5381-B – us Hoover Inst Photo [320]
SOCIALIST – 1-9 (all publ). 1919 – 1 reel – 1 – $65.00 – us UPA [335]
SOCIALIST – Huntington. West Virginia. and Labor Star. 1912-14 – 1 – us UMI [071]
SOCIALIST – London. 1902-22 – 3r – 1 – uk Microform Academic [335]
THE SOCIALIST – 1902-24 – 1 – uk World [072]
THE SOCIALIST – Edinburgh and Glasgow. Scotland. -m. Aug 1902-Feb 1924. (7 reels) – 1 – uk British Libr Newspaper [073]
THE SOCIALIST – England. The organ of the Sunderland Independent Labour Party. -m. 12 June 1894-Jan 1895. 10 ft – 1 – uk British Libr Newspaper [072]
SOCIALIST ACTION : OFFICIAL ORGAN OF THE SOCIALIST WORKERS' LEAGUE OF CANADA – (Includes c.1: v.1:no.1 (1939:Jan.3), v.2:no.5 (1939:Sept.); 1941:May; 1942:Apr) – Toronto, Ont.: The League, 19uu – 1 – CSUXALM4303-S – us Hoover Inst Photo [331]
SOCIALIST ACTION – Wellington, [N.Z.]: Published by K. Locke for the Socialist Action Pub. Association, 1969 – 1 – CSUXALM3092-S – us Hoover Inst Photo [320]
SOCIALIST AFFAIRS – London, UK. 1971-1990 – 10r – $500.00 – R63564 – us Library Micro [320]
SOCIALIST AND LABOUR THOUGHT IN BRITAIN SINCE 1884 – (Part 2: 1898-1902. Part 3: 1903-07. Part 4: 1908-11. Part 5: 1912-18. Part 6: 1919-25. Part 7: 1926-33. Part 8: 1934-45) – Pamphlets of Socialist and Reform Movements. Part 1: 1884-97 – 9 – us Primary [941]
SOCIALIST APPEAL – 1-3 2+3 (all publ). 1934-1937 – 4mf – 9 – $35.00 – us UPA [335]
SOCIALIST CALL – 1935-62 – 6r – 1 – us Ross [335]
SOCIALIST CALL – Chicago, 1935-62 – 1 – us NY Public [335]
SOCIALIST CALL – Chicago, 1937-52 (incompl newspaper), 1953-62 (incompl) – 1 – us Hoover Inst Photo [335]
SOCIALIST CALL – New York. v. 1-29, no. 1. Mar 23 1935-Spring 1962 – 1 – us NY Public [335]
SOCIALIST COLLECTIONS IN THE TAMIMENT LIBRARY, 1872-1956 – 68r – 1 – $4175.00 – us UMI [335]
SOCIALIST COMMENTARY *see* THE LEFT IN BRITAIN, PART 1
SOCIALIST CURRENT – vol.1, no.1, May 1956-. London: Socialist Current Group, 1956-...Marxist Journal of Labour Opinion" – 1 – us U.W. Library [941]
Socialist Labor Party *see* PROCEEDINGS
SOCIALIST LEADER – -w. v.1-67, no.13, Oct. 6, 1922-June 21, 1975. Leeds etc. Independent Labour Publications etc – 1 – us U.W. Library [073]
Socialist League *see*
– THE COMMONWEAL
SOCIALIST LEAGUER – (The Socialist) Journal of the Socialist League. London. -m. Jun 1934-Jan 1937. (23 ft) – 1 – uk British Libr Newspaper [073]
Socialist Party. Argentine Republic *see* LA VANGUARDIA
Socialist Party, Chicago *see* THE SOCIALIST WORLD
Socialist Party. Great Britain *see*
– SOCIALIST RECORD
– SOCIALIST STANDARD
SOCIALIST PARTY OF AMERICA PAPERS, 1897-1976 – (Base collection 1897-1963 142 reels $8750; Addendum 1963-76 38 reels $2380) – 180r complete collection – 1 – $11,130.00 complete collection – us UMI [335]
THE SOCIALIST PARTY OF THE UNITED STATES : PERSONAL PAPERS OF DARLINGTON HOOPES, 1917-1968 / Hoopes, Darlington; ed by Fileppeli, Ronald L – 1972 – 25r – 1 – $2,125.00 – S1868 – us Scholarly Res [335]
Socialist Party. U.S.A *see*
– AMERICAN SOCIALIST
– NEW YORK COMMUNIST
– PARTY BUILDER
SOCIALIST PRESS BULLETIN – (1941/42-1958/59 Can$100.00) – Toronto, 1941-1979 – 5 – Can$50.00y – cn Micromedia [335]
SOCIALIST RECORD : A MONTHLY JOURNAL OF INTERNAL AFFAIRS FOR MEMBERS OF THE BRITISH SOCIALIST PARTY / Socialist Party. Great Britain – (Series 1: no1-11 (all publ). 1912-1913. Series 2: no1-12 (all publ). 1913-16) – 1 reel – 1 – $65.00 – us UPA [335]
SOCIALIST REVIEW – 1-7 2+2 (all publ). 1932-1940 – 24mf – 9 – $120.00 – us UPA [335]
SOCIALIST REVIEW – -m. no.1, April 1978-. London, Socialist Workers Party – 1 – us U.W. Library [073]
SOCIALIST REVIEW – v. 8-. 1978- – 1,5,6,9 – us UMI [335]
THE SOCIALIST REVIEW – London, Maerz 1908-Febr 1913 – 3r – 1 – DM280.00 – gw Mikro Press [335]
THE SOCIALIST REVIEW – London. Mar 1908-Feb 1913. 6082-84 – 1 – DM280.00 – gw Mikro Press [072]
SOCIALIST REVOLUTION – v. 1-7. 1970-1974 – 1. ; 5,6,9 – apply; v.7$ – us UMI [335]
SOCIALIST SPIRIT – 1-2 2+6 (all publ). 1901-1903 – 7mf – 9 – $50.00 – us UPA [335]
SOCIALIST STANDARD / Socialist Party. Great Britain – London. -m. Sep. 1904-Dec. 1960. 8 reels – 1 – uk British Libr Newspaper [073]
SOCIALIST STANDARD *see* THE LEFT IN BRITAIN, PART 4
Socialist Tract Association. Detroit *see* TRACTS
THE SOCIALIST TRANSFORMATION OF AGRICULTURE: (THEORY AND PRACTICE) / Stanis, V F – Trans. from Russian by S. Vechor-Shcherbovich. Moscow: Progress Publishers, 1976. 238p. Bibliographical references – 1 – us U.W. Library [335]
Socialist Union Party *see* LABOR POWER
SOCIALIST VOICE – (v1-9 1977-85 Can$60.00y 1. Cont: Labour Challenge, 1977. Ceased 1988) – Montreal. v1-12. 1977-1988 – 1,9 – Can$20.00y – cn Micromedia [335]
SOCIALIST VOICE *see* LABOUR CHALLENGE
Socialist Workers Party *see*
– INTERNATIONAL SOCIALIST REVIEW
– NEW INTERNATIONAL
THE SOCIALIST WORLD / Socialist Party, Chicago – Chicago, 1920-25 (incompl) – 9 – us Hoover Inst Photo [335]
EL SOCIALISTA – Paris, Toulouse, 1944-47, 1952, 1955-57 (all incompl) – 1 – us Hoover Inst Photo [335]
EL SOCIALISTA / Partido Obrero Espanol – Madrid, 1936-39 (incompl) – 1 – us Hoover Inst Photo [335]
EL SOCIALISTA / Partido Socialista del Peru – Lima, no 40 1935 – 1 – us Hoover Inst Photo [335]
EL SOCIALISTA (1886-1986) : ORGANO DEL PARTIDO SOCIALISTA OBRERO ESPANOL / ed by Partido Socialista Obrero Espanol – Madrid: Editorial Pablo Iglesias, 1987 – 53r – 5 – Pta390,000 – sp Iglesias [331]
EL SOCIALISTA (PARTIDO SOCIALISTA OBRERO ESPANOL: 1977) – Madrid: s.n – 1 – us U.W. Library [073]
LE SOCIALISTE – Journal d'informations et d'action socialistes. no. 17-35. Paris. avr 1938-mars 1939 – 1 – fr A.C.R.P.P. [335]
LE SOCIALISTE – Journal socialiste parlementaire. Dir. Eugene Flambant. no. 13 14, 18-21. Cayene. janv-mai 1910 – 1 – fr A.C.R.P.P. [335]
LE SOCIALISTE : ORGANE DU PARTI OUVRIER – Paris, 1885-1923 – 1 – fr A.C.R.P.P. [335]
LE SOCIALISTE ARDENNAIS / La Federation des Travailleurs Socialistes des Ardennes – no. 499-641. Charleville. 1905-06 – 1 – fr A.C.R.P.P. [073]
LE SOCIALISTE DE L'ALLIER – Organe de concentration des forces socialistes. Montlucon. 1895-oct 1903 – 1 – fr A.C.R.P.P. [335]
LE SOCIALISTE DU MIDI – Organe des socialistes collectivistes de Toulouse. Toulouse. janv-juin 1894 – 1 – fr A.C.R.P.P. [335]
DIE SOCIALISTEN : DRAMA IN FUENF ACTEN / Walter, Hans – Wien: L Rosner, 1881 – 1r – 1 – us U.W. Library [820]
SOCIALISTICESKIJ VESTNIK / Rossijskaja Social-Demokraticeskaja Rabocaja Partija – Berlin, Paris, New York, 1921-65 – 1 – us Hoover Inst Photo [335]
SOCIALISTICNA ZARJA – Cleveland, OH, 1922 – 1mf or 1 reel – 1,9 – us I.H.R.C. [975]
Das Socialistische Bund *see* TURN-ZEITUNG
THE SOCIALIST'S CHURCH / Headlam, Stewart D – London: G. Allen, 1907 – 1mf – us A.T.L.A. [240]
SOCIALIZATION AND WORKAHOLISM : A LIFESTYLE PERSPECTIVE / Trueman, Andrea L – Dalhousie University, 1995 – 2mf – 9 – $8.00 – PSY1869 – us Microform Publ [306]
THE SOCIALIZATION OF BEGINNING PHYSICAL EDUCATION TEACHERS / Lee, Jae Y et al – 1993 – 4mf – 9 – $16.00 – us Microform Publ [150]
THE SOCIALIZED CHURCH : ADDRESSES BEFORE THE FIRST NATIONAL CONFERENCE OF THE SOCIAL WORKERS OF METHODISM, ST. LOUIS, NOVEMBER 17-19, 1908 / ed by Tippy, Worth M – New York: Eaton & Mains; Cincinnati: Jannings and Graham, c1909 – 1mf – us A.T.L.A. [240]
SOCIAL-POLITISCHE BLAETTER : ZUR UNTERHALTUNG UND BELEHRUNG FUER DIE DEUTSCHEN ARBEITER – Berlin, 1873-75 – 2r – 1 – Inquire at Mikrofilmarchiv for details – gw Misc Inst [360]
SOCIAL-POLITISCHE BLAETTER : ZUR UNTERHALTUNG UND BELEHRUNG FUER DIE DEUTSCHEN ARBEITER – Berlin, Germany. 1873-1874 – 1r – 1 – gw Mikrofilm [072]
SOCIAL-POLITISCHE BLAETTER ZUR UNTERHALTUNG UND BELEHRUNG FUER DIE DEUTSCHEN ARBEITER – Berlin, 1873-74 – 1r – 1 – DM80.00 – gw Mikro Press [072]
SOCIALPOLITISCHES CENTRALBLATT – Berlin, 1892-1895 – 2r – 1 – DM200.00 – gw Mikro Press [072]
SOCIALPOLITISCHES CENTRALBLATT – Berlin, 1892-sep 23 1895 – 2r – 1 – Inquire at Mikrofilmarchiv for details – gw Misc Inst [360]
SOCIALPOLITISCHES CENTRALBLATT – Berlin, Germany. 1892-23 Sept 1895 – 2r – 1 – gw Mikrofilm [072]
Sociedad Anonima Mirat *see* TARIFA DE PRECIOS
SOCIEDAD DE CAZADORES DE ALDEACENTENERA. REGLAMENTO / Aldeacentenera – Caceres: Tip. la Minerva Cacerena, s.a. (1939) – 1 – sp Bibl Santa Ana [946]
Sociedad de Geografia e Historia de Honduras. Tegucigalpa *see* REVISTA
LA SOCIEDAD DE ZACATECAS EN LOS ALBORES DEL REGIMEN COLONIAL / Davila Garibi, Jose Ignacio – Madrid: Razon y Fe, 1940 – 1 – sp Bibl Santa Ana [946]
Sociedad Economica Amigos del Pais *see*
– ESTATUTOS
– MEMORIA
Sociedad Economica de Amigos del Pais *see* REVISTA BIMESTRE CUBANA
Sociedad Economica de Amigos del Pais de Badajoz *see*
– EN MEMORIA DE RAMON
– MEMORIA DE LOS TRABAJOS EFECTUADOS POR LA MISMA DURANTE EL ANO 1889
SOCIEDAD EXTREMENA DE FOMENTO-REFORMA DE PROYECTO BANCO HIPITECARIO / Gonzalez, Rafael – 1866 – 9 – 1.50f – sp Bibl Santa Ana [332]
Sociedad Hipica Lebrera de Badajoz *see*
– 3 RAID HIPICO INTERNACIONAL. BADAJOZ-CACERES-BADAJOZ (14 Y 15 DE MARZO 1970)
– 4 RAID HIPICO INTERNACIONAL-BADAJOZ-CACERES-BADAJOZ (18-19 DE MARZO 1971)
Sociedad Mexicana de Historia Naturale *see* NATURALEZA
Sociedad rural Argentina. Buenos Aires *see* ANALES
LAS SOCIEDADES DE CREDITO Y LOS FERROCARRILES EXTREMENOS / Gonzalez Hernandez, Juan – 1864 – 9 – $1.50f – sp Bibl Santa Ana [380]
Sociedades Hispanas Confederadas de Ayuda a Espana *see* MEMORIA DEL CONGRESO NACIONAL
SOCIET JOURNAL OF GLASS PHYSICS AND CHEMISTRY *see* GLASS PHYSICS AND CHEMISTRY
Societa Chimica Italiano. Rome *see* RENDICONTI
Societa Italiana di Biologia Superimentale *see* BOLLETINO
LE SOCIETA STRANIERE IN ITALIA / Danieli, G – Roma, 1885 – 4mf – 1 – ILM-3763/1 – ne IDC [327]
Societa Toscana di Scienze Naturali *see* PROCESSI VERBALI
SOCIETAL UTILIZATION OF SCIENTIFIC AND TECHNOLOGICAL RESEARCH – 1981 – 32p – 9 – 92-3-101858-2 – fr UNESCO [360]
Societas Orientalis Batava *see* ACTA ORIENTALIA
Societe Belge d'Etudes Coloniales *see* BULLETIN
Societe Bienveillante St-Roch *see* BULLETIN DE LA SOCIETE BIENVEILLANTE ST-ROCH
Societe Chimique de France *see*
– BULLETIN
Societe d'Agriculture de Quebec *see* PRIX OFFERTS PAR LA SOCIETE D'AGRICULTURE DE QUEBEC, 1829-30
La Societe d'Agriculture du Bas-Canada *see* JOURNAL D'AGRICULTURE ET PROCEDES DE LA SOCIETE D'AGRICULTURE DU BAS-CANADA
Societe d'archeologie lorraine et du musee historique lorrain *see* JOURNAL
Societe de Biologie. Paris *see* COMPTES RENDUS
Societe de Chimie Biologique. Paris *see* BULLETIN
Societe de Colonisation Montarville *see* VALLEE DE LA LIEVRE, REGION DE L'OTTAWA: RAPPORT SOUMIS PAR P.B. BENOIT, PRESIDENT...LE 10 JANVIER 1884

Society of Jesus. Missouri Province *see* OSAGE MISSIONS
Society of Jesus. Philippine Islands *see* CARTAS DE LOS PADRES DE LA COMPANIA DE LA MISION DE FILIPINAS
Society of Liberian Authors *see* PUBLICATIONS OF THE SOCIETY OF LIBERIAN AUTHORS
SOCIETY OF MALAWI JOURNAL *see* NYASALAND JOURNAL
Society of Manufacturing Engineers *see* TECHNICAL PAPERS
SOCIETY OF MONTANA PIONEERS / Sanders, James U – Society of Montana Pioneers, 1899. Montana reel 4. (Cox Library Collection) – 5 – us Americana [978]
Society of Motion Picture and Television engineers *see* JOURNAL
Society of Oklahoma Indians *see* THE AMERICAN INDIAN
Society of Petroleum Engineers *see* SOCIETY OF PETROLEUM ENGINEERS TECHNICAL PAPERS
SOCIETY OF PETROLEUM ENGINEERS TECHNICAL PAPERS / Society of Petroleum Engineers – (Ca 8000 papers. Base collection 1950s to 1979 $3840; annual supplements 1980-88 $470 ea; supplement 1989 $455) – 9 – us UMI [660]
Society of Plastics Engineers *see* JOURNAL
Society of Plastics Industry of Canada *see*
- CANPLAST '76
- CANPLAST '77
- CANPLAST '79

Society of Research Administrators *see* JOURNAL
Society of Rheology *see* TRANSACTIONS
SOCIETY OF SEPARATISTS OF ZOAR, MS 1663 – (Account books, banking and financial papers, deeds, contracts, post office records, land patents, correspondence, sermons, and miscellaneous documents of this German Portestant religious community) – Zoar, Tuscarawas, OH. 1817-1927 – 6r – 1 – us Western Res [360]
Society of Solicitors in the Supreme Courts of Scotland. Council *see* REPORT BY THE COUNCIL OF THE SOCIETY OF SOLICITORS BEFORE THE SUPREME COURTS, UPON THE BILL (TO ABOLISH FEUDAL AND BURGAGE TENURE, AND TO AMEND THE LAW RELATING TO LAND RIGHTS IN SCOTLAND.)
Society of Telegraph Engineers and Electricians. London *see* JOURNAL
Society of the Cincinnati of the State of South Carolina *see* MINUTES
SOCILISMO E CULTURA / Poggi, Alfredo – Torino: P. Gobetti, 1925 – 1 – us U.W. Library [335]
DER SOCINIANISMUS : NACH SEINER STELLUNG IN DER GESAMTENTWICKLUNG DES CHRISTLICHEN GEISTES, NACH SEINEM HISTORISCHEN VERLAUF UND NACH SEINEM LEHRBEGRIFF / Fock, Otto – Kiel: Carl Schroeder, 1847 – 2mf – us A.T.L.A. [240]
SOCIO-ECONOMIC ANALYSIS AND PLANNING : CRITICAL CHOICE OF METHODOLOGIES – 1986 – 9 – 92-3-102391-8 – fr UNESCO [330]
SOCIO-ECONOMIC ASPECTS URBAN HYDROLOGY / Lindh, Gunnar – 1979 – 88p – 9 – 92-3-101702-0 – fr UNESCO [330]
SOCIO-ECONOMIC EFFECTS OF THE EVOLUTION OF NILE PERCH FISHERIES IN LAKE VICTORIA : A REVIEW – 1989 – 160p – it F.A.O. [338]
SOCIO-ECONOMIC INDICATORS FOR PLANNING : METHODOLOGICAL ASPECTS AND SELECTED EXAMPLES – 1981 – 9 – 92-3-101892-2 – fr UNESCO [360]
SOCIO-ECONOMIC INDICATORS RELATING TO THE AGRICULTURAL SECTOR AND RURAL DEVELOPMENT – 1984 – 110p – it F.A.O. [339]
SOCIOECONOMIC NEWSLETTER – v1-11. 1976-86 – 9 – $30.00 set – us Hein [330]
SOCIOECONOMIC NEWSLETTER *see* SOCIOECONOMIC STUDIES
SOCIO-ECONOMIC PLANNING SCIENCES – v1-1967- – 5,6,9 – us UMI [300]
SOCIOECONOMIC STUDIES – (Includes Journal of the Institute for Socioeconomic Studies, v1-10; Socioeconomic Newsletter, v1-10. 1976-85) – Institute for Socioeconomic Studies. Publications. Complete – 9 – $183.00 set – us Hein [300]
EL SOCIOGRAMA DE LA ESTRUCTURA INFORMAL / Buceta Facorro, Luis – Marzo de 1971. A. Moret, Linea XXI, 1973 – 1 – sp Bibl Santa Ana [946]
SOCIOLOGIA DEL AFRICA NEGRA / Elias de Tejada, Francisco – Madrid: Ediciones Rialp S.A., 1956 – sp Bibl Santa Ana [301]
SOCIOLOGICAL ANALYSIS IN AGRICULTURAL INVESTMENT PROJECT DESIGN – 1992 – 148p – it F.A.O. [332]
SOCIOLOGICAL FOCUS – (v1-18 1967-85 on reel $157.50. v19-27 1985-94 on mf $141.50) – Kent State University. v1-27. 1967-94 – 5,6 – $299.00 set – us Hein [300]
SOCIOLOGICAL FOCUS – (v.12-. 1979- 5,6,9) – v.1-. 1967- – 1 – us UMI [073]
SOCIOLOGICAL FORUM – v1-9. 1986-94 – 1,5 – $90.00v – us UMI [301]
SOCIOLOGICAL INQUIRY – (v.51-. 1981-. 5,6,9) – v.31-. 1961- – 1 – us UMI [300]
SOCIOLOGICAL INQUIRY *see* ALPHA KAPPA DELTAN
SOCIOLOGICAL METHODS AND RESEARCH – (v.8-. 1979-) – v.1-. 1972- – 1 – us UMI [073]
SOCIOLOGICAL MICROJOURNAL / ed by Svalastoga, K – (Cont as: Social Science Series. Publ by the Institute for Longitudinal Studies. Copenhagen v1-6 1984-1990) – Copenhagen. v1-19. 1967-85 – 108mf – 9 – H-352/2 + H-3020/1 – ne IDC [300]
SOCIOLOGICAL PERSPECTIVES – v26-. 1983- – 1,5,6,9 – us UMI [073]
SOCIOLOGICAL PRACTICE – v3-. 1979- – 1,5,6,9 – us UMI [073]
SOCIOLOGICAL QUARTERLY – v. 1-. 1960- – 1,5,6,9 – us UMI [300]
SOCIOLOGICAL QUARTERLY – v1-25. 1960-84 – 5,6 – $260.00 – us Hein [300]
SOCIOLOGICAL REVIEW – v1- 1908- 1; v21- 5,6; v24- 9 – us UMI [300]
SOCIOLOGICAL SPECTRUM / Mid-South Sociological Association – (v3-. 1983-. 5,6,9) – v1-. 1981- – 1 – us UMI [073]
SOCIOLOGICAL SYMPOSIUM – v1-31 1968-80 1; v22-31 5,6,9 – us UMI [300]
SOCIOLOGICAL THEORIES, RACE AND COLONIALISM – 1980 – 500p – 9 – 92-3-101635-0 – fr UNESCO [301]
SOCIOLOGICAL THEORY – (1985-. 5,6,9) – v1-. 1983- – 1 – us UMI [300]
SOCIOLOGIE DES BRAZZAVILLES NOIRES / Balandier, G – F50.00 – fr Ethnologie [307]
SOCIOLOGIE DU TRAVAIL – v. 1-10. Paris. 1959-68. Lacking: v. 9 (3) 1967. BH-1801 1 – 9 – ne IDC [073]
SOCIOLOGIE ELECTORALE : ESQUISSE D'UN BILAN GUIDE RECHERCHES / Goguel, F et al – F20.00 – fr Ethnologie [303]
SOCIOLOGIE ET DROIT SLAVES; REVUE TRIMESTRIELLE DE TESTES ET CRITIQUES SOCIOLOGIQUES ET JURIDIQUES RELATIFS AUX PAYS SLAVES – Paris. On film: v1-4; 1945-48. LL-032 – 1 – us L of C Photodup [340]
SOCIOLOGISTS GAY CAUCUS NEWSLETTER – New York. v11; 34, no.2; 40-. Running title: SGC Newsletter – 1 – us U.W. Library [305]
SOCIOLOGY – v1-10 1973-83 1; v6-10 5,6,9 – us UMI [300]
SOCIOLOGY AND RURAL LIFE SERIES / Mississippi. State University. Division of Sociology and Rural Life – v. 1-30. 1950-75 – 1,5,6 – us Spaulding [307]
SOCIOLOGY AND SOCIAL ANTHROPOLOGY IN ASIA AND THE PACIFIC – 9 – 92-3-102172-9 – fr UNESCO [301]
SOCIOLOGY AND SOCIAL RESEARCH – v1-1916- 1; v53- 5,6; v61- 9 – us UMI [300]
SOCIOLOGY AND SOCIAL RESEARCH / California. University of Southern California – Los Angeles. v. 1-33. 1916-49. Lacking: 1917, v. 2 (7); 1920, v. 4 (15); 1921-23, v. 6 (1, 2, 4, 6); v. 7 (2, 3, 6); v. 11 (2). BH-1817 1 – 145mf – 9 – ne IDC [300]
SOCIOLOGY AND SOCIAL RESEARCH: AN INTERNATIONAL JOURNAL – v. 1-49. 1916-1965 – 1 – us Princeton Micro [300]
SOCIOLOGY IN THE UNITED STATES OF AMERICA / Zetterberg, H L – UNESCO. 1956 – 4mf – 7 – uk Microform Academic [970]
SOCIOLOGY OF CANADIAN MENNONITES, HUTTENITES AND AMISH : A BIBLIOGRAPHY WITH ANNOTATIONS / ed by Smucker, Donovan E – 1977 – xvi/232p – 9 – $20.00 – 0-88920-175-7 – cn W.L.U. Press [305]
SOCIOLOGY OF EDUCATION – v1- 1927- 1; v41- 5,6; v48- 9 – us UMI [300]
SOCIOLOGY OF EDUCATION ABSTRACTS – 1964- 29v – 9 – £271.00 – 0038-0415 – uk Carfax [370]
SOCIOLOGY OF LEISURE AND SPORTS ABSTRACTS – v1-5. 1980-84 – 1,5,6,13 – sz Elsevier [073]
SOCIOLOGY OF WORK AND OCCUPATIONS – (v.7-. 1980-. 5,6,9) – v.1-. 1974- – 1 – us UMI [300]
SOCIOMETRY – (See also: Social Psychology) – v1-40. 1937-77 – 1. ; 5,6. ; 9 – apply; v.31-40.; v.39-40 – us UMI [300]
SOCIO-POLITICAL ASPECTS OF THE PALAVER IN SOME AFRICAN COUNTRIES – 1979 – 93p – 9 – 92-3-101641-5 – fr UNESCO [320]
SOCORRO JURIDICO CRISTIANO "ARZOBISPO OSCAR ROMERO" DE EL SALVADOR (SJC) = CHRISTIAN LEGAL AID "ARCHBISHOP OSCAR ROMERO" OF EL SALVADOR – San Salvador. 209 docs. 1980-1990 – 37mf – 9 – ne IDC [320]
SOCRATES AND CHRIST : A STUDY IN THE PHILOSOPHY OF RELIGION / Wenley, Robert Mark – (Includes bibliographical references) – Edinburgh: William Blackwood, 1889 – 1mf – 9 – 0-8370-6461-9 – 1986-0461 – us A.T.L.A. [240]
SOCRATES AND THE ANIMALS / Quarelli, Elena – Trans. from the Italian by Kathleen Speight. London: Hodder and Stoughton, (c1960). 160p – 1 – us U.W. Library [830]
SOD HA-NESHAMAH – Basle. 1609. BJ-43-114 – 9 – ne IDC [470]
SODA FOUNTAIN *see* FAST FOOD
SODA FOUNTAIN AND QUICK FOOD-SERVICE *see* FAST FOOD
SODA FOUNTAIN MAGAZINE *see* FAST FOOD
SODA FOUNTAIN SERVICE *see* FAST FOOD
Soden, H von *see* URKUNDEN ZUR ERSTEHUNGSGESCHICHTE DES DONATISMUS
Soden, Hans, Freiherr von *see*
- DIE CYPRIANISCHE BRIEFSAMMLUNG
- DAS LATEINISCHE NEUE TESTAMENT IN AFRIKA ZUR ZEIT CYPRIANS (T.U.U. 3-33)

Soden, Hermann *see*
- URCHRISTLICHE LITERATURGESCHICHTE: DIE SCHRIFTEN DES NEUEN TESTAMENTS
- DIE WICHTIGSTEN FRAGEN IM LEBEN JESU: FERIENKURSVORTRAEGE

Soderberg, Gary L *see* THE EFFECTS OF FIXED AND HINGED ANKLE FOOT ORTHOSES ON GAIT MYOELECTRIC ACTIVITY AND STANDING JOINT ALIGNMENT IN CHILDREN WITH CEREBRAL PALSY
SODERFORORTERNAS NYHETER – Stockholm, 1987-90 – 1 – sw Kungliga [072]
SODERHAMNS-HALSINGEKURIREN – Soderhamn, Sweden. 1967-78. Soderhamnskuriren, 1895-1955 – 237r – 1 – sw Kungliga [072]
SODERHAMNS-HALSINGEKURIREN – Soderhamn, Sweden. 1979-81 – 1 – sw Kungliga [072]
SODERHAMNSKURIREN *see* SODERHAMNS-HALSINGEKURIREN
SODERMANLANDS LANS TIDNING – Nykoping, Sweden. 1862-1952 – 1 – sw Kungliga [072]
SODERMANLANDS NYHETER – Nykoping, Sweden. 1893-1978 – 380r – 1 – sw Kungliga [072]
SODERMANLANDS NYHETER – Nykoping, Sweden. 1979- – 1 – sw Kungliga [072]
SODERNYHETERNA – Stockholm, Sweden. 1982-87 – 1 – sw Kungliga [072]
SODERNYHETERNA *see* HUDDINGEPOSTEN
SODERORT – Stockholm, Sweden. 1979-82. Soderposten – Soderposten – 1 – sw Kungliga [072]
SODERPOSTEN – Stockholm, Sweden. 1982-87 – 1 – sw Kungliga [072]
SODERTALJE ALLEHANDA – Sodertalje, Sweden. 1979-81 – 1 – sw Kungliga [072]
SODERTALJE TIDNING – Sodertalje, Sweden. 1891-1930 – 36r – 1 – sw Kungliga [072]
SODERTELGE TIDNING – Sodertalje, Sweden. 1861-80 – 3r – 1 – sw Kungliga [072]
SODERTIDNINGEN – Stockholm, Sweden. 1979-82 – 1 – sw Kungliga [072]
Sodko, N P *see* RUSSKAIA BIBLIOGRAFIIA, GOD PERVYI (1878)
SODRA DALARNES TIDNING – (Saters Tidning, 1979-82) – Borlange, Sweden. 1979- – 1 – sw Kungliga [072]
SODRA DALARNES TIDNING – (Tidning for Hedemora, Sater och Avesta eller Sodra Dalarnes Veckoblad 1880-87; Sodra Dalarnes Tidning 1887-1915) – Hedemora, Sweden – 28r – 1 – sw Kungliga [072]
SODRA ROSLAGEN – Norrtalje, 1988-94 – 1 – sw Kungliga [072]
SODRA ROSLAGSTIDNINGEN – Stockholm, Sweden. 1942 – 1 reel – 1 – sw Kungliga [072]
SOEARA INDONESIA – (Lacking: 1945, V.1(1-9, 11, 13-16)) – San Francisco: Perhimpoenan Indonesia, 1945 – 3mf – 9 – SE-440/1 – ne IDC [950]
SOEARA MADJILIS ISLAMIL A'LAA INDONESIA – (Lacking: 1945, V.3(18). Microfiche Nos 423-463) – Djakarta, 2603-2605.-1943-1945.-3v – 41mf – 9 – SE-2002/1 – ne IDC [260]
SOEARA MOESLIMIN INDONESIA – (Lacking: 1945, V.3(18)) – Djakarta, 1943-1945 – 36mf – 9 – SE-411/1 – ne IDC [950]
SOEARA TANI – (Lacking: 1946, V.1(1)) – Jogjakarta; Barisan Tani Indonesia, 1946-1947 – 1mf – 9 – SE-412/1 – ne IDC [950]
SOEARA ZAMAN; SJA'IR DAN PANTOEN PADA MASA PERANG INI / Takahashi, K – (Microfiche Nos 172-173) – Djakarta: Djawa Gunseikanbu, Hongyakusito, 2605. 7, 133p – 2mf – 9 – SE-2002/1 – ne IDC [950]
Soederblom, Nathan *see*
- DEN ALLMAENNA RELIGIONSHISTORIEN OCH DEN KYRKLIGA TEOLOGIEN
- DEN ENSKILDE OCH KYRKAN
- LES FRAVASHIS
- GUDSTRONS UPPKIMST
- HERDABREF TILL PRAESTERSKAPET OCH FOERSAMLINGARNA I UPPSALA AERKESTIFT
- DIE RELIGION UND DIE SOZIALE ENTWICKLUNG
- RELIGIONSPROBLEMET INOM KATOLICISM OCH PROTESTANTISM
- UR RELIGIONENS HISTORIA
- VATER, SOHN UND GEIST
- LA VIE FUTURE D'APRES LE MAZDEISME

SOEDERHAMNSKURIREN – Soederhamn, 1956-67 – 9 – sw Kungliga [072]
SOEDERKOEPINGS NYA TIDNING – Soederkoeping, 1862-79 – 9 – sw Kungliga [072]
SOEDERKOEPINGSPOSTEN – Soederkoeping, 1879-1948 – 9 – sw Kungliga [072]
SOEDRA HALLANDS TIDNING LAHOLMSPOSTEN – Laholm, Sweden. 1912 – 1 – sw Kungliga [072]
SOEDRA SVERIGE – Malmoe, 1898 – 9 – sw Kungliga [072]
SOEHNE DER HEIMAT : EIN EPISCHER BERICHT AUS UNSEREN TAGEN / Podewils, Clemens, Graf – Berlin: S Fischer, 1941 – 1r – 1 – us U.W. Library [430]
DIE SOEHNE DES HERRN BUDIWO : EINE DICHTUNG / Sperl, August – Muenchen: C H Beck, 1922 – 1r – 1 – us U.W. Library [810]
Soekarno *see* MOLUCCAS SPEECHES OF PRESIDENT SOEKARNO
SOEKARNO, PRESIDENT OF INDONESIA / Indonesia. Kementerian Penerangan – SE-10,578 1. 1958 – 9 – ne IDC [920]
Soell, Hartmut Diethelm *see* DIE SOZIALDEMOKRATISCHE ARBEITERBEWEGUNG IM REICHSLAND ELSASS-LOTHRINGEN 1871-1918
SOELOEH TENTARA – (Lacking: 1947(5, 11-13, 20-21)) – Jogjakarta, 1947-1948 – 11mf – 9 – SE-597/1 – ne IDC [950]
SOEMMTLICHE WERKE / Spielhagen, Friedrich – Neue vom Verfasser revidirte Ausgabe. Bd. I-III, V-X. Berlin, O. Janke, 187-. Film Mas C 601 – 1 – us H.U. Library [080]
SOEMO – (Microfiche No 170) – Djakarta; Kantor Pengadjaran, 2604 – 1mf – 9 – SE-2002/1 – ne IDC [950]
Soemodinoto, Soekanto *see* DUKUN AS REFERRER OF FAMILY PLANNING ACCEPTORS
SOENDAGEN – Goeteborg, 1884-85 – 9 – sw Kungliga [072]
SOENUMID – Luebeck. Germany. -w. 27 Oct 1945-29 Mar 1946, 11 Oct 1946-29 Oct 1948. (2 reels) – 1 – uk British Libr Newspaper [072]
SOERABAIASCH HANDELSBLAD, 1866-1917 / Netherlands. Royal Library. The Hague. Newspaper Department – (1866-75.-182mf.Dfl1,135.00; 1876-85.-260mf. Dfl1,625.00; 1886-95.-293mf.Dfl1,830.00; 1896-1900.-222mf. Dfl1,385.00; 1901-05.-298mf.Dfl1,860.00; 1906-10.-367mf.Dfl2,295.00; 1911-17.-432mf.Dfl2,700.00) – One of the earliest dailies of the Indies. KB003 – 2067mf – 9 – Dfl12,870.00 silver – ne MMF Publ [072]

Soergel, Albert *see* DICHTUNG UND DICHTER DER ZEIT
Soeria Nata Atmadja, R A A A *see* DE REGENTENPOSITIE
Soerjaningrat, R M *see* SOEWARDI
SOERMLANDSTIDNINGEN MED TROSA ANNONSBLAD – Eskilstuna, 1972 – 9 – sw Kungliga [072]
SOESTER ANZEIGER – Soest, Germany. 1992- – 10r per yr – 1 – gw Mikrofilm [072]
SOESTER KREISBLATT – Soest, Germany. 1032 (Nr 34)-26 Sept 1856 – 2r – 1 – gw Mikrofilm [072]
Soetadi, R *see* SEISMIC ZONES IN INDONESIA
Soetken Gerijts v. Rotterdamme *see* EEN NIEU GHEESTELIJCK LIEDT-BOECXKEN. WT DEN O. ENDE N.T. GHEMAECT
Soeurs de la Charite de Quebec. Academie *see* ARBRE HISTORIQUE DES DYNASTIES FRANCAISES
Soeurs de Sainte-Anne *see* DICTIONNAIRE BIOGRAPHIQUE DE MUSICIENS ET VOCABULAIRE DE TERMES MUSICAUX
LES SOEURS MISSIONNAIRES DE L'IMMACULEE-CONCEPTION, PREMIER INSTITUT MISSIONNAIRE D'ORIGINE CANADIENNE, 1902-1932 : BIBLIOGRAPHIE ANALYTIQUE / Pauline-Marie, Soeur – 1964. SEM105P4 – 5mf – 9 – cn Bibl Nat [240]
SOEWARDI : ALS IK EENS NEDERLANDER WAS...UITG. VAN HET INLANDSCH COMITE TOT HERDENKING VAN NEERLANDS HONDERDJARIGE VRIJHEID / Soerjaningrat, R M – Badoeng, 1913 – 1mf – 9 – SE-1428/1 – ne IDC [950]
Sofer, J *see* EDUT BI-YEHOSEF
Soffe, Emil *see* CHARLES SEALSFIELD (CARL POSTL)
SOFIA NEWS – (Lacking: 1973-74) – Sofia, Bulgaria. 1970-Jul 1991 – 12r – 1 – us L of C Photodup [949]
SOFIIA – Zhurnal iskusstva i literaturnyi. v. 1-6. M. 1914. BR-3763 2 – 8 – ne IDC [073]
SOFIISKA PRAVDA – Sofia, Bulgaria. 1956-69 – 9r – 1 – us L of C Photodup [949]
SOFIISKA PRAVDA – Sofia, Bulgaria. -tw. 1960-70. 11 reels – 1 – uk British Libr Newspaper [949]
Sofinov, PG *see* IZ ISTORII RUSSKOI DO REVOLIUTSIONNOI ARKHEOGRAFII
EIN SOFORTPROGRAMM ZUR BEHEBUNG DER ARBEITSLOSIGKEIT / Beckerath, Ulrich von – 9 – 1.00f – at Libertarian Micro [335]
SOFT DRINK INDUSTRY – (With Soft Drink Industry Annual Manual 1969-70) – v49-50 1970 – 9 – $5.00f – us Ross [660]
SOFT NEUROLOGICAL SIGNS IN CLUMSY CHILDREN : INDICATORS OF TIMING AND FORCE CONTROL DYSFUNCTION / Lundy-Ekman, Laurie & Woollacott, Marjorie H – 1990 – 2mf – 9 – $8.00 – us Microform Publ [150]
SOFTALK – v4. 1983-84 – 9 – us UMI [510]
SOFTALK FOR THE IBM PERSONAL COMPUTER – v2-3. 1983-84 – 9 – us UMI [000]
SOFTWARE – v.1-. 1981- – 1,5,6,9 – us UMI [510]
SOFTWARE CANADA – (1985- . 5,6,9) – v1- . 1982- – 1 – us UMI [073]
SOFTWARE CANADA – (Contained in: Canadian Datasystems) – Toronto, 1986-1989 – 9 – cn Micromedia [000]
SOFTWARE CANADA *see* CANADIAN DATASYSTEMS
SOFTWARE JOURNAL – U.S. ed. v1-. 1984- – 1,5,6,9 – us UMI [073]
SOFTWARE NEWS – v.1-. 1981- – 1,5,6,9 – us UMI [510]
SOFTWARE. PRACTICE AND EXPERIENCE – v. 1-. 1971- – 1,5,6,9 – us UMI [510]
SOFTWARE REVIEW: SR – v1-2. 1982-83 – 1 – us UMI [510]
SOGDICA / Henning, W B – 1940 – 1 – uk Microform Academic [490]
DER SOGENANNTE HISTORISCHE JESUS UND DER GESCHICHTLICHE, BIBLISCHE CHRISTUS / Kaehler, Martin – (Includes bibliographical references) – 2. erw. erl. Aufl. Leipzig: A Deichert (Georg Boehme), 1896 – 1mf – 9 – 0-8370-38243 – 1985-1824 – us A.T.L.A. [240]
DIE SOGENANNTE ILMENAUISCHE EMPOERUNG VON 1768 : EIN TRUEBER ABSCHNITT AUS ILMENAUS VORGOETHISCHER ZEIT / Voigt, Julius – (Includes bibliographical references) – Leipzig: Xenien-Verlag, 1912 – 1r – 1 – us U.W. Library [430]
DER SOGENANNTE PRAEDESTINATUS : EIN BEITRAG ZUR GESCHICHTE DES PELAGIANISMUS (T.U.U. 2-24/4) / Schubert, Hans von – Leipzig, 1903 – 3mf – 9 – ne Slangenburg [240]
DAS SOGENANNTE RELIGIONSGESPRAECH AM HOF DER SASANIDEN (T.U.U. 2-19/3A) / Brakte, E – Leipzig, 1899 – 5mf – 9 – ne Slangenburg [240]
DER SOGENANNTE SOPHRONIUS (T.U.U. 1-14/1B) / Gebhardt, Oscar von – Leipzig, 1896 – 2mf – 9 – ne Slangenburg [240]
DIE SOGENANNTEN SIEBENBUERGISCHEN EHEN... / Fuchs, W – Wien, 1889 – 3mf – 1 – ILM-3521/1 – ne IDC [327]
SOGLASHENII A S GERMANIE I ZAKLI UCHENNYE V BERLINE 6 MAI A 1921 GODA / Narodny i komissariat inostrannykh del – Moskva: Komissariat, 1921 – 1 – CSUX90-B5650 – us Hoover Inst Photo [340]
SOGNO D'UNA NOTTE D'ESTATE-A MIDSUMMER NIGHT'S DREAM / Shakespeare, William – In Italian. Introduzione e note di G.N. Giordano-Orsini. Firenze: G.C. Sansoni, 1934.xxxiii,233p – 1 – us U.W. Library [820]
Sohm, Rudolf *see*
– OUTLINES OF CHURCH HISTORY
– WESEN UND URSPRUNG DES KATHOLIZISMUS
DER SOHN : ROMAN AUS DEN BERGEN / Widmann, Ines – Stuttgart: J G Cotta, c1938 – 1r – 1 – us U.W. Library [830]
DER SOHN DER WILDNISS : DRAMATISCHES GEDICHT / Halm, Friedrich – 10. Aufl. Wien: C Gerold, 1896 – 1r – 1 – us U.W. Library [810]
DER SOHN DES MANITU : EINE ERZAEHLUNG VOM KAMPFE TECUMSEHS / Wittek, Erhard – Stuttgart: Kosmos, c1938 – 1r – 1 – us U.W. Library [830]
Sohrab, Mirza Ahmad *see* ABDUL BAHA IN EGYPT
THE SOIL – New York. v. 1, no. 1-5. Dec 1916-July 1917 – 1 – us NY Public [073]
SOIL AND FRESHWATER FISH CULTURE : SIMPLE METHODS FOR AQUACULTURE / Coche, A G – 1986 – 174p – it F.A.O. [639]
SOIL AND PLANT TESTING AND ANALYSIS – 1980 – 251p – it F.A.O. [631]
SOIL AND WATER CONSERVATION IN SEMI-ARID AREAS – 1987 – 185p – it F.A.O. [333]
SOIL AND WATER CONSERVATION NEWS – v1- 1980- – 1,5,6,9 – us UMI [333]
SOIL BIOLOGY AND BIOCHEMISTRY – (Back issues of journal available from UMI) – 12 issues/y. v25. 1993 – 9 – £472.00y – uk Elsevier Sci [574]
SOIL BIOLOGY AND BIOCHEMISTRY – v1- 1969- – 5,6,9 – us UMI [631]
SOIL CONSERVATION – v1- 1935- 1; v36- 5,6; v42- 9 – us UMI [333]
SOIL CONSERVATION AND MANAGEMENT IN DEVELOPING COUNTRIES – 1981 – 216p – it F.A.O. [631]
SOIL CONSERVATION FOR DEVELOPING COUNTRIES – 1981 – 104p – it F.A.O. [631]
SOIL CONSERVATION FOR SMALL FARMERS IN THE HUMID TROPICS – 1989 – 113p – it F.A.O. [631]
SOIL EROSION BY WATER : SOME MEASURES FOR ITS CONTROL ON CULTIVATED LANDS – 1978 – 284p – it F.A.O. [631]
SOIL EROSION BY WIND AND MEASURES FOR ITS CONTROL ON AGRICULTURAL LANDS – 1978 – 88p – it F.A.O. [631]
SOIL FERTILITY INVESTIGATIONS ON FARMERS' FIELDS – 1977 – 84p – it F.A.O. [631]
SOIL MANAGEMENT: COMPOST PRODUCTION AND USE IN TROPICAL AND SUBTROPICAL ENVIRONMENTS – 1987 – 193p – it F.A.O. [631]
SOIL MAP LEAFLET / South Carolina. Agricultural Experiment Station. Clemson – n.1-47. 1965-69 – 1,5 – us Spaulding [631]
SOIL MECHANICS AND FOUNDATION ENGINEERING – v1-31. 1964-94 – 1,5 – $65.00 – us UMI [624]
SOIL REPORT / Illinois. Agricultural Experiment Station – n.1-87. 1911-69 – 1, 5 – us Spaulding [631]
SOIL SCIENCE – v1-162. 1916-96 – 1,5,6,9 – $90.00r – us Williams [631]
Soil Science Society of America *see* PROCEEDINGS
SOIL SERIES / Minnesota. College of Agriculture – nos.1-90. 1943-73 – 1,5,6 – us Spaulding [631]
SOIL SOLARIZATION : PROCEEDINGS OF THE FIRST INTERNATIONAL CONFERENCE ON SOIL SOLARIZATION; AMMAN, 19-25 FEBRUARY 1990 – 1991 – 411p – it F.A.O. [631]
SOIL SURVEY INTERPRETATION FOR ENGINEERING PURPOSES – 1978 – 30p – it F.A.O. [624]
SOIL SURVEY INVESTIGATIONS FOR IRRIGATION – 1979 – 198p – it F.A.O. [631]
SOIL SURVEY SERIES / South Dakota. State University. Agricultural Experiment Station – nos.1-5. 1955-62 – 1,5,6 – us Spaulding [631]
SOIL & TILLAGE RESEARCH – v1-4. 1981-84 – 1,5,6,13 – sz Elsevier [631]
SOILLESS CULTURE FOR HORTICULTURAL CORP PRODUCTION – 1990 – 202p – it F.A.O. [580]
SOILS AND FERTILIZERS – Harpenden: Imperial Bureau of Social Science. v1-14. 1938-41 – 27mf – 9 – 5293c/2 – ne IDC [630]
SOILS AND FERTILIZERS – v1-17. 1938-54 – 1,5,6 – us Princeton Micro [631]
SOILS BULLETIN / Wisconsin. College of Agriculture. Dept. of Soils – 1959-Nov 1963, n.1-6 – 1,5 – us Spaulding [630]
SOILS OF THE ARID ZONES OF CHILE – 1966 – 96p – it F.A.O. [631]
SOI-MEME – Publication de litterature et d'art. no. 1-24 25. Paris. fevr 1917-janv fevr 1919 – 1 – fr A.C.R.P.P. [800]
LE SOIR – Bruxelles: s.n., 1949-sep 1988 – us Res Libr [072]
LE SOIR – (Ed. de Versailles. 22 mars-2 juin 1871. 1) – Politique et litteraire, puis Le seul Journal de Gauche du Soir. Paris.nov 1869-1871, juil-dec 1873, juil 1927-1928, 1930 – 1 – fr A.C.R.P.P. [072]
LE SOIR : GRAND FORMAT / ed by Beaugrand, Honore – Montreal, Canada. 22,26,27 jan 1883 – 1r – 1 – Can$25.00 – cn Can Microfilming [072]
LE SOIR – Montreal, Canada. 19 sep 1884 – 1r – 1 – Can$25.00 – cn Can Microfilming [072]
LE SOIR – Montreal, Canada. 24 avr-31 aut 1896 – 1r – 1 – Can$40.00 – cn Can Microfilming [072]
LE SOIR – Port-au-Prince. Sept 5 1944-May 31 1946. Incomplete – 1 – us NY Public [072]
LE SOIR (BRUSSELS, BELGIUM) – (Library has: v.28, no.206-207, 211-232; v.32, no.1-2, 9, 27; v.54, no.139-318; v.55-62. July 25-26, July 30-Aug. 20, 1914; Nov.18-19, 26, Dec. 14, 1918; June 14) – Bruxelles: Le Soir, 1887 – 1 – CSUX87-S390 – us Hoover Inst Photo [949]
LA SOIREE ORAGEUSE, COMEDIE ET UN ACTE ET EN PROSE, OP. 12 / Dalayrac, N – Paris: Pleyel, 179- – 1 – us Sibley [780]
LES SOIREES CANADIENNES – (Suivie de: Nouvelles soirees canadiennes) – Quebec: Brousseau, 1861-[1865] – 9 – cn C.I.H.M. [073]
LES SOIREES CANADIENNES *see* NOUVELLES SOUREES CANADIENNES
SOIREES DE FERNEY, OU, CONFIDENCES DE VOLTAIRE / Despreaux de la Condamine, S – Recueillies par un ami de ce grand homme. Paris: Dentu, 1802. XII – 9 – fr Hachette [920]
LES SOIREES DE PARIS – G. Apollinaire et J. Cerusse. no. 1-26 27. Paris. fevr 1912-juil aout 1914 – 1 – fr A.C.R.P.P. [073]
SOIR-REPUBLICAIN – Red. en chef Albert Camus. no. 1-117. Alger. sept 1939-janv 1940. mq no. 2 – 1 – fr A.C.R.P.P. [073]
Soiterus, M *see* DE BELLO PANNONICO, PER ILVSTRISSIMVM PRINCIPEM DOMINUM AC DOMINUM FREDERICUM COMITEM...
SOIUZ – Ekaterinodar, 1914 n1 – 1mf – 9 – COR-691/1 – ne IDC [334]
SOIUZ MOLODEZHI – Nr. 3. pri uchastii poetov "Gileia". Spb. 1913. BR-3610 2 – 8 – ne IDC [460]
SOIUZ POTREBITELEI – (Missing: 1904 n19; 1907 n10, 26, 39; 1915 n5; 1917 n6, 10; 1918 n27, 29-30; 1919 n1-2, 11; 1920 n1, 4, 6-7; 1921 n1-7, 10-11, 14; 1922 n1-6) – M., 1903-30 n5 – 470mf – 9 – COR-692/1 – ne IDC [334]
Soiuz rabochikh poligraficheskogo proizvodstva S SS R Leningradskii gubernskii otdel *see* PRAVLENIE
Soiuza Russkikh Sotsial'-Demokratov *see* RABOCHEE DELO
SOIUZNICHESKAIA INTERVENTSIIA NA DALNEM VOSTOKE I V SIBIRI : DOKLAD PISHONA / PEREVOD S FRANTSUZSKOGO P. IVANGORODSKOGO; REDAKTSIIA I PREDISLOVIE VL. VILENSKOGO-SIBIRIAKOVA / Chopin, Jules – Moskva: Gos. izd-vo, 1925 – 1 – CSUX88-B9106 – us Hoover Inst Photo [947]
SOIUZNOE STROITEL'STVO KOOPERATIVOV / Chaianov, A V – M., 1916 – 1mf – 9 – COR-140/1 – ne IDC [334]
SOIUZNOE STROITEL'STVO KOOPERATIVOV – M., 1916 – 1mf – 9 – COR-108/1 – ne IDC [334]
SOIUZY KOOPERATIVOV ROSSII : SPRAVOCHNYE SVEDENIIA PO MATERIALAM STATISTIKO-EKONOMICHESKOGO OTDELA SOVETA VSEROSSIISKIKH KOOPERATIVNYKH S'EZDOV NA 1 AVG 1919 G – M., 1919 – 5mf – 9 – COR-748/1 – ne IDC [310]
SOIUZY POTREBITEL'SKIKH OBSHCHESTVO : DLIA CHEGO ONI NUZHNY I KAK ONI POSTROENY / Nechaev, A I – Ed 2. M., 1929 – 2mf – 9 – COR-337/1 – ne IDC [334]
SOIXANTE ANS DE LIBERTE, 1837-97: SOUVENIRS PATRIOTIQUES PAR NOS MEILLEURS ECRIVAINS – Compile par Ant. Bissonnette. 1898?. 03586. (Pre-1900 Canadiana) – 9 – cn C.I.H.M. [971]
SOJOURNERS – (Cont: Post American) – v5-18. 1976-89 (complete) – 7r – 1 – ATLA S0280A – us A.T.L.A. [073]
SOJOURNERS – v5- . 1976- – 1,5,6,9 – us UMI [073]
SOJOURNERS *see* POST AMERICAN
Soko, B J *see* "STYLISTIQUE ET MESSAGES DANS LE VIMBUZA"
SOKOL – St. Louis, MO, May, December 1933; Jan.-July, Oct., Nov. 1934 – 1r – 1 – us I.H.R.C. [975]
SOKOL SOJEDINENIJA = FALCON OF THE GREEK CATHOLIC UNION – Homestead, PA: Greek Catholic Union of the USA, aug 30 1914-aug 17 1926 – us Res Libr [073]
Sokolov, A N *see* OCHERKI PO ISTORII RUSSKOI POEMY 18 I PERVOI POLOVINY 19 VEKA
Sokolov, A P *see* RUSSKAIA MORSKAIA BIBLIOTEKA 1701-1851. ISCHISLENIE I OPISANIE KNIG, RUKOPISEI I STATEI PO MORSKOMU DELU ZA 150 LET. 2-OE IZD
Sokolov, B S *see* GEOLOGY REVIEWS
Sokolov, Boris Matveevich *see* SKAZKI I PESNI BELOZERSKOGO KRAIA
Sokolov, K N *see* PRAVLENIE GENERALA DENIKINA
Sokolov, P *see* OBSHCHII TSERKOVNO-SLAVIANOROSSIISKII SLOVAR'
Sokolow, N *see*
– HA-ASIF
– SEFER HA-SHANAH
– SEFER HA-YOVEL LE-NAHUM SOKOLOW
Sokolowski, Emil *see* DIE BEGRIFFE GEIST UND LEBEN BEI PAULUS
SOKOTO PROVINCIAL GAZETTEER / Harris, P G – (Filmed with: Daniel, F de F A History of Katsina) – [s.l: s.n., 19-] – us Res Libr [960]
Sokowati, S *see* TNI AND CIVIC MISSION, AN ASPECT OF REGIONAL DEVELOPMENT
SOKRATES UND DAS ALTE CHRISTENTUM : VORTRAG / Geffcken, Johannes – Heidelberg: C. Winter, 1908 – 1mf – us A.T.L.A. [240]
SOKROVISHCHA DREVNEI PIS'MENNOSTI I STAROI PECHATI – Basic survey of 27 ms collections and seven collections of early printed books in ms division of State Historical Museum. BR-11,018/1 – 9 – ne IDC [090]
EL SOL – Curacao. Netherlands West Indies. 1910-1911 – 1 – us UMI [072]
EL SOL : DIARIO INDEPENDENTE – Madrid, Spain. 1 Dec 1917-1936 – 74r – 1 – us L of C Photodup [072]
EL SOL – Madrid, [nov 19-23 1930; 1931-oct 21 1936] – 23r – 1 – us Res Libr [072]
LE SOL – Roberval, 10 jun 1919 – 1r – 1 – Can$25.00 – cn Can Microfilming [072]
O SOL – Lisbon. No.1-8, 9 Mar 1976-27 Apr 1976. (Portuguese Revolution of 1974. Newspapers from Portugal publ. from 21 Feb 1971 to 15 Feb 1980, collected and filmed by University of Wisconsin-Madison libraries.) – 1 – us U.W. Library [072]

O SOL – Santos-Dumont, Jan-Dec 1934; Jul 1935-Oct 1936; May 1937; Jan-Jun, Oct-Nov 1938; Apr 1939; Feb 1940; Jan, Apr, Jun-Jul, Oct-Dec 1941; Jan-Feb, May-Jul 1942; Jan 1943-Oct 1944; Mar-Apr, Jul-Oct, Dec 1945; Jan-Mar 1946; Apr 1947-1 Apr 1951 – 1,5,6 – bl Biblioteca [072]

SOL DE LA MEDICINA QUE ALUMBRA A LOS QUE IGNORAN LA VERDADERA DOCTRINA... / Guerrero, J – Madrid, 1682 – 2mf – 9 – sp Cultura [610]

THE SOL FEINSTONE COLLECTION OF THE AMERICAN REVOLUTION / Feinstone, Sol – (With printed guide) – 1972 – 5r – 1 – $425.00 – S1849 – us Scholarly Res [975]

Sola, F *see*
- OBSERVACION Y SUMARIA RELACION DE LAS VIRUELAS
- PARECER ACERCA DE LA ESSENCIA Y CURA...GARROTILLO
- PARECER...ACERCA DE LOS POLVOS VENENOSOS DE MILAN

SOLAKZADE TARIHI / Celebi, Solakzade Mehmed Hemdemi – Istanbul, 1297 – 14mf – 9 – $47.25 – us MEDOC [949]

Solana y Gutierrez, Mateo *see*
- DON HERNANDO CORTES, MARQUES DEL VALLE DE OAJACE
- DON HERNANDO CORTES...MARQUES DEL VALLE DE OCIJACA

Solander, D *see* THE NATURAL HISTORY OF MANY CURIOUS AND UNCOMMON ZOOPHYTES

SOLANO AND NAPA COUNTIES, CALIFORNIA – 1884-1906. 260 maps. 10 towns. Sanborn Company Fire Insurance Maps – 1 – $46.00r – us Shkurkin [910]

Solano Bote, Jose *see* SENALES...NOCHE... ARMADA DEL REY

SOLANO COUNTY COURIER – Suisun, CA. Jan 1915-Jun 1937; 1940-43 – 9r – 1 – $450.00 – B03017 – us Library Micro [071]

SOLANO COUNTY HERALD – Benicia, CA. 1855-58 – 1r – 1 – $50.00 – B02052 – us Library Micro [071]

Solano de Figueroa y Altamirano, Juan *see*
- 25 SERMON...SAN JUAN DE LA MATA
- 25TH SERMON EN LA FESTIVIDAD DEL GLORIOSO PATRIARCA SAN JUAN DE LA MATA, FUNDADOR DE LA ORDEN DE LA SANTISIMA TRINIDAD...
- HISTORIA ECLESIASTICA DE LA CIUDAD Y OBISPADO DE BADAJOZ
- HISTORIA...DE MEDELLIN
- SAN JONAS
- SERMON DE SAN ROQUE
- SERMON...SAN IGNACIO DE LOYOLA
- SERMON...VIRGEN DE LA PIEDAD
- VIDA...MADRE ISABEL DE LA CRUZ

Solano, F I *see* NOVA INSTRUCCAO MUSICAL, OU THEORICA PRATICA DA MUSICA RYTHMICA

THE SOLANO HERALD – Suisun, CA. 1861-63 – 1r – 1 – $50.00 – C03542 – us Library Micro [071]

Solano Pedrero, Carlos *see* ASAMBLEA PLENARIA DEL CONSEJO ECONOMICO SINDICAL

THE SOLANO PRESS-WEEKLY – Suisun, CA. 1866-1868 – 1r – 1 – $50.00 – B03543 – us Library Micro [071]

SOLANO REPUBLICAN – Fairfield. Calif. -w. 1945-53 – 1 – us UMI [071]

SOLANO REPUBLICAN – Suisun, CA. 1862-68; 1870-89; 1891-1915; 1917; 1925 (incomplete) – 29r – 1 – $1,450.00 – B03018 – us Library Micro [071]

SOLANO/NAPA COUNTIES – 1910-20 – 10r – 1 – $500.00 – P00069 – us Library Micro [910]

SOLANORUM GENERUMQUE AFFINIUM SYNOPSIS / Dunal, M F – Monspelii. 1816. B-5911 2 – 8 – ne IDC [580]

SOLAR AGE – v1- 1976- – 1,5,6,9 – us UMI [621]

Solar, Antonio del *see* COMISION PROVINCIAL DE MONUMENTOS HISTORICOS Y ARTISTICOS DE BADAJOZ

SOLAR CELLS – v1-12. 1979-84 – 1,5,6,13 – sz Elsevier [621]

SOLAR DRYING OF FISH AND PADDY – 1989 – 59p – it F.A.O. [630]

SOLAR ENERGY – (Back issues of journal available from UMI) – 12 issues/y. v50-51. 1993 – 9 – £312.00y – uk Elsevier Sci [530]

SOLAR ENERGY / ed by Palz, W et al – 1983- – 1,5,9 – us Harwood [621]

SOLAR ENERGY – v1- 1957- – 5,6,9 – us UMI [621]

SOLAR ENERGY IN SMALL-SCALE MILK COLLECTION AND PROCESSING – 1983 – 120p – it F.A.O. [333]

SOLAR ENERGY MATERIALS – v1-11. 1979-84 – 1,5,6,13 – sz Elsevier [621]

SOLAR ENGINEERING – v1- Jan 1976-May 1976 – 1 – us UMI [621]

SOLAR ENGINEERING AND CONTRACTING – v1- 1982- – 1,5,6,9 – us UMI [621]

SOLAR ENGINEERING MAGAZINE – v1- 1976- – 1,5,6,9 – us UMI [621]

SOLAR HEATING AND COOLING – 1976-79 – 1 – us UMI [621]

SOLAR MAGAZINE – (1986- 1,5,6) – 1983- – 9 – us UMI [621]

SOLAR PHYSICS – (v91-. 1984-. 5,6,9) – v1-. 1967- – 1 – us UMI [073]

SOLAR SYSTEM RESEARCH – v1-28. 1967-94 – 1,5 – $65.00v – us UMI [520]

Solar y Maeztu, Jose del *see* PANORAMA SOCIAL

Solar y Taboada, Antonio *see*
- EL ADELANTADO HERNANDO DE SOTO
- ADICION DEL INVENTARIO DEL MUSEO DE LA COMISION PROVINCIAL DE MONUMENTOS HISTORICOS Y ARTISTICOS DE BADAJOZ
- LOS ALVARADOS EN EL – NUEVO MUNDO
- EL CORONEL DE CABALLERIA DON ANTONIO DEL SOLAR E IBANEZ
- EL DEBER Y LA PASION
- DON EUGENIO ESCOBAR PRIETO. APUNTES DE SU VIDA
- DON LORENZO SUAREZ DE FIGUEROA Y DE MENDOZA. NOTAS SOBRE SU DESCENDENCIA
- DON NARCISO DIAZ DE ESCOVAR. APUNTES DE SU VIDA
- DON RODRIGO DE TORRES, PRIMER MARQUES DE MATALLANA
- DONA MENCIA DE LOS NIDOS
- FIAT LUX
- INDICE DE LOS DOCUMENTOS QUE PRESENTO PARA INGRESAR EN EL REAL CUERPO...Y...ORDEN MILITAR DE MALTA...
- JUAN MARTIN ROCO. SENOR DE CAMPOFRIO
- MARINOS EXTREMNOS
- MEMORIAL QUE ELEVO A S.M. EN 1673 DON INIGO ANTONIO ARGUELLO CARVAJAL...
- MILITARES EXTREMENOS
- REGALA MANUSCRITOS DE ALCANTARA A LA REAL ACADEMIA DE LA HISTORIA
- LOS VALDIVIA

Solar y Taboada, Antonio del *see* PEDRO DE VALDIVIA CONQUITADOR DE CHILE

Solar y Taboada, Antonio et al *see* PIEDRAS AREMERAS DE LA PROVINCIA DE BADAJOZ

DIE SOLARE SEITE DES ALTTESTAMENTLICHEN GOTTESBEGRIFFES / Vollers, Karl – Leipzig: B.G. Teubner, 1906. 1 fiche – 9 – us A.T.L.A. [240]

Solari, A E *see* ELITES Y DESARROLLO EN AMERICA LATINA

Solberg, Thorvald *see* COPYRIGHT IN CONGRESS, 1789-1904

IL SOLCO – New York, NY. 1927-1928(?) – us I.H.R.C. [073]

O SOLDADO : ORGAM DOS INTERESSES DA GUARDA NACIONAL NO ESTADO DO AMAZONAS – Manaos, Amazonas. 5 Set-4 Out 1908 – 1,5,6 – bl Biblioteca [072]

UN SOLDADO DE LA CONQUISTA DE CHILE / Fernandez Duro, Cesareo – Madrid: Tip. Fortanet, 1899 – sp Bibl Santa Ana [972]

DER SOLDAT AUF DEM THRON : EIN BERICHT AUS DEM LEBEN DES ZWEITEN PREUSSENKOENIGS / Helke, Fritz – 3. und 4. Aufl. Berlin: Junge Generation Verlag, c1935 – 1r – 1 – us U.W. Library [920]

LE SOLDAT CITOYEN, OU VUES PATRIOTIQUES SUR LA MANIERE LA PLUS AVANTAGEUSE DE POURVOIR A LA DEFENSE DU ROYAUME / Servan de Gerbey, Joseph – 1780. iv, 640p. (Strategy of War Series) – 9 – fr Hachette [355]

SOLDAT UND KAEMPFER / Holm, Norbert – Berlin: Deutscher Wille, 1938 – 1r – 1 – us U.W. Library [830]

SOLDATEN DES KOENIGS : PREUSSISCHE NOVELLEN / Kier, Martin – Berlin: Brunnen-Verlag, c1943 – 1r – 1 – us U.W. Library [830]

DER SOLDATENEID : EINE ERZAEHLUNG / Tumler, Franz – Muenchen: A Langen, G Mueller, 1939 – 1r – 1 – us U.W. Library [830]

SOLDATS ET MISSIONAIRES AU CONGO DE 1891 A 1894 / Gochet, Alexis Marie – 1896. 240p. (Historical Studies Series) – 9 – 8.75 – fr Bibl Nationale [240]

SOLDATS ET MISSIONAIRES AU CONGO DE 1891 A 1894 / Gochet, Alexis Marie – 3. ed. [Lille]: Societe de Saint-Augustin, 1899 – us Res Libr [960]

SOLDATSKAIA BESEDA – Spb, 1858-67 – 8 – BR-1618 2 – ne IDC [355]

SOLDATY FRONTA I VOPROSY VO INY I MIRA / Fishgendler, Abram Markovich – Petrograd: "Kniga", [1918?] – 1 – CSUX88-B4784 – us Hoover Inst Photo [947]

THE SOLDIER OF CHRIST, OR, TALKS BEFORE CONFIRMATION / Loyola, Mary, Mother; ed by Thurston, Herbert – (Includes index) – London; New York: Burns and Oates, 1904 – 2mf – 9 – 0-8370-7485-1 – 1986-1485 – us A.T.L.A. [240]

SOLDIERS – v1- 1946- 1; v26- 5,6; v30- 9 – us UMI [355]

SOLDIERS AND CITIZENS ALBUM OF WISCONSIN / Grand Army Publishing Co – Biographical Record. Chicago: 1888. Vol. 1. Wisconsin Reel 1; Vol. 2. Wisconsin Reel 2. (The Cox Library Collection) – 5 – us Americana [978]

SOLDIERS' AND PATRIOTS' BIOGRAPHICAL ALBUM / Union Veteran Publishing Co – Chicago, 1892. Illinois Reel 6. (The Cox Library Collection) – 5 – us Americana [978]

SOLDIERS' AND SAILORS' CIVIL RELIEF ACT – Washington: GPO, 1985 – 1mf – 9 – $1.50 – LLMC 96-078B – us L.L.M.C. [340]

SOLDIERS' AND SAILORS' CIVIL RELIEF ACT OF 1940 AS AMENDED : SELECTED CASES AND MATERIALS – Washington: GPO, 1962 – 3mf – 9 – $4.50 – LLMC 96-078 – us L.L.M.C. [340]

SOLDIERS' BURIAL RECORDS / Wyandot County. Ohio. Board of County Commissioners – 1885-1899 – 1r – 1 – $32.50r – us Archival [324]

SOLDIERS DIED IN THE GREAT WAR – 1914-1919 – 1 – uk Manchester Libr [941]

SOLDIER'S DISCHARGE RECORDS / Allen County. Ohio. Recorder – 1865-1946 – 1r – 1 – $32.50r – us Archival [324]

SOLDIERS' DISCHARGE RECORDS / Defiance County. Ohio. Recorder – 1865-1937 – 1r – 1 – $32.50r – us Archival [324]

SOLDIERS' DISCHARGE RECORDS / Henry County. Ohio. Recorder – 1865-1945 – 2r – 1 – $32.50r – us Archival [324]

SOLDIERS' DISCHARGE RECORDS / Putnam County. Ohio. Recorder – 1861-1946 – 2r – 1 – $32.50r – us Archival [324]

SOLDIERS' DISCHARGE RECORDS / Wyandot County. Ohio. Recorder – 1865-1948 – 1r – 1 – $32.50r – us Archival [324]

THE SOLDIERS GAZETTE – Montreal, Canada. 10 nov 1915 – 1r – 1 – Can$25.00 – cn Can Microfilming [072]

SOLDIER'S GRAVE RECORD / Putnam County. Ohio. Recorder – 1949-1976 – 1r – 1 – $32.50r – us Archival [324]

SOLDIERS' GRAVE RECORD INDEX / Putnam County. Ohio. Recorder – 1943-1992 – 1r – 1 – $32.50r – us Archival [324]

SOLDIERS' GRAVE RECORDS / Henry County. Ohio. Recorder – 1835-1976 – 1r – 1 – $32.50r – us Archival [324]

SOLDIERS' GRAVE RECORDS / Wyandot County. Ohio. Recorder – 1782-1972 – 1r – 1 – $32.50r – us Archival [324]

SOLDIERS IN KING PHILIP'S WAR; BEING A CRITICAL ACCOUNT OF THAT WAR,... CONCISE HISTORY OF THE INDIAN WARS OF NEW ENGLAND FROM 1620-1677 / Bodge, George Madison – 1967. 3rd ed. Orig. publ., 1906. Indexed. 8 fiches. F-0866 – 9 – us A.G.L.L. [978]

SOLDIERS OF PERON : ARGENTINA'S MONTONEROS / Gillespie, Richard – Oxford [Oxfordshire]: Clarendon Press; New York: Oxford University Press, 1982 – 1 – CSUXADM8372-B – us Hoover Inst Photo [355]

SOLDIERS' RELIEF APPLIC. LTTRS / Ottawa County. Ohio. Auditor – 1861-1865 – 1r – 1 – $32.50r – us Archival [324]

SOLDIERS' RELIEF DISBURSEMENTS / Defiance County. Ohio. Auditor – 1919-1921 – 1r – 1 – $32.50r – us Archival [324]

A SOLDIER'S STORY / Calhoun, Alfred R – A monologue by Alfred R. Calhoun of New York City. 1895 – 1 – 18.00 – us L of C Photodup [830]

SOLDIERS' VOICE – (Library has v.1, no.1 (Dec. 1933)) – [United States: s.n.], 1933- – 1 – CSUX89-S94 – us Hoover Inst Photo [355]

IL SOLE 24 ORE – (Standing orders available) – Milano, 1965- – 1 – inquire – us Ross [072]

SOLE 24 ORE – 1965-1981 – 6 times per yr – 1 – L480,000 – sz Infoprint [072]

SOLE 24 ORE – 1982-1983 – 12 times per yr – 1 – L960,000 – sz Infoprint [072]

SOLE 24 ORE – 1988-1992 – 12 times per yr – 1 – L960,000 – sz Infoprint [072]

SOLE 24 ORE – 1988-1995 – 12 times per yr – 1 – L960,000 – sz Infoprint [072]

SOLE 24 ORE – (Also available on CD-ROM) – 1984-1987 – 6r per y – 5,6 – Sfr1,176.00 – sz Infoprint [072]

SOLE 24 ORE – (Also available on CD-ROM. 1980-94 on 35mm Sfr1,250.00) – 1980-1995 – 6r per y – 5,6 – F4,500.00 – sz Infoprint [072]

LE SOLEIL – 1970.$99.00; 1971-74.$148.50y; 1975-77.$148.50y 145.00y; AFI; 1 – 1 – us African Imprint [072]

LE SOLEIL – Dakar, Senegal: Societe senegalaise de presse et de publications, [jul 1970-dec 30 1981] – 48r – 1 – us Res Libr [072]

LE SOLEIL / ed by Pacaud, E et al – (1 mar 1975-30 jun 1983 172r Can$55.00. 1 jul 1983-30 avr 1991 94r Can$80.00. 1 mai 1991-31 dec 1992 40r Can$50.00) – Quebec, Canada. 28 dec 1896-28 fev 1975 – 447r – 1 – Can$70.00r – cn Can Microfilming [072]

LE SOLEIL – Paris. 28 fevr 1873-1911 – 1 – fr A.C.R.P.P. [073]

LE SOLEIL – Paris. oct 1865-sept 1867. Fusionne avec: La Chronique de Paris – 1 – fr A.C.R.P.P. [073]

LE SOLEIL – Vancouver, BC. v2 n15. 1 aut 1969-v8 n34. 19 dec 1975 – 3r – 1 – Can$55.00r – cn Can Microfilming [072]

LE SOLEIL *see*
- L'ELECTEUR
- THE SAINT LAWRENCE SUN

LE SOLEIL AU SAGUENAY – Chicoutimi, Canada. 1 avr 1946-29 sep 1973 – 60r – 1 – Can$60.00r – cn Can Microfilming [072]

LE SOLEIL D'AYLMER SUN – Aylmer, Canada. v2 n12. 28 aut 1975 – 1r – 1 – Can$25.00 – cn Can Microfilming [072]

LE SOLEIL DE L'OUEST – Winnipeg, Canada. v6 n7. 15 fev 1912 – 1r – 1 – Can$25.00 – cn Can Microfilming [072]

LE SOLEIL DU DIMANCHE – Suppl. hebdomadaire du Soleil. Paris. 1888-1914 – 1 – fr A.C.R.P.P. [073]

LE SOLEIL DU SAINT LAURENT *see* THE SAINT LAWRENCE SUN

Soleillet, Paul *see*
- L'AFRIQUE OCCIDENTALE
- RECIT D'UNE EXPLORATION COMMERCIALE EN ETHIOPIE...
- LES VOYAGES ET DECOUVERTES DE PAUL SOLEILLET DANS LE SAHARA ET DANS LE SOUDAN.

SOLEMNE NOVENA EN HONOR DE LA SANTISIMA VIRGEN DE LA LUZ, EXCELSA PATRONA DE MALPARTIDA DE PLASENCIA. 1962 – (Tambien ano 1976) – Plasencia: La Victoria, 1962 – 1 – sp Bibl Santa Ana [240]

SOLEMNE NOVENA EN HONOR DE LA SANTISIMA VIRGEN DE LA LUZ, EXCELSA PATRONA DE MALPARTIDA DE PLASENCIA. ANO 1960 – Plasencia: Imp. La Victoria, 1960 – sp Bibl Santa Ana [240]

Soleniere, Eugene de *see* ...LA FEMME COMPOSITEUR..

LA SOLENNE VICTORIA DI ANDREA DORIA : CONTRA LARMATA DEL TURCHO – N.p., 1532 – 1mf – 9 – H-8144/1 – ne IDC [956]

Soler Arques, Carlos *see*
- IDEAL DE FAMILIA...MEMORIA
- LECCIONES DE LENGUA FRANCESA
- NORTE Y MEDIODIA ...EXTREMADURA BAJA
- LAS REFORMAS Y LA SEGUNDA ENSENANZA
- RESUMEN DEL ESTADO...INSTITUTO DE BADAJOZ

Soler de los Rios, Antonio *see* ORACION... MAGESTAD...CABILDOS DE LA CIUDAD DE BADAJOZ...INFANTES

SOLFEGES OU NOUVELLE METHODE DE MUSIQUE PAR DEMANDES ET PAR REPONCES, DIVISEES EN DEUX PARTIES / Rodolphe, J J – Paris. BP-449 1 – 9 – ne IDC [780]

SOLGLIMTEN *see* MALMOTIDNINGEN
SOLIA – Detroit, Mich. 1936-1973 – 1 – us Res Libr [071]
Solichin Salam *see* SEKITAR WALP SANGA
SOLICITOR OF THE POST OFFICE OPINIONS / U.S. Postal Service – (v1-5 entitled: Opinions of the Assistant Attorney General for the Post Office) – v1-9. 1873-1951 (all publ) – 87mf – 9 – $130.00 – LLMC 81-237 – us L.L.M.C. [380]
SOLICITORS' JOURNAL – (Updates planned) – London. v1- 1857- – 9 – LLMC 84-674 – us L.L.M.C. [073]
SOLICITOR'S OPINIONS RELATING TO INDIAN AFFAIRS, 1917-1974 – Washington: Dept of the Interior, GPO. 2v. 1974 (all publ) – 24mf – 9 – $36.00 – LLMC 94-321 – us L.L.M.C. [340]
SOLICTOR'S UNPUBLISHED OPINIONS, 1955-1974 / U.S. Department of the Interior – 1955-74 (all publ) – 354mf – 9 – $531.00 – LLMC 82-506 – us L.L.M.C. [324]
SOLID STATE COMMUNICATIONS – (Back issues of journal available from UMI) – 48 issues/y. v85-88. 1993 – 9 – £930.00y – uk Elsevier Sci [530]
SOLID STATE COMMUNICATIONS – v1- 1963- – 5,6,9 – us UMI [621]
SOLID STATE ELECTRONICS – v1- 1960- – 5,6,9 – us UMI [530]
SOLID STATE IONICS – v1-14. 1980-84 – 1,5,6,13 – sz Elsevier [073]
SOLID STATE TECHNOLOGY – (v.24-. 1981-. 5,6,9) – v.11-. 1968- – 1 – us UMI [621]
SOLIDARIDAD HUMANA / Vital, Antonio Alonso – Caceres: Tip. Extremadura, 1978 – sp Bibl Santa Ana [946]
SOLIDARITA – Prague, Czechoslovakia. Jul 1929-Mar 1938 (incomplete) – 1r – 1 – us L of C Photodup [072]
SOLIDARITAET – Wien, Austria. 1949-55, 1960-61, 1964-66. Incomplete. Continues: Oesterreichische Arbeiter und Angestellte – 1 – us U.W. Library [331]
SOLIDARITAT – Liberec, Czechoslovakia. Oct 1932-Jun 1938 – 1r – 1 – us L of C Photodup [072]
SOLIDARITAT – Prague, Czechoslovakia. 30 Jul 1929; 1930-Jul 1931 – 1r – 1 – us L of C Photodup [072]
SOLIDARITE FRANCAISE – Hebdomadaire de combat. Dir. E. Reifenrath. no. 9-11, 21. Paris. avr-oct 1934 – 1 – fr A.C.R.P.P. [335]
SOLIDARITE FRANCAISE / Parti du Faisceau Francais – Dir. Jean Renard. no. 1, 8-14. Paris. janv-mai 1938 – 1 – fr A.C.R.P.P. [073]
SOLIDARITE NATIONALE / Parti du Faisceau Francais – Dir.-red. en chef Jean Renard. no. 18-21. Paris. juin-juil 1937 – 1 – fr A.C.R.P.P. [073]
SOLIDARITY / National Workers' Committee Movement – London. -m. Feb. 1917-May 1921. 40 feet – 1 – uk British Libr Newspaper [331]
SOLIDER'S GAZETTE – Montreal, Canada. -w. Nov 1915-Nov 1917. 2 reels – 1 – uk British Libr Newspaper [072]
SOLID-STATE ELECTRONICS – (Back issues of journal available from UMI) – 12 issues/y. v36. 1993 – 9 – £534.00y – uk Elsevier Sci [530]
Solie, J *see* MADEMOISELLE DE GUISE, OPERA-COMIQUE EN TROIS ACTES
Solier, A J J *see* MEMOIRE SUR QUELQUES POINTS DE LA PHYSIOLOGIE DES ALGUES
THE SOLILOQUIES OF ST AUGUSTINE / Augustine, Saint, Bishop of Hippo – Boston: Little, Brown, 1910 – 1mf – us A.T.L.A. [240]
SOLILOQUIOS AMOROSOS DE UN ALMA A DIOS / Padecopeo, Gabriel – Madrid: Imp. Prudencio Cuartero, 1863 – 1 – sp Bibl Santa Ana [810]
A SOLILOQUY ON THE ART OF MAN-FISHING / Boston, Thomas – Paisley: Alexander Gardner, 1900 – 1mf – 9 – 0-8370-7127-5 – 1986-1127 – us A.T.L.A. [240]
SOLIMANO / Hasse, J A – (Manuscript, vocal score) – 178- – 1 – us Sibley [780]
O SOLIMOES : ORGAO INDEPENDENTE, LITERARIO, NAO POLITICO PROPRIETARIO E UNICO RESPONSAVEL – Manacapuru, Amazonas. 16 Jul 1933 – 1,5,6 – bl Biblioteca [072]
SOLINGER KREIS-INTELLIGENZBLATT *see* DER VERKUENDIGER
SOLINGER TAGEBLATT *see* DER VERKUENDIGER
SOLINGER WOCHENBLATT *see* DER VERKUENDIGER
SOLINGER ZEITUNG *see* BERGISCHES VOLKSBLATT
Solinus, Caius Julius *see* THE EXCELLENT AND PLEASANT WORK COLLECTANEA RERUM MEMORABILIUM
Solis, Antonio de *see*
- HISTORIA DE LA COMQUISTA DE MEXICO... TOMO 3
- HISTORIA DE LA CONQUISTA DE MEXICO
- HISTORIA DE LA CONQUISTA DE MEXICO. TOMO 2

SOLIS E PVTEO EMERGENTIS, SIVE, DISSERTATIONIS CHYMIATECHNICAE LIBRI TRES / Rhenanus, Johann – Francofvrti: Imprensis A. Humij, 1613-15. 3v in 1. illus. With: dispvtationvm de medicina nova Philippi Paracelse pars prima by Thomas Erastus – 1 – us U.W. Library [540]
Solis Rivadeneira, Antonio de *see* HISTORIA DE LA CONQUISTA DE MEXICO
Solis Rivadeneyra, Antonio de *see*
- HISTORIA DE LA CONQUISTA DE MEJICO
- HISTORIA DE LA CONQUISTA, POBLACION U PROGRESOS DE LA MERICA SEPTENTRIONAL, CONOCIDA CON EL NOMBRE DE NUEVA ESPANA
- HISTORIA...MEJICO...NUEVA ESPANA
- OTUMBA RELACION DE LA BRILLANTE VICTORIA ALCANZADA POR HERNAN CORTES EN MEJICO POR DON...

Solis y Willancourt, Alfonso *see* POESIAS
SOLITAIRE AND PATIENCE; SEVENTY GAMES TO TEST THE CARD PLAYER'S SKILL AND MAKE A LONELY HOUR PASS QUICKLY / Hapgood, George – Philadelphia: Penn Publishing Co., 1913.191p – 1 – us U.W. Library [790]
THE SOLITARY : AND OTHER POEMS; THE CAVALIER: A PLAY / Whitehead, Charles – London: Bentley, 1849 – 1 roll – 1 – 1-55879-436-0 – uk Libr Preservation [800]
SOLL DEUTSCHLAND RUSTEN? DIE SPD ZUM WEHRBEITRAG / Erler, Fritz – Bonn, 1952 – 1 – DM30.00 – gw Mikro Press [943]
SOLL DIE REDE AUF IMMER EIN DUNKLER GESANG BLEIBEN / Schocher, Christian G – 1791 – 9 – us Sibley [780]
Sollberger *see* UR EXCAVATION TEXTS. (ROYAL INSCRIPTIONS, 5. 8)
SOLLEFTEÅ NYA TIDNING – Sollefteå, 1910-11 – 9 – sw Kungliga [072]
SOLLEFTEÅBLADET – OErnskoeldsvik, Sollefteå. 1895-1942 – 9 – sw Kungliga [072]
Solleysel, Jacques de *see* LE PARFAIT MARESCHAL, QUI ENSEIGNE A CONNOISTRE LA BEAUTE, LA BONTE ET LES DEFAUTS DES CHEVAUX
Solling, Gustav *see* DIUTISKA
Sollogub, B *see* UKAZATEL' LUCHSHIKH, PO OTZYVAM PECHATI, UCHEBNIKOV, NAGLIADNYKH UCHEBNYKH POSOBII I METODICHESKIKH RUKOVODSTV NA RUSSKOM I UKRAINSKOM IAZYKAKH
Solms-Laubach, H M C L F *see* DIE HEIMATH UND DER URSPRUNG DES CULTIVIRTEN MELONENBAUMES
SOLNECHNAIA PRIAZHA. IZBORNIK 1890-1918 / Bal'mont, K D – M. 1921. BR-539 2 – 8 – ne IDC [460]
SOLNECHNYI ZAIATS / Inber, Vera Mikhailovna – Moskva: Gos. izdvo, 1928 – 1 – CSUX88-B7296 – us Hoover Inst Photo [460]
Solneman, K H Z *see*
- DER BAHNBRECHER: JOHN HENRY MACKAY
- IDEAS ARCHIVES NO. 1
- DAS MANIFEST DER FREINHEIT UND DES FRIEDENS
- DER WELTVERBAND DER STAATENLOSEN UND DU

SOLNTSE (THE SUN) – Los Angeles, CA. No.7, 1938. No.9, 1940 (incomplete). The Independent Organ of the Universal Church of Christ – 1 – $15.84 – us Baptist [240]
SOLNTSE V GOSTIAKH U MAIAKOVSKOGO / Maiakovskii, Vladimir – New York. n.d. BR-1001 2 – 8 – ne IDC [460]
SOLO DIOS ES GRANDE : EL LIBRO DE LOS CASCALES / Cascales Munoz, Jose – Toledo, 1931; Madrid: Razon y Fe, 1931 – 1 – sp Bibl Santa Ana [240]
A SOLO FOR A FLUTE AND A BASS / Courteville, R – London(?): 1715(?) – 1 – us Sibley [780]
UN SOLO INTERES : EL DE TODOS LOS ARGENTINOS. DISCURSO PRONUNCIADO POR EL TENIENTE GENERAL JUAN PERON ANTE EL CONGRESO DEL PARTIDO JUSTICIALISTA...EL 18 DE AGOSTO DE 1973 / Peron, Juan Domingo – [Buenos Aires, 1973] – 1 – CSUXADP3208-B – us Hoover Inst Photo [320]
SOLO LA VERDAD NOS HARA LIBRES : ESTA ES LA VERDAD! / Peron, Juan Domingo – [Buenos Aires?, 1947?] – 1 – CSUXADL6493-B – us Hoover Inst Photo [972]
SOLO PARA MI LUGAR / Gabriel y Galan, Jose Maria – Caceres: Tip. Suc. de Alvarez, 1903 – sp Bibl Santa Ana [946]
SOLO REHABILITATION CENTRE / Indonesia. Departemen Penerangan – SE-3488 1. 1960? – 9 – ne IDC [324]
SOLO SONATAS OF THE BAROQUE – 134mf – 9 – MS-d – ne IDC [780]
Sologub, F *see*
- FIMIAMY
- IARYI GOD
- ISTLEVAIUSHCHIIA LICHINY
- KNIGA RAZLUK
- KNIGA SKAZOK
- MELKII BES
- NEBO GOLUBOE
- ODNA LIUBOV
- PLAMENNYI KRUG
- POBEDA SMERTI
- POLITICHESKIIA SKAZOCHKI
- POLITICHESKIIA SKAZOCHKI. IZD. "RODNAIA RECH'"
- SOBORNYI BLAGOVEST
- SOBRANIE SOCHINENII. 1-20
- SOBRANIE STIKHOV. (1897-1903)
- SOCHTENNYE DNI
- STIKHI
- STIKHOTVORENIIA
- SVIREL'
- ZAKLINATEL'NITSA ZMEI
- ZEMLIA RODNAIA
- ZHALO SMERTI

O SOLOGUBE: KRITIKA, STAT'I ZAMETKI / Chebotarevskaia, A – Izd. "Shipovnik". Spb. 1911. BR-3257 2 – 8 – ne IDC [460]
SOLOMON / Farrar, Frederic William – New York: Anson D.F. Randolph, 188?. 1 fiche – 9 – us A.T.L.A. [240]
SOLOMON : HIS LIFE AND TIMES / Farrar, Frederic William – (Includes bibliographical references) – New York: Anson D F Randolph, [188-?] – 1mf – 9 – 0-8370-9384-8 – 1986-3384 – us A.T.L.A. [920]
SOLOMON. A SERENATA, IN SCORE, TAKEN FROM THE CANTICLES / Boyce, W – Libretto by E. Moore. 1743 – 1 – us Sibley [780]
Solomon, George *see* THE JESUS OF HISTORY AND THE JESUS OF TRADITION IDENTIFIED
Solomon Islands. British. Ministry of Education and Cultural Affairs *see* TRIENNIAL REPORT 1974-1976
Solomon Islands. British. Protectorate *see*
- FIFTH DEVELOPMENT PLAN
- SIXTH DEVELOPMENT PLAN 1971-1973

SOLOMON R GUGGENHEIM MUSEUM CATALOGUE – (Individual titles not listed separately) – New York, 1953-1972 – 34 catalogues on 45mf – 9 – £380.00 – uk Chadwyck [700]
SOLOMON VALLEY PIONEER – Lindsey. Kan. 1870-73 – 1 – us UMI [071]
Solomon, Y M *see* YISHUV EREZ HA-KODESH
THE SOLOMONS NEW DRUM – Honiara. Trial issue & n1-66, 68-171, 173-360, 362. oct 1974, feb 1975-apr 1982 – r1-6 – 1 – PMB Doc415 – at Pacific Mss [072]
SOLOMON'S SONG : TRANSLATED AND EXPLAINED: IN THREE PARTS, 1. THE MANUDUCTION, 2. THE VERSION, 3. THE SUPPLEMENT / Withington, Leonard – Boston: J E Tilton, 1861 – 1mf – 9 – 0-8370-9348-1 – 1986-3348 – us A.T.L.A. [220]
SOLOMON'S TEMPLE: ITS HISTORY AND ITS STRUCTURE / Caldecott, William Shaw – London: Religious Tract Society, 1908. 1 fiche – 9 – us A.T.L.A. [270]
SOLOMON'S TEMPLE MISSIONARY BAPTIST CHURCH. KINGSPORT, TENNESSEE : CHURCH RECORDS – 1910-83 – 1 – 5.00 – us Baptist [240]
SOLOMONS TOK TOK / ed by Aitkin, George – Honiara, 1977-82 (gaps) – 1r – 1 – PMB Doc424 – at Pacific Mss [980]
Solorzano Pereira, Juan de *see*
- EMBLEMATA CENTUM, REGIO POLITICA
- POLITICA INDIANA, CORREGIDA POR... FRANCISCO RAMIRO DE VALENZUELA. 5 TOMOS

SOLOS FOR A GERMAN FLUTE, A HOBOY OR VIOLIN WITH A THOROUGH BASS FOR THE HARPSICHORD OR BASS VIOLIN / Quantz, Johann Joachim – London: I Walsh, [1739] – 1 – us Sibley [780]
Solov'ev, Vsevolod S *see*
- PIS'MA V. S. SOLOV'EVA. POD. RED. E. L. RADLOVA
- POSMERTNYI SBORNIK. RAZSKAZY, STIKHI, PUTEVYE OCHERKI
- SOBRANIE SOCHINENII
- SOBRANIE SOCHINENII TOM 7
- STIKHOTVORENIIA

Soloweyczyk, Elias *see* KOL KORE
Solsona y Baselga, Conrado *see* AYALA
LES SOLSTICES – Revue mensuelle de litterature et d'art. no. 1-3. Paris. 1er juin-1er aout 1917 – 1 – fr A.C.R.P.P. [800]
Soltau, George *see* PERSONAL WORK FOR CHRIST AND SOME EXPERIENCES
Soltau, Wilhelm *see*
- THE BIRTH OF JESUS CHRIST
- DAS FORTLEBEN DES HEIDENTUMS IN DER ALTCHRISTLICHEN KIRCHE
- DIE GEBURTSGESCHICHTE JESU CHRISTI
- HAT JESUS WUNDER GETAN?: EINE BIBLISCHE WIDERLEGUNG KIRCHLICHEN ABERGLAUBENS
- UNSERE EVANGELIEN: IHRE QUELLEN UND IHR QUELLENWERT VOM STANDPUNKT DES HISTORIKERS

LA SOLTERONA / Polipodio de Salamanca (Seud. Doncel y Ordaz) – 1882 – 9 – 1.50f – sp Bibl Santa Ana [830]
Sol'ts, A *see* REVOLIUTSIONNAIA ZAKONNOST' I NASHA KARATEL'NAIA POLITIKA
LA SOLUCION QUE ESPANA DA AL PROBLEMA DE SUS PRESOS POLITICOS / Perez del Pulgar, Jose Agustin – Valladolid, 1939. Fiche W1103. (Blodget Collection of Spanish Civil War Pamphlets) – 9 – us H.U. College Libr [946]
SOLUCIONES ARGENTINAS : ANALISIS DE LA REALIDAD POLITICA ECONOMICA NACIONAL / Boscovich, Nicolas – [2. e. Buenos Aires? prologo 1960] – 1 – CSUXADM9630-B – us Hoover Inst Photo [320]
SOLUTION FOR SOUTH AFRICA : A JEWISH VIEW / Katzew, Henry – Cape Town: Nasionale Boekhandel Bpk, [1955] – us Res Libr [960]
SOLUTION FOR THE IBERIAN PUZZLE; NOTES FOR A FURTHER STUDY / Gibernau, Jose – N.Y., 1943. Fiche W912. (Blodgett Collection of Spanish Civil War Pamphlets) – 9 – us H.U. College Libr [946]
SOLUTION GENERALE DU PROBLEME DE LA PHOTOGRAPHIE DES COULEURS / Cros, Charles – Paris: Gauthier-Villars, 1869. 12p. 1 fiche. (Art) – 9 – $6.00 – fr Bibl Nationale [770]
SOLUTIONS – 1984- – 1,5,6,9 – us UMI [073]
SOLVARNYI UKAZATEL'PO KNIGOVEDENIIU / Mez'er, A V – L. 1924. BR-11,219 1 – 9 – ne IDC [010]
SOLVENT EXTRACTION AND ION EXCHANGE – v1-. 1983- – 1,5,6,9 – us UMI [073]
SOLVESBORGSTIDNINGEN *see* BLEKINGE LANS TIDNING
SOLVING EDUCATIONAL PROBLEMS : THEORY AND REALITY OF INNOVATION IN DEVELOPING COUNTRIES / Havelock, R G & Huberman, A M – 1978 2nd ed 1983 – 308p – 9 – 92-3-101527-3 – fr UNESCO [370]
SOLVING THE COUNTRY CHURCH PROBLEM / Bricker, Garland A – Cincinnati: Jennings and Graham; New York: Eaton and Mains, c1913 – 1mf – us A.T.L.A. [240]
Solymosi, Frank *see* AN INVESTIGATION OF THE RELATIONSHIP BETWEEN MEASURES OF KINESTHESIS AND SLECTED ASPECTS OF PERFORMANCE IN BEGINNER SKIING
Somaize, A Baudeau, sieur de *see* LE GRAND DICTIONNAIRE DES PRETIEUSES
Somali Republic. The Ministry of Information and National Guidance *see* SOMALIA'S FIVE-YEAR PLAN 1974-1978
Somali Republic. Planning and Coordination Committee *see*
- DEVELOPMENT PROGRAMME 1971-1973
- FIRST FIVE YEAR PLAN, 1963-1967
- FIVE YEAR DEVELOPMENT PROGRAMME, 1974-1978

Somali Republic. Planning Commission *see* SHORT TERM DEVELOPMENT PROGRAMME, 1968-1970
SOMALIA : KOOBAHA ISTATISTIKADA/ STATISTICAL ABSTRACT / Somalia. Central Statistical Department – (Coll title: African Official Statistical Serials, 1867-1982) – 21mf – 9 – £175.00 – uk Chadwyck [960]
SOMALIA : (VICENDE E PROBLEMI) / Vecchi, Bernardo Valentino – Milano: O Maragoni, 1935 – us Res Libr [960]
Somalia. Central Statistical Department *see* SOMALIA
Somalia. Italian Administration *see* PLANS DE DEVELOPPEMENT ECONOMIQUE DE LA SOMALIE, 1954-1960
SOMALIA ITALIANA / Corni, Guido – Milano: Editoriale arte e storia, 1937 – us Res Libr [960]
LA SOMALIA ITALIANA NEI TRE ANNI DEL MIO GOVERNO. / Martino, Giacomo de – Rome. 1912 – 1 – us Res Libr [960]
SOMALIA SOCIOLOGY *see* PRINCIPLE DI DIRITTO CONSUETUDINARIO DELLA SOMALIA, ITALIANA MERIODINALE
SOMALIA'S FIVE-YEAR PLAN 1974-1978 / Somali Republic. The Ministry of Information and National Guidance – Mogadishu. Jun 1974. BD-1869 1 – 9 – ne IDC [338]
LA SOMALIE FRANCAISE / Aubert de la Rue, Edgar – Paris, 1939 – 1 – us Res Libr [960]
Somaliland *see*
– ANNUAL REVIEW OF DEVELOPMENT, 1957-1958
– ANNUAL REVIEW OF THE DEVELOPMENT PLAN, 1953
– ANNUAL REVIEW OF THE DEVELOPMENT PLAN, 1954
– REVIEW OF DEVELOPMENT, 1955-1957
– THE SOMALILAND GAZETTE
– THE SOMALILAND PROTECTORATE GAZETTE
Somaliland. French *see* JOURNAL OFICIEL...
SOMALILAND GAZETTE – (Includes: Somaliland. Italian: Bolletino Ufficiale, 1957-60) – 1957-63 – 1r – 1 – us Ross [960]
THE SOMALILAND GAZETTE / Somaliland – Hargeisa. June 26-July 5, 1960 – 1 – us NY Public [324]
Somaliland. Italian *see* BOLLETTINO UFFICIALE
THE SOMALILAND PROTECTORATE GAZETTE / Somaliland – Hargeisa. 1956-Jun. 1960 – 1 – us NY Public [960]
DIE SOMALI-SPRACHE / Reinish, Leo – Vienna. 1900-03. 3v – 1 – us Res Libr [470]
SOMATIC CELL AND MOLECULAR GENETICS – v1-20. 1975-94 – 1,5 – $80.00v – us UMI [575]
SOMATIC CELL GENETICS – v. 1- 1975- – 1,5,6 – us UMI [574]
A SOMATOGRAPHIC ANALYSIS OF YOUNG AND OLDER WOMEN BASED ON THE REFERENCE WOMAN / Romejko, Lynn C – 1989 – 188p 2mf – 9 – $8.00 – us Microform Publ [612]
SOMATOSENSORY RESEARCH – v1-. 1983- – 1,5,6,9 – us UMI [073]
SOMBORSKE NOVINE – Sombor, Yugoslavia. Mar 1961-1962 – 1r – 1 – us L of C Photodup [949]
EN LA SOMBRA / Hurtado, Antonio – 1870 – 9 – 1.50f – sp Bibl Santa Ana [830]
LA SOMBRA DE DONA ISABEL DE MERCADO / Munoz de San Pedro, Miguel – Badajoz: (Imp. Diputacion Provincial), 1970. Sep. Rev. Estudios Extremenos – 1 – sp Bibl Santa Ana [920]
LA SOMBRA DE HERNAN CORTES...NUEVA ESPANA / Rianzuela, Marques de – 1857 – 9 – 1.50f – sp Bibl Santa Ana [946]
LA SOMBRA DE NELSON / Fernandez de Moratin, Leandro – 1805 – 1mf – 9 – Pta1,000.00 – 84-7848-203-2 – sp Pentalfa [820]
SOMBRA, PENUMBRA Y LUZ EN LA EXTREMADURA / Lopez de la Viesca, Evaristo – Madrid: Ediciones del Centro, 1976 – 1 – sp Bibl Santa Ana [946]
SOMBRAS DE BARAUNAS / Sette, Mario – Porto. 1927 – 1 – us Res Libr [440]
LAS SOMBRAS DE LOYOLA / Salaverria, Jose Maria – Madrid. 1911 – 1 – us Res Libr [946]
SOMBRAS QUE SE HICIERON. !LUZ! / Sanchez-Arjona, Vicente – Sevilla: Imp. Zambrano, 1958 – 1 – sp Bibl Santa Ana [810]
SOMBRAS QUE SOFREM / Campos, Humberto de – 3a. ed. Rio de Janeiro. 1935 – 1 – us Res Libr [810]
SOMDET PHRA CHAO TAK SIN MAHARAT / Fels, Jacqueline de – Le roi de Thonburi. 1976 – 9 – fr Orientalistes [920]
SOME ACCOUNT OF THE ENGLISH STAGE, 1660-1830 / Genest, J – 6r – 1 – uk Microform Academic [790]
SOME ACCOUNT OF THE INSTITUTION, PLAN AND PRESENT STATE OF THE SOCIETY...LIST OF MEMBERS AND THE RULES AND ORDERS...TO WHICH IS ANNEXED, SOME PAPERS ON SUBJECTS OF NAVAL ARCHITECTURE / Society for the Improvement of Naval Architecture – 1792 – 9 – uk Libr Preservation [623]
SOME ACCOUNT OF THE INSTITUTION, PLAN AND PRESENT STATE OF THE SOCIETY... WITH THE PREMIUMS...LIST OF MEMBERS AND THE RULES AND ORDERS. TO WHICH IS ANNEXED, SOME PAPERS ON SUBJECTS OF NAVAL ARCHITECTURE, RECEIVED BY THE COMMITTEE / Society for the Improvement of Naval Architecture – London, 1792 – 1mf – 1 – 1-55879-140-X – uk Libr Preservation [620]
SOME ACCOUNT OF THE TRADE IN SLAVES FROM AFRICA... / Bandinel, J – London, 1842 – 4mf – 9 – ILM-1225/1 – ne IDC [340]
SOME ANCIENT ORIENTAL ACADEMIES / Rosenau, William – Baltimore: [s.n.], 1906 – 1mf – 9 – 0-8370-7578-5 – 1986-1578 – us A.T.L.A. [270]
SOME APPLICATIONS OF BEHAVIOURAL RESEARCH / Likert, R & Hayes, S P – UNESCO – 8mf – 7 – uk Microform Academic [300]
SOME ASPECT OF THE FINANCIAL POLICY OF THE DJAKARTA GOVERNMENT, ITS IMPACTS AND ITS RELATIONS TO THE DEMANDS PUT FORWARD BY THE P.R.R.I / Indonesia. Pemerintah Revolusioner Republik – SE-3582 1. 1957? – 9 – ne IDC [336]
SOME ASPECTS OF CANADIAN CONSTITUTIONALISM / Rand, Ivan Cleveland – Cambridge, Mass., Harvard, 1960. 33 p. LL-2296 – 1 – us L of C Photodup [340]
SOME ASPECTS OF HEALTH PROTECTION TO LOCAL AREAS IN INDONESIA / Indonesia. Ministry of Health – Johannes Leimena. 1953?. SE-6949-1 – 9 – ne IDC [610]
SOME ASPECTS OF LOCAL GOVERNMENT IN INDONESIA / Ulinski, John A – SE 10,994 1. 1954 – 9 – ne IDC [320]
SOME ASPECTS OF PRIMITIVE CHURCH LIFE / Bright, William – London; New York: Longmans, Green, 1898 – 1mf – us A.T.L.A. [240]
SOME ASPECTS OF PROFESSIONAL FREEDOM OF TEACHERS : AN INTERNATIONAL PILOT INQUIRY / Morris, Ben – 1977 – 213p – 9 – 92-3-101424-2 – fr UNESCO [370]
SOME ASPECTS OF RABBINIC THEOLOGY / Schechter, Solomon – (Includes bibliographical references and index) – New York:Macmillan, 1909 – 1mf – 9 – 0-8370-5078-2 – 1985-3078 – us A.T.L.A. [270]
SOME ASPECTS OF SPONTANEOUS TRANSMIGRATION IN INDONESIA / Djoko Santoso – SE-4754 1. 1956 – 9 – ne IDC [950]
SOME ASPECTS OF THE RELIGIOUS LIFE OF NEW ENGLAND : WITH SPECIAL REFERENCE TO CONGREGATIONALISTS / Walker, George Leon – New York: Silver, Burdett, 1897 – 1mf – us A.T.L.A. [240]
SOME BRIEF ANIMADVERSIONS UPON MR. ALLEN'S ESSAY, TO PROVE THE COMMON PRACTICE OF SINGING IN RHIME. TO BE A CHRISTIAN DUTY / Russell, William – London. 1696 – 1 – 5.00 – us Baptist [240]
SOME CANADIAN BIRDS: A BRIEF ACCOUNT OF SOME OF THE COMMON BIRDS OF EASTERN CANADA: FIRST SERIES – BIRDS OF FIELD AND GROVE / Chamberlain, Montague – Toronto: Copp, Clark. 1895. 00544. (Pre-1900 Canadiana) – 9 – cn C.I.H.M. [590]
SOME CANADIAN IRON ORES / Dewey, Fred Perkins – s.l., s.n., 1893?. 02652. (Pre-1900 Canadiana) – 9 – cn C.I.H.M. [622]
SOME CHAPTERS ON JUDAISM AND THE SCIENCE OF RELIGION / Grossmann, Louis – (Includes index) – New York:G.P. Putnam, 1889, c1888 – 1mf – 9 – 0-8370-3412-4 – 1985-1412 – us A.T.L.A. [270]
SOME CRITICAL AREAS CONCERNING TECHNICAL ASSISTANCE IN PUBLIC ADMINISTRATION FOR INDONESIA / Jones, Garth N – SE-3704 1. 1960? – 9 – ne IDC [321]
SOME CURRENT REPROGRAPHIC CONCERNS RELATED TO INTERLIBRARY LOAN / American Library Association – RLMS Micro-File Series, v. 4. 1977 – 9 – 8.00 – us L of C Photodup [770]
SOME DATA ON AGRICULTURAL STATISTICS IN LIBYA / Libya. Ministry of Agriculture and Animal Wealth. Agricultural Planning and Economics Department. Statistics Division – 1964 65. BNE-1006 1 – 9 – ne IDC [324]
SOME DATA ON THE POPULATION OF DJABRES: A VILLAGE IN CENTRAL JAVA / Jakarta. Universitas Indonesia – SE-2175 1. 1956 – 9 – ne IDC [310]
SOME DESCRIPTIVE NOTES ON FOREIGN ASSISTANCE IN INDONESIAN TECHNICAL EDUCATION / Ford Foundation. Indonesia – By Daniel S. Lev. 1961.SE-3333-1 – 9 – ne IDC [370]
SOME DOGMAS OF RELIGION / McTaggart, John McTaggart Ellis – London: Edward Arnold, 1906. 1 fiche – 9 – us A.T.L.A. [240]
SOME EARLY ITEMS CONCERNING VINCENNES, INDIANA FROM THE YEAR OF 1783-1790 / Indiana – Comp. by June B. Barekman, et al. Grants of land to the early settlers, and donations of land to the Militia men. 39p. SW16-0135 – 5 – us A.G.L.L. [920]
SOME EARLY RECORDS OF & RELATING TO THE TOWN OF WINDSOR, CT / Hartford County. Connecticut – 1639-1703. By Historical Society. Item D. 227p, indexed. SW16-0228 – 5 – us A.G.L.L. [920]
SOME ELEMENTS OF FORCEFULNESS IN THE COMPARISONS OF JESUS : WITH COMPARATIVE TABLES OF METAPHORS FROM THE DEUTERO-ISAIAH AND PAUL / Robinson, Benjamin Willard – (Includes bibliographical references) – 1904 – 1mf – 9 – 0-8370-6352-3 – 1986-0352 – us A.T.L.A. [220]
SOME ELEMENTS OF RELIGION: LENT LECTURES, 1870 / Liddon, Henry Parry – London: Longmans, Green, 1904. 1 fiche – 9 – us A.T.L.A. [240]
SOME ENGLISH CORRESPONDENTS OF GOETHE / Scott, D F S – (Includes bibliographical references) – London: Methuen, 1949 – 1r – 1 – us U.W. Library [920]
SOME ETHICAL PHASES OF ESKIMO CULTURE / Gilbertson, A N – BN 220 2. 1913-14 15 – 8 – ne IDC [306]
SOME FACTS CONCERNING THE UNIVERSITY OF INDONESIA / Jakarta. Universitas Indonesia – SE-3329 1. 14th February 1959 – 9 – ne IDC [370]
SOME FACTS IN THE HISTORY OF THE TWINING FAMILY / Twining, William H G – 2d ed. 1895; Supplement 1893; Part 3, 1896 – 1 – $50.00 – us Presbyterian [920]
SOME FACTS OF RELIGION AND OF LIFE : SERMONS / Tulloch, John – Edinburgh: William Blackwood, 1877 – 1mf – us A.T.L.A. [240]
SOME FARTHER REMARKS ON THE REV. MR. JOHN WESLEY'S LAST JOURNAL, TOGETHER WITH A FEW CONSIDERATIONS ON HIS 'FARTHER APPEAL',... / Church T – London, 1746 – 2mf – 9 – MP-330/1 – ne IDC [240]
SOME FEW GENERAL REMARKS ON FRACTURES AND DISLOCATIONS / Pott, P – M 121. 1768 – 9 – ne IDC [610]
SOME GENERAL AND THEORETICAL CONSIDERATIONS ON THE FISH PRODUCTION OF AFRICAN RIVERS – 1974 – 26p – it F.A.O. [639]
SOME GLIMPSES OF OCCULTISM, ANCIENT AND MODERN / Leadbeater, Charles Webster – 3rd ed. Krotona, CA: Theosophical Publishing House, 1919. 380p – 1 – us U.W. Library [150]
SOME IDEALS IN THE EDUCATION OF WOMEN / Hazard, Caroline – New York: Thomas Y Crowell, c1900 – 1mf – 9 – 0-8370-7544-0 – 1986-1544 – us A.T.L.A. [370]
SOME IMPROVEMENTS TO THE ART OF TEACHING / Walker, William – 1669. 268p. (English Linguistics Series 1500-1800) – 9 – us UMI [400]
SOME INFORMATION ABOUT GADJAH MADA UNIVERSITY / Indonesia. Jogjakarta – SE-3071 1 – 9 – ne IDC [370]
SOME INTERNATIONAL ELEMENTS IN MATRIMONIAL CAUSES / Conginsby, F C – London, 1931 – 1mf – 1 – ILM-3555/1 – ne IDC [327]
SOME JEWISH WITNESSES FOR CHRIST / Bernstein, A – (Includes bibliographical references) – London: Operative Jewish Convert's Institution, 1909 – 2mf – 9 – 0-8370-6802-9 – 1986-0802 – us A.T.L.A. [920]
SOME LESSONS OF THE REVISED VERSION OF THE NEW TESTAMENT / Westcott, Brooke Foss – New York: Edwin S. Gorham, 1903.1 fiche – 9 – us A.T.L.A. [240]
SOME LETTERS, NOTES AND DRAFTS ON HUMAN RIGHTS / Beckerath, Ulrich von – 9 – 1.00f – at Libertarian Micro [335]
SOME LITERARY RECOLLECTIONS / Payn, James – London: Smith, Elder, 1884 – 1 roll – 1 – 1-55879-473-5 – uk Libr Preservation [420]
SOME MEDICINAL FOREST PLANTS OF AFRICA AND LATIN AMERICA – 1986 – 271p – it F.A.O. [580]
SOME MODERN SUBSTITUTES FOR CHRISTIANITY : A CONSIDERATION OF THE CLAIMS OF THEOSOPHY, CHRISTIAN SCIENCE, SPIRITUALISM, SOCIALISM AND AGNOSTICISM, AND OF THE REASONS FOR DECLINING TO ACCEPT ANY ONE OF THESE SYSTEMS AS A SUBSTITUTE FOR CHRISTIANITY / Shinn, George Wolfe – New York: T. Whittaker, 1897, c1896 – 1mf – us A.T.L.A. [290]
SOME MORAL ASPECTS OF THE 'WOMAN MOVEMENT' / Rauschenbusch, Walter – (The Biblical World, v. 42, Oct. 1913, p. 195-199) – 9 – us A.T.L.A. [240]
SOME NEGLECTED ASPECTS OF GRESHAM'S LAW / Fetter, Frank Whitson – 1932. 16p – 9 – $1.00f – at Libertarian Micro [335]
SOME NOTES ON THE BOOK OF PSALMS / Cross, John A – (Includes index of psalms discussed) – London:Longmans, Green, 1884 – 1mf – 9 – 0-8370-2784-5 – 1985-0784 – us A.T.L.A. [220]
SOME NOTES ON THE RIDEAU CANAL: THE SOURCES OF ITS WATER SUPPLY, AND ITS EARLY HISTORY / Drummond, Andrew Thomas – s.l.: s.n., 1893?. 02771. (Pre-1900 Canadiana) – 9 – cn C.I.H.M. [971]
SOME NOVA SCOTIAN ILLUSTRATIONS OF DYNAMICAL GEOLOGY / Bailey, Loring Woart – 1898?. 05992. (Pre-1900 Canadiana) – 9 – cn C.I.H.M. [550]
SOME OF THE CAUSES OF MODERN RELIGIOUS SKEPTICISM : A LECTURE / Ryan, Patrick John – St Louis: B Herder, 1885 – 1mf – 9 – 0-8370-7014-7 – 1986-1014 – us A.T.L.A. [210]
SOME OLD EGYPTIAN LIBRARIANS / Richardson, Ernest Cushing – New York: Scribner, 1911 – 1mf – us A.T.L.A. [020]
SOME PAGES OF LEVANTINE HISTORY / Duckworth, H T F – London: A. Moring, [1906?] – 1mf – us A.T.L.A. [240]
SOME PAPERS GIVING AN ACCOUNT OF THE RISE AND PROGRESS OF METHODISM AT WEDNESBURY IN STAFFORDSHIRE AND OTHER PARISHES ADJACENT,... – London, 1744 – 1mf – 9 – MP-315/1 – ne IDC [240]
SOME PRINCIPLES OF LITERARY CRITICISM AND THEIR APPLICATION TO THE SYNOPTIC PROBLEM / Burton, E D – Chicago: University of Chicago, 1904. 1 fiche – 9 – us A.T.L.A. [220]
SOME PRINCIPLES OF LITURGICAL REFORM : A CONTRIBUTION TOWARDS THE REVISION OF THE BOOK OF COMMON PRAYER / Frere, Walter H – London: John Murray, 1911 – 1mf – us A.T.L.A. [240]
SOME PRINCIPLES OF MARITIME STRATEGY / Corbett, J Stafford – 1911 – 9 – $20.00 – uk Libr Preservation [355]
SOME PROBLEMS OF PHILOSOPHY / Alexander, Archibald – New York: Scribner, 1886 – 1mf – us A.T.L.A. [100]
SOME PROBLEMS OF STATE BUDGETING / Roesdi, Imam – Trans. by G. N. Jones. (Translation series in Indonesian finance administration). SE-10,236 1 – 9 – ne IDC [336]
SOME PROBLEMS OF THE PALESTINE MANDATE / Feinberg, N – Tel-Aviv, 1936 – 2mf – 1 – ILM-1998/1 – ne IDC [327]

SOME PROBLEMS PERTAINING TO THE EXAMINATION AND THE SELECTION OF PROSPECTIVE STUDENTS OF THE TEACHER TRAINING AND EDUCATIONAL SCIENCES, BANDUNG(ACADEMIC YEAR 1958/1959). SE-11,530/1. 1959 / Buchori, Mochtar – 9 – ne IDC [370]

SOME QUESTIONS AND AN APPEAL / Cohn, Michael A – New York, Independent Sacco-Vanzetti Committee 1927 11 p. LL-382 – 1 – us L of C Photodup [340]

SOME REASONS FOR OPPOSING THE AUTHOR OF THE SOUTH AFRICAN RESEARCHES, THE REV JOHN PHILIPS... : BY THE BRITISH IMMIGRANTS OF 1820 – (Filmed with: Moodie, Donald. Miscellaneous Writings...) – Cape Town: A S Robertson, 1836 – us Res Libr [960]

SOME REMARKS ON A DIALOGUE (PUBLISH'D BY MR. WESLEY) BETWEEN A PREDESTINARIAN AND HIS FRIEND,... – London, 1741 – 1mf – 9 – MP-289/1 – ne IDC [240]

SOME REMARKS ON A PAMPHLET INTITULED A LETTER TO A PERSON LATELY JOIN'D WITH THE PEOPLE CALL'D QUAKERS,... / Fry, J – Bristol, 1748 – 1mf – 9 – MP-334/1 – ne IDC [240]

SOME REMARKS ON THE PROBLEMS AND DIFFICULTIES BESETTING PRESENT-DAY INDONESIAN-JAPANESE RELATIONS / Lie, Tek Tjeng – SE-6503 1. 1968 – 9 – ne IDC [950]

SOME SALIENT POINTS IN THE SCIENCE OF THE EARTH / Dawson, John William – Montreal: W. Drysdale, 1893. 02609. (Pre-1900 Canadiana) – 9 – cn C.I.H.M. [550]

SOME SIMPLE METHODS FOR THE ASSESSMENT OF TROPICAL FISH STOCKS – 1983 – 60p – it F.A.O. [639]

SOME SIMPLE SONGS AND A FEW MORE AMBITIOUS ATTEMPTS / McGirt, James Ephraim – Philadelphia: G.F. Lasher, (1901). 72p.ill – 1 – us U.W. Library [830]

SOME SOCIAL PRINCIPLES OF ORESTES A. BROWNSON / Corrigan, Felicia – Washington: Catholic University of America, 1939. 130p – 1 – us U.W. Library [300]

SOME SOCIAL REMEDIES: SOCIALISM, ANARCH; HENRY GEORGISM AND THE LAND QUESTION, COMMUNISM, ETC / Tolstoy, Leo – Collected from the recent and unpublished writings of L. Tolstoy. Maldon, Essex, 1900. 40p – 1 – us U.W. Library [335]

SOME SOUTH INDIAN INSECTS / Fletcher, T B – Z-268 2. 1914 – 8 – ne IDC [590]

SOME STATISTICAL FEATURES OF THE FLORA OF ONTARIO & QUEBEC: AND A COMPARISON WITH THOSE OF THE UNITED STATES FLORA / Drummond, Andrew Thomas – s.l.: s.n., 1868?. 02772. (Pre-1900 Canadiana) – 9 – cn C.I.H.M. [580]

SOME SUDAN PRODUCE AND SECONDARY INDUSTRIES IN THE SUDAN / Sudan. Ministry of Commerce, Industry and Supply – 1956? BNE-7665 1 – 9 – ne IDC [380]

SOME TABLE TALK OF MR. JUSTICE HOLMES AND "THE MRS."...WITH CHRISTMAS GREETINGS FROM RICHARD WALDEN HALE / Holmes, Oliver Wendell, Jr – Boston: Getchell 1935. 17p. LL-492 – 1 – us L of C Photodup [340]

SOME TECHNICAL DETAILS OF THE STATUTES OF AN EMPLOYMENT BANK / Beckerath, Ulrich von – c1951 – 9 – 1.00f – at Libertarian Micro [335]

SOME THOUGHTS ON CHRISTOLOGY / Drummond, James – London: Philip Green, 1902. 1 fiche – 9 – us A.T.L.A. [240]

SOME THOUGHTS ON LIBYAN AGRICULTURAL PROGRAMS FOR 1959-1960 / Libya – 1959. BNE-1035 1 – 9 – ne IDC [630]

SOME THOUGHTS ON THE ATHANASIAN CREED / Robinson, J Armitage – London, New York: Longmans, Green, 1905 – 1mf – us A.T.L.A. [240]

SOME THOUGHTS ON THE CONSTITUTION OF RHODE ISLAND / Durfee, Thomas – Providence, Rider, 1884. 57 p. LL-1395 – 1 – us L of C Photodup [340]

SOME THOUGHTS ON THE TEXTUAL CRITICISM OF THE NEW TESTAMENT / Salmon, George – London: John Murray, 1897 – 1mf – 9 – 0-8370-5028-6 – 1985-3028 – us A.T.L.A. [220]

SOME TRIBAL GODS OF SOUTHERN NIGERIA / Egharevba, Jacob U – [s.l: s.n], 1951 – us Res Libr [290]

SOME WEMBA WORDS : SOME MEANINGS AND EXPLANATIONS / Goodall, Edward Basil Herbert – London, New York: Oxford UP, 1921 – us Res Libr [470]

SOME WORTHIES OF THE IRISH CHURCH : LECTURES / Stokes, George Thomas; ed by Lawlor, Hugh Jackson – London: Hodder and Stoughton, 1900 – 1mf – us A.T.L.A. [240]

Somel, Aksin *see* DAS GRUNDSCHULWESEN IN DEN PROVINZEN DES OSMANISCHEN REICHES WAEHREND DER HERRSCHAFTSPERIODE ABDUELHAMIDS 2 (1876-1908)

SOMERS TRACTS – British history from the end of the Middle Ages to the nineteenth century – 9 – us Primary [941]

THE SOMERS TRACTS – 1651-1716. 5 reels – 1 – $225.00 – us Trans-Media [941]

SOMERSET, 1822 : BRITISH ISLES CENSUS DIRECTORIES PROJECT, ENGLAND – (In prep) – at Vine [941]

SOMERSET, 1844 : BRITISH ISLES CENSUS DIRECTORIES PROJECT, ENGLAND – (In prep) – at Vine [941]

SOMERSET 1680-1892 – (Mf 1-3: Vital Records 1690-1855. Mf 4-5: Vitals Index 1690-1855. Mf 6-8: Town Records 1680-1830. Mf 9-12: Town Records 1790-1808. Mf 13-17: Town Records 1808-20. Mf 18-22: Town Records 1820-30. Mf 23-27: Birth Index 1844-1975. Mf 28-32: Marriage Index 1844-1975. Mf 33-35: Death Index 1844-1975. Mf 36-37: Births 1844-59. Mf 37: Marriages 1844-58. Mf 38: Deaths 1844-55. Mf 39-44: Births 1860-92. Mf 45-47: Marriages 1858-92. Mf 47-51: Deaths 1856-92. Mf 52: Deaths 1893-99) – (mf ed 1991) – 52mf – 9 – 0-87623-142-3 – us Holbrook [920]

SOMERSET (BRISTOL), 1793 : BRITISH ISLES CENSUS DIRECTORIES PROJECT, ENGLAND – at Vine [941]

SOMERSET (BRISTOL), 1824 : BRITISH ISLES CENSUS DIRECTORIES PROJECT, ENGLAND – (In prep) – at Vine [941]

SOMERSET (BRISTOL), 1826 : BRITISH ISLES CENSUS DIRECTORIES PROJECT, ENGLAND – (In prep) – at Vine [941]

SOMERSET (BRISTOL), 1841 : BRITISH ISLES CENSUS DIRECTORIES PROJECT, ENGLAND – (In prep) – at Vine [941]

SOMERSET (BRISTOL), 1846 : BRITISH ISLES CENSUS DIRECTORIES PROJECT, ENGLAND. VOL 266 – 3mf – 9 – A$21.00 – at Vine [941]

SOMERSET (BRISTOL), 1847 : BRITISH ISLES CENSUS DIRECTORIES PROJECT, ENGLAND – (In prep) – at Vine [941]

SOMERSET (BRISTOL), 1855 : BRITISH ISLES CENSUS DIRECTORIES PROJECT, ENGLAND – at Vine [941]

SOMERSET (BRISTOL), 1932 : BRITISH ISLES CENSUS DIRECTORIES PROJECT, ENGLAND – at Vine [941]

SOMERSET (BRISTOL AND CLIFTON), 1854 : BRITISH ISLES CENSUS DIRECTORIES PROJECT, ENGLAND – (In prep) – at Vine [941]

SOMERSET (BRISTOL AND CLIFTON), 1881 : BRITISH ISLES CENSUS DIRECTORIES PROJECT, ENGLAND – (In prep) – at Vine [941]

SOMERSET (BRISTOL, BATH, BRIDGEWATER AND FROME), 1805 : BRITISH ISLES CENSUS DIRECTORIES PROJECT, ENGLAND. VOL 162 – 1mf – 9 – A$9.00 – at Vine [941]

SOMERSET COUNTY GAZETTE – 1903-70, irregular – 41r – 1 – uk Microform Academic [072]

SOMERSET DEMOCRAT – Somerset, PA. -w 1889-1912. 8 rolls – 13 – $25.00r – us I.M.R. [071]

SOMERSET (EAST CENTRAL), 1850 : BRITISH ISLES CENSUS DIRECTORIES PROJECT, ENGLAND. VOL 107 – 1mf – 9 – A$9.00 – at Vine [941]

SOMERSET (EXC BRISTOL), 1830 : BRITISH ISLES CENSUS DIRECTORIES PROJECT, ENGLAND – at Vine [941]

SOMERSET (EXC BRISTOL), 1852 : BRITISH ISLES CENSUS DIRECTORIES PROJECT, ENGLAND. VOL 108 – 2mf – 9 – A$15.00 – at Vine [941]

SOMERSET (EXC BRISTOL), 1875 : BRITISH ISLES CENSUS DIRECTORIES PROJECT, ENGLAND. VOL 88 – 8mf – 9 – A$51.00 – at Vine [941]

SOMERSET (EXC BRISTOL), 1889 : BRITISH ISLES CENSUS DIRECTORIES PROJECT, ENGLAND. VOL 241 – 8mf – 9 – A$51.00 – at Vine [941]

SOMERSET FIRST BAPTIST CHURCH. SOMERSET, KENTUCKY : CHURCH RECORDS – 1863-1977 – 1 – 194.63 – us Baptist [240]

SOMERSET HERALD – Somerset, PA., 1900-1935 – 13 – $25.00r – us I.M.R. [071]

SOMERSET HILLS BAPTIST CHURCH. BERNARDSVILLE, NEW JERSEY : CHURCH RECORDS – 1964-69 – 1 – 5.13 – us Baptist [240]

SOMERSET (INC BRISTOL), 1861 : BRITISH ISLES CENSUS DIRECTORIES PROJECT, ENGLAND – at Vine [941]

SOMERSET (INC BRISTOL), 1894 : BRITISH ISLES CENSUS DIRECTORIES PROJECT, ENGLAND – at Vine [941]

SOMERSET (INC BRISTOL), 1902 : BRITISH ISLES CENSUS DIRECTORIES PROJECT, ENGLAND. VOL 155 – 16mf – 9 – A$99.00 – at Vine [941]

SOMERSET (INC BRISTOL), 1923 : BRITISH ISLES CENSUS DIRECTORIES PROJECT, ENGLAND. VOL 96 – 11mf – 9 – A$69.00 – at Vine [941]

SOMERSET (NORTH EAST), 1888 : BRITISH ISLES CENSUS DIRECTORIES PROJECT, ENGLAND – (In prep) – at Vine [941]

SOMERSET (NORTH WEST), 1850 : BRITISH ISLES CENSUS DIRECTORIES PROJECT, ENGLAND. VOL 109 – 1mf – 9 – A$9.00 – at Vine [941]

SOMERSET (SOUTH WEST), 1848 : BRITISH ISLES CENSUS DIRECTORIES PROJECT, ENGLAND. VOL 106 – 1mf – 9 – A$9.00 – at Vine [941]

SOMERSET WHIG/HERALD – Somerset, PA. -sw 1817-1847 – 13 – $25.00r – us I.M.R. [071]

Somerville, Andrew *see* LECTURES ON MISSIONS AND EVANGELISM

Somerville, David *see* ST. PAUL'S CONCEPTION OF CHRIST, OR, THE DOCTRINE OF THE SECOND ADAM

Somerville, J *see* OBSERVATIONS ON SHEEP, WOOL, PLOUGHS AND OXEN

SOMETHING ELSE / Bastiat, Frederic – 5p – 9 – 1.00f – at Libertarian Micro [335]

SOMETHING ON BATIK TRADE / Gabungan Koperasi Batik Indonesia – SE-5348 1. 1959 – 9 – ne IDC [380]

Somigli, Enzo *see* SHERPA ARCHITECTURE

SOMMARIE OFTE BY EEN VERGADERINGE VAN SOMMIGE SCHRIFTELIJCKE BEKENTENISSEN DES GHELOOFS, MITSGADERS EENIGHE WAERACHTIGE VERANTWOORDINGEN OP SOMMIGE SCHRIFTEN, VAN GELLIO FABRO ENDE JOANNE A LASCO VOORGESTELT / Simons, Menno – Ghedruckt tot Alckmaer, by Jacob de Meester, 1601. Hoorn, Jan Janszoon. 1600. BME-299 1 – 9 – ne IDC [240]

SOMMARIO DELLE CONCESSIONI FATTI DAL RE CHRISTIANISSIMO DI FRANCIA, ALLI VGONOTII, PER CONCLUDERE CON LORO LA PACE – Padoa, 1575 – 1mf – 9 – H-8200/1 – ne IDC [956]

Sommer, F *see* DIE AHHIJTAVIA-URKUNDEN

Sommer, Frank Henry *see* PROPERTY IN LAND

Sommer, Friedrich Tobias *see* THEORIE NEURONALER ASSOZIATIVSPEICHER

Sommerfelt, S C *see* SUPPLEMENTUM FLORAE LAPPONICAE QUAM EDITIT BY DR. G. WAHLENBERG

Sommerlad, Lloyd E *see* NATIONAL COMMUNICATION SYSTEMS

Sommermeyer, Edwin *see* HAUFFS "MEMOIREN DES SATAN"

EIN SOMMERNACHTSTRAUM, VON SHAKESPEARE. VIERHAENDIGER CLAVIERAUSZUG VON COMPONISTEN, OP.61 / Mendelssohn, Felix – Leipzig: Breitkopf, [1843?] – 1 – us Sibley [780]

SOMMERWANDERUNGEN UND WINTERFAHRTEN / Widmann, Joseph Viktor – Frauenfeld: J Huber, 1897 – 1r – 1 – us U.W. Library [910]

LE SOMMET – (Becomes: Le Sommet "Herault des Laurentides" 9 oct 1959-3 sep 1964. Becomes: Le Sommet, Echo des Laurentides 10 sep 1964-12 jul 1989) – Ste-Agathe et ses environs, Canada. 19 jun 1959-26 oct 1961 – 23r – 1 – Can$70.00r – cn Can Microfilming [072]

LE SOMMET, ECHO DES LAURENTIDES *see* LE SOMMET

LE SOMMET HERAULT DES LAURENTIDES *see* LE SOMMET

Sommi, Luis Victor *see* LOS CAPITALES YANQUIS EN LA ARGENTINA

SOMMIGE BELIJDINGHEN, SCHRIFTLIJCKE SENTBRIEUEN, ENDE TESTAMENTEN / Van Cuyck, J W – 1579. BME-206 1 – 9 – ne IDC [240]

SOMMIGE BRIEUEN, TESTAMENTEN, ENDE BELIJDINGEN / Verkindert, J – 1577. In den bundel martelaarsbrieven enz. van 1577. BME-200 1 – 9 – ne IDC [240]

SOMMIGE BRIEVEN OFTE BELIJDINGEN / Tollenaer, Joose de – Harlinghen, Peter Sebastiaensz. 1599. BME-209 1 – 9 – ne IDC [240]

SOMMIGHE NIEUWE SCHRIFTUERELICKE LIEDEKENS / Straten, F vander – Leyden F. vander Straten den Jongeren. Ghedruckt by V. Gaubisch. 1599. BME-353 2 – 8 – ne IDC [240]

Somner, William *see* DICTIONARIUM SAXONICA-LATINO-ANGLICUM

SOMOGYI NEPLAP – Kaposvar, Hungary. 1962-79 – 32r – 1 – us L of C Photodup [072]

SOMOS UNA NACION? *see* GEOGRAFIA ECONOMICO-SOCIAL ARGENTINA

SOMOSTROI PO KONSHINSKOMU SPISKU I PODOBNYM / ed by Orlov, Aleksandr Sergeevich – Moskva: Sinodal naia Tipografiia, 1908. 2v in 1. Illus. Facs.Text in Old Church Slavonic, Russian recension. 1 reel. 1264 – 1 – us U.W. Library [460]

THE SON OF MAN : STUDIES IN HIS LIFE AND TEACHINGS / Alexander, Gross – (Includes index) – Nashville, TN: Publ House of the M E Church, South, 1900, c1899 – 1mf – 9 – 0-8370-2061-1 – 1985-0061 – us A.T.L.A. [240]

SON OF MAN AMONG THE SONS OF MEN / Carpenter, William Boyd – London: Isbister, 1893. 1 fiche – 9 – us A.T.L.A. [240]

SON OF MAN: STUDIES IN HIS LIFE AND TEACHINGS / Gross, Alexander – Nashville: Methodist Episcopal Church Co., 1900.1 fiche – 9 – us A.T.L.A. [240]

THE SON OF TEMPERANCE – Brandford [Ont.: s.n., 1879-1881] (Toronto: Hunter, Rose) – 9 – cn C.I.H.M. [170]

THE SON OF TEMPERANCE – Renfrew, Ont.: W E Smallfield, [1892?-189- or 19–] – 9 – cn C.I.H.M. [170]

THE SON OF TEMPERANCE AND CANADIAN LITERARY GEM – (Cont: Canadian Son of Temperance and Literary Gem) – Toronto: A H St Germain, 1854 – 9 – cn C.I.H.M. [240]

THE SON OF TEMPERANCE AND CANADIAN LITERARY GEM *see* THE CANADIAN SON OF TEMPERANCE [AND] LITERARY GEM

Sonara. Mexico (State) *see* BOLETIN OFICIAL DEL GOBIERNO CONSTITUCIONAL DEL ESTADO DE SONARA

A SONATA, FOR THE HARPSICHORD WITH A TENOR OBLIGATO / Stamitz, K – (2 pts) – London: printed and sold by the author..., [1780?] – 1 – us Sibley [780]

SONATA FOR THE PIANO FORTE WITH AN ACCOMPANIMENT FOR A VIOLIN / Taylor, Raynor – Philadelphia: Printed for the Author 1797. MUSIC 3082, Item 12 – 1 – us L of C Photodup [780]

SONATA FOR THE PIANO FORTE, WITH AN ACCOMPANIMENT FOR A VIOLIN.. / Taylor, Raynor – 1797 – 9 – us Sibley [780]

SONATA NO. 1, G MINOR, OP. 45, "SONATA TRAGICA" / MacDowell, E – Leipzig: Breitkopf & Haertel, 1893 – 1 – us Sibley [780]

SONATA NO. 2, G MINOR, OP. 50, "SONATA EROICA" / MacDowell, E – Leipzig: Breitkopf & Haertel, 1895 – 1 – us Sibley [780]

SONATA NO. 3, OP. 57, "NORSE" / MacDowell, E – Boston: A.P. Schmitt, ca 1900 – 1 – us Sibley [780]

SONATA NO. 4, OP. 59, "KELTIC" / MacDowell, E – Boston: A P Schmitt, ca 1891 – 1 – us Sibley [780]

SONATA PER CLAVICEMBALO O PIANOFORTE CON UN VIOLINE O FLAUTO E VIOLONCELLO, OP. (33)/T. 6 / Clementi, M – (3 pts) – Vienna: Artaria, 1795 – 1 – us Sibley [780]

SONATA SOPRA SANCTA MARIA ORA PRO NOBIS. ARRANGED FOR SOPRANO, STRING QUARTET, AND PIANO BY L. TORRI : ORIGINALLY FOR CANTUS WITH 8 INSTRUMENTS [STRINGS AND BRASS] / Monteverdi, Claudio – (Sc and pts. Parts are for tenor, string quartet and harmonium) – Ms, Pisa: 1907? – 1 – us Sibley [780]

SONATA, VIOLONCELLO AND PIANO, NO. 2, OP. 99, F-DUR / Brahms, Johannes – (Score and parts) – Berlin: Simrock, 1887 – 1 – us Sibley [780]
SONATAS (1-6) 2VLNS, VC, THOROUGH-BASS; OUT OF GEMINIANIS SOLOS / Barsanti, F – London: B Cooke. 3pts. 173- – 1 – us Sibley [780]
SONATAS (16) COMPOSED FOR A VIOLIN AND A BASS VIOL OR HARPSICHORD / Pepusch, J C – 177? mss – 9 – us Sibley [780]
SONATAS FOR KEYBOARD AND VIOLIN : 1760-1820 – 162mf – 9 – MS-m – ne IDC [780]
SONATAS, HARPSICHORD, FLUTE AND VIOLONCELLO, OP. 4 / Hoffmeister, Franz A – (Bound in Wragg's Improved Flute Preceptor of 1806) – Berlin: 1791 – 1 – us Sibley [780]
SONATAS, HARPSICHORD, W. 49 / Bach, C P E – 1st ed. Nurnberg: Johann Ulrich Haffner – 1 – us Sibley [780]
SONATAS, PIANO, OP. 2, C MAJOR / Clementi, M – Wurtzbourg: J Demar, 1797? – 1 – us Sibley [780]
SONATAS, PIANO, VIOLIN, OP. 7 / Boieldieu, F – (Parts) – Paris: Cherubine, Mehu, et al... 180- – 1 – us Sibley [780]
SONATAS, VIOLIN AND PIANO, OP 16, WITH AN ACCOMPANYMENT FOR THE VIOLIN OR GERMAN FLUTE / Bach, Johann Christian – London: John Weicker, 178- – us Sibley [780]
SONATAS, VIOLIN ET CONTINUO, LER LIVRE / Senaille, J B – Paris: de la Chevardiere, [1760?] – 1 – us Sibley [780]
SONATE A VIOLINO CON VIOLA DI GAMBA O CEMBALO / Guerini, Francesco – Opera prima. (Score). 1760? – 9 – us Sibley [780]
SONATE A VIOLINO E VIOLINE O CEMBALO. / Corelli, Arcangelo – op. 5. 1700 – 9 – us Sibley [780]
SONATE A VIOLINO E VIOLONCELLO O CIMBALO : OPERA PRIMA / Tartini, Giuseppe – Amsterdam: M C LeCene, [1734] – 1 – us Sibley [780]
SONATE A VIOLINO SOLO E VIOLONCELLE A BASSO CONTINUO...OPERA PRIMO, LIBRO PRIMO / Birckenstock, J – Amsterdam: Roger & Michel Charles le Cene, No. 496, [1722] – 1 – us Sibley [780]
SONATE [C DUR], OP. 12 / Sinding, C – Kopenhagen: Hansen, [189-] – 1 – us Sibley [780]
SONATE FAVORITE POUR LE FORTEPIANO AVEC ACCOMP. DE VIOLON ET VIOLONCELLE, OP. 37 / Dussek, J L – (Parts) – Leipsic: Breitkopf & Hartel, 182- – 1 – us Sibley [780]
SONATE FOR PIANO, OP. 21 / Paderewski, Ignace Jan – Berlin: Bote & Book, 190- – 1 – us Sibley [780]
SONATE, GRANDE, POUR PIANOFORTE, OP. 44 / Dussek, J L – Paris: Pleyel, 181- – 1 – us Sibley [780]
SONATE PER CLAVICEMBALO OPIANOFORTE, CON VIOLINE O FLAUTO / Clementi, M – (3 pts) – Vienna: Artaria & Co, 1794 – 1 – us Sibley [780]
SONATE POUR LE FORTEPIANO, OP. 8 / Adam, Lucien – Paris: Pleyel, 179-? – 1 – us Sibley [780]
SONATE POUR LE PIANOFORTE AVEC ACCOMPAGNEMENT DE VIOLON ET VIOLONCELLE, OP. 47 / Reicha, A – (Pts.) – Leipsic: Breitkopf & Hartel, 1804 – 1 – us Sibley [780]
SONATE POUR LE VIOLON AVEC ACCOMPAGNEMENT DE BASSE / Jarnowick, JG – Paris: Boyer, [178-?] – 1 – us Sibley [780]
SONATE, TWO VIOLINS AND BASS / Festoni, A – London: Hodgeson, 1797? – 1 – us Sibley [780]
DIE SONATE VON GRIEG : ROMAN / Landesen, Wera von – Nuernberg: J L Schrag, 1944 – 1r – 1 – us U.W. Library [830]
SONATES, 3 POUR LE CLAVECIN OU PIANOFORTE AVEC FLUTE ET BASSE / Clementi, M – (Pts) – Offenbach s/M: Andre, ca 1785 – 1 – us Sibley [780]
SONATES, 12...TIRES DE TOUS SES OUVRAGES AND TRANSPORTES POUR LA FLUTE, DONT IL EN A 6 A 2 FL. AND A BASSE CONTINUE... / Corelli, Arcangelo – (Parts) – Amsterdam: Roger, c1703 – 1 – us Sibley [780]
SONATES, DEUX, POUR FORTEPIANO AVEC ACCOMP. DE VIOLON ET BASSE, OEUVRE POSTHUME / Dussek, J L – (Parts) – Paris: Naderman, 181- – 1 – us Sibley [780]
SONATES, DEUX, POUR LE PIANOFORTE AVEC VIOLON ET BASSE, OP. 34 / Dussek, J L – (Parts) – Leipsic: Breitkopf & Hartel, 182- – 1 – us Sibley [780]
SONATES, DEUX, POUR PIANOFORTE AVEC ACCOMPAGNEMENT DE VIOLON ET VIOLONCELLE...OEUVRE 61 / Steibelt, Daniel – (Parts) – A Offenbach s/M: chez Jean Andre, No. 2062 – 1 – us Sibley [780]
...SONATES FOR 2 VIOLINS AND VIOLONCELLO, OP. 1 / Desaubrys, J P – Manuscript, 177- – 1 – us Sibley [780]
SONATES POUR UNE FLUTE TRAVERSIERE ET UN VIOLINCELLE. / Dothel, Nicholas – II OEUVRE After 1750 – 9 – us Sibley [780]
SONATES, TROIS GRANDES, POUR PIANO, OP. 35 / Dussek, J L – Paris: Pleyel, 181- – 1 – us Sibley [780]
SONATES, TROIS. HEFT 1 OF REPERTOIRE DES CLAVECINISTES / Clementi, M – Zuric: J G Naigueli, [1803-10] – 1 – us Sibley [780]
SONATES, TROIS, OP. 29 / Dussek, J L – (Parts) – Mayence: B Schott, 1800 – 1 – us Sibley [780]
SONATES, TROIS, (PIANO SOLO) ET TROIS PRELUDES POUR LE PIANOFORTE AVEC ACCOMP. DE FLUTE, VIOLA ET VIOLONCELLO, OP. 31 / Dussek, J L – (Parts) – Leipsic: Breitkopf & Hartel, 1812 – 1 – us Sibley [780]
SONATES, TROIS, POUR LE CLAVECIN OU FORTEPIANO AVEC VIOLON AD LIB., OP. 13 / Dussek, J L – (Parts) – Paris: Sieber (pere), 181- – 1 – us Sibley [780]
SONATES, TROIS, POUR LE CLAVECIN OU LE FORTEPIANO AVEC ACCOMPAGNEMENT DE VIOLON, OP. 10 / Dussek, J L – (Parts) – Paris: Naderman, 180- – 1 – us Sibley [780]
SONATES, TROIS, POUR LE PIANOFORTE AVEC VIOLON ET VIOLONCELLE, OP. 21 / Dussek, J L – (Folio) – Bonn: N. Simrock, 1819? – 1 – us Sibley [780]
SONATINAS, TROIS, POUR LE PIANOFORTE AVEC ACCOMPAGNEMENT DE FLUTE OU VIOLON, OP. 72 / Steibelt, Daniel – (Score and part) – Paris: [Dunhan, 181-?] – 1 – us Sibley [780]
SONATINEN FUER PIANOFORTE ZU VIER HAENDEN.. / Schmitt, Jacob – Op. 209. 188-? – 9 – us Sibley [780]
Sonda, Amir *see*
– THE ECONOMY OF INDONESIA WITHIN THE LAST 150 YEARS, 1800-1950
– PEREKONOMIAN INDONESIA DIDALAM MASA 150 TAHUN, 1800-1950
SONDAGSNISSE – Stockholm, Sweden. 1862-1924 – 24r – 1 – sw Kungliga [073]
Sonder, O W *see* DIE ALGEN DES TROPISCHEN AUSTRALIENS
Sondley, F A *see* A HISTORY OF BUNCOMBE COUNTY
SONETOS / Botto, Antonio – Lisbon, 1938 – 1 – us Res Libr [810]
SONETOS AL CUARTO DE HORA / Sanchez-Arjona, Vicente – Sevilla: Graficas Tirvia, Tomo 1-4. 1959 – 1 – sp Bibl Santa Ana [810]
SONETOS INTRANSCENDENTES / Sanchez-Arjona, Vicente – Sevilla: Imp. Alvarez, Tomo 2. 1956 – 1 – sp Bibl Santa Ana [810]
SONETOS INTRANSCENDENTES / Sanchez-Arjona, Vicente – Sevilla: Imp. Alvarez, Tomo 3. 1956 – 1 – sp Bibl Santa Ana [810]
SONETOS INTRANSCENDENTES / Sanchez-Arjona, Vicente – Sevilla: Imp. Alvarez, Tomo 4. 1956 – 1 – sp Bibl Santa Ana [810]
SONETOS INTRANSCENDENTES QUE MIS TORPEZAS DAN !POR EVIDENTES! / Sanchez-Arjona, Vicente – Sevilla: Imp. Alvarez, Tomo 1. 1956 – 1 – sp Bibl Santa Ana [810]
SONETOS VULGARES / Sanchez-Arjona, Vicente – Sevilla: Imp. Alvarez, Tomo 1,2. 1956 – 1 – sp Bibl Santa Ana [810]
SONETOS VULGARES / Sanchez-Arjona, Vicente – Sevilla: Imp. Alvarez, Tomo 3-4. 1956 – 1 – sp Bibl Santa Ana [810]
SONETOS VULGARES / Sanchez-Arjona, Vicente – Sevilla: Imp. Alvarez, Tomo 5,6. 1956 – 1 – sp Bibl Santa Ana [810]
SONETOS VULGARES / Sanchez-Arjona, Vicente – Sevilla: Imp. Alvarez, Tomo 7-8. 1957 – 1 – sp Bibl Santa Ana [810]
DIE SONETTE AN EAD / Wildgans, Anton – Leipzig: L Staackmann, 1927 – 1r – 1 – us U.W. Library [810]
SONETTENGARTEN / Guenther, Johannes von – Heidelberg: H Meister, 1946 – 1r – 1 – us U.W. Library [810]
SONETTI AND CANZONI / Petrarca – 1416. Holkham ms. 519. Holkham Hall, Norfolk, England – 1 – uk Microform Academic [810]
SONETY SOLNTSA, MEDA I LUNY PESNIA MIROV / Bal'mont, K D – M. 1917. BR-540 2 – 8 – ne IDC [460]
SONETY SOLNTSA, MEDA I LUNY. PESNIA MIROV / Bal'mont, K D – Berlin. 1921. BR-541 2 – 8 – ne IDC [460]
SONG AFTER SORROW – (Some original pgs damaged. Cont by and flimed with: Leprosy Missions Digest) – v4-10. 1942-47 – 1r – 1 – ATLA S0722 – us A.T.L.A. [073]
SONG AFTER SORROW *see* LEPROSY MISSIONS DIGEST
SONG JINGSHI DANGAN SHILIAO, XIANFENG SHIYINIAN-TONGZHI ERNIAN – Archival materials on Song Jingshi, from the 11th year of Xianfeng's reign through the 2nd year of Tongzhi's reign, Feb 1861-Nov 1863. Comp. by the First Chinese Archive of History. 5 fiches. F/H101 – 9 – $36.00 – cc Microforms [950]
SONG JINGSHI QIYI SHILIAO – Historical materials relating to the uprising led by Song Jingshi. Comp. by Zheng Tiantig. 3 fiches. F-H80 – 9 – $17.50 – cc Microforms [950]
THE SONG JOURNAL – Detroit, New York City. v1-18 n2. 1871-74 – 1r – 1 – £60.00 – uk Chadwyck [780]
THE SONG MESSENGER OF THE NORTHWEST – Apr 1863-Oct 1875 – 1 – 395.00 – us Opus [073]
THE SONG OF LOS (COPY A) AND MILTON (COPY A) / Blake, William – 2r – 14 – uk Microform Academic [810]
SONG OF OUR SYRIAN GUEST / Knight, William Allen – Boston: Pilgrim Press, 1906. 1 fiche – 9 – us A.T.L.A. [240]
THE SONG OF SOLOMON : WITH INTRODUCTION AND NOTES / ed by Harper, Andrew – (Includes index) – Cambridge: University Press; New York: G P Putnam [distributor], 1907 – 1mf – 9 – 0-8370-3485-X – 1985-1485 – us A.T.L.A. [220]
THE SONG OF SOLOMON / Zoeckler, Otto – New York: Charles Scribner, 1870 – 1mf – 9 – 0-8370-6159-8 – 1986-0159 – us A.T.L.A. [220]
SONG OF SOLOMON AND THE LAMENTATIONS OF JEREMIAH / Adeney, Walter Frederic – New York: A.C. Armstrong, 1895. 1 fiche – 9 – us A.T.L.A. [270]
THE SONG OF SOLOMON AND THE LAMENTATIONS OF JEREMIAH / Adeney, Walter Frederic – New York: A C Armstrong, 1895 – 1mf – 9 – 0-8370-2053-0 – 1985-0053 – us A.T.L.A. [220]
THE SONG OF SOLOMON: COMPARED WITH OTHER PARTS OF SCRIPTURE / Newton, Adelaide Leaper – London: James Nisbet, 1850. 1 fiche – 9 – us A.T.L.A. [240]
THE SONG OF SOLOMON WITH INTRODUCTION AND NOTES – By Rev. Andrew Harper. Cambridge: University Press, 1907. 96p – 1 – us U.W. Library [240]
THE SONG OF SONGS : TRANSLATED FROM THE HEBREW: WITH A STUDY OF THE PLAN, THE AGE, AND THE CHARACTER OF THE POEM / Renan, Ernest – London: William M Thompson, [1860?] – 1mf – 1 – 0-8370-6342-6 – 1986-0342 – us A.T.L.A. [220]
THE SONG OF SONGS: A REVISED TRANSLATION WITH INTRODUCTION AND COMMENTARY / Thrupp, Joseph Francis – Cambridge: Macmillan, 1862. 1 fiche – 9 – us A.T.L.A. [240]
SONG OF SONGS TRANSLATED FROM THE HEBREW WITH OCCASIONAL NOTES / Daland, William C – Alfred Center: American Sabbath Tract, 1888. 1 fiche – 9 – us A.T.L.A. [220]
SONG OF THE U.E. LOYALIST AND YORK PIONEER / Date, Henry Harrington – s.l.: s.n., 1895. 02507. (Pre-1900 Canadiana) – 9 – cn C.I.H.M. [971]
Song, Qilai *see* THE USE OF HEART RATE AND PERCEIVED EXERTION TO PREDICT AEROBIC AND ANAEROBIC RESPONSES DURING WEIGHT LIFTING IN MALE AND FEMALE COLLEGE STUDENTS
Song, S *see* THE EFFECTS OF INSTRUCTIONS AND MOVEMENT REVERSALS ON THE ACCURACY AND KINEMATICS OF A RAPID SEQUENTIAL TAPPING MOVEMENT
SONG VICTORIES OF THE BLISS AND SANKEY HYMNS – Boston. 1877 – 1 – 5.88 – us Baptist [240]
SONGE DE J.J. ROUSSEAU. NOCTURNE POUR PIANO, COR OU VIOLON / Duvernoy, F – (Score and violin part) – Paris: Erard, 182- – 1 – us Sibley [780]
Songeon, R P *see* HISTOIRE DE LA BULGARIE DEPUIS LES ORIGINES JUSQU' A NOS JOURS, 485-1913
SONGS.. / Hodges, Ann M – Harmonized and published by Mr. Huellmandel. 1798 – 9 – us Sibley [780]
SONGS AND STORIES OF THE ALEUTS / Golder, F A – BN 225 2. 1907 – 8 – ne IDC [390]
SONGS CHIEFLY IN THE RURAL LANGUAGE OF SCOTLAND / Cunningham, Allan – 1813 – 1 – us I.U. Libraries [390]
SONGS FROM BERANGER / Beranger, Pierre Jean de – Trans. by Craven Langstroth Betts. New York: F. Stokes, 1888. 03574. (Pre-1900 Canadiana) – 9 – cn C.I.H.M. [810]
SONGS FROM THE HEARTS OF WOMEN: ONE HUNDRED FAMOUS HYMNS AND THEIR WRITERS / Smith, Nicholas – 1903 – 9 – us A.T.L.A. [240]
SONGS IN THE NEW OPERA CALL'D THE TEMPLE OF LOVE / Saggione, G – London: I Walsh and I Hare, [1706] – 1 – us Sibley [780]
SONGS IN THE NIGHT-WATCHES : FROM VOICES OLD AND NEW / Thompson, Helen Hills Strong – New York: Baker and Taylor, 1888 – 1mf – us A.T.L.A. [780]
SONGS OF A SUSSEX TRAMP / Croft-Cooke, Rupert – Steyning: The Vine Press, 1922. 25p. illus – 1 – us U.W. Library [941]
SONGS OF ALL SEASONS, CLIMES AND TIMES: A MOTLEY JINGLE OF JUMBLED RHYMES / Crawford, Mrs. John – Toronto: Rose, 1890. 02126. (Pre-1900 Canadiana) – 9 – cn C.I.H.M. [971]
SONGS OF EXPERIENCE / Blake, William – (Copy B) – 1r – 14 – uk Microform Academic [810]
SONGS OF INNOCENCE / Blake, William – (Copy B) – 1 reel – 14 – uk Microform Academic [810]
SONGS OF INNOCENCE AND EXPERIENCE / Blake, William – (Copy AA). Linnell-Riches – 1 reel – 14 – uk Microform Academic [810]
SONGS OF LIFE: A COLLECTION OF POEMS / Dewart, Edward Hartley – Toronto?: s.n., 1869 (Toronto: Dudley & Burns). 02650. (Pre-1900 Canadiana) – 9 – cn C.I.H.M. [810]
THE SONGS OF ROBERT BURNS / Burns, Robert – 1859 – 1 – us I.U. Libraries [810]
THE SONGS OF SCOTLAND – Edinburgh: Wood, 1848-50. Adapted to their appropriate melodies. Arr. with pianoforte accomp. by G.F. Graham et al. Illus. with historical, biographical, and critical notices. Inc. indexes of first lines – 1 – us I.U. Libraries [390]
SONGS OF THE CAVALIERS AND ROUNDHEADS, JACOBITE BALLADS, ETC / Thornbury, Walter – 1857 – 1 – us I.U. Libraries [390]
SONGS OF THE CHURCH / Pratt, J H – or Hymns and tunes for Christian worship. 1862 – 1 – 14.56 – us Baptist [240]
SONGS OF THE COPPER ESKIMOS / Jenness, D & Roberts, H – (Rep. of the Canad. Arct. Exp. 1913-18, v. 14. Ottawa. 1925). BN-274 2 – 8 – ne IDC [780]
SONGS OF THE HEBRIDES AND OTHER CELTIC SONGS FROM THE HIGHLANDS OF SCOTLAND – c1909-1925 – 1 – us I.U. Libraries [390]
SONGS OF THE PINES / Caldwell, James Ernest – Toronto: W. Briggs; Montreal: C. Coates; Halifax: S. Huestis, 1895. 00380. (Pre-1900 Canadiana) – 9 – cn C.I.H.M. [810]
SONGS OF TWO WORLDS. BY THE AUTHOR OF THE EPIC OF HADES / Morris, Lewis – London: C. Kegan Paul, 4th ed 1878 – 1 roll – 1 – 1-55879-554-5 – uk Libr Preservation [810]

THE SONGS UND BALLADS OF UHLAND : TRANSLATED FROM THE GERMAN / Uhland, Ludwig – London: Williams and Norgate, 1864 – 1r – 1 – us U.W. Library [780]
Sonin, M *see* IZMENENIIA PROFESSIONALNO-KVALIFIKATSIONNOI STRUKTURY ZHENSKOGO TRUDA I SEMIA
Sonis, F de *see* LETTRES DU COMTE ET DE LA COMTESSE DE FICQUELMONT A LA COMTESSE TIESENHAUSEN
SONN- UND FEIERTAGS-SONETTE / Gryphius, Andreas; ed by Welti, Heinrich – Halle a.S.: M Niemeyer, 1883 – 1r – 1 – us U.W. Library [810]
DIE SONNE – Peoria. Ill. 1879; 1882-1891 – 1 – us UMI [071]
DE SONNE-BLOEME, OFTE OVEREENKOMINGE VAN DEN MENSCHELIJKEN WILLE MET DEN GODTLIJCKEN / Drexelius, H – Antwerpen, 1687 – 7mf – 9 – ne IDC [700]
DER SONNENWIRTH : SCHWAEBISCHE VOLKSGESCHICHTE AUS DEM VORIGEN JAHRHUNDERT / Kurz, Hermann – Stuttgart: J G Cotta, 1880 – 1r – 1 – us U.W. Library [390]
Sonnerat, P *see* VOYAGE A LA NOUVELLE GUINEE
SONNETS FROM VENICE / Platen, August, Graf von – Madison, Wis.: [s.n.] 1914 – 1r – 1 – us U.W. Library [810]
THE SONNETS OF MICHAEL ANGELO BUONARROTI AND TOMMASO CAMPANELLA. / Michelangelo & Campanella, Tommaso – Trans. into rhymed English by John Addington Symonds. London: Smith, Elder and Co., 1878. viii,212p – 1 – us U.W. Library [810]
SONNETS TO LITERARY PERSONAGES / Platen, August, Graf von – Ithaca, NY: Andrus & Church, 1922 – 1r – 1 – us U.W. Library [810]
SONNETTE / Gryphius, Andreas; ed by Crone, Curt – Stuttgart: Reclam, 1949 – 1r – 1 – us U.W. Library [810]
SONNIGE HEIMAT : ERZAEHLUNGEN / Tremel-Eggert, Kuni – 11. Aufl. Muenchen: F Eher, 1943 – 1r – 1 – us U.W. Library [430]
EINE SONNIGE WELT : MAERCHEN UND GEDICHTE / Reinick, Robert – Muenchen: F Seybold, [1922?] – 1 – us U.W. Library [800]
Sonnini de Manoncourt, Charles N S *see*
- VOYAGE DANS LA HAUTE ET BASSE EGYPTE: FAIT PAR ORDRE DE L'ANCIEN GOUVERNEMENT ET CONTENANT DES OBSERVATIONS DE TOUS GENRES, AVEC UNE COLLECTION DE 40 PLANCHES GRAVEES PAR J.P.B. TARDIEU DESSINEES SUR LES LIEUX
- VOYAGE EN GRECE ET EN TURQUIE FAIT PAR ORDRE DE LOUIS XVI ET AVEC L'AUTORISATION DE LA COUR OTTOMANE AVEC UN VOLUME GRAND IN 40, CONTENANT UNE TRES BELLE CARTE COLORIEE ET DES PLANCHES GRAVEES EN TAILLE DOUCE

THE SONNINO PAPERS – 54r – 1 – $3740.00 – us UMI [945]
SONNOE TSARSTVO VELIKIKH NACHINANII / Zhirkevich, A V – (K stoletnemu iubileiu dnia rozhdeniia. I.P. Kornilova). Vil'na. 1911. BR-4572 2 – 8 – ne IDC [947]
SONNOE TSARSTVO VELIKIKH NACHINANII / Zhirkevich, A V – Vil'na, 1911 – 4mf – 9 – ne IDC [947]
DER SONNTAG – Bela Crkva, Yugoslavia. 1933-37 – 2r – 1 – us L of C Photodup [949]
DER SONNTAG *see* DEUTSCHE VOLKSZEITUNG
SONNTAG – 1970-1989 – 900mf – 1 – DM5,130.00 – gw Mikro Press [073]
SONNTAG – Berlin, 1946-49 – 2r – 1 – DM150.00 – gw Mikro Press [072]
SONNTAG – Berlin, Germany. -w. 19 March 1967-Dec 1976. 9 reels – 1 – uk British Libr Newspaper [072]
SONNTAG – Berlin, jul 7 1946-90 – 26r – 1 – Inquire at Mikrofilmarchiv for details – gw Misc Inst [072]
SONNTAG – East Berlin, Germany. 7 Jul 1946-1990 – 26r – 1 – gw Mikrofilm [073]
SONNTAG – -w. 1.- Jahrg; Juli 7, 1946-. Berlin, Aufbau-Verlag – 1 – us U.W. Library [949]
SONNTAGPOST *see* ABENDPOST
SONNTAGS BLATT DES ARBEITENDEN VOLKES IN KARLSRUHE *see* DER BOTE AUS KURPFALZ
SONNTAGSBLATT – Hamburg. Germany. -w. 7 Jan-30 Dec 1951. (1 reel) – 1 – uk British Libr Newspaper [072]
SONNTAGSBLATT DES BUFFALO VOLKSFREUND – Buffalo, NY. aug 25 1935-dec 10 1939 (incomplete) – 2r – 1 – Inquire at Mikrofilmarchiv for details – gw Misc Inst [072]
SONNTAGSBLATT DES WACHTER AM ERIE – (Sunday edition of this German language Republican newspaper) – Cleveland, Cuyahoga, OH. 5 Aug 1877-24 Sept 1893 – 7r – 1 – us Western Res [071]
SONNTAGS-BLATT FUER JEDERMANN AUS DEM VOLKE – Berlin, Germany. Apr 1868-1873 – 2r – 1 – gw Mikrofilm [073]
SONNTAGS-BLATT FUER JEDERMANN AUS DEM VOLKE – Berlin, mar 29 1868-73 – 2r – 1 – Inquire at Mikrofilmarchiv for details – gw Misc Inst [072]
SONNTAGSGAENGE / Wagner, Christian – 2. Aufl. Stuttgart: Greiner & Pfeiffer, 1887-90 – 1r – 1 – us U.W. Library [430]
DER SONNTAGSLUEGNER : ROMAN / Bauer, Josef Martin – Muenchen: Ehrenwirth, c1957 – 1r – 1 – us U.W. Library [830]
SONNTAGSMAGAZIN – Leipzig, Nov 1833-1834 – 1r – 1 – gw Mikrofilm [072]
SONNTAGSPOST – (Issues for 1904, 1906-97, 1939 filmed consecutively with: Abendpost (Chicago ed)) – Chicago: Abendpost Co, 1899-1950 (Chicago ed) – us Res Libr [071]
SONNTAGSPOST – Omaha, NE. -w. 16 Mar 1975-1 Apr 1979. In German – 1 – us NE Hist [071]
SONNTAGSPOST : SONNTAGSAUSGABE DER ABENDPOST/MILWAUKEE DEUTSCHE ZEITUNG, CHICAGO – Chicago, IL. 1972-85 – 11r – 1 – gw Mikrofilm [073]
DIE SONNTAGSPOST 150 PARIS, FR. NO 6 FEVR 1939 = LE COURRIER DU DIMANCHE : AUSLANDSDEUTSCHES ORGAN – (Only one issue publ) – 1 – fr A.C.R.P.P. [073]
DIE SONNTAGS-ZEITUNG – Heilbronn, Stuttgart. 1920-1943 – 4r – 1 – DM300.00 – gw Mikro Press [072]
DIE SONNTAGS-ZEITUNG *see* SUEDDEUTSCHE SONNTAGS-ZEITUNG
SONNTAGSZEITUNG FUER DEUTSCHLANDS FRAUEN – Berlin, Germany. 1900; 1902; 1905 – 3r – 1 – gw Mikrofilm [305]
SONNTAGSZEITUNG FUER DEUTSCHLANDS FRAUEN – (Cont by: Sonntags-Zeitung fuers deutsche Haus) – Berlin, 1900-07 – 1 – Inquire at Mikrofilmarchiv for details – gw Misc Inst [640]
SONNTAGS-ZEITUNG FUERS DEUTSCHE HAUS *see* SONNTAGSZEITUNG FUER DEUTSCHLANDS FRAUEN
DER SONNWENDHOF : VOLKSSCHAUSPIEL IN FUENF AUFZUEGEN / Mosenthal, Salomon Hermann von – 4. Aufl. Leipzig: J J Weber, 1896 – 1r – 1 – us U.W. Library [820]
SONNWILL : EINE ERZAEHLUNG AUS DER GERMANENZEIT / Auerswald, Annmarie von – Dresden: C C Meinhold, 1938 – 1r – 1 – us U.W. Library [830]
Sonolet, L *see* MOUSSA ET GI-GLA
SONOMA COUNTY – 1907-33; 1994- – 14+ r – 1 – $700.00 – P00125 – us Library Micro [910]
SONOMA COUNTY DEMOCRAT *see* SONOMA DEMOCRAT
SONOMA COUNTY INCLUDING PETALUMA AND SANTA ROSA – Sonoma Co, CA. 1895; 1903-1949 – 12r – 1 – $600.00 – D099 – us Library Micro [978]
SONOMA COUNTY JOURNAL – Petaluma. Calif. 1856-1864 – 1 – us UMI [071]
SONOMA COUNTY TRIBUNE – Healdsburg, CA. 1888-1890; 1891-1892 – 2r – 1 – $100.00 – B03239 – us Library Micro [071]
SONOMA COUNTY TRIBUNE *see* HEALDSBURG ENTERPRISE
SONOMA COUNTY-NORTH – 1992 – 5+ r – 1 – $250.00 – P00127 – us Library Micro [910]
SONOMA COUNTY-SOUTH – 1992-94 – 5r – 1 – $250.00 – P00126 – us Library Micro [910]
SONOMA DEMOCRAT – (Also known as: Sonoma County Democrat) – Santa Rosa, CA. 1857-95 – 24r – 1 – $1,200.00 – B02981 – us Library Micro [071]
SONOMA DEMOCRAT – Santa Rosa. Calif. -w. 1857-90 – 1 – us UMI [071]
SONOMA DEMOCRAT – Sonoma, CA. 1857-1890 – 20r – 1 – $10,000.00 – B06032 – us Library Micro [071]
THE SONOMA INDEX TRIBUNE – Sonoma, CA. 1885- – 129+ r – 1 BC02998 – $6,450.00 ($240.00y) – us Library Micro [071]
SONOMA STATE UNIVERSITY NEWSPAPER COLLECTION – (Titles include: The County Bugle; Sonoma State Carousel; Sonoma State Morning Glory; Sonoma State Star; Cotati Call; Key; Patchwork; The Sonoman; Sonoma State Stony Point Gazette; Steppes) – Rohnert Park, CA. 1970s – 18r – 1 – $900.00 – B05070 – us Library Micro [370]
SONOMA/LAKE/MENDOCINO COUNTIES – 1907-33 – 21r – 1 – $1,050.00 – P00128 – us Library Micro [910]
Sonora. Mexico (State) *see* BOLETIN OFICIAL
THE SONS OF ENGLAND RECORD – Toronto: [Sons of England Benefit Society, 1896?-19–] – 9 – cn C.I.H.M. [334]
SONS OF FIRE / Braddon, Mary Elizabeth – British Fiction Archive: Unit 5 – 9 – uk Bell [830]
SONS OF TEMPERANCE OF NORTH AMERICA, GRAND DIVISION OF NOVA SCOTIA *see* JOURNAL OF THE PROCEEDINGS OF THE GRAND DIVISION OF THE SONS OF TEMPERANCE OF THE PROVINCE OF NOVA SCOTIA AT THE QUARTERLY SESSION...
Sons of Temperance of North America. Grand Division of Nova Scotia *see* JOURNAL OF THE PROCEEDINGS OF THE GRAND DIVISION OF THE SONS OF TEMPERANCE OF THE PROVINCE OF NOVA SCOTIA AT THE QUARTERLY SESSION...
THE SONS OF TEMPERANCE RECORD – (Cont by: The Sons of Temperance Record and Prohibition Advocate) – Kettleby [Ont.]: Grand Division, Sons of Temperance of Ontario, [1897] – 9 – cn C.I.H.M. [073]
THE SONS OF TEMPERANCE RECORD *see* THE SONS OF TEMPERANCE RECORD AND PROHIBITION ADVOCATE
THE SONS OF TEMPERANCE RECORD AND PROHIBITION ADVOCATE – (Cont: The Sons of Temperance Record) – Toronto: [s.n., 1898-19–] – 9 – cn C.I.H.M. [073]
THE SONS OF TEMPERANCE RECORD AND PROHIBITION ADVOCATE *see* THE SONS OF TEMPERANCE RECORD
SONTETOS AL CUARTO DE HORA / Sanchez-Arjona, Vicente – Sevilla: Imp. Alvarez, Tomo 5-8. 1959 – 1 – sp Bibl Santa Ana [810]
Sonthonnax, L *see* ESSAI DE CLASSIFICATION DES LEPIDOPTERES PRODUCTEURS DE SOIE
SONUMID – Lubeck, Germany. Oct 1945-Mar 1946; Dertmold, 11 Oct 1946-29 Oct 1948 – 2r – 1 – us L of C Photodup [072]
SOOBSHCHENIIA SOVETSKOGO INFORMBIURO – Moscow. June 22, 1941-May 15, 1945, Vols. 1-8, plus index. 2989 pages – 1 – 35.00r – us Hoover Inst Photo [355]
Soolsma, Serge J *see* THE EFFECT OF INTERMITTENT HYPERBARIC OXYGENATION ON SHORT TERM RECOVERY FROM GRADE 2 MEDIAL COLLATERAL LIGAMENT INJURIES
Soothill, William Edward *see* A TYPICAL MISSION IN CHINA
SOPHIA – (1986- 5,6,9) – v1- 1962- – 1 – us UMI [100]
SOPHIA : A JOURNAL OF DISCUSSION IN PHILOSOPHICAL THEOLOGY – v1-31. 1962-92 (complete) – Inquire – 1 – ATLA S0393 – us A.T.L.A. [073]
SOPHIE LA ROCHE : DIE GROSSMUTTER DER BRENTANOS / Milch, Werner – (Includes bibliographical references) – Frankfurt a.M.: Societaets-Verlag, 1935 – 1r – 1 – us U.W. Library [920]
SOPHIE TAEUBER-ARP / Reunion des musees nationaux. Paris – 1964. 27 illus. 1 fiche – 9 – fr Réunion [700]
SOPHOCLES : TRANSLATED AND EXPLAINED BY JOHN SWINNERTON PHILLIMORE / Sophocles, Evangelinus Apostolides – New York: Longmans, Green and Co.; London: George Allen, 1902 – lxxxvi/215p – 1 – us U.W. Library [450]
Sophocles, Evangelinus Apostolides *see*
- GREEK LEXICON OF THE ROMAN AND BYZANTINE PERIODS
- GREEKS LEXICON OF THE ROMAN AND BYZANTINE PERIODES (FROM B.C. 146 TO A.D. 1100)
- SOPHOCLES

Sopikov, V S *see* OPYT ROSSIISKOI BIBLIOGRAFII, ILI POLNYI SLOVAR' SOCHINENII I PEREVODOV, NAPECHATANNYKH NA SLAVENSKOM I ROSSIISKOM IAZYKAKH, OT NACHALA ZAVEDENIIA TIPOGRAFII, DO 1813 GODA...
Soppitt, C A *see* AN HISTORICAL AND DESCRIPTIVE ACCOUNT OF THE KACHARI TRIBES IN THE NORTH CACHAR HILLS
SOQUEL TIMES – Soquel, CA. 1939-1941 – 1r – 1 – $50.00 – B06033 – us Library Micro [071]
SOR DEMONIO. (EN HONOR DE UN MARIDO HIDALGO Y METAFISICO / Trigo, Felipe – Madrid: Renacimiento, 1908 – sp Bibl Santa Ana [946]
SOR MARIANA DE LA PRESENTACION EJEMPLAR CLARISA CACERENA / Munoz de San Pedro, Miguel – Badajoz: Imp. Diputacion Prov., 1958. Sep. Est. Extr. – 1 – sp Bibl Santa Ana [946]
SORAIKWAN KINSHO – Chinese Paintings in the Collection of Abe Fusajiro. 1868-1937. 3 v. Osaka. 1930. BCH-534 2 – 8 – ne IDC [760]
Soranzo, L *see*
- ORATIONE...AD HENRICO 4. CHRISTIANISSIMO RE DI FRANCIA, E DI NAUARRA
- L'OTTOMANNO

Sorapan de Rieros, Juan *see* MEDICINA ESPANOLA...PROVECHOSA
Sorauer, P C H *see* HANDBUCH DER PFLANZER KRANKHEITEN
SORBY DIARIES, 1859-1908 – 2r – 1 – uk Microform Academic [920]
LA SORCELLERIE EN POITOU : GILLES DE RAIS / Huysmans, Joris-K – Paris: Libr. de la Tradition nationale, 1897 – 1 – F50.00 – fr Armell [130]
SORCIERS ET MAGICIENS / Gilbert, Emile – Moulins: Durond, 1895 – fr Armell [130]
SORCIERS, FETICHEURS ET GUERISSEURS DE LA COTE D'IVOIRE – HAUTE-VOLTA / Kerharo, J – Paris: Vigot, 1950 – 1 – F88.24 – fr Armell [130]
Sordi, Giovanni Pietro *see* TRACTATVS DE ALIMENTIS.
SOREARA MOESLIMIN INDONESIA – Djakarta. SE 411 1. 1943-1945. Lacking: v. 3(18), 1945 – 9 – ne IDC [073]
Sorel, A *see* PRECIS DU DROIT DES GENS...
THE SOREL ADVERTISER – Sorel, Canada. v1 n6. 24 nov 1868-v2 n31. 11 jun 1870 – 1r – 1 – Can$70.00 – cn Can Microfilming [072]
Sorel, Ch *see* LA BIBLIOTHEQUE FRANCOISE
THE SOREL NEWS – Sorel. v1 n40. 10 jan 1880-v2 n42. 31 dec 1880 – 1r – 1 – Can$65.00 – cn Can Microfilming [072]
THE SOREL PILOT – Sorel. v4 n1. 28 oct 1871-v12 n47. 18 dec 1880 – 1r – 1 – Can$75.00 – cn Can Microfilming [072]
LE SORELOIS – (v3 n54 31 jan 1882-28 jan 1943 9r Can$55.00r) – Sorel, Canada. v1 n96. 4 jan 1880-v2 n77. 28 dec 1880 – 1r – 1 – Can$60.00 – cn Can Microfilming [072]
LE SORELOIS ILLUSTRE – Sorel, Canada. 10e anniversaire. jul 1889 – 1r – 1 – Can$40.00 – cn Can Microfilming [072]
SOREVNOVATEL PROSVESHCHENIIA I BLAGOTVORENIIA – (Lacking: n2-3 1818) – Spb. v1 (1-3). 1818 – 8 – BR-3995 2 – ne IDC [947]
Sorge, G A *see*
- ANLEITUNG ZUM GENERALBASS UND ZUR COMPOSITION
- COMPENDIUM HARMONICUM
- GESPRAECH ZWISCHEN EINEM MUSICO THEORETICO
- GESPRAECH ZWISCHEN EINEM MUSICO THEORETICO UND EINEM STUDIOSO MUSICES VON DER PRAETORIANISCHEN
- DER IN DER RECHEN-UND MESSKUNST WOHLERFAHRNE ORGELBAUMEISTER/ WELCHER DIE BEHOERIGE WEITE UND LAENGE ALLER ORGEL PFEIFEN
- VORGEMACH DER MUSICALISCHEN COMPOSITION

SORGHUM NEWSLETTER – v. 1-19. 1958-76 – 1 – us UMI [630]
Sorhagen, L *see* DIE KLEINSCHMETTERLINGE DER MARK BRANDENBURG UND EINIGER ANGRENZENDEN LANDSCHAFTEN
Soria Sanchez, Valentin *see* MONASTERIOS DE JARANDILLA
Soriano Diaz, Antonio *see* VENDAVAL
Soriano Diaz, Eloy *see* RENUNCIACION
Soriano, Josefina P *see* NATIONAL LANGUAGE WORKBOOK FOR GRADE 6
Sorley, W R *see* THE DEVELOPMENT OF MODERN PHILOSOPHY
SORMLANDSBYGDEN – Flen, Sweden. 1979- – 1 – sw Kungliga [072]
SORMLANDSKURIREN *see* FOLKET

SORMLANDSPOSTEN – Eskilstuna, Sweden. 1893-1947 – 121r – 1 – sw Kungliga [072]
Sorof, Martin *see* DIE ENTSTEHUNG DER APOSTELGESCHICHTE: EINE KRITISCHE STUDIE
Sorokin, N *see* SOTSIAL'NOE STRAKHOVANIE; SBORNIK ZAKONODATEL'NYKH I DIREKTIVNYKH MATERIALOV
Sorosis Club. Defiance, Ohio *see* RECORDS
SORRISI ET CANZONI – 1986-1995 – 2r per y – 5,6 – Sfr642.00 – sz Infoprint [072]
O SORRISO : PERIODICO CRITICO, LITTERARIO E RECREATIVO – '(s.l.')-Sao Luis, Brazil. 22 Mar-24 May 1885 – 1,5,6 – bl Biblioteca [072]
SORROW / Reid, John – 1870 – 9 – us A.T.L.A. [240]
THE SORROW AND HOPE OF THE EGYPTIAN SUDAN : A SURVEY OF MISSIONARY CONDITIONS AND METHODS OF WORK IN THE EGYPTIAN SUDAN / Watson, Charles Roger – Philadelphia, Pa.: The Board of Foreign Missions of the United Presbyterian Church of North America, c1913 – 1mf – us A.T.L.A. [240]
SORROW OF THE WRITER ARNICHES FOR THE RUIN OF MADRID / Arniches, Carlos – Valencia, 193? Fiche W 728. (Blodgett Collection of Spanish Civil War Pamphlets) – 9 – us H.U. College Libr [946]
THE SORROWS OF SATAN / Corelli, Marie – British Fiction Archive: Unit 1 – 9 – uk Bell [830]
SORRY BUT YOU'RE WRONG ABOUT IT / Wiggam, Albert Edward – First ed. Indianapolis: The Bobbs-Merrill Co., c1931 – 1 – us U.W. Library [150]
Sortais, Gaston *see* PRECIS DE PHILOSOPHIE SCIENTIFIQUE ET DE PHILOSOPHIE MORALE
Sorte, C *see* OSSERVATIONI NELLA PITTURA
SOS – Berlin, may 1952-oct 1958 – 2r – 1 – Inquire at Mikrofilmarchiv for details – gw Misc Inst [072]
SOS FOR SPANISH DEMOCRACY – n.p., 193? Fiche W1165. (Blodgett Collection of Spanish Civil War Pamphlets) – 9 – us H.U. College Libr [946]
Sosa, Enrique *see* IGLESIA Y JUSTICIALISMO
Sosa, Estelredo J *see* DOCTRINA DE LA REVOLUCION DEL 4 DE JUNIO
Sosa Saa, Jose Thomas *see* ILUSTRISIMO SENOR DOCTOR JOSE ANTONIO PONTE. CARACAS, 1929
SOSIALISME INDONESIA DAN SJARAT-SJARAT PELAKSANAANNJA / Aidit, Dipa Nusantara – SE-10,248 1. 1962 – 9 – ne IDC [335]
SOSIALISME INDONESIA; PERKEMBANGAN TJITA2-NJA DAN KETEGASANNJA / Ruslan, Abdulgani – SE 4563 1. 1961 – 9 – ne IDC [335]
SOSIALISME INDONESIA; PERKEMBANGAN TJITA2NJA, KETEGASANNJA, SOSIALISME UTOPIA, SOSIALISME ILMIJAH / Ruslan, Abdulgani – SE 4050 1. 1963 – 9 – ne IDC [335]
SOSIALITAS SEBAGAI EKSISTENSIAL / Drijarkara, N – SE-4104 1. 1962 – 9 – ne IDC [140]
SOSIAWAN-PUTERA – Incomplete. SE 865 1. 1951-1963 – 9 – ne IDC [073]
Sosis, Y *see* GESHIKHTE FUN YIDISHE GEZELSHAFTLIEKHE SHTREMUNGEN IN RUSLAND
Sosrodirdjo, Surasno, raden *see* TRANSFORMATOR UNTUK PESAWAT PENERIMA RADIO; KONSTRUKSI, RENTJANA, DAN PEMBUATANNJA, OLEH R. SURASNO SOSRODIRDJO
Sostavlen Iuridichesko i chasti u NKVT *see* SBORNIK DEISTVUIUSHCHIKH DEKRETOV I POSTANOVLENII PO VNESHNE I TORGOVLE
Sostavlen Statisticheskim otdelom Moskovskogo soveta *see* SVODNYI STATISTICHESKII BIULLETEN PO GORODU MOSKVE I MOSKOVSKO I GUBERNII ZA...
sostavlena Osobo i komissie i po razsli edovanii u zlodi ei an i i bolshevikov,... *see* BOLSHEVIKI V TSARITSYNIE
SOSTAVLENIE KHOZIAISTVENNOGO PLANA V PROMYSLOVYKH TOVARISHCHESTVAKH I ARTELIAKH : KRATKOE RUKOVODSTVO / Khizhniakov, V V – M., 1929 – 2mf – 9 – COR-455/1 – ne IDC [334]
SOSTOIANIE OZIMYKH I IAROVYKH POSEVOV V SAMARSKOI GUBERNII K... – (Includes c1: 1919 July 15) – [Samara: Biuro], 19uu – 1 – CSUXAKZ1240-S – us Hoover Inst Photo [630]
SOSTOIANIE PROIZVODITELNYKH SIL I TENDENTSII I IKH RAZVITIIA V RAZNYKH OTRASLIAKH NARODNAGO KHOZIAISTVA SAMARSKOI GUBERNII / Baskin, G I – Samara: [Samarskoe gubernskoe statisticheskoe bi uro], 1918 – 1 – CSUX91-B1382 – us Hoover Inst Photo [947]
SOTA EYA YE YAPI – 1970-73.(American Indian Periodicals in the Princeton University Library). 5 fiches – 9 – $45.00 – us UPA [073]
SOTERIOLOGY OF THE NEW TESTAMENT / Du Bose, William Porcher – New York: Macmillan, 1899. 1 fiche – 9 – us A.T.L.A. [240]
SOTHEBY AND CO : CATALOGUES OF SALES, 1733-1980 / Sotheby and Co – (Section 1 1734-1850 $3955; Section 2 1851-1900 $8240; Section 3 1901-45 $8625; Section 4 1946-70 $9125; Section 5 1971-80 $4895) – 611r – 1 – $34,840.00 complete collection – us UMI [700]
Sotheby and Co *see* SOTHEBY AND CO
Sotheby's Bond Street Picture Departments *see* SOTHEBY'S PICTORIAL ARCHIVE
SOTHEBY'S PICTORIAL ARCHIVE / Sotheby's Bond Street Picture Departments – (Complete set of 6 coll in 10 binders. Individual titles also listed separately) – over 1129mf – $12,000.00 set – uk Mindata [700]
SOTHEBY'S PICTORIAL ARCHIVE *see*
- 19TH CENTURY EUROPEAN PAINTINGS AND DRAWINGS
- BRITISH PAINTINGS 1500 TO 1850
- BRITISH WATERCOLOURS AND DRAWINGS TO 1850
- MODERN BRITISH PAINTINGS DRAWINGS AND SCULPTURE
- OLD MASTER PAINTINGS
- VICTORIAN PAINTINGS WATERCOLOURS AND DRAWINGS

Sotillo de la Andrada. Ayuntamiento *see* FERIAS Y FIESTAS 1972
Soto, D de *see* COMMENTARIUM IN QUARTUM SENTENTIARUM
SOTO, DE IUSTITIA ET IURE. 1. 1967 Y SUAREZ, TRATADO DE LEYES...2, 1967 / Barrado Manzano, Arcangel – Madrid: Graf. Calleja, 1969 – 1 – sp Bibl Santa Ana [946]
Soto, J *see* LIBRO DE CONOCIMIENTO...DEL GARROTILLO
Soto Marne, Francisco *see*
- REFLEXIONES CRITICO-APOLOGETICAS. TOMO 1
- REFLEXIONES CRITICO-APOLOGETICAS. TOMO 2

Soto, P, de *see* TRACTATUS DE INSTITUTIONE SACERDOTUM, QUI SUB EPISCOPIS ANIMARUM CURAM GERUNT
Soto y Mancera, Felix *see*
- DISCURSO DE CLAUSURA PRONUNCIADO POR EL EXCMO. SR. OBISPO DE BADAJOZ EL...1907
- LECCIONES DE DOCTRINA CRISTIANA... CUARTA EDICION

Soto y Marne, Francisco de *see*
- COPIA DE LA RELACION...VIAGE...CADIZ A CARTAGENA DE INDIAS
- FLORILEGIO...IGLESIA...DIVIDIDO EN DISCURSOS
- ORIENTE, ZENITH Y OCASO
- REFLEXIONES CRITICO-APOLOGETICAS
- SERMON PANEGYRICO

Sotomayor, Damaso *see* EL SIGLO JEROGLIFICO AZTECA...1897
Sotomayor y Terrazas, Luis *see*
- TIEMPO PERDIDO
- TIEMPO PERDIDO, POESIAS

SOTOYME SCIMITAR *see* THE HEALDSBURG TRIBUNE
SOTOYOME SCIMITAR – Healdsburg, CA. 1920-1930 – 4r – 1 – $200.00 – B03240 – us Library Micro [071]
SOTSIAL-DEMOKRAT – Geneva. 1888, no. 1; 1890-1892, nos. 1-4 – 1 – 35.00r – us Hoover Inst Photo [335]
Sotsialdemokraticheskoi Rabochei Partii *see* IZVESTIIA ZAGRANICHNAGO SEKRETARIATA ORGANIZATSIONNAGO KOMITETA ROSSIISKOI
SOTSIALISTICHESKAI A SOVETSKAI A RESPUBLIKA / Eremeev, K – Moskva: Izd-vo Vseros. t sentr. ispolnitelnogo kom-ta, 1919 – 1 – CSUX89-B6632 – us Hoover Inst Photo [947]
SOTSIALISTICHESKAIA REKONSTRUKTSIIA I NAUKA : ORGAN TSNISA I TSENTEKHPROPA NKTP SSSR – (Includes c.1: 1933:no.2; 1934:no.5-7, 9; 1935:no.1-10; 1936:no.1-8) – Moskva: Izdvo NKTP SSSR, 1931-1936. 6v – 1 – CSUXAKY5700-S – us Hoover Inst Photo [335]
SOTSIALISTICHESKAIA ZAKONNOST'. ORGAN PROKURATURY SSSR / U.S.S.R. – Moscow. 1934-41 – 1 – us UMI [324]
SOTSIALISTICHESKII VESTNIK – Berlin, Paris, New York. 1924-1940. Gaps – 1 – 35.00r – us Hoover Inst Photo [335]
SOTSIALISTICHESKII VESTNIK – Paris. 1921-65. BR-4024 2 – 8 – ne IDC [073]
SOTSIALISTICHESKOE KHOZIAISTVO – Moscow. 1923, nos. 1-10; 1924, nos. 1-5; 1925, nos. 1-6; 1926, nos. 1-5; 1927, nos. 1-6; 1928, nos. 1-6; 1929, nos. 1-6; 1930, nos. 1-3 – 1 – 35.00r – us Hoover Inst Photo [072]
SOTSIALISTICHESKOE KHOZIAISTVO BASHKIRII – (Library has: 1932, no.3-9; 1933, no. 1-8; 1934, no. 1-6; 1935, no. 1-6; 1936, no. 3-6) – [Ufa]: izd. Gos. planovoi komissii Bashkirsko i A.S.S.R., 1932-1941. 10v – 1 – CSUX90-S38 – us Hoover Inst Photo [330]
SOTSIALISTICHESKOE KHOZIAISTVO TURKMENII – (Library has: 1936, no. 1-2) – Ashkhabad: [s.n.], 1934-1936. 3v – 1 – CSUX89-S616 – us Hoover Inst Photo [330]
SOTSIALISTICHESKOE KHOZIAISTVO ZAKAVKAZIA : ORGAN V ES'A ZSFSR – (Library has: Aug./Sept.-Nov./Dec. 1932) – Tiflis: Sovet, 1931-1936. 6v – 1 – CSUX89-S659 – us Hoover Inst Photo [330]
SOTSIALISTICHESKOE KHOZIAISTVO ZAPADNOI SIBIRI – (Library has: Jan.-Sep. 1932; Feb./Mar., June/July 1933; Jan.-Mar., June-Dec. 1934; Jan.-Sep. 1935; Feb.-June., Sept. 1936) – Novosibirsk: Izd. Kraiplana i Kraisovnarkhoza, 1932-1936. 5v – 1 – CSUX89-S791 – us Hoover Inst Photo [330]
SOTSIALISTICHESKOE PRAVOSOZNANIE I UGOLOVNOE PRAVO REVOLIUTSII / Cheltsov-Bebutov, M A – Kharkov, 1924. 92p. BR-9653/1 – 9 – ne IDC [360]
SOTSIALISTICHESKOE ZEMLEDELIE – Moscow, U.S.S.R. -d. 1 Jan 1934-31 Dec 1935; 1 Feb-27 Sept 1940. 5 reels – 1 – uk British Libr Newspaper [947]
SOTSIALISTICHESKOE ZEMLEDLIE – Moscow. U.S.S.R. 1931-1953 – 1 – us UMI [072]
SOTSIALISTIK QAZAQSTAN : QAZAQSTAN KOMMUNISTIK PARTII ASY ORTALYQ KOMITETININ G, QAZAQ SSR ZHOGHARGHY SOVETI, MEN MINISTRLER SOVETININ G ORGANY – (Includes c.1: 1945:June 30-1946:Jan.13) – Almaty: [s.n.], 1932 – 1 reel – 1 – CSUXANRO959-S – us Hoover Inst Photo [335]
DI SOTSIALISTISCHE LITERATUR AF IDISH – v. 2. Minsk. 1935. BJ-290-21 1 – 9 – ne IDC [335]
DOS SOTSIALISTISHE VORT = SOCIALIST WORD – Toronto, CN, 1941-1942 – 1r – 1 – Can$35.00 – cn Can Microfilming [072]
Sotsialistov-Revoliutsionerov Partii *see* DELO NARODA
Sotsialistov-Revoliutsionerov Partii. Petrogradskago oblastnago komiteta *see* ZEMLIA I VOLIA
SOTSIALISTRICHESKY TRUD – Socialist Labor. Moscow. U.S.S.R. 1961- – 1 – us UMI [073]
SOTSIALIZATSIIA ZEMLI / Litoshenko, LN – M., 1918 – 1mf – 9 – COR-208/1 – ne IDC [334]
SOTSIALNAIA GIGIENA : OBSHCHESTVENNAIA MEDITSINA I SOTSIALNAIA GIGIENA, KAK NAUKA I KAK PREDMET PREPODAVANIIA V VYSSHEI SHKOLE / Frenkel, Zakharii Grigorevich – Kharkov: "Nauchnai a mysl", 1923 – 1 – CSUX91-B4180 – us Hoover Inst Photo [360]
SOTSIALNAIA GIGIENA : OBSHCHESTVENNAIA MEDITSINA I SOTSIALNAIA GIGIENA, KAK NAUKA I KAK PREDMET PREPODAVANIIA V VYSSHEI SHKOLE / Frenkel, Zakharii Grigorevich – Kharkov: "Nauchnai a mysl", 1923 – 1 – CSUXADP9430-B – us Hoover Inst Photo [360]
SOTSIALNOE OBESPECHENIE : EZHEMESIACHNYI ZHURNAL MINISTERSTVA SOTSIALNOGO OBESPECHENII A RSFSR – (Includes Jan. 1959-. For latest issues context publisher) – Moskva: Ministerstvo, 1931- – 1 – CSUX90-S457 – us Hoover Inst Photo [360]
SOTSIAL'NOE STRAKHOVANIE; SBORNIK ZAKONODATEL'NYKH I DIREKTIVNYKH MATERIALOV / Kats, R R & Sorokin, N – 2nd ed. rev. Moscow, 1936. 498p. Collected legislative material relating to social insurance. First ed., 1935. BR-8802/1 – 9 – ne IDC [340]
SOTSIALNOE VOSPITANIE : NAUCHNO-PEDAGOGICHESKII ORGAN GLAV. UPRAVLENIIA SOTSIALNOGO VOSPITANII A I POLITICHESKOGO OBRAZOVANIIA DETEI RESPUBLIKI – (Library has June-July 1921) – Kostroma: Gos. izd-vo, 1921. 1v – 1 – CSUX89-S905 – us Hoover Inst Photo [370]
SOTSIALNYE OSNOVY KOOPERATSII / Tugan-Baranovskii, M I – M., 1916 – 6mf – 9 – COR-126/1 – ne IDC [334]
SOTSIOLOGICHESKAIA POETIKA / Arvatov, B – (Izd. "Federatsiia"). M. 1928. BR-1973 2 – 8 – ne IDC [410]
DI SOTSYALISTISHE SHTIME = THE SOCIALIST VOICE – (In Yiddish) – New York City, NY. v2 no10 15 Oct 1936-v4 no7 Nov 1938 – 1r – 1 – $25.00 – cn Can Microfilming [071]
SOTTISES DE LA SEMAINE – Par les freres Seguier. no. 1-32. paris. 1789-mai 1790 – 1 – fr A.C.R.P.P. [073]
SOTZIAL'DEMOKRAT – Paris. no. 2-55. 1909-1916. Incomplete – 1 – us NY Public [335]
Souance, C de *see*
- ICONOGRAPHIE DES PERROQUETS

Soubigon, P *see* L'ENSEIGNEMENT DE SAINT PAUL DANS LES EPITUS DE L'ANNEE LITURGIQUE, 1933
Souchon, Auguste *see* LA CRISE DE LA MAIN D'OEUVRE AGRICOLE EN FRANCE
Souchon, Paul *see* LA SERVITUDE AMOUREUSE DE JULIETTE DROUET A VICTOR HUGO
Souchy, Agustin *see*
- SPAIN
- THE TRAGIC WEEK IN MAY
- LA VERDAD SOBRE LOS SUCECOS EN LA RETAGUARDIA LEAL, LOS ACONTECIMIENTOS DE CATALUNA

LE SOUDAN EN 1894 / Guillaumet, Edouard – Paris, Albert Savine. 1895 – 9 – 5.00 – fr Orientalistes [960]
LE SOUDAN EN 1894: LA VERITE SUR TOMBOUCTOU; L'ESCLAVAGE AU SOUDAN / Guillaumet, Edouard – Paris. 1895 – 1 – us Res Libr [960]
LE SOUDAN FRANCAIS / Service d'Information – (Lacks two issues) – 1954-Apr. 12, 1958. – 1r – 1 – $49.50 – us African Imprint [960]
SOUDAN FRANCAIS : MONOGRAPHIE DE DJENNE; CERCLE ET VILLE / Monteil, Charles Victor – Tulle, France: J Mazeyrie, 1903 – us Res Libr [960]
LA SOUDANAISE ET SON AMANT; ROMAN / Francis-Boeuf, Jean – Paris. 1924 – 1 – us Res Libr [960]
SOUL FORCE – Atlanta, CA. 1969-1973 – 1r – 1 – $50.00 – R04144 – us Library Micro [071]
THE SOUL, HER SORROWS AND HER ASPIRATIONS : AN ESSAY TOWARDS THE NATURAL HISTORY OF THE SOUL, AS THE TRUE BASIS OF THEOLOGY / Newman, Francis William – London: J. Chapman, 1849 – 1 roll – 1 – 1-55879-501-4 – uk Libr Preservation [290]
THE SOUL OF LILITH / Corelli, Marie – British Fiction Archive: Unit 1 – 9 – uk Bell [830]
THE SOUL OF THE BANTU: A SYMPATHETIC STUDY OF THE MAGICO-RELIGIOUS PRACTICES AND BELIEFS / Willoughby, W C – Garden City. N.Y. 1928. BA-356 2 – 8 – ne IDC [290]
THE SOUL OF WOMAN UNDER SOCIALISM / Faust, Johanna – LA pamphlet, no.11, 1986. 4p – 9 – 1.00f – at Libertarian Micro [335]
SOUL PROBLEMS / Peck, George – 1875 – 9 – us A.T.L.A. [240]
Souleyet, FLA *see* HISTOIRE NATURELLE DES MOLLUSQUES PTEROPODES
Soulez *see* REFLEXIONS SUR L'ETUDE SOCIOLOGIQUE DES CENTRES SEMI-URBAINS DE LA COTE D'IVOIRE
Soulier, P *see*
- L'EXPLICATION DE L'EDIT DE NANTES DE M. BERNARD, AVEC DE NOUVELLES OBSERVATIONS...
- L'EXTRACTION DU SILEX EN EUROPE OCCIDENTALE

- HISTOIRE DES EDITS DE PACIFICATION ET DES MOYENS QUE LES PRETENDUS REFORMEZ ONT EMPLOYE POUR LES OBTENIR...
- HISTOIRE DU CALVINISME, CONTENANT SA NAISSANCE...

THE SOUL'S EXODUS AND PILGRIMAGE / Brown, James Baldwin – London: Smith, Elder, 1867 – 2mf – us A.T.L.A. [240]

THE SOULS OF BLACK FOLK : ESSAYS AND SKETCHES / DuBois, WE Burghard – Chicago: A.C. McClurg, 1903 – 1mf – us A.T.L.A. [240]

Soultrait, Georges de *see* DICTIONNAIRE TOPOGRAPHIQUE DU DEPARTEMENT DE LA NIEVRE: COMPRENANT LES NOMS DE LIEU ANCIENS ET MODERNES

SOUL-WINNING : A PROBLEM AND ITS SOLUTION / Carroll, Phidellia Patton – New York: Eaton & Mains; Cincinnati: Jennings & Graham, c1905 – 1mf – 9 – 0-8370-6030-3 – 1986-0030 – us A.T.L.A. [240]

Soumelis, Constantin G *see* PROJECT EVALUATION

SOUMISSION DES TRIBUS MUSULMANES DU TURKESTAN PAR LA CHINE (1757-1759) (APPENDICE TROIS LETTRES DE L'EMPEREUR K'IEN-LONG AU KHAN DE BADAKCHAN) / Lepage & Vissiere, A – (Revue de Monde Musulman XI. 1910). BU-761 2 – 8 – ne IDC [949]

SOUMISSIONS QUEBEC – Montreal. v1 n5. 15 jul 1974-4 nov 1974 – 1r – 1 – Can$35.00 – cn Can Microfilming [072]

SOUND ANATOMIZ'D IN A PHILOSOPHICAL ESSAY ON MUSICK / Turner, W – 1724 – 9 – us Sibley [190]

THE SOUND AND THE FURY – Concordance to the novel – 10mf – 9 – us UMI [420]

SOUND AND VISION – Toronto. v1-9. 1985-93 – 9 – Can$28.00y – cn Micromedia [621]

"SOUND CURRENCY" – 1896. On monetary history and monetary freedom. 5 fiches (24x) – 9 – 1.00f – at Libertarian Micro [320]

SOUND OF THE WORKING CLASSES – London, UK. 1842. -irr. 8 feet – 1 – uk British Libr Newspaper [072]

SOUND PRODUCTION : TECHNICAL NOTES FOR THE NON-TECHNICIAN / Roberts, Michael – 1986 – 9 – 92-3-102299-7 – fr UNESCO [620]

SOUND WAVE – London, England. -w. Jan 1907-Dec 1933. 22 1 2 reels – 1 – uk British Libr Newspaper [072]

SOUND WAVES – Logansport, IN. v7-14. 1903-07 – 1,5,6 – us Princeton Micro [073]

SOUNDEX INDEX TO CANADIAN BORDER ENTRIES THROUGH THE ST ALBANS, VERMONT, DISTRICT, 1895-1924 – 400r – 1 – M1461 – us Nat'l Archives [340]

SOUNDEX INDEX TO ENTRIES INTO THE ST ALBANS, VERMONT, DISTRICT THROUGH CANADIAN PACIFIC AND ATLANTIC PORTS, 1924-1952 – 98r – 1 – M1463 – us Nat'l Archives [340]

SOUNDINGS, AN INTERDISCIPLINARY JOURNAL – v1- 1917- 1; v53- 5,6; v58- 9 – us UMI [240]

Soupault, Philippe *see* LE BON APOTRE

LE SOUPER DES JACOBINS / Charlemagne, Armand – (French Theatre Series). Paris. Barba, an III. 1795 – 9 – fr Hachette [820]

LA SOURCE : HEBDO / ed by Harinegnies, Michael – Arvida, Canada. 5 avr 1972-v1 n24. 13 sep 1972 (incomplete) – 1r – 1 – Can$25.00 – cn Can Microfilming [072]

LA SOURCE – Mensuel d'education spirituelle, intellectuelle et litteraire. (V-XI, no. 37-89. Paris. 1934-fevr 1940. mq no. 67, 88 – 1 – fr A.C.R.P.P. [800]

SOURCE AND RELIABILITY OF DEMOGRAPHIC DATA IN INDONESIA / Bhatta, Jitandra Nath – SE-3683 1. 1961? – 9 – ne IDC [310]

A SOURCE BOOK FOR ANCIENT CHURCH HISTORY : FROM THE APOSTOLIC AGE TO THE CLOSE OF THE CONCILIAR PERIOD / Ayer, Joseph Cullen – New York: Charles Scribner, 1913 – 2mf – us A.T.L.A. [240]

SOURCE BOOK FOR THE INLAND FISHERY RESOURCES OF AFRICA – it F.A.O. [636]

SOURCE BOOK OF STATEMENTS OF INCOME, 1958-59 / U.S. Internal Revenue Service – U.S. Treasury Department, Internal Revenue Service, Statistics Division. Washington: The Service, 1960? – 1 – us U.W. Library [332]

SOURCE MATERIALS IN THE FIELD OF THEATRE – (Documents selected by Speech Association of America. Cataloging available) – 22r – 1 – $1635.00 – us UMI [790]

SOURCEBOOK FOR LITERACY WORK : PERSPECTIVE FROM THE GRASSROOTS / Bhola, H S – 1994 – 200p – 9 – 92-3-102947-9 – Co-publ with Jessica Kingsley/ UNESCO Publishing – fr UNESCO [370]

SOURCE-BOOK FOR VOLCANIC-HAZARDS ZONATION / Crandell, DR et al – 1984 – 97p – 9 – 92-3-102111-7 – fr UNESCO [360]

SOURCEBOOK OF KOREAN CIVILIZATION : VOL. 1 – FROM EARLY TIMES TO THE SIXTEENTH CENTURY / ed by Lee, Peter H – 1993 – 750p – 9 – 92-3-102848-0 – Co-published with Columbia University Press, which has exclusive sales rights in the USA and Canada – fr UNESCO [930]

THE SOURCEBOOK OF LIBRARY TECHNOLOGY 1994 EDITION – v1-23 (Library Technology Reports). Cum. ed.-1965-87. Includes Library Systems Newsletter, v6-7, 1986-87. ISSN: 0275-6811 – 9 – us A.L.A. [020]

THE SOURCES AND LITERATURE OF ENGLISH HISTORY / Gross, Ch. – London, 1900 – Dfl49.00 – ne Slangenburg [941]

THE SOURCES AND TEXT OF RICHARD WAGNER'S OPERA "DIE MEISTERSINGER VON NUERNBERG" / Bowen, Anna Maude – (Includes bibliography) – Munich: H Lueneburg, 1897 – 1r – 1 – us U.W. Library [790]

SOURCES BIBLIOGRAPHIQUES... CONGRES INTERNATIONAL DE DROIT COMMERCIAL D'ANVERS 1885 / Nyssens, A et al – Bruxelles, 1885 – 2mf – 9 – ILM-3909/1 – ne IDC [270]

LES SOURCES DE L'HISTOIRE DE FRANCE : 1E PARTIE: DES ORIGINES AUX GUERRES D'ITALIE (1494) – (v1: Epoque Primitive Paris 1901 Dfl22.00. v2: Epoque Feodale Paris 1902 Dfl25.00. v3: Les Capetiens Paris 1903 Dfl22.00. v4: Les Valois, 1328-1461 Paris 1904 Dfl28.00. v5: Les Valois, Louis 11 Et Charles 7 (1461-1494) 1904 Dfl28.00. v6: Table Generale Paris 1906 Dfl19.00) – ne Slangenburg [944]

LES SOURCES DE L'HISTOIRE DE FRANCE : 2E PARTIE: LE 16E SIECLE – (v1: Les Premieres Guerres d'Italie Paris 1906 Dfl19.00. v2: Francois 1 Et Henri 2 (1515-1559) Paris 1909 Dfl19.00. v3: Les Guerres De Religion (1559-1589) Paris 1912 Dfl25.00. v4: Henri 4 (1589-1610) Paris 1915 Dfl22.00) – ne Slangenburg [944]

LES SOURCES DE L'HISTOIRE DE FRANCE : 3E PARTIE: LE 17E SIECLE – (v1: Geographie Et Histoires Generales Paris 1913 Dfl25.00) – ne Slangenburg [944]

LES SOURCES DE L'HISTOIRE DE FRANCE / Molinier, Auguste – 1592 2. v. 1-6. 1901-1906 – 8 – ne IDC [025]

SOURCES DE L'HISTOIRE DE L'AFRIQUE AU SUD DU SAHARA DANS LES ARCHIVES ET BIBLIOTHEQUES FRANCAISES / International Council on Archives – (Guide to the Sources of the History of Africa). Index 3-4. Zug. 1976. BA-740 1 – 9 – ne IDC [960]

LES SOURCES DE L'HISTOIRE DU MONTANISME : TEXTES GRECS, LATINS, SYRIAQUES / Labriolle, Pierre de – Fribourg (Suisse): Librairie de l'Universite; Paris: Ernest Leroux, 1913. (Collectanea Friburgensia ; nouv. ser., fasc. 15: 24me de la collection) – 1mf – us A.T.L.A. [240]

LES SOURCES DU NIL, JOURNAL DE VOYAGE DU CAPITAINE JOHN HANNING SPEKE / Speke, John H – (African Library). Paris. Hachette. 1865 – 9 – fr Hachette [960]

LES SOURCES ET LE DEVELOPPEMENT DU RATIONALISME DANS LA LITTERATURE FRANCAISE DE LA RENAISSANCE (1533-1601) / Busson, H – Paris, 1922 – 12mf – 8 – ne Slangenburg [140]

SOURCES FOR THE CULTURE AND ETHNOLOGY OF NETHERLANDS NEW GUINEA (IRIAN JAYA) : THE ARCHIVE OF THE OFFICE OF POPULATION AFFAIRS, HOLLANDIA, 1951-1962 / General State Archives, The Hague – (Without "Memories van overgave" Dfl3,585. With printed inventory and concordance) – 1997 – 738mf – 9 – Dfl5,975.00 – ne MMF Publ [950]

SOURCES FOR THE HISTORY OF IRISH CIVILIZATION, ARTICLES IN IRISH PERIODICALS / Ireland. National Library; ed by Hayes, Richard J – 1970.-Approx. 271,000 entries 18 reels.-ISBN: 0-8161-1349-1; or 206mf.-ISBN: 0-8161-1750-0 – 1,9 – $1090.00 – uk Hall [941]

SOURCES FOR THE HISTORY OF THE BRITISH IN THE MIDDLE EAST / ed by Grimwood-Jones, Diana – A catalogue of the Private Papers Collection in the Middle East Centre, St. Anthony's College, Oxford 1979. 22 fiches. Printed booklet – 9 – £95.00 – uk Mansell Publ [956]

SOURCES FOR THE STUDY OF COLONIAL INDONESIA AND DUTCH COLONIAL POLICY : FROM VOC TO COLONIAL STATE, C. 1700-1850 – (Part 1: Collection of Nicolaus Engelhard, c. 1700-1838. 806mf.Dfl4,560.00; Part 2: Collection of Gerard Jan Chretien Schneither, 1788-1831. 417mf.Dfl2,360.00; Part 3:Collection of Count Johannes van den Bosch, 1807-1844. ca 604mf.Dfl3,420.00; Part 4: Collection of Jean Chretien baron Baud, 1804-1859. ca 978mf.Dfl5,535.00) – 4pts ca 2,805mf – 9 – Dfl14,995.00 set – ne MMF Publ [950]

LES SOURCES FRANCAISES DE GOLDSMITH / Sells, Arthur Lytton – Paris, E. Champion, 1924 – 1 – us U.W. Library [420]

SOURCES INEDITES DE L'HISTOIRE DU MAROC DE 1530 A 1845 / ed by Castries, H de – Paris, 1905. 2v – 15mf – NE-20146/1 – ne IDC [960]

SOURCES OF HISTORY IN THE PENTATEUCH: SIX LECTURES / Bartlett, Samuel Colcord – New York: A.D.F. Randolph, 1883.1 fiche – 9 – us A.T.L.A. [240]

SOURCES OF JAMAICAN HISTORY, 1655-1838 / Ingram, K E – 2v. Zug. 1976. BI-1132 1 – 9 – ne IDC [972]

SOURCES OF MASSACHUSETTS LEGAL HISTORY – 1628-1839 – 1 – us Primary [978]

SOURCES OF NEW TESTAMENT GREEK : OR, THE INFLUENCE OF THE SEPTUAGINT ON THE VOCABULARY OF THE NEW TESTAMENT / Kennedy, Harry Angus Alexander – (Includes index to Greek words) – Edinburgh: T & T Clark, 1895 – 1mf – 9 – 0-8370-9251-5 – 1986-3251 – us A.T.L.A. [450]

THE SOURCES OF OUR KNOWLEDGE OF THE LIFE OF JESUS / Wernle, Paul – London: Philip Green, 1907. 1 fiche – 9 – us A.T.L.A. [240]

SOURCES OF STATISTICS IN SYRIA: A REFERENCE MANUAL FOR RESEARCH WORK / Syria. Bureau des Documentations Syriennes et Arabes – A. A. Sharif. 1964. BNE-9730 1 – 9 – ne IDC [330]

SOURCES OF STRESS IN ATHLETES : A VALIDATION OF THE PRECOMPETITIVE STRESS INVENTORY / Cornelius, A E – 1991 – 2mf – 9 – $8.00 – us Microform Publ [150]

THE SOURCES OF THE MISSISSIPPI: THEIR DISCOVERIES, REAL AND PRETENDED: A REPORT READ BEFORE THE MINNESOTA HISTORICAL SOCIETY, FEBRUARY 8, 1887 / Baker, James Heaton – Saint Paul, MN: Brown, Treacy, 1887. 02484. (Pre-1900 Canadiana) – 9 – cn C.I.H.M. [910]

SOURCES SYRIAQUES, VOL 1 / Mingana – Leipzig, 1908 – 9mf – 8 – ne Slangenburg [240]

Souriau, Maurice Anatole *see* LOUIS 16 ET LA REVOLUTION

LE SOURIRE – Quebec, Canada. 8 mai 1904-v1 n118. 4 sep 1904 – 1r – 1 – Can$35.00 – cn Can Microfilming [072]

Sourisseau, George E *see* THE EFFECT OF AEROBIC EXERCISE ON THE RATE OF PROTEIN CATABOLISM DURING A SEVENTY-TWO HOUR FAST

Sournia, A *see* PHYTOPLANKTON MANUAL

SOUS LE FOULARD CREOLE : NOUVELLE REVUE ILLUSTREE DU FOLKLORE MARTINIQUAIS... / Nay-Reine, Lucien – Fort-de-France: Imp. du Gouvernement, 1938 – 1 – F132.83 – fr Armell [390]

Sousa Dias, Gastao *see* OS PORTUGUESES EM ANGOLA...

Sousa, L de *see* LES PORTUGAIS ET L'AFRIQUE DU NORD DE 1521-1557

Sousa, Octavio Tarquinio de *see* BERNARDO PEREIRA DE VASCONCELLOS E SEU TEMP

Sousberghe, Leon de *see* STRUCTURE DE PARENTE ET D'ALLIANCE D'APRES LES FORMULES PENDE (BA-PENDE, CONGO BELGE)

Soustelle, G *see* COLLECTION D'OBJETS DES INDIENS OTOMI ET D'ETHNIES APPARENTEES

Soustelle, J *see* COLLECTION D'OBJETS DES INDIENS OTOMI ET D'ETHNIES APPARENTEES

Soute, Gihon & Nesbet *see* THE ANNALS OF SAN FRANCISCO

Souter, A *see*
- PELAGIUS'S EXPOSITIONS OF THIRTEEN EPISTLES OF ST PAUL
- A STUDY OF AMBROSIASTER

SOUTES – Revue de culture revolutionnaire internationale. Fond. Luc Decaunes. no. 5-9; n.s., no. 1-2. Paris. oct 1936-janv 1938, oct 1952-juil 1953 – 1 – fr A.C.R.P.P. [335]

SOUTH – Cape Town, South Africa. 19 Mar 1987-18 Jan 1990 – 3r – 1, 16 diazo available – sa SA Libr [960]

SOUTH – Holly Springs. Miss. -w. 1902-19 – 1 – us UMI [071]

SOUTH AFRICA : FROM THE GREAT TREK TO THE UNION / Cana, Frank Richardson – London: Chapman & Hall, 1909 – us Res Libr [960]

SOUTH AFRICA : INTERNAL AFFAIRS AND FOREIGN AFFAIRS, 1945-1959 – (1945-59: 14r ISBN 0-89093-683-8. $1,665.00. 1950-54: 23r ISBN 0-89093-684-6. $2,740.00; 1955-59: 14r ISBN 1-55655-404-4. $1,665.00. With printed guides) – Series: Confidential US State Department Central Files – 1 – $5,770.00 set – us UPA [960]

SOUTH AFRICA : THE MAKING OF U.S. POLICY, 1962-1988 – (With 2-vol printed guide & index £630.00) – 439mf – 9 – £2,940.00 – uk Chadwyck [327]

SOUTH AFRICA : SOUTH AFRICAN STATISTICS 1968-1976 / South Africa. Department of Statistics – (Coll title: African Official Statistical Serials, 1867-1982) – 39mf – 9 – £7.00f (set £495.00 67 mf) – uk Chadwyck [960]

SOUTH AFRICA : STATISTICAL YEARBOOK 1964-1966 / South Africa. Department of Statistics – (Coll title: African Official Statistical Serials, 1867-1982) – 23mf – 9 – £7.00f (set £495.00 67mf) – uk Chadwyck [960]

SOUTH AFRICA / Trollope, Anthony – London: Chapman and Hall, 1878 – 1 roll – 1 – 1-55879-981-8 – uk Libr Preservation [910]

SOUTH AFRICA : UNION STATISTICS FOR FIFTY YEARS: JUBILEE ISSUE / South Africa. Office of Census and Statistics – (Coll title: African Official Statistical Serials, 1867-1982) – 9 – £7.00f (set £495.00 67mf) – uk Chadwyck [960]

South Africa *see*
- OFFICIAL GAZETTE
- OFFICIAL GAZETTE-STAATSKOERANT VAN DIE UNIE VAN SUID-AFRIKA
- SELECTED PAMPHLETS, HANDBOOKS, CONGRESS AND OTHER REPORTS RELATING TO SOUTH AFRICA

SOUTH AFRICA: A COLLECTION OF POLITICAL DOCUMENTS COVERING THE YEARS 1902-1963 – 1 – 35.00r – us Hoover Inst Photo [960]

South Africa. Agriculture and Forestry Dept *see* SCIENCE BULLETIN

South Africa. Bophuthatswana. Department of Education *see*
- REPORT 1972-1988
- A SURVEY OF THE DEVELOPMENT OF EDUCATION AMONG THE BATSWANA OF BOPHUTHATSWANA

South Africa. Bophuthatswana. National Education Committee *see* REPORT ...: EDUACTION FOR 'POPAGANO'

South Africa. Commission for the Socio-Economic Development of the Bantu Areas *see* VERSLAG VAN DIE KOMMISSIE VIR DIE SOSIO-EKONOMIESE ONTWIKKELING VAN DIE BANTOEGEBIEDE BINNE DIE UNIE VAN SUID-AFRIKA

South Africa. Commission of Inquiry into the Events in the District of Vereeniging *see* [MINUTES OF EVIDENCE AND EXHIBITS]

South Africa. Department of Education and Culture *see* ANNUAL REPORT 1984

South Africa. Department of Education and Training *see* ANNUAL REPORT 1982-1988

South Africa. Department of National Education *see* ANNUAL REPORT 1982-1989

South Africa. Department of Planning *see*
- ECONOMIC DEVELOPMENT PROGRAMME FOR THE REPUBLIC OF SOUTH AFRICA, 1964-69

– ECONOMIC DEVELOPMENT PROGRAMME FOR THE REPUBLIC OF SOUTH AFRICA, 1965-1970
– ECONOMIC DEVELOPMENT PROGRAMME FOR THE REPUBLIC OF SOUTH AFRICA, 1966-71
– ECONOMIC DEVELOPMENT PROGRAMME FOR THE REPUBLIC OF SOUTH AFRICA, 1968-1973
– ECONOMIC DEVELOPMENT PROGRAMME FOR THE REPUBLIC OF SOUTH AFRICA, 1972-1977

South Africa. Department of Statistics *see*
– SOUTH AFRICA

South Africa. Federation of Mining Unions *see* MISCELLANEOUS PAPERS FROM THE FILES OF THE FEDERATION

South Africa. Gazankulu. Department of Edcuation *see* ANNUAL REPORT 1974-1989

South Africa. High Commissioner *see* OFFICIAL GAZETTE

South Africa. Human Sciences Research Council. Institute for Educational Research *see* THE ROLE OF LANGUAGE IN BLACK EDUCATION

SOUTH AFRICA INSTITUTE OF RACE RELATIONS – 16r – 1 – sa Microfile [960]

SOUTH AFRICA; ITS HISTORY, HEROES AND WARS / Mackenzie, William Douglas – Chicago, Philadelphia: Monarch Book Co., c1899. 663p.illus – 1 – us U.W. Library [960]

South Africa. Kangwane. Department of Education and Culture *see* ANNUAL REPORT 1985-1988

South Africa. Kwa Zulu. Department of Education and Culture *see* ANNUAL REPORT 1977-1985

South Africa. Lebowa. Department of Education *see* ANNUAL REPORT 1976-1984

South Africa. Natives Representative Council *see* VERBATIM REPORT OF PROCEEDINGS

South Africa. Office of Census and Statistics *see* SOUTH AFRICA

South Africa. The Office of the Economic Adviser to the Prime Minister *see* ECONOMIC DEVELOPMENT PROGRAMME FOR THE REPUBLIC OF SOUTH AFRICA, 1974-1979

South Africa. Parliament. House of Assembly *see* DEBATES

South Africa. Signatory Association. Task Force on Education *see* BLACK EDUCATION IN SOUTH AFRICA

South Africa. State Library. Pretoria *see*
– PERIODICALS IN SOUTHERN AFRICAN LIBRARIES
– UNICAT

South Africa. Venda. Department of Education *see*
– ANNUAL REPORT 1979-1985
– EDUCATIONAL STATISTICS 1983-1985

SOUTH AFRICAN ADVERTISER AND MAIL – (Title varies: S A Commercial Advertiser, 1824-60. Merged with: Cape Standard to become Standard & Mail. Suspended: May 1824-Aug 1825; and Mar 1827-Oct 1828) – Cape Town, South Africa. 7 Jan 1824-29 Sept 1869 – 23r – 1, 16 diazo available at reduced price – sa SA Libr [072]

SOUTH AFRICAN ANNALS, 1652-1795 / Moodie, Donald – Pietermaritzburg. 1855 – 1 – us Res Libr [960]

SOUTH AFRICAN ARCHIVES: INDEX AND FINDING LISTS / United Society for the Propagation of the Gospel – 1 – uk Microform Academic [240]

SOUTH AFRICAN BAPTIST – Johannesburg. 1882, Aug 1894-1967 – 1 – 482.30 – us Baptist [240]

SOUTH AFRICAN CHARTERED ACCOUNTANT/ SUID-AFRIKAANSE GEOKTROOIEEDE REKENMEESTER – v1- 1965- 1; v12- 5,6,9 – us UMI [380]

SOUTH AFRICAN CHRONICLE – Cape Town, South Africa. 5 Jan-29 Mar 1844 – 1r – 1, 16 diazo available at reduced price – sa SA Libr [072]

SOUTH AFRICAN CHRONICLE AND MERCANTILE ADVERTISER – Cape Town, South Africa.18 Aug 1824-26 Dec 1826. 1 reel – 1, 16 diazo available at reduced price – sa SA Libr [072]

SOUTH AFRICAN CITIZEN *see* KIMBERLEY CITIZEN

SOUTH AFRICAN COMMERCIAL ADVERTISER *see* SOUTH AFRICAN ADVERTISER AND MAIL

SOUTH AFRICAN COUNCIL OF CHURCHES – Johannesburg. 33 docs. 1980-1991 – 22mf – 9 – ne IDC [240]

South African Institute of Mining and Metallurgy *see* JOURNAL

South African Institute of Race Relations *see*
– ANNUAL REPORT
– [MEMOS]
– [NEWSPAPER CLIPPINGS]
– PRESS CUTTING FILES, 1956-1967
– RECORDS RELATING TO THE JOINT COUNCILS OF EUROPEANS AND NATIVES

South African Institute of Race Relations Library *see* [CARD CATALOGUE (AUTHORS AND TITLES) OF THE INSTITUTE'S LIBRARY]

South African Institution of Engineers *see* JOURNAL

SOUTH AFRICAN JEWISH CHRONICLE – Cape Town, South Africa, 1902-1959 – 41r – 1,16 diazo also available – sa SA Libr [270]

SOUTH AFRICAN JOINT CATALOGUE OF MONOGRAPHS.. – 1971-94. Pretoria.State Library computerized catalogue of monographs in South African libraries – 17 – sa State Libr [025]

SOUTH AFRICAN JOURNAL OF MEDICAL SCIENCES – v. 18-32. 1953-1967 – 1,5,6 – us Princeton Micro [616]

SOUTH AFRICAN LABOUR BULLETIN – Johannesburg. 75 docs. 1980-1991 – 100mf – 9 – ne IDC [331]

SOUTH AFRICAN LAW JOURNAL – (Cont: Cape Law Journal (v1-16). Add vols as copyright expires) – v1-29. 1884-1912 – 157mf – 9 – $235.00 – LLMC 84-433 – us L.L.M.C. [073]

SOUTH AFRICAN LAW JOURNAL – (Title varies: v1-17 1884-1900 as Cape Law Journal) – v1-112. 1884-1995 – 9 – $1,492.00 set – us Hein [340]

SOUTH AFRICAN LAW REPORTS 1828-1946 – (Appellate Division Reports 1910-1946. R350.00; South West Africa Report. R161.00; Orange Free State Reports. R343.00; Eastern Districts and Griqualand Reports. R518.00; Natal Reports. R518.00; Cape Reports. R910.00; Transvaal Reports. R700.00) – 9 – R3,500.00 set – sa Juta [340]

SOUTH AFRICAN LIBRARY AFRICANA CATALOGUE / Pretoria State Library. South Africa – 1981 – 354mf – 9 – sa State Libr [025]

South African Library, Cape Town *see* INVENTORIES OF THE MANUSCRIPT COLLECTIONS

SOUTH AFRICAN LIBRARY CATALOGUES : CAPE TOWN, SOUTH AFRICAN LIBRARY. AFRICANA COLLECTION – 354mf – 9 – EA-3/1 – ne IDC [020]

SOUTH AFRICAN LIBRARY CATALOGUES : JOHANNESBURG, PUBLIC LIBRARY. STRANGE LIBRARY OF AFRICANA – 855mf – 9 – EA-1/1-Ea-2/1 – ne IDC [020]

THE SOUTH AFRICAN LITURGY : THE STORY OF THE REVISION OF THE RITE AND ITS CONSECRATION PRAYER / Hinchliff, P – Cape Town, 1959 – 2mf – 8 – Dfl9.00 – ne Slangenburg [240]

SOUTH AFRICAN MECHANICAL ENGINEER – v. 1-4. 1951-1955 – 1,5,6 – us Princeton Micro [621]

SOUTH AFRICAN MINING AND ENGINEERING JOURNAL – v8-71. 1910-1960 – 1 – us Princeton Micro [622]

SOUTH AFRICAN MISCELLANEOUS MANUSCRIPTS, 1911-1953 – [s.l: s.n., 196-?] – us Res Libr [960]

SOUTH AFRICAN NATIVE AFFAIRS COMMISSION, 1903-5 : REPORT, VOL 1-5 / Lagden, Godfrey – Cape Town: Government Printer, 1905 – 9 – sa SA Libr [324]

SOUTH AFRICAN NEWS – Cape Town, South Africa.2 May 1899-31 Oct 1914. 78 reels. Suspended: Oct 1901-Aug 1902 – 1, 16 diazo available at reduced price – sa SA Libr [072]

SOUTH AFRICAN OUTLOOK – 1870-1988. Continued annually. Continues: Kaffir-Christian Express and S.A. Outlook – 1 – uk World [240]

SOUTH AFRICAN OUTLOOK – Rondebosch. 110 docs. 1980-1991 – 36mf – 9 – ne IDC [960]

SOUTH AFRICAN OUTLOOK – Rondebosch. 90 docs. 1980-88 – 26mf – 9 – HRD-1281/1 – ne IDC [960]

SOUTH AFRICAN OUTLOOK – (Title varies: Kaffir Express, 1870-75. Christian Express, 1876-1921) – Lovedale, South Africa. 1 Oct 1870-1 Dec 1970 – 29r – 1,16 diazo available at reduced price – sa SA Libr [072]

SOUTH AFRICAN OUTLOOK *see* CHRISTIAN EXPRESS

SOUTH AFRICAN QUARTERLY – Cape Town. June Aug. 1914-Feb. 1926 – 1 – 35.00r – us Hoover Inst Photo [073]

THE SOUTH AFRICAN QUARTERLY JOURNAL *see*
– A LIST OF SOUTH AFRICAN INDIGENOUS PLANTS USED AS REMEDIES BY THE COLONISTS OF THE CAPE OF GOOD HOPE
– RULES AND REGULATIONS OF THE SOUTH AFRICAN INSTITUTE

SOUTH AFRICAN SCOTSMAN – Durban, South Africa. 1904 – 1 – sa State Libr [072]

SOUTH AFRICAN SHORT STORIES FROM 1945 TO THE PRESENT / ed by Hirson, Denis – 1994 – 248p – 9 – 92-3-102944-4 – fr UNESCO [830]

THE SOUTH AFRICAN SPECTATOR – Cape Town, South Africa.14 Jan 1901-6 Dec 1902. 1 reel – 1, 16 diazo available at reduced price – sa SA Libr [072]

SOUTH AFRICAN STRUGGLE / McCord, J J – Pretoria: J H de Bussy, 1952 – us Res Libr [960]

THE SOUTH AFRICAN TELEGRAPH – Cape Town, South Africa.1 Aug 1895-3 Sept 1896. 7 reels – 1, 16 diazo available at reduced price – sa SA Libr [072]

SOUTH AFRICAN TRIALS : COURT RECORDS OF VARIOUS APPEAL AND CRIMINAL CASES, MOSTLY ON CHARGES OF SABOTAGE OR POLITICAL OFFENSES, HEARD IN THE SUPREME COURT OF SOUTH AFRICA (APPELLATE DIVISION) AND OTHER COURTS – Pretoria, etc, 1951-66 – us Res Libr [340]

SOUTH AIKEN BAPTIST CHURCH. AIKEN COUNTY. SOUTH CAROLINA : CHURCH RECORDS – 1958-Jan 1973 – 1 – 102.50 – us Baptist [240]

THE SOUTH AMERICAN JOURNAL – London. v. 36-79. 1894-1915. Absorbed by Latin American World. (Scattered issues wanting) – 1 – 330.00 – us L of C Photodup [972]

South American Missionary Society. Archives *see* RECORDS

SOUTH AMERICAN PROBLEMS / Speer, Robert Elliott – New York: Student Volunteer Movement for Foreign Missions, 1912 – 1mf – us A.T.L.A. [972]

South Arabia. Ministry of Finance *see* DEVELOPMENT IN THE FEDERATION OF SOUTH ARABIA (1963-1966)

SOUTH ARCOT DISTRICT GAZETTEER / Francis, W – Madras. I-743 2. 1906 – 8 – ne IDC [072]

SOUTH ASIA GENERAL CATALOGUE – 685 titles – 9 – ne IDC [950]

SOUTH ASIA MICROFORM NEWSLETTER – v1, no.1. Feb 1964-v3, no.1. Feb 1966.3v. -q. Inter-University Committee on South Asia Scholarly Resources – 1 – us U.W. Library [950]

SOUTH ASIAN ART AND ARCHAEOLOGY – 195 titles – 9 – ne IDC [700]

SOUTH ASIAN ART PHOTOGRAPH COLLECTION / ed by Huntington, Susan L et al – (Part 1: Kushan period, Caves, and Gupta period 187 mf Dfl2,057.00; Part 2: Gandhara 75mf Dfl825.00; Part 3.1: Buddhist and Hindu Art of Eastern India and Bangladesh; Part 3.2 Islamic Monuments of Eastern India and Bangladesh 118mf Dfl1,298.00) – 9 – ne IDC [770]

SOUTH ASIAN LIBRARY AND RESEARCH NOTES – New Delhi; Educational Resources Center.Sept 1966-1969. -q. Continues: South Asia Microform Newsletter – 1 – us U.W. Library [950]

SOUTH ASIAN LIBRARY RESOURCES IN NORTH AMERICA / ed by Patterson, M L P – A survey prepared for the Boston Conference, 1974. (Bibliotheca Asiatica. v. 12). Zug. 1975. BI-1131 1 – 9 – ne IDC [950]

SOUTH ASIAN LIBRARY RESOURCES IN NORTH AMERICA / Patterson, M L P & Yanuck, M – Papers from the Boston Conference, 1974. (Bibliotheca Asiatica. v. 11). Zug. 1975. BI-1130 1 – 9 – ne IDC [950]

SOUTH ATLANTIC QUARTERLY – v1- 1902- 1; v70- 5,6; v74- 9 – us UMI [320]

SOUTH ATLANTIC QUARTERLY – v1-79. 1902-80 – inquire – us Ross [073]

SOUTH ATLANTIC REVIEW – v.46-. 1981- – 1,5,6,9 – us UMI [073]

SOUTH AUSTRALIAN *see* SOUTHERN AUSTRALIAN

SOUTH AUSTRALIAN ADVERTISER. (THE ADVERTISER.-THE ADVERTISER AND REGISTER) – Adelaide, Australia. Sep 1864-Jun 1953; Sep 1957-Dec 1975.-w,d. 937 reels – 1 – uk British Libr Newspaper [072]

SOUTH AUSTRALIAN CHRONICLE – London, England. -f, -w. 3 April 1852-3 Dec 1853. 1 reel – 1 – uk British Libr Newspaper [072]

SOUTH AUSTRALIAN GOVERNMENT GAZETTE / Australia. South – Adelaide. 1840-1969-. Incomplete – 1 – us NY Public [324]

SOUTH AUSTRALIAN WEEKLY CHRONICLE. (THE CHRONICLE) – Adelaide, Australia. 30 Mar 1861-31 Dec 1870; 2 Jan 1904-24 Jun 1922; 2 Jan 1930-30 Jul 1936 (imperfect).-w. 87mqn reels – 1 – uk British Libr Newspaper [072]

SOUTH AUSTRALIAN WEEKLY DISPATCH. (THE WEEKLY DISPATCH) – Adelaide, Australia. 2 Jul-31 Dec 1853; 1 Jul-30 Dec 1854; 7 Jul 1855-29 Dec 1855.-w. 2 reels – 1 – uk British Libr Newspaper [072]

SOUTH AUSTRALIAN WORKER – Adelaide, Australia. 9 Jan-13 Feb 1925; 28 May 1926-21 Oct 1927; 23 Mar-27 Dec 1928; 1929-24 Apr 1931; 23 Dec 1932.-w. 3 reels – 1 – uk British Libr Newspaper [072]

SOUTH BANK ADVERTISER – Middlesbrough, England. 10 Nov 1876-13 Dec 1884.-w. 4 reels – 1 – uk British Libr Newspaper [072]

SOUTH BANK EXPRESS. (SOUTH BANK STANDARD & EXPRESS) – Redcar, England. 27 Mar 1909-7 Sep 1940.-w. 23 reels – 1 – uk British Libr Newspaper [072]

SOUTH BANK NEWS – Middlesbrough, England. 5 Apr 1884-25 Jun 1887.-w. 2 reels – 1 – uk British Libr Newspaper [072]

SOUTH BAY : EL SEGUNDO, GARDENA, INGLEWOOD, LONG BEACH, PALOS VERDES, SAN PEDRO, TORRANCE, ETC. – 1939-50; 1975-78; 1980-85; 1987- – 39+ r – 1 – $1,950.00 – P00129 – us Library Micro [910]

SOUTH BAY DAILY BREEZE – (Cont: Redondo, Hermosa, Torrance Daily Breeze) – Redondo Beach, CA. 1909-1914; 1917-1918; 1920-1924; 1925-1985 – 701r – 1 – $35,050.00 – H04036 – us Library Micro [071]

SOUTH BAY-LONG BEACH (SPANISH) – 1992- – 3+ r – 1 – $150.00 – P00130 – us Library Micro [910]

SOUTH BAY-REDONDO : HERMOSA BEACH, PALOS VERDES, REDONDO BEACH, TORRANCE, ETC. – 1975-79 – 6r – 1 – $300.00 – P00131 – us Library Micro [910]

SOUTH BELTLINE BAPTIST CHURCH. RICHLAND COUNTY. SOUTH CAROLINA : CHURCH RECORDS – 1965-73. Deacons' Minutes. 1968-72. Trustees' Minutes. 1968-72 – 1 – 9.50 – us Baptist [240]

SOUTH BEND TRIBUNE – South Bend, Ind. 1873- – 1 – us UMI [071]

South Berwick, Maine. South Berwick Baptist Church *see* RECORDS

SOUTH BIRMINGHAM, MOSELEY AND BALSALL HEATH NEWS ETC *see* MOSELEY AND BALSALL HEATH NEWS ETC

SOUTH BIRMINGHAM NEWS *see* BEDMINSTER KNOWLE & BRISLINGTON RECORD

SOUTH BRANCH INTELLIGENCER – Romney. West Virginia. 1866-1896 – 1 – us UMI [071]

SOUTH BUCKS STANDARD ETC – High Wycombe, England. 23 May 1890-1910; 1912-30 Apr 1914. -w.20 1/2 reels – 1 – uk British Libr Newspaper [072]

SOUTH CAROLINA – 9r – 1 – $720.00 – us Scholarly Res [370]

SOUTH CAROLINA : CODE OF LAWS OF SOUTH CAROLINA – Rochester: Lawyers Cooperative Pub Co, 1977-Jun 1996 update – 9 – $1,061.00 set – us Hein [340]

SOUTH CAROLINA : SESSION LAWS OF AMERICAN STATES AND TERRITORIES – 1776-1995 – 9 – $2,454.00 set – us Hein [340]

South Carolina *see*
– CHARTS OF SOUTH CAROLINA BAPTIST CHURCHES BY ASSOCIATIONS
– LAND GRANTS
– REPORTS AND OPINIONS (A-G)
– REPORTS AND RESOLUTIONS, 1868-1900
– REPORTS, POST-NRS
– REPORTS, PRE-NRS

South Carolina. Agricultural Experiment Station. Clemson *see*
- AE SERIES
- THE AGRARIAN
- AGRICULTURAL CHEMICAL SERVICES SERIES
- AGRICULTURAL ENGINEERING RESEARCH SERIES
- AGRICULTURAL WEATHER RESEARCH SERIES
- AGRONOMY AND SOILS RESEARCH SERIES
- ANIMAL SCIENCE RESEARCH SERIES
- ANNUAL REPORT
- ANNUAL REPORT OF ECONOMICS POISONS ANALYSIS
- BULLETIN
- CIRCULAR
- CLIMATIC RESEARCH SERIES
- DAIRY RESEARCH SERIES
- ECONOMIC LEAFLET
- MISCELLANEOUS PUBLICATIONS
- RESEARCH SUMMARIES
- SOIL MAP LEAFLET
- SOUTH CAROLINA AGRICULTURAL RESEARCH
- SOUTH CAROLINA CROP AND LIVESTOCK REPORTING SERVICE: MONTHLY AGRICULTURAL REPORT
- TECHNICAL BULLETIN

South Carolina. Agricultural Experiment Station. Clemson. Dept. of Food Science and Biochemistry *see* RESEARCH SERIES

South Carolina. Agricultural Experiment Station. Clemson. Dept. of Seed Certification *see* RESEARCH SERIES

South Carolina. Agricultural Experiment Station. Clemson. Horticultural Dept *see* RESEARCH SERIES

South Carolina. Agricultural Experiment Station. Clemson. Poultry Science Dept *see* RESEARCH SERIES

SOUTH CAROLINA AGRICULTURAL RESEARCH / South Carolina. Agricultural Experiment Station. Clemson – n.1-16. 1954-69 – 1,5 – us Spaulding [630]

SOUTH CAROLINA ATTORNEY GENERAL REPORTS AND OPINIONS – (6 1870-1977 $350.00. 9 1978-1994 $147.50) – 1870-1994 – 6,9 – $497.50set – us Hein [340]

SOUTH CAROLINA BAPTIST – Anderson. 1866-68 – 1 – 18.09 – us Baptist [240]

SOUTH CAROLINA BAPTIST – Greenwood. 1898-1902. Later: Pittman and Gardner. Aug. 1905 changed to the Baptist Press, Greenwood, Union, S. C – 1 – 5.00 – us Baptist [240]

SOUTH CAROLINA BAR ASSSOCIATION TRANSACTIONS – (Lacking: 50th-53rd meetings 1943-47) – 1st to 49th annual meetings. 1885-1942 (all publ) – 23mf – 9 – $103.00 – LLMC 84-675 – us L.L.M.C. [073]

SOUTH CAROLINA BAR NEWS – (Supersedes Transcript of the South Carolina Bar) – v1-7. 1989-95 – 9 – $70.00 set – us Hein [340]

SOUTH CAROLINA BAR NEWS *see* TRANSCRIPT OF THE SOUTH CAROLINA BAR

South Carolina. Court of Admiralty *see* RECORDS, 1716-32

South Carolina. Court of Appeals *see* REPORTS OF CASES ARGUED AND DETERMINED IN THE COURT OF APPEALS OF SOUTH CAROLINA.

SOUTH CAROLINA COURT OF GENERAL SESSIONS, 1769-1776 / South Carolina. Department of Archives and History – M-14 – 2r – 1 – $75.00r – Out-of-state orders: us Scholarly Res – us SC Archives [340]

SOUTH CAROLINA CROP AND LIVESTOCK REPORTING SERVICE: MONTHLY AGRICULTURAL REPORT / South Carolina. Agricultural Experiment Station. Clemson – 1952-69 – 1,5 – us Spaulding [636]

South Carolina. Department of Archives and History *see*
- ACCOUNTS AUDITED OF CLAIMS GROWING OUT OF THE REVOLUTION IN SOUTH CAROLINA
- COUNTY AND DISTRICT RECORDS: ABBEVILLE COUNTY
- COUNTY AND DISTRICT RECORDS: AIKEN (CITY)
- COUNTY AND DISTRICT RECORDS: AIKEN COUNTY
- COUNTY AND DISTRICT RECORDS: ANDERSON COUNTY
- COUNTY AND DISTRICT RECORDS: BARNWELL COUNTY
- COUNTY AND DISTRICT RECORDS: BEAUFORT COUNTY
- COUNTY AND DISTRICT RECORDS: BERKELEY COUNTY
- COUNTY AND DISTRICT RECORDS: CAMDEN DISTRICT
- COUNTY AND DISTRICT RECORDS: CHARLESTON COUNTY
- COUNTY AND DISTRICT RECORDS: CHEROKEE COUNTY
- COUNTY AND DISTRICT RECORDS: CHESTER COUNTY
- COUNTY AND DISTRICT RECORDS: CHESTERFIELD COUNTY
- COUNTY AND DISTRICT RECORDS: CLARENDON COUNTY
- COUNTY AND DISTRICT RECORDS: COLLETON COUNTY
- COUNTY AND DISTRICT RECORDS: DARLINGTON COUNTY
- COUNTY AND DISTRICT RECORDS: DORCHESTER COUNTY
- COUNTY AND DISTRICT RECORDS: EAU CLAIRE (TOWN)
- COUNTY AND DISTRICT RECORDS: EDGEFIELD COUNTY
- COUNTY AND DISTRICT RECORDS: FAIRFIELD COUNTY
- COUNTY AND DISTRICT RECORDS: FLORENCE COUNTY
- COUNTY AND DISTRICT RECORDS: GEORGETOWN COUNTY
- COUNTY AND DISTRICT RECORDS: GREENVILLE COUNTY
- COUNTY AND DISTRICT RECORDS: HAMPTON COUNTY
- COUNTY AND DISTRICT RECORDS: HORRY COUNTY
- COUNTY AND DISTRICT RECORDS: IRMO (TOWN)
- COUNTY AND DISTRICT RECORDS: KERSHAW COUNTY
- COUNTY AND DISTRICT RECORDS: LANCASTER COUNTY
- COUNTY AND DISTRICT RECORDS: LAURENS COUNTY
- COUNTY AND DISTRICT RECORDS: LEE COUNTY
- COUNTY AND DISTRICT RECORDS: LEXINGTON COUNTY
- COUNTY AND DISTRICT RECORDS: LEXINGTON (TOWN)
- COUNTY AND DISTRICT RECORDS: MARION COUNTY
- COUNTY AND DISTRICT RECORDS: MARLBORO COUNTY
- COUNTY AND DISTRICT RECORDS: NEWBERRY COUNTY
- COUNTY AND DISTRICT RECORDS: NINETY SIX DISTRICT
- COUNTY AND DISTRICT RECORDS: OCONEE COUNTY
- COUNTY AND DISTRICT RECORDS: ORANGEBURG COUNTY
- COUNTY AND DISTRICT RECORDS: PICKENS COUNTY
- COUNTY AND DISTRICT RECORDS: PINCKNEY DISTRICT (YORK)
- COUNTY AND DISTRICT RECORDS: RICHLAND COUNTY
- COUNTY AND DISTRICT RECORDS: SALUDA COUNTY
- COUNTY AND DISTRICT RECORDS: SPARTANBURG COUNTY
- COUNTY AND DISTRICT RECORDS: SPARTANBURG (TOWN)
- COUNTY AND DISTRICT RECORDS: ST PAUL'S PARISH
- COUNTY AND DISTRICT RECORDS: ST STEPHEN'S PARISH
- COUNTY AND DISTRICT RECORDS: SUMTER COUNTY
- COUNTY AND DISTRICT RECORDS: UNION COUNTY
- COUNTY AND DISTRICT RECORDS: WILLIAMSBURG COUNTY
- COUNTY AND DISTRICT RECORDS: YORK COUNTY
- DUTIES ON TRADE AT CHARLESTON, 1784-89
- MEMORIALS OF SEVENTEENTH AND EIGHTEENTH CENTURY SOUTH CAROLINA LAND TITLES
- RECORDS IN THE BRITISH PUBLIC RECORDS OFFICE RELATING TO SOUTH CAROLINA, 1663-1782
- RECORDS OF THE PUBLIC TREASURERS OF SOUTH CAROLINA, 1725-76
- RECORDS OF THE SOUTH CAROLINA TREASURY, 1775-80
- SOUTH CAROLINA COURT OF GENERAL SESSIONS, 1769-1776
- SOUTH CAROLINA STATE PLATS, CHARLESTON SERIES, 1784-1860
- SOUTH CAROLINA TAX RETURNS, 1783-1800
- SOUTH CAROLINA TREASURY LEDGERS AND JOURNALS, 1783-91
- SOUTH CAROLINA TREASURY LEDGERS AND JOURNALS, 1791-1865
- SOUTH CAROLINA WILL TRANSCRIPTS, 1782-1868
- STATE FREE NEGRO CAPITATION TAX BOOKS, CHARLESTON, SC

SOUTH CAROLINA ENVIRONMENTAL LAW JOURNAL – v1-3. 1991-94 – 9 – $45.00 set – us Hein [340]

South Carolina. First Baptist Church *see* TWO CENTURIES

SOUTH CAROLINA HISTORICAL MAGAZINE – v1- 1900- 1; v77- 5,6,9 – us UMI [978]

SOUTH CAROLINA HISTORICAL MAGAZINE – South Carolina Historical Society. 1900-81. 82v. 267 fiches. Printed cumulative indexes available – 9 – us South Carolina Historical [073]

South Carolina Historical Society *see*
- COLLECTIONS
- PAMPHLETS

SOUTH CAROLINA LAW QUARTERLY *see* SOUTH CAROLINA LAW REVIEW

SOUTH CAROLINA LAW REVIEW – (v1-36 1948-85 on reel $465.00. v37-46 1985-95 on mf $223.00. Title varies: v1-14 1948-62 as South Carolina Law Quarterly) – v1-46. 1948-95 – 5,6,9 – $688.00 set – us Hein [340]

SOUTH CAROLINA LAWYER – (Supersedes Transcript of the South Carolina Bar) – v1-7. 1989-96 – 9 – $90.00 set – us Hein [340]

SOUTH CAROLINA LAWYER *see* TRANSCRIPT OF THE SOUTH CAROLINA BAR

South Carolina. Milita. First, Second and Third Regiment *see* TYPESCRIPT SERVICE RECORDS

South Carolina. Militia. Fourth Brigade *see*
- ACCOUNT BOOK
- RECORDS

South Carolina. Militia. German Fusiliers *see* MINUTES

South Carolina. Militia. Scottish Guard *see* RECORDS

South Carolina. Militia. Third Regiment *see* ORDER BOOK

SOUTH CAROLINA. MISCELLANEOUS NEWSPAPERS – (South-Carolina Weekly Gazette. Charleston, 1758-64. Chronicle of Liberty. Charleston. 1783. South-Carolina Weekly Advertiser. Charleston. 1783. South-Carolina Gazette. Columbia. 1792-93. Columbia Gazette. Columbia. 1794. Daily Evening Gazette. Charleston. 1795. Telegraphe. Charleston. 1795. Strength of the People. Charleston. 1809-10. Anti-Monarchist. Edgefield. 1811-15. Winyaw Intelligencer. Georgetown. 1817-20) – Sold as one unit – 3 – us Readex [071]

SOUTH CAROLINA NEWSPAPERS FROM THE ANTEBELLUM, CIVIL WAR, AND RECONSTRUCTION YEARS – (The Abbeville Press and Banner, 1869-1900 21r $1,785 D3275.P30. The Palmetto Standard, 1851-53 1r $85.00 D3275.P31. Rising Sun, 1858-65 1r $85.00 D3275.P32) – 1996 – 1 – Co-publ with South Carolina Library, University of South Carolina – us Scholarly Res [978]

SOUTH CAROLINA NEWSPAPERS FROM THE ANTEBELLUM, CIVIL WAR, AND RECONSTRUCTION YEARS – (Tri-Weekly South Carolinian 1849-65 2r $170 D3275.P17. Daily South Carolinian 1849-67 5r $425 D3275.P18. Charleston Tri-Weekly Courier 1832-70 5r $425 D3275.P19. Daily Southern Guardian 1858-70 2r $170 D3275.P10. Free South 1863-64, New South, 1862-66, 1895, Palmetto Herald 1864, Camp Kettle 1861-62, Hospital Transcript 1865 6 papers on 1r $85 D3275.P11. Keowee Courier 1849-88 5r $425 D3275.P12. Lancaster Ledger 1852-66 3r $225 D3275.P13. Laurensville Herald 1860-72 1r $85 D3275.P14. Mountaineer 1829-1904 4r $340 D3275.P15. Southern Enterprise 1854-70 2r $170 D3275.P16. Greenville -Enterprise 1870-72 1r $85 and the Enterprise and Mountaineer (Greenville) 1875-91 6r $510 D3275.P21. South Carolina Temperance Advocate 1839-47 2r $170 D3275.P22. Southern Chronical 1840-47 1r $85 D3275.P23. South-Carolina State Gazette and Columbia Advertiser, 1822, 1827-28, and the Southern Times and State Gazette 1830-38 1r $85 D3275.P24. Columbia Telescope 1815-39 2r $170 D3275.P25. Pendleton Messenger 1829-51 6r $510 D3275.P26. Camden Commercial Carrier 1837-38, and the Camden Confederate 1861-63 1r $85 D3275.P27. Pickens Sentinel 1875-94, 1903-07 4r $340 D3275.P28. Highland Sentinel 1840-43 and the Anderson Gazette 1846-48 1r $85 D3275.P29) – 1 – $75.00r – Co-publ with South Caroliniana Library, University of South Carolina – us Scholarly Res [978]

South Carolina. Orangeburg Association. First Union Division *see* EXECUTIVE BOARD MINUTES, 1883-86

South Carolina Post Offices and Postmasters *see* RESEARCH NOTES

South Carolina. Probate Court *see* MARRIAGE BONDS

South Carolina. St. Thomas and St. Denis Protestant Episcopal Church *see* RECORDS

South Carolina. State Bar Association *see* PROCEEDINGS

SOUTH CAROLINA STATE PLATS : CHARLESTON SERIES, 1784-1860; COLUMBIA SERIES, 1796-1868 – (13r index on 16mm) – South Carolina Department of Archives and History, 1995 – 29r – 1 – $3,570.00 – D3317 – us Scholarly Res [910]

SOUTH CAROLINA STATE PLATS, CHARLESTON SERIES, 1784-1860 / South Carolina. Department of Archives and History – Columbia Series, 1796-1868. M-10 – 30r – 1 – $75.00r – Out-of-state orders: us Scholarly Res – us SC Archives [025]

South Carolina. State Ports Authority *see* PHOTO ALBUM

South Carolina. Supreme Court *see*
- BAILEY'S CASES IN EQUITY
- BAILEY'S LAW REPORTS
- BAY'S LAW REPORTS
- BREVARD'S LAW REPORTS
- CHEVES' CASES IN EQUITY
- CHEVES' LAW REPORTS
- DESAUSSURE'S CASES IN EQUITY
- DUDLEY'S CASES IN EQUITY
- DUDLEY'S LAW REPORTS
- HARPER'S CASES IN EQUITY
- HARPER'S LAW REPORTS
- HILL'S CASES IN EQUITY
- HILL'S LAW REPORTS
- MCMULLAN'S CASES IN EQUITY
- MCMULLAN'S LAW REPORTS
- MCORD'S CASES IN EQUITY
- MCORD'S LAW REPORTS
- MILL'S CONSTITUTIONAL REPORTS
- NOTT AND M'CORD'S LAW REPORTS
- RICE'S CASES IN EQUITY
- RICE'S LAW REPORTS
- RICHARDSON'S CASES IN EQUITY
- RICHARDSON'S LAW REPORTS
- RICHARDSON'S LAW REPORTS, N.S.
- RILEY'S CASES IN EQUITY
- RILEY'S LAW REPORTS
- SOUTH CAROLINA SUPREME COURT REPORTS
- SPEER'S CASES IN EQUITY
- SPEER'S LAW REPORTS
- STROBHART'S CASES IN EQUITY
- STROBHART'S LAW REPORTS
- TREADWAY'S LAW REPORTS

SOUTH CAROLINA SUPREME COURT REPORTS / South Carolina. Supreme Court – (Pre-NRS: v1-25 1868-86 168mf $252.00. Updates planned) – v1-114. 1868-1920 – 786mf – 9 – $1,179.00 – LLMC 84-208 – us L.L.M.C. [340]

SOUTH CAROLINA TAX RETURNS, 1783-1800 / South Carolina. Department of Archives and History – M-15 – 2r – 1 – $75.00r – out-of-state orders: us Scholarly Res – us SC Archives [336]

SOUTH CAROLINA TAX RETURNS, 1783-1800 – South Carolina Department of Archives and History, 1995 – 2r – 1 – $170.00 – D3322 – us Scholarly Res [336]

SOUTH CAROLINA TREASURY LEDGERS AND JOURNALS, 1783-1791 – South Carolina Department of Archives and History, 1995 – 3r – 1 – $255.00 – D3312 – us Scholarly Res [332]

SOUTH CAROLINA TREASURY LEDGERS AND JOURNALS, 1783-91 / South Carolina. Department of Archives and History – (With index) – M-5 – 4r – 1 – $75.00r – Out-of-state orders: us Scholarly Res – us SC Archives [978]

SOUTH CAROLINA TREASURY LEDGERS AND JOURNALS, 1791-1865 / South Carolina. Department of Archives and History – M-7 – 12r – 1 – $75.00r – Out-of-state orders: us Scholarly Res – us SC Archives [978]

SOUTH CAROLINA TREASURY LEDGERS AND JOURNALS, 1791-1865 – South Carolina Department of Archives and History, 1995 – 12r – 1 – $1,020.00 – D3314 – us Scholarly Res [332]

South Carolina. Volunteers. Fourth Regiment *see* ORDER BOOK

SOUTH CAROLINA WILL TRANSCRIPTS, 1782-1868 / South Carolina. Department of Archives and History – Transcripts of all counties except Charleston (M-9) – 31r – 1 – $75.00r – Out-of-state orders: us Scholarly Res – us SC Archives [920]

SOUTH CAROLINA WILL TRANSCRIPTS, 1782-1868 – South Carolina: Department of Archives and History, 1995 – 21r – 1 – $1,785.00 – us Scholarly Res [920]

SOUTH CHINA MORNING POST – (Issues for Aug 8 1941-sep 29 1941 filmed with: South China Morning Post and the Hongkong Telegraph sep 30-nov 7 1945) – Hong Kong: A Cunningham, [1904-sep 1941] – us Res Libr [072]

THE SOUTH CHINA MORNING POST – (The South China Morning Post will soon be available on CD-ROM) – 1984- – 12-24r per y – 1 – inquire – us Ross [072]

SOUTH COUNTY JOURNAL – Wakefield. R.I. 1858-1859 – 1 – us UMI [071]

SOUTH DAKOTA : CODIFIED LAWS – Charlottesville: Michie Co, 1969-Jun 1996 update – 9 – $1,714.00 set – us Hein [340]

SOUTH DAKOTA : SESSION LAWS OF AMERICAN STATES AND TERRITORIES – 1890-1995 – 9 – $662.00 set – us Hein [340]

South Dakota *see*
- REPORTS AND OPINIONS (A-G)
- REPORTS, PRE-NRS

South Dakota. Agricultural Extension Service. Cooperative Extension Service *see*
- FACT SHEET
- SPECIAL REPORT
- SPECIAL SERIES

South Dakota. Agricultural Extension Service. State College of Agriculture and Mechanic Arts *see*
- AMONG OURSELVES
- CIRCULAR
- CIRCULAR LETTER
- DAKOTA ZEPHYR
- EXTENSION LEAFLET
- EXTENSION OFFSET CIRCULAR
- FARM AND RANCH ECONOMIC REVIEW
- FARM-HOME NEWS
- FOOD ECONOMY LEAFLET
- JUNIOR EXTENSION CIRCULAR
- MIMEOGRAPHED CIRCULAR
- READING IN THE HOME
- RURAL PROGRAM SERVICE
- SOUTH DAKOTA EXTENSION REVIEW
- SOUTH DAKOTA FARM HOME OUTLOOK
- SPECIAL EXTENSION CIRCULAR
- SUMMARY OF ACCOMPLISHMENTS
- SUMMARY OF IMPORTANT FARM BUREAU ACTIVITIES
- WAR FOOD SERIES

SOUTH DAKOTA ATTORNEY GENERAL REPORTS AND OPINIONS – (6 1889-1978 $280.00. 9 1979-1994 $70.00) – 1889-1994 – 6,9 – $350.00set – us Hein [340]

SOUTH DAKOTA BAPTIST BULLETIN – Sioux Falls, SD.SD Baptist Convention. 1908, 1910-64. Single reels available – 1 – $150.20 – us A.B.H.S. [240]

SOUTH DAKOTA BAR ASSOCIATION REPORTS – 1st to 32nd meetings, 1897-1932. All published. 84-676 – 9 – $44.00 – us L.L.M.C. [340]

SOUTH DAKOTA BAR ASSOCIATION REPORTS – (Includes 1st-2nd Annual Meetings of the State Bar of South Dakota, 1931-1932) – 1st-32nd Annual Meetings. 1897-1932 – 21mf – $94.00 – LLMC 84-676 – us L.L.M.C. [073]

SOUTH DAKOTA BAR JOURNAL – (Lacking: v6 p33-64) – v1-44. 1932-75 – 84mf – 9 – $378.00 – LLMC 84-677 – us L.L.M.C. [073]

SOUTH DAKOTA BIOGRAPHICAL RECORD-1899 / G.A. Ogle and Co – Chicago, 1899. South Dakota Reel 4. The Cox Library Collection – 5 – us Americana [978]

South Dakota. Emergency Relief Administration *see* SURVEY OF INDIAN RESERVATIONS

SOUTH DAKOTA EXTENSION REVIEW / South Dakota. Agricultural Extension Service. State College of Agriculture and Mechanic Arts – v.1-3. 1922-24 – 1,5,6 – us Spaulding [630]

SOUTH DAKOTA FARM AND HOME RESEARCH / South Dakota. State University. Agricultural Experiment Station – nos.1-25. 1949-74 – 1,5,6 – us Spaulding [630]

SOUTH DAKOTA FARM HOME OUTLOOK / South Dakota. Agricultural Extension Service. State College of Agriculture and Mechanic Arts – 1941 – 1,5,6 – us Spaulding [630]

SOUTH DAKOTA LAW REVIEW – (v1-30 1956-85 on reel $312.00. v31-39 1985-94 on mf $160.00) – v1-39. 1956-94 – 5,6,9 – $472.00 set – us Hein [340]

South Dakota. State Bar Association *see* PROCEEDINGS

SOUTH DAKOTA STATE BAR NEWSLETTER – 1974-1995 – 9 – $269.00 set – us Hein [340]

South Dakota. State Department of History *see* HISTORICAL COLLECTIONS OF SOUTH DAKOTA

South Dakota. State University. Agricultural Experiment Station *see*
- AES INFO SERIES
- AGRICULTURAL ECONOMICS PAMPHLETS
- AGRICULTURAL ENGINEERING PAMPHLET
- AGRONOMY PAMPHLET
- ANIMAL HUSBANDRY PAMPHLET
- ANNUAL REPORT
- AREA SHEEP DAY
- BULLETIN
- CATTLE FEEDERS' DAY
- CIRCULAR
- ENTOMOLOGY PAMPHLET
- HOME ECONOMICS PAMPHLET
- HORTICULTURE PAMPHLET
- MIMEOGRAPH PAMPHLET
- PLANT PATHOLOGY PAMPHLET
- POULTRY DAY
- RURAL SOCIOLOGY PAMPHLET
- SOIL SURVEY SERIES
- SOUTH DAKOTA FARM AND HOME RESEARCH
- SOUTHEAST SOUTH DAKOTA EXPERIMENT FARM PROGRESS REPORT
- STATION CHEMISTRY PAMPHLET
- SWINE DAY
- TECHNICAL BULLETIN

South Dakota. Supreme Court *see* SOUTH DAKOTA SUPREME COURT REPORTS

SOUTH DAKOTA SUPREME COURT REPORTS / South Dakota. Supreme Court – (Pre-NRS vols listed under Dakota Reports. Vols after 1928 still in copyright. Updates poss after year 2003) – v1-52. 1890-1928 – 156mf – 9 – $702.00 – LLMC 82-990 – us L.L.M.C. [340]

SOUTH DURHAM HERALD – West Hartlepool. 26 May 1866-3 Oct 1891.-w. 19mqn reels – 1 – uk British Libr Newspaper [072]

SOUTH EAST DISTRICT DEVELOPMENT PLAN 1989-1995 / Botswana. South East District – Gaborone, 1990 – 3mf – 9 – ne IDC [338]

SOUTH EAST LONDON AND KENTISH MERCURY *see* GREENWICH WOOLWICH AND DEPTFORD GAZETTE

SOUTH END REPORTER – Chicago. Ill. 1930-1967 – 1 – us UMI [071]

SOUTH ESSEX MAIL ETC – London, UK. 7 Apr 1888-16 May 1941; 7 May 1943.-w. 58 reels – 1 – uk British Libr Newspaper [072]

SOUTH FLORIDA BANNER – Homestead. Fl. 1912-1913 – 1 – us UMI [071]

SOUTH FLORIDA JEWISH TRIBUNE *see*
- BROWARD JEWISH WORLD
- PALM BEACH JEWISH WORLD

SOUTH FORK BAPTIST CHURCH. KENTUCKY : CHURCH RECORDS – Apr 1804-1955 – 1 – 48.87 – us Baptist [240]

SOUTH GEORGIA TIMES – Valdosta. Ga. -w. 1868-69 – 1 – us UMI [071]

SOUTH GLOUCESTERSHIRE GAZETTE – Bristol, England. Mar 1913-1914; Feb 1918-1919; 17 Apr-28 Aug, 6 Nov-25 Dec 1920; 1921-Mar 1935. -w. 15 reels – 1 – uk British Libr Newspaper [072]

SOUTH GRAND AVENUE BAPTIST CHURCH. SPRINGFIELD, ILLINOIS : CHURCH RECORDS – 1859-1954 – 1 – 71.28 – us Baptist [240]

SOUTH HADLEY 1730-1890 – (Mf 1: Index to Births & Deaths by Family 1712-1845. Mf 1-4: District & Town Meeting Minutes 1753-1825. Mf 5-8: Vital & Town Records 1712-1845. Mf 9-17: Marriages, Births, Deaths 1852-96. Mf 18-19: Birth Index 1843-96. Mf 20-21: Marriage Index 1843-96. Mf 22-23: Death Index 1844-96. Mf 24-26: Births, Marriages, Deaths 1891-96) – (mf ed 1984) – 26mf – 9 – 0-931248-67-1 – us Holbrook [920]

SOUTH HAMPSTEAD ADVERTISER – (St. John's Wood and South Hampstead Advertiser Hampstead and St. John's Wood Advertiser Hampstead News). London. -w. 1882-1971. (83 reels) – 1 – uk British Libr Newspaper [072]

SOUTH INDIA CHURCHMAN – Nov 1947-1991 (complete) – 8r – 1 – ATLA S0116 – us A.T.L.A. [073]

South India (Madras) Mission. Church Missionary Society *see* CORRESPONDENCE 1830-1865

SOUTH INDIA MISSIONARY CONFERENCE – 2D, Bangalore, 1879. The missionary conference: South India and Ceylon, 1879. 2 v. 1880 – 1 – us A.T.L.A. [240]

SOUTH INDIAN MISSIONS : CONTAINING GLIMPSES INTO THE LIVES AND CUSTOMS OF THE TAMIL PEOPLE / Sharrock, J A – Westminster: Society for the Propagation of the Gospel in Foreign Parts, 1910 – 1mf – us A.T.L.A. [305]

SOUTH INDIAN POLITY / Mahalingam, T V – Madras: University of Madras, 1955 – 1 – us U.W. Library [950]

SOUTH JERSEY REPUBLICAN – Hammonton. N.J. 1863-65; 1869-1871; 1875-1918 – 1 – us UMI [071]

SOUTH KANSAS TRIBUNE – Independence. Kansas. -w. 1876-1942 – 1 – us UMI [071]

SOUTH LAKE PRESS – Clermont. Fl. -w. 1928-1930 – 1 – us P.K. Yonge [071]

South London Botanical Institute *see* INDEX TO THE JOURNAL OF BOTANY, 1863-1942

SOUTH LONDON CHRONICLE – London, England. 19 Nov 1859-26 Feb 1876; 6 May 1876-1 Nov 1890; 5 Dec 1891-22 Apr 1893; 1 Mar 1895-19 Apr 1907 – 39 1/2r – 1 – uk British Libr Newspaper [072]

SOUTH LONDON JOURNAL – (South London Local Journal, 1856) – London, UK. 1856-71 – 16r – 1 – uk British Libr Newspaper [072]

SOUTH LONDON LOCAL JOURNAL *see* SOUTH LONDON JOURNAL

SOUTH LONDON MAIL – London, UK. 1888-1906 – 26r – 1 – uk British Libr Newspaper [072]

SOUTH LONDON NEWS ETC *see* LAMBETH AND SOUTHWARK ADVERTISER

SOUTH LONDON PRESS – (Lacking: Jul-Dec 1871) – London, England. 1865-1951; 1983- – 238+ r – 1 – uk British Libr Newspaper [072]

SOUTH LOS ANGELES BULLETIN – Los Angeles, CA. 1933-1945; 1948-1959; 1961-1983 – 66r – 1 – $3,300.00 – H04027 – us Library Micro [071]

SOUTH MACOMB NEWS – Mount Clemens. MI. Includes preds. -w. 1932-64 – 1 – us UMI [071]

SOUTH MACOMB PROGRESS – Utica. Mich. 1954-56 – 1 – us UMI [071]

South Manchurian Railway. North China Office *see* CHINTAO KINKO NI OKERU NOSON JITTAI CHOSA HOKOKU

South Manchurian Railway. North China Research Bureau *see* NOKA KEIZAI CHOSA HOKOKU

South Manchurian Railway. Shanghai *see* KONICHI MINZOKU TOITSU SENSEN UNDO SHI

SOUTH MEDIATON JOURNAL – Little Rock. Ark. 1964- – 1 – us UMI [071]

THE SOUTH MOLUCCAN CASE IN THE UNITED NATIONS MACHINERY / South Moluccas. (Republic). Dept. of Public Information – SE 1213 1. 1955 – 9 – ne IDC [950]

South Moluccas. (Republic). Dept. of Public Information *see*
- UN NOUVEAU COLONIALISME; DOCUMENT HISTORIQUE PUBLIE PAR LE GOUVERNEMENT DE LA REPUBLIQUE DES MOLUQUES DU SUD
- THE SOUTH MOLUCCAN CASE IN THE UNITED NATIONS MACHINERY

SOUTH NOTTINGHAM AND NOTTS GAZETTE – (South Nottingham Gazette & West Bridgford Gazette, 21 Sep 1901-25 Apr 1903) – England, 21 Sep 1901-25 Apr 1903; 11 Jan 1908-30 Dec 1910 – 2r – 1 – uk British Libr Newspaper [072]

SOUTH NOTTINGHAM GAZETTE AND WEST BRIDGFORD GAZETTE *see* SOUTH NOTTINGHAM AND NOTTS GAZETTE

SOUTH OCEANSIDE DIAMOND – California. 1888-91. Also: Valley Willow, 1889; Oceanside Vidette, 1891. 1 roll – 1 – 25.00 – uk Libr Preservation [071]

SOUTH OF INDIA OBSERVER – Ootacamund, India. Jan 1877-1893; 1897-1900; 1902-14 – 75r – 1 – uk British Libr Newspaper [072]

SOUTH OMAHA SUN – South Omaha, NE. -tw. Feb 1925-Sep 1926; Jan 1927-Jul 1933; Feb 1934-Nov 1935 – 1 – us NE Hist [071]

SOUTH OMAHA SUN – South Omaha, NE. -w. Dec 1951 to date – 1 – us NE Hist [071]

SOUTH OMAHA WASP – Omaha, NE. -w. Sep 1871-Mar 1872, scattered issues missing; Jan 1873-Dec 1875; May 1876-Dec 1886; Mar 1887; Jul 1887-May 1918 – 1 – us NE Hist [071]

SOUTH ONTARIO NEWS – Chino, CA. Nov 1978- – 15+ r – 1 – $750.00 ($50.00y) – R02109 – us Library Micro [071]

SOUTH OREGON EYE – Medford, OR. -w. 4 Jan 1899-25 Jan 1900. 1 roll – 1 – us U.O. Library [071]

SOUTH OREGON MONITOR – Medford OR. Dec 4 7 14 1894, Feb 8 12 15 19 1895 – 1 – us U.O. Library [071]

SOUTH OXFORDSHIRE CHRONICLE – 1987; Jan 8-Feb 26, Mar 1988-92; Jan 8 1993-Aug 1995 – 43r – 1 – uk British Libr Newspaper [072]

SOUTH OXFORDSHIRE COURIER – (Also known as: Courier South Oxfordshire) – 1986-96 – 22r – 1 – uk British Libr Newspaper [072]

SOUTH OXFORDSHIRE NEWS AND THAME AND WATLINGTON HERALD – England, 1 Jan 1887-19 May 1894 – 7r – 1 – uk British Libr Newspaper [072]

SOUTH PACIFIC JOURNAL OF TEACHER EDUCATION – 21v – 9 – £131.00 – 0311-2136 – uk Carfax [370]

SOUTH PACIFIC LAW REVIEW – v1 nos1-8. July 1948-June 1950 (all publ) – 1mf – $1.50 – LLMC 95-112 – us L.L.M.C. [073]

SOUTH PACIFIC MAIL – Valparaiso. Chile. -w and d. Jan 1914-Dec 1939. (60 reels) – 1 – uk British Libr Newspaper [072]

SOUTH PACIFIC MAIL – Valparaiso. Weekly. Jan 24 1918-Dec 28 1923 – 1 – us NY Public [072]

SOUTH PASADENA JOURNAL – Los Angeles. Calif. 1963-1964 – 1 – us UMI [071]

SOUTH PASADENA REVIEW – Pasadena, CA. 1956 – 38+ r – 1 – $1,900.00 ($50.00y) – H04057 – us Library Micro [071]

SOUTH PENINSULA JEWISH PRESS – Palo Alto, CA. 1981 – 1 – us A.J.P.C. [071]

South, R *see* MUSICA INCANTANS, SIVE POEMA EXPRIMENS MUSICAE VIRES

SOUTH REPORTER – Holly Springs. Miss. 1919-1966 – 1 – us UMI [071]

SOUTH SACRAMENTO NEWS – Sacramento, CA. 1983-1984 – 2r – 1 – $100.00 – B05058 – us Library Micro [071]

SOUTH SALEMITE – Salem, OR. -w. 4 Mar 1965-28 Apr 1966. 1 roll – 1 – us U.O. Library [071]

SOUTH SAN JOSE SUN – San Jose, CA. 1973-76 – 11r – 1 – $550.00 – B02890 – us Library Micro [071]

The South Sea Company *see* PAPERS

SOUTH SHIELDS EVANGELIST – England. -m. July 1874-Dec 1877. 1 2 reel – 1 – uk British Libr Newspaper [072]

THE SOUTH SHORE ADVERTISER AND WEEKLY REVIEW – St-Lambert, Canada. 14 avr 1915; v1 n4. 5 mai 1915 – 1r – 1 – Can$25.00 – cn Can Microfilming [072]

SOUTH SHORE AND BLACKPOOL GUARDIAN – England.30 Jan-2 Jul 1929; 12 Feb-2 Jul 1935; 2 Jan-10 Dec 1940; various dates between Jan 1941 and 1956. -w. 2 reels – 1 – uk British Libr Newspaper [072]

THE SOUTH SHORE ECHO DE LA RIVE SUD – St-Lambert, Canada. v30 n22. 3 jun 1954; v30 n25. 23 jun 1954; v38. 17 oct 1962 – 1r – 1 – Can$25.00 – cn Can Microfilming [072]

SOUTH SHORE GLEANER – Huntingdon, Canada. 16 aut 1919-7 jul 1923 – 1r – 1 – Can$45.00 – cn Can Microfilming [072]

SOUTH SHORE METRO EXPANSION RIVE SUD – St-Lambert, Canada. v39 n22. 2 jun 1976-v39 n28. 14 jul 1976 – 1r – 1 – Can$25.00 – cn Can Microfilming [072]
SOUTH SHORE NEWS – Ville Jacques-Cartier (Longueuil), Canada. v1 n7. 12 jul 1960 – 1r – 1 – Can$25.00 – cn Can Microfilming [072]
THE SOUTH SHORE NEWS – St-Lambert, Canada. 4 oct 1917-8 aut 1918 – 1r – 1 – Can$40.00 – cn Can Microfilming [072]
THE SOUTH SHORE PRESS – St-Lambert, Canada. v2 n91. 7 fev 1913-v6 n312. 30 mar 1917; ns: v1 n1. 29 aut 1929-v1 n28. 6 mar 1930 – 2r – 1 – Can$60.00r – cn Can Microfilming [072]
SOUTH SIDE BAPTIST CHURCH. PINE BLUFF, ARKANSAS : CHURCH RECORDS – 1936-70 – 1 – 162.81 – us Baptist [240]
SOUTH SIDE SENTINEL – Danbury, NE. -w. Sep. 1922-Oct. 1934 – 1 – us NE Hist [071]
South Sioux City. Dakota County, Nebraska *see* SOUTH SIOUX CITY NEWS
SOUTH SIOUX CITY MAIL – South Sioux City, NE. -w. Jun 1926-Dec 1927; Feb 1928-Oct 1937; Apr 1938-Feb 1951 – 1 – us NE Hist [071]
SOUTH SIOUX CITY NEWS / South Sioux City. Dakota County, Nebraska – Apr 1, 1887-Dec 28, 1888 – 1 – us NE Hist [071]
SOUTH SIOUX CITY PRESS – South Sioux City, NE. -w. Jul 1892; Dec 1892; Oct 1895-Feb 1896; May 1896-Dec 1897 – 1 – us NE Hist [071]
SOUTH SIOUX CITY STAR – South Sioux City, NE. -w. Jan 1918-Jun 1949; Jan 1950 to date – 1 – us NE Hist [071]
SOUTH SISKIYOU NEWS – Weed, CA. 1975-1976 – 3r – 1 – $150.00 – B03691 – us Library Micro [071]
SOUTH SLAV HERALD – Belgrade, Yugoslavia. -m. 23 Feb 1932-June 1940. Imperfect. 1 reel – 1 – uk British Libr Newspaper [949]
South Staffordshire Archaeological and Historical Society *see* TRANSACTIONS
SOUTH STAFFORDSHIRE EXAMINER – Wednesbury, England. 2 May-21 Nov 1874 – 36ft – 1 – uk British Libr Newspaper [072]
SOUTH STAR – Park Forest. Ill. 1972- – 1 – us UMI [071]
SOUTH TEXAS LAW JOURNAL *see* SOUTH TEXAS LAW REVIEW
SOUTH TEXAS LAW REVIEW – (v1-25 1954-84 on reel $255.00. v26-36 1985-95 on mf $281.00v. Title varies: v1-26 1954-85 as South Texas Law Journal) – v1-36. 1954-95 – 5,6,9 – $536.00 – us Hein [340]
SOUTH TILLAMOOK COUNTY NEWS – Cloverdale, OR. -bw. 27 Jun 1940-29 Jan 1942. 1 roll – 1 – us U.O. Library [071]
SOUTH TRINITY NUGGET – Hayfork, CA. 1984 – 1r – 1 – $50.00 – B03238 – us Library Micro [071]
SOUTH UMPQUA NEWS – Riddle, OR. -w. 23 Dec 1927-30 Jul 1942. 1 roll – 1 – us U.O. Library [071]
SOUTH UNION BAPTIST CHURCH. MAYWOOD, MISSOURI : CHURCH RECORDS – 1929, May, 1978 – 1 – 22.77 – us Baptist [240]
SOUTH VIETNAM IN STRUGGLE – NOS. 24-178. 20 Dec 1968-18 Dec 1972 – 1 – 25.00 – us L of C Photodup [950]
SOUTH WALES, 1822 : BRITISH ISLES CENSUS DIRECTORIES PROJECT, WALES – (In prep) – at Vine [941]
SOUTH WALES, 1830 : BRITISH ISLES CENSUS DIRECTORIES PROJECT, WALES. VOL 5 – 1mf – 9 – A$9.00 – at Vine [941]
SOUTH WALES, 1835 : BRITISH ISLES CENSUS DIRECTORIES PROJECT, WALES – at Vine [941]
SOUTH WALES, 1844 : BRITISH ISLES CENSUS DIRECTORIES PROJECT, WALES – (In prep) – at Vine [941]
SOUTH WALES, 1852 : BRITISH ISLES CENSUS DIRECTORIES PROJECT, WALES – at Vine [941]
SOUTH WALES, 1858 : BRITISH ISLES CENSUS DIRECTORIES PROJECT, WALES. VOL 2 – 2mf – 9 – A$15.00 – at Vine [941]
SOUTH WALES, 1880 : BRITISH ISLES CENSUS DIRECTORIES PROJECT, WALES. VOL 4 – 4mf – 9 – A$27.00 – at Vine [941]
SOUTH WALES, 1891 : BRITISH ISLES CENSUS DIRECTORIES PROJECT, WALES – at Vine [941]
SOUTH WALES CRITIC – Swansea, Wales. 22 May-5 Jun 1869 – 4ft – 1 – uk British Libr Newspaper [072]
SOUTH WALES ECHO – Cardiff, Wales. 1894; Jan-Jun 1896; 1897; 1912; 1950; 1983; 1986- – 251+ r – 1 – uk British Libr Newspaper [072]
SOUTH WALES OBSERVER – Pontardulais, Wales, UK. 6 Jul 1889-5 Feb 1892; 14 Oct-2 Dec 1892 – 2r – 1 – uk British Libr Newspaper [072]
SOUTH WALES REPORTER ETC – Merthyr Tydfil, Wales, UK. Mar-May 1837 – 1/2r – 1 – uk British Libr Newspaper [072]
SOUTH WALES TIMES AND STAR OF GWENT *see* MONMOUTH, GLAMORGAN AND BRECON HERALD
SOUTH WEST AREA COMBINED HEADQUARTERS LOG BOOK, CHRONOLOGICAL ORDER, 1941-1942 / South West Area Combined Headquarters, Western Australia – 8mf – 9 – CRS K809 – at Archives [920]
South West Area Combined Headquarters, Western Australia *see* SOUTH WEST AREA COMBINED HEADQUARTERS LOG BOOK, CHRONOLOGICAL ORDER, 1941-1942
SOUTH WEST SUFFOLK ECHO *see* THE ECHO
SOUTH WEST TIMES – Swakopmund, South West Africa. 1928-33 – 1 – sa State Libr [072]
THE SOUTH WESTERN ECHO – Riversdale, South Africa. 20 Aug 1892-25 Dec 1926. 16 reels – 1, 16 diazo available at reduced price – sa SA Libr [072]
SOUTH WESTERN HERALD – George, South Africa. 2 Jun 1971-23 Dec 1975. 10 reels – 1, 16 diazo available at reduced price – sa SA Libr [072]
SOUTH WESTERN HERALD *see* GEORGE AND KNYSNA HERALD
SOUTH WESTERN JEWISH CHRONICLE – Oklahoma City. Okl. 1956-64 – 1 – us A.J.P.C. [071]
THE SOUTH WESTERN PSALMIST / Dyer, Sidney – 1852 – 1 – 13.58 – us Baptist [240]
SOUTH WESTERN STAR – (Battersea and Clapham Star South West Star). London. -w. 1889-1972. (63 reels) – 1 – uk British Libr Newspaper [072]
South Yemen *see* REPORT TO THE GOVERNMENT OF SOUTHERN YEMEN ON THE INTRODUCTION OF HIDE, SKINS AND LEATHER IMPROVEMENT SERVICES AND THE REOPENING OF AN EXISTING TANNERY
South Yemen. Centre d'Etudes et de Documentation Economiques, Financieres et Sociales. Damascus *see* SOUTHERN YEMEN; ESTABLISHMENT OF A SOCIALIST REGIME IN A DECOLONIZED ECONOMY
South Yemen. Ministry of Finance *see* GENERAL BUDGET FOR THE FIFTH GOVERNORATE
South Yemen. Southern Yemen Ministry of Finance *see* GENERAL BUDGET 1968-1970
SOUTHAMPTON 1758-1890 – (Mf 1: Births & Deaths 1750-1800. Mf 2: Births 1750-1800. Mf 3: Births 1783-1856. Mf 4: Marriages 1790-1856; Out-of-Town Marriages 1761-99. Mf 5-6: Marriage Intentions 1758-1802. Mf 7-8: Marriage Intentions 1848-66. Mf 8: Deaths 1756-1857. Mf 9-10: Church Records 1743-1832. Mf 11-12: Church Records 1832-74. Mf 13: Births 1857-81. Mf 14: Births 1882-90; Marriages 1857-70. Mf 15: Marriages 1871-90; Deaths 1857-63. Mf 16: Deaths 1863-83. Mf 17: Deaths 1884-90) – (mf ed 1987) – 17mf – 9 – 0-87623-030-3 – us Holbrook [920]
SOUTHAMPTON AMUSEMENTS – England.21 Oct 1895-6 Apr 1912. -w. 13 1/2 reels – 1 – uk British Libr Newspaper [072]
SOUTHAMPTON AND DISTRICT PICTORIAL – England. -w. 10 April 1912-29 March 1916. 4 reels – 1 – uk British Libr Newspaper [072]
SOUTHAMPTON COUNTY CHRONICLE ETC – England.4 Apr 1822-4 Sept 1824. -w. 1 reel – 1 – uk British Libr Newspaper [072]
SOUTHAMPTON OBSERVER AND HAMPSHIRE NEWS *see* SOUTHAMPTON OBSERVER AND WINCHESTER NEWS
SOUTHAMPTON OBSERVER AND WINCHESTER NEWS – England, 1869-1900 (slightly imperfect) – 32r – 1 – uk British Libr Newspaper [072]
SOUTHAMPTON RECORD SOCIETY – (Coll title: Publications of the English Record Societies, 1835-1972...) – v1-20. 1905-41 – 86mf – 9 – £630.00 – uk Chadwyck [941]
SOUTHAMPTON RECORD SOCIETY RECORD SERIES – (Coll title: Publications of the English Record Societies, 1835-1972...) – v1-8. 1951-65 – 28mf – 9 – £235.00 – uk Chadwyck [941]
SOUTHBRIDGE 1816-1889 – 52mf – 9 – us Holbrook [920]
SOUTHEAST ASIA CATALOG / Cornell University. Libraries – 1976. 111,000 cards. 13 reels. ISBN 0-8161-1329-7 – 1 – $680.00 – uk Hall [950]
SOUTHEAST ASIA RESOURCE CENTER *see* ASIA RESOURCE CENTER
SOUTHEAST ASIA SUBJECT CATALOG / Library of Congress. Orientalia Division – 1972. 82,500 cards on 9 reels – 1 – $595.00 export $720.00 – 0-8161-1234-7 – uk Hall [950]
SOUTHEAST ASIA SUBJECT CATALOG / U.S. Library of Congress. Orientalia Division – 1972. 82,500 cards. 9 reels. ISBN 0-8161-1234-7 – 1 – $655.00 – uk Hall [950]
SOUTH-EAST ASIAN ART AND ARCHAEOLOGY – 99 titles – 9 – ne IDC [700]
SOUTHEAST ECONOMIST – Chicago. Ill. -w. 1951-53, 1955-63, 1969- – 1 – us UMI [330]
SOUTHEAST INDEX – Portland OR. Aug 25 1933 – 1 – us U.O. Library [071]
SOUTHEAST LINCOLN SUN – Lincoln, NE. -w. Nov 1961 to date – 1 – us NE Hist [071]
SOUTHEAST MISSOURIAN – Cape Girardeau. Mo. 1918- – 1 – us UMI [071]
SOUTHEAST PEDIATRICS – v1-. 1985- – 1,5,6,9 – us UMI [618]
SOUTHEAST SOUTH DAKOTA EXPERIMENT FARM PROGRESS REPORT / South Dakota. State University. Agricultural Experiment Station – nos.1-14. 1963-74 – 1,5,6 – us Spaulding [630]
SOUTHEASTERN LIBRARIAN – v1- 1951- 1; v26- 5,6,9 – us UMI [020]
SOUTHEASTERN REPORTER – (Add vols planned) – 1st series: v1-99. 1887-1919 – 1226mf – 9 – $1,839.00 – LLMC 79-404G – us L.L.M.C. [340]
SOUTHEASTERN SYMPOSIUM ON MISSILES AND AEROSPACE VEHICLE SCIENCES – 1969 – 30mf – 9 – $40.00 – 0-87703-229-7 – us Univelt [623]
SOUTHERN ACCENTS – (1985-. 5,6,9) – v1-. 1977- – 1 – us UMI [073]
SOUTHERN ADVOCATE – Ashland, Miss. 1915-21 – 1 – us UMI [071]
SOUTHERN ADVOCATE – Tampa. Fla. 1927-28 – 1 – us A.J.P.C. [071]
SOUTHERN AFRICA – 21 docs. 1980-83 – 8mf – 9 – HRD-1312/1 – ne IDC [960]
SOUTHERN AFRICAN BOOKS IN PRINT – 1995 – 9 – R480.00 – sa Books in Print [020]
SOUTHERN AFRICAN RESEARCH SERVICE (SARS) – Yeoville. 56 docs. 1980-1989 – 65mf – 9 – ne IDC [960]
SOUTHERN AGRICULTURIST *see* FARM AND RANCH
Southern Aid Society *see* CONSTITUTION AND ADDRESS TO THE CHRISTIAN PUBLIC
SOUTHERN AREA (SPANISH) : BELLFLOWER, DOWNEY, NORWALK, PARAMOUNT, ETC. – 1992- – 2+ r – 1 – $100.00 – P00132 – us Library Micro [910]
SOUTHERN AUSTRALIAN – (1838-41 imperfect) – Adelaide, Australia. June 1838-Dec 1841; 3,17,31 Jan, 4 Apr 1845; 4 Sep, 9 Oct, 29 Dec 1846; 13,23 April 1847; 3 Aug 1849 – 1r – 1 – uk British Libr Newspaper [072]
SOUTHERN BAPTIST – South Carolina. 1847-60 – 1 – 99.12 – us Baptist [240]
SOUTHERN BAPTIST ADVOCATE – Dallas, TX. v1-10. 1980-1991 – 1r – 1 – $48.08 – us Baptist [240]
SOUTHERN BAPTIST ALMANAC AND ANNUAL REGISTER / Graves, J R – 1850 – 1 – 5.00 – us Baptist [240]
SOUTHERN BAPTIST AND GENERAL INTELLIGENCER – South Carolina. 1835-36 – 1 – 36.68 – us Baptist [240]
Southern Baptist Association of Executives of Baptist Children's Homes *see* MINUTES
SOUTHERN BAPTIST CLIP SHEET – 1920-29; News Notes of General Activities of Southern Baptists for Ready Use – 1 – 5.00 – us Baptist [240]
Southern Baptist College. Walnut Ridge, Ark *see* CATALOGS AND COLLEGE RECORDS
Southern Baptist Convention *see*
- '70 ONWARD PREPARATION MATERIALS
- 75 MILLION CAMPAIGN
- ANNUALS
- BIOGRAPHICAL DATA FOR ELECTED OFFICERS AND MEMBERS OF BOARDS, COMMISSIONS, AND STANDING COMMITTEES
- INDEX TO ANNUALS OF SOUTHERN BAPTIST CONVENTION
- MANUSCRIPT PROCEEDINGS
- NEWSPAPER COVERAGE OF SESSIONS
- PERIODICAL INDEX
- PROCEEDINGS
- REGISTRATION CARDS
- REGISTRATION CARDS, 1961-68
- RESEARCH REPORTS ON HISTORY OF SBC AGENCIES
- STEWARDSHIP COMMISSION, FORWARD PROGRAM OF CHURCH FINANCE, 1956-60
- STEWARDSHIP COMMISSION, MATERIALS FROM MID-SOUTH AND FAR WEST CLINICS, 1956

THE SOUTHERN BAPTIST CONVENTION, 1845-1953 / Barnes, William W – Ms. 444p – 1 – 15.54 – us Baptist [240]
Southern Baptist Convention. Advisory Council on Work with Negroes *see* MINUTES, REPORTS, AND CORRESPONDENCE
Southern Baptist Convention. Annual Convention *see* SERMONS FROM PERSONAL FILES OF DR. PORTER ROUTH, EXECUTIVE SECRETARY-TREASURER OF THE SBC, 1951-79
Southern Baptist Convention. Education Commission *see* PUBLICATIONS
Southern Baptist Convention. Executive Committee *see*
- REPORTS: SURVEY OF THEOL. EDUCATION
- SOUTHERN BAPTIST PROGRAM OF STUDENT WORK: A STUDY

Southern Baptist Convention. Hospitals *see* SCRAPBOOK
Southern Baptist Foreign Mission Board *see* PERIODICALS
SOUTHERN BAPTIST HANDBOOK – Nashville. Tenn. 1921-54 – 1 – 413.63 – us Baptist [240]
SOUTHERN BAPTIST JOURNAL – Decatur, GA, Buchanan, GA, + Austin, TX. 1973-1989. v1-17, incomplete – 1r – 1 – $55.20 – us Baptist [240]
SOUTHERN BAPTIST JOURNAL *see* PERIODICALS
SOUTHERN BAPTIST MESSENGER – Georgia. Aug 1852-Mar 1862 – 1 – 23.38 – us Baptist [240]
SOUTHERN BAPTIST PERIODICAL INDEX – Author and Subj. index to 47 periodicals published by Southern Baptist Convention. Approx. 10,000 entries, 300p. Annual public. 1974- – 1 – us Baptist [240]
SOUTHERN BAPTIST PREACHER – Washington, GA., 1839-1841. Nos 1-12 – 1r – 1 – $6.96 – us Baptist [240]
SOUTHERN BAPTIST PROGRAM OF STUDENT WORK: A STUDY / Southern Baptist Convention. Executive Committee – 1968-69 – 1 – 42.21 – us Baptist [240]
SOUTHERN BAPTIST RECORD – 1878-96 (complete) – 5r – 1 – ATLA R0112 – us A.T.L.A. [073]
SOUTHERN BAPTIST REVIEW AND ECLECTIC MONTHLY – v. 1-7. 1855-61 – 1 – 139.93 – us Baptist [240]
Southern Baptist Seminary *see*
- SEMINARY MAGAZINE
- SEMINARY NEWS

SOUTHERN BAPTIST STATE CONVENTION ANNUALS – (Mexican Baptist Association: 1910, 1938, 1943-47. Negro Baptists: 1940-41. German Baptists: 1902-06, 1908-10) – Texas. 714p – 1 – 24.99 – us Baptist [240]
Southern Baptist Theological Seminary *see* CATALOGS AND COLLEGE RECORDS
SOUTHERN BAPTIST THEOLOGICAL SEMINARY, 1859-89 / Sampey, John R – 220p – 1 – 7.70 – us Baptist [240]
Southern Baptist Theological Seminary. Library *see*
- CARD CATALOGUE FILE
- CARD FILE OF BAPTIST MATERIALS

THE SOUTHERN BENCH AND BAR REVIEW – 1v. 1913 (all publ) – 9 – LLMC 82-959 – us L.L.M.C. [073]
SOUTHERN BULLETIN – Ireland.6 Jan-24 Feb 1923 – 1 – ie Microforms [072]
SOUTHERN CALIFORNIA BUSINESS – Los Angeles, CA. 1939-1982 – 6r – 1 – $300.00 – R03317 – us Library Micro [071]

SOUTHERN CALIFORNIA INDUSTRIAL NEWS – Los Angeles, CA. 1960-1982 – 15r – 1 – $750.00 – R03318 – us Library Micro [071]
SOUTHERN CALIFORNIA INTERDISCIPLINARY LAW JOURNAL – v1-3. 1992-94 – 9 – $40.00 set – us Hein [340]
SOUTHERN CALIFORNIA LAW REVIEW – (v1-58 1927-85 on reel or mf $813.00. v59-68 1986-95 on mf $319.00) – v1-68. 1927-95 – 5,6,9 – $1,132.00 set – us Hein [340]
SOUTHERN CALIFORNIA REVIEW OF LAW AND WOMEN'S STUDIES – v1-4. 1992-95 – 9 – $68.00 set – us Hein [340]
SOUTHERN CALIFORNIA TEAMSTERS – Los Angeles, CA. 1943-1985 – 19r – 1 – $950.00 – R03319 – us Library Micro [071]
SOUTHERN CHANGES – v.4-. 1981- – 1,5,6,9 – us UMI [073]
SOUTHERN CHURCHMAN – Richmond. Va. 1861-65 – 1 – us UMI [071]
SOUTHERN CHURCHMAN *see* PROPHETIC RELIGION / SOUTHERN CHURCHMAN
SOUTHERN CHURCHMAN / PROPHETIC RELIGION – 1937-55 (complete) – 1r – 1 – ATLA S0616 – us A.T.L.A. [073]
SOUTHERN COLLEGE PERSONNEL ASSOCIATION JOURNAL – (v.3-. 1980-81. 5,6,9) – v1- 1978-81 – 1 – us UMI [073]
SOUTHERN CONFEDERACY – Atlanta. Ga. -w. misc. issues to 1865. 1861-63 – 1 – us UMI [071]
SOUTHERN CONNECTICUT BUSINESS JOURNAL *see* FAIRFIELD COUNTY BUSINESS JOURNAL
SOUTHERN COOPERATIVE SERIES: BULLETIN / University of Georgia. Agricultural Experiment Station – No.148-283. 1970-82. 104 fiches – 9 – us Spaulding [630]
SOUTHERN COOS COUNTY AMERICAN – Myrtle Point, OR. -w. 1917-28 – 1 – 96.00 – us Oregon Hist [071]
SOUTHERN COOS COUNTY AMERICAN – Myrtle Point. Or. -w. 1917-38 – 1 – us UMI [071]
SOUTHERN CROSS – June, Apr 12 1884-Oct 25 1884 – 1 – at Pascoe [072]
SOUTHERN CROSS – Sydney, 1859-61 – 1r – 1 – A$35.00 silver A$30.00 vesicular – at Pascoe [072]
SOUTHERN DAILY ECHO – Southampton, England. 1889; Apr-Dec 1896; 1897-99; 1909-10; 1912-34; May-Sep 1940; 1949-72; 1976- – 455+ r – 1 – uk British Libr Newspaper [072]
SOUTHERN DAILY MAIL – Portsmouth, England. 1897-98 – 6r – 1 – uk British Libr Newspaper [072]
SOUTHERN DISTRICT DEVLOPMENT PLAN 1989-1995 / Botswana. Southern District – Gaborone, 1990 – 4mf – 9 – ne IDC [338]
SOUTHERN ECONOMIC JOURNAL – (v.37-1970- 5,6. v.42- 1975- 9) – v.1- 1933- – 1 – us UMI [330]
SOUTHERN ENTERPRISE – High Point. N.C. 1960-1962 – 1 – us UMI [071]
SOUTHERN ENTERPRISE – Thomasville. Ga. 1867-1876 – 1 – us UMI [071]
SOUTHERN EVENING ECHO *see* SOUTHERN DAILY ECHO
SOUTHERN FARM AND RANCH – 1984-85 – 1,5,6,9 – us UMI [630]
SOUTHERN FARM LEADER *see* SHARECROPPER'S VOICE, 1935-1937 : SOUTHERN FARM LEADER, 1936 : STFU NEWS, 1938-1939 : TENANT FARMER, 1941-1942 : FARM WORKER, 1943-1944 : FARM LABOR NEWS, 1946-1951 : THE UNION FARMER, 1952-1953 : AGRICULTURAL UNIONIST, 1952-1954
SOUTHERN FOLKLORE QUARTERLY – v1-1937- 1; v35- 5,6; v40- 9 – us UMI [390]
SOUTHERN FRONTIER / Commission on Interracial Cooperation – 1-6 (all publ). 1940-1945 – 4mf – 9 – $55.00 – us UPA [305]
THE SOUTHERN GENEALOGIST'S EXCHANGE QUARTERLY – (v1, 1957, Nos.1-4. Indexed. 5 fiches. F-0635. v3, 1961. Cumulative index, 1957-61. 3 fiches. F-0636. v3, 1962, Division 2, Issue nos.21-24. Indexed. 4 fiches. F-1831. v3, Part 1, 1961, Issue nos.17-20. Indexed, 1957-61. 3 fiches. F-1830) – 9 – us A.G.L.L. [920]
THE SOUTHERN HARMONY AND MUSICAL COMPANION / Walker, William – 1847 – 1 – 11.23 – us Baptist [240]
SOUTHERN HERALD – Liberty. Miss. 1943-1948 – 1 – us UMI [071]
SOUTHERN HEROES, OR, THE FRIENDS IN WAR TIME / Cartland, Fernando G – Cambridge: Riverside Press, 1895 – 2mf – us A.T.L.A. [240]
SOUTHERN HIGH. NEWS – Bowral – at Pascoe [980]
Southern Historical Society *see* – PAPERS
Southern Home Mission Board *see* PERIODICALS
SOUTHERN HOSPITALS – Years: 1933-1971 – 1,5,6 – us Princeton Micro [610]
SOUTHERN HUMANITIES REVIEW – v1- 1967- 1; v11- 5,6,9 – us UMI [000]
SOUTHERN HUMBOLT LIFE AND TIMES – Garberville, CA. 1987-1991 – 3r – 1 – $150.00 – B05037 – us Library Micro [071]
SOUTHERN ILLINOIS JEWISH COMMUNITY NEWS – East St. Louis, IL. 1972-84 – 1 – us A.J.P.C. [071]
SOUTHERN ILLINOIS UNIVERSITY LAW JOURNAL – 1976- 1; 1978- 5,6,9 – us UMI [340]
SOUTHERN ILLINOISAN – Carbondale. Ill. 1899- – 1 – us UMI [071]
SOUTHERN INDIAN STUDIES – 1949-73.(American Indian Periodicals in the Princeton University Library). 14 fiches – 9 – $70.00 – us UPA [073]
SOUTHERN INDUSTRY – Ireland.Apr-Dec 1889. -w. 1 reel – 1 – uk British Libr Newspaper [072]
SOUTHERN INTELLIGENCER – Chester. S.C. 1822-1922 – 1 – us UMI [071]
SOUTHERN INTELLIGENCER – South Carolina. 1822-23 – 1 – 8.96 – us Baptist [240]
THE SOUTHERN ISRAELITE – Atlanta. Ga. 1959-67 – 1 – us A.J.P.C. [071]
SOUTHERN JEWISH WEEKLY – Jacksonville. Fl. 1939-to date – 1 – us P.K. Yonge [073]
THE SOUTHERN JEWISH WEEKLY – Jacksonville. Fla. 1965-66 – 1 – us A.J.P.C. [071]
SOUTHERN JOURNAL OF APPLIED FORESTRY – (v.3-. 1979- 5,6,9) – v.1-. 1977- – 1 – us UMI [073]
SOUTHERN JOURNAL OF CRIMINAL JUSTICE – (1982-. 1,5,6,9) – v1-. 1975- – 1 – us UMI [073]
SOUTHERN JOURNAL OF CRIMINAL JUSTICE *see* AMERICAN JOURNAL OF CRIMINAL JUSTICE
SOUTHERN JOURNAL OF MUSIC – Louisville. v1 n1-14. 1867-68 – 1r – 1 – £60.00 – uk Chadwyck [780]
THE SOUTHERN LAW JOURNAL – (Cont by: The Southern Law Journal and Reporter) – Tusculoosa. v1-2. 1878-79 (all publ) – 14mf – 9 – $21.00 – LLMC 82-960 – us L.L.M.C. [073]
THE SOUTHERN LAW JOURNAL *see* THE SOUTHERN LAW JOURNAL AND REPORTER
THE SOUTHERN LAW JOURNAL AND REPORTER – (Cont: The Southern Law Journal) – ns: v1-2. 1879-81 (all publ) – 6mf – 9 – $27.00 – LLMC 82-961 – us L.L.M.C. [073]
THE SOUTHERN LAW JOURNAL AND REPORTER *see* THE SOUTHERN LAW JOURNAL
SOUTHERN LAW QUARTERLY *see* TULANE LAW REVIEW
THE SOUTHERN LAW REVIEW – Atlanta. 1v. 1901-02 (all publ) – 10mf – 9 – $15.00 – LLMC 82-963 – us L.L.M.C. [073]
THE SOUTHERN LAW REVIEW – Nashville. v1-3. ns v1-8, 1872-83 (all publ) – 42mf – 9 – $189.00 – LLMC 82-962 – us L.L.M.C. [073]
THE SOUTHERN LAW TIMES – (Lacking: v2) – v1-2. 1885-86 (all publ) – 9mf – 9 – $13.50 – LLMC 82-964 – us L.L.M.C. [073]
THE SOUTHERN LIBERTARIAN MESSENGER – 1974-79. Continued as: The Libertarian Messenger. Incomplete. 6 fiches (24x) – 9 – 1.00f – at Libertarian Micro [320]
SOUTHERN LITERARY JOURNAL – v1- 1968- 1; v4- 5,6; v10- 9 – us UMI [800]
SOUTHERN LITERARY MESSENGER – Journal of the Old South. 38v. 1834-64 – 9 – us Primary [073]
SOUTHERN LITERARY MESSENGER; DEVOTED TO EVERY DEPARTMENT OF LITERATURE, AND THE FINE ARTS – 1-38. August 1834-June 1864 – 1 – us UMI [073]
SOUTHERN LIVESTOCK JOURNAL – Starkville. Miss. 1880-1891 – 1 – us UMI [071]
SOUTHERN LIVING CLASSICS – v1-. 1985- – 1,5,6,9 – us UMI [073]
SOUTHERN MEDICAL JOURNAL – v1- 1908- 1; v68- 5,6,9 – us UMI [610]
SOUTHERN METHODISM IN KOREA.. / ed by Ryang, J S – 1929? – 1 – us A.T.L.A. [240]
SOUTHERN METHODIST ITINERANT – Parkersburg. West Virginia. 1856-60 – 1 – us UMI [071]
THE SOUTHERN MISSOURI ADVOCATE – Jackson, Missouri. Jan 20-Dec 29 1838 – 1r – 1 – us L of C Photodup [071]
SOUTHERN MOROCCO MISSION – Jul 1914-Dec 1959 (complete) – 1r – 1 – ATLA S0659 – us A.T.L.A. [073]
SOUTHERN MUSICAL ADVOCATE – Virginia, 1859-69 – 1 – £115.00 – uk Chadwyck [780]
SOUTHERN NEBRASKA REGISTER – Lincoln, NE. -w. Aug 1932 to date – 1 – us NE Hist [071]
SOUTHERN NEBRASKAN – Arago, NE. -w. Nov. 1860-Sep. 1872. Incomplete – 1 – us NE Hist [071]
SOUTHERN NEBRASKAN – Fairbury, NE. -w. May 1882; Dec 1882; Feb. 1883-Mar. 1883; Jun. 1883-Nov. 1883; Feb. 1885-Apr. 1885; Sep. 1885 – 1 – us NE Hist [071]
SOUTHERN NEWS ALMANAC – Birmingham. Ala. 1940-1941 – 1 – us UMI [071]
SOUTHERN NIGERIA CIVIL SERVICE LIST, WITH HANDBOOK / Nigeria – 1904, 1905, 1907 and 1913 – 1 – uk Microform Academic [960]
SOUTHERN OBSERVER – Nashville. Tenn. 1953-1965 – 1 – us UMI [071]
SOUTHERN OREGON GAZETTE – Jacksonville OR. Aug 22 1861-Mar 11 1862 – 1 – us U.O. Library [071]
SOUTHERN OREGON NEWS-REVIEW – (Set incl. Southern Oregon Miner and Jacksonville Miner) – Ashland, OR. -w. 1 Jan 1932-31 Jul 1952. – 6r – 1 – us U.O. Library [071]
SOUTHERN OREGON PRESS – Jacksonville OR. Jan 5-Aug 24 1867 – 1 – us U.O. Library [071]
SOUTHERN OREGON TRANSCRIPT – Medford OR. Mar 13 1888 – 1 – us U.O. Library [071]
SOUTHERN OREGON WEEKLY REVIEW – Grants Pass OR. Jan 12 1981-July 13 1982 – 1 – us U.O. Library [071]
SOUTHERN OREGONIAN – (Set incl. Southern Oregonian and Jacksonville Times (Medford)) – Medford, OR. -sw. 5 Aug 1902-30 Oct 1909. – 2r – 1 – us U.O. Library [071]
SOUTHERN OREGONIAN AND JACKSONVILLE TIMES – Medford OR. Aug 28 1907-Apr 14 1908 – 1 – us U.O. Library [071]
SOUTHERN PATRIOT – Mallow. Ireland. -w. 10 Feb-13 Mar 1844. (8 ft) – 1 – uk British Libr Newspaper [072]
SOUTHERN PATRIOT – v1-22. Dec 1942-1964 (complete) – 4r – 1 – ATLA S0095 – us A.T.L.A. [073]
THE SOUTHERN PATRIOT – Nashville. Tenn. 1951-1964 – 1 – us UMI [071]
THE SOUTHERN PATRIOT – New Orleans. La. 1965-1969 – 1 – us UMI [071]
THE SOUTHERN PREACHER / McIver, Colin – A collection of sermons, manuscripts of several eminent ministers of the gospel. 1824 – 1 – 14.98 – us Baptist [240]
SOUTHERN PRESBYTERIAN REVIEW – (Some pgs lacking) – v1-36. 1847-85 – 15r – 1 – ATLA S0501 – us A.T.L.A. [073]
THE SOUTHERN PSALMIST – 1871 – 1 – 26.60 – us Baptist [240]
THE SOUTHERN PSALMIST / Graves, J R & Pendleton, J M – 1859 – 1 – 25.76 – us Baptist [240]
SOUTHERN PULPIT – Richmond, VA. Jul 1882-Jun 1883. 870p – 1 – 30.45 – us Baptist [240]
SOUTHERN PUNCH – Richmond, VA. 15 Aug 1863-2 Oct 1864. 1 reel – 1 – us Western Res [071]
SOUTHERN QUAKERS AND SLAVERY : A STUDY IN INSTITUTIONAL HISTORY / Weeks, Stephen Beauregard – Baltimore: Johns Hopkins, 1896 – 1mf – us A.T.L.A. [976]
SOUTHERN QUARTERLY – v1- 1962- 1; v13- 5,6; v16- 9 – us UMI [978]
SOUTHERN REGIONAL COUNCIL PAPERS, 1944-1968 – (Price together with Association of Southern Women for the Prevention of Lynching, 1930-1942 plus Commission on Interracial Cooperation, 1919-1944 $18,985) – 225r – 1 – $14,450.00 – us UMI [977]
SOUTHERN RELIGIOUS TELEGRAPH – Richmond, VA. v3-4. 1824-26 – 1r – 1 – us Ross [071]
SOUTHERN REPORTER – 1 – £42.00r – uk Scot News [072]
SOUTHERN REPORTER – (Add vols planned) – 1st series: v1-81. 1887-1919 – 925mf – 9 – $1,387.00 – LLMC 79-404H – us L.L.M.C. [340]
SOUTHERN REPORTER – Sardis. Miss. 1902-1912; 1914-1952 – 1 – us UMI [071]
SOUTHERN REPORTER AND CORK COMMERCIAL COURIER – Cork. Ireland. -w. 1824; 1847. (2 reels) – 1 – uk British Libr Newspaper [072]
SOUTHERN REVIEW – (v7- 1971- 5,6 v12-1976- 9) – v1- 1935- – 1 – us UMI [420]
THE SOUTHERN REVIEW – 1867-79 – 1 – us UMI [073]
SOUTHERN REVIEW OF PUBLIC ADMINISTRATION – (v.4-. 1980- 5,6,9) – v.1-. 1977- – 1 – us UMI [073]
SOUTHERN RHODESIA CHURCH MAGAZINE – v2-6. 1937-69 (complete) – 1r – 1 – ATLA S0726B – us A.T.L.A. [073]
SOUTHERN SENTINEL – Ripley. Miss. 1905-1924; 1927-1952 – 1 – us UMI [071]
SOUTHERN SOCIOLOGIST – (v.11-. 1979-5,6,9) – v.1-. 1968- – 1 – us UMI [073]
SOUTHERN SPEECH COMMUNICATION JOURNAL – v1-51. 1935-85 – 12r – 1 – us Ross [410]
SOUTHERN SPEECH COMMUNICATION JOURNAL – (v.46-. 1980-. 5,6,9) – v.37-. 1971- – 1 – us UMI [400]
SOUTHERN SPEECH JOURNAL – v.1-. 1935- – 1 – us UMI [400]
SOUTHERN STAR – Hobart, Australia. Aug 1882-Aug 1883.-d. 2mqn reels – 1 – uk British Libr Newspaper [072]
SOUTHERN STAR AND LONDON AND BRIGHTON PATRIOT – London. -w. 19 Jan-12 Jul 1840. (1 reel) – 1 – uk British Libr Newspaper [072]
THE SOUTHERN STATES OF THE AMERICAN UNION : CONSIDERED IN THEIR RELATIONS TO THE CONSTITUTION OF THE UNITED STATES AND TO THE RESULTING UNION / Curry, J LM – Richmond, VA: B F Johnson Publ Co, 1895 – 3mf – 9 – $4.50 – LLMC 95-083 – us L.L.M.C. [323]
SOUTHERN TENANT FARMERS' UNION *see* HOWARD A. KESTER PAPERS, 1923-1972
Southern Tenant Farmers Union *see* SHARECROPPER'S VOICE, 1935-1937 : SOUTHERN FARM LEADER, 1936 : STFU NEWS, 1938-1939 : TENANT FARMER, 1941-1942 : FARM WORKER, 1943-1944 : FARM LABOR NEWS, 1946-1951 : THE UNION FARMER, 1952-1953 : AGRICULTURAL UNIONIST, 1952-1954
SOUTHERN TENANT FARMERS UNION PAPERS, 1934-1977 – (Base collection 1934-70 60r $4225; Supplement 1910-77 17r $1245) – 77r complete collection – 1 – $5470 complete collection – us UMI [977]
SOUTHERN UNIVERSITY LAW REVIEW – 1985-. Southern University School of Law – 1 – us UMI [073]
SOUTHERN WATCHMAN AND GENERAL INTELLIGENCER – South Carolina. 1837-38 – 1 – 8.82 – us Baptist [240]
SOUTHERN WOMEN AND THEIR FAMILIES IN THE 19TH CENTURY: PAPERS AND DIARIES : SERIES A: HOLDINGS OF THE SOUTHERN HISTORICAL COLLECTION.... / ed by Scott, Anne Firor & Chafe, William H – (All with printed guides. Pt 1: Mary Susan Ker Papers 1785-1923 25r $3,480 ISBN: 1-55655-294-7. Pt 2: Roach and Eggleston Family Papers 1830-1905 18r $2,515 ISBN 1-55655-295-5. Pt 3: Louisiana and Mississippi Collections 6r $840 ISBN 1-55655-296-3. Pt 4: The Nicholas Philip Trist Papers 17r $2,380 ISBN 1-55655-417-6. Pt 5: Alabama, South Carolina, Georgia, and Florida Collections 24r $3,345 ISBN 1-55655-418-4. Pt 6: Virginia 30r $4,180 ISBN 1-55655-419-2. Pt 7: Phillips and Spencer Family Collections 29r $4,000 ISBN 1-55655-462-1. Pt 8: North Carolina 36r $4,965 ISBN 1-55655-463-X) – University of North Carolina, Chapel Hill – 8pts – 1 – us UPA [305]
SOUTHERN WOMEN AND THEIR FAMILIES IN THE 19TH CENTURY: PAPERS AND DIARIES : SERIES B: HOLDINGS OF THE COLONIAL WILLIAMSBURG FOUNDATION LIBRARY: THE CARTER FAMILY PAPERS, 1888-1989 / ed by Scott, Anne Firor – (With printed guide) – 26r – 1 – $3,590.00 – 1-55655-485-0 – us UPA [305]

SOUTHERN WOMEN AND THEIR FAMILIES IN THE 19TH CENTURY: PAPERS AND DIARIES : SERIES C: HOLDINGS OF THE EARL GREGG SWEM LIBRARY, THE COLLEGE OF WILLIAM AND MARY IN VIRGINIA: MISCELLANEOUS COLLECTIONS, 1773-1938 / ed by Scott, Anne Firor – (With printed guide) – 22r – 1 – $3,035.00 – 1-55655-499-0 – us UPA [305]

SOUTHERN WOMEN AND THEIR FAMILIES IN THE 19TH CENTURY: PAPERS AND DIARIES : SERIES D: HOLDINGS OF THE VIRGINIA HISTORICAL SOCIETY / ed by Scott, Anne Firor & Chafe, William H – (Pt 1: Tidewater Virginia 21r $2,895 ISBN 1-55655-531-8. Pt 2: Richmond, Virginia 30r $4,140 ISBN 1-55655-532-6. Pt 3: Piedmont Virginia 54r $7,445 ISBN 1-55655-595-4. Pt 4: District of Columbia, Florida, Georgia, Kentucky, Louisiana, Maryland, Mississippi, Missouri and Tennessee 16r $2,205 ISBN 1-55655-596-2) – 4pts – 1 – us UPA [305]

SOUTHERN WOMEN AND THEIR FAMILIES IN THE 19TH CENTURY: PAPERS AND DIARIES : SERIES E: HOLDINGS OF THE LOUISIANA STATE UNIVERSITY / ed by Scott, Anne Firor – (All pts include printed guide) – 34r – 1 – $4,690.00 – 1-55655-653-5 – us UPA [305]

SOUTHERN WOMEN IN THE RECENT EDUCATIONAL MOVEMENT IN THE SOUTH / Mayo, A D – 1892 – 1 – $50.00 – us Presbyterian [370]

SOUTHERN WORKMAN / Hampton Normal and Agricultural Institute – Hampton, VA. v1-68. 1872-1939 – 17r – 1 – us Ross [331]

SOUTHERN WORKMAN – v. 1-68, no. 7. Jan 1872-Jul 1939 – 1 – 302.00 – us L of C Photodup [073]

SOUTHERN YEMEN; ESTABLISHMENT OF A SOCIALIST REGIME IN A DECOLONIZED ECONOMY / South Yemen. Centre d'Etudes et de Documentation Economiques, Financieres et Sociales. Damascus – 1970. BNE-9612 1 – 9 – ne IDC [335]

Southey, Caroline Bowles *see* THE POETICAL WORKS OF CAROLINE BOWLES SOUTHEY

Southey, Robert *see*
- THE CURSE OF KEHAMA
- THE DOCTOR
- ENGLISH SEAMEN
- JOAN OF ARC
- MADOC
- POEMS AND LETTERS TO WALTER SAVAGE LANDOR
- THE POETICAL WORKS OF ROBERT SOUTHEY
- RODERICK, THE LAST OF THE GOTHS
- A VISION OF JUDGEMENT

Southey, Thomas *see* CHRONOLOGICAL HISTORY OF THE WEST INDIES

Southgate, Horatio *see* NARRATIVE OF A VISIT TO THE SYRIAN (JACOBITE) CHURCH OF MESOPOTAMIA

SOUTHGATE SENTINEL – Lincoln Park. Mich. 1964- – 1 – us UMI [071]

SOUTHGATE SENTINEL – Wyandotte. Mich. -w. 1957-65 – 1 – us UMI [071]

SOUTH-INDIAN INSCRIPTIONS, TAMIL AND SANSKRIT,... : ARCHAEOLOGICAL SURVEY OF INDIA – (Missing: v18 1964/1965) – Madras. v1-20. 1890-1965 – 289mf – 9 – I-598/2 – ne IDC [490]

SOUTH-INDIAN TEMPLE INSCRIPTIONS / Madras – v1-3 (2). Madras. 1954-57. Lacking: 1954, v1. BI-797 2 – 8 – ne IDC [410]

SOUTHLAND DAILY NEWS – Invercargill, New Zealand. -d. 17 Jan 1963-27 Jan 1968. 14 reels – 1 – uk British Libr Newspaper [072]

SOUTHLAND TIMES – Invercargill, New Zealand. -d. Jan 1941-Aug 1972. Lacking Jan-June, Sept 1945; Sept 1950. 247 reels – 1 – uk British Libr Newspaper [072]

SOUTHSIDE BAPTIST CHURCH. ANDERSON COUNTY. SOUTH CAROLINA : CHURCH RECORDS – Sept 1925-Apr 1957, scattered. 290p – 1 – 13.05 – us Baptist [240]

SOUTHSIDE BAPTIST CHURCH. MORGAN COUNTY. DECATUR, ALABAMA : CHURCH RECORDS – 1911-60 – 1 – 44.80 – us Baptist [240]

SOUTHSIDE BAPTIST CHURCH. PALESTINE, TEXAS : CHURCH RECORDS – (History Brochure, 1940-1990) – Oct. 1944-Mar. 1965 – 1r – 1 – $42.66 – us Baptist [240]

SOUTHSIDE BAPTIST CHURCH. SAVANNAH, GOERGIA : CHURCH RECORDS – (2,058p) – 1965-1990 – 1 reel – 1 – $92.61 – us Baptist [240]

SOUTHSIDE BAPTIST CHURCH. TEMPE, ARIZONA : CHURCH RECORDS – Dec. 1962-64 – 1 – 8.28 – us Baptist [240]

SOUTHSIDE (CHESNEE MILLS). CHESNEE, SOUTH CAROLINA : CHURCH RECORDS – 1932-72 – 1 – 12.65 – us Baptist [240]

SOUTHSIDE CITIZEN – Richmond. Va. -w. 1954-59 – 1 – us UMI [071]

SOUTHSIDE HERALD – Richmond. Va. 1962-1963 – 1 – us UMI [071]

SOUTHSIDE NEWS – Richmond. Va. 1937-1941 – 1 – us UMI [071]

SOUTHSIDE SENTINEL – Urbana. Va. 1950- – 1 – us UMI [071]

SOUTHTOWN ECONOMIST – Chicago. Ill. -w. 1924-26, 1969- – 1 – us UMI [071]

SOUTHWARK MERCURY – London, UK. 1879-81. -w. 3 reels – 1 – uk British Libr Newspaper [072]

SOUTHWAYSIDE BAPTIST CHURCH. FORT WORTH, TEXAS : CHURCH RECORDS – 1952-Oct 1964 – 1 – 20.66 – us Baptist [240]

Southwest Africa. Legislative Assembly *see* VOTES AND PROCEEDINGS

SOUTHWEST BAPTIST CHURCH. WICHITA, KANSAS : CHURCH RECORDS – 1956-62 – 1 – 5.00 – us Baptist [240]

SOUTHWEST BUILDER AND CONTRACTOR – 1917-66. Pioneer engineering, building and architectural news magazine of the Western states – 209r; individualr available – 1 – $4180.00 – uk Libr Preservation [690]

SOUTHWEST CONTRACTOR AND MANUFACTURER / Engineers and Architects Association of Southern California – 1908-17. Individual rolls available – 16r – 1 – $320.00 – uk Libr Preservation [624]

SOUTHWEST ENTERPRISE – Bakersfield. Calif. 1956-1965 – 1 – us UMI [071]

SOUTHWEST GEORGIAN – Albany. Ga. 1945- – 1 – us UMI [071]

SOUTHWEST LEADER – Richfield. Kan. 1887-88 – 1 – us UMI [071]

SOUTHWEST LINCOLN SUN – Lincoln, NE. -w. Jan 1973 to date – 1 – us NE Hist [071]

SOUTHWEST OIL AND GAS WORLD *see*
- HART'S OIL AND GAS WORLD
- PACIFIC OIL AND GAS WORLD

SOUTHWEST OIL WORLD – v34- 1985- – 1,5,6,9 – us UMI. [660]

SOUTHWEST PORTLAND SHOPPER – Portland OR. Aug 9 1951 – 1 – us U.O. Library [071]

SOUTHWEST REVIEW – v1- 1915- 1; v56- 5,6; v60- 9 – us UMI [073]

SOUTH-WEST SUFFOLK ECHO. (HAVERHILL ECHO) – England. 25 Jan 1890-Dec 1975 (missing 1897).-w. 39 reels – 1 – uk British Libr Newspaper [072]

Southwest. Synod (United Pres. Ch. in the U.S.A.) *see* MINUTES, 1973-1974

SOUTHWEST TEXAS BAPTIST – 1925, 1929 – 1 – 9.73 – us Baptist [240]

SOUTHWEST TIMES – Beaverton, OR. -w. 1 May 1969-18 Dec 1975. 11 rolls – 1 – us U.O. Library [071]

SOUTHWEST TIMES – Portland OR. May 1 1969-Jan 25 1973 – 1 – us U.O. Library [071]

SOUTHWEST TIMES – Pulaski. Va. 1944-1966 – 1 – us UMI [071]

SOUTHWEST VIRGINIA ENTERPRISE – Wytheville. Va. 1970- – 1 – us UMI [071]

SOUTHWEST WAVE – Los Angeles. Calif. -w. 1967- – 1 – us UMI [071]

SOUTHWESTERN JOURNAL OF ANTHROPOLOGY – (See now: Journal of Anthropological Research) – 1-28. 1945-72 – 1 – us UMI [301]

SOUTHWESTERN JOURNAL OF SOCIAL EDUCATION – (1980- 5,6,9) – 1970- – 1 – us UMI [073]

SOUTHWESTERN JOURNAL OF THEOLOGY – Fort Worth. Texas. 1917-31, 1958-70. (1925-31 as Southwestern Evangel; NOT PUB. 1932-57) – 1 – 318.71 – us Baptist [240]

SOUTHWESTERN LAW JOURNAL *see* SMU LAW REVIEW

SOUTH-WESTERN METHODISM : A HISTORY OF THE M.E. CHURCH IN THE SOUTH-WEST FROM 1844 TO 1864... / Elliott, Charles; ed by Vernon, Leroy M – Cincinnati: Poe & Hitchock, 1868 – 2mf – 9 – us A.T.L.A. [240]

SOUTHWESTERN NATURALIST – v1- 1956- 1; v20- 5,6,9 – us UMI [574]

SOUTHWESTERN OREGON DAILY NEWS – (Set incl. Evening Record (Marshfield)) – Marshfield, OR. 2 Jan 1922-12 Apr 1940. – 16r – 1 – us U.O. Library [071]

SOUTHWESTERN RELIGIOUS LUMINARY – Mississippi. 1836-37 – 1 – 5.00 – us Baptist [240]

SOUTHWESTERN REPORTER – (Add vols planned) – 1st series: v1-214. 1886-1919 – 2698mf – 9 – $4,047.00 – LLMC 79-404I – us L.L.M.C. [340]

SOUTH-WESTERN STAR – Livingstone, Zambia. -f. 28 June 1961-24 July 1963. 1 reel – 1 – uk British Libr Newspaper [072]

SOUTHWESTERN UNIVERSITY LAW REVIEW – Los Angeles. v1-24. 1916-95 – 1,5,6 – $495.00 – us Hein [073]

SOUTHWICK 1771-1890 – (Mf 1: Vital Records 1771-1810. Mf 2: Vital Records 1771-1847. Mf 3: Births 1783-1850. Mf 4: Vital Records 1818-46. Mf 5-6: Vital Records 1818-46. Mf 7-8: Intentions 1875-1906. Mf 9: Births 1844-64. Mf 10: Vital Records 1844-76. Mf 11: Births 1868-90; Marriages 1859-62. Mf 12: Marriages & Deaths 1863-90. Mf 13: Deaths 1877-90) – (mf ed 1986) – 13mf – 9 – 0-931248-33-7 – us Holbrook [920]

Southworth, Edward Wells *see* A TREATISE ON THE NEW YORK MANUFACTURING CORPORATION ACT OF 1848, AND BUSINESS CORPORATION ACT OF 1875...2ND ED

Southworth, Emma Dorothy Eliza Nevitte *see*
- THE HIDDEN HAND
- RUTH, THE FAITHFUL BRIDE

SOUTINE / Reunion des musees nationaux. Paris – 1973. 58 illus. 2 fiches – 9 – fr Réunion [700]

Souto-Maior Fontes, Breno Augusto *see* LA PLANIFICATION URBAINE ET LE POUVOIR LOCAL

Souton, Arthur E *see* ILESHA – AND BEYOND!

LE SOUVENIR / ed by Belanger, Florent – Ville de Laval (Pont-Viau), Canada. 12 jan 1963 – 1r – 1 – Can$25.00 – cn Can Microfilming [072]

LE SOUVENIR – Montreal?: s.n., 1900-190-? – 9 – cn C.I.H.M. [240]

SOUVENIR, 1893 / Canadian Manufacturers' Association – Toronto: J. Murray, 1892. 00440. (Pre-1900 Canadiana) – 9 – cn C.I.H.M. [971]

SOUVENIR AND OFFICIAL PROGRAMME: FOURTEENTH ANNUAL CONVENTION...HELD IN MONTREAL, 15TH, 16TH, 17TH + 18TH OF OCTOBER, 1895 / Convention of the American Street Railway Association – Montreal?: s.n., 1895? (Montreal: Desbarats). 00795. (Pre-1900 Canadiana) – 9 – cn C.I.H.M. [971]

SOUVENIR D'ARTISTES – [Montreal?]: [s.n.], [1896?] ([Montreal]: Desbarats & cie, graveurs et imprimeurs). SEM105P1484 – 1mf – 9 – Can$2.25 – cn Bibl Nat [780]

SOUVENIR DE LA PERSEVERANCE DE MONTREAL – Montreal, 1872. 04278. (Pre-1900 Canadiana) – 9 – cn C.I.H.M. [971]

SOUVENIR DE MAISONNEUVE: ESQUISSE HISTORIQUE DE LA VILLE DE MONTREAL ET SEANCE D'INAUGURATION DU MONUMENT DE M. DE MAISONNEUVE, LE 1ER JUILLET, 1895 – Montreal: Desbarais & Cie., 1896. 02153. (Pre-1900 Canadiana) – 9 – cn C.I.H.M. [971]

SOUVENIR DE MON VOYAGE AUX ETATS-UNIS AT AU CANADA / Desache, Gaetan – s.l.: s.n., 1878? (Tours France: Bouserez). 03771. (Pre-1900 Canadiana) – 9 – cn C.I.H.M. [910]

SOUVENIR DE NOEL ET DU NOUVEL AN – Montreal, Canada. 1896 – 1r – 1 – Can$25.00 – cn Can Microfilming [390]

SOUVENIR DES ARDENNES, MAZURKA DE SALON / Gottschalk, L M – Mayence: Schotts Sohne, 188- – 1 – us Sibley [780]

SOUVENIR DU BANQUET LAURIER, BOSTON, MASS, HOTEL VENDOME MARDI, 17 NOVEMBRE 1891:...LES DISCOURS DES ORATEURS, LEURS PORTRAITS / Beaumont, R C de – Lowell, MA: National, 1892. 03527. (Pre-1900 Canadiana) – 9 – cn C.I.H.M. [971]

SOUVENIR NUMBER OF THE FOURTH ANNUAL CONVENTION... 1893 / Convention of the Canadian Association of Stationary Engineers – Held at Montreal, Quebec. s.l., s.n., 1893?. 02032. (Pre-1900 Canadiana) – 9 – cn C.I.H.M. [620]

SOUVENIR NUMBER OF THE ILLUSTRATED WAR NEWS : HISTORY OF RIEL'S SECOND REBELLION – Montreal, Jul 1885 – 1r – 1 – Can$25.00 – cn Can Microfilming [072]

SOUVENIR OF SETTLEMENT AND PROGRESS OF WILL COUNTY / Historical Directory Publishing Co – Chicago, 1884. (Illinois Reel 61). (The Cox Library Collection) – 5 – us Americana [978]

SOUVENIR OF THE UNION OF SOUTH AFRICA – (Filmed with: Rose-Innes, R W (Rev). John Brownlee, a Veteran Missionary and the Founder of King Williamstown) – Cape Town: South African Newspaper Co, [1910] – us Res Libr [960]

SOUVENIR PROGRAM AND 100-YEAR HISTORY / Bulloch County. Georgia. Macedonia Baptist Church – 1854-1954 – 1 – 5.00 – us Baptist [240]

SOUVENIR PROGRAM OF WILLIAMSON COUNTY CENTENNIAL (AUGUST 26-SEPTEMBER 1, 1929) / Herrin Daily Journal – Herrin, 1939. (Illinois Reel 63). (The Cox Library Collection) – 5 – us Americana [978]

SOUVENIR PROGRAMME...FROM JULY 6TH TO JULY 11TH, 1897 / Central Conference of American Rabbis. 18th: 1897: Montreal, Quebec – 1897? 04123. (Pre-1900 Canadiana) – 9 – cn C.I.H.M. [290]

SOUVENIRS DE LA LANGUE D'AUVERGNE / Mege, P – 1861 – 9 – fr I.C.S. [440]

SOUVENIRS DE LA MISSION MARCHAND / Baratier, Albert Ernest Augustin – Paris: Fayard, [1914-41] – us Res Libr [960]

SOUVENIRS DE LA MISSION SAVORGNAN DE BRAZZA / Brousseau, Georges – Paris: Societe d'Editions Geographiques, Maritimes et Coloniales, 1925 – us Res Libr [960]

SOUVENIRS DE VOYAGE / Gobineau, Joseph A – Nouv. ed. Paris: Grasset, 1922. SEM35P64 – 1r – 1 – Can$15.00 – cn Bibl Nat [830]

SOUVENIRS DU ROI DE ROME / Reunion des musees nationaux. Paris – 1932. 1 illus. 2 fiches – 9 – fr Réunion [700]

SOUVENIRS D'UN DEMI-SIECLE OU MEMOIRES POUR SERVIR A L'HISTOIRE CONTEMPORAINE / Barthe, Joseph Guillaume – Montreal: J. Chapleau, 1885. 03008. (Pre-1900 Canadiana) – 9 – cn C.I.H.M. [971]

SOUVENIRS D'UN GARIBALDIEN: CAMPAIGNE DE 1870-71 / Du Mesnil de Maricourt, Rene – Paris, 1892. 268p. (Historical Studies Series) – 9 – 9.00 – fr Bibl Nationale [900]

SOUVENIRS D'UN JEUNE FRANC-TIREUR / Muller, Eugene – Paris: Delagrave, 1884. 300p. 4 fiches. (Literature Collection) – 9 – 10.00 – fr Bibl Nationale [920]

SOUVENIRS D'UN SIBERIEN / Piotrowski, Rufin – (Russia – 19th C. series). 1870 – 9 – fr Hachette [947]

SOUVENIRS ENTOMOLOGIQUES / Fabre, J H – Paris, 1879. v1. Continued as: Nouveaux Souvenirs entomologiques, Paris, 1882, v2; Continued as: Souvenirs entomologiques, Paris, 1886-1900, v4-7. Z/1224/2 – 8 – ne IDC [590]

LES SOUVENIRS ET LA VIE INTIME DE LA BELLE OTERO / Otero, Caroline – Paris: Le Calame, 1926. 2v. (Les Femmes Collection) – 7mf – 9 – $17.00 – fr Bibl Nationale [830]

SOUVENIRS ET LEGENDES: CONFERENCE FAITE A L'INSTITUT CANADIEN DE QUEBEC / Chauveau, Pierre J O – Quebec?: A. Cote, 1877. 00594. (Pre-1900 Canadiana) – 9 – cn C.I.H.M. [971]

SOUVENIRS ET PERSPECTIVES; UNE DISCOURS, BARCELONE, 28 AOUT, 1938 / Prieto, Indalecio – Barcelona?, 1938. Fiche W1118. (Blodgett Collection of Spanish Civil War Pamphlets) – 9 – us H.U. College Libr [946]

SOUVENIRS ET REFLEXIONS: UN HAUT DIGNITAIRE DE LA FRANCMACONNERIE DE TRADITION REVELE DES SECRETS / Marsaudon, Yves – Paris: Vitiano, c1976. 413p. Illus. Incl. bibliog. references and index. 966 – 1r – 1 – us U.W. Library [920]

SOUVENIRS OF THE PAST WITH ILLUSTRATIONS: AN INSTRUCTIVE AND AMUSING WORK, GIVING A CORRECT ACCOUNT OF THE CUSTOMS AND HABITS OF THE PIONEERS OF CANADA AND THE SURROUNDING COUNTRY. / Baby, William Lewis – Windsor, Ont: 1896. 00813. (Pre-1900 Canadiana) – 9 – cn C.I.H.M. [971]

DIE SOUVERAENITAET / Heller, H - Berlin, Leipzig, 1927 - 2mf - 1 - ILM-2163/1 - ne IDC [327]
LA SOUVERAINETE DU PEUPLE - spec. no. 1-5. Paris. 1er-14 15 avr 1848. mq no. 4 - 1 - fr A.C.R.P.P. [335]
Souvestre, Emile *see* LES DERNIERS PAYSANS
Souvorof *see* L'ART DE VAINCRE, PRESENTE PAR LE GENERAL DRAGOMIROF
Souza, Jose Antonio Soares de *see* A VIDA DO VISCONDE DO URUGUAI (1807-1866)
Sovalov, A A *see* SEZONNOST RUSSKOGO EKSPORTA DO VO INY I V NSTOI ASHCHEE VREMI A
Sovd, G *see* BNMA ULSUIN ERUA5UA5GYN ERKH DEKH GEM BURUUGYN ZARIM ASUUDAL
A SOVEREIGN REMEDY FOR THE CURE OF HYPOCRISY AND BLIND ZEAL : EXTRACTED FROM THE SALUTARY PRECEPTS OF JESUS CHRIST, AND ADDRESSED TO THE SERIOUS CONSIDERATION OF THE PEOPLE CALLED METHODISTS - London, 1764 - 1mf - 9 - MP-427/1 - ne IDC [240]
THE SOVEREIGNTY OF THE BRITISH SEAS / Boroughs, J - Edinburgh, 1920 - 2mf - 9 - ILM-3892/1 - ne IDC [327]
THE SOVEREIGNTY OF THE SEA / Fulton, T W - Edinburgh, London, 1911 - 9mf - 1 - ILM-2198/1 - ne IDC [327]
Sovet narodnogo khozi a istva Severnogo ra iona *see* CHTO TAKOE SOVETY NARODNOGO KHOZIAISTVA I DLIA CHEGO ONI SOZDANY?
Sovet sezdov promyshlennosti i transporta *see* VESTNIK PROMYSHLENNOSTI, TORGOVLI I TRANSPORTA
SOVET TURKMENISTANY - (Includes c.1: 1945:July 17, 20-21, 27-Aug.7, 10-17, 21-Sept.11, 15-Oct.31; 1945:Nov.4-7, 13-Dec.4, 8-30) - Ashgabad: "Sovet Turkmenistany", 1920 - 1 reel - 1 - CSUXANR1639-S - us Hoover Inst Photo [335]
SOVETISH HEYMLAND *see* DI IDISHE GAS (EVREISKAIA ULITSA)
SOVETSKAI A RESPUBLIKA I KAZAKI / Ulianov, Ivan - Moskva: Gos. izdvo, 1920 - 1 - CSUX88-B7911 - us Hoover Inst Photo [947]
SOVETSKAI A SISTEMA ZA RABOTO I = THE SOVIET SYSTEM AT WORK : OTCHET O POEZDKE V SOVETSKUI U ROSSII U / Williams, Robert - Moskva: Gos. izdvo, 1921 - 1 - CSUX88-B5089 - us Hoover Inst Photo [335]
SOVETSKAI A TORGOVLI A = SOVIET TRADE / ed by Narodnogo komissariata vneshne i i vnutrenne i torgovli SSSR - (Library has: June-Dec. 1926, July-Aug. 1928, Jan.-May 1929, Apr., June 1930, Index for 1927; some issues missing) - Moskva: Izdvo Narkomtorga SSSR, -1931 - 1 - CSUX90-S516 - us Hoover Inst Photo [380]
SOVETSKAIA ANTROPOLOGIIA - v. 1-3. M. 1957-59. BR-1795 2 - 8 - ne IDC [301]
SOVETSKAIA ARKHEOGRAFIIA / Valk, S N - Leningrad, 1948. 289p. BR-10,774/1 - 9 - ne IDC [025]
SOVETSKAIA ARKHITEKTURA - v. 1-9. M. 1951-58. BR-3749 2 - 8 - ne IDC [720]
SOVETSKAIA BELORUSSIIA - (Backfile through 1998 $85r) - Belarus, 1999- - 6r per y standing order - 1 - us Ross [072]
SOVETSKAIA BIBLIOGRAFIA SBORNIK - U.S.S.R. 1933-41 - 1 - us UMI [010]
SOVETSKAIA ETNOGRAFII - (Missing: 1940-1945) - M., 1931-1964 - 496mf - 9 - R-2312/2 - ne IDC [947]
SOVETSKAIA FILARMONIA : BULLETIN - Moscow, 1928-29 - 7mf - 9 - us Ross [780]
SOVETSKAIA IUSTITSIIA - 1922-41 - 1 - 282.00 - us L of C Photodup [947]
SOVETSKAIA IUSTITSIIA *see* EZHENEDEL'NIK SOVETSKOI IUSTITSII
SOVETSKAIA KARELIIA - (Library has: 1931, no. 1-10; 1932, no. 1-4; 1933, no. 1-7; 1934, no. 1-4, 9-10; 1935, no. 1-3) - Petrozavodsk: Komissiia, 1929-1935. 7v - 1 - CSUX89-S655 - us Hoover Inst Photo [335]
SOVETSKAIA KINOKHRONIKA - 1918-25.Moscow, 1965. 152p. Lists newsreels from the period 1918-25 now in TsGAKFD SSSR. BR-10,826/1 - 9 - ne IDC [947]
SOVETSKAIA KNIZHNAIA TORGOVLIA - (Includes c.1: 1960-1963) - Moskva: "Iskusstvo", 1948 - 1 - CSUXAKZ0079-S - us Hoover Inst Photo [070]
SOVETSKAIA KOOPERATSIIA / Legeso, S & Faiershtein, M - M., 1925 - 2mf - 9 - COR-164/1 - ne IDC [334]
SOVETSKAIA KOOPERATSIIA / Shvetsov, A I - M., L., 1926 - 1mf - 9 - COR-241/1 - ne IDC [334]
SOVETSKAIA KUL'TURA - Prilozhenie k zhurnalu "Krasnaia Niva" za 1924 g. M. 1924. BR-10,448 1 - 9 - ne IDC [947]
SOVETSKAIA KULTURA - Moscow. U.S.S.R. 1961-1970 - 1 - us UMI [460]
SOVETSKAIA PECHAT' - Moscow, 1956-66.Lacking: 1956 (11-12).BR-10,453/1 - 9 - ne IDC [947]
SOVETSKAIA PECHAT' - Moscow. Journal of the Union of Journalists of the USSR. 1956-1966 - 1 - 35.00r - us Hoover Inst Photo [073]
SOVETSKAIA PEDAGOGIKA - (Includes c.1: 1938-1972, 1981:no.3-) - Moskva: Narkompros-Uchpedgiz, 1937- - 1 - CSUXAKY6115-S - us Hoover Inst Photo [370]
SOVETSKAIA ROSSIIA - Moscow: Sovetskaia Rossiia, 1956- - 2mf - 9 - $199.95y - us East View [320]
SOVETSKAIA SIBIR : ORGAN SIBIRSKOGO REVOLIUTS. KOMITETA, SIB. BIURO T S.K.R.K.P. (BOLSHEVIKOV), NOVONIKOL. GUBKOMA R.K.P. I GUBISPOLKOMA - (Includes c.1: 1941-1942; Lacks: 1941, no. 201, no. 263) - Novonikolaevsk: [s.n.], 1919 - 1 - CSUXADJ2702-S - us Hoover Inst Photo [335]
Sovetskaia sotsiologicheskaia assotsiatsiia *see*
- DINAMIKA IZMENENIIA POLOZHENIIA ZHENSHCHINY I SEMIA
SOVETSKAIA TORGOVLIA - (Includes c.1: 1956:no.2 Feb.-1966:no.12 (Dec.); 1967:no.6 June-1988:no.12 (Dec.)) - Moskva: Gostorgizdat, -1991 - 1 - CSUX89-S485 - us Hoover Inst Photo [380]
SOVETSKAIA TORGOVLIA / ed by Instituta ekonomiki Komakademii, T Sentrosoi uza SSSR i R.S.F.S.R. i Narkomsnaba SSSR - (Library has: Sept./Oct. 1931, Jan./Feb.-Nov./Dec. 1934, Jan.-Dec. 1935, Jan.-Nov./Dec. 1936, Jan.-July 1937) - Moskva: Izdvo "Snabzhenie, kooperatsiia, torgovlia", 1926-1937 - 1 - CSUX89-S548 - us Hoover Inst Photo [380]
SOVETSKAIA TORGOVLIA : ORGAN NARODNOGO KOMISSARIATA SNABZHENII A SSSR - (Library has: no. 1-6, 1931) - Moskva: Snabkoopgiz, 19uu - 1 - CSUX89-S563 - us Hoover Inst Photo [380]
SOVETSKAIA TORGOVLIA / Russia. Narodnyi Komissariat Snabzheniia - n2641-3742. 1935-39 - 4r - 1 - us Ross [947]
SOVETSKAIA TORGOVLYA - Moscow. U.S.S.R. 1961- - 1 - us UMI [380]
SOVETSKAIA UGOLOVNAIA REPRESSIIA / Aminova, I et al - Moscow, 1934. 222p. BR-9105 1 - 9 - ne IDC [340]
SOVETSKAIA UKRAINA - Kiev, 1951-61 (8). Continued by: Raduga. Kiev, 1961 (9-12)-1972. Lacking: 1951-55 (1-9,11-12); 1956 (1-12); 1958 (6); 1965 (1,11). BR-10,458/1 - 9 - ne IDC [947]
SOVETSKAYA BELORUSSIA - Minsk. Belorussia (U.S.S.R.). 1955- - 1 - us UMI [072]
SOVETSKAYA ESTONIA - Tallin, USSR. 1963-1980 - 18r - $900.00 - B63595 - us Library Micro [072]
SOVETSKAYA ESTONIA - Tallinn.Estonia (U.S.S.R.). 1955- - 1 - us UMI [072]
SOVETSKAYA KIRGIZIA - Frunze. Kirghiz (U.S.S.R.). 1955-70 - 1 - us UMI [072]
SOVETSKAYA LATVIA - Riga. Latvia (U.S.S.R.). 1955- - 1 - us UMI [072]
SOVETSKAYA LITVA - Vilna. Lithuania (U.S.S.R.). 1955- - 1 - us UMI [072]
SOVETSKAYA LITVA - Vilnius, 1955-1960 (incomplete) - 1 - us NY Public [947]
SOVETSKAYA MOLDAVIA - Kishinev. Moldavia (U.S.S.R.). 1955- - 1 - us UMI [072]
SOVETSKAYA MOLDAVIYA - Kishinev, 1955-1960 (incomplete) - 1 - us NY Public [947]
SOVETSKAYA MUZYKA - Moscow. U.S.S.R. 1961- - 1 - us UMI [073]
SOVETSKAYA PECHAT - Moscow. U.S.S.R. 1961- - 1 - us UMI [072]
SOVETSKAYA ROSSIYA - Moscow. U.S.S.R. 1957-1970 - 1 - us UMI [072]
SOVETSKAYA TORGOVLIA - Moscow. U.S.S.R. 1966- - 1 - us UMI [380]
SOVETSKAYA TORGOVLYA - Moscow, Jan 1935-Feb 1939 - 1 - us NY Public [947]
SOVETSKAYA YUSTITSIA - Moscow. U.S.S.R. 1961- - 1 - us UMI [323]
SOVETSKIE ARKHIVY - Moscow, 1966-75. Bimonthly publ. of the Main Archival Administration with coop. of Institute of Marxism-Leninism and Institute of History of the USSR. BR-10,756/1 - 9 - ne IDC [025]
SOVETSKIE ARKHIVY : ORGAN GLAVNOGO ARKHIVNOGO UPRAVLENIIA PRI SOVETE MINISTROV SSSR - (Includes 1966, no. 2-) - Moskva: Upr., 1966- - 1 - CSUX90-S475 - us Hoover Inst Photo [947]
SOVETSKIE ARKHIVY : ORGAN GLAVNOGO ARKHIVNOGO UPRAVLENIIA PRI SOVETE MINISTROV SSSR - (Includes c.1: 1966:no.2-) - Moskva: Upr., 1966-1991 - 1 - CSUX90-S474 - us Hoover Inst Photo [947]
SOVETSKIE ARKHIVY : ORGAN GLAVNOGO ARKHIVNOGO UPRAVLENIIA PRI SOVETE MINISTROV SSSR - (Includes c.1: 1966:no.2-) - Moskva: Upr., 1966-1991 - 1 - CSUXACQ6065-S - us Hoover Inst Photo [947]
SOVETSKIE AVTONOMNYE OBLASTI I RESPUBLIKI / Arkhippov, K A - Moscow, 1925. 123p. BR-9427 1 - 9 - ne IDC [340]
SOVETSKIE KHUDOZHESTVENNYE FIL'MY - Annotirovannyi katalog. Basic catalog of feature films and short produced in USSR between 1917 and 1963. Moscow, 1961-68. 4v.527p; 784p; 307p; 824p. BR-10,999/1 - 9 - ne IDC [790]
SOVETSKIE SUBTROPIKI : ORGAN GLAVNOGO UPRAVLENIIA SUBTROPICHESKIKH KULTUR NARKOMZEMA SOIUZA - (Library has: Sep.-Nov. 1934) - Moskva: Zhurnalno-gazetnoe obedinenie, 1934-1940. 7v - 1 - CSUX89-S781 - us Hoover Inst Photo [306]
SOVETSKIE VOENNO-UCHEBNYE ZAVEDENIIA ZA CHETYRE GODA 1918-1922 / Avinovitskii, I Akov Lazarevich - Moskva: Vysshi i voen. redatsionny i sovet, 1922 - 1 - CSUX88-B6937 - us Hoover Inst Photo [947]
SOVETSKII FOL'KLOR / ed by Krivosheeva, A - 1939. Russian folk literature - 1 - us I.U. Libraries [390]
SOVETSKII MUZEI - Moscow. 10v 1931-40 - 1 - $46.00 - us L of C Photodup [060]
SOVETSKII PATRIOT : PATRIOTE SOVIETIQUE - (Library has: no. 22-62 (Mar. 24, 1945-Dec. 28, 1945) - Paris: Patriote sovietique, 1945-. 1v - 1 - CSUX87-S204 - us Hoover Inst Photo [320]
SOVETSKII PATRIOT - U.S.S.R. 1958- - 1 - us UMI [072]
SOVETSKII SEVER / ed by Komitet sodeistviia narodnostiam severnykh okrain pri Prezidiume VT SIK - (Includes c.1: v.1 1929) - Moskva: Komitet, 1929- - 1 - CSUXAKZ2189-S - us Hoover Inst Photo [306]
SOVETSKII SOIUZ - Ezhemesiachnyi obshchestvenno-politicheskii illiustrirovannyi zhurnal. M. 1950-57. BR-3737 2 - 8 - ne IDC [947]
SOVETSKII SPORT - (Backfile through 1998 $85r) - 1999- - 1r per y - 1 - $80.00 standing order - us Ross [072]
SOVETSKII SPORT - Moscow, Mar 19 1946-63; 1965-76; 1980 - 42r - 1 - us L of C Photodup [072]
SOVETSKII TEATR - Russkii teatr, 1917-21. Dokumenty i materialy. Leningrad, 1968. 548p. Includes a detailed inventory of archival materials for theater history, p403-96. BR-10,747/1 - 9 - ne IDC [790]
SOVETSKII UGOLOVNYI PROTSESS / Cheltsov-Bebutov, M A - Kharkov, 1928. 2v. BR-9667/1 - 9 - ne IDC [360]
SOVETSKII VOIN - (Includes 1962, no.15-) - Moskva: Voenizdat, 194u - 1 - CSUX90-S542 - us Hoover Inst Photo [355]
SOVETSKII ZAGOTOVITEL' - 1931-39. v.5. n.18-v.13, n.31. Scattered issues missing - 1 - 113.00 - us L of C Photodup [073]
SOVETSKI-INDONEZIISKOE EKONOMICHESKOE SOTRUDNICHESTVO / Farizov, Ivan Omarovich - SE-10,390 1. 1964 - 9 - ne IDC [330]
SOVETSKIYE PROFSOYUZY - Moscow. U.S.S.R. 1961- - 1 - us UMI [330]
SOVETSKOE GOSUDARSTVO I PRAVO - Moscow. Title variation as follows: 1927-1929, Revoliutsiia prava; 1930-1931, Sovetskoe gosudarstvo i revoliutsiia prava; 1932-1938, Sovetskoe gosudarstvo. 1930-1971. Suspended May 1941-Dec. 1945 - 1 - 35.00r - us Hoover Inst Photo [072]
SOVETSKOE GOSUDARSTVO REVOLIUTSIIA PRAVA - (Cont. as: Sovetskoe gosudarstvo. M., 1932-1939; Cont. as: Sovetskoe gosudarstvo i pravo. M., 1940-1990(12); 1941, May-1945, December have not been published; published monthly 1930-32, 1940-52, and 1957 to date; 10 issues in 1956; bi-monthly 1933-39; 8 issues annually in 1953-55; Missing: 1936(6); Supplemented: 1972-1990(12). 405mf) - M., 1930-1931 - 9 - 2364/1 - ne IDC [340]
SOVETSKOE ISKUSSTVO - (Library has: Dec. 11, 1934; Feb. 5, 1935-Dec. 29, 1937; Jan. 4-Dec. 21, 1939; June 29, 1945-Dec. 15, 1951[many issues missing]) - Moskva: Zhurnalno-gazetnoe obedinenie, 1931-1953 - 1 - CSUX87-S255 - us Hoover Inst Photo [700]
SOVETSKOE ISKUSSTVO - Moscow, U.S.S.R. -w. Jan-Oct 1941; Nov 1944-April 1945; June 1945-June 1953. 4 reels - 1 - uk British Libr Newspaper [947]
SOVETSKOE KHLOPKOVODSTVO - Moscow, U.S.S.R. -sw. Jan-Dec 1951; Jan-March 1953. 1 reel - 1 - uk British Libr Newspaper [947]
SOVETSKOE KHOZIAISTVENHOE ZAKONODATEL'STVO.. / ed by Gintsburg, L Ia - Moscow, 1934. 2v. Collected normative materials on the administration of the national economy intended as a manual for law students.BR-9037/1 - 9 - ne IDC [340]
SOVETSKOE KOOPERATIVNOE ZAKONODATEL'STVO / Lur'e, GI - M. 4v. 1925 (Zaochnye kooperativnye kursy Tsentro soiuza No. 11) - 4mf - 9 - COR-298/1 - ne IDC [334]
SOVETSKOE PRAVO - Tallin, 1967-1988 - 128mf - 9 - ne IDC [340]
SOVETSKOE PRAVO - Zhurnal Instituta sovetskogo prava. 1922-28. BR-2432 2 - 8 - ne IDC [073]
SOVETSKOE PRAVO PERED INOSTRANNYMI SUDAMI / Kel'man, E I - Kharkov, 1928. 118p. BR-8473/1. Critique, with translations, of cases involving Soviet law in foreign courts - 9 - ne IDC [340]
SOVETSKOE PRAVO ZA RUBEZHEM / Kel'man, E I - Moscow, 1927. 94p. Analysis of the extraterritorial effect of Soviet decrees, with attention to foreign cases. BR-8474/1 - 9 - ne IDC [340]
SOVETSKOE PROMYSHLENNOE PRAVO / Karass, A V - Moscow, Leningrad, 1925.162p. State enterprise during NEP with normative materials appended to each chapter. BR-9407/1 - 9 - ne IDC [340]
SOVETSKOE STROITEL'STVO - Moskva. On film: v1-5; 1925-26. LL-081 - 1 - us L of C Photodup [340]
SOVETSKOE STROITEL'STVO / Russia. (1923-U.S.S.R.). Tsentral'nyi ispolnitel'nyi komitet - v. 1-12. 1926-37 - 1 - $139.00 - us L of C Photodup [330]
SOVETSKOE TRUDOVOE PRAVO / Grishin, Z Z - Moscow, 1936. 272p. Labor law textbook for Soviet law schools with extensive data on reforms of the mid-1930s. BR-8458/1 - 9 - ne IDC [340]
SOVETSKOE TRUDOVOE PRAVO / Kaminskaia, PD - 2nd ed. Kharkov, 1927. 472p. Enlarges coverage to include most union republic legislation, while lamenting continued absence of fundamental principles of labor legislation. BR-9366/1 - 9 - ne IDC [340]
SOVETSKOE TRUDOVOE PRAVO / Kaminskaia, PD - Khar'kov, 1925. 362p. Soviet labor law with extensive quotation of primary sources, especially Ukrainian, critical commentary on inconsistent normative acts, and references to foreign doctrine and law. BR-9363/1 - 9 - ne IDC [340]
SOVETSKOE TRUDOVOE PRAVO - Ukazatel' literatury 1917-1969. Kazan. 1971. BR-11,269 - 9 - ne IDC [340]
SOVETSKOE UGOLOVNOE PRAVO: BIBLIOGRAFIIA (1917-60) / Asknazii, F M & Marshalovas, N V - Moscow, 1961. 324p. BR-5707 1 - 9 - ne IDC [340]
SOVETSKOE VOENNO-UGOLOVNOE PRAVO / Chkhikvadze, V M - Moscow, 1948. 462p. Treatise on military-criminal law in U.S.S.R. Updates the 1941 volume. BR-8435/1 - 9 - ne IDC [947]
SOVETSKOE VOENNO-UGOLOVNOE PRAVO / Chkhikvadze, V M & Savitskii, M I - Moscow, 1941. 284p. Treatise on military crimes under Soviet criminal law. BR-9666/1 - 9 - ne IDC [340]

DEN SOVETSKOI PROPAGANDY : LOZUNGI – Moskva: Gos. izd-vo, 1919 – 1 – CSUX89-B6585 – us Hoover Inst Photo [320]
SOVETSKOYE GOSUDARSTVO I PRAVO – Moscow. U.S.S.R. 1930-41; 1945- – 1 – us UMI [340]
DIE SOVET-UNION 1917-1932 / Mehnert, K – Berlin, 1933 – 4mf – 9 – ne IDC [947]
SOVETY 1905 G / Babakhan, N – Moskva: "Moskovski i rabochi i", 1923 – 1 – CSUX88-B883 – us Hoover Inst Photo [947]
SOVETY DEPUTATOV TRUDY ASHCHIKHSYA – Moscow. U.S.S.R. 1961- – 1 – us UMI [335]
SOVETY I KOOPERATSIIA – Ivanovo-Voznesensk, 1928 n1-48 – 11mf – 9 – COR-690/1 – ne IDC [334]
SOVETY KAZAKHSTAN = THE SOVIET OF KAZAKHSTAN – (Comes in Russian) – 1990- – 1 – sz Infoprint [947]
SOVETY RABOCHIKH DEPUTATOV V 1905 GODU NA DONU I SEVERNOM KAVKAZE / Muzhev, I F – Nal'chik, 1962 – 1 – 35.00r – us Hoover Inst Photo [947]
LE SOVIET / La Federation Communiste des Soviets – no. 1-13. Paris. mars 1920-mai 1921 – 1 – fr A.C.R.P.P. [335]
SOVIET ANALYST – London, England, USSR. 1972-1983 – 7r – $350.00 – R63620 – us Library Micro [320]
SOVIET ANALYST – London, UK. 1972-1992 – 11r – $550.00 – R63608 – us Library Micro [320]
Soviet Antarctic Expedition *see* INFORMATION BULLETIN
SOVIET AUTOMATIC CONTROL – (v17. 1984. 5,6,9) – v1-17. 1968-84 – 1 – us UMI [629]
SOVIET AUTOMATION: PERSPECTIVES AND PROSPECTS / Baranson, Jack – 1987. 142p. ISBN:0-912338-62-8 – 9 – 29.50 – us Lomond [338]
SOVIET BIOGRAPHIC ARCHIVE, 1954-1985 – 2,812mf – 9 – £10,670.00 – Publ in association with Radio Free Europe, Radio Liberty Inc and the Hoover Institution – uk Chadwyck [920]
SOVIET ELECTROCHEMISTRY *see* RUSSIAN JOURNAL OF ELECTROCHEMISTRY
THE SOVIET ESTIMATE : U.S. ANALYSIS OF THE SOVIET UNION, 1947-1991 – (Printed guide & index only £630.00) – 1995 – Over 600 intelligence estimates and reports – 9 – £2,940.00 – uk Chadwyck [327]
SOVIET GENETICS *see* RUSSIAN JOURNAL OF GENETICS
SOVIET HYDROLOGY: SELECTED PAPERS – (v1-10. 1962-71. $20.00y; 1,5,6. v11. 1972. $40.00; 9. v12-14. 1973-75. $20.00y; 1,5,6. v15-16. 1976-77. $30.00y; 1,5,6. v17. 1978. $35.00; 1,5,6. v18-19. 1979-80. $40.00y; 1,5,6) – v1-19. 1962-80. Quarterly. In English – us A.G.U. [550]
SOVIET JEWISH AFFAIRS – v1- 1971- 1; v6- 5,6,9 – us UMI [270]
SOVIET JEWRY ACTION NEWSLETTER – (Lacking: v10 n1-2; v13 n1; 1981/82) – New York, New York. v8 n1 (Rosh Hashanah 1975)-Passover 1986 – 10ft – us A.J.P.C. [270]
SOVIET JOURNAL OF AUTOMATION AND INFORMATION SCIENCE – v18-. 1985- – 1,5,6,9 – us UMI [000]
SOVIET JOURNAL OF BIOORGANIC CHEMISTRY *see* RUSSIAN JOURNAL OF BIOORGANIC CHEMISTRY
SOVIET JOURNAL OF CHEMICAL PHYSICS – 1983- – 1,5,9 – in prep – us Gordon [073]
SOVIET JOURNAL OF COMMUNICATIONS TECHNOLOGY AND ELECTRONICS – v30-. 1985- – 1,5,6,9 – us UMI [621]
SOVIET JOURNAL OF COMPUTER AND SYSTEMS SCIENCES – v23-. 1985- – 1,5,6,9 – us UMI [073]
SOVIET JOURNAL OF COORDINATION CHEMISTRY *see* RUSSIAN JOURNAL OF COORDINATION CHEMISTRY
SOVIET JOURNAL OF ECOLOGY *see* RUSSIAN JOURNAL OF ECOLOGY
SOVIET JOURNAL OF OPTICAL TECHNOLOGY – English-language translation of Optiko-Mekhanicheskaya Promyshlennost, microfilm edition: available for back numbers – 850p per year – us Optical Soc [621]
SOVIET JOURNAL OF REMOTE SENSING / ed by Kondrateu, K YA – 1982- – 1,5,9 – us Harwood [530]
SOVIET LAW AND GOVERNMENT *see* RUSSIAN POLITICS AND LAW
SOVIET LIFE – v1- 1956- 1; v250- 5,6,9 – us UMI [360]
SOVIET LIGHTWAVE COMMUNICATIONS – v1-3. 1991-93. Publ. ceased – 1,5,6,9 – uk I.O.P. [530]
SOVIET MARRIAGE CODE / Russia. (1923- U.S.S.R.). Laws, Statutes, etc – Paris: Navarre 1933. 29p. LL-4216 – 1 – us L of C Photodup [340]
SOVIET MATERIALS SCIENCE *see* MATERIALS SCIENCE
SOVIET MATHEMATICS – v1-19. 1960-78 – 1 – us UMI [073]
SOVIET MATHEMATICS-DOKLADY – (1982-. 1,5,6,9) – v20-. 1979- – 1 – us UMI [073]
SOVIET PHYSICS JOURNAL *see* RUSSIAN PHYSICS JOURNAL
SOVIET PLANT PHYSIOLOGY *see* RUSSIAN JOURNAL OF PLANT PHYSIOLOGY
SOVIET POWDER METALLURGY AND METAL CERAMICS *see* POWDER METALLURGY AND METAL CERAMICS
SOVIET RADIOCHEMISTRY *see* RADIOCHEMISTRY
SOVIET REVIEW – v.1-. 1960- – 1,5,6,9 – us UMI [947]
SOVIET RUSSIA PICTORIAL – v1-9. no. 10 (all publ). 1919-1924 – 1 reel – 1 – $230.00 – us UPA [335]
SOVIET SHIPPING JOURNAL JAN. 1977- *see* MORSKO I FLOT (MOSKOW, R.S.F.S.R.: 1955)
SOVIET SOIL SCIENCE – (v16-. 1984-. 5,6,9) – 1958- – 1 – us UMI [631]
SOVIET SPACE PROGRAMS 1980-1985 – (v66 1987, Science and Technology) – 1987 – 9 – $45.00 – us Univelt [380]
SOVIET STATUTES AND DECISIONS *see* STATUTES AND DECISIONS
SOVIET STUDIES – Continued as Europe-Asia Studies – 9 – 0038-5859 – uk Carfax [947]
SOVIET UNION / U.S. Office of Strategic Services – (Soviet Union: 1950-61. Supplement. 1979. Series, Pt 11. $570.00) – 1977. Series: US State Department Intelligence and Research Reports, Pt 6 – 1 – $770.00 – us UPA [947]
Soviet Union *see*
- LAWS, ETC
- SBORNIK DEISTVUIUSHCHIKH DEKRETOV I POSTANOVLENII PO VNESHNE I TORGOVLE
- TREATIES, ETC

THE SOVIET UNION, 1919-1933 / U.S. Department of State – Series: Confidential U.S. Diplomatic Post Records: Russia and the Soviet Union, Part 2. 1983 – 1 – $8,255.00 – us UPA [947]
THE SOVIET UNION, 1919-44 : REPORTS / U.S. Military Intelligence – (1919-41: $1,030.00 ISBN 0-89093-660-9; 1941-44: 22r $2,200.00) – With printed guides – 1 – us UPA [355]
THE SOVIET UNION, 1934-1941 / U.S. Department of State – Series: Confidential U.S. Diplomatic Post Records: Russia and the Soviet Union, Part 3. 1983 – 1 – $6,600.00 – us UPA [947]
THE SOVIET UNION, 1946-76 / U.S. Central Intelligence Agency – 1982. Series: CIA Research Reports – 1 – $480.00 – us UPA [947]
THE SOVIET UNION, 1970-80 : SPECIAL STUDIES / ed by Kesaris, Paul – (Supplements: 1980-82. 8r $830.00 ISBN 0-89093-432-0; 1982-85. 9r $900.00 ISBN 0-89093-645-5; 1985-88. 10r $1,105.00 ISBN 1-55655-111-8; 1989-91. 13r $1,665.00 ISBN 1-55655-415-X. With printed guides) – 1981. 9 reels – 1 – $900.00 – 0-89093-385-5 – us UPA [320]
THE SOVIET UNION AND REPUBLICS OF THE FORMER U.S.S.R., 1992-94 SUPPLEMENT : SPECIAL STUDIES – 15r – 1 – $1,785.00 – 1-55655-533-4 – us UPA [320]
Soviet Union, Ministerstvo vooruzhennykh sil *see* PRIKAZ MINISTRA VOORUZHENNYKH SIL SOIUZA SSR
Soviet Union, Narodnyi komissariat snabzheniia *see* BIULLETEN NARODNOGO KOMISSARIATA SNABZHENIIA
Soviet Union, Sovet narodnykh komissarov *see*
- DEI ATELNOST SNK I STO, SVODNYE MATERIALY
- SVODNYE MATERIALY O DEIATELNOSTI SOVETA NARODNYKH KOMISSAROV SSSR I SOVETA TRUDA I OBORONY ZA...

Soviet Union, T Sentralnoe statisticheskoe upravlenie *see* STATISTICHESKOE OBOZRENIE
Soviet Union, Verkhovnyi Sovet *see*
- MATERIALY...VERKHOVNOGO SOVETA SSSR...
- STENOHRAFICHNY IZVIT ZASIDANNIA VERKHOVNOI RADI SRSR

Soviet Union, Vysshii sovet narodnogo khoziaistva *see*
- SBORNIK POSTANOVLENII I PRIKAZOV PO PROMYSHLENNOSTI

SOVIET WAR POSTERS, CA 1940-1945 : THE TASS POSTER SERIES FROM THE HALLWARD LIBRARY, UNIVERSITY OF NOTTINGHAM / ed by Spring, Derek – Marlborough: Adam Matthew Publications, 1991 – 1 b/w reel; 13mf; 1 colour reel – 1,9,14 – $875.00 – uk Matthew [740]
THE SOVIET WORLD 1948-1989 / Institute for Soviet and East European Studies. University of Amsterdam – (Includes printed guide. A unique bibliographical card file from over 300 selected Soviet and Western newspapers and periodicals) – 612mf – 9 – R-17017/1 – ne IDC [947]
THE SOVIETS AT WORK; THE INTERNATIONAL POSITION OF THE RUSSIAN SOVIET REPUBLIC AND THE FUNDAMENTAL PROBLEMS OF THE SOCIALIST REVOLUTION / Lenin, Vladimir Ilyich – 5th ed. New York: Rand School of Social Science, 1919. 48p – 1 – us U.W. Library [335]
LOS SOVIETS EN ESPANA: LA LUCHA POR EL PODER POR LA REPUBLIC OBRERA Y CAMPESINA EN ESPANA – Paris, 1935. Fiche W1169. (Blodgett Collection of Spanish Civil War Pamphlets) – 9 – us H.U. College Libr [946]
Sovitskii, D *see* RUSSKII GOMILET NACHALA 18 VEKA IOAKIM BOGOMOLEVSKII
SOVKHOZNAYA GAZETA – Moscow, U.S.S.R. - w. Jan 1950-April 1953. Imperfect. 3 reels – 1 – uk British Libr Newspaper [947]
LA SOVRANITA DEGLI STATI... / Casulli, A – Roma, 1932 – 3mf – 1 – ILM-2176/1 – ne IDC [327]
LA SOVRANITA DEGLI STATI SULLE ACQUE / Criscuolo, E – Napoli, 1886 – 1mf – 1 – ILM-2928/1 – ne IDC [327]
LA SOVRANITA TERRITORIALE... / Ghirardini, C – Cremona, 1913 – 1mf – 1 – ILM-2167/1 – ne IDC [327]
SOVREMENNAIA DEREVNIA V TSIFRAKH : EKONOMIKA I RAZNOOBRAZNYI BYT DEREVNI ZA REVOLIUTSIONNNYI PERIOD / Bol'shakov, A M – L., 1928 – 2mf – 9 – COR-464/1 – ne IDC [334]
SOVREMENNAIA KONNITSA / Golovin, Nikolai Nikolaevich – Belgrad: [s.n.], 1923 – 1 – CSUX89-B669 – us Hoover Inst Photo [320]
SOVREMENNAIA KOOPERATSIIA I EE ZADACHI / Miliutin, VP – M., 1925 – 1mf – 9 – COR-214/1 – ne IDC [334]
SOVREMENNAIA LETOPIS – M. 1861-71. B-1904 2 – 8 – ne IDC [520]
SOVREMENNAIA LITERATURA – Sbornik statei. Izd. Mysl'. (Blok, Belyi, Fors i dr.). L. 1925. BR-3342 2 – 8 – ne IDC [460]
SOVREMENNAIA ZAPADNOEVROPEISKAIA TSIVILIZATSIIA / Flerovskii, N – (Azbuka sotsial'nykh nauk). Londonskii fond vol'noi russkoi pressy. v. 10-12. London. 1894. BR-10.550 2 – 8 – ne IDC [947]
SOVREMENNAYA MUZYKA – Moscow. year 1-6, no. 32 1924-Mar 1929 – 1 – us NY Public [780]
SOVREMENNAYA ZHIZN' – 1906 – 1r – 1 – us Ross [073]
SOVREMENNIK – Ezhemesiachnyi zhurnal literatury, politiki, istorii, iskusstva i obshchestvennoi zhizni. Spb. 1911-15. Lacking: v. 6-9, 11-12, 1915. B-1199 2 – 8 – ne IDC [947]
SOVREMENNIK – Literaturnyi zhurnal. v. 1-44. Spb. 1836-46; Index. v. 1-113. 1847-66. B-1294 2 – 8 – ne IDC [460]
SOVREMENNIK – St. Petersburg. 1851-1862, Vols. 27-93. Missing: Vols. 30-48, 61-78 – 1 – 35.00r – us Hoover Inst Photo [073]
SOVREMENNIKI / Chukovskii, K – Portrety i etiudy. M. 1962. BR-2037 2 – 8 – ne IDC [460]
SOVREMENNOE OBOZRENIE – Zhurnal literaturnyi, nauchnyi i politicheskii. v. 1-6. Spb. 1868. B-1906 2 – 8 – ne IDC [320]
SOVREMENNOE POLOZHENIE I VOZMOZHNOE BUDUSHCHEE : AGRARNAIA PROBLEMA I EE RESHENIE BORIUSHCHIMISIA PARTIAMI: 3-IA DUMA, PRICHINI EE POIAVLENIIA I EE BUDUSHCHEE / Cherevanin, N – M., 1903. 246p – 3mf – 9 – ne IDC [320]
SOVREMENNOE POLOZHENIE I ZADACHI PARTII : PLATFORMA, VYRABOTANNAI A GRUPPO I BOLSHEVIKOV / Ide inai a gruppa Vpered – Paris: "Vpered", [1910?] – 1 – CSUX89-B5255 – us Hoover Inst Photo [320]
SOVREMENNOE SOSTOYANIE RAKOLO SEKTANTSTVA V KHARKOVSKOI EPARKII / Davidenko, Vasilii – The contemporary status of dissenting sectarianism in Kharkov Diocese. Kharkov, 1901 – 1 – 7.92 – us Baptist [240]
SOVREMENNOST' – Spb. v1-2. 1906 – 8 – BR-3768 2 – ne IDC [320]
SOVREMENNYE VOPROSY ORGANIZATSII I PRAKTIKI SEL'SKOKHOZIAISTVENNOI KOOPERATSII / Maslov, S L – L., 1925 – 1mf – 9 – COR-487/1 – ne IDC [334]
SOVREMENNYI TEATR I MUZYKA – St Petersburg, 1903 (weekly 17 issues publ) – 10mf – 9 – us Ross [780]
SOVREMENNYIA ZAPISKI – Ezhemesiachnyi literaturnyi i nauchnyi zhurnal. no. 1. Spb. 1906. BR-3767 2 – 8 – ne IDC [460]
SOVREMENNYIA ZAPISKI – Ezhemesiachnyi obshchestvenno-politicheskii i literaturnyi zhurnal. 1-70. Paris. 1920-40; Ukazatel'k. no. 1-65 za 1920-37 gg. Paris. n.d. BR-3750 2 – 8 – ne IDC [947]
SOVREMENNYIA ZAPISKI – Paris. 1920-1940 – 1 – 35.00r – us Hoover Inst Photo [073]
SOVREMENNYIA ZAPISKI – Paris. v. 1-70. 1920-40 – 1 – 295.00 – us L of C Photodup [940]
Sovsun, V *see* AKMEIZM ILI ADAMIZM
Soward, A M et al *see* GEOPHYSICAL AND ASTROPHYSICAL FLUID DYNAMICS
Sowell, Benjamin Luther *see* PIONEER PARSON
THE SOWER – Toronto: Bible and Tract Depot, [1891?-1926?] – 9 – cn C.I.H.M. [220]
THE SOWER IN THE WEST – Calgary, Alta.: Publ by the Gibson Print. Co, 1893?-189- or 19– – 9 – cn C.I.H.M. [240]
Sowerby *see* CONSTABLE'S ACCOUNTS, 1629-1866
SOWERBY BRIDGE CHRONICLE – England. -w. 1883-1914. (12 reels) – 1 – uk British Libr Newspaper [072]
Sowerby, G B *see*
- A CATALOGUE OF THE SHELLS CONTAINED IN THE COLLECTION OF THE LATE EARL OF TANKERVILLE
- THE CONCHOLOGICAL ILLUSTRATIONS
- A CONCHOLOGICAL MANUAL
- ILLUSTRATED INDEX OF BRITISH SHELLS
- MARINE SHELLS OF SOUTH AFRICA
- POPULAR BRITISH CONCHOLOGY
- THESAURUS CONCHYLIORUM, OR FIGURES AND DESCRIPTIONS OF RECENT SHELLS

Sowerby, J *see*
- GROSSBRITTANIENS. MINERAL-CONCHOLOGIE
- THE SUPPLEMENT TO ENGLISH BOTANY

THE SOWETAN – Johannesburg, South Africa. 21 Jan 1981- – 84r – 1 – sa Microfile [072]
DIE SOWJETISCHE HISTORIOGRAPHIE ZUR GESCHICHTE DER INTERNATIONALEN SOZIALDEMOKRATIE ZWISCHEN DEM ERSTEN UND DEM ZWEITEN WELTKRIEG / Peter, Hartmut Ruediger – 1992 – 1mf – 9 – DM75.00 – 3-89349-608-4 – gw Hänsel [320]
SOWJETRUSSLAND IM BILD – (Cont by: Sichel und Hammer, 1922 n1; AIZ Arbeiter-Illustrierte Zeitung, 1924. Publ in Berlin until mar 5 1933, then in Prague as: VI – Die Volks-Illustrierte) – Berlin, 1921-aug 12 1936 – 1 – Inquire at Mikrofilmarchiv for details – gw Misc Inst [770]
SOWJETRUSSLAND IM BILD – (Title changes: Sichel und Hammer, 1922; Arbeiter-Illustrierte Zeitung (AIZ), 1924) – Berlin-Prag. Nov 1924-12 Aug 1936 – 8r – 1 – gw Mikrofilm [072]
SOWJETWISSENSCHAFT – 1948-1989 – 1,037mf – 1 – DM5,910.90 – gw Mikro Press [500]
SOY UN POBRE PEREGRINO... / Juez Nieto, Antonio – Badajoz: Tip. Clasica, 1947 – sp Bibl Santa Ana [946]
Soyka, Josef *see* DAS BUCH UM ANTON WILDGANS
DER SOZIAL-DEMOKRAT *see* VORWAERTS
DER SOZIALDEMOKRAT – Berlin, Feb 1894-95 – 2r – 1 – DM150.00 – gw Mikro Press [072]
DER SOZIALDEMOKRAT – Berlin. Germany. -d. 3 Jun 1946-31 Dec 1949. (9 reels) – 1 – uk British Libr Newspaper [072]

DER SOZIALDEMOKRAT – Berlin, Germany. Feb 1894-1895 – 2r – 1 – gw Mikrofilm [072]

DER SOZIALDEMOKRAT – Berlin, jan 6 1891-feb 28 1933 – 1 – Inquire at Mikrofilmarchiv for details – gw Misc Inst [320]

DER SOZIALDEMOKRAT – Berlin. June 3 1946-Dec 1948 – 1 – $35.00r – us Hoover Inst Photo [072]

DER SOZIALDEMOKRAT – Bremen, 1907-10 – 1r – 1 – Inquire at Mikrofilmarchiv for details – gw Misc Inst [320]

DER SOZIALDEMOKRAT / Deutsche sozialdemokratische Arbeiter-partei in der CSR – Prague, 1934-38 (incompl) – 1 – us Hoover Inst Photo [335]

DER SOZIALDEMOKRAT : ORGAN DER DEUTSCHEN SOZIALDEMOKRATIE – Zuerich. 1880-Sep 1890 – 4r – 1 – gw Mikrofilm [072]

DER SOZIALDEMOKRAT : ZENTRAL-ORGAN DER DEUTSCHEN SOZIALDEMOKRATIE – Zurich: A Herter, dec 5 1880; sep-oct 20, nov 10-dec 1881; jan 1-26, feb 16-may 18, jun 8-nov, dec 14-21 1882; jan-mar, apr 5,19-26, may-sep 20, oct 4-11,25, nov 1-15,29, dec 1883; jan-mar 20, apr 3-may 22, jun 5-jul 24, aug 7-sep, oct 2,16-30, nov-dec 1884; jan-aug, spe 3-10,24, oct-dec 1885; jan, feb 4-11,25, mar-jun, jul 1-15,29, aug-dec 1887; jan-jul 28, aug 11-dec 1888; jan-oct 26, nov 9-dec 1889; jan-sep 27 1890 – us Res Libr [072]

DER SOZIALDEMOKRAT – Zuerich, Sep 1880-90 – 3r – 1 – DM225.00 – gw Mikro Press [072]

DER SOZIALDEMOKRAT *see* SOZIALDEMOKRAT

SOZIALDEMOKRAT – (Cont: Der Sozialdemokrat, -mar 5 1948. Cont by: BS, mar 10 1950; BS, Berliner Sozialdemokrat, mar 11 1950; Berliner Stadtblatt, mar 24 1950; BS – Das Berliner Stadtblatt, apr 1 1950; Berliner Sozialdemokrat, jun 3 1950; Stadtblatt, may 3 1951; Berliner Stimme, oct 20 1951) – Berlin, may-aug 1948, 1950-apr 29 1951, oct 20 1951-67 – 12r – 1 – Inquire at Mikrofilmarchiv for details – gw Misc Inst [072]

SOZIALDEMOKRAT : INTERNATIONALES ORGAN DER SOZIALDEMOKRATIE DEUTSCHER ZUNGE – Zurich, 1879-90 – 1r – 1 – us Ross [335]

SOZIALDEMOKRAT – London. Halbmonatschrift der Sudentendeutschen Sozialdemokratie. Apr. 1940-June 1949. Missing: nos. 8, 10, 1940; nos. 65, 72-73, 1945 – 1 – 35.00r – us Hoover Inst Photo [073]

SOZIALDEMOKRAT – Prag, Czechoslovakia. 17 Feb 1926-8 Mar 1933 – 1 – gw Mikrofilm [072]

SOZIALDEMOKRAT – Prague, Czechoslovakia. Sept 1921-Oct 1928; 1929- 1 Oct 1938 (scattered issues) – 16r – 1 – us L of C Photodup [072]

DIE SOZIALDEMOKRATISCHE ARBEITERBEWEGUNG IM REICHSLAND ELSASS-LOTHRINGEN 1871-1918 : EIN BEITRAG ZUR GESCHICHTE EINES EUROPAEISCHEN GRENZLANDES / Soell, Hartmut Diethelm – Heidelberg, 1963 – 9 – DM98.00 – 3-89349-284-4 – gw Hänsel [320]

Sozialdemokratische Arbeiterpartei Deutschoesterreichs *see*
- PROTOKOLL DES PARTEITAGES
- VERHANDLUNGEN

Sozialdemokratische Arbeiter-partei OEsterreichs/RSOE/SPOE *see*
- ARBEITER-ZEITUNG

SOZIALDEMOKRATISCHE BIBLIOTHEK – Gottingen-Zurich. no. 1-32, 34. 1885-1890 – 1 – us NY Public [335]

SOZIALDEMOKRATISCHE FELDPOST – Berlin, Germany. 15 May 1916-15 Nov 1918 – 1r – 1 – gw Mikrofilm [072]

SOZIALDEMOKRATISCHE FELDPOST – Berlin, may 15 1916-nov 15 1918 – 1r – 1 – Inquire at Mikrofilmarchiv for details – gw Misc Inst [320]

Sozialdemokratische Partei *see* SOZIALDEMOKRATISCHE PARTEIKORRESPONDENZ

Sozialdemokratische Partei der Schweiz *see* BERNER TAGWACHT

Sozialdemokratische Partei Deutschlands *see*
- BAYERN-2. PARTEITAG
- BAYERN-3. PARTEITAG
- BAYERN-4. PARTEITAG
- BAYERN-7. PARTEITAG
- BAYERN-8. PARTEITAG
- BAYERN-13. PARTEITAG
- GESCHAEFTSBERICHTE DER BEZIRKE/ LANDESVERBAENDE
- JAHRBUECHER
- MITTEILUNGSBLAETTER DER BEZIRKE-LANDESVERBAENDE
- PARTEIKONFERENZ
- PARTEITAGE
- PREUSSEN-PARTEITAG
- PROTOKOL DES VEREINIGUNG SPARTEITAGES DER SOZIALDEMOKRATISCHEN PARTEI DEUTSCHLANDS (SPD) UND DER KOMMUNISTISCHEN PARTEI DEUTSCHALNDS (KPD) AM 21. UND 22, APRIL 1946 IN DER STAATSOPER "ADMIRALSPALAST" IN BERLIN
- PROTOKOLLE, BERICHTE..
- PROTOKOLLE PARTEITAGE, PARTEIAUSSCHUSS
- SACHSEN-LANDESVERSAMMLUNG
- SACHSEN-LANDESVERSAMMLUNGEN
- SACHSEN-PARTEITAG
- SPD-PRESSEMITTEILUNGEN DER BUNDESTAGSFRAKTION
- SPD-PRESSEMITTEILUNGEN DES VORSTANDS
- VORWAERTS

Sozialdemokratische Partei Deutschlands. Parteitag *see* PROTOKOLL UEBER DIE VERHANDLUNGEN DES PARTEITAGES

Sozialdemokratische Partei Deutschlands (Sopade) *see* MITTEILUNGEN DES PARTEIVORSTANDES

SOZIALDEMOKRATISCHE PARTEIKORRESPONDENZ – Berlin, jul 19 1906-feb 6 1933 – 5r – 1 – Inquire at Mikrofilmarchiv for details – gw Misc Inst [320]

SOZIALDEMOKRATISCHE PARTEIKORRESPONDENZ / Sozialdemokratische Partei – Berlin, Jul 1906-1933 – 5r – 1 – DM400.00 – gw Mikro Press [320]

DIE SOZIALDEMOKRATISCHE PARTEIPRESSE DER KONZENTRATION – Berlin, 1924-29 – 1 – Inquire at Mikrofilmarchiv for details – gw Misc Inst [072]

Der Sozialdemokratischer Verein. Duisburg, Germany *see* MITTEILUNGSBLATT DES SOZIALDEMOKRATISCHEN VEREINS DUISBURG

SOZIALDEMOKRATISCHES MAGAZIN *see* VORWAERTS

SOZIALDEMOKRATISCHES REICHSTAGSHANDBUCH / Schippel, Max – Berlin: Buchhandlung Vorwaerts, (1902). x,1174p – 1 – us U.W. Library [320]

DER SOZIALE KATHOLIZISMUS IN DEUTSCHLAND BIS ZUM TODE KETTELERS / Franz, Albert – Moenchen-Gladbach, 1914 – 259p – 9 – DM48.00 – 3-89349-213-5 – gw Hänsel [240]

SOZIALE ORDNUNG : CHRISTLICH-DEMOKRATISCHE BLAETTER DER ARBEIT – Koenigswinter, 1951-68 – 2r – 1 – DM220.00 – gw Mikro Press [072]

SOZIALE ORDNUNG : CHRISTLICH-DEMOKRATISCHE BLAETTER DER ARBEIT – Koenigswinter, Germany. May 1951-1969 – 2r – 1 – gw Mikrofilm [360]

SOZIALE POLARITAET IN GOETHES KLASSIK / Jockers, Ernst – (Includes bibliographical references) – Philadelphia: [s.n.], 1942 – 1r – 1 – us U.W. Library [430]

SOZIALE PRAXIS – Berlin, 1895 (incomplete) – 1 – Inquire at Mikrofilmarchiv for details – gw Misc Inst [072]

SOZIALE PRAXIS – Berlin, Germany. 1895 (incomplete) – 1 – gw Mikrofilm [072]

SOZIALE PROBLEME IM DRAMA DES STURMES UND DRANGES : EINE LITERARHISTORISCHE STUDIE / Stockmeyer, Clara – (Includes bibliographical references) – Frankfurt am Main: M Diesterweg, 1922 – 1mf – 1 – us U.W. Library [430]

DIE SOZIALE UND PRAKTISCHE WEISHEIT DER SPRUECHE SALOMOS: VORTRAG / Krafft, H – Elberfeld: Buchh. Evang. Gesell., 1900. 1 fiche – 9 – us A.T.L.A. [240]

DIE SOZIALE UND VOLKSWIRTHSCHAFTLICHE GESEZGEBUNG DES ALTEN TESTAMENTS / Kuebel, Franz Eberhard – Wiesbaden: Julius Niedner, 1870.1 fiche – 9 – us A.T.L.A. [240]

SOZIALE WELT – v. 1-2. Goettingen. 1949-51. Lacking: v. 1 (1) 1949. BH-1819 1 – 9 – ne IDC [300]

SOZIALISMUS UND INDIVIDUALISMUS IM ALTEN TESTAMENT / Loehr, Max – Giessen: Alfred Toepelmann, 1906. 1 fiche – 9 – us A.T.L.A. [240]

DER SOZIALIST : ORGAN DER UNABHAENGIGEN SOZIALISTEN – Berlin, Germany. Oct 1898-Mar 1899 – 1 – gw Mikrofilm [072]

DER SOZIALIST : ORGAN DER UNABHAENGIGEN SOZIALISTEN – Berlin, nov 15 1891-92, mar 18 1893, 1894, sep 28 1895, oct 1898-mar 1899, 1909-15, 1915-16 (incomplete), 1918-22 – 1 – Inquire at Mikrofilmarchiv for details – gw Misc Inst [320]

SOZIALIST – (Lacks 1 issue) – New York. v1-8. 1885-92 (all publ) – 2r – 1 – us Ross [335]

DIE SOZIALISTIN – Stuttgart, Germany. 1919-1920 – 1r – 1 – gw Mikrofilm [072]

DER SOZIALISTISCHE AKADEMIKER : INTERNATIONALE REVUE DES SOZIALISMUS – (Title change: Sozialistische Monatshefte, 1897) – Berlin, Germany. 1897-13 Jan 1933 – 1 – gw Mikrofilm [073]

SOZIALISTISCHE AKTION : ORGAN DER SOZIALDEMOKRATISCHEN PARTEI DEUTSCHLANDS – Karlsbad (Karlovy Vary), Czechoslovakia. 29 Oct 1933-Mar 1938 – 1r – 1 – gw Mikrofilm [072]

SOZIALISTISCHE ARBEITER-ZEITUNG : SAZ – Breslau, Berlin. oct 1 1931-feb 28 1933 – 1 – Inquire at Mikrofilmarchiv for details – gw Misc Inst [335]

SOZIALISTISCHE BILDUNG – (Die Buecherwarte. Zeitschrift fuer sozialistische Buchkritik. 1926-Feb 1933. Missing: Nov 1931, Aug 1932. Sozialistische Erziehung. Organ der Reichsarbeitsgemeinschaft der Kinderfreunde und der Arbeitsgemeinschaft sozialdemokratischer Lehrer und Lehrerinnen Deutschlands. 1929-Nov 1932. Missing: May, 1930; Jan and Jul 1931; Dec 1932) – Berlin. Mit den Beilagen Buecherwarte und sozialistische Erziehung. Jan 1929-Feb 1933. Missing: Sept 1932 – 1 – 35.00r – us Hoover Inst Photo [073]

SOZIALISTISCHE DEMOKRATIE – Berlin, sep 1957-72 – 8r – 1 – Inquire at Mikrofilmarchiv for details – gw Misc Inst [072]

SOZIALISTISCHE DEMOKRATIE – East Berlin, Germany. Sep 1957-1972 – 8r – 1 – gw Mikrofilm [072]

Sozialistische Einheitspartei Deutschlands *see*
- PROTOKOLL...DES ERSTEN KULTURTAGES..
- REFERENTEN-MATERIAL

Sozialistische Einheitspartei Deutschlands. Parteikonferenz *see* PROTOKOLL DER VERHANDLUNGEN DER..

Sozialistische Einheitspartei Deutschlands. Parteitag *see* PROTOKOLL DER VERHANDLUNGEN...

SOZIALISTISCHE HEFTE – Wien, Sozialistische Partei Oesterreichs. v1- , 1945- . illus – 1 – us U.W. Library [073]

DER SOZIALISTISCHE KAMPF – (Cont by: Der Kampf, Prag) – Paris, France. 2 Jun 1938-1 Jun 1940 – 1r – 1 – gw Mikrofilm [072]

DER SOZIALISTISCHE KAMPF *see* DER KAMPF

SOZIALISTISCHE MITTEILUNGEN : NEWS FOR GERMAN SOCIALISTS IN ENGLAND – London, England. Jan 1940-Sep, Oct 1948 – 1r – 1 – gw Mikrofilm [072]

SOZIALISTISCHE MONATSHEFTE – Berlin, 1897-1933 – 20r – 1 – DM2,200.00 – gw Mikro Press [073]

SOZIALISTISCHE MONATSHEFTE : INTERNATIONALE REVUE DES SOZIALISMUS – (Cont: Der sozialistische Akademiker, -1896) – Berlin, 1896-33 – 1 – Inquire at Mikrofilmarchiv for details – gw Misc Inst [335]

SOZIALISTISCHE MONATSHEFTE *see* DER SOZIALISTISCHE AKADEMIKER

SOZIALISTISCHE NACHRICHTEN : ORGAN DER DEUTSCHEN SOZIALDEMOKRATISCHEN ARBEITER-PARTEI IN DER TSCHECHOSLOWAKISCHEN REPUBLIK – London, England. 6 Nov 1940-Jul, Aug 1945 – 1r – 1 – gw Mikrofilm [072]

SOZIALISTISCHE POLITIK UND WIRTSCHAFT – Berlin. 1923-1928 – 1r – 1 – gw Mikrofilm [335]

SOZIALISTISCHE POLITIK UND WIRTSCHAFT – Berlin, 1923-28 – 1r – 1 – DM200.00 – gw Mikro Press [072]

SOZIALISTISCHE POLITIK UND WIRTSCHAFT – Berlin, 1923-28 – 1r – 1 – Inquire at Mikrofilmarchiv for details – gw Misc Inst [335]

SOZIALISTISCHE REPUBLIK – Koeln, Germany. 1919-22 Feb 1933 – 1 – gw Mikrofilm [072]

SOZIALISTISCHE REPUBLIK – (Mit beilagen) – Koeln, Jan 1919-Feb 1933 – 24r – 1 – DM1,800.00 – gw Mikro Press [072]

SOZIALISTISCHE WARTE – (Vorlaeufer: JSK-Mitteilungsblatt) – Paris, 1934-40 – 2r – 1 – DM160.00 – gw Mikro Press [072]

SOZIALISTISCHE WARTE *see* ISK – MITTEILUNGSBLATT DES INTERNATIONALEN SOZIALISTISCHEN KAMPFBUNDES

SOZIALIST-REVOLUTIONAR – Paris, 1927-32 – 1 – us Hoover Inst Photo [335]

SOZIAL-PADAGOGIK – v2-25, 1960-83 – 1 – us A.T.L.A. [073]

SOZIAL-PAEDAGOGIK – v2-34. 1960-92 (complete) – Inquire – 1 – ATLA S0384 – us A.T.L.A. [073]

SOZIALPOLITISCHE LOESUNGSKONZEPTE ZUR ABSICHERUNG DES RISIKOS DER PFLEGEBEDUERFTIGKEIT : EIN LAENDERVERGLEICH OESTERREICH-DEUTSCHLAND / Haege, Christine – 1995 – 2mf – 9 – DM80.00 – 3-8267-2109-8 – gw Hänsel [360]

SOZIALPSYCHIATRISCHE DIENSTE IN BADEN-WUERTTEMBERG : ENTSTEHUNGSDETERMINANTEN, IMPLEMENTATION, ANSPRUCH UND REALITAET / Pfeifer, Thomas – 1994 – 2mf – DM 80.00 – 3-8267-2037-7 – gw Hänsel [360]

SOZIALSTRATEGIEN DER DEUTSCHEN ARBEITSFRONT / ed by Hepp, Michael – (Teil A: Jahrbuecher des Arbeitswissenschaftlichen Instituts der Deutschen Arbeitsfront, 1936-1940/4. Reprint in 6 Baenden ca 5259 Seiten DM2,780.00 ISBN 3-598-31572-4 Teil B: Denkschriften, Gutachten und Veroeffentlichungen des Arbeitswissenschaftlichen Instituts der Deutschen Arbeitsfront. 498 silver fiche DM4,620.00 ISBN 3-598-31572-4) – 1936-40. 1987-89 – 9 – DM7,200.00 repr and silver fiche ed – 3-598-31570-8 – gw Saur [331]

SOZIALSTRUKTUR UND DISZIPLINARINDIVIDUUM : ZU JOHANN HEINRICH WICHERNS FUERSORGE- UND ERZIEHUNGSKONZEPTION DES RAUHEN HAUSES / Anhorn, Roland – 1995 (2. Aufl.) – 3mf – 9 – DM98.00 – 3-8267-2228-0 – gw Hänsel [370]

SOZIO-SEMANTISCHE BESONDERHEITEN HISTORIOGRAPHISCHER FACHTEXTE DES ENGLISCHEN / Baumann, Klaus-Dieter – 1992 – 9 – DM98.00 – 3-89349-518-5 – gw Hänsel [410]

Sozomen, Edward Walford *see* THE ECCLESIASTICAL HISTORY OF SOZOMEN

SP BUNTIG : A POLITICAL BIOGRAPHY / Roux, Edward – Cape Town: [E Roux] dist by the African Bookman, 1944 – us Res Libr [920]

Spaar, Dieter *see* ARCHIVES OF PHYTOPATHOLOGY AND PLANT PROTECTION

SPACE : A DEVELOPING ROLE FOR EUROPE, 18TH EUROPEAN SPACE SYMPOSIUM – (Suppl to v54, Science and Technology) – 1984 – 5mf – 9 – $20.00 – 0-87703-195-9 – us Univelt [629]

SPACE : ENHANCING TECHNOLOGICAL LEADERSHIP – (Suppl to v44, Advances) – 1981 – 2mf – 9 – $10.00 – 0-87703-164-9 – us Univelt [629]

SPACE AS A NATIONAL RESOURCE – 1969 – 5mf – 9 – $15.00 – 0-87703-231-9 – us Univelt [300]

SPACE BUSINESS OPPORTUNITIES FOR THE NEXT DECADE – 1991 – 11mf – 9 – $50.00 – 0-87703-331-5 – us Univelt [338]

SPACE BUSINESS OPPORTUNITIES-2 : SPACE SYSTEMS AND TECHNOLOGY INITIATIVES – (Suppl to v80, Advances) – 1992 – 7mf – $60.00 – 0-87703-362-5 – us Univelt [338]

SPACE COMMERCE / ed by Ryan, Mike – 9,5,1 – us Gordon [629]

SPACE EDUCATION – v1-. 1982- – 1,5,6,9 – us UMI [073]

SPACE EXPLOITATION AND UTILIZATION – (Suppl to v60 Advances in the Astronautical Sciences) – 1986 – 2mf – 9 – $10.00 – 0-87703-256-4 – us Univelt [620]

SPACE EXPLORATION, SPACE SCIENCE, AND APPLICATIONS – 1970 – 17mf – 9 – $25.00 – 0-87703-236-X – us Univelt [620]

SPACE FLIGHT MECHANICS SPECIALIST SYMPOSIUM – (Suppl to v11, Science and Technology) – 1968 – 9mf – 9 – $15.00 – 0-87703-221-1 – us Univelt [629]

SPACE FLIGHT MECHANICS SPECIALISTS SYMPOSIUM – (v11 1967, Science and Technology) – 9 – $60.00 – us Univelt [629]

SPACE LIFE SCIENCES – v1-4. Mar 1968-73 – 1 – us UMI [574]
SPACE MANUFACTURING – (v53 1983, Advances) – 1983 – 9 – $50.00 – us Univelt [629]
SPACE OPERATIONS FOR THE 80S AND 90S : 30TH NATIONAL AAS CONFERENCE – 1984 – 3mf – 9 – $12.00 – 0-87703-196-7 – us Univelt [629]
SPACE PROJECTIONS – 1969 – 28mf – 9 – $35.00 – 0-87703-228-9 – us Univelt [629]
SPACE RESCUE AND SAFETY 1974 – (v37 1975, Science and Technology) – 9 – $25.00 – us Univelt [629]
SPACE SCIENCE REVIEWS – (v37-. 1984-. 5,6,9) – v1-. Jun 1962- – 1 – us UMI [629]
SPACE SHUTTLE : DAWN OF AN ERA – (Suppl to v41, Advances) – 1980 – 2mf – 9 – $10.00 – 0-87703-136-3 – us Univelt [629]
SPACE SHUTTLE MISSIONS OF THE 80'S – (Suppl to v32, Advances) – 1976 – 65mf – 9 – $65.00 – 0-87703-133-9 – us Univelt [629]
SPACE SOLAR POWER REVIEW – v1- 1980- – 5,6,9 – us UMI [621]
SPACE TECHNOLOGY – 1,5,69 – us UMI [600]
SPACE TECHNOLOGY AND EARTH PROBLEMS – (Suppl to v23, Science and Technology) – 1970 – 15mf – 9 – $20.00 – 0-87703-134-7 – us Univelt [629]
SPACE WORLD – (1968- 5,6. 1970- 9) – v. 1- 1960- – 1 – us UMI [629]
SPACE WORLD *see* AD ASTRA
SPACECRAFT AND SPACE TECHNOLOGY – 1970 – 25mf – 9 – $30.00 – 0-87703-235-1 – us Univelt [629]
SPACEFLIGHT DYNAMICS 1993 – (With v84, Advances comprises proceedings of the AAS/GSFC International Symposium held Apr 26-30 1993, Greenbelt, Maryland) – 1mf – 9 – $10.00 – us Univelt [629]
SPACEFLIGHT MECHANICS 1991 – (Suppl to v75, Advances) – 1991 – 7mf – 9 – $50.00 – 0-87703-340-4 – us Univelt [629]
SPACEFLIGHT MECHANICS 1992 – (Suppl to v79, Advances) – 1992 – 5mf – 9 – $40.00 – 0-87703-359-5 – us Univelt [629]
SPACEFLIGHT MECHANICS 1993 – (Suppl to v82, Advances) – 1993 – 2mf – $15.00 – 0-87703-369-2 – us Univelt [629]
SPACEFLIGHT MECHANICS 1995 – (Suppl to v89, Advances) – 1995 – 3mf – $15.00 – 0-87703-402-8 – us Univelt [629]
SPACEFLIGHT MECHANICS 1996 – (Suppl to v93, Advances) – 1996 – 3mf – $10.00 – 0-87703-415-X – us Univelt [629]
SPACELAB, SPACE PLATFORMS AND THE FUTURE – (Suppl to v49, Advances) – 1982 – 1mf – 9 – $10.00 – 0-87703-181-9 – us Univelt [629]
Spach, E *see*
- HISTOIRE NATURELLE DES VEAGEA1TAUX
- ILLUSTRATIONES PLANTARUM ORIENTALIUM

SPADE AND WHIP, AND BUCKS WEEKLY TIMES. (PEOPLE'S COURIER) – Aylesbury, England. 28 Feb-20 Jun 1874.-w. 13 ft – 1 – uk British Libr Newspaper [072]
Spael, Wilhelm *see* PUBLIZISTIK UND JOURNALISTIK UND IHRE ERSCHEINUNGSFORMEN BEI JOSEPH GOERRES (1798-1814)
SPAETE HEIMKEHR / Grabenhorst, Georg – Muenchen: A Langen/G Mueller, 1942, c1938 – 1r – 1 – us U.W. Library [430]
SPAETE KRONE : GEDICHTE / Weinheber, Josef – Muenchen: A Langen/G Mueller, 1936 – 1r – 1 – us U.W. Library [810]
Spaeth, H *see* DIE ENTWICKLUNG JESU: VORTRAG
SPAETLESE ALTER UND NEUER ANEKDOTEN / Schaefer, Wilhelm – Muenchen: A Langen, G Mueller, 1942 – 1r – 1 – us U.W. Library [430]
SPAETSOMMER : EINE GESCHICHTE AUS WIEN / Moeller, Karl von – 3. Aufl. Muenchen: F Eher, 1943 – 1r – 1 – us U.W. Library [830]
SPAETZEITEN UND SPAETZEITLICHKEIT : VORTRAEGE, GEHALTEN AUF DEM 2. INTERNATIONALEN GERMANISTENKONGRESS / ed by Internationaler Germanisten-Kongress – (One of the contributions in English. Includes bibliographical references) – Bern: Francke Verlag, c1962 – 1 – us U.W. Library [430]
Spaey, Jacques et al *see* SCIENCE FOR DEVELOPMENT
Spafford, Amos *see* CLEVELAND, OHIO, TAXES, MS V.F. O

SPAGNA INDOMITA / Opiso, Papirio – Napoli, 1945. Fiche W 1089. (Blodgett Collection of Spanish Civil War Pamphlets) – 9 – us H.U. College Libr [946]
Spahr *see* EARLY LIFE AND TIMES IN BOONE COUNTY
SPAHR, JOHN D., PAPERS – (A daily diary of Spahr's service in the 50th Ohio Volunteer Infantry regiment in 1865 during the Civil War, and financial and pension documents relating to family life) – 1865-1915 – 1r – I – us Western Res [976]
Spahr, K *see* DAS LEBEN DES HL. ROBERT VON MOLESME
SPAIN : ANUARIO ESTADISTICO DE ESPANA 1858-1867, 1912-1934, 1943-1970 / Spain. Instituto Nacional de Estadistica – (1970 not available. Coll title: European Official Statistical Serials, 1841-1984) – 504mf – 9 – £2,654.00 – uk Chadwyck [946]
SPAIN / Burns, Emile – London, 1936. Fiche W 769. (Blodgett Collection of Spanish Civil War Pamphlets) – 9 – us H.U. College Libr [946]
SPAIN / Cadden, Joseph – New York, 1936. Fiche W 1500. (Blodgett Collection of Spanish Civil War Pamphlets) – 9 – us H.U. College Libr [946]
SPAIN / Friends of Spanish Democracy – NY, 1936. Fiche W 1170. (Blodgett Collection of Spanish Civil War Pamphlets) – 9 – us H.U. College Libr [946]
SPAIN / Souchy, Agustin – N.Y., 1937. Fiche W1166. (Blodgett Collection of Spanish Civil War Pamphlets) – 9 – us H.U. College Libr [946]
Spain *see*
- BOLETIN OFICIAL DEL ESTADO
- BOLETIN OFICIAL DEL ESTADO - GACETA DE MADRID
- BOLETIN OFICIEL DEL ESTADO
- COLECCION DE DOCUMENTOS INEDITOS PARA LA HISTORIA DE ESPANA
- GACETA DE MADRID

SPAIN 1938 / Trade Union and Labour Party Members' Delegation to Spain – Report. London, 1938. Fiche W1232. (Blodgett Collection of Spanish Civil War Pamphlets) – 9 – us H.U. College Libr [946]
SPAIN AGAINST THE INVADERS; NAPOLEON 1808 HITLER AND MUSSOLINI 1936 – London, 1938. Fiche W1191. (Blodgett Collection of Spanish Civil War Pamphlets) – 9 – us H.U. College Libr [946]
SPAIN AND BRITAIN / Lloyd George, David – London, 1937. Fiche W1002. New York, 1937. Fiche W1003. (Blodgett Collection of Spanish Civil War Pamphlets) – 9 – us H.U. College Libr [946]
SPAIN AND THE CHRISTIAN FRONT: UBI CRUX IBI PATRIA / Lunn, Arnold – N.Y., 1937? Fiche W1007. (Blodgett Collection of Spanish Civil War Pamphlets) – 9 – us H.U. College Libr [946]
SPAIN AND THE WEST COUNTRY. LONDON, 1935 / Fraser, J Alban – Madrid: Razon y Fe, 1936 – 1 – sp Bibl Santa Ana [946]
SPAIN AND THE WORLD / Gibernau, Jose – n.p. 193? Fiche W913. (Blodgett Collection of Spanish Civil War Pamphlets) – 9 – us H.U. College Libr [946]
SPAIN AND THE WORLD – London, England. Revolt. -f. 11 Dec 1936-23 Dec 1938; 11 Feb-3 June 1939. 5 ft – 1 – uk British Libr Newspaper [072]
SPAIN AND THE WORLD. THE INNOCENT VICTIMS OF FASCIST BESTIALITY NEED YOUR SOLIDARITY – London, 1937. Fiche W960. (Blodgett Collection of Spanish Civil War Pamphlets) – 9 – us H.U. College Libr [946]
SPAIN AND US – London, 1936. Fiche W1192. (Blodgett Collection of Spanish Civil War Pamphlets) – 9 – us H.U. College Libr [946]
SPAIN AT WAR; FACTS AND PHOTOGRAPHS – London, 1938. Fiche W1193. (Blodgett Collection of Spanish Civil War Pamphlets) – 9 – us H.U. College Libr [946]
SPAIN, BATTLEGROUND OF DEMOCRACY / Herring, Hubert Clinton – N.Y., 1937. Fiche W943. (Blodgett Collection of Spanish Civil War Pamphlets) – 9 – us H.U. College Libr [946]
Spain. Canary Islands. Comisaria del Plan de Desarrollo Economico y Social *see* CANARIAS ANEXO AL PLAN DE DESARROLLO ECONOMICO Y SOCIAL

Spain. Comisaria del Plan de Desarrollo Economico *see* PLAN DE DESARROLLO ECONOMICO Y SOCIAL. 1964-1967
Spain. Comisaria del Plan de Desarrollo Economico y Social *see*
- DEVELOPMENT PLANS. PRODUCTIVIDAD ANEXO A1 PLAN 1964-1967. D 1200/1. 1964
- OBRAS Y SERVICIOS DE LAS CORPORACIONES LOCALES, SANIDAD Y ASSISTENCIA ANEXO AL PLAN. 1964/67
- PRODUCTIVIDAD ANEXO AL PLAN. 1964/67
- PROYECTO DEL 2 PLAN DE DESARROLLO ECONOMICO Y SOCIAL Y ANEXO
- TRANSFORMACION EN REGIADOS ANEXO AL PLAN. 1964-1967

Spain. Comisaria del Plan de Desarrollo Economico y Social. Comercio Exterior *see* ANEXO AL PLAN DE DESARROLLO. 1964/67
Spain. Comisaria del Plan de Desarrollo Economico y Social. Turismo y Servicios de Informacion *see* ANEXOS AL PLAN
Spain. Congreso de los Diputados *see* DIARIO DES LAS SESIONES DEL CONGRESO DE LOS DIPUTADOS
Spain. Consejo de Hacienda *see* SENTENCIA DEL PLEITO
Spain. Cortes, 1836-1837 *see* DIARIO DE SESIONES DE LAS CORTES CONSTITUYENTES
Spain. Cortes Constituyentes, 1869-1871 *see* DIARIO DE SESIONES DE LAS CORTES CONSTITUYENTES
SPAIN DEFENDS DEMOCRACY / Workers Library Publishers. New York – New York, 1936. Fiche W1257. (Blodgett Collection of Spanish Civil War Pamphlets) – 9 – us H.U. College Libr [946]
Spain. Direccion general de Obras publicas *see* ITINERARIO DE RIO GUADIANA Y TODOS SUS AFLUENTES
Spain. Direction general de estadistica *see* CENSO DE LA POBLACION DE ESPANA
Spain. Embajada. Argentine Republic *see* BREVE INFORME DE LA ACTIVIDAD DE LA OFICINA DE PRENSA Y PROPAGANDA DE LA REPRESENTACION DE ESPANA EN LA ARGENTINA DESDE EL MES DE SEPTIEMBRE DE 1937 HASTA EL DE AGOSTO DE 1938
Spain. Embajada. Great Britain *see*
- CATHOLIC AND PROTESTANT PRIESTS, FREEMASONS AND LIBERALS SHOT BY THE REBELS
- ITALIAN PRISONERS IN SPAIN

Spain. Embajada. United States *see*
- ASSASSINATION OF CATHOLIC PRIESTS IN THE DIOCESE OF BARCELONA, SPAIN, UNDER THE SO-CALLED SPANISH REPUBLIC, NOW THE SPANISH REPUBLIC IN EXILE
- THE GOVERNMENT AND ITS CARE OF CHILDREN
- THE GREAT HISTORICAL PROCESS AGAINST FASCISM
- HOW THE PEASANT LIVED IN SPAIN
- IS THE FASCIST REBELLION IN SPAIN A POPULAR MOVEMENT?
- REPORT ON SPAIN, OCTOBER 1946
- THE SPANISH QUESTION BEFORE THE UNITED NATIONS: AN OUTRAGE OF THE INTERNATIONAL LAW

SPAIN FIGHTS FOR VICTORY / Rust, William – London, 1938. Fiche W1152. (Blodgett Collection of Spanish Civil War Pamphlets) – 9 – us H.U. College Libr [946]
SPAIN ILLUSTRATED; A YEAR'S DEFENCE OF DEMOCRACY – London, 1937. Fiche W1187. (Blodgett Collection of Spanish Civil War Pamphlets) – 9 – us H.U. College Libr [946]
SPAIN IN CHAINS / Gil-Robles y Quinones, Jose Maria – N.Y., 1937. Fiche W915. (Blodgett Collection of Spanish Civil War Pamphlets) – 9 – us H.U. College Libr [946]
SPAIN IN FLAMES / Echeverria, Frederico de – NY, 1936. Fiche W 851. (Blodgett Collection of Spanish Civil War Pamphlets) – 9 – us H.U. College Libr [946]
SPAIN IN TORMENT / Medical Bureau to Aid Spanish Democracy. New York – N.Y., 1937. Fiche W 1194. (Blodgett Collection of Spanish Civil War Pamphlets) – 9 – us H.U. College Libr [946]
Spain. Instituto Nacional de Estadistica *see* SPAIN

SPAIN IS FIGHTING FOR CIVILIZATION / Merry del Val, Alfonso – N.Y., 1936? Fiche W 1047. (Blodgett Collection of Spanish Civil War Pamphlets) – 9 – us H.U. College Libr [946]
SPAIN IS FIGHTING FOR YOU / American Society for Technical Aid to Spanish Democracy – New York, 193? Fiche W 1195. (Blodgett Collection of Spanish Civil War Pamphlets) – 9 – us H.U. College Libr [946]
Spain. Laws, Statutes, etc *see*
- COLECCION DE TODAS LAS LEYES
- DISPOSICIONES COMPLEMENTARIAS DE LAS LEYES DE INDIAS
- INSTRUCCION PARA LA VISITA
- EL MARQUES DE USTARIZ
- ORDEN CIRCULAR RELATIVA..

Spain. Ministerio de Agricultura *see*
- 7 DE OCTUBRE: UNA NUEVA ERA EN EL CAMPO
- PARA QUE EL CAMPESINO TENGA TIERRAS, TRABAJO, LIBERTAD Y BIENESTAR

Spain. Ministerio de Comunicaciones, Transportes y Obras Publicas *see* APROVECHAMIENTO MAXIMO DE LOS RECURSOS NATURALES EN BENEFICIO DEL PUEBLO
Spain. Ministerio de Defensa Nacional *see* UN EJERCITO POPULAR Y DEMOCRATICO AL SERVICIO DEL PUEBLO
Spain. Ministerio de Estado *see*
- DOCUMENTOS. LO QUE HAN VISTO EN MADRID LOS PARLAMENTARIOS INGLESES
- LUCHAR POR LA PAZ Y LA SOLIDARIDAD ENTRE TODOS LOS PUEBLOS

Spain. Ministerio de Gobernacion *see* ASEGURAR UN REGIMEN DE LIBERTAD Y DEMOCRACIA
Spain. Ministerio de Hacienda y Economia *see* UTILIZACION DE LA RIQUEZA NACIONAL EN BENEFICIO DE PUEBLO
Spain. Ministerio de Instruccion publica y bellas artes *see* L'EFFORT CULTUREL DU PEUPLE ESPAGNOL EN ARMES
Spain. Ministerio de Instruccion Publica y Sanidad *see* LA REPUBLICA ES LA CULTURA PAR TODOS
Spain. Ministerio de Justicia *see* POR UNA JUSTICIA POPULAR, HUMANA Y DEMOCRATICA
Spain. Ministerio de Propaganda *see*
- 30 CARICATURAS DE LA GUERRA
- IGLESIAS BOMBARDEADAS POR LOS REBELES
- LOS NINOS CON LA REPUBLICA Y CON LA REACCION
- EL TRIBUNAL SUPREMO

Spain. Ministerio de ultramar *see* PRESUPUESTO GENERAL DE GASTOS E INGRESOS DE LAS ISLAS FILIPINAS
Spain. Ministerio del Interior *see*
- DISCURSO DEL GENERALISIMO. NO CABE TRANSACCION IDEALOGICA
- ESCUDO DEL ESTADO ESPANOL
- MENSAJE DEL GOBIERNO A ESPANA

SPAIN, PAST AND FUTURE: AN ADDRESS TO THE COSMOS SOCIETY, OXFORD, ON 15 MAY 1945 / Azcarate y Florez, Pablo de – London, 1945. Fiche W 744. (Blodgett Collection of Spanish Civil War Pamphlets) – 9 – us H.U. College Libr [946]
Spain. Presidencia del Consejo de Ministros *see* DEFENDER LA INDEPENDENCIA DE LA PATRIA
Spain. Servicio Informativo Espanol *see* BOMBARDMENT OF THE BRITISH EMBASSY IN MADRID
Spain. Servicio Nacional de Prensa y Propaganda *see* LA LECCION DEL PASADO. ESPANA SALVA A EUROPA DEL COMUNISMO, BIOGRAFIAS
Spain. Subcomisariado de Propaganda *see* NORTEAMERICA Y LA GUERRA DE ESPANA: DOS DISCURSOS EN TORNO A LA ENTREGA DE UNA BANDERA DE LOS SOCIALISTAS NORTEAMERICANOS
SPAIN, THE BATTLEFIELD OF CAPITALISM / Horup, Ellen – n.p., 1937. Fiche W947. (Blodgett Collection of Spanish Civil War Pamphlets) – 9 – us H.U. College Libr [946]
SPAIN: THE ELECTIONS OF FEBRUARY 16, 1936 – London, 1937? Fiches W1172, 1173. (Blodgett Collection of Spanish Civil War Pamphlets) – 9 – us H.U. College Libr [946]

SPAIN; THE SPANISH WAR IN PICTURES; LATEST PHOTOS OF SPAIN'S FIGHT FOR DEMOCRACY – N.Y., 193? Fiche W1190. (Blodgett Collection of Spanish Civil War Pamphlets) – 9 – us H.U. College Libr [946]

SPAIN, THE UNPOPULAR FRONT / Lunn, Arnold – London, 1937. Fiche W1008. (Blodgett Collection of Spanish Civil War Pamphlets) – 9 – us H.U. College Libr [946]

Spain. Tribunal Supremo *see*
- JURISPRUDENCIA CIVIL
- JURISPRUDENCIA CRIMINAL

SPAIN UNDER FRANCO / Phillips, A V – London, 1940. Fiche W1107. (Blodgett Collection of Spanish Civil War Pamphlets) – 9 – us H.U. College Libr [946]

SPAIN'S CIVIL WAR NOW AN INTERNATIONAL STRUGGLE FOR INDEPENDENCE – Washington, DC, 193? Fiche W1184. (Blodgett Collection of Spanish Civil War Pamphlets) – 9 – us H.U. College Libr [946]

SPAIN'S DEMOCRACY TALKS TO AMERICA / Ward, Harry F – N.Y., 1936. Fiche W1251. (Blodgett Collection of Spanish Civil War Pamphlets) – 9 – us H.U. College Libr [946]

SPAIN'S FUTURE SPEECH MADE AT THE MAISON DE CHIMIE, PARIS, FEB 22, 1937 / Ossorio, Angel – n.p., 1937. Fiche W1092. (Blodgett Collection of Spanish Civil War Pamphlets) – 9 – us H.U. College Libr [946]

SPAIN'S OCTOBER / Blache, Robert – New York, 1935. Fiche W 756. (Blodgett Collection of Spanish Civil War Pamphlets) – 9 – us H.U. College Libr [946]

SPAIN'S STRUGGLE AGAINST ANARCHISM AND COMMUNISM / Diez, Genadius – NY, 1936? Fiche W 832. (Blodgett Collection of Spanish Civil War Pamphlets) – 9 – us H.U. College Libr [946]

SPAIN'S WAR OF INDEPENDENCE – President Azana, Premier Negrin, Defense Minister Prieto, Alvarez del Vayo, Martinez Barrio and Portela Valladares put the case of the Spanish Republic before the world. Washington, DC, 1937. Fiche W1196. (Blodgett Collection of Spanish Civil War Pamphlets) – 9 – us H.U. College Libr [946]

SPAIN'S WAR OF INDEPENDENCE – Washington, DC, 1938. Fiche W1197. (Blodgett Collection of Spanish Civil War Pamphlets) – 9 – us H.U. College Libr [946]

Spalding, Albert G *see* AMERICA'S NATIONAL GAME

Spalding, Benedict Joseph *see* BIBLE HISTORY

SPALDING DEMOCRAT – Spalding, NE. -w. May 1914-May 1917 – 1 – us NE Hist [071]

SPALDING ENTERPRISE – Spalding, NE. -w. Jan 1901; Mar 1901-Apr 1903; Jun 1903; Jun 1904; Jun 1905; Jan 1908-Jun 1909; Feb 1915-Dec 1921; Jan 1924 to date – 1 – us NE Hist [071]

SPALDING FREE PRESS ETC – (Also known as: Lincolnshire Free Press; Lincolnshire Boston and Spalding Free Press) – 1850; Jan 3-Dec 26 1871; Jan 2-Sep 30 1872; Jan 6-Dec 1 1874; 1876; Jan 9-Dec 25 1877; 1878-81; 1889; 1950; 1986-89; Jul 1990-Sep 24 1991; Oct 1991-96 – 40 1/4r – 9 – uk British Libr Newspaper [072]

Spalding, Hugh Mortimer *see*
- AN ENCYCLOPEDIA OF LAW AND FORMS
- THE JURISDICTION AND PRACTICE AT LARGE IN CITY JUDGES', MAYORS', AND JUSTICES' COURTS OF THE STATE OF INDIANA...2ND ED
- A MANUAL OF STATUTES AND FORMS, AND A COMMENTARY UPON THE RIGHTS, DUTIES AND POWERS OF EXECUTORS AND ADMINISTRATORS OF THE STATE OF KANSAS
- SPALDING'S TREATISE: THE PRACTICE AND FORMS IN JUSTICES' COURTS FOR THE STATE OF KANSAS...3RD ED

Spalding, J A *see* ILLUSTRATED POPULAR BIOGRAPHY OF CONNECTICUT

Spalding, J L *see*
- APHORISMS AND REFLECTIONS
- EDUCATION AND THE HIGHER LIFE
- RELIGION AND ART, AND OTHER ESSAYS
- SOCIALISM AND LABOR
- THINGS OF THE MIND

Spalding, Martin John *see* SKETCHES OF THE LIFE, TIMES, AND CHARACTER OF THE RT. REV. BENEDICT JOSEPH FLAGET, FIRST BISHOP OF LOUISVILLE

SPALDING OFFICIAL BASEBALL GUIDE – 1877-80; 1882-86; 1888-90; 1892-1903 – 3r – 1 – $150.00 – B70090 – us Library Micro [790]

Spalding, Susan E *see* AESTHETIC STANDARDS IN OLD TIME DANCING IN SOUTHWEST VIRGINIA

Spalding, Thomas W *see* AN ANALYSIS OF ASSOCIATION BETWEEN RESPIRATION RATE AND FINGER TEMPERATURE IN NORMALS AND RAYNAUD'S SUBJECTS GIVEN THERMAL BIOFEEDBACK

Spalding, William A *see* HISTORY AND REMINISCENCES OF LOS ANGELES CITY AND COUNTY

SPALDING'S OFFICIAL BASEBALL GUIDE – 1878-1900. New York. 1878-1900 – 1 – us NY Public [790]

SPALDING'S OFFICIAL BASEBALL GUIDE – New York, 1878-1900 – 1r – 1 – us Ross [790]

SPALDING'S TREATISE: THE PRACTICE AND FORMS IN JUSTICES' COURTS FOR THE STATE OF KANSAS...3RD ED / Spalding, Hugh Mortimer – Topeka, Crane, 1890. 832 (i.e. 843) p. LL-1295 – 1 – us L of C Photodup [340]

Spallanzani, Lazzaro *see*
- EXPERIENCES POUR SERVIR A L'HISTOIRE DE LA GENERATION DES ANIMAUX ET DES PLANTES AVEC UNE EBAUCHE DE L'HISTOIRE DES ETRES ORGANISES AVANT LEUR FECONDATION, PAR SENEBIER
- PRODROMO DI UN'OPERA DA IMPRIMIRSI SOPRA LE RIPRODUZIONI ANIMALI

Spallholz, Julian E *see* JOURNAL OF NUTRITIONAL IMMUNOLOGY

Spamer, Earle E *see*
- GEOLOGY OF THE GRAND CANYON

SPANDAUER VOLKSBLATT – (Cont by: Volksblatt Berlin, jan 23 1981) – Berlin, 1947-mar 31 1955 (incomplete), 1956- – 1 – Inquire at Mikrofilmarchiv for details – gw Misc Inst [072]

SPANDAUER VOLKSBLATT – (Title change: Volksblatt Berlin, 23 Jan 1981) – West Berlin, Germany. 1976-1991 – 1 – gw Mikrofilm [072]

SPANDAUER ZEITUNG *see* HAVELLAENDISCHES ECHO

Spandugino, T *see* I COMMENTARI...DELL' ORIGINE DE PRINCIPI TURCHI, ET DE' CONSTUMI DI QUELLA NATIONE

SPANGA NYHETER – Stockholm, Sweden. 1949-54 – 2r – 1 – sw Kungliga [072]

Spangenberg, Bradford *see* SELECTIONS FROM THE HOME DEPARTMENT ESTABLISHMENTS, JUDICIAL AND PUBLIC FILES, 1908, 1918-1926, 1931-1932

Spangenberg, Johann *see*
- QUAESTIONES MUSICAE IN USUM SCHOLAE NORTHUSIANAE, PER IOANN. SPANG. HERDESS. COLLECTAE...
- QUESTIONES MUSICAE IN USUM SCHOLAE NORTHUSIANAE

SPANIEN-UND PORTUGAL-INDEX : BILDDOKUMENTATION ZUR KUNST IN SPANIEN UND PORTUGAL / ed by Bildarchiv Foto Marburg – Deutsches Dokumentationszentrum fuer Kunstgeschichte Philipps-Universitaet Marburg – 1995 – 298mf (1:24) – silver DM7,800.00 – 3-598-33633-0 – gw Saur [700]

DIE SPANISCHE INQUISITION UND DIE ALUMBRADOS. BERLIN-BONN, 1934 / Carrillo de Albornoz, A & Llorca, Bernardino – Madrid: Razon y Fe, 1935 – 1 – sp Bibl Santa Ana [320]

DIE SPANISCHE POLITIK IM WESTSAHARA-KONFLIKT : DER WEG INS DESASTER / Brummet, Stephan DH – 1991 – 130p – 9 – DM98.00 – 3-89349-438-3 – gw Hänsel [320]

SPANISH ARCHIVES OF NEW MEXICO SERIES 2 / New Mexico. State Records Center and Archives – (Guide included) – 1621-1821 – 23r – 1 – $15.00r – us NM Archives [978]

THE SPANISH CHURCH AND POLITICS / Langdon-Davies, John – London, 1937. Fiche W987. New York, 1938: Fiche W988. (Blodgett Collection of Spanish Civil War Pamphlets) – 9 – us H.U. College Libr [946]

SPANISH CIVIL WAR / Great Britain. Foreign Office – International committee for the application of the agreement regarding non-intervention in Spain, 1936-1939. (FO 849) – 24r – 1 – us Ross [946]

THE SPANISH CIVIL WAR / Gunther, John – NY, 1938. Fiche W935. (Blodgett Collection of Spanish Civil War Pamphlets) – 9 – us H.U. College Libr [946]

THE SPANISH CIVIL WAR COLLECTION – 3000 rare pamphlets selected by the University of California, San Diego, University Library – 1 – us Primary [080]

SPANISH COLONIZATION IN THE SOUTHWEST / Blackmar, Frank W – 1890 – 1r – 1 – $50.00 – B40142 – us Library Micro [978]

Spanish Committee in Defense of Democracy *see*
- DATES AND EVENTS
- INFORMATION BULLETIN

THE SPANISH CONQUEST IN AMERICA AND ITS RELATION TO THE HISTORY OF SLAVERY AND TO THE GOVERNMENT OF COLONIES / Helps, Arthur – London. 4v. 1855-61 – 1r – 1 – us Ross [976]

SPANISH CONTACT VERNACULARS IN THE PHILIPPINE ISLANDS / Whinnom, Keith – [Hong Kong]: Hong Kong UP, 1956 – us Res Libr [440]

SPANISH DEMOCRACY AND ITS REFUGEES: A NARRATIVE OF PERSONAL EXPERIENCE / Reissig, Herman F – n.p., 1939. Fiche W1131. (Blodgett Collection of Spanish Civil War Pamphlets) – 9 – us H.U. College Libr [946]

SPANISH DRAMA – 23,234mf – 9 – $66,235.00 $1,280.00y – us OmniSys [440]

SPANISH DRAMA OF THE GOLDEN AGE – Collection of plays – 1 – us Primary [440]

Spanish Government of East Florida *see* RECORDS

THE SPANISH GRAMMAR / Corro, Antonio del – 1590. 145p. (English Linguistics Series 1500-1800) – 9 – us UMI [440]

Spanish Guinea. (Spain). Comisaria del Plan de Desarrollo Economico y Social Guinea Ecuatorial *see* ANEXO AL PLAN DE DESARROLLO ECONOMICO Y SOCIAL, ANOS 1964-1967

THE SPANISH GYPSY, A POEM / Eliot, George – Edinburgh: William Blackwood, 1868 – 1 roll – 1 – 1-55879-939-7 – uk Libr Preservation [810]

Spanish Information Bureau. New York *see*
- AMERICAN DEMOCRACY VS. THE SPANISH HIERARCHY
- THE CRIME OF GUERNICA
- FRANCO'S MEIN KAMPF; THE FASCIST STATE IN REBEL SPAIN

SPANISH INSTITUTIONS OF THE SOUTHWEST / Blackmar, Frank W – 1891 – 1r – 1 – $50.00 – B40143 – us Library Micro [978]

SPANISH LEGAL DOCUMENTS (15TH-19TH CENTURIES) / U.S. Library of Congress. Law Library – 2597 items on 36 reels. Briefs, canon law, notarial instruments, opinions and judgments, law and statutes, misc. Index cards on introd. reel – 1 – 23.00r – us L of C Photodup [340]

SPANISH LIBERALS SPEAK ON THE COUNTER-REVOLUTION IN SPAIN – San Francisco, 1937. Fiche W1201. (Blodgett Collection of Spanish Civil War Pamphlets) – 9 – us H.U. College Libr [946]

SPANISH MISSION CHURCHES OF NEW MEXICO / Prince, Le Baron Bradford – Cedar Rapids, Iowa: Torch Press, 1915 – 1mf – us A.T.L.A. [240]

THE SPANISH MISSION OF GIORG... / Tate Lanning, John – Madrid: Razon y Fe, 1941 – 1 – sp Bibl Santa Ana [240]

SPANISH MYSTICS : A SEQUEL TO "MANY VOICES" / Tollemache, Marguerite – London: K. Paul, Trench, 1886 – 1mf – us A.T.L.A. [240]

SPANISH NEWS – n.p., 193? Fiche W1202. (Blodgett Collection of Spanish Civil War Pamphlets) – 9 – us H.U. College Libr [946]

THE SPANISH NEWS DIGEST – N.Y., 1937-38. Fiche W1203. (Blodgett Collection of Spanish Civil War Pamphlets) – 9 – us H.U. College Libr [946]

SPANISH NEWS SERVICES – N.Y., 1937. Fiche W1264. (Blodgett Collection of Spanish Civil War Pamphlets) – 9 – us H.U. College Libr [946]

THE SPANISH PEOPLE ARE FIGHTING OUR BATTLE / Friends of Spain – London, 193? Fiche W 1205. (Blodgett Collection of Spanish Civil War Pamphlets) – 9 – us H.U. College Libr [946]

SPANISH PLAYS COLLECTION – (Index Reel. Guides and Author Index. 15.50; 1) – More than 8,000 dramatic works pub. in Spain in the 19th and 20th cent. Descriptive cards and guides included. 161 reels – 1 – 3035.00 – us L of C Photodup [820]

SPANISH POLITICAL AND ECONOMIC TRANSITION GROUPS, 1940S-1980S – (With printed guide) – 1992 – 88r – 1 – $7,480.00 – D3283 – us Scholarly Res [320]

SPANISH PROFESSORS AND ARTISTS IN THE EMIGRATION / Comite Tecnico de Ayuda a los Espanoles en Mexico – Mexico, 1940? Fiche W 1206. (Blodgett Collection of Spanish Civil War Pamphlets) – 9 – us H.U. College Libr [946]

SPANISH PROTESTANTS IN THE SIXTEENTH CENTURY / Wilkens, C A – London: W. Heinemann, 1897 – 1mf – us A.T.L.A. [240]

THE SPANISH QUESTION BEFORE THE UNITED NATIONS: AN OUTRAGE OF THE INTERNATIONAL LAW / Spain. Embajada. United States – Washington, DC, 1946. Fiches W1207, 1208. (Blodgett Collection of Spanish Civil War Pamphlets) – 9 – us H.U. College Libr [946]

SPANISH RARE BOOKS OF THE GOLDEN AGE – 1472-1700 – 1 – us Primary [440]

THE SPANISH REBELS IN THE FIELD: WHY GENERAL FRANCO TAKES NO PRISONERS – n.p., 1938? Fiche W1209. (Blodgett Collection of Spanish Civil War Pamphlets) – 9 – us H.U. College Libr [946]

THE SPANISH REFORMERS : THEIR MEMORIES AND DWELLING-PLACES / Stoughton, John – London: Religious Tract Society, [1883?] – 1mf – us A.T.L.A. [240]

Spanish Refugee Relief Campaign Program Bureau *see* THE PILOT; A MANUAL OF DIRECTIONS

SPANISH REVOLUTION / United Libertarian Organizations – 1-2, no. 12 (all publ). 1936-38 – 1 reel – 1 – $65.00 – us UPA [335]

SPANISH REVOLUTION / Workers' Party of Marxist Unification – 1-2, no. 9 (all publ). 1936-37 – 2mf – 9 – $35.00 – us UPA [335]

SPANISH SAHARA = SAHARA ESPANOL: ANUARIO ESTADISTICO 1948-1950 : ANUARIO ESTADISTICO 1948-1950 / Spanish Sahara. Secretario General – (Coll title: African Official Statistical Serials, 1867-1982) – 8mf – 9 – £67.00 – uk Chadwyck [960]

Spanish Sahara. Secretario General *see* SPANISH SAHARA

THE SPANISH SCHOOLE-MASTER / Stepney, William – 1591. 266p. (English Linguistics Series 1500-1800) – 9 – us UMI [440]

THE SPANISH STRUGGLE FOR JUSTICIE IN THEIR CONQUEST OF AMERICA... / Hanke, Lewis – Madrid: Missionalia Hispanica, 1950 – 1 – sp Bibl Santa Ana [946]

THE SPANISH WAR AND LYING PROPAGANDA / Code, Joseph Bernard – NY, 1938. Fiche W 805. (Blodgett Collection of Spanish Civil War Pamphlets) – 9 – us H.U. College Libr [946]

THE SPANISH WAR: FOREIGN WINGS OVER THE BASQUE COUNTRY – London, 1937. Fiche W1211. (Blodgett Collection of Spanish Civil War Pamphlets) – 9 – us H.U. College Libr [946]

Spanish West Florida *see* ARCHIVES

SPANISH WOMEN WRITERS / ed by Palmer, Maria del Carmen Simon – (Pt 1: 16th-17th Century £1,830.00. Pt 2: 19th Century £4,680.00) – 2 pts 2,077mf – 9 – £7,180.00 set – uk Chadwyck [440]

SPANISH-BASQUE POLITICAL PERIODICALS : NAPARTARRA, ABERI, LEL OBRERO VASCO, GUDARI, EUSKADI ROJAY ERI, EUZKO DEYA, ALKARTU, NACIO VASCA, EUZKADI SOCIALISTA – 1r – 1 – $50.00 – U603005 – us Library Micro [073]

SPANJE HELPEN IS WERKEN VOOR DE VREDE – Amsterdam, 1938. Fiche W1495. (Blodgett Collection of Spanish Civil War Pamphlets) – 9 – us H.U. College Libr [946]

SPANNUNG IN DER ERZAEHLUNG / Lawson, Marjorie Frances – (Includes bibliographical references and index) – Bonn a. Rh.: L Roehrschied, 1934 – 1r – 1 – us U.W. Library [400]

SPARE RIB – London. Jul 1972-. -m – 1 – us U.W. Library [073]

SPARE RIB *see* SEXUAL POLITICS IN BRITAIN

SPARK – (Includes c.1: v.1:no.2 1974:Apr.-v.1:no.3 (1974:June); v.1:no.5 1974:Sept) – [Boston, Mass.: Party for Workers Power], 1974- – 1 – CSUX89-S112 – us Hoover Inst Photo [331]
THE SPARK – 1935-39 – 1 – uk Microform Academic [073]
THE SPARK – Cape Town, South Africa.1 Mar 1935-30 Jun 1939. 1 reel – 1, 16 diazo available at reduced price – sa SA Libr [072]
THE SPARK – Ireland.7 Feb 1915-23 Apr 1916 – 1 – ie Microforms [072]
SPARK PLUG *see* AUTO WORKER/THE SPARK PLUG
SPARKS – v1-8 no 1. Nov 1975-Jan 1983 (complete) – 1r – 1 – ATLA S0453 – us A.T.L.A. [073]
Sparks, Colin *see* NEW COMMUNICATION TECHNOLOGIES
SPARKS DAILY TRIBUNE – Sparks, NV. 1910- – 103+ r – 1 – $5,150.00 ($275.00y) – UN04754 – us Library Micro [071]
SPARKS HEADLIGHT – Sparks, NV. 21 Jan 1905 – 1r – 1 – $50.00 – U04751 – us Library Micro [071]
SPARLING AND BOLDEN LETTER BOOK, 1788-99 – BRRAM – 1 – uk Microform Academic [025]
Sparmann, A *see*
- SVENSK ORNITHOLOGIE
- A VOYAGE TO THE CAPE OF GOOD HOPE, TOWARDS THE ANTARCTIC POLAR CIRCLE AND AROUND THE WORLD FROM THE YEAR 1772 TO 1776
- A VOYAGE TO THE CAPE OF GOOD HOPE, TOWARDS THE ANTARCTIC POLAR CIRCLE, AND ROUND THE WORLD...1772, TO 1776

Sparrow, George *see* A CONDENSED INDEX TO THE MINOR LIENS FILED IN THE OFFICE OF THE CLERK OF KINGS COUNTY, NY.
Sparrow-Simpson, William John *see* ROMAN CATHOLIC OPPOSITION TO PAPAL INFALLIBILITY
Sparshott, T H *see* A NIKA-ENGLISH DICTIONARY.
SPARTACUS – Pour la culture revolutionnaire et l'action de masse. no. 1-10. Paris. dec 1934-sept 1935 – 1 – fr A.C.R.P.P. [335]
SPARTAKUS / ed by Kommunistische Partei Deutschlands, Spartakusbund – [Berlin: Kommunistische Partei Deutschlands], 1919-. 9 nos – 1 – CSUX88-S390 – us Hoover Inst Photo [320]
SPARTAN DAILY / San Jose State College – San Jose. Calif. 1943-58 – 1 – us UMI [370]
THE SPARTAN DAILY – (Title varies: The Normal Times 1909-20 1r $50.00. The College Times 1921-22 1r $50.00. State Teachers College Times 1922-26 1r $50.00. State College Times 1926-34 2r $50.00.) – San Jose, CA: San Jose SU – 41+ r – 1 – $2,050.00 ($100.00y) – B02891 – us Library Micro [370]
SPARTANBURG COUNTY / Landrum, J BO – Atlanta, Franklin Printing and Publishing Co., 1900. South Carolina Reel 3. (The Cox Library Collection) – 5 – us Americana [978]
SPARTANBURG FIRST BAPTIST CHURCH. SPARTANBURG, SOUTH CAROLINA : CHURCH RECORD BOOK OF WOMAN'S MISSIONARY UNION – 1884-May 1888 – 1 – $5.00 – us Baptist [240]
SPARTENSBURG SENTINEL – Spartensburg, PA. -w 1903-12. 3 rolls – 13 – $25.00r – us I.M.R. [071]
SPASENIE : ECOLOGICAL JOURNAL – (Backfile through 1998 $85r) – 1999- – 1r per y – 1 – $80.00 standing order – us Ross [574]
Spasovich, V D *see* SOCHINENIIA
Spasskii, S *see* MAIAKOVSKII I EGO SPUTNIKI
Spataro, Giovanni *see*
- AD REVERENDISSIMUM IN CHRISTO PATREM ET D.D. ANTONIUM GALEAZ. DE BENTIVOLIS SEDIS APOSTOLICAE PROTHONOTARIUM B.M. JOHANNIS SPADARII IN MUSICA HUMILIMI...
- TRACTATO DI MUSICA DI GIOVANNI SPARTARO MVSICO BOLOGNESE NEL QVALE SI TRACTA DE LA PERFECTIONE DE LA SESQVALTERA PRODVCTA IN LA MVSICA MENSVRATA EXDERCITATE...

LES SPATULES ET LES LISSOIRS AU PALEOLITHIQUE SUPERIEUR / Baudoux, P – 9 – F50.00 – fr Ethnologie [930]
Spaulding, George W *see* A TREATISE ON THE PUBLIC LAND SYSTEM OF THE UNITED STATES
Spaulding, Henry George *see* LESSONS ON THE GOSPEL OF LUKE WITH A COMMENTARY
Spayth, Henry *see* THE AMERICAN DRAUGHT PLAYER
SPCA JOURNAL – Halifax, NS: Nova Scotia Society for the Prevention of Cruelty to Animals, [1879-18– or 19–] – 9 – cn C.I.H.M. [170]
DAS SPD-KONZEPT DER "SOZIALEN GRUNDSICHERUNG" UNTER BESONDERER BERUECKSICHTIGUNG IHRER AUSWIRKUNG AUF DIE ARBEITSLOSENVERSICHERUNG (ALS STRATEGIE GEGEN "NEUE ARMUT") / Bleses, Peter – 1994 – 2mf – DM80.00 – 3-8267-2017-2 – gw Hänsel [320]
SPD-PRESSEMITTEILUNGEN DER BUNDESFRAKTION – Bonn, Germany. 1954-60 – 1 – gw Mikrofilm [072]
SPD-PRESSEMITTEILUNGEN DER BUNDESTAGSFRAKTION / Sozialdemokratische Partei Deutschlands – Bonn, 1954-1960 – 1 – DM300.00 – gw Mikro Press [943]
SPD-PRESSEMITTEILUNGEN DES VORSTANDES – Bonn, Germany. 1958-69 – 1 – gw Mikrofilm [072]
SPD-PRESSEMITTEILUNGEN DES VORSTANDS / Sozialdemokratische Partei Deutschlands – (1964-1969 16mm DM240.00) – Bonn, 1958-1963 – 1 – DM280.00 – gw Mikro Press [943]
SPEAKER AND GAVEL – v1- 1963- 1; v13- 5,6,9 – us UMI [370]
THE SPEAKER OF THE HOUSE OF REPRESENTATIVES / Follett, M P – N.Y.: Longmans, Green & Co, 1904 – 5mf – 9 – $7.50 – LLMC 92-153 – us L.L.M.C. [323]
SPEAKERS' CORNER : AN ANTHOLOGY / ed by Huggon, Jim – 1977. 139p 1 fiche (29x) – 9 – $1.00f – at Libertarian Micro [320]
THE SPEAKERS OF THE HOUSE OF COMMONS FROM THE EARLIEST TIMES TO THE PRESENT DAY / Dasent, A I – H-919 2. 1911 – 8 – ne IDC [941]
SPEAKING AT SCIENTIFIC MEETINGS = ORGANISATION DU MESSAGE DANS LES EXPOSES SCIENTIFIQUES : ORGANISING THE MESSAGE / Tripathi, Bansh R – 1991 – 9 – $6.00 – 92-9053-218-1 – et ILRI [500]
SPEAKING AT SCIENTIFIC MEETINGS = TECHNIQUES DE PRESENTATION ORALE DES EXPOSES SCIENTIFIQUES : ORAL PRESENTATION TECHNIQUES / Tripathi, Bansh R – 1991 – 9 – $6.00 – 92-9053-227-0 – et ILRI [500]
SPEAR – Lagos, Nigeria. v2-5. 1964-67 – 2r – 1 – us Ross [073]
Spear, Charles *see* ESSAYS ON THE PUNISHMENT OF DEATH
Spear, Samuel Thayer *see*
- THE BIBLE IN PUBLIC SCHOOLS
- THE LAW OF THE FEDERAL JUDICIARY.
- RELIGION AND THE STATE

Spearman, H R *see* BRITISH BURMA GAZETTEER
SPEC (NEW CARLISLE, QUEBEC) / Committee for Anglophone Social Action – New Carlisle; Gaspe: CASA. v1- 1975-. SEM35P223 – 14r – 1 – Can$788.00 – cn Bibl Nat [073]
Specht, Karl August *see* THEOLOGIE UND WISSENSCHAFT, ODER, ALTE UND NEUE WELTANSCHAUUNG
Specht, Thomas *see* DIE LEHRE VON DER KIRCHE NACH DEM H. AUGUSTIN
Spechtshart, Hugo of Reutlingen *see* FLORES MUSICAE
SPECIAL / Montana. Forest and Conservation Experiment Station. Missoula – nos.1-3. 1963-68 – 1,5,6 – us Spaulding [630]
SPECIAL BULLETIN / Connecticut. Agricultural Experiment Station. Storrs – (Unnumbered). 1931-49 – 1,5,6 – us Spaulding [630]
SPECIAL BULLETIN / Wisconsin. Agricultural Experiment Station – 1896-Mar 1948; n.1-12, Apr 1948-Jun 1968 – 1,5 – us Spaulding [630]
SPECIAL BULLETIN UNNUMBERED / Massachusetts. Agricultural Experiment Station – 1889-1919 – 1,5,6 – us Spaulding [630]
SPECIAL BULLETINS / U.S. Department of Labor. Women's Bureau – ns: 1-20. 1940-44 – 9 – $5.00f – us Ross [331]
SPECIAL BULLETINS, SPECIAL PROGRAMS, MISC. MEETINGS / Niagara Falls. New York. La Salle Baptist Church – 1954-59 – 1 – $5.67 – us Baptist [240]
SPECIAL CARE IN DENTISTRY – (1985-. 5,6,9) – v1-. 1981- – 1 – us UMI [617]
SPECIAL CHILDREN – v. 1-. 1974- – 1,5,6,9 – us UMI [370]
SPECIAL CIRCULAR / Wisconsin. Agricultural Extension Service – 1918-1956 – 1,5 – us Spaulding [630]
SPECIAL CIRCULAR / Wisconsin. Agricultural Extension Service – 1948-71.no.1-151; Revisions 1949-71 – 1,5 – us Spaulding [630]
SPECIAL COLLECTION / Career Guidance Foundation – Education Directory of College and Universities, Fulbright Grants and Study Abroad, Occupational Outlook Handbook, Association of Independent Colleges and Schools – 15mf – 9 – $19.00 – us Career [370]
SPECIAL COLLECTION OF THE NATIONAL LIBRARY OF CHINA – 78mf – $200.00 – us I.A.S.W.R. [280]
SPECIAL EDUCATION: FORWARD TRENDS – v1- 1974- 1; v3- 5,6,9 – us UMI [370]
SPECIAL EDUCATION IN THAILAND / Thailand. Ministry of Education – Bangkok, 1982 – 1mf – 9 – DE-301/1 – ne IDC [370]
SPECIAL EDUCATIONAL NEEDS ABSTRACTS – 1989- 5v – 9 – £197.00 – 0954-0822 – uk Carfax [370]
SPECIAL EXTENSION CIRCULAR / South Dakota. Agricultural Extension Service. State College of Agriculture and Mechanic Arts – nos.1-52. 1928-48 – 1,5,6 – us Spaulding [630]
"SPECIAL FILES" OF HEADQUARTERS, DIVISION OF THE MISSOURI, RELATING TO MILITARY OPERATIONS AND ADMINISTRATION, 1863-1885 – 16r – 1 – M1495 – us Nat'l Archives [355]
SPECIAL FILES OF THE OFFICE OF INDIAN AFFAIRS / U.S. Bureau of Indian Affairs – 1807-1904. 85 rolls. M574 – 1 – us Nat'l Archives [324]
SPECIAL FILES OF THE OFFICE OF INDIAN AFFAIRS, 1807-1904 / U.S. Bureau of Indian Affairs – 85 rolls. M574. Printed guide – 1 – us Nat'l Archives [324]
SPECIAL FOLDERS / Kentucky. Agricultural Extension Service – v. 1-52. 1964-69 – 1,5,6 – us Spaulding [630]
SPECIAL INDEX TO NUMBERED RECORDS IN THE WAR DEPARTMENT COLLECTION OF REVOLUTIONARY WAR RECORDS / U.S. War Department. Collection of Revolutionary War Records – 1775-83. 39 rolls. M847 – 1 – us Nat'l Archives [324]
SPECIAL ISSUE / Indonesia. Kementerian Penerangan – Incomplete. SE-373 1. 1958-1965 – 9 – ne IDC [320]
SPECIAL ISSUE; REFERENCE EDITION / Indonesia. Departemen Penerangan – Incomplete. SE-540 1. 1963-1964 – 9 – ne IDC [324]
SPECIAL ISSUES OF BAPTISTS, 1914-30 – Misc. reel of articles from books, periodicals and annuals, 1914-1930's. 350p – 1 – us Baptist [240]
THE SPECIAL LAW GOVERNING PUBLIC SERVICE CORPORATIONS. / Wyman, Bruce – New York, Baker, Voorhis, 1911. 2 v. LL-966 – 1 – us L of C Photodup [340]
SPECIAL LEAFLET / Alabama. Agricultural Experiment Station – 1935-56 – 1,5,6 – us Spaulding [630]
SPECIAL LEGISLATION FOR WOMEN / Johnsen, Julia Emily – New York, Wilson Co., 1926. 142 p. LL-1422 – 1 – us L of C Photodup [340]
SPECIAL LIBRARIES – v1- 1910- 1; v57- 5,6; v66- 9 – us UMI [020]
Special Libraries Association. Business and Finance Division *see* NEWSLETTER
SPECIAL MARKET STUDY. RELEASE NUMBER 1-41, DEC. 19, 1961-NOV. 8, 1963 / U.S. Securities and Exchange Commission – 9 – us UMI [336]
SPECIAL MARKET STUDY RELEASES – nos1-41. 19 Dec 1961-8 Nov 1963 (all publ) – 2mf – 9 – $3.00 – LLMC 89-006 – us L.L.M.C. [340]
SPECIAL NEEDS IN THE CLASSROOM : A TEACHER EDUCATION GUIDE – 1994 – 225p – 9 – 92-3-102934-7 – fr UNESCO [370]
SPECIAL NOTE. PRO MUNDI VITA – v.1-43. 1968-75 – 1 – us UMI [073]
SPECIAL NUMBER OF THE DOMINION ILLUSTRATED DEVOTED TO TORONTO, THE COMMERCIAL METROPOLIS OF ONTARIO – Montreal: Sabiston, 1892. 02733. (Pre-1900 Canadiana) – 9 – cn C.I.H.M. [971]
SPECIAL PAPERS, 1850-1888 / Boyce, James Petigru – (Account of administration of his father's estate). 344p – 1 – 12.04 – us Baptist [920]
SPECIAL PUBLICATION / Illinois. College of Agriculture – n.1-16. 1960-69 – 1,5 – us Spaulding [630]
SPECIAL PUBLICATION / University of Georgia. Agricultural Experiment Station – No.1-21.1974-82. 10 fiches – 9 – us Spaulding [630]
SPECIAL READINGS IN CONSERVATION – 1980 – 112p – it F.A.O. [550]
SPECIAL RELEASE ON CURRENT INDONESIAN AFFAIRS / Indonesia. Kementerian Penerangan – SE-374 1. 1957-1961. Lacking: 1960 – 9 – ne IDC [324]
SPECIAL REPORT / American Indian Press Association – (American Indian Periodicals in the Princeton University Library). 1 fiche – 9 – $45.00 – us UPA [305]
SPECIAL REPORT / Georgia. University. Department of Agriculture Economics – 1963-65 – 1,5 – us Spaulding [630]
SPECIAL REPORT / Iowa State University. Iowa Agriculture and Home Economics Experiment Station – No.1-86.1936-80 – 1,5 – us Spaulding [630]
SPECIAL REPORT / Minnesota. Agricultural Extension Service – nos.1-35. 1961-70 – 1,5,6 – us Spaulding [630]
SPECIAL REPORT / Nebraska. Agricultural Experiment Station. Lincoln – n.1-11. 1952-63 – 1,5 – us Spaulding [630]
SPECIAL REPORT / New Mexico State University. Agricultural Experiment Station – No.1-46.1971-82 – 1,5 – us Spaulding [630]
SPECIAL REPORT / South Dakota. Agricultural Extension Service. Cooperative Extension Service – nos.1-5. 1960-66 – 1,5,6 – us Spaulding [630]
SPECIAL REPORT. / Canada. Commissioners to Revise the Public General Statutes – Ottawa: Acland, 1928. 159p. LL-2328 – 1 – us L of C Photodup [340]
SPECIAL REPORT... EDUCATIONAL EXHIBITS AND CONVENTIONS AT THE WORLD'S INDUSTRIAL AND COTTON CENTENNIAL EXPOSITION, NEW ORLEANS, 1884-85 / U.S. Bureau of Education – Washington: GPO, 1886. 3v in 1.illus – 1 – us U.W. Library [370]
SPECIAL REPORT: ENTOMOLOGY / Virginia. Agricultural Experiment Station. Blacksburg – Dec 1937. 1 fiche – 9 – us Spaulding [630]
SPECIAL REPORT OCTOBER 1965 – JUNE 1976 / Hong Kong. University and Politechnic Grants Committee – Hong Kong, 1976 – 2mf – 9 – DE-185/1 – ne IDC [370]
SPECIAL REPORT OF THE MEASURES WHICH HAVE BEEN ADOPTED FOR THE ESTABLISHMENT OF A NORMAL SCHOOL / Canada. Departement de l'instruction publique pour le Haut-Canada – Montreal: Printed by Lovell and Gibson, 1847. SEM105P336 – 1mf – 9 – Can$2.25 – cn Bibl Nat [370]
SPECIAL REPORT ON THE SEPARATE SCHOOL PROVISIONS OF THE SCHOOL LAW OF UPPER CANADA / Canada. Departement de l'instruction publique pour le Haut-Canada – Toronto: Printed by John Lovell, 1858. SEM105P326 – 1mf – 9 – Can$2.25 – cn Bibl Nat [370]
SPECIAL REPORTS / University of Missouri. Agricultural Experiment Station – No.1-311. 1961-83 – 1,5 – us Spaulding [630]
SPECIAL RIVER BULLETIN / Colorado. Agricultural Experiment Station. Fort Collins – 1900-02 – 1,5,6 – us Spaulding [630]
SPECIAL RULES FOR THE CONDUCT AND GUIDANCE OF THE PERSONS ACTING IN THE MANAGEMENT AND OF ALL PERSONS EMPLOYED IN...THE ALBION MINES / Albion Mines. Nova Scotia – Halifax: Morning Herald Office, 1880. 06148. (Pre-1900 Canadiana) – 9 – cn C.I.H.M. [622]
SPECIAL SCIENTIFIC REPORTS FISHERIES / U.S. National Oceanic and Atmospheric Administration – Early part v1-67; later part v1-775. 1949-83. 1043 fiches – 9 – 1300.00 – us Updata [324]
SPECIAL SEED BULLETIN / North Dakota. Agricultural Experiment Station. Fargo – nos.1-2. 1909, 1913 – apply; – us Spaulding [631]

SPECIAL SERIES / South Dakota. Agricultural Extension Service. Cooperative Extension Service – nos.1-19B. 1970-74 – 1,5,6 – us Spaulding [630]

SPECIAL SERVICES IN THE SCHOOLS / ed by Maher, Charles A – v3- 1986- – 1, 9 ($135.00 in US $189.00 outside hardcopy subsc) – us Haworth [370]

Special Staff Office of the Japanese Army *see* CHOHATSU BUKKEN ICHIRANHYO

A SPECIAL STUDY OF ADMINISTRATION OF ELEMENTARY EDUCATION IN RELATION TO THE PROGRAMME OF UNIVERSALISATION IN ORISSA : REPORT / India. Orissa. National Institute of Educational Planning and Administration – New Delhi, 1979 – 4mf – 9 – DE-552/1 – ne IDC [370]

SPECIAL SUBJECT STUDIES REPORTS / National Science Council. Taiwan – Over 1200 titles – 1584mf – 9 – $1350.00 – ch Transmission [500]

Specialis, Nicolaus *see* DE GESTIS SICULORUM SUB FREDERICO 2 REGE

SPECIALIST SERVICE BULLETIN / New Mexico State University. Cooperative Extension Service – Series 400. 1970-82. Series 400 A-Z – 1,5 – us Spaulding [630]

SPECIALIZED LEADERSHIP TRAINING IN THE TENNESSEE TECH BAPTIST STUDENT UNION EXECUTIVE COUNCIL / Haskins, Dan D – 1981 – 1 – 5.00 – us Baptist [240]

SPECIALIZED TRANSPORTATION PLANNING AND PRACTICE – 1982- – 1,5,9 – us Gordon [620]

SPECIES ALGARUM / Kuetzing, F T – Lipsiae. 1849. B-643 2 – 8 – ne IDC [580]

SPECIES ALGARUM...GRYPHISWALDIAE / Agardh, C A – 1823-28. 2v. B-5271 2 – 8 – ne IDC [580]

SPECIES ASTRAGALORUM DESCRIPTAE ET ICONIBUS COLORATIS ILLUSTRATAE / Pallas, Peter Simon – Leipzig. 1800-03. B-5630 2 – 8 – ne IDC [580]

SPECIES ET ICONOGRAPHIE GENERIQUE DES ANIMAUX ARTICULES / Guerin-Meneville, Felix Edouard – Paris, 1843-49. Pt.1. Z/1319/2 – 8 – ne IDC [590]

SPECIES FILICUM / Hooker, W J – 5v. London. 1846-64. B-5209 2 – 8 – ne IDC [580]

SPECIES, GENERA ET ORDINES ALGARUM / Agardh, J G – 3v. Lundae. 1848-80. B-452 2 – 8 – ne IDC [580]

SPECIES GENERAL DES COLEOPTERES DE LA COLLECTION DE M. LE COMTE DEJEAN / Dejean, PF M A – Paris, 1825-31. 5v. Z-1179/2 – 8 – ne IDC [590]

SPECIES GRAMINUM ICONIBUS ET DESCRIPTIONIBUS ILLUSTRAVIT / Trinius, Carl Bernhard – Petropoli. 3v. 1823- 1828-36 – 37mf – 9 – ne IDC [580]

SPECIES HEPATHICARUM / Lindenberg, J B W & Gottsche, C M – 11 fasc. Bonnae. 1839-51. B-5192 2 – 8 – ne IDC [580]

SPECIES HEPATICARUM / Stephani, F – Geneva, 1900-1925. v. 1-6. B-75 2 – 8 – ne IDC [580]

SPECIES MUSCORUM FRONDOSORUM / Hedwig, J – Suppl. 1-4. Lipsiae. 1801, 1842. B-5022 2 – 8 – ne IDC [580]

SPECIES PLANTARUM / Linnaeus, Carl – 1764 – 2r £70.00 34mf £119.00 – 1,7 – uk Microform Academic [580]

SPECIES PLANTARUM / Linnaeus, Carl – 2v. ed. 2. Holmiae. 1762-63. B-175 2 – 8 – ne IDC [580]

SPECIES PLANTARUM / Linnaeus, Carl – 2v. Holmiae. 1753. B-181 2 – 8 – ne IDC [580]

SPECIES PLANTARUM: CURANTE C. L. WILLDENOW / Linnaeus, Carl – 6v. ed 5. Berolini. 1797-1830. B-403 2 – 8 – ne IDC [580]

SPECIES PLANTARUM: CUSANTE C. L. WILLDENOW / Linnaeus, Carl – 1810 – 10mf – 7 – uk Microform Academic [580]

SPECIES UMBELLIFERARUM MINUS COGNITAE, ILLUSTRATE / Sprengel, K P J – Halae. 1818. B-7138 1 – 9 – ne IDC [580]

SPECIFICATION FOR IDENTITY AND PURITY OF FOOD ADDITIVES : ANTICAKING AGENTS, BUFFERING AGENTS, SALTS, EMULSIFIERS, ENZYMES, EXTRACTION SOLVENTS, FLAVOURING AGENTS AND MISCELLANEOUS FOOD ADDITIVES. F.A.O./ WHO, ROME, 1984 – 1985 – 148p – it F.A.O. [660]

SPECIFICATIONS FOR IDENTITY AND PURITY OF BUFFERING AGENTS, SALTS, EMULSIFIERS, THICKENING AGENTS, STABILIZERS, FLAVOURING AGENTS, EXTRACTION SOLVENTS, SWEETENING AGENTS AND MISCELLANEOUS FOOD ADDITIVES – 1983 – 159p – it F.A.O. [660]

SPECIFICATIONS FOR IDENTITY AND PURITY OF BUFFERING AGENTS, SALTS, EMULSIFIERS, THICKENING AGENTS, STABILIZERS, FLAVOURING AGENTS, FOOD COLOURS, SWEETENING AGENTS AND MISCELLANEOUS FOOD ADDITIVES – 1982 – 242p – it F.A.O. [660]

SPECIFICATIONS FOR IDENTITY AND PURITY OF CARRIER SOLVENTS, EMULSIFIERS AND STABILIZERS ENZYME PREPARATIONS, FLAVOURING AGENTS, FOOD COLOURS, SWEETENING AGENTS AND OTHER FOOD ADDITIVES – 1981 – 265p – it F.A.O. [660]

SPECIFICATIONS FOR IDENTITY AND PURITY OF CERTAIN FOOD ADDITIVES : ANTIOXIDANTS, ENZYME PREPARATIONS, FLAVOURING AGENTS, FLAVOUR ENHANCERS, FOOD COLOURS, SWEETENING AGENTS, THICKENING AGENTS, MISCELLANEOUS FOOD ADDITIVES; 31ST AND 33RD SESSIONS OF JECFA, GENEVA 1987 AND 1988 – 1988 – 323p – it F.A.O. [660]

SPECIFICATIONS FOR IDENTITY AND PURITY OF CERTAIN FOOD ADDITIVES : ANTIOXIDANTS, FLAVOURING AGENTS, FOOD ACIDS AND SALTS, FOOD COLOURS, SWEETENERS, THICKENERS AND MISCELLANEOUS FOOD ADDITIVES. F.A.O./WHO, ROME, 1986 – 1986 – 172p – it F.A.O. [660]

SPECIFICATIONS FOR IDENTITY AND PURITY OF CERTAIN FOOD ADDITIVES : ENZYME PREPARATIONS AND IMMOBILIZING AGENTS, FLAVOURING AGENTS, FLOUR TREATMENT AGENTS, FOOD ACIDS AND SALTS, FOOD COLOURS, SWEETENERS, THICKENERS AND MISCELLANEOUS FOOD ADDITIVES. F.A.O./ WHO, GENEVA, 1985 – 1986 – 253p – it F.A.O. [660]

SPECIFICATIONS FOR IDENTITY AND PURITY OF CERTAIN FOOD ADDITIVES; EMULSIFIERS, ENZYME PREPARATIONS, FLAVOURING AGENTS, FOOD COLOURS, THICKENING AGENTS, MISCELLANEOUS FOOD ADDITIVES : 35TH SESSION OF JECFA, ROME 1989 – 1990 – 95p – it F.A.O. [660]

SPECIFICATIONS FOR IDENTITY AND PURITY OF FOOD COLOURS ENZYME PREPARATIONS AND OTHER FOOD ADDITIVES – 1978 – 98p – it F.A.O. [660]

SPECIFICATIONS FOR IDENTITY AND PURITY OF FOOD COLOURS, F.A.O./WHO, ROME, 1984 – 1984 – 207p – it F.A.O. [660]

SPECIFICATIONS FOR IDENTITY AND PURITY OF FOOD COLOURS, FLAVOURING AGENTS AND OTHER FOOD ADDITIVES : AS PREPARED BY THE 23RD SESSION OF THE JOINT F.A.O./W.H.O. EXPERT COMMITTEE ON FOOD ADDITIVES, GENEVA, 1979 – 1979 – 155p – it F.A.O. [660]

SPECIFICATIONS FOR IDENTITY AND PURITY OF THICKENING AGENTS, ANTICAKING AGENTS, ANTIMICROBIALS, ANTIOXIDANTS AND EMULSIFIERS : JOINT F.A.O./W.H.O. EXPERT COMMITTEE ON FOOD ADDITIVES – 1978 – 331p – it F.A.O. [660]

SPECIFICATIONS FOR IDENTITY AND PURTIY OF SWEETENING AGENTS, EMULSIFYING AGENTS, FLAVOURING AGENTS AND OTHER FOOD ADDITIVES – 1980 – 180p – it F.A.O. [660]

SPECIFICITY AND DYNAMICS OF AFRICAN NEGRO CULTURES – 1986 – 184p – 9 – 92-3-102317-9 – fr UNESCO [306]

SPECIFYING ENGINEER – (5,6,9 1985-) – v34- 1975- – 1 – us UMI [629]

SPECIFYING ENGINEER *see* ACTUAL SPECIFYING ENGINEER

SPECIMEN BOTANICUM / Blackstone, J – Londini. 1746. B-6453 2 – 8 – ne IDC [580]

SPECIMEN BOTANICUM DE GERANIIS / Burman, N L B – Lugduni Batavorum. 1759. B-5868 2 – 8 – ne IDC [580]

SPECIMEN BOTANICUM SISTENS DESCRIPTIONES ET ICONES / L'Heritier de Brutelle, C L Cornus – Parisiis, 1788; 1789 – 8 – B-6019 2 – ne IDC [580]

SPECIMEN DE PHOTO-GRAVURE DE L'IMPRIMERIE C. DARVEAU / Darveau, C – Quebec: Imp. Darveau, 1895. SEM105P341 – 1mf – 9 – Can$2.25 – cn Bibl Nat [760]

SPECIMEN HISTORIA PLANTARUM / Renealmus, P – Parisiis. 1611. B-7331 2 – 8 – ne IDC [580]

SPECIMEN INSECTORUM ULTERIORIS CALABRIAE / Petagna, V – Francofurti, Moguntiae, 1787. vi,46p. 1 pl. Z-1543- – 8 – ne IDC [590]

SPECIMEN JURIDICUM INAUGURALE DE JURE POSTLIMINII / Cock, C – Leiden, 1778 – 1mf – 1 – ILM-666/1 – ne IDC [327]

SPECIMEN MEDICINAE SINICAE,... / Boym, M P – Francofurti, 1682 – 3mf – 9 – ne IDC [610]

SPECIMEN OF A LICHENOGRAPHIA BRITANNICA / Turner, D & Borrier, W – or An attempt at a history of the British Lichens. Yarmouth. 1839. B-5460 2 – 8 – ne IDC [580]

A SPECIMEN OF PREACHING, AS PRACTISED AMONGST THE PEOPLE CALLED METHODISTS / Helme, J – London, 1762 – 1mf – 9 – MP-418/1 – ne IDC [240]

A SPECIMEN OF THE BOTANY OF NEW HOLLAND / Smith, J E – 485. 1793 – 9 – ne IDC [580]

SPECIMEN OF WELCH PREACHING – 1 – 5.00 – us Baptist [240]

SPECIMENS OF CUSTOM WORK / Journal Company Print. Lawrence, Kansas – 1859-61 – 1 – us KS Hist [070]

SPECIMENS OF DIALECTS : SHORT VOCABULARIES OF LANGUAGES, AND NOTES OF COUNTRIES AND CUSTOMS IN AFRICA / Clarke, John – Berwick-upon-Tweed: Cameron, 1848 – us Res Libr [470]

SPECIMENS OF ENGLISH DRAMATIC POETS, WHO LIVED ABOUT THE TIME OF SHAKESPEARE : WITH NOTES / Lamb, Charles – London: Printed for Longman, Hurst, Rees, and Orme, 1808 – 1 roll – 1 – 1-55879-656-8 – uk Libr Preservation [810]

SPECIMENS OF POPULAR POETRY OF PERSIA / Kuroghlu – 1842 – 1 – uk Microform Academic [810]

SPECIMENS OF THE BRITISH POETS : WITH BIOGRAPHICAL AND CRITICAL NOTICES, AND AN ESSAY ON ENGLISH POETRY / Campbell, Thomas – London: J. Murray, 1845 – 1 roll – 1 – 1-55879-644-4 – uk Libr Preservation [810]

SPECIMENS OF THE TABLE TALK OF THE LATE SAMUEL TAYLOR COLERIDGE / Coleridge, Samuel Taylor – London: J. Murray, 1835 – 1 roll – 1 – 1-55879-237-6 – uk Libr Preservation [800]

Speck, F G *see*
- BEOTHUK AND MICMAC. INDIAN NOTES AND MONOGRAPHS
- CENTRAL ESKIMO AND INDIAN DOT ORNAMENTATION. INDIAN NOTES, V. 2
- CULTURE PROBLEMS IN NORTHEASTERN NORTH AMERICA
- RIVER DESERT INDIANS OF QUEBEC

Speck, Hermann Berthold Georg *see* KATILINA IM DRAMA DER WELTLITERATUR

LE SPECTACLE DE LA VIE HUMAINE : OU LECONS DE SAGESSE, EXPRIME'1ES AVEC ART EN 103. TABLEAUX EN TAILLE DOUCE... / Clerc, Jean le – (together with: Das Schauspiel des menschlichen Lebens) – Den Haag, 1755 – 6mf – 9 – ne IDC [700]

O SPECTADOR BRASILEIRO : DIARIO POLITICO, LITTERARIO E COMMERCIAL – (Cont as: Jornal do Commercio) – Rio de Janeiro, 28 Jun 1824-21 May 1827. – 1,5,6 – bl Biblioteca [072]

LE SPECTATEUR – Hull, Canada. 4 mai 1889-v25 n3. 15 mai 1913 (incomplete) – 5r – 1 – Can$40.00r – cn Can Microfilming [072]

LE SPECTATEUR CANADIEN – (Cont by: The Canadian Spectator) – Montreal, Canada. Prosp. 7 avr 1813; v1 n2. 3 jun 1813-2 oct 1822 – 3r – 1 – Can$50.00r – cn Can Microfilming [072]

LE SPECTATEUR DU NORD – Journal politique, litteraire et moral. Hambourg. 1797-1802 (I-XXIV) – 1 – fr A.C.R.P.P. [800]

LE SPECTATEUR DU SUD DE LA FRANCE – no. 6. Toulouse. janv 1791 – 1 – fr A.C.R.P.P. [073]

LE SPECTATEUR FRANCAIS AU 19E SIECLE – Paris. 1805-12, 1828 (I-XII) – 1 – fr A.C.R.P.P. [073]

LE SPECTATEUR FRANCAIS DEPUIS LA RESTAURATION DU TRONE DE SAINT LOUIS ET DE HENRI 4 – Ou Varietes. Recueillies des meilleurs ecrits periodiques. Paris. 1814-17 (1-3). Remplace: Le Spectateur francais au 19e SIECLE – 1 – fr A.C.R.P.P. [800]

LE SPECTATEUR MILITAIRE – Paris. 1826-aout 1914 – 1 – fr A.C.R.P.P. [073]

SPECTATOR – (Arlington.) 1972-77 – 1 – us UMI [073]

SPECTATOR – London. v. 1-185. 1848-1950 – 1,5,6 – us Princeton Micro [700]

SPECTATOR – New York. N.Y. 1797-1820 – 3 – us Readex [073]

SPECTATOR – New York. N.Y. 1814-1815; 1877-1897; 1899-1943; 1944-1969 – 1 – us UMI [071]

SPECTATOR – Staunton. Va. 1869-1893 – 1 – us UMI [071]

SPECTATOR – v. 1-. 1930- – 1 – us UMI [360]

THE SPECTATOR – Hamilton, Ontario, CN. 1846- – 36r per yr – 1 – Can$53.00r – cn Commonwealth Micro [072]

THE SPECTATOR – Hayward, CA: Chabot College, 1974-75 – 1r – 1 – $50.00 – B02291 – us Library Micro [370]

THE SPECTATOR – London. nos. 1-635. 1711-1714 – 1 – us NY Public [073]

THE SPECTATOR – London. -w. 1828-35, 1852, 1854, 1856-65, 1907-27. (71 reels) – 1 – uk British Libr Newspaper [072]

THE SPECTATOR – Madras, India. -w. March 1844-Dec 1856. 27 reels – 1 – uk British Libr Newspaper [072]

THE SPECTATOR – Melbourne, Australia. -w. 1 July 1865-23 Feb 1867. Imperfect. 2 reels – 1 – uk British Libr Newspaper [072]

THE SPECTATOR – New York. 1801-April 4 1864. Incomplete. Not collated – 1 – us NY Public [071]

THE SPECTATOR – New York City, NY. v2 n132. 29 dec 1798 – 1r – 1 – Can$25.00 – cn Can Microfilming [071]

THE SPECTATOR – Ville St-Laurent (Montreal), Canada. v3 n2. 1 dec 1881-v4 n8. 27 avr 1883 – 1r – 1 – Can$40.00 – cn Can Microfilming [072]

Spectator Company. New York *see* CHARTERS OF AMERICAN LIFE INSURANCE COMPANIES.

SPECTATOR DAILY – Accra. Ghana. -d. Jan-Feb 1939, Jan 1953-Sep 1955. (Imperfect). (5 reels) – 1 – uk British Libr Newspaper [072]

THE SPECTATOR DAILY – Accra. Ghana. june 1-2, 24-26, 29, 1948 – 1 – us NY Public [072]

SPECTATOR (LONDON.) – (v224- 1970- 5,6 v234- 1975- 9) – v1- 1828- – 1 – us UMI [800]

SPECTATOR (WALGETT) – 1898-1939 – 9 – at Pascoe [072]

Spector, John Jacob *see* ESSAYS ON LABOUR LAW IN THE PROVINCE OF QUEBEC

SPECTRAL ANALYSIS OF RANDOM PROCESSES AND FIELDS / Konjaev, K V – 1975. Engl trans of Russian text orig. pub. in 1973 – ca 300p – 1,5,6,9 – $5.00 – us A.G.U. [530]

SPECTRE – Irvine, CA. 1966 – 1r – 1 – $50.00 – R02 – us Library Micro [071]

LE SPECTRE DU RAVIN. / Lacerte, E A Bourgeois – Montreal: Ed. E Garand, c1924. SEM105P70 – 2mf – 9 – Can$4.50 – cn Bibl Nat [830]

SPECTROCHIMICA ACTA – (Continued in Part A and B) – v1-22. 1939-66 – 5,6,9 – us UMI [540]

SPECTROCHIMICA ACTA: PART A – (Back issues of journal available from UMI) – Molecular Spectroscopy. 14 issues/y. v49. 1993 – 9 – £661.00y – uk Elsevier Sci [540]

SPECTROCHIMICA ACTA: PART A – Molecular Spectroscopy. v23- 1967- – 5,6,9 – us UMI [530]

SPECTROCHIMICA ACTA: PART B – Atomic Spectroscopy. v23- 1967- – 5,6,9 – us UMI [530]

SPECTROCHIMICA ACTA: PART B – (Back issues of journal available from UMI) – Atomic Spectroscopy. 14 issues/y. v48. 1993 – 9 – £750.00y – uk Elsevier Sci [540]

SPECTROCHIMICA ACTA REVIEWS – v1- 1978- – 5,6,9 – us UMI [530]

SPECTROSCOPY LETTERS – (v17-. 1984-. 5,6,9) – v1-. 1968- – 1 – us UMI [073]

SPECTRUM – v1- 1957- 1; v13- 5,6; v18- 9 – us UMI [073]

SPECTRUM – Irvine, CA. 1965-66 – 1r – 1 – $50.00 – R02312 – us Library Micro [071]

SPECTRUM : THE JOURNAL OF STATE GOVERNMENT – (Title varies: v1-65 No 3, 1926-92 as Journal of State Government) – v1-66. 1926-93 – 9 – $656.00 set – us Heln [350]

SPECTRUM – Rancho Cordova, CA. 1993 – 2+ r – 1 – $100.00 ($50.00y) – B06050 – us Library Micro [071]

SPECTRUM – Rancho Cordova, NV. 1990 – 4+ r – 1 – $200.00 ($50.00y) – U04875 – us Library Micro [071]

SPECULUM : A JOURNAL OF MEDIAEVAL STUDIES – Cambridge, Mass. v1-15. 1926-40 – 148mf – 9 – 308c/2 – ne IDC [420]

SPECULUM – (v.45- 1970- 5,6. v.50- 1975-9) – v.1- 1926- – 1 – us UMI [073]

SPECULUM BEATAE MARIAE VIRGINIS FR. CONRADI A SAXONIA / Conradus de Brunopoli – 1904 – 1 – us A.T.L.A. [240]

SPECULUM HISTORIALE : FESTSCHRIFT JOHANNES SPOERL – Muenchen, 1965 – Dfl49.00 – ne Slangenburg [240]

SPECULUM HUMANAE SALVATIONIS: MEDIEVAL COSTUMES – From the early 15th century ms. of Speculum Humanae Salvationis – 14 – uk Microform Academic [740]

SPECULUM LATINUM / Entick, John – 1728. 46p. (English Linguistics Series 1500-1800) – 9 – us UMI [450]

SPECULUM MAIUS / Belvacensis, Vincentius – (Tomus 1: Speculum Naturale. Duaci, 1624. 73mf; 2: id. Doctrinale. Duaci 1624. 47mf; 3: id. Morale. Duaci, 1624. 45mf; 4: id. Historiale. Duaci, 1624. 78mf) – 8 – ne Slangenburg [290]

SPECULUM SIMPLICIUM ANIMARUM / Porete, Margareta – 1986 – 4mf – 9 – Bf975.00 – 2-503-63692-6 – be Brepols [240]

SPECULUM TESTAMENTORUM... / Espino de Caceres, Diego – Medina del Campo: Juan de Canto, 1593 – 1 – sp Bibl Santa Ana [946]

SPECULUM TESTAMENTORUM; SIVE.. / Espino de Caceres, Diego – (1593 ed.1.50f; 9) – 1587 – 9 – 1.50f – sp Bibl Santa Ana [946]

SPECULUM VIRGINUM – 1991 – 10mf – 9 – Bf2,250.00 – 2-503-63052-9 – be Brepols [240]

Spedding *see* THE PHILOSOPHICAL WORKS OF FRANCIS BACON, BARON OF VERULAM, VISCOUNT ST ALBANS.

Spedding, James *see* REVIEWS AND DISCUSSIONS

Spee, P Friedrich von *see* ADVIS AUX CRIMINALISTES SUR LES ABUS QUI SE GLISSENT DANS LES PROCES DE SORCELLERIE

SPEECH AND DRAMA – (v. 27- 1978-5,6,9) – v. 1- 1951- – 1 – us UMI [400]

SPEECH AND HEARING SERVICES IN SCHOOLS – v.1-3. 1970. Continued by Journal of language, speech and hearing services in the schools – 1 – us UMI [370]

SPEECH AT AURORA: DELIVERED OCTOBER 3RD, 1874 ON THE OCCASION OF A MEETING OF THE REFORM PARTY OF NORTH YORK / Blake, Edward – By the Hon. Edward Blake. Montreal: Penny, Wilson, 1874. 00828. (Pre-1900 Canadiana) – 9 – cn C.I.H.M. [971]

SPEECH AT LONDON, SEPT. 19TH, 1900 / Cartwright, Richard – 1900? 03846. (Pre-1900 Canadiana) – 9 – cn C.I.H.M. [971]

SPEECH AT THE ALIARCHAM ACADEMY OF SOCIAL SCIENCES IN INDONESIA / P'Eng, Chen – SE-11,319 1. May 25, 1965 – 9 – ne IDC [300]

SPEECH BROADCAST BY THE CHAIRMAN OF THE B.F.O. ON FEB. 27, 1949 / Hamid 2, Sultan – SE-11,873 1 – 9 – ne IDC [956]

SPEECH BY THE HON. EDWARD BLAKE, Q.C., M.P., EX-PREMIER OF ONTARIO, CANADA, IN CONNECTION WITH THE FROME DIVISION LIBERAL ASSOCIATION, AND IN SUPPORTING A RESOLUTION OF CONFIDENCE IN MR. GLADSTONE'S GOVERNMENT...JANUARY 27TH, 1893 / Blake, Edward – Bath, England: Southwell and Goodwin, 1893? 00893. (Pre-1900 Canadiana) – 9 – cn C.I.H.M. [323]

SPEECH BY THE HONORABLE J. BLANCHET, SECRETARY OF THE PROVINCE OF QUEBEC, ON THE AUTONOMY OF THE PROVINCES / Blanchet, Jean Gervais Protais (1843-1908) – Quebec: L J Demers & Frere, 1884. SEM105P43 – 1mf – 9 – Can$2.25 – cn Bibl Nat [971]

A SPEECH DELIVERED AT THE SESSION OF JUNE 3RD, 1892, OF THE LEGISLATIVE ASSEMBLY OF THE PROVINCE OF QUEBEC / Beaubien, Louis – 1892. 05679. (Pre-1900 Canadiana) – 9 – cn C.I.H.M. [630]

SPEECH DELIVERED BEFORE THE ASSEMBLY OF THE LEAGUE OF NATIONS, 25 SEPTEMBER 1936 / Alvarez del Vayo, Julio – n.p. 1936? Fiche W 715. (Blodgett Collection of Spanish Civil War Pamphlets) – 9 – us H.U. College Libr [946]

SPEECH DELIVERED ...BEFORE THE LEGISLATIVE ASSEMBLY...PROVINCE OF QUEBEC, ON 4TH AND 5TH DECEMBER 1894 ON THE LOAN OF 27,632,647 FRANCS (3 PER CENT BONDS AT 77 FOR 60 YEARS) / Hall, John Smythe – 1894?. 05339. (Pre-1900 Canadiana) – 9 – cn C.I.H.M. [971]

A SPEECH DELIVERED BY HON. C. F. FRASER, COMMISSIONER OF PUBLIC WORKS IN THE LEGISLATIVE ASSEMBLY, MARCH 25TH, 1890, ON SEPARATE SCHOOLS AND THE POSITION OF THE ROMAN CATHOLIC ELECTORS WITH THE TWO POLITICAL PARTIES / Fraser, Christopher Findlay – s.l.: s.n., 1890 (Toronto: Hunter, Rose). 03174. (Pre-1900 Canadiana) – 9 – cn C.I.H.M. [971]

SPEECH DELIVERED IN THE LEGISLATIVE ASSEMBLY DURING THE DEBATE ON THE SUBJ / Dunkin, Christopher – Quebec: Hunter, Rose & Co, 1865. SEM105P646 – 1mf – 9 – Can$2.25 – cn Bibl Nat [971]

SPEECH DELIVERED IN THE REICHSTAG, FEBRUARY 20TH, 1938.. / Hitler, Adolf – (Berlin: M. Mueller & Sohn, 1938). 63p – 1 – us U.W. Library [943]

SPEECH DELIVERED ON SIXTH DIES NATALIS OF UNIVERSITAS INDONESIA, ON 2D FEB., 1956, AT BANDUNG, BY PROF. BAHDER DJOHAN / Jakarta. Universitas Indonesia – SE-11,022 1 – 9 – ne IDC [370]

SPEECH FOR THE MILITARY / Brembeck, Cole Speicher – In Indonesian. SE-10,306 1. 1959? – 9 – ne IDC [355]

SPEECH IN THE CANADIAN SENATE, MARCH 21, 1878 ON THE PUBLIC FINANCES OF THE DOMINION: THE FINANCIAL TRANSACTIONS OF THE MACKENZIE AND MACDONALD GOVERNMENTS CONTRACTED / Brown, George – Toronto: Office of the Globe Newspaper, 1878. 00312. (Pre-1900 Canadiana) – 9 – cn C.I.H.M. [971]

SPEECH MONOGRAPHS – (See now: Communications Monographs) – v1-42 1934-75 1; v38-42 5,6; v42- 9 – us UMI [400]

SPEECH OF HON. J. A. CHAPLEAU TO BLAME THE GOVERNMENT FOR HAVING ALLOWED THE EXECUTION OF LOUIS RIEL / Chapleau, Joseph Adolphe – Montreal: Imp. Gen., 1886. SEM105P38 – 1mf – 9 – Can$2.25 – cn Bibl Nat [971]

SPEECH OF JOHN CHARLTON, M.P. ON UNRESTRICTED RECIPROCITY WITH THE UNITED STATES: DELIVERED IN THE CANADIAN HOUSE OF COMMONS, THURSDAY, MARCH 7TH, 1889 / Charlton, John – Ottawa: A. Senecal for the Queen's Printer, 1889. 02965. (Pre-1900 Canadiana) – 9 – cn C.I.H.M. [971]

SPEECH OF JOHN CHARLTON, M.P. ON UNRESTRICTED RECIPROCITY WITH THE UNITED STATES: DELIVERED IN THE HOUSE OF COMMONS, FRIDAY, MARCH 16TH, 1888 / Charlton, John – Ottawa?, 1888? 02962. (Pre-1900 Canadiana) – 9 – cn C.I.H.M. [971]

SPEECH OF MR. J. D. EDGAR IN THE CANADIAN HOUSE OF COMMONS IN SUPPORT OF HIS MOTION FOR A COMMITTEE TO ENQUIRE INTO THE CHARGES AGAINST SIR ADOLPHE CARON, POSTMASTER GENERAL / Edgar, James David – Delivered April 27th, 1892. Ottawa?: s.n., 1892?. 04161. (Pre-1900 Canadiana) – 9 – cn C.I.H.M. [971]

SPEECH OF MR. N. F. DAVIN, M.P., ON HOME RULE FOR IRELAND, DELIVERED IN THE HOUSE OF COMMONS, OTTAWA, APRIL 22ND AND 26TH, 1887 / Davin, Nicholas Flood – s.l.: s.n., 1887. (Ottawa: McLean, Roger). 02591. (Pre-1900 Canadiana) – 9 – cn C.I.H.M. [971]

SPEECH OF N. F. DAVIN, M.P., ON THE ADDRESS, OTTAWA, FRIDAY 24TH MARCH, 1899 / Davin, Nicholas Flood – Ottawa: Queen's Printer, 1899. 03652. (Pre-1900 Canadiana) – 9 – cn C.I.H.M. [971]

SPEECH OF NICHOLAS FLOOD DAVIN, M.P., ON THE REVIEW OF THE FINANCIAL SITUATION: OTTAWA, TUESDAY, JULY 10, 1900 / Davin, Nicholas Flood – Ottawa?: s.n., 1900?. 0366l. (Pre-1900 Canadiana) – 9 – cn C.I.H.M. [971]

SPEECH OF SIR ADOLPHE CARON, M.P. ON THE REMEDIAL BILL, OTTAWA, WEDNESDAY, 4TH MARCH 1896 / Caron, Adolphe – Ottawa?, 1896? 02817. (Pre-1900 Canadiana) – 9 – cn C.I.H.M. [971]

SPEECH OF SIR ADOLPHE CARON ON THE EXECUTION OF LOUIS RIEL: OTTAWA, MARCH 17TH AND 18TH, 1886 / Caron, Adolphe – Ottawa: MacLean, Roger, 1886? 02818. ((Pre-1900 Canadiana) – 9 – cn C.I.H.M. [971]

SPEECH OF SIR RICHARD CARTWRIGHT AT INGERSOLL, NOV. 14TH, 1889 / Cartwright, Richard – 1889? 00505. (Pre-1900 Canadiana) – 9 – cn C.I.H.M. [971]

SPEECH OF THE HON. A.T. GALT, BRINGING DOWN THE FINANCIAL STATEMENT, AUGUST 29TH, 1865 / Canada. Ministere des Finances – s.l., s.n, 1865. SEM105P300 – 1mf – 9 – Can$2.25 – cn Bibl Nat [336]

SPEECH OF THE HON. A.T. GALT...ON INTRODUCING THE BUDGET OF 1862, TOGETHER WITH STATISTICAL AND FINANCIAL STATEMENTS / Canada. Ministere des Finances – Quebec: Printed by S Derbishire and G Desbarats, 1862. SEM105P301 – 1mf – 9 – Can$2.25 – cn Bibl Nat [336]

SPEECH OF THE HON. EDWARD BLAKE ON THE ADDRESS IN ANSWER TO THE SPEECH FROM THE THRONE: DELIVERED IN THE HOUSE OF COMMONS AT OTTAWA, ON FRIDAY, JAN. 30TH, 1885 / Blake, Edward – 12339. (Pre-1900 Canadiana) – 9 – cn C.I.H.M. [971]

SPEECH OF THE HONORABLE A.T. GALT...IN INTRODUCING THE BUDGET / Canada. Ministere des Finances – Ottawa: Printed by Hunter, Rose and Co, 1866. SEM105P299 – 1mf – 9 – Can$2.25 – cn Bibl Nat [336]

SPEECH OF THE HONORABLE EDWARD BLAKE, M.P.: DELIVERED IN THE HOUSE OF COMMONS OF CANADA ON THE MOTION FOR THE SECOND READING OF THE ORANGE INCORPORATION BILL, 17TH MARCH, 1884 / Blake, Edward – 1884? 00827. (Pre-1900 Canadiana) – 9 – cn C.I.H.M. [971]

SPEECH ON HOME RULE FOR IRELAND / Blake, Edward – Hon. E. Blake, Ottawa: MacLean, Roger, 1886. 02341. (Pre-1900 Canadiana) – 9 – cn C.I.H.M. [941]

SPEECH ON SEVENTH DIES NATALIS OF UNIVERSITAS INDONESIA ON FEB. 2ND, 1957, AT DJAKARTA, BY PROF. BAHDER DJOHAN / Jakarta. Universitas Indonesia – SE-3439 1 – 9 – ne IDC [370]

SPEECH ON THE 4TH DIES NATALIS OF THE UNIVERSITY OF INDONESIA ON FEB. 4, 1954 / Jakarta. Universitas Indonesia – Djakarta. Delivered by Supomo, Raden. SE-2036 1 – 9 – ne IDC [370]

SPEECH ON THE BRITISH COLUMBIA TARIFF, WEDNESDAY, 7TH MARCH, 1877 / Bunster, Arthur – Ottawa: MacLean Roger, 1877. 02012. (Pre-1900 Canadiana) – 9 – cn C.I.H.M. [971]

SPEECH ON THE BUDGET BY THE HON. P. BACHAND, TREASURER OF THE PROVINCE OF QUEBEC: DELIVERED IN THE LEGISLATIVE ASSEMBLY, QUEBEC, 18TH JUNE 1878 / Bachand, P – Quebec, 1879. 05684. (Pre-1900 Canadiana) – 9 – cn C.I.H.M. [971]

SPEECH ON THE BUDGET: DELIVERED IN THE HOUSE OF COMMONS, JULY 22ND., 1891 / Davin, Nicholas Flood – Regina: Leader Co., 1891. 02597. (Pre-1900 Canadiana) – 9 – cn C.I.H.M. [971]

SPEECH ON THE BUDGET: DELIVERED IN THE HOUSE OF COMMONS, OTTAWA, MARCH 29TH, 1892 / Davin, Nicholas Flood – Regina: Leader Co., 1892. 02596. (Pre-1900 Canadiana) – 9 – cn C.I.H.M. [971]

A SPEECH ON THE BUDGET, IN THE CANADIAN HOUSE OF COMMONS, ON THURSDAY, APRIL 5TH, 1883 / Foster, George Eulas – Ottawa?: s.n., 1883?. 05594. (Pre-1900 Canadiana) – 9 – cn C.I.H.M. [971]

A SPEECH ON THE CHARACTER OF THE RIGHT HON. WILLIAM PITT.. / Tomline, William Edward Pretyman – Trinity College Chapel, Cambridge, 17 Dec 1806. 23p – 1 – us U.W. Library [920]

SPEECH ON THE DRAFT FUNDAMENTAL LAW OF THE FIRST NATIONAL OVERALL DEVELOPMENT PLAN DELIVERED TO THE PRESIDENT OF INDONESIA ON 13 AUG. 1960 / Yamin, Muhammad – SE 2432 1 – 9 – ne IDC [338]

SPEECH ON THE FIFTH DIES NATALIS OF THE UNIVERSITY OF INDONESIA ON 10TH FEB., 1955 AT BANDUNG, BY PROF. BAHDER DJOHAN / Jakarta. Universitas Indonesia – SE-3330 1 – 9 – ne IDC [370]

SPEECH TEACHER – (1970-75. 5,6) – v1-24. 1952-75. Continued by: Communications Education – 1 – us UMI [370]

SPEECH TO THE CONFERENCE ON AMERICAN LIBRARY RESOURCES ON SOUTHERN ASIA IN WASHINGTON, D.C. ON NOV. 21, 1957 / Mukarto, Notowidigdo – SE-2235 1 – 9 – ne IDC [020]

SPEECH...1853 : THE CENTRAL AMERICAN TREATY CONCLUDED WITH GREAT BRITAIN...1850 / Clayton, J M – Washington, 1853 – 1mf – 1 – ILM-2433/1 – ne IDC [327]

SPEECH...DELIVERED AT ST LAURENT, COUNTY OF JACQUES CARTIER, ON THE 6TH SEPTEMBER, 1883 / Chapleau, Joseph Adolphe – 1883? 02855. (Pre-1900 Canadiana) – 9 – cn C.I.H.M. [971]

SPEECHES / Colombo Plan Conference of National Information Officers – Delegation from Indonesia. 2d, Bangkok. 5-8 Sept. 1960. SE-3322 1 – 9 – ne IDC [350]

SPEECHES, ADDRESSES, AND OCCASIONAL SERMONS / Parker, Theodore – Boston. 3v. 1861 – 1r – 1 – us Ross [975]

SPEECHES AND ADDRESSES / Magee, W C – London: Isbister, 1892 – 1mf – us A.T.L.A. [240]

SPEECHES AND DOCUMENTS ON INDIAN POLICY, 1750-1921 / ed by Keith, Arthur Berriedale – I-1067 1. 2v 1922 – 9 – ne IDC [950]

SPEECHES, ARGUMENTS AND MISCELLANEOUS PAPERS OF DAVID DUDLEY FIELD / ed by Sprague, A P – New York: D Appleton & Co. 3v. 1884-1890 – 18mf – 9 – $24.00 – LLMC 92-103 – us L.L.M.C. [340]

SPEECHES: DELIVERED BY HON. EDWARD BLAKE, THE LEADER OF THE LIBERAL PARTY: AND A SYNOPSIS OF THE DEBATE ON THE HOME RULE RESOLUTIONS IN THE HOUSE OF COMMONS / Blake, Edward – Toronto: C. Robinson, 1886. 00170. (Pre-1900 Canadiana) – 9 – cn C.I.H.M. [941]

SPEECHES, LECTURES AND LETTERS / Phillips, Wendell – (While Phillips was a successful lawyer, he achieved his widest fame as a leading abolitionist) – Boston: Lothrop, Lee & Shepard Co, 1863 – 6mf – 9 – $9.00 – LLMC 92-240 – us L.L.M.C. [340]

SPEECHES, LECTURES, AND LETTERS / Phillips, Wendell – Boston: Lee and Shepard, 1892. 2v – 1 – us U.W. Library [920]

SPEECHES, LITERARY AND SOCIAL. NOW FIRST COLLECTED : WITH CHAPTERS ON "CHARLES DICKENS AS A LETTER WRITER, POET, AND PUBLIC READER" / Dickens, Charles – London: John Camden Hotten, [1870] – 1 roll – 1 – 1-55879-424-7 – uk Libr Preservation [420]

SPEECHES OF DR HASTINGS KAMUZU BANDA, PRESIDENT OF MALAWI / Banda, Hastings K – [Chicago]: University of Chicago, Joseph Regenstein Library, Photodup Dept, [1980] – us Res Libr [850]

SPEECHES OF THE HOLY APOSTLES / Fraser, Donald – New York: Macmillan, 1882. 1 fiche – 9 – us A.T.L.A. [240]

THE SPEECHES OF THE HOLY APOSTLES / Fraser, Donald – New York:Macmillan, 1882 – 1mf – 9 – 0-8370-3184-2 – 1985-1184 – us A.T.L.A. [220]

SPEECHES OF THE HON. EDWARD BLAKE, M.P., ON THE NORTH-WEST TERRITORIES ACT, TUESDAY, 6TH MAY, 1890 / Blake, Edward – Ottawa: B. Chamberlin, 1890. 02337. (Pre-1900 Canadiana) – 9 – cn C.I.H.M. [971]
SPEECHES ON DIVERS OCCASIONS / Campbell, Alexander – Ottawa: A. Woodburn, 1885. 00996. (Pre-1900 Canadiana) – 9 – cn C.I.H.M. [971]
SPEECHES ON FREE TRADE / Cobden, Richard – 1903 ed.232p – 9 – 1.00f – at Libertarian Micro [380]
SPEECH...ON CANADIAN PACIFIC RAILWAY RESOLUTIONS, HOUSE OF COMMONS, 16TH JUNE 1885 / Chapleau, Joseph Adolphe – 1885. (Ottawa: MacLean, Roger), 1885. 02854. (Pre-1900 Canadiana) – 9 – cn C.I.H.M. [971]
SPEECH...ON JESUITS' ESTATES ACT: DELIVERED IN THE HOUSE OF COMMONS, OTTAWA ON THURSDAY, MARCH 28TH, 1889 / Charlton, John – 1889? 02120. (Pre-1900 Canadiana) – 9 – cn C.I.H.M. [971]
SPEECH...ON JESUITS' ESTATES ACT: DELIVERED IN THE HOUSE OF COMMONS, OTTAWA, ON TUESDAY, MARCH 26TH, 1889 / Colby, Charles Carroll – Ottawa?, 1889?. 03203. (Pre-1900 Canadiana) – 9 – cn C.I.H.M. [971]
SPEECH...ON THE BUDGET: DELIVERED IN THE HOUSE OF COMMONS, OTTAWA, FRIDAY, MARCH 28TH, 1890 / Charlton, John – Ottawa: Queen's Printer, 1890. 02963. (Pre-1900 Canadiana) – 9 – cn C.I.H.M. [971]
SPEECH...ON THE MOIETY SYSTEM, UNDERVALUATIONS AND ADMINISTRATION OF THE CUSTOMS / Bowell, Mackenzie – Ottawa: Printed for the Queen's printer by A. Senecal, 1889. 02527. (Pre-1900 Canadiana) – 9 – cn C.I.H.M. [971]
SPEECH...ON UNRESTRICTED RECIPROCITY DELIVERED IN THE HOUSE OF COMMONS, OTTAWA, ON TUESDAY, MARCH 19TH, 1889 / Cockburn, George Ralph Richardson – Ottawa: Queen's Printer, 1889. 03207. (Pre-1900 Canadiana) – 9 – cn C.I.H.M. [977]
SPEED'S ATLAS – 1611-12 – 1 – uk Microform Academic [910]
SPEEDY TRIAL ACT OF 1974 : LEGISLATIVE HISTORY OF TITLE 1 / Partridge, Anthony – Washington: Federal Judicial Center, Aug 1980 – 5mf – 9 – $7.50 – LLMC 94-359 – us L.L.M.C. [340]
Speelman, R P *see* ENTRETIENS D'UN MOIS DE MARIE
Speer *see* THE ENCYCLOPEDIA OF THE NEW WEST
Speer, Albert *see* PERSONAL PAPERS RE PNG
Speer, D *see*
– GRUND-RICHTIGER, KURTZ, LEICHT UND NOETHIGER, (JETZT WOHLVERMEHRTER) UNTERRICHT DER MUSICALISCHEN KUNST
– GRUND-RICHTIGER, KURTZ-, LEICHT- UND NOETHIGER, JETZT WOL-VERMEHRTER UNTERRICHT DER MUSICALISCHEN KUNST
– GRUND-RICHTIGER, KURTZ, LEICHT UND NOETHIGER UNTERRICHT DER MUSICALISCHEN KUNST
Speer, Emory *see* REMOVAL OF CAUSES FROM THE STATE OF FEDERAL COURTS, AN ANALYSIS OF THE LAW AS CHANGED BY ACT OF CONGRESS OF MARCH 3, 1887
SPEER PAMPHLET COLLECTION ON CHINESE MISSION : CARD CATALOGUE – New York, Union Theological Seminary – 11mf – 9 – ne IDC [950]
Speer, Robert Elliott *see*
– CHRISTIANITY AND THE NATIONS
– THE DEITY OF CHRIST
– A MEMORIAL OF HORACE TRACY PITKIN
– MISSIONARY PRINCIPLES AND PRACTICE
– MISSIONS AND MODERN HISTORY
– MISSIONS AND POLITICS IN ASIA
– MISSIONS IN SOUTH AMERICA
– PAUL, THE ALL-ROUND MAN
– PRESBYTERIAN FOREIGN MISSIONS
– SERVANTS OF THE KING
– SOUTH AMERICAN PROBLEMS
– STUDIES OF THE MAN CHRIST JESUS
– STUDIES OF THE MAN PAUL
Speer, William *see* THE GREAT REVIVAL OF 1800
SPEER'S CASES IN EQUITY / South Carolina. Supreme Court – (A Pre-NRS title) – 1v. 1842-1844 (all publ) – 8mf – 9 – $12.00 – LLMC 94-035 – us L.L.M.C. [340]
SPEER'S LAW REPORTS / South Carolina. Supreme Court – (A Pre-NRS title) – v1-2. 1842-1844 (all publ) – 16mf – 9 – $24.00 – LLMC 94-023 – us L.L.M.C. [340]
Speicher, Jacob *see* THE CONQUEST OF THE CROSS IN CHINA
Speidel, Ludwig *see* AUSGEWAEHLTE SCHRIFTEN
Speierer, Ludwig *see* DER STRAFRECHTLICHE SCHUTZ DES GESCHAFTSGEHEIMNISSES
Speisser, F L *see* GRAMMAIRE ELEMENTAIRE DE LA LANGUE VOLOFE
SPEKE AND THE NILE SOURCE / Speke, John Hanning – Edited by E. A. Loftus. Edinburgh Nelson 1954 – 1 – us U.W. Library [910]
Speke, John H *see* LES SOURCES DU NIL, JOURNAL DE VOYAGE DU CAPITAINE JOHN HANNING SPEKE
Speke, John Hanning *see* SPEKE AND THE NILE SOURCE
SPEKTRUM – Stockholm, Sweden. 1931-33 – 1 – sw Kungliga [073]
Speleers, L *see* LE PAPYRUS DE NEFER RENPET
THE SPELLING REFORM / March, Francis Andrew – Washington: Government Printing Office, 1893 – 1mf – 9 – 0-8370-8765-1 – 1986-2765 – us A.T.L.A. [420]
Spelling, Thomas Crisp *see*
– A TREATISE ON EXTRAORDINARY RELIEF IN EQUITY AND AT LAW. COVERING: PART I-INJUNCTION. PART II-HABEAS CORPUS.
– A TREATISE ON THE LAW OF PRIVATE CORPORATIONS.
Spelman, Henry *see* THE ENGLISH WORKS OF SIR HENRY SPELMAN, KT.
Spemann, Franz *see* VON DER RENAISSANCE ZU JESUS: BEKENNTNISSE EINES MODERNEN STUDENTEN
Spence, H Donald M *see*
– CLOISTER LIFE IN THE DAYS OF COEUR DE LION
– EARLY CHRISTIANITY AND PAGANISM
– THE EARLY CHRISTIANS IN ROME
– THE WHITE ROBE OF CHURCHES OF THE 11TH CENTURY
Spence, James Carmichael *see* THE CONSCIENCE OF THE KING
Spence, Thomas *see* THE GRAND REPOSITORY OF THE ENGLISH LANGUAGE
Spence, W *see* AN INTRODUCTION TO ENTOMOLOGY, OR, ELEMENTS OF THE NATURAL HISTORY OF INSECTS
Spence, Walter *see* BACK TO CHRIST
SPENCER 1744-1890 – 51mf – 9 – us Holbrook [920]
Spencer, A E *see* A HISTORY OF UGANDA LAND AND SURVEYS AND OF THE UGANDA LAND AND SURVEY DEPARTMENT
SPENCER ADVOCATE – Spencer, NE. -w. Jan 1896-May 1896, scattered issues missing; Jan 1908-Dec 1921; Jan 1924 to date – 1 – us NE Hist [071]
Spencer, Anna Garlin *see*
– BELL STREET CHAPEL DISCOURSES
– STATE CONTROL AND SOCIAL CARE OF THE VICIOUS AND DEPENDENT CLASSES
Spencer, Edgar A *see* HINTS FROM A LAWYER: OR, LEGAL ADVICE TO MEN AND WOMEN.
Spencer, Elihu *see* THE PIONEERS OF OUTAGAMIE COUNTY, WISCONSIN
Spencer Family (Kalida, Ohio) *see* PAPERS
Spencer, Herbert *see*
– APHORISMS, SELECTED BY JULIA R. GINGELL
– AN AUTOBIOGRAPHY
– THE DATA OF ETHICS
– ESSAYS
– FACTS AND COMMENTS
– ILLUSTRATIONS OF UNIVERSAL PROGRESS
– THE MAN VERSUS THE STATE
– THE PRINCIPLES OF SOCIOLOGY
– RECENT DISCUSSIONS IN SCIENCE, PHILOSOPHY, AND MORALS
– SOCIAL STATICS
– SOCIAL STATICS, ABRIDGED AND REVISED
– THE STUDY OF SOCIOLOGY
– UEBER DAS RECHT DEN STAAT ZU IGNORIEREN
– VARIOUS FRAGMENTS, TOGETHER WITH TWO ESSAYS FROM VOL. 1 OF HIS "ESSAYS"
Spencer, Ichabod Smith *see* EVIDENCES OF DIVINE REVELATION: IN A LETTER TO A JUDGE
Spencer, J H *see* A HISTORY OF KENTUCKY BAPTISTS
Spencer, Jesse Ames *see* PAPALISM VERSUS CATHOLIC TRUTH AND RIGHT
Spencer, John Henderson *see* FROM HIS BIRTH, 9 SEPT 1826 UNTIL AUG 1876
Spencer, Richard H *see* GENEALOGICAL AND MEMORIAL ENCYCLOPEDIA OF THE STATE OF MARYLAND
Spencer, Selden Palmer *see* LAWYERS AND LAWLESSNESS; AN ADDRESS DELIVERED BEFORE THE JOINT MEETING OF THE BAR ASSOCIATIONS OF ARKANSAS AND TEXAS, JULY 11, 1906, AT TEXARKANA
Spencer, Thomas *see* THE ART OF LOGICK
Spencer, William Gabriel *see* THE CHRISTIAN OUTLOOK: AN ADDRESS
Spencerport, New York. Ogden Baptist Church *see* RECORDS
SPENDEN VERZEICHNISSE = CHARITABLE RECORD – (In German) – Berlin, DE. v9 no3 14 Jan 1886-v15 no14 25 Dec 1890 – 1r – 1 – $35.00 – cn Can Microfilming [072]
SPENERSCHE ZEITUNG *see* BERLINISCHE NACHRICHTEN VON STAATS- UND GELEHRTEN SACHEN
Spengemann, Christof *see* DIE WAHRHEIT UBER ANNA BLUME; KRITIK DER KUNST, KRITIK DER KRITIK; KRITIK DER ZEIT
Spengler, Franz *see* SAMUEL UND SAUL
Spenle, E *see* NOVALIS DEVANT LA CRITIQUE
[Speranskii, M M] *see* A SUMMARY OF HISTORICAL SKETCHES ON THE FORMATION OF THE BODY OF THE RUSSIAN LAWS
Speranskii, M N *see*
– ISTORIIA RUSSKOI LITERATURY 19 VEKA. ZAPISKI SLUSHATELEI, REDAKTIROVANNIIA PROFESSOROM
– OPISANIE RUKOPISEI TVERSKAGO MUZEIA
Speranskii, N M *see* TAINOPIS' V IUGOSLAVIANSKIKH I RUSSKIKH PAMIATNIKAKH PIS'MA
Sperber, Eduard *see* RELIGIONSBUECHLEIN FUER DIE UNTERSTUFE EVANGELISCHER SCHULEN
Sperl, August *see*
– BURSCHEN HERAUS!
– PFALZGRAF PHILIPP LUDWIG VON NEUBURG, SEIN SOHN WOLFGANG WILHELM UND DIE JESUITEN
– DIE SOEHNE DES HERRN BUDIWO
Sperling, O *see* DE DANICAE LINGUAE,... COMMENTARIOLUS
Sperry, C S *see* THE LAWS AND USAGES OF MARITIME WARFARE
Spethmann, H *see* DER MAISTREIK 1924 IM RUHRBERGBAU
Spetia, A *see* BULLARII ROMANI CONTINUATIO
DAS SPEYERER DIOEZESANRITUALE VON 1512 BIS 1932 / Lamott, A – Speyer, 1961 – 5mf – 8 – Dfl22.00 – ne Slangenburg [240]
SPEYERER TAGESPOST – (Title change: Tagespost, 27 Jan 1981) – Speyer, Germany. 1981- – 7r per yr – 1 – gw Mikrofilm [072]
SPEYSIDE INVERNESS 1851 CENSUS INDEX : ARGYLL AND WEST SCOTLAND CENSUS INDEX, PART 7 / Gibson, Peter & Macinnes, John – 1995 – 2mf – 9 – A$19.95 – 0-646-23190-1 – at Seanachas [920]
SPHAERA MUNDI / Sanchez de las Brozas, Francisco – 1579 – 9 – 1.50f – sp Bibl Santa Ana [810]
SPHAERA MUNDI / Sanchez de las Brozas, Francisco – 1588 – 9 – 1.50f – sp Bibl Santa Ana [810]
THE SPHAGNACEAE OR PEAT-MOSSES OF EUROPE AND NORTH AMERICA / Braithwaite, R – 7511 2. 1880 – 8 – ne IDC [580]
SPHERE – v1-7 1972-78 – 1 – us UMI [640]
THE SPHERE AND RIGHTS OF WOMAN IN THE CHURCH / Presbyterian Church in the U.S.A. Synods. Virginia – 1899 – 9 – us A.T.L.A. [240]
LA SPHERE FEMININE = WOMEN'S SPHERE : ORGANE OFFICIEL DE L'ALLIANCE CANADIENNE POUR LE VOTE DES FEMMES DU QUEBEC – Westmount: l'Alliance canadienne..., 1931-. SEM105P1300 – 11mf – 9 – Can$24.75 – cn Bibl Nat [305]
THE SPHERE OF RELIGION : A CONSIDERATION OF ITS NATURE AND OF ITS INFLUENCE UPON THE PROGRESS OF CIVILIZATION / Hoffman, Frank Sargent – (Includes an index) – New York:G P Putnam, 1908 – 1mf – 9 – 0-8370-3617-8 – 1985-1617 – us A.T.L.A. [200]
SPHERE OF RELIGION: A CONSIDERATION OF ITS NATURE AND OF ITS INFLUENCE / Hoffman, Frank Sargent – New York: G.P. Putnam, 1908. 1 fiche – 9 – us A.T.L.A. [240]
SPHERE'S CUISINE – v7- 1978- – 1 – us UMI [640]
SPHINX : MONATSSCHRIFT FUER SEELEN- UND GEISTESLEBEN – Leipzig. v1-22. 1886-96 – 4r – 1 – us Ross [073]
SPHINX : REVUE CRITIQUE EMBRASSANT LE DOMAINE ENTIER DE L'EGYPTOLOGIE / ed by Piehl, K – Uppsala, Stockholm, v1-22. 1897-1931 – 50mf – 9 – NE-357/1 – ne IDC [930]
Spicer, Henry *see* JUDICIAL DRAMAS
SPICILEGIA ENTOMOLOGICA GENAVENSIA / Saussure, H de – Geneve, 1879-87.2 pts.Z-1596/2 – 8 – ne IDC [590]
SPICILEGIA ZOOLOGICA. / Pallas, Peter Simon – Berlin: G.A. Lange, 1767-80. 2v. 9 fiches. (Science Collection) – 9 – 22.00 – fr Bibl Nationale [590]
SPICILEGIUM BOTANICUM / Smith, J E – London, 1791-1792. B-5575 2 – 8 – ne IDC [580]
SPICILEGIUM FLORAE GERMANICAE / Schrader, H A – Hannoveranae. 1794. B-213 2 – 8 – ne IDC [580]
SPICILEGIUM FLORAE LIPSICAE / Schreber, J C D von – Lipsiae. 1771. B-5372 2 – 8 – ne IDC [580]
SPICILEGIUM FLORAE RUMELICAE ET BITHYNICAE EXHIBENS SYNOPSIN PLANTARUM / Grisebach, A – 2v. Brunsvigae. 1843-44. B-5941 2 – 8 – ne IDC [580]
SPICILEGIUM ROMANUM / ed by Mai, A – Romae. Tom 1-10. 1839-1844 – 133mf – 9 – Dfl483.00 – ne Slangenburg [999]
SPICILEGIUM SOLESMENSE / Pitra, J B – (Tomus 1 22mf. Tomus 2 21mf. Tomus 3 23mf. Tomus 4 21mf) – Paris, 1852-1858 – 9 – ne Slangenburg [240]
SPICILEGIUM SYRIACUM : CONTAINING REMAINS OF BARDESAN, MELITON, AMBROSE, AND MARA BAR SERAPION / Cureton, William – London: Rivingtons, 1855 – 1mf – us A.T.L.A. [240]
Spicker, Max *see* SUPPLEMENT TO THE HYMN BOOK FOR THE USE OF TEMPLE EMANU-EL
Spicq, C *see*
– AGAPE, DANS LE N.T
– ST. PAUL
– THEOLOGIE MORALE DU N.T
THE SPIDER BOOK / Comstock, J H – Z-2168 2. 1913 – 8 – ne IDC [590]
THE SPIDER CRABS OF AMERICA / Rathbun, M J – 2790 2. 1925 – 8 – ne IDC [590]
SPIDERS / Workman, T – v. 1: Malaysian Spiders. Z 2216 2. 1896 – 8 – ne IDC [590]
THE SPIDERS OF DORSET / Pickard-Cambridge, O – Z-2165 2.. 1879-1881 – 8 – ne IDC [590]
THE SPIDERS OF THE UNITED STATES / Heutz, N M – Z-2164 2. 1875 – 8 – ne IDC [590]
DE SPIEGEL – Amsterdam, Netherlands. -w. 22 Sept 1906-25 Sept 1920. 7 reels – 1 – uk British Libr Newspaper [949]
DER SPIEGEL – (1947- 150mf/y. Der Spiegel Index also available 1947-) – 1970- – 4r per y – 5 – inquire – us Ross [072]
DER SPIEGEL – (1947-1992 DM17,802.00 set DM490.00y; Index, 1947-1992 DM1,725.00 set DM40.00y; Index, 1993 DM42.00y) – 1993 – 9 – DM516.00y – gw IOS [943]
DER SPIEGEL – (Backfiles. 1) – Germany. 1947- – 1 – us Primary [072]
DER SPIEGEL – Hanover, Hamburg, Germany. -w. 1947-54; 1956. 18 reels – 1 – uk British Libr Newspaper [072]
DER SPIEGEL – v2-33. 1948-79 – 1,5,6 – us Princeton Micro [073]
SPIEGEL – 1 – F1,484.00 – sz Infoprint [073]
SPIEGEL – 1947-1957 – 1 – F742.00 – sz Infoprint [073]
SPIEGEL – 1958-1963 – 1 – F1,048.00 – sz Infoprint [073]
SPIEGEL – 1964-1975 – 1 – F1,528.00 – sz Infoprint [073]
SPIEGEL – 1970-1995 – 4 times per yr – 6 – F2,600.00 – sz Infoprint [072]
SPIEGEL – 1976-1994 – 1 – F2,052.00 – sz Infoprint [073]
SPIEGEL DER DEUGDEN EN KONSTEN : MET PRENTEN EN HAAR UYTLEGGING – Leiden, 1721 – 2mf – 9 – ne IDC [700]
SPIEGEL DER HAUSSUCHT. IESUS SYRACH GENAND... / Huberinus, Caspar – Nuernberg: [J. vom Berg & U. Neuber], 1556. [G.F.: 23.5] – 7mf – 9 – HUB-81/1 – ne IDC [240]

SPIEGEL DER HAUSSUCHT. IESUS SYRACH GENANDT... / Huberinus, Caspar – Nuernberg: [U. Neuber & J. vom Bergs Erben], 1567. [G.F.: 23.9] – 7mf – 9 – HUB-82/1 – ne IDC [240]

SPIEGEL DER HAUSTZUCHT, IHESUS SYRACH GENANT... / Huberinus, Caspar – [Nuernberg: Johann Daubmann], 1553. [G.F.: 23.1] – 13mf – 9 – HUB-53/1 – ne IDC [240]

Spiegel, F see AVESTA, DIE HEILIGEN SCHRIFTEN DER PARSEN...SAMMT DER HUZVARESCH-UEBERSETZUNG

SPIEGEL SONDER BEDROGH OFTE KENNISSE SYNS SELFS... / Pinamonti, G P – Antwerpen, 1733 – 2mf – 9 – ne IDC [700]

SPIEGEL VAN DEN OUDEN EN NIEUWEN TYD. BESTAENDE UYT SPREECK-WOORDEN... / Cats, J – Amsterdam, 1722 – 4mf – 9 – ne IDC [700]

SPIEGEL VAN DEN OUDEN EN NIEUWEN TYDT, BESTAANDE UYT SPREKWOORDEN... / Cats, J – Amsterdam, [c. 1690] – 4mf – 9 – ne IDC [700]

SPIEGEL VAN DEN OUDEN ENDE NIEUWEN TIJT / Cats, J – Dordrecht, 1635 – 6mf – 9 – ne IDC [700]

SPIEGEL VAN DEN OUDEN ENDE NIEUWER TIJDT / Cats, J – O 196. 1632 – 9 – ne IDC [760]

SPIEGEL VAN HET MENSELIJK BEDRYF / Luiken, J & Luiken, K – O 348. 1730 – 9 – ne IDC [240]

Spiegelberg, W see
- AEGYPTISCHE GRABSTEINE UND DENKSTEINE AUS SUEDDEUTSCHEN SAMMLUNGEN
- DIE AEGYPTISCHE SAMMLUNG DER MUSEUM-MEERMANNO-WESTREENIANUM
- DIE AEGYPTISCHE SAMMLUNG DES MUSEUM-MEERMANNO-WESTREENIANUM IM HAAG
- AEGYPTOLOGISCHE RANDGLOSSEN ZUM ALTEN TESTAMENT

SPIEGHEL DER WATERLANTSCHER WEDERDOOPEREN LEUGHENKON ONTDECKENDENDE DE ONGHEGRONDE ENDE LEUGHENACHTIGE BESCHULDINGHEN / Bisschop, P de – Rotterdam, J. van Waesberghe. 1597. BME-252 1 – 9 – ne IDC [240]

Spieghel, H L see
- HERTSPIEGHEL

SPIEL DER MAECHTE : EIN KAPITEL AUS GOETHES LEBEN UND GOETHES WELT / Hankamer, Paul – Stuttgart: R Wunderlich, 1947 – 1r – 1 – us U.W. Library [920]

SPIEL IN FLANDERN : EINE NOVELLE AUS DEM GROSSEN KRIEGE / Linker, Wilhelm – 10. Aufl. Guetersloh: C Bertelsmann, 1943 – 1r – 1 – us U.W. Library [830]

SPIEL MIT DER WIRKLICHKEIT : GESCHICHTE EINES JUNGEN MANNES IN DER GESELLSCHAFT DES VORKRIEGES / Hillard, Gustav – Hamburg: Hanseatische Verlagsanstalt, 1938 – 1r – 1 – us U.W. Library [920]

DAS SPIEL VON DEN DEUTSCHEN AHNEN / Mell, Max – Leipzig: Insel-Verlag, 1935 – 1r – 1 – us U.W. Library [820]

SPIELEREI : DREI STUECKE / Bahr, Hermann – Berlin: Buehnenverlag Ahn & Simrock, c1919 – 1r – 1 – us U.W. Library [820]

Spielhagen, Friedrich see
- IN REIH' UND GLIED
- DIE PHILOSOPHIN
- SOEMMTLICHE WERKE
- STURMFLUT
- THROUGH NIGHT TO LIGHT
- VERMISCHTE SCHRIFTEN, UND, AMERIKANISCHE GEDICHTE
- WAS DIE SCHWALBE SANG

Spielmann, Marion Harry see JOHN RUSKIN

DAS SPIELMANNSKIND – DER STUMME RATSHERR : NOVELLEN / Riehl, Wilhelm Heinrich; ed by Eaton, Abbie Fiske – (German text with introd etc in English) – Boston: D C Heath, 1908 – 1 – us U.W. Library [830]

Spier, Leslie see THE DISTRIBUTION OF KINSHIP SYSTEMS IN NORTH AMERICA

Spiero, Heinrich see
- ERNST ZAHN
- GESCHICHTE DER DEUTSCHEN FRAUENDICHTUNG SEIT 1800
- HERMEN
- PAUL HEYSE

Spies, Meinrad see TRACTATUS MUSICUS COMPOSITORIO-PRACTICUS

Spiesser, Fritz see DIE ZWEITE GENERATION

Spiller, Gustav see REPORT ON MORAL INSTRUCTION (GENERAL AND DENOMINATIONAL) AND ON MORAL TRAINING

Spillman, Jane Shadel see
- AMERICAN AND EUROPEAN PRESSED GLASS IN THE CORNING MUSEUM OF GLASS
- THE CUT AND ENGRAVED GLASS OF CORNING, 1868-1940
- DINING AT THE WHITE HOUSE
- GLASS FROM WORLD'S FAIRS, 1851-1904
- GLASSMAKING: AMERICA'S FIRST INDUSTRY

Spillsbury, William H see LINCOLN'S INN

Spilman, B W see COLLECTION

Spilsbery, John see A TREATISE CONCERNING THE LAWFULL SUBJECT OF BAPTISM

Spilsbury, William Holden see LINCOLN'S INN; ITS ANCIENT AND MODERN BUILDINGS, WITH AN ACCOUNT OF THE LIBRARY

SPILSBY STANDARD see LINCOLNSHIRE STANDARD (SPILSBY ED)

Spinden, H J see THE NEZ PERCE INDIANS

SPINDLAR FRAN NIKOBERERNA OCH ANDRA DELAR AF SODRA ASIEN. INSAMLADE UNDER AREN 1845-1847 / Thorell, T T T – (Kongl. Svenska Vet. Akad. Handlingar.). v. 24, nr. 2. Stockholm. 1891-92. BZ-2206 2 – 8 – ne IDC [590]

Spindler, Carl see
- DER INVALIDE
- DER JESUIT

Spindler, William see AUF DEM SCHLACHTFELDE VON CUSTOZZA

SPINE – v. 1-. 1976- – 1,5,6,9 – us UMI [617]

Spinelli, V see LE ALGHE MARINE DELLA SICILIA ORIENTALE

SPINES THESAURUS : A CONTROLLED AND STRUCTURED VOCABULARY FOR INFORMATION PROCESSING IN THE FIELD OF SCIENCE AND TECHNOLOGY FOR DEVELOPMENT / Padirac, B de et al – (English/French/Spanish/Portuguese) – 1988 – 2v/1122p – 9 – 92-3-102257-1 – fr UNESCO [500]

DIE SPINNEN AMERIKAS / Keyserling, Eduard von – Z-2177 2. 4 v. 1880-1893 – 8 – ne IDC [590]

DIE SPINNEN DEUTSCHLANDS / Boesenberg, F W – Z-2163 2. 1901-1903 – 8 – ne IDC [590]

Spinner, Heinrich see GOETHES TYPUSBEGRIFF

Spinniker, A see
- LEERZAME ZINNEBEELDEN
- VERVOLG DER LEERZAAME ZINNEBEELDEN, SPIEGEL DER BOETVAARDIGHEID...

SPINNSTUBE – Goettingen. aug 30, 1919-apr 1935 – 3r – 1 – gw Mikrofilm [640]

SPINNSTUBE see DEUTSCHE VOLKSWACHT

Spinola de Gironza, Araceli see
- DIOS SOBRE TODO
- IMPRESIONES INTIMAS
- POR MIS SENDEROS
- ROSAS Y ESPIGAS
- TODAVIA SUENO

Spinola, M see ESSAI MONOGRAPHIQUE SUR LES CLERITES. INSECTES COLEOPTERES

SPINOZA / Caird, John – Edinburgh: W. Blackwood, 1888 – 1mf – us A.T.L.A. [190]

SPINOZA : EIN DENKERLEBEN / Auerbach, Berthold – 7. Aufl. Stuttgart: J G Cotta, 1871 – 1 – us U.W. Library [920]

Spinoza, Benedictus de see
- OPERA POSTHUMA
- TRACTATUS THEOLOGICO-POLITICUS

THE SPINOZA BIBLIOGRAPHY / Columbia University; ed by Oko, Adolph S – 1964. 7000 entries – 1r – 1 – $85.00 – 0-8161-1539-7 – uk Hall [190]

SPINOZA, DESCARTES AND MAIMONIDES / Roth, L – Oxford. 1924. BJ-33-22 1 – 9 – ne IDC [180]

SPINOZA EN ZIJN KRING / Meinsma, KO – 's-Gravenhage. 1896. BJ-262-36 1 – 9 – ne IDC [190]

SPINOZA IM JUNGEN GOETHE / Hering, Robert – (Includes bibliographical references) – [S.l.: s.n.] Leipzig: Druck von Schmidt & Baumann, 1897 – 1r – 1 – us U.W. Library [430]

SPINOZAS BRIEFWECHSEL U. ANDERE DOKUMENTE / Bluwstein, J – Leipzig, 1916 – 7mf – 8 – ne Slangenburg [100]

SPIONZA DANS LES PAYS NEERLANDAIS DANS LE SECONDE MOITIE DU 17E SIECLE / Frances, Madeleine – Paris, 1937 – 7mf – 8 – ne Slangenburg [190]

THE SPIRIT – Punxsutawney, PA. -d 1930-1990 – 13 – $25.00r – us I.M.R. [071]

THE SPIRIT AND THE INCARNATION : IN THE LIGHT OF SCRIPTURE, SCIENCE, AND PRACTICAL NEED / Walker, William Lowe – 2nd rev ed. Edinburgh: T & T Clark, 1901 – 1mf – 9 – 0-8370-3929-0 – 1985-1929 – us A.T.L.A. [230]

THE SPIRIT IN THE WORD / McIntyre, David – London: Morgan & Scott, 1908 – 1mf – 9 – us A.T.L.A. [240]

THE SPIRIT IN THE WORD, OR, LETTERS...ON THE CANON...AND ITS INSPIRATION / Smith, Justin A – Chicago: Church & Goodman, 1863.1 fiche – 9 – us A.T.L.A. [240]

SPIRIT OF "76 – Tacoma, WA: Spirit of 76 Cooperative Pub Association. n1-19. dec 3 1898-apr 15 1899 – us Res Libr [073]

SPIRIT OF '76 – Washington. D.C. 1809-11 – 1,3 – us Readex [071]

THE SPIRIT OF AMERICAN GOVERNMENT : A STUDY OF THE CONSTITUTION, ITS ORIGINS, INFLUENCE AND RELATION TO DEMOCRACY / Smith, J Allen – (With index) – New York: Macmillan, 1915 – 5mf – 9 – $7.50 – LLMC 95-092 – us L.L.M.C. [323]

SPIRIT OF BERKS – Reading, PA., 1876-1881 – 13 – $25.00r – us I.M.R. [071]

THE SPIRIT OF BRITISH MISSIONS – Dedicated to the Church Missionary Society. 1815 – 1 – us A.T.L.A. [240]

THE SPIRIT OF CHRIST IN COMMON LIFE : ADDRESSES AND SERMONS / Bigg, Charles – London, New York: Longmans, Green, 1909 – 1mf – 9 – us A.T.L.A. [240]

THE SPIRIT OF CHRISTIANITY (CCC231) / Lo, Yun-yen – (In Chinese) – 1st ed. Hong Kong: Council on Christian Literature for Overseas Chinese, 1958 – 1r – 1 – 1984-6570 – us A.T.L.A. [240]

THE SPIRIT OF DEMOCRACY / Abbott, Lyman – Boston: Houghton, Mifflin, 1910 – 1mf – us A.T.L.A. [321]

THE SPIRIT OF GOD IN BIBLICAL LITERATURE : A STUDY IN THE HISTORY OF RELIGION / Wood, Irving Francis – (Includes indexes) – New York: A C Armstrong, 1904 – 1mf – 9 – 0-8370-5897-X – 1985-3897 – us A.T.L.A. [220]

THE SPIRIT OF JAPAN / Moule, G H – London: Church Missionary Society, 1913 – 1mf – us A.T.L.A. [240]

SPIRIT OF JEFFERSON – Charles Town. West Virginia. 1852-1947 – 1 – us UMI [071]

SPIRIT OF JEFFERSON FARMERS ADVOCATE – Charles Town. West Virginia. -w. 1948-66 – 1 – us UMI [071]

THE SPIRIT OF JUDAISM / Lazarus, Josephine – New York: Dodd, Mead, 1895. 1 fiche – 9 – us A.T.L.A. [270]

SPIRIT OF MAN: AN ESSAY IN CHRISTIAN PHILOSOPHY / Chandler, Arthur – London: Longmans, Green, 1891. 1 fiche – 9 – us A.T.L.A. [240]

SPIRIT OF MISSIONS – v1-104, 1836-1939 – 1 – us A.T.L.A. [073]

THE SPIRIT OF NEW ENGLAND / Swan, Fredrick W – (Focuses on local government) – New York/Chicago/Boston: Charles Scribner's Sons, 1920 – 1mf – 9 – $1.50 – LLMC 92-201 – us L.L.M.C. [340]

THE SPIRIT OF POWER : AS SET FORTH IN THE BOOK OF THE ACTS OF THE APOSTLES / Adamson, Thomas – Edinburgh: T & T Clark, 1897 – 1mf – 9 – 0-8370-2047-6 – 1985-0047 – us A.T.L.A. [220]

SPIRIT OF POWER: AS SET FORTH IN THE BOOK OF THE ACTS OF THE APOSTLES / Adamson, Thomas – Edinburgh: T. & T. Clark, 1897. 1 fiche – 9 – us A.T.L.A. [240]

THE SPIRIT OF SPORT – (Series: United States Olympic Academy, 3) – Brigham Young University at Provo, 1979 – 2mf – 9 – $8.00 – us Microform Publ [790]

SPIRIT OF THE AGE – London. -w. 1 Jul 1848-3 Mar 1849. (1 reel) – 1 – uk British Libr Newspaper [072]

SPIRIT OF THE AGE – Sacramento, CA. 1855-1858 – 2r – 1 – $100.00 – C03440 – us Library Micro [071]

THE SPIRIT OF THE AGE : OR CONTEMPORARY PORTRAITS / Hazlitt, William – London: Printed for Henry Colburn, 1825 – 1 roll – 1 – 1-55879-330-5 – uk Libr Preservation [920]

THE SPIRIT OF THE CHRISTIAN LIFE : SERMONS / Brooke, Stopford Augustus – London: C. Kegan Paul, 1881 – 1mf – us A.T.L.A. [240]

THE SPIRIT OF THE MARKETS AND PRODUCE ADVERTISER – Montreal: H Jones, [1847?-18–] – 9 – cn C.I.H.M. [380]

THE SPIRIT OF THE MARTYRS REVIVED IN THE DOCTRINES OF THE REVEREND MR. GEORGE WHITEFIELD AND THE JUDICIOUS AND FAITHFUL METHODISTS,... / Warne, J – London, 1740 – 2mf – 9 – MP-283/1 – ne IDC [240]

THE SPIRIT OF THE NORTH AND OTHER POEMS / Gunne, A Evelyn – Toronto: Imrie, Graham, 1900. 05132. (Pre-1900 Canadiana) – 9 – cn C.I.H.M. [810]

SPIRIT OF THE PILGRIMS – v. 1-6. 1828-1833 – 1,5,6 – us Princeton Micro [240]

SPIRIT OF THE TIMES – A Chronicle of the Turf, Agriculture, Field Sports, Literature and the Stage. New York. v. 6-31, no. 20. Feb 20 1836-June 22 1861 – 1 – us NY Public [630]

SPIRIT OF THE TIMES – (Also: Carlise Republican 1819-20; Chambersburg Democratic-Republican, 1815-17; Shippensburg Spirit of the Times, 1817. Sold as one unit) – Carlisle, PA. 1817-19. Also: Carlisle Republican, – 3 – us Readex [071]

SPIRIT OF THE TIMES – Batavia, NY: O Follett, 1821-25 – us Res Libr [071]

SPIRIT OF THE TIMES : A CHRONICLE OF THE TURF, AGRICULTURE, FIELD SPORTS, LITERATURE AND THE STAGE – New York. v6-31. 1836-61 – 13r – 1 – us Ross [790]

SPIRIT OF THE TIMES – New York City, NY. v18 n1. 26 feb 1848-v18 n52. 17 feb 1849 – 1r – 1 – Can$45.00 – cn Can Microfilming [071]

SPIRIT OF THE TIMES – Philadelphia, PA. -d 1838; 1839; 1840; 1841; 1842; 1843-1846; 1846-1848; 1849 – 13 – $25.00r – us I.M.R. [071]

THE SPIRIT PUNXSUTAWNEY – Punxsutawney, PA., 1983 – 13 – $25.00r – us I.M.R. [071]

THE SPIRIT-FILLED LIFE / MacNeil, John – New York: Fleming H Revell, 1896 – 1mf – 9 – 0-8370-2261-4 – 1985-0261 – us A.T.L.A. [240]

SPIRITISM AND RELIGION. / Liljencrantz, John – Lynchburg, VA: J.B. Bell & Co., 1918. 295p – 1 – us U.W. Library [150]

SPIRITISTEN UND THEOSOPHEN see DEUTSCHE REVUE

LO SPIRITO FOLETTO – Milan, Italy. -w. 6 June 1861-Dec 1885. 12 reels – 1 – uk British Libr Newspaper [072]

THE SPIRIT-RAPPER : AN AUTOBIOGRAPHIE / Brownson, Orestes Augustus – Boston: Little, Brown, 1854 – 1mf – 9 – 0-8370-7204-2 – 1986-1204 – us A.T.L.A. [130]

SPIRIT-RAPPING UNVEILED / Mattison, Hiram – 1855 – 9 – us A.T.L.A. [150]

A SPIRITUAL AWAKENING AMONG INDIA'S STUDENTS : ADDRESSES OF SIX STUDENT CONFERENCES OF THE STUDENT VOLUNTEER MOVEMENT HELD AT JAFFNA, BOMBAY, LAHORE, LUCKNOW, CALCUTTA, AND MADRAS – (Includes index) – Madras: Addison, 1896 – 1mf – 9 – 0-8370-6697-2 – 1986-0697 – us A.T.L.A. [240]

SPIRITUAL COUNTERFEITS PROJECT. NEWSLETTER.. – 1977-80 – 1 – us UMI [290]

SPIRITUAL DEVELOPMENT OF ST. PAUL / Matheson, George – New York:Thomas Whittaker, [1890?] – 1mf – 9 – 0-8370-4317-4 – 1985-2317 – us A.T.L.A. [220]

A SPIRITUAL, ECCLESIASTICAL AND HISTORICAL VIEW OF SLAVERY : FROM THE DAYS OF THE PATRIACH ABRAHAM, TO THE NINETEENTH CENTURY / Hopkins, John Henry – (A pro-slavery work by the Episcopal bishop of Vermont) – New York: W I Pooley & Co, 1864 – 4mf – 9 – $6.00 – LLMC 91-100 – us L.L.M.C. [306]

SPIRITUAL MELODY, CONTAINING THREE HUNDRED SACRED HYMNS / Keach, Benjamin – London. 1691 – 1 – 13.44 – us Baptist [240]

SPIRITUAL MILK, OR, CHRISTIAN INSTRUCTION FOR CHILDREN / Valdes, Juan de – London: Truebner, 1882 – 1mf – us A.T.L.A. [240]

SPIRITUAL MOBILIZATION – v13-15. May 1946-Oct 1949 (complete) – 1r – 1 – ATLA S0685C – us A.T.L.A. [073]

THE SPIRITUAL QUIXOTE : OR, THE SUMMER'S RAMBLE OF MR. GEOFFREY WILDGOOSE: A COMIC ROMANCE / Graves, R – (Missing: V.1-2) – London, 1773.-3v – 4mf – 9 – MP-484/1 – ne IDC [820]

SPIRITUAL REFORMERS IN THE 16TH AND 17TH CENTURIES / Jones, Rufus M – London: Macmillan, 1914 – 1mf – us A.T.L.A. [240]

THE SPIRITUAL RETURN OF CHRIST WITHIN THE CHURCH : PAPERS ON CHRISTIAN THEISM / De Bary, Richard – London: John Murray, 1907 – 1mf – 9 – 0-8370-4582-7 – 1985-2582 – us A.T.L.A. [240]

SPIRITUAL SABBATHISM / Lewis, Abram Herbert – Plainfield, N.J.: American Sabbath Tract Society, 1910 – 1mf – us A.T.L.A. [240]

SPIRITUAL STRUGGLES OF A ROMAN CATHOLIC : AN AUTOBIOGRAPHICAL SKETCH / Beaudry, Louis Napoleon – (Includes bibliographical references) – New York: Nelson & Phillips; Cincinnati: Hitchcock & Walden, 1875 – 1mf – 9 – 0-8370-8723-6 – 1986-2723 – us A.T.L.A. [240]

A SPIRITUAL TREASURY FOR THE CHILDREN OF GOD : CONSISTING OF A MEDITATION FOR EACH DAY IN THE YEAR, UPON SELECT TEXTS OF SCRIPTURE / Mason, William – (Includes index) – New York: American Tract Society, [18–] – 2mf – 9 – 0-8370-6274-8 – 1986-0274 – us A.T.L.A. [240]

SPIRITUAL UNIVERSE – Cleveland, OH, 9 Dec 1854-19 May 1855 – 1 reel – 1 – us Western Res [071]

SPIRITUAL UNIVERSE AND JOURNAL OF REFORM – Cleveland, OH, 24 Nov 1855-14 June 1856 – 1 reel – 1 – us Western Res [071]

SPIRITUALIST – Cleveland, OH, 14 Nov., 1857 – 1 reel – 1 – us Western Res [071]

THE SPIRO T. AGNEW CASE : THE INVESTIGATIVE AND LEGAL DOCUMENTS / Fay, Thomas F – (With printed guide) – 3r – 1 – $255.00 – D3259 – us Scholarly Res [340]

SPISKI IEARKHOV I NASTOIATELEI MONASTYREI / Stroev, P M – St. Petersburg, 1877. BR-10,064/2 – 8 – ne IDC [240]

SPISOK ARTELEI I TOVARISHCHESTV – CHLENOV LENINGRADSKOGO SOIUZA PROMYSLOVOI KOOPERATSII "PROIZVODSOIUZA" – L., 1927 – 1mf – 9 – COR-447/1 – ne IDC [334]

SPISOK CHLENOV IMP. AKADEMII NAUK (1725-1907) / Modzalevskii, B L – Spb. 1908. BR-8002 – 8 – ne IDC [947]

SPISOK GLAVNEISHIKH PERIODICHESKIKH IZDANII, IMEIUSHCHIKHSIA / St. Petersburg. University. Imperial Library – Spb. 1909. BR-4718 2 – 8 – ne IDC [020]

SPISOK GOSUDARSTVENNYKH MUZEEV SSSR (PO SOSTOIANIIU NA 1 IANVARIA 1968 GODS) / U.S.S.R. Ministerstva Kultury. RSFSR – (Nauchno-issledovatel'skii institut kul'tury Ministerstva kul'tury RSFSR). M. 1969. BR-11,309 1 – 9 – ne IDC [060]

SPISOK IZDANII PERESELENCHESKAGO UPRAVLENIIA – Spb. 1914. BR-7275 2 – 8 – ne IDC [947]

SPISOK IZDANII TSENTRAL'NAGO STATISTICHESKAGO KOMITETA MINISTERSTVA VNUTRENNYKH DEL, VYSHEDSHIKH S 1881 PO 1 APRELIA 1901 G – Spb. 1902. BR-5641 2 – 8 – ne IDC [310]

SPISOK IZDANNII, VYSHEDSHIKH V ROSSII. 1888-1907 – Spb. 1888-1908. Lacking: 1894. BR-4378 2 – 8 – ne IDC [010]

SPISOK KNIG O RUSSKIKH MONASTYRIAKH I TSERKVAKH / Gennadi, G – Spb. 1854. BR-5899 2 – 8 – ne IDC [240]

SPISOK KOOPERATIVNYKH SOIUZOV SSSR (SEL'SKOKHOZIAISTVENNYKH, KREDIT., PROMYSLOVYKH, LESN. I ZHIL.) NA 1-E IANV. 1926 G. – Ed 4. M., 1926 – 1mf – 9 – COR-275/1 – ne IDC [334]

SPISOK KOOPERATIVNYKH SOIUZOV SSSR (SEL'SKOKHOZIAISTVENNYKH, KREDITNYKH, PROMYSLOVYKH, LESNYKH) NA 1-E FEVRALIA 1925 GODA – Ed 3. M., 1925 – 1mf – 9 – COR-747/1 – ne IDC [334]

SPISOK KOOPERATIVNYKH SOIUZOV SSSR (TSENTRAL'NYKH, OBLASTNYKH, GUBERNSKIKH I RAIONNYKH) NA 1-E IIULIA 1923 G. – M., 1923 – 1mf – 9 – COR-746/1 – ne IDC [334]

SPISOK KOOPERATIVOV ARKHANGEL'SKOI GUBERNII – Arkhangel'sk, 1918 – 1mf – 9 – COR-749/1 – ne IDC [334]

SPISOK PAISHCHIKOV VSEROSSIISKOGO KOOPERATIVNOGO BANKA NA 1 FEVRALIA 1925 GODA – M., 1925 – 1mf – 9 – COR-403/1 – ne IDC [334]

SPISOK PERIODICHESKIKH IZDANII, VYKHODIASHCHIKH V ROSSII, S PEREVODOM ZAGLAVII NA FRANTSUZSKII IAZYK I S SOKRASHCHENIIAMI – Spb. 1907. BR-4419 2 – 8 – ne IDC [460]

SPISOK PERSIDSKIKH, TURETSKO-TATARSKIKH I ARABSKIKH RUKOPISEI BIBLIOTEKI PETROGRADSKOGO UNIVERSITETA / Romaskevich, A A – Leningrad, 1925, v1, p353-371. BR-10,920/1 – 9 – ne IDC [010]

SPISOK POVREMENNYKH IZDANII POLUCHAVSHIKHSIA. 1906-1911 GG / Moscow. University. Imperial Library – M. 1909. BR-4763 2 – 8 – ne IDC [020]

SPISOK POVREMENNYKH IZDANII POLUCHAVSKIKHSIA. 1906-1911 GG / Moscow. University. Imperial Library – M. 1911. BR-4764 2 – 8 – ne IDC [020]

SPISOK RUKOPISEI SEVANSKAGO MONASTYRIA / Marr, N Ia – Moscow, 1892. 63p. BR-7300/2 – 8 – ne IDC [240]

SPISOK RUSSKIKH I NEMNOGIKH INORODCHESKIKH NAZVANII RASTENII. DOPOLNENIE K "BOTANICHESKOMU SLOVARIU" / Gornitskii, KS – N. Annenkova. Khar'kov, 1886 – 1mf – 9 – R-4293/2 – ne IDC [580]

SPISOK RUSSKIKH POVREMENNYKH IZDANII S 1703 PO 1899 GOD. PRINADLEZHASHCHIKH BIBLIOTEKE IMP / Akademiia Nauk. Saint Petersburg – Spb. 1901. BR-7277 2 – 8 – ne IDC [020]

SPISOK RUSSKIM PAMIATNIKAM, SLUZHASHCHIM K SOSTAVLENIIU ISTORII KHUDOZHESTV I OTECHESTVENNOI PALEOGRAFII / Keppen, P – Moscow, 1822. BR-4678/2 – 8 – ne IDC [340]

SPISOK TADZHIKSKIKH, PERSIDSKIKH I TIURSKIKH RUKOPISEI VOSTOCHNOGO OTDELA BIBLIOTEKI LGU / Tagirdzhanov, A T – Moscow, 1967. 19p. BR-10,924/1 – 9 – ne IDC [025]

SPISOK UKAZATELEI K RUSSKIM PERIODICHESKIM IZDANIIAM 17-19 ST / Lisovskii, N M – 1903 – 8 – BR-4045 2 – ne IDC [073]

SPISOK ZAVEDENII PECHATI I KNIZHNOI TORGOVLI NAKHODIASHCHIKHSIA V VEDENII INSPEKTORSKAGO NADZORA V S.-PETERBURGE PO 1 APRELIA 1891 G – Spb. 1891. BR-4590 2 – 8 – ne IDC [947]

Spitta, Friedrich *see* DIE APOSTELGESCHICHTE: IHRE QUELLEN UND DEREN GESCHICHTLICHER WERT

Spitta, Heinrich *see* HELDENTOD: STUDIEN ZUR VERGLEICHENDEN PSYCHOLOGIE

Spitteler, Carl *see* SELECTED POEMS OF CARL SPITTELER

Spitzel, T G *see* DE RE LITERARIA SINENSIUM COMMENTARIUS,...

DIE SPITZHACKE : EIN PHANTASTISCHES ERLEBNIS / Hauptmann, Gerhart – Berlin: S Fischer, 1931, c1930 – 1r – 1 – us U.W. Library [830]

SPITZKUGELN : ZEIT-DISTICHEN / Hoffmann von Fallersleben, August Heinrich – Darmstadt: In Commission bei C W Leske, 1849 – 1r – 1 – us U.W. Library [810]

Spix, J B von *see* AVIUM SPECIES NOVAE, QUAS IN ITINERE PER BRASILIAM

SPLACE – Pattee, University Park, PA. 1989 – 18p 1mf – 9 – $0.50f – us Lawrence Pub [720]

SPLENDEUR DES COSTUMES DU MONDE / Institut d'Ethnologie. Museum National d'Histoire Naturelle. Paris – Commissaire: Monique de Fontanes – 9 – F200.00 – fr Ethnologie [390]

A SPLENDID SIN / Allen, Grant – New York: F. M. Buckles, 1899. 05070. (Pre-1900 Canadiana) – 9 – cn C.I.H.M. [830]

THE SPLENDOUR THAT WAS EGYPT / Murray, Margaret – Philosophical Library. 1949 – 9 – $12.00 – us I.R.C. [930]

Splettstoesser, W *see* DER HEIMKEHRENDE GATTE UND SEIN WEIB IN DER WELTLITTERATUR

"SPLINTERS." / Atchison, Topeka and Santa Fe Railway Company – 1 – us KS Hist [978]

Splitgerber, F L *see* ENUMERATIO FILICUM ET LYCOPODIACEARUM QUAS IN SURINAMO

SPLYWY ROSYJSKIE NA DUSZE POLSKA / Zdziechowski, Marian – Krakow, Krakowska Spolka Wydawnicza, 1920. 155p. Bibliog. footnotes – 1 – us U.W. Library [943]

Spoerl, J J *see* ACCURACY OF PERCEIVED HEAVINESS AND PERCEIVED JOINT PLACEMENT IN NORMAL AND INJURED SHOULDER JOINTS

Spofford, A R *see* THE LIBRARY OF WIT AND HUMOR, PROSE AND POETRY

Spofford, Harriet Prescott *see* HOUSE AND HEARTH

Spohr, Louis *see* SYMPHONIE NO. 10 FUER GROSSES ORCHESTER

Spohr, Ludwig *see* FAUST

SPOKEN ENGLISH – (v10-. 1977-. 5,6,9) – v. 1-. 1968- – 1 – us UMI [420]

THE SPOKEN WORD – Los Angeles, California. v. 1. no. 1- v. 3. no. 81. Oct. 20, 1934-July 31, 1937 – 1 – us NY Public [073]

SPOKESMAN – Roseburg, OR. 1 Jun 1906-26 Dec 1907. 1 roll – 1 – us U.O. Library [071]

SPOKESMAN – Spokane. Wash. -w. 1891-93 – 1 – us UMI [071]

THE SPOKESMAN / ed by McKenzie, Charles – Drummondville, Canada. 26 jun 1928-27 dec 1957 – 6r – 1 – Can$65.00r – cn Can Microfilming [072]

THE SPOKESMAN – San Francisco, CA. 1933-1935 – 1r – 1 – $50.00 – C03502 – us Library Micro [071]

SPOKESMAN-REVIEW – Spokane. Wash. 1884- – 1 – us UMI [071]

SPOKESMAN-REVIEW – Spokane. Wash. -w, sw. 1883-1929 – 1 – us UMI [071]

SPOKESMAN-REVIEW INDEX – Spokane.WA. 1887-1920 – 1 – us UMI [071]

LES SPOLIATIONS COLONIALES EN TUNISIE : AUTOUR DE L'AFFAIRE COUITEAS (DEBUT DU 20TH SIECLE) / Poitevin, C – F100.00 – fr Ethnologie [960]

Spon, Jacob *see*
- REPONSE A LA CRITIQUE PUBLIEE PAR M. GUILLET SUR LE VOYAGE DE GRECE DE JACOB SPON
- VOYAGE D'ITALIE, DE DALMATIE, DE GRECE ET DU LEVANT, FAIT AUX ANNEES 1675 ET 1676

Spondanus, H *see* GENERALE KERCKELYCKE HISTORIE VAN DEN GHEBOORTE ONZES H. IESU CHRISTI TOT HET IAER 1624. H. ROSWEYDUS

Sponsel, J U *see* ORGELHISTORIE

SPONTANEOUS KICKING IN INFANTS : A REPLICATION STUDY / Janzen, Tami M – 1989 – 97p 1mf – 9 – $4.00 – us Microform Publ [612]

Spontini *see*
- FERNAND CORTEZ OU LA CONQUETE DU MEXIQUE
- LA VESTALE

Spooner, E A *see* DIARY

Spooner, Edward *see* TEN MINUTES' READINGS IN THE BOOK OF GENESIS

Spooner Family *see* GENEALOGICAL MATERIAL, MS 1826

Spooner, Lysander *see* COLLECTED WORKS OF LYSANDER SPOONER

Spooner, W W *see* WESTCHESTER COUNTY

SPOR ALEMI – (Sahib-i Imtiyaz: Celebizade Said Tevfik, Sermuharriri: Burhaneddin. Nos. 1-7, 13-29 (5 Eyluel 1338-11 Nisan 1339[1922-1923])) – Istanbul: Halk Matbaasi, 1919-1928 – 7mf – 9 – $125.00 – us MEDOC [949]

LE SPORT – (Cont by: La Voix de Shawinigan, Grand-Mere 7 jun 1946-9 avr 1975. Absorbed by: La Voix Commerciale) – Shawinigan, Canada. 13 avr 1945-24 mai 1946 – 16r – 1 – Can$65.00r – cn Can Microfilming [072]

LE SPORT : HEBDO RECREATIF – Montreal, Canada. v2 n31. 29 dec 1939 – 1r – 1 – Can$25.00 – cn Can Microfilming [790]

LE SPORT *see* LE BULLETIN

O SPORT : ORGAM CRITICO, SPORTIVO E NOTICIOSO – Itacoatiara, Amazonas. 7 Set-7 Nov 1917 – 1,5,6 – bl Biblioteca [072]

O SPORT : ORGAO DE INTERESSES SPORTIVOS – Manoas, Amazonas. 31 Jul 1909-13 Maio 1911 – 1,5,6 – bl Biblioteca [072]

SPORT – Bratislava, Czechoslovakia. 1977-92 – 27r – 1 – us L of C Photodup [072]

SPORT – Katowice, Poland. -w. Aug 1952-Dec 1958. 7 reels – 1 – uk British Libr Newspaper [072]

SPORT : LITTERARIO ILLUSTRADO – Manoas, Amazonas. 1907 – 1,5,6 – bl Biblioteca [072]

SPORT – Montreal: J A Lowe, [1887-18– or 19–] – 9 – cn C.I.H.M. [790]

SPORT ACHIEVEMENT ORIENTATION OF MALE AND FEMALE INTERCOLLEGIATE ATHLETES, INTRAMURAL ATHLETES, AND NONATHLETES / Ruan, Nianyu & Murray, Mimi – 1993 – 2mf – 9 – $8.00 – us Microform Publ [150]

SPORT ADMINISTRATION PROGRAM DIRECTORS AT INSTITUTIONS OF HIGHER EDUCATION : A STUDY OF QUALIFICATIONS AS PERCEIVED BY SPORT ADMINISTRATION PROGRAM DIRECTORS AND SPORT MANAGEMENT PRACTITIONERS / Quinn, Ronald W – 1994 – 2mf – $8.00 – us Microform Publ [790]

SPORT AND OLYMPISM : A WAY OF LIFE – (Series: United States Olympic Academy, 2) – Illinois State University at Normal, 1978 – 2mf – 9 – $8.00 – us Microform Publ [790]

SPORT AND POETRY: AN EXPLORATION OF THE INTERRELATEDNESS OF WORDS AND ACTIONS / Resen, Ardis C – 1981 – 2mf – 9 – $8.00 – us Microform Publ [790]

SPORT DIVER – v1-8. 1977-84 – 1,5,6,9 – us UMI [790]

LE SPORT ILLUSTRE – Montreal: A Marion, [1899] – 9 – cn C.I.H.M. [790]

SPORT ILLUSTRE – Laprairie. v6 n7. 14 jan 1974 – 1r – 1 – Can$25.00 – cn Can Microfilming [072]

SPORT IM BILD – Berlin, 10 May 1895-4 Sep 1934 – 30r – DM2,250.00 – gw Mikro Press [790]

SPORT IM WORT – Berlin, 5 Jan-30 Mar 1900 – 1r – DM75.00 – gw Mikro Press [790]

SPORT LIFE – Philadelphia. v1-70. 1883-1922 – 27r – 1 – us Ross [790]

SPORT NATIONALISM IN THE MODERN OLYMPIC GAMES / Lee, J-Y – 1990 – 3mf – 9 – $12.00 – us Microform Publ [790]

SPORT PROGRAM EFFECTS ON PARTICIPANTS WITH MENTAL RETARDATION / Riggen, Katherine J & Ulrich, Dale A – 1992 – 2mf – 9 – $8.00 – us Microform Publ [150]

SPORT SOCIALIZATION OF CEREBRAL PALSIED ADOLESCENTS / Lugo, A M – 1991 – 3mf – 9 – $12.00 – us Microform Publ [150]

SPORT SOCIALIZATION OF URBAN COSTA RICAN CHILDREN / Pizarro, A – 1991 – 2mf – 9 – $8.00 – us Microform Publ [150]

SPORT SPONSORSHIP IN CANADA : A STUDY OF EXCHANGE BETWEEN CORPORATE SPONSORS AND SPORT GROUPS / Copeland, R P – 1991 – 3mf – 9 – $12.00 – us Microform Publ [790]

SPORT UND TECHNIK – Berlin, 1958-89 – 11r – 1 – Inquire at Mikrofilmarchiv for details – gw Misc Inst [790]

SPORT UND TECHNIK – Berlin, DE. 1958-89 – 11r – 1 – gw Mikrofilm [072]

SPORTBERICHT – Stuttgart, Germany. 4 Nov 1946-28 Dec 1960 – 11r – 1 – gw Mikrofilm [072]

SPORTING BULLETIN – Goldfield, NV. 29 Aug 1906 – 1r – 1 – $50.00 – U04561 – us Library Micro [071]

SPORTING CHRONICLE – 1880- – 1 – uk Manchester Libr [790]

SPORTING LIFE – London. -w. 1860-1967. (404mqn reels) – 1 – uk British Libr Newspaper [073]

SPORTING LIFE – Montreal, Canada. v1 n24. 15 jul 1889 – 1r – 1 – Can$25.00 – cn Can Microfilming [790]

SPORTING LIFE – Philadelphia. v. 1-6, 9-16, 31-34 and 62-66. no. 7. Apr 15 1883-Apr 7 1886, Apr 13 1887-Mar 28 1891, 1898-1900, 1914-1915 – 1 – us NY Public [790]

SPORTING LIFE, 1883-1917 – v1-68. 1883-1917 – 29r – 1 – $40.00r – us U.N.D. Archives [790]

SPORTING LIFE; THE LOYAL CHAMPION OF CLEAN SPORT – v.3-74, 1883-1917; 1922-26 – 1 – 598.00 – us L of C Photodup [790]

SPORTING MAGAZINE – London. -m. 1792-1870. (78 reels) – 1 – uk British Libr Newspaper [073]

SPORTING NEWS : THE BASE BALL PAPERS OF THE WORLD – St. Louis, MO. v56-114. 1914-42 – 20r – 1 – us Ross [790]

SPORTING NEWS – v.1-. 1886- – 1 – us UMI [790]

THE SPORTING NEWS, 1916-1972 – 70r – 1 – $2800.00 set $45.00r – us U.N.D. Archives [790]

SPORTING PRINTS / British Museum – (Includes printed catalogue) – 1993 – 8mf – 15 – $273.00 – 1-869934-62-8 – uk Emmett [760]

SPORTING REVIEW – London. -m. 1839-70. (32 reels) – 1 – uk British Libr Newspaper [073]

SPORTOWIEC – Warsaw, Poland. -w. July 1954-Dec 1958; Jan 1961-Dec 1962. 6 reels – 1 – uk British Libr Newspaper [072]
SPORTS ILLUSTRATED – (v. 30- 1969- 5,6,9) – v. 1- 1954- – 1 – us UMI [790]
SPORTS LAWYERS JOURNAL – v1-3. 1994-96 – 9 – $36.00set – us Hein [340]
SPORTS MEDICINE, TRAINING AND REHABILITATION : AN INTERNATIONAL JOURNAL / ed by Banister, Eric – 1,5,9 – us Gordon [617]
SPORTS MERCHANDISER – 1969- 1; 1975- 5,6,9 – us UMI [790]
SPORTS PERIODICALS – 1882-1922. All Outdoors; The Amateur Athlete; American Athlete and Cycle Trade Review; American Gymnasia and Athletic Record; Annals of Sporting and Fancy Gazette; Chicago Field; Illustrated Outdoor News; Western Field. Titles available seperately. See under title for price – 1 – $3,965.00 – us UPA [970]
THE SPORTSMAN – London. 1833-70; 1875-Aug 1882.-m. 53 reels – 1 – uk British Libr Newspaper [072]
THE SPORTSMAN – London. Aug 1865-Jun 1903; Jul 1908-Dec 1918. -d. 146mqn reels – 1 – uk British Libr Newspaper [072]
SPORTSNOW – v1-. 1983- – 1,5,6,9 – us UMI [073]
SPORTSTYLE – New York, Nov 1978- – 1 – $175.00y – us Fairchild Micro [790]
SPORTUNTERRICHT UND HOCHSCHULSPORT IN FRANKREICH / Becker, Werner – 1992 – 122p – 9 – DM98.00 – 3-89349-616-5 – gw Hänsel [790]
SPORY I RAZDELENIIA V RUSSKOM RASKOLE V PERVOI CHETVERTI 18 VEKA / Smirnov, P S – Spb. 1909. BR-7878 2 – 8 – ne IDC [947]
[LA SPOSA FIDELE] ROBERT UND KALLISTE. EIN OPERETTE IN 3 AUFZUGEN. NACH DEM INHALT UND KOMPOSITION DER SPOSA FELEL VON CHIARI... / Gugliehmi, P – (Score) – 178-? – 1 – us Sibley [780]
SPOT – Goettingen. apr 24, 1975-apr 1, 1977 – 1r – 1 – gw Mikrofilm [072]
SPOTLIGHT : AMERICAN YOUTH FOR DEMOCRACY – v1-3, no. 5 (all publ). 1943-1945 – 1 reel – 1 – $65.00 – us UPA [335]
SPOTLIGHT – (v6-13. 1980) – v2-13. 1976-81. Continues National Spotlight – 1 – us UMI [073]
SPOTLIGHT ON SPAIN / Huntz, Jack – London, 1936? Fiche W950. (Blodgett Collection of Spanish Civil War Pamphlets) – 9 – us H.U. College Libr [946]
SPOTS AND ROTS / Kentucky. Agricultural Extension Service – v. 1, no. 1-8. 1966 – 1,5,6 – us Spaulding [630]
SPOTS ON THE SUN, OR, THE PLUMB-LINE PAPERS : BEING A SERIES OF ESSAYS, OR CRITICAL EXAMINATIONS OF DIFFICULT PASSAGES OF SCRIPTURE / Hopkins, T M – New York: Rudd & Carleton, 1861 – 1mf – 9 – 0-8370-4864-8 – 1985-2864 – us A.T.L.A. [220]
SPOTSWOOD BAPTIST CHURCH. FREDERICKSBURG, VIRGINIA : CHURCH RECORDS – Feb 1956-Jun 1987 – 1 – 41.90 – us Baptist [240]
Spotts, David L *see* DIARIES
SPOTTVOGEL – Indianapolis. Ind. 1871-1918 – 1 – us UMI [071]
DIE SPRACHE DER MUTTER GOETHES : EIN BEITRAG ZUR GESCHICHTE DER RHEINISCHEN SCHRIFTSPRACHE IM 18. JAHRHUNDERT / Merkel, Bertha – (Includes bibliographical references) – Frankfurt am Main: M Diesterweg, [1938] – 1 – us U.W. Library [430]
DIE SPRACHE DER OPITZISCHEN GEDICHTSAMMLUNGEN VON 1624 UND 1625 : LAUTE, FLEXIONEN, BETONUNG / Baesecke, Georg – Braunschweig: J Krampe, 1899 – 1r – 1 – us U.W. Library [430]
DIE SPRACHE DER PRESSE UND DES PARLAMENTS / Silbermann, Josef – Kiel: Lipsius und Tischer, 1893 – 1r – 1 – us U.W. Library [070]
DIE SPRACHE DES JUNGEN HERDER IN IHREM VERHAELTNIS ZUR SCHRIFTSPRACHE : EIN BEITRAG ZUR GESCHICHTE DER NEUHOCHDEUTSCHEN SCHRIFTSPRACHE / Laengin, Theodor – (Includes bibliographical references) – Tauberbischofsheim: J Lang, 1891 – 1r – 1 – us U.W. Library [430]
SPRACHE, ERKENNTNIS UND HANDLUNG – "SPRACHINHALTSFORSCHUNG" UND "SPRACHPRAGMATIK" ALS EINANDER ERGAENZENDE WISSENSCHAFTEN / Hentschel, Ute – 1994 – 2mf – DM80.00 – 3-8267-2066-0 – gw Hänsel [400]
DIE SPRACHE IN RICHARD WAGNERS DICHTUNGEN / Wolzogen, Hans von – (Includes bibliographical references) – 4. Aufl. Leipzig: F Reinboth, [189-?] – 1 – us U.W. Library [430]
SPRACHE, REGEL UND SPIEL : DIE STELLUNG DES REGELBEGRIFFS IN DER SPAETPHILOSOPHIE LUDWIG WITTGENSTEINS / Moellmann, Margarete – Frankfurt a.M., 1977 – 2mf – 9 – DM62.00 – 3-89349-385-9 – gw Hänsel [190]
SPRACHFEHLER, WORTSPIELE, ETC. / Weber, Karl Friedrich – [S.l: s.n, 18–?] – 1r – 1 – us U.W. Library [430]
SPRACHKENNTNISSE UND DOLMETSCHERWESEN IM MISSIONARISCHEN UND DIPLOMATISCHEN VERKEHR ZWISCHEN ABENDLAND (PAEPSTLICHE KURIE) UND ORIENT IM 13 UND 14 JH / Altaner, Bruno – Ztschr. fuer Kirchengeschichte LV. 1936. p83-126. BU-716 2 – 8 – ne IDC [240]
DIE SPRACHLICHE BEHANDLUNG DES TEXTES IN DER PROBEBIBEL / Walter, Emil – Bernburg: Ad. Schmelzer, 1885. 1 fiche – 9 – us A.T.L.A. [240]
DIE SPRACHLICHEN VERSCHIEDENHEITEN IN DEN HEXATEUCHQUELLEN : EIN BEITRAG ZUM SPRACHBEWEIS IN DER LITERARKRITIK DES ALTEN TESTAMENTS / Kraeutlein, Jonathan – (Includes bibliography) – Leipzig: J C Hinrichs, 1908 – 1mf – 9 – 0-8370-3988-6 – 1985-1988 – us A.T.L.A. [220]
SPRACHLICHES HANDBUCH ZUR BIBLISCHEN VULGATA / Kaulen, Franz – Freiburg i.B.: Herder, 1904. 1 fiche – 9 – us A.T.L.A. [240]
DIE SPRACHRESTE DER DRAVAENOV-POLABEN IM HANNOEVERSCHEN / Rost, P – Leipzig. 1907. BR-5602 2 – 8 – ne IDC [400]
SPRACHWISSENSCHAFTLICHE UNTERSUCHUNGEN ZUM SEMITISCHEN / Barth, Jakob – Leipzig. 1907, 1911. BNE-466 1 – 9 – ne IDC [470]
Sprading, Charles *see* LIBERTY AND THE GREAT LIBERTARIANS
Sprague, A P *see* SPEECHES, ARGUMENTS AND MISCELLANEOUS PAPERS OF DAVID DUDLEY FIELD
Sprague, C P *see* WESTERN SHORE GAZETTEER AND COMMERCIAL DIRECTORY FOR CALIFORNIA
Sprague, Peley *see* SPRAGUE'S ADMIRALTY AND MARITIME DECISIONS IN THE DISTRICT OF MASSACHUSETTS, 1841-1864
Sprague, William Buell *see* THE LIFE OF JEDIDIAH MORSE, D.D.
Sprague, William Cyrus *see*
- LESSON SHEETS ON CRIMINAL LAW
- LESSONS ON AGENCY
- LESSONS ON PARTNERSHIP
- LESSONS ON SALES
- QUIZZER NO. 1...BEING QUESTIONS AND ANSWERS ON DOMESTIC RELATIONS.
- QUIZZER NO. 4...BEING QUESTIONS AND ANSWERS ON REAL PROPERTY...2ND ED
- QUIZZER NO. 14...BEING QUESTIONS AND ANSWERS ON SALES OF PERSONAL PROPERTY...5TH ED

SPRAGUE'S ADMIRALTY AND MARITIME DECISIONS IN THE DISTRICT OF MASSACHUSETTS, 1841-1864 / Sprague, Peley – Philadelphia: Johnson. v1-2. 1861-68 (all publ) – 11mf – 9 – $16.50 – LLMC 81-469 – us L.L.M.C. [324]
SPRAGUE'S HISTORY OF GRAND TRAVERSE AND LEELANAW COUNTIES – Indianapolis: B. F. Bowen and Co., 1903. Michigan Reel 10. (The Cox Library Collection) – 5 – us Americana [978]
SPRAGUE'S ILLUSTRATIVE CASES ON PERSONAL PROPERTY / Griffin, Levi Thomas – Detroit: Sprague Correspondence School of Law 1896. 202p. LL-78 – 1 – us L of C Photodup [340]
SPRAGUE'S ILLUSTRATIVE CASES UPON THE LAW OF EVIDENCE / Hughes, Thomas Welburn – Detroit: Sprague 1897. 141p. LL-1493 – 1 – us L of C Photodup [340]
Spratt, T *see* THE HISTORY OF THE ROYAL-SOCIETY
Spratt, T A B *see* TRAVELS IN LYCIA, MILYAS AND CIBYRATIS
SPRAVEDLNOST – Chicago: Bohemian Socialistic Pub Assoc of Chicago, [oct 18 1917-sep 20 1940] – 52r – 1 – us Res Libr [071]
SPRAVOCHNAIA KNIZHKA DLIA SEL'SKOKHOZIAISTVENNYKH I KREDITNYKH TOVARISHCHESTV – (Missing: No. 1) – M., 1923 – 4mf – 9 – COR-405/1 – ne IDC [334]
SPRAVOCHNAIA KNIZHKA DLIA SEL'SKOKHOZIAISTVENNYKH I SEL'SKOKHOZIAISTVENNYKH KREDITNYKH TOVARISHCHESTV / ed by Khizhniakov, V V – Ed 5. M., 1929 – 5mf – 9 – COR-515/1 – ne IDC [334]
SPRAVOCHNAIA KNIZHKA PO KOOPERATIVNYM ORGANIZATSIIAM, NAKHODIASHCHIMSIA V MOSKVE NA 1918 GOD – M. v1-2 n96. 1918 – 2mf – 9 – COR-753/1 – ne IDC [334]
SPRAVOCHNIK / Akademiia Nauk. SSSR Biblioteki – A.I. Chebotarev, Comp. Moscow, 1959. 323p. BR-11,311 1 – 1 – ne IDC [020]
SPRAVOCHNIK DLIA USTROITELEI I RUKOVODITELEI TRUDOVYKH ZEMLEDEL'CHESKIKH ARTELEI / Nikolaev, A A – M., 1918 – 2mf – 9 – COR-497/1 – ne IDC [334]
SPRAVOCHNIK. ESTESTVENNYE I FIZIKOMATEMATICHESKIE NAUKI / Davidenkova, N K; ed by Mankevich, A I – L. 1967. BR-11,301 1 – 9 – ne IDC [500]
SPRAVOCHNIK O RUSSKIKH KNIGAKH GRAZHDANSKOI PECHATI, IZD. V SVET S 1708 PO 1855 GOD. VYP. 1. A-ALLER / Serzhputovskii, I – Spb. 1909. BR-7253 2 – 8 – ne IDC [460]
SPRAVOCHNIK PARTIINOGO RABOTNIKA – Moscow, 1921-1935 – 1 – $35.00r – us Hoover Inst Photo [947]
SPRAVOCHNIK PO SEL'SKOKHOZIAISTVENNOI KOOPERATSII / ed by Ozeretskovskii, N E – M., 1922 – 1mf – 9 – COR-516/1 – ne IDC [334]
SPRAVOCHNIK PO SEL'SKOKHOZIAISTVENNOI PERIODICHESKOI PECHATI NA 1915-1916 G – Spb. 1915-16. BR-4420 2 – 8 – ne IDC [630]
SPRAVOCHNIK PO STROITELSTVU MOSKOVSKOI OBLASTI NA...GOD / Moskovskai a oblastnai a planovai a komissii a – (Includes c.1: 1929/1930) – Moskva: Stro isektor Mosoblplana, 1930- – 1 – CSUXAKY6540-S – us Hoover Inst Photo [710]
SPRAVOCHNIK PO ZAKONODATEL'STVU DLIA ISPOLNITEL'NYKH KOMITETOV SOVETOV DEPUTATOV TRUDIASHCHIKHSIA – Riga. 3v. 1970-1976 – 35mf – 9 – ne IDC [340]
SPRAVOCHNIK SOKRASHCHENII, PRINIATYKH V ISTORICHESKOI LITERATURE / Samorukova, N A; ed by Tikhomirov, M N – M. 1964. BR-11,332 1 – 9 – ne IDC [900]
SPRAVOCHNIK VOSTOCHNO-SIBIRSKOGO OBSHCHESTVA SELSKOGO KHOZIASTVA, PROMYSHLENNOSTI I TORGOVLI V ENISEISKOI GUBERNII – (Cont as: Sibirskaia Derevnia. Krasnoiarsk, 1913/14 (1 nov)-1917 n31. Missing: 1915 n1-21, 24; 1917 n3-12, 24-27) – Krasnoiarsk, 1912-13 n12 – 30mf – 9 – COR-687/1 – ne IDC [334]
SPRAVOCHNIK-PUTEVODITEL PO BIBLIOTEKE AKADEMII NAUK SSSR / Akademiia Nauk. SSSR – Ed. by G. A. Chebotarev, comp. by I. F. Grigor'eva, T. M. Koval'chuk and T. I. Skirpkina. M., L. 1959. BR-11,303 1 – 9 – ne IDC [000]
SPRAVOCHNIK-UKAZATEL' PECHATNYKH OPISANII SLAVIANO-RUSSKIKH RUKOPISEI – Moscow, 1963. 360p. Comprehensive bibliography of published catalogs and other descriptions of Slavic-Russian mss organized according to the repository where the collections are currently housed. BR-10,661/1 – 9 – ne IDC [947]
SPRAWA – London, UK. Dwutygodnik polskiego instytutu: Miecz ducha. 16 Jan 1944-28 Jan 1954 – 1 – uk British Libr Newspaper [072]
SPRAWOZDANIE / Poland – Z Zycia Mniejszasci Narodowych. Ministere de l'Interieur. Rapport sur la vie des minorites ethniques. Warszawa. janv-sept 1932, janv-sept 1933, oct 1934-sept 1935 – 1 – fr A.C.R.P.P. [073]
Sprawozdanie, C K *see* RADY SZKOLNEJ KRAJOWEJ
SPRAWOZDANIE STENOGRAFICZNE / Poland. (1918-). Senat – 1922-38 – 1 – 121.00 – us L of C Photodup [943]
SPRAWY MIEDZYNARODOWE – Warsaw. v. 5, 7-12. 1952, 1954-1959 – 1 – us NY Public [073]
SPRAWY NARODOWOSA1CIOWE – Warsaw. Jan. 1927-Dec. 1935; 1936-1939 (undated) – 1 – 35.00r – us Hoover Inst Photo [072]
SPRAY COURIER – Spray, OR. -w. 19 Oct 1907-14 Sept 1916. 1 roll – 1 – us U.O. Library [071]
SPRAY TECHNOLOGY AND MARKETING *see* AEROSOL AGE
DER SPRECHER *see* WESTPHAELISCHER ANZEIGER
Sprecher, Samuel P *see* INFIDELITY REFUTED BY INFIDELS
SPRECH-SAAL. (ORGAN DER PORZELLAN-, GLAS- UND THONWAAREN-INDUSTRIE) – Coburg, Germany. 1900-09.-w. 17 reels – 1 – uk British Libr Newspaper [073]
SPREEDUMA ISWILKUMS IS BALTIJAS BAPTISTU KONZILA (GADASAPULZES) PROTOKULEEM = AN EXTRACT OF A JUDGEMENT FROM THE MINUTES OF THE BALTIC BAPTIST COUNCIL/ANNUAL MEETING – Riga, 1884. Publ. No. 6347c. One of three items on reel. 146p – 1 – us Baptist [240]
SPREMNOST – Zagreb. Yugoslavia. -w. 6 Dec 1942-25 Feb 1945. (Very imperfect). (2 reels) – 1 – uk British Libr Newspaper [949]
Spreng, S P *see* THE LIFE AND LABORS OF JOHN SEYBERT
Sprengel, C K *see* DAS ENTDECKTE GEHEIMNISS DER NATUR IM BAU UND IN DER BEFRUCHTUNG DER BLUMEN
Sprengel, Hans Rolf *see* NATURANSCHAUUNG UND MALERISCHES EMPFINDEN BEI WILHELM HEINSE
Sprengel, K P J *see*
- ANLEITUNG ZUR KENNTNISS DER GEWAA5CHSE
- ANTIQUITATUM BOTANICARUM SPECIMEN PRIMUM
- DER BOTANISCHE GARTEN DER UNIVERSITAA5T ZU HALLE
- CAROLI LINNAEI...GENERA PLANTARUM
- FLORAE HALENSIS TENTAMEN NOVUM
- NEUE ENTDECKUNGEN IM GANZEN UMFANG DER PFLANZENKUNDE
- NOVI PROVENTUS HORTORUM HALENSIS ET BEROLENSIS
- PLANTARUM MINUS COGNITARUM PUGILLUS PRIMUS ET SECUNDUS
- PLANTARUM UMBELLIFERARUM
- SPECIES UMBELLIFERARUM MINUS COGNITAE, ILLUSTRATE

Sprengel, K P J et al *see* JAHRBUECHER DER GEWAECHSKUNDE
Sprengler, Joseph *see* GRILLPARZER, DER TRAGIKER DER SCHULD
Spriddle, Dean *see* A TEST OF THE VARIABILITY OF PRACTICE HYPOTHESIS
Spriewald, Ingeborg *see* HANS FOLZ
Sprigg, Joshua *see* ANGLIA REDIVIVA: ENGLANDS RECOVERY
SPRING – v1- 1982- – 1,5,6,9 – us UMI [640]
Spring, Agnes W *see* WILLIAM CHAPIN DEMING OF WYOMING
SPRING BRANCH BAPTIST CHURCH. BARNWELL COUNTY. SOUTH CAROLINA : CHURCH RECORDS – 1883-1923 – 1 – 9.90 – us Baptist [240]
SPRING BRANCH BAPTIST CHURCH. HORRY COUNTY. SOUTH CAROLINA : CHURCH RECORDS – 1832-99 – 1 – 29.07 – us Baptist [240]
SPRING CREEK BAPTIST CHURCH. ROME, GEORGIA : CHURCH RECORDS – Dec 1851 – Sept 1978. Incomplete – 1 – 60.75 – us Baptist [240]
SPRING DAYS : A REALISTIC NOVEL / Moore, George – London: Vizetelly, 1888 – 1 roll – 1 – 1-55879-772-6 – uk Libr Preservation [830]
Spring, Derek *see* SOVIET WAR POSTERS, CA 1940-1945
Spring, F A *see*
- ENUMERATIO LYCOPODINEARUM QUAS IN EJUSDEM PLANTARUM ORDINIS MONOGRAPHIA MOX EDENDA DESCRIPSIT
- MONOGRAPHIE DE LA FAMILLE DES LYCOPODIACEES

Spring, Gardiner *see* MEMOIR OF SAMUEL JOHN MILLS
SPRING HILL BAPTIST CHURCH. COLLETON COUNTY. SOUTH CAROLINA : CHURCH RECORDS – 1854-1880 – 1 reel – 1 – $5.00 – us Baptist [240]

SPRINGDALE FIRST BAPTIST CHURCH. SPRINGDALE, SOUTH CAROLINA : CHURCH RECORDS – 1959-72 – 1 – 8.91 – us Baptist [240]
Springer, F *see*
– THE CRINOIDEA FLEXIBILIA
– THE NORTH AMERICAN CRINOIDEA CAMERATA
Springer, Helen Emily (Chapman) *see* A HAND-BOOK OF CHIKARANGA
Springer, Judy B *see* POST RUNNING, POST-CYCLING, AND POST TRAINING RUNNING ECONOMY IN DUATHLETES
Springer, Rebecca Ruter *see* MARCUS AND MIRIAM
SPRINGER SEMINARS IN IMMUNOPATHOLOGY – v.1-4, 1978-81. ISSN:0344-4325 – 1,5,6,9,13 – 50.00v – us UMI [616]
SPRINGFIELD 1640-1894 – 138mf – 9 – 0-87623-048-6 – us Holbrook [920]
SPRINGFIELD BAPTIST CHURCH. BLACK BAPTI AUGUSTA, GEORGIA : CHURCH RECORDS – (Deacons' Meetings. May 1917-Nov 1925) – Dec 1888-Feb 1889; Aug 1896-Dec 1905; Aug 1916-May 1922 – 1 – 48.15 – us Baptist [240]
SPRINGFIELD BAPTIST CHURCH. ORANGEBURG COUNTY. SOUTH CAROLINA : CHURCH RECORDS – 1889-96, 1912-63, 1971-78 – 1 – $53.87 – us Baptist [240]
SPRINGFIELD COUNTY DIRECTORY 1867/68 / Samuel Bowles and Co – Springfield, 1867. Massachusetts Reel 5. The Cox Library Collection – 5 – us Americana [978]
SPRINGFIELD DAILY NEWS – Springfield, Mass. 1911- – 1 – us UMI [071]
SPRINGFIELD MONITOR – Springfield, NE. -w. Dec 1892; Jan 1896 to date – 1 – us NE Hist [071]
SPRINGFIELD NEWS – Springfield, OR. -sw,-w. 11 Jan, 12 July 1907; 18 Feb 1915-. – 1 – us U.O. Library [071]
Springfield. Presbytery (Assoc. Ref. Pres. Ch.) *see* MINUTES, 1850-58
SPRINGFIELD REPUBLICAN – Springfield, MA. 1850-70 – 1 – us UMI [071]
SPRINGFIELD STAR – Springfield, OR. -w. 5 Jul 1939-23 Oct 1939. 1 roll – 1 – us U.O. Library [071]
SPRINGFIELDER – v.23-40. 1959-76. Continued by yConcordia theological quarterly – 1 – us UMI [073]
SPRINGHAVEN / Blackmore, Richard Doddridge – British Fiction Archive: Unit 3 – 9 – uk Bell [830]
SPRINGHEAD BAPTIST CHURCH. PLANT CITY, FLORIDA : CHURCH RECORDS – 1905-60 – 1 – 10.53 – us Baptist [240]
SPRINGHILL BAPTIST CHURCH. CREAL SPRINGS, ILLINOIS : CHURCH RECORDS – (788p) – 1849-1983, incomplete – 1 reel – 1 – $35.46 – us Baptist [240]
SPRINGHILL BAPTIST CHURCH. MARENGO COUNTY. ALABAMA : CHURCH RECORDS – 1833-64 – 1 – 10.16 – us Baptist [240]
SPRINGS AND BRAKPAN ADVERTISER – Springs, South Africa. 1928-75 – 1 – sa State Libr [072]
"THE SPRINGS OF NATIONAL PROGRESS": A SPEECH IN THE OPERA HOUSE, BRANDON, FRIDAY, NOVEMBER 4TH, 1892, ON THE OCCASION OF A BANQUET TO THE HON. T. MAYNE DALY / Davin, Nicholas Flood – Delivered by Nicholas Flood Davin. s.l.: s.n., 1892?. 02598. (Pre-1900 Canadiana) – 9 – cn C.I.H.M. [971]
SPRINGS PRIMITIVE BAPTIST CHURCH. GREENVILLE COUNTY. SOUTH CAROLINA : CHURCH RECORDS – (394p) – 1834-1840, 1886-1948, 1964-1980 – 1 reel – 1 – $17.73 – us Baptist [240]
SPRINGTIME PLEASURES. FOR PIANO / VanLaer, C – Autograph ms, [18–?] – 1 – us Sibley [780]
SPRINGVIEW HERALD – Springview, NE. -w. Nov 1895-Jul 1898, scattered issues missing; Jul 1901-Sep 1902; Jan 1907 to date – 1 – us NE Hist [071]
SPRINGVILLE JOURNAL – Buffalo. N.Y. -w. 1867- – 1 – us UMI [071]
SPRINGWOOD SENTINEL – Dec 3 1959 – 1 – at Pascoe [072]
Sprink, Walter *see* DIE MONOLOGE IN DEN DRAMEN HEBBELS
Sprinzl, Josef *see* DIE THEOLOGIE DER APOSTOLISCHEN VAETER
THE SPRITE – Quebec: C E Holiwell, [1865] – 9 – cn C.I.H.M. [073]
THE SPRITE – Quebec, Canada. 7 jun 1865-v1 n5. 5 jul 1865 – 1r – 1 – Can$25.00 – cn Can Microfilming [072]
Spriwald, Dietmar *see* ZUR ANALYSE VON FARBTRENDS
SPROCAS PAPERS – 6r – 1 – sa Microfile [960]
Sprogle, Howard O *see* THE PHILADELPHIA POLICE, PAST AND PRESENT
SPRUCE GROVE EXAMINER – Spruce Grove, Alberta, CN. 1982-90 – 25r – 1 – cn Commonwealth Micro [072]
Spruce, R *see* CATALOGUS MUSCORUM FERE OMNIUM QUOS IN TERRIS AMAZONICIS ET ANDINIS
THE SPRUCE-GALL LOUSE: (CHERMES ABIETIS) / Brodie, William – Prepared for the Bureau of Forestry. Toronto: The Bureau, 1898?. 00881. (Pre-1900 Canadiana) – 9 – cn C.I.H.M. [634]
DIE SPRUECHE JESU DIE IN DEN KANONISCHEN EVANGELIEN NICHT UEBERLIEFERT SIND (T.U.U. 1-14/2) / Ropes, J -H – Leipzig, 1896 – 3mf – 9 – ne Slangenburg [240]
DIE SPRUECHE SALOMONIS : THEOLOGISCH-HOMILETISCH BEARBEITET / Zoeckler, Otto – 2. erg. umgearb. Aufl. Bielefeld: Velhagen & Klasing, 1896 – 1mf – 9 – 0-8370-5970-4 – 1985-3970 – us A.T.L.A. [220]
DIE SPRUECHE SALOMOS / Strack, Hermann Leberecht – Muenchen: C.H. Beck, 1899. 1 fiche – 9 – us A.T.L.A. [240]
Spry, W J *see* THE BRITISH COLEOPTERA DELINEATED: CONSISTING OF FIGURES OF ALL THE GENERA OF BRITISH BEETLES
SPUK UM MITTERNACHT : DIEBESKOMOEDIE / Wendler, Otto Bernhard – Leipzig: A Strauch, [1928] – 1r – 1 – us U.W. Library [820]
Spuler, A *see* UEBERSICHT DER LEPIDOPTEREN-FAUNA DES GROSSHERZOGTUMS BADEN
THE SPUR – London, England. -m. June 1914-April 1921. 41 ft – 1 – uk British Libr Newspaper [072]
DIE SPUR IM HAFEN : ROMAN / Vring, Georg von der – 6. Aufl. Guetersloh: C Bertelsmann, 1944 – 1r – 1 – us U.W. Library [830]
Spurgeon, Charles Haddon *see*
– C.H. SPURGEON'S AUTOBIOGRAPHY...
– COMMENTING AND COMMENTARIES: LECTURES
– MEMORIES OF STAMBOURNE
– THE SAINT AND HIS SAVIOUR
– SKETCH OF THE LIFE AND MINISTRY OF THE REV. C.H. SPURGEON: FROM ORIGINAL DOCUMENTS, INCLUDING ANECDOTES AND INCIDENTS OF TRAVEL.
SPURIOUS AND DOUBTFUL WORKS / Ovid – Groningae: in aedibus heredum P Noordhoff, [1928?] – 1 – us U.W. Library [450]
Spurrell, George James *see* NOTES ON THE HEBREW TEXT OF THE BOOK OF GENESIS
Spurzheim, Johann Gaspar *see*
– OBSERVATIONS ON THE DERANGED MANIFESTATIONS OF THE MIND AND INSANITY
– PHRENOLOGY, OR THE DOCTRINE OF THE MENTAL PHENOMENA
SPUTNIK AGITATORA – (Library has: 1938-1939, 1941, 1943, 1945-1947; many issues missing) – Moskva: Izdvo T SK VKP (b) "Pravda", 1936-1947. 12v – 1 – CSUX90-S193 – us Hoover Inst Photo [320]
SPUTNIK CHITATELIA – Ukazatel' obshchedostupnoi literatury. Spb. 1906. Available: (2-3, 8-9) 1906. BR-4335 2 – 8 – ne IDC [460]
SPUTNIK IZBIRATELIA NA 1906 G : OSVOBODITEL'NOE DVIZHENIE I SOVREMENNYE EGO FORMY – Spb., 1906. 804p – 3mf – 9 – ne IDC [320]
SPUTNIK KOMMUNISTA – Moscow. From 1921 to 1924 titled Kommunist. 1921-1926. Missing: no. 22, 1923; all but Jan., 1925; nos. 32, 33, 1926 – 1 – 35.00r – us Hoover Inst Photo [335]
SPUTNIK KOOPERATORA – M., 1924-25 n3 – 5mf – 9 – COR-693/1 – ne IDC [334]
SPUTNIK KOOPERATORA : V.1. SBORNIK DEKRETOV, POSTANOVLENII, INSTRUKTSII I TSIRKULIAROV PO VOPROSAM PRAKTICHESKOI RABOTY KOOPERATSII – Omsk, 1921 – 3mf – 9 – COR-754/1 – ne IDC [334]
SPUTNIK KUSTARIA : ZAKONY O KUSTARIAKH I REMESLENNIKAKH – Tula, 1926 – 3mf – 9 – COR-317/1 – ne IDC [334]
SPUTNIK KUSTARIA I REMESLENNIKA / ed by Artemev, E A – Ed 3. M., 1928 – 2mf – 9 – COR-318/1 – ne IDC [334]
SPUTNIK KUSTARIA, PROMYSLOVIKA I REMESLENNIKA : ZAPISNAIA KNIZHKAKALENDAR' NA 1930 G – M., 1930 – 3mf – 9 – COR-448/1 – ne IDC [334]
SPUTNIK SOVETSKOGO IURISTA / Institut sovetskogo prava – (Library has: Nov. 1922-July 1923) – Moskva: I Urid. izdvo Narkomi usta, 1922 – 1 – CSUX90-S197 – us Hoover Inst Photo [340]
Spyri, Johanna *see* HEIDI
Squair, John *see* THE TOWNSHIPS OF DARLINGTON AND CLARKE
SQUARE DEAL – Richmond. Va. 1915-54 – 1 – us UMI [071]
A SQUARE TALK TO YOUNG MEN ABOUT THE INSPIRATION OF THE BIBLE / Hastings, Horace Lorenzo – Boston: Scriptural Tract Repository, c1890 – 1mf – 9 – 0-8370-3521-X – 1985-1521 – us A.T.L.A. [220]
SQUARE TALK TO YOUNG MEN ABOUT THE INSPIRATION OF THE BIBLE / Hatings, Horace Lorenzo – Boston: Scriptural Tract Rep., 1890. 1 fiche – 9 – us A.T.L.A. [240]
SQUATTER SOVEREIGN – Atchison. Kan. 1855-57 – 1 – us UMI [071]
Squier, Ephraim George *see*
– EPHRAIM GEORGE SQUIER PAPERS, 1835-1872
– PAPERS
Squier, Miles Powell *see*
– THE BEING OF GOD
– REASON AND THE BIBLE
SQUIRREL HILL NEWS – Pittsburgh. Pa. -w. 1956, 1958-66 – 1 – us UMI [071]
S'RAUTA SUTRA OF APASTAMBA BELONGING TO THE TAITTIRIYA SAMHITA – 3v. Calcutta. 1882-1902. BI-501 2 – 8 – ne IDC [280]
S'RAUTA SUTRA OF A'S'VALA'YANA – Calcutta. 1874. BI-497 2 – 8 – ne IDC [280]
S'RAUTA SUTRA OF LATYAYANA – Calcutta. 1872. BI-500 2 – 8 – ne IDC [280]
SRAVNITEL'NYI ETIMOLOGICHESKII SLOVAR' LITERATURNOGO RUSSKOGO IAZYKA / Goriaev, N V – Ed.2. Tiflis, 1896 – 10mf – 9 – 956/2 – ne IDC [460]
SRBADIJA – New York, NY, 1921-1927 – 2r – 1 – us I.H.R.C. [978]
SRBOBRAN – Zagreb, Croatia.1884-1914. 2-3 times per week (-1900), daily (1900-14) – 1 – us U.W. Library [949]
SREDI KNIG – Ezhemesiachnyi kritiko-bibliograficheskii zhurnal. Spb. 1909. Available: (1-2) 1909. BR-4336 2 – 8 – ne IDC [010]
SREDI KNIG. OPYT OBZORA RUSSKIKH KNIZHNYKH BOGATSTV V SVIAZI S ISTORIEI NAUCHNOFILOSOFSKIKH I LITERATURNO-OBSHCHESTVENNYKH IDEI / Rubakin, N A – v1-3(1). ed 2. M. 1911-15. BR-7240 2 – 8 – ne IDC [100]
SREDI KOLLEKCIONEROV / Lazarevskij, I V – 1917 – 8 – R-4655 2 – ne IDC [947]
SREDI POLITKATORZHAN / Genkin, Iosif Isaevich – Moskva: Izd-vo Vses. ob-vo politkatorzhan i ssylno-poselent sev, 1930 – 1 – CSUX89-B7327 – us Hoover Inst Photo [947]
SREDNEVEKOV'E V RUKOPISIAKH PUBLICHNOI BIBLIOTEKI / Saltykov-Shchedrin Library; ed by Dobiash-Rozhdestvenskaia, O A – Analecta Medii Aevi. 3v. L. 1926-29. BR-10,858 1 – 9 – ne IDC [010]
SREDNIAIA AZIIA – Ezhemesiachnoe literaturnoistoricheskoe izdanie. Tashkent. 1910-11. Lacking: (3, 8) 1910. BR-1622 2 – 8 – ne IDC [460]
SREDNIAIA AZIIA – Nauchno-literaturnyi sbornik s Kalendarem na 1896 god. Pod. red. E.T. Smirnova. Tashkent. 1895. BR-15,002 1 – 9 – ne IDC [460]
Sredoje, Lalic *see* ARCHIVSKI FONDOMI U VOJVODINI
Sreznevskii, 1 *see* SKAZANIIA OB ANTIKHRISTE V SLAVIANSKIKH PEREVODAKH, S ZAMECHANIIAMI O SLAVIANSKIKH PEREVODAKH TVORENII SV. IPPOLITA
Sreznevskii, 2 *see*
– MATERIALY DLIA SLOVARIA
– MATERIALY DLIA SLOVARIA DREVNERUSSKOGO IAZYKA PO PIS'MENNYM PAMIATNIKAM
– SKAZANIIA O SVIATYKH BORISE I GLEBE
Sreznevskii, 6 *see*
– DREVNII SLAVIANSKII PEREVOD PSALTYRI. IZSLEDOVANIE EGO TEKSTA I IAZYKA PO RUKOPISIAM 11-14 V
– K ISTORII IZDANIIA IZVESTII I UCHENYKH ZAPISOK VTOROGO OTDELENIIA IMP. AKADEMII NAUK. (1852-1863)
– OPISANIE RUKOPISEI I KNIG, SOBRANNYKH DLIA IMP. AKADEMII NAUK V OLONETSKOM KRAE
– OTCHET OTDELENIIU RUSSKOGO IAZYKA SLOVESNOSTI IMP. AKADEMII NAUK O POEZDKE V OLONETSKUIU, VOLOGODSKUIU PERMSKUIU GUBERNII (IIUN' 1902 G.)
– SVEDENIIA O RUKOPISIAKH PECHATNYKH IZDANIIAKH I DRUGIKH PREDMETAKH, POSTUPIVSHIKH V RUKOPISNOE OTDELENIE BIBLIOTEKI IMP. AKADEMII NAUK V 1900-1903 GG
SRI CHAITANYA'S CONCEPT OF THEISTIC VEDANTA / Tirtha, Bhakti Vilas, Swami – 1st ed. Madras: Sree Gaudiya Math, 1964. x,192p. Bibliog. footnotes – 1 – us U.W. Library [280]
Sri Lanka *see* JANARAJAYE GASAT PATRAYA
Sri Lanka. University Grants Commission *see* BASIC STATISTICS ON UNIVERSITY EDUCATION IN SRI LANKA 1981-1982
SRI POESTAKA / Balai Pustaka, Djakarta – Weltevreden, 1919/20-1930. v1-12 – 71mf – 9 – ne IDC [999]
SRIS QUARTERLY – School Research Information Service. v.1-7. 1968-74. Continued by C E D R Quarterly – 1 – us UMI [073]
Srobar, V *see* CORRESPONDENCE
SRPSKA BIBLIOGRAFIJA ZA NOVIJU KNIZEVNOST, 1741-1867 / Novakovic, S – Beograd. 1869. BR-4362 2 – 8 – ne IDC [010]
SRPSKA KRALJEVSKA AKADEMIJA – v. 1-70. Godisnjak. 1887-1963; Beograd. 1888-1965. BR-5758 2 – 8 – ne IDC [947]
SRPSKE NOVINE / Serbia – Beograd. Title varies. On film: 1870-1918. LL-0114 – 1 – us L of C Photodup [340]
SRPSKE NOVINE – U Krfu: Izd. i Stampa drz. Stamparije kraljevine Srbije – 1 – us U.W. Library [073]
Srygley, F D *see* LIFE OF J.A. HARDING; TWO OLDEST LIVING COLLEGES; CHURCH OF CHRIST
SS LEITHEFT – Berlin, 1936-44 (incomplete) – 1 – Inquire at Mikrofilmarchiv for details – gw Misc Inst [320]
S.S. STEWART'S BANJO, GUITAR AND MANDOLIN JOURNAL – v. 2-18. 1883-1901. (Scattered issues lacking) – 1 – 35.00 – us L of C Photodup [780]
S.S. Wallihan and Co *see* ROCKY MOUNTAIN DIRECTORY AND COLORADO GAZETTEER
SSMM LOS REYES DE ESPANA EN LA DIPUTACION DE CACERES / Diputacion Provincial – 1977 – 1 – sp Bibl Santa Ana [946]
SSPC (STEEL STRUCTURES PAINTING COUNCIL) – Printed index. Updated every 60 days – 6,9 – us Info Handling [660]
SSSR OT SEZDA K SEZDU *see* OT SEZDA K SEZDU
SSSR V SISTEME MIROVOGO KHOZIAISTVA / Gorfinkel, E S; ed by Varga, E – Moskva: Izd-vo Kommunistichesko i akademii, 1929 – 1 – CSUX89-B3556 – us Hoover Inst Photo [947]
SSSR V T SIFRAKH V...GODU / Tsentralnoe statisticheskoe upravlenie pri Sovete Ministrov SSSR – (Includes c.1: 1965-1967, 1970-1989) – Moskva: Gosstatizdat, 1960- – 1 – CSUXAKY6211-S – us Hoover Inst Photo [310]
SST SUNDBYBERG SOLNA – Sundbyberg, Solna, Sweden. 1987-89 – 1 – sw Kungliga [072]
SSU FA KUNG PAO / China. Provisional Government of the Republic of China – Official gazette of the Judicial Council. Peking. 1938-40. Lacking (13-17) 1938-39. BCH-1081 1 – 9 – ne IDC [324]
SSU FA YUAN KUNG PAO / China. Judicial Yuan – Official gazette. Chunking, Nanking. 1932-48. Lacking: (108-652), (666-678), (692-821) 1934-45; 1946-48. BCH-1083 1 – 9 – ne IDC [324]
SSU-CH'UAN HSIANG-SHIH LU – List of successful candidates in the imperial examination in Szechwan province: 1885, 1893, 1900, 1901. 1 reel – 1 – 14.00 – us Chinese Res [950]

SSU-CH'UAN JIH-PAO – Chengtu, Szechwan, China. Szechwan Daily. Sep 1952-May 1953; Jan-May 1955; Apr, Sept-Dec 1956; Jan 1957-1960; Jul 1961-1963. 15 reels – 1 – 385.00 – us Chinese Res [072]

SSU-CH'UAN T'UNG-CHIH – 1733; 1736, 47, 1. BCH-690 2 – 8 – ne IDC [950]

Staab, Karl *see* DIE LEHRE VON DER STELLVERTRETENDEN GENUGTUUNG CHRISTI HISTORISCH-KRITISCH DARGESTELLT

Staal, Marguarite Jeanne Cordier de *see* MEMOIRS...WRITTEN BY HERSELF

STAAT- EN ZEDEKUNDIGE ZINNEPRENTEN, OF LEERZAME FABELEN : DIE VAN DEN HEERE LA COURT SPEELSWYZE GEVOLGT DOOR J. VAN HOOGSTRATEN / Hoogstraten, J van – Sole ed. Rotterdam, 1731 – 4mf – 9 – O-3087/1 – ne IDC [760]

DER STAAT, IDEEN ZU EINEM VERSUCH DIE GRENZEN DER WIRKSAMKEIT DES STAATES ZU BESTIMMEN / Humboldt, Wilhelm, Freiherr von – 1792. 1 fiche (29x) – 9 – 1.00f – at Libertarian Micro [320]

DIE STAAT TEEN ELIASER TUHADELENI AND 36 ANDER : REKORD VAN VERRIGTINGE IN DIE HOOGGEREGSHOF VAN SUID-AFRIKA (TRANSVAAL PROVINSIALE AFDELING) – [Pretoria?, 1967-68] – us Res Libr [340]

STAAT UND BUERGER – Breslau, 1889 – 1r – 1 – Inquire at Mikrofilmarchiv for details – gw Misc Inst [072]

STAAT UND BUERGER – Breslau (Wroclaw), Poland. 1889 – 1r – 1 – gw Mikrofilm [943]

DER STAAT UND DIE KATHOLISCHE KIRCHE IM GROSSHERZOGTHUM BADEN : SEIT DEM JAHRE 1860 / Friedberg, Emil – Leipzig: Duncker & Humblot, 1874 – 2mf – us A.T.L.A. [240]

STAAT UND KIRCHE IN DEN ARIANISCHEN KOENIGREICHEN UND IM REICHE CHLODWIGS : MIT EXKURSEN UEBER DAS AELTESTE EIGENKIRCHENWESEN / Schubert, Hans von – Muenchen: R. Oldenbourg, 1912 – 1mf – us A.T.L.A. [240]

STAAT UND RECHT – 1952-1989 – 1,247mf – 1 – DM7,107.90 – gw Mikro Press [340]

STAATKUNDIG EN STAATHUISHOUDKUNDIG JAARBOEKJE VOOR 1849-84 – v. 1-36. 1849?-84 – 1 – 105.00 – us L of C Photodup [949]

DAS STAATLICHE AUFSICHTSRECHT UEBER GEMEINDEN UND GEMEINDEVERBAENDE IN RECHTSVERGLEICHENDER DARSTELLUNG UNTER BERUECKSICHTIGUNG DER PREUSSISCHEN ENTWUERFE / Fachinger, Josef – Koeln, 1927 – 2mf – DM62.00 – 3-8267-3063-1 – gw Hänsel [340]

DAS STAATLICHE MISCHEHENRECHT IN PREUSSEN VOM ALLGEMEINEN LANDRECHT AN / Fonk, Friedrich Hermann – Bielefeld, 1961 – 191p – 9 – DM48.00 – 3-89349-059-0 – gw Hänsel [350]

STAATS ANZEIGER. WIESBADEN. 1959-1968 / Hesse – 1 – us NY Public [943]

STAATS- UND GELEHRTE ZEITUNG DES HAMBURGISCHEN UNPARTHEYISCHEN CORRESPONDENTEN – Hamburg, Germany. Hamburgischer Correspondent. -d. Jan 1850-March 1934. 606 reels – 1 – uk British Libr Newspaper [072]

STAATS- UND GELEHRTE ZEITUNG DES HAMBURGISCHEN UNPARTHEYISCHEN CORRESPONDENTEN *see* STAATS- UND GELEHRTE ZEITUNG DES HOLLSTEINISCHEN UNPARTHEYISCHEN CORRESPONDENTEN

STAATS- UND GELEHRTE ZEITUNG DES HOLLSTEINISCHEN UNPARTHEYISCHEN CORRESPONDENTEN – (Title change: Staats- und Gelehrte Zeitung des Hamburgischen unpartheyischen Correspondenten, 1873; Hamburgischer Correspondent, 1 Jan 1869) – Hamburg, Germany. 1721-Mar 1934 – 580r – 1 – gw Mikrofilm [072]

STAATS- UND GELEHRTE ZEITUNG DES KOENIGLICHEN DAENISCHEN UNPARTHEYISCHEN CORRESPONDENTEN – Hamburg-Altona, Germany. 1736 – 1r – 1 – gw Mikrofilm [072]

STAATS- UND GESELLSCHAFTS-LEXIKON (AEL, ABT 1;14) : NEUES CONVERSATIONS-LEXIKON / ed by Wagener, Herrmann – Berlin, 1859-1867 (mf ed 1993) – 116mf – 9 – DM1,480.00 – 3-89131-097-8 – gw Fischer [030]

DIE STAATS- UND SOZIAL-LEHREN DER FRANZOESISCHEN JANSENISTEN IM 17. JAHRHUNDERT / Honigsheim, Paul – Heidelberg: C. Pfeffer, 1914 – 1mf – us A.T.L.A. [320]

DIE STAATS- UND VOELKERRECHTLICHE STELLUNG AEGYPTENS / Gruenau, W von – Leipzig, 1903 – 4mf – 1 – ILM-1947/1 – ne IDC [327]

STAATS ZEITUNG – Portland. Or. 1893-1899 – 1 – us UMI [071]

DIE STAATSANGEHOERIGKEIT DER JURISTISCHEN PERSONEN... / Havestadt, J – Emsdetten i W, 1928 – 1mf – 1 – ILM-3465/1 – ne IDC [327]

STAATSANGEHOERIGKEITSFRAGEN IM SAARGEBIET / Geiersbach, H – Wuerzburg, 1934 – 1mf – 1 – ILM-3336/1 – ne IDC [327]

DER STAATS-ANZEIGER – Bismarck, ND. mar 1 1920-apr 19 1932 – 1 – Inquire at Mikrofilmarchiv for details – gw Misc Inst [072]

DIE STAATSAUFFASSUNG HEINRICH VON KLEISTS / Hoppe, Alfred – (Includes bibliographical references) – Bonn: Scheur, 1938 – 1r – 1 – us U.W. Library [430]

DIE STAATSAUFFASSUNG...DES ERASMUS... / Geldner, F – Berlin, 1930 – 2mf – 1 – ILM-918/1 – ne IDC [327]

STAATSBLAD – Netherlands, 1814-1984 – 9 – inquire – us Ross [072]

STAATSBLAD DER VEREENIGDE NEDERLANDEN – Den Haag. nos1-268. 1813-81. Register – 703mf – 9 – H-2031/1 – ne IDC [949]

STAATSBLAD VAN HET KONINKRIJK DER NEDERLANDEN / Netherlands. Laws, Statutes, etc – Amsterdam, 'S-Gravenhage. Available from 1814- . Official publication of laws and general administrative regulations – 9 – ne Sdu MICRO [324]

STAATSBLAD VAN OOST-INDONESIE : STAATSBLAD INDONESIA TIMUR – (In Indonesian and Dutch. Missing: 1949(1-47,51-53,56-58,60,61,68, 69,71,75-?); 1950(1-16,19-27,36,42-44,46,47)) – Makssar, 1949-50 – 12mf – 9 – SE-213/1 – ne IDC [950]

STAATSBUERGER ZEITUNG – Berlin, 1865-1914 (incomplete) – 165r – 1 – gw Mikrofilm [072]

STAATSBUERGER ZEITUNG – Berlin, jan-aug 1865, 1866-aug 1870, jan-apr 1871, jun 1871-78, apr 1879-mar 1885, jul 1885-92, apr-sep 1893, 1894-1914, feb-dec 1917, 1919-20, 1922-dec 4 1926 – 163r – 1 – Inquire at Mikrofilmarchiv for details – gw Misc Inst [943]

DIE STAATSBUERGERIN – Offenbach, Germany. -w. 3 Jan-13 June 1886. 11 ft – 1 – uk British Libr Newspaper [072]

STAATSCOURANT – Netherlands, 1814-1984 – 9 – inquire – us Ross [072]

STAATSCOURANT DER ZAR – Pretoria, South Africa. 1857-1900 – 1 – sa State Libr [072]

DAS STAATSINTERESSE ALS GRUNDLAGE DES VOELKERRECHTS / Birkas, G – Berlin, 1933 – 2mf – 9 – ILM-1728/1 – ne IDC [327]

STAATSKALENDER DER SCHWEIZERISCHEN EIDGENOSSENSCHAFT / Switzerland – Annual. Continued by: Eidgenoessischer Staatskanlender – 1 – us U.W. Library [949]

DIE STAATSLEHRE ADAM MUELLERS IN IHREM VERHAELTNIS ZUR DEUTSCHEN ROMANTIK / Aris, Reinhold – Tuebingen, 1929 – viii/64p – 9 – DM48.00 – 3-89349-058-2 – gw Hänsel [430]

DAS STAATS-LEXIKON : ENCYKLOPAEDIE DER SAEMMTLICHEN STAATSWISSENSCHAFTEN FUER ALLE STAENDE (AEL, ABT 1;15) / ed by Welcker, Karl & Rotteck, K von – Leipzig, 1856-1866 (mf ed 1993) – 61mf – 9 – DM980.00 – 3-89131-103-6 – gw Fischer [030]

DER STAATS-SOCIALIST – Berlin, dec 20 1877, 1878-80 – 1 – Inquire at Mikrofilmarchiv for details – gw Misc Inst [330]

DER STAATS-SOCIALIST – Berlin, Germany. 20 Dec 1877; 1878-80 – 1 – gw Mikrofilm [072]

STAATSVERTRAEGE ... / Bergbohm, C – Dorpat, 1877 – 2mf – 9 – ILM-130/1 – ne IDC [327]

STAATS-VORANSCHLAG FUER DIE IM REICHSRATHE VERTRETENEN KOENIGREICHE UND LAENDER / Austria. Finanz-Ministerium – 1869-1925. (1870; 1873; 1907, pt. 6; 1910, pt. 6; 1912, pt. 6 wanting) – 1 – 1,016.00 – us L of C Photodup [943]

STAATSWIRTSCHAFT / Auerswald, Hans von – 1808, Auszug: Kap. 3 & 4 des 3. Teils, 99p., ueber Steuerfundation und Bankfreiheit, beschraenkt durch Einloesungspflicht – 9 – 1.00f – at Libertarian Micro [335]

DIE STAATSZUGEHOERIGKEIT DER SCHIFFE... 1935 / Heijk, H – N.p., n.d. – 2mf – 1 – ILM-1665/1 – ne IDC [327]

DER STAB IN DER GERMANISCHEN RECHTSSYMBOLIK : ABAW.PPH 25/1 / Amira, K von – Muenchen, 1909 – Dfl22.00 – ne Slangenburg [240]

STABAT MATER / Winter, Peter van – (Orchestral score) – Manuscript, [179-?] – 1 – us Sibley [780]

STABAT MATER DOLOROSA. ANTOLOGIA DE LA SANTISIMA VIRGEN DE LOS DOLORES / Corredor Garcia, Antonio – Caceres: Edic. Cruzada Mariana, s.a. – 1 – sp Bibl Santa Ana [240]

Stabel, P *see* DE KLEINE STAD IN VLAANDEREN (14DE – 16DE EEUW)

STABILITAETS- UND SENSITIVITAETSANALYSE IN DER VEKTOROPTIMIERUNG / Klose, Juergen – 1993 – 1mf – 9 – DM60.00 – 3-89349-808-7 – gw Hänsel [570]

STABILITY OF EXPERIENCED FEMALE LIFTERS' HEART RATES ACROSS DAYS DURING AND AFTER PYRAMID EXERCISES OF BENCH PRESS AND PARALLEL SQUAT / Ritzer, Christine L – 1994 – 1mf – $4.00 – us Microform Publ [612]

STABILIZASYON PROJESI – [Istanbul]: Tuerk Ocaklari Merkez Heyeti Matbaasi, 1928 – 9 – $20.00 – us MEDOC [338]

DIE STABREIMENDEN WORTBINDUNGEN IN DEN DICHTUNGEN WALTER SCOTT'S / Opitz, Georg – 1995 – 1mf – 9 – DM48.00 – 3-8267-3149-2 – gw Hänsel [420]

Stach, Ilse von *see* GRISELDIS

STACHKA : TEORIIA STACHKI I ISTORIIA STACHECHNOGO DVIZHENIIA V ROSSII, 1905-1910 GG / Chermenskii, V D – Moskva: Kn-vo VT SSPS, 1928 – 1 – CSUX89-B7305 – us Hoover Inst Photo [947]

Stachlin, Carlos Maria *see* ASI ERA EL HERMANO AGUSTIN. UN JESUITA DESCONOCIDO. CINCUENTA ANOS DE HEROISMO CORONADOS POR EL MOCTIVIO. VIDA HEROICA DE AGUSTIN MARIA DIAZ ZAPATA...1869-1936

Stackhouse, J *see*
- NEREIS BRITANNICA
- TENTAMEN MARINO-CRYPTO-GAMICUM

Stackhouse, Perry J *see* CHICAGO AND THE BAPTISTS

Stackhouse, Thomas *see* REFLECTIONS ON THE NATURE AND PROPERTY OF LANGUAGES IN GENERAL

Stackpole, Everett Schermerhorn *see*
- THE EVIDENCE OF SALVATION
- PROPHECY
- PROPHECY, OR, SPEAKING FOR GOD

Stacks, John F *see* STRIPPING

Stacy, James *see*
- HISTORY OF THE PRESBYTERIAN CHURCH IN GEORGIA
- A HISTORY OF THE PRESBYTERIAN CHURCH IN GEORGIA

DE STAD PALEMBANG IN 1935 : 275 JAAR GELEDEN ALS EEN PHOENIX UIT HAAR ASCH HERREZEN / Wellan, J W I – Groningen, 1935 – 1mf – 9 – SE-1280/1 – ne IDC [950]

THE STADACONA PUNCH : CARICATURES – Quebec, Canada. 20 mai 1865 – 1r – 1 – Can$25.00 – cn Can Microfilming [072]

Stade, B *see* ZEITSCHRIFT FUER DIE ALTTESTAMENTLICHE WISSENSCHAFT

Stade, Bernhard *see* AUSGEWAHLTE AKADEMISCHE REDEN UND ABHANDLUNGEN

Stader Geschichts- und Heimatverein *see* ARCHIV

STADER TAGEBLATT – Stade, Germany. 1977- – ca 6r per yr – 1 – gw Mikrofilm [072]

STADIER PAA LIVETS VEI : STUDIER AF FORSKJELLIGE / Kierkegaard, Soren – Kjobenhavn: C.A. Reitzel, 1845 – 1mf – us A.T.L.A. [190]

Stadler, S *see* BEITRAEGE ZUR KENNTNISS DER NECTARIEN

STADT IM STURM / Malitz, Bruno – Berlin: W Limpert, 1943 – 1r – 1 – us U.W. Library [830]

STADT UND FESTUNG BELGERAD : ROMAN / Wehner, Josef Magnus – Hamburg: Hanseatische Verlagsanstalt, c1942 – 1r – 1 – us U.W. Library [830]

STADT- UND LAND BOTE – Birnbaum (Miedzychod), Poland. 1927-6 Aug 1939 – 1 – gw Mikrofilm [943]

DER STADT- UND LANDBOTE – Bielefeld, apr 5 1851-jul 29 1853 – 1 – Inquire at Mikrofilmarchiv for details – gw Misc Inst [072]

STADT- UND LANDBOTE – Birnbaum, apr 26 1927-aug 6 1939 – 10r – 1 – Inquire at Mikrofilmarchiv for details – gw Misc Inst [947]

STADT-AACHENER ZEITUNG *see* AACHENER ZEITUNG

Stadtbibliothek Mainz *see* DIE SCHRIFTEN DER MAINZER JAKOBINER UND IHRER GEGNER (1792-1802)

STADTBLATT *see* SOZIALDEMOKRAT

STADTENTWICKLUNGSPOLITIK IN DRESDEN : EIN FALLBEISPIEL AUS DEN NEUEN BUNDESLAENDERN / Fiolka, Marion – 1992 – 135p – 9 – DM98.00 – 3-89349-630-0 – gw Hänsel [350]

Stadtmueller, G *see* EINE GRIECHISCHE UEBERSETZUNG DES ITALIENISCHEN APOKALYPSENKOMMENTARS VON FEDERIGO DA VENEZIA O.P. (T.U.U. 4-48/2)

STADTRATH DONNING : LUSTSPIEL IN DREI AUFZUEGEN / Reitler, Marzellin Adalbert – Wien: Im Selbstverlage des Verfassers, 1883 – 1r – 1 – us U.W. Library [820]

STADTSANIERUNG KOELN-SEVERINSVIERTEL : DIE BEURTEILUNG VON SANIERUNGSKONZEPTION UND -MASSNAHMEN DURCH SCHUELERINNEN DER JAHRGANGSSTUFE 13 UNTER EINBEZIEHUNG DER "ARBEIT VOR ORT" / Drueke, Petra – 1992 – 206p – 9 – DM98.00 – 3-89349-570-3 – gw Hänsel [943]

STADTTEIL-UMSCHAU – Bremen, Germany. 1 Okt 1981- – 1 – gw Mikrofilm [072]

DER STADT-WAECHTER – Bielefeld, mar 30 1930-jun 28 1931 – 1 – Inquire at Mikrofilmarchiv for details – gw Misc Inst [072]

Staehelin, H *see* DIE GNOSTISCHEN QUELLEN HIPPLOYTIS (T.U.U. 1-6/3A)

Staehelin, Johann Jakob *see* DIE MESSIANISCHEN WEISSAGUNGEN DES ALTEN TESTAMENTS

Staehelin, Rudolf *see* HULDREICH ZWINGLI UND SEIN REFORMATIONSWERK

Staehler, Gerhard *see* UEBER DIE UMLAGERUNG VON ARYLSULFONSAEUREARYLESTERN IN ORTHO- UND PARA-OXYDIARYLSULFONE

DAS STAEHLERNE ABENTEUER : EIN JUNGENERLEBNIS UNSERER ZEIT / Sigleur, Johannes – Berlin: O Elsner, 1945 – 1r – 1 – us U.W. Library [943]

Staehlin, Friedrich *see* HEBEL UND KLEIST ALS MEISTER DER ANEKDOTE

Staehlin, Otto *see*
- CLEMENS ALEXANDRINUS UND DIE SEPTUAGINTA
- ZUR HANDSCHRIFTLICHEN UEBERLIEFERUNG DES CLEMENS ALEXANDRINUS (T.U.U. 2-20/4C)

Stael *see* LETTRES SUR LES OUVRAGES ET LA CARACTERE DE J.J. ROUSSEAU

Staerk, Willy *see*
- DAS ASSYRISCHE WELTREICH IM URTEIL DER PROPHETEN
- DAS DEUTERONOMIUM: SEIN INHALT UND SEINE LITERARISCHE FORM
- DIE ENTSTEHUNG DES ALTEN TESTAMENTES
- SUENDE UND GNADE: NACH DER VORSTELLUNG DES AELTEREN JUDENTUMS

THE STAFF – Hollywood, CA. 1971-1973 – 4r – 1 – $200.00 – R03246 – us Library Micro [071]

STAFF PAPER / Nebraska. College of Agriculture. Dept. of Agricultural Economics – n.1-8. 1969 – 1,5 – us Spaulding [630]

STAFF PAPER SERIES / Mississippi State University. Agricultural Experiment Station. Department of Agricultural Economics – No.1-61.1970-82. 1 reel – 1,5 – us Spaulding [630]

STAFF PAPER SERIES / University of Florida. Agricultural Experiment Station.Food and Resource Economics Department – No.1-227. 1975-82. 67 fiches – 9 – us Spaulding [630]

STAFF PAPER: SERIES / Wisconsin. College of Agricultural and Life Sciences. Dept. of Agricultural Economics – Oct 1965-Dec 1969, no.1-28 – 1,5 – us Spaulding [630]

STAFF PAPERS / International Monetary Fund – 1- 1950- – 1. ; 5,6. ; 9 – apply; v.18-; v.22- – us UMI [336]

STAFF PAPERS / Minnesota. College of Agriculture. Dept. of Agricultural and Applied Economics – 68-1 thru P69-26. 1968-69 – 1,5,6 – us Spaulding [630]

STAFF PAPERS / University of Kentucky. Department of Agricultural Economics – No.1-142. 1973-82. 37 fiches – 9 – us Spaulding [630]

STAFF REPORT EXECUTIVE SUMMARY / University of Florida. Agricultural Experiment Station.Food and Resource Economics Department – No.1-11.1977-81. 4 fiches – 9 – us Spaulding [650]

STAFF STUDY ON AMERICAN SAMOA : INFORMATION ON THE GOVERNMENT, ECONOMY, PUBLIC HEALTH, AND EDUCATION OF AMERICAN (EASTERN) SAMOA / American Samoa. US Congress – 86th Congress 2nd sess. Senate Comm on Interior & Insular Affairs. Washington: GPO, 1960 – 1mf – 9 – $1.50 – LLMC 82-100C Title 35 – us L.L.M.C. [327]

Stafford, Alfred *see* DIARY

STAFFORD COUNTY HERALD – Stafford. England. -w. Oct 1831-Nov 1832. (1 reel) – 1 – uk British Libr Newspaper [072]

Staffordshire *see*
- ADBASTON PARISH REGISTERS, 1600-1760, ASHLEY PARISH REGISTERS, 1581-1733, BIDDULPH PARISH REGISTERS, 1558-1755, BILSTON, ST LEONARD PARISH REGISTERS, 1684-1837
- AUSTREY, BRAILSFORD, CHURCH BROUGHTON, ETWALL, LONGSFORD, MARSTON MONTGOMERY PARISH REGISTERS

STAFFORDSHIRE, 1822 : BRITISH ISLES CENSUS DIRECTORIES PROJECT, ENGLAND – (In prep) – at Vine [941]

STAFFORDSHIRE, 1842 : BRITISH ISLES CENSUS DIRECTORIES PROJECT, ENGLAND – (In prep) – at Vine [941]

STAFFORDSHIRE, 1850 : BRITISH ISLES CENSUS DIRECTORIES PROJECT, ENGLAND – at Vine [941]

STAFFORDSHIRE, 1851 : BRITISH ISLES CENSUS DIRECTORIES PROJECT, ENGLAND. VOL 1 – 5mf – 9 – A$33.00 – at Vine [941]

STAFFORDSHIRE, 1862 : BRITISH ISLES CENSUS DIRECTORIES PROJECT, ENGLAND. VOL 258 – 3mf – 9 – A$21.00 – at Vine [941]

STAFFORDSHIRE, 1872 : BRITISH ISLES CENSUS DIRECTORIES PROJECT, ENGLAND. VOL 259 – 10mf – 9 – A$63.00 – at Vine [941]

STAFFORDSHIRE, 1900 : BRITISH ISLES CENSUS DIRECTORIES PROJECT, ENGLAND – at Vine [941]

STAFFORDSHIRE, 1924 : BRITISH ISLES CENSUS DIRECTORIES PROJECT, ENGLAND. VOL 202 – 12mf – 9 – A$75.00 – at Vine [941]

STAFFORDSHIRE (BURTON-UPON-TRENT), 1857 : BRITISH ISLES CENSUS DIRECTORIES PROJECT, ENGLAND. VOL 87 – 1mf – 9 – A$9.00 – at Vine [941]

STAFFORDSHIRE CERAMICS / Stoke on Trent Museum – (Ceramic items from Bronze Age to 1980s. Includes printed catalogue) – 25mf – 15 – $606.00 – 0-907696-21-X – uk Emmett [730]

STAFFORDSHIRE COURIER – Stoke-on-Trent, England. -d. 10 Nov 1890-9 May 1891. 1 reel – 1 – uk British Libr Newspaper [072]

STAFFORDSHIRE EVENING POST – Stoke-on-Trent, England. Staffordshire Post. -d. 26 June 1894-29 June 1895. 2 reels – 1 – uk British Libr Newspaper [072]

STAFFORDSHIRE EXAMINER – Lichfield & Wolverhampton, England. -w. 14 May 1836-17 Dec 1842. 3 reels – 1 – uk British Libr Newspaper [072]

STAFFORDSHIRE KNOT – (Potteries Free Press and Staffordshire Knot). Stoke-on-Trent. England. -w. 13 May 1882-26 Dec 1891 – 10r – 1 – uk British Libr Newspaper [941]

STAFFORDSHIRE (LEEK AND WOLVERHAMPTON) : BRITISH ISLES CENSUS DIRECTORIES PROJECT, ENGLAND – (In prep) – 1816 – at Vine [941]

STAFFORDSHIRE (LEEK, WALSALL AND WOLVERHAMPTON), 1805 : BRITISH ISLES CENSUS DIRECTORIES PROJECT, ENGLAND. VOL 182 – 1mf – 9 – A$9.00 – at Vine [941]

STAFFORDSHIRE MERCURY, POTTERY GAZETTE AND NEWCASTLE EXPRESS – (North Staffordshire Mercury Staffordshire Mercury). Stoke-on-Trent. England. -w. 2 Jan 1830-27 May 1848. (7 reels) – 1 – uk British Libr Newspaper [072]

STAFFORDSHIRE POTTERIES TELEGRAPH – Stoke-on-Trent. England. -w. Oct 1852-Feb 1855 – 2r – 1 – uk British Libr Newspaper [941]

STAFFORDSHIRE RECORD SOCIETY : COLLECTIONS FOR A HISTORY OF STAFFORDSHIRE – (1st series: v1-20 1880-1897 £685.00 NS: v21-34 1898-1909 £425.00 58mf. 3rd series: v35-71 1910-54 £960.00 152mf. 4th series: v72-77 1957-70 £135.00 16mf. Coll title: Publications of the English Record Societies, 1835-1972..) – 1st series: v1-20. 1880-1897 – 93mf – 9 – £685.00 – uk Chadwyck [941]

Staffordshire Record Society *see* COLLECTIONS FOR A HISTORY OF STAFFORDSHIRE

STAFFORDSHIRE SENTINEL – Stoke-on-Trent, England.1870-81. -w. 5 reels – 1 – uk British Libr Newspaper [072]

STAFFORDSHIRE (SOUTH), 1829 : BRITISH ISLES CENSUS DIRECTORIES PROJECT, ENGLAND. VOL 64 – 1mf – 9 – A$9.00 – at Vine [941]

STAFFORDSHIRE (SOUTH EAST), 1823 : BRITISH ISLES CENSUS DIRECTORIES PROJECT, ENGLAND. VOL 98 – 1mf – 9 – A$9.00 – at Vine [941]

STAFFORDSHIRE TIMES AND NEWCASTLE PIONEER – Newcastle-under-Lyme, England. 1795-2 Jan 1830; 1855-82. -w. 32 reels – 1 – uk British Libr Newspaper [072]

Stafleu, F A *see*
- BOTANY
- TAXONOMIC LITERATURE

STAGE / Theatre Guild, Inc – New York. v2-16. 1925-39 – 4r – 1 – us Ross [790]

STAGE *see* THEATRUM

STAGE AND TELEVISION TODAY – London, UK. 1978-1984 – 14r – $700.00 – R63609 – us Library Micro [790]

STAGES OF CHANGE FOR SMOKING CESSATION, ALCOHOL MODERATION, DIETARY FAT REDUCTION, AND EXERCISE ADOPTION IN A RURAL MINNESOTA COUNTY / Quanrud, Audrey M – University of Wisconsin-La Crosse – 1mf – 9 – HE 569 – us Microform Publ [613]

Stagg, John Weldon *see* CALVIN, TWISSE AND EDWARDS ON THE UNIVERSAL SALVATION OF THOSE DYING IN INFANCY

Stahl, A *see* LES RITUELS DE CONSTRUCTION DES PAYSANS ROUMAINS

Stahl, Andreas *see* UNTERSUCHUNGEN ZUR BEDEUTUNG DER EHESCHLIESSUNG FUER DEN VERLAUF SCHIZOPHRENER ERKRANKUNGEN

Stahl, Charles *see* INTERNATIONAL MIGRATION TODAY

Stahl, Ernst Leopold *see* DER HEBBELVEREIN IN HEIDELBERG

Stahl, Georg Ernst *see* ZUFALLIGE GEDANCKEN UND NUSZLICHE BEDENCKEN UBER DEN STREIT

Stahl, Hermann *see* TRAUM DER ERDE

Stahl, Johann Matthias *see* QUAESTIONES GRAMMATICAE AD THUCYDIDEM PERTINENTES

STAHL UND EISEN : ZEITSCHRIFT FUER DAS DEUTSCHE EISENHUETTENWESEN – v1-75 1881-1955 – 1,5,6 – us Princeton Micro [670]

DER STAHLHELM SENDER – Berlin. apr 29, 1932-34 n4 – 2r – 1 – gw Mikrofilm [072]

Stahr, Adolf Wilhelm Theodor *see*
- AUS DER JUGENDZEIT: LEBENSERINNERUNGEN
- KLEINE SCHRIFTEN ZUR LITTERATUR UND KUNST

Staiger, Emil *see*
- DIE KUNST DER INTERPRETATION
- STILWANDEL
- DIE ZEIT ALS EINBILDUNGSKRAFT DES DICHTERS

Staiger, Ralph C *see*
- ROADS TO READING
- TEACHING OF READING

STAIN TECHNOLOGY *see* BIOTECHNIC AND HISTOCHEMISTRY

STAINLESS STEEL – 1965- – 1 – us UMI [670]

Stainton, H T *see*
- INSECTA BRITANNICA: LEPIDOPTERA. TINEINA
- A MANUAL OF BRITISH BUTTERFLIES AND MOTHS

STAKHANOVSKI GLAS – Gabrovo, Bulgaria. Jun 1953-Jun 1955 – 1r – 1 – us L of C Photodup [949]

STAL – Moscow. U.S.S.R. 1936-40 – 1 – us UMI [670]

Stal, C *see*
- HEMIPTERA AFRICANA
- RECENSIO ORTHOPTERORUM

STALCUP'S STALL REVIEWED / McGhee, J C – Also: The Difference between Baptists and Landmark Missionary Baptists; Christian Union, or, the Problem Solved. 126p – 1 – 5.00 – us Baptist [240]

Staley, Kimberly T *see* EDUCATING THROUGH DANCE

Stalin, Iosif *see*
- DASAR-DASAR LENINISME
- MATERIALISME DIALEKTIK DAN HISTORI (SEPT. 1938)
- PRIKAZ MINISTRA VOORUZHENNYKH SIL SOIUZA SSR

STALINE CONTRE L'EUROPE / Bardoux, Jacques – Paris, 1937. Fiche W 797.1. (Blodgett Collection of Spanish Civil War Pamphlets) – 9 – us H.U. College Libr [946]

LE STALINISME EN ESPAGNE; TEMOIGNAGES DE MILITANTS REVOLUTIONNAIRES SAUVES DES PRISONS STALINIENNES / Landau, Katia – Paris, 1938. Fiche W985. (Blodgett Collection of Spanish Civil War Pamphlets) – 9 – us H.U. College Libr [946]

STALINSKO ZNAME – Varna, Bulgaria. Jul 1951-Oct 1956 – 6r – 1 – us L of C Photodup [949]

Stalker, James *see*
- THE ATONEMENT
- JOHN KNOX
- THE LIFE OF JESUS CHRIST
- THE LIFE OF ST PAUL
- THE TRIAL AND DEATH OF JESUS CHRIST: A DEVOTIONAL HISTORY OF OUR LORD'S PASSION
- THE TWO ST JOHNS OF THE NEW TESTAMENT

Stall, Sylvanus *see* METHODS OF CHURCH WORK

Stallo, John Bernard *see* GENERAL PRINCIPLES OF THE PHILOSOPHY OF NATURE

STALYBRIDGE REPORTER – England. 16 May 1874-Dec 1976 (missing 1897).-w. 123 reels – 1 – uk British Libr Newspaper [072]

Stambina, E Ia. *see* SUD I PROKURATURA LATVIISKOI SSR

STAMBOUL – Istanbul, Turkey. 16 Aug 1875-17 Oct 1914 – 83r – 1 – uk British Libr Newspaper [949]

STAMFORD ENTERPRISE – Stamford, NE. -w. Jan-Mar 1896 – 1 – us NE Hist [071]

STAMFORD MERCURY – England, 13 May-Dec 26 1717; 1718-92; 1834; 1847; 1854; 1873; 1876-80; 1883; 1901-02; 1904-11; 1913-96 – 221 1/4r – 1 – uk British Libr Newspaper [072]

STAMFORD NEWSLETTER – Stamford, Harlan County, Nebraska. 16 Feb 1967- . -w. Missing issues, some issues of poor quality – 1 – us NE Hist [071]

STAMFORD POST – Stamford, NE. -w. Aug 1907-Jan 1911 – 1 – us NE Hist [071]

STAMFORD STAR – Stamford, NE. -w. Dec 1914-Jan 1915; Apr 1915; Oct 1918-Apr 1964 – 1 – us NE Hist [071]

Stamitz, K *see*
- SIX QUARTETTOS, OP. 4
- SIX QUATUORS CONCERTANTES A UN VIOLON, DEUX ALTO ET VIOLONCELLE. OP. 2DA...
- A SONATA, FOR THE HARPSICHORD WITH A TENOR OBLIGATO
- THREE QUATUORS CONCERTANTES A UN VIOLON, DEUX ALTO, ET VIOLONCELLO... BOOK 1 [-2]

Stamm, Hermann *see*
- EIN BEITRAG ZU THEODOR STORM'S STIMMUNGSKUNST
- THEODOR STORM'S STIMMKUNGSKUNST

Stammler, Wolfgang *see*
- ANTI-XENIEN
- REALLEXIKON DER DEUTSCHEN LITERATURGESCHICHTE

THE STAMP ARGUS – St John, NB: R J Melvin, [1865] – 9 – cn C.I.H.M. [760]

STAMP COLLECTION – Los Angeles, CA. 1847-1911 – 1r – 1 – $50.00 – R04064 – us Library Micro [071]

THE STAMP COLLECTOR'S CHRONICLE – St John, N.B.: W.H. Bruce, [1872-1873] – 9 – cn C.I.H.M. [760]

THE STAMP COLLECTOR'S MONTHLY GAZETTE – Saint John, N.B.: G Stewart, [1865-1867] – 9 – cn C.I.H.M. [760]

THE STAMP COLLECTOR'S RECORD – Montreal: S.A. Taylor, [1864] – 9 – cn C.I.H.M. [760]

Stamp, D L *see* LONDON ESSAYS IN GEOGRAPHY

THE STAMP REPORTER – (Is absorbed by: Philatelic Advocate) – St Catharines, Ont: Bradley and Oswald, [1897-1899] – 9 – cn C.I.H.M. [760]

THE STAMP REPORTER *see* THE PHILATELIC AND ADVOCATE

LA STAMPA – 1867-1906 – 2 times per yr – 1 – L160,000 – sz Infoprint [072]

LA STAMPA – 1907-1942 – 3 times per yr – 1 – L240,000 – sz Infoprint [072]

LA STAMPA – 1943-1948 – Annual – 1 – L90,000 – sz Infoprint [072]

LA STAMPA – 1949-1955 – 3 times per yr – 1 – L240,000 – sz Infoprint [072]

LA STAMPA – 1956-1959 – 4 times per yr – 1 – L320,000 – sz Infoprint [072]

LA STAMPA – 1960-1977 – 6 times per yr – 1 – L480,000 – sz Infoprint [072]

LA STAMPA – (Yrly reel count varies. Also available on CD-ROM) – Torino, Italy, 1867- – 1 – inquire – us Ross [072]

STAMPA – Kansas City, Mo. 1921-1924 – 1 – app – us Res Libr [071]

STAMPA – Turin, Italy. 1956, 1960 – 1 – us Res Libr [072]

STAMPA E STAMPA SERA – (Also available on 35mm Sfr1,250.00) – 1970-1995 – 6r per y – 5,6 – Sfr1,176.00 – sz Infoprint [072]

STAMPA (GAZZETTA DEL PIEMONTE) – 1793-1860 – Annual – 1 – L100,000 – sz Infoprint [072]

STAMPA (LA) – 1978-1986 – 12 times per yr – 1 – L840,000 – sz Infoprint [072]

STAMPA (LA) – 1987 – 18 times per yr – 1 – L1,260,000 – sz Infoprint [072]

STAMPA (LA) – 1988 – 14 times per yr – 1 – L980,000 – sz Infoprint [072]

STAMPA (LA) – 1989 – 30 times per yr – 1 – L2,100,000 – sz Infoprint [072]

STAMPA (LA) – 1990 – 36 times per yr – 1 – L2,520,000 – sz Infoprint [072]

STAMPA (LA) – 1991 – 37 times per yr – 1 – L2,590,000 – sz Infoprint [072]

STAMPA (LA) – 1992 – 36 times per yr – 1 – L2,520,000 – sz Infoprint [072]

STAMPA (LA) – 1993 – 48 times per yr – 1 – L3,300,000 – sz Infoprint [072]

STAMPA RACCOLTA PER AUTORE – 1921-1982 – Cumul – 1 – L2,400,000 – sz Infoprint [072]

STAMPA SERA – 1931-1953 – 1 – L160,000 – sz Infoprint [072]

STAMPA SERA – 1954-1962 – 1 – L320,000 – sz Infoprint [072]

STAMPA SERA – 1963-1976 – 1 – L480,000 – sz Infoprint [072]

STAMPA SERA – 1977-1981 – 1 – L960,000 – sz Infoprint [072]

STAMPA SERA – 1982-1983 – 1 – L1,920,000 – sz Infoprint [072]

STAMPA SERA – 1984-1995 – 1 – L960,000 – sz Infoprint [072]

STAMPA SERA – Torino, Italy, 1931- – 1 – inquire – us Ross [072]

STAMPA SERA RACOLTA PER ARGOMENTO – 1973-1981 – Cumul – 1 – L2,080,000 – sz Infoprint [072]

LA STAMPA UNITA – Rochester. N.Y. 1920-1939 – 1 – us UMI [071]

LA STAMPA UNITA DI ROCHESTER – Rochester, NY: Rochester Alliance Press, 1923-25; 1932-33 – 5r – 1 – us Res Libr [071]

LA STAMPA-ITALIANA – Kansas City, MO. -w. 12 Jan 1918-20 Dec 1921 – 1 – us NE Hist [071]

STAMP-LORE – London, Ont: Commercial Print Co, [1896-1897] – 9 – cn C.I.H.M. [760]

Stampp, Kenneth M *see*
- RECORDS OF ANTE-BELLUM SOUTHERN PLANTATIONS FROM THE REVOLUTION THROUGH THE CIVIL WAR

STAMPS – (v186- 1979- 5,6,9) – v1- 1932- – 1 – us UMI [760]

Stanbridge, John *see* ACCEDENCE

LES STANCES. / Moreas, Jean – Paris: Mercure de France, 1905. 3 fiches. (Literature Collection) – 9 – 8.00 – fr Bibl Nationale [830]

STAND BY LOYALIST SPAIN THEY ARE STILL FIGHTING AMERICA MUST LIFT THE EMBARGO – Boston, 1939. Fiche W1212. (Blodgett Collection of Spanish Civil War Pamphlets) – 9 – us H.U. College Libr [946]
STAND DER FORSCHUNGSLEHRE AUF DEM GEBIETE DER WIRTSCHAFTSLEHRE DES LANDBAUES / Laur, Ernst – Brugg, 1951 – 1 – DM30.00 – gw Mikro Press [943]
STAND FAST CRAIG-ROYSTON: A NOVEL / Black, William – British Fiction Archive. Unit 4 – 9 – uk Bell [830]
DE STANDAARD – (Sunday Supplement. 1872-1876) – Amsterdam, 1872-1944 – 213r – 1 – SF-1/3 – ne IDC [072]
STANDARD – (1955-1992.-74r) – Elliott Lake, 1993 – 6r – 1 – cn Preston [971]
STANDARD – Aiken. S.C. 1915-1930 – 1 – us UMI [071]
STANDARD – Aiken. S.C. and South Cina Gazette. 1930-35 – 1 – us UMI [071]
STANDARD – Aliquippa. Pa. 1907-09 – 1 – us UMI [071]
STANDARD – Anaconda. Mont. 1889-1915; 1926-1928 – 1 – us UMI [071]
STANDARD – Bangkok, Thailand. Jun 1946-Jul 1949 (imperfect) – 5r – 1 – uk British Libr Newspaper [072]
STANDARD – Benton. Ill. -w. 1959- – 1 – us UMI [071]
STANDARD – Blind River, De1966-1975Ja – 8r – 1 – cn Preston [971]
STANDARD – Chester. S.C. 1854-1857 – 1 – us UMI [071]
STANDARD – Cornwall, 1886-1932 – 19r – 1 – cn Preston [971]
STANDARD – Cortland. N.Y. 1867-1900; 1967- – 1 – us UMI [071]
STANDARD : DAILY – (1891-1992.-843r) – St. Catharines, 1993 – 12r – 1 – cn Preston [971]
STANDARD – Emporia. Kan. 1890-1892 – 1 – us UMI [071]
STANDARD – Espanola, 1965-1979 – 15r – 1 – cn Preston [971]
STANDARD – Fallon. Nev. -w. 1949-58 – 1 – us UMI [071]
STANDARD – Fallon, NV. 1920-1947; 1949-1958 – 10r – 1 – $500.00 – N04527 – us Library Micro [071]
STANDARD – Fort Worth. Tex. 1876-77 – 1 – us UMI [071]
STANDARD – Greensburg. Ind. -w. 1868-70, 1890, 1893, 1897-98, 1902, 1904, 1907-10, 1912-25 – 1 – us UMI [071]
STANDARD – Hillsdale. Mich. 1859-1860; 1865-1897 – 1 – us UMI [071]
STANDARD – Illinois. Aug 1867-24 Jan 1920 – 1 – 1586.76 – us Baptist [240]
STANDARD – Kendallville. Ind. -w. 1873-1908 – 1 – us UMI [071]
STANDARD – Manistee. Mich. -w. 1871-74 – 1 – us UMI [071]
STANDARD – Markdale, 1983-1984 – 2r – 1 – cn Preston [971]
STANDARD – New York. v1-12. 1887-92 – 3r – 1 – us Ross [071]
STANDARD – North Kingston. R.I. -w. 1959- – 1 – us UMI [071]
STANDARD – Petersham, Jan 7 1899-Dec 31 1904 – 1 – at Pascoe [072]
STANDARD – Poplar. Mont. 1958-1959; 1966- – 1 – us UMI [071]
STANDARD – Portland, OR. -d. 1876-84 – 1 – $96.00 – us Oregon Hist [071]
STANDARD – Portland, OR. -w. 1876-84 – 1 – 96.00 – us Oregon Hist [071]
STANDARD – Rensselaer. Ind. 1879-1881 – 1 – us UMI [071]
STANDARD – Sikeston. Mo. 1913- – 1 – us UMI [071]
STANDARD – Somerset. Pa. 1894; 1904-1905 – 1 – us UMI [071]
STANDARD – Tupelo. Miss. 1873-1877 – 1 – us UMI [071]
STANDARD – (v.206-. 1980- 5,6,9) – v.1-. 1865- – 1 – us UMI [073]
STANDARD : WEEKLY – St. Catharines, 1896-1907 – 4r – 1 – cn Preston [971]
STANDARD – Wickford. R.I. -w. 1888-1958 – 1 – us UMI [071]
THE STANDARD / ed by Aubin, Napoleon & Rowen, W H – Quebec, Canada. v1 n2. 2 dec 1842 – 1r – 1 – Can$25.00 – cn Can Microfilming [072]
THE STANDARD : A BAPTIST NEWSPAPER – (Several mergers. Some pgs missing) – v1-67. 31 Aug 1853-24 Jan 1920 – 57r – 1 – ATLA S0194 – us A.T.L.A. [073]
THE STANDARD – Dar es Salaam. Tanzania. 1945-Apr 1972 – 66r – 1 – us L of C Photodup [072]
THE STANDARD : LARGE SIZE ILLUSTRATED SUPPLEMENTS – (5 aut 1922-28 oct 1923 1r Can$65.00) – Montreal. 23 sep 1905-v8 n52. 28 dec 1912 – 2r – 1 – Can$65.00 – cn Can Microfilming [072]
THE STANDARD – London, May 1827-Mar 1872; Jan 1875-Dec 1916 – 354r – 1 – uk British Libr Newspaper [072]
THE STANDARD – Milton, N.S.: [s.n. 1899-1900?] – 9 – cn C.I.H.M. [971]
THE STANDARD – Montreal, Canada. -w. Jan 1906-June 1922. 44 reels – 1 – uk British Libr Newspaper [072]
THE STANDARD – New York. (Henery George). v. 1-12, no. 9. Jan 8 1887-Aug 31 1892 – 1 – us NY Public [071]
THE STANDARD – New York, NY. -w. 8 Jan 1887-31 Aug 1892. 5 reels – 1 – uk British Libr Newspaper [071]
THE STANDARD – Toronto: Standard Pub. Co, [1878-187-?] – 9 – cn C.I.H.M. [971]
THE STANDARD – Wellington, New Zealand. v. 1-13, no. 25. Oct 9 1935-June 26 1947. Incomplete – 1 – us NY Public [072]
THE STANDARD – Wellington, NZ. Jan 1941-Sep 1952 – 12r – 1 – uk British Libr Newspaper [072]
STANDARD ALPHABET FOR REDUCING UNWRITTEN LANGUAGES AND FOREIGN GRAPHIC SYSTEMS TO A UNIFORM ORTHOGRAPHY IN EUROPEAN LETTERS / Lepsius, Richard – London: Seeleys, 1855 – us Res Libr [400]
DE STANDARD AMSTERDAM – Holland. Mich. 1906-1925; 1927-1929; 1931-1934 – 1 – us UMI [071]
STANDARD AND DIGGERS NEWS – Johannesburg. v25. 1899-1900 – 1r – 1 – us Ross [072]
STANDARD AND MAIL – Cape Town, South Africa.2 Oct 1869-30 Dec 1879. 21 reels – 1, 16 diazo available at reduced price – sa SA Libr [072]
STANDARD AND MAIL *see* SOUTH AFRICAN ADVERTISER AND MAIL
STANDARD AND POOR'S ANNUAL DIVIDEND RECORD – 1976- – 9 – 40.00y – us Standard & Poor's [336]
STANDARD AND POOR'S BOND GUIDE – 1980- – 9 – 75.00y – us Standard & Poor's [336]
STANDARD AND POOR'S CORPORATION RECORDS – Corporation descriptions and cumulative news service on 12,000 pages. 6 v. and index. Yearly update. Approx. 120 fiches – 9 – 839.00y – us Standard & Poor's [380]
STANDARD AND POOR'S DAILY STOCK PRICE RECORD – (NYSE. 310.00y; 9. ASE. 292.00y; STP; 9. OTC. 380.00y; STP; 9) – 1980- – us Standard & Poor's [380]
STANDARD AND POOR'S STOCK GUIDE – 1980- – 9 – 75.00y – us Standard & Poor's [336]
THE STANDARD AND RIVER PLATE NEWS – Buenos Aires. Argentina. -d. 1 Feb 1870-22 Jun 1872, 6-12 Feb 1873, 1-5 Mar, 17 Jun 1874-13 Jul 1936, 24 Jun 1939-31 May 1940, 7 Jan-14 Apr 1941, 23 Nov 1943-21 Feb 1944. (421 reels) – 1 – uk British Libr Newspaper [072]
STANDARD AND TRANSVAAL MINING CHRONICLE – Johannesburg, South Africa. 1887 – 1 – sa State Libr [072]
STANDARD DESIGN FOR SMALL-SCALE MODULAR SLAUGHTERHOUSES – 1988 – 191p – it F.A.O. [636]
STANDARD ENCYCLOPAEDIA OF PROCEDURE – Los Angeles, Chicago: L D Powell Co. v1-26 + suppl 1-3. 1911-20 (all publ) – 341mf – 9 – $511.00 – LLMC 94-281 – us L.L.M.C. [340]
STANDARD ENCYCLOPEDIA OF THE ALCOHOL PROBLEM – Ed. by Mary S. Higley. 1904, 1919-31 – 1 – us Ohio Hist [360]
STANDARD EXPLORATION PROJECT REPORT – v.1-8. 1974-76 – 1 – us UMI [550]
STANDARD FREEHOLDER – (1932-1992.-432r) – Cornwall, 1993 – 18r – 1 – cn Preston [971]
STANDARD GAUGE – Loup City, NE. -w. Mar 1908-Aug 1911 – 1 – us NE Hist [071]
Standard Genealogical Publishing Co *see* REPRESENTATIVE CITIZENS OF NORTHERN CALIFORNIA
STANDARD HISTORY OF ALLEGHENY COUNTY AND CITY OF PITTSBURGH / Wilson, Erasmus – Chicago, Goodspeed Publ. Co., 1899. Pennsylvania Reel 7. (The Cox Library Collection) – 5 – us Americana [978]
A STANDARD HISTORY OF ALLEN COUNTY / Rusler, William – 2v. Chicago: American Historical Society, 1921.Ohio Reel 13. (The Cox Library Collection) – 5 – us Americana [978]
A STANDARD HISTORY OF FULTON COUNTY / Reighard, Frank H – Chicago: Lewis Publ. Co., 1920. 2v. Ohio Reel 33. (The Cox Library Collection) – 5 – us Americana [978]
A STANDARD HISTORY OF JASPER AND NEWTON COUNTIES / Hamilton & Darrach – Biographical sketches. Chicago: Lewis Publ. Co., 1916. Vols. 1-2. Indiana Reel 16. (The Cox Library Collection) – 5 – us Americana [978]
STANDARD HISTORY OF KANSAS AND KANSANS / Connelley, William Elsey – Chicago: Lewis Publ. Co., 1918. v1-2, Kansas Reel 2. v3-5, Kansas Reel 3. (The Cox Library Collection) – 5 – us Americana [978]
A STANDARD HISTORY OF LAKE COUNTY AND THE CALUMET REGION / Howat, William F – Chicago: Lewis Publ. Co., 1915. Vol. 1, Indiana Reel 18; Vol. 2. Inidiana Reel 19. (The Cox Library Collection) – 5 – us Americana [978]
STANDARD HISTORY OF LORAIN COUNTY / Wright, G Frederick – Chicago: Lewis Publ. Co., 1916. Vol. 1. Ohio Reel 43; Vol. 2. Ohio Reel 44. (The Cox Library Collection) – 5 – us Americana [978]
A STANDARD HISTORY OF SPRINGFIELD AND CLARK COUNTY / Prince, Benjamin F – Chicago: American Historical Company, 1922. 2v.Ohio Reel 20. (The Cox Library Collection) – 5 – us Americana [978]
THE STANDARD OF EMPIRE – London, UK. n210. 24 May 1912 + suppl Empire Day – 1r – 1 – Can$25.00 – cn Can Microfilming [072]
Standard Remedies Publishing Company, Inc *see* COMPILATION OF LAWS WITH 1937 INSERTS; DIGEST OF STATE, FEDERAL AND CANADIAN LAWS, RELATING TO FOODS, DRUGS, PHARMACY.
STANDARD SENTINEL – Hazleton. Pa. 1935-1961 – 1 – us UMI [071]
STANDARD SPEAKER – Hazleton. Pa. 1962- – 1 – us UMI [071]
STANDARD TIME FOR THE UNITED STATES OF AMERICA, CANADA AND MEXICO / American Society of Civil Engineers – New York: The Society, 1882. 00794. (Pre-1900 Canadiana) – 9 – cn C.I.H.M. [520]
STANDARD TIME: REPLIES TO QUESTIONS SUBMITTED BY SPECIAL COMMITTEE.. / American Society of Civil Engineers – Ottawa: C. Mitchell, 1882. 02170. (Pre-1900 Canadiana) – 9 – cn C.I.H.M. [520]
STANDARD WEEKEND MAGAZINE – Montreal, 1952-1979 – 90r – 1 – cn Preston [971]
STANDARDISATION OF TONOMETERS / International Ophtalmological Congress 14, 1933 – 1mf – 9 – ne IDC [617]
STANDARDIZATION COMMITTEE / UN Economic Commission for Europe (ECE) – 1970-84 – E.55 F.54 R.53 – 9 – us U.N. Pubs [340]
STANDARDIZATION NEWS / American Society for Testing and Materials – Philadelphia. v1-5 1973-77 – 1,5,6 – us Princeton Micro [620]
STANDARDIZED DESIGNS FOR GRAIN STORES IN HOT DRY CLIMATES – 1985 – 142p – it F.A.O. [631]
STANDARDIZED PILOT MILK PLANTS / Hall, H S – 1976 – 104p – it F.A.O. [338]
STANDARD-REGISTER-LEADER – Sunnyvale. Calif. 1946-1970 – 1 – us UMI [071]
STANDARDS OF BUSINESS / Rice, Elwood E – Rice Leaders of the World Association, 1921 – 1mf – 9 – $1.50 – LLMC 91-070 – us L.L.M.C. [170]
STANDARD-STAR – New Rochelle. N.Y. 1931- – 1 – us UMI [071]
STANDARD-TIMES – New Bedford. Mass. 1850- – 1 – us UMI [071]
STANDARD-TIMES – San Angelo. Tex. (evening). 1911-12, 1915-18, 1931- – 1 – us UMI [071]
STANDARD-TIMES – San Angelo. Tex. (morning). 1928- – 1 – us UMI [071]
Standard-Vacuum Oil Company *see*
- HUBUNGAN INDONESIA DENGAN INDUSTRI MINJAK DUNIA
- PEKERDJA MINJAK DI INDONESIA. PENJUSUNAN BUKU INI DISELENGGARAKAN
- PETA-DJALAN INDONESIA
- SERBANEKA STANVAC
- SVPM, STANDARD-VACUUM PETROLEUM MAATSCHAPPIJ, 40 TAHUN KEMADJUAN, 1912-1952
- SVPM (STANDARD-VACUUM PETROLEUM MAATSCHAPPIJ), FORTY YEARS OF PROGRESS, 1912-1952

STANDART – 1993 – 1 – sz Infoprint [947]
STANDART – (1993-98 12r per y $1,020y) – 1999- – 12r per y – 1 – $960.00 – us Ross [072]
DIE STANDARTE : ROMAN / Lernet-Holenia, Alexander – 5. und 6. Aufl. Berlin: S Fischer, 1934 – 1r – 1 – us U.W. Library [830]
STANDES-RUNDSCHAU UND JAHRESBERICHT / Deutsche Angestelltenschaft. Gau Bayern – 1928-30. (Serial publications of German trade unions in the Memorial Library, University of Wisconsin-Madison.) – 1 – us U.W. Library [330]
STANDETH GOD WITHIN THE SHADOW / Jordan, David Starr – New York: Thomas Y Crowell, c1901 – 1mf – 9 – 0-8370-3799-9 – 1985-1799 – us A.T.L.A. [230]
STANDING COMMITTEE ON ROADS AND PUBLIC IMPROVEMENTS, 1831-1832 / Bas-Canada. Parlement. Chambre d'assemblee. Comite permanent sur les chemins et ameliorations publiques – [s.l.]: [s.n.], [1832?]. SEM105P1230 – 2mf – 9 – Can$4.50 – cn Bibl Nat [625]
Standing, Herbert F *see* THE CHILDREN OF MADAGASCAR
STANDING RULES AND REGULATIONS. / Canada. Parliament. Legislative Council – Kingston: Printed by G Desbarats & T Cary, 1841. SEM105P167 – 2mf – 9 – Can$4.50 – cn Bibl Nat [324]
STANDING RULES AND REGULATIONS.. / Canada. Bas-Canada. Parlement. Chambre d'Assemblee – Quebec: Printed by Neilson & Cowan, 1830. SEM105P104 – 2mf – 9 – Can$4.50 – cn Bibl Nat [324]
Standley, P C *see*
- FLORA OF NEW MEXICO
- LISTA PRELIMINAR DE LAS PLANTAS DE EL SALVADOR

DER STANDPUNKT – Meran, Bozen. aug 29 1947-may 14 1954 – 5r – 1 – gw Mikrofilm [072]
STANDPUNKT – (Some original pgs damaged) – 1973-90 – 6r – 1 – ATLA S0640 – us A.T.L.A. [073]
STANFIELD STANDARD – Stanfield OR. Oct 1 1909-Nov 18 1927 – 1 – us U.O. Library [071]
Stanford, A *see* LE CORPS ANDROGYNE. L'HABITAT AU BURUNDI
Stanford, Charles *see*
- THE ALTERNATIVES OF FAITH AND UNBELIEF
- JOSEPH ALLEINE
- PHILIP DODDRIDGE, D.D.
- SYMBOLS OF CHRIST

Stanford, Charles Stuart *see* A HANDBOOK OF THE ROMISH CONTROVERSY
STANFORD DAILY – Palo Alto. Calif. 1945-47; 1949-58 – 1 – us UMI [071]
STANFORD DAILY – Standford, CA. Stanford University: 1926-1947; 1949-1958; 1971-1972; 1987-1994 – 33r – 1 – $1,650.00 – BC03008 – us Library Micro [370]
STANFORD DAILY *see* THE DAILY PALO ALTO
STANFORD DAILY (STANFORD UNIVERSITY) – Palo Alto, CA. 1926-47; 1949-58; 1971-72 – 26r – 1 BC02603 – $1,300.00 – us Library Micro [370]
STANFORD ENVIRONMENTAL LAW ANNUAL *see* STANFORD ENVIRONMENTAL LAW JOURNAL
STANFORD ENVIRONMENTAL LAW JOURNAL – (None publ 1984-86. Title varies: v1-5 1978-83 as Stanford Environmental Law Annual) – v1-15. 1978-96 – 9 – $184.00 set – us Hein [340]
STANFORD LAW REVIEW – v1-48. 1948-96 – 1,5,6,9 – $1,620.00 – us Hein [073]
STANFORD LAWYER – v1-29. 1966-94 – 9 – $124.00 set – us Hein [340]
Stanford Research Institute *see* AREA HANDBOOK FOR LIBYA

Stanford University. Hoover Institution on War, Revolution, and Peace *see*
- THE LIBRARY CATALOGS OF THE HOOVER INSTITUTION ON WAR, REVOLUTION, AND PEACE

Stanford University. KZSU Radio Station *see* PROJECT SOUTH

Stang, C S *see* DAS SLAVISCHE UND BALTISCHE VERBUM

Stang, William *see* MEDULLA FUNDAMENTALIS THEOLOGIAE MORALIS

Stange, Carl *see*
- DAS DOGMA UND SEINE BEURTEILUNG IN DER NEUEREN DOGMENGESCHICHTE
- WAS IST SCHRIFTGEMAESS?: VORTRAG

Stanihursto, Guillermo *see*
- DIOS IMMORTAL..
- DIOS INMORTAL...PASION DE CRISTO
- VETERIS HOMINIS PER EXPENSA QUATUOR NOVISSIMA METAMORPHOSIS, ET NOVI GENESIS

Stanis, V F *see* THE SOCIALIST TRANSFORMATION OF AGRICULTURE: (THEORY AND PRACTICE)

Stanish, Heidi I *see* PREDICTION OF THE PHYSICAL ABILITY REQUIREMENT EVALUATION (PARE) SCORES USING STANDARD MEASURES OF PHYSICAL FITNESS

STANISLAUS COUNTY – 1989- – 9+ r – 1 – $450.00 – P00133 – us Library Micro [910]

STANISLAUS COUNTY, MODESTO AND TURLOCK – Stanislaus Co, CA. 1893; 1910-1950 – 39r – 1 – $1,950.00 – D100 – us Library Micro [978]

STANISLAUS COUNTY WEEKLY NEWS – Modesto, CA. 1870-71; 1874-76; 1884-1902; 1903-07; 1908-12 – 12r – 1 RB02472 – $600.00 – us Library Micro [071]

Stanislavskaia, A M *see* RUSSKO-ANGLIISKIE OTNOSHENIIA I PROBLEMY SREDIZEMNOMOR'IA (1798-1807)

Stankevich, V *see* SUD'BY NARODOV ROSSII

Stanley *see* MURRAY STANLEY GREAT WAR DIARY

Stanley, Arthur Penrhyn *see*
- COMMENTARY ON THE EPISTLES OF ST PAUL TO THE CORINTHIANS
- HISTORICAL MEMORIALS OF WESTMINSTER ABBEY
- THE HISTORY OF THE JEWISH CHURCH
- LECTURES ON THE HISTORY OF THE EASTERN CHURCH
- MEMOIRS OF EDWARD AND CATHERINE STANLEY
- SERMONS AND ESSAYS IN THE APOSTOLIC AGE
- SINAI AND PALESTINE IN CONNECTION WITH THEIR HISTORY

STANLEY FOUNDATION PUBLICATIONS – 1960-1980 – 9 – $235.00 set – 0-89941-424-9 – us Hein [327]

Stanley, G A V *see* MISCELLANEOUS PAPERS FOR THE PERIOD 1924-1965

Stanley, Henry Morton *see*
- CINQ ANNEES AU CONGO,1879-1884
- THE CONGO AND THE FOUNDING OF ITS FREE STATE
- DANS LES TENEBRES DE L'AFRIQUE, RECHERCHE, DELIVRANCE ET RETRAITE D'EMIN PACHA
- IN DARKEST AFRICA
- SLAVERY AND THE SLAVE TRADE IN AFRICA
- THROUGH THE DARK CONTINENT

Stanley, Linda S et al *see* THE DEVELOPMENT OF AN INSTRUMENT TO ASSESS THE ATTITUDES TOWARD CULTURAL DIVERSITY AND CULTURAL PLURALISM AMONG PRESERVICE PHYSICAL EDUCATION MAJORS

STANLEY NEWS & NORTH WEST DURHAM OBSERVER. (STANLEY NEWS. AUCKLAND & COUNTY CHRONICLE, ETC.-STANLEY & CHESTER-LE-STREET NEWS.-STANLEY NEWS & CONSETT CHRONICLE) – England. Sep 1912-1928.-w. 16 reels – 1 – uk British Libr Newspaper [072]

Stanley, William C *see* THE EFFECTS OF AGE AND ENDURANCE TRAINING ON RAT ADRENAL TISSUE

Stanley-Brown, R *see* SURVEY OF THE ARCHITECTURE OF COMPLETED PROJECTS OF THE PUBLIC WORKS ADMINISTRATION

STANLEYVILLOIS – Stanleyville, 1959(31 Dec)-1960(16 Jul) – 7r – 1 – AF-122/3 – ne IDC [960]

Stanner, W E H *see* REPORT ON FIELD WORK IN NORTH-CENTRAL AND NORTH AUSTRALIA 1934-1935

Stannus, Hugh Hutton *see* A HISTORY OF THE ORIGIN OF THE DOCTRINE OF THE TRINITY IN THE CHRISTIAN CHURCH

Stansbury, Charles F *see* THE BARRISTER

THE STANSTEAD ADVERTISER – Stanstead, Canada. v1 n3. avr 1887; v1 n5. jun 1887 – 1r – 1 – Can$25.00 – cn Can Microfilming [072]

STANSTEAD JOURNAL – (Cont by: The Journal 30 jun 1982-31 dec 1991) – Rock Island, Canada. 6 nov 1845-25 dec 1901; 2 jan 1902-23 jun 1982 – 10r – 1 – Can$75.00r – cn Can Microfilming [072]

STANSTEAD JOURNAL – Rock Island, Canada. 1845-1900 – 20r – 1 – $1,300.00 – cn Library Assoc [971]

STANSTEAD JOURNAL *see* THE JOURNAL

STANTON COUNTY NEWS – Pilger, NE. -w. Sep 1901-Nov 1936, scattered issues missing; May 1937-Sept 1943 – 1 – us NE Hist [071]

STANTON DEMOCRAT – Stanton, NE. -w. Sept 1895-Jan 1897; Mar-Jun 1897 – 1 – us NE Hist [071]

Stanton, Elizabeth Cady *see*
- PAPERS
- THE PAPERS OF ELIZABETH CADY STANTON AND SUSAN B. ANTHONY

Stanton, Elizabeth Cady et al *see* THE WOMAN'S BIBLE

Stanton, John L Jr *see* JOURNAL OF FOOD PRODUCTS MARKETING

Stanton, R L *see* THE CHURCH AND THE REBELLION

STANTON REGISTER – Stanton, NE. -w. (-sw 1901). Mar 1880-Dec 1895, scattered issues missing; Feb 1896-May 1898; Oct 1898-Jan 1901; Apr 1901-May 1913; Jul 1915 to date – 1 – us NE Hist [071]

Stanton, Vincent Henry *see*
- THE GOSPELS AS HISTORICAL DOCUMENTS
- THE JEWISH AND THE CHRISTIAN MESSIAH
- THE PLACE OF AUTHORITY IN MATTERS OF RELIGIOUS BELIEF

STANTON WEEKLY PICKET – Stanton, NE. Nov 1893; Oct 1895-May 1898; Jul 1898; Oct 1898-Dec 1900; Apr-Aug 1901; Oct 1901-Nov 1917; Jan 1918-Jan 1920; Apr 1920; Aug 1920 – 1 – us NE Hist [071]

Stanwood, Edward *see* MR. SPOONER'S ISLAND COMMUNITY

Stanyer, F M *see* HISTORY OF POINT ANO NUEVO, SAN MATEO COUNTY

Stap, A *see* L'IMMACULEE CONCEPTION

Stapel, H F *see* BIOGRAPHICAL HISTORY OF ATCHISON COUNTY

STAPELIAE NOVAE: OR A COLLECTION OF SEVERAL NEW SPECIES OF THAT GENUS / Masson, F – London, 1796 -1797. 24 pp., 41 pls. B-6059 1 – 9 – ne IDC [580]

Stapf, O *see* INDEX LONDINENSIS TO ILLUSTRATIONS OF FLOWERING PLANTS

Stapfer, Edmond *see*
- THE DEATH AND RESURRECTION OF JESUS CHRIST
- JESUS CHRIST BEFORE HIS MINISTRY
- JESUS CHRIST DURING HIS MINISTRY
- JESUS CHRIST PENDANT SON MINISTERE

STAPLE INN AND ITS STORY / Worsfold, Thomas Cato – London: H Rumpus, 1903 – 2mf – 9 – $3.00 – LLMC 84-318 – us L.L.M.C. [340]

STAPLEHURST SENTINEL – Staplehurst, NE. -w. Dec 1921-Jun 1923; Sept-Oct 1923 – 1 – us NE Hist [071]

Staples, Abram Penn *see* NOTES ON VIRGINIA CORPORATION LAWS

Staples, James R *see* THE EFFECTS OF INTERMITTENT HYPERBARIC OXYGEN ON PAIN PERCEPTION AN ECCENTRIC STRENGTH IN A HUMAN INJURY MODEL

Stapleton, A *see* FLASHLIGHTS ON EVANGELICAL HISTORY

STAPLETON ENTERPRISE – Stapleton, NE. -w. Jul 1912 to date – 1 – us NE Hist [071]

Stapleton, H E *see* MEMOIRS OF GAUR AND PANDUA

Stapleton, John Henry *see* MORAL BRIEFS

Stapleton, Thomas *see*
- OPERA OMNIA
- PROMPTUARIUM CATHOLICUM...

STAR – Anniston. Ala. 1900- – 1 – us UMI [071]

STAR – Auburn. Ind. 1932- – 1 – us UMI [071]

STAR – Aurora. Ill. 1921-24 – 1 – us UMI [071]

STAR – Aurora. Ill. -w. 1964-66 – 1 – us UMI [071]

STAR – Barneston. Neb. 1895-1903; 1905-1907 – 1 – us UMI [071]

STAR – Chicago Heights. Ill. -w. 1906- – 1 – us UMI [071]

STAR – Coronado. Kan. 1886-1887 – 1 – us UMI [071]

STAR – Crawfordsville. Ind. -w. 1872-97 – 1 – us UMI [071]

STAR – El Sereno. Calif. 1953-1964 – 1 – us UMI [071]

STAR – Elk City. Kan. 1884-1885 – 1 – us UMI [071]

STAR – Eskridge. KS. 1883-86 – 1 – us UMI [071]

STAR – Fredericksburg. Va. 1893-1926 – 1 – us UMI [071]

STAR – Fredericksburg. Va. -sw. 1898-1900 – 1 – us UMI [071]

STAR – Gervais. Or. -w. 1901-26 – 1 – us UMI [071]

STAR – Gettysburg. PA.-w. And Sentinel. 1867-1953 – 1 – us UMI [071]

STAR – Hammond. La. 1967- – 1 – us UMI [071]

STAR – Indianapolis. Ind. 1903- – 1 – us UMI [071]

STAR – Johannesburg, South Africa. 3 Apr 1889- – 2177r – 1 – sa Microfile [960]

STAR – Lima. Ohio. 1965-1966 – 1 – us UMI [071]

STAR – Lincoln. Neb. 1902- – 1 – us UMI [071]

STAR – Marion. Ohio. 1877- – 1 – us UMI [071]

STAR – Marion. Ohio. -w. 1885-1912 – 1 – us UMI [071]

STAR – Marion. S.C. -sw. 1948-57 – 1 – us UMI [071]

STAR – Marion. S.C. -w. 1852-59, 1862-1901, 1902-20, 1929-47, 1958- – 1 – us UMI [071]

STAR – Merced, CA. 1886-97; 1910-20 – 6r – 1 – $270.00 – B02452 – us Library Micro [071]

STAR – Meridian. Miss. 1898- – 1 – us UMI [071]

STAR – Minneapolis. Minn. Indexed. 1947- – 1 – us UMI [071]

STAR – Muncie. Ind. 1900- – 1 – us UMI [071]

STAR – Napoleon, Ohio. 1857-58 – 1r – 1 – $32.50r – us Archival [071]

STAR – Oneonta. N.Y. 1916-30; 1948- – 1 – us UMI [071]

STAR – Pawtucket. R.I. 1936-1937 – 1 – us UMI [071]

STAR – Peoria. Ill. 1951-55 – 1 – us UMI [071]

STAR – Port St. Joe. Fla. Jul 1970- – 1 – us P.K. Yonge [071]

STAR – Portland OR. Oct 28 1938, Sep 28 1939, Mar May 1957, May 9 16 1960 – 1 – us U.O. Library [071]

STAR – Portsmouth. Va. After 1955 filmed with Norfolk Ledger Star. 1879-1955 – 1 – us UMI [071]

STAR – Sandusky. Ohio. -w. 1900-04 – 1 – us UMI [071]

STAR – Santa Barbara. Calif. -w. 1951-62 – 1 – us UMI [071]

STAR – Sevierville. Tenn. -w. 1895-97 – 1 – us UMI [071]

STAR – Somerton. Ariz. 1917-20 – 1 – us UMI [071]

STAR – St. Helena. CA.-w. 1950-58 – 1 – us UMI [071]

STAR – Steubenville. Ohio. 1890-1897 – 1 – us UMI [071]

STAR – Terre Haute. Ind. 1948-1964; 1965- – 1 – us UMI [071]

STAR – Tiffin, Ohio. 1869-73 – 1r – 1 – $32.50r – us Archival [071]

STAR – (Title varies: Humboldt Star, Silver State 1925. Merged with: Battle Mountain-Scout 1962) – Winnemucca, NV. 1906-67 – 75r – 1 – $3,750.00 – UN04822 – us Library Micro [071]

STAR – Townsend. Mont. 1958-1959; 1966- – 1 – us UMI [071]

STAR – (v11-. 1984-. 5,6,9) – Nov 1975- – 1 – us UMI [073]

STAR – Waco. Neb. 1916-1918 – 1 – us UMI [071]

STAR – Whitehorse, Yukon, CN. 1901- – 12r per yr – 1 – cn Commonwealth Micro [072]

THE STAR – Bombay, India. Feb 1946-May 1947 – 1r – 1 – us L of C Photodup [072]

THE STAR – Ireland.5 Jan 1929-1930 – 1 – ie Microforms [072]

THE STAR – Johannesburg. South Africa. Nov. 25-26, Dec. 1, 1942 – 1 – us NY Public [072]

THE STAR – Kingston, Jamaica. -d. 2 Jan-29 May, 13 July 1959-21 July 1962. 11 reels – 1 – uk British Libr Newspaper [072]

THE STAR – London. -d. 17 Jan 1888-Dec 1924. (80 reels) – 1 – uk British Libr Newspaper [072]

THE STAR – (Philadelphia). 1906 – 1 – us A.J.P.C. [071]

STAR ADVERTISER – Redwood City, CA. Mar 1963 – 1r – 1 – $50.00 – B02683 – us Library Micro [071]

THE STAR ALMANAC : A CYCLOPEDIA OF FACTS AND FIGURES RELATING TO THE DOMINION OF CANADA...1893-96 – Montreal: publ by Hugh Graham, 1892-[1895]. SEM105P506 – 5mf – 9 – Can$11.25 – cn Bibl Nat [971]

STAR AND BANNER – Gettysburg, Pa. -w. 1862-64 – 1 – us Western Res [976]

THE STAR AND COMMERCIAL ADVERTISER = L'ETOILE ET JOURNAL DU COMMERCE / ed by Wilkie, D – Quebec, Canada. 5 dec 1827-4 dec 1830 – 1r – 1 – Can$35.00 – cn Can Microfilming [072]

THE STAR AND ENTERPRISE – Newville, PA., 1897-1906 – 13 – $25.00r – us I.M.R. [071]

STAR AND HERALD – (Jan 1910-Mar 1920 Weekly ed 5r. 1915-4 Oct 1987 383r) – Panama City, Panama. Dec 1901-27 Dec 1909 – 1r – 1 – us L of C Photodup [072]

STAR AND HERALD – Panama City, Panama. Aug 1916-Apr 1918. Afternoon ed – 5r – 1 – us L of C Photodup [072]

STAR AND HERALD – Panama City, Panama. Jan 2 1866-Nov 27 1867 – 1r – 1 – us L of C Photodup [072]

STAR AND HERALD : TRIWEEKLY EDITION – Panama City, Panama. June-Dec 1868 – 1r – 1 – us L of C Photodup [072]

STAR AND KANSAN – Independence. Kansas. 1876-1905 – 1 – us UMI [071]

STAR AND NEWS POST *see* STAR-NEWS

STAR AND TIMES – Kansas City. Mo. 1880- – 1 – us UMI [071]

STAR AND WHEATLAND HERALD – Marysville, CA. 1935-36 – 3r – 1 – $150.00 – B02434 – us Library Micro [071]

STAR AND WORKINGMANS GUARDIAN – Sydney, 1844-46 – 1r – 1 – A$31.00 silver A$27.00 vesicular – at Pascoe [072]

THE STAR. (BALLARAT STAR) – Ballarat, Australia. 22 Jan 1856-30 Jun 1859; 19 Jan 1885-29 Jun 1922 (imperfect).-w. 127mqn reels – 1 – uk British Libr Newspaper [072]

STAR CHAMBER CASES; SHOWING WHAT CASES PROPERLY BELONG TO THE COGNIZANCE OF THAT COURT / Crompton, Richard, 1573-99 – Boston, Soule and Bugbee, 1881. 57 p. LL-110 – 1 – us L of C Photodup [340]

STAR DEMOCRAT – Carlisle, PA., 1906-1908 – 13 – $25.00r – us I.M.R. [071]

STAR DEMOCRAT – Mifflintown, PA. -w 1908-1912. 7 rolls – 13 – $25.00r – us I.M.R. [071]

STAR DEMOCRAT – Portland OR. Oct 12 1939-Nov 1 1940, Feb 29 1940 – 1 – us U.O. Library [071]

STAR FARMER – Kansas City. Mo. -w. 1949-61 – 1 – us UMI [071]

STAR FREE PRESS – Ventura, CA. 1944-49; 1978- – 386+ r – 1 RC03071 – $19,300.00 ($650.00y) – us Library Micro [071]

STAR IN THE EAST : RECORD OF THE WORK....IN INDIA AND SOUTH AFRICA – (Lacking: 1920-21. 1924-33) – Jul 1919-64 – 3r – 1 – ATLA S0201 – us A.T.L.A. [073]

STAR (MELBOURNE) – 1933-1936. ST1-24 – 24r – 1 – at Corangamite [072]

STAR OF BETHLEHEM – Milwaukee. Wis. 1869-71 – 1 – us UMI [071]

STAR OF BRUNSWICK – Dublin. Ireland. -w. 29 Nov 1828-21 Nov 1829. (47 ft) – 1 – uk British Libr Newspaper [072]

STAR OF GWENT AND SOUTH WALES TIMES *see* MONMOUTH, GLAMORGAN AND BRECON HERALD

STAR OF INDIA – Bombay, India. -d. Sept 1870-Dec 1871. 7 reels – 1 – uk British Libr Newspaper [072]

STAR OF INDIA – Calcutta, India. Aug 1932-1948 – 42r – 1 – us L of C Photodup [072]

STAR OF INDIA – Calcutta, jan-may, jul-dec 17 1941; jan-may 1942; dec 31 1942-aug 13 1949 – us Res Libr [072]

STAR OF OUR LORD : OR, CHRIST JESUS, KING OF ALL WORLDS, BOTH OF TIME OR SPACE: WITH THOUGHTS ON INSPIRATION, AND THE ASTRONOMIC DOUBT AS TO CHRISTIANITY / Upham, Francis William – (Includes bibliographical references and index) – New York: Phillips & Hunt; Cincinnati: Hitchcock & Walden, c1873 – 1mf – 9 – 0-8370-6435-X – 1986-0435 – us A.T.L.A. [230]

STAR OF THE EAST – Ipswich, England. 1893-Jun 1910; Jul 1913-1968; 1978-Jun 1987. -d. 334 reels. Missing: 1897 – 1 – uk British Libr Newspaper [072]

THE STAR OF THE TWENTIETH CENTURY : SAINT JOSEPH, THE STORY OF HIS LIFE / De Ruyter, John A – Baltimore, MD: St Joseph's Seminary, c1894 – 1mf – 9 – 0-8370-6974-2 – 1986-0974 – us A.T.L.A. [920]

STAR OF THE VALLEY – Newville, PA., 1864-1875 – 13 – $25.00r – us I.M.R. [071]

STAR OF WEST AFRICA – Cape Coast. Ghana. -w. 14 Jan-25 Feb 1939. (18 ft) – 1 – uk British Libr Newspaper [072]

THE STAR OF WEST AFRICA – Cape Coast. Ghana. feb. 28; Oct. 16, 19, 30; Nov. 2, 1948 – 1 – us NY Public [072]

STAR OF ZION : AFRICAN METHODIST EPISCOPAL CHURCH IN AMERICA – (Damaged original. Lacking: some pgs) – 1884-1904; 1906-70 – 33r – 1 – ATLA S0186 – us A.T.L.A. [073]

THE STAR PHOENIX – Saskatoon, Saskatchewan, CN. 1902- – 24r per yr – 1 – Can$53.00r – cn Commonwealth Micro [072]

STAR ROOT – Garberville, CA. 1977-1982 – 1r – 1 – $50.00 – B03226 – us Library Micro [071]

STAR ROUTE JOURNAL – Redway, CA. 1987-1991 – 1r – 1 – $50.00 – B05048 – us Library Micro [073]

STAR ROUTE NEWS – Risingsun. Ohio. 1959- – 1 – us UMI [071]

THE STAR SPANGLED BANNER / Key, Francis Scott – 1840. Author's ink copy of the poem. At end: Washington Oct. 21-40. F S Key. One of the four extant holographs of the poem, the earliest with the author's signature. It was probably copied for Lewis Jacob Cist (1808-1885) and has become known as the "Cist copy." MUSIC 1046 – 1 – us L of C Photodup [780]

STAR WEEKLY – (Lacking: 1946, V.1(31); 1947, V.2(84); 1948, V.3(84, 117,120, 123-136, 138-154); 1949, V.4(157,p.9-20, 163-165,p.1-4, 166); 1950, V.5(210, 217, 235-236, 241); 1950-1951, V.5-6(257-286, 288, 291-293, 295, 297-298, 300, 307); 1952, V.7(318-319, 322-323, 325-330, 332-336, 341-342); 1953, V.8(395-403); 1960, V.15(745, 775)) – Djakarta, 1946-1961.-v1-16(823) – 888mf – 9 – SE-444/1 – ne IDC [072]

STARA UKRAINA / Chasopis Istorii i Kul'turi. (Naukove Tovaristvo imeni Shevchenka) – Lemberg, 1924-25 – 1r – 1 – us Ross [947]

STARA UKRAYINA – L'vov, 1924-1925 – 1 – us NY Public [947]

STAR-ADVOCATE – Titusville. Fl. $w, sw. 1890-1920, 1921, 1922-30, 1946- – 1 – us P.K. Yonge [071]

STARAIA MONETA – Numizmaticheskii Zhurnal. St. Petersburg, 1910-12. Lacking some issues. B-1494/2 – 8 – ne IDC [730]

STARAIA MOSKVA – Organ russkikh monarkhistov. v. 1-2. M. 1912-14. BR-3996 2 – 8 – ne IDC [947]

STARAIA MOSKVA / Pyliaev, M I – St. Petersburg, 1891. 575, 22p. BR-7794 2 – 8 – ne IDC [460]

STARAIA MOSKVA : RASSKAZY IZ BYLOI ZHIZNI PERVOPRESTOL'NOI STOLITZY / Pyliaev, M I – St Petersburg: A Suvorin Publ, 1891 – 12mf – 9 – $120.00 – us Ross [947]

STAR-BANNER – Ocala. Fl. 1874-76, 1885-92, 1895-42, 1947-Sept. 1954 – 1 – us P.K. Yonge [071]

STAR-BEACON – Ashtabula. Ohio. 1916- – 1 – us UMI [071]

STAR-BULLETIN – Honolulu. Hawaii. Final. 1912-54 – 1 – us UMI [071]

STAR-BULLETIN – Honolulu. Hawaii. Home. 1946- – 1 – us UMI [071]

STAR-BULLETIN – Honolulu. Hawaii. -sw. 1913-16, 1919 – 1 – us UMI [071]

Starchevskii, A V *see* RUSSKII OB IASNITEL'NYI SLOVAR' ZAKLIUCHAIUSHCHII V SEBE ODNI NEPONIATNYIA SLOVA RUSSKOGO KNIZHNOGO IAZYKA

STAR-CHRONICLE – Kemptville, Ontario, CN. 1908-13 – 2r – 1 – cn Commonwealth Micro [072]

STARCH-STAERKE : INTERNATIONAL JOURNAL FOR THE INVESTIGATION, PROCESSING AND USE OF CARBOHYDRATES AND THEIR DERIVATIVES – v1-48. 1949-96 – 1,5,6,13 – us V.C.H. [660]

STAR-COURIER – Kewanee. Ill. 1950- – 1 – us UMI [071]

STARDOCK – n2-3. 1969-70 – 2mf – 9 – $5.00f – us Ross [150]

STARE DECISIS : PRESENTED AT A SEMINAR FOR FEDERAL APPELLATE JUDGES, 13-16 MAY 1975 / Re, Edward D – Washington: FJC, 1975 – 1mf – 9 – $1.50 – LLMC 95-301 – us L.L.M.C. [340]

STAR-EXPONENT – Culpeper. Va. 1881; 1897-1966- – 1 – us UMI [071]

STAR-GAZETTE – Elmira. N.Y. and Advertiser. 1891- – 1 – us UMI [071]

STAR-HERALD – Scottsbluff. Neb. 1912- – 1 – us UMI [071]

STARINA I NOVIZNA : ISTORICHESKII SBORNIK, IZDAVAEMYI PRI OBSHCHESTVE REVNITELEI RUSSKOGO ISTORICHESKOGO PROSVESHCHENIIA V PAMIAT'IMP. ALEKSANDRA 3 – Spb. v1-22. 1897-1917 – 106mf – 9 – RET-20/1 – ne IDC [947]

STARINAR – Organ Srpskog arheoloskog drustva. S. 3, v. 1 (za 1922). Beograd. 1923. BR-5759 2 – 8 – ne IDC [073]

STARINNYE POMESHCHIKI NA SLUZHBE I DOMA. IZ SEMEINOI KHRONIKI (1578-1762) / Shchepkina, E – Spb. 1890. BR-10,530 1 – 9 – ne IDC [947]

STAR-JOURNAL – Ainsworth. NE. And pred. 1886-1963 – 1 – us UMI [071]

STAR-JOURNAL – Minneapolis. Minn. 1939-1943; 1944-1946 – 1 – us UMI [071]

STAR-JOURNAL – Pueblo. Col. 1946- – 1 – us UMI [071]

STAR-JOURNAL – Sandusky. Ohio. 1898-1941 – 1 – us UMI [071]

STARK COUNTY AND ITS PIONEERS / Shallenberger, E H – Cambridge: B. W. Seaton, Prairie Chief Office, 1876. Illinois Reel 55. (The Cox Library Collection) – 5 – us Americana [978]

Stark, James *see* THE WESTMINSTER CONFESSION OF FAITH CRITICALLY COMPARED WITH THE HOLY SCRIPTURES AND FOUND WANTING

STARK WIE DIE MARK : ROMAN / Stratz, Rudolph – Stuttgart: J G Cotta, 1923 – 1r – 1 – us U.W. Library [830]

Starke, Matthias *see*
- HEINRICH HEINES AUFFASSUNGEN VON DER GESCHICHTE UND DER REVOLUTION ALS IMPULSGEBENDEN ELEMENTEN DES FRANZOESISCHEN EXILS (1831-1848)
- DIE STUDIEN JACOB GRIMMS ZUR HERAUSBILDUNG UND ZU DEN MERKMALEN DES DEUTSCHEN MEISTERGESANGS IM REZEPTIONSGESCHICHTLICHEN KONTEXT

STARKE'S MONTREAL POCKET ALMANAC AND GENERAL REGISTER FOR...1858-59 – Montreal: J Starke and Co. SEM16P353 – 1r – 5 – Can$9.00 – cn Bibl Nat [910]

STARKE'S POCKET ALMANAC AND GENERAL REGISTER FOR... 1860-61 – Montreal: J Starke and Co. SEM16P354 – 1r – 5 – Can$73.00 – cn Bibl Nat [910]

Starkey, George *see* PYROTECHNY ASSERTED AND ILLUSTRATED, TO BE THE SUREST AND SAFEST MEANS FOR ARTS TRIUMPH OVER NATURES INFIRMITIES

Starkey, P H et al *see* ANIMAL TRACTION

Starkie, Thomas *see* A TREATISE ON THE LAW OF SLANDER AND LIBEL, AND INCIDENTALLY OF MALICIOUS PROSECUTIONS...FROM THE 2ND ENGLISH ED. OF 1830

STAR-LEDGER – Newark. N.J. 1945- – 1 – us UMI [071]

STARLING'S LAW OF THE HEART: ITS SIGNIFICANCE IN CHRONIC CONGESTIVE HEART FAILURE / Loe, Ping Kian – Summary in Indonesian and English. SE-10,690 1. 1961 – 9 – ne IDC [616]

STAR-NEWS – (Also known as: Star and News Post) – Pasadena, CA. 1894; 1911-23; 1925-56; historical headlines 1938-45 – 344r – 1 CH03388 – $17,200.00 – us Library Micro [071]

STAR-NEWS – National City, CA. 1968-1976; 1977-1979 – 93+ r – 1 – $4,650.00 ($190.00y) – H03350 – us Library Micro [071]

STAR-NEWS – National City. Calif. 1903-1959 – 1 – us UMI [071]

STAR-NEWS – Pasadena. Calif. 1951- – 1 – us UMI [071]

STAR-NEWS – Wilmington. N.C. 1949- – 1 – us UMI [071]

STAROBALGARSKI RAZKAZI / Ivanov, I – Sofiia. 1935. BR-3964 2 – 8 – ne IDC [940]

Starobin, Joseph Robert *see* THE LIFE AND DEATH OF AN AMERICAN HEROE; THE STORY OF DAVE DORAN

STAROE I NOVOE – Ezhemesiachnyi zhurnal russkoi stariny, prikladnykh khudozhestv, iskusstva i nauki. v. 1-4. Revel'. 1931-33. BR-3766 2 – 8 – ne IDC [073]

STAROE VREMIA – (Includes c.1: no.1 1923:Oct.8, no.33 (1924:Apr.24); no.54 1924:July 6-no.56 (1924:July 13); no.58 1924:July 20-no.61 (1924:July 31); no.63 1924:Aug.7; no.65 1) – Bielgrad: [s.n.], 1923- – 1 – CSUXADP4804-S – us Hoover Inst Photo [947]

STAROE ZHIT'E / Pyliaev, M I – St. Petersburg, 1892. 318p. BR-7795 2 – 8 – ne IDC [460]

STAROOBRIADCHESKAIA MUSL' – Ezhemesiachnyi zhurnal, posviashchennyi tserkovno-obshchestvennoi zhizni staroobradchestva. Kiev. 1910-16. Lacking: (9) 1912. B-1434 2 – 8 – ne IDC [073]

STAROOBRIADCHESKAIA MYSL – Moscow. 1910-16 – 1 – 92.00 – us L of C Photodup [947]

STAROOBRIADCHESKII PASTYR' – Ezhemesiachnyi dukhovnyi zhurnal. v. 1-12. M. 1913-14. BR-3997 2 – 8 – ne IDC [073]

STAROOBRIADETS – Ezhemesiachnyi zhurnal. Nizhnyi-Novgorod. 1906-07. Lacking: (3) 1906, (9) 1907. B-1443 2 – 8 – ne IDC [073]

STAROOBRIADTSY – Ezhemesiachnyi zhurnal. Organ tserkovno-obshchestvennoi zhizni staroobriadchestva. Nizhnii Novgorod. 1908-09. B-1909 2 – 8 – ne IDC [240]

STARORUSSKAIA POVEST' / Piksanov, N K – Petrograd, 1923 – 8 – BR-7770 2 – ne IDC [947]

STARO-UKRAINS'KA LEKSYKOHRAFIIA V II ZV'IAZKAKH Z ROSIIS'KOIU TA BILORUS'KOIU / Nimchuk, V V – Kyiv, 1980 – 4mf – 9 – R-14873/1 – ne IDC [460]

Starr, Frederick *see*
- BIBLIOGRAPHY OF CONGO LANGUAGES
- A BIBLIOGRAPHY OF CONGO LANGUAGES

Starr, H *see* INTERNATIONAL INTERACTIONS

STARS AND STRIPES – All editions – 1 – us NY Public [071]

STARS AND STRIPES – Auburn, CA. 1867-71 – 1r – 1 – $50.00 – B02033 – us Library Micro [071]

STARS AND STRIPES – (Individual listings also available) – All editions. 1918-19; 1942-67 – 218r – 1 – us Ross [071]

STARS AND STRIPES – London. England. 1918-1944 – 1 – us UMI [072]

STARS AND STRIPES – Washington, DC. 14 Jun 1919-2 Jan 1926 – 3r – 1 – us L of C Photodup [073]

THE STARS AND STRIPES : NEWSPAPER OF THE U.S. ARMED FORCES IN EUROPE, THE MEDITERRANEAN, AND NORTH AFRICA, 1942-1964 – 1989 – 138r – 1 – $3,174.00 set in US $30.00r outside – M1506 – us Nat'l Archives [355]

THE STARS AND STRIPES : NEWSPAPER OF THE U.S. ARMED FORCES IN THE PACIFIC, 1945-1963 – 1990 – 166r – 1 – $3,818.00 set in US $30.00r outside – M1624 – us Nat'l Archives [355]

THE STARS AND STRIPES : COMPLETE COLLECTION: WORLD WAR 1 – WORLD WAR 2 – POST-WORLD WAR 2 – (Individual colls and titles also listed separately) – 502r – 1 – $38,650.00 complete coll – us Ross [071]

THE STARS AND STRIPES : EUROPEAN EDITION – DARMSTADT, GERMANY – (Filming is ongoing at the State Historical Society of Wisconsin 10-18r annually $1350y annual subsc ca 18r) – sep 1973-dec 1998 – ca 285r – 1 – $22,800.00 set – us Ross [071]

STARS AND STRIPES AT SEA – v. 1-2, no. 5. June 26-July 7 1943 – 1 – us NY Public [071]

THE STARS AND STRIPES AT SEA (PWW2 COLL) – ([Publ on Landing Ship Tank 325 Anchored off Tunisia]) – v1 n1-v2 n5. jun 26-jul 7 1943 – 1r (reel 218) – 1 – $100.00r – us Ross [071]

THE STARS AND STRIPES, POST-WORLD WAR 2 (PWW2) – (Titles also listed individually) – 174r – 1 – $14,000.00 coll – us Ross [071]

THE STARS AND STRIPES (PWW2 COLL) : DAILY CHINA EDITION – SHANGHAI – (Includes: US Navy Suppl issued with v1 n26 oct 27 1945. Lacks: China Bowl Suppl issued with v1 n56, and Army Day Suppl issued with v1 n161) – v1 n1-167 sep 28 1945-apr 13 1946 – 1r (reel 45) – 1 – $100.00r – us Ross [071]

THE STARS AND STRIPES (PWW2 COLL) : EUROPEAN EDITION – (Includes: Olympic Souvenir issue 1948. Lacking: v15 n301 feb 15 1957; and v15 n335 mar 21 1957 as well as some issues in 1958, 1959, 1960) – v1 n1-v25 n362. dec 6 1946-apr 17 1967 – 91r (reels 127-217) – 1 – $100.00r – us Ross [071]

THE STARS AND STRIPES (PWW2 COLL) : WEEKEND – PFUNGSTADT, GERMANY – v1 n1-36 may 26 1946-jan 26 1947; v2 n1-v3 n5 feb2 1947-feb 28 1948; v3 n6-23 mar 6-jul 3 1948 – 3r (reels 123-125) – 1 – $100.00r – us Ross [071]

THE STARS AND STRIPES (PWW2 COLL) : WEEKLY COMICS – (Lacking: n9-12,14,16-20,22,24) – v2 n2-39. aug 4 1946-jun 29 1947 – 1r (reel 126) – 1 – $100.00r – us Ross [071]

THE STARS AND STRIPES (PWW2 COLL) : WEEKLY MAGAZINE SUPPLEMENT – CHINA EDITION – SHANGHAI – v1 n1-19. nov 3 1945-mar 1946 – 1r (reel 46) – 1 – $100.00r – us Ross [071]

THE STARS AND STRIPES, WORLD WAR 1 : THE OFFICIAL NEWSPAPER OF THE AEF – (Includes: The Star and Stripes – Pictorial Suppl – Victory Edition jun 13 1919. Liberty Loan Suppl sep 181918) – v1 n1-52 feb 8 1918-jan 31 1919; v2 n1-19 feb 7 1919-jun 13 1919 – 1r (reel 1) – 1 – $100.00r – us Ross [071]

THE STARS AND STRIPES, WORLD WAR 2 (WW2) – (Titles also listed individually) – 43r – 1 – $3,600.00 coll – us Ross [071]

THE STARS AND STRIPES (WW2 COLL) : AFRICA, MIDDLE EAST, PERSIAN GULF EDITION – (Lacking: v2 n3 jan 21 1944. Also includes: Special Invasion Ed publ for Armed Forces in the Cairo area jun 6 1944; and The Stars and Stripes – Extra aug 15 1945, "It's All Over!") – v1 n1-38 apr 16 1943-dec 1943; v2 n1-52 1944; v3 n1-51 jan-dec 21 1945 – 1r (reel 9) – 1 – $100.00r – us Ross [071]

THE STARS AND STRIPES (WW2 COLL) : ALGIERS DAILY EDITION – (Also includes: Extra sunday jul 11 1943 (Allied Landings on Sicily Carried Out Successfully)) – v1 n1-262 apr 1943-apr 14 1944; v2 n1-66 apr 17 1944-jul 15 1944 – 1r (reel 8) – 1 – $100.00r – us Ross [071]

THE STARS AND STRIPES (WW2 COLL) : CASABLANCA EDITION – (v1 n148-240 nov 27 1943-apr 2 1944 not publ. The Stars and Stripes, North Africa Ed served the Casablanca area for this period) – v1 n1-147, 241-262 may 19-nov 26 1943, apr 3-may 2 1944; v2 n1-58 may 3-jul 20 1944 – 1r (reel 11) – 1 – $100.00r – us Ross [071]

THE STARS AND STRIPES (WW2 COLL) : DAILY DIJON EDITION – v1 n49-56, 58-60. jan 22-feb 3 1945 – 13 (reel 33) – 1 – $100.00r – us Ross [071]

THE STARS AND STRIPES (WW2 COLL) : DAILY GERMAN EDITION – PFUNGSTADT – v1 n1-185 apr 5-oct 6 1945; v1 n186-357, v2 n1-13 oct 7 1945-apr 17 1946 – 2r (reels 36-37) – 1 – $100.00r – us Ross [071]

THE STARS AND STRIPES (WW2 COLL) : DAILY MIDDLE PACIFIC AREAS EDITION – HONOLULU – v1 n1-169 may 14 1945-nov 27 1945 incl Navy Day Suppl oct 27 1945; v1 n170-222 nov 28 1945-jan 30 1946 – 2r (reels 43-44) – 1 – $100.00r – us Ross [071]

THE STARS AND STRIPES (WW2 COLL) : DAILY NANCY EDITION – v1 n1-81. jan 22-apr 16 1945 – 1r (reel 35) – 1 – $100.00r – us Ross [071]

THE STARS AND STRIPES (WW2 COLL) : DAILY NEWSPAPER OF U.S. ARMED FORCES IN THE EUROPEAN THEATER OF OPERATIONS – BESANCON – v1 n1-68. sep 14-dec 1 1944 – 1r (reel 29) – 1 – $100.00r – us Ross [071]

THE STARS AND STRIPES (WW2 COLL) : DAILY NEWSPAPER OF U.S ARMED FORCES IN THE EUROPEAN THEATER – STRASBOURG – v1 n1-42. dec 4 1944-jan 20 1945 – 1r (reel 32) – 1 – $100.00r – us Ross [071]

THE STARS AND STRIPES (WW2 COLL) : EUROPEAN EDITION – ALTDORF, BAVARIA [SOUTHERN GERMAN EDITION] – (Also includes: Midweek – The Stars and Stripes Southern German Ed – Altdorf (weekly) v1 n1-22 aug 22 1945-jan 16 1946) – v1 n1-179 may 8-nov 3 1945 incl Victory ed aug 15 1945; v1 n180-230, v2 n1-143 nov 5 1945-may 24 1946; v2 n144-278 may 25-oct 7 1946; v2 n279-337 oct 8 1946-dec 5 1946 – 5r (reels 38-42) – 1 – $100.00r – us Ross [071]

THE STARS AND STRIPES (WW2 COLL) : FIFTH ARMY EDITION – (Also includes: The Stars and Stripes – Mediterranean Ed – Dry Run) n1-2 jul 27-aug 3 1944 "Combat Ed"; "The Ess and Ess", Rome v1 n1-13 aug 16 1945-jan 9 1946. Lacking n2,3,6,10,12; Picture Section, Stars and Stripes n1-3 (no date); Fifth Army – The Stars and Stripes – Combat Ed Italy v1 n1-33 oct 20 1943-nov 24 1943) – v1 n1-10. sep 6-sep 16 1943 – 1r (reel 13) – 1 – $100.00r – us Ross [071]

THE STARS AND STRIPES (WW2 COLL) : LIEGE EDITION – v1 n1-88. jan 20-apr 17 1945 – 1r (reel 34) – 1 – $100.00r – us Ross [071]

THE STARS AND STRIPES (WW2 COLL) : LONDON EDITION. NEWSPAPER OF THE U.S. ARMED FORCES IN THE EUROPEAN THEATER OF OPERATIONS – (Also includes: The Stars and Stripes Magazine jun 16 1945-oct 13 1945, Tomorrow dec 21 1944-may 26 1945 both issued wkly as separate sections of the London ed; and War Weekly jul 29 1943-may 31 1945) – v2 n1-29 apr 18 1942-oct 31 1942; v3 n1-268 nov 2 1942-sep 13 1943; v3 n269-310, v4 n1-226 sep 14 1943-jul 25 1944; v4 n227-311, v5 n1-141 jul 26 1944-apr 18 1945; v5 n142-294 apr 19 1945-oct 15 1945 incl ETO Victory suppl of may 8 1945 – 5r (reels 2-6) – 1 – $100.00r – us Ross [071]

THE STARS AND STRIPES (WW2 COLL) : MEDITERRANEAN EDITION – ALGIERS AND ROME – (Also includes: The Stars and Stripes (Mediterranean Ed) Naples v 2 n1-6 dec 20 1943-jan 17 1944) – v1 n1-52 dec 9 1942-dec 4 1943; v2 n1-81 dec 11 1943-jun 23 1945 – 1r (reel 7) – 1 – $100.00r – us Ross [071]

THE STARS AND STRIPES (WW2 COLL) : MEDITERRANEAN EDITION (DAILY) ROME – v1 n1-186 jun 5 1944-feb 13 1945; v1 n187-v2 n80 feb 14 1945-sep 12 1945; v2 n81-229 sep 13 1945-mar 3 1946; v2 n230-307 mar 5 1946-jun 2 1946 – 4r (reels 19-22) – 1 – $100.00r – us Ross [071]

THE STARS AND STRIPES (WW2 COLL) : MEDITERRANEAN EDITION – NAPLES – (Lacking: n175-183 jun 1-11 1945) – v1 n1-250 nov 10 1943-sep 2 1944; v1 n251-v2 n108 sep 4 1944-mar 15 1945; v2 n109-184 mar 16 1945-jun 12 1945 – 3r (reels 14-16) – 1 – $100.00r – us Ross [071]

THE STARS AND STRIPES (WW2 COLL) : MEDITERRANEAN WEEKLY EDITION – ROME – (Also includes: The Stars and Stripes – Western Europe Ed (Unofficial Newspaper of US Forces in the European Theater, Paris v1 n1-69 jul 4 1944-sep 22 1944; v1 n70-255 sep 23 1944-apr 1945; v1 n256-v2 n70 apr 9 1945-sep 18 1945; v2 n71-198 sep 19 1945-feb 1 1946. Also includes: Tomorrow v1 n1-23 dec 13 1944-may 23 1945; War Week oct 7 1944-may 27 1945; Stars and Stripes – Weekly Comics – Paris Ed v1 n-126 jul 30 1945-jan 27 1946) – v1 n1-53 nov 26 1944-nov 25 1945 – 5r (reels 23-27) – 1 – $100.00r – us Ross [071]

THE STARS AND STRIPES (WW2 COLL) : NORTH AFRICAN EDITION – v1 n-262 may 3 1943-may 2 1944; v2 n1-122 may 3 1944-nov 24 1944 – 1r (reel 10) – 1 – $100.00r – us Ross [071]

THE STARS AND STRIPES (WW2 COLL) : NORTHERN IRELAND EDITION – BELFAST – v1 n1-183. dec 6 1943-jul 8 1944 – 1r (reel 17) – 1 – $100.00r – us Ross [071]

THE STARS AND STRIPES (WW2 COLL) : SICILY EDITION – (Also includes: The Stars and Stripes – Grenoble aug 25 1944 publ by Bill Maudlin; and The Stars and Stripes – Mediterranean printed in France v1 n1-14 aug 29-sep 13 1944) – v1 n1-85. aug 12 1943-jun 2 1944 – 1r (reel 12) – 1 – $100.00r – us Ross [071]

THE STARS AND STRIPES (WW2 COLL) : SOUTHERN FRANCE EDITION – NICE, MARSEILLE – series 1: v1 n1-14 sep 29-oct 14 1944; series 2: v1 n1-126 oct 16 1944-mar 10 1945; series 3: v1 n1-201 mar 12-sep 30 1945 – 2r (reels 30-31) – 1 – $100.00r – us Ross [071]

THE STARS AND STRIPES (WW2 COLL) : TUNIS EDITION – TUNIS – v1 n1-48. dec 21 1943-jun 2 1944 – 1r – 1 – $100.00r – us Ross [071]

THE STARS AND STRIPES (WW2 COLL) : WEEKLY MAGAZINE – PARIS – v1 n1-34. jun 3 1945-jan 20 1946 – 1r (reel 28) – 1 – $100.00r – us Ross [071]

STARS AND THE EARTH : OR, THOUGHTS UPON SPACE, TIME, AND ETERNITY / Ansted, David Thomas – Boston: Noyes, Holmes, 1874 – 1mf – 9 – us A.T.L.A. [240]

THE STARS IN MYTH AND FACT / Scott, Oral E – Caldwell, ID: The Caxton Printers, 1947.374p. illus. plates, diag., charts – 1 – us U.W. Library [520]

STAR-SENTINEL – Hays. Kan. 1882-86 – 1 – us UMI [071]

STARSHINA-SERZHANT – (Library has: Aug.-Dec. 1962; Jan. 1963-Dec. 1971) – Moskva: [s.n.], 1960- – 1 – CSUX90-S105 – us Hoover Inst Photo [355]

STARSHIP *see* ALGOL

STAR-TELEGRAM – Fort Worth. Texas – 1 – us UMI [071]

STAR-TIMES – Staunton. Ill. 1906-1936 – 1 – us UMI [071]

STAR-TRIBUNE – Casper. Wyoming. 1966- – 1 – us UMI [071]

STARYE GODY = BYGONE YEARS – St Petersburg, 1907-16 – 141mf – 9 – $985.00 – us Ross [700]

STARYE GODY – Ezhemesiacknik dlia liubitelei iskusstva i stariny. Spb. 1907-16. B-1910 2 – 8 – ne IDC [073]

STARYE I NOVYE RELIGII TROPICHESKOI I IUZHNOI AFRIKI / Sharevskaia, B I – M. 1964. BR-2469 2 – 8 – ne IDC [290]

STARYI FOL'KLOR PRIBAIKAL'IA / ed by Gurevich, Aleksandr V – 1939. Russian folklore – 1 – us I.U. Libraries [390]

STARYI NARVSKII LISTOK – (Includes c.1: v.30:no.17=no.1229 1934:Feb. 8) – Narva: [Staryi narvskii listok], 1898 – 1 – CSUXADM8788-S – us Hoover Inst Photo [947]

STARYI PETERBURG. RAZSKAZY IZ BYLOI ZHIZNI STOLITSY / Pyliaev, M I – v1. St. Petersburg, n.d. 471p. BR-7793 2 – 8 – ne IDC [460]

STARYIA GNEZDA / Gorodetskii, S – Povesti i razskazy. (Izd. A. S. Suvozina). Spb. 1914. BR-1133 2 – 8 – ne IDC [460]

Stasov, V *see* GALLEREIA PETRA VELIKAGO V IMPERATORSKOI PUBLICHNOI BIBLIOTEKE

Stasov, Vladimir Vasil'evich *see*
– AVTOGRAFY MUZYKANTOV V IMPERATORSKOI PUBLICHNOI BIBLIOTEKE
– MATERIALY K BIBLIOGRAFII. OPISANIE RUKOPISEI

Stassen, Ingo *see* ELEKTROCHEMISCHE THERMOSPRAY-MASSENSPEKTROMETRIE

Stassen, Michael *see* DAS MIKROTUBULI-ASSOZIIERTE PROTEIN TYP 4 (MAP 4) DES HAUSHUHNS

STAT. REPORT OF STATE AND COUNTY EXTENSION WORKERS / Auburn University. Extension Service – 1958-64. 1 fiche – 9 – us Spaulding [630]

STAT TEEN J. A. THERON / Theron, Johannes Andreas, defendant – Record of trial in Johannesburg Magistrates Court, 1965-67 – 1 – us Res Libr [960]

STATE – Columbia. S.C. 1891- – 1 – us UMI [071]

STATE – Richmond. Va. 1876-1897 – 1 – us UMI [071]

THE STATE – Columbia, SC: The State Co Printers, 1892-1901; 1903-11 – 1r – 1 – us Res Libr [071]

THE STATE / Oppenheimer, Franz – 1914. 133p. Together with: Banking and The Social Problem a 1909 Pamphlet, by Henry Meulen, 17p; and The Production of Security, by Gustave de Molinari, 1849, 23p., Introd. by Murray Rothbard,trans. by J. Huston McCulloch. 1 fiche (24x) – 9 – 1.00f – at Libertarian Micro [320]

THE STATE AND ECONOMIC PLANNING / Eckermann, Lee – 1977, 16p – 9 – 1.00f – at Libertarian Micro [339]

STATE AND MIND – (See also: R T: A Journal of Radical Therapy; Rough Times) – v5- 1976- – 1,5,6,9 – us UMI [150]

STATE AND SOCIETY IN INDEPENDENT NORTH AFRICA / The Middle East Institute. Washington, D.C; ed by Brown, L C – (The James Terry Duce Memorial Series v. 1). 1966. BNE-522 1 – 9 – ne IDC [956]

STATE AND TERRITORIAL GENERAL STATUTES RELATING TO THE USE OF STREETS AND HIGHWAYS BY STREET RAILWAY, GAS, WATER AND ELECTRIC LIGHT COMPANIES / Cummins, James Sheldon – Chicago, Byllesby, 1905. 268 p. LL-164 – 1 – us L of C Photodup [340]

THE STATE AND THE UNIVERSITIES (1910-1943) / Cilliers, Andries Charl – Cape Town: Miller, [1944] – us Res Libr [370]

STATE ARCHIVE OF THE RUSSIAN FEDERATION (GARF): COLLECTION HELD AT PIROGOVSKAIA STREET, FOND R-393 PEOPLE'S COMMISSARIAT OF INTERNAL AFFAIRS (NKVD RSFSR) : OPIS 4: PRESS BUREAU 1917-1918 – Dela 1-128 – 26r – 1 – Reel nos 3.573-3.598 – uk Chadwyck [324]

STATE ARCHIVE OF THE RUSSIAN FEDERATION (GARF): COLLECTION HELD AT PIROGOVSKAIA STREET, FOND R-393 PEOPLE'S COMMISSARIAT OF INTERNAL AFFAIRS (NKVD RSFSR) : OPIS 5: LOCAL ECONOMY DEPARTMENT 1917-1919 – Dela 1-871 – 105r – 1 – uk Chadwyck [324]

STATE ARCHIVE OF THE RUSSIAN FEDERATION (GARF): DELA SERIES. COLLECTION HELD AT PIROGOVSKAIA STREET, FOND R-393 PEOPLE'S COMMISSARIAT OF INTERNAL AFFAIRS (NKVD RSF SR) : OPIS 20: SECRETARIAT, MARRIAGE REGISTRATION DEPARTMENT 1920 – Dela 1-180 – 21r – Reel nos 3.1144-3.1151; 3.1214-3.1226 – uk Chadwyck [324]

STATE ARCHIVE OF THE RUSSIAN FEDERATION (GARF): DELA SERIES. COLLECTION HELD AT PIROGOVSKAIA STREET, FOND R-393 PEOPLE'S COMMISSARIAT OF INTERNAL AFFAIRS (NKVD RSFSR) : OPIS 1: CHANCELLERY 1917-1919 – Dela 1-271 – 31r – 1 – Reel nos 3.396-3.426 – uk Chadwyck [324]

STATE ARCHIVE OF THE RUSSIAN FEDERATION (GARF): DELA SERIES. COLLECTION HELD AT PIROGOVSKAIA STREET, FOND R-393 PEOPLE'S COMMISSARIAT OF INTERNAL AFFAIRS (NKVD RSFSR) : OPIS 10: SECRETARIAT – Dela 1-112 – 13r – 1 – Reel nos 3.953-3.965 – uk Chadwyck [324]

STATE ARCHIVE OF THE RUSSIAN FEDERATION (GARF): DELA SERIES. COLLECTION HELD AT PIROGOVSKAIA STREET, FOND R-393 PEOPLE'S COMMISSARIAT OF INTERNAL AFFAIRS (NKVD RSFSR) : OPIS 11: ADMINISTRATION, MARRIAGE REGISTRATION AND FOREIGN DEPARTMENT 1919-1920 – Dela 1-400 – 46r – 1 – Reel nos 3.966-3.1004; 3.1163-3.1169 – uk Chadwyck [324]

STATE ARCHIVE OF THE RUSSIAN FEDERATION (GARF): DELA SERIES. COLLECTION HELD AT PIROGOVSKAIA STREET, FOND R-393 PEOPLE'S COMMISSARIAT OF INTERNAL AFFAIRS (NKVD RSFSR) : OPIS 12: PRESS INSTITUTE 1919-1920 – Dela 1-52 – 12r – 1 – Reel nos 3.1005-3.1016 – uk Chadwyck [324]

STATE ARCHIVE OF THE RUSSIAN FEDERATION (GARF): DELA SERIES. COLLECTION HELD AT PIROGOVSKAIA STREET, FOND R-393 PEOPLE'S COMMISSARIAT OF INTERNAL AFFAIRS (NKVD RSFSR) : OPIS 13: STATISTICS DEPARTMENT 1919 – Dela 1-627 – 310r – 1 – uk Chadwyck [324]

STATE ARCHIVE OF THE RUSSIAN FEDERATION (GARF): DELA SERIES. COLLECTION HELD AT PIROGOVSKAIA STREET, FOND R-393 PEOPLE'S COMMISSARIAT OF INTERNAL AFFAIRS (NKVD RSFSR) : OPIS 14: LOCAL ENTERPRISES DEPARTMENT 1919 – Dela 1-45 – 6r – 1 – Reel nos 3.1106-3.1111 – uk Chadwyck [324]

STATE ARCHIVE OF THE RUSSIAN FEDERATION (GARF): DELA SERIES. COLLECTION HELD AT PIROGOVSKAIA STREET, FOND R-393 PEOPLE'S COMMISSARIAT OF INTERNAL AFFAIRS (NKVD RSFSR) : OPIS 15: CHIEF ADMINISTRATION OF THE MILITIA (POLICE) 1919 – Dela 1-58 – 5r – 1 – Reel nos 3.1112-3.1116 – uk Chadwyck [324]

STATE ARCHIVE OF THE RUSSIAN FEDERATION (GARF): DELA SERIES. COLLECTION HELD AT PIROGOVSKAIA STREET, FOND R-393 PEOPLE'S COMMISSARIAT OF INTERNAL AFFAIRS (NKVD RSFSR) : OPIS 16: CRIMINAL INVESTIGATION DEPARTMENT 1918-1919 – Dela 1-64 – 10r – 1 – Reel nos 3.1117-3.1126 – uk Chadwyck [324]

STATE ARCHIVE OF THE RUSSIAN FEDERATION (GARF): DELA SERIES. COLLECTION HELD AT PIROGOVSKAIA STREET, FOND R-393 PEOPLE'S COMMISSARIAT OF INTERNAL AFFAIRS (NKVD RSFSR) : OPIS 18: FINANCIAL DEPARTMENT 1918-1919 – Dela 1-40 – 7r – 1 – Reel nos 3.1133-3.1139 – uk Chadwyck [324]

STATE ARCHIVE OF THE RUSSIAN FEDERATION (GARF): DELA SERIES. COLLECTION HELD AT PIROGOVSKAIA STREET, FOND R-393 PEOPLE'S COMMISSARIAT OF INTERNAL AFFAIRS (NKVD RSFSR) : OPIS 19: SECRETARIAT 1920 – Dela 1-34 – 4r – 1 – Reel nos 3.1140-3.1143 – uk Chadwyck [324]

STATE ARCHIVE OF THE RUSSIAN FEDERATION (GARF): DELA SERIES. COLLECTION HELD AT PIROGOVSKAIA STREET, FOND R-393 PEOPLE'S COMMISSARIAT OF INTERNAL AFFAIRS (NKVD RSFSR) : OPIS 2: ADMINISTRATIVE DEPARTMENT 1917-1919 – Dela 1-180 – 35r – 1 – Reel nos 3.427-3.461 – uk Chadwyck [324]

STATE ARCHIVE OF THE RUSSIAN FEDERATION (GARF): DELA SERIES. COLLECTION HELD AT PIROGOVSKAIA STREET, FOND R-393 PEOPLE'S COMMISSARIAT OF INTERNAL AFFAIRS (NKVD RSFSR) : OPIS 21: FOREIGN SUBDEPARTMENT 1920-1921 – Dela 1-330 – 152r – 1 – uk Chadwyck [324]

STATE ARCHIVE OF THE RUSSIAN FEDERATION (GARF): DELA SERIES. COLLECTION HELD AT PIROGOVSKAIA STREET, FOND R-393 PEOPLE'S COMMISSARIAT OF INTERNAL AFFAIRS (NKVD RSFSR) : OPIS 22: STATISTICS DEPARTMENT 1920-1921 – (Dela 1-277 78r. Dela 342-437 40r) – 1 – uk Chadwyck [324]

STATE ARCHIVE OF THE RUSSIAN FEDERATION (GARF): DELA SERIES. COLLECTION HELD AT PIROGOVSKAIA STREET, FOND R-393 PEOPLE'S COMMISSARIAT OF INTERNAL AFFAIRS (NKVD RSFSR) : OPIS 23: CHIEF ADMINISTRATION OF THE MILITIA (POLICE) 1919-1923 – Dela 1-218 – 16r – 1 – Reel nos 3.1278-3.1293 – uk Chadwyck [324]

STATE ARCHIVE OF THE RUSSIAN FEDERATION (GARF): DELA SERIES. COLLECTION HELD AT PIROGOVSKAIA STREET, FOND R-393 PEOPLE'S COMMISSARIAT OF INTERNAL AFFAIRS (NKVD RSFSR) : OPIS 24: STATISTICS DEPARTMENT 1920-1921 – Dela 1-74 – 18r – 1 – Reel nos 3.1294-3.1308; 3.1564-3.1566 – uk Chadwyck [324]

STATE ARCHIVE OF THE RUSSIAN FEDERATION (GARF): DELA SERIES. COLLECTION HELD AT PIROGOVSKAIA STREET, FOND R-393 PEOPLE'S COMMISSARIAT OF INTERNAL AFFAIRS (NKVD RSFSR) : OPIS 25: FINANCE AND SUPPLIES DEPARTMENT 1919-1920 – Dela 1-112 – 11r – 1 – Reel nos 3.1567-3.1577 – uk Chadwyck [324]

STATE ARCHIVE OF THE RUSSIAN FEDERATION (GARF): DELA SERIES. COLLECTION HELD AT PIROGOVSKAIA STREET, FOND R-393 PEOPLE'S COMMISSARIAT OF INTERNAL AFFAIRS (NKVD RSFSR) : OPIS 26: ADMINISTRATION OF AFFAIRS 1921 – Dela 1-80 – 14r – 1 – Reel nos 3.1578-3.1591 – uk Chadwyck [324]

STATE ARCHIVE OF THE RUSSIAN FEDERATION (GARF): DELA SERIES. COLLECTION HELD AT PIROGOVSKAIA STREET, FOND R-393 PEOPLE'S COMMISSARIAT OF INTERNAL AFFAIRS (NKVD RSFSR) : OPIS 27: ORGANISATION AND ADMINISTRATION DEPARTMENT 1921-1923 – (Dela 1-342 80r. Dela 432-1266 88r) – 1 – uk Chadwyck [324]

STATE ARCHIVE OF THE RUSSIAN FEDERATION (GARF): DELA SERIES. COLLECTION HELD AT PIROGOVSKAIA STREET, FOND R-393 PEOPLE'S COMMISSARIAT OF INTERNAL AFFAIRS (NKVD RSFSR) : OPIS 28: ORGANISATION AND ADMINISTRATION DEPARTMENT 1921-1922 – (Dela 1-57 17r reel nos 3.1779-3.1795. Dela 194-253 27r reel nos 3.1939-3.1965) – 1 – uk Chadwyck [324]

STATE ARCHIVE OF THE RUSSIAN FEDERATION (GARF): DELA SERIES. COLLECTION HELD AT PIROGOVSKAIA STREET, FOND R-393 PEOPLE'S COMMISSARIAT OF INTERNAL AFFAIRS (NKVD RSFSR) : OPIS 29: STATISTICS DEPARTMENT 1921-1922 – Dela 1-10 – 5r – 1 – Reel nos 3.1796-3.1800 – uk Chadwyck [324]

STATE ARCHIVE OF THE RUSSIAN FEDERATION (GARF): DELA SERIES. COLLECTION HELD AT PIROGOVSKAIA STREET, FOND R-393 PEOPLE'S COMMISSARIAT OF INTERNAL AFFAIRS (NKVD RSFSR) : OPIS 3: INFORMATION DEPARTMENT 1918 – Dela 1-629 – 233r – 1 – uk Chadwyck [324]

STATE ARCHIVE OF THE RUSSIAN FEDERATION (GARF): DELA SERIES. COLLECTION HELD AT PIROGOVSKAIA STREET, FOND R-393 PEOPLE'S COMMISSARIAT OF INTERNAL AFFAIRS (NKVD RSFSR) : OPIS 30: MARRIAGE REGISTRATION DEPARTMENT 1921-1922 – Dela 1-18 – 2r – 1 – Reel nos 3.1801-3.1802 – uk Chadwyck [324]

STATE ARCHIVE OF THE RUSSIAN FEDERATION (GARF): DELA SERIES. COLLECTION HELD AT PIROGOVSKAIA STREET, FOND R-393 PEOPLE'S COMMISSARIAT OF INTERNAL AFFAIRS (NKVD RSFSR) : OPIS 31: CHIEF ADMINISTRATION OF THE MILITIA (POLICE) 1921-1922 – Dela 337-705 – 18r – 1 – Reel nos 3.1966-3.1983 – uk Chadwyck [324]

STATE ARCHIVE OF THE RUSSIAN FEDERATION (GARF): DELA SERIES. COLLECTION HELD AT PIROGOVSKAIA STREET, FOND R-393 PEOPLE'S COMMISSARIAT OF INTERNAL AFFAIRS (NKVD RSFSR) : OPIS 32: ADMINISTRATION OF AFFAIRS 1921-1923 – Dela 1-144 – 12r – 1 – Reel nos 3.1984-3.1995 – uk Chadwyck [324]

STATE ARCHIVE OF THE RUSSIAN FEDERATION (GARF): DELA SERIES. COLLECTION HELD AT PIROGOVSKAIA STREET, FOND R-393 PEOPLE'S COMMISSARIAT OF INTERNAL AFFAIRS (NKVD RSFSR) : OPIS 33: ADMINISTRATIVE DEPARTMENT 1922-1923 – Dela 1-167 – 41r – 1 – Reel nos 3.1996-2036 – uk Chadwyck [324]

STATE ARCHIVE OF THE RUSSIAN FEDERATION (GARF): DELA SERIES. COLLECTION HELD AT PIROGOVSKAIA STREET, FOND R-393 PEOPLE'S COMMISSARIAT OF INTERNAL AFFAIRS (NKVD RSFSR) : OPIS 6: CHIEF ADMINISTRATION OF THE MILITIA (POLICE) 1917-1919 – Dela 1-141 – 14r – 1 – Reel nos 3.660-3.673 – uk Chadwyck [324]

STATE ARCHIVE OF THE RUSSIAN FEDERATION (GARF): DELA SERIES. COLLECTION HELD AT PIROGOVSKAIA STREET, FOND R-393 PEOPLE'S COMMISSARIAT OF INTERNAL AFFAIRS (NKVD RSFSR) : OPIS 64: ADMINISTRATIVE AND REGISTRATION DEPARTMENT 1926-1927 – (Dela 1-166 3r reel nos 3.1605-3.1620. Dela 167-173 1r reel no 3.686. Dela 174-203 7r reel nos 3.1621-3.1627. Dela 241-246 3r reel nos 3.687-3.689) – 1 – uk Chadwyck [324]

STATE ARCHIVE OF THE RUSSIAN FEDERATION (GARF): DELA SERIES. COLLECTION HELD AT PIROGOVSKAIA STREET, FOND R-393 PEOPLE'S COMMISSARIAT OF INTERNAL AFFAIRS (NKVD RSFSR) : OPIS 7: FOREIGN DEPARTMENT 1918-1919 – Dela 1-144 – 38r – 1 – Reel nos 3.674-3.685; 3.790-3.807; 3.940-3.947 – uk Chadwyck [324]

STATE ARCHIVE OF THE RUSSIAN FEDERATION (GARF): DELA SERIES. COLLECTION HELD AT PIROGOVSKAIA STREET, FOND R-393 PEOPLE'S COMMISSARIAT OF INTERNAL AFFAIRS (NKVD RSFSR) : OPIS 8: VETERINARY DEPARTMENT 1918-1919 – Dela 1-44 – 5r – 1 – Reel nos 3.808-3.809; 3.948-3.950 – uk Chadwyck [324]

STATE ARCHIVE OF THE RUSSIAN FEDERATION (GARF): DELA SERIES. COLLECTION HELD AT PIROGOVSKAIA STREET, FOND R-393 PEOPLE'S COMMISSARIAT OF INTERNAL AFFAIRS (NKVD RSFSR) : OPIS 9: FINANCIAL DEPARTMENT 1918 – Dela 1-23 – 2r – 1 – Reel nos 3.951-3.952 – uk Chadwyck [324]

STATE ARCHIVE OF THE RUSSIAN FEDERATION (GARF): DELA SERIES. COLLECTION HELD AT PIROGOVSKAIA STREET, FOND R-393 PEOPLE'S COMMISSARIAT OF INTERNAL AFFAIRS (NKVD RSFSR) : OPIS 90: TRADE UNION COMMITTEE 1918-1930 – Dela 1-331 – 34r – 1 – Reel nos 3.694-3.727 – uk Chadwyck [324]

STATE ARCHIVE OF THE RUSSIAN FEDERATION (GARF): OPIS SERIES : COLLECTION HELD AT BEREZHKOVSKAIA NABEREZHNAIA – 131r – 1 – Reel nos 3.169-3.228; 3.230-3.254; 3.350-3.395 – uk Chadwyck [324]

STATE ARCHIVE OF THE RUSSIAN FEDERATION (GARF): OPIS SERIES : COLLECTION HELD AT PIROGOVSKAIA STREET, FOND R-393 PEOPLE'S COMMISSARIAT OF INTERNAL AFFAIRS (NKVD RSFSR) – 264r – 1 – Reel nos 3.1-3.168; 3.255-3.349; 3.837 – uk Chadwyck [324]

STATE ARCHIVES-BAPTISTS / Germany. Kingdom of Prussia – MS. and printed materials on Baptists in German State Archives. 1840-1896 – 1 – 159.60 – us Baptist [240]

STATE ATTORNEY GENERAL REPORTS AND OPINIONS – (6/81-1996 no 3 update on mf $10,840.00 set. Updated bimonthly) – All opinions thru 6/81 on reel – 9,6 – $14,500.00 set – us Hein [340]

STATE AUDIT REPORTS / Fulton County. Ohio. Board of Education – 1921-1945 – 1r – 1 – $32.50r – us Archival [324]

THE STATE BANK OF THE U.S.S.R. : 1921-1926 / Gosudarstvenny i bank SSSR – Moscow: Financial and Economic Research Bureau of the State Bank, 1927 – 1 – CSUX91-B203 – us Hoover Inst Photo [332]

STATE BAR ASSOCIATION REPORTS – 1934-35 (all publ) – 3mf – 9 – $4.50 – LLMC 84-587 – us L.L.M.C. [073]

STATE BAR JOURNAL OF THE STATE BAR OF CALIFORNIA *see* CALIFORNIA STATE BAR JOURNAL

STATE BAR OF CALIFORNIA JOURNAL – v1-1926- 1; v50- 5,6,9 – us UMI [340]

STATE BAR OF NEW MEXICO BULLETIN AND ADVANCE OPINIONS *see* BAR BULLETIN

STATE BUDGET OF LEBANON / Lebanon – 17 v. 1947-75. Lacking: 1949 54; 1957; 1959 60; 1964. BNE-9669 1 – 9 – ne IDC [336]

STATE CAPITAL – Guthrie. Okl. 1891-92 – 1 – us UMI [071]

STATE CAPITOL REPORTER – Sacramento, CA. 1868-1870 – 5r – 1 – $250.00 – C03646 – us Library Micro [071]

STATE CENSUS / Atchison County. Kansas – (v12-13. V115-0002) – 1895. v9-11. V115-0001 – 1 – us A.G.L.L. [310]

STATE CENSUS, 1825 / Illinois. Census – Edwards and Fulton Counties. V122-0004 – 1 – us A.G.L.L. [310]

STATE CENSUS, 1830 / Illinois. Census – Morgan County. V122-0004 – 1 – us A.G.L.L. [310]

STATE CENSUS, 1835 / Illinois. Census – Fulton, Jasper and Morgan Counties. V122-0004 – 1 – us A.G.L.L. [310]

STATE CENSUS, 1840 / Illinois. Census – Alphabetical by county. V122-0001/V122-0003 – 1 – us A.G.L.L. [310]

STATE CENSUS, 1845 / Illinois. Census – Cass, Putnam and Tazewell Counties. V122-0004 – 1 – us A.G.L.L. [310]

STATE CENSUS, 1855 / Illinois. Census – Alphabetical by county. V122-0004 to V122-0019 – 1 – us A.G.L.L. [310]

STATE CENSUS, 1855 / Kansas.Census – All inclusive. V113-0001 – 1 – us A.G.L.L. [310]

STATE CENSUS, 1865 / Illinois. Census – Alpha by county. V122-0020 to V122-0040 – 1 – us A.G.L.L. [310]

STATE CENSUS, 1875 / Kansas.Census – Allen-Barber Co.V114-0001 – 1 – us A.G.L.L. [310]

STATE CENSUS, 1875 / Kansas.Census – Barton-Brown Co.V114-0002 – 1 – us A.G.L.L. [310]

STATE CENSUS, 1875 / Kansas.Census – Butler-Cherokee Co. V114-0003 – 1 – us A.G.L.L. [310]

STATE CENSUS, 1875 / Kansas.Census – Clay-Coffey Co. V114-0004 – 1 – us A.G.L.L. [310]

STATE CENSUS, 1875 / Kansas.Census – Cowley-Dickinson Co. V114-0005 – 1 – us A.G.L.L. [310]

STATE CENSUS, 1875 / Kansas.Census – Doniphan, Douglas Co. V114-0006 – 1 – us A.G.L.L. [310]

STATE CENSUS, 1875 / Kansas.Census – Edwards-Greewood Co. V114-0007 – 1 – us A.G.L.L. [310]

STATE CENSUS, 1875 / Kansas.Census – Harvey, Howard with Elk, Jackson Co. V114-0008 – 1 – us A.G.L.L. [310]

STATE CENSUS, 1875 / Kansas.Census – Jefferson-Johnson Co. V114-0009 – 1 – us A.G.L.L. [310]

STATE CENSUS, 1875 / Kansas.Census – Labette, Leavenworth (part) Co. V114-0010 – 1 – us A.G.L.L. [310]

STATE CENSUS, 1875 / Kansas.Census – Leavenworth (part)-Linn Co. V114-0011 – 1 – us A.G.L.L. [310]

STATE CENSUS, 1875 / Kansas.Census – Lyon-Marshall Co. V114-0012 – 1 – us A.G.L.L. [310]

STATE CENSUS, 1875 / Kansas.Census – Miami, Mitchell Co. V114-0013 – 1 – us A.G.L.L. [310]

STATE CENSUS, 1875 / Kansas.Census – Montgomery-Nemaha Co. V114-0014 – 1 – us A.G.L.L. [310]

STATE CENSUS, 1875 / Kansas.Census – Neosho-Osborne Co. V114-0015 – 1 – us A.G.L.L. [310]

STATE CENSUS, 1875 / Kansas.Census – Ottawa-Pottawatomie Co. V114-0016 – 1 – us A.G.L.L. [310]

STATE CENSUS, 1875 / Kansas.Census – Reno-Russell Co.V114-0017 – 1 – us A.G.L.L. [310]

STATE CENSUS, 1875 / Kansas.Census – Saline-Shawnee Co. V114-0018 – 1 – us A.G.L.L. [310]

STATE CENSUS, 1875 / Kansas.Census – Smith-Washington Co. V114-0019 – 1 – us A.G.L.L. [310]

STATE CENSUS, 1875 / Kansas.Census – Wilson-Wyandotte Co. V114-0020 – 1 – us A.G.L.L. [310]

STATE CENSUSES : THE COMPLETE COLLECTION OF ALL REPORTS AND SELECTED FOOTNOTES IN STATE CENSUSES – (Annotated bibliographies of censuses of population taken after the year 1790 by Henry J Dubester) – Washington: Library of Congress, 1948 – 703mf – 9 – $5.00f – us Ross [975]

STATE CHARITIES REPORT / Van Wert County. Ohio. Pleasant Township. Board of Trustees – 1897 – 1r – 1 – $32.50r – us Archival [324]

STATE COLLEGE TIMES *see* THE SPARTAN DAILY

STATE CONSTITUTIONAL CONVENTIONS ON MICROFICHE / U. S. – (Pt 1: State Constitutional Conventions, from Independence to Completion of the Present Union, 1776-1959 $7,795. Pt 2: State Constitutional Conventions, 1959-75 $2,495. Pt 3: State Constitutional Conventions, Revisions and Amendments, 1959-76 $995. Pt 4: State Constitutional Conventions, Commissions and Amendments, 1959-78 $9,570. Pt 5: State Constitutional Conventions, Commissions and Amendments, 1979-88 $4,550. Printed bibliographies also available: Pt 1; Pts 2-4 $350.00. Pt 5 $295.00. Subsets by state available) – Pts 1-5. 1776-1988 – 9 – us CIS [324]

STATE CONTROL AND SOCIAL CARE OF THE VICIOUS AND DEPENDENT CLASSES : WOMAN'S SHARE IN THE WORK / Spencer, Anna Garlin – (Excerpted from Transactions of the National Council of Women of the United States) – 1891 – 1r – 1 – us Western Res [360]

STATE CONTROL OF TRADE AND COMMERCE BY NATIONAL OR STATE AUTHORITY / Stickney, Albert – New York, Baker, Voorhis, 1897. 202 p. LL-1111 – 1 – us L of C Photodup [340]

STATE COURT JOURNAL – v1-18. 1977-1994 – 9 – $182.00 set – us Hein [340]

STATE DEMONSTRATION FARMS ANNUAL REPORT / North Dakota. Agricultural Experiment Station. Fargo – nos.1-12. 1907-17 – 1,5,6 – us Spaulding [630]

STATE DEPARTMENT REGISTERS OF CORRESPONDENCE, 1870-1906 / U.S. Department of State – M17 – 71r – 1 – us Nat'l Archives [975]

STATE DEPARTMENT TERRITORIAL PAPERS: MISSOURI, 1812-1820 / U.S. Department of State – RG 59. M1134. 1 roll – 1 – us Nat'l Archives [978]

STATE DEPT. TERRITORIAL PAPERS / U.S. Department of State – (Colorado Series, 1859-74. 1 roll. M3. Printed guide. Dakota, 1861-73. 1 roll. M309. Printed guide. Florida, 1777-1824. 11 rolls. M116. Idaho, 1863-72. 1 roll. M445. Printed guide. Kansas, 1854-61. 2 rolls. M218. Printed guide. Montana, 1864-72. 2 rolls. M356. Printed guide. Nebraska, 1854-67. 1 roll. M228. Printed guide. Nevada Series, 1861-64. 1 roll. M13. New Mexico, 1851-72. 4 rolls. T17. Oregon, 1848-58. 1 roll. M419. Orleans Series, 1764-1823. 13 rolls. T260. Territory Northwest of the River Ohio, 1787-1801. 1 roll. M470. Territory Southwest of the River Ohio, 1790-95. 1 roll. M471. Utah Series, 1853-73, 2 rolls. M12. Printed guide. Washington, 1854-72. 2 rolls. M26. Wyoming, 1868-73. 1 roll. M85) – Arizona, 1864-72. 1 roll. M342. Printed guide – 1 – us Nat'l Archives [324]

STATE DEVELOPMENT PLANS REVIEW OF PROGRESS / India. Planning Commission – New Delhi. 1958 – 9 – ne IDC [330]

STATE DIRECTED EMIGRATION: WITH PREFATORY LETTER FROM HIS EXCELLENCY THE RIGHT HON. THE EARL OF DUFFERIN. / Boyd, J F – Manchester: J. Heywood, 1883. 02526. (Pre-1900 Canadiana) – 9 – cn C.I.H.M. [971]

STATE DOCUMENTS / U. S. – 30,653mf – 9 – $86,850.00 – us OmniSys [324]

STATE DOCUMENTS RELATING TO LIBRARIES – 2,002mf – 9 – $7,500.00 – us OmniSys [020]

STATE ECONOMIST – Reno, NV. 14 Apr 1932 – 1r – 1 – $50.00 – U04717 – us Library Micro [071]

STATE EDUCATION DIRECTORIES / Career Guidance Foundation – Key education personnel in 50 states – 53mf – 9 – $89.00 – us Career [370]

STATE FINANCE ADMINISTRATION; FINANCE MANAGEMENT; ORGANIZATION OF SECOND-LEVEL AUTONOMOUS GOVERNMENT (BY SOEPARDI) / Arifin, Abudlrachman – Indonesian Finance Administration series – 9 – SE-2557-1 – ne IDC [336]

STATE FIVE-YEAR PLAN. FOR THE PERIOD 1971-1975, PT. 1-2 / U.S.S.R. – N. K. Baybokov. Trans. from Russian. Gosudarstvennyy. SSSR na 1971-1975 Gody. JPRS 56970-1-2. 1972. BD-1853 1 – 9 – ne IDC [338]

STATE FREE NEGRO CAPITATION TAX BOOKS, CHARLESTON, SC / South Carolina. Department of Archives and History – c1811-60. M-11 – 2r – 1 – $75.00r – Out-of-state orders: us Scholarly Res – us SC Archives [978]

STATE FREE NEGRO CAPITATION TAX BOOKS, CHARLESTON, SOUTH CAROLINA, CA 1811-1860 – South Carolina: Department of Archives and History, 1995 – 2r – 1 – $170.00 – us Scholarly Res [336]

STATE GAZETTE – Point Pleasant. West Virginia. 1908-26; 1932-46 – 1 – us UMI [071]

STATE GAZETTE – Providence, RI. 1796 – 1,3 – us Readex [071]

STATE GAZETTE – Trenton, NJ. 1847-50 – 1 – us Readex [071]

STATE GOVERNMENT – v1- 1926- 1; v42-5,6; 1975- 9 – us UMI [323]

STATE GOVERNMENT NEWS – v1-37. 1958-94 – 9 – $388.00 set – us Hein [340]

State Historical Co *see*
- HISTORY OF DAVIS COUNTY
- HISTORY OF MILLS COUNTY
- HISTORY OF TAYLOR COUNTY

THE STATE IN CONSTITUTIONAL AND INTERNATIONAL LAW / Crane, R T – Baltimore, 1907 – 1mf – 1 – ILM-1146/1 – ne IDC [327]

STATE IN GLOBAL PERSPECTIVE / ed by Kazancigil, Ali – 1986 – xx/300p – 9 – 92-3-102283-0 – Co-published with the Gower Publishing Company. Ltd, Aldershot, UK, who have exclusive rights in the UK and the USA – fr UNESCO [320]

THE STATE IN RELATION TO RAILWAYS / Acworth, W M – 1fiche (29x) – 9 – .60 per fiche (f); 1.00f – at Libertarian Micro [320]

STATE INDEX TO NON-GOVERNMENT MASTER FREQUENCY DATA BASE / U.S. National Technical Information Service – Quarterly. Contains by state, the transmitter location, frequency, service, call sign, licensee name and authorization for each station in that state – 9 – us N.T.I.S. [000]

STATE INSOLVENT LAWS / Moses, Raphel Jacob – New York: Baker-Voorhies, 1879. 497 1p. LL-502 – 1 – us L of C Photodup [340]

State Institute for War Documentation, Amsterdam *see* THE DUTCH UNDERGROUND PRESS, 1940-1945

STATE JOURNAL – Lansing. Mich. 1911- – 1 – us UMI [071]

STATE JOURNAL – Parkersburg. West Virginia. -w. 1869-1902 – 1 – us UMI [071]

STATE JOURNAL – Topeka. Kan. 1879- – 1 – us UMI [071]

STATE LABOR PROCEEDINGS : PHASE 1. 1885-1974 / AFL, CIO, and AFL-CIO. Conventions – (Middle Atlantic States $1,350.00; Middle Western States $3,915.00; New England States $990.00; Southern States $1,500.00; Southwestern States $1,190.00; Western and Pacific States $1,990.00) – All convention proceedings held in AFL-CIO Library – 3,765mf – 9 – $8,200.00 – us UPA [331]

STATE LABOR REPORTS / California – (Biennial Reports: Bureau of Labor Statistics $75.00; State Board of Arbitration $45.00) – 9 – us UPA [331]

STATE LABOR REPORTS / Colorado – (Bureau of Labor Statistics $75.00; State Board of Arbitration, Annual Report $45.00) – 9 – us UPA [331]

STATE LABOR REPORTS / Connecticut – (Bureau of Labor Statistics, Series 1: $45.00; Series 2: $150.00; Dept. of Factory Inspection $65.00) – 9 – us UPA [331]

STATE LABOR REPORTS : FROM THE FIRST REPORTS THROUGH 1900 – (See also indiv. states) – 9 – $5,915.00 set – us UPA [331]

STATE LABOR REPORTS / Idaho. Dept. of Immigration, Labor and Statistics – 9 – $45.00 – us UPA [331]

STATE LABOR REPORTS / Illinois – (Bureau of Labor Statistics, Biennial Report $130.00; Dept. of Factory Inspection, Annual Report $75.00; State Board of Arbitration, Annual Report $65.00) – 9 – us UPA [331]

STATE LABOR REPORTS / Indiana – (Bureau of Statistics, Report $330.00; Labor Commission, Biennial Report $45.00; State Bureau of Inspection, Annual Report $45.00) – 9 – us UPA [331]

STATE LABOR REPORTS / Iowa – (Bureau of Labor, Biennial Report $135.00; Mine Inspector, Report $80.00) – 9 – us UPA [330]

STATE LABOR REPORTS / Kansas – (Dept. of Labor and Industry, Report $265.00; State Labor Dept., Report of the Mine Inspection Section and the Mine Rescue Station $90.00) – 9 – us UPA [331]

STATE LABOR REPORTS / Kentucky. Dept. of Mines and Minerals – 9 – $145.00 – us UPA [331]

STATE LABOR REPORTS / Maine – (Bureau of Industrial and Labor Statistics, Annual Report $150.00; Secretary of State. Statistics of Industries and Finances $65.00) – 9 – us UPA [331]

STATE LABOR REPORTS / Maryland – (Bureau of Industrial Statistics and Information, Biennial Report $65.00; Bureau of Statistics and Information, Annual Report $100.00) – 9 – us UPA [331]

STATE LABOR REPORTS / Massachusetts – (Bureau of Statistics of Labor, Annual Report $360.00; Index to Reports, 1870-1889 $45.00; Bureau of Statistics $45.00; State Board of Arbitration and Conciliation, Annual Report $75.00) – 9 – us UPA [331]

STATE LABOR REPORTS / Michigan – (Bureau of Labor and Industrial Statistics, Annual Report $215.00; Dept. of Labor, Report of the Inspection of Factories $50.00) – 9 – us UPA [331]

STATE LABOR REPORTS / Minnesota. Dept. of Labor and Industry – Biennial Report – 9 – $125.00 – us UPA [331]

STATE LABOR REPORTS / Missouri – (Bureau of Labor Statistics, Annual Report $350.00; Division of Mine Inspection, Report $130.00) – 9 – us UPA [331]

STATE LABOR REPORTS / Montana. Bureau of Agriculture, Labor and Industry – (Annual Report) – 9 – $100.00 – us UPA [331]

STATE LABOR REPORTS / Nebraska. Dept. of Labor – 9 – $190.00 – us UPA [331]

STATE LABOR REPORTS / New Hampshire – (Bureau of Labor $90.00, Factory Inspection $45.00; Commissioners on Bureau of Labor Statistics $45.00) – 9 – us UPA [331]

STATE LABOR REPORTS / New Jersey – (Annual Reports: Bureau of Statistics of Labor and Industries $275.00; Dept. of Factory and Workshop Inspection $110.00; State Board of Arbitration $50.00) – 9 – us UPA [331]

STATE LABOR REPORTS / New York – (Annual Reports: Board of Mediation and Arbitration $185.00; Bureau of Factory Inspection $305.00; Bureau of Labor Statistics $490.00) – 9 – us UPA [331]

STATE LABOR REPORTS / North Carolina. Dept. of Labor and Printing – (Annual Report) – 9 – $195.00 – us UPA [331]

STATE LABOR REPORTS / North Dakota. Dept. of Agriculture and Labor – (Biennial Report) – 9 – $75.00 – us UPA [331]

STATE LABOR REPORTS / Ohio – (Annual Reports: Bureau of Labor Statistics $235.00; Dept. of Inspection of Workshops, Factories and Public Buildings $230.00; State Board of Arbitration $50.00) – 9 – us UPA [331]

STATE LABOR REPORTS / Pennsylvania – (Annual Reports: Bureau of Industrial Statistics $430.00; Dept. of Factory Inspector $115.00) – 9 – us UPA [331]

STATE LABOR REPORTS – Phase One. 58 titles from 30 states. From the first reports to 1900 – 9 – $5,915.00 – us UPA [331]

STATE LABOR REPORTS / Rhode Island. Bureau of Industrial Statistics – (Annual Report) – 9 – $125.00 – us UPA [331]

STATE LABOR REPORTS / Tennessee. Bureau of Labor, Statistics and Mines – (Annual Report) – 9 – $80.00 – us UPA [331]

STATE LABOR REPORTS / Virginia. Bureau of Labor and Industry – (Annual Report) – 9 – $50.00 – us UPA [331]

STATE LABOR REPORTS / Washington (State) – (Bureau of Labor, Biennial Report $45.00; Bureau of Statistics, Agriculture and Immigration $45.00; Factory, Mill and Railway Inspection, Biennial Report $45.00) – 9 – us UPA [331]

STATE LABOR REPORTS / West Virginia. Bureau of Labor Statistics – (Biennial Report) – 9 – $50.00 – us UPA [331]

STATE LABOR REPORTS / Wisconsin – (Biennial Reports: Bureau of Labor and Industrial Statistics $245.00; State Board of Arbitration and Conciliation $45.00) – 9 – us UPA [331]

STATE LAW INDEX – Washington: GPO. v1-12. 1925-48 (all publ) – 112mf – 9 – $168.00 – LLMC 78-072 – us L.L.M.C. [340]

STATE LEDGER – Jackson. Miss. 1884-1892 – 1 – us UMI [071]

State Library of New South Wales *see* SDYNEY MORNING HERALD INDEX

STATE LINE BAPTIST CHURCH. CHEROKEE COUNTY. SOUTH CAROLINA : CHURCH RECORDS – 1837-1972. Deacons' Minutes. 1971-Jan 1973 – 1 – 42.89 – us Baptist [240]

STATE LINE HERALD – Lakeview OR. Oct 25 1879 – 1 – us U.O. Library [071]

STATE NEWS – Whitesville. West Virginia. 1947-57 – 1 – us UMI [071]

STATE OF CONNECTICUT REGISTER AND MANUAL, 1884 / Cook, Elizur – Hartford, Brown and Gross, 1884. Connecticut Reel 2. (The Cox Library Collection) – 5 – us Americana [978]

STATE OF CONNECTICUT REGISTER AND MANUAL, 1910 / Connecticut – Hartford, 1910. Also: 1943. Connecticut Reel 2. (The Cox Library Collection) – 5 – us Americana [978]

STATE OF DEVELOPMENT POLICIES 1971-1980 / Malawi. Office of the President and Cabinet. Economic Planning Div – D-1528 1. 1971 – 9 – ne IDC [338]

STATE OF FOOD AND AGRICULTURE – it F.A.O. [630]

THE STATE OF MORALS AND OF SOCIETY IN THE EASTERN CHURCH IN THE TIME OF S. CHRYSOSTOM / Fremantle, S J – Oxford: E. Baxter, 1870 – 1mf – us A.T.L.A. [240]

STATE OF NEW YORK. FOURTH JUDICIAL DEPARTMENT. ATTORNEYS' DIRECTORY FOR 1872 / Walbridge, Arthur Dewey – Rochester, Democrat and Chronicle Book and Job Printing House, 1872. 25 p. LL-1360 – 1 – us L of C Photodup [340]

STATE OF SINGAPORE DEVELOPMENT PLAN, 1961-1964 / Singapore. Ministry of Finance – Singapore. 1961. BD-139 1 – 9 – ne IDC [336]

THE STATE OF SOCIETY IN FRANCE BEFORE THE REVOLUTION IN 1789 AND THE CAUSES WHICH LED TO THAT EVENT / Tocqueville, Alexis de – 1856. 319p. 1 fiche (29x) – 9 – 1.00f – at Libertarian Micro [320]

THE STATE OF SOCIETY IN FRANCE BEFORE THE REVOLUTION OF 1789: AND THE CAUSES WHICH LEAD TO THAT EVENT / Tocqueville, Alexis de – Trans. by Henry Reeve. 3rd ed. London: J. Murray, 1888. 303p – 1 – us U.W. Library [944]

STATE OF THE PHILIPPINE ISLANDS / Comyn, T de – London, 1821 – 5mf – 9 – ne IDC [950]

THE STATE OF VIRGINIA IN ACCOUNT WITH OFFICERS OF THE ARMY OF THE REVOLUTION. PRIVATE ACCOUNTS OF GENERAL CHARLES SCOTT / Virginia – 1 – $50.00 – us Presbyterian [975]

STATE OF WASHINGTON / Hines, Harvey Kimball – Chicago: Lewis Publ. Co., 1894. Washington reel 1. (Cox Library Collection) – 5 – us Americana [978]

STATE OWNED INSTITUTIONAL FARMS; ANNUAL REPORT / Mississippi State University. Cooperative Extension Service – 1947-69 – 1,5,6 – us Spaulding [630]

STATE PAPERS AND FAMILY DOCUMENTS/ COMMONPLACE BOOK / Heveningham, William – 17th cent. Holkham mss. 684, 685. Holkham Hall, Norfolk, England – 1 – uk Microform Academic [920]

STATE PAPERS AND TRACTS RELATING TO ENGLAND AND FRANCE FROM THE COLLECTION OF SIR EDWARD COKE AT HOLKHAM HALL – 15th cent. Holkham ms. 683. Holkham Hall, Norfolk, England – 1 – uk Microform Academic [941]

STATE PAPERS CONCERNING THE IRISH CHURCH IN THE TIME OF QUEEN ELIZABETH / ed by Brady, W Maziere – London: Longmans, Green, Reader & Dyer, 1868 – 1mf – us A.T.L.A. [240]

STATE PAPERS (FOREIGN) OF EDWARD 6TH, 1547-1553 / Great Britain. Public Record Office – (Orig. publ. by Michael Glazier Inc.) – 6r – 1 – $510.00 – D3261 – us Scholarly Res [941]

STATE PAPERS (FOREIGN) OF MARY 1ST, 1553-1558 / Great Britain. Public Record Office – (Orig. publ by Michael Glazier Inc.) – 5r – 1 – $425.00 – D3262 – us Scholarly Res [941]

STATE PAPERS MEDIEVAL AND OTHER RECORDS / Great Britain. Public Record Office – (Part 2: SC1, v33-64) – PRO Class SC1 (Ancient correspondence) 1175-1538. Part 1: SC1, v1-32 – 1 – us Primary [941]

THE STATE PAPERS OF QUEEN ANNE / Great Britain. Public Record Office – (With printed guide) – 15r – 1 – $1,275.00 – D3263 – us Scholarly Res [941]

State Printing Board *see* WISCONSIN BLUE BOOK, 1921

THE STATE PROHIBITIONIST – Sacramento, CA. 1883-85 – 1r – 1 – $50.00 – B02742 – us Library Micro [071]

STATE PROVISION FOR SOCIAL NEED : THE BEVERIDGE COMMITTEE REPORT ON THE WELFARE STATE (PUBLIC RECORD OFFICE CLASS PIN 8 AND CAB 87/76-82) – Marlborough: Adam Matthew Publications, 1991 – 26r – 1 – $3,100.00 – uk Matthew [360]

STATE RECORD – Topeka. KS. 1859-75; 1899-1908 – 1 – us UMI [071]

STATE REGISTER AND YEARBOOK OF FACTS – State of California. 1859 – 1r – 1 – $50.00 – D109 – us Library Micro [978]

STATE REPORTS ON CORRECTION AND PUNISHMENT, POVERTY AND PUBLIC WELFARE, PRIOR TO 1930 – (Reports by state available on request) – 64 titles for 11 states, 1833-1931 – 2591mf – 9 – $5.00f – us Ross [360]

STATE REPORTS, POST-NRS / Alabama – 1887-1920; 1911-18. 29 reels – 1 – $33.50r – us Trans-Media [340]

STATE REPORTS, POST-NRS / Arkansas – 1887-1971. 52 reels – 1 – $33.50r – us Trans-Media [340]

STATE REPORTS, POST-NRS / Illinois – 1886-1946. 69 reels – 1 – $33.50r – us Trans-Media [340]

STATE REPORTS, POST-NRS / Pennsylvania – 1885-1974. 71 reels – 1 – $33.50r – us Trans-Media [340]

STATE REPORTS, POST-NRS / Rhode Island – 1887-1980. 23 reels – 1 – $33.50r – us Trans-Media [340]

STATE REPORTS, PRE-NRS / Alaska – 1869-1937; 1887-1940. 5 reels – 1 – $35.00r – us Trans-Media [340]

STATE REPORTS, PRE-NRS / Oklahoma – 1890-93; 1908-09. 1 reel – 1 – $35.00 – us Trans-Media [340]

STATE REPUBLICAN – Eugene, OR. -w. 1 Jan 1862-11 Apr 1863. 1 roll – 1 – us U.O. Library [071]

STATE REPUBLICAN – Lansing. Mich. 1886-1910 – 1 – us UMI [071]

STATE RESOURCES – Oakland, CA. v1 n6. apr/may 1890 – 1r – 1 – Can$25.00 – cn Can Microfilming [071]

STATE RIGHTS DEMOCRAT – Albany, OR. -w. 21 Aug 1865-20 Apr 1900. 9 rolls – 1 – us U.O. Library [071]

STATE SECESSION DEBATES – (Complete records of debates for all states in which secession was an active issue. Individual states available) – 19r – 1 – us Ross [976]

STATE SENTINEL – Fayetteville. West Virginia. -w. 1936- – 1 – us UMI [071]

STATE SERVICE REPORT / New Hampshire. Agricultural Experiment Station – v. 1-30. 1960-69 – 1,5,6 – us Spaulding [630]

STATE SESSION LAWS – (1995-present $1,786.50. 1990-94 $9,964.00. 1985-89 $9,288.00. 1980-84 $7,455.00. 1975-79 $6,125.00. 1970-74 $5,353.00. 1965-69 $5,512.00. 1960-64 $3,644.00. Prior yrs also available in set. Updated monthly) – Backfile 1775-1996 no 8 update – 9 – $97,036.00 set – us Hein [324]

THE STATE SHOULD BELIEVE IN GOD / Indonesia. Departemen Agama – SE-11,167 1. 2d ed. 1965 – 9 – ne IDC [324]

STATE SLAVERY STATURES – (Guide only: $140.00 ISBN 1-55655-211-4) – $2,165.00 – 1-55655-122-3 – us UPA [305]

STATE SOCIALISM AND THE COLLAPSE IN AUSTRALIA / Fortescue, John William – 1894. 1 fiche (29x) – 9 – 1.00f – at Libertarian Micro [320]

STATE TEACHERS COLLEGE TIMES *see* THE SPARTAN DAILY

THE STATE THE ENEMY / Benn, Ernest J P – 1953. 2 fiches (29x) – 9 – 1.00f – at Libertarian Micro [320]

STATE TIMES – Baton Rouge. Louisiana. 1906- – 1 – us UMI [071]

STATE TIMES – Jackson. Miss. 1955-1961 – 1 – us UMI [071]

STATE TRADING CORPORATIONS IN INDONESIA: FIRST YEAR'S PERFORMANCE, 1961 / Panglaykim, J – In English and Indonesian. SE-3928 1. 1963 – 9 – ne IDC [380]

STATE UNDERWRITER – (1975-. 5,6,9) – 1967- – 1 – us UMI [336]

THE STATE VERSUS GONVILLE AUBIE FFRENCH-BEYTAGH IN THE SUPREME COURT OF SOUTH AFRICA (TRANSVAAL PROVINCIAL DIVISION) – Johannesburg: Microfile, [19–?] – us Res Libr [340]

THE STATE VERSUS WILSON WELILE CHIEF TWALA AND 10 OTHERS – Johannesburg: Microfile, [19–?] – us Res Libr [340]

STATE VS FILISBERTO TAIMO IN THE MAGISTRATE'S COURT FOR THE REGIONAL DIVISION, SOUTH TRANSVAAL : HELD AT JOHANNESBURG – (Filmed with: Setshedi, Isaac, defendant. The State versus Isaac Setshedi) – Johannesburg, 1965 – us Res Libr [340]

STATE VS ISAAC SETSHEDI : IN THE MAGISTRATE'S COURT FOR THE REGIONAL DIVISION OF THE TRANSVAAL, HELD AT JOHANNESBURG – (Filmed with: Taimo, Filisberto, defendant: State vs F Taimo) – Johannesburg, 1965 – us Res Libr [340]

STATE VS KADER HASSIM AND TWELVE OTHERS IN THE SUPREME COURT OF SOUTH AFRICA (NATAL PROVINCIAL DIVISION) – (Filmed with: Supreme Court of South Africa Provincial Division) – Johannesburg: Microfile [19–?] – us Res Libr [340]

STATE VS MASEMULA AND 15 OTHERS : [RECORD OF THE TRIAL IN THE SUPREME COURT OF SOUTH AFRICA, TRANSVAAL PROVINCIAL DIVISION] – (Filmed with: Ngakane, Pascal, defendant. State vs P N Ngekane...Durban, 1964) – n.p, 1963 – us Res Libr [340]

THE STATE VS. MESSACK VICTORY AND OTHERS, IN THE SUPREME COURT OF SOUTH AFRICA (APPELLATE DIVISION) / Victory, Messack – Johannesburg. 1970 – 1 – us Res Libr [960]

THE STATE VS. MESSACK VICTORY AND OTHERS, IN THE SUPREME COURT OF SOUTH AFRICA (SOUTH WEST AFRICA DIVISION) / Victory, Messack – Windhoek. 1969 – 1 – us Res Libr [960]

STATE VS. NELSON MANDELA, OCT. 1962 / Mandela, Nelson – In the Magistrate's Court for the regional division of Transvaal – 1 – us Res Libr [960]

STATE VS PASCAL NGKANE IN THE MAGISTRATE'S COURT FOR THE REGIONAL DIVISION : HELD AT PIETERMARITZBURG AND DURBAN. CHARGE: [SABOTAGE, ETC] – (Filmed with: Masemula, J K, defendant. State vs Masemula...[n.p., 1963]) – Durban, 1964 – us Res Libr [340]

THE STATE VS SOUTH AFRICAN ASSOCIATED NEWSPAPERS LTD AND L.O. GANDAR AND BENJAMIN POGRUND : IN THE SUPREME COURT OF SOUTH AFRICA (WITWATERSRAND LOCAL DIVISION) – (Brief inventory of contents available) – Johannesburg: Microfile, [19–?] – us Res Libr [340]

STATE WATER RESOURCES REPORTS / Arizona. State Water Commission – 1 – $50.00 – us UPA [333]

STATE WATER RESOURCES REPORTS / Connecticut. State Water Commission – 1 – $50.00 – us UPA [333]

STATE WATER RESOURCES REPORTS / Illinois – (Department of Public Works and Buildings, Division of Waterways $115.00; Rivers and Lakes Commission $30.00) – 1911-40 – 1 – us UPA [333]

STATE WATER RESOURCES REPORTS / Maine – (State Water Storage Commission $80.00; Water Power Commission $30.00) – 1910-13; 1919-22 – 1 – us UPA [333]

STATE WATER RESOURCES REPORTS / Massachusetts – (Metropolitan District Commission $140.00; Metropolitan Sewerage Commission $95.00; Metropolitan Water and Sewerage Board $285.00; Metropolitan Water Board $75.00) – 1889-1939 – 1 – us UPA [324]

STATE WATER RESOURCES REPORTS / New York – (Conservation Department, Division of Inland Water $870.00; Water Power Commission $45.00; State Water Supply Commission $160.00) – 1905-39 – 1 – us UPA [333]

STATE WATER RESOURCES REPORTS : SURFACE WATER SUPPLY OF NEW MEXICO / New Mexico. Engineering Department – 1st-14th. 1911-1931. All pub – 1 – $145.00 – us UPA [333]

STATE WATER RESOURCES REPORTS / Texas. Board of Water Engineers – 1st-14th. 1913-40 – 1 – $55.00 – us UPA [333]

STATE ZIONISM / Jabotinsky, V – Tel Aviv. 1934. BJ-28-9 1 – 9 – ne IDC [270]

Stateburg. South Carolina. Holy Cross Episcopal Church *see* REGISTERS

STATEHOOD AND NATIONHOOD – 1906-29 – 1 – us Ross [977]

STATEMENT BY AMBASSADOR PETER R ROSENBLATT : PERSONAL REPRESENTATIVE OF THE PRESIDENT OF THE U.S. FOR MICRONESIAN STATUS NEGOTIATIONS – (Typescript) – Koror, apr 30, 1979 – 1mf – 9 – $1.50 – LLMC 82-100G, Title 17 – us L.L.M.C. [327]

STATEMENT BY HIS MAJESTY'S GOVERNMENT IN THE UNITED KINGDOM / Great Britain. Colonial Office. Palestine – London. Nov 1938. BJ-28-85 1 – 9 – ne IDC [956]

STATEMENT BY PRES. SUKARNO BEFORE THE NON-ALIGNED CONFERENCE IN CAIRO / Sukarno, Pres. Indonesia – SE 10,542 1. Oct 6 1964 – 9 – ne IDC [950]

A STATEMENT CONCERNING THE FIRST YEAR'S ACTIVE WORK OF THE LEAGUE, AND ITS PURPOSES FOR THE IMMEDIATE FUTURE / ed by King, James M – New York: Central offices, 1891 – 1mf – 9 – 0-8370-7553-X – 1986-1553 – us A.T.L.A. [370]

STATEMENT EXHIBITING THE MORAL AND MATERIAL PROGRESS AND CONDITION OF INDIA – London, 1861-1937. v1-70 – 735mf – 8 – ne IDC [950]

STATEMENT MADE ON BEHALF OF HIS MAJESTY'S GOVERNMENT DURING THE YEAR 1918 IN REGARD TO THE FUTURE STATUS OF CERTAIN PARTS OF THE OTTOMAN EMPIRE / Great Britain. Foreign Office – London. 1939. BJ-28-90 1 – 9 – ne IDC [949]

STATEMENT OF BOOKS AND PAMPHLETS PUBLISHED IN THE SEVERAL DIVISIONS OF BRITISH BURMAH – Burma, 1868-1941 – 43mf – 9 – I-610/2 – ne IDC [950]

STATEMENT OF BOOKS PRINTED IN CEYLON AND REGISTERED UNDER ORDINANCE NO. 1 OF 1885 – (Missing: 1905(3)-1906(1); 1915(2-4)-1916(2)) – Ceylon, 1902-1921 – 33mf – I-609/2 – ne IDC [950]

STATEMENT OF DEVELOPMENT POLICIES 1971-1980 / Malawi. Economic Planning Division – Zomba. 1971. BD-1689 1 – 9 – ne IDC [338]

A STATEMENT OF DEVELOPMENT POLICIES AND PROGRAMMES 1973-1977 / Swaziland – Mbabane. BD-1746 1 – 9 – ne IDC [338]

STATEMENT OF EXTERNAL TRADE / Aden. Customs and Excise Department – 24 v. in 10. 1902-62. (lacking 1907 08-1916 17, 1918 19, 1930 31, 1933 34-1945, 1950 51). BNE-9607 1 – 9 – ne IDC [380]

STATEMENT OF GOALS / Council for Monetary Reform – 1984 – 9 – 1.00f – at Libertarian Micro [330]

STATEMENT OF HIS EXCELLENCY SUBANDRIO IN GENERAL ASSEMBLY OF UNITED NATIONS ON 9 OCT. 1961 / Indonesia. Permanent Mission to the United Nations – SE-5376 1 – 9 – ne IDC [950]

STATEMENT OF INFORMATION RELATING TO ACTS OF VIOLENCE / Great Britain. Colonial Office. Palestine – Presented to Parliament by the Secretary of State for the colonies. London. Jul 1946. BJ-28-99 1 – 9 – ne IDC [956]

STATEMENT OF MONEYS FURNISHED BY GOVERNMENT TO AID IN ERECTING SCHOOL HOUSES IN LOWER CANADA... – Toronto: Lovel & Gibson, 1851. SEM105P1688 – 1mf – 9 – Can$2.25 – cn Bibl Nat [350]

STATEMENT OF OBJECTIVES AND POLICIES OF THE TRUST TERRITORY OF THE PACIFIC ISLANDS (TTPI) / Goding, MW – 15 Feb 1962 – 1mf – 9 – $1.50 – LLMC 82-100F Title 98 – us L.L.M.C. [324]

STATEMENT OF PARTICULARS REGARDING BOOKS AND PERIODICALS PUBLISHED IN THE UNITED PROVINCES... – (Missing: 1919-1921; 1940(3)) – Allahabad, 1904-45 – 278mf – 9 – I-603/2 – ne IDC [950]

STATEMENT OF PAYMENTS MADE IN THE YEAR 1831, FOR A PROPOSITION OF THE COST OF SCHOOL HOUSES, ERECTED OR PURCHASED BY TRUSTEES AND FABRIQUES... – [Quebec]: [s.n.], [1831?]. SEM105P1163 – 1mf – 9 – Can$2.25 – cn Bibl Nat [306]

STATEMENT OF POLICY BY HIS MAJESTY'S GOVERNMENT IN THE UNITED KINGDOM PRESENTED BY THE SECRETARY OF STATE FOR THE COLONIES TO PARLIAMENT / Great Britain. Colonial Office. Palestine – London. Jul 1937. BJ-28-82 1 – 9 – ne IDC [956]

STATEMENT OF POLICY. MAY 1939 / Great Britain. Colonial Office. Palestine – London. 1939. BJ-28-88 1 – 9 – ne IDC [956]

STATEMENT OF SCHOOL FUNDS / Hancock County. Ohio. Biglick Township. Township Clerk – 1878 – 1r – 1 – $32.50r – us Archival [324]

STATEMENT OF THE AFFAIRS OF THE CORPORATION OF THE ECCLESIASTICS OF THE SEMINARY OF ST SULPICE, MONTREAL / Ecclesiastiques du Seminaire de St-Sulpice de Montreal – Quebec: printed by Rollo Campbell, 1853. SEM105P1780 – 1mf – 9 – Can$2.25 – cn Bibl Nat [240]

A STATEMENT OF THE NATURAL SOURCES OF THEOLOGY : WITH A DISCUSSION OF THEIR VALIDITY ON THE FIRST CHAPTER OF GENESIS / Hill, Thomas – Andover, W F Draper, 1877 – 1mf – 9 – 0-8370-3586-4 – 1985-1586 – us A.T.L.A. [210]

STATEMENT OF THE PUBLIC REVENUE AND EXPENDITURE OF LOWER CANADA FOR THE YEAR... / Bas-Canada – Quebec: s.n, 18–? -. SEM105P1340 – 5mf – 9 – Can$11.25 – cn Bibl Nat [336]

STATEMENT OF THE ZIONIST ORGANIZATION REGARDING PALESTINE / World Zionist Organization – Feb 1919. BJ-28-47 1 – 9 – ne IDC [956]

STATEMENT OF TOWNSHIP FUNDS / Hancock County. Ohio. Biglick Township. Township Clerk – 1890 – 1r – 1 – $32.50r – us Archival [324]

STATEMENT ON GOVERNMENT'S POLICY ON THE REORGANIZATION OF THE STRUCTURE OF PRIMARY AND SECONDARY EDUCATION : TABLED IN HONG KONG ... 23RD JANUARY 1963 / Hong Kong. Legislative Council – Hong Kong, 1963 – 1mf – 9 – DE-150/1 – ne IDC [370]

STATEMENT REGARDING THE BUILDING OF THE CHINESE HOSPITAL AT SHANHAE, [BY] THE COMMITTEE – Shanghae, 1848 – 1mf – 9 – ne IDC [360]

STATEMENT TO THE UNITED NATIONS IN GENERAL DEBATE OF 18TH SESSION OF GENERAL ASSEMBLY / Palar, LN – SE-4039 1. Sep 27 1963 – 9 – ne IDC [327]

STATEMENTS AND DOCUMENTS / World Zionist Organization – The Keren Hayesod Controversy in America. London. 1921. BJ-28-49 1 – 9 – ne IDC [270]

STATEMENTS AND SPEECHES / Canada. Department of External Affairs – 1946-86 – 9 – cn Micromedia [971]

STATEMENTS OF BIRTH AND DEATHS / Erie County. Ohio. Probate Court – 1890-1899 – 1r – 1 – $32.50r – us Archival [324]

STATEMENTS OF BIRTHS / Defiance County, Ohio. Probate Court – 1875-1877 – 1r – 1 – $32.50r – us Archival [324]

STATEMENTS OF BIRTHS AND DEATHS / Putnam County. Ohio. Probate Court – 1880-1882 – 1r – 1 – $32.50r – us Archival [324]

STATEMENTS OF BIRTHS AND DEATHS / Van Wert County. Ohio. Probate Court – 1867-1906 – 3r – 1 – $32.50r – us Archival [324]

STATEMENTS OF BIRTHS AND DEATHS / Wyandot County. Ohio. Probate Court – 1903-1908 – 2r – 1 – $32.50r – us Archival [324]

STATEMENTS OF DEATHS / Defiance County, Ohio. Probate Court – 1875-1877 – 1r – 1 – $32.50r – us Archival [324]

STATEMENTS OF FACT / Sandusky County. Ohio. County Home – 1921-1948 – 1r – 1 – $32.50r – us Archival [324]

STATEMENTS OF JAPANESE OFFICIALS ON WORLD WAR 2 / U.S. Army. General Headquarters. Far East Command – v1-4. 1949-50 – 1 – $82.00 – us L of C Photodup [950]

STATEMENTS, REPORTS AND ACCOUNTS.. / Compagnie du Grand Tronc – Toronto: Printed by Steward Derbishire and Georges Desbarats, 1857. SEM105P358 – 1mf – 9 – Can$2.25 – cn Bibl Nat [336]

STATEMENTS, REPORTS AND ACCOUNTS OF THE GRAND TRUNK RAILWAY COMPANY OF CANADA / Chemin de Fer du Grand Tronc – Toronto: Stewart Derbishire and George Desbarats..., 1857. SEM105P358 – 1mf – 9 – Can$2.25 – cn Bibl Nat [380]

STATEMENTS RESPECTING HOSPITALS IN CHINA / Parker, P – London, 1841 – 1mf – 9 – ne IDC [360]

STATEMENTS RESPECTING HOSPITALS IN CHINA, PRECEDED BY A LETTER TO JOHN ABERCROMBRIE,... / Parker, P – Glasgow, 1842 – 1mf – 9 – ne IDC [360]

STATEN ISLAND ADVANCE – Staten Island. N.Y. 1945- – 1 – us UMI [071]

STATES – New Orleans. La. 1916-58 – 1 – us UMI [071]

STATES – New Orleans. La. and Item. 1959- – 1 – us UMI [071]

States, Rebecca A *see* RESOLVING INDETERMINACY ASSOCIATED WITH JOINT-LEVEL MOTOR EQUIVALENCE IN PLANAR AIMED ARM MOVEMENTS

STATES' RIGHTS AND NATIONAL PROHIBITION / Stevenson, Archibald Ewing – New York, Clark Boardman, 1927. 157 p. LL-1536 – 1 – us L of C Photodup [340]

STATES-ITEM – New Orleans, LA. 1858-1980 – 1 – us UMI [071]

STATESMAN – Austin. Tex. 1871-30 Nov 1973 – 1 – us UMI [071]

STATESMAN – Calcutta, India. 1981-Jun 1995 – 105r – 1 – us L of C Photodup [072]

STATESMAN : DAILY EDITION – Calcutta, 1915-1941 – 203r – 1 – ne IDC [072]

STATESMAN – Delhi, India. Oct 1942-Mar 1956; Jul-Sept 1956; Apr 1957-Mar 1985; Jul 1985-Dec 1986 – 190r – 1 – us L of C Photodup [072]

STATESMAN – Ireland.1841-Oct 1846.-d. 6 reels – 1 – uk British Libr Newspaper [072]

STATESMAN – Karachi, PK. 1972-1979 – 7r – $350.00 – R04229 – us Library Micro [320]

STATESMAN – Martinsburg. West Virginia. 1874-1911 – 1 – us UMI [071]

STATESMAN – Walla Walla. Wash. -w. 1861-84 – 1 – us UMI [071]

STATESMAN – Yonkers. N.Y. 1863-1932 – 1 – us UMI [071]

THE STATESMAN – Calcutta, India. The Sunday Statesman. -d. Jan-Dec 1914; Jan 1939-April 1952. 83 reels – 1 – uk British Libr Newspaper [072]

THE STATESMAN – Calcutta, India. Weekly (overseas) edition. Jan 1951-Dec 1956; Jan 1959-Dec 1975. 18 reels – 1 – uk British Libr Newspaper [072]

THE STATESMAN – Calcutta: The Statesman Ltd, 1952-70 – us Res Libr [072]

THE STATESMAN – Port of Spain. Trinidad. -w. 24 Jun 1961-24 Aug 1962. (1 reel) – 1 – uk British Libr Newspaper [072]

THE STATESMAN – Toronto: Statesman Publishing. v1- 1918-. SEM35P169 – 1r – 1 – Can$66.00 – cn Bibl Nat [320]

STATESMAN AND FRIEND OF INDIA – Calcutta, India. 1877-85 – 34r – 1 – uk British Libr Newspaper [072]

THE STATESMAN AND FRIEND OF INDIA – 1941-51 – 1 – us Primary [072]

STATESMAN WEEKLY – Calcutta, India. 1954-Jun 1956; 23 Mar 1957-1984; 1985-87; 1989-Jul 1994 – 34r – 1 – us L of C Photodup [072]

STATESMAN-DEMOCRAT – Martinsburg. West Virginia. 1908-1913 – 1 – us UMI [071]

THE STATESMAN'S MANUAL; OR, THE BIBLE, THE BEST GUIDE TO POLITICAL SKILL AND FORESIGHT... / Coleridge, Samuel Taylor – London: Printed for Gale and Fenner, 1816 – 1 roll – 1 – 1-55879-325-9 – uk Libr Preservation [220]

THE STATE-WAR-NAVY COORDINATING COMMITTEE (SWNCC) AND STATE-ARMY-NAVY-AIR FORCE COORDINATING COMMITTEE (SANACC) CASE FILES, 1944-49 / ed by Claussen, Martin P – (With printed guide) – 1978 – 32r – 1 – $2,720.00 – S1869 – us Scholarly Res [335]

STATI I DOKLADY ZA 1918-1920 PO ORGANIZATSII RASPREDELENII A RABOCHEI SILY *see* ORGANIZATSIIA RASPREDELENIIA RABOCHEI SILY

STAT'I O RUSSKOI POEZII / Khodasevich, V – Spb. 1922. BR-702 2 – 8 – ne IDC [460]

STATIC RANGE OF MOTION, LEG POWER, AND LEG STRENGTH AS PREDICTORS OF DYNAMIC RANGE OF MOTION IN FEMALE BALLET DANCERS / Moscov, June G, Lacourse, Michael G – 1992 – 2mf – 9 – $8.00 – us Microform Publ [612]

STATION BULLETIN / Purdue University. Agricultural Experiment Station – N.s.No.1-415. 1973-83 – 1,5 – us Spaulding [630]

STATION CHEMISTRY PAMPHLET / South Dakota. State University. Agricultural Experiment Station – nos.1-2. 1943-44 – 1,5,6 – us Spaulding [630]

STATION CIRCULAR / New Hampshire. Agricultural Experiment Station – v. 1-82. 1908-50 – 1,5,6 – us Spaulding [630]

STATION ONEFREIT : ZWEI ERZAEHLUNGEN / Wittstock, Erwin – Muenchen: A Langen, G Mueller, 1936 – 1r – 1 – us U.W. Library [890]

DAS STATIONAERE KRANKENGUT DES JAHRES 1988 DER UNIVERSITAETSKLINIKEN FUER KINDER- UND JUGENDPSYCHIATRIE LUEBECK UND KINDERNEUROPSYCHIATRIE ROSTOCK – EINE VERGLEICHENDE ANALYSIERENDE STUDIE / Kraemer, Christoph – 1994 – 2mf – DM80.00 – 3-8267-2029-6 – gw Hänsel [618]

STATIONERY OFFICE CATALOGUES OF GOVERNMENT PUBLICATIONS, 1894-1970 AND CONSOLIDATED INDEXES TO GOVERNMENT PUBLICATIONS, 1936-1970 *see*
- ANNUAL CATALOGUES OF BRITISH OFFICIAL AND PARLIAMENTARY PUBLICATIONS, 1894-1909
- ANNUAL CATALOGUES OF BRITISH OFFICIAL AND PARLIAMENTARY PUBLICATIONS, 1910-1919

STATIST: A JOURNAL OF FINANCE, TRADE AND INDUSTRY – London. v. 99-165. 1922-1957 – 1,5,6 – us Princeton Micro [332]

STATISTICA GIUDIZIARIA CIVILE E COMMERCIALE / Italy. Istituto Centrale di Statistica – 1863-1939. (scattered parts wanting) – 1 – 180.00 – us L of C Photodup [945]

STATISTICAL ABSTRACT / Arabian Gulf Emirates. Abu-Dhabi. Directorate General of Planning and Coordination – 1v. 1969. BNE-10.004 1 – 9 – ne IDC [956]

STATISTICAL ABSTRACT / Kuwait. Central Statistical Office – 8v. in 5. 1964-75 76. (lacking 1969, 1973 74). BNE-9005 1 – 9 – ne IDC [310]

STATISTICAL ABSTRACT / Libya. Ministry of Economy and Trade. Census and Statistical Department – Tripoli. 1958-1974. BNE-506 1 – 9 – ne IDC [330]

STATISTICAL ABSTRACT, 1949-1978 / Syria. Central Bureau of Statistics – BNE-9693 1 – 9 – ne IDC [310]

STATISTICAL ABSTRACT 1967-1972 / Bahrain. Statistical Bureau – 5v. in 1. (lacking 1970). BNE-10,012 1 – 9 – ne IDC [956]

STATISTICAL ABSTRACT FOR BRITISH INDIA WITH STATISTICS, WHERE AVAILABLE RELATING TO CERTAIN INDIA STATES / India. Commercial Intelligence Department – v. 1 (1911 12-1920 21)-v. 19 (1936 37-1940 41). Calcutta. 1923-42. Lacking: v. 16. BI-487 2 – 8 – ne IDC [324]

STATISTICAL ABSTRACT FOR THE DEMOCRATIC REPUBLIC OF SUDAN / Sudan – 1970. BNE-7624 1 – 9 – ne IDC [310]

STATISTICAL ABSTRACT OF ISRAEL / Israel. Prime Minister's Office. Central Bureau of Statistics – Jerusalem, 1950-. Text also in Hebrew – 9 – 300.00; 10.00y – is I.T.T.I. [310]

STATISTICAL ABSTRACT OF ISRAEL / Israel. Prime Minister's Office. Central Bureau of Statistics – v. 1-26. 1949-75. BJ-81-4 1 – 9 – ne IDC [310]

STATISTICAL ABSTRACT OF LIBYA 1958-1962 / Libya. Ministry of National Economy – Tripoli. BNE-505 1 – 9 – ne IDC [330]

STATISTICAL ABSTRACT OF THE UNITED ARAB REPUBLIC, 1967-1972 / Egypt. U.A.R. Central Agency for Public Mobilisation and Statistics – Cairo. 1971. BNE-4613 1 – 9 – ne IDC [310]

STATISTICAL ABSTRACT OF THE UNITED STATES / U.S. Bureau of the Census – 1969- 1; 1975- 5,6; 1978- 4 x 6 in. 9 – us UMI [310]

STATISTICAL ABSTRACT OF THE UNITED STATES / U.S. Bureau of the Census – v. 1-94. 1878-1973 – 1,5,6 – us Princeton Micro [310]

STATISTICAL ABSTRACT RELATING TO BRITISH INDIA / India. Commercial Intelligence Department – v. 1. (1840-65)-36 (1891 92-1900 01). London. 1867-1902. BI-486 2 – 8 – ne IDC [324]

STATISTICAL ABSTRACTS : BUREAU OF THE CENSUS / U.S. Department of Commerce – (Updated as released) – Washington: GPO, 1st-115th. 1878-1995 – 9 – $1,980.00 set – 0-89941-199-1 – us Hein [310]

STATISTICAL ABSTRACTS / Indonesia. Biro Pusat Statistik – SE-159 1. 1955-1956. Lacking: 1955 – 9 – ne IDC [324]

STATISTICAL ACCOUNT OF BANFFSHIRE 1892 – 5mf – 9 – A$35.00 – at State Libr Vic [910]

STATISTICAL ACCOUNT OF SCOTLAND – 1791-1799 – 168mf – 9 – A$250.00 – at State Libr Vic [920]

STATISTICAL ACCOUNT OF UPPER CANADA, COMPILED WITH A VIEW TO A GRAND SYSTEM OF EMIGRATION / Gourlay, Robert – London: Simpkin and Marshall, 1822. SEM105P373 – 16mf – 9 – Can$36.00 – cn Bibl Nat [310]

STATISTICAL BULLETIN / Metropolitan Life Insurance Company – v1- 1920- 1; v51-5,6; v58- 9 – us UMI [336]

STATISTICAL BULLETIN / Syria. Ministry of Social Affairs and Labour – 5v. 1966-72. Lacking: 1967 68. BNE-9724 1 – 9 – ne IDC [338]

STATISTICAL BULLETIN FOR THE FISHERY COMMITTEE FOR THE EASTERN CENTRAL ATLANTIC (CECAF) : NOMINAL CATCHES 1977-1989 – 1991 – 335p – it F.A.O. [639]

STATISTICAL BULLETIN FOR THE GENERAL FISHERIES COUNCIL FOR THE MEDITERRANEAN (GFCM) : NOMINAL CATCHES 1977-1989 – 1992 – 225p – it F.A.O. [338]

STATISTICAL BULLETIN OF THE PHILIPPINE ISLANDS / Philippines. Bureau of Commerce – v. 1-12. 1918-29 – 1 – 21.00 – us L of C Photodup [950]

STATISTICAL BULLETINS / U.S. Department of Agriculture – Nos. 1-748. 1245 fiches – 9 – $1600.00 – us Updata [630]

STATISTICAL CLASSIFICATION FOR GOODS IMPORTED, EXPORTED, OR RE-EXPORTED / Sudan. Dept. of Statistics – 1963 – 9 – ne IDC [380]

STATISTICAL DATA – Tower Hill, Freetown: Central Statistics Office – 1r – $49.50 – us African Imprint [310]

STATISTICAL DATA 1976/77-1984/85 / Nigeria. Benue State. Ministry of Education – Makurdi, 1986 – 3mf – 9 – DE-644/1 – ne IDC [370]

STATISTICAL DATA PERTAINING TO THE COLONIAL PERIOD / Sjamsuddin, Sutan – In Indonesian. SE 6423 1. Inc. 1961 census figures – 9 – ne IDC [780]

STATISTICAL DATA RESULTING FROM A SURVEY OF FAMILY BUDGETS OF FAMILIES OF LOWER INCOME GROUPS IN THE URBAN AREA OF TRIPOLI DURING THE YEAR 1962 / Libya. Census and Statistical Department – Isha Limizaniyyat Al-Usrah Fi Madinat Tarablus, 1962. Tripoli. 1962. In Arabic. BNE-623 1 – 9 – ne IDC [310]

STATISTICAL HANDBOOK.. / Philippines. Department of Agriculture and Commerce – 1932. Manila: Bureau of Printing, 1933- – 1 – us U.W. Library [324]

STATISTICAL HANDBOOK OF THE UNITED ARAB REPUBLIC / Egypt. Central Agency for Public Mobilisation and Statistics – 1952-68$1952 1974. Lacking: 1952 56, 1952, 1969, 1970. BNE-4612 1 – 9 – ne IDC [310]

STATISTICAL HISTORY OF THE FIRST CENTURY OF AMERICAN METHODISM : WITH A SUMMARY OF THE ORIGIN AND PRESENT OPERATIONS OF OTHER DENOMINATIONS / Goss, C C – New York: Carlton & Porter, 1866 – 1mf – us A.T.L.A. [240]

STATISTICAL INDICATOR REPORTS – 1954-70 – 63mf – 9 – $5.00f – us Ross [310]

STATISTICAL INDICATORS / UN Economic Commission for Europe (ECE) – 1973-89 – E.474 – 9 – us U.N. Pubs [340]

STATISTICAL PAPERS SERIES *see*
- COMPENDIUM OF HUMAN SETTLEMENT STATISTICS
- COMPENDIUM OF SOCIAL STATISTICS

STATISTICAL PAPERS SERIES ON YOUTH AND THE DISABLED / United Nations – E.10 – 9 (ST/ESA/STAT/Ser.Y/1-3) – us U.N. Pubs [360]

STATISTICAL POCKET BOOK OF INDONESIA / Indonesia. Biro Pusat Statistik – SE-160 1. 1956-1967 – 9 – ne IDC [310]

STATISTICAL POCKETBOOK OF INDONESIA, 1941 / Dutch East Indies. Centraal Kantoor voor de Statistiek – SE-11,813 1. 1947 – 9 – ne IDC [310]

A STATISTICAL PORTRAIT / Egypt. Ministry of Economy – 1961? BNE-4659 1 – 9 – ne IDC [330]

STATISTICAL POWER FOR REPEATED MEASURES ANOVA / Potvin, Patrick J – University of British Columbia, 1996 – 2mf – 9 – $8.00 – PE 3666 – us Microform Publ [619]

STATISTICAL PROFILE OF EDUCATION IN BANGLADESH / Bangladesh. Ministry of Education – Dacca, 1978 – 2mf – 9 – DE-530/1 – ne IDC [370]

STATISTICAL PROFILE OF ZAMBIAN EDUCATION 1976-1978 / Zambia. Ministry of Education. Development and Planning Unit – Lusaka – 3mf – 9 – DE-492/1 – ne IDC [370]

STATISTICAL REFERENCE INDEX MICROFICHE LIBRARY – (American statistical publications from private, academic and state sources. Printed index available) – 1980- – 9 – Apply for prices – us CIS [310]

STATISTICAL RELEASES / U.S. Board of Governors of the Federal Reserve System – (With guidebook) – 1919-76 – 36r – 1 – us Ross [332]

STATISTICAL REPORT / Michigan. Insurance Bureau – 1870-1978. 648 fiches. (Harvard Law School Library Collection.) – 9 – $1.50f – us H.U. Law [336]

STATISTICAL REPORT ON THE FACTORY AND BUILDING PRODUCTION.. / New Zealand. Census and Statistics Office – 1933 34-1936 37. Wellington: Government Printer. Annual – 1 – us U.W. Library [310]

STATISTICAL REPORT ON THE FACTORY PRODUCTION.. / New Zealand. Census and Statistics Office – 1923 24-1925 26, 1927, 1929 30. Wellington: Government Printer. Annual – 1 – us U.W. Library [310]

STATISTICAL REPORT ON THE INDUSTRIAL MANUFACTURES.. / New Zealand. Census and Statistics Office – 1921 22-1922 23. Wellington: Government Printer. Annual. Filmed with later titles – 1 – us U.W. Library [310]

STATISTICAL REPORT ON TRADE AND SHIPPING.. / New Zealand. Census and Statistics Office – 1921-50-51. Wellington: Census and Statistics Office, (192?-195?). Annual. Title varies slightly. 1288 – 1 – us U.W. Library [380]

STATISTICAL REPORT, YEAR: 1954, 1955, 1956, 1957, 1958 / Indonesia – SE-5363 1. 1959 – 9 – ne IDC [310]

STATISTICAL SCIENCE – v1-. 1986- – 1,5,6,9 – us UMI [310]

STATISTICAL SERIES. RELEASE NUMBER 1-2635, AUG. 12, 1937-JAN. 31, 1973 / U.S. Securities and Exchange Commission – The series will continue in the Statistical Bulletin – 9 – us UMI [336]

STATISTICAL SOURCES ON THE HISTORY OF FRANCE. UNDER THE EMPIRE / ed by Perrot, Jean-Claude – 1803-13 – 9 – fr Hachette [944]

STATISTICAL SOURCES UNDER THE EMPIRE – 98 titles on 436 fiches – 9 – fr Hachette [944]

STATISTICAL SUMMARY, 1974/1975 / Saudi Arabia. Monetary Agency – 9 – ne IDC [339]

STATISTICAL SURVEY, 1948 / Syria. Ministry of Economy. Dept. of Statistics – BNE-11,514 1 – 9 – ne IDC [310]

STATISTICAL TABLES FOR BRITISH INDIA / India. Commercial Intelligence Department – v. 5-17. Calcutta. 1881-93. Cont. of: Miscellaneous statistics relating to British India. BI-482 2 – 8 – ne IDC [324]

STATISTICAL YEAR BOOK / Jordan. Department of Statistics – 1950-75. BNE-9779 1 – 9 – ne IDC [310]

STATISTICAL YEAR BOOK / Saudi Arabia. Central Department of Statistics – 1965-1976. BNE-6602 1 – 9 – ne IDC [324]

STATISTICAL YEARBOOK 1975 / Nigeria. Kaduna State. Ministry of Economic Planning and Rural Development – Kaduna, 1976 – 6mf – 9 – DE-107/1 – ne IDC [370]

STATISTICAL YEARBOOK FOR ASIA AND THE FAR EAST / United Nations – 1968-1972 – E/F.40 – 9 (E/CN.11/) – us U.N. Pubs [304]

STATISTICAL YEARBOOK FOR ASIA AND THE PACIFIC / United Nations – 155 fiches – 9 – $285.00; $1.90f – uk UNIMICRO [310]

STATISTICAL YEARBOOK FOR ASIA AND THE PACIFIC / United Nations – (1973-1975. E/CN.11/. E/F.30; 1976-1989. E/ESCAP/. E/F.136) – 9 – us U.N. Pubs [304]

STATISTICAL YEARBOOK FOR LATIN AMERICA / United Nations – (1975-1983. E/CEPAL/. E/S.89; 1984. LC/G. E/S.14) – 9 – us U.N. Pubs [330]

STATISTICAL YEARBOOK FOR LATIN AMERICA / United Nations – 88 fiches – 9 – 165.00; 1.90f – uk UNIMICRO [972]

STATISTICAL YEARBOOK FOR LATIN AMERICA AND THE CARIBBEAN / United Nations – 1985-1989 – E/S.77 – 9 (LC/G.) – us U.N. Pubs [330]

STATISTICHES JAHRBUCH DER STADT BERLIN / Berlin. Statistisches amt – 1873-1919, 1924-30 – 1 – 148.00 – us L of C Photodup [943]

STATISTICHESKAIA ZAPISKA O MOSKVE / Androsov, V – Moscow: S Selivanovsky's Printing-House, 1832 – 2mf – 9 – $25.00 – us Ross [947]

STATISTICHESKI EZHEGODNIK ROSSII / Russia. Tsentral'nyi Statisticheski Komitet – Leningrad, 1904-14 – 4r – 1 – us Ross [310]

STATISTICHESKI I BI ULLETEN *see* EVOLIUTSIIA OSNOVNYKH ELEMENTOV SELSKOGO KHOZIA ISTVA ODESSKOI GUBERNII

STATISTICHESKI I BI ULLETEN NO. 1 (OKT. 1924) *see* BIULLETEN SIBIRSKOGO STATISTICHESKOGO UPRAVLENII A

STATISTICHESKI I BIULLETEN = BULLETIN STATISTIQUE / T Sentralnoe statisticheskoe upravlenie, Kievskoe gubernskoe statisticheskoe biuro – (Includes c.1: no.1 1922:Jan.-no.8/12 (1922:Aug./Dec.)) – Kiev: Biuro, 1922- – 1 – CSUXAKY6350-S – us Hoover Inst Photo [304]

STATISTICHESKI I BIULLETEN / Sibirskoe kraevoe statisticheskoe biuro – (Includes c.1: no.1 1925:Oct.-no.3 (1926:Jan./Feb.)) – Novo-Nikolaevsk: [Biuro], 1925- – 1 – CSUXAKZ2417-S – us Hoover Inst Photo [304]

STATISTICHESKI I BIULLETEN PO GORODU KIEVU = BULETIN STATISTIQUE DE LA VILLE DE KIEFF – (Includes c.1: v.1 1918-v.4 (1920)) – Kiev: [Biuro], 1918-1920. 4v – 1 – CSUXAKZ0454-S – us Hoover Inst Photo [304]

STATISTICHESKI I EZHEGODNIK *see* STATYSTYCHNY SHTOGODNIK

STATISTICHESKI I LISTOK *see* STATYSTYCHNY LISTOK

STATISTICHESKI I OBZOR DEI ATELNOSTI MESTNYKH ADMINISTRATIVNYKH ORGANOV NARODNOGO KOMISSARIATA VNUTRENNIKH DEL RSFSR / Narodny i komissariat vnutrennikh del, Statisticheskoe biuro – (Library has: v3 (Oct./Dec. 1924)) – Moskva: Biuro, 1924 – 1 – CSUX90-S943 – us Hoover Inst Photo [304]

STATISTICHESKI I SBORNIK PO ARKHANGELSKO I GUBERNII ZA...GOD / Arkhangelski i gubernski i statisticheski i otdel – (Includes c.1: 1926) – Arkhangelsk: Otdel, 1924 – 1 – CSUXAKY6223-S – us Hoover Inst Photo [304]

STATISTICHESKI YEZHEGODNIK ROSSII / Russia. Tsentral'nyi Statisticheski Komitet – St Petersburg. year 1-11. 1904-1914 – 1 – us NY Public [310]

STATISTICHESKIE DANNYE PO SOTSIALNOMU STRAKHOVANII U V RSFSR ZA...POLUGODIE... / NKT–RSFSR, Glavnoe upravlenie sotsialnogo strakovaii a – (Includes c.1: 1927/1928) – Moskva: Voprosy truda, 1927 – 1 – CSUXAKZ2715-S – us Hoover Inst Photo [304]

STATISTICHESKII EZHEGODNIK. NA 1912 GOD – v. 1-3. Spb. 1912-14. BR-3999 2 – 8 – ne IDC [947]

Statisticheskii komitet Sodruzhestva Nezavisimykh Gosudarstv *see*
- ITOGI VSESOIUZNOI PEREPISI NASELENIIA 1989 GODA

STATISTICHESKII SPRAVOCHNIK / ed by Diadichenko, A N – St. Petersburg, 1906 – 1 – 35.00r – us Hoover Inst Photo [310]

STATISTICHESKII SPROVOCHNIK SSSR ZA 1928 GOD – M. 1929. BR-8167 1 – 9 – ne IDC [947]

STATISTICHESKII VESTNIK – Obshchestvo im. A.I. Chuprova dlia razrabotki obshchestvennykh nauk. M. 1914-16. BR-8168 2 – 8 – ne IDC [947]

STATISTICHESKII VREMENNIK ROSSIISKOI / Russia. Tsentralnyi Statisticheskii Komitet – 40v. 1871-89 – 1 – $140.00 – us L of C Photodup [310]

STATISTICHESKII VREMENNIK ROSSIISKOI IMPERII – S. 1, v. 1-25. 1858-66; S. 2, v. 1-25. 1871-84; S. 3, v. 1-25. 1884-90. Lacking: S. 1, v. 2-25; S. 3, v. 25. B-1911 2 – 8 – ne IDC [947]

STATISTICHESKOE OBOZRENIE – Moscow. U.S.S.R. 1927-30 – 1 – us UMI [073]

STATISTICHESKOE OBOZRENIE / Russia. (1923-U.S.S.R.). Tsentral'noe Statisticheskoe Upravlenie – Moscow. 4v. 1927-30 – 1 – $69.00 – us L of C Photodup [310]

STATISTICHESKOE OBOZRENIE = STATISTICAL REVIEW / Soviet Union, T Sentralnoe statisticheskoe upravlenie – (Includes c.1: 1927:Jan.-1929:Nov.; 1930:Feb., June-Dec)) – Moskva: T S.S.U. Soiuza SSR, 1927- – 1 – CSUXAKY5311-S – us Hoover Inst Photo [304]

THE STATISTICIAN – 1951- 42v – 9 – £238.00 – 0039-0526 – uk Carfax [310]

STATISTICKI GODISNJAK KREALJEVINE SRBIJE / Serbia. Uprava Drzavne Statistike – 1893-1908. 12v – 1 – 69.00 – us L of C Photodup [310]

STATISTICS : A JOURNAL OF THEORETICAL AND APPLIED STATISTICS / ed by Bunke, O – 9,5,1 – us Gordon [510]

STATISTICS ABSTRACT FOR THE PRINCIPAL FOREIGN COUNTRIES IN EACH YEAR 1860/72-1901/12 – (Coll title: British Government Publications...1801-1977, Empire and Foreign Countries) – 5r – 1 (£380.00 empire and foreign countries set of 7r) – uk Chadwyck [310]

STATISTICS AND GAZETTEER OF NEW HAMPSHIRE / Fogg, Alonzo J – Concord, D. L. Guernsey, 1874. New Hampshire Reel 1. (The Cox Library Collection) – 5 – us Americana [978]

STATISTICS AND STUDIES FOR AGRICULTURAL DEVELOPMENT PLANNING : A PHASED PROGRAMME – 1976 – 29p – it F.A.O. [510]

STATISTICS FOR ECONOMIC DEVELOPMENT PLANNING: EGYPTIAN REGION, UNITED ARAB REPUBLIC / Bog, P (United Nations Technical Assistance Administration) – 1958. BNE-4608 1 – 9 – ne IDC [338]

STATISTICS IN MEDICINE – v.1-. 1982- – 1,5,6,9 – us UMI [310]

STATISTICS OF BRITISH INDIA – Calcutta, 1908-22. v1, 1906-07 to v13, 1919-20.Continues: Financial and Commercial Statistics of British India (1904-07). Lacking: 1914-15, v8 (1-4); 1915-16, v8 (2); 1916-17, v8 (1). BI-485/2 – 8 – ne IDC [073]

STATISTICS OF BRITISH INDIA / India. Judicial and Administrative Department – Calcutta. 1879-1907. Lacking: 1885, 1902. BI-483 2 – 8 – ne IDC [324]

STATISTICS OF EDUCATION 1961-1976 – (Coll title: British Government Publications...1801-1977, Education) – 138mf – 9 (£970.00 education set of 152mf) – uk Chadwyck [370]

STATISTICS OF FOREIGN TRADE, 1960-1975 / Iraq. Central Statistical Organization – Lacking: 1964. BNE-2016 1 – 9 – ne IDC [338]

STATISTICS OF HIGHER EDUCATION IN THE KINGDOM OF SAUDI ARABIA 1983/84 / Saudi Arabia. Directorate General for the Development of Higher Education. Data Centre – (Arabic text and English summary) – Riyadh – 12mf – 9 – DE-631/1 – ne IDC [370]

STATISTICS OF SCIENCE AND TECHNOLOGY – (Coll title: British Government Publications...1801-1977, Science and Technology) – 6mf – 9 – £50.00 – uk Chadwyck [600]

STATISTICS OF THE FOREIGN TRADE OF SYRIA / Syria. Central Bureau of Statistics – 1964-74. BNE-9692 1 – 9 – ne IDC [310]

STATISTICS OF THE FOREIGN TRADE OF SYRIA DURING THE YEAR 1975 / Syria. Office of the Prime Minister. Central Bureau of Statistics – Damascus, 1976 – 9 – ne IDC [380]

STATISTICS OF THE MANUFACTURES AND COMMERCE OF LAKE MEMPHREMAGOG / Harrington, E – Stanstead: L R Robinson, 1864. SEM105P450 – 1mf – 9 – Can$2.25 – cn Bibl Nat [380]

STATISTICS OF THE POPULATION CENSUS, 1971 / Bahrain. Statistical Bureau – 1972. BNE-10.014 1 – 9 – ne IDC [310]

STATISTICS OF THE THIRD REICH ANALYSED, 1933-1944 – Official German Foreign Trade Statistics – 1 – us Primary [943]

STATISTICS OF TRADE THROUGHOUT U.K. PORTS 1976 AND 1977 – (Coll title: British Government Publications...1801-1977, Foreign Trade) – 8mf – 9 (£15,875.00 foreign trade set of 220r + 824mf) – uk Chadwyck [380]

STATISTICS OF WAGES AND WORKING HOURS IN EGYPT / Egypt. Statistical Department – 31 v. (in 28). 1942-60. Lacking: 1955 (Jul); 1956 57 (Jul-Jan); 1958 (Jan); 1959 (Jul); 1960 (Jul). BNE-4678 1 – 9 – ne IDC [310]

STATISTICS ON ACADEMIC STREAM OF EDUCATION BY PROVINCE 1975-1980 / Thailand. Ministry of Education. National Statistical Office – (In Thai and English. Missing: 1975-1977) – Bangkok – 14mf – 9 – DE-273/1 – ne IDC [370]

STATISTICS ON CROP PRODUCTION AND LAND USE IN THE SUDAN, 1955/1956-1965/1966 / Sudan. Dept. of Agriculture. Sharif Dishoni and Nasr El Din Mustafa – 1966. BNE-7607 1 – 9 – ne IDC [338]

STATISTICS ON HIGHER EDUCATION IN PAKISTAN 1973/74-1983/84 / Pakistan. University Grants Commission – Islamabad – 15mf – 9 – DE-571/1 – ne IDC [370]

STATISTICS ON SCHOOLS, PUPILS AND TEACHERS, 1957-58 / Indonesia. Kementerian Pendidikan – 1959?. SE-4613-1 – 9 – ne IDC [324]

STATISTICS ON TRADE / Kuwait. Customs and Port Dept – 1v. 1962. BNE-9013 1 – 9 – ne IDC [380]

STATISTICS ON UNIVERSITY EDUCATION 1968-1974 / Pakistan. Ministry of Education. Bureau of Educational Planning and Management – Islamabad, 1976 – 3mf – 9 – DE-569/1 – ne IDC [370]

STATISTICS ON WOMEN IN NEPAL / Nepal. Social Service National Co-ordination Council. Women Service Co-ordination Committee – Kathmandu, 1986 – 1mf – 9 – DE-620/1 – ne IDC [370]

STATISTICS: PART 2. DEMOGRAPHY / Bibliotheque Nationale – Population movements in France, the growth and decline of various regions during the nineteenth century. In French. 39 titles, available separately. 86 fiches – 9 – $97.00 – fr Bibl Nationale [310]

STATISTICS: PART 3. TOPOGRAPHY / Bibliotheque Nationale – Physical characteristics of the regions of France, by department and data on natural resources and industry. Mostly nineteenth century and including 3 studies on Europe. In French. 29 titles, available separately. 177 fiches – 9 – $438.00 – fr Bibl Nationale [310]

STATISTICS: PART I. MEDICAL STUDIES / Bibliotheque Nationale – 19th Century statistics on malnutrition, prostitution, hygiene, plague, cholera, birth and mortality rates, infant care, etc. In French. 70 titles, available separately. 221 fiches – 9 – 547.00 – fr Bibl Nationale [310]

STATISTICS REPORT / Arabian Gulf Emirates. Dubai. Port and Customs Dept – 1969$74. BNE-10.017 1 – 9 – ne IDC [310]

STATISTIEK VAN JAVA EN MADURA DOOR J.M. BEUSECHEM, 1836 – Arch. Kol. no.3042. BSD-112/1 mf.1-9 – 9 – ne IDC [950]

STATISTIK – Djakarta. SE 185 1. 1963-1967. Lacking: 1963-1964, v. 1; 1964-1966, v. 2 – 8 – ne IDC [310]

STATISTIK PEMERINTAH DAERAH ISTIMEWA JOGJAKARTA / Jogjakarta. Indonesia – 1958-63, v1-3; 1964-66, v1-3; 1967, v1-4; 1968, v1-4; 1969, v1-4; 1970, v1-3. TEN 1145.Lacking some issues. BSE-1719/1 – 9 – ne IDC [950]

STATISTIK PERDAGANGAN EKSPOR – Djakarta, Biro Pusat Statistik. 1955-56. Incomplete. In Indonesian; tables of contents and explanatory remarks also in English. Filmed with: ekspor – 1 – us U.W. Library [310]

STATISTIKA *see* STATYSTYKA

STATISTIKA GOSUDARSTVENNYKH NALOGOV I POSHLIN ZA...BIUDZHETNY I GOD / Narodny i komissariat finansov Soiuza SSR, Upravlenie gosudarstvenymi nalogami – (Includes c.1: 1923/1924-1924/1925) – Moskva: Finansovoe izdvo NKF SSSR, 1926- – 1 – CSUXAKZ6292-S – us Hoover Inst Photo [304]

STATISTIKA PROIZVEDENII PECHATI, VYSHEDSIKH V ROSSII 1910-1911, 1913-1915 – Spb. 1911-16. BR-4606 2 – 8 – ne IDC [947]

STATISTIKA PROIZVODSTV, OBLAGAEMYKH AKTSIZOM / Russia. Glavnoe Upravlenie Neukladnykh Sborov i Kazennoi Prodazhi pitei – 15v. 1897-1914 – 1 – $207.00 – us L of C Photodup [310]

STATISTIKA ROSSIISKOI IMPERII / Russia. Ministerstvo Vnutrennikh Del'. Tsentral'nyi statisticheskii komitet – v. 88, 91, 93. Dvizhenie Naseleniia v Evropeiskoi Rossii Za. 1908 G., v. 36; 1909 G., v. 91; 1910 G., v. 93 – 1 – 35.00r – us Hoover Inst Photo [324]

STATISTIKA ROSSIISKOI IMPERII / Russia. Ministerstvo vnutrennykh del'. Tsentral'nyi statisticheskii komitet – v. 79. St. Petersburg, 1913 – 1 – 35.00r – us Hoover Inst Photo [324]

STATISTIKA ROSSIISKOI IMPERII / Russia. Tsentralnyi Statisticheskii Komitet – v.1-92. 1887-1916. Very incomplete – 1 – $160.00 – us L of C Photodup [310]

STATISTIKA TRUDA / Narodny i komissariat truda – (Includes c.1: 1918:no.1 July 15-1919:no.11/12 (June 1/Aug.15)) – Moskva: Komissariat, 1918-1919. 2v – 1 – CSUX90-S29 – us Hoover Inst Photo [304]

STATISTIKA TRUDA : ORGAN T SENTRALNOGO BIURO STATISTIKI TRUDA VT SSPS, T SSU, NKT – (Includes c.1: 1922:no.1 Dec.1, 1923:no.3 (Feb.), 1923:no.5; 1925:no.1-1927:no.11/12) – Moskva: Izd. Vserossi iskogo t sentralnogo soveta profsoiuzov, 1922-1929 – 1 – CSUX89-S930 – us Hoover Inst Photo [304]

STATISTIKA VNESHNE I TORGOVLI SSSR / Narodny i komissariat vneshne i torgovli, Glavnoe tamozhennoe upravlenie – (Library has: Jan.-Dec. 1936; Jan.-Sep., Dec. 1937; Jan.-Dec. 1938) – Moskva: Vneshtorigizdat, 1936-1938 – 1 – CSUX89-S844 – us Hoover Inst Photo [304]

STATISTIQUE ADMINISTRATIVE ET MEDICALE DE L'ASILE PUBLIC DES ALIENEES DE LILLE, POUR LES ANNEES 1847 A 1851: RAPPORT? MR. LE PREFET DE DEPART. DU NORD / L'Herbon de Lussats & Gosselet, A – Lille, Lefebvre-Ducrocq, 1852 – 1mf – 9 – fr Bibl Nationale [310]

STATISTIQUE COMMERCIALE DU DEPARTEMENT D'INDRE ET LOIRE ET DES CINQ DEPARTEMENTS LIMITROPHES, MAINE ET LOIRE, SARTHE, LOIR ET CHER, INDRE ET VIENNE, TOURS / Moreau – 1811 – 9 – fr Hachette [944]

STATISTIQUE DE DEPARTEMENT DE SEINE-ET-MARNE / Dubarle, E – Paris: Verdiere, 1836. 3 fiches. (Statistics Series: Topography) – 9 – 8.00 – fr Bibl Nationale [944]

STATISTIQUE DE LA BATAVIE / Estienne, Emiland – an XI – 9 – fr Hachette [944]

STATISTIQUE DE LA FRANCE. INDUSTRIE RESULTATS GENERAUX DE L'ENQUETE EFFECTUEE DANS LES ANNEES 1861-1865 – (Condition of 19th C. French working class series). 1873 – 9 – fr Hachette [310]

STATISTIQUE DE L'ARRONDISSEMENT DE FALAISE / Galeron, Frederic & Brebisson, Alphonse de – Falaise: Bree, 1826-28. 2v. (Statistics Series: Topography) – 12mf – 9 – 30.00 – fr Bibl Nationale [944]

STATISTIQUE DE L'ENSEIGNEMENT SECONDAIRE DES GARCONS: ANNEE 1900 – Paris: Imp. nationale, 1900. 99p. 2 fiches. (Education Collection) – 9 – 6.00 – fr Bibl Nationale [370]

STATISTIQUE DE L'INDUSTRIE A PARIS RESULTANT DE L'ENQUETE FAITE PAR LA CHAMBRE DE COMMERCE POUR L'ANNEE 1860. RESULTATS GENERAUX – (Condition of 19th C. French working class series). 1864 – 9 – fr Hachette [310]

STATISTIQUE DE L'INDUSTRIE A PARIS, RESULTANT DE L'ENQUETE FAITE PAR LA CHAMBRE DE COMMERCE POUR LES ANNEES 1847-1848. RESULTATS GENERAUX / Chambre de Commerce de Paris – (Condition of 19th C. French working class series). 1851 – 9 – fr Hachette [025]

STATISTIQUE DE L'INDUSTRIE DE LA FRANCE / Moreau de Jonnes, Alexandre – Paris. 1856. (La Condition Ouvriere. Part Two.) – 9 – 12.50 – fr Bibl Nationale [360]

STATISTIQUE DES ETABLISSEMENTS DE BIENFAISANCE. RAPPORT A M. LE MINISTRE DE L'INTERIEUR SUR L'ADMINISTRATION DES MONTS-DE-PIETE, PAR AD. DE WATTEVILLE – (Condition of 19th C. French working class series). 1859 – 9 – fr Hachette [310]

STATISTIQUE DES MALADIES OBSERVEES PENDANT L'ANNEE 1850. / Laforgue, Henri – Toulouse, Donnal et Gibrac, 1851. 55 p. 1 fiche. (Statistics Series: Medical Studies) – 9 – 6.00 – fr Bibl Nationale [310]

STATISTIQUE DU COMMERCE EXTERIEUR / Syria. Direction Generale des Douanes – 19 v. 1950-71. Lacking: 1951 52; 1966. BNE-9697 – 9 – ne IDC [380]

STATISTIQUE DU COMMERCE EXTERIEUR DES ETATS DU LEVANT SOUS MANDAT FRANCAIS / Lebanon. Haut-Commissariat en Syrie et au Liban – 1937-38. BNE-9661 1 – 9 – ne IDC [380]

STATISTIQUE DU DEPARTEMENT DE GARD / Rivoire, Hector – Nimes: Ballivet et Fabre, 1842. 17 fiches. (Statistics Series: Topography) – 9 – 42.00 – fr Bibl Nationale [944]

STATISTIQUE DU DEPARTEMENT DE LA CHARENTE / Delaistre, Guillaume J – an X – 9 – fr Hachette [944]

STATISTIQUE DU DEPARTEMENT DE LA LOIRE-INFERIEURE / Huet de Coetlizan, Jean-Baptiste – an X – 9 – fr Hachette [944]

STATISTIQUE DU DEPARTEMENT DE LA LOZERE / Jerphanion, Gabriel J – an X – 9 – fr Hachette [944]

STATISTIQUE DU DEPARTEMENT DE LA MEUSE-INFERIEURE / Cavenne – an X – 9 – fr Hachette [944]

STATISTIQUE DU DEPARTEMENT DE LA ROER / Dorsch, Anton-Joseph – An XII – 9 – fr Hachette [944]

STATISTIQUE DU DEPARTEMENT DE LA SARTHE / Auvray, Louis M – an X – 9 – fr Hachette [944]

STATISTIQUE DU DEPARTEMENT DE LA VENDEE / Labretonniere, PL C – an IX – 9 – fr Hachette [944]

STATISTIQUE DU DEPARTEMENT DE L'AISNE / Dauchy, Luc J E – an X – 9 – fr Hachette [944]

STATISTIQUE DU DEPARTEMENT DE LOT-ET-GARONNE / Pieyre, Jean – an X – 9 – fr Hachette [944]

STATISTIQUE DU DEPARTEMENT DE SAMBRE-ET-MEUSE / Jardrinet – An X – 9 – fr Hachette [944]

STATISTIQUE DU DEPARTEMENT DES BASSES-PYRENEES / Serviez, Emmanuel G R de – an X – 9 – fr Hachette [944]

STATISTIQUE DU DEPARTEMENT DES BOUCHES DU RHONE / Eyguieres, Joseph E d' – an XI – 9 – fr Hachette [944]

STATISTIQUE DU DEPARTEMENT DES DEUX-NETHES / Herbouville, Charles J F d' – an X – 9 – fr Hachette [944]

STATISTIQUE DU DEPARTEMENT DES DEUX-SEVRES / Dupin, Claude FE – An IX – 9 – fr Hachette [944]

STATISTIQUE DU DEPARTEMENT D'ILLE ET VILAINE / Borie, Nicolas Y – an IX – 9 – fr Hachette [944]

STATISTIQUE DU DEPARTEMENT DU BAS-RHIN / Laumond, Jean C J – an X – 9 – fr Hachette [944]

STATISTIQUE DU DEPARTEMENT DU GOLO / Pietry – an X – 9 – fr Hachette [944]

STATISTIQUE DU DEPARTEMENT DU MONT-BLANC / Sauzay, Antoine de – an IX – 9 – fr Hachette [944]

STATISTIQUE DU DEPARTEMENT DU NORD / Dieudonne, Christophe – An XII – 9 – fr Hachette [944]

STATISTIQUE DU DEPARTEMENT DU TARN / Lamarque, Francois – an IX – 9 – fr Hachette [944]

STATISTIQUE DU DEPARTEMENT DU VAR / Noyon, CN – Draguignan: H. Bernard, 1838. 7 fiches.(Statistics Series: Topography) – 9 – 17.00 – fr Bibl Nationale [944]

STATISTIQUE DU SALAIRE DES OUVRIERS EN REPONSE A M. THIERS ET AUTRES ECONOMISTES DE LA MEME ECOLE / Perdiguier, Agricol – (Condition of 19th C. French working class series). 1849 – 9 – fr Hachette [310]

STATISTIQUE GENERALE DE LA FRANCE / Bossi, Giuseppe – Departement de l'Ain. 1808 – 9 – fr Hachette [944]

STATISTIQUE GENERALE DE LA FRANCE. DEPARTEMENT DE LA HAUTE-VIENNE / Texier-Olivier, Louis – 1808 – 9 – fr Hachette [944]

STATISTIQUE GENERALE DE LA FRANCE. DEPARTEMENT DU MONT-BLANC / Verneil-Puyraseau, Jean J – 1807 – 9 – fr Hachette [944]

STATISTIQUE GENERALE DE LA FRANCE. PRIX ET SALAIRES A DIVERSES EPOQUES (DE 1824 A 1857) – (Condition of 19th C. French working class series). 1864 – 9 – fr Hachette [330]

STATISTIQUE GENERALE DE LA FRANCE. SALAIRES ET COUT DE L'EXISTENCE A DIVERSES EPOQUES JUSQU'EN 1910 / France. Ministere du Travail et de la Prevoyance sociale – (Condition of 19th C. French working class series). 1911 – 9 – fr Hachette [310]

STATISTIQUE GENERALE DE L'ALGERIE / Algeria. Service de la Statistique Generale – 1888-1925 – 1 – 92.00 – us L of C Photodup [310]

STATISTIQUE MENSUELLE DU COMMERCE EXTERIEUR DE L'INDOCHINE / Indochina. French. Direction des douanes et regies – Jan 1935-Dec 1939 – 1 – 302.00 – us L of C Photodup [950]

STATISTIQUES DES BUDGETS FAMILIAUX DANS LA VILLE DE TRIPOLI / Libya. Ministere de l'Economique Nationale. Administration de statistique et de recensement – Tripoli. 1962. BNE-520 1 – 9 – ne IDC [339]

STATISTIQUES DES EXPORTATIONS DES PRODUITS CONTROLES, CAMPAGNE / Algeria. Office Algerien d'Action Commerciale – 5v. 1958-65. BNE-8663 1 – 9 – ne IDC [338]

STATISTIQUES DES SOCIETES ANONYMES TRAVAILLANT PRINCIPALEMENT EN EGYPTE / Egypt. Ministry of Finance – 2v. 1939-46. (lacking 1940-45). BNE-4662 1 – 9 – ne IDC [336]

STATISTIQUES DU COMMERCE EXTERIEUR / Lebanon. Direction Generale des Douanes – 22 v. (in 25). 1950-72. BNE-9656 1 – 9 – ne IDC [380]

STATISTIQUES DU COMMERCE EXTERIEUR DU LIBAN / Lebanon. Ministere du Plan – 1960-1968. Lacking: 1964 65; 1966, v. 3(2-3). BNE-9680 1 – 9 – ne IDC [324]

STATISTIQUES DU COMMERCE EXTERIEUR DU MAROC / Morocco. Office des Changes – 1966-77. BNE-3089 1 – 9 – ne IDC [380]

STATISTIQUES DU COMMERCE EXTERIEUR DU MAROC, ANNEES 1966-1970 / Morocco. Office des Changes – BNE-3088 1 – 9 – ne IDC [380]

LES STATISTIQUES DU TRAVAIL ET DES RESSOURCES HUMAINES DANS QUATRE PAYS CHOISIS / Algeria. Service des Statistiques Sociales – (U.S.A., France, Yougoslavie, Algerie). 1968. BNE-8742 1 – 9 – ne IDC [310]

STATISTIQUES TOURISTIQUES / Morocco. Ministere du Tourisme – 2v. 1969-71. (lacking 1970). BNE-3079 1 – 9 – ne IDC [338]

STATISTIQUES VITALES DES CATHOLIQUES DE MONTREAL POUR L'ANNEE 1874 / Choquet, A – Montreal?: J. Plinguet, 1875? 00633. (Pre-1900 Canadiana) – 9 – cn C.I.H.M. [240]

STATISTISCHE ERHEBUNGEN DES...FUER DIE ZEIT VOM 1. OKTOBER 1891 BIS 30 SEPTEMBER 1892 / Zentralverband der Maurer Deutschlands – Hamburg. 36p. tables. (Serial publications of German trade unions in the Memorial Library, University of Wisconsin-Madison.) – 1 – us U.W. Library [330]

STATISTISCHE METHODEN ZUR UNTERSUCHUNG VON ASSOZIATIONEN ZWISCHEN ANTIGENEN UND KRANKHEITEN / Niemann, Frank-Michael – 1995 – 2mf – 9 – DM80.00 – 3-8267-2193-4 – gw Hänsel [616]

STATISTISCHE UEBERSICHTEN UEBER WAARENVERKEHR UND ZOLL-ERTRAG IM DEUTSCHEN ZOLL-VEREINE FUER DAS JAHR.. – Berlin: G. Reimer. -ann – 1 – us U.W. Library [310]

STATISTISCHE UNTERSUCHUNGEN UEBER DIE ARBEITSKAEMPFE IN BORGBAU UND HUETTENINDUSTRIE DEUTSCHLANDS IN DER NACHKRIEGSZEIT / Boehm, Gotthold – Leipzig, 1938 – 1 – DM30.00 – gw Mikro Press [310]

STATISTISCHE UNTERSUCHUNGEN UEBER DIE VERWENDUNG DER FARBEN IN DEN DICHTUNGEN GOETHE'S / Franck, Ludwig – [S.l.: s.n.], 1909 (Giessen: Muenchow'sche Hof- und Universitaets-Druckerei) – 1r – 1 – us U.W. Library [430]

STATISTISCHE UNTERSUCHUNGEN ZUM ALTERS- UND GESCHLECHTSUNTERSCHIED IM KARIESBEFALL DER EINZELNEN ZAEHNE / Sergl, Hans Georg – 1995 – 1mf – 9 – DM60.00 – 3-8267-2183-7 – gw Hänsel [617]

STATISTISCHES JAHRBUCH / Hungary. Magyar Statisztikai Evkonyv – 1875-89; 1893-1915 – 6r – 1 – us Ross [310]

STATISTISCHES JAHRBUCH FUER DAS DEUTSCHE REICH – 1880-1942. Berlin: Puttkammer & Muhlbrecht, 1880-1942. 59v. illus – 1 – us U.W. Library [943]

STATISTISCHES JAHRBUCH FUER DAS DEUTSCHE REICH / Germany. Statistiches Reichsamt – v1-59 1880-1941/42 – 1 – $253.00 – us L of C Photodup [943]

STATISTISCHES JAHRBUCH FUER DAS DEUTSCHE REICH *see* GERMANY (FORMERLY FEDERAL REPUBLIK)

STATISTISCHES JAHRBUCH FUER DAS DEUTSCHE REICH SEIT 1880 / Statistisches Reichsamt – Berlin, 1910-42. Hildesheim, 1983 – 251mf – 9 – DM1,600.00 diazo DM1,900.00 silver – gw Olms [943]

STATISTISCHES JAHRBUCH FUER DAS LAND BADEN / Baden. Statistisches Landesamt – v. 1-34. 1868-1903 – 1 – 106.00 – us L of C Photodup [943]

STATISTISCHES JAHRBUCH FUER DIE BUNDESREPUBLIK DEUTSCHLAND *see* GERMANY (FORMERLY FEDERAL REPUBLIC)

STATISTISCHES JAHRBUCH FUR DAS KOENIGREICH BAYERN / Bavaria. Statistisches Landesamt – v. 1-26. 1894-1958 – 1 – 113.00 – us L of C Photodup [943]

STATISTISCHES KOMPENDIUM UBER DIE SOWJETISCHE BESATZUNGSZONE / Berlin. Germany. Deutsches Institut fur Wirtschaftsforschung – Berlin. Statistics under Allied Occupation, 1945-1955 – 1 – us U.W. Library [943]

Statistisches Reichsamt *see* STATISTISCHES JAHRBUCH FUER DAS DEUTSCHE REICH SEIT 1880

STATISTISCHES VERFAHREN UND NEURONALE NETZE ZUR DATENANALYSE IM MARKETING : EIN SYSTEMATISCHER VERGLEICH / Pietruska, Reinhard – 1994 – 2mf – 9 – DM80.00 – 3-89349-917-2 – gw Hänsel [650]

STATISZTIKAI SZEMLE / Hungary. Kozponti Statisztikai Hivatal – v. 1-6. 1923-28. (v. 3 wanting) – 1 – 45.00 – us L of C Photodup [943]

LO STATO GIURIDICO DELLA GENTE DELL'ARIA, DIRITTO INTERNAZIONALE ED INTERNO / Giannini, Amedeo – 2. ed. Roma: Soc. ed. del "Foro italiano", 1940. 92p. LL-4100 – 1 – us L of C Photodup [340]

LO STATO OPERAIO – Paris. v. 1-10, no. 12. Mar 1927-1936 – 1 – us NY Public [330]

STATSKIRKE OG FRIKIRKE : EN HISTORISK SKILDRING / Nielsen, Fredrik – Kobenhavn: K. Schonberg, 1883 – 1mf – us A.T.L.A. [240]

STATSTIDENDE – Copenhagen. v64-65. 1967-69 – 6r – 1 – us Ross [324]

STATSTIDENDE / Denmark – (Copenhagen). Apr. 1957-1966 – 1 – us NY Public [948]

STATSVETENSKAPLIGA INSTITUTIONEN I UPPSALA PRESSARKIVET US – (UT. Utrikes material. 1945-78. 196 reels) – Uppsala, Sweden. Svenskt material. 1945-78. 349 reels – 1 – sw Kungliga [300]

STATUE E GRUPPI, IN BRONZO E IN MARMO, CHE SONO IN FIRENZE ALLA VISTA DEL PUBBLICO... / Vascellini, G – Firenze, 1777 – 2mf – ne IDC [700]

THE STATUES IN THE BLOCK, AND OTHER POEMS / O'Reilly, John Boyle – 2nd ed. Boston: Roberts Brothers, 1881.110p – 1 – us U.W. Library [810]

THE STATUES OF THE APOSTLES OR CANONES ECCLESIASTICI / ed by Horner, J – London, 1904 – 9mf – 8 – ne Slangenburg [220]

STATUS / Morocco. Banque Nationale pour le Developpement Economique – BNE-3012 1 – 9 – ne IDC [330]

THE STATUS AND DEVELOPMENT OF EDUCATION IN THE KINGDOM OF SWAZILAND : EDUCATION AND TRAINING SECTOR REVIEW 1981 / Swaziland. Ministry of Education. Department of Economic Planning and Statistics – [Mbabane], 1981 – 5mf – 9 – DE-482/1 – ne IDC [370]

STATUS OF AFRICAN RESERVOIR FISHERIES – 1984 – 331p – it F.A.O. [338]

STATUS OF CADMIUM, LEAD, COBALT AND SELENIUM IN SOILS AND PLANTS OF THIRTY COUNTRIES – 1992 – 207p – it F.A.O. [631]

THE STATUS OF CONTINUOUS ECG MONITORING IN PHASE 2 CARDIAC REHABILITATION PROGRAMS / Finegan, Mark T – University of Wisconsin-La Crosse, 1995 – 1mf – 9 – PH 1492 – us Microform Publ [612]

THE STATUS OF DANCE IN KOREAN HIGHER EDUCATION / Kim, Kyunghee – Texan Woman's University, 1993 – 3mf – 9 – $12.00 – PE 3659 – us Microform Publ [790]

STATUS OF THE CONVENTION ON THE RIGHTS OF THE CHILD / United Nations – E.1 – 9 – us U.N. Pubs [320]

STATUS OF THE RUFOUS SCRUB-BIRD : HABITAT, GEOGRAPHICAL VARIATION AND ABUNDANCE / Ferrier, Simon – (BSc Hons Thesis) – microfiche – A$15.00 – at R.A.O.U. [590]

THE STATUS OF WOMEN IN INDIA : OR, A HAND-BOOK FOR HINDU SOCIAL REFORMERS / Shahani, Dayaran Gidumal – Bombay: Fort Printing Press, 1889. iv,cii,337,viiip – 1 – us U.W. Library [305]

THE STATUS QUO IN THE HOLY PLACES / Palestine – (L.G.A. Cust). Jerusalem. 1929. BJ-28-110 1 – 9 – ne IDC [956]

STATUT.. / Mansfeld'sche Kupferschieferbauende Gewerkschaft – 1851-52. 29p. By the authority of the Koeniglich Preussisches Mansfeldsches Berg-Amt. (Serial publications of German trade unions in the Memorial Library, University of Wisconsin-Madison.) – 1 – us U.W. Library [331]

STATUT DE L'ERREUR ET VARIATION LINGUISTIQUE : ELEMENTS D'ANALYSE SOCIOLINGUISTIQUE DE L'ANGLAIS DANS LA SALLE DE CLASSE BURKINABE / Sawadogo, Mahamadou – 1mf – 9 – 10237 – fr Atelier National [420]

LE STATUT INTERNATIONAL DE LA PALESTINE ORIENTALE / Ficheleff, S – Paris, 1932 – 2mf – 1 – ILM-1995/1 – ne IDC [327]

LE STATUT INTERNATIONAL DU CHEQUE / Bouteron, J – Paris, 1934 – 13mf – 9 – ILM-3284/1 – ne IDC [327]

STATUT INTERNATIONAL DU MAROC / Deloncle, L – Ed 2. Paris, 1912 – 4mf – 1 – ILM-1696/1 – ne IDC [327]

LE STATUT JURIDIQUE DES MINORITES... / Erdstein, D – Paris, 1932 – 3mf – 1 – ILM-1576/1 – ne IDC [327]

STATUT JURIDIQUE INTERNATIONAL DE L'EGYPTE / Chafik, H – Paris, 1928 – 3mf – 1 – ILM-1944/1 – ne IDC [327]

STATUT ORGANIQUE DE LA MONNAIE ET CREATION DE LA BANQUE CENTRALE DE SYRIE / Syria. Ministry of Finance – Promolgue par le Decret legislatif nr. 87 du mars 1953. Damas? BNE-9715 1 – 9 – ne IDC [336]

LE STATUT PERSONNEL ANGLAIS OU LA LOI DU DOMICILE / Dicey, A V – Paris. 2v. 1887-88 – 10mf – 1 – ILM-3962/1 – ne IDC [327]

STATUT VELIKOGO KNIAZHESTVA LITOVSKOGO – Vilna, 1588 – 17mf – 9 – ne IDC [340]

STATUTA CAPITULORUM GENERALIUM ORDINIS CISTERCIENSIS / Canivez, J-M – Louvain. 8v. 1933-1941 – v1-5 88mf; v7-8 35mf – 8 – Dfl501.00 – ne Slangenburg [240]

STATUTA ENDING 1330; REGISTRUM BREVIUM, ETC.; STATUTA FROM 1344-1388; NATURA BREVIUM; BREVIA PLACITATA ETC.; TENURES, NATURA BREVIUM, ETC / Holkham Hall. Norfolk. England – Holkham mss. 752, 753, 754, 755. 14th-15th centuries – 1 – uk Microform Academic [025]

STATUTA PROVINCIALIA ET SYNODALIA ECCLESIAE COLONIENSIS – Impr Per Joh. Koelhoff De Lubyck, 1482 – Dfl9.00 – ne Slangenburg [240]

STATUTA PROVINCIALIA ET SYNODALIA TRAJECTENSIA – Goude: Impr Per Gerardum Leeu, 1484 – Dfl13.00 – ne Slangenburg [240]

STATUTE LAWS OF THE COMMONWEALTH OF LIBERIA, AND PLAN OF CIVIL GOVERNMENT / Liberia. Laws, Statutes, etc – Monrovia? 1841? 16 p. LL-12015 – 1 – us L of C Photodup [340]

STATUTE OF BANK NEGARA INDONESIA / Indonesia. Bank Negara – SE-4786 1. 1963 – 9 – ne IDC [950]

THE STATUTE RAILROAD LAWS OF THE STATE OF NEW YORK. / Colby, John H – (Supplement Albany, 1883. 55 p) – Albany, Little, 1882. 718 p. LL-702 – 1 – us L of C Photodup [340]

STATUTEN EN HUISHOUDELIKJ REGLEMENT / Vaderlandsche Club – SE 816 1. 1933 – 9 – ne IDC [060]

STATUTES / Germany. Democratic Republic – Gesetzblatt. Berlin. Teil 1-3. 1951-1968 and Indexes – 1 – us NY Public [324]

STATUTES AND AMENDMENTS TO THE CODES OF THE TERRITORY OF GUAM, 1951-1952 / Bohn, John A – Agana: Gov of Guam, 6 Oct 1952 – 7mf – 9 – $10.50 – LLMC 82-100B Title 6 – us L.L.M.C. [324]

STATUTES AND CONSTITUTIONAL PROVISIONS OF THE STATES AND TERRITORIES OF THE UNITED STATES AND THE STATUTES OF ENGLAND ON LIBEL AND SLANDER. / Hatch, Azel Farnsworth – Brooklyn, NY: Eagle, 1895. 162p. LL-224 – 1 – us L of C Photodup [340]

STATUTES AND DECISIONS : THE LAWS OF THE USSR AND ITS SUCCESSOR STATES – (v1-21 1964-85 on reel $450.00. v22-31 1985-95 on mf $379.00. Title varies: v1-28 no 1 as Soviet Statutes and Decisions) – v1-31. 1964-95 – 5,6,9 – $829.00 – us Hein [340]

STATUTES AT LARGE / Ireland. Laws, Statutes, etc – 1310-1800. 8 reels – 1 – $300.00 – us Trans-Media [941]

STATUTES AT LARGE / U. S. Laws, Statutes, etc – (1972- . 5,6. 1977- . 9) – 1789- – 1 – us UMI [321]

STATUTES AT LARGE – v1-107 pt 3. 1789-1993 – 9 – $4,150.00 set – us Hein [340]

STATUTES AT LARGE FROM MAGNA CHARTA TO THE END OF THE ELEVENTH PARLIAMENT OF GREAT BRITAIN, ANNO 1761 / ed by Pickering, Danby – Cambridge. v28-42. 1767-1799 – 195mf – 9 – H-920/2 – ne IDC [941]

THE STATUTES AT LARGE, PASSED IN THE PARLIAMENTS HELD IN IRELAND : FROM THE THIRD YEAR OF EDWARD THE SECOND, A.D. 1310, TO THE FORTIETH YEAR OF GEORGE THE THIRD, A.D. 1800, INCLUSIVE / Ireland. Laws, Statutes, etc – v1-21. 1765-1801 – 1 – $770.00 – 0-89093-028-7 – us UPA [941]

THE STATUTES AT LARGE (PICKERING'S STATUTES), 1225-1869 : FROM THE MAGNA CARTA TO THE 33RD YEAR OF THE REIGN OF QUEEN VICTORIA / Great Britain. Laws, Statutes, etc; ed by Pickering, Danby – (Lacking: v100. Danby Pickering from which the series acquires its name edited v1-46) – v1-109 (all publ) – 909mf – 9 – $1,363.00 – LLMC 84-802 – us L.L.M.C. [324]

STATUTES D'ANGLETERRE / Great Britain. Laws, Statutes, etc – Holkham ms. 232.15th cent. Holkham Hall, Norfolk, England – 1 – uk Microform Academic [340]

THE STATUTES OF NEW SOUTH WALES OF RACTICAL UTILITY PASSED PRIOR TO 1894 AND STILL IN FORCE / Cockshott, H M & Lamb, S Ernest – Sydney/Brisbane: The Law Book Company of Australasia. 1v. 1904 – 8mf – 9 – $12.00 – LLMC 96-006 – us L.L.M.C. [323]

STATUTES OF THE REALM / Great Britain. Laws, Statutes, etc – 1215-1714. 7 reels – 1 – $300.00 – us Trans-Media [324]

STATUTES OF THE REALM – (Historical and bibliographical information about England, Ireland and Scotland) – 11v in 12bks. 1225-1713 – 5,6 – $280.00 set – us Hein [340]

STATUTES OF THE UNITED STATES RELATING TO REVENUE, COMMERCE, NAVIGATION, AND THE CURRENCY / Heyl, Lewis – Boston: Little, Brown, 1868. 960p. LL-1657 – 1 – us L of C Photodup [340]

STATUTES REGULATING JUDICATURE OF LOWER CANADA. / Canada. Laws, Statutes, etc – Kingston: Printed by S Derbishire & G Desbarats, 1843. SEM105P199 – 2mf – 9 – Can$4.50 – cn Bibl Nat [340]

STATUTES RELATING TO THE DUTIES OF JUSTICES OF THE PEACE IN LOWER CANADA / Canada. Laws, Statutes, etc – Quebec: Printed by Stewart Derbishire and George Desbarats, 1863. SEM105P143 – 3mf – 9 – Can$6.75 – cn Bibl Nat [340]

STATUTES...1652-1905 / Cape of Good Hope. Laws, Statutes, etc – Rev. 1906. 4v. LL-12012 – 1 – us L of C Photodup [340]

STATUTORUM...FAMILIA...OBSERVANTIAE... SANCTI FRANCISCI / Jimenez Samaniego, Jose – 1704 – 9 – 1.50f – sp Bibl Santa Ana [240]

STATUTORY ANNOTATIONS TO THE REVISED STATUTES OF CANADA, 1906, AND OTHER CANADIAN STATUTES (2D ED.) PROVIDING REFERENCES TO EVERY CHANGE MADE BY THE ANNUAL STATUTES FOR 1907, 1908, 1909, 1910, 1911, 1912, 1913 AND 1914 / Bligh, Harris Harding – Toronto, Carswell Co., 1914. 3 p. l., 2-67 numb. LL-2368 – 1 – us L of C Photodup [340]

THE STATUTORY CRIMINAL LAW OF GERMANY : WITH COMMENTS / Control Council for Germany – (A translation of the German criminal code of 1871 with amendments, together with the most important supplementary penal statutes and with the laws nos. 1 & 11 and Proclamation no) – Washington: War Dept, 1946 – 4mf – 9 – $6.00 – LLMC 96-076 – us L.L.M.C. [340]

THE STATUTORY JURISDICTION AND PRACTICE OF THE SUPREME COURT OF THE UNITED STATES. / Phillips, Philip – (Rev. ed. Washington: Morrison, 1878. 612p. LL-1179) – 2nd ed. Washington: Morrison, 1874. 512p. LL-1148 – 1 – us L of C Photodup [340]

STATUTORY REVISION OF THE LAWS OF NEW YORK AFFECTING MISCELLANEOUS CORPORATIONS, ENACTED IN 1892. / Hamilton, Andrew – (New York, Banks, 1897. 450 p. LL-1569. Albany, N.Y., Banks, 1906. 529 p. LL-824) – New York, Banks, 1893. 272 p. LL-666 – 1 – us L of C Photodup [340]

STATUTS CONCERNANT LES DEVOIRS DES JUGES DE PAIX DANS LE BAS-CANADA / Canada. Laws, Statutes, etc – Quebec: Imprimes par George Desbarats, 1863. SEM105P142 – 3mf – 9 – Can$6.75 – cn Bibl Nat [340]

STATUTS DE LA PROVINCE DE QUEBEC PASSES DANS LA PREMIERE ANNEE DU REGNE DE SA MAJESTE LE ROI GEORGE 6... / Quebec. Lois, etc. Extrait – Quebec: imprime par Redempti Paradis, 1937. SEM105P899 – 1mf – 9 – Can$2.25 – cn Bibl Nat [340]

STATUTS DE LA PROVINCE DU CANADA... 1852-1866 / Canada (Province) Lois, etc. – Quebec: Impr. par Stewart Derbishire & George Desbarats. SEM35P339 – 5r – 1 – Can$178.00 – cn Bibl Nat [340]

STATUTS ET REGLEMENTS DE LA COMPAGNIE / Club de Chasse et de Peche du Chenal-du-Moine – Montreal: Pigeon, 1891. 03201. (Pre-1900 Canadiana) – 9 – cn C.I.H.M. [060]

STATUTS ET REGLEMENTS DU BUREAU DE DIRECTION DE LA CORPORATION...PREPARES PAR UN COMITE DU BUREAU DE DIRECTION, APPROUVES ET SANCTIONNES A UNE ASSEMBLEE GENERALE TENUE LE 9 AVRIL 1890 / Corporation des Arpenteurs-Geometres de la Province de Quebec – Quebec: C. Darveau, 1890. 00247. (Pre-1900 Canadiana) – 9 – cn C.I.H.M. [971]

STATUTS, ORDONNANCES ET LETTRES PASTORALES POUR LES REGLEMENTS DE SON DIOCESE – Paris: S Langlois, 1703. SEM16P29 – 1r – 5 – Can$9.00 – cn Bibl Nat [240]

LES STATUTS PROVINCIAUX DU CANADA... / Canada (Province). Lois, etc. – v1 (1841)-1852? SEM35P338 – 3r – 1 – Can$144.00 – cn Bibl Nat [340]

STATUTS PROVINCIAUX DU CANADA, PASSES PAR SA TRES-EXCELLENTE MAJESTE, NOTRE SOUVERAINE DAME VICTORIA... VOL 3, 1RE SESS. 3E PARLT / Canada. (Province) – Montreal: Stewart Derbishire & George Desbarats, 1848. SEM105P900 – 1mf – 9 – Can$2.25 – cn Bibl Nat [971]

LES STATUTS REFONDUS DU CANADA / Canada. Laws, Statutes, etc – Toronto: Imprimes par Stewart Derbishire et Georges Desbarats, 1859. SEM105P137 – 16mf – 9 – Can$36.00 – cn Bibl Nat [324]

LES STATUTS REFONDUS POUR LE BAS-CANADA / Canada. Laws, Statutes, etc – Quebec: Imprimes par Stewart Derbishire et Georges Desbarats, 1861. SEM105P136 – 13mf – 9 – Can$29.25 – cn Bibl Nat [324]

STATUTS...PASSES DANS LA PREMIERE ANNEE DU REGNE DE SA MAJESTE LE ROI GEORGE 6...DEUXIEME SESSION DE LA VINGTIEME LEGISLATURE. / Canada. (Province). Laws, Statutes, etc – Quebec: Redempti Paradis, 1937. SEM105P899 – 1mf – 9 – Can$2.25 – cn Bibl Nat [340]

STATYSTYCHNY I BI ULETEN *see* BULLETIN STATISTIQUE (KIEVSKOE GUBERNSKOE STATISTICHESKOE BI URO)

STATYSTYCHNY LISTOK / T Sentralnai a statystychnai a uprava – (Includes c.1: 1926:no.1) – [Minsk: Uprava], 1925 – 1 – CSUXAKZ2165-S – us Hoover Inst Photo [304]

STATYSTYCHNY SHTOGODNIK / T Sentralnai a statystychnai a uprava – (Includes c.1: 1923/1924; 1924/1925:v.1-1924/1925:v.2:no.1) – Minsk: Uprava, 1925- – 1 – CSUXAKZ3937-S – us Hoover Inst Photo [304]

STATYSTYKA : EMIGRACYI POLSKIEJ I AUSTRO-WEGIERKIEJ DO STANOW ZJEDNOCZONYCH AMERYKI POLNOCNEJ / Caro, Leopold – Krakov, 1907 – 1r – 1 – us I.H.R.C. [320]

STATYSTYKA – (Includes c.1: v.1:no.1 1927:Oct.-v.1:no.3 (1927:Dec.)) – Minsk: Upravlenie, 1927 – 1 – CSUXAKZ1925-S – us Hoover Inst Photo [304]

Staudinger, O *see*
- CATALOG DER LEPIDOPTEREN EUROPA'S UND DER ANGRENZENDEN LAENDER
- EXOTISCHE SCHMETTERLINGE

Staudinger, Paul *see* IM HERZEN DER HAUSSALAENDER

Staudt-Bickel, Claudia *see* THERMODYNAMISCHE UNTERSUCHUNGEN ZUM EINSATZ DER PERVAPORATION IN TECHNISCHEN PROZESSEN

Stauffer, Henry *see* THE GREAT AWAKENING IN COLUMBUS, OHIO

STAVANGER AFTENBLAD – Norway, 1992- – 12r per y – 1 – inquire – us Ross [072]

STAVANGER BISPEDOMME – (Lacking some pgs) – 1968-85 – 2r – 1 – ATLA S0764 – us A.T.L.A. [073]

Stave, Erik *see*
- OM KALLORNA TILL 1526 ARS OFVERSATTNING AF NYA TESTAMENTET
- OM KALLORNA TILL 1541 ARS OFVERSATTNING AF NYA TESTAMENTET

LE STAVEGANZE DI AMORE / Cimarosa, D – Ms, 179? – 1 – us Sibley [780]

Staveley, E F *see* BRITISH SPIDERS

Stavenhagen, Rodolfo *see* THE ETHNIC QUESTION

Stavrianeas, Stasinos *see* THE EFFECT OF MUSCLE ISCHEMIA ON SARCOPLASMIC RETICULUM CA2+-ATPASE FUNCTION

STAWELL BOWLING CLUB INC. – 1893-1988. Minutes. SBC1-2 – 2r – 1 – at Corangamite [910]

STAWELL BOWLING CLUB INC. ASSOC. – 1952-1985. Minutes. SBCA1 – 1r – 1 – at Corangamite [910]

STAWELL NEWS – 1937-1961. STN1-25 – 25r – 1 – at Corangamite [072]

STAYTON MAIL – Stayton, OR. -w. 17 Dec 1896-. – 1 – us U.O. Library [071]

STAYTON SIFTINGS – Stayton OR. July 2 1910 – 1 – us U.O. Library [071]

STAYTON STANDARD – Stayton OR. Mar 29 1916-Feb 21 1917 – 1 – us U.O. Library [071]

STAYTON SUN – Stayton OR. Dec 19 1889 – 1 – us U.O. Library [071]

STAYTON TIMES – Stayton OR. July 21 1893, Jan 1 1897 – 1 – us U.O. Library [071]

STAZIONI SPERIMENTALI AGRARIE ITALIENE... – Turin. 16v. 1872-89 – 87mf – 9 – 8022/1 – ne IDC [630]

St-Barbe, Charles *see* A DIRECTORY OF THE NORTHERN PART OF THE SAANICH PENINSULA

Stchoukine, I *see* LA PEINTURE INDIENNE A L'EPOQUE DES GRANDS MOGHOLS

St-Claude-Marie, Soeur *see* L'ENSEIGNEMENT MENAGER AU CANADA FRANCAIS

St-Didier, Marie de *see* BIBLIOGRAPHIE DE MONSIEUR L'ABBE HENRI GRENIER, DOCTEUR EN PHILOSOPHIE, DOCTEUR EN THEOLOGIE, DOCTEUR EN DROIT CANON

Stead, D G *see* FISHES OF AUSTRALIA

Stead, W T *see* HOW NOT TO MAKE PEACE

Steadman, Hilda Mary *see* PAPERS, 1913-1975

STEAGUL ROSU – Bacau, Romania. 1962-Sept 1989 – 29r – 1 – us L of C Photodup [949]

STEAGUL ROSU – Bucharest, Romania. Mar 1954-1989 – 39r – 1 – us L of C Photodup [949]

STEAGUL ROSU – Petrosani, Romania. Mar 1958-1962 – 3r – 1 – us L of C Photodup [949]

STEAM LOCOMOTIVE DRAWINGS / Great Northern and Northern Pacific Railway Companies – 1r – 1 – $35.00r – us M.H.S. [625]

STEAM NAVIGATION AND ITS RELATION TO THE COMMERCE OF CANADA AND THE UNITED STATES / Croil, James – Toronto: W. Briggs; Montreal: Montreal News, 1898. 02131. (Pre-1900 Canadiana) – 9 – cn C.I.H.M. [971]

STEAM WARFARE IN THE PARANA : A NARRATIVE OF OPERATIONS BY THE COMBINED SQUADRONS OF ENGLAND AND FRANCE / Mackinnon, Lauchlan Bellingham – 2v 1848 – 9 – $40.00 – uk Libr Preservation [941]

STEAMBOATS AND STEAMBOATMEN OF THE UPPER MISSISSIPPI: DESCRIPTIVE, PERSONAL AND HISTORICAL / Merrick, George B – Articles published in the Saturday Evening Post, Burlington, Iowa, from 20 Sept 1913-24 Jan 1920 – 1r – 1 – $30.00 – us M.H.S. [978]

Ste-Antonie, Soeur *see* BIBLIOGRAPHIE CANADIENNE DES ARCHIVES MEDICALES D'UN HOPITAL, 1944-1950

Stearns, Ezra Scollay *see*
- GENEALOGICAL AND FAMILY HISTORY OF THE STATE OF NEW HAMPSHIRE
- HISTORY OF THE TOWN OF RINDGE 1736-1874

Stearns, Ezra Scollay et al *see* GENEALOGICAL AND FAMILY HISTORY OF NEW HAMPSHIRE

Stearns, George Luther *see* PAPERS OF GEORGE AND MARY STEARNS

Stearns, Mary E *see* PAPERS OF GEORGE AND MARY STEARNS

Stearns, Oakman S *see* INTRODUCTION TO THE BOOKS OF THE OLD TESTAMENT

Stearns, Oakman Sprague *see*
- INTRODUCTION TO THE...OLD TESTAMENT: WITH...ILLUSTRATIVE LITERATURE
- A SYLLABUS OF THE MESSIANIC PASSAGES IN THE OLD TESTAMENT

Stearns, Wallace Nelson *see*
- FRAGMENTS FROM GRAECO-JEWISH WRITERS
- A MANUAL OF PATROLOGY

STEAUA NOASTRA – New York, NY, 1912-1931 – 2r – 1 – us I.H.R.C. [978]

STEAUA ROSIE – Tirgu-Mures, Romania. 1962-Jul 1979 – 25r – 1 – us L of C Photodup [949]

Stebbing, Henry *see*
- A CAUTION AGAINST RELIGIOUS DELUSION
- AN EARNEST AND AFFECTIONATE ADDRESS TO THE PEOPLE CALLED METHODISTS

Stebbins, Rufus Phineas *see* A STUDY OF THE PENTATEUCH

Stech, Vaclav *see* STESTI ZLATEHO HROZNU: PREDMSTSKY ROMAN

STECHAEPFEL : EIN FRUEHLINGSGEDICHT / Ilgen, Pedro – Highland, IL: P Ilgen, [19–?] – 1r – 1 – us U.W. Library [810]

Steciak, David M *see* A COMPARISON OF SELECTED NEUROMUSCULAR AND KINEMATIC VARIABLES BEFORE AND AFTER LEARNING AN AIMING TASK

Steck, A *see* DISSERTATIO INAUGURALIS MEDICA DE SAGU

Steck, Franz Xaver *see* DIE LITURGIE DER KATHOLISCHE ARMENIER

Steck, Rudolf *see* DER GALATERBRIEF

Stedelijk Museum, Amsterdam *see* MALEVICH ARCHIVE

STEDSNAVN – 1939 – 1 – us I.U. Libraries [390]

Steedman, H F *see* ZOOPLANKTON FIXATION AND PRESERVATION

STEEL COMMITTEE / UN Economic Commission for Europe (ECE) – 1947-89 – E/F.664 E.486 F.604 R.663 – 9 – us U.N. Pubs [340]

Steel, David *see* THE ELEMENTS AND PRACTICE OF NAVAL ARCHITECTURE

STEEL IN THE USSR – v1- 1971- – 1,5,6,9 – us UMI [670]

Steel, John *see* SERMONS

STEEL LABOR : 1936-1955 / United Steel Workers of America – (Coll title: Labor Union Periodicals, Pt 1) – 3r – 1 – $405.00 – 1-55655-249-1 – us UPA [331]

STEEL LABOR – Indianapolis. Ind. 1959-1966 – 1 – us UMI [071]

Steel, William A *see* LEGISLATIVE SOUVENIR MANUAL 1895-1896

STEELE CITY NEWS – Steele City, NE. -w. Jan 1929-Jan 1940 – 1 – us NE Hist [071]

STEELE CITY PRESS – Steele City, NE. -w. Mar 1908; Oct 1908-Jul 1923; Nov 1923-Oct 1928 – 1 – us NE Hist [071]

STEELE CITY STANDARD – Steele City, NE. -w. Nov 1892; Oct 1895-Apr 1900 – 1 – us NE Hist [071]

Steele, Francesca Maria *see* MONASTERIES AND RELIGIOUS HOUSES OF GREAT BRITAIN AND IRELAND

Steele, James E *see* HISTORY OF CLAY COUNTY TO 1909

Steele, Joshua *see* AN ESSAY TOWARDS ESTABLISHING THE MELODY AND MEASURE OF SPEECH TO BE EXPRESSED AND PERPETUATED BY PECULIAR SYMBOLS

Steele, Kristy J *see* IDENTIFICATION OF BODY BUILT STEREOTYPES IN PREADOLESCENTS

Steele, Oliver Hazard Perry *see* AUTOBIOGRAPHY AND JEFFERSON LODGE MINUTES

Steele, Sherman *see* EQUITY JURISPRUDENCE.

STEELHEAD – Waldport, OR. -w. 20 Feb 1947-15 Jan 1948. 1 roll – 1 – us U.O. Library [071]

STEELTON ITEM – Steelton, PA. -w 1879-1885 – 13 – $25.00r – us I.M.R. [071]

STEELTON PRESS – Steelton, PA. -w 1903-1912 – 13 – $25.00r – us I.M.R. [071]

STEELTON REPORTER – Steelton, PA. -d,-w 1882-1912 – 13 – $25.00r – us I.M.R. [071]

Steenbergen, F van *see*
- LES OEUVRES ET LA DOCTRINE DE SIGER DE BRABANT
- SIGER DE BRABANT D'APRES SES OEUVRES INEDITES, VOL 1
- SIGER DE BRABANT D'APRES SES OEUVRES INEDITES, VOL 2

Steenis, C G G J van *see* FLORA MALESIANA

Steensby, H P *see*
- AN ANTHROPOGEOGRAPHICAL STUDY OF THE ORIGIN OF THE ESKIMO CULTURE
- CONTRIBUTIONS TO THE ETHNOLOGY AND ANTHROPOGEOGRAPHY OF THE POLAR ESKIMOS
- ETNOGRAFISKE OF ANTROPO-GEOGRAFISKE REJSETUDIER I NORD-GRONLAND
- OM ESKIMOKULTURENS OPRINDELSE

Steenstra, Peter Henry *see* THE BEING OF GOD AS UNITY AND TRINITY

Steenstrup, J J S *see* ON THE ALTERNATION OF GENERATIONS

Steeves, Sarah H *see* BOOK OF REMEMBERANCES OF MARION COUNTY PIONEERS

STEFAN GEORGES GEDICHTZYKLUS "PILGERFAHRTEN" IN EINZELANALYSEN / Lach, Friedrich – Frankfurt a.M., 1974 – 2mf – 9 – DM62.00 – 3-89349-639-4 – gw Hänsel [430]

STEFAN ZWEIG : EINE GEDENK-SCHRIFT / Zech, Paul – Buenos Aires: Quadriga Verlag, 1943 – 1r – 1 – us U.W. Library [430]

Stefani, Marie T *see* SHAKER COLLECTION, 1723-1952

Stefanini, Giuseppe *see* I POSSEDIMENTE ITALIANI IN AFRICA (LIBIA, ERITREA, SOMALIA)

Stefanini, Giuseppi *see* IN SOMALIA

Stefansson, Vilhjalmur *see*
- ARCTIC EXPEDITION DIARIES OF VILHJALMUR STEFANSSON
- ENCYCLOPEDIA ARCTICA
- THE FRIENDLY ARCTIC
- MY LIFE WITH THE ESKIMO
- PREHISTORIC AND PRESENT COMMERCE AMONG THE ARCTIC COAST ESKIMO
- THE STEFANSSON-ANDERSON ARCTIC EXPEDITION OF THE AMERICAN MUSEUM

THE STEFANSSON-ANDERSON ARCTIC EXPEDITION OF THE AMERICAN MUSEUM / Stefansson, Vilhjalmur – BN 404 2. 1919 – 8 – ne IDC [910]

Steffen, Hans-Michael *see* UNTERSUCHUNGEN ZUR REVALGISIERUNG UND ZUM ANTETORSIONSREZIDIV NACH INTERTROCHANTEREN OSTEOTOMIEN BEI KINDERN UND JUGENDLICHEN

Stefke, Elmar J *see* THE EFFECT OF EXERCISE INTENSITY ON THE EXTENT OF AND RECOVERY FROM FATIGUE OF LONG DURATION

Stegeman, B *see* HET OUDE KERSPEL WINTERSWIJK
Steger, Franz *see* ERGAENZUNGS-CONVERSATIONSLEXIKON (AEL, ABT 1;19)
Steglich, Friedrich August William *see* GUTACHTEN VON GEISTLICHEN DER DIOECES GRIMMA UEBER DIE VORGESCHLAGENE VERDRAENGUNG DER VOLLSTAENDIGEN BIBEL AUS UNSERN VOLKSSCHULEN
DER STEGLITZER – Berlin, 1956-78 (incomplete) – 1 – Inquire at Mikrofilmarchiv for details – gw Misc Inst [072]
STEGLITZER ANZEIGER – Berlin, 1888-90, 1905-06, 1914-17, jul 1-dec 31 1918, 1921-nov 30 1923, 1924-nov 16 1929, 1930-apr 30 1931, sep 1 1931-aug 31 1932, 1933-40, apr 22 1951-may 18 1952 – 1 – Inquire at Mikrofilmarchiv for details – gw Misc Inst [943]
STEGLITZER LOKAL-ANZEIGER – Berlin, 1954-80 (incomplete) – 1 – Inquire at Mikrofilmarchiv for details – gw Misc Inst [072]
Stegmuller, F *see* REPERTORIUM COMMENTARIORUM IN SENTENTIAS PETRI LOMBARDI
Steguweit, Heinz *see*
- FROHES LEBEN
- INS VOLLE MENSCHENLEBEN
- KLEINES PARADIES
- DER KOENIG MIT DEM HANDGEPAECK
- LEIERMANN UND FIEDELBOGEN
- MIT VERGNUEGTEN SINNEN

Stehr, Hermann *see*
- DAMIAN, ODER, DAS GROSSE SCHERMESSER
- GESAMMELTE WERKE
- DIE KRAEHEN
- DER SCHINDELMACHER

Steibelt, Daniel *see*
- CHAMBER MUSIC. SELECTIONS
- DOUZE BACCHANALES POUR LE FORTE-PIANO AVEC ACCOMPAGNEMENT DE TAMBOURIN..
- EXERCISIS, HUIT, AVEC LEUR DOIGTE POUR LE PIANOFORTE TIREES DE LA METHODE DE PIANO...2ND EDITION
- FANTAISIE AVEC NEUF VARIATIONS SUR UN AIR DES MISTERES D'ISIS:POUR LE PIANOFORTE...
- GRAND CONCERTO A LA CHASSE, OP. 64
- A GRAND CONCERTO FOR THE PIANOFORTE, OP. 33
- GRAND SONATA POUR PIANO, VIOLON, VIOLONCELLE OU BASSOON, OP. 69
- [LE JUGEMENT DU BERGER PARIS] A SELECTION OF FAVORITE AURS IN THE GRAND BALLET CALLED LE JUGEMENT DU BERGER PARIS AS PERFORMED... AT THE KING'S THEATRE
- LECONS, DOUZE, AVEC LEUR GOIGTE POUR LE PIANO-FORTE...
- SONATES, DEUX, POUR PIANOFORTE AVEC ACCOMPAGNEMENT DE VIOLON ET VIOLONCELLE...OEUVRE 61
- SONATINAS, TROIS, POUR LE PIANOFORTE AVEC ACCOMPAGNEMENT DE FLUTE OU VIOLON, OP. 72
- TROIS QUATUORS POUR DEUX VIOLONS, ALTO ET BASSE
- TROIS SONATES POUR LE FORTEPIANO AVEC ACCOMPAGNEMENT DE FLUTE OU VIOLON...OP. 39
- TROIS SONATES POUR LE PIANO FORTE AVEC ACCOMPAGNT. DE VIOLON ET VIOLONCELLE

Steig, Reinhold *see* NEUE KUNDE ZU HEINRICH VON KLEIST
Steiger, Ernst *see* DORNROSEN ERSTLINGSBLUETHEN DEUTSCHER LYRIK IN AMERIKA
DER STEIGERNDE STIL IN DER TRAGOEDIE FRIEDRICH HEBBELS / Schmidt, Hans – (Includes bibliographical references) – [S.l.: s.n.], 1910 (Dresden: Druck von C Heinrich) – 1r – 1 – us U.W. Library [430]
Stein, C F *see* STEIN'S DECISIONS
Stein, Gary L *see* THE RELAPSE PREVENTION MODEL AND EXERCISE MAINTENANCE BEHAVIOR
Stein, Guenther *see* CHUNGKING DAN YENAN
Stein, J P E F *see* CATALOGUS COLEOPTERORUM EUROPAE
Stein, M A *see* CATALOGUE OF THE SANSKRIT MSS IN THE RAGHUNATHA TEMPLE LIBRARY OF HIS HIGHNESS THE MAHARAJA OF JAMMU AND KASHMIR
Stein, Philipp *see* GOETHE-BRIEFE
Stein, S F N von *see*
- DER ORGANISMUS DER INFUSIONSTHIERE
- VERGLEICHENDE ANATOMIE UND PHYSIOLOGIE DER INSECTEN IN MONOGRAPHIEN BEARBEITET

STEIN UND MOERTEL : ZIEGEL- UND BAUINDUSTRIE – Berlin, Germany. Jan 1897-Dec 1909 – 7r – 1 – uk British Libr Newspaper [690]
STEINAUER STAR-POST – Steinauer, NE. -w. Nov 1895-Jan 1896; Mar 1896-May 1898; Mar-Dec 1899; Feb 1900-Jan 1901; Apr 1901-May 1925 – 1 – us NE Hist [071]
Steinbach, Pia *see* ZELLULAERE WIRKUNGEN VON ULTRASCHALLSTOSSWELLEN
Steinbeck, Johannes *see* DAS VERHAELTNIS VON THEOLOGIE UND ERKENNTNISTHEORIE
Steinbeck, John *see* JOHN STEINBECK COLLECTION
Steinberg, A *see* SIMON DUBNOV, L'HOMME ET SON OUEVRE
Steinberg, Johannes *see* DIE REYEN IN DEN TRAUERSPIELEN DES ANDREAS GRYPHIUS
Steinberger, Julius *see* LUCIANS EINFLUSS AUF WIELAND
Steinbrenner, Manfred *see*
- DADAISMUS UND RELIGION
- "FLUCHT AUS DER ZEIT?" ANARCHISMUS, KULTURKRITIK UND CHRISTLICHE MYSTIK – HUGO BALLS KONVERSIONEN
- THEORETISCHER ANARCHISMUS UND "IMITATIO CHRISTI"

Steinbrunner, Pamela J *see* ASSESSMENT TOOLS USED BY ELEMENTARY LEVEL ADAPTED PHYSICAL EDUCATORS IN WISCONSIN
Steinbuechel, Theodor *see* NIETZSCHE
Steincipher, John *see* CODE OF THE TRUST TERRITORY OF THE PACIFIC, 1970 REV
Steindler, Arthur *see* MECHANICS OF NORMAL AND PATHOLOGICAL LOCOMOTION IN MAN
Steindorff, G *see* DIE APOKALYPSE DES ELIAS (T.U.U. 2-17/3A)
Steinecke, Hartmut *see* ANTI-NAPOLEONISCHE PAMPHLETE
STEINER : THE TRIAL – 1r – $49.50 – us African Imprint [340]
Steiner, Emil *see* FRIEDRICH HAUGS EPIGRAMME UND IHRE QUELLEN
Steiner, Gustav *see* GOTTFRIED KELLER
Steiner, Herbert *see* VERZEICHNIS DER ERSTDRUCKE HOFMANNSTHALS
Steiner, Rudolf *see*
- GOETHE ALS VATER EINER NEUEN AESTHETIK
- GRUNDLINIEN EINER ERKENNTNISTHEORIE DER GOETHESCHEN WELTANSCHAUUNG MIT BESONDERER RUECKSICHT AUF SCHILLER

Steinfuehrer, W *see* DER GANZE PROLOG DES JOHANNESEVANGELIUMS IN SATZFOLGE UND -GLIEDERUNG WOERTLICHES CITAT AUS JESAIA
Steinhart, Edward I *see* INTERVIEWS FOR TRANSITION IN WESTERN UGANDA, 1891-1901
Steinhaus, Arthur H *see* CHRONIC EFFECTS OF EXERCISE
Steinhausen, Heinrich *see* IRMELA
Steinhorst, Ulrich H *see* PHARMACOLOGICAL TREATMENT OF INTRACOULAR PROLIFERATIVE EMTITIES
Steininger, Anton *see* TROTZ VERBOT NICHT TOT
Steininger, Wanda K *see* ATTITUDES TOWARD PHYSICAL ACTIVITY OF OBESE AND NON-OBESE CHILDREN AND THEIR PARENTS
DIE STEINKLOPFER / Saar, Ferdinand von; ed by Handschin, Charles Hart & Roedder, Edwin Carl – (German text with introd & notes in English) – New York: H Holt, 1906 – 1r – 1 – us U.W. Library [830]
Steinlein, A *see* BUNTE BLUETHEN
Steinmann, Alexander *see* ERSTE UNTERSUCHUNGEN UEBER BIODISTRIBUTION UND THERAPEUTISCHE EFFEKTE NEUARTIGER ALBUMIN-CYTOSTATIKA-KONJUGATE
Steinmann, Alphons *see* DIE ABFASSUNGSZEIT DES GALATERBRIEFES
Steinmann, Theophil *see* DIE GEISTIGE OFFENBARUNG GOTTES IN DER GESCHICHTLICHEN PERSON JESU
Steinmetz, Rudolf *see* DIE ZWEITE ROEMISCHE GEFANGENSCHAFT DES APOSTELS PAULUS
Steinmeyer, E *see* DIE ALTHOCHDEUTSCHEN GLOSSEN
Steinmeyer, Franz Ludwig *see*
- DIE GESCHICHTE DER AUFERWECKUNG DES LAZARUS
- THE HISTORY OF THE PASSION AND RESURRECTION OF OUR LORD
- THE MIRACLE OF OUR LORD IN RELATION TO MODERN CRITICISM
- DIE WUNDERTHATEN DES HERRN: ZUM ERWEISE DES GLAUBENS

Steinmueller, Paul *see* EINFUEHRUNG DER REFORMATION IN DIE KURMARK BRANDENBURG DURCH JOACHIM
Steinmueller Zierer, Maria *see* BAUERNSCHRITT
STEIN'S DECISIONS / Stein, C F – 1v. 1921-36 (all publ) – 6mf – 9 – $9.00 – LLMC 84-153 – us L.L.M.C. [340]
Steinschneider, M *see*
- DIE ARABISCHE LITERATUR DER JUDEN, EIN BEITRAG ZUR LITERATURGESCHICHTE DER ARABER GROSSENTEILS AUS HANDSCHRIFTLICHEN QUELLEN
- GESAMMELTE SCHRIFTEN
- HEBRAEISCHE BIBLIOGRAPHIE, BLAETTER FUER NEUERE UND AELTERE LITERATUR DES JUDENTHUMS...
- DIE HEBRAEISCHEN HANDSCHRIFTEN DER K. HOF- UND STAATSBIBLIOTHEK IN MUENCHEN, BESCHRIEBEN...
- DIE HEBRAEISCHEN UEBERSETZUNGEN DES MITTELALTERS UND DIE JUDEN ALS DOLMETSCHER, EIN BEITRAG ZUR LITERATURGESCHICHTE DES MITTELALTERS...
- KA'ARAT HA-KESEL
- POLEMISCHE UND APOLOGETISCHE LITERATUR IN ARABISCHER SPRACHE, ZWISCHEN MUSLIMEN, CHRISTEN UND JUDEN...
- RANGSTREITLITERATUR
- TEHILLAH LE-MOSHEH

Steinstra, Donna *see*
- DECIDING CASES WITHOUT ARGUMENT
- THE JOINT TRIAL CALENDARS IN THE WESTERN DISTRICT OF MISSOURI
- THE ROLE OF STAFF ATTORNEYS AND FACE-TO-FACE CONFERENCING IN NON-ARGUMENT DECISIONMAKING
- UNPUBLISHED DISPOSITIONS
- VISITING JUDGES IN FEDERAL DISTRICT COURTS

Steinthal, Heymann *see* ZUR GESCHICHTE SAULS UND DAWIDS
STEIRISCHE BEITRAEGE ZUR HYDROGEOLOGIE – v.25-33, 1973-81. Earlier vols. upon request. ISSN:0376-4826 – 1,5,6,9,13 – 34.00v – us UMI [550]
Stekel, Wilhelm *see* PECULIARITIES OF BEHAVIOR; WANDERING MANIA, DIPSOMANIA, CLEPTOMANIA, PYROMANIA AND ALLIED IMPULSIVE ACTS
Stekla, Herbert *see* DER REGRESSUS IN INFINITUM IN DER ARISTOTELISCHEN PHILOSOPHIE
Stelfox, A W *see* LAND AND FRESH-WATER MOLLUSCA (FROM CLARE ISLAND)
LA STELLA – Utica, NY, July-Dec. 1932 – 43mf or 1r – 1,9 – us I.H.R.C. [978]
Stella, C di *see* POSTE PER DIVERSE PARTI DEL MONDO, ...
STELLA LEADER – Stella, NE. -w. Apr-Jul 1894 – 1 – us NE Hist [071]
STELLA ME ABRIU A PORTA / Cruz, Eddy Diaz de – Port Alegre. 1942 – 1 – us Res Libr [972]
STELLALANDER, DE – Vryburg, South Africa. 2 Feb-31 Aug 1899. 1 reel – 1, 16 diazo available at reduced price – sa SA Libr [072]
STELLARIO : REVISTA DE ARTE – Curitiba, 15 Oct-Dec 1905; 1 Apr 1906 – 1,5,6 – bl Biblioteca [072]
Stellhorn, F W *see* THE ERROR OF MODERN MISSOURI
Stellman, Jeanne Mager *see* WOMEN AND HEALTH
DIE STELLUNG AEGYPTENS SEIT 1922 / Harnier, J A von – Regensburg, 1931 – 2mf – 1 – ILM-1942/1 – ne IDC [327]
DIE STELLUNG AUGUSTINS IN DER PUBLICISTIK DER GREGORIANISCHEN KIRCHENSTREITS / Mirbt, Carl – Leipzig: J.C. Hinrichs, 1888 – 1mf – us A.T.L.A. [240]
DIE STELLUNG CHRISTI IM LITURGISCHEN GEBET. L.T.Q 19/20 / Jungmann, J A – Muenster Westf., 1925 – 5mf – 8 – Dfl28.00 – ne Slangenburg [240]
DIE STELLUNG DER CONCILIEN, PAEPSTE UND BISCHOEFE : VOM HISTORISCHEN UND CANONISTISCHEN STANDPUNKTE: UND DIE PAEPSTLICHE CONSTITUTION VOM 18. JULI 1870 / Schulte, Johann Friedrich von – Prag: F Tempsky, 1871 – 2mf – 9 – 0-8370-8548-9 – 1986-2548 – us A.T.L.A. [240]
DIE STELLUNG DER FRAU IM LEBEN / Morgenstern, Lina (Bauer) et al – Kiel: Lipsius und Tischer, 1891 – 1r – 1 – us U.W. Library [170]
DIE STELLUNG DER KAISERLICHEN FRAUEN AUS DEM JULISCH-CLAUDISCHEN HAUSE / Sandels, Friedrich – Gießen, 1912 – 1mf – 9 – DM48.00 – 3-89349-355-7 – gw Hänsel [305]
DIE STELLUNG DER KONSTANZER BISCHOEFE ZU PAPST UND KAISER WAEHREND DES INVESTITURSTREITS / Hofmann, Ernst – Freiburg, 1930 – 1mf – 9 – DM48.00 – 3-89349-336-0 – gw Hänsel [240]
DIE STELLUNG DER LUTHERISCHEN KIRCHE DEUTSCHLANDS ZUR MISSION IM 17. JAHRHUNDERT / Groessel, Wolfgang – Leipzig-R.: O. Schmidt, 1895 – 1mf – us A.T.L.A. [240]
DIE STELLUNG DER PHILANTHROPISTEN ZUM RELIGIONSUNTERRICHT / Bahlcke, H – Meissen: C E Klinkicht, [1900] – 1mf – 9 – 0-8370-7524-6 – 1986-1524 – us A.T.L.A. [370]
DIE STELLUNG DER RELIGION IM GEISTESLEBEN / Kalweit, Paul – (Includes bibliographical references) – Leipzig: B G Teubner, 1908 – 1mf – 9 – 0-8370-3841-3 – 1985-1841 – us A.T.L.A. [200]
DIE STELLUNG DER RELIGION IM GEISTESLEBEN / Kalweit, Paul – (Includes bibliographical references) – Leipzig: B G Teubner, 1908 – 1mf – 9 – 0-8370-3841-3 – 1985-1841 – us A.T.L.A. [200]
DIE STELLUNG DER SCHWABEN ZU GOETHE / Thiess, Frank – Stuttgart: W Kohlhammer, 1915 – 1r – 1 – us U.W. Library [430]
DIE STELLUNG DES APOSTOLISCHEN SYMBOLS IM KIRCHLICHEN LEBEN DES MITTELALTERS 1 : SYMBOL UND KATECHUMENAT / Wiegand, F – Leipzig, 1899 – 7mf – 8 – ne Slangenburg [210]
DIE STELLUNG DES ERSTEN CLEMENSBRIEFES, INNERHALB DER ENTWICKLUNG DER ALTCHRISTLICHEN GEMEINDEVERFASSUNG UND DES KIRCHENRECHTS (T.U.U. 4-47/1) / Gerke, F – Leipzig, 1931 – 3mf – 9 – ne Slangenburg [240]
DIE STELLUNG DES EUROPAEISCHEN PARLAMENTS IN DER EUROPAEISCHEN WIRTSCHAFTSGEMEINSCHAFT BIS ZUR FUSION DER EXEKUTIVEN : DAS PROBLEM DER EINFLUSSNAHME AUF DEN ENTSCHEIDUNGSPROZESS / Sen, Asit Kumar – Heidelberg, 1969 – 9 – DM60.00 – 3-89349-283-6 – gw Hänsel [320]
DIE STELLUNG DES PROPHETEN JESAJA ZUR POLITIK SEINER ZEIT / Kuechler, Friedrich – Tuebingen: J.C.B. Mohr, 1906. 1 fiche – 9 – us A.T.L.A. [240]
DIE STELLUNG DES STAATES ZUR KIRCHE IN BEZUG AUF DEN RELIGIONSUNTERRICHT IN DER SCHULE IN PREUSSEN, ENGLAND UND DEN VEREINIGTEN STAATEN VON NORDAMERIKA / Brown, Elmer E – Halle: Ehrhardt Karras, 1890 – 1mf – 9 – 0-8370-7530-0 – 1986-1530 – us A.T.L.A. [370]
DIE STELLUNG DES THOMAS VON AQ. ZU AVENCEBROL : BGPHMA 3/3 / Wittmann, M – Muenster, 1990 – 2mf – 9 – ne Slangenburg [240]
DIE STELLUNG DES THOMAS VON AQ. ZU AVENCEBROL / Wittmann, M – Muenster, 1900 – 2mf – 8 – ne Slangenburg [100]
DIE STELLUNG DES URCHRISTENTUMS ZUM STAAT / Weinel, Heinrich – Tuebingen: Mohr, 1908 – 1mf – us A.T.L.A. [240]
DIE STELLUNG DES WEIBES ZU JAHWE-RELIGION UND -KULT / Loehr, Max – Leipzig: J.C. Hinrichs, 1908. 1 fiche – 9 – us A.T.L.A. [240]
DIE STELLUNG EZECHIELS IN DER ALTTESTAMENTLICHEN PROPHETIE / Arndt, Theodor – Berlin: A Haack, 1885 – 1mf – 9 – 0-8370-2114-6 – 1985-0114 – us A.T.L.A. [220]

DIE STELLVERTRETENDE BEDEUTUNG DER PERSON JESU CHRISTI / Cremer, Ernst - (Includes bibliographical references & index) - 2. neu bearb Aufl. Guetersloh: C Bertelsmann, 1900 - 1mf - 9 - 0-8370-2829-9 - 1985-0829 - us A.T.L.A. [240]
Stelter, Franz *see* DER KREIS NEUSTETTIN
STELTON FIRST BAPTIST CHURCH OF PISCATAWAY. STELTON, NEW JERSEY : CHURCH RECORDS - 1781-1855. 172p - 1 - 7.74 - us Baptist [240]
Stelzele, Charles *see*
- AMERICAN SOCIAL AND RELIGIOUS CONDITIONS
- CHRISTIANITY'S STORM CENTRE
- THE CHURCH AND LABOR
- THE CHURCH AND THE LABOR MOVEMENT
- THE GOSPEL OF LABOR
- MESSAGES TO WORKINGMEN
- THE WORKINGMAN AND SOCIAL PROBLEMS

Stelzer, Otto *see* GOETHE UND DIE BILDENDE KUNST
STEM UIT BELGIE *see* ECHO DE BELGIQUE (DE STEM UIT BELGIE)
Ste-Marthe-de-la-Trinite *see* BIO-BIBLIOGRAPHIE ANALYTIQUE DU REVEREND PERE LAURENT TREMBLAY, O.M.I., MISSIONNAIRE ECRIVAIN...
Ste-Martine, Soeur *see* BIBLIOGRAPHIE
Stemm, John D *see* EFFECTS OF AQUATIC SIMULATED AND DRY LAND PLYOMETRICS ON VERTICAL JUMP HEIGHT
Stemsrud, David Walter *see* STUDIEN ZUM STABVERHALTEN DES FINITIVEN VERBS IN DER ALTENGLISCHEN UND ALTSAECHSISCHEN STABREIMDICHTUNG
STENAHRAFICHNAI A SPRAVAZDACHA / Byelorussian S.S.R. Usebelaruski zezd saveta u rabochykh, si ali anskikh i chyrvona-arme iskikh d eputata u - (Includes c.1: v.9 1929) - Mensk: T SVK BSSR, 1927 - 1 - CSUXAKY6470-S - us Hoover Inst Photo [947]
STENARBETAREN - Kopenhamn, Malmo, Lysekil. Sweden. 1897-1921 - 1 reel - 1 - sw Kungliga [330]
Stenay, Victor de *see* LOUIS 17 VENGE: OU, LE DERNIER MOT DE L'HISTOIRE SUR LE VRAI DAUPHIN (BARON DE RICHEMONT)..
STENCIL BULLETIN / Wisconsin. Agricultural Experiment Station - Feb. 1948-Mar 1950,n.1-9 - 1,5 - us Spaulding [630]
STENCIL BULLETIN AND REVISIONS / Wisconsin. Agricultural Extension Service - Jul 1915-Mar 1931, nos.1-109 - 1,5 - us Spaulding [630]
STENCIL CIRCULAR AND REVISIONS / Wisconsin. Agricultural Extension Service - n.110-327. 1931-51 - 1,5 - us Spaulding [630]
Stendahl, K *see* THE SCHOOL OF ST MATTHEW AND ITS USE OF THE OLD TESTAMENT
Stender-Petersen, A *see* SLAVISCH-GERMANISCHE LEHNWORTKUNDE
Stendhal, Marie-Henri Beyle *see* D'UN NOUVEAU COMPLOT CONTRE LES INDUSTRIELS
Stendhal, M-Henri Beyle *see* MEMOIRES D'UN TOURISTE, T. 2
Stengel Georg *see* OVA PASCHALIA SACRO EMBLEMATE INSCRIPTA DESCRIPTAQUE
Stengel, Karl *see* DER EINHEITLICHE FESTELLUNGSBESCHEID
Stenger, Gerhard *see*
- GOETHE AND AUGUST VON KOETZEBUE
- GOETHE UND AUGUST VON KOTZEBUE

STEN'KA RAZIN / Kamenskii, V - Roman. M. 1916. BR-946 2 - 8 - ne IDC [947]
STENNAIA GAZETA GLAVPOLITPROSVETA A.S.S.R. - (Includes c.1: v.1:no.20 1921:Apr. 20) - Baku: [Glavpolitprosvet], 1921 - 1 - CSUXADM8130-S - us Hoover Inst Photo [320]
STENNAIA GAZETA LUZHSKOGO OTDELENIIA PETERB. BIURO ROSTA - (Includes c.1: no. 168=no.298 1921:Nov.6) - Luga: [Otdelenie], 19uu - 1 - CSUXADM8073-S - us Hoover Inst Photo [073]
STENNAIA GAZETA ROSTA - (Includes c.1: no.411 1920:Dec.16) - Moskva: ROSTA, 19uu - 1 - CSUXADM8102-S - us Hoover Inst Photo [073]
STENOGRAFICHESKI I OTCHET PLENARNYKH ZASEDANI I VSEROSSI ISKOGO SEZDA UPRAVLI AI USHCHIKH MESTNYMI UCHREZHDENII AMI GOSUDARSTVENNOGO BANKA, 19-22 DEKABRI A 1922 G / Gosudarstvenny i bank RSFSR. Vserossi iski i sezd upravli ai ushchikh mestnymi uchrezhdenii ami (1922: Moscow, R.S.F.S.R.) - Moskva: [s.n.], 1922 - 1 - CSUX91-B1223 - us Hoover Inst Photo [332]
STENOGRAFICHESKI I OTCHET...SESSII T SENTRALNOGO ISPOLNITELNOGO KOMITETA B.S.S.R... / Byelorussian S.S.R. TS entralny vykana uchny kamit et - (Includes c.1: 6 sozyv:4 sess ia 1925:Feb) - Minsk: T SIK, 1924 - 1 - CSUXAKY5565-S - us Hoover Inst Photo [947]
STENOGRAFICHESKI OTCHET / Vsesoiuznaia Kommunisticheskaya Partiia Bol'shevikov. S'ezd Rossiiskoi Kommunisticheskoi Partii (b) - S'ezd 7-18. 1918-1939. Petrograd etc - 1 - us NY Public [335]
STENOGRAFICHESKIE OTCHETY / Russia. Gosudarstvennyi Sovyet - Apr 28 1906-Feb 14 1917. 25v - 1 - 169.00 - us L of C Photodup [947]
STENOGRAFICHESKIE OTCHETY / S'ezd narodov Vostoka. 1st, Baku - 1-8 Sept. 1920 G. Petrograd, 1920 - 1 - 35.00r - us Hoover Inst Photo [335]
STENOGRAFICHESKIE OTCHETY MOSKOVSKOGO SOVETA RABOCHIKH I KRASNOARME ISKIKH DEPUTATOV / Moskovski i sovet rabochikh, kresti anskikh i krasnoarme iskikh deputatov - (Includes c.1: 1919-1921) - Moskva: [s.n.], 19uu - 1 - CSUXAKY9885-S - us Hoover Inst Photo [947]
STENOGRAFICHESKII OTCHET / Kommunisticheskaia Partiia Sovetskogo Soiuza - S'ezd: Stenograficheskii Otchet, 1918-39 - 4r - 1 - us Ross [335]
STENOGRAFICHESKII OTCHET / Russia. (1917-R.S.F.S.R.). S'ezd Sovetov - v. 2-16. 1917-35 - 1 - $59.00 - us L of C Photodup [947]
STENOGRAFICHESKII OTCHET / Trete Gubernskoe soveshchanie predsedatelei uispolkomov Tambovsko i gubernii - Tambov: Gos. izdvo, Tambovsk. otd., 1920 - 1 - CSUX91-B2152 - us Hoover Inst Photo [320]
STENOGRAFICHESKII OTCHET / U.S.S.R. S'Ezd Sovietov Soiuza Sovietskikh Sotsialisticheskikh Respublik - (Congress of the Union of Soviet Socialist Republics: Stenographic reports). 1922-36 - 3 - us Readex [324]
STENOGRAFICHESKII OTCHET / U.S.S.R. Zasedaniia Verkhovnogo Sovieta SSSR - (Congress...Meetings of the Supreme Soviet of the USSR: Stenographic reports). 1938-64 - 3 - us Readex [324]
STENOGRAFICHESKII OTCHET / Vserossiiskoe soveshchanie sovetov rabochikh i soldatskikh deputatov. Leningrad - 1917. Moscow, 1927 - 1 - 35.00r - us Hoover Inst Photo [335]
STENOGRAFICHESKII OTCHET / Vsesoiuznaia Kommunisticheskaia Partiia...S'ezd - Moscow, 1923-1939 - 3 - us Readex [947]
STENOGRAFICHESKII OTCHETY / Russia. Gosudarstvennaia duma, I-II - St. Petersburg, 1906-07.Stenographic records of the First and Second Convocations of the Russian State Duma. BR-238- - 8 - ne IDC [947]
STENOGRAFICHESKII OTCHETY / Russia. Gosudarstvennaia duma, III - St. Petersburg, 1908-12.Stenographic records of the Third convocation of the Russian State Duma. Sessions 1-5, with index and suppls. BR-4238/2 - 8 - ne IDC [947]
STENOGRAFICHESKII OTCHETY / Russia. Gosudarstvennaia duma, IV - St. Petersburg, 1912-17.Stenographic records of the Fourth convocation of the Russian State Duma, Sessions 1-5. Lacking: Session 4 (1915-16), v1 of the Annexes to the Stenog. Reports. BR-4239/2 - 8 - ne IDC [947]
STENOGRAFICHESKOE OTCHETY / Russia. Gosudarstvennaia Duma. I-IV - Apr. 27 May 10, 1906-Feb. 25 Mar. 11, 1917. Missing: 4 scattered stenograms - 1 - 35.00r - us Hoover Inst Photo [324]
STENOGRAFICZNE SPRAWOZDANIA / Galicia. Sejm - Lwow. 1861-1913 14 - 1 - 1,597.00 - us L of C Photodup [947]
LE STENOGRAPHE CANADIEN - Montreal: J de Larochelle, [1889-1910] - 9 - cn C.I.H.M. [650]
THE STENOGRAPHER'S AND TYPEWRITER'S COMPANION *see* THE STENOGRAPHER'S COMPANION
THE STENOGRAPHER'S COMPANION - (Cont: The Stenographer's and Typewriters Companion) - Montreal: R Goltman, [1898?-19-] - 9 - cn C.I.H.M. [650]
THE STENOGRAPHIC EXPERT / Bottome, Willard B - New York: self-published?, 1910 - 3mf - 9 - $4.50 - LLMC 91-067 - us L.L.M.C. [340]
STENOGRAPHIC RECORDS / Russia. Gosudarstvennyi Sovet. Upper House of the Imperial Russian Government Council - 21v 1906-17 - 3 - us Readex [947]
STENOGRAPHIC RECORDS OF THE DEBATES IN THE IMPERIAL DUMA / Russia - 36 v. 1906-1917 - 3 - us Readex [324]
STENOGRAPHISCHE / Prussia. Landtag. Herrenhaus - 1849 50-1916 18 - 1 - 1081.00 - us L of C Photodup [324]
STENOGRAPHISCHE BERICHT. STENOGRAFICKE ZPRAVY / Bohemia. Zemsky Snem - 1868-1908 - 1 - 377.00 - us L of C Photodup [943]
STENOGRAPHISCHE BERICHTE DES REICHSTAGS DER WEIMARER REPUBLIK 1919-1933 : 1.-9. WAHLPERIODE - (Including the stenographical reports of the Nazi-time) - Berlin, 1919-1933. Hildesheim, 1989 - 1396mf - 9 - DM9,900.00 diazo DM11,900.00 silver - gw Olms [320]
STENOGRAPHISCHE BERICHTE UBER DIE VERHANDLUNGEN / Prussia. Landtag. Zweite Kammer - 1849-1916 18 - 1 - 2576.00 - us L of C Photodup [324]
STENOGRAPHISCHE BERICHTE UEBER DIE SITZUNGEN DER BURGERSCHAFT ZU HAMBURG / Hamburg.Burgerschaft - Hamburg.1899-1952. 32 reels - 1 - 23.00r - us L of C Photodup [943]
STENOGRAPHISCHE BERICHTE UEBER DIE VERHANDLUNGEN / Prussia. Landtag. Haus der Abgeordneten - 1849-1916 18 - 1 - 2.318.00 - us L of C Photodup [943]
STENOGRAPHISCHE BERICHTE UEBER DIE VERHANDLUNGEN DES DEUTSCHEN REICHSTAGES, DES NORDDEUTSCHEN BUNDES, BZW. AB 1871 DES DEUTSCHEN REICHSTAGES 1867-1918 : 1.-13. LEGISLATURPERIODE - (With additions and amendments) - Berlin, 1867-1918. Hildesheim, 1985-87 - 2298mf+ 47 color slides - 9 - DM16,800.00 diazo DM19,800.00 silver - gw Olms [943]
STENOGRAPHISCHE BERICHTE UND ANLAGEN UEBER DIE VERHANDLUNGEN DES REICHSTAGES DES NORDDEUTSCHEN BUNDES / Germany. North German Confederation, 1866-70. Reichstag - 1867-70 - 1 - $92.00 - us L of C Photodup [324]
STENOGRAPHISCHE PROTOKOLLE / Bukovina. Landtag - v. 1-11. 1861-1912 13. v. 1, 7 and scattered issues wanting - 1 - 411.00 - us L of C Photodup [949]
STENOGRAPHISCHE PROTOKOLLE : SITZUNGEN DER PROVISORISCHEN NATIONALVERSAMMLUNG FUER DEUTSCHOESTERREICH 1918 UND 1919, DER KONSTITUIERENDEN NATIONALVERSAMMLUNG DER REPUBLIK OESTERREICH 1919 UND 1920, DES NATIONALRATES DER REPUBLIK OESTERREICH 1920-1934 UND DES BUNDESRATES 1926-34 - (Sitzungen 269mf Beilagen 504mf Index 39mf) - Wien. 71v. 1918-1934 - 812mf - 9 - DM5,200.00 diazo DM5,900.00 silver - gw Olms [320]
STENOGRAPHISCHE PROTOKOLLE. / Austria. Lower. Lantag - v.1-11. Wahlperiode, 1861-1919 20 - 1 - 1705.00 - us L of C Photodup [324]
STENOGRAPHISCHE PROTOKOLLE DER LANDTAGE DES KOENIGREICHS SACHSEN SOWIE DES SPAETEREN FREISTAATES SACHSEN 1833-1933 : DIE SITZUNGEN DER 1. UND 2. KAMMER - 4200mf - 9 - subsc: DM16,800.00 diazo DM21,000.00 silver - gw Olms [320]
STENOGRAPHISCHE PROTOKOLLE DES ABGEORDNETENHAUSES DES REICHSRATHES / Austria. Reichsrat. Abgeordnetenhaus - v. 1-22. 1862-1918. Issues wanting - 1 - 4,178.00 - us L of C Photodup [943]
STENOGRAPHISCHE PROTOKOLLE UEBER DIE SITZUNGEN DES HAUSES DER ABGEORDNETEN DES OESTERREICHISCHEN REICHSRATHES 1861-1918 - Wien, 1862-1920. Hildesheim, 1990 - 5229mf - 9 - DM23,800.00 diazo DM28,800.00 silver - gw Olms [320]
STENOGRAPHISCHE PROTOKOLLE UEBER DIE SITZUNGEN DES HERRENHAUSES DES OESTERREICHISCHEN REICHSRATES 1861-1918 - Wien, 1862-1918. Hildesheim, 1990 - 698mf - 9 - DM4,600.00 diazo DM5,400.00 silver - gw Olms [320]
STENOGRAPHISCHE PROTOKOLLE UEBER DIE SITZUNGEN DES OESTERREICHISCHEN REICHSRATHES / Austria. Herrenhaus - Vienna. 1869 70-1917 18. Incomplete - 1 - us NY Public [324]
STENOGRAPHISCHER BERICHT / Deutscher Werkmeister-Verband - Duesseldorf. v10, 26-27, 29-30. 1897-1932. (Serial publications of German trade unions in the Memorial Library, University of Wisconsin-Madison.) - 1 - us U.W. Library [330]
STENOGRAPHISCHER BERICHT.. / Deutscher Werkmeister-Verband - Duesseldorf. 1902, 1908, 1910. (Serial publications of German trade unions in the Memorial Library, University of Wisconsin-Madison.) - 1 - us U.W. Library [330]
STENOGRAPHISCHER BERICHT.. / Deutscher Werkmeister-verband - Duesseldorf. 1930. (Serial publications of German trade unions in the Memorial Library, University of Wisconsin-Madison.) - 1 - us U.W. Library [330]
STENOGRAPHISCHER BERICHT UEBER.. / Deutscher Webertag. 2nd. Berlin - Crimmitschau. 1872. 70p. (Serial publications of German trade unions in the Memorial Library, University of Wisconsin-Madison.) - 1 - us U.W. Library [330]
STENOGRAPHISCHER BERICHT UEBER DIE VERHANDLUNGEN.. / Deutscher Handwerks- und Gewerbekammertag. Koenigsberg - Aug 1926. s.l., s.n., 1926? 152p. (Serial publications of German trade unions in the Memorial Library, University of Wisconsin-Madison.) - 1 - us U.W. Library [330]
STENOGRAPHISCHER BERICHT UEBER DIE VERHANDLUNGEN DER DEUTSCHEN CONSTITUIERENDEN NATIONALVERSAMMLUNG ZU FRANKFURT 1848-49 / ed by Wigard, F - Leipzig und Frankfurt a.M., 1848-49. Hildesheim, 1985 - 78mf - 9 - DM650.00 diazo DM800.00 silver - gw Olms [943]
STENOHRAFICHNY IZVIT ZASIDANNIA VERKHOVNOI RADI SRSR / Soviet Union, Verkhovnyi Sovet - (Includes c.1: 1942:June 18) - [Moskva]: Sovet, 1938 - 1 - CSUXAKY5943-S - us Hoover Inst Photo [320]
Stensen, N *see*
- DE MUSCULIS ET GLANDULIS OBSERVATIONUM SPECIMEN
- OBSERVATIONES ANATOMICAE...

Stentrup, Ferdinandus Aloisius *see* DE FIDE
STENUNGSUNDSPOSTEN - Lysekil, Sweden. 1981- - 1 - sw Kungliga [072]
A STEP BY STEP GUIDE TO CONCERT PLANNING FOR DANCE IN SECONDARY EDUCATION / Branson, Sheri W - 1989 - 178p 2mf - 9 - $8.00 - us Microform Publ [790]
Stepan, J *see*
- KNEKTERYM OTAZKAM PRIPRANEHO RIZENI
- SKONCENI PRIPRAVNEHO RIZENI PODLE TRESTNIHO RADI CSSR

Stepankowsky, Vladimir *see* THE RUSSIAN PLOT TO SEIZE GALICIA (AUSTRIAN RUTHENIA)
Stepanov, N *see* POEZIIA BURZHUAZNOGO UPADKA
Stepanov, N L *see* RUSSKAIA BASNIA 18 I NACHALA 19 VEKA
Stepanovskii, I K *see*
- KOOPERATSIIA I VOLOGODSKOE ARTEL'NOE MASLODELIE
- RUSSKOE MOLOCHNOE KHOZIAISTVO I KOOPERATSIIA

STEPFAMILY BULLETIN - v1- 1981- - 1,5,6,9 - us UMI [306]
Stephan, Horst *see*
- DIE LEHRE SCHLEIERMACHERS VON DER ERLOESUNG
- LUTHER IN DEN WANDLUNGEN SEINER KIRCHE

Stephan, Oskar *see* BEITRAEGE ZUR ASKANISCHEN VOLKSKUNDE
Stephani, F *see*
- ICONES HEPATICARUM
- SPECIES HEPATICARUM

Stephanopoli de Comnene, Dimo et Nicolaos *see* VOYAGE DE DIMO ET NICOLO STEPHANOPOLI EN GRECE PENDANT LES ANNEES 5 ET 6 REDIGE PAR UN PROFESSEUR DU PRYTANEE SERIEYS
Stephanopoli-Comnene, M N *see* GUIZOT DEMASQUE
Stephanus Henricus *see*
- THESAURUS GRAECAE LINGUAE

Stephanus, Henricus *see*
- THESAURUS GRAECAE LINGUAE
- THESAURUS LINGUAE GRAECAE

Stephanus, R *see*
- DICTIONARIOLUM PUERORUM TRIBUS LINGUIS LATINA, GALLICA ET GERMANICA CONSCRIPTUM...
- DICTIONARIVM, SEV LATINAE LINGUAE THESAURUS,...

STEPHEN : A SOLDIER OF THE CROSS / Kingsley, Florence Morse – Philadelphia: Henry Altemus, 1898 – 1mf – 9 – 0-8370-3899-5 – 1985-1899 – us A.T.L.A. [830]

STEPHEN BAR SUDALI, THE SYRIAN MYSTIK / Frothingham, A L – Leyden, 1886 – 2mf – 8 – ne Slangenburg [240]

Stephen F. Austin University. School of Forestry *see* BULLETIN

Stephen F. Austin University. Texas Forest Service *see*
- CIRCULAR
- TF NEWS

STEPHEN GRAHAM'S NEWSLETTER – nos 1-38. 1940-43 (incomplete) – 1r – 1 – ATLA S0713E – us A.T.L.A. [073]

Stephen, Henry John *see* A TREATISE ON THE PRINCIPLES OF PLEADING IN CIVIL ACTIONS...3RD AMERICAN FROM THE 2ND LONDON ED

Stephen, James Fitzjames *see*
- A DIGEST OF THE LAW OF EVIDENCE... FROM THE 15TH ED. (1899)...WITH BOTH GENERAL AMERICAN NOTES AND NOTES ESPECIALLY ADAPTED TO THE STATE OF OHIO
- A GENERAL VIEW OF THE CRIMINAL LAW OF ENGLAND
- HORAE SABBATICAE

Stephen, Leslie *see*
- AN AGNOSTIC'S APOLOGY
- ESSAYS ON FREETHINKING AND PLAINSPEAKING
- HISTORY OF ENGLISH THOUGHT IN THE EIGHTEENTH CENTURY
- HOURS IN A LIBRARY
- LECTURES AND ESSAYS BY WILLIAM KINGDON CLIFFORD
- THE LIFE OF SIR JAMES FITZJAMES STEPHEN, BART., K.C.S.I.
- THE PLAYGROUND OF EUROPE
- THE SCIENCE OF ETHICS

Stephens, Alexander H *see* PAPERS

Stephens, Anthony et al *see* FESTSCHRIFT FOR RALPH FARRELL

Stephens, David Ellis *see* THE CREATIVE USE OF THE LORD'S SUPPER AS A TEACHING TOOL FOR THE DOCTRINE OF ATONEMENT

Stephens, Dawn E *see* GOAL ORIENTATION AND MORAL ATMOSPHERE IN YOUTH SPORT

Stephens, Edward *see* INFIDELITY DISARMED

Stephens, Frederic George *see* SIR EDWIN LANDSEER

Stephens, J *see* CHRONICLES OF WESLEYAN METHODISM, SECOND DEPARTMENT

Stephens, J F *see*
- ILLUSTRATIONS OF BRITISH ENTOMOLOGY...
- A MANUAL OF BRITISH COLEOPTERA, OR BEETLES...
- THE NOMENCLATURE OF BRITISH INSECTS...

Stephens, James C *see* MANAGING COMPLEXITY

Stephens, John Vant *see*
- THE CAUSES LEADING TO THE ORGANIZATION OF THE CUMBERLAND PRESBYTERIAN CHURCH
- THE PRESBYTERIAN CHURCHES

Stephens, W P *see* CANOE AND BOAT BUILDING

Stephens, William Richard Wood *see*
- THE ENGLISH CHURCH FROM THE NORMAN CONQUEST TO THE ACCESSION OF EDWARD 1 (1066-1272)
- HILDEBRAND AND HIS TIMES
- THE LIFE AND LETTERS OF WALTER FARQUHAR HOOK..
- MEMORIALS OF THE SOUTH SAXON SEE AND CATHEDRAL CHURCH OF CHICHESTER
- SAINT JOHN CHRYSOSTOM, HIS LIFE AND TIMES

Stephens, Winifred *see* WOMEN OF THE FRENCH REVOLUTION

Stephenson Family *see* DIARIES AND ACCOUNTS

Stephenson, P D *see* THE WOMAN QUESTION

Stephenson, Robert L *see* RIVER BASIN SURVEYS PAPERS

Stephenson, Sheryl L *see* IS THERE A RELATIONSHIP BETWEEN PRENATAL EXERCISE AND POSTPARTUM DEPRESSION

Stepney, William *see* THE SPANISH SCHOOLE-MASTER

Stepniak, S *see* NIHILISM AS IT IS, BEING STEPNIAK'S PSEUD. PAMPHLETS ..

STEPS IN THE DARK – Philadelphia:J.B. Lippincott, [1863?] – 1mf – 9 – 0-8370-5354-4 – 1985-3354 – us A.T.L.A. [240]

STEPS INTO THE BLESSED LIFE / Meyer, Frederick Brotherton – Philadelphia: Henry Altemus, c1896 – 1mf – 9 – 0-8370-7177-1 – 1986-1177 – us A.T.L.A. [240]

Stepun, F A *see*
- PAMIATI A. BELOGO
- VIACHESLAV IVANOV

STER – Gdynia, Poland. Feb 1952-Jun 1958 – 2r – 1 – uk British Libr Newspaper [947]

Sterbeeck, F van *see* THEATRUM FUNGORUM

DER STERBENDE NAPOLEON. UNVEROEFFENTLICHTES TAGEBUCH / Lowe, Hudson; ed by Fremaux, Paul – Berlin, 1911 – 9 – DM48.00 – 3-89349-278-X – gw Hänsel [920]

STEREO – (1978-. 5,6,9) – 1960- – 1 – us UMI [600]

STEREO REVIEW – (v26-49. 1971-84. 5,6. v34-49. 1975-84. 9) – v1-49. Feb 1958-1984 – 1 – us UMI [073]

LE STEREOMETRICON: CUBAGE DE TOUS LES CORPS PAR UNE SEULE ET MEME REGLE / Baillairge, Charles – Quebec: C. Darveau, 1884. 04356. (Pre-1900 Canadiana) – 9 – cn C.I.H.M. [510]

THE STEREOMETRICON: MEASUREMENT OF ALL SOLIDS BY ONE AND THE SAME RULE: UNIVERSAL APPLICATION OF THE PRISMOIDAL FORMULA / Baillairge, Charles – Montreal: J. Lovell, 1881. 04020. (Pre-1900 Canadiana) – 9 – cn C.I.H.M. [510]

THE STEREOMETRICON: SOLID GEOMETRY: STEREOMETRY, STEREOTOMY / Baillairge, Charles – 1896?. 03401. (Pre-1900 Canadiana) – 9 – cn C.I.H.M. [510]

STEREOTACTIC AND FUNCTIONAL NEUROSURGERY – v37-. 1975- – 1,5,9 – us UMI [617]

STEREO-VIDEO GUIDE – (Ceased v18 no 3 1989) – Toronto. v1-18. 1972-1989 – 9 – Can$20.00y – cn Micromedia [790]

Sterkel, Johann F X *see* RECUEIL DES 6. PIECES POUR LE CLAVECIN..

STERLING 1740-1900 – (Mf 1-8: Vital Records 1759-1873. Mf 9-10: Vital Records 1792-1866. Mf 11-15: Vital Records Index 1843-92. Mf 16-17: Births 1843-71; Marriages 1843-54. Mf 18: Deaths 1843-63. Mf 19: Births 1872-91. Mf 20-21: Marriages 1855-92. Mf 21-22: Deaths 1864-91. Mf 23-24: Birth Index 1893-1960. Mf 25-26: Marriage Index 1892-1959. Mf 27-28: Death Index 1893-1959. Mf 29: Deaths 1892-1905. Mf 30: Marriages 1892-1911. Mf 31: Births 1892-1900) – (mf ed 1992) – 31mf – 9 – 0-87623-141-5 – us Holbrook [920]

STERLING ACRES BAPTIST CHURCH. KANSAS CITY, MISSOURI : CHURCH RECORDS – Sept 1957-Feb 1974 – 1 – 28.08 – us Baptist [240]

STERLING EAGLE – Sterling, NE. -w. Sept 1895-Jul 1899 – 1 – us NE Hist [071]

STERLING RECORD – Sterling, NE. -w. Aug 1899-Jan 1904; Mar 1904; May 1904-Mar 1906 – 1 – us NE Hist [071]

STERLING SUN – Sterling, NE. -w. (-sw 1895-1910). Jul 1890-Aug 1895, scattered issues missing; Oct 1895-Nov 1912; Mar 1913-Oct 1945 – 1 – us NE Hist [071]

STERLINGTON FIRST BAPTIST CHURCH. STERLINGTON, LOUISIANA : CHURCH RECORDS – 1927-44 – 1 – 12.78 – us Baptist [240]

STERN – 1947-1993 – 9 – F1,583.00 – sz Infoprint [073]

STERN – (1948 150mf per y inquire for price) – Germany, 1974- – 4r per y – 5 – inquire – us Ross [072]

STERN – 1974-1995 – 4r per y – 5,6 – Sfr695.00 – sz Infoprint [073]

STERN – 1993 – 9 – DM490.00y – gw IOS [943]

STERN – v. 2-29 1949-76 – 1 – us UMI [000]

Stern, Adolf *see* DIE LETZTEN HUMANISTEN

DER STERN DER ERLOESUNG. 1-2-3 / Rosenzweig, F – 1930 – 11mf – 8 – ne Slangenburg [100]

DER STERN DES WESTENS : EPISCHES GEDICHT / Gugler, Julius – Milwaukee: Selbstverlag des Verfassers, 1900 – 1r – 1 – us U.W. Library [810]

Stern, E Mark *see* THE PSYCHOTHERAPY PATIENT

Stern, G H *see* MARRIAGE IN EARLY ISLAM

Stern, Henry A *see*
- THE CAPTIVE MISSIONARY
- DAWNINGS OF LIGHT IN THE EAST

Stern, Jakob E Molchow *see* IST DER PENTATEUCH VON MOSES VERFASST?

Stern, Nathan *see* THE JEWISH HISTORICO-CRITICAL SCHOOL OF THE NINETEENTH CENTURY

Sternaux, Ludwig Friedrich *see* GOETHE IN DORNBURG

Sternberg, G K *see* FLORA DER VORWELT

Sternberg, K M von *see*
- CATALOGUS PLANTARUM COMMENTARIORUM MATHIOLI IN DIOSCORIDEM
- REVISIO SAXIFRAGARUM ICONIBUS ILLUSTRATA

Sternberg, Lev J *see*
- GILJAKI, OROCI, GOL'DY, NEGIDAL'CY, AJMI...
- PERVOBYTNAJA RELIGIA V SVETE ETNOGRAFII...

Sterndale, R A *see* NATURAL HISTORY OF THE MAMMALIA OF INDIA AND CEYLON

Sterne, L *see* THE SERMONS OF MR. YORICK

Sterne, Simon *see* THE PREVENTION OF DEFECTIVE AND SLIPSHOD LEGISLATION

STERNE'SCHER HUMOR IN IMMERMANNS "MUENCHHAUSEN" : ALS BEITRAG ZUR GESCHICHTE DES DEUTSCHEN ROMANS / Bauer, Friedrich – Wien: C Reisser & M Werthner, 1896 – 1r – 1 – us U.W. Library [430]

STERN'S MARIA, A PATHETIC SONG... / Moulds, J – [Boston, s.n., ca. 1796] – 1 – us Sibley [780]

DER STERNSTEINHOF : DORFROMAN / Anzengruber, Ludwig – Philadelphia: Morwitz, [1890?] – 1r – 1 – us U.W. Library [830]

DER STERNSTEINHOF : ROMAN / Anzengruber, Ludwig – Leipzig: Breitkopf & Haertel, [19–] – 1r – 1 – us U.W. Library [830]

Sterrett, James Macbride *see*
- THE FREEDOM OF AUTHORITY
- REASON AND AUTHORITY IN RELIGION

Stesik, L N *see* GORENIE I VZRYV

STESTI ZLATEHO HROZNU: PREDMSTSKY ROMAN / Stech, Vaclav – Prague: J. Otto, 1915. Illus. by Artus Scheiner. 179p. With: Lacna srdce by M.A. Simacek, Prague: Unive, 1918 and Mistr Kampanus by Zikmund Winter, Chicago: Slavie, 1915 – 1 – us U.W. Library [460]

Ste-Suzanne, Soeur *see* BIO-BIBLIOGRAPHIE ANALYTIQUE DES ECRITS DU DOCTEUR WILFRID LEBLOND, PROFESSEUR TITULAIRE A L'UNIVERSITE LAVAL

Ste-Therese de Lisieux, Soeur *see* BIBLIOGRAPHIE SUR L'OPHTALMO-OTORHINO-LARYNGOLOGIE

STETSON KENNEDY COLLECTION : FROM THE HOLDINGS OF THE SCHOMBURG CENTER FOR RESEARCH IN BLACK CULTURE, MANUSCRIPTS, ARCHIVES AND RARE BOOKS DIVISION: THE NEW YORK PUBLIC LIBRARY, ASTOR, LENOX AND TILDEN FOUNDATIONS – (Guide sold separately for $20.00 which covers other Schomburg Center collections) – 1995 – ca 4r – 1 – ca $340.00 – 1167-6 – us L of C Photodup [920]

STETSON KENNEDY COLLECTION – (Guide sold separately $20.00 D3305.G6) – Schonburg Center, 1995 – 4r – 1 – $340.00 – D3305P26 – us Scholarly Res [975]

STETSON LAW REVIEW – v1-24. 1970-95 – 1,5,6 – $450.00 – us Hein [073]

Stetson University. DeLand, Florida *see* CATALOGS AND COLLEGE RECORDS

Stettenheim, Ludwig *see* SCHILLERS FRAGMENT

Stettheimer, Ettie *see* DIE URTEILSFREIHEIT ALS GRUNDLAGE DER RECHTFERTIGUNG DES RELIGIOESEN GLAUBENS

Stettner, Leo *see* DAS PHILOSOPHISCHE SYSTEM SHAFTESBURYS UND WIELANDS AGATHON

Steuart, J *see*
- AN INQUIRY INTO THE PRINCIPLES OF POLITICAL OECONOMY
- THE PRINCIPLES OF MONEY APPLIED TO THE PRESENT STATE OF THE COIN OF BENGAL

STEUBEN ADVOCATE – Ithaca. N.Y. 1944-1946 – 1 – us UMI [071]

STEUBEN COURIER – Bath. N.Y. 1876-1920 – 1 – us UMI [071]

STEUBEN COURIER – Ithaca. N.Y. 1876-1920 – 1 – us UMI [071]

STEUBEN FARMER'S ADVOCATE – Ithaca. N.Y. 1840-1925 – 1 – us UMI [071]

Steuben, Friedrich Wilhelm Baron von *see* THE PAPERS OF GENERAL FRIEDRICH WILHELM VON STEUBEN, 1777-1794

Steubenville. Presbytery (Pres. CH. in the U.S.A.) *see* MINUTES, 1833-1841

Steudel, E G *see*
- NOMENCLATOR BOTANICUS
- SYNOPSIS PLANTARUM GLUMACEARUM

Steuernagel, Carl *see*
- DIE ENTSTEHUNG DES DEUTERONOMISCHEN GESETZES
- DER RAHMEN DES DEUTERONOMIUMS

Steven, C von *see* VERZEICHNISS DER AUF DER TAURISCHEN HALBINSEL WILDWACHSENDEN PFLANZEN

STEVENAGE COMET – Luton, England. 1980- – 60+ r – 1 – uk British Libr Newspaper [072]

STEVENAGE GAZETTE – (Also known as: The Gazette (Stevenage)) – 1980-Mar 1984; Jul 1984-Sep 1987; 1988-Jun 22 1990; Jul 1990-92; Jan 8-Jun 25 1993; Jul 1993-Dec 23 1994; 1995-96 – 57 1/2r – 1 – uk British Libr Newspaper [072]

STEVENAGE GAZETTE – England, 1980-81 – 8r – 1 – uk British Libr Newspaper [072]

Stevens, Abel *see*
- AN APPEAL TO THE METHODIST EPISCOPAL CHURCH
- THE CENTENARY OF AMERICAN METHODISM
- A COMPENDIOUS HISTORY OF AMERICAN METHODISM
- AN ESSAY ON CHURCH POLITY
- ESSAYS ON THE PREACHING REQUIRED BY THE TIMES: AND THE BEST METHODS OF OBTAINING IT
- LIFE AND TIMES OF NATHAN BANGS, D.D.
- REMARKABLE EXAMPLES OF MORAL RECOVERY
- SUPPLEMENTARY HISTORY OF AMERICAN METHODISM

Stevens, Arnold William *see* AN OUTLINE HANDBOOK OF THE LIFE OF CHRIST

Stevens County. Kansas *see* MISCELLANEOUS RECORDS

STEVENS COUNTY REVEILLE – Colville. Wash. 1907-1909 – 1 – us UMI [071]

Stevens, Deborah A *see* A VALID AND RELIABLE INSTRUMENT FOR THE DIRECT MEASURE OF PERCEIVED BODY SIZE IN CHILDREN

Stevens, Edward Thomas *see* FLINT CHIPS. A GUIDE TO PRE-HISTORIC ARCHAEOLOGY, AS ILLUSTRATED BY THE COLLECTION IN THE BLACKMORE MUSEUM, SALISBURY

STEVENS FAMILY PAPERS, 1664-1959 – New Jersey Historical Society – 46r – 1 – $3405.00 – us UMI [920]

Stevens, Frank E *see* HISTORY OF LEE COUNTY

Stevens, G A *see* A LECTURE ON HEADS...

Stevens, George Barker *see*
- DOCTRINE AND LIFE
- THE JOHANNINE THEOLOGY
- THE JOHANNINE THEOLOGY...DOCTRINAL CONTENTS OF THE GOSPEL AND EPISTLES
- THE LIFE, LETTERS, AND JOURNALS OF THE REV. AND HON. PETER PARKER, M.D.
- THE MESSAGE OF THE APOSTLES
- THE PAULINE THEOLOGY...ORIGIN AND CORRELATION OF THE DOCTRINAL TEACHINGS
- A SHORT EXPOSITION OF THE EPISTLE TO THE GALATIANS...AS A TEXT-BOOK
- THE THEOLOGY OF THE NEW TESTAMENT

Stevens, H N *see* PTOLEMY'S GEOGRAPHY

Stevens, Hiram F *see* HISTORY OF THE BENCH AND BAR

Stevens, John H *see* MINNESOTA AND ITS PEOPLE AND EARLY HISTORY OF MINNEAPOLIS

Stevens, L C *see* CHURCH FINANCES

Stevens, Lewis T *see* HISTORY OF CAPE MAY COUNTY

Stevens, Michael E *see* THE VICTOR BERGER PAPERS

Stevens, Robert E *see* JOURNAL OF MINISTRY MARKETING AND MANAGEMENT

Stevens, S C *see* A COST/BENEFIT ANALYSIS OF DECLINING NUMBERS OF WOMEN COACHES

STEVENS TRANSCRIPTS / British Library – 1 – 2995.00 – uk World [025]

Stevens, W W *see* PAST AND PRESENT OF WILL COUNTY

Stevens, Walter B *see* ST. LOUIS: THE FOURTH CITY 1764-1909

Stevens White, Horatio *see* SELECTIONS FROM HEINE'S POEMS

Stevens, William *see*
- THE UNJUST JUDGE
- UNJUST JUDGE

Stevens, William Arnold *see* COMMENTARY ON THE EPISTLES TO THE THESSALONIANS

Stevens, William Bacon *see*
- A HISTORY OF GEORGIA, FROM ITS DISCOVERY BY EUROPEANS TO THE ADOPTION OF THE PRESENT CONSTITUTION IN 1798
- THE PARABLES OF THE NEW TESTAMENT PRACTICALLY UNFOLDED

Stevenson *see* CHRONICON ANGLICANUM (RS66)

Stevenson, A *see* THE VOCAL PRECEPTOR OR KEY TO SACRED MUSIC FROM CELEBRATED AUTHORS

Stevenson, Andrew *see* THE HISTORY OF THE CHURCH AND STATE OF SCOTLAND FROM THE ACCESSION OF K. CHARLES 1, TO THE RESTORATION OF K. CHARLES 2

Stevenson, Archibald Ewing *see* STATES' RIGHTS AND NATIONAL PROHIBITION

Stevenson, Francis Seymour *see* ROBERT GROSSETESTE, BISHOP OF LINCOLN

Stevenson, George J *see*
- METHODIST WORTHIES
- PASTOR C. H. SPURGEON

Stevenson, J *see*
- CHRONICON MONASTERII DE ABINGTON (RS2)
- HYMENOMYCETES BRITANNICI
- LETTERS AND PAPERS ILLUSTRATIVE OF THE WARS OF THE ENGLISH IN FRANCE DURING THE REIGN OF HENRY 6 (RS22)
- MYCOLOGIA SCOTICA
- NARRATIVES OF THE EXPULSION OF THE ENGLISH FROM NORMANDY, 1449-1450 (RS32)

Stevenson, J M *see* WOMAN'S PLACE IN ASSEMBLIES FOR PUBLIC WORSHIP

Stevenson, John R *see* THE EFFECTS OF STICK LENGTH ON THE KINEMATICS OF MAXIMAL VELOCITY THROWING IN LACROSSE

Stevenson, R F *see* THE MISSOURI SCHOOL DISTRICT COUNSELOR: A COMMENTARY ON THE SCHOOL LAW OF MISSOURI

Stevenson, Robert Louis *see*
- THE BLACK ARROW
- CATRIONA
- THE EBB TIDE
- FAMILIAR STUDIES OF MEN AND BOOKS
- A FOOTNOTE TO HISTORY
- AN INLAND VOYAGE
- ISLAND NIGHT'S ENTERTAINMENTS
- KIDNAPPED
- THE MASTER OF BALLANTRAE
- THE MERRY MEN
- NEW ARABIAN NIGHTS
- PRINCE OTTO
- ST. IVES
- THE SILVERADO SQUATTERS
- STRANGE CASE OF DR. JEKYLL AND MR. HYDE
- TRAVELS WITH A DONKEY IN THE CEVENNES
- TREASURE ISLAND
- VAILIMA LETTERS...
- VIRGINIBUS PUERISQUE
- WEIR OF HERMISTON
- THE WRECKER
- THE WRONG BOX

Stevenson, W B *see* THE CRUSADERS IN THE EAST

Stevenson, W H *see* THE CRAWFORD COLLECTION OF EARLY CHARTERS AND DOCUMENTS

Stevenson, William Fleming *see* PRAYING AND WORKING

Steves, Heinrich *see* FR. HEBBELS VERHAELTNIS ZU DEN POLITISCHEN UND SOZIALEN FRAGEN

Steward, J H *see* RECOLLECTIONS OF THE EARLY SETTLEMENT OF CARROLL COUNTY, INDIANA

STEWARD'S BOOK AND SELECTED ARTICLES FROM THE TRANSACTIONS / Shawnee Mission – undated – 1 – us KS Hist [920]

STEWARDSHIP AMONG BAPTISTS / Vail, Albert L – Philadelphia: American Baptist Publication Society, 1913 – 1mf – us A.T.L.A. [240]

STEWARDSHIP AND MISSIONS / Cook, Charles Augustus – [Philadelphia]: American Baptist Publ Society, c1908 – 1mf – 9 – 0-8370-6252-7 – 1986-0252 – us A.T.L.A. [240]

STEWARDSHIP COMMISSION, FORWARD PROGRAM OF CHURCH FINANCE, 1956-60 / Southern Baptist Convention – 778p – 1 – us Baptist [240]

STEWARDSHIP COMMISSION, MATERIALS FROM MID-SOUTH AND FAR WEST CLINICS, 1956 / Southern Baptist Convention – 182p – 1 – us Baptist [240]

STEWARDSHIP DEVELOPMENT MATERIALS / Hastings, Robert J – 1 – 189.35 – us Baptist [240]

Stewart, Alexander Morris *see*
- HANDBOOK OF CHRISTIAN EVIDENCES
- THE LIFE OF CHRIST
- THE TEMPTATION OF JESUS: A STUDY OF OUR LORD'S TRIAL IN THE WILDERNESS

STEWART AND PORTER'S REPORTS / Alabama. Supreme Court – (A Pre-NRS title) – Alabama. v1-5. 1831-34 (all publ) – 30mf – 9 – $45.00 – LLMC 91-045 – us L.L.M.C. [340]

Stewart, David *see* THE LAW OF HUSBAND AND WIFE

STEWART E. MCCLURE, SENATE SERVICE 1949-1973 : CHIEF CLERK, SENATE COMMITTEE ON LABOR, EDUCATION, AND PUBLIC WELFARE – 3mf – 9 – $15.00 – us Scholarly Res [320]

Stewart, Ethelbert *see* PAPERS

Stewart, G F *see* MARKETING EGGS AND POULTRY

Stewart, George W *see* PERSONAL PAPERS OF "THE FATHER OF SEQUOIA NATIONAL PARK, 1890-1930"

Stewart, I D *see* THE HISTORY OF THE FREEWILL BAPTISTS FOR HALF A CENTURY

Stewart, J L *see*
- THE FOREST FLORA OF NORTH-WEST AND CENTRAL INDIA
- ILLUSTRATIONS OF THE FOREST FLORA OF NORTH-WEST AND CENTRAL INDIA
- PUNJAB PLANTS, COMPRISING BOTANICAL AND VERNACULAR NAMES AND USES OF MOST OF THE TREES, SHRUBS AND HERBS OF ECONOMICAL VALUE

Stewart, J T *see* INDIANA COUNTY: HER PEOPLE, PAST AND PRESENT

Stewart, James *see* DAWN IN THE DARK CONTINENT

Stewart, James R *see* DIARY

STEWART OF LOVEDALE : THE LIFE OF JAMES STEWART, D.D., M.D., HON. F.R.G.S. / Wells, James – London: Hodder and Stoughton, [1908?] – 2mf – us A.T.L.A. [240]

STEWART OF LOVEDALE; THE LIFE OF JAMES STEWART. / Wells, James – London. 1909 – 1 – us Res Libr [920]

Stewart, Robert Laird *see*
- THE LAND OF ISRAEL
- SHELDON JACKSON

Stewart, Samuel James *see* THE GOSPEL OF LAW

Stewart, William H *see* HISTORY OF NORFOLK COUNTY

STEWART'S KENTUCKY HERALD – Lexington. Ky. 1795-1801 – 1 – us UMI [071]

STEWART'S LITERARY QUARTERLY MAGAZINE – (Cont by: Stewart's Quarterly) – St John, N.B.: G Stewart, [1867-1870?] – 9 – cn C.I.H.M. [420]

STEWART'S LITERARY QUARTERLY MAGAZINE *see* STEWART'S QUARTERLY

STEWART'S NOVA SCOTIA ADMIRALTY REPORTS / Nova Scotia. Canada – 1v. 1803-13 (all publ) – 7mf – 9 – $10.50 – LLMC 81-037 – us L.L.M.C. [340]

STEWART'S QUARTERLY – (Cont: Stewart's Literary Quarterly Magazine) – Saint John, N.B.: G Stewart, [1870-1872?] – 9 – cn C.I.H.M. [420]

STEWART'S QUARTERLY *see* STEWART'S LITERARY QUARTERLY MAGAZINE

STEWART'S REPORTS / Alabama. Supreme Court – (A Pre-NRS title) – Alabama. v1-3. 1827-31 (all publ) – 19mf – 9 – $28.50 – LLMC 91-044 – us L.L.M.C. [340]

STEWART'S TELEGRAPHIC DESPATCH AND DAILY ADVERTISER – Dublin, Ireland. 12 Nov 1832-17 Oct 1835 – 7r – 1 – uk British Libr Newspaper [072]

STFU NEWS *see* SHARECROPPER'S VOICE, 1935-1937 : SOUTHERN FARM LEADER, 1936 : STFU NEWS, 1938-1939 : TENANT FARMER, 1941-1942 : FARM WORKER, 1943-1944 : FARM LABOR NEWS, 1946-1951 : THE UNION FARMER, 1952-1953 : AGRICULTURAL UNIONIST, 1952-1954

St-Gilles, Marie de *see* BIBLIOGRAPHIE DE L'OEUVRE DE MADAME FRANCOISE GAUDET-SMET DE LA SOCIETE DES ECRIVAINS CANADIENS ET DU CERCLE DE FEMMES JOURNALISTES, ECRIVAIN DE PRESSE, RADIO ET T.V., SPECIALISTE EN ARTS DOMESTIQUES

STICHOTVORENIIA / Gumilev, Nikolai Sepanovich – Posmertnyi sbornik. S predisloviem. G. Ivanova. Ed. 2., izd., dopolnennoe. Petrograd. 1923. BR-3615 2 – 8 – ne IDC [460]

STICHOTVORENIIA / Voloshin, M – 1900-10. M., Izd. "Grif". M. 1910. BR-896 2 – 8 – ne IDC [460]

STICHTAGSAMMLUNG : DEUTSCHE TAGESPRESSE / ed by Schuetz – n.p, n.d. 1954, 1964, 1967, 1976, 1989 – 47r+89r+92r+106r+226r=560r – 1 – gw Mikrofilm [072]

STICHTELYKE RYMEN OP VERSCHEIDE STOFFEN, IN TWEE DEELEN / Huygen, Jan – Amsterdam, [1740] – 2mf – 9 – O-3232/1 – ne IDC [760]

STICHTELYKE RYMEN OP VERSCHEIDEN STOFFEN, WAAR VAN ONTRENT DE HELFT NOOIT VOOR-DEESEN GEDRUKT ZIJN / Huygen, Jan – 1st ed. Amsterdam, 1700 – 2mf – 9 – O-3231/1 – ne IDC [760]

STICHTELYKE ZINNEBEELDEN EN BYBEL-STOFFEN / Klinkhamer, G – Amsterdam, 1740 – 3mf – 9 – O-3099/1 – ne IDC [760]

STICHTELYKE ZINNEBEELDEN GEPAST OP DEUGDEN EN ONDEUGDEN, IN 57 TAFEREELEN VERTOOND / Houbraken, Arnold – Amsterdam, 1767 – 4mf – 9 – O-3090/1 – ne IDC [760]

STICHWORTE ZUR DEUTSCHEN LITERATUR = SAGGI E NOTE DI LETTERATURA TEDESCA : KRITISCHE NOTIZEN / Cases, Cesare – (Includes bibliographical references and index) – Wien: Europa Verlag, c1969 – 1 – us U.W. Library [430]

STICK DANCE. ESSAIS SUR LA FETE DES MORTS DES INDIENS KOYUKONS DE L'ALASKA / Marchiori, M – 9 – F70.00 – fr Ethnologie [306]

Stickelberger, Emanuel *see* DER REITER AUF DEM FAHLEN PFERD

Stickney, Albert *see* STATE CONTROL OF TRADE AND COMMERCE BY NATIONAL OR STATE AUTHORITY

STICKNEY, BENJAMIN F., PAPERS, MS 3450 – 1788-1830 – 1 reel – 1 – us Western Res [978]

Stieglitz, C L *see* ZEICHNUNGEN AUS DER SCHOENEN BAUKUNST ODER DARSTELLUNG IDEALISCHER UND AUSGEFUEHRTEN GEBAEUDE...

Stieler, Karl *see* EIN WINTER-IDYLL

Stier, G *see* DIE SCHLOSSKIRCHE ZU WITTENBERG

Stifler, James M *see*
- THE EPISTLE TO THE ROMANS
- AN INTRODUCTION TO THE STUDY OF THE ACTS OF THE APOSTLES

Stifter, Adalbert *see*
- ABDIAS
- BRIGITTA UND ANDERE ERZAEHLUNGEN
- ERZAEHLUNGEN
- DAS HEIDEDORF
- STUDIEN

STIFTLANDBOTE – Tirschenreuth, Germany. 1 Jun 1983- – 7r per yr – 1 – gw Mikrofilm [072]

DIE STIFTSHUETTE / Haarbeck, J – Elberfeld: Buch. Evang. Gesell., 1900. 1 fiche – 9 – us A.T.L.A. [240]

DIE STIFTSHUETTE IN BILD UND WORT / Neumann, Wilhelm – (Includes index of biblical texts cited) – Gotha: Friedrich Andreas Perthes, 1861 – 1mf – 9 – 0-8370-4571-1 – 1985-2571 – us A.T.L.A. [220]

Stiftung Archiv der Akademie der Kuenste Berlin *see* DER BESTAND PREUSSISCHE AKADEMIE DER KUENSTE – KAISERREICH, WEIMARER REPUBLIK, NATIONALSOZIALISMUS, NACHKRIEGSZEIT (1871-1955) TEIL 1

Stiftung Archiv der Parteien und Massenorganisationen der DDR im Bundesarchiv *see* TARNSCHRIFTEN 1933 BIS 1945

Stiftung Weimarer Klassik *see* INTERNATIONALE BIBLIOGRAPHIE ZUR DEUTSCHEN KLASSIK 1750-1850

Stigand, C H *see* CENTRAL AFRICAN GAME AND ITS SPOOR

STIKCHI I POEMY / Maiakovskii, Vladimir – Stat'i o stikhakh i poemakh. V. D. Duvakina. M. 1960. BR-998 2 – 8 – ne IDC [460]

STIKHI / Aseev, N – M. 1941. BR-911 2 – 8 – ne IDC [460]

STIKHI / Gippius, Z N – Dnevnik 1911-21. Berlin. 1922. BR-726 2 – 8 – ne IDC [460]

STIKHI / Gorodetskii, S – Moscow, 1964. BR-5970-2 – 8 – ne IDC [460]

STIKHI / Mandelstam, Osip E – Den' poezii 1962. M. 1962. BR-1167 2 – 8 – ne IDC [460]

STIKHI / Narbut, V – Kniga I. Spb. 1910. BR-1209 2 – 8 – ne IDC [460]

STIKHI / Sologub, F – Kniga pervaia. Spb. 1896. BR-879 2 – 8 – ne IDC [460]

STIKHI I PEREVODY / Voloshin, M – Berlin. 1923. BR-895 2 – 8 – ne IDC [460]

STIKHI I POEMY / Esenin, Sergei – M. 1931. BR-1062 2 – 8 – ne IDC [460]

STIKHI I POEMY / Kamenskii, V – Tiflis. 1945. BR-947 2 – 8 – ne IDC [460]

STIKHI I POEMY / Sluchevskii, K – Bol'shaia Seriia, Biblioteka Poeta. L. 1962. BR-3539 2 – 8 – ne IDC [460]

STIKHI O ROSSII / Belyi, A – Berlin. 1922. BR-601 – 8 – ne IDC [460]

STIKHI O ZAGRANITSE / Maiakovskii, Vladimir – M. 1950. BR-999 2 – 8 – ne IDC [460]

STIKHI, POEMY, PROZA / Maiakovskii, Vladimir – L. 1938. BR-1000 2 – 8 – ne IDC [460]

STIKHI V. BRIUSOVA I RUSSKII IAZYK / Shemshurin, A – M. 1908. BR-2120 2 – 8 – ne IDC [460]

STIKHOTVORENIIA / Akhmatova, A – M. 1958 – 8 – ne IDC [460]

STIKHOTVORENIIA / Annenskii, I F – L. 1939. BR-506 2 – 8 – ne IDC [460]

STIKHOTVORENIIA / Belyi, A – Izd. "Sovetskii pisatel'." (Biblioteka poeta. Malaia seriia). 1940. BR-602 2 – 8 – ne IDC [460]

STIKHOTVORENIIA / Esenin, Sergei – L. 1953. BR-1065 2 – 8 – ne IDC [460]

STIKHOTVORENIIA / Esenin, Sergei – M. 1933. BR-1063 2 – 8 – ne IDC [460]

STIKHOTVORENIIA / Esenin, Sergei – M. 1934. BR-1064 2 – 8 – ne IDC [460]

STIKHOTVORENIIA / Gorodetskii, S – 1905-1955. Leningrad. 1956. BR-1134 2 – 8 – ne IDC [460]

STIKHOTVORENIIA / Maiakovskii, Vladimir – v. 1. L. 1940. BR-1002 2 – 8 – ne IDC [460]

STIKHOTVORENIIA / Minskii, N – Ed. 2. Spb. 1887. BR-814 2 – 8 – ne IDC [460]

STIKHOTVORENIIA / Neledinskii-Meletskii, Iu. A – Spb. 1876. BR-7725 2 – 8 – ne IDC [460]

STIKHOTVORENIIA / Sologub, F – "Sovetskii Pisatel". (Biblioteka poeta, Malaia seriia). L. 1939. BR-881 2 – 8 – ne IDC [460]

STIKHOTVORENIIA / Solov'ev, Vsevolod S – ed. 3. Enlarged. M. 1900. BR-890 2 – 8 – ne IDC [190]

STIKHOTVORENIIA / Solov'ev, Vsevolod S – ed. 6 v1. M. 1915. BR-122 2 – 8 – ne IDC [190]

STIKHOTVORENIIA 1 POEMY / Pasternak, B – M. 1961. BR-1019 2 – 8 – ne IDC [460]

STIKHOTVORENIIA (1883-1887) / Merezhkovskii, Dimitrii – Spb. 1888. BR-791 2 – 8 – ne IDC [460]

STIKHOTVORENIIA 1909-1960 / Akhmatova, A – M. 1961. BR-1104 2 – 8 – ne IDC [460]

STIKHOTVORENIIA 1910-1925 / Esenin, Sergei – Paris. 1950. BR-1067 2 – 8 – ne IDC [460]

STIKHOTVORENIIA I POEMY / Aseev, N – 2v. M. 1959. BR-912 2 – 8 – ne IDC [460]

STIKHOTVORENIIA I POEMY / Esenin, Sergei – L. 1956. BR-1066 2 – 8 – ne IDC [460]

STIKHOTVORENIIA I POEMY / Khlebnikov, V – L. 1960. BR-929 2 – 8 – ne IDC [460]

STIKHOTVORENIIA I TRAGEDII / Annenskii, I F – Sovetskii pisatel'. (Biblioteka poeta. Bol'shaia seriia). 1959. BR-507 2 – 8 – ne IDC [460]

STIKHOTVORENIIA V ODNOM TOME / Pasternak, B – Ed. 2. L. 1935. BR-1021 2 – 8 – ne IDC [460]

STIKHOTVORENIIA V ODNOM TOME / Pasternak, B – L. 1933. BR-1020 2 – 8 – ne IDC [460]

STIL UND STILZUG IM KOMMUNIKATEN KONTEXT / Hoffmann, Michael – 1992 – 242p – 9 – DM98.00 – 3-89349-564-9 – gw Hänsel [430]

Stiler, Henry R *see* HISTORY OF KINGS COUNTY AND BROOKLYN 1683-1884

Stiles, Edward H *see* RECOLLECTIONS AND SKETCHES OF EARLY LAWYERS AND PUBLIC MEN OF IOWA

Stiles, Meredith Newcomb *see* THE WORLD'S WORK AND THE CALENDAR; TELLING THE STORY OF THE EVOLUTION OF THE JULIAN-GREGORIAN CALENDAR, OF HOW IT FAILED TO ANTICIPATE THE NEEDS OF A CHANGED CIVILIZATION...INTERNATIONAL UNDERTAKING TO IMPROVE IT

STILETTO – v1. no. 1-6 (monthly: all publ). 1900-01 – 1 reel – 1 – $55.00 – us UPA [360]
STILISTIK, RHETORIK, POETIK IN BEZUG AUF DIE BIBLISCHE LITTERATUR / Koenig, Eduard – (Includes indexes) – Leipzig: Dieterich, 1900 – 1mf – 9 – 0-8370-9708-8 – 1986-3708 – us A.T.L.A. [220]
STILISTIK, RHETORIK, POETIK IN BEZUG AUF DIE BIBLISCHE LITTERATUR KOMPARATIVISCH DARGESTELLT / Koenig, F E – Leipzig. 1900. BJ-412-12 1 – 9 – ne IDC [220]
STILL HOURS = STILLE STUNDEN / Rothe, Richard – (Includes index) – New York: Funk and Wagnalls, [187-?] – 1mf – 9 – 0-8370-9737-1 – 1986-3737 – us A.T.L.A. [240]
THE STILL LIFE OF THE MIDDLE TEMPLE : WITH SOME OF ITS TABLE TALK / Thorpe, William G – (Preceded by fifty years of reminiscences) – London: Richard Bentley, 1892 – 4mf – 9 – $6.00 – LLMC 84-316 – us L.L.M.C. [340]
STILLE DE L'ORATEUR – 1647 – 9 – fr I.C.S. [440]
Stille, H *see* GRUNDFRAGEN DER VERGLEICHENDEN TEKTONIK
Stiller, Christoph *see* ADAPTIVE BEAMFORMING APPLIED TO HYDROACOUSTIC COMMUNICATIONS
Stillman, William *see* AN ATTEMPT TO REMOVE ERROR, DESIGNED AS A LETTER TO A FRIEND ON THE IMPORTANT SUBJECT OF THE SABBATH
STILLWATER COUNTY DEMOCRAT – Columbus. Mont. 1914-1916 – 1 – us UMI [071]
STILLWATER ENTERPRISE – Absarokee. Mont. 1923-1933 – 1 – us UMI [071]
STILLWATER NEWS – Absarokee. Mont. 1952- – 1 – us UMI [071]
Stillwell, H E *see* PIONEERING IN BOLIVIA
STILTHEORIE UND RHETORIK DER ROEMER ALS GEGENSTAND DER IMITATIO IM BEREICH DES DEUTSCHEN HUMANISMUS : UNTERSUCHT BESONDERS AUF GRUND DER LATEINISCHEN SCHUELERGESPRAECHE BIS ZU ERASMUS' "COLLOQUIA FAMILIARIA" / Streckenbach, Gerhard – Berlin, 1932 – 1mf – DM48.00 – 3-8267-3053-4 – gw Hänsel [450]
STILWANDEL : STUDIEN ZUR VORGESCHICHTE DER GOETHEZEIT / Staiger, Emil – (Includes bibliographical references) – 1r – 1 – us U.W. Library [430]
STIMMBILDUNG – Stimmwissenschaftliche Blaetter fuer Kultur u. Kritik d. Kunstgesanges. v1-9. 1919-1931/32 – 1 – us Schnase [780]
DIE STIMME : JUEDISCHE ZEITUNG – Vienna. v1-10. 1928-1937? B358 (Leo Baeck Institute. German-Jewish Periodicals, Pt 1) – 1r – 1 – $75.00 – us UPA [270]
STIMME DER ARBEIT – Frankfurt Main, West Germany. 14 Sep 1946-25 Dec 1949 – 1r – 1 – gw Mikrofilm [073]
STIMME DER ARBEIT : ORGAN DES FREIEN GEWERKSCHAFTSBUNDES HESSEN – Frankfurt M., 1946-1949 – 1r – 1 – DM80.00 – gw Mikro Press [072]
Stimmel, Barry *see* JOURNAL OF ADDICTIVE DISEASES
STIMMEN AUS DER KATHOLISCHEN KIRCHE UEBER DIE KIRCHENFRAGEN DER GEGENWART – Muenchen: Rudolph Oldenbourg. 2v. 1870 – 3mf – 9 – 0-8370-8830-5 – 1986-2830 – us A.T.L.A. [240]
STIMMEN AUS MARIA LAACH – Bd 1,2 – 60mf – 9 – Dfl210.00 – ne Slangenburg [073]
DIE STIMMEN DER VOELKER UEBER DIE URGESCHICHTE : NACH GENESIS 1-11 / Pressel, Wilhelm – Hamburg: Rauhen Hauses, 1890 – 1mf – 9 – us A.T.L.A. [240]
STIMMEN DER ZEIT – (Band der Stimmen aus Maria Laach) – (Maria Laach). 1915, 1:88-1917, 1:92 – 57mf – 9 – Dfl200.00 – ne Slangenburg [073]
STIMMUNGEN: DREI VORTRAGSSTUECKE FUER VIOLONCELLO MIT KLAVIERBEGLEITUNG. OP. 22 : CONTAINS: 1. MELODIE; 2. ROMANZE; 3. SCHERZO / Thiessen, K – (Score and part) – Leipzig: Mersburger, [189-] – 1 – us Sibley [780]
STIMMVERBOTE IN DEN AKTIENRECHTEN DER EWG-STAATEN / Meyer-Giesow, Helmut – Bonn, 1966 – 1 – DM30.00 – gw Mikro Press [943]
Stimpson, Thomas Morrill *see* IN MEMORIAM
Stimpson, W *see* SHELLS OF NEW ENGLAND
Stimson, Frederic Jesup *see* GLOSSARY OF TECHNICAL TERMS, PHRASES, AND MAXIMS OF THE COMMON LAW
STIMULATOR – McCleary. Wash. -w. 1953-61 – 1 – us UMI [071]
Stinde, Julius *see*
- HUMORESKEN
- UT'N KNICK
Stintzing, R *see* ULRICH ZASIUS
Stirling, Edward *see* NICHOLAS NICKLEBY: A FARCE IN TWO ACTS, TAKEN FROM THE POPULAR WORK OF THAT NAME BY "BOZ"
Stirling, James Hutchison *see*
- JERROLD, TENNYSON AND MACAULAY
- PHILOSOPHY AND THEOLOGY
Stirling, John *see* A SYSTEM OF RHETORIC
STIRLING OBSERVER – 1 – £42.00r – uk Scot News [072]
STIRLINGSHIRE, 1837 : BRITISH ISLES CENSUS DIRECTORIES PROJECT, SCOTLAND. VOL 55 – 1mf – 9 – A$9.00 – at Vine [941]
Stirner, Max *see*
- THE EGO AND HIS OWN
- DER EINZIGE UND SEIN EIGENTUM
STIRPES AUSTRIACAE / Crantz, H J N von – Ed. 2. 2 v. Viennae. 1769 – 8 – ne IDC [580]
STIRPES AUSTRIACAE / Crantz, H J N von – Viennae, Lipsiae. 1762-67. B-5473 2 – 8 – ne IDC [580]
STIRPES NOVAE AUT MINUS COGNITAE / L'Heritier de Brutelle, C L Cornus – Paris, 1784-88; 1785-1805 – 8 – B-113 2 – ne IDC [580]
STIRPIUM RARIORUM MINUSQUE COGNITARUM / Bivona-Bernardi, A – Panormi. 1813-16. B-5470 2 – 8 – ne IDC [580]
STIRRING INCIDENTS IN THE LIFE OF A BRITISH SOLDIER / Faughnan, Thomas – Toront: Hunter, Rose, 1879. 03076. (Pre-1900 Canadiana) – 9 – cn C.I.H.M. [971]
STIRRING SCIENCE STORIES – v1 (all publ). 1941-42 – 1 reel – 1 – $60.00 – us UPA [830]
Stirton, J *see* NEW AND RARE LICHENS
Stitcher, Thomas P *see* THE EFFECTS OF GOAL SETTING ON PERFORMANCE ENHANCEMENT IN A COMPETITIVE ATHLETIC SETTING
STITHTON BAPTIST CHURCH. RADCLIFF, KENTUCKY : CHURCH RECORDS – 1889-1917, 1934-Apr 1968 – 1 – 22.95 – us Baptist [240]
Stizenberger, E *see*
- LICHENAEA AFRICANA
- LICHENES HELVETICI EORUMQUE STATIONES ET DISTRIBUTIO
St-Jean, Marie de *see* BIO-BIBLIOGRAPHIE CRITIQUE DE L'AVOCAT GEORGES BELLERIVE, 1859-1935
STJERNEN – Dannebrog, NE. -w. Dec. 1885-Dec. 1893 – 1 – us NE Hist [071]
St-John, Bernard *see* THE BLESSED VIRGIN IN THE NINETEENTH CENTURY
LE ST-MICHEL – (Includes: Hebdo Le St-Michel 18 nov 1969-4 jun 1974) – Montreal. v1 n6. 4 dec 1962-11 nov 1969 – 6r – 1 – Can$70.00 – cn Can Microfilming [072]
St-Nom-de-Jesus, Soeur *see* LES FAMILLES ROYALES ACTUELLES EN EUROPE
STO POETOV / Gusman, B – Literaturnye portrety s prilozheniem bibliografícheskogo ukazatelia russkoi poezii za poslednee desiatiletie. Tver'. 1923. BR-1292 2 – 8 – ne IDC [460]
STOA – (Cont by: Canadian Journal of Higher Education) – Winnipeg. v1-4. 1971-74 – 9 – Can$28.00y – cn Micromedia [370]
STOA – v.1-4. 1971-74. Continued by canadian journal of higher education La revue canadienne de l'enseignment superieur – 1 – us UMI [073]
STOA *see* CANADIAN JOURNAL OF HIGHER EDUCATION
Stobel, P *see* GIORNALE DI MALACOLOGIA
STOCHASTIC ANALYSIS AND APPLICATIONS – v1-. 1983- – 1,5,6,9 – us UMI [073]
STOCHASTIC MODELS – v1-. 1985- – 1,5,6,9 – us UMI [073]
STOCHASTIC PROCESSES AND THEIR APPLICATIONS – v1-18. 1973-84 – 1,5,6,13 – sz Elsevier [073]
STOCHASTICS / ed by Davis, M – 1,5,9 – us Gordon [510]
Stocher, Rhamanthus M *see* CENTENNIAL HISTORY OF SUSQUEHANNA COUNTY
STOCK CREEK BAPTIST CHURCH. KNOXVILLE, TENNESSEE : CHURCH RECORDS – 1821-Mar 1989. 1007p – 1 – 45.32 – us Baptist [240]
Stock, Eberhard *see* SCHILLERS VERHAELTNIS ZUR GESPROCHENEN SPRACHE
Stock, Eugene *see*
- THE ENGLISH CHURCH IN THE NINETEENTH CENTURY
- AN HEROIC BISHOP
- THE HISTORY OF THE CHURCH MISSIONARY SOCIETY, ITS ENVIRONMENT, ITS MEN AND ITS WORK
- A SHORT HANDBOOK OF MISSIONS
- THE STORY OF THE BIBLE
STOCK EXCHANGE DAILY OFFICIAL LISTS – 1967-Feb 1981 – 137r – uk Microform Academic [330]
STOCK EXCHANGE OFFICIAL INTELLIGENCE, 1899-1933 – 61r – 1 – uk Microform Academic [332]
STOCK EXCHANGE OFFICIAL YEARBOOK, 1875-1945 : PART 1: 1875-1895 – (Part 2: 1896-1910, 24r $2,100.00. Part 3: 1911-1921, 23r $2100.00. Part 4: 1922-1929, 24r $2,100.00. Part 5: 1930-1937, 24r $2,100.00. Part 6: 1938-1945, 24r $2,100) – Marlborough: Adam Matthew Publications, 1993 – 12r – 1 – $1,400.00 – uk Matthew [332]
THE STOCK EXCHANGE OFFICIAL YEARBOOK 1875-1945 – (Pt 1: 1875-1903; Pt 2: 1904-13; Pt 3: 1914-23; Pt 4: 1924-33) – 1 – us Primary [336]
STOCK EXCHANGE PRACTICES : HEARINGS BEFORE THE COMMITTEE ON BANKING AND CURRENCY, 73RD CONGRESS, FIRST SESSION, ON S. RES. 84, AND S. RES. 56 (73RD CONGRESS) / U.S. Congress. Senate. Committee on Banking and Currency – Washington. 20 pts in 9v. 1933-34 – 149mf – 9 – $5.00f – us Ross [336]
STOCK EXCHANGE PRACTICES : REPORT OF THE COMMITTEE ON BANKING AND CURRENCY PURSUANT TO S. RES. 84 / U.S. Congress. Senate. Committee on Banking and Currency – Washington, 1934 – 5mf – 9 – $5.00f – us Ross [332]
STOCK GROWER – Las Vegas. N.M. 1886-89 – 1 – us UMI [071]
STOCK MARKET REVIEW – London, UK. 20 Jul, 16 Nov, 7 Dec 1906 – 8ft – 1 – uk British Libr Newspaper [072]
Stock, Richard *see* A COMMENTARY UPON THE PROPHECY OF MALACHI
Stock, Robert B *see* TEEING OFF TOWARD THE NCAA CHAMPIONSHIP
Stock, Sarah Geraldina *see* THE STORY OF UGANDA
STOCKARD SUNDAY SCHOOL BOOKS. ATHENS, TEXAS : CHURCH RECORDS – 1909-26 – 1 – 5.67 – us Baptist [240]
Stockbauer, J *see* DIE KUNSTBESTREBUNGEN AM BAYERISCHEN HOFE UNTER DEN HERZOGEN ALBERT V UND WILHELM V
STOCKBRIDGE 1737-1887 – (Mf 1-32: Vital Records Index 1737-1983. Mf 33: Births 1737-91. Mf 34: 1792-1844. Mf 35: Marriages 1747-1811. Mf 36: Marriages 1812-41; Deaths 1740-1844. Mf 37: Vital Records 1737-1835. Mf 38: Births 1809-22. Mf 39: Births 1844-54. Mf 40: Births 1854-57; Marriages 1844-57; Out-of-Town Marriages 1758-97. Mf 40-41: Deaths 1844-57. Mf 42: Births 1857-78. Mf 43: Births 1879-87. Mf 43: Marriages 1857-61. Mf 44: Marriages 1863-83. Mf 45: Marriages 1883-88; Deaths 1857-76. Mf 46: Deaths 1876-87) – (mf ed 1983) – 46mf + 12 trays of index cards – 9 – 0-931248-51-5 – us Holbrook [920]
STOCKHOLM – Stockholm, Sweden. 1885-86 – 1 reel – 1 – sw Kungliga [072]
STOCKHOLM INTERNATIONAL PEACE RESEARCH INSTITUTE – 164mf – 9 – us UMI [320]
STOCKHOLMAREN – Stockholm, Sweden. 1980-81 – 1 – sw Kungliga [072]
STOCKHOLMISCHES MAGAZIN;. – Stockholm, 1754-56. v. 1-3 – 3 – us Readex [073]
STOCKHOLMS DAGBLAD – Stockholm, Sweden. 1824-1931 – 479r – 1 – sw Kungliga [072]
STOCKHOLMS FORSTADSBLAD *see* SUNDBYBERGS OCH SOLNA TIDNING
STOCKHOLMS LANS & SODERTALJE TIDNING – Sodertalje, Sweden. 1930-63 – 90r – 1 – sw Kungliga [072]
STOCKHOLMS LANS TIDNING – Sodertalje, Sweden. 1891. 1 reel; 1930. 2 reels – 1 – sw Kungliga [072]
STOCKHOLMSPOSTEN – Stockholm, Sweden. 1778-1800 – 6r – 1 – sw Kungliga [072]
STOCKHOLMSPOSTEN – Stockholm, Sweden. 1868-70 – 1 – sw Kungliga [072]
STOCKHOLMSTIDNINGEN – Stockholm, 1993- – 9 – sw Kungliga [072]
STOCKHOLMSTIDNINGEN – Stockholm, Sweden. 1889-1966 – 645r – 1 – sw Kungliga [072]
STOCKHOLMSTIDNINGEN – Stockholm, Sweden. 1981-84 – 1 – sw Kungliga [072]
STOCKING AND INTRODUCTION OF FISH IN LAKES AND RESERVOIRS IN THE ASEAN COUNTRIES – 1984 – 87p – it F.A.O. [639]
STOCKMAN – Wood Lake, NE. -w. Aug 1911-Dec 1941 – 1 – us NE Hist [071]
Stockmann, Alois *see* ZUM GOETHE-PROBLEM
Stockmayer, Otto *see* TRANSFORMATION
Stockmeyer, Clara *see* SOZIALE PROBLEME IM DRAMA DES STURMES UND DRANGES
Stockmeyer, Immanuel *see*
- DIE BERGPREDIGT JESU CHRISTI
- DER BRIEF DES JACOBUS: IN VIERZIG PREDIGTEN
STOCKPORT ADVERTISER – 1822-1980 – 1 – uk Manchester Libr [072]
STOCKPORT EXPRESS – Cheshire. 1932-38 11 reels; 1964 3 reels; 1966 3 reels – 17r – 1 – uk Microform Academic [072]
STOCKPORT MERCURY – England, 1849-25 Jul 1851 – 1r – 1 – uk British Libr Newspaper [072]
STOCKPORT TIMES – England. -w. 6 Oct 1893-11 May 1894. 40 ft – 1 – uk British Libr Newspaper [072]
STOCKTON – 1908-50; 1990- – 25+ r – 1 – $1,250.00 – P00134 – us Library Micro [910]
STOCKTON AND HARTLEPOOL MERCURY – Stockton-on-Tees. England. -w. 2 Jun 1855-13 Dec 1865. (10 reels) – 1 – uk British Libr Newspaper [072]
STOCKTON CITY DIRECTORIES – San Joaquin Co, CA. 1852; 1856; 1870-1874; 1876-1877; 1881-1905; 1936-1950 – 22r – 1 – $1,100.00 – D088 – us Library Micro [910]
Stockton, Doane *see* PRECIOUS SONGS
STOCKTON JOURNAL, SOUTH STOCKTON AND NORTON RECORD – England.16 Oct-31 Dec 1880; 1881-15 Nov 1884. -w. 4 reels – 1 – uk British Libr Newspaper [072]
Stockton, Kirkpatrick *see* PRECIOUS SONGS
Stockton, Lewis *see* MARRIAGE CONSIDERED FROM LEGAL AND ECCLESIASTICAL VIEWPOINTS, IN CONNECTION WITH THE RECENT NE TEMERE DECREE OF THE ROMAN CATHOLIC CHURCH
STOCKTON'S VICE-ADMIRALTY CASES / New Brunswick. Canada – 1v. 1877-91 (all publ) – 9mf – 9 – $13.50 – LLMC 81-028 – us L.L.M.C. [340]
Stockwell, Thomas B *see* A HISTORY OF PUBLIC EDUCATION IN RHODE ISLAND, FROM 1636 TO 1876
Stoddard, Dwight J *see* PROMINENT MEN OF CARBONDALE, SCRANTON, WILKES-BARRE, PITTSTON, HAZELTON, AND MONTROSE
Stoddard, Elliott Joseph *see*
- PRACTICE IN THE UNITED STATES PATENT OFFICE; A TABLE OF CASES.
- STODDART'S DIGEST OF PRACTICE IN THE U.S. PATENT OFFICE
Stoddard, Francis H *see* LIFE AND LETTERS OF CHARLES BUTLER
Stoddard, W H *see* PIONEER HISTORY OF TURNER COUNTY
Stoddart, Jane T *see* W. ROBERTSON NICOLL, LL.D.
STODDART'S DIGEST OF PRACTICE IN THE U.S. PATENT OFFICE : A TABLE OF CASES CONSTRUING AND DEFINING THE SEVERAL RULES OF PRACTICE AND CASES SUBSEQUENTLY CITED / Stoddard, Elliott Joseph – Detroit: Drake Law Book Co, 1907 (all publ) – 2mf – 9 – $3.00 – LLMC 84-337 – us L.L.M.C. [340]
Stodel, Emma J *see* OBLIGATORY EXERCISE AND PATHOGENIC WEIGHT CONTROL IN COLLEGE STUDENTS
Stoeber, August *see* DER AKTUAR SALZMANN
Stoecker, Adolf *see* REDEN UND AUFSAETZE
Stoecker, Gerhard *see* ARCHIVES OF NATURE CONSERVATION AND LANDSCAPE RESEARCH
Stoecker, Helene *see*
- MUTTERSCHUTZ (HQ 5)
- DIE NEUE GENERATION (HQ 6)

Stoeckl, Albert *see* DIE INFALLIBILITAET DES OBERHAUPTES DER KIRCHE UND DIE ZUSTIMMUNGSADRESSEN AN HERRN V. DOELLINGER, NAMENTLICH DIE MUENSTER'SCHE
Stoeckle, A *see* GESCHICHTE DER PHILOSOPHIE
Stoecklein, J et al *see* DER NEUE WELT BOTT
Stoelwijck, W van *see* EEN TROSTELIJCKE VERMANINGHE ENDE SEER SCHOON ONDERWYSINGHE VAN HET LYDEN ENDE HEERLICHEYT DER CHRISTENEN
Stoesel, Franz *see* APOLLONIOS RHODIOS: INTERPRETATIONEN ZUR ERZAEHLUNGSKUNST UND QUELLENVERWERTUNG
Stoess, Willi *see*
- DIE BEARBEITUNGEN DES "VERBRECHERS AUS VERLORENER EHRE"

Stoessel, C *see* KURZGEFASSTES MUSICALISCHES LEXICON...
Stoessel, J D *see* KURZGEFASSTES MUSICALISCHES LEXICON...
DER STOFF UND DIE QUELLE VON BAUERNFELDS LUSTSPIEL "DAS TAGEBUCH" / Kreisler, Emil – Wien: Selbstverlag des k k Erzherzog Rainer-Gymnasiums, 1907 – 1 – us U.W. Library [430]
STOFF- UND MOTIVGESCHICHTE DER DEUTSCHEN LITERATUR – (Each issue has also a distinctive title) – Berlin: W de Gruyter & Co, 1929 – 1r – 1 – us U.W. Library [430]
Stoffel, Georges *see* DICTIONNAIRE TOPOGRAPHIQUE DU DEPARTEMENT DE HAUT-RHIN
Stoffel, J *see* LESSINGS MINNA VON BARNHELM
STOIC AND CHRISTIAN IN THE SECOND CENTURY : A COMPARISON OF THE ETHICAL TEACHING OF MARCUS AURELIUS WITH THAT OF CONTEMPORARY AND ANTECEDENT CHRISTIANITY / Alston, Leonard – (Includes bibliographical references) – London; New York: Longmans, Green, 1906 – 1mf – 9 – 0-8370-6320-5 – 1986-0320 – us A.T.L.A. [170]
STOIC AND EPICUREAN / Hicks, R D – New York: Scribner, 1910 – 1mf – us A.T.L.A. [180]
STOICORUM VETERUM FRAGMENTA – (Collegit Ioannes ab Arnim. Vol 1 Zeno et Zenonis Discipili. Lipsiae, 1921. 5mf; Vol 2 Chrysippi Fragmenta, Logica et Physica. Lipsiae, 1903. 9mf; Vol 3 Chrysippi Fragmenta Moralia. Fragmenta Successorum Chrysippi, Lipsiae, 1903. 7mf; Vol 4 Indices Lipsiae, 1924. 6mf) – 8 – ne Slangenburg [100]
STOICS AND SAINTS : LECTURES ON THE LATER HEATHEN MORALISTS: AND ON SOME ASPECTS OF THE LIFE OF THE MEDIAEVAL CHURCH / Brown, James Baldwin – New York: Macmillan, 1893 – 1mf – us A.T.L.A. [240]
Stoke on Trent Museum *see* STAFFORDSHIRE CERAMICS
STOKE-ON-TRENT CITY TIMES – England. -w. 9 Nov 1935-31 Dec 1969. 37 reels – 1 – uk British Libr Newspaper [072]
Stokes, Francis Griffin *see* EPISTOLAE OBSCURORUM VIRORUM
Stokes, George Gabriel *see* NATURAL THEOLOGY
Stokes, George Thomas *see*
- THE ACTS OF THE APOSTLES
- IRELAND AND THE ANGLO-NORMAN CHURCH
- SOME WORTHIES OF THE IRISH CHURCH

Stokes, J *see* A BOTANICAL MATERIA MEDICA
Stokes, W *see*
- DISEASES OF THE HEART AND AORTA
- THE MARTYROLOGY OF GORMAN
- THE MARTYROLOGY OF OENGUS THE CULDEE
- TRIPARTITE LIFE OF PATRICK (RS89)

Stoklosa, S M *see* HOME COURT ADVANTAGE IN MEN'S AND WOMEN'S BIG TEN INTERCOLLEGIATE BASKETBALL
Stolarik, Mark *see* THE ROLE OF THE AMERICAN SLOVAKS
STOLBERG IN DEN ZWEI LETZTEN JAHRZEHNTEN SEINES LEBENS – Mainz: F Kirchheim, 1875 – 1r – 1 – us U.W. Library [920]
Stolberg, Michael *see* ONOMASTIKON MEDICINAE (AEL, ABT 3;9)
THE STOLEN BACILLUS : AND OTHER INCIDENTS / Wells, H G – London: Methuen, 1895 – 1 roll – 1 – 1-55879-775-0 – uk Libr Preservation [830]
STOLETIE SOBSTVENNOI EGO IMPERATORSKAGO VELICHESTVA KANTSELIARII / Stroev, V N – St Petersburg, 1912 – 8 – BR-4263 2 – ne IDC [947]
Stoliczka, F *see* CRETACEOUS FAUNA OF SOUTHERN INDIA
STOLIETIE VOENNOGO MINISTERSTVA, 1802-1902 / Russia. Voennoe Ministerstvo – St. Petersburg. 1902-14 – 1 – $437.00 – us L of C Photodup [947]
STOLITSA I USAD'BA – Zhurnal krasivoi zhizni. v. 1-73. Spb. 1913 14-1917. BR-4000 2 – 8 – ne IDC [073]
Stolk, C J *see* INDONESIA LANGKAH PERTAMA KE OLYMPIADE 15 HELSINKI, 1952
Stoll, Friedrich Albert Robert *see* JUNGENS, MAENNER UND MOTORE
Stolle, Carl *see* FRITZ STAVENHAGENS "MUDDER MEWS"
Stolow, Nathan *see* CONSERVATION STANDARDS FOR WORKS OF ART IN TRANSIT AND ON EXHIBITION
Stolpe, H J *see* UEBER DIE FORSCHUNGSERGEBNISSE DER SCHWEDISCHEN GROENLAND-EXPEDITION, 1899
Stolpe, Heinz *see* DIE AUFFASSUNG DES JUNGEN HERDER VOM MITTELALTER
Stolterfoht, J *see* HISTORIA VON DAVID GEOERGEN, EINEM HEILLOSEN MANN VND GOTTESLAESTERLICHEN ERTZ-KETZER
Stoltze, Friedrich *see* GEDICHTE IN HOCHDEUTSCHER MUNDART
STOLY RAZRIADNOGO PRIKAZA, PO KHRANIASCHIMSIA V MOSKOVSKOM ARKHIVE MINISTERSTVA IUSTITSII KNIGAM IKH / Zagoskin, N F – Kazan. 1878. PKG-B-83.2 BR-11,234 1 – 9 – ne IDC [947]
Stolypin, D A *see*
- 15-I DOKLAD V KOMISSIIU IMPERATORSKOGO MOSKOVSKOGO OBSHCHESTVA SEL'SKOGO KHOZIAISTVA PO VOPROSU O KHUTORAKH I SOVRENMENNYKH USLOVIIAKH KREST'IANSKOGO KHOZIAISTVA
- OB ORGANIZATSII NASHEGO SEL'SKOGO BYTA
- OB USTROISTVE ARENDNYKH KHUTOROV NA VLADEL'CHESKIKH ZEMLIAKH I KREST'IANSKOM KHOZIAISTVE VOOBSHCHE

STOLYPIN I TRET'IA DUMA / Avrekh, A I – M., 1968. 517p – 6mf – 9 – ne IDC [320]
Stolz, Friedrich *see* GESCHICHTE DER LATEINISCHEN SPRACHE
Stolz, J C *see* FLORE DES PLANTES QUI CROISSENT DANS LES DEA1PARTEMENTS DU HAUT- ET BAS-RHIN
Stolz, Joseph *see* FUNERAL AGENDA
Stone, Arthur F *see* THE VERMONT OF TODAY
Stone, Barton W *see* THE BIOGRAPHY OF ELD. BARTON WARREN STONE
THE STONE CHURCH BELL AND OTHER POEMS / Fairweather, George Edwin – St. John, N.B.: Barnes, 1895. 02941. (Pre-1900 Canadiana) – 9 – cn C.I.H.M. [810]
STONE COUNTY ENTERPRISE – Wiggins. Miss. 1936-1953 – 1 – us UMI [071]
STONE CREEK BAPTIST CHURCH. TWIGGS COUNTY. GEORGIA : CHURCH RECORDS – 1808-1954 – 1 – 63.00 – us Baptist [240]
Stone, Darwell *see*
- A HISTORY OF THE DOCTRINE OF THE HOLY EUCHARIST

Stone, E A *see* THE ABIDING COMFORTER... THE PERSON, THE PRESENCE, AND THE POWER OF THE HOLY SPIRIT
Stone, Elizabeth A *see* UINTA COUNTY – ITS PLACE IN HISTORY
Stone, Elizabeth C *see* OLD BABYLONIAN CONTRACTS FROM NIPPUR, VOL 1
Stone, J *see* THE SUDAN ECONOMY; INTRODUCTORY NOTES
Stone, J M *see*
- FAITHFUL UNTO DEATH
- STUDIES FROM COURT AND CLOISTER

Stone, James Samuel *see* READINGS IN CHURCH HISTORY
Stone, Jean Mary *see*
- ELEANOR LESLIE
- REFORMATION AND RENAISSANCE

Stone, John S *see*
- THE BEARINGS OF MODERN COMMERCE ON THE PROGRESS OF MODERN MISSIONS
- THE CHURCH UNIVERSAL
- THE CONTRAST, OR, THE EVANGELICAL AND TRACTARIAN SYSTEMS COMPARED IN THEIR STRUCTURE AND TENDENCIES

Stone, John Timothy *see* RECRUITING FOR CHRIST
THE STONE OF THE SUN AND THE FIRST CHAPTER OF HISTORY IN MEXICO / Palacios, Enrique Juan – University of Chicago Department of Anthropology Bulletin VI. 1921 – 1 – us Res Libr [930]
Stone, Randall A *see* A COMPARISON AMONG THE TRACK AND GRAB STARTS IN SWIMMING AND A STAND-UP RESPONSE TASK
Stonebraker, Beaumont E *see* PAST AND PRESENT OF CALHOUN COUNTY
Stonehouse, George Gordon Vigor *see* THE BOOK OF HABAKKUK
Stonehouse, Ned B *see*
- THE WITNESS OF LUKE TO CHRIST
- THE WITNESS OF MATTHEW AND MARK TO CHRIST

Stoner, K Lynn *see* THE WOMEN'S MOVEMENT IN CUBA, 1898-1958
STONE'S DUNEDIN AND INVERCARGILL DIRECTORY 1886 – 5mf – 9 – NZ$20.00 – 0-908797-14-1 – nz BAB [980]
STONE'S OTAGO AND SOUTHLAND DIRECTORY 1907 – (Towns, streets within the towns and country districts are listed alphabetically and residents named. There is a separate alphabetical list of householders, a trades directory etc.) – 8mf – 9 – NZ$32.00 – 0-908797-15-X – nz BAB [980]
STONE'S OTAGO AND SOUTHLAND DIRECTORY 1909 – (Towns, streets within the towns and country districts are listed alphabetically and residents named. There is a separate alphabetical list of householders, a trades directory etc.) – 9mf – 9 – NZ$36.00 – 0-908797-16-8 – nz BAB [980]
STONE'S OTAGO AND SOUTHLAND DIRECTORY 1915 – (Towns, streets within the towns and country districts are listed alphabetically and residents named. There is a separate alphabetical list of householders, a trades directory etc.) – 7mf – 9 – NZ$28.00 – 0-908797-17-6 – nz BAB [980]
STONES ROLLED AWAY, AND OTHER ADDRESSES TO YOUNG MEN / Drummond, Henry – New York: J. Pott, 1899 – 1mf – us A.T.L.A. [240]
STONEVILLE SERVICE SHEETS / Mississippi. Agricultural Experiment Station. State College – v. 1-431. 1927-55 – 1,5,6 – us Spaulding [630]
STONEY HILL BAPTIST CHURCH. RALEIGH ASSOCIATION. NORTH CAROLINA : CHURCH RECORDS – 1884-1914 – 1 – 11.70 – us Baptist [240]
STONINGTON, COUNTY OF NEW LONDON, CONNECTICUT / New London County. Connecticut – By Richard Anson Wheeler, 1900. Item D.History of town from 1649 to 1900 and geneal. register of Stonington families. Includes index, 735p. SW16-0111 – 5 – us A.G.L.L. [920]
STONY PLAIN REPORTER – Stony Plain, Alberta, CN. 1972-90 – 43r – 1 – cn Commonwealth Micro [072]
STONY POINT BAPTIST CHURCH. ALBANY, KENTUCKY : CHURCH RECORDS – 1884-Jul 1988. Lacking: 1900-22, 1924-35. 1045p – 1 – 47.03 – us Baptist [240]
Stony Ridge. Ohio. St. John's Evangelical Lutheran Church *see* RECORDS
STOP THE 22 X00. MILLION LEGAL TENDER CRIME / Zube, John – Also: the soft option: monetary freedom to stop inflation without causing unemployment. 1 fiche (24X) – 9 – 1.00f – at Libertarian Micro [320]
STOPA – v1-3 inc. 1910-1912 – 1 – us I.U. Libraries [073]
STOPANSKI VESNIK – Skopje, Yugoslavia. Jul 1964-1968 – 2r – 1 – us L of C Photodup [949]
Stopford, Jane L *see* EFFECTS OF CALORIC RESTRICTION AND RESISTIVE EXERCISE ON THE RESTING ENERGY EXPENDITURE OF WEIGHT-REDUCED OBESE WOMEN
Stopka, Christine *see*
- THE EFFECTS OF ENHANCED ECCENTRIC TRAINING ON IMPROVEMENT OF STRENGTH
- EFFECTS OF LOW-INTENSITY, PAIN-FREE EXERCISE ON MUSCLE METABOLISM IN PATIENTS WITH PERIPHERAL VASCULAR DISEASE EVALUATED BY 31P-NMR SPECTROSCOPY

Stopperka, Klaus *see* JOURNAL OF INFORMATION RECORDING MATERIALS
Stora, G *see* RECHERCHES DE BIONOMIE DESCRIPTIVE ET EXPERIMENTALE (IN VIVO ET IN VITRO) DANS QUELQUES BIOTOPES LITTORAUX SOUMIS A DES VARIATIONS NATURELLES OU ARTIFICIELLES DES CONDITIONS DU MILIEU (NOTAMMENT DANS L'ETANG DE BERRE ET LE GOLFE DE FOS)
Storace, S *see*
- BEAUX YEUX, AND JEUNES COEURS SOYEZ FIDELLES. THE FAVORITE FRENCH AIR AND GAVOTTE
- [LE NOZZE DI DORINA]. IO NON ERA

Storace, Stephen *see*
- THE HAUNTED TOWER: A COMIC OPERA IN THREE ACTS.
- LODOISKA: A MUSICAL ROMANCE IN THREE ACTS.
- MY GRANDMOTHER: A MUSICAL ENTERTAINMENT
- NO SONG, NO SUPPER: A COMIC OPERA IN TWO ACTS.
- THE SIEGE OF BELGRADE: AN OPERA IN THREE ACTS.
- THE THREE AND THE DEUCE: A MUSICAL ENTERTAINMENT.

STORBONDEN OG HAND SØNNER : EN FORTÅLLING FRA SCHWARZWALD / Auerbach, Berthold – Christiana: P T Malling, 1858 – 1r – 1 – us U.W. Library [830]
DER STORCH : ERZAEHLUNG / Schwarzkopf, Nikolaus – Muenchen: A Langen/G Mueller, 1942, c1938 – 1r – 1 – us U.W. Library [830]
Storch, N ? *see* DAS BIECHLIN ZAIGET AN WER DER LEBENDIG SEY AUFF ERDTRICH
Storch, N et al *see* EIN TZEYTLANG GESCHWIGNER CHRISTLICHER BRUEDER AUCH UM DIE WARHEIT WILLEN VERYAGT
Storck, Karl *see* DEUTSCHE LITERATURGESCHICHTE
Storck, Willy F *see* GOETHES FAUST UND DIE BILDENDE KUNST
STOREFRONT CLASSROOM – (v.7. 1979-80 5,6,9) – 1976-80. Continued by Utopian classroom – 1 – us UMI [073]
Storer, Bellamy *see* THE BIBLE IN THE COMMON SCHOOLS
Storer, D H *see* A SYNOPSIS OF THE FISHES OF NORTH AMERICA
Storey, Frederick Davis *see* THE HIGHER CRITICISM CROSS-EXAMINED: AN APPEAL AND A WARNING
Storey, Graham *see* CHARLES DICKENS RESEARCH COLLECTION
Storey, Henry W *see* HISTORY OF CAMBRIA COUNTY
Storey, Moorfield *see* CHARLES SUMMER
LA STORIA CALABRESE E LA DIMORA DEGLI EBREI IN CALABRIA / Dito, O – 1916. BJ-25-47 1 – 9 – ne IDC [945]
STORIA DEI SALMI E DELL'IDEA MESSIANICA / Minocchi, Salvatore – Firenze: Bib. Scientifico-Relig., 1904. 1 fiche – 9 – us A.T.L.A. [240]
STORIA DEL CODICE DI ALLEANZA DELLE NAZIONI... / Cervo, F – Napoli, 1878 – 1mf – 1 – ILM-1697/1 – ne IDC [327]
STORIA DEL DUOMO DI ORVIETO / Valle, G della – O 1046 1. 1791 – 9 – ne IDC [700]
STORIA DEL PATRIARCA S. BRUNONE E DEL SUO ORDINE CARTUSIANO / Tromby, B – Napoli. Tom 1-10. 1773-1779 – 276mf – 9 – Dfl966.00 – ne Slangenburg [240]
STORIA DELL ARTE ITALIANA / ed by Venturi, Adolfo – O 450. 7 v. in 10 pts. 1901-1915 – 314mf – 9 – ne IDC [945]
STORIA DELLA ARTE CRISTIANA NEI PRIMI OTTO SECOLI DELLA CHIESA / Garrucci, R – Prato. v1-6. 1873-1881 – 96mf – 8 – Dfl336.00 – ne Slangenburg [240]
STORIA DELLA COLONIZZAZIONE DELLA CIRENAICA / Narducci, Guglielmo – Milano: Editoriale arte e storia, 1942 – us Res Libr [960]
STORIA DELLA LETTERATURA RUSSA CONTEMPORANEA / Lo Gatto, E – R-1374 2. 1958 – 8 – ne IDC [460]
STORIA DELLA LETTERATURA TEDESCA MEDIOEVALE / Gruenanger, Carlo – Milano: Nuova Accademia Editrice, 1955 – 1r – 1 – us U.W. Library [430]

STORIA DELLA LITTERATURA LATINA CHRIST : 1: DALLE ORIGINE FINO AL TEMPO DI CONSTANTINO / Moricca, U – 1923 – 2mf – 8 – ne Slangenburg [240]
STORIA DELLA MUSICA / Martini, G – 1757-81.3v – 9 – us Sibley [780]
STORIA DELLA MUSICA / Martini, G – P 717. 3 v. 1757, 1770, 1781 – 9 – ne IDC [780]
STORIA DELLA SCULTURA / Cicognara, L – O-964 1. 7 v. 1823-1824 – 9 – ne IDC [730]
STORIA D'ETIOPIA : PARTE PRIMA: DALLE ORIGINI ALL'AVVENTO DELLA DINASTIA SALOMONIDE / Rossini, Carlo Conti – Pergamo, 1928 – 19mf – 8 – Dfl67.00 – ne Slangenburg [240]
STORIA DI ABELARDO E DEI SUOI TEMPI : DIVISA IN LIBRI QUATTRO / Tosti, Luigi – Napoli: Poliorama Pittoresco, 1851 – 1mf – 9 – 0-8370-6951-3 – 1986-0951 – us A.T.L.A. [920]
STORIED DOMAIN / Alter, J Cecil – (v3. Utah reel 3) – Chicago: American Historical Society, n.d. v1-2. Utah reel 2. (Cox Library Collection) – 5 – us Americana [978]
STORIES FROM THE EARLY WORLD / Fleming, Rachel M – 1923 – 1 – us I.U. Libraries [830]
STORIES FROM THE RABBIS / Isaacs, Abram S – New York: Charles L. Webster, 1893. 1 fiche – 9 – us A.T.L.A. [270]
STORIES OF ABU ZEID THE HILALI IN SHUWA ARABIC – London: Kegan Paul, Trench, Trubner, 1930 – us Res Libr [470]
THE STORIES OF GENESIS : SYLLABUS OF A COURSE OF TWELVE LECTURE STUDIES / Harper, William Rainey – (Includes bibliographies) – Chicago: University Press of Chicago: D C Heath, c1893 – 1mf – 9 – 0-8370-9391-0 – 1986-3391 – us A.T.L.A. [220]
STORIES OF GUERNSEY COUNTY / Wolfe, William G – Cambridge: 1943. Ohio Reel 35. (The Cox Library Collection) – 5 – us Americana [978]
STORIES OF INDIAN CHRISTIAN LIFE / Satthianadhan, Samuel – Madras: Srinivasa, Varadachari, 1898 – 1mf – us A.T.L.A. [306]
STORIES OF THE HIGH PRIESTS OF MEMPHIS / Griffith, FL L – Oxford, 1900. BNE-375/1 – 9 – ne IDC [290]
Stork, Hans-Walter *see* LEBEN JESU
Storke, Yda A *see*
– HISTORY OF CAYUGA COUNTY, 1789
– A MEMORIAL AND BIOGRAPHICAL HISTORY OF THE COUNTIES OF SANTA BARBARA, SAN LUIS OBISPO AND VENTURA, CALIFORNIA
STORM : AUSWAHL AUS SEINEN WERKEN / Storm, Theodor – Leipzig: Bibliographisches Institut, 1944 – 1 – us U.W. Library [430]
THE STORM, 1970 – Montreal: Bibliotheque Nationale du Quebec, 1973. SEM35P56 – 1r – 1 – Can$15.00 – cn Bibl Nat [830]
Storm, Gertrud *see*
– BRIEFE AN SEINE BRAUT
– BRIEFE AN SEINE FRAU
– BRIEFE AN SEINE FREUNDE HARTMUTH BRINKMANN UND WILHELM PETERSEN
– BRIEFE AN SEINE KINDER
– VERGILBTE BLAETTER AUS DER GRAUEN STADT
Storm, Theodor *see*
– AUF LEBEN UND TOD
– AUSGEWAEHLTE NOVELLEN
– EIN BEKENNTNIS
– BOETJER BASCH
– BRIEFE AN SEINE BRAUT
– BRIEFE AN SEINE FRAU
– BRIEFE AN SEINE FREUNDE HARTMUTH BRINKMANN UND WILHELM PETERSEN
– BRIEFE AN SEINE KINDER
– DER BRIEFWECHSEL ZWISCHEN THEODOR STORM UND GOTTFRIED KELLER
– ES KLINGT WIE EINE SAGE
– GEDICHTE
– IMMENSEE
– IMMENSEE; IM SONNENSCHEIN; EIN GRUENES BLATT; ABSEITS
– MENSCHENSCHICKSALE
– NOVELLEN
– NOVELLEN DER LIEBE
– DER SCHIMMELREITER
– STORM
– STORM-FONTANE
– THEODOR STORMS BRIEFE AN FRIEDRICH EGGERS
– THEODOR STORMS BRIEFE AN SEINEN FREUND GEORG LORENZEN
– THEODOR STORM'S SAEMMTLICHE SCHRIFTEN
– VON JUNGER LIEBE, LUST UND LEID
– WERKE
STORM-BELL / ed by Butler, Josephine E – London, 1898-1900 – 4mf – 9 – W-31/1 – ne IDC [941]
STORM-FONTANE : BRIEFE DER DICHTER UND ERINNERUNGEN VON THEODOR FONTANE / Storm, Theodor – (Includes bibliographical references and index) – Reinbeck bei Hamburg: Parus-Verlag, c1948 – 1r – 1 – us U.W. Library [920]
STORMKLOCKAN – Stockholm, Sweden. 1908-29 – 14r – 1 – sw Kungliga [072]
Stormont, Gil. R *see* HISTORY OF GIBSON COUNTY
Storms, G *see* ANGLO-SAXON MAGIC
STORNOWAY GAZETTE – 1 – £42.00r – uk Scot News [072]
Storr, Vernon F *see* THE DEVELOPMENT OF ENGLISH THEOLOGY IN THE NINETEENTH CENTURY, 1800-1860
Storrow, Edward *see* PROTESTANT MISSIONS IN PAGAN LANDS
Storrs, Richard Salter *see*
– ADDRESSES ON FOREIGN MISSIONS
– BERNARD OF CLAIRVAUX
– JOHN WYCLIFFE AND THE FIRST ENGLISH BIBLE
– THE PURITAN SCHEME OF NATIONAL GROWTH
– THE PURITAN SPIRIT
– THE RECOGNITION OF THE SUPERNATURAL IN LETTERS AND IN LIFE: AN ORATION
STORY HOUR LEADER – 1937-49 – 1 – 93.03 – us Baptist [240]
Story, Isaac A *see* MINUTES OF THE PROCEEDINGS OF A CONVENTION OF CHURCHES THAT FORMED THE FREEDOM ASSOCIATION OF UNITED BAPTISTS
Story, Joseph *see*
– COMMENTARIES ON EQUITY JURISPRUDENCE, AS ADMINISTERED IN ENGLAND AND AMERICA. 11TH ED
– COMMENTARIES ON EQUITY PLEADINGS, AND THE INCIDENTS THEREOF, ACCORDING TO THE PRACTICE OF THE COURTS OF EQUITY, OF ENGLAND AND AMERICA. 6TH ED
– COMMENTARIES ON THE CONFLICT OF LAWS, FOREIGN AND DOMESTIC, IN REGARD TO CONTRACTS, RIGHTS, AND REMEDIES, AND ESPECIALLY IN REGARD TO MARRIAGES, DIVORCE, WILLS, SUCCESSIONS, AND JUDGMENTS. 8TH ED
– COMMENTARIES ON THE CONSTITUTION OF THE UNITED STATES
– COMMENTARIES ON THE LAW OF AGENCY AS A BRANCH OF COMMERCIAL AND MARITIME JURISPRUDENCE...4TH ED
– COMMENTARIES ON THE LAW OF BAILMENTS, WITH ILLUSTRATIONS FROM THE CIVIL AND FOREIGN LAW. 8TH ED
THE STORY OF A CHINESE OXFORD MOVEMENT / Ku, Hung-Min – 2d ed. 1912 – 1 – us A.T.L.A. [240]
THE STORY OF A DARK PLOT : OR TYRANNY ON THE FRONTIER / A.L.O.C. – (Relates to troubles of the Temperance Movt in Canada) – Boston: The Warren Press, 1903 – 3mf – 9 – $4.50 – LLMC 96-042 – us L.L.M.C. [971]
STORY OF A GRAND DESIGN : UNESCO 1946-1993 / Conil-Lacoste, Michel – 1995 – 508p – 9 – 92-3-102878-2 – fr UNESCO [370]
THE STORY OF A ROMAN SOLDIER / Pearse, Mark Guy – 1899 – 9 – us A.T.L.A. [240]
THE STORY OF A SOUL, OR, THOUGHTS ON THE PARABLE OF THE PRODIGAL SON / Zabriskie, Francis Nicoll – New York: A.D.F. Randolph, 1872.1 fiche – 9 – us A.T.L.A. [240]
THE STORY OF ACADIA / Hannay, James – Kentville, N.S.: Dominion Atlantic Railway, 18–. 05355. (Pre-1900 Canadiana) – 9 – cn C.I.H.M. [971]
THE STORY OF AFRICA AND ITS EXPLORERS / Brown, Robert – v1-4. 1911 – 1r – 1 – us Ross [960]
THE STORY OF AMERICAN HISTORICAL FLASKS / McKearin, Helen – 1953. 70p., 90 illus. 1 fiche. Fiche no. 1032 – 9 – $2.50 – us Corning Mus [700]
THE STORY OF AMERICAN PRESSED GLASS OF THE LACY PERIOD 1825-1850 / Rose, James H – 1954. 163p., 41 illus. 3 fiche. Fiche no. 1042 – 9 – $6.25 – us Corning Mus [700]
STORY OF AN OLD TOWN / Demilt, A P – Omaha: Douglas Printing Co., 1902. Nebraska Reel 4. (The Cox Library Collection) – 5 – us Americana [978]
THE STORY OF ANCIENT IRISH CIVILISATION / Joyce, Patrick Weston – London: Longmans, Green; Dublin: M H Gill, 1907 – 1mf – 9 – 0-8370-6910-6 – 1986-0910 – us A.T.L.A. [941]
THE STORY OF BARBARA, HER SPLENDID MISERY AND HER GILDED CAGE / Braddon, Mary Elizabeth – British Fiction Archive: Unit 5 – 9 – uk Bell [830]
THE STORY OF BESSIE COSTRELL / Ward, Mary Augusta – British Fiction Archive: Unit 2 – 9 – uk Bell [830]
THE STORY OF BOHEMIA / Gregor, Frantiska – Cincinnati: Cranston & Curts; New York: Hunt & Eaton, 1895. 486p. illus – 1 – us U.W. Library [943]
THE STORY OF BUGUMA BAPTISTS / Roberson, Cecil F – History of beginning of SBC's mission work in Eastern Nigeria, West Africa; Nigerian Baptist Historical Materials; 58p – 1 – us Baptist [240]
THE STORY OF CANADA / Bourinot, John George – New York: G. Putnam; Toronto: Copp, Clark, 1896. 00222. (Pre-1900 Canadiana) – 9 – cn C.I.H.M. [971]
THE STORY OF CHALDEA FROM THE EARLIEST TIMES TO THE RISE OF ASSYRIA,. / Ragozin, Zenaide A – Treated as a general introduction to the study of ancient history. 2nd ed. rev. New York: G.P. Putnam, 1898. xx,381p. illus. maps – 1 – us U.W. Library [900]
THE STORY OF CHARLES STRANGE / Wood, Ellen – British Fiction Archive: Unit 1 – 9 – uk Bell [830]
THE STORY OF CHRISTIAN ENDEAVOR / Anderson, R P – Boston: United Society of Christian Endeavor, [1914?] – 1mf – us A.T.L.A. [240]
THE STORY OF COMMANDER ALLEN GARDINER, R.N.,WITH SKETCHES OF MISSIONARY WORK IN SOUTH AMERICA / Marsh, John W – 2d ed. 1868 – 1 – us A.T.L.A. [240]
THE STORY OF DANIEL : HIS LIFE AND TIMES / Hunter, Peter Hay – (Includes bibliographical references) – 4th ed. Edinburgh: Oliphant, Anderson, Ferrier, 1890 – 1mf – 9 – 0-8370-3695-X – 1985-1695 – us A.T.L.A. [220]
THE STORY OF DAYTON / Conover, Charlotte R – Dayton: The Greater Dayton Asso., 1917. Ohio Reel 51. (The Cox Library Collection) – 5 – us Americana [978]
THE STORY OF ELIZABETH / Ritchie, Anne Thackeray – London: Smith, Elder, 1863 – 1 roll – 1 – 1-55879-508-1 – uk Libr Preservation [830]
THE STORY OF ELIZABETH / Thackeray, Anne – British Fiction Archive: Unit 3 – 9 – uk Bell [830]
THE STORY OF ENGLAND BY ROBERT MANNING OF BRUNNE (RS87) / Robert Mannyng; ed by Furnivall, F J – (v1 1887 Dfl32.00. v2 1887 Dfl28.00) – ne Slangenburg [941]
THE STORY OF EUGENE DEBS, BY HENRY T. SCHNITTKIND (UNCLE HENRY) WITH INTRODUCTION BY ROMAIN ROLLAND / Thomas, Henry – Boston: National Educational Committee, Independent Workmen's Circle, 1929. 1 reel.1249 – 1 – us U.W. Library [330]
THE STORY OF FIFTY YEARS' MISSION WORK IN CHHOTA NAGPUR / Chatterton, Eyre – London: S.P.C.K., New York: E. & J.B. Young, 1901 – 1mf – us A.T.L.A. [240]
STORY OF GEORGETOWN / Rodway, James – Revised from a series of articles in the Argosy, 1903. 1903 – 1 – us UMI [972]
THE STORY OF GEORGIA AND THE GEORGIA PEOPLE, 1732 TO 1860 / Smith, George G – 2nd ed, 1900. 11 fiches. F-0090 – 9 – us A.G.L.L. [920]
THE STORY OF GLASS DECORATION / Corning Museum of Glass – Corning, NY. 1954. Fiche No. 1027 – 1mf – 9 – $2.50 plus $0.50 postage and handling plus N.Y. State sales tax as applicable – us Corning Mus [740]
THE STORY OF HOSEA'S MARRIAGE / Bewer, Julius August – [Chicago]: Uni of Chicago Press, [ca 1906] – 1mf – 9 – 0-8370-2326-2 – 1985-0326 – us A.T.L.A. [220]
THE STORY OF HOULTON: FROM THE PUBLIC RECORDS AND FROM THE EXPERIENCES OF ITS FOUNDERS, THEIR DESCENDANTS AND ASSOCIATES TO THE PRESENT TIME: ALSO ANNOUNCEMENTS OF ALL THE PROMINENT MERCHANTS AND MANUFACTURING INTERESTS / Barnes, Francis – Houlton, Me.: W. Smith, 1889. 02100. (Pre-1900 Canadiana) – 9 – cn C.I.H.M. [971]
STORY OF IOWA / Harsha, William J – 1890 – 1 – $50.00 – us Presbyterian [240]
THE STORY OF IRELAND / O'Grady, Standish – London: Methuen, 1894. 214p – 1 – us U.W. Library [941]
STORY OF ISRAEL (CCC6) / Chan, Shui – (In Chinese) – 1st ed. Hong Kong: Council on Christian Literature for Overseas Chinese, 1955 – 1r – 1 – 0-8370-1706-8 – 1984-6096 – us A.T.L.A. [240]
THE STORY OF JOHN FREDERIC OBERLIN / Beard, Augustus Field – Boston: Pilgrim Press, c1909 – 1mf – us A.T.L.A. [240]
THE STORY OF JOHN G. PATON TOLD FOR YOUNG FOLKS : OR, THIRTY YEARS AMONG SOUTH SEA CANNIBALS / ed by Paton, James – New York: A L Burt, 1898 – 2mf – 9 – 0-8370-6339-6 – 1986-0339 – us A.T.L.A. [920]
THE STORY OF LAURA SECORD, 1813 / Curzon, Sarah Anne – Toronto: Williamson & Co., 1891. 02249. (Pre-1900 Canadiana) – 9 – cn C.I.H.M. [971]
STORY OF LEE COUNTY, IOWA – v1. Ed. by Nelson C. Roberts and S. W. Moorehead, 1914.8 fiches. F-0138 – 9 – us A.G.L.L. [978]
THE STORY OF MADAGASCAR / Mears, John W – Philadelphia: Presbyterian Board of Publication, c1873 – 1mf – us A.T.L.A. [960]
THE STORY OF MARCUS WHITMAN : EARLY PROTESTANT MISSIONS IN THE NORTHWEST / Craighead, JG – Philadelphia: Presbyterian Board of Publication and Sabbath-School Work, 1895 – 1mf – us A.T.L.A. [240]
THE STORY OF MARY JONES AND HER BIBLE / Jones, Mary – 1882 – 1 – 6.09 – us Baptist [240]
THE STORY OF METHODISM THROUGHOUT THE WORLD, FROM THE BEGINNING TO THE PRESENT TIME;... / Hyde, A B – Springfield, Mass., 1889. xiv/827p – 9 – ne IDC [240]
THE STORY OF METHODIST UNION / Townsend, W J – London, [1906]. xiii/254p – 3mf – 9 – ne IDC [240]
THE STORY OF MY BECOMING A CHRISTIAN (CCC346) = KUEI I CHI TU TZU SHU / Yin, Tzu-heng – (In Chinese) – [s.l: s.n, 1931] – 1r – 1 – 1984-6685 – us A.T.L.A. [920]
THE STORY OF MY CONNECTION WITH THE CHINIQUY MOVEMENT IN MONTREAL, OF 1874-77, OR, A PRESBYTERIAN CHURCH ASSEMBLY REPORT CRITICISED / Court, William B – Montreal?: s.n., 1877?. 04182. (Pre-1900 Canadiana) – 9 – cn C.I.H.M. [971]
STORY OF MY LIFE / Loy, M – Columbus, Ohio: Lutheran Book Concern, 1905 – 2mf – us A.T.L.A. [240]
THE STORY OF MY LIFE / Taylor, Philip Meadows – British Fiction Archive: Unit 5 – 9 – uk Bell [830]
THE STORY OF NORTHERN RHODESIA / Bradley, Kenneth – 2nd ed. London: Longmans, Green, [1955] – Northern Rhodeisa and Nyasaland Joint Publications Bureau – us Res Libr [960]
THE STORY OF OKLAHOMA CITY / Kerr & Gainer – Chicago: S.J. Clarke Publ. Co., 1922. 3v. Oklahoma Reel 3. (The Cox Library Collection) – 5 – us Americana [978]
A STORY OF ONE SHORT LIFE, 1783-1818 / Stryker, Elisabeth G – Chicago: Woman's Presbyterian Board of Foreign Missions of the Northwest, c1888 – 1mf – 9 – 0-8370-6526-7 – 1986-0526 – us A.T.L.A. [920]
THE STORY OF OUR COLONIES: WITH SKETCHES OF THEIR PRESENT CONDITIONS / Bourne, Henry Richard Fox – London: J. Hogg, 1869. 00215. (Pre-1900 Canadiana) – 9 – cn C.I.H.M. [900]
STORY OF OUR ENGLISH BIBLE AND WHAT IT COST / Bayly, Mary – London: James Nisbet, (188?). 1 fiche – 9 – us A.T.L.A. [240]

THE STORY OF OUR ENGLISH BIBLE AND WHAT IT COST / Bayly, Mary – London: James Nisbet, [188-?] – 1mf – 9 – 0-8370-2217-7 – 1985-0217 – us A.T.L.A. [220]
THE STORY OF PARIS / Okey, Thomas – Illus. by Katherine Kimball. London: J.M. Dent, 1906 – 1 – us U.W. Library [944]
THE STORY OF PUNISHMENT; A RECORD OF MAN'S INHUMANITY TO MAN / Barnes, Harry Elmer – Boston: The Stratford Company, c1930. vii,292p – 1 – us U.W. Library [360]
THE STORY OF RELIGION IN ENGLAND / Herford, Brooke – 6th ed. With an index by H. R. Appleton. 1899 – 9 – us A.T.L.A. [240]
THE STORY OF SCOTLAND YARD / Dilnot, George – Boston, New York: Houghton, Mifflin & Co, 1927 – 4mf – 9 – $6.00 – LLMC 92-196 – us L.L.M.C. [360]
THE STORY OF SIGURD THE VOLSUNG AND THE FALL OF THE NIBLUNGS / Morris, William – London: Ellis and White, 1877, [1876] – 1 roll – 1 – 1-55879-596-0 – uk Libr Preservation [390]
THE STORY OF SONNY SAHIB / Duncan, Sara Jeannette – By Mrs. Everard Cotes. New York: S. Appleton, 1895. 05297. (Pre-1900 Canadiana) – 9 – cn C.I.H.M. [830]
STORY OF ST PAUL: COMPARISON OF ACTS & EPISTLES / Bacon, Benjamin Wisner – Boston: Houghton, Mifflin, 1904.1 fiche – 9 – us A.T.L.A. [240]
THE STORY OF THE ABRAHAM LINCOLN BATTALION, WRITTEN IN THE TRENCHES OF SPAIN – N.Y., 1937? Fiche W1213. (Blodgett Collection of Spanish Civil War Pamphlets) – 9 – us H.U. College Libr [946]
THE STORY OF THE AMERICAN BOARD : AN ACCOUNT OF THE FIRST HUNDRED YEARS OF THE AMERICAN BOARD OF COMMISSIONERS FOR FOREIGN MISSIONS / Strong, William Ellsworth – (Includes index) – Boston: Pilgrim Press: American Board of Commissioners for Foreign Missions, 1910 – 2mf – 9 – 0-8370-6705-7 – 1986-0705 – us A.T.L.A. [240]
THE STORY OF THE AMERICAN INDIAN: HIS ORIGIN, DEVELOPMENT, DECLINE AND DESTINY / Brooks, Elbridge Streeter – Boston: D. Lothrop, 1887. 03226. (Pre-1900 Canadiana) – 9 – cn C.I.H.M. [305]
THE STORY OF THE ANABAPTISTS / Pike, Edward Carey – (Includes index) – London: National Council of Evangelical Free Churches, 1904 – 1mf – 9 – 0-8370-8932-8 – 1986-2932 – us A.T.L.A. [240]
THE STORY OF THE ART OF MUSIC / Crowest, Frederick J – New York: D Appleton & Co, 1902 – us Res Libr [780]
THE STORY OF THE AUSTRALIAN CHURCH / Symonds, Edward – London: S.P.C.K.; New York: E. & J.B. Young, 1898 – 1mf – us A.T.L.A. [240]
STORY OF THE BEGINNING: GENESIS IN THE LIGHT OF RECENT RESEARCH / Green, Mrs. Frederic – London: Wells Gardner, Darton, 1905 – 9 – us A.T.L.A. [220]
THE STORY OF THE BIBLE / Stock, Eugene – (Includes bibliographical references and index) – New York: E P Dutton, [1906?] – 1mf – 9 – 0-8370-9186-1 – 1986-3186 – us A.T.L.A. [220]
STORY OF THE BIBLE IN POETRY AND SONG – Chicago: Elliot & Beezley, 1892.1 fiche – 9 – us A.T.L.A. [240]
THE STORY OF THE BIBLE IN POETRY AND SONG : BEING A NARRATIVE OF THE PRINCIPLE EVENTS OF THE BIBLE, AS TOLD BY THE POETS / ed by Dale, Daphne – Chicago: Ell[i]ot and Beezley, 1892 – 2mf – 9 – 0-8370-2251-7 – 1985-0251 – us A.T.L.A. [220]
THE STORY OF THE BIRKENHEAD: A RECORD OF BRITISH HEROISM / Addison, Albert Christopher – 1902 – 9 – $20.00 – uk Libr Preservation [941]
STORY OF THE CHILDHOOD AND PASSION OF THE LORD JESUS...IN THE WORDS OF THE EVANGELISTS / Klueh, John M – Chicago: J.M. Klueh, 1892. 1 fiche – 9 – us A.T.L.A. [240]
THE STORY OF THE CHINA INLAND MISSION / Guinness, Geraldine M – London: Morgan & Scott. 2v. 1893-94 – 4mf – 9 – 0-8370-6528-3 – 1986-0528 – us A.T.L.A. [240]
THE STORY OF THE CHURCH OF EGYPT : BEING AN OUTLINE OF THE HISTORY OF THE EGYPTIANS UNDER THEIR SUCCESSIVE MASTERS FROM THE ROMAN CONQUEST UNTIL NOW / Butcher, Edith Louisa – (Includes index) – London: Smith, Elder. 2v. 1897 – 4mf – 9 – 0-8370-7610-2 – 1986-1610 – us A.T.L.A. [230]
THE STORY OF THE CONGRESS : A RECORD OF GREAT THINGS SEEN AND HEARD IN CATHOLIC LONDON, SEPT 1908 – London: Burns & Oates, [1909?] – 1mf – 9 – 0-8370-6987-4 – 1986-0987 – us A.T.L.A. [240]
THE STORY OF THE EARTH AND MAN / Dawson, John William – Toronto: Copp Clark, 1873. 02610. (Pre-1900 Canadiana) – 9 – cn C.I.H.M. [560]
THE STORY OF THE ENGLISH BAPTISTS / Carlile, John C – London: J. Clarke, 1905 – 1mf – us A.T.L.A. [240]
THE STORY OF THE EVANGELIZATION SOCIETY / Wood, John – London: Evangelization Society, [1907?] – 1mf – us A.T.L.A. [240]
THE STORY OF THE FILIBUSTERS, TO WHICH IS ADDED THE LIFE OF COLONEL DAVID CROCKETT / Roche, James Jeffrey – London: T.F. Unwin, 1891. illus. xiii,373p. Double map – 1 – us U.W. Library [972]
THE STORY OF THE GOTHS, FROM THE EARLIEST TIMES TO THE END OF THE GOTHIC DOMINION IN SPAIN / Bradley, Henry – New York: G.P. Putnam; London: T. Fisher Unwin, 1891. xxii,376p. ill. map – 1 – us U.W. Library [900]
THE STORY OF THE GREAT DISASTER – San Francisco, Apr 18-21 1906 – 1r – 1 – $50.00 – B40326 – us Library Micro [978]
THE STORY OF THE GREAT WAR: SOME LESSONS FROM THE MAHABHARATA FOR THE USE OF HINDU STUDENTS IN THE SCHOOLS OF INDIA / Besant, Anne Wood – Adyar, Madras: Theosophical Publishing House, 1899. 3p,271p – 1 – us U.W. Library [940]
THE STORY OF THE HYMNS AND TUNES / Brown, Theron & Butterworth, Hezekiah – New York: Richard R. Smith, c1906 – 2mf – us A.T.L.A. [780]
THE STORY OF THE HYMNS, OR, HYMNS THAT HAVE A HISTORY / Butterworth, Hezekiah – 1875 – 1 – us A.T.L.A. [240]
THE STORY OF THE IMITATIO CHRISTI / Wheatley, Leonard Abercromby – London: E. Stock, 1891. xvi,236p. facsim – 1 – us U.W. Library [240]
THE STORY OF THE INNS OF COURT / Barton, Dunbar P – Boston: Houghton-Mifflin, 1924 – 4mf – 9 – $6.00 – LLMC 84-271 – us L.L.M.C. [340]
THE STORY OF THE IRISH BEFORE THE CONQUE FROM THE MYTHICAL PERIOD TO THE INVASION UNDER STRONGBOW / Ferguson, Mary Catharine Guinness – 3rd ed. rev. and enlg. Dublin: Sealy, Bryers & Walker, 1903. xvi,377p. maps – 1 – us U.W. Library [941]
STORY OF THE JEWISH REVOLT (CCC103) = KU YU T'AI KO MING SHIH YEN I / Chien, Yu-wan – (In Chinese) – 1st ed. Hong Kong: Council on Christian Literature for Overseas Chinese, 1957 – 1r – 1 – 1984-B500 – us A.T.L.A. [270]
A STORY OF THE LIFE AND TIMES OF JACQUES DE MOLAY / Haywood, H L – St Louis, MO: National Masonic Research Society, 1925 – 1mf – 9 – $1.50 – LLMC 92-180 – us L.L.M.C. [920]
THE STORY OF THE LIFE OF MACKAY OF UGANDA : PIONEER MISSIONARY / Harrison, Mrs J W – (Includes bibliographical references) – 6th ed. London: Hodder & Stoughton, 1898 – 1mf – 9 – 0-8370-6260-8 – 1986-0260 – us A.T.L.A. [920]
THE STORY OF THE L.M.S., 1795-1895 / Horne, Charles S – 2d rev. ed. 1895 – 1 – us A.T.L.A. [240]
STORY OF THE MANUSCRIPTS / Merrill, George Edmunds – Boston: D. Lothrop, 1881. 1 fiche – 9 – us A.T.L.A. [240]
STORY OF THE MAUMEE VALLEY AND TOLEDO AND THE SANDUSKY REGION / Van Tassel, Charles S – Chicago: S.J. Clarke Publ. Co., 1929. 2v. Ohio Reel 10. (The Cox Library Collection) – 5 – us Americana [978]
THE STORY OF THE NEGRO : THE RISE OF THE RACE FROM SLAVERY / Washington, Booker T – New York. v1. 1909 – 1r – 1 – us Ross [976]
THE STORY OF THE OLD CATHOLIC AND KINDRED MOVEMENTS : LEADING UP TO A UNION OF NATIONAL INDEPENDENT CHURCHES / Scarth, A M E – London: Simpkin, Marshall; Bath: R.E. Peach, 1883 – 1mf – us A.T.L.A. [240]
THE STORY OF THE PRAYER-BOOK IN THE OLD AND NEW WORLD AND THROUGHOUT THE ANGLICAN CHURCH / Dearmer, Percy – London, 1933 – 4mf – 8 – Dfl19.00 – ne Slangenburg [240]
THE STORY OF THE PSALMS / Van Dyke, Henry – New York: Charles Scribner, 1888 – 1mf – 9 – 0-8370-5634-9 – 1985-3634 – us A.T.L.A. [220]
THE STORY OF THE PSALTERS : A HISTORY OF THE METRICAL VERSIONS OF GREAT BRITAIN AND AMERICA FROM 1549 TO 1885 / Glass, Henry Alexander – London: Kegan Paul, Trench, 1888 – 1mf – us A.T.L.A. [240]
STORY OF THE RESURRECTION OF CHRIST TOLD ONCE MORE / Furness, William H – Philadelphia: Lippincott, 1885. 1 fiche – 9 – us A.T.L.A. [240]
THE STORY OF THE REVISED NEW TESTAMENT / Riddle, Matthew Brown – Philadelphia:Sunday School Times Co, c1908 – 1mf – 9 – 0-8370-4894-X – 1985-2894 – us A.T.L.A. [220]
THE STORY OF THE RHINEGOLD = DER RING DES NIBELUNGEN : TOLD FOR YOUNG PEOPLE / Chapin, Anna Alice – New York: Harper & Brothers, 1899 – 1 – us U.W. Library [790]
THE STORY OF THE RHINEGOLD : DER RING DES NIBELUNGEN, TOLD FOR YOUNG PEOPLE / Chapin, Anna Alice – New York: Harper & Brothers, 1899, c1897 – 1r – 1 – us U.W. Library [430]
THE STORY OF THE SCOTTISH COVENANTS IN OUTLINE / Fleming, David Hay – Edinburgh: Oliphant, Anderson & Ferrier, 1904 – 1mf – us A.T.L.A. [240]
THE STORY OF THE UGANDA PROTECTORATE / Lugard, Frederick John Dealtry – London: Horace Marshall & Son, n.d.. 175p – 1 – us U.W. Library [960]
THE STORY OF THE UNITED METHODIST CHURCH / ed by Smith, H et al – London, 1932. xi/406p – 5mf – 9 – ne IDC [240]
THE STORY OF THE UPPER CANADIAN REBELLION, LARGELY DERIVED FROM ORIGINAL SOURCES AND DOCUMENTS. VOL. 01 / Dent, John Charles – Toronto: C. Blackett Robinson, 1885. 05444. (Pre-1900 Canadiana) – 9 – cn C.I.H.M. [971]
THE STORY OF THE UPPER CANADIAN REBELLION, LARGELY DERIVED FROM ORIGINAL SOURCES AND DOCUMENTS. VOL. 02 / Dent, John Charles – Toronto: C. Blackett Robinson, 1885. 05445. (Pre-1900 Canadiana) – 9 – cn C.I.H.M. [971]
THE STORY OF THE WELSH REVIVAL : AS TOLD BY EYEWITNESSES TOGETHER WITH A SKETCH OF EVAN ROBERTS AND HIS MESSAGE TO THE WORLD / Goodrich, Arthur et al – New York: Fleming H Revell, c1905 – 1mf – 9 – 0-8370-6156-3 – 1986-0156 – us A.T.L.A. [240]
THE STORY OF THE WOMAN'S FOREIGN MISSIONARY SOCIETY OF THE METHODIST EPISCOPAL CHURCH, 1869-1895 / Baker, Frances J – Cincinnati: Cranston & Curts, 1896. 436p. 1 fiche – 9 – us A.T.L.A. [240]
THE STORY OF TURKEY / Lane-Poole, Stanley – New York: G.P. Putnam; London: T. Fisher Unwin, 1889, c1888 – 1mf – us A.T.L.A. [956]
THE STORY OF UGANDA : AND THE VICTORIA NYANZA MISSION / Stock, Sarah Geraldina – New York: Fleming H Revell, 1892 – 1mf – 9 – 0-8370-6619-0 – 1986-0619 – us A.T.L.A. [960]
THE STORY OF W.J.E. BENNETT : FOUNDER OF S. BARNABAS, PIMLICO, AND VICAR OF FROOME-SELWOOD: AND OF HIS PART IN THE OXFORD CHURCH MOVEMENT OF THE NINETEENTH CENTURY / Bennet, F – London, New York: Longmans, Green, 1909 – 1mf – us A.T.L.A. [920]
STORY TIME – (Succeeds The Child's Gem). 6 Oct 1929-61 – 1 – 241.57 – us Baptist [240]
Story, William Wetmore *see*
– LIFE AND STORY OF JOSEPH STORY
– STORY'S REPORTS OF CASES IN THE FIRST CIRCUIT, 1839-1845
THE STORY-CITY OF PITHOM AND THE ROUTE OF THE EXODUS (MEES NO 1) / Naville, E – London, 1885 – 3mf – 8 – Dfl13.00 – ne Slangenburg [910]
STORY'S REPORTS OF CASES IN THE FIRST CIRCUIT, 1839-1845 / Story, William Wetmore – Boston: Little-Brown. v1-3. 1851-55 (all publ) – 24mf – 9 – $36.00 – LLMC 81-470 – us L.L.M.C. [340]
Stosch, Georg *see*
– FUER HEILIGE GUETER: APHORISMEN ZUR GESCHICHTLICHEN RECHTFERTIGUNG DES ALTEN TESTAMENTS
– ST. PAULUS, DER APOSTEL: EINE APOLOGETISCHE STUDIE
Stössel, C *see* KURZTGEFASSTES MUSICALISCHES LEXICON
Stössel, J D *see* KURZTGEFASSTES MUSICALISCHES LEXICON
Stott, Peter *see* PLASMA PHYSICS AND CONTROLLED FUSION
Stottmeister, Frank *see* INFIZIERBARKEIT VERSCHIEDENER ERYTHROZYTENPOPULATONEN MIT MALARIA
STOUFFVILLE SUN – (1982-1992.-18r) – Stouffville, 1993 – 2r – 1 – cn Preston [971]
Stough *see* HISTORY OF HALL COUNTY
STOUGHTON 1709-1900 – (Mf 1-3: Vital Records 1709-61. Mf 4-15: Tax Lists 1728-51. Mf 16-18: Vital Records 1745-1800. Mf 19-21: Vital Records 1800-33. Mf 22-24: Births 1727-1847. Mf 24: Town Records 1878-84. Mf 25: Deaths 1723-1848. Mf 26-28: Marriages 1727-1851. Mf 29-31: Index Marriages 1727-1873. Mf 31: Index Intentions 1801-33. Mf 32: Marriages & Intents 1753-65. Mf 33-44: Intentions 1834-1904. Mf 45-47: Index: Births 1844-91. Mf 48-49: Index Marriages 1844-92. Mf 50-51: Index Deaths 1844-92. Mf 52-53: Vital Records 1844-51. Mf 54-59: Births 1851-91. Mf 60-64: Marriages 1852-91. Mf 65-71: Deaths 1852-91. Mf 72-76: Vital Records 1892-1903) – (mf ed 1991) – 76mf – 9 – 0-87623-125-3 – us Holbrook [920]
Stoughton, John *see*
– AGES OF CHRISTENDOM BEFORE THE REFORMATION
– CHURCH AND STATE TWO HUNDRED YEARS AGO
– FOOTPRINTS OF ITALIAN REFORMERS
– AN INTRODUCTION TO HISTORICAL THEOLOGY
– OUR ENGLISH BIBLE: ITS TRANSLATIONS AND TRANSLATORS
– THE SPANISH REFORMERS
– WILLIAM WILBERFORCE
Stoughton, John Alden *see* REFLECTIONS UPON THE "MEMORANDUM" OF THE HON. WM. H. WILLIAMS, REGARDING THE COMPENSATION OF JUDGES
Stoughton, Laurie J *see* PSYCHOLOGICAL PROFILES BEFORE AND AFTER 12 WEEKS OF WALKING OR EXERSTRIDER TRAINING IN ADULT WOMEN
STOURBRIDGE MERCURY – England. -w. 3 Jan 1862-29 May 1868, 2 Jul-24 Sep 1869. (3 reels) – 1 – uk British Libr Newspaper [072]
STOURBRIDGE SUN – England. -w. 29 Nov 1884-21 Mar 1885 – 1 – uk British Libr Newspaper [072]
STOURBRIDGE TIMES – England. -w. 5 Oct 1861-20 Dec 1862. (1 reel) – 1 – uk British Libr Newspaper [072]
Stout, B A *see* ENERGY FOR WORLD AGRICULTURE
Stout, George Frederick *see* ANALYTIC PSYCHOLOGY
Stout, Tom *see* MONTANA: ITS STORY AND BIOGRAPHY
STOVE MOUNTERS' AND RANGE WORKERS' JOURNAL : 1898-1955 / Stove Mounters International Union of North America – (Coll title: Labor Union Periodicals, Pt 1) – 7r – 1 – $945.00 – 1-55655-250-5 – us UPA [331]
Stove Mounters International Union of North America *see* STOVE MOUNTERS' AND RANGE WORKERS' JOURNAL
STOW 1669-1905 – (Mf 1-13: Vital Records 1679-1858. Mf 12: Out-of-Town Marriages 1695-1798. Mf 14-18: Intentions 1823-88. Mf 15-18: Vital Records 1796-1851. Mf 19-26: Church Records 1774-1879. Mf 27-35: Town Records 1669-1746. Mf 36-47: Proprietors 1718-1826. Mf 48-94: Town Records 1724-1911. Mf 95-113: Accounts 1775-1861. Mf 112-115: School Records 1843-69. Mf 116: Land Records 1654-1827; Muster Roll 1779. Mf 117: Indentures 1755-1818. Mf 118-123:

Military 1816-76. Mf 124-126: Town Records 1688-1864. Mf 127-149: Taxes 1742-1860. Mf 150-159: Mortgages 1835-97. Mf 160-164: Voters 1884-1934. Mf 165-171: Paupers 1807-1939. Mf 172-173: Intentions 1889-1928. Mf 174-175: Burials 1688-1981. Mf 176: Birth Index 1801-1900. Mf 177-178: Births 1801-55. Mf 178: Marriages 1844-56; Deaths 1818-55. Mf 179-186: Vitals 1842-1905) – (mf ed 1996) – 186mf – 9 – 0-87623-382-5 – us Holbrook [920]
Stow, Baron *see* VOLUNTARY ASSOCIATION THEIR USE AND ABUSE
Stowe, Harriet Beecher *see*
- FOOTSTEPS OF THE MASTER
- LADY BYRON VINDICATED
- WOMEN IN SACRED HISTORY: A SERIES OF SKETCHES DRAWN FROM SCRIPTURAL, HISTORICAL AND LEGENDARY SOURCES

THE STOWE MISSAL / Warner, G F – 2v. 1906-1915 – 4mf – 8 – ne Slangenburg [210]
Stowe, Stephen R *see* A COMPARISON OF BODY COMPOSITION CHANGES IN MODERATELY OBESE AND EXTREMELY OBESE WOMEN WHO EXPERIENCE THE SAME CALORIC DEFICIT
Stowell, Hugh *see* A MODEL FOR MEN OF BUSINESS, OR, THE CHRISTIAN LAYMAN CONTEMPLATED
Stowell, Joseph M *see* BACKGROUND AND HISTORY OF THE GENERAL ASSOCIATION OF REGULAR BAPTIST CHURCHES
STOWMARKET CHRONICLE & MERCURY. (STOWMARKET CHRONICLE) – England. Oct. 1963-Dec 1975; 1979. 1981. 22mqn reels – 1 – uk British Libr Newspaper [072]
St-Pierre, Jacqueline *see* BIBLIOGRAPHIE COLLECTIVE DES AUTEURS DE LA REGION DU SAGUENAY
STRABANE MORNING POST – Ireland. 7 Jan 1823-11 Apr 1837.-w. 5 reels – 1 – uk British Libr Newspaper [072]
Strachan, John *see* A SERMON, PREACHED AT YORK, UPPER CANADA ON THE THIRD OF JUNE, BEING THE DAY APPOINTED FOR A GENERAL THANKSGIVING
STRACHAN PRISON TRIAL – ((Case history)) – 3r – 1 – sa Microfile [960]
Strachey, J *see* INDEX TO THE ROLLS OF PARLIAMENT. 1278-1503
Strachey, Loe *see* NATIONAL WORKSHOPS
Strachey, R *see* CATALOGUE OF THE PLANTS OF KUMAON AND OF THE ADJACENT PORTIONS OF GARHWAL AND TIBET
Strachwitz, Moritz Graf *see* GEDICHTE
Strack, H L *see* CATALOG DER HEBRAEISCHEN BIBELHANDSCHRIFTEN DER KAISERLICHEN OEFFENTLICHEN BIBLIOTHEK IN ST PETERSBURG
Strack, Hermann Leberecht *see*
- ABODA ZARA: DER MISCHNATRAKTAT GOETZENDIENST
- DER BLUTABERGLAUBE BEI CHRISTEN UND JUDEN
- EINLEITUNG IN DAS ALTE TESTAMENT:... APOKRYPHEN UND PSEUDEPIGRAPHEN
- EINLEITUNG IN DEN TALMUD
- THE JEW AND HUMAN SACRIFICE
- JOMA: DER MISCHNATRAKTAT VERSOEHNUNGSTAG
- SCHABBATH: DER MISCHNATRAKTAT SABBATH
- DIE SPRUECHE SALOMOS

THE STRAD – 1921-92. Continued annually – 1 – £1,450.00 – uk World [073]
Strada, Jacobus de *see* EPITOME THESAVRI ANTIQVITATVM, HOC EST, IMPP. ROM. ORIENTALIUM ET OCCIDENTALIUM ICONUM EX ANTIQUIS NUMISMATIBUS QUAM FIDELISSIME DELINIATARUM
STRADNIEKU AVIZE – Petersburgh, De 1917 a 1918 – 1 reel – 1 – Sfr120.00 – sz Infoprint [947]
STRADNIEKU AVIZE – St Petersburg, 1917-18 – 1r – 1 – inquire – us Ross [072]
Straelen, J B van der *see* GESLAGT-LYSTE DER NAKOMELINGEN VAN DER VERMAERDEN CHRISTOFFEL PLANTIN
Straesser, E *see* QUINTET FOR CLARINET AND STRINGS, OP. 34
DIE STRAFBARKEIT EINER IN DEN KONSULARGEBIETEN BEGANGENEN BIGAMIE ... / Boenisch, H – Breslau, 1917 – 1mf – 9 – ILM-2080/1 – ne IDC [327]
Strafford, New Hampshire. Strafford and Barnstead Union Church *see* RECORDS
STRAFRECHTELIJKE ONTZETTING VAN RECHTEN... / Frikkers, C – Amsterdam, 1897 – 2mf – 1 – ILM-2030/1 – ne IDC [327]
DER STRAFRECHTLICHE BEGRIFF INLAND... / Harburger, H – Noerdlingen, 1878 – 1mf – 1 – ILM-2028/1 – ne IDC [327]
DER STRAFRECHTLICHE BEGRIFF INLAND... / Harburger, H – Noerdlingen, 1882 – 3mf – 1 – ILM-2001/1 – ne IDC [327]
DER STRAFRECHTLICHE SCHUTZ DES GESCHAFTSGEHEIMNISSES / Speierer, Ludwig – Munchen, 1926. 74 p. LL-4022 – 1 – us L of C Photodup [340]
DIE STRAFRECHTSPFLEGE IN AMERIKA / Hartmann, Adolf – Berlin: Vahlen, 1906. 335p. LL-561 – 1 – us L of C Photodup [340]
Strahlenberg, P J von *see*
- DAS NORD- UND OSTLICHE THEIL VON EUROPA, UND ASIA / IN SO WEIT SOLCHES DAS GANTZE RUSSISCHE REICH MIT SIBERIEN UN DER GROSSEN TATAREN IN SICH BEGREIFFET...
- DAS NORD-UND OSTLICHE THEIL VON EUROPA, UND ASIA

STRAHLENTHERAPIE – v. 1-113. 1912-60 – 1,5,6 – us Princeton Micro [615]
STRAIGHT GOODS – Portland OR. Feb 11 1928 – 1 – us U.O. Library [071]
STRAIGHT TALK – Ireland.8 Nov-28 Dec 1922 – 1 – ie Microforms [072]
Straight University. New Orleans University *see* CATALOGS, 1870-1935
STRAITS BUDGET – Kuala Lumpur. Federation of Malaysia. -w. 1956- – 1 – us UMI [072]
THE STRAITS BUDGET – Singapore: E A Snewin, may 31 1951-55 – 5r – 1 – us Res Libr [072]
THE STRAITS BUDGET – Singapore, Jul 1940-Feb 1942 – 3r – 1 – us L of C Photodup [072]
THE STRAITS ECHO – (Issues for nov 1-13 1976 filmed with: National Echo nov 15-30 1976) – Penang [Malaysia]: Straits Echo Press, Ltd, 1971-nov 13 1976 – us Res Libr [072]
THE STRAITS ECHO : TIMES OF MALAYSIA – (No Sunday issues filmed: Issue for jan 1 1968 filmed with: Straits Echo, Times of Malaya and Pinang Gazette jan 3-mar 1968) – Penang [Malaysia]: Straits Echo Press Ltd, 1953-68. [jun 1956-jan 1 1968 (53r)] – 1 – us Res Libr [072]
THE STRAITS ECHO : TIMES OF MALAYSIA AND PINANG GAZETTE – (Issues for jan 3-mar 1968 filmed with: Straits Echo, Times of Malaya jan 1 1968) – Penang [Malaysia]: Straits Echo Press Ltd, jan 3 1968-70 – us Res Libr [072]
STRAITS GUARDIAN – Singapore, 13 May, 3 Jun 1854 – 3ft – 1 – uk British Libr Newspaper [072]
STRAITS INDEPENDENT AND PENANG CHRONICLE – (8 May 1895-12 Feb 1896 not publ) – George Tonn, Malaysia. 13 Mar 1889-8 May 1895; 12, 19 Feb 1896 – 10r – 1 – uk British Libr Newspaper [072]
STRAITS MARITIME JOURNAL *see* PENANG MARITIME JOURNAL
STRAITS MARITIME JOURNAL AND GENERAL NEWS – George Town, Malaysia. 7 Dec 1894-31 Oct 1896 – 3r – 1 – uk British Libr Newspaper [072]
STRAITS OBSERVER – George Town, Malaysia. 15 Jun 1897-31 Jan 1898 – 1r – 1 – uk British Libr Newspaper [072]
STRAITS TIMES – 1984- – 62r per y – 1 – inquire – us Ross [072]
THE STRAITS TIMES – Singapore. 1845, 1848, 1852, 1883-1942, 1984-to date – 1 – uk Microform Academic [072]
THE STRAITS TIMES – Singapore: E A Murphy, 1956-81 – us Res Libr [072]
THE STRAITS TIMES – Singapore, Sept 1945-55; 1982-83 – 91r – 1 – us L of C Photodup [072]
Straker, David Augustus *see* COMPENDIUM OF EVIDENCE
Straker, David Augustus et al *see* SELECTED WORKS
Strakhov, A B *see* EAST SLAVIC ETHNOGRAPHY AND FOLKLORE
Strakhov, N *see* BOR'BA S ZAPADOM V NASHEI LITERATURE
STRALN = RAYS – (In Yiddish) – Kaunas, LT. v1 no2. 15 Jun 1938 – 1r – 1 – $20.00 – cn Can Microfilming [072]
Stralow, C R *see* ACUTE CARDIOVASCULAR RESPONSES OF CARDIAC PATIENTS TO DYNAMIC VARIABLE RESISTANCE EXERCISE OF VARYING INTENSITY
Strand, A E *see* A HISTORY OF THE NORWEGIANS OF ILLINOIS
DIE STRAND-UND STEPPENGEBIETE DER IBERISCHEN HALBINSEL UND DEREN VEGETATION / Willkomm, H M – Leipzig. 1852. B-5448 2 – 8 – ne IDC [580]
STRANG REPORTER – Strang, NE. -w. Sept 1892; Aug 1899; Apr 1901-Feb 1902; May-Oct 1902 – 1 – us NE Hist [071]
THE STRANGE ADVENTURES OF A HOUSE-BOAT / Black, William – British Fiction Archive: Unit 4 – 9 – uk Bell [830]
THE STRANGE ADVENTURES OF A PHAETON / Black, William – British Fiction Archive: Unit 4 – 9 – uk Bell [830]
STRANGE CASE OF DR. JEKYLL AND MR. HYDE / Stevenson, Robert Louis – London: Longmans, Green, 1886 – 1 roll – 1 – 1-55879-679-7 – uk Libr Preservation [830]
Strange, J *see* DIALOGUS MIRACULORUM
STRANGE LIBRARY OF AFRICANA: AUTHOR-TITLE CATALOGUE / Johannesburg Public LibraryPretoria State Library – 1978 – 473mf – 9 – sa State Libr [025]
STRANGE LIBRARY OF AFRICANA: SUBJECT CATALOGUE / Johannesburg Public LibraryPretoria State Library – 1980 – 382mf – 9 – sa State Libr [025]
THE STRANGE VISITATION / Corelli, Marie – British Fiction Archive: Unit 1 – 9 – uk Bell [830]
A STRANGE WORLD / Braddon, Mary Elizabeth – British Fiction Archive: Unit 5 – 9 – uk Bell [830]
STRANGER AND GUEST / Vincent, Marvin Richardson – New York: Anson D F Randolph, c1879 – 1mf – 9 – 0-8370-7434-7 – 1986-1434 – us A.T.L.A. [240]
STRANGERS AND PILGRIMS / Braddon, Mary Elizabeth – British Fiction Archive: Unit 5 – 9 – uk Bell [830]
STRANICHKA UZNIKA : BIULLETEN' – M., 1988-1991. Nos. 1-17 – 6mf – 9 – RI-4/1 – ne IDC [947]
STRANITSY ZHIVOI ISTORII – Moscow, 1961. 152p. Film and photographic materials. BR-10,741/1 – 9 – ne IDC [460]
Stranitzky, Joseph Anton *see* LUSTIGE REYSS-BESCHREIBUNG AUS SALTZBURG IN VERSCHIEDENE LAENDER
STRANNIK – Dukhovnyi zhurnal sovremennoi zhizni, nauki i literatury. Spb. 1860-1917. Lacking: v. 3 (9) 1890; v. 1 (4), v. 2 (6), v. 3 (10-12) 1899; v. 1 (2-4), v. 2-3, 1900; 1901-08; v. 1 (2-3), v. 3 (11-12) 1916; 1917. B-1912 2 – 8 – ne IDC [460]
STRANNIK / Veltman, A F – Moscow, 1831-32.v1-3. B-1467/2 – 8 – ne IDC [460]
STRANNITSA. POVEST' / Remizov, A – Petrograd, 1918. BR-848 2 – 8 – ne IDC [460]
Strano, Alessandro *see* THE RELATIONSHIP BETWEEN OBESITY MEASUREMENTS WITH SERUM LIPIDS, FAT INTAKE AND PHYSICAL ACTIVITY IN CHILDREN
Straparola, Giovanni Francesco *see* THE MOST DELECTABLE NIGHTS OF STRAPAROLA OF CARAVAGGIO
Strappini, Walter Diver *see* THE INWARD GOSPEL
Strashimirov, D T *see* ISTORIIA NA APRILSKOTO VUZSTANIE
STRASHNOE V REVOLIUTSII : PO LICHNYM VOSPOMINANII AM / Bonch-Bruevich, Vladimir Dmitrievich – Moskva: Akts. izd. o-vo "Ogonek", 1926 – 1 – CSUX88-B6753 – us Hoover Inst Photo [947]
STRASHNYE GODY / Bielogorskii, N – [S.l.]: "Rodina", [between 1943 and 1947] – 1 – CSUX88-B5277 – us Hoover Inst Photo [947]
Strassburg, Gottfried von *see* TRISTAN UND ISOLDE
DIE STRASSBURGER LITTERARISCHE "BESEGARD" : EINE SATIRE IN VIER ABSCHNITTEN / Halter, Eduard – Illstadt: [s.n.], 1899 – 1r – 1 – us U.W. Library [870]
STRASSBURGER POST – France, 18 Jan 1916-21 Nov 1918 (imperfect) – 10r – 1 – uk British Libr Newspaper [072]
DIE STRASSBURGER REFORMATOREN UND DIE GEWISSENSFREIHEIT / Paulus, Nikolaus – Freiburg im Breisgau, St. Louis, Mo.: Herder, 1895 – 1mf – us A.T.L.A. [943]
STRASSBURGER RUNDSCHAU – Strasbourg, France. 1901-14 – 1 – fr A.C.R.P.P. [072]
STRASSBURGER THEOLOGISCHE STUDIEN / ed by Ehrhard, A & Mueller, Eugen – (Bd. 1, Heft 4 u. 5. Ester Suppelementband) – 19mf – 8 – ne Slangenburg [290]
DIE STRASSE DES LEBENS : ROMAN / Tremel-Eggert, Kuni – Muenchen: F Eher, 1939 – 1r – 1 – us U.W. Library [830]
DIE STRASSE DES UNRECHTS : DES ROKOKO ANDERES GESICHT: ROMAN / Langer, Georg – Muenchen: F Eher, 1939 – 1r – 1 – us U.W. Library [830]
DIE STRASZBURGER LITURGISCHEN ORDNUNGEN IM ZEITALTER DER REFORMATION / Hubert, F – Goettingen, 1900 – 5mf – 8 – Dfl22.00 – ne Slangenburg [240]
STRATEGIC POINTS IN THE WORLD'S CONQUEST : THE UNIVERSITIES AND COLLEGES AS RELATED TO THE PROGRESS OF CHRISTIANITY / Mott, John Raleigh – New York: F.H. Revell, c1897 – 1mf – us A.T.L.A. [370]
STRATEGIE – (Also available on CD-ROM) – France. 1988-1995 – 2r per y – 5,6 – Sfr869.00 – sz Infoprint [944]
STRATEGIE, OBJET, ENSEIGNEMENT, ELEMENTS / Grouard, Auguste Antoine – Paris. L. Baudoin. 1895. vi, 85p. (Strategy of War Series) – 9 – fr Hachette [355]
STRATEGIE POUR L'ENSEIGNEMENT DE L'ANGLAIS DE L'INFORMATIQUE : DEMARCHE DIDACTIQUE INTEGRANT L'ORDINATEUR ET LE TRAITEMENT DE TEXTE / Dechet, Arlette – 4mf – 9 – 10422 – fr Atelier National [420]
STRATEGIES, APPROACHES AND SYSTEMS IN INTEGRATED WATERSHED MANAGEMENT – 1986 – 238p – it F.A.O. [631]
STRATEGIES FOR CROP INSURANCE PLANNING – 1990 – 167p – it F.A.O. [360]
STRATEGIES FOR ENDOGENOUS DEVELOPMENT / Tri, Huynh Cao et al – 1987 – x/309p – 9 – 92-3-102209-1 – Co-published with Oxford and IBH Publishing Co. PVT, Ltd, New Delhi, who have exclusive sales rights in India and in South-East Asia. Unesco has exclusive sales rights in the UK and USA – fr UNESCO [338]
STRATEGIES FOR LIBERTY / Buchanan, Martin L – 1985. 5p – 9 – 1.00f – at Libertarian Micro [335]
STRATEGISCHE ALLIANZEN : ANALYSE EINES INDUSTRIEOEKONOMISCHEN PHAENOMENS UND DESSEN WETTBEWERBSIMPLIKATIONEN / Gramberg, Frank – 1993 – 1mf – 9 – DM60.00 – 3-89349-754-4 – gw Hänsel [338]
STRATEGY – (Cont: Playback Strategy at v2 no 23 1991) – Toronto. v2-6. 1990/91-1994/95 – 1 – Can$85.00y – cn Micromedia [073]
STRATEGY / Svechin, A A – Minneapolis: East View Publications, 1992 – 7mf – 9 – $19.95 – 1-879944-00-6 – us East View [355]
STRATEGY *see* PLAYBACK STRATEGY
STRATEGY AND ART OF WAR FROM FEUDAL TIMES TO THE WORLD WARS / ed by Charney, J P – 66 French, German or English titles. Available by individual title also – 426mf – 9 – fr Hachette [355]
STRATEGY AND BASIC TARGETS OF LONG-TERM DEVELOPMENT AND THE THIRD FIVE-YEAR DEVELOPMENT PLAN / Turkey. Prime Ministry. State Planning Organization – Ankara. 1973. BD-2003 1 – 9 – ne IDC [338]
STRATEGY AND OBJECTIVES OF THE SECOND FIVE YEAR DEVELOPMENT PLAN (1968-1972) / Turkey. Devlet Planlama Teskilati – Ankara. 1967. BD-390 1 – 9 – ne IDC [338]
A STRATEGY FOR THE SOUTH EAST / Great Britain. South East Economic Planning Council – London. 1967 – 9 – ne IDC [338]
STRATEGY OF WAR SERIES *see* STRATEGY AND ART OF WAR FROM FEUDAL TIMES TO THE WORLD WARS
Straten, F vander *see* SOMMIGHE NIEUWE SCHRIFTUERELICKE LIEDEKENS
Stratford, Jessie P *see* BUTLER COUNTY'S EIGHTY YEARS 1885-1935
STRATFORD-ON-AVON NEWS – England, 5 Dec 1901-27 Nov 1902 – 62ft – 1 – uk British Libr Newspaper [072]
STRATFORD-UPON-AVON HERALD – England, 15 Jun 1866- – 187+ r – 1 – uk British Libr Newspaper [072]
STRATHAVEN TIMES AND HAMILTON NEWS – Scotland, UK. 4 Jan-27 Sep 1879 – 1/2r – 1 – uk British Libr Newspaper [072]

STRATHCONA PLAIN DEALER – Alberta, CN. Nov 1894-Dec 1912 – 5r – 1 – cn Commonwealth Micro [072]
STRATHEDEN ADVERTISER – Cupar, Scotland, UK. 6 Aug 1853-2 Jun 1855 – 23ft – 1 – uk British Libr Newspaper [072]
Strathern, Paul *see* SILK AND SPICE ROUTES
STRATHMORE / Ouida – British Fiction Archive: Unit 3 – 9 – uk Bell [830]
STRATHMORE STANDARD – Alberta, CN. Oct 1909-Dec 1948 – 13r – 1 – cn Commonwealth Micro [072]
STRATHROY-AGE DISPATCH – Ontario Prov., Canada. 1981- – 1 – cn Commonwealth Micro [072]
STRATHSPEY AND BADENOCH HERALD – 1 – £42.00r – uk Scot News [072]
STRATHSPEY HERALD AND GRANTOWN ADVERTISER – Grantown, Scotland, UK. 1907-83. -w. 33 reels – 1 – uk British Libr Newspaper [072]
Stratigos, Susan *see* WOMEN, HOUSEHOLDS AND CHANGE
STRATIGRAPHICAL SYSTEM OF ORGANIZED FOSSILS / Smith, W – G 113 2. 1817 – 8 – ne IDC [560]
STRATIOTIKA NEA – Athens. Greece. -w. 11 Nov 1951-8 May 1955. (Imperfect). (2 reels) – 1 – uk British Libr Newspaper [949]
STRATTON BOOSTER – Stratton, NE. -w. May 1959-May 1962 – 1 – us NE Hist [071]
Stratton, John F *see* MILITARY BAND MUSIC
STRATTON NEWS – Stratton, NE. -w. Aug 1911-Jan 1927; Aug-Sept 1927; Jan 1930-Oct 1957 – 1 – us NE Hist [071]
STRATTON SIGNAL – Stratton, NE. -w. Nov 1895; Mar 1896; Dec 1896-Feb 1898; Apr 1898-Feb 1899 – 1 – us NE Hist [071]
Stratz, Heinz *see* DER REGENMACHER VON TURKESTAN
Stratz, Rudolph *see* STARK WIE DIE MARK
STRAUBINGER TAGBLATT – Straubing, West Germany. 1976- – ca 11r per yr – 1 – gw Mikrofilm [072]
Strauch, A *see* CATALOGUE SYSTEMATIQUE DE TOUS LES COLEOPTERES DECRITS DANS LES ANNALES DE LA SOCIETE ENTOMOLOGIQUE DE FRANCE DEPUIS 1832 JUSQU'A 1859
Strauch, Alfons *see* DIE KOSMOGRAPHIE IN ARIOSTS ORLANDO FURIOSO
Straus, Oscar S *see* ROGER WILLIAMS
STRAUSS AS A PHILOSOPHICAL THINKER = PHILOSOPH STRAUSS : A REVIEW OF HIS BOOK "THE OLD FAITH AND THE NEW FAITH", AND A CONFUTATION OF ITS MATERIALISTIC VIEWS / Ulrici, Hermann – (In English. Includes bibliographical references and index) – Philadelphia: Smith, English; Edinburgh: T & T Clark, 1874 – 1mf – 9 – 0-8370-5598-9 – 1985-3598 – us A.T.L.A. [210]
Strauss, David Friedrich *see*
- DER ALTE UND DER NEUE GLAUBE: EIN BEKENNTNISS
- DER CHRISTUS DES GLAUBENS UN DER JESUS DER GESCHICHTE
- KLEINE SCHRIFTEN
- KLOPSTOCK'S JUGENDGESCHICHTE UND KLOPSTOCK UND DER MARKGRAF KARL FRIEDRICH VON BADEN
- THE LIFE OF JESUS CRITICALLY EXAMINED

Strauss, Eberhard *see* KAMERADEN UNTERM SPATEN
Strauss, Emil *see*
- DER ENGELWIRT: EINE SCHWABENGESCHICHTE
- FREUND HEIN
- DER LAUFEN
- PRINZ WIEDUWITT
- VATERLAND

STRAUSS: L'ANCIENNE ET LA NOUVELLE FOI / Vera, Augusto – Naples: Detken & Rocholl, 1873. 1 fiche – 9 – us A.T.L.A. [240]
Strauss, Richard *see*
- ARIADNE AUF NAXOS
- ELEKTRA
- INTERMEZZO

Strauss und Torney, Lulu von *see*
- BAUERNSTOLZ
- DER HOF AM BRINK
- JUDAS
- NEUE BALLADEN UND LIEDER
- REIF STEHT DIE SAAT

Strauss und Torney, Viktor Friedrich von *see* GUDRUN
Strausz, D F *see* DAS LEBEN JESU
STRAY FEATHERS : A JOURNAL OF ORNITHOLOGY FOR INDIA AND ITS DEPENDENCIES. – Calcutta, (1872) 1873-1888(-1899). v. 1-11. London. 1899. Index. BZ-2040 2 – 112mf – 8 – ne IDC [073]
STRAY LEAVES FROM AN ARCTIC JOURNAL / Osborn, Sh – BN 330 2. 1852 – 8 – ne IDC [910]
STRAY LEAVES FROM SCOTCH AND ENGLISH HISTORY: WITH THE LIFE OF SIR WILLIAM WALLACE, SCOTLAND'S PATRIOT, HERO, AND POLITICAL MARTYR / Glass, Charles Gordon – (Montreal: J. Lovell), 1873. 03448. (Pre-1900 Canadiana) – 9 – cn C.I.H.M. [941]
STRAY PAPERS : BEING STORIES, REVIEWS, VERSES AND SKETCHES (1821-1847). EDITED WITH AN INTRODUCTION AND NOTES BY LEWIS MELVILLE / Thackeray, William Makepeace – London: Hutchinson and Co., 1901 – 1 roll – 1 – 1-55879-616-9 – uk Libr Preservation [800]
THE STRAYED REVELLER : AND OTHER POEMS / Arnold, Matthew – London: B. Fellowes, 1849 – 1 roll – 1 – 1-55879-193-0 – uk Libr Preservation [810]
STRAZ – Scranton, PA, 1897-1898, 1900-1907, 1910, 1913, 1917, 1919-1937 – 10r – 1 – us I.H.R.C. [978]
STRAZ – Scranton, PA. The Guard. -w. 17 May 1951-7 July 1955. 3 reels – 1 – uk British Libr Newspaper [071]
STRAZ LIDU – Olomouc, Czechoslovakia. Jan 1953-Mar 1960 – 4r – 1 – us L of C Photodup [072]
STRAZ MIRU – Karlovy Vary, Czechoslovakia. 1955-Mar 1960 – 1r – 1 – us L of C Photodup [072]
STRAZ SEVERU – (Some issues lacking) – Liberec, Czechoslovakia. Aug 1945-Oct 1946 – 2r – 1 – us L of C Photodup [072]
STRAZNICA EWANGELICZNA – (Lacks: v10 1955. Cont by and filmed with: Zwiastun) – v1-15. 1946-60 – Inquire – ATLA S0382 – us A.T.L.A. [240]
STRAZNICA EWANGELICZNA *see* ZWIASTUN
STREAKS OF SQUATTER LIFE, AND FAR-WEST SCENES / Robb, John S – 1847 – 9 – $15.00 – us Scholars' Facs [830]
THE STREAMLET. A FAVORITE SONG / Shield, W – Philadelphia: printed by G E Blake [1804?] – 1 – us Sibley [780]
STREATHAM NEWS – London. 18 Jul 1891-2 Dec 1959.-w. 86mqn reels – 1 – uk British Libr Newspaper [072]
STREATHAM NEWS – Surrey, England.1983-84. -w. 7 reels – 1 – uk British Libr Newspaper [072]
Streck, Friedrich Karl *see* DIE ANGST IN DEN INTERPRETATIONEN DER EXISTENZPHILOSOPHIE UND DER TIEFENPSYCHOLOGIE
Streck, M *see* ASSURBANIPAL UND DIE LETZTEN ASSYRISCHEN KOENIGE
Streckenbach, Gerhard *see* STILTHEORIE UND RHETORIK DER ROEMER ALS GEGENSTAND DER IMITATIO IM BEREICH DES DEUTSCHEN HUMANISMUS
Strecker, G *see* DAS JUDENCHRISTENTUM IN DEN PSEUDOKLEMENTINEN (T.U.U. 5-70)
Strecker, H *see* BUTTERFLIES AND MOTHS OF NORTH AMERICA
Strecker, Otto A *see* ENTWICKLUNG IN EINER MONETAER GESTEUERTEN WELTWIRTSCHAFT
STREET AND INTERURBAN RAILWAY SYSTEMS IN OHIO, 1860-1946 / Wilson, Harriet E – 1 – us Ohio Hist [978]
STREET AND SMITH'S NEW YORK WEEKLY. (NEW YORK WEEKLY WELCOME) – New York. 28 May 1904-7 Aug 1915.-w. 12 reels – 1 – uk British Libr Newspaper [071]
Street, Arthur Leonard Howell *see* LEGAL DECISIONS AFFECTING COAL AND COKE; ABSTRACT OF DECISIONS OF AMERICAN COURTS
STREET DUST / Ouida – British Fiction Archive: Unit 3 – 9 – uk Bell [830]
STREET FOODS – 1989 – 100p – it F.A.O. [640]
STREET RAILROAD ACCIDENT LAW. / Nellis, Andrew J – Albany, N.Y.: Bender, 1904. 711p. LL-1507 – 1 – us L of C Photodup [340]
STREET RAILWAY REPORTS, ANNOTATED / ed by Gilbert, Frank G – (Reporting the electric railway and street railway decisions of the Federal and State Courts in the U.S. 150 Albany: M Bender. v1-8. 1903-13 (all publ)) – 89mf – 9 – $133.00 – LLMC 84-709 – us L.L.M.C. [340]
STREET RAILWAY SERVICE... – London [Ont]: London Street Railway Co, [1917?-19–?] – 9 – cn C.I.H.M. [380]
Street, Thomas Atkins *see* THE FOUNDATIONS OF LEGAL LIABILITY.
STREET TRADES PERMITS / Wisconsin. Industrial Commission. Statistical Dept – 1940-58. 4 fiches. (Harvard Law School Library Collection.) – 9 – 1.50f – us H.U. Law [331]
Streetsboro. Ohio. Congregational Church *see* CHURCH RECORDS, MS 3190
Streff, L L *see* A DETERMINATION OF MEMBER SATISFACTION AT THREE DIFFERENT TYPES OF FITNESS CENTER
LA STREGA / Ouida – British Fiction Archive: Unit 3 – 9 – uk Bell [830]
Strehlke, Friedrich *see* MARTIN OPITZ
Streibert, Jacob *see* THE DIFFICULTIES OF THE NEW HYPOTHESIS
DIE STREICHE DER SCHLIMMEN PAULETTE : ODER, DIE INSEL DER ENTTAEUSCHUNG: EIN ROMAN IN WEISS UND BLAU / Strobl, Karl Hans – Berlin: Ullstein, 1912 – 1r – 1 – us U.W. Library [830]
Streicher, Andreas *see* SCHILLERS FLUCHT
STREIFLICHTER / Hoffmann von Fallersleben, August Heinrich – Berlin: Franz Lipperheide, 1872 – 1r – 1 – us U.W. Library [810]
DER STREIK DER BERGLEUTE UND DIE SOZIALDEMOKRATIE – 1905 – 1 – DM30.00 – gw Mikro Press [331]
DIE STREIKJUSTIZ IM RUHRREVIER ODER MADAME JUSTITIA MIT VERBUNDENEN AUGEN – Bochum 1913 – 1 – DM30.00 – gw Mikro Press [331]
DAS STREIT BUECHLIN / Huberinus, Caspar – [Augsburg: Philipp Ulhart, 1541]. [G.F.: 15.1] – 3mf – 9 – HUB-37/1 – ne IDC [240]
Streit, R *see* BIBLIOTHECA MISSIONUM
DER STREIT UM DIE FREIHEIT DER MEERE ... / Boschan, R – Leipzig, 1919 – 1mf – 9 – ILM-2180/1 – ne IDC [327]
DER STREIT ZWISCHEN ERASMUS UND LUTHER UEBER DIE WILLENSFREIHEIT / Zickendraht, Karl – (Includes name index) – Leipzig: J C Hinrichs, 1909 – 1mf – 9 – 0-8370-5725-6 – 1985-3725 – us A.T.L.A. [120]
STREITS SCHLESISCHE PROVINZIALBLAETTER *see* SCHLESISCHE PROVINZIAL-BLAETTER
STREKOZA, RUSSIA – St Petersburg, 1875-82; 1884-1908 – 334mf – 9 – $1,990.00 – us Ross [790]
Strempel, J C F *see* FILICUM BEROLINENSIUM SYNOPSIS
Strenger, Hermann *see* STROM AUS DER ERDE
STRENGNAS TIDNING – Strangnas, Sweden. 1846-47. 1 reel. 1854-1920; 1955-63, 111 reels – 1 – sw Kungliga [072]
STRENGNAS TIDNING *see* ESKILSTUNAKURIREN
STRENGNAS WECKOBLAD – Strangnas, Sweden. 1825-28 – 1 reel – 1 – sw Kungliga [072]
STRENGNASBLADET – Strangnas, Sweden. 1848-53 – 2r – 1 – sw Kungliga [072]
STRENGTH AND BEAUTY / Miller, James Russell – New York: Thomas Y Crowell, c1899 – 1mf – 9 – 0-8370-7246-8 – 1986-1246 – us A.T.L.A. [240]
STRENGTH GAINS CONSEQUENT TO TEN WEEKS OF UNIVERSAL OR BOWFLEX TRAINING / Marquardt, Janis R & Porcari, John P – 1992 – 2mf – $8.00 – us Microform Publ [612]
STRENGTH GAINS THROUGH AQUATIC EXERCISE / Martin, Melanie M & Redmond, Charles J – 1992 – 2mf – $8.00 – us Microform Publ [612]
STRENGTH OF MATERIALS – v1-26. 1969-94 – 1,5 – $150.00v – us UMI [620]
STRENGTHEN NATIONAL UNITY AND COMMUNIST UNITY: DOCUMENTS OF THE THIRD PLENUM OF THE CENTRAL COMMITTEE OF THE COMMUNIST PARTY OF INDONESIA, END DECEMBER 1961 / Communist Party. Indonesia. Comite Central – SE-3512 1. 1962 – 9 – ne IDC [950]
STRENGTHENING COOPERATION BETWEEN ENGINEERING SCHOOLS AND INDUSTRY / Fishwick, Wilfred – 1983 – 167p – 9 – 92-3-101989-9 – fr UNESCO [620]
STRESS AND JOB SATISFACTION OF NURSE MANAGERS IN HOSPITAL SETTINGS / Pittman, Nancy & Cramer, Barbara J – 1992 – 1mf – $4.00 – us Microform Publ [150]
STRESS MEDICINE – v1-. 1985- – 1,5,6,9 – us UMI [616]
STRETFORD AND URMSTON NEWS TELEGRAPH – Cheshire. 1953-58 – 1 – uk Microform Academic [072]
STRETFORD COUNTY EXPRESS – Cheshire. 1959-65 – 1 – uk Microform Academic [072]
STRETFORD URMSTON EXPRESS – Cheshire. 1957-58 – 1 – uk Microform Academic [072]
STRETTON / Kingsley, Henry – British Fiction Archive: Unit 2 – 9 – uk Bell [830]
Strich, Fritz *see* KUNST UND LEBEN
THE STRICKEN DEER : OR, THE LIFE OF COWPER / Cecil, David – London: Constable and Co., 1929 – 1 roll – 1 – 1-55879-345-3 – uk Libr Preservation [420]
THE STRICKEN DEER: OR, THE LIFE OF COWPER / Cecil, David – London, Constable, 1929 – 1 – us U.W. Library [920]
Strickland, Hugh Edwin *see*
- MEMOIRS
- ORNITHOLOGICAL SYNONYMS

Strickland, W P *see*
- AUTOBIOGRAPHY OF PETER CARTWRIGHT
- AUTOBIOGRAPHY OF REV. JAMES B. FINLEY, OR, PIONEER LIFE IN THE WEST
- SKETCHES OF WESTERN METHODISM

Strickland, William Peter *see*
- THE GENIUS AND MISSION OF METHODISM
- HISTORY OF THE AMERICAN BIBLE SOCIETY
- HISTORY OF THE MISSIONS OF THE METHODIST EPISCOPAL CHURCH
- THE LIFE OF JACOB GRUBER
- THE PIONEER BISHOP, OR, THE LIFE AND TIMES OF FRANCIS ASBURY

STRICTLY WHOLESALING – (1984-. 5,6,9) – 1969- – 1 – us UMI [380]
STRICTURES ON DR. LIVINGSTON'S SYSTEM OF PENAL LAWS, PREPARED FOR THE STATE OF LOUISIANA / Lewis, Seth – New Orleans, Bloomfield, 1825. 67 p. LL-2400 – 1 – us L of C Photodup [340]
STRICTURES ON THE SUBSTANCE OF A SERMON PREACHED AT BALTIMORE... / Wesley, Charles – London, 1785 – 1mf – 9 – MP-550/1 – ne IDC [240]
Strieder, Friedrich Wilhelm et al *see* GRUNDLAGE ZU EINER HESSISCHEN GELEHRTEN- UND SCHRIFTSTELLER-GESCHICHTE
STRIGA : IMPROVED MANAGEMENT IN AFRICA – 1989 – 207p – it F.A.O. [650]
DE STRIJD OM DE KERK IN HET DERDE RIJK / Gurian, W – Amsterdam, 1936 – Dfl13.00 – ne Slangenburg [240]
DE STRIJENDE GEREFORMEERDE KERK : EEN STRIJDSCHRIFT, VOORAL TEGEN DE CHRISTELIJKE AFGESCHEIDENE KERK GERICHT / Linde, Antonius van der – Amsterdam: W. Clement: 1859 – 1mf – us A.T.L.A. [240]
THE STRIKE FILES OF THE U.S. DEPARTMENT OF JUSTICE, PART 1 : 1894-1920 – 9 – $2,200.00 – 1-55655-219-X – us UPA [331]
STRIKES AND AGREEMENTS FILE, 1898-1953 / American Federation of Labor – From holdings of State Historical Society of Wisconsin. (ALF Records, Pt 1) – 55r – 1 – $5,365.00 – us UPA [330]
Strindberg, August *see* PLAYS
THE STRING QUARTET : MINOR COMPOSERS BEFORE 1820 – 137mf – 9 – MS-p – ne IDC [780]
STRING QUARTET, B. 75 IN D MINOR, OP. 34 / Dvorak, A – Berlin: Schlesinger, 19– – 1 – us Sibley [780]
THE STRING QUARTETS OF HAYDN, BOCCHERINI, MOZART, PLEYEL AND BEETHOVEN – 142mf – 9 – MS-o – ne IDC [780]
STRING QUARTETS OP. 49 / Reicha, A – (Parts) – Leipzig: Breitkopf & Haertel, 186- – 1 – us Sibley [780]
THE STRING QUINTET : 1770-1820 – 150mf – 9 – MS-q – ne IDC [780]
THE STRING TRIO : 1760-1820 – 110mf – 9 – MS-l – ne IDC [780]

STRIPPING : THE SURFACE MINING OF AMERICA / Stacks, John F – 1r – 5,9 – $50.00 – us Library Micro [622]

STRIVE FOR THE VICTORY OF THE INDONESIAN REVOLUTION WITH THE WEAPON OF DIALECTICAL AND HISTORICAL MATERIALISM / Njoto – (Speech on June 3, 1964). SE-5249 1. 1965 – 9 – ne IDC [335]

Strivers *see* HISTORY OF ADAMS COUNTY

STRIVINGS FOR THE FAITH : A SERIES OF LECTURES – (Includes bibliographical references) – New York: A D F Randolph, 1875 – 1mf – 9 – 0-8370-5453-2 – 1985-3453 – us A.T.L.A. [230]

STRIX – Stockholm, Sweden. 1897-1924 – 13r – 1 – sw Kungliga [073]

Strobel, A *see* URSPRUNG UND GESCHICHTE DES FRUEHCHRISTLICHEN OSTERKALENDERS (T.U.U. 5-121)

Strobel, Otto *see* SKIZZEN UND ENTWUERFE ZUR RING-DICHTUNG

Strobel, P A *see* THE SALZBURGERS AND THEIR DESCENDANTS

STROBHART'S CASES IN EQUITY / South Carolina. Supreme Court – (A Pre-NRS title) – v1-4. 1846-1850 (all publ) – 18mf – 9 – $24.00 – LLMC 94-037 – us L.L.M.C. [340]

STROBHART'S LAW REPORTS / South Carolina. Supreme Court – (A Pre-NRS title) – v1-5. 1846-1850 (all publ) – 30mf – 9 – $45.00 – LLMC 94-025 – us L.L.M.C. [340]

Strobl, G *see* NEUE BEITRAEGE ZUR DIPTERENFAUNA DER BALKAN-HALBINSEL

Strobl, Karl Hans *see*
- ARNO HOLZ UND DIE JUENGSTDEUTSCHE BEWEGUNG
- DORF IM KAUKASUS
- DAS FRAUENHAUS VON BRESCIA
- KAISER ROTBART
- REX
- DIE STREICHE DER SCHLIMMEN PAULETTE
- TOTENHORN-SUEDWAND

Strobl, P G *see* DIPTERENFAUNA VON BOSNIEN, HERCEGOVINA UND DALMATIEN

Strode, William *see* THE FLOATING ISLAND..

Strodtmann, Adolf *see*
- BRIEFE VON UND AN GOTTFRIED AUGUST BUERGER
- GEDICHTE
- IMMORTELLEN HEINRICH HEINE'S
- LETZTE GEDICHTE UND GEDANKEN

Stroev, P M *see*
- BIBLIOGRAFICHESKII SLOVAR' I TSERKOVNYE K NEMU MATERIALY
- OBSTOIATEL'NOE OPISANIE SLAVIANO-ROSSIISKIKH RUKOPISEI, KHRANIASHCHIKHSIA...V BIBLIOTEKE...F.A. TOLSTOGO
- OBSTOIATEL'NOE OPISANIE STAROPECHATNYKH KNIG SLAVIANSKIKH I ROSSIISKIKHM KHRANIASHCHIKHSIA V BIBLIOTEKE...GRAFA F.A. TOLSTOVA
- OPISANIE RUKOPISEI MONASTYREI VOLOKOLAMSKOGO, NOVYI IERUSALIM, SAVVINA STOROZHEVSKOGO I PAFNUTIEVA BOROVSKOGO
- OPISANIE STAROPECHATNYKH KNIG SLAVIANSKIKH NAKHODIASHCHIKHSIA V BIBLIOTEKE...I.N. TSARSKAGO
- OPISANIE STAROPECHATNYKH KNIG SLAVIANSKIKH SLUZHASHCHEE DOPELNENIEM K OPISANIIAM BIBLIOTEK GRAFA F.A. TOLSTOVA I KUPTSA I.N. TSARSKAGO
- RUKOPISI SLAVIANSKIE I ROSSIISKIE, PRINADLEZHASHCHIE...IVANU NIKITICHU TSARSKOMU
- SPISKI IEARKHOV I NASTOIATELEI MONASTYREI

Stroev, S *see* OPISANIE PAMIATNIKOV SLAVIANO-RUSSKOI LITERATURY KHRANIASHCHIKHSIA V PUBLICHNYKH BIBLIOTEKAKH GERMANII I FRANTSII

Stroev, V N *see*
- BIRONOVSHCHINA I KABINET MINISTROV
- STOLETIE SOBSTVENNOI EGO IMPERATORSKAGO VELICHESTVA KANTSELIARII

St-Roger, Soeur *see* BIBLIOGRAPHIE

Strohm, Hans *see* UNTERSUCHUNGEN ZUR ENTWICKLUNGSGESCHICHTE DER ARISTOTELISCHEN METEOROLOGIE

Strohmeyer, Curt *see* MEIN SILBERGRAUER WEGGEFAEHRTE

STROITEL'NAIA GAZETA – Moscow. U.S.S.R. 1954- – 1 – us UMI [072]

STROITELNAIA PROMYSHLENNOST – (Library has: Jan.-Dec. 1931) – Moskva: Gos. nauchno-tekh. izdvo, 1923-1958. 36v – 1 – CSUX90-S461 – us Hoover Inst Photo [624]

STROKESTOWN DEMOCRAT – Ireland. -w. 1 March 1913-12 Sept 1914; 17 April 1915-8 April 1922; 14 Oct 1922-Dec 1927. 5 reels – 1 – uk British Libr Newspaper [072]

DER STROM : DRAMA IN DREI AUFZUEGEN / Halbe, Max – Berlin: G Bondi, 1904 – 1r – 1 – us U.W. Library [820]

DER STROM : NEUE GEDICHTE / Lissauer, Ernst – Jena: E Diederichs, 1912 – 1r – 1 – us U.W. Library [810]

STROM AUS DER ERDE : ROMAN EINES LEBENS / Strenger, Hermann – Stuttgart: Deutsche Verlags-Anstalt, 1942 – 1r – 1 – us U.W. Library [830]

STROMSBURG NEWS – Stromsburg, NE. -w. Jul 1890-Dec 1894, scattered issues missing; Oct 1895-Dec 1912; Apr 1913-Nov 1918 – 1 – us NE Hist [071]

DIE STROMSCHNELLEN DES YANGTZE / Vare, Daniele – Berlin: K H Bischoff, 1942 – 1r – 1 – us U.W. Library [830]

STROMSTADS TIDNING – Stromstad, Sweden. 1866-1918 – 1 – sw Kungliga [072]

STROMSTADS TIDNING – Uddevalla, Stromstad, Sweden. 1920- – 1 – sw Kungliga [072]

STROMSUNDS TIDNING – Ostersund, Sweden. 1906-17 – 14r – 1 – sw Kungliga [072]

Strong, Albert Ambrose *see* DRAMATIC AND MUSICAL LAW.

Strong, Augustus Hopkins *see*
- LECTURES ON THEOLOGY
- OUTLINES OF SYSTEMATIC THEOLOGY

Strong, Caleb *see* CALEB STRONG PAPERS, 1657-1818

STRONG DRINK: WHAT IT IS, AND WHAT IT DOES / Brown, Thomas Storrow – Montreal: W. Drysdale, 1884. 03729. (Pre-1900 Canadiana) – 9 – cn C.I.H.M. [360]

Strong, Elnathan Ellsworth *see* MISSION STORIES OF MANY LANDS

Strong, James *see*
- A COMPLETE HERMENEUTICAL MANUAL ON THE BOOK OF ECCLESIASTES
- EPITOME OF GREEK GRAMMAR
- PROPHET DANIEL
- THE TABERNACLE OF ISRAEL IN THE DESERT

Strong, Josiah *see*
- THE CHALLENGE OF THE CITY
- THE NEW ERA, OR, THE COMING KINGDOM
- THE NEW WORLD-LIFE
- THE NEW WORLD-RELIGION
- THE NEXT GREAT AWAKENING
- RELIGIOUS MOVEMENTS FOR SOCIAL BETTERMENT
- THE TIMES AND YOUNG MEN

Strong, Moses M *see* HISTORY OF THE TERRITORY OF WISCONSIN

Strong, Richard P *see* THE AFRICAN REPUBLIC OF LIBERIA AND THE BELGIAN CONGO

Strong, Robert *see* THE EPISCOPAL INVITATION

Strong, Theron George *see*
- JOSEPH H. CHOATE, NEW ENGLANDER, NEW YORKER, LAWYER, AMBASSADOR
- LANDMARKS OF A LAWYER'S LIFETIME

Strong, Thomas Banks *see*
- AUTHORITY IN THE CHURCH
- CHRISTIAN ETHICS
- A MANUAL OF THEOLOGY
- THE ORIGINS OF CHRISIANITY

Strong, William Ellsworth *see* THE STORY OF THE AMERICAN BOARD

Stroope, Sandra L *see* SOCIAL LOAFING AND CREW

STROPHANTHUS, NOVUM GENUS / Candolle, A P de – Parisiis. 1804. B-5871 2 – 8 – ne IDC [580]

THE STROPHIC STRUCTURE OF HABAKKUK / Kelly, Fred T – (Discussion in English; text in Hebrew. Includes bibliographical references) – Chicago: University of Chicago Press, 1902 – 1mf – 9 – 0-8370-9800-9 – 1986-3800 – us A.T.L.A. [470]

STROPHISCHE GEDICHTEN : UITG. E. ROMBOUTS EN N. DE PAEPE / Hadewijch – Zwolle, 1961 – 4mf – 8 – ne Slangenburg [810]

Stroppel, Robert *see* LITURGIE UND GEISTLICHE DICHTUNG ZWISCHEN 1050 UND 1300

Stroud, Frederick *see* THE JUDICIAL DICTIONARY OF WORDS AND PHRASES JUDICIALLY INTERPRETED

STROUD FREE PRESS – England. -w. 22 Nov 1850-15 June 1855. 1 1 2 reels – 1 – uk British Libr Newspaper [072]

STROUD NEWS – England. -w. 1877; 1880; 1891-93; 1900. 6 reels – 1 – uk British Libr Newspaper [072]

Stroud, William *see*
- THE PHYSICAL CAUSE OF THE DEATH OF CHRI..AND PRACTICE OF CHRISTIANITY
- THE PHYSICAL CAUSE OF THE DEATH OF CHRIST, AND ITS RELATION TO THE PRINCIPLES AND PRACTICE OF CHRISTIANITY

STROUDSBURG TIMES – Stroudsburg, PA. -w 1888-1910; 1918 – 13 – $25.00r – us I.M.R. [071]

Strozzi, G B *see* ESSEQUIE DEL SERENISSIMO DON FRANCESCO MEDICI GRAN DUCA DI TOSCANA 2

STRUCTURAL ADJUSTMENT AND HOUSEHOLD WELFARE IN RURAL AREAS : A MICRO-ECONOMIC PERSPECTIVE – 1991 – 64p – it F.A.O. [339]

STRUCTURAL ADJUSTMENT POLICY SEQUENCING IN SUB-SAHARAN AFRICA – 1991 – 137p – it F.A.O. [338]

STRUCTURAL AND OPERATIONAL ASPECTS OF PUBLIC (ESPECIALLY INDUSTRIAL) ENTERPRISES / Sadli, Mohammad – In Indonesia. SE 3586 1. 1959 – 9 – ne IDC [380]

STRUCTURAL AND SYSTEMATIC CONCHOLOGY; AN INTRODUCTION TO THE STUDY OF THE MOLLUSCA / Tryon, G WA – Z 840 2. 3 v. 1882-1884 – 8 – ne IDC [590]

STRUCTURAL CHEMISTRY – v1-5. 1990-94 – $80.00 – us UMI [540]

STRUCTURAL ENGINEERING PRACTICE, ANALYSIS, DESIGN, MANAGEMENT – v1-1982- – 1,5,6,9 – us UMI [620]

STRUCTURAL ENGINEERING REVIEW – 1,5,69 – us UMI [624]

STRUCTURE AGRAIRE ET ECONOMIE DE PLANTATION CHEZ LES ABE, DEPARTEMENT D'AGBOVILLE, COTE D'IVOIRE / Chaleard, J L – 9 – F150.00 – fr Ethnologie [306]

THE STRUCTURE AND AUTHORSHIP OF THE NEW TESTAMENT / Panin, Ivan – (Includes appendix) – Grafton, MA: [s.n., 188-?] – 1mf – 9 – 0-8370-4663-7 – 1985-2663 – us A.T.L.A. [220]

THE STRUCTURE AND DEVELOPMENT OF MOSSES AND FERNS / Campbell, D H – (Archegoniatae). Ed. 3. New York. 1918. B-5280 2 – 8 – ne IDC [580]

THE STRUCTURE AND DEVELOPMENT OF MOSSES AND FERNS / Campbell, D H – (Archegoniatae). London. 1895. B-7170 1 – 9 – ne IDC [580]

THE STRUCTURE AND HABITS OF SPIDERS / Emerton, J H – Z-2170 2. 1878 – 8 – ne IDC [590]

STRUCTURE AND SOCIAL CONTEXT OF NON-FORMAL TRAINING IN LUSAKA / Hoppers, W H ML – Lusaka, 1981 – 2mf – 9 – DE-314/1 – ne IDC [370]

STRUCTURE DE PARENTE ET D'ALLIANCE D'APRES LES FORMULES PENDE (BA-PENDE, CONGO BELGE) / Sousberghe, Leon de – [Bruxelles, 1955] – us Res Libr [306]

STRUCTURE, FORMATION ET REGENERATION DES ECAILLES D'UN POISSON TELEOSTEEN, HEMICHROMIS BIMACULATUS (PERCIFORME, CICHLIDE) / Sire, JY – 9 – F95.00 – fr Ethnologie [590]

LA STRUCTURE INTERNE DES PARTIS POLITIQUES AMERICAINS / Seurin, J L – 9 – F70.00 – fr Ethnologie [320]

THE STRUCTURE OF THE ENGLISH LANGUAGE / Sedger, John – 1798. 138p. (English Linguistics Series 1500-1800) – 9 – us UMI [420]

THE STRUCTURE OF THE OLD TESTAMENT: A SERIES OF POPULAR ESSAYS / Leathes, Stanley – Philadelphia: Smith, English, 1873. 1 fiche – 9 – us A.T.L.A. [240]

STRUCTURE OF WOOL FIBRE / Bowman, F H – 1908 – 8mf – 7 – uk Microform Academic [680]

STRUCTURE OF WORKING CAPITAL – National Council of Applied Economic Research. New Delhi: The Council, 1966. ix,83p – 1 – us U.W. Library [332]

STRUCTURES ASSISTING THE MIGRATIONS OF NON-SALMONID FISH : LATIN AMERICA – 1989 – 46p – it F.A.O. [623]

STRUCTURES ASSISTING THE MIGRATIONS OF NON-SALMONID FISH : USSR – 1989 – 104p – it F.A.O. [623]

STRUCTURES OF TECHNOLOGICAL EDUCATION AND CONTRIBUTING SOCIAL FACTORS / ed by Fishwick, Wilfred – 1988 – 231p – 9 – 92-3-102489-2 – fr UNESCO [370]

Struebe, Hermann *see* WILTFEBER, DER EWIGE DEUTSCHE; DIE GESCHICHTE EINES HEIMATSUCHERS

Struempfel, Emil *see* WAS JEDERMANN HEUTE VON DER MISSION WISSEN MUSS

A STRUGGLE FOR A SOUL AND OTHER STORIES OF LIFE AND WORK IN SOUTH INDIA / Hinkley, Edyth & Christlieb, Marie L – Philadelphia: Union, 1907 – 1mf – us A.T.L.A. [240]

THE STRUGGLE FOR LAW / Ihering, Rudolf von – Chicago: Callaghan, 1915 – 2mf – 9 – $3.00 – LLMC 95-202 – us L.L.M.C. [340]

THE STRUGGLE FOR LIBERTY IN SPAIN, 1840-1936 – London, 1936. Fiche W1214. (Blodgett Collection of Spanish Civil War Pamphlets) – 9 – us H.U. College Libr [946]

THE STRUGGLE FOR RELIGIOUS FREEDOM IN VIRGINIA : THE BAPTISTS / Thom, William Taylor – Baltimore: Johns Hopkins Press, 1900. (Johns Hopkins University studies in historical and political science ; ser. 18, nos. 10-11-12) – 1mf – us A.T.L.A. [240]

THE STRUGGLE OF PROTESTANT DISSENTERS FOR RELIGIOUS TOLERATION IN VIRGINIA / McIlwaine, Henry R – Baltimore: Johns Hopkins Press, 1894. (Johns Hopkins University studies in historical and political science; 12th ser., 4) – 1mf – us A.T.L.A. [240]

THE STRUGGLE WITH PURITANISM / Blaxland, Bruce – London: Methuen, 1910. (Handbooks of English church history; 5) – 1mf – us A.T.L.A. [240]

THE STRUGGLES FOR RELIGIOUS LIBERTY IN VIRGINIA / James, Charles F – 1900 – 1 – 9.94 – us Baptist [240]

Struker, Johannes *see* BEITRAEGE ZUR KRITISCHEN WUERDIGUNG DER DRAMATISCHEN DICHTUNGEN THEODOR KOERNERS

STRUKTUR, UMFELDBEDINGUNGEN UND MOTIVATIONEN BEI SCHUELERHANDBALLMANNSCHAFTEN (C, D-, E-JUGEND) DES KREISES BERGSTRASSE / Hofmann, Juergen – 1994 – 2mf – DM80.00 – 3-8267-2041-5 – gw Hänsel [790]

STRUKTUR UND AUFBAU AUSGEWAEHLTER STUECKE DARSTELLENDER MUSIK (TIERDARSTELLUNGEN) IN VERBINDUNG MIT INSTRUMENTENKUNDE / Drobnitzky-Eickhoff, Barbara – 1991 – 138p – 9 – DM98.00 – 3-89349-424-3 – gw Hänsel [370]

STRUKTUR UND FUNKTION DES SIGNALERKENNUNGSPARTIKELS (SRP) AUS ESCHERICHIA COLI / Lentzen, Georg – 1995 – 2mf – 9 – DM80.00 – 3-8267-2258-2 – gw Hänsel [574]

STRUKTURANALYSE AB INITIO SCHWACH STREUENDEN KRISTALLEN MIT SYNCHROTRONSTRAHLUNG / Herzig, Thomas – 1995 – 1mf – 9 – DM60.00 – 3-8267-2112-8 – gw Hänsel [550]

STRUKTURANALYSEN VON ROMANEN VIRGINIA WOOLFS / Walter, Margot – Bonn 1952 – 1 – DM30.00 – gw Mikro Press [420]

STRUKTUREN UND BEDINGUNGEN POLITISCHER PARTIZIPATION UND MITBESTIMMUNG IN DER KOMMUNALPOLITIK : EINE POLITIKWISSENSCHAFTLICHE ANALYSE RELEVANTER HANDLUNGSSPIELRAEUME KOMMUNALER SELBSTVERWALTUNG – DARGESTELLT AM BEISPIEL DES NORDRHEIN-WESTFAELISCHEN MITTELZENTRUMS BOCHOLT / Kloecker, Andreas – 1992 – 9 – DM98.00 – 3-89349-526-6 – gw Hänsel [320]

STRUKTURUNTERSUCHUNGEN AN SCHNECKENGALACTANEN MIT HILFE MONOKLONALER ANTIKOERPER UND SEQUENTIELLEM SMITH-ABBAU / Weymayr, Christian – 1993 – 2mf – 9 – DM98.00 – 3-89349-678-5 – gw Hänsel [574]

STRUKTURWANDEL ALS HERAUSFORDERUNG : KOMMUNALE WIRTSCHAFTSFOERDERUNG IN AHLEN/WESTFALEN 1986-1991. EINE POLITIKWISSENSCHAFTLICHE UNTERSUCHUNG ZUM BEITRAG DES POLITISCH-ADMINISTRATIVEN SYSTEMS ZUR BEWAELTIGUNG DER OEKONOMISCHEN KRISE EINER ZECHENSTADT / Schlueter,

Gerda – 1993 – 6mf – 9 – DM125.00 – 3-89349-840-0 – gw Hänsel [320]

STRUKTUURVERANDERINGEN IN NEDERLANDSCH-INDIE IN DE LAATSTE 25 JAAR / Cool, M F J – Rotterdam, 1941 – 1mf – 9 – ne IDC [320]

DIE "STRUKIERIERTE BIOGRAPHISCHE ANAMNESE FUER SCHMERZPATIENTEN" BEI PATIENTEN MIIT LUMBAGO-ISCHIALGIE-SYNDROMEN / Plessen, Kerstin von – 1995 – 2mf – 9 – DM80.00 – 3-8267-2167-5 – gw Hänsel [616]

Strumenskii, M *see* UKAZETS STARINNYKH RUKOPISEI

DE STRUNZ : EINE INDUSTRIE- UN BUERN-GESCHICHTE UT'N MOENSTERLANNE / Wibbelt, Augustin – 4. Aufl. Essen (Ruhr): Fredebeul und Koenen, 1920 – 1r – 1 – us U.W. Library [830]

Strunz, Franz *see* GOETHE ALS NATURFORSCHER

Strutt, Elizabeth *see* THE FEMININE SOUL

Struve, Burkhard Gotthelf *see* BURCARDI GOTTHELFFII STRUVII,...CORPUS HISTORIAE GERMANICAE.

Struyf, Ivon *see*
- LES BAKONGO DANS LEURS LEGENDES
- KONGOLEESCHE VERTELLINGEN

Stryjewski, Detlef *see* NMR-SPEKTROSKOPISCHE METHODEN ZUR DETEKTION VON METABOLITEN IM PHYSIOLOGISCHEN MEDIUM

STRYKER ADVANCE – Stryker, Ohio. 1975-76 – 1r – 1 – $32.50r – us Archival [071]

Stryker, Elisabeth G *see* A STORY OF ONE SHORT LIFE, 1783-1818

Stryker, Roy *see* ROY STRYKER PAPERS, 1912-72

Strype, John *see* HISTORICAL AND BIOGRAPHICAL WORKS

STSENA I MUZYKA – Odessa, 1903-05 (weekly during the theater season) – 7mf – 9 – us Ross [780]

STUART ADVOCATE – Stuart, NE. -w. Mar 1906-Feb 1907; Jan 1908; Mar 1908-Mar 1965 – 1 – us NE Hist [071]

Stuart, Jacobus *see* DE HOLLANDSCHE AFRIKANEN EN HUNNE REPUBLIEK IN ZUID-AFRIKA

Stuart, James *see*
- CATALOGUE OF THE LIBRARY OF THE LATE HON. SIR JAMES STUART, BART.,CHIEF JUSTICE OF LOWER CANADA
- COPY OF A MEMORIAL FROM JAMES STUART,...TO THE RIGHT HONORABLE LORD VISCOUNT GODERICH,.

Stuart, John *see* SIMONS AND STUART'S REPORTS

STUART LEDGER – Stuart, NE. -w. Dec 1887-Aug 1888, scattered issues missing; Jan 1896-Dec 1898; Mar 1899-May 1900; Jul 1900-Jan 1901; Apr-Nov 1901; Oct 1902-Mar 1903 – 1 – us NE Hist [071]

STUART MONARCHS: CORRESPONDENCE / Victoria and Albert Museum. London – 17th Century – 1 – uk Microform Academic [025]

Stuart, Moses *see*
- A COMMENTARY ON ECCLESIASTES
- A COMMENTARY ON THE BOOK OF PROVERBS
- A COMMENTARY ON THE EPISTLE TO THE ROMANS
- CRITICAL EXAMINATION OF SOME PASSAGES IN GENESIS 1
- CRITICAL HISTORY AND DEFENCE OF THE OLD TESTAMENT CANON
- A CRITICAL HISTORY AND DEFENCE OF THE OLD TESTAMENT CANON
- HAVE THE SACRED WRITERS ANYWHERE ASSERTED THAT THE SIN OR RIGHTEOUSNESS OF ONE IS IMPUTED TO ANOTHER?
- HINTS RESPECTING COMMENTARIES UPON THE SCRIPTURES
- LETTERS TO THE REV. WM. E. CHANNING, CONTAINING REMARKS ON HIS SERMON RECENTLY PREACHED AND PUBLISHED AT BALTIMORE
- MISCELLANIES
- ON THE ALLEGED OBSCURITY OF PROPHECY
- REVIEW OF THE EVIDENCES OF THE GENUINENESS OF THE GOSPELS

STUART ON THE OLD TESTAMENT / Noyes, George Rapall – (The Christian Examiner and Religious Miscellany, v. 40 (4th series, v. 5) Jan. 1846, p. 69-77) – 9 – us A.T.L.A. [240]

STUART PAPERS / Chiddingstone Castle, Kent. Denys Bower Collection – 3r – 1 – uk Microform Academic [025]

STUART PAPERS / Windsor Castle. Royal Archives – 1579-1823. 541v – 272r – 1 – uk Microform Academic [941]

STUART PAPERS INDEX – 4r – 1 – uk Microform Academic [324]

Stuart, R *see* CALENDONIA ROMANA

STUART'S LOWER CANADA COURT KING'S BENCH REPORTS / Canada. Quebec – 1v. 1810-35 (all publ) – 7mf – 9 – $11.50 – LLMC 81-088 – us L.L.M.C. [340]

STUART'S LOWER CANADA VICE-ADMIRALTY REPORTS / Canada. Quebec – v1-2. 1836-74 (all publ) – 10mf – 9 – $15.00 – LLMC 81-089 – us L.L.M.C. [340]

Stubbings, Frank H *see* MYCENAEAN POTTERY FROM THE LEVANT

Stubbs *see* EARLY SETTLERS OF ALABAMA

Stubbs, John William *see* THE HISTORY OF THE UNIVERSITY OF DUBLIN

Stubbs, W *see*
- CHRONICA MAGISTRI ROGERI DE HOUEDENE (RS51)
- THE CHRONICLE OF THE REIGNS OF HENRY 2 AND RICHARD 1, 1169-1192 (RS49)
- CHRONICLES AND MEMORIALS OF THE REIGN OF RICHARD 1 (RS38)
- CHRONICLES OF THE REIGNS OF EDWARD 1 AND EDWARD 2 (RS76)
- THE CONSTITUTIONAL HISTORY OF ENGLAND IN ITS ORIGIN AND DEVELOPMENT
- DE GESTIS REGUM ANGLORUM LIBRI QUINQUE
- THE HISTORICAL WORK OF MASTER RALPH DE DICETO, DEAN OF LONDON (RS68)
- HISTORICAL WORKS, THE CHRONICLE OF THE REIGNS OF STEPHEN, HENRY 2 AND RICHARD 1 (RS73)
- MEMORIALE FRATRIS WALTERI DE COVENTRIA (RS58)
- MEMORIALS OF ST DUNSTAN, ARCHBISHOP OF CANTERBURY (RS63)

Stubbs, William *see*
- COUNCILS AND ECCLESIASTICAL DOCUMENTS RELATING TO GREAT BRITAIN AND IRELAND
- ORDINATION ADDRESSES
- REGISTRUM SACRUM ANGLICANUM
- VISITATION CHARGES DELIVERED TO THE CLERGY AND CHURCHWARDENS OF THE DIOCESES OF CHESTER AND OXFORD

STUBE 118 : EIN HEITERER TATSACHENBERICHT AUS DEM LEBEN DER NEUEN REKRUTEN / Wendt, Hans – Berlin: Verlag "Die Wehrmacht", 1937 – 1r – 1 – us U.W. Library [430]

Stuchka, Petr Ivanovich *see*
- 13 LET BOR'BY ZA REVOLIUTSIONNO-MARKSISTSKUIU TEORIIU PRAVA
- ENTSIKLOPEDIIA GOSUDARSTVA I PRAVA
- GRAZDANSKOE PRAVO I PRAKTIKA EGO PRIMENENIIA
- KLASSOVOE GOSUDARSTVO I GRAZHDANSKOE PRAVO
- KURS SOVETSKOGO GRAZHDANSKOGO PRAVA
- REVOLIUTSIONNAIA ROL' PRAVA I GOSUDARSTAVA
- REVOLIUTSIONNAIA ROL' PRAVA I GOSUDARSTVA
- REVOLIUTSIONNAIA ROL' SOVETSKOGO PRAVA
- UCHENIE O GOSUDARSTVE I KONSTITUTSI RSFSR

Stucken, Eduard *see*
- BALLADEN
- GAWAN
- LANVAEL

Stuckenberg, John Henry Wilburn *see*
- THE AGE AND THE CHURCH
- CHRISTIAN SOCIOLOGY
- THE FINAL SCIENCE, OR, SPIRITUAL MATERIALISM
- GERMAN RATIONALISM
- THE HISTORY OF THE AUGSBURG CONFESSION
- THE SOCIAL PROBLEM
- SUNBURY AMERICAN AND SHAMOKIN JOURNAL
- TENDENCIES IN GERMAN THOUGHT

Stuckert, Franz *see*
- DAS DRAMA ZACHARIAS WERNERS
- THEODOR STORM

Stuckey, Ronald L *see*
- CATALOG OF THE MANUSCRIPT AND ARCHIVAL COLLECTIONS AND INDEX TO THE CORRESPONDENCE OF JOHN TORREY
- INDEX TO PLANT DISTRIBUTION MAPS IN NORTH AMERICAN PERIODICALS THROUGH 1972

Stucki, J W *see* ANTIQVITATUM CONVIVIALIVM LIBRI 3 IN QVIBVS HEBRAEORVM, GRAECORVM, ROMANORVM ALIARVMQVE NATIONVM ANTIQVA CONVIVIORVM GENERA...

STUD BOOK REGISTER / American Kennel Club – v. 1-34, 43-86. 1878-1917, 1926-69 – 1 – 2,941.00 – us L of C Photodup [636]

Studenskii, G A *see* BIUDZHET KREST'IANSKOGO KHOZIAISTVA

STUDENT ACTIVITIES – v12, no.1-. Sept 1983- – 1,5,6,9 – us UMI [073]

STUDENT ACTIVITIES PROGRAMMING – v1-1968- 1; v11- 5,6; v8- 9 – us UMI [370]

STUDENT ADVOCATE – 1-3 2+1 (all publ). 1936-1938 – 4mf – 9 – $35.00 – us UPA [370]

THE STUDENT AND INTELLECTUAL OBSERVER OF SCIENCE, LITERATURE, AND ART – London, 1868-71 – 3 – us Readex [500]

STUDENT COGNITION DURING MOTOR SKILL LEARNING / Langley, David Jet al – 1992 – 3mf – 9 – $12.00 – us Microform Publ [150]

STUDENT DIRECTORY OF THE FIRST AND SECOND INFANTRY BATTALIONS OF THE TWENTY-FIRST CLASS OF THE (NATIONALIST) CHINESE MILITARY ACADEMY / U.S. Office of the Chief of Military History – v. 1-2. 1969-70 – 1 – 52.00 – us L of C Photodup [950]

STUDENT IMPACT: FORUM OF THE STUDENT NATIONAL EDUCATION ASSOCIATION – -q. Introductory issue 1 Apr 1968; introductory issue 2 May-June 1968; v1 no 1 Oct 1968; v8 no2 Oct 1975. Washington, D.C.: Student National Education Association, National Commission on Teacher Education and Professional Standards of the National Education Association of the United States – 1 – us U.W. Library [370]

STUDENT LAW REVIEW, NEW YORK LAW SCHOOL *see* NEW YORK LAW SCHOOL LAW REVIEW

STUDENT LAWYER – (v.8-. Sep 1979- 5,6,9) – v.1-. Sep 1972- – 1 – us UMI [073]

STUDENT LAWYER (ABA) – v1-20. 1972-1992 – 9 – $310.00 set – us Hein [340]

THE STUDENT NONVIOLENT COORDINATING COMMITTEE PAPERS, 1959-1972 (SNCC) – 73r – 1 – $5480.00 – us UMI [360]

STUDENT POLITICS IN ARGENTINA : THE UNIVERSITY REFORM AND ITS EFFECTS, 1918-1964 / Walter, Richard J – New York: Basic Books, [1968] – 1 – CSUXADJ0979-B – us Hoover Inst Photo [320]

THE STUDENT RECORD – Reno, CA. University of Nevada: 1897-1900 (Scats) – 1r – 1 – $50.00 – U04719 – us Library Micro [370]

STUDENT REVIEW / National Student League – 1-5, no. 1 (all publ). 1931-35 – 6mf – 9 – $45.00 – us UPA [360]

STUDENT WORLD – v1-62. 1908-69 (complete) – Inquire – 1 – ATLA 1993-S521 – us A.T.L.A. [073]

STUDENTENSPIEGEL – (Lacking: 1947, V.1(1,p. 1-26)) – Batavia, 1947 – 1mf – 9 – SE-740/1 – ne IDC [370]

STUDENTS AND THE MISSIONARY PROBLEM : ADDRESSES DELIVERED AT THE INTERNATIONAL STUDENT MISSIONARY CONFERENCE, LONDON, JAN 2-6 1900 – (Includes index) – London: Student Volunteer Missionary Union, 1900 – 2mf – 9 – 0-8370-6504-6 – 1986-0504 – us A.T.L.A. [240]

STUDENTS ASK: WHERE IS THE CONSCIENCE OF AMERICA? – N.Y., n.d. Fiche W1216. (Blodgett Collection of Spanish Civil War Pamphlets) – 9 – us H.U. College Libr [946]

THE STUDENT'S BLACKSTONE / Blackstone, William – 10th ed. London, Clowes, 1887. 596 p. L.C. copy imperfect: title page wanting. LL-103 – 1 – us L of C Photodup [340]

THE STUDENTS' CHALLENGE TO THE CHURCHES : A PLEA FOR A FORWARD MOVEMENT IN WORLD EVANGELIZATION / Wishard, Luther Deloraine – Chicago: Fleming H Revell, c1899 – 1mf – 9 – 0-8370-6468-6 – 1986-0468 – us A.T.L.A. [240]

STUDENT'S CHRONICLE – (Lacking: nos 25-28,34) – nos 24-64. 1912-16 – 1r – 1 – ATLA S0714C – us A.T.L.A. [073]

STUDENTS FOR A DEMOCRATIC SOCIETY PAPERS, 1958-1970 – (With printed guide £32.00) – State Historical Society of Wisconsin – 41r – 1 – £2,460.00 – uk Chadwyck [975]

THE STUDENT'S GUIDE : BEING A CONCISE ACCOUNT OF HONORABLE SOCIETY OF LINCOLN'S INN; CONTAINING FORMS OF ADMISSION, KEEPING TERMS, PERFORMING EXCERCISES, CALL TO THE BAR, ADMISSION TO CHAMBERS.. / Lane, Thomas – London: I Gold, 1803 – 2mf – 9 – $3.00 – LLMC 84-301 – us L.L.M.C. [340]

THE STUDENT'S GUIDE THROUGH LINCOLN'S INN : WITH AN ACCOUNT OF THAT HONORABLE SOCIETY, FORMS OF ADMISSION.. / Lane, Thomas – 2nd ed. London: Ellerton & Byworth, 1805 – 3mf – 9 – $4.50 – LLMC 84-302 – us L.L.M.C. [340]

STUDENT'S HANDBOOK OF BRITISH HEPATICS / Macvicar, S M – 1926 – 7 – uk Microform Academic [580]

STUDENT'S HERALD – Manhattan. Kan. 1896-1912; 1914-1968 – 1 – us UMI [071]

THE STUDENTS' LAW LEXICON. / Cochran, William Cox – 2d ed. Cincinnati: Clarke, 1892. 348p. LL-1340 – 1 – us L of C Photodup [340]

THE STUDENT'S LEGAL ANALYSIS / Ford, Melbourne Haddock – Chicago: Myers, 1882. 255p. LL-356 – 1 – us L of C Photodup [340]

THE STUDENT'S LIFE OF JESUS / Gilbert, George Holley – (Includes index) – Chicago: Chicago Theological Seminary, 1896 – 1mf – 9 – 0-8370-3280-6 – 1985-1280 – us A.T.L.A. [240]

THE STUDENT'S LIFE OF PAUL / Gilbert, George Holley – (Includes appendixes & indexes) – New York: Macmillan, 1902, c1899 – 1mf – 9 – 0-8370-3281-4 – 1985-1281 – us A.T.L.A. [920]

THE STUDENT'S LIST OF BRITISH COLEOPTERA, WITH SYNOPTIC TABLES OF FAMILIES AND GENERA / Pascoe, F P – Z-1532 2. 1882 – 9 – ne IDC [590]

THE STUDENT'S MANUAL OF ORIENTAL HISTORY...THE ANCIENT HISTORY OF THE EAST TO THE COMMENCEMENT OF THE MEDIAN WARS / Lenormant, Francois – Philadelphia: J.P. Lippincott, 1869-70. 2v – 1 – us U.W. Library [900]

THE STUDENT'S MONTHLY – (Cont by: Lennoxville Magazine) – [Lennoxville, Quebec?: s.n. 1867?] – 9 – cn C.I.H.M. [370]

THE STUDENT'S MONTHLY *see* THE LENNOXVILLE MAGAZINE

STUDENTS, SCHOLARS AND SAINTS / Ginzberg, L – New York. 1928. BJ-100-4 1 – 9 – ne IDC [290]

Studer, Jacob H *see* COLUMBUS, ITS HISTORY, RESOURCES AND PROGRESS

Studer, T *see* FAUNE DES VERTEGRES DE LA SUISSE. V.2

STUDI ALGOLOGICI / Borzi, A – Messina-Palermo, 1883-1895 – 2 vols, 378p, 31pls – 8 – ne IDC [580]

STUDI CRITICI... / Anzilotti, D – N.p., 1898 – 4mf – 9 – ILM-413/1 – ne IDC [340]

STUDI DI LETTERATURA GRECA E TEDESCA / Traverso, Leone – Milano: Feltrinelli, 1961 – 1r – 1 – us U.W. Library [430]

STUDI E RICERCHE INTERNO A SAN GIOVANNI CRISOSTOMO / Xpycoctomika – Roma, 1908 – 30mf – 9 – ne Slangenburg [240]

STUDI ENTOMOLOGICI / Baudi di Selve, F & Trouqui, E – Torino, 1848. v1, 376p. 17pls. Z-1051/2 – 8 – ne IDC [590]

STUDI ETIOPICI... / Cerulli, Enrico – Roma: Instituto per l'oriente. v1-4. 1936- – us Res Libr [960]

STUDI ITALIANI DI FILOLOGIA CLASSICA – (N.S. v1-26. 1920-52. Dfl1,560.00; Dfl60.00v) – Firenze. v1-21. 1893-1915 – 5,9 – Dfl1,575.00; Dfl75.00v – ne Swets [450]

STUDI MICOLOGICI / Venturi, Adolfo – Brescia. 1842. B-6333 2 – 8 – ne IDC [580]

STUDI SUI SACRAMENTI AMMINISTRATI SECONDO IL RITO BIZANTINO / Meester, Placidus de – Roma, 1947 – 6mf – 8 – Dfl25.00 – ne Slangenburg [240]

STUDI SULLE MIXOFICEE / Borzi, A – (Nuovo giornale botanico Italiano, N.S., 1914-1917. v21-24) – 8 – ne IDC [580]

STUDIA CANONICA – (1985- . 5,6,9) – v1- . 1967- – 1 – us UMI [073]

STUDIA CANONICA – (v1-23 1967-90 Can$20.00y) – Ottawa. v1-28. 1967-94 – 9 – Can$28.00y – cn Micromedia [240]

STUDIA EVANGELICA : PAPERS PRESENTED TO THE INTERNATIONAL CONGRESS ON "THE FOUR GOSPELS" IN 1957 HELD AT CHRIST CHURCH, OXFORD (T.U.U. 5-73) / ed by Aland-Cross-Danielou – Berlin, 1959 – 14mf – 9 – ne Slangenburg [240]

STUDIA EVANGELICA : VOL. 6 + INDICES VOL. 1-6 (T.U.U. 5-112) / Livingstone, E A – Berlin, 1973 – 14mf – 9 – ne Slangenburg [240]

STUDIA EVANGELICA, VOL 2 (TUU 5-87) / Cross, F L – 12mf – 9 – ne Slangenburg [240]

STUDIA EVANGELICA, VOL 4 (TUU 5-102) / Cross, F L – Berlin, 1968 – 9mf – 9 – ne Slangenburg [240]

STUDIA EVANGELICA, VOL 5 (TUU 5-103) / Cross, F L – Berlin, 1968 – 6mf – 9 – ne Slangenburg [240]

STUDIA FENNICA – Collected works. 1933-61 – 1 – us I.U. Libraries [490]

STUDIA ISLAMICA – Dir. R. Brunschvig, J. Schacht. t. 1-36. Paris. 1953-72 – 5 – fr A.C.R.P.P. [260]

STUDIA LOGICA – (1985-. 5,6,9) – v1-. 1953- – 1 – us UMI [160]

STUDIA MYSTICA – (1985-. 5,6,9) – v1-. 1978- – 1 – us UMI [150]

STUDIA PANEGYRICA. COMMENTATIO ACADEMICA SCRIPSIT GUSTAVUS THORNELL / Thornell, Gustaf – Upsaliae, 1905. 58p – 1 – us U.W. Library [450]

STUDIA PATRISTICA : PAPERS PRESENTED TO THE SECOND INTERNATIONAL CONFERENCE ON PATRISTIC STUDIES HELD AT CHRIST CHURCH, OXFORD 1955 (T.U.U. 5-63+64) / ed by Aland, Kurt & Cross, F L – Berlin. v1-2. 1957 – 22mf – 9 – ne Slangenburg [240]

STUDIA PATRISTICA, VOL 3 PT 2 (TUU 5-88) : THE NEW TESTAMENT MESSAGE / Cross, F L – Berlin, 1964 – 9mf – 9 – ne Slangenburg [240]

STUDIA PATRISTICA, VOL 3 (TUU 5-78) / Cross, F L – Berlin, 1961 – 8mf – 9 – ne Slangenburg [240]

STUDIA PATRISTICA, VOL 4 (TUU 5-79) / Cross, FL – Berlin, 1961 – 10mf – 9 – ne Slangenburg [240]

STUDIA PATRISTICA, VOL 5 (TUU 5-80) / Cross, F L – Berlin, 1962 – 10mf – 9 – ne Slangenburg [240]

STUDIA PATRISTICA, VOL 6 (TUU 5-81) / Cross, F L – Berlin, 1962 – 10mf – 9 – ne Slangenburg [240]

STUDIA PATRISTICA, VOL 7 (TUU 5-92) / Cross, F L – Berlin, 1966 – 10mf – 9 – ne Slangenburg [240]

STUDIA PATRISTICA, VOL 8 (TUU 5-93) / Cross, F L – Berlin, 1966 – 8mf – 9 – ne Slangenburg [240]

STUDIA PATRISTICA, VOL 9 (TUU 5.94) / Cross, F L – Berlin, 1966 – 11mf – 9 – ne Slangenburg [240]

STUDIA PATRISTICA, VOL 10 (TUU 5-107) / Cross, F L – Berlin, 1970 – 8mf – 9 – ne Slangenburg [240]

STUDIA PATRISTICA, VOL 11 (TUU 5-108) / Cross, F L – Berlin, 1972 – 7mf – 9 – ne Slangenburg [240]

STUDIA PATRISTICA, VOL. 12 (T.U.U. BAND 5-115) / Livingstone, E A – 9mf – 9 – ne Slangenburg [240]

STUDIA PATRISTICA, VOL. 13 (T.U.U. BAND 5-116) / Livingstone, E A – 9mf – 9 – ne Slangenburg [240]

STUDIA PATRISTICA, VOL. 14 (T.U.U. BAND 5-117) / Livingstone, E A – 9mf – 9 – ne Slangenburg [240]

STUDIA PONTICA / Anderson, John George Clark & E Cumont – Bruxelles, 1903-1910. v. 1-3. BH-651 2 – 8 – ne IDC [073]

STUDIA SACRA : COMMENTARIES ON THE INTRODUCTORY VERSES OF ST JOHN'S GOSPEL, AND ON A PORTION OF ST PAUL'S EPISTLE TO THE ROMANS: WITH OTHER THEOLOGICAL PAPERS / Keble, John – (Includes appendix citing the Fathers on the doctrine of the Holy Spirit) – Oxford: James Parker, 1877 – 1mf – 9 – 0-8370-3859-6 – 1985-1859 – us A.T.L.A. [220]

STUDIA SINAITICA 2 : AN ARABIC VERSION OF THE EPISTLES OF ST. PAUL...9TH CENT. MOUNT SINAI / ed by Gibson, Margaret Dunlop – 5mf – 8 – ne Slangenburg [220]

STUDIA SINAITICA 11 : APOCRYPHA SYRIACA. THE PROTEVANGELIUM JACOBI AND TRANSITUS MARIAE / ed by Lewis, Agnes Smith – London, 1902 – 11mf – 8 – ne Slangenburg [220]

STUDIA THEOLOGICA – (1981-. 1,5,6,9) – v1-. 1947- – 1 – us UMI [073]

STUDIE- EN INFORMATIECENTRUM MENSENRECHTEN = NETHERLANDS INSTITUTE OF HUMAN RIGHTS – Utrecht. 57 docs. 1982-1991 – 63mf – 9 – ne IDC [320]

STUDIE OVER DE GEWOONTELIJKE STRAFBEPALINGEN TEGEN HET OVERSPEL BIJ DE BALUBA EN BA LULUA VAN KASAI / Caeneghem, E P R van – [Bruxelles: G van Campenhout, 1938] – us Res Libr [960]

DE STUDIE VAN HET INTERNATIONALE RECHT / Eysinga, W J M van – Leiden, 1912 – 1mf – 1 – ILM-1599/1 – ne IDC [327]

STUDIEN / Stifter, Adalbert; ed by Fuerst, Rudolf – Leipzig: Max Hesse, [1899?] – 1 – us U.W. Library [800]

STUDIEN EN BIJDRAGEN OP 'T GEBIED DER HISTORISCHE THEOLOGIE – (1885-: Archief voor Nederl. Kerkgeschiedenis; 1857-1866: Kerkhistorisch Archief) – 1(1870)-4(1880) – 25mf – 9 – Dfl210.00 – ne Slangenburg [073]

STUDIEN FUER TONKUENSTLER UND MUSIKFREUNDE...IN ZWEI THEILEN / ed by Reichardt, Johann F & Kunzen, F L A – 1793. Contains the periodicals: Musikalisches Wochenblatt, Nos. 1-24, 1791-2. Ed. by Kunzen, and Musikalische Monatschrifft, Nos. 1-6, July-December 1792, ed by Reichardt – 9 – us Sibley [780]

DIE STUDIEN JACOB GRIMMS ZUR HERAUSBILDUNG UND ZU DEN MERKMALEN DES DEUTSCHEN MEISTERGESANGS IM REZEPTIONSGESCHICHTLICHEN KONTEXT / Starke, Matthias – 1992 – 89p – 9 – DM75.00 – 3-89349-586-X – gw Hänsel [430]

STUDIEN UEBER BRASILIANISCHE FLECHTEN / Zahlbruckner, A – (Sitzungsber. K.Ak. Wiss. Wien. Math. Nat. Cl. v. 3, 1902). B-513 2 – 8 – ne IDC [580]

STUDIEN UEBER DEN ZUSAMMENHANG ZWISCHEN GESCHLACHTSREIFE UND WACHSTUM BEI LEBISTES / Svardson, G – (Medd. Undersoekn. Anst. Soetvattenfisk, no. 21). Stockholm. 1943. B-555 2 – 8 – ne IDC [590]

STUDIEN UEBER DIE DEM JOHANNES VON DAMASKUS ZUGESCHRIEBENEN PARALLELEN / Loofs, Friedrich – Halle a.S.: M. Niemeyer, 1892 – 1mf – us A.T.L.A. [240]

STUDIEN UEBER DIE DRAMEN CARL GUTZKOWS : 1. HINTERLASSENE DRAMENENTWUERFE – 2. EIN WEISSES BLATT / Houben, Heinrich Hubert – (Includes bibliographical references) – Jena: H Costenoble, 1899 – 1r – 1 – us U.W. Library [430]

STUDIEN UEBER DIE NATURWISSENSCHAFTLICHEN KENNTNISSE DER TALMUDISTEN / Bergel, Joseph – Leipzig: Wilhelm Friedrich, 1880 – 1mf – 9 – 0-8370-2284-3 – 1985-0284 – us A.T.L.A. [500]

STUDIEN UEBER DIE PROTOPLASMASTROEMUNG BEI DEN CHARACEEN / Hoermann, G – Jena. 1898. B-6377 2 – 8 – ne IDC [590]

STUDIEN UEBER DIE RASSISCHEN GRUNDLAGEN DES "STURM UND DRANG" / Mueller, Wilhelm – (Includes bibliographical references) – Berlin: Junker und Duennhaupt, 1938 – 1 – us U.W. Library [430]

STUDIEN UEBER DIE SPRACHE ABRAHAMS A SANTA CLARA : EIN BEITRAG ZUR GESCHICHTE DER DEUTSCHEN DRUCKSPRACHE IM 17. UND 18. JAHRHUNDERT / Blanckenburg, Curt – Halle a. S: M Niemeyer, 1897 – 1r – 1 – us U.W. Library [430]

STUDIEN UEBER HOMONYME WURZELN IM ARABISCHEN MIT BESONDERER BERUECKSICHTIGUNG DES MUCVGAM MAQAYIS AL-LUGA VON AHMAD IBN FARIS (GE 395/1005) / Ali, Khalid Ismail – Heidelberg, 1964 – 2mf – 9 – DM62.00 – 3-89349-741-2 – gw Hänsel [470]

STUDIEN UEBER JESCHU'A BEN JEHUDA / Schreiner, M – Berlin. 1900. BJ-33-13 1 – 9 – ne IDC [270]

STUDIEN UEBER SALOMON IBN GABIROL / Kaufmann, David – Budapest. 1899. BJ-33-16 1 – 9 – ne IDC [180]

STUDIEN UEBER ZACHARIAS WERNERS STIL / Degenhart, Friedrich – Eichstaett: Ph Broennersche Buchdruckerei, 1907 – 1r – 1 – us U.W. Library [790]

STUDIEN UEBER ZACHARIAS-APOKRYPHEN UND ZACHARIAS-LEGENDEN / Berendts, Alexander – Leipzig: A. Deichert, 1895 – 1mf – us A.T.L.A. [240]

STUDIEN UND BEITRAEGE ZUR ERKLAERUNG UND ZEITBESTIMMUNG COMMODIANS (T.U.U. 3-39/4A) / Martin, J – Leipzig, 1913 – 3mf – 9 – ne Slangenburg [240]

STUDIEN UND BEITRAEGE ZUR SCHWEIZERISCHEN KIRCHENGESCHICHTE / Fleischlin, B – Luzern. 3 Bde. 1902-1903 – Dfl140.00 – ne Slangenburg [240]

STUDIEN UND MITTEILUNGEN AUS DEM BENEDIKTINER- UND CISTERCIENSER-ORDEN – Salzburg, etc. Jahrg. 3-31; 1882-1910. Continued by Studien und Mitteilungen zur Geschichte des Benediktiner-Ordens und seiner Zweige. Film Mas C 287 – 1 – us H.U. Library [240]

STUDIEN UND MITTEILUNGEN ZUR GESCHICHTE DES BENEDIKTINER-ORDENS UND SEINER ZWEIGE – Salzburg, etc. Jahrg. 32-35; 1911-14 (also numbered n.s., v. 1-4). Continues Studien und Mitteilungen aus dem Benediktiner- und Cistercienser-Orden. Film Mas C 287 – 1 – us H.U. Library [240]

STUDIEN UND MITTEILUNGEN ZUR GESCHICHTE DES BENEDIKTINERORDENS UND SEINER ZWEIGE (SMBG) – Salzburg, spaeter Raigern u.a., 1880-1889 – 602mf – 9 – subsc: DM3,200.00 diazo DM3,900.00 silver – gw Olms [240]

STUDIEN UND TEXTE ZU ASTERIOS VON AMASEA (T.U.U. 3-40/1) / Bretz, A – Leipzig, 1914 – 2mf – 9 – ne Slangenburg [240]

STUDIEN ZU DEN ACTA APOSTOLORUM DER CHESTER BEATTY-PAPYRI / Kanter, Hermann – 1937 – 1 – us A.T.L.A. [240]

STUDIEN ZU DEN DICHTUNGEN ABRAHAMS BEN EZRA / Albrecht, K – (Zeitschrift der Deutschen Morgenlaend. Gesellschaft, v. 57). Leipzig. 1903. BJ-421-60 1 – 9 – ne IDC [470]

STUDIEN ZU DEN DICHTUNGEN JEHUDA HA-LEVI'S 1: UEBER DIE METRA DER VERSGEDICHTE / Brody, H – Berlin. 1895. BJ-421-24 1 – 9 – ne IDC [470]

STUDIEN ZU DEN KOMMENTAREN HIPPOLYTS ZUM BUCHE DANIEL UND HOHEN LIEDE (T.U.U. 2-16/2) / Bonwetsch, G N – Leipzig, 1897 – 2mf – 9 – ne Slangenburg [240]

STUDIEN ZU DEN PSEUDO-CLEMENTINEN NEBST EINEM ANHANGE : DIE AELTESTE ROEMISCHE BISCHOFSLISTE UND DIE PSEUDO-CLEMENTINEN (T.U.U. 4-46/1) / Schmidt, Carl – Leipzig, 1929 – 7mf – 9 – ne Slangenburg [240]

STUDIEN ZU EINER MONOGRAPHIE UEBER DEN BAROCKBILDHAUER MICHAEL ZUERN D.J. / Ludwig, Guenther – Frankfurt a.M., 1970 – 3mf – 9 – DM76.00 – 3-89349-373-5 – gw Hänsel [730]

STUDIEN ZU EUSEBS THEOPHANIE (T.U.U. 2-23/3) / Gressmann, H – Leipzig, 1903 – 4mf – 9 – ne Slangenburg [240]

STUDIEN ZU HEINES ROMANZERO / Herrmann, Helene – (Includes bibliographical references) – Berlin: Weidmann, 1906 – 1r – 1 – us U.W. Library [430]

STUDIEN ZU HEINRICH VON KLEIST / Schneider, Hermann – (Includes bibliographical references) – Berlin: Weidmann, 1915 – 1r – 1 – us U.W. Library [430]

STUDIEN ZU LESSINGS STIL IN DER HAMBURGISCHEN DRAMATURGIE / Waldberg, Maximilian R von – Berlin: W H Kuhl, 1882 – 1r – 1 – us U.W. Library [430]

STUDIEN ZU METHODIOS VON OLYMPOS (T.U.U. 5-69) / Buchheit, V – Berlin, 1958 – 4mf – 9 – ne Slangenburg [240]

STUDIEN ZU NICCOLO TRIBOLO / Aschoff, Wiebke – Frankfurt a.M., 1967 – 2mf – 9 – DM62.00 – 3-89349-683-1 – gw Hänsel [720]

STUDIEN ZU NICOLAES BERCHEM / Schaar, E – Koeln 1958 – 1 – DM30.00 – gw Mikro Press [920]

STUDIEN ZU THOMAS HARDY'S PROSASTIL / Aliesch, Peter – Bern, 1940 – 2mf – DM62.00 – 3-8267-3062-3 – gw Hänsel [420]

STUDIEN ZU THOMAS HARDY'S PROSASTIL / Aliesch, Peter – H-332 2. 1941 – 9 – ne IDC [420]

STUDIEN ZU WIELANDS ROMANE "PEREGRINUS PROTEUS" / Raab, Karl – (Includes bibliographical references) – Prag [i.e. Prague]: Selbstverlag, 1909 – 1r – 1 – us U.W. Library [410]

STUDIEN ZUM BUCHE TOBIT / Rosenmann, M – Berlin: Mayer & Mueller, 1894 – 1mf – 9 – 0-8370-7331-6 – 1986-1331 – us A.T.L.A. [220]

STUDIEN ZUM INTERNATIONALEN RECHT / Cybichowski, S – Berlin, 1912 – 1mf – 1 – ILM-3140/1 – ne IDC [327]

STUDIEN ZUM IRRTUM UEBER DIE UNRECHTMASSIGKEIT DES VERHALTENS / Schewe, Guenter – Hamburg 1956 – 1 – DM30.00 – gw Mikro Press [900]

STUDIEN ZUM NEUEN TESTAMENT UND ZUR PATRISTIK (T.U.U. 5-77) / Klostermann, Erich – Berlin, 1961 – 7mf – 9 – ne Slangenburg [220]

STUDIEN ZUM PROBLEM DER GEDICHTSAMMLUNG MIT EINGEHENDER UNTERSUCHUNG DER GEDICHTSAMMLUNG GOETHES UND TIECKS / Reitmeyer, Elisabeth – Bern, 1931 – 3mf – DM76.00 – 3-8267-3036-4 – gw Hänsel [430]

STUDIEN ZUM STABVERHALTEN DES FINITIVEN VERBS IN DER ALTENGLISCHEN UND ALTSAECHSISCHEN STABREIMDICHTUNG / Stemsrud, David Walter – Frankfurt a.M., 1970 – 2mf – 9 – DM62.00 – 3-89349-375-1 – gw Hänsel [420]

STUDIEN ZUM STIL VON GRIMMELSHAUSENS SIMPLICISSIMUS / Knauss, Heinz – (Includes bibliographical references) – Giessen: Published by the author, 1935 – 1r – 1 – us U.W. Library [430]

STUDIEN ZUR ALLGEMEINEN THEORIE DES WERTS / Weiss, Karl Fr. – Tuebingen, 1913 – 2mf – DM62.00 – 3-8267-3033-X – gw Hänsel [170]

STUDIEN ZUR APOSTELGESCHICHTE: KRITISCHE UNTERSUCHUNGEN DER VON TH. V. ZAHN REKONSTRUIERTEN "URAUSGABE DER APOSTELGESCHICHTE DES LUCAS." / Eisentraut, Englehard – Wuerzburg, Becker, 1924. xvii, 139 p. Film Mas 8419 – 1 – us H.U. Library [240]

STUDIEN ZUR BEURTEILUNG DES ABRAHAM A SANTA CLARA / Bianchi, Lorenzo – (Includes bibliographical references) – Heidelberg: Weiss, 1924 – 1r – 1 – us U.W. Library [430]

STUDIEN ZUR BIBLISCHEN THEOLOGIE : DER GOTTESNAME ADONAJ UND SEINE GESCHICHTE / Dalman, Gustaf – (Includes bibliographical references) – Berlin: H Reuther, 1889 – 1mf – 9 – 0-8370-6174-1 – 1986-0174 – us A.T.L.A. [220]

STUDIEN ZUR BRIEFLITERATUR DEUTSCHLANDS IM 11. JAHRHUNDERT (MGH SCHRIFTEN..: 1.BD) / Erdmann, C – 1938 – Dfl32.00 – ne Slangenburg [240]

STUDIEN ZUR CHRISTLICH-MITTELALTERLICHEN CHRONOLOGIE : DER 84-JAEHRIGE OSTERCYCLUS UND SEINE QUELLEN / Krusch, B – Leipzig, 1880 – 6mf – 8 – Dfl25.00 – ne Slangenburg [240]

STUDIEN ZUR CHRISTLICH-MITTELALTERLICHEN CHRONOLOGIE : DIE ENTSTEHUNG UNSERER HEUTIGEN ZEITRECHNUNG / Krusch, B – Berlin, 1938 – 3mf – 8 – Dfl13.00 – ne Slangenburg [240]

STUDIEN ZUR ENTWICKLUNG DER ITALIENISCHEN VIOLONCELLSONATE VON DEN ANFAENGEN BIS ZUR MITTE DES 18. JAHRHUNDERTS / Zingler, Ute – Frankfurt a.M., 1967 – 3mf – 9 – DM76.00 – 3-89349-711-0 – gw Hänsel [780]

STUDIEN ZUR FORMELHAFTIGKEIT DER MITTELALTERLICHEN DAENISCHEN VOLKSBALLADE / Holzapfel, Otto – Frankfurt a.M., 1969 – 2mf – DM62.00 – 3-89349-891-5 – gw Hänsel [490]

STUDIEN ZUR GESCHICHTE DER DEUTSCHEN PROSA IM 18. JAHRHUNDERT / Hafen, Hans – Zuerich, 1951 – 2mf – DM62.00 – 3-8267-3067-4 – gw Hänsel [430]

STUDIEN ZUR GESCHICHTE DER GESELLSCHAFT JESU : LOYOLA... / Boehmer, Heinrich – Bonn am Rhein: A. Falkenroth, 1914 – 2mf – us A.T.L.A. [240]

STUDIEN ZUR GESCHICHTE DES JUEDISCHEN GOTTESDIENSTES / Elbogen, I – Berlin. 1907. BJ-421-12 1 – 9 – ne IDC [270]

STUDIEN ZUR HETHITISCHEN SPRACHWISSENSCHAFT / Weidner, E F – (Leipziger semitistische studien. v. 7, pt. 1-2. Leipzig. 1915). Leipzig. 1917. BNE-20,119 1 – 9 – ne IDC [470]

STUDIEN ZUR KRITIK UND ERKLAERUNG DER BIBLISCHEN URGESCHICHTE, GEN. CAP. 1-11 : DREI ABHANDLUNGEN / Schrader, Eberhard – (Includes bibliographical references) – Zuerich:Meyer & Zeller, 1863 – 1mf – 9 – 0-8370-5148-7 – 1985-3148 – us A.T.L.A. [220]

STUDIEN ZUR LEHRE VON DER STAATENSUKZESSION / Barclay, T – Berlin, 1923 – 2mf – 9 – ILM-1514/1 – ne IDC [340]

STUDIEN ZUR METABOLISIERUNG UND ZUM INTRAZELLULAEREN WIRKMECHANISMUS TUMORRAFFINER RUTHENIUM(III)KOMPLEXE : METHODEN UND ANSAETZE ZUR WEITERENTWICKLUNG TUMORHEMMENDER RUTHENIUMVERBINDUNGEN / Hartmann, Markus – 1995 – 2mf – 9 – DM80.00 – 3-8267-2270-1 – gw Hänsel [540]

STUDIEN ZUR METAPHYSIK UND ERKENNTNISLEHRE WILHELMS VON OCKHAM / Hochstetter, E – Berlin, 1927 – 4mf – 8 – ne Slangenburg [110]

STUDIEN ZUR MUSIKWISSENSCHAFT. BEIHEFTE DER TONKUNST IN OESTERREICH – Leipzig Wien. P 622. v. 1-21. 1913-1934 – 61mf – 9 – ne IDC [780]

STUDIEN ZUR PFAHLDORFGESCHICHTE AUS FRIEDRICH THEODOR VISCHERS ROMAN "AUCH EINER" / Kuerbs, Harry – (Includes bibliographical references) – Borna: R Noske, 1914 – 1r – 1 – us U.W. Library [430]

STUDIEN ZUR SPRACHAUFFASSUNG GEORG CHRISTOPH LICHTENBERGS : VERSUCH EINER INTERPRETATION DER SPRACHPHILOSOPHISCHEN APHORISMEN / Jung, Rudolf – Frankfurt a.M., 1968 – 2mf – 9 – DM62.00 – 3-89349-386-7 – gw Hänsel [100]

STUDIEN ZUR SPRACHE DES JUNGEN GRILLPARZER : MIT BESONDRER BERUECKSICHTIGUNG DER "AHNFRAU" / Kuechling, Eduard Hermann – (Includes bibliographical references) – [S.l.: s.n.] 1900 (Leipzig: Druck von K H Scheithauer) – 1 – us U.W. Library [430]

STUDIEN ZUR STAATSANSCHAUUNG CALVINS : MIT BESONDERER BRUECKSICHTIGUNG SEINES SOUVERAENITAETSBEGRIFFS / Beyerhaus, Gisbert – Berlin: Trowitzsch, 1910. (Neue Studien zur Geschichte der Theologie und der Kirche; 7. Stueck) – 1mf – us A.T.L.A. [240]

STUDIEN ZUR SYNTAX DER BRIEFE DES HL. CYPRIAN / Schrijnen, J & Mohrmann, Chr. – (v1 1936 5mf. v2 1937 Lat. Christ. Primaeva, deel 5 en 6 4mf) – ne Slangenburg [240]

STUDIEN ZUR TEXTKRITIK DER VULGATA / Dobschuetz, Ernst von – (Includes appendix) – Leipzig: J C Hinrichs, 1894 – 1mf – 9 – 0-8370-2934-1 – 1985-0934 – us A.T.L.A. [220]

STUDIEN ZUR THEORIE DES UEBERSETZENS IM ZEITALTER DER DEUTSCHEN AUFKLAERUNG, 1730-1770 / Huber, Thomas – (Includes bibliographical references) – Meisenheim am Glan: A Hain, 1968 – 1r – 1 – us U.W. Library [430]

STUDIEN ZUR VORGESCHICHTE DER REFORMATION : AUS SCHLESISCHEN QUELLEN / Meyer, Arnold Oskar – Muenchen: R. Oldenbourg, 1903 – 1mf – us A.T.L.A. [943]

STUDIEN ZUR VORGOTISCHEN MOEBELFORM / Mueller, Gisela D – Frankfurt a.M., 1966 – 1mf – 9 – DM48.00 – 3-89349-793-5 – gw Hänsel [740]

STUDIENAUSGABEN ZUR NEUEREN DEUTSCHEN LITERATUR / Deutsche Akademie der Wissenschaften zu Berlin, Institut fuer deutsche Sprache und Literatur – (Each vol has also a special title) – Berlin: Akademie-Verlag, 1957 – 1 – us U.W. Library [430]

DIE STUDIENORDNUNG DER GESELLSCHAFT JESU : MIT EINER EINLEITUNG / Duhr, Bernhard – Freiburg im Breisgau; St. Louis, Mo.: Herder, 1896. (Bibliothek der katholischen Paedagogik; 9) – 1mf – us A.T.L.A. [240]

STUDIER I INTERNATIONELL FOERMYNDERSKAPSTRAETT / Heimer, E H – Uppsala, Stockholm, 1925 – 1mf – 1 – ILM-3033/1 – ne IDC [327]

STUDIER I SVENSK FOLKLORE / Norlind, Tobias – Lund: H. Ohlssons Boktryckeri. 1911. xxv, 432p. 16p of music. Inc. indexes. 1 reel – 1 – us I.U. Libraries [390]

STUDIER OEFVER MOSSORNAS BYGGNAD OCH UTVECKLING / Berggren, S – 2pts. Lund. 1867-71. B-1233 2 – 8 – ne IDC [580]

STUDIES – v1- 1912- 1; v65- 5,6,9 – us UMI [000]

STUDIES AND REPORTS..., 1941-46 / U.S. Office of Price Administration – 2rolls. M164 – 1 – us Nat'l Archives [324]

STUDIES BIBLICAL AND ORIENTAL / Turner, William – Edinburgh: Black, 1876. 2 fiches – 9 – us A.T.L.A. [240]

STUDIES FOR PERSONAL WORKERS / Johnston, Howard Agnew – New York: Association Press, 1916, c1903 – 1mf – 9 – 0-8370-6068-0 – 1986-0068 – us A.T.L.A. [240]

STUDIES FROM COURT AND CLOISTER : BEING ESSAYS, HISTORICAL AND LITERARY, DEALING MAINLY WITH SUBJECTS RELATING TO THE 16TH AND 17TH CENTURIES / Stone, J M – London: Sands, 1905 – 1mf – us A.T.L.A. [240]

STUDIES IN AFRICAN LAND USAGE IN NORTHERN RHODESIA / Allen, W – 3mf – 7 – uk Microform Academic [960]

STUDIES IN AMERICANISM = ETUDES SUR L'AMERICANISMEENGLISH : FATHER HECKER, IS HE A SAINT? / Maignen, Charles – (Includes index) – Rome:International Catholic Library, 1898 – 1mf – 9 – 0-8370-5948-8 – 1985-3948 – us A.T.L.A. [240]

STUDIES IN APPLIED MATHEMATICS – v. 1-46. 1921-1967 – 1,5,6 – us Princeton Micro [510]

STUDIES IN APPLIED MATHEMATICS – v1-71. 1922-84.Continues: Journal of Mathematics and Physics – 1,5,6,13 – sz Elsevier [510]

STUDIES IN ARABIAN FATALISM / Ringgren, H – Uppsala, 1955 – 5mf – 8 – ne Slangenburg [140]

STUDIES IN BIBLICAL LAW / Daube, D – 1947 – 9 – $12.00 – us I.R.C. [220]

STUDIES IN BIBLICAL LAW / Wiener, Harold Marcus – London: David Nutt, 1904. 1 fiche. 8370-5835-X – 9 – us A.T.L.A. [220]

STUDIES IN CANADIAN LITERATURE – Fredericton. v1-20. 1975-95 – 9 – Can$20.00y – cn Micromedia [420]

STUDIES IN CHINESE DIPLOMATIC HISTORY / Hsia, Ching-Lin – Shanghai, 1925 – 3mf – 1 – ILM-704/1 – ne IDC [327]

STUDIES IN CHRISTIAN ANTIQUITY *see*
- ANGELS AND DEMONS ACCORDING TO LACTANTIUS
- THE EUCHARISTIE DOCTRINE AND LITURGY OF THE MYSTAGOGICAL CATECHESE OF THEODORE OF MOPSUESTIA
- THE IMAGE OF GOD IN MAN ACCORDING TO CYRIL OF ALEXANDRIA
- IMPERIUM AND SACERDOTIUM ACCORDING TO ST BASIL THE GREAT
- MATER ECCLESIA
- OSSIUS OF CORDOVA
- THE PROBLEM OF DIVINE ANGER IN ARNOBIUS AND LACTANTIUS

STUDIES IN CHRISTIANITY / Bowne, Borden Parker – Boston: Houghton, Mifflin, 1909.1 fiche – 9 – us A.T.L.A. [240]

STUDIES IN CHURCH HISTORY : THE RISE OF THE TEMPORAL POWER, BENEFIT OF CLERGY, EXCOMMUNICATION, THE EARLY CHURCH AND SLAVERY / Lea, Henry Charles – Philadelphia: H.C. Lea's Son, 1883 – 2mf – us A.T.L.A. [240]

STUDIES IN COMPARATIVE INTERNATIONAL DEVELOPMENT – v1- 1965- 1; v10- 5,6,9 – us UMI [337]

STUDIES IN COMPARATIVE INTERNATIONAL DEVELOPMENT – 1985-. -q – 1 – us UMI [337]

STUDIES IN COMPARATIVE RELIGION – (v.13-. 1979- 5,6,9) – v.1-. 1967- – 1 – us UMI [230]

STUDIES IN CONTEMPORARY BIOGRAPHY / Bryce, James – New York: Macmillan, 1903 – 2mf – us A.T.L.A. [920]

STUDIES IN DANIEL / Wilson, Robert D – 1917 – 9 – $24.00 – us I.R.C. [220]

STUDIES IN DESIGN, EDUCATION AND CRAFT – 1968- 1; 1975- 5,6,9 – us UMI [740]

STUDIES IN EARLY CHURCH HISTORY : COLLECTED PAPERS / Turner, Cuthbert Hamilton – Oxford: Clarendon Press, 1912 – 1mf – us A.T.L.A. [240]

STUDIES IN EARLY ROMAN LITURGY / Frere, Walter H – (Vol 1: The Kalender, 1930; Vol 2: The Roman Gospel-Lecture, 1934; Vol 3: The Roman Epistle-Lecture, 1935) – London. v1-3. 1930-35 – 11mf – 8 – Dfl39.00 – ne Slangenburg [240]

STUDIES IN EASTERN HISTORY. CHRONICLES CONCERNING EARLY BABYLONIAN KINGS / King, L W – London. 1907. BNE-488 1 – 9 – ne IDC [930]

STUDIES IN EDUCATION DURING THE AGE OF THE RENAISSANCE, 1400-1600 / Woodward, William Harrison – 1 – us A.T.L.A. [370]

STUDIES IN EDUCATIONAL EVALUATION – v1- 1975- 1; v4- 5,6,9 – us UMI [370]

STUDIES IN EGYPTIAN SYNTAX / Gunn, B – Paris. 1924. BNE-494 1 – 9 – ne IDC [470]

STUDIES IN ENGLISH LITERATURE / Dennis, John – London: Edward Stanford, 1876 – 1 roll – 1 – 1-55879-759-9 – uk Libr Preservation [420]

STUDIES IN ENGLISH LITERATURE – (v.11-1971- 5,6. v.15- 1975- 9) – v.1- 1961- – 1 – us UMI [420]

STUDIES IN ENGLISH RELIGION IN THE SEVENTEENTH CENTURY : ST. MARGARET'S LECTURES 1903 / Henson, Hensley – London: J. Murray, 1903 – 1mf – us A.T.L.A. [240]

STUDIES IN EPHESIANS / Cocke, Alonzo Rice – Chicago: Fleming H Revell, c1892 – 1mf – 9 – 0-8370-2697-0 – 1985-0697 – us A.T.L.A. [220]

STUDIES IN EUROPEAN HISTORY : BEING ACADEMICAL ADDRESSES / Doellinger, Ignaz von – London: J. Murray, 1890 – 1mf – us A.T.L.A. [940]

STUDIES IN EVOLUTION / Beecher, C E – Z-314 2. 1901 – 9 – ne IDC [575]

STUDIES IN HEBREW PROPER NAMES / Gray, George Buchanan – 1896 – 1 – us A.T.L.A. [270]

STUDIES IN HIGHER EDUCATION – 1976-18v – 9 – £229.00 – 0307-5079 – uk Carfax [370]

STUDIES IN HISTORICAL AND POLITICAL SCIENCE / Johns Hopkins University – Series 18. nos. 10-12. Ed. by Herbert B. Adams. Thom, William T. The struggle for religious freedom in Virginia: the Baptists. 1900; Thomas David. The Virginia Baptist – 1 – 6.30 – us Baptist [240]

STUDIES IN HISTORY AND PHILOSOPHY OF SCIENCE – v1- 1970- – 5,6,9 – us UMI [500]

STUDIES IN HONOR OF JOHN ALBRECHT WALZ – (Includes bibliographical references) – Lancaster, PA: Lancaster Press, 1941 – 1 – us U.W. Library [370]

STUDIES IN INTERPRETATION : KEATS-CLOUGH-MATTHEW ARNOLD / Hudson, William Henry – New York, London: G.P. Putnam's Sons, 1896 – 1 roll – 1 – 1-55879-729-7 – uk Libr Preservation [420]

STUDIES IN JEWISH LITERATURE / Kohler, K – Berlin, 1913 – 9 – ne IDC [470]

STUDIES IN JEWISH THEOLOGY / Marmorstein, Arthur; ed by Rabbinowitz, J & Lew, M S – London, 1950 – 7mf – 8 – ne Slangenburg [270]

STUDIES IN JOHN THE SCOT (ERIGENA) : A PHILOSOPHER OF THE DARK AGES / Gardner, Alice – London; New York: Oxford University Press, 1900 – 1mf – us A.T.L.A. [180]

STUDIES IN JUDAISM: SECOND SERIES / Schechter, Solomon – Philadelphia: Jewish Publ. So. Am., 1908. 1 fiche – 9 – us A.T.L.A. [270]

STUDIES IN LAW AND ECONOMIC DEVELOPMENT *see* GEORGE WASHINGTON JOURNAL OF INTERNATIONAL LAW AND ECONOMICS

STUDIES IN LITERARY IMAGINATION – v.1-. 1968- – 1,5,6,9 – us UMI [410]

STUDIES IN LITERATURE / Morley, John – London, New York: Macmillan and Co., 1891 – 1 roll – 1 – 1-55879-532-4 – uk Libr Preservation [420]

STUDIES IN LITERATURE *see* HARTFORD STUDIES IN LITERATURE

STUDIES IN LOGIC / ed by Peirce, Charles Sanders – By members of Johns Hopkins University. Boston: Little, Brown and Co., 1883. 203p. illus. 2 maps – 1 – us U.W. Library [160]

STUDIES IN LUKE'S GOSPEL. FIRST SERIES / Robinson, Charles Seymour – New York: Century, 1889.1 fiche – 9 – us A.T.L.A. [240]

STUDIES IN MARITIME HISTORY / Cotter, Charles H – (v1: A History of Nautical Astronomical Tables £50.00; v2: A History of Ship Magnetism £45.00; v3: A Pathway to Perfect Sailing: A History of Dead Reckoning Navigation £40.00) – 9 – £115.00 – uk Mansell Publ [623]

STUDIES IN MARK'S GOSPEL / Robinson, Charles Seymour – New York: American Tract Society, 1888. 1 fiche – 9 – us A.T.L.A. [240]

STUDIES IN MATHEMATICS EDUCATION / ed by Morris, Robert – 9 – fr UNESCO [370]

STUDIES IN METHODS / United Nations – E.196 – 9 (ST/STAT/Ser.F/1-17/Rev.1; ST/ESA/STAT/Ser.F/18-51) – us U.N. Pubs [310]

STUDIES IN MODERN CHURCH HISTORY / Smith, Justin A – New Haven, Conn.: J.P. Cadman, 1887 – 1mf – us A.T.L.A. [240]

STUDIES IN MODERNISM / Fawkes, Alfred – London: Smith, Elder, 1913 – 2mf – us A.T.L.A. [900]

STUDIES IN MUSIC AND SUPPLEMENT – n1-4. 1967-70 – 12mf – 9 – $5.00f – us Ross [780]

STUDIES IN MUSLIM POLITICAL THOUGHT AND ADMINISTRATION / Sherwani, Haroon Khan – In Indonesian. SE 6421 1. 1964 – 9 – ne IDC [320]

STUDIES IN MYSTICAL RELIGION / Jones, Rufus M – London: Macmillan, 1909 – 2mf – us A.T.L.A. [200]

STUDIES IN NEW ENGLAND TRANSCENDENTALISM / Goddard, Harold Clarke – New York: Columbia University Press, 1908. (Columbia University studies in English; ser. 2, v2, no. 3) – 1mf – us A.T.L.A. [200]

STUDIES IN OLD TESTAMENT PROPHECY / Rowley, H H – Scribner's. 1950 – 9 – $10.00 – us I.R.C. [220]

STUDIES IN OPTIMISM : OR, SUBJECTS SUGGESTED BY THE HUMANISM AND HOPE OF THE TIMES / Penniman, Alford Brown – Adams, MA: Freeman Publ, 1902 – 1mf – 9 – 0-8370-5445-1 – 1985-3445 – us A.T.L.A. [240]

STUDIES IN PEERAGE AND FAMILY HISTORY / Round, J H – H 1158 2. 1901 – 8 – ne IDC [920]

STUDIES IN PHILOLOGY – v1- 1906- 1; v67-5,6; v73- 9 – us UMI [400]

STUDIES IN PHILOLOGY – (1929-1958. v26-55. Sfr972.00) – Chapel Hill, 1906-1940. v1-37 – 277mf – 8 – ne IDC [400]

STUDIES IN PHILOLOGY – v. 1-57. 1906-1960 – 1,5,6 – us Princeton Micro [400]

STUDIES IN POETRY AND PHILOSOPHY / Shairp, John Campbell – 6th ed. 1884 – 1 – us A.T.L.A. [410]

STUDIES IN PORTUGUESE LITERATURE / Bell, Aubrey FG – Oxford: B.H. Blackwell, 1914. xviii,247p – 1 – us U.W. Library [440]

STUDIES IN PRE-TIBBONIAN PHILOSOPHICAL TERMINOLOGY / Efros, II – I. Abraham bar Hiyya the Prince. (Jewish Quarterly Review, ns no 17). Philadelphia. 1926-27. BJ-33-2 1 – 9 – ne IDC [180]

STUDIES IN RECENT ADVENTISM / Sheldon, Henry Clay – New York: Abingdon, c1915 – 1mf – us A.T.L.A. [240]

STUDIES IN RELIGIOUS NURTURE / Ormer, Abraham Brower Bunn van – (Includes bibliographical references) – Philadelphia, PA: Lutheran Publ Society, c1908 – 1mf – 9 – 0-8370-8629-9 – 1986-2629 – us A.T.L.A. [370]

STUDIES IN SCIENCE EDUCATION – v1- 1974-1; v4- 5,6,9 – us UMI [370]

STUDIES IN SCOTTISH ECCLESIASTICAL HISTORY IN THE SEVENTEENTH AND EIGHTHEENTH CENTURIES / Kinloch, MG J – London: Simpkin, Marshall, Hamilton, Kent; Edinburgh: R. Grant, 1898 – 1mf – us A.T.L.A. [240]

STUDIES IN SCOTTISH HISTORY : CHIEFLY ECCLESIASTICAL / Innes, Alexander Taylor – London: Hodder and Stoughton, 1892 – 1mf – us A.T.L.A. [240]

STUDIES IN SECOND LANGUAGE ACQUISITION – (v.3-. 1980-. 5,6,9) – v.1-. 1977- – 1 – us UMI [400]

STUDIES IN SHORT FICTION – v1- 1963- 1; v11- 5,6; v13- 9 – us UMI [420]

STUDIES IN SOVIET THOUGHT – (v27-. 1984-. 5,6,9) – v1-. 1961- – 1 – us UMI [073]

STUDIES IN STATECRAFT / Butler, G – Cambridge, 1920 – 2mf – 9 – ILM-1173/1 – ne IDC [327]
STUDIES IN THE ACTS OF THE APOSTLES / Loomis, Benjamin Bloomfield – New York: Eaton & Mains, 1896. 1 fiche – 9 – us A.T.L.A. [240]
STUDIES IN THE ACTS OF THE APOSTLES / Robertson, William – New York:Fleming H Revell, [1902] – 1mf – 9 – 0-8370-4926-1 – 1985-2926 – us A.T.L.A. [220]
STUDIES IN THE ADMINISTRATION OF THE INDIANS IN NEW SPAIN. BERKELEY, 1934 / Byrd, Simpson Lesley – Madrid: Razon y Fe, 1936 – 1 – sp Bibl Santa Ana [350]
STUDIES IN THE ANTHROPOLOGY OF VISUAL COMMUNICATION – v.1-5. 1974-79. Continued by Studies in Visual Communication – 1 – us UMI [073]
STUDIES IN THE BOOK OF DANIEL / Wilson, Robert D – New York, 1917 – 8mf – 8 – ne Slangenburg [220]
STUDIES IN THE BRYOLOGY OF NEW ZEALAND / Dixon, H N – (New Zealand Institute. Bull. nr.3. Wellington, 1913-1929). 6 pts. BZ-2054 – 9 – ne IDC [590]
STUDIES IN THE CHRISTIAN EVIDENCES: BEING APOLOGETICS FOR THE TIMES / Mair, Alexander – Edinburgh: T.&T. Clark, 1894. 1 fiche – 9 – us A.T.L.A. [240]
STUDIES IN THE CIVIL, SOCIAL AND ECCLESIASTICAL HISTORY OF EARLY MARYLAND : LECTURES / Gambrall, Theodore C – New York: T. Whittaker, 1893 – 1mf – us A.T.L.A. [978]
STUDIES IN THE CL PSALMS...COINCIDENCES WITH THE INDEPENDENT SCRIPTURE HISTORIES / Fausset, A R – London: Christian Book Soc., (1876). 1 fiche – 9 – us A.T.L.A. [240]
STUDIES IN THE COPTIC (MANICHAEAN) PSALMBOOK. PROSODY AND MANDAEAN PARALLELS / Saeve-Soederbergh, T – Uppsala. 1949. BH-283 2 – 8 – ne IDC [240]
STUDIES IN THE CREATIVE WEEK / Boardman, George Dana – New York: D. Appleton, 1878. 1 fiche – 9 – us A.T.L.A. [240]
STUDIES IN THE CREATIVE WEEK / Boardman, George Dana – New York: D. Appleton, 1886. 338p – 1 – us U.W. Library [240]
STUDIES IN THE ENGLISH REFORMATION / Clarke, Henry Lowther – London: S.P.C.K.; New York: E.S. Gorham, 1912 – 1mf – us A.T.L.A. [240]
STUDIES IN THE EVANGELISATION OF SOUTH AFRICA / Gerdener, G B A – London; New York: Longmans, Green, 1911 – 1mf – us A.T.L.A. [960]
STUDIES IN THE FIELD AND FOREST / Flagg, Wilson – Boston: Little, Brown, 1857. vi,330p – 1 – us U.W. Library [574]
STUDIES IN THE FIRST BOOK OF SAMUEL: FOR THE USE OF...SECONDARY SCHOOLS / Willett, Herbert Lockwood – Chicago: University of Chicago, 1909. 1 fiche. 8370-5853-8 – 9 – us A.T.L.A. [240]
STUDIES IN THE FORTY DAYS BETWEEN CHRIST'S RESURRECTION AND ASCENSION / Lipscomb, Andrew Adgate – Nashville: South. Meth. Pub. House, 1885. 1 fiche – 9 – us A.T.L.A. [240]
STUDIES IN THE GOSPELS / Trench, Richard Chenevix – (Includes bibliographical references) – New York:Charles Scribner, 1867 – 1mf – 9 – 0-8370-5572-5 – 1985-3572 – us A.T.L.A. [220]
STUDIES IN THE HISTORY AND METHOD OF SCIENCE / ed by Singer, Ch – London, 1955 – Dfl35.00 – ne Slangenburg [500]
STUDIES IN THE HISTORY OF CHRISTIAN APOLOGETICS: NEW TESTAMENT AND POST-APOSTOLIC / Macgregor, James – Edinburgh: T. & T. Clark, 1894. 1 fiche – 9 – us A.T.L.A. [240]
STUDIES IN THE LECIDEA RIVULOSA GROUP / Magnusson, A H – (Goa5teborgs Kgl. Vertensk. Samh. Handlingar, s. 4, v. 29, nr. 4, 1925. 50 pp.). B-195 2 – 8 – ne IDC [580]
STUDIES IN THE LIFE OF CHRIST / Fairbairn, Andrew Martin – New York:D Appleton, 1882 – 1mf – 9 – 0-8370-3089-7 – 1985-1089 – us A.T.L.A. [240]
STUDIES IN THE LIFE OF ST. PAUL / Leacock, Arthur Gordner – New York: Young Men's Christian Association, 1907, c1906 – 1mf – 9 – 0-8370-9712-6 – 1986-3712 – us A.T.L.A. [920]
STUDIES IN THE MOSAIC INSTITUTIONS / Moorehead, William Gallogly – Dayton: W.J. Shuey, 1896. 1 fiche – 9 – us A.T.L.A. [240]
STUDIES IN THE MOUNTAIN INSTRUCTION / Boardman, George Dana – New York: D. Appleton, 1888. 1 fiche – 9 – us A.T.L.A. [240]
STUDIES IN THE NOVEL – v1- 1969- 1; v8-5,6,9 – us UMI [420]
STUDIES IN THE PHILOSOPHY OF RELIGION / Galloway, George – (Includes an index) – Edinburgh: William Blackwood, 1904 – 1mf – 9 – 0-8370-3227-X – 1985-1227 – us A.T.L.A. [200]
STUDIES IN THE PHILOSOPHY OF RELIGION AND HISTORY / Fairbairn, Andrew Martin – (Includes bibliographical references) – New York:Lovell, Adam, Wesson, [c1876] – 1mf – 9 – 0-8370-3090-0 – 1985-1090 – us A.T.L.A. [200]
STUDIES IN THE PROPHECY OF DANIEL / Crocker, William Andrew – Nashville, TN: Southern Methodist Publ House, 1885 – 1mf – 9 – 0-8370-2778-0 – 1985-0778 – us A.T.L.A. [220]
STUDIES IN THE PROPHECY OF JEREMIAH / Morgan, George Campbell – London, Edinburg, 1948 – 8 – ne Slangenburg [240]
STUDIES IN THE RENAISSANCE – New York. v1-21. 1954-74 – 2r or 66mf – inquire – us Ross [410]
STUDIES IN THE SERMON ON THE MOUNT / Lyttelton, Edward – London: Longmans, Green, 1905. 1 fiche – 9 – us A.T.L.A. [240]
STUDIES IN THE SOCIAL PROGRESS IN THE GOSPEL OF THE KINGDOM *see* SOCIAL PROGRESS
STUDIES IN THE SYNTAX OF THE LINDISFARNE GOSPELS / Callaway Jr., M – Baltimore, 1918 – Dfl22.00 – ne Slangenburg [220]
STUDIES IN THEOLOGIC DEFINITION UNDERLYING THE APOSTLES' AND NICENE CREEDS / Palmer, Frederic – (Includes bibliographical references and appendix) – New York: E P Dutton, 1895 – 1mf – 9 – 0-8370-4660-2 – 1985-2660 – us A.T.L.A. [220]
STUDIES IN VISUAL COMMUNICATION – v.6-1980- – 1,5,6,9 – us UMI [073]
STUDIES IN WALT WHITMAN'S LEAVES OF GRASS / ed by Warfel, Harry R – 1954 – 9 – 10.00 – us Scholars' Facs [420]
STUDIES IN WORSHIP MUSIC. FIRST SERIES : CHIEFLY AS REGARDS CONGREGATIONAL SINGING / Curwen, John Spencer – London: J Curwen, [1901?] – 2mf – us A.T.L.A. [780]
STUDIES IN WORSHIP MUSIC. SECOND SERIES / Curwen, John Spencer – London: J. Curwen, [1886?] – 1mf – us A.T.L.A. [780]
STUDIES IN ZECHARIAH / Gaebelein, Arno Clemens – 8th ed. New York: Francis E Fitch, c1911 – 1mf – 9 – 0-8370-6047-8 – 1986-0047 – us A.T.L.A. [220]
STUDIES IN ZEN / Suzuki, Daisetz Teitaro; ed by Humphreys, Christmas – New York: Philosophical Library, 1955 – 212p – 1 – us U.W. Library [280]
STUDIES OF ARIANISM : CHIEFLY REFERRING TO THE CHARACTER AND CHRONOLOGY OF THE REACTION WHICH FOLLOWED THE COUNCIL OF NICAEA / Gwatkin, Henry Melvill – Cambridge: D. Bell; London: G. Bell, 1900 – 1mf – us A.T.L.A. [240]
STUDIES OF CHARACTER FROM THE OLD TESTAMENT / Guthrie, Thomas – New York: Robert Carter, 188?.1 fiche – 9 – us A.T.L.A. [220]
STUDIES OF CREATION AND LIFE / Godet, Frederic Louis – 1882 – 9 – us A.T.L.A. [240]
STUDIES OF ENGLISH MYSTICS : ST. MARGARET'S LECTURES, 1905 / Inge, William Ralph – London: J. Murray, 1906 – 1 roll – 1 – 1-55879-389-5 – uk Libr Preservation [290]
STUDIES OF ENGLISH MYSTICS : ST. MARGARET'S LECTURES, 1905 / Inge, William Ralph – London: John Murray, 1906 – 1mf – us A.T.L.A. [240]
STUDIES OF FAMILIAR HYMNS / Benson, Louis F – Philadelphia: Westminster, 1903 – 1mf – us A.T.L.A. [780]
STUDIES OF GOOD AND EVIL : A SERIES OF ESSAYS UPON PROBLEMS OF PHILOSOPHY AND OF LIFE / Royce, Josiah – (Includes bibliographical references) – New York: D Appleton, 1899, c1898 – 1mf – 9 – 0-8370-6360-4 – 1986-0360 – us A.T.L.A. [210]
STUDIES OF INDO-PACIFIC EURYALIDS / Mortensen, T – (Viddensk. Modd. f. Dansk. Nat. Foer., v. 96). Koepenhagen. 1933. B-648 2 – 8 – ne IDC [980]
STUDIES OF SENSATION AND EVENT : POEMS / Jones, Ebenezer; ed by Shepherd, Richard Herne – London: Pickering and Co., 1879 – 1 roll – 1 – 1-55879-285-6 – uk Libr Preservation [810]
STUDIES OF THE BEHAVIOUR OF CERTAIN STREPTOPLIA DOVES AND THEIR HYBRIDS / Davies, Stephen – (PhD Thesis) – microfiche – A$15.00 – at R.A.O.U. [590]
STUDIES OF THE ENGLISH METRICAL PSALTER AT THE TIME OF THE REFORMATION / Illing, Robert – (I: English Metrical Psalter 1562. 3v. 1983 Adelaide. ISBN: 0-949302-05-8. 1 commentary. 194p. 2 transcriptions. 370p. 3 facsimiles. 334p; II: Est-Barley-Ravenscroft and the English Metrical Psalter. 1969 Adelaide. 44p. Est's Psalter. 2v. 1969, 1971 Adelaide. 1 commentary. 80p. 2 transc. 96p; III: Ravenscroft's Revision of Est's Psalter. 2v. 1985 Adelaide. ISBN: 0-949302-27-9. 1 intro. and transc. 124p. 2 facs. 116p; IV: Day's Companion to the English Metrical Psalter. 1948 London, 1961 Oxford, 1986 Adelaide. ISBN: 0-949302-24-2. 1 intro. and transc. 180p. 2 facs. 84p; V: Allison's Companion to the English Metrical Psalter. 1961 Oxford, 1985 Adelaide. The 4-part settings. 104p) – Adelaide, 1983. Set of 11 vols – 10mf – 9 – A$25.00 set – at Baillieu Libr [780]
STUDIES OF THE MAN CHRIST JESUS / Speer, Robert Elliott – New York: Fleming H. Revell, 1896. 1 fiche – 9 – us A.T.L.A. [240]
STUDIES OF THE MAN PAUL / Speer, Robert Elliott – New York: Fleming H. Revell, 1900. 1 fiche – 9 – us A.T.L.A. [240]
STUDIES OF THE MIND OF CHRIST / Adamson, Thomas – Edinburgh: T. & T. Clark, 1898. 1 fiche – 9 – us A.T.L.A. [240]
STUDIES OF THE OLD TESTAMENT / Phelps, Austin – 1879 – 9 – us A.T.L.A. [240]
STUDIES OF THE PORTRAIT OF CHRIST / Matheson, George – New York: A C Armstrong; London: Hodder & Stoughton, 1901 – 2mf – 9 – 0-8370-6275-6 – 1986-0275 – us A.T.L.A. [240]
STUDIES ON AGRARIAN REFORM AND RURAL POVERTY / Ghonemy, M R El et al – 1984 – 104p – it F.A.O. [360]
STUDIES ON BASA CUSTOMS : WHAT I HAVE HEARD AND WHAT I HAVE SEEN / Bot, S Pierre Njovk – [s.l: s.n., 19–? – us Res Libr [306]
STUDIES ON GROWTH, BODY COMPOSITION AND NUTRITION OF EMUS / Algar, D – (MSc Agric Thesis) – 1980 – microfiche – A$15.00 – at R.A.O.U. [590]
STUDIES ON NEOTROPICAL FAUNA AND ENVIRONMENT – Lisse. v3-25. 1961-90 – 5,9 – Dfl3,220.00; Dfl140.00v – ne Swets [590]
STUDIES ON SELECTED DEVELOPMENT PROBLEMS IN VARIOUS COUNTRIES IN THE MIDDLE EAST / UNESCO – New York. 1970. BNE-19.715 1 – 9 – ne IDC [338]
STUDIES ON THE AMERICAN PATENT SYSTEM : STUDIES NO 1-30, SENATE COMMITTEE ON THE JUDICIARY, SUBCOMMITTEE ON PATENTS, TRADEMARKS AND COPYRIGHTS / U.S. Congress – Washington: GPO, 1956-1963 – 33mf – 9 – $49.50 – LLMC 81-107 – us L.L.M.C. [340]
STUDIES ON THE BOOK OF PSALMS: THE STRUCTURAL CONNECTION OF THE BOOK OF PSALMS / Forbes, John – Edinburgh: T. & T. Clark, 1888. 1 fiche – 9 – us A.T.L.A. [240]
STUDIES ON THE EPISTLES / Godet, Frederic Louis – New York: E P Dutton, [1889?] – 1mf – 9 – 0-8370-3322-5 – 1985-1322 – us A.T.L.A. [220]
STUDIES ON THE FINANCING OF FISHERIES DEVELOPMENT IN WEST AFRICA – 1989 – 42p – it F.A.O. [332]
STUDIES ON THE MATERIAL CULTURE OF THE ESKIMO IN WEST GREENLAND / Porsild, M P – BN 350. 2. 1915 – 9 – ne IDC [306]
STUDIES ON THE NEW TESTAMENT / Godet, Frederic Louis – New York: E.P. Dutton, 1873. 1 fiche – 9 – us A.T.L.A. [240]
STUDIES ON THE OLD TESTAMENT / Godet, Frederic Louis – New York: E.P. Dutton, 1897. 1 fiche – 9 – us A.T.L.A. [240]
STUDIES ON THE PLATEAU TONGA OF NORTHERN RHODESIA – 2mf – 9 – uk Microform Academic [960]
STUDIES ON THE ROLE OF FISHERMEN'S ORGANIZATIONS IN FISHERIES MANAGEMENT – 1988 – 54p – it F.A.O. [650]
STUDIES ON THE SYRIAN EXPORTS: POTENTIALITIES AND CONDITIONS FOR INCREASE / Syria. Syrian Documentation Papers – 1969. BNE-9741 1 – 9 – ne IDC [380]
STUDIES ON THE TEACHING OF JESUS: AS RECORDED IN THE SYNOPTIC GOSPELS / Oldham, Joseph Houldsworth – London: British College, 1903. 1 fiche – 9 – us A.T.L.A. [240]
STUDIES ON THE VOLUME AND YIELD OF TROPICAL FOREST STANDS : DRY FOREST FORMATIONS – 1989 – 112p – it F.A.O. [634]
STUDIES ON VOLTAIRE AND THE EIGHTEENTH CENTURY : GENERAL INDEX TO VOLS 1-30 – Oxford. 1967 – 9 – $27.00 – uk Voltaire [440]
STUDIES ON WOMEN ABSTRACTS – 1983-11v – 9 – £244.50 – 0262-5644 – uk Carfax [305]
STUDII NAD POETICHNOIU TVORCHISTIU T. SHEVCHENKA / Kolessa, Filaret, 1871-1947 – 1939 – 1 – us I.U. Libraries [390]
STUDIO DI PITTURA, SCOLTURA, ET ARCHITETTURA NELLE CHIESE DI ROMA / Titi, F – O 1054 1. 1674 – 9 – ne IDC [945]
STUDIO INTERNATIONAL – London, 1893-1991. Continued annually. Continues: The Studio – 1,14 – £3,495.00 – uk World [700]
LE STUDIOLO D'ISABELLE D'ESTE / Reunion des Musees Nationaux. Paris – 1975 – 9 – fr Réunion [700]
STUDIUM BIBLICUM FRANCISCANUM : COLLECTIO MAIOR – Jerusalem. v1-16. 1941-64 – 135mf – 9 – H-2504/1 – ne IDC [220]
STUDIUM BIBLICUM FRANCISCANUM : LIBER ANNUUS – Jerusalem. v1-20. 1951-1970 – 127mf – 9 – H-2507/1 – ne IDC [220]
DAS STUDIUM DER HEBRAEISCHEN SPRACHE IN DEUTSCHLAND : VOM ENDE DES 25. BIS ZUR MITTE DES 26. JAHRHUNDERTS / Geiger, Ludwig – (Includes bibliographical references) – Breslau [Wroclaw]: Schletter, 1870 – 1mf – 9 – 0-8370-9145-4 – 1986-3145 – us A.T.L.A. [470]
DAS STUDIUM DER THEOLOGIE IN DER GEGENWART: ANLEITUNG FUER ANFAENGER / Schuster, Carl Fr. Th – Stuttgart: Greiner & Pfeiffer, 1892. 1 fiche – 9 – us A.T.L.A. [240]
STUDJ SULL'ARMONIA / Basevi, A – Firenze: G G Guidi, 1865 – 1 – us Sibley [780]
Studwell, William *see* MUSIC REFERENCE SERVICES QUARTERLY
STUDY / Oklahoma Territory and the National Archives – undated, "Oklahoma Territory and the National Archives: A Study of Federal Lands," by Berlin B. Chapman. See Chapman, Berlin B, MS 1369-1370 – 1 – us KS Hist [978]
STUDY ABROAD = ETUDES A L'ETRANGER – (Trilingual: English/French/Spanish) – 1993 – xxviii/1300p – 9 – Distribution exclusive en Suisse: Éditions Techniques Van Diermen – fr UNESCO [370]
STUDY ABROAD 1991/92/93/94 : INTERNATIONAL SCHOLARSHIPS AND COURSES – (English/French/Spanish) – 1991 – 1278p – 9 – 92-3-002715-4 – fr UNESCO [370]
A STUDY FOR QUALITY DEVELOPMENT OF PRIMARY EDUCATION, B.E. 2525-2534 / Thailand. National Primary Education Commission – 1983 – 2mf – 9 – DE-598/1 – ne IDC [370]
STUDY GUIDE, BLACK DENOMINATIONS / Turner, Maynard P, Jr – 36p – 1 – 5.00 – us Baptist [240]
A STUDY IN HUMAN NATURE / Abbott, Lyman – 1884 – 1 – us A.T.L.A. [240]
A STUDY IN THE PSYCHOLOGY OF RITUALISM / Henke, Frederick Goodrich – Chicago, Ill.: University of Chicago Press, c1910 – 1mf – us A.T.L.A. [150]

A STUDY OF ACCOUNTABILITY IN SECULAR EDUCATION IN THE UNITED STATES TO DETERMINE POSSIBLE PRINCIPLES FOR THEOLOGICAL EDUCATION AMONG SOUTHERN BAPTISTS / Neal, Bart C – 1981 – 1 – 8.64 – us Baptist [240]

THE STUDY OF AFRICAN SOCIETY / Wilson, G & Hunter, M – 1mf – 7 – uk Microform Academic [960]

A STUDY OF AMBROSIASTER / Souter, A – 1905 – 5mf – 9 – ne Slangenburg [240]

A STUDY OF ATTITUDES TOWARD HIGH SCHOOL ACADEMICS REPORTED BY CURRENT FOOTBALL PLAYERS ENROLLING AT SELECTED BIG TEN CONFERENCE UNIVERSITIES FROM 1985 THROUGH 1989 / Otten, Orvin G & Hansen, Gary F – 1991 – 2mf – 9 – $8.00 – us Microform Publ [150]

A STUDY OF AUTHORITY FROM A THEOLOGICAL PERSPECTIVE AND ITS IMPLICATIONS FOR BUCK RUN BAPTIST CHURCH / Howell, Gerald Emmett – 1982 – 1 – 5.28 – us Baptist [240]

A STUDY OF BIOMECHANICAL VARIABLES IN THE COUNTERMOVEMENT JUMP AND THE DROP JUMP PERFORMED BY FEMALE INTERCOLLEGIATE ATHLETES / Weston, Joan & Wilkerson, Jerry D – 1992 – 2mf – $8.00 – us Microform Publ [612]

THE STUDY OF CASES : A COURSE OF INSTRUCTION IN READING AND STATING REPORTED CASES, COMPOSING HEADNOTES AND BRIEFS, CRITICISING AND COMPARING AUTHORITIES AND COMPILING DIGESTS / Wambaugh, Eugene – Boston: Little, Brown & Co, 1894 – 4mf – 9 – $6.00 – LLMC 92-151 – us L.L.M.C. [340]

THE STUDY OF CASES / Wambaugh, Eugene – 2d ed. Boston, Little, Brown, 1894. 333 p. LL-1247 – 1 – us L of C Photodup [340]

A STUDY OF CHRISTIAN MISSIONS / Clarke, William Newton – New York: Charles Scribner, 1914, c1900 – 1mf – 9 – 0-8370-6660-3 – 1986-0660 – us A.T.L.A. [240]

A STUDY OF CLOUGH, ARNOLD, ROSSETTI AND MORRIS : WITH AN INTRODUCTION ON THE COURSE OF POETRY FROM 1822 TO 1852 / Brooke, Stopford Augustus – [London]: Sir Isaac Pitman, 1908 – 1 roll – 1 – 1-55879-421-2 – uk Libr Preservation [420]

A STUDY OF CODEX BEZAE / Harris, J R – 1891 – 5mf – 9 – ne Slangenburg [240]

STUDY OF COMPENSATION AND REHABILITATION PROCEDURES AND THEIR IMPACT ON REHABILITATION OF ROAD ACCIDENT VICTIMS IN ISRAEL / Israel. National Insurance Institute – By Arye Nizan. July 1975. 141 p. Bibliogr – 9 – 3.00 – is I.T.T.I. [324]

STUDY OF COST AND LIVING AND FAMILY BUDGET IN DAMASCUS FROM 1957 / Syria. Dept. of Statistics – 1959? BNE-9696 1 – 9 – ne IDC [310]

STUDY OF CULTURAL POLICY IN THE UNITED STATES / Mark, Charles C – 3rd ed 1973 – 9 – 92-3-100739-4 – fr UNESCO [975]

THE STUDY OF ECCLESIASTICAL HISTORY / Collins, William Edward – London; New York: Longmans, Green, 1903. (Handbooks for the clergy) – 1mf – us A.T.L.A. [240]

A STUDY OF ETHICAL PRINCIPLES / Seth, James – (Includes bibliographies and index) – 5th ed. New York: Charles Scribner, 1900 – 2mf – 9 – 0-8370-6374-4 – 1986-0374 – us A.T.L.A. [170]

STUDY OF FISH POPULATION BY CAPTURE DATA AND THE VALUE OF TAGGING EXPERIMENTS – 1974 – 75p – it F.A.O. [639]

A STUDY OF GRILLPARZER'S AHNFRAU / Klose, W H – (Includes bibliographical references) – [S.l.: s.n.] 1908 – 1r – 1 – us U.W. Library [430]

A STUDY OF HIGH SCHOOL TRACK AND FIELD OUTDOOR CHAMPIONSHIPS BASED ON THE EVENTS ENDORSED BY THE NATIONAL FEDERATION OF STATE HIGH SCHOOL ASSOCIATIONS / Titlebaum, Peter J & Jackson, Michael W – 1993 – 2mf – $8.00 – us Microform Publ [790]

A STUDY OF INDIVIDUAL DIFFERENCES IN BREATHING CAPACITY / Kelly, Helen G – 1933 – 3mf – 9 – $9.00 – us Microform Publ [612]

THE STUDY OF INTERNATIONAL LAW...1907 / Gregory, C N – N.p., n.d. – 1mf – 1 – ILM-1601/1 – ne IDC [327]

A STUDY OF LAND CLASSIFICATION IN THE FOUR PROVINCES OF HONAN, HUPEH, ANHWEI AND KIANGSI-SURVEY REPORTS ON THE RURAL ECONOMY IN THE FOUR PROVINCES OF HONAN, HUPEH, ANHWEI AND KIANGSI – No. 2. Nanking, 1936. 1 reel – 1 – 14.00 – us Chinese Res [950]

A STUDY OF MEASUREMENT AND EVALUATION PROCEDURES IN INDIANA ELEMENTARY PHYSICAL EDUCATION PROGRAMS / Minniear, T C – 1991 – 2mf – 9 – $8.00 – us Microform Publ [790]

STUDY OF METHODOLOGIES FOR FORECASTING AQUACULTURE DEVELOPMENT – 1984 – 53p – it F.A.O. [639]

A STUDY OF MULTI-DIMENSIONAL EVALUATION PROCESSES IN THE PROFESSIONAL PREPARATION OF ATHLETIC TRAINERS / Ciganek, David S – 1989 – 80p 1mf – 9 – $4.00 – us Microform Publ [617]

THE STUDY OF NATURE AND THE VISION OF GOD : WITH OTHER ESSAYS IN PHILOSOPHY / Blewett, George John – Toronto: W. Briggs, 1907 – 1mf – us A.T.L.A. [210]

A STUDY OF ORIGINS / Pressense, Edmond Dehault de – 1883 – 9 – us A.T.L.A. [240]

A STUDY OF PRIMARY SCHOOLING IN THAILAND : THE FINAL REPORT, A JOINT PROJECT / Thailand. National Education Commission – Bangkok, c. 1977 – 3mf – 9 – DE-306/1 – ne IDC [370]

THE STUDY OF PUBLIC ADMINISTRATION / Waldo, Dwight – (In Indonesian) – 1955 – 9 – SE-10,996 1 – ne IDC [950]

A STUDY OF SKILLED LABOR IN INDONESIA / Guthrie, Harold W – SE-2247 1. 1959 – 9 – ne IDC [305]

THE STUDY OF SOCIOLOGY / Spencer, Herbert – 1873. 453 p. 1 fiche (29x) – 9 – 1.00f – at Libertarian Micro [320]

A STUDY OF SOUTHERN BAPTIST VACATION BIBLE SCHOOL MUSIC AND ITS CORRELATION WITH EDUCATIONAL ORGANIZATION / Ball, Mary C – 1958 – 1 – 5.00 – us Baptist [240]

A STUDY OF SPINOZA / Martineau, James – London: Macmillan and Co., 1882 – xi/371 – 1 – us U.W. Library [190]

A STUDY OF STRATEGIC LESSONS LEARNED IN VIETNAM – (Guide also sold seperately for $10.00) – 1991 – 3r – 1 – $255.00 – S3277 – us Scholarly Res [355]

STUDY OF TEXAS AGRICULTURE AND AGRICULTURAL PROGRAMS AT TEXAS A & M UNIVERSITY / Texas A & M University. College of Agriculture – Section 1, pt.1-Section 5, pt.2.1966-67. 32 fiches – 9 – us Spaulding [370]

A STUDY OF THE AMERICAN NEGRO / Fisher, S J – Pittsburgh, 1909 – 1r – 1 – us Ross [975]

STUDY OF THE BOOK OF REVELATION / Finnell, Reuben A – Nashville: Pub. House M.E. Ch. So., 1903. 1 fiche – 9 – us A.T.L.A. [240]

A STUDY OF THE BREEDING BIOLOGY AND AGGRESSIVE BEHAVIOUR OF BLACK SWANS IN SOUTH-WESTERN AUSTRALIA / Tingay, Alan – (PhD Thesis) – 1980 – 9 – A$15.00 – at R.A.O.U. [590]

A STUDY OF THE BUSINESS OF THE FEDERAL COURTS. / American Law Institute. Philadelphia – Philadelphia, 1934. 2 v. LL-1464 – 1 – us L of C Photodup [340]

STUDY OF THE CONTRIBUTION OF POPULATION EDUCATION TO EDUCATIONAL RENEWAL AND INNOVATION IN EL SALVADOR, THE REPUBLIC OF KOREA, PHILIPPINES AND TUNISIA / UNESCO. International Study of the Conceptualization and Methodology of Population Education (ISCOMPE) – 1980 – 206p – 9 – fr UNESCO [370]

A STUDY OF THE DRAMA / Matthews, Brander – Boston: Houghton Mifflin, [1910] – 1 roll – 1 – 1-55879-368-2 – uk Libr Preservation [820]

A STUDY OF THE ESKIMO BOWS IN THE U.S. NATIONAL MUSEUM / Murdoch, John – BN 321 2. 1884 – 8 – ne IDC [306]

A STUDY OF THE ETHICS OF SPINOZA / Joachim, Harold Henry – New York: Russell & Russell, 1964 – 316p – 1 – us U.W. Library [170]

A STUDY OF THE EVALUATION OF TEACHER TRAINING IN THAILAND : TOWARD A MODEL FOR DEVELOPMENT / Suntornpithung, N – 1979 – 3mf – 9 – DE-285/1 – ne IDC [370]

A STUDY OF THE FUNCTIONS OF PHYSICAL EDUCATION IN HIGHER EDUCATION / Cobb, Louise S – 1943 – 4mf – 9 – $12.00 – us Microform Publ [790]

A STUDY OF THE GOSPEL SONG / Gold, Charles E – Thesis. 1953 – 1 – 5.48 – us Baptist [240]

A STUDY OF THE GUIDANCE CONSIDERED ESSENTIAL FOR TEACHER'S INTELLIGENT SELF-DIRECTION IN THE PROCESS OF SECURING EMPLOYMENT IN THE MIDDLE ATLANTIC STATES / Fisher, Charles A – Philadelphia, 1937 – 2mf – DM62.00 – 3-8267-3087-9 – gw Hänsel [370]

A STUDY OF THE MONEY QUESTION / Bilgram, Hugo – 1894, 1955. 55p. with 3p of notes by John Zube – 9 – 1.00f – at Libertarian Micro [335]

A STUDY OF THE PENTATEUCH : FOR POPULAR READING / Stebbins, Rufus Phineas – Boston: Geo H Ellis, 1881 – 1mf – 9 – 0-8370-9306-6 – 1986-3306 – us A.T.L.A. [220]

A STUDY OF THE PEOPLE OF MIDDLETOWN OF SICILIAN EXTRACTION / Sangree, Walter H & Hybaeum, Mel – May 1952 – 1r – 1 – us I.H.R.C. [306]

A STUDY OF THE PERCEIVED EFFECTS OF THE REPEAL OF THE PENNSYLVANIA INTERSCHOLASTIC ATHLETIC ASSOCIATION CONSTITUTIONAL BYLAW ARTICLE 11, SECTION 2 : ON SELECTED ASPECTS OF ADMINISTERING PENNSYLVANIA PUBLIC HIGH SCHOOL, INTERSCHOLASTIC, VARSITY ATHLETIC PROGRAMS / Goehringer, Diane M & Jackson, Michael – 1992 – 4mf – 9 – $16.00 – us Microform Publ [370]

STUDY OF THE REASONS FOR SUCCESS OR FAILURE OF SOIL CONSERVATION PROJECTS – 1991 – 73p – it F.A.O. [631]

A STUDY OF THE RELATIONSHIP BETWEEN SELFREPORTED STRESS-RELATED PHYSICAL SYMPTOMOLOGY AND SPIRITUAL WELLNESS / Davies, Courtney C – Brigham Young University, 1994 – 1mf – 9 – PSY 1883 – us Microform Publ [150]

STUDY OF THE RELATIONSHIP BETWEEN WATER QUALITY AND SEDIMENT TRANSPORT / Golterman, H L et al – 1983 – 231p – 9 – 92-3-102109-5 – fr UNESCO [550]

A STUDY OF THE RELATIONSHIP OF "WITHITNESS" TO ALT-PE AND MONITORING IN MIDDLE SCHOOL PHYSICAL EDUCATION / Johnston, B D – 1991 – 2mf – 9 – $8.00 – us Microform Publ [790]

STUDY OF THE SECOND FIVE-YEAR PLAN OF PAKISTAN / Pakistan. General Agreement on Tariffs and Trade – Geneva. 1962 – 9 – ne IDC [338]

A STUDY OF THE SOCIO-ETHICAL THOUGHT OF GEORGE ALBERT COE / Moon, Tony G – 1982 – 1 – $5.00 – us Baptist [170]

A STUDY OF THE UNIVERSITIES IN CHINA – (Hsueh-fu chi-wen). 1901-39. Comp. by Nan King Chu-pan She. Taipei. 1981. 11v. 4400p. 2 reels or 70 fiches – 1 $75.00; 9 $95.00 – ch Transmission [370]

A STUDY OF UPPER EXTREMITY STRENGTH AND ENDURANCE OF EDUCABLE MENTALLY RETARDED AND NON-RETARDED BOYS IN SELECTED ONTARIO SEPARATE SCHOOLS / Valiquette, John E – 1982 – 3mf – 9 – $12.00 – us Microform Publ [790]

A STUDY OF WESTERN RESERVE ARCHITECTURE AS TYPIFIED BY CHURCHES IN OHIO DURING THE PERIOD 1800-1860 / Wardell, John Wilford – (A thesis submitted to Kent State University for the degree of Master of Arts) – Kent, OH, 1951 – 1r – 1 – us Western Res [720]

STUDY ON FEDERAL REGULATIONS / U.S. Senate Committee on Governmental Operations – (Includes appendix) – Washington: GPO. v1-6. 1977-78 – 32mf – 9 – $48.00 – LLMC 81-105 – us L.L.M.C. [323]

A STUDY ON THE AUTONOMY OF EDUCATIONAL ADMINISTRATION / Korea. Korean Educational Development Institute – Seoul, 1988 – 2mf – 9 – DE-660/1 – ne IDC [370]

STUDY ON THE DYNAMICS, EVOLUTION AND CONSEQUENCES OF MIGRATIONS 2 : THREE CENTURIES OF SPATIAL MOBILITY IN FRANCE / Courgeau, Daniel – 1983 – 64p – 9 – 92-3-102086-2 – fr UNESCO [304]

A STUDY ON THE FIFTH REVISION OF THE GENERAL GUIDELINES OF THE KOREAN SCHOOL CURRICULUM / Korea. Korean Educational Development Institute – Seoul, 1988 – 2mf – 9 – DE-661/1 – ne IDC [370]

STUDY PAPERS / Baptist World Alliance – Single reels available – 1 – 78.40 – us A.B.H.S. [240]

STUDY PROJECT ON CHRISTIANITY IN APARTHEID SOCIETY – Dossiers v.1-5. General Documentation. Occasional papers v.1-11. 1969-73 – 1 – us Res Libr [240]

A STUDY TO INVESTIGATE THE PSYCHO-SOCIAL REASONS FOR THE TERMINATION OF ORGANIZED SPORT PARTICIPATION AS RELATED TO AGE / Reven, A L – 1990 – 1mf – 9 – $4.00 – us Microform Publ [150]

A STUDY: WITH CRITICAL AND EXPLANATORY NOTES OF ALFRED TENNYSON'S POEM THE PRINCESS / Dawson, Samuel Edward – Montreal: Dawson, 1882. 02615. (Pre-1900 Canadiana) – 9 – cn C.I.H.M. [420]

Stuebe, Rudolf *see* ZUR GESCHICHTE DES CHRISTENTUMS IN MITTEL-ASIEN BIS ZUR MONGOLISCHEN EROBERUNG

Stuebe, Rudolph *see* JUEDISCH-BABYLONISCHE ZAUBERTEXTE

EIN STUECK ERDE : ROMAN IN ZWEI BUECHERN / Franck, Hans – Hannover: A Sponboltz, 1944- – 1r – 1 – us U.W. Library [830]

Stueck, Patricia MO *see* PHYSICAL ACTIVITY PATTERNS AND CHARACTERISTICS OF HIGH SCHOOL STUDENTS IN A GOVERNOR'S HONORS PROGRAM

Stueirzinger, J J *see* LE PELERINAGE DE VIE HUMAINE

Stuelcken, A *see* ATHANASIANA (T.U.U. 2-19/4)

Stueler, A *see* SCHRIFTLEHRE UND NATURWISSENSCHAFT: NEUN VORLESUNGEN, IM WINTER 1868

Stuelpner, Kurt *see* DER TOTE IN BRAUCH UND GLAUBEN DER MADAGASSEN

Stuerenburg, E *see* ALTE BEKANNTE AUS DEM NEW YORKER DEUTSCHEN VIERTEL

DER STUERMER – Nuernberg, 1923-45 – 8r – 1 – DM640.00 – gw Mikro Press [072]

DER STUERMER – Nuernberg, Germany. 1923-1945 – 8r – 1 – gw Mikrofilm [072]

DER STUERMER – Nuernberg. v1, no.1-v13, no.52.20 Apr 1923-33. Missing: v2, no.20, Aug 1924 – 1 – 35.00r – us Hoover Inst Photo [072]

STUERMISCHER SEPTEMBER : DAS SCHICKSAL EINER PARISER STRAFVERTEIDIGERIN / Lorei, Madlen – Berlin: K Curtius, c1943 – 1r – 1 – us U.W. Library [830]

Stuewer, W *see* DIE PATROZINIEN IM KOELNER GROSZARCHIDIAKONAT XANTEN

STUFF / St Joseph's College – Rensselaer. Ind. 1938- – 1 – us UMI [370]

STUFFED CROCODILE – London. v1-4. 1972-78 – 9 – Can$37.00y – cn Micromedia [073]

STUKKEN BETR. DE DIACONIE DER VREEMDELINGEN TE EMDEN 1560-1576 (DE WERKEN..1,2) / ed by Toorenbergen, J J van – Utrecht, 1876 – Dfl13.00 – ne Slangenburg [240]

Stuler, Lesley R *see* THE IMPACT OF THERAPEUTIC HORSEBACK RIDING ON THE SELF-CONCEPT AND RIDING PERFORMANCE OF CHILDREN AND ADOLESCENTS WITH DISABILITIES

STULTIFERA NAVIS NARRAGONICE PROFECTIONIS NUMQUAM SATIS LAUDATA NAVIS / Brant, S – O-1022. 1498 – 9 – ne IDC [623]

Stumbaugh, T A *see* THE EFFECTS OF THE KIDS' CONNECTION PROGRAM ON SIXTH GRADERS' DRUG KNOWLEDGE AND SELF-CONCEPT

STUMBLING STONES REMOVED FROM THE WORD OF GOD / Pierson, Arthur Tappan – New York: Baker & Taylor, 1891. 1 fiche – 9 – us A.T.L.A. [240]

Stump, Joseph *see* LIFE OF PHILIP MELANCHTHON

Stumpf, J C *see* SIX DUETTOS FOR TWO VIOLINS, OP. 18

Stumpf, R K P *see* L'ATTITUDE RELIGIEUSE DES LYCEENS DANS UNE VILLE DU WEST-CAMEROON, 1967-72. LE COMPARTIMENTAGE DES LANGUES ET LA FORMATION D'UNE LANGUE CULTUELLE

STUNDE DER STERNE : KUENSTLERNOVELLEN / Hohlbaum, Robert – Stuttgart: Verlag Deutsche Volksbuecher, 1942 – 1r – 1 – us U.W. Library [830]

DIE STUNDE HEIDELBERGS : EINE ERZAEHLUNG / Ponten, Josef – Muenchen: A Langen-G Mueller, 1935 – 1r – 1 – us U.W. Library [430]

THE STUNDIST IN SIBERIAN EXILE AND OTHER POEMS / Fetler, V A – London & Chicago, 1922. Filmed with: Otverzhenie boga (St. Petersburg, 1908), and, Rasti ili Umalyatsya (St. Petersburg, 1908) – 1 – 7.74 – us Baptist [240]

Stupperich, Robert *see* UNIONSVERHANDLUNGEN ZWISCHEN KATHOLIKEN UND PROTESTANTEN IN DEN JAHREN 1530-1540

STURBRIDGE 1723-1891 – (Mf 1: Births & Deaths 1723-88. Mf 2: Births & Deaths 1788-1823. Mf 3: Births & Deaths 1823-44; Out-of-Town Marriages 1736-99. Mf 3-5: Marriages & Intentions 1736-1844. Mf 5-6: Marriage Intentions 1845-61. Mf 7-8: Births 1860-85. Mf 9: Births 1885-91, Marriages 1860-69. Mf 10: Marriages 1869-89. Mf 11: Marriages 1890-91, Deaths 1860-74. Mf 12-13: Deaths 1874-91. Mf 14: Birth Index 1860-91. Mf 15: Marriage Index 1860-91. Mf 16: Death Index 1860-91) – (mf ed 1986) – 16mf – 9 – 0-87623-017-6 – us Holbrook [920]

Sturgess, Gary *see* A SUBMISSION TO THE MINISTER OF POLICE ON THE PROPOSED AMENDMENTS TO THE FIREARMS ACT (1927-67)

Sturgess, Philip *see* THEORIE ET PRATIQUE DE LA NARRATIVITE

Sturleson, Snorre. (Sturlusen) *see* EDDA, DEUXIEME PARTIE: TRACTATUS PHILOGICUS ET ADDIMENTA EX LODICIBUS MANUSCRIPTIS

DER STURM – Berlin. v. 1-21. no. 3. Mar 1910-1932 – 1 – us NY Public [073]

STURM – Berlin. v1-21. 1910-32 – 3r – 1 – us Ross [073]

DER STURM AUF LANGEMARCK : VON EINEM DER DABEI WAR / Thimmermann, Hermann – 5. Aufl. Muenchen: Knorr & Hirth, 1938 – 1r – 1 – us U.W. Library [830]

Sturm, J *see* BRYOLOGIA GERMANICA

Sturm, J W *see*
- DEUTSCHLAND FLORA
- ENUMERATIO PLANTARUM VASCULARIUM CRYPTOGAMICARUM CHILENSIUM. EIN BEITRAG ZUR FARN-FLORA CHILE'S

Sturm, L *see* LE VERITABLE VAUBAN, SE MONTRANT AU LIEU DU FAUX VAUBAN

Sturm, L C *see* KURTZE VORSTELLUNG DER GANTZEN CIVIL-BAU-KUNST, WORINNEN ERSTLICH DIE VORNEHMSTEN KUNSTWOERTER, ...

Sturm, Stefan *see*
- DER BLUEHENDE BAUM
- DAS GLUECK DIESES SOMMERS
- KAMERADEN
- VERLIEBTE ODERFAHRT
- WILDENGRUND

STURM UND DRANG : KRITISCHE SCHRIFTEN / ed by Loewenthal, Erich – (Includes bibliographical references and index) – Heidelberg: Verlag L Schneider, 1949 – 1 – us U.W. Library [430]

STURMBLATT – Berlin, 1865 – 1 – Inquire at Mikrofilmarchiv for details – gw Misc Inst [072]

DER STURMER – (In German) – Nuremberg, DE. no46 11 Nov 1943-v- no-(no7) 17 Feb 1944 – 1r – 1 – $25.00 – cn Can Microfilming [072]

STURMFLUT : ROMAN IN SECHS BUECHERN / Spielhagen, Friedrich – Leipzig: L Staackmann, 1877 – 1r – 1 – us U.W. Library [830]

STURMVOGEL UND NACHTIGALL : NEUE GEDICHTE / Waelti, C – Bern: Jent & Reinert, 1850 – 1r – 1 – us U.W. Library [810]

Sturtevant, Edgar H *see* A COMPARATIVE GRAMMAR OF THE HITTITE LANGUAGE

STUTTGART FIRST BAPTIST CHURCH. STUTTGART, ARKANSAS : CHURCH RECORDS – Jan 1938-Feb 1981. 3844p – 1 – 172.98 – us Baptist [240]

STUTTGARTER NACHRICHTEN – (Also available: Wuerttembergische Nachrichten, nov 2 1953-mar 31 1958. Also Bereichsausgaben available: BOEBLINGEN, aug 5 1948-apr 16 1951, 6r; ESSLINGEN, oct 14 1947-oct 31 1953, 14r; LUDWIGSBURG, oct 16 1947-oct 31 1953, 14r; NUERTINGEN, nov 1 1948-apr 30 1951, 6r; WAIBLINGEN, aug 2 1948-jun 6 1951, 6r) – Stuttgart, oct 16 1947- – 1 – Inquire at Mikrofilmarchiv for details – gw Misc Inst [072]

STUTTGARTER NACHRICHTEN – Esslingen a. Neckar, Germany. 14 Okt 1947-31 Okt 1953 – 13r – 1 – gw Mikrofilm [072]

STUTTGARTER NACHRICHTEN – Stuttgart, dec 1973, jan 2-oct 19 1986 – 6r – 1 – gw Mikrofilm [072]

STUTTGARTER NACHRICHTEN / ed by Wuerttembergische Nachrichten – Boeblingen, Germany. 1976- – ca 11r per yr – 1 – gw Mikrofilm [072]

STUTTGARTER STIMME : HERAUSGEBEN VON DER AMERIKANISCHEN ARMEE FUER DIE DEUTSCHE ZIVILVEVOELKERUNG – Germany, Aug-Sep 1945 – 1r – 1 – DM80.00 – gw Mikro Press [072]

STUTTGARTER ZEITUNG – Esslingen, Germany. 9 Apr 1947-31 Dec 1951 – 9r – 1 – gw Mikrofilm [072]

STUTTGARTER ZEITUNG – Germany, 29 Sep 1945-1 Oct 1947; 17 Jan 1948-29 Nov 1952 (imperfect) – 26r – 1 – uk British Libr Newspaper [072]

STUTTGARTER ZEITUNG – Stuttgart, 1945-1966 – 111r – 1 – DM8,325.00 – gw Mikro Press [943]

STUTTGARTER ZEITUNG – Stuttgart, Germany. 1961-91 – 455r – 1 – us L of C Photodup [072]

STUTTGARTER ZEITUNG – Stuttgart, Germany. 1967- – ca 11r per yr – 1 – gw Mikrofilm [072]

STUTTGARTER ZEITUNG – Stuttgart, jan 2 1975-apr 28 1976. aug 19 1978-79 – 27r – 1 – gw Mikrofilm [072]

Stutz, Ulrich *see*
- DIE KATHOLISCHE KIRCHE UND IHR RECHT IN DEN PREUSSISCHEN RHEINLANDEN
- DIE THATSACHEN DES GLAUBENS: VORTRAEGE

Stuve, Bernard et al *see* HISTORY OF ILLINOIS 1673-1873

STUW – Weltevreden, 1930-1933.-v1-4 – 30mf – 9 – SE-324/1 – ne IDC [950]

Stuxberg, A J *see* SVERIGES OCH NORGES FISKAR

Styczynska-Jurewicz, E et al *see* CULTIVATION OF FISH FRY AND ITS LIVE FOOD

Styger, Paul *see* DIE ALTCHRISTLICHE GRABESKUNST

STYLE – 1908- 1; 1975- 5,6,9 – us UMI [073]

STYLE AND LINGUISTICS; AN INAUGURAL LECTURE DELIVERED IN THE UNIV. OF INDONESIA ON 31STOCT. 1959 / Lott, Bernard – SE-3910 1. 1960 – 9 – ne IDC [400]

"STYLISTIQUE ET MESSAGES DANS LE VIMBUZA" / Soko, B J – Chants des cultes de possession recueillis dans les regions de Mzimba et Rumphi (Malawi) – 9 – F160.00 – fr Ethnologie [306]

SU ALCUNE IMPORTANTI QUESTIONI DI DIRITTO PENALE INTERNAZIONALE / Baldassarri, A – Roma, 1910 – 1mf – 9 – ILM-2067/1 – ne IDC [340]

Su, Hsueh-Lin *see* THE OLD TESTAMENT AND THE CHINESE CLASSICAL BOOKS (CCC285)

Su, I *see* MODERN INDONESIAN SHORT STORIES

SU POSICION EN LA HISTORIA DE LA FILOSOFIA DEL ESTADO EUROPEA / Schmitt, Carl – Madrid: Centro de intercambio intelectual Germano-Espanol, 1930 – sp Bibl Santa Ana [100]

SUAKHILI-RUSSKII SLOVAR' : SWAHILI-RUSSIAN DICTIONARY / ed by Ol'derogge, D A – Moscow, 1961 – 10mf – 9 – R-2463/1 – ne IDC [490]

SUARA MUHAMMADIJAH – Djakarta. Incomplete. SE 419 1. 1925-1968 – 9 – ne IDC [073]

SUARA PERTI – Djakarta. SE 424 1. v. 1-30. 1937-1965. Lacking: v. 1-29; 1937-1964 – 9 – ne IDC [073]

SUARA SBBT – Djakarta. SE 426 1. 1952-1960. Lacking: v. 1-8; 1952-1959 – 9 – ne IDC [073]

SUARA TANI – Jogjakarta. Incomplete. SE 429 1. 1950-1964 – 9 – ne IDC [073]

LOS SUAREZ DE FIGUEROA, DE FERIA Y ZAFRA / Figueroa y Melgar, Alfonso de – Badajoz: Dip. Provincial, 1974. Sep. REE – 1 – sp Bibl Santa Ana [390]

Suarez de Figueroa, Diego *see*
- CAMINO DEL CIELO
- HISTORIA DE BADAJOZ
- HISTORIA DE LA CIUDAD DE BADAJOZ...
- NASON, P. OVIDIO. LIBROS 4, 5 Y 6
- P. OVIDIO NASON. DE EL REMEDIO DEL AMOR IMPURO
- P. OVIDIO NASON. EPISTOLAS DE LAS HEROIDAS
- P. OVIDIO NASON.COMENTO DEL...NASON
- P. OVIDIO NASON.DE EL...AMOR
- P. OVIDIO NASON.EPISTOLAS...HERODIAS
- P. OVIDIO NASON.FASTOS

Suarez, F *see* TRACTATUS DE LEGIBUS AC DEO LEGISLATORE IN DECEM LIBROS DISTRIBUTUS...

Suarez, Gabriel *see*
- MANIFESTACION HECHA POR EL SINDICO
- MANIFESTACION...AYUNTAMIENTO...BADAJOZ

Suarez Murillo, Marcos *see* EXTREMADURA Y SUS HOMBRES. LAS ESCUELAS PARROQUIALES DE LOS SANTOS

Suarez Quintero, Valentin *see*
- INSTITUTO DE 2ND...CURSO 1898 A 1899
- MEMORIA...INSTITUTO DE BADAJOZ

Suau, Pierre *see* MERE MARIA DE JESUS EMILIE D'OULTREMONT

Suavi, Ali *see* MINISTRY AND SPECIAL INTEREST SALNAME

SUB CORONA : SERMONS / ed by Cowan, Henry & Hastings, James – Edinburgh: T. & T. Clark, 1915 – 1mf – us A.T.L.A. [240]

Subagijo, I N *see* BUNG KARNO

Subandrio *see*
- COLLECTED SPEECHES DELIVERED WHILE AMBASSADOR OF REP. OF INDONESIA TO COURT OF ST JAMES
- THE ESSENCE OF NATIONAL INDEPENDENCE AND THE REVOLUTION OF MANKIND
- INDONESIA ON THE MARCH
- OPENING ADDRESS AT MEETING OF MINISTERS IN PREPARATION OF THE SECOND ASIAN-AFRICAN CONFERENCE, DJAKARTA
- LA POLITIQUE ETRANGERE D'INDONESIE. INDONSIA'S FOREIGN POLICY
- PRESENT-DAY INDONESIAN-AMERICAN RELATIONSHIP

Sub-Collector of Customs, Burnie *see*
- REGISTER OF BRITISH SHIPS

Sub-Collector of Customs, Cairns *see* REGISTER OF BRITISH SHIPS

Sub-Collector of Customs, Darwin *see*
- REGISTER OF BRITISH SHIPS

Sub-Collector of Customs, Devonport *see*
- REGISTER OF BRITISH SHIPS

Sub-Collector of Customs, Geelong *see* REGISTER OF BRITISH SHIPS

Sub-Collector of Customs, Gladstone *see*
- REGISTER OF BRITISH SHIPS

Sub-Collector of Customs, Launceston *see*
- APPROPRIATION BOOK FOR OFFICIAL NUMBERS OF BRITISH REGISTERED SHIPS, 1855-1982
- REGISTERS OF BRITISH SHIPPING, 1846-1982

Sub-Collector of Customs, Maryborough *see*
- REGISTER OF BRITISH SHIPS

Sub-Collector of Customs, Newcastle *see*
- CREW AND PASSENGER LISTS, PORT OF NEWCASTLE, INWARDS AND OUTWARDS, 1865-1884
- REGISTER OF BRITISH SHIPS

Sub-Collector of Customs, Port Fairy *see* REGISTER OF BRITISH SHIPS

Sub-Collector of Customs, Port Kembla *see*
- REGISTER OF BRITISH SHIPS

Sub-Collector of Customs, Portland *see* REGISTER OF BRITISH SHIPS

Sub-Collector of Customs, Rockhampton *see*
- REGISTER OF BRITISH SHIPS

Sub-Collector of Customs, Townsville *see*
- REGISTER OF BRITISH SHIPS

Subcomision de monumentos *see* ACTA DE LA SESION DE 9 DE DICIEMBRE DE 1918

SUB-COMMISSION ON PREVENTION DISCRIMINATION AND PROTECTION OF MINORITIES / United Nations. Commission on Human Rights – (1st – 27th Sessions: 1947-1975, E.500 F.511; 28th – 41st Sessions: 1976-1989, E.744 F.682 R.344 S.463) – 9 – us U.N. Pubs [320]

THE SUBCONSCIOUS SELF AND ITS RELATION TO EDUCATION AND HEALTH / Waldstein, Louis – London: G. Richards, 1897. 171p – 1 – us U.W. Library [150]

SUB-DISTRICT DIRECTORS MINUTES / Hancock County. Ohio. Biglick Township. Board of Education – 1899-1911 – 1r – 1 – $32.50r – us Archival [324]

SUBDIVISIONS DU BAS CANADA, EN PAROISSES ET TOWNSHIPS, DEPUIS 1853 / Canada. Parliament. Legislative Assembly – Quebec: Imprime par Thompson et Cie, 1860. SEM105P125 – 1mf – 9 – Can$2.25 – cn Bibl Nat [324]

SUBDIVISIONS DU BAS-CANADA EN PAROISSES ET TOWNSHIPS, EN REPONSE A L'ADRESSE CI-JOINTE DE L'ASSEMBLEE LEGISLATIVE, 1853 – Quebec: imprime par E R Frechette, 1853. SEM105P1280 – 2mf – 9 – Can$4.50 – cn Bibl Nat [324]

Subekti *see* HUKUM PEMBUKTIAN

Subercaseaux, Guillermo *see* EL PAPEL MONEDA

SUBH-I AZADIGAN – (Shumarah-'i 958-1564 (3 Khurdad 1362-18 Urdibisht 1364[24 May 1983-8 May 1985]). Partial issues: Shumarah-'i 1005, 1029, 1051, 1094, 1096, 1104-5, 1108-15, 1129-1132, 1143-47, 1149, 1152, 1154, 1163-64, 1167-68, 1171-76, 1178, 1180-82, 1184-90, 1192-99, 1379, 1414, 1443, 1425, 1477, 1499, 1501-02, 1517-18, 1525, 1536, 1541, 1545-47. Missing issues: Shumarah-'i 970-71, 976, 998-99, 1012-13, 1018-22, 1040-42, 1071-72, 1080, 1082, 1200-1378, 1380-1409, 1411-12, 1415-16, 1419, 1422, 1425-26, 1429-30, 1432, 1434, 1438, 1444, 1446-48, 1450-63, 1465-71, 1480, 1489, 1491-94, 1497, 1503-16, 1519-23, 1527, 1551, 1553, 1555, 1561-63) – Tehran – 3r – 1 – $50.00 – us MEDOC [950]

SUBJECT AND TRIBAL INDEXES : AND AUTHOR CATALOGUE – 428mf – 9 – $2,890.00 – 0-907006-89-2 – uk Mindata [305]

SUBJECT BIBLIOGRAPHY ON ISLAM IN MALAYSIA / Sulaimon, Zainon – Sydney: BISA, 1988 – 1mf – 9 – A$10.00 – 0-86758-278-2 – at BISA [290]

SUBJECT CATALOG / California. University. Berkeley. East Asiatic Library – (First suppl., 1973. 28,200 cards. 2 reels. $265.00 ISBN 0-8161-1415-3) – uk Hall [950]

SUBJECT CATALOG / Harvard University. Graduate School of Business Administration. Baker Library – (First suppl., 1974.-30,500 cards 2 reels. $130.00 ISBN: 0-8161-1440-4) – 1971.-228,000 cards 10 reels.-ISBN: 0-8161-1228-2 – 1 – $1170.00 – uk Hall [380]

SUBJECT CATALOG / New York Academy of Medicine. Library – (First suppl., 1974. 57,500 cards. 8 reels. $545.00 ISBN 0-8161-1273-8) – 1969. 646,000 cards. 34 reels. ISBN 0-8161-1460-9 – 1 – $3550.00 – uk Hall [610]

SUBJECT CATALOG / U.S. Library of Congress – (1975-82. Annual) – Quinquennia: 1950-54; 1955-59; 1960-64; 1965-69; 1970-74 – 9 – us Advanced Libr [010]

SUBJECT CATALOG OF THE ARTHUR LAKES LIBRARY OF THE COLORADO SCHOOL OF MINES / Colorado School of Mines – (Available on microfilm by request) – 1977. 80,300 cards – 9 – $595.00 export $720.00 – uk Hall [622]

SUBJECT CATALOG OF THE DEPARTMENT LIBRARY / U.S. Department of Health, Education and Welfare. Library – (First Suppl., 1973. 61,700 cards. 8 reels. $440.00 ISBN 0-8161-1348-3) – 1965. 363,000 cards. 40 reels. ISBN 0-8161-1347-5 – 1 – $2060.00 – uk Hall [310]

SUBJECT CATALOG OF THE LIBRARY OF THE NEW YORK ACADEMY OF MEDICINE / New York Academy of Medicine – (First Supplement, 1974. 57,500 cards 8 reels. $495.00 export $598.00 – ISBN 0-8161-1273-8) – 1969. 646,000 cards on 34 reels – 1 – $3,225.00 export $3,900.00 – 0-8161-1460-9 – uk Hall [610]

SUBJECT CATALOG OF THE WORLD WAR 1 COLLECTION / New York Public Library. Research Libraries – 1961. 61,300 cards. 4 reels. ISBN 0-8161-1424-2 – 1 – $310.00 – uk Hall [900]

SUBJECT CATALOG, SHELF LIST, SHELF LIST OF DOCUMENTS AND REPORTS / California. University.San Diego. Scripps Institution of Oceanography – (First suppl., 1973.-20,900 cards 1 reel. $120.00 ISBN: 0-8161-1423-4; Second Suppl., Subject Catalog, 1980.-14,800 cards 1 reel. $180.00 ISBN: 0-8161-1406-4) – 1 – uk Hall [910]

SUBJECT CATALOG...THE HISTORY OF THE ISTHMUS OF PANAMA AS IT APPLIES TO INTEROCEANIC TRANSPORTATION / Panama Canal Zone Museum. Library – 1964.-7100 cards 1 reel.-ISBN: 0-8161-1371-8 – 1 – $90.00 – uk Hall [972]
SUBJECT CATALOGUE OF ACCESSIONS, TO 1950 / Great Britain. Colonial Office Library – 1 – uk Microform Academic [025]
SUBJECT FILE OF THE CONFEDERATE STATES NAVY – 1861-65. 61 rolls. M1091 – 1 – us Nat'l Archives [324]
SUBJECT GUIDE TO BOOKS IN PRINT ON MICROFICHE – (Entire non-fiction database of American titles under 77,000 Library of Congress subject headings) – Quarterly – 9 – Apply – 0-8352-3691-9 – us Bowker [010]
SUBJECT HEADINGS / New York Public Library.Theatre Collection – 1 – us NY Public [020]
THE SUBJECT OF MISSIONS CONSIDERED UNDER THREE NEW ASPECTS : THE CHURCH AND MISSIONS, THE REPRESENTATION OF THE SCIENCE OF MISSIONS AT THE UNIVERSITIES, COMMERCE AND THE CHURCH / Plath, Karl Heinrich Christian – Edinburgh: T. & T. Clark, 1873 – 1mf – us A.T.L.A. [240]
SUBJECT-AUTHOR-TITLE CATALOG OF SELECTED PUBLICATIONS OF THE FEDERAL GOVERNMENT, CA 1900-CA 1950 – 64r – 1 – T1203 – us Nat'l Archives [010]
SUBJECT-INDEX TO THE ANNUAL REPORTS ON SOUTH-INDIAN EPIGRAPHY FROM 1887-1936 / Krishnamacharlu, C R – Calcutta, 1940 – 3mf – 9 – ne IDC [490]
DIE SUBJEKTIVE DIAGNOSTISCHE VALENZ VON INTELLIGENZTESTS / Haase, Henning – Frankfurt a.M., 1969 – 3mf – 9 – DM76.00 – 3-89349-649-1 – gw Hänsel [150]
DER SUBJEKTIVISMUS IN DER MODERNEN THEOLOGIE UND SEIN ANRECHT / Polstorff, Friedrich – Guetersloh: C. Bertelsmann, 1893. 1 fiche – 9 – us A.T.L.A. [240]
LA SUBLEVACION DE CATALUNA. ANTECEDENTES DE UNOS TITULOS DEL REINO / Siete Iglesias, Antonio de – Madrid, s.i. Julio-Agosto, 1957 – 1 – sp Bibl Santa Ana [946]
SUBLEVACION EN CURUZ U CUATIA / Hume, Rolando – Santa Fe: Argentina Libreria y Editorial Castellv i, [1962] – 1 – CSUXADJ7528-B – us Hoover Inst Photo [320]
SUBLIMITY FARMERS REVIEW – Sublimity OR. July 28 1910 – 1 – us U.O. Library [071]
SUBMARINE TELEGRAPHS: THEIR HISTORY, CONSTRUCTION AND WORKING: FOUND IN PART ON WUENSCHENDORFF'S "TRAITE DE TELEGRAPHIE SOUS-MARINE". / Bright, Charles – London: C. Lockwood, 1898. 00867. (Pre-1900 Canadiana) – 9 – cn C.I.H.M. [380]
SUBMARINER – Issue Nos. 11-15 Fall 1943-Winter 44-45 – 5mf – 15 – $31,95 – us Comics [760]
SUBMARINER – Issue Nos. 1-5 Spring 1941-Spring 1942 – 5mf – 15 – $31,95 – us Comics [760]
SUBMARINER – Issue Nos. 16-20 Spring 1945-Summer 1946 – 5mf – 15 – $31,95 – us Comics [760]
SUBMARINER – Issue Nos. 21-25 Fall 1946-Spring 1948 – 5mf – 15 – $31,95 – us Comics [760]
SUBMARINER – Issue Nos. 6-10 Summer 1942-Summer 43 – 5mf – 15 – $31,95 – us Comics [760]
A SUBMAXIMAL ONE-MILE TRACK JOG TO ESTIMATE VO2MAX IN FIT MEN AND WOMEN, AGES 30-39 YEARS / Etchie, Michael P & Fisher, A Garth – 1992 – 1mf – $4.00 – us Microform Publ [612]
A SUBMAXIMAL TREADMILL WALKING PROTOCOL FOR PREDICTING MAXIMAL OXYGEN CONSUMPTION / Landle, K M – 1991 – 1mf – 9 – $4.00 – us Microform Publ [612]
A SUBMISSION TO THE MINISTER OF POLICE ON THE PROPOSED AMENDMENTS TO THE FIREARMS ACT (1927-67) / Sturgess, Gary – A Progress Party Paper of 1977. With: Local Financing for Local Government, A Progress Party Discussion Paper. 1 fiche (29x) – 9 – 1.00f – at Libertarian Micro [320]
SUBPLEMENTO AL TESORO POETICO CASTELLANO DEL SIGLO 19 / Gomez Bravo, Vicente – Madrid: La Difusora del Libro, 1959 – 9 – sp Bibl Santa Ana [810]
Subronto, K Atmodjo *see* KEMERDEKAAN INDONESIA; KUMPULAN PERTAMA
SUBSCRIBERS REAL ESTATE DIRECTORY – (Cont by: Halifax and Provincial Real Estate Register) – [Halifax, N.S.?]: F.C. Wakefield, [187-?-1877?] – 9 – cn C.I.H.M. [333]
SUBSCRIBERS REAL ESTATE DIRECTORY *see* HALIFAX AND PROVINCIAL REAL ESTATE REGISTER
SUBSCRIPTION BOOKS BULLETIN – v1-27. 1930-56 – 1 – us UMI [073]
A SUBSCRIPTION SERVICE FOR STATE STATUTES AND CODES OF ALL 50 STATES – 1988 – 9 – us Hein [340]
SUBSCRIPTIONS TO CANADIAN NATIONAL FUND FOR THE RELIEF OF THE DISTRESS IN INDIA:. / Canadian India Famine Fund – Ottawa: Govt. Print. Bureau, 1897. 02039. (Pre-1900 Canadiana) – 9 – cn C.I.H.M. [360]
Subsecretaria de Turismo *see* BADAJOZ. DATOS INFORMATIVOS
Subsecretaria de turismo *see* DATOS INFORMATIVOS
Subsecretariade Turismo *see* MERIDA
SUBSIDIA AD COGNOSCENDUM GRAECORUM SERMONEM VULGAREM E PENTATEUCHI VERSIONE ALEXANDRINE REPETITA / Anz, Henricus – (Includes bibliographical references) – Halis Saxonum: Max Niemeyer, 1894 – 1mf – 9 – 0-8370-9281-7 – 1986-3281 – us A.T.L.A. [220]
SUBSIDIARY LEGISLATION - SUPPLEMENT / Ghana – 1957-59 – 1 – us NY Public [960]
SUB-STANCE – 1971- 1; 1976- 5,6,9 – us UMI [800]
SUB-STANCE – Three issues per year, 1971-1976; -q., 1977. no.1-. Madison, Wis., Sub-Stance, Inc. 1971- – 1 – us U.W. Library [420]
SUBSTANCE AND ALCOHOL ACTIONS/ MISUSE *see* ALCOHOL AND DRUG RESEARCH
SUBSTANCE AND ALCOHOL MISUSE – v. 1-. 1980- – 5,6,9 – us UMI [610]
THE SUBSTANCE AND DEVELOPMENT OF PRESERVICE TEACHERS' KNOWLEDGE DURING A FIELD-BASED ELEMENTARY PHYSICAL EDUCATION METHODS COURSE / Rovegno, Inez C – 1989 – 230p 3mf – 9 – $12.00 – us Microform Publ [370]
SUBSTANCE AND SHOW / King, Thomas Starr – 1877 – 9 – us A.T.L.A. [240]
SUBSTANCE OF AN ADDRESS...AT A MEETING OF THE FRIENDS OF THE CHINESE ASSOCIATION, IN AID OF THE MEDICAL MISSIONARY SOCIETY IN CHINA / Hobson, B – Hackney, 1846 – 1mf – 9 – ne IDC [610]
THE SUBSTANCE OF FAITH ALLIED WITH SCIENCE : A CATECHISM FOR PARENTS AND TEACHERS / Lodge, Oliver – New York: Harper, 1907 – 1mf – 9 – 0-8370-4289-5 – 1985-2289 – us A.T.L.A. [210]
SUBSTANCE OF SEVERAL COURSES / Crotch, William – 1831 – 9 – us Sibley [780]
SUBSTITUTE OR, ENTOMOLOGICAL EXCHANGE FACILITATOR AND ENTOMOLOGIST'S FIRESIDE COMPANION FOR 1856-1857 – London. nos1-20. 1857 – 4mf – 9 – Z-1004/2 – ne IDC [590]
SUBSTITUTED LIABILITIES / Dixon, S F – Philadelphia, Childs, 1862. 188 p. LL-268 – 1 – us L of C Photodup [340]
LES SUBSTITUTIONS FIDEI-COMMISSAIRES EN DROIT ANNAMITE HUONG-HOA. / Tran-van-Lieu – Paris, Les Presses modernes, 1927. 130 p. L.C. copy imperfect: p. 21-22. LL-10020 – 1 – us L of C Photodup [340]
SUBUD / Subuh Sumohadiwidjojo, Muhammad – From original poem in High Javanese into bahasa Indonesian; English translation by Subud Committee for Great Britain. Head of title: The way of submission to the will of God. SE 2344 1. 1959 – 9 – ne IDC [290]
Subuh Sumohadiwidjojo, Muhammad *see* SUBUD
SUBURBAN – Eugene, OR. -w. 9 Apr 1964-3 Aug 1964. 1 roll – 1 – us U.O. Library [071]
THE SUBURBAN – Montreal, Canada. 1 mar 1963-v2 n1. 20 mar 1964 – 1r – 1 – cn Can Microfilming [072]
SUBURBAN NEWS – Farmers Branch. Tex. 1970- – 1 – us UMI [071]
SUBURBAN NEWSPAPERS – Sacramento. Calif. 1967- – 1 – us UMI [071]
SUBURBAN PRESS – Genoa, Ohio, 1975-1990 – 13r – 1 – $32.50r – us Archival [978]
SUBURBAN REPORTER – Vienna. Ohio. 1961-1962 – 1 – us UMI [071]
SUBURBAN STAR – Chicago. Ill. 1931-1932 – 1 – us UMI [071]
SUBURBAN STAR – Chicago. Ill. (Blue Island Edition). 1930-32 – 1 – us UMI [071]
SUBURBAN TELEGRAPH – Newtown, Nov 2 1878-Mar 4 1882 – 1 – at Pascoe [072]
SUBURBAN TRENDS – Riverdale. N.J. -w. 1973- – 1 – us UMI [071]
O SUBURBIO : ORGAO NOTICIOSO E DOS INTERESSES DE BEBEDOURO – Maceio, Alagoas. 22 Abr 1909 – 1,5,6 – bl Biblioteca [072]
SUBVERSIVE ACTIVITIES CONTROL BOARD REPORTS / U.S. Subversive Activities Control Board – (With index/digest) – 4v. 1950-56 (all publ) – 36mf – 9 – $54.00 – LLMC 81-242 – us L.L.M.C. [324]
LE SUCCES – Journal des illustrations dramatiques. Paris. Ed. bimens. oct 1848-49. Publ. parallelement a: Le Succes. Journal-programme des theatres et des illustrations dramatiques. Ed. quot. janv-mai 1849 – 1 – fr A.C.R.P.P. [410]
SUCCESS – 1985-. -m – 1 – us UMI [073]
SUCCESS – (v31-. 1984-. 5,6,9) – v28-. Mar 1981- – 1 – us UMI [073]
THE SUCCESS AND FAILURE OF THE CHURCH (CCC282) / Shih, Tao-hung – (In Chinese) – 1st ed. Hong Kong: Council on Christian Literature for Overseas Chinese, 1964 – 1r – 1 – 1984-6621 – us A.T.L.A. [240]
SUCCESS UNLIMITED – Chicago. v1-20. 1954-73 – 5r – 1 – us Ross [073]
SUCCESS UNLIMITED – v1-28. 1954-81 – 1 – us UMI [073]
SUCCESSAO DO ESTRANGEIRO NO BRASIL / Ferraz Alvim, O – Sao Paulo, 1934 – 1mf – 1 – ILM-2964/1 – ne IDC [327]
SUCCESSFUL BOOKSELLING : A MANAGEMENT TRAINING COURSE – 1993 – 197p – 9 – 92-3-102838-3 – Co-published with Book House Training Centre – fr UNESCO [650]
SUCCESSFUL EXECUTIVE – (Cont: Executive, 1986. Ceased 1987) – Don Mills, v1. 1986-87 – 9 – Can$37.00 – cn Micromedia [650]
SUCCESSFUL EXECUTIVE *see* EXECUTIVE
SUCCESSFUL FARMING – (v. 67- 1969- 5,6. v. 68- 1970- 9) – v. 1- 1902- – 1 – us UMI [630]
SUCCESSFUL FARMING. OHIO EDITION – (1986-. 1,5,6) – 1965- – 9 – us UMI [630]
SUCCESSFUL IRRIGATION : PLANNING, DEVELOPMENT, MANAGEMENT / Hagan, R M et al – 1982 – 53p – it F.A.O. [631]
SUCCESSFUL TEACHING; FIFTEEN STUDIES BY PRACTICAL TEACHERS, PRIZE-WINNERS IN THE NATIONAL EDUCATIONAL CONTEST OF 1905 – Introd. by James M. Greenwood. New York, London: Funk & Wagnalls, 1906. 198p – 1 – us U.W. Library [370]
SUCCESSFUL VERMONTERS-GAZETTER OF CALEDONIA, ESSEX, AND ORLEANS COUNTIES / Jeffrey, William H – Burke, Historical Publishing Co., 1904. Vermont Reel 6. (The Cox Library Collection) – 5 – us Americana [978]
SUCCESSFUL WOMAN – v3-. 1981- – 9 – us UMI [650]
THE SUCCESSION OF THE PRELATES AND MEMBERS OF THE CATHEDRAL BODIES IN IRELAND, VOL 3 : THE PROVINCE OF ULSTER / Cotton, Henry – (Includes index) – Dublin:Hodges and Smith, 1849 – 1mf – 9 – 0-8370-3495-7 – 1985-1495 – us A.T.L.A. [240]
THE SUCCESSION OF THE PRELATES AND MEMBERS OF THE CATHEDRAL BODIES IN IRELAND, VOL 4 : THE PROVINCE OF CONNAUGHT / Cotton, Henry – (Includes appendix of consecrations of Irish prelates and index) – Dublin:Hodges and Smith, 1850 – 1mf – 9 – 0-8370-3493-0 – 1985-1493 – us A.T.L.A. [240]
THE SUCCESSION OF THE PRELATES AND MEMBERS OF THE CATHEDRAL BODIES OF IRELAND, VOL 1 : THE PROVINCE OF MUNSTER / Cotton, Henry – (Includes index) – 2nd corr enl ed. Dublin:Hodges and Smith, 1851 – 2mf – 9 – 0-8370-3509-0 – 1985-1509 – us A.T.L.A. [240]
LE SUCCESSIONI NEL DIRITTO INTERNAZIONALE... / Ciolfi, E – Roma, 1905 – 2mf – 1 – ILM-3657/1 – ne IDC [327]
LE SUCCESSIONI SECONDO IL DIRITTO INTERNAZIONALE PRIVATO ITALIANO / Bellegotti, L – Pisa, 1892 – 2mf – 9 – ILM-3318/1 – ne IDC [327]
LES SUCCESSIONS EN DROIT FRANCO-SUISSE / Chatenay, C – Lausanne 1922 – 2mf – 1 – ILM-3115/1 – ne IDC [327]
LES SUCCESSIONS EN DROIT INTERNATIONAL PRIVE... / Ausbourg, A d' – Paris, 1912 – 3mf – 9 – ILM-3194/1 – ne IDC [340]
LA SUCESION ANTE EL DERECHO INTERNACIONAL PRIVADO / Faundes Rivera, H – Santiago de Chile, 1929 – 2mf – 1 – ILM-2956/1 – ne IDC [327]
SUCESION DE EXTRANJEROS... / Flores, R – Mexico, 1897 – 1mf – 1 – ILM-948/1 – ne IDC [327]
LAS SUCESIONES EN EL DERECHO INTERNACIONAL PRIVADO...REPUBLICA ARGENTINA / Diez Mieres, A – Madrid, 1927 – 1mf – 1 – ILM-2958/1 – ne IDC [327]
LOS SUCESOS DE BARCELONA: RELACION DOCUMENTAL DE LAS TRAGICAS JORNADAS DE LA SEMANA DE MAYO DE 1937 / Confederacion Nacional de Trabajo. Spain – Valencia, 1937. Fiche W 1217. (Blodgett Collection of Spanish Civil War Pamphlets) – 9 – us H.U. College Libr [946]
LOS SUCESOS DE MAYO EN BARACELONA. RELATO AUTENTICO / Confederacion Nacional de Trabajo. Spain – NY, 1937. Fiche W 1498. (Blodgett Collection of Spanish Civil War Pamphlets) – 9 – us H.U. College Libr [946]
SUCH IS LIFE : A PLAY IN FIVE ACTS / Wedekind, Frank – Philadelphia: Brown, 1912 – 1r – 1 – us U.W. Library [820]
SUCHASNA UKRAINA – Munich, Germany. 7 Jan 1951-25 Dec 1960 – 3r – 1 – uk British Libr Newspaper [947]
SUCHEN WIR EINEN NEUEN GOTT? / Classen, Walther – Tuebingen: J C B Mohr (Paul Siebeck), 1907 – 1mf – 9 – 0-8370-2676-8 – 1985-0676 – us A.T.L.A. [240]
Suchodolski, Bogdan et al *see* INTERNATIONAL BUREAU OF EDUCATION IN THE SERVICE OF EDUCATIONAL DEVELOPMENT
Suchy, Anke *see* AKTIONSARTEN MIT GRADUIERENDER SEMANTIK IN DER RUSSISCHEN SPRACHE DER GEGENWART
Suchy, Joerg *see* DAS GROTESKE IN DER FRUEHEN PROSA V.A. KAVERINS (1920-1931)
SUCINTA ESPOSCION SIC DOCUMENTADA DE LOS NOBLES HECHOS, GRANDES SERVICIOS Y PADECIMIENTOS DEL TENIENTE GENERAL MARQUES DE CASA-PIZARRO – 185?. Argentinian War of Independence, 1810-17 – 1 – us U.W. Library [972]
SUCINTA...MANICOMIO DEL CARMEN DE MERIDA / Fadon Sanchez, Antonio – 1885 – 9 – 1.50f – sp Bibl Santa Ana [610]
Suckow, Georg Adolph *see* ANFANGSGRUNDE DER OKONOMISCHEN UND TECHNISCHEN CHYMIE
Sucquet, A *see* DEN WECH DES EEUWICH LEVENS BESCHREVEN INT LATIJN...
LE SUCRE EN ALGERIE / Algeria. Chambre de Commerce et d'Industrie d'Alger – 1969. BNE-8704 1 – 9 – ne IDC [338]
Sucre, Luis Alberto *see*
– COBERNADORES Y CAPITANES GENERALES DE VENEZUELA
– HISTORIAL GENEALOGICO DEL LIBERTADOR
Sucre. Venezuela (District) *see* GACETA MUNICIPAL
Sucre. Venezuela (State) *see* GACETA OFICIAL DEL ESTADO
LE SUD / ed by Rouillard, Jean-Baptiste – Sorel, Canada. 1 dec 1887-9 avr 1892 – 5r – 1 – Can$50.00r – cn Can Microfilming [072]
SUD – Revue mensuelle de litterature et d'art. Alger. dec 1931-avr 1935 – 1 – fr A.C.R.P.P. [800]
SUD I PROKURATURA LATVIISKOI SSR / Stambina, E Ia. – Riga, 1962 – 3mf – 9 – ne IDC [340]
SUD I RASKOLI' NIKISEKTANTY = THE COURT AND SCHISMATICS-SECTARIANS / Bobrishchev-Pushkin, Aleksandr M – St. Petersburg, 1902. 234p – 1 – us Baptist [240]

SUD NAD DELEGATKOI : DELO PO OBVINENIIU DELEGATKI TIKHONOVOI, NE VYPOLNIVSHEI SVOEGO PROLETARSKOGO DOLGA / Glebova, N – 3e izd., ispr. Moskva: Gos. izd-vo., 1926 – 1 – CSUX89-B1529 – us Hoover Inst Photo [947]

SUDA HALKALAR / Camlibel, Faruk Nafiz – Istanbul: Sani'i Nefisi Matbaasi, 1928 – $39.00 – us MEDOC [470]

Sudan *see*
- DEVELOPMENT BUDGETS
- EXPLANATORY MEMORANDUM ON DEVELOPMENT BUDGETS
- FIVE YEAR DEVELOPMENT PLAN 1970/71 TO 1974/75
- JOURNAL OFFICIEL DE LA REPUBLIQUE SOUDANAISE
- A REPORT ON THE SAMPLE CENSUS OF AGRICULTURE FOR THE YEAR 1964/1965 IN THE NORTHERN AND KHARTOUM PROVINCES OF SUDAN
- REPORT TO THE GOVERNMENT OF THE REPUBLIC OF THE SUDAN ON A PRODUCTIVITY MISSION
- REPORT TO THE GOVERNMENT OF THE REPUBLIC OF THE SUDAN ON THE DEVELOPMENT OF A SOCIAL INSURANCE SCHEME
- REPORT TO THE GOVERNMENT OF THE SUDAN ON THE DEVELOPMENT OF CO-OPERATIVES
- REPORT TO THE GOVERNMENT OF THE SUDAN ON THE REGULATION OF EMPLOYMENT OF DOCK WORKERS: REGULATIONS IN SAFETY AND HEALTH
- STATISTICAL ABSTRACT FOR THE DEMOCRATIC REPUBLIC OF SUDAN
- THE SUDAN, A RECORD OF PROGRESS, 1898-1947

THE SUDAN : A SHORT COMPENDIUM OF FACTS AND FIGURES ABOUT THE LAND OF DARKNESS / Kumm, Hermann Karl Wilhelm – (Includes appendix) – 2nd ed. London: Marshall, [1907?] – 1mf – 9 – 0-8370-6134-2 – 1986-0134 – us A.T.L.A. [960]

THE SUDAN, A RECORD OF PROGRESS, 1898-1947 / Sudan – 1948. BNE-7689 1 – 9 – ne IDC [338]

Sudan. Bank of Sudan *see*
- FOREIGN TRADE STATISTICAL DIGEST
- REPORT 1960-1972

Sudan. Commercial bank *see* REPORT OF THE BOARD OF DIRECTORS

Sudan. Commission on Coordination between Central and Local Government *see* REPORT

Sudan. Currency Board *see* REPORT

Sudan. Dept. of Agriculture *see*
- AGRICULTURAL STATISTICS: BULLETIN
- ANNUAL REPORT

Sudan. Dept. of Agriculture. Sharif Dishoni and Nasr El Din Mustafa *see* STATISTICS ON CROP PRODUCTION AND LAND USE IN THE SUDAN, 1955/1956-1965/1966

Sudan. Dept. of Cooperation *see* ANNUAL REPORT

Sudan. Dept. of Land Use and Rural Water Development *see* ANNUAL REPORT 1955/1956-1963/1964

Sudan. Dept. of Statistics *see*
- THE 1953 PILOT POPULATION CENSUS FOR THE FIRST POPULATION CENSUS IN SUDAN
- CAPITAL FORMATION AND INCREASE IN NATIONAL INCOME IN SUDAN IN 1955/1959
- FIRST POPULATION CENSUS OF SUDAN, 1955/1956
- FIRST POPULATION CENSUS OF SUDAN. 1955/1956. FINAL REPORT
- FOREIGN TRADE AND INTERNAL STATISTICS
- FOREIGN TRADE REPORT. (WITH SOME INTERNAL STATISTICS), 1946-1954
- FOREIGN TRADE STATISTICS
- THE HOUSE-HOLD BUDGET SURVEY IN THE GEZIRA-MANAGIL AREA
- INTERNAL STATISTICS
- NATIONAL INCOME OF SUDAN
- A REPORT ON THE CENSUS OF PUMP SCHEMES, JUN-AUG 1963
- A REPORT ON THE SAMPLE CENSUS OF AGRICULTURE FOR THE YEAR 1964-1965 IN THE BLUE NILE PROVINCE OF THE SUDAN
- STATISTICAL CLASSIFICATION FOR GOODS IMPORTED, EXPORTED, OR RE-EXPORTED
- SUDAN IMPORT CLASSIFIED ACCORDING TO END-USE, 1950-1959, WITH INFORMATION FOR 1960
- WADI HALFA SOCIAL AND ECONOMIC SURVEY: REPORT ON THE INCOME AND EXPENDITURE SURVEY, INCLUDING RESULTS OF A LIVESTOCK SURVEY

SUDAN DEVELOPMENT PROGRAMME, 1951-1956 / Sudan. Finance Dept. Development Branch – D 1480 1. 1953 – 9 – ne IDC [336]

THE SUDAN DEVELOPMENT PROGRAMME, 1951/1956 / Sudan. Finance Department – 1953. BNE-7635 1 – 9 – ne IDC [336]

Sudan. Economic Planning Secretariat *see*
- THE TEN YEAR PLAN OF ECONOMIC AND SOCIAL DEVELOPMENT, 1961/1962-1970/1971
- THE TEN YEAR PLAN OF ECONOMIC AND SOCIAL DEVELOPMENT, 1961/62-1970/71

THE SUDAN ECONOMY; INTRODUCTORY NOTES / Stone, J – 1953. BNE-7686 1 – 9 – ne IDC [960]

Sudan. FAO *see*
- HIDES, SKINS AND LEATHER DEVELOPMENT AND TRAINING PROJECT. FINAL REPORT
- LAND AND WATER RESOURCES SURVEY IN THE JEBEL MARRA AREA. FINAL REPORT
- REPORT TO THE FOOD AND AGRICULTURE ORGANISATION OF THE UNITED NATIONS

Sudan. Finance Department *see*
- ANNUAL REVIEW OF THE FIVE YEAR DEVELOPMENT PLAN; THE DEVELOPMENT BUDGET
- DEVELOPMENT BUDGETS ESTIMATES, 1946/1951 AND 1951/1956 PROGRAMMES
- THE SUDAN DEVELOPMENT PROGRAMME, 1951/1956

Sudan. Finance Dept. Development Branch *see* SUDAN DEVELOPMENT PROGRAMME, 1951-1956

Sudan. Forests Department *see* REPORT

Sudan. Gezira Board *see*
- ANNUAL REPORT AND STATEMENT OF ACCOUNTS
- THE GEZIRA SCHEME FROM WITHIN: A COLLECTION OF ARTICLES BY HEADS OF DEPARTMENTS
- SOCIAL DEVELOPMENT IN THE GEZIRA, 1950-1960

SUDAN HERALD *see* SUNDAN DAILY HERALD

SUDAN IMPORT CLASSIFIED ACCORDING TO END-USE, 1950-1959, WITH INFORMATION FOR 1960 / Sudan. Dept. of Statistics – 1961. BNE-7625 1 – 9 – ne IDC [310]

Sudan. Industrial Bank *see*
- ANNUAL REPORTS
- THE INDUSTRIAL BANK OF SUDAN, 17 NOV 1961

Sudan. Institute of Public Administration *see* PROCEEDINGS OF THE ROUND TABLE 1961-1964

Sudan. Intelligence Department *see* KORDOFAN AND THE REGION TO THE WEST OF THE WHITE NILE

Sudan. Ministry of Agriculture *see* ANNUAL REPORT 1953/1955

Sudan. Ministry of Commerce, Industry and Supply *see*
- GOVERNMENT POLICY TOWARDS THE ENCOURAGEMENT OF LOCAL AND FOREIGN CAPITAL IN THE FIELD OF INDUSTRY AND ITS ATTITUDE TOWARDS FOREIGN CAPITAL IN GENERAL
- SOME SUDAN PRODUCE AND SECONDARY INDUSTRIES IN THE SUDAN

Sudan. Ministry of Education *see* EDUCATIONAL STATISTICS, 1965/66-1984/85

Sudan. Ministry of Finance and Economics *see*
- FINANCIAL AND ECONOMIC REVIEW; SPECIAL SUPPLEMENT: 1966/1967 BUDGET
- MEMORANDUM ON THE BUDGET ESTIMATES OF THE REPUBLIC OF SUDAN
- REVIEW OF THE ECONOMY; A SUPPLEMENT TO THE 1967/1968 BUDGET

Sudan. Ministry of Irrigation and Hydroelectric Power *see*
- ANNUAL REPORT
- IRRIGATION BY GRAVITY FROM THE RIVER ATBARA

Sudan. Ministry of Irrigation and Hydroelectric power *see* REPORT ON THE NILE VALLEY PLAN

Sudan. Ministry of Planning *see* THE FIVE YEAR PLAN OF ECONOMIC AND SOCIAL DEVELOPMENT FOR THE PERIOD 1970/1971-1974/1975

Sudan. Ministry of Social Affairs *see*
- FIRST POPULATION CENSUS OF SUDAN, 1955/1956 INTERIM REPORT
- THE MANAGIL EXTENSION

Sudan. Ministry of Treasury *see* ESTIMATES OF REVENUE AND EXPENDITURE FOR CURRENT AND DEVELOPMENT BUDGET FOR THE FISCAL YEAR

Sudan. National Agricultural Extension Seminar for Sudan *see* SEMINAR PROCEEDINGS

SUDAN NOTES AND RECORDS – Khartoum, 1918-1965. v1-46 – 259mf – 8 – ne IDC [960]

Sudan. Philosophical Society of the Sudan *see* THE POPULATION OF SUDAN

Sudan. Southern Development Investigation Team *see* NATURAL RESOURCES AND DEVELOPMENT POTENTIAL IN THE SOUTHERN PROVINCES OF THE SUDAN; A PRELIMINARY REPORT, 1954

Sudan. Southern Region. Regional Ministry of Education and Guidance *see* EDUCATION STATISTICS 1978/79-1981/82

Sudan. Survey Department *see* ANNUAL REPORTS

SUDAN TIMES – Khartoum, Sudan. July 1986-June 1989 – 6r – 1 – us L of C Photodup [072]

Sudan. U.N. Bureau of Social Affairs *see* POPULATION GROWTH AND MANPOWER IN THE SUDAN: A JOINT STUDY BY THE UNITED NATIONS AND THE GOVERNMENT OF THE SUDAN

SUDAN WITNESS – v8-18. 1957-68 (complete) – 1r – 1 – ATLA S0726C – us A.T.L.A. [073]

A SUDANESE KINGDOM : AN ETHNOGRAPHICAL STUDY OF THE JUKUN SPEAKING PEOPLES OF NIGERIA / Meek, Charles Kingsley – London: Paul, Trench, Trubner, 1931 – us Res Libr [305]

Sudarmo, R *see* PANDANGAN KITAB SUTJI BIJBEL TENTANG PEKERDJAAN

Sudarsono, R P *see* SIDANG MAHKAMAH TENTERA AGUNG DALAM PEMERIKSAAN PROCES SUDARSONO CS; STENOGRAFISCH VERSLAG

Sudau, Guenter *see* DIE RELIGIOESE GEDANKENWELT DER JAPANER IM SPIEGEL IHRES SPRICHWORTS

SUD'BA BLOKA / Nemerovskaia, O & Vol'pe, Ts. – Izd. Pisatelei. L. 1930. BR-1456 2 – 8 – ne IDC [920]

SUDBA ROSSII : OPYTY PO PSIKHOLOGII VOINY I NATSIONALNOSTI / Berdiaev, N A – Moskva: Izd. G.A. Lemana i S.I. Sakharova, 1918 – 1 – CSUX88-B9776 – us Hoover Inst Photo [947]

O SUD'BE OGNENNOI / Remizov, A – Petrograd, n.d. BR-828 2 – 8 – ne IDC [460]

SUDBURY MERCURY – Ipswich, England. 14 Aug- – 24+ r – 1 – uk British Libr Newspaper [072]

THE SUDBURY MINING JOURNAL – Sudbury, Ont: A McCharles, [1890?-189- or 19–] – 9 – cn C.I.H.M. [622]

SUDBURY SCENE – Sudbury, 1961-1964 – 2r – 1 – cn Preston [971]

SUDBURY STAR – (1910-1992.-578r) – Sudbury, 1993 – 14r – 1 – cn Preston [971]

SUDBURY STAR EDITORIAL PAGES – Sudbury, 1960-1976 – 7r – 1 – cn Preston [971]

SUD'BY KAPITALIZMA V. ROSSII / Vorontsov, V P – Spb. 1882. BR-10.646 2 – 8 – ne IDC [330]

SUD'BY NARODOV ROSSII / Stankevich, V – Berlin. 1921. B-1533 2 – 8 – ne IDC [947]

SUDDEUTSCHE MONATSHEFTE – Munich, Leipzig. 1904-36. 1985 – 99 fiches (1:42) – 9 – diazo DM1,880.00 – 3-598-30670-9 – gw Saur [073]

SUDDEUTSCHE ZEITUNG – (Munich), 1945- – ca 20r per y – 1 – us Ross [072]

SUDDEUTSCHE ZEITUNG – Munich: Verlag der Suddeutschen Zeitung, 1953-81 – us Res Libr [072]

SUDEBNAIA GAZETA – (Missing: 1882(1-3); 1883(30, 38, 47); 1884; 1886; 1887(48); 1891(16,27)) – Spb., 1882-1892 – 198mf – 9 – R-18364/1 – ne IDC [947]

SUDEBNAJA PRAKTIKA VERCHOVNOGO SUDA SSSR – Moskva. R 2433 1. 1946-1956 – 9 – ne IDC [947]

SUDEBNIK GOSUDARIA TSARIA I VELIKAGO KNIAZIA IOANNA VASIL'EVICHA, I NEKOTORYE SEGO GOSUDARIA I BLIZHNIKH EGO PREEMNIKOV UKAZY / Tatishchev, V N – ed. 2. Moskva. 1786. R-8044 2 – 8 – ne IDC [947]

SUDEBNIK GOSUDARIA TSARIA I VELIKAGO KNIAZIA IONNA VASIL'EVICHA, I NEKOTORYE SEGO GOSUDARIA I BLIZHNIKH EGO PREEMNIKOV UKAZY – Ed.2. Moscow, 1876. 276p. BR-8044/2 – 8 – ne IDC [947]

Sudendorf, Hans *see* BERENGARIUS TURONENSIS, ODER, EINE SAMMLUNG IHN BETREFFENDER BRIEFE

Sudermann, Daniel *see* CENTURIA SIMILITUDINUN. 100 GLEICHNUSSEN IN WELCHEN DURCH VORSTELLUNG LEIBLICHER FIGUREN. LEHREN FURGEBILDET WERDEN: VORNEHMLICH AUSS H. SCHRIFT

Sudermann, Hermann *see*
- ES WAR
- FRAU SORGE

SUDERMANN'S TREATMENT OF VERSE / Cannon, Harry Sharp – (Includes bibliographical references) – Tuebingen: H Laupp, 1922 – 1r – 1 – us U.W. Library [430]

SUDETENDEUTSCHE LANDBOTE – Bruenn (Brno), Czechoslovakia. 15 Dec 1927,1928-9 Dec 1933 – 1 – gw Mikrofilm [072]

SUDETENDEUTSCHE TAGESZEITUNG, TETSCHEN-BODENBACHER ZEITUNG – Decin, Czechoslovakia. Aug 1941-Mar 1945 (incomplete) – 3r – 1 – us L of C Photodup [072]

SUDETENDEUTSCHE VOLKSZEITUNG – Bruenn, 1930-sep 16 1933 – 2r – 1 – Inquire at Mikrofilmarchiv for details – gw Misc Inst [943]

SUDETENDEUTSCHE VOLKSZEITUNG – Bruenn (Brno), Czechoslovakia. 1930-16 Sep 1933 – 2r – 1 – gw Mikrofilm [072]

SUDETENDEUTSCHE ZEITUNG – Muenchen. 1954-1960 – 7r – 1 – gw Mikrofilm [072]

SUDETENDEUTSCHE ZEITUNG – Munich, Germany. Jan 1954-Dec 1960 – 7r – 1 – uk British Libr Newspaper [072]

SUDETENDEUTSCHER LANDBOTE – Bruenn, dec 15 1927?-dec 9 1933 – 1 – Inquire at Mikrofilmarchiv for details – gw Misc Inst [943]

SUDETENDEUTSCHER LANDBUND – Asch, mar 5 1930-32 – 1r – 1 – Dist. gw Mikrofilm – gw Misc Inst [943]

SUDETENDEUTSCHER LANDBUND – Bruenn, 1934 – 1 – Inquire at Mikrofilmarchiv for details – gw Misc Inst [943]

SUDETENDEUTSCHES WOCHENBLATT – Duchcov, Czechoslovakia. Sept-Dec 1933 – 1r – 1 – us L of C Photodup [072]

SUDETENDEUTSCHES WOCHENBLATT – Dux (Duchcov), Czechoslovakia. 23 Sep-2 Dec 1933 – 1r – 1 – gw Mikrofilm [072]

Sudharnoto *see* ASIA AFRIKA BERSATU

LE SUDISTE = THE SOUTHERNER – Laprairie, Canada. 17 aut 1966-19 avr 1967 – 1r – 1 – Can$35.00 – cn Can Microfilming [072]

LE SUDISTE – St-Hubert, Canada. 18 mai 1966 – 1r – 1 – Can$25.00 – cn Can Microfilming [072]

SUDOUSTROISTVO SSSR; UCHEBNIK DLIA IURIDICHESKIKH SHKOL / Golunskii, Sergei Aleksandrovich – Moskva: Iurid. izd-vo, 1946. 194p. LL-4102 – 1 – us L of C Photodup [340]

Sudworth, G B *see* FOREST TREES OF THE PACIFIC SLOPE

SUEDBOEHMISCHE VOLKSZEITUNG – Budweis (Ceske Budejovice), Czechoslovakia. 20 Mar 1920-29 Dec 1935; 1937-25 Sept 1938 – 15r – 1 – gw Mikrofilm [072]

SUEDBOEHMISCHE VOLKSZEITUNG – Budweis, mar 20 1920-dec 29 1935, 1937-sep 25 1938 – 15r – 1 – Inquire at Mikrofilmarchiv for details – gw Misc Inst [943]

SUEDDEUTSCHE FILMZEITUNG *see* DEUTSCHE FILMZEITUNG

SUEDDEUTSCHE KINEMATOGRAPHEN-ZEITUNG – Muenchen, 1916, jan-jun 1918 – 1 – gw Mikrofilm [790]

SUEDDEUTSCHE MITTEILUNGEN – Heidelberg, Germany. 16 Jun-1 Sep 1945 – 1r – 1 – gw Mikrofilm [072]

SUEDDEUTSCHE MITTEILUNGEN – Heidelberg, Jun-Sep 1945 – 1r – 1 – DM80.00 – gw Mikro Press [072]

SUEDDEUTSCHE MONATSHEFTE – Munich. Jan. 1904-Sept. 1936 gaps – 1 – 35.00r – us Hoover Inst Photo [073]

SUEDDEUTSCHE SONNTAGS-ZEITUNG – (Title change: Die Sonntags-Zeitung, 1 Oct 1922;) – Heilbronn-Stuttgart, Germany. 20 Feb 1921-4 Jan 1925; Mar 1925-20 Jun 1937 – 5r – 1 – gw Mikrofilm [072]

SUEDDEUTSCHE ZEITUNG – 1945-1995 – 18 times per yr – 1 – DM900.00 – sz Infoprint [072]

SUEDDEUTSCHE ZEITUNG – (1965-84 272r DM19,040.00. 1985-91 118r DM8,260.00. 1992-94 60r DM4,500.00) – Muenchen, 1945-64 – 82r – 1 – DM5,740.00 (Subsc 1995 DM1,200.00) – gw Mikro Press [072]

SUEDDEUTSCHE ZEITUNG – Muenchen. 1992- – 20r per yr – 1 – gw Mikrofilm [072]

SUEDDEUTSCHE ZEITUNG – Muenchen, jan 2 1974-may 12 1978, aug 3 1978-79 – 74r – 1 – gw Mikrofilm [072]

SUEDDEUTSCHE ZEITUNG – Munich. DE. 4 Dec 1945-Dec 1952 (incomplete) – 25r – 1 – uk British Libr Newspaper [072]

SUEDDEUTSCHE ZEITUNG FUER KIRCHE UND STAAT – Freiburg, DE. 1847-31 Dec 1848 – 2r – 1 – gw Mikrofilm [072]

SUEDDEUTSCHE ZEITUNG – MAGAZIN – 1990-1993 – 16r – 1 – DM1,200.00 (1995 subsc DM180.00) – gw Mikro Press [943]

SUEDDEUTSCHE ZEITUNG MAGAZIN – 1990-1995 – 3 times per yr – 1 – DM210.00 – sz Infoprint [072]

SUEDDEUTSCHE ZEITUNG, MUENCHEN *see*
– MUENCHNER NEUESTE NACHRICHTEN

SUEDDEUTSCHER RUNDFUNK : AUSGABE B FUER WUERTTEMBERG UND BADEN – Stuttgart, sep 28 1924-dec 23 1928 – 10r – 1 – gw Mikrofilm [790]

SUEDDEUTSCHER RUNDFUNK – AUSGABE A: MUENCHEN *see* BAYERISCHE RADIO-ZEITUNG UND BAYERNFUNK

SUEDEN UND NORDEN : EINE BAYRISCHE GESCHICHTE AUS DEM KRIEGSJAHR 1866 / Schmid, Herman – Leipzig: Pallas-Verlag, [18–?] – 1 – us U.W. Library [830]

SUEDERLAENDER TAGEBLATT – Plettenberg, Germany. 1992- – 7r per yr – 1 – gw Mikrofilm [072]

DER SUEDFRANZOESISCHE SAGENKREIS UND SEINE PROBLEME / Becker, Philipp August – 1898 – 1 – us I.U. Libraries [390]

SUEDFUNK – Stuttgart, dec 18 1927-35 – 8r – 1 – gw Mikrofilm [790]

SUEDHANNOVERSCHER ANZEIGER – (Bereichsausgabe der Hannoverschen Allgemeinen Zeitung) – Goettingen. aug 25-oct 26, 1949 – 1r – 1 – gw Mikrofilm [072]

SUEDHESSISCHE POST – Heppenheim, Germany. 1 Sep 1978-1989 – 72r – 1 – gw Mikrofilm [072]

SUEDKURIER – Konstanz, Germany. 1968- – ca 8r per yr – 1 – gw Mikrofilm [072]

SUEDMAEHREN BLATT – Bruenn, jun 25 1921-may 26 1923 – 1r – 1 – Inquire at Mikrofilmarchiv for details – gw Misc Inst [943]

SUEDMAEHRER BLATT – Bruenn (Brno), Czechoslovakia. 25 Jun 1921-26 Mai 1923 – 1r – 1 – gw Mikrofilm [072]

DIE SUEDMARK – Graz. 1920, nos. 1, 3, 4, 6-10; 1921, nos. 2-6; 1922, nos. 1, 6, 10-12; 1923, nos. 1-8, 10-12 – 1 – 35.00r – us Hoover Inst Photo [073]

SUED-OST – Hermannstadt (Sibiu), Rumaenien. 12 Nov 1935-16 Jul 1939 – 5r – 1 – gw Mikrofilm [949]

DIE SUEDPOLEXPEDITION DES KAPITAENS SCOTT : SPIEL IN DREI TEILEN / Goering, Reinhard – Berlin: Propylaen Verlag, c1929 – 1r – 1 – us U.W. Library [820]

SUEDPREUSSISCHE ZEITUNG – Posen, 1794-1846 – 9 – gw Olms [072]

SUEDSLAWISCHE BIBELANSTALT IN URACH AND TUEBINGEN – Imprints and mss. from the Uracher Bibelanstalt of Primus Truber – 9 – ne IDC [240]

SUEDWEST – Swakopmund, South West Africa. 1910-15 – 1 – sa State Libr [072]

DER SUEDWESTBOTE – Windhoek, South West Africa. 1903-15 – 1 – sa State Libr [072]

SUEDWESTDEUTSCHE RUNDFUNK-ZEITUNG – Frankfurt/Main. oct 3, 1925-may 31, 1941 – 20r – 1 – gw Mikrofilm [073]

SUEDWEST-PRESSE *see*
– HEIDENHEIMER ZEITUNG
– SCHWAEBISCHE DONAU-ZEITUNG

SUEDWEST-PRESSE/STEINLACH-BOTE – Tuebingen, Germany. 2 Jan 1980- – 1 – gw Mikrofilm [072]

SUELE-I EDEB – Istanbul: Ahenk Matbaasi, 1896-1897 – 9 – $95.00 – us MEDOC [956]

Sueleyman, Nazif *see* FUZULI

Sueleyman, Sihabeddin *see* YENI OSMANLI TARIH EDEBIYATI

SUELEYMANNAME / Karacelebizade, Abduelaziz – Cairo: Bulak, 1248 [1832] – 30mf – 9 – $50.00 – us MEDOC [949]

DER SUELFMEISTER : EINE ALTE STADTGESCHICHTE / Wolff, Julius – Berlin: G Grote'sche Verlagsbuchhandlung, 1893 – 1r – 1 – us U.W. Library [830]

DIE SUENDE IM ALTEN ISRAEL / Bennewitz, Fritz – Leipzig: A. Deichert, 1907. 1 fiche – 9 – us A.T.L.A. [270]

SUENDE UND ERLOESUNG : NACH BIBLISCHER UND BABYLONISCHER ANSCHAUUNG / Hehn, Johannes – (Includes bibliographical references) – Leipzig: J C Hinrichs, 1903 – 1mf – 9 – 0-8370-3546-5 – 1985-1546 – us A.T.L.A. [220]

SUENDE UND GNADE: NACH DER VORSTELLUNG DES AELTEREN JUDENTUMS / Staerk, Willy – Tuebingen: J.C.B. Mohr, 1905. 1 fiche – 9 – us A.T.L.A. [270]

DIE SUENDE WIDER DEN HEILIGEN GEIST : UND DIE DARAUS GEZOGENEN DOGMATISCHEN UND ETHISCHEN FOLGERUNGEN: EINE EXEGETISCH-DOGMATISCHE ABHANDLUNG / Schaf, Philipp – Halle: J.F. Lippert, 1841 – 1mf – us A.T.L.A. [240]

DIE SUENDLOSIGKEIT JESU: EINE APOLOGETISCHE BETRACHTUNG / Ullmann, Karl – Gotha: F.A. Perthes, 1863. 1 fiche – 9 – us A.T.L.A. [240]

SUENGUE – (Continued as Ileri) – Manastir: Neyyir-i Hakikat Matbaasi. Sahib-i Imtiyaz: Matli Ziya; Mueduer-i Mes'ul: Hamdi, 1910-1911 – 9 – $25.00 – us MEDOC [956]

Suenner, Tobias *see*
– GEDAECHTNISEFFEKTE BEI NICHTLINEAREN OSZILLATOREN
– INSTABILITAETEN, BIFURKATIONEN UND CHAOS FUER EINEN DREIDIMENSIONALEN VAN DER POL OSZILLATOR

EL SUENO DE LUCIANO Y LA TABLA DE CEBES / Florez Canseco, Casimiro – 1778 – 1mf – 9 – Pta1,000.00 – 84-7848-141-9 – sp Pentalfa [440]

EL SUENO ES VIDA / Grillparzer, Franz – Wien: Bergland Verlag, 1968 – 1 – sp Bibl Santa Ana [946]

SUENO MISTICO EXPLICACION / Diez Lopez, Juan – 1886 – 9 – 1.50f – sp Bibl Santa Ana [946]

SUENO REALIZADO. POESIAS / Lopez Ledesma, Jose – Madrid: Imp. Samaran, 1953 – 1 – sp Bibl Santa Ana [810]

LOS SUENOS DE MI PRIMA AURELIA / Garcia Lorca, Federico – MS DE 1936. Fragmento – 1mf – 9 – sp Cultura [830]

SUENOS Y REALIDADES / Hurtado, Antonio – 1886 – 9 – 1.50f – sp Bibl Santa Ana [830]

Suepke, H F W *see* BEITRAGE ZU EINFACH-PRAKTISCHEN PRUFUNGEN VERSCHIEDENER HANDELSWAREN

DIE SUERAG – Offenburg, mar 6 1927-may 25 1941; 1950-51 – 15r – 1 – gw Mikrofilm [072]

SUERUR-I MUEVERRIH / Tevfik, Ebuezziya – Kostantiniye: Matbaai-i Ebuezziya, 1305 [1888] – $15.00 – us MEDOC [956]

SUES – Mueduer: Selami Izzet, Mehmed Rauf. Istanbul: Tanin Matbaasi, Amidi Matbaasi. Sene 1-2, sayi 1-55 (1339-1340 [1922-1923]) – 15mf – 9 – $150.00 – us MEDOC [949]

Sueß, Hermann *see* WAGENSEIL COLLECTION

SUESSWASSER-DIATOMACEEN UND DESMIDIACEEN VON DER INSEL BANKA / Grunow, A – Leipzig. 1865. B-27 2 – 8 – ne IDC [580]

DIE SUESSWASSER-FLORA DEUTSCHLANDS, OESTERREICHS UND DER SCHWEIZ / Pascher, A – v. 1-7, 9-10 (v. 8 not pub.). Jena. 1913. B-1072 2 – 8 – ne IDC [580]

DIE SUESSWASSER-FLORA (VON DEUTSCHLAND, OSTERREICH UND DER SCHWEIZ) / Pascher, A – 4r – 1 – uk Microform Academic [580]

DIE SUESWASSER-DIATOMACEEN / Rabenhorst, G L – (Bacillarien) fuer Freunde der Mikroskopie. Leipzig. 1853. B-6398 2 – 8 – ne IDC [580]

SUEVARILERE MAHSUS MALUMAT VE TERBIYE-I ASKERIYE / Faik, Mehmet – Istanbul: Mekteb-i Funuen-i Harbi, 1315 [1898] – $85.00 – us MEDOC [956]

THE SUEZ CANAL / Hallberg, C W – New York, London, 1931 – 5mf – 1 – ILM-1818/1 – ne IDC [327]

THE SUEZ CANAL COMPANY AND THE DECISION TAKEN BY THE EGYPTIAN GOVERNMENT ON 26 JUL 1956 / Egypt. Compagnie Universelle du Canal Maritime de Suez – 2v. Paris. 1956. BNE-4619 1 – 9 – ne IDC [338]

THE SUEZ CANAL; NOTES AND STATISTICS / Egypt. Compagnie Universelle du Canal Maritime de Suez – 1952. BNE-4620 1 – 9 – ne IDC [380]

SUEZ CANAL REPORT / Egypt. U.A.R. Suez Canal Authority – 1957-65, BNE-4680 1 – 9 – ne IDC [956]

DER SUEZKANAL / Birk, A & Mueller-Hamburg, K H – Hamburg, 1925 – 2mf – 9 – ILM-2213/1 – ne IDC [327]

DER SUEZKANAL / Dedreux, R – Tuebingen, 1918 – 2mf – 1 – ILM-2199/1 – ne IDC [327]

THE SUFFERING SERVANT IN DEUTERO-ISAIAH / North, C R – Oxford. 1956 – 9 – $10.00 – us I.R.C. [220]

THE SUFFICIENCY OF THE GOSPEL FOR THE SALVATION OF SOCIETY / Mathews, Shailer – 1911 – 1 – 5.00 – us Baptist [240]

SUFFOLK, 1823 : BRITISH ISLES CENSUS DIRECTORIES PROJECT, ENGLAND. VOL 214 – 1mf – 9 – A$9.00 – at Vine [941]

SUFFOLK, 1830 : BRITISH ISLES CENSUS DIRECTORIES PROJECT, ENGLAND – at Vine [941]

SUFFOLK, 1839 : BRITISH ISLES CENSUS DIRECTORIES PROJECT, ENGLAND – at Vine [941]

SUFFOLK, 1844 : BRITISH ISLES CENSUS DIRECTORIES PROJECT, ENGLAND. VOL 20 – 5mf – 9 – A$33.00 – at Vine [941]

SUFFOLK, 1846 : BRITISH ISLES CENSUS DIRECTORIES PROJECT, ENGLAND – at Vine [941]

SUFFOLK, 1850 : BRITISH ISLES CENSUS DIRECTORIES PROJECT, ENGLAND. VOL 82 – 2mf – 9 – A$15.00 – at Vine [941]

SUFFOLK, 1855 : BRITISH ISLES CENSUS DIRECTORIES PROJECT, ENGLAND – at Vine [941]

SUFFOLK, 1858 : BRITISH ISLES CENSUS DIRECTORIES PROJECT, ENGLAND – at Vine [941]

SUFFOLK, 1864 : BRITISH ISLES CENSUS DIRECTORIES PROJECT, ENGLAND. VOL 240 – 4mf – 9 – A$27.00 – at Vine [941]

SUFFOLK, 1874 : BRITISH ISLES CENSUS DIRECTORIES PROJECT, ENGLAND – at Vine [941]

SUFFOLK, 1883 : BRITISH ISLES CENSUS DIRECTORIES PROJECT, ENGLAND. VOL 34 – 5mf – 9 – A$33.00 – at Vine [941]

SUFFOLK, 1896 : BRITISH ISLES CENSUS DIRECTORIES PROJECT, ENGLAND. VOL 12 – 7mf – 9 – A$45.00 – at Vine [941]

SUFFOLK, 1900 : BRITISH ISLES CENSUS DIRECTORIES PROJECT, ENGLAND – at Vine [941]

SUFFOLK, 1908 : BRITISH ISLES CENSUS DIRECTORIES PROJECT, ENGLAND – at Vine [941]

SUFFOLK, 1912 : BRITISH ISLES CENSUS DIRECTORIES PROJECT, ENGLAND – at Vine [941]

SUFFOLK, 1925 : BRITISH ISLES CENSUS DIRECTORIES PROJECT, ENGLAND – at Vine [941]

Suffolk. England *see* QUARTER SESSIONS ORDER BOOKS, 1639-1872

SUFFOLK (IPSWICH), 1805 : BRITISH ISLES CENSUS DIRECTORIES PROJECT, ENGLAND. VOL 178 – 1mf – 9 – A$9.00 – at Vine [941]

SUFFOLK MERCURY – Ipswich, England. Ipswich Mercury. -w. 1978-80. 6 reels – 1 – uk British Libr Newspaper [072]

Suffolk. Presbytery (Pres. Ch. in the U.S.A.) *see* MINUTES, 1747-1789

SUFFOLK TRANSNATIONAL LAW JOURNAL – v1-16. 1977-93 – 1,5,6 – $225.00 – us Hein [073]

SUFFOLK UNIVERSITY LAW REVIEW – v1-26. 1967-92 – 1,5,6 – $900.00 – us Hein [073]

LE SUFFRAGE DES FEMMES / Academie des Sciences Morales et Politiques – Joran, Paris. 1913 – 1 – fr A.C.R.P.P. [320]

THE SUFFRAGETTE / Women's Social and Political Union – (Britannia). London. -w. Oct. 1912-Dec. 1918. 3 reels – 1 – uk British Libr Newspaper [320]

SUFFRAGIST – v. 1-9, no. 1. 15 Nov 1913-Jan Feb 1921 – 1 – $67.00 – us L of C Photodup [320]

SUFFRAGIST : A WEEKLY JOURNAL DEVOTED TO THE INTERESTS OF COLORED CITIZENS – New York, 1880 – 1r – 1 – us Ross [320]

SUFLER – Russia, 1878-86 – 5r – 1 – $400.00 – us Ross [330]

SUGAR : MAJOR TRADE AND STABILIZATION ISSUES IN THE EIGHTIES – 1985 – 40p – it F.A.O. [380]

SUGAR CANE – v1- 1983- – 1,5,6,9 – us UMI [631]

THE SUGAR CONVENTION / Farrer, Thomas Henry – London, New York: Cassell & Co., Ltd., 1889. viii,135p.Published for the Cobden Club – 1 – us U.W. Library [330]

SUGAR JOURNAL AND TROPICAL CULTIVATOR – Mackay, Australia. 15 Feb 1896-15 Mar 1905.-m. 4mqn reels – 1 – uk British Libr Newspaper [072]

SUGAR PINE PRESS – Westwood, CA. 1946-1954 – 4r – 1 – $200.00 – B03097 – us Library Micro [071]

SUGAR PRODUCTION POTENTIALS IN THE REPUBLIC OF THE SUDAN / Tudor Engineering Company. San Francisco – 1958. BNE-7691 1 – 9 – ne IDC [338]

SUGAR TECHNOLOGY REVIEWS – v1-12 1969-84 – 1,5,6,13 – sz Elsevier [660]

SUGARCANE AS FEED – 1988 – 323p – it F.A.O. [636]

SUGAR-CANE DISEASES : A GUIDE FOR FIELD IDENTIFICATION – 1988 – 152p – it F.A.O. [631]

SUGARCREEK BUDGET – Lancaster. Pa. 1890-1910 – 1 – us UMI [071]

Sugden, Edward Burtneshaw *see*
– A CONCISE AND PRACTICAL TREATISE OF THE LAW OF VENDORS AND PURCHASERS OF ESTATES
– A PRACTICAL TREATISE OF POWERS

Sugenheim, Samuel *see* GESCHICHTE DER ENTSTEHUNG UND AUSBILDUNG DES KIRCHENSTAATES

SUGERENCIAS PARA QUE HAYA TIERRAS, TRABAJO, PAZ Y ABUNDANCIA PARA TODOS... – Caceres: Imp. La Minerva, 1958 – 1 – sp Bibl Santa Ana [946]

SUGGESTED EMENDATIONS OF THE AUTHORIZED ENGLISH VERSION OF THE OLD TESTAMENT / Riggs, Elias – (Includes index) – Andover:Warren F. Draper, 1873 – 1mf – 9 – 0-8370-4908-3 – 1985-2908 – us A.T.L.A. [220]

A SUGGESTED METHOD OF COMPLIANCE WITH THE DAVIS AMENDMENT TO THE RADIO LAW / Caldwell, Louis Goldsborough – Chicago? 1928. 42p. LL-229 – 1 – us L of C Photodup [340]

SUGGESTED STATE LEGISLATION – v1-53. 1941-94 – 9 – $535.00 set – us Hein [340]

SUGGESTIONS FOR COUNTY PLAN OF WORK / Auburn University. Extension Service – 1947-68 – 1,5,6 – us Spaulding [630]

SUGGESTIONS FOR THE FORMATION OF A MEDICAL MISSIONARY SOCIETY, OFFERED TO THE CONSIDERATION OF ALL CHRISTIAN NATIONS, MORE ESPECIALLY TO THE KINDRED NATIONS OF ENGLAND AND THE UNITED STATES OF AMERICA / Colledge, T R et al – Canton, 1836 – 1mf – 9 – ne IDC [610]

SUGGESTIONS ON THE TEACHING OF HISTORY / Hieronymus, Saint – UNESCO – 7 – uk Microform Academic [370]

Sugondo Sumodiredjo *see* MEREK PERUSAHAAN DAN PERNIAGAAN

SUGORO – (Microfiche No 171) – Pentjak: Tjetakan kedoea, 2605 – 1mf – 9 – SE-2002/1 – ne IDC [950]

Suhadji Hadibroto *see* A COMPARATIVE STUDY OF AMERICAN AND DUTCH ACCOUNTANCY AND THEIR IMPACT ON THE PROFESSION IN INDONESIA

Suhardiman *see* SAPTA AKSI

Suharsono *see*
– A SHORT GUIDE TO THE PRAMBANAN COMPLEX
– A SHORT GUIDE TO THE SANCTUARY OF BARABUDUR

Suhr, J N von *see* BEITRAAGE ZUR ALGENKUNDE. VRATISLAVIAE, BONNAE, 1841

SUI FUNGHI SAGGIO GENERALE. CON TAVOLE IN RAME ED UNA DESCRIZIONE E TAVOLA SINOTTICA DE FUNGHI MANGERECCI PIU COMMUNI D'ITALIA / Larber, G – v. 1, v. 2. Bassano. 1829. B-5287 2 – 8 – ne IDC [580]

SUI MUTAMENTI DEL RAPPORTI PATRIMONIALI FRA CONIUGI... / Anzilotti, D – Firenze, 1899 – 3mf – 9 – ILM-3640/1 – ne IDC [340]

SUICIDE – v. 5. 1975 – 1 – us UMI [150]

SUICIDE AMONG THE AMERICAN INDIANS / U.S. Public Health Service – 1969 – 9 – $5.00f – us Ross [360]

SUICIDE AND LIFE-THREATENING BEHAVIOR – v. 6-. 1976- – 1,5,6,9 – us UMI [150]

SUICIDE OR SURVIVAL? : THE CHALLENGE OF THE YEAR 2000 – 1978 – 192p – 9 – 92-3-101534-6 – fr UNESCO [303]

DIE SUIDERSTEM – Cape Town, South Africa.8 Oct 1936-30 Jun 1950. 83 reels – 1, 16 diazo available at reduced price – sa SA Libr [072]
SUID-WES NUUSBLAD – Windhoek, South West Africa. 1919-25 – 1 – sa State Libr [072]
SUIDWES-AFRIKANER – Windhoek, South West Africa. 1927-50 – 1 – sa State Libr [072]
SUIKER : EEN SCHETS VAN PRODUCTIE, HANDEL EN VERBRUIK, IN VERBAND OOK MET DE BRUSSELSCHE CONVENTIE / Schoepp, F – Groningen, 1908 – 2mf – 9 – ILM-866/1 – ne IDC [338]
LA SUISSE – 1980-1994 – 6r per y – 6 – Sfr1,176.00 – sz Infoprint [073]
THE SUITABILITY AND RELIABILITY OF THE PHYSICAL BEST FITNESS TEST WITH SELECTED SPECIAL POPULATIONS / Forbus, W R – 1990 – 2mf – 9 – $8.00 – us Microform Publ [790]
SUITE DE LA CLEF – ou Journal historique sur les matieres du tems. Paris. 1734, 1768 – 1 – fr A.C.R.P.P. [944]
SUITE DE LA GRAMMAIRE FRANCAISE SUR UN PLAN NOUVEAU OU TRAITE PHILOSOPHIQUE ET PRATIQUE D'ELOQUENCE / Buffier, Cl – (Linguistics series). 1728 – 9 – fr Hachette [440]
SUITE DE LA GRAMMAIRE FRANCOISE / Buffier, Cl – 1728 – 9 – fr I.C.S. [440]
SUITE DE LA PANHYPOCRISIADE OU LE SPECTACLE INFERNAL DU DIX-NEUVIEME SIECLE / Lemercier, Nepomucene – Paris: G. Doyen, 1832. xvi,119p. 2 fiches. (Literature Collection) – 9 – 6.00 – fr Bibl Nationale [810]
SUITE DES REMARQUES NOUVELLES SUR LA LANGUE FRANCOISE / Bouhours, D – 1692 – 9 – fr I.C.S. [440]
SUITE DU MEMOIRE DE M. LORANGER, CONTENANT SA REPLIQUE DEVANT LA COUR SEIGNEURIALE / Loranger, Thomas Jean Jacques – Montreal: Senecal et Daniel..., 1856. SEM105P271 – 1mf – 9 – Can$2.25 – cn Bibl Nat [971]
SUITE DU NEPTUNE FRANCOIS OU ATLAS NOUVEAU DES CARTES MARINES. / Fremont d'Ablancourt, Nicolas – Amsterdam: Chez Pierre Mortier..., 1700. SEM35P171 – 1r – 1 – Can$15.00 – cn Bibl Nat [910]
SUITE DU VOYAGE DE LEVANT: DANS LAQUELLE APRES PLUSIEURS REMARQUES TRES SINGULIERES SUR DES PARTICULARITEZ DE L'EGYPTE, DE LA SYRIE, DE LA MESOPOTAMIE, DE L'EUPHRATE ET DU TIGRE... / Thevenot, Jean – Paris, C. Angot, 1674, xxii-392-18 p. French Voyagers in the Mediterranean 16th to 18th Centuries. 5964 – 9 – fr Hachette [910]
SUITE POUR PIANO, OP. 10 / Enesco, G – Paris: Enoch & Co, 192- – 1 – us Sibley [780]
Sujoldzic, A et al *see* ETUDE ANTHROPOLOGIQUE DE L'ILE D'OLIB. GEOMORPHOLOGIE, ETHNO-HISTOIRE, DEMOGRAPHIE
Sujunus, R M *see* BEBERAPA SEGI DASAR KEDJAHATAN
THE SUK : THEIR LANGUAGE AND FOLKLORE / Beech, Mervyn Worcester Howard – Oxford: Clarendon Press, 1911 – us Res Libr [305]
Sukadis Sosroprawiro, R *see*
- DJAGUNG
- KATJANG TANAH

Sukanto, Bustaman *see* HUBUNGAN DIPONEGORO-SENTOT
Sukarno *see* "SHAPING AND RESHAPING" INDONESIA; MANGGALANG MASSAAKSI REVOLUSIONER MENUDJU MASJARAKAT ADIL DAN MAKMUR
SUKARNO; EEN AUTOBIOGRAFIE UIT DE MOND VAN DE PRESIDENT, OPGETEKEND DOOR CINDY ADAMS / Sukarno, Pres. Indonesia – SE 6262 1. 1967 – 9 – ne IDC [025]
Sukarno, Pres. Indonesia *see*
- AFTER TEN YEARS, STILL: ONWARD, NEVER RETREAT
- AGAMA ADALAH UNSUR MUTLAK DIDALAM NATION BUILDING
- AMALKAN ILMU DARIPADA KEHIDUPAN SEHARI-HARI (THE SCHOOL OF LIFE) AMANAT PADA PERINGATAN HARI SARDJANA KE-4, 30 SEPT. 1963
- AMANAH PRESIDEN
- AMANAT POLITIK PRESIDEN/PEMIMPIN BESAR REVOLUSI
- ASIAN PROBLEMS SOLVED BY ASIANS
- BE IN HARMONY WITH THE WILL OF GOD
- BELORONG IMPERIALISME
- THE BIRTH OF PANTJASILA; AN OUTLINE OF FIVE PRINCIPLES OF INDONESIAN STATE
- BUNG KARNO KITA; SEBUAH SKETSA
- BUNG KARNO, PENJAMBUNG LIDAH RAKJAT INDONESIA. (AUTOBIOGRAPHY)
- BUNG KARNO: SUKARNO
- DEKON; DEKLARASI EKONOMI, DISAMPAIKAN TGL. 28 MARET 1963
- DIBAWAH BENDERA REVOLUSI
- DJADIKAN INDONESIA POROS THE NEW EMERGING FORCES
- DJAKARTA CHARTER OBLIGATES THE LAW OF SHARIAT UPON ITS ADHERENTS
- DJANGAN MENDERITA TANI-PHOBI
- DOA RESTU P.J.M. PRESIDEN R.I. PADA UPATJARA PENTJANGKULAN PERTAMA DALAM USAHA SELF-SUPPORTING BERAS DI RENGASDENGKLOK, KRAWANG
- EVER UPWARD, NEVER GO DOWN
- THE FIFTH FREEDOM IS OUR WEAPON
- FLY ON, RADJAWALI
- GANEFO SUATU KEHARUSAN SEDJARAH
- GERAKAN KEBERSIHAN NASIONAL
- THE HOLY QURAN REMOLDS MANKIND
- IF YOU WANT TO SEARCH GOD, READ THE HOLY QUR'AN
- IMPERIALISME DAN KAPITALISME SERTA IMPERIALISME DI INDONESIA
- INDONESIA IN BRIEF
- INDONESIA, KAMI SIAP
- INDONESIA, PILIHLAH DEMOKRASIMU JANG SEDJATI
- INDONESIA'S POLITICAL MANIFESTO 1959-1964
- INDONESIA'S VIEWS ON EN H BOMB TESTS
- KAPITALISME DAN IMPERIALISME ADALAH DJAHAT
- KEBEBASAN JANG KELIMA ADALAH SENDJATA KITA; SALAH SATU PEDOMAN PELAKSANAAN MANIPOL
- KETIGA KALINJA 17 AGOESTOES
- KIKIS HABIS TIAP-TIAP PERBUATAN KONTRA-REVOLUSIONER
- LAHIRNJA PANTJA-SILA
- LAHIRNJA PANTJASILA; THE BIRTH OF PANTJASILA. OUTLINE OF FIVE PRINCIPLES OF THE INDONESIAN STATE
- LECTURE BEFORE STUDENTS OF PADJADJARAN UNIV. IN BANDUNG
- LET US BECOME THE VEHICLE OF HISTORY
- MANIFESTO POLITIK
- MARCH OF OUR REVOLUTION
- MARHAEN DAN PROLETAR
- MARHAENISME; ADJARAN BAPAK MARHAENISME BUNG KARNO
- MARHAENISME PERDJUANGKAN DAN AMALKAN DITENGAHTENGAH MARHAEN
- NASIONALISME, ISLAMISME DAN MARXISME
- NEVER LEAVE HISTORY
- PANTJA SILA, THE BASIS OF THE STATE OF THE REPUBLIC OF INDONESIA
- PANTJAWARSA MANIPOL
- PRESIDENT SUKARNO'S MESSAGE TO THE NATION ON THE SIXTH ANNIVERSARY OF INDONESIAN INDEPENDENCE
- RADIO SPEECH DELIVERED ON SEPT. 19, 1948 ON THE MADIUM COUP
- REACH TO THE STARS A YEAR OF SELF-RELIANCE
- THE REDISCOVERY OF OUR REVOLUTION
- REFLECTIONS SUR LA REVOLUTION INDONESIENNE
- REFLECTIONS UPON THE INDONESIAN REVOLUTION
- THE RESOUNDING VOICE OF THE INDONESIAN REVOLUTION
- REVOLUSI OKTOBER DAN KEBANGUNAN RAKJAT ASIA
- SOAL HIDUP ATAU MATI
- STATEMENT BY PRES. SUKARNO BEFORE THE NON-ALIGNED CONFERENCE IN CAIRO
- SUKARNO; EEN AUTOBIOGRAFIE UIT DE MOND VAN DE PRESIDENT, OPGETEKEND DOOR CINDY ADAMS
- SUMMARY OF THE INDONESIAN POLICY REGARDING PRODUCTION SHARING ARRANGEMENTS
- TAHUN KEMENANGAN; A YEAR OF TRIUMPH
- TAHUN KEMENANGAN; PIDATO PJM. PRESIDEN/PANGLIMA TERTINGGI/PEMIMPIN BESAR REVOLUSI INDONESIA PADA HARI ULANG TAHUN KEMERDEKAAN REPUBLIK INDONESIA PADA TANGGAL 17 AUGUSTUS 1962
- TAHUN TANTANGAN. A YEAR OF CHALLENGE
- TAHUN "VIVERE PERICOLOSO."
- TAHUN "VIVERE PERICOLOSO," TAVIP
- TESTAMENT POLITIK IR. SOEKARNO
- TJAPAILAH BINTANG-BINTANG DILANGIT (TAHUN BERDIKARI)
- TO BUILD THE WORLD ANEW
- TO PRESERVE THE REPUBLIC WE HAVE PROCLAIMED; CONCEPT OF PRESIDENT SUKARNO
- TRITUNGGAL: RE-SO-PIM, REVOLUSI, SOSIALISME, PIMPINAN NASIONAL
- WEDJANGAN REVOLUSI; KARYA BUNG KARNO. SEBUAH KAMUS ILMU PERDJUANGAN UNTUK RAKJAT
- A YEAR OF CHALLENGE
- A YEAR OF LIVING DANGEROUSLY

Sukawati, Tjokorde Gde Rake *see* BALI, AN EARTHLY VALLEY OF PEACE
Sukirno, Adhy *see* MA'HUAN TERKENAL DENGAN SUNAN AMPEL KETUA WALI SANGA
Sukria *see* RASIAH NU GORENG PATUT; KARNADI ANEMER BANGKONG
SUL DE ALAGOAS : ORGAM CONSAGRADO AOS INTERESSES SOCIAES – Penedeo, Alagoas. 27 Maio, Jul, 11 Nov 1896 – 1,5,6 – bl Biblioteca [072]
O SUL DE MINAS – Campanha, 23 Sept 1859-13 May 1860 – 1,5,6 – bl Biblioteca [072]
O SUL DE MINAS : SEMANARIO POLITICO, INDUSTRIAL E LITTERARIO – Campanha, 2 Dec 1877 – 1,5,6 – bl Biblioteca [072]
SUL DE MINAS : SEMINARIO INDEPENDENTE E NOTICIOSO – Campanha, 26 Jul 1936; 14 Nov 1937 – 1,5,6 – bl Biblioteca [072]
SUL MATRIMONIO... / Axerio, E – Torino, 1902 – 1mf – 9 – ILM-3645/1 – ne IDC [340]
SUL PROGRETTO DI UNA LEGGE INTERNAZIONALE SUL DIRITTO CAMBIARIO / Bologna. Camera di Commercio ed Arti – Bologna, 1891 – 1mf – 9 – ILM-3936/1 – ne IDC [327]
SUL QUESTIONARIO PROPOSTO DAL SOCIO PROF. GIANTURCO... / Fiore, P – Napoli, 1902 – 1mf – 1 – ILM-3967/1 – ne IDC [327]
Sulaimon, Zainon *see* SUBJECT BIBLIOGRAPHY ON ISLAM IN MALAYSIA
SULAMITH : A METRICAL ROMANCE / Osmond, Samuel McClurg – Philadelphia: Jas B Rodgers, 1892 – 1mf – 9 – 0-8370-4645-9 – 1985-2645 – us A.T.L.A. [810]
SULAMITH – (New York). 1889-90 – 1 – us A.J.P.C. [073]
SULAMITH – (St. Louis). 1880-81 – 1 – us A.J.P.C. [073]
SULAMITH : EINE ZEITSCHRIFT ZUR BEFOERDERUNG DER KULTUR UND HUMANITAET UNTER DER JUEDISCHEN NATION – Leipzig, Dessau. v1-9. 1806-37; 1845-48. Complete. B362 (Leo Baeck Institute. German-Jewish Periodicals, Pt 2) – 3r – 1 – $205.00 – us UPA [270]
Sulardjo Pontjosutirto *see* LAPORAN ETHNOGRAFI DARI DAERAHKABUPATEN WANASABA
Sulchan, M *see* SEDJARAH PEMBANGUNAN JAJASAN BADAN WAKAF SEMARANG
Suleiman, A H et al *see* EVALUATION OF SHUGOR, DUBASI AND WATISH SUBTYPES OF SUDAN DESERT SHEEP AT THE EL-HUDA NATIONAL SHEEP RESEARCH STATION, GEZIRA PROVINCE, SUDAN
SULFUR LETTERS / ed by Senning, A – 1982- – 1,5,9 – us Harwood [660]
SULFUR REPORTS / ed by Senning, A – 1980- – 320p per v – 1,5,9 – us Harwood [660]
Sulger-Gebing, Emil *see*
- GERHART HAUPTMANN
- HUGO VON HOFMANNSTHAL

Sulgrove, B R *see* HISTORY OF MARION COUNTY AND INDIANAPOLIS
Sulivan, Henry North *see* LIFE AND LETTERS OF THE LATE ADMIRAL SIR B.J. SULIVAN, K.C.B., 1810-90
SULLA CONTROVERSIA DEL DIVORZIO IN ITALIA / Fiore, P – Torino, 1891 – 1mf – 1 – ILM-2990/1 – ne IDC [327]
SULLA LIBERTA DEI MARI / Breganze, G – Milano, 1857 – 1mf – 1 – ILM-2493/1 – ne IDC [327]
SULLA LITISPENDENZA E SUL CONFLITTO DEI GIUDICATO... / Gatti, A – Pistoia, 1905 – 1mf – 1 – ILM-2405/1 – ne IDC [327]
SULLAM – Jerusalem. 1949-64. BJ-91-80 1 – 9 – ne IDC [470]
SULL'ARTICOLO 8 DELLE DISPOSIZIONI GENERALI DEL CODICE CIVILE ITALIANO / Fiore, P – Torino, 1901 – 1mf – 1 – ILM-3663/1 – ne IDC [327]
SULL'IMMACOLATO CONCEPIMENTO DI MARIA = A POLEMICAL TREATISE ON THE IMMACULATE CONCEPTION OF THE BLESSED VIRGIN / Lambruschini, Luigi – (In English. Includes bibliographical references) – New York: D & J Sadlier, 1855 – 1mf – 9 – 0-8370-7228-X – 1986-1228 – us A.T.L.A. [240]
Sullivan, Alexander Martin *see* NEW IRELAND
Sullivan, C Glenn *see* A MINISTRY INVOLVING OLDER WIDOWS IN THE OAKHURST BAPTIST CHURCH, CLARKSDALE, MISSISSIPPI
SULLIVAN GAZETTE – Dushore, PA. -w 1889-1905 – 13 – $25.00r – us I.M.R. [071]
Sullivan, Jeremiah *see* CUMBERLAND AND WESTMORELAND, ANCIENT AND MODERN
Sullivan, John J *see* AMERICAN BUSINESS LAW
Sullivan, John P, Jr *see* AN EXAMINATION OF THE VALIDITY OF THE PROFILE OF MOOD STATES (POMS) IN THE ASSESSMENT OF MENTAL HEALTH IN ATHLETES
Sullivan, Maurice J *see* NEVADA'S GOLDEN STARS
SULLIVAN REPUBLICAN – Laporte, PA. -w 1889-1896 – 13 – $25.00r – us I.M.R. [071]
SULLIVAN REVIEW – Dushore. Pa. -w. 1879-1924, 1941, 1958-68 – 1 – us UMI [071]
THE SULLIVAN REVIEW – Dushore, PA. 1975. 1 roll – 13 – $25.00r – us I.M.R. [071]
Sullivan, William *see*
- LETTERS TO HIS HOLINESS POPE PIUS 10
- THE PRIEST

Sullivan's Island. South Carolina. Chapel of the Holy Cross *see* RECORDS
Sullivant, W S *see*
- ICONES MUSCORUM
- ICONES MUSCORUM, SUPPLEMENT
- MUSCI ALLEGHANIENSES SIVE ENUMERATIO

SULLOM VOE SCENE – 1977-1993 – 1. 122-125 – £42.00r – uk Scot News [622]
Sully, James *see* AN ESSAY ON LAUGHTER; ITS FORMS, ITS CAUSES, ITS DEVELOPMENT AND ITS VALUE
O SUL-MINEIRO : ORGAM DOS INTERESSES DO MUNICIPIO – Villa Nepomuceno, 12 May-Jun, Oct 1918; Jan-Feb, Apr-Aug, Oct-Dec 1919; Jan, Mar-May, Jul-Aug, Nov 1920; Jan, Mar-31 Oct 1921 – 1,5,6 – bl Biblioteca [072]
O SULMINEIRO : DIARIO ILLUSTRADO – Pouso Alegre, 12 Oct 1914; Apr-29 May 1915 – 1,5,6 – bl Biblioteca [072]
SUL..."OGGETTO DI NORME DI DIRITTO INTERNAZIONALE PRIVATO" / Enriques, G – Firenze, 1936 – 1mf – 1 – ILM-2483/1 – ne IDC [327]
SULPHUR SPRING BAPTIST CHURCH. FRANKLIN, KENTUCKY : CHURCH RECORDS – 1893-1933. Records. 1934-63 – 1 – 55.98 – us Baptist [240]
SULPHUR SPRING BAPTIST CHURCH. JONESBORO, TENNESSEE : CHURCH RECORDS – 1876-1952 – 1 – 63.36 – us Baptist [240]
Sulphur Springs. Ohio. St. Paul Lutheran Church *see* RECORDS
Sulphur Springs.Ohio. Hope United Church of Christ *see* RECORDS
LES SULPICIENS ET LES PRETRES DES MISSIONS-ETRANGERES EN ACADIE, 1676-1762 / Casgrain, Henri-Raymond – Quebec: Pruneau & Kirouac, 1897. 00530. (Pre-1900 Canadiana) – 9 – cn C.I.H.M. [240]
SULTAN AZIN'IN HAL'I VE INTIHARI / Nureddin, Tevfik – Istanbul: Karabet Matbaasi, 1324 [1909] – $10.00 – us MEDOC [956]
Sulte, Benjamin *see*
- HISTOIRE DE LA MILICE CANADIENNE-FRANCAISE, 1760-1897
- LES MARCHES DE LA VILLE DES TROIS-RIVIERES

SULU STAR – Philippines. Jolo Sulu. 1959- – 1 – us UMI [072]
SULUH INDONESIA – Djakarta. Indonesia. (Daily). 1954-66 – 1 – us UMI [072]
SULUH INDONESIA – Jogjakarta. Indonesia. (Jogjakarta Ed.). 1965-66 – 1 – us UMI [072]
SULUH MARHAEN – Jogjakarta. Indonesia. 1966- – 1 – us UMI [072]
Sulzbach, A *see* DICHTERKLAENGE AUS SPANIENS BESSEREN TAGEN
Sulzberger, Mayer *see* THE AM HA-ARETZ
Sulzer, Johann Georg *see* ALLGEMEINE THEORIE DER SCHOENEN KUENSTE

THE SUM OF THE PARTS: SHARING THE RESPONSIBILITY FOR BIBLIOGRAPHIC CONTROL / Daval, Nicola – Minutes of the meeting of the Association of Research Libraries. 103d, Chapel Hill, NC, 19-20 Oct 1983. ED 244-630 – 9 – 0.91 – us EDRS [070]

SUMA DE GEOGRAPHIA QUE TRATA DE TODOS LOS PARTIDOS E PROVINCIAS DEL MUNDO... / Fernandez de Enciso, M – Sevilla, 1519 – 3mf – 9 – sp Cultura [946]

Suman, Hasibuan *see* PERTJOBAAN SETIA

Sumantri Praptokusumo *see*
- FRAGMENTA SOCIALIA
- TOWARDS RAISING THE STANDARD OF LIVING IN INDONESIA

Sumardi Atmaprawira *see* MENGISI "PANTJA WARDHANA," SISTIM PENDIDIKAN INDONESIA

Sumardjo *see* BUNG KARNO SEBAGAI AHLI SEDJARAH

Sumarga *see* PEACE CORPS

SUMARIO DE LA NATURAL Y GENERAL HISTORIA DE LAS INDIAS / Fernandez de Oviedo Valdes, Gonzalo – Madrid: Espasa Calpe, S.A., 1978 – 1 – sp Bibl Santa Ana [950]

Sumarsidik *see* USAHA GOTONG ROJONG MASJARAKAT DESA BODJONEGORO; LAPORAN

Sumarto, M D *see* TANAH AIRKU DARI ZAMAN KE ZAMAN

Sumartono *see* INDONESIA UNDER FASCISM

SUMATRA POST, 1898-1923 – Medan, 1924 – 1mf – 9 – SE-1448/1 – ne IDC [950]

SUMATRA POST, 1898-1940 / Netherlands. Royal Library. The Hague. Newspaper Department – (1898-1902. 189mf. Dfl1,180.00; 1903-07. 271mf. Dfl1,695.00; 1908-12. 304mf. Dfl1,900.00; 1913-17. 325mf. Dfl2,030.00; 1918-22. 352mf. Dfl2,200.00; 1923-27. 372mf. Dfl2,325.00; 1928-32. 410mf. Dfl2,560.00; 1933-37. 385mf. Dfl2,405.00; 1938-40. 156mf. Dfl975.00) – KB006 – 2764mf – 9 – Dfl16,280.00 silver – ne MMF Publ [072]

Sumberg, J E *see*
- GLIRICIDIA SEPIUM (JACQ.) STEUD
- SHEEP AND GOATS IN HUMID WEST AFRICA

SUMERIAN AND BABYLONIAN PSALMS / Langdon, S – Paris. 1909. BNE-20,005 1 – 9 – ne IDC [290]

SUMERIAN LITURGICAL TEXTS / Langdon, S – University of Pennsylvania, The University Museum, Publications of the Babylonian Section. v. 10, nr. 2, 4. Philadelphia. 1917. BNE-425 1 – 9 – ne IDC [200]

SUMERIAN MYTHOLOGY / Kramer, SN – 1944 – 9 – $10.00 – us I.R.C. [930]

SUMERIAN RELIGIOUS TEXTS / Chiera, E – (Crozer Theological Seminary, Babylonian Publ., v. 1). Upland. 1924. BNE-449 1 – 9 – ne IDC [290]

SUMERISCH-BABYLONISCHE HYMNEN NACH THONTAFELN GRIECHISCHER ZEIT / Reisner, George A – (Koen. Mus. Berlin. Mitt. Orient. Sammlungen. heft X). Berlin. 1896. BNE-457 1 – 9 – ne IDC [290]

SUMERISCH-BABYLONISCHE TAMMUZLIEDER / Zimmern, Heinrich – Leipzig. 1907. BNE-20,039 1 – 9 – ne IDC [930]

DIE SUMERISCHE FRAGE / Weissbach, Franz Heinrich – (Includes indexes) – Leipzig: J C Hinrichs, 1898 – 1mf – 9 – 0-8370-8631-0 – 1986-2631 – us A.T.L.A. [470]

SUMERISCHE STUDIEN / Haupt, Paul – (Includes bibliographical references) – Leipzig: Breitkopf & Haertel, 1879 – 1mf – 9 – 0-8370-8519-5 – 1986-2519 – us A.T.L.A. [470]

Sumintawikarta, Sadikin *see* THE IMPROVEMENT OF AGRICULTURE RESEARCH ESTABLISHMENTS IN INDONESIA

SUMMA AUREA IN 4 LIBROS SENTENT / Altissiodorensis, Guillermus – Parisiis, 1500 – 13mf – 8 – ne Slangenburg [240]

SUMMA DE ARTE PRAEDICANDI / Chobham, Thomas de – 1988 – 9mf – 9 – Bf1,775.00 – 2-503-63822-8 – be Brepols [240]

[SUMMA DE CONFESSIONE] : COMPILATIO PRAESENS / Petrus Pictaviensis; ed by Longere, J – 1980 – 3mf – 9 – Bf3,000.00 – 2-503-03511-6 – be Brepols [450]

SUMMA DE ECCLESIA / Turrecremata, J de – Venetiis, 1561 – 10mf – 9 – CA-92/1 – ne IDC [240]

SUMMA DOCTRINAE CHRISTIANAE IN USUM DOCENTIUM / Weninger, Francis Xavier – Oeniponte [Innsbruck]: Feliciani Rauch, 1844 – 1mf – 9 – 0-8370-6872-X – 1986-0872 – us A.T.L.A. [240]

SUMMA EXPONIBILIUM MAGISTRI GASPARIS LAX ARAGONENSIS / Lax, Gaspar – Zaragoza: P. Bardouyn, 1529 – 1 – us U.W. Library [190]

SUMMA PARVORUM LOGICALIUM / Lax, Gaspar – Zaragoza, 1532 – 1 – us U.W. Library [160]

SUMMA PHILOSOPHIAE SCHOLASTICAE ET SCOTISTICAE... / Dupasquier, S – Patavii. 4v. 1705 – 25mf – 9 – CA-14/1 – ne IDC [100]

SUMMA PLANTARUM / Vitman, F – 6v. Mediolani. 1789-92; Suppl. 1802. B-921 2 – 8 – ne IDC [580]

SUMMA SUPER CODICEM / Azzo – c1300. Holkham ms. 206.Holkham Hall, Norfolk, England – 1 – uk Microform Academic [760]

SUMMA THEOLOGICA / Aquinas, Thomas – Ed. nova. New York: Benziger Bros., 1875. 8v – 1 – us U.W. Library [240]

SUMMA THEOLOGICA / Henricus A Gandovo – Ferrariae. Tomus 1-4. 1642-1646 – 67mf – 8 – ne Slangenburg [240]

SUMMA THEOLOGICA AB HIERONYMUS SCARPARIO : NOVITER EDITA. TOMUS 1-4 / Gandavo, Henricus A – Ferrariae, 1642-1646 – 46mf – 8 – ne Slangenburg [240]

SUMMA VEGETABILIUM SCANDINAVIAE / Fries, E M – Holmiae. 1846-49. B-1263 2 – 8 – ne IDC [580]

SUMMA...D. THOMAE AQUINATIS...IN ORDINEM CURSUS PHILOSOPHICI ACCOMMODATA / Alamanni, C – Parisiis. 2v. 1639-40 – 15mf – 9 – CA-1/1 – ne IDC [100]

SUMMAE SYLVESTRINAE PARS 1-2 / Prieras, S – 1619. 2v – 30mf – 8 – ne Slangenburg [290]

AIN SUMMARI DER TUERCKISCHEN BOTTSCHAFFT WERBUNG AN DIE HERRSCHAFFT ZU VENEDIG, ... – Venedig, 1537 – 1mf – 9 – H-8145/1 – ne IDC [956]

SUMMARIES OF ILLICIT TRANSACTIONS AND SEIZURES / United Nations. Commission on Narcotic Drugs – 1947-1984 – E.213 F.210 S.123 – 9 (E/NS) – us U.N. Pubs [360]

SUMMARIES OF SELECTED JAPANESE MAGAZINES / U.S. Embassy. Tokyo, Japan – 1952- – 1 – 20.00y – us L of C Photodup [073]

SUMMARIES OF THE INDUSTRIAL DEVELOPMENT PLANS OF THIRTY COUNTRIES / United Nations – UNIDO IPPD. 3v. New York. 1970. BD-1802 1 – 9 – ne IDC [338]

A SUMMARY ACCOUNT OF THE MAJOR ACTIVITIES OF THE GOVERNMENT OF INDIA IN ITS VARIOUS DEPARTMENTS – (Filmed with: India. Imperial Record Dept: List of the Heads of Administrations in India and of the India Office in England) – [s.l: s.n.,], 1946 – us Res Libr [950]

SUMMARY AND ANALYSIS OF THE 1984 COMPACT OF FREE ASSOCIATION – Koror: Belau Pacific Center, jun 1984 – 1mf – 9 – $1.50 – LLMC 82-100G, Title 28 – us L.L.M.C. [327]

SUMMARY JUDGEMENT PRACTICE IN THREE DISTRICT COURTS / Cecil, Joe S & Douglas, C R – Washington: FJC, 1987 – 1mf – 9 – $1.50 – LLMC 95-338 – us L.L.M.C. [340]

SUMMARY JURY TRIALS IN THE NORTHERN DISTRICT OF OHIO / Jacoubovitch, M-Daniel & Moore, Carl M – Washington: FJC, May 1982 – 2mf – 9 – $3.00 – LLMC 95-351 – us L.L.M.C. [340]

SUMMARY OF ACCOMPLISHMENTS / South Dakota. Agricultural Extension Service. State College of Agriculture and Mechanic Arts – 1953 – 1,5,6 – us Spaulding [630]

SUMMARY OF AGRICULTURE ACTIVITIES / U.S. Operations Mission to Indonesia – SE 11,632 1. 1957 – 9 – ne IDC [630]

SUMMARY OF AIRWORTHINESS DIRECTIVES, VOLS 1 AND 2 / U.S. Federal Aviation Administration – 2v. Basis manual, including update no 1 and 25 cumulative indexes and updates annually – 96mf – 9 – $186.00y in US $232.00 outside – S-N 950-054-00000-0. Sub-List ID: SADM 1996 – us Gov't Printing [324]

SUMMARY OF CHURCH DISCIPLINE; DRAWN UP BY THE DIRECTION OF THE DOVER BAPTIST ASSOCIATION, VA / Baptist Association – 1824 – 1 – 5.00 – us Baptist [240]

A SUMMARY OF CHURCH-DISCIPLINE / Charleston Association. South Carolina – 2nd ed. 1794 – 1 – 5.00 – us Baptist [240]

SUMMARY OF CONTRIBUTIONS TO THE NATIONAL DEBATE ON EDUCATION REFORM / Zambia. Ministry of Education – (Missing: v3) – Lusaka. 3v. 1977 – 4mf – 9 – DE-500/1 – ne IDC [370]

A SUMMARY OF CURRENT EDUCATION / Nigeria. Ondo State. Ministry of Finance and Economic Development – Akure, 1978 – 1mf – 9 – DE-120/1 – ne IDC [370]

A SUMMARY OF CURRENT EDUCATION STATISTICS 1976-1977 / Nigeria. Oyo State. Ministry of Finance and Economic Planning. Statistics Division – Ibadan, 1978 – 1mf – 9 – DE-122/1 – ne IDC [370]

A SUMMARY OF CURRENT EDUCATION STATISTICS 1976/77-1987 / Nigeria. Oyo State. Ministry of Economic Planning. Statistics Division – (Missing: 1978/79-1982/83; 1984/85-1986/87) – Ibadan – 4mf – 9 – DE-459/1 – ne IDC [370]

SUMMARY OF EGYPTIAN STUDIES; FINAL REPORT TO U.S. GOVERNMENT INTERNATIONAL COOPERATION ADMINISTRATION / Little, A.D., Inc. – 1956. BNE-4642 1 – 9 – ne IDC [956]

A SUMMARY OF EQUITY PLEADING / Langdell, Christopher Columbus – Cambridge Mass. Sever, 1877. 130 p. LL-1137 – 1 – us L of C Photodup [340]

SUMMARY OF EVIDENCE / International Military Tribunal for the Far East – Tokyo. Various pagination. LL-027 – 1 – us L of C Photodup [340]

SUMMARY OF EXTERNAL TRADE STATISTICS / Libya. Ministry of Economy and Trade. Census and Statistical Department – Tripoli. 1966, 1967, 1970, 1971. BNE-610 1 – 9 – ne IDC [310]

SUMMARY OF FOREIGN TRADE STATISTICS 1963-1966 / Saudi Arabia. Central Department of Statistics – 3v. in 1. BNE-6603 1 – 9 – ne IDC [324]

SUMMARY OF FUTURE POLITICAL FUTURE STATUS TALKS / Joint Committee on Future Status [TTPI (U.S.)] – n.a, n.p, oct 1973 – 1mf – 9 – $1.50 – LLMC 82-100F, Title 54 – us L.L.M.C. [323]

A SUMMARY OF HISTORICAL SKETCHES ON THE FORMATION OF THE BODY OF THE RUSSIAN LAWS / [Speranskii, M M] – Spb., 1841 – 171, vi p – 9 – ne IDC [340]

SUMMARY OF IMPORTANT FARM BUREAU ACTIVITIES / South Dakota. Agricultural Extension Service. State College of Agriculture and Mechanic Arts – 1919-21 – 1,5,6 – us Spaulding [630]

SUMMARY OF LECTURE AT CEREMONY OF THE 8TH DIES NATALIS OF THE UNIVERSITY OF INDONESIA / Jakarta. Universitas Indonesia – SE-3647 1. 1958 – 9 – ne IDC [370]

A SUMMARY OF METHODIST LAW AND DISCIPLINE; BEING A NEW EDITION OF 'THE LARGE MINUTES' / Simon, J S – 4th ed. London, 1915. xvi/831p – 9mf – 9 – ne IDC [240]

SUMMARY OF MONITORING INFORMATION RECEIVED BY THE BR / ed by International Telecommunication Union – (Available in French, English and Spanish) – 1992- . updated quarterly – 9 – Sfr59.00 – sz I.T.U. [380]

A SUMMARY OF PAPERS READ AT DIFFERENT TIMES...ROYAL SOCIETY OF CANADA, CANADIAN ASSOCIATION OF CIVIL ENGINEERS: AND ARCHITECTS, AND LITERARY AND SCIENTIFIC SOCIETIES.. / Baillairge, Charles – 1903?. 07439. (Pre-1900 Canadiana) – 9 – cn C.I.H.M. [624]

SUMMARY OF PROCEEDINGS, 1936 / Orissa. India (State). Advisory Council – v. 1-2. Orissa-Cuttack. 1936. BI-50 2 – 6mf – 8 – ne IDC [324]

SUMMARY OF PROCEEDINGS AND SELECTED PAPERS. SYMPOSIUM ON THE PLANNING AND IMPLEMENTATION OF FISHERIES MANAGEMENT AND DEVELOPMENT PROGRAMS IN AFRICA. LUSAKA, 1985 – 1986 – 160p – it F.A.O. [338]

SUMMARY OF RECOMMENDATIONS / United Nations. Special Committee on Palestine – Jerusalem. 1947. BJ-28-158 1 – 9 – ne IDC [956]

SUMMARY OF REPORT / Palestine Royal Commission – (Official Communique no. 9 37). 1937. BJ-28-42 1 – 9 – ne IDC [324]

SUMMARY OF SALES OF PERSONAL PROPERTY / Molleson, Stanley Holcomb – Cooperstown, N.Y.: Crist, Scott & Parshall, 1901. 76p. LL-222 – 1 – us L of C Photodup [340]

SUMMARY OF SPECIAL COMMERCIAL DECISIONS AFFECTING THE BANKER, FROM THE REPORTS OF THE HIGHEST COURTS OF THE SEVERAL STATES / McMaster, James Smith – New York, Evening Post Job Printing House, 1896. 56 p. LL-272 – 1 – us L of C Photodup [340]

SUMMARY OF THE 5TH NATIONAL DEVELOPMENT PLAN 1973-1978 / Iran. Iran Plan and Budget organization – June. 1973. BD-1804 1 – 9 – ne IDC [956]

SUMMARY OF THE ANNUAL REPORT FOR 1950 OF THE INSTITUTE FOR LINGUISTIC AND CULTURAL RESEARCH / Jakarta. Universitas Indonesia – SE-3784 1. 1950 – 9 – ne IDC [370]

SUMMARY OF THE ANNUAL REPORT FOR 1951 OF THE INSTITUTE FOR LINGUISTIC AND CULTURAL RESEARCH / Jakarta. Universitas Indonesia – SE-4101 1. 1951 – 9 – ne IDC [370]

SUMMARY OF THE EVOLUTION OF PLANNING INSTITUTIONS ON LIBYA / Libya. Ministry of Planning and Development – 1965. BNE-713 1 – 9 – ne IDC [338]

SUMMARY OF THE FIRST FIVE-YEAR ECONOMIC PLAN, 1962-1966 / Korea. South. Economic Planning Board – Seoul. 1962. BD-501 1 – 9 – ne IDC [338]

SUMMARY OF THE FULFILMENT OF THE FIRST FIVE-YEAR PLAN FOR THE DEVELOPMENT OF THE NATIONAL ECONOMY OF THE USSR / U.S.S.R. Gosudarstvennaia Planovaia Komissiia – M. 1933. BD-212 1 – 9 – ne IDC [338]

A SUMMARY OF THE GERMAN MONETARY FREEDOM SCHOOL / Beckerath, Ulrich von – 9 – 1.00f – at Libertarian Micro [335]

SUMMARY OF THE INDONESIAN POLICY REGARDING PRODUCTION SHARING ARRANGEMENTS / Sukarno, Pres. Indonesia – SE 3185 1. 1962 – 9 – ne IDC [324]

SUMMARY OF THE LAW OF NEGOTIABLE INSTRUMENTS / Levin, Robert – Philadelphia, Brown & Levin, 1939. 52, 1 p. LL-630 – 1 – us L of C Photodup [340]

A SUMMARY OF THE LAW OF PATENTS AND OF EXTENSION OF PATENTS / Wordsworth, Charles Favell Forth – London,Benning, 1853. 140 p. LL-1678 – 1 – us L of C Photodup [340]

SUMMARY OF THE LAW OF PLEADING, PRACTICE AND EVIDENCE IN THE STATE OF NEW YORK. / Medina, Harold Raymond – 10th ed. New York 1933. 189p. LL-623 – 1 – us L of C Photodup [340]

A SUMMARY OF THE LAW OF PRIVATE CORPORATIONS / Tompkins, Leslie Jay – New York, Baker, Voorhis, 1904. 264 p. LL-1474 – 1 – us L of C Photodup [340]

SUMMARY OF THE MID-TERM EVALUATION OF THE 5TH EDUCATION PROJECT (1980-1982) / Thailand. National Education Commission. Educational Planning Division – Bangkok, 1983 – 1mf – 9 – DE-593/1 – ne IDC [370]

SUMMARY OF THE NETHERLANDS CENTRAL ECONOMIC PLAN, 1967 / Netherlands. Centraal Planbureau – The Hague. 1967. BD-1702 1 – 9 – ne IDC [338]

SUMMARY OF THE NETHERLANDS CENTRAL ECONOMIC PLAN, 1968 / Netherlands. Centraal Planbureau – The Hague. 1968. BD-1703 1 – 9 – ne IDC [338]

SUMMARY OF THE NETHERLANDS CENTRAL ECONOMIC PLAN, 1969 / Netherlands. Centraal Planbureau – The Hague. 1969. BD-1704 1 – 9 – ne IDC [338]

SUMMARY OF THE NETHERLANDS CENTRAL ECONOMIC PLAN, 1973 / Netherlands. Centraal Planbureau – The Hague. 1973. BD-1707 1 – 9 – ne IDC [338]

A SUMMARY OF THE NEW FERNS WHICH HAVE BEEN DISCOVERED OR DESCRIBED SINCE 1874 / Baker, J G – (Annals of Botany, v. 5. 1891). Oxford. 1892. B-7155 1 – 9 – ne IDC [580]

SUMMARY OF THE ORGANIZED DISCUSSION ON THE ECONOMIC EVALUATION OF SPORT FISHING (1967-1968, DUBLIN) – 1973 – 27p – it F.A.O. [338]

SUMMARY OF THE REPORT OF THE COMMISSION FOR THE SOCIO-ECONOMIC DEVELOPMENT OF THE BANTU AREAS WITHIN THE UNION OF SOUTH AFRICA – (Filmed with: South Africa...Verslag...) – [s.l: s.n.], 1955 – us Res Libr [300]

A SUMMARY OF THE SECOND FIVE-YEAR DEVELOPMENT PLAN OF TURKEY (1968-1972) / Turkey. Devlet Planlama Teskilati – v1. Economic planning. Ankara. 1967 – 9 – ne IDC [338]

SUMMARY OF THE SECOND FIVE-YEAR PLAN (1967-1971) / Thailand. National Economic Development Board – Bangkok. 1966. BD-774 – 9 – ne IDC [338]

SUMMARY OF THE SEVEN YEAR PLAN FOR ECONOMIC DEVELOPMENT, 1964-1970 / Jordan – Amman. 1964. BD-282 1 – 9 – ne IDC [338]

A SUMMARY OF THE THIRD FIVE YEAR DEVELOPMENT PLAN 1973-1977 / Turkey. Prime Ministry. State Planning Organization – Ankara. 1973. BD-2002 1 – 9 – ne IDC [338]

SUMMARY OF THE YUGOSLAV PRESS / U.S. British Legation – US British Legation: 1960-30 Jun 1972 – 153r – 1 – us L of C Photodup [949]

A SUMMARY OF TORTS / Erwin, Frank Alexander – New York, Erwin 1899. 159 p. LL-245 – 1 – us L of C Photodup [340]

SUMMARY OF UNITED STATES ASSISTANCE TO JORDAN / U.S. General Accounting Office – Report to the Congress of the Department of State and the Agency of international development. 1973. BNE-9818 1 – 9 – ne IDC [956]

SUMMARY RECORD OF THE U.S.-MICRONESIA ROUNDTABLE CONFERENCE ON THE FUTURE POLITICAL STATUS OF THE TRUST TERRITORY OF THE PACIFIC : HELD ON GUAM, JUL 1977 / Off of Micronesian Status Negotiations – Washington: Off of Micronesian Status Negotiations, 1977 – 1mf – 9 – $1.50 – LLMC 82-100F, Title 59 – us L.L.M.C. [323]

SUMMARY RECORDS OF MAIN COMMITTEES OF THE GENERAL ASSEMBLY : AD HOC COMMITTEE OF THE WHOLE ASSEMBLY / United Nations – 12th Sess. – 18th Sess., 1957-1963 – E.7 F.7 S.7 – 9 (A/AC. /PV. or SR) – us U.N. Pubs [324]

SUMMARY RECORDS OF MAIN COMMITTEES OF THE GENERAL ASSEMBLY : AD HOC POLICITAL COMMITTEE / United Nations – (3rd Sess.: A/AC. /SR. 1948/1949. E/F.17 S.10; 4th Sess. 10th Spec. Sess.: A/AC. /SR. 1949-1955. E.49 F.52 S.52) – 9 – us U.N. Pubs [324]

SUMMARY RECORDS OF MAIN COMMITTEES OF THE GENERAL ASSEMBLY : FIFTH COMMITTEE / United Nations – (1st Sess. – 3rd Sess.: A/C.5/session/SR. 1946-1948. E/F.55 S.29; 4th Sess. – 44th Sess.: A/C.5/session/SR. 1949-1989. E.568 F.670 S.569) – 9 – us U.N. Pubs [324]

SUMMARY RECORDS OF MAIN COMMITTEES OF THE GENERAL ASSEMBLY : FIRST COMMITTEE / United Nations – (1st Sess. – 3rd Sess.: A/C.1/session/PV. 1946-1948. E/F.63 S.34; 4th Sess. 44th Sess.: A/C.1/PV. 1949-1989. E.1203 F.1143 S.1085) – 9 – us U.N. Pubs [324]

SUMMARY RECORDS OF MAIN COMMITTEES OF THE GENERAL ASSEMBLY : FOURTH COMMITTEE / United Nations – (1st Sess. – 3rd Sess.: A/C.4/session/SR. 1946-1948. E/F.31 S.18; 4th Sess. – 44th Sess.: A/C.4/session/SR. 1949-1989. E.417 F.416 S.428) – 9 – us U.N. Pubs [324]

SUMMARY RECORDS OF MAIN COMMITTEES OF THE GENERAL ASSEMBLY : GENERAL COMMITTEE / United Nations – (1st Sess. – 3rd Sess.: A/BUR/session/SR. 1946-1949. E/F.14 S.10; 4th Sess. – 43rd Sess.: A/BUR/session/SR. 1949-1988. E.55 F.56 S.55) – 9 – us U.N. Pubs [324]

SUMMARY RECORDS OF MAIN COMMITTEES OF THE GENERAL ASSEMBLY : JOINT FIRST AND SIXTH COMMITTEES / United Nations – 1st Sess., 1946 – E/F.3 S.2 – 9 (A/C.1 and 6/SR) – us U.N. Pubs [324]

SUMMARY RECORDS OF MAIN COMMITTEES OF THE GENERAL ASSEMBLY : JOINT SECOND AND THIRD COMMITTEES / United Nations – (1st Sess. – 3rd Sess.: A/C.2 and 3/SR. 1946-1948. E/F.10 S.6; 4th Sess. – 6th Sess.: A/C.2 and 3/SR. 1949-1951/52. E.6 F.6 S.6) – 9 – us U.N. Pubs [324]

SUMMARY RECORDS OF MAIN COMMITTEES OF THE GENERAL ASSEMBLY : SECOND COMMITTEE / United Nations – (1st Sess. – 3rd Sess.: A/C.2/session/SR. 1946-1948. E/F.18 S.12; 4th Sess. – 44th Sess.: A/C.2/session/SR. 1949-1989. E.523 F.536 S.533) – 9 – us U.N. Pubs [324]

SUMMARY RECORDS OF MAIN COMMITTEES OF THE GENERAL ASSEMBLY : SIXTH COMMITTEE / United Nations – (1st Sess. – 3rd Sess.: A/C.6/session/SR. 1946-1948. E/F.36 S.10; 4th Sess. – 44th Sess.: A/C.6/session/SR. 1949-1989. E.475 F.482 S.481) – 9 – us U.N. Pubs [324]

SUMMARY RECORDS OF MAIN COMMITTEES OF THE GENERAL ASSEMBLY : SPECIAL POLITICAL COMMITTEE / United Nations – 11th Sess. – 44th Sess., 1956-1989 – E.405 F.403 S.377 – 9 (A/SPC/session/SR. or PV) – us U.N. Pubs [324]

SUMMARY RECORDS OF MAIN COMMITTEES OF THE GENERAL ASSEMBLY : THIRD COMMITTEE / United Nations – (1st Sess. – 3rd Sess.: A/C.3/session/SR. 1946-1948. E/F.48 S.18; 4th Sess. – 44th Sess.: A/C.3/session/SR. 1949-1989. E.625 F.633 S.630) – 9 – us U.N. Pubs [324]

SUMMARY RECORDS OF PLENARY MEETINGS / UN – (10th-15th sess: E/SR 1950-53 mf: E.60 F.62; 16th- 63rd sess; Year 1978, 1987 E/Year/SR 1950-1987 mf: E.269 F.283 S.278; Years 1986, 1987, v1 are not yet available) – 1st-9th sess – E/F.91 – 9 – E/SR. 1946-49 – us U.N. Pubs [340]

SUMMARY REPORT: MATERIALS USED AND PRODUCTION OF RUBBER REMILLING MILLS / Indonesia. Biro Pusat Statistik – SE-6937 1 – 9 – ne IDC [670]

SUMMARY REPORTS IN ALL CASES REPORTED TO CONGRESS AS DISALLOWED UNDER THE ACT OF MARCH 3, 1871. / U.S. Commissioners of Claims – Washington, Govt. Print. Off., 1876-81. 4v. LL-152 – 1 – us L of C Photodup [340]

SUMMARY TRANSLATION OF THE NIGER REPUBLIC'S ECONOMIC AND SOCIAL DEVELOPMENT PLAN: INTERIM PLAN, 1961-1963 / Niger – D-1387 1. 1962 – 9 – ne IDC [338]

A SUMMARY VIEW OF THE DOCTRINES OF METHODISM, OCCASIONED BY THE LATE PERSECUTION OF THE METHODISTS AT NORWICH,... / Perronet, Charles – Bristol, 1752 – 1mf – 9 – MP-362/1 – ne IDC [240]

A SUMMARY VIEW OF THE RIGHTS OF BRITISH AMERICA / Jefferson, Thomas – 9 – 5.00 – us Scholars' Facs [975]

SUMMATION OF NONMILITARY ACTIVITIES IN JAPAN AND KOREA, 1945-1948 – 1983 – 8 rolls – 9 – $600.00 – Dist. us Scholarly Res – Published in cooperation with the Center of Military History – us L of C Photodup [320]

SUMMATION OF NONMILITARY ACTIVITIES IN JAPAN AND KOREA, 1945-48 / Supreme Command for the Allied Powers. Headquarters – 8r – 1 – $680.00 – S1667 – Co-publ with the U.S. Army Center of Military History – us Scholarly Res [355]

AIN SUMME AINS GANTZEN CHRISTLICHEN LEBENS / Fridberger, B – 1525. BME-37 1 – 9 – ne IDC [240]

SUMMER BREEZE – Ashland, NE. -d. Jul. 1895-Aug. 1895; Jun. 1896-Jul. 1896 – 1 – us NE Hist [071]

SUMMER BREEZE – Ashland. Neb. 1895-1896 – 1 – us UMI [071]

SUMMER EMERALD – Eugene OR. June 23-Aug 8 1950, June 20 1962-June 24 1971 – 1 – us U.O. Library [071]

A SUMMER IN NORWAY; WITH NOTES ON THE INDUSTRIES, HABITS, CUSTOMS AND PECULIARITIES OF THE PEOPLE. / Caton, John Dean – Chicago: Jansen, McClurg and Co., 1875. 401p. ill – 1 – us U.W. Library [910]

A SUMMER SEARCH FOR SIR JOHN FRANKIN / Inglefield, E A – BN-266 2. 1853 – 8 – ne IDC [910]

SUMMER SIGNAL – Portland OR. June 18-July 25 1945 – 1 – us U.O. Library [071]

SUMMER SUN – Eugene OR. June 25 1918-July 30 1919, June 27 1923-Aug 4 1939, June 20 1951-Aug 4 1961 – 1 – us U.O. Library [071]

SUMMER TOURS / Canadian Pacific Railway Company. Passenger Department – Montreal: The Company, 1887. 02071. (Pre-1900 Canadiana) – 9 – cn C.I.H.M. [910]

Summers, Ewing *see* GENEALOGICAL AND FAMILY HISTORY OF EASTERN OHIO

Summers, Lewis P *see* ANNALS OF SOUTH WEST VIRGINIA

Summers, Montague *see* THE HISTORY OF WITCHCRAFT AND DEMONOLOGY

Summers, Thomas Osmond *see*
- COMMENTARY ON THE ACTS OF THE APOSTLES
- THE EPISTLE OF PAUL, THE APOSTLE, TO THE ROMANS

Summers, W H *see*
- HISTORY OF THE CONGREGATIONAL CHURCHES IN THE BERKS, SOUTH OXON AND SOUTH BUCKS ASSOCIATION
- THE LOLLARDS OF THE CHILTERN HILLS

SUMMERSIDE PROGRESS – Summerside, Canada. 1866-69; 1872 – 1 reel – 1 – $68.00 – cn Library Assoc [971]

Summerton. South Carolina. St. Matthias Episcopal Church *see* REGISTER

SUMMERVILLE BAPTIST CHURCH. DORCHESTER COUNTY, SOUTH CAROLINA : CHURCH RECORDS – 1896-Feb. 1986 – 2r – 1 – $104.81 – us Baptist [240]

THE SUMMIT LOOKOUT – Weed, CA. 1913-14 – 1r – 1 – $50.00 – B03091 – us Library Micro [071]

THE SUMMONS TO A LARGER EVANGELISM (CCC255) / Mott, J R – (In Chinese) – Shanghai: National Christian Council of China, 1929 – 1r – 1 – 1984-6594 – us A.T.L.A. [240]

SUMMUM ARGENTORATENSIUM TEMPLUM / Schadaeus, O – O 1042 1. 1617 – 9 – ne IDC [700]

SUMMUM ARGENTORATENSIUM TEMPLUM... / Schadaeus, O – Strassburg, 1617 – 9 – ne IDC [730]

Sumner, A T *see*
- A HANDBOOK OF THE MENDE LANGUAGE
- A HANDBOOK OF THE SHERBO LANGUAGE
- A HANDBOOK OF THE TEMNE LANGUAGE

Sumner, Charles *see*
- PAPERS OF CHARLES SUMNER
- SUMNER'S REPORTS OF CASES IN THE FIRST CIRCUIT, 1829-1839

SUMNER COUNTY DEMOCRAT – Wellington. Kan. 1877-1881 – 1 – us UMI [071]

SUMNER COUNTY PRESS – Wellington. Kan. 1873-1892 – 1 – us UMI [071]

SUMNER COUNTY STANDARD – Wellington. Kan. 1884-1896 – 1 – us UMI [071]

SUMNER COUNTY STAR – Wellington. Kan. 1895-1909 – 1 – us UMI [071]

SUMNER NEWS – Sumner, NE. -w. Jun 1914-Aug 1939 – 1 – us NE Hist [071]

Sumner, Robert *see* THE UNITY OF GOVERNMENT IN THE CHURCH OF CHRIST

Sumner, Shelley et al *see* THE ARNO PRESS REPRINT

Sumner Town Company. Kansas *see* RECORD OF LOTS SOLD

Sumner, William Graham *see*
- BUECHER DER KOENIGE
- THE CHALLENGE OF FACTS AND OTHER ESSAYS
- THE FORGOTTEN MAN AND OTHER ESSAYS
- A HISTORY OF AMERICAN CURRENCY.
- SELECTED ESSAYS

SUMNER'S REPORTS OF CASES IN THE FIRST CIRCUIT, 1829-1839 / Sumner, Charles – Boston: Hilliard & Gray. v1-3. 1836-41 (all publ) – 21mf – 9 – $31.50 – LLMC 81-471 – us L.L.M.C. [340]

Sumodiwirjo, Teko *see* SEKOLAH TINGGI RAKJAT. FOLK HIGH SCHOOL

Sumosaputro, Sumantri *see* SERAT TUNTUNAN TJAKING PAKELIRAN PADALANGAN RINGGIT PURWA LAMPAHAN: DONORODJO, DENING R.M. SOEMANTRI SOEMOSAPOETRO

SUMPTER MINER – Sumpter OR. Sep 13 1899-Apr 12 1905 – 1 – us U.O. Library [071]

SUMPTER MINER – Sumpter, OR. -w. 1899-1905 – 1 – 96.00 – us Oregon Hist [071]

SUMPTER NEWS – Sumpter, OR. -w. 26 Feb 1897-29 Jul 1899; 6 Mar, 3 Apr 1897 – 1r – 1 – us U.O. Library [071]

SUMPTER VALLEY NEWS – Sumpter OR. June 2 1902 – 1 – us U.O. Library [071]

SUMPTER-BAKER CITY-SUMPTER MINER – Or. and Inland Empire Miner. 1900-1905 – 1 – us UMI [071]

SUMTER COUNTY TIMES – Bushnell. Fl. -w. 1938, 1939, 1941, 1955- – 1 – us P.K. Yonge [071]

SUN – 1888-1902. S1-14 – 14r – 1 – at Corangamite [072]

SUN – (1977-1992.-68r) – Swift Current, 1993 – 6r – 1 – cn Preston [971]

SUN – Alameda, CA. 1965-67 – 1r – 1 – $50.00 – B02006 – us Library Micro [071]

SUN – (Also known as: Morning Sun) – Las Vegas, NV. 1951-1971 – 377r – 1 – ¶18,850.00 – N04612 – us Library Micro [071]

SUN – Aurora. Neb. 1885-1904; 1908-1926 – 1 – us UMI [071]

SUN – Austin, NV. 1933-34 – 1r – 1 – $50.00 – U04405 – us Library Micro [071]

SUN – Bessemer. Ala. -w. 1963- – 1 – us UMI [071]

SUN – Bremerton. Wash. 1938- – 1 – us UMI [071]

SUN – Brisbane, CA. 1937-38 – 1r – 1 – $50.00 – B02079 – us Library Micro [071]

SUN : CENTRAL EDITION – San Jose, CA. 1973-76 – 11r – 1 – $550.00 – B02892 – us Library Micro [071]

SUN – Clarence. Iowa. 1901-1962 – 1 – us UMI [071]

SUN – Clearwater. Fl. 1925- – 1 – us UMI [071]

SUN – (Cont by: Contra Costa Sun) – Lafayette, CA. 1957-62; 1963-80 – 43r – 1 – $2,150.00 – B02330 – us Library Micro [071]

SUN – Corsicana. Tex. 1966- – 1 – us UMI [071]

SUN – (Details on request) – Sydney – 1 – at Pascoe [072]

SUN – Dixon. Ill. -w. 1872-73, 1882-83, 1888-89 – 1 – us UMI [071]

SUN – Durham. N.C. 1929-1946; 1970- – 1 – us UMI [071]

SUN – Emporia. Kan. 1878-1897 – 1 – us UMI [071]

SUN – Enid. Okl. -w. 1898-99 – 1 – us UMI [071]

SUN – Gary. Ind. 1923-29 – 1 – us UMI [071]

SUN – Goldfield, NV. 1905-06 – 1r – 1 – $50.00 – U04562 – us Library Micro [071]

SUN – Greenville. Tenn. 1957-1963 – 1 – us UMI [071]

SUN – Harris. Kan. 1909-1911 – 1 – us UMI [071]

SUN – Jackson. Tenn. 1936- – 1 – us UMI [071]

SUN – Joliet. Ill. 1874-75 – 1 – us UMI [071]

SUN – Joliet. Ill. -w. 1878, 1881 – 1 – us UMI [071]

SUN – Kearney, NE. -w. Jul 1895-Feb 1900 – 1 – us NE Hist [071]

SUN – Las Vegas. Nev. 1951- – 1 – us UMI [071]

SUN – Laurens. Iowa. -w. 1963-72, 1973- – 1 – us UMI [071]

SUN – Lewiston. Maine. 1953- – 1 – us UMI [071]

SUN – London, 1964-67; 1982- – 260+ r – 1 – uk British Libr Newspaper [072]

SUN – London: Odham Press, [sep 15 1964-1981] – 157r – 1 – us Res Libr [072]

SUN – Lowell. Mass. 1878- – 1 – us UMI [071]

SUN – Marshfield, OR. -w. 12 Feb 1891-15 Jun 1944. – 5r – 1 – us U.O. Library [071]

SUN – Midland. Mich. 1881-1927 – 1 – us UMI [071]

SUN – Moraga, CA. 1973-1980 – 15r – 1 – $750.00 – B02487 – us Library Micro [071]

SUN – Morro Bay. Calif. -w. 1956-67 – 1 – us UMI [071]

SUN – New York. N.Y. 1946-49 – 1 – us UMI [071]

SUN – Norwich. N.Y. 1891-1945 – 1 – us UMI [071]

SUN – Parsons. Kan. 1881- – 1 – us UMI [071]

SUN – Parsons. Kan. -w. 1871-1908 – 1 – us UMI [071]

SUN – Pawtucket. RI. And preds. 1883-93; 1897 – 1 – us UMI [071]

SUN – Pittsburgh. Pa. 1906-1927 – 1 – us UMI [071]

SUN – Pittsfield. Massachusetts. 1800-1820 – 1,3 – us Readex [071]

SUN – Portland, OR. -d. 15 Oct 1894-3 Aug 1895. 2 rolls – 1 – us U.O. Library [071]

SUN – Rosamond. Calif. 1952-1956 – 1 – us UMI [071]

SUN – San Bernardino, CA. 1952 – 953+ r – 1 – $47,650.00 ($1,080.00y) – R03463 – us Library Micro [071]

SUN – San Francisco, CA. 1910 – 1r – 1 – $50.00 – C03501 – us Library Micro [071]

SUN – Santa Clara, CA. 1973-80 – 13r – 1 – $650.00 – B02948 – us Library Micro [071]

SUN – (See: Sun, Lafayette) – Moraga, CA. 1973-80 – 15r – 1 – $750.00 – B02487 – us Library Micro [071]

SUN – (See: Sun, Lafayette) – Orinda, CA. 1973-80 – 15r – 1 – $750.00 – B02559 – us Library Micro [071]

SUN – (Set incl. East Side Post (Portland)) – Portland, OR. -w. 6 Jan 1950-25 Oct 1951 – 1r – 1 – us U.O. Library [071]

SUN – Sheridan. Or. -w. 1901-07, 1908-62 – 1 – us UMI [071]

SUN – Solano Beach, CA. 1990 – 8+ r – 1 – $400.00 ($100.00y) – H04072 – us Library Micro [071]

SUN – Springfield. Ohio. 1894- – 1 – us UMI [071]

SUN – Sterling. Neb. 1890-1945 – 1 – us UMI [071]

SUN – Summit. Miss. 1941- – 1 – us UMI [071]

SUN – Tonopah, NV. May 1904-10 – 7r – 1 – $350.00 – U04771 – us Library Micro [071]

SUN – Utica. Neb. 1892-1955 – 1 – us UMI [071]

SUN – Wallowa. Or. -w. 1915-42 – 1 – us UMI [071]

SUN – Waukegan. Ill. 1898-1930 – 1 – us UMI [071]

SUN – Yuma. Ariz. -w. 1914-25, 1931 – 1 – us UMI [071]

SUN *see*
- SUN

THE SUN – Athelstan, Canada. v1 n1. 9 fev 1885-v3 n23. 3 nov 1887 – 1r – 1 – Can$45.00 – cn Can Microfilming [072]

THE SUN – Cape Town, South Africa.26 Aug 1932-28 Sept 1956. 23 reels – 1, 16 diazo available at reduced price – sa SA Libr [072]

THE SUN – Georgetown, Guyana. 12 Nov 1960-23 Dec 1961; 6-27 Jan 1962; 9 Mar 1963-23 Apr 1966 (imperfect) – 1r – 1 – uk British Libr Newspaper [072]

THE SUN – Jacksonville. Fl. Nov. 1905-Nov. 1906 – 1 – us P.K. Yonge [071]

THE SUN – London, 1801-76 – 257r – 1 – uk British Libr Newspaper [072]

THE SUN – Melbourne, Australia. 28 Jul 1893-24 Jun 1898 – 5r – 1 – uk British Libr Newspaper [072]

THE SUN – Montreal, Canada. v1 n19. 14 jun 1853 – 1r – 1 – Can$25.00 – cn Can Microfilming [072]

THE SUN – New York. Morning ed. 1833-1947 – 549r – 1 – us Ross [071]

THE SUN – New York. School pages. 1926-Jan 4 1950 – 1 – us NY Public [370]

THE SUN – New York. Sept 3 1833-Dec 1840; Jan 1870-Dec 1947 – 1 – us NY Public [071]

THE SUN – Red Oak. Iowa. 1885-1954 – 1 – us UMI [071]

THE SUN – St. John, Canada. -d. May 1907-March 1910. 15 1 2 reels – 1 – uk British Libr Newspaper [072]

THE SUN – St. John's, Antigua. 27 Mar 1911-17 Nov 1916; 11 Feb-24 Apr 1918; 16 Jun-17 Dec 1919; 10 Feb-30 Apr, 28 Oct 1920 (imperfect).-d. 8 reels – 1 – uk British Libr Newspaper [072]

THE SUN – Sydney, Australia. 1 Jul 1910-26 Aug 1919; 13 Oct 1919-30 Jun 1922; 1 Jan 1952-27 Oct 1954.-d. 98 reels – 1 – uk British Libr Newspaper [072]

SUN AND ADVERTISER – Halifax, Canada. 1862-67 – 6r – 1 – $390.00 – cn Library Assoc [971]

SUN AND KING WILLIAM'S TOWN GAZETTE – King William's Town, South Africa. 9 Dec 1874-7 Aug 1875. 1 reel – 1, 16 diazo available at reduced price – sa SA Libr [072]

SUN AND NORTH BEND NEWS – North Bend OR. July 6 1967-Sep 25 1969 – 1 – us U.O. Library [071]

SUN AT WORK IN BRITAIN – 1974- – 5,6,9 – us UMI [621]

SUN BEAM – Kenesaw. Neb. and Kenesaw Progress. 1914-38 – 1 – us UMI [071]

THE SUN BEAM – Toronto: [s.n. 1892-189- or 19–] – 9 – cn C.I.H.M. [240]

SUN BRITISH COLUMBIA DIRECTORY, 1934 – Vancouver, BC: Sun Directories, 1934 – 2r – 1 – Can$70.00r – cn U.B.C. Preserve [971]

SUN CITY NEWS – Sun City, CA. 1962-93 – 48r – 1 – $2,400.00 – R03020 – us Library Micro [071]

SUN CITY WEEK – Sun City, CA. 1990 – 1+ r – 1 – $50.00 ($50.00y) – R04126 – us Library Micro [071]

SUN ENTERPRISE – Monmouth, OR. 16 May 1979+ – 1 – us U.O. Library [071]

Sun Grain Association. Risingsun, Ohio *see* RECORDS

Sun, Hui-lan *see* NEW PARENTS (CCC227)

SUN INSURANCE FIRE POLICY REGISTERS AND THE ROYAL EXCHANGE ASSURANCE RECORDS / Guildhall Library, London – (Microfiche index is available for £130.00) – 1775-87. 80 reels with printed guide – £2,995.00 – uk World [332]

SUN MOUNTAIN SENTINEL – Virginia City, NV. 1964-65 – 1r – 1 – $50.00 – U04796 – us Library Micro [071]

SUN NEWS – North Bend OR. Oct 2 1969-Apr 30 1970 – 1 – us U.O. Library [071]

SUN NEWS-PICTORIAL – Melbourne, Australia. -d. 1 Jan 1969-27 Nov 1970. 21 reels – 1 – uk British Libr Newspaper [072]

THE SUN OF SARATOGA: A ROMANCE OF BURGOYNE'S SURRENDER / Altsheler, Joseph Alexander – New York: D. Appleton, 1897. 00927. (Pre-1900 Canadiana) – 9 – cn C.I.H.M. [971]

SUN POST – Lakewood. Ohio. 1966- – 1 – us UMI [071]

SUN SENTINEL – Pompano Beach. Fl. 1960- – 1 – us UMI [071]

SUN SHOPPER – Coachella, CA. 1971-1977 – 2r – 1 – $100.00 – R03185 – us Library Micro [071]

SUN SUPERIOR EXPRESS – Superior. Neb. 1895-1961 – 1 – us UMI [071]

The Sun. Synod (United Pres. Ch. in the U.S.A.) *see* MINUTES, 1972-1974

SUN TIMES – (Cont: The Times) – Morgan Hill, CA. 1901-30 – 9 – 1 – $450.00 – B02490 – us Library Micro [071]

Sun Yat-San Institute for Advancement of Culture and Education *see* CHUNG-SHAN WEN-HUA CHIAO-YU-KUAN CHI-K'AM

SUN ZHONGSHAN YU XINHAI GEMING SHILIAO ZHUANJI – Special collection of historical materials: Sun Yat-Sen and the Revolution of 1911. Comp. by the Research Office of Historical and Literary Materials, Guangdong province.4 fiches. F-H103 – 9 – $18.00 – cc Microforms [950]

SUN-ADVERTISER – Mountain View, CA. 1973-75 – 3r – 1 – $150.00 – B02503 – us Library Micro [071]

SUNAN KALIDJAGA / Jogjakarta. Indonesia. Institut Agama Islam Negeri – Progress Report, 1385-1387, 1965-67. 39p. BSE-6491/1 – 9 – ne IDC [959]

Sunardhi Shs *see* KOPERASI RAKJAT DESA (K.R.D.) PRIMER

Sunardjo Haditjaroko *see* RAMAYANA; OUR NATIONAL READER

Sunaria, R M *see* ICHTISAR RINGKAS TENTANG RIWAJAT SOSIAL-EKONOMIS INDONESIA

Sunaria, Sanyatavijaya Kalapaking *see* PEMANDANGAN SOCIOLOGISCH TENTANG PEROBAHAN DALAM MASJARAKAT

Sunarko, R *see* DASAR-DASAR UMUM TATANEGARA

Sunarno, Sisworahardjo *see* TAPAKING TEPA-TULUS; ANDARAN NGELMU KASAMPURNAN TJUNDUKE LAN NGELMU KALAHIRAN MINANGKA PANGGAJUH KARAHAJON

Sunarto Hadiwidjojo, R *see* SEWINDU PEMBANGUNAN DESA. CIVIL ADMINISTRATION AND EIGHT YEARS OF VILLAGE ADMINISTRATION

THE SUNBEAM – (Cont by: Playmate) – Toronto: Methodist Book and Pub. House, [1880-1906] – 9 – cn C.I.H.M. [240]

THE SUNBEAM – Montreal, Canada. v1 n2. dec 1891; v2 n2. dec 1892 – 1r – 1 – Can$25.00 – cn Can Microfilming [072]

SUNBEAM RECORDS / Taylor, George Baxton – 1887-96.195p – 1 – 6.82 – us Baptist [240]

SUN-BULLETIN – Binghamton. N.Y. 1957- – 1 – us UMI [071]

SUN-BULLETIN – Morro Bay, CA. 1949- – 90+ r – 1 – $4,500.00 ($100.00y) – H04053 – us Library Micro [071]

THE SUNBURY AMERICAN – Sunbury, PA. -w 1850-92; 1899-1901. 10 rolls – 13 – $25.00r – us I.M.R. [071]

SUNBURY AMERICAN AND SHAMOKIN JOURNAL / ed by Stuckenberg, John Henry Wilburn – Sunbury, PA. -w 1840-50. 3 rolls – 13 – $25.00r – us I.M.R. [071]

THE SUNBURY DAILY – Sunbury, PA. -d 1873-1903. 3 rolls – 13 – $25.00r – us I.M.R. [071]

SUNBURY GAZETTE – Sunbury, PA. -w 1844-1876. 7 rolls – 13 – $25.00r – us I.M.R. [071]

SUNBURY GAZETTE AND AMERICAN – Sunbury, PA., 1876-1879 – 13 – $25.00r – us I.M.R. [071]

SUNBURY GAZETTE AND MINER'S REGISTER – Sunbury, PA. 1838-44. 1 roll – 13 – $25.00r – us I.M.R. [071]

SUNBURY NEWS – 1892-1910. SN1-5 – 5r – 1 – at Corangamite [072]

THE SUNBURY WEEKLY NEWS – Sunbury, PA. -w 1881-92 – 3 rolls – 13 – $25.00r – us I.M.R. [071]

SUN-COMMERCIAL – Vincennes. Ind. 1964- – 1 – us UMI [071]

SUNDAN DAILY HERALD – (1941 very imperfect) – Khartoum, Sudan. 3 Jan 1941-30 Mar 1952 – 18r – 1 – uk British Libr Newspaper [072]

SUNDAY ADVERTISER – Boston. Mass. 1952- – 1 – us UMI [071]

SUNDAY CHRONICLE – Los Angeles, CA. 1987 – 6+ r – 1 – $300.00 ($50.00y) – R04065 – us Library Micro [071]

SUNDAY CITIZEN AND REYNOLDS NEWS – (Issues for sep 23-dec 1962 filmed with: Reynolds News and Sunday Citizen. jan-sep 16 1962. Issues for jan-feb 14 1965 filmed with: Sunday Citizen (London, 1965)) – London: Cooperative Press Ltd, sep 23 1962-feb 14 1965 – us Res Libr [072]

SUNDAY COURIER – Evansville. Ind. and Journal. 1931-34 – 1 – us UMI [071]

SUNDAY COURIER – Poughkeepsie. N.Y. 1872-1942 – 1 – us UMI [071]

SUNDAY CRITIC – Logansport. Ind. 1884-1886 – 1 – us UMI [071]

SUNDAY DEMOCRAT – Flint. Mich. 1876-1885 – 1 – us UMI [071]

SUNDAY DISPATCH – Providence. R.I. 1882-1883 – 1 – us UMI [071]

THE SUNDAY EPISTLES SIMPLY EXPLAINED. FOREWORD BY...LONDON / Messenguer, E – Burgos: Razon y Fe, 1938 – 1 – sp Bibl Santa Ana [240]

SUNDAY EXPONENT TELEGRAM – Clarksburg. West Virginia. 1952-1962 – 1 – us UMI [071]

SUNDAY EXPRESS – 1960-74 – 1 – us UMI [073]

SUNDAY EXPRESS – Lagos, Nigeria. 8 Nov-27 Dec 1959; 8 Jan-26 Nov 1961; 6 Jan 1963-17 Jan, 11 Apr-21 Nov 1965 (imperfect) – 4r – 1 – uk British Libr Newspaper [072]

SUNDAY EXPRESS – London, 1919-67; 1986- – 102+ r – 1 – uk British Libr Newspaper [072]

SUNDAY EXPRESS – London, Great Britain – 1960- 1; 1975- 5,6,9 – us UMI [072]

SUNDAY EXPRESS *see*
- POPULAR NEWSPAPERS DURING WORLD WAR 1
- POPULAR NEWSPAPERS DURING WORLD WAR 2

SUNDAY GAZETTE – Atlantic City. N.J. 1891-1921 – 1 – us UMI [071]

SUNDAY GLEANER – Kingston, Jamaica. Jan 1958-Dec 1961 – 10r – 1 – uk British Libr Newspaper [072]

SUNDAY GRAPHIC – 1927-1946 – 1 – uk Manchester Libr [072]

SUNDAY HERALD – London, UK. 1920. -w. 1 reel – 1 – uk British Libr Newspaper [072]

SUNDAY HERALD – Montreal, Jl1913-1913De – 1r – 1 – cn Preston [971]

SUNDAY INDEPENDENT – 1906-1980 – 103r – 1 – ie Microforms [941]

SUNDAY INDEPENDENT – Ireland.-d. 1906- – 1 – PS27.50r – ie European Micro [072]

SUNDAY INDEPENDENT – Santa Monica, CA. 1952-1958 – 4r – 1 – $200.00 – R03525 – us Library Micro [071]

SUNDAY JOURNAL – Napa. Calif. -w. 1950-56 – 1 – us UMI [071]

SUNDAY JOURNAL – Utica. N.Y. 1894-1902 – 1 – us UMI [071]

SUNDAY LEGISLATION : ITS HISTORY TO THE PRESENT TIME AND ITS RESULTS / Lewis, Abram Herbert – New York: D. Appleton, 1902 – 1mf – us A.T.L.A. [340]

"SUNDAY LOLLIPOPS" – [Toronto?: s.n. 1875?-18–?] – 9 – cn C.I.H.M. [240]

SUNDAY MAGAZINE – St. Louis. 5 Mar 1905-11 Apr 1915 (imperfect).-w. 10 reels – 1 – uk British Libr Newspaper [071]

SUNDAY MAIL – Harare, Zimbabwe (Formerly Salisbury, Rhodesia). 1 Jun 1950- – 106r – 1 – sa Microfile [960]

SUNDAY MERCURY – Philadelphia, PA. -w 1866-1876 – 13 – $25.00r – us I.M.R. [071]

SUNDAY MERCURY – Portland, OR. 1889-90. Incomplete – 1 – 17.00 – us Oregon Hist [071]

SUNDAY MERCURY – Portland OR. July 8 29 1883, Nov 9 23 1889, June 4 7 21 1931 + – 1 – us U.O. Library [071]

THE SUNDAY MERCURY – New York. Oct 10 1841; Apr 10 1859-Nov 13 1870; June 18 1876-Feb 14 1892. Not collated – 1 – us NY Public [071]

SUNDAY MIRROR – Singapore. -w. 18 Nov 1928-28 Apr 1929. (39 ft) – 1 – uk British Libr Newspaper [072]

THE SUNDAY MORNING – Montreal, Canada. 24 avr 1892-v1 n5. 22 mai 1892 – 1r – 1 – Can$25.00 – cn Can Microfilming [072]

SUNDAY MORNING BEE – North Bend OR. Jan 23-July 10 1926 – 1 – us U.O. Library [071]

SUNDAY MORNING CALL – Atchison. Kan. 1880-1883 – 1 – us UMI [071]

SUNDAY MORNING CALL – Battle Creek. Mich. 1884-1886 – 1 – us UMI [071]

SUNDAY MORNING TRANSCRIPT – Providence. R.I. 1881-1884 – 1 – us UMI [071]

SUNDAY NEWS – Bulawayo, Rhodesia. 1 Jun 1950- – 64r – 1 – sa Microfile [960]

SUNDAY NEWS – Dar-es-Salaam, Tanzania. -w. 7 Nov 1954-1 Jan 1969. 27 reels – 1 – uk British Libr Newspaper [072]

SUNDAY NEWS – Kuala Lumpur. Malaysia. -w. 18 Nov 1945-27 Jul 1947. (1 reel) – 1 – uk British Libr Newspaper [072]

SUNDAY NEWS – Lancaster. Pa. 1923-1940; 1946- – 1 – us UMI [071]

SUNDAY NEWS – Lancaster, PA., 1951 – 13 – $25.00r – us I.M.R. [071]

SUNDAY NEWS : MAPLE RIDGE, NORTH BURNABY, PORT MOODY, PORT COQUITLAM, PITT MEADOWS – British Columbia, CN. 1985-89 – 18r – 1 – cn Commonwealth Micro [072]

SUNDAY NEWS – Sydney, Australia. 18 Jan 1920-25 Jun 1922.-w. 25 reels – 1 – uk British Libr Newspaper [072]

SUNDAY NEWS – Wilkes Barre. Pa. 1884-1899 – 1 – us UMI [071]

SUNDAY OBSERVER – (Dublin Observer). Dublin. Ireland. -w. 11 Dec 1831-16 Jan 1836. (6 reels) – 1 – uk British Libr Newspaper [072]

SUNDAY PATRIOT-NEWS – Harrisburg. Pa. 1949- – 1 – us UMI [071]

SUNDAY PIONEER – Lucknow, India. -w. 6 Jan 1952-10 Jan 1954; 21 July 1957-27 Dec 1959; 3 July 1960-Dec 1975. 21 reels – 1 – uk British Libr Newspaper [072]

SUNDAY POST – Lagos, Nigeria. -w. Jan 1963-Dec 1965. 2 reels – 1 – uk British Libr Newspaper [072]

SUNDAY PRESS – 1978-1980 – 24r – 1 – ie Microforms [941]

SUNDAY PRESS – Asbury Park. N.J. 1920- – 1 – us UMI [071]

SUNDAY PRESS – Atlantic City. N.J. 1891- – 1 – us UMI [071]

SUNDAY PRESS – Ireland.-d. 1978- – 1 – PS27.50r – ie European Micro [072]

SUNDAY RAMPARTS – San Francisco, CA. 1966-67 – 1r – 1 – $50.00 – C02856 – us Library Micro [071]

SUNDAY RECORD – Independence OR. Apr 21-May 12 1895 – 1 – us U.O. Library [071]

SUNDAY REGISTER – Sandusky. Ohio. 1884-98 – 1 – us UMI [071]

THE SUNDAY SCHOOL BANNER – v27-32. 1937-42 (incomplete) – 1r – 1 – ATLA 1994-S037 – us A.T.L.A. [073]

SUNDAY SCHOOL BUILDER – 1912-61. (Superintendent's Quarterly. 1912-20) – 1 – 941.85 – us Baptist [240]

SUNDAY SCHOOL EXTENSION QUARTERLY – 1959-61 – 1 – 22.54 – us Baptist [240]

SUNDAY SCHOOL GUARDIAN – Toronto: Wesleyan-Methodist Book Room, [1846?-1854] – 9 – cn C.I.H.M. [240]

SUNDAY SCHOOL HELPER – St. John, N.B.: [s.n. 1891?-189- or 19–] – 9 – cn C.I.H.M. [240]

SUNDAY SCHOOL HYMNBOOK – 19th ed. 1827 – 1 – 5.00 – us Baptist [240]

SUNDAY SCHOOL INTERMEDIATE PUPIL – 1930-61. Formerly Intermediate Quarterly, 1930-49. 5,764p – 1 – 201.74 – us Baptist [240]
SUNDAY SCHOOL LESSONS FOR THE DEAF – 1957-61 – 1 – 28.21 – us Baptist [240]
THE SUNDAY SCHOOL MAN OF THE SOUTH / McCullagh, Joseph H – 1889 – 1 – 6.86 – us Baptist [240]
SUNDAY SCHOOL MARRIED YOUNG PEOPLE – 1956-61 – 1 – $38.99 – us Baptist [306]
SUNDAY SCHOOL STATISTICS / Texas Baptist Association – Information from each association in the State, 1891-93. 301p – 1 – 10.53 – us Baptist [240]
SUNDAY SCHOOL TIMES – 1-109. 1859-1967 – 1 – us UMI [240]
THE SUNDAY SCHOOL UNION, ITS HISTORY AND WORK / Watson, William H – 1781-1854 – 1 – 7.98 – us Baptist [240]
SUNDAY SCHOOL YOUNG ADULTS – 1956-61 – 1 – $38.71 – us Baptist [240]
SUNDAY SCHOOL YOUNG PEOPLE – 1915-61. (Formerly: Advanced Quarterly. 1915-35; Sunday School Young People's Quarterly. 1936-56) – 1 – 242.34 – us Baptist [240]
SUNDAY SCHOOL YOUNG PEOPLE AND ADULTS – 1919-44. (Formerly: The Organized Class. 1919-20) – 1 – 355.32 – us Baptist [240]
SUNDAY STAR – Wilmington. Del. 1881-1954 – 1 – us UMI [071]
SUNDAY STATESMAN – India. 1939-1952 – 1 – uk British Libr Newspaper [072]
SUNDAY SUN – Sydney, Australia. (Sunday edition of The Sun). 26 Dec 1909-25 Jun 1922.-w. 25 reels – 1 – uk British Libr Newspaper [072]
THE SUNDAY SUN – Baltimore. Md. 1927-1937 – 1 – us UMI [071]
SUNDAY TELEGRAM – Elmira. N.Y. 1880-1899; 1903-1921; 1924-1950 – 1 – us UMI [071]
SUNDAY TELEGRAM – Newburgh. N.Y. 1889-1915 – 1 – us UMI [071]
SUNDAY TELEGRAM – Portland. Maine. -w. 1892-1946 – 1 – us UMI [071]
SUNDAY TELEGRAM – Providence. R.I. 1878-1879; 1882-1885 – 1 – us UMI [071]
SUNDAY TELEGRAPH – 1962-1973 – 1 – F1,877.00 – sz Infoprint [072]
SUNDAY TELEGRAPH – Feb 1961-Dec – 1 – F1,877.00 – sz Infoprint [072]
SUNDAY TELEGRAPH – London. -w. 1961-67. (18 reels) – 1 – uk British Libr Newspaper [072]
THE SUNDAY TELEGRAPH – London. 1961- – 1 – us Primary [072]
SUNDAY TELEPHONE – Barnsley, England. Barnsley Monthly Telephone. -m. July-Nov 1900. 12 ft – 1 – uk British Libr Newspaper [072]
SUNDAY: THE MAGAZINE FOR THE LORD'S DAY – (1986- . 5,6,9) – v55- . 1969- – 1 – us UMI [073]
SUNDAY TIMES – 1822-1925 – 1 – F873.00 – sz Infoprint [072]
SUNDAY TIMES – 1926-1939 – 1 – F1,528.00 – sz Infoprint [072]
SUNDAY TIMES – 1940-1952 – 1 – F873.00 – sz Infoprint [072]
SUNDAY TIMES – 1953-1957 – 1 – F1,528.00 – sz Infoprint [072]
SUNDAY TIMES – 1958 – 1 – F2,881.00 – sz Infoprint [072]
SUNDAY TIMES – 1959-1986 – 1 – F3,405.00 – sz Infoprint [072]
SUNDAY TIMES – 1987-1994 – 1 – F4,409.00 – sz Infoprint [072]
SUNDAY TIMES – Cumberland. Md. -w. 1925-31 – 1 – us UMI [071]
SUNDAY TIMES – Johannesburg, South Africa. 4 Mar 1906- – 512r – 1 – sa Microfile [960]
SUNDAY TIMES – Johannesburg, South Africa, 7 Jul 1922-27 Mar 1938 – 65r – 1,16 diazo available – sa SA Libr [960]
SUNDAY TIMES – Johannesburg. South Africa. -w. Jun 1914-Jun 1922. (16 reels) – 1 – uk British Libr Newspaper [072]
SUNDAY TIMES – Lafayette. Ind. 1895; 1898-1900; 1904-1905; 1914 – 1 – us UMI [071]
SUNDAY TIMES – London. -w. 1890-1927. (54 reels) – 1 – uk British Libr Newspaper [072]
SUNDAY TIMES – Perth, Australia. -w. 14 Nov 1915-28 Sept 1919; 28 Aug 1921-25 June 1922. 11 reels – 1 – uk British Libr Newspaper [072]
SUNDAY TIMES – Portland. Maine. 1890-99 – 1 – us UMI [071]
SUNDAY TIMES – Singapore, 1984- – 6r per y – 1 – inquire – us Ross [072]
SUNDAY TIMES – Subscription – 1 – F3,231.00 – sz Infoprint [072]
SUNDAY TIMES – Sydney, Australia. 20 Sep 1914-13 Jan 1929.-w. 34 reels – 1 – uk British Libr Newspaper [072]
SUNDAY TIMES – Toledo. Ohio. 1930-48 – 1 – us UMI [071]
SUNDAY TIMES – Trenton. N.J. and Advertiser. 1883- – 1 – us UMI [071]
THE SUNDAY TIMES – London. England. 1822- – 1 – us Primary [072]
THE SUNDAY TIMES – Oshkosh. Wis. 1967 – 1 – us UMI [071]
THE SUNDAY TIMES – Singapore. Jul 1957-63; 1965 – 9r – 1 – us L of C Photodup [072]
SUNDAY TIMES OF MALTA – Valletta, Malta. -w. 1941-52; 1954-72. 32 reels – 1 – uk British Libr Newspaper [072]
SUNDAY TIMES OF ZAMBIA – Formerly: Zambia News. Lusaka, Zambia. 7 Mar 1965-31 Dec 1972 – 12 rolls – 1 – sa Microfile [960]
SUNDAY TRANSCRIPT – (Library has: v.86,no.34-v.101,no.30; Mar. 25, 1934-Sept. 12, 1937; many issues are missing or mutilated) – Philadelphia, Pa.: Johnson, Greene & Co., 1847-1937. 101v – 1 – CSUX87-S430 – us Hoover Inst Photo [978]
SUNDAY TRIBUNE – (Now filmed with Daily News) – Durban, South Africa. 5 Jan 1969-26 May 1991 end – 155r – 1 – sa Microfile [960]
SUNDAY TRIBUNE – Utica. N.Y. 1877-1922 – 1 – us UMI [071]
SUNDAY VINDICATOR – Youngstown. Ohio. 1896-1916 – 1 – us UMI [071]
SUNDAY WELCOME – Portland OR. Dec 21 1879, May 7 1882, May 14 1927, June 28 1930 – 1 – us U.O. Library [071]
SUNDAY WORKER – London. -w. 15 Mar 1925-1 Dec 1929. (5 reels) – 1 – uk British Libr Newspaper [331]
SUNDAY WORKER – New York. N.Y. (Pa. edition). 1942-56 – 1 – us UMI [071]
SUNDAYS IN YOHO: TWELVE STORIES FOR CHILDREN AND THEIR FRIENDS / Campbell, Mary Helen – Montreal: W. Drysdale, 1884. 00391. (Pre-1900 Canadiana) – 9 – cn C.I.H.M. [830]
THE SUNDAY-SCHOOL : ITS ORIGIN, MISSION, METHODS, AND AUXILIARIES / Trumbull, Henry Clay – Philadelphia: J.D. Wattles, 1888 – 1mf – us A.T.L.A. [240]
SUNDAY-SCHOOL BANNER FOR TEACHERS AND YOUNG PEOPLE – Toronto: W Briggs, [1897?-1905?] – 9 – cn C.I.H.M. [240]
SUNDAY-SCHOOL CONVENTIONS: THEIR OBJECTS AND IMPORTANCE, AND THE BEST METHODS OF CONDUCTING THEM. TWO PRIZE ESSAYS / Bell, George – By George Bell and John Wood. Toronto: Lovell & Gibson, 1867. 05685. (Pre-1900 Canadiana) – 9 – cn C.I.H.M. [240]
THE SUNDAY-SCHOOL IN THE DEVELOPMENT OF THE AMERICAN CHURCH / Michael, Oscar S – Milwaukee: Young Churchman, 1904 – 1mf – us A.T.L.A. [370]
SUNDAY-SCHOOL MOVEMENTS IN AMERICA / Brown, Marianna C – New York: Fleming H. Revell, c1901 – 1mf – us A.T.L.A. [240]
SUNDAZ – (Includes index) – Santa Cruz, CA. Nov 1970-May 1976 – 6r – 1 – $300.00 – B02962 – us Library Micro [071]
SUNDBYBERGS OCH SOLNA TIDNING – Stockholm, Sweden. 1979-87 – 1 – sw Kungliga [072]
SUNDBYBERGS OCH SOLNA TIDNING – (Stockholms Forstadsblad, 1920-62. Sundybergs och Solna Tidning, 1962-78) – Stockholm, Sweden. 1900-19 – 77r – 1 – sw Kungliga [072]
SUN-DEMOCRAT – Paducah. Ky. 1949- – 1 – us UMI [071]
SUNDERLAND 1778-1908 – (Mf 1: Births 1686-1805; Deaths 1720-1806. Mf 1-2: Marriages 1720-1843. Mf 2: Births 1755-1803; Intentions 1789-1835. Mf 2: Earmarks. Mf 3-4: Births 1699-1862. Mf 4: Deaths 1721-1877. Mf 4-5: Out-of-Town Marriages 1720-99. Mf 5: Marriages 1720-1843. Mf 5: Unrecorded Intentions 1790-1822+. Mf 6-7: Births 1858-90. Mf 8-9: Marriages 1858-90. Mf 10-11: Deaths 1858-90) – (mf ed 1987) – 11mf – 0-931248-50-7 – us Holbrook [920]
SUNDERLAND AND DURHAM COUNTY HERALD – Tyne and Wear. 1839-51, 1853-67, 1869 and 1876 – 1 – uk Microform Academic [072]
SUNDERLAND BEACON – Tyne and Wear. 1838-39 – 1 – uk Microform Academic [072]
SUNDERLAND DAILY ECHO – England. -d. Dec 1873-Dec 1875, Jan 1880-Dec 1885. (16 reels) – 1 – uk British Libr Newspaper [072]
SUNDERLAND DAILY ECHO – Tyne and Wear – 50r – 1 – uk Microform Academic [072]
SUNDERLAND DAILY ECHO AND SHIPPING GAZETTE – 1 – uk Microform Academic [072]
SUNDERLAND ECHO – (After 1993 under Echo and Sports Echo) – Dec 22 1873-77; 1880-85; 1889; 1898; 1910; May 1911-Aug 1912; 1913-Mar 1915; May 1915-19; 1932-Jun 20 1959; Aug-Dec 1959; 1985-Jun 1993 – 305r – 1 – uk British Libr Newspaper [072]
SUNDERLAND ECHO *see* ECHO AND SPORTS ECHO
SUNDERLAND ECHO AND SHIPPING GAZETTE – England.1932-39. -d. 48 reels – 1 – uk British Libr Newspaper [072]
Sunderland, Edson Read *see* CASES ON COMMON LAW PLEADING. 2ND ED
SUNDERLAND HERALD AND DAILY POST – Tyne and Wear. 1894, 1895 and 1897 – 9r – 1 – uk Microform Academic [072]
SUNDERLAND LOCAL NEWSPAPERS – Tyne and Wear. 1831-32 – 1 – uk Microform Academic [072]
SUNDERLAND NEWS – England. -w. 5 Jul 1851-19 May 1855. (3 reels) – 1 – uk British Libr Newspaper [072]
SUNDERLAND TIMES – Tyne and Wear. 1868, 1870-76 – 9r – 1 – uk Microform Academic [072]
SUNDERLAND WEEKLY ECHO AND TIMES – Tyne and Wear. 1881-84 and 1894-96 – 9r – 1 – uk Microform Academic [072]
Sundevall, C *see* A HISTORY OF SCANDINAVIAN FISHES
Sundevall, C J *see*
– CONSPECTUM AVIUM PICINARUM
– METHODI NATURALIS AVIUM DISPONENDARUM TENTAMEN
Sundman, G et al *see* FINLANDS FISKAR
Sundquist, Robert D *see* THE COMPARATIVE EFFECTIVENESS OF STATIC STRETCHING AND PROPRIOCEPTIVE NEUROMUSCULAR FACILITATION STRETCHING TECHNIQUES IN INCREASING HIP FLEXION RANGE OF MOTION
SUNDRE ROUND-UP – Alberta. Canada. 1960-68 – 1 – cn Commonwealth Micro [072]
SUNDRY TRIALS – 13r – 1 – sa Microfile [960]
SUNDSVALLS DAGBLAD – Sundsvall, 1898-1902 – 9 – sw Kungliga [072]
SUNDSVALLS TIDNING – (Alfwar och Skamt, 1841-43; Nytt Allvar och Skamt, 1844-51; Norrlandska Korrespondenten, 1851-73; Sundsvalls Tidning Norrlandska Korrespondenten, 1873-79; Sundsvalls Tidning, 1880-1978) – Sundsvall, Sweden – 555r – 1 – sw Kungliga [072]
SUNDSVALLS TIDNING – Sundsvall, Sweden. 1979- – 1 – sw Kungliga [072]
SUNDSVALLS TIDNING NORRLANDSKA KORRESPONDENTEN *see* SUNDSVALLS TIDNING
SUNDSVALLSPOSTEN – Sundsvall, Sweden. 1859-1921 – 79r – 1 – sw Kungliga [072]
SUNDSVALLSPOSTEN – Sundsvall, Sweden. 1922-62 – 1 – sw Kungliga [072]
Sundt, Christine L *see* VISUAL RESOURCES
Sune Benagages, Juan *see* FRASEOLOGIA DE CERVANTES
SUN-EAGLE – Enid. Okl. -w. 1899-1900 – 1 – us UMI [071]
THE SUNFLOWER TOCSIN – Indianola. Miss. 1895-1897; 1915-1927 – 1 – us UMI [071]
SUNG CHI-SHA TSANG – A.D. 1231-1322 repr 1935 – 2,558mf – $1,100.00 – us I.A.S.W.R. [280]
Sung, Il-je *see* THINKING AND EDUCATION
SUN-HERALD – Colusa. Calif. 1933-1934; 1941-1944; 1949- – 1 – us UMI [071]
SUN-HERALD – Sydney, Australia. -d. 11 Oct 1953-Dec 1975. 117 reels – 1 – uk British Libr Newspaper [072]
Sunjana, P D B *see* DINKARD
SUN-JOURNAL – Brooksville. Fl. -w. 1935-42, 1946, 1948, Oct 1950- – 1 – us P.K. Yonge [071]
THE SUNKEN BELL. / Hauptmann, Gerhart – Trans. by C. M. Meltzer. New York, 1907 1 – us Res Libr [820]
SUNLAND – (Los Angeles). 1925 – 1 – us A.J.P.C. [071]
SUNNDAG UN WERDAG : GEDICHTE, SPRUECHE UND GESCHICHTEN IN ODENWAELDER MUNDART / Volk, Georg – Giessen: E Roth, [18–?] – 1r – 1 – us U.W. Library [390]
SUNNERBOTIDNINGEN – Vaxjo, Sweden. 1982-84 – 1 – sw Kungliga [072]
SUN-NEWS – Virginia Beach. Va. -w. 1956- – 1 – us UMI [071]
SUNNY SLOPE : SONGS AND STORIES / Morse, Annie E – New York: Nelson & Phillips; Cincinnati: Hitchcock & Waldon, c1866 – 1mf – 9 – 0-8370-7314-6 – 1986-1314 – us A.T.L.A. [240]
SUNNYSIDE GAZETTE – Portland, OR. -w. 18 Aug 1917-10 Apr 1943. 4 rolls – 1 – us U.O. Library [071]
SUNNYVALE STANDARD AND REGISTER LEADER – Sunnyvale, CA. 1908-09; 1913-24; 1929-31; 1935-66 – 99r – 1 BC03023 – $4,950.00 – us Library Micro [071]
SUNNYVALE/SANTA CLARA COUNTY – 1941 – 1r – 1 – $50.00 – P00135 – us Library Micro [910]
THE SUNOLIAN – Sunol, CA. 1981-1984 – 1r – 1 – $50.00 – B03544 – us Library Micro [071]
SUNRAYSIA DAILY – 1940-1978. SD1-140 – 155mf – at Corangamite [072]
SUNRISE – 1972- 1; 1975- 5,6,9 – us UMI [300]
SUNRISE: A STORY OF THESE TIMES / Black, William – British Fiction Archive: Unit 4 – 9 – uk Bell [830]
SUNRISE IN THE SUNRISE KINGDOM / Forest, J H de – (Includes index) – rev ed. New York: Missionary Educ Movt of the US and Canada, 1912, c1909 – 1mf – 9 – 0-8370-6486-4 – 1986-0486 – us A.T.L.A. [950]
THE SUNRISE KINGDOM : OR, LIFE AND SCENES IN JAPAN: AND WOMAN'S WORK FOR WOMAN THERE / Carrothers, Julia D – Philadelphia: Presbyterian Board of Publ, c1879 – 1mf – 9 – 0-8370-6169-5 – 1985-0169 – us A.T.L.A. [950]
SUNSET (CENTRAL EDITION) – (v. 144- 1970- 5,6. v. 146- 1971- 9) – v. 1- 1898- – 1 – us UMI [073]
SUNSET (DESERT EDITION) – (v. 146- 1971- 5,6. v. 150- 1973- 9) – v. 131- 1963- – 1 – us UMI [073]
SUNSET (PACIFIC NORTHWEST EDITION) – (v. 146- 1971- 5,6. v. 150- 1973- 9) – v. 124- 1932- – 1 – us UMI [073]
SUNSET SECOND BAPTIST CHURCH. PICKENS COUNTY. SUNSET, SOUTH CAROLINA : CHURCH RECORDS – 1795-1938, 1944-70 – 1 – 28.40 – us Baptist [240]
SUNSET (SOUTHERN CALIFORNIA/HAWAII EDITION) – (1971- 5,6. 1973- 9) – 1932- – 1 – us UMI [073]
SUNSETS ON THE HEBREW MOUNTAINS / Macduff, John Ross – New York: Robert Carter, 1862. 1 fiche – 9 – us A.T.L.A. [270]
SUNSHINE – (Cont by: Sunshine Magazine) – Montreal: Sun Life Assurance Company of Canada, [1896?-191-] – 9 – cn C.I.H.M. [360]
SUNSHINE – Paradise, NV. May 1906 – 1r – 1 – $50.00 – U04639 – us Library Micro [071]
SUNSHINE ADVOCATE – 1924-1970. SA1-28 – 28r – 1 – at Corangamite [072]
SUNSHINE AND HEALTH / American Sunbathing Association – May's Landing, NJ. v2-4. 1933-35 – 1r – 1 – us Ross [613]
SUNSHINE, FRUIT AND FLOWERS, SAN JOSE, CALIFORNIA / Shortridge, Charles – Santa Clara Co, 1896 – 1r – 1 – $50.00 – B40262 – us Library Micro [978]
SUNSHINE IN THOUGHT / Leland, Charles G – 1862 – 9 – $15.00 – us Scholars' Facs [190]
SUNSHINE MAGAZINE *see* SUNSHINE
SUNSHINE STATE AGRICULTURAL RESEARCH REPORT / Florida. Agricultural Experiment Station – v. 1-14. 1956-1969 – 1,5,6 – us Spaulding [630]
SUNSHINE STATE AGRICULTURAL RESEARCH REPORT / University of Florida. Agricultural Experiment Station – 15/1-23/1. 1970-79. 1 reel – 1, 5 – us Spaulding [630]

SUNSHINE VALLEY NEWS – Biggs, CA. 1910-16 – 2r – 1 – $100.00 – B02068 – us Library Micro [071]
SUN-STANDARD – Blue Island. Ill. 1918-1930; 1932-1967 – 1 – us UMI [071]
SUN-STANDARD – Chicago. Ill. -w. 1969- – 1 – us UMI [071]
SUN-STAR – Merced. Calif. 1938- – 1 – us UMI [071]
SUN-TATTLER – Hollywood. Fla. 1942- – 1 – us UMI [071]
SUN-TELEGRAPH – Pittsburgh. Pa. 1027-1960 – 1 – us UMI [071]
SUN-TIMES – Chicago, IL 1948- – 1 – us UMI [071]
SUN-TIMES INDEX – Chicago, IL 1979- – 1 – us UMI [071]
Suntornpithung, N *see* A STUDY OF THE EVALUATION OF TEACHER TRAINING IN THAILAND
SUNTRACKS – 1971-80.(American Indian Periodicals in the Princeton University Library). 11 fiches – 9 – $45.00 – us UPA [073]
SUN-UP AND OTHER POEMS / Ridge, Lola – New York: B.W. Huebsch, 1920. 93p – 1 – us U.W. Library [810]
SUNWORLD – v.1- 1976- – 5,6,9 – us UMI [073]
SUNYATSENIA : JOURNAL OF THE BOTANICAL INSTITUTE, COLLEGE OF AGRICULTURE SUN YATSEN UNIV – Canton, Hongkong. v1-7. 1930-48 – 33mf – 9 – 8150/1 – ne IDC [580]
SUOMALAISEN KIRJALLISUUDEN HISTORIA / Krohn, Julius – 2v, complete. 1883-84. About the Kalevala, the Finnish national epic – 1 – us I.U. Libraries [390]
SUOMEN KANSAN SATUJA JA TARINOITA / ed by Salmelainen, Eero – v1-4, complete. 1852-76. Finnish tales – 1 – us I.U. Libraries [390]
SUOMEN LAHETYSSANOMAT – (Some original pgs damaged) – 1970-90 – 6r – 1 – ATLA S0392 – us A.T.L.A. [073]
SUOMEN VIRALLINEN LEHTI / Finland – Helsinki. 1958-1967 – 1 – us NY Public [324]
SUOMEN VIRALLINEN LEHTI – Helsinki, 1968-69 – 3r – 1 – us Ross [072]
SUOMEN-SOSIALIDEMOKRAATTI – (In mf 1961-62) – Helsinki, 1939-41, 1946 (all incompl) – 1 – us Hoover Inst Photo [335]
Suomi, Rory *see* EFFECTS OF A LOWER LIMB STRENGTH TRAINING PROGRAM ON BALANCE MEASURES IN MEN WITH MENTAL RETARDATION
Supardi *see*
- ADJUR-ADJER
- HUTAN-REBOISASI MEMPERTINGGI KEMAKMURAN

Supardo *see*
- BUKU PELADJARAN EKONOMI UMUM AND INDONESIA
- MANUSIA DAN MASJARAKAT BARU INDONESIA (CIVICS)

Suparma, Satiadiredja *see* BETERNAK LEBAH
Suparto, R *see* KESESATAN HAKIM (RECHTERLIJKE DWALING)
SUPER 4 LIBROS SENTENTIARUM 1-2-3-4 + TABULAE 1-4 ET CENTILOGIUM THEOLOGICUM / Occam, Guillelmus de – Lyon, 1495-1496 – 31mf – 8 – ne Slangenburg [240]
Super, Charles William *see*
- BETWEEN HEATHENISM AND CHRISTIANITY
- A HISTORY OF THE GERMAN LANGUAGE

SUPER HEBDO DE L'ESTRIE *see* L'ESTRIEN REGIONAL
SUPERCONDUCTIVITY REVIEW / ed by Kumar, Pradeep – 1,5,9 – us Gordon [530]
SUPERCONDUCTOR SCIENCE AND TECHNOLOGY – v1-. 1988- – 1,5,6,9 – £244.00 – uk I.O.P. [530]
SUPERFICIES ET PRODUCTIONS, STATISTIQUES AGRICOLES / Algeria. Ministere de l'Agriculture – 17 v. in 5. 1959-70. (lacking 1961-63). BNE-8658 1 – 9 – ne IDC [630]
Superintendant Indian Museum *see* MEMOIRS OF THE INDIAN MUSEUM
SUPERINTENDENT VISITATION REC. / Fulton County, Ohio. York Township. Board of Education – 1893-1894 – 1r – 1 – $32.50r – us Archival [324]
SUPERINTENDENT'S ANNUAL NARRATIVE AND STATISTICAL REPORTS FROM FIELD JURISDICTIONS OF THE BUREAU OF INDIAN AFFAIRS / U.S. Bureau of Indian Affairs – 1907-38. 174 rolls. M1011 – 1 – us Nat'l Archives [324]
SUPERIOR COURT DECISIONS / Georgia – 2pts. 1842-1843 (all publ) – 5mf – 9 – $7.50 – LLMC 91-034 – us L.L.M.C. [340]
SUPERIOR DAILY JOURNAL – Superior, NE. Feb 1893; Oct 1895-Feb 1896; Apr 1896-Jun 1898; Jan 1899-Oct 1902 – 1 – us NE Hist [071]
SUPERIOR EXPRESS – Superior, NE. -w. Feb 1900-Feb 1902; Mar 1908 to date – 1 – us NE Hist [071]
SUPERIOR SUN – Superior, NE. -w. Nov 1895-Feb 1896; May 1896-Jul 1897; Dec 1897-Feb 1900 – 1 – us NE Hist [071]
SUPERIOR WEEKLY JOURNAL – Superior, NE. (-sw 1914). Mar 1892; Jul 1892; Jan-May 1895; Jul 1895-Jan 1951 – 1 – us NE Hist [071]
SUPERMAN – Issue Nos. 11-15 Jul 1941-Apr 1942 – 5mf – 15 – $31,95 – us Comics [760]
SUPERMAN – Issue Nos. 1-5 Summer 39-Summer 40 – 5mf – 15 – $31,95 – us Comics [760]
SUPERMAN – Issue Nos. 16-20 May 1942-Feb 1943 – 5mf – 15 – $31,95 – us Comics [760]
SUPERMAN – Issue Nos. 21-25 Mar 1943-Dec 1943 – 5mf – 15 – $31,95 – us Comics [760]
SUPERMAN – Issue Nos. 26-30 Jan 1944-Oct 1944 – 5mf – 15 – $31,95 – us Comics [760]
SUPERMAN – Issue Nos. 31-35 Nov 1944-Aug 1945 – 5mf – 15 – $31,95 – us Comics [760]
SUPERMAN – Issue Nos. 36-40 Sept 1945-May 1946 – 5mf – 15 – $31,95 – us Comics [760]
SUPERMAN – Issue Nos. 41-45 Jul 1946-Apr 1947 – 5mf – 15 – $31,95 – us Comics [760]
SUPERMAN – Issue Nos. 46-50 May 1947-Feb 1948 – 5mf – 15 – $31,95 – us Comics [760]
SUPERMAN – Issue Nos. 51-55 Mar 1948-Dec 1948 – 5mf – 15 – $31,95 – us Comics [760]
SUPERMAN – Issue Nos. 56-60 Jan 1949-Oct 1949 – 5mf – 15 – $31,95 – us Comics [760]
SUPERMAN – Issue Nos. 6-10 Sept 1940-Jun 1941 – 5mf – 15 – $31,95 – us Comics [760]
SUPERMAN – Issue Nos. 61-65 Nov-Dec 1949-Jul-Aug 1950 – 5mf – 15 – $31.95 – us Comics [760]
SUPERMAN – Issue Nos. 66-70 Sep-Oct 1950-May-June 1951 – 5mf – 15 – $31.95 – us Comics [760]
SUPERMAN – Issue Nos. 71-75 Jul-Aug 1951-Mar-Apr 1952 – 5mf – 15 – $31.95 – us Comics [760]
SUPERMAN – Issue Nos. 76-80 May-Jun 1952-Jan-Feb 1953 – 5mf – 15 – $31.95 – us Comics [760]
SUPERMAN – Issue Nos. 81-85 Mar-Apr 1953-Nov-Dec 1953 – 5mf – 15 – $31.95 – us Comics [760]
SUPERMAN – Issue Nos. 86-90 Jan 1954-Jul 1954 – 5mf – 15 – $31.95 – us Comics [760]
SUPERMAN – Issue Nos. 91-95 Aug 1954-Feb 1955 – 5mf – 15 – $31.95 – us Comics [760]
SUPERMAN – Issue Nos. 96-100 Mar 1955-Sept 1955 – 5mf – 15 – $31.95 – us Comics [760]
SUPERMARKET NEWS – New York, 1953- – 1 – $175.00y – us Fairchild Micro [650]
THE SUPERNATURAL : AN ADDRESS DELIVERED BEFORE THE ALUMNI OF BANGOR THEOLOGICAL SEMINARY, MAY 18, 1898, ON "THE RELATION OF NATURE AND THE SUPERNATURAL TO THE CHRISTIAN THOUGHT OF TODAY" / Abbott, Lyman – NY: Harold J Howland, 1899 – 1mf – 9 – 0-8370-2028-X – 1985-0028 – us A.T.L.A. [210]
SUPERNATURAL: AN ADDRESS / Abbott, Lyman – New York: Harold J. Howland, 1899. 1 fiche – 9 – us A.T.L.A. [130]
SUPERNATURAL ELEMENT IN OUR LORD'S EARTHLY LIFE / Chase, Frederic Henry – London: Macmillan, 1903.1 fiche – 9 – us A.T.L.A. [240]
THE SUPERNATURAL FACTOR IN RELIGIOUS REVIVALS / Townsend, Luther Tracy – Boston: Lee and Shepard, 1877 – 1mf – us A.T.L.A. [210]
THE SUPERNATURAL GIFTS OF THE SPIRIT / Erskine, Thomas; ed by Carter, R Kelso – Philadelphia, Pa.: Office of "Words of Faith", 1883 – 1mf – us A.T.L.A. [210]
THE SUPERNATURAL IN CHRISTIANITY : WITH SPECIAL REFERENCE TO STATEMENTS IN THE RECENT GIFFORD LECTURES / Rainy, Robert – Edinburgh: T & T Clark; New York: Charles Scribner [distributor], 1894 – 1mf – 9 – 0-8370-4831-1 – 1985-2831 – us A.T.L.A. [240]
THE SUPERNATURAL IN RELATION TO THE NATURAL / McCosh, James – New York:Robert Carter, 1862 – 1mf – 9 – 0-8370-4347-6 – 1985-2347 – us A.T.L.A. [230]
SUPERNATURAL RELIGION: AN INQUIRY INTO THE REALITY OF DIVINE REVELATION / Cassels, Walter Richard – 6th ed. Toronto, Chicago: Rose-Belford Pub. Co., 1879. 1115p – 1 – us U.W. Library [130]
SUPERNATURAL REVELATION, OR, FIRST PRINCIPLES OF MORAL THEOLOGY / Birks, Thomas Rawson – London: Macmillan, 1879.1 fiche – 9 – us A.T.L.A. [130]
LA SUPERSTICION DEL DIVORCIO / Chesterton, GK – Madrid: Razon y Fe, 1932 – 1 – sp Bibl Santa Ana [390]
SUPERSTICIONES EXTREMENAS. PROLOGO DE URBANO GONZALEZ SERRANO / Hurtado de Mendoza, Publio – Caceres: Tip. Enc. y Lib. de Jimenez, 1902 – 1 – sp Bibl Santa Ana [946]
SUPERVISION – v35- 1,5,6; v38- 9 – us UMI [650]
SUPERVISION IN DER STATIONAEREN ALTENPFLEGE – UEBERLEGUNGEN ZUR SICHERUNG DER PFLEGEQUALITAET / Tempels, Holger – 1994 – 2mf – DM80.00 – 3-8267-2012-1 – gw Hänsel [360]
SUPERVISOR NURSE – (1972-81. 1,5,6,9) – v1-12. 1970-81 – 1 – us UMI [073]
SUPERVISORY MANAGEMENT – v1- 1955- 1; v15- 5,6; v20- 9 – us UMI [650]
SUPER-ZEITUNG – Berlin, may 2 1991-jul 24 1992 – 5r – 1 – Inquire at Mikrofilmarchiv for details – gw Misc Inst [072]
SUPER-ZEITUNG – Berlin-Ost, 1991-1992 – 5r – 1 – DM375.00 – gw Mikro Press [943]
Suphan, Bernhard *see* HERDERS SAEMMTLICHE WERKE
SUPHAPBURUT – Bangkok, Thailand. 1946-49 – 7r – 1 – us L of C Photodup [072]
Suphawibul, M *see* COMPETENCIES FOR ADAPTED PHYSICAL EDUCATORS IN THAILAND
Supjan, Iskandar *see* PITUDUH PAWULANG BASA
SUPLEMENTO A LA QUINOLOGIA, EN EL QUAL SE AUMENTAN LAS ESPECIES DE QUINA NUEVAMENTE DESCUBIERTAS EN EL PERU... / Ruiz Lopez, Hipolito & Pavon y Jimenez, Jose Antonio – Madrid, 1801 – 2mf – 9 – ne IDC [580]
SUPLEMENTO AL ARTICULO DE TRIGUEROS / Sempere y Guarinos, Juan – 1790 – 9 – 1.50f – sp Bibl Santa Ana [946]
SUPLEMENTO DOMINICAL DE EL NACIONAL – Mexico City, MX. 1947-1968 – 15r – $750.00 – R04224 – us Library Micro [072]
SUPLEMENTO LITERARIO DO ESTADO DE S. PAULO – (Suppl to: O Estado de Sao Paulo) – Sao Paulo, Oct 1956-Dec 1980 – 1,5,6 – bl Biblioteca [072]
SUPLEMENTO LITERARIO DO ESTADO DE S. PAULO. JORNAL CORRENTE *see* O ESTADO DE S. PAULO
SUPLEMENTO LITERARIO DO MINAS GERAIS – (Cont of: Jornal Corrente) – Minas Gerais, Sep-Dec 1966- – 1,5,6 – bl Biblioteca [072]
SUPLEMENTO...GRAMATICA DE ANTONIO DE NEBRIJA / Leon, Juan Manuel – 1837 – 9 – 1.50f – sp Bibl Santa Ana [440]
SUPLICA GENERAL Y ULTIMA QUE INSINUA A LA...VILLA DE MADRID...(SOBRE LA LIMONA) / Belvis Trejo, A – SL, SA – 1mf – 9 – sp Cultura [946]
SUPLICA QUE HIZO AL REY LA PROVINCIA DE EXTREMADURA SOBRE EL PLEITO CON LOS GANADORES TRASUMANTES / Paino y Hurtado, Vicente – S.L., s.i., s.a. – 1 – sp Bibl Santa Ana [946]
Supomo *see*
- THE BANDUNG CONFERENCE FROM THE HISTORICAL POINT OF VIEW
- HUBUNGAN ANTARA INTENSITY DAN DJARAK EPICENTER
- INDONESIA FACING PROBLEMS OF NEW LIFE AND REINTEGRATION
- PETUNDJUK PRACTICUM KIMIA UNTUK S.P.M.A

Supomo Pudjosudarmo *see* INDONESIAN INFLUENCE ON JAVANESE
Suponev, N A *see* ZADACHI KOOPERATSII
SUPPLEMENT A LA PREMIERE EDITION DU MANUEL LEXIQUE / Prevost, Abbe – 1755 – 9 – fr I.C.S. [440]
SUPPLEMENT AU CONTRAT SOCIAL / Gudin de la Brenellerie, Paul P – Paris, Maradan et Perlet. 1791 – 9 – fr Hachette [190]
SUPPLEMENT AU DICTIONNAIRE CHINOIS-LATIN DU P. BASILE DE GLEMONA... / Klaproth, J H – Paris, 1819 – 5mf – ne IDC [480]
SUPPLEMENT AU DICTIONNAIRE DE L'ACADEMIE FRANCAISE / Raymond, F – 6E ED. 1836 – 9 – fr I.C.S. [440]
SUPPLEMENT AU DICTIONNAIRE DES LANGUES FRANCAISE ET ALLEMANDE DE L'ABBE MOZIN / Peschier, A – 1863 – 9 – fr I.C.S. [440]
SUPPLEMENT AU GRAND DICTIONNAIRE HISTORIQUE, GENEALOGIQUE, GEOGRAPHIQUE, ETC.. / Moreri, Louis – Paris: Jacques Vincent. SEM35P203 – 1r – 1 – Can$63.00 – cn Bibl Nat [900]
SUPPLEMENT AU "PIONNIER" : DISCOURS DE L'HON. ADOLPHE CHAPLEAU RE: VENTE DU CHEMIN DE FER QMOO – Sherbrooke, 27/28 mar 1882 – 1r – 1 – Can$20.00 – cn Can Microfilming [072]
SUPPLEMENT AU TRAITTE DES AYDES – Paris. 1643. 523p. (Historical Studies Series) – 9 – 18.00 – fr Bibl Nationale [900]
SUPPLEMENT AUX DICTIONNAIRES DES SCIENCES, DES ARTS ET DES METIERS – 2nd ed. 4v. 1778-79 – 2r – 1 – $150.00 – us OmniSys [500]
SUPPLEMENT AUX ERREURS DE VOLTAIRE OU REFUTATION COMPLETE DE SON TRAITE SUR LA TOLERANCE / Loisson, H M – Liege. J. Tutot. Paris. Valade. 1779 – 9 – fr Hachette [190]
SUPPLEMENT AUX LIVRES D'HEURES : MANUSCRITS DE LA BIBLIOTHEQUE NATIONALE / Leroquais, Victor – (Planches, 2mf) – Macon, 1943 – 3mf – 8 – Dfl22.00 – ne Slangenburg [240]
A SUPPLEMENT INDEX TO PASSENGER LISTS OF VESSELS ARRIVING AT ATLANTIC AND GULF COAST PORTS (EXCLUDING NEW YORK), 1820-74 / U.S. Bureau of the Customs – 188 rolls. M334. Printed guide – 5 – us Nat'l Archives [324]
THE SUPPLEMENT TO ENGLISH BOTANY / Sowerby, J – 7727 1. 4v. plus part of v5. 1831-1865 – 9 – ne IDC [580]
SUPPLEMENT TO "NOTES OF MY LIFE" 1879, AND "MR. GLADSTONE", 1886 / Denison, George Anthony – Oxford: James Parker, 1893 – 1mf – us A.T.L.A. [240]
SUPPLEMENT TO SELECTIONS OF CHINA MAINLAND MAGAZINES / U.S. Consulate General. Hong Kong – 1965-21 Oct 1969 – 1 – $35.00 – us L of C Photodup [950]
SUPPLEMENT TO SURVEY OF CHINA MAINLAND PRESS / U.S. Consulate General. Hong Kong – 1960-69; 1970- – 1 – $128.00 – us L of C Photodup [950]
SUPPLEMENT TO THE HYMN BOOK FOR THE USE OF TEMPLE EMANU-EL / Spicker, Max – New York: Temple Emanu-El, 1906.1 fiche – 9 – us A.T.L.A. [780]
SUPPLEMENT TO THE MONTHLY BULLETIN OF STATISTICS : DEFINITIONS AND EXPLANATORY NOTES / United Nations – 1948; 1950; 1954 and 1963 – E.17 F.15 – 9 – us U.N. Pubs [310]
SUPPLEMENT TO THE STATISTICAL YEARBOOK AND MONTHLY BULLETIN OF STATISTICS / United Nations – (1972.74.17.2. ST/ESA/STAT/Ser.Q/Supp.1. E.8 F.10; 1977.78.17.10. ST/ESA/STAT/Ser.S/Supp.2. E.8 F.10) – 9 – us U.N. Pubs [310]
SUPPLEMENT TO THE STATISTICAL YEARBOOK AND THE MBS / United Nations – (1972 (74.17.2). ST/ESA/STAT/Ser.Q/Supp.1. E.8 F.10; 1977 (78.17.10). ST/ESA/STAT/Ser.S/Supp.2. E.8 F.10) – 9 – us U.N. Pubs [310]
SUPPLEMENT ZU DEN ASSYRISCHEN WOERTERBUECHERN / Meissner, B – Leiden, 1898 – 3mf – ne IDC [470]
SUPPLEMENT ZUR ELFTEN AUFLAGE DES CONVERSATIONS-LEXIKONS (AEL, ABT 1; 35.20) – Leipzig. 2 Bde. 1872-73 (mf ed 1997) – 11mf – 9 – DM250.00 – 3-89131-269-5 – gw Fischer [943]

SUPPLEMENTA TOM. 16-25 (MGH 5: 30.BD. PARS 1) – (Pars 2. Supplementa Tom. 1-15 1934) – 1896 – Dfl154.00 – ne Slangenburg [240]
SUPPLEMENTARY CATALOGUE OF BOOKS ADDED TO THE COLLECTION ON THE HISTORY OF AMERICA, DURING THE YEAR 1848 / Canada. Parliament. Legislative Assembly. Library – Montreal: Lovell and Gibson, 1849. SEM105P220 – 1mf – 9 – Can$2.25 – cn Bibl Nat [971]
SUPPLEMENTARY HISTORY OF AMERICAN METHODISM : A CONTINUATION OF THE AUTHOR'S ABRIDGED HISTORY OF AMERICAN METHODISM / Stevens, Abel – New York: Eaton & Mains; Cincinnati: Curts & Jennings, c1899 – 1mf – us A.T.L.A. [240]
SUPPLEMENTARY MEMORANDUM / Palestine – By the Government of Palestine, including Notes on Evidence given to the United Nations Special Committee on Palestine up to the 12th July, 1947. Jersualem. 1947. BJ-28-97 1 – 9 – ne IDC [956]
SUPPLEMENTARY MEMORANDUM ON ACTS OF ARAB AGGRESSION TO ALTER BY FORCE THE SETTLEMENT ON THE FUTURE GOVERNMENT OF PALESTINE / Jewish Agency for Palestine. Lake Success, New York – Submitted to the United Nations Palestine Commission. 1948. BJ-28-160 1 – 9 – ne IDC [956]
SUPPLEMENTARY NOTES ON WALRUS AND NARWHAL IVORY / Laufer, B – (T'oung pao, v. 17). Leide. 1916. BU-524 2 – 8 – ne IDC [380]
SUPPLEMENTARY OBSERVATIONS UPON THE PROCEEDINGS OF THE HOUSE OF ASSEMBLY IN THIS PROVINCE / Aristides – Montreal Herald, 1814. SEM16P4 – 1r – 5 – Can$9.00 – cn Bibl Nat [323]
SUPPLEMENTARY REPORT OF THE QUEBEC CORPORATION ENGINEER OF THE NORTH SHORE RAILWAY / Baillairge, Charles – Presented 12th February, 1875. Quebec, 1875. 05669. (Pre-1900 Canadiana) – 9 – cn C.I.H.M. [971]
SUPPLEMENTARY VOLUME OF PERSONAL HISTORY AND REMINISCENCE OF KANSAS – Chicago, 1912. Part 1, Kansas Reel 1. Part 2, Kansas Reel 2. (The Cox Library Collection) – 5 – us Americana [978]
SUPPLEMENTBAND ZUM CONVERSATIONS-LEXIKON FUER DIE BESITZER DER ERSTEN, ZWEITEN UND DRITTEN AUFLAGE (AEL, ABT 1; 35.7) – Leipzig, 1818 (mf ed 1997) – 7mf – 9 – DM180.00 – 3-89131-257-1 – gw Fischer [943]
SUPPLEMENTE ZU SCHILLERS WERKEN AUS SEINEM NACHLASS : NACHLESE ZU SCHILLERS WERKEN NEBST VARIANTENSAMMLUNG / ed by Hoffmeister, Karl – Stuttgart: J G Cotta, 1858 – 1r – 1 – us U.W. Library [430]
SUPPLEMENTE ZUM CONVERSATIONS-LEXIKON FUER DIE BESITZER DER ERSTEN, ZWEITEN, DRITTEN UND VIERTEN AUFLAGE (AEL, ABT 1; 35.9) – 4 Abtlg. Leipzig, 1819-20 (mf ed 1997) – 12mf – 9 – DM290.00 – 3-89131-259-8 – gw Fischer [943]
SUPPLEMENT...FLORA VON N.O. CELEBES,... / Koorders, SH – (Lacking: 1918(1); 1922(1-2)) – Batavia, 1918-1922 – 1mf – 9 – ne IDC [580]
SUPPLEMENTUM FLORAE LAPPONICAE QUAM EDITIT BY DR. G. WAHLENBERG / Sommerfelt, S C – Christianiae, 1826. 331 pp., 3 pls. B-6187 1 – 9 – ne IDC [580]
SUPPLEMENTUM PLANTARUM SUCCULENTARUM / Haworth, A H – Londini. 1819. B-5048 2 – 8 – ne IDC [580]
SUPPLEMENTUM PLANTARUM SYSTEMATIS VEGETABILIUM / Linnaeus, Carl – Brunsvigae. 1781. B-174 2 – 8 – ne IDC [580]
SUPPLEMENTUM TENTAMINIS PTERIDOGRAPHIAE / Presl, C B – 1845 – 8mf – 7 – uk Microform Academic [580]
SUPPLY AND DISTRIBUTION OF OIL PRODUCTS IN INDONESIA – SE 3564 1. 1958? – 9 – ne IDC [338]
SUPPORTER – (Weekly Federalist newspaper) – Chillicothe, OH. oct 6, 1808-jan 17, 1821 – 5r – 1 – us Western Res [071]
SUPPORTER & SCIOTO GAZETTE – (Weekly National Republican newspaper) – Chillicothe, OH. feb 21, 1821-feb 9, 1827 – 3r – 1 – us Western Res [071]
THE SUPPOSED HEBRAISMS IN THE GRAMMAR OF THE BIBLICAL ARAMAIC / Powell, Herbert Harry – (Includes bibliographical references) – Berkeley: University of California, 1907 – 1mf – 9 – 0-8370-7184-4 – 1986-1184 – us A.T.L.A. [470]
SUPPRESSED POEMS OF ALFRED LORD TENNYSON, 1830-1862... / Tennyson, Alfred, Lord; ed by Thomson, J C – Warwick [Eng.]: J. Thomson; New York: Harper, 1904 – 1 roll – 1 – 1-55879-808-0 – uk Libr Preservation [810]
SUPPRESSIO VERI, OR THE DANGERS OF THE PRESS / Wright, Vincent – Together with "A foreign correspondent speaks." London, 1939? Fiche W1259. (Blodgett Collection of Spanish Civil War Pamphlets) – 9 – us H.U. College Libr [946]
THE SUPPRESSION OF THE AFRICAN SLAVE-TRADE TO THE UNITED STATES OF AMERICA, 1638-1870 / Du Bois, WE B – New York: Longmans, Green, 1896 – 1mf – us A.T.L.A. [976]
SUPRACONFESSIONNEL DE L'EGLISE DU SILENCE = CATACOMBES, SUPRACONFESSIONAL MESSENGER OF THE CHURCH OF SILENCE / Catacombes, Messager – Courbevoie. 86 docs. 1980-1991 – 31mf – 9 – ne IDC [320]
SUPRAMOLECULAR CHEMISTRY / ed by Atwood, Jerry L & Gokel, George W – 9,5,1 – us Gordon [540]
Suprapti, I N *see* DJEDJAK DYNAMICA MASJARAKAT
THE SUPREMACY AND SUFFICIENCY OF JESUS CHRIST OUR LORD...IN...THE EPISTLE TO THE HEBREWS / Mathieson, J E – Edinburgh: William Blackwood, 1897. 1 fiche – 9 – us A.T.L.A. [240]
SUPREMACY OF THE SPIRITUAL / Knowles, Edward Randall – s.l.: s.n., 1892. 1 fiche – 9 – us A.T.L.A. [240]
Supreme Command for the Allied Powers *see* THE HISTORY OF INTELLIGENCE ACTIVITIES UNDER GENERAL DOUGLAS MACARTHUR, 1942-1950
Supreme Command for the Allied Powers. Headquarters *see*
- THE POLITICAL REORIENTATION OF JAPAN, 1945-48
- SUMMATION OF NONMILITARY ACTIVITIES IN JAPAN AND KOREA, 1945-48

Supreme Commander for the Allied Powers *see*
- PREPARATORY MATERIAL FOR THE REVISION OF JAPANESE CIVIL LAW PREPARED IN THE HEADQUARTERS OF THE AMERICAN MILITARY GOVERNMENT FOR JAPAN
- SCAP DIRECTIVES TO THE IMPERIAL JAPANESE GOVERNMENT

SUPREME COMMANDER FOR THE ALLIED POWERS HISTORICAL MONOGRAPHS, 1945-1951 – (Printed guide sold separately for $15.00) – 1989 – 13r – 1 – $1,105.00 – S1676 – us Scholarly Res [975]
Supreme Commander for the Allied Powers. International Prosecution Section *see* ANALYSIS OF DOCUMENTARY EVIDENCE
SUPREME COURT AND CONGRESS / Mid-west Debate Bureau – Jacksonville, IL, 1935. 1v. LL-261 – 1 – us L of C Photodup [340]
SUPREME COURT JUDGEMENTS, 1922-1955, 1960-1972 – 8r – $396.00 – us African Imprint [340]
Supreme Court of New South Wales, District Registry, Port Phillip *see* REGISTER OF PATENTS AND (FROM 19 FEB. 1851) REGISTER OF CERTIFICATES OF NATURALIZATION VOLUME OF ENROLLED CERTIFICATES WITH INDEX, 1847-1852
SUPREME COURT OF THE UNITED STATES : U.S. REPORTS / U.S. Supreme Court – Washington: GPO, 1-503. 1790-1992 – 9 – $6,044.00 set; $15.00v – us Hein [340]
THE SUPREME COURT OF THE UNITED STATES / Maury, William Arden – Washington, D.C.: Morrison, 1881. 31p. LL-191 – 1 – us L of C Photodup [340]
SUPREME COURT OF THE U.S. HEARINGS AND REPORTS ON SUCCESSFUL AND UNSUCCESSFUL NOMINATIONS OF SUPREME COURT JUSTICES BY THE SENATE JUDICIARY COMMITTEE / ed by Mersky, Roy M & Jacobstein, J Myron – (With suppl) – v1-1. 1983 – 9 – $205.00 set – 0-930342-48-8 – us Hein [340]
Supreme Court of Victoria *see* REGISTERS OF CERTIFICATES OF NATURALIZATION
THE SUPREME COURT REPORTER – (Title part of: National Reporter System publ by West Pub Co. Updates planned) – v1-38. 1882-1919 – 394mf – 9 – $591.00 – LLMC 79-404A – us L.L.M.C. [340]
SUPREME COURT REPORTS / Canada. Supreme Court – v1-64. 1876-1922. Continued by: Canada Law Reports: Supreme Court. 81-301 – 9 – $340.00 – us L.L.M.C. [340]
SUPREME COURT REVIEW – (1979- 5,6,9) – 1960- – 1 – us UMI [073]
LA SUPRESION DEL JUEGO / Bayle, Constantino – Madrid: Razon y Fe, 1924 – 1 – sp Bibl Santa Ana [946]
EL SUR DE EXTREMADURA – Llerena, 1879 – 5 – sp Bibl Santa Ana [073]
SUR LA COTE – Beauport, Canada. v1 n9. 11 nov 1954 – 1r – 1 – Can$25.00 – cn Can Microfilming [072]
SUR LA COTE D'AFRIQUE : VILLES, BROUSSES, FLEUVES ET PROBLEMES DE L'OUEST AFRICAIN / d'Anfreville de la salle – Paris: E LaRose, 1912 – us Res Libr [910]
SUR LA DUREE MOYENNE DES MALADIES AUX DIFFERENS AGES / Villerme, Louis Rene – Reprod. d'un extrait des Annales d'Hygiene publique et de Medecine legale. v2, 1829. p241-66. 1 fiche.(Statistics Series: Medical Studies) – 9 – 6.00 – fr Bibl Nationale [310]
SUR LA FORMATION DES JARDINS / Duchesne, Antoine Nicolas – Paris. Dorez, 1775. 8 fol. 104p. (Architecture Series) – 9 – fr Hachette [720]
SUR LA LOI DU MARIAGE, LA LOI DU DIVORCE ET LE SYSTEME DE L'ADOPTATION – Paris. Les Directeurs de l'Imprimerie du Cercle Social – 9 – fr Hachette [321]
SUR LA PRETENDUE DEGENERESCENCE DE LA POPULATION FRANCAISE / Broca, Paul – Paris, E. Martinet, 1867, 55 p. 1 fiche. (Statistics Series: Demography) – 9 – 6.00 – fr Bibl Nationale [310]
SUR LA RELIGION SAINT-SIMONIENNE / Lagrue – Nancy, impr. de Dard, 1832, 64 p. Les Saint-Simoniens, 1825-1834. 6935 – 9 – fr Hachette [335]
SUR LA ROUTE DE BERTHIER – Berthier, Canada. 16 jan 1948-v5 n2. 3 jul 1952 – 1r – 1 – Can$35.00 – cn Can Microfilming [072]
SUR L'AMELIORATION DU SORT DES TRAVAILLEURS. DE L'ASSOCIATION DES OUVRIERS. NECESSITE D'UNE NOUVELLE ENQUETE INDUSTRIELLE ET MODELES DE STATUTS POUR UNE CAISSE DE SECOURS ET DE RETRAITES / Molher, Edmond – (Condition of 19th C. French working class series). 1849 – 9 – fr Hachette [331]
SUR LE HAUT-CONGO / Coquilhat, Camille – (African Library). Paris. J. Lebegue. 1888 – 9 – fr Hachette [960]
SUR LE HAUT-CONGO / Coquilhat, Camille – Ed. by J. Lebegue et Cie. Paris. 1888 – 9 – 15.00 – fr Orientalistes [960]
SUR LE PARCOURS DU CHEMIN DE FER DU LAC SAINT-JEAN: 1ERE CONFERENCE FAITE A LA SALLE VICTORIA, LE 31 MARS, 1886 / Buies, Arthur – Quebec: A. Cote, 1886. 00364. (Pre-1900 Canadiana) – 9 – cn C.I.H.M. [971]
SUR LES AINO / Rosny, Leon de – Extrait des comptes-rendus de Congres International des sciences geographiques. Paris: Imprimerie E. Martinet. 1878 – 9 – 5.00 – fr Orientalistes [305]
SUR LES ANCIENS RECENSEMENTS DE LA POPULATION BELGE / Quetelet, Adolphe Lambert Jacques – Bruxelles, M. Hayez, 1847. 38 p. 1 fiche. (Statistics Series: Demography) – 9 – $6.50 – fr Bibl Nationale [310]
SUR LES CITES OUVRIERES / Villerme, Louis Rene – (Condition of 19th C. French working class series). 1850 – 9 – fr Hachette [305]
SUR LES CYSTOSEIRA ADRIATIQUES. LEUR MORPHOLOGIE, ECOLOGIE ET EVOLUTION / Ercegovicz, A – Split. 1952. B-668 2 – 8 – ne IDC [580]
SUR LES ENVELOPPES FLORALES DES VEGETAUX MONOCOTYLEDONS / Boreau, A – (Mem. Soc. Linneenne). v. 6. Paris. 1827. B-5109 2 – 8 – ne IDC [580]
SUR LES GOUVERNEMENTS EN GENERAL ET EN PARTICULIER SUR CELUI QUI NOUS CONVIENT / Auger, Athanase – Paris. Imp. du Cercle Social. s.d – 9 – fr Hachette [321]
SUR LES PISTES DU DESERT / Lehuraux, Leon Joseph – Paris: Plon, [1928] – us Res Libr [960]
SUR LES PRINCIPES FONDAMENTAUX DE LA THEORIE DES NOMBRES ET DE LA GEOMETRIE / Laurent, Paul-Mathieu – Evreux: C. Herrisey, 1902. 68p.1 fiche. (Science Collection) – 9 – 6.00 – fr Bibl Nationale [510]
SUR LES ROUTES DE SYRIE... / Gontaut Biron, R de – Paris, 1928 – 3mf – 1 – ILM-2156/1 – ne IDC [327]
SUR LES ROUTES DU SUDAN / Baillaud, Emile – Toulouse: E Privat, 1902 – us Res Libr [910]
SUR L'HOMME ET LE DEVELOPPEMENT DE SES FACULTES OU ESSAI DE PHYSIQUE SOCIALE / Quetelet, Adolphe Lambert Jacques – Paris: Bachelier, 1835. 327p. 8 fiches. (Statistics Series: Medical Studies) – 9 – 20.00 – fr Bibl Nationale [310]
SUR QUELQUES MYRIONEMACOOS / Sauvageau, C – (Ann. Sci. Nat. Bot. Ser. 8, v. 5). Paris. 1897. B-678 2 – 8 – ne IDC [580]
Surabaya, Java *see* LAPORAN KEPADA DEWAN PERWAKILAN RAKJAT DAERAH
Suradi, Bintang *see*
- CONTEMPORARY PROGRESSIVE INDONESIAN POETRY
- INDONESIA SINGS OF AFRO-ASIA

Suradji, D *see*
- REFLEKSI DJIWA; DJEMPUTAN TJERITA-TJERITA PENDEK DAN DRAMA
- ULAR; DUA DRAMA DAN DUA TJERITA PENDEK

SURA-YI UEMMET – Paris, Cairo, Istanbul: Osmanli Ittihad ve Terakki Cemiyeti, Hilal Matbaasi. Sahib-i Imtiyaz: Dr. Bahaddin Sakir; Mueduerue: Mustafa Asim, 1902-1910 – 9 – $25.00 – us MEDOC [956]
SURAYYA – (v.1, no. 8-21, 23, 26-27 (19 Sha'ban 1316-17 Zu'l-qa'dah 1316[27 Dec 1898-18 Mar 1899]); v.2, no. 3-4, 11, 13, 18, 21 (1 Rajab 1317-13 Zu'l-hijjah 1317[4 Nov 1899-7 Apr 1900]); v.6, no.5-6 (14 Jumadi al-avval 1322-28 Jumadi al-avval 1322[31 Jul 1904-11 Aug 1904])) – Cairo, Tehran, Kashan – 1 – us MEDOC [950]
Surburg, Paul R *see* EFFECTS OF A LOWER LIMB STRENGTH TRAINING PROGRAM ON BALANCE MEASURES IN MEN WITH MENTAL RETARDATION
EL SURCO DE LA SANGRE / Alvarez Lencero, Luis – Guadalajara, 1953 – sp Bibl Santa Ana [946]
Surdam, T Janet *see*
- BIBLE (CCC289)
- EXAMPLE (CCC287)
- FRIENDS (CCC288)
- JESUS (CCC291)
- LOVE OTHERS AS YOURSELF (CCC286)
- SERVE ONE ANOTHER (CCC290)

THE SURE FOUNDATION, OR, THOUGHTS ON THE BELIEVER'S SAFETY / Boys, Ernest – Chicago: Fleming H. Revell, 18–. 1 fiche – 9 – us A.T.L.A. [240]
LES SURESTARIES... / Barbay, G – Paris, 1909 – 1mf – 9 – ILM-3446/1 – ne IDC [340]
SURF (DAILY) – Santa Cruz, CA. 1883-84; 1885-1918 – 61r – 1 – $3,050.00 – B02963 – us Library Micro [071]
SURF (WEEKLY) – Santa Cruz, CA. 1891; 1892; 1896-99; 1919 – 5r – 1 – $250.00 – B02964 – us Library Micro [071]
SURFACE AND INTERFACE ANALYSIS: SIA – (1982-. 1,5,6,9) – v1-. 1979- – 1 – us UMI [073]
SURFACE MINING AND RECLAMATION APPEALS BOARD DECISIONS / U.S. Department of the Interior – v1-5. 1978-1983 (all publ) – 20mf – 9 – $30.00 – LLMC 82-210 – us L.L.M.C. [324]
SURFACE SCIENCE – v1-138. 1964-84 – 1,5,6,13 – sz Elsevier [073]
SURFACE SCIENCE LETTERS – v1-5. 1980-84 – 1,5,6,13 – sz Elsevier [073]
SURFACE SCIENCE REPORTS – v1-4. 1981-84 – 1,5,6,13 – sz Elsevier [540]
SURFACE TECHNOLOGY – v1-23. 1972-84 – 1,5,6,13 – sz Elsevier [073]
SURFACE WATER AND GROUNDWATER INTERACTION : A CONTRIBUTION TO THE INTERNATIONAL HYDROLOGICAL PROGRAMME / ed by Wright, C E – 1980 – 123p – 9 – 92-3-101862-0 – fr UNESCO [550]
SURFCOMBER – Del Mar, CA. 1958-1983; 1984 – 50+ r – 1 – $2,500.00 ($75.00y) – H03198 – us Library Micro [071]

THE SURGEONS MATE OR MILITARY AND DOMESTIQUE SURGERY / Woodall, J – M 80. 1639 – 9 – ne IDC [617]
SURGEON'S ORDER AND LETTER BOOK / U.S. Army. Cavalry, Kansas Volunteer. 15th Regiment – 1863-65 – 1 – us KS Hist [324]
SURGERY, GYNECOLOGY AND OBSTETRICS – An international magazine. v1-101. 1905-55. Plus abstracts – 1,5,6 – us Princeton Micro [610]
SURGERY, GYNECOLOGY AND OBSTETRICS – (v. 124- 1967- 5,6; v. 130- 1970- 9) – v. 1- 1905- – 1 – us UMI [618]
SURGICAL BUSINESS *see* HEALTH INDUSTRY TODAY
SURGICAL FORUM – (v.30-. 1979- 5,6,9) – v.1-. 1950- – 1 – us UMI [617]
SURGICAL FORUM / American College of Surgeons – Chicago. v1-48 1950- 1*; v30-48 1979- 5*; v30-48 1979- 9 – 1,5,9 – D12442 – us UMI [617]
SURGICAL NEUROLOGY – v19-22. 1982-84 – 1,5,6,13 – sz Elsevier [617]
SURGICAL OBSERVATIONS ON THE CONSTITUTIONAL ORIGIN AND TREATMENT OF LOCAL DISEASES AND ON ANEURISMS / Abernethy, J – M-149. 1809 – 9 – ne IDC [617]
SURGICAL RESEARCH COMMUNICATIONS / ed by Leaper, D J – 9,5,1 – us Harwood [617]
SURGICAL ROUNDS – 1978- – 1,5,6,9 – us UMI [617]
SUR-I ISRAFIL – (Shumarah-'i 1-32 (17 Rabi al-Akhir 1325-20 Jumada al-avval 1326[30 May 1907-12 Jul 1908])) – 1 reel 150 Tehran: Pesarsiyan, 1907-1909 – 1 – $45.00 – us MEDOC [950]
Suria, J *see* CATALOGO GENERAL DEL ARCHIVO ARQUIDIOCESANO DE CARACAS, 1964
SUR-I-ISRAFIL – Tehran: Khayaban-e Nasri Kitab-Khanah tarbiyet, may 30 1907-jun 1 1908 – us Res Libr [072]
Surin, P Jean J Le *see* LETTRE ESCRITE A MONSIEUR L'EVESQUE DE POICTIERS PAR UN DES PERES JESUITES QUI EXORCISENT A LOUDON
SURINAAMSCHE COURANT – Surinam. 1804-1885 – 1 – us UMI [072]
SURINAM : JAACIJFERS VOOR SURINAME 1956-1965 / Surinam. Algemeen Bureau voor de Statistiek – (Coll title: Latin American and Caribbean Official Statistical Serials, 1821-1982) – 7mf – 9 – £60.00 – uk Chadwyck [972]
Surinam *see*
- ECONOMIC PLANS
- GOUVERNEMENTS ADVERTENTIEBLAD

Surinam. Algemeen Bureau voor de Statistiek *see* SURINAM
Surinam. (Netherlands). Stichting Planbureau Suriname *see*
- BIJLAGE BEHORENDE BIJ TWEEDE VIJFJARENPLAN 1972-1976
- NATIONAAL ONTWIKKELINGSPLAN SURINAME RAAMWERK VOOR HET TWEEDE VIJFJARENPLAN 1972-1976

SURINAME – Surinam. South America. 1872-1961 – 1 – us UMI [072]
SURINAME-PARAMARIBO – Surinam. 1886-1967 – 1 – us UMI [072]
Surius, L *see*
- DE PROBATIS SANCTORUM HISTORIIS
- DE PROBATIS SANCTORUM. HISTORIIS, PARTIM EX TOMIS ALOYSII LIPOMANI

Surius, L et al *see* CONCILIA OMNIA, TUM GENERALIA, TUM PROVINCIALIA ATQUE PARTICULARIA
Surja Anjakrakusuma, Prabu *see* SERAT NITISASTRA
Surjo Untoro, S *see* MANUSIA SOSIALIS INDONESIA
LE SURMALE, ROMAN MODERNE / Jarry, Alfred – Paris, ed. de la Revue Blanche, 1902. 248p. 3 fiches. (Literature Collection) – 9 – 8.00 – fr Bibl Nationale [830]
SURNAMES OF THE UNITED KINGDOM : A CONCISE ETYMOLOGICAL DICTIONARY / Harrison & Pulling – London: Eton Press, 1912-1918. 3v – 7mf – 9 – A$21.00 – at State Libr Vic [920]
Suroso Purwamihardjo, R *see* ENGLISH-GRAMMAR UNTUK SEKOLAH LANDJUTAN PERTAMA
SURPLUS REVENUES AND CANADIAN RELATIONS / Barker, Wharton – Philadelphia? 1887? 03366. (Pre-1900 Canadiana) – 9 – cn C.I.H.M. [971]
SURPRISE – Creighton, NE. -w. Apr. 1896-Oct. 1896 – 1 – us NE Hist [071]
THE SURPRISE BOOSTER – Surprise, NE. -w. 2 Nov 1933-26 Aug 1937. Many issues discolored & mutilated. Scattered issues missing – 1 – us NE Hist [071]
SURPRISE ENTERPRISE – Surprise, NE. -w. Sept 1914; Dec 1915-Nov 1921 – 1 – us NE Hist [071]
SURPRISE HERALD – Surprise, NE. -w. Mar 1896-Jun 1898; Jul 1899; Oct 1899-Oct 1900 – 1 – us NE Hist [071]
THE SURPRISE TIMES – Surprise, NE. -w, -sw. 8 May 1930-26 Jan 1933.Issues missing – 1 – us NE Hist [071]
SURPRISE VALLEY JOURNAL – Cedarville, CA. Aug 1952-Feb 1958 – 2r – 1 – $100.00 – B02102 – us Library Micro [073]
SURPRISE VALLEY RECORD – Cedarville, CA. Apr 1906-Feb 1937 – 7r – 1 – $350.00 – B02103 – us Library Micro [071]
SURREALISM : SUBJECT COLLECTIONS – (Individual titles not listed separately) – 60 catalogues on 82mf – 9 – £600.00 – uk Chadwyck [750]
LE SURREALISME AU SERVICE DE LA REVOLUTION – Paris, 1930-33 – 1r – 1 – £60.00 – uk Chadwyck [750]
SURREALISME ET ANARCHISME / Ferrua, Pietro – 1982 – 9 – 1.00f – at Libertarian Micro [335]
SURRENDER AT APPOMATTOX – 1 – us Ross [976]
THE SURRENDER OF NAPOLEON; BEING THE NARRATIVE OF THE SURRENDER OF BUONAPARTE AND OF HIS RESIDENCE ON BOARD H.M.S. BELLEROPHON / Maitland, Frederick Lewis – With a detail of the principal events that occurred in that ship between the 24th of May and the 8th of August, 1815. New ed. 1904 – 9 – $20.00 – uk Libr Preservation [941]
SURREY, 1823 : BRITISH ISLES CENSUS DIRECTORIES PROJECT, ENGLAND. VOL 212 – 1mf – 9 – A$9.00 – at Vine [941]
SURREY, 1839 : BRITISH ISLES CENSUS DIRECTORIES PROJECT, ENGLAND. VOL 15 – 2mf – 9 – A$15.00 – at Vine [941]
SURREY, 1846 : BRITISH ISLES CENSUS DIRECTORIES PROJECT, ENGLAND. VOL 227 – 7mf – 9 – A$45.00 – at Vine [941]
SURREY, 1855 : BRITISH ISLES CENSUS DIRECTORIES PROJECT, ENGLAND. VOL 253 – 8mf – 9 – A$51.00 – at Vine [941]
SURREY, 1862 : BRITISH ISLES CENSUS DIRECTORIES PROJECT, ENGLAND – (In prep) – at Vine [941]
SURREY, 1895 : BRITISH ISLES CENSUS DIRECTORIES PROJECT, ENGLAND. VOL 248 – 11mf – 9 – A$69.00 – at Vine [941]
SURREY ADVERTISER – Guildford, England. Apr 1864-16 Nov 1867; 1872-74; 1876-77; Jan-Jun 1895; Jan-Nov 1898; Jan-Jun 1909; Jan-Jun 1918; Jul-Dec 1923. -w. 10 reels – 1 – uk British Libr Newspaper [072]
SURREY, COMET AND GENERAL ADVERTISER – London, England. -w. Kingston upon Thames Aug 1854-Dec 1873; Jan 1926-Dec 1939. 55 reels – 1 – uk British Libr Newspaper [072]
SURREY COMET AND GENERAL ADVERTISER. SATURDAY EDITION – London. Kingston-upon-Thames, England. 1940-45.-w. 6 reels – 1 – uk British Libr Newspaper [072]
SURREY COMET AND GENERAL ADVERTISER. WEDNESDAY EDITION – London. Kingston-upon-Thames, England. 1940-45.-w. 4mqn reels – 1 – uk British Libr Newspaper [072]
SURREY GAZETTE – Surrey, British Columbia, CN. Mar 1917-Oct 1929 – 2r – 1 – cn Commonwealth Micro [072]
SURREY INDEPENDENT AND WIMBLEDON MERCURY – (Surrey Independent and Mid-Surrey Standard). London. -w. 18 Mar 1882-9 Sep 1905. (9 reels) – 1 – uk British Libr Newspaper [072]
SURREY LEADER – Surrey, B. C., Canada. Jul 1929- – 1 – cn Commonwealth Micro [072]
SURREY STREET MAPS / British Ordnance Survey – 1994 – 9mf – 15 – $55.50 – us Comics [941]
SURREY (SUTTON), 1880 : BRITISH ISLES CENSUS DIRECTORIES PROJECT, ENGLAND – at Vine [941]
SURREY TIMES – Surrey, British Columbia, CN. Apr-Oct 1895 – 1r – 1 – cn Commonwealth Micro [072]
Surridge, Brewster Joseph *see* REPORT ON CO-OPERATION IN THE FEDERATION OF MALAYA
Surtees, Robert Smith *see* HANDLEY CROSS
SURTEES SOCIETY – (Coll title: Publications of the English Record Societies, 1835-1972...) – v1-181. 1835-1966 – 747mf – 9 – £3,920.00 – uk Chadwyck [420]
SURUSH – (Includes special issues: Winter 1360, Summer 1361, Winter 1361, Spring 1363, Spring 1364, Missing issue: 204. New filming includes everything except nos 14-26, 28-31, 34, 38, 40-42, 44-50, 52-59, 63-74, 77-79, 81-103, 105-109) – Tehran. Sal-i I, shumarah-'i 1- sal-i 8, shumarah-'i 369 (13 Urdibihisht. 1358-11 Bahman 1365 [2 May 1979-31 Nov 1987] – $750.00 – us MEDOC [956]
SURUSH – (Sal-i 1, shumarah-'i 14-sal-i 3, shumarah-'i 115 (13 Murdad 1358-11 Mihr 1360[4 Aug 1979-3 Oct 1981]). Missing issues: 27, 32, 33, 35-37, 39, 43, 51, 60, 62, 75-76, 80, 104, 110-114) – Tehran – 5r – 1 – $250.00 – us MEDOC [950]
SURVEILLANCE OF RADICALS IN THE UNITED STATES, 1917-41 : REPORTS / U.S. Military Intelligence – (With printed guide) – 34r – 1 – $3,275.00 – 0-89093-682-X – us UPA [355]
SURVEY – 85-88. 1949-1952 – 1 – us UMI [360]
SURVEY – New York. v.22-88. 1909-52 – 1,5,6 – 22661.00 – us Princeton Micro [073]
SURVEY : SOCIAL WELFARE PERIODICALS – (Includes Charities, 3) – 1-88 2+5 (all publ). 1897-1952 – 822mf – 9 – $2,855.00 – us UPA [360]
A SURVEY ANALYSIS OF DANCE WELLNESSRELATED CURRICULA IN AMERICAN HIGHER EDUCATION / Cardinal, Marita K & Hilsendager, Sarah A – 1993 – 3mf – $12.00 – us Microform Publ [790]
SURVEY AND ANALYSIS OF TEACHER-TRAINING ACTIVITIES IN POPULATION EDUCATION, FAMILY LIFE EDUCATION AND SEX EDUCATION / UNESCO. International Study of the Conceptualization and Methodology of Population Education (ISCOMPE) – 1980 – 119p – 9 – fr UNESCO [370]
THE SURVEY ASSOCIATE RECORDS, PART 1 – The Forget-Me-Not Files – 57r with printed guide – 1 – $5,485.00 – 0-89093-523-8 – us UPA [360]
THE SURVEY ASSOCIATE RECORDS, PART 2 – Editorial Files – 19r with printed guide – 1 – $1,830.00 – 0-89093-524-6 – us UPA [360]
THE SURVEY ASSOCIATE RECORDS, PART 3 – Corporate and Financial Records – 5r with printed guide – 1 – $480.00 – 0-89093-528-9 – us UPA [360]
SURVEY GRAPHIC *see* SURVEY
SURVEY MIDMONTHLY *see* SURVEY
SURVEY OF AGRICULTURAL LAND IRRIGATED BY ARTESIAN WELLS / Jordan. Department of Statistics – 3v. in 2. 1971-77. Lacking: 1975-76. BNE-9780 1 – 9 – ne IDC [310]
SURVEY OF ANESTHESIOLOGY – v1-40. 1957-96 – 1,5,6,9 – $80.00r – us Williams [617]
SURVEY OF AQUATIC PROGRAMS AND AQUATIC FACILITY ACCESSIBILITY FEATURES AVAILABLE TO AND UTILIZED BY PHYSICALLY HANDICAPPED STUDENTS AT FOUR-YEAR PENNSYLVANIA COLLEGES AND UNIVERSITIES / Gunning, Mary Jo & Jackson, Michael W – 1991 – 2mf – 9 – $8.00 – us Microform Publ [790]
SURVEY OF CHINA MAINLAND PRESS / U.S. Consulate General. Hong Kong – 1 Nov 1950-74; 1975- – 1 – $3,218.00 – us L of C Photodup [950]
SURVEY OF CONDITIONS OF THE INDIANS IN THE UNITED STATES / U.S. Congress. Senate. Committee on Indian Affairs – v1-41. 1928-43 – 1 – $770.00 – 0-89093-004-X – us UPA [977]
SURVEY OF CONDITIONS OF THE INDIANS OF THE UNITED STATES / U.S. Congress. Senate. Committee on Indian Affairs – v. 1-41. 1929-44 – 1 – 194.00 – us L of C Photodup [360]
A SURVEY OF CORPORATE FITNESS PROGRAMS / Walker, Sheila – 1981 – 1mf – 9 – $4.00 – us Microform Publ [613]
SURVEY OF CURRENT BUSINESS – (v. 49-1969- 5,6. v. 55- 1975- 9) – v. 1- 1921- – 1 – us UMI [650]
A SURVEY OF DIVISION 1 ATHLETIC ADMINISTRATOR'S COMPETENCY DIMENSIONS FOR ADMINISTRATION AND MENTORING / Fager, Karl E & Terry, Lawrence R – 1991 – 1mf – $4.00 – us Microform Publ [790]
A SURVEY OF DIVISION 2 ATHLETIC AND PHYSICAL EDUCATION FISCAL TRENDS FOR THE NEXT TWENTY YEARS / Johnson, Jay R & Bhaneman, Carl P – 1992 – 2mf – 9 – $8.00 – us Microform Publ [370]
A SURVEY OF FAMILY CONDITIONS WITH SPECIAL REFERENCE TO HOUSING NEEDS, ORLANDO TOWNSHIP, JOHANNESBURG / Eberhardt, Jacqueline – Johannesburg: City of Johannesburg, Non-European Affairs Dept, [1949?] – us Res Libr [360]
SURVEY OF INDIAN RESERVATIONS / South Dakota. Emergency Relief Administration – This collection, which was compiled during the Great Depression but was never published, includes observations of Indian life on major reservations. ca 1935 – 1 – $295.00 – 0-89093-011-2 – us UPA [977]
SURVEY OF INDONESIA FOR LONG VEGETABLE FIBER DEVELOPMENT / Dempsey, James M – SE-5505 1. 1961 – 9 – ne IDC [630]
SURVEY OF LOCAL PLANNING IN MARYLAND / Parsarew, Isadore Alvin – Baltimore, 1948. LL-1376 – 1 – us L of C Photodup [340]
SURVEY OF METHODIST RECORDS [...CONNEXIONAL COMMITTEES, RESIDENTIAL SCHOOLS AND COLLEGES,... / Himsworth, Sheila J – N.p., 1978 – 1mf – 9 – Df15.00 – ne IDC [240]
SURVEY OF MOTOR VEHICLE USE, AUSTRALIA : DATA SERVICE – 9 – at Statistics [304]
SURVEY OF PALESTINE / United Nations. Special Committee on Palestine – Notes compiled for the information of the United Nations Special Committee on Palestine, Jun 1947. Supplementl. United Nations Special Committee on Palestine. II. Palestine-Mandate. III. Palestine Politics and Government. Jerusalem. 1947. BJ-28-123 1 – 9 – ne IDC [956]
A SURVEY OF PALESTINE PREPARED IN DEC 1945 AND JAN 1946 FOR THE INFORMATION OF THE ANGLO-AMERICAN COMMITTEE OF INQUIRY / Palestine. Chief Secretary's Office – 5v. Jerusalem. 1946. BJ-28-122 1 – 9 – ne IDC [956]
SURVEY OF PROGRESS, 1960 / Afghanistan. Ministry of Planning – BD-730 1 – 9 – ne IDC [339]
SURVEY OF PROGRESS, 1961-62 / Afghanistan. Ministry of Planning – 1v. Kabul. 1963. BD-731 1 – 9 – ne IDC [339]
SURVEY OF SOCIAL STATISTICS *see* COMPENDIUM OF SOCIAL STATISTICS
A SURVEY OF SOME PHASES OF ADMINISTRATION FACULTY OF ECONOMICS, UNIV. OF INDONESIA / Shontz, Howard B – Including class schedules and course catalogue of Univ. of California. SE 4567 1. 1963 – 9 – ne IDC [370]
A SURVEY OF TELEFACSIMILE USE IN LIBRARIES IN THE UNITED STATES / American Library Association – 1976 – 9 – 8.00 – us L of C Photodup [770]
SURVEY OF THE ARCHITECTURE OF COMPLETED PROJECTS OF THE PUBLIC WORKS ADMINISTRATION / Short, C W & Stanley-Brown, R – (Companion to the "Historic American Buildings Survey") – 1939 – 66mf – 9 – £285.00 – uk Chadwyck [720]
A SURVEY OF THE ATTITUDES ON EDUCATION IN KOREA / Korea. Korean Educational Development Institute – Seoul, 1988 – 2mf – 9 – DE-662/1 – ne IDC [370]
A SURVEY OF THE DESIRED EDUCATIONAL PREPARATION AND EMPLOYMENT MARKET FOR HIGH SCHOOL ATHLETIC TRAINERS IN METROPOLITAN WASHINGTON, DC AS PERCEIVED BY HIGH SCHOOL ATHLETIC DIRECTORS / Howard, Eric C & Jackson, Michael – 1992 – 2mf – 9 – $8.00 – us Microform Publ [790]
A SURVEY OF THE DEVELOPMENT OF EDUCATION AMONG THE BATSWANA OF BOPHUTHATSWANA / Lekhela, E P – 1972 – 1mf – 9 – DE-109/1 – ne IDC [370]

A SURVEY OF THE ETHNOGRAPHY OF AFRICA AND THE FORMER RACIAL AND TRIBAL MIGRATIONS IN THAT CONTINENT / Johnston, Sir Harry Hamilton – London, 1913 – 1 – us Res Libr [305]
SURVEY OF THE FUTURE OF THE SUEZ CANAL / Egypt. Compagnie Universelle du Canal Maritime du Suez – 1v. 1956-57. BNE-4621 1 – 9 – ne IDC [380]
SURVEY OF THE LAWS OF THE MEMBER STATES ON PAYMENT OF MAINTENANCE BETWEEN DIVORCED SPOUSES / Council of Europe. Directorate of Legal Affairs – Strasbourg, 1974. 61 p. LL-4210 – 1 – us L of C Photodup [340]
A SURVEY OF THE PRINCIPLES OF CONTEMPORARY AMERICAN NONLITURGICAL CHURCH MUSIC / Quinn, Eugene F – 1962 – 1 – 17.92 – us Baptist [240]
SURVEY OF THE SOMERSET PROPERTIES OF THE DUCHY OF CORNWALL, 1611 / Norden – Ms. From Royal Library, Windsor Castle – 1 – uk Microform Academic [941]
SURVEY OF WOOD RESIDUE IN ALABAMA / Auburn University. Extension Service – 1966, 1973. 1 reel – 1, 5 – us Spaulding [630]
SURVEY OPERATIONS IN UNADMINISTRATED AREAS OF ASSAM AND BURMA, 1935-1936. REPORT / Bull, L C – BSE-74 2 – 8 – ne IDC [950]
SURVEY SERIES. RELEASE NUMBER 1-161, JULY 31, 1940-AUG. 3, 1949 / U.S. Securities and Exchange Commission – 9 – us UMI [336]
SURVEY SERIES RELEASES – nos1-161. 31 Jul 1940-3 Aug 1949 (all publ) – 20mf – 9 – $30.00 – LLMC 89-002 – us L.L.M.C. [340]
SURVEYING AND MAPPING – v4- 1944- – 1,5,6,9 – us UMI [520]
SURVEYING AND MAPPING *see* BULLETIN
SURVEYING THE SPANISH WAR; LIBERALISM AND COMMUNISM / Maranon, Gregorio – N.Y., 1937? Fiche W 1023. (Blodgett Collection of Spanish Civil War Pamphlets) – 9 – us H.U. College Libr [946]
SURVEYS IN HIGH ENERGY PHYSICS / ed by Kaidalov, A B et al – 1979- – 1,5,9 – us Harwood [530]
SURVIVAL INTERNATIONAL – London, Washington D.C. 234 docs. 1980-1991 – 60mf – 9 – ne IDC [320]
SURVIVALS IN CHRISTIANITY : STUDIES IN THE THEOLOGY OF DIVINE IMMANENCE: SPECIAL LECTURES / Wood, Charles James – New York: Macmillan, 1893 – 1mf – 9 – 0-8370-6471-6 – 1986-0471 – us A.T.L.A. [240]
LA SURVIVANCE : ORGANE OFFICIEL DE L'ASSOCIATION CANADIENNE-FRANCAISE DE L'ALBERTA – (Cont by: Le Franco-Albertain) – Edmonton, Alberta. 16 nov 1928-8 nov 1967 – 14r – 1 – Can$55.00r – cn Can Microfilming [072]
Suryati *see*
– MASAKAN INDONESIA, ASIA, BROPAH
– MASAKAN INDONESIA MODERN
SUSAN A. NEWMAN DIARY *see* NEWMAN, SUSAN A., DIARY
SUSAN HOPLEY : OR, THE ADVENTURES OF A MAID-SERVANT / Crowe, Catherine – Edinburg: William Tait; Glasgow: W.S. Orr..., 1842 – 1 roll – 1 – 1-55879-451-4 – uk Libr Preservation [830]
Susanta Tirtapradja *see* NAJAKA LALANA
Susanto Tirtoprodjo *see* SEDJARAH PERGARAKAN NASIONAL INDONESIA; RINGKASAN DARI SERI TJEREMAH DIMUKA "KURSUS PENJEGARAN" DARI DEPARTEMEN LUAR NEGERI DALAM BULAN2 MEI
Susemihl, E *see* DIE VOEGEL EUROPAS
Susemihl, J C *see* DIE VOEGEL EUROPAS
Susin, M *see* LERIDA. ARCHIVO HISTORICO PROVINCIAL INVENTARIO DE PROTOCOLOS NOTARIALES
THE SUSPENDING POWER AND THE WRIT OF HABEAS CORPUS / Johnston, James F – Philadelphia, Campbell, 1862. 48 p. LL-1370 – 1 – us L of C Photodup [340]
SUSQUEHANNA REGISTER AND NORTH FARMER – Susquehanna, PA., 1844 – 13 – $25.00r – us I.M.R. [071]
Susquehanna. Synod (Pres. Ch. in the U.S.A. New School) *see* MINUTES, 1853-1869
SUSSEX, 1823 : BRITISH ISLES CENSUS DIRECTORIES PROJECT, ENGLAND. VOL 217 – 1mf – 9 – A$9.00 – at Vine [941]
SUSSEX, 1839 : BRITISH ISLES CENSUS DIRECTORIES PROJECT, ENGLAND. VOL 16 – 2mf – 9 – A$15.00 – at Vine [941]
SUSSEX, 1846 : BRITISH ISLES CENSUS DIRECTORIES PROJECT, ENGLAND – at Vine [941]
SUSSEX, 1855 : BRITISH ISLES CENSUS DIRECTORIES PROJECT, ENGLAND. VOL 254 – 9mf – 9 – A$57.00 – at Vine [941]
SUSSEX, 1858 : BRITISH ISLES CENSUS DIRECTORIES PROJECT, ENGLAND. VOL 39 – 4mf – 9 – A$27.00 – at Vine [941]
SUSSEX, 1862 : BRITISH ISLES CENSUS DIRECTORIES PROJECT, ENGLAND – (In prep) – at Vine [941]
SUSSEX, 1871 : BRITISH ISLES CENSUS DIRECTORIES PROJECT, ENGLAND – at Vine [941]
SUSSEX, 1895 : BRITISH ISLES CENSUS DIRECTORIES PROJECT, ENGLAND – at Vine [941]
SUSSEX, 1913 : BRITISH ISLES CENSUS DIRECTORIES PROJECT, ENGLAND – at Vine [941]
SUSSEX ARCHAEOLOGICAL COLLECTIONS – London. v1-61. 1848-1920 – 379mf – 9 – H-888/2 – ne IDC [930]
SUSSEX (CHICHESTER), 1805 : BRITISH ISLES CENSUS DIRECTORIES PROJECT, ENGLAND. VOL 174 – 1mf – 9 – A$9.00 – at Vine [941]
SUSSEX DAILY NEWS – Sussex. 1881-1952 – 14r – 1 – uk Microform Academic [072]
SUSSEX RECORD SOCIETY – (Coll title: Publications of the English Record Societies, 1835-1972...) – v1-70. 1902-70 – 228mf – 9 – £1,435.00 – uk Chadwyck [941]
SUSSEX WEEKLY ADVERTISER – Sussex. 1749-1822. Incomplete – 14r – 1 – uk Microform Academic [072]
SUSSEX-SURRY DISPATCH – Waverly. Va. 1947- – 1 – us UMI [071]
Sussman, Marvin B *see* MARRIAGE AND FAMILY REVIEW
SUSTAINABLE AGRICULTURAL PRODUCTION : IMPLICATIONS FOR INTERNATIONAL AGRICULTURAL RESEARCH – 1989 – 154p – it F.A.O. [338]
SUSTAINABLE DEVELOPMENT AND ENVIRONMENTAL MANAGEMENT OF SMALL ISLANDS / ed by Beller, W et al – 1990 – 9 – 92-3-102670-4 – Co-published with Parthenon Publishing – fr UNESCO [333]
SUSTAINABLE INVESTMENT AND RESOURCE USE – 200p – 9 – 92-3-102748-4 – fr UNESCO [333]
SUSTAINABLE PRODUCTION FROM LIVESTOCK IN SUB-SAHARAN AFRICA : ILCA'S PROGRAMME PLANS AND FUNDING REQUIREMENTS, 1989-1993 – 1988 – 9 – free – 92-9053-149-5 – et ILRI [636]
SUSTANCIA : REVISTA DE CULTURA SUPERIOR – Tucuman: Talleires "La raza". v1-5 n1-18. jun 1939-1946 – us Res Libr [972]
Susto, Juan Antonio *see* PANAMA EN EL ARCHIVO DE INDIAS
SUSYALISM – (Shumarah-'i 1-18 (Bahman 1342-Bahman 1345[Dec 1963-Dec 1966])) – [S.l.]: Jami'ah-'i Susyalist'ha-yi Irani dar Urupa – 1 reel – 1 – $35.00 – us MEDOC [950]
SUSYALISM (MAJALLAH) – (Dawrah-'i 2: shumarah-'i 1-7 (Urdibihisht 1343-Mihr 1345[May 1964-Oct 1966])) – [S.l.]: Jami'ah-'i Susyalist'ha-yi Irani dar Urupa – 1 reel – 1 – $35.00 – us MEDOC [950]
Sutadi, R *see* SEISMIC ZONES IN INDONESIA
Sutaine, Ger *see* PLAN D'ETUDES ET D'EDUCATION, AVEC UN DISCOURS SUR L'EDUCATION
Sutardjo, Nurdjana *see* A GENERAL OUTLINE OF THE INDONESIAN YOUTH MOVEMENTS IN PREWAR TIME
Sutarman *see* INDONESIAN CHEMICAL NOMENCLATURE
Sutarti, Christina *see* ASIAN AGRICULTURAL RESEARCH AND DEVELOPMENT
Sutherland, Alexander *see*
– METHODISM IN CANADA
– THE METHODIST CHURCH AND MISSIONS IN CANADA AND NEWFOUNDLAND
SUTHERLAND COURIER-TIMES – Sutherland, NE. -w. May 1897 to date – 1 – us NE Hist [071]
Sutherland, George *see* CONSTITUTIONAL POWER AND WORLD AFFAIRS
Sutherland, J *see* HORTUS MEDICUS
Sutherland, J A *see* THE NINETEENTH CENTURY LITERATURE SPECIALIST COLLECTION
Sutherland, Jabez Gridley *see* A TREATISE ON THE LAW OF DAMAGES, EMBRACING AN ELEMENTARY EXPOSITION OF THE LAW AND ALSO OF ITS APPLICATION TO PARTICULAR SUBJECTS OF CONTRACT AND TORT. 3D ED
Sutherland, James *see* TALKS ON LIVING SUBJECTS: THE CREATION, THE BIBLE... EVILS AND...CURE OF INTEMPERANCE
Sutherland, John *see*
– ORIGINAL MATTER CONTAINED IN LIEUT-COLONEL SUTHERLAND'S MEMOIR ON THE KAFFERS, HOTTENTOTS, AND BOSJEMANS OF SOUTH AFRICA, HEADS 1ST AND 2ND
– PUBLISHERS' CIRCULAR 1837-1900
Sutherland, Laroy *see* TRANCE, AND CORRELATIVE PHENOMENON
Sutherland, P C *see* JOURNAL OF A VOYAGE IN BAFFIN'S BAY AND BARROW STRAITS
Sutherland, Richard *see* THE PARAQUAT REPORT, A HIT-AND-RUN HERBICIDE
Sutherland, William *see* THE SHIPBUILDER'S ASSISTANT, OR MARINE ARCHITECTURE
SUTHERLANDSHIRE, 1837 : BRITISH ISLES CENSUS DIRECTORIES PROJECT, SCOTLAND. VOL 56 – 1mf – 9 – A$9.00 – at Vine [941]
SUTHERLANDSHIRE, 1852 : BRITISH ISLES CENSUS DIRECTORIES PROJECT, SCOTLAND. VOL 19 – 1mf – 9 – A$9.00 – at Vine [941]
SUTHERLIN STAR – Sutherlin, OR. -w. 5 Nov 1920-11 Nov 1921. 1 roll – 1 – us U.O. Library [071]
SUTHERLIN SUN – Sutherlin OR. July 29 1910-July 27 1951 – 1 – us U.O. Library [071]
SUTHERLIN SUN OAKLAND TRIBUNE – Sutherlin OR. Aug 3 1951-May 27 1959 – 1 – us U.O. Library [071]
SUTHERLIN SUN-TRIBUNE – Sutherlin, OR. -w. 4 June 1959-. – 1 – us U.O. Library [071]
Sutigna, Daeng *see* GEMBIRA BERNJANJI
Sutjipto Wirjosunparto, R M *see* GLIMPSES OF CULTURAL HISTORY OF INDONESIA
Sutjipto Wirjosuparto, R M *see* DARI LIMA ZAMAN PENDJADJAHAN MENUDJU ZAMAN KEMERDEKAAN; BUKU PELADJARAN SEDJARAH INDONESIA UNTUK SEKOLAH MENEGAH ATAS BAGIAN A.B. DAN C
Sutlive, Vinson H, 3rd *see* EFFECT OF PRACTICE SCHEDULE VARIATION ON THE ACQUISITION, RETENTION, AND TRANSFER OF AN APPLIED MOTOR SKILL BY CHILDREN WITH AND WITHOUT MENTAL RETARDATION
Sutoko Djojosubroto *see* PANTJA SILA PEMBENTUK KESATUAN BANGSA. INDONESIA
Sutomo *see*
– KEMANA BEKAS PEJUANG BERSENDJATA?
– KENANGAN BAHAGIA
– KINI TERSERAH PADA BUNG KARNO
– KO-ORDINASI DALAM REPUBLIK INDONESIA
– OPEN LETTER TO PRES. EISENHOWER
Sutomo, S Honggowongso *see* PEMBANGUNAN MASJARAKAT DESA DI INDONESIA
Sutrisno, C *see* ON THE DIURNAL VARIATION OF AIR TEMPERATURE
SUTRO MEXICAN PAMPHLET COLLECTION – (This coll is the largest of its kind in the world, covering the period 1680-1880. Pamphlets cover all aspects of Mexican life; political, religious, literary, economic, scientific and others. Also included are annual reports of the ministries, rare sermons and unique runs of periodicals such as El Iris) – 161r – 1,5 – $8,050.00 coll + index (Index $165.00 3r B61001) – B61000 – us Library Micro [972]
SUTTER COUNTY – Sutter Co, CA: Thompson & West, 1879 – 1r – 1 – $50.00 – B40280 – us Library Micro [978]
SUTTER COUNTY, 1925-1949 – 24r – 1 – $1,200.00 – D101 – us Library Micro [978]
SUTTER COUNTY FARMER – Yuba City, CA. 1881-1933 – 17r – 1 – $850.00 – B03127 – us Library Micro [630]
SUTTER COUNTY PAPERS : SENTINEL, FARMER AND BANNER – 1867-1868 – 1r – 5 – $50.00 – B06011 – us Library Micro [071]
SUTTER INDEPENDENT – Yuba City, CA. 1893-1935 – 23r – 1 – $1,150.00 – B03128 – us Library Micro [071]
SUTTERTOWN NEWS – Sacramento, CA. 1977-1989 – 8r – 1 – $400.00 – B05059 – us Library Micro [071]
SUTTER/YUBA COUNTIES – 1992- – 3+ r – 1 – $150.00 – P00142 – us Library Micro [910]
Suttie, Ian Dishart *see* THE ORIGINS OF LOVE AND HATE
Suttner, Bertha von *see*
– DIE WAFFEN NIEDER
– WHEN THOUGHTS WILL SOAR
SUTTON 1720-1825 – (Mf 1: Church Records 1720-1822. Mf 2: Church Records 1729-1826; Marriages 1766-1825; Deaths 1769-88, 1796-98. Mf 3: Church Records 1734-93; Baptisms 1728-1826. Mf 4: Parish Records 1743-60. Mf 5: Parish Records 1750-71. Mf 6: Parish Records 1772-73; Inventory of Church Records) – (mf ed 1993) – 6mf – 9 – us Holbrook [920]
Sutton, Amos *see* ORISSA AND ITS EVANGELIZATION
SUTTON AND CHEAM HERALD – London. -w. 21 Jun 1957-Dec 1965. (12 reels) – 1 – uk British Libr Newspaper [072]
SUTTON AND CHEAM WEEKLY RECORD – London, England. -w. 6 Aug 1909-30 Dec 1910. 65 ft – 1 – uk British Libr Newspaper [072]
Sutton, Anthony *see* WARS AND REVOLUTIONS
SUTTON COLDFIELD AND ERDINGTON NEWS – England. -w. 1 Jan-31 Dec 1870; 6 Jan 1877-2 Dec 1882; 11 Aug 1883-19 July 1884. 7 reels – 1 – uk British Libr Newspaper [072]
SUTTON COLDFIELD AND ERDINGTON TIMES – England. -w. 31 March 1883-9 Feb 1901. Lacking 1896. 16 reels – 1 – uk British Libr Newspaper [072]
SUTTON COLDFIELD NEWS – England. -w. 10 Feb 1900-Dec 1912. 13 reels – 1 – uk British Libr Newspaper [072]
SUTTON HERALD – London. -w. 3 Aug 1878-26 Dec 1885. (5 reels) – 1 – uk British Libr Newspaper [072]
SUTTON JOURNAL – London, England. -w. 30 Sept 1863-25 Dec 1902. Lacking 1897. 18 reels – 1 – uk British Libr Newspaper [072]
SUTTON NEWS – Sutton, NE. -w. Sept 1895-Aug 1905; Oct 1905; Dec 1905-Feb 1936 – 1 – us NE Hist [071]
SUTTON PIONEER – Sutton, Canada. 16 oct 1879 – 1r – 1 – Can$25.00 – cn Can Microfilming [072]
SUTTON REGISTER – Sutton, NE. -w. Mar 1881; Oct 1881; Jul 1887; Sept 1889-Dec 1891; Jan 1894-Dec 1896; Jan 1899-Dec 1917; Feb 1925-Dec 1942 – 1 – us NE Hist [071]
Sutton's Hospital. Charterhouse *see* THE ASSEMBLY ORDER BOOKS
Suviranta, Antti *see* THE ROLE OF THE MEMBER STATES IN THE UNIFICATION WORK OF THE INTERNATIONAL LABOUR ORGANIZATION
SUVORIN : CITY DIRECTORIES OF ST PETERSBURG/LENINGRAD, 1892-1940 – (1: St Petersburg Address Books 1892-1902 261mf $1,300. 2: All Petersburg 1894-1917 773mf $3,800. 3: All Leningrad 1922-40 (not publ for 1936-39) 380mf $1,900) – 1993 – 1414mf – 9 – $6,500.00 coll – us Ross [910]
Suvorov, Alexandr Vasil'evich *see* OPIS' DOKUMENTAL'NYKH MATERIALOV ARKHIVNOGO FONDA NO.43
SUVOROV V RODNOI POEZII / ed by Petrov, P V – Sbornik pesen, legend, predanii, od, poslanii i drugikh stikhotvorenii XVII-XIX stoletti. Spb. 1900. BR-7764 2 – 8 – ne IDC [460]
SUVOROVETS – (Includes c.1: 1948:Sept.24-Oct.8, 22-1951:Sept.22, Oct.6-Dec.29) – Buenos Aires: Suvorovskii soiuz, 1948- – 1 reel – 1 – CSUXANR0124-S – us Hoover Inst Photo [355]
Suwalski, I *see* KENESET HA-GEDOLAH
SUWANNEE DEMOCRAT – Live Oak. Fl. -w. 1906-1910, 1928-1930, 1932- – 1 – us P.K. Yonge [071]
Suwardi, Idris *see*
– NAPOLEON DIMEDAN ASMARA
– TERBUNUHNJA PRESIDEN KENNEDY
Suwardjo *see* BALAI PENDIDIKAN MASJARAKAT DESA; B.P.M.D. VILLAGE EDUCATIONAL CENTER
Suyematsu, Kencho *see* THE RISEN SUN
Suys, E *see* LA SAGESSE D'ANI. TEXTE, TRADUCTION ET COMMENTAIRE
EN SUYUERLIJCKE BEWIJSREDEN VAN GODES WOORT / Joris, David – BME-373 1 – 9 – ne IDC [240]
Suzdal'tsev, K K *see* KOOPERATSIIA I PROSVESHCHENIE

SUZETTE: LIVRE DE LECTURE COURANTE A L'USAGE DES JEUNES FILLES / Halt, Marie Malezieux – Paris: P. Delaplaine, 1888. 328p. (Literature Collection) – 4mf – 9 – $10.00 – fr Bibl Nationale [830]

SUZHDENIYA I TOLKI SHTUNDISTOV I OPROVERZHENIE IKH / Leonov, Ioann – Opinions and Doctrine on the Stundists and Their Refutation. Kiev, 1890. One of 13 titles on reel – 1 – 86.44 – us Baptist [240]

Suzor, L T *see*
- CODE MILITAIRE
- TABLEAU SYNOPTIQUE DES EVOLUTIONS D'UN BATAILLON ACCOMPAGNE DE PLANCHES

Suzuki, Daisetz Teitaro *see* STUDIES IN ZEN

SV. LOVRENC AND SMIHEL CHURCHES – Dolenjsko, Slovenia, 1905-1950 – 1 reel – 1 – us I.H.R.C. [240]

SVABU KAPRICO / Eglitis, Anslavs – 1951. 252p. illus – 1 – us U.W. Library [830]

Svalastoga, K *see* SOCIOLOGICAL MICROJOURNAL

Svardson, G *see* STUDIEN UEBER DEN ZUSAMMENHANG ZWISCHEN GESCHLACHTSREIFE UND WACHSTUM BEI LEBISTES

SVARI – Riga. year 3 no. 29- year 9 no. 51. July 7 1922-Dec 21 1928 – 1 – us NY Public [999]

SVATOSLAVICH. VRAZHII PITOMETS / Veltman, A F – Moscow, 1835. v1-2. B-1468/2 – 8 – ne IDC [460]

SVCCESSI DELL' ARMATA DELLA M^{TA} C^{CA} DESTINATA ALL' IMPRESA DI TRIPOLI DI BARBERIA, DELLA PRESA DELLE GERBE, E PROGRESSI DELL' ARMATA TURCHESCA, ... / Cirni, AF – Fiorenza, 1560 – 2mf – 9 – H-8296/1 – ne IDC [956]

SVCCESSI DELLA ARMATA DELLA MAESTA' CATOLICA DESTINATA ALL' IMPRESA DI TRIPOLI DI BARBERIA, DELLA PRESA DELLE GERBE, E PROGRESSI DELL' ARMATA TURCHESCA, ... / Cirni, AF – Vinegia, 1560 – 2mf – 9 – H-8295/1 – ne IDC [956]

SVCCESSIO APOSTOLICA. DAT IS, NAECOMINGHE, OFT DE NAETREDINGHE DER / Meulen, J P vander – Alcmaer, J. de Meester. 1600. BME-260 1 – 9 – ne IDC [240]

SVCCESSO DELLA FELICE VITTORIA, CHE HA CONSEGUITO L'ARMATA CHRISTIANA, CONTRA LA TURCHESCA – N.p., [1571] – 1mf – 9 – H-8185/1 – ne IDC [956]

SVEA – Worcester, CA. 1903-1954 – 104r – 1 – $5,200.00 – R04379 – us Library Micro [071]

SVEA – Worchester, MA. 1898-1902 – 4r – 1 – sw Kungliga [071]

SVEA: TIDSKRIFT FOR VETENSKAP OCH KONST – Upsala, 1818-31 – 3 – us Readex [073]

Svechin, A A *see* STRATEGY

Svechina, A *see* BOEVYE DEISTVIIA VTOROOCHEREDNYKH CHASTEI V MIROVUIU VOINU

SVEDENIE O SLAVIANSKIKH RUKOPISIAKH, POSTUPIVSHIKH IZ KNIGOKHRANILISHCHA SVIATO-TROITSKOI SERGIEVOI LAVRY V BIBLIOTEKU TROITSKOI DUKHOVNOI SEMINARII V 1747 G. (NYNE NAKHODIASHCHIKHSIA V BIBLIOTEKE MOSKOVSKOI DUKHOVNOI AKADEMII) / Leonid, Arkhimandrit – 2v. M. 1884-87. BR-7295 2 – 8 – ne IDC [010]

SVEDENIIA O NEBOL'SHIKH SOBRANIIAKH SLAVIANO-RUSSKIKH RUKOPISEI V SSSR / Rogov, A I – Moscow, 1962. 298p. BR-10,662/1 – 9 – ne IDC [025]

SVEDENIIA O RUKOPISIAKH PECHATNYKH IZDANIIAKH I DRUGIKH PREDMETAKH, POSTUPIVSHIKH V RUKOPISNOE OTDELENIE BIBLIOTEKI IMP. AKADEMII NAUK V 1900-1903 GG / Sreznevskii, 6 – St. Petersburg, 1902-05. BR-7335/2 – 8 – ne IDC [500]

SVEDOK = THE WITNESS – v60-78. 1966-84 (complete) – 3r – 1 – ATLA S0349 – us A.T.L.A. [240]

Svehla, B G *see* GRIP STRENGTH PROFILES OF ELEMENTARY AGED MALES AND FEMALES

Sveistrup, Heidi *see* CONTRIBUTIONS OF THE VISUAL AND SOMATOSENSORY PERCEPTUAL SYSTEMS TO THE DEVELOPMENT OF POSTURAL CONTROL IN INFANTS

SVEN ROS'EN OCH HANS INSATS I FRIHETS-TIDENS RADIKALA PIETISM / Linderholm, Emanuel – Uppsala & Stockholm: Almquist & Wiksells, 1911 – 1 – us U.W. Library [948]

SVENSK BOTANIK / ed by Palmstruch, J W – v. 1-8. Stockholm. 1802-19; v. 9-11. Upsala. 1823-43. B-5631 2 – 59mf – 8 – ne IDC [580]

SVENSK BOTANISK LITERATUR / Krok, T O B N – Lund. 1859-1906. B-5199 2 – 8 – ne IDC [580]

SVENSK BOTANISK TIDSKRIFT 1907-1932 – (Index v1-20 1907-26) – Stockholm, Uppsala. v1-26. 1908-32/33 – 162mf – 9 – 8575/1 – ne IDC [580]

SVENSK EKONOMI, 1960-1965 / Sweden. Finansdepartementet – 2v. Stockholm. 1962 – 9 – ne IDC [336]

SVENSK EKONOMI 1966-1970 MED UTBLICK MOT 1980. 1965 ARS LANGTIDSUTREDNING / Sweden. Finansdepartementet – (The Swedish Economy 1966-1970 with an Outlook for 1980. 1965 Long-Term Planning Commission). 8 v. Stockholm. 1966. BD-1752 1 – 9 – ne IDC [336]

SVENSK EKONOMI 1971-1975 MED UTBLICK MOT 1990. 1970 ARS LANGTIDSUTREDNING HUVUDRAPPORT / Sweden. Finansdepartementet – (The Swedish economy 1971-1975 and the General outlook up to 1990. Report by the 1970 Long-Term Planning Commission). Stockholm. 1970. BD-1753 1 – 9 – ne IDC [336]

SVENSK HANDELSTIDNING – Stockholm, Sweden. 1918-28 – 1 – sw Kungliga [072]

SVENSK LITTERATURTIDNING – Uppsala, Sweden. 1813 – 1 reel – 1 – sw Kungliga [410]

SVENSK MISSIONSTIDSKRIFT – v1-80. 1913-22 (complete) – 12r – 1 – ATLA 1993-S522 – us A.T.L.A. [073]

SVENSK ORNITHOLOGIE / Sparmann, A – Z 1935. 1806 – 9 – ne IDC [590]

SVENSK PASTORALTIDSKRIFT – (Lacks some pgs) – Uppsala, 1959-93 – 35r – 1 – ATLA S0461 – us A.T.L.A. [073]

SVENSK TEOLOGISK KVARTALSKRIFT – v1-26. 1925-50 (complete) – Inquire – 1 – ATLA 1993-S523 – us A.T.L.A. [073]

SVENSKA AMERIKANAREN – Chicago, IL. 1866-1939 – 73r – 1 – sw Kungliga [071]

SVENSKA AMERIKANSKA POSTEN – Minneapolis & St. Paul, MN. 1885-97, 1901-40 – 63r – 1 – sw Kungliga [071]

SVENSKA AMERIKANSKA TRIBUNEN – Superior, WI. 1904-20 – 16r – 1 – sw Kungliga [071]

SVENSKA DAGBLADET – Stockholm, 1952-53 – 24r – 1 – us Res Libr [072]

SVENSKA DAGBLADET – Stockholm, Sweden. 1884-1978. 1058 reels. Newsbills, 1966-78. 13 reels – 1 – sw Kungliga [072]

SVENSKA DAGBLADET – Stockholm, Sweden. 1979- – 1 – sw Kungliga [072]

SVENSKA FARM-JOURNALEN – Omaha, NE. -sm. Oct 1907-15 Mar 1910. The Swedish Agricultural Magazine – 1 – us NE Hist [630]

SVENSKA FOLKETS TRIBUN – Wahoo, NE. -w. 12 Feb. 1884-26 Aug 1884. In Swedish – 1 – us NE Hist [071]

SVENSKA FORNSANGER – 1834-42 – 1 – us I.U. Libraries [390]

Svenska Hjaelpkommitten for Spanien *see*
- FORTECKNING OVER TALARE OCH MATERIAL TILL DE LOKALA SPANIENKOMMITTEERNA, AUGUSTI 1937
- KORTFATTAD REDOGORELSE OVER ARBETET, DESS ORGANISATION OCH UTVECKLING SAMT RAPPORT FRAN KOMMITTENS REVISORER

SVENSKA JERUSALEMFORENINGENS TIDSKRIFT – 1965-88 (complete) – 2r – 1 – ATLA S0671 – us A.T.L.A. [073]

SVENSKA JOURNALEN – Omaha, NE. -w. 25 Sept 1890-28 Jan 1954. Title varies – 1 – us NE Hist [071]

DEN SVENSKA KYRKANS UTVECKLING : FRAN S:T BERNHARDS TIDEVARV TILL INNOCENTIUS III:S: EN UNDERSOEKNING / Westman, Knut B – Stockholm: P.A. Norstedt, [1915?] – 1mf – us A.T.L.A. [240]

SVENSKA LINNEE SAELLSKAPETS ARSSKRIFT – (Missing: v1 1918) – Uppsala. v1-15. 1918-32 – 32mf – 9 – 8576/1 – ne IDC [073]

DEN SVENSKA MISSIONEN I OST-AFRIKA / Beskov, Gustaf E – 2v. 1884-87 – 1 – us A.T.L.A. [240]

SVENSKA MORGONBLADET – (Svenska Morgonbladet, 1890-1956. Morgonbladet, 1957-58) – Stockholm, Sweden – 376r – 1 – sw Kungliga [072]

SVENSKA POSTEN – Omaha, NE. -w. 9 Dec 1893-4 Sep 1894. In Swedish – 1 – us NE Hist [071]

SVENSKA POSTEN – Seattle, WA. and Oregon Posten. Portland, OR. -w. 1930-39 – 1 – $96.00 – us Oregon Hist [071]

SVENSKA POSTEN – Seattle WA. Jan 30 1936-Dec 28 1939 – 1 – us U.O. Library [071]

SVENSKA PRESSEN – Omaha, NE. -w. 16 Apr 1903-17 Apr 1906. In Swedish – 1 – us NE Hist [071]

SVENSKA REPUBLIKANEN – Galesburg & Chicago, IL. 1896-98 – 1 reel – 1 – sw Kungliga [071]

SVENSKA STANDARET/SVENSKA STANDARET OCH NYA VECKO-POSTEN – Chicago.Swedish Baptist Churches in America. 1916, 1929-36. Single reels available – 1 – 173,00 – us A.B.H.S. [073]

SVENSKA TIDNINGEN – Stockholm, Sweden. 1851-59 – 30r – 1 – sw Kungliga [072]

SVENSKA VETENSKAPS ACADEMIENS HANDLINGAR – Stockholm, 1739-1941 – 2758mf – 9 – H-542c/2 – ne IDC [948]

Svenska Vetenskapsakademien, Stockholm *see*
- HANDLINGAR
- DER KONIGL

SVENSKA VETENSKAPS-AKADEMIENS HANDLINGAR : BIHANG – Stockholm, v1-28. 1872/1973-1902/1903 – 562mf – 9 – 7670/2 – ne IDC [948]

DEN SVENSKE FOLKSOCIALISTEN – Stockholm, 1939-50 – 9 – sw Kungliga [072]

DEN SVENSKE NATIONALSOCIALISTEN – Stockholm, 1933-39 – 9 – sw Kungliga [072]

SVENSKT LANGTIDSPROGRAM 1947-1952/53 / Sweden. Handelsdepartementet – Stockholm. 1948. BD-395 1 – 9 – ne IDC [338]

Sverdrup, Jacobo *see* LES ROBINSONS DU SPITZBERG

SVERIGENYTT – Stockholm, Sweden. 1979- – 1 – sw Kungliga [072]

SVERIGES OCH NORGES FISKAR / Stuxberg, A J – Z 2133 2. 1895 – 8 – ne IDC [590]

SVERIGES OCH NORGES FISKARNE FAUNA / Lilljeborg, W – 2135 2. 3 v. 1881-1891 – 8 – ne IDC [590]

SVERIGES OFFICIELLA STATISTIK. SOCIAL – STATISTIK. KOOPERATIV VERKSAMHET I SVERIGE / Sweden. Statistiska Centralbyraan – Stockholm. 1908 10-1937 – 1 – us NY Public [330]

Sveriges Socialdemokratiska Arbetareparti *see*
- SOCIAL-DEMOKRATEN

SVET = THE WORLD – Cleveland: Svet Print & Pub Co, 1911-39. [dec 18 1917-jun 1918; jan-jun 3 1939 (3r)] – 1 – us Res Libr [071]

SVET I ZVUK – St. Petersburg, Russia. n1-12. 1905 – 8mf – 9 – $50.00 – us Ross [780]

SVET I ZVUK *see* GRAMMOFON I FONOGRAF

SVET I ZVUK – St Petersburg. n1-12. 1905 (monthly) – 8mf – 9 – $50.00 – us Ross [780]

SVET SOCIALIZMU – Bratislava, Czechoslovakia. -w. 22 Dec 1960-31 Jan 1963. Imperfect. 2 reels – 1 – uk British Libr Newspaper [072]

SVET SOVETU – Prague. Czechoslovakia. -w. 21 Dec 1960-12 Jun 1963. (Imperfect). (2 reels) – 1 – uk British Libr Newspaper [072]

SVET VECHERNII / Ivanov, V – Stikhi (with an introduction by Sir Maurice Bowra). Clarendon press. Oxford. 1962. BR-744 2 – 8 – ne IDC [460]

SVET-AMERICAN – Cleveland: Tiskarska a Vydavatelska Spolecnost "Svet", jun 5 1939-jul 1 1950 – us Res Libr [071]

Svetlov, F *see* OCHEREDNYE ZADACHI MAKSIMALIZMA

SVETLYI CHAS. IZBRANNYE STIKHI / Bal'mont, K D – Paris. 1921. BR-542 2 – 8 – ne IDC [460]

SVETOVNA VOJNA – New York, NY, 1914 – 2mf or 1 reel – 1,9 – us I.H.R.C. [975]

SVETOZOR – Prague, Czechoslovakia. -w. 13 July 1867-15 Dec 1899; 27 April-1 Oct 1909. 26 reels – 1 – uk British Libr Newspaper [072]

SVEUCILISTNI ZAKONI I PROVEDBENA NAREDBA O DRZAVNIM ISPITIMA / Dalmatia. Laws, Statutes, etc – U Zagrebu, Tiskarski zavod "Narodnih novinah," 1895. 67 p. LL-4032 – 1 – us L of C Photodup [340]

SVF : FACHORGAN FUER TEXTILVEREDLUNG – v14-20 1959-65 – 1,5,6 – us Princeton Micro [670]

SVIET = LIGHT – (Library has from between v. 22, no. 34-v. 48, no. 52 (Aug. 30, 1918-Dec. 13, 1945; scattered issues only for v22, no. 34-v35, no. 52) – Wilkes Barre, Pa.: Russian Orthodox Catholic Mutual Aid Society of U.S.A., 1897- – 1 – CSUX86-S595 – us Hoover Inst Photo [240]

SVIJET – (Cont: Oslobodenje Svijet) – Sarajevo, Yugoslavia. May 1958-1960; 1962 – 3r – 1 – us L of C Photodup [949]

SVILUPPO E ORGANIZZAZIONE – v57-62. 1980 – 1,5,6,9 – us UMI [073]

SVIREL' / Sologub, F – Russkie berzherety. Petrograd. 1922. BR-882 2 – 8 – ne IDC [460]

SVIREL' PANA – Moscow, 1913-14 (bimonthly) – 3mf – 9 – us Ross [780]

Svirin, A N *see* ISKUSSTVO KNIGI DREVNEI RUSI

SVIT = THE LIGHT – Wilkes-Barre, PA, 1918, 1911-1924, 1927-1928, 1931-1944, 1946-1948, 1953-1954, 1965-1971, 1973-1975 – 44r – 1 – us I.H.R.C. [978]

SVOBODA – Chicago, 1930, 1935 – 2mf or 1 reel – 9,1 – us I.H.R.C. [975]

SVOBODA = LIBERTY – Jersey City, NJ: Ruthenian National Association, 1915-jun 1941; jan 2-dec 1992 – us Res Libr [071]

SVOBODA = LIBERTY – New York: Nicholas Lipchak. v1 n1-4. may 8-jun 15 1944 – us Res Libr [073]

SVOBODA – Prague, Czechoslovakia. May 1957-Jun 1966 (incomplete) – 7r – 1 – us L of C Photodup [072]

SVOBODA – Sofia, Bulgaria. Jul 1892-93; Sept 1944-Jan 1945 – 2r – 1 – us L of C Photodup [949]

SVOBODA – Warsaw, Poland. Jul-Nov 1921 – 1r – 1 – us L of C Photodup [943]

Svoboda, Jan *see* MAGNETIC AND ELECTRICAL SEPARATION

SVOBODA LA LIBERTE – Sofia, Bulgaria. Oct 1886-1891 – 3r – 1 – us L of C Photodup [949]

O SVOBODE RUSSKOI PECHATI / Gradovskii, A – Posmertnoe izdanie. Spb, 1906 – 9 – BR-10 507 1 – ne IDC [947]

SVOBODEN NAROD – Sofia, Bulgaria. Sept 1945-Apr 1947 – 3r – 1 – us L of C Photodup [949]

SVOBODNAIA MYSL – Geneva. Aug.-Dec. 1899, nos. 1-5; Apr.-Dec. 1900, nos. 4-12; Jan. Mar.-Apr. Sept. 1901, nos. 13-16 – 1 – 35.00r – us Hoover Inst Photo [072]

SVOBODNE CESKOSLOVENSKO – Prague, Czechoslovakia. Jun 1945-1946 – 2r – 1 – us L of C Photodup [072]

SVOBODNE SLOVO – Prague, Czechoslovakia. -d. July 1945-May 1947; Oct 1951-Dec 1970. 43 reels – 1 – uk British Libr Newspaper [072]

SVOBODNE SLOVO – Prague, Czechoslovakia. May 1945-1993 – 82r – 1 – us L of C Photodup [072]

SVOBODNO SLOVO – Sofia, Bulgaria. Jan-Sept 1894 – 1r – 1 – us L of C Photodup [949]

SVOBODNOE MYSL' = FREE THOUGHT – Onex, Switzerland. 1899, Nos 1-5; 1900, Nos19-1, 1-16. Missing: 1900, nos2,4. Tolstoyan periodical.With: Razvet. Geneva, Switzerland. 1904, 1-9. Marxist periodical – 1 – 22.80 – us Baptist [240]

Svobodny, Dolly *see*
- THE ALVINA TREUT BURROWS RESEARCH COLLECTION ON COMPOSITION
- EARL RANKIN COLLECTION ON CLOZE PROCEDURE
- THE JOHN A. LENT COLLECTION ON ASIAN MASS COMMUNICATIONS
- JOHN F. KENNEDY ASSASSINATION
- THE MARTIN KLING TARGETED READING COLLECTION
- THE RICHARD HODGES RESEARCH COLLECTION ON SPELLING
- WILLIAM S. GRAY RESEARCH COLLECTION IN READING

SVOBODNY SMER – Plzen, Czechoslovakia. Jun-Nov 1945 – 1r – 1 – us L of C Photodup [072]

SVOBODNYE NOVOSTI – (Backfile through 1998 $85r) – Belarus, 1999- – 1r per y standing order – 1 – us Ross [072]

SVOD 260 AZBUK I OBRAZTSOV KIRILITSY. IZ SNIMKOV RUKOPISEI X-XVIII VEKOV RUSSKOI IUGO-SLAVIANSKIKH / Trusevich, Ia – Izbornik. St. Petersburg, 1905, Pt.1-2.BR-10,365/1 – 9 – ne IDC [947]
SVOD OTCHESTOV FABRICHNYKH INSPEKTOROV ZA 1900-1914 / Russia. Ministerstvo torgovli i promyshiennosti. Otdiel promyshiennosti – 1902-15 – 1 – $55.00 – us L of C Photodup [338]
SVOD SVEDENII O DEIATEL'NOSTI POTREBITEL'NYKH OBSHCHESTV V ROSSII VOOBSHCHE I ZA 1903 GOD V CHASTNOSTI / Totomiants, V F – Spb., 1905 – 2mf – 9 – COR-121/1 – ne IDC [334]
SVOD TRUDOV MIESTNYKH KOMITETOV PO 49 GUBERNIIAM EVROPEISKOI ROSSII / Russia. Osoboe Soveshohanie o Nuzhdakh Sel'Skokhoziaistvennai Promyshlennosti – St. Petersburg. 23v. 1903-05 – 1 – $46.00 – us L of C Photodup [330]
SVOD VYSOCHAISHIKH OTMETOK PO VSEPODDANEISHIM OTCHETAM GENERAL-GUBERNATOROV / Russia. Crown – St Petersburg. 1881-1893 – 1 – us NY Public [947]
SVODKA PO NARODNOMU KOMISSARIATU IUSTITSII U.S.S.R. / Ukraine, Narodnyi komisariat iustytsii – (Includes c.1: no.1 1921:Jan./Feb.) – Kharkov: Otdel publikatsii zakonov N.K. I U., 1921- – 1 – CSUXAKZ4022-S – us Hoover Inst Photo [320]
SVODNYE MATERIALY O DEIATELNOSTI SOVETA NARODNYKH KOMISSAROV SSSR I SOVETA TRUDA I OBORONY ZA... / Soviet Union, Sovet narodnykh komissarov – (Includes c.1: 1924/1925-1927/1928) – Moskva: [Informatsionnoe biuro Upravleniia delami Sovnarkoma i STO SSSR], 1925-1928. 4v – 1 – CSUXAKY6413-S – us Hoover Inst Photo [340]
SVODNYI BALANS PO KRYMSKOI MESTNOI TRESTIROVANNOI GOSPROMYSHLENNOSTI,...I KOOPERATSII ZA 1924-1925 OPERATSIONNYI GOD – Simferopol', 1926 – 6mf – 9 – COR-745/1 – ne IDC [334]
SVODNYI STATISTICHESKII BIULLETEN PO GORODU MOSKVE I MOSKOVSKO I GUBERNII ZA... = BULLETIN STATISTIQUE RECAPITULATIF DE LA VILLE ET DU GOUVERNEMENT DE MOSCOU / Sostavlen Statisticheskim otdelom Moskovskogo soveta – (Includes c.1: 1927) – Moskva: Sovet, 19uu – 1 – CSUXAKZ2521-S – us Hoover Inst Photo [310]
SVORNOST – (Filmed consecutively with: Nedelni svornost nov 28 1932-may 14 1942) – Chicago: [s.n.], 1875 – us Res Libr [071]
SVPM, STANDARD-VACUUM PETROLEUM MAATSCHAPPIJ, 40 TAHUN KEMADJUAN, 1912-1952 / Standard-Vacuum Oil Company – SE 5920 1. 1953 – 9 – ne IDC [660]
SVPM (STANDARD-VACUUM PETROLEUM MAATSCHAPPIJ), FORTY YEARS OF PROGRESS, 1912-1952 / Standard-Vacuum Oil Company – SE 3523 1. 1953 – 9 – ne IDC [660]
SWA PIONIER – Windhoek, S.W.A.1976-77 – 1 – sa State Libr [072]
Swaan, J S *see* TOT STREELING VAN HET OOG EN VOEDSEL VOOR HET HART
SWADESAMITRAN – Madras, India. Sept 1946-11 Aug 1977 – 70r – 1 – us L of C Photodup [072]
SWADHINATA – Calcutta, India. 1952-54; 1956 – 5r – 1 – us L of C Photodup [072]
Swagerty, William R *see* PAPERS OF THE ST LOUIS FUR TRADE
Swaim, David G *see* LETTERS, MS 3263
Swain, G W *see* THE INDIVIDUAL
Swaine, S A *see* FAITHFUL MEN
Swainson, Charles Anthony *see*
– THE CREEDS OF THE CHURCH
– THE GREEK LITURGIES
Swainson, H *see* THE CHURCH OF SANCTA SOPHIA CONSTANTINOPLE
Swainson, W *see*
– BIRDS OF WESTERN AFRICA
– EXOTIC CONCHOLOGY
– ON THE NATURAL HISTORY AND CLASSIFICATION OF BIRDS
– A TREATISE ON MALACOLOGY; OR THE NATURAL CLASSIFICATION OF SHELLS AND SHELLFISH
– A TREATISE ON THE GEOGRAPHY AND CLASSIFICATION OF ANIMALS
SWAKOPMUNDER ECHO – Swakopmund, South West Africa. 1916 – 1 – sa State Libr [072]
SWAKOPMUNDER ZEITUNG – Swakopmund, South West Africa. 1911-38 – 1 – sa State Libr [072]
Swallow, T *see* DISRUPTIONS AND SECESSIONS IN METHODISM
Swamikannu Pillai, L D *see* AN INDIAN EPHEMERIS, A.D. 700 TO A.D. 1999
Swammerdam, Jan *see*
– BIBLIA NATURAE; SIVE HISTORIA INSECTORUM
– THE BOOK OF NATURE OR THE HISTORY OF INSECTS.
– EPHEMERI VITA
– HISTOIRE GENERALE DES INSECTES
– MIRACULUM NATURAE
SWAMPLAND RECORDS, 1852-1874 / Illinois County Records – Edwards-White Co. V141-0091 – 1 – us A.G.L.L. [978]
Swan, Frederick R *see* THE IMMANENCE OF CHRIST IN MODERN LIFE
Swan, Fredrick W *see* THE SPIRIT OF NEW ENGLAND
SWAN HILL GUARDIAN – 1901-1950. SG1-67 – 67r – 1 – at Corangamite [072]
SWAN HILL SHIRE RATES – 1863-1899 – 246mf – 9 – at Corangamite [980]
SWAN HILL SHIRE VARIOUS MINUTES – 1881-1946 – 69mf – 9 – at Corangamite [350]
Swan, Joseph Rockwell *see*
– A NEW TREATISE ON THE LAW RELATING TO THE POWERS AND DUTIES OF JUSTICES OF THE PEACE AND CONSTABLES IN THE STATE OF KANSAS...REVISED TO CONFORM TO THE STATUTES IN FORCE 1872
– A TREATISE ON THE LAWS OF OHIO PERTAINING TO THE POWERS AND DUTIES OF, AND PRACTICE BEFORE, JUSTICES OF THE PEACE...17TH ED
Swan, Peter L *see* ON BUYING A JOB, THE REGULATION OF TAXI CABS IN CANBERRA
SWANAGE TIMES AND DIRECTORY – England.6 Sept 1919-1936. -w.17 1/4 reels – 1 – uk British Libr Newspaper [072]
DER SWANGERN FRAWEN / Roesslin, E – M 162. 1513 – 9 – ne IDC [890]
Swank, James M *see* CAMBRIA COUNTY PIONEERS
Swann, H K *see* A BIBLIOGRAPHY OF BRITISH ORNITHOLOGY...
Swann, Peter et al *see* ECONOMICS OF INNOVATION AND NEW TECHNOLOGY
SWANSEA AND NEATH ADVERTISER – (Swansea and South Wales Advertising Journal Sept-Dec 1853) – Wales, UK. 3 Jan 1849-1 Mar 1852; 22 Sept-29 Dec 1853 – 1r – 1 – uk British Libr Newspaper [072]
SWANSEA AND SOUTH WALES ADVERTISING JOURNAL *see* SWANSEA AND NEATH ADVERTISER
SWANTON BAPTIST CHURCH. SWANTON, VERMONT : CHURCH RECORDS – 1796-1840 – 1 – 11.61 – us Baptist [240]
Swanton, E W *see* THE MOLLUSCA OF SOMERSET (LAND, FRESHWATER, ESTUARINE AND MARINE)
SWANTON ECHO – Swanton, NE. -w. Mar-Apr 1895; Jul 1895-Jun 1896 – 1 – us NE Hist [071]
SWANTON ENTERPRISE – Swanton, Ohio. 1922- – 31r – 1 – $32.50r – us Archival [071]
SWANTON ITEMS – Swanton, NE. -w. Nov 1896-May 1897 – 1 – us NE Hist [071]
Swanton, J R *see*
– CONTRIBUTIONS TO THE ETHNOLOGY OF THE HAIDA
– SOCIAL CONDITION, BELIEFS, AND LINGUSTIC RELATIONSHIP OF THE TLINGIT INDIANS
SWANTON NEWS – Swanton, NE. -w. Mar 1893-Apr 1895; Jan 1898-Nov 1902; Jan 1903-Sept 1907; Oct 1908-Feb 1911 – 1 – us NE Hist [071]
Swars, Ewald *see* DAS DORF AM MEER
SWARTHMORE COLLEGE PEACE COLLECTION *see*
– THE PAPERS OF EDWIN DOAK MEAD AND LUCIA AMES MEAD, 1876-1936
– THE PAPERS OF EMILY GREENE BALCH, 1875-1961
– THE PAPERS OF HANNAH CLOTHIER HULL, 1889-1958
Swarthmore College Peace Collection Staff. Woman's Peace Party *see* COLLECTED RECORDS OF THE WOMAN'S PEACE PARTY, 1914-20
Swartling, Karl *see* FYRTIOFEMTE PSALMEN AF PSALTAREN OFVERSATTNING MED ANMARKNINGAR
Swartz, C *see* SYNOPSIS FILICUM
Swartz, Clarence B *see* WHAT IS MUTUALISM?
Swartz, O P *see*
– DISPOSITIO SYSTEMATICA MUSCORUM FRONDOSORUM SUECIAE
– FLORA INDIAE OCCIDENTALIS
– ICONES PLANTARUM INCOGNITARUM QUAS IN INDIA OCCIDENTALI
– METHODUS MUSCORUM ILLUSTRATA
– NOVA GENERA ET SPECIES PLANTARUM SEU PRODROMUS DESCRIPTIONUM VEGETABILIUM
– OBSERVATIONES BOTANICAE
– SYNOPSIS FILICUM EARUM ET SPECIES SYSTEMATICE COMPLECTENS
Swayne, William Shuckburgh *see* AN INQUIRY INTO THE NATURE OF OUR LORD'S KNOWLEDGE AS MAN
THE SWAZI / Kuper, Hilda – London: International African Insitute, 1952 – us Res Libr [305]
THE SWAZI / Marwick, B A – An ethnographic account of the natives of the Swaziland Protectorate. (Cambridge University Press). Cambridge. 1940. BA-365 2 – 8 – ne IDC [960]
SWAZILAND : ANNUAL STATISTICAL BULLETIN 1966-1976 / Swaziland. Central Statistical Office – (1969 not publ. Coll title: African Official Statistical Serials, 1867-1982) – 16mf – 9 – £135.00 – uk Chadwyck [960]
Swaziland *see*
– GOVERNMENT DOCUMENTS, 1880-1972
– GOVERNMENT GAZETTE
– POST INDEPENDENCE DEVELOPMENT PLAN
– SECOND NATIONAL DEVELOPMENT PLAN, 1973-1977
– A STATEMENT OF DEVELOPMENT POLICIES AND PROGRAMMES 1973-1977
Swaziland. Central Statistical Office *see*
– EDUCATION STATISTICS 1968/69-1987
– SWAZILAND
Swaziland. Economic Planning Office *see*
– DEVELOPMENT PLAN 1990/91-1992/93
– DEVELOPMENT PLAN 1991/92-1993/94
– DEVELOPMENT PLAN 1992/93-1994/95
SWAZILAND EXPEDITION, 1888-90 ; ZULULAND CAMPAIGN, 1888-90 / Baden-Powell, R S S – 2 fiche + 3 fiche – 9 – sa SA Libr [960]
Swaziland Labour Department *see* FILE NOTE
Swaziland. Ministry of Education *see*
– ANNUAL REPORT 1955-1984/85
– CURRENT TRENDS IN EDUCATIONAL POLICY
– EDUCATIONAL DEVELOPMENT
Swaziland. Ministry of Education. Department of Economic Planning and Statistics *see* THE STATUS AND DEVELOPMENT OF EDUCATION IN THE KINGDOM OF SWAZILAND
Swaziland. Ministry of Education. Education Planning Section *see* A FINANCIAL AND STATISTICAL ANALYSIS OF SWAZILAND'S EDUCATIONAL SYSTEM, WITH PROJECTIONS TO 1986
Swaziland. National Education Commission *see* REPORT ... 1975
Swaziland. (United Kingdom) *see* DEVELOPMENT PLAN PROPOSALS, 1965-1968
Swaziland. United Kingdom *see* DEVELOPMENT PLAN, 1960-1964
Sweany, Lisa *see* COMPARISON OF FACTORS AFFECTING THE CAREER PATHS OF MALE AND FEMALE DIRECTORS OF INTERCOLLEGIATE ATHLETICS
SWEDEN = STATISTICAL ABSTRACT OF SWEDEN 1914-1965 : STATISTISK ARSBOK FOER SVERIGE 1914-1965 / Sweden. Statistiska Centralbyran – (Coll title: European Official Statistical Serials, 1841-1984) – 260mf – 9 – £4.00f (set £2,225.00 424mf) – uk Chadwyck [948]
SWEDEN : STATISTISK TIDSKRIFT 1860-1913 / Sweden. Kungl. Statistika Centralbyraan – (Coll title: European Official Statistical Serials, 1841-1984) – 164mf – 9 – £5.00f (set £2,225.00 424mf) – uk Chadwyck [948]
Sweden. Finansdepartementet *see*
– BALANSERAD EXPANSION. BETANKANDE AVGIVET AV 1955 ARS LANGTIDSUTREDNING
– SVENSK EKONOMI, 1960-1965
– SVENSK EKONOMI 1966-1970 MED UTBLICK MOT 1980. 1965 ARS LANGTIDSUTREDNING
– SVENSK EKONOMI 1971-1975 MED UTBLICK MOT 1990. 1970 ARS LANGTIDSUTREDNING HUVUDRAPPORT
Sweden. Finansdepartementet. 1950 ars Langtidsutredning *see* EKONOMISKT LANGTIDSPROGRAM, 1951-1955
Sweden. Handelsdepartementet *see* SVENSKT LANGTIDSPROGRAM 1947-1952/53
Sweden. Kungl. Statistika Centralbyraan *see* SWEDEN
Sweden. Long-Term Planning Commission *see* THE SWEDISH ECONOMY 1961-1965
Sweden. Ministry of Finance *see*
– THE SWEDISH ECONOMY 1966-1970 AND THE GENERAL OUTLOOK FOR THE SEVENTIES
– THE SWEDISH ECONOMY 1971-1975 AND THE GENERAL OUTLOOK UP TO 1990
Sweden. Statistika Centralbyraan *see* SVERIGES OFFICIELLA STATISTIK. SOCIAL – STATISTIK. KOOPERATIV VERKSAMHET I SVERIGE
Sweden. Statistika centralbyran *see* FOLKRAKNINGEN DEN 1 NOV 1960
Sweden. Statistiska Centralbyran *see* SWEDEN
SWEDENBORG : EN STUDIE OEFVER HANS UTVEKCLING TILL MYSTIKER OCH ANDESKADARE / Lamm, Martin – Stockholm: Hogo Geber, 1915 – 1mf – us A.T.L.A. [240]
Swedenborg, Emanuel von *see* OPERA VARIA
SWEDISH BAPTIST YEARBOOK – 1856-1961 – 1 – 602.70 – us Baptist [240]
THE SWEDISH ECONOMY 1961-1965 / Sweden. Long-Term Planning Commission – D 1209 1. 1963 – 9 – ne IDC [330]
THE SWEDISH ECONOMY 1966-1970 AND THE GENERAL OUTLOOK FOR THE SEVENTIES / Sweden. Ministry of Finance – D 1210 1. 1966 – 9 – ne IDC [330]
THE SWEDISH ECONOMY 1971-1975 AND THE GENERAL OUTLOOK UP TO 1990 / Sweden. Ministry of Finance – D 1211 1. 1971 – 9 – ne IDC [330]
THE SWEDISH ELEMENT IN ILLINOIS / Olson, Ernest W – Chicago: Swedish-American Biographical Assoc., 1917. Illinois Reel 10. (The Cox Library Collection) – 5 – us Americana [978]
THE SWEDISH ELEMENT IN OMAHA / Nelson, OM – Omaha: Morrell Printers, 1935. Nebraska Reel 8.(The Cox Library Collection) – 5 – us Americana [978]
SWEDISH FOLK-LORE / Hofberg, Herman – Trans. by W.H. Myers. Chicago, New York: Belford, Clarke & Co., 1888 – 1 – us U.W. Library [390]
THE SWEDISH SETTLEMENTS ON THE DELAWARE : THEIR HISTORY AND RELATION TO THE INDIANS, DUTCH AND ENGLISH, 1638-1664 / Johnson, Amandus – [Philadelphia?]: University of Pennsylvania, 1911 – 3mf – us A.T.L.A. [305]
THE SWEDISH SETTLEMENTS ON THE DELAWARE, 1638-1664 – 2v. By Amandus Johnson, 1969. Orig. publ., 1911. Indexes in v2. F-0852 and F-0853 – 9 – us A.G.L.L. [920]
Sweerts, C *see*
– MENGELZANGEN EN ZINNEBEELDEN
– ZEDE- EN ZINNEBEELDEN OVER KONING DAVIDS HARPZANGEN, NEVENS DAAR OP TOEGEPASTE ZIEL-ZUCHTEN
– ZEDE-EN ZINNEBEELDEN OVER KONING DAVIDS HARPGEZANGEN
Sweerts, H *see* ALLE DE GEDICHTEN VAN HIERONYMUS SWEERTS
SWEET AND MAXWELL'S GUIDE TO LAW REPORTS AND STATUTES. / Sweet & Maxwell, Ltd. London – Toronto, Carswell, 1929. 70 p. LL-2230 – 1 – us L of C Photodup [340]
Sweet, Henry *see*
– A PRIMER OF PHONETICS
– A PRIMER OF SPOKEN ENGLISH
SWEET HOME FIRST BAPTIST CHURCH. SWEET HOME, OREGON : CHURCH RECORDS – Jun 1943-Sep 1962 – 1 – 24.12 – us Baptist [240]
Sweet, Louis Matthews *see*
– THE BIRTH AND INFANCY OF JESUS CHRIST: ACCORDING TO THE GOSPEL NARRATIVES
– ROMAN EMPEROR WORSHIP
Sweet & Maxwell, Ltd. London *see* SWEET AND MAXWELL'S GUIDE TO LAW REPORTS AND STATUTES.
Sweet, R *see*
– FLORA AUSTRALASICA
– GERANIACEAE
– GERANIACEAE. THE NATURAL ORDER OF GERANIA

- HORTUS BRITANNICUS
- HORTUS SUBURBANUS LONDINENSIS: OR A CATALOGUE OF PLANTS
- THE NATURAL ORDER OF CISTUS

SWEET SINGERS OF WALES : A STORY OF WELSH HYMNS AND THEIR AUTHORS / Lewis, Howell Elvet – London: Religious Tract Society, [1889?] – 1mf – us A.T.L.A. [240]

Sweet, William Warren *see* THE METHODIST EPISCOPAL CHURCH AND THE CIVIL WAR

SWEET'S ARCHITECTURAL CATALOGUES – 1906-49 – 2,334mf – 9 – $11,345.00 – us UPA [720]

SWEETWATER / Faldbakken, Knut – 1994 – 184p – 9 – 92-3-102936-3 – Co-Published with Peter Owen Publishers, London, Which Has Exclusive Sales Rights in the UK – fr UNESCO [830]

SWEETWATER BAPTIST CHURCH (ALIAS MT. LEBANON). NORTH AUGUSTA, SOUTH CAROLINA : CHURCH RECORDS – 1832-1966. Cemetary Financial Records. 1897-1920 – 1 – 49.32 – us Baptist [240]

SWENSK WECKOTIDNING – Stockholm, Sweden. 1893-94 – 1 – sw Kungliga [072]

DEN SWENSKE REPUBLIKANEN I NORRA AMERIKA – Galva & Chicago, IL. 1856-58 – 1 reel – 1 – sw Kungliga [071]

Swete, Henry Barclay *see*
- THE APOSTLES' CREED
- THE APPEARANCES OF OUR LORD AFTER THE PASSION:...EARLIEST CHRISTIAN TRADITION
- CHURCH SERVICES AND SERVICE-BOOKS BEFORE THE REFORMATION
- ENGLAND VERSUS ROME
- ESSAYS ON SOME BIBLICAL QUESTIONS OF THE DAY
- THE GOSPEL ACCORDING TO ST MARK
- THE HOLY SPIRIT IN THE NEW TESTAMENT
- AN INTRODUCTION TO THE OLD TESTAMENT IN GREEK
- ON THE EARLY HISTORY OF THE DOCTRINE OF THE HOLY SPIRIT
- ON THE HISTORY OF THE DOCTRINE OF THE PROCESSION OF THE HOLY SPIRIT
- PATRISTIC STUDY
- THE PSALMS OF SOLOMON
- TWO CAMBRIDGE DIVINES OF THE SEVENTEENTH CENTURY

SWIASEK I PARAFJA A SWIADOMOSC NARODOWA EMIGRANTA / Chalasinski, Jozef – Poznan-Warszawa, 1936 – 2r – 1 – us I.H.R.C. [304]

SWIASTUN – v1-34, 1946-79. Continues: Straznica Ewangeliczna – 1 – us A.T.L.A. [073]

SWIAT – Warsaw, Poland. v3-6, 1953-56 – 1 – us I.U. Libraries [073]

SWIAT I POLSKA – Warsaw, Poland. -w. May 1957-March 1959. 3 reels – 1 – uk British Libr Newspaper [943]

SWIAT I POLSKA – Warsaw. v. 1, no. 1-v. 3, no. 46. Nov 17 1946-Nov 14 1948 – 1 – us NY Public [072]

Swieten, Jan van *see* DE LUITENANT-GENERAAL J. VAN SWIETEN CONTRA DEN LUITENANT-GENERAAL G. M. VERSPYCK

SWIFT CREEK BAPTIST CHURCH. DARLINGTON COUNTY. SOUTH CAROLINA : CHURCH RECORDS – 1852-1940 – 1 – 17.08 – us Baptist [240]

SWIFT CURRENT SUN – (Some missing issues) – Swift Current, Alberta, CN. Apr 1904-1967 – 77r – 1 – cn Commonwealth Micro [072]

Swift, Ernest John *see* MR. SWIFT, VICE-PRES. OF THE AMERICAN RED CROSS, GIVES HIS IMPRESSIONS OF REPUBLICAN SPAIN

Swift, Jonathan *see* A PROPOSAL FOR CORRECTING, IMPROVING AND ASCERTAINING THE ENGLISH TONGUE

Swift, Lindsay *see* BROOK FARM

SWIFTCREEK BAPTIST CHURCH. PAMICO ASSOCIATION. NORTH CAROLINA : CHURCH RECORDS – 1808-49 – 1 – 6.57 – us Baptist [240]

SWIMMING AND LIFE-SAVING / Andrews, William – Toronto: W. Briggs, 1889. 04208. (Pre-1900 Canadiana) – 9 – cn C.I.H.M. [790]

A SWIMMING PROTOCOL FOR DETERMINATION OF INDIVIDUAL ANAEROBIC THRESHOLD / Hein, Michael S – 1988 – 129p 2mf – 9 – $8.00 – us Microform Publ [617]

SWIMMING TECHNIQUE – v1- 1964- 1; v14-5,6,9 – us UMI [790]

Swinburne, Algernon Charles *see*
- A CENTURY OF ROUNDELS
- A MIDSUMMER HOLIDAY AND OTHER POEMS
- WILLIAM BLAKE

Swindell, Frank G *see* A SHORT HISTORY OF ST ANDREW'S CATHEDRAL, SINGAPORE

SWINDON ADVERTISER – England. -sw and w. Jan 1858-Sep 1869, Jun 1873-Dec 1960. (174 reels) – 1 – uk British Libr Newspaper [072]

SWINE DAY / South Dakota. State University. Agricultural Experiment Station – nos.1-8. 1958-74 – 1,5,6 – us Spaulding [636]

SWINE FEEDERS' DAY / Minnesota. College of Agriculture. Institute of Agriculture – nos.31-37. 1953-59 – 1,5,6 – us Spaulding [636]

SWINE SHORT COURSE PROCEEDINGS / Texas A & M University. Department of Animal Science – 1957-82.21 fiches – 9 – us Spaulding [636]

Swineshead, Richard *see* CALCULATIONES NOUITER EMENDATE ATQUE REUISE. QUAESTIO INSUPER DE REACTIONE IUXTA ARISTOTELIS SENTENTIAM COMMENTATORIS

Swing, Albert Temple *see* JAMES HARRIS FAIRCHILD, OR, SIXTY-EIGHT YEARS WITH A CHRISTIAN COLLEGE

Swing, David *see* THE WORLD'S EDITION OF THE GREAT PRESBYTERIAN CONFLICT, PATTON VS. SWING

SWINGING SIXTIES : FASHION IN BRITAIN FROM 1960 TO 1969 – (In 2 sections: by designer and chronologically. Indexes by name, date, etc. Pt 4 of series "Fashion, Costume and Uniforms") – 1984 – 27 colour mf – 15 – $532.00 – 0-907696-15-5 – uk Emmett [740]

Swinhoe, C *see*
- A CATALOGUE OF THE MOTHS OF INDIA
- LEPIDOPTERA INDICA

Swinney, James Oswald *see* ECCE FILIUS

Swisher *see* HISTORY OF HAMPSHIRE COUNTY

Swiss Chiropractors' Association *see* ANNALS

Switalski, B W *see* DAS CHALCIDIUS KOMMENTAR ZU PLATOS TIMAEUS

SWITZERLAND = ANNUAIRE STATISTIQUE DE LA SUISSE 1891-1965 : STATISTISCHES JAHRBUCH DER SCHWEIZ 1891-1965 / Switzerland. Eidgenoessisches Statistisches Amt – (Coll title: European Official Statistical Serials, 1841-1984) – 402mf – 9 – £2,110.00 – uk Chadwyck [949]

Switzerland *see* STAATSKALENDER DER SCHWEIZERISCHEN EIDGENOSSENSCHAFT

Switzerland. Eidgenoessisches Statistisches Amt *see* SWITZERLAND

Switzerland. Laws, Statutes, etc *see*
- BUNDESGESETZ UBER DAS VERFAHREN BEI DEM BUNDESGERICHTE IN BURGERLICHEN RECHTSSTRETIGKEITEN
- LANDWIRTSCHAFTLICHE GESETZGEBUNG DES BUNDES
- LOI FEDERALE SUR L'ORGANISATION JUDICIAIRE FEDERALE

SWITZERLAND'S FOUR NATIONAL LANGUAGES / Doka, Carl – 13p – 9 – 1.00f – at Libertarian Micro [320]

Swobada, A *see* HARMONIELEHRE

Swope, Gilbert E *see* HISTORY OF THE BIG SPRING PRESBYTERIAN CHURCH, NEWVILLE, PA., 1737-1898

THE SWORD AND GARMENT / Townsend, Luther Tracy – Boston: Lee and Shepard, 1871 – 1mf – us A.T.L.A. [240]

THE SWORD AND THE KEYS : CIVIL AND SPIRITUAL JURISDICTIONS, THEIR UNION AND DIFFERENCE / Joyce, James Wayland – London: Sold at the office of the English Church Union, 1881 – 1mf – us A.T.L.A. [240]

THE SWORD AND THE TROWEL – London, England.1865-91; 1893-97 1908-09, 1921, 1922, 1926, 1930, 1952.Single reels available – 1 – 453.70 – us A.B.H.S. [073]

SWORD AND TROWEL – 1868-94 – 1 – $378.00 – us UMI [240]

THE SWORD OF THE LORD – (Some pgs missing) – v1-34. 28 Sep 1934-1968 – 11r – 1 – ATLA S0163 – us A.T.L.A. [073]

THE SWORD OF TRUTH : AND HARBINGER OF PEACE – South Lebanon, ME: G J Adams. [v1 n1-v4 n8]. sep 15 1862-jun 15 1867 – us Res Libr [073]

SWORD OF TRUTH AND HARBINGER OF PEACE – v. 1-3. 1862-1866 – 1 – us UMI [240]

Swynnerton, C F M *see* SHORT CUTS BY BIRDS TO NECTARIES

Sy, Amadou Abel *see* LA GESTE TIEDO

SYCAMORE LEADER – Sycamore, Ohio. 1900-38 – 13r – 1 – $32.50r – us Archival [071]

SYDENHAM AND PENGE GAZETTE – London. -w. 1873-1945. (71 reels) – 1 – uk British Libr Newspaper [072]

Sydenham, T *see*
- OBSERVATIONES MEDICAE CIRCA MORBORUM AUCTORUM HISTORIAM ET CURATIONEM
- TRACTATUS DE PODAGRA ET HYDROPE

SYDENHAM TIMES – London, UK. 1862-28 Sept 1869; 4 Jan-18 Oct 1870; 9 Jan 1872; 6 May 1873; 6 Jan 1874-28 Aug 1883. -w. 17 3/4 reels – 1 – uk British Libr Newspaper [072]

SYDHALLAND – Laholm, Sweden. 1893-1932 – 63r – 1 – sw Kungliga [072]

Sydney Chamber of Commerce *see* COMMERCE

SYDNEY CHRONICLE – Sydney, 1839-48 – 4r – 1 – A$123.00 silver A$106.00 vesicular – at Pascoe [072]

SYDNEY DAILY ADVERTISER – Sydney, 1848 – 1r – 1 – A$31.00 silver A$27.00 vesicular – at Pascoe [072]

SYDNEY GAZETTE – Australia. -w. March 1803-Feb 1807; Jan 1810-Dec 1831; Jan 1837-Nov 1840. 13 1 2 reels – 1 – uk British Libr Newspaper [072]

SYDNEY GAZETTE AND NSW ADVERTISER – Sydney, 1803-42 – 18r – 1 – A$558.00 silver A$486.00 vesicular – at Pascoe [072]

SYDNEY HERALD – Sydney. Australia. (Sidney Morning Herald). -d; -w. Jun 1841-49; 1910-11. (35mqn reels) – 1 – uk British Libr Newspaper [072]

SYDNEY JEWISH NEWS – 1939-1970 – 17r – 1 – at Pascoe [072]

SYDNEY LAW REVIEW – (1978-. 5,6,9) – v. 1-. 1953- – 1 – us UMI [340]

SYDNEY MAIL – Sydney, 1860-1938 – 147r – 1 – A$4,410.00 silver A$3,822.00 vesicular – at Pascoe [072]

SYDNEY MAIL – Sydney, Australia. 1 Jan 1887-22 Jun 1922; 1 Jan 1930-17 Jun 1931; 6 Jan 1932-31 Aug 1938.-d. 120 reels – 1 – uk British Libr Newspaper [072]

SYDNEY MAIL INDEX / Mitchell Library. New South Wales – Details on request – 9 – at Pascoe [020]

SYDNEY MONITOR – Sydney, 1826-41 – 8r – 1 – A$270.00 silver A$230.00 vesicular – at Pascoe [072]

SYDNEY MORNING HERALD – (Current issues avail on subscription) – Sydney, 1831- – 1,443r – 1 – at Pascoe [072]

THE SYDNEY MORNING HERALD – 1842- – 36r per y – 1 – inquire – us Ross [072]

THE SYDNEY MORNING HERALD – (Issues for 1952-oct 4 1953 filmed consecutively with: Sunday Herald; for oct 11 1953-jul 12 1964 with: Sun-Herald) – Sydney, NSW: John Fairfax & Sons, jul 1938-1985 – us Res Libr [072]

SYDNEY MORNING HERALD INDEX – (Apply to publ for details) – 1900-14 – 9 – at Pascoe [020]

SYDNEY MORNING HERALD INDEX / Mitchell Library. New South Wales – Oct 1961-Feb 1962. Apr 1963-Dec 1978 – 9 – at Pascoe [072]

SYDNEY MORNING HERALD QUARTERLY INDEX – (Apply to publ for details) – 1927-61 – 9 – at Pascoe [020]

SYDNEY PUNCH – Sydney, 1956-57 – 1r – 1 – A$31.00 silver A$27.00 vesicular – at Pascoe [072]

SYDNEY STOCK AND STATION JOURNAL – Australia. 24 Jan 1893-27 Apr, 21 Sep 1917; 19 Dec 1919-30 Jun 1922.-w. 34 reels – 1 – uk British Libr Newspaper [072]

SYDNEY STOCK AND STATION JOURNAL ILLUSTRATED MONTHLY – Australia. -m. March-July 1907. 15 ft – 1 – uk British Libr Newspaper [073]

SYDNEY TIMES – Sydney, 1834-64 – 1r – 1 – A$35.00 silver A$30.00 vesicular – at Pascoe [072]

SYDNEY TRADE REVIEW AND PRICES CURRENT – Australia. -m. 25 May 1894-16 Sept 1911. 2 reels – 1 – uk British Libr Newspaper [072]

SYDOSTRA SVERIGES DAGBLAD – (Blekinge Folkblad, 1903-21; Sydostra Sveriges Dagblad, 1921-73; Sydostran, 1973-78) – Karlskrona, Sweden – 359r – 1 – sw Kungliga [072]

SYDOSTRA SVERIGES DAGBLAD, POST 1979 *see* SYDOSTRAN

SYDOSTRAN – Karlskrona, Sweden. 1979- – 1 – sw Kungliga [072]

SYDOSTRAN 1973-1978 *see* SYDOSTRA SVERIGES DAGBLAD

Sydow, Achim *see* SYSTEMS ANALYSIS MODELLING SIMULATION

Sydow, H *see* MONOGRAPHIA UREDINEARUM

Sydow, P *see*
- DIE BISHER BEKANNTEN EUROPAA5ISCHEN CHARACEEN
- MONOGRAPHIA UREDINEARUM
- THESAURUS LITERATURAE MYCOLOGICAE ET LICHENOLOGICAE

SYDSVENSKA DAGBLADET – Malmo, Sweden. 1979- – 1 – sw Kungliga [072]

SYDSVENSKA DAGBLADET *see* SYDSVENSKA DAGBLADET SNALLPOSTEN

SYDSVENSKA DAGBLADET SNALLPOSTEN – (Snallposten, 1848-71; Sydsvenska Dagbladet, 1870-71; Sydsvenska Dagbladet Snallposten, 1872-1978) – Malmo, Sweden – 1136r – 1 – sw Kungliga [072]

Syed Ali Asgar Bilgrami, A *see* LANDMARKS OF THE DECCAN. A COMPREHENSIVE GUIDE TO THE ARCHAEOLOGICAL REMAINS

SYGNALY – London, UK. May 1968-Jul 1969 – 1 – uk British Libr Newspaper [072]

SYGNALY – Warsaw, Poland. -w. Dec 1951; Feb 1952-Dec 1965. 13 reels – 1 – uk British Libr Newspaper [947]

Sykes, E R *see* DIGESTA MALACOLOGICA

Sykes, Meredith H *see* MANUAL ON SYSTEMS OF INVENTORYING IMMOVABLE CULTURAL PROPERTY

Sylburgius, F *see* SARACENIA, SIUE MOAMETHICA

LE SYLLABUS = SYLLABUS ERRORUM : TEXTE OFFICIEL ET QUELQUES NOTES / Pius 9, Pope – Geneve: [s.n.], 1873 – 1mf – 9 – 0-8370-8800-3 – 1986-2800 – us A.T.L.A. [240]

SYLLABUS DER VORLESUNGEN UEBER SPECIELLE UND MEDICINISCH-PHARMACEUTISCHE BOTANIK. ED. 8 / Engler, H G A – Berlin, 1919 – 5mf – 9 – ne IDC [615]

SYLLABUS MUSCORUM IN ITALIA ET IN INSULIS CIRCUMSTANTIBUS HUCUSQUE COGNITORUM / Notaris, G de – Taurini. 1838. B-5319 2 – 8 – ne IDC [580]

SYLLABUS OF A COURSE OF FOUR LECTURES ON THE HISTORY AND AUTHORITY OF THE HOLY SCRIPTURES IN THE CHURCH / Buchanan, Edgar Simmons – Sevenoaks: J Salmon, 1905 – 1mf – 9 – 0-8370-2503-6 – 1985-0503 – us A.T.L.A. [220]

SYLLABUS OF LECTURES ON APOSTOLIC HISTORY AND LITERATURE : PRINTED FOR THE USE OF THE SENIOR CLASS IN PRINCETON THEOLOGICAL SEMINARY / Hodge, Caspar Wistar – Princeton:Princeton Press, 1887 – 1mf – 9 – 0-8370-3604-6 – 1985-1604 – us A.T.L.A. [220]

A SYLLABUS OF OLD TESTAMENT HISTORY : OUTLINES AND LITERATURE FOR PRIVATE STUDY AND THE CLASS ROOM / Price, Ira Maurice – (Includes indexes) – 7th rev ed. New York: Fleming H Revell, c1908 – 1mf – 9 – 0-8370-9302-3 – 1986-3302 – us A.T.L.A. [220]

A SYLLABUS OF THE AMERICAN SOCIAL DANCE SILVER LEVEL TECHNIQUE / Holman, Sharon S – Brigham Young University, 1994 – 2mf – 9 – $8.00 – PE 3652 – us Microform Publ [790]

SYLLABUS OF THE DOCUMENTS..."RYMER'S FOEDERA" / Hardy, T D – London, 1869 – 19mf – 1 – ILM-2460/1 – ne IDC [327]

SYLLABUS OF THE HON. HENRY D. HARLAN'S LECTURES ON THE LAW OF DOMESTIC RELATIONS / Harlan, Henry David – Baltimore: King, 1898. 244p. LL-240 – 1 – us L of C Photodup [340]

A SYLLABUS OF THE MESSIANIC PASSAGES IN THE OLD TESTAMENT / Stearns, Oakman Sprague – (Includes bibliographies) – Boston: Percival T Bartlett, 1884 – 1mf – 9 – 0-8370-5379-X – 1985-3379 – us A.T.L.A. [220]

SYLLABUS OF THIRTY-ONE LESSONS ON NEW TESTAMENT GREEK SYNTAX / Robertson, A T – Louisville, KY: [s.n.], 1900 – 1mf – 9 – 0-8370-9173-X – 1986-3173 – us A.T.L.A. [450]
SYLLABUS OF TWO COURSES OF LECTURES / Rodger, James George – Yokohama: Fukuin, 1909. 1 fiche – 9 – us A.T.L.A. [240]
SYLLOGE ALGARUM / De Toni – (v. 4; S3. 4.00f; 7) – v. 1-6 – 1,7 – uk Microform Academic [580]
SYLLOGE ALGARUM OMNIUM HUCUSQUE COGNITARUM / Toni, G B de – v. 1 (1-2), 2 (1-3), 3, 4 (1-4), 5, 6. Padua. 1889-1924. B-461 2 – 8 – ne IDC [580]
SYLLOGE FLORAE EUROPAEAE, SEU PLANTARUM VASCULARIUM EUROPAE INDIGENARUM ENUMERATIO / Nyman, CF – Oerebro. 1854-55; supplement. Oerebro. 1865. B-649 2 – 8 – ne IDC [580]
SYLLOGE FUNGORUM OMNIUM HUCUSQUE COGNITORUM / ed by Saccardo, P A – Patavii. v1-25. 1882-1931 – 483mf – 9 – 5395/2 – ne IDC [580]
SYLLOGE GENERUM SPECIERUMQUE CRYPTOGAMARUM / Montagne, J P F C – Paris, 1856. 498 pp. B-591 2 – 8 – ne IDC [580]
SYLLOGE INSCRIPTIONUM ROMANARUM / Finestres de Monsalvo, Jose – 1762 – 1mf – 9 – Pta1,000.00 – 84-7848-035-8 – sp Pentalfa [440]
SYLLOGE JUNGERMANNIDEARUM EUROPAE INDIGENARUM / Dumortier, B C J – Tornaci Nerviorum. 1831. B-5315 2 – 8 – ne IDC [580]
SYLLOGE MINUTIARUM LEXICI / Mentzel, C – Norimbergae, 1685 – 1mf – ne IDC [450]
SYLLOGE PLANTARUM NOVARUM ITEMQUE MINUS COGNITARUM / Hornschuch, C F – 2v. Ratisbonae. 1824-28. B-7290 2 – 8 – ne IDC [580]
SYLLOGE PLANTARUM VASCULARIUM FLORAE NEAPOLITANAE HUCUSQUE DETECTARUM / Tenore, M – appendix quarta; Napoli. 1831; appendix quinta. Napoli. 1842. B-5761 2 – 8 – ne IDC [580]
LA SYLPHIDE – Litterature, beaux-arts, modes. Red. en chef de Villemessant. Paris. nov 1839-65 – 1 – fr A.C.R.P.P. [800]
O SYLPHO : PERIODICO FLUMINENSE – Rio de Janeiro, 6 Aug-1 Nov 1823 – 1,5,6 – bl Biblioteca [072]
SYLVA SYLVARUM / Bacon, Francis – Ed. 6. M-295 2. 1651 – 8 – ne IDC [500]
SYLVA TELLURIANA / Rafinesque-Schmaltz, Constantine S – Philadelphia. 1838. B-8117 1 – 9 – ne IDC [580]
SYLVAN LAKE NEWS – Alberta, CN. Sept 1922-1955 – 8r – 1 – cn Commonwealth Micro [072]
SYLVANIA HERALD – Sylvania, Ohio. 1910- – 21r – 1 – $32.50r – us Archival [071]
Sylvania United Church of Christ (Sylvania, Ohio) *see* RECORDS
SYLVES NOIRES / Calve, Adolphe (Azal pseud) – Paris: H Daragon, 1901 – us Res Libr [960]
Sylvester, Nathaniel B *see*
– HISTORY OF RENSSELAER COUNTY
– HISTORY OF SARATOGA COUNTY
– HISTORY OF ULSTER COUNTY
Sylvester, Nathaniel B et al *see* HISTORY OF SARATOGA COUNTY
SYLVIA : OR, THE MAY QUEEN. A LYRICAL DRAMA / Darley, George – London: Published for John Taylor by James Duncan and sold by J.A. Hessey and John Hatchard and Son, 1827 – 1 roll – 1 – 1-55879-360-7 – uk Libr Preservation [820]
SYLVIA CIRCLE BAPTIST CHURCH. YORK COUNTY. SOUTH CAROLINA : CHURCH RECORDS – 1955-59, 1964-72 – 1 – 5.36 – us Baptist [240]
SYLVIA PORTER'S PERSONAL FINANCE MAGAZINE – v1-. 1983- – 1,5,6,9 – us UMI [073]
Sylvis, Robin *see* CAREER SATISFACTION OF DENTAL HYGIENISTS PERFORMING EXPANDED FUNCTIONS AS COMPARED TO DENTAL HYGIENISTS PERFORMING ONLY TRADITIONAL DUTIES
Sylvius, Aeneas *see* COMMENTARIA (LIBRI 13)
Sylvius, Dit Jacques Dubois *see* IN LINGUAM GALLICAM ISAGOGE
DAS SYMBOL DES FISCHES UND DIE FISCHDENKMAELER DER ROEMISCHEN KATAKOMBEN / Achelis, Hans – Marburg: N.G. Elwert, 1888 – 1mf – us A.T.L.A. [240]
THE SYMBOL OF LIBERIA / Simpson, C L – A 588 2. 1961 – 8 – ne IDC [960]
SYMBOLA CHRISTIANA QUIBUS IDEA HOMINIS CHRISTIANI EXPRIMITUR / Philotheus – Leiden, 1682 – 4mf – 9 – ne IDC [700]
SYMBOLA DIVINA ET HUMANA PONTIFICUM IMPERATORUM REGUM : ACCESSIT BREVIS, ET FACILIS ISAGOGE JACOBI TYPOTII / Typotius, J – Tomus primus. Editio altera. Amsterdam, 1690 – 5mf – 9 – O-3217/1 – ne IDC [760]
SYMBOLA FAUNAE INSECTORUM HELVETIAE / Hagenbach, J J – Basileae, 1822. Z/1324/2 – 8 – ne IDC [590]
SYMBOLA HEROICA / Pietrasancta, S – O-1256 1. 1682 – 9 – ne IDC [760]
SYMBOLA HEROICA M. CLAUDII PARADINI, BELLIIOCENSIS CANONICI / Paradin, Claude & Simeoni, G – Leiden, 1600 – 4mf – 9 – ne IDC [700]
SYMBOLA VARIA DIVERSORUM PRINCIPUM, ARCHIDUCUM, DUCUM, COMITUM ET MARCHIONUM TOTIUS ITALIAE : CUM FACILI ISAGOGE D. ANSELMI DE BOOT BRUGENSIS, SAC. CAES. MAJEST. AULAE MEDICI / Typotius, J – Amsterdam, 1686 – 6mf – 9 – O-3219/1 – ne IDC [760]
SYMBOLA VARIA DIVERSORUM PRINCIPUM, ARCHIDUCUM, DUCUM, COMITUM ET MARCHIONUM TOTIUS ITALIAE : CUM FACILI ISAGOGE D. ANSELMI DE BOOT BRUGENSIS, SAC. CAES. MAJEST. AULAE MEDICI / Typotius, J – Arnhem, 1681 (1697) – 5mf – 9 – O-3184/1 – ne IDC [760]
SYMBOLAE AD FLORAM ARGENTINAM / Grisebach, A – 1878 – 1 reel – 7 – uk Microform Academic [580]
SYMBOLAE AD ORTHOPTERORUM QUORUNDAM OECONOMIAM / Goldfuss, F – Bonnae, 1843. vi,24p,1pl. Z/1297/2 – 8 – ne IDC [590]
SYMBOLAE ANTILLANAE, SEU FUNDAMENTA FLORAE INDIAE OCCIDENTALIS / Urban, I – 9v. Berlin. 1898-1928. B-597 2 – 8 – ne IDC [580]
SYMBOLAE BOTANICAE / Presl, K B – 2v. Pragae. 1830-58. B-275 2 – 8 – ne IDC [580]
SYMBOLAE BOTANICAE / Vahl, M – 3v. Havniae. 1790-94. B-5052 2 – 8 – ne IDC [580]
SYMBOLAE GASTEROMYCORUM AD ILLUSTRANDAM FLORAM SVECICAM / Fries, E M – Lund. 1817-18. B-5925 2 – 8 – ne IDC [580]
SYMBOLAE LITTERARIAE / Gori, A F – O-1043 1. 5 v. 1748-1752 – 9 – ne IDC [450]
SYMBOLAE MYCOLOGICAE. BEITRAEGE ZUR KENNTNISS DER RHEINISCHEN PILZE / Fuckel, KWG L – Wiesbaden. 1869. B-6269 2 – 8 – ne IDC [580]
SYMBOLAE SINICAE / ed by Handel-Mazzetti, H – 7pts. Wien. 1929-37. B-635 2 – 37mf – 8 – ne IDC [480]
SYMBOLARUM AD VITAM ET DOCTRINAM LAELII SOCINI / Illgen, Christianus Fridericus – Lipsiae: Frid. Christ. Guil. Vogelii, 1826 – 1mf – us A.T.L.A. [240]
SYMBOLE EIS TO DIETHNES POLNIKON DIKAION / [Gardikas, K G] – Athens, 1923 – 1mf – 1 – ILM-2765/1 – ne IDC [327]
THE SYMBOLIC LIFE OF MAN / Mukerjee, Radhakamal – Bombay: Hind Kitabs (1959) – xii/294p – 1 – us U.W. Library [180]
THE SYMBOLIC PARABLES OF THE CHURCH, THE WORLD, AND THE ANTICHRIST – Edinburgh: T. & T. Clark, 1877. 1 fiche – 9 – us A.T.L.A. [240]
SYMBOLIK : ODER, DARSTELLUNG DER DOGMATISCHEN GEGENSAETZE DER KATHOLIKEN UND PROTESTANTEN NACH IHREN OEFFENTLICHEN BEKENNTNISSCHRIFTEN [SIC] / Moehler, Johann Adam – (Includes bibliographical references) – 10., unveraenderte Original-Aufl. Mainz: Florian Kupferberg, 1888 – 2mf – 9 – 0-8370-7250-6 – 1986-1250 – us A.T.L.A. [230]
SYMBOLIK : VERGLEICHENDE DARSTELLUNG DER CHRISTLICHEN HAUPTKIRCHEN NACH IHREM GRUNDZUGE UND IHREN WESENTLICHEN LEBENSAEUSSERUNGEN / Mueller, Ernst Friedrich Karl – Erlangen: A. Deichert, 1896 – 2mf – us A.T.L.A. [240]
SYMBOLIK DER ROEMISCH-KATHOLISCHEN KIRCHE / Baier, A H – (Includes bibliographical references) – Greifswald: C A Koch. 2v. 1854 – 2mf – 9 – 0-8370-8321-4 – 1986-2321 – us A.T.L.A. [240]
DIE SYMBOLIK IN GERH. HAUPTMANNS MAERCHENDRAMA DIE VERSUNKENE GLOCKE / Ramiew, H – Mainz: Commissionsverlag von H Quasthoff, 1897 – 1r – 1 – us U.W. Library [430]
SYMBOLIK, ODER, CHRISTLICHE KONFESSIONSKUNDE / Loofs, Friedrich – Tuebingen: J.C.B. Mohr, 1902. (Grundriss der theologischen Wissenschaften; 4. T., 4. Bd.) – 1mf – us A.T.L.A. [240]
DIE SYMBOLISCHEN BUECHER DER EVANGELISCH-LUTHERISCHEN KIRCHE : MIT DEN SAECHSISCHEN VISITATIONS-ARTIKELN, EINEM VERZEICHNIS ABWEICHENDER LESARTEN, HISTORISCHEN EINLEITUNGEN UND AUSFUEHRLICHEN REGISTERN / ed by Mueller, Johann Tobias – (In German and Latin. Includes indexes) – 10. Aufl. Guetersloh: C Bertelsmann, 1907 – 3mf – 9 – 0-8370-8698-1 – 1986-2698 – us A.T.L.A. [240]
DIE SYMBOLISCHEN BUECHER DER EVANGELISCH-LUTHERISCHEN KIRCHE, DEUTSCH UND LATEINISCH / Lutheran Church.Book of Concord – Stuttgart: S.G. Liesching, 1869 – 1 – us U.W. Library [240]
SYMBOLISM : SUBJECT COLLECTIONS – (Individual titles not listed separately) – 30 catalogues on 51mf – 9 – £375.00 – uk Chadwyck [750]
THE SYMBOLISM OF COLOUR / Conroy, Ellen – Philadelphia: David McKay Company, (1928). v,66p. Printed in Great Britain – 1 – us U.W. Library [150]
THE SYMBOLISM OF SOLOMON'S TEMPLE / Peake, T De Witt – Cincinnati: Cranston & Curts, 1896. 1 fiche – 9 – us A.T.L.A. [240]
SYMBOLISM OF THE SAINTS / Ditchfield, P H – London: Mowbray, 1910. (The Arts of the church; 7) – 1mf – us A.T.L.A. [240]
SYMBOLISM; OR, EXPOSITION OF THE DOCTRINAL DIFFERENCES BETWEEN CATHOLICS AND PROTESTANTS, AS EVIDENCED BY THEIR SYMBOLICAL WRITINGS / Moehler, Johann Adam – 1844 – 1 – us A.T.L.A. [240]
LE SYMBOLISME DU NOM ET L'ART DE DONNER DES NOMS AUX HOMMES / Mahend Betind, P – (Etude faite chez les Banen du Cameroun) – 9 – F50.00 – fr Ethnologie [306]
LE SYMBOLISTE – Journal hebdomadaire. no. 1-4. Paris. oct-nov 1886 – 1 – fr A.C.R.P.P. [073]
SYMBOLORUM HEROICORUM LIBER SINGULARIS / Reusner, N – O 1263 1. 1608 – 9 – ne IDC [760]
SYMBOLS OF CHRIST / Stanford, Charles – London: Jackson, Walford, 1865. 1 fiche – 9 – us A.T.L.A. [240]
SYMEON VON MESOPOTANIEN (T.U.U. 4-55/1) / Doerries, H – Leipzig, 1941 – 8mf – 9 – ne Slangenburg [240]
Symington, Alexander MacLeod *see* THE APOSTLES OF OUR LORD: PRACTICAL STUDIES
Symington, Andrew *see* ELEMENTS OF DIVINE TRUTH
Symmachus, Q.A *see* EPISTOLAE FAMILIARES
Symmes, John Cleves *see* SYMZONIA: A VOYAGE OF DISCOVERY
SYMMICTA LICHENUM NOVORUM VEL MINUS COGNITORUM / Massalongo, A B – Veronae, 1855. 134 pp. B-586 2 – 8 – ne IDC [580]
SYMMICTA SIVE OPUSCULA GRAECA ET LATINA (CBH 30,5) / Allatius, L – Venetiis, 1733 – Dfl30.00 – ne Slangenburg [930]
Symonds, Edward *see* THE STORY OF THE AUSTRALIAN CHURCH
Symons, Craig *see* PATROL AND NATIVE LOCAL GOVERNMENT SURVEY REPORTS
Symons, J *see* SYNOPSIS PLANTARUM INSULIS BRITANNICIS INDIGENARUM
Symons, Menno *see* OPERA OMNIA THEOLOGICA
Symphoiren, D *see* LA REGLE DE S. BENOIT MEDITEE
SYMPHONIA, 2 VIOLINS, VIOLA AND CELLO, B-FLAT MAJOR, F MAJOR, F MINOR / Pergolesi, G B – 9 – us Sibley [780]
SYMPHONIE / Rueter, H – Manuscript, [18–] – 1 – us Sibley [780]
SYMPHONIE / Rueter, H – Ms, [18–] – 1 – us Sibley [780]
SYMPHONIE IN DREI SAETZEN : NOVELLEN / Hohlbaum, Robert – Wien: Wiener Verlagsgesellschaft, 1943 – 1r – 1 – us U.W. Library [830]
SYMPHONIE NO. 10 FUER GROSSES ORCHESTER / Spohr, Louis – (Never published manuscript) – [1856] – 1 – us Sibley [780]
SYMPHONY NO. 1, OP. 25, IN F : YOUTH AND LIFE / Hadley, H – Ms score, [1897] – 5 – us Sibley [780]
SYMPHONY NO. 2, OP. 30, IN F MINOR : THE FOUR SEASONS / Hadley, H – Ms score, [1899] – 5 – us Sibley [780]
SYMPHONY NO. 76 IN E-FLAT MAJOR ARR. FOR FORTEPIANO, 2 VIOLINS, ALTO AND BASSE / Haydn, Joseph – (Piano part only) – Paris: Boyer, 180- – 1 – us Sibley [780]
SYMPHONY NO. 94, "THE SURPRISE" ANDANTE PER CLAVICEMBALO & PIANOFORTE / Haydn, Joseph – Vienna: Artaria, 1794 – 1 – us Sibley [780]
SYMPOSIA / Faraday Society. London – Nos. 1-4. 1967-1970 – 1,5,6 – us Princeton Micro [621]
SYMPOSIA / Society for General Microbiology – nos 1-10, 12 – 4mf – 9 – uk Microform Academic [576]
SYMPOSIUM – (v.34-36. 1980-83. 5,6,9) – v.1-36. 1946-83 – 1 – us UMI [073]
THE SYMPOSIUM – Concord, New Hampshire. v. 1-4, no. 4. Jan 1930-Oct 1933 – 1 – us NY Public [073]
SYMPOSIUM ARISTOTELICUM – 1st (1957)- Goeteborg, 1960- – 1 – us U.W. Library [180]
SYMPOSIUM ON CHINESE CULTURE / ed by Zen, S H, Chen – (China Institute of Pacific Relations). Shanghai. 1931. BCH-864 2 – 8 – ne IDC [000]
SYMPOSIUM ON LAND TENURE IN RELATION TO ECONOMIC DEVELOPMENT : A REPORT OF THE CONFERENCE HELD AT THE UNIVERSITY OF THE SOUTHERN PACIFIC, LAUCALA BAY, SUVA, FIJI, SEP 1-12, 1969 – Noumea, New Caledonia: The Southern Pacific Commission, sep 1969 – 1mf – 9 – $1.50 – LLMC 82-100F, Title 77 – us L.L.M.C. [980]
SYMPOSIUM ON RIVER AND FLOODPLAIN FISHERIES IN AFRICA (1977, BUJUMBURA, BURUNDI) – 1978 – 390p – it F.A.O. [639]
SYMPOSIUM ON THE DEVELOPMENT AND MANAGEMENT OF FISHERIES IN SMALL WATER BODIES (SUMMARY OF PROCEEDINGS, AND SELECTED PAPERS) : ACCRA, 1987 – 1989 – 195p – it F.A.O. [338]
Symposium sur les Repercussions Sociales de l'Industrialisation dans la Province de Quebec. *see* ESSAIS SUR LE QUEBEC CONTEMPORAIN
SYMZONIA: A VOYAGE OF DISCOVERY / Symmes, John Cleves – 1820 – 9 – $15.00 – us Scholars' Facs [830]
SYN – Baden-Baden, 1965-67 – 1r – 1 – £60.00 – uk Chadwyck [700]
SYN OTECHESTVA = SIEN OTECHESTVA – (Filmed with: Prikarpatskaia Rus and Srpska straza) – New York: Rodnaya Rech Pub Corp Inc, nov 13 1918-mar 16 1920 – 1r – 1 – us Res Libr [073]
SYN OTECHESTVA – Zhurnal politicheskii, uchenyi i literaturnyi. Spb., 1856-1861. Lacking: 1861, v. 1-52. B-1924 2 – 8 – ne IDC [320]
DIE SYNAGOGALE POESIE DES MITTELALTERS / Zunz, L – Ed. 2. Frankfurt am Main. 1920. BJ-421-7 1 – 9 – ne IDC [470]
SYNAGOGAL-POESIEEN: HEBRAEISCHE TEXTE MIT DER DEUTSCHEN UEBERTRAGUNG... DES MITTELALTERS / Zunz, L – Berlin: Louis Gerschel, 1884 – 9 – us A.T.L.A. [270]
DE SYNAGOGEN TE UTRECHT / Zwarts, J – Utrecht. 1926. BJ-262-78 1 – 9 – ne IDC [270]
SYNAGOGUE AND THE CHURCH: BEING A CONTRIBUTION TO THE APOLOGETICS OF JUDAISM / Goodman, Paul – London: George Routledge, (1908). 1 fiche – 9 – us A.T.L.A. [270]
"SYNANON ESPOSE" PULITZER PRIZE WINNING SERIES BY THE POINT REYES LIGHT – Marin Co, Feb 1978-3 May 1979 – 1r – 1 – $50.00 – B40230 – us Library Micro [978]
SYNANON EXPOSE *see* POINT REYES LIGHT
SYNC – (1983-. 1,5,6,9) – v1-. 1981- – 1 – us UMI [073]

Syncellus, Georgius *see*
- CHRONOGRAPHIA
- CORPUS SCRIPTORUM HISTORIAE BYZANTINAE (CSHB 12, 13)

SYNCHRONISCH-DIACHRONISCHE UNTERSUCHUNGEN ZUR ZEICHENSETZUNG IN ENGLISCHEN TEXTEN / Bergien, Angelika – 1993 – 2mf – 9 – DM98.00 – 3-89349-646-7 – gw Hänsel [420]

SYNCHROTRON RADIATION NEWS / ed by Frahm, Ronald et al – 9,5,1 – us Gordon [530]

SYNCRISIS, OR, THE MOST NATURAL AND EASY METHOD OF LEARNING LATIN / Coles, Elisha – 1677. 71p. (English Linguistics Series 1500-1800) – 9 – us UMI [450]

SYNDERNAS FOERLATELSE / Aulen, Gustaf – Uppsala: Sveriges Kristliga Studentroerelses Foerlag, [1915] – 1mf – us A.T.L.A. [240]

SYNDICALISME / CF TC – no. 1-47. Paris. 1936-fevr mars 1940. mq no. 7, 9, 11-12, 19, 23, 25, 28, 35, 40-41, 43, 46 – 1 – fr A.C.R.P.P. [073]

SYNDICALISME – C.F.D.T.Dir., Laurent Lucas. Paris. 1968-1993 – 1 – fr A.C.R.P.P. [335]

SYNDICALISME – Paris. Nov. 4, 1944-Nov. 24, 1949. Missing: Nov. 28 and Dec. 3, 1944 – 1 – 35.00r – us Hoover Inst Photo [335]

LE SYNDICALISME CHRETIEN / CF TC – no. 111-134. Paris. oct 1933-janv 1936. mq no. 127 – 1 – fr A.C.R.P.P. [073]

LE SYNDICALISME CONTRE L'ETAT / Louis, Paul – Paris. 1910. (La Condition Ouvriere. Part Two.) – 9 – 10.00 – fr Bibl Nationale [360]

SYNDICALISME EXPRESS : PRESSE ETUDIANTE NATIONALE – Montreal. no special. mai 1965 – 1r – 1 – Can$25.00 – cn Can Microfilming [072]

LE SYNDICALISME REVOLUTIONNAIRE – no. 1-15. Paris. dec 1921-22 – 1 – fr A.C.R.P.P. [335]

LE SYNDICALISME REVOLUTIONNAIRE: PAUL DELESALLE / Maitron, Jean – Paris. 1952. (La Condition Ouvriere. Part Two.) – 9 – 5.00 – fr Bibl Nationale [360]

SYNDICALIST – 1-3 (all publ). 1910-1913 – 1mf – 9 – $65.00 – us UPA [335]

THE SYNDICALIST – London. -m. Jan 1912-Aug 1914. (19 ft) – 1 – uk British Libr Newspaper [331]

Syndicat regional unitaire des mineurs *see* BULLETIN OFFICIEL

SYNDICATS – Hebdomadaire du monde du travail. no. 1-188. Paris. oct 1936-juin 1940 – 1 – fr A.C.R.P.P. [331]

LES SYNDICATS AUX ETATS-UNIS : LEUR FORCE ET LEUR ORIGINALITE / Waline, P – F50.00 – fr Ethnologie [331]

Syndicats Independants et des Oeuvres Sociales de Meurthe-et-Moselle *see* LA LORRAINE SOCIALE

DER SYNDIKALIST – Berlin, Germany. 1918-1927; 1931 (incomplete) – 2r – 1 – gw Mikrofilm [072]

SYNDIKALISTEN – Malmo, Sweden. 1911-21 – 7r – 1 – sw Kungliga [072]

DAS SYNEDRION IN JERUSALEM UND DAS GROSSE BETH-DIN IN DER QUADERKAMMER DES JERUSALEMISCHEN TEMPELS / Buechler, Adolf – (Includes index) – Wien: Alfred Hoelder, 1902 – 1mf – 9 – 0-8370-2517-6 – 1985-0517 – us A.T.L.A. [270]

SYNESIOS VON KYRENE : EIN KOMMENTAR ZU SEINEM "DION" (T.U.U. 5-71) / Treu, K – Berlin, 1958 – 4mf – 9 – ne Slangenburg [240]

SYNESIUS OF CYRENE : PHILOSOPHER AND BISHOP / Gardner, Alice – London: S.P.C.K.; New York: E.& J.B. Young, 1886. (The Fathers for English readers) – 1mf – us A.T.L.A. [240]

SYNESIUS, THE HELLENE / Crawford, W S – London: Rivingtons, 1901 – 2mf – us A.T.L.A. [180]

Synge, John Millington *see* THE ARAN ISLANDS

SYNODALIA – Journal of Convocation. 1852-57 – 1 – uk Microform Academic [073]

DE SYNODE IN HET OUDE BISDOM DOORNIK GESITUEERD IN DE EUROPESE ONTWIKKELING / Lambecht, D – Gent, 1976 – Dfl119.00 – ne Slangenburg [240]

DE SYNODE TE EMDEN IN 1571 / Janssen, H Q. – Harderwijk: M.C. Bronsveld, 1871 – 1mf – us A.T.L.A. [240]

SYNODICON ORIENTALE OU RECUEIL DES SYNODES NESTORIENS / ed by Chabot, J B – Paris, 1902 – 18mf – 8 – Dfl63.00 – ne Slangenburg [240]

SYNODICON SIVE PANDECTAE CANONUM APOSTOLORUM ET CONCILIORUM AB ECCLESIA GRAECA RECEPTORUM / ed by Beveregio, G – Oxonii. Tom 1-2. 1672 – Dfl235.00 – ne Slangenburg [240]

SYNODO DEL OBISPADO DE PLASENCIA / Jimenez Samaniego, Jose – 1692 – 9 – 1.50f – sp Bibl Santa Ana [240]

SYNODO...OBISPADO DE PLASENCIA / Plasencia. (Spain). Diocesis – 1692 – 9 – 1.50f – sp Bibl Santa Ana [240]

DIE SYNONYMA DES WAHREN UND GUTEN IN DEN SEMITISCHEN SPRACHEN / Ryssel, Victor – (Includes bibliographical references and index) – Leipzig: Alfred Lorentz, 1872 – 1mf – 9 – 0-8370-9176-4 – 1986-3176 – us A.T.L.A. [470]

SYNONYMES / Vivier, G du – 1569 – 9 – fr I.C.S. [440]

SYNONYMES FRANCOIS / Girard – 1769 – 9 – fr I.C.S. [440]

SYNONYMES FRANCOIS / Girard – 3e ed. 1741 – 9 – fr I.C.S. [440]

SYNONYMIA INSECTORUM / Schoenherr, C J – Stockholm, Skara, 1806-1817. 4v.,app. Z-1616/2 – 8 – ne IDC [590]

A SYNONYMIC CATALOGUE OF DIURNAL LEPIDOPTERA / Kirby, W F – Supplement-Appendix. London, 1871. v,883p. Z-1392/2 – 8 – ne IDC [590]

A SYNONYMIC CATALOGUE OF LEPIDOPTERA HETEOCERA / Kirby, W F – v1: Sphinges and Bombyces. London, Berlin, 1892. xii,951p. Z-1397/2 – 8 – ne IDC [590]

A SYNONYMIC CATALOGUE OF NEUROPTERA ODONATA, OR DRAGONFLIES / Kirby, W F – London, Berlin, 1890. ix,202p. Z-1396/2 – 8 – ne IDC [590]

SYNOPSIS ALGARUM / Zanardini, G A M – Taurini. 1841. B-5007 2 – 8 – ne IDC [580]

SYNOPSIS ALGARUM SCANDINAVIAE / Agardh, C A – 1817 – 4mf – 7 – uk Microform Academic [580]

SYNOPSIS ALGARUM SCANDINAVIAE / Agardh, C A – Lundae. 1817. B-7405 1 – 9 – ne IDC [580]

SYNOPSIS ANALYTIQUE DE LA FLORE DES ENVIRONS DE PARIS / Cosson, E SC & Saint-Pierre, Dde – Ed. 2. Paris. 1859. B-7296 1 – 9 – ne IDC [580]

SYNOPSIS AND A TEACHER'S GUIDE ENTITLED TEACHER'S RESOURCES FOR SYNOPSIS – Pre-sub issue and v1. 1969-70 – 19mf – 9 – $5.00f – us Ross [370]

SYNOPSIS AROIDEARUM / Schott, H W – Vindobonae. 1856. B-1032 2 – 8 – ne IDC [580]

SYNOPSIS AVIUM. NOUVEAU MANUEL D'ORNITHOLOGIE / DuBois, A – Z-2069 2. 2 v. 1899-1904 – 8 – ne IDC [590]

SYNOPSIS AVIUM TANAGRINARUM / Sclater, P L – (Zool. Soc. London. Proc., v. 24, London, 1858). Z-1916 2 – 8 – ne IDC [590]

SYNOPSIS CONIFERARUM / Endlicher, S L – Sangalli. 1847. B-5357 2 – 8 – ne IDC [580]

SYNOPSIS DER LAUBMOOSE MECKLENBURGS / Fiedler, K F B – Schwerin. 1844. B-6201 2 – 8 – ne IDC [580]

SYNOPSIS DER MITTELEUROPAEISCHEN FLORA / Ascherson, P F A & Graebner, C O R – Leipzig, 1896-1938. v1-12. B-5428 2 – 8 – ne IDC [580]

SYNOPSIS DES DIATOMEES DE BELGIQUE / Heurck, H F van – Anvers. 1885; Texte. 1880-83. B-6374 2 – 8 – ne IDC [580]

SYNOPSIS DIATOMEARUM / Kuetzing, F T – (Linnaea, v. 8). Halle. 1834. B-7142 1 – 9 – ne IDC [580]

SYNOPSIS DU GENRE ARTHONIA / Nylander, W – (Mem. Soc. Imp. Sci. Nat. Cherbourg, v. 4, 1856). B-5195 2 – 8 – ne IDC [580]

SYNOPSIS FILICUM / Hooker, W J & Baker, JG – London. 1868. B-6457 2 – 8 – ne IDC [580]

SYNOPSIS FILICUM / Swartz, C – 1806 – 9mf – 7 – uk Microform Academic [580]

SYNOPSIS FILICUM AFRICAE AUSTRALIS / Pappe, CW L & Rawson, R W – Cape Town. 1858. B-7240 1 – 9 – ne IDC [580]

SYNOPSIS FILICUM EARUM ET SPECIES SYSTEMATICE COMPLECTENS / Swartz, O P – Kiliae, 1806, 445 pp., 5 pls. B-5577 2 – 8 – ne IDC [580]

SYNOPSIS FLORAE GERMANICAE ET HELVETICAE / Koch, W D J – ed. 2. 2 PTS. Lipsiae. 1843-45. B-7328 1 – 9 – ne IDC [580]

SYNOPSIS FLORAE GERMANICAE ET HELVETICAE / Koch, W D J – Francofurti. 1835-37. B-5985 2 – 8 – ne IDC [580]

SYNOPSIS FUNGORUM CAROLINAE SUPERIORIS SECUNDUM OBSERVATIONES / Schweinitz, L D von – Leipzig. 1822. B-6313 1 – 9 – ne IDC [580]

SYNOPSIS GENERIS LUPINI / Agardh, J G – Lundae. 1835. B-7131 1 – 9 – ne IDC [580]

SYNOPSIS GENERUM COMPOSITARUM / Lessing, C F – Berolini. 1832. B-1270 2 – 8 – ne IDC [580]

SYNOPSIS HEPATICARUM / Gottsche, C M et al – Hamburgi. 1844-47. B-6160 2 – 8 – ne IDC [580]

SYNOPSIS HEPATICARUM EUROPAEARUM / Lindenberg, J B W – Nova Acta Acad. Caes. Leop. v. 16. suppl. Carol. Bonnae. 1829. B-2328 2 – 8 – ne IDC [580]

SYNOPSIS HEPATICARUM JAVANICARUM... / Sande Lacoste, C M v.d. – Amstelaedami, 1856- . 112p, 22pls – 4mf – 9 – ne IDC [580]

SYNOPSIS HYMENOPHYLLA CEARUM, MONOGRAPHIAE HUJUS ORDINIS PRODROMUS / Bosch, R B van den – (Mededeelingen Rijksherbarium). no. 17. 1913. B-7165 1 – 9 – ne IDC [580]

SYNOPSIS HYMENOPTEROLOGIAE SCANDINAVICAE / Dahlbom, A G – Lund, 1839-40. 21, 104p. 5pls.Z-1169/2 – 8 – ne IDC [590]

SYNOPSIS JUGERMANNIARUM IN GERMANIA / Ekart, T P – Coburgi. 1832. B-6519 2 – 8 – ne IDC [580]

SYNOPSIS JUNCORUM RITE COGNITORUM. AD INAUGURANDUM EIUSDEM PLANTARUM GENERIS MONOGRAPHIAM / Meyer, E H F – Goettingen. 1822. B-209 2 – 8 – ne IDC [580]

SYNOPSIS JURIS CANONICI PER EROTEMATA DIGESTI ET ENUCLEATI. / Andre, Valere – Lovanii, typis Guilielmi Strychwant sub aurea lampade, 1695. 308 8 p. LL-4063 – 1 – us L of C Photodup [340]

SYNOPSIS LUZULARUM / Meyer, E H F – Gottingae, 1823. 66 pp. B-199 2 – 8 – ne IDC [580]

SYNOPSIS METHODICA ANIMALIUM QUADRUPEDUM ET SERPENTINI GENERIS / Ray, J – Londini, 1693 – 7mf – 9 – ne IDC [590]

SYNOPSIS METHODICA FUNGORUM SISTENS ENUMERATIONEM OMNIUM HUCUSQUE DETECTARUM SPECIERUM, CUM BREVIBUS DESCRIPTIONIBUS SELECTIS / Persoon, C H – PTS. 1-2. Gottingae. 1801. B-5023 2 – 8 – ne IDC [580]

SYNOPSIS METHODICA LICHENUM / Acharius, E – Lundae. 1814. B-516 2 – 8 – ne IDC [580]

SYNOPSIS METHODICA LICHENUM / Nylander, W – 2v. Parisiis. 1858-60. B-6224 2 – 8 – ne IDC [580]

SYNOPSIS METHODICA STIRPIUM BRITANNICARUM / Ray, J – Londini. 1690. BM-393 1 – 9 – ne IDC [580]

SYNOPSIS MOLLUSCORUM EXTRAMARINORUM REGIONIS PALAEARCTICAE / Westerlund, C A – Pt. 1. Lundae. 1897. BZ-865 2 – 8 – ne IDC [590]

SYNOPSIS MOLLUSCORUM EXTRAMARINORUM SCANDINAVIAE / Westerlund, C A – Z 864 2. 1897 – 8 – ne IDC [590]

SYNOPSIS MOLLUSCORUM IN REGIONE PALAEARCTICA / Westerlund, C A – Z 866 2. 1901 – 8 – ne IDC [590]

SYNOPSIS MOLLUSCORUM MARINORUM DANIAE / Moerch, O A L – Z-673 2. 1871 – 8 – ne IDC [590]

SYNOPSIS MUSCORUM EUROPAEORUM / Schimper, W P – Stuttgartiae. 1860. B-5004 2 – 8 – ne IDC [580]

SYNOPSIS MUSCORUM FRONDOSORUM OMNIUM HUCUSQUE COGNITORUM / Mueller, K A F W – Berlin, (1848) 1849-1851. 2 pts. B-6086 2 – 8 – ne IDC [580]

SYNOPSIS MUSICAE NOVAE. OMNINO VERAE ATQUE METHODICAE UNIVERSAE / Lippius, J – P 371. 1612 – 9 – ne IDC [780]

SYNOPSIS OF A COURSE OF LECTURES ON PLEADING AT COMMON LAW, DELIVERED IN THE DEPARTMENT OF LAW, UNIVERSITY OF PENNSYLVANIA, FIRST TERM, 1889-90 / Pepper, George Wharton – Philadelphia: Sickler, 1890. 40p. LL-1226 – 1 – us L of C Photodup [340]

SYNOPSIS OF BIOLOGICAL DATA ON SCALLOPS : CHLAMYS (AEQUIPECTEN) OPERCULARIS (LINNAEUS), ARGOPECTEN IRRADIANS (LAMARCK), ARGOPECTEN GIBBUS (LINNAEUS) – 1976 – 44p – it F.A.O. [590]

SYNOPSIS OF BIOLOGICAL DATA ON THE EEL ANGUILLA ANGUILLA, (LINNAEUS, 1758) – 1984 – 81p – it F.A.O. [590]

SYNOPSIS OF BIOLOGICAL DATA ON THE GRASS CARP CTENOPHARYNGODON IDELLA (CUVIER AND VALENCIENNES, 1844) – 1983 2nd print 1984 – 90p – it F.A.O. [590]

SYNOPSIS OF BIOLOGICAL DATA ON THE GREEN TURTLE CHELONIA MYDAS (LYNNAEUS, 1758) – 1971 – 71p – it F.A.O. [590]

SYNOPSIS OF BIOLOGICAL DATA ON THE HAWKSBILL TURTLE ERETMOCHELYS IMBRICATA (LINNAEUS, 1766) – 1983 – 82p – it F.A.O. [590]

SYNOPSIS OF BIOLOGICAL DATA ON THE LUMPSUCKER CYCLOPTERUS LUMPUS (LINNAEUS, 1758) – 1985 – 40p – it F.A.O. [590]

SYNOPSIS OF BIOLOGICAL DATA ON THE NORTHERN PIKE, ESOX LUCIUS – 1988 – 187p – it F.A.O. [590]

SYNOPSIS OF BIOLOGICAL DATA ON THE NORWAY LOBSTER, NEPHROPS NORVEGICUS – 1975 – 97p – it F.A.O. [590]

SYNOPSIS OF BIOLOGICAL DATA ON THE SCHOOL SHARK GALEORHINUS AUSTRALIS (MACLEAY, 1881) – 1984 – 48p – it F.A.O. [590]

SYNOPSIS OF BIOLOGICAL DATA ON THE SEAWEED GENERA, GELIDIUM AND PTEROCLADIA (RHODOPHITA) – 1988 – 61p – it F.A.O. [580]

SYNOPSIS OF BIOLOGICAL DATA ON THE WALLEYE STIZOSTEDION V. VITREUM (MITCHILL 1818) – 1981 – 147p – it F.A.O. [590]

SYNOPSIS OF BIOLOGICAL DATA ON THE WESTERN ROCK LOBSTER PANULIRUS CYGNUS (GEORGE, 1962) – 1980 – 69p – it F.A.O. [590]

SYNOPSIS OF BIOLOGICAL DATA ON THE WHITEMOUTH CROACKER, MICROPOGONIAS FURNIERI – 1988 – 41p – it F.A.O. [590]

SYNOPSIS OF ELEMENTARY LAW (SUBSTANTIVE AND REMEDIAL) AND THE LAW OF PERSONAL PROPERTY. / McClain, Emlin – Iowa City, 1891. 6 pamphlets. LL-343 – 1 – us L of C Photodup [340]

SYNOPSIS OF LECTURES DELIVERED IN THE LAW DEPARTMENT OF IOWA STATE UNIVERSITY, ON EQUITY JURISPRUDENCE, AS ADMINISTERED IN THE SAME COURTS WITH COMMON LAW / Hammond, William Gardiner – Iowa City: Lee, 1875. 84p. LL-432 – 1 – us L of C Photodup [340]

SYNOPSIS OF LECTURES DELIVERED IN THE LAW DEPARTMENT OF IOWA STATE UNIVERSITY, ON THE LAW OF REAL PROPERTY / Hammond, William Gardiner – Iowa City: Lee, 1875. 100p. LL-816 – 1 – us L of C Photodup [340]

SYNOPSIS OF QUADRUPEDS / Pennant, T – 2491 2. 1771 – 8 – ne IDC [590]

SYNOPSIS OF SUNDRY DECISIONS OF THE TREASURY DEPARTMENT, 1868-1898 : COVERING TREASURY DECISIONS NOS 1-240467 / U.S. Department of the Treasury – (Cont by: Treasury Decisions, 1899-1966) – Washington: GPO. 34bks. 1869-98 (all publ) – 226mf – 9 – $339.00 – LLMC 84-365C – us L.L.M.C. [340]

SYNOPSIS OF THE AMERICAN FIRS / Engelmann, G – 7538 2. 1878 – 8 – ne IDC [580]

A SYNOPSIS OF THE BIRDS OF NORTH AMERICA / Audubon, John James – Z-333 2. 1839 – 8 – ne IDC [760]

A SYNOPSIS OF THE BRITISH DIATOMACEAE / Smith, W – 6405. 2 V. 1853-1856 – 9 – ne IDC [580]

SYNOPSIS OF THE BRITISH FUCI / Dawson Turner, A M – 1802 – 10mf – 7 – uk Microform Academic [580]

SYNOPSIS OF THE CACTEAE OF THE UNITED STATES / Engelmann, G – 7534 2. 1856 – 8 – ne IDC [580]

SYNOPSIS OF THE CHANGES IN THE LAW EFFECTED BY THE CIVIL CODE OF LOWER CANADA / McCord, T – Ottawa: G E Desbarats, 1866. SEM105P429 – 1mf – 9 – Can$2.25 – cn Bibl Nat [340]

A SYNOPSIS OF THE CLASSIFICATION OF THE BRITISH PALAEOZOIC ROCKS... WITH A SYSTEMATIC DESCRIPTION OF THE BRITISH PALAEOZOIC FOSSILS IN THE GEOLOGICAL MUSEUM OF THE UNIVERSITY OF CAMBRIDGE / Sedgwick, A & Maccooy, F – Cambridge, 1854. Z-2228/1 – 9 – ne IDC [560]

SYNOPSIS OF THE DALBERGIAE, A TRIBE OF THE LEGUMINOSAE / Bentham, G – (Journal and Proceedings Linnean Soc.). v. 4, suppl. London. 1860. B-2254 2 – 8 – ne IDC [580]

SYNOPSIS OF THE ELEMENTARY SCHOOL CURRICULUM B.E. 2521 (A.D. 1978) / Thailand. Ministry of Education – Bangkok, c. 1978 – 1mf – 9 – DE-311/1 – ne IDC [370]

SYNOPSIS OF THE FAMILIES AND GENERA OF THE HYMENOPTERA OF AMERICA, NORTH OF MEXICO / Cresson, E T – Philadelphia, 1887. vi,350p. (Trans. Amer. Entom. Soc. Suppl. Vol). Z-1151/2 – 8 – ne IDC [590]

SYNOPSIS OF THE FAMILY TELLINIDAE AND OF THE NORTH AMERICAN SPECIES / Dall, W H – Proc. U.S. Nat. Mus., 1900. v23, p285-326, pls. 2-4. Z-2234/1 – 9 – ne IDC [590]

A SYNOPSIS OF THE FISHES OF CHINA / Fowler, H W – Z-188 2. 1956 – 8 – ne IDC [590]

A SYNOPSIS OF THE FISHES OF NORTH AMERICA / Storer, D H – 2143 2. 1846 – 8 – ne IDC [590]

SYNOPSIS OF THE FLORA OF COLORADO / Porter, T C & Coulter, J M – 7606 2. 1874 – 8 – ne IDC [580]

A SYNOPSIS OF THE GENUS ARTHONIA / Willey, H – New Bedford. 1890. B-716 2 – 8 – ne IDC [580]

SYNOPSIS OF THE GEOLOGY OF MONTREAL / Ami, Henry Marc – Montreal: Canada Engraving & Lithographing Co., 1897. 07060. (Pre-1900 Canadiana) – 9 – cn C.I.H.M. [550]

A SYNOPSIS OF THE NORTH AMERICAN LICHENS / Tuckerman, E – 7635 2. 2 pts. 1882-1888 – 8 – ne IDC [580]

A SYNOPSIS OF THE QUEENSLAND FLORA / Bailey, F M – Suppl. 1-3. Brisbane. 1886-90. B-7406 1 – 9 – ne IDC [580]

SYNOPSIS OF THE SPECIES OF INSECTS BELONGING TO THE FAMILY OF PHASMIDAE / Gray, G R – London, 1835. 48p. Z/1305/2 – 8 – ne IDC [590]

SYNOPSIS PAPISMI : OR, A GENERAL VIEW OF THE PAPACY: WITH CONFUTATIONS OF ROMISH ERRORS FROM THE SCRIPTURES, FATHERS, COUNCILS, ETC, ETC / Willet, Andrew – (Includes bibliographical references and index) – New ed. London: The Society, 1852 – 10mf – 9 – 0-8370-8398-2 – 1986-2398 – us A.T.L.A. [240]

SYNOPSIS PITTOSPOREARUM / Putterlick, A – Wien. 1839. B-5647 2 – 8 – ne IDC [580]

SYNOPSIS PLANTARUM / Dietrich, D N F – 5v. Vimariae. 1839-52. B-5203 2 – 8 – ne IDC [580]

SYNOPSIS PLANTARUM / Persoon, C H – 2v. Paris. 1805-07. B-429 2 – 8 – ne IDC [580]

SYNOPSIS PLANTARUM ACOTYLEDONEARUM / Todaro, A – Panormi. 1866. B-5172 2 – 8 – ne IDC [580]

SYNOPSIS PLANTARUM AEQUATORIENSIUM / Jameson, W – 2v. Quinto. 1865. B-836 2 – 8 – ne IDC [580]

SYNOPSIS PLANTARUM AEQUINOCTIALIUM ORBIS NOVI / Kunth, C S – (Voyage de Humboldt et Bonpland, pt. 6: Botanique). 4 v. Paris. 1822-25. BN-458 2 – 8 – ne IDC [580]

SYNOPSIS PLANTARUM DIAPHORICARUM / Rosenthal, D A – Erlangen, 1862 – 15mf – 9 – ne IDC [615]

SYNOPSIS PLANTARUM FOSSILIUM / Unger, F J A N – 5008 2. 1845 – 8 – ne IDC [560]

SYNOPSIS PLANTARUM GERMANIAE / Honckeny, G A – 2v. Berolini. 1792-93. B-908 2 – 8 – ne IDC [580]

SYNOPSIS PLANTARUM GLUMACEARUM / Steudel, E G – 2v. Stuttgartiae. 1854-55. B-2303 2 – 8 – ne IDC [580]

SYNOPSIS PLANTARUM HORTI BOTANICI TAURINENSIS / Balbis, G B – Turin. 1801. B-5537 2 – 8 – ne IDC [580]

SYNOPSIS PLANTARUM IN AUSTRIA PROVINCIISQUE ADJACENTIBUS SPONTE CRESCENTIUM / Host, N T – Vindobonae. 1797. B-651 2 – 8 – ne IDC [580]

SYNOPSIS PLANTARUM IN FLORA GALLICA DESCRIPTIORUM / Lamarck, J B A P M de & Candolle, A P de – Paris. 1806. B-6004 2 – 8 – ne IDC [580]

SYNOPSIS PLANTARUM INSULIS BRITANNICIS INDIGENARUM / Symons, J – 5168. 1798 – 9 – ne IDC [580]

SYNOPSIS PLANTARUM, QUAS IN ITINERE AD PLAGAM AEQUINOCTIALEM ORBIS NOVI / Humboldt, Alexander von & Bonpland, A J A & Kunth, CS – 4v. Paris. 1822-25. B-5253 2 – 8 – ne IDC [580]

SYNOPSIS PLANTARUM SUCCULENTARUM / Haworth, A H – Londini. 1812. B-5047 2 – 8 – ne IDC [580]

SYNOPSIS PROVISOIRE DES SOLEN (MOLLUSQUES LAMELLIBRANCHES) / Fischer-Piette, Edouard – Laboratoire de Biologie des Invertebres marins et Malacologie, Museum d'Histoire naturelle. Paris, 1976. 196p. Illus. – 9 – F70.00 – fr Ethnologie [590]

SYNOPSIS STIRPIUM INDIGENARUM ARAGONIAE / Asso y Del Rio, I J de – Massiliae. 1779. B-5536 2 – 8 – ne IDC [580]

THE SYNOPTIC GOSPELS : TOGETHER WITH A CHAPTER ON THE TEXTCRITICISM OF THE NEW TESTAMENT / Cary, George Lovell – (Includes index to biblical references) – New York: G P Putnam, 1900 – 1mf – 9 – 0-8370-2601-6 – 1985-0601 – us A.T.L.A. [220]

SYNOPTIC GOSPELS: TOGETHER WITH A CHAPTER ON THE TEXT-CRITICISM OF THE NEW TESTAMENT / Cary, George Lovell – New York: Putnam, 1900. 1 fiche – 9 – us A.T.L.A. [240]

A SYNOPTICAL CATALOGUE OF BRITISH BIRDS / Forster, T I M – Z-1756 2. 1817 – 8 – ne IDC [590]

SYNOPTICAL FLORA OF NORTH AMERICA / Gray, A – 7548 1. 2 v. 1878-1897 – 9 – ne IDC [580]

A SYNOPTICAL INDEX OF THE CONSOLIDATED STATUTES OF CANADA AND UPPER CANADA, WITH NOTICES OF THE LATER ACTS WHICH AFFECT THEM; INCLUDING THE SESSION OF 1864 / Canada. Laws, Statutes, etc – Toronto: Chewett, 1865. 479p. LL-2388 – 1 – us L of C Photodup [340]

SYNOPTISCHE ERKLAERUNG DER DREI ERSTEN EVANGELIEN / Sevin, Hermann – Wiesbaden: Julius Niedner, 1873.1 fiche – 9 – us A.T.L.A. [240]

DIE SYNOPTISCHE FRAGE / Wernle, Paul – Freiburg i.B.: J C B Mohr (Paul Siebeck), 1899 – 1mf – 9 – 0-8370-6463-5 – 1986-0463 – us A.T.L.A. [220]

SYNOPTISCHE UEBERLIEFERUNG BEI DEN APOSTOLISCHEN VAETERN (T.U.U. 5-65) / Koester, H – Berlin, 1957 – 5mf – 9 – ne Slangenburg [240]

DIE SYNOPTISCHEN EVANGELIEN NACH DER FORM IHRES INHALTES / Holsten, Carl – Heidelberg: Karl Groos, 1885. 1 fiche – 9 – us A.T.L.A. [240]

SYNTAGMA GRAMMATICUM, OR AN EASIE AND METHODICALL EXPLANATION OF LILLIES GRAMMAR / Granger, Thomas – 1616. 243p. (English Linguistics Series 1500-1800) – 9 – us UMI [420]

SYNTAGMA MUSICUM EX VETERUM ET RECENTIORUM ECCLESIASTICORUM AUTOREM LECTIONE / Praetorius, Michael – 1615-19 – 9 – us Sibley [780]

SYNTAGMA MUSICUM EX VETERUM ET RECENTIORUM. MUSICAE ARTIS OBSERVATIONE / Praetorius, Michael – Creutzbergensi. 1615-20. BP-737 1 – 9 – ne IDC [780]

THE SYNTAX AND SYNONYMS OF THE GREEK TESTAMENT / Webster, William – (Includes bibliographical references and indexes) – London: Rivingtons, 1864 – 1mf – 9 – 0-8370-9198-5 – 1986-3198 – us A.T.L.A. [450]

SYNTAX DER WENDISCHEN SPRACHE IN DER OBERLAUSITZ / Liebsch, G – Bautzen. 1884. BR-5594 2 – 9 – ne IDC [460]

DIE SYNTAX DES AUTORS DER CHRONIK VERGLICHEN MIT DER SEINER QUELLEN BEIHEFTE ZUR ZEITSCH. F. D. ALTTESTAMENTLICHE WISSENSCHAFT XVI / Kropat, A – Giessen. 1909. BJ-412-13 1 – 9 – ne IDC [470]

DIE SYNTAX DES NOMENS BEI GEORG RUDOLF WECKHERLIN / Zeller, Gustav – Tuebingen, 1905 – 1mf – 9 – DM48.00 – 3-89349-308-5 – gw Hänsel [430]

SYNTAX OF THE MOODS AND TENSES IN NEW TESTAMENT GREEK / Burton, Ernest De Witt – (Includes indexes) – 2nd rev enl ed. Chicago: University Press of Chicago, 1893, c1892 – 1mf – 9 – 0-8370-9282-5 – 1986-3282 – us A.T.L.A. [450]

SYNTAX OF THE MOODS AND TENSES OF NEW TESTAMENT GREEK / Burton, Ernest De Witt – 1898 – 9 – $10.00 – us I.R.C. [240]

LA SYNTAXE DU VERBE SUMERIEN / Langdon, Stephen – (In French, Sumerian, and English) – Paris: Paul Geuthner, 1907 – 1mf – 9 – 0-8370-8585-3 – 1986-2585 – us A.T.L.A. [470]

SYNTHESE – (v58-. 1984-. 5,6,9) – v1-. 1936- – 1 – us UMI [073]

LA SYNTHESE DOCTRINALE DE ROGER BACON / Carton, R – Paris, 1924 – 3mf – 8 – ne Slangenburg [190]

SYNTHESIS AND REACTIVITY IN INORGANIC AND METAL-ORGANIC CHEMISTRY – (v14-. 1984-. 5,6,9) – v4-. 1974- – 1 – us UMI [073]

SYNTHESIS IN INORGANIC AND METAL-ORGANIC CHEMISTRY – v1-3. 1971-73 – 1 – us UMI [073]

SYNTHETIC COMMUNICATIONS – (v14-. 1984-. 5,6,9) – v1-. 1971- – 1 – us UMI [073]

SYNTHETIC METALS – v1-9. 1979-84 – 1,5,6,13 – sz Elsevier [670]

DIE SYNTHETISCHE EVOLUTIONSTHEORIE UND IHRE KRITIKER / Gallas, Heidrun – 1994 – 2mf – DM80.00 – 3-8267-2003-2 – gw Hänsel [575]

SYONAN SHIMBUN – Engl ed. Singapore, Feb 1942-Sept 1945 – 3r – 1 – us L of C Photodup [072]

SYONAN SINBUN – Singapore MY. Dec 8 1943-Apr 22 1944 – 1 – us U.O. Library [071]

SYONAN TIMES – Singapore MY. Feb 23 1943-Dec 5 1943 – 1 – us U.O. Library [071]

SYONAN TIMES – Syona, OR. 23 Feb 1943-22 Apr 1944. 1 roll – 1 – us U.O. Library [071]

SYPHILIS ET REGLEMENTATION DE LA PROSTITUTION / Deck, Louis – Paris: Carre, Naud, 1898. 93p. (Les Femmes Collection) – 2mf – 9 – $6.00 – fr Bibl Nationale [613]

SYPHILIS SIVE MORBUS GALLICUS / Fracastoro, G – M-53. 1530 – 9 – ne IDC [610]

SYRACUSE AND ITS ENVIRONS / Chase, Franklin N – New York, Lewis Historical Publ. Co., 1924. Vols. 1-3. New York Reel 27. (The Cox Library Collection) – 5 – us Americana [978]

SYRACUSE DEMOCRAT – Syracuse, NE. -w. Jul 1896-Dec 1902; Apr 1903-Apr 1917 – 1 – us NE Hist [071]

SYRACUSE HERALD-JOURNAL – Syracuse, NY. 1893-1912. 1945- – 1 – us UMI [071]

SYRACUSE JEWISH OBSERVER – Syracuse, NY. 1 Nov 1979- . English. Continued: Federation News – 1 – us A.J.P.C. [071]

SYRACUSE JOURNAL – Syracuse, NE. -w. Oct-Nov 1888; Jan 1897-Dec 1898, scattered issues missing – 1 – us NE Hist [071]

SYRACUSE JOURNAL-DEMOCRAT – Syracuse, NE. -w. (-sw 1896-97). Feb 1878-Jan 1901; Apr 1901-Dec 1907; Mar 1908; May 1908; Jun 1910 to date – 1 – us NE Hist [071]

SYRACUSE LAW REVIEW – (v1-35 1949-84 on reel or mf $970.00. v36-46 1985-96 on mf $255.00) – v1-46. 1949-96 – 5,6,9 – $1,225.00 set – us Hein [340]

SYRIA : REVUE D'ART ORIENTAL ET D'ARCHEOLOGIE – 1(1920)-31(1954) – 484mf – 9 – Dfl1,694.00 – ne Slangenburg [073]

Syria *see*
- AL-JARIDAH AL-RASMIYAH
- BUDGET GENERAL DE L'EXERCISE, 1970-1971
- CODE FISCAL SYRIEN: CODE PERMANENT
- DOCUMENTS PERTAINING TO THE POLITICAL AND ECONOMIC RELATIONS BETWEEN SYRIA AND LEBANON 1943-1950
- MEDITERRANEAN DEVELOPMENT PROJECT: UNITED ARAB REPUBLIC, SYRIAN REGION, COUNTRY REPORT
- TROISIEME PLAN QUINQUENNAL DE DEVELOPPEMENT ECONOMIQUE ET SOCIAL, 1971-1975

SYRIA AND EGYPT : FROM THE TEL EL AMERINA LETTERS / Petrie, William Matthew Flinders – New York, 1898 – 1r – 1 – us Ross [956]

Syria. Banque Agricole de Syrie *see* GENERAL ADMINISTRATION AND AUDITOR'S REPORTS

Syria. Banque Centrale de Syrie *see* RAPPORT

Syria. Bureau des Documentations Syriennes et Arabes *see* SOURCES OF STATISTICS IN SYRIA: A REFERENCE MANUAL FOR RESEARCH WORK

Syria. Central Bureau of Statistics *see*
- CONTRIBUTION OF BOTH PUBLIC AND PRIVATE SECTORS TO THE ECONOMIC INDICATORS FOR 1970 AT 1963 CONSTANT PRICES
- OUTLINE OF THE ECONOMIC AND SOCIAL CHANGES IN THE SYRIAN ARAB REPUBLIC DURING 1950-1970
- STATISTICAL ABSTRACT, 1949-1978
- STATISTICS OF THE FOREIGN TRADE OF SYRIA

Syria. Dept. of Statistics *see*
- FOREIGN TRADE STATISTICS
- NATIONAL INCOME ESTIMATES OF SYRIA
- STUDY OF COST AND LIVING AND FAMILY BUDGET IN DAMASCUS FROM 1957

Syria. Direction Generale des Douanes *see* STATISTIQUE DU COMMERCE EXTERIEUR

Syria. Directorate-General of Information *see* ECONOMY OF SYRIA IN FACTS AND FIGURES

Syria. Economic Development Organisation *see* ECONOMIC DEVELOPMENT PLAN, 1958-1967

Syria. Economic Development Organization *see* REPORT ON ECONOMIC DEVELOPMENT PLAN, 1958-1967

Syria. Government Planning Agency *see* SECOND FIVE YEAR PLAN FOR ECONOMIC AND SOCIAL DEVELOPMENT, 1966-1970

Syria. Industrial Bank in the Syrian region *see*
- ANNUAL REPORT 1959-1965
- GUIDE PRATIQUE DES OPERATIONS DE LA BANQUE INDUSTRIELLE

Syria. Industrial bank in the Syrian region *see* LOI DE FONDATION ET STATUTS

Syria. Ministry of Economy and Treasury *see*
- THE BUDGET REPORT
- FINANCIAL AND ECONOMIC LEGISLATION ISSUED BY THE CENTRAL MINISTRIES OF ECONOMY AND TREASURY

Syria. Ministry of Economy. Dept. of Statistics *see* STATISTICAL SURVEY, 1948

Syria. Ministry of Finance *see*
- COLLECTION OF SYRIAN LAWS AND FINANCIAL TEXTS
- CONVENTIONS MADE BETWEEN THE GOVERNMENT OF THE SYRIAN REPUBLIC AND THE IRAQ PETROLEUM COMPANY LTD, THE 11TH
- GENERAL BUDGET, SUPPLEMENTARY AND INDEPENDENT BUDGETS
- REPORT OF THE SYRIAN CHAMBER OF DEPUTIES REGARDING THE FINANCIAL STATE OF THE NATION DURING TEN YEARS
- STATUT ORGANIQUE DE LA MONNAIE ET CREATION DE LA BANQUE CENTRALE DE SYRIE

Syria. Ministry of Planning *see*
- ANNUAL REPORT ON THE ECONOMIC AND SOCIAL DEVELOPMENT PLAN 1960/1961
- ANNUAL REPORT ON THE ECONOMIC AND SOCIAL DEVELOPMENT PLAN 1960-1961: IMPLEMENTATION REPORT ON THE FIRST FIVE-YEAR PLAN 1960-1965
- IMPLEMENTATION REPORT ON THE FIRST FIVE YEAR PLAN
- IMPLEMENTATION REPORT ON THE FOURTH STAGE PLAN, JAN-DEC 1964, OF THE FIRST FIVE YEARS DEVELOPMENT PLAN
- IMPLEMENTATION REPORT ON THE THIRD STAGE PLAN, JUL 1962-DEC 1963 OF THE FIRST YEAR DEVELOPMENT PLAN
- SECOND ANNUAL REPORT ON THE ECONOMIC AND SOCIAL DEVELOPMENT PLAN OF SYRIA, 1961-1962
- SECOND FIVE YEAR PLAN 1966-1970 (BASIC ELEMENTS)
- THE SYRIAN FIVE-YEAR PLAN FOR ECONOMIC AND SOCIAL DEVELOPMENT, 1960/1961-1964/1965
- THE SYRIAN FIVE-YEAR PLAN FOR ECONOMIC AND SOCIAL DEVELOPMENT, 1960/61-1964/65

Syria. Ministry of Social Affairs and Labour *see* STATISTICAL BULLETIN

Syria. Office Arabe de Presse et de Documentation *see*
- LES BUDGETS DE DEVELOPPEMENT EN R.A.S., 1967-1968-1969
- RAPPORT SUR L'ECONOMIE SYRIENNE
- RECUEIL DES STATISTIQUES SYRIENNES COMPAREES, 1928-1968
- THIRD FIVE-YEAR PLAN FOR ECONOMIC AND SOCIAL DEVELOPMENT IN THE SYRIAN ARAB REPUBLIC

Syria. Office of Foreign Exchange *see* ANNUAL REPORT ON OPERATIONS. 1952-1954

Syria. Office of the Prime Minister. Central Bureau of Statistics *see* STATISTICS OF THE FOREIGN TRADE OF SYRIA DURING THE YEAR 1975

SYRIA. REVUE D'ART ORIENTAL ET D'ARCHEOLOGIE – v. 10-22. Paris. 1929-41. BNE-332 1 – 105mf – 9 – ne IDC [930]

Syria. State Planning Organization *see* INVESTMENT EFFECTIVENESS IN INDUSTRIAL SECTOR IN THE SYRIAN ARAB REPUBLIC

Syria. Syrian Documentation Papers *see*
- EVALUATION OF THE ACHIEVEMENTS OF THE 2ND
- THE PRESENT STATUS OF ALL THE PROJECTS OF DEVELOPMENT IN SYRIA AND ALL NECESSARY FIGURES AND STATISTICS AS IN MAY 1970
- STUDIES ON THE SYRIAN EXPORTS: POTENTIALITIES AND CONDITIONS FOR INCREASE
- THE SYRIAN CONSOLIDATED GENERAL BUDGET FOR 1970
- TEXTILE INDUSTRY IN SYRIA

THE SYRIAC CHRONICLE KNOWN AS THAT OF ZACHARIAH OF MITYLENE – Trans. into English by F.J. Hamilton and E.W. Brooks. 1899 – 1 – us A.T.L.A. [240]

SYRIAC DICTIONARY / Payne-Smith, Robert – 1903 – 9 – $21.00 – us I.R.C. [470]

SYRIAC ROOT-BOOK : CONTAINING ALL THE ROOTS IN THE SYRIAC LANGUAGE / Young, Robert – Edinburgh: George Adam Young; London: S W Partridge, [18–?] – 1mf – 9 – 0-8370-7358-8 – 1986-1358 – us A.T.L.A. [470]

SYRIAE DESCRIPTIO / Postel, G – [Paris], 1540 – 1mf – 9 – H-8264/1 – ne IDC [956]

Syrian Arab Republic *see* THIRD FIVE YEAR PLAN FOR ECONOMIC AND SOCIAL DEVELOPMENT

THE SYRIAN CONSOLIDATED GENERAL BUDGET FOR 1970 / Syria. Syrian Documentation Papers – 1970. BNE-9739 1 – 9 – ne IDC [350]

THE SYRIAN FIVE-YEAR PLAN FOR ECONOMIC AND SOCIAL DEVELOPMENT, 1960/1961-1964/1965 / Syria. Ministry of Planning – BNE-9721 1 – 9 – ne IDC [338]

THE SYRIAN FIVE-YEAR PLAN FOR ECONOMIC AND SOCIAL DEVELOPMENT, 1960/61-1964/65 / Syria. Ministry of Planning – Damascus. 1961. BD-151 1 – 9 – ne IDC [338]

SYRIAN HOME LIFE / Jessup, Henry Harris; ed by Riley, Isaac – New York: Dodd & Mead, 1874. viii,366p – 1 – us U.W. Library [640]

SYRIAN HOME-LIFE / Riley, Isaac – New York: Dodd & Mead, c1874 – 1mf – us A.T.L.A. [306]

THE SYRIAN WORLD – New York, NY, July 1926-Nov. 15, 1935 – 4r – 1 – us I.H.R.C. [978]

LA SYRIE DU NORD A L'EPOQUE DES CROISADES ET LA PRINCIPAUTE FRANQUE D'ANTIOCHE / Cahen, C – Paris, 1940. 768p. BU-656/2 – 8 – ne IDC [900]

LA SYRINX DANS LES REGIONS ANDINES DE BOLIVIE / Girault, L – 9 – F90.00 – fr Ethnologie [780]

DIE SYRISCHE DIDASKALIA / ed by Achelis, Hans & Flemming, J – Leipzig: J.C. Hinrichs, 1904. (Die AEltesten Quellen des orientalischen Kirchenrechts; 2. Buch. Texte und Untersuchungen zur Geschichte der altchristlichen Literatur; der ganzen Reihe 25. Bd., 2. Heft. n.F., 10. Bd., 2. Heft) – 1mf – us A.T.L.A. [956]

DIE SYRISCHE DIDASKALIA (T.U.U. 2-25/2) / Achelis, Hans & Flemming, J – Leipzig, 1904 – 6mf – 9 – ne Slangenburg [240]

DIE SYRISCHE UEBERSETZUNG DER ZWOELF KLEINEN PROPHETEN / Seboek, Mark – 1887 – 9 – $10.00 – us I.R.C. [220]

DIE SYRISCHE UEBERSETZUNG DER ZWOELF KLEINEN PROPHETEN / Seboek, Mark – Wroclau: Preuss & Juenger, 1887.1 fiche – 9 – us A.T.L.A. [240]

DIE SYRISCHE UEBERSETZUNG DES ERSTEN BUCHES SAMUELIS UND...MT., 70 UND TRG / Schwartz, Emanuel – Berlin: H. Itzkowski, 1896. 1 fiche – 9 – us A.T.L.A. [220]

DIE SYRISCHEN CLEMENTINEN (T.U.U. 4-48/3) / Frankenberg, W – Leipzig, 1937 – 7mf – 9 – ne Slangenburg [240]

DIE SYRISCHEN KANONES DER SYNODEN VON NICAEA BIS CHALCEDON : NEBST EINIGEN ZUGEHOERIGEN DOKUMENTEN / ed by Schulthess, Friedrich – Berlin: Weidmann, 1908. (Abhandlungen der Koeniglichen Gesellschaft der Wissenschaften zu Goettingen. Philologisch-historische Klasse ; n.F., Bd. 10, Nro. 2) – 1mf – us A.T.L.A. [240]

DAS SYRISCH-MONOPHYSITISCHE MOENCHTUM IM TUR-AB(H)DIN VON SEINEN ANFAENGEN BIS ZUR MITTE DES 12. JAHRHUNDERTS / Krueger, Paul – Muenster i.W., 1937 – 2mf – 8 – Dfl9.00 – ne Slangenburg [240]

SYRISCH-NESTORIANISCHE GRABINSCHRIFTEN AUS SEMIRJETSCHIE / Chwolson, D A – Nebst einer Beilage ueber das tuerkische Sprachmaterial dieser Grabinschriften vom Akademiker Dr. W. Radloff. Memoires de l'Academie Imp. des Sciences. VIIe serie, XXXVIII no 8. Spb. 1890. BU-711 2 – 8 – ne IDC [410]

Syrkin, N *see*
- DIE JUDENFRAGE UND DER SOZIALISTISCHE JUDENSTAAT
- KITVEI NAHMAN SYRKIN

Syrku, P *see* OPISANIE BUMAG EPISKOPA PORFIRIIA USPENSKOGO, POZHERTVOVANNYKH IM V BIBLIOTEKU IMP. AKADEMII NAUK PO ZAVESHCHANIIU

SYRLIN / Ouida – British Fiction Archive: Unit 3 – 9 – uk Bell [830]

THE SYRO-LATIN TEXT OF THE GOSPELS / Chase, Frederic Henry – London: Macmillan, 1895.1 fiche – 9 – us A.T.L.A. [240]

SYSTEM – (v4- 1976- 5,6,9) – v1- 1973- – 1 – us UMI [370]

SYSTEM 5 : AN INFORMATION PROCESSING APPROACH TO TEACHING TENNIS / Allam, Paul F W – University of North Carolina at Chapel Hill, 1995 – 1mf – 9 – $4.00 – PE3581 – us Microform Publ [370]

SYSTEM AND CONTROL LETTERS – v1-4. 1981-84 – 1,5,6,13 – sz Elsevier [073]

SYSTEM DER ASTERIDEN / Mueller, J & Troschel, F H – 2680 2. 1842 – 8 – ne IDC [580]

SYSTEM DER CHRISTLICHEN WAHRHEIT / Frank, Franz H R – 2v. 1885-1886 – 1 – us A.T.L.A. [240]

SYSTEM DER ORNITHOLOGIE WESTAFRICAS / Hartlaub, C JG – Bremen, 1857. BZ/1796/2 – 8 – ne IDC [590]

DAS SYSTEM DER PILZE UND SCHWAEMME / Nees von Esenbeck, C G D – Wua5rzburg, 1816. xxxvi, 334 pp., 46 pls. B-6093 1 – 9 – ne IDC [580]

SYSTEM DER URWELTLICHEN KONCHYLIEN DURCH DIAGNOSE / Bronn, H G – Z-446 2. 1824 – 8 – ne IDC [560]

SYSTEM OF CHRISTIAN ETHICS / Dorner, Isaak August – Edinburgh: T. & T. Clark, 1887. xx,616p. 2 fiches – 9 – us A.T.L.A. [170]

SYSTEM OF CHRISTIAN ETHICS / Harless, G C Adolf von – Edinburgh: T. & T. Clark, 1868 – 2mf – us A.T.L.A. [170]

SYSTEM OF ECONOMIC CONTRADICTIONS / Proudhon, Pierre-Joseph – Trans. by B. R. Tucker in "Radic. Review". 3 fiches (29x) – 9 – 1.00f – at Libertarian Micro [320]

THE SYSTEM OF EDUCATION IN THAILAND / Thailand. National Education Commission – Bangkok, 1981 – 1mf – 9 – DE-592/1 – ne IDC [370]

THE SYSTEM OF EDUCATION OF THE JEWISH COMMUNITY IN PALESTINE: REPORT / Great Britain. Colonial Office. Palestine – Colonial no. 201. London. 1946. BJ-28-113 1 – 9 – ne IDC [324]

A SYSTEM OF ETHICS / Paulsen, Friedrich – New York: Charles Scribner, 1899 – 723p 2mf – 9 – us A.T.L.A. [170]

A SYSTEM OF LOGIC / Reid, Thomas – 1763 – 1 – us Res Libr [160]

A SYSTEM OF LOGIC, RATIOCINATIVE AND INDUCTIVE : BEING A CONNECTED VIEW OF THE PRINCIPLES OF EVIDENCE AND THE METHODS OF SCIENTIFIC INVESTIGATION / Mill, John Stuart – London: Longmans, Green, Reader, and Dyer, 7th ed 1868 – 2 rolls – 1 – 1-55879-798-X – uk Libr Preservation [160]

A SYSTEM OF MORAL PHILOSOPHY...PUBLISHED BY HIS SON...TO WHICH IS PREFIXED SOME ACCOUNT OF THE LIFE, WRITINGS AND CHARACTER OF THE AUTHOR BY W. LEECHMAN / Hutcheson, F – London, 1755 – 9mf – 9 – ne IDC [170]

A SYSTEM OF RHETORIC / Stirling, John – 1733. 31.p. (English Linguistics Series 1500-1800) – 9 – us UMI [400]

THE SYSTEM OF THE WORLD / Laplace, Pierre Simon de – Translated from the French by J. Pond. London: Printed for R. Phillips, 1809 – 1 – us U.W. Library [520]

THE SYSTEM OF THEOLOGY CONTAINED IN THE WESTMINSTER SHORTER CATECHISM : OPENED AND EXPLAINED / Hodge, Archibald Alexander – (Includes index) – New York: A C Armstrong, 1888 – 1mf – 9 – 0-8370-4865-6 – 1985-2865 – us A.T.L.A. [240]

SYSTEM THEOLOGISCHER ERKENNTNISLEHRE / Dunkmann, Karl – Leipzig: A. Deichert, 1909. 1 fiche – 9 – us A.T.L.A. [240]

EIN SYSTEM ZUR ERFASSUNG UND AUSWERTUNG PERIODISCH WIEDERKEHRENDER SIGNALE BEI PHYSIKALISCHEN EXPERIMENTEN / Radloff, Hans-Henning – 1995 – 2mf – 9 – DM80.00 – 3-8267-2232-9 – gw Hänsel [530]

SYSTEMA ALGARUM / Agardh, C A – 1824 – 1 – uk Microform Academic [580]

SYSTEMA ALGARUM / Agardh, C A – Lund. 1824. B-5272 2 – 8 – ne IDC [580]

SYSTEMA AVIUM / Wagler, J G – Z 1955. 1827 – 9 – ne IDC [590]

SYSTEMA COSMICUM, 1663; SYSTEMA COSMICUM, 1635; NOV-ANTIQUA, 1636 / Galilei, Galileo – 1 – uk Microform Academic [520]

SYSTEMA, GENERA, SPECIES PLANTARUM UNO VOLUMINE. EDITIO CRITICA / Linnaeus, Carl – Ed. by H. E. Richter. Leipzig. 1835. B-7137 2 – 8 – ne IDC [580]

SYSTEMA GRAMMATICUM / Farnaby, Thomas – 1641. 150p. (English Linguistics Series 1500-1800) – 9 – us UMI [400]

SYSTEMA HISTORICO-CHRONOLOGICUM ECCLESIARUM SLAVONICARUM / Regenvolscius, A – Trajecti Ad Rhenum, 1652 – Dfl32.00 – ne Slangenburg [240]

SYSTEMA INSECTORUM / Gistl, J von N FX. – Monachii,Bernae., 1837-39. 132p,1pl. Z/1290/2 – 8 – ne IDC [590]

SYSTEMA LICHENUM / Eschweiler, F G – Norimbergae. 1824. B-572 2 – 8 – ne IDC [580]

SYSTEMA LICHENUM GERMANIAE / Koerber, G W – Breslau. 1855. B-6170 2 – 8 – ne IDC [580]

SYSTEMA MATERIAE MEDICAE VEGETABILIS BRASILIENSIS / Martius, Karl Friedrich Philipp von – Lipsiae, 1843 – 2mf – 9 – ne IDC [615]

SYSTEMA MYCOLOGICUM / Fries, E M – v. 1. Gryphiswaldae. 1821; v. 2. Gryphiswaldae. 1823; v. 3. Gryphiswaldae. 1829; Supplementa. 1830-32. B-5021 2 – 8 – ne IDC [580]

SYSTEMA NATURAE / Linnaeus, Carl – 2v. ed. 10. Holmiae. 1758-59. B-740 2 – 8 – ne IDC [580]

SYSTEMA NATURAE / Linnaeus, Carl – Aucta, reformata, cura J. F. Gmelin. B-440 2. 3 v. 1788-1793 – 8 – ne IDC [574]

SYSTEMA NATURAE, EDITIO DUODECIMA, 12 REFORMATA / Linnaeus, Carl – 3v. Holmiae. 1766-68. BZ-318 2 – 8 – ne IDC [580]

SYSTEMA NATURAE. LUGDUNI BATAVORUM / Linnaeus, Carl – B-182 2. 1735 – 8 – ne IDC [574]

SYSTEMA ORBIS VEGETABILIS / Fries, E M – Lundae. 1825. B-576 2 – 8 – ne IDC [580]

SYSTEMA ORNITHOLOGIAE, SIVE INDEX ORNITHOLOGICUS / Latham, J – 2097 2. 1809 – 8 – ne IDC [590]

SYSTEMA PIPERACEARUM / Miquel, F A W – Roterodami, 1843-1844. 575 pp. B-6073 2 – 8 – ne IDC [580]

SYSTEMA PLANTARUM EUROPAE EXHIBENS CHARACTERES NATURALES GENERUM / Gilibert, Jean Emmanuel – (Fundamenta botanica. v. 5-7). 7 v. Coloniae Allobrogum. 1785-87. B-178 2 – 8 – ne IDC [580]

SYSTEMA PLANTARUM GENERALE EX FRUCTIFICATIONE / Heister, L – Helmstadii. 1748. B-855 2 – 8 – ne IDC [580]

SYSTEMA PLANTARUM SECUNDUM CLASSES, ORDINES, GENERA SPECIES CUM CHARACTERIBUS / Linnaeus, Carl – Editio novissima. Ed. by J. J. Reichard. 4 pts. Francofurti ad Moenum. 1779-80. B-7657 2 – 8 – ne IDC [580]

SYSTEMA RHYNGOTORUM SECUNDUM ORDINES, GENERA, SPECIES / Fabricius, J C – Z-160 2. 1803 – 8 – ne IDC [615]

SYSTEMA VEGETABILIUM / Linnaeus, Carl – curantibus J. J. Roemer et J. A. Schultoc. Systematis Vegetabilium. 3 v. Stuttgardtiae. 1822-27. 7 v. Stuttgardtiae. 1817-30. B-238 2 – 8 – ne IDC [580]

SYSTEMA VEGETABILIUM / Linnaeus, Carl – ed. 13. Gottingae, Gothae, 1774. 4. 844 pp. B-176 2 – 8 – ne IDC [580]

SYSTEMA VEGETABILIUM / Linnaeus, Carl – Edita a J. A. Murray. ed. 14. Goettingae. 1784. B-2249 2 – 8 – ne IDC [580]

SYSTEMA VEGETABILIUM. CURANTE C. SPRENGEL / Linnaeus, Carl – Ed. 16. 5 v. and suppl. Gottingae. 1825-28. B-459 2 – 8 – ne IDC [580]

SYSTEMA VEGETABILIUM FLORAE PERUVIANAE ET CHILENSIS / Ruiz Lopez, Hipolito & Pavon y Jimenez, Jose Antonio – Madrid, 1798 – 8mf – 9 – ne IDC [580]

A SYSTEMATIC ARRANGEMENT OF BRITISH PLANTS / Withering, W – 5487. 4 V. Ed. 4. 1801 – 9 – ne IDC [580]

SYSTEMATIC BENEVOLENCE : A SERMON / Schaff, Philip – Mercersburg, Pa.: P.A. Rice, 1852 – 1mf – us A.T.L.A. [240]

SYSTEMATIC CARD CATALOGUE : MAIN CATALOGUE, AND 1981-1985 SUPPLEMENT / Documentation Office for East European Law (DBOER), University of Leiden; ed by Pries, A – (Includes printed guide) – 88mf – 9 – R-1608/1 – ne IDC [020]

A SYSTEMATIC CATALOGUE OF THE FLOWERING PLANTS AND FERNS INDIGENOUS TO, OR GROWING WILD IN CEYLON / Trimen, H – Journ. Ceylon Branch R. Asiatic Soc., v. 9 (nr. 30)). Colombo. 1885. B-7272 1 – 9 – ne IDC [580]

SYSTEMATIC GIVING: THE CHURCH'S SAFEGUARD AGAINST NINETEENTH CENTURY EVILS / Cook, Charles Augustus – Toronto: W. Briggs; Montreal: c. Coates; Halifax, N.S.: S. Huestis, 1888. 00317. (Pre-1900 Canadiana) – 9 – cn C.I.H.M. [971]

SYSTEMATIC INDEX OF INTERNATIONAL WATER RESOURCES TREATIES, DECLARATIONS, ACTS AND CASES BY BASIN – 1978 – 511p – it F.A.O. [333]

SYSTEMATIC INDEX OF INTERNATIONAL WATER RESOURCES TREATIES, DECLARATIONS, ACTS AND CASES, BY BASIN. VOL 2 – 1984 – 365p – it F.A.O. [340]

SYSTEMATIC LIST OF THE TREES, SHRUBS AND WOODY CLIMBERS OF THE BOMBAY PRESIDENCY / Talbot, W A – Bombay. 1894. B-5169 2 – 8 – ne IDC [580]

SYSTEMATIC MORAL EDUCATION: WITH DAILY LESSONS IN ETHICS / Clark, John King – New York: A S Barnes, 1911 – 1mf – 9 – 0-8370-8495-4 – 1986-2495 – us A.T.L.A. [230]

A SYSTEMATIC SURVEY OF THE ORGANIC COLOURING MATTERS, FOUNDED ON THE GERMAN OF DR. G. SCHULTZ AND P. JULIUS / Green, Arthur George – 2nd ed. rev. and enl. London, New York: Macmillan, 1904. x,280p – 1 – us U.W. Library [540]

SYSTEMATIC THEOLOGY / Foster, Robert Verrell – Nashville, Tenn.: Cumberland Presbyterian Publishing House, 1898 – 2mf – us A.T.L.A. [240]

SYSTEMATIC THEOLOGY (CCC147) = CHIAO I SHEN HSUEH / Hayes, W M – (In Chinese. v2 2nd ed 1933) – Shanghai: Christian Literature Society. 2v. 1930-1933 – 1r – 1 – 1984-B500 – us A.T.L.A. [240]

A SYSTEMATIC VIEW OF THE SCIENCE OF JURISPRUDENCE / Amos, Sheldon – London: Longmans, Green & Co, 1872 – 6mf – 9 – $9.00 – LLMC 95-179 – us L.L.M.C. [340]

SYSTEMATIC ZOOLOGY – (v25-. 1976-. 5,6,9) – v. 1-. 1952- – 1 – us UMI [590]

DIE SYSTEMATIK... / Bulmerincq, A von – Dorpat, 1858 – 4mf – 1 – ILM-136/1 – ne IDC [327]

SYSTEMATISCHE EINLEITUNG IN DIE MUSICALISCHE SETZKUNST / Alembert, Jean Le Rond d' – 1757 – 9 – us Sibley [780]

SYSTEMATISCHE MODULATIONSLEHRE ALS GRUNDLAGE DER MUSIKALISCHE FORMENLEHRE / Riemann, H – Hamburg: Richter, 1887 – 1 – us Sibley [780]

SYSTEMATISCHE THEOLOGIE / Warren, William Fairfield – (Includes bibliographical references) – Bremen: Verlag des Tractathauses; Cincinnatti, OH: Poe & Hitchcock, [1865?] – 1mf – 9 – 0-8370-5698-5 – 1985-3698 – us A.T.L.A. [240]

SYSTEMATISCHE UBERSICHT DER VOEGEL BAYERNS / Jackel, A J – Muenchen, Leipzig. 1891. Z-1810 2 – 8 – ne IDC [590]

SYSTEMATISCHE UEBERSICHT DER VOEGEL NORD OST AFRIKA S / Heuglin, M Th. von – (Repr. Akad. der Wissensch. Wien. Sitzungsber. Math. Naturw. Classe). Wien. 1836. Z-1802 2 – 8 – ne IDC [590]

SYSTEMATISCHE UEBERSICHT DER VOEGEL NORDOSTAFRIKAS / Rueppell, E – Frankfurt a.Main. 1845. Z-1898 2 – 8 – ne IDC [590]

SYSTEMATISCHE ZUSAMMENSTELLUNG DER TEXTE DER FRIEDENSVERTRAEGE 1792-1913 / Corpus pacificationum – Berlin, 1924 – 11mf – 9 – ne IDC [943]

SYSTEMATISCHER GRUNDRIS DER ALLGEMEINEN EXPERIMENTAL-CHEMIE ZUM GEBRAUCH SEINER VORLESUNGER ENTWORFEN / Hermbstadt, Sigismund Friedrich – Berlin, 1791 – 1 – us U.W. Library [540]

SYSTEMATISCHER KATALOG... – gw Olms [020]

SYSTEMATISCHES CONCHYLIEN-CABINET / Martini, F H W & Chemnitz, J H; ed by Kuester, H C – (New and revised edition) – Nueremberg, 1837-1920 – 614 mf – 9 – 2165/2 – ne IDC [943]

SYSTEMATISCHES VERZEICHNIS... / Koorders-Schumacher, A – Buitenzorg, Batavia, 1910-1913 [-1914] – 23mf – 9 – ne IDC [580]

SYSTEMATISCHES VERZEICHNISS DER IM INDUSCHEN ARCHIPEL IN. 1842-1848 GESAMMELTEN SOWIE DER AUS JAPAN EMPFANGENEN PFLANZEN / Zollinger, H – Zuerich. 1854-55. B-5823 2 – 8 – ne IDC [580]

SYSTEMATISCHES VERZEICHNISS DER PFLANZEN WELCHE IN DER GEGEND UM ERFURT GEFUNDEN WERDEN / Bernhardi, J J – Erfurt. 1800. B-5509 2 – 8 – ne IDC [580]

SYSTEMATISCHES VERZEICHNISS DER VON H. ZOLLINGER IN 1842-1844 AUF JAVA GESAMMELTEN PFLANZEN, NEBST KURZER BESCHREIBUNG DER NEUEN GATTUNGEN UND ARTEN / Moritzi, A – Solothurn, 1845-1846. 144 pp. B-6132 2 – 3mf – 8 – ne IDC [580]

LE SYSTEME CONTINENTAL ET LA SUISSE... / Cerenville, B de – Lausanne, 1906 – 4mf – 1 – ILM-857/1 – ne IDC [327]

LE SYSTEME DE CREDIT FONCIER, FONCTIONNEMENT DE CETTE INSTITUTION EN EUROPE / Macaulay, George Henry – s.l.: Desbarats et Derbishire, 1863. SEM105P222 – 1mf – 9 – Can$2.25 – cn Bibl Nat [336]

LE SYSTEME DE FORMATION EN COTE D'IVOIRE : FLUX D'ENTREE, EVOLUTION DES EFFECTIFS: (RESUME) / Ivory Coast. Office National de Formation Professionnelle – [Abidjan], 1986 – 1mf – 9 – DE-616/1 – ne IDC [370]

SYSTEME DE LA NATURE, OU DES LOIS DU MONDE PHYSIQUE ET DU MONDE MORAL / Holbach, Paul-Thiry d' – (D'Holbach series). 1770 – 9 – fr Hachette [170]

SYSTEME DE PRONONCIATION FIGUREE / Montmignon, J B – 1785 – 9 – fr I.C.S. [440]

SYSTEME DE TELEGRAPHES ET DE SEMAPHORES A L'USAGE DE LA MARINE, DANS LE GOLFE ST LAURENT: LETTERS DE L'HONORABLE PIERRE FORTIN / Fortin, Pierre – Quebec: "Canadien", 1876. 05588. (Pre-1900 Canadiana) – 9 – cn C.I.H.M. [971]

SYSTEME ET STRUCTURE BANCAIRES EN ALGERIE / Algeria. Ministere de l'Information et de la Culture – 1971. BNE-8733 1 – 9 – ne IDC [332]

SYSTEME GENERAL DES OPERATIONS MILITAIRES DE LA CAMPAGNE PROCHAINE / Carnot, Hippolyte; ed by Charavay – Extrait de correspondance generale de Carnot. Paris. Impr. Nat. 1907. v.4. p.279-283. (Strategy of War Series) – 9 – fr Hachette [355]

LE SYSTEME JURIDIQUE DE LA SOCIETE DES NATIONS POUR LA PREVENTION DE LA GUERRE / Barandon, P – Paris, 1933 – 5mf – 9 – ILM-4013/1 – ne IDC [340]

SYSTEME MARITIME ET POLITIQUE DES EUROPEENS,... / Arnould, A M – Paris, 1797 – 4mf – 9 – ILM-630/1 – ne IDC [340]

A SYSTEME OF ANATOMY / Collins, S – M 328. 2 v. 1685 – 9 – ne IDC [611]

SYSTEME PROTECTEUR : OU, DE LA NECESSITE D'UNE REFORME DU TARIF CANADIEN / Beausoleil, Cleophas – Montreal: Nouveau-Monde, 1871. 03029. (Pre-1900 Canadiana) – 9 – cn C.I.H.M. [971]

SYSTEME SILURIEN DU CENTRE DE LA BOHEME / ed by Barrande, J – Prague, Paris, 1852-1911 – 392mf – 9 – 2527/2 – ne IDC [943]

SYSTEME SOCIAL. OU PRINCIPES NATURELS DE LA MORAL ET DE LA POLITIQUE. AVEC UN EXAMEN DE L'INFLUENCE DU GOUVERNEMENT SUR LES MOEURS / Holbach, Paul-Thiry d' – (D'Holbach series). 1773 – 9 – fr Hachette [170]

LES SYSTEMES DE REPRESENTATION DANS LES CONTES DU VETALA / Desormonts, M – 9 – F70.00 – fr Ethnologie [306]

LES SYSTEMES DE TRANSPORTATION ET DE MAIN-D'OEUVRE PENALE AUX COLONIES DANS LE DROIT FRANCAIS / Declareuil, Jean – Toulouse, Fournier, 1927. 189 p. LL-12007 – 1 – us L of C Photodup [340]

SYSTEMISCHES DENKEN / Dillinger, Stefan – 1994 – 2mf – DM80.00 – 3-8267-2049-0 – gw Hänsel [370]

SYSTEMS ANALYSIS MODELLING SIMULATION / ed by Sydow, Achim – 9,5,1 – us Gordon [000]

SYSTEMS AND COMPUTERS IN JAPAN – v16-. 1985- – 1,5,6,9 – us UMI [073]

SYSTEMS AND SOFTWARE – v1-. 1982- – 1,5,6,9 – us UMI [073]

SYSTEMS, COMPUTERS, CONTROLS – (v15-. 1984-. 5,6,9) – v1-15. 1970-84 – 1 – us UMI [073]

SYSTEMS OF BUDDHISTIC THOUGHT / Yamakami, Sogen – Calcutta: University of Calcutta, 1912. 315p – 1 – us U.W. Library [280]

SYSTEMS PRACTICE – v1-7. 1988-94 – 1,5 – $80.00v – us UMI [000]

SYSTEMS RESEARCH AND INFORMATION SCIENCE / ed by Johnson, L – 9,5,1 – us Gordon [000]

SYSTEMS, SCIENCES AND MODELLING / ed by Ruberti, A – 1984 – 159p – 9 – 92-3-102138-9 – fr UNESCO [600]

SYSTEMS, TECHNOLOGY AND SCIENCE FOR LAW ENFORCEMENT AND SECURITY – (v7-. 1975-. 5,6,9) – v. 1-. 1969- – 1 – us UMI [360]

SYSTOLIC BLOOD PRESSURE VERSUS HEART RATE TO PREDICT STEADY-STATE OXYGEN UPTAKE IN MALE CYCLISTS / Roberts, Scott O – 1987 – 125p 2mf – 9 – $8.00 – us Microform Publ [612]

Syunyaev, R A *see* ASTROPHYSICS AND SPACE PHYSICS REVIEWS

SYUU HOOKOOKAI... / Panitya Pasar Malam – Pertjetakan Hookookai, 2605. 24p – 125mf – 9 – ne IDC [950]

SZABAD FOLD – Budapest. 1951- – 1 – 23.00r – us L of C Photodup [073]

SZABAD FOLD – Budapest, Hungary. -w. Dec 1956-Dec 1975. 21 reels – 1 – uk British Libr Newspaper [072]

SZABAD IFJUSAG – Budapest. Hungary. -d. 3 Dec 1952-21 Oct 1956. (Imperfect). (14 reels) – 1 – uk British Libr Newspaper [072]

SZABAD NEP – Budapest, Hungary. 1946-Jun 1954; Jan-Oct 1956 – 17r – 1 – us L of C Photodup [072]

SZABAD SZO – Timisoara, Romania. 1967-73; Jul 1975-76 – 10r – 1 – us L of C Photodup [949]

SZABAD SZO – Titre francais: La Libre parole. Paris. dec 1935-fevr 1938 – 1 – fr A.C.R.P.P. [073]

SZABADSAG – Cleveland: "Szabadsag" Co, nov 12 1891-sep 9 1897 – 3r – 1 – us Res Libr [071]

Szabolcs, I *see* REVIEW OF RESEARCH ON SALT-AFFECTED SOILS

Szadkowski, Karin *see* DIE KIELER SPROTTEN

Szakonyi, Robert *see* HOW TO SUCCESSFULLY KEEP R&D PROJECTS ON TRACK

Szameitat, Max *see* BIBLIOGRAPHIE DES MEMELLANDES

Szawleski, Mieczyslaw *see* WYCHODZTWO POLSKIE W STANACH ZJEDNOCZONYCH AMERYKI

Szczodrowski, Daniel F *see* A COMPARATIVE STUDY ON THE EFFECTIVENESS OF PREVENTIVE KNEE BRACES

Szekely-Lulofs, M H *see* TJOET NJA DIN. DE GESCHIEDENIS VAN EEN ATJEHSE VORSTIN

SZENISCHE BAUWEISE DES ERZAEHLERS EICHENDORFF NACH DEM OPERNVORBILD GLUCKS UND MOZARTS / Siara, Norbert – Frankfurt a.M., 1973 – 3mf – 9 – DM76.00 – 3-89349-389-1 – gw Hänsel [430]

UM SZEPTER UND KRONEN : ZEITROMAN / Samarow, Gregor – (1st of a series of "Zeitromane" which includes Europaeische Minen und Gegenminen 1874; Zwei Kaiserkronen 1875; Kreuz und Schwert 1875; Held und Kaiser 1876) – 3. Aufl. Stuttgart: E Hallberger, 1873 – 1r – 1 – us U.W. Library [830]

SZKOLNICTWO – Nowy Sacz, Galicia, 1891-1895 – 2r – 1 – us I.H.R.C. [947]

SZOLNOK MEGYEI NEPLAP – Szolnok, Hungary. 1962-78; 1980-May 1987 – 49r – 1 – us L of C Photodup [072]

Szondi, Peter *see* SATZ UND GEGENSATZ

SZOVETKEZET – Budapest. 1950- – 1 – 23.00r – us L of C Photodup [330]

SZTANDAR LUDU – Lublin, Poland. May 1952-1990 – 76r – 1 – us L of C Photodup [947]

SZTANDAR MLODYCH – Warsaw, Poland. Nov 1950-1951; 1956-1993 (scattered issues) – 82r – 1 – us L of C Photodup [943]

SZTANDAR POLSKI – (Consists of scattered issues) – Bay City, MI, April 1917-May 1925 – 1r – 1 – us I.H.R.C. [978]

Szymanowski, K *see* 2. SONATE, OP. 21, PIANO SOLO

Szymanzig, Max *see* IMMERMANNS "TRISTAN UND ISOLDE"

Szyrocki, Marian *see* DIE DEUTSCHE LITERATUR DES BAROCK

Szyszylowicz, I *see* POLYPETALAE THALAMIFLORAE ET DISCIFLORAE REHMANNIANAE. ROZPRAWY I SPRAWOZDANIA

T. DE WITT TALMAGE : HIS LIFE AND WORK: BIOGRAPHICAL EDITION / ed by Banks, Louis Albert – [S.l.: s.n.], c1902 (Philadelphia; J.C. Winston) – 2mf – us A.T.L.A. [240]

A T E N *see* BULLETIN D'INFORMATION DE L'A.T.E.N

T. Eaton Co. Ltd *see* MAIL ORDER CATALOGUES

'T GEOPENDE, EN BEREIDWILLIGE HERTE, NA DEN HEERE JESUS... / Boekholt, J – Amsterdam, 1693 – 3mf – 9 – ne IDC [700]

T Sentralnai a statystychnai a uprava *see*
- STATYSTYCHNY LISTOK
- STATYSTYCHNY SHTOGODNIK

T Sentralnoe statisticheskoe upravlenie, Kievskoe gubernskoe statisticheskoe biuro *see* STATISTICHESKI I BIULLETEN

T Sentralnoe statisticheskoe upravlenie pri Sovete Ministrov SSSR *see* CHISLENNOST SKOTA V SSSR

T Sentralnoe statisticheskoe upravlenie RSFSR, Sektor sotsialno i statistiki *see* ESTESTVENNOE DVIZHENIE NASELENII A RSFSR ZA 1926 GOD

T Sentralnoe statisticheskoe upravlenie SSSR, Sektor statistiki promyshlennosti *see* FABRICHNO-ZAVODSKAIA PROMYSHLENNOST SSSR V 1925/26 GODU

T Sentralnoe statisticheskoe upravlenie SSSR, Sektor statistiki truda, Sekt sii a obshche i statistiki *see* BI UDZHETY RABOCHIKH I SLUZHASHCHIKH

T Sentralny i ispolnitelnyi komitet Soiuza SSRTsentralnaia izbiratelnaia komissiia T SIK Soiuza SSSR *see* VYBORY V SOVETY V SOIUZE SSR

T Sentralny i komitet Rossi isko i kommunistichesko i partii (bolshevikov) *see* EDINY I PARTI INY I BILET

T S.K.R.K.P.(bolsh.) *see* INSTRUKTSIIA ORGANIZATSII AM R.K.P. BOLSHEVIKOV O EDINOM PARTI INOM BILETE

T SU SSSR, Statisticheskoe upravlenie Belorussko i SSR *see* DOSTIZHENIIA SOVETSKOI BELORUSSII ZA 40 LET

T SU SSSR, T Sentralnoe statisticheskoe upravlenie pri Sovete Ministrov Armi ansko i SSR *see* EKONOMIKA I KULTURA ARMENII K 50-LETII U VELIKOGO OKTI ABRI A

TA GONG BAO – China. Various titles and places of publication. Jun 1902-1966. D47 – 9 – 2400.00 – cc Globe [072]

TA HSUEH YUAN KUNG PAO / China. Ministry of Education – Gazette. Nanking. v.1, n.1-9.Jan-Sep 1928. 1 reel – 1 – 18.70 – us Chinese Res [324]

TA INFORMATIONS – (v1-5 as: Traduction automatique) – v1-22. 1960-80 – 5,9 – Dfl880.00 Dfl40.00v – ne Swets [073]

TA KUNG PAO – Hong Kong, Aug 1938-Dec 1941; Mar 1948-1991 – 216r – 1 – us L of C Photodup [072]

TA KUNG PAO – Hong Kong: [s.n., dec 1951-55] – us Res Libr [072]

TAA, THERMAL ANALYSIS ABSTRACTS – (1982-. 1,5,6,9) – v6-. 1977- – 1 – us UMI [073]

Taaffe, John *see* THE HISTORY OF THE HOLY, MILITARY, SOVEREIGN ORDER OF ST. JOHN OF JERUSALEM

TABADUL-I NAZAR BAYN-I SAZMAN-I CHIRIK'HA-YI FADA'I-I KHALQ VA GURUH-I ITTIHAD-I KUMUNISTI – Daftar [0]-3 (winter 1975-summer 1977) – 1 reel – 1 – $30.00 – us MEDOC [950]

DER TABAK-ARBEITER – Bremen, 1913 (incomplete) – 1r – 1 – Inquire at Mikrofilmarchiv for details – gw Misc Inst [331]

TABAKARBEITER-ZEITUNG – Duesseldorf, 1906-1933 – 4r – 1 – DM320.00 – gw Mikro Press [072]

THE TABAKAT-U-NASIRI/A GENERAL HISTORY OF THE MUHAMMADAN DYNASTIES OF ASIA INCLUDING HINDUSTAN. FROM A.H. 194(810 A.D.) TO A.H. 658(1260 A.H.) AND THE IRRUPTION... / Raverty, H G – London, 1881 – LXIV, 1296, XXVIp – 8 – ne IDC [950]

TABAQAA8T-I-AKBARIA8 / Niza' Muddin Ahmad – B. De, Transl. Bibliotheca Indica Series. Calcutta, 1927-1939. v. 1-3. BI-779 2 – 8 – ne IDC [490]

TABAQAT-I-AKBARI / Niza' Muddin Ahmad – (Bibliotheca Indica series: Persian). Calcutta. 1913. BI-778 2 – 8 – ne IDC [490]

Tabaraud, M M *see* DE LA PHILOSOPHIE DE LA HENRIADE

Tabari *see*
- CHRONIQUE

TABELLEN EN PLATEN VOOR DE JAVAANSCHE ORCHIDEEN / Blume, C L – Batavia, 1825. 15p. 5 pls. B-5459/2 – 2mf – 8 – ne IDC [580]

TABELLEN ZUR DEUTSCHEN LITERATURGESCHICHTE / Schmitt, Fritz – Berlin: Junker und Duennhaupt, 1935 – 1r – 1 – us U.W. Library [430]

TABELLEN ZUR NEUTESTAMENTLICHEN ZEITGESCHICHTE : MIT EINER UEBERSICHT UEBER DIE CODICES, IN DENEN DIE NEUTESTAMENTLICHEN SCHRIFTEN BEZEUGT SIND / Vollert, Wilhelm – Leipzig: A Deichert, 1897 – 1mf – 9 – 0-8370-9331-7 – 1986-3331 – us A.T.L.A. [220]

Taber, Henry Moorehouse *see* FAITH OR FACT

THE TABERNACLE : ITS HISTORY AND STRUCTURE / Caldecott, William Shaw – (Includes index) – Philadelphia:Union Press, 1904 – 1mf – 9 – 0-8370-2570-2 – 1985-0570 – us A.T.L.A. [220]

TABERNACLE BAPTIST CHURCH. CARROLLTON, GEORGIA : CHURCH RECORDS – 1899-1933, 1937-63 – 1 – 38.52 – us Baptist [240]

THE TABERNACLE IN THE WILDERNESS : THE SHADOW OF HEAVENLY THINGS / Rhind, William Graeme – (Includes bibliographical references & appendix) – 5th rev ed. London: W H Broom, 1860 – 1mf – 9 – 0-8370-4887-7 – 1985-2887 – us A.T.L.A. [240]

THE TABERNACLE OF ISRAEL IN THE DESERT / Strong, James – Providence: Harris, Jones, 1888.1 fiche – 9 – us A.T.L.A. [240]

Tablan, Andrea Amor *see* MGA PAMARAAN SA PAGTUTURO NG WIKANG PILIPINO PARA SA KOLEHIYO

TABLAS BOTANICAS / Gomez Ortega, Casimiro – 1783 – 1mf – 9 – Pta1,000.00 – 84-7848-134-6 – sp Pentalfa [580]

TABLAS DE REDUCCIONES Y EQUIVALENCIAS DEL ANTIGUO SISTEMA DE PESAS / Camara, Ezequiel Enrique – 1871 – 9 – $1.50f – sp Bibl Santa Ana [930]

TABLAS REFORMADAS SEGUN EL CALENDARIO GREGORIANO / Jimenez Arias, Diego – 1644 – 9 – 1.50f – sp Bibl Santa Ana [240]

[TABLATURE FOR THE GUITAR AND LUTE] – Ms of the 2nd half of the 17th century – 1 – us Sibley [780]

TABLATURE FOR THE LUTE – Ms: early 18th century – 1 – us Sibley [780]

THE TABLE : JOURNAL OF THE SOCIETY OF CLERKS-AT THE TABLE IN COMMONWEALTH PARLIAMENTS – London. v1-54. 1932-86 – 57mf – 9 – $256.00 – LLMC 84-678 – us L.L.M.C. [073]

A TABLE ALPHABETICALL OF HARD USUAL ENGLISH WORDES / Cawdrey, Robert – 1604 – 9 – 10.00 – us Scholars' Facs [420]

TABLE ANALYTIQUE DES ARCHIVES DE MONTREAL, 1651-1694 – Montreal, Canada. 1v. 1890 – 1r – 1 – Can$25.00 – cn Can Microfilming [025]

TABLE ANALYTIQUE DU CODE CIVIL DU BAS CANADA – Ottawa: G.E. Desbarats, 1867. SEM105P431 – 2mf – 9 – Can$4.50 – cn Bibl Nat [340]

TABLE ANALYTIQUE ET RAISONNEE DE L'ENCYCLOPEDIE / Diderot, Denis – 1780 – 9 – fr I.C.S. [030]

TABLE CHRONOGRAPHIQUE DE L'ESTAT DU CHRISTIANISME / Gaultier, J – Lyon, 1673 – 18mf – 9 – CA-133/1 – ne IDC [240]

TABLE CHRONOLOGIQUE DES TRAITES CONCLUS PAR LA LETTONIE / Latvia – N.p., n.d. – 1mf – 9 – ILM-3928/1 – ne IDC [947]

TABLE DES MATIERES DES NOMS DE LIEUX ET DES NOMS DE PERSONNES CONTENUS DAUS LES PROCES-VERBAUX DES SEANCES DEPUIS LE 5 MAI 1789 JUSQU'AU 30 SEPTEMBRE 1791 / France. Parlement. Assemblee Constituante – 1 – fr A.C.R.P.P. [324]

TABLE GENERALE DES MATIERES DU PROCES-VERBAL / France. Parlement. Assemblee Nationale – 1792 – 1 – fr A.C.R.P.P. [324]

LA TABLE LATINE D'HERACLEE (LA PRETENDUE LEX JULIA MUNICIPALIS) / Legras, Henri – Paris, Rousseau, 1907. 400 2 p. LL-4019 – 1 – us L of C Photodup [340]

TABLE OF CASES AND INDEX TO THE NOTES IN AMERICAN DECISIONS AND REPORTS – San Francisco: Bancroft-Whitney, 1888 (all publ) – 3mf – 9 – $3.00 – LLMC 78-038F – us L.L.M.C. [340]

TABLE OF CASES DECIDED BY THE N.L.R.B / U.S. National Labor Relations Board – (Includes suppls for v268-289. Lacking: v224-267. Updates planned) – 4bks. v1-223 – 26mf – 9 – $39.00 – LLMC 80-209 – us L.L.M.C. [324]

A TABLE OF CASES IN THE REPORTS OF THE STATE OF CONNECTICUT 1785-1876, WHICH HAVE BEEN CITED, EXPLAINED, LIMITED, DOUBTED, OR OVERRULED IN SUBSEQUENT DECISIONS / Sharswood, George – Philadelphia: Johnson, 1878. 199p. LL-1557 – 1 – us L of C Photodup [340]

TABLE OF FEES / Bas-Canada. Cour du Banc du Roi – [S.l.]: [s.n.], [1830?] – 1mf – 9 – Can$2.25 – cn Bibl Nat [340]

TABLE OF MEASURED DISTANCES AND POST FARES BETWEEN QUEBEC AND MONTREAL... – [S.l.: s.n., 1799 ?]. SEM105P1403 – 1mf – 9 – Can$2.25 – cn Bibl Nat [380]

A TABLE OF WRITTEN LAW JUDICIALLY CONSIDERED BY THE SUPREME COURT OF THE STRAIGHTS SETTLEMENTS AND ON APPEAL THEREFROM, 1808-1898 / Koek, Edwin Rowland – Singapore, American Mission Press, 1900. 48 p. LL-10010 – 1 – us L of C Photodup [340]

TABLE PREPARED BY THE SUPERINTENDENT OF EDUCATION FOR LOWER CANADA, SHOWING THE COUNTIES WHICH HAVE RECEIVED SUMS OF MONEY FOR THE CONSTRUCTION OF SCHOOL HOUSES / Canada. Bas-Canada. Bureau de l'Education – Montreal: Lovell and Gibson, 1847. SEM105P940 – 1mf – 9 – Can$2.25 – cn Bibl Nat [370]

TABLE ROCK ARGUS – Table Rock, NE. -w. May 1883; Jul-Nov 1883; Jul 1884; Sept 1884-May 1885; Jun 1892; Oct 1895 to date – 1 – us NE Hist [071]

TABLE ROCK HERALD – Table Rock, NE. -w. Apr 1893-Nov 1894 – 1 – us NE Hist [071]

TABLE ROCK SENTINEL – Jacksonville OR. Jan 5-Dec 6 1856, May 24 Dec 6 1856 – 1 – us U.O. Library [071]

LA TABLE RONDE – Paris. Revue europeenne de recherche chretienne. 1948-59 – 1 – fr A.C.R.P.P. [240]

TABLE TALK : AND OTHER POEMS / Cowper, William – London: Printed for John Sharpe, by C. Whittingham, Chiswick, 1817 – 1 roll – 1 – 1-55879-311-9 – uk Libr Preservation [810]

TABLE TALK – Melbourne, Australia. 21 Oct 1892-5 Dec 1901; 27 Feb 1902-29 Jun 1922.-w. 51 reels – 1 – uk British Libr Newspaper [072]

THE TABLE TALK OF MARTIN LUTHER / Hazlitt, William – London. 1856 – 1 – 17.85 – us Baptist [240]

TABLEAU ALPHABETIQUE DES CITES, VILLES, VILLAGES, PAROISSES ET CANTONS DANS CHAQUE COMTE DE LA PROVINCE DE QUEBEC / Glackemeyer, Edouard Claude – (Quebec: J. Langlais), 1889. 03447. (Pre-1900 Canadiana) – 9 – cn C.I.H.M. [971]

TABLEAU COMPARATIF POUR CHACUN DES DEPARTEMENTS DE LA FRANCE CONTINENTALE ET DES RESULTATS STATISTIQUES RELATIFS A LEUR POPULATION. / Villot, Frederic & Villerme, Louis Rene – Reprod. d'un extrait du Bulletin des Sciences geographiques. v6, 1825. p7-16. 1 fiche. (Statistics Series: Demography) – 9 – 6.00 – fr Bibl Nationale [310]

TABLEAU DE L'ECOLE DE BOTANIQUE DU MUSEUM D'HISTOIRE NATURELLE / Desfontaines, R L – Paris. 1804 – 8 – ne IDC [580]

TABLEAU DE L'ETAT ACTUEL DE L'INSTRUCTION PRIMAIRE EN FRANCE, RAPPORT PRESENTE AU ROI PAR M. VILLEMAIN, MINISTRE DE L'INSTRUCTION PUBLIQUE, LE – ler Novembre 1841. (Condition of 19th C. French working class series) – 9 – fr Hachette [370]

TABLEAU DE L'ETAT PHYSIQUE ET MORAL DES OUVRIERS EMPLOYES DANS LES MANUFACTURES DE COTON, DE LAINE ET DE SOIE / Villerme, Louis Rene – (Condition of 19th C. French working class series). 1840 – 9 – fr Hachette [360]

TABLEAU DE L'INCONSTANCE DES MAUVAIS ANGES ET DEMONS OU IL EST AMPLEMENT TRAICTE DES SORCIERS ET DE SORCELERIE / L'Ancre, Pierre de – Paris. 1612 – 9 – fr Hachette [360]

TABLEAU DE L'INSTRUCTION PRIMAIRE EN FRANCE, D'APRES LES RAPPORTS DES 490 INSPECTEURS CHARGES DE VISITER TOUTES LES ECOLES DE FRANCE EN 1833 / Lorain – (Condition of 19th C. French working class series). 1837 – 9 – fr Hachette [370]

TABLEAU DE SITUATION DU DEPARTEMENT DE L'ALLIER / Huguet, Jean A – an X – 9 – fr Hachette [944]

TABLEAU DES ARANEIDES / Walckenaer, C A – Z 2212 2. 1805 – 8 – ne IDC [590]

TABLEAU DES GENRES DE VEGETAUX FOSSILES / Brongniart, A T – 1849 – 3mf – 7 – uk Microform Academic [560]

TABLEAU DES PARTIS POLITIQUES DE L'AFRIQUE AU SUD DU SAHARA / Decraene, P – F70.00 – fr Ethnologie [320]

TABLEAU DES SAINTS, OU EXAMEN DE L'ESPRIT, DE LA CONDUITE, DES MAXIMES ET DU MERITE DES PERSONNAGES QUE LE CHRISTIANISME REVERE ET PROPOSE POUR MODELE / Holbach, Paul-Thiry d' – (D'Holbach series). 1770 – 9 – fr Hachette [240]

TABLEAU DES VARIETES DE LA VIE HUMAINE: AVEC LES AVANTAGES ET LES DESAVANTAGES DE CHAQUE CONSTITUTION ET DES AVIS. / Daignan, Guillaume – Paris, 1786. 2 v. xxiii, 389, 386 p. 10 fiches. (Statistics Series: Medical Studies) – 9 – 25.00 – fr Bibl Nationale [310]

TABLEAU DU COMMERCE DE LA GRECE, FORME D'APRES UNE ANNEE MOYENNE, DEPUIS 1787 JUSQU'EN 1797, PAR FELIX-BEAUJOUR, EX-CONSUL EN GRECE / Beaujour, Louis Auguste Felix de – Paris, A.-A. Renouard, 1800, 2 v., 338-8 plus 333 p. French Voyagers in the Mediterranean 16th to 18th Centuries. 5993-94 – 9 – fr Hachette [944]

TABLEAU DU REGNE VEGETAL SELON LA METHODE DE JUSSIEU / Ventenat, E P – 4v. Paris. 1799. B-5790 2 – 8 – ne IDC [580]

TABLEAU DU SURINTENDANT D'EDUCATION DU BAS-CANADA, INDIQUANT LES COMTES QUI ONT RECU DES SOMMES D'ARGENT POUR LA CONSTRUCTION DE MAISONS D'ECOLE. / Canada. Bas-Canada. Bureau de l'Education – Montreal: Lovell et Gibson, 1847. SEM105P942 – 1mf – 9 – Can$2.25 – cn Bibl Nat [370]

TABLEAU D'UN COLLEGE EN ACTIVITE / Major, J F – Bar-le-Duc. impr. Moucheron et Duval. 1790. 6770 – 9 – fr Hachette [370]

TABLEAU ENCYCLOPEDIQUE ET METHODIQUE DES TROIS REGNES DE LA NATURE BOTANIQUE / ed by Lamarck, J B A P M de & Poiret, J L M – (Supplement pl. 1-1000) – Paris. v1-3. 1791-1823 – 94mf – ne IDC [580]

TABLEAU GENERALE DE L'EMPIRE OTHOMAN, DIVISE EN DEUX PARTIES / Ohsson, M C d' – H-436 2. 7 v. in 8. 1788-1824 – 8 – ne IDC [949]

TABLEAU GEOGRAPHIQUE DE LA VEGETATION PRIMITIVE DANS LA PROVINCE DE MINAS GERAES / Saint-Hilaire, A F C P de – Paris. 1837. B-5562 2 – 8 – ne IDC [580]

TABLEAU HISTORIQUE, POLITIQUE, ET MODERNE DE L'EMPIRE OTTOMAN / Eton, William – Paris, Tavernier, an VII 1798-99, 2 t. en 1 v., iv-xxii-352 plus 320 p. French Voyagers in the Mediterranean 16th to 18th Centuries. 5979 – 9 – fr Hachette [949]

TABLEAU PHILOSOPHIQUE DU GENRE HUMAIN / Borde, Charles – (D'Holbach series). 1767 – 9 – fr Hachette [190]

LE TABLEAU PRETENDU DE LA PENITENCE – Rouen. 1699 – 9 – fr Hachette [360]

TABLEAU STATISTIQUE / Dyle. France (Department) – Par M.D.B. Bruxelles: E. Flon, An XIII – 9 – fr Hachette [944]

TABLEAU STATISTIQUE DE L'EUROPE / Beaufort, Secretaire de Legation – Paris: Didot fils aine, 1787-88.1 fiche. (Statistics Series: Topography) – 9 – 6.00 – fr Bibl Nationale [944]

TABLEAU STATISTIQUE DU DEPARTEMENT DE L'AUBE / Brusle de Valsuzenay, Claude L – an X – 9 – fr Hachette [944]

TABLEAU STATISTIQUE DU DEPARTEMENT DE L'OURTHE / Desmousseaux, Antoine F – an X – 9 – fr Hachette [944]

TABLEAU STATISTIQUE DU DEPARTEMENT DES VOSGES / Desgouttes, Zacharie H – An X – 9 – fr Hachette [944]

TABLEAU STATISTIQUE DU DEPARTEMENT DU GERS / Balguerie – an X – 9 – fr Hachette [944]

TABLEAU STATISTIQUE ET POLITIQUE DES DEUX CANADAS / Lebrun, Isidore – Paris: Treuttel et Wurtz, 1833. SEM105P915 – 6mf – 9 – Can$13.50 – cn Bibl Nat [320]

TABLEAU SYNOPTIQUE DES EVOLUTIONS D'UN BATAILLON ACCOMPAGNE DE PLANCHES / Suzor, L T – Quebec: Desbarats et Derbishire, [1862]. SEM105P1287 – 2mf – 9 – Can$4.50 – cn Bibl Nat [623]

TABLEAUX ANALYTIQUES ET DICHOTOMIQUES DE TOUS LES GENRES ET ESPECES DE LICHENS DECRITS DANS LE LICHENOGRAPHIA SCANDINAVICA DE TH. M. FRIES / Olivier, H – Autheuil. 1881. B-7097 1 – 9 – ne IDC [580]

TABLEAUX DE EDMOND-J. MASSICOTTE / Massicotte, Edmond-Joseph – [Quebec (Province)?: s.n., 1930?] ([Laprairie: Imprimerie du Sacre-Coeur]). SEM105P1701 – 1mf – 9 – Can$2.25 – cn Bibl Nat [700]

TABLEAUX ET SCENES DE LA VIE DES ANIMAUX / Lesbazeilles, Eugene – Paris: Hachette, 1882. 189p. 2 fiches.(Miscellaneous Selections) – 9 – 6.00 – fr Bibl Nationale [590]

TABLEAUX STATISTIQUES DE L'EPIDEMIE CHOLERIQUE A PARIS PENDANT LES MOIS DE SEPT, OCTOBRE, NOVEMBRE ET DECEMBRE 1865 – Paris: P. Dupont, 1872. 538p. 10 fiches. (Statistics Series: Medical Studies) – 9 – 25.00 – fr Bibl Nationale [310]

TABLEAUX STATISTIQUES RELATIFS A L'ECONOMIE FRANCAISE ET L'ECONOMIE MONDIALE / Jeanneney, J M – F50.00 – fr Ethnologie [339]

TABLEAUX SYNOPTIQUES DES LEPIDOPTERES D'EUROPE / Villiers, F de & Guenee, A – Paris, Londres, 1835. v1, iii,147p. 1 pl. Z-1687/2 – 8 – ne IDC [590]

TABLES ANNUELLES / France – 1871-1965 – 1 – fr A.C.R.P.P. [944]

TABLES GENERALES DES TRAVAUX CONTENUS DANS LES MEMOIRES DE L'ACADEMIE – Paris. 1881; v1-14. 1795-1815; v1-40. 1816-78 – 3mf – 9 – 472/2 – ne IDC [944]

TABLES GIVING THE NUMBER OF DAYS FROM ONE DATE TO ANOTHER / Dorais, O Emile – Three Rivers, Que.: s.n., 1890 (Three Rivers, Que.: A. Genest). 02739. (Pre-1900 Canadiana) – 9 – cn C.I.H.M. [971]

TABLES ON AGRICULTURAL STATISTICS / Jordan. Ministry of Economy – 1955 – 9 – ne IDC [310]

TABLET : A CATHOLIC WEEKLY – Brooklyn, NY. 1970-71 – 2r – 1 – us Ross [240]

THE TABLET – London. -w. May 1840-Jul 1842. (4 reels) – 1 – uk British Libr Newspaper [072]

THE TABLET – v. 39, no. 44-65, no. 49. 3 Jan 1948-28 Dec 1972 – 1 – us NY Public [073]

TABLET OF THE TIMES – Bennington, VT. 1797. Also: Epitome of the World, Bennington, 1807; World, Bennington, 1807-09; Green-Mountain Farmer, Bennington, 1809-16. Sold as one unit – 3 – us Readex [071]

TABLE-TALK : OR ORIGINAL ESSAYS / Hazlitt, William – London: John Warren, 1821-22 – 1 roll – 1 – 1-55879-240-6 – uk Libr Preservation [840]

THE TABLE-TALK OF JOHN SELDEN / Singer, S W – London: Reeves & Turner, 1890 – 4mf – 9 – $6.00 – LLMC 91-071 – us L.L.M.C. [340]

THE TABLE-TALK OF SHIRLEY : REMINISCENCES OF AND LETTERS FROM FROUDE, THACKERAY, DISRAELI, BROWNING, ROSSETTI, KINGSLEY, BAYNES, HUXLEY, TYNDALL AND OTHERS / Skelton, John – Edinburgh, London: W. Blackwood, 1895 – 1 roll – 1 – 1-55879-762-9 – uk Libr Preservation [860]

TABLETTES UNIVERSELLES – Repertoire des evenements, des nouvelles, et de tout ce qui concerne l'histoire, les sciences, la litterature et les arts, avec une bibliographie generale. Dir. J.-B. Gouriet. no. 1-68. Paris. oct 1820-mars 1824 – 1 – fr A.C.R.P.P. [900]

Tabor, Britton H *see* SKEPTICISM ASSAILED

TABOR MELODIES / Evans, Robert – Toronto: S. Rose, 1878. 02927. (Pre-1900 Canadiana) – 9 – cn C.I.H.M. [971]

TABOR'S TEACHINGS : OR, THE VEIL LIFTED: A GLIMPSE OF CHRIST'S GLORY AND INTERCOURSE WITH HIS PEOPLE FOR EVER / Author of Heaven our home – Edinburgh: William P Nimmo, 1865 – 1mf – 9 – 0-8370-2438-2 – 1985-0438 – us A.T.L.A. [240]

Tabourot, Etienne *see* LES BIGARRURES ET TOUCHES DU SEIGNEUR DES ACCORDS. (E.T.) AVEC LES APOPHTEGMES DU SIEUR GAULARD LES ESCRAIGNES DIJONNOISES

TABULA AFFINITATUM REGNI VEGETABILIS / Batsch, A J G C – Wimariae. B-5838 2 – 8 – ne IDC [580]

TABULA ANALYTICA FUNGORUM IN EPICRISI, SEU SYNOPSI HYMENOMYCETUM FRIESIANA DESCRIPTORUM / Trogg, J G – Bernae. 1846. B-6330 2 – 8 – ne IDC [580]

TABULAE ANATOMICAE / Eustacchi, B – Romae, 1714 – 6mf – ne IDC [611]

TABULAE BOTANICAE ELEMENTARES QUATOR PRIORES SIVE ICONES PARTIUM / Cyrillus, D – Neapoli. 1790 – 8 – ne IDC [580]

TABULAE GREGORIANAE MOTUUM OCTAUAE SPHAERAE AC LUMINARIUM AD USUM CALENDARIJ ECCLESIASTICI / Moleti, Giuseppe – Gregorian Calendar, Calendar reform – 1 – us U.W. Library [520]

TABULAE PHYCOLOGICAE / Kuetzing, F T – 19 v. Nordhausen. 1845-1869-71. Index. B-762 2 – 8 – ne IDC [580]

TABULAE PHYCOLOGICAE ODER ABBILDUNGEN DER TANGE / Kuetzing, F T – 1845-71 – 85mf – 7 – uk Microform Academic [580]

A TABULAR ANALYSIS OF THE LAW OF AGENCY / Minning, Arthur C – Cincinnati: Anderson, 1903. LL-1206 – 1 – us L of C Photodup [340]

TABY NYHETER – Stockholm, Sweden. 1945-46 – 1 reel – 1 – sw Kungliga [072]

TABY TIDNING – Stockholm, Sweden. 1940-41 – 1 reel – 1 – sw Kungliga [072]

TABYPOSTEN – Stockholm, Sweden. 1924-25 – 1 reel – 1 – sw Kungliga [072]

DU TAC AU TAC: REPONSES AUX OBJECTIONS MODERNES CONTRE LA RELIGION / Augier, Ernest – 9th ed. Paris: P. Letmielleux, 1908 – 1 – us U.W. Library [240]

TAC UET-TEVARIH / Sadeddin – Istanbul, 1279 [1802].-2v – 22mf – 9 – $52.50 – us MEDOC [949]

O TACAPE : LITTERARIO, SCIENTIFICO E NOTICIOSO – Parintins, Amazonas. 15 Nov 1902-18 Jun 1904 – 1,5,6 – bl Biblioteca [072]

Tachdijian. A *see* VOCABULAIRE D'ACCESSION A L'INFORMATION

Tache, Archbishop *see* PASTORAL LETTER DECLARING THE DECREES OF THE FIRST COUNCIL OF ST BONIFACE

Tache, Joseph C *see*
- LES SABLONS (L'ILE DU SABLE) ET L'ILE SAINT-BARNABE
- TROIS LEGENDES DE MON PAYS

Tache, Louis-H et al *see* L'OPINION PUBLIQUE

LA TACHE NOIRE – I, no. 1-5; II, no. 6-20. Paris. mars 1871, fevr-dec 1872 – 1 – fr A.C.R.P.P. [073]

Tachereau, J-F *see* LA GAZETTE D'ARTHABASKA

TA-CHUNG-HUA – The Great China Magazine. v. 1-2. Shanghai. 1915-16. BCH-344 2 – 8 – ne IDC [073]

TACOMA: ITS HISTORY AND ITS BUILDERS / Hunt, Herbert – Chicago: S.J. Clarke Publ. Co., 1916. v1-3. Washington reel 4.(Cox Library Collection) – 5 – us Americana [978]

TACOMIAN – Tacoma. Wash. -w. 1892-93 – 1 – us UMI [071]

TACT IN COURT / Donovan, Joseph Wesley – 6th ed. Rochester, N.Y., Williamson, 1898. 188 p. LL-483 – 1 – us L of C Photodup [340]

TACTICAL AND TECHNICAL TRENDS IN ARTILLERY FOR INSTRUCTION – (See also: Artillery Trends and Field Artilleryman) – v1-5. 1957-58 – 1 – us UMI [355]

TACTICAL MISSION REPORTS OF THE 20TH AND 21ST BOMBER COMMANDS, 1945 / U. S. Strategic Bombing Survey – RG 243. M1159. 6 rolls – 1 – us Nat'l Archives [355]

LA TACTIQUE AU TREIZIEME SIECLE / Delpech, Henri – Montpellier, Paris, 1885-86. 2v. (Historical Studies Series) – 9 – 33.00 – fr Bibl Nationale [900]

LA TACTIQUE DANS LE SOUDAN; QUELQUES COMBATS ET EPISODES DE GUERRES REMARQUABLES / Peroz, Marie Etienne – Paris. 1890 – 1 – us Res Libr [960]

TACTOLOGY : THE SCIENCE OF PERSONAL WORK / Young, William Henry – Athens, GA: How Publishing; London: Elliot Stock, 1905, c1902 – 1mf – 9 – 0-8370-7359-6 – 1986-1359 – us A.T.L.A. [240]

Taczanowski, W *see*
- FAUNE ORNITHOLOGIQUE DE LA SIBERIE ORIENTALE
- ORNITHOLOGIE DU PEROU

Tadra, F *see* ZUR KAISERWAHL 1619

TADZHIKSKO-PERSIDSKIE I TIURKSKIE RUKOPISI VOSTOCHNOGO FAKUL'TETA LGU / Tagirdzhanov, A T – BR-10,922/1 – 9 – ne IDC [025]

TAEGLICHE RUNDSCHAU : BEILAGE: BILDER RUNDSCHAU – (Cont by: Neue Taegliche Rundschau, dec 1, 1924. Taegliche Rundschau, feb 1, 1925) – Berlin. jan 8-jun 10, 1928 – 1r – 1 – gw Mikrofilm [072]

TAEGLICHE RUNDSCHAU – Berlin, 1945-1955 – 19r – 1 – DM1,740.00 – gw Mikro Press [072]

TAEGLICHE RUNDSCHAU – Berlin, Germany. 1881-1933 (incomplete) – 286r – 1 – gw Mikrofilm [072]

TAEGLICHE RUNDSCHAU – Berlin, Germany. -d. 8-12 Aug, 27 Sept-10 Oct 1914; 1 April 1916-7 Aug 1919. 21 reels – 1 – uk British Libr Newspaper [072]

TAEGLICHE RUNDSCHAU – Berlin, may 15 1945-jun 30 1955 – 19r – 1 – Inquire at Mikrofilmarchiv for details – gw Misc Inst [072]

TAEGLICHE RUNDSCHAU – (Cont by: Neue Taegliche Rundschau, dec 1 1924; Taegliche Rundschau, feb 1 1925. Also suppl available: Bilder Rundschau, jan 8-jun 10 1928, 1r; Unterhaltungsbeilage, jan 2-sep 29 1922, 1r) – Berlin, sep 1 1881-jul 8 1933 – 1 – Inquire at Mikrofilmarchiv for details – gw Misc Inst [943]

TAEGLICHE RUNDSCHAU – East Berlin, Germany. 19 Mai 1945-Jun 1955 – 19r – 1 – gw Mikrofilm [072]

TAEGLICHER ANZEIGER – Holzminden, Germany. 1977- – ca 6r per yr – 1 – gw Mikrofilm [072]

TAEGLICHER ANZEIGER *see* BAMBERGER TAGBLATT

TAEGLICHER BALTIMORE CORRESPONDENT *see* BALTIMORE CORRESPONDENT

TAEGLICHER PEORIA DEMOKRAT – Peoria. Ill. 1891, 1894, 1898-1906, 1907-14 – 1 – us UMI [071]

TAEGLICHER TELEGRAM – Indianapolis. Ind. 1865-1918 – 1 – us UMI [071]

Taeglichsbeck, D *see* DIE BELEGSCHAFT DER BERGWERKE UND SALINEN IM OBERAMTSBEZIRK DORTMUND NACH DER ZAHLUNG VOM 16. 12. 1893

DIE TAENZERIN UND ANDERE ERZAEHLUNGEN / Bang, Hermann Joachim – Berlin: Otto Janke, c1901 – 1r – 1 – us U.W. Library [830]

TAES NEWS / Texas A & M University. Agricultural Experiment Station – No.43-56. 1970-82 – 1,5 – us Spaulding [630]

DIE TAETIGKEIT DES KINDES IN DER SPIELTHERAPIE / Chow, Sergio et al – 1994 – 7mf – DM130.00 – 3-8267-2031-8 – gw Hänsel [150]

TAEUBCHEN IM NEST, 1860 : ELEGIEN / Beck, Karl – 2. Aufl. Wien: J P Gotthard, 1869 – 1 – us U.W. Library [810]

Taeubler, Eugen *see* MITTEILUNGEN DES GESAMTARCHIVS DER DEUTSCHEN JUDEN

DIE TAEUFERBEWEGUNG IN DER GRAFSCHAFT OLDENBURG-DELMENHORST UND DER HERRSCHAFT JEVER ZUR ZEIT DER REFORMATION : EINE KIRCHENGESCHICHTLICHE STUDIE / Schauenburg, L – (Includes bibliographical references) – Oldenburg: Gerhard Stalling, 1888 – 1mf – 9 – 0-8370-8941-7 – 1986-2941 – us A.T.L.A. [240]

DIE TAEUFERBEWEGUNG IN THUERINGEN VON 1526-1584 : NAMENS DES VEREINS FUER THUERINGISCHE GESCHICHTE UND ALTERTUMSKUNDE HERAUSGEGEBEN VON DER THUERINGISCHEN HISTORISCHEN KOMMISSION / Wappler, Paul – Jena: Gustav Fischer, 1913 – 2mf – us A.T.L.A. [240]

TA-FENG – "The Typhoon Magazine". nos. 1-101. Hongkong. 1938-41. Fortnightly. BCH-345 – 9 – ne IDC [073]

TAFEREEL VAN OVERDEFTIGE ZINNEBEELDEN / Zaunslifer, P – O 468. 1722 – 9 – ne IDC [760]

TAFEREELEN – Amsterdam. v1-3. 1860-62 – 15mf – 9 – J-261-110/1 – ne IDC [949]

Taffin, I *see* ONDERWIJSINGHE, TEGHENS DE DWALINGHE DER WEDERDOOPEREN

TAFSIER MUCHTASOR : TAFSIER QURAN UNTUK SEKOLAH LANDJUTAN / Idries, Iskandar – 1960 – 9 – SE-6333 1 – ne IDC [370]

TAFSIR SINAR / Ahmad, H A Malik – v1 only.In Indonesian and Arabic. SE-4906-1. 1963 – 9 – ne IDC [950]

TAFSIRAN UNDANG-UNDANG POKOK AGRARIA / Gouw, Giok Siong – SE-4757 1. 1963 – 9 – ne IDC [950]

TAFSIRAN-TAFSIRAN ALKITAB INDJIL JAHJA / Verkuyl, Johannes – SE 5165 1. 1963 – 9 – ne IDC [950]

TAFSIRAN-TAFSIRAN ALKITAB INDJIL MATIUS / Riedel, K – SE-5125 1. 1963 – 9 – ne IDC [950]

TAFT CITY DIRECTORIES – Kern Co, CA. 1926; 1949 – 2r – 1 – $100.00 – D045 – us Library Micro [910]

Taft, Robert *see*
- CORRESPONDENCE WITH WILLIAM HENRY JACKSON
- NOTES
- RECORDS

Taft, William H *see* PAPERS

Taft, Z *see* BIOGRAPHICAL SKETCHES OF THE LIVES AND PUBLIC MINISTRY OF VARIOUS HOLY WOMEN,...IN WHICH ARE INCLUDED SEVERAL LETTERS FROM THE REV. J. WESLEY NEVER BEFORE PUBLISHED

TAFT'S COMPILATION OF SENATE ELECTION CASES, 1789-1913 – (1789-1885 by George S. Taft. Cont to 1893 by George P. Furber. Cont to 1903 by George M. Buck. Cont to 1913 by Charles A. Webb & Herbert R. Pierce) – Washington: GPO. Senate doc no 1036 62nd Congress 3rd Session. 1v. 1913 (all publ) – 9 – LLMC 95-124 – us L.L.M.C. [340]

DER TAG – (Also suppl available: Bilder Tag, apr 2 1950-feb 24 1952) – Berlin, mar 23 1948-mar 31 1963 – 1 – Inquire at Mikrofilmarchiv for details – gw Misc Inst [072]

DER TAG – Aussig, mar 24 1927-sep 16 1933 (incomplete) – 8r – 1 – Dist. gw Mikrofilm – gw Misc Inst [943]

DER TAG : BEILAGE: BILDER TAG – Berlin. apr 2, 1950-feb 24, 1952 – 1 – gw Mikrofilm [072]

DER TAG – Berlin. Germany. -d. 23 Mar 1948-31 Dec 1957. (28 reels) – 1 – uk British Libr Newspaper [072]

DER TAG – Czernowitz (Cernauti), Rumaenien. 1 May 1932-30 Sep 1933 – 2r – 1 – gw Mikrofilm [949]

DER TAG – Duchcov, Czechoslovakia. Mar 1919-Oct 1924; Oct 1932-Sept 1933 – 4r – 1 – us L of C Photodup [072]

DER TAG : MODERNE ILLUSTRIERTE ZEITUNG – Berlin, Germany. 8 Jan 1901-21 Oct 1934 – 151r – 1 – gw Mikrofilm [072]

DER TAG : MODERNE ILLUSTRIERTE ZEITUNG. AUSGABE A – (Also available: Ausgabe B, jul-dec 25 1921, 1r) – Berlin, jan 8 1901-oct 21 1934 – 151r – 1 – Inquire at Mikrofilmarchiv for details – gw Misc Inst [943]

DER TAG – Usti Nad Labem, Czechoslovakia. 14 Mar 1931; Jan-Oct 1932 – 1r – 1 – us L of C Photodup [072]

DER TAG. AUSGABE B *see* DER TAG

DER TAG DES DEUTSCHEN : KRIEGSGEDICHTE / Presber, Rudolf – 13. Aufl. Stuttgart: Deutsche Verlags-Anstalt, c1914 – 1 – us U.W. Library [810]

DER TAG: ILLUSTRIERTE UNTERHALTUNGSBEILAGE – Berlin. v. 1-6; 1914-1920. Film Mas C 723 – 1 – us H.U. Library [073]

TAG IN KAPERNAUM = A DAY IN CAPERNAUM / Delitzsch, Franz – (In English) – NY: Funk & Wagnalls, 1892, c1887 – 1mf – 9 – 0-8370-2867-1 – 1985-0867 – us A.T.L.A. [240]

TAG UND DAEMMERUNG : APHORISMEN, SCHRIFTEN, BRIEFE, TAGEBUECHER / Lichtenberg, Georg Christoph; ed by Vincent, Ernst – (Includes bibliographical references & indexes) – 5. erw. Aufl. Leipzig: Dieterich, 1944 – 1 – us U.W. Library [880]

TAGBLAT – Lemberg. Mar 30 1904-Apr 1905; 1906-1911. Not collated – 1 – us NY Public [073]

TAGBLAT – (Yiddish daily) – Lwow, PL. v4 no206 29 Oct 1907-v11 no155 5 Jul 1914 – 1r – 1 – $25.00 – cn Can Microfilming [072]

TAGBLATT = DAILY – (In Yiddish) – Lemberg, DE. no155 5 Jul 1914-v4 no206 29 Oct 1914 – 1r – 1 – $25.00 – cn Can Microfilming [072]

TAGBLATT BRUEXER VOLKSZEITUNG *see* DEUTSCHE VOLKSZEITUNG

TAGBLATT DER STADT BAMBERG *see* BAMBERGER TAGBLATT

TAGEBLATT *see* HEIDELBERGER GENERAL-ANZEIGER

TAGEBLATT DER STADT BAMBERG – Bamberg, Germany. 1848-49 – 2r – 1 – gw Mikrofilm [072]

TAGEBLATT FUER NORD-CHINA – Tientsin, China. 19 Jul 1914-28 Oct 1915 – 1r – 1 – gw Mikrofilm [072]

TAGEBLATT FUER NORDCHINA – Tientsin. 1914-15. KCHF-2-3 – 1 – ne IDC [072]

TAGEBLATT JOURNAL D'ESCH – Esch/Alzette, Luxemburg. 1972- – 1 – gw Mikrofilm [949]

DAS TAGEBUCH – (Cont by: Das neue Tagebuch, 1933) – Berlin, Muenchen, Paris, Amsterdam. jul 1 1933-may 11 1940 – 4r – 1 – Inquire at Mikrofilmarchiv for details – gw Misc Inst [072]

DAS TAGEBUCH : GEDICHTE / Greiner, Leo – 2., verm. Aufl. Muenchen: G Mueller, 1912 – 1r – 1 – us U.W. Library [810]

DAS TAGEBUCH (1810) : VIER UNTERDRUECKTE ROEMISCHE ELEGIEN... / Goethe, Johann Wolfgang von – (Includes bibliographical references) – Leipzig; A Weigel, 1904 – 1r – 1 – us U.W. Library [920]

TAGEBUCH DER MERKWUERDIGEN STAATSBEGEBENHEITEN – Braunschweig, dec 7-13 1782, jan 1-jun 30 1783 – 1r – 1 – Inquire at Mikrofilmarchiv for details – gw Misc Inst [943]

TAGEBUCH EINER REISE NACH DEN KUESTEN DES ADRIATISCHEN MEERES UND DEN GEBIRGEN VON KRAIN, VORZUEGLICH IN BOTANISCHER UND ENTOMOLOGISCHER HINSICHT / Hoppe, DH & Hornschuch, F – Regensburg. 1818. B-5198 2 – 8 – ne IDC [580]

TAGEBUCH EINES LESERS : BEMERKUNGEN UND AUFSAETZE ZUR LITERATUR / Weber, Werner – (Includes index) – Olten, Freiburg im Breisgau: Walter-Verlag, 1965 – 1r – 1 – us U.W. Library [430]

DAS TAGEBUCH KAISER KARL'S 7. AUS DER ZEIT DES OESTERREICHISCHEN ERBFOLGEKRIEGS / ed by Heigel, K T – Muenchen, 1883 – 3mf – 9 – ne IDC [943]

TAGEBUECHER / Varnhagen von Ense, Karl August – (At head of title: Aus dem Nachlass Varnhagen's von Ense) – Leipzig: F A Brockhaus, 1861-62 – 4r – 1 – us U.W. Library [880]

DIE TAGEBUECHER DES DICHTERS ZACHARIAS WERNER / ed by Floeck, Oswald – (Includes bibliographical references and index) – Leipzig: K W Hiersemann. 2v. 1939-40 – 1 – us U.W. Library [920]

DIE TAGEBUECHER DES GRAFEN AUGUST VON PLATEN = DIARIES / Platen, August, Graf von – Stuttgart: J G Gotta Nachfolger, 1896-1900 – 1r – 1 – us U.W. Library [920]

TAGEBUECHER VON FRIEDRICH VON GENTZ / ed by Ense, K A Varnhagen von – Leipzig, 1861 – 4mf – 9 – ne IDC [943]

TAGEBUECHER VON FRIEDRICH VON GENTZ (1829-1831) / ed by Fournier, A & Winkler A – Zuerich, Leipzig, Wien, 1920 – 5mf – 9 – ne IDC [943]

TAGES ANZEIGER – (Also available on CD-ROM) – Switzerland. 1988-1995 – 12r per y – 5,6 – Sfr1,176.00 (diazo) – sz Infoprint [949]

TAGESBOTE – Brno, Czechoslovakia. Jul 1938-Feb 1939 – 2r – 1 – us L of C Photodup [072]

TAGES-CHRONIK – (Cont by: Bremer Tages-Chronik, jan 2 1851) – Bremen, jul 2 1849-may 20 1851 – 2r – 1 – Inquire at Mikrofilmarchiv for details – gw Misc Inst [943]

TAGES-CHRONIK – (Title change: Bremer Tages-Chronik, 2 Jan 1851) – Bremen, Germany. 2 Jul 1849-20 May 1851 – 2r – 1 – gw Mikrofilm [072]

TAGESPOST – (Cont by: Bruenner Tagespost, 1929) – Bruenn, 1923-sep 1933 – 12r – 1 – Inquire at Mikrofilmarchiv for details – gw Misc Inst [943]

TAGESPOST – (Title change: Bruenner Tagespost, Jan 1929) – Bruenn (Brno), Czechoslovakia. Jan 1923-Sept 1933 – 12r – 1 – gw Mikrofilm [072]

TAGESPOST *see* SPEYERER TAGESPOST

DER TAGESSPIEGEL – Berlin, sep 27 1945- – 1 – Inquire at Mikrofilmarchiv for details – gw Misc Inst [072]

DER TAGESSPIEGEL – Berlin. sep 27, 1945-68 – 76r – 1 – gw Mikrofilm [072]

DER TAGESSPIEGEL – Berlin: Tagesspiegel GmbH, sep 27 1945-1981 – us Res Libr [072]

DIE TAGESZEITUNG *see* DIE ABENDZEITUNG

DIE TAGESZEITUNG (TAZ) – (Also available: Ausgabe Berlin-Ost/DDR/Berliner Ausgabe, feb 26 1990-dec 23 1991) – Berlin, Frankfurt/Main. Sep 22 1978- – 1 – Inquire at Mikrofilmarchiv for details – gw Misc Inst [072]

DIE TAGESZEITUNG (TAZ) : AUSGABE BREMEN – Bremen, oct 1 1990- – 1 – Inquire at Mikrofilmarchiv for details – gw Misc Inst [072]

DIE TAGESZEITUNG (TAZ) – Frankfurt/Main-Berlin, Germany. 2 Sep 1978-1993 – ca 3r per yr – 1 – gw Mikrofilm [072]

Taggard, Genevieve *see*
- THE COMPLETE WORKS OF GENEVIEVE TAGGARD
- COMPLETE WORKS OF GENEVIEVE TAGGARD

TAGHUT – (Continued by (and boxed with): Asghar Aga. Sal-i 1: shumarah-'i 1-22 (5 Murdad 1358-8 Day 1358[27 Jul 1979-29 Dec 1979])) – London, 1979- – 1 reel – 1 – $105.00 – us MEDOC [950]
Tagirdzhanov, A T *see*
- RUKOPISNYI FOND VOSTOCHNOGO FAKUL'TETA LGU I EGO IZUCHENIE
- SPISOK TADZHIKSKIKH, PERSIDSKIKH I TIURSKIKH RUKOPISEI VOSTOCHNOGO OTDELA BIBLIOTEKI LGU
- TADZHIKSKO-PERSIDSKIE I TIURKSKIE RUKOPISI VOSTOCHNOGO FAKUL'TETA LGU

TAGLICHE RUNDSCHAU – Berlin, Germany. Sept 1881-Jun 1928; Jun 1945-1948; Jul-Dec 1950 – 135r – 1 – us L of C Photodup [072]
TAGLICHER CLEVELAND ANZEIGER : DAILY GERMAN LANGUAGE NEWSPAPER – Cleveland, OH. 5 Aug 1872-30 Sept 1876 – 6r – 1 – us Western Res [071]
Taglioretti, Graciela *see* WOMEN AND WORK IN URUGUAY
Tagore, Saumyendranath *see* REVOLUTION AND QUIT INDIA
TAGSBLATT DER STADT BAMBERG *see* BAMBERGER TAGBLATT
TAGUMPAY NG MANGGAGAWA / Honorio, Cirilo S – Maynila: J. Martinez, 1925. 79p – 1 – us U.W. Library [360]
Tahir, Bursali Mehmed *see*
- MESAYIHI OSMANIYEDEN SEKIZ ZATIN TERCEME-I AHVALT
- OSMANLI MUEELLIFLERI

Tahir, Mehmed *see* KATIP CELEBI
TAHITI / Adams, Henry – 1901 – 9 – 15.00 – us Scholars' Facs [980]
TAHKEMONI – Ed. by B. M. Lewin. v. 1-2. Berlin. 1910-11. BJ-100-188 1 – 9 – ne IDC [956]
TAHOE DAILY TRIBUNE – South Lake Tahoe, CA. Jun 1961- – 223+ r – 1 – $11,150.00 ($450.00y) – N03003 – us Library Micro [071]
TAHOE TATTLER – Tahoe City, CA. 1935-36; 1937-41 – 2r – 1 – $100.00 – C03033 – us Library Micro [071]
TAHOE WORLD – Tahoe City, CA, NV. 1969 – 35+ r – 1 – $1,750.00 ($240.00y) – N03034 – us Library Micro [071]
TAHRIR USUL LI UQLIDAS = EUCLID'S ELEMENTS OF GEOMETRY / Euclid – Rome, 1594 – 8mf – 9 – H-8436/1 – ne IDC [510]
TAHSILAT-I 'UMUMIYEYI NATIK IHSAIYAT-I MALIYE MECMUASI / Maliye, Nezareti – (Published monthly in French and Ottoman; Temmuz 1327-Subat 1327[Jul 1911-Feb. 1912], 1. sene, no.5-12.-19mf. $90.00; Mart 1328-Subat 1328[Mar 1912-Feb 1913], 2. sene, no 1-12.-28mf. $105.00; Mart 1329-Subat 1329[Mar 1913-Feb 1914], 3. sene, no. 1-12.-28mf. $105.00; Eyluel 1330-Subat 1330[Sep 1914-Feb 1915], 4. sene, no. 7-12.-19mf. $90.00) – us MEDOC [350]
Tahsin-Al-Din *see* QISSEH I KAMRUP VA KALA (ADVENTURES OF KAMRUP)
Tahu, Hector *see* AN INVESTIGATION INTO PAIN THRESHOLD, PAIN TOLERANCE AND AUGMENTATION REDUCTION LEVELS AMONG RUGBY PLAYERS
TAHUN KEMENANGAN; A YEAR OF TRIUMPH / Sukarno, Pres. Indonesia – SE 3591 1. Address on 17 Augustus 1962 – 9 – ne IDC [324]
TAHUN KEMENANGAN; PIDATO PJM. PRESIDEN/PANGLIMA TERTINGGI/PEMIMPIN BESAR REVOLUSI INDONESIA PADA HARI ULANG TAHUN KEMERDEKAAN REPUBLIK INDONESIA PADA TANGGAL 17 AUGUSTUS 1962 / Sukarno, Pres. Indonesia – SE 4066 1 – 9 – ne IDC [324]
TAHUN TANTANGAN. A YEAR OF CHALLENGE / Sukarno, Pres. Indonesia – SE 1223 1. 1958 – 9 – ne IDC [025]
TAHUN "VIVERE PERICOLOSO." / Sukarno, Pres. Indonesia – Speech on 17 Aug. 1964. SE 10,422 1. 1964 – 9 – ne IDC [324]
TAHUN "VIVERE PERICOLOSO," TAVIP = A YEAR OF LIVING DANGEROUSLY / Sukarno, Pres. Indonesia – SE 5276 1. Speech on 17 August 1964 – 9 – ne IDC [324]
TAI, CHIH-LI. SSU-CH'UAN PAO-LU YUN-TUNG SHIH-LIAO – Documents on Protests to Ssuchuan Railroad Building. 1959. BCH-955 2 – 8 – ne IDC [950]
TAIBAI = THE SATIRIST – Sept 1934-Sept 1935. 1 reel. M-C49 – 1 – $45.00 – cc Microforms [073]
TAICOLE O EL SACRIFICIO GLADIATORIO / Mendoza y Gonzalez, Luis de – 1834 – 9 – 1.50f – sp Bibl Santa Ana [830]
Taieb, M *see* L'INDUSTRIE DE LA CHAUSSURE AU MAROC
TAIFA EMPYA – Kampala, Uganda. -d. June 1964-Dec 1969. 13 reels – 1 – uk British Libr Newspaper [072]
TAIKA KEIZAI SHIRYO – Tokyo, Nov. 1937. v.1-5. Economic materials on China. In Japanese. 1 reel – 1 – 18.70 – us Chinese Res [330]
TAILLE ET CULTURE DU ROSIER: SUIVIES DE LA TAILLE DES ARBUTES D'AGREMENT / Forney, Eugene – Paris: A. Goin, 1882. 216p. 3 fiches. (Miscellaneous Selections) – 9 – 8.00 – fr Bibl Nationale [631]
THE TAILLESS BATRACHIANS OF EUROPE / Boulenger, G A – 1897-98 – 1 reel 12mf – 1,7 – uk Microform Academic [590]
TAILOR – London, UK. 6 Oct 1866-1867. -w. 1 reel – 1 – uk British Libr Newspaper [072]
TAILOR'S SYSTEM FOR CUTTING SHAKER GARMENTS / Eads, Harvey L – 1849-50 – 1r – 1 – us Ohio Hist [740]
TAIN AND SURROUNDS 1851 CENSUS INDEX : ARGYLL AND WESDT SCOTLAND CENSUS INDEX, PART 11 / Macinnes, John & Gibson, Peter – 1996 – 2mf – 9 – A$19.95 – 0-9586638-2-3 – at Seanachas [920]
TAINA TREKH / Merezhkovskii, Dimitrii – Egipet i Vavilon. Prague. 1925. BR-792 2 – 8 – ne IDC [460]
TAINA ZAPADA / Merezhkovskii, Dimitrii – Atlantida-Evropa. 2 v. Beograd. 1930. BR-793 2 – 8 – ne IDC [460]
Taine, Hippolyte *see* NOTES ON ENGLAND...
TAINOPIS' V IUGOSLAVIANSKIKH I RUSSKIKH PAMIATNIKAKH PIS'MA / Speranskii, N M – Entsiklopediia Slavianskoi Filologii. Leningrad, 1929. v4(3). BR-10,378/1 – 9 – ne IDC [460]
TAIPENG WEEKLY RECORD – Malaysia. -w. 4 Mar-20 Dec 1935. (55 ft) – 1 – uk British Libr Newspaper [072]
TAIPING TIANGUO GEMING SHIQI GUANGXI NONGMIN QIYI ZILIAO, 1-2 – Materials on peasant uprisings in Guangxi province during the Taiping Rebellion, v1-2. 1 reel. M-H98 – 5 – $40.00 – cc Microforms [950]
TAIPING TIANGUO SHILIAO – Historical materials on the Taiping Rebellion. Comp. by Jin Yufo, Tian Yuqing. 6 fiches. F-H90 – 9 – $27.00 – cc Microforms [950]
TAIPING TIANGUO SHILIAO CONGBIAN JIANJI, 1-6 – Abridged serials of historical materials on the Taiping Rebellion, v1-6. Comp. by the Museum of the Taiping Rebellion. 1 reel. M-H91 – 5 – 30.00 – cc Microforms [950]
TAIPING TIANGUO SHILIAO ZHUANJI – Special collection of historical materials on the Taiping Rebellion. Comp. by the Suzhou Museum. 7 fiches.F-H95 – 9 – $31.50 – cc Microforms [950]
TAIPING TIANGUO WENSHU HUIBIAN – Documents and dispatches of the Taiping Rebellion. Comp. by the Museum of the Taiping Rebellion. 7 fiches. F-H93 – 9 – $49.00 – cc Microforms [950]
TAIPING TIANGUO YINSHU – Documents under the seal of the Taiping Rebellion. Comp. by the Museum of the Taiping Rebellion. 1 reel. M-H94 – 5 – 30.00 – cc Microforms [950]
TAIPING TIANGUO ZILIAO HUIBIAN – Collection of materials on the Taiping Rebellion, 1-6. Comp. by the Museum of the Taiping Rebellion. 1 reel. M/H92 – 5 – $40.00 – cc Microforms [950]
T'AI-P'ING-YANG – "The Pacific Ocean". 4 v. Shanghai. 1917-25. Lacking: v. 2 (2, 4, 11-12) 1920-21; v. 3 (4-6) 1921-22. BCH-346 1 – 9 – ne IDC [910]
Taira, Ellen Dunleavey *see* PHYSICAL AND OCCUPATIONAL THERAPY IN GERIATRICS
TAIRIKU NENKAU / China – Shanghai. 1940-45. Continental yearbook in Japanese. 3 reels – 1 – 56.10 – us Chinese Res [950]
TAIRIKU NIPPO = THE CONTINENTAL DAILY NEWS – Vancouver, BC. 1908-1941 – 68r – 1 – Can$65.00r – cn U.B.C. Preserve [072]
TAISHO SHINSHU DAIZO-KYO – v. 1-84, V. 1-12. Tokio. 1924-34. BCH-1001 1 – 9 – ne IDC [073]
TAISHO SHOWA KYOIKU TOKEI SHIRYO = EDUCATIONAL STATISTICS OF THE RESPECTIVE PREFECTURES OF JAPAN IN THE TAISHO AND SHOWA ERAS / Japan. Prefectures – 1913-45 – 120r – 1 – Y792,000.00 – ja Yushodo [370]
TAISHO SHOWA NENKAN FUKEN TOKEISHO SHUSEI = COMPLETE COLLECTION OF THE STATISTICAL ANNUALS OF THE RESPECTIVE PREFECTURES OF JAPAN IN THE TAISHO AND SHOWA ERAS, 1913-1945 – All of the annual statistical report of the 47 pref., totaling 4,480cps. 1,100,000p – 636r – 1 – Y4,140,000.00 – ja Yushodo [950]
TAISHO SHOWA-KI KEIZAI TOKEI SHIRYO = SOURCE MATERIALS OF THE ECONOMIC STATISTICS OF JAPAN IN THE TAISHO AND SHOWA ERAS / Japan – (Economic Statistics of Japan. 1918-40; 41. Monetary Statistics 1926; 35-1928; 39. (Hypothec Bank of Japan). Annual Reports of Prices 1900; 25-1939. (Ministry of Commerce and Industry). Annual Reports of Wages 1900; 29-1939. (Ministry of Commerce and Industry). Annual Abstracts of Labor Statistics 1926-39. (Statistical Bureau of the Cabinet). Survey of Principal Industries 1921-22. (Dept. of Agric. and Comm.). Annual Reports of Companies. 1920-45. (Ministry of Comm. and Ind.). Annual Survey of Exchanges 1913-41. (Ministry of Comm. and Ind.). Lacks a few years. Annual Survey of Shipping 1918-34. (Ministry of Communications). Annual Reports of Iron Industry. 1917-43; 48. (Ministry of Commerce and Industry). Annual Reports of Mining Industry. 1906-41; 45. (Ministry of Commerce and Industry). Annual Reports of Rices 1926-38. (Ministry of Agric. and Forestry). Annual Survey of Fertilizers 1920-40. (Ministry of Agric. and Forestry). Annual Reports of Silk Cocoons 1911-38. (Ministry of Agric. and Forestry). Annual Reports of Raw Silk and Floss Silk 1911-37. (Ministry of Agric. and Forestry). Lacks 2 yrs. Annual Survey of Forests 1927-35 (Ministry of Agric. and Forestry). Annual Reports of Aquatic Products 1898; 1908-25. (Dept. of Agric. and Commerce). Lacks 1 vol. Annual Survey of Industrial Guild. 1903-40 (Ministry of Agric. and Forestry). Annual Reports of Colonial Affairs 1928-39 (Dept. of Overseas Affairs)) – 65r – 1 – Y594,000.00 – ja Yushodo [310]
Tait, Arthur James *see* LECTURE OUTLINES ON THE THIRTY-NINE ARTICLES
Tait, James *see* MIND IN MATTER
TAIWAN DOCUMENTS SERIES / Bank of Taiwan. Economic Research Bureau – Taipei, 1951-72. 596v. Approx. 90,000p. 40 reels – 5 – 1450.00 – ch Transmission [950]
TAIWAN SHIN SHENG DAILY NEWS – Taipei, Taiwan. 1962-83. 88 reels – 1 – 4400.00 – ch Transmission [072]
TAIWAN SOTOKUFU TOKEISHO / China. Republic of China – (Taiwan Statistical Abstract). 1898-1942 – 1 – 605.00 – us L of C Photodup [950]
TAIWAN STATISTICAL ABSTRACTS, 1897-1942 – (In Japanese) – 15r – 1 – $525.00 set in US $40.00r outside – L9400099 – Dist. us Scholarly Res – us L of C Photodup [304]
TAIWAN'S OPPOSITION MAGAZINES 1975-1986 – 847mf – 9 – ne IDC [320]
TAIYANGNENG XUEBAO – Acta Energiae Solaris Sinica. In Chinese but English abstracts to the main articles. F p137 – 9 – $4.50f – cc Microforms [073]
TAIYUAN GONGXUEYUAN XUEBAO – Journal of Taiyuan Institute of Technology. In Chinese but English abstracts to the main articles. F p193 – 9 – $4.50f – cc Microforms [073]
TAIYUAN RIBAO = TAIYUAN DAILY – China. 1983-. M-D43 – 1 reel/y – 1 – $55.00r – cc Microforms [072]
TAIYUAN RIBAO – (Taiyuan Daily). China. Feb 1935-Aug 1937. M B12 – 8r – 1 – $360.00 – cc Microforms [072]
TAK – v1-2. 1937-1938 – 1 – us I.U. Libraries [073]
TAK BYLO : PUT MOEI ZHIZNI / Dmitrieva, Valentina Iovovna – Moskva: Molodai a gvardii a, 1930 – 1 – CSUX88-B560 – us Hoover Inst Photo [920]
Takahashi, K *see* SOEARA ZAMAN; SJA'IR DAN PANTOEN PADA MASA PERANG INI
Takao, SH *see* RELIABILITY OF PEAK TORQUE VALUES FOR SHOULDER INTERNAL AND EXTERNAL ROTATION DURING ECCENTRIC AND CONCENTRIC LOADING USING THE KIN-COM 125E ISOKINETIC DYNAMOMETER
Takato, A *see* DARI SEKOLAH KEMEDAN PERANG
Takekoshi, Yosaburo *see*
- THE ECONOMIC ASPECTS OF THE HISTORY OF THE CIVILIZATION OF JAPAN
- JAPANESE RULE IN FORMOSA

TAKEN AT THE FLOOD / Braddon, Mary Elizabeth – British Fiction Archive: Unit 5 – 9 – uk Bell [830]
Taki, Mir *see* CONSEILS AUX MAUVAIS POETES
TAKING AGRICULTURAL CENSUS : GUIDELINES SUPPLEMENTING THE PROGRAMME FOR THE 1980 WORLD CENSUS OF AGRICULTURE – 1978 – 135p – it F.A.O. [630]
TAKING DRUDGERY OUT OF SCHOOL-TOWARDS AN UNINHIBITED FUTURE / Cohen, David – 2p, 1971 – 9 – 1.00f – at Libertarian Micro [370]
THE TAKING OF LOUISBURG, 1745 / Drake, Samuel Adams – Boston: Lee and Shepard, 1891. 02758. (Pre-1900 Canadiana) – 9 – cn C.I.H.M. [971]
TAKKANOT HA-IZVONOT BI-YERUSHALAYIM / Rivlin, E – v. 5. Azkarah. 1937. BJ-27-56 1 – 9 – ne IDC [270]
TAKKANOT YESHIVAT "HAVERIM MAKSHIVIM" BI-YERUSHALAYIM / Schischa, A – v. 3. Yerushalayim. 1950. BJ-27-73 1 – 9 – ne IDC [270]
TAKKANOT ZIBBUR VE-SIDREI MISHPAT / Rivlin, E – v. 2. Ha-Mishpat ha-Ivri. 1927. BJ-27-64 1 – 9 – ne IDC [270]
TAKVIM-I VEKA'YI – Istanbul, Nos. 1-400 (25 Cumada evvel, 1247-13 Rebiuelevvel, 1265 [1 Nov 1831-6 Feb 1849]); nos. 201-427 (15 Rebiuelahir-30 Zilhicce, 1327 [22 Nisan-30 Kanun-i evvel, 1325 M (7 May 1909-12 Jan 1910)]) – 3r – 1 – $750.00 – us MEDOC [949]
TAL OROT / Luzzatto, S D – 81 poems. Przemysl. 1881. BJ-421-35 1 – 9 – ne IDC [810]
Tal, T *see* ORANJEBLOESEMS
DAS TAL VON LAUSA UND DURON / Tumler, Franz – Muenchen: A Langen, G Mueller, 1935 – 1r – 1 – us U.W. Library [830]
Taladoire, E *see* LES TERRAINS DE JEU DE BALLE DE L'AIRE MAYA
TALANTA – (Back issues of journal available from UMI) – 12 issues/y. v40. 1993 – 9 – £530.00y – uk Elsevier Sci [540]
TALANTA – v1- 1954- – 5,6,9 – us UMI [500]
Talavan. Ayuntamiento *see* FIESTAS PATRONALES 1971
Talavera, Fr. Gabriel *see* HISTORIA...GUADALUPE
TALAVERA LA VIEJA. LAPIDA / Fita, Fidel – Madrid: Fortanet, 1912. B.R.A.H. 61. p. 460 – 1 – sp Bibl Santa Ana [946]
Talavera y Garces, Mariano *see* APUNTES DE HISTORIA ECLESIASTICA DE VENEZUELA. CARACAS, 1929
THE TALBA / Bray, Anna Eliza – British Fiction Archive: Unit 2 – 9 – uk Bell [830]
Talba, Aly *see* UNE CONTRIBUTION A L'ETUDE DES PARTIS POLITIQUES NIGERIENS: LE TEMOIGNAGE DE ADAMOU MAYAKI
Talbot, Bernadette *see* BIBLIOGRAPHIE ANALYTIQUE DE RENEE DES ORMES
TALBOT BOROUGH RATES – 1877-1915 – 1r – 1 – at Corangamite [910]
Talbot, George *see* TALBOT PAPERS: CORRESPONDENCE AND PAPERS OF GEORGE, SIXTH EARL OF SHREWSBURY (1528-1590)
Talbot, James F *see* POPE LEO 13
Talbot, P A *see* IN THE SHADOW OF THE BUSH
TALBOT PAPERS: CORRESPONDENCE AND PAPERS OF GEORGE, SIXTH EARL OF SHREWSBURY (1528-1590) / Talbot, George – From the Archives of the Marquess of Bath, Longleat. 1574-1608 – 2r – 1 – uk Microform Academic [920]
Talbot, Reginald Thomas *see* OUR BIBLE
TALBOT SHIRE RATES – 1868-1919 – 2r – 1 – at Corangamite [910]
Talbot, Theodore *see* LETTERS
Talbot, W A *see* SYSTEMATIC LIST OF THE TREES, SHRUBS AND WOODY CLIMBERS OF THE BOMBAY PRESIDENCY

Talbot, William Henry Fox *see* CONTRIBUTIONS TOWARDS A GLOSSARY OF THE ASSYRIAN LANGUAGE

A TALE OF THE HOUSE OF THE WOLFINGS : AND ALL THE KINDREDS OF THE MARK, WRITTEN IN PROSE AND IN VERSE / Morris, William – London: Reeves & Turner, 1889 – 1 roll – 1 – 1-55879-400-X – uk Libr Preservation [830]

TALE OF THREE CENTURIES – Sussex County. Waverly, Sussex County School Board, 1942. Virginia Reel 5. (The Cox Library Collection) – 5 – us Americana [978]

TALEBE DEFTERI – (Mueessis ve Muedueruе: Muallim Ahmed Halid. Nos. 27, 37-38, 40-54 (22 Mayis 1330[1914]-30 Mayis 1918)) – Istanbul: Necm-i Istikbal Matbaasi, 1913-1919 – 5mf – 9 – $85.00 – us MEDOC [949]

TALENT NEWS – Talent, OR. -w. 14 Jan 1892-15 Jul 1894. 1 roll – 1 – us U.O. Library [071]

TALES / Zschokke, Heinrich – New York: G P Putnam's Sons [1890?] – 1r – 1 – us U.W. Library [830]

TALES AND NOVELS / Edgeworth, Maria – London: Printed for Baldwin and Cradock; Liverpool: G. and J. Robinson, 1832-33 – 9 rolls – 1 – 1-55879-063-2 – uk Libr Preservation [830]

TALES AND SKETCHES. BY THE ETTRICK SHEPHERD. INCLUDING THE BROWNIE OF BODSBECK, WINTER EVENING TALES, SHEPHERD'S CALENDAR... / Hogg, James – Glasgow: Blackie & Son, 1837 – 3 rolls – 1 – 1-55879-018-7 – uk Libr Preservation [830]

TALES AND TRADITIONS OF THE ESKIMOES / Rink, H J; ed by Brown, Robert – BH 176 2. 1875 – 8 – ne IDC [306]

TALES BY LEIGH HUNT : NOW FIRST COLLECTED WITH A PREFATORY MEMOIR BY WILLIAM KNIGHT / Hunt, Leigh – London: William Paterson & Co., 1891 – 1 roll – 1 – 1-55879-720-3 – uk Libr Preservation [830]

TALES FOR CHILDREN, BK 1 (CCC326) / ed by Woman's Messenger Staff – (In Chinese) – Hong Kong: Bible Book and Tract Depot for Council on Christian Literature for Overseas Chinese, 1953 – 1r – 1 – 1984-6665 – us A.T.L.A. [390]

TALES FOR CHRISTMAS EVE / Broughton, Rhoda – British Fiction Archive: Unit 4 – 9 – uk Bell [830]

TALES FOR FIFTEEN / Cooper, James Fenimore – 1823 – 9 – $15.00 – us Scholars' Facs [830]

TALES FROM KODIAK ISLAND / Golder, F A – BN 226 2. 1903 – 8 – ne IDC [390]

TALES FROM MUSAEUS, TIECK, RICHTER / Carlyle, Thomas – Trans. from the German by Thomas Carlyle. People's ed. London: Chapman and Hall, 1874. 2v – 1 – us U.W. Library [450]

TALES FROM THE GERMAN OF HEINRICH ZSCHOKKE / Zschokke, Heinrich; ed by Godwin, Parke – New York: Wiley and Putnam, 1845 – 1r – 1 – us U.W. Library [830]

TALES FROM THE TALMUD / Montague, E R – Edinburgh: William Blackwood, 1906. 1 fiche – 9 – us A.T.L.A. [270]

TALES FROM THE TELLING HOUSE (SLAIN BY THE DOONES) / Blackmore, Richard Doddridge – British Fiction Archive: Unit 3 – 9 – uk Bell [830]

TALES OF A GRANDFATHER : BEING STORIES TAKEN FROM SCOTTISH HISTORY / Scott, Walter – Edinburgh: Printed for Cadell and Co.; London: Simpkin and Marshall; Dublin: John Cumming, 1828 – 1 roll – 1 – 1-55879-271-6 – uk Libr Preservation [830]

TALES OF A GRANDFATHER / Scott, Walter – Edinburgh: Cadell; London: Simpkin and Marshall; Dublin: John Cumming, 2nd ser 1829 – 2 rolls – 1 – 1-55879-247-3 – uk Libr Preservation [830]

TALES OF OLD TRAVEL RE-NARRATED / Kingsley, Henry – British Fiction Archive: Unit 2 – 9 – uk Bell [830]

TALES OF SPACE AND TIME / Wells, H G – New York: Doubleday & McClure, 1899 – 1 roll – 1 – 1-55879-927-3 – uk Libr Preservation [830]

TALES OF THE EAST – 1812 – 1 – us I.U. Libraries [390]

THE TALES OF THE GENII, OR, THE DELIGHTFUL LESSONS OF HORAM THE SON OF ASMAR / Morell, Charles, Sir – 1882 – 1 – us I.U. Libraries [390]

TALES OF THE KLONDYKE / Ellis, T Mullett – Toronto: Copp Clark, 1898. 02909. (Pre-1900 Canadiana) – 9 – cn C.I.H.M. [830]

TALES OF THE ST LAWRENCE / Chapin, Gardner B – (Montreal: J. Lovell, 1873). 00562. (Pre-1900 Canadiana) – 9 – cn C.I.H.M. [971]

TALES OF UNREST / Conrad, Joseph – London: T. Fisher Unwin, 1898 – 1 roll – 1 – 1-55879-681-9 – uk Libr Preservation [830]

TALES OF UNREST / Conrad, Joseph – London: T. Fisher Unwin, 1898. 297p – 1 – us U.W. Library [830]

TALESTRI, REGINA DELLE AMAZZONI / Maria Antonia Walpurgis – 1765. Dramma per Musica – 9 – us Sibley [780]

Talfourd, Thomas Noon *see* TRAGEDIES

Taliaferro, Lawrence *see* PAPERS

TALIB : EIN KREIS MORGENLAENDISCHER GESCHICHTEN / Arnold, Paul Johannes – Tuebingen: Alexander Fischer, 1925 – 1r – 1 – us U.W. Library [830]

EL TALISMAN / Mendoza, Luis de – 1857 – 9 – 1.50f – sp Bibl Santa Ana [830]

THE TALISMAN, A GRAND OPERA IN THREE ACTS...LIB A. MATTHISON / Balfe, MW – London: Duff & Stewart, 1874? – 1 – us Sibley [780]

THE TALISMAN OF UNITY : A SERMON IN BEHALF OF CHURCH CONSOLIDATION / Huntington, William Reed – New York: T. Whittaker, 1899 – 1mf – us A.T.L.A. [240]

A TALK ABOUT WINE: WHAT IT IS, ITS USE AND ITS ABUSE / Crawford, G – s.l.: s.n., 1878 (London, Ont.: Free Press). 00757. (Pre-1900 Canadiana) – 9 – cn C.I.H.M. [640]

THE TALKING DEAF MAN / Amman, J – 1694. 137p. (English Linguistics Series 1500-1800) – 9 – us UMI [400]

TALKING MACHINE NEWS – London, England. -w. May 1903-Nov 1908. 5 reels – 1 – uk British Libr Newspaper [072]

TALKING MACHINE NEWS, 1903-1935 – 196mf – 9 – Dfl3,300.00 – M394 – ne MMF Publ [780]

TALKING MACHINE NEWS & SLIDE LINES – London, England. Talking Machine & Wireless News. -w. Dec 1908-Dec 1928. 12 1 2 reels – 1 – uk British Libr Newspaper [380]

TALKING MACHINE WORLD – New York. v. 1-26. 1905-1930 – 1 – us NY Public [600]

TALKS ON CHRISTIAN FAITH (CCC339) / Wu, Yao-tsung – (In Chinese) – Shanghai: Association Press of China, 1950 – 1r – 1 – 1984-6678 – us A.T.L.A. [240]

TALKS ON LIVING SUBJECTS: THE CREATION, THE BIBLE...EVILS AND...CURE OF INTEMPERANCE / Sutherland, James – Chicago: Fleming H. Revell, 1886. 1 fiche – 9 – us A.T.L.A. [240]

TALKS TO YOUNG CHRISTIANS (CCC315) = HSIEH KEI TS'ING NIEN TI CHI TU T'U / Wang, Ming-tao – (In Chinese) – Peiping: Spiritual Food Quarterly, 1948 – 1r – 1 – 1984-6654 – us A.T.L.A. [240]

TALKS WITH SOCRATES ABOUT LIFE : TRANSLATIONS FROM THE GORGIAS AND THE REPUBLIC OF PLATO / Plato – New York: Scribner, 1886. Ellen F. Mason, trans – xvii/176p – 1 – us U.W. Library [450]

TALLAHATCHIAN – Charleston. Miss. 1904-1905 – 1 – us UMI [071]

TALLAHATCHIE HERALD – Charleston. Miss. 1905-1910 – 1 – us UMI [071]

TALLASSEE FIRST BAPTIST CHURCH. TALLASSEE, ALABAMA = TALLASSEE, ALABAMA. FIRST BAPTIST CHURCH : CHURCH RECORDS – 1825-1989. History by David Bentley, 83p – 1 – $5.00 – us Baptist [240]

Tallemant, P *see* REMARQUES ET DECISIONS DE L'ACADEMIE FRANCOISE

TALLER ESCUELA-SINDICAL "VIRGEN DEL PUERTO" / Obra Sindical de Formacion Profesional. Organizacion Sindicazl – Plasencia: Imprenta y Libraria Montero, 1962 – 1 – sp Bibl Santa Ana [780]

TALLERES PUBLICOS IN COSTA RICA : OEFFENTLICHE WERKSTAETTEN FUER AUSBILDUNG UND PRODUKTION ZUR BERUFLICHEN BILDUNG IM INFORMELLEN SEKTOR. EXKURSIONSBERICHT / Weitzenegger, Karsten – 1992 – 1mf – 9 – DM38.00 – 3-89349-520-7 – gw Hänsel [370]

Talleyrand, Henri de *see* DOCUMENTS LE CONCERNANT CONSERVES A LA BIBLIOTHEQUE MUNICIPALE DE NANTES

Talleyrand-Perigord, Charles Maurice de *see*
- MEMOIRS OF THE PRINCE DE TALLEYRAND
- RAPPORT SUR L'INSTRUCTION PUBLIQUE, FAIT AU NOM DU COMITE DE CONSTITUTION, LES 10, 11 ET 19 SEPTEMBRE 1791

TALLEYRAND'S BRIEFWECHSEL MIT KOENIG LUDWIG 18. WAEHREND DES WIENER CONGRESSES / ed by Pallain, G – (Index) – Leipzig, Paris, 1881 – 5mf – 9 – ne IDC [943]

Tallgren, A M *see* ZUR OST-EUROPAEISCHEN ARCHAEOLOGIE

Tallqvist, K *see*
- AKKADISCHE GOETTEREPITHETA
- DER ASSYRISCHE GOTT

Tallmadge, Nathaniel P *see* PAPERS OF NATHANIEL P. TALLMADGE

Tallon, Eugene *see* LEGISLATION SUR LE TRAVAIL DES ENFANTS DANS LES MANUFACTURES. RECUEIL DES DOCUMENTS PARLEMENTAIRES, LEGISLATIFS ET STATISTIQUES

Tally, Elizabeth *see* THE EFFECTS OF REWARDS ON INTRINSIC MOTIVATIONS OF EXERCISERS AND NONEXERCISERS

Talmage, James Edward *see*
- THE GREAT APOSTASY
- THE HOUSE OF THE LORD

TALMAGE TOPICS – Talmage, NE. -w. Jun 1967-Aug 1973 – 1 – us NE Hist [071]

TALMAGE TRIBUNE – Talmage, NE. -w. Sept 1886; Dec 1895; Feb 1899-Oct 1902, scattered issues missing; Jan 1904-Apr 1905; Jan 1907-Oct 1942; May 1946-Mar 1960 – 1 – us NE Hist [071]

Tal'man, E M *see* ISTORIIA ARKHEOGRAFII V DOREVOLIUTSIONNOI ROSSII

DER TALMUD : SEIN WESEN, SEINE BEDEUTUNG UND SEINE GESCHICHTE / Bernfeld, Simon – Berlin:S. Calvary, 1900 – 1mf – 9 – 0-8370-2295-9 – 1985-0295 – us A.T.L.A. [270]

LE TALMUD : EXPOSE SYNTHETIQUE DU TALMUD ET DE L'ENSEIGNEMENT DES RABBINS SUR L'ETHIQUE, LA RELIGION, LES COUTUMES ET LA JURISPRUDENCE / Cohen, A – Paris, 1933 – 8mf – 8 – ne Slangenburg [270]

THE TALMUD / Darmesteter, Arsene – Philadelphia: Jewish Publ. Soc., 191-.1 fiche – 9 – us A.T.L.A. [270]

THE TALMUD / Pick, Bernhard – 1876. 1 fiche – 9 – us A.T.L.A. [270]

TALMUD. BAVA BATRA – Collection of hidushim, etc. to Bava batra – 1 – us U.W. Library [270]

TALMUD BAVLI AL PI KITVEI YAD U-DEFUSIM RISHONIM / ed by Pereferkovich, N – Massekhet Berakhot. St. Petersburg. 1909. BJ-32-15 1 – 9 – ne IDC [270]

THE TALMUD EDITIONS OF DANIEL BOMBERG : A COMPREHENSIVE COLLECTION OF ALL TRACTATES OF THE FOUR EDITIONS BY BOMBERG, VENICE 1520-1549 / ed by Rosenthal, A – (Complete coll will consist of 3pts) – 175mf – 9 – ne IDC [270]

DER TALMUD: EIN VORTRAG / Cohn, Tobias – Wien: Herzfeld & Bauer, 1866. 1 fiche – 9 – us A.T.L.A. [270]

THE TALMUD: WHAT IT IS AND WHAT IT KNOWS ABOUT JESUS AND HIS FOLLOWERS / Pick, Bernhard – New York: John B. Alden, 1887. 1 fiche – 9 – us A.T.L.A. [270]

TALMUDAH SHEL KEISARIN: YERUSHALMI, MASSEKHET NEZIKIN / Lieberman, S – (Supplement to vTarbiz, year 2, issue 4). Jerusalem. 1931. BJ-32-18 1 – 9 – ne IDC [270]

TALMUDISCHE CHRESTOMATHIE: MIT ANMERKUNGEN, SCHOLIEN UND GLOSSAR – Leipzig: J.A. Barth, 1884 – 1mf – 9 – us A.T.L.A. [270]

TALOUSPOLITIIKAN PERUSOHJELMA / Finland. Talouspoliitiinen Suunnitteluneuvosto – (Basic program for the economic policy). Helsinki. 1954 – 9 – ne IDC [330]

TALPIYOTH – Berdichef. v1. 1895 – 1r – 1 – us Ross [073]

TALPIYOTH – Berdychev. v. 1. 1895. Includes Lewik, J. B. Shebet m'jehuda – 1 – us NY Public [073]

LE TAM TU KINH. LE LIVRE DES PHRASES DE TROIS CARACTERES – Texte chinois et traduction A. Des Michels. 1882 – 9 – fr Orientalistes [480]

Tamamuro, Fumio *see* SHAJI TORISHIRABE RUISAN

TAMAN PENGADJAR : SOERAT BOELANAN AKAN GOENA... – Semarang, 1899-1912.-v1-13 – 60mf – 9 – SE-20,006/1 – ne IDC [950]

TAMAN-INDRYA, KINDERGARTEN / Dewantara, Ki Hadjar – SE-4248 1. 1959 – 9 – ne IDC [950]

Tamar, D *see* SHETEI IGGAROT AL ZEFAT ME-ET RABBI TEHUDAH ARYEH MI-MODENA

TAMARACK REVIEW – (v1-84 1956-82 Can$20.00y 9) – Toronto. v1-67. 1956-75 – 5,9 – cn Micromedia [073]

Tamarati, Michel *see* L'EGLISE GEORGIENNE

Tamari, Ittai Joseph *see* HEBRAEISCHE SCHRIFTGESTALTUNG IN DEUTSCHLAND VON DER JAHRHUNDERTWENDE BIS ZUM AUSBRUCH DES ZWEITEN WELTKRIEGES UNTER BESONDERER BERUECKSICHTIGUNG DER "FRANK-RUEHL"-LETTERN

Tamarit de Plaza *see* CONTESTACION AL INFORME...JOAQUIN MUNOZ BUENO...LINEA FERREA...CACERES

Tamaulipas. Mexico *see* PERIODICO OFICIAL

Tamayo de Salazar, Juan *see*
- ANAMNESIS SIVE COMMEMORATIO
- SAN EPITACIO...TUY...MARTIR DE PLASENCIA
- TRUINFO...CATOLICAS...DIEGO DE ARCE

Tamayo Zamora, B *see* ANTOLOGIA DE AUTORES CLASICOS EXTRANJEROS

O TAMBOR : ORGAO REPUBLICANO – Diamantina, 13 Jul-7 Aug 1890 – 1,5,6 – bl Biblioteca [072]

TAMBOUR – Paris. no. 1-8. Feb 1929-June 1930 – 1 – us NY Public [999]

TAMIL AND SANSKRIT INSCRIPTIONS / Burgess, J – Nates'a S'astri (Transl.) (Archaeological Survey of Southern India, v16). Madras, 1886. BI-796 2 – 8 – ne IDC [410]

TAMIL CULTURE : A QUATERLY REVIEW DEDICATED TO THE STUDY AND DIFFUSION OF TAMILIANA. – v. 1-12. Tuticorin. 1952-66. BI-298 2 – 88mf – 8 – ne IDC [306]

TAMIL GRAMMAR : DESIGNED FOR USE IN COLLEGES AND SCHOOLS / Lazarus, John – Madras, 1878 – us Res Libr [490]

TAMIL INFORMATION CENTRE – London. 96 docs. 1983-1991 – 15mf – 9 – ne IDC [490]

TAMIL NESAN – Kuala Lumpur, Malaysia. In Tamil. -w. 10 Sept 1924-Dec 1932. 13 reels – 1 – uk British Libr Newspaper [072]

TAMMS FIRST BAPTIST CHURCH. TAMMS, ILLINOIS : CHURCH RECORDS – May 1944-Sept 1983 – 1 – 44.37 – us Baptist [240]

O TAMOIO – Rio de Janeiro, 12 Aug-11 Nov 1823 – 1,5,6 – bl Biblioteca [072]

TAMORA REGISTER – Tamora, NE. -w. Nov 1893-May 1898, scattered issues missing; Sept 1899-Jan 1901; Apr 1901-Sept 1902; Nov 1902; Jan-Dec 1903; Jan 1908-Mar 1909 – 1 – us NE Hist [071]

TAMPA TIMES – Tampa, FL. 1912- – 1 – us UMI [071]

TAMPA TRIBUNE – Tampa, FL. 1895- – 1 – us UMI [071]

TAMPON LABELING AND ITS EFFECT ON FEMALE ADOLESCENTS' KNOWLEDGE OF TAMPON ABSORBENCY, KNOWLEDGE OF TOXIC SHOCK SYNDROME AND TAMPON USAGE PATTERNS / Hanrahan, Susan N & Ruzek, Sheryl – 1992 – 4mf – 9 – $16.00 – us Microform Publ [613]

LE TAM-TAM – Magasin hebdomadaire de litterature, d'arts, de sciences et d'industrie; feuilleton d'annonces permanentes. Paris. 1840-47 – 1 – fr A.C.R.P.P. [400]

LE TAM-TAM DE L'OUTAOUAIS – Saint Andre Avellin. v1 no 1-8. 1979. SEM35P246 – 1r – 1 – Can$15.00 – cn Bibl Nat [072]

THE TAMWORTH COURT ROLLS / Borough of Tamworth, Staffs; ed by University of Keele – (Complete record of medieval manorial Court, from 1284 to 15th C.) – 1987 – 80 colour mf – 15 – $3,200.00 – 0-907716-50-4 – uk Mindata [941]

TAMWORTH MINERS' EXAMINER AND WORKING MEN'S JOURNAL – (Tamworth Examiner). England. -w. 13 Sep 1873-15 Jan 1876. (2 reels) – 1 – uk British Libr Newspaper [331]

TAN – Ankara, 1923 – 9 – $10.00 – us MEDOC [956]
Tan, An Djien *see* CRITICISMS OF THE NEUMARK TREATMENT OF THE AGRICULTURAL SECTOR IN ESTIMATING THE NATIONAL INCOME OF INDONESIA
TAN DAN BAO – Dir. politique Tran-Van-Minh. no. 2-78. Saigon. 18 nov 1924-20 fevr 1925. mq no. 39 – 1 – fr A.C.R.P.P. [950]
Tan, Eng Kie *see* POKOK DASAR CONTRACT BRIDGE. MENURUT POINT COUNT METHOD DARI CHARLES H. GOREN
Tan, Goan Tiang *see* ARTI DAN TUDJUAN DEMOGRAFI
Tan, Hian Kie *see* BATJAAN POKOK TUNTUK AKUNTANSI KETATALAKSANAAN
Tan Malaka *see*
- DARI IR. SOEKARNO SAMPAI KE PRESIDEN SOEKARNO
- GERPOLEK: GERILA POLITIK EOKONOMI
- ISLAM DALAM TINDJAUAN MA-DI-LOG. (MATERIALISME-DIALEKTIKA-LOGIKA)
- MADILOG: MATERIALISM-DISLEKTIKA-LOGIKA
- MENUDJU REPUBLIK INDONESIA (KARJA 1924)
- PARI; PARTAI REPOEBLIK INDONESIA
- POLITIK
- RENTJANA EKONOMI
- THESIS

TAN MALAKA, 1897-1949 : MADILOG: MATERIALISM-DIALEKTIKA-LOGIKA – Djakarta, Widjaya, 1951 – 5mf – 9 – SEM-14,777 – 14,781/1 – ne IDC [950]
TAN MALAKKA EN TAMIN MOETEN VRIJ – Amsterdam, 1933 – 1mf – 9 – SE-1288/1 – ne IDC [950]
Tan, Siew Eng *see* CHINESE KUNGFU STORIES IN INDONESIAN
TAN THE KY – no. 2-142. Saigon. 2 nov 1926-30 avr 1927. mq no. 4, 47 – 1 – fr A.C.R.P.P. [950]
Tana-Bogoraza, V G *see* EVREISKOE MESTECHKO V REVOLIUTSII
TANAGRA : AN IDYL OF GREECE / Kinkel, Gottfried – New York: G P Putnam's sons, 1893 – 1 – us U.W. Library [830]
TANAH AIR KITA: A PICTORIAL INTRODUCTION TO INDONESIA / Indonesia – Niels A. Douwes Dekker. 1963. SE-10,797-1 – 9 – ne IDC [950]
TANAH AIRKU DARI ZAMAN KE ZAMAN / Sumarto, M D – SE 4487 v. 2 only. 1952 – 9 – ne IDC [950]
Tanaka, Migaku *see* HISTORIC CITY OF NARA
TANAMASOANDRO *see* NY TANAMASOANDRO
Tananarive *see* NY FANDROSOAM-BAOVAO
TANCREDI. OPERA SERIE IN DUE ATTI. ACT 1, GERMAN / Rossini, G – Copyist MS, after 1816 – 1 – us Sibley [780]
Tanera, Karl *see* SENHORA ANNINHA
Taney, R B *see* TANEY'S REPORTS OF CASES IN THE FOURTH CIRCUIT, 1836-1851
Taneyhill, Richard H *see* THE LEATHERWOOD GOD
TANEY'S REPORTS OF CASES IN THE FOURTH CIRCUIT, 1836-1851 / Taney, R B – Philadelphia: Kay. 1v. 1871 (all publ) – 8mf – 9 – $12.00 – LLMC 81-472 – us L.L.M.C. [340]
Tang, R *see* LES COSTUMES DANS L'OPERA DE PEKIN
Tanganyika *see*
- ANNUAL REPORT OF THE DEVELOPMENT ORGANIZATION 1949
- ANNUAL REPORT OF THE DEVELOPMENT ORGANIZATION 1950
- ANNUAL REPORT OF THE DEVELOPMENT ORGANIZATION 1951
- ANNUAL REPORT ON DEVELOPMENT 1952
- ANNUAL REPORT ON DEVELOPMENT 1953
- ANNUAL REPORT ON DEVELOPMENT 1954
- ANNUAL REPORT ON DEVELOPMENT 1955
- THE DEVELOPMENT PLAN REPORT FOR THE YEAR 1947
- THE DEVELOPMENT PLAN REPORT FOR THE YEAR 1948
- GOVERNMENT PUBLICATIONS
- A REVIEW OF DEVELOPMENT PLANS IN THE SOUTHERN PROVINCE, 1953

Tanganyika. Development Commission *see* TEN YEAR DEVELOPMENT AND WELFARE PLAN OF TANGANYIKA, 1947-1956
TANGANYIKA NOTES AND RECORDS – Dar es Salaam. v1-63. 1936-64 – 189mf – 9 – A-391/2 – ne IDC [960]
TANGANYIKA OPINION – Dar-es-Salaam, Tanzania. -w. Jan 1941-Dec 1944; May 1945-Dec 1946; April-Nov 1947. 7 reels – 1 – uk British Libr Newspaper [072]
THE TANGANYIKA OPINION – Dar-es-Salaam. Tanganyika Territory. mar. 11, 18, 1932 – 1 – us NY Public [072]
TANGANYIKA REGIONAL AND DISTRICT BOOKS – 1 – us Res Libr [960]
TANGANYIKA STANDARD – Dar-es-Salaam, Tanzania. -d. Jan 1941-Dec 1944; May 1945-Oct 1954; Jan 1957-Dec 1961. 38 reels – 1 – uk British Libr Newspaper [072]
TANGANYIKA TERRITORY GAZETTE – Tanganyika. v41-43. 1960-62 – 3r – 1 – us Ross [324]
TANGIBLE TESTS FOR A YOUNG MAN'S FAITH / MacKinnon, Albert Glenthorne – Cincinnati: Jennings & Graham, 1907. 1 fiche – 9 – us A.T.L.A. [240]
TANGLED ENDS / Ardagh, Alice Maud – Toronto, Montreal, Halifax, 1888. 03969. (Pre-1900 Canadiana) – 9 – cn C.I.H.M. [830]
Tanguay, Cyprien *see*
- A TRAVERS LES REGISTRES
- DICTIONNAIRE GENEALOGIQUE DES FAMILLES CANADIENNES DEPUIS LA FONDATION DE LA COLONIE JUSQU'A NOS JOURS
- MONSEIGNEUR DE LAUBERIVIERE, CINQUIEME EVEQUE DE QUEBEC, 1739-1740

Tanguay, Marthe *see* BIBLIOGRAPHIE ANALYTIQUE DES TRAVAUX DE PAUL-ANTOINE GIGUERE, DIRECTEUR DU DEPARTEMENT DE CHIMIE, FACULTE DES SCIENCES, UNIVERSITE LAVAL
TANGUT STUDIES / Grinstead, E D – Working notes on texts from Kharakhoto, the "dead city" of NW China. The General's Garden. The Book of Filial Piety in standard script. Indexes to Buddhist and Taoist literature. Leiden, 1967. 10 vols. BCH-878 2 – 8 – ne IDC [306]
TANGUTSKIE RUKOPISI I KSILOGRAFY – Spisok otozhdestvlennykh i opredelennykh tangutskikh rukopisei i ksilografov kollektsii Instituta narodov Azii AN SSSR.Moscow, 1963. 171p. BR-10,987/1 – 9 – ne IDC [025]
TANGWEERS: LIFE AND ADVENTURE AMONG GENTLE SAVAGES / Bell, Charles Napier – London: E. Arnold, 1899. 03551. (Pre-1900 Canadiana) – 9 – cn C.I.H.M. [306]
TANI MUKTI – Bandung. Incomplete. SE 846 1. 1948-1962 – 9 – ne IDC [073]
TANIS / Flinders Petrie, W M et al – London, 1885-1888. 2pts. Nebesheh (Am) and Defenneh (Tahpanhes). (Second and Fourth Memoir Egypt Exploration Fund) – 9 – ne IDC [956]
TANIS / Petrie, William Matthew Flinders – 2v. 1885, 1888 – 9 – $10.00 – us I.R.C. [930]
TANIS (MEES NO 2) : PART 1, 1883-1884 / Flinders Petrie, W M – London, 1885 – 5mf – 8 – Dfl22.00 – ne Slangenburg [910]
TANIS (MEES VOL 5) : PART 2. NEBESHEH (AM) AND DEFENNEH (TAHPANHES) / Flinders Petrie, W M – London, 1888 – 13mf – 8 – Dfl46.00 – ne Slangenburg [930]
TANJA DJAWAB: ANGKATAN 45 / Maat, R H – SE-4442 1. v. 1 only – 9 – ne IDC [073]
TANKER TIMES – Bangor. Maine. 1956-57 – 1 – us UMI [071]
TANKER TIMES – Bangor, Maine. Aug 18, 1955-Jan 29, 1960 – 1 – us Res Libr [071]
Tankersley. Yorkshire *see* PARISH REGISTERS
Tann, Jennifer *see* INDUSTRIAL REVOLUTION: A DOCUMENTARY HISTORY
Tannenhill, Deborah *see* ANALYSIS OF THE INSTRUCTIONAL ECOLOGY IN TUTORIAL TENNIS SETTINGS
Tanner, B T *see* AN OUTLINE OF OUR HISTORY AND GOVERNMENT FOR AFRICAN METHODIST CHURCHMEN
Tanner, David A *see* WEIGHT AND BODY COMPOSITION CHANGES AS A FUNCTION OF DIET DURING A MOUNTAINEERING EXPEDITION
Tanner, Henry *see* HISTORY OF THE RISE AND PROGRESS OF THE ALTON RIOTS, CULMINATING IN THE DEATH OF REV. ELIJAH P. LOVEJOY, 7 NOV 1837
TANNERS BAPTIST CHURCH. WARREN COUNTY. NORTH CAROLINA : CHURCH RECORDS – 1828-63 – 1 – 6.57 – us Baptist [240]
TANNER'S INDEX TO THE BISHOPS' REGISTERS / Norwich. (Diocese) – 17th century. Ms – 2r – 1 – uk Microform Academic [240]
Tannery, J *see* ELEMENTS DE LA THEORIE DES FONCTIONS ELLIPTIQUES
TANNHAEUSER : EIN MINNESANG / Wolff, Julius – 9., unveraend. Aufl. Berlin: G. Grote'sche Verlagsbuchhandlung. 2v. 1884 – 1 – us U.W. Library [780]
TANNHAEUSER : EIN MINNESANG / Wolff, Julius – Berlin: G Grote, 1880 – 1r – 1 – us U.W. Library [780]
TANNHAEUSER : UND DER SAENGERKRIEG AUF WARTBURG: HANDLUNG IN DREI AUFZUEGEN / Wagner, Richard – (With: Der fliegende Hollaender) – Berlin: A Fuerstner, [18–?] – 1r – 1 – us U.W. Library [790]
TANNHAEUSER UND DER SAENGERKRIEG AUF WARTBURG : HANDLUNG IN DREI AUFZUEGEN / Wagner, Richard – Berlin: A Fuerstner, [18–?] – 1 – us U.W. Library [780]
Tanquerey, Adolphe *see* ADDITAMENTA AD SYNOPSIM THEOLOGIAE PRO ANNO 1908
Tans de Monsalve, Agustin *see* OBSERVACIONES DIRIGIDAS A DEMOSTRAR LA JUSTICIA DEL RECURSO DE SUPLICA
Tansil, Charles C *see* DOCUMENTS ILLUSTRATIVE OF THE FORMATION OF THE UNION OF THE AMERICAN STATES
Tansill, William R *see* AMERICAN SAMOA
Tan'sur, W *see* [THE ROYAL MELODY COMPLEAT]
TANT QU'IL FAIT JOUR – 1961-78 (complete) – 1r – 1 – ATLA S0597 – us A.T.L.A. [073]
TANTRAS.MAHANIRVANA TANTRA – Prose English trans. of Mahanirvana Tantram. Calcutta: Elysium Press, 1900. 315p – 1 – us U.W. Library [280]
TANTUR NEWSLETTER – v6-27. 1973-85 (complete) – Inquire – 1 – ATLA S0779 – us A.T.L.A. [073]
TANU RABBANAN BI-LESHON GEMARA – 16th or 17th century?. BJ-43-115 1 – 9 – ne IDC [470]
TANVEER – Lucknow, India. Sept-Dec 1950 – 1r – 1 – us L of C Photodup [072]
TANZ UND RECHT / Panzer, Marianne – (Includes bibliographical references) – Frankfurt am Main: M Diesterweg, 1938 – 1r – 1 – us U.W. Library [790]
Tanzania *see*
- THE ANNUAL PLAN FOR 1972-73
- ECONOMIC PLANS
- SECOND FIVE-YEAR PLAN FOR ECONOMIC AND SOCIAL DEVELOPMENT 1ST

Tanzania. Bureau of Statistics *see* EDUCATION AND TRAINING STATISTICS 1986
TANZANIA (FORMERLY TANGANYIKA AND ZANZIBAR) : STATISTICAL ABSTRACT 1938-1970 / Tanzania (formerly Tanganyika and Zanzibar). East African High Commission. East African Statistical Department. Tanganyika Office – (1953, 1967-69 not publ. Coll title: African Official Statistical Serials, 1867-1982) – 28mf – 9 – £235.00 – uk Chadwyck [960]
Tanzania (formerly Tanganyika and Zanzibar). East African High Commission. East African Statistical Department. Tanganyika Office *see* TANZANIA (FORMERLY TANGANYIKA AND ZANZIBAR)
Tanzania. International Institut for Educational Planning *see* THE TANZANIA LITERACY PROGRAMME
THE TANZANIA LITERACY PROGRAMME : A VIEW FROM BELOW: REPORT OF AN IIEP RESEARCH REVIEW WORKSHOP HELD AT MOROGORO, TANZANIA, 10-12 OCTOBER 1990 / Tanzania. International Institut for Educational Planning – Paris, 1991 – 1mf – 9 – DE-674/1 – ne IDC [370]
Tanzania. Ministry of Economic Affairs and Dev. Planning *see* FIRST YEAR PROGRESS REPORT ON THE FIVE YEAR DEVELOPMENT PLAN (PUBLIC SECTOR) 1 JUL 1964 TO 30 JUN 1965
Tanzania. Ministry of Education *see* BASIC EDUCATION STATISTICS IN TANZANIA (BEST) 1981-1985
Tanzania. National Development Corporation *see* THREE YEAR INVESTMENT AND DEVELOPMENT PLAN (1975 TO 1977)
TAO CHIAO SHIH, VOL 1 (CCC197) / Hsu, Ti-shan – (In Chinese) – [s.l: s.n, 1934] – 1r – 1 – 1984-B500 – us A.T.L.A. [240]
TAO HUAI WEI YUAN HUI PAN NIEN K'AN / Hwai River Comm – Bulletin. Nanking. 1936-47. Available: (4-5) 1940-(12-13) 1944. BCH-1084 1 – 9 – ne IDC [073]
TAO TE CHING (CCC211) / Lao-tzu – (In Chinese) – 1940 – 1r – 1 – 1984-B500 – us A.T.L.A. [280]
LE TAON : HUMORISTIQUE ET ILLUSTRE / ed by Charlebois, CH-T – Montreal, Canada. 1 jan 1903; jul 1907-fev 1910 – 1r – 1 – Can$40.00 – cn Can Microfilming [073]
THE TAOS NEWS – Santa Fe. N.M. 1970- – 1 – us UMI [071]
Tao-shing, Chang *see* RUSSIA, CHINA AND THE CHINESE EASTERN RAILWAY
TAP CHI CONG SAN = REVIEW OF COMMUNISM : CO QUAN LY LUAN VA CHINH TRI CUA DANG CONG SAN VIET-NAM – Hanoi: Dang cong san Viet-nam. v23 n253-v27 n318 1977-jun 1982; v27 n319-v32 n372 jul 1982-1986 – us Res Libr [320]
TAP CHI NAM-KY KHUYEN HOC-HOI – no. 1. Saigon. 20 fevr 1926 – 1 – fr A.C.R.P.P. [073]
TAP CHI QUAN DOI NHAN DAN – [Hanoi]: Tap chil ly luan quan su chinh tri cua cac luc luo ng vu trang nhan dan viet-nam. [v16 n183-v26 n308] 1972-jun 1982; v26 n309-v30 n359 jul 1982-sep 1986; v30 n360-362 oct-dec 1986 – us Res Libr [072]
TAP CHI VAN HOC – Hanoi. aout-dec 1963, 1965-66 – 1 – fr A.C.R.P.P. [073]
TAP CHI VAN HOC – [Hanoi]: Vien van hoc, Uy ban khoa hoc xa hoi Vietnam, aug 1963-1966 – 4r – 1 – us Res Libr [072]
TAP LUAT LE VE TU PHAP, THEO CAC VAN DA CONG BO DEN NGAY 10/7/1957 = COMPENDIUM OF LAWS AND REGULATIONS ON THE JUDICIARY, ACCORDING TO DOCUMENTS PROMULGATED UP TO JULY 10, 1957 / Ministry of Justice – Hanoi, 1957, 1960 – 4mf – 9 SEL-106/1 – ne IDC [340]
TAPAKING TEPA-TULUS; ANDARAN NGELMU KASAMPURNAN TJUNDUKE LAN NGELMU KALAHIRAN MINANGKA PANGGAJUH KARAHAJON / Sunarno, Sisworahardjo – SE 4215 1. 1961 – 9 – ne IDC [950]
TAPESTRY – Irvine, CA. 1984-1986 – 1r – 1 – $50.00 – R04039 – us Library Micro [071]
DAS TAPFERE SCHNEIDERLEIN : FUER DIE MAERCHENSPIELE DER KUENSTLERISCHEN VOLKSBUEHNE NACH DEM MAERCHEN DER GEBRUEDER GRIMM IN HANDLUNG UND REIM GEBRACHT / Guembel-Seiling, Max – Leipzig: Breitkopf & Haertel, 1918 – 1r – 1 – us U.W. Library [820]
Tapia *see* LAS ESCRITURAS...TAPIA
Tapia, Gregorio de *see* COPILACION...ORDEN...SANTIAGO DEL ESPADA
TAPOL, THE INDONESIA HUMAN RIGHTS CAMPAIGN – Thornton Heath. 94 docs. 1980-1991 – 41mf – 9 – ne IDC [320]
TAPP JOURNAL – Montreal, Canada. v5 n2. 15 avr 1942; 15 jul 1942 – 1r – 1 – Can$25.00 – cn Can Microfilming [073]
Tappan, Benjamin *see*
- BENJAMIN TAPPAN PAPERS
- PAPERS

Tappan, Lewis *see*
- THE LIFE OF ARTHUR TAPPAN
- PAPERS

TAPPAN'S COMMON PLEAS REPORTS / Cleveland. Ohio. Fifth Circuit Court – 1v. 1816-19 (all publ) – 2mf – 9 – $3.00 – LLMC 84-186 – us L.L.M.C. [340]
Tappert, W *see* DAS VERBOT DER QUINTEN-PARALLELEN
TAPPI / Technical Association of the Pulp and Paper Industry – v1-66 1918-83. Continues: T.A.P.P.I. Bulletin and Technical Association Papers – 1,5,6 – us Princeton Micro [670]
TAPPI (TECHNICAL ASSOCIATION OF THE PULP & PAPER INDUSTRY) – Standards. Printed index. Updated every 60 days – 6,9 – us Info Handling [670]
TAQUIMETRO : MODELO UNICO / Sanchez, Lozano – Clases ABC, 1908 – sp Bibl Santa Ana [946]
TAQZIR PISQE DIN SHEL BET HA-MISHPAT HA-ELYON / Israel. Ministry of Justice. Supreme Court – (Summary of Judgements of the Supreme Court). 1966-76. BJ-81-39 1 – 9 – ne IDC [340]
TAR HEEL ECONOMIST / North Carolina. State University. Raleigh. Agricultural Extension Service – Aug 1952-69 – 1,5 – us Spaulding [330]
TAR HEEL ECONOMIST / North Carolina State University.Agricultural Extension Service – 1970-82.1 reel – 1,5 – us Spaulding [630]
Tar River Association. North Carolina *see* MS. RECORDS
TARA: A MAHRATTA TALE / Taylor, Philip Meadows – British Fiction Archive: Unit 5 – 9 – uk Bell [830]

TARADALE EXPRESS – (Incomplete) – 1872-1882 – 1mf – 1 – at Corangamite [980]
Tarafa, Francisco *see* CRONICA DE CAVALLERS CATALANS
TARA-NOUA – Bucharest, Romania. -d. 2 Feb-27 March 1920. 1 reel – 1 – uk British Libr Newspaper [949]
TARAQQI – (Missing issues: 16-23) – Tehran: Sal-i 1, shumarah-i 2-24 (20 Safar 1325-12 Rajab 1325 [4 April 1907-21 August 1907]) – 1 reel – 1 – $65.00 – us MEDOC [950]
TARAS SHEVCHENKO : UKRANIAN POET, 1814-61 / Novichenko, Leonid – 1986 – 134p – 9 – 92-3-102051-X – fr UNESCO [460]
O TARAUACA : ORGAO DE DIVULGACAO DA PREFEITURA MUNICIPAL – Tarauaca, Acre. 29 Fev, 17 Out 1976 – 1,5,6 – bl Biblioteca [072]
O TARAUACA : ORGAO DOS INTERESSES DO DEPARTAMENTO – Seabra, Acre. 11-25 Out 1914 – 1,5,6 – bl Biblioteca [072]
Tarbell, Ida Minerva *see* THE EARLY LIFE OF ABRAHAM LINCOLN..
TARBIZ – v. 1-44. 1930-75; Index v. 1-30. BJ-100-190 1 – 9 – ne IDC [073]
TARBUS PUSAKA / Ali, Is. – SE-5027 1 – 9 – ne IDC [950]
TARBUT – v. 1-3. Warsaw. 1922-24. Education. BJ-291-34 1 – 9 – ne IDC [370]
Tarchi, A *see*
- [ALESSANDRO NELLE INDIE. OVERTURE; ARR.] OPERA OVERTURES ADAPTED FOR THE HARPSICHORD OR PIANO FORTE WITH AN ACCOOMPANIMENT FOR A VIOLIN. NUMBER 6
- [VIRGINIA] IDOL MIO QUEST'ALMA AMANT...
- [VIRGINIA] NON LAGRIMAR BEN MIO

A TARDE – Juiz de Fora, 17 Nov 1956; Oct 1958; 25 Oct 1960 – 1,5,6 – bl Biblioteca [072]
A TARDE – Lisbon. No.1-128. 1 Oct 1979-14 Feb 1980. Incomplete. (Portuguese Revolution of 1974. Newspapers from Portugal publ. from 21 Feb 1971 to 15 Feb 1980, collected and filmed by University of Wisconsin-Madison libraries.) – 1 – us U.W. Library [072]
A TARDE – Manaos, Amazonas. Jul 1915 – 1,5,6 – bl Biblioteca [072]
TARDES DE LA QUINTA...CRISTIANO / Ganderias, Perfecto – 1828 – 9 – 1.50f – sp Bibl Santa Ana [240]
Tardi, D *see* FORTUNAT. ETUDE SUR UN DERNIER REPRESENTANT DE LA POESIE LATINE DANS LA GAULE MEROVINGIENNE
Tardie, Gregory B *see* THE EFFECTS OF BODY SEGMENT LENGTH AND HEAD POSITION UPON SIT AND REACH FLEXIBILITY PERFORMANCE
Tardieu, Ambroise *see*
- DICTIONNAIRE D'HYGIENE PUBLIQUE ET DE SALUBRITE (AEL, ABT 3;24)
- ETUDE MEDICO-LEGALE SUR L'INFANTICIDE

Tardieu, Amedee-Eugene *see* SENEGAMBIE ET GUINEE
Tardieu, E *see* L'ENNUI, ETUDE PSYCHOLOGIQUE
THE TARDIGRADE FAUNA OF GREENLAND / Petersen, B – 6196 2. 1951 – 9 – ne IDC [590]
Tardivel, Jules-Paul *see* LA VERITE
Tardivel, Paul *see* LA DEFENSE
Tarducci, A *see* IL TVRCO VINCIBILE IN VNGARIA. CON MEDIOCRI AIUTI DI GERMANIA, ...
TAREAS DE ORGANIZACION Y TRABAJO PRACTICO DEL PARTIDO / Checa, Pedro – Madrid, 1938. Fiche W 795. (Blodgett Collection of Spanish Civil War Pamphlets) – 9 – us H.U. College Libr [946]
TARGET – (Lacks: no 306 1980. nos 312-330 1980-81. Ceased publ) – Nairobi. nos 253-355. 1968-81 – 3r – 1 – ATLA S0596 – us A.T.L.A. [073]
TARGET MARKETING *see* ZIP TARGET MARKETING
TARGETS AND OUTLINE OF THE 4-YEAR DEVELOPMENT PLAN, 1963-67 / Israel. Economic Planning Authority – Jerusalem. 1962 – 9 – ne IDC [338]
Targioni-Tozzetti, G *see* CATALOGUS VEGETABILIUM MUSEI SUI
Targioni-Tozzetti, O *see* INSTITUZIONI BOTANICHE
TARGUM SHEL HAMESH MEGILLOT BI-LESHON ASHKENAZ – Freiburg. c.1584. Cowley. BJ-43-116 1 – 9 – ne IDC [470]
THE TARGUMS ON THE BOOKS OF RUTH AND JONAH / Crane, Oliver Turnbull – New York: Jenkins & McCowan, 1886. 1 fiche – 9 – us A.T.L.A. [240]
TARIF DES DROITS DE DOUANE: DROITS D'IMPORTATION / Morocco. Administration des Douanes et Impots Indirects – Ed. 2. 1961. BNE-3002 1 – 9 – ne IDC [380]
TARIFA DE HONORARIOS MINIMOS APROBADA POR JUNTA DE GOBIERNO: SESION ORDINARIA DEL 12-2-80 / Colegio Oficial de Ayudantes Tecnicos Sanitarios – Caceres: Tip. Extremadura, 1980 – 1 – sp Bibl Santa Ana [628]
TARIFA DE PRECIOS / Sociedad Anonima Mirat – Caceres: Imprenta Moderna, 1961 – 1 – sp Bibl Santa Ana [380]
TARIFAS Y ORDENANZAS PARA LA EXACCION DE ARBITRIOS E IMPUESTOS MUNICIPALES, APROBADAS PARA EL EJERCICIO ECONOMICO DE 1924-25 / Badajoz – Badajoz: La Minerva Extremena, 1924 – sp Bibl Santa Ana [330]
TARIFF BOOK OF THE NEW INDONESIAN CUSTOMS IMPORT DUTIES AND CLASSIFICATION OF IMPORT COMMODITIES IN GROUP 1,2,3 / Indonesia. Laws, Statutes, etc – SE-4805 1. 1963 – 9 – ne IDC [380]
TARIFF MAKERS, THEIR AIMS AND METHODS / Cobden Club – The Cobden Club's reply to Mr. Chamberlain. 1909 – 9 – 1.00f – at Libertarian Micro [331]
TARIFF REVIEW – New York, 1889-1930 – 14r – 1 – us Ross [380]
DIE TARIFLICHEN LOHNGARANTIEN DES AKKORDWEBERS IN DER DEUTSCHEN TEXTIL-INDUSTRIE / Oehler, Rolf – 1994 – 1mf – 9 – DM48.00 – 3-8267-3008-9 – gw Hänsel [340]
TARIFVERTRAGE DES DEUTSCHEN.. / Deutscher Holzarbeiter-Verband. Berlin – Berlin. 1913-14. (Serial publications of German trade unions in the Memorial Library, University of Wisconsin-Madison.) – 1 – us U.W. Library [330]
TARIHCE-I ERZURUM YAHUT HEMSERILERE ARMAGAN / Nusret, Mehmed – Istanbul: Ali Suekrue Matbaasi, 1338 [1922] – $16.00 – us MEDOC [956]
TARIH-I ASKERI-YI OSMANI / Cevat Pasa, Ahmet – Istanbul: Kirk Anbar Matbaasi, 1299 [1882] – 9 – $45.00 – us MEDOC [956]
TARIH-I 'ATA / Ata, Tayyarzade Ahmed – 30mf – 9 – $63.00 – us MEDOC [949]
TARIH-I CEVDET / Pasa, Ahmet Cevdet – Istanbul: Matbaa-i Amire, 1309.-2v – 13mf – 9 – $50.00 – us MEDOC [949]
TARIH-I CEVRI CELEBI / Celebi, Ibrahim Cevri – Istanbul: Sueleyman Efendi Matba'asi, 1291-1292 [1873-1874].-2v – 30mf – 9 – $50.00 – us MEDOC [949]
TARIH-I DEVLET-I ALIYYE-I 'OSMANIYYE / Efendi, Hayrullah – Istanbul, 1217 [1854].-Books 1-15 – 36mf – 9 – $68.25 – us MEDOC [949]
TARIH-I GILMANI / Halife, Mehmet – Istanbul: Orhaniye Matbaasi, 1340 [1924] – 9 – $35.00 – us MEDOC [956]
TARIH-I IZZI / Izzi, Sueleyman – Istanbul: Mueteferrika, 1199 [1784] – 7mf – 9 – $26.25 – us MEDOC [320]
TARIH-I KAMANICE / Nabi – [Istanbul]: Tercueman-i Ahval Matbaasi, 1281 [1864] – 9 – $65.00 – us MEDOC [956]
TARIH-I LUTFI / Aktepe, M Muenir – (Set includes: 9 volumes: V. 1-8 in Ottoman) – 33mf – 9 – $165.00 – us MEDOC [949]
TARIH-I NA'IMA / Na'ima, Mustafa – Istanbul: Ibrahim Mueteferrika Matba'asi, 2v – 30mf – 9 – $375.00 – us MEDOC [949]
TARIH-I NA'IMA / Na'ima, Mustafa – Istanbul, [n.d.].-6v – 30mf – 9 – $525.00 – us MEDOC [949]
TARIH-I NEFIS / Efendi, Mustafa – Istanbul, [1863] – 2mf – 9 – $10.50 – us MEDOC [949]
TARIH-I OSMANI / Cevat Pasa, Ahmet – Istanbul: Ceride-i Askeri Matbaasi, 1296 [1879] – 9 – $65.00 – us MEDOC [956]
TARIH-I OSMANI / Nabi – 9 – $65.00 – us MEDOC [956]
TARIH-I 'OSMANI ENCUEMENI MECMU'ASI – (96 fascicles and 11 supplements in Ottoman script plus 5 fascicle new series in Latin script. A scholarly historical review issued by the Institute of Ottoman Historical Studies) – Istanbul, 1910-1931 – 71mf – 9 – $107.50 – us MEDOC [949]
TARIH-I PECEVI / Pecevi, Ibrahim – Istanbul: Matba'a-i Amire, 1281-1283 [1865-1867] – 2v 30mf – 9 – $225.00 – us MEDOC [949]
TARIH-I RASIT / Efendi, Rasit – (Vol. 6 by Asim Efendi Kuecuekcelebizade) – Istanbul: Matbaa-i Amiri, 1282 [1865] – 9 – $400.00 – us MEDOC [956]
TARIH-I SAMI VE SAKIR VE SUBHI / Sarni, Mustafa et al – Kostantiniye [Istanbul], 1198 [1784] – 9 – $125.00 – us MEDOC [956]
TARIH-I SANIZADE / Sanizade, Mehmed Ataullah – Istanbul: Ceride-i Havadis Matba'asi, 1290-1291 – 4v 19mf – 9 – $300.00 – us MEDOC [949]
TARIH-I SELANIKI / Efendi, Selaniki Mustafa – Istanbul: Matba'a-i 'Amire, 1281 [1864] – 30mf – 9 – $100.00 – us MEDOC [949]
TARIH-I SIYASI DEVLET-I ALIYE-I OSMANIYE / Pasa, Kamil – [Istanbul]: Matbaa-i Ahmet Ihsan, 1327H [1909] – 9 – $90.00 – us MEDOC [956]
TARIH-I VAHHABIYUN / Sabri, Eyueb – Istanbul: Kirk Anbar Matbaasi, 1296 [1879] – $65.00 – us MEDOC [956]
Tarihi ve Ictimai Tedkikat *see* KUERDLER
Tarik, Tevfik *see* YENI ADLI KANUNU
TARIKH AL-TAMADDUN AL-HADITH / Seignobos, Charles – Egypt, 1909 – 1 – us U.W. Library [470]
TARIKH-I-FEROZ SHAHI / Ziaa Al-din Barni – (Bibliotheca Indica: Coll. Oriental Works). Calcutta. 1862. BI-758 2 – 8 – ne IDC [490]
TARIKH-I-FIROZ SHAHI / Shamasira'j'afif – Bibliotheca Indica series: Persian. Calcutta, 1891. BI-759 2 – 8 – ne IDC [490]
Tariol, J *see* NOTICIAS DE EL CAPHE...
TARJUMAN AL-ASHWAQ / Ibn Al-Arabi – 1911 – 1 – uk Microform Academic [470]
Tarkalankara, Krsna *see* THE DAYA-CRANA-SANGRAHA, AN ORIGINAL TREATISE ON THE HINDOO LAW OF INHERITANCE
TARLETON PAPERS: AMERICAN MATERIAL / Liverpool. Record Office – BRRAM. 18th Century – 1 – uk Microform Academic [970]
Tarleton, W W *see* A COLLECTION OF PRIVATE ACTS OF PRACTICAL UTILITY IN FORCE IN NEW SOUTH WALES
TARNAGULLA AND LLANELLY COURIER – (WITH TC: 1) – 1869. TLC1 with TC1, Tarnagulla Courier – 1r – 1 – at Corangamite [072]
TARNAGULLA COURIER – (WITH TLC: 1) – 1869. TC1 with TLC1, Tarnagulla & Llanelly Courier – 1r – 1 – at Corangamite [072]
THE TARNISHED GOLDEN DOOR : CIVIL RIGHTS ISSUES IN IMMIGRATION / U.S. Commission on Civil Rights – Washington: GPO, 1980. LLMC 94-333 – 2mf – 9 – $3.00 – us L.L.M.C. [320]
Tarnow, Johannes *see* IN PROPHETAM HOSEAM COMMENTARIUS
TARNSCHRIFTEN 1933 BIS 1945 / ed by K.G. Saur Verlag; Stiftung Archiv der Parteien und Massenorganisationen der DDR im Bundesarchiv – (Includes bibliiography and accompanying issue "Bibliographie der Tarnschriften 1933 bis 1945" von Heinz Gittig ISBN: 3-598-11224-6. Free to subscribers to the mf ed) – (mf ed 1997) – ca 190mf (1:24) – 9 – silver DM4,800.00 – 3-598-32016-7 – gw Saur [320]
TAROMBO-MARGA NI SUKU BATAK / Hutagalung, Wasinton – SE-4671 1. 1961 – 9 – ne IDC [950]
TARPON SPRINGS LEADER – Tarpon Springs. Fla. 1921-36, 1938-47, Jul 1948-54, 1956- – 1 – us P.K. Yonge [071]
TARPON-BEACON – Pass Christian. Miss. 1936-1953 – 1 – us UMI [071]
Tarte, Joseph Israel *see* DELAPIDATION SIC DES FONDS PUBLICS: 12,000 POUR LA FAMILLE JOLY. JOB HONTEUX
Tartini, G *see*
- DE PRINCIPI DELL'ARMONIA MUSICALE CONTENUTA NEL DIATONICO GENERE
- SIX SOLOS FOR A VIOLIN WITH A THOROUGH BASS FOR THE HARPSICHORD
- TRAITE DES AGREMENS DE LA MUSIQUE..
- TRATTATO DI MUSICA SECONDO LA VERA SCIENZA DELL' ARMONIA
- LE TRILLE DU DIABLE

Tartini, Giuseppe *see* SONATE A VIOLINO E VIOLONCELLO O CIMBALO
Tartu. Esti Rahva Muuseum *see* AASTARAAMAT
TASCHENATLAS ZUR FLORA VON NORD- UND MITTELDEUTSCHLAND / Potonie, R – Jena, 1923 – 5mf – ne IDC [580]
TASCHENBUCH DER DEUTSCHEN VOEGELKUNDE / Meyer, B & Wolf, J – 3v. 1810-22 – 9 – Z 1856. – ne IDC [590]
TASCHENBUCH FUER DIE GESAMMTE MINERALOGIE / ed by Leonhard, C C von – Frankfurt am Main. v1-23. 1807-29 – 316mf – 9 – 2543/2 – ne IDC [550]
TASCHENBUCH FUER DIE GESAMMTE MINERALOGIE, MIT HINSICHT AUF DIE NEUESTEN ENTDECKUNGEN – Frankfurt am Main, 1807-29 – 3 – us Readex [550]
TASCHENBUCH FUER FREIMAURER – Goethen. 7v. 1798-1805 – 37mf – 9 – VR-2.12/1 – ne IDC [360]
TASCHENKALENDER ZUR BELEHRENDEN UNTERHALTUNG FUER DIE JUGEND UND IHRE FREUNDE – Bayreuth, 1796, 1798 – 1r – 1 – Dist. gw Mikrofilm – gw Misc Inst [370]
Taschereau, Jean Thomas *see* REPORT FROM THE SPECIAL COMMITTEE...
Tascon Alvarez, Luis *see* APORTACIONES AL CONOCIMIENTO DE LAS COMUNIDADES SILICICOLAS DE POA BULBOSA EN LA PROVINCIA DE LEON
TASHLUM ABUDRAHAM / Prinz, E L – Berlin. 1900. BJ-421-36 1 – 9 – ne IDC [470]
THE TASK : A POEM, IN SIX BOOKS. TO WHICH ARE ADDED AN EPISTLE TO JOSEPH HILL, ESQ., TIROCINIUM, OR A REVIEW OF SCHOOLS, AND THE HISTORY OF JOHN GILPIN / Cowper, William – London: Printed for J. Johnson, 1785 – 1 roll – 1 – 1-55879-847-1 – uk Libr Preservation [810]
TASK ACCOUNT ABILITY IN SCHOOL PHYSICAL EDUCATION AND SPORTS SETTINGS / Hastie, Peter A & Saunders, John – 1990 – 4mf – 9 – $16.00 – us Microform Publ [790]
TASK FORCE DETAINEES FOR THE PHILIPPINES – Manila. 221 docs. 1980-1991 – 83mf – 9 – ne IDC [320]
TASK FORCE ON FELON IDENTIFICATION IN FIREARM SALES REPORT TO THE A.G. : ON SYSTEMS FOR IDENTIFYING FELONS WHO ATTEMPT TO PURCHASE FIREARMS / Department of Justice, Office of Justice Programs – Washington: n.p., Oct 1989 (all publ) – 2mf – 9 – $3.00 – LLMC 95-014 – us L.L.M.C. [340]
THE TASK WORTH WHILE : OR, THE DIVINE PHILOSOPHY OF MISSIONS / Mabie, Henry Clay – Philadelphia: Griffith & Rowland Press, 1910 – 1mf – 9 – 0-8370-6212-8 – 1986-0212 – us A.T.L.A. [240]
Tasmania *see* TASMANIA GOVERNMENT GAZETTE
Tasmania. Australia. Parliament *see*
- HOUSE OF ASSEMBLY
- LEGISLATIVE COUNCIL

TASMANIA GOVERNMENT GAZETTE / Tasmania – Hobart. 1958-69 – 1 – us NY Public [980]
TASMANIAN DAILY NEWS – Hobart, Australia. May 1855-Jun 1858.-d. 9 reels – 1 – uk British Libr Newspaper [072]
TASMANIAN MAGAZINE & MASONIC REGISTER – Hobart 1849 – 1r – 1 – A$31.00 silver A$27.00 vesicular – at Pascoe [072]
TASMANIAN MAIL – 1982-1987 – 12r – 1 – at Pascoe [072]
TASMANIAN MAIL. (ILLUSTRATED TASMANIAN MAIL) – Hobart, Australia. 10 Sep 1892-27 Jun 1935.-d. 212 reels – 1 – uk British Libr Newspaper [072]
TASMANIAN NEWS – Hobart, Australia. 17 Jan 1884-31 Dec 1868.-w. 11 reels – 1 – uk British Libr Newspaper [072]
TASMANIAN TRIBUNE. (THE TRIBUNE) – Hobart, Australia. Nov 1874-Oct 1879.-w. 2mqn reels – 1 – uk British Libr Newspaper [072]
TASMANIAN UNIVERSITY LAW REVIEW – v.1. 1958-63. Continued by University of Tasmania law review – 1 – us UMI [340]
Tasse, Didace *see* REPONSE...AUX CORRESPONDANCES ET AU PAMPHLET DE ALEXANDRE DUFRESNE..
Tasse, Joseph *see* VOLTAIRE, MADAME DE POMPADOUR ET QUELQUES ARPENTS DE NEIGE
Tassi, F *see* BULLETINO DEL LABORATORIO BOTANICO DELLA R. UNIVERSITA DI SIENA
Tassin, R *see*
- NOUVEAU TRAITE DE DIPLOMATIQUE

Tasso, H *see* DELLA REALTA, AND PERFETTIONE DELLE IMPRESE
Tasso, Torquato *see* JERUSALEM DELIVREE: POEME HEROIQUE

TASSO UND SEIN GEFOLGE / Geisel, Judith Charlotte – (Includes bibliographical references) – [S.l.: s.n.], 1911 – 1r – 1 – us U.W. Library [440]
Tassy, M Garcin de *see*
- LES AUTEURS HINDOUSTANIS ET LEURS OUVRAGES
- LES FEMMES POETES DANS L'INDE
- HISTOIRE DE LA LITTERATURE HINDOUI ET HINDOUSTANI
- HISTOIRE DE LA LITTERATURE HINDOUIE ET HINDOUSTANI

TASVIR-I EFKAR – (Nos. 102-300 (6 Haziran 1280-12 Mayis 1281[1864-1865])) – Istanbul: Matbaa-i Tasvir-i Efkar Gazetesi. Sahibi: Sinasi, Sahib-i Imtiyaz Vekili: Rasid, 1862-1871 – 14mf – 9 – $200.00 – us MEDOC [949]
DI TAT – (In Hebrew. Missing: 1938, 1939) – Warsaw. v1-2. 1938-1939. Irgun Zeva'i Le'umoni – 1r – 1 – J-292-77/3 – ne IDC [072]
DIE TAT : ANTIFASCHISTISCHE WOCHENZEITUNG – (Cont by: Deutsche Volkszeitung, Duesseldorf) – Frankfurt, Germany. 29 Jan 1966-23 Sep 1983 – 1 – gw Mikrofilm [073]
DIE TAT – Frankfurt-Main, 1966-1983 – 17r – 1 – DM1,275.00 – gw Mikro Press [072]
DIE TAT – Jena/Leipzig, 1909-24. apr 1925-42. mar-apr 1943 – 14r – 1 – gw Mikrofilm [072]
DIE TAT : EINE VERGESSENE GESCHICHTE / Schulze-Smidt, Bernhardine – Dresden: C Reissner, [19–?] – 1r – 1 – us U.W. Library [830]
DIE TAT – Zuerich, Switzerland. Apr 1945-1977 – 1 – gw Mikrofilm [949]
TATA NEGARA REPUBLIK INDONESIA / Rachman, R A – SE-10,183 1. 1954? – 9 – ne IDC [320]
TATALAKSANA PRODUKSI; PRODUCTION MANAGEMENT JOGJAKARTA, FAKULTAS EKONOMI, UNIVERSITAS GADJAH MADA, 1963 / Gazali – SE-4337 1 – 9 – ne IDC [338]
Tatarchukov, O N *see* RABOCHII I KOOPERATSIIA
TATATJARA. ANGGITANIPOEN KJAI TOEWIN NJAI PADMASOESASTRA; DIPOEN BIJANTOE DATENG BAGOES NGARPAH / Wirapustaka, N – (Microfiche Nos 179-181) – Djakarta, Bale Poestaka, 2604 – 3mf – 9 – SE-2002/1 – ne IDC [950]
TATE COUNTY DEMOCRAT – Senatobia. Miss. 1941-1953 – 1 – us UMI [071]
Tate Gallery. London *see* THE INDEX TO THE TATE GALLERY ARCHIVE
Tate Lanning, John *see* THE SPANISH MISSION OF GIORG...
Tate, N *see* A DUKE AND NO DUKE
Tate, R S *see* PETIT DE BACHAUMONT
TATERE OG NATMANDSFOLK I DANMARK / Dyrlund, Folmer – 1872 – 1 – us I.U. Libraries [390]
Tatham, E *see* A SERMON SUITABLE TO THE TIMES, PREACHED AT ST MARY'S OXFORD ON SUNDAY THE 18TH OF NOVEMBER,...
Tatham, G B *see* THE PURITANS IN POWER
Tatham, Geoffrey Bulmer *see* DR. JOHN WALKER AND THE SUFFERINGS OF THE CLERGY
TATIANI ORATIO AD GRAECOS / Schwartz, Eduard – Leipzig, 1888 – 2mf – 9 – ne Slangenburg [240]
TATIANI ORATIO AD GRAECOS / Schwartz, Eduard – Leipzig: J.C. Hinrichs, 1888. (Texte und Untersuchungen zur Geschichte der altchristlichen Literatur; 4. Bd., Heft 1) – 1mf – us A.T.L.A. [240]
TATIGKEITSBERICHT / Zentralverband der Angestellten. Ortsgruppe Gross-Berlin – Berlin. 1928 29. (Serial publications of German trade unions in the Memorial Library, University of Wisconsin-Madison.) – 1 – us U.W. Library [330]
Tatishchev, V N *see*
- LEKSIKON ROSSIISKOI, ISTORICHESKOI, GEOGRAFICHESKOI POLITICHESKOI I GRAZHDANSKOI
- SUDEBNIK GOSUDARIA TSARIA I VELIKAGO KNIAZIA IOANNA VASIL'EVICHA, I NEKOTORYE SEGO GOSUDARIA I BLIZHNIKH EGO PREEMNIKOV UKAZY

TATLER – Fostoria, Ohio. 1892 – 1r – 1 – $32.50r – us Archival [071]
TATLER – Tahoe. Calif. -w. 1937-41 – 1 – us UMI [071]
THE TATLER – London. -f. 24 Feb 1877-19 Jan 1878. (1 reel) – 1 – uk British Libr Newspaper [072]
THE TATLER – Melbourne: George Robertson & Company, August 1897 – September 1898; Robert Thompson, September-October 1898 – 16mf – 9 – A$40.00 – at State Libr Vic [072]
Tatman, Sandra L *see* BIOGRAPHICAL DICTIONARY OF PHILADELPHIA ARCHITECTS: 1700-1930
Taton, Rene *see* HISTORY OF SCIENCE IN FRANCE: 17TH-19TH CENTURIES
TATRA PRESSE – Kaesmark (Kesmarok), Czechoslovakia. 1 Jun-21 Dec 1929; 11 Jan-7 Sep 1930 – 1r – 1 – gw Mikrofilm [072]
TATSACHEN DES SITTLICHEN LEBENS = THE FACTS OF THE MORAL LIFE / Wundt, Wilhelm Max – (In English. Includes bibliographical references and index) – London: Swan Sonnenschein; New York: Macmillan, 1902 – 1mf – 9 – 0-8370-6635-2 – 1986-0635 – us A.T.L.A. [230]
TATTLER – Medford OR. June 9 1934 – 1 – us U.O. Library [071]
TATTVARTHADHIGAMASUTRA.ENGLISH AND SANSKRIT / Umasvati – A treatise on the essential principles of Jainism. Edited with introd. trans., notes and commentary in English by J.L. Jaini.1920. xix,210p – 1 – us U.W. Library [280]
Tau, Max *see* GESAMMELTE WERKE
Taube, Otto Freiherr von *see* LEBENSERINNERUNGEN DES ALTEN MANNES IN BRIEFEN AN SEINEN BRUDER GERHARD
DER TAUBSTUMMENFREUND – Berlin, oct 1872-mar 1882, jan 1883, jan 1884, 1885-99 – 1 – Inquire at Mikrofilmarchiv for details – gw Misc Inst [360]
Tauchid, Mochammad *see* PERGURUAN PARTIKELIR, KEDUDUKAN DAN TUGASNJA DALAM MASARAKAT DULU, SEKARANG DAN DIMASA DATANG
DAS TAUFBUCH DER AETHIOPISCHEN KIRCHE / Trumpp, E – (BAW.PP. 8) – 3rd ed. Abth. S. 148-183 – 1mf – 8 – Dfl6.00 – ne Slangenburg [240]
Tauler, Johannes *see*
- GHEESTELYCKE SERMOONEN
- THE HISTORY AND LIFE OF THE REVEREND DOCTOR JOHN TAULER OF STRASBOURG; WITH TWENTY-FIVE OF HIS SERMONS (TEMP. 1340)
- PREDIGTEN
- THE SERMONS AND CONFERENCES OF JOHN TAULER.

TAULERS BEKEHRUNG / Denifle, Heinrich – Strassburg: K.J. Truebner, 1879 – 1mf – us A.T.L.A. [240]
EL TAUMATURGO CATALAN BEATO SALVADOR DE HORTA / Foguet, Juan; ed by Bayle, Constantino – Madrid: Razon y Fe, 1928 – 9 – sp Bibl Santa Ana [946]
TAU'N LUSTIGEN STEEBEL : 'NE ABENTUIERLICHE VERTELLUNGE / Henze, Wilhelm – Bad Pyrmont: F Gersbach, 1925 – 1r – 1 – us U.W. Library [830]
Taunay, Alfonso de E *see* RIO DE JANEIRO DE ANTANHO
TAUNTON AND BRIDGEWATER JOURNAL ETC – England.21 Nov 1812; 11 Sept 1813; 30 Apr 1814; 27 Apr 1816. -irr. 9 feet – 1 – uk British Libr Newspaper [072]
TAUNTON DAILY GAZETTE – Taunton. Massachusetts. 1978- – 1 – us UMI [071]
Taunton, Ethelred L *see*
- THE LAW OF THE CHURCH
- THOMAS WOLSEY

Taunton, Ethelred Luke *see* THE LITTLE OFFICE OF OUR LADY
TAUNUS-ZEITUNG : BA DER FRANKFURTER NEUEN PRESSE FUER DEN HOCHTAUNUSKREIS – Bad Homburg-Frankfurt/Main, Germany. 1978- – ca 8r per yr – 1 – gw Mikrofilm [072]
LA TAUPE ROUGE : GROUPE MARXISTE REVOLUTIONNAIRE – Montreal: le Groupe, 1972-75. SEM35P198 – 1r – 1 – Can$18.00 – cn Bibl Nat [320]
LE TAUREAU : ANTI-HOUDE ILLUSTRE – Montreal, Canada. 26 avr 1930-v1 n4. 8 mai 1930 – 1r – 1 – Can$25.00 – cn Can Microfilming [072]
Taurinius, Zacharias *see* VOYAGE DANS L'INTERIEUR DE L'AFRIQUE DEPUIS LE CAP DE BONNE-ESPERANCE, A TRAVERS LA CAFRERIE, LES ROYAUMES DE MATAMAN, DE MASSI, DE MONOEMUGI, DE MUSCHAKO, ETC.
DER TAURUS : GEDICHTE / Juenger, Friedrich Georg – Hamburg: Hanseatische Verlagsanstalt, 1937 – 1r – 1 – us U.W. Library [810]
TAUSCH ENTTAEUSCHT : LUSTSPIEL IN FUENF AUFZUEGEN / Jordan, Wilhelm – 2. Aufl. Frankfurt a.M.: W Jordan, 1884 – 1r – 1 – us U.W. Library [820]
DAS TAUSENDJAEHRIGE REICH / Hadorn, W – Berlin: E. Runge, 1915 – 1mf – us A.T.L.A. [240]
Tausin, H *see* DICTIONNAIRE DES DEVISES ECCLESIASTIQUES
Tauxier, Louis *see* LE NOIR DE BONDOUKOU
Tavel, F von *see* VERGLEICHENDE MORPHOLOGIE DER PILZE
Tavel, Rudolf von *see*
- D'FROU KAETHELI UND IHRI BUEBE
- GOETTI UND GOTTELI
- DER HOUPME LOMBACH
- JAE GAELL, SO GEIT'S:
- DER SCHTAERN VO BUEBEBAERG
- VOM WERT DER TRADITION

Taverne, E R M *see* ARCHITECTURAL HISTORY
Tavernier, Jean-Baptiste *see*
- NOUVELLE RELATION DE L'INTERIEUR DU SERRAIL DU GRAND SEIGNEUR CONTENANT PLUSIEURS SINGULARITEZ QUI JUSQU'ICI N'ONT POINT ESTE MISES EN LUMIERE
- RECUEIL DE PLUSIEURS RELATIONS ET TRAITEZ SINGULIERS ET CURIEUX QUI N'ONT POINT ESTE MIS DANS SES SIX PREMIERS VOYAGES
- LES SIX VOYAGES EN TURQUIE, EN PERSE, ET AUX INDES, PENDANT L'ESPACE DE QUARANTE ANS, ET PAR TOUTES LES ROUTES QUE L'ON PEUT TENIR

Tavernier, Y et al *see* L'UNIVERS POLITIQUE DES PAYSANS DANS LA FRANCE CONTEMPORAINE
TAVETA CHRONICLE – Mahoo, Taveta. 1895-1901 – 1 – uk Microform Academic [073]
TAWFIK AI-HAKIM – The Collector. A modern one-act play. Transl. by Shafik Megally. Zug, 1974. BNE-382/1 – 9 – ne IDC [820]
TAWFIQ – (Sal-i 37, shumarah-'i 1-sal-i 50, shumarah-'i 12 (28 Isfand 1336-18 Khurdad 1350[19 Mar 1957-8 June 1971]). Missing issues: Sal-i 21, 26, 27, 31-36; Sali 28 shumarah-'i 1-19) – Tehran – 6r – 1 – $200.00 – us MEDOC [950]
Tawil, A *see* ETUDE SUR LA NATIONALITE DE LA FEMME ETRANGERE QUI EPOUSE UN SUJET OTTOMAN
Tawiow, J H *see* OZAR HA-MESHALIM VE-HA-PITGAMIM
Tawney, T H *see* THE KATHAKOSA (OR TREASURY OF STORIES)
TAX ADVISER – v1-26. 1970-95 – 9 – $620.00 set – us Hein [336]
THE TAX ANALYSTS MICROFICHE DATABASE – 3 databases – $1,999.00y – us Tax [336]
TAX CONVENTIONS OF THE UNITED STATES : LEGISLATIVE HISTORY / U.S. Congress. Joint Committee on Internal Revenue Taxation – Washington: GPO. 4v. 1962 – 50mf – 9 – $75.00 – LLMC 81-108 – us L.L.M.C. [323]
TAX COURT REPORTS / U.S. Tax Court – (Updated as released) – Washington: GPO, v1-104. 1942-95 – 9 – $1,760.00 set – 0-89941-237-8 – us Hein [340]
TAX COURT REPORTS *see* BOARD OF TAX APPEALS, REPORTS
TAX DEPRECIATION AND THE NEED FOR THE RESERVE RATIO TEST / Pollock, Richard Leo – Washington: GPO, 1964 – 2mf – 9 – $3.00 – LLMC 82-709 – us L.L.M.C. [336]
TAX DUPLICATE / Erie County. Ohio. Treasurer – 1849 – 1r – 1 – $32.50r – us Archival [324]
TAX DUPLICATE / Ottawa County. Ohio. Treasurer – 1843 – 1r – 1 – $32.50r – us Archival [324]
TAX DUPLICATES / Cuyahoga County. Ohio. Auditor – 1819, 1823-69. 56 reels – 1 – us Western Res [336]
TAX DUPLICATES / Hancock County. Ohio. Treasurer – 1844-1883 – 24r – 1 – $32.50r – us Archival [324]
TAX DUPLICATES / Huron County. Ohio. Treasurer – 1822-1825 – 1r – 1 – $32.50r – us Archival [324]
TAX DUPLICATES / Van Wert County. Ohio Treasurer – 1840-1841 – 1r – 1 – $32.50r – us Archival [324]
TAX DUPLICATES / Williams County, Ohio. Treasurer – 1851-1875 – 11r – 1 – $32.50r – us Archival [324]
TAX DUPLICATES / Williams County. Ohio. Treasurer – 1876-1905 – 23r – 1 – $32.50r – us Archival [324]
TAX DUPLICATES / Wood County. Ohio. Treasurer – 1851-1860 – 7r – 1 – $32.50r – us Archival [324]
TAX FOUNDATION ARCHIVE PUBLICATIONS AND SERIALS – Backfile 1937-1987 – 9 – $2,095.00 set – us Hein [332]
TAX INSTITUTE (UNIVERSITY OF SOUTHERN CALIFORNIA) : MAJOR TAX PLANNING – v1-43. 1948-91 – 1,5,6 – $1,080.00 – us Hein [073]
TAX LAW REVIEW – v1-48. 1945-93 – 1,5,6 – $630.00 – us Hein [073]
TAX LAWYER (ABA) – (Title varies: v1-20, 1947-67 as American Bar Association Section of Taxation. Bulletin) – v1-46. 1947-93 – 9 – $770.00 set – us Hein [340]
TAX LAWYER (ABA) – v1-48. 1947-95 – 1,5,6 – $1,080.00 – us Hein [073]
TAX LEVIES / Allen County. Ohio. Auditor – 1879-1883 – 1r – 1 – $32.50r – us Archival [324]
TAX LEVIES / Hancock County, Ohio. Biglick Township. Board of Trustees – 1944-1988 – 1r – 1 – $32.50r – us Archival [324]
TAX LIST / Williams County, Ohio. Auditor – 1829 – 1r – 1 – $32.50r – us Archival [324]
TAX LISTS : 1782-1860 / Bucks County. Pennsylvania – (1782-1846 26r $2,210 S1811. 1847-60 50r $4,250 S1812) – 76r – 1 – $6,460.00 – us Scholarly Res [336]
TAX LISTS / Erie County. Ohio. Auditor – 1838-1843 – 2r – 1 – $32.50r – us Archival [324]
TAX LISTS / Hancock County. Ohio. Auditor – 1841 – 2r – 1 – $32.50r – us Archival [324]
TAX LISTS / Huron County. Ohio. Auditor – 1818-1841 – 10r – 1 – $32.50r – us Archival [324]
TAX LISTS / Ottawa County. Ohio. Auditor – 1840-1848 – 2r – 1 – $32.50r – us Archival [324]
TAX MAPS / Allen County. Ohio. Auditor – 1870 – 2r – 1 – $32.50r – us Archival [324]
TAX PLANNING IDEAS – (v.26-. 1979- 5,6,9) – v.1-. 1954- – 1 – us UMI [073]
TAX REFERENCE MANUALS / Massachusetts. Comptroller's Division – 1948-76. 24 fiches. (Harvard Law School Library Collection.) – 9 – 1.50f – us H.U. Law [324]
TAX REFORM, 1978 : LEGISLATIVE HISTORY OF THE REVENUE ACT OF 1978 – 9v in 14bks – 9 – $348.00 set – 0-89941-565-2 – us Hein [336]
TAX REFORM 1984 : THE LAW, HEARINGS, DEBATES, REPORTS AND RELATED DOCUMENTS / ed by Reams, Bernard D Jr – 20v – 9 – $515.00 set – 0-89941-669-1 – us Hein [336]
TAX REFORM STUDIES AND PROPOSALS / U.S. Treasury Department. Office of Tax Analysis – Joint pub. for the House Ways & Means Comm. and the Senate Finance Comm., 91st Cong., 1st session. 4v. GPO, 1969. (AALS-Recommended Law Books, "A" rated.) 82-706 – 9 – $16.00 – us L.L.M.C. [336]
TAX ROLLS FOR THE TENTH PENNY OF 1543 – 313mf – 9 – Dfl3600.00 – ne MMF Publ [336]
TAX SAVINGS FOR CAR OWNERS / Mitchell, Stanley – Washington: Car Life Annuals, 1954 66p. LL-195 – 1 – us L of C Photodup [340]
THE TAXATION CRY – 1891?. 03695. (Pre-1900 Canadiana) – 9 – cn C.I.H.M. [971]
TAXATION FOR ACCOUNTANTS – v1- 1966- 1; v19- 5,6,9 – us UMI [650]
TAXATION FOR LAWYERS – v1- 1972- 1; v7- 5,6,9 – us UMI [336]
TAXATION, INFLATION AND THE ROLE OF GOVERNMENT / Friedman, M et al – C.I.S. 2 fiches (29x) – 9 – $1.00f – at Libertarian Micro [320]
TAXATION IS ROBBERY / Brooks, David M – 1p – 9 – $1.00f – at Libertarian Micro [335]
THE TAXATION OF CORPORATIONS AND PERSONAL INCOME IN NEW YORK / Powell, Henry Montefiore – (Supplement. New York: Boardman, 1920. 401, 681p. LL-1282) – Rev. ed. New York: Boardman, 1919. 400p. L.C. copy imperfect: supplement wanting. LL-1282 – 1 – us L of C Photodup [340]
TAXATION OF INCOME FLOWING THROUGH LIFE INSURANCE COMPANIES / U.S. Department of the Treasury – By Thomas Neubig & Eugene Steuerle, Office of Tax Analysis. Washington: GPO, 1984. 88-008 – 9 – us L.L.M.C. [336]

LA TAXE DES PAUVRES A ABBEVILLE EN 1588, PRECEDEE D'UNE ETUDE SUR L'ASSISTANCE PUBLIQUE AVANT CETTE EPOQUE / Brandt de Galametz, Rodolphe M – Abbeville. 1884. (La Condition Ouvriere. Part Two.) – 9 – 6.00 – fr Bibl Nationale [360]
LE TAXE DIRECTE: LIBERAUX EN FAVEUR DE SON IMPOSITION – 1891?. 03680. (Pre-1900 Canadiana) – 9 – cn C.I.H.M. [971]
TAXES – v1- 1923- 1; v49- 5,6; v54- 9 – us UMI [336]
TAXES, AIDS AND SHARED TAXES IN WISCONSIN MUNICIPALITIES / Wisconsin. Dept. of Revenue – 1964-78. 27 fiches. (Harvard Law School Library Collection.) – 9 – 1.50f – us H.U. Law [336]
LES TAXES: COMMENT ELLES SE REPARTISSENT: CONTRIBUTIONS DU RICHE ET DU PAUVRE – 1891?. 03679. (Pre-1900 Canadiana) – 9 – cn C.I.H.M. [971]
TAXES OF... *see*
- CLEVELAND, OHIO, TAXES, MS V.F. O
- CLEVELAND, OHIO, TAXES, MS V.F.O.
- FRANKLIN, OHIO, TAXES, MS V.F.O.
- HUDSON, OHIO, TAXES, MS V.F.O.
- MIDDLEFIELD, OHIO, TAXES, MS V.F.O.
- PAINSVILLE, OHIO, TAXES, MS V.F. O
- PAINSVILLE, OHIO, TAXES, MS V.F.O.
- POLAND, OHIO, TAXES, MS V.F.O.
- RICHFIELD, OHIO, TAXES, MS V.F. O
- RICHFIELD, OHIO, TAXES, MS V.F.O.
- SALEM, OHIO, TAXES, MS V.F.O.
- VERNON, OHIO, TAXES, MS V.F. O
- VERNON, OHIO, TAXES, MS V.F.O.
- WARREN, OHIO, TAXES, MS V.F. O
- WARREN, OHIO, TAXES, MS V.F.O.
- YOUNGSTOWN, OHIO, TAXES, MS V.F.O.

TAXING LAND AND ECONOMIC DEVELOPMENT / Crotty, R – 1982, 14p – 9 – 1.00f – at Libertarian Micro [336]
TAXING TIMES – Sacramento, CA. 1978-1988 – 1r – 1 – $50.00 – C03646 – us Library Micro [071]
Taxonera, Luciano de *see* GODOY. PRINCIPE DE LA PAZ Y DE BASSANO
TAXONOMIC LITERATURE : A SELECTIVE GUIDE TO BOTANICAL PUBLICATIONS WITH DATES, COMMENTARIES AND TYPES / Stafleu, F A – Zug, 1967 – 10mf – Published in cooperation with the IAPT – ne IDC [580]
TAXONOMIC LITERATURE / Stafleu, F A – Selective guide to botanical publications with dates, commentaries and types. 7674 1. 1967 – 9 – ne IDC [570]
TAXONOMIE, BIOLOGIE ET BIOGEOGRAPHIE DES COPEPODES PELAGIQUES RECOLTES AU COURS DE LA CAMPAGNE MD 03 DU "MARION DUFRESNE" (ILES CROZET, KERGUELEN ET HEARD) / Seret, C – Paris. 1979. 187p. 53p annexes – 9 – F90.00 – fr Ethnologie [590]
TAXPAYER – Salem OR. Jan 1922 – 1 – us U.O. Library [071]
TAXPAYER REVOLT IN FRANCE: THE NATIONAL TAXPAYERS' FEDERATION / Hoisington, William A, Jr – 1928-1939. Hoover Institution Press, 1973. Manuscript in Microfilm Series 2+3. 212 pp – 1 – 35.00r – us Hoover Inst Photo [944]
TAXPAYERS' GUARDIAN : TRUMBULL WEEKLY INDEPENDENT NEWSPAPER – Warren, OH. 24 Oct 1888-17 Apr 1889 – 1r – 1 – us Western Res [071]
TAYIJLAR GECIDI – Istanbul, Matbaa-i Amire, 1335 [1919] – $30.00 – us MEDOC [470]
Tayler, William Elfe *see* POPERY
Taylor *see*
- CITY AND COUNTY OF SAN DIEGO
- WASHINGTON WEST OF THE CASCADES

Taylor, A W *see* 31-PHOSPHOROUS, NUCLEAR MAGNETIC RESONANCE SPECTROSCOPY STUDIES OF EXERCISING HUMAN MUSCLE
Taylor, Alfred S *see* ON POISONS IN RELATION TO MEDICAL JURISPRUDENCE AND MEDICINE
Taylor, B *see* ANTROPOLOGIJA
TAYLOR BAPTIST CHURCH. TAYLOR, LOUISIANA : CHURCH RECORDS – Oct 1909-83 – 1 – 23.76 – us Baptist [240]
Taylor, Bayard *see* TRAVELS IN ARABIA, COMPILED AND ARRANGED BY BAYARD TAYLOR
Taylor, C *see* SAYINGS OF THE JEWISH FATHERS
Taylor, Charles W *see*
- BENCH AND BAR OF CALIFORNIA
- THE BENCH AND BAR OF INDIANA

TAYLOR CLARION – Taylor, NE. -w. Jul 1883; Sept 1884; Apr-Aug 1888, scattered issues missing; Jun 1892; Aug 1895 to date – 1 – us NE Hist [071]
TAYLOR COUNTY NEWS – (See also: News Herald. Perry. Fl) – Perry. Fl. 1919-May 1920, 1931-Aug 1958 – 1 – us P.K. Yonge [071]
Taylor, D H *see* 1956 POPULATION CENSUS, 8TH APRIL 1956
Taylor, David Henry *see* THE LIFE OF PAUL
Taylor, Edward Fairfax *see* CHURCH AND STATE
Taylor, Esten C *see* INDEX TO SOUTH CAROLINA PLEADING AND PRACTICE FORMS
TAYLOR FIRST BAPTIST CHURCH. GREENVILLE COUNTY. SOUTH CAROLINA : CHURCH RECORDS – (Formerly Chick's Springs. 426p) – 1864-1917 – 1 reel – 1 – $19.17 – us Baptist [240]
Taylor, Frank Johnson *see* THE APOSTLE OF PATIENCE AND PRACTICE:...EXPOSITION OF THE EPISTLE OF ST JAMES
Taylor Funeral Home (Oakwood, Ohio) *see* FUNERAL HOME RECORDS
Taylor, G W *see* FERROELECTRICS
Taylor, George Baxton *see*
- HANDWRITTEN DIARIES
- SUNBEAM RECORDS

Taylor, George W *see*
- FERROELECTRICS LETTERS SECTION
- INTEGRATED FERROELECTRICS

Taylor, Graham *see* RELIGION IN SOCIAL ACTION
Taylor, H Boyce *see* NEWS AND TRUTHS
Taylor, Hannis *see*
- THE ORIGIN AND GROWTH OF THE AMERICAN CONSTITUTION
- THE ORIGIN AND GROWTH OF THE ENGLISH CONSTITUTION

Taylor, Henry Osborn *see*
- THE CLASSICAL HERITAGE OF THE MIDDLE AGES
- DELIVERANCE
- A TREATISE ON THE LAW OF PRIVATE CORPORATIONS. 2D ED

Taylor, Howard (Mrs) *see*
- IN THE FAR EAST
- ONE OF CHINA'S SCHOLARS

Taylor, Irwin *see* A GENERAL TREATISE ON KANSAS PLEADING AND PRACTICE UNDER THE CODE OF CIVIL PROCEDURE
Taylor, Isaac *see*
- CONSIDERATIONS ON THE PENTATEUCH
- FANATICISM. BY THE AUTHOR OF NATURAL HISTORY OF ENTHUSIASM
- LOYOLA: AND JESUITISM IN ITS RUDIMENTS
- LOYOLA AND JESUITISM IN ITS RUDIMENTS
- WESLEY, AND METHODISM
- WORDS AND PLACES

Taylor, IT *see* CAVALCADE OF JACKSON COUNTY
Taylor, J *see*
- DESIGNS FOR SHOP-FRONTS AND DOOR-CASES
- THE KIRKSTALL ABBEY CHRONICALS, VOL 62
- A REPLY TO THE REVEREND MR. JOHN WESLEY'S 'REMARKS ON THE SCRIPTURE-DOCTRINE OF ORIGINAL SIN';...

Taylor, J B *see* ELDER LOTT CARY BIOGRAPHY
Taylor, J E *see* NOTES ON THE RUINS OF MUQEYER
Taylor, James B *see* MEMOIR OF REV. LUTHER RICE, ONE OF THE FIRST AMERICAN MISSIONARIES TO THE EAST
Taylor, James Hudson *see*
- DAYS OF BLESSING IN INLAND CHINA
- SEPARATION AND SERVICE, OR, THOUGHTS ON NUMBERS VI,VII

Taylor, James W *see* PAPERS
Taylor, Jeremy *see* THE SERMONS..
Taylor, John *see*
- HISTORY OF CLEAR CREEK BAPTIST CHURCH, KENTUCKY
- A HISTORY OF TEN BAPTIST CHURCHES, KENTUCKY-VIRGINIA
- THE MASSORETIC TEXT AND THE ANCIENT VERSIONS OF THE BOOK OF MICAH
- THOUGHTS ON MISSIONS AND BIOGRAPHIES OF BAPTIST PREACHERS

Taylor, John Francis *see* OWEN ROE O'NEILL
Taylor, John Neilson *see* A TREATISE ON THE AMERICAN LAW OF LANDLORD AND TENANT..., 4TH ED
Taylor, Joseph *see* APPARITIONS, OR, THE MYSTERY OF GHOSTS, HOBGOBLINS, AND HAUNTED HOUSES DEVELOPED
Taylor, L *see* DESIGNS FOR SHOP-FRONTS AND DOOR-CASES
Taylor, Lewis N *see* NEGRO EDUCATION IN KENTUCKY
Taylor, Marshall William *see* THE LIFE, TRAVELS, LABORS, AND HELPERS OF MRS. AMANDA SMITH: THE FAMOUS NEGRO MISSIONARY EVANGELIST
Taylor, N *see* FLORA OF THE VICINITY OF NEW YORK
Taylor, Nathaniel *see* CONCIO AD CLERUM: A SERMON DELIVERED IN THE CHAPEL OF YALE COLLEGE, 10 SEP 1828
Taylor, O W *see* INDEX TO EARLY TENNESSEE BAPTISTS
Taylor, Philip Meadows *see*
- CONFESSIONS OF A THUG
- A NOBLE QUEEN: A ROMANCE OF INDIAN HISTORY
- RALPH DARNELL
- SEETA
- THE STORY OF MY LIFE
- TARA: A MAHRATTA TALE
- TIPPOO SULTAUN: A TALE OF THE MYSORE WAR

Taylor, Raynor *see*
- AMERICA AND BRITTANIA. PEACE. A NEW MARCH
- THE AMERICAN TAR: INDEPENDENT AND FREE
- EN VERITE
- RONDO FOR THE FORTE PIANO
- SIX SOLOS FOR THE VIOLONCELLO
- SONATA FOR THE PIANO FORTE, WITH AN ACCOMPANIMENT FOR A VIOLIN..
- SONATA FOR THE PIANO FORTE WITH AN ACCOMPANIMENT FOR A VIOLIN
- 'TIS ALL A JOKE

Taylor, T *see*
- MUSCOLOGIA BRITANNICA
- NEW LICHENS, PRINCIPALLY FROM THE HERBARIUM OF W. J. HOOKER

Taylor, Telford *see* FINAL REPORT ON NUERNBERG WAR CRIMES TRIALS
Taylor, Theodore W *see*
- AMERICAN INDIAN POLICY
- FEDERAL PUBLIC POLICY: PERSONAL ACCOUNTS OF TEN SENIOR FEDERAL CIVIL SERVICE EXECUTIVES

Taylor, Thomas *see*
- CORNWALL PARISH REGISTERS. MARRIAGES
- A DISSERTATION ON THE PHILOSOPHY OF ARISTOTLE, IN FOUR BOOKS

Taylor, Tom *see* AUTOBIOGRAPHICAL RECOLLECTIONS
Taylor, Vincent *see* THE FORMATION OF THE GOSPEL TRADITION
Taylor, W F *see* ROMANISTS DISQUALIFIED FOR CIVIL POWER
Taylor, William A *see*
- CENTENNIAL HISTORY OF COLUMBUS AND FRANKLIN COUNTIES
- OHIO STATESMEN AND HUNDRED YEAR BOOK 1788-1892

Taylor, William M et al *see* GOD'S WORD
Taylor, William MacKergo *see*
- CHRISTIAN ADVENTURES IN SOUTH AFRICA
- DANIEL THE BELOVED
- THE ELECTION OF GRACE
- FOUR YEARS' CAMPAIGN IN INDIA
- JESUS AT THE WELL, JOHN 4, 1-42
- JOHN KNOX
- THE MIRACLES: HELPS TO FAITH, NOT HINDRANCES
- THE MODEL PREACHER
- ORIENTAL HISTORICAL MANUSCRIPTS IN THE TAMIL LANGUAGE
- PAULINE METHODS OF MISSIONARY WORK
- PETER, THE APOSTLE
- RUTH THE GLEANER; AND ESTHER THE QUEEN

Taylor, William Mackergo *see*
- THE GOSPEL MIRACLES IN THEIR RELATION TO CHRIST AND CHRISTIANITY
- MOSES THE LAW-GIVER

Taylor, Zachary *see* PAPERS
TAYLOR'S UPPER CANADA KING'S BENCH REPORTS / Ontario. Canada – 1v. 1823-97 (all publ) – 6mf – 9 – $9.00 – LLMC 81-052 – us L.L.M.C. [340]
TAYLORSVILLE FIRST BAPTIST CHURCH. TAYLORSVILLE, KENTUCKY : CHURCH RECORDS – 1828-1910, 1925-Oct 1984 – 1 – 87.39 – us Baptist [240]
DOS TAYTSH ESRIM VE-ARBA – Hanau. c.1625-30. Cowley. BJ-43-117 1 – 9 – ne IDC [270]
Tazi, Abdelhadi *see* EDUCATION IN THE ARAB STATES IN THE LIGHT OF THE 1977 ABU DHABI CONFERENCE
TC RESMI GAZETE : THE OFFICIAL GAZETTE OF THE TURKISH REPUBLIC – [Ankara], 1926-1972 – us MEDOC [956]
TC RESMI GAZETTE – Ankara, Turkey, 1950-69 – 32r – 1 – us Ross [324]
TC RESMI GAZETTE / Turkey – Ankara. LL-12050 – 1 – us L of C Photodup [340]
Tchadaie, Pierre *see* OEUVRES CHOISIES, PUBLIEES POUR LA PREMIERE FOIS PAR GAGARIN
Tchaikovsky, Peter Ilyich *see*
- MUZYKAL'NOE NASLEDIE CHAIKOVSKOGO
- OPIS' DOKUMENTAL'NYKH MATERIALOV LICHNOGO FONDA NO. 905

Tcheraz, M *see* POETES ARMENIENS, BEDROS TOURIAN, GAMAR-KATHIPA, SAIATH-NOVA, GUEVORK DOKOKHIANTZ, MIKAEL NALBANDIANTZ CORENE DE LUSIGNAN
Tchernichowsky, S *see*
- ALILOT GILGAMESH
- IMMANUEL HA-ROMI
- SHIREI ANACREON
- SIPPURIM

Tchernovitz, H *see* BENEI MOSHEH U-TEKUFATAM
Tchoume, Mezan *see* ETUDE DE LA VEGETATION ADVENTICE DES PALMERAIES
TE ALABAMOS SENOR – Caceres: Imp. T. Rodriguez, 1971 – 1 – sp Bibl Santa Ana [946]
TE DEMU LANDANUS. LA BATALLA DE TERUEL... / Garcia Sanchez, Federico – Madrid: Razon y Fe, 1940 – sp Bibl Santa Ana [946]
TE DEUM / Handel, George Frederic – Manuscript, [17–?] – 1 – us Sibley [780]
TE DEUM...ALS QUELLEN ZU HANDEL'S SAUL, ALLEGRO... / Urio, F – (Series: Denkmaeler der Tonkunst, 5) – Bergedorf bei Hamburg: Weissenborn, 1871 – 1 – us Sibley [780]
TE LI LE / Kruchenykh, A & Khlebnikov, V – (Stikhi i risunki). Spb. 1914. BR-962 2 – 8 – ne IDC [460]
TEA PROCESSING – 1974 repr 1978 – 214p – it F.A.O. [660]
TEACHER – 1892-1961 – 1 – 1965.88 – us Baptist [240]
TEACHER – v. 1- 1963- – 1 – us UMI [370]
TEACHER – (v. 86- 1968- 5,6. v. 93- 1975-9) – v. 1- 1893- – 1 – us UMI [370]
THE TEACHER – 1872- – 1 – uk World [370]
THE TEACHER – (New York). 1894 – 1 – us A.J.P.C. [370]
THE TEACHER AND THE DYNAMICS OF NATION BUILDING : MODERNISATION SEMINAR / Singapore. Singapore Teachers' Union – Singapore, 1971 – 1mf – 9 – DE-269/1 – ne IDC [370]
TEACHER (BC) – (Cont: B.C. Teacher 1988/89) – Vancouver. v1-7. 1988/89-1994/95 – 1 – Can$60.00y – cn Micromedia [370]
TEACHER EDUCATION AND SPECIAL EDUCATION – (v.4-. 1981-. 5,6,9) – v.1-. 1977- – 1 – us UMI [370]
TEACHER EDUCATOR – v1- 1965- 1; v12- 5,6,9 – us UMI [073]
A TEACHER OF THE VIOLIN / Shorthouse, Joseph Henry – British Fiction Archive: Unit 1 – 9 – uk Bell [830]
TEACHER-LIBRARIAN TODAY *see* ALBERTA LEARNING RESOURCES JOURNAL
TEACHERS AND WRITERS COLLABORATIVE NEWSLETTER – v. 1-7. 1974-76 – 1 – us UMI [370]
TEACHERS AND WRITERS MAGAZINE – v. 8-. 1976- – 1,5,6,9 – us UMI [370]
TEACHERS AND YOUTH LEADERS: REPORT OF THE COMMITTEE APPOINTED BY THE PRESIDENT OF THE BOARD OF EDUCATION TO CONSIDER THE SUPPLY, RECRUITMENT AND TRAINING OF TEACHERS AND YOUTH LEADERS / Great Britain. Ministry of Education – 1944. McNair Report – 2mf – 9 – uk Microform Academic [324]
TEACHERS' APPLICATION LETTERS / Hancock County. Ohio. Biglick Township. Board of Education – 1893-1902 – 1r – 1 – $32.50r – us Archival [324]
THE TEACHERS' ASSISTANT – Toronto: Pub. for the Sunday-School Committee of the Diocese of Toronto at the Church Book Room, [1886?-19–] – 9 – cn C.I.H.M. [240]
TEACHERS' BELIEFS ABOUT PURPOSES AS REFLECTED IN TEACHING PRACTICES : A STUDY IN ELEMENTARY SCHOOL PHYSICAL EDUCATION / Roberts, E L – 1990 – 4mf – 9 – $16.00 – us Microform Publ [790]

TEACHERS' BOOK OF OLD TESTAMENT HEROES : A COURSE OF STUDY, BEAUTIFYING AND GLORIFYING THE MORAL AND RELIGIOUS QUALITIES OF OLD TESTAMENT CHARACTERS / Keedy, John Lincoln – Boston, MA: Graded Sunday School Pub Co, c1906 – 1mf – 9 – 0-8370-9479-8 – 1986-3479 – us A.T.L.A. [220]

TEACHERS' CERTIFICATES / Hancock County. Ohio. Biglick Township. Board of Education – 1867-1904 – 1r – 1 – $32.50r – us Archival [324]

TEACHERS COLLEGE RECORD – v. 1- 1900-1; v. 70-1968- 5,6; v. 77- 1975- 9 – us UMI [370]

TEACHERS' CONTRACTS / Hancock County. Ohio. Biglick Township. Board of Education – 1898-1904 – 1r – 1 – $32.50r – us Archival [324]

TEACHERS' CONTRACTS / Ottawa County. Ohio. Carroll Township. Board of Education – 1900-1913 – 1r – 1 – $32.50r – us Archival [324]

TEACHERS GUIDE TO THE EDUCATION OF SPANISH SPEAKING CHILDREN / California State Govt – 1952 – 1r – 1 – $50.00 – C63009 – us Library Micro [370]

TEACHER'S MANUAL OF NATURE LESSONS FOR THE COMMON SCHOOLS / Brittain, John – Saint John, N. B.: J. McMillan, 1896. 00306. (Pre-1900 Canadiana) – 9 – cn C.I.H.M. [574]

TEACHER'S MODEL AND THE MODEL TEACHER / Groser, William H – London: Sunday School Union, (1878). 1 fiche – 9 – us A.T.L.A. [240]

THE TEACHER'S MODEL AND THE MODEL TEACHER : OR, THOUGHTS ON THE EDUCATIONAL ASPECTS OF OUR LORD'S TEACHING / Groser, William Howse – London:Sunday School Union ; New York:Thomas Nelson, [1878] – 1mf – 9 – 0-8370-3407-8 – 1985-1407 – us A.T.L.A. [240]

THE TEACHERS' MONTHLY – [Toronto: Published under authority of the General Assembly, 1895?-19–] – 9 – cn C.I.H.M. [240]

TEACHERS' MONTHLY TERM REPORTS / Hancock County. Ohio. Biglick Township. Board of Education – 1884-1905 – 1r – 1 – $32.50r – us Archival [324]

THE TEACHERS' PREPARATION LEAFLET – St. John, N.B.: General Assembly's Sabbath School Committee, Presbyterian Church in Canada, [1894-189- or 19–] – 9 – cn C.I.H.M. [240]

TEACHERS RECORDS / Bloomfield. Kansas. Public Schools – 1888-96 – 1 – us KS Hist [025]

TEACHERS' REGISTER / Wabaunsee County. Kansas. School District 2 – 1856-77 – 1 – us KS Hist [978]

TEACHERS' REPORT TO TWP. CLERK / Hancock County. Ohio. Biglick Township. Board of Education – 1864-1888 – 1r – 1 – $32.50r – us Archival [324]

TEACHERS' SERVICE VERIFICATION / Hancock County. Ohio. Biglick Township. Board of Education – 1862-1884 – 1r – 1 – $32.50r – us Archival [324]

TEACHER'S STUDY GUIDE ON THE BIOLOGY OF HUMAN POPULATIONS: ASIA / UNESCO. International Study of the Conceptualization and Methodology of Population Education (ISCOMPE) – 1975 – 439p – 9 – 92-3-101279-7 – fr UNESCO [573]

THE TEACHER'S TEXT BOOK / Forrester, Alexander – Halifax, N.S.: A. & W. Mackinlay, 1867. 03155. (Pre-1900 Canadiana) – 9 – cn C.I.H.M. [971]

TEACHER-WRITER – v.1-. Jul 1978- – 1,5,6,9 – us UMI [370]

TEACHING AGRICULTURE / Wisconsin. College of Agricultural and Life Sciences. Dept. of Agricultural and Extension Education – Nov 1955-Nov 1969 – 1,5 – us Spaulding [370]

TEACHING AIDS IN HYDROLOGY / ed by Jowitt, P W – 2nd ed 1985 – 174p – 9 – 92-3-102304-7 – fr UNESCO [550]

TEACHING AND COMPUTERS – v1-. 1983- – 1,5,6,9 – us UMI [073]

TEACHING AND RESEARCH IN INTERNATIONAL LAW IN ASIA AND THE PACIFIC – 1985 – 264p – 9 – 92-3-102395-0 – fr UNESCO [340]

TEACHING AND RESEARCH IN PHILOSOPHY : ASIA AND THE PACIFIC – 1986 – 430p – 9 – 92-3-102389-6 – fr UNESCO [370]

TEACHING AND RESEARCH IN PHILOSOPHY: AFRICA – 1984 – 9 – 92-3-102124-9 – fr UNESCO [370]

TEACHING AND TEACHER EDUCATION – v1-1985- – 5,6,9 – us UMI [370]

TEACHING AT A DISTANCE – v. 1-. 1974- – 1,5,6,9 – us UMI [370]

TEACHING ENGLISH – v.10. Jan 1968 – 1 – us UMI [370]

TEACHING ENGLISH IN THE TWO YEAR COLLEGE – v1- 1974- 1; v3- 5,6,9 – us UMI [370]

TEACHING EXCEPTIONAL CHILDREN – (v.13-. 1980- 5,6) – v.1-. 1968- – 1 – us UMI [073]

TEACHING HISTORY – (v20-. 1978-. 5,6,9) – London. v1-. 1969- – 1 – us UMI [900]

TEACHING HISTORY – (v9-. 1975-. 5,6,9) – Rozelle.v1-. 1960- – 1 – us UMI [370]

TEACHING, LEARNING, COMPUTING: TLC – 1983-84 – 9 – us UMI [510]

TEACHING METHODS IN THE SOVIET SCHOOL / Zverez, I D – 1983 – 116p – 9 – 92-3-102126-5 – fr UNESCO [370]

THE TEACHING OF CITIZENSHIP / Hughes, Edwin Holt – (Includes bibliographical references and index) – Boston: W A Wilde, c1909 – 1mf – 9 – 0-8370-8831-3 – 1986-2831 – us A.T.L.A. [320]

TEACHING OF JESUS / Jackson, George – New York: A.C. Armstrong, 1903. 1 fiche – 9 – us A.T.L.A. [240]

THE TEACHING OF JESUS : IN EIGHTEEN SECTIONS / Horton, Robert Forman – New York: Dodd Mead, 1895 – 1mf – 9 – 0-8370-3670-4 – 1985-1670 – us A.T.L.A. [240]

THE TEACHING OF JESUS / Jackson, George – New York: A C Armstrong, 1903 – 1mf – 9 – 0-8370-3740-9 – 1985-1740 – us A.T.L.A. [240]

THE TEACHING OF JESUS : STUDIES IN ITS FORM AND CONTENT / Manson, T W – Cambridge, 1963 – 7mf – 8 – ne Slangenburg [220]

THE TEACHING OF JESUS ABOUT THE FUTURE: ACCORDING TO THE SYNOPTIC GOSPELS / Sharman, Henry Burton – Chicago: University of Chicago Press, 1909. 1 fiche – 9 – us A.T.L.A. [240]

THE TEACHING OF JESUS CONCERNING CHRISTIAN CONDUCT / Zenos, Andrew Constantinides – New York: American Tract Soc., 1905. 1 fiche – 9 – us A.T.L.A. [240]

TEACHING OF JESUS CONCERNING THE FUTURE LIFE / Beecher, Willis Judson – New York: American Tract Society, 1906. 1 fiche – 9 – us A.T.L.A. [240]

THE TEACHING OF JESUS CONCERNING THE FUTURE LIFE / Beecher, Willis Judson – (Includes indexes) – NY: American Tract Society, c1906 – 1mf – 9 – 0-8370-2242-8 – 1985-0242 – us A.T.L.A. [240]

THE TEACHING OF JESUS CONCERNING THE KINGDOM OF GOD AND THE CHURCH / Vos, Geerhardus – New York: American Tract Society, 1903. 1 fiche – 9 – us A.T.L.A. [240]

TEACHING OF JESUS: READINGS ON THE GOOD LIFE / Fenn, William Wallace – Cambridge: Caustic-Claflin, 1906. 1 fiche – 9 – us A.T.L.A. [240]

THE TEACHING OF OUR LORD : ITS AUTHORITY AND ITS THEMES / Cole, David – New York: Reformed Church in America, 1900 – 1mf – 9 – 0-8370-2707-1 – 1985-0707 – us A.T.L.A. [240]

TEACHING OF PSYCHOLOGY – (v3-. 1976-. 5,6,9) – v. 1- 1974- – 1 – us UMI [150]

TEACHING OF READING / ed by Staiger, Ralph C – 1973 – 213p – 9 – 92-3-101027-1 – fr UNESCO [370]

TEACHING OF ST JOHN THE APOSTLE TO THE CHURCHES OF ASIA AND THE WORLD / Hewit, Augustine Francis – New York: Catholic Book Exchange, 1895 – 1mf – 9 – 0-8370-3581-3 – 1985-1581 – us A.T.L.A. [220]

THE TEACHING OF THE GOSPEL OF JOHN / Smith, Jonathan Ritchie – New York: Fleming H. Revell, 1903. 1 fiche – 9 – us A.T.L.A. [240]

TEACHING OF THE TWELVE APOSTLES – Edited with a translation, introduction and notes, by Roswell D. Hitchcock and Francis Brown. 1885 – 1 – us A.T.L.A. [240]

TEACHING OF THE TWELVE APOSTLES – Two lectures on an ancient church manual discovered at Constantinople, given by C. Taylor. 1886 – 1 – us A.T.L.A. [240]

THE TEACHING OF THE TWELVE APOSTLES; DIDACHE TON DODEKA APOSTOLON, OR, THE OLDEST CHURCH MANUAL : THE DIDACHE AND KINDRED DOCUMENTS IN THE ORIGINAL, WITH TRANSLATIONS AND DISCUSSIONS OF POST-APOSTOLIC TEACHING / Schaff, Philip – New York: Funk and Wagnalls, 1889, c1885 – 1mf – us A.T.L.A. [240]

TEACHING POLITICAL SCIENCE – (v.8. 1980-5,6,9) – v.1-. 1973- – 1 – us UMI [320]

TEACHING SCHOOL MATHEMATICS / Servais, W & Varga, T – 1971 – 308p – 9 – 92-3-100884-6 – fr UNESCO [370]

TEACHING SOCIOLOGY – (1983-. 1,5,6,9) – v1-. 1973- – 1 – us UMI [073]

THE TEACHINGS OF DANTE / Dinsmore, Charles Allen – Boston: Houghton, Mifflin, 1901 – 1mf – us A.T.L.A. [180]

THE TEACHINGS OF THE BOOKS : OR, THE LITERARY STRUCTURE AND SPIRITUAL INTERPRETATION OF THE BOOKS OF THE NEW TESTAMENT / Willett, Herbert Lockwood & Campbell, James Mann – 2nd ed. Chicago:Fleming H. Revell, 1901, c1899 – 1mf – 9 – 0-8370-5854-6 – 1985-3854 – us A.T.L.A. [220]

TEAGARDENS RECORDER AND DENTON RECORDER – Denton. Mont. 1924-1949 – 1 – us UMI [071]

Teague, E B *see* RECORDS OF SAMUEL HENDERSON AND E. B. TEAGUE

Teague, E P *see* AN OUTLINE PICTURE OF THE BAPTIST DENOMINATION IN ALABAMA; AUTOBIOGRAPHY OF REV. ELDER BURDER TEAGUE, 1820-1902

Teague, Edward H *see* ART REFERENCE SERVICES QUARTERLY

Teague, H A *see* HISTORY OF SANDY CREEK BAPTIST ASSOCIATION, NORTH CAROLINA

Teague, S L *see* THE EFFECTS OF WEIGHT LOSS ON PLASMA CHOLESTEROL AND LIPOPROTEINS AMONG FEMALE PARTICIPANTS IN A RESIDENTIAL WELLNESS PROGRAM

THE TEAK FORESTS OF TJEPU; HISTORY OF THE MANAGEMENT AND ITS WORKING PLANS / Indonesia. Forest Service – SE-5534 1. 1957? – 9 – ne IDC [634]

TEAM-BASED ATTITUDE : THEORY DEVELOPMENT, INVENTORY CONSTRUCTION, AND PSYCHOMETRIC ANALYSIS / Twist, Pete W & Schutz, Robert – 1991 – 2mf – 9 – $8.00 – us Microform Publ [150]

TEAMING UP, BUT ONLY JUST IN TIME / Cranswick, Kester – On TEAM and JIT organization development. 2p – 9 – 1.00f – at Libertarian Micro [335]

THE TEAPOT DOME DOCUMENTS – (An original microform collection which contains testimony, grand jury material, briefs, evidence, correspondence, hearings, and archival records concerning the background to and the prosecution of the Teapot Dome scandal of the 1920's. With printed guide) – 7r – 1 – $675.00 – 0-89093-003-1 – us UPA [324]

TEARIF-I MUESLIMIN – Istanbul: Necm-i Istikbal Matbaasi; Karagoez Matbaasi, 1910. Sahipleri: Ahmed Taceddin, Yakup Kemal; Mueduer-i Mesul: Osman Cudi. Nos. 1-32 (2 Nisan-19 Kanunisani 1326 [1910]) – $65.00 – us MEDOC [073]

TEARS OF JESUS OF NAZARETH / Duncan, William C – New York: Sheldon & Co., 1860. 1 fiche – 9 – us A.T.L.A. [240]

TEATER UN RADIO VELT = THEATER AND RADIO WORLD – (In Yiddish) – New York City, NY. v1 no2 Oct 1935-Nov 1935 – 1r – 1 – $25.00 – cn Can Microfilming [071]

TEATR – Moscow. U.S.S.R. 1961- – 1 – us UMI [790]

TEATR : SBORNIK STATEI – 1908 – 1r – 1 – us Ross [790]

TEATR – Sbornik Statei. St Petersburg, 1908 – 1 – us NY Public [790]

TEATR I DRAMATURGIIA = THEATER AND DRAMA – Moscow. n1-9 1933; n1-12 1934; n1-12 1935; n1-12 1936 – 62mf – 9 – $430.00 – us Ross [790]

TEATR I KINO / Maiakovskii, Vladimir – 2v. M. 1954. BR-1003 2 – 8 – ne IDC [460]

TEATR I MUZYKA – Dokumenty i materialy. Moscow, Leningrad, 1963.194p. BR-10,743/1 – 9 – ne IDC [790]

TEATR I MUZYKA – Moscow, 1922-23 (weekly) – 22mf – 9 – us Ross [780]

TEATR I MUZYKA – Vladivostok, 1912-13 (weekly 10 issues publ) – 2mf – 9 – us Ross [780]

TEATR I STUDIA – Moscow, 1922 – 2mf – 9 – $50.00 – us Ross [790]

TEATRAL'NAIA MOSKVA = THEATRICAL MOSCOW – Moscow. n1-55. 1921-22 – 25mf – 9 – $175.00 – us Ross [790]

TEATRAL'NAIA ROSSIA – MUZYKAL'NYI MIR – St Petersburg, 1904-05 (weekly 46 issues publ) – 14mf – 9 – us Ross [780]

TEATRAL'NOE NASLEDIE – Sbornik pervyi Leningrad, 1934. 278p.BR-10,926/1 – 9 – ne IDC [790]

TEATRAL'NYE MUZEI V SSSR – Moscow, 1969. 173p. BR-10,748/1 – 9 – ne IDC [790]

TEATRAL'NYI OKTIABR' – Sbornik, 1926 – 1r – 1 – us Ross [790]

TEATRAL'NYI OKTYABR' – Sbornik 1. Leningrad Moscow. 1926 – 1 – us NY Public [790]

IL TEATRO ALLA MODA / Marcello, Benedetto – C.1720 – 2 – us Sibley [780]

UN TEATRO ARGENTINO PARA LA NUEVA ARGENTINA / Castillo, Catulo – [Buenos Aires: s.n., 1953] – 1 – CSUXADP9668-B – us Hoover Inst Photo [790]

TEATRO CRITICO UNIVERSAL. TOMO 1 / Feijoo Montenegro, Benito J – 1726 – 2mf – 9 – Pta1,500.00 – 84-85422-96-1 – sp Pentalfa [440]

TEATRO CRITICO UNIVERSAL. TOMO 2 / Feijoo Montenegro, Benito J – 1728 – 2mf – 9 – Pta1,500.00 – 84-85422-97-X – sp Pentalfa [440]

TEATRO CRITICO UNIVERSAL. TOMO 3 / Feijoo Montenegro, Benito J – 1729 – 2mf – 9 – Pta1,500.00 – 84-85422-98-8 – sp Pentalfa [440]

TEATRO CRITICO UNIVERSAL. TOMO 4 / Feijoo Montenegro, Benito J – 1730 – 2mf – 9 – Pta1,500.00 – 84-85422-99-6 – sp Pentalfa [440]

TEATRO CRITICO UNIVERSAL. TOMO 5 / Feijoo Montenegro, Benito J – 1733 – 2mf – 9 – Pta1,500.00 – 84-7848-000-5 – sp Pentalfa [440]

TEATRO CRITICO UNIVERSAL. TOMO 6 / Feijoo Montenegro, Benito J – 1734 – 2mf – 9 – Pta1,500.00 – 84-7848-001-3 – sp Pentalfa [440]

TEATRO CRITICO UNIVERSAL. TOMO 7 / Feijoo Montenegro, Benito J – 1736 – 2mf – 9 – Pta1,500.00 – 84-7848-002-1 – sp Pentalfa [440]

TEATRO CRITICO UNIVERSAL. TOMO 8 / Feijoo Montenegro, Benito J – 1739 – 2mf – 9 – Pta1,500.00 – 84-7848-003-X – sp Pentalfa [440]

TEATRO DE LA ELOCUENCIA ESPANOLA. TOMO 1 / Capmany Montpalau, Antonio – 1786 – 2mf – 9 – Pta1,500.00 – 84-7848-055-2 – sp Pentalfa [790]

TEATRO DE LA ELOCUENCIA ESPANOLA. TOMO 2 / Capmany Montpalau, Antonio – 1786 – 2mf – 9 – Pta1,500.00 – 84-7848-056-0 – sp Pentalfa [790]

TEATRO DE LA ELOCUENCIA ESPANOLA. TOMO 3 / Capmany Montpalau, Antonio – 1787 – 2mf – 9 – Pta1,500.00 – 84-7848-057-9 – sp Pentalfa [790]

TEATRO DE LA ELOCUENCIA ESPANOLA. TOMO 4 / Capmany Montpalau, Antonio – 1788 – 2mf – 9 – Pta1,500.00 – 84-7848-058-7 – sp Pentalfa [790]

TEATRO DE LA ELOCUENCIA ESPANOLA. TOMO 5 / Capmany Montpalau, Antonio – 1794 – 2mf – 9 – Pta1,500.00 – 84-7848-059-5 – sp Pentalfa [790]

TEATRO DE LAS GRANDEZAS DE LA VILLA DE MADRID / Avila, G G d' – O-1057. 1623 – 9 – ne IDC [720]

TEATRO D'IMPRESE / Ferro, G – O-609 1. 1623 – 9 – ne IDC [760]

TEATRO ESPANOL ANTERIOR A LOPE DE VEGA / Bohl de Faber, Juan N – 1832 – 9 – 1.50f – sp Bibl Santa Ana [440]

EL TEATRO, ESPECTACULO LITERARIO / Sassone, Felipe – Madrid. 1930 – 1 – us Res Libr [790]

EL TEATRO INDIGENA DE AMERICA / Bayle, Constantino – Madrid: Razon y Fe, 1946 – 1 – sp Bibl Santa Ana [790]

TEATRO INFANTIL / Carballo, Julio – (1898 ed) – 1895 – 9 – 1.50f – sp Bibl Santa Ana [790]

TEATRO MEXICANO / Vetancourt, Agustin de – 1698 – 9 – 1.50f – sp Bibl Santa Ana [790]

TEATRO NACIONAL... / Fernandez, Placido Jose – Caracas, 1929; Madrid: Razon y Fe, 1931 – 1 – sp Bibl Santa Ana [790]

EL TEATRO ROMANO DE MERIDA / Melida, Jose Ramon – Madrid: Imp. de la Rev. de Arch. Bib. y Museos, 1915 – 1 – sp Bibl Santa Ana [790]
EL TEATRO TAGALO / Barrantes Moreno, Vicente – 1889 – 9 – 1.50f – sp Bibl Santa Ana [820]
TEATRY V DNI REVOLIUTSII 1917 / Bezpalov, Vasilii F – Leningrad: "Academia", 1927 – 1 – CSUX88-B6111 – us Hoover Inst Photo [790]
Tebekin, D A *see* BORBA ZA USTANOVLENIE I UPROCHENIE SOVETSKOI VLASTI V IAKUTII
TEBIWA – (v18-. 1975-. 5,6,9) – v. 1-. 1958- – 1 – us UMI [073]
TECH AIR – (v31-. 1975-. 5,6,9) – v. 1-. 1945- – 1 – us UMI [629]
TECH AIR *see* AEROSPACE
THE TECHAER'S HANDBOOK / Nigeria. Lagos State. Ministry of Education and Community Development. School Service Board – Lagos, 1971 – 1mf – 9 – DE-110/1 – ne IDC [370]
Techen, Friedrich *see* HANSERECESSE
Techen, Ludwig *see* ZWEI GOETTINGER MACHZORHANDSCHRIFTEN
TECHNICAL AND ECONOMIC CRITERIA FOR MEDIA SELECTION AND PLANNING IN EDUCATIONAL INSTITUTIONS – 1984 – 81p – 9 – 92-3-102234-2 – fr UNESCO [370]
Technical Association of the Pulp and Paper Industry *see* TAPPI
TECHNICAL BOOKS AND MONOGRAPHS / U.S. Department of Energy – 1958-79. Includes publications of DoE and its predecessors – 23mf – 9 – $50.00 – us Updata [621]
TECHNICAL BRIEFS / U.S. National Aeronautics and Space Administration – 1976- – 1,5,6,9 – us UMI [073]
TECHNICAL BULLETIN / Clemson University. Agricultural Experiment Station – No.1035-1086. 1970-82. 1 reel – 1,5 – us Spaulding [630]
TECHNICAL BULLETIN / Colorado. Agricultural Experiment Station. Fort Collins – nos.1-108. 1932-69 – 1,5,6 – us Spaulding [630]
TECHNICAL BULLETIN / Georgia. Agricultural Experiment Station. Athens – n.s. v. 1-57. 1952-66 – 1,5,6 – us Spaulding [630]
TECHNICAL BULLETIN / Georgia. Experiment Station. Athens – v.1. 1 fiche – 9 – us Spaulding [630]
TECHNICAL BULLETIN / Georgia. Experiment Station. Experiment – n.1-3. 1 fiche – 9 – us Spaulding [630]
TECHNICAL BULLETIN / Louisiana State University. Agricultural Experiment Station – No.101. Feb 1978. 1 reel – 1,5 – us Spaulding [630]
TECHNICAL BULLETIN / Maine. Agricultural Experiment Station – v. 1-40. 1962-69 – 1,5,6 – us Spaulding [630]
TECHNICAL BULLETIN / Massachusetts. Agricultural Experiment Station – v. 1-15. 1903-28 – 1,5,6 – us Spaulding [630]
TECHNICAL BULLETIN / Minnesota. University. Agricultural Experiment Station. St. Paul – nos.1-34. 1921-25 – 1,5,6 – us Spaulding [630]
TECHNICAL BULLETIN / Mississippi. Agricultural Experiment Station. State College – v. 1-56. 1892-69 – 1,5,6 – us Spaulding [630]
TECHNICAL BULLETIN / Mississippi State University. Agricultural Experiment Station. Agricultural and Forestry Experiment Station – No.57-113. 1970-82 – 1,5 – us Spaulding [630]
TECHNICAL BULLETIN / New Hampshire. Agricultural Experiment Station – v. 1-108. 1901-66 – 1,5,6 – us Spaulding [630]
TECHNICAL BULLETIN / North Carolina. Agricultural Experiment Station. Raleigh – n.1-196. Jul 1891-1969 – 1,5 – us Spaulding [630]
TECHNICAL BULLETIN / North Carolina State University.Agricultural Experiment Station – No.197-273 – 1,5 – us Spaulding [630]
TECHNICAL BULLETIN / North Carolina State University.Department of Soil science. International Soil Fertility Evaluation and Improvement Program – No.1-7. 1965-73. 5 fiches – 9 – us Spaulding [630]
TECHNICAL BULLETIN / Oklahoma State University. Agricultural Experiment Station – T130-T158. 1970-82 – 1,5 – us Spaulding [630]
TECHNICAL BULLETIN / South Carolina. Agricultural Experiment Station. Clemson – n.1001-1034. 1961-69 – 1,5 – us Spaulding [630]
TECHNICAL BULLETIN / South Dakota. State University. Agricultural Experiment Station – nos.1-41. 1939-74 – 1,5,6 – us Spaulding [630]
TECHNICAL BULLETIN / U.S. Department of Agriculture – Nos. 1-1092. 1927-1954 – 1,5,6 – us Princeton Micro [630]
TECHNICAL BULLETIN / Virginia. Agricultural Experiment Station. Blacksburg – n.1-181. Apr 1915-Jul 1965 – 1,5 – us Spaulding [630]
TECHNICAL BULLETIN / Washington. Agricultural Experiment Station – nos.1-79. 1950-74 – 1,5,6 – us Spaulding [630]
TECHNICAL BULLETINS / U.S. Department of Agriculture – Nos. 1-1722. 1927-86. 2083 fiches – 9 – $3000.00 – us Updata [630]
TECHNICAL DRAWINGS OF MUSICAL INSTRUMENTS – 1995 – 575mf – 9 – Dfl4,865.00 – M390 – ne MMF Publ [780]
TECHNICAL EDUCATION AND TRAINING ABSTRACTS – 1960- 33v – 9 – £197.00 – 0966-162X – uk Carfax [370]
TECHNICAL EDUCATION IN BANGLADESH : CAPACITY AND UTILIZATION / Bangladesh. National Foundation for Research on Human Resource Development – Dacca, 1979 – 3mf – 9 – DE-534/1 – ne IDC [370]
TECHNICAL EDUCATION NEWS – v1- 1941- 1; v37- 5,6,9 – us UMI [370]
TECHNICAL EDUCATION OF THE PEOPLE IN UNTECHNICAL LANGUAGE / Baillairge, Charles – Read...May 1894. 00067. (Pre-1900 Canadiana) – 9 – cn C.I.H.M. [370]
TECHNICAL EDUCATION SURVEY TEAM. REPORT,BY. R. L. BARLOGA. SE 11,630/1. 1955 / U.S. Agency for International Development – 9 – ne IDC [324]
TECHNICAL FORESTRY EDUCATION : DESIGN AND IMPLEMENTATION – 1984 – 133p – it F.A.O. [634]
TECHNICAL GUIDELINE FOR CEREAL SEED TESTING – 1983 – 140p – it F.A.O. [631]
TECHNICAL GUIDELINE FOR SORGHUM AND MILLET SEED PRODUCTION – 1982 – 119p – it F.A.O. [631]
TECHNICAL GUIDELINE ON SEED POTATO MICROPROPAGATION AND MULTIPLICATION – 1986 – 61p – it F.A.O. [631]
TECHNICAL GUIDELINES FOR MAIZE AND SEED TECHNOLOGY – 1982 – 211p – it F.A.O. [630]
TECHNICAL GUIDELINES FOR MUSHROOM GROWING IN THE TROPICS – 1990 – 170p – it F.A.O. [631]
TECHNICAL GUIDELINES FOR VEGETABLE SEED TECHNOLOGY : A TECHNICAL GUIDE OF VEGETABLE SEED PRODUCTION, PROCESSING, STORAGE AND QUALITY CONTROL – 1980 – 185p – it F.A.O. [630]
TECHNICAL HANDBOOK ON SYMBIOTIC NITROGEN FIXATION, LEGUME RHIZOBIUM – 1983 – 185p – it F.A.O. [631]
TECHNICAL MEMORANDUMS / U.S. National Advisory Committee on Aeronautics – No.1-1441 – 1 – 828.00 – us L of C Photodup [629]
TECHNICAL MIMEOGRAPH PAPER / Georgia. Coastal Plain Experiment Station. Tifton – v. 1-6. 1949-52 – 1,5,6 – us Spaulding [630]
TECHNICAL MONOGRAPH / Texas A & M University. Agricultural Experiment Station – No.7-10.1970-80. 1 reel – 1,5 – us Spaulding [630]
TECHNICAL OIL MISSION *see* PRELIMINARY CLASSIFIED INDEX OF TECHNICAL OIL MISSION REPORTS
Technical Oil Mission *see* REPORTS
TECHNICAL PAPER / Clemson University. Department of Forestry – No.1-15.1973-82. 7 fiches – 9 – us Spaulding [630]
TECHNICAL PAPER / University of Florida. Florida Sea Grant Program – No.1-25.1978-82. 41 fiches – 9 – us Spaulding [639]
TECHNICAL PAPERS / American Congress on Surveying and Mapping – (Proceeding of the American Congress on Surveying and Mapping annual meeting. Cont by: Technical papers of the...Annual Meeting of the American Congress on Surveying and Mapping) – Falls Church. v40-42. 1980-82* – 1 – D12486.02 – us UMI [520]
TECHNICAL PAPERS / American Congress on Surveying and Mapping – v40- 1980- – 1,5,6,9 – us UMI [520]
TECHNICAL PAPERS / Society of Manufacturing Engineers – (Subsc receive new papers 4 times per yr detailing the latest theories, applications and innovations in manufacturing) – 1977- – 1mf per paper. No of papers per yr varies – 9 – $725.00y – us S.M.E. [670]
TECHNICAL PAPERS / U.S. Bureau of Mines – Nos 1-727. 1911-48 – 1,5,6 – $22,374.00 – us Princeton Micro [622]
TECHNICAL PAPERS / American Congress on Surveying and Mapping Fall Technical Meeting – (Cont in pt: American Congress on Surveying and Mapping Joint proceeding of the American Society of Photogrammetry; American Congress on Surveying and Mapping. Cont by: ASP-ACSM Fall Technical meeting. Technical papers of the American Congress on Surveying and Mapping) – Falls Church. oct 1980* – 1 – D16421 – us UMI [520]
TECHNICAL PAPERS, INSTITUTE CONFERENCE AND CONVENTION / American Institute of Industrial Engineers – (Cont by: Proceedings. Institute of Industrial Engineers. Former titles: American Institute of Industrial Engineers conference proceedings (1954-1968)) – New York. 1954-may 1973 1; 1971-may 1973 5 – 1,5 – D3181 – us UMI [620]
TECHNICAL PAPERS OF THE AMERICAN CONGRESS ON SURVEYING AND MAPPING *see* ANNUAL MEETING OF THE AMERICAN CONGRESS ON SURVEYING AND MAPPING
TECHNICAL PAPERS OF THE AMERICAN SOCIETY OF PHOTOGRAMMETRY, FALL TECHNICAL MEETING AND AMERICAN CONGRESS ON SURVEYING AND MAPPING *see* JOINT PROCEEDINGS
TECHNICAL PAPERS OF THE ANNUAL MEETING OF THE AMERICAN CONGRESS ON SURVEYING AND MAPPING *see* PROCEEDINGS
TECHNICAL PAPERS OF THE...ANNUAL MEETING OF THE AMERICAN CONGRESS ON SURVEYING AND MAPPING *see* TECHNICAL PAPERS
TECHNICAL PAPERS ON THE AMERICAN CONGRESS ON SURVEYING AND MAPPING FALL TECHNICAL MEETING *see* JOINT PROCEEDINGS
TECHNICAL PHYSICS – v1- 1956- – 1,5,6 – us A.I.P. [530]
TECHNICAL PHYSICS LETTERS – v1- 1975- – 1,5,6 – us A.I.P. [530]
TECHNICAL PHYSICS OF THE U.S.S.R – v. 1-5. 1934-1938 – 1 – us Princeton Micro [530]
TECHNICAL PROBLEMS IN FORECASTING THE POPULATION OF LIBYA / Libya – Statistical Paper no. 7. BNE-501 1 – 9 – ne IDC [310]
TECHNICAL REPORT ON A STUDY OF THE AGROCLIMATOLOGY OF THE HUMID TROPICS OF SOUTHEAST ASIA (F.A.O./UNESCO/WMO) – 1962 – 259p – it F.A.O. [550]
TECHNICAL REPORTS / U.S. National Marine Fisheries Service (NOAA) – Nos. 1-45. 1984-86. 57 fiches – 9 – 130.00 – us Updata [324]
TECHNICAL REPORTS OF THE SPECIAL STUDY COMMITTEE ON TECHNICAL EDUCATION / Indonesia. Panitia Chusus Penjelidikan Pendidikan Tehnik – (2 year Cooperative Study). SE-2510 1. 2 v. 1958-1960. 1960 – 9 – ne IDC [370]
TECHNICAL SERVICES QUARTERLY : NEW TRENDS IN COMPUTERS, AUTOMATION AND ADVANCED TECHNOLOGIES IN THE TECHNICAL OPERATION OF LIBRARIES AND INFORMATION CENTERS / ed by Pitkin, Gary M – v1- 1983- – 1, 9 ($175.00 in US $245.00 outside hardcopy subsc) – us Haworth [020]
TECHNICAL TRANSLATIONS – v. 1-18. 1959-1967 – 1,5,6 – us Princeton Micro [600]
THE TECHNICAL WRITING TEACHER – (1983-. 1,5,6,9) – v1-. 1974- – 1 – us UMI [073]
TECHNICALITIES – (1983-. 1,5,6,9) – v1-. 1980- – 1 – us UMI [073]
TECHNICKE NOVINY – Prague, Czechoslovakia. Technicky tydenik. -w. May 1953-Jan 1956; Jan 1957-Dec 1970. 13 reels – 1 – uk British Libr Newspaper [072]
TECHNIK CHOETBAH, TOENTOENAN NGARANG CHOETBAH DJOEM'AH, DENING M. 'AFWAN SHD(JAVANESE OR ARABIC) SE-5290/1. 1947 / Abubakar, H – 9 – ne IDC [950]
TECHNIKUNTERSTUETZUNG FUER VIRTUELLE UNTERNEHMEN 1500 1995 / Detering, Soeren – 2mf – 9 – DM80.00 – 3-8267-2121-7 – gw Hänsel [000]
TECHNIQUE : REVUE INDUSTRIELLE / INDUSTRIAL REVIEW – Montreal, fev 1926-avr 1969 – 11r – 1 – Can$45.00r – cn Can Microfilming [073]
LA TECHNIQUE DES TRAVAUX – Revue bimestrielle des procedes modernes de construction. Paris. 1970-73 – 5 – fr A.C.R.P.P. [600]
LA TECHNIQUE MODERNE – Revue universelle des sciences appliquees a l'industrie. Paris. 1950-72 – 5 – fr A.C.R.P.P. [600]
TECHNIQUE MODERNE: CONSTRUCTION – v5-9 1950-54 – 1 – us UMI [690]
TECHNIQUES *see* VOCATIONAL EDUCATION JOURNAL
LES TECHNIQUES DE DECOR CERAMIQUE / Balfet, H. et al – Essai de nomenclature et de definitions – 9 – F20.00 – fr Ethnologie [740]
TECHNIQUES DE TRANSFORMATION DU LAIT FERMENTE / O'Connor, C B & Tripathi, B R – 1992 – 9 – $6.00 – 92-9053-501-6 – et ILRI [630]
TECHNIQUES ET CULTURE DES NOMADES BAXTYARI D'IRAN / Digard, J P – 9 – F70.00 – fr Ethnologie [306]
TECHNIQUES IN ORTHOPAEDICS: TIO – v1- . 1986- – 1,5,6,9 – us UMI [617]
TECHNISCHE HOCHSCHULE DARMSTADT : FESTSCHRIFT – 25 JAHRE. FACHGEBIET MASCHINENELEMENTE UND MECHANIK / Raab, Walter; ed by Doersam, Edgar – 1994 – 1mf – DM60.00 – 3-8267-2034-2 – gw Hänsel [620]
TECHNISCHE MITTEILUNGEN – v3-33. 1925-55 – 1,5,6 – us Princeton Micro [600]
TECHNOLOGIC PAPERS / U.S. National Bureau of Standards – (Now: JOURNAL OF RESEARCH OF THE NATIONAL BUREAU OF STANDARDS). v. 16-22. 1921-1928 – 1,5,6 – us Princeton Micro [324]
TECHNOLOGICAL CHANGE IN PRINTING AND PUBLISHING / ed by Hattery, Lowell H & Bush, George P – 1973. 275p. Focuses on computers in typesetting, printing and binding; simulation as an aid to planning; video editing; microfilm publishing – 9 – us Lomond [680]
TECHNOLOGICAL FORECASTING AND SOCIAL CHANGE – v1-26. 1969-84 – 1,5,6,13 – sz Elsevier [073]
TECHNOLOGICAL PAPERS / U.S. National Bureau of Standards – v1-370 1910-28 – 1 – us Princeton Micro [380]
TECHNOLOGIES FOR RURAL DEVELOPMENT : BASED ON AN EXPERT MEETING ON NEW MODALITIES FOR THE ACTION OF UNESCO IN THE FIELD ON TECHNOLOGIES FOR RURAL DEVELOPMENT, BRUSSELS, 1980 – 1981 – 9 – 92-3-101971-6 – fr UNESCO [600]
TECHNOLOGISCHES WOERTERBUCH ODER ALPHABETISCHE ERKLAERUNGEN ALLER NUETZLICHEN MECHANISCHEN KUENSTE, MANUFAKTUREN.. / Jacobson, Johann Carl Gottfried – Berlin. 8v. 1781-95. Suppl. by G.E. Rosenthal – 68mf – 9 – subsc: DM400.00 diazo DM490.00 silver – gw Olms [600]
TECHNOLOGY – London. Great Britain. 1958-1961 – 1 – us UMI [072]
TECHNOLOGY – v.1-. 1981- – 1,5,6,9 – us UMI [600]
TECHNOLOGY ANALYSIS AND STRATEGIC MANAGEMENT – 1989- 5v – 9 – £184.00 – 0953-7325 – uk Carfax [650]
TECHNOLOGY AND COPYRIGHT / Bush, George P – Annotated bibliog. and source materials.1972. 454p. ISBN: 0-912338-04-0 – 9 – 9.50 – us Lomond [340]
TECHNOLOGY AND COPYRIGHT: SOURCES AND MATERIALS / ed by Bush, George P & Dreyfuss, Robert H – 1979. 2nd ed. rev. 552p. ISBN: 0-912338-18-0 – 9 – 15.50 – us Lomond [600]
TECHNOLOGY AND COPYRIGHT: SOURCES AND SELECTED MATERIALS / ed by Hattery, Lowell H & Schaefer, Mary Tonne – 3rd ed. 1988. ISBN: 0-912338-64-4 – 9 – 19.50 – us Lomond [600]
TECHNOLOGY AND CULTURE – v1- 1959- 1; v12- 5,6; v18- 1977- 9 – us UMI [900]
TECHNOLOGY APPLICATIONS GAP : OVERCOMING CONSTRAINTS TO SMALL-FARM DEVELOPMENT – 1986 – 150p – it F.A.O. [307]
TECHNOLOGY ASSESSMENT – 1972 – 1,5,9 – us Gordon [600]

TECHNOLOGY ASSESSMENT : REVIEW AND IMPLICATIONS FOR DEVELOPING COUNTRIES / Wad, Atul & Radnor, Michael – 184 – 72p – 9 – 92-3-102276-8 – fr UNESCO [306]
TECHNOLOGY & COPYRIGHT: RESOURCES ON LAW, PRACTICE, OPINION / ed by Hattery, Lowell H & Schaefer, Mary Tonne – 3rd ed – 9 – us Lomond [600]
TECHNOLOGY DIFFUSION / Hough, Granville W – Federal programs and procedures.1975 406p. ISBN: 0-912338-06-7 – 9 – 12.50 – us Lomond [600]
TECHNOLOGY FOR THE PRODUCTION OF PROTEIN FOODS FROM COTTONSEED FLOUR – 1971 repr 1977 – 42p – it F.A.O. [660]
TECHNOLOGY ILLUSTRATED – 1981- – 1,5,6,9 – us UMI [600]
TECHNOLOGY IN SOCIETY. AN INTERNATIONAL JOURNAL – v1- 1979- – 5,6,9 – us UMI [600]
TECHNOLOGY OF PRODUCTION OF EDIBLE FLOURS AND PROTEIN PRODUCTS FROM SOYBEAN – 1971 repr 1979 – 158p – it F.A.O. [660]
TECHNOLOGY OF TRADITIONAL MILK PRODUCTS IN DEVELOPING COUNTRIES – 1990 – 348p – it F.A.O. [636]
TECHNOLOGY REVIEW – (v.74- 1971- 5,6. v.78- 1975- 9) – v.1- 1899- – 1 – us UMI [073]
TECHNOLOGY TRANSFER AND COMMUNICATION / ed by Hancock, Alan – 1984 – 385p – 9 – 92-3-102176-1 – fr UNESCO [303]
TECHNOLOGY UTILIZATION IDEAS FOR THE 70S AND BEYOND – (v26 1971, Science and Technology) – 1971 – 9 – $30.00 – us Univelt [620]
TECHNOLOGY WEEK – v. 1-11. 1956-1962 – 1,5,6 – us Princeton Micro [600]
TECHNOMETRICS – v1- 1959- 1; v13- 5,6; v19- 9 – us UMI [600]
TECHTRENDS – v30, no.2-. Feb 1985- – 1,5,6,9 – us UMI [073]
TECKLENBURGS HEIMATKALENDER – Goettingen, 1910-41 – 2r – 1 – gw Mikrofilm [943]
TECNICA DE INVESTIGACION... / Altamira, Rafael – Madrid: Razon y Fe, 1940 – 1 – sp Bibl Santa Ana [946]
TECNICA Y PERITACION CALIGRAFICA / Alcanzar Anguita, Eufrasio – Guadalajara: Imp. del Suc. de A. Concha, 1915 – 1 – sp Bibl Santa Ana [740]
TECNICH POCHTZIN, HIJA DE MOTECZUMA (?1510?-1550) / Lopez de Meneses, Amada – Madrid, 1948. Sep. Rev. de Indias. no 31-32 (Enero-Junio, 1948). pp. 471-495 – 1 – sp Bibl Santa Ana [946]
Tecnicos Empresarios promotores de Empresas *see*
– MEMORIA, 1976
– MEMORIA EJERCICIO 1975
EL TECOLOTE – San Francisco, CA. Aug 1970- – 13+ r – 1 – $650.00 ($50.00y) – B02815a – us Library Micro [071]
TECTONA – Djakarta, 1908-1932.-v1-25 – 401mf – 9 – SE-350/1 – ne IDC [073]
TECTONICS – Pattee, University Park, PA, 1990 – 17p 1 card – 9 – us Lawrence Pub [720]
TECTONICS – (v11 1992 $280.00. v12 1993 $308.00. v13 1994 $330.00. v14 1995 $380.00) – v1- 1982- Bimonthly – us A.G.U. [550]
TECTONOPHYSICS – v1-110. 1964-84 – 1,5,6,13 – sz Elsevier [073]
TECUMSEH CHIEFTAIN – Tecumseh, NE. - w. Sept 1873-Oct 1875, scattered issues missing; Sept 1876-Aug 1878; Jan 1881-Dec 1885; Jan 1887 to date – 1 – us NE Hist [071]
Tecumseh. Kansas. Tecumseh Methodist Church *see* RECORDS
TECZA – v4. 1930 – 1 – us I.U. Libraries [073]
LES TEDDA DU TIBESTI ET LE PROBLEME DE SURVIE / Lopatinsky, O – 9 – F120.00 – fr Ethnologie [306]
TEDDY ASHTON'S JOURNAL – (Northern Weekly & Teddy Ashton's Journal 1899) – England, 22 May 1896-25 Dec 1897; 1898-1903; 1 Oct 1904; 7 Jan-30 Dec 1905; 1906; 5 Jan 1907-29 Feb 1908 – 10r – 1 – uk British Libr Newspaper [072]
Tedeschi, Paolo *see* GUADALAJARA, 8-23 MARZO, 1937
Tedrick, Raymond E Ted *see* MUSIC

TEDRISAT-I IBTIDAIYYE MECMUASI [TEDRISAT MECMUASI] – (Yayimliyan: Maarif Nezareti Dar-uel Muallimin Hey'et-i T'limiyesi. Nos. 5-6, 8-11, 14-21, 23-26, 28, 33, 57, 59-61, 63, 65, 67 (15 Haziran 1326-Mayis 1341[1910-1925])) – Istanbul: Matbaa-i Amire, 1910-1926 – 29mf – 9 – $425.00 – us MEDOC [949]
TEEING OFF TOWARD THE NCAA CHAMPIONSHIP : FACTORS DETERMINING SUCCESS IN MALE COLLEGIATE GOLFERS / Stock, Robert B – University of Southern Mississippi, 1995 – 1mf – 9 – $4.00 – PE3621 – us Microform Publ [370]
Teele, A K *see* THE HISTORY OF MILTON, MASS. 1640 TO 1887
TEEN GENERATION MAGAZINE – (v1-2 1940-1942 Can$60.00 1. Cont by: TG Magazine at v49 1989. v1-2 publ under the title: Canadian High News) – Toronto. v1-48. 1940/41-1988 – 1,9 – Can$20.00y – cn Micromedia [305]
TEEN GENERATION MAGAZINE *see* TG MAGAZINE
TEES-SIDE WEEKLY HERALD – England.1904-27 Apr 1918. -w.14 reels – 1 – uk British Libr Newspaper [072]
Teetaert, Amedee *see* LA CONFESSION AUX LAIQUES DANS L'EGLISE LATINE DEPUIS LE VILLE
THE TEETOTAL TYRANT: BEING ILLUSTRATIONS OF TEETOTAL METHODS UNDER A PROHIBITORY LIQUOR LAW: TOGETHER WITH REMARKS ON THE PRESENT POSITION IN GREAT BRITAIN / Down, T C – London: J. Phillips, 1895. 02752. (Pre-1900 Canadiana) – 9 – cn C.I.H.M. [971]
Teetz, Ferdinand *see*
– DAS LIED VON DER GLOCKE
– SCHILLERS LIED VON DER GLOCKE
Tefft, Benjamin F *see* METHODISM SUCCESSFUL, AND THE INTERNAL CAUSES OF ITS SUCCESS..
Tefft House. Topeka, Kansas *see* LEDGER
TEFILLAH MI-KOL HA-SHANAH – Amsterdam. 1650. BJ-43-120 1 – 9 – ne IDC [956]
TEFILLAH MI-KOL HA-SHANAH – Cracow. 1594. BJ-43-118 1 – 9 – ne IDC [270]
Tegeler, Ernst *see* DER BOCHUMER ARZT DR. CARL ARNOLD KORTUM, DER DICHTER DER JOBSIADE
TEGEN DEN STROOM / Altmann, Otto – Den Haag: D A Daamen, [19–] – 1r – 1 – us U.W. Library [943]
TEGEN-SPRAECK ENDE WEDERLEGH. OVER T' PUNCT DER WEERELTLIJCKE MIJDINGHE – Door I. M. K. Haerlem, G. Rooman. 1598. BME-227 1 – 9 – ne IDC [240]
DIE TEGERNSEE BRIEFSAMMLUNG (FROUMUND) (MGH EPISTOLAE 4: 3.BD) – 1925 – Dfl19.00 – ne Slangenburg [240]
TEGGS MONTHLY MAGAZINE – Melbourne, 1836 – 1r – 1 – A$31.00 silver A$27.00 vesicular – at Pascoe [073]
TEGHENBERICHT – Op een Laster ende Scheltboecxken gheintituleert, Dauid Georis wt Hollandt, des Ertzketters waerachtige Historie. wtgheghaen int Jaer, 1559. 1584. BME-268 1 – 9 – ne IDC [240]
TEGHENS DE WEDERDOOPERS, SES BOECKEN, NV EERST WT DE LATIJNSCHE TALE IN NEDERDUYTSCH OUERGESTELT, D. G. NICOLAJ DIE DAER BY GHEUOECHT HEEFT DE WEDERLEGGINGHE DER LEERINGEN V. MENNO SYMONS, DIERICK PHILIPS, ADAM PASTOR, HENDRICK NICLAES / Bullingerus, H – Embden. 1569. BME-120 1 – 9 – ne IDC [240]
Tegland, Karl *see* MEDIATION IN THE WESTERN DISTRICT OF WASHINGTON
TEHACHAPI NEWS – Tehachapi, CA. 1928-39; 1941-53; 1956-58 – 14r – 1 – $700.00 – C03035 – us Library Micro [071]
TEHAMA COUNTY REPORTER – Gerber, CA. 1953-63 – 3r – 1 – $150.00 – B02272 – us Library Micro [071]
TEHAMA COUNTY REPUBLICAN – Red Bluff, CA. 1918-1919 – 1r – 1 – $50.00 – B02665 – us Library Micro [071]
TEHAMA COUNTY VETERAN – Red Bluff, CA. 1945-46 – 1r – 1 – $50.00 – B02666 – us Library Micro [071]
TEHAMA/GLENN COUNTIES – 1916-33; 1992- – 20+ r – 1 – $1,000.00 – P00033 – us Library Micro [910]
DOS TEHILIM BUKH – Cracow. 1586. Cowley. BJ-43-121 1 – 9 – ne IDC [270]
TEHILLAH LE-MOSHEH / Steinschneider, M – Festschrift. M. Steinschneider. Leipzig. 1896. BJ-100-66 1 – 9 – ne IDC [290]

TEHILLIM – Cracow. 1598. Cowley. BJ-43-123 1 – 9 – ne IDC [270]
TEHILLIM – Mantua. 1562. Cowley. BJ-43-122 1 – 9 – ne IDC [270]
TEHINNAH ZU – Sam Hayyim. Prague. 1590. BJ-43-124 1 – 9 – ne IDC [270]
TEHINNOT – Amsterdam. 1648. BJ-43-126 1 – 9 – ne IDC [270]
TEHINNOT – Amsterdam. 1650. BJ-43-127 1 – 9 – ne IDC [270]
TEHIYAT HA-NEFESH = THE SOUL REVIVED – New York, NY. 1971-72 – 1 – us A.J.P.C. [071]
Teichert, Gerard *see* MUSEUMS AND CHILDREN
Teichmann, Alfred *see* SAVONAROLA IN DER DEUTSCHEN DICHTUNG
TEIGNMOUTH WESTERN GUARDIAN – Totnes, England.1904-07. -w. 4 reels – 1 – uk British Libr Newspaper [072]
TEIKOKU BUNGAKU – Japan, 1895-1921 – 15r – 1 – inquire – us Ross [950]
TEIKOKU GIKAI GIJIROKU = PROCEEDINGS OF THE IMPERIAL DIET OF JAPAN, 1890-1947: THE HOUSE OF PEERS AND REPRESENTATIVES, 1ST-92ND SESSION – 85r and Index in 2r – 1 – Y792,000.00 – ja Yushodo [336]
Teilhard de Chardin, J *see* LA GUINEE SUPERIEURE ET SES MISSIONS
TEILHARD REVIEW – v1- 1966- 1; v10- 1975- 5,6,9 – us UMI [240]
THE TEILHARD REVIEW AND JOURNAL OF CREATIVE EVOLUTION – v17, no.1-. Spring 1982- – 1,5,6,9 – us UMI [575]
Teixeira, Antonio *see* DISCURSO PRONUNCIADO...SOBRE EL PROYECTO DE REFORMA AGRARIA
TEJ – Delhi, India. Mar-18 Oct 1953; 1962-Jun 1966 – 11r – 1 – us L of C Photodup [072]
TEJ WEEKLY – Delhi, India. 18 Apr 1944-18 Dec 1945; 1947-53; 11 Feb 1957-19 Dec 1960; 1961 – 11r – 1 – us L of C Photodup [072]
EL TEJADO DE VIDRIO / Lopez de Ayala, Adelardo – Madrid: R. Velasco, Impresor, 5th ed 1902 – sp Bibl Santa Ana [946]
Tejado, Gabino *see*
– EL CATOLICISMO LIBERAL
– RESPUESTAS CLARAS...CONTRA LA RELIGION
– VICTIMAS Y VERDUGOS
Tejeda. Ayuntamiento *see* ORDENANZAS MUNICIPALES
Tejero Garcia, Angel *see* ESTUDIO SINTETICO SOBRE LA IGLESIA EN LA CONSTITUCION
TEKAMAH JOURNAL – Tekamah, NE. -w. Feb 1900-Aug 1918 – 1 – us NE Hist [071]
TEKELI OU LE SIEGE DE MONTGATZ / Guilbert de Pixerecourt – (French Theatre Series). Paris. Barba, an XII. 1804 – 9 – fr Hachette [820]
TEKHNICHESKIE IZVESTIIA : ORGAN TEKHNICHESKOGO KOMITETA SOVETA NARODNOGO KHOZIAISTVA SEVERNOGO RAIONA – Petrograd: Komitet, 1918-1919. 2v – 1 – CSUX89-S856 – us Hoover Inst Photo [600]
TEKHNICHESKO DELO – Sofia, Bulgaria. Nov 20 1956-Nov 15 1957; Jan 5-Dec 30 1961 – 2r – 1 – us L of C Photodup [072]
TEKHNICHESKOE NORMIROVANIE V PROMYSLOVOI KOOPERATSII : POLOZHENIIA I INSTRUKTSII – M., 1931 – 1mf – 9 – COR-450/1 – ne IDC [334]
TEKHNIKA : ORGAN VYSSHAGO SOVIETA NARODNAGO KHOZIAISTVA – (Library has: nos. 1-2, 4, 1918; nos. 10-13, 1919) – Moskva: Izdatelskaia Sektsiia organizatsii Proizvodstv, 1918-1919. 2v – 1 – CSUX89-S977 – us Hoover Inst Photo [600]
TEKHNIKA I VOORUZHENIE : ORGAN NACHALNIKA VOORUZHENII RKKA – (Includes June-July, Sept.-Dec. 1935; Aug.-Oct., Dec. 1936; Jan., June 1937; Nov. 1938; Jan. 1966-Dec. 1971; July 1979-) – Moskva: Gos. voen. izdvo, 1932- – 1 – CSUX90-S401 – us Hoover Inst Photo [623]
TEKHNIKA STIKHA / Shengeli, G – Ed 2. 1960 – 8 – BR-2121 2 – ne IDC [810]
TEKHNIKA-MOLODYOZHI – Moscow. U.S.S.R. 1961- – 1 – us UMI [073]
TEKIRDAG – Tekirdag: Vilayet Matbaasi. Sahibi: Mehmed Saki. No. 1 (3 Kanunievvel 1341 [1925]) – 9 – $10.00 – us MEDOC [956]
TEKNICHESKO DELO – Sofia, Bulgaria. -w. 25 Feb 1951-1 Jan 1955. 1 reel – 1 – uk British Libr Newspaper [949]

TEKUSHCHAIA LITERATURA / Berkovskii, N I – M. 1930. BR-1997 2 – 8 – ne IDC [460]
TELANG: A MA'ANJAN DAJAK VILLAGE OF CENTRAL KALIMANTAN / Hudson, Alfred B – SE-10,567 1. 1965 – 9 – ne IDC [950]
TELE BILD MIT RADIO – Saarbruecken, 1952-nov 11 1955 – 8r – 1 – gw Mikrofilm [790]
TELECOMMUNICATIONS – 1981-. Global ed – 1,5,6,9 – us UMI [380]
TELECOMMUNICATIONS – International Edition – v1- 1967- 1; v11- 5,6,9 – apply; v.11- – us UMI [621]
TELECOMMUNICATIONS AND ENGINEERING – (v39-. 1984-. 5,6,9) – v1-. 1964- – 1 – us UMI [073]
TELECOMMUNICATIONS. NORTH AMERICAN EDITION – v15-. 1981- – 1,5,6,9 – us UMI [073]
TELECOMMUNICATIONS POLICY – (v7-. 1983-. 5,6,9) – v1-. Dec 1976- – 1 – us UMI [073]
TELEFOONGIDS *see* PENUNDJUK TELEPON, MEDAN
DOS TELEGRAF – Warsaw. v1. 1906 – 1r – 1 – J-92-18/3 – ne IDC [072]
DER TELEGRAF – Berlin, 1953-55 (9r); 1956-jun 1972 (73r) – 1 – us Res Libr [072]
TELEGRAF : BEILAGE: BILD DER ZEIT/BERLIN IM BILD – (Cont: Der Berliner, since may 1 1946) – Berlin, jul 9 1950-oct 28 1951 – 1 – gw Mikrofilm [072]
TELEGRAF – Berlin, 1969-1972 – 16r – 1 – DM1,200.00 – gw Mikro Press [072]
TELEGRAF – Berlin. Germany. -d. 22 Mar 1946-31 Dec 1954. (45 reels) – 1 – uk British Libr Newspaper [072]
TELEGRAF – Berlin, Germany. May-Jul 1952 – 1r – 1 – us L of C Photodup [072]
TELEGRAF : DEUTSCHLANDAUSGABE – (Cont: Der Berliner, since may 1 1946) – Berlin, nov 19 1946-sep 30 1949 – 1 – Dist. gw Mikrofilm – gw Misc Inst [943]
TELEGRAF *see*
– DER BERLINER
EL TELEGRAFO – Guayaquil, Ecuador: [s.n., 1938-39] – 16r – 1 – us Res Libr [072]
TELEGRAM – Bloom. Kan. 1888-1889 – 1 – us UMI [071]
TELEGRAM – Clarksburg. West Virginia. -w. 1890-98, 1900-05, 1907-12 – 1 – us UMI [071]
TELEGRAM – Eau Claire. Wis. 1896-1904 – 1 – us UMI [071]
TELEGRAM – Eau Claire. Wis. -w. 1897-1905 – 1 – us UMI [071]
TELEGRAM – Elyria. Ohio. 1907-19 – 1 – us UMI [071]
TELEGRAM – Garden City. Kan. 1955- – 1 – us UMI [071]
TELEGRAM – Norton. Kan. 1920-1947; 1951- – 1 – us UMI [071]
TELEGRAM – Norton. Kan. -w. 1906-18 – 1 – us UMI [071]
TELEGRAM – Providence. R.I. -w. 1899-1906 – 1 – us UMI [071]
TELEGRAM – Richmond. Ind. 1895-1897 – 1 – us UMI [071]
TELEGRAM – Rocky Mount. N.C. 1971- – 1 – us UMI [071]
TELEGRAM – San Luis Obispo. Calif. 1908-1939 – 1 – us UMI [071]
THE TELEGRAM – Adrian. Mich. 1893- – 1 – us UMI [071]
THE TELEGRAM – New York. Sept 24 1867-Dec 31 1926 – 1 – us NY Public [071]
TELEGRAM AND POST – Bridgeport. Conn. 1918-1929; 1947- – 1 – us UMI [071]
TELEGRAM OBSERVER – Sherbrooke, Canada. ns: 12 jan 1961-v95 n41. 9 sep 1965 – 2r – 1 – Can$70.00r – cn Can Microfilming [072]
TELEGRAM TRIBUNE – San Luis Obispo, CA. 1869- – 580+ r – 1 RC02911 – $29,000.00 ($420.00y) – us Library Micro [071]
LE TELEGRAMME DE BREST ET DE L'OUEST – Morlaix, France.Journal republicain du matin. Toutes eds. oct 1962-juin 1986 – 1 – fr A.C.R.P.P. [072]
TELEGRAMME DE PARIS – Dir. J. Dauer. Paris. fevr 1955-mai juin 1962 – 1 – fr A.C.R.P.P. [073]
TELEGRAMS COLLECTED BY THE OFFICE OF THE SECRETARY OF WAR / U.S. Secretary of War – Bound, 1861-82. 282 rolls. M473 – 1 – us Nat'l Archives [324]

TELEGRAMS COLLECTED BY THE OFFICE OF THE SECRETARY...(UNBOUND), 1860-70 / U.S. War Department. Office of the Secretary – 454 rolls. M504. Printed guide – 1 – us Nat'l Archives [324]
TELEGRAMS RECEIVED BY THE CONFEDERATE SECRETARY OF WAR, 1861-65 / U.S. War Department. Confederate Records – 19 rolls. M618. Printed guide – 1 – us Nat'l Archives [324]
TELEGRAMS SENT BY THE CONFEDERATE SECRETARY OF WAR, 1861-65 / U.S. War Department. Confederate Records – 1roll. M524. Printed guide – 1 – us Nat'l Archives [324]
TELEGRAMS SENT BY THE SECRETARY OF THE TREASURY (XA SERIES), 1850-74 / U.S. Treasury Department – 3rolls. M738. Printed guide – 1 – us Nat'l Archives [336]
TELEGRAM-TRIBUNE – San Luis Obispo. Calif. 1939- – 1 – us UMI [071]
TELEGRAPH – Alton. Ill. and Democratic Review. -W. 1836-53 – 1 – us UMI [071]
TELEGRAPH – Alton. Ill. -w. 1854-1902 – 1 – us UMI [071]
TELEGRAPH – Aurora. Neb. 1878-1879 – 1 – us UMI [071]
TELEGRAPH – Bremen, 1859-63 – 5r – 1 – Inquire at Mikrofilmarchiv for details – gw Misc Inst [943]
TELEGRAPH – Bremen, Germany. 1859-63 – 5r – 1 – gw Mikrofilm [072]
TELEGRAPH – Brownsville. Pa. 1927- – 1 – us UMI [071]
TELEGRAPH – Burlington. Iowa. 1851-1855 – 1 – us UMI [071]
TELEGRAPH – Calcutta, India. Jul 1982-Jul 1995 – 134r – 1 – us L of C Photodup [072]
TELEGRAPH – Dixon. IL. And Herald.-w. 1869-73 – 1 – us UMI [071]
TELEGRAPH – Dixon. Ill. and Lee County Herald. 1851-57 – 1 – us UMI [071]
TELEGRAPH – Dixon. Ill. -w. 1873-81 – 1 – us UMI [071]
TELEGRAPH – Folsom. Calif. -w. 1874-87, 1889-1933, 1956-58 – 1 – us UMI [071]
TELEGRAPH – Grass Valley. Calif. 1854-1858 – 1 – us UMI [071]
TELEGRAPH – Hamilton. Ohio. 1848-1917 – 1 – us UMI [071]
TELEGRAPH – Newburgh. N.Y. 1862-1870; 1874 – 1 – us UMI [071]
TELEGRAPH – Newburgh. N.Y. -w. 1831-67 – 1 – us UMI [071]
TELEGRAPH – North Platte. NE. -w. 1899-1927; 1942-66 – 1 – us UMI [071]
TELEGRAPH – North Platte. Neb. 1881- – 1 – us UMI [071]
TELEGRAPH – Pittsburgh. Pa. -w. 1847-1848; 1875-1880 – 1 – us UMI [071]
TELEGRAPH – Rome. N.Y. 1834-1837 – 1 – us UMI [071]
TELEGRAPH – Seattle. Wash. 1890-1894 – 1 – us UMI [071]
TELEGRAPH – Sharon. Pa. -w. 1894-1914 – 1 – us UMI [071]
TELEGRAPH – Sidney. Neb. 1876-1898; 1900-1963 – 1 – us UMI [071]
TELEGRAPH – (Weekly independent newspaper) – Painesville, OH. july 6, 1830-aug 2, 1831 – 1r – 1 – us Western Res [071]
TELEGRAPH – (Weekly Whig newspaper) – Painesville, OH. nov 23, 1842-oct 15, 1845 – 2r – 1 – us Western Res [071]
THE TELEGRAPH – Norwich. N.Y. and Chronicle. 1868-71 – 1 – us UMI [071]
THE TELEGRAPH – Painesville. Ohio. and Telegraph Republican. 1822- – 1 – us UMI [071]
THE TELEGRAPH – Philadelphia. Pa. 1898-99 – 1 – us A.J.P.C. [071]
THE TELEGRAPH – Quebec, Canada. v1 n33. 10 jun 1867 – 1r – 1 – Can$25.00 – cn Can Microfilming [072]
THE TELEGRAPH – Sacramento, CA. 1976 – 1r – 1 – $50.00 – C02743 – us Library Micro [071]
TELEGRAPH AND ARGUS – Bradford, Yorkshire. 1975-77; 1981-to date – 1 – uk Microform Academic [072]
TELEGRAPH AND POLITICAL REVIEW – St. John's, Canada. 1862-73 – 2r – 1 – $136.00 – cn Library Assoc [971]
TELEGRAPH AND SANTA CLARA COUNTY REGISTER – San Jose, CA. 1853-60 – 3r – 1 – $150.00 – B02893 – us Library Micro [071]
TELEGRAPH AND TELEPHONE AGE – v. 27-71. 1910-1953 – 1,5,6 – us Princeton Micro [600]
TELEGRAPH AND TRIBUNE – Indianapolis. Ind. 1907-1918 – 1 – us UMI [071]
TELEGRAPH & ARGUS – Bradford, England. 1964-76. -d. 156 reels – 1 – uk British Libr Newspaper [072]
THE TELEGRAPH. (BRISBANE TELEGRAPH) – Brisbane, Australia. 1 Jan 1884-31 Dec 1888; 5 Apr 1911-30 Jun 1922; 1 Jan 1952-29 Jun 1968 (missing Apr 1952, May 1966).-d. 302 reels – 1 – uk British Libr Newspaper [072]
TELEGRAPH & GUARDIAN. (DAILY TELEGRAPH) – Kingston, Jamaica. 8 Jan 1910-25 May 1912 (imperfect).-d. 5 reels – 1 – uk British Libr Newspaper [072]
THE TELEGRAPH OR, CONNAUGHT RANGER – Castlegbar, Ireland. Connaught Telegraph. -w. 22 Sept 1830-31 Aug 1870; 13 May 1876-Dec 1947. 93 1 2 reels – 1 – uk British Libr Newspaper [072]
LE TELEGRAPHE – Paris. juil-dec 1882 – 1 – fr A.C.R.P.P. [073]
LE TELEGRAPHE = THE TELEGRAPH – Quebec, Canada. 20 mar-3 jun 1837 – 1r – 1 – Can$40.00 – cn Can Microfilming [072]
TELEGRAPH-HERALD – Dubuque. Iowa. 1860- – 1 – us UMI [071]
TELEGRAPHIC SIGNALS, OR MARINE VOCABULARY; WITH OBSERVATIONS ON SIGNAL FLAGS, AND THE BEST MODE OF APPLYING THEM / Popham, Home Riggs – 1812 – 9 – $20.00 – uk Libr Preservation [380]
THE TELEGRAPH-JOURNAL – St John, New Brunswick, CN. 1970- – 12r per yr – 1 – Can$55.00r – cn Commonwealth Micro [072]
O TELEGRAPHO : PERIODICO CRITICO E JOCO-SERIO – Maceio, Alagoas. 1 Fev-31 Mar 1877 – 1,5,6 – bl Biblioteca [072]
O TELEGRAPHO – Sao Luiz, 28 Dec 1876. Oct, Dec 1877. Aug, Dec 1878. May-Jul 1880. Apr 1881. Jun, Sep, Dec 1882. May, Jul, 7 Dec 1883 – 1,5,6 – bl Biblioteca [072]
TELEGRAPH/ORANGEVALE NEWS – Folsom, CA. 1980 – 28+ r – 1 – $1,400.00 ($100.00y) – H04078 – us Library Micro [071]
LE TELE-JOURNAL / ed by Lalonde, Pierre – Montreal, 13/19 jan 1969-v1 n37. 29 sep 1969 – 1r – 1 – Can$40.00 – cn Can Microfilming [380]
Telemann, G M *see*
– PREUSSISCHE KRIEGSLIEDER IN DER FELDZUGEN 1756 UND 1757 VON EINEM GRENADIER
– UNTERRICHT IM GENERALBASS-SPIELEN AUF. DER ORGEL ODER SONST EINEM CLAVIER-INSTRUMENTE
TELEMAQUE / Egville, J d' – London: Birchall, 180- – 1 – us Sibley [780]
TELEMARKETING UPDATE; DIRECTORY OF SCRIPT PRESENTATIONS – 1992 – 9 – $49.95 – us Continnuus [650]
TELEMATICS AND INFORMATICS – v1- 1984- – 5,6,9 – us UMI [000]
TELEPHE EN 12 LIVRES / Pechmeja, Jean de – (Utopias in the Enlightenment series). 1784 – 9 – fr Hachette [830]
THE TELEPHONE – Conway. S.C. 1880 – 1 – us UMI [071]
THE TELEPHONE – Moncton, N.B.: J.S. Cowie, [1884-18– or 19–] – 9 – cn C.I.H.M. [170]
TELEPHONE AND TELEGRAPH JOURNAL – v. 1-20. 1914-1933 – 1,5,6 – us Princeton Micro [380]
TELEPHONE BOOK (DUTCH) / Netherlands – Updated twenty times a year – 9 – ne Sdu MICRO [380]
TELEPHONE ENGINEER AND MANAGEMENT – (Formerly: Telephone Engineer). v. 1-45. 1909-1941 – 1,5,6 – us Princeton Micro [621]
TELEPHONE MAGAZINE – v. 1-25. 1893-1905 – 1,5,6 – us Princeton Micro [380]
TELEPHONE NEWS – 1980- – 1,5,6,9 – us UMI [380]
TELEPHONE-REGISTER – McMinnville. Or. -w. 1893-1953 – 1 – us UMI [071]
TELEPHONE-REGISTER – McMinnville, OR. -w. 1893-1953 – 1 – 706.00 – us Oregon Hist [071]
TELEPHONE-REGISTER – McMinnville, OR. -w. 21 Nov 1889 – 30 Dec 1897. – 1 – us U.O. Library [071]
TELEPHONY, THE AMERICAN TELEPHONE JOURNAL – v. 1-150. 1901-56 – 1,5,6 – us Princeton Micro [621]
TELE-RADIOMONDE – Montreal: Telemonde Inc. v24-47. 1962-85. SEM35P98 – 41r – 1 – Can$2,080.00 – cn Bibl Nat [072]
TELERAMA – France. 1988-1995 – 3r per y – 5,6 – Sfr695.00 – sz Infoprint [790]
TELESALES SCRIPT PRESENTATIONS DIRECTORY / Dasta Notes Staff – Denver, Co., 1991 – 1mf – 9 – $25.00 – 0-911569-91-X – us Continnuus [338]
THE TELESCOPE – London. -w. 12 Dec 1824-11 Dec 1825. (32 ft) – 1 – uk British Libr Newspaper [072]
TELESCOPE-MESSENGER – v113-129, 1947-63. Title varies – 1 – us A.T.L.A. [073]
THE TELESCOPIC MESSENGER – (Supersedes: Religious Telescope, 1834-1946) – v113-129. 1947-63 (complete) – 17r – 1 – ATLA S0082 – us A.T.L.A. [073]
TELE-SOLEIL – Quebec, 7-14 mar 1981-7 jan 1982 – 1r – 1 – Can$40.00 – cn Can Microfilming [072]
TELEVIDENIE I RADIOVESHCHANIE – Moscow, 1970-90 – 257mf – 9 – $1,700.00 – us Ross [790]
TELEVISION. : THE JOURNAL OF THE ROYAL TELEVISION SOCIETY / Royal Television Society – 1928-83 – 12r – 1 – £755.00 £65.00r – uk Chadwyck [621]
TELEVISION AND CHILDREN – (1983-. 1,5,6,9) – v3-. 1980- – 1 – us UMI [380]
TELEVISION AND RURAL ADULT EDUCATION / Dumazedier, Joffre – UNESCO. 1956 – 8mf – 7 – uk Microform Academic [370]
TELEVISION EN EL CUARTO DE ESTAR / Perez Lozano, Jose Maria – Madrid: PPC, 1966 – 1 – sp Bibl Santa Ana [380]
THE TELEVISION ERA – 1942-71. (From Kine Weekly 1907-71) – 1 – uk World [380]
TELEVISION/RADIO AGE – v1- 1953- 1; v25- 5,6,9 – us UMI [621]
TELFAIR AVENUE BAPTIST CHURCH, MISSION OF FIRST SOUTHERN BAPTIST CHURCH, NORTH HOLLYWOOD. SUN VALLEY, CALIFORNIA : CHURCH RECORDS – 1953-64 – 1 – 7.43 – us Baptist [240]
Telford, Thomas *see* REPORTS, PAPERS, ETC. RELATING TO THE PUBLIC WORKS
TELHAMED OU ENTRETIENS D'UN PHILOSOPHE INDIEN AVEC UN MISSIONAIRE FRANCAIS SUR LA DIMINUTION DE LA MER, LA FORMATION DE LA TERRE, L'ORIGINE DE L'HOMME / Maillet, Benoit de – D'apres Barbier. Amsterdam: L'Honore et Fils, 1748. (Philosophy Collection; Religion Series) – 6mf – 9 – $18.00 – fr Bibl Nationale [190]
THE TELL AMARNA TABLETS = TELL EL-AMARNA TABLETS – (Includes index) – 2nd ed. [London?]: A P Watt, 1894 – 1mf – 9 – 0-8370-7452-5 – 1986-1452 – us A.T.L.A. [930]
TELL EL AMARNA / Petrie, William Matthew Flinders – Methuen and Co., 1894 – 9 – $10.00 – us I.R.C. [930]
THE TELL EL-AMARNA TABLETS / ed by Mercer, Samuel A B – Macmillan, 1939 – 9 – $30.00 – us I.R.C. [930]
TELL HASSUNA / Lloyd, Seton – 1945 – 9 – $10.00 – us I.R.C. [930]
Tell, Torcuato S di et al *see* ARGENTINA, SOCIEDAD DE MASAS
TELL UQAIR / Lloyd, Seton – 1943 – 9 – $10.00 – us I.R.C. [930]
Telle, J A *see* LES GRAMMAIRIENS FRANCAIS
THE TELL-EL-AMARNA-LETTERS = TELL EL-AMARNA TABLETS / Winckler, Hugo – (In English and Akkadian) – New York: Lemcke & Buechner; Berlin: Reuther & Reichard, 1896 – 2mf – 9 – 0-8370-7517-3 – 1986-1517 – us A.T.L.A. [470]
Tellenbach, Gerd *see* GOETHES GESCHICHTLICHER SINN
TELLIAMED, OU ENTRETIENS D'UN PHILOSOPHE INDIEN AVEC UN MISSIONAIRE FRANCAIS SUR LA DIMINUTION DE LA MER, LA FORMATION DE LA TERRE, L'ORIGINE DE L'HOMME / Maillet, Benoit de – Amsterdam, 1748, 2 tomes, 208 plus 231 p. Histoire des Sciences XVIIe-XIXe Siecles. 7932 3 – 9 – fr Hachette [577]
Tellier, G *see* AUTOUR DE KITA
TELLS OF EXPLOITS AS REBEL DESERTER – n.p., n.d. Fiche W1223. (Blodgett Collection of Spanish Civil War Pamphlets) – 9 – us H.U. College Libr [946]
Tel'man, I *see* DVISTI SVIDKIV
Telmann, Fritz *see* DIE GUTEN CHRISTEN
Telmon, Soeur *see* BIO-BIBLIOGRAPHIE DE LA R.S. GABRIEL-LALEMANT, S.G.C., B.A., B.ED., CONSEILLERE PEDAGOGIQUE AU SECRETARIAT NATIONALE DE LA J.E.C. A MONTREAL
Telting, A *see* BEZOEK AAN EEN NEDERLANDSCHE STAD IN DE XIVE EEUW
A TELUGU-ENGLISH CLASSICAL DICTIONARY : A VOCABULARY FROM PANCHATNATRA, MITRABHEDAMU, BK 1, VEMANA'S FIRST 50 STANZAS, AND NALOPAKHYANAM, THE WHOLE / Holler, P – Rajahmundry: Printed at Vivekavardhani Press, 1900 – us Res Libr [490]
TELUGU-ENGLISH DICTIONARY / Brown, Charles Philip – New ed. 1903 – 1 – us A.T.L.A. [490]
TELUK GONG / Lukman, Karmani – SE-4884 1. 1964 – 9 – ne IDC [950]
TEMAS ALEMAES / Erwin, Theodor – (Includes bibliographical references) – Sao Paulo: Conselho Estadual de Cultura, Commissao de Literatura, [1965] – 1 – us U.W. Library [440]
TEMASA – (Sahibi: Seyyid Tahir, Mueduer-i Mes'ul: Sueleyman Tevfik. No. 21 (1 Nisan 1336[1920])) – Istanbul: Kader Matbaasi, 1918-1920 – 1mf – 9 – $12.00 – us MEDOC [949]
TEMASA – (Sahibi ve Mueessisi: Melih Fikret, Mueduer-i Mes'ul ve Sermuharriri: Mehmed Raif. No. 3 (4 Eyluel 1324[1908])) – Istanbul, 1908-? – 1mf – 9 – $12.00 – us MEDOC [949]
TEMATIKA ISSLEDOVANII PO DOKUMENTAL'NYM MATERIALAM / U.S.S.R. Tsentral'nykh Gosudarstvennykh Arkhivakh SSSR – 12v. Spravochnik. M. 1964-74. Glavnoe arkhivnoe upravlenie PKG-B-0.5 BR-11,316 1 – 9 – ne IDC [324]
TEMBULAND NEWS – (Filming in progress) – Elliott, South Africa, 26 Feb 1907-22 Dec 1922 – 11r – 1,16 diazo also available – sa SA Libr [960]
TEMECULA WEEK – Temecula, CA. 1989 – 2+ r – 1 – $100.00 ($100.00y) – R04129 – us Library Micro [071]
TEMISKAMING SPEAKER – Ontario, CN. 1941- – 2r per yr – 1 – Can$55.00r – cn Commonwealth Micro [072]
Temminck, C J *see* VERHANDELINGEN OVER DE NATUURLIJKE GESCHIEDENIS DER NEDERLANDSCHE OVERZEESCHE BEZITTINGEN,...
Temminck, C J *see* NOUVEAU RECUEIL DE PLANCHES COLORIEES D'OISEAUX
TEMNYE ALLEI / Bunin, Ivan Alekseevich – Paris: La Presse francaise et etrangere, (c1946). 324p.In Cyrillic characters – 1 – us U.W. Library [947]
TEMOIGNAGE CHRETIEN – Paris. aout 1944-86 – 1 – fr A.C.R.P.P. [240]
TEMOINS DE L'HOMME : LA CONDITION HUMAINE DANS LA LITTERATURE CONTEMPORAINE / Simon, P H – F50.00 – fr Ethnologie [440]
TEMORA HERALD AND MINING JOURNAL – Apr 21 1882-Apr 6 1883 – 1 – at Pascoe [072]
TEMORA INDEPENDENT – Dec 30 1896-Dec 29 1906 – 1 – at Pascoe [072]
TEMORA STAR – Sep 7 1881-Aug 10 1883; Jan 4 1899-Dec 29 1906 – 1 – at Pascoe [072]
TEMOTIMES – Temiscamingue, Canada. 6 jan 1950; v23 n22. 2 jun 1972 – 1r – 1 – Can$25.00 – cn Can Microfilming [072]
DER TEMPELHOFER – Berlin, 1947-52 – 1 – Inquire at Mikrofilmarchiv for details – gw Misc Inst [072]
Tempels, Holger *see* SUPERVISION IN DER STATIONAEREN ALTENPFLEGE – UEBERLEGUNGEN ZUR SICHERUNG DER PFLEGEQUALITAET
DIE TEMPELSAENGER IM ALTEN TESTAMENT: EIN VERSUCH / Koeberle, Justus – Erlangen: Fr. Junge, 1899. 1 fiche – 9 – us A.T.L.A. [240]
TEMPERANCE AND PROHIBITION COLLECTION / Ohio Historical Society – (vAmerican nvIssue. n National ed. Jan 1900-Dec 1933. 11 rolls. American Issue Publishing Company. vPapers, n1911-39, 1950. 17 rolls. vAmerican nvPatriot. n Apr 1912-Aug 1916. 2 rolls. Anti-Saloon League of America. vPapers, n1880, 1894-1938. 17 rolls. Anti-Saloon League of the District of Columbia. vPapers, n1902-28. 3 rolls. Anti-Saloon League of Ohio. vPapers, n1894-95, 1902-33. 8 rolls. Cherrington, Ernest H. vPapers, n1900-50. 110 rolls. Intercollegiate Prohibition Association. vPapers, n1885-1940,

1963. 7 rolls. McBride, F. Scott. vPapers, n1924-26. 15 rolls. Mid-Nineteenth Century Series, 1830-75. (24 small collections). 2 rolls. vNational nvDaily. n Jun 1915-Dec 1916. 2 rolls. vNew nvRepublic. n Jan 1913-Dec 1916. 1 roll. Office of Gen. Council, Legislative Superintendent of the Anti-Saloon League of America. vPapers. n 15 rolls. Prohibition Party. vPapers, n1868-1933. 2 rolls. Russell, Howard H. vPapers, n1842-1946. 8 rolls. Scientific Temperance Federation. Papers, 1881-1934. 67 rolls. Standard Encyclopedia of the Alcohol Problem. 1904, 1919-31. 5 rolls. Steuart, Thomas J. vPapers, n1927-33. 10 ROLLS. vTemperance nvMinute nvbook nof Hillsboro, Ohio, 1873-82. 1 roll. vUnion nvSignal. n Jan 1883-Dec 1933. 37 rolls. W.C.T.U. (Woman's Christian Temperance Union). vPapers, n1853-1939. 49 rolls. World League Against Alcoholism. vPapers, n1900-36. 28 rolls) – Series Listings: – 1 – us Ohio Hist [978]

TEMPERANCE AND PROHIBITION PAPERS, 1830-1933 / ed by Bordin, Ruth M – (With printed guide £47.00. Series available separately: The Records of Organizations: Mid.Nineteenth Century Temperance Movt 1830-75 £154; Prohibition Party 1868-1933 £154; Woman's Christian Temperance Union 1853-1939 £2,700; Intercollegiate Prohibition Assoc 1892-1963 £500; Ohio Anti-Saloon League 1893-1933 £540; District of Columbia Anti-Saloon League 1902-28 £230; Anti-Saloon League of America 1894-1938 £1,050; Office of General Counsel & Legislative Superintendent, Anti-Saloon League of America 1883-1933 £940; Scientific Temperance Federation 1881-1934 £3,640; American Issue Publ Co 1909-34 £1,050; World League Against Alcoholism 1900-37 £1,765; Standard Encyclopedia of the Alcohol Problem 1904-30 £380. Archives & Papers of Individuals: Ernest Hurst Cherrington 1877-1950 £5,955; Francis Scott McBride 1872-1955 £940; Howard Hyde Russell 1855-1946 £550; Thomas Justin Steuart £710. Periodicals: American Issue 1900-33 £700; American Patriot 1912-16 £155; National Daily 1915-16 £155; New Republic 1913-16 £78; Union Signal 1883-1933 £2,095) – From the Michigan Historical Collections, Ohio Historical Society, Woman's Christian Temperance Union, Westerville Public Library – 424r – 13 – £22,990.00 – uk Chadwyck [360]

TEMPERANCE MINUTE BOOKS – Ed. by Charles A. Isetts. Hillsboro, Ohio. 1873-82 – 1 – us Ohio Hist [360]

THE TEMPERANCE MONITOR – [Quebec?: s.n. 1831-183-?] – 9 – cn C.I.H.M. [170]

TEMPERANCE STANDARD BEARERS OF THE NINETEENTH CENTURY: A BIOGRAPHICAL AND STATISTICAL TEMPERANCE DICTIONARY / Winskill, Peter T – Liverpool: Peter T. Winskill, 1898. 2v – 1 – us U.W. Library [920]

TEMPERANCE STAR – Portland OR. Nov 21 1874, Aug 12 1875 – 1 – us U.O. Library [071]

[THE TEMPEST] COME UNTO THESE YELLOW SANDS / Purcell, Henry – London: Birchall, 1795? – 1 – us Sibley [780]

TEMPESTA : TRAUERSPIEL IN FUENF ACTEN / Saar, Ferdinand von – Heidelberg: Georg Weiss, 1881 – 1r – 1 – us U.W. Library [820]

THE TEMPLAR QUARTERLY – Hamilton [Ont]: Templar Pub. House, [1895-189- or 19–] – 9 – cn C.I.H.M. [170]

TEMPLARKURIREN – Stockholm, 1922-38 – 9 – sw Kungliga [072]

THE TEMPLE – Louisville, KY. 1909-10 – 1 – us A.J.P.C. [071]

TEMPLE BAPTIST CHURCH. KINGS MOUNTAIN, NORTH CAROLINA : CHURCH RECORDS – 1945-63 – 1 – 23.67 – us Baptist [240]

TEMPLE BAR – A London Magazine for Town and Country Readers. v. 1-134. Dec 1860-Dec 1906 – 1 – 747.00 – us L of C Photodup [073]

Temple Church, Saline County, KS *see* RECORDS

TEMPLE ENVIRONMENTAL LAW AND TECHNOLOGY JOURNAL – (Title varies: v1-2 1982-83 as Outlook Environmental Law Journal) – v1-14. 1982-95 – 1,9 – $124.00 set – us Hein [340]

THE TEMPLE IN THE TIME OF CHRIST AS RESTORED BY HEROD / Butler, Carlos A – New York: Carlos A. Butler, 1900. 1 fiche – 9 – us A.T.L.A. [240]

TEMPLE INTERNATIONAL AND COMPARATIVE LAW – v1-9. 1985-95 – 9 – $99.00set – us Hein [340]

TEMPLE LAW QUARTERLY / Temple University – v1-52, 1927-79 – 1,5 – 600.00 – us Gaunt [370]

TEMPLE LAW QUARTERLY *see* TEMPLE LAW REVIEW

TEMPLE LAW REVIEW – (Title varies: v1-61 1927-87 as Temple Law Quarterly) – v1-68. 1927-1995 – 9 – Inquire – us Hein [340]

THE TEMPLE OF DEIR EL BAHARI (MEES VOL 12) : ITS PLAN, ITS FOUNDERS AND ITS FIRST EXPLORERS / Naville, E – London, 1894 – 3mf – 8 – Dfl13.00 – ne Slangenburg [720]

THE TEMPLE OF IMPOSTURE : A POEM / Combe, William – London, 1778 – 1mf – 9 – MP-532/1 – ne IDC [810]

THE TEMPLE OF JERUSALEM / Parrot, Andre – S.C.M. Press, 1957 – 9 – $10.00 – us I.R.C. [270]

TEMPLE OF REASON – New York, NY. 1800-01. Also: Temple of Reason, Philadelphia, 1801-03. Sold as one unit – 3 – us Readex [290]

TEMPLE OF THE HEIGHTS – Cleveland, OH, 7/5/1891-5/30/1920 – 1r – 1 – us I.H.R.C. [270]

THE TEMPLE OF THE NINETIES / Alexander, Gilchrist G – London: Hodge & Co, 1938 – 4mf – 9 – $6.00 – LLMC 84-270 – us L.L.M.C. [340]

TEMPLE POLITICAL AND CIVIL RIGHTS LAW REVIEW – v1-4. 1992-95 – 9 – $557.00 set – us Hein [340]

Temple, Richard *see* LIFE OF SIR JOHN HAWLEY GLOVER

Temple, Sarah *see* FIRST FIVE HUNDRED YEARS

Temple University *see* TEMPLE LAW QUARTERLY

THE TEMPLE...IN THE TIME OF OUR SAVIOUR / Fisher, Elliot D – Rock Island: Kramer, 1901. 1 fiche – 9 – us A.T.L.A. [240]

Templeman, A B *see* ENGINEERING OPTIMIZATION

TEMPLES AND TOMBS OF ANCIENT NUBIA : THE INTERNATIONAL RESCUE CAMPAIGN AT ABU SIMBEL, PHILAE AND OTHER SITES / ed by Saeve-Soederbergh, Torgny – 1987 – 9 – 92-3-102383-7 – Co-published with Thames and Hudson, London, who have exclusive sales rights in the UK and USA – fr UNESCO [720]

TEMPLES AT TRICHINOPOLY / India. Preservation of National Monuments; ed by Cole, H H – Calcutta, 1884. BI-689 2 – 8 – ne IDC [720]

TEMPLES OF THE JEWS AND OTHER BUILDINGS IN THE HARAM AREA OF JERUSALEM / Fergusson, James – London: John Murray, 1878. 1 fiche – 9 – us A.T.L.A. [270]

TEMPLETON 1760-1895 – 51mf – 9 – us Holbrook [920]

Templeton, John Stewart *see* A LAYMAN'S MIND ON CREED AND CHURCH

TEMPLETON TIMES – (Also known as: Eaglet Times, Atascadero Times) – Templeton, CA. 1913-1921 – 2r – 1 – $100.00 – C03548 – us Library Micro [071]

LES TEMPLIERS / Raynouard – (French Theatre Series). Paris. Giguet et Michaud, an XIII. 1805 – 9 – fr Hachette [820]

EL TEMPLO DE AMMON Y LOS PITAGORICOS / Gonzalez Alonso, Diego – 1839 – 9 – 1.50f – sp Bibl Santa Ana [930]

EL TEMPLO DE SANTA EULALIA DE MERIDA / Monsalud, Marques de – Madrid: Est. Tip. Fortanet, 1907. B.R.A.H. Tomo 50, 1907, pp. 442-456 – 1 – sp Bibl Santa Ana [240]

IL TEMPO – 1987-1995 – 6r per y – 5,6 – Sfr1,176.00 – sz Infoprint [072]

O TEMPO – Itabira, 25 Jan 1891 – 1,5,6 – bl Biblioteca [072]

O TEMPO – Maceio, Alagoas. 14 Abr 1860 – 1,5,6 – bl Biblioteca [072]

O TEMPO : ORGAM INDEPENDENTE E NOTICIOSO, DEDICADO AOS INTERESSES DA ZONA DO RIO DOCE – Caratinga, 21 Jul-21 Dec 1933 – 1,5,6 – bl Biblioteca [072]

O TEMPO : ORGAO DEDICADO AOS INTERESSES DO MUNICIPIO – Queluz de Minas, 8 Feb 1928-22 Jan 1930 – 1,5,6 – bl Biblioteca [072]

O TEMPO : ORGAO DO PARTIDO CONSERVADOR – '(s.l.')-Sao Luis, Brazil. 5 Jan 1880-29 Aug 1881 – 1,5,6 – bl Biblioteca [072]

O TEMPO – Sao Paulo, Brazil. 1930; Jan-Apr, Jul-Aug. Oct 1931 – 1 – bl Biblioteca [072]

TEMPO – Berlin, 1928-33 – 15r – 1 – gw Mikrofilm [072]

TEMPO – Berlin, 1928-33 – 15r – 1 – Inquire at Mikrofilmarchiv for details – gw Misc Inst [072]

TEMPO : IN PACE WITH THE CHANGING CHURCH – v1-3 no 2, 15 Oct 19968-1970 (complete) – 1r – 1 – ATLA S0200 – us A.T.L.A. [073]

TEMPO – Lisbon. No.7-248. 10 Jul 1975-7 Feb 1980. Incomplete. (Portuguese Revolution of 1974. Newspapers from Portugal publ. from 21 Feb 1971 to 15 Feb 1980, collected and filmed by University of Wisconsin-Madison libraries.) – 1 – us U.W. Library [072]

TEMPO BRASILEIRO – Rio de Janeiro, BL. 1962-1970 – 1r – $50.00 – R04183 – us Library Micro [073]

TEMPO; THE MODERN MUSICAL NEWSMAGAZINE – Los Angeles. v. 3, no. 11-4, no. 12; 6, no. 1-3. May 1936-Jun 1937; Jul-Sep 1938 – 1 – us NY Public [780]

TEMPORAL AND SPATIAL AGRICULTURAL DEVELOPMENT IN THE SUDAN – 1989 – 98p – it F.A.O. [630]

TEMPORAL POWER / Corelli, Marie – British Fiction Archive: Unit 1 – 9 – uk Bell [830]

TEMPORARY ADMINISTRATIVE CONFERENCE OF THE UNITED STATES : 1953 REPORT – Washington: GPO, 1955 (all publ) – 2mf – 9 – $3.00 – LLMC 82-208 – us L.L.M.C. [324]

TEMPORARY ADMINISTRATIVE CONFERENCE OF THE U.S. : 1961 REPORTS / Administrative Conference of the U.S. (ACUS). Subcomm on Administrative Practice and Procedure od the Senate Judiciary Committee – Washington: GPO. no 24 88th Congress 1st session. 1963 – 5mf – 9 – $7.50 – LLMC 82-209 – us L.L.M.C. [324]

THE TEMPORARY AND THE PERMANENT IN NEW TESTAMENT REVELATION / Nichols, Harry Peirce – (Includes bibliographical references) – New York: Thomas Whittaker, c1905 – 1mf – 9 – 0-8370-4583-5 – 1985-2583 – us A.T.L.A. [220]

TEMPORARY NATIONAL ECONOMIC COMMITTEE; INVESTIGATION OF CONCENTRATION OF ECONOMIC POWER : "O'MAHONEY COMMITTEE HEARINGS – Washington: GPO. v1-13 + monographs. 1938-41 (all publ) – 250mf – 9 – $375.00 – LLMC 81-243 – us L.L.M.C. [324]

LE TEMPOREL DE LA SITUATION FINANCIERE DES ETABLISSEMENTS DE L'ORDRE DE CLUNY DU 12E AU 14E SIECLE / Valous, G de – 1935 – Dfl22.00 – ne Slangenburg [240]

LE TEMPS – Journal des progres politiques, scientifiques, litteraires et industriels. Fond. Jacques Coste. Paris. 15 oct 1829-17 juin 1842. AR. Jo. 781 – 1 – fr A.C.R.P.P. [944]

LE TEMPS / ed by Marchand, Felix-Gabriel – Montreal, Canada. 7 jul-15 oct 1883 – 1r – 1 – Can$35.00 – cn Can Microfilming [072]

LE TEMPS – Paris. France. Jan 1919-Nov 1942 – 1 – 35.00r – us Hoover Inst Photo [073]

LE TEMPS – Paris, France. Journal de la Republique progressive. Red. en chef Xavier Durrieu. Ed. du matin. 1er mars-12 dec 1849 – 1 – fr A.C.R.P.P. [944]

LE TEMPS – Paris, France. Journal quotidien politique et litteraire. 25 avr 1861-30 nov 1942 – 1 – fr A.C.R.P.P. [944]

LE TEMPS – Paris: Impr Schiller, [1861-1942]. jun 30 1938-jun 4 1940 – 1 – us Res Libr [072]

LE TEMPS – Port-au-Prince. Haiti. apr. 6, 1929-Dec. 1931; May 1, 3, 1935 – 1 – us NY Public [072]

LE TEMPS – Quebec, Canada. 13-27 avr 1882 – 1r – 1 – Can$25.00 – cn Can Microfilming [072]

LE TEMPS : QUOTIDIEN – Ottawa, Ontario. vA n1. 3 nov 1894-31 dec 1915 – 41r – 1 – Can$60.00r – cn Can Microfilming [072]

LE TEMPS : REFORMISTE – Montreal, Canada. 18 jul 1838-30 oct 1838 – 1r – 1 – Can$30.00 – cn Can Microfilming [072]

LE TEMPS : UNION NATIONALE – (Cont by: Le Temps Nouveau 15 oct 1969-21 oct 1971. Cont by: L'Unite 11 nov 1971-22 jul 1973. Cont by: Le Temps fev-jul 1973) – Quebec, Canada. 8 nov 1940-2 aut 1969 – 14r – 1 – Can$55.00r – cn Can Microfilming [072]

LE TEMPS *see* LE TEMPS

LE TEMPS DE MONTREAL : SUPPLEMENT ILLUSTRE DU SAMEDI – Montreal Canada. v1 n3. 15 nov 1919 – 1r – 1 – Can$25.00 – cn Can Microfilming [072]

LE TEMPS NOUVEAU *see* LE TEMPS

LES TEMPS NOUVEAUX – Supplement litteraire. Paris. mai 1895-juil 1914 – 1 – fr A.C.R.P.P. [800]

TEMPS NOUVEAUX D'AFRIQUE – Usumbura: [1957-may 1962] – 6r – 1 – us Res Libr [073]

LE TEMPS PERDU, OU LES ECOLES PUBLIQUES / Maubert de Gouvest, Jean-Henri – Amsterdam: Fr. Changuion, 1765. 146p. 2 fiches. (Education Collection) – 9 – 6.00 – fr Bibl Nationale [370]

LE TEMPS PERDU OU LES ECOLES PUBLIQUES, CONSIDERATIONS D'UN PATRIOTE SUR L'EDUCATION DE LA PREMIERE JEUNESSE EN FRANCE AVEC L'IDEE D'UN NOUVEAU COLLEGE ET LE PRECIS DE L'INSTRUCTION QUI Y SERAIT DONNEE / Maubert De Gouvest, Jean-Henri – Amsterdam. Fr. Changuion. 1765. 6773 – 9 – fr Hachette [944]

TEMPS PRESENT – no. 1-133. Paris. nov 1937-juin 1940; n.s., no. 1-126 127. 26 aout 1944-24 janv 1947 – 1 – fr A.C.R.P.P. [944]

THE TEMPTATION OF CHRIST / Barrett, George Slatyer – New York: Macmillan, 1883 – 1mf – 9 – 0-8370-2185-5 – 1985-0185 – us A.T.L.A. [240]

THE TEMPTATION OF JESUS: A STUDY OF OUR LORD'S TRIAL IN THE WILDERNESS / Stewart, Alexander Morris – London: Andrew Melrose, 1903. 1 fiche – 9 – us A.T.L.A. [240]

TEMPTATION OF OUR LORD...AS RELATED TO...MINISTRY AND AS A REVELATION OF HIS PERSON / Knight, Henry JC – London: Longmans, Green, 1907. 1 fiche – 9 – us A.T.L.A. [240]

TEMPTED TO UNBELIEF / Burr, Enoch Fitch – New York: American Tract Society, 1882. 1 fiche – 9 – us A.T.L.A. [240]

TEMPUS – (New York Times Weekly Review, 1983-86) – Stockholm, Sweden. 1980- – 1 – sw Kungliga [072]

TEN CAMEOS FROM DARKEST AFRICA : STORIES OF PIONEER WORK AMONG COLOURED AND AFRICAN BLIND / Blaxall, Arthur William – [Lovedale, South Africa]: Lovedale Press, [1937] – us Res Libr [960]

TEN COMMANDMENTS / Dale, Robert William – London: Hodder & Stoughton, 1885. 1 fiche – 9 – us A.T.L.A. [240]

THE TEN COMMANDMENTS / Dale, Robert William – 5th ed. London:Hodder and Stoughton, 1885 – 1mf – 9 – 0-8370-2805-1 – 1985-0805 – us A.T.L.A. [220]

THE TEN COMMANDMENTS AND THE LORD'S PRAYER : A SOCIOLOGICAL STUDY / Schenck, Ferdinand Schureman – New York:Funk & Wagnalls, 1902 – 1mf – 9 – 0-8370-5083-9 – 1985-3083 – us A.T.L.A. [220]

TEN COMMANDMENTS EXPLAINED IN SERMONIC LECTURES / Dallmann, William Henry – Pittsburgh: Amer. Luth. Pub. Board, 1900. 1 fiche – 9 – us A.T.L.A. [240]

TEN DIARIES AND OTHER UNPUBLISHED WORKS IN MANUSCRIPT. / Backus, Isaac – 1724-1806. 1885p – 1 – 65.97 – us Baptist [920]

Ten Hoor, George J *see* BILDER AUS DER SCHWEIZ

TEN HUMAN RIGHTS POINTS FROM THEIR 1971 WORK, A CONSTITUTION FOR A MORAL GOVERNMENT / Anderson, Jack & Miles, Perry – 9 – 1.00f – at Libertarian Micro [320]

TEN LECTURES ON THE MARTYRS / Allard, Paul – New York: Benziger, 1907. (The International Catholic library; v.3) – 1mf – us A.T.L.A. [240]

TEN MAKERS OF MODERN PROTESTANT THOUGHT: SCHWEITZER, RAUSCHENBUSCH, TEMPLE, KIERKEGAARD, BARTH, BRUNNER, NIEBUHR, TILLICH, BULTMANN, BUBER / ed by Hunt, George Laird – 1958 – 1 – us A.T.L.A. [240]

TEN MINUTES' READINGS IN THE BOOK OF GENESIS / Spooner, Edward – London: Hamilton, Adams, 1870.1 fiche – 9 – us A.T.L.A. [240]
TEN MONTHS IN BRAZIL: WITH INCIDENTS OF VOYAGES AND TRAVELS, DESCRIPTIONS OF SCENERY AND CHARACTER, NOTICES OF COMMERCE. / Codman, John – Boston: Lee and Shepard, 1867. 208p. plates – 1 – us U.W. Library [910]
TEN NEQUDOTH OF THE TORAH...THE EXTRAORDINARY POINTS OF THE PENTATEUCH / Butin, Romain F – Baltimore: J.H. Furst, 1906. 1 fiche – 9 – us A.T.L.A. [270]
TEN' OT PAL'MY / Gumilev, Nikolai Sepanovich – Rasskazy. Petrograd. 1922. BR-1157 2 – 8 – ne IDC [460]
TEN PERSONAL STUDIES / Ward, Wilfrid Philip – London, New York: Longmans, Green, 1908 – 1mf – us A.T.L.A. [240]
TEN STUDIES ON ASPECTS AND PROBLEMS OF THE CARIBBEAN DEFENSE COMMAND DURING THE EARLY AND MID 1940'S / U.S. Army. Caribbean Army. Caribbean Defense Command. Historical Section – 1945-48. 11 v. charts, maps. 2 reels – 1 – 38.00 – us L of C Photodup [355]
TEN TALKS ON THE APOSTLES' CREED (CCC322) / Wei, Chuo-ming – (In Chinese) – 1st HK ed. Hong Kong: Council on Christian Literature for Overseas Chinese, 1955 – 1r – 1 – 1984-6661 – us A.T.L.A. [220]
TEN THEOPHANIES: THE APPEARANCES OF OUR LORD TO MEN BEFORE HIS BIRTH / Baker, William M – New York: A.D.F. Randolph, 1883.1 fiche – 9 – us A.T.L.A. [240]
TEN THOUSAND THINGS RELATING TO CHINA AND THE CHINESE : AN EPITOME OF THE GENIUS, GOVERNMENT, HISTORY, LITERATURE, AGRICULTURE, ARTS... OF THE CELESTIAL EMPIRE,... / Langdon, W B – London, 1842 – 4mf – 9 – ne IDC [950]
TEN TOWNS MESSENGER – England. 1836-38 – 1 – uk Microform Academic [072]
TEN WORKS ON MILITARY HISTORY / Palat, Barthelemy Edmond Pierre Lehautcourt – (Bibliographie generale de la guerre de 1870-71. Paris, etc., Berger-Levrault & cie., 1896. viii, 581 p.. Campagne de l'est en 1870-1871. Paris, etc., Berger-Levrault & cie., 1896. 2 v. (Author's pseud., "Pierre Lehautcourt," at head of title.). Campagne de la Loire en 1870-1871, Josnes, Vendome, Le Mans. Paris, etc., Berger-Levrault & cie., 1895. 444 p. (Pseud. at head of title.). Campagne du Nord en 1870-1871; la defense nationale dans le Nord de la France. Nouv. ed. Paris, etc., Berger-Levrault et cie., 1897. viii, 348 p. (Pseud. at head of title.). Une grande question d'histoire et de psychologie. Bazaine et nos desastres en 1870. Paris, Chapelot, 1913. 2 v. La guerre de 1870-1871. Paris, A. Fontemoing, 1900. 27 p. (Bibliotheque de bibliographies critiques, pub. par la Societe des etudes historiques, 5). Histoire de la guerre de 1870-1871. I. ptie.: La guerre de 1870. Paris, Nancy, Berger-Levrault & cie., 1901-08. 7 v. (Pseud. at head of title.). Les origines de la guerre de 1870. La candidature Hohenzollern 1868-1870. Paris, etc., Berger-Levrault, 1912. xv, 664p. (pseud. at head of title.). Siege de Paris. Paris, etc., Berger-Levrault & cie., 1898. 3 v. (Pseud. at head of title.). La strategie de Moltke en 1870. Paris, Nancy, Berger-Levrault & cie., 1907. vii, 392 p) – Film Mas C422 – 1 – us H.U. Library [355]
TEN YEAR DEVELOPMENT AND WELFARE PLAN OF TANGANYIKA, 1947-1956 / Tanganyika. Development Commission – D 1487 1. 1946 – 9 – ne IDC [338]
TEN YEAR DEVELOPMENT PLAN (1947-1956) / Rhodesia. Northern – D-1402 1. 1947 – 9 – ne IDC [338]
TEN YEAR NATIONAL HEALTH PLAN, 1967-1976 / Liberia. National Public Health Service – Monrovia. 1967. BD-1872 1 – 9 – ne IDC [360]
THE TEN YEAR PLAN OF ECONOMIC AND SOCIAL DEVELOPMENT, 1961/1962-1970/1971 / Sudan. Economic Planning Secretariat – 1962. BNE-7632 1 – 9 – ne IDC [338]
THE TEN YEAR PLAN OF ECONOMIC AND SOCIAL DEVELOPMENT, 1961/62-1970/71 / Sudan. Economic Planning Secretariat – Khartoum. 1962. BD-370 1 – 9 – ne IDC [338]
A TEN YEAR PROGRAMME OF DEVELOPMENT / Cyprus. Secretariat – D-1028 1. 1946-1955 – 9 – ne IDC [338]
TEN YEARS IN A PORTSMOUTH SLUM / Dolling, Robert R – London: Swan Sonnenschein, 1896 – 1mf – us A.T.L.A. [240]
TEN YEARS IN BURMA / Smith, Julius – Cincinnati: Jennings & Pye; New York: Eaton & Mains, c1902 – 1mf – 9 – 0-8370-6521-6 – 1986-0521 – us A.T.L.A. [920]
TEN YEARS IN EQUATORIA AND THE RETURN WITH EMIN PASHA / Casati, Gaetano – 2v. 1891 – 1r – 1 – us Ross [960]
TEN YEARS IN EQUATORIA AND THE RETURN WITH EMIN PASHA / Casati, Gaetano – Trans. from the original Italian...London, 1891 – 1 – us Res Libr [910]
TEN YEARS IN NEVADA: OR, LIFE ON THE PACIFIC COAST / Mathews, M M – Buffalo, New York: Baker, Jones and Co., 1880. Nevada reel 1. (Cox Library Collection) – 5 – us Americana [978]
TEN YEARS OF DEVELOPMENT AND PROGRESS IN EDUCATION 1966-1976 / Malawi. Ministry of Education – Limbe, 1976 – 1mf – 9 – DE-449/1 – ne IDC [370]
TEN YEARS OF PREACHER-LIFE : CHAPTERS FROM AN AUTOBIOGRAPHY / Milburn, William Henry – New York: Derby & Jackson, 1859 – 1mf – us A.T.L.A. [240]
TEN YEARS OF UPPER CANADA IN PEACE AND WAR, 1805-1815: BEING THE RIDOUT LETTERS / Ridout, Thomas – Toronto: W. Briggs, 1890. 02885. (Pre-1900 Canadiana) – 9 – cn C.I.H.M. [971]
Tena Fernandez, Juan *see*
– CONSIDERACIONES SOBRE LOS DOLORES DE LA SANTISIMA VIRGEN MARIA. PRIMER DOLOR
– DIVULGACION HISTORICA FRANCISCO PIZARRO
– FRANCISCO PIZARRO 2° EDICION
– HISTORIA DE SANTA MARIA DE LA VICTORIA
A TENABLE THEORY OF BIBLICAL INSPIRATION: AN ADDRESS / Wood, Irving Francis – Quaker Hill: Quaker Hill Conf., 1902. 1 fiche – 9 – us A.T.L.A. [240]
LES TENAILLES – no. 1. Paris. nov 1921 – 1 – fr A.C.R.P.P. [073]
TENANT FARMER *see* SHARECROPPER'S VOICE, 1935-1937 : SOUTHERN FARM LEADER, 1936 : STFU NEWS, 1938-1939 : TENANT FARMER, 1941-1942 : FARM WORKER, 1943-1944 : FARM LABOR NEWS, 1946-1951 : THE UNION FARMER, 1952-1953 : AGRICULTURAL UNIONIST, 1952-1954
THE TENANT OF WILDFELL HALL / Bront, Anne – London: T.C. Newby, 1848 – 2 rolls – 1 – 1-55879-102-7 – uk Libr Preservation [830]
TENBY AND PEMBROKESHIRE CHRONICLE – Wales, UK. 7 Feb 1946-1 Oct 1947. -w. 1 reel – 1 – uk British Libr Newspaper [072]
TENCH COXE PAPERS, 1638-1896 / Coxe, Tench – 122r – 1 – $6860.00 – us UMI [920]
TENDANCES ET PERSPECTIVES DE L'AGRICULTURE ET DE L'ELEVAGE EN AFRIQUE SUB-SAHARIENNE / Mongolfier-Kouevi, C de & Vlavonou, A – 1983 – 9 – $5.00 – 92-9053-173-8 – et ILRI [630]
Tende, G de *see* REGLES DE LA TRADUCTION
TENDENCIAS Y GUPOS POLITICOS EN LA REALIDAD ARGENTINA / Castagno, Antonio – [Buenos Aires]: Editorial Universitaria de Buenos Aires, [2nd ed 1972, c1971] – 1 – CSUXADL7073-B – us Hoover Inst Photo [320]
TENDENCIES IN GERMAN THOUGHT / Stuckenberg, John Henry Wilburn – Hartford: Student Publishing Co., 1896 – 1mf – us A.T.L.A. [100]
THE TENDENCIES OF MODERN THEOLOGY / Banks, John Shaw – London: C.H. Kelly, 1897 – 1mf – us A.T.L.A. [240]
LA TENDERIE AUX GRIVES CHEZ LES ARDENNAIS DU PLATEAU / Jamin, J – Essai d'ethno-biologie – 9 – F60.00 – fr Ethnologie [305]
TENDRES CHOSES: POESIES CANADIENNES / Chevrier, Rodolphe – Montreal: J. P. Bedard, 1892. 00605. (Pre-1900 Canadiana) – 9 – cn C.I.H.M. [810]
THE TENEMENT-HOUSE ACT OF NEW JERSEY, 1904, WITH INDEX / Rockwell, William Locke – Newark: Soney & Sage, 1904. 65p. LL-957 – 1 – us L of C Photodup [340]
Tenenbaum, Samuel *see* WHY MEN HATE
Teng, Shu-kun *see* OUT OF THE DEPTHS (CCC292)
TENG T'A *see* LIGHTHOUSE
T'ENG-YUEH CHOU-CHIH – 1790, 13. Lacking: ch. 13. BCH-678 2 – 8 – ne IDC [950]
EL TENIENTE APOLOGISTA UNIVERSAL / Habela Patino, Eugenio – 1788 – 9 – 1.50f – sp Bibl Santa Ana [830]
LOS TENIENTES DE NAVIO JORGE JUAN Y SANTACILIA Y ANTONIO DE ULLOA Y DE LA TORRE G.Y. LA MEDICION DEL MERIDIANO... / Guillen, Julio F – Madrid: Razon y Fe, 1939 – 1 – sp Bibl Santa Ana [946]
Tennant, Frederick Robert *see* THE ORIGIN AND PROPAGATION OF SIN
Tennent, Gilbert *see*
– SERMONS, 1742-1763
– THOUGHTS ON EXTEMPORE PREACHING
Tennent, Gilbert et al *see* SERMONS AND ESSAYS
Tennent, J E *see*
– CEYLON, AN ACCOUNT OF THE ISLAND PHYSICAL, HISTORICAL, AND TOPOGRAPHICAL WITH NOTICES OF ITS NATURAL HISTORY, ANTIQUITIES AND PRODUCTIONS
– SKETCHES OF THE NATURAL HISTORY OF CEYLON
Tennent, Sylvia R *see* AN EVALUATION OF THE EFFECTS OF A SMOKING PREVENTION PROGRAM ON MIDDLE SCHOOL STUDENTS' KNOWLEDGE AND ATTITUDES CONCERNING CIGARETTE SMOKING
Tennent, William *see* COMMUNION SERMON MANUSCRIPTS
TENNESSEAN – Nashville. Tenn. 1949- – 1 – us UMI [071]
TENNESSEE – 24r – 1 – $1,920.00 – us Scholarly Res [370]
TENNESSEE : CODE ANNOTATED – Charlottesville: Michie Co, 1956-Jun 1996 update – 9 – $2,420.00 set – us Hein [340]
TENNESSEE : SESSION LAWS OF AMERICAN STATES AND TERRITORIES – 1792-1995 – 9 – $2,723.00 set – us Hein [340]
Tennessee *see*
– REPORTS AND OPINIONS (A-G)
– REPORTS, POST-NRS
– REPORTS, PRE-NRS
TENNESSEE ATTORNEY GENERAL REPORTS AND OPINIONS – (6 1875-1931, 1911-1980 $70.00. 9 v10 1980-1995 $922.00. 1932-70 not available) – 1875-1995 – 6,9 – $992.00 set – us Hein [340]
Tennessee. Baptist Associations *see* ANNUALS
Tennessee Baptist Church Library Convention *see* MINUTES, APR 13-15, 1972
Tennessee Baptist Missionary and Educational Convention *see* ANNUALS
TENNESSEE BAR ASSOCIATION PROCEEDINGS – 1st to 54th annual meetings. 1882-1935 (all publ) – 95mf – 9 – $427.00 – LLMC 84-679 – us L.L.M.C. [073]
TENNESSEE BAR JOURNAL – v1-30. 1965-94 – 9 – $276.00 set – us Hein [340]
Tennessee. Bureau of Labor, Statistics and Mines *see* STATE LABOR REPORTS
Tennessee. Central. Baptist Associations *see* ANNUALS
TENNESSEE EDUCATION – v1- 1971- 1; v7- 5,6,9 – us UMI [073]
TENNESSEE EXTENSION REVIEW / Tennessee. University. Agricultural Extension Service – n.1-51.May 1918-1969 – 1,5 – us Spaulding [630]
TENNESSEE EXTENSION REVIEW / University of Tennessee.Agricultural Extension Service – No.51-54. 1970-72. 1 reel – 1,5 – us Spaulding [630]
TENNESSEE FARM AND HOME SCIENCE PROGRESS REPORT / Tennessee. University. Agricultural Experiment Station – n.1-72. 1952-69 – 1,5 – us Spaulding [630]
TENNESSEE FARM AND HOME SCIENCE PROGRESS REPORT / University of Tennessee.Agricultural Experiment Station – No.73-124. 1970-82 – 1,5 – us Spaulding [630]
TENNESSEE FARMER / Tennessee. University. College of Agriculture – v.1-60. Oct 1906-summer 1964 – 1,5 – us Spaulding [630]
TENNESSEE HISTORICAL QUARTERLY – v31-1972- 1; v35- 5,6,9 – us UMI [978]
TENNESSEE HISTORICAL QUARTERLY – v. 1-5. 1942-1946 – 1,5,6 – us Princeton Micro [073]
THE TENNESSEE JUSTICE'S MANUAL AND CIVIL OFFICER'S GUIDE / Mitchell, James Coffield – Nashville: Mitchell and Norvell, 1834. 534p. LL-1286 – 1 – us L of C Photodup [340]
TENNESSEE LAW REVIEW – (v1-52 1922-85 on reel $720.00. v53-62 1986-95 on mf $209.00) – v1-62. 1922-95 – 5,6,9 – $929.00 set – us Hein [340]
THE TENNESSEE MANUAL OF CHANCERY PRACTICE / Hicks, Wesley Jones – (Addenda. Knoxville, Tenn.: Press and Herald Steam Book & Job Office, 1871. 307 1p. LL-487) – Knoxville: " Whig" Steam Book and Job Office, 1870. 538p. LL-487 – 1 – us L of C Photodup [340]
Tennessee Nurses Association *see* BULLETIN
TENNESSEE PIONEER BAPTIST PREACHERS / Burnett, James J – 1775-1875 – 1 – 20.51 – us Baptist [240]
TENNESSEE RIDGE BAPTIST CHURCH. HOUSTON COUNTY. TENNESSEE : CHURCH RECORDS – 1915-68 – 1 – 11.61 – us Baptist [240]
Tennessee. State Bar Association *see* PROCEEDINGS
Tennessee State Nurses' Association *see* BULLETIN
Tennessee. Supreme Court *see*
– COOPER'S CHANCERY REPORTS
– HIGGIN'S COURT OF CIVIL APPEALS REPORTS
– SHANNON'S UNREPORTED CASES
– TENNESSEE SUPREME COURT REPORTS
– THOMPSON'S UNREPORTED CASES
– WRIGHT'S CHANCERY APPEALS DECISIONS
TENNESSEE SUPREME COURT REPORTS / Tennessee. Supreme Court – (Pre-NRS: v1-84 1791-1886 664mf $996.00. Updates planned) – v1-142. 1791-1920 – 1164mf – 9 – $1,746.00 – LLMC 82-991 – us L.L.M.C. [340]
TENNESSEE SUPREME COURT REPORTS *see*
– COOPER'S CHANCERY REPORTS
– HIGGIN'S COURT OF CIVIL APPEALS REPORTS
– SHANNON'S UNREPORTED CASES
– THOMPSON'S UNREPORTED CASES
– WRIGHT'S CHANCERY APPEALS DECISIONS
Tennessee. University. Agricultural Experiment Station *see*
– AGRICULTURAL ECONOMICS CIRCULAR
– ANIMAL HUSBANDRY: VETERINARY SCIENCE PROGRESS REPORTS
– ANNUAL REPORT
– BULLETIN
– CIRCULAR
– CIRCULAR OF INFORMATION
– MISCELLANEOUS BULLETINS
– PRESS BULLETIN
– REPORT OF COOPERATIVE AND EXTENSION WORK IN AGRICULTURE IN MIDDLE TENNESSEE
– RURAL RESEARCH SERIES: MONOGRAPHS
– TENNESSEE FARM AND HOME SCIENCE PROGRESS REPORT
Tennessee. University. Agricultural Experiment Station and Extension Service *see* FARM ECONOMICS CIRCULAR
Tennessee. University. Agricultural Extension Service *see*
– ANNUAL REPORT
– COMMUNITY RESOURCE DEVELOPMENT NEWSLETTER
– LEAFLET
– PUBLICATION
– TENNESSEE EXTENSION REVIEW
Tennessee. University. Agriculture Department *see* REPORT
Tennessee. University. College of Agriculture *see* TENNESSEE FARMER
Tenney *see* MEMORIAL RECORD OF THE FATHERS OF WISCONSIN
Tenney, Horace Kent *see* PRACTICE COURSE, UNIVERSITY OF CHICAGO LAW SCHOOL
TENNIS – (1979-. 9. 1982-. 5,6) – 1965 – 1 – us UMI [073]
TENNIS RACKET COEFFICIENT OF RESTITUTION UNDER STATIC AND DYNAMIC CONDITIONS / Kern, Jack C – Texas Woman's University, 1994 – 2mf – 9 – $8.00 – PE 3658 – us Microform Publ [612]

DER TENNISSPORT TENNIS UND GOLF – Heidelberg, 10 Apr-18 Dec 1924; 1 Jan 1935-15 Mar 1943 – 8r – DM600.00 – gw Mikro Press [790]

Tennodrac, M J *see* L'ANTIQUITE EROTIQUE

Tennyson, Alfred, Lord *see*
- THE DEATH OF OENONE
- DEMETER AND OTHER POEMS
- ENOCH ARDEN, ETC.
- THE FORESTERS
- HAROLD
- IDYLLS OF THE KING
- MAUD
- THE PRINCESS
- QUEEN MARY
- A SELECTION FROM THE WORKS OF ALFRED TENNYSON, D.C.L., POET LAUREATE
- SUPPRESSED POEMS OF ALFRED LORD TENNYSON, 1830-1862...
- TIRESIAS AND OTHER POEMS

TENNYSON AS A RELIGIOUS TEACHER / Masterman, Charles FG – London: Methuen, 1899 – 1mf – us A.T.L.A. [240]

TENNYSON AS A RELIGIOUS TEACHER / Masterman, Charles FG – London: Methuen, 1900 – 1 roll – 1 – 1-55879-423-9 – uk Libr Preservation [200]

TENNYSON, RUSKIN, MILL AND OTHER LITERARY ESTIMATES / Harrison, Frederic – London, New York: Macmillan, 1899 – 1 roll – 1 – 1-55879-538-3 – uk Libr Preservation [420]

Tenon, Jacques Rene *see* MEMOIRES SUR LES HOPITAUX DE PARIS

DER TENOR VON TRAPANI : NOVELLE / Thiess, Frank – Leipzig: Reclam, 1942 – 1r – 1 – us U.W. Library [830]

Tenore, M *see*
- FLORA NAPOLITANA
- SYLLOGE PLANTARUM VASCULARIUM FLORAE NEAPOLITANAE HUCUSQUE DETECTARUM

Tenorio Cordero de Santoyo, Miguel *see* DISCURSOS

Tenorio de Leon, A *see* ATOMOS QUE NUEVAMENTE SE HAN DESCUBIERTO CON LAS LUCES DE APOLO, EN LA CONTROVERSIA...

Tenorio, Igor *see* LAW AND CYBERNETICS

TENRIKYO – Tenri-city, Japan, 1962-93 (complete) – 2r – 1 – ATLA S0625 – us A.T.L.A. [073]

TENTAMEN : ORGAM DOS ALUMNOS DO GYMNASIO AMAZONESE – Manaos, Amazonas. 1 Maio 1909 – 1,5,6 – bl Biblioteca [072]

TENTAMEN – Serro, 21 Aug 1890 – 1,5,6 – bl Biblioteca [072]

TENTAMEN DISPOSITIONIS METHODICAE FUNGORUM IN CLASSES. ORDINES GENERA ET FAMILIAS CUM SUPPLEMENTO ADJECTO / Persoon, C H – Lipsiae. 1797. B-6295 2 – 8 – ne IDC [580]

TENTAMEN EX IURISPRUDENTIA NATURALI / Comes de Blumegen, F H – Viennae, 1774 – 1mf – 1 – ILM-1090/1 – ne IDC [327]

TENTAMEN FLORA GEDANENSIS METHODO SEXUALI ACCOMODATAE / Reyger, G – 2v. Dantisci. 1764-66. B-220 2 – 8 – ne IDC [580]

TENTAMEN FLORAE ABYSINICAE; SEU ENUMERATIO PLANTARUM. / Richard, Achille – In Lefebvre, C.T. Voyage en Abyssinie. Paris. 1847-51. Pt.3. v.4-5 – 1 – us Res Libr [580]

TENTAMEN FLORAE BOHEMIAE / Pohl, J B E – 2pts. Praha. 1809-14. B-5640 2 – 8 – ne IDC [580]

TENTAMEN FLORAE GERMANICAE / Roth, A W – 3v. Lipsiae. 1788-1800. B-502 2 – 8 – ne IDC [580]

TENTAMEN FLORAE NEPALENSIS / Wallich, N – Calcutta-Serampore. 1824-26. B-5799 2 – 8 – ne IDC [580]

TENTAMEN HISTORIAE LICHENUM ET PRAESERTIM PRUSSICORUM / Hagen, C G – Regionmonti. 1782. B-1078 2 – 8 – ne IDC [580]

TENTAMEN HYDROPHYOLOGIAE DENICAW / Lyngbye, H C – 1819 – 1 – uk Microform Academic [580]

TENTAMEN HYDROPHYTOLOGIAE DANICAE / Lyngbye, H C – Hafniae, 1819 – 8 – ne IDC [580]

TENTAMEN MARINO-CRYPTO-GAMICUM / Stackhouse, J – (Mem. Soc. Naturalistes de Moscou, v. 2, 1809). B-1510 2 – 8 – ne IDC [580]

TENTAMEN METHODI MUSCORUM / Greville, R K & Walker-Arnott, G A – or A new arrangement of the genera of mosses. (Mem. Wernerian Nat. Hist. Soc., v. 4. 1821-22). B-5066 – 8 – ne IDC [580]

TENTAMEN MONOGRAPHIAE GENERIS PAPAVER / Elkan, L – Regimontii Borussorum. 1839. B-5123 2 – 8 – ne IDC [580]

TENTAMEN MYCOLOGIUM SEU AMANITARUM ILLUSTRATIO / Vittadini, C – Mediolani. 1826. B-358 2 – 8 – ne IDC [580]

TENTAMEN NOVAE THEORIAE MUSICAE EX CERTISSIMIS HARMONIAE PRINCIPIIS DILUCIDE EXPOSITAE / Euler, Leonhard – 1739 – 2 – us Sibley [780]

TENTAMEN PTERIDOGRAPHIAE / Presl, C B – 1836 – 8mf – 7 – uk Microform Academic [580]

TENTAMEN PTERIDOGRAPHIAE, SEU GENERA FILICACEARUM / Presl, K B – Prague. 1836. Supplementum Tentaminis Pteridographiae. Prague. 1845. B-5207 2 – 8 – ne IDC [580]

TENTAMEN ROSARUM MONOGRAPHIAE / Regel, E A von – St. Petersburgh. 1877. B-5152 2 – 8 – ne IDC [580]

TENTANG DIALEKTIKA / Lenin, Vladimir Ilyich – SE-2631 1. 1958 – 9 – ne IDC [335]

TENTANG KOPERASI / Lenin, Vladimir Ilyich – SE-4543 1. 1960 – 9 – ne IDC [335]

TENTANG MARXISME / Aidit, Dipa Nusantara – SE-6693 1. 1963 – 9 – ne IDC [335]

TENTANG OTORITET / Engels, Friedrich – Trans. of Von Der Autoritaet. SE-4523 1. 1960 – 9 – ne IDC [335]

TENTANG SENI DAN SASTERA / Mao, Tse-tung – SE-3489 1. 1963 – 9 – ne IDC [324]

TENTARA : PEMATANG SIANTAR, MARKAS DIPISI 4, BAHAGIAN PENERANGAN, TENTARA REPOEBLIK INDONESIA – (Lacking: 1946, V.1(1-2)) – 1946.-v1-3 – 1mf – 9 – SE-105/1 – ne IDC [950]

TENTARA NASIONAL INDONESIA / Nasution, Abdul Haris – SE-4817 1. v. 1 only. 1963- – 9 – ne IDC [320]

LES TENTATIONS / Routier, Simone – Paris: Edition de la Caravelle, 1934. SEM16P199 – 1r – 5 – Can$9.00 – cn Bibl Nat [830]

TENTATIVA...LECCION DE DON VICENTE GARCIA DE LA HUERTA / Guerrero, Placido – 1785 – 9 – $1.50f – sp Bibl Santa Ana [946]

TENTATIVE D'ENLEVEMENT DE LA SOEUR MARY BASIL – 191? SEM105P55 – 2mf – 9 – Can$4.50 – cn Bibl Nat [240]

A TENTATIVE LIST OF THE FLOWERING PLANTS, FERNS, ETC., KNOWN TO OCCUR IN. CORNWALL, INCLUDING THE SCILLY ISLES / Davey, F H – Penryn. 1902 – 9 – ne IDC [580]

A TENTATIVE LIST OF TREATY COLLECTIONS – Washington, 1919 – 2mf – 9 – ILM-2258/1 – ne IDC [327]

A TENTATIVE STRATEGY OF DEVELOPMENT FOR LIBYA / Glinstra Bleeker, R J P van – (Continued). Paper nr. 16. Tripoli, Libya. 29 Sep 1964. BNE-702 1 – 9 – ne IDC [338]

A TENTATIVE STRATEGY OF DEVELOPMENT FOR LIBYA / Glinstra Bleeker, R J P van – (Continued). Paper nr. 19. Tripoli, Libya. 18 Nov 1974. BNE-604 1 – 9 – ne IDC [338]

TENTERDEN NEWS – Kent, England. 15 Sept, 20 Dec 1938. -irr. 11 feet – 1 – uk British Libr Newspaper [072]

TENTERFIELD COURIER – Jan 5 1914-Dec 31 1914 – 1 – at Pascoe [072]

TENTERFIELD STAR – Jan 6 1894-Dec 25 1897 – 9 – at Pascoe [072]

TENTH CENSUS OF THE UNITED STATES / U.S. Bureau of the Census – 1880. 1454 rolls. T9 – 1 – us Nat'l Archives [324]

TENTH INTERNATIONAL CONGRESS OF GERONTOLOGY / Israel. National Insurance Institute – 22-27 June 1975. Jerusalem. 125 p – 9 – 3.00 – is I.T.T.I. [324]

THE TENTH MUSE AND FROM THE MANUSCRIPTS, MEDITATIONS DIVINE AND MORALL, TOGETHER WITH LETTERS AND OCCASIONAL PIECES / Bradstreet, Anne – 1650 – 9 – 20.00 – us Scholars' Facs [880]

TENTUDIA / Calera de Leon, Ayuntamiento – Calera de Leon-Fiestas de septiembre: Badajoz, Ayu. de Calera de Leon.Hermandad Sindical de Labradores y ganaderos, 1974 – 1 – sp Bibl Santa Ana [390]

TENTUDIA. FIESTAS DE SEPTIEMBRE 1973 / Calera de Leon – Calera de Leon: Hermandad de la Santisima Virgen de Tentudia, 1973 – sp Bibl Santa Ana [390]

TENTUDIA. REVISTA DE FERIAS Y FIESTAS DE 1975 / Calera de Leon – sp Bibl Santa Ana [390]

TENTUDIA. REVISTA OFICIAL DE FIESTAS, 1972 / Calera de Leon – Zafra: Tipografia Castro, 1972 – sp Bibl Santa Ana [390]

Tentzel, W *see* DE VETERIS RECENTISQ. ECCLESIAE HYMNO

Tentzel, Wilhelm Ernst *see* MONATLICHE UNTERREDUNGEN EINIGER GUTEN FREUNDE VON ALLERHAND BUECHERN UND ANDERN ANNEHMLICHEN GESCHICHTEN

TENU'AT HA-HASKALAH BE-EREZ-YISRA'EL BA-ME'AH HA-19 / Hanani, Y – Jerusalem. 1949. BJ-27-31 1 – 9 – ne IDC [270]

TENUITVOERLEGGING VAN BUITENLANDSCHE ARBITRALE VONNISSEN / Bijleveld, C G – Amsterdam, 1921 – 1mf – 9 – ILM-2097/1 – ne IDC [327]

TENY SOA FANALAN' ANDRO / Societe des Missions Evangeliques – no. 1-13, 24. Tananarive. 1866-69 – 1 – fr A.C.R.P.P. [240]

TEN-YEAR DEVELOPMENT PLAN; 1946-1956 / Barbados – D-945 1 – 9 – ne IDC [338]

THE TEN-YEAR PLAN / Ceylon. Planning Council – Colombo. 1959. BD-374 1 – 9 – ne IDC [324]

TEN-YEAR PLAN, 1962-1971 / Jamaica. Central Planning Unit – D-1107 1. 1962 – 9 – ne IDC [338]

TEN-YEAR PLAN OF DEVELOPMENT (1946/47-1955/56) / Jamaica – D-1344 1. 1947 – 9 – ne IDC [338]

TEN-YEAR PLAN OF DEVELOPMENT AND WELFARE FOR NIGERIA / Nigeria – 1946 – 9 – ne IDC [338]

TEN-YEAR PLAN OF ECONOMIC AND SOCIAL DEVELOPMENT FOR SIERRA LEONE, 1962/63-1971/72 / Sierra Leone – Freetown. 1962 – 9 – ne IDC [338]

Teodorovich, I A *see* PERSPEKTIVY RAZVITIIA SEL'SKOGO KHOZIAISTVA SSSR

TEOFANIA O MANISFETACION DE DIOS EN LAS CRIATURAS / Serrano Serrano, Ildefonso – Badajoz: Uceda Hermanos, 1904 – 1 – sp Bibl Santa Ana [240]

Teo-Koh, Sock M *see* RELATIONSHIP BETWEEN PEAK VO2 AND PERFORMANCE ON THE ROCKPORT FITNESS WALKING TEST OF ADOLESCENT MALES WITH MENTAL RETARDATION

TEOLOGIA Y VIDA – (v.22-. 1981-. 5,6,9) – v.1-. 1960- – 1 – us UMI [240]

TEOLOGISK TIDSSKRIFT (1899) – v1-9. 1899-Oct 1907 (complete) – 1r – 1 – ATLA S0237 – us A.T.L.A. [073]

TEORETICHESKIE PROBLEMY SOVREMENNOI SOVETSKOI KOOPERATSII : DISKUSSIIA V KOOPERATIVNOI SEKTSII – M., 1930 – 1mf – 9 – COR-222/1 – ne IDC [334]

TEORI EKONOMI NASIONAL; KUMPULAN BATJAAN / ed by Djanin, Arief – In English. SE-5347 1. 1965 – 9 – ne IDC [338]

TEORIA DE LA SOCIEDAD SEGUN DE BONALD Y DONOSO CORTES / Lozano, Miguel – Badajoz: Imp. Dip. Provincial, 1963 – sp Bibl Santa Ana [301]

TEORIA DEL CONOCIMINETO Y ONTOLOGIA / Frutos Cortes, Eugenio – Barcelona: Ediciones SPES S.A., 1942 – sp Bibl Santa Ana [120]

TEORIA DEL TRABAJO / Moreno Torrado, Luis – Badajoz: Tip y Lib. de A. Arqueros, 1915 – 1 – sp Bibl Santa Ana [331]

TEORIA I PRAKTIKA KOOPERATIVNOGO DVIZHENIIA / Nikolaev, A A – M. 2v. 1908-1909 – 3mf – 9 – COR-78/1 – ne IDC [334]

TEORIA Y METODO DEL CONOCIMIENTO DE SISTEMAS POR SU COMPORTAMIENTO / Perez Garcia, Augusto – 2mf – 9 – Pta1,500.00 – 84-85422-59-7 – sp Pentalfa [100]

TEORIA Y PRACTICA DE LA LIBERCION ECONOMICA, SOCIAL Y POLITICA DE LA REPUBLICA; DISCURSOS PRONUNCIADOS POR EL PRESIDENTE DE LA NACION Y POR MARIA EVA DURATE DE PERON / Peron, Juan Domingo – Buenos Aires: Senado de la Nacion, 1949 – 1 – CSUXAHZ3468-B – us Hoover Inst Photo [320]

TEORIA Y PRACTICA DE LA PINTURA / Palomino de Castro & Velasco, A – Madrid, 1724 – 17mf – 9 – sp Cultura [750]

LE TEORICA DEI MANDATI INTERNAZIONALI / Ferri, C E – Torino, 1927 – 5mf – 1 – ILM-2138/1 – ne IDC [327]

TEORICA Y PRACTICA DE GUERRA / Mendoza, B – Madrid, 1595 – 5mf – 9 – sp Cultura [355]

TEORIIA, ISTORIIA I PRAKTIKA POTREBITEL'SKOI KOOPERATSII / Totomiants, V F – Ed 3. Spb., 1913 – 1mf – 9 – COR-123/1 – ne IDC [334]

TEORIIA KOOPERATSII : KURS LEKTSII, CHIT. V UN-TE I KOMMER. IN-TE / Totomiants, V F – M., 1918 – 3mf – 9 – COR-277/1 – ne IDC [334]

TEORIIA KOOPERATSII : ZAOCHNYE KOOPKURSY TSENTROSOIUZA. NO. 8 / Popov, N I – M., 1927 – 3mf – 9 – COR-271/1 – ne IDC [334]

EL TEOSOFISMO. BARCELONA, 1928 / Tusquets, Juan; ed by Bayle, Constantino – Madrid: Razon y Fe, 1929 – 9 – sp Bibl Santa Ana [240]

DIE TEPLER BIBELUBERSETZUNG : EINE ZWEITE KRITIK / Jostes, Franz – Munster I/W: Heinrich Schoningh, 1886 – 1mf – 9 – 0-8370-3805-7 – 1985-1805 – us A.T.L.A. [220]

TER HERKENNING – 1973-92 (complete) – Inquire – 1 – ATLA S0615 – us A.T.L.A. [073]

Ter Minassiantz, E *see* DIE ARMENISCHE KIRCHE IN IHREN BEZIEHUNGEN ZU DEN SYRISCHEN KIRCHEN BIS ZUM ENDE DES 13. JAHRHUNDERTS (T.U.U. 2-26/4)

Teram, A *see* MEMOIRES D'UNE PETROLEUSE

Teran, Juan B *see* LA SALUD DE LA AMERICA ESPANOLA. PARIS, 1926

TERANG EXPRESS – 1921-1994 – 76mf – 9 – at Corangamite [980]

TERAPIA – 1915-1977 – 1. 1975-1977; ; 5,6,9 – us UMI [610]

TERAS BAHASA; PELADJARAN BAHASA INDONESIA UNTUK SEKOLAH LANDJUTAN PERTAMA DAN JANG SEDERADJAT DENGAN ITU / Sjahrul Sjarif – SE 3944 1. v. 1 only. 1962- – 9 – ne IDC [950]

TERATOLOGY – Philadelphia. v1-20. 1968-76 – 5,9 – Dfl1,600.00; Dfl80.00v – ne Swets [616]

THE TERATOLOGY OF FISHES / Gemmill, J F – Z-2104 2. 1912 – 8 – ne IDC [590]

TERBUNUHNJA PRESIDEN KENNEDY / Suwardi, Idris – SE 10,427 1. 1964 – 9 – ne IDC [920]

TERCEIRO PLANO DE FOMENTO, 1968-73 / Cape Verde Islands – D-999-1 – 9 – ne IDC [338]

TERCER CENSO DE LA REPUBLICA DE VENEZUELA, TOMO 2, 4. ANO 1891, 1890 – 19mf – 9 – sp Cultura [304]

TERCER CENTENARIO DE LA CANONIZACION DE SAN PEDRO DE ALCANTARA (1669-28 DE ABRIL-1969) / Barrado Manzano, Arcangel – Madrid: Graf. Calleja, 1969 – 1 – sp Bibl Santa Ana [240]

TERCER CUADERNO DE LOS INVENTOS CERES / Alvarez Guerra, Andres – 1828 – 9 – 1.50f – sp Bibl Santa Ana [999]

TERCER MUNDO – Mexico, MX. 1986-1987 – 2r – $200.00 – R04219 – us Library Micro [073]

TERCERA PARTE DE LOS SERMONES Y DISCURSOS QUE CONTIENE DESDE EL...SERMON EN LA FERIA SEGUNDA.. / Caceres y Sotomayor, Antonio – 1612 – 9 – 1.50f – sp Bibl Santa Ana [240]

LA TERCERA POSICION EN LA PREDICA Y EL EJEMPLO DE PERON / Peron, Juan Domingo – Buenos Aires: [Presidencia de la Nacion, Subsecretaria de Informaciones], 1951 – 1 – CSUXADH9079-B – us Hoover Inst Photo [320]

"LA TERCERA POSICION IDEOLOGICA" Y APRECIACIONES SOBRE EL RETORNO DE PERON / Ferla, Salvador – Buenos Aires: Ediciones Meridiano, c1974 – 1 – CSUXAGP8732-B – us Hoover Inst Photo [320]

LA TERCERA POSICION Y LA NEUTRALIZACION ARGENTINA / Disandro, Carlos A – Buenos Aires: Ediciones Patria Libre, 1984 – 1 – CSUXADL7479-B – us Hoover Inst Photo [972]

TERCERO LIBRO DE LAS GUERRAS CIVILES... DE QUITO / Cieza Leon, Pedro de – 1877 – 9 – 1.50f – sp Bibl Santa Ana [972]

TERCERO PLANO DIRECTOR DE DESENVOLVIMENTO ECONOMICA E SOCIAL DO NORDESTE, 1966-68 / Brazil. Superintendencia do Desenvolvimento do Nordeste - Recife. 1966 - 9 - ne IDC [338]

EL TERCIO. BANDERAS IRLANDESAS : THE BATTLE GENERAL IDEA / Tercio, El - Caceres: Tip. La Minerva, S.A. (hacia 1937) - 1 - sp Bibl Santa Ana [355]

EL TERCIO. BANDERAS IRLANDESAS : DEFINITIONS / Tercio, El - Caceres: Tip. La Minerva Cacerena, s.a. (hacia 1937) - 1 - sp Bibl Santa Ana [355]

EL TERCIO. BANDERAS IRLANDESAS : THE DUFIES OF THE SQUAD-CORPORAL (RIFLE-BOMBER) / Tercio, El - Caceres: Tip. La Minerva cacerena, s.a. (hacia 1937) - 1 - sp Bibl Santa Ana [355]

EL TERCIO. BANDERAS IRLANDESAS : INSTRUCTION FOR MACHINE-GUNNER / Tercio, El - Caceres: Tip. La Minerva Extremena, s.a. (hacia 1937) - 1 - sp Bibl Santa Ana [355]

EL TERCIO. BANDERAS IRLANDESAS : PLATOON COMBAT / Tercio, El - Caceres: Tip. La Minerva Cacerena, s.a. (hacia 1937) - 1 - sp Bibl Santa Ana [355]

EL TERCIO. BANDERAS IRLANDESAS : THE PLATOON SERGEANT'S DUTIES / Tercio, El - Caceres: Tip. La Minerva Cacerena, s.a. (hacia 1937) - 1 - sp Bibl Santa Ana [355]

Tercio, El *see*
- EL TERCIO. BANDERAS IRLANDESAS

TERCUEMAN - Bahcesaray, Crimea. Muharriri: Ismail Gasprenski [Gaspirali], 1882-1917. Nos. 21 (19 Zilhicca 1312 [1896]), 135 (27 Reced 1331 [1915]) - 9 - $25.00 - us MEDOC [956]

TERCUEMAN : TAGESZEITUNG FUER TUERKEN IN EUROPA - Neu-Isenburg, Germany. 1 Sep 1978- - ca 4r per yr - 1 - gw Mikrofilm [072]

TERENCE VINCENT POWDERLY PAPERS, 1864-1937; THE JOHN WILLIAM HAYES PAPERS, 1880-1921 / Powderly, Terence Vincent & Hayes, John William - (Leaders of the labor union the Knights of Labor) - 109r - 1 - $7315.00 - us UMI [920]

Terenteva, L *see* ETNICHESKIE PROTSESSY I SEMIA

Terentius *see* COMMOEDIAE, ETC

Teresa of Avila, St *see* THE INTERIOR CASTLE

Terlitza, Victor *see* GRILLPARZERS "AHNFRAU" UND DIE SCHICKSALSIDEE

TERMAS DE MONTEMAYOR / Pesado Blanco, Sergio - Caceres: Tip. Enc. y Lib. Jimenez, 1902 - 1 - sp Bibl Santa Ana [946]

TERMAS DE SAN HILARIO / Perez Jimenez, Nicolas - 1892 - 9 - 1.50f - sp Bibl Santa Ana [830]

Terme, J F *see* HISTOIRE DES ENFANTS TROUVES, NOUVELLE EDITION REVUE ET AUGMENTEE

Ter-Mekerttschian, K *see* DES HEILIGEN IRENAEUS SCHRIFT ZUM ERWEISE DER APOSTOLISCHEN VERKUENDIGUNG (T.U.U. 3-31/1)

Ter-Mekerttschian, Karapet *see* DES HEILIGEN IRENAEUS SCHRIFT ZUM ERWEISE DER APOSTOLISCHEN VERKUENDIGUNG

TERMES DE PARENTE DANS UNE POPULATION SCOLARISEE DE LA BANLIEUE PARISIENNE / Delaporte, Y - 9 - FF20.00 - fr Ethnologie [306]

TERMINAL - Richmond, CA. 1906-30 - 4r - 1 BC02699 - $200.00 - us Library Micro [071]

TERMINAL AND TRAFFIC OPERATIONS TRAINING PROGRAM (FOR INDONESIAN CARGO PERSONNEL) / U.S. Agency for International Development - SE 4969 1 - 9 - ne IDC [324]

TERMINAL REPORT: RECENT U.S. DEVELOPMENTS : CONCLUSIONS AND RECOMMENDATIONS FOR THE GRAPHIC ARTS AND ALLIED INDUSTRIES OF THE REPUBLIC OF INDONESIA TO THE AGENCY FOR INTERNATIONAL DEVELOPMENT AND THE GOVERNMENT OF THE REPUBLIC OF INDONESIA / Crockett, William D - SE-5499 1. 1962 - 9 - ne IDC [760]

Ter-Minassiantz, E *see* IRENAEUS GEGEN DIE HAERETIKER

Ter-Minassiantz, Erwand *see* DES HEILIGEN IRENAEUS SCHRIFT ZUM ERWEISE DER APOSTOLISCHEN VERKUENDIGUNG

DER TERMINISTISCHE STREIT : EIN BILD THEOLOGISCHEN LEBENS AUS DEN GRAENZJAHREN DES SIEBENZEHNTEN UND ACHTZEHNTEN JAHRHUNDERTS / Hesse, Friedrich Hermann - Giessen: J Ricker, 1877 - 9 - 0-8370-8579-9 - 1986-2579 - us A.T.L.A. [240]

TERMINOLOGIA MEDICA E SUE VOCI NELLA LINGUA SOMALA / Maino, Mario - Alessandria, Italy: Tip Ferrari, Ocella, 1953 - us Res Libr [610]

TERMINOLOGICAL PROBLEMS INVOLVED IN THE PROCESS OF EXCHANGE OF NEW TECHNOLOGY BETWEEN DEVELOPING AND DEVELOPED COUNTRIES / Sager, JC & Nkwenti-Azeh, Blaise - 1989 - 37p - 9 - 92-3-102559-7 - fr UNESCO [600]

TERMINOLOGICHESKII SLOVAR' CHASTNYKH AKTOV MOSKOVSKOGO GOSUDARSTVA / Andreev, A I - Petrograd. 1922. B-293/2 - 2mf - 8 - ne IDC [340]

DIE TERMINOLOGIE DER WIEDERGEBURT UND VERWANDTER ERLEBNISSE IN DER AELTESTEN KIRCHE (T.U.U. 3-42/3B) / Harnack, Adolf von - Leipzig, 1918 - 1mf - 9 - ne Slangenburg [240]

TERMINOLOGIE GEOGRAPHIQUE MAURE / Leriche, Albert - Saint-Louis, Senegal: Centre IFAN, 1955 - us Res Libr [910]

TERMINOLOGIIA PRAVA - M., 1926 - 2mf - 9 - R-9123/1 - ne IDC [340]

TERMINOLOGY BULLETINS / United Nations - (Covering: Air-Water Pollution, Tobacco, Navigation, Housing, Nuclear Tests, Timber, Transport and Storage of Gas, Steel, Coal, Mining, Food and Agriculture, Industry, Disarmament, Environment, Cartography, Human Rights, Terminology, etc) - 1969-1984 - E/F.76 - 9 (ST/CS/SER.F/) - us U.N. Pubs [300]

TERMINOLOGY OF SPECIAL EDUCATION - (English/French/Spanish/Russian) - 2nd ed 1983 - 167p - 9 - 92-3-002127-X - fr UNESCO [370]

TERMINOLOGY OF THE INTERNAL REVENUE CODE OF 1954 / U.S. Congress. Joint Committee on Internal Revenue Taxation - Washington: GPO. 1v. 1956 - 2mf - 9 - $3.00 - LLMC 82-703 - us L.L.M.C. [340]

TERMITENLEBEN AUF CEYLON / Escherich, K L - Jena. 1911. BZ-219 2 - 8 - ne IDC [590]

TERMS OF COMMUNION AGREED UPON BY THE SCOTS METHODISTS, BUT GENERALLY KNOWN BY THE SPECIOUS DENOMINATION OF THE PRESBYTERY OF RELIEF, THEIR OWN EXPLANATION OF SAID TERMS, WITH REMARKS UPON BOTH;... / Bennett, Thomas - Edinburgh, 2nd ed 1778 - 1mf - 9 - MP-525/1 - ne IDC [240]

THE TERMS OF COMMUNION AT THE LORD'S TABLE *see* COMMUNION

TERMS OF ENVIRONMENT RELATED TO AGRICULTURE - 1979 - 178p - it F.A.O. [630]

Terner, F G *see* VOSPOMINANIIA ZHIZNI F. G. TERNERA

Ternisien, T de *see* ESSAI SUR L'ACCLIMATATION DE QUELQUES FOUGEA6RES ET LYCOPODES EXOTIQUES

TERNISTYI PUT K SVOBODIE : BORBA PROTIV SAMODERZHAVNYKH PORIADKOV PRO TSARIAKH IZ DOMA ROMANOVYKH: ISTORICHESKIE OCHERKI / Efrusi, E; ed by Breshko-Breshkovsko, Ekaterina Konstantinova et al - Moskva: Moskovskoe izd-vo "Zemli a i voli a" partii sotsialistov-revoliutsionerov, 1918 - 1 - CSUX88-B2844 - us Hoover Inst Photo [947]

TEROENGA - Paramaribo. v1-25. 1939-64 - 67mf - 9 - J-261-111/1 - ne IDC [972]

TERPINEN-4-OL ALS VERHALTENSSTEUERNDER DUFTSTOFF VON FICHTENBORKENKAE-FERN / Reddemann, Joachim Karl Adolf - 1993 - 1mf - 9 - DM48.00 - 3-89349-670-X - gw Hänsel [574]

TERPISCHORE. SELECTIONS. IM CLAVIERAUSZUG / Breitkopf, C - Leipzig: Breitkopfischen Buchhandlung, 179- - 1 - us Sibley [780]

Terpresa *see*
- ESTATUTOS DE...
- MEMORIA 1971
- MEMORIA 1972

O TERPSICHORE : DEDICADO AS GENTIS SENHORITAS E SOCIOS DO TERPSICHORE CLUB - Manaos, Amazonas. 13 Fev 1909 - 1,5,6 - bl Biblioteca [072]

LA TERRA - Stockton, CA, 1907 - 6mf or 1r - 1,9 - us I.H.R.C. [978]

TERRA BELLA NEWS - Terra Bella, CA. 1911-44 (various dates) - 1r - 1 - $50.00 - B03036 - us Library Micro [071]

TERRA DO UORO - Nova Lima, 15 Aug 1959 - 1,5,6 - bl Biblioteca [072]

LES TERRAINS DE JEU DE BALLE DE L'AIRE MAYA / Taladoire, E - 9 - F60.00 - fr Ethnologie [306]

THE TERRANIAN NATIONAL CONSTITUTION / Barnes - 3rd draft, 1972.75 human rights articles - 9 - 1.00f - at Libertarian Micro [335]

Terrasson, Jean *see*
- DISSERTATION CRITIQUE SUR L'ILIADE D'HOMERE
- SETHOS: HISTOIRE OU VIE TIREE DES MONUMENS ANECDOTES DE L'ANCIENNE EGYPTE: TRADUITE D'UN MANUSCRIT GREC

LA TERRE / Communist Party. France - Hebdomadaire paysan. Dir. politique, Waldeck-Rochet. Paris. 7 oct 1944-1993 - 1 - fr A.C.R.P.P. [073]

LA TERRE DE CHEZ-NOUS : LE SEUL HEBDOMADAIRE AGRICOLE D'EXPRESSION FRANCAISE EN AMERIQUE / ed by Filion, Gerard - Montreal, Canada. 1 fev 1927-26 dec 1991 - 47r - 1 - Can$75.00r - cn Can Microfilming [072]

TERRE DE MORT : SOUDAN ET DAHOMEY / Vigne d'Octon, Paul - Paris: Lemerre, 1892 - us Res Libr [960]

TERRE DES HOMMES - no. 1-23. Paris. sept 1945-mars 1946 - 1 - fr A.C.R.P.P. [073]

TERRE LIBRE - Organe d'action syndicale. Paris. nov dec 1909-mars 1912, dec 1913-mai 1914 - 1 - fr A.C.R.P.P. [073]

LA TERRE PATERNELLE / Lacombe, Patrice - (Also: Le Chien d'Or by A.S. Soulard and L'Ile Saint-Barnabe by J.C. Tache) - Nouv. ed. Montreal: Beauchemin, 1924. SEM16P154 - 5 - Can$9.00 - cn Bibl Nat [830]

TERRELL FIRST BAPTIST CHURCH. TERRELL, TEXAS : CHURCH RECORDS - 1879-1982 - 1 - 189.81 - us Baptist [240]

Terrell, Henry *see* CRIMES BY NATIONAL BANK OFFICERS AND AGENTS UNDER SECTIONS 5208 AND 5209 REVISED STATUTES OF THE UNITED STATES

Terrell, Mary Church *see* PAPERS

Terreros Pando, Esteban *see* PALEOGRAFIA ESPANOLA

TERRES BOISEES DANS ONTARIO: DE 20 CENTS A 50 CENTS DE L'ACRE, TOUT LE LONG DE LA VOIE DU CHEMIN DE FER PACIFIQUE - Montreal: La Cie. du Pacifique canadien, 1888.00729.(Pre-1900 Canadiana) - 9 - cn C.I.H.M. [971]

TERRESTRIAL HEAT FLOW / Lee, W H K - 1965 - 9 - $10.00 - us A.G.U. [550]

LA TERRIBLE ET MERVEILLEUSE VIE DE ROBERT LE DIABLE LEQUEL APRES FUT HOMME DE BIEN - Troyes: J. Oudot, 1741 - fr Armell [944]

A TERRIBLE TEMPTATION / Reade, Charles L - British Fiction Archive: Unit 2 - 9 - uk Bell [830]

Terrien, Jacques *see* RECHERCHES HISTORIQUES SUR CETTE TRADITION QUE LA MORT DANS LA COMPAGNIE DE JESUS EST UN GAGE CERTAIN DE PREDESTINATION

LE TERRIER DES MUTATIONS DES SEIGNEURIES DE VAUDREUIL AND RIGAUD, 1781-1872 - Montreal: Bibliotheque nationale du Quebec, 1986. SEM35P279 - 1r - 1 - Can$54.00 - cn Bibl Nat [971]

TERRIERS, DEEDS, PARTICULARS, ETC / Holkham Hall. Norfolk. England - 1 - uk Microform Academic [025]

Terrill, Robert H *see* PAPERS

LE TERRITOIRE DU DEPARTEMENT DE LA MOSELLE: HISTOIRE ET STATISTIQUE / Chastellux, Louis Emmanuel de - Metz, V. Maline, 1860. xix, 232 p. 3 fiches. (Statistics Series: Topography) - 9 - 8.00 - fr Bibl Nationale [944]

TERRITOIRE DU NORD-QUEST : RAPPORTS DE PROGRES, AUSSI UN RAPPORT PRELIMINAIRE ET UN RAPPORT GENERAL SUR L'EXPEDITION D'EXPLORATION DE L'ASSINNIBOINE ET DE LA SASKATCHEWAN.. / Hind, Henry Youle - Toronto: John Lovell, 1859. SEM105P283 - 4mf - 9 - Can$9.00 - cn Bibl Nat [910]

TERRITORIAL ARCHIVES OF NEW MEXICO : 1846-1912 / New Mexico. State Records Center and Archives - Guide, National Historical Publication Commission, 1974 - 189r - $15.00r - us NM Archives [978]

TERRITORIAL CASE FILES OF THE U.S. DISTRICT COURTS OF UTAH, 1870-1896 - 38r - 1 - M1401 - us Nat'l Archives [340]

TERRITORIAL ENTERPRISE - Carson Valley, NV. 1859 - 1r - 1 - $50.00 - U04474 - us Library Micro [071]

TERRITORIAL ENTERPRISE - Carson Valley, UT. Jan 1859 - 1r - 1 - $50.00 - U05300 - us Library Micro [071]

TERRITORIAL ENTERPRISE - Virginia City. Nev. 1952- - 1 - us UMI [071]

TERRITORIAL ENTERPRISE - Virginia City, NV. 1940 - 1r - 1 - $50.00 - B06070 - us Library Micro [071]

TERRITORIAL ENTERPRISE - Virginia City, NV. Jun 1861-1913; 1901-16 - 33r - 1 - $1,650.00 - U04798 - us Library Micro [071]

TERRITORIAL ENTERPRISE AND VIRGINIA CITY NEWS - Virginia City, NV. 1952-1970 - 13r - 1 - $650.00 - UN04797 - us Library Micro [071]

THE TERRITORIAL MAGAZINE - Verulam, South Africa. 1938-46 - 2r - 1,16 diazo available - sa SA Libr [072]

TERRITORIAL NEWS - (Title varies: Umtata Herald, 1882-1904) - East London, South Africa. 6 Jan 1905-27 Feb 1974 - 53r - 1 - sa SA Libr [072]

TERRITORIAL PAPERS: HAWAII / U.S. Department of the Interior - 1898-1907. 4 rolls. M827 - 1 - us Nat'l Archives [324]

TERRITORIAL PAPERS, INDEXED / U. S. - (v2-3, The Territory Northwest of the River Ohio, 1787-1803. M721-0002. v4, The Territory South of the River Ohio, 1790-1896. M721-0003. v5-6, The Territory of Mississippi, 1809-1817. M721-0004. v7-8, The Territory of Indiana, 1800-1816. M721-0005. v9, The Territory of Orleans, 1803-1812. M721-0006. v10-11, The Territory of Michigan, 1805-1829. M721-0007. v12, The Territory of Michigan, 1829-1837. M721-0008. v13-15, The Territory of Louisiana, Missouri, 1803-1821. M721-0009. v16-17, The Territory of Illinois, 1809-1818. M721-0010. v18, The Territory of Alabama, 1817-1819. M721-0011. v19-20, The Territory of Arkansas, 1819-1829. M721-0012. v21, The Territory of Arkansas, 1829-1836. M721-0013. v22-23, The Territory of Florida, 1821-1828. M721-0014. v24-25, The Territory of Florida, 1828-1839. M721-0015. v26 1968, The Territory of Florida, 1839-1845. M721-0016) - 1 - us A.G.L.L. [978]

THE TERRITORIAL PAPERS OF THE UNITED STATES / U.S. Department of State; ed by Carter, Clarence E - (Covers Northwest, Southwest, Mississippi, Indiana, New Orleans, Michigan, Louisiana, Missouri, Alabama, Arkansas, Florida, and Wisconsin Territories) - 28bks - 282mf - 9 - $423.00 - LLMC 78-076 - us L.L.M.C. [324]

THE TERRITORIAL PAPERS OF THE UNITED STATES: IOWA, 1838-1846 / U.S. Department of State - 102r - 1 - M325 - us Nat'l Archives [324]

TERRITORIAL PAPERS OF THE UNITED STATES SENATE, 1789-1873 / U.S. Congress. Senate - (With printed guide) - 20r - 1 - M200 - us Nat'l Archives [324]

THE TERRITORIAL PAPERS OF THE UNITED STATES: THE TERRITORY OF MINNESOTA, 1849-1858 / U.S. Department of State - 14r - 1 - M1050 - us Nat'l Archives [324]

THE TERRITORIAL PAPERS OF THE UNITED STATES: THE TERRITORY OF OREGON, 1848-1859 / U.S. Department of State - 12r - 1 - M1049 - us Nat'l Archives [324]

THE TERRITORIAL PAPERS OF THE U.S / U.S. National Archives and Records Service - 15 rolls. M721. Printed guide - 1 - us Nat'l Archives [324]

TERRITORIAL PAPERS: OKLAHOMA / U.S. Department of the Interior - 1889-1912. 5 rolls. M828 - 1 - us Nat'l Archives [324]

THE TERRITORIAL REGISTER / Trust Territory of the Pacific Islands. (U.S.) - (Publ monthly) - Saipan: Registrar of Corporations, Office of the Attorney General. v1-2. 1974-79 - 10mf - 9 - $15.00 - LLMC 82-100F Title 4 - us L.L.M.C. [324]

TERRITORIAL SEA *see* TERRITORIAL SEA JOURNAL

THE TERRITORIAL SEA / Bustamante y Sirven, A S de - New York, 1930 - 3mf - 1 - ILM-2432/1 - ne IDC [327]

TERRITORIAL SEA JOURNAL – (Supersedes Territorial Sea. Superseded by Ocean and Coastal Law) – University of Maine. v1-2. 1990-91 (all publ) – 9 – $27.00 set – us Hein [340]
TERRITORIAL USE RIGHTS AND ECONOMIC EFFICIENCY : THE CASE OF THE PHILIPPINE FISHING CONCESSIONS – 1984 2nd print 1985 – 25p – it F.A.O. [340]
TERRITORIAL USE RIGHTS IN MARINE FISHERIES : DEFINITIONS AND CONDITIONS – 1992 – 16p – it F.A.O. [340]
TERRITORIAL WATERS AND OCEAN FISHERY RIGHTS / Haynes, T H – London: Spottiswoode & Co., 1893. 05524. (Pre-1900 Canadiana) – 9 – cn C.I.H.M. [900]
TERRITORIES LAW REPORTS / Northwest Territories. Canada – v1-7. 1885-1907 – 43mf – 9 – $64.00 – LLMC 81-033 – us L.L.M.C. [340]
TERRITORIO ACTUAL Y DIVISION POLITICA DE LA NACION ARGENTINA / Dagnino, Carlos – Buenos Aires, 1948 – 1 – CSUXADQ6996-B – us Hoover Inst Photo [320]
TERRITORY TIMES AND GAZETTE NAME INDEX 1876 – 1988 – 1mf – 9 – A$5.00 – 0-949124-37-0 – item 8 – at G.S.N.T. [072]
LE TERROIR : REVUE DE L'ECOLE LITTERAIRE – (Index by authors' names) – Montreal, Canada. 1909 – 1 – Can$30.00 – cn Can Microfilming [073]
TERROR IN SPAIN: HOW THE COMMUNIST INTERNATIONAL HAS DESTROYED WORKING CLASS UNITY, UNDERMINED THE FIGHT AGAINST FRANCO, AND SUPPRESSED THE SOCIAL REVOLUTION / McGovern, John – London, 1937? Fiche W1009. (Blodgett Collection of Spanish Civil War Pamphlets) – 9 – us H.U. College Libr [946]
TERROR OF THE ESTATE OF LORD THOMAS FAUCONBERG / Fauconberg, Thomas – 1 – uk Microform Academic [941]
TERROR SOBRE ESPANA / Zapirain, Luis – Mexico, 1940. Fiche W1261. (Blodgett Collection of Spanish Civil War Pamphlets) – 9 – us H.U. College Libr [946]
TERRORISM : AN INTERNATIONAL RESOURCE FILE / ed by Alexander, Yonah – (Documents 1986-88 $780.00 ea; documents 1980-85 backfile $1650) – 9 – $4925.00 complete collection to 1988 – us UMI [360]
TERRORISM – v. 1- 1977- – 1,5,6,9 – us UMI [300]
TERRORISM IN INDIA *see*
– POLITICAL TROUBLE IN INDIA, 1907-1917
– POLITICO-CRIMINAL WHO'S WHO
TERRORISM IN INDIA, 1917-1936 / India. Intelligence Bureau. Home Department – (Filmed with: Political Trouble in India, 1907-17; and Politico-Criminal Who's Who) – [s.l: s.n.], 1937 – us Res Libr [303]
TERRORISM SLIM / U.S. National Institute of Justice NCJRS – (1986 suppl. 76 documents, indexed. $86.00) – 1969-1981. 142 full-text documents, indexed – 9 – $125.00 – us N.C.J.R.S. [360]
TERRORISM: SPECIAL STUDIES : BASIC SET, 1975-1985 – (1st suppl 1985-88 5r $580.00 ISBN 1-55655-108-8. 2nd suppl 1989-91 3r $375.00 ISBN 1-55655-425-7. 3rd suppl 1992-95 4r $500.00 ISBN 1-55655-540-7. All with printed guides) – 5r – 1 – $580.00 set – 0-89093-493-2 – us UPA [320]
Terry, Garnet *see* AN AFFECTIONATE ADDRESS TO THE MEMBERS OF THE METHODIST SOCIETY, IN LEEDS AND ELSEWHERE, RESPECTING THE LATE TRANSACTIONS AT BRISTOL;...
Terry, Lawrence A *see* VALIDATION OF A CYCLE ERGOMETER VO2MAX PREDICTION EQUATION FOR NONSEDENTARY COLLEGE-AGE WOMEN
Terry, Lawrence R *see* A SURVEY OF DIVISION 1 ATHLETIC ADMINISTRATOR'S COMPETENCY DIMENSIONS FOR ADMINISTRATION AND MENTORING
Terry, Milton Spenser *see*
– BIBLICAL APOCALYPTICS
– CHRONICLES AND THE MOSAIC LEGISLATION
– MOSES AND THE PROPHETS:...SOME OF THE POSITIONS OF MODERN BIBLICAL CRITICISM
– THE NEW APOLOGETIC:...METHODS OF MEETING...ATTACKS UPON THE CHRISTIAN RELIGION
– THE PROPHECIES OF DANIEL
Terskoi, An *see* S KINOAPPARATOM PO SSSR

DIE TERTIAERFLORA AUF DER INSEL JAVA,... / Goeppert, H R – 's-Gravenhage, 1854[-1857] – 4mf – 9 – ne IDC [580]
TERTIARY AND UPPER CRETACEOUS FAUNA OF WESTERN INDIA / Duncan, P M & Sladen, WP – (Mem. geol. Surv. of India; paleont. Ind.). v. 1. Calcutta. 1871-74. BG-159 2 – 8 – ne IDC [590]
TERTIUS ARTICULUS QUE... / Gonzalez de Carreras, Diego & Zambrano Villalobos, Sebastian – S.l., s.i. s.a. Hacia 1612 – 1 – sp Bibl Santa Ana [946]
TERTIUS LIBER MOYSIS, QVI INSCRIBITVR LEVITICVS. ADDITA ENARRATIONE / Chytraeus, D – Vitebergae, 1575 – 6mf – 9 – ne IDC [240]
TERTULLIAN'S GEGEN DIE JUDEN AUF EINHEIT, ECHTHEIT, ENTSTEHUNG / Noeldechen, Ernst – Leipzig: J.C. Hinrichs, 1894. (Texte und Untersuchungen zur Geschichte der altchristlichen Literatur; 12. Bd., Heft 2) – 1mf – us A.T.L.A. [240]
TERTULLIAN'S GEGEN DIE JUDEN (T.U.U. 1-12/2A) / Noeldechen, Ernst – Leipzig, 1894 – 2mf – 9 – ne Slangenburg [240]
TERUEL EN EL SIGLO 15. LA VIDA ECONOMICA Y LA CUESTION MONETARIA / Floriano Cumbreno, Antonio C – Madrid: Tip. Arch. Bibliot. y Museos, 1926 – 1 – sp Bibl Santa Ana [330]
Terzi, Arduino *see*
– LA CHIESA NUOVA IN AISSI...
– CRONOLOGIA DELLA VITA DI S. FRANCESCO
Tesauro, Emanuel *see*
– FILOSOFIA MORAL DERIVADA DE ARISTOTELES
– FILOSOFIA MORAL, DERIVADA DE LA ALTA FUENTE DEL GRANDE ARISTOTELES
Teschaner, C *see* ARIFAUNA Y FLORA. NOS COSTUMES, SUPERSTICOES E LENDAS BRASILEIRAS E AMERICANAS...
Teschner, Pamela J S *see* COMPARATIVE ANALYSIS OF FACTORS INFLUENCING PARTICIPATION IN AN EMPLOYEE HEALTH PROMOTION PROGRAM, INCLUDING CHARACTERIZATIONS OF PARTICIPANTS AND NONPARTICIPANTS
Teselkin, Avenir Stepanovich *see* KAMUS PELADJARAN INDONESIA-RUSIA; 7000 KATA
TESERA ROMANA DE PLOMO EXTREMENA, QUE POSEE DON ANTONIO VIVES / Fita, Fidel – Madrid: Fortanet, 1913. B.R.A.H. 62. pp. 480-482 – 1 – sp Bibl Santa Ana [440]
TESHUVAH GELUYAH LE-MO"L HA-HAVAZZELET – (La-Levanon, 5635). 1875. BJ-27-220 1 – 9 – ne IDC [956]
TESHUVAH LI-TESHUVAH – (Havazzelet, Jerusalem, 5635). 1875. BJ-27-207 1 – 9 – ne IDC [956]
Tesi, P *see* INTRODUCTION A L'ETUDE DES SERRURES BAMBARA
TESIS / Gil, M – Mexico, 1900 – 1mf – 1 – ILM-3719/1 – ne IDC [327]
Teske, Hermann *see* ZEHNTAUSEND MANN DIE ZOGEN INS MANOEVER
TESL CANADA JOURNAL – Winnipeg. v1-11. 1984-1993/94 – 9 – Can$20.00y – cn Micromedia [073]
TESNOPISECKE ZPRAVY O SCHUZICH / Czechoslovakia. Narodni shromazdeni. Senat – Praha. 26 May 1920-17 Dec 1938.16 reels – 1 – 23.00r – us L of C Photodup [943]
TESOL QUARTERLY – Teachers of English to Speakers of Other Languages – v1- 1967-1; v9- 5,6,9 – us UMI [400]
TESORO DE ALISEDA / Melida, Jose Ramon – Madrid: Fototipias de Hanser y Menet, 1921 – 1 – sp Bibl Santa Ana [946]
EL TESORO DE DOBAIDE / Mendez Pereira, Octavio – Madrid: Ed.Nuestra Raza.Talleres Tip.A.F. – 1 – sp Bibl Santa Ana [946]
TESORO DE INDULGENCIAS...DEL SUFRAGIO... NIMES – 1885 – 9 – 1.50f – sp Bibl Santa Ana [240]
TESORO DE LA ALISEDA / Melida, Jose Ramon – Madrid: Fortanet, 1920. B.R.A.H. 76. pp. 479-480 – 1 – sp Bibl Santa Ana [946]
TESORO DE LA ALISEDA / Melida, Jose Ramon – Madrid: Tip. Rev. Arch. Bibliot. y Museos, 1926 – 1 – sp Bibl Santa Ana [946]
TESORO DE LA VERDADERA CIRUGIA... / Hidalgo de Aguero, B – Barcelona, 1624 – 11mf – 9 – sp Cultura [617]

TESORO DE LAS EXCELENCIAS Y UTILIDADES DE LA MEDICINA Y ESPEJO DEL PRUDENTE Y SABIO MEDICO... / Aroza, D – Lerida, 1668 – 7mf – 9 – sp Cultura [610]
IL TESORO ILLUMINATO DI TUTTI I TUONI DI CANTO FIGURATO.. / Aiguino da Brescia, Illuminato – 1581 – 9 – us Sibley [780]
IL TESORO ILLVMINATO DI TVTTI I TVONI DI CANTO FIGVRATO, CON ALCVNI BELLISSIMI SECRETI / Aiguino, T – Venetia, appresso Giovanni Varisco. 1631. BP-633 1 – 9 – ne IDC [780]
TESORO POETICO CASTELLANO DEL SIGLO 19 / Gomez Bravo, Vicente – Madrid: Graficas Nebrija, 1954 – 1 – sp Bibl Santa Ana [810]
TESOROS DEL PASADO ARGENTINO... / Cabrera, Pablo – Madrid: Razon y Fe, 1927 – 1 – sp Bibl Santa Ana [972]
A TESOURA : COMPLETA NEUTRALIDADE NA LUTA DOS PARTIDOS POLITICOS – Corumba, 1 Jul 1878 – 1,5,6 – bl Biblioteca [072]
A TESOURA : ORGAM INTRANSIGENTE DA LIGA CONTRA O ALCOOL – S. Felippe, Amazonas. Abr. 1908 – 1,5,6 – bl Biblioteca [072]
TESS OF THE D'URBERVILLES : A PURE WOMAN FAITHFULLY PRESENTED / Hardy, Thomas – [London]: James R. Osgood, McIlvaine, [1893] – 1 roll – 1 – uk Libr Preservation [830]
Tessier, A *see* LE RAPATRIEMENT
Tessier, Albert *see* ALBERT TESSIER ET SON OEUVRE
Tessier, G J *see* LE REVEIL
TEST CASE ON THE ORDINATION OF WOMEN: APPEALED FROM THE NEW ENGLAND CONFERENCE TO GENERAL CONFERENCE / Oliver, Ann – 1880 – 9 – us A.T.L.A. [240]
A TEST OF THE VARIABILITY OF PRACTICE HYPOTHESIS : THE ACQUISITION OF A GROSS MOTOR SKILL / Spriddle, Dean & Sinclair, Gary D – 1993 – 1mf – 9 – $4.00 – us Microform Publ [150]
LA TESTA DI MERIDA CENNI SULLA CRITICA ICONOGRAFICA / Ferri, Silvia – 1935 – 1 – sp Bibl Santa Ana [946]
Testa, G M R *see* DE INHOUD DER OVEREENKOMSTEN IN HET INTERNATIONAAL PRIVAATRECHT
Testa, I de *see* RECUEIL DES TRAITES DE LA PORTE OTTOMANE
TESTACEA MUSEI CAESAREI VINDOBONENSIS / Born, I von – Vienna, 1780 – 24mf – ne IDC [590]
TESTACEA UTRIUSQUE SICILIAE EORUMQUE HISTORIA ET ANATOME / Poli, G S – Z 190 2. 3 v. 1791-1827 – 8 – ne IDC [580]
TESTAMENT (DAT NIEUWE) ONS LIEFS HEEREN JESU CHRISTI – Gedr. na de Copye v. Nic. Biestkens. (Emden, W. Geylliaert). 1563. BME-333 1 – 9 – ne IDC [240]
LE TESTAMENT DE LA LIBERTE / Constant, Alphonse Louis – Paris: J. Frey, 1848. 219p. 3 fiches. (Political Science Collection) – 9 – 8.00 – fr Bibl Nationale [320]
TESTAMENT DE MARIE-ANTOINETTE, REINE DE FRANCE(...) / Poudra, Jean-G – Lucon, Nantes: Mellinet-Malassis, 1817 – fr Armell [944]
THE TESTAMENT OF ABRAHAM : WITH AN APPENDIX BY W.E. BARNES / ed by James, M R – 1892 – 3mf – 9 – ne Slangenburg [220]
THE TESTAMENT OF JOHN DAVIDSON / Davidson, John – London: Grant Richards, 1908 – 1 roll – 1 – 1-55879-463-8 – uk Libr Preservation [810]
TESTAMENT POLITIK IR. SOEKARNO / Sukarno, Pres. Indonesia – SE 2140 1. 1946 – 9 – ne IDC [025]
DAS TESTAMENT UNSERES HERRN UND DIE VERWANDTEN SCHRIFTEN / Funk, Franz Xaver – Mainz: F. Kirchheim, 1901 – 1mf – us A.T.L.A. [220]
TESTAMENTA XII PATRIARCHARUM: AD FIDEM CODICIS CANTABRIGIENSIS EDITA / Sinker, Robert – Cambridge: Deighton, Bell, 1869.1 fiche – 9 – us A.T.L.A. [240]
DE TESTAMENTEN DER TWAALF PATRIARCHEN / Hengel, Wessel Albertus van – (Includes bibliographical references) – Amsterdam: Ten Brink & de Vries, 1860 – 1mf – 9 – 0-8370-3560-0 – 1985-1560 – us A.T.L.A. [220]

TESTAMENTO DE D. RODRIGO PEREZ, ARCEDIANO EN 1550 DE LA ARCHIDIOCESIS DE LIMA / Martin Gil, Tomas – Badajoz: Tip. La Alianza, 1935 – 1 – sp Bibl Santa Ana [320]
EL TESTAMENTO DE FRANCISCO PIZARRO, CONQUISTADOR DE PERU / Porras Barrenechea, Paul – Madrid, 1936 – 1 – sp Bibl Santa Ana [920]
TESTAMENTO DE HERNAN CORTES / Cuevas, Manuel – Mexico: Imp. del Asilo Patricio Sanz, 1925 – sp Bibl Santa Ana [920]
EL TESTAMENTO DE PIZARRO / Porras Barrenechea, Paul – Paris: Imp. Les Presses Moderenes, 1936. Cuad. Hª del Peru, Documentos Ineditos 1 Cuaderno no 1 – sp Bibl Santa Ana [920]
EL TESTAMENTO DE PIZARRO DE 1539 / Porras Barrenechea, Paul – Madrid: Revista de Indias, 1941 – 1 – sp Bibl Santa Ana [946]
TESTAMENTO DEL CARDENAL CISNEROS (ANNO 1513) – Alcala de H. – 1r – 5,6 – sp Cultura [240]
TESTAMENTOS CANONIGOS. ANIVERSARIOS (SIECLE 14). BULAS. (SIECLE 17-18) – Albarracin – 1r – 5,6 – sp Cultura [240]
TESTAMENTUM DOMINI NOSTRI JESU CHRISTI / Rahmani, Ignace Efraem 2 – 1989 – 8mf – 9 – ne Slangenburg [240]
TESTAMENTVM NOVVM...EST AUTEM INTERPRETATIO SYRIACA NOUI TESTAMENTI, ...AVTORE IMMANVELE TREMELLIO, ...CUIUS ETIAM GRAMMMATICA CHALDAICA ET SYRA CALCI OPERIS ADJECTA EST / ed by Tremellius, Immanuel – [Geneva], 1569 – 39mf – 9 – H-8437/1 – ne IDC [220]
Testelin, H *see* SENTIMENS DES PLUS HABILES PEINTRES DU TEMPS, SUR LA PRATIQUE DE LA PEINTURE
TESTIMONIAL FOR JOHN CARTER, ENGLISH ORGANIST, BY HIS COLLEAGUES, PUPIL, CLERGY, AND OTHER ASSOCIATES – (33 letters pasted in a scrapbook) – England, before 1853, Quebec after that date – 2mf – 9 – us Sibley [780]
TESTIMONIAL OF RESPECT OF THE BAR OF NEW YORK, TO THE MEMORY OF ALEXANDER W. BRADFORD, ESQ / New York. Bar of the City of New York – New York: Baker and Godwin, 1868. 23p. LL-942 – 1 – us L of C Photodup [340]
TESTIMONIES OF AMERICAN STATESMEN AND JURISTS TO THE TRUTHS OF CHRISTIANITY / Wilson, Henry – Boston: American Tract Society, 1866. 1 fiche – 9 – us A.T.L.A. [240]
TESTIMONIES TO THE DIVINE AUTHORITY AND INSPIRATION OF THE HOLY SCRIPTURES / McCaul, Alexander – London: Rivingtons, 1862. 1 fiche – 9 – us A.T.L.A. [240]
TESTIMONIO DE CARINO Y RESPETO QUE EL PUEBLO OFRECE A SU HIJO ADOPTIVO DR. D. EZEQUIEL FERNANDEZ SANTANA. LOS SANTOS DE MAIMONA. 27 DE MAYO DE 1917 – Madrid: Tip. Artistica, 1917 – sp Bibl Santa Ana [946]
EL TESTIMONIO DE LAS PIEDRAS-DISCURSO / Fernandez Valbuena, Ramiro – 1891 – 9 – 1.50f – sp Bibl Santa Ana [240]
TESTIMONY FROM THE WORD AGAINST DIVINITY DEGREES IN THE UNIVERSITY / Dell, William – 1816 – 1 – 5.00 – us Baptist [240]
TESTIMONY OF CHRIST TO CHRISTIANITY / Bayne, Peter – New York: F.H. Revell, 1904. 1 fiche – 9 – us A.T.L.A. [240]
THE TESTIMONY OF CHRIST TO CHRISTIANITY / Bayne, Peter – New York: Fleming H Revell, c1904 – 1mf – 9 – 0-8370-2218-5 – 1985-0218 – us A.T.L.A. [230]
TESTIMONY OF EMINENT WITNESSES FOR THE BIBLE...FOR THE SPECIAL BENEFIT OF YOUNG MEN – New York: G.C. Rand & Avery, 1866. 1 fiche – 9 – us A.T.L.A. [240]
THE TESTIMONY OF JUSTIN MARTYR TO EARLY CHRISTIANITY : LECTURES / Purves, George Tybout – New York: Anson D.F. Randolph, c1889 – 1mf – us A.T.L.A. [240]
THE TESTIMONY OF THE BIBLE CONCERNING...DESTRUCTIVE CRITICISM / Wishard, Samuel Ellis – Los Angeles: Johnson & Haney, 1909. 1 fiche – 9 – us A.T.L.A. [240]

THE TESTIMONY OF THE CATACOMBS AND OF OTHER MONUMENTS OF CHRISTIAN ART : FROM THE SECOND TO THE EIGHTEENTH CENTURY, CONCERNING QUESTIONS OF DOCTRINE NOW DISPUTED IN THE CHURCH / Marriott, Wharton B – London: Hatchards, 1870 – 1mf – us A.T.L.A. [240]

TESTING STRENGTH AND POWER : AN INVESTIGATION OF THE RELIABILITY, VALIDITY AND APPROPRIATE USE OF ISOMETRIC ISOKINETIC, AND ISOINERTIAL TESTS OF MUSCULAR FUNCTION / Murphy, Aron J – Southern Cross University, 1996 – 4mf – 9 – $16.00 – PE 3664 – us Microform Publ [612]

TESTING THE VALIDITY OF THE NEAR INFRARED BODY COMPOSITION TECHNIQUE IN CHILDREN / Appleton, R J – 1990 – 1mf – 9 – $4.00 – us Microform Publ [790]

TESTOSTERONE AND PHYSICAL ACTIVITY : A META-ANALYSIS / Arce, Joan C & Jensen, Barbara E – 1992 – 2mf – $8.00 – us Microform Publ [612]

TEST-RETEST STUDY OF THE BIODEX CLOSED KINETIC CHAIN ATTACHMENT FOR THE UPPER EXTREMITY / Gorman, Monica E – 1994 – 1mf – $4.00 – us Microform Publ [612]

TESTS IN MICROFICHE – (A collection of unpublished research instruments in education and psychology. 21 sets (A-U) of ca 25-100 tests each. Annotated indexes. New sets issued annually. Individual tests available) – 9 – ca $150.00 set; $11.00 per test – us E.T.S. [370]

THE TESTS OF LIFE: A STUDY OF THE FIRST EPISTLE OF ST JOHN / Law, Robert – Edinburgh: T. & T. Clark, 1909. 1 fiche – 9 – us A.T.L.A. [240]

TESTS OF TRUTH:...ON THE TEACHINGS OF NATURE AND REVEALED RELIGION / Dyer, David – New York: Broughton & Wyman, 1866. 1 fiche – 9 – us A.T.L.A. [240]

TESVIK – Koestence (Kostanza). Sahib-i Imtiyaz: Abduelhakim Bekir; Sermuharriri: Mehmed Niyazi, 1909. No. 2 (19 Haziran 1909) – 9 – $25.00 – us MEDOC [956]

Tetermann, A *see* ESTI BAPTISTI...25 JUUBELI AASTA MALESTUSETS

TETON CHRONICLE – Choteau. Mont. 1898; 1900-1901 – 1 – us UMI [071]

TETON COUNTY MONTANA – Cut Bank. Mont. 1911-1950 – 1 – us UMI [071]

TETRADYMUS / Toland, John – (Contains: 1. Hodegus...; 2. Clidophorus...; 3. Hypatia...; 4. Mangoneutes...) – London, 1720 – 7mf – 8 – ne Slangenburg [100]

TETRAHEDRON : INTERNATIONAL JOURNAL OF ANALYTICAL CHEMISTRY – (Combined with Bioorganic & Medicinal Chemistry Letters and Tetrahedron Letters, 124 issues/y. £5,775.00y. Back issues of journal available from UMI) – Includes Tetrahedron: Asymmetry. 60 issues/y. v49. 1993 – 9 – £2,788.00y – uk Elsevier Sci [540]

TETRAHEDRON – v1- 1957- – 5,6,9 – us UMI [540]

TETRAHEDRON LETTERS – 1959- – 5,6,9 – us UMI [540]

TETRAHEDRON LETTERS – (Combined with Bioorganic & Medicinal Chemistry Letters, 64 issues/y £2,964.00y and with Tetrahedron and Tetrahedron: Asymmetry, 124 issues/y £5,775.00y. Back issues of journal available from UMI) – 52 issues/y. v34. 1993 – 9 – £2,465.00y – uk Elsevier Sci [540]

TETRATEUCHUS SIVE COMMENTARIUS IN SANCTA JESU CHRISTI EVANGELIA / Jansenius, Corn. – Ed. 2a. Lovanii, 1659 – 16mf – 8 – ne Slangenburg [220]

Tettamanzi, Fabricio *see* BREVE METODO PER FONDATAMENTE, E CON FACILITA APPRENDERE IL CANTO FERMO..

Tetteh, S N *see* GHANA AGRICULTURE, 1890-1962

Tetterman, Andres *see* LUULETUSED JA AUTOBIOGRAAFIA

Tetu, Henri *see* MANDEMENTS, LETTRES PASTORALES ET CIRCULAIRES DES EVEQUES DE QUEBEC

Tetu, Theophile *see* REPORTS OF PIERRE FORTIN AND THEOPHILE TETU...IN COMMAND OF THE EXPEDITION FOR THE PROTECTION OF THE FISHERIES IN THE GULF OF ST LAWRENCE... 1867

TE'UDAH BE-YISRAEL / Levinsohn, I B – Vilna, Grodno. 1828. BJ-422-46 1 – 9 – ne IDC [180]

TE'UDAH MIN HA-DOR HA-RISHON SHEL MEGORESHEI SEFARAD BI-ZEFAT / Benayahu, M – Sefer S. Assaf. 1953. BJ-27-62 1 – 9 – ne IDC [956]

TE'UDOT LE-TOLEDOT HA-YISHUV BE-HEVRON / Yaari, A – v. 32. Sinay. 1953. BJ-27-65 1 – 9 – ne IDC [956]

TE'UDOT TURKIYYOT AL YEHUDEI ZEFAT BA-MEAH HA-16 / Heyd, U – v. 5. Yerushalayim. 1955. BJ-27-59 1 – 9 – ne IDC [270]

DIE TEUETSCH SPRAACH : ALLE WOERTER... MIT GUETEM LATEIN... VERTOLMETSCHT... DICTIONARIUM GERMANICOLATINUM... / Maler, J – Tiguri: Christoph Froschouer, 1561 – 12mf – ne IDC [430]

TEUFELSMUELLER : BEZIEHUNGEN UND DEUTUNGEN / Culmann, Hellmut – Pirmasens: W Neumann, 1926 – 1r – 1 – us U.W. Library [700]

Teulet, A et al *see*
- INVENTAIRES ET DOCUMENTS PUBLIES PAR ORDRE DE L'EMPEREUR
- INVENTAIRES ET DOCUMENTS PUBLIES PAR ORDRE DE L'EMPEREUR. LAYETTES DU TRESOR DES CHARTES

TEUNGKU TJHI'DI TIRO : OLEH TEUNGKOE ISMAIL JAKOEB / Ismail Ja'kub, T – Tjetakan 1, Medan ? Nafi-Peutoea Hoesin 2605. 113p – 51-52mf – 9 – ne IDC [920]

DER TEUTSCHE DIOGENES – Danzig (Gdansk), Poland. 1736-1737 – 2r – 1 – gw Mikrofilm [943]

DER TEUTSCHE EDITOREN-KONGRESS ZU CINCINNATI : ODER, DAS GEBROCHENE HERZ / Heinzen, Karl Peter – Boston: Selbstverlag des Verfassers, 1872 – 1r – 1 – us U.W. Library [071]

TEUTSCHER BEOBACHTER – Stuttgart, Germany. 10 Aug 1822-12 Jun 1823 – 1r – 1 – gw Mikrofilm [072]

TEUTSCHLAND UND DIE REVOLUTION / Goerres, Joseph – Koblenz, 1819 – 9 – DM48.00 – 3-89349-246-1 – gw Hänsel [943]

TEVARIH-I AL-I OSMAN / Pasa, Luetfi – Istanbul: Matbaa-i Amire, 1341 [1925] – 9 – $85.00 – us MEDOC [956]

TEVARIH-I AL-I OSMAN [ASIKPASAZADE TARIHI] / Asikpasazade; ed by Giese, Friedrich – Leipzig: Otto Harrassowitz, 1929 – 9 – us MEDOC [956]

TEVARIH-I AL-I OSMAN [ASIKPASAZADE TARIHI] / Asikpasazade – Istanbul: Matbaa-yi Amiri, 1332 [1914] – 9 – $85.00 – us MEDOC [956]

LE TEVECOIS : AU SERVICE DU SAGUENAY/ LAC ST-JEAN ET DE CHIBOUGAMAU-CHAPAIS / Quebec. (Province). Direction Generale de l'Education Permanente – [Quebec]: Ministere de l'Education. no 1-6. 1969. SEM35P38 – 1r – 1 – Can$15.00 – cn Bibl Nat [073]

Tevfik *see*
- DIVANCE
- UFAK MECMU'A-'I SI'IR

Tevfik, Ebuezziya *see*
- 1297 [1880] SENE-I HICRIYESINE MAHSUS SALNAME-I KAMERI
- SUERUR-I MUEVERRIH

Tevfik, Neyzen *see* HIC!

TEVIJA – Riga (1941-44), Liepaja (1944-45), 1941-45 – 8r – 1 – $560.00 – us Ross [072]

TEVIJA, RIGA, + LIEPAJA – De 1941 a 1945; De 1944 a 1945 – 9r – 1 – Sfr1,080.00 – sz Infoprint [947]

TEVISKES ZIBURIAI – Toronto, Canada. -w. 1971-75; 1977-78. 4 reels – 1 – uk British Libr Newspaper [072]

TEVISKES ZIBURIAL – (In Lithuanian) – Canada, 1958- – 1 – cn Commonwealth Micro [072]

Tevo, Z *see* IL MUSICO TESTORE DEL P. BAC ZACCARIA TEVO

TEVU'OT HA-AREZ. JERUSALEM / Schwarz, Y – 1845. BJ-27-39 1 – 9 – ne IDC [910]

Teweles, Heinrich *see* GOETHE UND DIE JUDEN

TEWKESBURY JOURNAL ETC – England.Jan-Jun 1982. -w. 1 1/2 reels – 1 – uk British Libr Newspaper [072]

TEXAN – Grand Prairie. Tex. 1908-1911; 1919-1932; 1934-1937; 1952- – 1 – us UMI [071]

TEXANS WHO WORE GRAY / Johnson, Sid S – Texas Reel 13. (The Cox Library Collection) – 5 – us Americana [978]

TEXANS WHO'S WHO / Acheson, Gambrell, Toomey, Acheson, Jr – Dallas: Texian Co., 1937. Texas Reel 13. (The Cox Library Collection) – 5 – us Americana [978]

TEXAS – 8r – 1 – $640.00 – us Scholarly Res [370]

TEXAS : SESSION LAWS OF AMERICAN STATES AND TERRITORIES – 1824-1995 – 9 – $2,285.00 set – us Hein [340]

TEXAS : VERNON'S ANNOTATED TEXAS STATUTES – St Paul: West Pub Co, 1925-Jan 1996 update – 9 – $2,850.00 set – us Hein [340]

TEXAS : VERNON'S ANNOTATED TEXAS STATUTES. SUPPLEMENT – St Paul: West Pub Co, superseded pocket parts 1988-95 – 9 – $2,750.00 set; $340.00y – us Hein [340]

Texas *see*
- REPORTS AND OPINIONS (A-G)
- REPORTS, POST-NRS
- REPORTS, PRE-NRS
- TEXAS CIVIL APPEALS REPORTS

TEXAS A AND M AGRICULTURIST / Texas A & M University. College of Agriculture.Department of Agricultural Economics – 28/1-29/3. 1970-82 – 1r – 1,5 – us Spaulding [630]

Texas A & M University. Agricultural Experiment Station *see*
- ANNUAL REPORT
- MISCELLANEOUS PUBLICATIONS
- PROGRESS REPORT
- RESEARCH IN TEXAS
- RESEARCH MONOGRAPH
- TAES NEWS
- TECHNICAL MONOGRAPH

Texas A & M University. Agricultural Experiment Station and Agricultural Extension Service *see*
- BULLETIN
- CENTER FOR ENERGY AND MINERAL RESOURCES: ALCOHOL-FUEL SYMPOSIUM
- LEAFLET
- PASTURE AND FORAGE CROPS: SHORT COURSE PROCEEDINGS
- TEXAS CONFERENCE ON INSECT, PLANT DISEASE, WEED AND BRUSH CONTROL

Texas A & M University. Agricultural Extension Service *see*
- ANNUAL REPORT
- DAIRY SHORT COURSE PROCEEDINGS
- PROCEEDINGS TURKEY INDUSTRY DAY
- TEXAS AGRICULTURAL PROGRESS

Texas A & M University. Agricultural Market Research and Development Center *see* INDUSTRY, INFORMATION, RESEARCH AND TECHNICAL REPORT

Texas A & M University. College of Agriculture *see*
- ANNUAL REPORT
- STUDY OF TEXAS AGRICULTURE AND AGRICULTURAL PROGRAMS AT TEXAS A & M UNIVERSITY

Texas A & M University. College of Agriculture.Department of Agricultural Economics *see*
- DEPARTMENTAL INFORMATION REPORT
- DEPARTMENTAL TECHNICAL REPORT
- TEXAS A AND M AGRICULTURIST

Texas A & M University. Department of Animal Science *see*
- DEPARTMENTAL TECHNICAL REPORT
- HORSE SHORT COURSE PROCEEDINGS
- SWINE SHORT COURSE PROCEEDINGS

Texas A & M University. Department of Entomology *see* DEPARTMENTAL TECHNICAL REPORT

Texas A & M University. Department of Forest Science *see* FOREST SCIENCE RESEARCH NOTES

Texas A & M University. Department of Poultry Science *see*
- COMMERCIAL EGG CLINIC COMPENDIUM
- DEPARTMENTAL INFORMATION REPORT
- TEXAS GAME BIRD CONFERENCE

Texas A & M University. Department of Recreation and Parks *see*
- DEPARTMENTAL INFORMATION REPORT
- DEPARTMENTAL TECHNICAL REPORT
- VISITING LECTURE SERIES

Texas A & M University. Department of Soil and Crop Sciences *see* DEPARTMENTAL INFORMATION REPORT; DEPARTMENTAL TECHNICAL REPORT; PROGRESS REPORT

Texas A & M University. Forest Service *see* PUBLICATION

TEXAS AGRICULTURAL PROGRESS / Texas A & M University. Agricultural Extension Service – v16,no.1-v26,no.3. 1970-80. 1 reel – 1,5 – us Spaulding [630]

TEXAS AS PROVINCE AND REPUBLIC: 1795-1845 – Based on Thomas Streeter's Bibliography of Texas, 1795-1845 – 1 – us Primary [975]

TEXAS ATTORNEY GENERAL REPORTS AND OPINIONS – (6 1840-1970 $315.00. 9 1971-1995 + indexes $840.00) – 1840-1995 and Indexes (1971-1994) – 6,9 – $1,195.00 set – us Hein [340]

TEXAS BAPTIST – 7 Mar 1855-61 – 1 – 68.81 – us Baptist [240]

TEXAS BAPTIST – Abilene. 13 Jan 1876-1883; Texas Baptist and Herald. 1884-1906 – 1 – 769.12 – us Baptist [240]

Texas Baptist Association *see* SUNDAY SCHOOL STATISTICS

Texas. Baptist Associations *see* PAPERS

Texas Baptist Oral History Consortium *see* MEMOIRS

TEXAS BAPTIST-HERALD – Houston/Dallas. 1869-70, 1887-88, 1901-08. Single reels available – 1 – 185.00 – us A.B.H.S. [073]

TEXAS BAR ASSOCIATION PROCEEDINGS – (Lacking: 13th, 14th (p273-76); 25th, 39th, 40th, 42nd, 44th & 51st meetings) – 1st to 58th annual meetings. 1882-1939 (all publ) – 59mf – 9 – $220.00 – LLMC 84-680 – us L.L.M.C. [073]

TEXAS BAR JOURNAL – (v1-47 1938-84 on reel or mf $660.00. v48-58 1985-95 on mf $254.00) – v1-58. 1938-95 – 5,6,9 – $914.00 set – us Hein [340]

Texas. Board of Water Engineers *see* STATE WATER RESOURCES REPORTS

Texas. Civil Appeals Court *see*
- THE TEXAS COURT REPORTER
- THE TEXAS LAW REPORTER
- WHITE AND WILSON'S REPORTS

TEXAS CIVIL APPEALS REPORTS / Texas – (No Pre-NRS vols) – v1-63. 1892-1911 (all publ) – 418mf – 9 – $627.00 – LLMC 84-209 – us L.L.M.C. [340]

TEXAS CIVIL APPEALS REPORTS *see*
- THE TEXAS COURT REPORTER
- THE TEXAS LAW REPORTER
- WHITE AND WILSON'S REPORTS

TEXAS CIVIL FORM BOOK. / Moffett, Jonas William – 4th ed. Austin: Gammel, 1915. 1061p. LL-22 – 1 – us L of C Photodup [340]

TEXAS CONFERENCE ON INSECT, PLANT DISEASE, WEED AND BRUSH CONTROL / Texas A & M University. Agricultural Experiment Station and Agricultural Extension Service – No.1-5. 1969-72. 13 fiches – 9 – us Spaulding [580]

Texas. County Commissioners *see* COUNTY COMMISSIONERS' LEGAL GUIDE, (FOR THE STATE OF TEXAS).

TEXAS COURT OF APPEALS REPORTS – (Cont by: Texas Criminal Appeals Reports) – v1-30. 1876-1892 – 266mf – 9 – $399.00 – LLMC 80-818 – us L.L.M.C. [340]

TEXAS COURT OF APPEALS REPORTS *see* TEXAS CRIMINAL APPEALS REPORTS

THE TEXAS COURT REPORTER / Texas. Civil Appeals Court – v1-20. 1900-1908 (all publ) – 250mf – 9 – $375.00 – LLMC 91-021 – us L.L.M.C. [340]

TEXAS CRIMINAL APPEALS REPORTS – (Cont: Texas Court of Appeals Reports. Updates planned) – v1-85. 1892-1919 – 719mf – 9 – $1,078.00 – LLMC 80-818 – us L.L.M.C. [340]

TEXAS CRIMINAL APPEALS REPORTS *see* TEXAS COURT OF APPEALS REPORTS

TEXAS ENVIRONMENTAL LAW JOURNAL – v1-24. 1976-95 – 9 – us Hein [340]

Texas. Fort Stockton *see* HEADQUARTERS RECORDS

TEXAS GAME BIRD CONFERENCE / Texas A & M University. Department of Poultry Science – No.1-7. 1969-83. 6 fiches – 9 – us Spaulding [639]

Texas Graduate Nurses Association *see* BULLETIN

TEXAS HISTORICAL AND BIOGRAPHICAL MAGAZINE – v. 1-2. 1891-92 – 1 – 53.41 – us Baptist [240]

TEXAS HOSPITALS – (v.35-. 1979- 5,6,9) – v.1-. 1945- – 1 – us UMI [073]

TEXAS INTELLECTUAL PROPERTY LAW JOURNAL – v1-3. 1992-1995 – 9 – $30.00set – us Hein [340]

TEXAS INTERNATIONAL LAW FORUM *see* TEXAS INTERNATIONAL LAW JOURNAL

TEXAS INTERNATIONAL LAW JOURNAL – (v1-19 1965-84 on reel $215.00. v20-30 1985-95 on mf $196.00. Title varies: v1 no 1 1965 as Texas University International Law Society Journal. v1 no 2-v6 1965-70 as Texas International Law Forum. With index v1-10 1965-75) – v1-30. 1965-94 – 5,6,9 – $435.00 set – us Hein [340]

THE TEXAS JEWISH HERALD – Houston, TX. 1925-38 – 1 – us A.J.P.C. [071]
THE TEXAS JEWISH POST – Ft. Worth Dallas. Texas. 1963-67 – 1 – us A.J.P.C. [071]
TEXAS JEWISH VOICE – Houston, TX. 1937 – 1 – us A.J.P.C. [071]
TEXAS JOURNAL OF WOMEN AND THE LAW – v1-5. 1992-96 – 5,6,9 – $67.00 set – us Hein [340]
TEXAS LAND TITLES; AN ESSAY ON DEFECTS IN TEXAS TITLES, AND REMEDIES THEREFOR / Snood, S G – Austin, Johns, 1885. 48 p. LL-1396 – 1 – us L of C Photodup [340]
TEXAS LAW AND LEGISLATION *see* SMU LAW REVIEW
THE TEXAS LAW REPORTER / Texas. Civil Appeals Court – v1-3. 1882-1884 (all publ) – 24mf – 9 – $36.00 – LLMC 92-412 – us L.L.M.C. [340]
TEXAS LAW REVIEW – v1-6. 1883-1886 (all publ) – 34mf – $51.00 – LLMC 90-329 – us L.L.M.C. [073]
TEXAS LAW REVIEW – v1-74. 1922-96 – 1,5,6,9 – $2,115.00 – us Hein [073]
TEXAS LIBRARY JOURNAL – (1983-. 1,5,6,9) – v26-. 1950- – 1 – us UMI [073]
TEXAS MONTHLY – 1973- – 9 – us UMI [073]
TEXAS NURSING – (1984-. 5,6,9) – v47-. 1973- – 1 – us UMI [610]
THE TEXAS OBSERVER – (1983-. 5,6,9) – v. 46-. 1954- – 1 – us UMI [320]
TEXAS PERSONNEL AND GUIDANCE ASSOCIATION JOURNAL *see* TPGA JOURNAL
Texas. Presbytery (Cum. Pres. Ch.) *see* MINUTES, 1837-1906
TEXAS QUARTERLY – v.1-21. 1958-78 – 1 – us UMI [073]
TEXAS REPORTS ON BIOLOGY AND MEDICINE – v1- 1943- 1; v33- 5,6,9 – us UMI [574]
TEXAS REPORTS ON BIOLOGY AND MEDICINE – v1-13. 1943-55 – 1,5,6 – us Princeton Micro [574]
THE TEXAS REPUBLIC – San Antonio. Tex. 1908-1921 – 1 – us UMI [071]
A TEXAS SCRAP BOOK / Baker, D W C – New York, Chicago and New Orleans: A.S. Barnes and Co., n.d. Texas Reel 5. (The Cox Library Collection) – 5 – us Americana [978]
TEXAS SOUTHERN INTRAMURAL LAW REVIEW *see* THURGOOD MARSHALL LAW REVIEW
TEXAS SOUTHERN UNIVERSITY LAW REVIEW *see* THURGOOD MARSHALL LAW REVIEW
Texas. State Bar Association *see* PROCEEDINGS
TEXAS STATE GAZETTE – Austin. Aug 25 1849-Aug 16 1851 – 1 – us NY Public [071]
Texas. Supreme Court *see*
- DALLAM'S REPORTS
- KING'S CONFLICTING CIVIL CASES IN THE TEXAS REPORTS
- POSEY'S UNREPORTED CASES
- ROBARD'S CONSCRIPT CASES
- ROSE'S NOTES ON THE TEXAS REPORTS, 1910 ED.
- TEXAS SUPREME COURT REPORTS

TEXAS SUPREME COURT REPORTS / Texas. Supreme Court – (Pre-NRS: v1-65 1846-86 512mf $768.00. Suppl vol for v25. Updates planned) – v1-109. 1846-1919 – 880mf – 9 – $1,320.00 – LLMC 80-817 – us L.L.M.C. [340]
Texas. Synod (Pres. Ch. in the U.S.A.) *see* MINUTES, 1878-1957
TEXAS TECH JOURNAL OF EDUCATION – (1981-. 1,5,6,9) – v1-. 1974- – 1 – us UMI [073]
TEXAS TECH LAW REVIEW – (v1-15 1969-84 on reel $249.00. v16-26 1985-95 on mf $291.00) – v1-26. 1969-95 – 5,6,9 – $540.00 set – us Hein [340]
TEXAS: THE COUNTRY AND ITS MEN / Daniell, L E – Historical-biographical-descriptive. Texas Reel 6. (The Cox Library Collection) – 5 – us Americana [978]
TEXAS: THE RISE, PROGRESS, AND PROSPECTS OF THE REPUBLIC OF TEXAS / Kennedy, William – Ft. Worth: Molyneaux Craftsman Inc., 1925. Texas Reel 3. (The Cox Library Collection) – 5 – us Americana [978]
TEXAS TRIBUNE – Dallas. 25 Jan 1941-29 Dec 1945. 3 reels – 1 – us I.H.R.C. [071]
TEXAS TRIBUNE – Dallas, TX. Jan 1941-Dec 1945 – 3r – 1 – us I.H.R.C. [071]
TEXAS UNDER MANY FLAGS / Wharton, Clarence R – Chicago: American Historical Society, 1930. v1-3, Texas Reel 3.v4-5, Texas Reel 4. (The Cox Library Collection) – 5 – us Americana [978]
Texas. University at Austin *see* CATALOG OF THE LATIN AMERICAN COLLECTION
TEXAS UNIVERSITY INTERNATIONAL LAW SOCIETY JOURNAL *see* TEXAS INTERNATIONAL LAW JOURNAL
Texas. University of Texas at Austin. Barker Texas History Center *see* BEXAR ARCHIVES: 1717-1836
TEXASPOSTEN – Austin, TX. 1898-1935, 1940-64 – 43r – 1 – sw Kungliga [071]
Texeyro de Valcarcel, Francisco J *see* DISQUISICION...INSTITUCION...MONTES DE PIEDAD
Texier, Edmond Auguste *see* L'ANE D'OR: RECUEIL SATIRIQUE
Texier, Paul *see* LE PORT DE SAIGON.
Texier-Olivier, Louis *see* STATISTIQUE GENERALE DE LA FRANCE. DEPARTEMENT DE LA HAUTE-VIENNE
TEXT AND TEACHER'S MANUAL : FUNCTIONAL LITERACY AND FAMILY LIFE PLANNING PROJECT / Thailand. Ministry of Education. Adult Education Division – Bangkok, [1975] – 3mf – 9 – DE-310/1 – ne IDC [370]
TEXT AUS DER VELKD – 1978-93 (complete) – 1r – 1 – ATLA S0913 – us A.T.L.A. [073]
TEXT BOOK OF LAMBA GRAMMAR / Doke, Clement Martin – Johannesburg, Witwatersrand, 1936 – us Res Libr [470]
A TEXT BOOK OF NORTH-SEMITIC INSCRIPTIONS / Cooke, G A – Oxford, 1903 – 9 – $15.00 – us I.R.C. [410]
A TEXT BOOK ON THE METHOD OF LEAST SQUARES / Merriman, Mansfield – New York: J. Wiley & Sons, 1884.viii,194p. Tables, Diagrs. 1 reel. 1293 – 1 – us U.W. Library [510]
DER TEXT DER BUECHER SAMUELIS / Wellhausen, Julius – (Includes bibliographical references) – Goettingen: Vandenhoeck und Ruprecht, 1871 – 1mf – 9 – 0-8370-6458-9 – 1986-0458 – us A.T.L.A. [220]
DER TEXT DER THESSALONICHERBRIEF : SAMT TEXTKRITISCHEM APPARAT UND KOMMENTAR: NEBST EINER UNTERSUCHUNG DER INDIVIDUALITAET UND DER VERWANDTSCHAFT DER TEXTZEUGEN DER PAULINISCHEN BRIEFE / Zimmer, Friedrich – (In German and Greek. Includes index) – 2. Aufl. Quedlinburg: Chr Friedr Vieweg, 1893 – 1mf – 9 – 0-8370-9679-0 – 1986-3679 – us A.T.L.A. [220]
DER TEXT DES BUCHES HIOB: ERSTES HEFT-KAPITEL I-XIV / Beer, Georg – Marburg: N.G. Elwert, 1895. 1 fiche – 9 – us A.T.L.A. [240]
TEXT OF LABOUR LEGISLATION AMENDMENTS ENACTED IN 1972 CONCERNING THE COMPULSORY SOCIAL PROTECTION OF WORKERS IN LIBYA / Libya. National Social Insurance Institution – Laws, Statutes, etc. Social Insurance Law nr.53 of 1957 as amended. Tripoli. 1972. BNE-908 1 – 9 – ne IDC [360]
TEXT OF PRESIDENTIAL REGULATION NO. 10 OF 1959, UNDER WHICH ALIEN RETAILERS ARE BANNED IN RURAL AREA I / Indonesia. President. (Sukarno) – SE-2186 1. 1959 – 9 – ne IDC [380]
TEXT OF THE CONSTITUTION OF THE COMMONWEALTH OF PUERTO RICO : APPROVED BY THE CONSTITUTIONAL CONVENTION OF PUERTO RICO, FEBRUARY 6 1952 / Fernos-Isern, A – Washington: GPO, 1952 – 1mf – 9 – $1.50 – LLMC 92-407 – us L.L.M.C. [324]
THE TEXT OF THE OLD TESTAMENT CONSIDERED / Davidson, Samuel – 1859 – 9 – us A.T.L.A. [240]
TEXT OF THE TRUSTEESHIP AGREEMENT : APPROVED BY THE SECURITY COUNCIL / U.N. Trusteeship – New York, 2 Apr 1947 – 1mf – 9 – $1.50 – LLMC 82-100F Title 18 – us L.L.M.C. [324]
TEXT- UND QUELLENSTUDIEN ZU DEM ANONYMEN MITTELDEUTSCHEN GEDICHT VON DEN SIEBEN WEISEN MEISTERN / Massey, Isabella – Marburg, 1913 – 1mf – DM48.00 – 3-8267-3095-X – gw Hänsel [430]
TEXT ZU DEN ILLUSTRATIONEN AUS REUTER'S WERKEN : NEBST EINER BIOGRAPHIE DES DICHTERS / Witt, R de & Kolbe, E – Berlin-Schoeneberg: P Oestergaard, [1904?] – 1r – 1 – us U.W. Library [430]
TEXT ZU MEINHOLD'S DEUTSCHEN MAERCHENBILDERN : DORNROESCHEN / Lehmensick, Fritz – (Includes bibliographical references) – Dresden: C C Meinhold [1878?] – 1r – 1 – us U.W. Library [390]
DIE TEXTBEZEUGUNG DER VITA CONSTANTINI DES EUSEBIUS VON CAESAREA (T.U.U. 5-84) / Winkelmann, F – 4mf – 9 – ne Slangenburg [240]
A TEXT-BOOK OF CHURCH HISTORY / Gieseler, Johann Carl Ludwig – Trans. from 4th rev. German ed. by Samuel Davidson, rev. and ed. by Henry B. Smith. New American ed. New York: Harper etc., 1857-80. 5v – 1 – us U.W. Library [240]
TEXT-BOOK OF CHURCH HISTORY / Kurtz, Johann Heinrich – Rev., with Corrections and Additions from the 7th German ed. 1884 – 1 – us A.T.L.A. [240]
TEXTBOOK OF INDONESIAN / Indonesia. Kementerian Pendidikan – SE-2131 1 – 9 – ne IDC [490]
A TEXT-BOOK OF POPERY : COMPRISING A BRIEF HISTORY OF THE COUNCIL OF TRENT, A TRANSLATION OF ITS DOCTRINAL DECREES, AND COPIOUS EXTRACTS FROM THE CATECHISM PUBLISHED BY ITS AUTHORITY / Cramp, John Mockett – New York: D. Appleton, 1831 – 2mf – us A.T.L.A. [240]
TEXTDICHTERREGISTER DER MUSIKABTEILUNG – 25mf – 9 – DM200.00 diazo DM230.00 silver – gw Olms [780]
TEXTE UND ARBEITEN : BEITRAEGE ZUR ERGRUENDUNG DES AELTEREN LATEINISCHEN CHRISTLICHEN SCHRIFTTUMS UND GOTTESDIENST BEURON. HEFT 1-54 UND 4 BEIHEFTE. 1917-1964 – 9 – Dfl490.00 – ne Slangenburg [240]
TEXTE UND UNTERSUCHUNGEN ZUR GESCHICHTE DER ALTCHRISTLICHEN LITERATUR – 1.Reihe: 1-5.Reihe, 114 – 9 – Dfl4,032.00 – ne Slangenburg [240]
TEXTE UND UNTERSUCHUNGEN ZUR GESCHICHTE DER ALTCHRISTLICHEN LITERATUR – (Index. Missing: v20; v25(1)) – Leipzig. v1-46. 1883-1930 – 394mf – 9 – H-2913/1 – ne IDC [240]
TEXTE UND UNTERSUCHUNGEN ZUR GESCHICHTE DER ALTCHRISTLICHEN LITERATUR *see*
- DIE ABFASSUNGSZEIT DER SCHRIFTEN TERTULLIANS (T.U.U. 1-5/2A)
- ACTA SS. NEREI ET ACHILLEI (T.U.U. 1-11/2)
- DIE ACTEN DES KARPUS, DES PAPYLUS UND DER AGATHONIKE (T.U.U. 1-3/4B)
- DIE AELTESTEN QUELLEN DES ORIENTALISCHEN KIRCHENRECHTES (T.U.U. 1-6/4
- AGRAPHA AUSSERCANONISCHE EVANGELIENFRAGMENTE (T.U.U. 1-5/4A)
- AGRAPHA AUSSERCANONISCHE PARALLELTEXTE ZU DEN EVANGELIEN
- AGRAPHA AUSSERCANONISCHE SCHRIFTFRAGMENTE (T.U.U. 2-30/3.4.)
- DIE AKTEN DER EDESSENISCHEN BEKENNER CURJAS, SAMONAS UND ABIBOS (T.U.U. 3-37/2)
- ALBERT EHRHARD UND DIE ERFORSCHUNG DER GRIECHISCH-BYZANTINISCHEN HAGIOGRAPHIE (T.U.U. 5-111)
- ALTCHRISTLICHE LITURGISCHE STUECKE AUS DER KIRCHE AEGYPTENS (T.U.U. 2-17/3B1)
- DER ALTE ANFANG UND DIE URSPRUENGLICHE FORM VON CYPRIANS SCHRIFT AD DONATUM (T.U.U. 2-19/1C)
- DIE ALTEN LATEINISCHEN THOMASAKTEN (T.U.U. 5-122)
- DIE ALTEN PETRUSAKTEN IM ZUSAMMENHANG MIT DER APOKRYPHEN APOSTELLITTERATUR (T.U.U. 2-24/1)
- DIE ALTERCATIO SIMONIS JUDAEI ET THEOPHILI CHRISTIANI UND DIE ACTA ARCHELAI UND DAS DIATERSSARON TATIANS (T.U.U. 1-1/3)
- ANALECTA ZUR AELTESTEN GESCHICHTE DES CHRISTENTUMS IN ROM (T.U.U. 2-28/2B)
- L'ANCIENNE VERSION LATINE DES QUESTIONS SUR LA GENESE DE PHILON D'ALEXANDRIE
- DER ANGEBLICHE EVANGELIENKOMMENTAR DES THEOPHILIUS VON ANTIOCHIEN (T.U.U. 1-1/4B)
- APHRAHAT'S DES PERSISCHEN WEISEN HOMILIEN (T.U.T. 1-3/4A)
- DIE APOKALYPSE DES ELIAS (T.U.U. 2-17/3A)
- APOLLINARIOS VON LAODICEA (T.U.U. 1-7/3.4.)
- DIE APOLOGIE DES ARISTIDES (T.U.U. 1-9/1B)
- DAS APOSTELDECRET NACH SEINER AUSSERCANONISCHEN TEXTGESTALT (T.U.U. 2-28/3)
- DIE APOSTELGESCHICHTE (T.U.U. 1-9/3.4.)
- ARMENISCHE IRENAEUSFRAGMENTE (T.U.U. 3-36/3)
- DIE ARMENISCHE KIRCHE IN IHREN BEZIEHUNGEN ZU DEN SYRISCHEN KIRCHEN BIS ZUM ENDE DES 13. JAHRHUNDERTS (T.U.U. 2-26/4)
- ATHANASIANA (T.U.U. 2-19/4)
- ATHENAGORAE LIBELLUS PRO CHRISTIANIS RECENSUIT E. SCHWARTZ (T.U.U.-1-4/2)
- DIE BEIDEN GRIECHISCHEN KLEMENTINEN-EPITOMEN UND IHRE ANHAENGE (T.U.U. 5-90)
- BEITRAEGE ZUR TEXTKRITIK VON ORIGENES' JOHANNESCOMMENTAR (T.U.U. 2-28/2A)
- DER BENANBRIEF
- DIE BERLINER HANDSCHRIFT DER SAHIDISCHEN APOSTELGESCHICHTE (T.U.U. 5-109)
- BIBLIOGRAPHIE ZUR JUEDISCH-HELLENISTISCHEN UND INTERTESTAMENTARISCHEN LITERATUR 1900-1965 (T.U.U. 5-106)
- EINE BISHER NICHT ERKANNTE SCHRIFT DES PAPSTES SIXTUS 2 (T.U.U. 1-13/1A)
- EINE BISHER NICHT ERKANNTE SCHRIFT NOVATIANS (T.U.U. 1-13/4B)
- EINE BISHER UNBEKANNTE VERSION DES ERSTEN TEILES DER "APOSTELLEHRE" (T.U.U. 1-13/1B)
- DIE BRIEFE DES LIBANIUS (T.U.U. 2-30/1.2)
- DIE BRIEFE DES SEXTUS JULIUS AFRICANUS AN ARISTIDES UDN ORIGENES (T.U.U. 3-34/3)
- BRUCHSTUECKE DES EVANGELIUMS UND DER APOKALYPSE DES PETRUS (T.U.U. 1-9/2)
- DAS BUCH HENOCH
- DIE BUECHER DER GEHEIMNISSE HENOCHS (T.U.U. 3-44/2)
- DIE CHRISTOLOGIE DER APOKALYPSE DES JOHANNES (T.U.U. 5-85)
- CHRISTUSBILDER
- DIE CHRONIK DES HIPPOLYTOS IN MATRITENSIS GRAECUS 121 (T.U.U. 2-29/1)
- DER CHRONOGRAPH AUS DEM ZEHNTEN JAHRE ANTONINS (T.U.U. 1-12/1A)
- DER CODEX D IN DER APOSTELGESCHICHTE (T.U.U. 2-17/1)
- CYPRIAN UND DER ROEMISCHE PRIMAT (T.U.U. 3-35/1)
- DIE CYPRIANISCHE BRIEFSAMMLUNG
- DAS DECRETUM GELASIANUM (T.U.U. 3-38/4)
- DEI APOLOGIE DES ARISTIDES (T.U.U. 1-4/3)
- DES H. EUSTATHIUS BEURTHEILING DES ORIGENES (T.U.U. 1-2/4)
- DES HEILIGEN IRENAEUS SCHRIFT ZUM ERWEISE DER APOSTOLISCHEN VERKUENDIGUNG (T.U.U. 3-31/1)
- DER DIALOG BEI DEN CHRISTLICHEN SCHRIFTSTELLERN DER ERSTEN VIER JAHRHUNDERTE (T.U.U. 5-96)
- DIDASCALIAE APOSTOLORUM CANONUM ECCLESIASTICORUM TRADITIONIS APOSTOLICAE
- DIDYMUS, DER BLINDE VON ALEXANDRIA (T.U.U. 2-29/3)
- DIODOR VAN TARSUS
- DREI GEORGISCH ERHALTENE SCHRIFTEN VON HIPPOLYTUS
- DREI WENIG BEACHTETE CYPRIANISCHE SCHRIFTEN UND DIE "ACTA PAULI" (T.U.U. 2-19/3B)
- DIE ECHTHEIT DES ZWEITEN THESSALONICHERBRIEFS (T.U.U. 2-24/2)
- DAS EDICT DES ANTONIUS PIUS (T.U.U. 1-13/4A)
- DER ERSTE CLEMENSBRIEF IN ALTKOPTISCHER UEBERSETZUNG (T.U.U. 3-32/1)
- DER ERSTE CLEMENSBRIEF (T.U.U. 2-20/1)
- EUSEBIUS KIRCHENGESCHICHTE BUCH 6 UND 7 AUS DEM ARMENISCHEN UEBERSETZT (T.U.U. 2-22/3)
- EUSEBIUS SCHRIFT PERI TOON TOPIKOON ONOMATOON (T.U.U. 2-23/2B)
- EUSTATHIUS
- DIE EVANGELIEN DES MATTHAEUS UND DES MARCUS (T.U.U. 1-1/4A)
- DAS EVANGELIENFRAGMENT VON FAJJUM (T.U.U. 1-5/4B)

- DAS EVANGELIUM NACH THOMAS (T.U.U. 5-101)
- DIE EVANGLIENZITATE DES ORIGENES (T.U.U. 3-34/2A)
- FORM UND UEBERLIEFERUNG DER LUKAS-HOMILIEN DES ORIGENES (T.U.U. 4-47/3)
- FORMEN UND MOTIVE IN DEN APOKRYPHEN APOSTELGESCHICHTEN (T.U.U. 4-48/1)
- FORTSCHRIFT UND VOLLENDUNG BEI PHILO VON ALEXANDRIEN (T.U.U. 4-49/1)
- FRAGMENT EINER SCHRIFT DES MAERTYRER-BISCHOFS PETRUS VON ALEXANDRIEN (T.U.U. 2-20/4B)
- FRAGMENTE DER HOMILIEN DES CYRILL VON ALEXANDRIEN ZUM LUKASEVANGELIUM (T.U.U. 3-34/1B)
- FRAGMENTE VORNICAENISCHER KIRCHENVAETER AUS DEN SACRA PARALLELA (T.U.U. 2-20/2)
- DIE FRAU IM ROEMISCHEN CHRISTENPROCESS (T.U.U. 2-28/4C)
- DER GEFAELSCHTE BRIEF DES BISCHOFS THEONAS AN DEN OBERKAMMERHERRN LUCIAN (T.U.U. 2-24/3C)
- DIE GESCHICHTE DER DOGMATISCHEN FLORILEGIEN VOM 5.-8. JAHRHUNDERT (T.U.U. 2-28/1)
- DIE GESCHICHTE VON JOSEPH DEM ZIMMERMANN (T.U.U. 5-56)
- GESPRAECHE JESU MIT SEINEN JUENGERN NACH DER AUFERSTEHUNG
- GNOSTISCHE SCHRIFTEN IN KOPTISCHER SPRACHE AUS DEM CODEX BRUCIANUS (T.U.U. 1-8/1.2.)
- DIE GNOSTISCHEN QUELLEN HIPPLOYTIS (T.U.U. 1-6/3A)
- DIE GNOSTISCHEN SCHRIFTEN DES KOPTISCHEN PAPYRUS BEROLINENSIS 8502 (T.U.U. 5-60)
- GRIECHISCHE EXCERPTE AUS HOMILIEN DES ORIGENES (T.U.U. 1-12/3B)
- DIE GRIECHISCHE UEBERSETZUNG DER VIRI INLUSTRES DES HIERONYMUS (T.U.U. 1-13/3)
- DIE GRIECHISCHE UEBERSETZUNG DES APOLOGETICUS TERTULLIAN'S (T.U.U. 1-8/4A)
- EINE GRIECHISCHE UEBERSETZUNG DES ITALIENISCHEN APOKALYPSENKOMMENTARS VON FEDERIGO DA VENEZIA O.P. (T.U.U. 4-48/2)
- GRIECHISCHE ZAUBERPAPYRI UND DAS GEMEINDE- UND DANKGEBET IM 1. KLEMENSBRIEFE (T.U.U. 3-34/2B)
- DIE GRIECHISCHEN HANDSCHRIFTEN DES NEUEN TESTAMENTS IN DER UDSSR (T.U.U. 5-91)
- DIE GWYNN'SCHEN CAJUS- UND HIPPOLYTUS-FRAGMENTE (T.U.U. 1-6/3C)
- DIE HANDSCHRIFTEN, AUSGABEN UND UEBERSETZUNGEN VON IAMBLICHOS DE MYSTERIIS
- DIE HANDSCHRIFTLICHE UEBERLIEFERUNG DER SOGENANNTEN HISTORIA TRIPARTITA DES EPIPHANIUS-CASSIDOR (T.U.U. 5-59)
- DIE HANDSCHRIFTLICHE UEBERLIEFERUNG DER ZACHARIAS- UND JOHANNES-APOKRYPHEN (T.U.U. 2-26/3A)
- DIE HANDSCHRIFTLICHE UEBERLIEFERUNG DES EPIPHANIUS (T.U.U. 3-36/2)
- DIE HARMONISTIK IM EVANGELIENTEXT IN CODEX CANTABRIGIENSIS (T.U.U. 3-36/1A)
- DER HEBRAEERBRIEF IN ZEITGESCHICHTLICHER BELEUCHTUNG (T.U.U. 3-35/3)
- DAS HEBRAER-EVANGELIUM (T.U.U. 1-5/3)
- HIERONYMUS LIBER DE VIRIS INLUSTRIBUS
- HIPPOLYTOS' CAPITEL GEGEN DIE MAGIER
- HIPPOLYTS DANIELCOMMENTAR (T.U.U. 3-38/1B)
- HIPPOLYTS KOMMENTAR ZUM HOHENLIED AUF GRUND VON N. MARRS AUSGABE DES GRUSINISCHEN TEXTES (T.U.U.2-23/2C)
- HIPPOLYTS SCHRIFT UEBER DIE SEGNUNGEN JAKOBS (T.U.U. 3-38/1A)
- HIPPOLYTSSTUDIEN (T.U.U. 2-16/4)
- HOMER IN DER FRUEHCHRISTLICHEN LITERATUR BIS JUSTININ (T.U.U. 5-105)
- DIE HYPOTIPOSEN DES THEOGNOST (T.U.U. 2-24/3B)
- IGNATIUS VON ANTIOCHIEN ALS CHRIST UND THEOLOGE (T.U.U. 1-12/3A)
- IGNATIUS VON ANTIOCHIEN UND DIE PAULUSBRIEFE (T.U.U. 5-99)
- DAS INDULGENZ-EDICT DES ROEMISCHEN BISCHOFS KALLIST (T.U.U. 1-11/3)
- DIE INTERPRETATION DES NEUEN TESTAMENTS IN DER VALENTINIANISCHEN GNOSIS (T.U.U. 3-37/3)
- IOVIANUS
- IRENAEUS GEGEN DIE HAERETIKER
- IST DIE REDE DES PAULUS IN ATHEN EIN URSPRUENGLICHER BESTANDTEIL DER APOSTELGESCHICHTE (T.U.U. 3-39/1A)
- JEREMIA IM FRUEHJUDENTUM UND URCHRISTENTUM (T.U.U. 5-118)
- DIE JOHANNES-APOKALYPSE (T.U.U. 1.7/1)
- DAS JOHANNES-EVANGELIUM NACH DER PARAPHRASE DES NONNUS PANOPOLITANUS (T.U.U. 2-23/4)
- JOHANNES-KOMMENTARE AUS DER GRIECHISCHEN KIRCHE (T.U.U. 5-89)
- DAS JUDENCHRISTENTUM IN DEN PSEUDOKLEMENTINEN (T.U.U. 5-70)
- JUDENTUM UND JUDENCHRISTENTUM IM JUSTINS DIALOG MIT TRYPHO (T.U.U. 3-39/1B)
- EIN JUEDISCH-CHRISTLICHES PSALMBUCH AUS DEM ERSTEN JAHRHUNDERT (T.U.U. 3-35/4)
- JULIAN VON ECLANUM (T.U.U. 1-15/3A)
- DIE KATHOLISCHEN BRIEFE (T.U.U. 1-8/3)
- DAS KERYGMA PETRI (T.U.U. 1-11/1)
- DER KETZER-KATALOG DES BISCHOFS MARUTA VON MAIPHERKAT (T.U.U. 2-19/1B)
- DIE KIRCHENGESCHICHTE DER NICEPHORUS CALLISTUS XANTHOPUPOS UND IHRE QUELLEN (T.U.U. 5-98)
- DIE KIRCHENGESCHICHTE DES EUSEBIUS (T.U.U. 2-21/2)
- DER KIRCHENGESCHICHTLICHE ERTRAG DER EXEGETISCHEN ARBEITEN DES ORIGENES
- KLEINE SCHRIFTEN 1
- KLEINE SCHRIFTEN 2
- KLEINE SCHRIFTEN 3
- KLEINE SCHRIFTEN (T.U.U. 5-83)
- DER KLEMENSROMAN UND SEINE GRIECHISCHEN QUELLEN (T.U.U. 3-40/2)
- KOMPOSITON UND ENTSTEHUNGSZEIT DER ORACULA SIBYLLINA (T.U.U. 2-23/1)
- KOPTISCHE AKTEN ZUM EPHESINISCHEN KONZIL VON JAHRE 431 (T.U.U. 2-26/2)
- DER KOPTISCHE TEXT DER KIRCHENORDNUNG HIPPOLYTS (T.U.U. 5-58)
- KRITIK DES NEUEN TESTAMENTS VON EINEM GRIECHISCHEN PHILOSOPHEN DES 3. JAHRHUNDERTS (T.U.U. 3-37/4)
- KRITISCHE BEITRAEGE ZU DEN CONSTANTIN-SCHRIFTEN DES EUSEBIUS (T.U.U. 3-36/4)
- KYRILLOS VON SKYTHOPOLIS (T.U.U. 4-49/2)
- DAS LATEINISCHE NEUE TESTAMENT IN AFRIKA ZUR ZEIT CYPRIANS (T.U.U. 3-33)
- DAS LEBEN CYPRIANS VON PONTIUS
- DAS LEBEN DES HEILIGEN SYMEON STYLITES (T.U.U. 3-32/4)
- DIE LEHRE DER ZWOELF APOSTEL (T.U.U. 1-2/1.2.)
- LEONTIUS VON BYZANZ 1.
- DER LITURGISCHE PAPYRUS VON DER-BALYZEH
- LOGOS SOTERIAS PROS TEN PARTHENON (DE VIRGINITATE)
- DIE LUKASKATENE DES NIKETAS VON HERAKLEIA (T.U.U. 2-22/4)
- LUKIAN VON SAMOSATA UND DAS NEUE TESTAMENT
- MARCION
- DAS MARTYRIUM DES HEILIGEN ABO VON TIFLIS (T.U.U. 2-28/4B)
- EIN MARTYROLOGIUM DER CHRISTLICHEN GEMEINDE ZU ROM (T.U.U. 2-21/3)
- MATERIAL RE-CREATION IN THE APOSTOLIC FATHERS (T.U.U. 5-100)
- MATTHAEUS-KOMMENTARE AUS DER GRIECHISCHEN KIRCHE (T.U.U. 5-61)
- MEDICINISCHES AUS DER AELTESTEN KIRCHENGESCHICHTE (T.U.U. 1-8/4B)
- MONARCHIANISCHE PROLOGE ZU DEN VIER EVANGELIEN (T.U.U. 1-15/1)
- DIE MOTIVIERUNG DER ASKESE IN DER ALTEN KIRCHE UND DER URSPRUNG DES MOENCHTUMS (T.U.U. 5.95)
- MYSTERIENGLAUBE UND GNOSIS IN CORPUS HERMETICUM 13 (T.U.U. 5-110)
- NACHLESE ZUR UEBERLIEFERUNG DER MATTHAEUSERKLAERUNG DES ORIGENES (T.U.U. 4-47/4)
- NEUE FRAGMENTE DES PAPIAS, HEGESIPPUS UND PIERIUS (T.U.U. 1-5/2B)
- NEUE FRAGMENTE UND UNTERSUCHUNGEN ZU DEN JUDENCHRISTLICHEN EVANGELIEN (T.U.U. 3-37/1)
- NEUE HOMILIEN DES MAKARIUS/SYMEON
- NEUE STUDIEN ZU MARCION (T.U.U. 3-44/4)
- NONNENSPIEGEL UND MOENCHSSPIEGEL DES EUAGRIOS PONTIKOS (T.U.U. 3-39/4B)
- DIE OFFENBARUNG JOHANNIS (T.U.U. 1-2/3)
- ONOMASTICA SACRA
- DIE PALAESTINISCHEN MAERTYRER DES EUSEBIUS VON CAESAREA (T.U.U. 1-14/4)
- PASSIO S. THECLAE VIRGINIS
- PATRISTISCHE MISCELLEN (T.U.U. 2-20/3B)
- DER PAULINISMUS DES IRENAEUS (T.U.U. 1-6/2)
- DER PAULINISMUS UND DIE LOGIA JESU (T.U.U. 2-27)
- PAULUS VON SAMOSATA (T.U.U. 3-44/5)
- DIE PFAFF'SCHEN IRENAEUS-FRAGMENTE ALS FAELSCHUNGEN PFAFFS (T.U.U. 2-20/3A)
- PLOTIN'S STELLUNG ZUM GNOSTICISMUS UND KIRCHLICHEN CHRISTENTUM (T.U.U. 2-20/4A)
- DIE PREDIGT UND DAS BRIEFFRAGMENT DES ARISTIDES (T.U.U. 1-12/2B)
- DER PROCES UND DIE ACTA APOLLONII (T.U.U. 1-15/2)
- PROPHETEN- UND APOSTELLEGENDEN (T.U.U.3-31-/3)
- DIE PSALMEN SALOMO'S (T.U.U. 1-13/2)
- DER PSEUDOCYPRIANISCHE TRACTAT DE ALEATORBUS (T.U.U. 1-5/1)
- DER PSEUDOCYPRIANISCHE TRAKTAT DE SINGULARITATE CLERICORUM
- PSEUDO-CYPRIANUS DE 12 ABUSIVES SAECULI (T.U.U. 3-34/1A)
- DIE PSEUDOKLEMENTINEN
- DIE QUELLEN DER SOGENANNTEN APOSTOLISCHEN KIRCHENORDNUNG (T.U.U. 1-2/5)
- DIE QUELLEN DER SYNOPTISCHEN UEBERLIEFERUNG (T.U.U. 3-32/3)
- DER ROEMERBRIEFTEXT DES ORIGENES (T.U.U. 3-44/3)
- DIE SACRA PARALLELA DES JOHANNES DAMASCENUS (T.U.U. 2-16/1)
- SAIDISCHE AUSZUEGE AUS DEM 8. BUCHE DER APOSTOLISCHEN KONSTITUTIONEN (T.U.U. 2-26/1B)
- SCHENUTE VON ATRIPE UND DIE ENTSTEHUNG DES NATIONAL AEGYPTISCHEN CHRISTENTUMS (T.U.U. 2-25/1)
- DER SCHOLIEN-KOMMENTAR DAS ORIGENES ZUR APOKALYPSE JOHANNIS (T.U.U. 3-38/3)
- SIEBEN NEUE BRUCHSTUECKE DER SYLLOGISMEN DES APELLES (T.U.U. 1-6/3B)
- DER SOGENANNTE PRAEDESTINATUS
- DAS SOGENANNTE RELIGIONSGESPRAECH AM HOF DER SASANIDEN (T.U.U. 2-19/3A)
- DER SOGENANNTE SOPHRONIUS (T.U.U. 1-14/1B)
- DIE SPRUECHE JESU DIE IN DEN KANONISCHEN EVANGELIEN NICHT UEBERLIEFERT SIND (T.U.U. 1-14/2)
- DIE STELLUNG DES ERSTEN CLEMENSBRIEFES, INNERHALB DER ENTWICKLUNG DER ALTCHRISTLICHEN GEMEINDEVERFASSUNG UND DES KIRCHENRECHTS (T.U.U. 4-47/1)
- STUDIA EVANGELICA
- STUDIA EVANGELICA, VOL 2 (TUU 5-87)
- STUDIA EVANGELICA, VOL 4 (TUU 5-102)
- STUDIA EVANGELICA, VOL 5 (TUU 5-103)
- STUDIA PATRISTICA
- STUDIA PATRISTICA, VOL 3 PT 2 (TUU 5-88)
- STUDIA PATRISTICA, VOL 3 (TUU 5-78)
- STUDIA PATRISTICA, VOL 4 (TUU 5-79)
- STUDIA PATRISTICA, VOL 5 (TUU 5-80)
- STUDIA PATRISTICA, VOL 6 (TUU 5-81)
- STUDIA PATRISTICA, VOL 7 (TUU 5-92)
- STUDIA PATRISTICA, VOL 8 (TUU 5-93)
- STUDIA PATRISTICA, VOL 9 (TUU 5.94)
- STUDIA PATRISTICA, VOL 10 (TUU 5-107)
- STUDIA PATRISTICA, VOL 11 (TUU 5-108)
- STUDIA PATRISTICA, VOL. 12 (T.U.U. BAND 5-115)
- STUDIA PATRISTICA, VOL. 13 (T.U.U. BAND 5-116)
- STUDIA PATRISTICA, VOL. 14 (T.U.U. BAND 5-117)
- STUDIEN UND BEITRAEGE ZUR ERKLAERUNG UND ZEITBESTIMMUNG COMMODIANS (T.U.U. 3-39/4A)
- STUDIEN UND TEXTE ZU ASTERIOS VON AMASEA (T.U.U. 3-40/1)
- STUDIEN ZU DEN KOMMENTAREN HIPPOLYTS ZUM BUCHE DANIEL UND HOHEN LIEDE (T.U.U. 2-16/2)
- STUDIEN ZU DEN PSEUDO-CLEMENTINEN NEBST EINEM ANHANGE
- STUDIEN ZU EUSEBS THEOPHANIE (T.U.U. 2-23/3)
- STUDIEN ZU METHODIOS VON OLYMPOS (T.U.U. 5-69)
- STUDIEN ZUM NEUEN TESTAMENT UND ZUR PATRISTIK (T.U.U. 5-77)
- SYMEON VON MESOPOTANIEN (T.U.U. 4-55/1)
- SYNESIOS VON KYRENE
- SYNOPTISCHE UEBERLIEFERUNG BEI DEN APOSTOLISCHEN VAETERN (T.U.U. 5-65)
- DIE SYRISCHE DIDASKALIA (T.U.U. 2-25/2)
- DIE SYRISCHEN CLEMENTINEN (T.U.U. 4-48/3)
- TATIANI ORATIO AD GRAECOS
- DIE TERMINOLOGIE DER WIEDERGEBURT UND VERWANDTER ERLEBNISSE IN DER AELTESTEN KIRCHE (T.U.U. 3-42/3B)
- TERTULLIAN'S GEGEN DIE JUDEN (T.U.U. 1-12/2A)
- DIE TEXTBEZEUGUNG DER VITA CONSTANTINI DES EUSEBIUS VON CAESAREA (T.U.U. 5-84)
- TEXTKRITIK DER PAULINISCHEN BRIEFE (T.U.U. 1-14/3)
- TEXTKRITIK DER VIER EVANGELIEN (T.U.U. 2-19/2)
- EINE TEXTKRITISCHE ARBEIT DES ZEHNTEN BEZW. SECHSTEN JAHRHUNDERTS (T.U.U. 2-17/4)
- TEXTKRITISCHE STUDIEN ZUM NEUEN TESTAMENT (T.U.U. 1-11/4)
- DIE TEXTUEBERLIEFERUNG DER BUECHER DES ORIGENES GEGEN CELSUS (T.U.U. 1-6/1)
- THEOPHILUS VON ANTIOCHIEN ADVERSUS MARCIONEM (T.U.U. 4-46/2)
- DER THORA-AUSLEGE ARISTOBULOS (T.U.U. 5-86)
- TISCHGEBETE UND ABENDMAHLSGEBETE IN DER ALTCHRISTLICHEN UND IN DER GRIECHISCHEN KIRCHE (T.U.U. 2-29/2B)
- TITUS VON BOSTRA STUDIEN ZU DESSEN LUKASHOMILIEN (T.U.U. 2-21/1)
- DIE TODESTAGE DER APOSTEL PAULUS UND PETRUS (T.U.U. 2-19/1A)
- LA TRADITION MANUSCRITE DE SOZOMENE (T.U.U. 3-32/2B)
- UEBER DAS GNOSTISCHE BUCH PISTIS-SOPHIA. BROT UND WASSER
- UEBER DEN DRITTEN JOHANNESBRIEF (T.U.U. 1-15/3B)
- UEBER DES DIDYMUS VON ALEXANDRIEN IN EPISTOLAS CANONICAS ENARRATIO (T.U.U. 2-28/2C)
- UEBER DIE BIBLIOTHEKEN DER METEORISCHEN UND OSSA-OLYMPISCHEN KLOESTER (T.U.U. 2-26/3B)
- UEBER VERLORENE BRIEFE UND ACTENSTUECKE DIE SICH AUS DER CYPRIANISCHEN BRIEFSAMMLUNG ERMITTELN LASSEN (T.U.U. 2-23/2A)
- DIE UEBERLIEFERUNG DER GRIECHISCHEN APOLOGETEN (T.U.U. 1-1/1.2.)
- DIE UEBERLIEFERUNG DER JEREMIA-HOMILIEN DES ORIGENES (T.U.U. 2-16/3)
- UEBERLIEFERUNG UND BESTAND DER HAGIOGRAPHISCHEN UND HOMILIETISCHEN LITERATUR DER GRIECHISCHEN KIRCHE VON DEN ANFAENGEN BIS ZUM ENDE DES 16. JAHRHUNDERTS
- UEBERLIEFERUNG UND TEXTGESCHICHTE DER LATEINISCHEN ORIGENESHOMILIEN ZUM ALTEN TESTAMENT (T.U.U. 3-42/1)
- DIE UNTER HIPPOLYTS NAMEN UEBERLIEFERTE SCHRIFT UEBER DEN GLAUBEN (T.U.U. 3-31/2A)
- UNTERSUCHUNGEN UEBER DIE ALTTESTAMENTLICHEN ZITATE BEI LUKAS (T.U.U. 5-104)
- UNTERSUCHUNGEN UEBER DIE EDESSENISCHE CHRONIK (T.U.U. 1-9/1A)
- UNTERSUCHUNGEN ZU NILUS DEM ASKETEN (T.U.U. 3-42/2)
- UNTERSUCHUNGEN ZUR GESCHICHTE DER GRIECHISCHEN VATERUNSER-EXEGESE (T.U.U. 3-40/3)
- UNTERSUCHUNGEN ZUR KOSMOLOGIE DES HELLENISTISCHEN UND PALAESTINISCHEN JUDENTUMS (T.U.U. 5-97)
- URKUNDEN AUS DEM ANTIMONTANISTISCHEN KAMPFE DES ABENDLANDES (T.U.U. 1-12/4A)
- URSPRUNG UND GESCHICHTE DES FRUEHCHRISTLICHEN OSTERKALENDERS (T.U.U. 5-121)
- VINCENZ VON LERIN UND GENNADIUS (T.U.U. 3-31/2B)
- VIRGINES CHRISTI (T.U.U. 3-31/2C)
- DIE VORSTELLUNG VOM SCHOEPFUNGSMITTLER IM HELLENISTISCHEN JUDENTUM UND URCHRISTENTUM (T.U.U. 5-82)
- DER VORWURF DES ATHEISMUS IN DEN DREI ERSTEN JAHRHUNDERTEN (T.U.U. 2-28/4A)
- DER WAHRE GNOSTIKER NACH CLEMENS ALEXANDRINUS (T.U.U. 5-57)
- DIE ZEUGNISSE VOM CHRISTENTUM IM SLAVISCHEN "DE BELLO JUDAICO" DES JOSEPHUS (T.U.U. 2-29/4)
- ZU DEN SCHRIFTEN DES MAKARIOS VON MAGNESIA (T.U.U. 3-31/4)
- ZUR ABERCIUS-INSCHRIFT (T.U.U. 1-12/4B)
- ZUR BARDESANISCHEN GNOSIS (T.U.U. 3-34/4)
- ZUR ERKLAERUNG UND TEXTKRITIK DES 1. BUCHES TERTULLIANS, "ADVERSUS

MARCIONEM" (T.U.U. 3-38/2)
- ZUR FRAGE NACH DEM URSPRUNG DES GNOSTIZISMUS (T.U.U. 1-15/4)
- ZUR HANDSCHRIFTLICHEN UEBERLIEFERUNG DES CLEMENS ALEXANDRINUS (T.U.U. 2-20/4C)
- ZUR TEXTGESCHICHTE DER CIVITAS DEI AUGUSTINS (T.U.U. 3-32/2A)
- ZUR TEXTGESCHICHTE UND ERKLAERUNG VON TERTULLIANS APOLOGETIKUM (T.U.U. 3-40/4)
- ZUR UEBERLIEFERUNG DER MATTHAEUSERKLAERUNG DES ORIGENES (T.U.U. 4-47/2)
- ZUR UEBERLIEFERUNG DES PHILOSTORGIOS (T.U.U. 2-17/3B2)
- ZUR UEBERLIEFERUNGSGESCHICHTE DER ALTCHRISTLICHEN LITTERATUR (T.U.U. 1-12/1B)
- DIE ZWEITE APOKALYPSE DES JACOBUS AUS NAG-MAMMADI-CODEX 5 (T.U.U. 5-119)

TEXTE ZUR ASSYRISCH-BABYLONISCHEN RELIGION / Jensen, P – Berlin. 1915. BNE-20,057 1 – 9 – ne IDC [290]

TEXTES D'AUTEURS GRECS ET LATINS RELATIFS A L'EXTREME ORIENT, DEPUIS LE IVE SIECLE AVANT J.C. JUSQU'AU XIVE SIECLE / Coedes, G – Paris, 1910. illus. BU-527/2 – 8 – ne IDC [950]

TEXTES D'INTERET GENERAL / France – 1957-67, 1971-72 – 1 – fr A.C.R.P.P. [944]

TEXTES D'INTERET GENERAL. PREPARATIONS DU VIEPLAN / France – Loi no. 70-588 du 9 juillet 1970 portant. Laws, Statutes, etc. Jul 1970. BD-1568 1 – 9 – ne IDC [338]

TEXTES DIVERS RELATIFS A L'HISTOIRE DE L'ASSYRIE / Nassouhi, E – (Mitteilungen der altorientalischen gesellschaft. v. 3, pt. 1-2). Leipzig. 1927. BNE-20,102 1 – 9 – ne IDC [930]

TEXTES ET MONUMENTS FIGURES RELATIFS AUX MYSTERES DE MITRA PUBLIES AVEC UNE INTRODUCTION CRITIQUE / Cumont, Franz – 2v. Bruxelles, 1896-99. BH.P-24 – 9 – ne IDC [290]

TEXTES FONDAMENTAUX DES INSTITUTIONS MAGHREBINES / Algeria. Maghreb Permanent Consultative Committee – Tunis. 1966? BNE-8656 1 – 9 – ne IDC [330]

TEXTES LEGITATIFS TOUCHANT LE CENOBITISME EGYPTIEN / Kozman, Fr. – Roma, 1935 – 2mf – 8 – Dfl9.00 – ne Slangenburg [240]

TEXTES ORAUX ORDOS, RECUEILLIS ET PUBLIES AVEC INTRODUCTION, NOTES MORPHOLOGIQUES, COMMENTAIRES ET GLOSSAIRE / Mostaert, Antoine – Peip'ing: Cura Universitatis Catholicae Pekini, 1937 – 1 – us U.W. Library [480]

TEXTES RELIGIEUX ASSYRIENS ET BABYLONIENS / Martin, Francois – (Text in French and Akkadian. Commentary in French. Includes bibliographical references) – Paris: Emile Bouillon, 1900 – 1mf – 9 – 0-8370-8451-2 – 1986-2451 – us A.T.L.A. [470]

TEXTGESCHICHTE DER REGULA S. BENEDICTI / Traube, L & Plenkers, H – Muenchen, 1910 – 5mf – 8 – Dfl22.00 – ne Slangenburg [240]

TEXTILARBEITER-ZEITUNG *see*
- CHRISTLICHER TEXTILARBEITER
- CHRISTLICHER TEXTIL-ARBEITER/ TEXTILARBEITER-ZEITUNG

TEXTILE BULLETIN – 1911-71 – 1,5,6 – us Princeton Micro [670]

TEXTILE DESIGNS 1840-1985 / Victoria and Albert Museum. London – (Over 2,000 designs for woven and printed textiles, embroidery and carpets. Includes printed index and catalogue) – 25 colour mf – 15 – $646.00 – 0-907696-07-4 – uk Emmett [740]

TEXTILE INDUSTRIE – v63-73 1961-71 – 1,5,6 – us Princeton Micro [338]

TEXTILE INDUSTRIES – v9- 1904- 1; v135-5,6; v141- 9 – us UMI [338]

TEXTILE INDUSTRIES – v124-148 1960-84 – 1,5,6 – us Princeton Micro [338]

TEXTILE INDUSTRY IN SYRIA / Syria. Syrian Documentation Papers – 1970 – 9 – ne IDC [338]

TEXTILE MANUFACTURER AND KNITTING WORLD – v102- 1975- – 1,5,6,9 – us UMI [680]

TEXTILE MONTH – (See also: Man-Made Textiles) – 1968- 1; 1976- 5,6,9 – us UMI [670]

Textile Museum. Washington, DC.Arthur D. Jenkins Library *see* RUG AND TEXTILE ARTS: A PERIODICAL INDEX, 1890-1982

TEXTILE PRODUCTS AND PROCESSES – v1-1978- – 1,5,6,9 – us UMI [670]

TEXTILE WORKERS IN BRAZIL AND ARGENTINA : A STUDY OF THE INTERRELATIONSHIPS BETWEEN WORK AND HOUSEHOLDS / Acero, Liliana – 9 – $14.00 – 92-808-0753-6 – ja U.N. Univ [331]

TEXTILE WORLD – v6- 1893- 1; v116- 5,6; v125- 9 – us UMI [670]

TEXTILES / Victoria and Albert Museum. London – (Almost 10,000 reproductions) – 166mf – 9 – $890.00 – 0-907006-10-8 – uk Mindata [740]

TEXTILES, COSTUME AND JEWELRY (TIAM, PT 1) – (With printed catalogue ISBN: 0-914146-62-9 £14) – 57mf – 15 – £1,040.00 – uk Chadwyck [740]

LES TEXTILES ET LE VETEMENT DANS LA CULTURE MOCHICA (PEROU) / Hocquenghem, Anne Marie – 9 – F70.00 – fr Ethnologie [740]

TEXTILES, WEAVING, EMBROIDERY AND COSTUME : ARCHITECTURE, APPLIED ARTS, STUDIO ARTS – (Individual titles not listed separately) – 85 catalogues on 111mf – 9 – £700.00 – uk Chadwyck [740]

TEXTIL-ZEITUNG – Berlin, Germany. -w. 1900-1909; Nov 1916-June 1919. 3 reels – 1 – uk British Libr Newspaper [072]

TEXTKONSTITUIERENDE GRAMMATISCHE KATEGORIEN IN ENGLISCHEN FACHTEXTEN DER HUMANMEDIZIN / Nestmann, Ralf – Leipzig, 1985 – 2mf – DM62.00 – 3-89349-913-X – gw Hänsel [611]

TEXTKRITIK DER PAULINISCHEN BRIEFE (T.U.U. 1-14/3) / Weiss, Bernhard – Leipzig, 1896 – 3mf – 9 – ne Slangenburg [240]

TEXTKRITIK DER VIER EVANGELIEN (T.U.U. 2-19/2) / Weiss, Bernhard – Leipzig, 1899 – 4mf – 9 – ne Slangenburg [240]

EINE TEXTKRITISCHE ARBEIT DES ZEHNTEN BEZW. SECHSTEN JAHRHUNDERTS (T.U.U. 2-17/4) / Goltz, Eduard von der – Leipzig, 1899 – 2mf – 9 – ne Slangenburg [240]

TEXTKRITISCHE STUDIEN ZUM NEUEN TESTAMENT (T.U.U. 1-11/4) / Bousset, Wilhelm – Leipzig, 1893 – 3mf – 9 – ne Slangenburg [240]

TEXTKRITISCHE UNTERSUCHUNGEN ZU OTTES "ERACLIUS" / Frey, Winfried – Frankfurt a.M., 1970 – 3mf – 9 – DM76.00 – 3-89349-394-8 – gw Hänsel [430]

TEXTKRITISCHE UNTERSUCHUNGEN ZUR LEX RIBVARIA (MGH SCHRIFTEN..: 5.BD) / Buchner, R – 1940 – Dfl22.00 – ne Slangenburg [240]

TEXTO DE DERECHO MARITIMO INTERNATIONAL... / Alamo, Gutierrez del & Garcia, J – Madrid, 1931 – 4mf – 1 – ILM-1504/1 – ne IDC [327]

TEXTO INTEGRO DEL DISCURSO PRONUNCIADO POR DON MANUEL AZANA DIAZ EL DIA 21 DE ENERO DE 1937 EN EL SALON DE SESIONES DEL AYUNTAMIENTO DE VALENCIA / Azana, Manuel – Madrid, 1937. Fiche W 742. (Blodgett Collection of Spanish Civil War Pamphlets) – 9 – us H.U. College Libr [946]

TEXTO INTERGRO DE LOS DISCURSOS PRONUNCIADOS ANTE LOS MICROFONOS DEL MINISTERIO DE LA GUERRA Y DEL PARTIDO COMUNISTA / Ossorio, Angel – Madrid, 1936. Fiche W1508. (Blodgett Collection of Spanish Civil War Pamphlets) – 9 – us H.U. College Libr [946]

Textor, Robert B *see* NOTES ON INDONESIAN VILLAGERS' PARTICIPATION IN PROGRAMS TO MODERNIZE RURAL LIFE

TEXTOS DE FILOSOFIA (PRIMER CURSO). INTRODUCCION A LA FILOSOFIA / Marquez, Gabino – Madrid: Editoria Bibliografica Espanola, 4th ed 1945 – sp Bibl Santa Ana [100]

TEXTS AND STUDIES : CONTRIBUTIONS TO BIBLICAL AND PATRISTIC LITERATURE / ed by Robinson, D – (With Index) – v1-9. 1891-1922 – 71mf – 9 – H-2914/1 – ne IDC [220]

TEXTS EXPLAINED, OR, HELPS TO UNDERSTAND THE NEW TESTAMENT / Farrar, Frederic William – New York: Dodd, Mead, 1899. 1 fiche – 9 – us A.T.L.A. [240]

DIE TEXTUEBERLIEFERUNG DER BUECHER DES ORIGENES GEGEN CELSUS (T.U.U. 1-6/1) / Koetschau, Paul – Leipzig, 1889 – 3mf – 9 – ne Slangenburg [240]

TEXTURE OF CRYSTALLINE SOLIDS – 1972 – 1,5,9 – us Gordon [500]

TEXTURES AND MICROSTRUCTURES / ed by Bunge, H J – 1982 – 1,5,9 – us Gordon [500]

TEXTUS HEBRAICI EMENDATIONES QUIBUS IN VETERE TESTAMENTO NEERLANDICE VERTENDO / Oort, Henricus – Leiden: E.J.Brill, 1900.1 fiche – 9 – us A.T.L.A. [240]

TEXTUS SENTENTIALE CUM CONCLUSIONIBUS MAGISTRI HENRICI GORICHEM / Lombardus, Petrus – Basileae, 1502 – 22mf – 8 – no Slangenburg [240]

TEXTUS SENTENTIALE PETRI LOMBARDI CUM CONCLUSIONIBUS MAGISTRI HENRICI GORICHEM / Henricus, Magister Gorichem – Basileae, 1502 – 22mf – 8 – ne Slangenburg [240]

TEXTVERWALTUNG ALS AUFGABE DER MENSCH-COMPUTER-INTERAKTION : EINFLUSS SUBJEKTIVER EPISODISCHER GEDAECHTNISSTRUKTUREN AUF DAS KODIEREN UND WIEDERFINDEN VON TEXTDATEIEN / Gindert, Christine – 1995 – 3mf – 9 – DM98.00 – 3-8267-2227-2 – gw Hänsel [150]

Teyler. Foundation *see* CATALOGUE DE LA BIBLIOTHEQUE

TEYLER'S THEOLOGISCH TIJDSCHRIFT – v1-9. 1903-11 (complete) – 3r – 1 – ATLA 1994-S522 – us A.T.L.A. [073]

Teyler's tweede genootschap, Haarlem *see* VERHANDELINGEN

Teynard, Felix *see* EGYPT AND NUBIA, THE MOST INTERESTING SITES AND MONUMENTS

A TEZOURA : SEMANARIO CRITICO E NOTICIOSO – Manaos, Amazonas. 9 Out-12 Dez 1909 – 1,5,6 – bl Biblioteca [072]

TF NEWS / Stephen F. Austin University. Texas Forest Service – No.49-61. 1970-82. 1 reel – 1,5 – us Spaulding [630]

TG MAGAZINE – (Cont: Teen Generation Magazine at v49 1989) – Toronto. v49-54. 1989-94 – 9 – Can$20.00y – cn Micromedia [305]

TG MAGAZINE *see* TEEN GENERATION MAGAZINE

TGETUYGENISSE ENDE DE NAEGHELAETEN SCHRIFTEN VAN CHRISTIAEN RIJCEN GHEDRUCKT T' HAERLEM, BY MY GILLIS ROOMAN / Rijcen, Chr – Anno 1588. Haerlem, F. Soete, 1588. BME-208 1 – 9 – ne IDC [240]

TH INTERNATIONAL LAW OF BILLS AND CHECKS / Conant, C A – Philadelphia, 1913 – 1mf – 1 – ILM-3382/1 – ne IDC [327]

O THABOR – Sao Paulo, Brazil. Apr-Aug 1883; 1884-1885; Jan-feb 1886; Jan-Sept 1887 – 1 – bl Biblioteca [072]

THACHER'S CRIMINAL CASES / Massachusetts. Supreme Court – 1v. 1823-43 (all publ) – 8mf – 9 – $12.00 – LLMC 84-160 – us L.L.M.C. [340]

Thackeray, Anne *see*
- BLACKSTICK PAPERS
- BLUEBEARD'S KEYS
- FIVE OLD FRIENDS
- FROM THE PORCH
- MISS ANGEL
- MISS WILLIAMSON'S DIVAGATIONS
- MRS. DYMOND
- OLD KENSINGTON
- THE STORY OF ELIZABETH
- TO ESTHER
- TOILERS AND SPINSTERS
- THE VILLAGE ON THE CLIFF

A THACKERAY DICTIONARY : THE CHARACTERS AND SCENES OF THE NOVELS AND SHORT STORIES ALPHABETICALLY ARRANGED / Mudge, Isadore Gilbert & Sears, M Earl – London: G. Routledge and Sons, limited; New York: E.P. Dutton and Co., 1910 – 1 roll – 1 – 1-55879-747-5 – uk Libr Preservation [420]

Thackeray, Henry St John *see*
- A GRAMMAR OF THE SEPTUAGINT
- THE RELATION OF ST. PAUL TO CONTEMPORARY JEWISH THOUGHT

Thackeray, William Makepeace *see*
- THE BOOK OF SNOBS
- A COLLECTION OF LETTERS OF THACKERAY 1847-1855...
- EARLY AND LATE PAPERS. HITHERTO UNCOLLECTED
- THE HISTORY OF HENRY ESMOND, ESQ.
- THE KICKLEBURYS ON THE RHINE BY MR. M.A. TITMARSH
- LOVEL THE WIDOWER
- THE NEWCOMES
- REBECCA AND ROWENA
- THE ROSE AND THE RING
- ROUNDABOUT PAPERS
- STRAY PAPERS
- VANITY FAIR
- THE VIRGINIANS

THADDEUS HYATT PAPERS / Hyatt, Thaddeus – 1843-1898. In Kansas State Historical Society. Guide – 1 – us KS Hist [920]

THADDEUS STEVENS / McCall, Samuel W – Boston & NY: Houghton, Mifflin & Co, 1899 – 5mf – 9 – $7.50 – LLMC 96-032 – us L.L.M.C. [975]

THE THADDEUS STEVENS PAPERS / ed by Wilson Palmer, Beverly – (With guide) – 1993 – 12r – 1 – $960.00 – S3281 – Dist. us Scholarly Res – us Nat'l Archives [976]

THAI CHRONICLE – Bangkok, Thailand. 1939 – 1r – 1 – us L of C Photodup [072]

THAI EDUCATION IN BRIEF 1980-1982 / Thailand. Ministry of Education – (Missing: 1981) – Bangkok, 1980-1983 – 2mf – 9 – DE-298/1 – ne IDC [370]

THAI LANNA – Lampang, Thailand. 1969-77; 1981-83 – 8r – 1 – us L of C Photodup [072]

THAI TAK SIN – Hai Yai, Thailand. 1969-77; Jul 1979-Jun 1984 – 13r – 1 – us L of C Photodup [072]

Thailand *see*
- THE NATIONAL ECONOMIC DEVELOPMENT PROGRAMME, B.E. 2504 2506 (1961-1966)
- PRAMUAN RATSADAKON CHABAB SOMBUN: PHAK L WA DUAI TUABOTKOTMAI

Thailand. Department of Teacher Training *see*
- AN INTRODUCTION TO THE DEPARTMENT OF TEACHER TRAINING 1976-1979
- RESEARCH REPORT ON AN EVALUATION OF TEACHER TRAINING CUM EDUCATION EXTENSION PROJECT

Thailand. Department of Teacher Training. Supervisory Unit *see* A STUDY OF THE EVALUATION OF TEACHER TRAINING IN THAILAND

THE THAILAND FUNCTIONAL LITERACY AND FAMILY LIFE PLANNING PROGRAM / Thailand. Ministry of Education. Adult Education Division – 1976 – 1mf – 9 – DE-291/1 – ne IDC [370]

THAILAND IN THE 90S / Thailand. Office of the Prime Minister – Bangkok, 1991 – 3mf – 9 – ne IDC [338]

Thailand. Laws, Statutes, etc *see*
- CODE PENAL DU ROYAUME DE SIAM PROMULGUE LE LER JUIN 1908, ENTRE EN VIGEUR LE 22 SEPTEMBRE 1908
- DRAFT CIVIL AND COMMERCIAL CODE FOR THE KINGDOM OF SIAM. BOOK ON OBLIGATIONS
- LAW ON NAVIGATION IN SIAMESE WATERS. IN FORCE SEPTEMBER 1ST, 1905
- THE PENAL CODE FOR THE KINGDOM OF SIAM (DRAFT VERSION.) R.S. 127 (1908)

Thailand. Ministry of Education *see*
- THE CHANGING ROLE OF THE TEACHER AND ITS INFLUENCE ON PREPARATION FOR THE PROFESSION AND ON IN-SERVICE TRAINING IN THAILAND
- COUNTRY REPORT THAILAND
- THE CURRICULUM DEVELOPMENT CENTRE OF THAILAND
- THE DEPARTMENT OF TEACHER TRAINING
- EDUCATION FOR THE BLIND IN THAILAND
- EDUCATIONAL DEVELOPMENT IN THAILAND
- FUNCTIONAL LITERACY PROGRAM FOR HILL TRIBE GROUPS
- A HISTORY OF THAI EDUCATION
- INTRODUCING THE MINISTRY OF EDUCATION
- MINISTRY OF EDUCATION THAILAND
- NATIONAL CASE STUDIES ON THE DEVELOPMENT OF OUT-OF SCHOOL POPULATION EDUCATION PROGRAMMES
- NATIONAL EDUCATION SCHEME 1977
- NON-FORMAL EDUCATION FOR NATIONAL HARMONY AND DEVELOPMENT
- SPECIAL EDUCATION IN THAILAND
- SYNOPSIS OF THE ELEMENTARY SCHOOL CURRICULUM B.E. 2521 (A.D. 1978)
- THAI EDUCATION IN BRIEF 1980-1982
- THE THIRD FIVE YEAR EDUCATIONAL PLAN
- WALKING TEACHER FUNCTIONAL LITERACY PROGRAM FOR HILL TRIBE GROUPS 1976-1981

Thailand. Ministry of Education. Adult Education Division *see*
- ADULT EDUCATION IN THAILAND
- FUNCTIONAL LITERACY TEACHER TRAINING HANDBOOK
- TEXT AND TEACHER'S MANUAL

- THE THAILAND FUNCTIONAL LITERACY AND FAMILY LIFE PLANNING PROGRAM

Thailand. Ministry of Education. Department of Educational Techniques *see* AN INTRODUCTION TO THE DEPARTMENT OF EDUCATIONAL TECHNIQUE

Thailand. Ministry of Education. Department of General Education *see* THAILAND'S WALKING TEACHER PROJECT FOR FUNCTIONAL LITERACY

Thailand. Ministry of Education. Department of Non-Formal Education *see* LITERACY SITUATION IN THAILAND

Thailand. Ministry of Education. Department of Secondary Education *see* PLAN OF OPERATION

Thailand. Ministry of Education. Department of Vocational Education *see*
- AREA VOCATIONAL CENTRES
- COUNTRY REPORT THAILAND; ...

Thailand. Ministry of Education. Division of Eductional Information *see* NATIONAL SCHEME OF EDUCATION B.E. 2503 (1960 A.D.)

Thailand. Ministry of Education. National Statistical Office *see* STATISTICS ON ACADEMIC STREAM OF EDUCATION BY PROVINCE 1975-1980

Thailand. Ministry of Education. National Statistical Office and Educational Planning Office *see* FINAL REPORT ON EDUCATION STATISTICS 1972-1980

Thailand. Ministry of Education. Planning Division *see* DEVELOPMENT ISSUES, NATIONAL OBJECTIVES AND EDUCATIONAL POLICIES 1982-1986

Thailand. National Economic and Social Development Board *see* SEVENTH NATIONAL ECONOMIC AND SOCIAL DEVELOPMENT PLAN (1992-1996)

Thailand. National Economic and Social Development Board Office of the Prime Minister *see* THE THIRD NATIONAL ECONOMIC AND SOCIAL DEVELOPMENT PLAN (1972-1976)

Thailand. National Economic Development Board *see*
- EDUCATIONAL PLANNING AT THE LOCAL LEVEL
- NATIONAL ECONOMIC DEVELOPMENT PLAN 1961-1966 SECOND PHASE, 1964-1966
- NATIONAL ECONOMIC DEVELOPMENT PLAN 1961-1966(REV.). D 1215/1
- THE NORTHEAST DEVELOPMENT PLAN, 1962-1966
- PERFORMANCE EVALUATION OF DEVELOPMENT IN THAILAND FOR 1965 UNDER THE NATIONAL ECONOMIC DEVELOPMENT PLAN, 1961-1966
- THE SECOND NATIONAL ECONOMIC AND SOCIAL DEVELOPMENT PLAN, 1967-1971
- SECONDARY EDUCATION, MANPOWER AND EDUCATIONAL PLANNING IN THAILAND
- SUMMARY OF THE SECOND FIVE-YEAR PLAN (1967-1971)
- THIRD NATIONAL ECONOMIC AND SOCIAL DEVELOPMENT PLAN, 1972-1976

Thailand. National Education Commission *see*
- THE DROP-OUT PROBLEM IN THAILAND
- EDUCATIONAL SIMULATION MODEL
- AN EVALUATIVE STUDY OF PRIMARY SCHOOL EFFICIENCY IN THAILAND
- THE ILLITERATE POPULATION OF THAILAND 1957-1980
- OPPORTUNITY OF CONTINUATION TO LOWER SECONDARY EDUCATION
- A RESEARCH REPORT ON THE HIGHER EDUCATION
- A STUDY OF PRIMARY SCHOOLING IN THAILAND
- THE SYSTEM OF EDUCATION IN THAILAND

Thailand. National Education Commission and National Youth Bureau *see* PERSPECTIVE POLICIES AND PLANNING FOR THE DEVELOPMENT OF CHILDREN

Thailand. National Education Commission. Educational Planning Division *see*
- EVALUATION REPORT
- SUMMARY OF THE MID-TERM EVALUATION OF THE 5TH EDUCATION PROJECT (1980-1982)

Thailand. National Education Commission. Macro Planning Section *see* THE ESSENCE OF THE FIFTH FIVE YEAR EDUCATIONAL DEVELOPMENT PLAN (1982-1986)

Thailand. National Primary Education Commission *see*
- ASPECTS OF PRIMARY EDUCATION IN THAILAND
- A STUDY FOR QUALITY DEVELOPMENT OF PRIMARY EDUCATION, B.E. 2525-2534

Thailand. National Youth Promotion and Coordination Committee *see* PERSPECTIVE POLICIES AND PLANNING FOR THE DEVELOPMENT OF YOUTH, AGE 15-25 YEARS

Thailand. Office of the National Education Council *see* REPORT [OF] THE JOINT HIGHER EDUCATION ENTRANCE EXAMINATION 1967/68-1975/76

Thailand. Office of the Prime Minister *see* THAILAND IN THE 90S

Thailand. Office of University Affairs *see* EDUCATIONAL REPORT

THAILAND OUTLOOK *see* THE SIAM OUTLOOK

Thailand. Sapha Phutaen Rasadon *see* RAINGAN KANPRACHOOM SAPHA PHUTAEN RASADON

Thailand. Treaties, etc *see* KHWAM TOK LONG TRAIPHAKHI...KHAO THAI...TRIPARTITE AGREEMENT BETWEEN THE GOVERNMENTS OF SIAM, THE UNITED STATES OF AMERICA AND THE UNITED KINGDOM OF GREAT BRITAIN AND NORTHERN IRELAND.

THAILAND'S WALKING TEACHER PROJECT FOR FUNCTIONAL LITERACY / Galadee, M – 1981 – 1mf – 9 – DE-599/1 – ne IDC [370]

Thakurda, Purshottamdas *see* PAPERS, 1917?-1957

Thalbitzer, W *see*
- THE ABSOLUTIVE AND THE RELATIVE IN ESKIMO
- THE AMMASSALIK ESKIMO
- THE CULTIC DEITIES OF THE INUIT (ESKIMO)
- ESKIMO. HANDBOOK OF THE AMERICAN INDIAN LANGUAGES
- ET MANUSKRIPT AF RASMUS RASK OM ALEUTERNES SPROG. SAMMENLIGNET MED GRONLAENDERNES
- DER ETHNOGRAPHISCHE ZUSAMMENHANG DER ESKIMO GROENLWNDS MIT DENEN DER HUDSONBAI
- FRA GRONLANDSFORSKNINGENS FORSTE DAGE
- IS THERE ANY CONNECTION BETWEEN THE ESKIMO LANGUAGE AND THE URALIAN
- DIE KULTISCHEN GOTTHEITEN DER ESKIMOS
- ON THE PHONETIC TRANSCRIPTION OF INDIAN LANGUAGES
- OSTGRONLANDSKE STEMMER
- A PHONETICAL STUDY OF THE ESKIMO LANGUAGE

THALIA / ed by Schiller, Friedrich von – (Siehe auch: Neue Thalia) – Leipzig, 1787-91. Hildesheim, 1977 – 25mf – 9 – DM220.00 diazo DM250.00 silver – gw Olms [430]

Thalmann, Marianne *see* HENRIK IBSEN, EIN ERLEBNIS DER DEUTSCHEN

Thalmayr, Franz *see*
- GOETHE UND DAS CLASSISCHE ALTERTHUM
- UEBER WIELANDS CLASSICITAET, SPRACHE UND STIL

DER THALMUD VOR DEM SCHWURGERICHT AM ENDE DES XIX. JAHRHUNDERTS / Pressel, Wilhelm – Leipzig: Doerffling & Franke, 1893. 1 fiche – 9 – us A.T.L.A. [270]

THE THALTAN INDIANS / Emmons, G T – BN 202. 2. 1911 – 8 – ne IDC [305]

THAME GAZETTE & OXFORDSHIRE & BUCKS ADVERTISER – England. 1857-69, 1912.-w. 9 reels – 1 – uk British Libr Newspaper [072]

Thames Navigation Commission *see* THAMES NAVIGATION COMMISSIONER'S RECORDS, 1771-1867

THAMES NAVIGATION COMMISSIONER'S RECORDS, 1771-1867 / Thames Navigation Commission – 6r – 1 – uk Microform Academic [623]

THAMESIDE MAIL – Southend-on-Sea, England. Dagenham edition. -w. 3 Oct-28 Dec 1928. 23 ft – 1 – uk British Libr Newspaper [072]

THANATOLOGY TODAY – v.1-. 1979- – 1,5,6,9 – us UMI [360]

THE THANATOPHIDIA OF INDIA / Fayrer, J – A description of the venomous snakes of the Indian Peninsula. London. 1872. B-2127 2 – 8 – ne IDC [590]

THANATOS – (1986-. 1,5,6) – 1981- – 9 – us UMI [616]

THAN-CHUNG – Saigon. 1929-mars 1930 – 1 – fr A.C.R.P.P. [073]

THANET TIMES – Margate, England. -w. Oct 1958-Dec 1979. 31 reels – 1 – uk British Libr Newspaper [072]

THANH-NGHE-TINH TAN VAN – Vinh. aout 1930-33 – 1 – fr A.C.R.P.P. [073]

THANH-NGHI TUAN BAO – Fond. Doan-ke-Thien. no. 1-120. Hanoi. avr 1941-mai 1945 – 1 – fr A.C.R.P.P. [073]

THANH-NIEN – Tribune du peuple annamite. Hanoi. 10 oct-28 nov 1933, 21 janv-26 nov 1934 – 1 – fr A.C.R.P.P. [073]

THANH-NIEN TAN TIEN – 16 no. Saigon. janv-aout 1929 – 1 – fr A.C.R.P.P. [073]

THANNER KREISBLATT – Thann, France. 1879-1914 – 1 – fr A.C.R.P.P. [072]

Thapar, B K *see* RECENT ARCHAEOLOGICAL DISCOVERIES IN INDIA

THARGUM JONATHAN BEN USIEEL ZUM PENTATEUCH / Ginsburger, M – Berlin. 1903. BNE-20,007 1 – 9 – ne IDC [270]

THARRAQAH UND SUNAMITH : DAS HOHE LIED, IN SEINEM GESCHICHTLICHEN UND LANDSCHAFTLICHEN HINTERGRUNDE / Noack, Ludwig – (Includes bibliographical references) – Leipzig: Fues (R Reisland), 1869 – 1mf – 9 – 0-8370-6289-6 – 1986-0289 – us A.T.L.A. [220]

THASSILO : TRAGOEDIE IN FUENF ACTEN / Saar, Ferdinand von – Heidelberg: Georg Weiss, 1886 – 1r – 1 – us U.W. Library [820]

THAT CHARACTER CALLED GOD / Arrigoni, Enrico – 183p. 1 fiche (29x) – 9 – 1.00f – at Libertarian Micro [320]

THAT PSEUDO-JUDICIAL DECLARATION OF 1888 / Warren, William Fairfield – (The Methodist Review, v. 78, Jan. 1896, p. 81-86) – 9 – us A.T.L.A. [240]

Thatcher, Erastus *see*
- A DIGEST OF STATUTES, EQUITY RULES, AND DECISIONS, UPON THE JURISDICTION, PLEADINGS, AND PRACTICE OF THE CIRCUIT COURTS OF THE UNITED STATES
- A DIGEST OF STATUTES, RULES, AND DECISIONS RELATIVE TO THE JURISDICTION AND PRACTICE OF THE SUPREME COURT OF THE UNITED STATES 1790-1879

Thatcher, Griffithes Wheeler *see* JUDGES AND RUTH: INTRODUCTION, REVISED VERSION WITH NOTES

Thatcher, Oliver Joseph *see*
- THE IDEAS THAT HAVE INFLUENCED CIVILIZATION, IN THE ORIGINAL DOCUMENTS
- A SKETCH OF THE HISTORY OF THE APOSTOLIC CHURCH

Thatcher, Samuel Cooper *see* REVIEW OF THE CONSTITUTION AND ASSOCIATE STATUTES OF THE THEOLOGICAL SEMINARY IN ANDOVER

THAT'S SHOW BUSINESS – v. 1. 1971-76 – 1 – 145.00 – cn McLaren [790]

DIE THATSACHEN DES GLAUBENS: VORTRAEGE / Stutz, Ulrich – Zuerich: Bei Franz Hanke, 1865. 1 fiche – 9 – us A.T.L.A. [240]

Thausing, Moriz *see* DUERERS BRIEFE, TAGEBUECHER UND REIME

Thaxter, R *see*
- CONTRIBUTIONS TOWARDS A MONOGRAPH OF THE LABOULBENIACEAE
- THE ENTOMOPHTHOREAE OF THE UNITED STATES

Thayer, Amos Madden *see* JURISDICTION OF THE FEDERAL COURTS. REV. ED

Thayer, Charles Snow *see* UEBER DAS VERHAELTNISS DER PSALMEN ZU JEREMIA

Thayer, Christopher Toppan *see* AN ADDRESS DELIVERED IN THE FIRST PARISH, BEVERLY, OCTOBER 2, 1867, ON THE TWO-HUNDREDTH ANNIVERSARY OF ITS FORMATION

THAYER COUNTY BANNER-ARGUS – Bruning, NE. -w. Jan. 1973.- – 1 – us NE Hist [071]

THAYER COUNTY BANNER-JOURNAL – Bruning, NE. -w. Oct. 1930-Dec. 1972 – 1 – us NE Hist [071]

THAYER COUNTY SENTINEL – Hebron, NE. -w. Aug 1876; Jan 1879-Jun 1880, scattered issues missing – 1 – us NE Hist [071]

Thayer, Eli *see* PAPERS OF ELI THAYER

Thayer, Ezra Ripley *see* OBSERVATONS ON THE LAW OF EVIDENCE

Thayer, J H *see* THE AUTHORSHIP OF THE FOURTH GOSPEL

Thayer, James Bradley *see* CASES ON CONSTITUTIONAL LAW

Thayer, Ralph Noyes *see* THE BRITISH PROTECTORATES AND THE UNION OF SOUTH AFRICA 1930-1950

Thayer, Wade W *see* THAYER'S DIGEST OF HAWAII SUPREME COURT DEC

Thayer, William M *see* MARVELS OF THE NEW WEST

THAYER'S DIGEST OF HAWAII SUPREME COURT DEC / Thayer, Wade W – (Covers v1-22 1847-1915) – Honolulu: Paradise Press, 1916 – 10mf – 9 – $15.00 – LLMC 90-002 – us L.L.M.C. [340]

THBY RN EL ESTUDIO DE LA BAJA ATMOSFERA EN UN NUCLEO URBANO / Gutierrez Alonso, Paulino – 1mf – 9 – Pta1,000.00 – 84-85422-14-7 – sp Pentalfa [550]

LE THE – ou Le Journal des dix-huit puis ou Le Controleur general. Bertin d'Antilly. Paris. avr-sept 1797, juil-aout 1799 – 1 – fr A.C.R.P.P. [073]

Theal, George McCall *see* RECORDS OF THE CAPE COLONY

THEATER – (See also: Yale Theater) – v9-1977- – 1,5,6,9 – us UMI [790]

THEATER : EIN WIENER ROMAN / Bahr, Hermann – Berlin: S Fischer, [19–?] – 1r – 1 – us U.W. Library [830]

THEATER DER ZEIT – 1970-1983 – 349mf – 1 – DM1,989.30 – gw Mikro Press [790]

THEATER HERALD – Reno, NV. 1921-22 – 1r – 1 – $50.00 – U04721 – us Library Micro [071]

THEATER HEUTE – Velbert, Hannover. 1960-1973 – 13r – 1 – DM975.00 – gw Mikro Press [072]

THEATER JOURNALS COLLECTION : FROM THE CENTRAL SCIENTIFIC LIBRARY OF THE THEATER UNION OF RUSSIA ON MICROFICHE – (Individual pts & titles also listed) – 3pts 17 titles 805mf – 9 – $4,400.00 coll – us Ross [790]

THEATER JOURNALS COLLECTION, PT 1 : FROM THE CENTRAL SCIENTIFIC LIBRARY OF THE THEATER UNION OF RUSSIA ON MICROFICHE – (Individual titles also listed) – 4 titles 40mf – 9 – $300.00 coll – us Ross [790]

THEATER JOURNALS COLLECTION, PT 2 : FROM THE CENTRAL SCIENTIFIC LIBRARY OF THE THEATER UNION OF RUSSIA ON MICROFICHE – (Individual titles also listed) – 6 titles 140mf – 9 – $850.00 coll – us Ross [790]

THEATER JOURNALS COLLECTION, PT 3 : FROM THE CENTRAL SCIENTIFIC LIBRARY OF THE THEATER UNION OF RUSSIA ON MICROFICHE – (Individual titles also listed) – 7 titles 625mf – 9 – $3,700.00 coll – us Ross [790]

THEATER JOURNALS FROM THE CENTRAL SCIENTIFIC LIBRARY OF THE THEATER UNION OF RUSSIA ON MICROFICHE, PT 1 *see*
- ERMITAZH
- KURANTY
- SEM'DNEI MKT
- VESTNIK TEATRA

THEATER JOURNALS FROM THE CENTRAL SCIENTIFIC LIBRARY OF THE THEATER UNION OF RUSSIA ON MICROFICHE, PT 2 *see*
- AFISHA TIM
- IGRA
- PROLETARSKAIA KUL'TURA
- RABOCHII I ZRITEL'
- TEATR I DRAMATURGIIA
- TEATRAL'NAIA MOSKVA

THEATER JOURNALS FROM THE CENTRAL SCIENTIFIC LIBRARY OF THE THEATER UNION OF RUSSIA ON MICROFICHE, PT 3 *see*
- EKRAN
- KHUDOZHESTVENNII TRUD
- KHUDOZHNIK I ZRITEL'
- LIUBOV' K TREM APELSINAM
- RABOCHII I TEATR
- TEATR I STUDIA
- TELEVIDENIE I RADIOVESHCHANIE

DER THEATER SPIGEL UND THEATER FRAYND = THEATRICAL MIRROR – (In Yiddish) – New York City, NY. v1 no1 1909-v1 no5 1910 – 1r – 1 – $30.00 – cn Can Microfilming [071]

THEATERUNTERNEHMEN ZWISCHEN KUNST, KOMMERZ UND POLITIK : ASPEKTE ZUR THEATERGESCHICHTE IN OST- UND WESTPREUSSEN IM SPAETEN 19. UND FRUEHEN 20. JAHRHUNDERT MIT REGESTENWERKEN ALS ANHANG / Eickenroth, Manuela P – 1995 – 2+2mf – 9 – DM112.00 – 3-8267-2255-8 – gw Hänsel [790]

THEATRALISCHES WOCHENBLATT – Hamburg, DE. 1774; 1775 – 1r – 1 – gw Mikrofilm [072]

LE THEATRE – [Quebec?: Theatre de Quebec, 1894-1895?] – 9 – cn C.I.H.M. [790]

THEATRE / Nadal, Augustin – Paris: Briasson, 1738. 5 fiches. (Literature Collection) – 9 – 12.00 – fr Bibl Nationale [790]

THEATRE 1948-1972 (PVB 1895-1977, PT 3) – (With printed bibliography & subject index) – 100mf – 9 – £425.00 – uk Chadwyck [790]

THEATRE ARTS – 1-48. 1916-64 – 1 – us UMI [790]

THEATRE ARTS – v. 1-29. 1916-1945 – 1 – us Princeton Micro [790]

THEATRE ARTS MAGAZINE – New York. v1-7. 1916-23 – 29mf – 9 – 333/2 – ne IDC [790]

LE THEATRE AU JAPON / Benazet, Alexandre – Ses rapports avec les cultes locaux. Paris, Ernest Leroux. 1901 – 9 – 10.00 – fr Orientalistes [790]

LE THEATRE CLASSIQUE EN ANGLETERRE, DANS L'AGE DE JOHN DRYDEN / Harvey-Jellie, W Raymond – Montreal: Librarie Beauchemin Ltee, (1932). SEM105P77 – 2mf – 9 – Can$4.50 – cn Bibl Nat [420]

THEATRE COMMUNICATIONS GROUP *see* PLAYBILLS

THEATRE COSTUME DESIGNS / Victoria and Albert Museum. London – (Four centuries of original costume designs including work by AE Chalon, Wilhelm, Leon Bakst and Edward Gordon Craig. Includes printed catalogue) – 1983 – 38 colour mf – 15 – $699.00 – 0-907696-10-4 – uk Emmett [740]

THEATRE CRAFTS – v1- 1967- 1; v5- 5,6; v9- 9 – us UMI [790]

THEATRE D'AMOUR – N.p., n.d. – 1mf – 9 – ne IDC [790]

LE THEATRE DE VOLTAIRE / Flaubert, Gustave; ed by Besterman, Theodore – (Studies on Voltaire and the eighteenth century, v50-51) – Oxford. 1967 – 9 – $81.00 – 0-7294-0151-0 – uk Voltaire [820]

LE THEATRE DES BONS ENGINS, AUQUEL SONT CONTENUZ CENT EMBLEMES MORAULX / La Perriere, Guillaume de – 1539 – 9 – 15.00 – us Scholars' Facs [810]

THEATRE DU MONDE, CONTENANT DIVERS EXCELLENS TABLEAUX DE LA VIE HUMAINE / Goulart, S – Amsterdam, 1657 – 2mf – 9 – ne IDC [700]

THEATRE ET DESTIN : LA SIGNIFICATION DE LA RENAISSANCE DRAMATIQUE EN FRANCE AU 20E SIECLE / Simon, P H – 1959 – F60.00 – fr Ethnologie [440]

A THEATRE FOR VOLUPTUOUS WORLDLINGS / Noot, Jan van der – 1569 – 9 – $20.00 – us Scholars' Facs [430]

Theatre Guild, Inc *see* STAGE

THEATRE HISTORY IN CANADA – (Cont by: Theatre Research in Canada at v13 1992) – Toronto. v1-12. 1980-91 – 9 – Can$20.00y – cn Micromedia [790]

THEATRE HISTORY SERIES NO 1 *see* THE ANNIE HORNIMAN COLLECTION

THEATRE HISTORY SERIES NO 2 *see* THE BASIL DEAN COLLECTION

THEATRE HISTORY SERIES NO 3 *see* THE HUGH HUNT COLLECTION

THEATRE HISTORY SERIES NO 4 *see* THE SIR JOHN GIELGUD ARCHIVE

THEATRE HISTORY SERIES NO 5 *see* THE GEORGE R SIMS COLLECTION OF PLAYSCRIPTS

THEATRE HISTORY SERIES NO 6 *see* PERFORMANCE SITES OF THE ANCIENT WORLD

THEATRE INEDIT-LE ROSSIGNOL, RABELAIS, CRETE-ROUGE HELENE / Delair, Paul – Paris: P. Ollendorff, 1899. vii,365p. 4 fiches. (Literature Collection) – 9 – 10.00 – fr Bibl Nationale [820]

THEATRE JOURNAL – v31- 1979- – 1,5,6,9 – us UMI [790]

THEATRE LYRIQUE / Le Brun, A-L – 1712 – 9 – us Sibley [780]

THE THEATRE MAGAZINE – New York. v1-53. 1901-31 – 11r – 1 – us Ross [790]

Theatre Museum. London *see* PLAYBILLS AND PROGRAMMES FROM LONDON THEATRES, 1801-1900

Theatre MuseumVictoria & Albert Museum. London *see* PROMPT BOOKS IN THE THEATRE MUSEUM, LONDON

THEATRE RECORDS *see* SHAKESPEARE AT STRATFORD-UPON-AVON

THEATRE RESEARCH IN CANADA *see* THEATRE HISTORY IN CANADA

THEATRE RESEARCH INTERNATIONAL – v. 1- 1975- – 1,5,6,9 – us UMI [790]

THEATRE SET DESIGNS / Victoria and Albert Museum. London – (Includes printed catalogue) – 1984 – 26 colour mf – 15 – $494.00 – 0-907696-19-8 – uk Emmett [790]

THEATRE, STAGE, COSTUME : ARCHITECTURE, APPLIED ARTS, STUDIO ARTS – (Individual titles not listed separately) – 55 catalogues on 70mf – 9 – £515.00 – uk Chadwyck [790]

THEATRE SURVEY – v1- 1960- 1; v16- 5,6; v17- 9 – us UMI [790]

THEATRE WORKSHOP – (New Theatre League). New York. v. 1-2. no. 1. Oct 1936-June 1938 – 1 – us NY Public [790]

LES THEATRES DE PARIS ET LEUR REPERTOIRE: THEATRE DE L'ODEON 1797-1900 / Lecomte, L H – 4 fiches. (Recueils documentaires des Arts du Spectacle) – 9 – 10.00 – fr Bibl Nationale [440]

LES THEATRES DES BOULEVARDS: 1789-1848 / Albert, Maurice – Paris, 1902. 381p. 4 fiches. (Literature Collection) – 9 – 10.00 – fr Bibl Nationale [790]

THEATRI MACHINARUM / Bartolus, A – pt. 6. Musica Mathematica. Altenburg. 1614. BR-636 – 9 – ne IDC [780]

THEATRICAL AND MUSICAL GUIDE – London. -m. Nov 1884-Jan 1886. (1 reel) – 1 – uk British Libr Newspaper [790]

THE THEATRICAL SONGSTER – (New York). 1905-09 – 1 – us A.J.P.C. [780]

THEATRICAL TIMES – London. -m. Oct 1883-Jun 1884. (21 ft) – 1 – uk British Libr Newspaper [790]

THEATRICAL WORLD – London. -w. Oct 1881-Apr 1882. (39 ft) – 1 – uk British Libr Newspaper [790]

O THEATRO – Manaos, Amazonas. 30 Jun-11 Ago 1906 – 1,5,6 – bl Biblioteca [072]

THEATRO DE LA TIERRA UNIVERSAL / Ortello, A – Amberes, 1588 – 8mf – 9 – sp Cultura [910]

THEATRO ECCLESIASTICO EM QUE SE ACHAO MUITOS DOCUMENTOS DE CANTOCHAO / Rosario, D. do – Oitava impressao. Lisboa. 1786. BP-451 1 – 9 – ne IDC [780]

THEATRO HESPANOL. TOMO 1 / Garcia de la Huerta, Vicente – 1785 – 2mf – 9 – Pta1,500.00 – 84-7848-176-1 – sp Pentalfa [790]

THEATRO HESPANOL. TOMO 2 / Garcia de la Huerta, Vicente – 1785 – 2mf – 9 – Pta1,500.00 – 84-7848-177-X – sp Pentalfa [790]

THEATRO HESPANOL. TOMO 3 / Garcia de la Huerta, Vicente – 1785 – 2mf – 9 – Pta1,500.00 – 84-7848-178-8 – sp Pentalfa [790]

THEATRO HESPANOL. TOMO 4 / Garcia de la Huerta, Vicente – 1785 – 2mf – 9 – Pta1,500.00 – 84-7848-179-6 – sp Pentalfa [790]

THEATRUM : THE THEATRE MAGAZINE – (Cont by: Stage at no 43 1995) – Toronto. nos 1-41. 1985/86-1994/95 – 9 – Can$20.00y – cn Micromedia [790]

THEATRUM BOTANICUM / Parkinson, J – London. 1640. BM-386 2 – 8 – ne IDC [580]

THEATRUM CHEMICUM, PRAECIPUOS SELECTORUM AUCTORUM TRACTATUS DE CHEMIAE ET LAPIDIS PHILOSOPHICI... – Strasbourg, Zetzneri. 6v. 1659-1661 – 55mf – 9 – O-1958/1 – ne IDC [540]

THEATRUM EUROPAEUM – 1646-1738 – 1 – 571.00 – us L of C Photodup [790]

THEATRUM FUNGORUM / Sterbeeck, F van – Antwerpen, 1675. 396, 20 pp., 36 pls. B-5288 2 – 8 – ne IDC [580]

THEATRUM OMNIUM SCIENTIARUM / Cacace, Giovanni Battista – O-187. 1650 – 9 – ne IDC [500]

THEATRUM STULTORUM JOCOSERIUM / Leenheer, J de – O 821. 1669 – 9 – ne IDC [450]

THEATRUM VETERUM RHETORUM, ORATORUM, DECLAMATORUM, QUOS IN GRAECIA NOMINABANT...EXPOSITUM LIBRIS QUINQUE / Cressolles, Loius de – Venetiis, 1735 – 7mf – 8 – ne Slangenburg [450]

THEATRUM VITAE HUMANAE / Boissard, J J – O-558 1. 1596 – 9 – ne IDC [450]

THEBES FIRST BAPTIST CHURCH. THEBES, ILLINOIS : CHURCH RECORDS – Aug 1869-Feb 1883; Jun 1887-Jul 1902; May 1909-Apr 1984.Formerly called Union Church, Sexton Creek, Thebes Baptist Church, Thebes Missionary Baptist Church – 1 – 54.81 – us Baptist [240]

THEDFORD BANNER – Thedford, NE. -w. Jan 1973-May 1974 – 1 – us NE Hist [071]

THEDFORD BANNER – Thedford, NE. -w. Jul-Oct 1894, scattered issues missing; Nov 1895-Dec 1897 – 1 – us NE Hist [071]

THEDFORD TRIBUNE – Thedford, NE. -w. Dec 1892; Jan 1894-Jul 1894, scattered issues missing – 1 – us NE Hist [071]

Thee, Marek *see* ARMAMENTS, ARMS CONTROL AND DISARMAMENT

Theiner, A *see*
- ANNALES ECCLESIASTICI
- MONUMENTS HISTORIQUES RELATIFS AUX REGNES D'ALEXIS MICHAELOWITCH, FEODOR 3 ET PIERRE LE GRAND, CZARS DE RUSSIE

THEIR CALL TO SERVICE : A STUDY IN THE PARTNERSHIP OF BUSINESS AND RELIGION / Howard, Philip E – Philadelphia: Westminster Press, 1915 – 1mf – us A.T.L.A. [240]

THEISM / Bowne, Borden Parker – New York: American Book, 1902 – 1mf – 9 – us A.T.L.A. [200]

THEISM : THE NATION'S NEED: AN ADDRESS / Mourbhunj, Sri Ram Chandra Bhanja Deo – (Presented to the All-India Theistic Conference, Calcutta, Dec 1906) – Mourbhunj: [s.n.], 1906 (Calcutta: Gupta, Mukherjee) – 1mf – 9 – 0-8370-2630-X – 1985-0630 – us A.T.L.A. [290]

THEISM: A SURVEY OF THE PATHS THAT LEAD TO GOD...IN...THE HISTORY OF PHILOSOPHY / Tigert, John James – Nashville: M.E. Church So. Pub. H., 1902. 1 fiche – 9 – us A.T.L.A. [240]

THEISM AND CHRISTIANITY : SIX SERMONS PREACHED BY THE REQUEST OF THE CHRISTIAN EVIDENCE SOCIETY AT ST. JAMES'S CHURCH, PICCADILLY, ON SUNDAY AFTERNOONS AFTER EASTER, 1878 – London: Christian Evidence Committee of the S P C K, [1878?] – 1mf – 9 – 0-8370-5581-4 – 1985-3581 – us A.T.L.A. [230]

THEISM AND THE CHRISTIAN FAITH : LECTURES / Everett, Charles Carroll; ed by Hale, Edward – New York: Macmillan, 1909 – 2mf – us A.T.L.A. [240]

THEISM IN THE LIGHT OF PRESENT SCIENCE AND PHILOSOPHY / Iverach, James – (Includes index) – New York: Macmillan, 1899 – 1mf – 9 – 0-8370-3737-9 – 1985-1737 – us A.T.L.A. [210]

THEISM OR AGNOSTICISM: AN ESSAY ON THE GROUNDS OF BELIEF IN GOD / Maitland, Brownlow – London: S.P.C.K., 1878. 1 fiche – 9 – us A.T.L.A. [240]

THEISM: THE NATION'S NEED: AN ADDRESS / Chandra Bhanja Deo, Maharaja – Mourbhunj, 1906.1 fiche – 9 – us A.T.L.A. [240]

THE THEISTIC ARGUMENT : AS AFFECTED BY RECENT THEORIES: A COURSE OF LECTURES DELIVERED AT THE LOWELL INSITUTE IN BOSTON / Diman, Jeremiah Lewis – (Includes index of names) – Boston: Houghton, Mifflin, 1882, c1881 – 1mf – 9 – 0-8370-2921-X – 1985-0921 – us A.T.L.A. [210]

THE THEISTIC CONCEPTION OF THE WORLD : AN ESSAY IN OPPOSITION TO CERTAIN TENDENCIES OF MODERN THOUGHT / Cocker, Benjamin Franklin – (Includes index) – New York: Harper, 1875 – 1mf – 9 – 0-8370-2698-9 – 1985-0698 – us A.T.L.A. [210]

THEISTIC CONCEPTION OF THE WORLD: AN ESSAY IN OPPOSITION TO CERTAIN TENDENCIES / Cocker, Benjamin – New York: Harper, 1875. 1 fiche – 9 – us A.T.L.A. [240]

Thelis, Claude-Antoine de *see*
- MEMOIRES CONCERNANT LES ECOLES NATIONALES
- PLAN D'EDUCATION NATIONALE, EN FAVEUR DES PAUVRES ENFANS DE LA CAMPAGNE

THELMA / Corelli, Marie – British Fiction Archive: Unit 1 – 9 – uk Bell [830]

THELOGIA (SIC) PECTORIS : OUTLINES OF RELIGIOUS FAITH AND DOCTRINE / Hodgson, James Muscutt – Edinburgh: T. & T. Clark, 1898 – 1mf – 9 – us A.T.L.A. [240]

THELOGISCHE RUNDSCHAU – Alte Folge: 1(1897)-20(1917) – 134mf – 9 – Dfl469.00 – ne Slangenburg [073]

Thelwall, John *see* THE POETICAL RECREATIONS OF THE CHAMPION, AND HIS LITERARY CORRESPONDENTS. WITH A SELECTION OF ESSAYS, LITERARY AND CRITICAL, WHICH HAVE APPEARED IN THE CHAMPION NEWSPAPER

DIE THEMATIK "ILLUSION UND WIRKLICHKEIT" IN TENNESSEE WILLIAMS' DRAMEN "THE GLASS MENAGERIE" UND "A STREETCAR NAMED DESIRE" / Ettinger-Hengstebeck, Ingrid – 1995 – 2mf – 9 – DM80.00 – 3-8267-2243-4 – gw Hänsel [420]

THEME D'HARMONIE, 100 : [2EME LIVRE]...OP. 71 / D'Indy, V – Paris: Rousanez, c1919 – 1 – us Sibley [780]

THEMELIOS – (1986- . 5,6,9) – v1- . 1962- – 1 – us UMI [073]

THEMENBEHANDLUNG IM FREMDSPRACHENUNTERRICHTLICHEN DISKURS : LEHREN UND LERNEN DURCH THEMATISCHE AKTIVITAETEN IM KONVERSATIONSUNTERRICHT AN KOREANISCHEN UNIVERSITAETEN / Ha, Su-Guen – 1993 – 3mf – 9 – DM98.00 – 3-89349-740-4 – gw Hänsel [400]

LA THEMIS – Montreal, Canada. fev 1879-v3 n12. jan 1882 – 1r – 1 – Can$30.00 – cn Can Microfilming [072]

Themudo Quiros, Florencio *see* PROCURADORES DE LOS TRIBUNALES EJERCIENTES EN ESPANA

THEO VAN DOESBURG ARCHIVE / Netherlands Office for Fine Arts – (Includes printed guide and two binders) – 441mf – 9 – ne IDC [700]

Theobald, A *see* UEBER'S OHR GEHAUEN

THEOBALD THAMER : DER REPRAESENTANT UND VORGAENGER MODERNER GEISTESRICHTUNG IN DEM REFORMATIONSZEITALTER: EINE HISTORISCHE MONOGRAPHIE / Neander, August – Berlin: C.G. Luederitz, 1842 – 1mf – us A.T.L.A. [240]

Theobald, W *see*
- CATALOGUE OF THE LAND AND FRESHWATER SHELLS OF BRITISH INDIA
- CATALOGUE OF THE RECENT SHELLS IN THE MUSEUM ASIATIC SOCIETY OF BENGAL
- CONCHOLOGIA INDICA
- DESCRIPTIVE CATALOGUE OF THE REPTILES OF BRITISH INDIA
- ON INDIAN OOLOGY

Theobald, William F *see*
- THE ECONOMIC EFFECTS OF GOVERNMENT ASSISTANCE IN COMMERCIAL RESORT DEVELOPMENT
- PARTICIPANTS BENEFITS ASSESSMENT AT A CAMPUS RECREATIONAL FACILITY

THE THEOCRACY OF ISRAEL / Rupert, Greenberry G – Oklahoma City: Union, 1902. 1 fiche – 9 – us A.T.L.A. [240]

LA THEOCRATIE A GENEVE AU TEMPS DE CALVIN / Choisy, Eugene – Geneve: Ch. Eggimann, [ca. 1897] – 1mf – us A.T.L.A. [949]

THEODICEA O LA RELIGION NATURAL... / Pereyra, L – Madrid, SA – 10mf – 9 – sp Cultura [290]

THEODOR BEZA / Baum, Johann Wilhelm – Leipzig: Weidmann, 1843-1852 – 4mf – us A.T.L.A. [240]

THEODOR BEZA : LEBEN UND AUSGEWAEHLTE SCHRIFTEN / Heppe, Heinrich – Elberfeld: R.L. Friderichs, 1861. (Leben und ausgewaehlte Schriften der Vaeter und Begruender der reformirten Kirchen; 6. T.) – 1mf – us A.T.L.A. [240]

THEODOR CHRISTLIEB, D.D.: OF BONN / Christlieb, Theodor – New York: A.C. Armstrong, 1892 – 2mf – us A.T.L.A. [240]

THEODOR FONTANES ENGERE WELT : AUS DEM NACHLASS / ed by Krammer, Mario – Berlin: A Collignon, 1920 – 1r – 1 – us U.W. Library [430]

THEODOR FONTANES ROMAN "DER STECHLIN" / Behrend, Erich – (Includes bibliographical references) – Marburg a.L.: N G Elwert, 1929 – 1r – 1 – us U.W. Library [430]

Theodor, Hugo *see* DIE KOMISCHEN ELEMENTE DER ALTFRANZOESISCHEN CHANSONS DE GESTE

THEODOR KOERNER / Berger, Karl – (Includes index) – Bielefeld: Velhagen & Klasing, 1912 – 1 – us U.W. Library [430]

THEODOR KOERNER : DICHTER UND FREIHEITSHELD / Loeffler, Fritz – Dresden: Verlag Heimatwerk Sachsen, v. Baensch Stiftung, 1938 – 1r – 1 – us U.W. Library [920]

THEODOR KOERNER : SEIN LEBEN UND SEINE DICHTUNGEN / Kohut, Adolph – (Mit zahlreichen ungedruckten Gedichten und Briefen von und an Theodor Koerner und Familie Koerner. Includes bibliographical references) – Berlin: A Slottko, 1891 – 1 – us U.W. Library [430]

THEODOR KOERNER / Zipper, Albert – Leipzig: P Reclam, 1900 – 1r – 1 – us U.W. Library [920]

THEODOR KOERNER UND DIE SEINEN / Peschel, Emil & Wildenow, Eugen – (Includes bibliographical references and index) – Leipzig: E A Seemann, 1898 – 1 – us U.W. Library [430]

THEODOR KOERNERS BRIEFWECHSEL MIT DEN SEINEN / Koerner, Theodor; ed by Weldler-Steinberg, A – Leipzig: Quelle & Meyer, 1910 – 1 – us U.W. Library [860]

THEODOR KOERNER'S TAGEBUCH UND KRIEGSLIEDER AUS DEM JAHRE 1813 : MIT DEM BILDNISS THEODOR KOERNER'S, ABBILDUNG SEINER GRABSTAETTE, SOWIE SECHS AUTOTYPIRTEN GEDICHTEN UND EINEM BRIEFE THEODOR KOERNER'S / ed by Peschel, W Emil – Freiburg i.B.: F E Fehsenfeld, 1893 – 1r – 1 – us U.W. Library [920]

THEODOR MUNDT UND SEINE BEZIEHUNGEN ZUM JUNGEN DEUTSCHLAND / Draeger, Otto – (Includes bibliographical references) – Marburg a.L.: N G Elwert, 1909 – 1r – 1 – us U.W. Library [943]

THEODOR STORM : EIN BILD SEINES LEBENS UND SCHAFFENS / Wehl, Feodor von – Altona: A C Reher, 1888 – 1r – 1 – us U.W. Library [920]

THEODOR STORM : DER DICHTER IN SEINEM WERK / Stuckert, Franz – (Includes bibliographical references) – 2. ueberarb. Aufl. Tuebingen: M Niemeyer, 1952 – 1 – us U.W. Library [430]

THEODOR STORM : EINIGE ZUEGE ZU SEINEM BILDE / Wedde, Johannes – Hamburg: H Gruening, 1888 – 1r – 1 – us U.W. Library [430]

THEODOR STORM : SEIN LEBEN UND SEINE DICHTUNG / Schuetze, Paul – Berlin: Gebrueder Paetel, 1887 – 1r – 1 – us U.W. Library [430]

THEODOR STORM UND DER MODERNE REALISMUS / Biese, Alfred – Berlin: R Eckstein, 1888 – 1r – 1 – us U.W. Library [430]

THEODOR STORMS BRIEFE AN FRIEDRICH EGGERS : MIT EINER LEBENSSKIZZE VON F. EGGERS UND GEDICHTPROBEN / Storm, Theodor; ed by Seidel, Wolfgang – (Includes bibliographical references) – Berlin: K Curtius, 1911 – 1r – 1 – us U.W. Library [920]

THEODOR STORMS BRIEFE AN SEINEN FREUND GEORG LORENZEN / Storm, Theodor – [S.l.: s.n.], 1923 – 1 – us U.W. Library [920]

THEODOR STORMS ERZAEHLUNG "AQUIS SUBMERSUS" / Mueller, Thea – (Includes bibliographical references (8th-10th prelim. pages)) – Marburg a.L.: N G Elwert, 1925 – 1r – 1 – us U.W. Library [430]

THEODOR STORMS ERZAEHLUNGSKUNST IN IHRER ENTWICKLUNG / Eichentopf, Hans – (Includes bibliographical references (3rd prelim. leaf)) – Marburg a.L.: N G Elwert, 1908 – 1r – 1 – us U.W. Library [430]

THEODOR STORM'S SAEMMTLICHE SCHRIFTEN / Storm, Theodor – 1. Gesammtausg. Braunschweig: G Westermann, 1868 – 1 – us U.W. Library [800]

THEODOR STORM'S STIMMKUNGSKUNST / Stamm, Hermann – Eckernfoerde, 1914 – 1mf – DM48.00 – 3-8267-3086-0 – gw Hänsel [430]

THEODORA SPECIOSA, IN NEUES PFLANZENGESCHLACHT / Medikus, F K – Mannheim. 1786. B-8135 1 – 9 – ne IDC [580]

THEODORE : OR, THE SKEPTIC'S CONVERSION / De Wette, Wilhelm Martin Leberecht – Boston: Hilliard, Gray, 1841 – 1r – 1 – us U.W. Library [430]

THEODORE 2, LE NOUVEL EMPIRE D'ABYSSINIE ET LES INTERETS FRANCAIS DANS LE SUD DE LA MER ROUGE / Lejean, Guillaume M – (African Library). Paris. Amyot. 1865 – 9 – fr Hachette [960]

THEODORE AND WILFRITH : LECTURES DELIVERED IN ST. PAUL'S IN DECEMBER 1896 / Browne, G F – London: S.P.C.K.; New York: E.& J.B. Young, 1897 – 1mf – us A.T.L.A. [240]

THEODORE BEZA : THE COUNSELLOR OF THE FRENCH REFORMATION, 1519-1605 / Baird, Henry Martyn – New York: G.P. Putnam, 1899. (Heroes of the Reformation; v4) – 1mf – us A.T.L.A. [240]

THEODORE E. BURTON PAPERS *see* BURTON, THEODORE E., PAPERS, MS 3469

Theodore Harris Institute. Pineville, Kentucky *see* FIRST ANNUAL CATALOG, 1901-02

THEODORE OF STUDIUM : HIS LIFE AND TIMES / Gardner, Alice – London: E. Arnold, 1905 – 1mf – us A.T.L.A. [240]

THEODORE PARKER PAPERS, 1826-1862 / Parker, Theodore – Massachusetts Historical Society – 4r – 1 – $305.00 – us UMI [920]

THEODORE THORNTON MUNGER : NEW ENGLAND MINISTER / Bacon, Benjamin Wisner – New Haven: Yale University Press, 1913 – 1mf – us A.T.L.A. [240]

THEODORE WILLIAM DWIGHT MICROFILM COLLECTION – (Manuscripts, articles, lectures, letters, printed and photographic materials from one of the great early American law teachers and founders of Columbia Law School) – 1r – 5,6 – $250.00 set – us Hein [340]

THEODORI PRODROMI COMMENTARIOS IN CARMINA SACRA MELODORUM COSMAE HIEROSOLYMITANI ET IOANNIS DAMASCENI / Prodromus, Theodore – Romae: Ex Bibliotheca Vaticana, 1888 – 1mf – us A.T.L.A. [240]

THEODORIC THE GOTH : THE BARBARIAN CHAMPION OF CIVILIZATION / Hodgkin, Thomas – New York: G.P. Putnam, 1891. (Heroes of the nations) – 2mf – us A.T.L.A. [240]

Theodorico, Guillelmus a S *see* EXPOSITIO IM EPISTOLAM AD ROMANOS

Theodorus of Mopsuestia *see* IN EPISTOLAS B. PAULI COMMENTARII

THEODORUS STUDITES : MARTYRBRIEFE AUS DER OSTKIRCHE – Mainz, 1931 – Dfl13.00 – ne Slangenburg [240]

THEODRIC : A DOMESTIC TALE, AND OTHER POEMS / Campbell, Thomas – London: Published for Longman, Hurst, Rees, Orme, Brown, and Green by S. and R. Bentley, 1824 – 1 roll – 1 – 1-55879-310-0 – uk Libr Preservation [810]

Theodule, Fr *see* DICTEES GRADUEES ET ANALYSES

THEODULFE : EVEQUE D'ORLEANS ET ABBE DE FLEURY-SUR-LOIRE / Baunard, Louis – Orleans: Gatineau, 1860 – 1mf – us A.T.L.A. [240]

Theoharis, Athan *see*
- THE "DO NOT FILE" FILE
- FBI AMERICAN LEGION CONTACT PROGRAM
- FBI FILE ON THE COMMITTEE FOR PUBLIC JUSTICE
- FBI FILING AND RECORDS PROCEDURES
- FBI MANUALS OF INSTRUCTION, INVESTIGATIVE PROCEDURES, AND GUIDELINES, 1927-1978
- FBI WIRETAPS, BUGS, AND BREAK-INS
- THE J. EDGAR HOOVER OFFICIAL AND CONFIDENTIAL FILE
- THE LOUIS NICHOLS OFFICIAL AND CONFIDENTIAL FILE AND THE CLYDE TOLSON PERSONAL FILE

THEOKRISIS : IDEEN UEBER GOTT UND WELT ZUR VERSOEHNUNG DES THEISMUS UND PANTHEISMUS / Buehler, Adolph – Berlin: Nicolai (O Parthess), 1861 – 1mf – 9 – 0-8370-2520-6 – 1985-0520l – us A.T.L.A. [210]

THEOKRISIS: IDEEN UEBER GOTT UND WELT / Buehler, Adolph – Berlin: Nicolai, 1861. 1 fiche – 9 – us A.T.L.A. [240]

THEOLOGIA / Abaelardus, Petrus – 1988 – 17mf – 9 – Bf1,975.00 – 2-503-63112-6 – be Brepols [240]

THEOLOGIA DOGMATICA CHRISTANORUM ORIENTALIUM / Jugie, Martin – Parisiis, 1926-1935.-5v – 53mf – 8 – ne Slangenburg [240]

THEOLOGIA DOGMATICO-POLEMICA... / Sardagna, C – Ratisbonae. 8v. 1770-71 – 49mf – 9 – CA-58/1 – ne IDC [240]

THEOLOGIA DOGMATICO-SCHOLASTICA... / Gener, J B – Romae. 6v. 1767-77 – 35mf – 9 – CA-49/1 – ne IDC [240]

THEOLOGIA FENNICA – v3-7. 1943-63 (complete) – Inquire – 1 – ATLA S0887 – us A.T.L.A. [073]

THEOLOGIA MORALIS... / Busenbaum, H; ed by Croix, C la – Coloniae Agrippinae. 9v. 1707 – 86mf – 9 – CA-46/1 – ne IDC [240]

THEOLOGIA MORALIS AD MENTEM DD : SERAPHICI, ET SUBTILIS CONCINNATA... / Mastrius, B – Venetiis, 1671 – 19mf – 9 – CA-23/1 – ne IDC [240]

THEOLOGIA MORALIS, LIBER QUINTUS DE SACRAMENTIS, ET SACRIFICIO, NOVAE LEGIS / Laymann, P – Monachii, 1625 – 5mf – 9 – CA-66/1 – ne IDC [240]

THEOLOGIA NATURALIS : SIVE, PHILOSOPHIA DE DEO: IN USUM SCHOLARUM / Boedder, Bernard – (Includes index) – Friburgi Brisgoviae [Freiburg i.B.]; S Ludovici Americae [St Louis]: Herder, 1900 – 1mf – 9 – 0-8370-6964-5 – 1986-0964 – us A.T.L.A. [210]

THEOLOGIA NATURALIS SIVE ENTIS INCREATI ET CREATI INTRA SUPREMAM ABSTRACTIONEM EX NATURAE LUNINE INVESTIGATIO / Raynaudus, T – Lugduni, 1622 – 12mf – 9 – CA-43/1 – ne IDC [210]

THEOLOGIA POLEMICA... / Burghaber, A – Freiburgi Helvetiorum, 1678 – 20mf – 9 – CA-45/1 – ne IDC [240]

THEOLOGIA POLEMICA... / Pichler, V – Augustae Vindelicorum. 2v. 1737 – 18mf – 9 – CA-55/1 – ne IDC [240]

THEOLOGIA SCHOLASTICA MORALI-POLEMICA... / Panger, M – Augustae Vindelicorum. 4v. 1732 – 35mf – 9 – CA-26/1 – ne IDC [240]

THEOLOGIA TRIPARTITA UNIVERSA... / Arsdekin, R – Dilingae. 3v. 1693-94 – 13mf – 9 – CA-44/1 – ne IDC [240]

THEOLOGIAE SCHOLASTICAE / Reding, A – Einsiedeln. 10v. 1667 – 68mf – 9 – CA-56/1 – ne IDC [240]

THEOLOGICA DOGMATICA ORTHODOXA / Palmieri, A – Florentiae, 1911-1913.-2v – 21mf – 8 – ne Slangenburg [290]

THEOLOGICA EVANGELICA – (1986- . 5,6,9) – v1- . 1968- – 1 – us UMI [073]

THE THEOLOGICAL ASPECT OF REFORMED JUDAISM / Margolis, Max Leopold – Baltimore: Friedenwald, 1904. 1 fiche – 9 – us A.T.L.A. [270]

THEOLOGICAL EDUCATION IN AMERICA : BULLETIN – New Haven. nos 1-5. 1954-56 (complete) – 1r – 1 – ATLA B0049 – us A.T.L.A. [073]

THEOLOGICAL ENCYCLOPAEDIA : AN INTRODUCTION TO THE STUDY OF THEOLOGY / Davies, Edward Owen – (Includes bibliographies) – London:Hodder and Stoughton, 1905 – 1mf – 9 – 0-8370-2839-6 – 1985-0839 – us A.T.L.A. [240]

THEOLOGICAL ENCYCLOPAEDIA *see* PROLEGOMENA TO SYSTEMATIC THEOLOGY

THEOLOGICAL ESSAYS / Shedd, William Greenough Thayer – (Includes bibliographical references) – New York: Scribner, Armstrong, 1877 – 1mf – 9 – 0-8370-56098 – 1985-3609 – us A.T.L.A. [240]

THEOLOGICAL FORUM – v1-7. 1929- Oct 1935 (complete) – 1r – 1 – ATLA S0236 – us A.T.L.A. [073]

THE THEOLOGICAL INSTRUCTOR – Toronto: [s.n. 1873-1874] – 9 – cn C.I.H.M. [240]

THEOLOGICAL MAGAZINE OF THE EVANGELICAL SYNOD OF NORTH AMERICA – v1-62. 1873-Nov 1934 (complete) – 10r – 1 – ATLA S0090 – us A.T.L.A. [073]

THEOLOGICAL MISCELLANY 1 – (Presbyterian Church: The Act and Testimony of the Minority 1835 J D Blair. Sermons Collected.... W C Davis. The Gospel Plan...Doctrines of Salvation.... G Duffield. Spiritual Life, or, Regeneration.... S Harker. Predestination Consistent.... Benjamin B Warfield. On the Revision of the Confession of Faith) – 1 – $50.00 – us Presbyterian [240]

THEOLOGICAL MISCELLANY 2 – (E. Erskine. The Stone Rejected.... E. Erskine. A Narrative and State of the Proceedings of the Judicatures.... E. Erskine. A Review of the Narrative and State of the Proceedings of the Judicatures.... E. Erskine. A Testimony to the Doctrine, Worship, Government.... E. Erskine. Reasons by Mr. Ebenezer Erskine...Why They have not Acceded.) – 1 – $50.00 – us Presbyterian [240]

THEOLOGICAL MISCELLANY 3 – Presbyterian Church officers. 59 pamphlets – 1 – $50.00 – us Presbyterian [240]

THE THEOLOGICAL MONTHLY – (Cont: The British and Foreign Evangelical Review) – [Toronto: Bain, 1889?-1891] – 9 – cn C.I.H.M. [240]

THEOLOGICAL PROPAEDEUTIC : A GENERAL INTRODUCTION TO THE STUDY OF THEOLOGY, EXEGETICAL, HISTORICAL, SYSTEMATIC, AND PRACTICAL: INCLUDING ENCYCLOPAEDIA, METHODOLOGY, AND BIBLIOGRAPHY / Schaff, Philip – New York: Scribner, 1904, c1893 – 2mf – us A.T.L.A. [240]

THEOLOGICAL QUARTERLY; NANKING SEMINARY REVIEW = SHEN HSUEH CHIN – (Lacking: v1-10) – v11-26. 1925-50 – 3r – 1 – ATLA S0311 – us A.T.L.A. [073]

Theological Seminary. Evangelical and Reformed Church *see* THEOLOGICAL SEMINARY OF THE EVANGELICAL AND REFORMED CHURCH

THEOLOGICAL SEMINARY OF THE EVANGELICAL AND REFORMED CHURCH : BULLETIN / Theological Seminary. Evangelical and Reformed Church – v1-28. 1930-57 (complete) – 5r – 1 – ATLA S0140 – us A.T.L.A. [240]

Theological Seminary of the Evangelical and Reformed Church *see* BULLETIN

THE THEOLOGICAL SIGNIFICANCE OF CITY EVANGELISM / Nelson, James M – Princeton. 1945 – 1 – us A.T.L.A. [240]

Theological Students Fellowship *see* TSF NEWS AND REVIEWS

THEOLOGICAL STUDIES – v1- 1940- 1; v36- 5,6,9 – us UMI [240]

A THEOLOGICAL UNDERSTANDING OF ANGER WITHIN GRIEF / Edgar, John Henry – 1981 – 1 – 5.00 – us Baptist [240]

THEOLOGICAL UNREST: DISCUSSIONS IN SCIENCE AND RELIGION / Froude, James Anthony – New York: A.S. Barnes, 1880. 1 fiche – 9 – us A.T.L.A. [240]

THEOLOGIE DE LA VIE MONASTIQUE D'APRES QUELQUES GRANDS MOINES DES EPOQUES MODERNE ET CONTEMPORAINE – 1961 – Dfl19.00 – ne Slangenburg [240]

LA THEOLOGIE DE L'EPITRE AUX HEBREUX / Menegoz, Eugene – Paris: Fischbacher, 1894. 1 fiche – 9 – us A.T.L.A. [240]

LA THEOLOGIE DE S. CYRILLE D'ALEXANDRIE D'APRES S. THOMAS D'AQUIN / Renaudin, P – Tongerloo, 1937 – 2mf – 9 – ne Slangenburg [240]

DIE THEOLOGIE DER APOSTOLISCHEN VAETER : EINE DOGMENGESCHICHTLICHE MONOGRAPHIE / Sprinzl, Josef – Wien: W. Braumueller, 1880 – 1mf – us A.T.L.A. [240]

THEOLOGIE DER GEGENWART – v1-33. 1958-90 (complete) – 6r – 1 – ATLA S0844 – us A.T.L.A. [073]

DIE THEOLOGIE DER PROPHETEN ALS GRUNDLAGE FUER...DER ISRAELITISCHEN RELIGION / Duhm, Bernhard – Bonn: Adolph Marcus, 1875. 1 fiche – 9 – us A.T.L.A. [270]

DIE THEOLOGIE DES ALTEN TESTAMENTS : IN IHRER GESCHICHTLICHEN ENTWICKLUNG DARGESTELLT VON AUGUST KAYSER / Kayser, August – (Includes index) – Strassburg: C F Schmidt, 1886 – 1mf – 9 – 0-8370-9706-1 – 1986-3706 – us A.T.L.A. [220]

THEOLOGIE DES ALTEN TESTAMENTS / Koenig, Eduard – Kritisch und vergleichend dargestellt. 1922 – 1 – us A.T.L.A. [240]

DIE THEOLOGIE DES HEILIGEN IGNATIUS : DES APOSTELSCHUELERS UND BISCHOFS VON ANTIOCHIEN / Nirschl, Joseph – Mainz: F. Kirchheim, 1880 – 2mf – us A.T.L.A. [240]

DIE THEOLOGIE DES JOHANNES DUNS SCOTUS / Seeberg, Reinhold – Leipzig, 1900 – 12mf – 8 – ne Slangenburg [290]

DIE THEOLOGIE DES JOHANNES DUNS SCOTUS / Seeberg, Reinhold – Leipzig, 1900 – 12mf – 8 – ne Slangenburg [290]

THEOLOGIE MORALE DU N.T / Spicq, C – Paris, 1965. 2v – 17mf – 8 – ne Slangenburg [240]

THEOLOGIE PORTATIVE OU DICTIONNAIRE ABREGE DE LA RELIGION CHRETIENNE / Holbach, Paul-Thiry d' – (D'Holbach series). 1768 – 9 – fr Hachette [240]

THEOLOGIE U. PHILOSOPHIE ALS MANUSKRIPT VERVIELFAELTIGT / Heidegger, M – 1mf – 8 – ne Slangenburg [290]

THEOLOGIE UND GESCHICHTSWISSENSCHAFT: REDE BEI ANTRITT DES REKTORATS / Pfleiderer, Otto – Berlin: Julius Becker, 1894. 1 fiche – 9 – us A.T.L.A. [240]

THEOLOGIE UND GLAUBE – 1(1909)-35(1943) – 442mf – 9 – Dfl1,547.00 – ne Slangenburg [073]
THEOLOGIE UND GLAUBE – Paderborn. v1-35. 1909-1943 – 442mf – 9 – ne IDC [210]
THEOLOGIE UND METAPHYSIK / Ritschl, Albrecht Benjamin – Bonn, A. Marcus, 1887. 68 p. Film Mas 8956 – 1 – us H.U. Library [110]
THEOLOGIE UND METAPHYSIK : DAS VERHAELTNIS DER THEOLOGIE ZUR MODERNEN ERKENNTNISTHEORIE UND PSYCHOLOGIE / Wobbermin, Georg – (Includes bibliographical references and name index) – Berlin: Alexander Duncker, 1901 – 1mf – 9 – 0-8370-6470-8 – 1986-0470 – us A.T.L.A. [110]
THEOLOGIE UND RELIGIONSGESCHICHTE : FUENF VORLESUNGEN / Reischle, Max – (Includes name index) – Tuebingen: J C B Mohr, 1904 – 1mf – 9 – 0-8370-6313-2 – 1985-0313 – us A.T.L.A. [200]
THEOLOGIE UND RELIGIONSWISSENSCHAFT / Heinrici, Carl Friedrich Georg – Leipzig: Duerr, 1902 – 1mf – 9 – 0-8370-3551-1 – 1985-1551 – us A.T.L.A. [240]
THEOLOGIE UND WISSENSCHAFT, ODER, ALTE UND NEUE WELTANSCHAUUNG / Specht, Karl August – Gotha: Stollberg, 1893. 1 fiche – 9 – us A.T.L.A. [240]
THEOLOGISCH TIJDSCHRIFT – v1-53. 1867-1919 (complete) – 23r – 1 – ATLA 1994-S540 – us A.T.L.A. [073]
THEOLOGISCHE ABHANDLUNGEN – Carl von Weizsaecker zu seinem siebzigsten Geburtstage 11. Dec. 1892, gewidmet von Adolf Harnack. 1892 – 1 – us A.T.L.A. [073]
THEOLOGISCHE AUFSAETZE / Sack, Karl Heinrich – Gera: C.B. Griesbach, 1876. 1 fiche – 9 – us A.T.L.A. [240]
THEOLOGISCHE BLAETTER – 1(1922)-21(1942) – 127mf – 9 – Dfl445.00 – ne Slangenburg [073]
THEOLOGISCHE BLAETTER – Leipzig. v1-21. 1922-1942 – 127mf – 9 – ne IDC [240]
THEOLOGISCHE ENCYCLOPAEDIE / Rothe, Richard – Wittenberg: Herman Koelling, 1880. 1 fiche – 9 – us A.T.L.A. [240]
THEOLOGISCHE ENCYKLOPAEDIE / Heinrici, Carl Friedrich Georg – (Includes bibliographies & indexes) – Freiburg i.B: J C B Mohr, 1893 – 1mf – 9 – 0-8370-3552-X – 1985-1552 – us A.T.L.A. [240]
DIE THEOLOGISCHE ERKENNTNIS- UND EINLEITUNGSLEHRE DES H. THOMAS VON AQUIN / Grabmann, M – Freiburg (Sw.), 1948 – 7mf – 8 – ne Slangenburg [120]
THEOLOGISCHE JAHRBUECHER – Tuebingen, 1(1842)-16(1857) – 178mf – 9 – Dfl623.00 – ne Slangenburg [073]
THEOLOGISCHE JAHRBUECHER, IN VERBINDUNG MIT MEHREREN GELEHRTEN – Tuebingen. v1-16. 1842-57 – 178mf – 9 – Dfl1,246.00 – us A.T.L.A. [073]
THEOLOGISCHE LITERATURZEITUNG – 1(1876)-85(1960) – 841mf – 9 – Dfl2,944.00 – ne Slangenburg [072]
THEOLOGISCHE LITERATURZEITUNG – Leipzig, Berlin. v1-85. 1876-1960 – 841mf – 9 – ne IDC [240]
THEOLOGISCHE QUARTALSCHRIFT – 1(1819)-126(1946) – 723mf – 9 – Dfl2,531.00 – ne Slangenburg [073]
THEOLOGISCHE QUARTALSCHRIFT – Tuebingen etc. v1-126. 1819-1946 – 723mf – 9 – ne IDC [240]
THEOLOGISCHE REVUE – 1(1902)-29(1930) – 219mf – 9 – Dfl767.00 – ne Slangenburg [073]
THEOLOGISCHE REVUE – Muenster. v1-29. 1902-1930 – 219mf – 9 – ne IDC [240]
THEOLOGISCHE RUNDSCHAU – Freiburg i.B, Tuebingen. v1-20. 1897-1917 – 134mf – 9 – ne IDC [240]
DIE THEOLOGISCHE SCHULE ALBRECHT RITCHLS / Ecke, Gustav – Berlin: Reuther & Reichard, 1897 (Die Theologische Schule Albrecht Ritschls und die evangelische Kirche der Gegenwart / von Gustav Ecke; 1. Bd.) – 1mf – us A.T.L.A. [240]
THEOLOGISCHE STUDIEN – Utrecht, 1(1883)-5(1887) – 48mf – 9 – Dfl168.00 – ne Slangenburg [073]
THEOLOGISCHE STUDIEN – Utrecht. v1-5. 1883-1887 – 48mf – 9 – ne IDC [240]
THEOLOGISCHE STUDIEN – v1-35. 1883-1917 (complete) – 12r – 1 – ATLA 1994-S517 – us A.T.L.A. [073]
THEOLOGISCHE STUDIEN UND KRITIKEN – 1(1828)-109(1941) – 1,472mf – 9 – Dfl5,512.00 – ne Slangenburg [073]
THEOLOGISCHE STUDIEN UND KRITIKEN – Hamburg. v1-109. 1828-1941 – 1472mf – 9 – ne IDC [240]
THEOLOGISCHE WERKEN / Camphuysen, DR – Amsterdam, 1672 – 15mf – 8 – ne Slangenburg [290]
THEOLOGISCHE ZEITBLAETTER = THEOLOGICAL MAGAZINE – v1-8. 1911-18 (complete) – 2r – 1 – ATLA S0261 – us A.T.L.A. [073]
THEOLOGISCHE ZEITBLAETTER (1882) – v1-29 no 6. 1882-1910 (complete) – 6r – 1 – ATLA S0260 – us A.T.L.A. [073]
THEOLOGISCHE ZEITSCHRIFT – Basel, 1(1945)-16(1960) – 145mf – 9 – Dfl508.00 – ne Slangenburg [073]
THEOLOGISCHE ZEITSCHRIFT – Berlin, 1(1819)-3(1822) – 13mf – 9 – Dfl46.00 – ne Slangenburg [073]
THEOLOGISCHE ZEITSCHRIFT – (Lacking: 4(1863). Continuation of: Kirchliche Zeitschrift) – Schwerin, 1(1860)-5(1864). – 9 – Dfl298.00 – ne Slangenburg [073]
THEOLOGISCHE ZEITSCHRIFT – Schwerin. v1-5. 1860-1864 – 85mf – 9 – ne IDC [240]
THEOLOGISCHE ZEITSCHRIFT – Wien, Triest. v1-5. 1813-1817 – 40mf – 9 – ne IDC [240]
THEOLOGISCHE ZEITSCHRIFT – Wien u.Triest, 1(1813)-5(1817) – 40mf – 9 – Dfl40.00 – ne Slangenburg [073]
THEOLOGISCHE ZEITSCRIFT 1500 BASEL. V1-16. 1945-1960 – 145mf – 9 – ne IDC [240]
THEOLOGISCH-HOMILETISCHES BIBELWERK. ALTEN TESTAMENTES 12 *see* DIE SPRUECHE SALOMONIS
THEOLOGISCH-HOMILETISCHES BIBELWERK. NEUEN TESTAMENTES *see* DIE BRIEFE PETRI UND DER BRIEF JUDAE
THEOLOGISCH-PRAKTISCHE MONATSSCHRIFT – Muenchen, etc. Bd. 1-25; 1891-1915. Centralorgan der Katholischen Geistlichkeit Bayerns. Film Mas C 291 – 1 – us H.U. Library [240]
THEOLOGISK TIDSSKRAFT / Norsk Luthersk Kirche in Amerika – v1-12:1, Oct 1917-Oct 1928. 2 reels – 1 – us A.T.L.A. [073]
THEOLOGORUM SAXONICORUM CONSENSUS REPETITUS FIDEI VERE LUTHERANAE / Henke, Ernst Ludwig Theodor – Marburgi: Typis Elwerti Academicis, 1846 – 1mf – us A.T.L.A. [240]
THE THEOLOGUE – Halifax [N.S.: Students of Pine Hill College, 1889-1919] – 9 – cn C.I.H.M. [370]
THEOLOGY – 1920-to date – 1,9 – uk Microform Academic [073]
THEOLOGY / Miller, John – (Includes index) – Princeton, NJ: Evangelical Reform Publication Co, 1887 – 1mf – 9 – 0-8370-5917-8 – 1985-3917 – us A.T.L.A. [240]
THEOLOGY AND ETHICS OF THE HEBREWS / Duff, Archibald – New York: Charles Scribner, 1902. 1 fiche – 9 – us A.T.L.A. [270]
THEOLOGY AND LIFE – (Supersedes: THEOLOGICAL SEMINARY OF THE EVANGELICAL AND REFORMED CHURCH: BULLETIN). v. 1-9. 1958-1966 – 1,5,6 – us Princeton Micro [240]
THEOLOGY AND THE SOCIAL CONSCIOUSNESS : A STUDY OF THE RELATIONS OF THE SOCIAL CONSCIOUSNESS TO THEOLOGY / King, Henry Churchill – (Includes bibliographical references and index) – New York:Macmillan, 1902 – 1mf – 9 – 0-8370-4474-X – 1985-2474 – us A.T.L.A. [240]
THEOLOGY AND TRUTH / Marshall, Newton Herbert – London: James Clarke, 1906. 1 fiche. 8370-4286-0 – 9 – us A.T.L.A. [240]
THEOLOGY AS A SCIENCE, INVOLVING AN INFINITE ELEMENT : INAUGURAL ADDRESS / Girardeau, John Lafayette – (Includes appendix) – Columbia: Presbyterian Publ House, 1876 – 1mf – 9 – 0-8370-3296-2 – 1985-1296 – us A.T.L.A. [210]
THEOLOGY AS SCIENCE: AND ITS PRESENT POSITION AND PROSPECTS IN THE REFORMED CHURCH / Hastie, William – Glasgow: James MacLehose, 1899. 1 fiche – 9 – us A.T.L.A. [240]
THEOLOGY IN THE ENGLISH POETS : COWPER, COLERIDGE, WORDSWORTH AND BURNS / Brooke, Stopford Augustus – London: Henry S. King, 1874 – 1mf – us A.T.L.A. [240]
THE THEOLOGY OF AN EVOLUTIONIST / Abbott, Lyman – Boston: Houghton, Mifflin, 1897.1 fiche – 9 – us A.T.L.A. [240]
THE THEOLOGY OF CHRIST FROM HIS OWN WORDS / Thompson, Joseph Parrish – New York: Scribner, Armstrong, 1873. 1 fiche – 9 – us A.T.L.A. [240]
THE THEOLOGY OF CIVILIZATION / Dole, Charles Fletcher – New York: Thomas Y Crowell, c1899 – 1mf – 9 – 0-8370-8662-0 – 1986-2662 – us A.T.L.A. [240]
THE THEOLOGY OF CONFORMATION IN THE RELATION TO BAPTISM / Dix, G – Westminster, 1953 – 1mf – 8 – ne Slangenburg [240]
THEOLOGY OF EVOLUTION: A LECTURE / Cope, Edward Drinker – Philadelphia: Arnold, 1887. 1 fiche – 9 – us A.T.L.A. [240]
THE THEOLOGY OF FATHERHOOD : PSYCHOLOGICALLY, METAPHYSICALLY, AND ETHICALLY CONSIDERED: A NEW THEOLOGY IN WHICH IS DEVELOPED A NEW THEORY OF ORIGINAL SIN, ATONEMENT, JUSTIFICATION, ETC / Kinnebrew, J H – Nashville, TN: Southern Methodist Publ House, 1883 – 1mf – 9 – 0-8370-4452-9 – 1985-2452 – us A.T.L.A. [240]
THE THEOLOGY OF HOLINESS / Clark, Dougan – Boston: McDonald & Gill, 1893 – 1mf – us A.T.L.A. [240]
THE THEOLOGY OF J.R. GRAVES AND ITS INFLUENCE ON SOUTHERN BAPTIST LIFE / Patterson, T A – 1944 – 1 – 11.84 – us Baptist [240]
THE THEOLOGY OF KARL BARTH (CCC76) = PA TE TI TSUNG CHIAO SSU HSIANG / Chao, Tzu-ch'en – (In Chinese) – Shanghai: Association Press of China, 1939 – 1r – 1 – 1984-B500 – us A.T.L.A. [240]
THE THEOLOGY OF LUTHER IN ITS HISTORIAL DEVELOPMENT AND INNER HARMONY / Koestlin, Julius – Philadelphia: Lutheran Publication Society, c1897 – 3mf – us A.T.L.A. [240]
THE THEOLOGY OF NEW ENGLAND : AN ATTEMPT TO EXHIBIT THE DOCTRINES NOW PREVALENT IN THE ORTHODOX CONGREGATIONAL CHURCHES OF NEW ENGLAND / Wallace, David A – Boston: Crocker and Brewster, 1856 – 1mf – us A.T.L.A. [240]
THE THEOLOGY OF THE APOSTLES PETER AND PAUL IN THEIR OWN WORDS / Schultze, Augustus – Bethlehem: Comenius Press, 1896.1 fiche – 9 – us A.T.L.A. [240]
THE THEOLOGY OF THE EPISTLE TO THE HEBREWS : WITH A CRITICAL INTRODUCTION / Milligan, George – (Includes index) – Edinburgh:T & T Clark, 1899 – 1mf – 9 – 0-8370-4437-5 – 1985-2437 – us A.T.L.A. [220]
THEOLOGY OF THE HEBREW CHRISTIANS / Rendall, Frederic – London: Macmillan, 1886.1 fiche – 9 – us A.T.L.A. [240]
THE THEOLOGY OF THE NEW TESTAMENT / Stevens, George Barker – New York: Charles Scribner, 1910. 619p.2 fiches – 9 – us A.T.L.A. [240]
THEOLOGY OF THE NEW TESTAMENT / Adeney, Walter Frederic – New York: T. Whittaker, n.d. 1 fiche – 9 – us A.T.L.A. [240]
THE THEOLOGY OF THE OLD TESTAMENT / Davidson, Andrew Bruce; ed by Salmond, Stewart Dingwall Fordyce – (Includes indexes) – New York: Charles Scribner, 1904 – 2mf – 9 – 0-8370-9457-7 – 1986-3457 – us A.T.L.A. [220]
THEOLOGY OF THE OLD TESTAMENT / Oehler, G F – Zondervan, 1883. Trans. by G.E. Day – 9 – $21.00 – us I.R.C. [220]
THEOLOGY OF THE OLD TESTAMENT / Piepenbring, Charles – New York: Thomas Y. Crowell, 1893. 1 fiche – 9 – us A.T.L.A. [220]
THEOLOGY OLD AND NEW / Cobb, William Frederick – New York: E P Dutton, [1902] – 1mf – 9 – 0-8370-2693-8 – 1985-0693 – us A.T.L.A. [240]
THEOLOGY: THE PHILOSOPHY OF RELIGION / Buck, William Calmes – 1857 – 1 – 18.13 – us Baptist [240]
THEOLOGY TODAY – v1-21. Apr 1944-65 (complete) – 11r – 1 – ATLA S0112 – us A.T.L.A. [073]
THEOLOTREMEAE ET GRAPHIDEAE NOVAE QUAS PRAESERTIM EX HB. REG. KEWENSIS / Mueller, J A – (Journ. Linn. Soc., Botany, London, 1895, v. 30, p. 451-463). B-624 2 – 8 – ne IDC [580]
THEOMONISM TRUE : GOD AND THE UNIVERSE IN MODERN LIGHT: A SEQUEL TO HAECKEL'S MONISM FALSE / Ballard, Frank – London: C.H. Kelly, [1906?] – 2mf – us A.T.L.A. [210]
Theophanes Continuatus et al *see* CORPUS SCRIPTORUM HISTORIAE BYZANTINAE (CSHB 33)
Theophanis *see*
– CHRONOGRAPHIA
– CHRONOGRAPHIA (CSHB 39, 40)
THEOPHILO OTTONI : SEMANARIO LIBERAL, DA CIDADE DO PARAISO, MINAS GERAIS – Theophilo Ottoni, 11 Aug 1878 – 1,5,6 – bl Biblioteca [072]
Theophilus, J *see* EENEN SENDTBRIEF AEN DIERCK VOLKERTZ CORNHERT: OP SYN BOECK GHENAEMPT: KLEYN MUNSTER, WTGEGHAEN TEGHENS DIE SCHRIFTEN VAN DAVID JORIS
THEOPHILUS PRESBYTER SCHEDULA DIVERSARUM ARTIUM / Ilg, A – (Quellenschriften fuer kunstgeschichte. v. 7. Wien. 1874). BO-517g 1 – 9 – ne IDC [700]
THEOPHILUS VON ANTIOCHIEN ADVERSUS MARCIONEM (T.U.U. 4-46/2) / Loofs, Friedrich – Leipzig, 1930 – 8mf – 9 – ne Slangenburg [240]
Theophraste *see* TRAITE DES PIERRES...
THEOPNEUSTIC OU INSPIRATION PLENIERE DES SAINTES ECRITURES / Gaussen, L – 2e ed Paris-Londres 1842 – 10mf – 8 – ne Slangenburg [220]
THEOREMATA PHYSICO-THEORICA MEDICO-PRACTICA, CHIRURGICO-MECHANICA... / Marcia et Faenes, G – Valencia, 1746 – 1mf – 9 – sp Cultura [617]
THEOREME – 1985- – 1,5,6,9 – us UMI [073]
Theoret, C *see*
– CODE MUNICIPAL DE LA PROVINCE DE QUEBEC ANNOTE MIS AU COURANT DE LA LEGISLATION ET DE LA JURISPRUDENCE
– LA LOI DE CONCILIATION
THEORETICA CHIMICA ACTA – v. 1-58. 1962-80 – 1,5,9 – 10,353.00 – us UMI [073]
THEORETICAL AND APPLIED GENETICS – v. 17 18-58. 1946 47-80 – 1,5,9 – 4851.00 – us UMI [073]
THEORETICAL AND APPLIED GENETICS *see* ZUECHTER
THEORETICAL AND EXPERIMENTAL CHEMISTRY – v1-30. 1965-94 – 1,5 – $80.00v – us UMI [540]
THEORETICAL AND MATHEMATICAL PHYSICS – v1-101. 1969-94 – 1,5 – $60.00v – us UMI [530]
THEORETICAL AND PRACTICAL SYSTEM OF BOOK-KEEPING BY SINGLE AND DOUBLE ENTRY: CONTAINING SEVEN SETS FULLY ILLUSTRATED: PRESENTING A GOOD COURSE OF MERCANTILE TRAINING: WITH NUMEROUS EXERCISES AND USEFUL FORMS FOR PRACTICAL USE : TO WHICH ARE ADDED A SHORT COMPENDIUM OF COMMERCIAL LAW, IN REFERENCE TO CONTRACTS AND NEGOTIABLE PAPER: AND A VOCABULARY OF MERCANTILE TERMS WITH THEIR EQUIVALENT IN FRENCH / Deblois, Isidore Gregoire – s.l.: s.n., 1887 (St. Anne de la Pocatiere, Quebec: F. H. Proulx). 02618. (Pre-1900 Canadiana) – 9 – cn C.I.H.M. [971]
THEORETICAL COMPUTER SCIENCE – v1-34. 1975-84 – 1,5,6,13 – sz Elsevier [073]
THEORETICAL FOUNDATIONS OF CHEMICAL ENGINEERING – v1-27. 1967-93 – 1,5 – $65.00v – us UMI [660]
THEORETICAL MEDICINE – v4-. Feb 1983- – 1,5,6,9 – us UMI [073]
DIE THEORETISCHEN AUFFASSUNGEN VOM ERFOLG DER VOLKSWIRTSCHAFT / Ihme, Gertrud – 1995 – 1mf – 9 – DM48.00 – 3-8267-3161-1 – gw Hänsel [330]
THEORETISCHER ANARCHISMUS UND "IMITATIO CHRISTI" : ZUR BEDEUTUNG DER EINFLUSSNAME MICHAIL BAKUNIN AUF DAS WERK HUGO BALLS / Steinbrenner, Manfred – 1994 – 1mf – 9 – DM60.00 – 3-89349-881-8 – gw Hänsel [100]
THEORETISCH-PRAKTISCHES HANDBUCH DER CHIRURGIE : MIT EINSCHLUSS DER SYPHILITISCHEN UND AUGEN-KRANKHEITEN (AEL, ABT 3;22) / ed by Rust, Johann Nepomuk – Berlin, Wien. 17 bde. 1830-1836 (mf ed 1995) – 85mf – 9 – DM1,690.00 – 3-89131-218-0 – gw Fischer [610]
THEORIA SYSTEMATIS PLANTARUM / Agardh, J G – Lundae. 1858. B-5218 2 – 8 – ne IDC [580]

THEORICA MUSICE FRANCHINI GAFURI LAUDENSIS / Gaffurio, Franchino – 1492 – 9 – us Sibley [780]

THEORICA MUSICE FRANCHINI GAFURI LAUDENSIS / Gaffurius, F – P 680. 1492 – 9 – ne IDC [780]

THEORIE DE LA FIGURE DE LA TERRE, TIREE DES PRINCIPES DE L'HYDROSTATIQUE / Clairaut, Alexis-Claude – Paris, David fils, 1743, xl, 310 p. Histoire des Sciences XVIIe-XIXe Siecles. 7968 – 9 – fr Hachette [550]

THEORIE DE LA GUERRE / Joly de Maizeroy, P G – Lausanne. 1777. cxiii, 365p. pl. (Strategy of War Series) – 9 – fr Hachette [355]

THEORIE DE LA PROPRIETE / Proudhon, Pierre-Joseph – 1871. 246p. Together with: In Defence of Property, a selection from the "Slogans for Liberty" File of Libertarian Microfiche Publishing. Compiled by John Zube. 1981. 27p. 1 fiche (24x) – 9 – 1.00f – at Libertarian Micro [320]

LA THEORIE DE L'INTUITION DANS...DE HUSSERL / Levinas, Emmanuel – Paris, 1930 – 3mf – 8 – ne Slangenburg [120]

THEORIE DER MERKANTILRECHNUNG / Held, Georg – Wiesbaden, 1960 – 1 – DM30.00 – gw Mikro Press [332]

DIE THEORIE DER OBJEKTBEZIEHUNGEN IN DER PSYCHOANALYSE : EINE PHILOSOPHISCHE UNTERSUCHUNG / Toegel, Manuel – Frankfurt a.M., 1978 – 3mf – 9 – DM76.00 – 3-89349-369-7 – gw Hänsel [150]

THEORIE DER STAATENVERBINDUNGEN / Brie, S – Stuttgart, 1886 – 2mf – 1 – ILM-1684/1 – ne IDC [327]

THEORIE DES FONCTIONS ANALYTIQUES CONTENANT LES PRINCIPES DU CALCUL DIFFERENTIEL / Lagrange, Joseph Louis de – Paris, an V, vii, 276 p. Histoire des Sciences XVIIe-XIXe Siecles. 7985 – 9 – fr Hachette [510]

THEORIE DES GROSSEN KRIEGE / Willisen, Karl Wilhelm von – Berlin. Duncker. 1840-68. 4v. (Strategy of War Series) – 9 – fr Hachette [355]

THEORIE DES JARDINS / Morel, Jean Marie – Paris. Pissot, 1776. 8 fol., 404p., pl. (Architecture Series) – 9 – fr Hachette [720]

LA THEORIE DES SONGES / Richard, Jerome – (French Precursors of Psychiatry Series). Paris. les freres Estienne. 1766 – 9 – fr Hachette [150]

THEORIE DES VOELKERRECHTS / Bergbohm, K – Leipzig, 1901 – 1mf – 9 – ILM-2117/1 – ne IDC [327]

THEORIE DU "MERVEILLEUX" DANS LA LITTERATURE FRANCAISE ET CANADIENNE / Lesage, Jules S – Quebec: Leger Brousseau..., 1902. SEM105P489 – 1mf – 9 – Can$2.25 – cn Bibl Nat [440]

THEORIE D'UNE EDUCATION REPUBLICAINE / Serane, Philippe – Paris. 1774. 6786 – 9 – fr Hachette [320]

THEORIE ELEMENTAIRE DE LA STATISTIQUE / Donnant, Denis Francois – (French Socialist Congresses Series). Paris. Valade. 1805 – 9 – fr Hachette [310]

LA THEORIE ET LA PRATIQUE DE COUPE DES PIERRES ET DES BOIS. / Frezier, AF – and DISSERTATION SUR LES ORDRES D'ARCHITECTURE. Strasbourg, J. D. Doulsseker; Paris, C. A. Jombert, 1737-39. 3 v. in 4 fol., illus. (Architecture Series) – 9 – fr Hachette [720]

LA THEORIE ET LA PRATIQUE DU JARDINAGE / Dezallier d'Argenville, Antoine Joseph – Paris, J. Mariette, 1709. (Architecture Series) – 9 – fr Hachette [720]

THEORIE ET PRATIQUE DE LA NARRATIVITE : PREMIERE PARTIE: THEORIE. DEUXIEME PARTIE: PRATIQUE / Sturgess, Philip – 2mf – 9 – 10053 – fr Atelier National [420]

THEORIE ET PRATIQUE DE LA PIETE FILIALE CHEZ LES CHINOIS / Hoogers, J – (Anthropos 5, 1-15, 1910). BCH-936 2 – 8 – ne IDC [306]

THEORIE GENERALE... / Hepp, F – Paris, 1914 – 2mf – 1 – ILM-546/1 – ne IDC [327]

THEORIE GENERALE DU DROIT / Dabin, Jean – Bruxelles, Establissements Émile Bruylant, 1944. 276 p. LL-4096 – 1 – us L of C Photodup [340]

THEORIE NEURONALER ASSOZIATIVSPEICHER : LOKALES LERNEN UND ITERATIVES RETRIEVAL VON INFORMATION / Sommer, Friedrich Tobias – 1994 – 1mf – DM60.00 – 3-89349-901-6 – gw Hänsel [621]

THEORIE PSYCHOLOGIQUE DE L'ESPACE / Dunan, C – H-522 2. 1895 – 8 – ne IDC [150]

THEORIE UND PRAXIS REGIONALER KOMMUNIKATION : EIN POLITIKWISSENSCHAFTLICHER BEITRAG ZUR ANALYSE REGIONALER MEDIENANGEBOTE UNTER BESONDERER BERUECKSICHTIGUNG LOKALER UND REGIONALER FERNSEHBERICHTERSTATTUNG / Kloecker, Andreas – 1992 – 628p – 9 – DM148.00 – 3-89349-478-2 – gw Hänsel [380]

THEORIES AND CRITICISMS OF SIR HENRY MAINE / Evans, Morgan O – London: Stevens & Haynes, 1896 – 2mf – 9 – $3.00 – LLMC 95-184 – us L.L.M.C. [340]

THE THEORIES OF DARWIN AND THEIR RELATION TO PHILOSOPHY, RELIGION, AND MORALITY / Schmid, Rudolf – Chicago: Jansen, McClurg, 1883. 1 fiche – 9 – us A.T.L.A. [240]

THEORIES OF THE WILL IN THE HISTORY OF PHILOSOPHY / Alexander, Archibald – New York: C. Scribner's Sons, 1898. ix,357p. Includes bibliographic footnotes and index – 1 – us U.W. Library [120]

THEORIES OF THE WILL IN THE HISTORY OF PHILOSOPHY / Alexander, Archibald – New York: Scribner, 1898 – 1mf – us A.T.L.A. [100]

THE THEORY AND COMPLETE DOCTRINE OF GENERAL PERON / Peron, Juan Domingo – [Buenos Aires]: Dept. of Information for Abroad, Ministry for Foreign Affairs and Worship, 1946 – 1 – CSUXAJB7846-B – us Hoover Inst Photo [320]

THEORY AND DECISION – (v16-. 1984-. 5,6,9) – v1-. Oct 1970- – 1 – us UMI [073]

THE THEORY AND PRACTICE OF FINDING THE LONGITUDE AT SEA OR LAND. TO WHICH ARE ADDED VARIOUS METHODS OF DETERMINING THE LATITUDE OF A PLACE AND VARIATION OF THE COMPASS, WITH NEW TABLES / Mackay, Andrew – 3rd ed., improved and enlarged. 2v. 1810 – 9 – $40.00 – uk Libr Preservation [623]

THEORY AND PRACTICE OF MUSICAL COMPOSITION / Marx, A B – New York: Mason Brothers, 1853 – 1 – us Sibley [780]

THE THEORY AND PRACTICE OF SHIP BUILDING / White, Thomas – 1848 – 9 – uk Libr Preservation [623]

THEORY AND RESEARCH IN SOCIAL EDUCATION – v1- 1973- 1; v5- 5,6,9 – us UMI [370]

THEORY AND SOCIETY – v1-13. 1974-84 – 1,5,6,13 – sz Elsevier [073]

THEORY INTO PRACTICE – v1- 1962- 1; v9-5,6; v14- 9 – us UMI [370]

A THEORY OF CONDUCT / Alexander, Archibald – New York: Scribner, 1890 – 1mf – us A.T.L.A. [100]

THEORY OF CURRICULUM CONTENT IN THE USSR / Kraevskij, V V & Lerner, IY – 1984 – 113p – 9 – 92-3-102128-1 – fr UNESCO [370]

THE THEORY OF GOOD AND EVIL : A TREATISE ON MORAL PHILOSOPHY / Rashdall, Hastings – Oxford: Clarendon Press, 1907 – 2v 2mf – 9 – us A.T.L.A. [170]

THEORY OF GROUPS OF FINITE ORDER / Burnside, William – Cambridge: University Press, 1897. xvi,388p. diagr – 1 – us U.W. Library [510]

THE THEORY OF INTERNATIONAL TRADE / Bastable, CF – 1897 – 9 – 1.00f – at Libertarian Micro [335]

THE THEORY OF LANGUAGE / Beattie, James – 1788. 404p. (English Linguistics Series 1500-1800) – 9 – us UMI [400]

THE THEORY OF LEGAL DUTIES AND RIGHTS : AN INTRODUCTION TO ANALYTICAL JURISPRUDENCE / Hearn, William E – Melbourne/London: John Ferres/ Truebner & Co, 1883 – 5mf – 9 – $7.50 – LLMC 95-196 – us L.L.M.C. [340]

THE THEORY OF MORALS / Janet, Paul – New York: Charles Scribner's Sons, 1900 – 6mf – 9 – $9.00 – LLMC 92-135 – us L.L.M.C. [170]

THEORY OF PROBABILITY AND ITS APPLICATIONS – v1- . 1957- – 1,5,6,13 – us S.I.A.M. [510]

THEORY OF THE EARTH, WITH PROOFS AND ILLUSTRATIONS / Hutton, J – G-109 2. 1795 – 8 – ne IDC [550]

A THEORY OF THE LABOR MOVEMENT / Perlman, Selig – In Indonesian. SE-8593 1. 1956 – 9 – ne IDC [360]

THE THEORY OF THE STATE / Bluntschli, J K – Oxford. 1885 – 9mf – 9 – ILM-684/1 – ne IDC [327]

THEORY OF THOUGHT AND KNOWLEDGE / Bowne, Borden Parker – New York: Harper, 1897 – 1mf – us A.T.L.A. [120]

THE THEORY OF TOLERATION UNDER THE LATER STUARTS / Seaton, A A – Cambridge: University Press, 1911 – 1mf – us A.T.L.A. [240]

THEOSOPHIA / Arboreus, Ioan. – Parisiis. v1-3. 1540-1553 – 45mf – 8 – ne Slangenburg [240]

THEOSOPHICAL REVIEW – (Cont: Lucifer) – v1-43. Sep 1887-Feb 1909 (complete) – 15r – 1 – ATLA S0278 – us A.T.L.A. [073]

THEOSOPHY, OR, PSYCHOLOGICAL RELIGION : THE GIFFORD LECTURES DELIVERED BEFORE THE UNIVERSITY OF GLASGOW IN 1892 / Mueller, Friedrich Max – (Includes index) – London; New York: Longmans, Green, 1893 – 2mf – 9 – 0-8370-9492-5 – 1986-3492 – us A.T.L.A. [290]

DIE THERAPEUTEN...IHRE STELLUNG IN DER GESCHICHTE DER ASKESE...DE VITA CONTEMPLATIVA / Lucius, Paul Ernst – Strassburg: C.F. Schmidt, 1879. 1 fiche – 9 – us A.T.L.A. [240]

THERAPEUTIC POTENTIAL OF THE OUTWARD BOUND PROCESS: AN EVALUATION OF A TREATMENT PROGRAM FOR JUVENILE DELINQUENTS / Wright, Alan N – 1982 – 2mf – 9 – $8.00 – us Microform Publ [790]

THERAPEUTISCHE UMSCHAU – v1-26. 1944-69 – 1,5,6 – us Princeton Micro [073]

THERAPIE – v1- 1946- 1; v32- 5,6,9 – us UMI [615]

THERAPIE – v. 19-30, 32. 1964-1975, 1977 – 1,5,6 – us Princeton Micro [610]

THERAPIE DER GEGENWART – v45-113.1904-73 – 1,5,6 – us Princeton Micro [610]

Therese du Carmel, Soeur *see* BIBLIOGRAPHIE ANALYTIQUE DE MONSEIGNEUR FELIX-ANTOINE SAVARD, PROFESSEUR DE POESIE FRANCAISE A L'UNIVERSITE LAVAL

THERIOGENOLOGY – (1982-. 1,5,6,9) – v1-. 1974- – 1 – us UMI [073]

THERIOTROPHIUM SEDELYCKE LUST-WARANDE OFT TWEEDE DEEL VAN HET SEDELYCK-VERMAECK-TONNEEL VERTHOONENDE DOOR SINNE-BEELDEN DEN LEERSAEMEN HANDEL VAN DE ONREDELIJCKE DIEREN, AEN DE VERKEERDE, EN BEESTAERDIGHE WERELDT / Moons, J – Antwerpen, 1678 – 7mf – 9 – O-3133/1 – ne IDC [760]

THERMAE ARCHINCAE (CARMEN) / Lopez de Ayala, Ignacio – 1777 – 1mf – 9 – Pta1,000.00 – 84-7848-200-8 – sp Pentalfa [946]

THERMAL ANALYSIS ABSTRACTS – v1-5. 1972-76 – 1 – us UMI [073]

THERMAL PHYSICS REVIEWS / ed by Scheindlin, A E & Fortov, V E – 9,5,1 – us Harwood [530]

THERMOCHIMICA ACTA – v1-78. 1970-84 – 1,5,6,13 – sz Elsevier [073]

THERMODYNAMISCHE UNTERSUCHUNGEN ZUM EINSATZ DER PERVAPORATION IN TECHNISCHEN PROZESSEN / Staudt-Bickel, Claudia – 1995 – 2mf – 9 – DM80.00 – 3-8267-2166-7 – gw Hänsel [540]

THERMOMETRE DU JOUR – Par une societe de gens de lettres, amis de la Constitution. no. 1-602. Paris. aout 1791-aout 1793 – 1 – fr A.C.R.P.P. [073]

Theron, Johannes Andreas, defendant *see* STAT TEEN J. A. THERON

THERON TRIAL – ((Case history)) – 5r – 1 – sa Microfile [970]

THERSITES : DIE ERINNERUNGEN DES DEUTSCH-BALTISCHEN JOURNALISTEN GARLIEB MERKEL / Merkel, Garlieb; ed by Mueller-Jabusch, Maximilian – (Includes index) – Berlin: Deutsche Verlagsgesellschaft fuer Politik und Geschichte, 1921 – 1r – 1 – us U.W. Library [920]

THESAURARIUM TRILINGUE PUBLICUM: BEING AN INTRODUCTION TO ENGLISH, LATIN AND GREEK – Anon. 1689. 180p. (English Linguistics Series 1500-1800) – 9 – us UMI [420]

THESAURI CONCIONATORUM / Trujillo, Thomas de – 1583 – 9 – 1.50f – sp Bibl Santa Ana [810]

Thesauro, Manuel *see* FILOSOFIA MORAL DERIVADA DE LA ALTA...DEL GRANDE ARISTOTELES. TRADUCIDA EN ESPANOL D. IUAN LUIS DE ORLEANS...

THESAURUS – (Formerly: Instituto Caro y Cuervo. Boletin) – v6-7. 1950-51 – 1 – us UMI [054]

THESAURUS AMPHILOCHII ICONIENSIS / ed by Coulie, B – 1994 – 9mf – 9 – Bf4,000.00 – 2-503-50374-8 – be Brepols [450]

THESAURUS ANECDOTORUM NOVISSIMUS / Pez, Bern. – Augustae-Vindelicorum. Pars 1-6. 1721-1729 – 290mf – 8 – Dfl1,015.00 – ne Slangenburg [240]

THESAURUS ANTIQUITATUM SACRARUM / Hugolinus, B – Venetiis. v1-34. 1744-1769 – 1260mf – 9 – Dfl4,410.00 – ne Slangenburg [030]

THESAURUS AUGUSTINIANUS : SERIES A: FORMAE – 1989 – 248mf – 9 – Bf35,000.00 set – 1-865-00031-0 – be Brepols [240]

THESAURUS BAUMIANUS. VERZEICHNIS DER BRIEFE UND AKTENSTUECKE. KAISERLICHE UNIVERSITAETS- UND LANDESBIBLIOTHEK STRASSBURG / Ficker, J – Strassburg, 1905 – 4mf – 9 – ne IDC [240]

THESAURUS CAPENSIS / Harvey, W H – or Illustrations of the South African flora. 2 v. Dublin. 1859-63. B-5948 2 – 8 – ne IDC [580]

THESAURUS CASSIANI – 1992 – 22mf – 9 – Bf9,950.00 – 2-503-50270-9 – be Brepols [450]

THESAURUS CONCHYLIORUM, OR FIGURES AND DESCRIPTIONS OF RECENT SHELLS / ed by Sowerby, G B – 2505 2. London 5v. 1842-, 1847-1887 – 99mf – 8 – ne IDC [590]

THESAURUS CONCILIORUM OECUMENICORUM ET GENERALIUM ECCLESIAE CATHOLICAE – 1996 – 15mf – 9 – Bf13,250.00 – 2-503-50529-5 – be Brepols [240]

THESAURUS DEVONICO-CARBONIFERUS. THE FLORA AND FAUNA OF THE DEVONIAN AND CARBONIFEROUS PERIODS / Bigsby, J J – London, 1878 – 8mf – 9 – ne IDC [574]

THESAURUS ET ARMAMENTARIUM MEDIOCHYMICUM. / Mynsicht, Adrian von – Venice: J.G. Hertz, 1718. 452,166,36p. Inc. index. With: Elements of Chemistry xHerman Boerhaave; The art of curing diseases by expectation xGidean Harvey – 1 – us U.W. Library [610]

THESAURUS FRATRIS SALIMBENE DE ADAM : SERIES A-B: FORMAE ET LEMMATA / ed by Beguin, P – 1992 – 27mf – 9 – Bf9,950.00 set – 2-503-50293-8 – be Brepols [450]

THESAURUS GRAECAE LINGUAE / ed by Stephanus Henricus – 645 2. Paris 8v. in 9. 1831-1865 – 281mf – 8 – ne IDC [450]

THESAURUS GRAECAE LINGUAE / Stephanus, Henricus – London, 1816-1828 – 201mf – 8 – ne Slangenburg [450]

THESAURUS GRAECAE LINGUAE / ed by Stephanus Henricus – Paris. 8v. 1831-1865 – 281mf – ne IDC [450]

THESAURUS GRAECITATIS MONASTICAE / Wagenaar, Chr. – Slangenburg, 1986 – 179mf – 9 – Dfl627.00 – ne Slangenburg [450]

THESAURUS HOTTINGERIANUS : A COLLECTION OF PAPERS ON THE HISTORY OF THE REFORMATION AND ON SWISS AND FOREIGN ECCLESIASTICAL HISTORY IN GENERAL / ed by Buesser, F – (Alphabetical index of correspondents 59mf. Inventory of manuscripts 8mf. Both indexes can be purchased loose) – 1,229mf – 9 – ne IDC [943]

THESAURUS INSCRIPTIONUM AEGYPTIACARUM / Brugsch, H – Altaegyptische Inschriften gesammelt, uebertragen, erklaert und autographiert von Heinrich Brugsch. 6v. Leipzig. 1883-91. BNE-456 1 – 9 – ne IDC [410]

THESAURUS INSCRIPTIONUM AEGYPTIACARUM. ALTAEGYPTISCHE INSCHRIFTEN GESAMMELT, UEBERTRAGEN, ERKLAERT UND AUTOGRAPHIERT VON HEINRICH BRUGSCH / Brugsch, H – Leipzig. 6v. 1883-1891 – 30mf – 9 – ne IDC [930]

THESAURUS IOHANNIS CASSIANI : SERIES A: FORMAE – 1992 – 22mf – 9 – Bf9,950.00 set – be Brepols [240]

THESAURUS LEONTII PRESBYTERI CONSTANTINOPOLITANI / ed by Noret, J – 1992 – 8mf – 9 – Bf3,500.00 – 2-503-50263-6 – be Brepols [240]
THESAURUS LIBRORUM SENTENTIARUM PETRI LOMBARDI : SERIES A: FORMAE / ed by Hamesse, J – 1991 – 25mf – 9 – Bf7,950.00 set – 1-865-00081-7 – be Brepols [450]
THESAURUS LINGUAE ARMENICAE, ANTIQUAE ET HODIERNAE,... / Schroeder, J J – Amsterdam, 1711 – 6mf – ne IDC [460]
THESAURUS LINGUAE GRAECAE / Stephanus, Henricus – Londini in aedibus Valpianis, 1810-1825. 9v – 9 – Bf11,900.00 set – 1-799-00102-4 – be Brepols [450]
THESAURUS LINGUAE LATINAE – (1904, Index A-Z) – Leipzig. v1-7(1). 1900-1934 – 107mf – 9 – 334c/1 – ne IDC [450]
THESAURUS LINGUAE ROMANAE ET BRITAINICAE / Cooper, Thomas – 1565. 1832p. (English Linguistics Series 1500-1800) – 9 – us UMI [450]
THESAURUS LINGUARUM ASIAE ET EUROPAE HARMONICUS... / Rudbeck, O – Uppsala, 1733 – 1mf – 9 – ne IDC [400]
THESAURUS LITERATURAE BOTANICAE / Pritzel, G A – Lipsiae, 1872-[1877] – 20mf – ne IDC [580]
THESAURUS LITERATURAE BOTANICAE... / Pritzel, G A – Lipsiae, 1851 – 19mf – ne IDC [580]
THESAURUS LITERATURAE MYCOLOGICAE ET LICHENOLOGICAE / Lindau, G & Sydow, P – Berlin. 5v. 1908-1917 – 69mf – ne IDC [580]
THESAURUS LOGICUS : MICROFICHE-EDITION ZUR GESCHICHTE DER LOGIK / ed by Risse, Wilhelm – (Pt 1: 1472-1520 68 titles. Pt 2: 1521-1600 71 titles. Pt 3: 1601-1700 68 titles. Pt 4: 1701-1800 69 titles. Each part available separately for DM2,500.00 diazo DM2,900.00 silver) – 1275mf – 9 – subsc: DM8,400.00 diazo DM9,900.00 silver – gw Olms [160]
THESAURUS MARII VICTORINI : SERIES A: FORMAE – 1993 – 21mf – 9 – Bf8,500.00 set – 2-503-50335-7 – be Brepols [240]
THESAURUS NOVUS ANECDOTORUM / Martene, Edmond & Durand, U – Lutetiae Parisiorum. v1-5. 1717 – 219mf – 9 – Dfl798.00 – ne Slangenburg [030]
THESAURUS ORNITHOLOGIAE / Giebel, CG A – Leipzig, 1872-77. 3v,appendix. Z/1763/2 – 8 – ne IDC [590]
THESAURUS PHILOLOGICUS CRITICUS LINGUAE HEBRAEAE ET CHALDAEAE V.T. / Genesius, W – Lipsiae, 1835 – 70mf – 8 – ne Slangenburg [470]
THESAURUS PHILOLOGICUS CRITICUS LINGUAE HEBRAEAE ET CHALDAEAE V.T. / Gesenius, G – Lipsiae, 1829 – 57mf – 8 – ne Slangenburg [470]
THESAURUS PHILOLOGICUS CRITICUS LINGUAE HEBRAICAE ET CHALDAICAE VETERIS TESTAMENTI / Gesenius, W – Lipsiae, 1835 – 9 – Dfl2,447.00 – ne IDC [470]
THESAURUS PHILOSOPHORUM SEU DISTINCTIONES ET AXIOMATA PHILOSOPHICA / Reeb, Georg – Paris: P. Letheilleux, 1891 (Philosophy Collection) – 377p 4mf – 9 – $10.00 – fr Bibl Nationale [100]
THESAURUS POLYGLOTTUS / Megister, J – In French. (Linguistic series). 1603 – 9 – fr Hachette [400]
THESAURUS PSEUDO-DIONYSII : VERSIONES LATINAE CUM TEXTU GRAECO – 1995 – 103mf – 9 – Bf19,950.00 – 2-503-50457-4 – be Brepols [240]
THESAURUS PSEUDO-DIONYSII AREOPAGITAE : TEXTUS GRAECUS CUM TRANSLATIONIBUS LATINIS / ed by Nasta, M – 1993 – 46mf – 9 – Bf12,500.00 – 2-503-50344-6 – be Brepols [450]
THESAURUS PSEUDO-NONNI QUONDAM PANOPOLITANI, PARAPHRASIS EVANGELII S. IOANNIS / ed by Coulie, B & Sherry, L F – 1995 – 7mf – 9 – Bf3,750.00 – 2-503-50458-2 – be Brepols [450]
THESAURUS RESOLUTIONUM SACRAE CONGREGATIONS CONCILII – Roma. v1-168. 1718-1910 – 2350mf – 9 – ne IDC [240]
THESAURUS RESOLUTIONUM SACRAE CONGREGATIONS COUNCILII – 1(1718)-168(1910) – 2,350mf – 9 – Dfl8,225.00 – ne Slangenburg [073]
THESAURUS SANCTI AMBROSII – 1994 – 87mf – 9 – Bf19,950.00 – 2-503-50395-0 – be Brepols [450]
THESAURUS SANCTI BERNARDI CLARAEVALLENSIS : SERIES A: FORMAE – 1987 – 80mf – 9 – Bf17,500.00 set – 2-503-61419-1 – be Brepols [240]
THESAURUS SANCTI GREGORII MAGNI : SERIES A: FORMAE – 1986 – 100mf – 9 – Bf17,500.00 set – 1-865-00011-6 – be Brepols [240]
THESAURUS SANCTI GREGORII NAZIANZENI : CARMINA, CHRISTUS PATIENS, VITA / ed by Mossay, J & Coulie, B – 1991 – 30mf – 9 – Bf9,950.00 – 1-475-00021-9 – be Brepols [240]
THESAURUS SANCTI GREGORII NAZIANZENI : ORIATIONES, EPISTULAE, TESTAMENTUM / ed by Mossay, J – 1990 – 50mf – 9 – Bf12,500.00 – 1-475-00011-1 – be Brepols [220]
THESAURUS SANCTI HIERONYMI : SERIES A: FORMAE – 1990 – 150mf – 9 – Bf27,500.00 set – 1-865-00061-2 – be Brepols [240]
THESAURUS SYRIACUS / ed by Smith, R Payne – Oxford. Tomus 1, 2 and Suppl. 1879 – 138mf – 9 – ne Slangenburg [240]
THESAURUS THOMAS A KEMPIS / ed by Chandler, Peleg W – 1994 – 47mf – 9 – Bf12,500.00 – 2-503-50413-2 – be Brepols [450]
THESAVRVS GRAECAE LINGVAE,... / Estienne, Henri – Genevae, 1572 – 73mf – ne IDC [450]
THESAVRVS PAVPERVM; EINN FURTREFLICHE VND VOLKOMNE HAUSSAPOTECK / Brunschwig, Hieronymus – Franckfurt, C. Egenolff, 1537 – 1 – us U.W. Library [540]
THESE AMERICANS SAY "LIFT THE EMBARGO AGAINST REPUBLICAN SPAIN" – N.Y., 1939? Fiche W1224. (Blodgett Collection of Spanish Civil War Pamphlets) – 9 – us H.U. College Libr [946]
THESE POUR LA LICENCE / ed by Helie, Arthur – Paris: Lacour, 1853 – fr Armell [944]
THESE POUR LE DOCTORAT / Castier, G A – Douai, 1884 – 5mf – 1 – ILM-3914/1 – ne IDC [327]
THESEE / Lully, Jean-Baptiste – Paris: Academie Royale de Musique, 1711 – 1 – us Sibley [780]
THESES AND DISSERTATIONS ON SOUTHEAST ASIA. INTERNATIONAL BIBLIOGRAPHY IN SOCIAL SCIENCES, EDUCATION, AND FINE ARTS / Sardesai, D R – SE 520. 1970 – 9 – ne IDC [010]
THESES, CHRISTVM IESVM ESSE MORTVVM PRO PECCATIS TOTIVS GENERIS HVMANI... / Huber, S – Tvbingae, 1592 – 4mf – ne IDC [240]
THESES DE JURE BELLI / Chemnitius, M – Rostock, 1623 – 1mf – 1 – ILM-1063/1 – ne IDC [327]
THESES IN CATHEDRAE HIPPOCRATIS CONCURSU... / Barrichina, P – Valencia, 1772 – 1mf – 9 – sp Cultura [610]
THESES PHYSICO-MEDICAS DISPUTATIONI PROPONIT IN PETITIONE BOTANICAE CATHEDRAE / Manez, E – Valencia, 1794 – 9 – sp Cultura [615]
THESES SEV COMMVNES LOCI TOTIUS REI MEDICAE. ITEM, DE VSV PHARMACORUM, DEQUE ARTIFICIO SUPPRESSAM ALUUM CIENDI, LIBER / Brunfels, Otto – Argentorati, 1532 – 1 – us U.W. Library [615]
THESIS / Aldredge, Robert Croom – 1936. Title: Weather Observers and Observations at Charleston, South Carolina, 1670-1871. 4 fiches – 9 – us South Carolina Historical [610]
THESIS / Tan Malaka – SE 12,145 1. 1946 – 9 – ne IDC [320]
LE THESMOGRAPHE, OU IDEES D'UN HONNETE HOMME SUR UN PROJET DE REGLEMENT, PROPOSE A TOUTES LES NATIONS DE L'EUROPE POUR OPERER UNE REFORME GENERALES DES LOIS; AVEC DES NOTES HISTORIQUES / Retif de la Bretonne, Nicolas Edme – (Utopias in the Enlightenment series). 1789 – 9 – fr Hachette [830]
A THESOURA : ORGAO CRITICO E NOTICIOSO – Penedo, Alagoas. 1 Out-10 Dez 1911 – 1,5,6 – bl Biblioteca [072]
THESSALONIANS AND GALATIANS / Adeney, Walter Frederic – Edinburgh: Jack, (1902?). 1 fiche – 9 – us A.T.L.A. [240]
THESSALONIANS AND GALATIANS : INTRODUCTION, AUTHORIZED VERSION, REVISED VERSION WITH NOTES, INDEX, AND MAP / ed by Adeney, Walter Frederic – (Includes index) – Edinburgh: T C & E C Jack, [1902?] – 1mf – 9 – 0-8370-2055-7 – 1985-0055 – us A.T.L.A. [220]
Theuriet, Andre *see* HISTOIRES GALANTES ET MELANCOLIQUES
Theuriet, Claude Adhemar, dit Andre *see* POESIES RUSTIQUES
Thevenot, Jean *see*
- RELATION D'UN VOYAGE FAIT AU LEVANT DANS LAQUELLE IL EST CURIEUSEMENT TRAITE DES ETATS SUJETS AU GRAND SEIGNEUR, DES MOEURS, RELIGIONS, FORCE, GOUVERNEMENTS, POLITIQUES, LANGUE...
- SUITE DU VOYAGE DE LEVANT: DANS LAQUELLE APRES PLUSIEURS REMARQUES TRES SINGULIERES SUR DES PARTICULARITEZ DE L'EGYPTE, DE LA SYRIE, DE LA MESOPOTAMIE, DE L'EUPHRATE ET DU TIGRE...
- TROISIEME PARTIE DES VOYAGES DE M. DE THEVENOT: CONTENANT LA RELATION DE L'INDOSTAN, DES NOUVEAUX MOGOLS, ET DES AUTRES PEUPLES ET PAYS DES INDES

Thevet, A *see* COSMOGRAPHIE DE LEVANT
THEWRUNGS SPIEGEL DARINNEN GEWIESEN WIRD WOHER THEWRUNG KOEME VND WARUMB... / Engel, A – Hamburg, 1598 – 2mf – 9 – ne IDC [240]
THEY MUST, OR, GOD AND THE SOCIAL DEMOCRACY : A FRANK WORD TO CHRISTIAN MEN AND WOMEN / Kutter, Hermann; ed by Weeks, Rufus W – Chicago: Co-operative Printing Co., c1908 – 1mf – us A.T.L.A. [240]
Thiam, Mamadou Cherif *see* INTRODUCTION A L'ETUDE D'UN GENRE SATIRICO-LAUDATIF
Thiault, M *see* DU BORNAGE EN DROIT ROMAIN
Thibaudeau, Antoine-C *see* ANTOINE THIBAUDEAU
Thibault, Anna-Marie Duval *see* LES DEUX TESTAMENTS
Thibault, Jehan *see* DECLARATION DE LA DIGNITE DES PLANETES [...]
Thibault, Priscille *see* BIBLIOGRAPHIE ANALYTIQUE DE L'OEUVRE DE MGR ARTHUR MAHEUX, P.D., ARCHIVISTE DU SEMINAIRE DE QUEBEC, MEMBRE DE LA SOCIETE ROYALE DU CANADA
Thibaut, Pierre *see*
- COURS DE CHYMIE, AUGMENTE DE LA COMPOSITION DU BAUME VERT VULNERAIRE, AVEC SON EMPLASTRE STIPTIQUE, DU FEBRIFUGE DE F. DELBOE SYLVIVS..
- COVRS DE CHYMIE

Thibert, A *see* ENGLISH-ESKIMO, ESKIMO-ENGLISH DICTIONARY
Thibert, Marguerite *see* LE FEMINISME DANS LE SOCIALISME FRANCAIS, DE 1830 A 1850
Thibodeau, Laura *see* COMPARISON OF ANDROGYNY LEVELS IN TEAM AND INDIVIDUAL SPORT FEMALE ATHLETES
Thicknesse, P *see* A SKETCH OF THE LIFE AND PAINTINGS OF THOMAS GAINSBORGOUGH
Thiebault, D *see*
- ESSAI SUR LE STYLE
- TRAITE DU STYLE

Thiel, Georg *see* DIE NEUE GEIGE
Thiele, Herbert *see* FRIEDRICH HOELDERLIN
Thiemann, Georg *see* SCHILLER UND GOETHE IN DEN XENIEN
Thieme, Karl *see*
- JESUS UND SEINE PREDIGT: EIN VOLKSHOCHSCHULKURSUS
- EINE KATHOLISCHE BELEUCHTUNG DER AUGSBURGISCHEN KONFESSION

THIEN SUNG YIT PO – Djakarta. Indonesia. -d. Nov 1948-Mar 1949. (1 reel) – 1 – uk British Libr Newspaper [072]
Thienon, C *see* VOYAGE PITTORESQUE DANS LE BOCAGE DE LA VENDEE OU VUES DE CLISSON [...] DESSINEES [...]
Thierry, J *see* DICTIONAIRE FRANCOIS LATIN
Thierry, S *see* LE POPIL, OBJET RITUEL CAMBODGIEN
Thiers, Jean B *see* TRAITE DES SUPERTITIONS SELON L'ECRITURE SAINTE, LES DECRETS DES CONCILES, ET LES SENTIMENS DES SAINTS PERES, ET DES THEOLOGIENS
Thiersch, Curt *see* BRIEFE DES DREISTOECKIGEN HAUSBESITZERS MISTER SCHORSCH DOBBELJUH HUTZELBERGER AN DIE "MISSISSIPPI BLAETTER"
Thiersch, Heinrich Wilhelm Josias *see* A HISTORY OF THE CHRISTIAN CHURCH IN THE APOSTOLIC TIMES
Thierstein, Johann R *see* NOVALIS UND DER PIETISMUS
Thiery, Avocat *see*
- CATECHISME NATIONAL
- LE DERNIER CRI DE LA VERITE SUR LA REVOLUTION FRANCAISE
- ELOGE DE J.J. ROUSSEAU, QUI A CONCOURU POUR LE PRIX D'ELOQUENCE DE L'ACADEMIE FRANCAISE, EN L'ANNEE 1791
- FETE CHAMPETRE CELEBREE A MONTMORENCY EN L'HONNEUR DE J.-J. ROUSSEAU
- PRINCIPES DE J.J. ROUSSEAU POUR L'EDUCATION DES ENFANTS
- LE ROI ET SES MINISTRES
- VOYAGE A ERMENONVILLE
- LES VRAIS PRINCIPES CONSTITUTIONNELS

Thiery, Jean-Paul *see* CELL ADHESION AND COMMUNICATION
Thiess, Frank *see*
- ABSCHIED VOM PARADIES
- THE DEVIL'S SHADOW
- FAREWELL TO PARADISE
- DIE STELLUNG DER SCHWABEN ZU GOETHE
- DER TENOR VON TRAPANI
- TSUSHIMA

Thiess, Karl *see* DER VERBAND DEUTSCHER JOURNALISTEN- UND SCHRIFTSTELLERVEREINE UND DIE BESCHLUESSE SEINER DELEGIERTENTAGE, 1895 BIS 1904
Thiessen, K *see* STIMMUNGEN: DREI VORTRAGSSTUECKE FUER VIOLONCELLO MIT KLAVIERBEGLEITUNG. OP. 22
THIETMARI MERSEBURGENSIS EPISCOPI CHRONICON (MGH 6: 9.BD) / ed by Holtzmann, R – 1935 – Dfl42.00 – ne Slangenburg [240]
THIETMARI MERSEBURGENSIS EPISCOPI CHRONICON (MGH 7: 54.BD) – 1889 – Dfl25.00 – ne Slangenburg [240]
Thigpen, Lydia K *see* EFFECTS OF STATICALLY PERFORMED TOE TOUCH STRETCHES ON TORQUE PRODUCTION OF THE HAMSTRING AND QUADRICEPS MUSCLE GROUPS
Thikoetter, Julius *see* IDEAL UND LEBEN
Thilo, C A *see* SCHLEIERMACHERS RELIGIONSPHILOSOPHIE
Thilo, Martin *see* DAS HOHELIED NEU UEBERSETZT UND AESTHETISCHSITTLICH BEURTEILT
Thimmermann, Hermann *see* DER STURM AUF LANGEMARCK
THIN SOLID FILMS – v1-122. 1967-84 – 1,5,6,13 – sz Elsevier [073]
THINGS AS THEY ARE : MISSION WORK IN SOUTHERN INDIA / Carmichael, Amy – New York: Fleming H Revell, [1903] – 1mf – 9 – 0-8370-6402-3 – 1986-0402 – us A.T.L.A. [240]
THE THINGS I AM FOR / Belknap, Paul A – A USIC pamphlet.4p – 9 – 1.00f – at Libertarian Micro [335]
THINGS I HAVE SEEN AND PEOPLE I HAVE KNOWN / Sala, George Augustus – London, Paris: Cassell, 1894 – 1 roll – 1 – 1-55879-960-5 – uk Libr Preservation [920]
THINGS JAPANESE; BEING NOTES ON VARIOUS SUBJECTS CONNECTED WITH JAPAN FOR THE USE OF TRAVELLERS AND OTHERS / Chamberlain, Basil Hall – 2nd ed. rev. and enl. London: K. Paul, Trench, Trubner, 1891. 503p – 1 – us U.W. Library [910]
THINGS NEW AND OLD (CCC125) = WEN KU CHIH HSIN / Feng, Shang-li – (In Chinese) – 1st. ed. Hong Kong: Council on Christian Literature for Overseas Chinese, 1964 – 1r – 1 – 1984-B500 – us A.T.L.A. [240]
THINGS OF THE MIND / Spalding, J L – Chicago: A.C. McClurg, 1901, c1894 – 1mf – us A.T.L.A. [240]
THE THINGS THAT ARE CAESARS, A DEFENCE OF WEALTH / Morrison Walker, Guy – 1919. 1 fiche (29x) – 9 – 1.00f – at Libertarian Micro [320]
THINGS TO COME / ed by Bullinger, W & Bowker, H C – July 1894-December 1915 – 63mf – 9 – $175.00 – us Schnappsburg [240]

THINKING AHEAD : UNESCO AND THE CHALLENGES OF TODAY AND TOMORROW – 1977 – 363p – 9 – 92-3-101525-7 – fr UNESCO [303]
THINKING AND DOING : YOUTH AND A NEW INTERNATIONAL ECONOMIC ORDER / Day, Barbara Bruehl – 1980 – 96p – 9 – 92-3-101841-8 – fr UNESCO [330]
THINKING AND EDUCATION / Korea. Korean Educational Development Institute; ed by Sung, Il-je – Seoul, 1988 – 2mf – 9 – DE-659/1 – ne IDC [370]
Thio, Goan Loo *see* PENUNTUN PRAKTIS UNTUK PEMBUATAN KARET
Thipphakonrawong (Kham), Chao Phraya *see* RUANG PHRA PATHOMCHEDI
THIRD BIANNUAL REVIEW OF THE CAPITAL EXPENDITURE PROGRAMME, 1957-62 / Mauritius – (Sessional Paper no. 7 of 1959). Port Louis. 1959 – 9 – ne IDC [338]
THE THIRD BOOK OF READING LESSONS / Brothers of the Christian Schools – Montreal: publ for the Christian Brothers by D & J Sadlier & Company, 1864. SEM105P1676 – 5mf – 9 – Can$11.25 – cn Bibl Nat [240]
THIRD BRANCH ADMINISTRATIVE OFFICE OF THE U.S. COURTS – Washington: GPO. v1-27. 1968-95 – 9 – $161.00 set – us Hein [340]
THIRD CENSUS OF THE UNITED STATES / U.S. Bureau of the Census – 1810. 71 rolls. M252 – 1 – us Nat'l Archives [324]
A THIRD CHAPTER ON THE RULE IN MINOT'S CASE / Sargent, John Osborne – New York: Putnam's, 1874. 48p. LL-1380 – 1 – us L of C Photodup [340]
THE THIRD COMMANDMENT / Coffin, Fulton Johnson – Norwood, MA: Norwood Press, [ca 1898] – 1mf – 9 – 0-8370-2700-4 – 1985-0700 – us A.T.L.A. [220]
THIRD DEVELOPMENT PLAN FOR MALTESE ISLANDS 1969-74 / Malta. Office of the Prime Minister – 9 – ne IDC [338]
THIRD DEVELOPMENT PROGRAMME 1971/72-1973/74 / Gambia – D-1545 1. 1971 – 9 – ne IDC [338]
THIRD FIVE YEAR DEVELOPMENT PLAN, 1961-1965 / Ethiopia – D-880 1. 1968 – 9 – ne IDC [338]
THIRD FIVE YEAR DEVELOPMENT PLAN 1971-1976 / Cameroon – 1 – $39.50 – us African Imprint [338]
THE THIRD FIVE YEAR ECONOMIC AND SOCIAL PLAN OF AFGHANISTAN, 1967-1971 / Afghanistan. Ministry of Planning – Kabul. 1967. BD-350 1 – 9 – ne IDC [338]
THE THIRD FIVE YEAR EDUCATIONAL PLAN : FOREIGN LOAN AND GRANT REQUIREMENTS OF THE MINISTRY OF EDUCATION 1972-1976 / Thailand. Ministry of Education – Bangkok, 1971 – 3mf – 9 – DE-276/1 – ne IDC [370]
THIRD FIVE YEAR PLAN / India. Planning Commission – New Delhi. 1961 – 9 – ne IDC [338]
THE THIRD FIVE YEAR PLAN (1965-1970) / Pakistan – Karachi. 1965 – 9 – ne IDC [338]
THIRD FIVE YEAR PLAN, 1969-1973 / Trinidad and Tobago – D 901 1. 1970 – 9 – ne IDC [338]
THIRD FIVE YEAR PLAN A DRAFT OUTLINE / India. Planning Commission – New Delhi. 1960 – 9 – ne IDC [338]
THIRD FIVE YEAR PLAN FOR ECONOMIC AND SOCIAL DEVELOPMENT / Syrian Arab Republic – D 1212 1. 1971-1975 – 9 – ne IDC [338]
THIRD FIVE YEAR PLAN PROGRESS REPORT, 1961-66 / Rajasthan. India (State). Directorate of Economics and Statistics – Jaipur. 1967 – 9 – ne IDC [338]
THIRD FIVE YEAR PLAN PROGRESS REPORT, 1962-63 / Rajasthan. India (State). Directorate of Economics and Statistics – Jaipur. 1963 – 9 – ne IDC [338]
THIRD FIVE YEAR PLAN PROGRESS REPORT, 1963-64 / Rajasthan. India (State). Directorate of Economics and Statistics – Jaipur. 1964 – 9 – ne IDC [338]
THIRD FIVE YEAR PLAN PROGRESS REPORT, 1964-65 / Rajasthan. India (State). Directorate of Economics and Statistics – Jaipur. 1966 – 9 – ne IDC [338]
THIRD FIVE YEAR PLAN SUMMARY OF DRAFT OUTLINE / India. Ministry of Information and Broadcasting – Delhi. 1961. BD-512 1 – 9 – ne IDC [380]
THIRD FIVE-YEAR DEVELOPMENT PLAN LAW / Iran – D-1098 1. Dated Sept. 6, 1962 – 9 – ne IDC [340]
THIRD FIVE-YEAR ECONOMIC DEVELOPMENT PLAN 1972-1976 / Korea. South – Feb 1971. BD-1683 1 – 9 – ne IDC [338]
THE THIRD FIVE-YEAR PLAN (1972-1976) / Cyprus. Planning Bureau – Nicosia. 1973. BD-2014 1 – 9 – ne IDC [338]
THIRD FIVE-YEAR PLAN FOR ECONOMIC AND SOCIAL DEVELOPMENT IN THE SYRIAN ARAB REPUBLIC / Syria. Office Arabe de Presse et de Documentation – 1971-75. 1971. BNE-9729 1 – 9 – ne IDC [338]
THIRD FOUR-YEAR DEVELOPMENT PLAN OF TAIWAN 1961-1964 / China. Republic. Ministry of Economic Affairs. Industrial Planning and Coordination Group – D-1021 1 – 9 – ne IDC [338]
THIRD NATIONAL DEVELOPMENT PLAN, 1975-1980 / Nigeria. Central Planning Office – 2v. Lagos. 1975. BD-1818 1 – 9 – ne IDC [338]
THE THIRD NATIONAL ECONOMIC AND SOCIAL DEVELOPMENT PLAN (1972-1976) / Thailand. National Economic and Social Development Board Office of the Prime Minister – Bangkok, Thailand. BD-1851 1 – 9 – ne IDC [338]
THIRD NATIONAL ECONOMIC AND SOCIAL DEVELOPMENT PLAN, 1972-1976 / Thailand. National Economic Development Board – Bangkok. Oct 1971. BD-1756 1 – 9 – ne IDC [338]
THE THIRD PART OF THE ECCLESIASTICAL HISTORY OF JOHN, BISHOP OF EPHESUS / Cureton, William – Oxford, 1853 – Dfl39.00 – ne Slangenburg [240]
THE THIRD PART OF THE ECCLESIASTICAL HISTORY OF JOHN, BISHOP OF EPHESUS / Joannes, Bischof von Ephesus – Trans. from the original Syriac by R. Payne Smith. 1860 – 1 – us A.T.L.A. [240]
(THIRD PART OF THE) MUSICIAN'S COMPANION / Howe, Elias – containing 40 setts of cotillions arranged with figures, and a large number of popular marches, quick steps, waltzes, hornpipes, contra dances, songs, &c. &c. several of which are in three parts–first, second, & bass, for the flute, violin, clarionett, bass-viol, &c., containing in all over 500 pieces of music, more than 150 of which are original, or have neve before been published in this country. Boston: Elias Howe, Jr., 1844. MUSIC 1898, Item 4 – 1 – us L of C Photodup [780]
THE THIRD PLAN, 1965-70 / Nepal. National Planning Council – Kathmandu. 1964 – 9 – ne IDC [338]
THIRD PROGRESS REPORT ON THE ECONOMIC PROGRAMME, 1955-60 / Nigeria – (Sessional Paper no. 1 of 1959). Lagos. 1959 – 9 – ne IDC [338]
THIRD PROGRESS REPORT ON THE RECONSTRUCTION AND DEVELOPMENT PROGRAMME 1960-65 FOR THE PERIOD 1962-63 / Mauritius – (Sessional Paper No. 5 of 1963). Port Louis. 1963. BD-447 1 – 9 – ne IDC [338]
THIRD PROGRESS REPORT TO THE MEMBERS OF THE COUNCIL OF THE ASIAN GAMES FEDERATION BY THE ORGANIZING COMMITTEE – SE-5785 1. 4th, Djakarta, 1962 – 9 – ne IDC [025]
THIRD REICH: RECORDS AND DOCUMENTS – 69r – 1 – uk Microform Academic [943]
THE THIRD REPORT... : COURT PROCEEDINGS AND THE LANGUAGE OF THE LAW / Hong Kong. Chinese Language Committee – Hong Kong, 1971 – 1mf – 9 – DE-161/1 – ne IDC [370]
THIRD REPORT OF THE COMMISSION CHARGED WITH THE REVISION AND AMENDMENT OF THE CODE OF CIVIL PROCEDURE OF LOWER CANADA / Quebec Province – Quebec: Morning Chronicle Steam Print, 1895. SEM105P1518 – 2mf – 9 – Can$4.50 – cn Bibl Nat [340]
THIRD REPORT OF THE STANDING COMMITTEE OF GRIEVANCES... / Bas-Canada. Parlement. Chambre d'Assemblee. Comite Permanent des Griefs – [s.l.]: [s.n.], [1831]. SEM105P1317 – 5mf – 9 – Can$11.25 – cn Bibl Nat [971]
THIRD THURSDAY / University of Tennessee.Institute of Agriculture – 1982. 1 reel – 1,5 – us Spaulding [630]
THIRD WAY – (1985- . 5,6,9) – v1- . 1977- – 1 – us UMI [073]
THIRD WORLD PLANNING REVIEW – v1-1979- – 1,5,6,9 – us UMI [338]
THIRD WORLD QUARTERLY – 1979-to date – 9 – uk Microform Academic [073]
THIRD WORLD QUARTERLY : JOURNAL OF EMERGING AREAS – 1990- 14v – 9 – £121.00 – 0143-6597 – uk Carfax [338]
THIRTEEN NOVELS / Langenscheidt, Paul – (v.1 Arme kleine Eva 1922. v.2 Beate. c 1920. v.3 Blondes Gift. 1922. v.4 Du bist mein. 1922. v.5 Eine dumme Geschichte. 1922?. v.6 Graf Cohn. 1922. v.7 Ich hab'Dich lieb 1922?. v.8 Kanaillen. 1922. v.9 Mutter, hilf mir. 1922. v.10 Der Sprung ins Dunkle, 1922. v.11 Um nichts 1922. v.12 Taumel. 1922.. v.13 Die weisse Nacht. c 1914) – Berlin, P. Langenscheidt. 13 v. Film Mas C 474 – 1 – us H.U. Library [830]
THIRTY DRAFTS OF GUINEA / Smith, W – 1749 – 2mf – 7 – uk Microform Academic [910]
THIRTY STRANGE STORIES / Wells, H G – New York: Edward Arnold, 1897 – 1 roll – 1 – 1-55879-928-1 – uk Libr Preservation [830]
THIRTY STUDIES IN THE REVELATION OF JESUS CHRIST TO JOHN / White, Wilbert Webster – New York: Fleming H. Revell, 1898. 1 fiche. 8370-5824-4 – 9 – us A.T.L.A. [240]
THIRTY YEARS FROM HOME; OR, A VOICE FROM THE MAIN DECK / Leech, Samuel – With notes by Ebenezer Collins. 1851 – 9 – $20.00 – uk Libr Preservation [920]
THIRTY YEARS' MUSICAL RECOLLECTIONS / Chorley, Henry Fothergill – London: Hurst and Blackett, 1862 – 1 roll – 1 – 1-55879-270-8 – uk Libr Preservation [780]
THIRTY YEARS OF NEW GLASS, 1957-1987 / Frantz, Susanne K – 1987. 6p. 2 color, 1 b/w illus. Fiche No. 9981 – 1mf – 9 – $2.50 – us Corning Mus [700]
THIRTY YEARS OF ORIENTAL STUDIES : ISSUED IN COMMEMORATION OF THIRTY YEARS OF ACTIVITY OF THE ORIENTAL CLUB OF PHILADELPHIA / ed by Kent, Roland Grubb – (Includes bibliographies) – Philadelphia: [s.n.], 1918 – 1mf – 9 – 0-8370-7073-2 – 1986-1073 – us A.T.L.A. [930]
THIRTY YEARS WITH THE MEXICANS: IN PEACE AND REVOLUTION / Case, Alden Buell – New York, Chicago: Fleming H. Revell Co., c1917 – 1 – us U.W. Library [390]
THE THIRTY-NINE ARTICLES : THEIR HISTORY AND EXPLANATION / Kidd, B J – New York: J. Pott, 1899 (Oxford church text books) – 1mf – us A.T.L.A. [240]
THIRTY-SIX YEARS OF A SEAFARING LIFE / Bechervaise, John – 1839 – 9 – $20.00 – uk Libr Preservation [920]
THIRTY-THREE METAL PRODUCING – v15-1977- – 1,5,6,9 – us UMI [670]
THIS BREAD IS MINE / Lefevre, Robert – 1960. 4 fiches (24x) – 9 – 1.00f – at Libertarian Micro [320]
THIS CANADA OF OURS AND OTHER POEMS / Edgar, James David – Toronto: W. Briggs; Montreal: C. W. Coates; Halifax: S. F. Huestis, 1893. 02882. (Pre-1900 Canadiana) – 9 – cn C.I.H.M. [810]
THIS DO : SIX ESSAYS IN PRACTICE / Horton, Robert Forman – 4th ed. London: James Clarke, 1893 – 1mf – 9 – 0-8370-7222-0 – 1986-1222 – us A.T.L.A. [240]
THIS INDENTURE...BETWEEN THE CHICAGO AND CANADA SOUTHERN RAILWAY COMPANY...AND ANDREW T. HALL...AND KENYON COX 111 TRUSTEES / Chicago and Canada Southern Railway Company – 1872? 02991. (Pre-1900 Canadiana) – 9 – cn C.I.H.M. [380]
THIS IS LAS VEGAS – Las Vegas, NV. 1961 – 1r – 1 – $50.00 – U04910 – us Library Micro [071]
THIS IS NORTHERN NIGERIA : BACKGROUND TO AN INVITATION / Kirk-Greene, Anthony Hamilton Millard – Kaduna: Northern Nigeria Govt Printer, 1955 – us Res Libr [960]
THIS IS OUR CONCERN; A STATEMENT TO AMERICAN SOCIAL WORKERS ON THEIR STAKE IN THE CIVIL WAR IN SPAIN / McMillen, Wayne – N.Y., 1937. Fiche W1013. (Blodgett Collection of Spanish Civil War Pamphlets) – 9 – us H.U. College Libr [946]
THIS MAGAZINE – (v7-12 1973-79 Can$115.00. v13-16 1979-83 Can$60.00y. v17-19 1983-86 Can$50. 00y. v20-29 1986-96 Can$20.00y. Cont: This Magazine is About Schools at v7 19) – Toronto. v7-28. 1973/74-1994/95 – 1,5,9 – Price varies – cn Micromedia [370]
THIS MAGAZINE *see* THIS MAGAZINE IS ABOUT SCHOOLS
THIS MAGAZINE IS ABOUT SCHOOLS – (Cont by: This Magazine at v7 1973/74) – Toronto. v1-6. 1966/67-1972/73 – 1 – Can$115.00 – cn Micromedia [370]
THIS MAGAZINE IS ABOUT SCHOOLS *see* THIS MAGAZINE
THIS MONTH IN VERMONT EXTENSION / Vermont. Agricultural Extension Service – 1964-69 – 1,5,6 – us Spaulding [630]
THIS QUARTER – Paris etc. v. 1-5. no. 2. Spring 1925-Dec 1932 – 1 – us NY Public [073]
THIS QUARTER – Paris. v1-5. 1925-32 – 2r – 1 – us Ross [073]
THIS THEY REMEMBERED, 1861-1865 / Reese, Gussie – 1965. Comp. from old copies of The Oglethorpe Echo. 4 fiches. F-1987 – 9 – us A.G.L.L. [978]
THIS WEEK – Fresno, CA. 1983-1993 – 61r – 1 – $3,050.00 – R03222 – us Library Micro [071]
THIS WEEK AND ENTERPRISE – (Se1990-1992.-7r) – Yorkton, 1993 – 4r – 1 – cn Preston [971]
THIS WEEK IN BUSINESS – Montreal, 16/22 jan 1988-2 jun 1990f (The Gazette, Montreal) – 4r – 1 – Can$75.00 – cn Can Microfilming [072]
THIS WEEK NEWS AND REVIEW – Eureka, CA. 1988 – 1r – 1 – $50.00 – B05034 – us Library Micro [071]
THIS WEEK/WEEKEND – Oshawa, 1980-1981 – 12r – 1 – cn Preston [971]
THIS WORLD – (1985-. 5,6,9) – No.1-. 1982- – 1 – us UMI [073]
Thiselton-Dyer, W T *see* FLORA OF TROPICAL AFRICA
Thoburn, James Mills *see*
- THE CHRISTIAN CONQUEST OF INDIA
- THE DEACONESSS AND HER VOCATION
- INDIA AND MALAYSIA
- MISSIONARY ADDRESSES

Thode, Henry *see*
- GOETHE DER BILDNER
- KUNST, RELIGION UND KULTUR

Thoerner, Th. de *see* ETUDES SUR LA QUESTION DE L'ABOLITION DE SERVAGE EN RUSSIE, PAR UN CONTEMPORAIN
THOI LUAM – Saigon. South Vietnam. 1964-66 – 1 – us UMI [072]
THOI MOI – Hanoi: [s.n., dec 31 1967-jan 25 1968 – 1r – 1 – us Res Libr [072]
THO'I-BAO – Tuan bao ra ngay thu' ba. No1-143. Hanoi. 6 avr 1937-26 mars 1938. mq No39-40. No1-2. 29 aout-5 sept 1938 – 1 – fr A.C.R.P.P. [073]
Thoinan, Ern *see* LES HOTTETERRE ET LES CHEDEVILLES CELEBRES JOUERS ET FRACTEURS DE FLUTES, HAUTBOIS, BASSOONS ET MUSETTES DES 17E ET 18E SIECLES, AVEC PORTRAITS ET FAC-SIMILES
Tholal, Pundit Bishambhar Nath *see* HISTORY OF THE SOMBANSI RAJ AND THE ESTATE OF PARTABGARH IN OUDH
THOLOMEI LUCENSIS ANNALES (MGH 6: 8.BD) / ed by Schmeidler, B – 1930 – Dfl30.00 – ne Slangenburg [240]
Tholuck, August *see*
- DAS ALTE TESTAMENT IM NEUEN TESTAMENT: UEBER DIE CITATE DES ALTEN TESTAMENTS IM NEUEN TESTAMENT UND UEBER DEN OPFER- UND PRIESTERBEGRIFF IM ALTEN UND NEUEN TESTAMENTE
- DER GEIST DER LUTHERISCHEN THEOLOGEN WITTENBERGS IM VERLAUFE DES 17. JAHRHUNDERTS
- GESCHICHTE DES RATIONALISMUS. ERSTE ABTHEILUNG, GESCHICHTE DES PIETISMUS UND DES ERSTEN STADIUMS DER AUFKLAERUNG
- DIE PROPHETEN UND IHRE WEISSAGUNGEN

Thom, Adam *see* THE SETTLER
Thom, William Taylor *see*
- SHAKESPEARE AND CHAUCER EXAMINATIONS
- THE STRUGGLE FOR RELIGIOUS FREEDOM IN VIRGINIA

Thoma, Hans *see*
- GEDICHTE UND GEDANKEN
- JAHRBUCH DER SEELE

Thoma, Ludwig *see*
- ERINNERUNGEN
- GELAEHMTE SCHWINGEN
- HEILIGE NACHT
- DER RUEPP

THOMAE AQUINITATIS OPERA OMNIA : INDICES TABULA AUREA MAGISTRI PETRI DE BERGOMO O.P. – Paris, 1880 – 33mf – 8 – ne Slangenburg [240]

THOMAE BARTHOLINI ACTA MEDICA ET PHILOSOPHICA HAFNIENSIA / Bartholin, Thomas – Hafniae. v1-5 1673-80 – 3 – us Readex [610]
Thomas *see* CENTENNIAL HISTORY OF RUSH COUNTY
THOMAS A. KEMPIS AND THE BROTHERS OF COMMON LIFE / Kettlewell, Samuel – London: K. Paul, Trench, 1882 – 3mf – us A.T.L.A. [240]
THOMAS A. KEMPIS AND THE BROTHERS OF THE COMMON LIFE / Kettlewell, Samuel – New York: G.P. Putnam, 1882. 2v – 1 – us U.W. Library [240]
Thomas a S Joseph *see* CURSUS PHILOSOPHICUS AD USUM STUDENTIUM TOTIUS ORDINIS MINORAM
THE THOMAS ADDIS EMMET AND THEODORUS BAILEY MYERS HISTORICAL EARLY AMERICAN AUTOGRAPHS COLLECTIONS – (Emmet ca 7r $595 D3337. Myers ca 13r $1,105 D3338. With guides) – Rare Books and Manuscripts Division: The New York Public Library, Astor, Lenox and Tilden Foundations 1995 – 1 – us Scholarly Res [976]
Thomas, Adrienne *see* VIKTORIA
Thomas, Alfred B *see* AFTER CORONADO, SPANISH EXPLORATION NORTHEAST OF NEW MEXICO, 1696-1727. DOCUMENTS FROM THE ARCHIVES OF SPAIN, MEXICO AND NEW MEXICO...NORMAN, 1935
Thomas, Anita C *see* PRIMARY AND SECONDARY CARDIOVASCULAR DISEASE RISK FACTORS AND THEIR CORRELATIONS WITH WAIST-TO-HIP RATIO AND BODY MASS INDEX IN NORTH CAROLINA DEPARTMENT OF CORRECTION EMPLOYEES
Thomas, Anneliese *see* DON CARLOS UND HAMLET
Thomas, Antoine Leonard *see* OEUVRES COMPLETES DE THOMAS...PRECEDEES D'UNE NOTICE SUR LA VIE ET LES OUVRAGES DE L'AUTEUR PAR M. CARET
Thomas Aquinas, Saint *see* SELECTIONS
Thomas, Arad *see* PIONEER HISTORY OF ORLEANS COUNTY
Thomas, Armstrong *see* PRAYERS AND INSTRUCTIONS, WITH FORMS
Thomas, Arthur G *see* WHEAT FROM THE FIELDS OF BOAZ
Thomas, Augusta (Dodge) *see* PRAIRIE CHILDREN
Thomas, Augustus *see* THE PRINT OF MY REMEMBRANCE
THOMAS BECKET : ARCHBISHOP OF CANTERBURY / Hutton, William Holden – London: I. Pitman, 1910. (Makers of national history) – 1mf – us A.T.L.A. [240]
THOMAS BECKET (RS65) = THOMAS SAGA ERKIBYSKUPS : A LIFE OF ARCHBISHOP THOMAS BECKET / ed by Magnusson, Eiriker – (In Icelandic, with English transl, notes and glossary. v1 1875 Dfl35.00. v2 1883 Dfl49.00) – ne Slangenburg [920]
Thomas Beckington *see* MEMORIALS OF THE REIGN OF KING HENRY 6 (RS56)
Thomas, Benjamin F *see*
- GOODWIN'S TOWN OFFICER
- OPINION AS TO THE VALIDITY OF THE TAX ON THE NON-RESIDENT STOCKHOLDERS OF THE NATIONAL BANKS

THOMAS BRADWARDINUS U. SEINE LEHRE V. D. MENSCHL. WILLENSFREIHEIT : BGPHMA 5/2 / Hahn, S – Muenster, 1905 – 1mf – 9 – ne Slangenburg [240]
THOMAS BURKE PAPERS / Burke, Thomas – 1763-1852. University of North Carolina Library. Guide – 1 – $90.00 – us U.N.C. Southern Hist [920]
THOMAS CAMPANELLA : EIN REFORMER DER AUSGEHENDEN RENAISSANCE / Kvacala, Jan – Berlin: Trowitzsch, 1909 – 1mf – us A.T.L.A. [240]
THOMAS CAMPBELL / Hadden, James Cuthbert – Edinburgh, London: Oliphant, Anderson & Ferrier, [1899] – 1 roll – 1 – 1-55879-672-X – uk Libr Preservation [920]
THOMAS CARLYLE / Macpherson, Hector Carsewell – London: Oliphant, Anderson & Ferrier, [1896] – 1 roll – 1 – 1-55879-356-9 – uk Libr Preservation [940]
Thomas, Catherine *see* MORPHOLOGIE DE LA KAHANI CHEZ PREMCAND
THOMAS CHALMERS / Blaikie, William Garden – New York: Charles Scribner, [1896?] (Famous Scots series) – 1mf – us A.T.L.A. [240]
THOMAS CHALMERS : HIS LIFE AND ITS LESSONS / Walker, Norman Lockhart – London: T. Nelson, 1880 – 1mf – us A.T.L.A. [240]
Thomas Cook et fils *see* DELEGATION EN FRANCE DE LA SOCIETE SAINT-JEAN-BAPTISTE ET DE LA SOCIETE HISTORIQUE DE MONTREAL
THOMAS CORNEILLE GRAMMAIRIEN / Sautebin, G – 1897 – 9 – fr I.C.S. [920]
THOMAS COUNTY CAT – Colby. Kan. 1885-91 – 1 – us UMI [071]
THOMAS COUNTY CLIPPER – Seneca, NE. -w. Jun 1914; Jan 1920-Feb 1927; Apr 1927-Sep 1928, scattered issues missing – 1 – us NE Hist [071]
THOMAS COUNTY HERALD-CLIPPER – Thedford, NE. -w. Apr 1910; Nov 1911-Oct 1946; Jan 1947-Mar 1952; Aug 1957; Nov 1959-Sept 1969 – 1 – us NE Hist [071]
THOMAS CRANMER / Mason, Arthur James – London: Methuen, 1898. (Leaders of religion) – 1mf – us A.T.L.A. [240]
THOMAS CRANMER AND THE ENGLISH REFORMATION, 1489-1556 / Pollard, Albert Frederick – New York: G.P. Putnam, 1904 – 2mf – us A.T.L.A. [240]
Thomas, David Y *see* ARKANSAS AND ITS PEOPLE
THOMAS DAVIS: THE MEMOIRS OF AN IRISH PATRIOT, 1840-1846 / Duffy, Charles Gavan – London: K. Paul, Trench, Truebner and Co. Ltd. 1890. 398p. With: Shakespeare Criticism by C.N. Menon. 1 reel. 1186. .PR.-apply; UWM; 1 – us U.W. Library [941]
Thomas de Burton *see* CHRONICA MONASTERII DE MELSA, A FUNDATIONE USQUE AD ANNUM 1396 (RS43)
Thomas de Papia *see* DIALOGUS DE GESTIS SANCTORUM FRATRUM MINORUM AUCTORE FR. THOMA DE PAPIA
THOMAS DE QUINCEY UND JOHN WILSON (CHRISTOPHER NORTH) IHRE LITERARISCHEN UND PERSOENLICHEN BEZIEHUNGEN / Cramer, Maria – Muenster/ Westf., 1929 – 1mf – DM48.00 – 3-8267-3064-X – gw Hänsel [420]
THOMAS DER PERLENFISCHER : ROMAN / Kuekelhaus, Heinz – Berlin: F A Herbig, 1941 – 1r – 1 – us U.W. Library [430]
Thomas, E D *see* A NEW AND CHOICE SELECTION OF HYMNS AND SPIRITUAL SONGS
THE THOMAS E. WATSON PAPERS – 1991 – 34r – 1 – $3,740.00 – 1-55655-291-2 – us UPA [320]
THE THOMAS EAKINS COLLECTION IN THE HIRSHHORN MUSEUM AND SCULPTURE GARDEN / Smithsonian Institution – (142p accompanying text) – 1979 – 2 color mf – 15 – $39.00r – us Chicago [700]
Thomas, Edward Beers *see* NEGLIGENCE; RULES–DECISIONS–OPINIONS. 2D ED
Thomas, Eric-Jean *see* IMMIGRANT WORKERS IN EUROPE
THOMAS EWING JR. PAPERS / Ewing, Thomas, Jr – 1856-1908. In Kansas State Historical Society. Guide – 1 – us KS Hist [920]
Thomas, F W *see* TIBETAN DOCUMENTS CONCERNING CHINESE TURKESTAN
THOMAS GUTHRIE / Smeaton, Oliphant – Edinburgh: Oliphant Anderson & Ferrier, [1900?] – 1mf – us A.T.L.A. [240]
THOMAS HANDASYD PERKINS PAPERS, 1789-1892 / Perkins, Thomas Handasyd – Massachusetts Historical Society – 17r – 1 – $1295.00 – us UMI [920]
THOMAS HARDY AS MAN, WRITER AND PHILOSOPHER : AN APPRECIATION WITH A SWEDISH HARDY BIBLIOGRAPHY / Zachrisson, R E – Stockholm, 1928 – 1mf – 9 – ne IDC [420]
THOMAS HARDY UND DIE BIBEL. EIN BEITRAG ZUR ENGLISCHEN LITERATUR-UND KULTURGESCHICHTE / Meusel, M – H-337 2. 1937 – 8 – ne IDC [420]
Thomas, Harold Beken *see* A HISTORY OF UGANDA LAND AND SURVEYS AND OF THE UGANDA LAND AND SURVEY DEPARTMENT
THOMAS HARRISON, REGICIDE AND MAJOR-GENERAL / De Wesselow, Charles Hare Simpkinson – London: J.M. Dent; New York: E.P. Dutton & Co., 1905. xv,304p – 1 – us U.W. Library [920]
Thomas, Henry *see* THE STORY OF EUGENE DEBS, BY HENRY T. SCHNITTKIND (UNCLE HENRY) WITH INTRODUCTION BY ROMAIN ROLLAND
Thomas, Henry F *see* A 20TH CENTURY HISTORY OF ALLEGAN COUNTY
THOMAS HOOD : HIS LIFE AND TIMES / Jerrold, Walter – New York: John Lane Company, 1909 – 1 roll – 1 – 1-55879-724-6 – uk Libr Preservation [920]
THOMAS HOOKER : PREACHER, FOUNDER, DEMOCRAT / Walker, George Leon – New York: Dodd, Mead, c1891 – 1mf – us A.T.L.A. [240]
Thomas, J *see* TWO LETTERS TO THE REV. THOMAS COKE, LL.D., CURATE OF SOUTH PETHERTON, WRITTEN WITH A FRIENDLY INTENTION OF CONVINCING HIM OF SOME GROSS ERRORS IN HIS CLERICAL CONDUCT
THOMAS JEFFERSON / Morse, John T, Jr. – Boston & NY: Houghton, Mifflin & Co, 1898? – 4mf – 9 – $6.00 – LLMC 96-036 – us L.L.M.C. [975]
THOMAS JEFFERSON PAPERS – 65r – 1 – $2,275.00 – Dist. us Scholarly Res – us L of C Photodup [975]
THOMAS JEFFERSON PAPERS, 1705-1827 / Jefferson, Thomas – Massachusetts Historical Society – 16r – 1 – $1210.00 – us UMI [920]
THOMAS JEFFERSON'S MARCH / Emrich, George – Philadelphia: G. Willig 1801. MUSIC 3082, Item 4 – 1 – us L of C Photodup [780]
Thomas, Jerry R *see* THE RELATIONSHIP BETWEEN KNOWLEDGE AND EXPERTISE IN BREASTSTROKE SWIMMING
Thomas, Jesse Burgess *see* THE OLD BIBLE AND THE NEW SCIENCE: AN ESSAY AND FOUR LECTURES
Thomas, Joe Milton *see* A PLAN FOR PREPARING A CONGREGATION FOR THE CONSTRUCTION OF A CHURCH BUILDING
Thomas, John *see* JOHN THOMAS PAPERS, 1693-1839
Thomas, John Lilburn *see* THE LAW OF CONSTRUCTIVE CONTEMPT. THE SHEPHERD CASE REVIEWED
Thomas, John Martin *see* THE CHRISTIAN FAITH AND THE OLD TESTAMENT
Thomas, Johnny D *see* A COMPARATIVE ANALYSIS OF THE LEADERSHIP STYLES OF HEAD FOOTBALL COACHES FROM TADITIONALLY BLACK AND WHITE UNIVERSITIES AND COLLEGES
Thomas, Joseph Llewelyn *see* JOURNEYS AMONG THE GENTLE JAPS IN THE SUMMER OF 1895, WITH A SPECIAL CHAPTER ON THE RELIGIONS OF JAPAN
Thomas, Keith Johnston *see* PERSONAL POWER
THOMAS LAKE HARRIS AND THE BROTHERHOOD OF THE NEW LIFE, 1854-1942 – 14r – 1 – $1050.00 – us UMI [360]
THOMAS M. COOLEY LAW REVIEW – v1-12. 1982-95 – 9 – $213.00 set – us Hein [340]
Thomas, M R O *see* THE BOOK OF ANTELOPES
THOMAS MATULESIA, HET HOOFD DER OPSTANDELINGEN OP HET EILAND HONIMOA, NA DE OVERNAME VAN HET BESTUUR DER MOLUKKEN DOOR DEN LANDVOOGD J.A. VAN MIDDELKOOP IN 1817 / Doren, J B J van – Amsterdam, 1857 – 5mf – 9 – ne IDC [950]
THOMAS MUENZER IN ZWICKAU UND DIE "ZWICKAUER PROPHETEN" / Wappler, Paul – Zwickau: Firma Zwickauer Zeitung, 1908 – 1mf – us A.T.L.A. [240]
THOMAS MURNER UND DIE DEUTSCHE REFORMATION / Kawerau, Waldemar – Halle: Verein fuer Reformationsgeschichte, 1891. ([Schriften des Vereins fuer Reformationsgeschichte; Bd. 32]) – 1mf – us A.T.L.A. [240]
THOMAS MURNER UND DIE KIRCHE DES MITTELALTERS / Kawerau, Waldemar – Halle: Verein fuer Reformationsgeschichte, 1890. ([Schriften des Vereins fuer Reformationsgeschichte; Bd. 30]) – 1mf – us A.T.L.A. [240]
Thomas, Murray *see* LANGUAGE USE AMONG PUPILS IN BANDUNG, INDONESIA
Thomas Of Elmham *see* HISTORIA MONASTERII S. AUGUSTINI CANTUARIENSIS BY THOMAS OF ELMHAM, FORMERLY MONK AND TREASURER OF THAT FOUNDATION (RS8)
THOMAS OTWAY. WITH AN INTROD. AND NOTES BY THE HON. RODEN NOEL / Otway, Thomas – London: Unwin; New York: Scribner's, 1903. 392p – 1 – us U.W. Library [920]
Thomas, P J *see* INDEX OF ALL ESTATES IN PROBATE IN SAN FRANCISCO 1850-1888
THE THOMAS PENN PAPERS / Penn, Thomas; ed by Kilbourne, John D – (With guide) – 1972 – 10r – 1 – $850.00 – S1619 – us Scholarly Res [920]
THOMAS PLATTER AND THE EDUCATIONAL RENAISSANCE OF THE SIXTEENTH CENTURY / Monroe, Paul – New York: D. Appleton, 1904. (International education series; v57) – 1mf – us A.T.L.A. [940]
Thomas, PR *see* THE EFFECT OF PRE-COMPETITIVE PRACTICE ON THE ACTIVATION AND MOOD OF HIGH SCHOOL FOOTBALL PLAYERS
Thomas, R S *see* A COMPARISON OF THREE WARM-UP PROTOCOLS ON POWER OUTPUT IN THE WINGATE ANAEROBIC TEST
THOMAS' REGISTER – 1905- – 1 – us Primary [330]
Thomas, Robert Gibbes *see* WILLIAM MOULTRIE: ARMS AND THE MAN
Thomas, Tammy R *see* EFFECT OF SLIDE BOARD TRAINING AS A COMPONENT OF PRE-SEASON CONDITIONING ON CONCENTRIC AND ECCENTRIC QUADRICEPS PEAK TORQUE, VERTICAL JUMP HEIGHT, AND AGILITY
Thomas, Thomas *see* DICTIONARIUM LINGUAE LATINAE ET ANGLICANAE
THOMAS TORSTEN : ROMAN / Ahlers, Rudolf – Braunschweig: G Westermann, c1937 – 1r – 1 – us U.W. Library [830]
THOMAS T.U.P. CHARLTON'S REPORTS / Georgia. Supreme Court – (A Pre-NRS title) – 1v. 1805-1810 (all publ) – 4mf – 9 – $6.00 – LLMC 91-032 – us L.L.M.C. [340]
THOMAS VON KEMPEN, DER PREDIGER DER NACHFOLGE CHRISTI / Baehring, Bernhard – Berlin: H. Schultze, 1849 – 1mf – us A.T.L.A. [240]
Thomas, W Cave *see* THE CONFORMATION OF THE MATERIAL BY THE SPIRITUAL
Thomas Walsingam *see* YPODIGMA NEUSTRIE (CHRONIA..7)
Thomas Walsingham *see*
- GESTA ABBATUM MONASTERII S. ALBANI (CHRONIA..4)
- HISTORIA ANGLICANA (CHRONIA..1)

Thomas, William *see* PRINCIPAL RULES OF THE ITALIAN GRAMMAR
Thomas, William Hannibal *see* THE AMERICAN NEGRO
THOMAS WOLSEY : LEGATE AND REFORMER / Taunton, Ethelred L – London, New York: J. Lane, 1902 – 1mf – us A.T.L.A. [240]
Thomasio, J M *see* OPERA OMNIA
Thomasius *see* OPERA OMNIA
Thomasius, Christian *see*
- AUSERLESENE ANMERCKUNGEN UEBER ALLERHAND WICHTIGE MATERIEN UND SCHRIFTEN
- MONATSGESPRAECHE

Thomasius, J M *see* INSTITUTIONES THEOLOGICAE ANTIQUORUM PATRUM
THOMASON TRACTS – 22,000 items representing 80 percent of works published 1640-60 in England – 256r – 1 – $19,130 – us UMI [090]
Thomassin, B A *see* PEUPLEMENTS DES SEDIMENTS CORALLIENS DE LA REGION DE TULEAR (S.W. DE MADAGASCAR) ET LEUR INSERTION DANS LE CONTEXTE COTIER INDO-PACIFIQUE
Thome, S *see*
- O EQUADOR
- FLORA VON DEUTSCHLAND, OESTERREICH UND DER SCHWEIZ

THOMIST – (1985- . 5,6,9) – v1- . 1939- – 1 – us UMI [073]
Thompson *see* GRUNDY COUNTY DIRECTORY
Thompson, A C *see*
- DISCOURSE COMMEMORATIVE OF REV. RUFUS ANDERSON, D.D., LL.D.
- FUTURE PROBATION AND FOREIGN MISSIONS

Thompson, Abram Warren *see* THE LAW OF THE FARM.
Thompson, Albert Edward *see* A CENTURY OF JEWISH MISS[I]ONS
THOMPSON AND COOK'S SUPREME COURT REPORTS / New York. (State). Supreme Court – v1-6. 1873-75 (all publ) – 53mf – 9 – $79.00 – LLMC 80-008 – us L.L.M.C. [340]
Thompson, Augustus Charles *see*
- FOREIGN MISSIONS
- MORAVIAN MISSIONS
- MORNING HOURS IN PATMOS
- PROTESTANT MISSIONS

Thompson, Augustus Charles et al *see* MODERN APOSTLES OF MISSIONARY BYWAYS
Thompson, B *see* TWO STUDIES IN AFRICAN NUTRITION
Thompson, C Bertrand *see* THE CHURCHES AND THE WAGE EARNERS
Thompson, Charles L *see* THE PRESBYTERIANS
Thompson, Charles Nebeker *see* A TREATISE ON THE LAW OF BUILDING AND LOAN ASSOCIATIONS...2ND ED
THOMPSON CREEK BAPTIST CHURCH. CHESTERFIELD COUNTY. SOUTH CAROLINA : CHURCH RECORDS – 1955-1977 – 1 – 22.50 – us Baptist [240]
Thompson, David *see* THE CROSS OF JESUS, OR, HEAVEN ON EARTH TO ME
Thompson, E M *see*
- CHRONICON ANGLIAE (RS64)
- CONTINUATIO CHRONICARUM (RS93)
- CUSTOMARY OF THE BENEDICTINE MONASTERIES OF ST AUGUSTINE, CANTERBURY AND ST PETER, WESTMINSTER, VOL 1
- CUSTOMARY OF THE BENEDICTINE MONASTERIES OF ST AUGUSTINE, CANTERBURY AND ST PETER, WESTMINSTER, VOL. 2
- HANDBOOK OF GREEK AND LATIN PALAEOGRAPHY
- INTRODUCTION TO GREEK AND LATIN PALEOGRAPHY

Thompson, Ed Porter *see* HISTORY OF THE ORPHAN BRIGADE
Thompson, Edward Healy *see* THE UNITY OF THE EPISCOPATE
Thompson, Effie Freeman *see* METANOEO AND METAMELEI IN GREEK LITERATURE UNTIL 100 A.D.
Thompson, Elbert Nevius Sebring *see* ESSAYS ON MILTON
Thompson, Emmanuel *see* EL CONFLICTO DE ESPANA ANTE EL MUNDO CRISTIANO REPUBLICA, MONARQUIA, FASCISMO Y JUSTICIA DE UNA CAUSA
Thompson, Garrett William *see* AN INQUIRY INTO THE SOURCES OF CHARLES SEALSFIELD'S NOVEL MORTON, ODER, DIE GROSSE TOUR
Thompson, George *see* THOMPSON IN AFRICA: OR, AN ACCOUNT OF THE MISSIONARY LABORS, SUFFERINGS, TRAVELS, AND OBSERVATIONS...IN WESTERN AFRICA, AT THE MENDI MISSION
Thompson, Helen Hills Strong *see*
- SONGS IN THE NIGHT-WATCHES
- THE WOMAN QUESTION

Thompson, Hugh H *see* DIRECTORY OF THE CITY OF NEVADA AND GRASS VALLEY
Thompson, Hugh Miller *see*
- COPY
- MORE "COPY"
- THE WORLD AND THE KINGDOM
- THE WORLD AND THE LOGOS

THOMPSON IN AFRICA : OR, AN ACCOUNT OF THE MISSIONARY LABORS, SUFFERINGS, TRAVELS, AND OBSERVATIONS, OF GEORGE THOMPSON IN WESTERN AFRICA, AT THE MENDI MISSION – [2nd ed]. New York: [s.n.], 1852, c1851 – 1mf – 9 – 0-8370-6625-5 – 1986-0625 – us A.T.L.A. [920]
THOMPSON IN AFRICA: OR, AN ACCOUNT OF THE MISSIONARY LABORS, SUFFERINGS, TRAVELS, AND OBSERVATIONS...IN WESTERN AFRICA, AT THE MENDI MISSION / Thompson, George – 2nd ed. New York: Printed for the author, 1852.356p. Illus. Fold. map – 1 – us U.W. Library [910]
Thompson, J D *see* THE CHURCH THAT FOUND HERSELF
Thompson, Mrs. J Frank *see* HISTORY OF BEAVER CREEK BAPTIST CHURCH
Thompson, James *see*
- DIARIES
- THE WARS OF RELIGION IN FRANCE, 1559-1576

Thompson, John S D *see* DISCOURS SUR LA QUESTION RIEL, PRONONCE LE 22 MARS 1886 A LA CHAMBRE DES COMMUNES
Thompson, Joseph Parrish *see*
- CHRISTIANITY AND EMANCIPATION, OR, THE TEACHINGS AND THE INFLUENCE OF THE BIBLE AGAINST SLAVERY
- CHURCH AND STATE IN THE UNITED STATES
- THE EARLY WITNESSES, OR, PIETY AND PREACHING OF THE MIDDLE AGES
- MAN IN GENESIS AND IN GEOLOGY
- MEMOIR OF REV. DAVID TAPPAN STODDARD
- A MEMOIR OF THE LATE TIMOTHY DWIGHT
- THE MORAL UNITY OF THE HUMAN RACE
- SHALL OUR COMMON SCHOOLS BE DESTROYED?
- THE THEOLOGY OF CHRIST FROM HIS OWN WORDS
- THE WORKMAN

Thompson, Laura *see* 'LETTERS FROM FIJI, 1933-34'
Thompson, Maurice *see*
- THE ETHICS OF LITERARY ART
- HOOSIER MOSAICS

Thompson, Patrick *see* THE HISTORY OF THE NEGRO BAPTISTS IN MISSISSIPPI
Thompson, R C *see*
- A DICTIONARY OF ASSYRIAN CHEMISTRY AND GEOLOGY
- THE PRISMS OF ESARHADDON AND ASHURBANIPAL FOUND AT NINEVEH 1927 AND 1928
- THE SCULPTURES AND INSCRIPTIONS OF DARIUS 1, KING OF PERSIA, 548-485 BC

Thompson, R E *see* THE LATIN HYMN-WRITERS AND THEIR HYMNS
Thompson, Ralph Wardlaw *see* BRITISH FOREIGN MISSIONS, 1837-97
Thompson, Reginald Campbell *see* THE REPORTS OF THE MAGICIANS AND ASTROLOGERS OF NINEVEH AND BABYLON IN THE BRITISH MUSEUM
Thompson, Robert Ellis *see*
- THE HAND OF GOD IN AMERICAN HISTORY
- THE HISTORIC EPISCOPATE
- A HISTORY OF THE PRESBYTERIAN CHURCHES IN THE UNITED STATES

Thompson, Seymour Dwight *see*
- COMMENTARIES ON THE LAW OF NEGLIGENCE IN ALL RELATIONS.
- THE LAW OF ELECTRICITY
- A TREATISE ON HOMESTEAD AND EXEMPTION LAWS
- A TREATISE ON THE LAW OF TRIALS IN ACTIONS CIVIL AND CRIMINAL. 2D ED
- A TREATISE ON THE LIABILITY OF STOCKHOLDERS IN CORPORATIONS

Thompson, Stith *see* THE RETURN FROM THE DEAD IN POPULAR TALES AND BALLADS
Thompson, T H *see* OFFICIAL HISTORICAL ATLAS MAPS OF FRESNO COUNTY
Thompson, Thomas *see* TRAVELS AND VOYAGES
Thompson, W *see* CATALOGUE OF THE LAND AND FRESH-WATER MOLLUSCA OF IRELAND
Thompson & West *see* HISTORY OF NEVADA COUNTY
Thompson, William Goodrich *see*
- BRIEF-MAKING
- METHOD OF ANALYSIS AND USE OF SYMBOLS IN BRIEF-MAKING

THOMPSON'S BANK NOTE AND COMMERCIAL RECORDER *see* AMERICAN BANKER
THOMPSON'S COMPLEAT TUTOR FOR THE VIOLIN. TO WHICH IS ADDED A FAVORITE COLLECTION OF AIRS, MARCHES, MINUETS, SONG TUNES AND DUETS – London. BP-486 1 – 9 – ne IDC [780]
THOMPSON'S HYMN TO THE SEASONS / Barber, R of N – (Score) – London: Presto, 1785 – 1 – us Sibley [780]
THOMPSON'S MIRROR OF PARLIAMENT – Quebec: S Thompson, [1860] – 9 – cn C.I.H.M. [320]
THOMPSON'S MIRROR OF PARLIAMENT *see* LE MIROIR DU PARLEMENT
THOMPSON'S NATIONAL BANK CASES *see* NATIONAL BANK CASES
THOMPSON'S UNREPORTED CASES / Tennessee. Supreme Court – (A Pre-NRS title) – 1v. 1847-1869 (all publ) – 4mf – 9 – $6.00 – LLMC 91-038 – us L.L.M.C. [340]
Thoms, Craig S *see* THE WORKING MAN'S CHRIST
THOM'S OFFICIAL DUBLIN DIRECTORY – 1904 – 38mf – 9 – Ir£25.00 – ie Microforms [910]
Thomson, A T *see* MEMOIRS OF VISCOUNTESS SUNDON, MISTRESS OF THE ROBES TO QUEEN CAROLINE, CONSORT OF GEORGE 2; INCLUDING LETTERS FROM THE MOST CELEBRATED PEOPLE.
THOMSON BROS. BOOKSTORE MONTHLY – Vancouver: [s.n. 1882?-18– or 19–] – 9 – cn C.I.H.M. [020]
Thomson, C G *see*
- HYMENOPTERA SCANDINAVIAE
- OPUSCULA ENTOMOLOGICA
- SKANDINAVIENS HYMENOPTERA

Thomson, Charles *see* CHARLES THOMSON PAPERS
Thomson, Clara Linklater *see* GEORGE ELIOT
Thomson, Clement R *see* THOMSON-BAILE-STREANE GENEALOGY, MS VF/T
Thomson, Edward A *see*
- EVIDENCES OF REVEALED RELIGION
- THE FOUR EVANGELISTS

Thomson, Erik *see*
- BALTISCHE BIBLIOGRAPHIE
- GESCHICHTE DER DOMSCHULE ZU REVAL

Thomson, G M *see* THE FERNS AND FERN ALLIES OF NEW ZEALAND
Thomson, J C *see* SUPPRESSED POEMS OF ALFRED LORD TENNYSON, 1830-1862...
Thomson, James *see*
- THE CITY OF DREADFUL NIGHT
- LETTERS ON THE MORAL AND RELIGIOUS STATE OF SOUTH AMERICA
- SHELLEY
- THROUGH MASAI LAND
- A VOICE FROM THE NILE

Thomson, James H *see* LOUISIANA TODAY
Thomson, K S *see* ENGLISH LAW AND PRACTICE RELATING TO ESTATES OF PERSONS DYING DOMICILED ABROAD...
Thomson, Katherine Byerley *see* MEMOIRS OF THE JACOBITES OF 1715 AND 1745
Thomson, N *see* COLUMBIA AND THE UNITED STATES
Thomson, Peter G., Publisher *see* SOCIETY BLUE BOOK AND FAMILY DIRECTORY
Thomson, Richard *see* AN HISTORICAL ESSAY ON THE MAGNA CHARTA OF KING JOHN.
Thomson, Shirley P *see*
- CALIFORNIA CEMETRY INSCRIPTION SOURCES
- MISSOURI CEMETRY INSCRIPTION SOURCES

Thomson, T *see* FLORA INDICA
Thomson, T D *see* DOMASI COMMUNITY DEVELOPMENT SCHEME, 1949-54
Thomson, T R H *see*
- A NARRATIVE OF THE EXPEDITION TO THE RIVER NIGER IN 1841
- A NARRATIVE OF THE EXPEDITION TO THE RIVER NIGER IN 1841 UNDER THE COMMAND OF CAPTAIN H.D. TROTTER

Thomson, Thomas *see* THE RISE AND FALL OF PAPACY
Thomson, W Burns *see* A MEMOIR OF WILLIAM JACKSON ELMSLIE..., LATE MEDICAL MISSIONARY, C.M.S., KASHMIR
Thomson, W R *see* THE BURDEN OF THE LORD
Thomson, William *see* AIDS TO FAITH
Thomson, William Duncan *see* THE CHRISTIAN MIRACLES AND THE CONCLUSIONS OF SCIENCE
Thomson, William Hanna *see* THE PARABLES BY THE LAKE: THE PARABLES AND THEIR HOME
THOMSON-BAILE-STREANE GENEALOGY, MS VF/T / Thomson, Clement R – (Accounts of the histories of these Irish and English families, which immigrated to the American colonies, and the Thomson family's involvement in abolitionism, religion, and the Civil War) – Cadiz, Harrison, OH. 1600-1880 – 1r – 1 – us Western Res [920]
Thomssen, George Nicholas *see* SAMUEL HEBICH OF INDIA
THONINDUSTRIE-ZEITUNG – Berlin, Germany. -w. 1898-1901; 1904-1909. 19 1 2 reels – 1 – uk British Libr Newspaper [072]
Thonning, P *see* HERBARIUM
Thonstad, Tore *see* ANALYSING AND PROJECTING SCHOOL ENROLLMENT IN DEVELOPING COUNTRIES
Thopdschian, Hagob *see* POLITISCHE UND KIRCHENGESCHICHTE ARMENIENS UNTER ASOT 1. UND SMBAT 1.
Thor, George, Astromagus *see* AN EASIE INTRODUCTION TO THE PHILOSOPHERS MAGICAL GOLD; TO WHICH IS ADDED, ZOROASTER'S CANE; AS ALSO JOHN PONTANUS EPISTLE UPON THE MINERAL FIRE
DER THORA-AUSLEGE ARISTOBULOS (T.U.U. 5-86) / Walter, N – Berlin, 1964 – 6mf – 9 – ne Slangenburg [240]
Thorbecke, Franz *see* IM HOCHLAND VON MITTEL-KAMERUN
Thorburn, Lyndal *see* VOCAL MIMICRY IN THE SUPERB LYREBIRD
Thorburn, Thomas James *see* A CRITICAL EXAMINATION OF...EVIDENCES FOR THE DOCTRINE OF THE VIRGIN BIRTH
Thorell, T T T *see*
- DESCRIPTIVE CATALOGUE OF THE SPIDERS OF BURMA
- ON EUROPEAN SPIDERS
- RECENSIO CRITICA ARANEARUM SUECICARUM
- REMARKS ON SYNONYMS OF EUROPEAN SPIDERS
- SPINDLAR FRAN NIKOBERERNA OCH ANDRA DELAR AF SODRA ASIEN. INSAMLADE UNDER AREN 1845-1847

THORESBY SOCIETY – (Coll title: Publications of the English Record Societies, 1835-1972...) – v1-45. 1891-19567 – 209mf – 9 – £1,315.00 – uk Chadwyck [941]
The Thoresby Society *see* THE KIRKSTALL ABBEY CHRONICALS, VOL 62
Thoret, Jacques *see* ATIEKWA. UN VILLAGE DE COTE D'IVOIRE
Thoret, Jean-Claude *see* LES DJIMINI. ELEMENTS D'ORGANISATION SOCIALE
Thorland, William G *see*
- CURRENT TRENDS IN THE RECONSTRUCTION AND REHABILITATION OF THE ANTERIOR CRUCIATE LIGAMENT
- PHYSIOLOGICAL DISCRIMINATORS OF ROWING PERFORMANCE IN MALE, CLUB ROWERS

Thormaehlen, Anton *see* LENZBLUETHEN UND HERBSTBLAETTER
Thormann, Isabelle *see* WIRTSCHAFTSENGLISCH
A THORN IN THE FLESH / Broughton, Rhoda – British Fiction Archive: Unit 4 – 9 – uk Bell [830]
Thorn, J H *see* THE TRAVAIL OF A SOUL
Thornbury, Walter *see*
- THE LIFE OF J.M.W. TURNER, R.A.
- SONGS OF THE CAVALIERS AND ROUNDHEADS, JACOBITE BALLADS, ETC

Thorndike, Edward Lee *see* ANIMAL INTELLIGENCE; EXPERIMENTAL STUDIES
Thornell, Gustaf *see* STUDIA PANEGYRICA. COMMENTATIO ACADEMICA SCRIPSIT GUSTAVUS THORNELL
DAS THORNER BLUTGERICHT 1724 / Jacobi, Franz – Halle: Verein fuer Reformationsgeschichte, 1896. (Schriften des Vereins fuer Reformationsgeschichte; 13. Jahrg., Schrift 51 u. 52) 8250 240 – 1mf – us A.T.L.A. [943]
THORNHILL LIBERAL – Ontario, CN. 1975- – 2r per yr – 1 – Can$57.00r – cn Commonwealth Micro [072]
Thorning, Joseph Francis *see* MERCY AND JUSTICE
Thornton, Anna Maria (Brodeau) *see* DIARIES
Thornton, Douglas Montagu *see* AFRICA WAITING
Thornton, New Hampshire.Thornton Baptist Church *see* RECORDS
Thornton, New Hampshire.Thornton Free Will Baptist Church *see* RECORDS
Thornton, Samuel *see* SAMUEL THORNTON SEA ATLAS
Thornton, William Wheeler *see*
- THE LAW OF RAILROAD FENCES AND PRIVATE CROSSINGS.
- PAPERS

Thorold, John *see* EXTRACTS OF LETTERS RELATING TO METHODISTS AND MORAVIANS
THOROTON SOCIETY : RECORD SERIES – (Coll title: Publications of the English Record Societies, 1835-1972) – v1-17. 1903-56 – 45mf – 9 – £380.00 – uk Chadwyck [941]
THOROUGH-BASS MADE EASY / Pasquali, N – 1757 – 9 – us Sibley [780]
Thorp *see* EARLY HISTORY OF MICHIGAN
Thorpe, B *see*
- ANCIENT LAWS AND INSTITUTES OF ENGLAND
- ANGLO-SAXON CHRONICLE (RS23)

Thorpe, Benjamin *see* NORTHERN MYTHOLOGY, COMPRISING THE PRINCIPAL POPULAR TRADITIONS AND SUPERSTITIONS OF SCANDINAVIA, NORTH GERMANY, AND THE NETHERLANDS
Thorpe, C *see* BRITISH MARINE CONCHOLOGY
Thorpe, Francis F *see* CONSTITUTIONAL HISTORY OF THE AMERICAN PEOPLE
Thorpe, Francis N *see*
- A COURSE IN CIVIL GOVERNMENT
- FEDERAL AND STATE CONSTITUTIONS

Thorpe, Francis Newton *see*
- CONSTITUTIONAL HISTORY OF THE UNITED STATES, 1765-1895
- THE ESSENTIALS OF AMERICAN CONSTITUTIONAL LAW
- THE FEDERAL AND STATE CONSTITUTIONS, COLONIAL CHARTERS, AND OTHER ORGANIC LAWS OF THE STATE, TERRITORIES, AND COLONIES.
- THORPE'S CONSTITUTIONS

Thorpe, Patricia M *see* PALLIATIVE CARE

Thorpe, William G *see*
- MIDDLE TEMPLE TALK
- THE STILL LIFE OF THE MIDDLE TEMPLE

THORPE'S CONSTITUTIONS : FEDERAL AND STATE CONSTITUTIONS, COLONIAL CHARTERS, AND OTHER ORGANIC LAWS OF THE STATES, TERRITORIES AND COLONIES OF THE UNITED STATES / ed by Thorpe, Francis Newton – Washington: GPO. v1-7. 1909 – 49mf – 9 – $73.00 – LLMC 82-713 – us L.L.M.C. [323]

Thory, C A *see*
- PRODROME DE LA MONOGRAPHIE DES ESPECES ET VARIETES CONNUES DU GENRE ROSIER
- ROSA CANDOLLEANA, SEU DESCRIPTIO NOVAE SPECIEI GENERIS ROSAE
- ROSA REDUTEA, SEU DESCRIPTIO NOVAE SPECIEI GENERIS ROSAE

THOSE PERPLEXING ARGENTINES / Bruce, James – New York: Longmans, Green, 1953 – 1 – CSUXADH0382-B – us Hoover Inst Photo [306]

THOU ART THE MAN / Braddon, Mary Elizabeth – British Fiction Archive: Unit 5 – 9 – uk Bell [830]

THOU ART THE MAN / Douglas, George – Toronto: W. Briggs; Montreal: C. Coates; Halifax: S. Huestis, 1895. 02743. (Pre-1900 Canadiana) – 9 – cn C.I.H.M. [971]

Thou, Jacques A de *see* HISTOIRE DE MARTHE BROSSIER PRETENDUE POSSEDEE TIREE DU LATIN

THE THOUGHT OF BLAISE PASCAL / Molinier, Auguste – C. Kegan Paul, trans. London: G. Bell and Sons, 1905 – xv/356p – 1 – us U.W. Library [190]

THOUGHTS AND CONCLUSIONS OF A MAN OF YEARS: CONCERNING CHURCHES AND CHURCH CONNECTION / Carroll, John – Toronto: W. Briggs, 1879. 00491. (Pre-1900 Canadiana) – 9 – cn C.I.H.M. [240]

THOUGHTS BY THE WAY / Cox, Edward – Toronto?: s.n., 1886 (Toronto: C. Blackett Robinson). 00269. (Pre-1900 Canadiana) – 9 – cn C.I.H.M. [971]

THOUGHTS CONCERNING THE METHODISTS AND THE ESTABLISHED CLERGY / Croft, G – London, 1795 – 1mf – 9 – MP-592/1 – ne IDC [240]

THOUGHTS, CRITICAL AND PRACTICAL, ON THE BOOK OF DANIEL / Smith, Uriah – Battle Creek: Seventh-Day Adv., 1881. 1 fiche – 9 – us A.T.L.A. [240]

THE THOUGHTS OF THE EMPEROR / Marcus Aurelius, Emperor of Rome – Trans. by George Long. 2nd ed., rev. and corr. London: G. Bell, 1880. 216p – 1 – us U.W. Library [450]

THE THOUGHTS OF THE EMPEROR / Marcus Aurelius, Emperor of Rome – Trans. by George Long. Boston: Little, Brown, 1890 – 296p – 1 – us U.W. Library [450]

THOUGHTS ON DANCING OCCASIONED BY SOME LATE TRANSACTIONS AMONG THE PEOPLE CALLED METHODISTS / Davis, M – London, 1791 – 1mf – 9 – MP-574/1 – ne IDC [240]

THOUGHTS ON EDUCATION : SPEECHES AND SERMONS / Creighton, Mandell; ed by Creighton, Louise – London; New York: Longmans, Green, 1902 – 1mf – us A.T.L.A. [240]

THOUGHTS ON EXTEMPORE PREACHING / Tennent, Gilbert – c.1762 – 1 – $50.00 – us Presbyterian [240]

THOUGHTS ON HIGH THEMES: BEING A COLLECTION OF SERMONS FROM THE MSS. OF THE LATE REV. JAMES GEORGE / George, James – Toronto: J. Campbell, 1874. 03327. (Pre-1900 Canadiana) – 9 – cn C.I.H.M. [240]

THOUGHTS ON MAN, HIS NATURE, PRODUCTIONS, AND DISCOVERIES : INTERSPERSED WITH SOME PARTICULARS RESPECTING THE AUTHOR / Godwin, William – London: Effingham Wilson, 1831 – 1 roll – 1 – 1-55879-323-2 – uk Libr Preservation [120]

THOUGHTS ON MISSIONS AND BIOGRAPHIES OF BAPTIST PREACHERS / Taylor, John – 1820 – 1 – 5.00 – us Baptist [240]

THOUGHTS ON OUTLINE, SCULPTURE, AND THE SYSTEM THAT GUIDED THE ANCIENT ARTISTS IN COMPOSING THEIR FIGURES AND GROUPES / Cumberland, G – O-1146 1. 1796 – 9 – ne IDC [930]

THOUGHTS ON PHILOSOPHY AND THEOLOGY / Abbott, Albert Holden – Two essays read before the Philosophical Society of the University of Toronto and the Knox College Literary and Theological Society respectively. 1896. 00004. (Pre-1900 Canadiana) – 9 – cn C.I.H.M. [100]

THOUGHTS ON RECENT SCIENTIFIC CONCLUSIONS: AND THEIR RELATION TO RELIGION – London: Strahan, 1872. 1 fiche – 9 – us A.T.L.A. [240]

THOUGHTS ON RELIGION / Romanes, George John; ed by Gore, Charles – 3rd ed. Chicago: Open Court, 1897 – 1mf – 9 – 0-8370-4960-1 – 1985-2960 – us A.T.L.A. [210]

THOUGHTS ON REVELATION : WITH SPECIAL REFERENCE TO THE PRESENT TIME / Campbell, John McLeod – 2nd ed. London:Macmillan, 1874 – 1mf – 9 – 0-8370-2576-1 – 1985-0576 – us A.T.L.A. [210]

THOUGHTS ON THE DEATH OF LITTLE CHILDREN / Prime, Samuel Irenaeus – New York: A.D.F. Randolph, 1852 – 1mf – us A.T.L.A. [240]

THOUGHTS ON THE HOLY GOSPELS : HOW THEY CAME TO BE IN MANNER AND FORM AS THEY ARE / Upham, Francis William – (Includes index) – New York: Phillips & Hunt; Cincinnati: Walden & Stowe, 1881 – 1mf – 9 – 0-8370-9323-6 – 1986-3323 – us A.T.L.A. [220]

THOUGHTS ON THE ORIGIN AND ON THE MOST RATIONAL AND NATURAL METHOD OF TEACHING THE LANGUAGES / Williams, John – 1783. 77p. (English Linguistics Series 1500-1800) – 9 – us UMI [400]

THOUGHTS...IMPROVING THE CONDITION OF THE SLAVES... / Clarkson, T – London, 1823 – 1mf – 1 – ILM-1219/1 – ne IDC [327]

Thouret, Michel Augustin *see* RECHERCHES ET DOUTES SUR LE MAGNETISME ANIMAL

THOZHILALI – Trichur, India. Jul-Sept 1966 – 1r – 1 – us L of C Photodup [072]

Thrall, Homer S *see* PICTORIAL HISTORY OF TEXAS

THREAT OF MODERN WARFARE TO MAN AND HIS ENVIRONMENT : AN ANNOTATED BIBLIOGRAPHY – 1979 – 9 – 92-3-101608-3 – fr UNESCO [320]

THE THREE AND THE DEUCE: A MUSICAL ENTERTAINMENT. / Storace, Stephen – (Vocal score). 1795 – 9 – us Sibley [780]

THREE BOOKS CONCERNING THE CHURCH / Loehe, Wilhelm – Reading, Pa.: Pilger, 1908 – 1mf – us A.T.L.A. [240]

THREE BOOKS OF ACCULT PHILOSOPHY / Agippa von Nettesheim, Heinrich Cornelius – 1651. Translated out of Latin into English by J. F. London. Elias Ashmole's copy, with his signature and notes – 1 – us U.W. Library [130]

THREE BOOKS ON FISHING (1599-1659) – Associated with the Complete angler (1653) by Izaak Walton – 9 – 15.00 – us Scholars' Facs [840]

THREE CENTURIES OF ENGLISH AND AMERICAN PLAYS, 1500-1830 – Over 5000 plays. Also sold in units – 3,9 – us Readex [820]

THE THREE CHANCELLORS, OR, SKETCHES OF THE LIVES OF WILLIAM OF WYKEHAM, WILLIAM OF WAYNFLETE, AND SIR THOMAS MORE / Drane, Augusta Theodosia – London: Burns and Lambert, [1860?] – 1mf – us A.T.L.A. [240]

THE THREE COLLECTIONS: HERSTORY; WOMEN AND HEALTH-MENTAL HEALTH; WOMEN AND LAW / Women's History Research Center – (Herstory. 1956-74. 90 reels. May be ordered separately. Guide available. $44.00r silver. $3,790.00 silver; Women and Health-Mental Health. 1968-74. 14 reels. May be ordered separately. Guide available. $44.00r silver. $604.00 silver; Women and Law. 1968-74. 40 reels. May be ordered separately. Guide available. $44.00r silver. $1,738.00 silver) – 1 – $5,852.00 – us Women's Hist [305]

THREE CORONATION ORDERS / Wickham Legg, J – 1900 – 4mf – 8 – Dfl19.00 – ne Slangenburg [390]

THREE DIVERTIMENTOS (FOR THE PIANO) / Carr, Benjamin – (No. 18 of the Musical Journal for the Piano-forte). Baltimore: J. Carr 1800. MUSIC 123, Item 8 – 1 – us L of C Photodup [780]

THREE ERAS OF REVIVALS IN THE UNITED STATES / Marvin, Abijah Perkins – (Bibliotheca sacra, v. 16, no. 62, April 1859, p. 279-301) – 9 – us A.T.L.A. [240]

THREE EXACT PIECES.. / Fiorvanti, Leonardo – London, 1652 – 1 – us U.W. Library [880]

THREE FACILES SONATINAS POUR LE CLAVECIN AVEC VIOLON AD LIB / Wanhal, J B – (Parts) – Vienne: Artaria & Co, 182- – 1 – us Sibley [780]

THREE FAVORITE SYMPHONIES / Bach, Johann Christian – In eight parts. Op. 21 (Op. 9). 178? – 9 – us Sibley [780]

THREE FEATHERS: A NOVEL / Black, William – British Fiction Archive: Unit 4 – 9 – uk Bell [830]

THREE FORKS OF BACON CREEK BAPTIST CHURCH. LYNN ASSOCIATION. KENTUCKY : CHURCH RECORDS – 1818-1968 – 1 – $64.98 – us Baptist [240]

THREE GREAT CENTURIES OF VENETIAN GLASS – 1958. Introd. by Paul N. Perrot. 116p, 133 illus. 3 fiche. Fiche no. 388 – 9 – $6.25 – us Corning Mus [700]

THREE GREAT PROTESTS AGAINST TRIAL OF CIVILIANS BY MILITARY COMMISSIONS / Robinson, Ira Ellsworth – Charleston, W. Va.: Kanawha 19- . 79 1p. LL-26 – 1 – us L of C Photodup [340]

THREE GREAT TEACHERS OF OUR OWN TIME : BEING AN ATTEMPT TO DEDUCE THE SPIRIT AND PURPOSE ANIMATING CARLYLE, TENNYSON, AND RUSKIN / Japp, Alexander Hay – London: Smith, Elder, 1865 – 1 roll – 1 – 1-55879-607-X – uk Libr Preservation [420]

THREE GUARDIANS OF SUPERNATURAL RELIGION : THE BEDELL LECTURES FOR 1899 / Dix, Morgan – New York: E.S. Gorham, 1901 – 1mf – us A.T.L.A. [210]

THREE HUNDRED YEARS OF THE EPISCOPAL CHURCH IN AMERICA / Hodges, George – Philadelphia: Published for the Missionary Thank Offering Committee by G.W. Jacobs, 1906 – 1mf – us A.T.L.A. [240]

THREE IRISH LITERARY AND DRAMATIC JOURNALS – 1899-1939 – 1r – 1 – us Ross [420]

THREE LECTURES ON THE CHURCH OF SCOTLAND : WITH ESPECIAL REFERENCE TO THE DEAN OF WESTMINSTER'S RECENT COURSE ON THAT SUBJECT / Rainy, Robert – Edinburgh: J. Maclaren, 1872 – 1mf – us A.T.L.A. [240]

THREE LETTERS TO ELLEN KEY / Rilke, Clara – 295 2. (Mss). Mar. 22, 1904-Oct. 1904 – 8 – ne IDC [920]

THREE LETTERS TO THE REV. MR. WESLEY, CONTAINING REMARKS ON A PIECE LATELY PUBLISHED... / Kingsford, W – Canterbury, 1789 – 1mf – 9 – MP-562/1 – ne IDC [240]

THREE LETTERS...TO THE REV. J. FLETCHER, VICAR OF MADELEY, IN THE YEAR 1773, SETTING FORTH MR. HILL'S REASONS FOR DECLINING ANY FURTHER CONTROVERSY RELATIVE TO MR. WESLEY'S PRINCIPLES / Hill, Richard – Shrewsbury, [1774] – 1mf – 9 – MP-492/1 – ne IDC [240]

THREE LISTS OF BIBLE-TRANSLATIONS ACTUALLY ACCOMPLISHED : CORRECTED UP TO AUG 1, 1890: 1. ALPHABETICAL, 2. GEOGRAPHICAL, 3. LINGUISTIC / Cust, Robert Needham – (Includes index) – London: Elliot Stock, 1890 – 1mf – 9 – 0-8370-9135-7 – 1986-3135 – us A.T.L.A. [220]

THREE MARTYRS OF THE NINETEENTH CENTURY / Charles, Elizabeth Rundle – Studies from the lives of Livingstone, Gordon, and Patteson...1886 – 1 – us A.T.L.A. [920]

THREE MEMOIRS ON IRIDECTOMY IN CERTAIN FORMS OF IRITIS, CHOROIDITIS AND GLAUCOMA / Graefe, A von – London, 1859 – 3mf – 9 – ne IDC [617]

THREE MONTHS OF TRUCE ON JAVA AND SUMATRA / United Nations. Security Council. Representative from the Netherlands – Documents submitted in the period 17 Jan. 1948 up to 30 April 1948. SE 12,162 1. 1948? – 9 – ne IDC [950]

THE THREE MRS. JUDSONS: THE CELEBRATED FEMALE MISSIONARIES / Hartley, Cecil B – 9 – us A.T.L.A. [240]

THREE NEEDED REFORMS IN CRIMINAL PROCEDURE: AN ADDRESS BEFORE THE ILLINOIS STATES ATTORNEYS' ASSOCIATION AT CHICAGO, DECEMBER 28TH, 1915 / Harker, Oliver Albert – Urbana: University of Illinois 1916. 14p. LL-545 – 1 – us L of C Photodup [340]

THREE ORIGINAL DUETTS FOR TWO PERFORMERS ON THE PIANO-FORTE OR HARPSICHORD / Pleyel, Ignaz J – Op. 20. ca.1790 – 9 – us Sibley [780]

THREE PAMPHLETS / Meulen, Henry – y monetary reform proposals; free banking; Individualist anarchism. Also: the soul of man under socialism by Oscar Wilde. 1 fiche – 9 – 1.00f – at Libertarian Micro [320]

THE THREE PERILS OF WOMAN : OR, LOVE, LEASING, AND JEALOUSY, A SERIES OF DOMESTIC SCOTTISH TALES / Hogg, James – London: Longman, Hurst, Rees, Orme, Brown, and Green, 1823 – 2 rolls – 1 – 1-55879-132-9 – uk Libr Preservation [830]

THREE PERSIAN DIALECTS / Lambton, A K S – 1938 – 1 – uk Microform Academic [470]

THREE PRIMERS PUT FORTH IN THE REIGN OF HENRY 8TH / Burton, E – Oxford, 1834 – 8mf – 8 – Dfl30.00 – ne Slangenburg [240]

THE THREE PROPHETIC DAYS OF MATTHEW 12:40 OR JESUS AND JONAS / Hailey, O L – 1 – 5.00 – us Baptist [240]

THREE QUARTETTS FOR FLUTE, VIOLIN, TENOR, AND VIOLINCELLO / Viotti, Giovanni B – op. 22. 1805? – 9 – us Sibley [780]

THREE QUATUORS CONCERTANTES A UN VIOLON, DEUX ALTO, ET VIOLONCELLO... BOOK 1 [-2] / Stamitz, K – (8 pts) – London: printed and sold by J Bland No 45 Holborn, [ca 1793] – 1 – us Sibley [780]

THREE REASONS WHY I AM A BAPTIST / Pendleton, J M – 1856 – 1 – 7.77 – us Baptist [240]

THREE RONDOS FOR THE PIANO FORTE OR HARPSICHORD / Brown, William – Philadelphia, The Author 1787. MUSIC 3082, Item 1 – 1 – us L of C Photodup [780]

THE THREE RYLANDS: A HUNDRED YEARS OF VARIOUS CHRISTIAN SERVICE / Culross, James – With intro. by W. Ryland D. Atkins. 1897 – 1 – 5.00 – us Baptist [240]

THREE SISTERS – Barlow, OR. -w. 16 Jun 1892-9 Jul 1896. 1 roll – 1 – us U.O. Library [071]

THREE SONATAS FOR THE PIANO FORTE, OPUS 5 / Hewitt, James – New York: Printed for the Author 1796. MUSIC 123, Item 5 – 1 – us L of C Photodup [780]

THREE SONATAS FOR THE PIANOFORTE WITH OR WITHOUT THE ADDITIONAL KEYS AND AN ACCOMPANYMENT FOR A FLUTE OR A VIOLIN / Mazzinghi, J – London: G. Goulding – 1 – us Sibley [780]

THREE SONATINAS, OP. 14 / Kambra, K – London: Bland and Weller, 179- – 1 – us Sibley [780]

THREE TRACTS RELATIVE TO SPANISH AND PORTUGUEZE AFFAIRS ... / Bentham, J – London, 1821 – 1mf – 9 – ILM-2550/1 – ne IDC [327]

THE THREE TRIBES HERALD – 1960-79.(American Indian Periodicals in the Princeton University Library). 6 fiches – 9 – $45.00 – us UPA [073]

THREE VIEWS OF THE PUBLIC SCHOOL QUESTION / Wylie, David Gourley – Philadelphia: MacCalla, [1890?] – 1mf – 9 – 0-8370-8638-8 – 1986-2638 – us A.T.L.A. [370]

THREE VISITS TO MADAGASCAR DURING THE YEARS 1853,1854-1856.. / Ellis, William – Illus. by woodcuts from photos. New York: Harper & Brothers, 1859. xv, 514p. Plates, ports., map – 1 – us U.W. Library [910]

THE THREE VOYAGES.. / Frobisher, M – N 214. 1867 – 9 – ne IDC [910]

THE THREE WAYFARERS / Hardy, Thomas – 1893 – 9 – 5.00 – us Scholars' Facs [830]

THREE YEAR DEVELOPMENT PLAN 1973-1975 / Jordan. National Planning Council – Amman. 1972. BD-2023 1 – 9 – ne IDC [956]

THREE YEAR DEVELOPMENT PLANS, 1972-1975. FIRST YEAR DEVELOPMENT BUDGET, 1972-1973 / Libya. Ministry of Planning. Development Plans. 1972-1975 – 1972? BNE-714 1 – 9 – ne IDC [956]

THREE YEAR INVESTMENT AND DEVELOPMENT PLAN (1975 TO 1977) / Tanzania. National Development Corporation – BD-1855 1 – 9 – ne IDC [338]

THE THREE YEAR PLAN (1962-1965) / Nepal. National Planning Council – Kathmandu. 1963. BD-133 1 – 9 – ne IDC [338]

THREE YEAR PLAN, 1965-1967 / Morocco. Delegation Generale a la Promotion Nationale et au Plan – 1965. BNE-3030 1 – 9 – ne IDC [338]

THREE YEAR PLAN, DEPT. OF AGRICULTURE / Indonesia. Kementerian Pertanian – SE-11,540 1. 1960 – 9 – ne IDC [630]

THREE YEAR PLAN FOR ECONOMIC AND SOCIAL DEVELOPMENT, 1963-65 / Brazil. Presidencia de Republica – Rio de Janeiro. 1962. BD-618 1 – 9 – ne IDC [338]

THREE YEARS OF ARCTIC SERVICE / Greeley, A W – BN 231 2. 2 v. 1886 – 8 – ne IDC [910]

THREE YEARS OF ECONOMIC AND TECHNICAL COOPERATION / U. S. Operations Mission to Morocco – 1960. BNE-3106 1 – 9 – ne IDC [338]

THREE YEARS OF EXTENSION WORK IN AGRICULTURE AND HOME ECONOMICS IN VIRGINIA / Virginia. Polytechnic Institute. Extension Division – 2mf – 9 – us Spaulding [630]

THREE YEARS OF STRUGGLE IN SPAIN, 1936-39; THE SPANISH REVOLUTIONARY UNIONS SPEAK – London, 1939. Fiche W1227. (Blodgett Collection of Spanish Civil War Pamphlets) – 9 – us H.U. College Libr [946]

THREE-DIMENSIONAL KINEMATIC AND KINETIC ANALYSIS OF TWO COMMON KICKING TECHNIQUES IN SOCCER / Levanon, Jacob – Indiana University, 1995 – 2mf – 9 – $8.00 – PE3607 – us Microform Publ [612]

THE THREEFOLD FELLOWSHIP AND THE THREEFOLD ASSURANCE : AN ESSAY IN TWO PARTS / Palmer, Benjamin Morgan – Richmond, VA: Presbyterian Committee of Publication, c1902 – 1mf – 9 – 0-8370-3956-8 – 1985-1956 – us A.T.L.A. [210]

THE THREEFOLD GRACE OF THE HOLY TRINITY / Egar, John Hodson – Philadelphia: J B Lippincott, 1870 – 1mf – 9 – 0-8370-3686-0 – 1985-1686 – us A.T.L.A. [240]

THREEPENNY REVIEW – v.1-. 1980- – 1,5,6,9 – us UMI [410]

THREE-SELF MOVEMENT (CCC304) = SUO WEI SAN-TZU YUN-TUNG / Wang, Chang-Chih – (In Chinese) – [s.l: s.n], 1952 – 1r – 1 – 1984-6643 – us A.T.L.A. [180]

THREE-YEAR ECONOMIC DEVELOPMENT PLAN (1960-1962) / Korea. South. Economic Development Council – D-1113 1. 1960 – 9 – ne IDC [338]

THREE-YEAR PRODUCTION PROGRAM(FY 1957-1959). LOCSIN, SENATOR JOSE C. IN: NATIONAL ECONOMIC COUNCIL / Philippines – Five-Year Economic and Social Development Program for FY 1957-1961. Manila. 1957. BD-1731 1 – 9 – ne IDC [338]

THREE-YEAR PROGRAM OF ECONOMIC AND SOCIAL DEVELOPMENT (FY 1959-60 TO FY 1961-62) / Philippines. National Economic Council – Manila. 1959 – 9 – ne IDC [338]

THRENODIARVM SANCTAE CRVCIS SALUTIFERAM PASSIONIS D.N.I.C. RECORDATIONEM, CONTINVATIO HISTORICA... / Besler, Samuel – Vratislaviae ex officina typographica Baumanniana, [1612] – 1 – us Sibley [780]

THRESHING RECORDS / Blymer and Sons (Hancock County, Ohio) – 1894-1912 – 1r – 1 – $32.50r – us Archival [978]

THRESOR DE LA LANGUE FRANCOYSE / Nicot, J – 1606 – 9 – fr I.C.S. [440]

THRESOR DE L'ELOQUENCE FRANCOYSE / Behourt, J – 1619 – 9 – fr I.C.S. [440]

THRESOR DE L'HISTOIRE DES LANGUES DE CEST UNIVERS / Duret, C – 1613 – 9 – fr I.C.S. [400]

LE THRESOR DES PARTERRES DE L'UNIVERS / Loris, D – Geneve: E. Gamonet, 1629. 200 pl. (Architecture Series) – 9 – fr Hachette [720]

THRESOR DES TROIS LANGUES, ESPAGNOLE, FRANCOISE ET ITALIENNE / Oudin, C – 1627 – 9 – fr I.C.S. [440]

THRESOR DES TROIS LANGUES, FRANCOISE, ITALIENNE, ET ESPAGNOLLE / Victor, H – 1609 – 9 – fr I.C.S. [440]

THRIFT / Smiles, Samuel – London: John Murray, 1875. xi,384p – 1 – us U.W. Library [336]

THRILLING AND INSTRUCTIVE DEVELOPMENTS : AN EXPERIENCE OF FIFTEEN YEARS AS ROMAN CATHOLIC CLERGYMAN AND PRIEST / Czechowski, Michael Belina – Boston: M B Czechowski, 1862 – 1mf – 9 – 0-8370-8732-5 – 1986-2732 – us A.T.L.A. [920]

THRILLING FACTS FROM MISSIONARY FIELDS / Uncle Josephus – 1853 – 1 – 15.89 – us Baptist [240]

Throgmorton, W P *see* HISTORY OF FRANKLIN ASSOCIATION (ILLINOIS) OF UNITED BAPTISTS

THROMBOSIS RESEARCH – v1- 1972- – 5,6,9 – us UMI [610]

THE THRONE OF ELOQUENCE: GREAT PREACHERS, ANCIENT AND MODERN / Hood, Edwin Paxton – 1885 – 1 – us A.T.L.A. [240]

THE THRONE ROOM OF MERENPTAH / Fisher, Clarence S – University of Pennsylvania Museum Journal: Mar 1921 – 9 – $10.00 – us I.R.C. [930]

Throop, James Addison *see* ANCESTRAL CHARTS OF GEORGE ADDISON THROOP, DEBORAH GOLDSMITH

Throop, Montgomery Hunt, 1827-92 *see* A TREATISE ON THE VALIDITY OF VERBAL AGREEMENTS.

THROUGH A GLASS, DARKLY : FUNCTIONAL ILLITERACY IN INDUSTRIALIZED COUNTRIES / Velis, Jean-Pierre – 1990 – 137p – 9 – 92-3-102651-8 – fr UNESCO [360]

THROUGH CANADA IN 1878 / Ewen, Robert – Hawick Scotland: "Express" Office, 1878?. 05494. (Pre-1900 Canadiana) – 9 – cn C.I.H.M. [910]

THROUGH CHRIST TO GOD : A STUDY IN SCIENTIFIC THEOLOGY / Beet, Joseph Agar – (Includes general index) – 4th ed. London:Hodder and Stoughton, 1901 – 1mf – 9 – 0-8370-3070-6 – 1985-1070 – us A.T.L.A. [240]

THROUGH CITIES AND PRAIRIE LANDS: SKETCHES OF AN AMERICAN TOUR / Hardy, Mary Anne Duffus – London: Chapman and Hall, 1881. 05362. (Pre-1900 Canadiana) – 9 – cn C.I.H.M. [910]

THROUGH EVOLUTION TO THE LIVING GOD / Cohu, J R – Oxford: J. Parker, 1912 – 1mf – us A.T.L.A. [240]

THROUGH JAPANESE EYES / ed by Tolischus, Otto David – New York: Reynal & Hitchcock, 1945 – 1 – us U.W. Library [950]

THROUGH MASAI LAND / Thomson, James – Rev. ed. London. 1895. BA-351 2 – 8 – ne IDC [960]

THROUGH NATURE TO GOD / Fiske, John – Boston: Houghton, Mifflin, 1899.1 fiche – 9 – us A.T.L.A. [240]

THROUGH NIGHT TO LIGHT : A NOVEL / Spielhagen, Friedrich – Rev ed. New York: H Holt, 1978 – 1r – 1 – us U.W. Library [830]

THROUGH SCIENCE TO FAITH / Smyth, Newman – New York: Charles Scribner, 1902. 1 fiche – 9 – us A.T.L.A. [240]

THROUGH SCYLLA AND CHARYBDIS : OR, THE OLD THEOLOGY AND THE NEW / Tyrrell, George – (Includes bibliographical references) – London; New York: Longmans, Green, 1907 – 1mf – 9 – 0-8370-8478-4 – 1986-2478 – us A.T.L.A. [240]

THROUGH THE BARREN GROUND OF NORTH-EASTERN CANADA TO THE ARCTIC COAST / Hanbury, D T – BN 239 2. 1903 – 8 – ne IDC [910]

THROUGH THE DARK CONTINENT : OR, THE SOURCES OF THE NILE, AROUND THE GREAT LAKES OF EQUATORIAL AFRICA, AND DOWN THE LIVINGSTONE RIVER TO THE ATLANTIC OCEAN / Stanley, Henry Morton – London. 2v. 1878 – 1r – 1 – us Ross [960]

THROUGH THE DARK CONTINENT / Stanley, Henry Morton – A 159 2. 2 v. 1878 – 8 – ne IDC [910]

THROUGH THE DARK CONTINENT / Stanley, Henry Morton – New York, 1878 – 1 – us Res Libr [960]

THROUGH THE ETERNAL SPIRIT : A BIBLICAL STUDY ON THE HOLY GHOST / Cumming, James Elder – (Includes indexes) – Chicago:Fleming H. Revell, c1896 – 1mf – 9 – 0-8370-2786-1 – 1985-0786 – us A.T.L.A. [220]

THROUGH THE GOLD-FIELDS OF ALASKA TO BERING STRAITS / De Windt, Harry – London: Chatto & Windus, 1898. 02653. (Pre-1900 Canadiana) – 9 – cn C.I.H.M. [910]

THROUGH TWO DECADES / Wolff, Theodor – E.W. Dickes, trans. xiv,324p. London: W. Heinemann, (1936) – 1 – us U.W. Library [943]

THROUGH UGANDA TO MOUNT ELGON / Purvis, John Bremner – (Includes index) – New York: American Tract Society, [1909] – 1mf – 9 – 0-8370-6770-7 – 1986-0770 – us A.T.L.A. [960]

THRU THE JOURNAL FOR EMPLOYMENT AND TRAINING PROFESSIONALS – v. 1-. 1979$ – 1,5,6,9 – us UMI [650]

Thrupp, Joseph Francis *see* THE SONG OF SONGS: A REVISED TRANSLATION WITH INTRODUCTION AND COMMENTARY

Thuanus, Iac. Aug. *see* HISTORIARUM SUI TEMPORIS AB ANNO DOMINI 1543 USQUE AD ANNUM 1607 LIBRI 138

Thudichum, Friedrich *see* DIE WAHREN LEHREN JESU

THUDO HANOI – [Hanoi: s.n., jul-sep 1967; dec 29 1967-jan 25 1968 – 1r – 1 – us Res Libr [072]

Thuemen, F K A von *see*
- FUNGI POMICOLI
- DIE PILZE DER OBSTGEWAECHSE
- DIE PILZE DES WEINSTOCKES

Thuemmler, Curt *see* ZUM VATER UNSER HEINRICHS VON KROLEWIZ

Thuerheim, A *see* BRIEFE DES GRAFEN MERCY-ARGENTEAU...

THUERINGENS KOENIGSHAUS : SEIN FLUCH UND FALL, ERZAEHLENDES GEDICHT IN SECHS GESAENGEN, AUS DEM NACHLASSE DES DICHTERS / Bechstein, Ludwig – (Includes bibliographical references) – Leipzig: Wigand, 1865 – 1 – us U.W. Library [890]

THUERINGER GAUZEITUNG *see* DER DEUTSCHE AAR

THUERINGER GAUZEITUNG-DER NATIONALSOZIALIST *see*
- DER DEUTSCHE AAR
- MITTELDEUTSCHE ZEITUNG

THUERINGER NEUESTE NACHRICHTEN – Weimar, East Germany. Aug 1954-12 May 1990 – 59r – 1 – gw Mikrofilm [072]

THUERINGER RAETHSEL UND CHARADEN / Moebius, Paul – 1881 – 1 – us I.U. Libraries [390]

THUERINGER TAGEBLATT – Weimar, East Germany. 1955-1990 – 71r – 1 – gw Mikrofilm [072]

THUERINGER TAGEBUCH : 66. AUFL. STUTTGART: GREINER UND PFEIFFER, [19–?] / Lienhard, Friedrich – (Includes bibliographical references) – 1r – 1 – us U.W. Library [910]

THUERINGER VOLK – Weimar, Gera. Apr 1946-47 – 2r – 1 – DM150.00 – gw Mikro Press [072]

THUERINGER VOLKSZEITUNG – Hildburghausen, Weimar. Nov 1945-Apr 1946 – 1r – 1 – DM840.00 – gw Mikro Press [072]

THUERINGER VOLKSZEITUNG – Hildburghausen-Weimar, Germany. 17 Nov 1945-6 Apr 1946 (incomplete) – 1 – gw Mikrofilm [072]

THUERINGISCHE LANDESZEITUNG – Weimar, 1946 – 1r – 1 – DM80.00 – gw Mikro Press [072]

THUERINGISCHE LANDESZEITUNG : WEIMARER TAGESPOST – Weimar, East Germany. 1992- – 6r per yr – 1 – gw Mikrofilm [072]

THUERINGISCHE STAATSZEITUNG *see* DER DEUTSCHE AAR

Thuillier, J L *see* LA FLORE DES ENVIRONS DE PARIS

THULE EXPEDITION, 5TH *see*
- IGLULIK AND CARIBOU ESKIMO TEXTS
- INTELLECTUAL CULTURE OF THE COPPER ESKIMO
- INTELLECTUAL CULTURE OF THE IGLULIK ESKIMOS
- THE NETSILIK ESKIMOS
- OBSERVATIONS ON THE INTELLECTUAL CULTURE OF THE CARIBOU ESKIMOS
- PRELIMINARY REPORT OF THE FIFTH THULE EXPEDITION

Thum, Rudolf *see* MENSCH UND CHRIST: DREI ABHANDLUNGEN

Thumb, Albert *see* DIE GRIECHISCHE SPRACHE IM ZEITALTER DES HELLENISMUS

Thun, Alphons *see* DIE INDUSTRIE AM NIEDERRHEIN BAND 2

Thunberg, C P *see*
- AMPELIS
- DISSERTATIO MEDICA INAUGURALIS DE CARYOPHYLLIS AROMATICIS
- DISSERTATIONES ACADEMICAE UPSALIAE HABITAE
- DISSERTATIONES BOTANICAE
- FAUNA BRASILIENSIS, QUAM. PRAESIDE C. P. THUNBERG
- FAUNA CAYANENSIS
- FAUNA CHINENSIS
- FAUNA JAPONICA CONTINUATIO
- FLORA CAPENSIS
- FLORA CAPENSIS, SISTENS PLANTAS
- FLORA JAPONICA
- HERBARIUM
- HORTI UPSALIENSIS PLANTAE CULTAE 1780-1800
- ICONES PLANTARUM JAPONICARUM
- NOVA GENERA PLANTARUM
- PLANTARUM BRASILIENSIUM
- PRODROMUS PLANTARUM CAPENSIUM, QUAS IN PROMONTORIO BONAE SPEI AFRICES, ANNIS 1772-1775 COLLEGIT
- VOYAGES AU JAPON

Thunberg, Charles-Pierre *see* VOYAGE EN AFRIQUE ET EN ASIE, PRINCIPALEMENT AU JAPON, PENDANT LES ANNEES 1770-1779

THUNBERG CORRESPONDENCE / Uppsala University Library, Stockholm – (A-HJO available on microfiche) – 440mf – 9 – ne IDC [580]

THUNDER – British Guyana. 1967- – 1 – us UMI [072]

THUNDER BAY HISTORICAL SOCIETY PAPERS AND ANNUAL REPORTS : 1908-1928, 1967 – (Includes index in mf. Index by F Brent Scollie also available separately in paper Can$12.00 ISBN: 0-920119-24-7) – Thunder Bay Historical Museum Society, 1908-28, 1967 (mf ed 1996) – 23mf – 9 – Can$15.00 – cn Thunder Bay [910]

THE THUNDERBOLT / Canadian Union of Fascists – Official Organ. v1,no.4-v2,no.1. 20 Jul 1937-Jan 1938 – 1 – 45.00 – cn McLaren [320]

THE THUNDERBOLT : AN EPISODE IN THE HISTORY OF A PROVINCIAL FAMILY. IN FOUR ACTS / Pinero, Arthur Wing – London: W. Heinemann, 1909 – 1 roll – 1 – 1-55879-469-7 – uk Libr Preservation [820]

THUNDERSTREAK – Bangor, Maine. Aug 19, 1953-April 7, 1955 – 1 – us Res Libr [071]

THUNENS ISOLIERTER STAAT / Petersen, Asmus – Berlin, 1944 – 1 – DM30.00 – gw Mikro Press [943]

Thurau, Gustav *see* SINGEN UND SAGEN

Thureau-Dangin, Paul *see*
- CATHOLICISME EN ANGLETERRE AU 19E SIECLE
- NEWMAN CATHOLIQUE

Thuren, Hj *see* ON THE ESKIMO MUSIC IN GREENLAND

Thuren, Hjalmar *see* DANS OG KVADDIGINING PAA FAEROERNE

Thuret, G *see*
- ETUDES PHYCOLOGIQUES
- NOTES ALGOLOGIQUES

THURGOOD MARSHALL LAW REVIEW – (Title varies: v1 1970-71 as Texas Southern Intramural Law Reviews. v2-6 1972-81 as Texas Southern University Law Review) – Texas Southern University. v1-20. 1970-95 – 9 – $218.00 set – us Hein [340]

THURIYA (SUN) – Rangoon, Burma. Jul 1911-Oct 1954 (incomplete) – 150r – 1 – us L of C Photodup [072]

Thurloe, John *see* PAPERS OF JOHN THURLOE

Thurn, R Payer von *see* JOHANN FAUST

Thurneisser zum Thurn, Leonard *see* QVINTA ESSENTIA

THURNIER BUCH... / Ruexner, G – Franckfurt am Mayn, 1566. (Cuts by J. Amman) – 9 – ne IDC [700]

Thurot, Ch *see* DE LA PRONONCIATION FRANCAISE DEPUIS LE COMMENCEMENT DU XVIE

Thursfield, James R *see* THE NAVY AND THE NATION; OR, NAVAL WARFARE AND IMPERIAL DEFENCE

Thurston, E *see* CASTES AND TRIBES OF SOUTHERN INDIA

Thurston, Herbert *see*
- THE HOLY YEAR OF JUBILEE
- THE SOLDIER OF CHRIST, OR, TALKS BEFORE CONFIRMATION

THURSTON MAIL – Thurston, NE. -w. Oct 1912-Jul 1915 – 1 – us NE Hist [071]

THURSTON'S BUSINESS AND RESIDENT DIRECTORY – State of California. 1911 – 1r – 1 – $50.00 – D113 – us Library Micro [380]

THE THUTMOSID SUCCESSION / Edgerton, W F – 1933 – 9 – $10.00 – us I.R.C. [930]

Thwaites, G H K *see* ENUMERATIO PLANTARUM ZEYLANICAE. ASSISTED. J. D. HOOKER

Thwaites, R G *see* JESUIT RELATIONS, AND ALLIED DOCUMENTS

Thwaites, Reuben Gold *see*
- THE COLONIES, 1492-1950
- FATHER MARQUETTE

Thyen, Yvonne *see* ZUSAMMENHAENGE ZWISCHEN SOZIALSTUKTUR UND BELASTUNG BEI WEIBLICHEN HAUSMEERSCHWEINCHEN (CAVIA APEREA F. PORCELLUS)

THYNNE PAPERS / Bath. Archives (Marquess). Longleat – c.1542-1780. Longleat. v. 1-100 plus 72 books and index – 61r – 1 – uk Microform Academic [025]

THYNNE PAPERS: INDEX / Bath. Archives (Marquess). Longleat – 1 – uk Microform Academic [025]

TI AAR BLANDT OASTGROANLANDS HEDNINGER / Ruettel, F C – Koabenhavn, Kristiania, 1917. 253 pp., ills., map. BN-378 2 – 8 – ne IDC [910]

TI PROFESSIONAL COMPUTING – 1984- – 1,5,6,9 – us UMI [510]

TIAN DI HUI, 1-2: QINGSHI ZILIAO CONGKAN – Historical materials on the Qing Dynasty. Series: Heaven and Earth Society, 1-2. Comp. by the Institute of Qing Dynasty History, People's University. 9 fiches.F-H79 – 9 – $40.00 – cc Microforms [950]

Tian, Han Swie *see* BIJDRAGE TOT DE KENNIS VAN HET FAMILIE- EN ERFRECHT DER CHINEEZEN IN NEDERLANDSCH-INDIE

TIANJIN GONGREN BAO = JOURNAL OF TIANJIN WORKERS – China. 2 issues a week.1985-. M-D88 – 1 – $55.00r – cc Microforms [072]

TIANJIN RIBAO – (1979-86, 1r/y; 1987- , 2r/y) – Tianjin Daily. China. In Chinese. Current subscription. Annual delivery. Backfiles supplied on request. M/D16 – 1 – $55.00r – cc Microforms [072]

TIANJING DAXUE XUEBAO – Journal of Tianjing University. In Chinese but English abstracts to the main articles. F 72 – 9 – 4.00f – cc Microforms [073]

TIANTI WULI XUEBAO – Acta Astrophysica Sinica. In Chinese but English abstracts to the main articles. F p78 – 9 – 4.00f – cc Microforms [073]

TIANWEN XUEBAO – Acta Astronomica Sinica. In Chinese but English abstracts to the main articles. F p48 – 9 – 4.00f – cc Microforms [073]

T'IAO-LI – Collection of laws and regulations 1753-1820. v. 1-204. Emp. Taou Kwang. v. 1-41. 1821-38. BCH-832 2 – 8 – ne IDC [340]

Tiarko Fourche, J A *see* LES COMMUNICATIONS DES INDIGENES DU KASAI AVEC LES AMES DES MORTS

TIAZHELAIA LIRA / Khodasevich, V – Chetvertaia kniga stikhov. Berlin. 1923. BR-703 2 – 8 – ne IDC [460]

Tiberghien, G *see* ENSAYO TEORICO E HISTORICO SOBRE LA GENERACION DE LOS CONOCIMIENTOS HUMANOS

TIBET AND THE TIBETANS / Sandberg, Graham – London: Society for Promoting Christian Knowledge, 1906.ix,333p – 1 – us U.W. Library [950]

TIBETAN COLLECTIONS, SET 1 – (Author catalog. 16mf. $16.00) – PL480-SFC. 7,844mf – 9 – $4,000.00 – us I.A.S.W.R. [280]

TIBETAN COLLECTIONS, SET 2 – (Author catalog. 3mf. $3.00) – PL480-SFC. 2,664mf – 9 – $1,300.00 – us I.A.S.W.R. [280]

TIBETAN COLLECTIONS, SET 3 – (Author catalog. 3mf. $3.00) – PL480-SFC. 2,125mf – 9 – $1,065.00 – us I.A.S.W.R. [280]

TIBETAN COLLECTIONS, SET 4 – (Author catalog. 3mf. $3.00) – PL480-SFC. 2,607mf – 9 – $1,300.00 – us I.A.S.W.R. [280]

TIBETAN COLLECTIONS, SET 5 – (Author catalog. 2mf. $2.00) – PL480-SFC. 1,890mf – 9 – $1,000.00 – us I.A.S.W.R. [280]

TIBETAN COLLECTIONS, SET 6 – (Author catalog. 2mf. $2.00) – PL480-SFC. 2,109mf – 9 – $1,065.00 – us I.A.S.W.R. [280]

TIBETAN COLLECTIONS, SET 7 – (Author catalog. 2mf. $2.00) – PL480-SFC. 2,094mf – 9 – $1,050.00 – us I.A.S.W.R. [280]

TIBETAN COLLECTIONS, SET 8 – (Author catalog. 2mf. $2.00) – PL480-SFC. 1,674mf – 9 – $900.00 – us I.A.S.W.R. [280]

TIBETAN COLLECTIONS, SET 9 – (Author catalog. 3mf. $3.00) – PL480-SFC. 3,190mf – 9 – $1,600.00 – us I.A.S.W.R. [280]

TIBETAN COLLECTIONS, SET 10 – (Author catalog. 1mf. $1.00) – PL480-SFC. 1,125mf – 9 – $700.00 – us I.A.S.W.R. [280]

TIBETAN COLLECTIONS, SET 11 – (Author catalog. 2mf. $2.00) – PL480-SFC. 1984. 2,373mf – 9 – $1,600.00 – us I.A.S.W.R. [280]

TIBETAN COLLECTIONS, SET 12 – (Author catalog. 2mf. $2.00) – PL480-SFC. 1985. 3,975mf – 9 – $2,800.00 – us I.A.S.W.R. [280]

TIBETAN COLLECTIONS, SET 13 – (Author catalog available.2mf.$2.00) – PL480-SFC. 1986 – 2608mf – 9 – $1,800.00 – us I.A.S.W.R. [280]

TIBETAN DOCUMENTS CONCERNING CHINESE TURKESTAN / Thomas, F W – I. Ha-za. JRAS. 1927. BU-586 2 – 8 – ne IDC [950]

TIBETAN-ENGLISH DICTIONARY / Das, Sarat Chandra – 18mf – 9 – $20.00 – us I.A.S.W.R. [480]

A TIBETAN-ENGLISH DICTIONARY WITH SANSKRIT SYNONYMS / Das, Sarat Chandra – Rev ed 1902 – 18mf – $20.00 – us I.A.S.W.R. [420]

TIBETANISCHE MAERCHEN – Berlin: A. Juncker Verlag, 1923. 224p. For the most part translated from Kanjur and Tanjur. 1 reel – 1 – us I.U. Libraries [390]

TIBETSKII SKAZ / Remizov, A – Berlin. 1922. BR-821 2 – 8 – ne IDC [480]

TIBETSKO-RUSSKY SLOVAR'... / Schmidt, I J – Spb., 1843 – 14mf – 9 – HT-1084/1 – ne IDC [040]

TIBOOBURRA TELEGRAPH – May 13 1890-Apr 28 1891 – 1 – at Pascoe [072]

Tiburcio, Luis *see* EDUCATION, ADJUSTMENT AND RECONSTRUCTION

Tibus, A *see* GRUENDUNGSGESCHICHTE DER STIFTER...DES ALTEN BISTUMS MUENSTER

TICARET BORSALARI HAKKINDA MEVZUAT KANUNIYE VE NIZAMIYE – Istanbul: Yeni Matbaasi, 1927 – 9 – $50.00 – us MEDOC [380]

TICARET GAZETESI – Izmir: Ticaret Gazetesi Yurdu, 1922-1928 – 9 – $10.00 – us MEDOC [956]

TICARET VE SANAYI ODALARI KANUNU – Istanbul: Vatan Matbaasi, 1341 [1925] – 9 – $20.00 – us MEDOC [380]

TICHBOURNE NEWS AND ANTI OPPRESSION JOURNAL – London, UK. 1872. -w. 9 feet – 1 – uk British Libr Newspaper [072]

TI-CHENG YUEH-K'AN – "Journal of Land Economics". 5 v. Nanking. 1933-37. Lacking: v. 5 (4-12) 1937. BCH-347 1 – 9 – ne IDC [073]

Tichenor, Isaac Taylor *see* DIARY

THE TICKLER – Philadelphia. Pa. 1807-1813 – 1,3 – us Readex [071]

Ticknor, Anna *see* THE TRAVEL JOURNALS OF GEORGE AND ANNA TICKNOR

Ticknor, George *see*
- LIFE, LETTERS AND JOURNALS OF GEORGE TICKNOR
- THE TRAVEL JOURNALS OF GEORGE AND ANNA TICKNOR

TICKS AND TICK-BORNE DISEASES : SELECTED ARTICLES FROM THE WORLD ANIMAL REVIEW – 1983 – 81p – it F.A.O. [590]

Ticozzi, S *see*
- DIZIONARIO DEL PITTORI DAL RINNOVAMENTO DELLO BELLE ARTI FINO AL 1800
- DIZZIONARIO DEI PITTORI DAL RINNEVAMENTO DELLE BELLE ARTI FINO AL 1800
- VITE DEI PITTORI VECELLI DI CADORE

TIDEHVERV – (Lacking: v19 1945. v24 1950) – 1933-90 – 7r – 1 – ATLA S0633 – us A.T.L.A. [073]

Tideman, Wilhelm *see* FRIEDRICH HEBBEL UND DIE GEGENWART

TIDEN – Stockholm, Sweden. 1883-86 – 3r – 1 – sw Kungliga [072]

TIDENS TECKEN – Battle Creek, MI. 14 Jan 1903-10 Aug 1915. Title Varies – 1 – us NE Hist [071]

TIDERAKNINGEN – 1934 – 1 – us I.U. Libraries [390]

TIDEVARVET – Stockholm, Sweden. 1923-36 – 5r – 1 – sw Kungliga [073]

TIDEWATER NEWS – Franklin. Va. 1951-60 – 1 – us UMI [071]

TIDEWATER REVIEW – West Point. Va. -w. 1929- – 1 – us UMI [071]

THE TIDINGS – Los Angeles, CA. 1895 – 94+ r – 1 – $4,700.00 ($50.00y) – H03323 – us Library Micro [071]

TIDINGS – Ashland. Or. -sw, w, d. 1890-1900, 1912-52 – 1 – us UMI [071]

TIDINGS – Chicago.Women's Baptist Home Mission Society. 1881-1911. Single reels available – 1 – 200.00 – us A.B.H.S. [073]

TIDINGS AND SHARP PARK BREAKERS – Pacifica, CA. 1958-59 – 1r – 1 – $50.00 – B02585 – us Library Micro [071]

TIDINGS FROM JAPAN – v4-7. 1901-04 (complete) – 1r – 1 – ATLA S0717D – us A.T.L.A. [073]

Tidner, E *see* DIDASCALIAE APOSTOLORUM CANONUM ECCLESIASTICORUM TRADITIONIS APOSTOLICAE

TIDNING FOER HEDEMORA, SAETER OCH AVESTA – Hedemora, 1880-87 – 9 – sw Kungliga [072]

TIDNING FOER STOCKHOLMS LAEN – Norrtaelje, 1840 – 9 – sw Kungliga [072]

TIDNING FOR AMALS STAD OCH DALSLAND – Amal, Sweden. 1849-51, 1879 – 2r – 1 – sw Kungliga [072]

TIDNING FOR HEDEMORA *see* SODRA DALARNES TIDNING

TIDNING FOR LEVERANSER TILL STATEN *see* POST-OCH INRIKES TIDNINGAR

TIDNING FOR SKARABORGS LAN *see* MARIESTADS WECKOBLAD

TIDNING FOR WESTER- OCH NORRBOTTENS LAN – Umea, Sweden. 1844-47 – 1 reel – 1 – sw Kungliga [072]

TIDNING FRAN FALKOPINGS STAD OCH FALBYGDEN *see* FALKOPINGS TIDNING

TIDNINGEN I ARVIDSJAUR – Arvidsjaur, 1993- – 9 – sw Kungliga [072]

TIDNINGEN OES – Nykoeping, 1992 – 9 – sw Kungliga [072]

TIDNINGEN SOEDERMALM – Stockholm, 1988-90 – 1 – sw Kungliga [072]

TIDNINGEN SOEDERMALM – Stockholm, 1993- – 9 – sw Kungliga [072]

TIDSKRIFT FOER KIRKE OG SAMFUND – Red Wing, MN. 1912-16 (complete) – 1r – 1 – ATLA S0242 – us A.T.L.A. [073]

TIDSKRIFT FOER KRISTEN TRO OCH FORKUNNELSE – (Lacking some issues) – 1949-91 – Inquire – 1 – ATLA S0742 – us A.T.L.A. [073]

TIDSKRIFT FOER MATEMATIK OCH FYSIK – Upsala. v1-5. 1868-75 – 3 – us Readex [510]

TIDSKRIFT FOER TEOLOGI OCH KIRKLIGA FRAGOR – (Cont: Tidskrift S.E.L.) – v1-19. 1899-1917 (incomplete) – 4r – 1 – ATLA S0149 – us A.T.L.A. [073]

TIDSKRIFT FOR KVINDER I DE TRE NORDISKE RIGER – no.1-18, 1882-83. Nr. 1, 5 jan 1882-. s.l.: s.n., 1882- – 1 – us U.W. Library [948]

TIDSKRIFT S.E.L. *see* TIDSKRIFT FOER TEOLOGI OCH KIRKLIGA FRAGOR

TIDSSKRIFT FOR NATURVIDENSKABERNE – Kjobenhavn, 1822-28 – 3 – us Readex [500]

Tidwell, D D *see* A HISTORY OF THE BAPTIST AT IREDELL, TEXAS

TIE – 1944-56 – 1 – 45.99 – us Baptist [240]

TIECK AND SOLGER : THE COMPLETE CORRESPONDENCE / Matenko, Percy – New York: B Westermann, 1933 – 1r – 1 – us U.W. Library [430]

Tieck, Ludwig *see*
- AUSGEWAEHLTE KRITISCHE SCHRIFTEN
- A MORTE DE CAMOES
- VITTORIA ACCOROMBONA

TIECK UND SHAKESPEARE : EIN BEITRAG ZUR GESCHICHTE DER SHAKESPEAREOMANIE IN DEUTSCHLAND / Zelak, Dominik – (Includes bibliographical references) – Tarnopol: Podolische Buchdruckerei, 1900 – 1r – 1 – us U.W. Library [420]

TIECK'S ESSAY ON THE BOYDELL SHAKESPEARE GALLERY / Danton, George H – (Includes bibliographical references) – [s.l.: s.n.] (Indianapolis: F J Hecker, printer), 1912 – 1r – 1 – us U.W. Library [430]

TIECKS WILLIAM LOVELL : EIN BEITRAG ZUR GEISTESGESCHICHTE DES 18. JAHRHUNDERTS / Wuestling, Fritz – (Includes bibliographical references) – Halle a.S.: M Niemeyer, 1912 – 1r – 1 – us U.W. Library [430]

TIEDAO XUEBAO – Journal of Railway. In Chinese but English abstracts to the main articles. F p135 – 9 – $3.50f – cc Microforms [073]

Tiedeman, Christopher Gustavus *see*
- THE AMERICAN LAW OF REAL PROPERTY. 3D ED
- AN ELEMENTARY TREATISE ON THE AMERICAN LAW OF REAL PROPERTY
- A TREATISE ON THE LAW OF BILLS AND NOTES, CHECKS, INCLUDING THE TEST OF THE NEGOTIABLE INSTRUMENTS LAW OF NEW YORK, CONNECTICUT, COLORADO, FLORIDA, VIRGINIA, MARYLAND, AND THE DISTRICT OF COLUMBIA

Tiefenthal, Fr. Salesius *see* DANIEL

TIEFGLUTH : DICHTUNGEN / Ilgen, Pedro – St Louis, MO: J Meyer, [1906?] – 1r – 1 – us U.W. Library [810]

TIEFURT / Wahl, Hans – Leipzig: J J Weber, [1929] – 1r – 1 – us U.W. Library [943]

T'IEH TAO KUNG PAO / China. Ministry of Railways – Official gazette. Nanking. 1928-37. Lacking: (12-61), (65-131) 1929-30; (144-145), (174-180) 1931; (495) 1933; (770), (866-875) 1934; (1613-?) 1936 37. BCH-1086 1 – 9 – ne IDC [380]

T'IEH TAO PAN YUEH K'AN / China. Ministry of Railways – Semi-monthly bulletin. 2 v. Nanking. 1936-37. BCH-1087 1 – 9 – ne IDC [380]

Tiele, Cornelis Petrus *see* DE VRUCHT DER ASSYRIOLOGIE VOOR DE VERGELIJKENDE GESCHIEDENIS DER GODSDIENSTEN

Tiele, Cornelius Petrus *see*
- GRUNDZUEGE DER RELIGIONSWISSENSCHAFT
- HISTORY OF THE EGYPTIAN RELIGION

Tielmans, Henri *see* LE LAC SAINT-JEAN

Tieman, James G *see* THE EFFECT OF ACUTE EXERCISE ON STATE ANXIETY AND ACOUSTIC STARTLE EYEBLINK RESPONSE IN PHYSICALLY ACTIVE AND INACTIVE MEN

EL TIEMPO – Bogota, CK. 1971-1993 – 276r – $13,800.00 – R060501 – us Library Micro [072]

EL TIEMPO – Caceres, 1911-1914 – 5 – sp Bibl Santa Ana [073]

EL TIEMPO – Madrid, Spain. -d. 1 Jan 1872-22 May 1874. 5 reels – 1 – uk British Libr Newspaper [072]

EL TIEMPO DE CUYO – Mendoza. Argentina. -d. 1 Mar 1960-26 Jan 1963. (28 reels) – 1 – uk British Libr Newspaper [072]

TIEMPO PERDIDO / Sotomayor y Terrazas, Luis – 1885 – 9 – 1.50f – sp Bibl Santa Ana [830]

TIEMPO PERDIDO, POESIAS / Sotomayor y Terrazas, Luis – Fregenal? – 1 – sp Bibl Santa Ana [440]

TIEN FENG CHOU KAN TZU LIAO SHIH (CC293) : CHIEH LOU FAN KO MING FEN TZU WANG MING-TAO TI FAN TUNG YEN LUN – (In Chinese) – [s.l: s.n, 1955] – 1r – 1 – 1984-6632 – us A.T.L.A. [240]

TIEN FENG CHOU KAN TZU LIAO SHIH (CCC294) : KUNG SU CHIEH FA WANG MING-TAO FAN KO MING CHI TUAN – (In Chinese) – [s.l: s.n, 1955] – 1r – 1 – 1984-6633 – us A.T.L.A. [240]

Tiendrebeogo, Yamba *see* CONTES DU LARHALLE, SUIVIS D'UN RECUEIL DE PROVERBES ET DE DEVISES DU PAYS MOSSI

TIENG-DAN – La Voix du peuple. no. 1-1766. Hue. aout 1927-24 avr 1943 – 1 – fr A.C.R.P.P. [073]

TIENG-TRE – Xuat-ban ngay thu' hai. Hanoi. 11 nov 1935-19 janv 1937 – 1 – fr A.C.R.P.P. [073]

T'IEN-HSIA MONTHLY – v. 1-10. Shanghai. 1935-40. Lacking: v. 10 (1) 1940. BCH-177 2 – 8 – ne IDC [073]

TIENJARENPLAN 1962-1971 / Curacao. (Netherlands) – D-1280 1 – 9 – ne IDC [338]

TIENJARENPLAN CURACAO / Netherlands Antilles – 14 v. Willemstad. 1962 – 9 – ne IDC [338]

Tiepolo, G *see*
- CANZONE...PER LA FELICISSIMA VITTORIA NAUALE CONTRA TURCHI
- TRE SORELLE CORONE DI SONETTI...

TIEREXPERIMENTELLE UNTERSUCHUNGEN ZUR FRAGE DER FUNKTIONELLEN ANPASSUNG IM KAUSYSTEM / Sergl, Hans Georg – 1995 – 2mf – 9 – DM80.00 – 3-8267-2182-9 – gw Hänsel [617]

TIERISCHE LANDESZEITUNG – Trier, Germany. -d. 12 Jan 1916-30 June 1919; 29 Oct 1949-30 Sept 1951. Imperfect. 12 reels – 1 – uk British Libr Newspaper [072]

TIERPS NYHETER – Enkoeping, 1930 – 9 – sw Kungliga [072]

TIERPS NYHETER – Tierp, 1932-33 – 9 – sw Kungliga [072]

TIERRA DE JAGUARES / Wast, Hugo – Buenos Aires, 1931; Madrid: Razon y Fe, 1932 – 1 – sp Bibl Santa Ana [830]

TIERRA VASCA – Buenos Aires. Argentina. -m. Jul 1956-Oct 1960. (1 reel) – 1 – uk British Libr Newspaper [072]

TIERRA Y MUJER O LAZARA LA PROFETISA / Caba, Pedro – Barcelona: S.L.C., 1945 – sp Bibl Santa Ana [946]

LAS TIERRAS NEGRAS DEL EXTREMO SUR DE ESPANA Y SUS YACIMIENTOS POLEOLITICOS / Hernandez Pacheco, Eduardo – Madrid, 1915 – 1 – sp Bibl Santa Ana [560]

LAS TIERRAS PARDAS. CANTOS A EXTREMADURA POR... / Ramirez Lopez Uria, Jose – Madrid: Imp. Torrent, 1923 – 1 – sp Bibl Santa Ana [946]

TIERZUCHT IM POMMERN : 19. UND 20. JAHRHUNDERT / Oertzen-Strehlow, Heinrich Ulrich von – (Includes bibliographical references) – Wuerzburg: Holzner Verlag, 1969 – 10r – 1 – us U.W. Library [943]

TIESA – Vilna, U.S.S.R. -d. 1961-70. 29 reels – 1 – uk British Libr Newspaper [947]

Tievant, S *see* LA DIFFERENCIATION SEXUELLE DANS LES RITES DE PASSAGE DE LA VIE QUOTIDIENNE EN ARIEGE

TIFERET SEIVAH, JUBELSCHRIFT. L. ZUNZ / Zunz, L – Berlin. 1884. BJ-100-64 1 – 9 – ne IDC [956]

TIFERET YISRA'EL, FESTSCHRIFT. ISRAEL LEWY / Lewy, I – Breslau. 1911. BJ-100-65 1 – 9 – ne IDC [920]

Tiffany, Alexander Ralston *see*
- A TREATISE ON THE POWERS AND DUTIES OF JUSTICES OF THE PEACE IN THE STATE OF MICHIGAN, UNDER CHAPTER NINETY-THREE OF THE REVISED STATUTES OF 1846, BEING CHAPTER THIRTY-FOUR OF THE COMPILED LAWS OF 1897...10TH ED
- A TREATISE ON THE POWERS AND DUTIES OF JUSTICES OF THE PEACE, IN THE STATE OF MICHIGAN, UNDER CHAPTER NINETY-THREE OF THE REVISED STATUTES OF 1846, BEING CHAPTER TWO HUNDRED AND FORTY-NINE OF HOWELL'S ANNOTATED STATUTES OF 1883. 9TH ED

Tiffany, Charles C *see* A HISTORY OF THE PROTESTANT EPISCOPAL CHURCH IN THE UNITED STATES

Tiffany, Francis Buchanan *see* DEATH BY WRONGFUL ACT...2ND ED

Tiffany, Herbert Thorndike *see*
- OUTLINES OF REAL PROPERTY
- A TREATISE ON THE LAW OF LANDLORD AND TENANT

Tiffany, Walter Checkley *see* HANDBOOK ON THE LAW OF PERSONS AND DOMESTIC RELATIONS. 2D ED

TIFFANY'S TRANSCRIPT APPEALS / Greene, JG – 2nd ed. v1-7. 1867-98 (all publ) – 34mf – 9 – $51.00 – LLMC 80-049 – us L.L.M.C. [340]

TIFFIN DAILY TRIBUNE – Tiffin, Ohio. 1921-33 – 29r – 1 – $32.50r – us Archival [071]

TIFFIN DAILY TRIBUNE AND HERALD – Tiffin, Ohio. 1887-1921 – 69r – 1 – $32.50r – us Archival [071]

TIFFIN GAZETTE – Tiffin, Ohio. 1839-42 – 1r – 1 – $32.50r – us Archival [071]

TIFFIN NEWS – Tiffin, Ohio. 1888-1902 – 5r – 1 – $32.50r – us Archival [071]

Tiffin. Ohio. First Lutheran Church *see* RECORDS

Tiffin. Ohio. First Presbyterian Church *see* RECORDS

Tiffin. Ohio. St. John's United Church of Christ *see* RECORDS

Tiffin. Ohio. St. Paul's Methodist Church *see* RECORDS

Tiffin. Ohio. Trinity United Church of Christ *see* RECORDS

DIE TIFFIN PRESSE – Tiffin, Ohio. 1891-94 – 2r – 1 – $32.50r – us Archival [071]

TIFFIN WEEKLY TRIBUNE – Tiffin, Ohio. 1856-1919 – 25r – 1 – $32.50r – us Archival [071]

TIGA PUTERA MEMBELA IBU DAN TANAH AIR; TJERITA DIMASA PERDJUANGAN KEMERDEKAAN UNTUK ANAK-ANAK BERUMUR 12 TAHUN KEATAS / Dahlan, Nursiah – SE-5050 1. 1963 – 9 – ne IDC [950]

TIGARD NEWS – Tigard OR. Dec 20 27 1951 – 1 – us U.O. Library [071]

TIGARD SENTINEL – Tigard, OR. -w. 1 Aug 1924-26 June 1951. – 6r – 1 – us U.O. Library [071]

TIGARD TIMES – Tigard, OR. -w. 23 Jan 1958-. – 1 – us U.O. Library [071]

Tiger, Lionel Samuel *see* BUREAUCRACY IN GHANA

TIGER PRESS – Kuala Lumpur, Malaysia. -d. 4 Sept 1959-14 Nov 1961. 9 reels – 1 – uk British Libr Newspaper [072]

TIGER TALK – Alexandria. La. (USAF base). 1953- – 1 – us UMI [071]

DER TIGER UND DIE HARFE : ROMAN AUS DEM SCHLESISCHEN BAROCK / Pauly, Charlotte E – Hamburg: H Goverts, 1944 – 1r – 1 – us U.W. Library [830]

Tigert, John James *see* THEISM: A SURVEY OF THE PATHS THAT LEAD TO GOD...IN... THE HISTORY OF PHILOSOPHY

Tigrini, O *see* IL COMPENDIO DELLA MUSICA NEL QUALE BREVEMENTE SI TRATTA DELL'ARTE DEL CONTRAPUNTO

TIHRAN-I MUSAVVAR – (Missing issue 22) – Tihran, No. 1-30, 8 Azar 1357-26 Murdad 1358 [29 November 1978-17 August 1979] – 1 reel – 1 – $95.00 – us MEDOC [950]

TI-HSUEH TSA-CHIH – "The Geological Journal". 26 v. Peiping. 1910-37. Lacking: v. 2 (18-24) 1911; v. 8 (2, 4) 1917; v. 9 (1-3, 6-8) 1918; v. 13 (10-12) 1922; v. 17 (1-2) 1929; v. 18 (1-2) 1930; v. 19 (2) 1931; v. 25 (3) 1936; v. 26, 1937. BCH-348 1 – 9 – ne IDC [910]

TI-I HUI CHUNG-KUO NIEN-CHIEN – (The China Yearbook, no. 1). 1924 – 1 – 40.00 – us Chinese Res [950]

TIJARAT MISR AL KHARIJIA (FOREIGN TRADE OF EGYPT) / Egypt. Ministry of Commerce and Industry – Saleh Mikhail. 1947. BNE-4657 1 – 9 – ne IDC [380]

DE TIJD – Bloemfontein. South Africa. 1862-75 – 1 – sa State Libr [072]

TIJDSCHRIFT VOOR NEDERLANDSCH INDIE – Batavia, 1838-1902 – .01mf – 9 – SE-20112/1 – ne IDC [950]

TIJDSCHRIFT / ed by Vereeniging ter beoefening der Joodsche Wetenschappen – Rotterdam. v1(1-2). 1869 – 8mf – 9 – J-261-114/1 – ne IDC [073]

TIJDSCHRIFT OVER PLANTENZIEKTEN – (Index) – Wageningen. v1-26. 1885-1920 – 103mf – 9 – 7369/1 – ne IDC [580]

TIJDSCHRIFT VOOR DEN VOORUITSTREVENDE JAVAAN – Amsterdam, 1909-1910.-5 pts – 4mf – 9 – SE-20,011/1 – ne IDC [073]

TIJDSCHRIFT VOOR HET BINNENLANDSCH BESTUUR – (Including a printed index by E.E. van Delden: Klein repertorium. Amsterdam, 1986-1987. 3 vols) – Batavia, 1888-1917.-v1-53 – 464mf – 9 – SE-33/1 – ne IDC [073]

TIJDSCHRIFT VOOR INDISCHE TAAL-, LAND-EN VOLKENKUNDE – (Lacking: 1958, V.86(p. 1-500)) – Batavia, 1853-1958.-v1-86. Index, 1908-1959 – 917mf – 9 – SE-16/1 – ne IDC [073]

TIJDSCHRIFT VOOR NATUURLIJKE GESCHIEDENIS EN PHYSIOLOGIE – Amsterdam, 1834-36; Leiden, 1837-45 – 3 – us Readex [574]

TIJDSCHRIFT VOOR NATUURLIJKE GESCHIEDENIS EN PHYSIOLOGIE / ed by Hoeven, v.d. & Vriese, de – Amsterdam, Leiden. v1-12. 1834-1845 – 111mf – 9 – 7145/2 – ne IDC [500]

TIJDSCHRIFT VOOR NEDERLANDSCH INDIE – n.s. (S5) 1-5, n. (S6), 1, 1897-1902 – 1 – us Res Libr [073]

TIJDSCHRIFT VOOR NOORDBRABANTSCHE GESCHIEDENIS, TAAL-EN LET-TERKUNDE – 1(1883/84)-3(1885/86) – 11mf – 8 – ne Slangenburg [949]

TIJDSCHRIFT VOOR OPPERVLAKTE TECHNIEKEN VAN METALEN – 1-15. 1957-71. Continued as" yBelgisch-Tijdschrift voor Oppervlaktetechnieken Van Matalen – 1 – us UMI [073]

TIJDSCHRIFT VOOR OPPERVLAKTETECHNIEKEN VAN MATERIALEN – v.25-. Jan 1981- – 1,5,6,9 – us UMI [073]

TIJDSCHRIFT VOOR PHILOSOPHIE – 1(1939)-2(1940) – 7mf – 9 – Dfl28.00 – ne Slangenburg [073]

LAS TIJERAS – Villafranca de los Barros, 1900 – 5 – sp Bibl Santa Ana [946]

Tikhivinskii, Pavel *see* RAZGOVOR PROVOSLAVNOGO S SHTUNCISTOM OB ISTINNOI VERE

Tikhomirov, M N *see*
- ISTOCHNIKOVEDENIE ISTORII SSSR
- KRATKIE ZAMETKI O LETOPISNYKH PROIZVEDENIIAKH V RUKOPISNYKH SOBRANIIAKH MOSKVY
- NOVOGORODSKIE GRAMOTY NA BERESTE (IZ RASKOPOK 1951 G.)
- OPIS' DOKUMENTAL'NYKH MATERIALOV LICHNOGO FONDA NO. 1996
- SPRAVOCHNIK SOKRASHCHENII, PRINIATYKH V ISTORICHESKOI LITERATURE

Tikhomirov, P *see* BEZBOZHIE POBEDIT

Tikhomirov, V A *see* DESIAT' LET SOVETSKOI KOOPERATSII

Tikhonov, D I *see* VOSTOCHNYE RUKOPISI INSTITUTA VOSTOKOVEDENIIA AKADEMII NAUK SSSR

Tikhonov, Nikolai *see* BRAGA

Tikhonravov, N S *see* RUSSKAIA PALEOGRAFIA

TIKKUNEI SHABBAT – Prague. c.1650? BJ-43-129 1 – 9 – ne IDC [270]

TIKVATH-ISRAEL – Scheveningen. v1-21. 1917-40 – 93mf – 9 – J-261-112/1 – ne IDC [270]

O TIL : CONSAGRADO AS FAMILIAS PERIODICO RECREATIVO – Coimbra, 23 Jul 1893 – 1,5,6 – bl Biblioteca [072]

TIL KARAKTERISTIK AF N.F.S. GRUNDTVIG / Roenning, F – Kobenhavn: Schonberg, [1915?] – 1mf – us A.T.L.A. [240]

Til, S van *see* DICHT-, SING- UND SPIEL-KUN..

Tilak, Bal Gangadhar *see* VEDIC CHRONOLOGY AND VEDANGA JYOTISHA: CONTAINING ALSO CHALDEAN AND INDIAN VEDAS AND OTHER MISCELLANEOUS ESSAYS

TILDEN CITIZEN – Tilden, NE. -w. Jan 1893-May 1907, scattered issues missing; Jun 1919-Dec 1920; Jan 1923-Sept 1926; Jan 1927 to date – 1 – us NE Hist [071]

TILDEN NEWS – Tilden, NE. -w. Mar 1891-Feb 1896, scattered issues missing; May 1896-May 1905 – 1 – us NE Hist [071]

Tilemann, Hero *see* DAS ZWEITE BUCH DER MEDIZINISCHEN BRIEFE DES ZUERICHER PHILOSOPHEN UND ARZTES KONRAD GESSNER

TILEMANN HESSHUSIUS : EIN STREITTHEOLOG DER LUTHERSKIRCHE / Wilkens, C A – Leipzig: Breitkopf und Haertel, 1860 – 1mf – us A.T.L.A. [240]

TI-LI – (Geography). v. 1-5. Peipei, Szechuan, Nanking. 1941-48. BCH-810 2 – 8 – ne IDC [910]

TI-LI CHI-K'AN – (Geographic Quarterly). v. 1-4. Peipei, Chungking. 1946. BCH-811 2 – 8 – ne IDC [910]

TILL ALGERNESS SYSTEMATIK / Agardh, J G – (Nya bidrag. Lunds Universitets Arsskrift). v. 1-6. 1872-88. B-5514 2 – 8 – ne IDC [580]

TILL BELYSNING AF DEN LUTHERSKA KYRKOIDEN : DESS HISTORIA OCH DESS VAERDE / Aulen, Gustaf – Uppsala: Almqvist & Wiksell, 1912 – 1mf – us A.T.L.A. [240]

TILL EULENSPIEGEL : NARRENSPIEL IN DREI TEILEN / Lienhard, Friedrich – 3. durchgearb. Aufl. Leipzig: G H Meyer, 1902 – 1r – 1 – us U.W. Library [820]

TILL HEMBYGDEN – v1-89. 1904-92 (complete) – Inquire – 1 – ATLA S0514 – us A.T.L.A. [073]

Till, W *see*
- DIE GNOSTISCHEN SCHRIFTEN DES KOPTISCHEN PAPYRUS BEROLINENSIS 8502 (T.U.U. 5-60)
- DER KOPTISCHE TEXT DER KIRCHENORDNUNG HIPPOLYTS (T.U.U. 5-58)

TILLAGE SYSTEMS FOR SOIL AND WATER CONSERVATION – 1984 – 296p – it F.A.O. [631]

TILLAMOOK COUNTY NEWS – (Set incl. Garibaldi News; Garibaldi Rockaway News; North Tillamook County News (Garibaldi)) – Garibaldi, OR. -w. 24 July 1947-13 Feb 1958. – 9r – 1 – us U.O. Library [071]

TILLAMOOK HEADLIGHT – Tillamook, OR. -w. 8 Jun 1888-30 Dec 1932. 9 rolls – 1 – us U.O. Library [071]

TILLAMOOK HEADLIGHT-HERALD – Tillamook, OR. -w. 1934-52 – 1 – 216.00 – us Oregon Hist [071]

TILLAMOOK HERALD – Tillamook, OR. -w. 1904-34. Incomplete – 1 – 192.00 – us Oregon Hist [071]

TILLAMOOK HERALD – Tillamook, OR. -w. 24 Sept 1896-2 June 1933 – 1 – us U.O. Library [071]

THE TILLER – Larned. KS. And Toiler. 1905-10, 1929-32 – 1 – us UMI [071]

TILLER – Arvin. Calif. 1954-1959 – 1 – us UMI [071]

TILLER BOOSTER – Arvin. Calif. 1960-1967 – 1 – us UMI [071]

Tilley, Steven *see* INDEX TO THE JOURNALS OF THE CONTINENTAL CONGRESS, 1774-1789

Tillier, S *see* MORPHOLOGIE COMPAREE, PHYLOGENIE ET CLASSIFICATION DES GASTEROPODES PULMONES STYLOMMATOPHORES (MOLLUSCA)

TILLMAN BAPTIST CHURCH (FORMERLY: SAVIN GROVE). JASPER COUNTY. SOUTH CAROLINA : CHURCH RECORDS – 1883-88, 1897-1912, 1951-76 – 1 – $9.28 – us Baptist [240]

Tillmann-Nonnenkamp, Tilke *see* "MACHT RUHESTAND KRANK?"

TILLSONBURG NEWS – Tillsonburg, Ontario, CN. 1923-79 – 75r – 1 – cn Commonwealth Micro [072]

Tilly, William *see* SIXTEEN SERMONS, ALL (EXCEPT ONE) PREACH'D BEFORE THE UNIVERSITY OF OXFORD, AT ST MARY'S UPON SEVERAL OCCASIONS LONDON

TILSIT-RAGNIT : STADT UND LANDKREIS: EIN OSTPREUSSISCHES HEIMATBUCH / ed by Brix, Fritz – (Includes bibliographical references and indexes) – Wuerzburg: Holzner Verlag, 1971 – 1 – us U.W. Library [910]

TIMANDRA : TRAUERSPIEL IN FUENF AUFZUEGEN / Wilbrandt, Adolf von – Stuttgart: J G Cotta, 1903 – 1r – 1 – us U.W. Library [820]

TIMARIT BOOKS – (In Icelandic) – Canada, 1919-68 – 8r – 1 – cn Commonwealth Micro [072]

Timayenis, Telemachus Thomas *see* THE MODERN GREEK

TIMBER COMMITTEE / UN Economic Commission for Europe (ECE) – 1947-89 – E/F.667 E.1194 F.925 R.871 – 9 – us U.N. Pubs [340]

Timber Development Association *see* RESEARCH REPORT

TIMBER TECHNOLOGY – 1955-61 – 7r – 1 – uk Microform Academic [073]

TIMBER TRADES JOURNAL AND WOODWORKING MACHINERY – 1873- 1; 1975- 5,6,9 – us UMI [634]

TIMBER TRENDS AND PROSPECTS IN AFRICA – 1967 – 90p – it F.A.O. [670]

TIMBOUCTOU, VOYAGE AU MAROC, AU SAHARA ET AU SOUDAN / Lenz, Oscar – Paris, Hachette. 1886 – 9 – 25.00 – fr Orientalistes [910]

O TIMBRE ALAGOANO : THRONO, CONSTITUICAO, LIBERDADE E ORDEM – Maceio, Alagoas. 1 Jul 1852 – 1,5,6 – bl Biblioteca [072]

TIMBRE ASTURIANO. HISTORIA...VIDA...SANTA EULALIA DE MERIDA / Quiros y Benavides, Felipe Bernardo – 1672 – 9 – $1.50f – sp Bibl Santa Ana [240]

Timbs, John *see*
- ANCESTRAL STORIES AND TRADITIONS OF GREAT FAMILIES ILLUSTRATIVE OF ENGLISH HISTORY
- ANECDOTE LIVES OF WITS AND HUMOURISTS

TIME – 1- 1923- – 1,5,6,9 – us UMI [073]

TIME – 1931- – 1 – us UMI [071]

TIME – Greenwich. Conn. 1952- – 1 – us UMI [071]

TIME AND FREE WILL = ESSAI SUR LES DONNEES IMMEDIATES DE LA CONSCIENCE : AN ESSAY ON THE IMMEDIATE DATA OF CONSCIOUSNESS / Bergson, Henri – (Includes bibliographical references and index) – London: Swan Sonnenschein; New York: Macmillan, 1910 – 1mf – 9 – 0-8370-9764-9 – 1986-3764 – us A.T.L.A. [120]
TIME AND MOTION STUDY – 1952-57 – 76mf – 7 – uk Microform Academic [650]
TIME AND THE PHILOSOPHIES : AT THE CROSSROADS OF CULTURES / Aguessy, H et al – 1977 – 256p – 9 – 92-3-101396-3 – fr UNESCO [100]
TIME AND THE SCIENCES / ed by Greenaway, Frank et al – 1979 – 182p – 9 – 92-3-101657-1 – fr UNESCO [500]
TIME AND TIDE – 1984- – 1,5,6,9 – us UMI [072]
TIME AND TIDE – London. -w. 14 May 1920-Dec 1942. (34 reels) – 1 – uk British Libr Newspaper [072]
TIME AND TIDE – v1-59. 1920-79 – 1 – us UMI [072]
TIME AND TIDE BY WEARE AND TYNE : TWENTY-FIVE LETTERS TO A WORKING MAN OF SUNDERLAND ON THE LAW OF WORK / Ruskin, John – London: Smith, Elder and Co., 1867 – 1 roll – 1 – 1-55879-716-5 – uk Libr Preservation [860]
TIME AUSTRALIA – (Details on Request) – July 1986- – 9 – at Pascoe [072]
THE TIME COURSE OF PULMONARY DIFFUSION CAPACITY CHANGES FOLLOWING MAXIMAL EXERCISE / Sheel, Andrew W – University of British Columbia, 1995 – 1mf – 9 – $4.00 – PH1476 – us Microform Publ [612]
THE TIME COURSE OF THE REPEATED BOUT EFFECT OF ECCENTRIC EXERCISE ON DELAYED ONSET MUSCLE SORENESS / Cleary, Michelle A – 1994 – 1mf – $4.00 – us Microform Publ [617]
TIME ED. CHICAGO – 1923-1994 – 6,1 – sz Infoprint [071]
TIME FLIES : A READING DIARY / Rossetti, Christina – Boston: Roberts Brothers, 1886 – 1 roll – 1 – 1-55879-778-5 – uk Libr Preservation [890]
TIME FRAMES : SOURCES IN CANADIAN HISTORY – (Series 2 1911-21) – Series 1. 1896-1910 – 9 – cn Micromedia [971]
TIME INDEX – 1973-1977 – 1 – sz Infoprint [071]
TIME MAGAZINE – 1994 – 1 – sz Infoprint [073]
TIME MOTION ANALYSIS OF THE SKATING CHARACTERISTICS OF PROFESSIONAL ICE HOCKEY PLAYERS / Bracko, Michael R & Hill, Larry T – 1992 – 2mf – $8.00 – us Microform Publ [790]
TIME SERIES OF OCEAN MEASUREMENTS – 9 – fr UNESCO [550]
TIME SERIES OF SCHOOL POPULATION STATISTICS 1964/65, 1969/70 AND 1974/75-1979/80 / Gambia. Ministry of Economic Planning and Industrial Development – Banjul, 1980 – 1mf – 9 – DE-426/1 – ne IDC [370]
TIME TABLE: UPPER LAKE EXPRESS STEAMSHIPS OF THE CANADIAN PACIFIC RAILWAY / Canadian Pacific Railway Company – 1892. 00437. (Pre-1900 Canadiana) – 9 – cn C.I.H.M. [380]
TIMEHRI / The Royal Agriculture and Commercial Society of British Guiana – 1882-99 – 1 – us UMI [630]
TIMELY NOTE ON SOIL AND CROPS / Kentucky. Agricultural Extension Service – 1937-61 – 1,5,6 – us Spaulding [630]
THE TIMES – Bryan. Ohio. 1961- – 1 – us UMI [071]
THE TIMES = LE COURS DU TEMPS – Quebec. Prospectus. v1 n1. 23 jun 1794-v1 n52. 27 jul 1795 – 1r – 1 – Can$35.00 – cn Can Microfilming [072]
THE TIMES – Fairfield. Mont. 1923-1941; 1956-1957; 1966- – 1 – us UMI [071]
THE TIMES – Kingstown, St. Vincent. 20 Jun 1901-18 Jun 1914; 13 Aug 1914-1 Jan 1925; 5 Mar 1925-24 Jun 1926; 8 Jan 1930-30 Jul 1938; 7 Jan 1939-28 Dec 1946; 5 Apr-13 Dec 1947 (imperfect).-w 22 reels – 1 – uk British Libr Newspaper [072]
THE TIMES – Lehighton, PA., 1972-1977 – 13 – $25.00r – us I.M.R. [071]
THE TIMES – London, England. n4298. 3 oct 1798-n9554. 22 jun 1815; n6609. 10 jan 1806 (Funeral of Lord Nelson) – 1r – 1 – Can$30.00 – cn Can Microfilming [072]
THE TIMES – London, England.1785- . Index available – 1 – us Primary [072]
THE TIMES – Medicine Hat, Canada. -w. Nov 1904-Feb 1916. 4 1 2 reels – 1 – uk British Libr Newspaper [072]
THE TIMES – Montreal, Canada. 13 sep 1884-3 oct 1885 – 1r – 1 – Can$50.00 – cn Can Microfilming [072]
THE TIMES – Newville, PA. 1904-07. 1 roll – 13 – $25.00r – us I.M.R. [071]
THE TIMES – Noblesville. Ind. 1904-1907 – 1 – us UMI [071]
THE TIMES – Philadelphia, PA. 1875-1898 – 13 – $25.00r – us I.M.R. [071]
THE TIMES – Quebec, Canada. 24 nov 1881-2 jan 1882 – 1r – 1 – Can$40.00 – cn Can Microfilming [072]
THE TIMES – Sacramento, CA. 1894 – 1r – 1 – $50.00 – B0344 – us Library Micro [071]
THE TIMES – San Mateo, CA. 1901-76; 1977- – 1073+ r – 1 – $53,650.00 ($800.00) – B02922 – us Library Micro [071]
THE TIMES – Williamsport, PA., 1884-1897 – 13 – $25.00r – us I.M.R. [071]
THE TIMES *see* SUN TIMES
TIMES – 1785-1828 – 1 – F1,746.00 – sz Infoprint [072]
TIMES – 1829-1847 – 1 – F2,314.00 – sz Infoprint [072]
TIMES – 1848-1907 – 1 – F3,231.00 – sz Infoprint [072]
TIMES – 1908-1939 – 1 – F5,282.00 – sz Infoprint [072]
TIMES – 1940-1952 – 1 – F3,318.00 – sz Infoprint [072]
TIMES – 1953-1966 – 1 – F5,282.00 – sz Infoprint [072]
TIMES – 1967-1994 – 1 – F8,949.00 – sz Infoprint [072]
TIMES – (1990-1992.-10r) – Nanaimo, 1993 – 4r – 1 – cn Preston [971]
TIMES – (1993.-24r; Jl1940-1940De.-1r; Jl1946-1975.-196r; 1922-1932.-23r) – Oshawa, 1976-1992 – 207r – 1 – cn Preston [971]
TIMES – Adrian. Mich. 1867-1914 – 1 – us UMI [071]
TIMES – Alderson. West Virginia. 1951-1960 – 1 – us UMI [071]
TIMES – Alliance. Neb. 1891-1922 – 1 – us UMI [071]
TIMES – Allyn. Wash. 1889-1891 – 1 – us UMI [071]
TIMES – (Also known as: Daily Times) – Los Gatos, CA. 1936-59 – 27r – 1 BC02405 – $1,350.00 – us Library Micro [071]
TIMES – Anchorage. Alaska. 1970- – 1 – us UMI [071]
TIMES – Apalachicola. Fl. -w. 1947- – 1 – us P.K. Yonge [071]
TIMES – Asheville. N.C. 1916- – 1 – us UMI [071]
TIMES – Augusta. Mont. 1915-1918 – 1 – us UMI [071]
TIMES – Axtell. Neb. 1896-1953 – 1 – us UMI [071]
TIMES – Bahamas. -sw. 1874-94 – 1 – us UMI [072]
TIMES – Barbados. 1863-1873; 1875-1876; 1884-1895 – 1 – us UMI [072]
TIMES – Barrington. R.I. 1958- – 1 – us UMI [071]
TIMES – Basin. Mont. 1894-1895; 1897-1900 – 1 – us UMI [071]
TIMES – Baxter Springs. Kan. 1878-80 – 1 – us UMI [071]
TIMES – Bay City. Mich. 1889-1909; 1915- – 1 – us UMI [071]
TIMES – Bayonne. N.J. 1881-95 – 1 – us UMI [071]
TIMES – Beemer. Neb. 1886-1947 – 1 – us UMI [071]
TIMES – Benson. Neb. 1907-1963 – 1 – us UMI [071]
TIMES – Billings. Mont. -w. 1891-1914, 1924-59, 1966-67 – 1 – us UMI [071]
TIMES – Boston, MA. 1807-08. Also: Boston Spectator, 1814-15; Boston Weekly Reports, 1819-20; Ladies' Port Folio, 1820; Agricultural Intelligencer, 1820. Sold as one unit – 3 – us Readex [071]
TIMES – Bridger. Mont. 1911-1948; 1956-1957 – 1 – us UMI [071]
TIMES – Buttonwillow. Calif. 1959-1967 – 1 – us UMI [071]
TIMES – Caldwell. KS. -w. 1886-87 – 1 – us UMI [071]
TIMES – Cambridge. Ohio. 1917-1919 – 1 – us UMI [071]
TIMES – Canton. Miss. 1902-1904 – 1 – us UMI [071]
TIMES – Carmi. Ill. 1958- – 1 – us UMI [071]
TIMES – Cherokee. Iowa. 1953- – 1 – us UMI [071]
TIMES – Clay Center. Kan. 1886-88 – 1 – us UMI [071]
TIMES – Clay Center. Kan. -w. 1882-1955 – 1 – us UMI [071]
TIMES – Corpus Christi. Tex. (evening). 1921- – 1 – us UMI [071]
TIMES – Coshocton. Ohio. -w. 1906-09 – 1 – us UMI [071]
TIMES – Cullman. Ala. 1953- – 1 – us UMI [071]
TIMES – Davenport. Iowa. 1887-1964 – 1 – us UMI [071]
TIMES – Detroit. Mich. 1900-60 – 1 – us UMI [071]
TIMES – Divide City, NV. 1919 (scats) – 1r – 1 – $50.00 – W04490 – us Library Micro [071]
TIMES – Dodge City. Kan. -w. 1876-82 – 1 – us UMI [071]
TIMES – Dowagiac. Mich. -w. 1887, 1894, 1898, 1904-05 – 1 – us UMI [071]
TIMES – Dubuque. Iowa. 1857-1905 – 1 – us UMI [071]
TIMES – El Dorado. Kan. 1920-1929 – 1 – us UMI [071]
TIMES – Escalon. Calif. -w. 1943-58 – 1 – us UMI [071]
TIMES – Everett. Wash. 1892-1896 – 1 – us UMI [071]
TIMES – Fairmont. West Virginia. 1903- – 1 – us UMI [071]
TIMES – Fairview. Mont. 1915-1917 – 1 – us UMI [071]
TIMES – Florence. Ala. 1924- – 1 – us UMI [071]
TIMES – Florence. Ala. -w. 1915, 1917-23 – 1 – us UMI [071]
TIMES – Florence, OR. -w. 4 Sept 1925-29 Oct 1926. 1 roll – 1 – us U.O. Library [071]
TIMES – Forest Grove. Or. -w. 1899-1909 – 1 – us UMI [071]
TIMES – Forsyth. Mont. 1895-1910 – 1 – us UMI [071]
TIMES – Fort Lauderdale. Fl. 1940-1942 – 1 – us UMI [071]
TIMES – Fostoria, Ohio. 1891-95 – 4r – 1 – $32.50r – us Archival [071]
TIMES – Fresno, CA. 1865 – 1r – 1 – $50.00 – B056028 – us Library Micro [071]
TIMES – Fulton. N.Y. 1882-1890; 1903-1906 – 1 – us UMI [071]
TIMES – Gadsden. Ala. 1955- – 1 – us UMI [071]
TIMES – Gainesville. Ga. 1947- – 1 – us UMI [071]
TIMES – Genoa. Neb. 1902-1926 – 1 – us UMI [071]
TIMES – Gerardstown. West Virginia. 1898-1905 – 1 – us UMI [071]
TIMES – Gettysburg. Pa. 1909- – 1 – us UMI [071]
TIMES – Glasgow. Mont. 1925-1927; 1929-1932 – 1 – us UMI [071]
TIMES – Glens Falls. N.Y. 1964- – 1 – us UMI [071]
TIMES – Gold Hill, OR. -w. 3 Jan 1952-23 Apr 1953. 1 roll – 1 – us U.O. Library [071]
TIMES – Gothenburg. Neb. 1896- – 1 – us UMI [071]
TIMES – Grand Rapids. Mich. -w. 1906-21 – 1 – us UMI [071]
TIMES – Granite, NV. 17 Apr, 1 May 1908 – 1r – 1 – $50.00 – U04569 – us Library Micro [071]
TIMES – Granville. Ohio. 1880-1918; 1925-1941 – 1 – us UMI [071]
TIMES – Green Springs, Ohio. 1891-95 – 1r – 1 – $32.50r – us Archival [071]
TIMES – Greenville. Miss. 1905-1910 – 1 – us UMI [071]
TIMES – Hammond. Ind. 1906- – 1 – us UMI [071]
TIMES – Harlowtown. Mont. 1958-1959; 1966- – 1 – us UMI [071]
TIMES – Harrison. Ark. -w. 1911-38 – 1 – us UMI [071]
TIMES – Hartford. Conn. 1839; 1841-1871; 1873- – 1 – us UMI [071]
TIMES – Hartford. Conn. -sw. 1835-38 – 1 – us UMI [071]
TIMES – Hartford. Conn. -tw. 1840-42, 1845 – 1 – us UMI [071]
TIMES – Hartford. Conn. -w. 1817-19, 1828-35, 1837-62, 1864-73, 1875-84, 1886-99 – 1 – us UMI [071]
TIMES – Hays. Kan. 1880-1887 – 1 – us UMI [071]
TIMES – Helena. Mont. 1950-1954; 1956-1957 – 1 – us UMI [071]
TIMES – Hobart. Ind. 1911-1930 – 1 – us UMI [071]
TIMES – Howard. R.I. 1885-1905 – 1 – us UMI [071]
TIMES – Hubbell, NE. -w. Dec 1892-Dec 1896, scattered issues missing; Mar-May 1897; Sep 1897-May 1899, Jul-Sep 1899 – 1 – us NE Hist [071]
TIMES – Hudson. Ohio. 1930-1958 – 1 – us UMI [071]
TIMES – Indianapolis. Ind. 1943-1965 – 1 – us UMI [071]
TIMES – Kenton, Ohio, 1956-1957 – 6r – 1 – $32.50r – us Archival [978]
TIMES – Kenton. Ohio. 1958- – 1 – us UMI [071]
TIMES – Kingsport. Tenn. 1916-1944; 1945- – 1 – us UMI [071]
TIMES – Kittanning. PA.-w. 1880-98, 1911 – 1 – us UMI [071]
TIMES – Las Vegas, NV. 1932 – 1r – 1 – $50.00 – U04613 – us Library Micro [071]
TIMES – Leavenworth. Kan. 1868- – 1 – us UMI [071]
TIMES – Leavenworth. Kan. -w. 1870-1918 – 1 – us UMI [071]
TIMES – Loon Lake. Wash. 1911-1913 – 1 – us UMI [071]
TIMES – Los Angeles. Calif. Indexed. 1881- – 1 – us UMI [071]
TIMES – Los Gatos. Calif. 1945-53 – 1 – us UMI [071]
TIMES – Loyalton, CA. Feb-Oct 1942 – 1r – 1 – $50.00 – B02414 – us Library Micro [071]
TIMES – Manhattan, NV. Jul-Dec 1907 – 1r – 1 – $50.00 – U04633 – us Library Micro [071]
TIMES – Manistee. Mich. -w. 1871-86 – 1 – us UMI [071]
TIMES – Mannington. West Virginia. 1929-1947 – 1 – us UMI [071]
TIMES – Marshfield. Wis. 1882-1919 – 1 – us UMI [071]
TIMES – Martins Ferry. Ohio. 1891-1892; 1926-1943 – 1 – us UMI [071]
TIMES – Metropolis. Ill. 1876-1879 – 1 – us UMI [071]
TIMES – Millbrook. KS. -w. 1879-89 – 1 – us UMI [071]
TIMES – Minden, NV. 1936-42 – 3r – 1 – $150.00 – U04628 – us Library Micro [071]
TIMES – Mishawaka. Ind. 1961-1966- – 1 – us UMI [071]
TIMES – Missoula. Mont. 1951-1959; 1966- – 1 – us UMI [071]
TIMES – Mobile. Ala. 1933-1939 – 1 – us UMI [071]
TIMES – Mountain City, NV. Jan-May 1898 – 1r – 1 – $50.00 – U04631 – us Library Micro [071]
TIMES – Natchez. Miss. 1949-1961 – 1 – us UMI [071]
TIMES – Neosho. Mo. 1892-96; 1901-1910; 1913-1944 – 1 – us UMI [071]
TIMES – Ness City. Kan. 1880-1891 – 1 – us UMI [071]
TIMES – Nettleton. Miss. 1950-1954 – 1 – us UMI [071]
TIMES – New Castle. Ind. 1909-1930 – 1 – us UMI [071]
TIMES – New Castle. Neb. 1895-1944 – 1 – us UMI [071]
TIMES – New Philadelphia. Ohio. 1886-1894; 1903; 1967- – 1 – us UMI [071]
TIMES – Niles. Ohio. 1933- – 1 – us UMI [071]
TIMES – Northport. Wash. 1917-1918 – 1 – us UMI [071]
TIMES – Oklahoma City. Okl. 1907- – 1 – us UMI [071]
TIMES – Olney. IL. 1857-59 – 1 – us UMI [071]
TIMES – Olneyville. R.I. 1888-1917; 1918-1924; 1926-1932; 1935-1937 – 1 – us UMI [071]
TIMES – Omaha. Neb. -w. 1857-59 – 1 – us UMI [071]
TIMES – Oskaloosa. Kan. 1891-1916 – 1 – us UMI [071]
TIMES – Ottawa. Ill. 1903- – 1 – us UMI [071]
TIMES – Palo Alto. Calif. 1945-1961 – 1 – us UMI [071]
TIMES – Paola. Kan. -w. 1882-1903 – 1 – us UMI [071]
TIMES – Parkersburg. West Virginia. -w. 1865-72 – 1 – us UMI [071]

TIMES – Pembroke, 1930-1931 – 1r – 1 – cn Preston [971]
TIMES – Perry County. Pa. 1966-1968 – 1 – us UMI [071]
TIMES – Peterborough, 1872-1914 – 36r – 1 – cn Preston [971]
TIMES – Philadelphia. Pa. -w. 1877-88 – 1 – us UMI [071]
TIMES – Pittsburgh. Pa. 1877-1888 – 1 – us UMI [071]
TIMES – Placerville. Calif. -w. 1941-57 – 1 – us UMI [071]
TIMES – Port Huron. Mich. 1872-1910 – 1 – us UMI [071]
TIMES – Port Huron. Mich. -w. 1869-72, 1875 – 1 – us UMI [071]
TIMES – Portland OR. Nov 25 1911-Nov 1 1912, Apr 21 May 12 26 June 17 1938, July 1 28, Aug 11 18 Sep 15 1938, Sep 22 1938, Dec 16 1948 + – 1 – us U.O. Library [071]
TIMES – Portland OR. Oct 28 Nov 18 1948, Jan 6 Feb 3 10 25 Mar 10 1949 + – 1 – us U.O. Library [071]
TIMES – Portland, OR. -w. 25 Nov 1911-1 Nov 1912. 1 roll – 1 – us U.O. Library [071]
TIMES – Portsmouth. Ohio. 1894- – 1 – us UMI [071]
TIMES – Portsmouth. Ohio. -w. 1858-1914 – 1 – us UMI [071]
TIMES – Providence. R.I. 1877-1879 – 1 – us UMI [071]
TIMES – Raleigh. N.C. 1903- – 1 – us UMI [071]
TIMES – Rancho Santa Fe, CA. 1986 – 16+ r – 1 – $800.00 ($100.00y) – H04069 – us Library Micro [071]
TIMES – Reno, NV. Jan-Sep 1882 – 1r – 1 – $50.00 – U04720 – us Library Micro [071]
TIMES – Roanoke. Va. 1890- – 1 – us UMI [071]
TIMES – Rogue River, OR. -w. 8 Nov 1951-29 Sept 1972. 8 rolls – 1 – us U.O. Library [071]
TIMES – Roxbury. N.Y. 1895-1951 – 1 – us UMI [071]
TIMES – Salisbury. Md. 1924- – 1 – us UMI [071]
TIMES – San Mateo. Calif. 1946-53 –11 – us UMI [071]
TIMES – Sandakan-North. Malaysia. Eng Ed. Borneo. Borneo. 1962-64 – 1 – us UMI [072]
TIMES – Santa Maria. Calif. 1900-1934; 1956- – 1 – us UMI [071]
TIMES – Scranton. Pa. 1895- – 1 – us UMI [071]
TIMES – Seattle. Wash. 1886-1889- – 1 – us UMI [071]
TIMES – Seattle.WA. -w. 1897-1902 – 1 – us UMI [071]
TIMES – Sebastopol. Calif. 1968- – 1 – us UMI [071]
TIMES – Seymour. Ind. 1862-1881 – 1 – us UMI [071]
TIMES – Shelby. Mont. 1966- – 1 – us UMI [071]
TIMES – Spokane. Wash. 1929-1931 – 1 – us UMI [071]
TIMES – Spokane. Wash. -w. 1879-82 – 1 – us UMI [071]
TIMES – St. Albans. West Virginia. 1959-60 – 1 – us UMI [071]
TIMES – St. Cloud. MN. 1928-47; 1953- – 1 – us UMI [071]
TIMES – St. Petersburg. FL. 1901- – 1 – us UMI [071]
TIMES – Stratford, 1876-1891 – 4r – 1 – cn Preston [971]
TIMES – Subscription – 1 – F7,072.00 – sz Infoprint [072]
TIMES – Temple City. Calif. -w. 1973- – 1 – us UMI [071]
TIMES – Temple. Tex. -w. 1886-99 – 1 – us UMI [071]
TIMES – Thomasville. N.C. 1971- – 1 – us UMI [071]
TIMES – Three Rivers. Mich. 1908-11 – 1 – us UMI [071]
TIMES – Toledo. Ohio. 1970- – 1 – us UMI [071]
TIMES – Toronto. 27 Mar-11 Sep 1919 – 1 – 145.00 – cn McLaren [072]
TIMES – Trenton. N.J. -w. 1883-87, 1891 – 1 – us UMI [071]
TIMES – Troy. Kan. 1886-1901 – 1 – us UMI [071]
TIMES – Troy. N.Y. 1851-1934 – 1 – us UMI [071]
TIMES – Troy. Ohio. 1831-1871 – 1 – us UMI [071]
TIMES – Tylertown. Miss. 1915-1922; 1936-1960 – 1 – us UMI [071]
TIMES – Union City. Pa. 1957-1969 – 1 – us UMI [071]
TIMES – Union City. Pa. and Enterprise. -W. 1882-1916, 1926-58 – 1 – us UMI [071]
TIMES – University Place, NE. -w. May 1896-May 1899, scattered issues missing – 1 – us NE Hist [071]
TIMES – Valdosta. Ga. -w. 1875-1905 – 1 – us UMI [071]
TIMES – Vallejo, CA. Mar-Sept 1891 – 1r – 1 – $50.00 – B03066 – us Library Micro [071]
TIMES – Vallejo. Calif. 1910-1922 – 1 – us UMI [071]
TIMES – Waitsburg. Wash. -d, w. 1881- – 1 – us UMI [071]
TIMES – Warren. R.I. -w. 1961-63 – 1 – us UMI [071]
TIMES – Warsaw. Ind. 1882-1949 – 1 – us UMI [071]
TIMES – Watertown. Wis. 1956- – 1 – us UMI [071]
TIMES – (Weekly general newspaper) – Lorain, OH. oct 7, 1976-dec 30, 1982 – 4r – 1 – us Western Res [071]
TIMES – West Valley. Calif. -w. 1966- – 1 – us UMI [071]
TIMES – Westerly. R.I. 1901-1935 – 1 – us UMI [071]
TIMES – Wilkes-Barre. Pa. 1892-1907 – 1 – us UMI [071]
TIMES – Wilkes-Barre. Pa. -w. 1896-1903 – 1 – us UMI [071]
TIMES – Willard. Ohio. 1971- – 1 – us UMI [071]
TIMES – Winnett. Mont. 1956-1959; 1966- – 1 – us UMI [071]
TIMES – Winona. Miss. 1915-1953 – 1 – us UMI [071]
TIMES – (With Clifton Hill Gazette) – 1938-1939 – at Corangamite [072]
TIMES – Yerington, NV. 7 Oct 1907 – 13r – 1 – $650.00 – U04829 – us Library Micro [071]
TIMES – York. Neb. 1886-1912 – 1 – us UMI [071]
TIMES – York. Neb. -w. 1892-93 – 1 – us UMI [071]
TIMES *see* THE UITENHAGE TIMES
TIMES ADVOCATE – Escondido, CA. 1912- – 838+ r – 1 RC02204 – $41,900.00 ($1,440.00y) – us Library Micro [071]
THE TIMES AND COUNTRY RECORD – Richmond, Canada. v12 n41. 10 jul 1891-v22 n27. 20 avr 1900 – 1r – 1 – Can$30.00 – cn Can Microfilming [072]
THE TIMES AND DAILY COMMERCIAL ADVERTISER – Montreal, Canada. v1 n4. 13 mar 1841-v6 n110. 8 aut 1846 (incomplete) – 1r – 1 – Can$40.00 – cn Can Microfilming [072]
TIMES AND DEMOCRAT – Orangeburg. S.C. 1879- – 1 – us UMI [071]
TIMES AND EXPOSITOR – Adrian. Mich. -w, sw, tw. 1865-1911 – 1 – us UMI [071]
TIMES AND GAZETTE *see* SAN MATEO COUNTY GAZETTE
TIMES AND GENERAL COMMERCIAL GAZETTE – St. John's, Canada. 1832-95 – 20r – 1 – $1,300.00 – cn Library Assoc [971]
TIMES AND HARTFORD ADVERTISER – Hartford. Conn. 1820-1822; 1824-1828 – 1 – us UMI [071]
TIMES AND NEWS LEADER – San Mateo, CA. 1930-57; Feb 1962 – 2r – 1 – $100.00 – B02924 – us Library Micro [071]
TIMES AND SEASONS – Nauvoo, IL. v1-6. 1839-46 – 1r – 1 – us Ross [071]
TIMES AND SEASONS – Nauvoo, Ill. v. 1-6. Nov 1839-Feb 15 1846 – 1 – us NY Public [073]
THE TIMES AND YOUNG MEN / Strong, Josiah – New York: Baker and Taylor, c1901 – 1mf – us A.T.L.A. [240]
TIMES COLONIST – Victoria, CN. 1858- – 24r per yr – 1 – Can$53.00r – cn Commonwealth Micro [072]
TIMES (DAILY) – (Cont by: Peninsula Times Tribune) – Palo Alto, CA. 1902-79 – 543r – 1 – $27,150.00 – B02604 – us Library Micro [071]
TIMES DEMOCRAT – Stroudsburg, PA. -w 1918 – 13 – $25.00r – us I.M.R. [071]
TIMES EDUCATINAL SUPPLEMENT – 1966-1977 – 1 – F2,881.00 – sz Infoprint [072]
TIMES EDUCATIONAL SUPPLEMENT – 1910-1955 – 1 – F698.00 – sz Infoprint [072]
TIMES EDUCATIONAL SUPPLEMENT – 1956-1965 – 1 – F 1,441.00 – sz Infoprint [072]
TIMES EDUCATIONAL SUPPLEMENT – 1978-1979 – 1 – F2,881.00 – sz Infoprint [072]
TIMES EDUCATIONAL SUPPLEMENT – 1980-1994 – 1 – F2,881.00 – sz Infoprint [072]
TIMES EDUCATIONAL SUPPLEMENT – (Backfiles. 1) – 1910- . Not published Nov 1978-Nov 1979 – 1 – us Primary [370]
TIMES EDUCATIONAL SUPPLEMENT – Subscription – 1 – F2,445.00 – sz Infoprint [072]
TIMES ENGINEERING AND TRATE SUPPLEMENT – 1905-1967 – Cumul – 1 – F23,138.00 – sz Infoprint [072]
TIMES FOR UITENHAGE *see* THE UITENHAGE TIMES
TIMES GAZETTE – (Also known as: County Gazette) – San Mateo, CA. 1877-1931 – 12r – 1 – $600.00 – B02923 – us Library Micro [071]
TIMES GAZETTE – Redwood City, CA. 1944-56 – 7r – 1 – $350.00 – C02684 – us Library Micro [071]
TIMES HERALD-RECORD – Middletown. N.Y. 1961- – 1 – us UMI [071]
TIMES HIGHER EDUCATION SUPPLEMENT – 1973-1977 – 1 – F1,222.00 – sz Infoprint [072]
TIMES HIGHER EDUCATION SUPPLEMENT – 1978-1979 – 1 – F1,222.00 – sz Infoprint [072]
TIMES HIGHER EDUCATION SUPPLEMENT – 1980-1994 – 1 – F1,222.00 – sz Infoprint [072]
TIMES HIGHER EDUCATION SUPPLEMENT – (Backfiles. 1) – 1971- – 1 – us Primary [370]
TIMES HIGHER EDUCATION SUPPLEMENT – Oct 1971-1972 – Cumul – 1 – F1,222.00 – sz Infoprint [072]
TIMES HIGHER EDUCATION SUPPLEMENT SUBSCRIPTION – 1995 – 1 – F917.00 – sz Infoprint [072]
TIMES INDEX – 1791-1860 – Cumul – F16,240.00 – sz Infoprint [072]
TIMES INDEX – 1861-1905 – F2,663.00 – sz Infoprint [072]
TIMES INDEX – 1906-1973 – F1,965.00 – sz Infoprint [072]
TIMES INDEX – 1906-1976 – 1 – F34,706.00 – sz Infoprint [072]
TIMES INDEX – 1974-1994 – F3,449.00 – sz Infoprint [072]
TIMES INDEX SUBSCRIPTION – 1995- – F4,628.00 – sz Infoprint [072]
TIMES INTELLIGENCE FILES/UNIT 1 – 1906-1978 – 1 – F18,161.00 – sz Infoprint [072]
TIMES INTELLIGENCE FILES/UNIT 2 – 1906-1971 – 1 – F12,835.00 – sz Infoprint [072]
TIMES INTELLIGENCE FILES/UNIT 3 – 1939-1945 – 1 – F11,438.00 – sz Infoprint [072]
TIMES JOURNAL – Albany, CA. 1979-1984 – 5r – 1 – $250.00 – B06010 – us Library Micro [073]
TIMES JOURNAL – Castroville, CA. Jun 1950-52; 1954-58 – 2r – 1 – $100.00 – B02098 – us Library Micro [071]
TIMES JOURNAL – Forsyth. Mont. 1911-1941 – 1 – us UMI [071]
TIMES JOURNAL *see* CASTROVILLE-TIMES
TIMES JOURNAL-CASTROVILLE TIMES *see* NORTH COUNTY NEWS
TIME'S LAUGHINGSTOCKS AND OTHER VERSES / Hardy, Thomas – London: Macmillan, 1909 – 1 roll – 1 – 1-55879-475-1 – uk Libr Preservation [810]
THE TIMES LAW REPORTS / Great Britain. England – (Updates planned) – London: George E Wright/The Times Publ Co. v1-41. 1884/85-1924/25 – 323mf – 9 – $484.00 – LLMC 95-227 – us L.L.M.C. [324]
TIMES LEHIGHTON – Lehighton, PA., 1983-1984 – 13 – $25.00r – us I.M.R. [071]
TIMES LITERARY SUPPLEMENT – 1902-1977 – 1 – F698.00 – sz Infoprint [072]
TIMES LITERARY SUPPLEMENT – 1978-1979 – 1 – F873.00 – sz Infoprint [072]
TIMES LITERARY SUPPLEMENT – 1980-1994 – 1 – F1,310.00 – sz Infoprint [072]
TIMES LITERARY SUPPLEMENT – (Backfiles. 1) – 1902- . Not published Nov 1978-Nov 1979; Index available – 1 – us Primary [420]
TIMES LITERARY SUPPLEMENT – Subscription – 1 – F1,091.00 – sz Infoprint [072]
THE TIMES, LIVERMORE *see* PLEASANTON TIMES
TIMES, LIVERMORE *see* VALLEY TIMES
The Times. London *see*
– HISTORY THROUGH THE TIMES; A COLLECTION OF LEADING ARTICLES ON IMPORTANT EVENTS, 1800-1937..
– INDEX TO EVENTS RELATING TO INDIA AND THE EAST REFERRED TO IN "THE TIMES" BETWEEN THE YEARS 1850 AND 1889 INCLUSIVE
TIMES: NATAL AND SOUTH-EAST AFRICA – Pietermaritzburg, South Africa. 1856 – 1 – sa State Libr [072]
TIMES NEWS – (1975-1992.-211r) – Thunder Bay, 1993 – 12r – 1 – cn Preston [971]
TIMES NEWS – Lehighton, PA. -d 1881-1991; 1967-1968; 1971-1975; 1986-1988 – 13 – $25.00r – us I.M.R. [071]
TIMES NEWS AND RECORD – Lehighton, PA. -w 1968-1969; 1970 – 13 – $25.00r – us I.M.R. [071]
THE TIMES OF ARGENTINA; WEEKLY SHIPPING JOURNAL – Buenos Aires. Ano 30, n. 1530-ano 53, n. 3101. 1 Jan 1923-20-Dec 1952. (Scattered issues wanting). Commercial and industrial gazette, banking and railway monitor – 1 – 672.00 – us L of C Photodup [972]
TIMES OF BURMA – Rangoon, Burma. 1 Jan 1899-10 mar 1900; 23 Jun 1900-30 Dec 1905; 2, 8-13 Jan 1906.-w,sw,d. 7mqn reels – 1 – uk British Libr Newspaper [072]
TIMES OF BURMA – Rangoon, Burma. (Weekly summary). 20 Jan 1906-20 Jul 1907.-w. 1 reel – 1 – uk British Libr Newspaper [072]
THE TIMES OF CHRIST / Muirhead, Lewis Andrew – Edinburgh: T. & T. Clark, 1907. 1 fiche – 9 – us A.T.L.A. [240]
TIMES OF CYPRUS – Nicosia, Cyprus. -d. 30 May-26 Oct 1955; 20 May 1957-28 Aug 1960. Imperfect. 11 reels – 1 – uk British Libr Newspaper [072]
THE TIMES OF HAVANA – Havana. Cuba. 1957-60 – 1 – us UMI [072]
THE TIMES OF HAVANA – Havana. Cuba. American Edition. 1960-1965 – 1 – us UMI [072]
THE TIMES OF INDIA – Bombay. 1861-89 – 92r – 1 – uk Microform Academic [072]
TIMES OF INDIA – Ahmedabad, India. Feb-Dec 1968; 1981-1994 – 93r – 1 – us L of C Photodup [072]
TIMES OF INDIA – Bombay. India. -d. 18 May 1861-1881; Mar 1911-Apr 1915 – 1 – uk British Libr Newspaper [072]
TIMES OF INDIA – New Delhi, India. 1962-1989 – 170r – 1 – us L of C Photodup [072]
TIMES OF INDIA OVERLAND SUMMARY – India. -w. Jan 1862-Dec 1869. 4 reels – 1 – uk British Libr Newspaper [072]
THE TIMES OF INDONESIA – Djakarta, Indonesia: Times Pub Co, [1952-60]. may 5 1952-55 (8r); 1956-oct 1960 (10r) – 1 – us Res Libr [072]
TIMES OF MALTA – Malta. 1939-1945 – 20r – 1 – uk Microform Academic [072]
TIMES OF MALTA – Valletta, Malta. -d. Jan 1941-Dec 1972. 116 reels – 1 – uk British Libr Newspaper [072]
TIMES OF MESOPOTAMIA – Basrah, Iraq. -d. 11 July 1921-30 Dec 1922. Imperfect. 3 reels – 1 – uk British Libr Newspaper [072]
TIMES OF MOROCCO – Tangier. Morocco. -w. 5 Jul 1884-2 Mar 1893. (2 reels) – 1 – uk British Libr Newspaper [072]
THE TIMES OF NATAL – Pietermaritzburg, South Africa. 1865-1926 – 1 – sa State Libr [072]
TIMES OF SWAZILAND – Mbabane, Swaziland. 1897-1977 – 1 – sa State Libr [072]
THE TIMES OF THE AMERICAS – Cuba. 1965- – 1 – us UMI [072]
TIMES OF THE AMERICAS – (v. 10- 1977-5,6,9) – v. 1-. 1957- – 1 – us UMI [073]
TIMES OF THE AMERICAS – Washington, DC. v10-26. 1966-82 – 8r – 1 – us Ross [071]
THE TIMES OF VIETNAM – (Filmed consecutively with: Times of Viet Nam magazine) – Saigon: Nguyen-Lau, [1960-nov 1 1963] – 12r – 1 – us Res Libr [072]
THE TIMES OF VIETNAM – Saigon: Dong-Nam-A, may 6-nov 1/ 1956 – 1r – 1 – us Res Libr [072]

TIMES OF ZAMBIA – (Formerly 'Northern News') – Ndolo, Zambia. 3 Jan 1956-30 June 1965 1-63 63 rolls; 1 July 1965-30 Dec 19 70 64-96 33 rolls – 99 rolls – 1 – sa Microfile [960]
TIMES OF ZAMBIA AND SUNDAY TIMES – 1972-74.$198.00y; 1975-81.$198.00y; Jan.-Dec. 1982.$198.00; Jan.-Dec. 1983.$198.00; Jan.-Dec. 1984.$198.00; Jan.-Dec. 1985.$198.00 – us African Imprint [072]
TIMES ON SUNDAY (NATIONAL TIMES) – (Details on Request) – 1981- – 9 – at Pascoe [072]
TIMES PHILADELPHIA – Philadelphia, PA., 1898-1902 – 13 – $25.00r – us I.M.R. [071]
TIMES PICAYNE – Riverside, CA. 1974 – 1r – 1 – $50.00 – R03418 – us Library Micro [071]
TIMES PRESS RECORDER – Arroyo Grande, CA. 1983- – 71+ r – 1 – $3,350.00 ($325.00y) – R04005 – us Library Micro [071]
TIMES RECORDER – Zanesville. Ohio. 1885- – 1 – us UMI [071]
THE TIMES RUSSIAN SUPPLEMENT – London. Dec 1911-Jan 1917. (1 reel) – 1 – uk British Libr Newspaper [947]
TIMES SENTINEL – Red Bluff, CA. 1935-38 – 1r – 1 – $50.00 – B02667 – us Library Micro [071]
TIMES STAR *see* DAILY MORNING TIMES
TIMES TRIBUNE – (Cont: Palo Alto Times Tribune) – Peninsula, CA. 1979-1993 – 336 – 1 – $16,800.00 – B02602 – us Library Micro [071]
TIMES (WEEKLY) – Palo Alto, CA. 1893-1905 – 9r – 1 – $450.00 – B0205 – us Library Micro [071]
TIMES WEEKLY – New Delhi, India. Aug 1970-1974 – 5r – 1 – us L of C Photodup [072]
TIMES WEEKLY MAIL – Bangkok. Thailand. 1898-1941 – 1 – us UMI [072]
TIMES-AGE – Coshocton. Ohio. -w. 1914 – 1 – us UMI [071]
TIMES-BONANZA – Tonopah. Nev. -w. 1949- – 1 – us UMI [071]
TIMES-BONANZA AND GOLDFIELD NEWS – (Also known as: Daily Times and Bonanza) – Tonopah, NV. 1917; 1930 – 72+ r – 1 – $3,600.00 ($90.00y) – U04765 – us Library Micro [071]
TIMES-CHRONICLE EXPRESS *see* THE UITENHAGE TIMES
TIMES-DELTA – Visalia. Calif. 1928- – 1 – us UMI [071]
TIMES-DEMOCRAT – Davenport. Iowa. 1964- – 1 – us UMI [071]
TIMES-DEMOCRAT – Tunica. Miss. 1941-1954 – 1 – us UMI [071]
TIMES-DEMOCRAT (DAILY) – Lima, Ohio. 1896-1898 – 3r – 1 – $32.50r – us Archival [071]
TIMES-DEMOCRAT (SEMI-WEEKLY) – Lima, Ohio. 1903-1908 – 3r – 1 – $32.50r – us Archival [071]
TIMES-ENTERPRISE – Albert Lea. Minn. 1907-21 – 1 – us UMI [071]
TIMES-ENTERPRISE – Thomasville. GA. And preds. 1873- – 1 – us UMI [071]
TIMES-ENTERPRISE – Thomasville. Ga. -sw. 1913-22, 1931 – 1 – us UMI [071]
TIMES-GAZETTE – Ashland. Ohio. 1919- – 1 – us UMI [071]
TIMES-GAZETTE – Redwood City. Calif. -w. 1950-56 – 1 – us UMI [071]
TIMES-GAZETTE – Warren. R.I. 1964- – 1 – us UMI [071]
TIMES-HERALD – Lorain. Ohio. 1901-1932 – 1 – us UMI [071]
TIMES-HERALD – Middletown. N.Y. 1932-1957 – 1 – us UMI [071]
TIMES-HERALD – Newport News. Va. 1908- – 1 – us UMI [071]
TIMES-HERALD – Olean. N.Y. 1932- – 1 – us UMI [071]
TIMES-HERALD – Port Huron. Mich. 1910- – 1 – us UMI [071]
TIMES-HERALD – Vallejo. Calif. 1910-1923; 1951- – 1 – us UMI [071]
TIMES-JOURNAL – (1950-1992.-344r; 1993.-12r; 1908-1928.-96r) – St. Thomas, 1932-1939 – 42r – 1 – cn Preston [971]
TIMES-JOURNAL – Condon, OR. -w. 3 Oct 1975-. – 1 – us U.O. Library [071]
TIMES-JOURNAL – Dubuque. Iowa. 1906-27 – 1 – us UMI [071]
TIMES-JOURNAL – Oklahoma City. Okl. 1901-07 – 1 – us UMI [071]
TIMES-JOURNAL – Oklahoma City. Okl. -w. 1901-04 – 1 – us UMI [071]
TIMES-JOURNAL – Selma. Ala. 1927, 1941-54; 1956- – 1 – us UMI [071]
TIMES-JOURNAL – Vineland. N.J. 1876- – 1 – us UMI [071]
TIMES-LEADER – McLeansboro. Ill. -w. 1961- – 1 – us UMI [071]
TIMES-LEADER – Martins Ferry. Ohio. 1943- – 1 – us UMI [071]
TIMES-LEADER-NEWS – Wilkes-Barre. Pa. 1909- – 1 – us UMI [071]
TIMES-MIRROR – Warren. Pa. 1901- – 1 – us UMI [071]
TIMES-MOUNTAINEER – (Set incl. Weekly Mountaineer (The Dalles)) – The Dalles, OR. -w. 4 June 1894-18 Aug 1903. – 6r – 1 – us U.O. Library [071]
TIMES-NEWS – Hendersonville. N.C. 1957- – 1 – us UMI [071]
TIMES-NEWS – Jackson. N.C. 1955- – 1 – us UMI [071]
TIMES-NEWS – Jim Thorpe. Pa. 1956- – 1 – us UMI [071]
TIMES-OBSERVER – (Also known as: Observer, Saratoga. See Saratoga and Los Gatos Weekly Times) – Saratogo, CA. 1955-90 – 75r – 1 – $3,750.00 – B02409 – us Library Micro [071]
TIMES-OBSERVER – Los Gatos. Calif. 1960- – 1 – us UMI [071]
TIMES-OBSERVER *see* OBSERVER
The Times-Picayune *see* WHO'S WHO IN LOUISIANA AND MISSISSIPPI
TIMES-PICAYUNE – New Orleans, LA. 1837- – 1 – us UMI [071]
TIMES-PICAYUNE INDEX – New Orleans. Louisiana. 1972- – 1 – us UMI [071]
TIMES-PICAYUNE STATES ITEM INDEX – New Orleans. LA. 1837- – 1 – us UMI [071]
TIMES-POST – Houston. Miss. 1936-1951 – 1 – us UMI [071]
TIMES-PRESS – Akron. Ohio. 1925-1938 – 1 – us UMI [071]
TIMES-PRESS – Middletown. N.Y. 1906-1923; 1925-1932; 1934-1941 – 1 – us UMI [071]
TIMES-PRESS – Streator. Ill. 1927- – 1 – us UMI [071]
THE TIMES-RECORD – Spencer. West Virginia. 1934-1952; 1958- – 1 – us UMI [071]
TIMES-REGISTER – Salem. Va. 1909; 1934- – 1 – us UMI [071]
TIMES-REPORTER – Dover. Ohio. 1968- – 1 – us UMI [071]
THE TIMES-REPUBLICAN – Corydon, IA. 1967-81 – 1 – us UMI [071]
TIMES-REPUBLICAN – Hayes Center, NE. -w. Apr 1885-Apr 1886; Jun 1888-Nov 1902; Mar 1903-Dec 1917; Dec 1918; Oct 1919; Dec 1919 to date – 1 – us NE Hist [071]
TIMES-REVIEW – Tuscarora, NV. 1880-1903 (broken series) – 17r – 1 – $850.00 – U04774 – us Library Micro [071]
TIMES-SENTINEL – Manistee. Mich. -w. 1890-93 – 1 – us UMI [071]
TIMES-STANDARD – Eureka. Calif. evening. 1967- – 1 – us UMI [071]
TIMES-STAR – Alameda. Calif. 1943-58 – 1 – us UMI [071]
TIMES-STAR – Sedan. Kan. and pred. -w. 1876-1902 – 1 – us UMI [071]
TIMES-TRIBUNE – Beaver City, NE. -w. Jul. 1876-Jan. 1894. Incomplete; Aug. 1895-May 1898; Jul. 1898-Oct. 1898; Nov. 1898-Dec. 1900; Apr. 1901-Dec. 1910; Jan. 1913- – 1 – us NE Hist [071]
TIMES-TRIBUNE – Beaver City. Neb. 1876-1960 – 1 – us UMI [071]
TIMES-TRIBUNE – Norfolk. Neb. 1896-1909 – 1 – us UMI [071]
TIMES-TRIBUNE – Selinsgrove. Pa. 1954- – 1 – us UMI [071]
TIMES-UNION – Albany. N.Y. 1900- – 1 – us UMI [071]
TIMES-UNION – Rochester. N.Y. 1918- – 1 – us UMI [071]
TIMES-UNION – Warsaw. Ind. 1949-1968 – 1 – us UMI [071]
TIMES-WEST VIRGINIAN – Fairmont. West Virginia. 1940-1954 – 1 – us UMI [071]
A TIME-TABLE, WITH NOTES OF THE WESTBOUND TRANSCONTINENTAL TRAIN: THE GREAT LAKES ROUTE: TORONTO AND CHICAGO LINE / Canadian Pacific Railway Company – Montreal: C.P.R., 1887. 00435. (Pre-1900 Canadiana) – 9 – cn C.I.H.M. [380]
Timiriazev, Kliment Arkad'evich *see* CHARLZ DARVIN I EGO UCHENIE
TIMM DER TOLPATSCH : ERZAEHLUNG AUS DEM KRIEG 1914-1918 / Klaehn, Friedrich Joachim – Muenchen: F Eher, 1943 – 1r – 1 – us U.W. Library [830]
TIMM KROEGER / Falke, Gustav – Hamburg: A Janssen, 1906 – 1r – 1 – us U.W. Library [920]
Timmerman, H *see* EEN CORTE BEKENTENISSE ENDE GRONDIGE AENWYSINGE WT DER H. SCHRIFT
Timmermans, I A *see* EMBLEMATA AMATORIA
Timmons, Scott A *see* INCREASING VERTICAL JUMP
TIMMONSVILLE FIRST BAPTIST CHURCH. TIMMONSVILLE, SOUTH CAROLINA : CHURCH RECORDS – 1912-17, 1928-36, 1938-72 – 1 – 16.38 – us Baptist [240]
TIMOLEON / Chenier, Marie-Joseph & Chenier, Mehul – (French Theatre Series). Paris. Maradan et Desenne, an III. 1794 – 9 – fr Hachette [820]
Timor *see*
– BOLETIM OFICIAL DILL
– ECONOMIC PLANS
Timoshenko, Mikhail *see* ZA UBEZHDENIE: IZ VOSPOMINANII SSYL'NAGO
TIMOTHY PICKERING PAPERS, 1758-1829 / Pickering, Timothy – Massachusetts Historical Society – 69r – 1 – $5210.00 – us UMI [920]
Timrot, L *see* SBORNIK ZAKONODATEL'NYKH MATERIALOV, INSTRUKTSII I RAZ"IASNENII PO KOOPERATSII INVALIDOV
Timur *see* MEMOIRS BY HIMSELF
TINATTANTI – Cennai, India. Jul 1966-Aug 1994 – 163r – 1 – us L of C Photodup [072]
Tindall, H D *see* FRUITS AND VEGETABLES IN WEST AFRICA
TINDJEUAN MASE'ELAH PERBURUHAN – Djekarta. 1958- . Monthly (irr.) – 1 – us U.W. Library [073]
Tineo, V *see*
– CATALOGUS PLANTARUM HORTI REGII PANORMITANI AD ANNUM 1827
– PLANTARUM RARIORUM SICILIAE MINUS COGNITARUM
– PLANTARUM RARIORUM SICILIAE PUGILLUS PRIMUS
TINERETUL LIBER *see* SCINTEIA TINERETULUI
TING-AN HSIEN-CHIH – 1878, 10, 1. BCH-637 2 – 8 – ne IDC [950]
Tingay, Alan *see* STUDY OF THE BREEDING BIOLOGY AND AGGRESSIVE BEHAVIOUR OF BLACK SWANS IN SOUTH-WESTERN AUSTRALIA
Tingay, Susan *see* SOCIAL BEHAVIOUR AND VOCALISATIONS OF AUSTRALIAN MAGPIE LARKS IN SOUTH-WESTERN AUSTRALIA
TINGZHAN TANPAN ZILIAO – Materials on the Armistice talks. Comp. by Zhuo Zhaoheng. 6 fiches. F-H144 – 9 – $27.00 – cc Microforms [950]
Tinkham, George H *see* HISTORY OF STANISLAUS COUNTY
Tinkham, Sandra Shaffer *see* THE INDEX OF AMERICAN DESIGN (TIAM)
TINLEY PARK STAR TRIBUNE – Chicago Heights. Ill. 1972- – 1 – us UMI [071]
Tinoco de Castilla *see* PINCELADAS EN CUADROS DE AYER, DE HOY Y DESIEMPRE
LE TINTAMARRE – Journal de litterature, de theatres, de musique, de modes et d'industrie. Paris. mars 1843-46 – 1 – fr A.C.R.P.P. [410]
DE TINTINNABULIS / Magius, H – P 384. New ed 1664 – 9 – ne IDC [780]
DE TINTINNABULIS LIBER POSTUMUS / Magius, H – P 385. 1689 – 9 – ne IDC [780]
DE TINTINNABULIS LIBER POSTVMVS / Maggi, Girolamo – Hanovia: C Marnium & I Aubrii, 1608 – 1 – us Sibley [780]
TIN-TU'C – Co'-quan mat tran binh-dan. No1-43. Hanoi. 2 avr-19 oct 1938 – 1 – fr A.C.R.P.P. [073]
TINY POULTRY TRIBUNE *see* FARM SUPPLIER
EL TIO JUAN – Llerena, 1871 – 5 – sp Bibl Santa Ana [073]
TIOGA COUNTY : OUR COUNTY AND ITS PEOPLE / W.S. Ferguson and Co – Elmira. New York Reel 35. The Cox Library Collection – 5 – us Americana [978]
TIP TOP WEEKLY – New York. no. 1-848. Apr 18 1896-July 13 1912. Incomplete – 1 – us NY Public [073]
Tiphaigne de la Roche, Charles-Francois *see*
– AMILEC, OU LA GRAINE D'HOMMES QUI SERT A PEUPLER LES PLANETES PAR L'A.D.P
– L'EMPIRE DE ZAZIRIS SUR LES HUMAINS OU LA ZAZIROCRATIE
– GIPHANTIE
Tippelskirch, Dorothee C von *see* "LIEBE VON FREMD ZU FREMD..."
TIPPERARY ADVOCATE – Nenagh, Ireland.Mar 1858-Sept 1869. -w. 4 reels – 1 – uk British Libr Newspaper [072]
TIPPERARY CONSTITUTION – Clonmel. Ireland. -w. 4 Dec 1835-30 May 1848. (12 reels) – 1 – uk British Libr Newspaper [072]
TIPPERARY EXAMINER ETC – (Limerick, Tipperary and Waterford Examiner, 1860) – Clonmel, Ireland. 17 Apr 1858-1860 – 3r – 1 – uk British Libr Newspaper [072]
TIPPERARY FREE PRESS – Clonmel, Ireland. 1851-Jul 1881. -w. 30 1/2 reels – 1 – uk British Libr Newspaper [072]
TIPPERARY LEADER – Thurles, Ireland. -w. 23 Sept 1882-25 April 1885. 1 reel – 1 – uk British Libr Newspaper [072]
TIPPERARY LEADER – Thurles, Ireland. -w. 27 Jan 1855-29 March 1856. 1 reel – 1 – uk British Libr Newspaper [072]
TIPPERARY NATIONALIST – Clonmel, Ireland. -w. 11 May 1889-1 Feb 1890. 41 ft – 1 – uk British Libr Newspaper [072]
TIPPERARY STAR – 1909-1980 – ca 72r – 1 – ie Microforms [941]
TIPPERARY STAR – Tipperary, Ireland. -d.1909-86. 98 reels – 1 – PS27.50r – ie European Micro [072]
TIPPERARY VINDICATOR – Nenagh, Ireland.1844-49; 26 Apr 1859-31 Oct 1871. -w.18 1/2 reels – 1 – uk British Libr Newspaper [072]
TIPPERARY WEEKLY NEWS – Ireland.Jan-Feb 1858. -w. 14 feet – 1 – uk British Libr Newspaper [072]
TIPPOO SULTAUN: A TALE OF THE MYSORE WAR / Taylor, Philip Meadows – British Fiction Archive: Unit 5 – 9 – us Bell [830]
Tippy, Worth M *see* THE SOCIALIZED CHURCH
TIPTON HERALD – England. -w. 1965-74. (19 reels) – 1 – uk British Libr Newspaper [072]
TIPTON HERALD – West Midlands. 1913-65 – 35r – 1 – uk Microform Academic [072]
EIN TIR – London, UK. Oct 1926-Apr 1929 – 1 – uk British Libr Newspaper [072]
TIRADAS EXTRAORDINARIAS PUNTUABLES PARA EL PRIMER CAMPEONATO RUTA DE LA PLATA. 1971 / Club Polideportivo de Tiro Puerto de los Castanos (Caceres) – Plasencia: Talleres Graficos Sanguino, 1971 – 1 – sp Bibl Santa Ana [946]
O TIRADENTES : PERIODICO NATIVISTA – Corumba, 7 Set 1897 – 1,5,6 – bl Biblioteca [072]
TIRADES, SIONIAE INTROTIUM MISSARUM EX PROSARUM... / Demantius, C – (9 parts) – Fribergae: Hoffman, 1619 – 1 – us Sibley [780]
Tirado, Juan *see* EPITOME HISTORIAL...JUAN DE LA PUEBLA
Tiran, Michel *see* QUELLES RESSOURCES DOCUMENTAIRES POUR L'EDUCATION AU DEVELOPPEMENT ET A LA FRANCOPHONIE?
TIRE SCIENCE AND TECHNOLOGY – v1-1973- 1; v6- 5,6,9 – us UMI [600]
TIRES – 1919-42. Continued by Tires Service Station – 1 – us UMI [380]
TIRES SERVICE STATION – 1942-52. Continued by Tires: TBA Merchandising – 1 – us UMI [380]
TIRES: TBA MERCHANDISING – 1953-59. Continued by yModern Tire Dealer – 1 – us UMI [380]
TIRESIAS AND OTHER POEMS / Tennyson, Alfred, Lord – London: Macmillan, 1885 – 1 roll – 1 – 1-55879-504-9 – uk Libr Preservation [810]
TIRO AMAZONENSE : JORNAL MENSAL DE PROPAGANDA – Manaos, Amazonas. 13 Maio-11 Jun 1909 – 1,5,6 – bl Biblioteca [072]
Tiro, Hasan Muhammad *see*
– NEO-COLONIALISM IN INDONESIA
– THE POLITICAL FUTURE OF THE INDONESIAN ARCHIPELAGO; A MANIFESTO
Tiro. Ohio. Oakland Lutheran Church *see* RECORDS
Tirtaamidjaja, Husein *see* POKOK-POKOK HUKUM PERNIAGAAN

Tirtaamidjaja, Nusjirwan *see* KULIAH KERDJA HUKUM INTERNASIONAL; PEMBAHASAN BUKU: STARKE 'AN INTRODUCTION TO INTERNATIONAL LAW,' TAHUN

Tirtayasa, I G N *see* BIBLIOGRAPHY OF SOCIAL ASPECTS OF AGRICULTURE IN BALI

Tirtha, Bhakti Vilas, Swami *see* SRI CHAITANYA'S CONCEPT OF THEISTIC VEDANTA

Tirtodiningrat, D *see* SEKITAR PERATURAN PEMERINTAH PENGGANTI UNDANG UNDANG TAHUN 1960 NO. 19 TENTANG PERUSAHAAN NEGARA

Tirtodiningrat, R M T *see* ICHTISAR HUKUM PERDATA DAN HUKUM DAGANG

TIRUMALAI-TIRUPATI DEVASTHANAM EPIGRAPHICAL SERIES : INSCRIPTIONS AND EPIGRAPHICAL GLOSSARY. – v.1-6 (2). Madras. 1930-38. BI-786 2 – 104mf – 8 – ne IDC [410]

'TIS ALL A JOKE / Taylor, Raynor – Voice and piano. 1793? – 9 – us Sibley [780]

TISAB TING, OR, THE ELECTRIC KISS / Fergus, Dyjan – Toronto: Hunter, Rose, 1896. 03089. (Pre-1900 Canadiana) – 9 – cn C.I.H.M. [971]

TISBURY 1669-1900 – (Mf 1-11: Town Records 1669-1864. Mf 12: Town Records 1672-83. Mf 13-18: Town Records 1682-1829. Mf 19-23: Town Meetings 1806-38. Mf 24-30: Town Records 1838-64. Mf 31-41: Town Records 1864-91. Mf 42-52: Vitals 1677-1832 (35mm). Mf 42-48: Family Records 1677-1829. Mf 42-52: Marriages 1719-1832. Mf 45-52: Intentions 1793-1832. Mf 53-55: Vitals 1677-1832 (16mm). Mf 53-55: Vital Records 1677-1832. Mf 56: Vital Records 1831-38. Mf 57-60: Intentions 1833-1905. Mf 61: Vital Records 1837-44. Mf 62: Births 1773-1867. Mf 63: Marriages & Deaths 1844-54. Mf 64-65: Deaths 1855-89. Mf 65-67: Marriages 1853-1900. Mf 68: Births 1807-73. Mf 69: Vital Records 1708-1882. Mf 70: Deaths 1890-1904. Mf 71-72: Births 1868-1904) – (mf ed 1994) – 72mf – 9 – 0-87623-194-6 – us Holbrook [920]

Tischendorf, Constantin *see* NOVUM TESTAMENTUM GRAECE

Tischendorf, Constantin von *see*
- ANECDOTA SACRA ET PROFANA EX ORIENTE ET OCCIDENTE ALLATA, SIVE, NOTITIA CODICUM GRAECORUM, ARABICORUM, SYRIACORUM, COPTICORUM, HEBRAICORUM, AETHIOPICORUM, LATINORUM
- CONLATIO CRITICA CODICIS SINAITICI CUM TEXTU ELZEVIRIANO
- ORIGIN OF THE FOUR GOSPELS
- WANN WURDEN UNSERE EVANGELIEN VERFASST

Tischendorf, G von *see* HABEN WIR DEN AECHTEN SCHRIFTTEXT DER EVANGELISTEN UND APOSTEL?

TISCHGEBETE UND ABENDMAHLSGEBETE IN DER ALTCHIRSTLICHEN UND IN DER GRIECHISCHEN KIRCHE / Goltz, Eduard von der – Leipzig: J.C. Hinrichs, 1905. (Texte und Untersuchungen zur Geschichte der altchristlichen Literatur; der ganzen Reihe 29. Bd., Heft 2b: n.F., 14. Bd., Heft 2b) – 1mf – us A.T.L.A. [240]

TISCHGEBETE UND ABENDMAHLSGEBETE IN DER ALTCHRISTLICHEN UND IN DER GRIECHISCHEN KIRCHE (T.U.U. 2-29/2B) / Goltz, Eduard von der – Leipzig, 1905 – 1mf – 9 – ne Slangenburg [240]

Tischhauser, Christian *see* GESCHICHTE DER EVANGEL. KIRCHE DEUTSCHLANDS

Tischler, Hermann *see* DIE DOPPELBEARBEITUNGEN DER "RAEUBER", DES "FIESCO" UND DES "DON CARLOS" VON SCHILLER

TISKY K TESNOPISECKYM ZPRAVAM O SCHUZICH / Czechoslovakia. Narodni shromazdeni. Senat – Praha. 1920-38.27 reels – 1 – 23.00r – us L of C Photodup [943]

TISKY K TESNOPISECKYM ZPRAVAM O SCHUZICH POSLANECKE SNEMOVNY NARODNIHO SHROMAZDONI.. / Czechoslovakia. Narodni shromazdeni Poslanecka snemova – Praha. 1920-38.55 reels – 1 – 23.00r – us L of C Photodup [943]

LE TISSAGE DE LA SOIE DANS LE BAS-DAUPHINE / Jouanny, Joseph – Grenoble. 1931. (La Condition Ouvriere. Part Two.) – 9 – 5.00 – fr Bibl Nationale [360]

TISSAGE QUECHUA CONTEMPORAIN, REGION DE CUZCO, PEROU / Mangeot, C – 9 – F80.00 – fr Ethnologie [972]

Tissandier, Gaston *see* RECREACIONES... FISICA Y QUIMICA

Tissier, Bertrandus *see* BIBLIOTHECA PATRUM CISTERCIENSIUM

Tissot, Charles Joseph *see* DE TRITONIDE LACU, THESES DIVIONONSI LITTERARUM FACULTATI PROPONETRE, EX TYPIS J.E. RABUTOT

TISSUE AND CELL – v1- 1969- 1; v8- 5,6,9 – us UMI [574]

TISSUE CULTURE ASSOCIATION. TCA MANUAL – v1-5. 1975-79 – 1 – us UMI [612]

TISSUE CULTURE OF SELECTED TROPICAL FRUIT PLANTS – 1987 – 132p – it F.A.O. [634]

TISSUE DEGRADATION MARKERS AND SUBJECTIVE REPORTS OF PAIN AS A RESULT OF ECCENTRIC MUSCULAR CONTRACTIONS / Geisler, PR – 1990 – 1mf – 9 – $4.00 – us Microform Publ [612]

TISSUS ET NOUVEAUTES – Montreal: A. et H. Loinais, [1900?-19–] – 9 – cn C.I.H.M. [640]

LES TISSUS OSSEUX DES OSTEICHTHYENS: STRUCTURE, GENESE, CROISSANCE ET EVOLUTION / Meunier, F J – 9 – F70.00 – fr Ethnologie [590]

TISZATAJ – Szeged. 1947-56, 1961-64 – 1 – 46.00 – us L of C Photodup [073]

TITAN TIMES *see* DAILY TITAN

Titcomb, Jonathan Holt *see* GLADIUS ECCLESIAE

Titcomb, Timothy *see* LETTERS TO THE JONESES

TITERES DE CACHIPORRA / Garcia Lorca, Federico – MS DE 1922 – 9 – sp Cultura [830]

Titford, W J *see* SKETCHES TOWARDS A HORTUS BOTANICUS AMERICANUS

THE TITHE IN SCRIPTURE / Lansdell, Henry – Being chapters from "The sacred tenth" with a revised bibliography on tithe-paying and systematic and proportionate giving. 1908 – 1 – us A.T.L.A. [240]

Titi, F *see*
- NUOVO STUDIO DI PITTURA, SCOLTURA, ED ARCHITETTURA NELLE CHIESE DI ROMA
- STUDIO DI PITTURA, SCOLTURA, ET ARCHITETTURA NELLE CHIESE DI ROMA

TITI LUCRETI CARI, PHILOSOPHI ET.. / Lucretius Carus, Titus – 1631. Includes dictionaries and indexes by Daniel Pareus, 1605-35. Scipione Capece, d1551? – 1 – us U.W. Library [450]

Titiano Vecellio *see* BREVE COMPENDIO DELLA VITA DEL FAMOSO TITIANO VECELLIO DI CADORE

TITLE TO REAL AND LEASEHOLD ESTATES AND LIENS / Frank, Eli – Baltimore: Baltimore City Printing and Binding Co., 1912. 348p. LL-239 – 1 – us L of C Photodup [340]

Titlebaum, Peter J *see* A STUDY OF HIGH SCHOOL TRACK AND FIELD OUTDOOR CHAMPIONSHIPS BASED ON THE EVENTS ENDORSED BY THE NATIONAL FEDERATION OF STATE HIGH SCHOOL ASSOCIATIONS

TITLES 7 AND 11 OF CIVIL RIGHTS ACT OF 1964 AND THE EQUAL EMPLOYMENT OPPORTUNITY ACT OF 1972 – Microfiche ed. US National Relations Board. 2v in 3bks – 9 – $95.00 set – 0-89941-196-7 – us Hein [340]

TITLES AND DOCUMENTS RELATIVE TO THE SEIGNIORIAL TENURE, REQUIRED BY AN ADDRESS OF THE LEGISLATIVE ASSEMBLY, 1851 – Quebec: E R Frechette, 1852. SEM105P252 – 3mf – 9 – Can$6.75 – cn Bibl Nat [340]

THE TITLES OF OUR LORD : A SERIES OF SKETCHES FOR EVERY SUNDAY IN THE CHRISTIAN YEAR / Hill, Rowley – London: James Nisbet, 1870 – 1mf – 9 – 0-8370-3585-6 – 1985-1585 – us A.T.L.A. [240]

TITLES ON COLOUR MICROFICHE : MASTER DRAWINGS / Royal Library. Windsor Castle – (149 drawings, from Leonardo to Augustus John. 316 colour images, including details. With printed index) – 1986 – 8 colour mf – 15 – $260.00 – 0-907716-41-5 – uk Mindata [740]

TITLES TO REAL ESTATE IN THE STATE OF NEW YORK / Gerard, James Watson – New York: Baker, Voorhis, 1869. 400p. LL-814 – 1 – us L of C Photodup [340]

TITO : ERZAEHLUNG AUS DEM TESSIN / Zahn, Ernst – Stuttgart: J Engelhorn, 1927 – 1r – 1 – us U.W. Library [890]

TITO IN INDONESIA / Indonesia. Kementerian Penerangan – SE-2189 1. 1959 – 9 – ne IDC [335]

Titon du Tillet, Evrard *see* DESCRIPTION DU PARNASSE FRANCOIS

Titov, A A *see*
- OPISANIE SLAVIANO-RUSSKIKH RUKOPISEI, NAKHODIASHCHIKHSIA V SOBRANII... A.A. TITOVA
- RUKOPISI SLAVIANSKIE I RUSSKIE, PRINADLEZHASHCHIE...I.A. VAKHRAMEEVU

TITRES, ANOBLISSEMENTS ET PAIRIES DE LA RESTAURATION – Paris, 1901-1906. 6v – 7mf – 9 – F210.00 – fr F.F.G. [920]

TITRES ET CONFIRMATIONS DE TITRES 1830-1908 – Paris, 1909 – 2mf – 9 – F60.00 – fr F.F.G. [920]

TITTLESHALL COURT ROLLS – 1200-1300. Holkham Hall, Norfolk, England – 1 – uk Microform Academic [941]

LOS TITULOS NOBILIARIOS DE LOS GODOY EN LA DOCUMENTACION DEL ARCHIVO HISTORICO NACIONAL / Munoz de San Pedro, Miguel – Badajoz: Imp. Diputacion Prov., 1967. Separata Revista Estudios Extremenos – 1 – sp Bibl Santa Ana [946]

TITULOS Y GRANDEZAS DE MARIA / Garcia Garces, Narciso – Madrid: Razon y Fe, 1944 – 1 – sp Bibl Santa Ana [240]

TITULOS Y GRANDEZAS DEL REINO, SEGUNDA PARTE. TITULOS DE LA CORONA DE ARAGON HASTA LA MUERTE DE FERNANDO EL, CATOLICO / Siete Iglesias, Antonio de – Madrid, s.i. 1958 – 1 – sp Bibl Santa Ana [946]

TITULOS Y GRANDEZAS DEL REYNO. TITULOS DE LA CORONA DE CASTILLA, CONCEDIDOS POR LOS REYES DE CASTILLA, HASTA LA MUERTE DE FERNANDO 5 EL CATOLICO. 1516 / Siete Iglesias, Antonio de – Madrid: Hidalguia, 1956 – 1 – sp Bibl Santa Ana [946]

TITUS COAN : A MEMORIAL / Coan, Lydia Bingham – (Includes bibliographical references) – Chicago: Fleming H Revell, c1884 – 1mf – 9 – 0-8370-6570-4 – 1986-0570 – us A.T.L.A. [920]

TITUS VON BOSTRA STUDIEN ZU DESSEN LUKASHOMILIEN (T.U.U. 2-21/1) / Sickenberger, J – Leipzig, 1901 – 4mf – 9 – ne Slangenburg [240]

TIUTCHEV V POETICHESKOI KUL'TURE RUSSKOGO SIMVOLIZMA / Gudzii, N – Akademiia nauk. Izvestiia po russkomu iazyku i slovesnosti. v. 3, nr. 2. 1930. BR-3269 2 – 8 – ne IDC [460]

Tiutrimov, IM *see* GRAZHDANSKOE PRAVO

TIV 1967- *see* TEKHNIKA I VOORUZHENIE

TIVERTON FIRST BAPTIST CHURCH (DARTMOUTH, OLD STONE CHURCH). TIVERTON, RHODE ISLAND : CHURCH RECORDS – 1752-1956. 1426p – 1 – 64.17 – us Baptist [240]

TIVERTON GAZETTE AND EAST DEVON HERALD – England.1860-66. -w. 5 reels – 1 – uk British Libr Newspaper [072]

TIYO SOGA / Chalmers, John Aitken – A Page Of South African mission work. 1877 – 1 – us A.T.L.A. [240]

TIYU BAO *see* ZHONGGUO TIYU BAO

Tjadens, Herbert *see* YOKO UND DIE PHILOSOPHEN

TJAHAJA – (Microfiche No 176) – Bandoeng, 2602 – 1mf – 9 – SE-2002/1 – ne IDC [950]

Tjahjaningsih, S *see* DUA KERINDUAN DAN TJERITA PENDEK LAINNJA

Tjahya, T S *see* GATOTKATJA GANDRUNG

Tjan, Thay-an *see* COMPARATIVE STUDY ON THREE COUNTRIES WITH REGARD TO THEIR ECONOMIC STRUCTURE AND LONG TERM DEVELOPMENT. A STUDY IN THE BEHAVIOR OF FAMILY CONSUMPTION EXPENDITURE ON HOUSEHOLD DURABLE EQUIPMENT

TJAPAILAH BINTANG-BINTANG DILANGIT (TAHUN BERDIKARI) / Sukarno, Pres. Indonesia – SE 5147 1. Speech on 17 Agustus 1965 – 9 – ne IDC [324]

TJARA BEKERDJA EFISIEN / Liang Gie – SE 5155 1. 1962 – 9 – ne IDC [950]

TJARA MERAWAT DAN MEMADJUKAN: 1 WARUNG DAN 2 TOKO / Silahi, Inan – SE 5627 1. 1952 – 9 – ne IDC [950]

TJARETAH PANDJAHTANDARAN / Adi Koro, Raden Pandji – Batavia: Landsdrukkerij, 1879. Text and t.p. in Madurese with added t.p. in Dutch – 1 – us U.W. Library [490]

TJARIOS NENG OMAH / Ach-San – SE-5170 1. 1965 – 9 – ne IDC [950]

Tjarly, S T *see* GELANGGANG REPOLUSI; 10 TAHUN PROKLAMASI

TJATATAN DI SUMATERA / Radjab, Muhammad – SE-4956 1. 1958 – 9 – ne IDC [950]

TJATATAN PERUNDINGAN HAL MAKANAN – Semarang, 1950 – 9 – SE-5133 1 – ne IDC [640]

TJC NEWS – (Vol. 1, no. 1 (Nov. 1979); comes on a reel with other titles) – Tucson, Arizona – 1 – us A.J.P.C. [978]

TJERITA – Djakarta. SE 807 1. 1957-1958 – 9 – ne IDC [950]

TJERITA PENDEK TIONG HOA – (Magic carpet book). SE 5157 1. v. 1-2 only – 9 – ne IDC [950]

TJERMIN DOENIA – (Lacking: 1947-1948. V.1(1-?(March); 1948, V.2(5-6, 9, 11-12); 1949, V.3(1)) – Makassar, 1947-1949 – 14mf – 9 – SE-972/1 – ne IDC [950]

Tjhio, Jan Seng *see* BUKU PENUNTUN UNTUK PEMBANTU AKUNTAN

TJINTA TANAH AIR / Iskandar, N S – Tjetakan kedoea 2. 2605. 147p – 49-50mf – 9 – ne IDC [950]

Tjipto Mangunkusomo *see* PERGERAKAN DI INDIA. DENGAN KATA PENGANTAR SOEKARNO

Tjirebon, Java *see* PEKAN INDUSTRI NASIONAL, 1961

Tjiung Wanara *see* TJIUNG WANARA: SEBUAH TJERITA PANTUN SUNDA

TJIUNG WANARA: SEBUAH TJERITA PANTUN SUNDA / Tjiung Wanara – SE 4497 1.m 1961 – 9 – ne IDC [950]

Tjoa, Sik Ien *see* PERGERAKAN KAUM BURUH: CAUSERIE TJOA SEK IEN DALAM KONGRES SERIKAT BURUH KEHUTANAN, 16 OKT. 1949

TJOET NJA DIN. DE GESCHIEDENIS VAN EEN ATJEHSE VORSTIN / Szekely-Lulofs, M H – Amsterdam, 1948 – 3mf – 9 – SE-1596/1 – ne IDC [950]

Tjokroaminoto, Umar Said *see* ISLAM DAN SOSIALISME

TLALOC (CELUI QUI FAIT GERMER) ET SES SUBORDONNES LES TLALOQUE / Gueusquin, M F – 9 – F50.00 – fr Ethnologie [290]

Tlaxcala. Mexico *see*
- PERIODICO OFICIAL

DIE TLINKIT-INDIANER / Krause, A – BN 285 2. 1885 – 8 – ne IDC [305]

TMPM: TSCHERMAKS MINERALOGISCHE UND PETROGRAPHISCHE MITTEILUNGEN – v1-29 1948-81. ISSN:0041-3763 – 1,5,6,9,13 – $113.00v – us UMI [550]

TNI AND CIVIC MISSION, AN ASPECT OF REGIONAL DEVELOPMENT / Sokowati, S – SE 5636 1. 1963 – 9 – ne IDC [360]

TO ALL PEOPLE / Moody, Dwight Lyman – 1877 – 9 – us A.T.L.A. [240]

TO BEMA – Athens, Greece. -d. May 1965-Dec 1970. 34 reels – 1 – uk British Libr Newspaper [949]

TO BUILD THE WORLD ANEW / Sukarno, Pres. Indonesia – SE 6247 1. Address at the 15th General Assembly of the UN on Sep 30 1960 – 9 – ne IDC [950]

TO EACH HIS OWN / Chipman, Lauchlan – 1977, 9p – 9 – 1.00f – at Libertarian Micro [335]

TO ESTHER / Thackeray, Anne – British Fiction Archive: Unit 3 – 9 – uk Bell [830]

TO FREE OR FREEZE, THAT IS THE QUESTION / Read, Leonard E – 1972. 224p. 1 fiche (24x) – 9 – 1.00f – at Libertarian Micro [320]

TO HIS ROYAL HIGHNESS GEORGES AUGUSTUS FREDERICK,...THIS TOPOGRAPHICAL MAP OF THE PROVINCE OF LOWER CANADA / Bouchette, Joseph – London: W Faden, 1815. SEM35P155 – 1r – 1 – Can$15.00 – cn Bibl Nat [910]

TO KUMASI WITH SCOTT : A DESCRIPTION OF A JOURNEY FROM LIVERPOOL TO KUMASSI WITH THE ASHANTI EXPEDITION, 1895-96 / Musgrave, George Clarke – London: Wightman, 1896 – us Res Libr [910]

TO PARTICIPATE – NOT JUST YOUR RIGHT BUT YOUR DUTY / Duncan, Bruce – 1fiche (29x) – 9 – 1.00f – at Libertarian Micro [320]

TO PRESERVE THE REPUBLIC WE HAVE PROCLAIMED; CONCEPT OF PRESIDENT SUKARNO / Sukarno, Pres. Indonesia – SE 1232 1. Address to whole Indonesian nation on Feb. 21, 1957 – 9 – ne IDC [324]

TO ROME AND BACK / Capes, J M – London: Smith, Elder, 1873 – 1mf – us A.T.L.A. [240]

TO SAFEGUARD THE BANNER OF THE REVOLUTION / Nasution, Abdul Haris – SE-11,310 1. 1964 – 9 – ne IDC [335]
TO TALER VED ALTERGANGEN OM FREDAGEN / Kierkegaard, Soren – Kjobenhavn: C.A. Reitzel, 1851 – 1mf – us A.T.L.A. [190]
TO TALER VED ALTERGANGEN OM FREDAGEN / Kierkegaard, Soren – Kjobenhavn: C.A. Reitzel, 1852 – 1mf – us A.T.L.A. [190]
TO THE AMERICAN PEOPLE / Apacible, G – Toronto?: s.n. 1900?. 04050. (Pre-1900 Canadiana) – 9 – cn C.I.H.M. [971]
TO THE BITTER END / Braddon, Mary Elizabeth – British Fiction Archive: Unit 5 – 9 – uk Bell [830]
TO THE CLERGY AND LAITY OF THE DIOCESE, HEALTH AND BENEDICTION IN THE LORD / O'Brien, Archbishop – Halifax?, 1892?. 05109. (Pre-1900 Canadiana) – 9 – cn C.I.H.M. [240]
TO THE CLERGY AND LAITY OF THE DIOCESE, HEALTH AND BENEDICTION IN THE LORD / O'Brien, Archbishop – Halifax?, 1893?. 05110. (Pre-1900 Canadiana) – 9 – cn C.I.H.M. [240]
TO THE CLERGY AND LAITY OF THE DIOCESE, HEALTH AND BENEDICTION IN THE LORD / O'Brien, Archbishop – Halifax?, 1895?. 05112. (Pre-1900 Canadiana) – 9 – cn C.I.H.M. [240]
TO THE CLERGY AND LAITY OF THE DIOCESE OF HALIFAX, HEALTH AND BENEDICTION IN THE LORD / O'Brien, Archbishop – Halifax?, 1884?. 05106. (Pre-1900 Canadiana) – 9 – cn C.I.H.M. [240]
TO THE CLERGY AND LAITY OF THE DIOCESE OF HALIFAX, HEALTH AND BENEDICTION IN THE LORD / O'Brien, Archbishop – Halifax?, 1885?. 05I07. (Pre-1900 Canadiana) – 9 – cn C.I.H.M. [240]
TO THE CLERGY, RELIGIOUS ORDERS AND LAITY OF THE DIOCESE, HEALTH AND BENEDICTION IN THE LORD / O'Brien, Archbishop – Halifax?, 1891?. 05108. (Pre-1900 Canadiana) – 9 – cn C.I.H.M. [240]
TO THE CLERGY, RELIGIOUS ORDERS AND LAITY OF THE DIOCESE, HEALTH AND BENEDICTION IN THE LORD / O'Brien, Archbishop – Halifax?, 1894?. 05111. (Pre-1900 Canadiana) – 9 – cn C.I.H.M. [240]
TO THE CLERGY, RELIGIOUS ORDERS AND LAITY OF THE DIOCESE, HEALTH AND BENEDICTION IN THE LORD / O'Brien, Archbishop – Halifax?, 1896?. 05113. (Pre-1900 Canadiana) – 9 – cn C.I.H.M. [240]
TO THE ELECTORS OF THE COUNTY OF STANSTEAD : POSTER / Webster, J J – Stanstead, Canada. 9 sep 1878 – 1r – 1 – Can$25.00 – cn Can Microfilming [971]
TO THE FIRST AMERICANS / U.S. Public Health Service – 1969 – 9 – $5.00f – us Ross [360]
TO THE INTELLECTUALS OF AMERICA WHO SIGNED THE PETITION TO GENERAL FRANCO, APPEARING IN THE AMERICAN PRESS OF SEPTEMBER NINTH, ASKING HIM TO SPARE THE LIVES OF 2,000 PRISONERS REPORTEDLY AWAITING TRIAL IN SANTANDER – Malaga, 1937? Fiche W1228. (Blodgett Collection of Spanish Civil War Pamphlets) – 9 – us H.U. College Libr [946]
TO THE POINT INTERNATIONAL – v1-5 1974-78 1; v3-5 5,6,9 – us UMI [320]
TO THE REFORMERS OF THE UNITED STATES AND ELSEWHERE... / Smolnikar, Andrew B – 1847 – 1r – 1 – us Western Res [240]
TO THE RIGHT HONOURABLE CHARLES POULETT THOMSON, GOVERNOR GENERAL OF HER MAJESTY'S PROVINCES IN NORTH AMERICA / Chatham – 1839. SEM105P657 – 1mf – 9 – Can$2.25 – cn Bibl Nat [971]
TO THE SHAREHOLDERS / Canadian Pacific Railway Company – Montreal: The Company, 1887. 00452. (Pre-1900 Canadiana) – 9 – cn C.I.H.M. [380]
TO THE YOUTH (CCC201) = KAO TS'ING NIEN / Woo, Y K – (In Chinese) – Shanghai: Association Press of China, 1928 – 1r – 1 – 1984-B500 – us A.T.L.A. [305]
TO VEMA – (Yrly reel count varies) – [Greece], 1989- – 1 – inquire – us Ross [072]
THE A TO Z SMALL BUSINESS REFERENCE ENCYCLOPEDIA-WORD MAPPING EDITION / Center for Self-Sufficiency Staff – 1992 – 9 – $29.50 – us Continnuus [650]
TOA KEIZAI KENKYU = JOURNAL OF THE EAST ASIAN ECONOMIC STUDY / ed by Institute of Chinese Economics, Yamaguchi College of Commerce, Japan – (In Japanese) – v1-29. 1917-1945 – 28r – 1 – Y150,000.00 – ja Yushodo [330]
Toadobunkai, Tokyo *see* SHINA SYO-BETSU ZENSHI
Toaldo, Gina-Lee *see* EFFECTS OF (ALPHA)-ADRENERGIC STIMULATION ON SR CA2+ ATPASE AND NA/CA MRNA EXPRESSION IN CULTURED NEONATAL RAT VENTRICULAR MYOCYTES
THE TOBA BATAK LANGUAGE: INTRODUCTION GRAMMAR AND SENTENCE PATTERNS / Pedersen, Paul B – SE-5587 1. 2v. in 1. 1965 – 9 – ne IDC [490]
Tobac, Edouard *see* LE PROBLEME DE LA JUSTIFICATION DANS SAINT PAUL
TOBACCO : SUPPLY, DEMAND AND TRADE PROJECTIONS, 1995 AND 2000 – 1990 – 77p – it F.A.O. [338]
TOBACCO ABSTRACTS / North Carolina. Agricultural Experiment Station. Raleigh – n.1-13. Dec 1956-69 – 1,5 – us Spaulding [630]
TOBACCO ABSTRACTS / North Carolina State University.Agricultural Experiment Station and Agricultural Research Service – No.14-25. 1970-82 – 1,5 – us Spaulding [630]
TOBACCO AND YOUTH – 1906 – 1r – 1 – us Ross [360]
TOBACCO PLAINS JOURNAL – Dewey. MT. 1903-09 – 1 – us UMI [071]
TOBACCO VALLEY NEWS – Eureka. Mont. 1966- – 1 – us UMI [071]
THE TOBACCO WORKER, 1897-1924, 1940-1943 / Tobacco Workers International Union – (Coll title: Labor Union Periodicals, Pt 3) – 1996 – 5r – 1 – $675.00 – 1-55655-614-4 – us UPA [331]
Tobacco Workers International Union *see* THE TOBACCO WORKER, 1897-1924, 1940-1943
TOBAGO GAZETTE – Tobago. 1871-1889; 1891-1898 – 1 – us UMI [072]
Tobar Donoso, Julio *see*
- LA INSTRUCCION PUBLICA EN EL ECUADOR DE 1830 A 1930
- PROBLEMAS ESCOLARES

Tobasco. Mexico *see* PERIODICO OFICIAL
TOBERNE OU LE PECHEUR SUEDOIS / Patrat & Bruni – French Theatre Series. Paris. Huet, an VI. 1797 – 9 – fr Hachette [820]
Tobia, Manuel Maria *see* PROSPECTO... COLEGIO...SAN MARTIN
TOBIAS EXPRESS – Tobias, NE. -w. Oct 1895-Sept 1907; Jan 1908-Dec 1910; Jan 1914-Dec 1921; Apr-Oct 1922 – 1 – us NE Hist [071]
TOBIAS NEWS – Tobias, NE. -w. Dec 1923-Feb 1927 – 1 – us NE Hist [071]
TOBIAS TIMES – Tobias, NE. -w. Jun 1927-Dec 1951 – 1 – us NE Hist [071]
TOBIAS TRIBUNE – Tobias, NE. -w. Jul 1883-Apr 1895; Jul-Nov 1895 – 1 – us NE Hist [071]
TOBIAS WEEKLY INDEX – Tobias, NE. Mar-Apr 1889; Jul 1889-Oct 1890 – 1 – us NE Hist [071]
Tobing, Ph. O L *see* CONTRIBUTIONS TO THE STUDY OF THE INDONESIAN IDENTITY
Tobler, A *see* LE VERS FRANCAIS ANCIEN ET MODERNE
Tobler, T *see* BIBLIOGRAPHIA GEOGRAPHICA PALAESTINAE
LA TOCA DO BAIXAO DAS MULHERES I, UN ABRI PEINT DE L'AIRE DE SAO RAIMUNDO NONATO, SUD-EST DU PIAUI, BRESIL / Monzon, S – 9 – F60.00 – fr Ethnologie [306]
LA TOCA DO BARRO, UN ABRI PEINT DE LA SERRA DA CAPIVARA, ETAT DU PIAUI, BRESIL / Monzon, S et al – 9 – Fr90.00 – fr Ethnologie [306]
LA TOCA DO ESTEVO 3, UN ABRI PEINT DE LA REGION DE SAO JOAO VERMELHO, ETAT DU PIAUI, BRESIL / Monzon, S et al – 9 – Fr60.00 – fr Ethnologie [306]
O TOCANTINS : JORNAL NOTICIOSO – [s.l.]-TO, Brazil. 6 Jan, Abr, Set-Dez 1855; Jan-Mar 1856; Set-22 Out 1857 – 1 – bl Biblioteca [073]
TOCCATA, HARPSICHORD, S. 913, D MINOR / Bach, Johann Sebastian – Lipsia: Hoffmeister, 1801 – 1 – us Sibley [780]
TOCCATE DI CHITARRIGLIA, PARTE TERZA...OVE CON CINQUE BELLISIMI ORDINI DESCRITTA SI VEDE UNA FACILLISSIMA REGOLA PER APPRENDERE IL MODO DI SUONARE LA CHITARRIGLIA DI SPAGNE / Pesori, S – Verona: Andrea & Fratelli Rossi, [ca 1660] – 1 – us Sibley [780]
Tocco, Gil *see* ACTION INFORMATIQUE
TOCHI KEIZAI SHIRYO = LANDED ECONOMIC SYSTEMS OF JAPAN BEFORE THE AGRARIAN REFORM OF 1947 / Japan. Ministry of Agriculture and Forestry – Reports, papers, statistics of farmer practice, land system, tenancy dispute and arbitration, agric. products, etc – 110r – 1 – Y1,188,000.00 – ja Yushodo [630]
DIE TOCHTER DES HERREN FABRICIUS : SCHAUSPIEL IN 4 AUFZUEGEN / Wilbrandt, Adolf von – 2. Aufl. Stuttgart: J G Cotta, 1901 – 1r – 1 – us U.W. Library [820]
DIE TOCHTER DES HERRN FABRICIUS : SCHAUSPIEL IN DREI AUFZUEGEN / Wilbrandt, Adolf von – Wien: L Rosner, 1883 – 1r – 1 – us U.W. Library [820]
DIE TOCHTER DES WUCHERERS : SCHAUSPIEL MIT GESANG IN FUENF ACTEN VON L. ANZENGRUBER / Anzengruber, Ludwig – Wien: L Rosner, 1873 – 1r – 1 – us U.W. Library [820]
DIE TOCHTER TROMSEES : ROMAN / Augustiny, Waldemar – Hamburg: Deutsche Hausbuecherei, c1938 – 1r – 1 – us U.W. Library [830]
Tocqueville, Alexis de *see*
- MEMOIRE SUR LE PAUPERISME
- RAPPORT FAIT AU NOM DE LA COMMISSION CHARGEE D'EXAMINER LA PROPOSITION DE M. DE TRACY, RELATIVE AUX ESCLAVES DES COLONIES. SEANCE DU 23 JUILLET, 1839
- THE STATE OF SOCIETY IN FRANCE BEFORE THE REVOLUTION IN 1789 AND THE CAUSES WHICH LED TO THAT EVENT
- THE STATE OF SOCIETY IN FRANCE BEFORE THE REVOLUTION OF 1789: AND THE CAUSES WHICH LEAD TO THAT EVENT

THE TOCSIN – Minneapolis. v. 1, no. 1-44. Aug 4 1898-June 3 1899. Incomplete – 1 – us NY Public [073]
LE TOCSIN, SUR LA PERMANENCE DE LA GARDE NATIONALE / Guffroy, Armand B J – Paris, Desray. 1789 – 9 – fr Hachette [321]
TOCUMWAL GUARDIAN – Feb 14 1908-Dec 24 1926; Jan 6 1933-Dec 27 1956 – 1 – at Pascoe [072]
TOCUMWAL TIMES – 1894-1895. TT1 – 1r – 1 – at Corangamite [072]
TOCUMWAL TIMES – Jan 4 1894-Apr 4 1895 – 1 – at Pascoe [072]
DER TOD AN DER GRENZE : AFRIKANISCHE ERZAEHLUNGEN / Kaempffer, Adolf – Bayreuth: Gauverlag Bayreuth, 1943 – 1r – 1 – us U.W. Library [830]
DER TOD DES EMPEDOKLES / Hoelderlin, Friedrich; ed by Scholz, Wilhelm von – Leipzig: Insel-Verlag, 1920 – 1r – 1 – us U.W. Library [820]
DER TOD DES MEISTERS : ZUM ZEHNTEN JAHRESTAG / Schenk von Stauffenberg, Alexander, Graf – [Ueberlingen]: Delfinverlag, 1948 – 1r – 1 – us U.W. Library [810]
DER TOD DES TIZIAN : EIN DRAMATISCHES FRAGMENT / Hofmannsthal, Hugo von – Berlin: Schuster & Loeffler, 1901 – 1r – 1 – us U.W. Library [820]
DER TOD FUHR IM ZUG : DEN AKTEN DER KRIMINALPOLIZEI NACHERZAEHLT VON AXEL ALT / Alt, Axel – Berlin-Grunewald: H Hillger, c1944 – 1r – 1 – us U.W. Library [830]
TOD, SEELENGLAUBE UND SEELENKULT IM ALTEN ISRAEL : EINE RELIGIONSGESCHICHTLICHE UNTERSUCHUNG / Frey, Johannes – Leipzig: A Deichert, 1898 – Includes bibliographical references – 9 – 0-8370-3196-6 – 1985-1196 – us A.T.L.A. [270]
Todaro, A *see* SYNOPSIS PLANTARUM ACOTYLEDONEARUM
Todaro, Julie Beth *see* COMMUNITY AND JUNIOR COLLEGE LIBRARIES
Todaro, R Elaine *see* THE PERCEIVED INFLUENCE OF PARTICIPATION IN INTRAMURAL SPORTS ON PURPOSE, INTERPERSONAL RELATIONSHIP, AND AUTONOMY
THE TODAS / Rivers, W H R – London. 1906. BI-1142 1 – 9 – ne IDC [306]
TODAVIA SUENO / Spinola de Gironza, Araceli – Madrid: Graficas Nebrija, 1964 – 1 – sp Bibl Santa Ana [946]
TO-DAY : THE MONTHLY MAGAZINE OF SCIENTIFIC SOCIALISM – London. ns: v1-11. 1884-89 – 1r – 1 – us Ross [073]
TO-DAY – Ottawa, 1977-1978 – 8r – 1 – cn Preston [971]
TODAY – Aspen. Colo. 1971- – 1 – us UMI [071]
TODAY – Chicago. Ill. 1969- – 1 – us UMI [071]
TODAY – Cocoa. Fl. 1966- – 1 – us UMI [071]
TODAY – (Cont by: San Bruno Herald) – San Francisco, CA. 1976-79 – 7r – 1 – $350.00 – B02861 – us Library Micro [978]
TODAY : THE MONTHLY MAGAZINE OF SCIENTIFIC SOCIALISM – (Series 1: no1-5 (all publ). 1883. Series 2: v1-11 (all and last publ). 1883-89) – 2r – 1 – $205.00 – us UPA [335]
TODAY MAGAZINE – (Cont: Canadian Weekend, 1980. Ceased 1982) – Toronto, 1980-82 – 9 – Can$46.00y – cn Micromedia [073]
TODAY MAGAZINE *see* CANADIAN WEEKEND
TODAY-ANGLO JEWISH MONTHLY – (In Jewish) – Canada, 1944-48 – 6r – 1 – cn Commonwealth Micro [072]
TODAY'S CHRISTIAN WOMAN – (1985-5,6,9) – v1- 1978- – 1 – us UMI [240]
TODAY'S EDUCATION – Annual ed. v71-1982- – 1,5,6,9 – us UMI [073]
TODAY'S EDUCATION – Educational support ed. v71-. 1983- – 1,5,6,9 – us UMI [073]
TODAY'S EDUCATION – Elementary Edition. v. 69-. 1980- – 1,5,6,9 – us UMI [073]
TODAY'S EDUCATION – General ed. v69-71. 1980-82 – 1,5,6,9 – us UMI [073]
TODAY'S EDUCATION – Higher Education Edition. v71-. 1983- – 1,5,6,9 – us UMI [073]
TODAY'S EDUCATION – Mathematics science ed. v.70-. 1981- – 1,5,6,9 – us UMI [370]
TODAY'S EDUCATION – Social Studies Edition. v. 69-. 1980- – 1,5,6,9 – us UMI [073]
TODAY'S EDUCATION – (v. 58- 1969- 5,6. v. 59- 1970- 9) – v. 1- 1913- – 1 – us UMI [370]
TODAY'S EDUCATION – Vocational career education ed. v.70-. 1981- – 1,5,6,9 – us UMI [370]
TODAY'S HEALTH – (See now: Family Health) – v1-54 1923-76 1; v45-54 5,6,9 – us UMI [610]
TODAY'S HEALTH *see* FAMILY HEALTH
TODAY'S MAGAZINE *see* CANADIAN MAGAZINE
TODAY'S OR NURSE – (1983-. 1,5,6,9) – v1-. 1979- – 1 – us UMI [073]
TODAY'S SECRETARY – v6-84 1903-82 1; v71-84 5,6; v78-84 9 – us UMI [650]
TODAY'S SUPERVISOR – v46-. 1982- – 1,5,6,9 – us UMI [650]
Todd, Alfred *see*
- TRAITE SUR LES FORMALITES A SUIVRE POUR OBTENIR OU CONTESTER LA PASSATION DE BILLS PRIVES DANS LE PARLEMENT DU CANADA.
- A TREATISE ON THE PROCEEDINGS TO BE ADOPTED IN CONDUCTING OR OPPOSING PRIVATES SIC BILLS IN THE PARLIAMENT OF CANADA.

Todd, Charles B *see* THE HISTORY OF REDDING, CONNECTICUT
Todd, H J *see* CATALOGUE OF THE ARCHIEPISCOPAL MANUSCRIPTS IN LAMBETH PALACE LIBRARY
Todd, Hiram C *see* DIGEST OF THE LAW OF IMPEACHMENT
Todd, J H *see* WAR OF THE GAEDHIL WITH THE GAIL (RS48)
Todd, James Cameron *see* POLITICS AND RELIGION IN ANCIENT ISRAEL
Todd, James Henthorn *see* ST. PATRICK APOSTLE OF IRELAND
Todd, John *see*
- CHARACTER OF GOD
- WOMAN'S RIGHTS

Todd, John P *see* JOURNALS AND ESSAYS
Todd, M K *see* EFFECT OF AGE AND THIRTY MINUTES OF EXERCISE ON PROSTACYCLIN THROMBOXANE A2 RATIOS AND CIRCULATING CONCENTRATIONS OF PROSTACYCLIN AND THROMBOXANE A2
Todd, Mabel Loomis *see*
- POEMS

DIE TODESTAGE DER APOSTEL PAULUS UND PETRUS (T.U.U. 2-19/1A) / Erbes, C – Leipzig, 1899 – 3mf – 9 – ne Slangenburg [240]

TODO POR CRISTO Y CRISTO POR TODOS / Macias Lorenzo, Angel – Caceres: Imp. La Minerva, 1953 – sp Bibl Santa Ana [946]
TODOFUKEN TOKEISHO SHUSEI = COMPLETE COLLECTION OF THE STATISTICAL ANNUALS OF THE RESPECTIVE PREFECTURES OF JAPAN IN THE SHOWA ERA, 1947-1972 – All of the annual statistical reports of the 47 pref., totaling 1,220v 470,000p – 320r – 1 – Y2,850,000.00 – ja Yushodo [950]
TODOS SUS DISCURSOS, MENSAJES Y CONFERENCIAS COMPLETOS, 1973-1974 / Peron, Juan Domingo – Buenos Aires: [Editorial de la Reconstruccion, 1974]. 2v – 1 – CSUXADJ0735-B – us Hoover Inst Photo [320]
DER TODTENDANTZ DURCH ALLE STENDE VNND GESCHLECHT DER MENSCHEN... / Huberinus, Caspar – [Koeln: Arnold Birckmanns Erben], 1557. [G.F.: 5.27] – 1mf – 9 – HUB-23/1 – ne IDC [240]
DIE TODTENFELDER VON SIBIRIEN, ODER DAS GEHEIMNISS DES RUSSISCHEN KAISERSCHLOSSES / Falk, Victor von – Sensations-Roman. Bearb. nach Mittheilungen und Angaben eines vornehmen Russen, der zwanzig Jahre in Siberien geschnachtet hat. Neu durchgesehene verb. Aufl. Berlin, Weichert 1900?. 3 v. Film Mas C 442 – 1 – us H.U. Library [323]
TODTEN-TANZ / Merian, Maria Sibylla – O-1252 1. 1649 – 9 – ne IDC [760]
TOEDJOEAN NIPPON KE INDONESIA / Sakura – (Microfiche No 147) – Boekit Tinggi, Pertjetakan Agam, 2602 – 1mf – 9 – SE-2002/1 – ne IDC [950]
Toegel, Friedrich *see* DAS PROBLEM DER ERZIEHUNG BEI GOTTFRIED KELLER
Toegel, Manuel *see* DIE THEORIE DER OBJEKTBEZIEHUNGEN IN DER PSYCHOANALYSE
DE TOEKOMST – The Hague, Netherlands. -w. 3 April 1915-28 Dec 1918. 4 reels – 1 – uk British Libr Newspaper [949]
TOELZER KURIER : HEIMATBLATT DES MUENCHNER MERKUR – Bad Toelz, Germany. 1 Sept 1978- – ca 14r per yr – 1 – gw Mikrofilm [072]
Toennies, Ferdinand *see* DIE SITTE
Toepke, G *see* DIE MATRIKEL DER UNIVERSITAET HEIDELBERG VON 1386 BIS 1662
Toeppen, Max *see* GESCHICHTE MASURENS
DE TOESTAND DER NEDERLANDSCHE KATHOLIEKEN TEN TIJDE DER REPUBLIEK / Knuttel, Willem Pieter Cornelis – 's-Gravenhage: M. Nijhoff, 1892-1894 – 2mf – us A.T.L.A. [240]
TOESTLOES-NAHWOELNOEK, OR, CARRIER REVIEW – Stuart's Lake, BC: s.n, 1891-189- or 19– – 9 – cn C.I.H.M. [073]
Toffteen, Olof Alfred *see* THE HISTORIC EXODUS
TOFIELD MERCURY – Alberta, CN. 1985- – 1r per yr – 1 – Can$57.00r – cn Commonwealth Micro [072]
Tofino de San Miguel, Vicente *see* DERROTERO...COSTAS DE ESPANA...ATLANTICO
DER TOG = THE DAY – (In Yiddish) – New York City, NY. v24 no8275 11 Sep 1937-v33 no11999 30 Nov 1947 (Birth of Israel Issue) – 1r – 1 – $30.00 – cn Can Microfilming [071]
DER TOG = THE DAY – (In Yiddish) – St-Petersburg, RU. v1 no21 [26 Jan 1904-15 Apr 1904] v1 no73 – 1r – 1 – $25.00 – cn Can Microfilming [072]
TOG PALACE MANUSCRIPT OF THE TIBETAN KANJUR – C. Namgyal Tarusergar, Leh, Ladakh, 1975-1978 – 1,810mf – $965.00 – us I.A.S.W.R. [090]
TOG PALACE MANUSCRIPT OF THE TIBETAN KANJUR – (Includes table of contents) – 1810mf – 9 – $965.00 – us I.A.S.W.R. [280]
DER TOG STRAYKER = THE DAILY STRIKER – (In Yiddish) – New York City, NY. v1 no7. 1941 – 1r – 1 – $25.00 – cn Can Microfilming [071]
AN T-OGLACH – Dublin, Ireland. 15 Aug 1918-29 Dec 1923 – 1 – ie Microforms [072]
Togliatti, Palmiro *see* LAS CARACTERISTICAS DE LA REVOLUCION ESPANOLA
TOGO : ANNUAIRE STATISTIQUE DU TOGO 1966-1973 / Togo. Direction de la Statistique – (Coll title: African Official Statistical Serials, 1867-1982) – 15mf – 9 – £125.00 – uk Chadwyck [960]
Togo *see*
- LE 2EME PLAN QUINQUENNAL 1917-1975
- ECONOMIE ET PLAN DE DEVELOPPEMENT, REPUBLIQUE TOGOLAISE
- JOURNAL OFFICIEL
- LE PARTIE OPERATIONS PREVUES AU PLAN EN 1966-1967
- PLAN QUINQUENNAL DE DEVELOPPEMENT, 1966-1970

Togo. Direction de la Statistique *see* TOGO
Togo. Europaeischer Wirtschaftsgemeinschaft *see* PLAN FUER DIE WIRTSCHAFTLICHE UND SOZIALE ENTWICKLUNG, 1966-1970
Toha, Mohtar *see* DAERAH TAK BERTUAN; SEBUAH EPOS REVOLUSI
TOHFUT-UL-MUJAH IDEEN / Zain-al-Din, Al-Ma'Bari – 1833 – 1 – uk Microform Academic [470]
Tohir, Kaslan Abdullah *see* EKONOMI SELAJANG PANDANG
Tohme, Georges *see* CULTURAL DEVELOPMENT AND ENVIRONMENT
TOHO GAKUHO – Journal of Oriental Studies. v. 1-15 (2). Tokyo. 1931-44. BCH-867 2 – 8 – ne IDC [470]
TOHO GAKUHO – Journal of Oriental Studies. v. 1-39. Kyoto. 1931-68. Lacking: v. 13 (1-2) 1942. BCH-866 2 – 8 – ne IDC [470]
TOHOKU JOURNAL OF EXPERIMENTAL MEDICINE – v1-105 1920-71 – 1,5,6 – us Princeton Micro [619]
Tohoku University *see* SCIENCE REPORTS OF THE RESEARCH INSTITUTE
THE TOILER – Ireland.4 Oct 1913-10 Dec 1914 – 1 – ie Microforms [072]
THE TOILER *see* THE OHIO SOCIALIST, 1919 : THE TOILER, 1919-1922 : THE WORKER, 1922
TOILER : A MONTHLY REVIEW OF INTERNATIONAL SYNDICALISM – v1-3, no. 1 (all publ). 1913-1915 – 1 reel – 1 – $65.00 – us UPA [335]
TOILERS AND SPINSTERS / Thackeray, Anne – British Fiction Archive: Unit 3 – 9 – uk Bell [830]
TOIRE-LIKHT = TORAH-LIGHT – (Yiddish bi-weekly) – Warsaw, PL. no7. 8 Apr 1938 – 1r – 1 – $25.00 – cn Can Microfilming [072]
EL TOISON (SIC) ROTO / Hurtado, Antonio – 1865 – 9 – 1.50f – sp Bibl Santa Ana [830]
TOKEN ECONOMY WITHIN AN ADAPTED PHYSICAL EDUCATION PROGRAM TO MODIFY UNCOOPERATIVE BEHAVIOR OF TRAINABLE MENTALLY RETARDED TEENAGERS / Ozols, M A – 1990 – 2mf – 9 – $8.00 – us Microform Publ [150]
LE "TOKHARIEN B", LANGUE DE KOUTCHA / Levi, S – S. 11. v. 2. JA. 1913. BU-622 2 – 8 – ne IDC [470]
Tokmakov, I F *see*
- BIBLIOTEKI MOSKOVSKOGO GLAVNOGO ARKHIVA MINISTERSTVA INOSTRANNYKH DEL, KATALOG DELAM I RUKOPISAM APTEKARSKOGO PRIKAZA I INYM, OTNOSIASHCHIMSIA K MEDITSINE S 15-GO STOLETIIA
- BIBLIOTEKI MOSKOVSKOGO GLAVNOGO ARKHIVA MINISTERSTVA INOSTRANNYKH DEL, KATALOG RUKOPISIAM, OTNOSIASCHIMSIA DO MOSKVY, MOSKOVSKOI GUBERNII, IKH TSERKVEI I MONASTYREI
- BIBLIOTEKI MOSKOVSKOGO GLAVNOGO ARKHIVA MINISTERSTVA INOSTRANNYKH DEL, KATALOG RUKOPISIAM, OTNOSIASHCHIMSIA DO TSERKOVNOI ISTORII
- BIBLIOTEKI MOSKOVSKOGO GLAVNOGO ARKHIVA MINISTERSTVA INOSTRANNYKH DEL. KATALOG RUKOPISIAM, PECHATNYM KNIGAM, GEOGRAFICHESKIM KARTAM, PLANAM I VIDAM, OTNOSIASHCHIMSIA DO VLADIMIRSKOI GUBERNII, I EE SVIATNI, S 16 STOLETIIA
- BIBLIOTEKI MOSKOVSKOGO GLAVNOGO ARKHIVA MINISTERSTVA INOSTRANNYKH DEL, KATALOG RUKOPISIAM PO IURISPRUDENTSII S 12 PO 19 STOLETIE
- SBORNIK I UKAZATEL' DOKUMENTOV I RUKOPISEI, OTNOSIASHCHIKHSIA K KAZANSKOI GUBERNII I KHRANIASHCHIKHSIA V MOSKOVSKOM GLAVNOM ARKHIVE MINISTERSTVA INOSTRANNYKH DEL I EGO BIBLIOTEKE

Tokmanov, I F *see* UKAZATEL'MATERIALOV PO ISTORII POCHT V ROSSII
TOKOH2 AMERIKA. (CHIEFLY PORTS) / U.S. Information Service, Djakarta – SE 4971 1 – 9 – ne IDC [324]
Tokoro, Isao *see* REIGI RUITEN
TOKSOEZ – Adana, 1924 – 9 – $10.00 – us MEDOC [956]
Tokugawa Institute of Forestry, Tokyo *see* NIHON RINSEISHI CHOSA SHIRYO
Tokutomi, Kenjiro *see* PLUTOT LA MORT
TOKYO ECONOMIC MAGAZINE – 1879-1923 – 80r – 1 – inquire – us Ross [330]
TOKYO NIROKU SHIMBUN – Tokyo, Japan. March-Aug 1904 – 1 – us Res Libr [072]
TOKYO SHIMBUN – October 1942-December 1994 – 597r – 1 – Y5,970,000 – ja Japan Micro [950]
TOKYO SHIMBUN – Tokyo, 1942-84 – 380r – 1 – inquire – us Ross [072]
TOKYO TIMES – Japan. -w. 6 Jan 1877-26 Jun 1880. (3 reels) – 1 – uk British Libr Newspaper [072]
Tokyo University. General Library *see*
- OHRAI-MONO BUNRUI SHUSEI
- SHACHIKU CHIKUREI CHIJU COLLECTION OF RENGA (LINKED VERSE) AND HAIKAI-SHO (17 SYLLABLED VERSE)

Toland, John *see*
- LETTRES PHILOSOPHIQUES SUR L'ORIGINE DES PREJUGES DU DOGME DE L'IMMORTALITE DE L'AME, DE L'IDOLATRIE ET DE LA SUPERSTITION; SUR LE SYSTEME DE SPINOZA ET SUR L'ORIGINE DU MOUVEMENT DANS LA MATIERE
- LE NAZAREEN OU LE CHRISTIANISME DES JUIFS, DES GENTILS ET DES MAHOMETANS
- NAZARENUS OR, JEWISH, GENTILE, AND MAHOMETAN CHRISTIANITY
- TETRADYMUS

TOLD IN THE TWILIGHT / Wood, Ellen – British Fiction Archive: Unit 1 – 9 – uk Bell [830]
TOLEDO AND LUCAS COUNTY 1623-1923 / Killits, John M – Chicago: S. J. Clarke Publ. Co., 1923. Vols. 1-3. Ohio Reel 45. (The Cox Library Collection) – 5 – us Americana [978]
TOLEDO. ARCHIVO DE LA CATEDRAL. SELLOS ECLESIASTICOS DEL ARCHIVO DE LA CATEDRAL DE TOLEDO (1099-1792) / Aroz Pascual, L – 21mf – 9 – sp Cultura [025]
Toledo Blade (Toledo, Ohio) *see* NEWSPAPER INDEX
TOLEDO EXPRESS – Toledo, Ohio. 1856-1913 – 61r – 1 – $32.50r – us Archival [071]
Toledo, Francisco de *see*
- COMMENTARII ET ANNOTATIONES IN EPISTOLAM B. PAULI APOSTOLI AD ROMANOS
- COMMENTARII IN PRIMA 12 CAPITA...EVANGELII SECUNDAM LUCAM
- IN SACROSANCTUM JOANNIS EVANGELIUM COMMENTARII
- INSTRUCTIO SACERDOTUM LOCUPLETISSIMA

TOLEDO HEROLD – Toledo, Ohio. 1907 – 1r – 1 – $32.50r – us Archival [071]
TOLEDO ISRAELITE – Toledo, Ohio. 1938 – 1r – 1 – $32.50r – us Archival [071]
TOLEDO JEWISH NEWS – Toledo, OH. 1969-85 – 1 – us A.J.P.C. [071]
TOLEDO JEWISH NEWS – Toledo, Ohio. 1951- – 6r – 1 – $32.50r – us Archival [071]
TOLEDO JEWISH TIMES – Toledo, Ohio. 1938-48 – 1r – 1 – $32.50r – us Archival [071]
Toledo, Jose de *see* CONSULTA... UNIVERSIDAD DE SALAMANCA...CENSURAS IMPUESTAS...P. CACERES
Toledo Museum of Art (Toledo, Ohio) *see* SCRAPBOOKS
TOLEDO NEWS-BEE – Toledo, Ohio. 1890-1903 – 14r – 1 – $32.50r – us Archival [071]
Toledo, Ohio *see* DIARIES
Toledo. Ohio. Broadway United Methodist Church *see* RECORDS
Toledo. Ohio. Epworth United Methodist Church *see* RECORDS
Toledo. Ohio. First United Church of Christ *see* RECORDS
Toledo. Ohio. Salem Lutheran Church *see* RECORDS
Toledo. Ohio. St. Paul's Evangelical Lutheran Church *see* RECORDS
TOLEDO REPORTER – Toledo OR. Jan 25 1906 – 1 – us U.O. Library [071]
TOLEDO SUNDAY JOURNAL – Toledo, Ohio. 1876-1907 – 1r – 1 – $32.50r – us Archival [071]
TOLEDO TIMES – Toledo, Ohio. 1900-50 – 217r – 1 – $32.50r – us Archival [071]
TOLEDO TRIBUNE – Toledo, Ohio. 1899-1900 – 1r – 1 – $32.50r – us Archival [071]
TOLEDO TRIBUNE – Toledo, Ohio. 1932 – 1r – 1 – $32.50r – us Archival [071]
TOLEDOT AHAVA AHAT / Smolenskin, M (Smilansky) – Warsaw. 1911. BJ-422-87 – 9 – ne IDC [470]
TOLEDOT HAKHMEI YERUSHALAYIM / Frumkin, A L – Jersualem. 4pts. 1928-1930 – 16mf – ne IDC [956]
TOLEDOT HA-R. ZERAHYAH HA-LEVI / Reifmann, J – Prague. 1853. BJ-421-64 1 – 9 – ne IDC [270]
TOLEDOT HA-TEVA / Abramowitsch, S J – v. 1. Leipzig. 1862; v. 2. Zhitomir. 1866; v. 3. Vilna. 1873. BJ-422-2 1 – 9 – ne IDC [470]
TOLEDOT HA-YISHUV U-MEKOMAN BA-HISTORIYYAH HA-YISRE'ELIT HA-KELALIT / Dinur, B – (ha-Kinnus ha-Olami le-Madda'ei ha-Yahadut). pt. 1. Jerusalem. 1952. BJ-27-4 1 – 9 – ne IDC [956]
TOLEDOT HEVRAT MARBEI HA-HASKALAH BE-YISRA'EL / Rosenthal, J L – St. Petersburg. 1885, 1890. BJ-290-12 1 – 9 – ne IDC [270]
LE TOLERANT OU LA TOLERANCE MORALE ET RELIGIEUSE / Demoustier – (French Theatre Series). Paris. Huet. s.d – 9 – fr Hachette [820]
TOLERANZ UND INTOLERANZ IM ZEITALTER DER REFORMATION / Voelker, Karl – Leipzig: J.C. Hinrichs, 1912 – 1mf – us A.T.L.A. [940]
THE TOLERATION ACT OF 1689 : A CONTRIBUTION TO THE HISTORY OF RELIGIOUS LIBERTY / Schaff, Philip – London: J. Nisbet, 1888 – 1mf – us A.T.L.A. [320]
Toletus, Franciscus *see*
- COMMENTARIA UNA CUM QUAESTIONIBUS, IN UNIVERSAM ARISTOTELIS LOGICAM
- COMMENTARII IN SACROSANCTUM IESU CHRISTI D.N. EVANGELIUM SECUNDUM LUCAM
- IN SACROSANCTUM IOANNIS EVANGELIUM COMMENTARIE
- THE MONASTIC BREVIARY OF HYDE ABBEY, WINCHESTER, VOL 3, 4, 6
- A TREATISE OF LITHOTOMY

Tolhurst, J B L *see*
- THE CUSTOMARY OF THE CATHEDRAL CHURCH OF NORWICH
- THE MONASTIC BREVIARY OF HYDE ABBEY
- THE ORDINAL AND CUSTOMERY OF THE ABBEY OF SAINT MARY, YORK, BY THE ABBESS OF STANBROOK (LAURENTIA MCLACHLAN)
- THE ORDINALE AND CUSTOMARY OF THE BENEDICTINE NUNS OF BARKING ABBEY

Tolischus, Otto David *see* THROUGH JAPANESE EYES
TOLK, DE – Paarl, South Africa. 11 Aug 1882-30 Dec 85. 1 reel – 1, 16 diazo available at reduced price – sa SA Libr [072]
TOL'KO LIUBOV' / Bal'mont, K D – Ed. 2. M. 1908. BR-544 2 – 8 – ne IDC [460]
TOL'KO LIUBOV'. SEMITSVETNIK / Bal'mont, K D – M. 1903. BR-543 2 – 8 – ne IDC [460]
TOLKOVYI SLOVAR' ZHIVOGO VELIKORUSSKOGO IAZYKA = VLADIMIR DAL'S INTERPRETIVE DICTIONARY OF THE LIVING GREAT RUSSIAN LANGUAGE / Dal', V I; ed by Courtenay, Baudouin de – 4th ed. St Petersburg, Moscow: M Wolf Publ. v1-4. 1912 – 44mf – 9 – $290.00 – us Ross [460]
TOLLAND 1843-1900 – (Mf 1: Marriage Index Cards 1843-1982. Mf 2: Birth Index Cards 1844-1982, A-S. Mf 3: Birth Index Cards 1844-1982, S-W. Mf 4: Death Index Cards 1843-1982, A-T. Mf 5: Death Index Cards 1843-1982, T-W. Mf 6: Births 1844-65, Marriages 1843-65. Mf 7: Deaths 1843-65. Mf 8: Deaths 1866-1987. Mf 9: Marriages 1866-1987. Mf 10: Births 1866-1900) – (mf ed 1988) – 10mf – 9 – 0-87623-088-5 – us Holbrook [920]
DER TOLLE BOMBERG : EIN WESTFAELISCHER SCHELMENROMAN / Winckler, Josef – Stuttgart: Deutsche Verlags-Anstalt, [1934?] – 1r – 1 – us U.W. Library [830]
Tollemache, Marguerite *see*
- FRENCH JANSENISTS
- MANY VOICES
- SPANISH MYSTICS

Tollenaer, Joose de *see* SOMMIGE BRIEVEN OFTE BELIJDINGEN
EIN TOLLER EINFALL : SCHWANK IN VIER AUFZUEGEN / Laufs, Carl – Leipzig: P Reclam, [18–?] – 1r – 1 – us U.W. Library [820]
Toller, Ernst *see*
- DIE BLINDE GOETTIN
- GEDICHTE DER GEFANGENEN
- VORMORGEN

Toller, Thomas Northcote *see* OUTLINES OF THE HISTORY OF THE ENGLISH LANGUAGE
Tollet, Casimir *see* LES HOPITAUX MODERNES AU XIXE SIECLE
Tollinton, Richard Bartram *see* CLEMENT OF ALEXANDRIA, A STUDY IN CHRISTIAN LIBERALISM
Tolman, William Howe *see* SOCIAL ENGINEERING: A RECORD OF THINGS DONE BY AMERICAN INDUSTRIALISTS EMPLOYING UPWARDS OF ONE AND ONE-HALF MILLION OF PEOPLE
TOLNA MEGYEI NEPUJSAG – Szekszard, Hungary. Feb 1959-70 – 21r – 1 – us L of C Photodup [072]
Tolson Memorial Museum. Huddersfield *see* POLITICAL PAMPHLETS
Tolstoi, Lev N *see* KEMBALI KEPADA TJINTA KASIHMU
Tolstoi, Lev N et al *see* O KOOPERATSII
TOLSTOI UND DAS NEUE TESTAMENT / Ackermann, Johannes – Leipzig, 1927 – 2mf – 9 – DM62.00 – 3-89349-338-7 – gw Hänsel [220]
Tolstoy, Leo *see*
- IN PURSUIT OF HAPPINESS
- SOME SOCIAL REMEDIES: SOCIALISM, ANARCH; HENRY GEORGISM AND THE LAND QUESTION, COMMUNISM, ETC
- WHAT IS TO BE DONE? LIFE

THE TOM HARRISSON MASS-OBSERVATION ARCHIVE – (Part 2: 1942-49) – Part 1, the File Reports, 1937-41 – 9 – us Primary [025]
TOM L. JOHNSON PAPERS *see* JOHNSON, TOM L., PAPERS, MS 4021
TOM L. JOHNSON PAPERS, SERIES 1, MS 3651 / Johnson, Tom L – 1901-08. Correspondence, memoranda, clippings, legal papers – 1 – us Western Res [920]
TOM (TEXT ON MICROFORM) – Monthly cumulative index (Sept-May) of 125 periodicals most often used in high school libraries, plus an integrated microfiche collection containing cover-to-cover film for 55 of these periodicals – 5,9 – us I.A.C. [073]
TOM, UNLIMITED: A STORY FOR CHILDREN / Allen, Grant – London: Grant Richards, 1897. 05082. (Pre-1900 Canadiana) – 9 – cn C.I.H.M. [830]
TOMA DE POSESION DE ACADEMICO. NOTICIA / Monsalud, Marques de – Madrid: Portanet, 1900. B.R.A.H. 36, 1900, pp. 521-522 – sp Bibl Santa Ana [946]
Tomac, Dragutin *see* USTAV I BRACNO PRAVO
TOMAHAWK – Portland OR. Dec 26 1893 – 1 – us U.O. Library [071]
Tomas Navarro, Domingo *see* EL REGALO DE BODA
Tomas, Pascual *see* DISCURSO EN EL "GRAN PRICE" DE BARCELONA, EL DIA 17 DE ENERO DE 1937
Tomasic, Dinko A *see* AMERICANS FROM CROATIA
TOMB OF JAHANGIR AT SHAHDARA NEAR LAHORE / India. Preservation of National Monuments; ed by Cole, H H – Calcutta, 1884. BI-688 2 – 8 – ne IDC [720]
THE TOMB OF TUT-ANKH-AMEN, 3 / Carter, Howard – Cassell, 1933 – 9 – $12.00 – us I.R.C. [900]
LE TOMBEAU DE REKHMARA, PREFET DE THEBES SOUS LA 17E / Virey, P H – Dynastie. H 395 2. 1894 – 8 – ne IDC [930]
LES TOMBEAUX MODERNES, CHAPELLES, CROIX, MAUSOLEES, PIERRES TOMBALES, SARCOPHAGES, STELES. / Chabat, Pierre – Paris, 1890. 16p., 50 pl. (Architecture Series) – 9 – fr Hachette [720]
LES TOMBES FLAMEJANTS / Gassol, Ventura – NY, 193? Fiche W 909. (Blodgett Collection of Spanish Civil War Pamphlets) – 9 – us H.U. College Libr [946]
LA TOMBOLA – Saint-Jean [Quebec: s.n., 1889?-189- ou 19–] – 9 – cn C.I.H.M. [170]
TOMBOLA – Montreal: Le Club independant ouvrier, [1898-189- ou 19–] – 9 – cn C.I.H.M. [360]
LA TOMBOLA QUOTIDIENNE – St-Jean, Canada. v2 n1. 30 sep 1890 – 1r – 1 – Can$25.00 – cn Can Microfilming [072]
TOMBS OF THE COURTIERS AND OXYRHYNKHOS / Petrie, William Matthew Flinders – 1925 – 9 – $10.00 – us I.R.C. [930]
THE TOMBS OF THE POPES = GRABDENKMAELER DER PAPSTE : LANDMARKS IN PAPAL HISTORY / Gregorovius, Ferdinand – (Includes index) – Westminster: Archibald Constable, 1903 – 1mf – 9 – 0-8370-8819-4 – 1986-2819 – us A.T.L.A. [920]
TOMBSTONE INSCRIPTIONS / Charleston. South Carolina. First (Scots) Presbyterian Church – 1888. Chronologically arranged.5 fiches – 9 – us South Carolina Historical [978]
TOMBSTONE INSCRIPTIONS / Charleston. South Carolina. Unitarian Church – 1777-86. 2 fiches – 2mf – 9 – us South Carolina Historical [920]
TOMBSTONE INSCRIPTIONS OF SNYDER COUNTY / Wagenseller, George W – Middleburgh, Wagenseller Publishing Co., 1904. Pennsylvania Reel 38. (The Cox Library Collection) – 5 – us Americana [978]
Tomkins, Henry George *see* THE LIFE AND TIMES OF JOSEPH IN THE LIGHT OF EGYPTIAN LORE
Tomkinson, Laura E *see* TWENTY YEARS' HISTORY: OF THE WOMAN'S HOME MISSIONARY SOCIETY OF THE METHODIST EPISCOPAL CHURCH, 1880-1900
Tomlin, Jacob *see* CRITICAL REMARKS ON DR. TREGELLES' GREEK TEXT OF THE REVELATION
Tomline, William Edward Pretyman *see* A SPEECH ON THE CHARACTER OF THE RIGHT HON. WILLIAM PITT..
Tomlins, Thomas Edlyne *see* THE LAW DICTIONARY
Tomlinson, H M *see* GALLIONS REACH. LEIPZIG, 1928
Tommasini, Gabriel *see* LA CIVILIZACION CRISTIANA DEL CHOCO (1554-1810)
TOMMY AND GRIZEL / Barrie, James Matthew – London: Cassell, 1900 – 1 roll – 1 – uk Libr Preservation [830]
TOMO OCTAVO DE LAS ESCRITURAS DE TAPIA – 1621 – 1 – sp Bibl Santa Ana [946]
TOMO QUINTO DE LAS ESCRITURAS DE TAPIA – 1631 – 1 – sp Bibl Santa Ana [946]
TOMO SEGUNDO DE LAS ESCRITURAS DE TAPIA – 1620 – 1 – sp Bibl Santa Ana [946]
TOMO SEXTO DE LAS ESCRITURAS DE TAPIA – 1627 – 1 – sp Bibl Santa Ana [946]
TOMO TERCERO DE LAS ESCRITURAS DE TAPIA – 1621 – 1 – sp Bibl Santa Ana [946]
TOMORI – Tirana, Albania.Sept 1940-Feb 1941 – 1r – 1 – us L of C Photodup [949]
Tompkins, D A *see* HISTORY OF MECKLENBURG COUNTY AND THE CITY OF CHARLOTTE 1749-1903
Tompkins, Leslie Jay *see* A SUMMARY OF THE LAW OF PRIVATE CORPORATIONS
TOMPKINSVILLE BAPTIST CHURCH (FORMERLY: MILL CREEK BAPTIST CHURCH). KENTUCKY : CHURCH RECORDS – 1799-1953 – 1 – 40.23 – us Baptist [240]
TOM'S CREEK BAPTIST CHURCH. LIBERTY ASSOCIATION. DAVIDSON COUNTY. NORTH CAROLINA : CHURCH RECORDS – 1808-91 – 1 – 12.06 – us Baptist [240]
Tomsinskii, S G *see*
- BOR'BA KLASSOV I PARTII V 1-I GOSUDARSTVENNOI DUME
- BOR'BA KLASSOV I PARTII VO VTOROI GOSUDARSTVENNOI DUME

TOMVS QVARTVS ANNOTATIONVM LUCAE LOSSII, IN NOVVM TESTAMENTUM IESV CHRISTI NAZARENI,...CONTINENS NARRATIONEM ACTORUM APOSTOLICORUM...A CAPITE TERTIODECIMO USQUE AD FINEM... / Lossius, L – Franc., 1558. V.4 – 8mf – ne IDC [240]
Tonawanda. New York. Amherst Baptist Church *see* AMHERST ANNOUNCER (NEWSLETTER) AND BULLETINS
TONBRIDGE FREE PRESS – England. -w. 18 Mar 1871-27 Aug 1971. (Wanting 1879). (100 reels) – 1 – uk British Libr Newspaper [072]
TONBRIDGE MISCELLANY – England. -m. Jan 1854-Dec 1855. 20 ft – 1 – uk British Libr Newspaper [072]
TONBRIDGE TELEGRAPH – England. -w. 19 Dec 1863-Dec 1872. 3 reels – 1 – uk British Libr Newspaper [072]
Tonci, S *see* DESCRIZIONE REGIONATA DELLA GALLERIA DORIA PRECEDUTA DA UN BREVE SAGGIO DI PITTURA
TONES AND OVERTONES – Montgomery, AL. v1-3. 1953-56 – 1r – 1 – us Ross [780]
Tong, Hollington Kong *see* AUTOBIOGRAPHY OF HOLLINGTON K. TONG (CCC302)
TONG JI DAXUE XUEBAO – Journal of Tong-Ji University. In Chinese but English abstracts to the main articles. F p174 – 9 – 4.00f – cc Microforms [073]
TONG MUC LUC LUAT LE CUA NUOC VIET NAM DAN CHU CONG HOA = GENERAL INDEX OF LAWS AND REGULATIONS OF THE DEMOCRATIC REPUBLIC OF VIET NAM / Legal Bureau, the Prime Minister's Office – (Includes subject-matter analytical indexes) – v1-3. 1945-68 – 7mf – 9 SEL-102/1 – ne IDC [340]
Tonga *see* DEVELOPMENT PLAN
TONGA GOVERNMENT GAZETTE – Tonga, 1955-67 – 3r – 1 – us Ross [324]
Tonga. Ministry of Education *see* REPORT 1965-1980
Tonga. Ministry of Justice *see*
- ARCHIVES OF THE TONGAN JUDICIARY, 1905-1995
- TONGATAPU REGISTRY

TONGATAPU REGISTRY : MARRIAGE CERTIFICATES, 1892-1899, 1903-1909 / Tonga. Ministry of Justice – 3r – 1 – PMB1086 – at Pacific Mss [920]
TONGOAN DICTIONARY AND OTHER VANUATU LANGUAGE MATERIAL / Miller, Rev. J Graham – c 1941 – 1r – 1 – at Pacific Mss [490]
THE TONGUE – (Cont: Anthill) – Irvine, CA: UC Irvine, 1966 – 1r – 1 – $50.00 – R02314 – us Library Micro [370]
THE TONGUE *see* ANTHILL
TONGUE OF FIRE: THE TRUE POWER OF CHRISTIANITY / Arthur, William – New York: Harper & Brothers, 1893. 1 fiche – 9 – us A.T.L.A. [240]
TONGXIN XUEBAO – Journal of China Institute of Communications. In Chinese but English abstracts to the main articles. F p92 – 9 – $4.50f – cc Microforms [073]
Toni, G B de *see*
- L'ALGARUM ZANARDINI. WITH BIOGRAPHY OF G. A. M. ZANARDINI BY G. MENEGHINI
- ALGHI DI AUSTRALIA, TASMANIA E NUOVA ZELANDA RACCOLTE DAL G. CAPRA NEL 1908-1909
- SYLLOGE ALGARUM OMNIUM HUCUSQUE COGNITARUM

TONIO KROEGER / Mann, Thomas – Berlin: Fischer, 1921 – 1r – 1 – us U.W. Library [830]
Toniolo, A *see* RIDENTE AMORE, THE FAVORITE RONDO IN THE OPERA 2 MARCHESE TULIPANO (BY PAISIELLO)
LE TONKIN: EXPLORATION DU MEKONG / Dumoulin, Stephane – Illus. de Dick de Lonlay. 4eme ed. Paris: C. Delagrave, (1888?). 396p. 1 reel.1247 – 1 – us U.W. Library [910]
Tonnelat, Ernest *see* LES FRERES GRIMM
TONOLOGISCHE SCHETS VAN HET TSHILUBA (KAYASI, BELGISCH KONGO) / Burssens, Amaat – Antwerpen: de Sikkel, 1939 – us Res Libr [470]
TONOMETRIE / Raoult, Francois Marie – Evreux, C. Herissey, 1900. 115p. 2 fiches. (Science Collection) – 9 – 6.00 – fr Bibl Nationale [530]
THE TONOPAH MINER – Butler, NV. Jul-Dec 1906 – 1r – 1 – $50.00 – U04428 – us Library Micro [071]
TONOPAH MINING RECORD AND REPORTER – Tonopah, NV. 1925-32 (broken series) – 2r – 1 – $100.00 – us Library Micro [071]
TONTEMBOANSCHE TEKSTEN / Schwarz, J A T – Leiden, 1907.-3v – 20mf – 9 – SE-1623/1 – ne IDC [950]
TONTEMBOANSCH-NEDERLANDSCH WOORDENBOEK MET NEDERLANDSCH-TONTEMBOANSCH REGISTER / Schwarz, J A T – Leiden, 1908 – 12mf – ne IDC [490]
TONTEMBOANSCH-NEDERLANDSCH WOORDENBOEK MET NEDERLANDSCH-TONTEMBOANSCH REGISTER / Schwarz, J A T – Leiden. SE 97/1. 1908 – 12mf – 9 – ne IDC [430]
Tonti, Henri de *see* DERNIERES DECOUVERTES DANS L'AMERIQUE SEPTENTRIONALE DE M. DE LA SALLE
Tontogany. Ohio. First United Presbyterian Church *see* RECORDS
DER TONWILLE – Leipzig, AU. 1922-1924 – 1r – $50.00 – R63597 – us Library Micro [072]
DER TONWILLE – Vienna. v1-3. 1922-1924 – 1 – us NY Public [943]
TONWISSENSCHAFT UND TONSETZKUNST / Vogler, Georg Joseph – 1776 – 2 – us Sibley [780]
TONWISSENSCHAFT UND TONSETZKUNST / Vogler, Georg Joseph – Mannheim. 1776. BP-770 1 – 9 – ne IDC [780]
TOO PROUD TO SERVE – 1956-60. Alaska Native Brotherhood. (American Indian Periodicals in the Princeton University Library) – 1mf – 9 – $45.00 – us UPA [305]
Tooke, Charles Wesley *see* CASES ON THE LAW OF MUNICIPAL CORPORATIONS
Tooke, John Horne *see* THE DIVERSIONS OF PURLEY
TOOLS, HARDWARE, FIREARMS AND VEHICLES (TIAM PT 4) – (With printed catalogue ISBN: 0-914146-68-8 £30) – 16mf – 15 – £410.00 – uk Chadwyck [680]
TOOLS OF THE GLASSMAKER – 1981. 16p, 26 illus. 1 fiche. Fiche no. 6685 – 9 – $2.50 – us Corning Mus [700]
Toomey, Glenn *see* BAPTIST CHURCHES OF EAST TENNESSEE
Toon, C J *see* BODY PART IDENTIFICATION AND COMPREHENSION OF SPATIAL PREPOSITIONS IN HANDICAPPED AND NONHANDICAPPED PRESCHOOL CHILDREN
Toone, William *see* THE MAGISTRATE'S MANUAL...4TH ED
TOONKUN WEEKBLAD GEWIJD AAN DE BELANGEN VAN HET MUZIEKLEVEN – P 623. Amsterdam v.1-14. 1905-1918 – 146mf – 9 – ne IDC [780]
TOONNEEL DES MENSCHELIKKEN LEVENS / Vondel, J van den – Amsterdam, 1661 – 2mf – 9 – ne IDC [700]
TOONNEEL DES MENSCHELIKKEN LEVENS, OF DE VERNIEUWDE GULDEN WINKEL : WAER IN, DOOR POETISCHE, HISTORISCHE, MORALE EN SCHRIFTUURLIKKE LEERINGEN, DEN MENSCHE VERTOONT WERDT, HOEDANIGH HY ZIJN LEVEN, HANDEL, EN WANDEL, ZEDIGLIK, EERBAERLIK EN VERMAKELIK SAL OVERBRENGEN / Vondel, J van den – Amsterdam, 1655 – 2mf – 9 – O-3196/1 – ne IDC [760]
TOONNEEL DES MENSCHELYKEN LEVENS : OF DE VERNIEUWDE GULDEN WINKEL; WAAR IN DOOR POETISCHE, HISTORISCHE, MORALE, EN SCHRIFTUURLIJKE LEERINGEN, DEN MENSCHE VERTOONT WERD, HOEDANIG HY ZIJN LEVEN, HANDEL, EN WANDEL, ZEDIGLIJK, EERBAARLIJK EN VERMAKELIJK ZAL OVERBRENGEN / Vondel, J van den – Amsterdam, 1699 – 2mf – 9 – O-3198/1 – ne IDC [760]
Toorenbergen, J J van *see*
- ACTEN VAN DE CLASSICALE EN SYNODALE VERGADERINGEN DER VERSCHILLENDEN GEMEENTEN IN HET LAND VAN CLEEF, STICHT VAN KEULEN EN AKEN 1571-1589 (DE WERKEN..2,2)
- ACTEN VAN DE COLLOQUIA DER NEDERLANSCHE GEMEENTEN IN ENGELAND 1575-1624 (DE WERKEN..2,1)
- BRIEVEN UIT ONDERSCHEIDENE KERKELIJKE ARCHIEVEN (DE WERKEN..3,2)
- BRIEVEN UIT ONDERSCHEIDENE KERKELIJKE ARCHIEVEN (DE WERKEN..3,4)
- BRIEVEN UIT ONDERSCHEIDENE KERKELIJKE ARCHIEVEN (DE WERKEN..3,5)
- GESCHIEDENISSEN ENDE HANDELINGEN.DER NEDERDUYTSCHE NATIE IN ENGELANT (DE WERKEN..3,1)
- STUKKEN BETR. DE DIACONIE DER VREEMDELINGEN TE EMDEN 1560-1576 (DE WERKEN..1,2)

Toornenbergen, J J van *see* DE SYMBOLISCHE SHRIFTEN DER NED. HERV. KERK
Toornenebergen, J van *see* ACTEN VAN DE CLASS. EN SYNOD. VERG. DER VERSCH. GEMEENTEN IN HET LAND VAN CLEEF

Tooth, M *see*
- JOURNALS, 1796-1807, 1813-1814, 1832-1833, 1837-1842
- POCKET-BOOKS AND DIARIES, 1799, 1801-1812, 1815, 1818-1831

TOOWOOMBA CHRONICLE – 1 – F3,660.00 – sz Infoprint [072]

TOOWOOMBA CHRONICLE – (Current issues avail on subscription) – Brisbane, 1979- – 214r – 1 – at Pascoe [072]

TOOZUK-I-JEHANGEEREE / Jahangir – Ghazeepore, 1863-1864. BI-768 2 – 8 – ne IDC [490]

THE TOP 250 / Career Guidance Foundation – Catalogs from the top-rated 250 academic centers from all 50 states – 225mf – 9 – $258.00 – us Career [370]

Top, Alexander *see* THE OLIVE LEAFE: OR, UNIVERSALL ABCE

TOP MANAGEMENT IN EGYPT: ITS STRUCTURE, QUALITY AND PROBLEMS / Farid, S M – (RAND Corporation). 1970. BNE-4629 1 – 9 – ne IDC [650]

TOP OF THE NEWS – (v. 27- 1970- 5,6. v. 33- 1976- 9) – v. 1- 1942- – 1 – us UMI [020]

TOP SECRET STUDIES ON U.S. COMMUNICATIONS INTELLIGENCE DURING WORLD WAR 2 / ed by National Security Agency – (Pt 1, Pacific Theater: 47r. $5,175.00. ISBN: 1-55655-181-9; Pt 2, European Theater: 5r. $550.00. ISBN: 1-55655-182-7; Pt 3, Organization and Administration. 7r. $770.00. ISBN: 1-55655-183-5) – 1 – $6,170.00 set – us UPA [355]

Topeka. Kansas. Clerk *see* COW AND DAIRY REGISTER

Topeka. Kansas. Fire Marshal *see* RECORD OF BUILDING AND OTHER PERMITS ISSUED IN THE CITY OF TOPEKA

Topeka. Kansas. First Baptist Church *see* RECORDS

Topeka. Kansas. First Congregational Church *see* RECORDS

Topeka. Kansas. First Presbyterian Church *see* RECORDS

Topeka, Kansas. John Knox United Presbyterian Church *see* RECORDS

Topeka. Kansas. Kansas Avenue United Methodist Church *see* RECORDS

Topeka. Kansas. Third United Presbyterian Church *see* RECORDS

Topeka. Kansas. Wanamaker Road Baptist Church *see* RECORDS

Topencharov, Vladimir *see* KHRISTO BOTEV

Tophel, Gustave *see*
- L'OEUVRE DU SAINT-ESPRIT DANS L'HOMME
- THE SEVEN CHURCHES OF ASIA: SEVEN DISCOURSES
- THE WORK OF THE HOLY SPIRIT IN MAN

TOPIC – (Cont: BMR Comment. Ceased 1980) – Toronto. v1-13. 1977-80 – 9 – Can$20.00y – cn Micromedia [600]

TOPICAL INDEX TO MAYFLOWER DESCENDANT 1620-1937 : NEW SAILS FOR AN OLD SHIP / Holbrook, Jay Mack – (Index arranges names & documents topically, with references to every vol and pg where they appear) – (mf ed 1994) – 1mf – 9 – us Holbrook [920]

TOPICAL STUDIES IN OCEANOGRAPHY *see* DEEP SEA RESEARCH

TOPICS – Columbia, NV. 1908-09 – 1r – 1 – $50.00 – U04480 – us Library Micro [071]

TOPICS – Pioneer, NV. Feb-Jul 1909 – 1r – 1 – $50.00 – U04650 – us Library Micro [071]

TOPICS IN ACUTE CARE AND TRAUMA REHABILITATION – v1- . 1986- – 1,5,6,9 – us UMI [073]

TOPICS IN AMERICAN HISTORY SERIES – (Rise and Fall of Sen Joseph R McCarthy 23mf $104.50 S1911.P3. Election of 1948 19mf $98.50 S1911.P1. Origins of the Cold War 17mf $95.50 S1911.P2. Rout of the 1932 Bonus Army from Washington 13mf $89.50 S1911.P4. Trial and Execution of Nicola Sacco and Bartolomeo Vanzetti 16mf $94.00 S1911.P5. All with printed guide) – 9 – S1911.P1-S1911.P5 – us Scholarly Res [320]

TOPICS IN CLINICAL NURSING – v.1-. 1979- – 1,5,6,9 – us UMI [073]

TOPICS IN CLINICAL NUTRITION – 1985- – 1,5,6,9 – us UMI [613]

TOPICS IN EARLY CHILDHOOD SPECIAL EDUCATION – v.1-. 1981- – 1,5,6,9 – us UMI [073]

TOPICS IN EMERGENCY MEDICINE – v.1-. 1979- – 1,5,6,9 – us UMI [073]

TOPICS IN GERIATRIC REHABILITATION – 1985- – 1,5,6,9 – us UMI [618]

TOPICS IN HEALTH CARE FINANCING – (v7- 1980- 5,6,9) – v1- 1974- – 1 – us UMI [336]

TOPICS IN HEALTH RECORD MANAGEMENT – v.1-. 1980- – 1,5,6,9 – us UMI [073]

TOPICS IN HOSPITAL LAW – 1985- – 1,5,6,9 – us UMI [340]

TOPICS IN HOSPITAL PHARMACY MANAGEMENT – v.1-. 1981- – 1,5,6,9 – us UMI [073]

TOPICS IN LANGUAGE DISORDERS – v.1-. 1980- – 1,5,6,9 – us UMI [400]

TOPICS IN LEARNING AND LEARNING DISABILITIES: TL AND LD – v.1-. 1981- – 1,5,6,9 – us UMI [073]

Topinard, Paul *see* LES OSSEMENTS DE SPY ET L'ETHNOGRAPHIE DE LA TUNISIE

Toplady, Augustus Montague *see*
- A CAVEAT AGAINST UNSOUND DOCTRINES, BEING THE SUBSTANCE OF A SERMON PREACHED IN THE PARISH CHURCH OF ST ANN, BLACKFRYARS, ON SUNDAY, APRIL 29, 1770
- THE CHURCH OF ENGLAND VINDICATED FROM THE CHARGE OF ARMINIANISM AND THE CASE OF ARMINIAN SUBSCRIPTION PARTICULARLY CONSIDERED,...
- FREE-WILL AND MERIT FAIRLY EXAMINED
- HISTORIC PROOF OF THE DOCTRINAL CALVINISM OF THE CHURCH OF ENGLAND,...
- A LETTER TO THE REV. MR. JOHN WESLEY RELATIVE TO HIS PRETENDED ABRIDGMENT OF ZANCHIUS ON PREDESTINATION
- MORE WORK FOR MR. JOHN WESLEY
- AN OLD FOX TARR'D AND FEATHER'D, OCCASIONED BY WHAT IS CALLED MR. JOHN WESLEY'S 'CALM ADDRESS TO OUR AMERICAN COLONIES'
- THE REVEREND MR. TOPLADY'S DYING AVOWAL OF HIS RELIGIOUS SENTIMENTS
- THE SCHEME OF CHRISTIAN AND PHILOSOPHICAL NECESSITY ASSERTED, IN OPPOSITION TO MR. JOHN WESLEY'S TRACT ON THAT SUBJECT;...
- THE WORKS...

TOPLIVNOE DELO / Glavnoe upravlenie po toplivu – (Library has: Oct., 1921) – Moskva: R.V.T s., 1921-1923 – 1 – CSUX89-S640 – us Hoover Inst Photo [621]

TOPLIVNYI EZHEGODNIK *see* TOPLIVNYI EZHEGODNIK PETROGRADA NA...

TOPLIVNYI EZHEGODNIK PETROGRADA NA... / Petrogradski i sovet narodnogo khozia istva – (Includes c.1: 1921; 1921 suppl) – Petrograd: Gos. izdvo, 1921-1922. 2v – 1 – CUSXAKY5929-S – us Hoover Inst Photo [621]

TOPO-CRONOGRAFIA DEL VIAGGIO DANTESCO / Agnelli, Giovanni – Milan: U. Hoepli, 1891. 159p. 15f. de pl. 3mf (Literature Collection) – 9 – $8.00 – fr Bibl Nationale [440]

TOPOGRADIIA KLADOV SEREBRIANYKH I ZOLOTYKH SLITKOV / Ilin, A A – St Petersburg: Gos. izd-vo, 1921 – us Res Libr [930]

TOPOGRAFIA HIPOCRATICA O DESCRIPCION DE LA EPIDEMIA DE CALENTURAS TERCIANAS INTERMITENTES MALIGNAS...EN LA ALCARRIA DEIDE 1784 / Ibanez, F – Madrid, 1745 – 5mf – 9 – sp Cultura [614]

TOPOGRAFISCHE UND NATURWISSENSCHAFTLICHE REISEN DURCH JAVA / Junghuhn, F W – Magdeburg, Rotterdam, Amsterdam, 1845 – 6mf – 9 – ne IDC [910]

A TOPOGRAPHICAL CATALOGUE OF THE PRIVATE TOMBS OF THEBES / Gardiner, A H, Weigall, A E P – London, 1913 – 2mf – 9 – ne IDC [930]

TOPOGRAPHICAL DICTIONARY OF 2885 ENGLISH EMIGRANTS TO NEW ENGLAND, 1620-1650 – By Charles Edward Banks, 1957.Item E. Orig. ed., indexed, and publ. by Elijah Ellsworth Brownell in 1937. Indexed, 295p. SW16-0079 – 5 – us A.G.L.L. [978]

A TOPOGRAPHICAL DICTIONARY OF IRELAND / Lewis, Samuel – 1830. 2v. 15 fiches – 9 – Ir£18.00 – ie Microforms [941]

TOPOGRAPHICAL DICTIONARY OF IRELAND / Lewis, Samuel – 2nd ed 1947 – 15 mf – Ir£15.00 – ie Microforms [910]

A TOPOGRAPHICAL DICTIONARY OF THE PROVINCE OF LOWER CANADA / Bouchette, Joseph – London: Publ by Henry Colburn and Richard Bentley, 1831. SEM16P297 – 1r – 5 – Can$9.00 – cn Bibl Nat [971]

TOPOGRAPHICAL LIBRARY OF GREAT BRITAIN. THE BRITISH TRAVELLERS' GUIDE; OR, POCKET COUNTY DIRECTORY / Cooke, George Alexander – London: Brimmer, n.d..24v. maps – 1 – us U.W. Library [910]

A TOPOGRAPHICAL LIST OF THE INSCRIPTIONS OF THE MADRAS PRESIDENCY / Rangacharya, V – v1-3. Madras, 1919. BI-696 2 – 8 – ne IDC [410]

TOPOGRAPHIE DE LA FRANCE – (Ile de France. 17 reels. 1) – Paris. Maps dating back to 17th cent. 67 reels. Also, drawings, engravings, lithographs, post cards, press clippings, photographs. Collection offered in geographical segments. (Collections of the Department of Prints and Photographs) – 1 – fr Bibl Nationale [944]

TOPOGRAPHIE DE LA VILLE DE NISMES ET DE SA BANLIEUE / Vincens-Planchut, Jean Cesar & Jean Baptiste Theodore Baumes – Nismes: Vve. Velle, 1802. xxiv,588p. 7 fiches.(Statistics Series: Topography) – 9 – 17.00 – fr Bibl Nationale [944]

TOPOGRAPHIE ET STATISTIQUE MEDICALES DE LA VILLE ET DE LA COMMUNE D'AUTUN / Guyton, Louis Marie – Autun: M. Dejussieu et L. Villedey, 1852. xvi,303p. 4 fiches. (Statistics Series: Medical Studies). (Statistics Series: Topography) – 9 – 10.00 – fr Bibl Nationale [310]

TOPOGRAPHIE HISTORIQUE, STATISTIQUE ET MEDICALE DE L'ARRONDISSEMENT DE LILLE. / Dupont, Jean Baptiste – Paris: Delarue, 1833. 377p. 4 fiches. (Statistics Series: Medical Studies). (Statistics Series: Topography) – 10.00; 0BN; 9 – fr Bibl Nationale [310]

TOPOGRAPHIE PHYSIQUE ET MEDICALE DE LA VILLE DE STRASBOURG / Graffenauer, Jean Philippe – Strasbourg: F.G. Levrault, 1816.4 fiches. (Statistics Series: Medical Studies). (Statistics Series: Topography) – 9 – 10.00 – fr Bibl Nationale [310]

TOPOGRAPHIE RURALE ET MEDICALE DE LA PARTIE MERIDIONALE DES DEPARTEMENTS DE LA MANCHE ET DU CALVADOS / Roussel, Gilles – an VIII – 9 – fr Hachette [944]

TOPOGRAPHISCHES VERZEICHNISS DER PFLANZENSAMMLUNG VON C. F. ECKLON / Ecklon, C F – Esslingen. 1827. B-5917 2 – 8 – ne IDC [580]

TOPOGRAPHISCH-HISTORISCH LEXICON ZU DEN SCHRIFTEN DES FLAVIUS JOSEPHUS / Boettger, Gustav – Leipzig: L. Fernau, 1879. 1 fiche – 9 – us A.T.L.A. [270]

TOPOGRAPHY FOR FRESHWATER FISH CULTURE : TOPOGRAPHICAL SURVEYS – 1989 – 266p – it F.A.O. [639]

TOPOGRAPHY FOR FRESHWATER FISH CULTURE : TOPOGRAPHICAL TOOLS – 1988 – 328p – it F.A.O. [639]

TOPOI – (v3-. 1984-. 5,6,9) – v1-. Dec 1982- – 1 – us UMI [073]

TOPOLOGY – v1- 1962- – 5,6,9 – us UMI [510]

TOPOLOGY AND ITS APPLICATIONS – v1-18. 1971-84 – 1,5,6,13 – sz Elsevier [073]

TOPONIMIA PATAGONICA DE ETIMOLOGIA ARAUCANA / Peron, Juan Domingo – Buenos Aires: [Direccion General de Cultura del Ministerio de Educacion de la Nacion], 1950 – 1 – CSUXADQ7363-B – us Hoover Inst Photo [972]

TOPSFIELD 1645-1905 – (Mf 1-4: Vital Records 1645-1751. Mf 5-6: Vital Records 1800-57. Mf 7-17: Vital Records & Index 1743-1833. Mf 18-22: Intentions & Marriages 1674-1886. Mf 23-24: Proprietor Records 1714-91. Mf 25-46: Town Records 1675-1810. Mf 47-54: Military Records 1775-1872. Mf 55-60: Rateables & Residents 1805-63. Mf 61-62: School Census 1888-98. Mf 63: Pauper Register 1888-1938. Mf 64-68: Births, Marriages, Deaths 1843-64. Mf 69-70: Marriage Intentions 1887-1905. Mf 71-74: Births, Marriages, Deaths 1860-1905) – (mf ed 1990) – 74mf – 0-87623-109-1 – us Holbrook [920]

DAS TOR DER FREUDE : ROMAN VOM STERBEN DES NIKOLAUS VON CUES / Kirschweng, Johannes – 2. Aufl. [Bonn]: Verlag der Buchgemeinde Bonn, 1946 – 1r – 1 – us U.W. Library [830]

THE TORA OF MOSES: BEING A CRITICAL STUDY OF DEUTERONOMY : ITS SEPARATION INTO TWO COPIES OF THE TORA: A REFUTATION OF HIGHER CRITICISM / Martin, William Wallace – Nashville, TN: Publ House of the M E Church, South: Barbee & Smith, agents, 1900 – 1mf – 9 – 0-8370-4303-4 – 1985-2303 – us A.T.L.A. [220]

Torabi, Mohammad R *see* PRESCHOOL CHILDREN'S ASSESSMENT OF HEALTH VALUE RELATED TO SELECTED NONHEALTH VALUES

TORAH SUCCESS PROGRAM – Staten Island, NY. Parashas Bamidbar 14 May 1984. Many issues missing – 1 – us A.J.P.C. [071]

Toranskii, M G *see* FORMY I METODY KOLLEKTIVNOGO INSTRUKTIROVANIIA V KOOPERATSII

TORAT HA-LASHON BE-HITPATTEHUTAH / Schneider, Sznejder, Mordecai Bezalel – (A grammar of the Hebrew "Language in its Evolution". Part I: Introduction and Grammar. Vilna. 1922-25. Part II: Syntax. Vilna. 1939. BJ-412-17 1 – 9 – ne IDC [470]

Torbert, William Sydenham *see*
- DIGEST OF PATENT AND TRADE-MARK CASES DECIDED BY THE COURT OF APPEALS OF THE DISTRICT OF COLUMBIA.
- TORBERT'S TABLE OF CASES IN THE TRINITY SERIES

TORBERT'S TABLE OF CASES IN THE TRINITY SERIES / Torbert, William Sydenham – San Francisco: Bancroft-Whitney. 1v. 1905 (all publ) – 8mf – 9 – $12.00 – LLMC 78-038D – us L.L.M.C. [340]

THE TORCH – 1950-52, 1954 (all incompl) – 1 – us Hoover Inst Photo [072]

THE TORCH – Bridgetown. Barbados. -w. 4 Jan 1958-20 Aug 1960. (2 reels) – 1 – uk British Libr Newspaper [072]

THE TORCH – Cape Town, South Africa. 1946-63. 7 reels – 1, 16 diazo available at reduced price – sa SA Libr [072]

THE TORCH – (Torch of Anarchy). A revolutionary journal of anarchist-communism. London. -m. Aug 1894-Jun 1896. (33 ft) – 1 – uk British Libr Newspaper [073]

TORCH – St John, NB: J S Knowles, [1877-1878] – 9 – cn C.I.H.M. [070]

TORCH LAKE TIME – Lake Linden. Mich. 1893-1900 – 1 – us UMI [071]

Torchi, Luigi *see* L'ARTE MUSICALE IN ITALIA

THE TORCHLIGHT – Hagerstown. Md. -w and sw. 1834, 1846-47 – 1 – us UMI [071]

TORCHLIGHT – Xenia. OH. And pred. -w. 1839-88 – 1 – us UMI [071]

THE TORCHLIGHT AND PUBLIC ADVERTISER – Hagerstown. Md. 1821-1831; 1842-1846 – 1 – us UMI [071]

Torczyner, Harry *see* LACHISH I, THE LACHISH LETTERS

Torday, E *see* CAUSERIES CONGOLAISES

Torell, O M *see* BIDRAG TILL SPITSBERGENS MOLLUSKFAUNA

Torelli, L *see* SECOLI AGOSTINIANI, OVERO HISTORIA GENERALE DEL SACRO ORDINE EREMITANO DEL GRAN DOTTORE DI SANTA CHIESE S. AVRELIO AGOSTINO

Torello, William A *see* JOURNAL OF TURFGRASS MANAGEMENT

TOREN *see* HA-TOREN

TORFIANAIA PROMYSHLENNOST – (Library has: July-Oct. 1945) – Moskva: Gosenegoizdat, 1941- – 1 – CSUX89-S785 – us Hoover Inst Photo [630]

Torge, Paul *see* SEELENGLAUBE UND UNSTERBLICHKEITSHOFFNUNG IM ALTEN TESTAMENT

TORGOVAIA ENTSIKLOPEDIIA : SPRAVOCHNIK I RUKOVODSTVO PO ORGANIZATSII, PRAKTIKE I TEKHNIKE TORGOVLI. SOVETSKOE ZAKONODATEL'STVO PO TORGOVOMU OBOROTU – (v1: Sovetskoe zakonodatel'stvo po torgovomu oborotu. (Ocherk vazhneishikh pravil). Mebel', M.A. (Ed). M., 1925. v2: Vnutrenniaia torgovlia. M., 1925. v3: Finansy i otchetnost'. Veitsman, R.Ia., Nekrasov, N.V. and A.I. Shvetsov (Eds). M., 1924. v4: Sladkoe khoziaistvo, transport i tovarovedenie. Nikitinskii, Ia. Ia. and D.N. Buchinskii (Eds). M., 1924. v5: Vneshniaia torgovlia. Kaufman, M.Ia. (Ed). M., 1924) – M. 5v. 1924-25 – 24mf – 9 – COR-755/1 – ne IDC [334]

TORGOVAIA ENTSIKLOPEDIIA : SPRAVOCHNIK I RUKOVODSTVO PO ORGANIZATSSII, PRAKTIKE I TEKHNIKE TORGOVLI. SOVETSKOE ZAKONODATEL'STVO PO TORGOVOMU OBOROTU – (V.1. Sovetskoe zakonodatel'stvo po torgovomu oborotu. (Ocherk vazhneishikh pravil). Mebel', M.A. M., 1925. Shvetsov. M., 1924; V.4: Sladkoe khoziaistvo, transport i tovarovedenie. Nikitinskii, Ia.Ia. and D.N. Buchinskii. M., 1924. V.5: Vneshniaia torgovlia. Kaufman, M.Ia. M., 1924) – M., 1924-1925. 5 vols – 24mf – 9 – COR-755/1 – ne IDC [340]

TORGOVAIA GAZETA – (Backfile through 1998 $85r) – 1999- – 2r per y – 1 – $160.00 standing order – us Ross [072]

TORGOVO PROMYSHLENNAIA GAZETTA – Moscow. nos. 44-302. 1922-29 – 1 – 320.00 – us L of C Photodup [947]

TORGOVO-PROMUISHLENNAYA GAZETA – Leningrad. USSR. -d. 2 May-13 Dec 1917. (2 reels) – 1 – uk British Libr Newspaper [072]

TORGOVO-PROMUISHLENNAYA GAZETA – (Za industrialisatsiyu Industriya Chernaya metallurgiya). Moscow. -d. Jan-Dec 1925, Apr-Dec 1926, Jul 1927-Mar, Jul-Sep 1932, Jan-Sep 1933, Jan 1934, Jan 1935-Dec 1940. (1925, 1933, 1940 very imperfect) – 38r – 1 – uk British Libr Newspaper [660]

TORGOVY I BIULLETEN = HANDELSBULLETIN : EZHENEDELNIK TORGOVOGO PREDSTAVITELSTVA S.S.S.R. V GERMANII – (Includes c.1: v.4:no.25 1925:June 20-v.4:no.26; v.4:no.30-v.4:no.31; v.4:no.37-v.4:no.40, v.4:no.43; v.6:no.15 1927:Apr.9) – [Berlin: Izd. Informatsionnogo otdela Torgpredstva SSSR v Germanii], 1922 – 1 – CSUXAKY9942-S – us Hoover Inst Photo [338]

"TORHEIT" UND "RAETSEL" IM NEUEN TESTAMENT / Gibb, H O – Stuttgart, 1941 – 2mf – 8 – ne Slangenburg [220]

TORIBIO ALFONSO DE MOGROVEJO, SEGUNDO ARZOBISPO DE LIMA... / Leturia, Pedro S – Madrid: Razon y Fe, 1940 – sp Bibl Santa Ana [240]

Toribiong, Johnson *see* LAND OWNERSHIP IN MICRONESIA

Torija, J *see* BREVE TRATADO DE TODO GENERO DE BOBEDAS ASI REGULARES COMO IRREGULARES...

Torley Duwel, C L *see* BULLETIN DE L'INSTITUT INTERMEDIAIRE INTERNATIONAL

LA TORMENTA QUE VIENE DE ORIENTE / Bayle, Constantino – Madrid: Razon y Fe, 1931 – 1 – sp Bibl Santa Ana [950]

Tormo, Elias *see*
- ISIS Y SERAPIS EN LA ESPANA PAGANA
- RESUMEN DEL HISTORICO ESTUDIO DE LA ESCULTURA ESPANOLA. LA ESCULTURA ESPANOLA EN LA ANTIGUEDAD

Tornavascas. Ayuntamiento *see* FIESTAS... SEPTIEMBRE 1960

Tornius, Valerian *see* DIE EMPFINDSAMEN IN DARMSTADT

Toro, Alfonso *see*
- UN CRIMEN DE HERNANDO CORTES. LA MUERTE DE DONA CATALINA XUARES MARCAYDA (ESTUDIO HISTORICO Y MEDICO LEGAL)
- DON CONSTITUYENTES DEL ANO 1824. BIOGRAFIAS DE DON MIGUEL RAMOS ARIZPE Y D. LORENZO ZAVALA, MEXICO. MUSEO NACIONAL DE ARQUEOLOGIA, 1925

Toro, Luis de *see* DESCRIPCION DE LA CIUDAD Y OBISPADO DE PLASENCIA POR...

THE TORONTO CHRISTIAN OBSERVER – (Cont: Christian Observer) – Toronto: A T McCord and J. Pyper, [1853?-18–?] – 9 – cn C.I.H.M. [240]

TORONTO CITIZEN – Toronto.v1-5. 1970-74 – 1 – 125.00 – cn McLaren [072]

TORONTO DAILY MAIL – Canada. -d. 1881-83; 1885-95. 72 1 2 reels – 1 – uk British Libr Newspaper [072]

TORONTO DAILY MAIL – Toronto, Canada. 1872-95 – 85r – 1 – $5,525.00 – cn Library Assoc [971]

TORONTO DAILY NEWS – 2May 1881-26 Mar 1919 – 1 – 8495.00 – cn McLaren [072]

TORONTO DAILY TELEGRAPH – Toronto, Canada. 1866-72 – 13r – 1 – $845.00 – cn Library Assoc [971]

TORONTO DIOCESAN CHRONICLE – Toronto?: s.n., 1897?-189- or 19– – 9 – cn C.I.H.M. [240]

TORONTO DIOCESAN GAZETTE – (Cont: Church of England. Diocese of Toronto. Synod. Journal of the Synod of the Church of England and Ireland in the Diocese of Toronto. Cont by: Church of England. Diocese of Toronto. Synod. Journal of the Incorporated Synod of the Church of England in the Diocese of Toronto) – Toronto: Publ under direction of the Synod of the Diocese of Canada [1874-1878] – 9 – cn C.I.H.M. [240]

TORONTO FREE PRESS – Toronto.14 Jul 1973-2 Feb 1974. Continues: Guerilla – 1 – 65.00 – cn McLaren [072]

THE TORONTO GAZETTE – Toronto: [s.n., 1874?-18–?] – 9 – cn C.I.H.M. [910]

TORONTO GLOBE *see* THE EXAMINER

TORONTO GLOBE AND MAIL *see* THE GLOBE AND MAIL

THE TORONTO JEWISH PRESS – Downsview, Ont., Canada.1978-79 – 1 – us A.J.P.C. [072]

TORONTO JOURNAL OF PHILATELY – Toronto: Toronto Philately Pub Co, [1892] – 9 – cn C.I.H.M. [760]

TORONTO LIFE – Toronto, 1976-85; v20-29. 1986-1995/96 – 9 – Price varies – cn Micromedia [910]

TORONTO MARKET REVIEW AND WEEKLY PRICE CURRENT – Toronto]: E Wiman, [1857?-18– or 19– – 9 – cn C.I.H.M. [338]

TORONTO MEETING 1897: PRELIMINARY PROGRAMME WITH MAPS AND ILLUSTRATIONS / British Association for the Advancement of Science. Canada – Issued by the Publication Committee of the Toronto Local Executive...Toronto, 1896. 02832. (Pre-1900 Canadiana) – 9 – cn C.I.H.M. [971]

TORONTO NATIVE TIMES – (v1-5 1970-74. v6-9 1975-78. v10-12 1979-81 Can$115.00 per block. Ceased) – Toronto. v1-12. 1970-81 – 1 – cn Micromedia [910]

TORONTO OF TODAY: WITH A GLANCE AT THE PAST / Adam, Graeme Mercer – Toronto: W. Bryce, 1887. 00773. (Pre-1900 Canadiana) – 9 – cn C.I.H.M. [910]

TORONTO, OLD AND NEW: A MEMORIAL VOLUME...TO MARK THE HUNDREDTH ANNIVERSARY OF THE PASSING OF THE CONSTITUTIONAL ACT OF 1791. / Adam, Graeme Mercer – Introd. by Henry Scadding. Toronto: Mail Print. Co. 1891. 00774. (Pre-1900 Canadiana) – 9 – cn C.I.H.M. [971]

TORONTO PERIODICAL JOURNAL, OR, WESLEYAN METHODIST – (Cont by: The Wesleyan Methodist) – Toronto: J C Ballantyne, [1845] – 9 – cn C.I.H.M. [240]

TORONTO PERIODICAL JOURNAL, OR, WESLEYAN METHODIST *see* THE WESLEYAN METHODIST

THE TORONTO PHILATELIC JOURNAL – Toronto: W S Weatherston, [1894] – 9 – cn C.I.H.M. [760]

TORONTO PHILATELIC JOURNAL – Toronto: G A Lowe, [1885-1888] – 9 – cn C.I.H.M. [760]

TORONTO REVIEW OF CONTEMPORARY WRITING ABROAD – v12- 1993/94- – 9 – Can$20.00y – cn Micromedia [420]

TORONTO REVIEW OF CONTEMPORARY WRITING ABROAD *see* TORONTO SOUTH ASIAN REVIEW

TORONTO SATURDAY NIGHT – Canada. -w. 3 Dec 1887-23 Nov 1907; 15 Feb 1908-12 March 1910. Imperfect. 26 1 2 reels – 1 – uk British Libr Newspaper [072]

THE TORONTO SCHOOL JOURNAL – Toronto: [s.n., 1888?-18– or 19–] – 9 – cn C.I.H.M. [370]

TORONTO SOUTH ASIAN REVIEW – (Cont by: Toronto Review of Contemporary Writing Abroad at v12 1993/94) – Toronto. v1-11. 1982/83-1992/93 – 9 – Can$20.00y – cn Micromedia [400]

TORONTO SPECIAL LIBRARIES BULLETIN – 1941-57 – 1r – 1 – $68.00 – cn Library Assoc [971]

THE TORONTO SPECIMEN – Toronto: J T Johnston, [188- or 189–189- or 19–] – 9 – cn C.I.H.M. [680]

THE TORONTO STAMP – Toronto: J H Lowe, [1894] – 9 – cn C.I.H.M. [760]

TORONTO STAR – (1993, Sub SP.-24r; 1993, Sub VP.-24r; 1971-1992.-399r) – Toronto, 1971-1992 – 399r – 1 – cn Preston [971]

TORONTO STAR – (1993, Sub SP.-48r; 1993, Sub VP.-48r; 1892-1992.-2057r) – Toronto, 1892-1992 – 2057r – 1 – cn Preston [971]

TORONTO STAR CANADIAN MAGAZINE – Toronto, 1962-1973 – 38r – 1 – cn Preston [971]

TORONTO STAR, TRANSCRIPT, AND GENERAL ADVERTISER – 1843-46 – 1 – 245.00 – cn McLaren [072]

TORONTO STAR WEEKLY – Toronto, 1910-1968 – 313r – 1 – cn Preston [971]

TORONTO STOCK EXCHANGE DAILY BULLETIN – 1982-85 – 9 – cn Micromedia [332]

TORONTO STOCK EXCHANGE DAILY RECORD – Montreal, 1977-1989 – 1 – Can$200.00y – cn Micromedia [332]

TORONTO STOCK EXCHANGE REVIEW – Toronto. v1-60. 1934-94 – 1,9 – Price varies – cn Micromedia [332]

TORONTO SUN – (1971-1992.-847r) – Toronto, 1993 – 60r – 1 – cn Preston [971]

TORONTO TELEGRAM – (Filming complete to 1954) – Toronto, Ontario, CN. Jan 1876-Oct 1971 – 1 – cn Commonwealth Micro [072]

TORONTO TELEGRAM CLIPPING FILES – Includes subject index – 9 – cn Commonwealth Micro [072]

THE TORONTO UNITARIAN – Toronto: D Rose, [1893-189- or 19–] – 9 – cn C.I.H.M. [240]

TORONTO WEEKLY GRAPHIC – Toronto: W N Sears, [1877?-18– or 19–] – 9 – cn C.I.H.M. [073]

THE TORONTO WEEKLY MAIL – Toronto, Canada. v9 n458. 7 jan 1881-v17 n55. 17 jan 1889 – 1r – 1 – Can$30.00 – cn Can Microfilming [072]

TORONTO WORLD – Toronto, Canada. 1880-1921 – 177r – 1 – $11,505.00 – cn Library Assoc [971]

TORONTOER ZEITUNG – (In German) – Canada, 1960-76 – 17r – 1 – cn Commonwealth Micro [072]

LOS TOROS ANTE LA IGLESIA Y LA MORAL. BILBAO, 1945 / Pereda, Julian – Madrid: Razon y Fe, 1946 – 1 – sp Bibl Santa Ana [240]

TOROS EN EXTREMADURA. AMPLIOS DETALLES DE LOS ESPECTACULOS TAURINOS CELEBRADOS EN LAS PLAZAS DE ESTA REGION DURANTE LA TEMPORADA DE 1969 / Garcia Flores, Juan Felipe (Don Felipe) – Badajoz: Tip. Clasica, 1970 – 1 – sp Bibl Santa Ana [790]

TORPEDOES AND TORPEDO VESSELS / Armstrong, George Elliot – 2nd ed. rev. 1901 – 9 – $20.00 – uk Libr Preservation [355]

LOS TORPEDOS EN LA GUERRA MARITIMA / Albarran, Ramon – 1875 – 9 – 1.50f – sp Bibl Santa Ana [355]

TORQUAY TIMES – England.17 Jul 1869-1911; 1921-33. -w. 53 1/2 reels.Missing: 20 Jul 1872-21 Feb 1873; 1896 – 1 – uk British Libr Newspaper [072]

TORQUEMADA AND THE SPANISH INQUISITION : A HISTORY / Sabatini, Rafael – New York: Brentano's, 1913 – 1mf – us A.T.L.A. [946]

TORQUEMADA ET L'INQUISITION / Molenes, Emile de – Paris. 1897. 236p. (Religion series) – 9 – 9.00 – fr Bibl Nationale [240]

Torquemada, Juan de *see* PRIMERA...VEINTIUN LIBROS RITUALES...INDIANA

Torr, Cecil *see* ANCIENT SHIPS

TORRANCE DAILY BREEZE *see* SOUTH BAY DAILY BREEZE

TORRANCE HERALD – (Cont by: Torrance Press Herald) – Torrance, CA. 1960-72 – 46r – 1 – $2,300.00 – C03037 – us Library Micro [071]

TORRANCE LIFESTYLE – Torrance, CA. 1986 – 48+ r – 1 – $2,400.00 ($300.00y) – H04074 – us Library Micro [071]

TORRANCE PRESS HERALD – Torrance, CA. 1970-1982; 1983 – 56r – 1 – $2,800.00 – H03553 – us Library Micro [071]

TORRANCE PRESS HERALD *see* TORRANCE HERALD

Torrance, Thomas F *see*
- THE DOCTRINE OF GRACE IN OUR APOSTOLIC FATHERS
- THE DOCTRINE OF GRACE IN THE APOSTOLIC FATHERS

TORRE DE BUJACO. PASACALLE PARA RONDALLA SOBRE MOTIVOS EXTREMENOS / Sanchez Loro, Domingo – Caceres: Publicaciones del Departamento de Seminarios de la Jefatura Provincial del Moviemiento, 1953 – 1 – sp Bibl Santa Ana [946]

Torre de Miguel Sesmero *see* ORDENANZAS MUNICIPALES

Torre Isunza de Hita, Pedro *see*
- ADICION A UN FOLLETO
- IMPRESIONES DE UN VIAJE POR DON... DEDICADAS A LOS JOVENES ESTUDIANTES DE LAS ESCUELAS DEL AVE MARIA DE LA CIUDAD DE DON BENITO
- RECUERDOS Y DATOS HISTORICOS DE LA CIUDAD DE D.BENITO
- VARIOS JUICIOS...
- VARIOS JUICIOS CRITICOS EMITIDOS POR LA PRENSA DE GRAN CIRCULACION Y PRIVADAMENTE SOBRE LA LABOR CIENTIFICA Y LITERARIA DE RAMON DE TORRE ISUNZA CON ANOTACIONES DE SU HERMANO D. PEDRO Y APENDICE

Torre Isunza de Hita, Ramon *see*
- FILOSOFIA CRISTIANA. TOMO 2: PROLEGOMENOS
- TRABAJOS INEDITOS DE...EDITATOS POR SU HERMANO D. PEDRO
- TRABAJOS POSTUMOS DE...
- TRABAJOS POSTUMOS DE...EDITADOS POR SU HERMANO D. PEDRO

Torre, Joao de *see* OLIVENCA ILLUSTRADA... MARIA DA CRUZ

TORRE MANUSCRIPTS, 1690-94 FROM YORK MINSTER LIBRARY / York Minster Library – 5r – 1 – uk Microform Academic [240]

Torre Naharro, Bartolome de *see* PROPALLADIA AND OTHER WORKS OF...

Torre Revello, Jose *see*
- ADICION A LA RELACION DESCRIPTIVA DE LOS MAPAS PLANOS...ARCHIVO GENERAL DE INDIAS
- EL ARCHIVO GENERAL DE INDIAS DE SEVILLA
- LOS ARTISTAS PINTORES DE LA EXPEDICION MALASPINA. BUENOS AIRES, 1944
- ESTECO Y CONCEPCION DEL BERMEJO. DOS CIUDADES DESAPARECIDAS. BUENOS AIRES, 1943
- EL GREMIO DE PLATEROS EN LAS INDIAS OCCIDENTALES
- JUAN JOSE DE VERTIZ Y SALADO, GOBERNADOR Y VIRREY DE BUENOS AIRES. ENSAYO BASADO EN DOCUMENTOS INEDITOS DEL ARCHIVO GENERAL DE INDIAS

Torre Yfranco Romero, Lucas de *see* DON DIEGO HURTADO DE MENDOZA NO FUE EL AUTOR DE "LA GUERRA DE GRANADA". APUNTES PARA UN LIBRO

Torrecillas de la Tiesa. Ayuntamiento *see* FERIAS Y FIESTAS. SEPTIEMBRE, 1961

Torrejoncillo. Ayuntamiento *see*
- AMIGOS DE LA ROMERIA DE SAN PEDRO 1975
- AMIGOS DE LA ROMERIA DE SAN PEDRO 1977
- AMIGOS DE LA ROMERIA DE SAN PEDRO, 1978
- FIESTAS EN HONOR DEL EMIGRANTE. 1971
- PROGRAMA DE FESTEJOS EN HONOR DEL EMIGRANTE 1972

Torrejoncillo. El Pechin *see* FIESTAS 1977

Torrejoncillo, Francisco de *see* CENTINELA CONTRA JUDIOS

TORRENT CONTROL TERMINOLOGY – 1981 – 165p – it F.A.O. [550]

Torrente Ballester, Gonzalo *see* ANTECEDENTES HISTORICOS DE LA SUBVERSION UNIVERSAL

Torreorgaz, Marques de *see* POESIAS

Torres Aguilar-Amat, Salvador *see* ELOGIO... JOSE MORENO NIETO

Torres Balbas, Leopoldo *see* LA ALCAZABA ALMOHADE DE BADAJOZ

Torres Cabrera, Marques de *see* PAGINAS DE EXTREMADURA. VILLANUEVA DE LA SERENA

TORRES DE HIDALGOS CACERENOS / Velo Nieto, Gervasio – Madrid, 1954 – 1 – sp Bibl Santa Ana [946]

LAS TORRES DEL SALVADOR Y DE SAN MARTIN Y TECHUMBRE DE LA CATEDRAL DE TERUEL (INFORME) / Monsalud, Marques de – Madrid: Est. Tip. Fortanet, 1908. B.R.A.H. 52, 1908, pp336-339 – 1 – sp Bibl Santa Ana [946]

Torres Gonzalez de la Laguna, Miguel *see* MARQUES DE TORRES CABRERA. NARRACIONES Y POESIAS

Torres, Jose Maria de la *see* LO QUE FUIMOS Y LO QUE SOMOS: O, LA HABANA ANTIGUA Y MODERNA

Torres Lanzas, Pedro see CATALOGO DE LOS DOCUMENTOS RELATIVOS A LAS ISLAS FILIPINAS EXISTENTES EN EL ARCHIVO DE INDIAS DE SEVILLA (1592-1602). BARCELONA, 1928

Torres, Luis de see
- HERNANDO CORTES
- HERNANDO CORTES (CONQUISTADOR DE MEJICO)

Torres, Manuel de see
- ALEGACION...DEHESA DE LA SERENA... PLEITO...MARQUES DE PERALES
- MEMORIAL AJUSTADO...MARQUES DE PERALES

Torres Martin, Ramon see
- ALGO SOBRE LOS DISCIPULOS Y SEGUIDORES DE ZURBARAN (1)
- ALGO SOBRE LOS DISCIPULOS Y SEGUIDORES DE ZURBARAN (2)
- BLAS DE LEDESMA, UN PINTOR RECIEN DESCUBIERTO

Torres Martinez Bravo, Joseph de see
- REGLAS GENERALES DE ACOMPANAR, EN ORGANO, CLAVICORDIO, Y HARPA, CON SOLO SABER CANTAR LA PARTE, O UN BAXO EN CANTO FIGURADO
- REGLAS GENERALES DE ACOMPANAR, EN ORGANO, CLAVICORDIO, Y HARPA, CON SOLO SABER CANTAR LA PARTE, O UN BAXO EN CANTO FIGURADO...ANADIDO AORA UN NUEVO TRATADO..

Torres Naharro, Bartolome see
- COMEDIA TROFEA
- HIMENEA. TESTO, INTRODUZIONE E NOTE DI ANNAMARIA GALLINA
- PROPALLADIA AND OTHER WORKS...
- PROPALLADIA AND OTHER WORKS OF...

Torres, P see LIBRO QUE TRATA DE LA ENFERMEDAD DE LAS BUBAS

TORRES STRAITS PILOT – Port Kennedy, Australia. 27 Feb 1897-21 Mar 1914 (1903-07 very imperfect).-w. 4 reels – 1 – uk British Libr Newspaper [072]

Torres Tapia, Alfonso see CRONICA DE LA ORDEN DE ALCANTARA

Torres y Lanzas, Pedro see
- CATALOGO DE LOS DOCUMENTOS RELATIVOS A LAS ISLAS FILIPINAS...

TORREY AND ALEXANDER : THE STORY OF A WORLD-WIDE REVIVAL : A RECORD AND STUDY OF THE WORK AND PERSONALITY OF THE EVANGELISTS R.A. TORREY, D.D., AND CHARLES M. ALEXANDER / Davis, T B – New York: Fleming H. Revell, c1905 – 1mf – us A.T.L.A. [240]

Torrey Botanical Club. New York see INDEX TO AMERICAN BOTANICAL LITERATURE, 1886-1966

Torrey, Charles Cutler see THE COMPOSITION AND HISTORICAL VALUE OF EZRA-NEHEMIAH

Torrey, Charles W see WOMAN'S SPHERE IN THE CHURCH

Torrey, Clarence Almon see NEW ENGLAND MARRIAGES PRIOR TO 1700

Torrey, J see
- CATALOGUE OF NORTH-AMERICAN GENERA OF PLANTS
- A CATALOGUE OF PLANTS, GROWING SPONTANEOUSLY WITHIN 30 MILES OF THE CITY OF NEW YORK
- A FLORA OF NORTH AMERICA
- FLORA OF THE NORTHERN AND MIDDLE SECTIONS OF THE UNITED STATES
- MONOGRAPH OF NORTH AMERICAN CYPERACEAE

Torrey, N L see VOLTAIRE'S CATALOGUE OF HIS LIBRARY AT FERNEY

Torrey, Reuben Archer see
- HOW TO BRING MEN TO CHRIST
- REAL SALVATION AND WHOLE-HEARTED SERVICE
- REVIVAL ADDRESSES

Torrijos y Gomez, Ramon see CARTA PASTORAL

TORRIJOS Y LA EUCARISTIA / Elviro Meseguer, Francisco – Toledo: Imprenta DE LA Diputacion Provincial, 1960 – 1 – sp Bibl Santa Ana [946]

Torrington, F W see
- APPENDICES TO VOTES AND PROCEEDINGS, 1817-1890 AND REPORTS OF THE SELECT COMMITTEES ON PUBLIC PETITIONS, 1833-1900
- DIVISION LISTS, 1836-1909

Torrington, William F see TREATY SERIES: 1892-1985

Torrund, Jassy see VON EINEM, DER SEINE AHNEN SUCHEN GING

TORT AND INSURANCE LAW JOURNAL (ABA) – (Title varies: v1-20 1965-85 as The Forum (ABA)) – v1-30. 1965-95 – 9 – $465.00 set – us Hein [340]

Tortoriti, G see SIX SONATAS FOR TWO VIOLINS AND A THOROUGH-BASS

TORVENY A MAGYAR NEPKOZTARSASAG ELSO OTEVES NEPGAZDASAGI TERVEROL / Hungary. Az Oteves Tervvel a Szocializmus Fele – Budapest. 1950. BD-714 1 – 9 – ne IDC [943]

TORVENYJAVASLAT A KOZIGAZGATAS ES AZ ONKORMANYZAT RENDEZERSEROL A VARMEGYEKBEN / Hungary. Laws, Statutes, etc – n.p. 1891 84,51p. LL-4074 – 1 – us L of C Photodup [340]

THE TORY – 1892-97 – 1 – uk Microform Academic [073]

Tory, G see CHAMP FLEURY AUQUEL EST CONTENU L'ART ET SCIENCE DE LA DEUE ET VRAYE PROPORTION DES LETTRES ATTIQUES

TORYISM IN THE CANADIAN CONFEDERATION / Carrick, John – 1886. 00473. (Pre-1900 Canadiana) – 9 – cn C.I.H.M. [971]

TOSCANELLO IN MUSICA. CANONICO DA RIMINI. NUOVAMENTE STAMPATO CON L'AGGIUNTA DA LUI FATTA ET CON DILIGENTIA CORRETTO / Aron, Pietro – 1529 – 9 – us Sibley [780]

Toscano, R see IL VERO ET SVPERBO APPARATO...PER LA GRANDE ALLEGREZZA HAUUTA, PER LA VITORIA DE' CHRISTIANI IN ONOR DE LA SANTISSIMA LEGA

Toscano, Salvador see ARTE PRECOLOMBINO EN MEXICO Y EN LA AMERICA CENTRAL

LE TOSCIN MARITIME CONTRE LE PRETENTION DES ROIS D'ANGLETERRE, A L'EMPIRE DE LA MER / Grave, P de la – Paris, [179-?] – 1mf – 1 – ILM-706/1 – ne IDC [327]

TOSHOKAN ZASSHI – The Library Journal. Tokyo. 1907-15. BCH-507 2 – 8 – ne IDC [073]

Tosi, P see OPINIONI DE' CANTORI ANTICHI, E MODERNI O SIENO OSSERVAZIONI SOPRA IL CANTO FIGURATO

Tosi, Pierfrancesco see ANLEITUNG ZUR SINGKUN.

EL TOSTADO. OPERA OMNIA...(ANNO 1596) / Madrigal, Alfonso de – Caceres – 1r – 9 – sp Cultura [946]

EL TOSTADO. OPERA OMNIA...(ANNO 1596) / Madrigal, Alfonso de – Caceres – 1r – 5,6 – sp Cultura [946]

Tosti, Luigi see STORIA DI ABELARDO E DEI SUOI TEMPI

Tosun, Hueseyin see MIDHAT PASA'NIN SURIYE LAYIHASI

TOT STREELING VAN HET OOG EN VOEDSEL VOOR HET HART / Swaan, J S – Utrecht, 1813 – 2mf – 9 – ne IDC [700]

TOTAL QUALITY MANAGEMENT – 1992- 4v – 9 – £188.50 – 0954-4127 – uk Carfax [650]

THE TOTALITARIAN NIGHTMARE / Arrigoni, Enrico – 286p. 1 fiche (29x) – 9 – 1.00f – at Libertarian Micro [320]

DER TOTE GAST : ZWEI ERZAEHLUNGEN / Zschokke, Heinrich; ed by Limmer, Rupert – Bayreuth: Gauverlag Bayreuth, 1944 – 1r – 1 – us U.W. Library [830]

DER TOTE IN BRAUCH UND GLAUBEN DER MADAGASSEN / Stuelpner, Kurt – Leipzig. 1929. (Studien zur Voelkerkunde. Bd.3) – 1 – us Res Libr [390]

DER TOTE TAG : DRAMA IN FUENF AKTEN / Barlach, Ernst – Berlin: P Cassirer, 1912 – 1r – 1 – us U.W. Library [820]

LE TOTEMISME : ETUDE D'ETHNOGRAPHIE COMPAREE / Frazer, James George – Paris: Schleicher, 1898 – fr Armell [301]

TOTENHORN-SUEDWAND : EIN ROMAN AUS OESTERREICHS BERGEN / Strobl, Karl Hans – Berlin: Vier Falken Verlag, 1939 – 1 – us U.W. Library [830]

TOTENKULT BEI DEN SERBEN / Matic, Tioslav – Leipzig, 1940 – 1mf – 9 – DM48.00 – 3-89349-353-0 – gw Hänsel [130]

TOTENTANZ IM LIVLAND : ROMAN / Vegesack, Siegfried von – Berlin: Universitas, c1935 – 1r – 1 – us U.W. Library [830]

DER TOTENWALD : EIN BERICHT / Wiechert, Ernst Emil – Berlin: Aufbau-Verlag, 1947 – 1r – 1 – us U.W. Library [830]

DER TOTENWALD : EIN BERICHT / Wiechert, Ernst Emil – Muenchen: K Desch, [1946?] – 1 – us U.W. Library [830]

DER TOTENWALD : EIN BERICHT / Wiechert, Ernst Emil – Zuerich: Rascher Verlag, 1948 – 1r – 1 – us U.W. Library [830]

Toth, Tihamez see FORMACION RELIGIOSA DE JOVENES. 2ND ED. TRAD. DE ANTONIO SANCHO NEBOT

TOTIUS LATINITATIS LEXICON / ed by Forcellini, Aeq – 646 2. Prati. 6 vols. 1858-1875 – 180mf – 8 – ne IDC [450]

TOTIUS TERRAE SANCTAE VRBIVMQVE ET QVICQVID IN EIS MEMORIA DIGNUM ACTUM GESTUMUE FUIT: ... / Brioneus, M – Parisiis, 1540 – 2mf – 9 – H-8260/1 – ne IDC [956]

TOTNES TIMES – England.1870-1935. -w. 50 1/2 reels – 1 – uk British Libr Newspaper [072]

Totomiants, V F see
- KOOPERATSIIA I BOR'BA S DOROGOVIZNOI
- KOOPERATSIIA V RUSSKOI DEREVNE
- MOSHCH' KOOPERATSII
- POTREBITEL'NYE OBSHCHESTVA
- SEL'SKOKHOZIAISTVENNAIA KOOPERATSIIA
- SVOD SVEDENII O DEIATEL'NOSTI POTREBITEL'NYKH OBSHCHESTV V ROSSII VOOBSHCHE I ZA 1903 GOD V CHASTNOSTI
- TEORIIA, ISTORIIA I PRAKTIKA POTREBITEL'SKOI KOOPERATSII
- TEORIIA KOOPERATSII
- UCHASTIE I PRIBYLI I RABOCHEE AKTSIONERSTVO (KOPARTNERSHIP)
- UCHASTIE V PRIBYLI I KOPARTNERSHIP

Tottie, J see TWO CHARGES DELIVERED TO THE CLERGY OF THE DIOCESE OF WORCESTER IN THE YEARS 1763 AND 1766,...

Totzke, Steffen see UNTERSUCHUNGEN ZUR RUSSISCHEN HISTORISCHEN WORTBILDUNG AM BEISPIEL DER WORTBILDUNGSKATEGORIEN "NOMINA AGENTIS" UND "NOMINA INSTRUMENTI" IN DER PERIODE VOM 11.-17. JAHRHUNDERT

TOU ANATOLIKOU NOMIMOU BIBLIA... – [Paris], 1573 – 4mf – 9 – H-8195/1 – ne IDC [956]

TOUCHSTONE – Sydney, 1869-70 – 1r – 1 – A$35.00 silver A$30.00 vesicular – at Pascoe [072]

Toulmin Smith, J see LOCAL SELF-GOVERNMENT AND CENTRALIZATION

Toulmin Smith, Lucy see THE ITINERARY OF JOHN LELAND IN OR ABOUT THE YEARS 1535-1543

Toulmouche, A see RECHERCHES STATISTIQUES SUR L'HYGIENE ET LA MORTALITE DE LA VILLE DE RENNES

TOULOUSE-LAUTREC. 50E ANNIVERSAIRE DE SA MORT / Reunion des musees nationaux. Paris – 1951. 16 illus. 2 fiches – 9 – fr Réunion [750]

T'OUNG PAO : ARCHIVES POUR SERVIR A L'ETUDE DE HISTOIRE, DES LANGUES, DE LA GEOGRAPHIE ET DE L'ETHNOGRAPHIE DE L'ASIE ORIENTALE – Leiden. v1-10. 1890-99; S2 v1-35. 1900-1939/40 – 464mf – 9 – ne IDC [950]

Toupin, JoS see LE COURRIER DE MONTMAGNY

TOUR DIARIES AND ARTICLES ON ASSAM / Mills, J P – (Manuscript and typescript, 1924-1936). BSE-75 – 8 – ne IDC [910]

LE TOUR DU MONDE – Collection of all articles from 1860 to 1913 on African exploration. 185 titles in French – 9 – fr Hachette [960]

LE TOUR DU MONDE – Selected articles on Africa, 1860-1913. (Afrique: Sub-Collection) – 9 – fr Hachette [960]

TOUR IN ARRACAN / Jenkins, F & Pemberton, R B – (Manuscript). 1831. BSE-77 2 – 8 – ne IDC [910]

TOUR NOTES BY J. P. MILLS / Mills, J P – 4pts. Shillong. 1943-46. BSE-76 2 – 8 – ne IDC [910]

A TOUR THROUGH UPPER AND LOWER CANADA / Ogden, John Cosens (1751-1800) – Litchfield, 1799. SEM105P16 – 2mf – 9 – Can$4.50 – cn Bibl Nat [910]

Touraine see
- BIOGRAPHIE TOURANGELLE
- NOBILIAIRE DE TOURAINE
- PAROISSES ET FAMILLES DE TOURAINE

TOURCOING / Belloc, Hilaire – (In english) – London: Swift, 1912 – 1 – F74.96 – fr Armell [830]

TOURCOING-CENTRE : JOURNAL DU COMITE DES FETES – Mensuel Tourcoing (Nord), mars 1932-aout 1939 – 1r – 1 – F50.00 – fr Armell [073]

Toure, A S see L'ENSEIGNEMENT ET L'EDUCATION EN REPUBLIQUE DE GUINEE

Toure, Ahmed Sekou see
- CINQUIEME CONFERENCE ECONOMIQUE NATIONALE
- L'ECOLE GUINEENNE
- L'ECOLE POUR LA VIE
- LA FEMME DANS LA SOCIETE
- HOMMAGE A MAFORY BANGOURA
- L'INFORMATION REVOLUTIONNAIRE
- L'ISLAM AU SERVICE DU PEUPLE

Toure, El Hadj Seydou N see MIGRATIONS ET DEVELOPPEMENT AGRICOLE DANS LE NORD DU SENEGAL (GUUTA TOORO)

Toure, O see MOUVEMENTS DE POPULATIONS ET PROJETS DE DEVELOPPEMENT DES ECONOMIES RURALES DE LA HAUTE-GAMBIE

TOURENOPTIMIERUNG IM HANDEL / Hillert, Freimut – 1992 – 95p – 9 – DM75.00 – 3-89349-524-X – gw Hänsel [000]

Tourgee, Albion W see ALBION W. TOURGEE PAPERS

Tourgueniev, Nicolas Ivanovitch see
- UN DERNIER MOT SUR L'EMANCIPATION DES SERFS EN RUSSIE
- LA RUSSIE ET LES RUSSES

TOURISM : TRANSNATIONAL CORPORATIONS AND CULTURAL IDENTITIES / Ascher, Francois – 1986 – 103p – 9 – 92-3-102095-1 – fr UNESCO [910]

TOURISM MARKETING ON THE WORLD WIDE WEB : A STUDY OF STATE, PROVINCIAL AND TERRITORIAL WEBSITE DEVELOPMENT AND PERCEIVED USEFULNESS / Burns, Martha J – Purdue University, 1996 – 1mf – 9 – RC 496 – us Microform Publ [650]

TOURISME : REVUE – Montreal, avr 1980-31 mar 1991 – 6r – 1 – Can$65.00 – cn Can Microfilming [073]

TOURISMUSENTWICKLUNG IN NIZZA / Freitag, Britta – 1994 – 2mf – DM80.00 – 3-89349-898-2 – gw Hänsel [338]

THE TOURIST – Anti-slavery periodical – 1 – uk World [305]

TOURIST GUIDE TO CENTRAL JAVA – Inc. maps. In English and Indonesian. SE 2187 1 – 9 – ne IDC [950]

TOURIST TRAVEL MOTIVATIONS AND SATISFACTION STUDY OF CHINA/ YANGZTE RIVER ADVENTURE TOURS / Shi, Shaoping & Godbey, Geoffrey C – 1993 – 2mf – 9 – $8.00 – us Microform Publ [790]

LE TOURISTE – Montreal, Canada. mai/jun 1907 and one undated issue – 1r – 1 – Can$25.00 – cn Can Microfilming [073]

LE TOURISTE – Murray Bay, Canada. 3 jul 1885 – 1r – 1 – Can$25.00 – cn Can Microfilming [910]

TOURIST'S GUIDE DU TOURISTE: QUEBEC ET OTTAWA VIA Q.M. D. ET O – Montreal: L. Frechet, 1879. 04265. (Pre-1900 Canadiana) – 9 – cn C.I.H.M. [910]

Tournebize, F see HISTOIRE POLITIQUE ET RELIGIEUSE DE L'ARMENIE

Tournefort, Joseph Pitton de see
- COROLLARIUM INSTITUTIONUM REI HERBARIAE IN QUO PLANTAE 1356 IN ORIENTALIBUS REGIONIBUS OBSERVATAE
- HERBARIUM
- INSTITUTIONES REI HERBARIAE
- RELATION D'UN VOYAGE DU LEVANT FAIT PAR ORDRE DU ROY

Tourneux, M see LES MANUSCRITS DE DIDEROT CONSERVES EN RUSSIE. CATALOGUE

TOURO ENVIRONMENTAL LAW JOURNAL – v1. 1994 – 9 – $35.00 – us Hein [340]

TOURO INTERNATIONAL LAW REVIEW – (Title varies: v1-4. 1988-1993, as Touro Journal of Transnational Law) – v1-5. 1988-1994 – 9 – $50.00set – us Hein [340]

TOURO JOURNAL OF TRANSNATIONAL LAW see TOURO INTERNATIONAL LAW REVIEW

Touroff, N see SEFER TUROV

Touron, Antoine see SKETCHES OF ILLUSTRIOUS DOMINICANS

TOURS IN WALES / Pennant, T – H-1134 2. v. 1-3. 1883 – 8 – ne IDC [941]

TOURS, WALKS, AND SIGHTS OF BALI; PRACTICAL GLIMPSES OF BALI FOR THE TOURIST / Indonesia: Bali – SE-3188 1 – 9 – ne IDC [950]

A TOUS LES REPUBLICAINS DE FRANCE SUR LA SOCIETE DES JACOBINS DE PARIS / Brissot De Warville, Jacques-Pierre – Paris. Imp. du Cercle Social. 1792 – 9 – fr Hachette [321]

Tousignant, J Laureat see BIBLIOGRAPHIE DU COMTE DE LOTBINIERE

Toussaint see A.M. ENFANTIN

Toussaint, A *see*
- BIBLIOGRAPHY OF MAURITIUS, (1502-1954)
- SELECT BIBLIOGRAPHY OF MAURITIUS

Toussaint, Alice *see* REVEREND PERE UBALD VILLENEUVE, O.M.I., AUMONIER NATIONAL DE L'ASSOCIATION LACORDAIRE ET SAINTE-JEANNE D'ARC DU CANADA

Toussaint-Samson, Adele *see* UNE PARISIENNE AU BRESIL

Toustain, Ch *see*
- NOUVEAU TRAITE DE DIPLOMATIQUE

TOUT PAR TOUT – Trois-Pistoles, mar 1980-4 dec 1984f – 1r – 1 – Can$70.00 – cn Can Microfilming [072]

LE TOUT PETIT – [Montreal?: s.n., 1896] – 9 – cn C.I.H.M. [200]

TOUTANKHAMON ET SON TEMPS / Reunion des Musees Nationaux. Paris – 1967 – 9 – fr Réunion [700]

Toutant, Thomas *see* BIO-BIBLIOGRAPHIE DU REVEREND PERE JOSEPH-FRANCOIS RICHARD, S.J.

TOUTE LA FRANCE – (Library has: v.1, no.1-v.4, no.77; Aug. 1941-Aug.1944) – Paris: Toute la France, 1941- – 1 – CSUX86-S187 – us Hoover Inst Photo [944]

TOUTE L'EDITION – Paris, France. -w. 24 June 1933-15 May 1940. 7 reels – 1 – uk British Libr Newspaper [072]

TOUTES LES LYRES: ANTHOLOGIE DES POETES CONTEMPORAINS; POEMES DE HENRI ALLORGE...(ET AL) – Avec biographies critiques par Georges Beauglais. Paris: Gastein-Serge, 19??. Illus. 1 reel.1286 – 1 – us U.W. Library [810]

Touzard, Jules *see* LE LIVRE D'AMOS

Tov, Emanuel *see*
- THE DEAD SEA SCROLLS
- THE DEAD SEA SCROLLS ON MICROFICHE

Tovar, Antonio *see* PROCESOS INQUISITORIALES CONTRA FRANCISCO SANCHEZ DE LAS BROZAS

TOVARICHESTVA POLNYE, NA VERE, KREDITNYE, SSUDO-SBEREGATEL'NYE, TRUDOVYE I S PEREMENNYM KAPITALOM : AKTSIONERNYE I PAEVYE KOMPANII: ZAKON I PRAKTIKA S SENATSKIMI RAZOOIASNENIIAMI / Gorbachev, I A – M., 1910 – 8mf – 9 – COR-116/1 – ne IDC [334]

Tovarishchestvo MO Vol'f. Leningrad *see* IZVIESTIIA PO LITERATURIE, NAUKAMI BIBLIOGRAFII

TOVAROVEDENIE : POSOBIE DLIA KOOPERATIVNYKH SHKOL I KURSOV / Klassen, N – Khar'kov, 1918 – 4mf – 9 – COR-254/1 – ne IDC [334]

TOVERI – Astoria, OR. -d. 9 Dec 1916-31 Dec 1927. – 19r – 1 – us U.O. Library [071]

Tovote, Heinz *see* MUTTER

TOWALIGA BAPTIST CHURCH. BUTTS COUNTY. GEORGIA : CHURCH RECORDS – 1899-1959 – 1 – 14.04 – us Baptist [240]

TOWANDA DAILY REVIEW – Towanda, PA., 1914-1919 – 13 – $25.00r – us I.M.R. [071]

THE TOWANDA JOURNAL – Towanda, PA., 1874-1875 – 13 – $25.00r – us I.M.R. [071]

TOWARD A NEW CENTURY – 1865-1917 – 1 – us Ross [978]

TOWARD A THEOLOGY OF MARRIAGE AND FAMILY MINISTRY: A PRACTICUM DEVELOPMENT IN A PASTORAL COUNSELING CENTER. 1982 / Click, Barry Clinton – 1 – $5.00 – us Baptist [240]

TOWARD IMPROVED MULTILEVEL PLANNING FOR AGRICULTURAL AND RURAL DEVELOPMENT IN ASIA AND THE PACIFIC – 1985 – 119p – it F.A.O. [338]

TOWARDS A CULTURAL POLICY FOR HONDURAS / Quesada, Alba Alonso de – 1978 – 9 – 92-3-101520-6 – fr UNESCO [972]

TOWARDS A LIBERTARIAN THEORY OF FASCISM / Blankertz, Stefan – 1986, LA Historical Notes, No.1, 4p – 9 – 1.00f – at Libertarian Micro [335]

TOWARDS A NEW INTERNATIONAL ECONOMIC ORDER / Bedjaoui, Mohammed – 1979 – 287p – 9 – 92-3-101670-9 – fr UNESCO [330]

TOWARDS A NEW LEAGUE / Brailsford, H N – London, 1936 – 1mf – 1 – ILM-4011/1 – ne IDC [327]

TOWARDS A PEOPLE'S ARMY / Nasution, Abdul Haris – SE-4452 1. 1964 – 9 – ne IDC [355]

TOWARDS A TEXT OF THE METAMORPHOSIS OF OVID. PROLEGOMENA; APPARATUS CRITICUS; LACTANTIUS / Slater, D A – Oxford. 1927. B-306 2 – 8 – ne IDC [450]

TOWARDS LIFELONG EDUCATION : A NEW ROLE FOR HIGHER EDUCATION INSTITUTIONS / Williams, Gareth – 1977 – 188p – 9 – 92-3-101449-8 – fr UNESCO [370]

TOWARDS NEW GOALS FOR SECONDARY EDUCATION IN THE COOPERATIVE REPUBLIC OF GUYANA / Guyana. Ministry of Education and Social Development – Georgetown, 1975 – 1mf – 9 – DE-519/1 – ne IDC [370]

TOWARDS RAISING THE STANDARD OF LIVING IN INDONESIA / Sumantri Praptokusumo – SE 3592 1. 1952 – 9 – ne IDC [360]

TOWARDS REALISTIC COMMUNICATION POLICIES : RECENT TRENDS AND IDEAS COMPILED AND ANALYSED / ed by Lee, John A R – 1976 – 60p – 9 – 92-3-101295-9 – fr UNESCO [380]

TOWARDS SOCIAL REFORM / Barnett, Canon Samuel Augustus – New York: Macmillan, 1909 – 1mf – us A.T.L.A. [360]

TOWARDS SOCIAL WELFARE IN INDONESIA / Indonesia. Kementerian Sosial – SE-1145 1. 1954 – 9 – ne IDC [360]

TOWARDS THE FULL UTILIZATION OF THE WATERS OF THE NILE; PAST, PRESENT AND FUTURE POLICY / Helmy, S – 1955. BNE-7647 1 – 9 – ne IDC [333]

TOWARDS WHOLENESS – 1972-86 (complete) – 1r – 1 – ATLA S0805 – us A.T.L.A. [073]

TOWARZYSTWO NAUKOWE W TORUNIU – v1-. 1878-. illus. -irr. In Polish; summaries in French or German – 1 – us U.W. Library [073]

TOWER – May 1976-27 Jul 1980. 1050p – 1 – 36.75 – us Baptist [240]

TOWER HAMLETS INDEPENDENT – (East London Advertiser Boroughs of Stepney and Poplar, and East London Advertiser Boroughs of Poplar and Stepney and East London Advertiser). London. -w. 17 Nov 1866-Feb 1945. (47 reels) – 1 – uk British Libr Newspaper [072]

TOWER HILL CEMETERY REGISTER – 1856-1989. THC1-2 – 2r – 1 – at Corangamite [910]

THE TOWER OF LONDON : A HISTORICAL ROMANCE / Ainsworth, William Harrison – London: Richard Bentley, 1840 – 1 roll – 1 – 1-55879-636-3 – uk Libr Preservation [830]

THE TOWER OF TADDEO / Ouida – British Fiction Archive: Unit 3 – 9 – uk Bell [830]

Towers, J *see* A LETTER TO THE REV. MR. JOHN WESLEY IN ANSWER TO HIS LATE PAMPHLET ENTITLED 'FREE THOUGHTS ON THE PRESENT STATE OF PUBLIC AFFAIRS'

Towle, Eleanor A *see*
- ALEXANDER HERIOT MACKONOCHIE
- JOHN MASON NEALE, D.D.

THE TOWN AND CITY OF WATERBURY FROM THE ABORIGINAL PERIOD TO THE YEAR 1895 / Anderson, Joseph – New Haven: Price and Lee Co., 1896. Vols. 1-2. (Connecticut Reel 5); Vol. 3. (Connecticut Reel 6). (The Cox Library Collection) – 5 – us Americana [978]

TOWN AND COUNTRY – London, 1847-1902 – 7r – 1 – us Ross [073]

TOWN AND COUNTRY – Providence. R.I. 1875-1879 – 1 – us UMI [071]

TOWN AND COUNTRY – San Francisco, May 1962-Sep 1963 – 1r – 1 – $50.00 – B40321 – us Library Micro [978]

TOWN AND COUNTRY – Toronto: J Watson, [1880?-18– or 19–] – 9 – cn C.I.H.M. [790]

TOWN AND COUNTRY CHURCH LEADERS CONFERENCE / Wisconsin. Agricultural Extension Service – 1963-66 – 1,5 – us Spaulding [240]

TOWN AND COUNTRY PLANNING – (v. 43-1975- 5,6,9) – v. 1- 1932- – 1 – us UMI [323]

Town and Country Planning Association. London, England *see* MINUTES OF THE TOWN AND COUNTRY PLANNING ASSOCIATION

TOWN AND COUNTRY SERMONS / Kingsley, Charles – 2nd ed. London: Macmillan, 1868 – 1mf – 9 – 0-8370-7470-3 – 1986-1470 – us A.T.L.A. [240]

TOWN AND TRADE – Ashford, Kent, England. 27 Jan 1910-8 Jul 1911.-w. 1/4 reels – 1 – uk British Libr Newspaper [072]

TOWN CREEK BAPTIST CHURCH. AIKEN COUNTY. SOUTH CAROLINA : CHURCH RECORDS – 1903-83 – 1 – 33.71 – us Baptist [240]

THE TOWN CRIER – Corning. N.Y. 1963-1965 – 1 – us UMI [071]

TOWN CRIER – 1994-1995 – 1r – 1 – at Corangamite [072]

TOWN CRIER – Georgetown, CA. 1961-72 – 4r – 1 – $200.00 – C02269 – us Library Micro [071]

TOWN CRIER – Los Altos, CA. 1973-76 – 11r – 1 – $550.00 – B02366 – us Library Micro [071]

TOWN CRIER / Zuni Day School – Oct 1941. (American Indian Periodicals in the Princeton University Library). 1 fiche – 9 – $45.00 – us UPA [305]

TOWN NEWS – Pompano Beach. Fl. 1950-1963 – 1 – us UMI [071]

TOWN OF MOUNT ROYAL WEEKLY POST – Ville Mont-Royal, Canada. v8 n19. 9 mai 1946-8 aut 1991 – 13r – 1 – Can$75.00r – cn Can Microfilming [072]

TOWN PLANNING – v1-10, no. 3. Oct 1920-Jun 1931 – 1 – cn Precision [710]

Town Planning Institute. London, England *see*
- MINUTES OF THE TOWN PLANNING INSTITUTE
- PAPERS AND DISCUSSIONS OF THE ROYAL TOWN PLANNING INSTITUTE

TOWN PLANNING REVIEW – v1-. 1910- – 9 – $5.00f – us Ross [710]

TOWN TALK – Alexandria. La. 1883-85; 1892; 1895- – 1 – us UMI [071]

TOWN TALK – Alexandria. La. -w. 1883-1957 – 1 – us UMI [071]

TOWN TALK – London. v1. 1858-59 – 1r – 1 – us Ross [072]

TOWN TALK – Portland OR. Feb 24 1934 – 1 – us U.O. Library [071]

THE TOWN TIMES – Ville Mont-Royal, Canada. 4 avr 1968; v1 n8. 29 aut 1968 – 1r – 1 – Can$25.00 – cn Can Microfilming [072]

TOWN TOPICS – Portland OR. May 12 1899, Jan 16 1903 – 1 – us U.O. Library [071]

TOWNE CRYER – Oklahoma City. Okl. 1955-59 – 1 – us UMI [071]

Towner, A *see* CHEMUNG COUNTY

TOWNLAND INDEX 1904 – 11 mf – Ir£9.00 – ie Microforms [910]

TOWNSEND 1726-1890 – 52mf – 9 – us Holbrook [920]

Townsend, Ann Albertson *see* MEMOIR OF ELIZABETH NEWPORT

Townsend, Calvin *see* A COMPENDIUM OF COMMERCIAL LAW

Townsend, Luther Tracy *see*
- ADAM AND EVE
- BIBLE AND SCIENCE
- BIBLE THEOLOGY AND MODERN THOUGHT
- CLERICAL POLITICS IN THE METHODIST EPISCOPAL CHURCH
- ELEMENTS OF GENERAL AND CHRISTIAN THEOLOGY
- EVOLUTION OR CREATION:...SCIENTIFIC AND SCRIPTURAL THEORIES OF CREATION
- THE MOSAIC RECORD AND MODERN SCIENCE
- THE SUPERNATURAL FACTOR IN RELIGIOUS REVIVALS
- THE SWORD AND GARMENT

Townsend, W J *see*
- A HANDBOOK FOR THE METHODIST NEW CONNEXION
- THE STORY OF METHODIST UNION

Townsend, W J et al *see* A NEW HISTORY OF METHODISM

Townsend, William John *see*
- MADAGASCAR
- ROBERT MORRISON

Townshend, Charles *see* PAPERS FROM THE BUCCLEUCH AND QUEENSBURY MUNIMENTS

TOWNSHIP AND BOROUGH / Maitland, Frederick William – H-1173 2. 1898 – 8 – ne IDC [941]

THE TOWNSHIP BONDS OF MISSOURI, UNDER THE ACT OF MARCH 23RD, 1868 / Bacon, Thomas – Hannibal, Hannibal Clipper, 1877. 141 p. LL-714 – 1 – us L of C Photodup [340]

TOWNSHIP HALL PLANS / Hancock County. Ohio. Biglick Township. Township Clerk – 1r – 1 – $32.50r – us Archival [324]

TOWNSHIP INCORPORATION RECORDS / Huron County. Ohio. Board of County Commissioners – 1819-1827 – 1r – 1 – $32.50r – us Archival [324]

THE TOWNSHIP OF SCARBORO 1796-1896 / ed by Boyle, David – Toronto: W. Briggs, 1896. 00983. (Pre-1900 Canadiana) – 9 – cn C.I.H.M. [971]

TOWNSHIP PLATS OF SELECTED STATES / U.S. General Land Office – 67 rolls. T1234 – 1 – us Nat'l Archives [310]

THE TOWNSHIP REFORMER – Stanbridge, Canada. v1 n5. 20 dec 1836-v1 n44. 21 nov 1837 (incomplete) – 1r – 1 – Can$35.00 – cn Can Microfilming [072]

TOWNSHIP SCHOOL RECORD / Monroe County. Mich, Bedford Township. Board of Education – 1895-1899 – 1r – 1 – $32.50r – us Archival [324]

THE TOWNSHIPS OF DARLINGTON AND CLARKE / Squair, John – Including Bowmanville and Newcastle. Toronto, 1927. Canada reel 5. (Cox Library Collection) – 5 – us Americana [971]

TOWNSHIPS SUN – Ayers' Cliff (Waterville & Lennoxville), Canada. 8 fev 1974-dec 1991 – 5r – 1 – Can$75.00r – cn Can Microfilming [072]

TOWNSVILLE DAILY BULLETIN – Australia. 3 Dec 1885; 10, 11 May, 1 Oct 1887-31; Dec 1888 – 3r – 1 – uk British Libr Newspaper [980]

TOWNSVILLE HERALD – (North Queensland Herald). Australia. -w. 10 Jul 1886-28 Nov 1908, 30 Jan 1909-21 Oct 1911. (65 reels) – 1 – uk British Libr Newspaper [072]

TOWN-TALK – Toronto: [s.n., 1884?-18–] – 9 – cn C.I.H.M. [073]

TOXIC SUBSTANCES CONTROL ACT, 1976 : LEGISLATIVE HISTORY / Environment and Natural Resources Policy Division of the Library of Congress – Washington: GPO, 1976 – 9mf – 9 – $13.50 – LLMC 90-357 – us L.L.M.C. [340]

TOXIC SUBSTANCES CONTROL ACT TEST SUBMISSIONS DATABASE (TSCATS) / U.S. National Technical Information Service – Ad hoc reports produced by E.P.A – 9 – us N.T.I.S. [360]

TOXIC SUBSTANCES JOURNAL – v.1-. 1979- – 1,5,6,9 – us UMI [540]

TOXICOLOGICAL AND ENVIRONMENTAL CHEMISTRY REVIEWS / ed by Hutzinger, O – 1972 – 1,5,9 – us Gordon [540]

TOXICOLOGY – v1-33. 1973-84 – 1,5,6,13 – sz Elsevier [073]

TOXICOLOGY ABSTRACTS – Monthly – 9 – us C.S.A. [615]

TOXICOLOGY IN VITRO – 1,5,69 – us UMI [616]

TOXICOLOGY LETTERS – v1-23. 1977-84 – 1,5,6,13 – sz Elsevier [073]

TOXICOMANIES / Quebec. (Province). Office de la prevention et du traitement de l'alcoolisme et des autres toxicomanies – Quebec: l'Office. v1-13. 1968-1980. SEM16P242 – 2r – 5 – Can$44.00 – cn Bibl Nat [360]

TOXICON – v1- 1962- – 5,6,9 – us UMI [540]

TOXIN / Ouida – British Fiction Archive: Unit 3 – 9 – uk Bell [830]

Toxopeus, Hendrik Jan *see* KARAKTER EN HERKOMST VAN DEN JACOBUSBRIEF

Toy, C H *see* BUECHER SAMUELIS

Toy, Crawford Howell *see*
- THE HISTORY OF THE RELIGION OF ISRAEL
- JUDAISM AND CHRISTIANITY: A SKETCH OF THE PROGRESS OF THOUGHT
- QUOTATIONS IN THE NEW TESTAMENT

TOYRE LID – Cracow. 1631-56. BJ-43-132 1 – 9 – ne IDC [470]

TOYRE LID – Prague. 1605-15. BJ-43-130 1 – 9 – ne IDC [470]

TOYS – Nov 1970-Nov 1977 – 1 – us UMI [790]

TOYS AND BICYCLES – Jul 1936-Jul 1940 – 1 – us UMI [790]

TOYS AND MUSICAL INSTRUMENTS (TIAM, PT 10) – (With printed catalogue ISBN: 0-914146-80-7 £30) – 21mf – 15 – £430.00 – uk Chadwyck [740]

TOYS AND NOVELTIES – 1909-36 – 1 – us UMI [790]

TOYS AND NOVELTIES – Aug 1940-Oct 1970 – 1 – us UMI [790]

TOYS, HOBBIES AND CRAFTS – (v81- 1981- 5,6,9) – Dec 1977- – 1 – us UMI [790]

Toyuela, Nicolas Perez *see* INDICE DE LOS PRIVILEGIOS DE LA CIUDAD (ANNO 1655)

Tozaka, Job *see* DIARIES

TOZAOT EREZ YISRA'EL – Amsterdam. 1649. BJ-43-133 1 – 9 – ne IDC [470]

Tozer, Henry Fanshawe *see*
- THE CHURCH AND THE EASTERN EMPIRE
- A HISTORY OF ANCIENT GEOGRAPHY

TPGA JOURNAL –[l] (v7- 1979- 5,6,9) – v1-1972 – 1 – us UMI [073]

TP'S WEEKLY – London. v. 1-27, no. 703. Nov. 14 1902-Apr 29 1916 – 1 – us NY Public [073]

TRA GLI EROI I MARTIRI DELLA LIBERTA / Estella – Madrid, 1937. Fiche W 864. (Blodgett Collection of Spanish Civil War Pamphlets) – 9 – us H.U. College Libr [946]

LOS TRABAJADORES, EL SENOR PERON Y EL PARTIDO SOCIALISTA : PERON ES PROGRESISTA O RETROGRADO? / Ghioldi, Americo – Buenos Aires: Editorial La Vanguardia, [2nd ed 1951] – 1 – CSUXAGP8737-B – us Hoover Inst Photo [320]

LOS TRABAJADORES EN FUNCI ON SOCIAL / Juarez, Juan C – Buenos Aires: Libro de Edici on Argentina, 1947 – 9 – us Hoover Inst Photo [972]

LOS TRABAJADORES SE EMANCIPAN – [Buenos Aires? Servicio Internacional Publicaciones Argentinas] 1952 – 9 – us Hoover Inst Photo [972]

TRABAJO – Havana. May 1960-Dec. 1964 – 1 – 35.00r – us Hoover Inst Photo [972]

TRABAJO DE BASE / Congreso Internacional de Folklore – 1960 – 1 – us I.U. Libraries [390]

EL TRABAJO DE LOS COMISARIOS POLITICOS / Clavego, P – Madrid, 1937? Fiche W 803. (Blodgett Collection of Spanish Civil War Pamphlets) – 9 – us H.U. College Libr [946]

TRABAJOS INEDITOS DE...EDITATOS POR SU HERMANO D. PEDRO / Torre Isunza de Hita, Ramon – Cabra: Tip. Manuel Cordon, 1920 – sp Bibl Santa Ana [440]

TRABAJOS POSTUMOS DE... / Torre Isunza de Hita, Ramon – Cabra: Tip. de Manuel Cordon Moriel, 1922 – 1 – sp Bibl Santa Ana [946]

TRABAJOS POSTUMOS DE...EDITADOS POR SU HERMANO D. PEDRO / Torre Isunza de Hita, Ramon – Cabra: Tip. M. Cordon, 2nd ed 1920 – sp Bibl Santa Ana [440]

TRABAJOS Y FIESTAS DE UN PUEBLO ESPANOL / Munoz de Dieste, Carmen – Plasencia: Imp. La Victoria, 1961 – 1 – sp Bibl Santa Ana [390]

O TRABALHADOR TEXTIL – Sao Paulo, Brazil. 1956-1958 – 1 – bl Biblioteca [072]

O TRABALHISTA – Manaus, Amazonas. Jun 1982 – 1,5,6 – bl Biblioteca [072]

O TRABALHO : ORGAM DA ESCOLA PROFISSIONAL "DELFIM MOREIRA" E APRENDIZADO AGRICOLA "EDUARDO DO AMARAL" – Pouso Alegre, 24 Mar 1927 – 1,5,6 – bl Biblioteca [072]

O TRABALHO : ORGAO DO COMMERCIO, DA LAVOURA E DOS INTERESSES SOCIAES – Pao d'Assucar, Alagoas. 10 Set, Dez 1882; Fev, Maio 1883; Ago 1884; Jan-Mar, Out 1885; Out 1886; Maio, Nov 1888; Fev 1889; Ago 1892; Jun 1893; Mar, Jun, Dez 1895; Jan 1896-Dez 1897; Jun, Set, 5 Nov 1898 – 1,5,6 – bl Biblioteca [072]

O TRABALHO – Patos de Minas, Brazil. Sept-Dec 1905; Mar-Jul, Nov-Dec 1906; Jan-Nov 1907; Jan-Mar, May, Jul-Nov 1908 – 1 – bl Biblioteca [072]

TRABALHOS NAUTICOS DOS PORTUGUEZES NOS SECULOS 16 E 17 : PARTE 1: MARINHARIA / Viterbo, Sousa – Lisboa: Academia Real des Sciencias, 1898 – fr Armell [355]

Trabert, George Henry *see* HISTORICAL SKETCH OF THE MISSION OF THE GENERAL COUNCIL OF THE EVANGELICAL LUTHERAN CHURCH, AMONG THE TELUGUS OF INDIA

Traboulsi, I *see* L'AGRICULTURE SYRIENNE ENTRE LES DEUX GUERRES

TRACE CREEK BAPTIST CHURCH. DENVER, TENNESSEE : CHURCH RECORDS – 1847-1967 – 1 – 49.41 – us Baptist [240]

TRACE ELEMENTS IN SOILS AND AGRICULTURE – 1979 – 70p – it F.A.O. [631]

TRACER STUDY OF KADUNA STATE PRIMARY / POST SCHOOL-LEAVERS 1977-1978 EDUCATIONAL YEAR / Nigeria. Kaduna State. Ministry of Economic Development. Statistics Division – Kaduna, 1978 – 1mf – 9 – DE-108/1 – ne IDC [370]

TRACES OF GREEK PHILOSOPHY AND ROMAN LAW IN THE NEW TESTAMENT / Hicks, Edward – London: S.P.C.K., 1896. 1 fiche – 9 – us A.T.L.A. [240]

TRACES OF THE PLAN OF OUR BEING / Mansfield, Lewis William – New York: E. & J.B. Young, 1884.1 fiche – 9 – us A.T.L.A. [240]

TRACH NHIEM CUA NHAN DAN VA CAN BO, DOI VOI CHINH QUYEN CACH MANG = RESPONSIBILITY OF THE PEOPLE AND THE CADRE TOWARDS THE REVOLUTIONARY GOVERNMENT / Ho, Chi Minh – (Collection of speeches) – 1971 – 1mf – 9 SEL-124/1 – ne IDC [340]

TRACK TECHNIQUE – 1960-81, 1983- 1; 1976-81, 1983- 5,6; 1975-81, 1983 9 – us UMI [790]

TRACK'S END; BEING THE NARRATIVE OF JUDSON PITCHER'S STRANGE WINTER SPENT THERE AS TOLD BY HIMSELF / Carruth, Hayden – Illus. by Clifford Carleton. New York and London: Harper & Brothers, 1911. 7,leaves, 229p.map – 1 – us U.W. Library [830]

TRACTADO CONTRA EL MAL SERPENTINO QUE VULGARMENTE EN ESPANA ES LLAMADO BUBAS / Diaz de Isla, R – Sevilla, 1539 – 2mf – 9 – sp Cultura [610]

TRACTADO DELAS DROGAS, Y MEDICINAS DE LAS INDIAS ORIENTALES,... / Acosta, C – Burgos, 1578 – 6mf – 9 – H-8350/1 – ne IDC [615]

TRACTADO EN EL QUE SE EXPLICA LA ESENCIA Y NATURALEZA DE LA ENFERMEDAD (QUE LLAMAN IANDRES) / Valdivia, A – Sevilla, 1601 – 7mf – 9 – sp Cultura [615]

TRACTARIAN PAMPHLETS AT PUSEY HOUSE: THE HALIFAX AND CHURCH SUB-COLLECTIONS / Pusey House – 1 – £2,750.00 – uk World [240]

TRACTATE OF EDUCATION / Milton, John; ed by Morris, Edward Ellis – (Includes bibliographical references) – London; New York: Macmillan, 1895 – 1mf – 9 – 0-8370-7567-X – 1986-1567 – us A.T.L.A. [370]

A TRACTATE ON THE RULE OF PRACTICE IN ENGLISH LAW, EMBODYING WHAT IS KNOWN AS THE EQUITABLE DOCTRINE OF ELECTION. / Flood, John Charles Henry – London: Maxwell, 1880. 34p. LL-1675 – 1 – us L of C Photodup [340]

TRACTATIONES THEOLOGICAE / Ursinus, Zach – Neustadii, 1587-1589 – 37mf – 8 – ne Slangenburg [290]

TRACTATIONES THEOLOGICAE... / Beza, Theodor – Geneve, 1582-.-3v – 41mf – 8 – ne Slangenburg [290]

TRACTATO DI MUSICA DI GIOVANNI SPARTARO MVSICO BOLOGNESE NEL QVALE SI TRACTA DE LA PERFECTIONE DE LA SESQVALTERA PRODVCTA IN LA MVSICA MENSVRATA EXDERCITATE... / Spataro, Giovanni – Impressa in Vinegia per Maetro Bernardino de Vitali el di octano del mese di ottobre M.D.31., [1531] – 1 – us Sibley [780]

TRACTATUS / Leo – 1987 – 10mf – 9 – Bf1,650.00 – 2-503-61382-9 – be Brepols [240]

TRACTATUS (CCSL 138-138A) / Leo Magnus – 1987 – 6mf – 9 – Bf975.00 – 2-503-71382-3 – be Brepols [240]

TRACTATUS DE BEATISSIMA VIRGINE MARIA MATRE DEI / Lepicier, Alexius Maria – (Includes bibliographical references and index) – Parisiis: P Lethielleux, [1901?] – 2mf – 9 – 0-8370-8836-4 – 1986-2836 – us A.T.L.A. [240]

TRACTATUS DE CURIA PISANA.. / Acevedo, Alfonso de – 9 – 1.50f – sp Bibl Santa Ana [340]

TRACTATUS DE DEO UNO ET TRINO (CCC198) = T'IEN CHU SAN WEI IH T'I LUN / Hsu, Tsung-che – (In Chinese) – [s.l: s.n, 1930] – 1r – 1 – 1984-B500 – us A.T.L.A. [240]

TRACTATUS DE GRATIA / Jungmann, Bernardus – (Includes bibliographical references and index) – Editio 5. Ratisbonae [Regensburg]; Neo Eboraci [New York]: Friderici Pustet, 1882 – 1mf – 9 – 0-8370-4551-7 – 1985-2551 – us A.T.L.A. [240]

TRACTATUS DE INSTITUTIONE SACERDOTUM, QUI SUB EPISCOPIS ANIMARUM CURAM GERUNT / Soto, P, de – Dilingae, 1560 – 10mf – 9 – CA-90/1 – ne IDC [240]

TRACTATUS DE IURAMENTO CONFIRMATORIO / Gutierrez, Juan – (1607. 1.50f; 9) – 1586 – 9 – 1.50f – sp Bibl Santa Ana [240]

TRACTATUS DE LEGATO / Chokier, I A – Cologne, 1624 – 2mf – 1 – ILM-616/1 – ne IDC [327]

TRACTATUS DE LEGIBUS AC DEO LEGISLATORE IN DECEM LIBROS DISTRIBUTUS... / Suarez, F – Coimbra, 1612 – 22mf – 9 – sp Cultura [340]

TRACTATUS DE LIBERTATIBUS ECCLESIAE GALLICANAE / Charlas, A – Editio Tertia. Romae. v1-3. 1720 – Dfl180.00 – ne Slangenburg [240]

TRACTATUS DE NOVISSIMIS / Jungmann, Bernardus – (Includes bibliographical references and index) – Editio 3. Ratisbonae [Regensburg]; Neo Eboraci [New York]: Friderici Pustet, 1885 – 1mf – 9 – 0-8370-4531-2 – 1985-2531 – us A.T.L.A. [210]

TRACTATUS DE PACE AUCTORE FR. GILBERTO DE TORNACO / Guibert de Tournai – 1 – us A.T.L.A. [240]

TRACTATUS DE PATRIARCHIS CONSTANTINOPOLITANIS (CBH 32) / Cuperi, G – Venetiis, 1751 – Dfl42.00 – ne Slangenburg [240]

TRACTATUS DE PENITENTIIS (I. 1500) / Benavente, Juan Alfonso de – Avila – 2r – 5,6 – sp Cultura [240]

TRACTATUS DE PESTE AC FEBRIBUS CUM PUNCTICULIS VULGO TAVARDILLO / Carmona, Juan – 1582 – 9 – 1.50f – sp Bibl Santa Ana [946]

TRACTATUS DE PESTE...AC FEBRIBUS CUM PUNCTICULIS VULGO TABARDILLO / Carmona, Juan – Sevilla, 1582 – 5mf – 9 – sp Cultura [616]

TRACTATUS DE PODAGRA ET HYDROPE / Sydenham, T – Londini, 1683 – 4mf – 9 – ne IDC [616]

TRACTATUS DE SEPTEM DONIS SPIRITUS SANCTI 15TH / Bernardino, S – Ms 231 U.B. Nijmegen – 6mf – 8 – ne Slangenburg [240]

TRACTATUS DE SPIRITU DEI / Haller, Benedictus – Antverpiae, 1662 – 2mf – 8 – Dfl9.00 – ne Slangenburg [240]

TRACTATUS DE VERA RELIGIONE / Jungmann, Bernardus – (Includes bibliographical references and index) – Editio 3. Ratisbonae [Regensburg]; Neo Eboraci [New York]: Friderici Pustet, 1886 – 1mf – 9 – 0-8370-4530-4 – 1985-2530 – us A.T.L.A. [230]

TRACTATUS DE VERBO INCARNATO / Jungmann, Bernardus – (Includes bibliographical references and index) – Editio 4. Ratisbonae [Regensburg]; Neo Eboraci [New York]: Friderici Pustet, 1884 – 1mf – 9 – 0-8370-4561-4 – 1985-2561 – us A.T.L.A. [240]

TRACTATUS DUO / Mayow, J – M 379. 1669 – 9 – ne IDC [610]

TRACTATUS GULIELMI HENTISBERI DE SENSU COPOSITO ET DIVISO / Hentisberus, Gulielmus – 15th Century – 1 – uk Microform Academic [180]

TRACTATUS MUSICUS COMPOSITORIO-PRACTICUS / Spies, Meinrad – Das ist, Musicalischer Tractat. Augsburg. 1745. BP-763 1 – 9 – ne IDC [780]

TRACTATUS NOVUS DE TUTELIS CURIS MINORUM / Gutierrez, Juan – 1730 – 9 – 1.50f – sp Bibl Santa Ana [240]

TRACTATUS PHYSICUS DE EFFECTIBUS MUSICES IN CORPUS ANIMATUM / Albrecht, J W – 1734 – 9 – us Sibley [780]

TRACTATUS QUINQUE MEDICO-PHYSICI / Mayow, J – M214. 1674 – 9 – ne IDC [610]

TRACTATUS THEOLOGICI IN PRIMUM SENTENTIARUM LIBRUM... / Hermann, A – Coloniae, 1690 – 11mf – 9 – CA-18/1 – ne IDC [240]

TRACTATUS THEOLOGICO-POLITICUS / Spinoza, Benedictus de – A theological and political treatise, showing that freedom of thought and of discussion may not only be granted with safety to religion and the peace of the state, but cannot be denied without danger to both the public peace and true piety. From the Latin. 2d ed. 1868 – 1 – us A.T.L.A. [240]

TRACTATUS...JURAMENTO / Gutierrez, Juan – 1730 – 9 – 1.50f – sp Bibl Santa Ana [946]

TRACTATVS APOLOGETICVS INTEGRITATEM SOCIETATIS DE ROSEA CRVCE DEFENDENS / Fludd, Robert – Lugduni Batavorum, 1617 – 1 – us U.W. Library [240]

TRACTATVS DE ALIMENTIS. / Sordi, Giovanni Pietro – Venetiis, apud Damianum Zenarium, 1620. 48 p. l., 881 numb. iln. LL-4201 – 1 – us L of C Photodup [340]

TRACTATVS DE PACE, TREVGA, VERBO DATO ALICVI PRINCIPE... / Gvazzini, S – Maceratae, 1670 – 8mf – 1 – ILM-977/1 – ne IDC [327]

TRACTATVS SEPTEM DE LAPIDE PHILOSOPHICO / Balbian, Joost van – Lugduno-Bat., 1599 – 1 – us U.W. Library [190]

A TRACTE CONTAINING THE ARTES OF CURIOUS PAINTINGE CARUINGE BUILDINGE / Lomazzo, G P – O-1005. 1598 – 9 – ne IDC [700]

TRACTS / Socialist Tract Association. Detroit – n1-7 – 1r – 1 – us Ross [335]

TRACTS AND MISCELLANEOUS CRITICISMS OF THE LATE RICHARD PORSON, ESQ. REGIUS GREEK PROFESSOR IN THE UNIVERSITY OF CAMBRIDGE / Porson, Richard; ed by Kidd, Thomas – London: Printed by R. and A. Taylor for Payne and Foss, 1815 – 1 roll – 1 – 1-55879-650-9 – uk Libr Preservation [450]

TRACTS AND TREATISES, 1613-1769 / Ireland – 1 – uk Microform Academic [941]

TRACTS AND TREATISES OF JOHN DE WYCLIFFE : WITH SELECTIONS AND TRANSLATIONS FROM HIS MANUSCRIPTS AND LATIN WORKS / Wycliffe, John; ed by Vaughn, Robert – London: Printed for the Society by Blackburn and Pardon, 1845 – 1mf – us A.T.L.A. [240]

TRACTS FOR PRIESTS AND PEOPLE – Boston: Walker, Wise, 1862 – 1mf – 9 – 0-8370-4684-X – 1985-2684 – us A.T.L.A. [230]

THE TRACTS OF CLEMENT MAYDESTON WITH THE REMAINS OF CAXTON'S ORDINALE / Wordworth, C – 1894 – 6mf – 8 – Dfl25.00 – ne Slangenburg [240]

TRACTS OF MR. THOMAS HOBBS, OF MALMSBURY CONTAINING: I. BEHEMOTH, THE HISTORY OF THE CAUSES OF THE CIVIL WARS OF ENGLAND FROM 1640 TO 1660 / Hobbes, Thomas – London. W. Crooke, 1682. 339p. illus. (Strategy of War Series) – 9 – fr Hachette [355]

TRACTS ON LIBERTY OF CONSCIENCE *see* PUBLICATIONS

TRACTS ON THE MASS / Wickham Legg, J – 1904 – 5mf – 8 – ne Slangenburg [210]

TRACTS RELATING TO THE REFORMATION / Calvin, Jean – 3v. 1844-1851 – 9 – us A.T.L.A. [240]

TRACY – 1992- – 3+ r – 1 – $150.00 – P00136 – us Library Micro [910]

Tracy, Joseph *see*
- COLONIZATION AND MISSIONS
- THE GREAT AWAKENING

Tracy, Michael L *see* CARDIORESPIRATORY RESPONSES OF CONTROLLED FREQUENCY BREATHING DURING SUBMAXIMAL EXERCISE

TRACY PRESS – Tracy, CA. 1909-47; 1949- – 154+ r – 1 – $7,700.00 ($360.00) – B03038 – us Library Micro [071]

TRADADO JURIDICO-POLITICO SOBRE PRESSAS DE MAR, ... / Abreu, F J de – Cadiz, n.d. – 5mf – 9 – ILM-1012/1 – ne IDC [340]

TRADE – it F.A.O. [380]

TRADE AGREEMENT BETWEEN UNITED STATES AND ARGENTINA *see* RECIPROCAL TRADE AGREEMENT BETWEEN UNITED STATES AND ARGENTINA

TRADE AND COMMERCE – (v1-61 1908-69 Can$4,000.00 5) – Winnipeg. v1-89. 1908-94 – 5,9 – Can$28.00y – cn Micromedia [380]

TRADE AND INDUSTRY IN MALAYSIA : A SUBJECT INDEX TO SELECT REFERENCE SOURCES 1975-1985 / Siti Zakiah, Aman – 1986 – A$10.00 – 0-86758-199-9 – at BISA [380]

THE TRADE BULLETIN – Montreal, Canada. v15 n27. 4 jun 1897 – 1r – 1 – Can$25.00 – cn Can Microfilming [380]

TRADE CARDS IN THE BRITISH MUSEUM / British Museum. London – (The Banks Collection of Trade Cards 19r $1,450.00 ISBN: 0-907006-78-7. The Heal Collection of Trade Cards 27r $2,100.00 ISBN: 0-907006 83-3) – 46r – 1 – uk Mindata [380]

TRADE CATALOGS : TRANSPORTATION / The Hagley Museum and Library – $4,955.00 – 1-55655-200-9 – us UPA [380]

TRADE CATALOGUES / Corning Museum of Glass – (US Catalogs $10,170.00 set: Bottles and Druggists' Glassware $620.00; Cut Glass $1,725.00; Flat Glass $1,090.00; Laboratory Ware $460.00; Lighting Glassware $1,665.00; Tableware $5,460.00; Foreign Catalogs $7,065.00 set: Bottles and Druggists' Glassware $355.00; Cut Glass $395.00; Flat Glass $710.00; Laboratory Ware $525.00; Lighting Glassware $895.00; Tableware $4,785.00. Guide only $210.00) – ca 2300 titles – 9 – $15,885.00 set – 0-88354-076-2 – us UPA [740]

TRADE CATALOGUES / Winterthur Museum – (Part 1: ISBN 0-88354-025-8. $13,461.00. Guide only $95.00; Part 2: ISBN 1-55655-207-6. $11,230.00. Guide only $95.00) – 3,605mf – 9 – us UPA [740]

TRADE CATALOGUES IN THE VICTORIA AND ALBERT MUSEUM / Victoria and Albert Museum. London – (British and European trade catalogues from 18th to 20th C. Three sections: domestic goods, fashion items, and commercial-industrial products) – 322mf – 9 – $1,680.00 – 0-907006-68-X – uk Mindata [380]

TRADE COMMITTEE / UN Economic Commission for Europe (ECE) – 1947-89 – E/F.19 E.1065 F.890 R.836 – 9 – us U.N. Pubs [340]

TRADE DIRECTORY OF INDONESIA / Dutch East Indies. Departement van Economische Zaken – SE-11,815 1. 1949 – 9 – ne IDC [324]

TRADE IN FOREST PRODUCTS : A STUDY OF THE BARRIERS FACED BY THE DEVELOPING COUNTRIES – 1988 – 149p – it F.A.O. [380]

TRADE JOURNAL AND REVIEW – Montreal, Canada. 1 fev 1884 – 1r – 1 – Can$25.00 – cn Can Microfilming [380]

TRADE LANES – Portland, OR. -w. 7 Apr 1932-31 Aug 1942. 2 rolls – 1 – us U.O. Library [071]

TRADE MARKS JOURNAL / Israel. State Records – Jerusalem. 1949-. -m – 9 – 360.00; 12.00y – is I.T.T.I. [340]

TRADE MARKS SUPPLEMENT TO THE GOVERNMENT GAZETTE / Sabah – Jesselton. Oct. 24, 1963-Dec. 22, 1964 – 1 – us NY Public [324]

TRADE MARKS SUPPLEMENT TO THE GOVERNMENT GAZETTE. JESSELTON. 1954-AUG. 1, 1963 / North Borneo. (United Kingdom) – 1 – us NY Public [340]

THE TRADE RELATIONS OF THE FARMERS OF NOVA SCOTIA / Elliot, James Rupert – Saint John, N.B.: Knodell, 1887. 02906. (Pre-1900 Canadiana) – 9 – cn C.I.H.M. [971]

THE TRADE REVIEW – (Merged with: The Intercolonial Journal of Commerce. Merged to become: The Trade Review and Intercolonial Journal of Commerce) – Montreal: W B Cordier, [1865-1866] – 9 – cn C.I.H.M. [380]

THE TRADE REVIEW – Winnepeg: Henderson, Main, [1881?-18– or 19–] – 9 – cn C.I.H.M. [380]

TRADE REVIEW *see*
- MARITIME TRADE REVIEW
- THE TRADE REVIEW AND INTERCOLONIAL JOURNAL OF COMMERCE

THE TRADE REVIEW AND INTERCOLONIAL JOURNAL OF COMMERCE – (Is absorbed by: Canadian Monetary Times amd Insurance Chronicle. Merger of: Trade Review (Montreal, Quebec). Merger of: The Intercolonial Journal of Commerce) – Montreal: M Longmoore, [1866-1870] – 9 – cn C.I.H.M. [380]

THE TRADE REVIEW AND INTERCOLONIAL JOURNAL OF COMMERCE *see* THE TRADE REVIEW

TRADE ROUTES AND COMMERCE OF THE ROMAN EMPIRE / Charlesworth, M P – Index. Cambridge. 1924. BA-619 2 – 8 – ne IDC [930]

TRADE UNION – Atchison. Kan. 1885-1886 – 1 – us UMI [071]

Trade Union and Labour Party Members' Delegation to Spain *see* SPAIN 1938

Trade Union Council of South Africa *see* ARCHIVE RECORDS

TRADE UNION COURIER – (Library has: v.19, no.19-22, 25; v.20, no.1, 3 (Nov. 10, 1954-March 16, 1955) – New York, N.Y.: Trade Union Courier Ltd., 19uu – 1 – CSUX89-S101 – us Hoover Inst Photo [331]

TRADE UNION COURIER AND THE FOOD ORGANIZER MAR. 1938-JAN. 1939 *see* TRADE UNION COURIER

TRADE UNION WORKER – London. -m. Jan 1916-Apr 1918. (1 reel) – 1 – uk British Libr Newspaper [331]

TRADE UNIONIST – London, England. -m. Nov 1915-Nov 1916. 8 ft – 1 – uk British Libr Newspaper [331]

TRADE UNIONIST – London. -w. 4 Apr 1891-19 Mar 1892. (1 reel) – 1 – uk British Libr Newspaper [331]

TRADE UNIONS IN CYRENAICA / Libya. Federation of Libya – 1961. BNE-1212 1 – 9 – ne IDC [331]

TRADE WITH CANADA: ADDRESS...BEFORE THE COMMITTEE ON WAYS AND MEANS, MARCH 3, 1890 / Butterworth, Benjamin – Washington: GPO, 1890. 02004. (Pre-1900 Canadiana) – 9 – cn C.I.H.M. [380]

THE TRADEMARK REPORTER – (Add vols planned) – New York: Trade-Mark Association. v1-10. 1911-1920 – 64mf – 9 – $96.00 – LLMC 90-330 – us L.L.M.C. [340]

TRADEMARK REPORTER – v1- 1911- 1; v60-5,6; v66- 9 – us UMI [380]

TRADE-MARKS / Chapman, Clowry – New York: Harper, 1930. 166p. LL-232 – 1 – us L of C Photodup [340]

TRADE-MARKS / Shoemaker, William David – Washington, DC: Williams, 1931. 2v. LL-1125 – 1 – us L of C Photodup [340]

TRADEMARKS AND COPYRIGHTS STUDIES / U.S. Congress. Senate. Committee on the Judiciary. Subcommittee on Patents – Washington: GPO. nos 1-30. 1956-63 – 33mf – 9 – $49.50 – LLMC 81-107 – us L.L.M.C. [340]

THE TRADER – (Cont by: The Trader and Canadian Jeweler) – Toronto: Trader Pub. Co., [1879-188-] – 9 – cn C.I.H.M. [380]

THE TRADER – Freetown. Sierra Leone. -m. Jan-Apr 1891. (5 ft) – 1 – uk British Libr Newspaper [072]

THE TRADER *see* THE TRADER AND CANADIAN JEWELER

TRADER – Monterey. Calif. -w. 1940-51 – 1 – us UMI [071]

THE TRADER AND CANADIAN JEWELER – (Cont: The Trader. Cont by: Canadian Jeweler) – Toronto: Trader Pub Co, [1887?-1958] – 9 – cn C.I.H.M. [380]

THE TRADER AND CANADIAN JEWELER *see* THE TRADER

TRADER AND CANADIAN JEWELLER – 1878-Jun 1958 – 1 – us UMI [730]

TRADER AND CANADIAN JEWELLER *see* CANADIAN JEWELLER

THE TRADER'S GUIDE, AND BUSINESS MAN'S LEGAL COMPANION, CONTAINING THE LAWS OF TRADE. / Butts, Isaac Ridler – Boston, Butts 1868? 138 p. L.C. copy imperfect. All after p. 138 wanting. LL-311 – 1 – us L of C Photodup [340]

Trades and Labour Congress *see* JOURNAL

TRADES AND PROFESSIONS / Palmer, George Herbert – Boston, New York: Houghton, Mifflin Co., c1914. xii,35p – 1 – us U.W. Library [370]

TRADES CHRONICLE – London, UK. 1854. -w. 10 feet – 1 – uk British Libr Newspaper [072]

Trades Council. Aberdeen *see* MINUTES, REPORTS, CORRESPONDENCE

Trades Council. Belfast *see* MINUTES, REPORTS, CORRRESPONDENCE, ETC

Trades Council. Bradford. England *see* MINUTES, REPORTS, CORRESPONDENCE, ETC

Trades Council. Dublin *see* PAPERS

Trades Council. Edinburgh *see* MINUTES, REPORTS, CORRESPONDENCE, ETC

Trades Council. Glasgow *see* MINUTES, REPORTS, CORRESPONDENCE, ETC

TRADES COUNCIL UNION NEWS – St Louis. v. 1-26. Oct. 1917-Aug 1941 – 1 – us NY Public [330]

TRADES' NEWSPAPER AND MECHANICS' WEEKLY JOURNAL – London, England. Trades' Free Press – Weekly Free Press. -w. 17 July 1825-2 April 1831. 3 reels – 1 – uk British Libr Newspaper [072]

Trades Union Congress *see*
- NO UNITED FRONT WITH COMMUNISM
- PARLIAMENTARY COMMITTEE MINUTES (1888-1921) AND REPORTS (1908-19)

Trades Union Congress (Great Britain) *see* ANNUAL REPORTS

TRADICION CONCEPTISTA EN LA PROVINCIA BETICA / Alvarez, Arturo – Sevilla: Imp. Provincial, 1958. Sep. Archivo Hispalense, 2nd epoca, no 87 – sp Bibl Santa Ana [946]

LA TRADICION PORTUENSE DE BOLIVIA / Baldivia Galdo, Jose Maria – La Paz. 1951 – 1 – us Res Libr [972]

TRADICION Y... / Mangarriello, Ma Esther – Madrid: Graf. Calleja, 1967 – 1 – sp Bibl Santa Ana [946]

TRADICIONALES FERIAS Y FIESTAS DE PRIMAVERA, 1978 / Alcantara. Ayuntamiento – Caceres: Imp. La Minerva, 1978 – sp Bibl Santa Ana [390]

TRADICIONALES FERIAS Y FIESTAS DE PRIMAVERA...1979 / Alcantara. Ayuntamiento – Caceres: La Minerva, 1979 – 1 – sp Bibl Santa Ana [390]

TRADICIONALES FIESTAS DE LA REAL VILLA EN HONOR DE SUS PATRONOS SAN FULGENCIO Y SANTA FLORENTINA. AGOSTO 1972 – Caceres: Imp. La Minerva, 1972 – 1 – sp Bibl Santa Ana [240]

TRADICIONALES FIESTAS EN HONOR DE LA SANTISIMA VIRGEN DE NAVELONGA / Cilleros. Ayuntamiento – Caceres: Tip. La Minerva, 1979 – 1 – sp Bibl Santa Ana [390]

TRADICIONALES FIESTAS EN HONOR DE LA SANTISIMA VIRGEN DE NAVELONGA, 1978 / Cilleros. Ayuntamiento – Caceres: Tip. La Minerva, 1978 – sp Bibl Santa Ana [390]

TRADICIONALES FIESTAS EN HONOR DE SAN SEBASTIAN PATRONO DE ACEHUCHE, 1975 – Caceres: Tip. La Minerva – 1 – sp Bibl Santa Ana [240]

TRADICIONES DE BUENOS AIRES / Obligado, Pastor S – v1, 3-10. 1888-1978 – 1 – us I.U. Libraries [390]

TRADICIONES POPULAIRES – 1885 – 1 – us I.U. Libraries [390]

TRADICIONES Y MEMORIAS HISTORIALES DE DON GONZALO DE STUNIGA / Alonso Chacon, Joseph – Madrid: Imp. Real, 1727 – 1 – sp Bibl Santa Ana [946]

TRADING POST OF ROGER WILLIAMS WITH THOSE OF JOHN WILCOX AND RICHARD SMITH / Chapin, Howard M – 1933 – 1 – 5.00 – us Baptist [240]

TRADITIO – 1(1943)-16(1960) – 214mf – 9 – Dfl749.00 – ne Slangenburg [073]

TRADITION – v1- 1958- 1; v16- 5,6,9 – us UMI [390]

TRADITION AND DEVELOPMENT IN AFRICA TODAY – 1990 – 138p – 9 – 92-3-102653-4 – fr UNESCO [306]

TRADITION, DIVERSIFICATION, AND ECONOMIC DEVELOPMENT / Senegal – A World Bank Country Economic Report. Washington. 1974. BD-1865 1 – 9 – ne IDC [330]

LA TRADITION MANUSCRITE DE SOZOMENE (T.U.U. 3-32/2B) / Bidez, J – Leipzig, 1908 – 2mf – 9 – ne Slangenburg [240]

LA TRADITION PEULE DES ANIMAUX D'ATTACHE / Laya, D – 9 – F90.00 – fr Ethnologie [306]

TRADITION UND TRADENTEN IN DEN SCHULEN PALAESTINAS UND BABYLONIENS / Bacher, Wilhelm – Leipzig, 1914 – 12mf – 8 – ne Slangenburg [260]

TRADITION UND URSPRUENGLICHKEIT : AKTEN DES 3. INTERNATIONALEN GERMANISTENKONGRESSES / ed by Internationaler Germanisten-Kongress – (Includes bibliographical references) – Bern: Francke Verlag, c1966 – 1 – us U.W. Library [430]

TRADITIONAL AND NON-TRADITIONAL FOODS / Fernando, R – 1981 – 156p – it F.A.O. [640]

TRADITIONAL BALLAD AIRS – 1876-81 – 1 – us I.U. Libraries [390]

TRADITIONAL BASEBALL WEIGHT TRAINING VERSUS POWER WEIGHT TRAINING : EFFECTS ON BAT VELOCITY / Schwendel, P J – 1991 – 2mf – 9 – $8.00 – us Microform Publ [790]

TRADITIONAL CHEESEMAKING MANUAL / O'Connor, C B – 1993 – 9 – $12.00 – et ILRI [630]

TRADITIONAL CULTURES OF THE WORLD PROGRAM / Human Relations Area Files – 1988. 95 cultural files constituting a research sample – 9 – 14,500.00; apply – us H.R.A.F. [301]

TRADITIONAL FOOD PLANTS : A RESOURCE BOOK FOR PROMOTING THE EXPLOITATION AND CONSUMPTION OF FOOD PLANTS IN ARID, SEMI-ARID AND SUB-HUMID LANDS OF EASTERN AFRICA – 1988 – 603p – it F.A.O. [631]

TRADITIONAL FOODS IN THE NEAR EAST – 1991 – 181p – it F.A.O. [640]

TRADITIONAL MANAGEMENT OF SEAWEEDS IN THE DISTRICT OF LEON – 1984 – 57p – it F.A.O. [639]

TRADITIONAL POST-HARVEST TECHNOLOGY OF PERISHABLE TROPICAL STAPLES – 1984 – 89p – it F.A.O. [660]

THE TRADITIONAL TEXT OF THE HOLY GOSPELS VINDICATED AND ESTABLISHED BY THE LATE JOHN WILLIAM BURGON / Burgon, John William – 1896 – 1 – us A.T.L.A. [240]

TRADITIONARY STORIES OF OLD FAMILIES, AND LEGENDARY ILLUSTRATIONS OF FAMILY HISTORY / Pickens, Andrew – With notes, historical and biographical.London: Longman, Rees, Orme, Brown, Green & Longman, 1833. 2v. illus – 1 – us U.W. Library [920]

TRADITIONEN ZUR CHARAKTERISTIK OESTERREICHS : SEINES STAATS- UND VOLKSLEBENS UNTER FRANZ 1. / Schoenholz, F A von – Muenchen. 2v. 1914 – 10mf – 9 – ne IDC [943]

TRADITIONS AND BELIEFS OF ANCIENT ISRAEL / Cheyne, Thomas Kelly – (Includes bibliographical references and indexes) – London: Adam and Charles Black, 1907 – 2mf – 9 – 0-8370-9454-2 – 1986-3454 – us A.T.L.A. [220]

TRADITIONS ET MUTATIONS DANS UN VILLAGE IVOIRIEN DE PALMERAIE / Manso Mangou-Eyi, J M – 9 – F60.00 – fr Ethnologie [305]

TRADITIONS HISTORIQUES ET LEGENDAIRES DU SOUDAN OCCIDENTAL : TRADUITES D'UN MANUSCRIT ARABE INEDIT / Delafosse, Maurice – ([Filmed with: Doulte, Edmond. L'Islam algerien...]) – Paris: Comite de l'Afrique francaise, 1913 – us Res Libr [960]

TRADITIONS INDIENNES DU CANADA NORD-OUE V. 23, XVII, 521P / Petitot, E – BN 343 2. 1886 – 8 – ne IDC [306]

TRADITIONS OF PALESTINE, OR, SCENES IN THE HOLY LAND IN THE DAYS OF CHRIST / Sargent, Moses H – Boston: Graves & Yound, 1863. 1 fiche – 9 – us A.T.L.A. [240]

TRADITIONS POPULAIRES, CROYANCES, SUPERSTITIEUSES.. / Richard, Nicolas Louis Antoine – 1848 – 1 – us I.U. Libraries [390]

LE TRADIZIONI POPOLARI DI S. STEFANO DI CALCINAIA / Gubernatis, Alessandro de – 1894 – 1 – us I.U. Libraries [390]

LA TRADUCCION AUTOMATICA / Regales Serna, Antonio – 2mf – 9 – Pta1,500.00 – 84-85422-25-2 – sp Pentalfa [400]

TRADUCCION DE LOS AFORISMOS DE HIPOCRATES / Sedeno de Meca, A – Madrid, 1699 – 6mf – 9 – sp Cultura [610]

LAS TRADUCCIONES DE "CALILA E DIMNA" / Penzol, Pedro – 1931 – 1 – us I.U. Libraries [810]

TRADUCION EN VERSO DEL SALMO L. DE DAVID. MISERERE MEI DEUS / Vera e Isla Fernandez, Fernando de la – Madrid: Gomez Fuentenebro, 1879 – 1 – sp Bibl Santa Ana [946]

TRADUCTION AUTOMATIQUE *see* TA INFORMATIONS

LA TRADUCTION DE L'ANCIEN TESTAMENT DE LEFEVRE D'ETAPLES / Laune, Alfred – Le Cateau: J. Roland, 1895. 1 fiche – 9 – us A.T.L.A. [240]

Traegardh, I *see* MONOGRAPHIE DER ARKTISCHEN ACARIDEN

Traenckner, Chr *see* DIE BIBLISCHE POESIE

TRAENEN : UNTERSUCHUNGEN UEBER DAS WEINEN IN DER DEUTSCHEN SPRACHE UND LITERATUR DES MITTELALTERS / Weinand, Heinz Gerd – (Includes bibliographical references) – Bonn: B Bouvier, 1958 – 1r – 1 – us U.W. Library [430]

Traetta, T *see*
- I TRINDARIDI
- IPPOLITA ED ARICIA. [DRAMMA IN CINQUE ATTI]
- ...SIROE, OPERA DI...[DRAMMA PER MUSICA DA RAPPRESENTARSI NEL NUOVE TEATRO DI CORTE...NEL CARNOVALE 1767. LA POESIA E DEL SIGNOR ABBATE PIETRO METASTASIO...

TRAEUME / Huch, Friedrich – Berlin: S Fischer, 1904 – 1r – 1 – us U.W. Library [800]

TRAFALGAR ECHOES – Montreal, 1918-. SEM16P364 – 3r – 5 – Can$91.00 – cn Bibl Nat [073]

TRAFFIC ENGINEERING AND CONTROL – v1-1960- 1; v17- 5,6,9 – us UMI [629]

TRAFFIC MANAGEMENT – (1984-. 5,6,9) – v1-. 1962- – 1 – us UMI [380]

TRAFFIC QUARTERLY – (v.33- 1979- 5,6,9) – v.1-. 1947- – 1 – us UMI [380]

TRAFFIC WORLD – v1- 1907- 1; v145- 5,6; v161- 9 – us UMI [600]

TRAGEDIA / Urcullu, Jose de Moctezuma – 1818 – 9 – 1.50f – sp Bibl Santa Ana [440]

LA TRAGEDIA DE LAS DICTADURAS LATINOAMERICANAS Y CUATRO PROBLEMAS ARGENTINOS / Lubertino, Jose – Buenos Aires: [Editorial Gure], 1956 – 9 – us Hoover Inst Photo [972]

LA TRAGEDIA DE RIBADELAGO / Escudero Gonzalez, Jose – Merida: Imp. Juan Rejas Lopez, 1959 – sp Bibl Santa Ana [946]

TRAGEDIA JOSEPHINE / Carvajal, Micael – Paris: Les presses Universitairs, 1932 – 1 – sp Bibl Santa Ana [946]

LA TRAGEDIE DE L'ESPAGNE – Bruxelles, 1936? Fiche W1233. (Blodgett Collection of Spanish Civil War Pamphlets) – 9 – us H.U. College Libr [946]

TRAGEDIE, SOGNI E MISTERI, DI GABRIELE D'ANNUNZIO / Annunzio, Gabriele d' – Milano: A. Mondadori. 1940. Con un avvertimento di Renato Simoni – 1 – us U.W. Library [920]

TRAGEDIES : TO WHICH ARE ADDED A FEW SONNETS AND VERSES / Talfourd, Thomas Noon – London: Edward Moxon, 1844 – 1 roll – 1 – 1-55879-278-3 – uk Libr Preservation [820]

TRAGEDIIA TVORCHESTVA. DOSTOEVSKII I TOLSTOI / Belyi, A – M. 1911. BR-603 2 – 8 – ne IDC [460]

TRAGEDY IN EAST TIMOR – 1992 – sz I.C.J. [320]

THE TRAGEDY OF SPAIN / Rocker, Rudolf – N.Y., 1937. Fiche W1145. (Blodgett Collection of Spanish Civil War Pamphlets) – 9 – us H.U. College Libr [946]

THE TRAGEDY OF SPAIN / Vollenhoven, M W R van – London, 1938 – 1 – sp Bibl Santa Ana [946]

Trager, Oliver *see* EDITORIALS ON FILE

THE TRAGIC WEEK IN MAY / Souchy, Agustin – Barcelona, 1937. Fiche W1167. (Blodgett Collection of Spanish Civil War Pamphlets) – 9 – us H.U. College Libr [946]

DIE TRAGIK DER DEM LEBEN NICHT GEWACHSENEN INNERLICHKEIT IN DEN WERKEN GERHART HAUPTMANNS / Engert, Horst – (Includes bibliographical references) – Leipzig: C G Roeder, 1910 – 1r – 1 – us U.W. Library [430]

DIE TRAGIK DES ORPHISCHEN DICHTERS : EIN GEISTESGESCHICHTLICHER VERSUCH UEBER HOELDERLIN / Michel, Ernst – Mainz: Matthias-Gruenewald-Verlag, 1922 – 1r – 1 – us U.W. Library [430]

DIE TRAGISCHEN PROBLEME DES STRUENSEE-STOFFES : EINE BETRACHTUNG DER HEBBELSCHEN ABHANDLUNG / Erler, Otto – Leipzig: H Haessel, 1916 – 1r – 1 – us U.W. Library [430]

TRAGIZM LOSOW POLSKI / Giertych, Jedrzej – 343p. Pelplin Nakt. ksieg., 1937 – 1 – us U.W. Library [943]

TRAICTE DE LA GRAMAIRE FRANCOISE / Estienne, Robert – 1569 – 9 – fr I.C.S. [440]

TRAICTE DES MANIERES DE GRAVER EN TAILLE-DOUCE / Bosse, Abraham – O-170. 1645 – 9 – ne IDC [760]

TRAICTE DES MARQUES DE POSSEDEZ ET LA PREUVE DE LA VERITABLE POSSESSION DES RELIGIEUSES DE LOUVIERS / Pietre, Simon – Rouen. 1644 – 9 – fr Hachette [360]

Traiecti, Jacobus *see* NARRATIO DE INCHOATIONE DOMUS CLERICORUM IN ZWOLLIS

Trail, J C M *see*
- SAHIWAL CATTLE
- SMALL RUMINANT BREED PRODUCTIVITY IN AFRICA

Trail, J C M et al *see* PRODUCTIVITY OF BORAN CATTLE MAINTAINED BY CHEMOPROPHYLAXIS UNDER TRYPANOSOMIASIS RISK

Trail, JC M et al *see* TRYPANOTOLERANT LIVESTOCK IN WEST AND CENTRAL AFRICA

THE TRAIL OF THE LOUP / Foght, H W – History of the Loup river region. 1906.Nebraska Reel 10. (The Cox Library Collection) – 5 – us Americana [978]

TRAIL OF THE REV. ALEXANDER FLETCHER, A.M. : BEFORE THE LORD CHIEF JUSTICE OF COMMON SENSE AND A SPECIAL JURY – London: Knight & Lacey, 1825 – 2mf – 9 – $3.00 – LLMC 91-088 – us L.L.M.C. [340]

THE TRAIL OF THE SERPENT, OR THE SECRET OF THE HEATH / Braddon, Mary Elizabeth – Formerly: Three Times Dead. British Fiction Archive: Unit 5 – 9 – uk Bell [830]

TRAILBLAZER : INDEX AND QUARTERLY BULLETIN OF THE PIONEERS OF SANTA CLARA COUNTY – Santa Clara, Washington, DC. Agnew, Abraham-Wright's Station: 1961-1972 – 1r – 1 – $50.00 – B06010 – us Library Micro [978]

TRAILER LIFE – 1976- – 9 – us UMI [073]

Traill, Henry Duff *see*
- THE NEW FICTION
- SHAFTESBURY (THE FIRST EARL)

Train, Arthur Cheney *see* THE JURY SYSTEM–DEFECTS AND PROPOSED REMEDIES

TRAINED MANPOWER FOR AGRICULTURAL AND RURAL DEVELOPMENT – 2nd ed 1980 – 132p – it F.A.O. [331]

TRAINING AIDS DIGEST – v1- 1976- 1; v2- 5,6,9 – us UMI [360]

TRAINING AMENORRHEA IN COLLEGE ATHLETES / Hall, Teri-Christine R – 1982 – 1mf – 9 – $4.00 – us Microform Publ [790]

TRAINING AND EXTENSION IN THE COOPERATIVE MOVEMENT / Laidlaw, Alexander Fraser – 1978 – 78p – it F.A.O. [370]

TRAINING AND METHODS SERIES / Wisconsin. Land Tenure Center – 1964-69. n.1-10 – 1,5 – us Spaulding [630]

TRAINING FOR AGRICULTURE AND RURAL DEVELOPMENT – it F.A.O. [370]

TRAINING FOR MASS COMMUNICATION – 1975 – 44p – 9 – 92-3-101234-7 – fr UNESCO [380]

TRAINING HOME ECONOMICS FOR RURAL DEVELOPMENT : REPORT OF A GLOBAL STUDY ON DEVELOPMENT OF CRITERIA FOR ESTABLISHING TRAINING INSTITUTIONS FOR HOME ECONOMICS STAFF IN RURAL DEVELOPMENT – 1978 – 125p – it F.A.O. [370]

TRAINING MANUAL FOR EMBRYO TRANSFER IN CATTLE – 1991 – 176p – it F.A.O. [636]

TRAINING MANUAL FOR EMBRYO TRANSFER IN WATER-BUFFALOES – 1991 – 68p – it F.A.O. [636]

TRAINING MANUAL ON ARTIFICIAL INSEMINATION IN SHEEP AND GOATS – 1991 – 250p – it F.A.O. [636]

THE TRAINING OF A PRIEST : AN ESSAY ON CLERICAL EDUCATION / Smith, John Talbot – New York: Longmans, Green, 1908 – 1mf – us A.T.L.A. [370]

TRAINING OF TEACHER EDUCATORS – 1983 – 39p – 9 – 92-3-101936-8 – fr UNESCO [370]

THE TRAINING OF TEACHERS : WITH SUPPLEMENT, PRESENTATION AND DISCUSSION OF THE REPORT IN THE CONFERENCE ON 22ND JUNE 1910 – (Includes indexes) – Edinburgh: Publ for the World Missionary Conference by Oliphant, Anderson & Ferrier; New York: Fleming H Revell, [1910?] – 1mf – 9 – 0-8370-6479-1 – 1986-0479 – us A.T.L.A. [370]

TRAINING OFFICER – (v.17-. 1981-. 5,6,9) – v.1-. 1965- – 1 – us UMI [073]

A TRAINING PROGRAM FOR VOLUNTEER LEADERS AT THE FIRST BAPTIST CHURCH, ALMA, GEORGIA / Haygood, Benjamin Iverson – 1981 – 1 – 5.44 – us Baptist [240]

TRAINING SCHOOL BULLETIN – v1-71 1904-74 1; v68-71 5,6 – us UMI [360]

TRAINING UNION QUARTERLY FOR THE DEAF – 1961 – 1 – 6.72 – us Baptist [240]

TRAINMAN NEWS – Cleveland. Ohio. 1959-1966 – 1 – us UMI [071]

TRAINS – 1940-51. Continued by Trains and Travel – 1 – us UMI [073]

TRAINS – 1954-55 – 1 – us UMI [073]

TRAINS AND TRAVEL – 1951-54. Continued by Trains – 1 – us UMI [073]

LE TRAIT D'UNION : COMMERCIAL ET LITTERAIRE / ed by Labelle, J H A – St-Jerome, Canada. v1 n39. 21 dec 1928-16 oct 1931 – 1r – 1 – Can$60.00 – cn Can Microfilming [072]

LE TRAIT D'UNION – Dolbeau, Canada. 27 jan-3 mar 1950 – 1r – 1 – Can$30.00 – cn Can Microfilming [072]

LE TRAIT D'UNION : ENTRE EMPLOYEURS ET EMPLOYES – Montreal, Canada. 1ere serie: v1 n1. 1 fev 1887-v7 n2. 26 sep 1896; 2e serie: v1 n3. 27 nov 1897-v1 n6. 18 dec 1897 – 1r – 1 – Can$35.00 – cn Can Microfilming [331]

LE TRAIT D'UNION – Montreal: H Roullaud et G de Martigny, [1897-189- ou 19–] – 9 – cn C.I.H.M. [306]

LE TRAIT D'UNION – Quebec. v1 n1. 1 dec 1945-avr/mai 1949 – 1r – 1 – Can$40.00 – cn Can Microfilming [072]

TRAITE ANALYTIQUE DE LA FOLIE ET DES MOYENS DE LA GUERIR / Amard, Louis Victor Frederic – (French Precursors of Psychiatry Series). Lyon. impr. Ballanche. 1807 – 9 – fr Hachette [150]

LE TRAITE BRYAN-CHAMORRO... / Castejon-Fiallos, M – Paris, 1925 – 2mf – 1 – ILM-2310/1 – ne IDC [327]

TRAITE CLASSIQUE D'ECONOMIE POLITIQUE: SELON LA DOCTRINE DE LEON XIII: AVEC APPLICATIONS AU CANADA / Baillairge, Frederic Alexandre – Joliette, Bureau de l'Etudiant, du Couvent et de la Famille. 1892. 00087. (Pre-1900 Canadiana) – 9 – cn C.I.H.M. [330]

TRAITE CLINIQUE ET THERAPEUTIQUE DE L'HYSTERIE / Briquet, Pierre de – (French Precursors of Psychiatry Series). Paris. J. B. Bailliere. 1859 – 9 – fr Hachette [150]

TRAITE COMPLET DE LA NAVIGATION CONTENANT LES PROPOSITIONS ET PRATIQUES DE GEOMETRIE, UN TRAITE DE LA SPHERE ET D'ASTRONOMIE. / Bouguer, M Pierre – Paris: Chez Claude Jombert et chez l'Auteur, 1706. SEM105PP953 – 4mf – 9 – $9.00 – cn Bibl Nat [623]

TRAITE COMPLET DE L'HYPOCHONDRIE / Brachet, Jean-Louis – (French Precursors of Psychiatry Series). Paris. J. B. Bailliere et Germer Bailliere; Lyon, C. Savy. 1844 – 9 – fr Hachette [150]

LE TRAITE CONTRE LES BOGOMILES / Cosmas Le Pretre; ed by Puech, H- & Vaillant, A – Paris, 1945 – Dfl25.00 – ne Slangenburg [240]

TRAITE D'ARCHITECTURE / Reynaud, Francois Leonce – Premiere Partie: Art de Batir. Deuxieme Partie: Composition des Edifices. Paris: Dalmont, 1860-63. 4v in 4 fol. dont 2 de pl. (Architecture Series) – 9 – fr Hachette [720]

TRAITE D'ARCHITECTURE. / Le Clerc, Sebastien – Paris, P. Giffard, 1714. 2v. in 4 dont un album de planches. (Architecture Series) – 9 – fr Hachette [720]

TRAITE D'ARCHITECTURE OU PROPORTIONS DES TROIS ORDRES GRECS. / Antoine, Jean – Treves: Imp. de son Altesse Serenissime, 1768. illus. (Architecture Series) – 9 – fr Hachette [720]

TRAITE D'ARCHITECTURE PRATIQUE / Monroy, Jean Francois – Paris. Prault, 1785. 8 fol., viii, 367p., pl. (Architecture Series) – 9 – fr Hachette [720]

TRAITE D'ARCHITECTURE RURALE / Perthuis de Laillevault, L – Paris. Dea1terville, 1810. 4 fol., 263p., pl. (Architecture Series) – 9 – fr Hachette [720]

TRAITE DE BOTANIQUE MEDICALE PHANEROGAMIQUE / Baillon, H E – Paris, 1883-1884 – 17mf – 9 – ne IDC [615]

TRAITE DE COMPOSITION / Bordier, L-C – 1770 – 9 – us Sibley [780]

TRAITE DE COMPOSITION MUSICALE / Fux, J J – 1773-75 – 9 – us Sibley [780]

TRAITE DE DROIT... / Carnazza Amaro, G – Paris, 1880-1882 – 14mf – 1 – ILM-369/1 – ne IDC [327]

TRAITE DE DROIT CONVENTIONNEL INTERNATIONAL CONCERNANT LA PROPRIETE INDUSTRIELLE / Plaisant, Marcel – Paris: Sirey, 1949. 422p. LL-4082 – 1 – us L of C Photodup [340]

TRAITE DE DROIT INTERNATIONAL PUBLIC / Fauchille, P – Ed 8. Paris. 2v. 1921-22 – 45mf – 1 – ILM-163/1 – ne IDC [327]

TRAITE DE DROIT PENAL INTERNATIONAL... / Fiore, P – Paris. 2v. 1880 – 11mf – 1 – ILM-2022/1 – ne IDC [327]

LE TRAITE DE DROIT PUBLIC D'IBN TAIMIYA / Laoust, Henri – Beyrouth, 1948 – 5mf – 8 – ne Slangenburg [260]

LE TRAITE DE DROIT PUBLIC D'IBN TAIMIYA / Laoust, Henri – Beyrouth, 1948 – Dfl22.00 – ne Slangenburg [260]

TRAITE DE GEOGRAPHIE ET DE STATISTIQUE MEDICALE ET DES MALADIES ENDEMIQUES / Boudin, Jean Christian Marc Francois Joseph – Paris: J.B. Bailliere et fils, 1857. illus. 15 fiches.(Statistics Series: Medical Studies) – 9 – 37.50 – fr Bibl Nationale [310]

TRAITE DE GEOLOGIE / Lapparent, Albert A – 5th ed. Paris: Masson. 3v. 1906. SEM35P70 – 1r – 1 – Can$60.00 – cn Bibl Nat [550]

TRAITE DE LA BASSE SOUS LE CHANT / Langle, H F M – c.1798 – 9 – us Sibley [780]

TRAITE DE LA COMPOSITION DE MUSIQUE / Nivers, G G de – P 416. 1667 – 9 – ne IDC [780]

TRAITE DE LA COMPOSITION DE MUSIQUE / Nivers, G G de – Trad. en flamand by E. Roger. P 417. 1697 – 9 – ne IDC [780]

TRAITE DE LA CONFIRMITE DU FRANCAIS AVEC LE GREC / Estienne, Henri – (Linguistic series). 1565 – 9 – fr Hachette [450]

TRAITE DE LA CONSTRUCTION ORATOIRE / Le Batteux – 1763 – 9 – fr I.C.S. [440]

TRAITE DE LA DANSE / Giraudet, E – Paris: [Imprimerie A. veutin], 187-? – 1 – us Sibley [780]

TRAITE DE LA DEFENSE DES PLACES / Vauban, Sebastien Le Prestre de – Paris: Chez Charles-Antoine Jombert, pere, 1769. SEM16P94 – 1r – 5 – Can$11.00 – cn Bibl Nat [355]

TRAITE DE LA FORMATION MECANIQUE DES LANGUES / Brosses, Charles de – (Linguistics series). 2 v. 1767 – 9 – fr Hachette [400]

TRAITE DE LA FORMATION MECHANIQUE DES LANGUES / Brosses, Charles de – 1765 – 9 – fr I.C.S. [400]

TRAITE DE LA FORMATION MECHANIQUE DES LANGUES, ET DES PRINCIPES PHYSIQUES DE L'ETYMOLOGIE / Brosses, Charles de – Paris. 2v. 1765 – 13mf – 9 – ne IDC [400]

TRAITE DE LA MANIERE D'ENSEIGNER A LIRE / Boulliette, Abbe – 1878 – 9 – fr I.C.S. [370]

TRAITE DE LA MUSETTE.. / Borjon de Scellery, Charles-Emmanuel – 1672 – 2 – us Sibley [780]

TRAITE DE LA MUSIQUE THEORIQUE ET PRATIQUE CONTENANT LES PRECEPTES DE LA COMPOSITION / Parran, A – 1646 – 9 – us Sibley [780]

TRAITE DE LA PEINTURE / Cennini, C – O-984 1. 1858 – 9 – ne IDC [760]

TRAITE DE LA PERSPECTIVE PRATIQUE AVEC DES REMARQUES SUR L'ARCHITECTURE. / Courtonne, J – Paris, J. Vincent, 1725. 16, 116p., ill. (Architecture Series) – 9 – fr Hachette [720]

TRAITE DE LA PERTE ET DE LA RESTITUTION DES TITRES AU PORTEUR ... / Bezard-Falgas, J – Paris, 1923 – 7mf – 9 – ILM-3265/1 – ne IDC [327]

TRAITE DE LA POESIE FRANCAISE / Mourgues, Le P Michel – 1724 – 9 – fr I.C.S. [440]

TRAITE DE LA PRONONCIATION / Dubroca, L – 1824 – 9 – fr I.C.S. [440]

TRAITE DE LA PROSODIE FRANCOISE / Olivet, P J d' – 1736 – 9 – fr I.C.S. [440]

TRAITE DE LA PROSODIE FRANCOISE / Olivet, P J d' – 1760 – 9 – fr I.C.S. [440]

TRAITE DE LA VIOLE / Rousseau, Jean-Jacques – Paris. 1687. BP-752 1 – 9 – ne IDC [780]

TRAITE DE LA VIOLE.. / Rousseau, Jean-Jacques – 1687 – 2 – us Sibley [780]

TRAITE DE L'ANTIMOINE CONTENANT L'ANALYSE CHYMIQUE / Lemery, Nicolas – Paris: J. Boudot, 1707. 7 fiches. (Science Collection) – 9 – $17.00 – fr Bibl Nationale [540]

TRAITE DE L'ARCHITECTURE / Catherinot, Nicolas – 10 mars 1688. 24p. (Architecture Series) – 9 – fr Hachette [720]

TRAITE DE L'ARCHITECTURE SUIVANT VITRUVE / Mauclerc, Julien – Paris. P. Daret. 1648. 8p., 50 pl. (Architecture Series) – 9 – fr Hachette [720]

TRAITE DE L'ARRANGEMENT DES MOTS / Le Batteux – 1783 – 9 – fr I.C.S. [440]

TRAITE DE L'ART METALIQUE / Barba, Alvaro Alonso – Paris: Chez Andre Knapen, 1730. SEM105P950 – 4mf – 9 – $9.00 – cn Bibl Nat [670]

TRAITE ... DE L'EXTRADITION ... / Bernard, P – Paris. 2v. 1883 – 13mf – 9 – ILM-939/1 – ne IDC [327]

TRAITE DE L'HARMONIE REDUITE A SES PRINCIPES NATURELS / Rameau, Jean-Phillippe – 1722 – 9 – us Sibley [780]

TRAITE DE L'ORTHOGRAPHE / Lesclache, L de – 1669 – 9 – fr I.C.S. [440]

TRAITE DE L'ORTHOGRAPHE / Mauconduit, De – 1669 – 9 – fr I.C.S. [440]

TRAITE DE L'ORTHOGRAPHE FRANCOISE / Le Roy, C – 1747 – 9 – fr I.C.S. [440]

TRAITE DE MECANIQUE DES POIDS SOUTENUS PAR DES PUISSASNCES SUR LES PLANS INCLINES / Roberval, Gilles de – Paris, 1636, 36 p. Histoire des Sciences XVIIe-XIXe Siecles. 7961 – 9 – fr Hachette [530]

TRAITE DE MUSIQUE CONCERNANT LES TONS, LES HARMONIES, LES ACCORDS ET LE DISCOURS MUSICAL / Bemetzrieder, A – Contains: Exemples du traite de Musique. . 1776 – 9 – us Sibley [780]

TRAITE DE MUSIQUE, CONCERNANT LES TONS, LES HARMONIES, LES ACCORDS ET LE DISCOURS MUSICAL / Bemetzrieder, A – Paris. 1776. BP-161 1 – 9 – ne IDC [780]

TRAITE DE MUSIQUE, POUR BIEN ET FACILEMENT APPRENDRE A CHANTER ET COMPOSER, TANT POUR LES VOIX QUE POUR LES INSTRUMENTS / La Voye, M de – 1656 – 9 – us Sibley [780]

TRAITE DE NEUTRALITE CONCLU A LONDRES LE SEIZIEME NOVEMBRE 1686, ENTRE LES ROYS DE FRANCE ET D'ANGLETERRE, TOUCHANT LES PAYS DES DEUX ROYS EN AMERIQUE / France. Treaties, etc – Paris: Frederic Leonard, 1689. SEM16P40 – 1r – 5 – Can$9.00 – cn Bibl Nat [941]

LE TRAITE "DE UNITATE FORMAE" DE GILLES DE LESSINES / Wulf, M de – 1901 – 8mf – 8 – ne Slangenburg [100]

TRAITE DE VERSIFICATION FRANCAISE / Quicherat, L M – 2e ed. 1850 – 9 – fr I.C.S. [440]

LE TRAITE DE WALTER DE BIBBESWORTH SUR LA LANGUE FRANCAISE / Bibbesworth, Walter de – 14eme siecle. (Linguistics Series). 1929 – 9 – fr Hachette [440]

TRAITE DES ACCORDS.. / Roussier, Pierre-Joseph – 1764 – 2 – us Sibley [780]

TRAITE DES AGREMENS DE LA MUSIQUE.. / Tartini, G – 1771 – 2 – us Sibley [780]

TRAITE DES ARBRES ET ARBUSTES / Duhamel du Monceau, H L – Ed. 2. Paris. 1800-01-1819. B-726 2 – 8 – ne IDC [580]

TRAITE DES ARBRES ET ARBUSTES / Duhamel du Monceau, Henri Louis – 2v. Paris. 1755 – 8 – ne IDC [580]

TRAITE DES ARBRES FRUITIERS: CONTENANT LEUR FIGURE, LEUR DESCRIPTION, LEUR CULTURE... / Duhamel du Monceau, M – Paris: Chez Saillant, libraire: Desaint, libraire, 1768. SEM35P324 – 1r – 1 – Can$41.00 – cn Bibl Nat [631]

LA TRAITE DES BLANCS; ROMANS DE MOEURS COLONIALES / Mathey, Michel – Paris. 1902 – 1 – us Res Libr [960]

TRAITE DES CAUSES SECONDES / Tritheme, Jean – Paris: Chamuel, 1897. 149p. 2 fiches. (Science Collection) – 9 – 6.00 – fr Bibl Nationale [500]

TRAITE DES CENSURES EN FRANCAIS: D'APRES LE DROIT NOUVEAU ETABLI PAR LA BULLE "APOSTOLICAE SEDIS." / Condis, Pierre – 1884. 300p. (Religion series) – 9 – 12.00 – fr Bibl Nationale [240]

TRAITE DES CHAMPIGNONS / Paulet, J J – 2v. Paris. 1793. Lacking: atlas consisting of 217 plates. B-5634 2 – 8 – ne IDC [580]

TRAITE DES CINQ ORDRES D'ARCHITECTURE. / Le Muet, Pierre – Paris. F. Langlois, 1645. 6, 229p., illus. (Architecture Series) – 9 – fr Hachette [720]

TRAITE DES DEGENERESCENCES PHYSIQUES, INTELLECTUELLES ET MORALES DE L'ESPECE HUMAINE ET DES CAUSES QUI PRODUISENT CES VARIETES MALADIVES / Morel, Benedict A – (French Precursors of Psychiatry Series). Paris. J. B. Bailliere. 1857 – 9 – fr Hachette [616]

TRAITE DES ENERGUMENES, SUIVY D'UN DISCOURS SUR LA POSSESSION DE MARTHE BROSSIER / Alexis, Leon d' – Troyes. 1599 – 9 – fr Hachette [360]

TRAITE DES ETUDES MONASTIQUES / Mobillon, Jean – Paris, 1691 – 16mf – 8 – Dfl56.00 – ne Slangenburg [240]

TRAITE DES FOUGERES DE L'AMERIQUE / Plumier, C – Paris. 1705. B-7245 1 – 9 – ne IDC [580]

TRAITE DES LANGUES / Frain du Tremblay, J – 1703 – 9 – fr I.C.S. [400]

TRAITE DES LANGUES OU L'ON DONNE DES PRINCIPES ET DES REGLES POUR JUGER DU MERITE ET DE L'EXCELLENCE DE CHAQUE LANGUE ET EN PARTICULIER DE LA LANGUE FRANCAISE / Frain du Tremblay, J – (Linguistic series). 1703 – 9 – fr Hachette [400]

TRAITE DES MALADIES DES OS / Petit, J L – M 119. 2 v. 1723 – 9 – ne IDC [611]

TRAITE DES MANIERES DE DESSINER LES ORDRES DE L'ARCHITECTURE ANTIQUE / Bosse, Abraham – Paris, 1664. 44 ff., ill. (Architecture Series) – 9 – fr Hachette [720]

LA TRAITE DES NEGRES ET LA CROISADE AFRICAINE. / Gochet, Alexis Marie – Liege. 1889 – 1 – us Res Libr [960]

LA TRAITE DES NEGRES; OU, DEUX MARINS AU SENEGAL / Enduran, Ludoix – Lille, 1868 – 1 – us Res Libr [960]

TRAITE DES ORDRES D'ARCHITECTURE / Potain – Part 1. Paris. Jombert, 1747. 4 fol., 96p., ill. (Architecture Series) – 9 – fr Hachette [720]

TRAITE DES PIERRES... / Theophraste – Paris: Herissant, 1754 – 1 – F158.45 – fr Armell [944]

TRAITE DES PONTS, OU IL EST PARLE DE CEUX DES ROMAINS / Gautier, Hubert – Paris: A. Cailleau, 1716. illus. (Architecture Series) – 9 – fr Hachette [720]

TRAITE DES SUPERTITIONS SELON L'ECRITURE SAINTE, LES DECRETS DES CONCILES, ET LES SENTIMENS DES SAINTS PERES, ET DES THEOLOGIENS / Thiers, Jean B – Paris: Antoine Dezallier, 1679. SEM16P89 – 1r – 5 – Can$9.00 – cn Bibl Nat [240]

TRAITE D'HARMONIE ET DE MODULATION / Langle, H F M – c.1797 – 9 – us Sibley [780]

TRAITE D'HYGIENE PUBLIQUE ET PRIVEE / Levi, Michel – Paris, J.B. Bailliere et fils, 1869. 2 v. x, 912; 968 p. 20 fiches. (Statistics Series: Medical Studies) – 9 – 50.00 – fr Bibl Nationale [310]

TRAITE D'HYGIENE PUBLIQUE ET PRIVEE / Levy, Michel – Paris. 1869. (La Condition Ouvriere. Part Two.) – 9 – 50.00 – fr Bibl Nationale [360]

TRAITE D'ICONOGRAPHIE CHRETIENNE / Barbier de Montault, X. – 2V. O-1231 1. 1890 – 9 – ne IDC [240]

TRAITE D'INSECTOLOGIE... / Bonnet, C – Paris, 1745 – 2pts – 8 – ne IDC [590]

TRAITE DU BEAU ESSENTIEL DANS LES ARTS AVEC UN TRAITE DES PROPORTIONS HARMONIQUES., ET LES CINQ ORDRES D'ARCHITECTURE / Briseux, C E – O-176. 1752 – 9 – ne IDC [700]

TRAITE DU CALCUL CONJECTURAL OU L'ART DE RAISONNER SUR LES CHOSES FUTURES ET INCONNUES / Parisot, Sabastien Antoine – Paris: Vve. Bernard, F. Didot, Courcier, 1810. 7 fiches. (Science Collection) – 9 – 17.00 – fr Bibl Nationale [510]

TRAITE DU CONTREPOINT ET DE LA FUGUE, CONTENANT L'EXPOSE ANALYTIQUE DES REGLES... / Fetis, Francois J – Paris: E Troupenas et c'e, 1846 – 1 – us Sibley [780]

TRAITE DU DROIT INTERNATIONAL... / Foelix, J J G – Paris, 1866 – 12mf – 1 – ILM-520/1 – ne IDC [327]

TRAITE DU JARDINAGE SELON LES RAISONS DE LA NATURE ET DE L'ART. / Boyceau de la Barraudier, J – Paris, M. Vanlochom, 1638. 87p. pl. (Architecture Series) – 9 – fr Hachette [720]

TRAITE DU JUGE COMPETENT DES AMBASSADEURS,... / Bynkershoek, C – The Hague, 1723 – 4mf – 1 – ILM-659/1 – ne IDC [327]

TRAITE DU MELO-DRAME, OU REFLEXIONS SUR LA MUSIQUE DRAMATIQUE / Garcins, L – P 288 1. 1772 – 9 – ne IDC [780]

TRAITE DU RECITATIF / Grimarest, J L le Gallois – 1707 – 9 – fr I.C.S. [440]

TRAITE DU RECITATIF DANS LA LECTURE / Le Gallois, J-L – 1707 – 9 – us Sibley [780]

TRAITE DU RIS / Joubert, L – 1579 – 9 – fr I.C.S. [630]

TRAITE DU STYLE / Thiebault, D – Nouv. ed. 1801 – 9 – fr I.C.S. [440]

TRAITE ELEMENTAIRE D'ANATOMIE, DE PHYSIOLOGIE ET D'HYGIENE PRIVEE : DESTINE AUX ECOLES PRIMAIRES / Prevost, Paul E – Montreal, 1902. SEM105P523 – 2mf – 9 – Can$4.50 – cn Bibl Nat [611]

TRAITE ELEMENTAIRE DE DROIT CIVIL EGYPTIEN INDIGENE ET MIXTE COMPARE AVEC LE DROIT FRANCAIS, CONFORME AUX PROGRAMMES DE L'ECOLE KHEDIVIALE ET DES FACULTES FRANCAISES DE DROIT / Grandmoulin, J – Rennes: Librairie Thanoux, 1912. 2v. LL-12026 – 1 – us L of C Photodup [340]

TRAITE ELEMENTAIRE DE PHYSIQUE : REDIGE CONFORMEMENT AU PROGRAMME DE L'UNIVERSITE LAVAL / Simard, Henri – Quebec, 1903. SEM105P1645 – 7mf – 9 – Can$15.75 – cn Bibl Nat [370]

TRAITE ELEMENTAIRE D'HYGIENE PRIVEE / Desroches, J Israel – Montreal?: s.n., 1889 (Montreal: W. F. Daniel). 02670. (Pre-1900 Canadiana) – 9 – cn C.I.H.M. [971]

TRAITE ENTOMOLOGIQUE ET PATHOLOGIQUE DE LA GALE DE L'HOMME / Bourguignon, H – Paris, 1854. 168p, 10pls (Mem.pres.Acad.Sci. Paris, v12) – 8 – ne IDC [590]

LE TRAITE "ERUDITIO REGUM ET PRINCIPUM" DE GUIBERT DE TOURNAI / De Poorter, A – 1914 – 4mf – 8 – ne Slangenburg [100]

TRAITE ESCLAVAGE ET CONTESTATION EN FRANCE (1744-1848) – (Following authors from this series are also listed separately in this Directory:. Barnave, A.P.J.M. Belu, C. Bouet-Willaumez, E. Broglie, A. Ch. L.V., duc de. Conseil Colonial de Bourbon. Deboys, Jacques. Du Puynode, Gustave. Expose General. Frossart, Benjamin-Sigismond. Gasparin, Agenor de. Granier de Cassagnac. Gregoire, Abbe Henri-Baptiste. Jacquemart, Nicolas-Francois. Jollivet, Th. M. Ad. Lamiral, Dominique-Harcourt. Limochel, F. Malouet, Pierre-Victor. Martyrologe colonial, No. 1-3. Metral, Antoine. France. Ministere de la Marine et des Colonies. Moreau de Jonnes, Alexandre. Morenas. Pelletan, Jean-Gabriel. Petit. Petit de Barancourt. Rouvellat de Cussas. Sanchamau, J.B. Schoelcher, Victor. Sismondi, Simonde de. Tocqueville, Alexis de) – (Slave Trade and Abolitionism in France series). 18th and 19th Century works, economic and social reports and French abolitionist writings. In French. Titles also available individually; inquire. 1744-1848 – 9 – fr Hachette [360]

TRAITE GENERAL DE VERSIFICATION FRANCAISE / Becq de Fouquieres, L – 1879 – 9 – fr I.C.S. [440]

TRAITE GENERAL D'OOLOGIE ORNITHOLOGIQUE / Murs, M A P O 'des – Z 1972. 1860 – 9 – ne IDC [590]

TRAITE GENERAL DU STILE / Mauvillon, E de – 1751 – 9 – fr I.C.S. [440]

TRAITE HISTORIQUE DES PLANTES QUI CROISSENT DANS LA LORRAINE ET LET TROIS EVECHES, CONTENANT LEUR DESCRIPTION, LEUR FIGURE, LEUR CULTURE LEUR ANALYSE, LEURS PROPRIETES, TANT POUR LA MEDICINE, QUE POUR LES ARTS ET METIERS / Buchoz, P J – v. 1-10. Paris-Nancy. 1762-70. B-5864 2 – 8 – ne IDC [580]

TRAITE HISTORIQUE ET CRITIQUE SUR L'ORIGINE ET LES PROGRES DES CARACTERES DE FONTE POUR L'IMPRESSION DE LA MUSIQUE.. / Fournier, Pierre-Simon – 1765 – 2 – us Sibley [780]

TRAITE JURIDICO-POLITIQUE SUR LES PRISES MARITIMES, ... / Abreu, F J de – Ed 2. Paris, 1802 – 7mf – 9 – ILM-1155/1 – ne IDC [340]

UN TRAITE MANICHEEN RETROUVE EN CHINE / ed by Chavannes, E & Pelliot, P – (Journal Asiatique. S. 10, v. 18. 1911; S. 11, v. 1. 1913). Paris. BU-599 2 – 8 – ne IDC [290]

TRAITE MEDICO-PHILOSOPHIQUE SUR L'ALIENATION MENTALE OU LA MANIE / Pinel, P – M 120 – 9 – ne IDC [150]

LA TRAITE ORIENTALE / Berlioux, Etienne-Felix – Paris, Librairie de Guillaumin et Cie. 1870 – 9 – 10.00 – fr Orientalistes [950]

TRAITE PHILOSOPHIQUE ET PHYSIOLOGIQUE DE L'HEREDITE NATURELLE DANS LES ETATS DE SANTE ET DE MALADIE DU SYSTEME NERVEUX / Lucas, Prosper – Paris, t. I, 1847; t. II. 1850, 1586 p. Histoire des Sciences XVIIe-XIXe Siecles. 7943 4 – 9 – fr Hachette [616]

TRAITE PRATIQUE D'ENTOMOLOGIE ET DE PATHOLOGIE COMPAREES DE LA PSORE / Delafond, O & Bourguignon, H – Paris, 1862. 646p. 7 pls. (Mem. pres. Acad. Sci. Paris. v16). Z-1181/2 – 8 – ne IDC [590]

TRAITE PRATIQUE DES MALADIES VENERIENNES / Ricord, P – Paris, 1838 – 14mf – 9 – ne IDC [616]

TRAITE SUR LA MUSIQUE ET SUR LES MOYENS D'EN PERFECTIONNER L'EXPRESSION / Le Pileu d'Apligny – P 366. 1779.m – 9 – ne IDC [780]

TRAITE SUR LA POESIE ET LA MUSIQUE DES HEBREAUX / Du Contant de La Molette, P – 1781 – 9 – us Sibley [780]

TRAITE SUR LA POESIE ET LA MUSIQUE DES HEBREUX / Contant de la Molette, P du – Pour servir d'Introduction aux Psaumes expliques. Paris. 1781. BP-672 1 – 9 – ne IDC [780]

TRAITE SUR LE GOVERNEMENT DES ESCLAVES / Petit – (Slave Trade and Abolitionism in France series). 1777 – 9 – fr Hachette [305]

TRAITE SUR L'ELEVAGE ET LES MALADIES DES BESTIAUX / Couture, Joseph Alphonse – Quebec: J A Langlois, librarie-editeur, 1884. SEM105P34 – 3mf – 9 – Can$6.75 – cn Bibl Nat [636]

TRAITE SUR L'ELEVAGE ET LES MALADIES DES BESTIAUX / Couture, Joseph Alphonse – Quebec: J. Langlais, 1882. 00261. (Pre-1900 Canadiana) – 9 – cn C.I.H.M. [971]

TRAITE SUR LES FORMALITES A SUIVRE POUR OBTENIR OU CONTESTER LA PASSATION DE BILLS PRIVES DANS LE PARLEMENT DU CANADA. / Todd, Alfred – 3rd ed. Ottawa: Publie par John Durie et fils, 1868. SEM105P99 – 2mf – 9 – Can$4.50 – cn Bibl Nat [323]

TRAITE THEORETIQUE ET PRATIQUE DES OPERATIONS DE BANQUE / Courcelle Seneuil, JG – Paris, 1853. 488p. Free Banking Series – 9 – 1.00f – at Libertarian Micro [332]

TRAITE THEORIQUE ET PRATIQUE DE LA NATURALISATION / Folleville, D de – Paris, 1880 – 9mf – 1 – ILM-3540/1 – ne IDC [327]

TRAITE THEORIQUE ET PRATIQUE DE L'ART DE BATIR / Rondelet, Jean Baptiste – Paris. 1802-17. 7v. in 4 fol., ill., pl. (Architecture Series) – 9 – fr Hachette [720]

TRAITE TOUCHANT LE COMMUN USAGE DE L'ESCRITURE FRANCOISE / Meigret, Louis – 1542 – 9 – fr I.C.S. [440]

LES TRAITES DE COMMERCE ... / Boiteau, P – Paris, 1863 – 7mf – 9 – ILM-1758/1 – ne IDC [327]

TRAITES ET CONVENTIONS EN VIGUEUR ENTRE LA FRANCE ET LES PUISSANCES ETRANGERES / ed by Basdevant, J – Paris. 4v. 1918-1921 – 36mf – 9 – ILM-2932/1 – ne IDC [320]

LES TRAITES PASSES LE 28 MAI 1902 ... / Billard, A – Paris, 1910 – 2mf – 9 – ILM-1100/1 – ne IDC [327]

TRAITES RELIGIEUX, PHILOSOPHIQUES ET MORAUX, EXTRAITS DES OEUVRES D'ISAAC DE NINIVE (7 SIECLE) PAR IBN AS-SALT (9 SIECLE) / Sbath, P – Le Caire, 1934 – 3mf – 9 – ne Slangenburg [240]

TRAITES SUR LA MUSIQUE / Rousseau, Jean-Jacques – Geneve. 1781. BP-753 1 – 9 – ne IDC [780]

TRAITEZ DE PAIX CONCLUS ENTRE S. M. LE ROY DE FRANCE ET LES INDIENS DU CANADA / France. Treaties, etc – Paris: Sebastien Mabre-Cramoisy, 1667. SEM16P41 – 1r – 5 – Can$9.00 – cn Bibl Nat [944]

TRAITS AND CONFIDENCES / Lawless, Emily – British Fiction Archive: Unit 4 – 9 – uk Bell [830]

TRAITS OPPOSITIONNELS ET TRAITS CONTRASTIFS EN KASSIM / Bonvini, Kassim – 1974 – 9 – fr Orientalistes [470]

TRAITTE DES ELEMENS CHYMIQUES, OV EST DONNE AVX CVRIEVX DE L'ART, LA CONNAISANCE DES SELS, DISSOLUANS, MENSTRUES, FONDANS ET PRECIPITANS / Marsigny, Jean Charle de – Rouen, 1671 – 1 – us U.W. Library [540]

TRAITTE DES HERESIES, CONTENANT LES CAUSES DES HERESIES, LES MOEURS ET ARTIFICES... / Abelly, L – Paris, 1661 – 4mf – 9 – CA-113/1 – ne IDC [240]

TRAITTE DES IUSTES CAUSES DE LA SEPARATION DES PROTESTANS D'AVEC L'EGLISE ROMAINE / Drelincourt, C – [Paris], 1649 – 7mf – 9 – CA-126/1 – ne IDC [240]

TRAITTE DU SAINCT SACREMENT DE L'EUCHARISTIE,... / Du Perron, JD – Paris, 1622 – 20mf – 9 – CA-131/1 – ne IDC [240]
TRAITTE QUI CONTIENT LA METHODE LA PLUS FACILE... / Richelieu, (A J Du Plessis) – Paris, 1657 – 9mf – 9 – CA-145/1 – ne IDC [240]
UN TRAJE A MEDIDA DE LOS ALCALDES / Montero de Espinosa y de la Barrera, Francisco – Almendralejo: Felix Bote, 1938 – 1 – sp Bibl Santa Ana [946]
Trakhtenberga, I A *see* KAPITALY GOSUDARSTVENNO I TORGOVLI SSSR
TRAKTAT UEBER DIE HINFUEHRUNG DER KLEINEN ZU CHRISTUS : HUGO VON ST. VIKTOR, DAS LEHRBUCH / Gerson, Joh. – Paderborn, 1896 – 5mf – 8 – ne Slangenburg [240]
TRALEE CHRONICLE – Ireland. 18 Mar 1843-20 May 1881 (missing Nov, Dec 1848).-w. 29 reels – 1 – uk British Libr Newspaper [072]
TRALEE MERCURY – Ireland. -w. 14 Feb 1829-31 Dec 1836, 18 Feb 1837-20 Jul 1839. (10 reels) – 1 – uk British Libr Newspaper [072]
LE TRAMWAY – Montreal, Canada. 26 mar 1927 – 1r – 1 – Can$25.00 – cn Can Microfilming [072]
Tramway Institute *see* RAILWAY AND TRAMWAY EXPRESS
TRANAS TIDNING *see* SMALANDSTIDNINGEN
TRANÅS TIDNING – Skaenninge, 1879-80 – 9 – sw Kungliga [072]
TRANASPOSTEN – Tranas, 1918- – 1 – sw Kungliga [072]
TRANCE, AND CORRELATIVE PHENOMENON / Sutherland, Laroy – (Published by James Walker at the office of The Liberal) – Chicago: The Liberal, 1868 – 1r – 1 – us Western Res [130]
TRANSACTION OF THE ZOOLOGICAL SOCIETY OF LONDON – London. v1-20. 1835-1915; v1-10. Index – 350mf – 9 – Z-2219/1 – ne IDC [590]
TRANSACTIONS / American Association of Cost Engineers (AACE) – (5,6,9 1975-) – 1967- – 1 – us UMI [650]
TRANSACTIONS / American Fisheries Society – (Former titles: Proceedings of the American Fish Culturists' Association (1872-1875); Transactions of the American Fish Culturists' Association (1876-1877); Transactions of the American Fish-Cultural Association (1878-1884); Transactions of the American Fisheries Society (1885-1896); Minutes of the American Fisheries Society (1897-1898); Proceedings of the American Fisheries Society (1899)) – Lawrence. cum index v1-82 1872-1952; v1-75 1872-1945 – 1 – D2258 – us UMI [630]
TRANSACTIONS / American Fisheries Society – v. 1-20. 1870-1891 – 1,5,6 – us Princeton Micro [639]
TRANSACTIONS / American Foundrymen's Society. New York – v53-56, 59-68. 1945-1948, 1951-1960 – 1,5,6 – us Princeton Micro [670]
TRANSACTIONS / American Institute of Electrical Engineers – New York. v69-76 Parts I-III 1950-57 – 1 – us NY Public [621]
TRANSACTIONS / American Institute of Mining and Metallurgical Engineers – (Cont by: American Institute of Mining, Metallurgical and Petroleum Engineers transactions. Former titles: Transactions of the American Institute of Mining Engineers (may 1871-feb 1918)) – New York. v140-172. 1940-1947 – 1 – D588 – us UMI [660]
TRANSACTIONS / American Institute of Mining, Metallurgical and Petroleum Engineers – v1-204. 1871-1955 – 1, 5, 6 – $1537.00 – us Princeton Micro [622]
TRANSACTIONS / American Mathematical Society – (1972- . 5,6. 1976- . 9) – 1-1900- – 1 – us UMI [510]
TRANSACTIONS / American Mathematical Society – v. 1-60. 1900-1946 – 1,5,6 – us Princeton Micro [510]
TRANSACTIONS / American Microscopical Society – v. 1-79. 1878-1960 – 1 – us Princeton Micro [500]
TRANSACTIONS / American Philosophical Society – (1971- 5,6; 1975- 9) – v1- 1789- – 1 – us UMI [100]
TRANSACTIONS / American Society for Metals – v1-62 1920-1969 – 1,5,6 – us Princeton Micro [670]
TRANSACTIONS / American Society of Civil Engineers – v1- 1872- 1; v139- 6; v141-1976- 9 – us UMI [624]
TRANSACTIONS / American Society of Mechanical Engineers – Series E, Journal of Applied Mechanics. v1-17. 1933-50. Continues: Journal of Applied Mechanics – 1,5,6 – us Princeton Micro [621]
TRANSACTIONS / American Society of Mechanical Engineers – v1-80. 1880-1958 – 1 – us UMI [621]
TRANSACTIONS / ASHRAE (American Society of Heating, Refrigerating and Air-Conditioning Engineers) – (v78- 5,6. v80- 9) – v1-1895- – 1 – us UMI [621]
TRANSACTIONS / Association of Military Surgeons of the National Guard of the U.S – v.1-3. 1891-93. Continued by: Proceedings of the Annual Meeting – 1 – us UMI [610]
TRANSACTIONS / Cambridge Philosophical Society – 1822-1928 – 11r – 1 – uk Microform Academic [100]
TRANSACTIONS / Congregational Historical Society – 1901-22. 3185p – 1 – us Baptist [240]
TRANSACTIONS / Connecticut Academy of Arts and Sciences – v1-24 1966-?0 – 1 – us Res Libr [500]
TRANSACTIONS / The Cumberland and Westmoreland Antiquarian and Archaeological Society – 1 reel – 1 – uk Microform Academic [930]
TRANSACTIONS / Diesel Engineers and Users Associations. Including Gas Turbines – 1912-83 – 1 – us UMI [621]
TRANSACTIONS / Durham and Northumberland Parish Register Society – 1898-1926 – 3r – 1 – uk Microform Academic [920]
TRANSACTIONS / Essex Field Club – v.1-. 1880- – 1 – us UMI [580]
TRANSACTIONS / Faraday Society. London – v. 1-67. 1905-1971 – 1,5,6 – us Princeton Micro [540]
TRANSACTIONS / Geological Society of South Africa – v1- 1896- 1; v80- 1977- 5,6,9 – us UMI [550]
TRANSACTIONS / Greenwich and Lewisham Antiquarian Society – 1905-81. With printed index. Continued annually – 1 – uk World [941]
TRANSACTIONS / Huguenot Society of South Carolina – 1889-1981. 72 fiches – 9 – us South Carolina Historical [240]
TRANSACTIONS / Institute of Marine Engineers – 1889-1992. Continued annually – 1 – £2,500.00 – uk World [623]
TRANSACTIONS / Institute of Welding – v1-3 1938-1940 – 1 – us Princeton Micro [670]
TRANSACTIONS / Institution of Chemical Engineers – v1- 1923- – 1,5,6,9 – apply; v54- – us UMI [660]
TRANSACTIONS / Institution of Chemical Engineers – v1-24. 1923-46 – 1,5,6 – us Princeton Micro [660]
TRANSACTIONS / Institution of Diesel and Gas Turbine Engineers – 1984- – 1,5,6,9 – us UMI [621]
TRANSACTIONS / Institution of Naval Architects – v31-61 1890-1919 – 1,5,6 – us Princeton Micro [623]
TRANSACTIONS / I.S.A. (Instrument Society of America) – v1- 1962- – 1,5,6,9 – us UMI [600]
TRANSACTIONS / Lichfield and South Staffordshire Archaeological and Historical Society – v3-9 1961-68 – 1 – us UMI [930]
TRANSACTIONS / Lichfield Archaeological and Historical Society – v1-2 1959-61 – 1 – us UMI [930]
TRANSACTIONS / Linnean Society, London – 1791-1875 – 3 – us Readex [580]
TRANSACTIONS / Literary and Historical Society of Quebec – v6-28 1863-1906. ns v29-30 1910-24 – 1 – cn Precision [971]
TRANSACTIONS / London and Middlesex Archaeological Society – (1980- 5,6,9) – 1856- – 1 – us UMI [930]
TRANSACTIONS / Medical Society of London – (v98- 1984- 5,6,9) – v13- 1889- – 1 – us UMI [610]
TRANSACTIONS / National Council of Women of the United States; ed by Avery, Rachel Foster – 1891 – 9 – us A.T.L.A. [360]
TRANSACTIONS / Natural History Society of Northumberland, Durham, and Newcastle-upon-Tyne – 1831-38 – 3 – us Readex [580]
TRANSACTIONS / Newcomen Society – (1963-1986. vol: 36-58 5 reels £35.00r) – 1920-63 – 11r – 1 – uk Microform Academic [600]
TRANSACTIONS / Oriental Ceramic Society – 1929-30 – 13mf – 7 – uk Microform Academic [740]
TRANSACTIONS / Pennsylvania Academy of Ophthalmology and Otolaryngology – (v33-1980- 5,6,9) – v1- 1948- – 1 – us UMI [610]
TRANSACTIONS : PROCEEDINGS OF THE ANNUAL MEETING / American Foundrymen's Society – (Former titles: Journal of the American Foundrymen's Association (jul 1896-jun 1903); Transactions of the American Foundrymen's Association (jun 1904-1947)) – Chicago. v1-105 jul 1896-1; v78-105 1970- 5*; v82-105 1974- 9 – 1,5,9 – D404 – us UMI [670]
TRANSACTIONS / Protestant Episcopal Church. South Carolina (Diocese) – 1795-ca.1870. 7 fiches – 9 – us South Carolina Historical [025]
TRANSACTIONS / Radnorshire Society – v1-1931- 1; v45- 5,6,9 – us UMI [941]
TRANSACTIONS / Royal Asiatic Society – 1823-30 – 2r – 1 – uk Microform Academic [950]
TRANSACTIONS / Royal Asiatic Society of Great Britain and Ireland. Korea Branch, Seoul – 1900-40 – 1 – us UMI [950]
TRANSACTIONS / Royal Historical Society – 1-14 1869-1900 – 1 – us UMI [900]
TRANSACTIONS / Royal Microscopical Society, London – 1844-52 – 3 – us Readex [580]
TRANSACTIONS / Royal Society of Edinburgh – v1-59 1783-1939 – 1,5,6 – $22,752.00 – us Princeton Micro [500]
TRANSACTIONS / S P W L A Annual Logging Symposium – (v.21-. 1980- 5,6,9) – v.1-. 1960- – 1 – us UMI [073]
TRANSACTIONS / Society of Rheology – v. 1-21. 1957-1977 – 1,5,6,9 – us UMI [530]
TRANSACTIONS / South Staffordshire Archaeological and Historical Society – (v22- 1980- 5,6,9) – v10- 1968- – 1 – us UMI [930]
TRANSACTIONS / Worcestershire Archaeological Society – (v7- 1930- 5,6,9) – v1- 1923- – 1 – us UMI [930]
TRANSACTIONS.. / American Society for Artificial Internal Organs – v1-31. 1955-85 – 1 – us UMI [073]
TRANSACTIONS / American Mathematical Society – Providence. cum index v1-160 1900-oct 1971; v1-364 1900- 1; v163-364 jan 1972- 5; v201-364 jan 1975 – 1,5,9 – D3258 – us UMI [510]
TRANSACTIONS. 2D SER. BOTANY / Linnean Society, London – 1880-1922 – 3 – us Readex [580]
TRANSACTIONS. 2D SER. ZOOLOGY / Linnean Society, London – 1879 i.e.1875-1936 – 3 – us Readex [590]
TRANSACTIONS, 1893-1984 / The Bronte Society – (Include printed and fiche index) – 80mf – 9 – $325.00 – us UPA [420]
TRANSACTIONS AND JOURNAL / Plastics Institute. London – v22-35. 1954-67 – 1 – us Princeton Micro [600]
TRANSACTIONS AND JOURNALS / Plastics Institute. London – 1932-60 – 9r – 1 – uk Microform Academic [660]
TRANSACTIONS AND PROCEEDINGS / American Philological Association – v. 1-40. 1869-1909 – 1 – us Princeton Micro [400]
TRANSACTIONS AND PROCEEDINGS / Glasgow. Natural History Society – n.s. v.1-8. 1883-1908 – 1,5,6 – 2277.00 – us Princeton Micro [580]
TRANSACTIONS AND PROCEEDINGS / Natural History Society of Glasgow – v1-8. 1883-1908 – 1,5,6 – us Princeton Micro [580]
TRANSACTIONS AND PROCEEDINGS / Royal Society of Canada – v46- 1952- 1; v9- 5,6; v15- 9 – us UMI [971]
TRANSACTIONS AND PROCEEDINGS OF THE BOTANICAL SOCIETY OF EDINBURGH – Edinburgh. v1-32. 1844-1939 – 285mf – 9 – 7672c/2 – ne IDC [580]
TRANSACTIONS AND PROCEEDINGS OF THE MODERN LANGUAGE ASSOCIATION OF AMERICA – Baltimore. v1-3. 1886-88 – 22mf – 9 – H-687/2 – ne IDC [400]
THE TRANSACTIONS AND PROCEEDINGS... FROM 1837 TO 1840 / London Electrical Society – London, 1841 – 3 – us Readex [621]
TRANSACTIONS AND STUDIES OF THE COLLEGE OF PHYSICIANS OF PHILADELPHIA – (With printed guide) – 1793-1971 – 19r – 1 – $1,615.00 – S1872 – us Scholarly Res [610]
TRANSACTIONS (A.S.M.E.) / American Society of Mechanical Engineers – v1-80. 1880-1958 – 1,5,6 – us Princeton Micro [621]
TRANSACTIONS FOR THE YEAR 1936 / Illinois State Historical Society – Proceedings of the annual meeting. F-1296 – 4mf – 9 – us A.G.L.L. [978]
TRANSACTIONS, OBJETS DE COMMERCE / Binger, Louis Gustave – Paris. 1890 – 9 – 5.00 – fr Orientalistes [960]
TRANSACTIONS OF THE AMERICAN FISH CULTURISTS' ASSOCIATION *see* TRANSACTIONS
TRANSACTIONS OF THE AMERICAN FISH-CULTURAL ASSOCIATION *see* TRANSACTIONS
TRANSACTIONS OF THE AMERICAN FISHERIES SOCIETY *see* TRANSACTIONS
TRANSACTIONS OF THE AMERICAN FOUNDRYMEN'S ASSOCIATION *see* TRANSACTIONS
TRANSACTIONS OF THE AMERICAN INSTITUTE OF MINING ENGINEERS *see* TRANSACTIONS
TRANSACTIONS OF THE AMERICAN MATHEMATICAL SOCIETY – (Index) – v1-48. 1900-1940 – 511mf – 9 – 2216c/2 – ne IDC [510]
TRANSACTIONS OF THE AMERICAN SOCIETY OF MECHANICAL ENGINEERS – New York. v42-63. 1920-41 – 820mf – 9 – 605c/2 – ne IDC [621]
TRANSACTIONS OF THE ASIATIC SOCIETY OF JAPAN – (Missing: v19(p1-36). 1891) – Yokohama, Tokyo. v1-50. 1872-1922 – 395mf – 9 – CH-200/2 – ne IDC [950]
TRANSACTIONS OF THE BOMBAY GEOGRAPHIC SOCIETY / Bombay Geographic Society – v1-19. Bombay. 1836-73. Index v1-17. BI-542 2 – 135mf – 8 – ne IDC [910]
TRANSACTIONS OF THE BOMBAY LITERARY SOCIETY / Bombay Literary Society – v1-3. Bombay. 1819-23. BI-124 2 – 29mf – 8 – ne IDC [410]
TRANSACTIONS OF THE BRITISH MYCOLOGICAL SOCIETY – Worcester, Cambridge. v1-25. 1897-1941 – 181mf – 9 – 5402c/2 – ne IDC [580]
TRANSACTIONS OF THE CANADIAN INSTITUTE / Canadian Institute – (Cont by: Royal Canadian Institute. Transactions of the Royal Canadian Institute) – Toronto: Printed for the Canadian Institute by Copp, Clark, [1890-1913] – 9 – cn C.I.H.M. [971]
TRANSACTIONS OF THE CHINA-MEDICAL-CHIRURGICAL SOCIETY, FOR THE YEARS 1845-1846 – Hongkong, 1846 – 1mf – 9 – ne IDC [060]
TRANSACTIONS OF THE CITY OF LONDON ENTOMOLOGICAL AND NATURAL HISTORY SOCIETY – London, 1891-1920 – 44mf – 9 – Z-1005/2 – ne IDC [500]
TRANSACTIONS OF THE ENTOMOLOGICAL SOCIETY OF LONDON / Entomological Society of London – v. 1-5. London. 1836-49; v.1-5. N.S. 1850-61; v. 1-5. S.3 1862-67; 1868-1920. BZ-1006 2 – 850mf – 8 – ne IDC [590]
TRANSACTIONS OF THE ENTOMOLOGICAL SOCIETY OF NEW SOUTH WALES – Sydney, London. v1-2. [1862]-1866-1873 – 15mf – 9 – Z-1007/2 – ne IDC [590]
TRANSACTIONS OF THE FARADAY SOCIETY – London. v26-36. 1930-40 – 280mf – 9 – 747c/2 – ne IDC [630]
TRANSACTIONS OF THE FIRST INTERNATIONAL CONGRESS ON THE ENLIGHTENMENT – Oxford. 1963 – 9 – $225.00 – 0-7294-0079-4 – uk Voltaire [190]
TRANSACTIONS OF THE HORTICULTURAL SOCIETY OF LONDON – London. v1-7. 1812-30; S2: v1-3. 1835-48 – 120mf – 9 – 7468/1 – ne IDC [630]
TRANSACTIONS OF THE JEWISH HISTORICAL SOCIETY OF ENGLAND / Jewish Historical Society of England – London, 1893-1940. v1-14. Index. BHC-799 2 – 108mf – 8 – ne IDC [270]
TRANSACTIONS OF THE KOREA BRANCH OF THE ROYAL ASIATIC SOCIETY – Seoul. v1-41. 1900-64 – 111mf – 9 – CH-993/2 – ne IDC [950]

TRANSACTIONS OF THE LINNEAN SOCIETY – London. S1: Botany, Zoology. v1-30. 1791-1875; S2: Botany. v1-9. 1880-1916 – 687mf – 9 – 7125/2 – ne IDC [500]

TRANSACTIONS OF THE LINNEAN SOCIETY – London. S2: Zoology. v1-19. 1876-1926/36 – 337mf – 9 – Z-254/2 – ne IDC [590]

TRANSACTIONS OF THE LONDON METHODIST PARSONS, IN THREE POETICAL EPISTLES – London, 1792 – 1mf – 9 – MP-580/1 – ne IDC [240]

TRANSACTIONS OF THE MCLEAN COUNTY HISTORICAL SOCIETY / McLean County Historical Society – War Record of McLean County. Bloomington, 1899. (Illinois Reel 45). (The Cox Library Collection) – 5 – us Americana [978]

TRANSACTIONS OF THE MISSIONARY SOCIETY – Ed2. London, 1795-1832 – 50mf – 9 – H-2756/1 – ne IDC [240]

TRANSACTIONS OF THE NEWCOMEN SOCIETY, 1963-1986 – October 1990, M.A.P. West Yorkshire – 5r – 1 – uk Microform Academic [600]

TRANSACTIONS OF THE NEW-YORK ECCLESIOLOGICAL SOCIETY / Hopkins, John Henry – New York: D. Dana, Jr., 1857 – 1mf – us A.T.L.A. [240]

TRANSACTIONS OF THE ROYAL ASIATIC SOCIETY OF GREAT BRITAIN AND IRELAND / Royal Asiatic Society of Great Britain and Ireland – 1823-35. v1-3. London. 1827-35. BI-546 2 – 49mf – 8 – ne IDC [950]

TRANSACTIONS OF THE ROYAL CANADIAN INSTITUTE *see* TRANSACTIONS OF THE CANADIAN INSTITUTE

TRANSACTIONS OF THE ROYAL HISTORICAL SOCIETY / ed by Rogers, C – London. v1-10. 1869-82; N.S.: v1-20. 1884-1906; S3: v1-11. 1907-17; S4: v1-23. 1918-41 – 394mf – 9 – H-579c/2 – ne IDC [941]

TRANSACTIONS OF THE ROYAL INSTITUTE OF BRITISH ARCHITECTS / Royal Institute of British Architects – 1835-93 – 1 – £825.00 – uk World [720]

TRANSACTIONS OF THE SOCIETY OF BIBLICAL ARCHAEOLOGY – London. 9v. 1872-86 – 68mf – 9 – NE-358/1 – ne IDC [220]

TRANSACTIONS OF THE YORKSHIRE DIALECT SOCIETY / Yorkshire Dialect Society – Bradford, 1898-1935/39. H-1779/1 – 31mf – 9 – ne IDC [420]

TRANSAFRICA FORUM – 1985- – 1 – us UMI [073]

TRANSATLANTIC REVIEW – Paris. etc. v. 1-2, no. 6. Jan 1924-Jan 1925 – 1 – us NY Public [073]

TRANSATLANTISCHE STIMMEN : EIN LIEDERCYKLUS AUS AMERIKA / Hopp, Ernst Otto – Stuttgart: J G Cotta, 1876 – 1r – 1 – us U.W. Library [780]

TRANSCENDENCIA EMOCIONAL DE LA LECTURA : CONFERENCIA...NAVAL MORAL DE LA MATA, AL DIA 1 DE MAYO DE 1927 / Blazquez Marcos, Jose – Navalmoral de Tip. de Joaquin S. Oliva, 1927 – 1 – sp Bibl Santa Ana [946]

THE TRANSCENDENT VALUE OF MAN: A SERMON DELIVERED BEFORE ST ANDREW'S SOCIETY IN KNOX CHURCH, OTTAWA ON SUNDAY EVENING, NOVEMBER 29TH, 1891 / Farries, Francis Wallace – Ottawa: s.n., 1891 (Ottawa: A. Woodburn). 03055. (Pre-1900 Canadiana) – 9 – cn C.I.H.M. [971]

TRANSCENDENTAL PROBLEMS OF PHILOSOPHICAL THOUGHT / Dooyeweerd, H – Grand Rapids, 1948 – 2mf – 8 – ne Slangenburg [100]

TRANSCENDENTALISM IN NEW ENGLAND : A HISTORY / Frothingham, Octavius Brooks – New York: G.P. Putnam, 1876 – 1mf – us A.T.L.A. [140]

TRANSCENDENTALISM, WITH PRELUDES ON CURRENT EVENTS / Cook, Joseph – Boston: J.R. Osgood, 1878, c1877 – 1mf – us A.T.L.A. [140]

TRANSCRIBED REPORTS AND COMMUNICATIONS TRANSMITTED BY THE EXECUTIVE BRANCH TO THE U.S. SENATE, 1789-1819, AND TRANSCRIBED REPORTS OF SENATE COMMITTEES, 1798-1817 / U.S. Senate – 4r – 1 – M1257 – us Nat'l Archives [324]

TRANSCRIBED REPORTS OF COMMITTEES OF THE U.S. SENATE, 1817-1827 / U.S. Senate – 2r – 1 – M1256 – us Nat'l Archives [324]

TRANSCRIBED TREATIES AND CONVENTIONS APPROVED BY THE U.S. SENATE, 1789-1836 / U.S. Senate – 2r – 1 – M1258 – us Nat'l Archives [324]

TRANSCRIPCION PALEOGRAFICA Y VERSION CASTELLANA DE LA CARTA DE POBLACION O FUERO LATINO DE CACERES / Floriano Cumbreno, Antonio C – Caceres: Tip. Carcia Flioriano, 1929 – sp Bibl Santa Ana [560]

THE TRANSCRIPT – Seattle. Wash. 1964-66 – 1 – us A.J.P.C. [071]

TRANSCRIPT – Bayard. Neb. 1896-1902; 1909-1958 – 1 – us UMI [071]

TRANSCRIPT – Concord, CA. 1905-07; 1909-10; 1910-23; 1925-26; 1928-30; 1936-37; 1951-82 – 156r – 1 – $7,800.00 – B02135 – us Library Micro [071]

TRANSCRIPT – Dresden. Ohio. 1897-1900; 1913-1932; 1933-1940; 1941-1946 – 1 – us UMI [071]

TRANSCRIPT – East Providence. R.I. 1947-1948 – 1 – us UMI [071]

TRANSCRIPT – Leoti. Kansas. 1887-1890 – 1 – us UMI [071]

TRANSCRIPT – Little Falls. Minn. 1964- – 1 – us UMI [071]

TRANSCRIPT – Olympia. Wash. -w. 1867-85 – 1 – us UMI [071]

TRANSCRIPT – Sacramento, CA. 1850-51 – 2r – 1 – $100.00 – C02745 – us Library Micro [071]

TRANSCRIPT – Sacramento. Calif. -w. 1850-51 – 1 – us UMI [071]

TRANSCRIPT OF PROCEEDINGS / International Military Tribunal for the Far East – n.p. On film: 7 Jan and 1 Oct 1947. LL-064 – 1 – us L of C Photodup [340]

TRANSCRIPT OF RECORD AND PROCEEDINGS IN THE COURTS OF LOWER CANADA APPEALED FROM IN A CAUSE BETWEEN GIDEON ROBERT AND OTHERS / Canada. Supreme Court for Lower Canada – Montreal: Le Pays Book and Job Printing Office, 1862. SEM105P436 – 4mf – 9 – Can$9.00 – cn Bibl Nat [340]

TRANSCRIPT OF RECORD AND PROCEEDINGS IN THE COURTS OF LOWER CANADA, APPEALED FROM IN A CAUSE BETWEEN HARLOW MINOR [I.E.] MINER, APPELLANT; AND FRANCIS C. GILMOUR RESPONDENT – Montreal: J Starke & Co, printers, [1858?]. SEM105P1350 – 6mf – 9 – Can$13.50 – cn Bibl Nat [340]

TRANSCRIPT OF RECORD AND PROCEEDINGS IN THE COURTS OF LOWER CANADA, APPEALED FROM IN A CAUSE BETWEEN ZEPHIR DORION, APPELLANT, AND ALEXANDRE EDOUARD KIERZKOWSKI; RESPONDENT.. / Canada. Supreme Court for Lower Canada – Montreal: Printed by Louis Perrault and Co, s.d.. SEM105P351 – 3mf – 9 – Can$6.75 – cn Bibl Nat [340]

TRANSCRIPT OF THE SOUTH CAROLINA BAR – (Superseded by South Carolina Bar News and South Carolina Lawyer) – v1-33. 1955-89 – 9 – $195.00 set – us Hein [340]

TRANSCRIPT OF THE SOUTH CAROLINA BAR *see*
- SOUTH CAROLINA BAR NEWS
- SOUTH CAROLINA LAWYER

TRANSCRIPT RECORDS / Charleston County. South Carolina. St. Andrew's Episcopal Church – 1714-1899. 8 fiches – 9 – us South Carolina Historical [240]

TRANSCRIPT SHOPPER – Concord, CA. 1933-51 (broken file) – 6r – 1 – $300.00 – B02136 – us Library Micro [071]

TRANSCRIPTS / Yorkshire Parish Register Society – 23r – 1 – uk Microform Academic [920]

TRANSCRIPTS AND FILES OF THE PARIS PEACE TALKS ON VIETNAM, 1968-73 / U.S. Department of State – 1982 – 1 – $1,320.00 – 0-89093-399-5 – us UPA [950]

TRANSCRIPTS AND STUDIES / Dowden, Edward – London: K. Paul, Trench & Co., 1888 – 1 roll – 1 – 1-55879-512-X – uk Libr Preservation [999]

TRANSCRIPTS AND SUMMARIES OF THE TRIAL OF ROLF STEINER / Khartoum. Press Centre, People's Court – 1971 – 1 – 39.50 – us African Imprint [323]

TRANSCRIPTS OF DEBATES / Ireland. Parliament. House of Commons – 82 v. 1776-89 – 1 – 202.00 – us L of C Photodup [025]

TRANSCRIPTS OF HEARINGS / Canada. National Energy Board – 1 – cn Micromedia [621]

TRANSCRIPTS OF ORAL EXPERT TESTIMONY PRESENTED BEFORE THE INDIAN CLAIMS COMMISSION / U.S. Indian Claims Commission – (Suppl. 1. 77 titles. $1,420.00) – 429 titles. 1,398mf. With printed index – 9 – $4,540.00 – us UPA [305]

TRANSCRIPTS OF PUBLIC HEARINGS / Canada. Royal Commission on Newspapers – 1981-82 – 9 – cn Micromedia [324]

TRANSCRIPTS OF RECORDS / Dundee. Scotland. St. Andrew's Roman Catholic Cathedral – 1795-1838 – 1 – uk Microform Academic [240]

TRANSCRIPTS OF THE MALCOLM X ASSASSINATION TRIAL – (With guide) – 1993 – 3r – 1 – $255.00 – S3297 – us Scholarly Res [340]

TRANSCRIPTS OF THREE REGISTERS OF PASSENGERS FROM GREAT YARMOUTH TO HOLLAND AND NEW ENGLAND – 1637-1639. By Charles Boardman Jewson. Indexed. 2 fiches. F-0626 – 9 – us A.G.L.L. [920]

TRANSDEX – (International information index and document delivery. Access to materials published outside the US and translated into English. Parts available) – 9 – $4420.00 complete 1989 collection; monthly index $855.00 – us UMI [000]

TRANSFER RECORDS / Fulton County. Ohio. Auditor – 1850-1854 – 1r – 1 – $32.50r – us Archival [324]

TRANSFER RECORDS / Putnam County. Ohio. Auditor – 1873-1874 – 1r – 1 – us Archival [324]

TRANSFER RECORDS / Putnam County. Ohio. Auditor – 1873-1874 – 1r – 1 – $32.50r – us Archival [324]

TRANSFER RECORDS / Van Wert County. Ohio. Auditor – 1820-1852 – 1r – 1 – $32.50r – us Archival [324]

TRANSFIGURATION OF CHRIST / Gunsaulus, Frank Wakeley – New York: Fleming H. Revell, 1907 – 9 – us A.T.L.A. [240]

THE TRANSFIGURATION OF LIFE / Clarke, James Freeman – Boston: American Unitarian Association, 1909 – 1mf – us A.T.L.A. [240]

TRANSFORMACION EN REGIADOS ANEXO AL PLAN. 1964-1967 / Spain. Comisaria del Plan de Desarrollo Economico y Social – Madrid. 1964 – 9 – ne IDC [338]

TRANSFORMATION / Stockmayer, Otto – London: Bethshan Book-Room, 1909. 1 fiche – 9 – us A.T.L.A. [240]

TRANSFORMATION DE L'ESPACE RURAL DANS LE FRONT PIONNIER DU SUD-OUEST IVOIRIEN / Lena, P – 9 – F100.00 – fr Ethnologie [306]

THE TRANSFORMATION OF HAWAII : HOW AMERICAN MISSIONARIES GAVE A CHRISTIAN NATION TO THE WORLD / Brain, Belle Marvel – New York: Fleming H Revell, c1898 – 1mf – 9 – 0-8370-6805-3 – 1986-0805 – us A.T.L.A. [975]

LES TRANSFORMATIONS DE LA PUISSANCE PUBLIQUE. LES SYNDICATS DE FONCTIONNAIRES / Leroy, Maxime – Paris. 1907. (La Condition Ouvriere. Part Two.) – 9 – 7.50 – fr Bibl Nationale [360]

DER TRANSFORMATIONSPROZEß IN DER EHEMALIGEN SOWJETUNION : ASPEKTE EINES HISTORISCHEN SYSTEMZUSAMMENBRUCHS / Lierow, Ralf – 1994 – 3mf – DM98.00 – 3-8267-2077-6 – gw Hänsel [335]

TRANSFORMATOR UNTUK PESAWAT PENERIMA RADIO; KONSTRUKSI, RENTJANA, DAN PEMBUATANNJA, OLEH R. SURASNO SOSRODIRDJO / Sosrodirdjo, Surasno, raden – Djakarta, Technipress [1958?] 76p, illus – 9 – ne IDC [620]

TRANSFUSION SCIENCE – 1,5,69 – us UMI [610]

TRANSGENICS : BIOLOGICAL ANALYSIS THROUGH DNA TRANSFER / ed by Lewis, Robert E Jr – 1,5,9 – us Gordon [575]

TRANSICION DE ESTADOS A NACIONES EN LATINO-AMERICA / Hillekamps, Karl Heinz – Buenos Aires: Ediciones Pleamer, [1965] – 1 – CSUXADQ3293-B – us Hoover Inst Photo [320]

IL TRANSILVANO DIALOGO SOPRA IL VERO MODO DI SONAR ORGANI, E ISTROMENTI DA PENNA / Diruta, Girolamo – Pt. 1 only. 1625 – 9 – us Sibley [780]

TRANSIT JOURNAL – v. 1-86. 1884-1942 – 1,5,6 – us Princeton Micro [629]

TRANSIT JOURNAL NEWS – New York, NY. -w. 14 Dec 1935-26 Dec 1942. 4 reels – 1 – uk British Libr Newspaper [071]

TRANSITION – n1-27. 1927-38 – 1 – us Ross [073]

TRANSITION – Paris. no. 1-27. April 1927-Spring 1938 – 1 – us NY Public [999]

TRANSITION FROM TECHNICAL AND VOCATIONAL SCHOOLS TO WORK : A SUMMARY REPORT OF AN INTERNATIONAL SYMPOSIUM AND 17 COUNTRY REPORTS – 1983 – 100p – 9 – 92-3-102030-7 – fr UNESCO [370]

THE TRANSITION TO SOCIALISM IN AFRICA, CONFERENCE PAPERS – May 1982. University of Leeds – 5mf – 9 – uk Microform Academic [335]

TRANSITIONAL PLAN FOR SOCIAL AND ECONOMIC DEVELOPMENT / Botswana – Gaberones. 1966 – 9 – ne IDC [338]

Transkei (South Africa). Territorial Authority *see* PROCEEDINGS AND REPORTS OF SELECT COMMITTEES

Transkeian Territories. General Council *see* PROCEEDINGS AND REPORTS OF SELECT COMMITTEES

TRANSLANTIC REVIEW – v. 1-60. 1959-77 – 1 – us UMI [800]

TRANSLATIO SYRA PESCITTO VETERIS TESTAMENTI / ed by Cerani, Antonio Maria – 2 v. in 1. 1876 – 1 – us A.T.L.A. [240]

A TRANSLATION OF LUKE'S GOSPEL / Robertson, A T – 1923. 248p – 1 – 8.68 – us Baptist [240]

TRANSLATION OF REPORT ON THE GENERAL CENSUS OF THE POPULATION OF PORTUGUESE INDIA, TAKEN ON THE 17 FEB 1881 / India – Trans. by N. R. Oliver. Bombay. 1882. BI-563 – 8 – ne IDC [310]

A TRANSLATION OF THE GOSPELS – Andrews Norton. 2 v. 1855-1856 – 1 – us A.T.L.A. [240]

TRANSLATION OF THE LAW OF WATERS IN FORCE IN THE ISLAND OF PUERTO RICO : ADAPTED FROM A TRANSLATION OF THE LAW OF WATERS IN FORCE IN THE ISLAND OF CUBA...WITH ANNOTATIONS OF AMENDMENTS MADE THERETO BY ACTS OF MARCH 12 1903 AND MARCH 9 1905 – n.p., n.d. – 1mf – 9 – $1.50 – LLMC 92-320 – us L.L.M.C. [327]

TRANSLATION UNIT PRESS REVIEW – (Missing: 1966(20-29, 49); 1967(209); 1969(234-237); 1970(29, 136, 185, 209); 1972(142, 216, 231-233)) – U.S. Embassy, Indonesia, 1965-73(4) – 437mf – 9 – SE-579/1 – ne IDC [070]

TRANSLATIONS / U.S. Joint Publications Research Service – (Soviet Union. China-Asia. Eastern Europe. Africa-Latin America) – Indexed in Transdex – 1 – us UMI [010]

TRANSLATIONS INTO ENGLISH AND LATIN / Calverley, Charles Stuart – Cambridge: Deighton, Bell, 1886 – 1 roll – 1 – 1-55879-535-9 – uk Libr Preservation [800]

TRANSLATIONS OF RADIO BROADCASTS OF COMMUNIST HSIN HUA STATION, NORTH SHENSI / U.S. Consulate General.Peiping, China – Nov 1947-Jul 1949 – 1 – 23.00r – us L of C Photodup [950]

TRANSLATIONS OF STATISTICAL AND CENSUS REPORTS OF TEXAS, 1782-1836 / Institute of Texan Cultures. Library – Demographic, statistical and qualitative data. Also: Sources Documenting the Black in Texas, 1603-1803. Gen'l. mss. with information on business and personal contracts, dowries, successions, slavery, criminal and civil proceedings. 3 rolls – 1 – $70.00 – us TX Culture [310]

THE TRANSLATORS REVIVED: THE AUTHORS OF THE ENGLISH...BIBLE / McClure, Alexander Wilson – New York: Charles Scribner, 1853. 1 fiche – 9 – us A.T.L.A. [240]

TRANSMISSION AND DISTRIBUTION – (v.31-. 1979$ 5,6,9) – 1956- – 1 – us UMI [600]

TRANSMISSION OF THE TEXT OF THE NEW TESTAMENT / Drummond, James – London: Sunday School Assoc., 1909. 1 fiche – 9 – us A.T.L.A. [240]

TRANSNATIONAL COMMUNICATION AND CULTURAL INDUSTRIES / Guback, Thomas & Varis, Tapio – 1982 – 55p – 9 – 92-3-101882-5 – fr UNESCO [302]

TRANSNATIONAL CORPORATIONS AND ENDOGENOUS DEVELOPMENT / Reiffers, Jean-Louis & Cartapanis, Andre – 1982 – 280p – 9 – 92-3-101853-1 – fr UNESCO [338]

TRANSNATIONAL DATA REPORT – v4-7. 1981-84 – 1,5,6,13 – sz Elsevier [073]

TRANSNATIONAL LAW AND CONTEMPORARY PROBLEMS – University of Iowa. v1-5. 1991-1995 – 9 – $80.00set – us Hein [340]

TRANSNATIONAL MENTAL HEALTH RESEARCH NEWSLETTER – v18-23. 1976-81 – 1,5,6,9 – us UMI [616]

TRANSPLANTATION – v1-62. 1963-96 – 1,5,6,9 – $110.00r – us Williams [617]

TRANSPORT COMMITTEE / UN Economic Commission for Europe (ECE) – 1947-89 – E/F.416 E.5506 F.5257 R.4602 – 9 – us U.N. Pubs [340]

Transport Holding Company *see* ANNUAL REPORT AND STATEMENT OF ACCOUNTS

TRANSPORT IN POROUS MEDIA – v1-. 1986- – 1,5,6,9 – us UMI [380]

TRANSPORT OF LIVE FISH : A REVIEW – 1986 – 62p – it F.A.O. [380]

TRANSPORT STATISTICS GREAT BRITAIN 1964/74-1967/77 – (Coll title: British Government Publications...1801-1977, Transport) – 12mf – 9 (£590.00 transport set of 12mf + 9r) – uk Chadwyck [380]

TRANSPORT THEORY AND STATISTICAL PHYSICS – (v13-. 1984-. 5,6,9) – v1-. 1971- – 1 – us UMI [073]

TRANSPORT TOPICS – 1935- – 1 – us UMI [380]

TRANSPORT WORKER – Liverpool. England. -m. Aug 1911-Mar 1912. (18 ft) – 1 – uk British Libr Newspaper [072]

TRANSPORTATION – v1-13. 1972-84 – 1,5,6,13 – sz Elsevier [073]

TRANSPORTATION AND DISTRIBUTION *see* HANDLING AND SHIPPING MANAGEMENT

TRANSPORTATION BUSINESS – (Incorporated in: Cargo Express at v12 no 4 1991) – Toronto. v9-11. 1989-91 – 5 – Can$50.00y – cn Micromedia [380]

TRANSPORTATION BUSINESS *see* CARGO EXPRESS

Transportation Dept., Federal Aviation Administration, Aviation Standards National Field Office, Engineering and Manufacturing Branch *see* PARTS MANUFACTURER APPROVALS, 1992

TRANSPORTATION ET COLONISATION PENALE / Pierret, G – Paris: La Tribune des Colonies et des Protectorats, 1892. 106p. LL-12006 – 1 – us L of C Photodup [340]

TRANSPORTATION LAW JOURNAL – (v1-13 1969-84 on reel $135.00. v14-23 1985-96 on mf $159.00) – v1-23. 1969-96 – 5,6,9 – $294.00 set – us Hein [340]

TRANSPORTATION LAW JOURNAL – (v.12-. 1980- 5,6,9) – v.1-. 1969- – 1 – us UMI [340]

TRANSPORTATION OF DANGEROUS GOODS ACT AND REGULATIONS / Canada. Laws, Statutes, etc – (Standing order. T19-1EM) – YX76-T19-1-EM – 9 – Can$9.00 – cn Communication [380]

TRANSPORTATION PLANNING AND TECHNOLOGY / ed by Gillingwater, D – 1972 – 1,5,9 – us Gordon [380]

TRANSPORTATION PRACTITIONERS' JOURNAL – (v1-52 1933-85 on reel $830.00. v53-62 1985-95 on mf $312.00. Title varies: v1-51 1933-84 as I.C.C. Practitioners' Journal) – v1-62. 1933-95 – 5,6,9 – $1,040.00 set – us Hein [340]

TRANSPORTATION PRACTITIONERS' JOURNAL *see* JOURNAL OF TRANSPORTATION LAW, LOGISTICS AND POLICY

TRANSPORTATION RESEARCH – (Individual subscriptions. 6 issues/y. £226.00y. Back issues of journal available from UMI) – Part A: Policy and Practice; Part B: Methodological; Part C: Emerging Technologies. 12 issues/y. v27. 1993 – 9 – £472.00y – uk Elsevier Sci [380]

TRANSPORTATION RESEARCH : PART A, GENERAL – v13- 1979- – 5,6,9 – us UMI [380]

TRANSPORTATION RESEARCH – v1- 1967- – 5,6,9 – us UMI [380]

TRANSPORTATION SCIENCE – (1985-. 5,6,9) – v1-. 1967- – 1 – us UMI [380]

TRANSPORTEN GLAS – (Some issues lacking) – Sofia, Bulgaria. 1951-61 – 5r – 1 – us L of C Photodup [949]

TRANSPORTS & TARIFS; REGIME ADMINISTRATIF DES VOIES DE COMMUNICATION, CONDITIONS TECHNIQUES ET COMMERCIALES DES TRANSPORTS. / Colson, Leon Clement – (Suppl. annuel a la deuxieme ed. Paris, 1906. 45p. 1) – 2e ed. Paris: J. Rothschild, 1898 – 1 – us U.W. Library [380]

TRANSPOSITIONS DE MUSIQUE.. / Frere, Alexandre – CA. 1708 – 2 – us Sibley [780]

THE TRANSVAAL – Lydenburg. South Africa. 1893-99 – 1 – sa State Libr [072]

Transvaal *see* GOVERNMENT GAZETTE

LE TRANSVAAL (1652-1899). / Porier, Jules – Paris. 1900 – 1 – us Res Libr [960]

TRANSVAAL ADVERTISER – Pretoria. South Africa. 1882-1907 – 1 – sa State Libr [072]

TRANSVAAL ADVOCATE AND COMMERCIAL ADVERTISER – Potchefstroom, South Africa. 1869-77 – 1 – sa State Libr [072]

THE TRANSVAAL AND BECHUANALAND / Clark, Gavin Brown – 2nd ed. London: Juta, Heelis, [1883] – us Res Libr [960]

TRANSVAAL ARGUS – Johannesburg. South Africa. 1894 – 1 – sa State Libr [072]

TRANSVAAL ARGUS – Potchefstroom. South Africa. 1866-69 – 1 – sa State Libr [072]

TRANSVAAL ARGUS – Potchefstroom, South Africa. May 1866-May 1869 – 1 – us Res Libr [072]

TRANSVAAL ARGUS – Pretoria. South Africa. 1875-81 – 1 – sa State Libr [072]

Transvaal. (Colony). Native Affairs Department *see* SHORT HISTORY OF THE NATIVE TRIBES OF THE TRANSVAAL

TRANSVAAL CRITIC – Johannesburg. South Africa. 1896-1919 – 1 – sa State Libr [072]

TRANSVAAL GOVERNMENT GAZETTE – Pretoria, South Africa. 1900-10 – 1 – sa State Libr [072]

TRANSVAAL INDEPENDENT – Johannesburg. South Africa. 1896 – 1 – sa State Libr [072]

TRANSVAAL LEADER – Johannesburg. South Africa. 1899-1915 – 1 – sa State Libr [072]

TRANSVAAL LEADER WEEKLY – Johannesburg, South Africa, 1904-1909 – 9r – 1 – sa State Libr [960]

TRANSVAAL MINER – Beatty, NV. 1906 – 1r – 1 – $50.00 – U04414 – us Library Micro [622]

Transvaal. Native Affairs Department *see* LAWS AND REGULATIONS, ETC...SPECIALLY RELATING TO THE NATIVE POPULATION OF THE TRANSVAAL

DE TRANSVAAL: NIEUWS EN ADVERTENTIEBLAD – Potchefstroom, South Africa. 1877-1881 – 1 – sa State Libr [072]

TRANSVAAL, REPORT OF THE AUDITOR OF ACCOUNTS. PRETORIA, 1910-27 – 1 reel – 9 – sa SA Libr [324]

TRANSVAAL RURAL ACTION COMMITTEE (TRAC) – Cape Town. 27 docs. 1983-1990 – 7mf – 9 – ne IDC [960]

TRANSVAAL TIMES AND OBSERVER – Pretoria, South Africa. Jan-Apr 1893 – 1 – sa State Libr [072]

TRANSVAAL TIMES (OBSERVER) – Pretoria, South Africa, 1893 – 1 – sa State Libr [072]

DIE TRANSVALER *see* VADERLAND

TRANSVALER – (Formerly 'Vaderland') – Johannesburg, South Africa. 3 Jan 1965-11 Oct 1988 end 291 rolls; 12 Oct 1988-23 April 1993 end 44 rolls – 335 rolls – 1 – sa Microfile [960]

TRANSVALER – Pretoria, South Africa. 24 Nov 1937-10 April 1991 end – 452r – 1 – sa Microfile [960]

Transylvania University. Kentucky *see* ITS ORIGIN, RISE, DECLINE AND FALL

Tran-van-Lieu *see* LES SUBSTITUTIONS FIDEI-COMMISSAIRES EN DROIT ANNAMITE HUONG-HOA.

Traore, M B *see* SOCIETE INITIATIQUE ET REGULATION SOCIALE CHEZ LES MALINKE ET LES BAMBARA DU MALI

Trapeznikov, I F *see* KREDIT I KREDITNYE OPERATSII V SEL'SKOKHOZIAISTVENNYKH KOOPERATIVAKH

Trapp, J *see*
- THE NATURE, FOLLY, SIN AND DANGER OF BEING RIGHTEOUS OVER-MUCH, WITH A PARTICULAR VIEW TO THE DOCTRINES AND PRACTICES OF CERTAIN MODERN ENTHUSIASTS;...
- THE NATURE, USEFULNESS AND REGULATION OF RELIGIOUS ZEAL
- A REPLY TO MR. LAW'S 'EARNEST AND SERIOUS ANSWER' (AS IT IS CALLED) TO DR. TRAPP'S DISCOURSE OF THE 'FOLLY, SIN AND DANGER OF BEING RIGHTEOUS OVER-MUCH'
- THE TRUE SPIRIT OF THE METHODISTS AND THEIR ALLIES (WHETHER OTHER ENTHUSIASTS, PAPISTS, DEISTS, QUAKERS OR ATHEISTS) FULLY LAID OPEN;...

LE TRAPPEUR – St-Boniface, Manitoba. 13 avr 1887-v1 n2. 20 avr 1887 – 1r – 1 – Can$30.00 – cn Can Microfilming [072]

Traquair, R H *see* A MONOGRAPH OF THE FISHES OF THE OLD RED SANDSTONE OF BRITAIN

TRARALGON RECORD – 1901-1932 – 25r – 1 – at Corangamite [072]

TRASCENDENCIA DE LA TERCERA POSICION / Cascella, Armando – [Buenos Aires?]: Ministerio de la Educacion de la Nacion. Direcci on General de Cultura, 1952 – 1 – CSUXADQ6410-B – us Hoover Inst Photo [370]

TRASLACION DE CUERPOS REALES DE GRANADA A SAN LORENZO DEL ESCORIAL Y DE VALLADOLID A GRANADA / T'Serclaes, Duque de – Madrid: Fortanet, 1912. B.R.A.H. 60, 1912 – sp Bibl Santa Ana [946]

TRASLADO DEL TESTAMENTO DEL REY JUAN 1 DE ARAGON (SIECLE 15) – Barcelona – 1r – 5,6 – sp Cultura [946]

EL TRASPORTE TERRESTRE Y MIXTO EN EL DERECHO INTERNACIONAL PRIVADO, EL TRATADO DE DERECHO COMERCIAL TERRESTRE INTERNACIONAL DE MONTEVIDEO DEL 9 I.E. 19 DE MARZO DE 1940 / Lazcano, Carlos Alberto – Buenos Aires, Impr. de la Univ., 1945. 86 p. LL-8013 – 1 – us L of C Photodup [340]

TRATADO BREVE DE FLEBOTOMIA (SANGRIA) / Perez de Bustos, D – Madrid, 1630 – 2mf – 9 – sp Cultura [615]

TRATADO BREVE DE LA CURACION DEL GARROTILLO / Gil y de Pina, J – Zaragoza, 1636 – 2mf – 9 – sp Cultura [616]

TRATADO BREVE DE LA PESTE / Paredes – Cordoba, 1601 – 1mf – 9 – sp Cultura [614]

TRATADO BREVE Y COMPENDIOSO SOBRE LA MARAVILLOSA OBRA DE LA BOCA Y DENTADURA / Martinez de Castrillo, F – Valladolid, 1570 – 6mf – 9 – sp Cultura [610]

TRATADO BREVE Y PARECER ACERCA DEL METHODO DE CURAR CON SANGRIAS... / Estelrique, I – Jerez de La Frontera, 1654 – 1mf – 9 – sp Cultura [600]

TRATADO COMPLETO DE LA FLEBOTOMIA U OPERACIONES DE LA SANGRIA / Fernandez del Valle, J – Madrid, 1794 – 6mf – 9 – sp Cultura [610]

TRATADO COMPLETO DE LAS CALENTURAS FUNDADO SOBRE LAS LEYES DE LA INFLAMACION... / Pereyra, L – Madrid, 1768 – 5mf – 9 – sp Cultura [615]

TRATADO DE ARITMETICA Y ALGEBRA / Mateos Rodrigo, Gonzalo – Serradilla (Caceres): Edit. Sanchez Rodrigo, 1929 – 1 – sp Bibl Santa Ana [510]

TRATADO DE ARMAS Y EXPLOSIVOS / Pedroso, Nicolas Ignacio – Badajoz: Graficas Jimenez, 1961 – sp Bibl Santa Ana [350]

TRATADO DE CALENTURAS / Piquer, Andres – 1768, 3rd ed – 1mf – 9 – Pta1,000.00 – 84-7848-286-5 – sp Pentalfa [340]

TRATADO DE CONSTRUCCION CIVIL / Ger y Lobez, Florencio – 1897 – 9 – $1.50 – sp Bibl Santa Ana [624]

TRATADO DE CONSTRUCCION CIVIL. ATLAS / Ger y Lobez, Florencio – 1897 – 9 – $1.50 – sp Bibl Santa Ana [624]

TRATADO DE DERECHO MERCANTIL INTERNACIONAL / Gual Villalbi, P – Madrid, 1913 – 7mf – 1 – ILM-3759/1 – ne IDC [327]

TRATADO DE DERECHO PENAL INTERNACIONAL Y DE LA EXTRADICION / Fiore, P – Madrid, 1880 – 6mf – 1 – ILM-2261/1 – ne IDC [327]

TRATADO DE ENFERMEDADES ENDEMICAS EPIDEMICAS CONTAGIOSAS A TODA ESPECIE DE GANADO / Montes, J – Madrid, 1789 – 6mf – 9 – sp Cultura [630]

TRATADO DE FIEBRES MALIGNAS... / Garcia Hernandez, F – Madrid, 1747 – 7mf – 9 – sp Cultura [616]

TRATADO DE LA ACCION DE EL ORADOR, U DE LA PRONUNCIACION Y DEL GESTO, OBRA MUY NECESARIA PARA TODOS LOS QUE SE DEDICAN A HABLAR EN PUBLICO / Le Faucheur, Michel – Madrid: Sancha, 1784 – 1 – us U.W. Library [410]

TRATADO DE LA CAZA DEL PERDIGON / Ruiz Campos, Manuel – Tip. La Economica, 1901 – sp Bibl Santa Ana [946]

TRATADO DE LA ORACION / Pedro de Alcantara, Saint – (1738 ed.1.50f; 9. 1587 ed.1.50f; BSA; 9. 1665 ed.1.50f; BSA; 9) – 1882 – 9 – 1.50f – sp Bibl Santa Ana [410]

TRATADO DE LA ORACION / Pedro de Alcantara, Saint – Salamanca: Establecimiento Tipografico de Calatrava, 1926 – 1 – sp Bibl Santa Ana [240]

TRATADO DE LA ORACION Y LA MEDITACION / Pedro de Alcantara, Saint – Medina del Campo: Francisco del Canto, 1587 – 1 – sp Bibl Santa Ana [240]

TRATADO DE LA ORACION Y MEDITACION / Alcantara, San Pedro de – Buenos Aires: Francisco A. Colombo, 1938 – 1 – sp Bibl Santa Ana [946]

TRATADO DE LA ORACION Y MEDITACION / Pedro de Alcantara, Saint – Cuarta edicion. Le sigue un pequeno devocionario por Fr. Andres de Ocerin-Jauregui. Madrid. Hijos de Gregorio del Amo, 1933 – 1 – sp Bibl Santa Ana [240]

TRATADO DE LA ORACION Y MEDITACION / Pedro de Alcantara, Saint – Sevilla: Andrea Pescioni y Juan de Leon, 1587 – 1 – sp Bibl Santa Ana [240]

TRATADO DE LA ORACION Y MEDITACION. CON BREVE INTRODUCCION Y UN TRATADO DE LOS TRES VOTOS DE LA RELIGION POR FRAY GERONYMO DE FERRERA / Pedro de Alcantara, Saint – Barcelona: Ioseph Forcada, 1665 – 1 – sp Bibl Santa Ana [240]

TRATADO DE LAS AGUAS MEDICINALES DE SALAM-BIR (8S.A.). TRAD. M. PIZZI / Agmer-Ben-Ab-Dala – 1mf – 9 – Pta1,000.00 – 84-7848-280-6 – sp Pentalfa [610]

TRATADO DE LAS ASFIXIAS O MUERTES ASFIXIANTES / Amaya Delgado, Manuel – 1818 – 9 – 1.50f – sp Bibl Santa Ana [610]

TRATADO DE LAS CALENTURAS SEGUN LA OBSERVACION Y EL MECANISMO / Piquer, Andres – Valencia, 1751 – 5mf – 9 – sp Cultura [615]

TRATADO DE LAS DROGAS Y MEDICINAS DE LAS INDIAS ORIENTALES CON SUS PLANTAS... / Acosta, C – Burgos, 1578 – 9mf – 9 – sp Cultura [615]

TRATADO DE LAS ENFERMEDADES EPIDEMICAS, PUTRIDAS, MALIGNAS, CONTAGIOSAS... / Lavedan, A – Madrid, 1802 – 13mf – 9 – sp Cultura [614]

TRATADO DE LAS INFLAMACIONES INTERNAS EXPLICADO POR LAS LEYES MECANICAS / Reyes, R – Salamanca, 1754 – 6mf – 9 – sp Cultura [615]

TRATADO DE LAS OBLIGACIONES DEL HOMBRE / Escoiquiz, Juan de – 1855 – 9 – 1.50f – sp Bibl Santa Ana [946]

TRATADO DE LAS QUALIDADES QUE LA NIEVE TIENE A PREDOMINIO... / Mirez Carvajal, C – Malaga, 1650 – 1mf – 9 – sp Cultura [615]

TRATADO DE LAS VIRTUDES Y EXCELENCIAS DE LOS BANOS DE TIERMAS / Velazquez, P – Pamplona, 1624 – 2mf – 9 – sp Cultura [615]

TRATADO DE LOS ERRORES DE PAFIVIO Y DE LAS OTRAS DE LA ESCUELA DIALECTICA / Sanchez de las Brozas, Francisco – Madrid: Sucesores de Rivadeneyra S.A., 1922 – 1 – sp Bibl Santa Ana [946]

TRATADO DE LOURENCO MARQUES : SUA HISTORIA PARLAMENTAR, SEU VALOR TECHNICO E SOCIAL, SUA CONCLUSAO / Ponte e Horta, Jose Maria da – (Filmed with: Barahona e Costa, Henrique Cesar da Silva: Apontamentos para a historia de guerra de Zambezia 1871-75; and others) – Lisboa: Impr Nacional, 1882 – us Res Libr [960]

TRATADO DE METAFISICA / Perez de la Mata, Antonio – Madrid: Impr. de T. Fortanet, 1877 – 1 – us U.W. Library [110]

TRATADO DE PESTE, DONDE SE CONTIENEN LAS CAUSAS, PRESERVACION Y CURA / Jimenez de Savariego, J – Antequera, 1602 – 7mf – 9 – sp Cultura [614]

TRATADO DE PESTE, SUS CAUSAS Y CURACION... / Biana, J – Malaga, 1637 – 4mf – 9 – sp Cultura [616]

TRATADO DE RARAS Y PEREGRINAS YERVAS / Murillo y Velarde Jurado, T – Madrid, 1674 – 2mf – 9 – sp Cultura [615]

TRATADO DE RE MILITARI... / Salazar, D – Alcala de Henares, 1536 – 3mf – 9 – sp Cultura [355]

TRATADO DE UTRECHT / Giraud, C – Paris, 1847 – 3mf – 1 – ILM-2592/1 – ne IDC [327]

TRATADO DEL CUYDADO QUE SE DEVE TENER DE LOS PRESOS PROBRES / Sandoval, B – Toledo, 1564 – 2mf – 9 – sp Cultura [616]

TRATADO DEL GARROTILLO MALIGNO ULCERADO O ANGINA MALIGNA GANGRENOSA... / Pascual y Rubio, J – Valencia, 1784 – 1mf – 9 – sp Cultura [616]

TRATADO DEL USO DE LA QUINA / Salazar, T – Madrid, 1791 – 7mf – 9 – sp Cultura [615]

TRATADO DEL...LINAJE DE VERA...SIERRA BRAVA / Velazquez de Mena – 1617 – 9 – 1.50f – sp Bibl Santa Ana [946]

TRATADO ELEMENTAL DE ARITMETICA / Luna y Gomez, Sergio – Badajoz: Tip. y Libreria Antonio Arqueros, 5th ed 1932 – 1 – sp Bibl Santa Ana [520]

TRATADO ELEMENTAL DE HIGIENE / Diaz Villar Martinez, Juan Manuel – 1896 – 9 – 1.50f – sp Bibl Santa Ana [610]

TRATADO ELEMENTAL DE HIGIENE COMPARADA DEL HOMBRE Y DE LOS ANIMALES DOMESTICOS / Diaz Villar Martinez, Juan Manuel – Madrid: Imprenta de los hijos de R. Alvarez, 1915.-v2 – 1 – sp Bibl Santa Ana [610]

TRATADO ELEMENTAL DE HIGIENE COMPARADA DEL HOMBRE Y LOS ANIMALES DOMESTICOS / Diaz de Villar y Martinez, Juan M – Madrid: Imprenta de Eduar do Arias, 2nd ed 1908.-v1 – 1 – sp Bibl Santa Ana [610]

TRATADO ELEMENTAL DE HISTORIA NATURAL / Aguas Monreal, Mariano – 1890 – 9 – 1.50f – sp Bibl Santa Ana [574]

TRATADO HISTORICO Y FISIOLOGICO...SOBRE LA GENERACION, EL HOMBRE Y LA MUJER / Hurtado de Mendoza, M – Madrid, 1821 – 6mf – 9 – sp Cultura [612]

EL TRATADO INEDITO "DE FIDE QUAE REVELANDA ERAT" / Ozaeta, Jose Maria OS A – Madrid: Imprenta, 1965 – 1 – sp Bibl Santa Ana [946]

TRATADO IURIDICO-POLITICO DEL CONTRA-BANDO / Gonzalez de Salcedo, P – Madrid, 1654 – 5mf – 1 – ILM-787/1 – ne IDC [327]

TRATADO LLAMADO EL DESEO...ESPEJO DE RELIGIOSO – 1554 – 9 – 1.50f – sp Bibl Santa Ana [240]

TRATADO PASTORAL...PROPIEDADES DEL BUEN PASTOR / Ovando, Juan de – 1601 – 9 – 1.50f – sp Bibl Santa Ana [240]

TRATADO PRACTICO DE LAS SANGRIAS / Nunez de Acosta, D – Jerez, 1653 – 3mf – 9 – sp Cultura [610]

TRATADO PRACTICO SOBRE EL MAL ROJO DEL CERDO / Gimenez de la Torre, Pelayo – Caceres: Tip. La Minerva, 1911 – 1 – sp Bibl Santa Ana [946]

TRATADO RELIGIOSO...ANTIGUEDADES DE ESTREMADURA / Viu, Jose de – 1853 – 9 – $1.50f – sp Bibl Santa Ana [946]

TRATADO REPARTIDO EN CINCO PARTES...(SOBRE)...PESTE... / Nunez, A – Coimbra, 1601 – 7mf – 9 – sp Cultura [616]

EL TRATADO SOBRE BELICE Y LA DOCTRINA MONROE / Gonzalez Gutierez, E – Mexico, 1894 – 1mf – 1 – ILM-1809/1 – ne IDC [327]

TRATADO SOBRE EL ARTE DE LA TINTURA / Fernandez, Luis – 1778 – 1mf – 9 – Pta1,000.00 – 84-7848-231-8 – sp Pentalfa [340]

TRATADO SOBRE EL LAUDANO OPIATO... / Barrionuevo, G – Toledo, 1648 – 1mf – 9 – sp Cultura [615]

TRATADO SUBTILISSIMO DE ARITMETICA Y GEOMETRIA... / Ortega, J – Sevilla, 2534 – 8mf – 9 – sp Cultura [510]

TRATADO TEORICO Y PRACTICO DE LAS HERNIAS EN GENERAL Y DE LAS ESTRANGULADAS / Fernandez del Valle, J – Madrid, 1803 – 4mf – 9 – sp Cultura [610]

TRATADO UNIVERSAL...(SOBRE) LA PESTE... / Munez de Castro, J – Madrid, 1648 – 1mf – 9 – sp Cultura [614]

TRATADO...DE LA ESENCIA, CAUSAS Y CURACIONES DE LOS BUBONES Y CARBUNCOS... / Escobar, M – Alcala, 1600 – 5mf – 9 – sp Cultura [616]

TRATADO...DE LA FACULTAD MEDICAMENTOSA QUE SE HALLA EN EL AGUA DE LOS BANOS... / Ferrer de Esparza, T – Zaragoza, 1634 – 4mf – 9 – sp Cultura [615]

TRATADO...LINAJE DE LA VERA / Puente, Francisco de la – 1635 – 9 – 1.50f – sp Bibl Santa Ana [340]

TRATADOS DA TERRA E GENTE DO BRASIL / Cardim, Fernao – Rio de Janeiro: Leite, 1925 – fr Armell [972]

TRATADOS DA TERRA E GENTE DO BRASIL / Cardim, Fernao – Sao Paulo, 1939 – 7mf – 8 – ne Slangenburg [972]

TRATADOS, HISTORICOS POLITICOS, ETHICOS, Y RELIGIOSOS DE LA MONARCHIA DE CHINA / Fernandez Navarette, D – Madrid, 1676 – 10mf – 9 – ne IDC [950]

TRATADOS PARA LA SUCESION DEL REINO DE ARAGON (SIECLE 14-15) – Barcelona – 1r – 5,6 – sp Cultura [946]

TRATADO...TISIS...HIGIENE / Lozano Ponce de Leon, Pablo – 1897 – 9 – 1.50f – sp Bibl Santa Ana [610]

TRATTATO DE COSTVMI ET VITA DE TURCHI, ... / Menavino, G A – Firenze, 1548 – 3mf – 9 – H-8280/1 – ne IDC [956]

TRATTATO DELL' ARTE DE LA PITTURA, SCOLTURA ET ARCHITETTURA / Lomazzo, G P – O 344. 1584 – 9 – ne IDC [700]

TRATTATO DELLA GVERRA, ET DELL' VNIONE DE' PRINCIPI CHRISTIANI CONTRA I TURCHI, ET GLI ALTRI INFEDELI / Filiarchi, C – Vinetia, 1572 – 2mf – 9 – H-8324/1 – ne IDC [956]

TRATTATO DELLA NATURA ET COGNITIONE DI TUTTI GLI TUONI DI CANTO FIGURATO / Aron, Pietro – 1525 – 9 – us Sibley [780]

TRATTATO DELLA NATURA ET COGNITIONE DI TUTTI GLI TUONI DI CANTO FIGURATO NO DA ALTRUI PIU SCRITTI / Aaron, P – P-105. 1525 – 9 – ne IDC [780]

TRATTATO DELLA PITTURA / Cennini, C – O 980. 1821 – 9 – ne IDC [760]

TRATTATO DELL'INGRATITUDINE – 15th century. Holkham MS. 533. Holkham Hall, Norfolk, England – 1 – uk Microform Academic [180]

TRATTATO DI DIRITTO COMMERCIALE INTERNAZIONALE... / Diena, G – Firenze. 3v. 1900-05 – 20mf – 1 – ILM-3654/1 – ne IDC [327]

TRATTATO DI MUSICA SECONDO LA VERA SCIENZA DELL' ARMONIA / Tartini, G – Padova. 1754. BP-765 1 – 9 – ne IDC [780]

TRATTATO SOPRA LE FUGHE MUSICALI. CORREDATO DA. FRANCESCO ANTONIO VALLOTI / Sabbatini, L A – 2v. Venezia. 1802. BP-459 1 – 9 – ne IDC [780]

TRATTATO...SOPRA IL SUCCESSO DELLA GUERRA, ...CONTRA...TURCO... / Papadopoli, N – N.p., [1571] – 1mf – 9 – H-8321/1 – ne IDC [956]

TRATTENIMENTI SULLE VERNICI, ED ALTRE MATERIE UTILI. / Agricola, F – c. 1788 – 5 – us Sibley [780]

Trattinick, L *see*
- FLORA DES OESTERREICHISCHEN KAISERTHUMES
- GENERA PLANTARUM METHODO NATURALI DISPOSITA
- ROSACEARUM MONOGRAPHIA

TRATTO DEL BALLO NOBILE DI GIAMBATISTA DUFORTE INDIRIZZATO ALL'ECCELENZE DELLE SIGNORE DAME, E DE'SIGNORI CAVALERI, NAPOLETANI / Dufort, Giovanni Battista – Napoli: Nella Stamperia di F Mosca, 1728 – 1 – us Sibley [780]

Traube, L *see*
- TEXTGESCHICHTE DER REGULA S. BENEDICTI
- VORLESUNGEN UND ABHANDLUNGEN

DIE TRAUER- UND TROSTGEDICHTE IN DER ROMISCHEN LITERATUR / Estere-Forriol, Jose – 1 – DM30.00 – gw Mikro Press [450]

TRAUERN : EINE VORAUSSETZUNG FUER DIE SELBSTWERDUNG DES MENSCHEN / Dueerkob, Monika – 1994 – 2mf – DM80.00 – 3-89349-886-9 – gw Hänsel [230]

DAS TRAUERSPIEL IN TYROL : EIN DRAMATISCHES GEDICHT IN FUENF AUFZUEGEN / Immermann, Karl Leberecht – Hamburg: Hoffmann und Campe, 1828 – 1r – 1 – us U.W. Library [820]

TRAUM DER ERDE : ROMAN / Stahl, Hermann – Hamburg: Hanseatische Verlagsanstalt, c1936 – 1r – 1 – us U.W. Library [830]

TRAUM IM FEBRUAR : ERZAEHLUNG / Wittek, Erhard – Dresden: W Heyne, c1939 – 1r – 1 – us U.W. Library [830]

TRAUMA QUARTERLY – v1-. 1984- – 1,5,6,9 – us UMI [617]

Traumann, Ernst *see* ZU GOETHE'S LEBEN UND WERKEN

DIE TRAUMDEUTUNG / Freud, Sigmund – 2. verm. Aufl. Leipzig: F Deuticke, 1909 – us Res Libr [150]

DER TRAUMGLAUBE DER ANTIKE: EIN HISTORISCHER VERSUCH / Hey, Friedrich Oskar – Muenchen, 1908. 40p – 1 – us U.W. Library [943]

DAS TRAUMMOTIV IN ALTDEUTSCHER DICHTUNG : BIS CIRCA 1250 / Beneze, Emil – 1995 – 1mf – 9 – DM48.00 – 3-8267-3122-0 – gw Hänsel [430]

TRAUNSTEINER WOCHENBLATT – Traunstein, Germany. 1978- – ca 7r per yr – 1 – gw Mikrofilm [072]

Trautmann, Karl *see* OBERAMMERGAU UND SEIN PASSIONSSPIEL

Trautmann, O *see* IM HERERO- UND HOTTENTOTTENLAND

Trautmann, R *see* DIE ALTPREUSSISCHEN SPRACHDENKMAELER

Trautmann, Rene *see*
- BOULOU
- LA DIVINATION A LA COTE DES ESCLAVES ET A MADAGASCAR

Trautner, Eduard *see* DER MORD AM POLIZEIAGENTEN BLAU

Trauttwein von Belle, E *see* WILHELM VON ORANIEN

Trautvetter, E R *see* PLANTARUM IMAGINES ET DESCRIPTIONES FLORAM RUSSICAM ILLUSTRATES

LE TRAVAIL : CHANSON DES TRAVAILLEURS AVEC MUSIQUE – Montreal, Canada. numero unique. 7 sep 1891 – 1r – 1 – Can$25.00 – cn Can Microfilming [780]

LE TRAVAIL – Organe de la renovation sociale. no. 1-3. Lyon. juin-sept 1841 – 1 – fr A.C.R.P.P. [335]

LE TRAVAIL – Organe des associations ouvrieres. no. 19, 25, 28. Paris. oct-dec 1869 – 1 – fr A.C.R.P.P. [331]

LE TRAVAIL – v. 23-36. 1947-1960 – 1 – us NY Public [331]

LE TRAVAIL *see* LA VIE SYNDICALE (C.S.N.)

LE TRAVAIL DES ENFANTS ET DES FILLES MINEURES DANS L'INDUSTRIE. LOI DU 19 MAI 1874. REGLEMENTS D'ADMINISTRATION PUBLIQUE, CIRCULAIRES, INSTRUCTIONS MINISTERIELLES, DECISIONS JUDICIARIES REUNIS ET COMMENTES / Bouquet, Louis – (Condition of 19th C. French working class series). 1885 – 9 – fr Hachette [331]

LE TRAVAIL DES FEMMES AU XIXE SIECLE / Leroy-Beaulieu, P – (Condition of 19th C. French working class series). 1873 – 9 – fr Hachette [360]

LE TRAVAIL DES MILITANTS (C.S.N.) – Montreal, Canada. mar 1968-v2 n6. sep 1969 – 1r – 1 – Can$30.00 – cn Can Microfilming [072]

LE TRAVAIL EN FRANCE. MONOGRAPHIES PROFESSIONNELLES / Barberet, J – (Condition of 19th C. French working class series). 1866-90 – 9 – fr Hachette [380]

TRAVAIL ET EMPLOI – 1992-1995 – 8 times per yr – 9 – F1,280.00 – sz Infoprint [331]

LE TRAVAIL ET LES OUVRIERS SOUS LA IIIE / Audiganne, A – Republique. (Condition of 19th C. French working class series). 1873 – 9 – fr Hachette [305]

LE TRAVAIL ET LES TECHNIQUES – Paris. 1948. (La Condition Ouvriere. Part Two.) – 9 – 5.00 – fr Bibl Nationale [360]

TRAVAIL ET METHODES – Revue des techniques nouvelles au service de l'entreprise. Paris. 1970-83 – 1 – fr A.C.R.P.P. [600]

TRAVAIL ET PROFESSION D'OUTRE-MER – Dir. C. Gombeyre. Paris. 1958-61, 1966 – 1 – fr A.C.R.P.P. [073]

TRAVAIL ET PROLETARIAT / Brissac, Henri – No. 9. Paris. 1886. (La Condition Ouvriere. Part Two.) – 9 – 2.50 – fr Bibl Nationale [360]

TRAVAIL ET SURMENAGE / Pierrot, Marc – Paris. 1911. (La Condition Ouvriere. Part Two.) – 9 – 2.50 – fr Bibl Nationale [360]

LE TRAVAIL: HEBDOMADAIRE POLITIQUE ET ECONOMIQUE – no. 1-30. Hanoi. 16 sept 1936-16 avr 1937 – 1 – fr A.C.R.P.P. [073]

LE TRAVAIL: JOURNAL DES INTERETS MORAUX ET MATERIELS DES CLASSES OUVRIERES – no. 1-12. Paris. janv-sept 1842 – 1 – fr A.C.R.P.P. [073]

LE TRAVAIL: JOURNAL LITTERAIRE ET SCIENTIFIQUE – no. 1-9. Paris. dec 1861-mars 1862 – 1 – fr A.C.R.P.P. [073]

LE TRAVAIL (MONTREAL, QUEBEC, 1912) : ORGANE DE LA CLASSE OUVRIERE – Montreal: [s.n.], 1912-. SEM35P39 – 1r – 1 – Can$15.00 – cn Bibl Nat [072]

THE TRAVAIL OF A SOUL / Thorn, J H – 1920 – 1 – 5.00 – us Baptist [240]

TRAVAIL SUR L'EDUCATION PUBLIQUE, TROUVE DANS LES PAPIERS DE MIRABEAU L'AINE, PUBLIE PAR P. J. G. CABANIS / Mirabeau, Honore-Gabriel de Riqueti – Paris. Impr. nationale. 1791. 6775 – 9 – fr Hachette [305]

LE TRAVAILLE DU STYLE CHEZ SAINT FRANCOIS DE SALES / Vincent, Francis – Paris. 1923. 115p. (Religion series) – 9 – 6.00 – fr Bibl Nationale [240]

LE TRAVAILLEUR / La Federation du Nord. (S.F.I.O.) – Lille. juil 1900-juin 1914 – 1 – fr A.C.R.P.P. [073]

LE TRAVAILLEUR : INDEPENDANT / ed by Potvin, D – Chicoutimi, Canada. 25 mai 1905-20 jun 1912 – 2r – 1 – Can$50.00r – cn Can Microfilming [072]

LE TRAVAILLEUR – Montreal, Canada. v2 n1. 1 fev 1946-v2 n35. 6 sep 1946 – 1r – 1 – Can$30.00 – cn Can Microfilming [072]

LE TRAVAILLEUR / Parti Ouvrier de la Region Nord – Lille. sept 1891-avr 1895 – 1 – fr A.C.R.P.P. [073]

LE TRAVAILLEUR – Quebec, Canada. 4 avr 1912 – 1r – 1 – Can$25.00 – cn Can Microfilming [072]

LE TRAVAILLEUR – Worcester, MA. 10 sep 1931-nov 1978 – 8r – 1 – Can$65.00r – cn Can Microfilming [071]

LE TRAVAILLEUR – Worcester, MA. v8 n55. 28 avr 1882-v19 n21. 31 dec 1892 – 3r – 1 – Can$70.00r – cn Can Microfilming [071]

LE TRAVAILLEUR ALGERIEN – Red. en chef R. Raffi. Alger. 1949-50, 1952-mai 1956 – 1 – fr A.C.R.P.P. [073]

TRAVAILLEUR CANADIEN – (Filmed with the english version "Canadian Labour" from v21 1976) – Ottawa. v16-20. 1971-75 – 5 – Can$100.00 – cn Micromedia [331]

LE TRAVAILLEUR DE L'ALLIER ET DE LA CREUSE – no. 2-29. Moulins. 22 mai-27 nov 1851. mq no. 1, 4 – 1 – fr A.C.R.P.P. [073]

LE TRAVAILLEUR DE LEVIS – Levis, Canada. 17 fev 1890; 19 fev 1890-23 jul 1892 – 1r – 1 – Can$45.00 – cn Can Microfilming [072]

LE TRAVAILLEUR DE LOT-ET-GARONNE ET DU GERS – Marmande. 7 janv 1922-26 dec 1931. Contient egalement: La Voix paysanne. no. 115-223. 8 avr 1922-17 mai 1924 – 1 – fr A.C.R.P.P. [073]

LE TRAVAILLEUR DU LAC MEGANTIC / ed by Vachon, Seraphin – Agnes (Lac Megantic), Canada. 3 fev 1898-3 fev 1899 – 1r – 1 – Can$45.00 – cn Can Microfilming [072]

LE TRAVAILLEUR DU SOUS-SOL / La Federation Nationale des Travailleurs du Sous-sol et Parties Similaires (Mineurs, Miniers et Ardoisiens) – Section francaise de l'Internationale miniere. Paris. sept 1919-sept oct 1939 – 1 – fr A.C.R.P.P. [073]

LE TRAVAILLEUR ET LE PROGRES SOCIAL UNIS – Marseille. 1851 – 1 – fr A.C.R.P.P. [073]

LE TRAVAILLEUR ILLUSTRE – Montreal: A Corbeil, 1887. SEM35P185 – 1r – 1 – Can$15.00 – cn Bibl Nat [073]

LE TRAVAILLEUR ILLUSTRE – Montreal, Canada. v1 n4. 4 jun 1887 – 1r – 1 – Can$25.00 – cn Can Microfilming [072]

LE TRAVAILLEUR ILLUSTRE – Quebec, Canada. 19 oct 1878 – 1r – 1 – Can$25.00 – cn Can Microfilming [072]

LE TRAVAILLEUR: REVUE SOCIALISTE REVOLUTIONNAIRE – I, no. 1-8; II, no. 1-4. Geneve. mai 1877-avr mai 1878 – 1 – fr A.C.R.P.P. [335]

LE TRAVAILLEUR RURAL / La Federation des Syndicats de Cultivateurs de la Region de Moulins – Secretaire de la redaction Emile Guillaumin. no. 1-24. Ygrande (Allier). fevr 1906-11. suivi de: Compte rendu annuel de la Federation des syndicats des travailleurs de la terre 1912-1913 – 1 – fr A.C.R.P.P. [073]

TRAVAILLEURS ET MARCHANDS DANS L'ANCIENNE FRANCE / Hauser, Henri – Paris. 1920. (La Condition Ouvriere. Part Two.) – 9 – 7.50 – fr Bibl Nationale [360]

TRAVA-MURAVA. SKAZ I VELICHANIE / Remizov, A – Berlin, 1922. 190, (2)p. BR-850 2 – 8 – ne IDC [460]

TRAVANCORE – Trivandrum. pt 4. 1911 – us Res Libr [310]

TRAVANCORE ARCHAEOLOGICAL SERIES – v.1-13. Madras. 1910-12. BI-653 2 – 13mf – 8 – ne IDC [930]

THE TRAVANCORE STATE MANUAL / Nagame, A V – 3v. Trivandrum. 1906. B-772 2 – 8 – ne IDC [321]

Travassos, Mario *see* INTRODUCAO A GEOGRAFIA DAS COMUNICACOES BRASILEIROS

Travassos Valdez, Francisco *see* SIX YEARS OF A TRAVELLER'S LIFE IN WESTERN AFRICA

TRAVAUX / Cercle Linguistique de Prague – v1-8. 1929-39. Lacking: v5(1), 1934. 2271/2 – 8 – ne IDC [400]

LES TRAVAUX DE LA MISSION SONT ORDONNES DE LA FACON SUIVANTE – Strasbourg, impr. de Mme Silberman, s.d., 1 feuille. Pourquoi nous venons. Ce que nous apportons. Strasbourg, Silberman, s.d., 8 p. Reponse a quelques objections. Strasbourg, impr. Silberman, 1831, 16 p. Les Saint-Simoniens, 1825-1834. 6939 – 9 – fr Hachette [335]

LES TRAVAUX DE MARS / Mallet, A – Paris, 1672 – 5mf – 9 – sp Cultura [355]

TRAVAUX DU 1ER CONGRES.. / Congres International de folklore – 1938 – 1 – us I.U. Libraries [390]

TRAVAUX DU LABORATOIRE DE GEOLOGIE DE LA FACULTE DES SCIENCES DE LYON – v1-39. 1921-40 – 78mf – 9 – 6116c/2 – ne IDC [550]

TRAVAUX ET MEMOIRES DE L'UNIVERSITE D'ABIDJAN – (Africa series sub-collection). Works on linguistics, anthropology, geography, science, medicine – 9 – fr Hachette [370]

TRAVAUX ET MEMOIRES DE L'UNIVERSITE D'ABIDJAN – Works on linguistics, anthropology, geography, science, medicine. (Afrique: Sub-Collection) – 9 – fr Hachette [400]

TRAVAUX HISTORIQUES PUBLIES DEPUIS TRENTE ANS PAR LE DR. N.E. DIONNE.. / Dionne, Narcisse Eutrope – Quebec: Laflamme et Proulx, 1909. SEM105P502 – 1mf – 9 – Can$2.25 – cn Bibl Nat [900]

TRAVAUX PARLEMENTAIRES / Congo. Chambre des Deputes. Kinshasa/Kalina – 1965. BA-664/1 – 9 – ne IDC [960]

TRAVAUX SCIENTIFIQUES DES MEDECINS DE L'HOPITAL SAINT-MICHEL-ARCHANGE ET DE LA CLINIQUE ROY-ROUSSEAU, 1930-1950 : BIBLIOGRAPHIE ANALYTIQUE / Rouen, Marie-de – 1963. SEM105P4 – 3mf – 91 – Can$6.75 – cn Bibl Nat [610]

THE TRAVEILER / Turler, Jerome – 1575 – 9 – 15.00 – us Scholars' Facs [910]

TRAVEL / Bibliotheque Nationale – Series. Six travelogues of trips within France, Argentina, England and Carthage, during the 19th century. Titles available separately – 9 – 44.00 – fr Bibl Nationale [910]

TRAVEL – (v136-. 1971-. 5,6,9) – v. 1- 1901- – 1 – us UMI [910]

TRAVEL ACCOUNT / Brisbane, William – 1801-ca.1805. 7 fiches – 9 – us South Carolina Historical [910]

TRAVEL AND ADVENTURE IN THE TERRITORY OF ALASKA / Whymper, F – BN 452 2. 1868 – 8 – ne IDC [910]

TRAVEL AND CULTURE SHOCK ADAPTATION AMONG CHINESE STUDENTS AT THE PENNSYLVANIA STATE UNIVERSITY / Yang, M-C – 1991 – 2mf – 9 – $8.00 – us Microform Publ [150]

TRAVEL DIARIES / Jackson, Sheldon – 1890-1900 – 1 – $50.00 – us Presbyterian [910]

TRAVEL DIARY / Allen, Mary Montcrieff – 1835-37.Europe and the Middle East. 12 fiches – 9 – us South Carolina Historical [910]

TRAVEL JOURNALS / Michoutouchkine, Nicolai – sep 1953-jan 1956 – 3r – 1 – PMB 1134 – at Pacific Mss [910]

THE TRAVEL JOURNALS OF GEORGE AND ANNA TICKNOR / Ticknor, George & Ticknor, Anna – 5r – 1 – $150.00 set – us Dartmouth [910]

THE TRAVEL JOURNALS OF GEORGE AND ANNA TICKNOR, 1815-1819 – (Critical observations of 19th-century Europe through the eyes of an American couple) – 1 – $370.00 – us UMI [910]

TRAVEL NOTES / Manigault, Charles Izard – 1818-22, 1827-30, 1847-48. 4 fiches – 9 – us South Carolina Historical [910]

TRAVEL WEEKLY – v1-48. 1958-84 – 1 – us UMI [910]

TRAVELER – Arkansas City. Kan. 1888- – 1 – us UMI [071]

TRAVELER – Arkansas City. KS. And Republican Traveler. -w. 1876-1908 – 1 – us UMI [071]

TRAVELER – St. Joseph. MI.-w. 1859-63, 1865-66 – 1 – us UMI [071]

THE TRAVELER'S DICTIONARY FOR ILLINOIS / Peck, John M – 1839 – 1 – 5.25 – us Baptist [978]

TRAVELER'S LEXICON FOR INDONESIA – Masa Baru, Ltd, Bandung. SE 2962 1. 1961 – 9 – ne IDC [490]

TRAVELERS' RAILWAY GUIDE – Pocket edition of the Official Railway Guide. Eastern Section. 1883-1919 – 1 – us NY Public [073]

TRAVELLER – London, UK. 1819-20. -d. 6 reels – 1 – uk British Libr Newspaper [072]

THE TRAVELLER IN AFRICA: CONTAINING SOME ACCOUNT OF THE ANTIQUITIES, NATURAL CURIOSITIES, AND INHABITANTS OF SUCH PARTS OF THAT CONTINENT AND ITS ISLANDS...EXPLORED BY EUROPEANS / Wakefield, Priscilla Bell – London: Darton, Harvey, and Darton, 1814. vi,374p. 1 fold. map – 1 – us U.W. Library [910]

THE TRAVELLER IN ASIA:... / Wakefield, Priscilla Bell – London, 1817 – 3mf – 9 – ne IDC [910]

TRAVELLER'S GUIDE TO THE BELGIAN CONGO AND RUANDA-URUNDI / Belgium.Office du Tourisme du Congo belge et du Ruanda-Urundi – 2nd ed. Brussels, 1956.xxxviii,790p. illus. plates.maps – 1 – us U.W. Library [910]

THE TRAVELLER'S GUIDE TO THE HUDSON RIVER, SARATOGA SPRINGS, LAKE GEORGE, FALLS OF NIAGARA AND THOUSAND ISLANDS / Disturnell, John – New York: American News Co., 1864. 04303. (Pre-1900 Canadiana) – 9 – cn C.I.H.M. [910]

TRAVELLING SKETCHES / Trollope, Anthony – London: Chapman and Hall, 1866 – 1 roll – 1 – 1-55879-893-5 – uk Libr Preservation [910]

TRAVELS – (Brings together works previously scattered through a number of catalogues. A 2nd catalogue continues the project with new material, including a section of missionary travels) – 1025 titles – 9 – ne IDC [910]

TRAVELS / Ibn Batutah – 1829 – 1 – uk Microform Academic [910]

TRAVELS AMONGST THE GREAT ANDES OF THE EQUATOR / Whymper, Edward – 2nd ed. London: J. Murray, 1892. xxii,456p. illus., maps – 1 – us U.W. Library [910]

TRAVELS AND ADVENTURES IN THE PROVINCE OF ASSAM, DURING A RESIDENCE OF FOURTEEN YEARS / Butler, J – London. 1855. BSE-69 2 – 8 – ne IDC [910]

TRAVELS AND DISCOVERIES IN AFRICA / Denham, D & Clapperton, Hugh – 1826 – 9mf – 7 – uk Microform Academic [910]

TRAVELS AND DISCOVERIES IN NORTH AND CENTRAL AFRICA / Barth, Heinrich – 5v. London. 1857-58. BA-275 2 – 66mf – 8 – ne IDC [910]

TRAVELS AND DISCOVERIES IN NORTH AND CENTRAL AFRICA / Barth, Heinrich – v1-5. 1890 – 1r – 1 – us Ross [910]

TRAVELS AND DISCOVERIES IN NORTHERN AND CENTRAL AFRICA / Denham, D – 4v. London. 1813. BA-303 2 – 8 – ne IDC [956]

TRAVELS AND EXPLORATIONS OF / Clarke, Wm. H – 1854-58 – 1 – 11.58 – us Baptist [910]

TRAVELS AND RESEARCHES AMONG THE LAKES AND MOUNTAINS OF EASTERN AND CENTRAL AFRICA : FROM THE JOURNALS OF THE LATE J FREDERIC ELTON / ed by Cotterill, H B – London: Murray, 1879 – us Res Libr [910]

TRAVELS AND RESEARCHES IN ASIA MINOR: MORE PARTICULARLY IN THE PROVINCE OF LYCIA / Fellows, Charles – London: Murray, 1852. xvi,510p.Includes index – 1 – us U.W. Library [910]

TRAVELS AND RESEARCHES IN CHALDAEA AND SUSIANA / Loftus, W K – London. 1857. BNE-414 1 – 9 – ne IDC [930]

TRAVELS AND VOYAGES / Keith, G & Thompson, Thomas – 1748-56. From the Archives of USPG – 1 – uk Microform Academic [240]

TRAVELS IN ABYSSINIA AND NUBIA, 1768-1773 : TO DISCOVER THE SOURCE OF THE NILE / Bruce, James – (Reduced from the original work by J Morison Clingan) – 2nd ed. Edinburgh: A & C Black, 1873 – us Res Libr [910]

TRAVELS IN ABYSSINIA AND THE GALLA COUNTRY : WITH AN ACCOUNT OF A MISSION TO RAS ALI IN 1848 / Plowden, Walter Chichele; ed by Plowden, Trevor Chichele – London: Longmans, Green & Co, 1868 – us Res Libr [910]

TRAVELS IN AFRICA PERFORMED DURING THE YEARS 1785, 1786 AND 1787 / Golbery, Sylvain M X de – 2v. London. 1803. BA-308 2 – 8 – ne IDC [910]

TRAVELS IN AMERICA: WITH SPECIAL REFERENCE TO THE PROVINCE OF ONTARIO AS A HOME FOR WORKING MEN / Easton, George – Glasgow, J. Marr, 1871. 02815. (Pre-1900 Canadiana) – 9 – cn C.I.H.M. [910]

TRAVELS IN ARABIA, COMPILED AND ARRANGED BY BAYARD TAYLOR / Taylor, Bayard – Rev. by Thomas Stevens. New York: Scribners, 1892. vi,296p. illus – 1 – us U.W. Library [910]

TRAVELS IN BRAZIL IN THE YEARS 1809 TO 1815 / Koster, Henry – London. 2v. 1817 – 1r – 1 – us Ross [910]

TRAVELS IN EGYPT, ARABIA, PETRAEA, AND THE HOLY LAND / Olin, Stephen – 2v. 1856 – 9 – us A.T.L.A. [910]

TRAVELS IN EUROPE, ASIA AND AFRICA / Evliya, Chelebi – 1834-50 – 1 – uk Microform Academic [910]

TRAVELS IN FAITH FROM TRADITION TO REASON / Adams, Robert Chamblet – New York: G P Putnam, 1884 – 1mf – 9 – 0-8370-2044-1 – 1985-0044 – us A.T.L.A. [210]

TRAVELS IN KORDOFAN; EMBRACING A DESCRIPTION OF THAT PROVINCE OF EGYPT, AND OF SOME OF THE BORDERING COUNTRIES. / Pallme, Ignatius – London: J. Madden and Co., 1844.356p – 1 – us U.W. Library [910]

TRAVELS IN LYCIA, MILYAS AND CIBYRATIS / Spratt, T A B & Forbes, E A – London, 1847. B-7391 1 – 9 – ne IDC [910]

TRAVELS IN NORTH AND CENTRAL CHINA / Birch, John Grant – London: Hurst and Blackett Ltd., 1902. xvi,379p. illus., plates – 1 – us U.W. Library [910]

TRAVELS IN PALESTINE: THROUGH THE COUNTRIES OF BASHAN AND GILEAD, EAST OF THE RIVER JORDAN.. / Buckingham, James Silk – London: Longman, Hurst, Rees, Orme, and Brown, 1822. 2v. ill – 1 – us U.W. Library [910]

TRAVELS IN SOUTH AFRICA / Campbell, J – London. 1815. BA-148 2 – 8 – ne IDC [910]

TRAVELS IN SOUTH-EASTERN ASIA, EMBRACING HINDUSTAN, MALAYA, SIAM, AND CHINA / Malcom, H – London. 2v. 1839 – 8mf – 9 – ne IDC [910]

TRAVELS IN SOUTHERN AFRICA IN THE YEARS 1803, 1804, 1805 AND 1806 / Lichtenstein, Hinrich – London. 2v. 1812 – 1r – 1 – us Ross [910]

TRAVELS IN THE AIR / ed by Glaisher, James – London: Bentley, 1871. 118 illus. xiii,398p. 12 plates – 1 – us U.W. Library [910]

TRAVELS IN THE CONFEDERATE STATES – Selected titles from E.M. Coulter's Travels in the Confederate States. 485v – 9 – us Primary [978]

TRAVELS IN THE EAST INDIAN ARCHIPELAGO / Bickmore, A S – London, 1868 – 7mf – 9 – ne IDC [910]

TRAVELS IN THE GREAT DESERT OF SAHARA / Richardson, J – 2v. London. 1848. BA-348 2 – 8 – ne IDC [910]

TRAVELS IN THE HIMALAYAN PROVINCES OF HINDUSTAN AND THE PANJAB, IN LADAKH & KASHMIR, IN PESHAWAR, KABUL, KUNDUZ, & BOKHARA, 1819-25. / Moorcraft, William – From original journals and correspondence, by Horace Hayman Wilson. London: J. Murray, 1841. 2v. illus – 1 – us U.W. Library [910]

TRAVELS IN THE INTERIOR OF AFRICA / Mollien, Gaspard T – London. 1820. BA-341 2 – 8 – ne IDC [910]

TRAVELS IN THE INTERIOR OF AFRICA / Park, Mungo – 1795, 1796 and 1797 – 9mf – 7 – uk Microform Academic [910]

TRAVELS IN THE INTERIOR OF AFRICA FROM THE CAPE OF GOOD HOPE TO MOROCCO / Damberger, Christian F – 2v. London. 1801. BA-140 2 – 8 – ne IDC [956]

TRAVELS IN THE INTERIOR OF SOUTH AFRICA / Chapman – 2v. London. 1868. BA-166 3 – 8 – ne IDC [910]

TRAVELS IN THE INTERIOR OF SOUTHERN AFRICA / Burchell, W J – London. 1822-24. B-5263 2 – 8 – ne IDC [910]

TRAVELS IN THE NEW SOUTH 1 AND 2 – Life in the post-Civil War South, 1865-1900, 1900-55. 611v – 9 – us Primary [978]

TRAVELS IN THE OLD SOUTH 1, 2, 3 – 1607-1860. 1149v – 9 – us Primary [978]

TRAVELS IN THE TIMANEE, KOORANKO, AND SOOLIMA COUNTRIES IN WESTERN AFRICA / Laing, Alexander G – London. 1825. BA-329 2 – 8 – ne IDC [910]

TRAVELS IN THE TRACK OF THE TEN THOUSAND GREEKS.. / Ainsworth, William Francis – London: J.W. Parker, 1844. xv,248p. fold. map – 1 – us U.W. Library [910]

TRAVELS IN THE WEST AND SOUTHWEST – American history from the end of the Civil War to the 1920s – 9 – us Primary [910]

TRAVELS IN VARIOUS COUNTRIES OF EUROPE, ASIA AND AFRICA / Clarke, E D – v. 1. London. 1810; v. 2, sect. 1-3. London. 1812-16; v. 3, sect. 1-2. London. 1819-23. B-5587 2 – 8 – ne IDC [910]

TRAVELS IN WEST AFRICA, CONGO FRANCAIS, CORISCO AND CAMEROON / Kingsley, M H – London. 1897. BA-324 2 – 8 – ne IDC [910]

TRAVELS INTO BOKHARA; BEING THE ACCOUNT OF A JOURNEY FROM INDIA TO CABOOL / Burnes, A – Z-263 2. 3 v. 1834 – 8 – ne IDC [910]

TRAVELS INTO THE INLAND PARTS OF AFRICA / Moore, F – London. 1738. BA-114 2 – 8 – ne IDC [910]

TRAVELS INTO...EUROPE AND ASIA,.. / Avril, P – London, 1693. 191+178pp. KHT-696-1 – 9 – ne IDC [910]

THE TRAVELS, OBSERVATIONS, AND EXPERIENCE OF A YANKEE STONECUTTER / Greenough, Horatio – 1852 – 9 – 15.00 – us Scholars' Facs [760]

TRAVELS THROUGH BARBARY : IN A SERIES OF LETTERS, WRITTEN FROM NUMIDIA, IN THE YEARS 1785 AND 1786 AND CONTAINING AN ACCOUNT OF THE CUSTOMS AND MANNERS OF THE MOORS, AND BEDOUIN ARABS – London: C Forster, [1791?] – us Res Libr [910]

TRAVELS THROUGH CENTRAL AFRICA TO TIMBUCTOO / Caillie, R – 2v. London. 1830. BA-289 2 – 8 – ne IDC [910]

TRAVELS THROUGH NORTH AND SOUTH CAROLINA, GEORGIA, EAST AND WEST FLORIDA / Bartram, W – Philadelphia. 1791. B-5835 2 – 8 – ne IDC [910]

TRAVELS THROUGH THAT PART OF NORTH AMERICA FORMERLY CALLED LOUISIANA / Bossu, N – Trans. from the French by J. R. Forster, illus. with Notes to Natural History; A Flora Americae Septentrionalis; An Abstract from Peter Loefling's travels. 2 V. London. 1771. B-2289 2 – 8 – ne IDC [910]

TRAVELS TO DISCOVER THE SOURCE OF THE NILE, IN THE YEARS 1768-1773 / Bruce, James – 5v. 1790 – 2r – 1 – us Ross [960]

TRAVELS WITH A DONKEY IN THE CEVENNES / Stevenson, Robert Louis – London: C. Kegan Paul & Co., 1879 – 1 roll – 1 – 1-55879-813-7 – uk Libr Preservation [830]

A TRAVERS L'ARMENIE RUSSE... / Chantre, B – Paris: Hachette, 1893 – 1 – F187.86 – fr Armell [910]

TRAVERS MADGE / Herford, Brooke – 1868 – 9 – us A.T.L.A. [240]

Travers, Nicolas *see*
– CONCILIA PROVINCIAE TURONENSIS
– HISTOIRE CIVILE, POLITIQUE ET RELIGIEUSE DE LA VILLE ET DU COMTE DE NANTES...

TRAVERSE BAY EAGLE – Traverse City. Mich. 1898-1901 – 1 – us UMI [071]

Traverso, Leone *see* STUDI DI LETTERATURA GRECA E TEDESCA

Traversy, Paul *see* BIBLIOGRAPHIE DE L'OEUVRE MUSICALE DU FRERE BARNABE, S.C., DOCTEUR EN MUSIQUE, MEMBRE DE LA SOCIETE DES COMPOSITEURS CANADIENS

TRAVESSIA DA AFRICA PELO DR LACERDA E ALMEIDA : EDICAO ACRESCIDA DO DIARIO DA VIAGEM DE MOCAMBIQUE PARA OS RIOS DE SENA E DO DIARIO – [Lisboa?]: Divisao de Publ e Biblioteca Agencia geral das Colonias, 1936 – us Res Libr [910]

Trawick, A M *see*
– THE CITY CHURCH AND ITS SOCIAL MISSION
– THE NEW VOICE IN RACE ADJUSTMENTS

LA TRAYECTORIA HOSPITALARIA DE LA ARMADA ESPANOLA. MADRID, 1944 / Clavijo y Clavijo, Salvador – Madrid: Razon y Fe, 1946 – 1 – sp Bibl Santa Ana [350]

TRE QUARTETTI PER DUE VIOLINI, VIOLA E VIOLONCELLO / Gyrowetz, Adalbert – opera 47. ca.1798 – 9 – us Sibley [780]

TRE SONATE E UNA TOCCATA PER IL CEMBALO / Piccinni, Nicolo – 178-? – 9 – us Sibley [780]

TRE SORELLE CORONE DI SONETTI... : SOPRA LA FELICISSIMA VITTORIA NAUALE / Tiepolo, G – Vinegia, 1572 – 1mf – 9 – H-8335/1 – ne IDC [945]

TRE TALER VED TAENKTE LEILIGHEDER / Kierkegaard, Soren – Kjobenhavn: C.A. Reitzel, 1845 – 1mf – us A.T.L.A. [190]

Treacher, W H *see* REPORT ON BRITISH NORTH BORNEO FROM 1 JUL TO 31 DEC 1882

Treacy, James J *see* TRIBUTES OF PROTESTANT WRITERS TO THE TRUTH AND BEAUTY OF CATHOLICITY

TREADWAY'S LAW REPORTS / South Carolina. Supreme Court – (A Pre-NRS title) – v1-2. 1812-1816 (all publ) – 11mf – 9 – $16.50 – LLMC 94-011 – us L.L.M.C. [340]

TREASON TRIAL – 47r – 1 – sa Microfile [960]

TREASON TRIAL 1970: DAVID LANDSANA AND ELEVEN OTHERS / Sierra Leone. Court of Appeals – 4r – 1 – $198.00 – us African Imprint [340]

A TREASTISE ON THE LAW OF OFFICIAL BONDS AND OTHER PENAL BONDS / Murfree, William Law – St Louis: Review, 1885. 646p. LL-554 – 1 – us L of C Photodup [340]

TREASURE ISLAND / Stevenson, Robert Louis – London, New York: Cassell & Company, 1883 – 1 roll – 1 – 1-55879-700-9 – uk Libr Preservation [830]

THE TREASURE OF HEAVEN / Corelli, Marie – British Fiction Archive: Unit 1 – 9 – uk Bell [830]

THE TREASURE OF PEYRE GAILLARD / Bennett, John – Typescript novel ca.1905. Issued by Century in 1906. 5 fiches – 9 – us South Carolina Historical [830]

THE TREASURE OF THREE EGYPTIAN PRINCESSES / Winlock, H E – 1948 – 9 – $10.00 – us I.R.C. [930]

TREASURER'S EXAMINATION RECORD / Allen County. Ohio. Probate Court – 1894-1906 – 1r – 1 – $32.50r – us Archival [324]

TREASURES OF HOLKHAM HALL LIBRARY / Holkham Hall. Norfolk. England – Selections of Mss. illuminations – 14 – uk Microform Academic [941]

A TREASURIE OR STOREHOUSE OF SIMILES / Cawdrey, Robert – 1600. 885p. (English Linguistics Series 1500-1800) – 9 – us UMI [420]

TREASURY BULLETIN / U.S. Treasury Department – (Earlier vols entitled: Bulletin of the Treasury. Lacking: 1939-42. Updates available) – 1939-Sept 1992 – 847mf – 9 – $1,270.00 – LLMC 81-218 – us L.L.M.C. [336]

TREASURY DECISIONS, 1899-1966 : COVERING TREASURY DECISIONS NO 20468-56557 / U.S. Treasury Department – (Later coverage by: Customs Bulletin. IRS Cumulative Bulletin) – v1 101 (all publ) – 1006mf – 9 – $1,509.00 – LLMC 78-234A – us L.L.M.C. [336]

TREASURY DECISIONS, 1899-1966 *see* SYNOPSIS OF SUNDRY DECISIONS OF THE TREASURY DEPARTMENT, 1868-1898

TREASURY DECISIONS, INTERNAL REVENUE : 1898-1942 / U.S. Treasury Department – all publ – 189mf – 9 – $283.00 – LLMC 78-044 – us L.L.M.C. [336]

TREASURY DECISIONS, INTERNAL REVENUE, 1898-1942 *see*
– DIGEST OF DECISIONS UNDER THE CUSTOMS REVENUE LAWS
– DIGEST OF INCOME TAX RULINGS

TREASURY DEPARTMENT EMPLOYEE CARICATURES / U.S. Library of Congress. Prints and Photographs Division – 107 drawings and momentos satirize staff working during late 19th and early 20th centuries. 1 reel. P&P9549 – 1 – 23.00r – us L of C Photodup [080]

THE TREASURY OF AMERICAN SACRED SONG : WITH NOTES EXPLANATORY AND BIOGRAPHICAL / Horder, W Garrett – London, New York: H. Frowde, 1900 – 1mf – us A.T.L.A. [780]

TREASURY PAPERS : SERIES ONE: PAPERS OF THE ECONOMIC SECTION, 1941-1961 – (Part 1: T230/1-36 12r $1,500. Part 2: T230/37-73 ca 12r $1,500. Part 3: T230/74-109 ca 12r $1,500. Part 4: T230/110-145 ca 12r $1,500) – Marlborough: Adam Matthew Publications, 1993 – 1 – uk Matthew [336]

Treat, John Harvey *see* THE CATHOLIC FAITH

TREATIES / Canada. Department of External Affairs – 1928- – 9 – cn Micromedia [971]

TREATIES AND ACTS OF CONGRESS RELATING TO THE PANAMA CANAL : ANNOTATED / McGuigan, J J – (With suppls 1-20 1922-34) – Mount Hope, CZ: Panama Canal Press, 1922 – 7mf – 9 – $10.50 – LLMC 82-100D Title 14 – us L.L.M.C. [340]

TREATIES AND ACTS OF CONGRESS RELATING TO THE PANAMA CANAL – Washington: GPO, 1917 – 3mf – 9 – $4.50 – LLMC 82-100D Title 22 – us L.L.M.C. [324]

TREATIES AND CONVENTIONS CONCLUDED BETWEEN THE U.S. AND OTHER POWERS SINCE JULY 4 1776 / U.S. Department of State – 2bks. J C B Davis 1873; John H Haswell 1889 eds (all publ) – 27mf – 9 – $40.50 – LLMC 80-915 – us L.L.M.C. [975]

TREATIES AND CORRESPONDENCE,...TO BOTH HOUSES OF PARLIAMENT,... – London, 1809 – 3mf – 9 – ILM-621/1 – ne IDC [327]

TREATIES AND ENGAGEMENTS AFFECTING THE MALAY STATES AND BORNEO / ed by Maxwell, William G – Reel 4001. 1924 – 1 – ja CEACS [950]

TREATIES AND OTHER INTERNATIONAL ACTS OF THE UNITED STATES / U.S. Department of State – (This series superseded: The Treaty Series. The Executive Agreement Series) – Nos 1501-10981. 1945-79 (all publ) – 2248mf – 9 – $3,372.00 – LLMC 80-908 – us L.L.M.C. [975]

TREATIES AND OTHER INTERNATIONAL ACTS OF THE UNITED STATES *see* THE EXECUTIVE AGREEMENT SERIES

TREATIES BETWEEN THE UNITED STATES OF AMERICA AND CHINA, JAPAN, LEWCHEW AND SIAM,... – Hongkong; 1862 – 2mf – 9 – ILM-2930/1 – ne IDC [327]

TREATIES, ETC : SBORNIK DE ISTVUI USHCHIKH TORGOVYKH DOGOVOROV I INYKH KHOZI A ISTVENNYKH SOGLASHENI I SSSR, ZAKLI UCHENNYKH S INOSTRANNYMI GOSUDARSTVAMI / Soviet Union; ed by Narodny i komissariat po inostrannym delam – (Includes c.1: v.1 1935:July 15) – Moskva: Izd. NKID, 1935- – 1 – CSUXALJ8239-S – us Hoover Inst Photo [340]

TREATIES, ETC : SBORNIK DE ISTVUI USHCHIKH TORGOVYKH DOGOVOROV I INYKH KHOZI A ISTVENNYKH SOGLASHENI I SSSR, ZAKLI UCHENNYKH S INOSTRANNYMI GOSUDARSTVAMI / Soviet Union; ed by Narodny i komissariat po inostrannym delam – Moskva: Izd. NKID, 1935- – 1 – CSUXALJ8241-S – us Hoover Inst Photo [340]

TREATIES, ETC. RUSSIAN S.F.S.R., 1921 MAY 6 *see* SOGLASHENII A S GERMANIE I ZAKLI UCHENNYE V BERLINE 6 MAI A 1921 GODA

TREATIES, ETC. SOVIET UNION, 1920 FEB. 2 = MIRNY I DOGOVOR MEZHDU ROSSIE I I ESTONIE I – [Tartus: Bergamann'i Trukikoda, 1920] – 1 – CSUX91-B217 – us Hoover Inst Photo [340]

TREATIES, ETC. SOVIET UNION, 1921 SEPTEMBER 27 *see* VREMENNOE SOGLASHCHENIE [SIC] MEZHDU ROSSIE I I FINLANDIE I O SPLAVE LESNYKH MATERIALOV PO REKAM MINALANIOKI I TULEMANIOKI

TREATIES GOVERNING LAND WARFARE – (This pamphlet serves as a suppl to FM 27-10...Contains: Hague and Geneva Conventions) – Washington: GPO, 1970 – 4mf – 9 – $6.00 – LLMC 96-098 – us L.L.M.C. [340]

TREATIES IN FORCE / U.S. Department of State – (None publ 1957. Lacking: 1991. Upadates planned) – 1955-93 (annual) – 159mf – 9 – $239.00 – LLMC 80-918 – us L.L.M.C. [977]

TREATING STRAW FOR ANIMAL FEEDING : AN ASSESSMENT OF ITS TECHNICAL AND ECONOMIC FEASIBILITY – 1978 – 84p – it F.A.O. [636]

A TREATISE ADAPTED TO THE LAW AND PRACTICE OF THE SUPERIOR COURTS, AND OF TRIAL JUSTICES, DISTRICT, POLICE, AND MUNICIPAL COURTS, IN CRIMINAL CASES / Heard, Franklin Fiske – Boston: Little, Brown, 1879. 863p. LL-322 – 1 – us L of C Photodup [340]

A TREATISE, ANALYTICAL, CRITICAL AND HISTORICAL, ON SUCCESSIONS / Cross, Kimball Allyn – New Orleans, 1891. 580 p. LL-609 – 1 – us L of C Photodup [340]

A TREATISE CONCERNING THE LAWFULL SUBJECT OF BAPTISM / Spilsbery, John – London. 1652 – 1 – 5.00 – us Baptist [240]

A TREATISE CONCERNING THE LAWFULNESS OF INSTRUMENTAL MUSICK IN HOLY OFFICES / Dodwell, H – 1700 – 9 – us Sibley [780]

A TREATISE CONCERNING THE LAWFULNESS OF INSTRUMENTAL MUSICK IN HOLY OFFICES / Dodwell, H – To which is prefixed, a preface in Vindication of Mr. Newte's Sermon. Ed. 2. London. 1700. BP-241 1 – 9 – ne IDC [240]

A TREATISE EXPLANATORY OF THE PRINCIPLES CONSTITUTING THE PRACTICE AND THEORY OF THE VIOLONCELLO... / MacDonald, John – London: Monzani & Co, [1811] – 1 – us Sibley [780]

A TREATISE OF ENGLISH PARTICLES / Walker, William – 1655. 296p. (English Linguistics Series 1500-1800) – 9 – us UMI [420]

A TREATISE OF EQUITY / Ballow, Henry – 4th Amer. ed. Brookfield, Mass., Merriam, 1835. 2 v. in 1. LL-1070 – 1 – us L of C Photodup [340]

A TREATISE OF GOOD TASTE IN THE ART OF MUSICK / Geminiani, Francesco – 1749 – 9 – us Sibley [780]

A TREATISE OF JUSTIFYING FAITH / Fraser, James – Edinburgh, 1749 – 1 – us A.T.L.A. [240]

A TREATISE OF LITHOTOMY / Toletus, Franciscus – M 412. 1683 – 9 – ne IDC [616]

A TREATISE OF MUSIC, CONTAINING THE PRINCIPLES OF COMPOSITION / Rameau, Jean-Phillippe – Trans. into English. 1752 – 9 – us Sibley [780]

A TREATISE OF MUSICK, SPECULATIVE, PRACTICAL, AND HISTORICAL / Malcolm, A – 1721 – 9 – us Sibley [780]

A TREATISE OF ONE HUNDRED AND THIRTEENE DISEASES OF THE EYES AND EYE-LIDDES / Banister, R – 1622. M-299 – 9 – ne IDC [617]

A TREATISE OF SCHEMES AND TROPES 1550 BY RICHARD SHERRY AND HIS TRANSLATION OF / Sherry, Richard – The Education of children BY Desiderius Erasmus – 9 – $15.00 – us Scholars' Facs [410]

A TREATISE OF STOPS, POINTS OR PAUSES – Anon. 1680. 35p. (English Linguistics 1500-1800) – 9 – us UMI [420]

A TREATISE OF THE ASTHMA / Floyer, J – M-52. 4 pts. 1698 – 9 – ne IDC [610]

A TREATISE OF THE LAW OF BILLS OF EXCHANGE, PROMISSORY NOTES, BANK-NOTES AND CHECKS / Byles, John Barnard – 12th ed., with notes from the 6th American ed. London: Sweet, 1876. 580p. LL-107 – 1 – us L of C Photodup [340]

A TREATISE OF THE LAW OF LANDLORD AND TENANT APPLICABLE TO THE DOMINION OF CANADA / Clarko, Samuel Robinson – Toronto: Carswell, 1895. 00673. (Pre-1900 Canadiana) – 9 – cn C.I.H.M. [340]

A TREATISE OF THE LAW RELATIVE TO MERCHANT SHIPS AND SEAMEN. / Abbott, Charles – 2nd Amer. from the 3rd London ed. Newburyport, Little, 1810. 656 p. LL-463 – 1 – us L of C Photodup [340]

A TREATISE OF THE LAW RELATIVE TO MERCHANT SHIPS AND SEAMEN. / Abbott, Charles – 7th Eng. ed., 5th Amer. ed., Boston, Little & Brown, 1846. 1004 p. LL-804 – 1 – us L of C Photodup [340]

A TREATISE OF THE NATURAL GROUND AND PRINCIPLES OF HARMONY / Holder, W – P 325. 1731 – 9 – ne IDC [780]

A TREATISE OF THE RICKETS / Glisson, F – Trans. by Armin. M 358. 1651 – 9 – ne IDC [610]

A TREATISE OF THE SACRAMENTS / Bedford, Thomas – 1638 – 1 – $50.00 – us Presbyterian [240]

A TREATISE OF THE SCURVY / Lind, J – M 66. 1753 – 9 – ne IDC [610]

A TREATISE ON AMERICAN BUSINESS LAW, WITH ILLUSTRATIVE CASES. – Chicago, Walton School of Commerce, 1916-21. 7 v. LL-1331 – 1 – us L of C Photodup [340]

A TREATISE ON CHATTEL MORTGAGES FOR ILLINOIS / Hammon, Louis Lougee – St. Paul: Keefe-Davidson, 1901. 424p. LL-915 – 1 – us L of C Photodup [340]

A TREATISE ON CONTEMPT INCLUDING CIVIL AND CRIMINAL CONTEMPTS OF JUDICIAL TRIBUNALS, JUSTICES OF THE PEACE. / Rapalje, Stewart – New York, Strouse, 1884. 273 p. LL-1491 – 1 – us L of C Photodup [340]

A TREATISE ON CONTRACTS FOR FUTURE DELIVERY AND COMMERCIAL WAGERS, INCLUDING "OPTIONS," "FUTURES," AND "SHORT SALES." / Dewey, Thomas Henry – New York, Baker, Voorhis, 1886. 385 p. LL-514 – 1 – us L of C Photodup [340]

A TREATISE ON CONTRACTS, TORTS, DAMAGES, EVIDENCE, AND PRACTICE AND PROCEDURE IN CIVIL CASES...IN THE STATE OF ILLINOIS / Moore, Ira M – (4th ed. Chicago: Callaghan, 1900. 2v. LL-248) – 3rd ed. Chicago: Callaghan, 1889. 1532p. LL-657 – 1 – us L of C Photodup [340]

A TREATISE ON CONTRACTS, WITHIN THE JURISDICTION OF COURTS OF EQUITY / Newland, John – Philadelphia: Warner, 1821. 31, 543p. LL-1671 – 1 – us L of C Photodup [340]

A TREATISE ON COURTS-MARTIAL : TO WHICH IS ADDED AN ESSAY ON MILITARY PUNISHMENTS AND REWARDS / Adye, Stephen P – London: J Murray, 1786 – 3mf – 9 – $4.50 – LLMC 88-107 – us L.L.M.C. [340]

A TREATISE ON CRIMES AND MISDEMEANORS / Russell, William Oldnall – 7th American ed. from the 3rd London ed. Philadelphia: Johnson, 1853. 2v. LL-1144 – 1 – us L of C Photodup [340]

A TREATISE ON CRIMINAL LAW / Wharton, Francis A – 9th ed. Philadelphia, Kay, 1885. 2 v. LL-1615 – 1 – us L of C Photodup [340]

A TREATISE ON CRIMINAL LAW AND CRIMINAL PROCEDURE. / Chadman, Charles Erehart – Chicago: Drake, 1906. 333p. LL-674 – 1 – us L of C Photodup [340]

A TREATISE ON CRIMINAL LAW AND PRACTICE: COMPRISING GENERALLY THE STATUTES OF MISSOURI. / Kelley, Henry Smith – St. Joseph, St. Joseph Steam Printing Co., 1876. 570 p. LL-289 – 1 – us L of C Photodup [340]

A TREATISE ON CRIMINAL LAW AS APPLICABLE TO THE DOMINION OF CANADA / Clarke, Samuel Robinson – Toronto: R. Carswell, 1872. 00671. (Pre-1900 Canadiana) – 9 – cn C.I.H.M. [360]

A TREATISE ON CRIMINAL PLEADING AND PRACTICE. 8TH ED / Wharton, Francis A – Philadelphia, Kay, 1880. 804 p. LL-1533 – 1 – us L of C Photodup [340]

A TREATISE ON CRIMINAL PROCEDURE / Rapalje, Stewart – San Francisco. Bancroft-Whitney, 1889. 715 p. LL-1166 – 1 – us L of C Photodup [340]

A TREATISE ON DENTAL JURISPRUDENCE FOR DENTISTS AND LAWYERS. / Rehfuss, William F – Philadelphia, Wilmington Dental Mfg. Co., 1892. 468 p. LL-1053 – 1 – us L of C Photodup [340]

A TREATISE ON ELECTRIC LAW, COVERING THE LAW GOVERNING ALL ELECTRIC CORPORATIONS, USES AND APPLIANCES. / Joyce, Joseph Asbury – New York, Banks Law Publishing Co., 1900. 1133 p. LL-180 – 1 – us L of C Photodup [340]

A TREATISE ON EQUITY JURISPRUDENCE / Willard, John – Rev., cor., and enl. Albany, N.Y., Banks, 1903. 1077 p. LL-1015 – 1 – us L of C Photodup [340]

A TREATISE ON EVERYDAY LAW / Gerin-Lajoie, Marie – Montreal: Lovell, 1902. 203p. LL-2270 – 1 – us L of C Photodup [340]

A TREATISE ON EXTRADITION AND INTERSTATE RENDITION / Moore, John Bassett – Boston: Boston Book Co., 1891. 2v. LL-577 – 1 – us L of C Photodup [340]

A TREATISE ON EXTRAORDINARY LEGAL REMEDIES, EMBRACING MANDAMUS, QUO WARRANTO AND PROHIBITION / High, James Lambert – 3d ed. Chicago: Callaghan, 1896. 861p. LL-520 – 1 – us L of C Photodup [340]

A TREATISE ON EXTRAORDINARY RELIEF IN EQUITY AND AT LAW. COVERING: PART I-INJUNCTION. PART II-HABEAS CORPUS. / Spelling, Thomas Crisp – Boston, Little, Brown, 1893. 2 v. LL-1163 – 1 – us L of C Photodup [340]

A TREATISE ON FACTS; OR, THE WEIGHT AND VALUE OF EVIDENCE / Moore, Charles Church – Northport, Long Island, N.Y.: Thompson, 1908. 2v LL-587 – 1 – us L of C Photodup [340]

A TREATISE ON FEDERAL TAXES. / Black, Henry Campbell – (Supplement, 4th ed. Kansas City, MO, 1920. 157 p. Cumulative Supplement. Kansas City, MO, 1921. 252 p. 1922 Supplement. Kansas City, MO, 1922. 194 p) – 4th ed. Kansas City, Mo., Vernon, 1919. 704 p. LL-156 – 1 – us L of C Photodup [340]

A TREATISE ON FRAUDULENT CONVEYANCES AND CREDITORS' BILLS. / Wait, Frederick Scott – (3d ed. New York, Baker, Voorhis, 1897. 834 p. LL-1321. 1) – New York, Baker, Voorhis, 1884. 741 p. LL-1323 – 1 – us L of C Photodup [340]

A TREATISE ON GONORRHOEA VIRULENTA AND LUES VENEREA / Bell, B – 2V. M-38. 1793 – 9 – ne IDC [610]

A TREATISE ON HARMONY / Day, A – London: Cramer, Beale, and Co, 1845 – 1 – us Sibley [780]

A TREATISE ON HARMONY / Pepusch, J C – 1731. The second edition alter'd, enlarg'd, and illustrated – 9 – us Sibley [780]

A TREATISE ON HARMONY: CONTAINING THE CHIEF RULES FOR COMPOSING IN TWO, THREE, AND FOUR PARTS / Pepusch, J C – P 735. 1731 – 9 – ne IDC [780]

A TREATISE ON HOMESTEAD AND EXEMPTION LAWS / Thompson, Seymour Dwight – St Louis: F H Thompson & Co, 1878 – 9mf – 9 – $13.50 – LLMC 95-054 – us L.L.M.C. [340]

A TREATISE ON INSPIRATION, IN WHICH THE PRETENCE TO EXTRAORDINARY INSPIRATION IS CONSIDERED AND CLEARLY AND FULLY REFUTED – York, 1799 – 1mf – 9 – MP-597/1 – ne IDC [240]

A TREATISE ON INSTRUCTIONS TO JURIES IN CIVIL AND CRIMINAL CASES. / Blashfield, De Witt Clinton – St. Paul, Keefe-Davidson, 1902. 1068 p. LL-596 – 1 – us L of C Photodup [340]

A TREATISE ON INTERNATIONAL LAW... / Hall, W E – Oxford, 1884 – 9mf – 1 – ILM-106/1 – ne IDC [327]

A TREATISE ON JUSTIFICATION, OR THE DISPUTATIO DE JUSTITIA HABITUALI ET ACTUALI / Davenant, John – 1631. Trans. from Latin. 2v 1844-46 – 1 – us A.T.L.A. [120]

A TREATISE ON LOGIC, OR, THE LAWS OF PURE THOUGHT : COMPRISING BOTH THE ARISTOTELIC AND HAMILTONIAN ANALYSES OF LOGICAL FORMS, AND SOME CHAPTERS OF APPLIED LOGIC / Bowen, Francis – Cambridge: Sever and Francis, 1864 – 2mf – us A.T.L.A. [160]

A TREATISE ON MADNESS / Battie, William – London: J Whiston and B White, 1758 – 2mf – 9 – $3.00 – LLMC 92-235 – us L.L.M.C. [340]

A TREATISE ON MALACOLOGY; OR THE NATURAL CLASSIFICATION OF SHELLS AND SHELLFISH / Swainson, W – Z 825 2. 1840 – 8 – ne IDC [590]

A TREATISE ON MILITARY LAW : AND THE JURISDICTION, CONSTITUTION, AND PROCEDURE OF MILITARY COURTS, WITH A SUMMARY OF THE RULES OF EVIDENCE AS APPLICABLE TO SUCH COURTS / Ives, Rollin A – 2nd ed, NY: D van Nostrand, 1881 – 5mf – 9 – $7.50 – LLMC 96-075 – us L.L.M.C. [340]

A TREATISE ON MILITARY LAW AND THE PRACTICE OF COURTS-MARTIAL / Benet, Stephen Vincent – 4th ed. New York, Van Nostrand, 1864. 389 p. LL-1547 – 1 – us L of C Photodup [340]

TREATISE ON NAVAL COURTS-MARTIAL / Delafons, John – London: P Steel, 1805 – 5mf – 9 – $7.50 – LLMC 89-021 – us L.L.M.C. [340]

A TREATISE ON NAVIGATION BY STEAM: COMPRISING A HISTORY OF THE STEAM ENGINE : AN ESSAY TOWARDS A SYSTEM OF NAVAL TACTICS PECULIAR TO STEAM NAVIGATION / Ross, John – 2pts. 2nd ed. 1837 – 9 – $20.00 – uk Libr Preservation [623]

A TREATISE ON PAINTING / Cennini, C – O-983 1. 1844 – 9 – ne IDC [750]

A TREATISE ON PLEADING, AND PARTIES TO ACTIONS. / Chitty, Joseph – (14th Amer. ed. from the 6th London ed. Springfield, MA: Merriam, 1872. 3v. LL-682) – 13th Amer. ed. from the 6th London ed. Springfield, MA: Merriam, 1859. 3v. LL-1181 – 1 – us L of C Photodup [340]

A TREATISE ON PLEADING, AND PARTIES TO ACTIONS, WITH SECOND AND THIRD VOLUMES, CONTAINING PRECEDENTS OF PLEADINGS, AND AN APPENDIX OF FORMS / Chitty, Joseph – v1-3. 1844 – 1 – $95.00 – 0-89093-033-3 – us UPA [941]

A TREATISE ON PLEADING AND PRACTICE IN EQUITY IN THE COURTS OF THE UNITED STATES. / Foster, Roger – Boston: Boston Book Co., 1890. 822p. LL-766 – 1 – us L of C Photodup [340]

A TREATISE ON PLEADING AND PRACTICE IN THE COURTS OF RECORD OF NEW YORK. / Nichols, Clark Asahel – (1909 Suppl. St. Paul: Keefe-Davidson, 1909. 500p. LL-639. 1914 Suppl. New York: Banks, 1914. 801p. LL-639) – Albany: Bender, 1904-08. 5v. LL-639 – 1 – us L of C Photodup [340]

A TREATISE ON PLEADING AND PRACTICE UNDER THE CODE OF CIVIL PROCEDURE / Maxwell, Samuel – (3rd ed. Lincoln, Neb.: Journal Co., 1883. 802p. LL-484) – Lincoln, Neb.: Journal Co., 1880. 618p. LL-797 – 1 – us L of C Photodup [340]

A TREATISE ON PRACTICAL NAVIGATION AND SEAMANSHIP / Nichelson, William – 1796 – 9 – $20.00 – uk Libr Preservation [623]

A TREATISE ON PRACTICAL SEAMANSHIP / Hutchinson, William – 1777 – 9 – $20.00 – uk Libr Preservation [623]

A TREATISE ON PRACTICE IN THE COURTS OF COMMON PLEAS OF PENNSYLVANIA / Brewster, Frederick Carroll – 2d ed. Philadelphia, Kay, 1896. 2 v. LL-633 – 1 – us L of C Photodup [340]

A TREATISE ON PRACTICE IN THE COURTS OF PENNSYLVANIA / Brewster, Frederick Carroll – Philadelphia, Bisel, 1891. 2 v. LL-720 – 1 – us L of C Photodup [340]

A TREATISE ON PRIVATE CORPORATIONS. / Smith, William Wharton – Philadelphia, Rees, Welsh, 1889. 69 p. LL-98 – 1 – us L of C Photodup [340]

A TREATISE ON RELICS / Calvin, John – Edinburgh: Johnstone and Hunter, 1854 – 1mf – us A.T.L.A. [240]

A TREATISE ON RUPTURES / Pott, P – M 73. 1756 – 9 – ne IDC [610]

A TREATISE ON STOCK AND STOCKHOLDERS, COVERING WATERED STOCK, TRUSTS, CONSOLIDATIONS AND HOLDING COMPANIES / Helliwell, Arthur Llewellyn – St. Paul: Keefe-Davidson, 1903. 1071p. LL-529 – 1 – us L of C Photodup [340]

A TREATISE ON STOCK WITHOUT PAR VALUE OF ORDINARY BUSINESS CORPORATIONS / Wickersham, Cornelius Wendell – Albany, N.Y., Bender, 1927. 188 p. LL-1266 – 1 – us L of C Photodup [340]

A TREATISE ON THE ADMISSIBILITY OF PAROLE EVIDENCE IN RESPECT TO WRITTEN INSTRUMENTS / Browne, Irving – New York, Strouse, 1893. 494 p. LL-1418 – 1 – us L of C Photodup [340]

A TREATISE ON THE AMERICAN LAW OF ELECTIONS / McCrary, George Washington – 4th ed. Chicago: Callaghan, 1897. 608p LL-295 – 1 – us L of C Photodup [340]

A TREATISE ON THE AMERICAN LAW OF LANDLORD AND TENANT..., 4TH ED / Taylor, John Neilson – (5th ed. Boston, Little, Brown, 1869. 736 p. LL-1029. 1. 6th ed. Boston, Little, Brown, 1873. 769 p. LL-1032. 1) – Boston, Little, Brown, 1866. 739 1 p. LL-1031 – 1 – us L of C Photodup [340]

A TREATISE ON THE AMERICAN LAW OF REAL PROPERTY / Washburn, Emory – 3d ed. Boston Little, Brown, 1868. 3 v. LL-818 – 1 – us L of C Photodup [340]

A TREATISE ON THE ANGLO-AMERICAN SYSTEM OF EVIDENCE IN TRIALS AT COMMON LAW...2ND ED / Wigmore, John Henry – (A supplement. 1923-1933. Boston, 1934. 1395 p) – Boston, Little, Brown, 1923. 5 v. LL-1436 – 1 – us L of C Photodup [340]

A TREATISE ON THE ART OF MUSIC / Jones, W – (Signed by author) – Colchester: W Keymar, 1784 – 1 – us Sibley [780]

A TREATISE ON THE AUGUSTINIAN DOCTRINE OF PREDESTINATION / Mozley, James Bowling – (Includes bibliographical references) – 2nd ed. New York: E P Dutton, 1878 – 1mf – 9 – 0-8370-4022-1 – 1985-2022 – us A.T.L.A. [240]

A TREATISE ON THE BANKRUPTCY LAW OF THE UNITED STATES / Remington, Harold – Charlottesville, Va.: Michie, 1908-10. 3v. LL-564 – 1 – us L of C Photodup [340]

TREATISE ON THE BLOOD, INFLAMMATION AND GUNSHOT WOUNDS / Hunter, J – M-62. 1794 – 9 – ne IDC [610]

A TREATISE ON THE BRITISH FRESHWATER ALGAE / West, G S & Fritsch, F E – 7139. 1927 – 9 – ne IDC [580]

A TREATISE ON THE CIVIL JURISDICTION OF JUSTICE OF THE PEACE, IN THE STATE OF TEXAS, INCLUDING FORMS OF PROCESS / Sayles, John – 4th ed. St. Louis: Gilbert, 1984. 741 (i.e. 939)p. LL-1662 – 1 – us L of C Photodup [340]

A TREATISE ON THE CIVIL JURISDICTION OF JUSTICES OF THE PEACE, AND THE POWERS AND DUTIES OF CONSTABLES, IN THE STATE OF ILLINOIS / Moore, Ira M – Chicago: Callaghan, 1875. 1020p. LL-833 – 1 – us L of C Photodup [340]

A TREATISE ON THE CIVIL JURISDICTION OF JUSTICES OF THE PEACE IN THE STATE OF NEW-YORK / Cowen, Esek, 1787-1844 – (3rd ed., Albany, Gould, 1844. 2 v. LL-646) – 2d ed. Albany, Gould, 1841. 2 v. LL-1481 – 1 – us L of C Photodup [340]

A TREATISE ON THE COMMON AND STATUTE LAW OF THE STATE OF NEW YORK RELATING TO INSOLVENT DEBTORS. / Bishop, James Lord – (A supplement to the treatise on insolvent debtors. New York, 1888. 92 p. LL-1435) – 2nd ed. New York, Baker, Voorhis, 1884. 575 p – 1 – us L of C Photodup [340]

A TREATISE ON THE COMMON SOLE (SOLEA VULGARIS) / Cunningham, J T – Z-2093 2. 1890 – 8 – ne IDC [590]

A TREATISE ON THE CONSTITUTION AND JURISDICTION OF THE UNITED STATES COURTS ON PLEADING, PRACTICE AND PROCEDURE THEREIN. / Garland, Augustus Hill – Philadelphia: Johnson, 1898. 2v. LL-169 – 1 – us L of C Photodup [340]

A TREATISE ON THE CONSTITUTIONAL LIMITATIONS : WHICH REST UPON THE LEGISLATIVE POWER OF THE STATES OF THE AMERICAN UNION / Cooley, Thomas M – 7th ed. Boston: Little, Brown, 1903 – 12mf – 9 – $18.00 – LLMC95-059 – us L.L.M.C. [323]

A TREATISE ON THE CONSTITUTIONAL LIMITATIONS : WHICH REST UPON THE LEGISLATIVE POWER OF THE STATES OF THE AMERICAN UNION / Cooley, Thomas McIntyre – Boston: Little, Brown, 1868 – 8mf – 9 – $12.00 – LLMC 95-056 – us L.L.M.C. [323]

A TREATISE ON THE CONSTRUCTION OF LIMITATIONS IN WHICH THE WORDS "ISSUE" AND "CHILD" OCCUR, AND ON THE STATUTE 1 VICTORIA, C. 26, S. 29 / Prior, John V – London: Saunders and Benning, 1839. 203p. LL-1683 – 1 – us L of C Photodup [340]

A TREATISE ON THE CONSTRUCTION OR INTERPRETATION OF COMMERCIAL AND TRADE CONTRACTS / Jones, Dwight Arven – New York, Baker, Voorhis, 1886. 554 p. LL-402 – 1 – us L of C Photodup [340]

A TREATISE ON THE CRIMINAL LAW OF THE UNITED STATES / Wharton, Francis A – 6th and rev. ed. Philadelphia, Kay, 1868. 3 v. LL-1631 – 1 – us L of C Photodup [340]

A TREATISE ON THE DISEASES OF THE HEART AND GREAT VESSELS / Hope, J – M 60. 1832 – 9 – ne IDC [616]

A TREATISE ON THE DOCTRINES OF RES ADJUDICATA AND STARE DECISIS / Wells, John Cleland – (Des Moines, Ia., Mills, 1879. 621 p. LL 757. 1) – Des Moines, Ia., Mills, 1878. 621 p. LL-1489 – 1 – us L of C Photodup [340]

A TREATISE ON THE ELEMENTS OF LAW / Lee, J Ross – Ada, O., Wagner, 1886. 395 p. LL-423 – 1 – us L of C Photodup [340]

A TREATISE ON THE FEDERAL CORPORATION TAX LAW. / Frost, Thomas Gold – Albany, N.Y.: Bender, 1911. 321p. LL-1256 – 1 – us L of C Photodup [340]

A TREATISE ON THE FEDERAL CORPORATION TAX LAW OF 1909. / Machen, Arthur Webster – Boston, Little, Brown, 1910. 269 p. LL-1261 – 1 – us L of C Photodup [340]

A TREATISE ON THE FOREIGN POWERS... / Hall, W E – Oxford, 1894 – 4mf – 1 – ILM-183/1 – ne IDC [327]

A TREATISE ON THE GEOGRAPHY AND CLASSIFICATION OF ANIMALS / Swainson, W – 2055 2. 1835 – 8 – ne IDC [590]

A TREATISE ON THE HIGH OPERATION FOR THE STONE / Cheselden, W – M 46. 1723 – 9 – ne IDC [617]

A TREATISE ON THE INSPIRATION OF THE HOLY SCRIPTURES / Elliott, Charles – (Includes a subject index) – Edinburgh: T & T Clark, 1877 – 1mf – 9 – 0-8370-3057-9 – 1985-1057 – us A.T.L.A. [220]

TREATISE ON THE INSPIRATION OF THE HOLY SCRIPTURES / Elliott, Charles – Edinburgh: T.&T. Clark, 1877. 1 fiche – 9 – us A.T.L.A. [240]

A TREATISE ON THE INVESTIGATION OF TITLES TO REAL ESTATE IN ONTARIO: WITH A PRECEDENT FOR AN ABSTRACT / Armour, Edward Douglas – Toronto: Carswell, 1887. 00023. (Pre-1900 Canadiana) – 9 – cn C.I.H.M. [340]

A TREATISE ON THE JURISDICTION AND PROCEEDINGS OF JUSTICES OF THE PEACE IN CIVIL SUITS / Griffith, William – 1st ed. Burlington N.J. Elderkin & Miller, 1796. 272 21p. LL-1691 – 1 – us L of C Photodup [340]

A TREATISE ON THE JURISDICTION OF CIVIL AND CRIMINAL PROCEEDINGS IN THE COURT FOR THE TRIAL OF SMALL CAUSES IN NEW JERSEY / Honeyman, Abraham Van Doren – Somerville N.J.: Honeyman & Rowe, 1876. 539 1p. LL-537 – 1 – us L of C Photodup [340]

A TREATISE ON THE LAW AND PRACTICE IN JUSTICES' COURTS, AS DETERMINED BY THE STATUTES AND DECISIONS OF THE STATES OF CALIFORNIA, COLORADO, NEVADA, AND OREGON... / Cowdery, Jabez Franklin – (Supplement. San Francisco, 1900. 589 p) – San Francisco, Bancroft-Whitney, 1889. 2 v. LL-68 – 1 – us L of C Photodup [340]

A TREATISE ON THE LAW AND PRACTICE OF VOLUNTARY ASSIGNMENTS FOR THE BENEFIT OF CREDITORS. / Burrill, Alexander Mansfield – New York, Voorhies, 1853. 623 p. LL-1460 – 1 – us L of C Photodup [340]

A TREATISE ON THE LAW AND PROCEEDINGS IN BANKRUPTCY / Loveland, Franklin Olds – 2nd ed. Cincinnati, Anderson, 1904. 1422 p. LL-21 – 1 – us L of C Photodup [340]

TREATISE ON THE LAW GOVERNING NUISANCES. / Joyce, Joseph Asbury – Albany, N.Y., Bender, 1906. 866 p. LL-252 – 1 – us L of C Photodup [340]

A TREATISE ON THE LAW OF ATTACHMENTS IN CIVIL CASES. / Kneeland, Stillman Foster – New York, Diossy, 1884. 722 p. LL-746 – 1 – us L of C Photodup [340]

A TREATISE ON THE LAW OF BAILMENTS, INCLUDING CARRIERS, INNKEEPERS, AND PLEDGE / Schouler, James – 2d ed. Boston: Little, Brown, 1887. 795p. LL-1313 – 1 – us L of C Photodup [340]

A TREATISE ON THE LAW OF BANKS AND BANKING / Morse, John Torrey – 4th ed. Boston: Little, Brown, 1903. 2v. LL-827 – I – us L of C Photodup [340]

A TREATISE ON THE LAW OF BILLS AND NOTES, CHECKS, INCLUDING THE TEST OF THE NEGOTIABLE INSTRUMENTS LAW OF NEW YORK, CONNECTICUT, COLORADO, FLORIDA, VIRGINIA, MARYLAND, AND THE DISTRICT OF COLUMBIA / Tiedeman, Christopher Gustavus – St. Louis, Thomas, 1898. 621 p. LL-1115 – 1 – us L of C Photodup [340]

A TREATISE ON THE LAW OF BILLS OF EXCHANGE, CHECKS ON BANKERS, PROMISSORY NOTES, BANKERS' CASH NOTES, AND BANKNOTES / Chitty, Joseph – London: Brooke and Rider etc. 1799. 286p. LL-11 – 1 – us L of C Photodup [340]

A TREATISE ON THE LAW OF BUILDING AND BUILDINGS. / Lloyd, Augustus Parlett – Boston, Houghton, Mifflin, 1888. 618 p. LL-805 – 1 – us L of C Photodup [340]

A TREATISE ON THE LAW OF BUILDING AND LOAN ASSOCIATIONS...2ND ED / Thompson, Charles Nebeker – Chicago, Callaghan, 1899. 832 p. LL-1122 – 1 – us L of C Photodup [340]

A TREATISE ON THE LAW OF CASEMENTS / Gale, Charles James – (5th ed. London: Sweet, 1876. 760p. LL-113) – New York: Halsted and Voorhies, 1840. 352p. LL-460 – 1 – us L of C Photodup [340]

A TREATISE ON THE LAW OF CHATTEL MORTGAGES / Pingrey, Darius Harlan – Jersey City, N.J.: Linn, 1891. 767p. LL-1119 – 1 – us L of C Photodup [340]

A TREATISE ON THE LAW OF CITIZENSHIP IN THE UNITED STATES / Webster, Prentiss – Albany, 1891 – 4mf – 9 – ILM-3162/1 – us L of C Photodup [340]

A TREATISE ON THE LAW OF COMMERCIAL PAPER. / Randolph, Joseph Fitz – Jersey City, N.J., Linn, 1886-88. 3 v. LL-1503 – 1 – us L of C Photodup [340]

A TREATISE ON THE LAW OF CONTRACTS. / Addison, Charles Greenstreet – 2nd Amer. from the 4th Eng. ed. Philadelphia, Small, 1857. 1264 p. LL-842 – 1 – us L of C Photodup [340]

TREATISE ON THE LAW OF CORPORATIONS: GENERAL AND LOCAL, PUBLIC AND PRIVATE; AGGREGATE AND SOLE / Potter, Platt – New York: Banks, 1879. 2v. LL-558 – 1 – us L of C Photodup [340]

A TREATISE ON THE LAW OF CORPORATIONS IN NEW YORK, INCLUDING THE BUSINESS COPORATIONS LAW. / Rosbrook, Alden Ivan – (3d ed. Albany: Bender, 1926. 1769p. LL-1307) – Albany: Bender, 1923. 1707p. LL-1407 – 1 – us L of C Photodup [340]

A TREATISE ON THE LAW OF COURT PRACTICE AND PROCEDURE, CIVIL AND CRIMINAL. / Kinkead, Edgar Benton – Cincinnati, Anderson, 1900. 734 p. LL-655 – 1 – us L of C Photodup [340]

A TREATISE ON THE LAW OF CRIMES / Clark, William Lawrence – 2d ed. St. Paul: Keefe-Davidson, 1905. 906p. LL-736 – 1 – us L of C Photodup [340]

A TREATISE ON THE LAW OF DAMAGES, EMBRACING AN ELEMENTARY EXPOSITION OF THE LAW AND ALSO OF ITS APPLICATION TO PARTICULAR SUBJECTS OF CONTRACT AND TORT. 3D ED / Sutherland, Jabez Gridley – Chicago, Callaghan, 1903-04. 4 v. LL-1010 – 1 – us L of C Photodup [340]

A TREATISE ON THE LAW OF DOMESTIC RELATIONS / Rodgers, William Champ – Chicago: Flood, 1899. 900p. LL-1688 – 1 – us L of C Photodup [340]

A TREATISE ON THE LAW OF EMINENT DOMAIN IN THE UNITED STATES / Lewis, John – 2nd ed. Chicago, Callaghan, 1900. 2v. LL-186 – 1 – us L of C Photodup [340]

A TREATISE ON THE LAW OF EMPLOYERS' LIABILITY ACTS / Reno, Conrad – Boston: Houghton, Mifflin, 1896. 423p. LL-1042 – 1 – us L of C Photodup [340]

A TREATISE ON THE LAW OF EMPLOYERS' LIABILITY ACTS OF NEW YORK, MASSACHUSETTS, INDIANA, ALABAMA, COLORADO, AND ENGLAND / Reno, Conrad – 2d ed. Indianapolis: Bowen-Merrill, 1903. 623p. LL-1113 – 1 – us L of C Photodup [340]

A TREATISE ON THE LAW OF EVIDENCE / Greenleaf, Simon – (3rd ed., Boston: Little and Brown, 1846-56. 3v. LL-778. 4th ed., Boston: Little and Brown, 1848-57. 3v. LL-594. 7th ed., Boston: Little, Brown, 1854-58. 2v. LL-1403. 9th ed., Boston: Little, Brown, 1858-63. 2v. v.3 not pub. in this ed. LL-1476. 10th ed., Boston: Little, Brown, 1860-68. 2v. LL-660. 13th ed., Boston: Little, Brown, 1876. 3v. LL-1445. 15th ed., Boston: Little, Brown, 1892. 3v. LL-1477. Philadelphia: Welsh, 1896. 3v. LL-1446. 16th ed., Boston: Little, Brown, 1899. 3v. LL-1480) – 2d ed. Boston: Little and Brown, 1844-53. 3v. LL-586 – 1 – us L of C Photodup [340]

A TREATISE ON THE LAW OF EVIDENCE / Phillipps, Samuel March – (6th Amer. ed. from the 9th London ed. New York: Banks, Gould, 1849-50. 5v. LL-230. 5th Amer. ed. New York: Banks. 1868. 3v. LL-1447) – 2nd. Amer. ed., from the 3rd London ed. New York: Gould and Banks, 1820-22. 2v. LL-504 – 1 – us L of C Photodup [340]

A TREATISE ON THE LAW OF EXECUTIONS IN CIVIL CASES, AND OF PROCEEDINGS IN AID AND RESTRAINT THEREOF / Freeman, Abraham Clark – (3rd ed., San Francisco: Bancroft-Whitney, 1900. 3v. LL-1448) – San Francisco: Whitney, 1876. 947p. LL-758 – 1 – us L of C Photodup [340]

A TREATISE ON THE LAW OF EXECUTORS, ADMINISTRATORS AND GUARDIANS / Reese, William Miller – Atlanta, Ga., Harrison, 1880. 431 p. LL-1291 – 1 – us L of C Photodup [340]

A TREATISE ON THE LAW OF EXTRAORDINARY, INDUSTRIAL AND INTERSTATE CONTRACTS / Pingrey, Darius Harlan – Albany, New York: Bender, 1905. 944p. LL-1420 – 1 – us L of C Photodup [340]

A TREATISE ON THE LAW OF IDENTIFICATION, A SEPARATE BRANCH OF THE LAW OF EVIDENCE / Harris, George Emrick – Albany: Parsons, 1892. 507p. LL-588 – 1 – us L of C Photodup [340]

A TREATISE ON THE LAW OF INJUNCTIONS / Henley, Robert Henley Eden – 1st Amer. ed. Albany: Gould, 1822. 336p. LL-1637 – 1 – us L of C Photodup [340]

A TREATISE ON THE LAW OF INJUNCTIONS, AS ADMINISTERED IN THE COURTS OF THE UNITED STATES AND ENGLAND / High, James Lambert – (2d ed. Chicago: Callaghan, 1880. 2v. LL-760. 4th ed. Chicago: Callaghan, 1905. 2v. LL-959) – Chicago: Callaghan, 1873. 642p. LL-982 – 1 – us L of C Photodup [340]

A TREATISE ON THE LAW OF INSTRUCTIONS TO JURIES IN CIVIL AND CRIMINAL CASES. / Randall, Henry Edward – Kansas City, Mo., Vernon, 1922. 5 v. LL-1538 – 1 – us L of C Photodup [340]

A TREATISE ON THE LAW OF INSTRUCTIONS TO JURIES IN CIVIL CASES. / McQuillin, Eugene – St. Louis, Gilbert, 1906. 1195 p. LL-703 – 1 – us L of C Photodup [340]

A TREATISE ON THE LAW OF INSURANCE / Clarke, Samuel Robinson – Toronto: Printed and published at the office of the Monetary Times, 1873. 00672. (Pre-1900 Canadiana) – 9 – cn C.I.H.M. [336]

A TREATISE ON THE LAW OF INSURANCE / Phillips, Willard – (4th ed. Boston: Little, Brown, 1854. 2v. LL-1126. 5th ed. New York: Hurd and Houghton, 1867. 2v. LL-1129) – 2nd ed. Boston: Little and Brown, 1840. 2v. LL-1120 – 1 – us L of C Photodup [340]

TREATISE ON THE LAW OF INSURANCE / Marshall, Samuel – Boston: Daniel Johnson. 2v. 1805 – 8mf – 9 – $12.00 – LLMC 92-107 – us L.L.M.C. [340]

A TREATISE ON THE LAW OF JUDGMENTS, INCLUDING THE DOCTRINE OF RES JUDICATA / Black, Henry Campbell – St. Paul, West, 1891. 2 v. LL-735 – 1 – us L of C Photodup [340]

A TREATISE ON THE LAW OF LANDLORD AND TENANT / Tiffany, Herbert Thorndike – Chicago, Callaghan, 1912. 2 v. LL-1430 – 1 – us L of C Photodup [340]

A TREATISE ON THE LAW OF LANDLORD AND TENANT. / Jones, Leonard Augustus – Indianapolis, Bobbs-Merrill Co., 1906. 925 p. LL-762 – 1 – us L of C Photodup [340]

A TREATISE ON THE LAW OF LANDLORD AND TENANT. / Underhill, Harry Clay – Chicago, Flood, 1909. 2 v. LL-1302 – 1 – us L of C Photodup [340]

A TREATISE ON THE LAW OF LANDLORD AND TENANT WITH SPECIAL REFERENCE TO THE AMERICAN LAW / Gear, Hiram Lewis – San Francisco: Bancroft-Whitney, 1888. 819p. LL-1695 – 1 – us L of C Photodup [340]

A TREATISE ON THE LAW OF LIENS / Overton, Daniel Y – Albany: Banks, 1883. 817p. LL-1121 – 1 – us L of C Photodup [340]

A TREATISE ON THE LAW OF LIENS, COMMON LAW, STATUTORY, EQUITABLE AND MARITIME / Jones, Leonard Augustus – (2nd ed. Boston, Houghton, Mifflin, 1894. 2 v. LL-90) – Boston, Houghton, Mifflin, 1888. 2 v. LL-91 – 1 – us L of C Photodup [340]

A TREATISE ON THE LAW OF MARINE INSURANCE AND GENERAL AVERAGE / Parsons, Theophilus – Boston: Little, Brown, 1868. 2v. LL-946 – 1 – us L of C Photodup [340]

A TREATISE ON THE LAW OF MASTER AND SERVANT / Wood, Horace Gay – Albany, N.Y., Parsons, 1877. 956 p. LL-1107 – 1 – us L of C Photodup [340]

A TREATISE ON THE LAW OF MECHANICS' LIENS AND BUILDING CONTRACTS WITH ANNOTATED FORMS / Bloom, Solomon – (Supplement. San Francisco, 1912. 431 p. LL-810. 1) – San Francisco, Bender-Moss, 1910. 1048 p – 1 – us L of C Photodup [340]

A TREATISE ON THE LAW OF MORTGAGES OF REAL PROPERTY / Jones, Leonard Augustus – (6th ed. Indianapolis. Bobbs-Merrill Co. 1904. 2 v. LL-748) – 4th ed. Boston, Houghton, Mifflin, 1889. 2 v. LL-856 – 1 – us L of C Photodup [340]

A TREATISE ON THE LAW OF MORTGAGES ON PERSONAL PROPERTY / Jones, Leonard Augustus – (4th ed. Boston, Houghton, Mifflin, 1894. 886 p. LL-405) – 3d ed. Boston, Houghton, Mifflin, 1888. 804 p. LL-20 – 1 – us L of C Photodup [340]

A TREATISE ON THE LAW OF NATURALIZATION OF THE UNITED STATES / Dyne, F van – Washington, 1907 – 6mf – 1 – ILM-3197/1 – ne IDC [327]

A TREATISE ON THE LAW OF NAVIGABLE RIVERS / Houck, Louis – Boston: Little, Brown, 1868. 235p. LL-177 – 1 – us L of C Photodup [340]

A TREATISE ON THE LAW OF NEGLIGENCE / Shearman, Thomas Gaskell – (6th ed. New York: Baker, Voorhis, 1913. 3v. LL-1150) – 4th ed. New York: Baker, Voorhis, 1888. 2v. LL-1441 – 1 – us L of C Photodup [340]

A TREATISE ON THE LAW OF NEGOTIABLE INSTRUMENTS, INCLUDING BILLS OF EXCHANGE; PROMISSORY NOTES; NEGOTIABLE BONDS AND COUPONS. / Dabin, Jean – (6th ed., New York, Baker, Voorhis, 1914. 2 v. LL-913. 7th ed., New York, Baker, Voorhis, 1933. 3 v. LL-286) – 3d ed. New York, Baker, Voorhis, 1882. 2 v. LL-822 – 1 – us L of C Photodup [340]

A TREATISE ON THE LAW OF NEW TRIALS IN CASES CIVIL AND CRIMINAL / Graham, David – 2d ed. New York: Banks, Gould, 1855. 3v. LL-742 – 1 – us L of C Photodup [340]

A TREATISE ON THE LAW OF PARTNERSHIP / Lindley, Nathaniel Lindley – 5th ed. Boston, Edson, 1888. 2 v. LL-534 – 1 – us L of C Photodup [340]

A TREATISE ON THE LAW OF PARTNERSHIP / Parsons, Theophilus – Boston: Little, Brown, 1867. 653,1p. LL-25 – 1 – us L of C Photodup [340]

A TREATISE ON THE LAW OF PARTNERSHIP / Shumaker, Walter Adams – (2d ed. St. Paul: Keefe-Davidson, 1905. 366p. LL-1159) – St. Paul: Keefe-Davidson, 1901. 499p. LL-1158 – 1 – us L of C Photodup [340]

A TREATISE ON THE LAW OF PATENTS FOR USEFUL INVENTIONS, AS ENACTED AND ADMINISTERED IN THE UNITED STATES OF AMERICA / Curtis, Charles Ticknor – 3d ed. Boston, Little, Brown, 1867. 631 p. LL-16 – 1 – us L of C Photodup [340]

A TREATISE ON THE LAW OF PLEDGES, INCLUDING COLLATERAL SECURITIES / Jones, Leonard Augustus – Boston, Houghton, Mifflin, 1883. 601 p. LL-450 – 1 – us L of C Photodup [340]

A TREATISE ON THE LAW OF PRINCIPAL AND AGENT, CHIEFLY WITH REFERENCE TO MERCANTILE TRANSACTIONS / Paley, William – 3d American ed. New York: Banks, Gould, 1847. 461 (i.e., 685)p. LL-249 – 1 – us L of C Photodup [340]

A TREATISE ON THE LAW OF PRIVATE CORPORATIONS. / Spelling, Thomas Crisp – New York, Strouse, 1892. 2 v. LL-1146 – 1 – us L of C Photodup [340]

A TREATISE ON THE LAW OF PRIVATE CORPORATIONS. 2D ED / Taylor, Henry Osborn – Philadelphia, Kay., 1888. 883 p. LL-525 – 1 – us L of C Photodup [340]

A TREATISE ON THE LAW OF PRIVATE CORPORATIONS...ENLARGEMENT, REVISION AND RECONSTRUCTION OF BEACH ON PRIVATE CORPORATIONS / Purdy, James Hart – Chicago: Flood, 1905. 3v. LL-1160 – 1 – us L of C Photodup [340]

A TREATISE ON THE LAW OF PROHIBITION. / Lloyd, Morgan – London, Benning, 1819. 127 p. LL-116 – 1 – us L of C Photodup [340]

A TREATISE ON THE LAW OF RAILROADS / Pierce, Edward Lillie – Boston: Little, Brown, 1881. 575p. LL-1051 – 1 – us L of C Photodup [340]

A TREATISE ON THE LAW OF REAL PROPERTY / Hawley, John Gardner – Detroit: Collector Publishing Co., 1900. 593p. LL-765 – 1 – us L of C Photodup [340]

A TREATISE ON THE LAW OF REAL PROPERTY / Reeves, Alfred Gandy – Boston, Little, Brown, 1909. 2 v. LL-1024 – 1 – us L of C Photodup [340]

A TREATISE ON THE LAW OF REAL PROPERTY / Walsh, William Francis – New York, Baker, Voorhis, 1915. 858 p. LL-1334 – 1 – us L of C Photodup [340]

A TREATISE ON THE LAW OF SALE OF PERSONAL PROPERTY / Mechem, Floyd Russell – Chicago: Callaghan, 1901. 2v. LL-299 – 1 – us L of C Photodup [340]

A TREATISE ON THE LAW OF SHERIFFS AND OTHER MINISTERIAL OFFICERS / Murfree, William Law – 2nd ed. St. Louis: Gilbert, 1890. 758 (i.e. 1010), 1007-1064p. LL-198 – 1 – us L of C Photodup [340]

A TREATISE ON THE LAW OF SLANDER AND LIBEL, AND INCIDENTALLY OF MALICIOUS PROSECUTIONS...FROM THE 2ND ENGLISH ED. OF 1830 / Starkie, Thomas – Hartford, Conn., Wendell, 1858. 2 v. LL-1124 – 1 – us L of C Photodup [340]

A TREATISE ON THE LAW OF STOCK-BROKERS AND STOCK EXCHANGES. / Dos Passos, John Randolph – (2nd ed. New York, Banks, 1905. 2 v. LL-945) – New York, Harper, 1882. 1043 p. LL-301 – 1 – us L of C Photodup [340]

A TREATISE ON THE LAW OF SUITS BY ATTACHMENT IN THE UNITED STATES / Drake, Charles Daniel – 3d ed. Boston, Little, Brown, 1866. 613 p. LL-745 – 1 – us L of C Photodup [340]

A TREATISE ON THE LAW OF TAX TITLES. / Black, Henry Campbell – St. Louis, Stevenson, 1888. 425 p. LL-395 – 1 – us L of C Photodup [340]

A TREATISE ON THE LAW OF TAXATION AS IMPOSED BY THE STATES AND THEIR MUNICIPALITIES. / Burroughs, William Henry – New York, Baker, Voorhis, 1877. 751 p. Includes Supp. New York, 1883. 126 p. LL-1461 – 1 – us L of C Photodup [340]

A TREATISE ON THE LAW OF TAXATION, INCLUDING THE LAW OF LOCAL ASSESSMENTS / Cooley, Thomas McIntyre – (2d ed. Chicago, Callaghan, 1886. 991 p. LL-704) – Chicago, Callaghan, 1881. 741 p. LL-406 – 1 – us L of C Photodup [340]

A TREATISE ON THE LAW OF THE DOMESTIC RELATIONS : EMBRACING HUSBAND AND WIFE, PARENT AND CHILD / Schouler, James – Boston: Little, Brown, 1870. 670p. LL-1080 – 1 – us L of C Photodup [340]

A TREATISE ON THE LAW OF THE PROTESTANT EPISCOPAL CHURCH IN THE U.S. / Hoffman, Murray – New York: Stanford & Swords, 1850 – 5mf – 9 – $7.50 – LLMC 92-123 – us L.L.M.C. [340]

A TREATISE ON THE LAW OF TORTS, OR THE WRONGS WHICH ARISE INDEPENDENT OF CONTRACT / Cooley, Thomas McIntyre – Chicago: Callaghan, 1880. 755p. LL-1027 – 1 – us L of C Photodup [340]

A TREATISE ON THE LAW OF TRIALS IN ACTIONS CIVIL AND CRIMINAL. 2D ED / Thompson, Seymour Dwight – Chicago, Flood, 19??. 4 v. LL-1444 – 1 – us L of C Photodup [340]

A TREATISE ON THE LAW OF TRUSTS AND TRUSTEES / Perry, Jairus Ware – (6th ed. Boston: Little, Brown, 1911. 2v. LL-329) – Boston: Little, Brown, 1889. 2v. LL-349 – 1 – us L of C Photodup [340]

A TREATISE ON THE LAW OF WAR / Bynkershoek, C van – Philadelphia, 1810 – 3mf – 1 – ILM-695/1 – ne IDC [327]

A TREATISE ON THE LAW OF WATERS, INCLUDING RIPARIAN RIGHTS, AND PUBLIC AND PRIVATE RIGHTS IN WATERS TIDAL AND INLAND / Gould, John Melvile – 3d ed. Chicago: Callaghan, 1900. 956p. LL-731 – 1 – us L of C Photodup [340]

A TREATISE ON THE LAW RELATING TO BILLS, NOTES, CHEQUES AND IOU'S / Clarke, Samuel Robinson – Toronto: R. Carswell, 1875. 00674. (Pre-1900 Canadiana) – 9 – cn C.I.H.M. [336]

A TREATISE ON THE LAW RELATING TO ELECTRICITY / Croswell, Simon Greenleaf – Boston, Little, Brown, 1895. 765 p. LL-163 – 1 – us L of C Photodup [340]

A TREATISE ON THE LAW RELATING TO REAL ESTATE IN PENNSYLVANIA / Nicholson, Vincint De Witt – 3d and rec. ed. Philadelphia: Bisel, 1929. 773p. LL-952 – 1 – us L of C Photodup [340]

A TREATISE ON THE LAW RELATING TO THE CUSTODY OF INFANTS, INCLUDING PRACTICE AND FORMS / Hocheimer, Lewis – 2nd ed. Baltimore: Scrimger, 1891. 167p. LL-430 – 1 – us L of C Photodup [340]

A TREATISE ON THE LAW RELATING TO THE OFFICE AND DUTIES OF NOTARIES PUBLIC THROUGHOUT THE UNITED STATES. / Proffatt, John – San Francisco: Whitney, 1877. 360p. LL-1170 – 1 – us L of C Photodup [340]

A TREATISE ON THE LAW RELATING TO THE POWERS AND DUTIES OF JUSTICES OF THE PEACE, CONSTABLES, ETC., ETC., IN THE STATE OF MISSOURI. / Kelley, Henry Smith – (4th ed. St. Louis, Gilbert Book Co., 1901. 886 p. LL-716) – St. Louis, Gilbert Book Co., 1890. 868 p. LL-709 – 1 – us L of C Photodup [340]

A TREATISE ON THE LAWS OF COMMERCE AND MANUFACTURES, AND THE CONTRACTS RELATING THERETO, WITH AN APPENDIX OF TREATIES, STATUTES, AND PRECEDENTS / Chitty, Joseph – v1-4. 1824 – 1 – $95.00 – 0-89093-034-1 – us UPA [941]

A TREATISE ON THE LAWS OF OHIO PERTAINING TO THE POWERS AND DUTIES OF, AND PRACTICE BEFORE, JUSTICES OF THE PEACE...17TH ED / Swan, Joseph Rockwell – (19th ed. Cincinnati, Clarke, 1903. 1062 p. LL-1339. 1. 20th ed. Cincinnati, Clarke, 1903. 1062 p. LL-1509. 1) – Cincinnati, Clarke, 1898. 1062 p. LL-1335 – 1 – us L of C Photodup [340]

A TREATISE ON THE LAWS OF THE STATE OF NEW YORK RELATING TO THE POOR, INSANE, IDIOTS AND HABITUAL DRUNKARDS. / Knapp, Clark D – Rochester, Williamson & Higbie, 1887. 894 p. LL-843 – 1 – us L of C Photodup [340]

A TREATISE ON THE LAWS REGULATING THE MANUFACTURE AND SALE OF INTOXICATING LIQUORS / Black, Henry Campbell – St. Paul, West, 1892. 711 p. LL-593 – 1 – us L of C Photodup [340]

A TREATISE ON THE LEGAL AND EQUITABLE RIGHTS OF MARRIED WOMEN / Cord, William H – (2nd ed. Philadelphia: Kay, 1885. 2v. LL-907) – Philadelphia: Kay, 1861. 796p. LL-832 – 1 – us L of C Photodup [306]

A TREATISE ON THE LEGAL REMEDIES OF MANDAMUS AND PROHIBITION, HABEAS CORPUS, CERTIORARI AND QUO WARRANTO / Wood, Horace Gay – (2nd Ed. Albany, NY., Little, 1891. 276 p. LL-1284. 1) – Albany, N.Y., Little, 1880. 278 p. LL-1604 – 1 – us L of C Photodup [340]

A TREATISE ON THE LIABILITY OF STOCKHOLDERS IN CORPORATIONS / Thompson, Seymour Dwight – St. Louis, Thomas, 1879. 528 p. LL-1140 – 1 – us L of C Photodup [340]

A TREATISE ON THE LIMITATION OF ACTIONS AT LAW AND IN EQUITY / Wood, Horace Gay – Boston, Soule 1882 913 p. LL-928 – 1 – us L of C Photodup [340]

A TREATISE ON THE MANAGEMENT OF DISEASE IN SHEEP / MacKenzie, C S – 1809 – 7 – uk Microform Academic [636]

A TREATISE ON THE MEASURE OF DAMAGES / Sedgwick, Theodore – (9th ed., rev., rearranged and enl. by Arthur G. Sedgwick and Joseph H. Beale. New York: Baker, Voorhis, 1920. 4v. LL-1012) – 9th ed., rev., rearranged, and enl. by Arthur G. Sedgwick and Joseph H. Beale. New York: Baker, Voorhis, 1912. 4v. LL-1537 – 1 – us L of C Photodup [340]

A TREATISE ON THE MEASURE OF DAMAGES / Sedgwick, Theodore – New York: Baker, Voorhis, 1874. 827p. LL-1014 – 1 – us L of C Photodup [340]

A TREATISE ON THE MECHANIC'S LIEN LAW OF THE STATE OF ILLINOIS, AS IN FORCE MARCH 1, 1894, SO FAR AS THE SAME RELATES TO REAL ESTATE / Coleman, Julius Archer – Chicago, Wait, 1894. 281 p. LL-63 – 1 – us L of C Photodup [340]

A TREATISE ON THE MODERN LAW OF CONTRACTS. / Beach, Charles Fisk – Indianapolis, Bowen-Merrill, 1896. 2 v. LL-1314 – 1 – us L of C Photodup [340]

TREATISE ON THE NATIONALITY OF CORPORATIONS / Arminjon, P – Washington, 1907 – 1mf – 9 – ILM-3753/1 – ne IDC [340]

A TREATISE ON THE NEGLIGENCE OF MUNICIPAL CORPORATIONS / Jones, Dwight Arven – New York, Baker, Voorhis, 1892. 588 p. LL-255 – 1 – us L of C Photodup [340]

A TREATISE ON THE NEW YORK MANUFACTURING CORPORATION ACT OF 1848, AND BUSINESS CORPORATION ACT OF 1875...2ND ED / Southworth, Edward Wells – New York, Baker, Voorhis, 1890. 2 380 p. LL-1324 – 1 – us L of C Photodup [340]

A TREATISE ON THE ORGANIZATION AND JURISDICTION OF THE SUPREME, CIRCUIT AND DISTRICT COURTS OF THE UNITED STATES. / Conkling, Alfred – 2d ed. New York, Gould, Banks, 1842. 634 p. LL-161 – 1 – us L of C Photodup [340]

A TREATISE ON THE ORGANIZATION, JURISDICTION AND PRACTICE OF THE COURTS OF THE UNITED STATES / Conkling, Alfred – (4th ed. Albany, N.Y., Little, 1864. 882 p. LL-407. 1. 5th ed. Albany, N.Y., Little, 1870. 946 p. LL-1414. 1) – 3d ed. Albany, 1856. 926 p. LL-160 – 1 – us L of C Photodup [340]

A TREATISE ON THE PLEADINGS IN SUITS IN THE COURT OF CHANCERY, BY ENGLISH BILL. THE 4TH ED. WITH ADDITIONAL REFERENCES AND NOTES, BY GEORGE JEREMY...3RD AMER. ED. WITH NOTES AND REFERENCES, BY CHARLES EDWARDS. / Redesdale, John Freeman-Mitford – New York, Voorhies, 1833. 401 28 p. LL-1667 – 1 – us L of C Photodup [340]

A TREATISE ON THE POLICE OF THE METROPOLIS : CONTAINING A DETAIL OF THE VARIOUS CRIMES AND MISDEMEANORS... / Colquhoun, P – London, 6th ed 1800 – 8mf – 9 – ne IDC [360]

A TREATISE ON THE POWERS AND DUTIES OF JUSTICES OF THE PEACE IN CIVIL, CRIMINAL AND SPECIAL CASES IN THE STATE OF IOWA. / Conklin, Charles H – 3d ed. Des Moines, Mills, 1880. 917 p. LL-801 – 1 – us L of C Photodup [340]

A TREATISE ON THE POWERS AND DUTIES OF JUSTICES OF THE PEACE IN THE STATE OF MICHIGAN, UNDER CHAPTER NINETY-THREE OF THE REVISED STATUTES OF 1846, BEING CHAPTER THIRTY-FOUR OF THE COMPILED LAWS OF 1897...10TH ED / Tiffany, Alexander Ralston – Chicago, Callaghan, 1905. 1012 p. LL-1309 – 1 – us L of C Photodup [340]

A TREATISE ON THE POWERS AND DUTIES OF JUSTICES OF THE PEACE, IN THE STATE OF MICHIGAN, UNDER CHAPTER NINETY-THREE OF THE REVISED STATUTES OF 1846, BEING CHAPTER TWO HUNDRED AND FORTY-NINE OF HOWELL'S ANNOTATED STATUTES OF 1883. 9TH ED / Tiffany, Alexander Ralston – Detroit, Richmond & Backus, 1894. 922 p. LL-1312 – 1 – us L of C Photodup [340]

A TREATISE ON THE POWERS AND DUTIES OF JUSTICES OF THE PEACE, MAYORS, MARSHALS, AND CONSTABLES IN THE STATE OF INDIANA. / McDonald, David – New ed. Cincinnati, Clarke Co., 1896. 1063 p. LL-783 – 1 – us L of C Photodup [340]

A TREATISE ON THE POWERS AND DUTIES OF JUSTICES OF THE PEACE, SHERIFFS, CORONERS, AND CONSTABLES, IN THE STATE OF NEBRASKA / Maxwell, Samuel – (5th ed. Lincoln, Neb.: State Journal Co., 1888. 880p. LL-835) – 4th ed. Lincoln, Neb.: State Journal Co., 1884. 692p. LL-830 – 1 – us L of C Photodup [340]

A TREATISE ON THE PRACTICE OF THE COURTS OF THE STATE OF NEW YORK. / Monell, Claudius L – Albany: Gould, Banks and Gould, 1849. 575p. LL-621 – 1 – us L of C Photodup [340]

A TREATISE ON THE PRINCIPLES AND PRACTICE GOVERNING THE TRIAL OF TITLE TO LAND. / Sedgwick, Arthur George – New York: Baker, Voorhis, 1882. 696p. LL-1028 – 1 – us L of C Photodup [340]

A TREATISE ON THE PRINCIPLES AND PRACTICE OF MILITARY LAW / Kennedy, Vans – Bombay: American Mission Press, 1832 – 4mf – 9 – $6.00 – LLMC 96-092 – us L.L.M.C. [340]

A TREATISE ON THE PRINCIPLES AND PRACTICE OF MILITARY LAW / Kennedy, Vans – rev ed. Bombay: American Mission Press, 1847 – 5mf – 9 – $7.50 – LLMC 89-026 – us L.L.M.C. [340]

A TREATISE ON THE PRINCIPLES AND PRACTICE OF THE ACTION OF EJECTMENT AND STATUTORY SUBSTITUTES / Warvelle, George William – Chicago, Flood, 1905. 679 p. LL-1483 – 1 – us L of C Photodup [340]

A TREATISE ON THE PRINCIPLES OF PLEADING, IN CIVIL ACTION / Gould, James – (4th ed., Albany: Gould, 1876. 502p. LL-480) – 2d ed. New York: Collins, 1836. 536p. LL-1186 – 1 – us L of C Photodup [340]

A TREATISE ON THE PRINCIPLES OF PLEADING IN CIVIL ACTIONS...3RD AMERICAN FROM THE 2ND LONDON ED / Stephen, Henry John – Washington, D.C., Morrison, 1875. xvii, 398, xciv p. LL-1187 – 1 – us L of C Photodup [340]

A TREATISE ON THE PROCEEDINGS TO BE ADOPTED IN CONDUCTING OR OPPOSING PRIVATES SIC BILLS IN THE PARLIAMENT OF CANADA. / Todd, Alfred – 2nd ed. Montreal: Printed by John Lovell, 1862. SEM105P98 – 2mf – 9 – Can$4.50 – cn Bibl Nat [323]

A TREATISE ON THE PUBLIC LAND SYSTEM OF THE UNITED STATES / Spaulding, George W – San Francisco, Bancroft, 1884. 523 p. LL-1177 – 1 – us L of C Photodup [340]

A TREATISE ON THE RIGHT OF PROPERTY IN TIDE WATERS AND IN THE SOIL AND SHORES THREROF / Angell, Joseph Kinnicut – 2d ed. Boston, Little and Brown, 1847. xvi, 295, cxlvi, 463- 475 p. LL 787 – 1 – us L of C Photodup [340]

A TREATISE ON THE RIGHT USE OF THE FATHERS IN THE DECISION OF CONTROVERSIES EXISTING AT THIS DAY IN RELIGION / Daille, John; ed by Jekyll, G – London: William White, 1841 – 1mf – us A.T.L.A. [240]

A TREATISE ON THE RULES FOR THE SELECTION OF THE PARTIES TO AN ACTION / Dicey, Albert Venn – 2d Amer. ed. Jersey City, Linn, 1886. 559 p. LL-741 – 1 – us L of C Photodup [340]

A TREATISE ON THE SCRIPTURE DOCTRINE OF ORIGINAL SIN : WITH EXPLANATORY NOTES / Boardman, Henry Augustus – Philadelphia: Presbyterian Board of Publication, c1839 – 1mf – us A.T.L.A. [240]

A TREATISE ON THE STATUTE OF LIMITATIONS / Ballantine, William – Albany, Packard, 1829. 592 p. LL-906 – 1 – us L of C Photodup [340]

A TREATISE ON THE SYSTEM OF EVIDENCE IN TRIALS AT COMMON LAW. / Wigmore, John Henry – (A supplement. Boston, 1908. 458p. 1p. A supplement. 2nd Ed. Boston, 1915. 935p) – Boston, Little, Brown, 1904-05. 4 v. LL-1424 – 1 – us L of C Photodup [340]

A TREATISE ON THE USE OF THE TENSES IN HEBREW AND SOME OTHER SYNTACTICAL QUESTIONS / Driver, Samuel Rolles – (Includes index) – 3rd rev ed. Oxford: Clarendon Press, 1892 – 1mf – 9 – 0-8370-9139-X – 1986-3139 – us A.T.L.A. [470]

A TREATISE ON THE VALIDITY OF VERBAL AGREEMENTS. / Throop, Montgomery Hunt, 1827-92 – In two volumes. Vol. 1. Albany, N.Y., Parsons, 1870. 794 p. LL-1002 – 1 – us L of C Photodup [340]

A TREATISE ON THE VENEREAL DISEASE / Hunter, J – M-63. 1786 – 9 – ne IDC [616]

A TREATISE ON THE WEALTH, POWER AND RESOURCES OF THE BRITISH EMPIRE... / Colquhoun, P – London, 1814 – 11mf – 9 – ne IDC [330]

A TREATISE ON TRIAL BY JURY, INCLUDING QUESTIONS OF LAW AND FACT / Proffatt, John – San Francisco: Whitney, 1877. 608p. LL-1184 – 1 – us L of C Photodup [340]

A TREATISE ON USURY AND USURY LAWS / Bolles, John Augustus – Boston, Munroe, 1837. 75 p. LL-2324 – 1 – us L of C Photodup [340]

A TREATISE ON WILLS / Jarman, Thomas – The 5th Amer. from the 4th Eng. ed. Boston, Little, Brown, 1881. 2 v. LL-772 – 1 – us L of C Photodup [340]

A TREATISE UPON BAPTIST CHURCH JURISPRUDENCE / Marshall, Edward P – 1897 – 1 – 19.88 – us Baptist [240]

A TREATISE UPON SOME OF THE GENERAL PRINCIPLES OF THE LAW. / Wait, William – Albany, Gould, 1885. 4v. LL-671 – 1 – us L of C Photodup [340]

A TREATISE UPON SOME OF THE GENERAL PRINCIPLES OF THE LAW. / Wait, William – (Supplement.Volume VIII. ...Albany, 1888.669p. Supplement. Chicago. Wait, 1894. 1501 p. A general index. Chicago, Wait, 1895. 653 p. A general index. Albany, Gould, 1882. 547p. A general index. Albany, Gould, 1885. 547 p) – Albany, Gould, 1877-79. 7 v. LL-1648 – 1 – us L of C Photodup [340]

A TREATISE UPON THE LAW OF TELEGRAPHS; WITH AN APPENDIX, CONTAINING THE GENERAL STATUTORY PROVISIONS OF ENGLAND, CANADA, THE UNITED STATES. / Scott, William L – Boston: Little, Brown, 1868. 535p. LL-1692 – 1 – us L of C Photodup [340]

A TREATISE UPON THE UNITED STATES COURTS. / Abbott, Benjamin Vaughan – (3rd ed., New York, Ward & Peloubet, 1877. 2v. LL-847) – New York, Diossy, 1869-71. 2v. LL-352 – 1 – us L of C Photodup [340]

THE TREATMENT OF CATARACT / Smith, H – M 430. 1910 – 9 – ne IDC [615]

THE TREATMENT OF THE REMAINS AT THE EUCHARIST AFTER HOLY COMMUNION AND THE TIME OF THE ABLUTIONS / Lockton, W – Cambridge, 1920 – 5mf – 8 – Dfl22.00 – ne Slangenburg [240]

TREATY INFORMATION BULLETIN / U.S. Department of State – (Includes 2 index vols) – nos 1-117. 1929-39 (all publ) – 58mf – 9 – $87.00 – LLMC 80-904 – us L.L.M.C. [975]

TREATY LAW MANUAL / Foundation for Study of Treaty Law – Washington 1954?. 61p. LL-2236 – 1 – us L of C Photodup [340]

TREATY OF 1826 BETWEEN PANAMA AND THE UNITED STATES : NOTES OF THE FOREIGN MINISTER OF PANAMA – Panama: Ministerio de Educacion, 1826 – 1r – 1 – $65.00 – us Ross [327]

THE TREATY OF ST GERMAIN : A DOCUMENTARY HISTORY OF ITS TERRITORIAL AND POLITICAL CAUSES / ed by Almond, Nina & Lutz, Ralph H – 1935. 712p – 1 – 35.00r – us Hoover Inst Photo [940]

THE TREATY OF WASHINGTON / Cushing, Caleb – New York: Harper, 1873. 02251. (Pre-1900 Canadiana) – 9 – cn C.I.H.M. [971]

THE TREATY SERIES / U.S. Department of State – (Lacking: nos 489-547; 549-563; 565-601; 603-653; 655-657) – nos 489-994. Jan 1908-45 (all publ) – 9 – LLMC 80-914 – us L.L.M.C. [975]

THE TREATY SERIES *see*
– THE EXECUTIVE AGREEMENT SERIES
– TREATIES AND OTHER INTERNATIONAL ACTS OF THE UNITED STATES

TREATY SERIES / United Nations – v1- – 8265mf – 9 – $15,705.00; $1.90f – uk UNIMICRO [900]

TREATY SERIES / United Nations – v1-1000 with indexes – 145r – 1 – $6,600.00 – us Trans-Media [340]

TREATY SERIES: 1892-1985 / United Kingdom; ed by Torrington, William F – Combined micro and hard copy coverage of the major Treaty Series – 42r – 1 – $2150.00 – us Trans-Media [941]

THE TREATY-MAKING POWER OF THE UNITED STATES / Butler, C H – New York, 1902 – 8mf – 1 – ILM-722/1 – ne IDC [327]

Trebilcock, Clive *see* BUSINESS AND FINANCIAL PAPERS, 1780-1939

Trebin, A A *see* SLAVIANO-RUSSKIIA STAROPECHATNYIA KNIGI DREVNEKHRANIKISHCH G. ZHITOMIRA

Trebitsch, R *see* BEI DEN ESKIMOS IN WEST-GROENLAND

TREBNIK – New York, NY. 1961. BR-10,364/1 – 9 – ne IDC [947]

Trebutien, G S *see* JOURNAL OF EUGENIE DE GUERIN

Trechsel, Jo *see* MICHAELIS DE CESENA, FRATRIS, LIBELLI

Trede, Paul *see*
- ABEL
- LENA ELLERBROK
- UT BROCHDOERP

TREDEGAR PAPERS – From National Library of Wales. BRRAM – 7r – 1 – uk Microform Academic [970]

Trediakovskii, V K *see* RAZGOVOR MEZHDU CHUZHESTRANNYM CHELOVEKOM I ROSSIISKIM OB ORFOGRAFII STARINNOI I NOVOI I O VSEM CHTO PRINADLEZHIT K SEI MATERII

A TREE FOR POVERTY : SOMALI POETRY AND PROSE / ed by Laurence, Margaret – Nairobi: Eagle Press, 1954 – us Res Libr [800]

TREE GROWING BY RURAL PEOPLE – 1986 3rd print 1987 – 139p – it F.A.O. [634]

THE TREE OF LIFE : OR, REDEMPTION, AND ITS FRUITS IN GRACE AND GLORY / Shepheard, H – 2nd ed. London: James Nisbet, 1866 – 1mf – 9 – 0-8370-7336-7 – 1986-1336 – us A.T.L.A. [230]

THE TREE OF LIFE : A STUDY OF RELIGION / Crawley, Alfred Ernest – (Incudes index) – London: Hutchinson, 1905 – 1mf – 9 – 0-8370-2774-8 – 1985-0774 – us A.T.L.A. [200]

TREE PLANTING PRACTICES IN AFRICAN SAVANNAS – 1981 – 185p – it F.A.O. [634]

THE TREES OF CALIFORNIA / Jepson, W L – 7566 2. 1923 – 8 – ne IDC [580]

TREES, SHRUBS AND VINES... / Parkhurst, H E – New York, 1903 – 5mf – 9 – ne IDC [615]

Treese, Joel D *see* BLACK AMERICANS IN CONGRESS 1870-1989

THE TREESEARCHER – v6-7, 1964-65. Indexed.4 fiches. F-0055 – 9 – us A.G.L.L. [920]

TREFFPUNKT WIESBADEN / Windecker, W C – Berlin: Schuetzen Verlag, c1943 – 1r – 1 – us U.W. Library [943]

Treffry, Philippe *see* BIO-BIBLIOGRAPHIE DE DAMASE POTVIN

Tregelles, Samuel Prideaux *see*
- HEADS OF HEBREW GRAMMAR
- THE HISTORIC EVIDENCE OF THE AUTHORSHIP AND TRANSMISSION OF THE BOOKS OF THE NEW TESTAMENT

Trego, Joseph Harrington *see*
- DIARIES
- DIARY

TREINTA ANOS DE RESTAURACION MONUMENTAL EN CACERES / Gonzalez Valcarcel, Jose Manuel – Badajoz: Dip. Provincial, 1970. Sep. REE – 1 – sp Bibl Santa Ana [946]

TREINTA SONETOS / Sanchez-Arjona, Vicente – Sevilla: Imp.y Pap. Casa de la Vega, 1935 – 1 – sp Bibl Santa Ana [810]

Treitel, Leopold *see* DIE ALEXANDRINISCHE UEBERSETZUNG DES BUCHES HOSEA, HEFT 1

TREIZE PIECES POUR PIANOFORTE A QUATRE MAINS... / Wanhal, J B – Offenbach: Chez Jean Andre, 1821-22 – 1 – us Sibley [780]

Trejo, Gutierre *see* IN SACRO...HUOR EVANGELIA

Trejo, Luis de *see* ADVERTENCIAS Y OBLIGACIONES...REJON

TREJO PANIAGUA, ANTONIO (VICARIO DE LA ORDEN Y OBISPO DE CARTAGENA) EN LA INMACULADA EN LA LITERATURA FRANCISCANO-ESPANOLA / Uribe, Angel – Archivo Ibero Americano, 1955 – 1 – sp Bibl Santa Ana [240]

Trejo Placentini *see* PARADISUS DELITIARUM PAULI

TREK – Port Elizabeth, Cape Town, Johannesburg, South Africa. 1936-1952 – 1 – sa State Libr [072]

TRELAWNEY OF THE "WELLS" : A COMEDIETTA IN FOUR ACTS / Pinero, Arthur Wing – London: W. Heinemann, 1899, [c1897] – 1 roll – 1 – 1-55879-369-0 – uk Libr Preservation [820]

TRELAWNY AND PUBLIC ADVERTISER – Falmouth. Jamaica. -w. 2 Jan 1871-29 Dec 1887. (13 reels) – 1 – uk British Libr Newspaper [072]

Trelawny, Edward John *see* LETTERS OF EDWARD JOHN TRELAWNY. EDITED WITH A BRIEF INTRODUCTION AND NOTES BY H. BUXTON FORMAN, C.B.

TRELAWNY OF TRELAWNE / Bray, Anna Eliza – British Fiction Archive: Unit 2 – 9 – uk Bell [830]

TRELLEBORGS ALLEHANDA – Trelleborg, Sweden. 1876-1978 – 271r – 1 – sw Kungliga [072]

TRELLEBORGS ALLEHANDA – Trelleborg, Sweden. 1979- – 1 – sw Kungliga [072]

Trelles, Oscar M *see*
- FEDERAL RULES OF EVIDENCE
- IMMIGRATION AND NATIONALITY ACTS

TRELLIS – (v3. 1975-79. 9) – v. 1-3. 1973-79 – 1,5,6 – us UMI [410]

Trembath, James F *see* A FIRST ACCOUNT OF LABOUR ORGANISATION IN SOUTH AFRICA

Tremblay, Ernest *see* RIEL

Tremblay, F et al *see* LE LAC SAINT-JEAN

Tremblay, Remi *see* PIERRE QUI ROULE

Tremblay, U. *see* LA DEFENSE

Tremblay-Boily, Germaine *see* FLAMBEAU SAGUENEEN, MONSIEUR L'ABBE CHARLES-ELZEAR TREMBLAY

Tremearne, Arthur John Newman *see* THE BAN OF THE BORI; DEMONS AND DEMON-DANCING IN WEST AND NORTH AFRICA

Tremel-Eggert, Kuni *see*
- DER SCHMIED VON HASSBERG
- SONNIGE HEIMAT
- DIE STRASSE DES LEBENS

Tremellius, Immanuel *see* TESTAMENTVM NOVVM...EST AUTEM INTERPRETATIO SYRIACA NOUI TESTAMENTI, ...AVTORE IMMANVELE TREMELLIO, ...CUIUS ETIAM GRAMMMATICA CHALDAICA ET SYRA CALCI OPERIS ADJECTA EST

Tremler, Wenzel *see* O FREUNDSCHAFT!

TREMONIA – Dortmund, Germany. 1887-Jun 1878; 1879-1880; 1882; 1884-Jun 1904; 1905-1914; 1 April 1915-30 Sep 1922; 12 Jul-29 Sep 1923; 1924-30 Sep 1925; Nov 1925-Mar 1928; 13 Apr-31 Dec 1928; 1 Mar-29 Jun 1929; 1930-Aug 1933; Nov 1933-30 Apr 1938; 1939-30 Jun 1940; 1 Oct 1940-7 Apr 1945 (incomplete) – 1 – gw Mikrofilm [072]

TREMTIS – Memmingen. Germany. -w and m. 4 Jul 1950-22 Oct 1953. (1 reel) – 1 – uk British Libr Newspaper [072]

THE TRENCH AND CAMP – (Army newspaper) – Palo Alto, CA. Mar-Aug 1918 (5 issues only) – 1r – 1 – $50.00 – B02606 – us Library Micro [071]

TRENCH AND CAMP – Battle Creek. Mich. 1917-1918 – 1 – us UMI [071]

Trench, Maria *see* JAMES SKINNER

Trench, Richard Chenevix *see*
- COMMENTARY ON THE EPISTLES TO THE SEVEN CHURCHES IN ASIA
- COMMENTARY ON THE EPISTLES TO...ASIA: REVELATION 2, 3
- THE FITNESS OF HOLY SCRIPTURE FOR UNFOLDING THE SPIRITUAL LIFE OF MEN; 2
- ON THE AUTHORIZED VERSION OF THE NEW TESTAMENT
- STUDIES IN THE GOSPELS

Trenck, Friedrich von der *see* THE LIFE OF BARON FREDERICK TRENCK: CONTAINING HIS ADVENTURES, AND ALSO HIS EXCESSIVE SUFFERINGS DURING TEN YEARS IMPRISONMENT

Trenckner, V *see* THE MILINDAPANHO

TREND – (Backfile through 1998 $85r) – Slovakia, 1999- – 4r per y – 1 – $320.00 standing order – us Ross [072]

TREND – (Every issue has a detailed summary in English. Please inquire to publisher) – 1991-1995 – 1 – sz Infoprint [330]

TRENDS AND DEVELOPMENT OF TECHNICAL AND VOCATIONAL EDUCATION – 1990 – 73p – 9 – fr UNESCO [370]

TRENDS IN ASBESTOS LITIGATION / Willging, Thomas E – Washington: FJC, 1987 – 2mf – 9 – $3.00 – LLMC 95-355 – us L.L.M.C. [340]

TRENDS IN BIOCHEMICAL SCIENCES – v1-9. 1976-84 – 1,5,6,13 – sz Elsevier [073]

TRENDS IN EDUCATION – 1966-80 – 79mf – 9 – uk Microform Academic [073]

TRENDS IN ENGINEERING – v1- 1948- – 1,5,6,9 – us UMI [620]

TRENDS IN ETHNIC GROUP RELATIONS IN ASIA AND OCEANIA – 1979 – 292p – 9 – 92-3-101603-2 – fr UNESCO [305]

TRENDS IN JEWISH EDUCATION – (Boston, Mass.). Spr.- 1984; Winter 1984/85; Fall 1985; Fall/Winter 1986; Spr./Summer 1987; Winter 1988; [Spr. 1988] – 5ft – us A.J.P.C. [270]

TRENDS IN LIBYAN IMPORTS AND EXPORTS, 1962-1968 / Libya. Ministry of Planning and Development. Census and Statistical Department – BNE-618 1 – 9 – ne IDC [380]

TRENDS IN NEUROSCIENCES – v1-7. 1978-84 – 1,5,6,13 – sz Elsevier [616]

TRENDS IN PHARMACOLOGICAL SCIENCES – v1-5. 1980-84 – 1,5,6,13 – sz Elsevier [073]

TRENDS OF EXPENDITURE ON EDUCATION 1968/69-1978/79 / India. Department of Education – New Delhi, 1980 – 3mf – 9 – DE-537/1 – ne IDC [370]

Trenker, Luis *see*
- BERGE IN FLAMMEN
- LEUCHTENDES LAND
- DER REBELL

DIE TRENNUNG VON KIRCHE UND STAAT : EIN VORTRAG / Hauck, Albert – Leipzig: J.C. Hinrichs, 1912 – 1mf – us A.T.L.A. [200]

DIE TRENNUNG VON STAAT UND KIRCHE IN FRANKREICH UND DER FRANZOESISCHE PROTESTANTISMUS / Luettge, Willy – Tuebingen: Mohr, 1912 – 1mf – us A.T.L.A. [240]

TRENT ADVOCATE – Trenton, 1889-1900 – 1r – 1 – cn Preston [971]

TRENT VALLEY ADVOCATE – Trenton, 1880-1887 – 2r – 1 – cn Preston [971]

TRENTE ANS DE CAFE-CONCERT : SOUVENIRS RECUEILLIS / Paulus, J – Paris: Societe d'edition et de publications, [191-?] – 1 – us Sibley [780]

TRENTE ANS DE VIE NATIONALE / La Vergne, Armand – Montreal, 1935. SEM105P747 – 3mf – 9 – Can$6.75 – cn Bibl Nat [971]

TRENTE MOIS AU CONTINENT MYSTERIEUX : GABON-CONGO ET COTE OCCIDENTALE D'AFRIQUE / Payeur-Didelot – Paris: B Levrault, 1899 – us Res Libr [960]

TRENTE-SEPTIEME RAPPORT DU COMITE DES BILLS PRIVES : BILL DE LA PAROISSE DES TROIS-RIVIERES / Canada. Parliament. Legislative Assembly – Quebec: Imprimerie de Louis Perrault, 1853. SEM105P162 – 1mf – 9 – Can$2.25 – cn Bibl Nat [324]

Trentini, Albert *see* GOETHE

Trentino-Alto Adige. Italy *see* BOLLETINO UFFICIALE

TRENTON BAPTIST CHURCH. KENTUCKY : CHURCH RECORDS – 1823-44 – 1 – 34.47 – us Baptist [240]

TRENTON COURIER – Trenton, 1867-1919 – 17r – 1 – cn Preston [971]

TRENTON FIRST BAPTIST CHURCH. TRENTON, TENNESSEE : CHURCH RECORDS – (266p) – Aug 1850-Oct 1878 – 1 reel – 1 – $11.97 – us Baptist [240]

TRENTON REPUBLICAN – Trenton, NE. -w. Feb 1904-Mar 1905 – 1 – us NE Hist [071]

TRENTON TORPEDO – Trenton, NE. -w. Oct 1885; Dec 1885-Jul 1887 – 1 – us NE Hist [071]

TRENTONIAN – Trenton. N.J. 1964- – 1 – us UMI [071]

TRENTONIAN AND TRI-COUNTY NEWS – (1993.-10r; 1957-1975.-59r) – Trenton, 1976-1992 – 130r – 1 – cn Preston [971]

Trepanier, V et al *see* LE BLOC

Trepman, Paul *see* VOKHNBLAT

Trepper, Terry S *see* JOURNAL OF FAMILY PSYCHOTHERAPY

Treptow, Alfred *see* DER BESTIRNTE HIMMEL UEBER MIR

AIN TRERVE WARNUNG VOR DER KUENFFTIGEN STRAFF GOTTES / Huberinus, Caspar – [Augsburg: Philipp Ulhart, Vorrede 1. Mai 1535]. [G.F.: 13.2] – 1mf – 9 – HUB-33/1 – ne IDC [240]

LE TRES ANCIEN DROIT MONASTIQUE DE L'OCCIDENT / Mclaughin, T P – 1936 – Dfl25.00 – ne Slangenburg [240]

TRES ANOS DE LUCHA / Diaz, Jose – Prologo de Santiago Carrillo. Barcelona: Laia, 1978 – 1 – us U.W. Library [946]

TRES CONQUISTADORES Y POBLADORES DE LA NUEVA ESPANA : CHRISTOBAL MARTIN MILLAN DE GAMBOA, ANDRES DE TAPIA, JERONIMO LOPEZ... / Bayle, Constantino – Mexico, 1927; Madrid: Razon y Fe, 1932 – 1 – sp Bibl Santa Ana [910]

TRES DICURSOS DE...CACERES / Pinar, Blas – Diputacion Provincial de Caceres: S. Culturales, 1959 – 1 – sp Bibl Santa Ana [946]

TRES DIPUTADOS DEL CAPITULO PRIVADO DE LA SAN GERONIMO / Fachenetti, Cesar – 1642 – 9 – 1.50f – sp Bibl Santa Ana [946]

TRES DISCURSOS DEL MINISTRO DE RELACIONES EXTERIORES Y CULTO DE LA REPUBLICA ARGENTINA, JUAN I. COOKE, SOBRE ASPECTOS DE LA POLITICA EXTERIOR DEL PAIS / Argentina. Ministerio de Relaciones Exteriores y Culto – [Buenos Aires]: Ministerio de Relaciones Exteriores y Culto, Direcci on de Informaci on al Exterior, [1946] – 1 – CSUXAJB7853-B – us Hoover Inst Photo [320]

TRES FARMACEUTICOS EXTREMENOS / Vegas Fabian, Gonzalo – Madrid: Graficas Valera, 1949 – sp Bibl Santa Ana [946]

TRES JOYEUSE PLAISANTE ET RECREATIVE HISTOIRE COMPOSEE PAR LE LOYAL SERVITEUR...GENTIL SEIGNEUR DE BAYART – Paris. 1837. p.479-607. (Strategy of War Series) – 9 – fr Hachette [355]

TRES LAPIDAS VISIGODAS DE MERIDA / Fita, Fidel – Madrid: Fortanet, 1886. B.R.A.H. IX, pp. 396-401, 1 lam – sp Bibl Santa Ana [946]

TRES PROBLEMAS Y EL FUTURO ECONOMICO DE ESPANA : CONFERENCIA PRONUNCIADA EN EL SALON DE ACTOS DE LA CAJA DE AHORROS Y M. DE P. DE CACERES, EL DIA DE LA INAUGURACION 30 DE OCTUBRE 1976 / Coronel de Palma, Luis – Caceres: Tip. Extremadura, 1976 – 1 – sp Bibl Santa Ana [330]

LAS TRES REINAS / Espronceda, Jose de – 1853 – 9 – $1.50f – sp Bibl Santa Ana [830]

TRES REVOLUCIONES MILITARES / Peron, Juan Domingo – Buenos Aires: Ediciones Corac, 1972 – 1 – CSUXADJ1872-B – us Hoover Inst Photo [972]

TRES REVOLUCIONES MILITARES / Peron, Juan Domingo – [Buenos Aires]: Escorpion, 1963 – 1 – CSUXADJ1923-B – us Hoover Inst Photo [972]

Tresal, Joseph *see* LES ORIGINES DU SCHISME ANGLICAN (1509-1571)

Tresckow, Hans von *see* VON FUERSTEN UND ANDEREN STERBLICHEN ERINNERUNGEN EINES KRIMINALKOMISSARS

Tresco, Carlo *see* AUTOBIOGRAPHY

LES TRES-MERVEILLEUSES VICTOIRES DES FEMMES DU NOUVEAU MONDE / Postel, Guillaume – Paris: chez Jehan Ruelle, 1533. SEM16P254 – 1r – 5 – Can$9.00 – cn Bibl Nat [390]

LE TRESOR / Andrieux – (French Theatre Series). Paris. Mme Masson, an XII. 1804 – 9 – fr Hachette [820]

LE TRESOR DES FAMILLES / ed by Frechette, O – Quebec, Canada. 1 mai 1883 – 1r – 1 – Can$25.00 – cn Can Microfilming [640]

LE TRESOR DES FAMILLES, OU, RECUEIL CLASSIQUE ET COMERICAL, FRANCAIS ET ANGLAIS, POUR LES ELEVES DE TOUT AGE ET DE TOUT DEGRE = THE FAMILY TREASURE, OR, CLASSIC AND COMMERICAL COLLECTIONS, FRENCH AND ENGLISH, FOR STUDENTS OF EVERY AGE AND OF ALL CLASSES – Quebec?: s.n., 1858-18– ou 19– – 9 – cn C.I.H.M. [110]

TRESOR DES RECHERCHES ET ANTIQUITES GAULOISES ET FRANCOISES / Borel, P – 1655 – 9 – fr I.C.S. [930]

TRESORS D'ART SUEDOIS / Reunion des musees nationaux. Paris – 1963. 1 fiche – 9 – fr Réunion [700]

TRESORS DE LA PEINTURE ESPAGNOLE / Reunion des musees nationaux. Paris – 1963. 153 illus. 4 fiches – 9 – fr Réunion [700]
TRESORS DU MUSEE DE BAGDAD DES ORIGINES A L'ISLAM / Reunion des musees nationaux. Paris – 1966. 140 illus. 2 fiches – 9 – fr Réunion [700]
Trespalacios y Mier, J *see* DISCURSO SOBRE QUE LOS NINOS EXPOSITOS CONSIGAN EN LAS INCLUSAS EL FIN DE ESTOS ESTABLECIMIENTOS
O TRES-PONTANO : ORGAM IMPARCIAL, LITTERARIO, NOTICIOSO E AGRICOLA – Tres Pontas, 27 Jun-Jul 1897; 9-13 Jul 1902 – 1,5,6 – bl Biblioteca [072]
Tress, R C *see* REPORT ON THE FINANCES OF ADEN COLONY
Tresti, Flaminio *see* MESSE, A QUATTRO VOCI...LIBRO PRIMO...NUOVAMENTE DATI IN LUCE
Trete Gubernskoe soveshchanie predsedatelei uispolkomov Tambovsko i gubernii *see* STENOGRAFICHESKII OTCHET
O TRET'EI KNIGE EZDRY. OPYT IZSLEDOVANIIA O KNIGAKH APOKRIFICHESKIKH / Shavrov, M – Spb. 1861. BR-4078 2 – 8 – ne IDC [460]
TRETIA GODOVSHCHINA OKTIABRSKOI REVOLIUTSII : SOVETSKAIA VLAST I EE ZLYEVRAGI / Divilkovskii, A – Moskva: Gos. izd-vo, 1920 – 1 – CSUX88-B7903 – us Hoover Inst Photo [947]
TRET'IA KNIGA RAZSKAZOV / Gippius, Z N – Spb. 1902. BR-727 2 – 8 – ne IDC [460]
Tret'iakov, Vitalii *see* NEZAVISIMAIA GAZETA
LE TRETTE DE LA GRAMMERE FRANCOEZE / Meigret, Louis – 1888 – 9 – fr I.C.S. [440]
Tretter, M J *see* PITHY BIT ARITHMETIC APPLIED TO THE COMPUTATION OF SOME ELEMENTARY TRANSCENDENTAL AND SPECIAL FUNCTIONS
Treu, K *see*
– DIE GRIECHISCHEN HANDSCHRIFTEN DES NEUEN TESTAMENTS IN DER UDSSR (T.U.U. 5-91)
– SYNESIOS VON KYRENE
DER TREUE JOHANNES : MAERCHENSPIEL NACH DEM GLEICHNAMIGEN MAERCHEN DER GEBRUEDER GRIMM IN HANDLUNG UND REIME GEBRACHT / Guembel-Seiling, Max – Leipzig: Breitkopf & Haertel, 1918 – 1r – 1 – us U.W. Library [820]
Treue, William *see* PREUSSISCHE STATISTIK
DER TREUE ZIONS-WAECHTER – Organ zur Wahrung der Interessen des orthodoxen Judenthums. Hamburg-Altona. v1-10. 1845-1854. B368 (Leo Baeck Institute. German-Jewish Periodicals, Pt 1) – 1r – 1 – $75.00 – us UPA [270]
Treuenfels, A *see* ISRAELITISCHE WOCHEN-SCHRIFT
Treugold, Fritz *see* SADRACH A.B. DNEGO
TREULICHER UNTERRICHT IM GENERAL-BASS / Kellner, David – 1732 – 9 – us Sibley [780]
TREULICHER UNTERRICHT IM GENERAL-BASS / Kellner, David & Bach, C P E – P 340 – 9 – ne IDC [780]
Treutler, A *see* DIE VERJAEHRUNGSEINREDE...
Treutler, Amand *see* HERDERS DRAMATISCHE DICHTUNGEN
TREVELYN HOLD / Wood, Ellen – British Fiction Archive: Unit 1 – 9 – uk Bell [830]
Treves, R *see* ZAH VE-ADOM
Trevillano, Salvador *see* LA VIDA INTENSA. VENCIDO
Trevor, George *see* TYPES AND THE ANTITYPE
Trevor, J *see* A SHORT HISTORY OF THE DONATISTS;...
Trevoux *see*
– DICTIONNAIRE UNIVERSEL FRANCOIS ET LATIN
Trew, C J *see*
– CEDRORUM LIBANI HISTORIA
– HERBARIUM BLACKWELLIANUM. VERMEHRTES UND VERBESSERTES BLACKWELLISCHES KRAEUTER-BUCH
– HORTUS NITIDISSIMUS
– PLANTAE RARIORES, QUAS MAXIMAM PARTEM IPSE IN HORTO DOMESTICO COLUIT
– PLANTAE SELECTAE. PINXIT G. D. EHRET
TREWMAN'S EXETER FLYING POST – England. -w. 8 Nov 1804; 3 Jan 1805; 1 Jan 1807-Dec 1832. 8 1 2 reels – 1 – uk British Libr Newspaper [072]
Trexler, James G *see* THE IMMEDIATE EFFECT OF CONCURRENT VISUAL FEEDBACK ON BEGINNING TARGETS ARCHERS
TRGOVINSKI PREGLED – Belgrade, Yugoslavia. Jun 1951-1952 – 1r – 1 – us L of C Photodup [949]
TRI CITY NEWS – Sherwood OR. Oct 11 1951-Feb 3 1966 – 1 – us U.O. Library [071]
TRI CITY POST *see* BERKELEY POST
TRI DUSHI (STIKHI N. L'VOVOI, A. ACHMATOVOI, M. MORAVSKOI) / Gizetti, A – Ezhemesiachnyi zhurnal, 12. 1915. BR-3657 2 – 8 – ne IDC [460]
Tri, Huynh Cao *see* PARTICIPATIVE ADMINISTRATION AND ENDOGENOUS DEVELOPMENT
Tri, Huynh Cao et al *see* STRATEGIES FOR ENDOGENOUS DEVELOPMENT
TRI RASTSVETA. DRAMA / Bal'mont, K D – Spb. 1907. BR-545 2 – 8 – ne IDC [460]
TRI RECHI O PROMYSLOVOI KOOPERATSII NA 6 SOBRANII UPOLNOMOCHENNYKH VSEKOMPOMSOIUZA, IIUN' 1928 G. / Rudzutak, Ia.E, et al – M., 1929 – 1mf – 9 – COR-191/1 – ne IDC [334]
TRI SVETOCHA = THE THREE LAMPS / Prokanov, Ivan S – St. Petersburg, 1909. Raduga; 8p added to reel of 274p – 1 – 11.28 – us Baptist [240]
TRI TAN – no. 1-212. Hanoi. 3 juin 1941-22 nov 1945. mq no. 30, 45, 57, 79, 177, 187 – 1 – fr A.C.R.P.P. [073]
TRI TSARIA / Otsup, N – Paris. 1958. BR-1218 2 – 8 – ne IDC [460]
TRI WEEKLY ADVERTISER – Umatilla OR. Apr 25 1865 – 1 – us U.O. Library [071]
TRIA GENERA PLANTARUM NOVA, EX HORTO BOTANICO VIENNENSI / Jacquin, J F – (Nova Acta Helvetia. v. 1. 1787. B-1088 2 – 8 – ne IDC [580]
TRIAL – v1-31. 1964-95 – 9 – $624.00 set – us Hein [340]
THE TRIAL AND DEATH OF JESUS CHRIST: A DEVOTIONAL HISTORY OF OUR LORD'S PASSION / Stalker, James – New York: Hodder & Stoughton, 1894. 1 fiche – 9 – us A.T.L.A. [240]
THE TRIAL AT BAR OF SIR ROGER C.D. TICHBORNE – 3r – 1 – $255.00 – S1871 – us Scholarly Res [340]
(A TRIAL) BALLOON – Midland. Mich. 1931-32 – 1 – us UMI [071]
TRIAL BRIEF AND DOCUMENT BOOKS / U.S. World War Two War Crimes Records – T991 – 1r – 1 – us Nat'l Archives [940]
TRIAL BY JURY. ADDRESSES OF MR. JACOB MARKS. / Marks, Jacob – New York: O'Brien, 1894. 36p. LL-681 – 1 – us L of C Photodup [340]
TRIAL BY JURY IN CONTEMPT PROCEEDINGS / Bartlett, Charles Lafayette – Washington Govt. Print. Off., 1900 8 p. LL-643 – 1 – us L of C Photodup [340]
TRIAL DIPLOMACY JOURNAL – v.1-. 1978- – 1,5,6,9 – us UMI [327]
TRIAL DIPLOMACY JOURNAL – v1-15. 1978-1992 – 9 – $85.00set – us Hein [340]
TRIAL DOCKETS / Huron County. Ohio. Supreme Court – 1821-1882 – 1r – 1 – $32.50r – us Archival [340]
TRIAL LAWYER'S GUIDE – (1980- 5,6,9) – 1957- – 1 – us UMI [073]
TRIAL LAWYERS GUIDE – (v1-28 1957-84 on reel $342.00. v29-38 1985-94 on mf $243.00. Index 1957-90) – v1-38. 1957-94 – 5,6,9 – $585.00 set – us Hein [340]
TRIAL LAWYER'S QUARTERLY – (v.14-. 1979-5,6,9) – v.1-. 1964- – 1 – us UMI [073]
TRIAL OF 37 SOUTH WEST AFRICA TERRORISTS – ((Case history)) – 1 reel – 1 – sa Microfile [960]
TRIAL OF AARON BURR AND HERMAN BLENNERHASSET, 1808 / U.S. District Courts – 1roll – 1 – T265 – us Nat'l Archives [324]
TRIAL OF ANDREW JOHNSON – Washington, 1868 – 1r – 1 – us Ross [976]
TRIAL OF, BEFORE THE FIRST BAPTIST CHURCH OF NASHVILLE, TENNESSEE / Graves, J R – 1858 – 1 – 5.00 – us Baptist [240]
TRIAL OF DANIEL M'COOK, ESQ., CLERK OF THE COURT OF COMMON PLEAS OF CARROLL COUNTY, ON ARTICLES OF IMPEACHMENT FOR BREACH OF GOOD BEHAVIOUR IN OFFICE / M'Cook, Daniel – Cincinnati, Hefley, Hubbell, 1839. 72 p. LL-2344 – 1 – us L of C Photodup [340]
THE TRIAL OF FRANK JAMES FOR MURDER / Miller, George, Jr – Kansas City, MO: Miller, 1898. 348p. LL-518 – 1 – us L of C Photodup [340]
TRIAL OF IMPEACHMENT OF LEVI HUBBELL, JUDGE OF THE SECOND JUDICIAL CIRCUIT, BY THE SENATE OF THE STATE OF WISCONSIN, JUNE 1853 / Hubbell, Levi – Madison? Brown, 1853. 820p. LL-1263 – 1 – us L of C Photodup [340]
THE TRIAL OF JESUS / Rosadi, Giovanni – New York: Dodd, Mead, 1905. 1 fiche – 9 – us A.T.L.A. [240]
THE TRIAL OF JESUS CHRIST : A LEGAL MONOGRAPH / Innes, Alexander Taylor – (Includes bibliographical references) – Edinburgh: T & T Clark; New York: Imported by Charles Scribner, 1899 – 1mf – 9 – 0-8370-3728-X – 1985-1728 – us A.T.L.A. [240]
TRIAL OF JESUS CHRIST / Innes, Alexander Taylor – Edinburgh: T. & T. Clark, 1899. 1 fiche – 9 – us A.T.L.A. [240]
TRIAL OF JESUS: FROM JEWISH SOURCES / Drucker, Aaron P – New York: Bloch Publishing, 1907. 1 fiche – 9 – us A.T.L.A. [240]
TRIAL OF JOHN H. REICKLES...FOR THE HOMICIDE OF HENRY LINSTEDT, IN THE CITY OF CHARLESTON – Charleston, S.C., Walker, Evans, 1858. 95 p. LL-1100 – 1 – us L of C Photodup [340]
TRIAL OF K. KASSIM AND 12 OTHERS – 9r – 1 – sa Microfile [960]
TRIAL OF LIEUTENANT GENERAL JOHN WHITELOCKE, COMMANDER IN CHIEF OF THE EXPEDITION AGAINST BUENOS AYRES / Whitelocke, John – London, Tipper etc. 1808. 214, 12 p. LL-31 – 1 – us L of C Photodup [340]
THE TRIAL OF MAHARAJA NANDA KUMAR : A NARRATIVE OF A JUDICIAL MURDER / Beveridge, Henry – Calcutta: Thacker, Spink, 1886 – 1r – 1 – us U.W. Library [360]
TRIAL OF MAJOR WAR CRIMINALS / International Military Tribunal – Nuremberg. Official Record. 14 Nov 1945-1 Oct 1946. 42v – 9r – 1 – $400.00 – us Trans-Media [340]
TRIAL OF MAJOR WAR CRIMINALS / International Military Tribunal for the Far East – Tokyo. 6 reels – 1 – $300.00 – us Trans-Media [340]
TRIAL OF MAJOR WAR CRIMINALS BEFORE THE INTERNATIONAL MILITARY TRIBUNAL, NUREMBERG / International Military Tribunal – Nuremberg, 14 Nov 1945-1 Oct 1946. Blue series – 267 fiches – 9 – $815.00 – us UPA [340]
THE TRIAL OF MR. WHITEFIELD'S SPIRIT; IN SOME REMARKS UPON HIS FOURTH JOURNAL,... / Weller, S – London, 1740 – 1mf – 9 – MP-275/1 – ne IDC [240]
TRIAL OF ROBERT MANGALISO SOBUKWE – 1 reel – 1 – sa Microfile [960]
TRIAL OF SETH COOPER AND EIGHT OTHERS – 9r – 1 – sa Microfile [960]
TRIAL OF SOUTH WEST AFRICA TERRORISTS (MESSACK VICTORY AND OTHERS) – 3r – 1 – sa Microfile [960]
THE TRIAL OF THE CONSTITUTION / Fisher, Sidney G – New York: J B Lippincott, 1862 – 4mf – 9 – $6.00 – LLMC 95-090 – us L.L.M.C. [323]
TRIAL OF THE DEAN OF JOHANNESBURG (GONVILLE AUBIL FFRENCH-BEYTACH) – 7r – 1 – sa Microfile [960]
THE TRIAL OF THE REV. DAVID SWING BEFORE THE PRESBYTERY OF CHICAGO – Chicago: Jansen, McClurg, 1874 – 1mf – us A.T.L.A. [240]
THE TRIAL OF THE WITNESSES OF THE RESURRECTION OF JESUS / Sherlock, James (Thomas?) – Philadelphia; Presbyterian Board of Publications, n.d. – 3mf – 9 – $4.50 – LLMC 91-091 – us L.L.M.C. [340]
THE TRIAL OF TRAIECHO KOSTOV AND HIS GROUP / Kostov, T – Sofia. 1949. BR-3884 2 – 8 – ne IDC [947]
TRIAL W.W.C. TWALA AND 10 OTHERS – 5r – 1 – sa Microfile [960]
TRIALS OF CAPT. JOSEPH J. KNAPP, JR., AND GEORGE CROWNINSHIELD, ESQ., FOR THE MURDER OF CAPT. JOSEPH WHITE, OF SALEM, ON THE NIGHT OF THE SIXTH OF APRIL, 1830 – Boston, Ellms, 1830. 32 p. LL-2401 – 1 – us L of C Photodup [340]
TRIALS OF THE HEART / Bray, Anna Eliza – British Fiction Archive: Unit 2 – 9 – uk Bell [830]
TRIALS OF WAR CRIMINALS BEFORE THE NUREMBERG MILITARY TRIBUNALS UNDER CONTROL COUNCIL LAW NO.10 / International Military Tribunal – Nuremberg, Oct 1946-Apr 1949. Green series – 187 fiches – 9 – $560.00 – us UPA [340]
Triana, Beverly F *see* MENSTRUAL DYSFUNCTION IN RUNNERS
Triana, J J *see* NUEVOS JENEROS I ESPECIES DE PLANTAS PARA LA FLORANEO-GRANADINA
Triandhy, A S *see* 1001 (I.E. SERIBU SATU)
O TRIANGULO – Uberaba, 12 Nov-Dec 1947; Apr-Jun, Aug 1948; Mar, Jul 1949; Sept 1950; 10 Jul 1951 – 1,5,6 – bl Biblioteca [072]
O TRIANGULO – Uberlandia, Brazil. Nov 1957; Dec 1960; May, Nov 1962; Mar-Dec 1978; Jan-May 1979 – 1 – bl Biblioteca [072]
DIE TRIARIER : H. LEO, DR. P. MARHEINECKE, DR. K. BRUNO / Goerres, Joseph – Regensburg: G.J. Manz, 1838 – 1mf – us A.T.L.A. [240]
THE TRIBAL SPOKESMAN – 1969-75.(American Indian Periodicals in the Princeton University Library). 9 fiches – 9 – $50.00 – us UPA [305]
TRIBAL SPOKESMAN – Sacramento, CA. 1968-79 (broken file) – 1r – 1 – $50.00 – B02744 – us Library Micro [071]
TRIBAL STUDIES IN NORTHERN NIGERIA / Meek, Charles Kingsley – London: Paul, Trench, Trubner. 2v. 1931 – us Res Libr [305]
THE TRIBES AND CASTES OF BENGAL; NORTH WESTERN PROVINCES, AND PUNJAB / Risley, H H – 2v. Anthropometric data; 2 v. Ethnographic glossary. Calcutta. 1891, 1892. BI-592 2 – 8 – ne IDC [306]
THE TRIBES AND CASTES OF BOMBAY / Enthoven, R E – 3v. Bombay. 1920-22. BI-479 2 – 8 – ne IDC [306]
THE TRIBES AND CASTES OF THE CENTRAL PROVINCES OF INDIA / Russell, R V & Lal, H – 4v. London. 1916. BI-595 2 – 8 – ne IDC [306]
THE TRIBES AND CASTES OF THE NORTHWESTERN PROVINCES AND OUDH / Crooke, W – 4v. Calcutta. 1896. BI-478 2 – 8 – ne IDC [306]
THE TRIBES OF THE ASHANTI HINTERLAND / Rattray, R S – 2v. Oxford. 1932. BA-367 2 – 8 – ne IDC [306]
THE TRIBES OF THE PACIFIC COAST OF NORTH AMERICA / Kroeber, A L – BN 287 2. 1917 – 8 – ne IDC [970]
TRIBINA – Skoplje, Yugoslavia. -w. 16 Feb 1966-19 Dec 1968. 3 reels – 1 – uk British Libr Newspaper [949]
TRIBOLOGIE UND SCHMIERUNGSTECHNIK – v30- 1983- – 1,5,6,9 – us UMI [620]
LE TRIBOULET – Ottawa: O. McDonnell, [1879-188? ou 189-?] – 9 – cn C.I.H.M. [073]
LE TRIBOULET – Ottawa, Ontario. 1 nov 1879-v1 n4. 29 nov 1879 – 1r – 1 – Can$35.00 – cn Can Microfilming [072]
LE TRIBOULET – Paris. nov 1878-1921 – 1 – fr A.C.R.P.P. [073]
LA TRIBU KONKOMBA DU NORD TOGO / Froelich, Jean Claude – Dakar. 1954 – 1 – us Res Libr [306]
TRIBUENE : ORGAN DES FDGB – (Cont: Die Freie Gewerkschaft, since 1947) – Berlin, jul 1980-sep 23 1991 – 1 – Dist. gw Mikrofilm – gw Misc Inst [072]
TRIBUENE *see* DIE FREIE GEWERKSCHAFT
TRIBUENE DER DEMOKRATIE – (Bereichsausgabe der Hamburger Volkszeitung) – Bremen, 1947-50 (many issues missing) – 1r – 1 – Inquire at Mikrofilmarchiv for details – gw Misc Inst [072]
LES TRIBULATIONS D'UN CHINOIS EN CHINE / Verne, Jules – Paris: J. Hetzel, 1879. 316p. 4 fiches. (Literature Collection) – 9 – 10.00 – fr Bibl Nationale [830]
THE TRIBULATIONS OF THE CHURCH IN CHINA, A.D. 1900 (CCC240) : NATIVES AND FOREIGNERS / MacGillivray, D – (In Chinese) – Shanghai: Society for the Diffusion of Christian and General Knowledge among the Chinese. 2v. 1901 – 1r – 1 – 1984-6579 – us A.T.L.A. [240]
LE TRIBUN – (23 missing numbers) – Angers (Maine-et-Loire), March 1848 – Nov. 1851 – 1r – fr Armell [331]
LE TRIBUN DU PEUPLE – Organe des travailleurs puis de la Montagne. no. 1-5. 16-30 mars 1848. Elements repris par: La Montagne de la fraternite. no. 1-4. 5-14 mai 1848. Paris – 1 – fr A.C.R.P.P. [331]

LE TRIBUN DU PEUPLE – Paris. au Bureau du Cercle Social. Redacteur: Nicolas de Bonneville – 9 – fr Hachette [321]
LE TRIBUN DU PEUPLE ET L'AMI DES DEFENSEURS DE LA PATRIE – no. 1-89. Paris. sept 1797-janv 1798 – 1 – fr A.C.R.P.P. [073]
A TRIBUNA : JORNAL DEDICADO AOS INTERESSES MORAES E MATERIAES DA PROVINCIA – Cuiaba, 7 Nov 1885-Dec 1888; Apr-Aug 1889; Jan-4 May 1890 – 1,5,6 – bl Biblioteca [072]
A TRIBUNA – Manacapuru, Amazonas. 14-21 Dez 1902 – 1,5,6 – bl Biblioteca [072]
A TRIBUNA : ORGAM DE ALUMNOS DO GYMNASIO AMAZONENSE – Manaus, Amazonas. 19 Jan-22 Jul 1911 – 1,5,6 – bl Biblioteca [072]
A TRIBUNA : ORGAO DO PARTIDO REPUBLICANO FEDERAL DE ALAGOAS – Maceio, Alagoas. 7-10 Set 1896; 21 Maio 1897 – 1,5,6 – bl Biblioteca [072]
A TRIBUNA – Parintins, Amazonas. 8 Nov 1969 – 1,5,6 – bl Biblioteca [072]
A TRIBUNA – Rio Pomba, Brazil. Jun-Dec 1934 – 1 – bl Biblioteca [072]
A TRIBUNA – S. Joao d'el-Rei, 28 Jul 1919; Oct, Dec 1920; Jan-3 Apr 1927 – 1,5,6 – bl Biblioteca [072]
A TRIBUNA – Santos, Brazil. Aug 1900-May 1945. Incomplete except 1907, 1911, 1914-16 complete – 1 – bl Biblioteca [072]
A TRIBUNA – Uberlandia, Brazil. Jul 1923-Sept 1944. Widely scattered issues except 1937 and 1941 complete – 1 – bl Biblioteca [072]
LA TRIBUNA – Asuncion, Paraguay. 1956-sep 1983 – us Res Libr [072]
LA TRIBUNA – Panama City, Panama. 28 Oct 1931-28 Oct 1933 – 1r – 1 – us L of C Photodup [072]
LA TRIBUNA – Rome, Italy. -d. 25 Sept 1914-21 Aug 1943. Including La Tribuna coloniale. 7 Dec 1918-4 Jan 1919. 83 reels – 1 – uk British Libr Newspaper [072]
TRIBUNA – Cluj, Romania. -w. 1958-70. 9 reels – 1 – uk British Libr Newspaper [949]
TRIBUNA – (Library has: Nov. 15, 1936) – Moskva: Izdvo "Der- Emes", 1928-1937. 10v – 1 – CSUX89-S795 – us Hoover Inst Photo [947]
TRIBUNA – Rumaenien, 1976-1991 – 16r – DM1,200.00 – gw Mikro Press [949]
TRIBUNA – San Luis, MX. 1975- – 168+ r – $8,400.00 ($445.00y) – R04160 – us Library Micro [072]
A TRIBUNA ACADEMICA : ORGAM DE ALUMNOS DA UNIVERSIDADE DE MANAOS – Manaos, Amazonas. 23 Jun-23 Jul 1911 – 1,5,6 – bl Biblioteca [072]
TRIBUNA DE FRUTAL – Frutal, 19 Nov 1944 – 1,5,6 – bl Biblioteca [072]
TRIBUNA DE LAVRAS – Lavras, 23 Mar-Dec 1969; Jan 1972-Mar 1975; Aug 1976-Dec 1977; Jan-Dec 1979; Jan-25 Dec 1982 – 1,5,6 – bl Biblioteca [072]
TRIBUNA DE OURO PRETO : ORGAO DO MOVIMENTO NACIONALISTA DE OURO PRETO – Ouro Preto, 1 Jan 1960 – 1,5,6 – bl Biblioteca [072]
TRIBUNA DE OURO PRETO – Ouro Preto, 3 Jun 1945-3 Jan 1948 – 1,5,6 – bl Biblioteca [072]
TRIBUNA DE PARINTINS – Parintins, Amazonas. Ago 1981 – 1,5,6 – bl Biblioteca [072]
TRIBUNA DE PATOS – Patos de Minas, Brazil. May 1953 – 1 – bl Biblioteca [072]
LA TRIBUNA DI UTICA – Utica, NY, 1912 – 3mf or 1r – 1,9 – us I.H.R.C. [978]
TRIBUNA DO CAIXEIRO : ORGAO DE PROPAGANDA E DEFESA DOS INTERESSES DA CLASSE – Manaus, Amazonas. 21 Abr 1908-11 Nov 1909 – 1,5,6 – bl Biblioteca [072]
TRIBUNA DO MUCURI – Teofilo Otoni, 5 Aug 1969 – 1,5,6 – bl Biblioteca [072]
TRIBUNA DO OESTE – Bambui, Brazil. Apr-May 1955 – 1 – bl Biblioteca [072]
TRIBUNA DO POVO – Rio Branco, Acre. 26 Maio, Set 1957; Mar 1958; Mar, Jun-Jul 1959 – 1,5,6 – bl Biblioteca [072]
TRIBUNA DO POVO – Uberaba, 5 Feb-7 Nov 1894 – 1,5,6 – bl Biblioteca [072]
TRIBUNA DO SUL – Sao Sebastiao do Paraiso, 6 Sept 1915 – 1,5,6 – bl Biblioteca [072]
LA TRIBUNA ITALIANA – (Filmed with: The Texas Tribune, jun 22 1940) – Dallas, TX: C S Papa & L E Adin, dec 8 1917-jun 15 1940 – us Res Libr [071]
LA TRIBUNA ITALIANA – Portland, OR. 8 Mar 1912-16 Dec 1932. 7 rolls – 1 – us U.O. Library [071]
LA TRIBUNA ITALIANA – Portland, OR. -w. 1911-32 – 1 – 192.00 – us Oregon Hist [071]
LA TRIBUNA ITALIANA TRANS-ATLANTICA – Chicago, mar 22 1913; [oct 17 1914-1922]; 1917-32 – us Res Libr [071]
TRIBUNA LIBERAL : JORNAL POLITICO E LITTERARIO – Sao Paulo, 17 May 1867 – 1,5,6 – bl Biblioteca [072]
TRIBUNA NARODOWA = PEOPLE'S TRIBUNE – (In Yiddish) – Krakow, PL. v3 no13(no112) 27 Mar 1927-v3 no21 29 May 1936 – 1r – 1 – $35.00 – cn Can Microfilming [072]
TRIBUNA POPULAR : JORNAL IMPARCIAL, NOTICIOSO E LITTERARIO – Maceio, Alagoas. 10 Ago-21 Set 1881 – 1,5,6 – bl Biblioteca [072]
TRIBUNA POPULAR – Penedo, Alagoas. 18 Jul-Ago 1897; Set 1898; Ago, 1 Nov 1899 – 1,5,6 – bl Biblioteca [072]
TRIBUNA POPULAR : PERIODICO COMMERCIAL, AGRICOLA, LITTERARIO E NOTICIOSO – Maceio, Alagoas. 3 Out, Dez 1887; Mar, Maio-23 Jun 1888 – 1,5,6 – bl Biblioteca [072]
TRIBUNA POPULAR – Sao Joao del-Rei, Brazil. Sept 1895 – 1 – bl Biblioteca [072]
TRIBUNA ROJA – Bogota, CK. – 1r – $50.00 – R04194 – us Library Micro [320]
TRIBUNA VARGINHENSE – Varginha, Brazil. Dec 1977; 1978; Jan-Mar 1979 – 1 – bl Biblioteca [072]
THE TRIBUNAL – Published by the No-Conscription Fellowship. London. -w. 8 Mar 1916-8 Jan 1920. (64 ft) – 1 – uk British Libr Newspaper [073]
EL TRIBUNAL DEL SANTO OFICIO EN ARAGON / Floriano Cumbreno, Antonio C – Madrid: Tip. Rev. Archivo y Bibliot. y Museos, 1925 – 1 – sp Bibl Santa Ana [946]
EL TRIBUNAL DEL SANTO OFICIO EN ARAGON ESTABLECIMIENTO DE LA INQUISICION EN TERUEL / Floriano Cumbreno, Antonio C – Madrid: Rev. Arch. Bibliot. y Museos, 1925 – 1 – sp Bibl Santa Ana [946]
LE TRIBUNAL MUSULMAN / Savvas, Pasha – Paris: Marchal et Billard, 1902. 180p. LL-12032 – 1 – us L of C Photodup [340]
EL TRIBUNAL SUPREMO / Spain. Ministerio de Propaganda – n.p., 1937? Fiche W1234. (Blodgett Collection of Spanish Civil War Pamphlets) – 9 – us H.U. College Libr [946]
IL TRIBUNALE DELL'AMMIRAGLIATO E CONSOLATO [1783-1808] / Gentile, E – Napoli, 1909 – 1mf – 1 – ILM-1644/1 – ne IDC [327]
LOS TRIBUNALES DE MENORES EN LOS ESTADOS UNIDOS DE AMERICA / Mena, Anselmo – Mexico: Imprenta de la Secretaria Mexico de relaciones exteriores, 1933. 49p. LL-476 – 1 – us L of C Photodup [340]
TRIBUNALES Y ABOGADOS CACERENOS / Hurtado de Mendoza, Publio – Caceres: Tip. Enc. y Lib. de Luciano Jimenez Merino, 1910 – sp Bibl Santa Ana [946]
LA TRIBUNE / ed by David, Laurent Oliver – Montreal, Canada. 23 oct 1880-3 mai 1884 – 1r – 1 – Can$40.00 – cn Can Microfilming [072]
LA TRIBUNE – Journal republicain socialiste. Dir. F. Trebois. Paris. 2 juin 1876-27 mars 1877 – 1 – fr A.C.R.P.P. [335]
LA TRIBUNE – Kinshasa, 1967 (May 29-Dec 30) – 2r – 9 – AF-105/3 – ne IDC [072]
LA TRIBUNE – Organe des syndicats de mineurs du Pas-de-Calais, du Nord et d'Anzin. Lens. 1929-avr 1940 – 1 – fr A.C.R.P.P. [331]
LA TRIBUNE – Quebec, Canada. 25 aut 1863-22 aut 1864 – 1r – 1 – Can$40.00 – cn Can Microfilming [072]
LA TRIBUNE – Quebec, Canada. 6 nov 1886-v1 n12. 4 dec 1886 – 1r – 1 – Can$25.00 – cn Can Microfilming [072]
LA TRIBUNE : QUOTIDIEN / ed by Nicol, Jacob & Desruisseaux, Paul – (Numea1ros souvenirs de fondation; editions speciales economiques, touristiques, etc.; cahiers historiques des paroisses des Cantons de l'Est 4r Can$75.00) – Sherbrooke, Canada. 21 fev 1910-30 nov 1992 – 403r – 1 – Can$75.00r – cn Can Microfilming [072]
LA TRIBUNE – St-Hyacinthe, Canada. 16 mar 1888-29 dec 1922 – 10r – 1 – Can$65.00r – cn Can Microfilming [072]
LA TRIBUNE – Woonsocket. R.I. 1896-1934 – 1 – us UMI [071]
LA TRIBUNE – Woonsocket, RI. v58 n141. 16 dec 1925-v64 n36. 11 fev 1929 – 1r – 1 – Can$25.00 – cn Can Microfilming [071]
THE TRIBUNE – Ambala, India. -w. Jan 1884-Dec 1885. 1 reel – 1 – uk British Libr Newspaper [072]
THE TRIBUNE – Concord. N.C. 1907- – 1 – us UMI [071]
THE TRIBUNE – Dublin. Ireland. -w. 21 Jun 1834-3 Jan 1835. (40 ft) – 1 – uk British Libr Newspaper [072]
THE TRIBUNE – Georgetown, Guyana. -w. 5 Jan 1930-26 Sept 1937. 4 reels – 1 – uk British Libr Newspaper [072]
THE TRIBUNE – Ireland.12 Mar-31 Dec 1926 – 1 – ie Microforms [072]
THE TRIBUNE – London. -d. 15 Jan 1906-7 Feb 1908. (13 reels) – 1 – uk British Libr Newspaper [072]
THE TRIBUNE – Sacramento, CA. 1928-1931 – 1r – 1 – $50.00 – C03436 – us Library Micro [071]
THE TRIBUNE = LA TRIBUNE – Montreal, Canada. 18 sep 1872 – 1r – 1 – Can$20.00 – cn Can Microfilming [072]
THE TRIBUNE *see* OAKLAND TRIBUNE
TRIBUNE – 1894-1906 – 2r – 1 – at Corangamite [072]
TRIBUNE – (1993.-2r; 1888-1905.-1r) – Stouffville, 1916-1992 – 70r – 1 – cn Preston [971]
TRIBUNE – (Also known as: Morning Tribune) – Las Vegas, NV. 1943-44 – 3r – 1 – $150.00 – U04615 – us Library Micro [978]
TRIBUNE – Ambala, India. May 1948-Jun 1985 – 243r – 1 – us L of C Photodup [072]
TRIBUNE – Arcadia, Calif. (includes BULLETIN and NEWS to 1961). Arcadia. Calif. 1931- – 1 – us UMI [071]
TRIBUNE – Arcadia. Calif. w. 1931-35 – 1 – us UMI [071]
TRIBUNE – Bay City. Mich. 1895-1915 – 1 – us UMI [071]
TRIBUNE – Beatrice, NE. -w. Aug. 1895-Apr. 1897; Jun. 1897-Oct. 1897; Aug. 1898-Oct. 1898 – 1 – us NE Hist [071]
TRIBUNE – Bismarck. N.D. 1970- – 1 – us UMI [071]
TRIBUNE – Blair, NE. -w. Jun. 1908-Nov. 1917 – 1 – us NE Hist [071]
TRIBUNE – Bloomington. Ind. 1967-1968 – 1 – us UMI [071]
TRIBUNE – Burwell. Neb. 1899-1917; 1918-1938; 1939-1963 – 1 – us UMI [071]
TRIBUNE – Chanute. Kan. 1892- – 1 – us UMI [071]
TRIBUNE – Chicago. Ill. Indexed. 1849- – 1 – us UMI [071]
TRIBUNE – Chicago.IL. Paris ed.1917-34 – 1 – us UMI [071]
TRIBUNE – Clarksburg. West Virginia. 1895-1896 – 1 – us UMI [071]
TRIBUNE – Cocoa. Fl. 1917-1969 – 1 – us UMI [071]
TRIBUNE – Coshocton. Ohio. 1881-1888; 1909- – 1 – us UMI [071]
TRIBUNE – Cullman. Ala. 1890-1891 – 1 – us UMI [071]
TRIBUNE – Cut Bank. Mont. 1913-1915 – 1 – us UMI [071]
TRIBUNE – Davenport. IA. -w. 1888-93 – 1 – us UMI [071]
TRIBUNE – Des Moines. Iowa. 1907- – 1 – us UMI [071]
TRIBUNE – Dixon. Calif. -w. 1943-58 – 1 – us UMI [071]
TRIBUNE – Dominica. 1924-1951 – 1 – us UMI [072]
TRIBUNE – Dunsmuir, CA. 1926-27 – 1r – 1 – $50.00 – B02189 – us Library Micro [071]
TRIBUNE – Elmore, Ohio. 1902-3 – 1r – 1 – $32.50r – us Archival [071]
TRIBUNE – Fairfield. Iowa. 1879-1904; 1908-1920- – 1 – us UMI [071]
TRIBUNE – Falls City. Neb. 1904-1911 – 1 – us UMI [071]
TRIBUNE – Fort Scott. Kan. and predecessors. -d. 1869- – 1 – us UMI [071]
TRIBUNE – Fremont.NE. -sw. 1868-1917 – 1 – us UMI [071]
TRIBUNE – Froid. Mont. 1911-1916; 1923-1942 – 1 – us UMI [071]
TRIBUNE – Gallipolis. Ohio. 1895- – 1 – us UMI [071]
TRIBUNE – Gary. Ind. -w. 1907-12 – 1 – us UMI [071]
TRIBUNE – Gildford. Mont. 1922-1924 – 1 – us UMI [071]
TRIBUNE – Grand Haven. Mich. 1891- – 1 – us UMI [071]
TRIBUNE – Great Bend. Kan. -w. 1887-1915 – 1 – us UMI [071]
TRIBUNE – Great Falls. Mont. 1953- – 1 – us UMI [071]
TRIBUNE – Great Falls. Mont. -w. 1885-89 – 1 – us UMI [071]
TRIBUNE – Greeley. Col. 1908- – 1 – us UMI [071]
TRIBUNE – Greeley. Col. -w. 1870-1911 – 1 – us UMI [071]
TRIBUNE – Greeley. Kan. 1880-1881 – 1 – us UMI [071]
TRIBUNE – Hardin. Mont. 1908-1924 – 1 – us UMI [071]
TRIBUNE – Harlan. Iowa. -w. 1951- – 1 – us UMI [071]
TRIBUNE – Harvey. Ill. 1930- – 1 – us UMI [071]
TRIBUNE – Healdsburg. Calif. -w. 1945-58 – 1 – us UMI [071]
TRIBUNE – Hibbing. Minn. 1899- – 1 – us UMI [071]
TRIBUNE – Hinsdale. Mont. 1958-1959; 1966- – 1 – us UMI [071]
TRIBUNE – Hornellsville. N.Y. -d. 1852-80 – 1 – us UMI [071]
TRIBUNE – Ironton. Ohio. 1949- – 1 – us UMI [071]
TRIBUNE – Jackson. Mich. 1926-1936 – 1 – us UMI [071]
TRIBUNE – Johnstown. Pa. 1873-1952 – 1 – us UMI [071]
TRIBUNE – Johnstown. PA. -w. 1864-1917 – 1 – us UMI [071]
TRIBUNE – Jordan. Mont. 1958-1959; 1966- – 1 – us UMI [071]
TRIBUNE – Junction City. Kan. 1873-1902 – 1 – us UMI [071]
TRIBUNE – Kent. Ohio. -w. 1915-28 – 1 – us UMI [071]
TRIBUNE – Kokomo. Ind. 1860- – 1 – us UMI [071]
TRIBUNE – La Crosse. WI. 1905- – 1 – us UMI [071]
TRIBUNE – Lewiston. Id. -w and sw and predecessor. 1892-95 – 1 – us UMI [071]
TRIBUNE – Liberty. Mo. -w. 1846-52 – 1 – us UMI [071]
TRIBUNE – London. England. 1937- – 1 – us UMI [072]
TRIBUNE – London, England.1951- . biweekly, weekly. Continues: Tribune for Victory and Socialism – 1 – us U.W. Library [072]
TRIBUNE – London. -w. Jan 1937-Dec 1970. (24mqn reels) – 1 – uk British Libr Newspaper [072]
TRIBUNE – Los Angeles. Calif. -w. 1946-56 – 1 – us UMI [071]
TRIBUNE – Lovelock, NV. 1898-1912 – 12r – 1 – $600.00 – U04625 – us Library Micro [071]
TRIBUNE – Lowell. Ind. -w. 1916- – 1 – us UMI [071]
TRIBUNE – McCook. Neb. -w. 1882-1926, 1933-36 – 1 – us UMI [071]
TRIBUNE – Madera. Calif. 1960- – 1 – us UMI [071]
TRIBUNE – Meadville. Pa. 1955- – 1 – us UMI [071]
TRIBUNE – Minneapolis. Minn. 1867- – 1 – us UMI [071]
TRIBUNE – Modesto, CA. 1931-33; 1935; 1938-Feb 1967 – 26r – 1 – $1,300.00 – B02473 – us Library Micro [071]
TRIBUNE – New York. N.Y. 1841-1924 – 1 – us UMI [071]
TRIBUNE – New York. N.Y. -w. 1850-52, 1855-65 – 1 – us UMI [071]
TRIBUNE – North Platte. Neb. 1885-1957 – 1 – us UMI [071]
TRIBUNE – Oakland. Calif. 1874-1926; 1946- – 1 – us UMI [071]
TRIBUNE – Omaha. Neb. -w. 1870-71 – 1 – us UMI [071]
TRIBUNE – Ottawa, 1854-1862 – 3r – 1 – cn Preston [971]
TRIBUNE – Pendleton. Or. 1885-1911; 1919-1923 – 1 – us UMI [071]
TRIBUNE – Philadelphia. Pa. 1932- – 1 – us UMI [071]
TRIBUNE – Port Orford. OR. 1901-24 – 1 – us UMI [071]

TRIBUNE – Pratt. Kan. 1955- – 1 – us UMI [071]
TRIBUNE – Prineville OR. Dec 7 1950-Sep 17 1953 – 1 – us U.O. Library [071]
TRIBUNE – Redwood City. Calif. 1945-53 – 1 – us UMI [071]
TRIBUNE – Rome. Ga. 1900-1902 – 1 – us UMI [071]
TRIBUNE – Rome. Ga. -w. 1887-88 – 1 – us UMI [071]
TRIBUNE – Roscoe. Kan. 1880-81 – 1 – us UMI [071]
TRIBUNE – Royal Oak. Mich. -w. 1877-1925 – 1 – us UMI [071]
TRIBUNE – San Jose, CA. 1854-62 – 4r – 1 – $200.00 – B02895 – us Library Micro [071]
TRIBUNE – San Luis Obispo. Calif. 1879-1888; 1896-1907; 1921; 1925-1926 – 1 – us UMI [071]
TRIBUNE – San Luis Obispo. Calif. -w. 1896-1903 – 1 – us UMI [071]
TRIBUNE – San Marino, CA. 1977 – 17+ r – 1 – $850.00 ($50.00y) – H04063 – us Library Micro [071]
TRIBUNE – Seattle. Wash. 1867-1878 – 1 – us UMI [071]
TRIBUNE – Seymour. Ind. 1921- – 1 – us UMI [071]
TRIBUNE – South Holland. Ill. 1959- – 1 – us UMI [071]
TRIBUNE – Sparks. Nev. -w. 1949- – 1 – us UMI [071]
TRIBUNE – Stella. Neb. 1883-1893 – 1 – us UMI [071]
TRIBUNE – Tacoma. Wash. 1908-1913 – 1 – us UMI [071]
TRIBUNE – Terre Haute. Ind. 1948- – 1 – us UMI [071]
TRIBUNE – Terry. Mont. 1958-1959; 1966- – 1 – us UMI [071]
TRIBUNE – Three Rivers. Mich. -w. 1878- – 1 – us UMI [071]
TRIBUNE – Tribune, CA. 1872-74 – 1r – 1 – $50.00 – C02454 – us Library Micro [071]
TRIBUNE – Tulsa. Okl. 1920- – 1 – us UMI [071]
TRIBUNE – Turlock. Calif. -w. 1911-16, 1943-55 – 1 – us UMI [071]
TRIBUNE – Union City. Wash. 1890-1893 – 1 – us UMI [071]
TRIBUNE – Vallejo, CA. 1914-15 – 6r – 1 – $300.00 – B03068 – us Library Micro [071]
TRIBUNE – Vallejo. Calif. 1914-1915 – 1 – us UMI [071]
TRIBUNE – Wisconsin Rapids. Wis. 1920- – 1 – us UMI [071]
TRIBUNE – Wyandotte. Mich. -w. 1945-61 – 1 – us UMI [071]
TRIBUNE AND HENDERSON HERALD – Las Vegas, NV. 5, 12 Jul 1946 – 1r – 1 – $50.00 – U04614 – us Library Micro [978]
TRIBUNE AND HERALD – Greensburg, PA., 1875-1908 – 13 – $25.00r – us I.M.R. [071]
TRIBUNE AND NEWS OF THE WEEK – Sydney, Australia. -w. 21 March 1884-28 June 1889. 11 reels – 1 – uk British Libr Newspaper [072]
TRIBUNE (BERLINE EDITION) – Berlin, Germany. Jul 1961-1976 – 34r – 1 – us L of C Photodup [072]
LA TRIBUNE CANADIENNE / ed by Ruant, F – Montreal, Canada. jun 1885 – 1r – 1 – Can$25.00 – cn Can Microfilming [072]
LA TRIBUNE D'ARGENTEUIL – Lachute, Canada. v13 n18. 14 jan 1943 – 1r – 1 – Can$25.00 – cn Can Microfilming [072]
TRIBUNE DE FRANCE – Hebdomadaire de la reconstitution francaise. Dir. Robert Suel. no. 1-31. Paris. fevr-sept 1939 – 1 – fr A.C.R.P.P. [073]
LA TRIBUNE DE GENEVE – 1887- – 6r per y – 5 – inquire – us Ross [072]
LA TRIBUNE DE GENEVE – 1887-1995 – 6r per y – 5,6 – Sfr1,176.00 – sz Infoprint [943]
TRIBUNE DE GENEVE – Geneve, jun 1978-jan 3 1982 – 43r – 1 – us Res Libr [072]
LA TRIBUNE DE HULL – Hull, Canada. v1 n1. 17 nov 1960-v1 n6. 22 dec 1960 – 1r – 1 – Can$25.00 – cn Can Microfilming [072]
LA TRIBUNE DE HULL – Hull: Editions de l'Outaouais inc. v1-4. 1960-64. SEM35P264 – 2r – 1 – Can$97.00 – cn Bibl Nat [072]
LA TRIBUNE DE LA GIRONDE – Bordeaux, France. Journal quotidien, politique, commercial, agricole, scientifique et litteraire. 15 oct 1848-2 dec 1851 – 1 – fr A.C.R.P.P. [072]
LA TRIBUNE DE LA REGION HULL-OTTAWA – Hull: '(s.n.)' v4 nos 17-33. 1964. SEM35P270 – 1r – 1 – Can$15.00 – cn Bibl Nat [072]
LA TRIBUNE DE L'EST – no. 1-37. Lons-le-Saunier. 29 juil-3 dec 1851. mq no. 3, 23, 27 – 1 – fr A.C.R.P.P. [073]
LA TRIBUNE DE LEVIS-METRO – (Merged with: Le Peuple Courier, Montmagny, 21 sep 1900) – Levis, Canada. v28 n1. 6 jan 1971-23 jul 1975 – 4r – 1 – Can$60.00r – cn Can Microfilming [072]
LA TRIBUNE DE L'EXPANSION – France. 1988-1992 – 3r per y – 5,6 – Sfr1,069.00 – sz Infoprint [944]
TRIBUNE DE SAINT-GERVAIS: REVUE DE LA SCHOLA CANTORUM / Schola Cantorum – v. 1-26. 1895-1929 – 1 – 101.00 – us L of C Photodup [780]
TRIBUNE DE ST. GERVAIS / Schola Cantorum – Revue de la Schola Cantorum. v1-26. 1895-1929 – 1 – us Schnase [780]
TRIBUNE DEFOSSES – 1992-1992 – 1 times per yr – 6 – F1,600.00 – sz Infoprint [072]
TRIBUNE DEFOSSES – 1994-1995 – 6 times per yr – 6 – F6,500.00 – sz Infoprint [072]
TRIBUNE DEMOCRAT – Johnstown. Pa. 1952- – 1 – us UMI [071]
LA TRIBUNE DES CHEMINOTS / La Federation Nationale des Travailleurs des Chemins de Fer. C.G.T. – no. 1-595. Paris. mars 1917-1er janv 1940 – 1 – fr A.C.R.P.P. [073]
LA TRIBUNE DES COPAINS – Montreal, jul-nov 1976 – 1r – 1 – Can$25.00 – cn Can Microfilming [072]
LA TRIBUNE DES DEPARTEMENS – puis La Tribune politique et litteraire; La Tribune du Mouvement; La Tribune politique et litteraire. Journal politique, commercial et litteraire. Paris. 8 juin 1829-13 avr 1834, 12 aout 1834-11 mai 1835 – 1 – fr A.C.R.P.P. [073]
LA TRIBUNE DES FEMMES – suite de: La Femme libre puis nouvelle. Paris. 1832-33 (I-II) – 1 – fr A.C.R.P.P. [073]
LA TRIBUNE DES FONCTIONNAIRES ET DES RETRAITES / La Federation Generale des Functionnaires – Paris. avr 1913-31, 1933-36, 1938-18 mai 1940 – 1 – fr A.C.R.P.P. [073]
LA TRIBUNE DES NATIONS – Geneva, Paris. -w. 2 Jan 1936-31 May 1940; 14 Sept-9 Nov 1945; 12 May 1950-4 Dec 1953. 7 reels – 1 – uk British Libr Newspaper [949]
LA TRIBUNE DU JURA – no. 1-23, 45-46, 77-80, 90, 94, 99-100, 103-105. Lons-le-Saunier. 11 avr-21 dec 1850 – 1 – fr A.C.R.P.P. [073]
LA TRIBUNE FRANCAISE – Journal quotidien. Dir. politique Jules Guerin. Paris. 1er sept 1902-29 sept 1903 – 1 – fr A.C.R.P.P. [073]
LA TRIBUNE FRANCAISE, POLITIQUE ET LITTERAIRE – Hebdomadaire. Red. Eugene Pelletan. no. 1-106. Paris. juin 1868-janv 1870 – 1 – fr A.C.R.P.P. [072]
TRIBUNE (INC AUSTRALIAN COMMUNIST, THE COMMUNIST, WORKERS WEEKLY) – 1920-1976 – 23r – 9 – at Pascoe [072]
TRIBUNE INDEX – New York. N.Y. 1875-1906 – 1 – us UMI [071]
LA TRIBUNE INDIGENE / Parti Constitutionnaliste Indochinois – Saigon. aout 1917-janv 1925 – 1 – fr A.C.R.P.P. [073]
LA TRIBUNE INDIGENE ALGERIENNE – Organe de defense et de revendications des indigenes algeriens. Alger. nov 1927-mars avr 1931 – 1 – fr A.C.R.P.P. [073]
LA TRIBUNE INDOCHINOISE / Parti Constitutionnaliste Indochinois – Saigon. aout 1926-oct 1942 – 1 – fr A.C.R.P.P. [073]
LA TRIBUNE JUIVE – Paris, France. -w. 12 March 1920-8 Dec 1924. 2 reels – 1 – uk British Libr Newspaper [072]
LA TRIBUNE LIBRE = THE FREE TRIBUNE – Montreal, Canada. v1 n8. 20 jun 1872-v1 n11. 11 jul 1872 – 1r – 1 – Can$25.00 – cn Can Microfilming [072]
LA TRIBUNE LIBRE – Montreal, Canada. v1 n2. 21 dec 1933; v1 n3. 28 dec 1933 – 1r – 1 – Can$25.00 – cn Can Microfilming [072]
LA TRIBUNE (MONTREAL, QUEBEC 1880) – Montreal: '(s.n.)'. v1-4. 1880-1884. SEM35P92 – 1r – 1 – Can$42.00 – cn Bibl Nat [072]
TRIBUNE NEWS EXTRA – San Gabriel, CA. 1985 – 1r – 1 – $50.00 – R04103 – us Library Micro [071]
LA TRIBUNE OUVRIERE – Paraissant le dimanche. Sciences, arts, industrie, litterature. no. 1-4. Paris. juin 1865 – 1 – fr A.C.R.P.P. [073]
LA TRIBUNE (QUEBEC, QUEBEC 1886) – Quebec: '(s.n.)' v1 no 1-12 1886. SEM35P93 – 1r – 1 – Can$15.00 – cn Bibl Nat [072]
LA TRIBUNE REPUBLICAINE – Saint-Etienne. 1er oct 1943-19 20 aout 1944 – 1 – fr A.C.R.P.P. [073]
TRIBUNE REPUBLICAN – Meadville. Pa. 1884-1955 – 1 – us UMI [071]
THE TRIBUNE REVIEW – Butte. Mont. 1898; 1919-1920 – 1 – us UMI [071]
TRIBUNE SOCIALISTE – (Library wants 113 issues) – Paris: Parti socialiste unifi ee, 1960-1982 – 1 – CSUX85-S415 – us Hoover Inst Photo [320]
TRIBUNE-HERALD – Casper. Wyoming. 1917- – 1 – us UMI [071]
TRIBUNE-HERALD – Hardin. Mont. 1925-1947; 1956-1959; 1966- – 1 – us UMI [071]
TRIBUNE-MESSENGER – South Haven. Mich. 1903-1917 – 1 – us UMI [071]
TRIBUNE-PRESS – Gouverneur. N.Y. -w. 1929- – 1 – us UMI [071]
TRIBUNE-REVIEW – Greensburg. Pa. 1956- – 1 – us UMI [071]
TRIBUNE-SENTINEL – Grant, NE. -w. Dec 1897-Oct 1901, scattered issues missing; Jan 1908-Jan 1918; May-Jul 1918; Oct 1918 to date – 1 – us NE Hist [071]
TRIBUNE-SENTINEL – Grant. Neb. and pred. 1897-1962 – 1 – us UMI [071]
IL TRIBUNO – Newark, NJ, 1908 – 1mf or 1r – 1,9 – us I.H.R.C. [978]
O TRIBUNO DO POVO – Rio de Janeiro, 18 Dec 1830-6 Mar 1832 – 1,5,6 – bl Biblioteca [072]
TRIBUNO DO POVO : ORGAO DO CLUB UNIAO CAERENSE – Manaos, Amazonas. 12 Jan 1890 – 1,5,6 – bl Biblioteca [072]
TRIBUNO DO POVO : ORGAO DO PARTIDO NACIONAL – Maceio, Alagoas. 23 Set-20 Out 1887 – 1,5,6 – bl Biblioteca [072]
A TRIBUTE TO PERSIA – 1972. 19p. 30 illus. 1 fiche. Fiche no. 1030 – 9 – $2.50 – us Corning Mus [700]
TRIBUTES OF PROTESTANT WRITERS TO THE TRUTH AND BEAUTY OF CATHOLICITY / Treacy, James J – (Includes index) – New York: Fr Pustet, c1885 – 1mf – 9 – 0-8370-7271-9 – 1986-1271 – us A.T.L.A. [230]
TRICHOMANES / Copeland, E B – 1933 – 9mf – 7 – uk Microform Academic [580]
TRICHOPTERA / Ulmer, G von – 2425 2. 1907 – 8 – ne IDC [580]
DIE TRICHOPTEREN DES BALTISCHEN BERNSTEINS / Ulmer, G von – Koenigsberg. n10. 1912 – 7mf – 9 – ne IDC [574]
Tricht, J *see* EEN NUT ENDE PROFITELIJCK BOECXKEN. AENGAENDE DE VERCLARINGHE DER MENSCHWERDINGE ONS HEEREN JESU CHRISTI
TRI-CITIES DAILY – Sheffield. Ala. 1955- – 1 – us UMI [071]
TRI-CITY HERALD – Tri-Cities, WA. 1947 – 637+ r – 1 – $31,850.00 ($680.00y) – R04155 – us Library Micro [071]
TRI-CITY NEWS – British Columbia, CN. 1989-1991 – 12r – 1 – cn Commonwealth Micro [072]
TRI-CITY NEWS : COQUITLAM, PORT COQUITLAM, PORT MOODY – British Columbia, CN. May 1985-Dec 1986 – 3r – 1 – cn Commonwealth Micro [072]
TRI-CITY NEWS : WEDNESDAY EDITION – British Columbia, CN. 1987-89 – 14r – 1 – cn Commonwealth Micro [072]
TRI-CITY PROGRESS – Utica. Mich. 1961-1964 – 1 – us UMI [071]
TRI-CITY PROGRESS – Warren. Mich. -w. 1957-1964 – 1 – us UMI [071]
TRI-CITY SCRIBE – (East Moline, Ill.) v1 n1 (28 Nov 1920)-v12 n13 (13 June 1932) – 40ft – us A.J.P.C. [270]
TRI-CITY TIMES – Sherwood, OR. -w. 10 Feb 1966 – 5 Aug 1973. Set incl. Tri-City News (Sherwood) – 15r – 1 – us U.O. Library [071]
TRI-CITY TRIBUNE – Cozad, NE. -sw. Jun. 1967- – 1 – us NE Hist [071]
TRICONTINENTAL BULLETIN – Havana, CU. 1966-1972 – 2r – $100.00 – R04207 – us Library Micro [073]
TRICONTINENTAL MAGAZINE – Havana, CU. 1967-1968 – 1r – $50.00 – R04208 – us Library Micro [073]
TRICONTINENTAL NEWS SERVICE – Chicago, IL. 1972-74 – 2r – 1 – $100.00 – R04303 – us Library Micro [071]
TRICOTRIN / Ouida – British Fiction Archive: Unit 3 – 9 – uk Bell [830]
TRI-COUNTY AMERICAN – Frazeyesburg. Ohio. 1926-1930 – 1 – us UMI [071]
TRI-COUNTY BULLETIN – Grand Rapids, Ohio, 1898-1914 – 1r – 1 – $32.50r – us Archival [978]
TRI-COUNTY EXPRESS – Fernley, NV. 1988-1992 – 5r – 1 – $250.00 – U04842 – us Library Micro [071]
TRI-COUNTY HERALD – Fairborn. Ohio. -w. 1930-41 – 1 – us UMI [071]
TRI-COUNTY HERALD NEWS – Weston. Ohio. 1950-1953 – 1 – us UMI [071]
TRI-COUNTY HERALD-NEWS – Weston, Ohio. 1949 – 3r – 1 – $32.50r – us Archival [071]
TRI-COUNTY HERALD-NEWS – Weston, Ohio, 1949-1953 – 3rs – 1 – $32.50r – us Archival [978]
TRI-COUNTY NEWS – Columbus. Mont. 1901-1909 – 1 – us UMI [071]
TRI-COUNTY NEWS – Grand Rapids, Ohio, 1915-1949 – 11r – 1 – $32.50r – us Archival [978]
TRI-COUNTY NEWS : WEEKLY GENERAL NEWSPAPER – Newton Falls, OH. 10 June 1915 – 1r – 1 – us Western Res [071]
TRI-COUNTY NEWS – (Weekly Republican newspaper) – Newton Falls, OH. mar 9, 1899-aug 22, 1918 – 1r – 1 – us Western Res [071]
TRI-COUNTY NEWS – Weston. Ohio. 1934-1948 – 1 – us UMI [071]
TRI-COUNTY SHOPPER – McMinnville, OR. -w. 19 Apr 1948 – 26 Mar 1953. 1 roll – 1 – us U.O. Library [071]
TRI-COUNTY TIMES – Lynch, NE. -w. Apr 1972-Jul 1974 – 1 – us NE Hist [071]
TRIDUO...PATRIARCA S. JOSE...DEVOTO... REIMPRESION – 1898 – 9 – 1.50f – sp Bibl Santa Ana [240]
A TRIENNAL CATALOGUE OF MANUSCRIPTS, COLLECTED DURING THE TRIENNIUM... TO... FOR THE GOVERNMENT ORIENTAL MSS LIBRARY, MADRAS – Madras, 1910-1958 – 177mf – 9 – ne IDC [090]
TRIENNIAL REPORT 1974-1976 / Solomon Islands. British. Ministry of Education and Cultural Affairs – 2mf – 9 – DE-609/1 – ne IDC [370]
TRIENNIAL SURVEY AND ANNUAL REPORT 1961/63-1984 / Kenya. Ministry of Education – (Missing: 1978-1983) – Nairobi – 25mf – 9 – DE-439/1 – ne IDC [370]
TRIENNIUM PHILOLOGICUM ODER GRUNDZUEGE DER PHILOLOGISCHEN WISSENSCHAFTEN FUER JUENGER DER PHILOLOGIE ZUR WIEDERHOLUNG UND SELBSTPRUEFUNG BEARB. VON WILHELM FREUND / Freund, Wilhelm – 1-VI. Semester-Abth. 2. verb Aufl. Leipzig, W. Violet, 1879-85. 6 v. in 5. Film Mas 9097 – 1 – us H.U. Library [400]
TRIERER THEOLOGISCHES ZEITSCHRIFT – 1(1899)-64(1955) – 63mf – 9 – Dfl221.00 – ne Slangenburg [073]
TRIERISCHER VOLKSFREUND – Trier, Germany. 1968- – ca 8r per yr – 1 – gw Mikrofilm [072]
TRIERSCHE ZEITUNG – Trier, 1842-1850 – 12r – 1 – DM900.00 – gw Mikro Press [072]
TRIER'SCHER VOLKSBOTE *see* DER KATHOLISCHE VOLKSBOTE
TRIESTE STATE ARCHIVES – 1863-1922 – 6r – 1 – us I.H.R.C. [324]
Trietsch, D, Winz, L *see* OST UND WEST
Triewald, M *see* A SHORT DESCRIPTION OF THE ATMOSPHERIC ENGINE, 1734
TRIFERTES SAGANI, OR, IMMORTAL DISSOLVENT: BEING A BRIEF BUT CANDID DISCOURCE OF THE MATTER AND MANNER OF PREPARING THE LIQUOR ALKAHEST OF HELMONT, THE GREAT HILECH OF PAROCELSUS.. / Conti, Luigi de – Cleidophorus Mystagogus. London. Printed by W. Pearson for T. Ballard, 1705 – 1 – us U.W. Library [610]
TRIFET'S MONTHLY GALAXY OF MUSIC – Boston, 1887-94 – 1 – £60.00 – uk Chadwyck [780]

LE TRIFLUVIEN : EDITION SEMI-QUOTIDIENNE – Trois-Rivieres, v10 n1. 3 jan 1877-31 dec 1877 – 1r – 1 – Can$60.00 – cn Can Microfilming [072]
LE TRIFLUVIEN – Trois-Rivieres, Canada. 31 oct 1888- -19 jun 1908 – 8r – 1 – Can$45.00r – cn Can Microfilming [072]
LE TRIFLUVIEN – Trois-Rivieres, Canada. 4 mai 1917-v4 n16. 15 oct 1920 – 1r – 1 – Can$45.00 – cn Can Microfilming [072]
Triggle, David J *see* PHARMACEUTICAL NEWS
Triggs, A *see*
- AN ALPHABETICAL AND CHRONOLOGICAL ARRANGEMENT OF THE WESLEYAN METHODIST MINISTERS AND PREACHERS ON TRIAL IN CONNEXION WITH THE BRITISH AND IRISH CONFERENCES; ...FROM THE COMMENCEMENT OF THEIR ITINERANCY TO...1912; ...
- AN ALPHABETICAL AND CHRONOLOGICAL ARRANGEMENT OF THE WESLEYAN METHODIST MINISTERS AND PREACHERS ON TRIAL IN CONNEXION WITH THE BRITISH AND IRISH CONFERENCES; ...FROM THE COMMENCEMENT OF THEIR ITINERANCY TO...1916; ...
- ALPHABETICAL AND CHRONOLOGICAL ARRANGEMENTS OF THE WESLEYAN METHODIST MINISTERS AND PROBATIONERS IN CONNEXION WITH THE BRITISH AND IRISH CONFERENCES; ...FROM THE COMMENCEMENT OF THEIR ITINERANCY TO...1922

Trigo, Felipe *see*
- ALMA EN LOS LABIOS
- LA ALTISIMA
- ASI PAGA EL DIABLO...
- LA BRUTA (HEROES DE AHORA)
- EN CAMISA ROSA. LAS SONATAS DEL OTONO
- CRISIS DE LA CIVILIZACION. LA GUERRA EUROPEA
- CUENTOS INGENUOS
- EN LOS ANDAMIOS
- LAS EVAS DEL PARAISO
- JARRAPELLEJOS
- EL MEDICO RURAL
- EL PAPA DE LAS BELLEZAS. LA SOMBRA. EL NAUFRAGO. A TODO HONOR
- LAS POSADAS DEL AMOR. MI PRIMA ME ODIA. ADEMAS DEL FRAC. MI MEDIA NARANJA
- LA SED DE AMAR
- SOCIALISMO INDIVIDUALISTA (INDICE PARA SU ESTUDIO ANTROPOLOGICO)
- SOR DEMONIO. (EN HONOR DE UN MARIDO HIDALGO Y METAFISICO

Trigueros, Candido Maria *see* LA RIADA
THE TRI-LEMMA / Graves, J R – 1860 – 1 – 5.67 – us Baptist [240]
TRILINGUAL DICTIONARY OF FISHERIES TECHNOLOGICAL TERMS : CURING – 1980 – 85p – it F.A.O. [639]
TRI-LINGUAL REVIEW – Cheltenham, UK. 30 Apr-21 Dec 1908 – 1 – uk British Libr Newspaper [072]
TRILINGUE DE TRES ARTS DE LAS TRES LENGUAS : CASTELLANA, LATINA Y GRIEGA, TODAS EN ROMANCE / Correas, Gonzalo – Salamanca: Antonia Ramirez, 1627 – 1 – sp Bibl Santa Ana [440]
TRILINGUE DE TRES...CASTELLANA, LATINA Y GRIEGA / Correas, Gonzalo – 1627 – 9 – 1.50f – sp Bibl Santa Ana [440]
Trilla y Munoz, A *see*
- PERFECTO PRACTICANTE, CIRUJANO Y DE MORBO GALICO
- PERFECTO PRACTICANTE MEDICO Y NUEVA LUZ DE FACIL ENSENANZA

LE TRILLE DU DIABLE / Tartini, G & Kreisler, F – (From binder's collection, score and part) – [c1905-c1915] – 1 – us Sibley [780]
Trilles, H *see*
- L'AME DU PYGMEE D'AFRIQUE
- CHEZ LES FANG AU QUINZE ANNEES DE SEJOUR AU CONGO FRANCAIS
- MILLES LIEUS DANS L'INCONNU

Trilling, W *see* WAS HALTET IHR VON JESUS?
Trimen *see* MEDICINAL PLANTS
Trimen, H *see* A SYSTEMATIC CATALOGUE OF THE FLOWERING PLANTS AND FERNS INDIGENOUS TO, OR GROWING WILD IN CEYLON
Trimen, H A *see* HANDBOOK TO THE FLORA OF CEYLON
TRIMESTRE DE RIBEIRO DE CAMPOS – Aracaju, 18 May 1882 – 1,5,6 – bl Biblioteca [072]
Trincant, Louis *see* HISTOIRE GENEALOGIQUE DE LA MAISON DU BELLAY...
Trindade, Paula da *see* CONQUISTA ESPIRITUAL DO ORIENTE...INTRODUCAO E NOTAS DE F. FELIX LOPES, 3 PARTE. LISBOA, 1967
Trine, Ralph Waldo *see* THE MAN WHO KNEW; HOW HE BROUGHT THE GOOD NEWS THAT THE KINGDOM OF GOD IS WITHIN US, AND THAT WE MAY PUT OURSELVES IN TUNE WITH THE CENTRE OF LIFE
TRINIDAD AND TOBAGO : ANNUAL STATISTICAL DIGEST 1935/51-1973/74 / Trinidad and Tobago. Central Statistical Office – (Coll title: Latin American and Caribbean Official Statistical Serials, 1821-1982) – 59mf – 9 – £435.00 – uk Chadwyck [972]
Trinidad and Tobago *see*
- DRAFT DEVELOPMENT PROGRAMME, 1970
- DRAFT DEVELOPMENT PROGRAMME, 1971
- DRAFT PLAN FOR EDUCATIONAL DEVELOPMENT IN TRINIDAD AND TOBAGO 1968-1983
- DRAFT THIRD FIVE-YEAR PLAN, 1969-1973
- FIVE YEAR DEVELOPMENT PROGRAMME, 1958-1962
- FIVE YEAR ECONOMIC PROGRAMME 1950-1955
- FIVE-YEAR DEVELOPMENT PROGRAMME, 1958-1962 1958 REPORT
- PROGRAMME OF DEVELOPMENT PROJECTS FOR THE YEAR 1963
- SECOND FIVE-YEAR PLAN 1964-1968, MODIFICATIONS TO DRAFT PLAN AS APPROVED BY PARLIAMENT, NOV 1963
- THIRD FIVE YEAR PLAN, 1969-1973
- TRINIDAD AND TOBAGO GAZETTE

Trinidad and Tobago. Central Statistical Office *see* TRINIDAD AND TOBAGO
Trinidad and Tobago. Central Statistical Office. Education Statistical Section *see* EDUCATION BULLETINS 1974/75-1975/76(1)
Trinidad and Tobago. Economic Planning and Developpement Dept *see* FIVE YEAR DEVELOPMENT PROGRAMME, 1958-1962 PROJECTS FOR 1959
Trinidad and Tobago. Economic Planning Division *see* FIVE-YEAR DEVELOPMENT PROGRAMME 1958-1962 REPORT OF THE PREMIER ON DEVELOPMENT PROJECTS FOR THE YEAR 1960
TRINIDAD AND TOBAGO GAZETTE / Trinidad and Tobago – Port-of-Spain. Sept. 3, 1962-1968 – 1 – us NY Public [972]
TRINIDAD AND TOBAGO GAZETTE – Trinidad and Tobago, 1957-69 – 14r – 1 – us Ross [324]
Trinidad and Tobago. National Planning Commission *see* DRAFT SECOND FIVE-YEAR PLAN, 1964-1968
TRINIDAD CHRONICLE – Port of Spain. Trinidad. 1960-62 – 1 – us UMI [072]
TRINIDAD CHRONICLE – Port of Spain. Trinidad. and Port of Spain Gazette. 1825-1956 – 1 – us UMI [072]
TRINIDAD CHRONICLE – Port of Spain. Trinidad. -d. 1 Jul 1956-28 aug 1959. (22 reels) – 1 – uk British Libr Newspaper [072]
TRINIDAD GAZETTE – Port of Spain. Trinidad. 1820-1822 – 1 – us UMI [072]
Trinidad. Governor *see* GOVERNOR'S DISPATCHES
TRINIDAD GUARDIAN – Port of Spain. Trinidad. 1917- – 1 – us UMI [072]
Trinidad, Juan de la *see* CRONICA...SAN GABRIEL
TRINIDAD ROYAL GAZETTE – Port of Spain. Trinidad. 1835-1899 – 1 – us UMI [072]
DIE TRINITAETSLEHRE DES BOETHIUS / Schurr, V – Paderborn, 1935 – 5mf – 8 – ne Slangenburg [240]
TRINITARIAN THEOLOGY – v5-6 nos 1-2. 1948-49 (complete) – Inquire – 1 – ATLA 1993-S517 – us A.T.L.A. [073]
DIE TRINITARISCHE LEHRDIFFERENZ ZWISCHEN DER ABENDLAENDISCHEN UND DER MORGENLAENDISCHEN KIRCHE : EINE DOGMENGESCHICHTLICHE UNTERSUCHUNG / Langen, Joseph – Bonn: Eduard Weber, 1876 – 1mf – us A.T.L.A. [240]
THE TRINITY / Burris, F Holiday – Chicago: S.C. Griggs, 1874 – 1mf – 9 – 0-8370-3042-0 – 1985-1042 – us A.T.L.A. [240]
TRINITY APOCALYPSE / Trinity College. Cambridge – (13th century). c.1230. Ms R.16.2 – 1 reel – 14 – uk Microform Academic [240]
TRINITY BAPTIST CHURCH. BENSON, NORTH CAROLINA : CHURCH RECORDS – 1880-1958. Minutes. 1880-Sep 1967 – 1 – 12.42 – us Baptist [240]
TRINITY BAPTIST CHURCH. MOULTRIE, GEORGIA : CHURCH RECORDS – 1953-86 – 1 – 21.69 – us Baptist [978]
TRINITY BAPTIST CHURCH. PORT ARTHUR, TEXAS : CHURCH RECORDS – 1928-75 – 1 – 10.80 – us Baptist [240]
TRINITY BAPTIST CHURCH. SENECA, SOUTH CAROLINA : CHURCH RECORDS – 1953-72 – 1 – 37.80 – us Baptist [240]
TRINITY BAPTIST CHURCH. SPRINGFIELD, OREGON : CHURCH RECORDS – Sep 1940-80 – 1 – 44.37 – us Baptist [240]
TRINITY BAPTIST CHURCH. VANCOUVER, WASHINGTON : CHURCH RECORDS – 4Jun-May 1973 – 1 – 35.82 – us Baptist [240]
Trinity College. Cambridge *see*
- THE MEDIAEVAL MANUSCRIPTS
- THE MEDIAEVAL MANUSCRIPTS, SECTION 1
- THE MEDIAEVAL MANUSCRIPTS, SECTION 2
- THE MEDIAEVAL MANUSCRIPTS, SECTION 3
- THE MEDIAEVAL MANUSCRIPTS, SECTION 4
- MEDIAEVAL MANUSCRIPTS, SECTION 5
- MEDIAEVAL MANUSCRIPTS, SECTION 6
- THE MEDIAEVAL MANUSCRIPTS, SECTION 7
- THE MEDIAEVAL MANUSCRIPTS, SECTION 8
- TRINITY APOCALYPSE

Trinity College. Dublin *see* THE COLLECTION OF MEDIAEVAL AND RENAISSANCE MANUSCRIPTS
Trinity College. Dublin. Library *see* PRINTED CATALOGUE
TRINITY DAILY JOURNAL – Weaverville. Calif. 1938-42 – 1 – us UMI [071]
TRINITY GOSPELS – Anglo-Saxon ms. made at Canterbury in the late 10th or early 1lth cent – 1 reel – 14 – uk Microform Academic [240]
TRINITY JOURNAL – Weaverville, CA. 1856- – 62+ r – 1 – $3,100.00 ($50.00y) – B03089 – us Library Micro [073]
TRINITY JOURNAL – Weaverville. Calif. -w. 1954- – 1 – us UMI [071]
Trinity Lutheran Church, Bender Hill Community, Russel County, KS *see* RECORDS
Trinity Lutheran Church (Jenera, Ohio) *see* RECORDS
Trinity Lutheran Church, Lehigh, KS *see* CHURCH BOOK
Trinity Lutheran Church (Middle Point, Ohio) *see* RECORDS
Trinity Lutheran Church, Otis, KS *see* KIRCHENBUCHS AND MINUTE BOOK
Trinity. Presbytery (Cum. Pres. Ch.) *see* MINUTES, 1869-1901
TRINITY SERIES : AMERICAN DECISIONS, AMERICAN REPORTS, AMERICAN STATES REPORTS – (American Decisions: v1-10 + digest 1760-1869. American Reports: v1-6 + dige st 1868-87. American State Reports: v1-140 1886-1911) – Law Library Microfilm Corporation. 300v + Digest – 9 – $4,800.00 set – us Hein [340]
TRINITY SERIES, AMERICAN DECISIONS 1760-1869 WITH DIGEST 1760-1789 – 35 reels – 1 – $38.00r – us Trans-Media [340]
TRINITY SERIES, AMERICAN REPORTS 1870-1887 – 22 reels – 1 – $38.00r – us Trans-Media [340]
TRINITY SERIES, AMERICAN STATE REPORTS 1887-1911 – 55 reels – 1 – $38.00r – us Trans-Media [340]
TRINITY SERIES, NOTES ON AMERICAN DECISIONS – 12 reels – 1 – $38.00r – us Trans-Media [340]
TRINITY SERIES, PART 1 *see* AMERICAN DECISIONS
TRINITY SERIES, PART 2 *see* AMERICAN REPORTS
TRINITY SERIES, PART 3 *see* AMERICAN STATE REPORTS
TRINITY SERIES, RAPALJE DIGEST – 3 reels – 1 – $38.00r – us Trans-Media [340]
TRINITY STUDIES – v1-2. 1971-72 – 1 – us UMI [240]
TRINITY TIMES – Weaverville, CA. Dec 1854-Sep 1855 – 1r – 1 – $50.00 – B03088 – us Library Micro [071]
TRINITY UNIVERSITY REVIEW *see* ROUGE ET NOIR
TRINITY/SHASTA/TEHAMA – 1909-19 – 10r – 1 – $500.00 – P00146 – us Library Micro [910]
Trinius, Carl Bernhard *see*
- AGROSTIDEA 3.
- CLAVIS AGROSTOGRAPHIAE ANTIQUIORIS
- DE GRAMINIBUS PANICEIS
- FUNDAMENTA AGROSTOGRAPHIAE SIVE THEORIA CONSTRUCTIONIS FLORIS GRAMINEI.....
- SPECIES GRAMINUM ICONIBUS ET DESCRIPTIONIBUS ILLUSTRAVIT

Trinkaus, Stephan *see* "DEM TRAUM FOLGEN"
TRINTA DE MARCO – Maceio, Alagoas. 30 Mar 1897; 30 Mar 1898 – 1,5,6 – bl Biblioteca [072]
TRINTIY UNIVERSITY REVIEW – (Cont: Rouge et noir) – Toronto: Students of Trinity College, [1888?-1973] – 9 – cn C.I.H.M. [370]
TRIO IN A MOLL FUER PIANOFORTE, VIOLINE UND VIOLONCELLO, OP. 24 / Henselt, A – Leipzig: Schuberth, [18-] – 1 – us Sibley [780]
TRIO IN A MOLL, OP. 188, FOR PIANOFORTE, OBOE AND HORN / Reinecke, C – (Score and parts) – Leipzig: Breitkopf & Haertel, [1887] – 1 – us Sibley [780]
TRIO '(IN CIS MOLL] FUER KLAVIER, VIOLINE UND VIOLA [ODER VIOLONCELL], OP. 46... / Zellner, J – (Score and parts) – Leipzig: M Brockhaus, [1890] – us Sibley [780]
TRIO NR. 3, B DUR / Bargiel, Woldemar – (Score and parts) – Leipzig, New York: Breitkopf & Haertel, [189-?] – 1 – us Sibley [780]
TRIO POUR LE FORTE PIANO AVEC ACCOMP. DE VIOLON ET VIOLONCELLE OBLIGEE, OP. 2 / Demonchau, C – (Parts) – Paris: Cochet, 179- – 1 – us Sibley [780]
TRIO POUR UN VIOLON, ALTO, ET BASSE / Rey, J – (Pts.) – Paris: Cousineau, 180- – 1 – us Sibley [780]
TRIO SONATAS OF THE BAROQUE – 99mf – 9 – MS-e – ne IDC [780]
TRIO SONATAS, OP 1 / Barbella, E – (3 pts) – London: Oswald for the author, 176- – 1 – us Sibley [780]
TRIO SONATAS, OP 1 / Barbella, E – London: Welcker, 176- – 1 – us Sibley [780]
[TRIO SONATAS, OP. 1 AND 2, SELECTIONS] / Corelli, Arcangelo – (Manuscript of Ist violin part only on empty pages of another manuscript) – 1 – us Sibley [780]
TRIO SONATAS, VIOLINS AND CONTINUO, OP. 1-4 / Corelli, Arcangelo – (Early 18th century manuscript (probably copied from one of the Editiones by E Roger, Amsterdam). 3 parts) – Amsterdam – 1 – us Sibley [780]
[TRIO SONATAS, Z.790-810] SONATAS OF THREE PARTS, TWO VIOLINS AND BASSE, TO THE ORGAN OR HARPSICHORD / Purcell, Henry – Manuscript, late 17th or early 18th century – 1 – us Sibley [780]
LA TRIOMPHANTE VICTOIRE DE LA VIERGE MARIE SUR SEPT MALINS ESPRITS / Benedicti, Le P Jean – Lyon. 1611 – 9 – fr Hachette [360]
LE TRIOMPHE DE LA FOY CATHOLIQUE / Marcel, J – Lyon, 1625 – 10mf – 9 – CA-138/1 – ne IDC [240]
LE TRIOMPHE DE LA LANGUE FRANCOISE / Raillet, Ph.M – 1664 – 9 – fr I.C.S. [440]
LE TRIOMPHE DE MARIE SOUS LE PONTIFICAT DE PIE 9 : OU, L'IMMACULEE CONCEPTION ET LA SAINTE MONTAGNE DE LA SALETTE – Nouv ed. Tournai: H Casterman, 1863 – 1mf – 9 – 0-8370-8377-X – 1986-2377 – us A.T.L.A. [240]
LE TRIOMPHE DE TRAJAN / Esmenard, Lesueur & Esmenard, Persuis – French Theatre Series. Paris. Impr. de Ballard. 1807 – 9 – fr Hachette [820]
TRIOMPHE DU ST-SIEGE ET DE L'EGLISE; OU, LES NOVATEURS MODERNES COMBATTUS AVEC LEURS PROPRES ARMES / Gregorius 16, Pope – Par Maur Cappellari, actuellement Gregoire XVI; traduit de l'italien par M. L'Abbe Jammes. 2v in 1. 1834 – 1 – us A.T.L.A. [240]
LES TRIOMPHES DE LOUIS LE JUSTE, 13E DU NOM, ROY DE FRANCE... / Valdor, Jean – Paris: A. Estienne, 1649 – fr Armell [944]
TRIONFI / Petrarca – With Tacitus, Annales et Historiae. 14th and 15th cents. Holkham MSS. 520, 359, 573. Holkham Hall, Norfolk, England – 1 reel – 1 – uk Microform Academic [810]
TRIONFI E COMPITI DEL NUOVO DIRITTO INTERNAZIONALE... / Cimbali, E – Campobasso, 1916 – 1mf – 1 – ILM-1744/1 – ne IDC [327]
IL TRIONFO DELLA FEDELTA.. / Maria Antonia Walpurgis – 1756. Dramma pastorale per musica. Score and parts – 9 – us Sibley [780]

TRIONFO DI CHRISTO PER LA VITTORIA CONTRA TVRCHI... / Magno, C – Venetia, 1571 – 1mf – 9 – H-8172/1 – ne IDC [956]

TRIOS FOR 2 VIOLINS AND A BASS – (Trios by: anon, Barbella(2), Wagerseil(5), bousso (6)) – Ms pts – 1 – us Sibley [780]

TRIOS GRANDS QUINTETTI, OP. 92, NO. 1 / Reicha, A – (Parts) – Paris: Pacini, 182- – 1 – us Sibley [780]

TRIOS (S VLN, VC)...OP. 3 / Antes, J – London: I Bland, 179- – 1 – us Sibley [780]

TRIOS, SEI, 2 VIOLINS ET VIOLONCELLO, OP.3 / Ricci, P – (3 pts.) – Den Haag: Hummel, 1770 – 1 – us Sibley [780]

TRIOS, SIX, FOR VIOLINS OR GERMAN FLUTES AND A BASS. / Magherini – 177-? – 9 – us Sibley [780]

TRIOS, VIOLINS AND VIOLONCELLO, G. 83-94, G. 89-94 / Boccherini, Luigi – Venezia: Luigi Marescalchi, ca 1775 – 1 – us Sibley [780]

TRIOS, VIOLINS & VIOLONCELLO, G. 83-88 / Boccherini, Luigi – Ms – 1 – us Sibley [780]

TRIO-SONATAS, 2 VIOLINS AND CONTINUO / Lidarti, C – (3 pts in 3 vols) – London: Welker, 176- – 1 – us Sibley [780]

TRIO-SONATAS, 2 VLNS AND CONT., OP. 3 / Campioni, C – (Apparently printed from same plates as Walsh publication. 3 pts) – London: Printed for Wm Randall – 1 – us Sibley [780]

TRIOSONATEN FUER 2 VIOLINEN, VIOLONCELLO UND BASSO CONTINUO / Pepusch, J C – 177? 12 sonatas in four parts, mss. copy – 9 – us Sibley [780]

Trip, Ch. J *see* PAULUS

THE TRIP HAMMER – v. 1. 1885-86 – 1 – 65.00 – cn McLaren [073]

A TRIP ON THE THA-ANNE RIVER, HUDSON BAY / Lofthouse, J – BN 295 2. 1899 – 8 – ne IDC [971]

A TRIP ROUND THE WORLD IN 1887-8 / Caine, William Sproston – Illus. by John Pedder, H. Sheppard Dale, George Bickham and the author. London: G. Routledge, 1888. 02002. (Pre-1900 Canadiana) – 9 – cn C.I.H.M. [910]

TRIP TO PORTSMOUTH. OVERTURE AND DANCES; WITH TRANSPOSITIONS FOR THE GERMAN FLUTE AND GUITAR / Arne, T A – London: Longman, Lukey & Co – 1 – us Sibley [780]

A TRIP TO THE TROPICS AND HOME THROUGH AMERICA / Argyll, John Douglas Sutherland Campbell, Duke of – London: Hurst and Blackett, 1867. 00046. (Pre-1900 Canadiana) – 9 – cn C.I.H.M. [910]

A TRIP UP THE VOLGA TO THE FAIR OF NIJNI-NOVGOROD / Munro-Butler-Johnstone, Henry Alexander – 2nd ed. Oxford: J. Parker and Co., 1876. Map and 12 illus – 1 – us U.W. Library [910]

TRIPARTITE LIFE OF PATRICK (RS89) : WITH OTHER DOCUMENTS RELATING TO THAT SAINT WITH TRANSLATIONS AND INDEXES / ed by Stokes, W – (v1 1888 Dfl30.00. v2 1888 Dfl28.00) – ne Slangenburg [920]

Tripathi, B R *see*
- INTRODUCTION A L'ETUDE DU LAIT
- AN INTRODUCTION TO MILK
- MILK PROCESSING TECHNIQUES
- TECHNIQUES DE TRANSFORMATION DU LAIT FERMENTE

Tripathi, Bansh R *see*
- LA REDACTION DES ARTICLES SCIENTIFIQUES
- ROLES OF VISUALS IN SCIENTIFIC PRESENTATIONS
- SPEAKING AT SCIENTIFIC MEETINGS
- WRITING A SCIENTIFIC PAPER

TRIPLE A – (Details on Request) – Oct 1985-Feb 1989 – 9 – at Pascoe [072]

TRIPLE TRADER – v.1-. 1979- – 1,5,6,9 – us UMI [073]

TRIPLE TRADITION OF THE EXODUS / Bacon, Benjamin Wisner – Hartford: Student Pub. Co., 1894. 1 fiche – 9 – us A.T.L.A. [240]

THE TRIPLICATE – Crescent City, CA. 1912- – 96+ r – 1 BC02149 – $4,800.00 ($160.00y) – us Library Micro [071]

TRIPOLI DAL 1510 AL 1850 / Bergna, Costanzo – Tripoli: "Nuove arti grafiche", [1925] – us Res Libr [960]

TRIPOLI INVENTORY REPORT / Libya. Ministry of Planning and Development – Tripoli. 11 v. BNE-1301 1 – 9 – ne IDC [330]

LA TRIPOLITAINE : LES ROUTES DU SOUDAN / Fournel, Marc – Paris: Challamel A., 1887 – 1 – F141.37 – fr Armell [380]

TRIPOLITANIA / Tumiati, Domenico – Milano: F Treves, 1905 – us Res Libr [960]

TRIPOS IN THREE DISCOURSES / Hobbes, Thomas – The first, Human nature: the second, De Corpore politico: the third, Of liberty and necessity. To which are added several other tracts. 1840 – 1 – us A.T.L.A. [190]

Tripp, April *see* ATTITUDES OF CHILDREN IN INTEGRATED AND SEGREGATED PHYSICAL EDUCATION PROGRAMS TOWARD PEERS WITH DISABLING CONDITIONS

Tripp, Bartlett *see* MY TRIP TO SAMOA

Trippault, L *see* CELT-HELLENISME

TRIPTIKH / Esenin, Sergei – Poemy. Berlin. 1920. BR-1068 2 – 8 – ne IDC [460]

TRIPURA GAZETTE / Tripura. India – Agartala. Sept. 16, 1962-1966 – 1 – us NY Public [950]

Tripura. India *see* TRIPURA GAZETTE

TRIPURA TIMES – Agartala, India. Jan 1968; 1970-82; 1983; 1987-94 – 14r – 1 – us L of C Photodup [072]

Trismegistus, Hermes *see* DE TRIGINTA SEX DECANIS

Tristan, Flore Celestine *see*
- PEREGRINATION D'UN PARIA: 1833-1834
- UNION OUVRIERE

TRISTAN UND ISOLDE : EIN GEDICHT IN ROMANZEN / Immermann, Karl Leberecht – Berlin: G Hempel, [18–] – 1r – 1 – us U.W. Library [810]

TRISTAN UND ISOLDE : NEU BEARBEITET VON WILHELM HERTZ / Strassburg, Gottfried von – 6. Aufl. Stuttgart; Berlin: J G Cotta, 1911 – 1 – us U.W. Library [830]

TRISTAN UND ISOLDE / Porges, Heinrich – Leipzig: Breitkopf & Haertel, 1906 – 1r – 1 – us U.W. Library [790]

TRISTAN UND ISOLDE / Wagner, Richard – (With: Lohengrin Leipzig,[18–?]) – Leipzig: Breitkopf und Haertel, [18–?] – 1r – 1 – us U.W. Library [790]

[TRISTAN UND ISOLDE]. EINLEITUNG, ARRANGED FOR ORGAN BY E. LEMARE / Wagner, R & LeMare, E – New York: Schirmer, 1909 – 1 – us Sibley [780]

TRISTAN UND ISOLDE IN DER FRANZOESISCHEN UND DEUTSCHEN DICHTUNG DES MITTELALTERS UND DER NEUZEIT / Golther, Wolfgang – (Includes bibliographical references) – Berlin: W de Gruyter & Co, 1929 – 2r – 1 – us U.W. Library [410]

Tristan Valentin, G *see* DE CLERICO MEDICO CURIOSA DISCEPTATIO, SIVE INTERPRETATIO AD TESTUM...

TRISTANA / Perez Galdos, Benito – Madrid, 1892. 252p – 1 – us U.W. Library [820]

TRI-STATE ALLIANCE – Pioneer, Ohio. 1891-1974 – 25r – 1 – $32.50r – us Archival [071]

TRI-STATE FARMER – Kimball, NE. -w. Oct 1923-Feb 1925 – 1 – us NE Hist [071]

TRI-STATE FARMER – Kimball. Neb. 1923-1925 – 1 – us UMI [071]

TRISTIA / Mandelstam, Osip E – Spb. Berlin. 1922. BR-1169 2 – 8 – ne IDC [460]

Tristram, Henry Baker *see*
- EASTERN CUSTOMS IN BIBLE LANDS
- THE NATURAL HISTORY OF THE BIBLE

TRISTRANT UND ISALDE / Oberge, Eilhart von – ca 30p + 4 color mf – ca DM520.00 – 3-89219-019-4 – gw Lengenfelder [830]

Tritheme, Jean *see*
- OPERA PIA ET SPIRITUALIA...
- TRAITE DES CAUSES SECONDES

Trithemius, J *see*
- AD MONACHOS DEHORTATIONES
- DE ORTU ET PROGRESSU ORDINIS...DE MONTE CARMELO
- EXHORTATIONES AD MONACHOS
- IN REGULAM DIVI BENEDICTI COMMENTARIUS
- OPERA HISTORICA

TRI-TOWN TIMES – Fernley. Nev. 1957-58 – 1 – us UMI [071]

TRI-TOWN TIMES – Fernley, NV. 1957-1958; 1965 – 1r – 1 – $50.00 – N04531 – us Library Micro [071]

TRI-TOWN TIMES – Silver Springs, NV. 1957-1958; 1965 – 1r – 1 – $50.00 – N04740 – us Library Micro [071]

TRI-TOWN TIMES – Wadsworth, NV. 1957-1958; 1965 – 1r – 1 – $50.00 – N04802 – us Library Micro [071]

TRI-TOWNS TODAY/TRADER – Kirkland Lake, Ma1990-1991De – 2r – 1 – cn Preston [071]

Tritto, G *see* PERCHE SE MIO TU SEI. (FROM LA BELLA PESCATRICE)

TRITUNGGAL: RE-SO-PIM, REVOLUSI, SOSIALISME, PIMPINAN NASIONAL / Sukarno, Pres. Indonesia – SE 3841 1. Speech on 17 Agustus 1961 – 9 – ne IDC [324]

TRIUMF – Uppsala, Sweden. Trumf 1889-91; Triumf 1891-97 – 5r – 1 – sw Kungliga [073]

DER TRIUMPH DER CHRISTLICHEN PHILOSOPHIE / Fischer, Engelbert Lorenz – Mainz: Franz Kirchheim, 1900 – 1mf – 9 – us A.T.L.A. [240]

THE TRIUMPH OF PEACE / Shirley, J – A masque, presented by the Foure Honourable Houses, or Innes of Court... at White Hall February the third, 1633. 1633 – 9 – us Sibley [780]

THE TRIUMPH OF RELIGIOUS LIBERTY OVER THE SPIRIT OF PERSECUTION, BEING AN ACCOUNT OF THE TRIALS OF SEVERAL PERSONS FOR AN OUTRAGEOUS AND UNPROVOKED PERSECUTION AT GREAT BARDFIELD IN THE COUNTY OF ESSEX,... – London, 1795 – 1mf – 9 – MP-590/1 – ne IDC [240]

TRIUMPH OF THE WILL : A DOCUMENTARY HISTORY – (With printed guide) – 1r – 1 – $115.00 – us UPA [790]

TRIUMPHANT SONGS / Excell, Edwin O – Chicago. 1887-96. 5v – 1 – 23.00 – us L of C Photodup [780]

DAS TRIUMPHIRENDE PERPETUUM MOBILE ORFFYREANUM / Bessler, Johann Ernst Elias – Cassel, 1719 – 1 – us U.W. Library [890]

O TRIUMPHO : JORNAL CRITICO E LITTERARIO – Manaus, Amazonas. 24 Nov 1901 – 1,5,6 – bl Biblioteca [072]

TRIUMPHO : FOLHA COMMERCIAL DO RIO NEGRO – S. Joaquim/Rio Negro, Amazonas. 7 Maio-Ago, Dez 1899; Jan-Ago 1900; Nov-Dez 1901; Abr-10 Jun 1902 – 1,5,6 – bl Biblioteca [072]

TRIUMPHO DA LEGITIMIDADE – Rio de Janeiro, 9 Dec 1825-28 Jan 1826 – 1,5,6 – bl Biblioteca [072]

TRIUMPHO DEL GOVIERNO POPULAR, Y DE LA ANTIGUEDAD HOLANDESA / Barrios, D L de – Amsterdam. 1683. BJ-262-5 1 – 9 – ne IDC [321]

EL TRIUMPHO VINDICADO DE LA CALUMNIA, IMPOSTURA E IGNORANCIA CONTRA LA MEDICINA... / Gil Sanz, J – Cadiz, 1730 – 2mf – 9 – sp Cultura [610]

TRIUMPHOS DEL AMOR DE DIOS / Juan de los Angeles – 1590 – 9 – 1.50f – sp Bibl Santa Ana [240]

TRIUMPHS OF THE BIBLE : WITH THE TESTIMONY OF SCIENCE TO ITS TRUTH / Tullidge Henry – (Includes bibliographical references) – New York:Charles Scribner, 1863 – 1mf – 9 – 0-8370-5584-9 – 1985-3584 – us A.T.L.A. [220]

O TRIUNFO – Laranjeiras, Brazil. Jan-Nov 1844. Incomplete – 1 – bl Biblioteca [072]

EL TRIUNFO DE LA MORAL CRISTIANA / Calzada, Bernardo Maria de – 1788 – 1mf – 9 – Pta1,000.00 – 84-7848-197-4 – sp Pentalfa [240]

TRIUNFO DEL AMOR / Isla, Jose Francisco – 1746 – 1mf – 9 – Pta1,000.00 – 84-7848-248-2 – sp Pentalfa [946]

TRI-VALLEY : ALAMO, DANVILLE, DUBLIN, LIVERMORE PLEASANTON, SAN RAMON, ETC. – 1992- – 5+ r – 1 – $250.00 – P00137 – us Library Micro [910]

THE TRI-VALLEY HERALD : SAN RAMON VALLEY – San Ramon, CA. 1987- – 42+ r – 1 – $2,100.00 ($600.00y) – B03681 – us Library Micro [071]

TRI-VALLEY HERALD – Dublin, CA. 1974 – 273+ r – 1 – $13,650.00 – B02180 – us Library Micro [071]

TRI-VALLEY HERALD – Pleasanton, CA. 1987- – 42+ r – 1 – $2,100.00 ($600.00y) – B02636 – us Library Micro [071]

TRI-VALLEY HERALD – (See San Ramon) – Livermore, CA. 1987- – 42+ r – 1 – $2,100.00 ($600.00y) – B02354 – us Library Micro [071]

TRI-VALLEY HERALD AND NEWS – Livermore, CA. Jan-Oct 1973 – 12r – 1 – $600.00 – B02355 – us Library Micro [071]

TRI-VALLEY HERALD AND NEWS *see* HERALD NEWS

TRI-VALLEY NEWS – (Cont by: The News) – Livermore, CA. 1973-81 – 101r – 1 – $5,050.00 – B02356 – us Library Micro [071]

TRI-VALLEY NEWS – (Cont by: The News) – San Ramon, CA. 1973-81 – 101r – 1 – $5,050.00 – B02932 – us Library Micro [071]

TRI-VALLEY NEWS – (Cont by: The News, Livermore) – Pleasanton, CA. 1973-81 – 101r – 1 – $5,050.00 – B02636 – us Library Micro [071]

TRI-VALLEY NEWS – (Cont: The News) – Dublin, CA. Dec 1974-Mar 1981 – 88r – 1 – $4,400.00 – B02182 – us Library Micro [071]

TRI-VALLEY NEWS – Danville, CA. Sep 1973-Mar 1980 – 95r – 1 – $4,750.00 – B02161 – us Library Micro [071]

TRI-VALLEY NEWS – (See Livermore) – Alamo, CA. 1973-80 – 80r – 1 – $4,000.00 – B02005 – us Library Micro [071]

TRI-VALLEY NEWS *see*
- THE NEWS
- VILLAGE PIONEER

TRI-VALLEY NEWS, LIVERMORE *see* VILLAGE PIONEER

TRIVENI – A Journal of the Indian Renaissance. v. 1-32. Masulipatam. 1928-64. Lacking: v. 6 (4-6), v. 8-12 (4, 6, 9, 11-12), v. 13 (2-12)-v. 18, v. 30. BI-119 2 – 8 – ne IDC [945]

TRIVENI : A JOURNAL OF THE INDIAN RENAISSANCE – (Missing: v6(4-6); v8-12(4, 6, 9, 11-12); v13(2-12)-v18; v30) – Masulipatam. v1-32. 1928-64 – 201mf – 9 – I-119/2 – ne IDC [073]

Trivet, Nicholas *see* COMMENTARY ON THE DE CONSOLATIONE PHILOSOPHIAE BY BOETHIUS

Trivino, Enrique *see* REGLAMENTO DE LA CONGREGACION DE MADRES CRISTIANAS, CANONICAMENTE ERIGIDA EN LA IGLESIA DEL I.C. DE MARIA. 1914

Trivino y Forte, Rogelio *see* PLUMAZOS

TRI-WEEKLY – Delphos, Ohio. 1894 – 1r – 1 – $32.50r – us Archival [071]

TRI-WEEKLY ASTORIAN – Astoria, OR. 1 Jul 1873-31 Jan 1874. – 1r – 1 – us U.O. Library [071]

TRI-WEEKLY COLUSA SUN – Colusa, CA. 1916-19 – 3r – 1 – $150.00 – C02129 – us Library Micro [071]

TRI-WEEKLY COLUSA SUN – Colusa. Calif. 1905-1906; 1918 – 1 – us UMI [071]

TRI-WEEKLY JOURNAL – Susquehanna, PA., 1890-1906 – 13 – $25.00r – us I.M.R. [071]

TRI-WEEKLY LEADER – Fremont, NE. Nov. 1895-Jul. 1903 – 1 – us NE Hist [071]

TRI-WEEKLY OBSERVER – Pensacola, FL. Aug 4 1866 – 1r – 1 – us Western Res [071]

TRI-WEEKLY REPUBLICAN – Corvallis, OR. 21 Jun 1909-17 Jun 1910. 1 roll – 1 – us U.O. Library [071]

TRI-WEEKLY REPUBLICAN – Lansing. Mich. 1880-1884 – 1 – us UMI [071]

TRI-WEEKLY STANDARD – Eureka, NV. 1885-86 – 2r – 1 – $100.00 – U04518 – us Library Micro [071]

TRI-WEEKLY TELEGRAM – Adrian. Mich. 1901-1902 – 1 – us UMI [071]

TRO KARLEK HOPP – Uddevalla, Sweden. 1841-44 – 1 reel – 1 – sw Kungliga [073]

TROBAR – 1-5. Brooklyn, N.Y.: Robert Kelly, c1960-1964. "A magazine of the new poetry" – 1 – us U.W. Library [440]

Trobriand, Philippe R D de K, Comte de *see* LE REBELLE

A TROCA : ORGAO CRITICO, LITTERARIO E NOTICIOSO – Maceio, Alagoas. 3 Abr-19 Out 1892 – 1,5,6 – bl Biblioteca [072]

Trochain, Jean-Louis *see* CONTRIBUTIONS A L'ETUDE DE LA VEGETATION DU SENEGAL

LAS TROCHAS / Moreno Marquez, Victor – Madrid: Estacion de Fitopatologia Agricola, 1941. Publicacion no 12 – 1 – sp Bibl Santa Ana [630]

LES TROCHILIDEES, OU LES COLIBRIS / Lesson, R P – Z 1832. 1832-1833 – 9 – ne IDC [590]

Trochon, Charles *see*
- ESSAI SUR L'HISTOIRE DE LA BIBLE DANS LA FRANCE CHRETIENNE AU MOYEN AGE
- LA QUESTION DU VASE DE SANG
- RICHARD SIMON ET LA CRITIQUE BIBLIQUE

Trochu, Francisco *see* VIDA DEL CURA DE ARS BARCELONA, 1929

O TROCISTA : LITTERARIO, NOTICIOSO E HUMORISTICO – Maceio, Alagoas. 26 Set 1898; Mar, Nov-Dez 1899; Dez 1900; Abr, Jun, Ago 1902; 3 Maio 1903 – 1,5,6 – bl Biblioteca [072]

Troeger, K W *see* MYSTERIENGLAUBE UND GNOSIS IN CORPUS HERMETICUM 13 (T.U.U. 5-110)

Troeltsch, Ernst *see*
- DER HISTORISMUS UND SEINE UEBERWINDUNG: FUENF VORTRAEGE
- PROTESTANTISM AND PROGRESS
- RICHARD ROTHE

Troemel, Paul Friedrich *see* SCHILLER-BIBLIOTHEK

DIE TROERINNEN : NACH DER TRAGOEDIE DES EURIPIDES UEBERSETZT VON FRANZ WERFEL / Euripides – Muenchen: K Wolff, 1923 – 1 – us U.W. Library [820]

EYNE TROESTELIJKE VERMANINGE VAN DAT LIJDEN, CRUYZE, VND VERUOLGINGE DER HEYLIGEN / Simons, Menno – BME-278 1 – 9 – ne IDC [240]

AIN TROESTLICHE SERMO VON DER VRSTENDT CHRISTI... / Huberinus, Caspar – [Augsburg: H. Steiner], 1525. [G.F.: 8.1] – 1mf – 9 – HUB-26/1 – ne IDC [240]

TROESTUNG AUSS GOETTLICHER SCHRIFFT... / Huberinus, Caspar – Frankfurt a.M.: Cyriacus Jacob, 1541. [G.F.: 4.4] – 1mf – 9 – HUB-72/1 – ne IDC [240]

Trog, Carl *see* RHEINLANDS WUNDERHORN: SAGEN, GESCHICHTEN UND LEGENDEN, AUCH RAENKE UND SCHWAENKE, AUS DEN ALTEN RITTERBURGEN KLOESTERN UND STAEDTEN DER RHEINUFER UND DES RHEINGEBIETES, VON DEN QUELLEN BIS ZUR MUENDUNG DES STROMES

Trogg, J G *see*
- DIE SCHWAEMME DES WALDES ALS NAHRUNGSMITTEL
- TABULA ANALYTICA FUNGORUM IN EPICRISI, SEU SYNOPSI HYMENOMYCETUM FRIESIANA DESCRIPTORUM

TROGUS POMPEIUS / Seel, Otto – Pompei Trogi fragmenta. Lipsiae: In aedibus B.G. Teubneri, 1956. xxxiii,208p. Includes index – 1 – us U.W. Library [930]

Trogus, Pompeius *see* GIVSTINO HISTORICO...

Troianovskogo, A et al *see* EKSPORT, IMPORT I KONTSESSII SOIUZA S.S.R:

TROIS AIRS VARIES POUR LE VIOLON AVEC ACCOMPAGNEMENT DE BASSE / Durand, A – (Parts) – Paris: Momigny, ca 1800 – 1 – us Sibley [780]

TROIS ANS DE REALISATION DU PROGRAMME D'EQUIPEMENT, 1949-1952 / Morocco. Division du Commerce et de la Marine Marchande – Rabat. 1952. BD-534 1 – 9 – ne IDC [380]

TROIS ARTISTES BRITANNIQUES: ROBERT ADAMS, HUBERT DALWOOD, RICHARDS / Reunion des musees nationaux. Paris – 1963. 6 illus. 1 fiche – 9 – fr Réunion [700]

TROIS ARTISTES ETRANGERS : ROBERT SHERARD / Grassal, Georges – Paris: Tricon, 1901 – fr Armell [700]

LES TROIS COMBATS DU LONG-SAULT / Guindon, Arthur – Montreal: Bibliotheque de l'Action francaise, 1923. SEM105P1466 – 1mf – 9 – Can$2.25 – cn Bibl Nat [971]

TROIS CONCERTANT, SIX, POUR DEUX VIOLONS ET BASSE. OP. 3 / Kuchler, J – (3 parts) – Paris: Mme Berault, 176- – 1 – us Sibley [780]

TROIS CONTES SAUVAGES / Lacasse, Zacharie – Quebec: Imp. de "La Verite"..., 1882. SEM105P453 – 1mf – 9 – Can$2.25 – cn Bibl Nat [830]

TROIS DISCOURS POUR LA RELIGION CATHOLIQUE / Richeome, L – Bourdeaus, 1597 – 7mf – 9 – CA-147/1 – ne IDC [240]

TROIS DOCTEURS : E.Z. MASSICOTTE, LITT. D., AEGIDIUS FAUTEUX, LITT. D., J.B. LAGACE, UNIV. D / Morin, Victor – Montreal, 1936. SEM105P754 – 1mf – 9 – Can$2.25 – cn Bibl Nat [920]

TROIS DOCUMENTS SUR MACHECOUL EN 1793, MICROFILMES ENSEMBLE = 3 DOCUMENTS ABOUT MACHECOUL IN 1793, MICROFILMED TOGETHER – (Martin, Gaston. – Les Blancs a Machecoul (mars-avril 1793). – Paris: Imp. de la cour d'appel, 1925; Extrait du proces-verbal des seances des trois corps administratifs de Rennes, reunis; suivi du recit des horreurs qui ont ete commises a Machecoul(...) – Rennes: Robiquet, 1793 – J.-P.-M. Sotin, administrateur du departement de la Loire-Inferieure, a ses concitoyens. Nantes: malassis, 1793) – fr Armell [944]

TROIS DUOS CONCERTANS POUR DEUX VIOLONS / Fleury, C – Paris: Momigny, 181- – 1 – us Sibley [780]

TROIS DUOS CONCERTANTS POUR DEUX VIOLONS... / Durand, A – (Parts) – Paris: Momigny, 180-? – 1 – us Sibley [780]

TROIS DUOS POUR DEUX VIOLONS : DUETS, VIOLINS, OP 18, NO 1 / Fodor, J – Paris: Imbault, 180? – 1 – us Sibley [780]

TROIS DUOS POUR DEUX VIOLONS : DUETS, VIOLINS, OP 18, NO 2 / Fodor, J – Paris: Imbault, 180- – 1 – us Sibley [780]

TROIS ETUDES / Cote, Thomas – (Also: Causerie Sociale, un Peuple Martyr, un Duel) – Levis: P-G Roy, 1891. SEM105P32 – 1mf – 9 – Can$2.25 – cn Bibl Nat [944]

TROIS ETUDES / Cote, Thomas – Levis Quebec: P. Roy, 1891. 00582. (Pre-1900 Canadiana) – 9 – cn C.I.H.M. [971]

TROIS GRAND QUATUOR CONCERTANS POUR DEUX VIOLONS, ALTO ET BASSE / Lickl, G – (Parts) – Paris: Imbault, [ca 1800] – 1 – us Sibley [780]

TROIS GRANDES SONATES POUR HARPE AVEC VIOLON ET VIOLONCELLE, OP. 18 / Ferrari, G G – Paris: Sieber, 183- – 1 – us Sibley [780]

TROIS GRANDS DUOS, A QUATRE MAINS / Rauzzini, V – Ms, 177- – 1 – us Sibley [780]

TROIS GRANDS QUATUORS CONCERTANS POUR DEUX VIOLONS, ALTO ET VIOLONCELLO...OP. 42 / Gyrowetz, Adalbert – Paris: Sieber pere, [1684] – 2mf – 9 – us Sibley [780]

LES TROIS HARMONIES, CHANSONS ET POESIES / Constant, Alphonse Louis – Paris: Fellens et Dufour, 1845. iv,316p. 4 fiches. (Literature Collection) – 9 – 10.00 – fr Bibl Nationale [810]

TROIS HEROS DE LA COLONIE DE MONTREAL / Dupuy, Paul – Montreal: Cadieux & Derome, 1887. 04139. (Pre-1900 Canadiana) – 9 – cn C.I.H.M. [971]

TROIS LEGENDES DE MON PAYS / Tache, Joseph C – Montreal: Librairie Saint-Joseph, 1884. SEM16P87 – 1r – 5 – Can$9.00 – cn Bibl Nat [830]

TROIS LETTRES ADRESSEES A R. LAFLAMME DE LA VILLE DE MONTREAL:...APPEL AU TRIBUNAL DE L'OPINION PUBLIQUE / Kierzkowski, Leon – Montreal?, 1873.02580.(Pre-1900 Canadiana) – 9 – cn C.I.H.M. [971]

LES TROIS MARTEAUX – no. 1. Toulouse. janv 1920. Collection privee – 1 – fr A.C.R.P.P. [073]

TROIS MOIS AUX NOUVELLES-HEBRIDES / Glaumont, G – 9 – F60.00 – fr Ethnologie [306]

TROIS MOIS DE CAPTIVITE AU DAHOMEY / Chaudoin, E – Paris, Librairie Hachette et Cie. 1891 – 9 – 12.50 – fr Orientalistes [960]

LES TROIS NIVEAUX DE L'ANALYSE PHONEMATIQUE DE L'AGNI DU MORONOU: LANGUE KWA DE LA COTE D'IVOIRE / Quaireau, A – 9 – F40.00 – fr Ethnologie [490]

TROIS NOCTURNES EN TROIS LIVRAISONS... / Jadin, L – Paris: Janet et Cotelle, [182-?] – 1 – us Sibley [780]

TROIS PIECES COMIQUES: PROPRES A ETRE JOUEES DAN LES COLLEGES, MAISONS D'EDUCATION, ET SUR TOUT THEATRE / Doin, Ernest – Montreal: C. Payette, 1871. 04293. (Pre-1900 Canadiana) – 9 – cn C.I.H.M. [820]

TROIS PRIMITIFS: LES GRUNEWALD DU MUSEE DE COLMAR, LE MAITRE DE FLEMMALLE ET LA FLORENTINE DU MUSEE DE FRANCFORT SUR LE MAIN / Huysmans, Joris Karl – Two fiches. (Literature Collection) – 9 – $6.00 – fr Bibl Nationale [750]

TROIS QUATOURS CONCERTANS, OP. 15 / Amon, J A – Offenbach: J Andre, 180- – 1 – us Sibley [780]

TROIS QUATOURS, OP. 1 / Arnaud, P – Paris: Sr Sieber, 178- – 1 – us Sibley [780]

TROIS QUATOURS POUR FLUTE...OP. 42 / Amon, J A – Vienne: Bureau d'Arts et d'Industrie, 180- – 1 – us Sibley [780]

TROIS QUATUORS / Alday, P – (Parts) – Paris: Pleyel, ca 1797 – 1 – us Sibley [780]

TROIS QUATUORS / Bliesener, J – (Parts) – Bruxelles: Weissenbruch, 179- – us Sibley [780]

TROIS QUATUORS / Duval, J – (Parts) – Bruxelles: Weissenbruch, 18– – 1 – us Sibley [780]

TROIS QUATUORS. 2E LIVRE / Widekehr, J – (Parts) – Paris: Pleyel, 179- – 1 – us Sibley [780]

TROIS QUATUORS CONCERTANS / Walter, G A – Paris: Boyer et Nadermann, 182- – 1 – us Sibley [780]

TROIS QUATUORS CONCERTANS POUR DEUX VIOLONS, ALTO ET BASSE : OEUVRE 33 ET 2 LIVRE DE QUATUOR... / Kozeluch, L – Paris: Sieber, 1791 – 1 – us Sibley [780]

TROIS QUATUORS CONCERTANT POUR FLUTE, VIOLON, ALTO, ET VIOLONCELLE.. / Hoffmeister, Franz A – Oeuvre 29. Parts. 179-? – 9 – us Sibley [780]

TROIS QUATUORS, OP. 13 / Eberl, A – (Parts) – Vienne: Molla, ca 1800 – 1 – us Sibley [780]

TROIS QUATUORS, OP.1 / Momigny, J-J – Paris: au Magazin de Musique et d'Instruments – 1 – us Sibley [780]

TROIS QUATUORS OP.6 / Roesler, J – (Pts.) – Leipzig: Breitkopf & Hartel, 179- – 1 – us Sibley [780]

TROIS QUATUORS POUR DEUX VIOLONS, ALTO ET BASSE / Steibelt, Daniel – Paris: Naderman, [181-?] – 1 – us Sibley [780]

TROIS QUATUORS POUR FLUTE, VIOLON, ALTO, ET BASSE, OP. 1 / Porta, B – (Parts) – Paris: Decombe, 178- – 1 – us Sibley [780]

TROIS QUATUORS POUR FLUTE, VIOLON, ALTO, ET BASSE, OP. 20 / Gyrowetz, Adalbert – (parts) – Paris: Sieber fils, 1793 – 1 – us Sibley [780]

TROIS QUATUORS POUR FLUTE, VIOLON, ALTO ET VIOLONCELLE...OEUVRE 78 / Mozart, Wolfgang Amadeus – Arrangements of K. 497, 548 and 498. Parts. 1799 – 9 – us Sibley [780]

TROIS QUATUORS POUR FLUTE, VIOLON, VIOLA ET VIOLONCELLE / Viotti, Giovanni B – Oeuvre 22. Parts. 179-? – 9 – us Sibley [780]

TROIS QUATUORS POUR FLUTE, VIOLON, VIOLE ET VIOLONCELLE.. / Schneider, Georg A – Op. 47. Parts. 181-? – 9 – us Sibley [780]

TROIS QUATUORS POUR FLUTE...OP. 42 / Amon, J A – Offenbach: Jean Andre, 182- – 1 – us Sibley [780]

TROIS QUATUORS POUR LA FLUTE, VLN, VLA, VC, OP. 40 / Brandl, J – (Parts) – Offenbach s/M: Andre, 181- – 1 – us Sibley [780]

TROIS QUATUORS...OP. 1 / Distler, J – (Parts) – Paris: Pleyel, ca 1795 – 1 – us Sibley [780]

TROIS QUATUORS...OP. 11 / Eler, A – (Parts) – Paris: Erard, 1795? – 1 – us Sibley [780]

TROIS QUESTIONS CAPITALES:... / Defourny, P – Paris, 1872 – 1mf – 1 – ILM-489/1 – ne IDC [327]

Trois Rivieres. Canada. Archives Judiciaires *see* GREFFE DES NOTAIRES (1648-1668)

Trois Rivieres. Canada. Bishop. Archives *see* "REGISTRE DES TREPASSEZ" (1634-1679)

TROIS ROMANCES AVEC ACCOMPAGNEMENT DE PIANO OU HARPE...OEUVRE 5... / Garat, P J – (Also contains 36 other works various composers publ between 1797 and 1810) – Paris: Chez M Erard, Rue du Mail, No 37 [between 1789? and 1802?] – 1 – us Sibley [780]

LES TROIS ROSES – Revue d'art. Dir. Justin-Frantz Simon. no. 1-12. Grenoble. juin 1918-avr mai 1919 – 1 – fr A.C.R.P.P. [700]

TROIS SCANDALES: L'AFFAIRE LOCKWOOD, L'AFFAIRE WHELAN, L'AFFAIRE LANGLAIS – 1892?. 03193. (Pre-1900 Canadiana) – 9 – cn C.I.H.M. [971]

TROIS SEXTUORS POUR DEUX VIOLONS, DEUX ALTOS, VIOLONCELLE ET BASSE, OP. 13, N.2 / Altbrechtsberger, J G – Vienne: Au Bureau d'Arts et d'Industrie, [180-?] – 1 – us Sibley [780]

TROIS SEXTUORS POUR DEUX VIOLONS, DEUX ALTOS VIONLONCELLE ET BASSE, OP. 13, N.1 / Albrechtsberger, Johann G – Vienne: Bureau d'Arts et d'Industrie, [180-?] – 1 – us Sibley [780]

TROIS SONATAS, A QUATRE MAINS POUR CLAVECIN OU FORTE-PIANO ARR. FROM "DUETS, VIOLINS, B. 519-21" / Pleyel, Ignaz J – Paris: Boyer, [181-?] – 1 – us Sibley [780]

TROIS SONATAS POUR LE CLAVECIN OU PIANOFORTE AVEC VIOLON OBLIGE... / Lance, Chevalier de la – (Piano part only) – Paris: Richomme, [182-?] – 1 – us Sibley [780]

TROIS SONATES POUR FORTEPIANO AVEC ACCOMPAGNEMENT DE VIOLON AD LIB / Rigel, H J – (Piano part only) – Paris: Naderman, 183- – 1 – us Sibley [780]

TROIS SONATES POUR LE FORTE PIANO ACCOMP. D'UN VIOLON / Amon, J A – Paris: Richault, 180- – 1 – us Sibley [780]

TROIS SONATES POUR LE FORTEPIANO AVEC ACCOMPAGNEMENT DE FLUTE OU VIOLON...OP. 39 / Steibelt, Daniel – Paris: Freres Gaveaux, [182-?] – 1 – us Sibley [780]

TROIS SONATES POUR LE PIANO FORTE AVEC ACCOMPAGNT. DE VIOLON ET VIOLONCELLE / Steibelt, Daniel – Tirees de l'oeuvre 35. 181? – 1 – us Sibley [780]

TROIS SONATES POUR LE PIANO-FORTE A DIFFERENTS ACCOMPAGNEMENTS AD LIBITUM : 1ER SONATE: AVEC VIOLON ET VIOLONCELLE; 2EM SONATE: AVEC ALTO ET VIOLONCELLE; 3E SONATE: AVEC UNVIOLON ET 2 CORS – (Pts) – Chez: I C Gombart et Comp, [179-?] – 1 – us Sibley [780]

TROIS SONATES POUR LE PIANO-FORTE A DIFFERENTS ACCOMPAGNEMENTS AD LIBITUM : 1ER SONATE: AVEC VIOLON ET VIOLONCELLE; 2EM SONATE: AVEC ALTO ET VIOLONCELLE; 3EM SONATE: AVEC UNVIOLON ET 2 CORS – (Parts) – Chez I C: Gombart et Comp, [179-?] – 1 – us Sibley [780]

TROIS SONATES POUR LE PIANOFORTE AVEC ACCOMP. DE VIOLON ET VIOLONCELLE, NO. 3 / Himmel, F H – (Parts) – Berlin: F S Lischke, 180- – 1 – us Sibley [780]

TROIS SONATES POUR LE PIANOFORTE AVEC ACCOMP. DE VIOLON ET VIOLONCELLE, NO. 11 / Himmel, F H – (parts) – Berlin: F S Lischke, 180- – 1 – us Sibley [780]

TROIS SONATES POUR LE PIANOFORTE AVEC ACCOMP. DE VIOLON ET VIOLONCELLE, OP. 16 NO. 3 / Himmel, F H – (Piano part only) – Berlin: F S Lischke, 180- – 1 – us Sibley [780]

TROIS SONATES POUR LE PIANO-FORTE AVEC ACCOMPAGNEMENT DE VIOLON ET VIOLONCELLE OBLIGES / Amon, J A – Mayence: B Schott, 182- – 1 – us Sibley [780]

TROIS SONATES POUR LE PIANOFORTE AVEC ACCOMPAGNEMENT D'UN VIOLON OU FLUTE ET VIOLONCELLE / Gyrowetz, Adalbert – Offenbach: J Andre, ca 1800 – 1 – us Sibley [780]

TROIS SONATES POUR LE PIANOFORTE AVEC ACCOMPAGT. DE FLUTE ET VIOLONCELLE OBLIGES, OP. 48 / Amon, J A – Paris: Richault, 182- – 1 – us Sibley [780]

TROIS SONATES POUR LE VIOLON AVEC ACCOMPAGNEMENT DE BASSE / Kreutzer, R – Paris: Cherubini, Nehul..., [184-?] – 1 – us Sibley [780]

TROIS SONATES POUR PIANO-FORTE AVEC ACCOMPAGNEMENT DE VIOLON OU FLUTE ET VIOLONCELLE / Gyrowetz, Adalbert – Op. 55. ca. 1800 – 9 – us Sibley [780]

TROIS SONATES POUR PIANOFORTE AVEC VIOLON ET VIOLONCELL OBLIGES / Becvarovsky, A – Offenbach s/M: J Andre, 180- – 1 – us Sibley [780]

TROIS TRIOS (2 VLNS, VC) / Eler, A – (Parts) – Paris: Pleyel, ca 1804 – 1 – us Sibley [780]

TROIS TRIOS CONCERTANS POUR VIOLON, ALTO ET BASSE...OP. 8 / Amon, J A – Paris: Pleyel, 180- – 1 – us Sibley [780]

TROIS TRIOS CONCERTANTES POUR VIOLON, ALTO ET VIOLONCELLE / Lickl, G – (Separate parts) – Augsbourg: Gombart, [179-?] – 1 – us Sibley [780]

TROIS TRIOS FOR VIOLON, ALTO ET VIOLONCELLE / Dahmen, J A – (Parts) – Paris: Erard, 180- – 1 – us Sibley [780]

TROIS TRIOS, OP. 6 / Barni, C – (Parts) – Paris: Leduc, 180- – us Sibley [780]

TROIS TRIOS POUR DEUX VIOLONS, ALTO ET BASSE, OEUVRE 2E DE TROIS / Jadin, H – Paris: Cochet, [179-?] – 5 – us Sibley [780]

TROIS TRIOS POUR DEUX VIOLONS ET BASSE, OEUVRE 1ER DE TROIS / Jadin, H – Paris: Cochet, [179-?] – us Sibley [780]

TROIS TRIOS POUR DEUX VIOLONS ET BASSE, OEUVRE 37. / Hoffmeister, Franz A – Paris: Sieber pere et fils, [179-?] – 5 – us Sibley [780]

TROIS TRIOS POUR PIANO ET STRINGS, OP. 23 / Woelfl, J – (Trio 1 only) – Offenbach s/M: Andre, 1803 – 1 – us Sibley [780]

TROIS TRIOS PROGRESSIVE POUR DEUX VIOLONS ET VIOLONCELL, [OP. 28], LIV. 2 / Hoffmeister, Franz A – Bonn: N Simrock, [1804 or 1805] – 5 – us Sibley [780]

TROIS TRIOS PROGRESSIVE POUR DEUX VIOLONS ET VIOLONCELLO, LIV. 1 / Hoffmeister, Franz A – Bonn: N Simrock, [1804 or 1805] – 5 – us Sibley [780]

TROIS TYPES DE L'HABITANT CANADIEN-FRANCAIS / Gerin, Leon – s.l., s.n., 18–. 05769. (Pre-1900 Canadiana) – 9 – cn C.I.H.M. [971]

TROIS VOYAGES DANS L'AFRIQUE OCCIDENTALE : SENEGAL-GAMBIE-CASAMANCE-GABON-OGOOUE / Marche, Alfred – Paris: L Hatchette, 1879 – us Res Libr [910]

LA TROISIEME CONFERENCE DE LA PAIX / Arnaud, Enrico – Berne, 1913 – 1mf – 9 – ILM-4064/1 – ne IDC [340]

LA TROISIEME EXPEDITION BELGE AU PAYS NOIR / Becker, Jerome – (African Library). Bruxelles. J. Lebegue. s.d. 1800 – 9 – fr Hachette [960]

TROISIEME PARTIE DES VOYAGES DE M. DE THEVENOT: CONTENANT LA RELATION DE L'INDOSTAN, DES NOUVEAUX MOGOLS, ET DES AUTRES PEUPLES ET PAYS DES INDES / Thevenot, Jean – Paris, C. Barbin, 1684, xxii-338-19 p. French Voyagers in the Mediterranean 16th to 18th Centuries. 5965 – 9 – fr Hachette [944]

TROISIEME PLAN QUADRIENNAL / French Equatorial Africa – D-1054 1. 1958-1962: section commune – 9 – ne IDC [338]

TROISIEME PLAN QUADRIENNAL DE DEVELOPPEMENT ECONOMIQUE ET SOCIAL, 1958-1962 / Ivory Coast. Ministere du Plan – D-1103 1. 1958 – 9 – ne IDC [338]

TROISIEME PLAN QUADRIENNAL DU CAMEROON, 1958-1962 / Cameroon – Yaounde. 1958. BD-273 1 – 9 – ne IDC [380]

TROISIEME PLAN QUINQUENNAL DE DEVELOPPEMENT ECONOMIQUE ET SOCIAL, 1971-1975 / Syria – (Recueil des lois et de la legislation financiere de la Republique Arabe Syrienne). 1971 – 9 – ne IDC [338]

TROISIEME PLAN QUINQUENNAL DE DEVELOPPEMENT ECONOMIQUE ET SOCIAL, 1971-1976 / Cameroon. Ministere du Plan et de l'Amenagement du Territoire – (Third Five-Year Plan of Economic and Social Development). l'Imprimerie Nationale. Yaounde. 1972. BD-1627 1 – 9 – ne IDC [338]

TROISIEME RAPPORT DE LA COMMISSION CHARGEE DE REVISER ET DE MODIFIER LE CODE DE PROCEDURE CIVILE DU BAS-CANADA / Quebec Province – Quebec: imprime par Leger Brousseau, 1895. SEM105P1515 – 2mf – 9 – Can$4.50 – cn Bibl Nat [340]

TROISIEME RAPPORT DU COMITE PERMANENT DES GRIEFS... / Bas-Canada. Parlement. Chambre d'Assemblee. Comite Permanent des Griefs – [s.l.]: [s.n.], [1831]. SEM105P1318 – 5mf – 9 – Can$11.25 – cn Bibl Nat [971]

TROISIEME RAPPORT ET DELIBERATIONS DU COMITE SPECIAL.. / Canada. Parliament. Legislative Assembly. Special Committee – Quebec: Louis Perrault, 1851. SEM105P257 – 2mf – 9 – Can$4.50 – cn Bibl Nat [323]

TROISIEME TRIO EN LA MIMEUR...OP. 26 / Lalo, E – (Score and parts) – Paris: Durand, 187- – 1 – us Sibley [780]

TROISIEME VOYAGE DE J. LINDEN / Linden, J J & Planchon, J E – Premiere partie. Botanique Plantae Columbianae. Bruxelles. 1863. B-6022 2 – 8 – ne IDC [580]

TROJANERKRIEG / Wuerzburg, Konrad von – 30p + 10 color mf – DM690.00 – 3-89219-015-1 – gw Lengenfelder [700]

Troll, Alfred *see* DER KIRCHENVORSTAND NACH DEM RECHTE DER EVANGELISCH-LUTHERISCHEN LANDESKIRCHE DES KOENIGREICHS SACHSEN

TROLLHATTAN – Trollhattan, Sweden. 1906-07 – 2r – 1 – sw Kungliga [072]

TROLLHATTAN – Trollhattan, Sweden. 1979-85 – 1 – sw Kungliga [072]

TROLLHATTANS TIDNING – Trollhattan, Sweden. 1985- – 1 – sw Kungliga [072]

TROLLHATTANS TIDNING – Uddevalla, Sweden. 1891-1901 – 10r – 1 – sw Kungliga [072]

Trollope, Adolphus *see* PAUL THE POPE AND PAUL THE FRIAR

Trollope, Anthony *see*
- CASTLE RICHMOND
- THE CLAVERINGS
- CLERGYMEN OF THE CHURCH OF ENGLAND
- THE GOLDEN LION OF GRANPERE
- HARRY HEATHCOTE OF GANGOIL
- HUNTING SKETCHES: REPRINTED FROM THE "PALL MALL GAZETTE"
- THE KELLYS AND THE O'KELLYS; OR, LANDLORDS AND TENANTS
- LADY ANNA
- LINDA TRESSEL
- LORD PALMERSTON
- LOTTA SCHMIDT
- NORTH AMERICA
- AN OLD MAN'S LOVE
- THE PRIME MINISTER
- RACHEL RAY
- RALPH THE HEIR
- SIR HARRY HOTSPUR OF HUMBLETHWAITE
- SOUTH AFRICA
- TRAVELLING SKETCHES
- THE WEST INDIES AND THE SPANISH MAIN
- WHY FRAU FROHMANN RAISED HER PRICES

Trollope, Frances Milton *see*
- ONE FAULT
- THE WIDOW MARRIED

Trollope, Thomas Adolphus *see*
- HISTORY OF THE COMMONWEALTH OF FLORENCE, FROM THE EARLIEST INDEPENDENCE OF THE COMMUNE TO THE FALL OF THE REPUBLIC IN 1531
- THE PAPAL CONCLAVES

A TROMBETA : ORGAO DE PROPAGANDA DO CLUB CHILE – Manaos, Amazonas. 13 Jun-1 Ago 1913 – 1,5,6 – bl Biblioteca [072]

A TROMBETA : PERIODICO INDEPENDENTE, POPULAR, NOTICIOSO, CRITICO E JOCO-SERIO – Maceio, Alagoas. 1-8 Nov 1888; 13 Maio 1889 – 1,5,6 – bl Biblioteca [072]

LA TROMBETTA DE TOGNON – N.p., [1571] – 1mf – 9 – H-8186/1 – ne IDC [956]

Tromby, B *see* STORIA DEL PATRIARCA S. BRUNONE E DEL SUO ORDINE CARTUSIANO

DIE TROMMEL – (Cont: Der junge Pionier) – Berlin, feb 2 1950-90 – 24r – 1 – Inquire at Mikrofilmarchiv for details – gw Misc Inst [370]

DIE TROMMEL : S.A.-GEDICHTE / Anacker, Heinrich – Muenchen: Zentralverlag der NSDAP, F Eher, 1936 – 1r – 1 – us U.W. Library [810]

TROMMEL – (Cont: Der junge Pionier) – Berlin, DE. Feb 2 1950-90 – 24r – 1 – gw Mikrofilm [072]

DIE TROMMEL DER NEUEN JUGEND – Hamburg, DE. 1933-Mar 1934 – 1 – gw Mikrofilm [072]

Trommer, Gert F *see*
- DAS ARGON-RESONANZKONTINUUM IM VAKUUM-ULTRAVIOLETTEN SPEKTRALBEREICH ZWISCHEN 50 MM UND 78.7NM
- METHODEN ZUR BERECHNUNG OPTIMIERTER BRECHZAHLPROFILE VON MONOMODEFASERN FUER DIE UEBERTRAGUNG HOECHSTER DATENRATEN

TROMPERT MASJARKAT – Surabaja. Indonesia. 1957-1965 – 1 – us UMI [072]

TROMPETA EVANGELICA.. / Blazquez del Barco, Juan – 1724 – 9 – 1.50f – sp Bibl Santa Ana [240]

TROMPETA EVANGELICA, ALFANGE.. / Blazquez del Barco, Juan – 1723 – 9 – 1.50f – sp Bibl Santa Ana [240]

DER TROMPETER VON SAEKKINGEN : EIN SANG VOM OBERRHEIN / Scheffel, Joseph Viktor von – 267. Aufl. Stuttgart: A Bonz, 1904 – 1r – 1 – us U.W. Library [810]

DER TROMPETER VON SAEKKINGEN : EIN SANG VOM OBERRHEIN / Scheffel, Joseph Viktor von – 38. Aufl. Stuttgart: J B Metzler, 1875 – 1r – 1 – us U.W. Library [810]

DER TROMPETER VON SAEKKINGEN : EIN SANG VOM OBERRHEIN / Scheffel, Joseph Viktor von; ed by Manz, Gustav – Berlin: Deutsche Bibliothek, [19-?] – 1r – 1 – us U.W. Library [780]

LA TROMPETTE : HUMORISTIQUE – Saint Sauveur de Quebec, Canada. 12 fev 1885 – 1r – 1 – Can$25.00 – cn Can Microfilming [072]

LA TROMPETTE DE LA METEMPSYCOSE UNIVERSITAIRE / Beausoleil, Joseph Maxime – Montreal, 1889. 03531. (Pre-1900 Canadiana) – 9 – cn C.I.H.M. [971]

TRONUS CUPIDINIS SIVE EMBLEMATA AMATORIA. P.T.L. – (An interleaved copy) – Utrecht, c1618 – 4mf – 9 – O-3024/1 – ne IDC [760]

TROON TIMES – 1 – £42.00r – uk Scot News [072]

TROOPS OUT – v1,no1- . Oct 1977- . Paper of the United Troops Out Movement – 1 – us U.W. Library [073]

TROPENMEDIZIN UND PARASITOLOGIE – v25-1974- 1,5,6; v26- 9 – us UMI [590]

TROPENMEDIZIN UND PARASITOLOGIE *see* ZEITSCHRIFT FUER TROPENMEDIZIN UND PARASITOLOGIE

DES TROPES / Du Marsais, C – 1730 – 9 – fr I.C.S. [400]

DES TROPES / Du Marsais, C – 1818 – 9 – fr I.C.S. [400]

TROPFEN IN'S MEER / Zimmermann, Paul – 1875 – 1 – us A.T.L.A. [240]

TROPI CARMINUM : LIBER HYMNORUM / Balbulus & Notkerus – ca 40p + 6 color mf – ca DM650.00 – 3-89219-020-8 – gw Lengenfelder [090]

O TROPICAL – Cruzerio Do Sul, Acre. 14 Maio 1972 – 1,5,6 – bl Biblioteca [072]

TROPICAL AGRICULTURE – (1982-. 1,5,6,9) – v1-. 1924- – 1 – us UMI [630]

TROPICAL AND SUB-TROPICAL APICULTURE – 1986 – 298p – it F.A.O. [636]

A TROPICAL DEPENDENCY / Lugard, F L – London. 1906. BA-337 2 – 8 – ne IDC [900]

TROPICAL DISEASES BULLETIN – v. 1-71. 1912-1974 – 1,5,6 – us Princeton Micro [616]

TROPICAL DOCTOR – (1983-. 1,5,6,9) – v1-. 1971- – 1 – us UMI [073]

TROPICAL FEEDS : FEED INFORMATION SUMMARIES AND NUTRITIVE VALUES / Goehl, Bo – 1981 – 529p – it F.A.O. [631]

TROPICAL FORAGE LEGUMES – 2nd rev exp ed 1988 – 692p – it F.A.O. [634]

TROPICAL FOREST RESOURCES – 1982 – 117p – it F.A.O. [634]

TROPICAL FORESTRY ACTION PLAN : COMMITTEE ON FOREST DEVELOPMENT IN THE TROPICS – 1985 2nd print 1986 – 168p – it F.A.O. [338]

TROPICAL FORESTS, PEOPLE AND FOOD : BIOCULTURAL INTERACTIONS AND APPLICATIONS TO DEVELOPMENT / ed by Hladik, C M et al – 1993 – 852p – 9 – 92-3-102879-0 – Co-published with Parthenon, which has exclusive sales rights in the UK – fr UNESCO [306]

TROPICAL GRASSES – 1990 – 832p – it F.A.O. [580]

TROPICAL GRAZING LAND ECOSYSTEMS : A STATE-OF-KNOWLEDGE REPORT / UNESCO et al – 1979 – 655p – 9 – 92-3-101625-3 – fr UNESCO [574]

TROPICAL HOME GARDENS / ed by Landauer, Kathleen & Brazil, Mark – 9 – $12.00 – 92-808-0732-3 – ja U.N. Univ [630]

TROPICAL NEWS – Fort Myers. Fl. 1920-31 – 1 – us UMI [071]

TROPICAL PASTURE SEED PRODUCTION – 1981 – 156p – it F.A.O. [338]

TROPICAL PEST MANAGEMENT *see* PANS

TROPICAL RAIN FORESTS OF CENTRAL AMERICA – 1993 – 9 – 92-3-102682-8 – fr UNESCO [972]

TROPICAL SHRIMP FISHERIES : TYPES OF FISHING GEAR USED AND THEIR SELECTIVITY – 1990 – 82p – it F.A.O. [639]

TROPICAL TUNA : SURFACE FISHERIES IN THE INDIAN OCEAN – 1989 – 240p – it F.A.O. [639]

TROPIQUES – Aime Cesaire, Rene Menil. no. 1-13 14. Fort-de-France. avr 1941-sept 1945 – 1 – fr A.C.R.P.P. [073]

TROPISCHE GROENTEN GETEELD EN IN HET 'T WILD GROEIENDE GEWASSEN, DIE DOOR DE INDISCHE BEVOLKING WORDEN GEGETEN / Ochse, J J – 1925. B-8313 1 – 3mf – 9 – ne IDC [580]

TROPOLOGIA: A KEY TO OPEN SCRIPTURE-METAPHORS / Keach, Benjamin – 4books. London. 1681 – 1 – 36.75 – us Baptist [240]

TROSA ANNONSBLAD – Trosa, 1920-71 – 9 – sw Kungliga [072]

TROSA TIDNING – (Gnesta Tidning, 1980-81) – Trosa, Sweden. 1979-82 – 1 – sw Kungliga [072]

TROSA TIDNING – Trosa, 1974-78 – 9 – sw Kungliga [072]

Troschel, F H *see* SYSTEM DER ASTERIDEN

Trosien, E *see* LESSING'S NATHAN DER WEISE

TROSSINGER ZEITUNG : BA DER SCHWAEBISCHEN ZEITUNG – Trossingen-Leutkirch, Germany. 2 Jan 1975- – 116r (1975-1990) – 1 – gw Mikrofilm [072]

Trost, Stewart G *see* THE EFFECT OF SUBSTRATE UTILIZATION, MANIPULATED BY NICOTINIC ACID, ON EXCESS POSTEXERCISE OXYGEN CONSUMPTION

TROSTBERGER TAGBLATT – Trostberg, West Germany. 1976- – ca 6r per yr – 1 – gw Mikrofilm [072]

EEN TROSTELIJCKE VERMANINGHE ENDE SEER SCHOON ONDERWYSINGHE VAN HET LYDEN ENDE HEERLICHEYT DER CHRISTENEN / Stoelwijck, W van – 1558. BME-169 1 – 9 – ne IDC [240]

DAS TROSTSCHREIBEN DES APOSTELS PAULUS AN DIE HEBRAEER KRITISCH WIEDERHERGESTELLT UND SPRACHLICH, ARCHAEOLOGISCH UND BIBLISCH-THEOLOGISCH ERLAEUTERT / Biesenthal, Johannes Heinrich Raphael – (Includes indexes) – Leipzig: Fernau, 1878 – 1mf – 9 – 0-8370-2339-4 – 1985-0339 – us A.T.L.A. [220]

TROSTUNG AUSS GOETTLICHER GESCHRIFFT / Huberinus, Caspar – Frankfurt a. Main: Christian Egenolph, [1531]. [G.F.: 2.1] – 1mf – 9 – HUB-64/1 – ne IDC [240]

TROSVITTNET – 19 Sep 1935-27 Nov 1941 (complete) – 4r – 1 – ATLA S0489 – us A.T.L.A. [073]

Trotha, Oberst von *see* MEINE BEREISUNG VON DEUTSCH-OSTAFRICA

TROTS ALLT – Stockholm, Sweden. 1939-46, 1948, 1950-52 – 5r – 1 – sw Kungliga [073]

Trotskii, L *see*
- LITERATURA I REVOLIUTSIIA
- NASHI POLITICHESKIIA ZADACHI
- SOCHINENIIA GOSIZDAT

Trotskyi, M *see* IAK PRYISHLO V ROSII DO REVOLIUTSII

TROTSKYISM IN LATIN AMERICA / Alexander, Robert Jackson – Stanford, Calif.: Hoover Institution Press, Stanford University, [1973] – 1 – CSUXAHZ6157-B – us Hoover Inst Photo [335]

Trott, Nicholas *see*
- JURY CHARGES
- WRITINGS ON PIRATES

Trotter, L B C *see* HISTOLOGY OF BRITISH MOSSES

Trottier, Guy N *see* LES ECRITS DE MONSEIGNEUR ARTHUR ROBERT, P.A., V.G.

Trottier, Irenee *see* BIO-BIBLIOGRAPHIE DE MGR JOSEPH-CLOVIS K.-LAFLAMME

TROTZ VERBOT NICHT TOT : BILDER AUS DEM ILLEGALEN KAMPF UM OESTERREICHS DEUTSCHE HEIMAT / Steininger, Anton – Graz: L Stocker, 1942 – 1r – 1 – us U.W. Library [943]

Trouchaud, J P *see*
- BILAN DE L'OPERATION SECTEURS PILOTES EN MOYENNE COTE D'IVOIRE, 1959-1968
- ESSAI DE VIVISION REGIONALE EN COTE D'IVOIRE
- PROPOSITIONS POUR UN CADRE REGIONAL DE PLANIFICATION EN COTE D'IVOIRE TRAVAUX PREPARATOIRES AU PLAN, 1971-1975
- ZONE RURALE DE SAN PEDRO. ENQUETES DEMOGRAPHIQUES

Troullidis, Thomas *see* DER HANDLUNGSSPIELRAUM DER ZENTRALBANK VON GRIECHENLAND UND SEIN EINFLUSS AUF DAS INFLATIONSNIVEAU DER GRIECHISCHEN VOLKSWIRTSCHAFT

Trouqui, E *see* STUDI ENTOMOLOGICI

TROUSER PRESS – v6-11. 1979-84 – 9 – us UMI [600]

Trouve *see* PAUSANIAS

DIE TROUVEREHANDSCHRIFT R. DIE HANDSCHRIFT PARIS, BIBL. NAT. FR. 1591 / Schubert, Johann – Frankfurt a.M., 1963 – 3mf – 9 – DM76.00 – 3-89349-725-0 – gw Hänsel [410]

O TROVAO : ORGAO DEDICADO AS PESSOAS QUE NAO SOFFREM PINDAHIBA – Curityba, 10 May-3 Jun 1888 – 1,5,6 – bl Biblioteca [072]

TROVAROMA (SUPPL.REPUBB.) – 1987-1995 – 1r per y – 5,6 – Sfr454.00 – sz Infoprint [072]
TROWBRIDGE ADVERTISER – (Trowbridge & North Wilts Advertiser 1860-80. Wiltshire Times 1950-62. Wiltshire Times & News (West Wilts ed.) 1962-70. Wiltshire Times & Trowbridge Advertiser 1880-1949) – England, 1855-73; May-Dec 1874; 1875-88; 1890-97; 1899-1963 – 109r – 1 – uk British Libr Newspaper [072]
TROWBRIDGE AND NORTH WILTS ADVERTISER *see* TROWBRIDGE ADVERTISER
TROZOS DE LITERATURA DE AUTORES EXTREMENOS / Castelo, Garcia – 1891 – 9 – 1.50f – sp Bibl Santa Ana [800]
TROZOS LATINOS – Villafranca de los Barros: Imp. Rodriguez, 1937 – 1 – sp Bibl Santa Ana [450]
TROZOS SELECTOS...CLASICOS LATINOS / Franco y Lozano, Francisco et al – 1890 – 9 – $1.50f – sp Bibl Santa Ana [450]
Trubeckoj, N S *see* DAS MORPHOLOGISCHE SYSTEM DER RUSSISCHEN SPRACHE
Trucchi, Ernesto *see* ESPOSIZIONE DELLA DIVINA COMMEDIA DI DANTE-ALIGHIERI
TRUCK AND OFF-HIGHWAY INDUSTRIES – v. 1-. 1979- – 1,5,6,9 – us UMI [380]
TRUCK FLEET – (Cont: Bus and Truck Transport at v63 1987. Ceased v64 1988) – Toronto. v63-64. 1987-88 – 9 – Can$28.00y – cn Micromedia [380]
TRUCK FLEET *see* BUS AND TRUCK TRANSPORT
TRUCKEE BASIN AND LAKE TAHOE CITY DIRECTORIES – Placer Co, CA. 1883-1885 – 2r – 1 – $100.00 – D076 – us Library Micro [910]
TRUCKEE BASIN AND LAKE TAHOE CITY DIRECTORY – State of Nevada. 1884-1885 – 1r – 1 – $50.00 – D076 – us Library Micro [910]
TRUD – (Backfile through 1998 $85r) – Russia, 1999- – 4r per y – 1 – $320.00 standing order – us Ross [072]
TRUD – (Missing: 1970) – Sofia, Bulgaria. Dec 1946-76 – 35r – 1 – us L of C Photodup [949]
TRUD – Moscow. 24 Feb-Dec 1921; Jul 1928-Dec 1932. (14mqn reels) – 1 – uk British Libr Newspaper [072]
TRUD – Moscow: Gazeta professional'nykh soiuzov, 1921- – 2mf – 9 – $199.95y – us East View [320]
TRUD – Moscow. USSR. 19 Feb 1921-1952 – 59r – 1 – us L of C Photodup [947]
TRUD – Moscow, USSR. 1952-1953; 1962-1981 – 21r – $1,050.00 – B63592 – us Library Micro [072]
TRUD – Moscow. U.S.S.R. 1953- – 1 – us UMI [073]
TRUD – Pg., 1916-17 n10 – 6mf – 9 – COR-696/1 – ne IDC [334]
TRUD – Sofia, 1976-1991 – 16r – 1 – DM1,200.00 – gw Mikro Press [949]
TRUD – Sofia, Bulgaria. -d. June 1959-Dec 1970. 23 reels – 1 – uk British Libr Newspaper [949]
TRUD – (Standing order available from De 1994 +. 2r per year. Sfr225.00y) – Avant 1993 – 2r – 1 – Sfr240.00 – sz Infoprint [947]
TRUD I KHOZIA ISTVO / Ekonomicheskoe soveshchanie Tatarsko i ASSR – (Library has: Feb-Mar. 1925; Jan. 1926) – Kazan: Izd. Ekonomsoveshchaniia TSSR, 1921- – 1 – CSUX89-S830 – us Hoover Inst Photo [330]
TRUDBENIK – Skoplje, Yugoslavia. -w. 1958-70. 11 reels – 1 – uk British Libr Newspaper [949]
Trudeau, Romuald *see* MES TABLETTES 1820-1848
Trudel, F-X *see* L'ETENDARD
TRUDOVOE EDINENIE *see* ARTEL'NOE DELO
TRUDOVOE KAZACHESTVO / Kazachiago Komiteta pri T S.I.K.S.R.K.S. i K.D. – (Library has: 1918, nos. 2-3, 5-15. 1:s1 1918, nos. 39-41, 44-45, 48, 50-52 not located) – Moskva: Kazachii Komitet pri T S.I.K., 191u – 1 – CSUX89-S963 – us Hoover Inst Photo [073]
TRUDOVOE KHOZIAISTVO / Narodny i komissariat zemledeliia – Kharkov: Vseukrainskoe gos. izdvo, 1920. 1v – 1 – CSUX89-S946 – us Hoover Inst Photo [331]
TRUDOVOE PRAVO. CHAST'L / Voitinskii, I S – Diktatura burzhuazii i trudovoe pravo. Moscow, 1934. 224p. BR-8534/1 – 9 – ne IDC [340]
TRUDOVYE ARTELI : PRAKTICHESKII KOMMENTARII / Tsypin, Ia.; ed by Danilovaia, E N – M., 1930 – 2mf – 9 – COR-456/1 – ne IDC [334]
TRUDOVYE ARTELI : PRAKTICHESKII KOMMENTARII K POSTANOVLENIIU VTSIK I SNK RSFSR OT 30 IANV. 1928 G. "O TRUDOVYKH ARTELIAKH" / Movchanovskii, BF & Dement'ev, B A – M., 1929 – 2mf – 9 – COR-435/1 – ne IDC [334]
TRUDOVYE KONFLIKTY V SSSR / Avdeev, Petr Nikolaevich – Moskva: Voprosy truda, 1928 – 1 – CSUX89-B7289 – us Hoover Inst Photo [947]
TRUDY / Gosudarstvennaia Publichnaia biblioteka im. M.E. Saltykova-Shchedrina – Leningrad, 1957-64. v1-12 (4-15). BR-10,849/1 – 9 – ne IDC [010]
TRUDY / Gosudarstvennyi Istoricheski Muzei. Moscow – v1-5, 8-9, 14 1926-1929, 1938-1941. ns no 1 1935 – 1 – us NY Public [947]
TRUDY / Russia. (1923-U.S.S.R.). Tsentral'noe Statisticheskoe Upravlenie – 1918-27. Moscow. v. 3, n. 6-7; v. 6, n. 1-2; v. 10, no. 3; v. 13; v. 19, n. 4; v. 20, pt. 3; v. 30, n. 4 wanting – 1 – $336.00 – us L of C Photodup [947]
TRUDY / Russia. Tsentral'noe Statisticheskoe Upravlenie – Moscow. 1920-1927. v. 1-35. Incomplete – 1 – us NY Public [310]
TRUDY / Russia. Tsentral'noe Statisticheskoe Upravlenie – Moscow. v1-35. 1919-28 – 11r – 1 – us Ross [947]
TRUDY / U.S.S.R. Tsentral'noe statisticheskoe upravlenie – 35 V. 1920-27 – 1 – 336.00 – us L of C Photodup [310]
TRUDY / Vsesoiuznoie Obshchestvo Polikatorzhan in Ssyl'no-Poselentzev. Kruzhok Narodovol'tzev – Moscow. v1-3. 1928-1930 – 1 – us NY Public [947]
TRUDY / Vsesoiuznyi Iuridicheskii Zaochnyi Institut. Moscow – Moscow, 1961-. Available: v1, 4, 7-8. (1961-67). BR-8639 1 – 9 – ne IDC [340]
TRUDY 1-GO VSEROSSIISKOGO S"EZDA RABOCHEIKOOPERATSII. V1 : DOKLADY I PRENIIA O TSENTRE RABOCHEI KOOPERATSII – Pg., 1918 – 1mf – 9 – COR-364/1 – ne IDC [334]
TRUDY ARKHANGEL'SKOGO GUBERNSKOGO STATISTICHESKOGO KOMITETA, ZA 1865-1869 GG – (Missing: 1866; 1867-1868, v1; 1869) – Arkhangel'sk, 1866-1869 – 12mf – 9 – RET-21/1 – ne IDC [947]
TRUDY ARKHANGEL'SKOGO GUBERNSKOGO STATISTICHESKOGO KOMITETA, ZA 1865-1869 GG. – (Missing: 1866; 1867-1868 v1; 1869) – Arkhangel'sk, 1866-1869 – 12mf – 9 – ne IDC [947]
TRUDY ARKHEOLOGICHESKIKH S"EZDOV V ROSSII 1869-1911 – M., Odessa, 1910-1916 – 408mf – 9 – ne IDC [930]
TRUDY ARKHEOLOGICHESKIKH S"EZDOV V ROSSII 1869-1911 – (S"ezd 1 v Moskve, 1869. M., 1871 v1-2; S"ezd 2 v Sanktpeterburge, 1872. Spb., 1876-1881 v1-2; S"ezd 3 v Kieve, 1874. Kiev, 1878 v1-2; S"ezd 4 v Kazani, 1877. Kazan', 1884-1891 v1-2; S"ezd 5 v Tiflise, 1881. M., 1887 v1; S"ezd 6 v Odesse, 1884. Odessa, 1886-1889 v1-4; S"ezd 7 v Iaroslave, 1887. M., 1890-1892 v1-3; S"ezd 8 v Moskve, 1890. Spb., 1892 v1; M., 1895-1897 v2-4; S"ezd 9 v Vil'ne, 1893. M., 1895-1897 v1-2; S"ezd 10 v Rige, 1896. M., 1899 v1; Riga, 1899 v2; M., 1900 v3; S"ezd 11 v Kieve, 1899. M., 1901-1902 v1-2; S"ezd 12 v Khar'kove, 1902. M., 1905 v1-3; S"ezd 13 v Ekaterinoslave, 1905. M., 1907-1908 v1-2; S"ezd 14 v Chernigove, 1908. M., 1910-1911 v1-3; S"ezd 15 v Novgorode, 1911. M., 1914-1916 v1-2) – M., Odessa, 1910-1916 – 408mf – 9 – R-17104/1-2 – ne IDC [947]
TRUDY ARKHIVA AKADEMII NAUK SSSR – Moscow, Leningrad, 1933-74. 25v. BR-10,949/1 – 9 – ne IDC [500]
TRUDY CHREZVYCHAINAGO VSEROSSIISKAGO SOIEZDA RABTONIKOV VODNAGO TRANSPORTA RESPUBLIKI: 14-27 FEVRALI A 1918 G – Petrograd: T Sentralny i komitet Soi ezda, 1918 – 1 – CSUX91-B2637 – us Hoover Inst Photo [331]
TRUDY DESIATOGO ARKHEOLOGICHESKOGO S"EZDA V RIGE / Archaeological Conference. Tenth. Riga – 3v. M. 1896, 1899-1900. PKG- BR-9833 1 – 9 – ne IDC [930]
TRUDY ETNOGRAFICHESKO-STATISTICHESKOI EKSPEDITSII V ZAPODNO-RUSSKII KRAI, SNARIAZHENNOI IMP. RUSSKIM GEOGRAFICHESKIM OBSHCHESTVOM. LUGO-ZAPADNYI OTDEL / Chuvinskii, P P – Spb. 7v. 1872-1878 – 48mf – 9 – RET-22/1 – ne IDC [947]
TRUDY FILOLOGICHESKIIA RAZYSKANIIA / Grot, Ia. K – v. 1-5 (v. 1, Ed. 4). Spb. 1899-1903. BR-6039 2 – 8 – ne IDC [460]
TRUDY GOSUDARSTVEHHOGO RUMIANTSEVSKOGO MUZEIA – Moscow, 1923-24. 5v. BR-11,042/1 – 9 – ne IDC [073]
TRUDY GUBERNSKIKH ARKHIVNYKH UCHENYKH KOMISII *see*
– TRUDY KURSKOI ARKHIVNOI UCHENOI KOMISII
– TRUDY ORLOVSKOI ARKHIVNOI UCHENOI KOMISII
– TRUDY PENZENSKOI ARKHIVNOI UCHENOI KOMISII
– TRUDY TUL'SKOI ARKHIVNOI UCHENOI KOMISII
TRUDY HIDROBIOLOHICHNO I STANTSIL = TRAVAUX DE LA STATION HYDROBIOLOGIGSUE (SIC) – No.7-19. Kyiv: Vyd-vo Ukrainskoi Akademii nauk, 1934-40. 13v. -irr – 1 – us U.W. Library [500]
TRUDY I DNI – Moscow. v. 1-8. 1912-1916 – 1 – us NY Public [073]
TRUDY I DNI – Moscow. v1-8. 1912-16 – 1r – 1 – us Ross [073]
TRUDY I DNI PUSHKINA / Lerner, N O – Ed. 2. Spb. 1910. BR-7131 2 – 8 – ne IDC [460]
TRUDY INSTRUKTORSKOGO SOVESHCHANIIA PO SCHETOVODSTVU SEL'SKOKHOZIAISTVENNYKH KOOPERATIVOV – Moscow, 1925 – 2mf – 9 – COR-519/1 – ne IDC [334]
TRUDY IURIDICHESKAGO OBSHCHESTVA, SOSTOIASCHCHAGO PRI IMP. KAZANSKOM UNIVERSITETE / Kazan Universitet. Russia – Kazan, 1901-05. 1900-04 available. Scholarly papers on law published by the University. BR-4012/2 – 8 – ne IDC [340]
TRUDY KOMISSII PO ISSLEDOVANIIU TOPLIV DLIA AVTOMOBILE I *see* TRUDY KOMISSII PO ISSLEDOVANIIU TOPLIV DLIA DVIGATELE I VNUTRENNEGO SGORANIIA PRI PETROGRADSKOM OTDELENII NAUCHNOTEKHNICHESKOGO OTDELA V.S.N.KH.
TRUDY KOMISSII PO ISSLEDOVANIIU TOPLIV DLIA DVIGATELE I VNUTRENNEGO SGORANIIA PRI PETROGRADSKOM OTDELENII NAUCHNOTEKHNICHESKOGO OTDELA V.S.N.KH. – (Includes c.1: v.1-2 1919) – Petrograd: Izdatelski i otdel Soveta narodnogo khoziaistva Severnogo ra iona, 1919. 2v – 1 – CSUXAKY6301-S – us Hoover Inst Photo [621]
TRUDY KOMISSII PO IZYSKANIIU NOVYKH ISTOCHNIKOV VODOSNABZHENIIA G. MOSKVY = TRAVAUX DE LA COMMISSION TECHNIQUE POUR LES RECHERCHES DES NOUVELLES SOURCES D'ALIMENTATION EN EAU POTABLE DE LA VILLE DE MOSCOU / Moskovskoe kommunalnoe khoziaistvo, Upravlenie vodoprovodom – (Includes c.1: v.1 1927) – Moskva: Moskovskoe kommunalnoe khoziaistvo, 1927- – 1 – CSUXAKZ1498-S – us Hoover Inst Photo [333]
TRUDY KOMISSII PO PODGOTOVKE ZEMEL'NOI REFORMY / Russia. (1917-Provisional Government). Glavnyi Zemel'nyi Komitet – Petrograd, 1917-1918. 5 vols. in 1 – 1 – 35.00r – us Hoover Inst Photo [324]
TRUDY KURSKOI ARKHIVNOI UCHENOI KOMISII – 1911, 1915 – 15mf – 9 – $90.00 – us Ross [025]
TRUDY KURSKOI GUBERNSKOI UCHENOI ARKHIVNOI KOMISSII – Kursk. v1(1-2). 1911 – 6mf – 9 – ne IDC [947]
TRUDY KURSKOI GUBERNSKOI UCHENOI ARKHIVNOI KOMISSII – Kursk. v1(1-2). 1911 – 6mf – 9 – RET-24/1 – ne IDC [947]
TRUDY MIESTNYKH KOMITETOV O NUZHDAKH SEL'SKOKHOZIAISTVENNOI PROMYSHLENNOSTI / Russia. Osoboe soveshchanie o nuzhdakh sel'skokhoziaistvennoi promsyshlennosti – 58 v. 1903 – 1 – $395.00 – us L of C Photodup [330]
TRUDY MOSKOVSKOGO GOSUDARSTVENNOGO ISTORIKO-ARKHIVNOGO INSTITUTA – Moscow, 1939-72.v1-29.BR-10,757/1 – 9 – ne IDC [947]
TRUDY MOSKOVSKOGO NUMIZMATICHESKOGO OBSHCHESTVA – Moscow, 1898-1905. v1-3. B-1934/2 – 8 – ne IDC [730]
TRUDY MOSKOVSKOGO PREDVARITEL'NOGO KOMITETA X ARKHEOLOGICHESKOGO S'EZDA V RIGE / Archaeological Conference. Tenth. Riga. Moscow Organizing Committee – 2v. Moskva. 1895-96. BR-9834 1 – 9 – ne IDC [930]
TRUDY NAUCHNOI KONFERENTSII PO VOPROSAM ARKHIVNOGO DELA V SSSR – Moscow, 1965. 2v. BR-10,760/1 – 9 – ne IDC [025]
TRUDY NUMIZMATICHESKOI KOMISSII – Gosudarstvennoi Akademii Istorii Material'noi Kul'tury. Petrograd, 1921-27. v1-6. BR-3424/2 – 8 – ne IDC [730]
TRUDY NUMIZMATICHESKOI KOMISSII – St Petersburg: Gos. izd-vo, 1921-27. v1 1921 – us Res Libr [730]
TRUDY OBSHCHESTVA ESTESTVOISPYTATELEI PRI IMPERATORSKOM KAZANSKOM UNIVESITETIE – v1- 1871- – 1 – us U.W. Library [500]
TRUDY OBSHCHESTVA ISSLEDOVATELEI VOLYNI – (Missing: v1,3,5,12) – Zhitomir. v1-13. 1902-1915 – 43mf – 9 – 1580/2 – ne IDC [947]
TRUDY ORLOVSKOI ARKHIVNOI UCHENOI KOMISII – 1885-1905 – 49mf – 9 – $290.00 – us Ross [025]
TRUDY PENZENSKOI ARKHIVNOI UCHENOI KOMISII – 1903-04, 1906 – 14mf – 9 – $85.00 – us Ross [025]
TRUDY PERVAGO EKONOMICHESKAGO SIEZDA MOSKOVSKAGO PROMYSHLENNAGO RAIONA / Ekonomicheski i si ezd Moskovskogo promyshlennago ra iona (1st: 1917: Moscow (RSFSR) – Moskva: Izd. Moskovskago ra ionnago ekonomicheskago komiteta, 1918 – 1 – CSUX88-B7688 – us Hoover Inst Photo [330]
TRUDY PO AVTOMATICHESKOI SVARKE POD FLYUSOM / Akademiia Nauk. URSR. Kiev. Instytut Elektrozvaryuvannya – 1948-1949, Sbornik 4-8, 1960, 1962, 1967 – 1 – us NY Public [073]
TRUDY PSKOVSKOGO ARKHEOLOGICHESKOGO OBSHCHESTVA, ZA 1901-1916 GG – (Missing: 1905 Pt3) – Pskov. 12pts. 1902-1916 – 30mf – 9 – RET-25/1 – ne IDC [947]
TRUDY PUBLICHNOI BIBLIOTEKI SSSR IMENI V.I. LENINA – Moscow, 1928-34. v1-3. BR-11,044/1 – 9 – ne IDC [020]
TRUDY SARATOVSKOI UCHENOI ARKHIVNOI KOMISSII – v. 1-33. Saratov. 1888-1916. Lacking: v. 2-19. B-1500 2 – 8 – ne IDC [025]
TRUDY SEKTSII PROMYSHLENNOSTI I TOVAROOBMENA / ed by N.K.F. – (Includes c.1: v.1 1920) – Moskva: N.K.F., 1920- – 1 – CSUXAKZ3063-S – us Hoover Inst Photo [338]
TRUDY SELSKO-KHOZIAISTVENNOI SEKTSII / N.K.F., Institut ekonomicheskikh issledovanii – (Includes c.1: v.1 1921) – Petrograd: Institut, 1921- – 1 – CSUXAKZ0032-S – us Hoover Inst Photo [330]
TRUDY TSENTRAL'NOGO I GUBERNSKIKH STATISTICHESKIKH KOMITETOV : BIBLIOGRAFICHESKII UKAZATEL' KNIG I ZAKLIUCHAIUSHCHIKHSIA V NIKH STATEI / Mezhov, VI – Spb., 1873 – 3mf – 9 – R-7169/2 – ne IDC [947]
TRUDY TUL'SKOI ARKHIVNOI UCHENOI KOMISII – 1915 – 19mf – 9 – $110.00 – us Ross [025]
TRUDY...VSEROSSIISKAGO SIEZDA SOVIETOV NARODNAGO KHOZIAISTVA / Vysshii soviet narodnago khoziaistva – (Includes c.1: v.1 1918:May/June-v.2 (1918:Dec.); v.4 1921:May) – Moskva: [Soviet], 1918- – 1 – CSUXAKZ3871-S – us Hoover Inst Photo [330]
TRUDY...VSEROSSIISKOGO SEZDA SOVETOV NARODNOGO KHOZIAISTVA *see* TRUDY...VSEROSSIISKAGO SIEZDA SOVIETOV NARODNAGO KHOZIAISTVA
THE TRUE AMERICAN – 3 Jun 1845-18 Mar 1846 – 1 – $60.00 – us OmniSys [071]
THE TRUE AMERICAN / Coe, Joseph – (Anthology of American constitutional documents and important addresses by leading founding figures) – Concord, NH: I S Boyd, 1840 – 5mf – 9 – $7.50 – LLMC 92-189 – us L.L.M.C. [323]
TRUE AMERICAN – Leesburg, VA. 1798-1800. Also: Washingtonian, 1808-20; Genius of Liberty, 1817-20. Sold as one unit – 1,3 – us Readex [071]

TRUE AMERICAN – Youngstown. Ohio. and Mahoning Register. 1855-75 – 1 – us UMI [071]
A TRUE AND FAITHFUL RELATION.. / Dee, John – London, 1659 – 1 – us U.W. Library [540]
THE TRUE AND FALSE THEORY OF EVOLUTION / Giles, Chauncey – Philadelphia: William H Alden, c1887 – 1mf – 9 – 0-8370-3283-0 – 1985-1283 – us A.T.L.A. [210]
A TRUE AND PARTICULAR NARRATIVE OF THE DISTURBANCES AND OUTRAGES THAT HAVE BEEN COMMITTED IN THE CITY OF NORWICH SINCE NOVEMBER TO THE PRESENT TIME;... – London, 1752 – 1mf – 9 – MP-363/1 – ne IDC [240]
THE TRUE AND READIE WAY TO LEARNE THE LATINE TONGUE / Hartlib, Samuel – 1654. 66p. (English Linguistics Series 1500-1800) – 9 – us UMI [450]
THE TRUE AND THE FALSE INFALLIBILITY OF THE POPES = WAHRE UND DIE FALSCHE UNFEHLBARKEIT DER PAPSTE : A CONTROVERSIAL REPLY TO DR. SCHULTE / Fessler, Joseph – (In English. Includes index) – New York: Catholic Publication Society, 1875 – 1mf – 9 – 0-8370-8506-3 – 1986-2506 – us A.T.L.A. [240]
THE TRUE BLUE-LAWS OF CONNECTICUT AND NEW HAVEN AND THE FALSE BLUE-LAWS INVENTED BY THE REVEREND SAMUEL PETERS : TO WHICH ARE ADDED SPECIMENS OF THE LAWS AND JUDICIAL PROCEEDINGS OF OTHER COLONIES AND SOME BLUE-LAWS OF ENGLAND / ed by Trumbull, J Hammond – Hartford, CT: American Publishing Co, 1876 – 4mf – 9 – $6.00 – LLMC 91-504 – us L.L.M.C. [340]
THE TRUE BRITON – London, England. -d. 18, 31 July, 11, 20, 26 Aug, 1 Sept 1801; Jan 1802-Dec 1803. 2 reels – 1 – uk British Libr Newspaper [072]
THE TRUE CATHOLIC – (Some original pgs damaged) – v1-10. 2nd series: v1-4. May 1842-1856 – 7r – 1 – ATLA S0130 – us A.T.L.A. [073]
TRUE CAUSE OF ALL CONTENTION, STRIFE, AND CIVIL WAR IN CHRISTIAN COMMUNITIES / Hopkins, Daniel C – New York: M W Dodd, 1862 – 1mf – 9 – 0-8370-4863-X – 1985-2863 – us A.T.L.A. [240]
THE TRUE CHARACTER OF THE REV. MR. WHITEFIELD, IN A LETTER FROM A DEIST IN LONDON TO HIS FRIEND IN THE COUNTRY,... – London, 1739 – 1mf – 9 – MP-255/1 – ne IDC [240]
THE TRUE CHRISTIAN LIFE AND HOW TO ATTAIN IT / Fernald, Woodbury M – 1874 – 9 – us A.T.L.A. [240]
TRUE CHRISTIANITY : A TREATISE ON SINCERE REPENTANCE, TRUE FAITH, THE HOLY WALK OF THE TRUE CHRISTIAN, ETC. / Arndt, Johann – Philadelphia: Lutheran Book Store, 1868 – 2mf – us A.T.L.A. [240]
TRUE CIVILIZATION, AN IMMEDIATE NECESSITY AND THE LAST GROUND FOR HOPE FOR MANKIND / Warren, Josiah – 1863. 189p. 1 fiche (24x) – 9 – 1.00f – at Libertarian Micro [320]
THE TRUE CONCEPT OF LITERATURE; EIGHT REPRINTED AND TWO ORIGINAL ARTICLES. SAN ANTONIO: MISSION PRESS 1948. 110P. WITH: CLASSIC FRENCH PLAYS/JOYNES, EDWARD SOUTHEY / App, Austin Joseph – 1 – us U.W. Library [410]
TRUE DAY STAR – 1845 – 1 – us UMI [240]
A TRUE DESCRIPTION OF THE MIGHTY KINGDOMS OF JAPAN AND SIAM : WITH INTRODUCTION, NOTES AND APPENDIXES / Caron, Francois & Schouten, Joost – (Repr from the English ed of 1663) – London: Argonaut Press, 1935 – us Res Libr [950]
A TRUE ECCLESIASTICAL HISTORY FROM MOSES TO THE TIME OF MARTIN LUTHER: IN VERSE / Hobbes, Thomas – From the Latin original.London: Printed for E. Curll, 1722. 187p. Includes index – 1 – us U.W. Library [240]
TRUE EVANGELISM : OR, WINNING SOULS BY PRAYER / Chafer, Lewis Sperry – (Includes indexes) – Rev ed. Chicago, IL: Moody Press, c1919 – 1mf – 9 – 0-8370-6482-1 – 1986-0482 – us A.T.L.A. [240]
THE TRUE FAITH OF OUR FOREFATHERS / Augustinis, Aemilius M de – (Includes index of authorities quoted) – New York: American News, c1880 – 2mf – 9 – 0-8370-6961-0 – 1986-0961 – us A.T.L.A. [230]
TRUE FISSURE – Candelaria, NV. 1881-86 – 2r – 1 – $100.00 – U04435 – us Library Micro [071]
THE TRUE GOD : A MODERN SUMMARY OF THE RELATIONS OF THEISM TO NATURALISM, MONISM, PLURALISM, AND PANTHEISM / Ballard, Frank – New York:Eaton & Mains, [c1907] – 1mf – 9 – 0-8370-2174-X – 1985-0174 – us A.T.L.A. [210]
TRUE GOD: A MODERN SUMMARY OF THE RELATIONS OF THEISM TO NATURALISM... PANTHEISM / Ballard, Frank – New York: Eaton & Mains, 1907 – 1mf – 9 – us A.T.L.A. [240]
THE TRUE HISTORY OF THE CONQUEST OF NEW SPAIN / Diaz del Castillo, Bernal – Mexico: Genaro Garica, 1908 – sp Bibl Santa Ana [946]
THE TRUE KNIGHT OF BRITISH COLUMBIA – Vancouver: T A Spink, [1898-1900] – 9 – cn C.I.H.M. [360]
TRUE LIGHT – Fairfield, NE. -w. Jan. 1899-Feb. 1900 – 1 – us NE Hist [071]
TRUE LIGHT REVIEW = CHEN KUANG – (In Chinese) – v24-34. 1925-35 (complete) – 5r – 1 – ATLA S0298 – us A.T.L.A. [073]
THE TRUE METHOD OF LEARNING THE LATIN TONGUE BY THE ENGLISH – Anon. 1696. 169p. (English Linguistics Series 1500-1800) – 9 – us UMI [450]
TRUE PATRIOT – Cuba. N.Y. 1866-1893 – 1 – us UMI [071]
A TRUE PICTURE OF THE EFFECTS OF INTEMPERANCE / Adams, Henry – Yarmouth, N.S.: C. Carey, 1888. 06149. (Pre-1900 Canadiana) – 9 – cn C.I.H.M. [360]
TRUE POLITICAL ECONOMY / Sharpe, John – Pamphlet. 1 fiche (29x) – 9 – 1.00f – at Libertarian Micro [320]
THE TRUE PRESBYTERIAN – Louisville, KY. v1-2. 1862-1864 – 1 – $50.00 – us Presbyterian [240]
TRUE PRESS – Pittsburgh. Pa. 1858-1861 – 1 – us UMI [071]
TRUE SCOTSMAN – Edinburgh. Scotland. -w. Oct 1838-Mar 1841. (2 reels) – 1 – uk British Libr Newspaper [072]
THE TRUE SPIRIT OF THE METHODISTS AND THEIR ALLIES (WHETHER OTHER ENTHUSIASTS, PAPISTS, DEISTS, QUAKERS OR ATHEISTS) FULLY LAID OPEN;... / Trapp, J – London, 1740 – 2mf – 9 – MP-271/1 – ne IDC [240]
TRUE STORIES OF NEW ENGLAND CAPTIVES CARRIED TO CANADA DURING THE OLD FRENCH AND INDIAN WARS / Baker, Charlotte Alice – Greenfield, MA: E. Hall, 1897. 02485. (Pre-1900 Canadiana) – 9 – cn C.I.H.M. [971]
THE TRUE STORY OF JOHN SMYTH, THE SE-BAPTIST : AS TOLD BY HIMSELF AND HIS CONTEMPORARIES... / Dexter, Henry Martyn – Boston: Lee and Shepard, 1881 – 1mf – us A.T.L.A. [240]
THE TRUE STORY OF ROBERT BROWNE (1550?-1633) FATHER OF CONGREGATIONALISM : INCLUDING VARIOUS POINTS HITHERTO UNKNOWN OR MISUNDERSTOOD : WITH SOME ACCOUNT OF THE DEVELOPMENT OF HIS RELIGIOUS VIEWS... / Burrage, Champlin – Oxford: Printed by Horace Hart at the University Press; London: H. Frowde, 1906 – 1mf – us A.T.L.A. [240]
THE TRUE STORY OF THE CATHOLIC HIERARCHY DEPOSED BY QUEEN ELIZABETH : WITH FULLER MEMOIRS OF ITS LAST TWO SURVIVORS / Bridgett, T F & Knox, T F – London: Burns & Oates; New York: Catholic Publication Society, [1889?] – 1mf – us A.T.L.A. [240]
THE TRUE STORY OF THE VATICAN COUNCIL / Manning, Henry Edward – London: Henry S King, 1877 – 1mf – 9 – 0-8370-8449-0 – 1986-2449 – us A.T.L.A. [240]
TRUE SUN – London. -d. Mar 1832-Dec 1837. (19 reels) – 1 – uk British Libr Newspaper [072]
TRUE SUN – New York, New York. July 14 1843; Jan 13 1844-Dec 30 1844; 1845-1847; Feb 21-Dec 1848 – 6r – 1 – us L of C Photodup [071]
TRUE TABLET – (The Tablet). London. -w. 1842-1914. (173 reels) – 1 – uk British Libr Newspaper [072]
TRUE UNION – 8Dec 1849-10 Nov 1857. (lacking v. 2 and 3, 1851-52); Southern Baptist Chronicle. 19 Jun 1847-25 May 1850 – 1 – 78.33 – us Baptist [240]
TRUE UNION – Baltimore, MD. Maryland Baptist Union Assoc. 1849-61. Single reels available – 1 – 132.80 – us A.B.H.S. [073]
THE TRUE VINE : OR, THE ANALOGIES OF OUR LORD'S ALLEGORY / Macmillan, Hugh – 4th ed. London:Macmillan, 1879 – 1mf – 9 – 0-8370-4248-8 – 1985-2248 – us A.T.L.A. [220]
THE TRUE WESLEYAN *see* WESLEYAN ADVOCATE
THE TRUE WITNESS : CATHOLIC CHRONICLE / ed by Clerk, E – Montreal, Canada. 16 aut 1850-28 jul 1910 – 19r – 1 – Can$50.00r – cn Can Microfilming [072]
THE TRUE WOMAN / Fulton, Justin Dewey – 1869 – 9 – us A.T.L.A. [240]
THE TRUE WOMAN, OR, LIFE AND HAPPINESS AT HOME AND ABROAD / Peck, Jesse Truesdell – c1857 – 9 – us A.T.L.A. [240]
Trueba, Alfonso *see*
– HERNAN CORTES. LIBERTADOR DEL INDIO
– HERNANDO CORTES. LIBERTADOR DEL INDIO
Trueba, Antonio de *see* NUEVOS CUENTOS POPULARES
Trueblood, Alva Curtis *see* LETTERS
Trueman, Andrea L *see* SOCIALIZATION AND WORKAHOLISM
TRUEMAN'S NEW BRUNSWICK EQUITY CASES / New Brunswick. Canada – 1v. 1876-93 (all publ) – 7mf – 9 – $11.50 – LLMC 81-029 – us L.L.M.C. [340]
Truempelmann, August *see* LUTHER UND SEINE ZEIT
Truestedt, Haro *see* BRUECKENKOPF
Truett Memorial Baptist Church *see* BRIEF HISTORY AND TENTH ANNIVERSARY SERVICES
TRUINFO...CATOLICAS...DIEGO DE ARCE / Tamayo de Salazar, Juan – 1648 – 9 – 1.50f – sp Bibl Santa Ana [240]
Trujillo *see*
– CONCURSO LITERARIO DE TRUJILLO ORGANIZADO POR LA COMISION DE FIESTAS PARA SOLUCIONAR LA INAUGURACION DEL MONUMENTO A PIZARRO, LEVAN TADO...VDA. DE D. CARLOS RUMSEY
– FIESTA DE NUESTRA SENORA, DE LA VICTORIA
– FIESTAS DE LA SANTISIMA VIRGEN DE LA VENDIMIA
– FIESTAS DE SU PATRONA LA VIRGEN DE LA VICTORIA
Trujillo, Antonio de *see*
– ARISTARCO...PADRE SAN FRANCISCO
– SATISFACION RELIGIOSA...SAN FRANCISCO
– VARONES HEROYCOS...SAN GABRIEL
Trujillo. Ayuntamiento *see*
– FERIAS Y FIESTAS DE JUNIO, 1960
– ORDENANZAS MUNICIPALES
– PROGRAMA DE FESTEJOS QUE EN HONOR DE SU PATRONA LA SANTISIMA VIRGEN DEL ROSARIO, CELEBRA LA BARRIADA DE HUERTAS DE ANIMAS 1971
TRUJILLO (CACERES) / Caceres. Junta Provincial de Turismo – (Texto tambien en frances, aleman, ingles) – Madrid: sucesos de Rivadeneyra, s.a. – sp Bibl Santa Ana [910]
Trujillo. Centro de Ensenanza Media y Profesional Garcia de Paredes *see* 10 ANOS DE ENSENANZA LABORAL EN TRUJIULLO
TRUJILLO, CUNA DE CONQUISTADORES. MONTANCHEZ, EL BALCON DE EXTREMADURA / Junta Provincial de Turismo – 1 – sp Bibl Santa Ana [946]
TRUJILLO. DECLARACION DE MONUMENTO HISTORICO-ARTISTICO DE SU CASTILLO / Castaneda, Vicente – Madrid: Tip. de la Rev. de Archivos, Bibliotecas y Museos, 1925. B.R.A.H. 87, p. 278 – sp Bibl Santa Ana [946]
Trujillo, Diego de *see* RELACION DEL DESCUBRIMIENTO DEL REYNO DEL PERU
TRUJILLO EN FIESTAS / Caja de Ahorros de Plasencia – Trujillo: Imp. Gexme, 1980 – 1 – sp Bibl Santa Ana [390]
Trujillo, Fray Thomas *see* CANCIONES QUADRAGESIMALES QUADRUPLICES
TRUJILLO. MERCADO REGIONAL DE GANADOS – Plasencia: Tip. Sanguino, 1979 – 1 – sp Bibl Santa Ana [946]
TRUJILLO. SEMANA SANTA. 1963. LA DIVINA TRAGEDIA – Caceres: Imp. Moderna, 1963 – 1 – sp Bibl Santa Ana [946]
Trujillo, Thomas de *see*
– CANCIONES...GUADALUPE...ADVENTU
– THESAURI CONCIONATORUM
TRUJILLO Y EL PRINCIPIO DE UNIDAD NACIONAL / Rodriguez Victoria, Armando – Ciudad Trujillo. 1945 – 1 – us Res Libr [972]
TRUJILLO Y SU TIERRA : HISTORIA, MONUMENTOS E HIJOS ILUSTRES / Naranjo Alonso, Clodoaldo – Trujillo: Tip. Sobrino de B. Pena, Tomo 1. 1922 – 1 – sp Bibl Santa Ana [946]
Truman, Harry S *see* POTSDAM CONFERENCE DOCUMENTS
Truman, J Henry *see* AMERICAN RAILWAY REPORTS
Trumbauer, Walter H R *see* GERHART HAUPTMANN AND JOHN GALSWORTHY
TRUMBULL COUNTY DEMOCRAT : WEEKLY DEMOCRATIC NEWSPAPER – Warren, OH. 6 Aug 1839, 16 Jun and 21 Jul 1840 – 1r – 1 – us Western Res [071]
TRUMBULL COUNTY NEWS : GENERAL NEWSPAPER – Niles, OH. 24 Mar 1876 – 1r – 1 – us Western Res [071]
TRUMBULL COUNTY, OHIO, TAXES, MS V.F. 0 – (Tax rate bill with names of residents, range and town in which their property was located, and amounts due, Aug 19 1803) – 1803 – 1r – 1 – us Western Res [978]
TRUMBULL COUNTY WHIG : WEEKLY WHIG NEWSPAPER – Warren, OH. 23 Oct 1848-17 Oct 1851 – 1r – 1 – us Western Res [071]
THE TRUMBULL DEMOCRAT – Warren. Pa. 1850-1851 – 1 – us UMI [071]
TRUMBULL DEMOCRAT : WEEKLY DEMOCRATIC NEWSPAPER – Warren, OH. 13 Jul 1841-30 Jan 1862 – 1r – 1 – us Western Res [071]
TRUMBULL DEMOCRAT : WEEKLY DEMOCRATIC NEWSPAPER – Warren, OH. 2 May 1843 and 15 Jan 1849 – 1r – 1 – us Western Res [071]
Trumbull, Henry Clay *see*
– THE COVENANT OF SALT
– KADESH-BARNEA
– A MODEL SUPERINTENDENT
– MY FOUR RELIGIOUS TEACHERS
– OLD TIME STUDENT VOLUNTEERS
– THE SUNDAY-SCHOOL
– WAR MEMORIES OF AN ARMY CHAPLAIN
Trumbull, Henry Clay et al *see* HINTS ON BIBLE STUDY
Trumbull, J Hammond *see*
– THE MEMORIAL HISTORY OF HARTFORD COUNTY, CONNECTICUT, 1633-1884
– THE TRUE BLUE-LAWS OF CONNECTICUT AND NEW HAVEN AND THE FALSE BLUE-LAWS INVENTED BY THE REVEREND SAMUEL PETERS
Trumbull, John *see* M'FINGAL
Trumbull, Jonathan *see* PAPERS, MS 2347
Trumbull, Lyman *see* PAPERS
Trumbull. Presbytery (Pres. Ch. in the USA. New School) *see* MINUTES, 1827-1870
Trumbull, William *see* EVOLUTION AND RELIGION
TRUMF *see* TRIUMF
TRUMP OF FAME : WEEKLY GENERAL NEWSPAPER – Warren, OH. 9 Jun 1812-27 Sept 1816 – 1r – 1 – us Western Res [071]
TRUMPET – McCook, NE. -w. Dec 1884-Dec 1885 – 1 – us NE Hist [071]
THE TRUMPETER : A ROMANCE OF THE RHINE / Scheffel, Joseph Viktor von – Edinburgh: London: W Blackwood, 1893 – 1r – 1 – us U.W. Library [810]
Trumpp, E *see* DAS TAUFBUCH DER AETHIOPISCHEN KIRCHE
TRU-NEWS – Henderson, NV. 1964 – 1r – 1 – $50.00 – U04847 – us Library Micro [071]
TRUNG-BAC TAN VAN – Grand quotidien d'information illustre en langue annamite. Hanoi. fevr 1922-avr 1941 – 1 – fr A.C.R.P.P. [072]
TRUNG-BAC TAN VAN CHU NHAT – avr 1940-sept 1945 – 1 – fr A.C.R.P.P. [073]
TRUNG-KY VE SINH CHI NAM – Moniteur de l'hygiene de l'Annam. no. 1-10. Hue. mars-dec 1930 – 1 – fr A.C.R.P.P. [073]
TRURO 1702-1890 – 35mf – 9 – us Holbrook [920]
TRURO CITY SHOPPER – Falmouth, England. 1985-Nov 1986. -w. 3 reels – 1 – uk British Libr Newspaper [072]
Trusevich, Ia *see* SVOD 260 AZBUK I OBRAZTSOV KIRILITSY. IZ SNIMKOV RUKOPISEI X-XVIII VEKOV RUSSKOI IUGO-SLAVIANSKIKH
Trusler, John *see* THE DIFFERENCE BETWEEN WORDS

LE TRUST DE L'ELECTRICITE, MENACE POUR LA SECURITE SOCIALE / Hamel, Philippe – Montreal: Le Devoir, 1937. SEM16P146 – 1r – 5 – Can$9.00 – cn Bibl Nat [336]
TRUST INDENTURE ACT OF 1939. RELEASE NUMBER 1-336, JAN. 23, 1940-JAN. 19, 1973 / U.S. Securities and Exchange Commission – 9 – us UMI [336]
TRUST INDENTURE ACT OF 1939 RELEASES / U.S. Securities and Exchange Commission – nos 1-336. 23 Jan 1940-19 Jan 1973 (all publ) – 19mf – 9 – $28.50 – LLMC 84-361 – us L.L.M.C. [340]
THE TRUST TERRITORY COURT REPORTS : 1951-1988 – Oxford, NH: Equity Publ Co, 1969-88 (all publ) – 64mf – 9 – $96.00 – LLMC 82-100F Title 25 – us L.L.M.C. [324]
Trust Territory of the Pacific *see* FOREIGN INVESTMENT LAWS AND REGULATIONS
TRUST TERRITORY OF THE PACIFIC ISLANDS NAVAL ADMINISTRATION : HANDBOOK ON THE TRUST TERRITORY OF THE PACIFIC ISLANDS / School of Administration, Hoover Institute, Stanford University – (A handbook for use in training and administration) – Washington: GPO, 1948 – 5mf – 9 – $7.50 – LLMC 82-100F Title 19 – us L.L.M.C. [324]
TRUST TERRITORY OF THE PACIFIC ISLANDS NAVAL ADMINISTRATION : INTERIM REGULATIONS / Trust Territory of the Pacific Islands. (U.S.) – n.p., 1947? – 2mf – 9 – $3.00 – LLMC 82-100F Title 1 – us L.L.M.C. [324]
TRUST TERRITORY OF THE PACIFIC ISLANDS NAVAL ADMINISTRATION : MONTHLY/ QUARTERLY REPORTS – 1 Jan 1947-30 Jun 1950 – 20mf – 9 – $30.00 – LLMC 82-100F Title 86 – us L.L.M.C. [324]
Trust Territory of the Pacific Islands. (U.S.). Secretariat d'Etat au Plan et a l'Economie Nationale *see*
- RAPPORT SUR LE BUDGET ECONOMIQUE DE L'ANNEE 1966
- RAPPORT SUR LE BUDGET ECONOMIQUE DE L'ANNEE 1967

Trust Territory of the Pacific Islands (U.S.) *see* THE MICRONESIAN REPORTER
Trust Territory of the Pacific Islands. (U.S.) *see*
- CODE OF REGULATIONS OF THE TTPI
- LAND TENURE PATTERNS IN THE TRUST TERRITORY OF THE PACIFIC
- MANUAL OF ADMINISTRATION OF THE TRUST TERRITORY OF THE PACIFIC ISLANDS
- RULES AND REGULATIONS FOR ADMINISTRATION AND OPERATION OF CONSTABULARY
- THE TERRITORIAL REGISTER
- TRUST TERRITORY OF THE PACIFIC ISLANDS NAVAL ADMINISTRATION
- UNITED STATES NAVAL ADMINISTRATION OF THE TTPI

Trust Territory of the Pacific Islands (U.S.) Div of Land Management *see* LAND MANAGEMENT CONFERENCE PROCEEDINGS
THE TRUSTEE – (Ceased v61 no 2 1991) – Edmonton. v58-61. 1988-91 – 9 – Can$20.00y – cn Micromedia [370]
TRUSTEE MINUTES / Porter Academy. Charleston, South Carolina – 1877-1955. 16 fiches – 9 – us South Carolina Historical [025]
TRUSTEES AND ADVISORY COMMITTEE MINUTES / Paducah. Kentucky. Jonathan Creek Baptist Assembly – 1956-66. 174p – 1 – us Baptist [240]
A TRUSTEE'S HANDBOOK / Loring, Augustus Peabody – 3rd ed. Boston, Little, Brown, 1907. 224 p. LL-337 – 1 – us L of C Photodup [340]
TRUSTEES MINUTES / Hancock County, Ohio. Cass Township. Township Clerk – 1906-1966 – 1r – 1 – $32.50r – us Archival [324]
TRUSTEES MINUTES / Wood County. Ohio. Pemberville. Village Cemetery Association – 1896-1993 – 1r – 1 – $32.50r – us Archival [324]
TRUSTEES' MINUTES / Chester, Pennsylvania. Crozer Theological Seminary – (Faculty Minutes, 1867-1970. Crozer Foundation, Records, 1965-70) – 1867-1970 – 1 – 130.70 – us A.B.H.S. [240]
Trustees of St. Augustine's College *see* OCCASIONAL PAPERS FROM ST AUGUSTINE'S COLLEGE, CANTERBURY, 1853-1935
TRUSTEES QUARTERLY REVIEW – Brisbane, Australia. -q. 1909-20. 4 reels – 1 – uk British Libr Newspaper [073]
TRUSTEES RECORDS / Burlington, Vermont. Gove Hill Christian Association – 1966-75 – 1 – 15.50 – us A.B.H.S. [240]
TRUSTEESHIP COUNCIL / United Nations – 935mf – 9 – $1600.00; $1.90f – uk UNIMICRO [900]
TRUSTEESHIP TERMINATION : COMMENTS / Advisory Council on Historic Preservation – (Various pagination) – n.p, aug 25, 1981 – 2mf – 9 – $3.00 – LLMC 82-100F, Title 112 – us L.L.M.C. [323]
TRUSTEESSHIP COUNCIL OFFICIAL RECORDS : ANNEXES/SESSIONAL FASCICLES / United Nations – (1st Sess. – 5th Sess.: 1947-1949. E/F.32; 6th Sess. – 52nd Sess.: 1950-1985. E.121 F.103; 1st Spec. Sess. – 2nd Spec. Sess.: 1949. E/F.2; 3rd Spec. Sess. – 15th Spec. Sess.: 1950-1982. E.10; No Annexes issued for 11th-13th Special Sessions) – 9 – us U.N. Pubs [324]
TRUSTEESSHIP COUNCIL OFFICIAL RECORDS : RESOLUTIONS AND DECISIONS / United Nations – (1st Sess. – 53rd Sess.: T/RES/-; T/ 1947-1986. E/F.68 S.57; 1st Spec. Sess. – 16th Spec. Sess.: T/RES/-; T/ 1949-1986. E/F.12 S.12) – 9 – us U.N. Pubs [324]
TRUSTEESSHIP COUNCIL OFFICIAL RECORDS : SUPPLEMENTS AND SPECIAL SUPPLEMENTS / United Nations – (1st Sess. – 54th Sess.: T/ 1947-1987. E/F.93 E.114 F.116 S.57; 1st Spec. Sess. – 18th Spec. Sess.: T/-1949-1986. E/F.12 E.4 F.4 S.12; No supplements issued for the 1st, 3rd, 4th, 6th and 12th Special Sessions) – 9 – us U.N. Pubs [324]
TRUSTEESSHIP COUNCIL OFFICIAL RECORDS : VERBATIM RECORDS OF PLENARY MEETINGS / United Nations – (1st Sess. – 5th Sess.: T/SR. or T/PV. 1947-1949. E/ F.64; 6th Sess. – 35th Sess.: T/SR. 1950-1968. E.176 F.185; 1st Spec. Sess. 2nd Spec. Sess.: T/SR. 1949. E/F.3; 3rd Spec. Sess. – 13th Spec. Sess.: T/SR. 1950-1967. E.12 F.12; After 35th Session, no further Plenary Mtg. to the Official Records of the Council have been issued) – 9 – us U.N. Pubs [324]
TRUSTS AND ESTATES – v1- 1904- 1; v110-5,6; v114- 9 – us UMI [336]
LOS TRUSTS YANQUIS CONTRA LA ARGENTINA / Fuchs, Jaime – Buenos Aires: Editorial Fundamentos, 1951 – 1 – CSUXADH5675-B – us Hoover Inst Photo [332]
THE TRUSTWORTHINESS OF BORDER BALLADS : AS EXEMPLIFIED BY "JAMIE TELFER I' THE FAIR DODHEAD" AND OTHER BALLADS / Elliot, William Fitzwilliam – Edinburgh: William Blackwood, 1906 – 1 roll – 1 – 1-55879-524-3 – uk Libr Preservation [420]
TRUTEN' / Novikov, N I – 1769-70. (Ed. 3 by P. A. Efremova). Spb. 1865. BR-5782 2 – 8 – ne IDC [460]
THE TRUTH – Montreal, Canada. 27 nov 1917; 18 dec 1917 – 1r – 1 – Can$35.00 – cn Can Microfilming [072]
THE TRUTH – New York. N.Y. 1894-95 – 1 – us A.J.P.C. [071]
TRUTH – Bridgetown. Barbados. -w. 2 Jul 1960-2 Jan 1965, 2 Oct 1965-30 Jul 1966. (Imperfect). (3 reels) – 1 – uk British Libr Newspaper [072]
TRUTH – (Cont by: Truth for the People) – Toronto: S.F. Wilson, [18–1884] – 9 – cn C.I.H.M. [072]
TRUTH – (Cont: Truth for the People) – Toronto: S F Wilson, [between 1886 and 1890-189 or 19–] – 9 – cn C.I.H.M. [072]
TRUTH – Elkhart. Ind. 1902- – 1 – us UMI [071]
TRUTH – London. 1877-99.-w. 58 reels – 1 – uk British Libr Newspaper [072]
TRUTH – Ness City. Kan. 1883-1884 – 1 – us UMI [071]
TRUTH – New York. July 6 1880-Jan 4 1884. Incomplete – 1 – us NY Public [071]
TRUTH – New York. n204-1421. 1880-84 – 4r – 1 – us Ross [071]
TRUTH *see*
- TRUTH FOR THE PEOPLE
- THE WATCHWORD
- WATCHWORD AND TRUTH, 1897-1921

TRUTH, 1875-1897 – 1875-1897 – 96mf – 9 – $275.00 – us Schnappsburg [220]
THE TRUTH ABOUT BARCELONA / Brockway, Fenner – London, 1937? Fiche W 764. (Blodgett Collection of Spanish Civil War Pamphlets) – 9 – us H.U. College Libr [946]
TRUTH ABOUT PALESTINE: A REPLY TO THE PALESTINE ARAB DELEGATION / Zionist Organization. London – 1922. BJ-28-127 1 – 9 – ne IDC [956]
THE TRUTH ABOUT SPAIN / Goebbels, Joseph – Nuernberg, 1937. Fiche W923. (Blodgett Collection of Spanish Civil War Pamphlets) – 9 – us H.U. College Libr [946]
THE TRUTH ABOUT SPAIN / Rocker, Rudolf – N.Y., 193? Fiche W1146. (Blodgett Collection of Spanish Civil War Pamphlets) – 9 – us H.U. College Libr [946]
THE TRUTH ABOUT THE BARCELONA EVENTS / Lambda – N.Y., 1937? Fiche W983. (Blodgett Collection of Spanish Civil War Pamphlets) – 9 – us H.U. College Libr [946]
THE TRUTH ABOUT THE PILGRIMS – By Francis R. Stoddard 1952. Item H. Indexed, 206p. SW16-0092 – 5 – us A.G.L.L. [978]
THE TRUTH ABOUT WEST IRIAN / Indonesia. Kementerian Penerangan – SE-3155 1. 1956? – 9 – ne IDC [324]
TRUTH AND COUNTER TRUTH / Richey, Thomas – New York: Pott & Amery, 1869 – 1mf – 9 – 0-8370-5280-7 – 1985-3280 – us A.T.L.A. [240]
TRUTH AND ERROR, OR, LETTERS TO A FRIEND ON SOME OF THE CONTROVERSIES OF THE DAY / Bonar, Horatius – New York: Robert Carter, 1850.1 fiche – 9 – us A.T.L.A. [240]
TRUTH AND FALSEHOOD IN RELIGION : SIX LECTURES / Inge, William Ralph – (Includes bibliographical references) – 2nd ed. New York:E P Dutton, 1906 – 1mf – 9 – 0-8370-4607-6 – 1985-2607 – us A.T.L.A. [240]
TRUTH AND GRACE, OR, THE WORKS OF MARY JANE GRAHAM / Graham, Mary Jane – Philadelphia: A. Kirkpatrick, 1868 – 9 – us A.T.L.A. [920]
TRUTH AND LIFE IN JESUS : SERMONS PREACHED IN THE MECHANICS' INSTITUTION, DAVID STREET, MANCHESTER, OCT, NOV AND DEC 1859... / Harris, Thomas Lake – New York: New Church Pub Association, 1860 – 1mf – 9 – 0-8370-7385-5 – 1986-1385 – us A.T.L.A. [240]
TRUTH AND REALITY : AN INTRODUCTION TO THE THEORY OF KNOWLEDGE / Boodin, John Elof – New York: Macmillan, 1911 – 1mf – us A.T.L.A. [120]
TRUTH AND REALITY WITH SPECIAL REFERENCE TO RELIGION : OR, A PLEA FOR THE UNITY OF THE SPIRIT AND THE UNITY OF LIFE IN ALL ITS MANIFESTATIONS / Smyth, John – (Includes bibliographical references) – Edinburgh: T & T Clark, 1901 – 1mf – 9 – 0-8370-6386-8 – 1986-0386 – us A.T.L.A. [110]
TRUTH DEFENDED : OR, THE AWFUL SOVEREIGNTY AND RIGHTEOUSNESS OF GOD (AS DISPLAY'D IN ETERNAL ELECTION, PARTICULAR REDEMPTION, AND C.) VINDICATED... / Ridgway, E – London, 1741 – 1mf – 9 – MP-294/1 – ne IDC [240]
TRUTH DEFENDED AND CLEARED FROM MISTAKES AND MISREPRESENTATIONS, IN A DIALOGUE BETWEEN ONE MISINFORMED AND AN ADVOCATE FOR THE TRUTH,... / Cudworth, W – London, 1746 – 1mf – 9 – MP-328/1 – ne IDC [240]
TRUTH EXPLODED : OR: THE ART OF LYNG AND SWEARING MADE EASY,... – Bath, 1782 – 1mf – 9 – MP-545/1 – ne IDC [240]
TRUTH FOR THE PEOPLE – (Cont: Truth. Cont by: Truth) – Toronto: S F Wilson, [1884-between 1886 and 1890] – 9 – cn C.I.H.M. [072]
TRUTH FOR THE PEOPLE *see*
- TRUTH

TRUTH (MELBOURNE) – 1987-1994. T1-23 – 42r – 1 – at Corangamite [072]
THE TRUTH OF SCRIPTURE : IN CONNECTION WITH REVELATION, INSPIRATION, AND THE CANON / Given, John James – (Includes appendix) – Edinburgh: T & T Clark, 1881 – 1mf – 9 – 0-8370-3301-2 – 1985-1301 – us A.T.L.A. [220]
THE TRUTH OF THE BIBLE : EVIDENCE FROM THE MOSAIC AND OTHER RECORDS OF CREATION, THE ORIGIN AND ANTIQUITY OF MAN, THE SCIENCE OF SCRIPTURE AND FROM THE ARCHAEOLOGY OF DIFFERENT NATIONS OF THE EARTH / Savile, Bourchier Wrey – (Includes bibliographical references and index) – London: Longmans, Green, 1871 – 1mf – 9 – 0-8370-9417-8 – 1986-3417 – us A.T.L.A. [220]
TRUTH "SANS PEUR" / ed by Larivee, Louis – Montreal, Canada. 2 mai 1914 – 1r – 1 – Can$25.00 – cn Can Microfilming [072]
THE TRUTH SEEKER – Bradford. 1894-1915. Irreg – 1 – uk Microform Academic [100]
TRUTH SEEKER – v. 1. 1854-1855 – 1 – us UMI [240]
TRUTH SEEKER: A MAGAZINE FOR FREETHINKERS – New York. v. 1-38. 1873-1911 – 1 – 592.00 – us L of C Photodup [073]
A TRUTH THAT IS NEWS – Ireland.1932 – 1 – ie Microforms [072]
TRUTH WAR ISSUE – Ireland.5 Jul-22 Aug 1922 – 1 – ie Microforms [072]
TRUTHS FOR THE PEOPLE : OR, SEVERAL POINTS IN THEOLOGY PLAINLY STATED, FOR BEGINNERS / Plumer, William Swan – NY: American Tract Society, c1875 – 1mf – 9 – 0-8370-5478-8 – 1985-3478 – us A.T.L.A. [240]
TRUYEN TICH VIET-NAM / Le Huong – (Saigon?): Mot Nhom Van-Hdu, (1970). 312p – 1 – us U.W. Library [950]
Truyol, A *see* METODOLOGIA DEL DERECHO (ORDENACION CRITICA DE LAS PRINCIPALES DIRECCIONES METODOLOGICAS). MADRID, 1945
Truyol Serra, A *see*
- EL HEGELISMO JURIDICO ESPANOL. MADRID, 1944
- EL RACISMO. BREVE HISTORIA DE SUS DOCTRINAS

TRUZHENIK – Kaunas, U.S.S.R. -d. 14 Jan-1 June 1941. Imperfect. 46 ft – 1 – uk British Libr Newspaper [947]
TRUZHENIK – (Missing: 1909 n3-24) – Spb., 1908-10 n1 – 7mf – 9 – COR-699/1 – ne IDC [334]
TRUZHENIK – (Missing: 1920 n1) – Irkutsk, 1920 n1-2 – 1mf – 9 – COR-698/1 – ne IDC [334]
TRUZHENITSA SEVERNOGO KAVKAZA – Rostov-na-Donu, 1925 n1-8; 1926 n1-8; 1927 n2-12 – 16mf – 9 – $100.00 – us Ross [305]
TRY – 1929-40. (Name change: The Challenge. 1929-38) – 1 – 185.50 – us Baptist [240]
TRYBUNA – (Backfile through 1998 $85r) – Poland, 1999- – 4r per y – 1 – $320.00 standing order – us Ross [072]
TRYBUNA LITERACKA – Warsaw. Poland. -w. Nov 1957-Jun 1959. (1 reel) – 1 – uk British Libr Newspaper [943]
TRYBUNA MAZOWIECKA – Warsaw, Poland. -d. Sept 1955-Dec 1958. 10 reels – 1 – uk British Libr Newspaper [943]
TRYBUNA MAZOWIECKA – Warsaw, Poland. Jul 1956-1960; 1962-Jun 1970 – 26r – 1 – us L of C Photodup [943]
TRYBUNA OPOLSKA – Opole, Poland. 1953-Jan 1976 – 43r – 1 – us L of C Photodup [943]
TRYBUNA OPOLSKA – Opole, Poland. -d. Sept 1955-Dec 1958. 7 reels – 1 – uk British Libr Newspaper [943]
TRYBUNA POMORSKA – Bydgoszcz, Poland. Aug-Nov 1945 – 1r – 1 – us L of C Photodup [943]
TRYBUNA ROBOTNICZA – (Cont by: Trybuna Slaska in 1990) – Katowice, Poland. Mar 1945-Jun 1946; Sept 1949-1992 (scattered issues) – 84r – 1 – us L of C Photodup [943]
TRYBUNA SLASKA *see* TRYBUNA ROBOTNICZA
TRYBUNA WOLNOSCI – Warsaw. Poland. -w. 6 Apr 1950-27 Jan 1957. (7 reels) – 1 – uk British Libr Newspaper [943]
TRYBUNU LUDU : ORGAN KOMITETU CENTRALNEGO POLSKIEJ ZJEDNOCZONEJ PARTII ROBOTNICZEJ – Warszawa: "Prasa", dec 16 1948-jan 27/28 1990 – us Res Libr [072]
Tryon, G W *see* THE COMPLETE WRITINGS OF C.S. RAFINESQUE ON RECENT AND FOSSIL CONCHOLOGY
Tryon, G W A *see* MANUAL OF CONCHOLOGY
Tryon, G WA *see*
- A MONOGRAPH OF THE TERRESTRIAL MOLLUSCA INHABITING THE UNITED STATES
- STRUCTURAL AND SYSTEMATIC CONCHOLOGY; AN INTRODUCTION TO THE STUDY OF THE MOLLUSCA

TRYON GRAPHIC – Tryon, NE. -w. Jun 1892-Oct 1903, scattered issues missing; May 1914-Nov 1919; Feb 1920-Mar 1922, scattered issues missing; Jul 1922 to date – 1 – us NE Hist [071]

TRYPANOTOLERANT CATTLE AND LIVESTOCK DEVELOPMENT IN WEST AND CENTRAL AFRICA – it F.A.O. [639]

TRYPANOTOLERANT LIVESTOCK IN WEST AND CENTRAL AFRICA – it F.A.O. [636]

TRYPANOTOLERANT LIVESTOCK IN WEST AND CENTRAL AFRICA = LE BETAIL TRYPANOTOLERANT D'AFRIQUE OCCIDENTALE ET CENTRALE. TOME 2: SITUATIONS NATIONALES : VOL 2. COUNTRY STUDIES / Lhoste, P & Mason IL – 1979 – 9 – $12.00 – 92-9053-126-6 – et ILRI [636]

TRYPANOTOLERANT LIVESTOCK IN WEST AND CENTRAL AFRICA = LE BETAIL TRYPANOTOLERANT D'AFRIQUE OCCIDENTALE ET CENTRALE. TOME 3: BILAN D'UNE DECENNIE : VOL 3. A DECADE'S RESULTS / Hoste, C H et al – 1992 – 9 – Free – 92-9053-230-0 – et ILRI [636]

TRYPANOTOLERANT LIVESTOCK IN WEST AND CENTRAL AFRICA = TRYPANOTOLERANT D'AFRIQUE OCCIDENTALE ET CENTRALE. TOME 1: SITUATION GENERALE : VOL 1. GENERAL STUDY / Trail, JC M et al – 1979 – 9 – $9.00 – 92-9053-125-8 – et ILRI [636]

TSA ASZI – 1974-78.(American Indian Periodicals in the Princeton University Library). 9 fiches – 9 – $45.00 – us UPA [305]

TS'AI CHENG KUNG PAO – Official gazette of the Ministry of Finance. Nanking. 1927-37. Lacking: (1-2) 1927; (48) 1931; (53-111) 1932-37. BCH-1088 1 – 9 – ne IDC [950]

TS'AI CHENG PU KUNG PAO – (Official Gazette of the Ministry of Finance). 6 v. Chungking. 1940-45. Lacking: v. 1, 1940; v. 2 (1-14, 21, 23, 24) 1941; v. 3 (1-14, 21, 22) 1942; v. 6 (13-24) 1945. BCH-1089 1 – 9 – ne IDC [336]

TSAI CHENG SHUO MING SHU – Descriptions of financial administration. Comp. by Ching-chi Hsueh Hui. Peking, 1915. Reel 1: Chihli, Fengtien, Kiangsu $18.70. Reel 2: Anhwei, Kiangsi, Shantung. $17.60. Reel 3: Shansi, Honan. $22.00. Reel 4: Shensi, Kansu $18.70. Reel 5: Singkiang, Fukien, Szechwan, Chekiang. $2,215.40. Reel 6: Kwangtung. $17.60. Reel 7: Kwangsi. $18.70. Reel 8: Yunan, Kweichow. $13.20. Reel 9: Kirin, Heilungkiang, Hupeh, Hunan. $17.60 – 1 – $159.50 – us Chinese Res [336]

TSAI-SHENG – "The National Renaissance". 4 v. Peiping. 1932-37; n.s., nrs. 1-251. 1938-49. Lacking: v. 2 (2-12) 1933; 1934-37; (1-77) 1938-41; (80-82, 84-90) 1942; (92-103) 1942-46; (251) 1949. BCH-351 1 – 9 – ne IDC [073]

TSALA EA BATHO – Kimberley, South Africa. 9 Jul 1910-24 Jul 1915. 1 reel. Title varies: Tsala ea Becoana, 1910-12 – 1, 16 diazo available at reduced price – sa SA Libr [072]

TS'AN I YUAN I SHIH LU / China. Provisional Legislative Assembly – Journal of Proceedings. Nanking. Jan-Apr 1912 – 1 – 5.00 – us Chinese Res [324]

TS'AN I YUAN KUNG PAO / China. Parliament. Upper House – Gazette. Peking. Apr-Jul 1913. n.1-13. 3 reels – 1 – 43.00 – us Chinese Res [324]

Tsan, Ju-kun *see* HSIAO CHING TONG KAO (CCC295)

Tsang, Mun C *see* COST ANALYSIS OF EDUCATIONAL INCLUSION OF MARGINALIZED POPULATIONS

Tsanga and Ige *see* A PARALEGAL TRAINER'S MANUAL FOR AFRICA

TS'ANG-WU HSIEN-CHIH – 1871, 18, 1. BCH-652 2 – 8 – ne IDC [950]

Tsao, E-Shu *see* WATER-BASED RECREATIONISTS' PREFERENCES FOR DIRECT/INDIRECT MANAGEMENT STRATEGIES BY VISITOR CHARACTERISTICS, PAST EXPERIENCES, AND PERCEIVED SITE PROBLEMS

Tsao, Hsin-ming *see* WHY I FOLLOW JESUS (CCC296)

TSAR' IKSION. TRAGEDIIA V PIATI DEISTVIIAKH / Annenskii, I F – Spb. 1902. BR-500 2 – 8 – ne IDC [460]

LE TSAR NICOLAS ET LA SAINTE RUSSIE / Gallet de Kulture, Achille – (Russia – 19th C. series). 1855 – 9 – fr Hachette [947]

TSAREVICH ALEKSEI / Merezhkovskii, Dimitrii – Tragediia v. 5 deistviiakh. Prague. n.d. BR-754 2 – 8 – ne IDC [920]

TSAREVICH ALEKSEI PETROVICH PO SVIDETEL'STVAM' VNOV' OTKRYTYM / Pogodin, M P – Chteniia v Imp. Obshchestve istorii i drevnostei rossiiskikh pri Moskovskom universitete. M. 1861. BR-8300 2(1369) – 8 – ne IDC [920]

TSARSKII VIESTNIK – Belgrade, Yugoslavia. 30 Nov 1930; Aug 1934-Jul 1940 – 2r – 1 – us L of C Photodup [949]

TSARSTVO ANTIKHRISTA / Merezhkovskii, Dimitrii – Munich. 1922. BR-755 2 – 8 – ne IDC [240]

DI TSAYT = THE JEWISH TIMES – (In Yiddish. Daily) – London, GB. v34 no10,129 24 Apr 1947-v38 no11,162 24 Sep 1950 – 1r – 1 – $25.00 – cn Can Microfilming [072]

DI TSAYT = TIME – (In Yiddish) – Kaunas, LT. v1 no28. 16 Oct 1932 – 1r – 1 – $25.00 – cn Can Microfilming [072]

DI TSAYT = THE TIMES – (In Yiddish) – Czestochowa, PL. v2 no2 13 Jan 1928-v3 no38 27 Sep 1929 – 1r – 1 – $25.00 – cn Can Microfilming [072]

TSAYT = THE JEWISH TIMES – Los Angeles, CA.1921-23 – 1 – us A.J.P.C. [071]

TSAYT = TIME – (In Yiddish) – Vilnius, LT. no396 3 May 1927-no3492 6 Aug 1937 – 1r – 1 – $25.00 – cn Can Microfilming [072]

DER TSAYT-GEYST = SPIRIT OF THE AGE – (In Yiddish) – New York City, NY. v1 no1 1 Sep 1905-v2 no109 27 Dec 1907 – 2r – 1 – $60.00 – cn Can Microfilming [071]

Tschackert, Paul *see*
- DIE ENTSTEHUNG DER LUTHERISCHEN UND DER REFORMIERTEN KIRCHENLEHRE
- EVANGELISCHE POLEMIK GEGEN DIE ROEMISCHE KIRCHE
- HERZOG ALBRECHT VON PREUSSEN ALS REFORMATORISCHE PERSOENLICHKEIT
- PAUL SPERATUS VON ROETLEN
- PETER VON AILLI (PETRUS DE ALLIACO)

Tschaikovsky, Pl *see*
- CONCERTO NO. 1, OP. 23
- ROMEO ET JULIETTE, OVERTURE-FANTASIE
- SIX MORCEAUX POUR PIANO, OP. 19
- SIX MORCEAUX POUR PIANO, OP. 21

TSCHECHISCH-DEUTSCHES GESPRAECHSBUCH / Smetanka, Emil – Berlin und Leipzig: W. de Grunter, 1922.154p – 1 – us U.W. Library [460]

DAS TSCHECHOSLOVAKISCHE NATIONALITAETENRECHT. (TSCHECHOSL. QUELLEN UND DOKUMENTE. NO. 7) / Sobota, E – Transl. by J. Kalfus. Prague. 1931. BR-5131 2 – 8 – ne IDC [943]

Tschersig, Hubert *see* DAS GASEL IN DER DEUTSCHEN DICHTUNG UND DAS GASEL BEI PLATEN

TSCH'ONG HUANG, DER SCHUTZGOTT DER STADTE IN CHINA / Volpert, P A – Anthropos 5. 1910. BCH-937 2 – 8 – ne IDC [290]

TSEIDO LADOREG – Amsterdam, 1935(1-2) – 1mf – 9 – J-261-113/1 – ne IDC [949]

TSEL' TVORCHESTVA / Erberg, K – M. 1913. BR-2058 2 – 8 – ne IDC [460]

LES TSELTALES: DES PAIENS SUPERFICIELLEMENT CHRISTIANISES OU DES CATHOLIQUES-MAYAS? / Maurer-Avalos, E – Mexique – 9 – F130.00 – fr Ethnologie [290]

TSEMENT – (Library has: March 1945) – Leningrad: Izdvo litry po stroitlstvu, 1933- – 1 – CSUX89-S924 – us Hoover Inst Photo [624]

Tseng, Pao-sun *see* EXPERIMENTS IN PERSONAL RELIGION (CCC297)

Tsentralne statystychne upravlinnia USRR *see* TSENZOVA PROMYSLOVIST UKRAINY V...

Tsentralnoe statisticheskoe upravlenie pri Sovete Ministrov SSSR *see* SSSR V T SIFRAKH V...GODU

TSENTRAL'NOE STATISTICHESKOE UPRAVLENIE, VESTNIK STATISTKI / U.S.S.R. – Moscow. 1919-29 – 1 – us UMI [310]

TSENTRAL'NYE BANKI KOOPERATIVNOGO KREDITA / Antsyferov, A N – Ed.3. Pg., 1919 – 3mf – 9 – COR-370/1 – ne IDC [334]

TSENTRAL'NYE BANKI KOOPERATIVNOGO KREDITA / Antsyferov, A N – Khar'kov, 1916 – 4mf – 9 – COR-4/1 – ne IDC [334]

Tsentral'nyi Gosudarstvennyi Arkhiv Drevnikh Aktov *see* PUTEVODITEL'

Tsentral'nyi Gosudarstvennyi Arkhiv Krasnoi Armii *see* PUTEVODITEL'

Tsentral'nyi Gosudarstvennyi Arkhiv Literatury i Iskusstva SSSR *see* PUTEVODITEL'

Tsentral'nyi Gosudarstvennyi Arkhiv Literatury i Isskusstva SSSR *see* PUTEVODITEL'

Tsentral'nyi Gosudarstvennyi Arkhiv Oktiabr'skoi Revoliutsii i Sotsialisticheskogo Stroitel'stva *see* PUTEVODITEL'

TSENTRAL'NYI GOSUDARSTVENNYI ISTORICHESKII ARKHIV LATVIISKOI SSR. KRATKII SPRAVOCHNIK / Ryzhov, N N et al – Riga. pt1: (1220-1918). 1980 – 2mf – 9 – ne IDC [460]

TSENTRAL'NYI GOSUDARSTVENNYI ISTORICHESKII ARKHIV SSSR V G. LENINGRADE. UCHEBNOE POSOBIE / Dremina, G A & Kuznetsova, T V – Moscow, 1959. 64p. BR-10,721/1 – 9 – ne IDC [947]

Tsentral'nyi Gosudarstvennyi Istoricheskii Arkhiv SSSR v Leningrade *see* PUTEVODITEL'

Tsentral'nyi Gosudarstvennyi Literaturnyi Arkhiv SSSR *see* PUTEVODITEL'

Tsentral'nyi Gsudarstvennyi Arkhiv Literatury i Iskusstva S SS R *see* PUTEVODITEL'

TSENTRAL'NYI ISPOLNITEL'NYI KOMITET SOIUZA SOVETSKIKH SOTSIALISTICHESKIKH RESPUBLIK (TSIK): STENOGRAFICHESKII OTCHET / U.S.S.R. – 1922-37 – 1 – us UMI [324]

TSENTRAL'NYI OBLASTNOI KOOPERATIVNYI BANK / Lur'e, E S – Ed.2. M., 1919 – 2mf – 9 – COR-389/1 – ne IDC [334]

TSENZOVA PROMYSLOVIST UKRAINY V... / Tsentralne statystychne upravlinnia USRR – (Includes c.1: 1925/1926-1928/1929) – Kharkiv: [Upravlinnia], 19uu – 1 – CSUXAKY6382-S – us Hoover Inst Photo [310]

T'SERCLAES ANUNCIA UN PREMIO / Perez de Guzman, Juan – Madrid: Fortanet, 1916. B.R.A.H. 69, p. 197 – sp Bibl Santa Ana [946]

T'Serclaes, Duque de *see*
- DOCUMENTOS DE LAS FUNDACIONES RELIGIOSAS Y BENEFICAS DE LA VILLA DE ALMONTE, POR LORENZO CRUZ DE FUENTES
- GENEALOGIA DE LA CASA DE URRIES, DEL MARQUES DE VELILLA DE EBRO
- HISTORIA DE LA DIOCESIS DE SIGUENZA Y DE SUS OBISPOS, POR TORIBIO MINGUELLA Y ARNEDO
- HISTORIAL DE FISTAS Y DONATIVOS, INDICE DE CABALLEROS Y REGLAMENTO DE UNIFORMIDAD DE LA REAL MAESTRANZA DE CABALLERIA DE SEVILLA, POR DON PEDRO LEON Y MANJON
- NOMBRES CLAROS DE EXTREMADURA, POR ANGELES MORAN MARQUEZ
- PREMIO A LA VIRTUD
- PREMIO A LA VIRTUD 1923
- REIVINDICACIONES HISTORICAS. VIRIATO NO FUE PORTUGUES, DE ANSELMO ARENAS LOPEZ
- TRASLACION DE CUERPOS REALES DE GRANADA A SAN LORENZO DEL ESCORIAL Y DE VALLADOLID A GRANADA
- EL VALLE DE RUISENADA, POR MIGUEL DE ASUA Y CAMPOS

T'Serclaes, Duque de et al *see* PREMIO DE LA FUNDACION LOUBAT 1929

T'SERCLAES, DUQUE DE. FIRMA LA PROPUESTA DE ACADEMICO DEL DUQUE DE ALBA / Perez de Guzman, Juan – Madrid: Fortanet, 1918. B.R.A.H. 72, p. 176 – sp Bibl Santa Ana [946]

T'SERCLAES FIRMA LA CANDIDATURA DEL MARQUES DE SAN JUAN DE PIEDRAS ALTAS / Vega de Hoz, Baron de – Madrid: Fortanet, 1917. B.R.A.H. 71, pp. 538 – sp Bibl Santa Ana [946]

TSERKOV' I GOSUDARSTVO PO ZAKONODATEL' STVU R.S.F.S.R. SBORNIK UZAKONENII I RASPORAZHENII A RAZ'IASNENIIAMI V OTDELA NKIU, POD REDAKTSEI P. A. KRASIKOVA / Russia. (1917-R.S.F.S.R.). Laws, Statutes, etc – Moskva: Iuridicheskoe izdatel' stvo Narkomiusta, 1923. 100p. LL-4086 – 1 – us L of C Photodup [340]

TSERKOVNIKI I SEKTANSKIE VOZHAKI NA SLUZHBE FASHISTSKIKH RAZVEDOK / Shestakoza, M – Moscow, 1938. Clergymen and Sectarian Leaders in the Service of the Fascist Secret Service. One of 13 titles by Soviet authors on reel – 1 – 74.32 – us Baptist [240]

TSERKOVNIKI I SEKTANTI NA SLUZHBE U KULAKI = CHURCHMEN AND SECTARIANS IN THE SERVICE OF KULAKS / Rostovtsev, A – Moscow, 1930. One of 13 titles by Soviet authors on reel – 1 – 74.32 – us Baptist [240]

TSERKOVNIKI I SEKTANTI V BOR'BE PROTIV KUL'TURNOI REVOLYUTSEE / Chudnovtsev, M – Churchmen and Sectarians in the Struggle against the Cultural Revolution. Moscow, 1930. One of 13 titles by Soviet authors on reel – 1 – 74.32 – us Baptist [240]

TSERKOVNO-OBSHCHESTVENNYI VESTNIK – (Missing: 1874-1878; 1879(10, 23-24, 28-29, 33, 35, 37-39, 111, 114, 139, 149, 155); 1880(7, 116, 122, 152); 1881(21-25, 34, p.3-4; 37-38, 81, 88-89, 97-100, 105, 107, 110, 137, 139, 141, 151); 1882-1886) – Spb., 1874-1886 – 89mf – 9 – R-18407/1 – ne IDC [947]

TSERKOVNYE BOGATSTVA I GOLOD V ROSII / Gorev, Mikhail – Moskva: Giz., 1922 – 1 – CSUX89-B2717 – us Hoover Inst Photo [947]

TSERKOVNYE VIEDOMOSTI – St. Petersburg. 1909, 1911, 1912, 1914, 1917 – 1 – 92.00 – us L of C Photodup [240]

TSERKOVNYI VIESTNIK – St. Petersburg. 1907-08, 1911, 1914, 1916, 1917 – 1 – 69.00 – us L of C Photodup [240]

TSERKOVNYYA VODOMOSTI = SUBJECT INDEX – Part I, Alfavitno-Predmetnyi...1888-97; Part II, Alfavitno-Predmetnyi... 1898-1919 – 1 – 21.20 – us Baptist [240]

TSESAREVICH PAVEL PETROVICH (1754-1796) / Kobeko, D M – Ed. 3. Spb. 1887. BR-6058 2 – 8 – ne IDC [920]

TSEZARIZM POD MASKO I REVOLIUTSII : PO POVODU KNIGI PROF. N. USTRI ALOVA "POD ZNAKAM REVOLIUTSII" / Bukharin, Nikolai Ivanovich – Moskva: Izd. Gazety "Pravdy", 1925 – 1 – CSUX88-B1793 – us Hoover Inst Photo [947]

TSF NEWS AND REVIEWS / Theological Students Fellowship – (v2. 1978-79. $10.00. v3. 1979-80. $10.00. v4. 1980-81. TSF bulletin. $12.00. v5. 1981-82. TSF bulletin. $12.00) – v1-9. 1978-86 – 9 – us I.R.C. [073]

TS-HEBDO FEB. 1979-OCT. 1982 *see* TRIBUNE SOCIALISTE

TSHERNOVITSER BLETER : TSHERNOVITSER LEAVES – (In Yiddish) – Cernauti, RM. v4 no132 25 Nov 1932-v5 no182 23 May 1934 – 1r – 1 – $25.00 – cn Can Microfilming [072]

TSHISTEKIIGAN TSHE APATSTATS IRNUTS – SEM105P491 – 1mf – 9 – Can$2.25 – cn Bibl Nat [073]

Tsiavlovskii, M *see* 1814-4 IIULIA 1914. PUSHKIN V PECHATI. 1814-1837. KHRONOLOGICHESKII UKAZATEL' PROIZVEDENII PUSHKINA, NAPCCHATANNYKH PRI EGO ZHIZNI

TSIMSHIAN MYTHOLOGY / Boas, Franz – BN 145 2. 1916 – 8 – ne IDC [390]

Tsinberg, S L *see* ISTORIIA EVREISKOI PECHATI V ROSSII V SVIAZI S OBSHCHESTVENNYMI TECHENIIAMI

TSING HUA JOURNAL OF CHINESE STUDIES – Taipei, Taiwan. Available: n.s. 1, nr. 3, n.s. 4, nr. 2, 1958-64. BCH-178 2 – 8 – ne IDC [073]

Tsingevatov, I A *see* KOOPERATSIIA V SOVETSKOI DEEREVNE

TSINGTAUER NEUESTE NACHRICHTEN – Tsingtau (Tsingtao), China. 1 Oct 1904; 1 Nov 1904-31 Dec 1904; 1905-11 Jun 1914 – 25r – 1 – gw Mikrofilm [072]

TSINGTAUER NEUSTE NACHRICHTEN – Tsingtau. 1904-14. KCHF-4-3 – 1 – ne IDC [072]

TSINIKI / Mariengof, A – Berlin. 1928. BR-1078 2 – 8 – ne IDC [460]

TSIONIST = THE ZIONIST – New York, NY. 1900 – 1 – us A.J.P.C. [071]

TSIONISTICHE BLETER = ZIONIST LEAVES – (In Yiddish) – Warsaw, PL. v4 no22 29 Mar 1922-v5 no20 20 Sep 1929 – 1r – 1 – $30.00 – cn Can Microfilming [070]

DI TSIONISTICHE WOCH – (In Yiddish) – Lwow, PL. no43 19 Dec 1933-v4 no99 25 Jan 1935 – 1r – 1 – $30.00 – cn Can Microfilming [072]

TSIONISTISHE BLETER = ZIONIST LEAVES – (Yiddish weekly) – Miedzyrzec, PL. v4 no22 29 Mar 1929-v5 no20 20 Sep 1929 – 1r – 1 – $25.00 – cn Can Microfilming [072]

DI TSIONISTISHE VOKH – (In Yiddish) – Lwow, PL. v3 no43 29 Dec 1933-v4 no99 25 Jan 1935 – 1r – 1 – $25.00 – cn Can Microfilming [072]

TSIRKULI ARY NARODNOGO KOMISSARIATA VNUTRENNIKH DEL / Russian S.F.S.R. Narodnyi komissariat vnutrennikh del – (Includes c.1: no. 1/7 1921:Jan.-no. 15/39 (1921: Jan.); no. 61/64 1921:Feb.-no. 66/75 (1921:Feb./Mar.); no.87/100 1921:Mar./ Apr) – [S.l.: Komissariat], 1921- – 1 – CSUXAKY5901-S – us Hoover Inst Photo [320]

TSIRKULIARNYE RASPORIAZHENIIA NARODNOGO KOMISSARIATA I USTITSII / Russian S.F.S.R. Narodnyi komissariati ustitsii – [Moskva]: Komissariat, 1920-1921. 2v – 1 – CSUX89-S642 – us Hoover Inst Photo [320]

Tsitron, A *see*
– 72 DNIA PERVOGO RUSKOGO PARLAMENTA
– 103 DNIA VTOROI DUMY

TSIYONISTISHE SHTIME = ZIONIST VOICE – (In Yiddish) – Munich, DE. v3 no93 22 Dec 1948-no123 30 Dec. 1949 – 1r – 1 – $35.00 – cn Can Microfilming [072]

T'sogart, Aigidius *see* DEN GULDEN SONNEN WYSER OFT HOROLOGIE VAN DE PASSIE ONS HEEREN IESU CHRISTI

TSON-KHA-PA BLO-BZAN-GRAGS-PA – The Lam rim chen mo of the incomparable Tsong-kha-pa...1972. Reprinted from 1842 edition. 2 vols – 1 – us Res Libr [280]

Tsountas, Chrestos *see* THE MYCENAEAN AGE

TSU DER GESHIKHTE FUN DER YIDISHER PRESE = THE HISTORY OF THE JEWISH PRESS IN RUSSIA AND POLAND / Druk, D – (In Yiddish) – Warsaw, PL. 1920 – 1r – 1 – $25.00 – cn Can Microfilming [072]

Tsu, P N *see* THE LORD'S PRAYER AND ORIENTALISM (CCC113)

Tsuboi, Kiyotari *see* HISTORIC CITY OF NARA

TSUI YING CHUNG HSUEH SHU PAN SHE (CCC298) = SU CHOU SSU LI TSUI YING CHUNG HSUEH HSIAO SSU SHIH CHOU CHI NIEN KAN : 40TH ANNIVERSARY PUBLICATION OF THE VINCENT MILLER ACADEMY – (In Chinese) – Shanghai: Mercury Press, 1933 – 1r – 1984-6637 – us A.T.L.A. [370]

TSUI-CHIN SHANG-HAI CHIN-JUNG SHIH, TI-SAN PAN – Recent financial history of Shanghai, 3rd ed. Comp. and pub. by Hsu Chi-ch'ing. Shanghai, 1932. 2v. Tables. Detailed statistical information for each bank is given, covering the years 1927-31. 1 reel – 1 – 30.00 – us Chinese Res [950]

TSUM ZIG = FORWARD TO VICTORY – (In Yiddish) – Bergen-Belsen (British Zone), DE. Only issue: 1946 – 1r – 1 – $25.00 – cn Can Microfilming [072]

TSUNG I YUAN KUNG PAO / China. Parliament. Lower House – Gazette. Peking. n.1-72. Apr-Oct 1913. Lacking:n. 65-72. 2 reels – 1 – 37.50 – us Chinese Res [950]

TSUNG I YUAN KUNG PAO FU LU, TI I TZU HUI I SU CHI LU / China. Parliament. Lower House – Gazette: Appendix-Parliamentary Debates of the First Session. Peking. n.1-82. Apr-Oct 1913. Lacking: ns.17, 19-24, 35, 78-82. 2 reels – 1 – 37.50 – us Chinese Res [950]

TS'UNG-HUA HSIEN-CHIH – 1730, 5. Lacking: prefaces: ch. 1. BCH-594 2 – 8 – ne IDC [950]

Tsung-tung, Chang *see* DER KULT DER SHANG-DYNASTIE IM SPIEGEL DER ORAKELINSCHRIFTEN

TSUSHIMA : DER ROMAN EINES SEEKRIEGES / Thiess, Frank – Berlin: P Zsolnay, 1936 – 1r – 1 – us U.W. Library [830]

TSUZAMEN = TOGETHER – (Quarterly) – Brooklyn, NY. v6. 1935 – 1r – Can$25.00 – cn Can Microfilming [071]

TSVAY SHEYNE GETLEKHE LIDER – Prague. c.1650? BJ-43-134 1 – 9 – ne IDC [810]

DER TSVAYG = THE BRANCH – (In Yiddish. Monthly) – Philadelphia, PA. Jun-Jul 1919 – 1r – 1 – $25.00 – cn Can Microfilming [071]

TSVEITER ALVEISRUSISHER TSUZAMENFOR FUN YIDISHE POYERIM : STENOGRAFISHER BARIKHT, YANVAR 1928 YOR. 2-HI USEBELARUSKI ZEZD I A UR EI A USI ALI AN – Minsk: Oisgabe fun der Natskomisiye bam Ts.A.K. fun Veisrusland, 1928 – 1 – CSUX91-B4019 – us Hoover Inst Photo [947]

TSVETNAIA KLEI / Kruchenykh, A – 1916. BR-960 2 – 8 – ne IDC [460]

TSVETUSHCHII POSOKH / Gorodetskii, S – Verenitsa vos'mistishii. Izd. Griadushchii den'. Spb. 1914. BR-1120 2 – 8 – ne IDC [460]

Tsypin, Ia. *see* TRUDOVYE ARTELI

Tsypkin, S *see* OKTIABR'SKAIA REVOLIUTSIIA I GRAZHDANSKAIA VOINA NA DAL'NEM VOSTOKE; 1917-1922 GG

[/TTPI (U.S.)/] *see* PAPERS OF THE FUTURE POLITICAL STATUS NEGOTIATIONS

TU BEDAWIE : AN ELEMENTARY HANDBOOK FOR THE USE OF SUDAN GOVERNMENT OFFICIALS / Roper, E M – Hertford, England, [1930] – us Res Libr [350]

TU, EN PRESENCIA / Sanchez-Arjona, Vicente – Sevilla: Imp. Carlos Acuna, 1944 – 1 – sp Bibl Santa Ana [810]

TU, EN PRESENCIA / Sanchez-Arjona, Vicente – Sevilla: Imp. Crufer, 2nd ed 1958 – 1 – sp Bibl Santa Ana [810]

TU PARROQUIA – Plasencia (Parroquia de San Nicolas), 1941-1947 – 5 – sp Bibl Santa Ana [073]

Tu, Yu-ching *see* CHRISTIANITY AND THE NEW PHYSICS (CCC299)

Tuaillon, Georges *see* L'AFRIQUE OCCIDENTALE FRANCAISE

TUALATIN NEWS – Tualatin OR. Apr 2-July 16 1915 – 1 – us U.O. Library [071]

TUALATIN VALLEY NEWS – Sherwood OR. Nov 12 1915-Dec 13 1918 – 1 – us U.O. Library [071]

TUALATIN VALLEY TIMES – Tualatin Valley, OR. -w. 13 May 1949-30 Jun 1950. 1 roll – 1 – us U.O. Library [071]

TUAM HERALD – Ireland. -w. May 1837-Nov 1877, Feb 1884-Dec 1909, Jan 1911-Dec 1923; Jan 1938-1965. (48 reels) – 1 – uk British Libr Newspaper [072]

TUAM NEWS & WESTERN ADVERTISER – Ireland. -w. 17 March, 2 June 1871-25 July 1873; 11 April 1884-31 Jan 1896. 5 reels – 1 – uk British Libr Newspaper [072]

TUANJIE BAO = UNITY WEEKLY – China. 1983-. M-D33 – 1 reel/y – 1 – $28.00r – cc Microforms [072]

TUBERCLE – (v.60-. 1979- 5,6,9) – v.1-. 1919- – 1 – us UMI [073]

LA TUBERCULOSE ET L'HABITATION URBAINE / Graux, Lucien – Paris. 1905. (La Condition Ouvriere. Part Two.) – 9 – 2.50 – fr Bibl Nationale [360]

Tubergen, C G van *see* NEW BULBOUS AND TUBEROUS ROOTED PLANTS

TUBERKULEZ / Narodnyi komissariat zdravookhraneniia, Sektsiia borby s tuberkulezom – (Includes c.1: no.1 1922) – Moskva: Komissariat, 1922- – 1 – CSUXAKZ0184-S – us Hoover Inst Photo [616]

Tubeuf, C von *see*
– PFLANZENKRANKHEITEN DURCH KRYPROGAME PARASITEN VERURSACHT
– SAMEN, FRUECHTE UND KEIMLINGE

Tubingen. Universitat. Juristische Facultat *see* FESTGABE HERRN DR. RUDOLPH VON JHERING ZUM DOKTORJUBILAUM AM 6, AUGUST 1892

TUBMAN, HARRIET – 1 – us Ross [976]

Tuch, Friedrich *see* EIN UND ZWANZIG SINAITISCHE INSCHRIFTEN

TUCHTORDENINGE DER STADT MUNSTER THO VNDERHOLDENE CHRISTLIKE TUCHT VNDE EERBARICHEYT – 1533. BME-148 1 – 9 – ne IDC [240]

Tuck, C E *see* PAST AND PRESENT OF GREENE COUNTY

Tucker, Abraham *see* VOCAL SOUNDS

Tucker, Alfred Robert *see* EIGHTEEN YEARS IN UGANDA & EAST AFRICA

Tucker, B R *see*
– INSTEAD OF A BOOK
– LIBERTY

Tucker, E *see* HISTORY OF RANDOLPH COUNTY

Tucker, George F *see* NOTES ON THE REVISED STATUTES OF THE U.S.

Tucker, H W *see* MEMOIR OF THE LIFE AND EPISCOPATE OF EDWARD FIELD

Tucker, Henry George *see* LIMITATIONS ON THE TREATY-MAKING POWER UNDER THE CONSTITUTION OF THE UNITED STATES

Tucker, Henry Holcombe *see* THE GOSPEL IN ENOCH, OR, TRUTH IN THE CONCRETE

Tucker, Henry ST George *see* THE CONSTITUTION OF THE UNITED STATES

Tucker, Henry William *see* UNDER HIS BANNER

Tucker, Hugh Clarence *see* THE BIBLE IN BRAZIL

Tucker, J *see*
– A BRIEF HISTORY OF THE PRINCIPLES OF METHODISM,...
– AN ESSAY ON THE ADVANTAGES AND DISADVANTAGES WHICH RESPECTIVELY ATTEND FRANCE AND GREAT BRITAIN WITH REGARD TO TRADE...
– SIX SERMONS ON IMPORTANT SUBJECTS

Tucker, John Randolph *see*
– THE CONSTITUTION OF THE UNITED STATES

Tucker, Marcia *see* ROBERT MORRIS

Tucker, Willard D *see* HISTORICAL AND BIOGRAPHICAL STATISTICAL RECORD OF GRATIOT COUNTY

Tucker, William H *see* HISTORY OF HARTFORD, JULY 4, 1761-APRIL 4, 1889

Tucker, William Jewett *see* COLLECTED ADDRESSES AND WRITINGS

Tuckerman, E *see*
– AN ENUMERATION OF NORTH AMERICAN LICHENES
– A SYNOPSIS OF THE NORTH AMERICAN LICHENS

TUCKER'S SELECT NEWFOUNDLAND CASES / Newfoundland. Canada – 1v. 1817-28 (all publ) – 7mf – 9 – $11.50 – LLMC 81-031 – us L.L.M.C. [340]

Tuckey, James Kingston *see*
– THE EXPEDITION TO THE RIVER ZAIRE
– NARRATIVE OF AN EXPEDITION TO EXPLORE THE RIVER ZAIRE, USUALLY CALLED THE CONGO.
– NARRATIVE OF AN EXPEDITION TO EXPLORE THE RIVER ZAIRE USUALLY CALLED THE CONGO IN SOUTH AFRICA IN 1816
– RELATION D'UNE EXPEDITION. POUR RECONNOITRE LE ZAIRE

Tuckey, Janet *see* JOAN OF ARC, THE MAID

TUDA I OBRATNO / Maiakovskii, Vladimir – M. 1930. BR-1005 2 – 8 – ne IDC [460]

TUDA I OBRATNO / Maiakovskii, Vladimir – Stikhi i ocherki. M. 1936. BR-1006 2 – 8 – ne IDC [460]

TU-DO – Hanoi. North Vietnam. 1962- – 1 – us UMI [072]

TU-DO – South Vietnam. 1962-1966 – 1 – us UMI [072]

TUDOR AND STUART MANUSCRIPTS / British Library. Harleian Collection – (Part 2. The most important of v261-390. Part 3. The most important of v396-736. Part 4. The most important of v737-1325. Part 5. The most important of v1326-1926. Part 6. The most important of v1927-2366. Part 7. The most important of v2367-4111. Part 8. The most important of v4112-4312. Part 9. The most important of v4313-4628) – Part 1. The most important volumes selected from the Harleian Collection of manuscripts. v1-260 – 1 – us Primary [025]

Tudor Engineering Company. San Francisco *see* SUGAR PRODUCTION POTENTIALS IN THE REPUBLIC OF THE SUDAN

THE TUEBINGEN SCHOOL AND ITS ANTECEDENTS: A REVIEW OF THE HISTORY AND PRESENT CONDITION OF MODERN THEOLOGY / Mackay, R W – 1843 – 9 – us A.T.L.A. [240]

TUEBINGER CHRONIK – (Cont by: Schwaebisches Tagblatt, sep 21 1945) – Tuebingen, jun 18-dec 31 1848 – 1r – 1 – gw Mikrofilm [943]

DIE TUEBINGER SCHULE UND IHRE STELLUNG ZUR GEGENWART / Baur, Ferdinand Christian – Tuebingen: L.Fr. Fues, 1860 – 1mf – us A.T.L.A. [240]

TUEBINGER ZEITSCHRIFT FUER THEOLOGIE – 1828-1948 (complete) – 6r – 1 – ATLA S0117 – us A.T.L.A. [073]

Tuegel, Ludwig *see*
– DER BROOK
– FRAU GESKE AUF TRUBERNES
– DIE FREUNDSCHAFT
– PFERDEMUSIK
– SANKT BLEHK

TUERCEMIZ – Istanbul: Matbaa-i Orhaniye, 1917 – $35.00 – us MEDOC [470]

TUERCHEN BUCHLEIN : WIE SICH PREDIGER UND LEIEN HALTEN SOLLEN, SO DER TUERCK DAS DEUDSCHE LAND VBERFALLEN WUERDE / Brentz, J the elder – Wittemberg, 1537 – 1mf – 9 – H-8248/1 – ne IDC [956]

TUERCKISCHE HISTORIEN : VON DER TUERCKEN ANKUNFFT, REGIERUNG, KOENIGEN VND KEYSERN, KRIEGEN, SCHLACHTEN, VICTORIEN VND SIGEN WIDER CHRISTEN VND HEIDEN – Franckfurt am Mayn. 4pts. 1563 – 6mf – 9 – H-8162/1 – ne IDC [956]

TUERK AMACI / Tuerk Kueltuer Birligi Dergisidir – Istanbul: 1942-43. Sahip ve Mueduerue: A Çaferoglu. No. 1-8 (Temmuz 1942-Subat 1943) – $150.00 – us MEDOC [073]

Tuerk, Daniel G *see*
– ANWEISUNG ZUM GENERALBASSSPIELEN HALLE
– KLAVIERSCHULE, ODER ANWEISUNG ZUM KLAVIERSPIELEN FUER LEHRER UND LERNEDE...
– KLAVIERSCHULE, ODER ANWEISUNG ZUM KLAVIERSPIELEN FUER LEHRER UND LERNENDE
– KURZE ANWEISUNG ZUM GENERALBASSPIELEN...
– KURZE ANWEISUNG ZUM KLAVIERSPIELEN
– VON DEN WICHTIGSTEN PFLICHTEN EINES ORGANISTEN

TUERK DERNEGI – Istanbul: Matbaa-i Hayriye ve Suerekasi, 1912-13 – $40.00 – us MEDOC [956]

TUERK GUERMUEK TA'RIFE-YI UMUMIYESINE MUTEALIK KANUN – Istanbul: Matbaa-yi Osmaniye, 1926 – 9 – $50.00 – us MEDOC [380]

Tuerk Kueltuer Birligi Dergisidir *see* TUERK AMACI

TUERK MEDENIYET TARIHI / Goekalp, Ziya – Istanbul: Matbaa-yi Amire, 1341 [1925] – $45.00 – us MEDOC [956]

TUERK OCAKLARI 1927 SENESI KURULTAY ZABITLERI / Kurultay, Dorduncu – Ankara, 1928 – $125.00 – us MEDOC [956]

TUERK OCAKLARI KONGRESI/KURULTAYI – Ankara, 1341 [1924], 1. kongresi. – 2mf. $85.00; Istanbul, [1926], 3. kurultay. – 4mf. $85.00; Ankara, [1928], 4. kurultay. – 8mf. $85.00; Ankara, [1930], 5. kurultay. – 7mf. $85.00 – 9 – us MEDOC [949]

TUERK SADASI – Sofia. Sahib ve Muharriri: Ahmed Fazil, 1913-19? – 9 – $25.00 – us MEDOC [956]

TUERK SOEZUE – Adana, 1924-19? – 9 – $10.00 – us MEDOC [956]

TUERK SOEZUE – Istanbul: Tanin Matbaasi, 1914 – 9 – $65.00 – us MEDOC [956]

TUERKCE NINNILER / Kunos, Ignatz – Istanbul: kitaphane-yi Hilmi, 1341[1925] – $30.00 – us MEDOC [470]

TUERKI-I SULTAN VELED – Istanbul, 1341 – 2mf – 9 – $12.00 – us MEDOC [949]

TUERKISCHE TRAUERSPIELE : IBRAHIM BASSA, IBRAHIM SULTAN / Lohenstein, Daniel Casper von; ed by Just, Klaus Guenther – (Includes bibliographical references) – Stuttgart: Hiersemann, 1953 – 1 – us U.W. Library [820]

TUERKISCHES BIOGRAPHISCHES ARCHIV = TURKISH BIOGRAPHICAL ARCHIVE / Sauer, Jutta – 1999 – ca 380mf (1:24) in 12 installments – 9 – diazo ca DM18,600.00 (silver ca DM20,400.00) – 3-598-34270-5 – silver ISBN: 3-598-34271-3 – gw Saur [920]

TUERKIYE CUMHURIYETI DEVLET SALNAMESI – 1926-1927 – $97.50 – us MEDOC [956]

TUERKIYE CUMHURIYETI DEVLET YILLIGI – 1929-1930 – $97.50 – us MEDOC [956]

TUERKIYE EDEBIYAT MECMU'ASI – Sene 1, cilt 1-6 (1339-1340) – 3mf – 9 – $31.50 – us MEDOC [949]

TUERKIYE HALK MEKTEBLERI MECMUASI – (Mueduer-i Mes'ul: Nureddin Nazif. Nos. 1-3, 22-24, 26-27, 35-39 (23 Nisan 1339-30 Mart 1341[1923-1925]) – Istanbul: Necm-i Istikbal Matbaasi, 1923-1925 – 4mf – 9 – $65.00 – us MEDOC [949]

TUERKIYE SEYR-I SEFAIN IDARESI REHBERI, 1927 – Istanbul: Ahmed Ihsan Matbaasi, 1927 – 9 – $75.00 – us MEDOC [956]

TUERKIYE TARIHI / Koepruelue, Mehmet Fuat – Istanbul: Kanaat Kitaphanesi, 1923 – 9 – us MEDOC [956]

TUERKIYE'NIN SIHHI-I ICTIMAI COGRAFYASI : GAZI AINTAB VILAYETI – Istanbul, 1926 – 9 – $35.00 – us MEDOC [956]

TUERKIYE'NIN SIHHI-I ICTIMAI COGRAFYASI : GELIBOLU VILAYETI – Istanbul, 1925 – 9 – $35.00 – us MEDOC [956]

TUERKIYE'NIN SIHHI-I ICTIMAI COGRAFYASI : ZONGULDAK SANCAGI – Ankara, 1922 – 9 – $35.00 – us MEDOC [956]

TUERKIYE-NIN SIHHI-I ICTIMAI COGRAFYASI : KONYA VILAYETI – Ankara, 1922 – 9 – $35.00 – us MEDOC [956]

TUERKIYE-NIN SIHHI-I ICTIMAI COGRAFYASI : URFA VILAYETI – Istanbul, 1925 – 9 – $35.00 – us MEDOC [956]

TUERKIYE'NIN SIHHI-I ICTIMAI COGRAFYASI HAMIDABAD (ISPARTA) SANCAGI – Ankara, 1922 – 9 – $35.00 – us MEDOC [956]

TUERKIYE'NIN SIHHI-I ICTIMAI COGRAFYASI. KANGIRI VILAYETI – Istanbul, 1926 – 9 – $35.00 – us MEDOC [956]

TUERKIYE'NIN SIHHI-I ICTIMAI COGRAFYASI. KIRK KILISE (KIRKLARELI) VILAYETI – Istanbul, 1925 – 9 – $35.00 – us MEDOC [956]

TUERKIYE'NIN SIHII-I ICTIMAI COGRAFYASI : CATALCA VILAYETI – Istanbul, 1925 – 9 – $35.00 – us MEDOC [956]

TUESDAY – (Also called: Tuesday Magazine) – Chicago. v1-6. 1965-71 – 72mf – 9 – $5.00f – us Ross [073]

TUESDAY EXPRESS – Ashford, Kent, England. -w. 22 Sept 1903-7 March 1916; 16 July 1918-Dec 1973. 47 reels – 1 – uk British Libr Newspaper [072]

TUESDAY MAGAZINE *see* TUESDAY

THE TUESDAY MORNING MUSIC CLUB : FOUNDED 1902; CONSTITUTIONS AND BY-LAWS – rev 1979. n.p., n.d. – 1mf – 9 – $1.50 – LLMC 96-044 – us L.L.M.C. [360]

TUESDAY NEWS – Lindsay, CA. 1931-1943 – 5r – 1 – $250.00 – C03610 – us Library Micro [071]

TUESDAY STUDY CLUB RECORDS – (Constitutions, minutes, programs, histories, clippings, and photographs of this Catholic woman's club, devoted to the study and discussion of scholarly topics and the support of a women's scholarship fund) – Cleveland, Cuyahoga, OH. 1914-95 – 2r – 1 – us Western Res [360]

TUFAN (TUFAN-I SAL) – (Sal-i 1-7 (Murdad 1348-Murdad 1353[Jul 1969-Jul 1974])) – Italy: Sazman-i Marksisti Lininisti-i Tufan – 1 reel – 1 – $30.00 – us MEDOC [950]

Tufnell, Olga *see* LACHISH

Tufts James H *see* ETHICS

Tufts, John *see* AN INTRODUCTION TO THE SINGING OF PSALM-TUNES, IN A PLAIN AND EASY METHOD

Tugan-Baranovskii, M I *see*
- EKONOMICHESKAIA PRIRODA KOOPERATIVOV I IKH KLASSIFIKATSIIA
- O KOOPERATIVNOM IDEALE
- SOTSIALNYE OSNOVY KOOPERATSII

TUGAS – Medan. Incomplete. SE 974 1. 1959-1967 – 9 – ne IDC [073]

TUHFAT AL-WUZARA : DER WESIRS-SPIEGEL EINES UNBEKANNTEN KOMPILATORS / Heinecke, Regina – Frankfurt a.M., 1972 – 2mf – 9 – DM62.00 – 3-89349-729-3 – gw Hänsel [260]

TUHFE-I 'ASIM – Bulak, 1254 – 1mf – 9 – $6.00 – us MEDOC [949]

TUHFE-I VEHBI / Vehbi, Suembulzade – Istanbul, 1256 [1840] – $18.00 – us MEDOC [470]

TUHFET EL-KIBARF I ESFAR EL-BIHAR / Katip Celebi – Istanbul: Muteferrika Matbaasi, 1141. BNE-100/1 – 9 – ne IDC [949]

Tuilovoni, Setareki *see* PAPERS, 1946-1987

Tuin, H van der *see* GUIDELINES ON THE STUDY OF SEAWATER INTRUSION INTO RIVERS

Tuite, Thomas *see* THE OXFORD SPELLING-BOOK

Tukhacheskii, M N *see* BUDUSHCHAIA VOINA

TUKOPISI V.G. BELINSKOGO / Saltykov-Shchedrin Library – Opisanie. Comp. by R. B. Zaborova. L. 1952. GPB PKG-F-67 BR-10,897 1 – 9 – ne IDC [460]

TULANE CIVIL LAW FORUM *see* TULANE EUROPEAN AND CIVIL LAW FORUM

TULANE ENVIRONMENTAL LAW JOURNAL – v1-8. 1988-1995 – 9 – $102.00 set – us Hein [340]

TULANE EUROPEAN AND CIVIL LAW FORUM – (Title varies: v1-7 1976-92 as Tulane Civil Law Forum. None publ 1977-87) – v1-10. 1973-95 – 9 – $132.00 set – us Hein [340]

TULANE JOURNAL OF INTERNATIONAL AND COMPARATIVE LAW – v1-3. 1993-95 – 9 – $45.00 set – us Hein [340]

TULANE LAW REVIEW – v1-52 1916-78 1; v51-52 5,6,9 – us UMI [340]

TULANE LAW REVIEW – (v1-3 are called "Southern Law Quarterly." The publication then lapsed for a decade, resuming again in 1929 as the "Tulane Law Review." LLMC will resume filming and annual delivery of the out-of-copyright volumes of this title in 2004) – v1-3. 1916-18 – 13mf – $19.50 – LLMC 95-141 – us L.L.M.C. [073]

TULANE LAW REVIEW – v1-70. 1916-96 – 1,5,6,9 – $1,755.00 – us Hein [073]

TULANE LAW REVIEW *see* TULANE LAW REVIEW

TULANE MARITIME LAW JOURNAL – (Cont: Maritime Lawyer) – v1-16. 1975-92 – 1,5,6 – $180.00 – us Hein [073]

TULANE STUDIES IN ENGLISH – v.2-18. 1950-70 – 1 – us UMI [420]

TULANE TAX INSTITUTE – v25-41. 1975-91 – 9 – $320.00 set – us Hein [340]

Tulane University. New Orleans *see*
- CATALOG OF THE LATIN AMERICAN LIBRARY OF THE TULANE UNIVERSITY LIBRARY

Tulane University. New Orleans. Latin American Library *see* CATALOG OF THE LATIN AMERICAN COLLECTION

TULARE ADVANCE REGISTER : SPECIAL EDITION – 1r – 1 – $50.00 – B40285b – us Library Micro [978]

TULARE ADVANCE-REGISTER – Tulare, CA. 1882-1921; 1927-1981; 1984 – 325+ r – 1 – $16,250.00 ($165.00y) – HC03555 – us Library Micro [071]

TULARE COUNTY HISTORICAL SOCIETY NEWSLETTER – Tulare Co, Oct 1968-Mar 1971 – 1r – 1 – $50.00 – B40285 – us Library Micro [978]

TULARE COUNTY INCLUDING TULARE CITY, PORTERVILLE AND VISALIA – Tulare Co, CA. 1888; 1892; 1900; 1904-1950 – 23r – 1 – $1,150.00 – D102 – us Library Micro [978]

TULARE COUNTY NEWS – Visalia, CA. 16 Jan 1896 – 1r – 1 – $50.00 – B03077 – us Library Micro [071]

TULARE COUNTY RECORD AND FRESNO EXAMINER – Visalia, CA. 1859 – 1r – 1 – $50.00 – C03566 – us Library Micro [071]

TULARE COUNTY SCHOOL : 100 YEARS / Hamm, Katherine – Tulare Co, 1961 – 1r – 1 – $50.00 – B40283 – us Library Micro [370]

TULARE COUNTY TIMES – Visalia, CA. 1868-1916 – 13r – 1 – $650.00 – B03078 – us Library Micro [071]

TULARE COUNTY TIMES – Visalia. Calif. -w. 1869-1916 – 1 – us UMI [071]

TULARE DAILY TIMES – Tulare, CA. 1894-1898; 1931-32 – 8r – 1 BC03042 – $400.00 – us Library Micro [071]

TULARE VALLEY CITIZEN – Tulare, CA. 1894-98 – 1r – 1 – $50.00 – B03041 – us Library Micro [071]

"TULARE'S FIRST 100 YEARS 1872-1972" – 1r – 1 – $50.00 – B40285a – us Library Micro [978]

Tulasne, C *see* SELECTA FUNGORUM CARPOLOGIA

Tulasne, LR *see*
- FUNGI HYPOGAEI. HISTOIRE ET MONOGRAPHIE DES CHAMPIGNONS HYPOGES
- SELECTA FUNGORUM CARPOLOGIA

TULELAKE REPORTER – Alturas, CA. 1935-63; 1965- – 33+ r – 1 – $1,650.00 ($50.00y) – B02013 – us Library Micro [071]

TULLAMORE AND KING'S CO. INDEPENDENT – Athlone, Ireland. 1912-19. -w.7 reels – 1 – uk British Libr Newspaper [072]

Tuller *see* PIONEERS AND BUSINESSMEN OF TODAY

Tullidge, Edward W *see*
- HISTORY OF SALT LAKE CITY AND ITS FOUNDERS
- TULLIDGE'S HISTORIES

Tullidge Henry *see* TRIUMPHS OF THE BIBLE

TULLIDGE'S HISTORIES / Tullidge, Edward W – Salt Lake City: Press of Juvenile Instructor, 1889. Utah reel 3. (Cox Library Collection) – 5 – us Americana [978]

Tulloch, John *see*
- THE CHRIST OF THE GOSPELS AND THE CHRIST OF MODERN CRITICISM
- THE CHRIST OF THE GOSPELS AND THE CHRIST OF MODERN CRITICISM...M. RENAN'S VIE DE JESUS
- LUTHER AND OTHER LEADERS OF THE REFORMATION
- MODERN THEORIES IN PHILOSOPHY AND RELIGION
- MOVEMENTS OF RELIGIOUS THOUGHT IN BRITAIN DURING THE NINETEENTH CENTURY
- POSITION AND PROSPECTS OF THE CHURCH OF SCOTLAND
- PROGRESS OF RELIGIOUS THOUGHT IN SCOTLAND
- SOME FACTS OF RELIGION AND OF LIFE

Tullock, Gordon *see* THE RHETORIC AND REALITY OF INCOME DISTRIBUTION

Tulou, J L *see* FANTASIE POUR FLUTE AVEC ACCOMPAGNEMENT DE PIANO... OP. 29...

TULSA – 1959- 1; v54- 5,6,9 – us UMI [380]

TULSA LAW JOURNAL – v1- 1964- 1; v11- 5,6,9 – us UMI [340]

Tulsa, Oklahoma *see* MISCELLANEOUS EARLY NEWSPAPERS

TUL'U – Istanbul: Mahmud Bey Matbaasi, 1884. Mueessis ve Muharriri: M Nuri. Nos. 1-9 (31 Temmuz-31 Tesrinisani 1300 [1884]) – $30.00 – us MEDOC [073]

UNA TUMBA HISPANO-VISIGODA EXCEPCIONAL HALLADA EN EL TURUNUELO : MEDELLIN (BADAJOZ) / Perez Martin, Maria Jesus – Madrid: Tip. y Ed. Maestre, 1961 – 1 – sp Bibl Santa Ana [946]

TUMBARUMBA TIMES – Apr 25 1913-Dec 18 1920 – 9 – at Pascoe [072]

TUMBO ANTIGUO (SIECLE 13) / Montes, San Pedro de – Astorga – 1r – 5,6 – sp Cultura [946]

Tumiati, Domenico *see* TRIPOLITANIA

Tumler, Franz *see*
- IM JAHRE 38
- DER SOLDATENEID
- DAS TAL VON LAUSA UND DURON

TUMOR BIOLOGY – v8-. 1987- – 1,5,9 – us UMI [616]

TUMORI – v1- 1911- 1; v60- 5,6; v61- 9 – us UMI [610]

TUMU GONGCHENG XUEBAO – China Civil Engineering Journal. In Chinese, with English abstracts to the main articles. 52p – 9 – $4.00f – cc Microforms [624]

TUNBRIDGE WELLS GAZETTE. (COUNTIES GAZETTE) – England. 6 Jul 1855-24 Sep 1869; 6 Jun 1873-3 Nov 1893.-w. 28mqn reels – 1 – uk British Libr Newspaper [072]

TUNBRIDGE WELLS JOURNAL – England. -w. 1862-1904. 30 reels – 1 – uk British Libr Newspaper [072]

TUNDRA TIMES – 1962-76.(American Indian Periodicals in the Princeton University Library). 109 fiches – 9 – $445.00 – us UPA [305]

THE TUNEER'S POLKA / Esputa, J – Washington: Hilbus & Hitz, 1855. MUSIC 3082, Item 5 – 1 – us L of C Photodup [780]

T'UNG CHI CHI-PAO – "Quarterly Journal of Statistics". pts. 1-8. Nanking. 1935-36. BCH-358 1 – 9 – ne IDC [073]

Tung, Ching-an *see* COLLECTION OF THE TEACHINGS OF FAMOUS CHINESE (CCC300)

Tung, Hsien-Kuang *see* THE DEVELOPMENT OF CHRISTIANITY IN TAIWAN (CCC301)

TUNG WAH TIMES – (Chinese language) – Sydney, Jun 1898-Jan 7 1914 – 1 – at Pascoe [072]

T'UNG-AN HSIEN-CHIH – 1767. 30, 1. BCH-565 2 – 8 – ne IDC [950]

T'UNG-AN HSIEN-CHIH – 1767. 42, 1, 7. Lacking: ch. 8-30. BCH-567 2 – 8 – ne IDC [950]

T'UNG-AN HSIEN-CHIH – 1798, 30, 1. Lacking: 5-8, 14-30. BCH-566 2 – 8 – ne IDC [950]

TUNG-AN HSIEN-CHIH – 1823; 1825, 4. Lacking: ch. 1; 4. BCH-643 2 – 8 – ne IDC [950]

T'UNG-CHI YUEH-PAO – The Statistical Monthly.Nanking, Chungking, 1929-48. Lacking: 1929, v1 (3); 1937 (34); 1942 (65). BCH-359/1 – 9 – ne IDC [310]

TUNG-FANG TSA-CHIH – The Eastern Miscellany. v. 1-35. Shanghai. 1904-38. semi monthly; index. 1904-48. Lacking: v. 4 (3, 6); v. 5 (1-4); v. 6-13; v. 21 (3, 23); v. 22 (7-12); v. 28 (8); v. 32, 1935. BCH-357 2 – 8 – ne IDC [073]

TUNG-KUAN HSIEN-CHIH – 1798, 46. BCH-593 2 – 8 – ne IDC [950]

T'UNG-LIANG HSIEN-CHIH – 1875, 16. BCH-717 2 – 8 – ne IDC [950]

TUNG-PEI JIH PAO – Shenyang, China. Northeast Daily. 15 Mar 1949-1950; Aug-Oct 1951 (loose issues); Apr-May, Oct 1952-Aug 1954. 5 reels – 1 – 112.00 – us Chinese Res [072]

T'UNG-SHENG YUEH-K'AN – (Harmonious Voice Monthly). v. 1-3 (1-11). Nanking. 1940-44. BCH-812 2 – 8 – ne IDC [073]

TUNG-WEN NEWSPAPER = T'UNG WEN PAO – no 452. 7 Jun 1911 (complete) – 1r – 1 – ATLA S0296Q – us A.T.L.A. [073]

THE TUNICATA, WITH AN ACCOUNT OF THE BRITISH SPECIES / Berrill, N J – Ray Society. 1946-50 – 1,7 – uk Microform Academic [580]

TUNISIA : ANNUAIRE STATISTIQUE DE LA TUNISIE 1940-1971 / Tunisia. Service des Statistiques – (Coll title: African Official Statistical Serials, 1867-1982) – 107mf – 9 – £1,025.00 – uk Chadwyck [960]

TUNISIA : STATISTIQUE GENERALE DE LA TUNISIE 1913-1939 / Tunisia. Direction des Affaires Economiques – (Coll title: African Official Statistical Serials, 1867-1982) – 107mf – 9 – £1,025.00 – uk Chadwyck [960]

Tunisia *see*
- AL-RA'ID AL-RASMI.
- JOURNAL OFFICIEL
- PLAN 1969-1972
- QUATRIEME PLAN DE DEVELOPPEMENT ECONOMIQUE ET SOCIAL. 1973-1976

Tunisia. Direction des Affaires Economiques *see* TUNISIA

Tunisia. Ministere du Plan *see*
- NOTE RELATIVE AUX TRAVAUX PREPARATOIRES DU IVE PLAN 1973-76
- RAPPORT SUR LE BUDGET ECONOMIQUE DE L'ANNEE 1973

Tunisia. Ministere, du Plan et du Developpement Regional *see* SEMINAIRE NATIONAL POPULATION ET DEVELOPPEMENT

Tunisia. Secretariat d'Etat au Plan *see* PLAN QUADRIENNAL, 1965-1968

Tunisia. Secretariat d'Etat au Plan et a l'Econ. Nationale *see* RAPPORT D'EXECUTION DU PLAN TRIENNAL, 1962-1964

Tunisia. Secretariat d'Etat au Plan et a l'Economie Nationale *see*
- PLAN DE DEVELOPPEMENT ECONOMIQUE ET SOCIAL
- RAPPORT SUR LE BUDGET ECONOMIQUE DE L'ANNEE 1968
- RAPPORT SUR LE BUDGET ECONOMIQUE DE L'ANNEE 1969
- RAPPORT SUR LE BUDGET ECONOMIQUE DE L'ANNEE 1970

Tunisia. Secretariat d'Etat au Plan et aux Finances *see*
- PERSPECTIVES DECENNALES DE DEVELOPPEMENT, 1962-1971
- PLAN TRIENNAL TABLEAU DETAILLE DES INVESTISSEMENTS, 1962-1964

Tunisia. Secretariat d'Etat aux Plan et aux Finances *see* PLAN TRIENNAL, 1962-1964

Tunisia. Service des Statistiques *see* TUNISIA

LA TUNISIE – Mescara. 1883. 16p. (Travel Series) – 9 – 3.00 – fr Bibl Nationale [910]

TUNKANNOCK EXAMINER – Tunkannock, PA., 1979-1980 – 13 – $25.00r – us I.M.R. [071]

TUNKHANNOCK NEW AGE – Tunkhannock, PA. -w 1969-1970; 1971-1979 – 13 – $25.00r – us I.M.R. [071]

TUNKHANNOCK REPUBLICAN – Tunkhannock, PA. -w 1889-1940; 1962-1968 – 13 – $25.00r – us I.M.R. [071]

TUNNELLING AND UNDERGROUND SPACE TECHNOLOGY – v1- 1986- – 5,6,9 – us UMI [574]

TUNNELLING AND UNDERGROUND SPACE TECHNOLOGY *see* ADVANCES IN TUNNELLING TECHNOLOGY AND SURFACE USE

TUNNELS AND TUNNELLING – v1- 1969- 1; v8- 5,6,9 – us UMI [624]

TUNTUNAN UNTUK DACTYLOSCOPISCH BUREAU DARI A.V.R.O.S / Algemeene Vereeniging van Rubberplanters ter Oostkust van Sumatra – SE-10,200 1. 1953 – 9 – ne IDC [630]

Tuohy, Anthony R *see* ALBUM HISTORICO DE LA PRIMERA ASAMBLEA FILIPINA

TUOLUMNE CITY NEWS – Tuolumne, CA. 1868-70 – 1r – 1 – $50.00 – B03043 – us Library Micro [071]

TUOLUMNE COUNTY – Tuolumne Co, CA. 1893 – 1r – 1 – $50.00 – D104 – us Library Micro [978]

TUOLUMNE INDEPENDENT – Sonora, CA. 1872-1916 – 19r – 1 – $950.00 – C03654 – us Library Micro [071]

TUOLUMNE INDEPENDENT *see* UNION DEMOCRAT

TUOLUMNE PROSPECTOR – Groveland, CA. 1901-1904 – 1r – 1 – $50.00 – C03603 – us Library Micro [071]
TU'O'NG-LAI TAP-CHI – Revue de l'avenir. No1-3. Nhatrang. 1934; No3-13. 1937 – 1 – fr A.C.R.P.P. [073]
TUPAMBAE Y MASOLLER, EL CAUDILLO Y SUS GLORIAS – Montevideo. 1905 – 1 – us Res Libr [972]
Tupikov, N M *see* SLOVAR' DREVNE-RUSSKIKH LICHNYKH SOBSTVENNYKH IMEN
Tupper, H A *see* TWO CENTURIES OF THE FIRST BAPTIST CHURCH OF SOUTH CAROLINA
Tupper, Kerr B *see* GLADSTONE AND OTHER ADDRESSES
Tupper, Martin Farquhar *see*
- MY LIFE AS AN AUTHOR
- PROVERBIAL PHILOSOPHY. IN FOUR SERIES, NOW FIRST COMPLETE

LA TUQUE – La Tuque, Canada. 24 nov-v1 n2. 9 dec 1911 – 1r – 1 – Can$25.00 – cn Can Microfilming [072]
Turaev, B *see* EFIOPSKIE RUKOPISI V ST PETERBURGE
TURANG XUEBAO – (Acta Pedologica Sinica). In Chinese, with English abstracts to the main articles. F p43 – 9 – $4.50f – cc Microforms [305]
Turberville, Arthur C *see* TYPES OF THE SAINTLY LIFE
Turbetskoi, E N *see* LEKTSII PO ISOTRII FILOSOFII PRAVA
TURBO MACHINERY INTERNATIONAL – v. 18-. 1977- – 1,5,6,9 – us UMI [073]
TURBULENCE IN GEOPHYSICS – 1962 – 9 – $10.00 – us A.G.U. [550]
TURBULENCE IN GEOPHYSICS : SYMPOSIUM ON FUNDAMENTAL PROBLEMS IN TURBULENCE AND THEIR RELATION TO GEOPHYSICS – 1962. Reprinted from the Journal of Geophysical Research. 235p – 1,5,6,9 – $5.00 – us A.G.U. [550]
TURCHICE SPURCITIE... – Paris, 1514 – 2mf – 9 – H-8219/1 – ne IDC [956]
TURCICARUM RERVM COMMENTARIVS / Giovio, P – Parisiis, 1539 – 1mf – 9 – H-8259/1 – ne IDC [956]
Turcotte, Fernande *see* LES BIBLIOTHEQUES PAROISSIALES
Turczaninov, N S *see* FLORA BAICALENSI-DAHURICA
Turdeanu, E *see* LA LITTERATURE BULGARE DU 14E SIECLE ET SA DIFFUSION DANS LES PAYS ROUMAINS
Turek, Ludwig *see* EIN PROLET ERZAEHLT
Turenne, Henri de la Tour d'Auvergne *see* MEMOIRES: EXTRAIT DU TOME 2 D'HISTOIRE DE HENRI DE LA TOUR D'AUVERGNE
TURFANDA MI YOKSA TURFA MI? / Mizanci, Mehmed Murad – Istanbul: Mahmud Bey Matbaasi, 1308 [1891] – $100.00 – us MEDOC [470]
DAS TURFANGEBIET / Fuchs, W – Seine aeusseren Geschichte bis in die T'ang-Zeit. (OZ.XIII is N.F. III). 1926. BU-614 2 – 8 – ne IDC [950]
Turgenev, Ivan Sergeevich *see*
- OPIS DOKUMENTAL'NYKH MATERIALOV LICHNOGO FONDA NO.509
- RUKOPISI, PEREPISKA I DOKUMENTY

Turgeon, Marguerite *see* BIO-BIBLIOGRAPHIE DE ROGER LEMELIN
TURHAND KIRTLAND PAPERS, MS 3237 / Kirtland, Turhand – 1794-1880. 11 reels – 1 – us Western Res [920]
THE TURK AND THE GREEK; OR, CREEDS, RACES, SOCIETY AND SCENERY IN TURKEY, GREECE, AND THE ISLES OF GREECE / Benjamin, Samuel Greene Wheeler – New York: Hurd and Houghton, 1867. vii,268p. With: Midrash Hasirot Ve-Yiterot. 1 reel. 1251 – 1 – us U.W. Library [949]
Turk, Joanne C *see* COLLEGIATE COACHES' KNOWLEDGE OF EATING DISORDERS
TURKESTAN DOWN TO THE MONGOL INVASION / Barthold, W – (Ed. 9. E.J.W. Gibb Memorial Series, N.S.V., 1928, XIX, 513p) – 8 – ne IDC [956]
"TURKESTANSKII AL'BOM." / U.S. Library of Congress. Prints and Photographs Division – 1220 captioned photographs, small number of maps and drawings. Turkestan in the 1870's. The region's archaeological heritage, ethnography, industry, and history. 1 reel. P&P11688 – 1 – 23.00r – us L of C Photodup [080]
Turkey *see* TC RESMI GAZETTE
TURKEY AND THE ARMENIAN ATROCITIES....WITH AN INTROD. BY MISS FRANCES E. WILLARD / Bliss, Edwin Munsell – c1896 – 1 – us A.T.L.A. [956]
Turkey. Basbakanlik Devlet Planlama Teskilati *see*
- 1972 YILI PROGRAMI, IKINCI BES YIL 1968-1972
- DEVELOPMENT PLANS
- UCUNCU BES YILLIK KALKINMA PLANI (1973-1977) BUYUME MODELI VE COZUMLERI

TURKEY CREEK BAPTIST CHURCH. ABBEVILLE COUNTY. SOUTH CAROLINA : CHURCH RECORDS – 1785-1909 – 1 – 22.01 – us Baptist [240]
Turkey. Devlet Planlama Teskilati *see*
- DRAFT PROGRAM FOR 1962 FOR TRANSITION INTO THE PLAN-PERIOD
- DRAFT PROGRAM FOR THE YEAR 1962 FOR TRANSITION INTO THE PLAN-PERIOD IMPLEMENTATION PLAN
- FIRST FIVE YEAR DEVELOPMENT PLAN, 1963-1967
- IKINCI BES YIL 1968-1972, 1968 YILI PROGRAMI
- IKINCI BES YIL 1968-1972, 1969 YILI PROGRAMI
- IKINCI BES YIL 1968-1972, 1970 YILI PROGRAMI
- KALKINMA PLANI UCUNCU BES YIL (1973-1977), 1973 YILI PROGRAMI
- STRATEGY AND OBJECTIVES OF THE SECOND FIVE YEAR DEVELOPMENT PLAN (1968-1972)
- A SUMMARY OF THE SECOND FIVE-YEAR DEVELOPMENT PLAN OF TURKEY (1968-1972)
- YENI STRATEJI VE KALKINMA PLANI UCUNCU BES YIL 1973-1977

TURKEY IN EUROPE, BY ODYSSEUS PSEUD / Eliot, Charles Norton Edgecumbe – London: Edward Arnold, 1900. 475p. 2 fold. maps – 1 – us U.W. Library [949]
Turkey. Laws, Statutes, etc *see* THE MEDJELLE OR OTTOMAN CIVIL LAW
Turkey. Prime Ministry. State Planning Organization *see*
- STRATEGY AND BASIC TARGETS OF LONG-TERM DEVELOPMENT AND THE THIRD FIVE-YEAR DEVELOPMENT PLAN
- A SUMMARY OF THE THIRD FIVE YEAR DEVELOPMENT PLAN 1973-1977

Turkey. State Planning Organization *see* DEVELOPMENT PLAN, FIRST FIVE YEARS (1963-1967), 1963 ANNUAL PROGRAM
TURKEY WORLD – v1- 1926- 1; v52- 5,6,9 – us UMI [636]
THE TURKISH CONSTITUTION PROCLAIMED UNDER MIDHAT PASHA / Khatti, Humayum Sharif – 1880 – 1r – 1 – us Ross [323]
THE TURKISH CONSTITUTION PROCLAIMED UNDER MIDHAT PASHA / Khatti, Humayum Sharif – Constantinople, 1880 – 1 – us NY Public [949]
TURKISTAN: NOTES OF A JOURNEY IN RUSSIAN TURKISTAN, KHOKAND, BUKHARA, AND KULDJA / Schuyler, Eugene – New York: Scribner, Armstrong & Co., 1876. 2v. illus – 1 – us U.W. Library [950]
TURKIYE IKTISAT GAZETESI – Istanbul, Turkey. Jan 1953-Sept 10 1956; April 13 1969-Dec 27 1979 – 7r – 1 – us L of C Photodup [072]
TURKMENSKAYA ISKRA – Ashkhabad. Turkmen (U.S.S.R.). 1955-70 – 1 – us UMI [072]
TURKMENSKAYA ISKRA – Ashkhabad, U.S.S.R. -d. Jan 1951-Dec 1952; July 1953-July 1954; Jan 1955-Dec 1958; July 1960-Dec 1968. 34 reels – 1 – uk British Libr Newspaper [947]
Turler, Jerome *see* THE TRAVEILER
TURLOCK – 1927-44 – 17r – 1 – $850.00 – P00138 – us Library Micro [910]
TURLOCK TRIBUNE – Turlock, CA. 1919-55 – 28r – 1 – $1,400.00 – B03044 – us Library Micro [071]
DER TURM – Bielefeld, jul 1 1920-may 27 1934 – 1 – Inquire at Mikrofilmarchiv for details – gw Misc Inst [072]
Turmel *see* SAINT JEROME
Turmel, Joseph *see*
- HISTOIRE DU DOGME DE LA PAPAUTE
- HISTOIRE DU DOGME DU PECHE ORIGINEL
- LA SAINTE VIERGE DANS L'HISTOIRE

TURMOLUS?. ANTIGUEDADES DESCUBIERTAS Y OTRAS YA CONOCIDAS / Sanguino y Michel, Juan – Caceres: Tip. Enc. y Lib. Jimenez, 1906 – 1 – sp Bibl Santa Ana [946]
Turnbull, John *see* A VOYAGE AROUND THE WORLD IN THE YEARS 1800-04; IN WHICH THE AUTHOR VISITED MADEIRA, THE BRAZILS, CAPE OF GOOD HOPE.
Turnbull, Shann *see* DEMOCRATIZING THE WEALTH OF NATIONS FROM NEW MONEY SOURCES AND PROFIT MOTIVES
Turnbull, W B *see* THE BUIK OF THE CHRONICLES OF SCOTLAND (RS6)
Turner *see* HISTORY OF EDGECOMBE COUNTY
Turner, A J *see* THE LEGISLATIVE MANUAL FOR THE STATE OF WISCONSIN
Turner, A P *see* A MODEL FOR DEVELOPING EFFECTIVE DECISION-MAKING DURING GAME PARTICIPATION
THE TURNER BEQUEST / British Museum. Department of Prints and Drawings – 43r – 1 – uk Microform Academic [700]
Turner, Cuthbert Hamilton *see* STUDIES IN EARLY CHURCH HISTORY
Turner, D *see*
- THE FORAGE PLANTS OF AUSTRALIA
- FUCI, SIVE PLANTARUM FUCORUM GENERI A BOTANICIS
- MUSCOLOGIAE HIBERNICAE SPICILEGIUM
- SPECIMEN OF A LICHENOGRAPHIA BRITANNICA

Turner, D H *see* THE MISSAL OF THE NEW MINISTER, WINCHESTER
Turner, Edward Raymond *see* THE NEGRO IN PENNSYLVANIA
Turner, F *see* AUSTRALIAN GRASSES AND PASTURE PLANTS
Turner, Frederick C *see* JUAN PERON AND THE RESHAPING OF ARGENTINA
Turner, Frederick Storrs *see* THE QUAKERS
Turner, J B *see* AN ANSWER TO THE DIFFICULTIES IN BISHOP COLENSO'S BOOK ON THE PENTATEUCH
Turner, J Horsfall *see* THE REVEREND OLIVER HEYWOOD, B.A. 1630-1702
Turner, John Mallord William *see* DRAWINGS AND WATERCOLOURS
Turner, Jonathan Baldwin *see* THE ONLY GOOD THING IN ALL THE WORLDS
Turner, L M *see*
- ETHNOLOGY OF THE UNGAVA DISTRICT, HUDSON BAY TERRITORY
- ON THE INDIANS AND ESKIMOS OF THE UNGAVA DISTRICT, LABRADOR

Turner, Maynard P, Jr *see* STUDY GUIDE, BLACK DENOMINATIONS
Turner, Paul E *see* PHYSICAL PRACTICE, MENTAL IMAGERY, AND RELAXATION, RELATED TO MOTOR SKILL ACQUISITION
Turner, Robert J *see* THE LAW AND PRACTICE UNDER THE ACT FOR QUIETING TITLES TO REAL ESTATE IN UPPER CANADA
Turner, S *see* AN ACCOUNT OF AN EMBASSY TO THE COURT OF THE TESHOO LAMA, IN TIBET; ...
TURNER TRIBUNE – Turner, OR. -w. 18 Aug 1921-4 Aug 1938. 2 rolls – 1 – us U.O. Library [071]
Turner, V W *see* NDEMBU DIVINATION, ITS SYMBOLISM AND TECHNIQUES
Turner, W *see*
- THE HERBAL
- SOUND ANATOMIZ'D IN A PHILOSOPHICAL ESSAY ON MUSICK

Turner, William *see*
- A BOOK OF WINES
- THE FIRST AND SECONDE PARTES OF THE HERBAL OF WILLIAM TURNER...
- STUDIES BIBLICAL AND ORIENTAL

TURNER'S WEEKLY – Saskatoon, Saskatchewan, CN. Sept 1918-Sept 1920 – 3r – 1 – cn Commonwealth Micro [072]
TURNING POINTS OF ENGLISH CHURCH HISTORY / Cutts, Edward L – London: S.P.C.K.; New York: E. & J.B. Young, 1895 – 1mf – us A.T.L.A. [240]
TURNPIKE GATE. COMIC OPERA IN 2 ACTS / Mazzinghi, J – London: Goulding, Phipps & D'Almaine, 1799 – 1 – us Sibley [780]
TURN-ZEITUNG / Das Socialistische Bund – Organ des Socialistischen Turnerbundes. New York. Jahrg. 1, no. 1, Jahrg. 3, no. 61. Nov. 15, 1851-Oct. 15, 1854 – 1 – us NY Public [073]
Turonensis, Beringerius *see* RESCRIPTUM CONTRA LANFRANNUM
Turonensis, Gregorius *see* LIBRI MIRACULORUM ALIAQUE OPERA MINORA
Turpaev, T M *see* PHYSIOLOGY AND GENERAL BIOLOGY REVIEWS
Turpie, David McCalman *see*
- THE NEW TESTAMENT VIEW OF THE OLD
- THE OLD TESTAMENT IN THE NEW

Turpin, M *see* HISTORY OF THE KINGDOM OF SIAM AND OF THE REVOLUTIONS THAT HAVE CAUSED THE OVERTHROW OF THE EMPIRE, UP TO A.D. 1770
Turpin, P J F *see* FLORE PARISIENNE
Turquet de Mayerne, T *see* MEDICINAL COUNCELS
Turquetil, A *see* NOTES SUR LES ESQUIMAUX DE BAIE HUDSON
LA TURQUIE – Istanbul. Turkey. -d. 7-13 Mar 1867; 16 Aug 1870- 30 Sept 1875. (11 reels) – 1 – uk British Libr Newspaper [949]
LA TURQUIE A TRAVERS QUELQUES RECITS DE VOYAGEURS FRANCAIS DE LA FIN DU 17EME SIECLE / Gregoire, Henri Baptiste – 9 – F60.00 – fr Ethnologie [949]
LA TURQUIE EN 1873 / Caston, Alfred de – (In French) – [n.p.], [n.d.] – 10mf – 9 – $75.00 – us MEDOC [949]
LA TURQUIE KEMALISTE – Ankara: Ministere de l'Interieur, Nos. 1-49 (June 1943-Mar 1948) – 40mf – 9 – $225.00 – us MEDOC [949]
Turra, A *see* FLORA ITALICAE PRODROMUS
Turrecremata, J de *see* SUMMA DE ECCLESIA
TURRIFF ADVERTISER – 1 – £42.00r – uk Scot News [072]
Turton W *see* A MANUAL OF THE LAND AND FRESHWATER SHELLS OF THE BRITISH ISLANDS
Turton, W *see* A CONCHOLOGICAL DICTIONARY OF THE BRITISH ISLANDS
TURTON'S LAND DEEDS OF THE NORTH ISLAND – (An Epitome of Official Documents Relative to Native Affairs and Land Purchases in the North Island of New Zealand...1883. Maori Deeds of Land Purchases in the North Island of New Zealand...1877-8, 2v. Maori Deeds of Old Private Land Purchases in New Zealand, 1815 to 1840...1882. Plans of Land Purchases in the North Island of New Zealand...1877-8. 2v) – 1990 – 39mf – 9 – NZ$49.95 – 0-477-07430-8 – nz Nat'l Libr [980]
THE TUSCAN ATHENAEUM – Florence. no. 1-13. Oct 30 1847-Jan 22 1848 – 1 – us NY Public [072]
TUSCAN CITIES / Howells, William Dean – Illus. from Joseph Pennell and others. Boston: Ticknor, 1886 c1885. v,251p. illus – 1 – us U.W. Library [945]
TUSCAN SCULPTORS: ... : THEIR LIVES, WORKS, AND TIMES, WITH ILLUSTRATIONS FROM ORIGINAL DRAWINGS AND PHOTOGRAPHS / Perkins, C C – London, 1864 – 19mf – ne IDC [730]
TUSCAN SCULPTORS: THEIR LIVES, WORKS AND TIMES / Perkins, C C – O-1168 1 – 9 – ne IDC [920]
THE TUSCUMBIAN – Tuscumbia, AL: Robert W Briggs, sep 1 1824-jan 17 1827 – us Res Libr [071]
TUSHKAHOMMAN – 1935-36. (American Indian Periodicals in the Princeton University Library). 1 reel – 1 – $75.00 – us UPA [305]
T'U-SHU P'ING-LUN – Book Review. v. 1-2 (12). Nanking. 1932-34. monthly. BCH-355 – 8 – ne IDC [073]
TU-SHU TSA-CHIH – Readers' Magazine. Shanghai, 1931-33. 3v. -m. Lacking: 1933, v3 (3-4).BCH-354/1 – 9 – ne IDC [480]
TUSHUGUANGXUE JIKAN = LIBRARY SCIENCE QUARTERLY – Mar 1926-Jun 1937. 6 reels. M-C40 – 1 – $270.00 – cc Microforms [073]
TUSKEGEE BAPTIST CHURCH. TUSKEGEE, ALABAMA : CHURCH RECORDS – 1852-74 – 1 – 15.48 – us Baptist [240]
Tuskegee Institute. Agricultural Experiment Station *see* BULLETIN
TUSKEGEE INSTITUTE NEWS CLIPPING FILE, 1899-1966 – 252r – 1 – $15,120.00 – us UMI [360]
TUSKEGEE MESSENGER – v1-12, no. 12 (all publ). 1924-26 – 2r – 1 – $185.00 – us UPA [976]
Tuskegee Normal and Industrial Institute. Experiment Station *see* BULLETIN
Tuson, Penelope *see* BRITISH POLICY IN ASIA: INDIA OFFICE MEMORANDA
Tusquets, Juan *see*
- ORIGENES DE LA REVOLUCION ESPANOLA
- EL TEOSOFISMO. BARCELONA, 1928

Tussac, F R de *see*
- CRI DES COLONS CONTRE UN OUVRAGE DE M. L'EVEQUE ET SENATEUR GREGOIRE, AYANT POUR TITRE DE LA LITERATURE DES NEGRES, OU REFUTATION DES INCULPATIONS CALOMNIEUSES FAITES AUX COLONS PAR L'AUTEUR, ET PAR LES AUTRES PHILOSOPHES NEGROPHILES, TELS QUE RAYNAL
- FLORE DES ANTILLES

Tussekiah Baptist Church *see* BICENTENNIAL

TUTA...MEDICATIO PRO LIENTERICIS... / Cerdan, F – Valencia, 1756 – 1mf – 9 – sp Cultura [610]

Tutcher, W J *see* FLORA OF KWANTUNG AND HONGKONG (CHINA)

TUTELA Y DIGNIFICACION DEL TRABAJO / Hernandez Gil, Fernando – Caceres: Tip. El Noticiero, s.a. 1950 – sp Bibl Santa Ana [946]

LA TUTELA...DISCURSO Y CONTESTACION... / Crehuet, Diego Maria – Madrid: Reus, 1921 – sp Bibl Santa Ana [946]

THE TUTOR, OR A NEW ENGLISH AND BENGALEE WORK / Miller, John – 1797. 180p. (English Linguistics Series 1500-1800) – 9 – us UMI [490]

THE TUTOR TO TRUE ENGLISH / Care, Henry – 1687. 121p. (English Linguistics Series 1500-1800) – 9 – us UMI [420]

Tutschek, C *see* DICTIONARY OF THE GALLA LANGUAGE

Tutt, J W *see* ENTOMOLOGIST'S RECORD AND JOURNAL OF VARIATION

Tuttar, H *see* EESTI BAPTISMI AJALUGU: I. ARKAMISE AEG

TUTTI HAN TORTO / Scrofani, Saverio – Italy, 1793. 2 fiches – 9 – $45.00 – us UPA [944]

Tuttle, Charles R *see*
- GENERAL HISTORY OF THE STATE OF MICHIGAN
- ILLUSTRATED HISTORY OF THE STATE OF WISCONSIN

TUTTO LIBRI – 1975-1995 – Once per yr – 1 – L100,000 – sz Infoprint [072]

TUTTO LIBRI – (Standing orders available) – Torino, Italy, 1975- – 1 – inquire – us Ross [072]

TUTTO SPORT – 1978-1983 – 1 – sz Infoprint [072]

Tuuk, H N van der *see* KAWI-BALINEESCH-NEDERLANDSCH WOORDENBOEK...

TUV YERUSHALAYIM / Farhi, I – Jerusalem. 1843. BJ-27-51 1 – 9 – ne IDC [956]

TUYEN HUAN – Hanoi, Vietnam. 1966-Jun3 1970, 1972 – 1 – us Res Libr [072]

TUZUK-I-JAHANGIRI / Jahangir – A. Rogers (Transl.) London, 1909-1914. (Oriental Translation Fund). 2 vols. BI-769 2 – 8 – ne IDC [800]

TV FERNSEH-WOCHE *see* WESTFUNK

TV HEBDO – Montreal: Editions Cousins. v1-1960-. SEM16P301 – 62r – 5 – cn Bibl Nat [073]

TV HOEREN UND SEHEN *see* WESTFUNK

TV TRANSLATORS ENGINEERING DATA BASE IN ORDER BY STATE, CHANNEL, CALL / U.S. National Technical Information Service – Monthly – 9 – us N.T.I.S. [000]

TV TRANSLATORS ENGINEERING DATA BASE IN ORDER BY STATE, CITY, CHANNEL / U.S. National Technical Information Service – Monthly – 9 – us N.T.I.S. [000]

TV TRANSNATIONALIZATION – EUROPE AND ASIA / ed by Sepstrup, Preben & Goonasekera, Anura – 1995 – 95p – 9 – 92-3-103035-3 – fr UNESCO [380]

TVC *see* VUE

TV-CONTACT – (Cont by: TV-Courier, jan 7, 1967 (Mainz). FFF-Courier, 1967 (Hamburg). TV-Courier, 1970. Publ in Wiesbaden since 1976. Lots of suppl) – Berlin. jan 20, 1961-dec 22, 1988 – 25r – 1 – gw Mikrofilm [073]

TV-CONTACT – (Cont by: TV-Courier, Mainz, jan 7 1967; FFF-Courier, Hamburg, 1967; TV-Courier, 1970, publ in Wiesbaden since 1976. Filmed with many suppl. This suppl is seperately available: AV-Echo, mar 20-oct 30 1978, mar 12-dec 3 1979, mar 3-jul 23 1980, aug 11-nov 30 1981) – Berlin, jan 16 1978-dec 22 1988 – 1 – Inquire at Mikrofilmarchiv for details – gw Misc Inst [790]

TV-COURIER *see*
- TV-CONTACT

TVERSKIIA EPARKHIAL'NYIA VIEDOMOSTI – Tver, Russia. 1877-Feb 6, 1917 – 1 – us Res Libr [072]

TVERSKOI KOOPERATOR – Tver', 1917-20 n5 – 30mf – 9 – COR-694/1 – ne IDC [334]

TVMVLTVVM ANABAPTISTARVM LIBER VNVS / Hortensius, L – Basileae, J. Oporinus. 1548. BME-166 1 – 9 – ne IDC [240]

T-VO SKOROPECHATNI A.A. LEBENSON / Lebenson, A A – Istorich. ocherk i opisanie masterskikh 1881-1903. M. 1903. BR-4577 2 – 8 – ne IDC [920]

TVORBA – Prague, Czechoslovakia. -w. Sept 1969-Dec 1970. 2 reels – 1 – uk British Libr Newspaper [072]

TVORCHESKOE NASLEDIE M.A. BALAKIREVA / Saltykov-Shchedrin Library – Katalog proizvedenii. Comp. by A. S. Liapunova. 3 v. L. 1960. PKG-F-66 BR-10,896 1 – 9 – ne IDC [780]

TVORCHESTVO FONVIZINA / Pigarev, K V – 1954 – 8 – BR-7768 2 – ne IDC [947]

TVORCHESTVO MAIAKOVSKOGO 1917-1924 GG / Metchenko, A – M. 1954. BR-1430 2 – 8 – ne IDC [460]

TVORCHESTVO MAIAKOVSKOGO 1925-1930 GG / Metchenko, A – M. 1961. BR-1431 2 – 8 – ne IDC [460]

TVORENIIA / Kheraskov, M M – Vnov' ispravlenyia i dopolnenyia. v. 1-12. M. 1796-1803. Lacking: v. 6, 8-11. BR-6005 2 – 8 – ne IDC [073]

TVORENIIA OTTSOV TSERKVI V DREVNE-RUSSKOI PIS'MENNOSTI / Arkhangel'skii, A S – Kazan', 1889-90. v.1-4. Br-4060 2 – 8 – ne IDC [460]

TVORENIIA OTTSOV TSERKVI V DREVNE-RUSSKOI PIS'MENNOSTI. OBOZRENIE RUKOPISNAGO MATERIALA. (K IZUCHENIIU DREVNE-RUSSKOI LITERATURY) / Arkhangel'skii, A S – St. Petersburg, 1888. BR-4088 2 – 8 – ne IDC [460]

TVORENIIA SVIATYKH OTTSOV V RUSSKOM PEREVODE – (Missing: 1849, V.10(p. 344-End); 1851, V.18(p. 404-End); 1854, V.24(p. 396-End); 1858, V.31(p. 226-End); Supplemented: 1849, V.9-10; 1851, V.18; 1854, V.24; 1858, V.31. 33mf) – M., 1843-1891. v1-57 – 9 – 1941/2 – ne IDC [947]

TVORTSI NA BALGARSKOTO VUZRAZHDANE / Arnaudov, M P – Sofiia, 1942 – 8 – BR-3846 2 – ne IDC [947]

TVORTSY KOOPERATSII I IKH DUMY : SBORNIK KRATKIKH BIOGRAFII VYDAIUSHCHIKHSIA KOOPERATOROV S VYDERZHKAMI IZ IKH STATEI I RECHEI – M., 1919 – 4mf – 9 – COR-115/1 – ne IDC [334]

TVRCICORVM TYRANNORVM QVI INDE VSQVE AB OTOMANNO REBUS TURCICIS PRAEFUERUNT, ... / Campanus, J – Pragae, 1597 – 1mf – 9 – H-8392/1 – ne IDC [956]

IL TVRCO VINCIBILE IN VNGARIA. CON MEDIOCRI AIUTI DI GERMANIA, ... / Tarducci, A – 2mf – 9 – H-8413/1 – ne IDC [956]

TVRCOGRAECIAE LIBRI OCTO A'MARTINO CRVSIO, IN ACADEMIA TYBINGENSI GRAECO ET LATINO PROFESSORE, VTRAQUE LINGUA EDITA / Crusius, M – Basileae, 1584 – 11mf – 9 – H-8363/1 – ne IDC [956]

THE TVVOO BOOKES OF FRANCIS BACON OF THE PROFICIENCE AND ADUANCEMENT OF LEARNING, DIUINE AND HUMANE / Bacon, Francis – London: Printed for Henrie Tomes, 1605. 45, 118 leaves. 1st ed – 1 – us U.W. Library [190]

TWAALF REDENEERINGEN OVER NUTTIGE MUZIKAALE ONDERWERPEN. MET 20 CIERLYCKE OP KOPER GESNEDENE NOOTEN-PLATEN EN MET EEN VOLLEDIG REGISTER / Lustig, Johann Wilhelm – Amsterdam. BP-381 1 – 9 – ne IDC [780]

TWANAS – Santa Cruz, CA. 1979-1984 – 1r – 1 – $50.00 – B03518 – us Library Micro [071]

Twardovski, Hans Heinrich von *see* DER RASENDE PEGASUS

TWEE SCHONE BRIEUEN. WT DER GHEVANCKENISSE / Verstralen, H – 1577. BME-201 1 – 9 – ne IDC [240]

Tweed, Boss *see* BOSS TWEED IN COURT

Tweed, R D *see* FRESHWATER ALGAE OF SIERRA LEONE

HET TWEEDE BOECK DER CHRISTLIJCKER SENDBRIEUEN / Joris, David – Brieven van 1549-56. BME-383 1 – 9 – ne IDC [240]

DAT TWEEDE HANDT-BOECXKEN. DEN INNERLIJCKEN WTTRECK OF GEESTELIJCKE PELGRIMAGIE, CORTELIJCK WTGHESPROKEN / Joris, David – BME-381 1 – 9 – ne IDC [240]

Twells, L *see* TWENTY-FOUR SERMONS PREACH'D AT THE PARISH CHURCH OF ST MARY LE BOW, LONDON, IN THE YEARS 1739, 1740, 1741...

TWELVE ANTHEMS AND A MORNING AND EVENING SERVICE WITH EIGHT ANTHEMS / Kent, J – (2v. (v.2: revised and arranged by Joseph Corfe; imprint: printed for the editor.]) – London: Birchall and Andrews, [1783?] – 1 – us Sibley [780]

TWELVE CONCERTOS IN SIX PARTS FOR A GERMAN FLUTE, TWO VIOLINS, A TENOR, WITH A THOROUGH BASS...OPERA TERZA / Hasse, J A – c. 1741 – 9 – us Sibley [780]

TWELVE EASY DUETS FOR TWO FLUTES / Nielson, L C – (Parts) – London: Goulding, D'Almaine, Potter & Co, 1800 – 1 – us Sibley [780]

TWELVE FAVORITE NEW COUNTRY DANCES FOR THE VIOLIN, HARP OR PIANOFORTE / Edwards, T – London: Author; Longman & Broderip, 1786 – 1 – us Sibley [780]

TWELVE FAVORITE PIECES. ARRANGED FOR THE PIANO FORTE OR HARPSICHORD / Reinagle, Alexander – Philadelphia: Printed for A. Reinagle 1787?. MUSIC 1468 – 1 – us L of C Photodup [780]

TWELVE GREAT ACTORS / Robins, Edward – New York, London: G.P. Putnam's Sons, 1900. xiv,474p – 1 – us U.W. Library [920]

TWELVE LECTURES TO YOUNG MEN, ON VARIOUS IMPORTANT SUBJECTS / Beecher, Henry Ward – rev ed. New York: D Appleton, 1898, c1879 – 1mf – 9 – 0-8370-9763-0 – 1986-3763 – us A.T.L.A. [240]

THE TWELVE MINOR PROPHETS / Orelli, Conrad von – Edinburgh: T. & T. Clark, 1897. 1 fiche – 9 – us A.T.L.A. [240]

THE TWELVE MINOR PROPHETS / Smith, George Adam – 1896 – 9 – $36.00 – us I.R.C. [220]

TWELVE MINUETS AND TWELVE DANCES FOR A VIOLIN, HAUTBOY, AND HARPSICHORD / Dabney, M – London: Thompson, 176- – 1 – us Sibley [780]

TWELVE PIECES OF HARMONY FOR...MILITARY BRASS BANDS OF SEVENTEEN INSTRUMENTS / Eaton, E K – New York: Firth & Hall, 1846. "All the pieces in this sett with the single exception of No. 10, may be played by a band of eight instruments." In parts. MUSIC 1983, Item 2 – 1 – us L of C Photodup [780]

TWELVE PIONEER MISSIONARIES / Smith, George Adam – London, New York: Thomas Nelson, 1900 – 1mf – us A.T.L.A. [240]

TWELVE SELECT SERMONS / Moody, Dwight Lyman – Chicago: F H Revell, 1881, c1880 – 1mf – 9 – 0-8370-9405-4 – 1986-3405 – us A.T.L.A. [240]

TWELVE SERMONS / Mann, Horace – Boston: Ticknor and Fields, 1861, c1860 – 1mf – us A.T.L.A. [240]

TWELVE SOLOS FOR A GERMAN FLUTE OR VIOLIN, WITH A THOROUGH BASS FOR THE HARPSICHORD OR VIOLONCELLE... / Vinci, L – London: I Walsh, [ca 1746] – 1 – us Sibley [780]

TWELVE TALES: WITH A HEADPIECE, TAILPIECE, AND AN INTERMEZZO: BEING SELECT STORIES / Allen, Grant – London: G. Richards, 1899. 05083. (Pre-1900 Canadiana) – 9 – cn C.I.H.M. [830]

TWELVE TALKS ON CHRISTIANITY (CCC156) = CHI TU CHIAO SHIH ERH CHIANG / Ho, Shih-ming – (In Chinese) – 1st ed. Hong Kong: Council on Christian Literature for Overseas Chinese, 1955 – 1r – 1 – 1984-B500 – us A.T.L.A. [240]

TWELVE YEARS OF A SOLDIER'S LIFE IN INDIA: BEING EXTRACTS FROM THE LETTERS OF THE LATE MAJOR W.S.R. HODSON. / Hodson, William Stephen Raikes – Ed. by his brother, Rev. George H. Hodson. 3rd & enl. ed. London: J.W. Parker & Son, 1859. xix,412p – 1 – us U.W. Library [950]

TWENTIETH ANNIVERSARY PUBLICATION OF THE UNION GIRLS' SCHOOL, HANGCHOW (CCC139) = HUNG TAO ER SHIH CHOU CHI NIEN K'AN / Union Girls' School (Hangchow, China) – (In Chinese) – [s.l: s.n, 1932] – 1r – 1 – 1984-B500 – us A.T.L.A. [370]

TWENTIETH CENTURY – v1-179 1877-1972 1; v178-179 5,6 – us UMI [300]

TWENTIETH CENTURY – v. 1-179. 1877-1972 – 1,5,6 us Princeton Micro [320]

TWENTIETH CENTURY ART – (Individual titles not listed separately) – 669 catalogues on 787mf – 9 – £4,130.00 – uk Chadwyck [700]

TWENTIETH CENTURY COMPOSERS, PART 1 : THE MANUSCRIPTS OF SIR MICHAEL TIPPETT, SIR ARTHUR BLISS AND GERALD FINZI – 1 – us Primary [780]

TWENTIETH CENTURY FARMER – Omaha, NE. -w. Sep 1871-Mar 1872, scattered issues missing; Jan 1873-Dec 1875; May 1876-Dec 1886; Mar 1887; Jul 1887-May 1918 – 1 – us NE Hist [071]

TWENTIETH CENTURY HISTORY AND BIOGRAPHICAL RECORD OF CRAWFORD COUNTY / Home Authors (sic) – Chicago: Lewis Publ. Co., 1905. Kansas Reel 8. (The Cox Library Collection) – 5 – us Americana [978]

A TWENTIETH CENTURY HISTORY AND BIOGRAPHICAL RECORD OF NORTH AND WEST TEXAS / Paddock, BB – Chicago: Lewis Publ. Co., 1906. v1, Texas Reel 7. v2, Texas Reel 8. (The Cox Library Collection) – 5 – us Americana [978]

A TWENTIETH CENTURY HISTORY OF SOUTHWEST TEXAS – Chicago, New York, Los Angeles, 1907. 2v. Texas Reel 9. (The Cox Library Collection) – 5 – us Americana [978]

TWENTIETH CENTURY IMPRESSIONS OF NATAL : ITS PEOPLE, COMMERCE, INDUSTRIES AND RESOURCES – Natal: Lloyd's Greater Britain Pub, 1906 – us Res Libr [960]

TWENTIETH CENTURY IMPRESSIONS OF THE ORANGE RIVER COLONY : ITS HISTORY, PEOPLE, COMMERCE, INDUSTRIES AND RESOURCES – Pretoria, State Library, 1978. Orig. publ., Natal: Lloyd's Greater Britain Publishing Company, 1906. (Microfiche Reprint Series no.3). 17 fiche, 1 printed booklet – 9 – sa State Libr [960]

TWENTIETH CENTURY INTERPRETATION OF PAUL'S EPISTLE TO THE EPHESIANS / Bender, Henry Richard – Cincinnati: Western Methodist Book Concern, 1905 – 1mf – 9 – 0-8370-2260-6 – 1985-0260 – us A.T.L.A. [220]

TWENTIETH CENTURY LEGAL TREATISES – 9 – us Primary [340]

TWENTIETH CENTURY LITERATURE – v1-1955- 1; v17- 5,6; v21- 9 – us UMI [410]

TWENTIETH CENTURY POLITICAL EPHEMERA. PART 1, SOUTH AFRICA / Institute of Commonwealth Studies. University of London – African Series. Pamphlets, etc. issued by political parties (95mf), trade unions (39mf) and pressure groups (49mf) – 9 – £750.00 – uk Altair [320]

TWENTIETH CENTURY POLITICAL EPHEMERA. PART 2, CENTRAL AFRICA / Institute of Commonwealth Studies. University of London – African Series. Pamphlets etc. issued by political parties, trade unions and pressure groups – 111mf – 9 – £450.00 – uk Altair [320]

TWENTIETH CENTURY POLITICAL EPHEMERA: PART 3, EAST AFRICA / Institute of Commonwealth Studies. University of London – African Studies. Pamphlets etc. Issued by Political Parties, Trade Unions and Pressure Groups – 69mf – 9 – £275.00 – uk Altair [320]

TWENTIETH CENTURY POLITICAL EPHEMERA: PART 4, WEST AFRICA / ed by Institute of Commonwealth Studies. University of London – African Studies. Pamphlets etc. Issued by Political Parties, Trade Unions and Pressure Groups – 60mf – 9 – £240.00 – uk Altair [320]

TWENTIETH CENTURY RELIGIOUS PERIODICALS COLLECTION – Selected, with emphasis on "third-world" countries – 1 – £3,500.00 – uk World [073]

TWENTIETH CENTURY THEATRE PERIODICALS – Part One: The Playgoer, 1901-1904, and Play Pictorial, 1902-39 – 1 – us Primary [790]

TWENTIETH-CENTURY EUROPEAN PAINTINGS : A. JAMES SPEYER / Donnell, Courtney Graham – (82p accompanying text) – 1980 – 4 color mf – 15 – $72.00f – 0-226-68804-6 – us Chicago [750]

TWENTY CHARGES AGAINST THE METHODISTS ANSWERED BY THE WORD OF GOD, FOR THEIR ENCOURAGEMENT AND CONVICTION OF THEIR ENEMIES / Barnes, J – Carmarthen, 1764 – 1mf – 9 – MP-429/1 – ne IDC [240]

TWENTY YEARS AMONG THE MEXICANS : A NARRATIVE OF MISSIONARY LABOR / Rankin, Melinda – St Louis: Christian Pub, c1875 – 1mf – 9 – 0-8370-6602-6 – 1986-0602 – us A.T.L.A. [240]

TWENTY YEARS' HISTORY: OF THE WOMAN'S HOME MISSIONARY SOCIETY OF THE METHODIST EPISCOPAL CHURCH, 1880-1900 / Tomkinson, Laura E – 1903 – 9 – us A.T.L.A. [240]

TWENTY YEARS OF CONGRESS : FROM LINCOLN TO GARFIELD / Blaine, James Gillespie – (With a review of the events which lead to the political revolution of 1860) – Norwich, CT. 2v. 1884-86 – 1r – 1 – us Ross [976]

TWENTY YEARS OF PIONEER MISSIONS IN NYASALAND : A HISTORY OF MORAVIAN MISSIONS IN GERMAN EAST AFRICA / Hamilton, J Taylor – Bethlehem, Pa.: Society for Propagating the Gospel, 1912 – 1mf – us A.T.L.A. [240]

TWENTY-FIVE SERMONS: A MEMORIAL OF TWENTY-FIVE YEARS' MINISTRY / Cordner, John – s.l.: s.n., 1868 (Montreal: J. Lovell). 00239. (Pre-1900 Canadiana) – 9 – cn C.I.H.M. [971]

TWENTY-FIVE YEARS IN SEVENTEEN PRISONS. THE LIFE STORY OF AN EX-CONVICT. – London. 1903 – 1 – us Res Libr [920]

TWENTY-FIVE YEARS OF PRESBYTERIAN...HUNGARIANS; OUR MAGYAR PRESBYTERIANS / Dikovics, John – 9 – $50.00 – us Presbyterian [240]

TWENTY-FIVE YEARS OF THE JEWISH NATIONAL FUND / Jewish National Fund (Keren Kayemeth Leisrael) – Jerusalem. BJ-28-37 1 – 9 – ne IDC [956]

TWENTY-FOUR SERMONS PREACH'D AT THE PARISH CHURCH OF ST MARY LE BOW, LONDON, IN THE YEARS 1739, 1740, 1741... : AND EIGHT SERMONS PREACH'D AT THE CATHEDRAL CHURCH OF ST. PAUL IN THE YEARS 1738 AND 1739... / Twells, L – London, 1743.-2v – 5mf – 9 – MP-301/1 – ne IDC [240]

TWENTY-ONE YEARS IN S. GEORGE'S MISSION : AN ACCOUNT OF ITS ORIGIN, PROGRESS, AND WORKS OF CHARITY; WITH AN APPENDIX / Lowder, CF – London: Rivingtons, 1877 – 1mf – us A.T.L.A. [240]

Twesten, A *see* MATTHIAS FLACIUS ILLYRICUS

TWI MANUSCRIPTS, 1855-1907 / Christaller, Johann Gottlieb – Basel: Walter Rentsch, 1977 – us Res Libr [090]

TWICE A WEEK COURANT – Delphos. Ohio. 1908- – 1 – us UMI [071]

TWICE A WEEK GUARD – Eugene OR. Oct 3 1910-Mar 5 1914 – 1 – us U.O. Library [071]

TWICE AROUND THE WORLD WITH ALEXANDER, PRINCE OF GOSPEL SINGERS / Davis, George T B – New York: Christian Herald, c1907 – 1mf – us A.T.L.A. [240]

TWICE BOUGHT, A TALE OF THE OREGON GOLD FIELDS / Ballantyne, Robert Michael – London: J. Nisbet, 1884?. 07479. (Pre-1900 Canadiana) – 9 – cn C.I.H.M. [830]

TWICE TAKEN: AN HISTORICAL ROMANCE OF THE MARITIME BRITISH PROVINCES / Hall, Charles Winslow – Boston: Lee and Shephard, 1867. 05335. (Pre-1900 Canadiana) – 9 – cn C.I.H.M. [830]

TWICKENHAM AND BARNES HERALD *see* RICHMOND HERALD

TWIGS – 1973- 1,5,6; 1975- 9 – us UMI [410]

TWILIGHT COUNTRY / Faldbakken, Knut – 1993 – 216p – 9 – 92-3-102855-3 – Co-published with Peter Owen, which has exclusive sales rights in the UK – fr UNESCO [830]

THE TWILIGHT OF FAITH / Frame, Elizabeth – Toronto: Hunter, Rose, 1872. 03169. (Pre-1900 Canadiana) – 9 – cn C.I.H.M. [971]

TWIN CITY NEWS – New Philadelphia. Ohio. 1899-1900 – 1 – us UMI [071]

TWIN CITY NEWS-RECORD – Neenah-Menasha. Wis. 1961- – 1 – us UMI [071]

TWIN CITY POST – Palmer, NE. -w. Mar 1972 to date – 1 – us NE Hist [071]

TWIN CITY TIMES – Port Alberni, British Columbia, CN. Jan 1966-Nov 1967 – 3r – 1 – cn Commonwealth Micro [072]

TWIN-CITY TIMES – Gering, NE. -w. Oct 1913-Nov 1914 – 1 – us NE Hist [071]

Twing, Mary A E *see* WOMAN'S WORK IN THE AMERICAN CHURCH

Twining, William H G *see* SOME FACTS IN THE HISTORY OF THE TWINING FAMILY

Twiss, Travers *see*
- BLACK BOOK OF THE ADMIRALITY (RS55)
- HENRICI DE BRACTON DE LEGIBUS ET CONSUETUDINES ANGLIAE LIBRI QUINQUE IN VARIOS TRACTATUS DISTINCTI (RS70)

Twist, Pete W *see* TEAM-BASED ATTITUDE

Twitchell, Ralph E *see* THE LEADING FACTS OF NEW MEXICAN HISTORY

TWO ADDRESSES DELIVERED BY ALUMNI OF FISK UNIVERSITY : IN CONNECTION WITH THE ANNIVERSARY EXERCISES OF THEIR ALMA MATER, JUNE, 1898 – (W E B Dubois on "Careers Open to College-Bred Negroes" and Rev H H Proctor on "The Fisk Idea") – 1898 – 1r – 1 – us Ross [370]

TWO ADMIRALS: ADMIRAL OF THE FLEET SIR FAIRFAX MORESBY, G.C.B. (1786-1877), AND HIS SON, JOHN MORESBY : A RECORD OF LIFE AND SERVICE IN THE BRITISH NAVY FOR A HUNDRED YEARS / Moresby, John – 1909 – 9 – $20.00 – uk Libr Preservation [920]

TWO ANCIENT CHRISTOLOGIES / Sellers, Robert Victor – A study in the Christological thought of the schools of Alexandria and Antioch in the early history of Chrjstian doctrine. 1940 – 1 – us A.T.L.A. [240]

TWO ASPECTS OF TRUSTEESHIP : PRESENTED TO THE FIRST TRUSTEESHIP COUNCIL / US Dept of State – Dept of State publ 2850, 1947 – 1mf – 9 – $1.50 – LLMC 82-100F Title 95 – us L.L.M.C. [324]

THE TWO BABYLONS / Hislop, Alexander – 1862 – 1 – us Res Libr [900]

TWO BOOKLETS RELATIVE TO THE BEGINNINGS OF SOUTHERN BAPTIST MISSIONS IN NIAGARA FALLS, NY, 1953-59 / Boroughs, R Zig – 1 – 5.00 – us Baptist [240]

THE TWO BOOKS OF THE KINGS : IN THE REVISED VERSION / Barnes, William Emery – (Includes index) – Cambridge: University Press, 1908 – 1mf – 9 – 0-8370-6007-9 – 1986-0007 – us A.T.L.A. [220]

TWO CAMBRIDGE DIVINES OF THE SEVENTEENTH CENTURY : LECTURES / Swete, Henry Barclay – London: S.P.C.K., 1913 – 1mf – us A.T.L.A. [240]

TWO CAMPAIGNS : MADAGASCAR AND ASHANTEE / Burleigh, Bennet – London, 1896 – 1r – 1 – us Ross [355]

TWO CENTURIES / South Carolina. First Baptist Church – 1683-1883. Supp. ed. by H. A. Tupper – 1 – 12.74 – us Baptist [240]

TWO CENTURIES OF BRITISH PERIODICALS, 1732-1914 / ed by Fader, Daniel & Bornstein, George – (Reproduces 22 periodicals. AACR1 cataloging available) – 266r – 1 – $16,710.00 – us UMI [073]

TWO CENTURIES OF THE FIRST BAPTIST CHURCH OF SOUTH CAROLINA / Tupper, H A – 1683-1883. With Supplement. 364p – 1 – 12.74 – us Baptist [240]

TWO CHARGES DELIVERED TO THE CLERGY OF THE DIOCESE OF WORCESTER IN THE YEARS 1763 AND 1766,... : [AND] A CHARGE RELATIVE TO THE ARTICLES OF THE CHURCH OF ENGLAND DELIVERED / Tottie, J – [Oxford, 1766] – 1mf – 9 – MP-440/1 – ne IDC [240]

TWO CURRICULAR SETTINGS OF A HIV EDUCATION UNIT RELATED TO SECONDARY SCHOOL STUDENTS' HIV KNOWLEDGE AND ATTITUDE / Clark, JK – 1991 – 2mf – 9 – $8.00 – us Microform Publ [370]

TWO DECADES OF EDUCATION IN RAJASTHAN 1950-1971 / India. Rajasthan. Directorate of Primary and Secondary Education – Bikaner, 1971 – 1mf – 9 – DE-555/1 – ne IDC [370]

TWO DUETTS FOR ONE PERFORMER / Brooks, J – London: Author, 1800? – 1 – us Sibley [780]

THE TWO EMPIRES : THE CHURCH AND THE WORLD / Westcott, Brooke Foss – London: Macmillan, 1909 – 1mf – us A.T.L.A. [240]

THE TWO EPISTLES OF PAUL TO TIMOTHY = PASTORALBRIEFE / Oosterzee, Johannes Jacobus van – (In English. Includes bibliographies) – New York: Charles Scribner, c1868 – 1mf – 9 – 0-8370-6769-3 – 1986-0769 – us A.T.L.A. [220]

TWO ESSAYS ELUCIDATING THE GEOMETRICAL PRINCIPLES OF GOTHIC ARCHITECTURE / Wallen, W – O 1138 1. 1842 – 9 – ne IDC [720]

TWO ESSAYS ON BIBLICAL AND ON ECCLESIASTICAL MIRACLES / Newman, John Henry – 9th ed. London: Longmans, Green, 1890 – 1mf – 9 – 0-8370-4575-4 – 1985-2575 – us A.T.L.A. [220]

TWO FIFTEENTH CENTURY COOKERY-BOOKS / ed by Austin, Thomas – London: N. Trubner. 1888. Harleian ms. 279 (c. 1430), & Harleian ms. 4016 (c. 1450), with extracts from Ashmole ms. 1429, Laud. ms. 553, & Douce ms. 55. Early English Text Society, Original Series, no 91. 151 p – 1r – 1 – us U.W. Library [640]

TWO FRONTIER CHURCHES: A PAPER READ BEFORE THE CANADIAN INSTITUTE AT NIAGARA, ON THE 2ND DAY OF JULY, 1890? / Carnochan, Janet – 02821. (Pre-1900 Canadiana) – 9 – cn C.I.H.M. [240]

THE TWO GREAT COMMANDMENTS / Dewey, Orville – 1876 – 9 – us A.T.L.A. [240]

THE TWO HAGUE CONFERENCES / Choate, J H – London, 1913 – 2mf – 1 – ILM-4086/1 – ne IDC [327]

TWO KNAPSACKS: A NOVEL OF CANADIAN SUMMER LIFE / Campbell, John – Toronto: Williamson, 1892. 00387. (Pre-1900 Canadiana) – 9 – cn C.I.H.M. [830]

TWO LECTURES ON THE CONNECTION BETWEEN THE BIBLICAL AND PHYSICAL HISTORY OF MAN / Nott, Josiah Clark – Delivered...Louisiana University, Dec 1848. New York: Bartlett and Welford, 1849.146p – 1 – us U.W. Library [910]

TWO LECTURES ON THEISM : DELIVERED ON THE OCCASION OF THE SESQUICENTENNIAL CELEBRATION OF PRINCETON UNIVERSITY / Seth Pringle-Pattison, Andrew – New York: Charles Scribner, 1897 – 1mf – 9 – 0-8370-5231-9 – 1985-3231 – us A.T.L.A. [210]

TWO LETTER BOOKS / The Wakefield Opera House. Yorkshire – 1892-96 – 2r – 1 – uk Microform Academic [780]

TWO LETTERS CONCERNING THE METHODISTS, ONE TO THE RT. REV. THE LORD B—P OF M—H, THE OTHER TO HIS LORDSHIP'S V—R G—L / Booker, M – Dublin, 1751 – 1mf – 9 – MP-355/1 – ne IDC [240]

TWO LETTERS OF MR. GEORGE WHITEFIELD UPON THE FALSE CHRISTS AND FALSE PROPHETS, WORKERS OF INIQUITY, MATT. VII. 15, 23,... – London, 1756 – 1mf – 9 – MP-370/1 – ne IDC [240]

TWO LETTERS TO THE LORD BISHOP OF ONTARIO ON THE QUESTION, IS LAY BAPTISM VALID? / Forest, Charles – Ottawa: Citizen Printing and Publishing Co., 1876. 03149. (Pre-1900 Canadiana) – 9 – cn C.I.H.M. [971]

TWO LETTERS TO THE REV. THOMAS COKE, LL.D., CURATE OF SOUTH PETHERTON, WRITTEN WITH A FRIENDLY INTENTION OF CONVINCING HIM OF SOME GROSS ERRORS IN HIS CLERICAL CONDUCT / Thomas, J – London, 1777 – 1mf – 9 – MP-521/1 – ne IDC [240]

TWO LITTLE WOODEN SHOES / Ouida – British Fiction Archive: Unit 3 – 9 – uk Bell [830]

TWO MILE SWAMP BAPTIST CHURCH. ORANGEBURG COUNTY. SOUTH CAROLINA : CHURCH RECORDS – 1844-80, 1964-84. 450p – 1 – $20.25 – us Baptist [240]

TWO MILLIONS / Butler, William A – New York: D Appleton & Co, 1858 – 1mf – 9 – $1.50 – LLMC 91-017 – us L.L.M.C. [810]

TWO MINDS WITH BUT A SINGLE THOUGHT : ADOLF HITLER AND FRANCISCO FRANCO / ed by Reissig, Herman F – N.Y. 1938? Fiche W 1130. Blodgett Collection of Spanish Civil War Pamphlets – 9 – us H.U. College Libr [946]

TWO NOTEBOOKS OF THOMAS CARLYLE FROM 23D MARCH, 1822, TO 16TH MAY, 1832 / Carlyle, Thomas; ed by Norton, Charles Eliot – New York: The Grolier Club, 1898 – 1 roll – 1 – 1-55879-839-0 – uk Libr Preservation [800]

TWO NOVELS AND A COLLECTION OF KPELLE TALES / Sankawulo, Wilton – 1 – $39.50 – us African Imprint [830]

TWO OFFENDERS / Ouida – British Fiction Archive: Unit 3 – 9 – uk Bell [830]

THE TWO PRODIGALS / Vincent, Marvin Richardson – New York: A.D.F. Randolph, 1876.1 fiche – 9 – us A.T.L.A. [240]

TWO REDISCOVERED WORKS OF ANCIENT CHRISTIAN LITERATURE : GREGORY OF NYSSA AND MACARIUS / Jaeger, W – Leiden, 1954 – 8mf – 8 – ne Slangenburg [240]

TWO SERMONS / Boardman, Henry Augustus – Philadelphia: Inquirer Book and Job Print, 1873 – 1mf – us A.T.L.A. [240]

THE TWO ST JOHNS OF THE NEW TESTAMENT / Stalker, James – New York: American Tract Society, 1895. 1 fiche – 9 – us A.T.L.A. [240]

TWO STUDIES IN AFRICAN NUTRITION / Thompson, B – 2mf – 7 – uk Microform Academic [613]

TWO STUDIES ON ETHNIC GROUP RELATIONS IN AFRICA : SENEGAL, THE UNITED REPUBLIC OF TANZANIA – 1974 – 156p – 9 – 92-3-101101-4 – fr UNESCO [305]

TWO STUDIES ON UNEMPLOYMENT AMONG EDUCATED YOUNG PEOPLE = DEUX ETUDES SUR LE CHOMAGE DES JEUNES INSTRUITS / Morio, Simone & Zoctizoum, Yarrise – 1980 – 9 – 92-3-101618-0 – fr UNESCO [331]

TWO SWORDS / Dalton, L H – In Indonesian. SE-11,259 1. 1964 – 9 – ne IDC [950]

TWO TASKS OF ALLIED FORCES IN INDONESIA FULFILLED / Indonesia. Kementerian Penerangan – SE-11,923 1. 1946 – 9 – ne IDC [324]

TWO TEXTS IN THE LANGUAGE OF TONGOA ISLAND IN THE SHEPHERD ISLANDS GROUP, VANUATU : NATULAKEANA NI NAWASIANA NI TUAI [THE BEGINNING OF WORK LONG AGO] AND RANGINATULATEAN WAINA TEATERE ERUUMAI [IN THE BEGINNING WHEN WHITE PEOPLE FIRST CAME] / Fak-Ao Tinapua Mata, Dick – 1944 – 1r – 1 – PMB 1125 – at Pacific Mss [490]

TWO THOUSAND YEARS OF MISSIONS BEFORE CAREY : BASED UPON AND EMBODYING MANY OF THE EARLIEST EXTANT ACCOUNTS / Barnes, Lemuel Call – (Includes index) – Chicago: Christian Culture Press, 1900 – 2mf – 9 – 0-8370-6242-X – 1986-0242 – us A.T.L.A. [240]

TWO TREATISES CONCERNING THE PRESERVATION OF EYESIGHT / Bailey, W – M-296. 1616 – 9 – ne IDC [615]

TWO VISITS TO THE TEA COUNTRIES OF CHINA AND THE BRITISH TEA PLANTATIONS IN THE HIMALAYA; WITH A NARRATIVE OF ADVENTURES, AND...DESCRIPTION OF THE TEA PLANT. / Fortune, Robert – 3rd ed. London: J. Murray, 1853. 2v. illus., plates, map – 1 – us U.W. Library [950]

TWO WORLDS ARE OURS / Macmillan, Hugh – London:Macmillan, 1880 – 1mf – 9 – 0-8370-4249-6 – 1985-2249 – us A.T.L.A. [210]

THE TWO WORLDS WEEKLY SUPPLEMENT – Maryborough, Australia. -w. 30 June 1876-5 July 1878. 1 reel – 1 – uk British Libr Newspaper [072]

TWO YEARS IN HELL OR TWENTY MONTHS IN THE PRISON PENS OF THE NORTH, 24 JUN 1865 / Rowan, W H – 1 – 5.00 – us Baptist [978]

TWO YEARS OF AMERICAN AID TO SPAIN / Medical Bureau and North American Committee to Aid Spanish Democracy – N.Y., 1938? Fiche W 1039. (Blodgett Collection of Spanish Civil War Pamphlets) – 9 – us H.U. College Libr [946]

TWO YEARS OF AMERICAN AID TO SPAIN / Medical Bureau and North American Committee to Aid Spanish Democracy – N.Y. 1938? Fiche W1039. (Blodgett Collection of Spanish Civil War Pamphlets) – 9 – us H.U. College Libr [946]

TWO YEARS OF HEROIC STRUGGLE OF THE SPANISH PEOPLE / Dimitrov, Georgi – NY, 1938. Fiche W 839. (Blodgett Collection of Spanish Civil War Pamphlets) – 9 – us H.U. College Libr [946]

TWOFOLD BAY MAGNET – Jun 5 1908-Oct 23 1911 – 1 – at Pascoe [072]

THE TWOFOLD LIFE : OR, CHRIST'S WORK FOR US AND CHRIST'S WORK IN US / Gordon, Adoniram Judson – New York: Fleming H Revell, c1883 – 1mf – 9 – 0-8370-9287-6 – 1986-3287 – us A.T.L.A. [240]

TWONDER-BOECK: WAER IN DAT VAN DER WERLDT AEN VERSLOTEN GHEOPENBAERT IS. OPT NIEUW GHECORRIGEERT VNDE VERMEERDERT BY DEN AUTHEUR SELUE / Joris, David – 1551. BME-363 1 – 9 – ne IDC [240]
TWONDERBOECK. WIE EEN DIE ICK, SEYT DIE HERE, SENDEN SAL ONTFANGT IN MINEN NAEM, DY ONTFANGT MY / Joris, David – Deventer, Dirk van Borne. 1542. BME-362 1 – 9 – ne IDC [240]
TWO-YEAR COLLEGE MATHEMATICS JOURNAL – v1- 1970- 1; v6- 5,6 – us UMI [510]
TWO-YEAR PLAN OF ECONOMIC DEVELOPMENT FOR BURMA / Burma. Economic Planning Board – Rangoon. 1948 – 9 – ne IDC [338]
TWP. TRUSTEES RELIEF RECORDS / Wood County. Ohio. County Home – 1856-1858 – 1r – 1 – $32.50r – us Archival [324]
Tyack, G S *see* LORE AND LEGEND OF THE ENGLISH CHURCH
THE TYBO WEEKLY SUN – Tybo, NV. 13 Sep 1879 – 1r – 1 – $50.00 – U04775 – us Library Micro [071]
TYCHO BRAHE'S SCIENTIFIC ACHIEVEMENTS / Dreyer, J L E – 1890 – 10mf – 7 – uk Microform Academic [500]
TYDENNI HLASATEL – Chicago, Ill. July 20, 1892-July 1893 – 1 – app – us Res Libr [071]
Tyerman, J *see* FREETHOUGHT VINDICATED, OR, INFIDEL CHRISTIANITY V. HONEST UNBELIEF
Tyerman, L *see* THE OXFORD METHODISTS
TYGER RIVER BAPTIST CHURCH. GREENVILLE COUNTY. TAYLORS, SOUTH CAROLINA : CHURCH RECORDS – (1,401p) – 1801-1911, 1958-1990 – 2r – 1 – $63.05 – us Baptist [240]
TYGODNIK ILLUSTROWANY – Warsaw, 1898-1938 – 16r – 1 – us Ross [073]
TYGODNIK ILLUSTROWANY – Warsaw. 1898-1938. Incomplete – 1 – us NY Public [073]
TYGODNIK ILUSTROWANY – London, UK. 15 May 1949-16 Mar 1952 – 1 – uk British Libr Newspaper [072]
TYGODNIK MORSKI – Szczecin, Poland. -w. July 1958-Dec 1970. 13 reels – 1 – uk British Libr Newspaper [947]
TYGODNIK POLSKI – London, UK. 16 Mar 1946-24 Oct 1950 – 1 – uk British Libr Newspaper [072]
TYGODNIK POLSKI – London, UK. 27 Jan-22 Dec 1918 – 1 – uk British Libr Newspaper [072]
TYGODNIK POLSKI – New York, NY. -w. 17 Jan 1943-1 June 1947. 3 reels – 1 – uk British Libr Newspaper [071]
TYGODNIK POWSZECHNY – (1995-98 2r per y $170. 1945-94 1r per two y $85r) – Poland, 1999- – 2r per y – 1 – $160.00 standing order – us Ross [072]
TYGODNIK POWSZECHNY – Cracow, Poland. -w. Oct 1948-May 1956; Jan 1957-Dec 1970. 19 reels – 1 – uk British Libr Newspaper [943]
TYGODNIK SOLIDARNOSC – (1993 1r $85. 1994-98 2r per y $170y) – Poland, 1999- – 2r per y – 1 – $160.00 standing order – us Ross [072]
TYGODNIK WARSZAWSKI – Warsaw. Poland. -w. 26 May-25 Dec 1946, 5 Jul 1947-5 Sep 1948. (2 reels) – 1 – uk British Libr Newspaper [943]
TYGODNIK ZACHODNI – Poznan. Poland. -w. Dec 1956-Mar 1957, Jan-Dec 1958. (1 reel) – 1 – uk British Libr Newspaper [072]
Tyler, B B et al *see* A HISTORY OF THE DISCIPLES OF CHRIST, THE SOCIETY OF FRIENDS, THE UNITED BRETHREN IN CHRIST AND THE EVANGELICAL ASSOCIATION
Tyler, Bennet *see*
- THE DOCTRINE OF THE SAINT'S PERSEVERANCE, VINDICATED AND ESTABLISHED, 1820
- LETTERS ON THE ORIGIN AND PROGRESS OF THE NEW HAVEN THEOLOGY

Tyler, Charles Mellen *see* BASES OF RELIGIOUS BELIEF
TYLER COUNTY JOURNAL – Sistersville. West Virginia. -w. 1903-49, 1955-64 – 1 – us UMI [071]
TYLER COUNTY STAR – Middlebourne. West Virginia. 1877-1917 – 1 – us UMI [071]
TYLER DEMOCRAT – Sistersville. West Virginia. 1888 – 1 – us UMI [071]
Tyler, George W *see* HISTORY OF BELL COUNTY
Tyler, John *see* PAPERS
Tyler, John M *see* GROWTH AND EDUCATION
Tyler, Lyon G *see* ENCYCLOPEDIA OF VIRGINIA BIOGRAPHY
Tyler, Moses Coit *see* PATRICK HENRY
TYLER STAR-NEWS – Middlebourne. West Virginia. 1900-1908; 1909; 1911-1914; 1916-1937 – apply; 2UM; 1 – us UMI [071]
TYLER STAR-NEWS – Sistersville. West Virginia. 1958-1965 – 1 – us UMI [071]
Tyler, Thomas *see*
- CHRIST THE LORD: THE REVEALER OF GOD...WITH A REPLY TO BISHOP COLENSO ...JEHOVAH
- JEHOVAH, THE REDEEMER GOD

Tyler, William Seymour *see* MEMOIR OF REV. HENRY LOBDELL, M.D., LATE MISSIONARY OF THE AMERICAN BOARD AT MOSUL
TYLER'S REPORTS / Vermont. Supreme Court – (A Pre-NRS title) – v1-2. 1800-1803 (all publ) – 13mf – 9 – $19.50 – LLMC 90-309 – us L.L.M.C. [340]
Tylor, Charles *see*
- THE CAMISARDS
- EARLY CHURCH HISTORY

Tylor, Charles, Backhouse, Edward *see* WITNESSES FOR CHRIST AND MEMORIALS OF CHURCH LIFE FROM THE FOURTH TO THE THIRTEENTH CENTURY
Tylor, J J *see* WALL DRAWINGS AND MONUMENTS OF EL KAB
Tymme, Thomas *see* A DIALOGVE PHILOSOPHICALL
Tymms, Thomas Vincent *see* THE MYSTERY OF GOD
Tynan, Katharine *see* BALLADS AND LYRICS
TYNDALE BULLETIN – 1956-90 (complete) – 3r – 1 – ATLA S0629 – us A.T.L.A. [073]
Tyndall, John *see*
- FARADAY AS A DISCOVERER
- THE GLACIERS OF THE ALPS
- HOURS OF EXERCISE IN THE ALPS

TYNE CHYLDE / Parker, Joseph – 1886 – 9 – us A.T.L.A. [240]
TYNEMOUTH GAZETTE ETC – England.24 Jun-24 Sept 1870; 24 Jan 1871-3 Aug 1872. -w. 1 1/2 reels – 1 – uk British Libr Newspaper [072]
TYNEMOUTH GUARDIAN – North Shields, England. 13 Jul-30 Nov 1861. -w. 1/4 reel – 1 – uk British Libr Newspaper [072]
TYNEMOUTH SENTINEL ETC – England.Mar 1895-1897; Mar-Dec 1898; Mar-Dec 1899. -w. 1/4 reel – 1 – uk British Libr Newspaper [072]
TYNESIDE DAILY ECHO – (Tyneside Echo). Newcastle-upon-Tyne. England. -d. 20 Jan 1880-30 Aug 1888. (17 reels) – 1 – uk British Libr Newspaper [072]
TYNESIDE WEEKLY NEWS – Tynemouth, England. -w. 4 Dec 1908-22 Jan 1909. 13 ft – 1 – uk British Libr Newspaper [072]
TYPE AND PRESS – Toronto: Miller & Richard, [1898?-189- or 19–] – 9 – cn C.I.H.M. [680]
TYPE CERTIFICATE DATA SHEETS AND SPECIFICATIONS / U.S. Department of Transportation – v1-6. 1994. Basic manual and 11 cumulative updates issued monthly – 9 – $117.00y in US $146.25 outside – S-N 950-053-00000-3. Sub-list ID-TCDSM – us Gov't Printing [324]
TYPE HERBARIUM OF MUSEUM BOTANICUM HAUNIENSE – Copenhagen – 240mf – 9 – 2204/2 – ne IDC [580]
TYPE OF THE TIMES – A Journal of the Writing and Spelling Reform. Cincinnati. v. 1-12. July 1848-Dec 1859; & Shorthand suppl. v. 1-4, no. 2. 1850-1854. Cincinnati – 1 – us NY Public [370]
TYPE OF THE TIMES : A JOURNAL OF THE WRITING AND SPELLING REFORM – Cincinnati, 1848-59 – 3r – 1 – us Ross [420]
TYPED TRAVEL DIARY / Ross, Mary Jane – 1892-1902. 10 fiches – 9 – us South Carolina Historical [910]
TYPES AND CONDITIONS OF AFRO-AMERICANS IN 1900 – (photos) – 1 – 20.00 – us L of C Photodup [977]
TYPES AND SPECIAL COLLECTIONS OF THE HERBARIUM OF THE ACADEMY OF NATURAL SCIENCES OF PHILADELPHIA – (Lewis and Clark Herbaria 4mf £32.00. A.B. Lambert Herbaria 19mf £160.00. Benjamin Smith Barton Herbaria 47mf £380.00. Henry Muhlenberg Herbaria 87mf £700.00. Index £260.00) – 474mf – 9 – £2,865.00 – uk Chadwyck [580]
TYPES AND THE ANTITYPE : LECTURES DELIVERED IN LENT 1862 AND 1863 / Trevor, George – London:J. & C. Mozley; Oxford. J.H. & James Parker, 1864 – 1mf – 9 – 0-8370-5573-3 – 1985-3573 – us A.T.L.A. [240]
TYPES OF AMERICAN CHARACTER / Bradford, Gamaliel – New York: Macmillan, 1895. ix,210p. Reprinted in part from the Atlantic Monthly – 1 – us U.W. Library [305]
TYPES OF CHRISTIAN SAINTLINESS / Inge, William Ralph – London; New York: Longmans, Green, 1915 – 1mf – us A.T.L.A. [240]
TYPES OF ETHICAL THEORY / Martineau, James – (Includes index) – 3rd rev ed. Oxford: Clarendon Press, 1901 – 4mf – 9 – 0-8370-6218-7 – 1986-0218 – us A.T.L.A. [170]
THE TYPES OF GENESIS BRIEFLY CONSIDERED AS REVEALING THE DEVELOPMENT OF HUMAN NATURE / Jukes, Andrew John – (Includes index) – 4th ed. New York: Thomas Whittaker, [1857?] – 2mf – 9 – 0-8370-3821-9 – 1985-1821 – us A.T.L.A. [200]
TYPES OF JEWISH-PALESTINIAN PIETY FROM 70 B.C.E. TO 70 C.E. : THE ANCIENT PIOUS MEN / Buechler, A – New York, 1968 – 5mf – 8 – ne Slangenburg [270]
TYPES OF MODERN THEOLOGY; SCHLEIERMACHER TO BARTH / Mackintosh, Hugh Ross – London: Nisbet and Co., ltd., (1952). vii,333,(1)p. First publ., 1937 – 1 – us U.W. Library [240]
TYPES OF THE SAINTLY LIFE / Turberville, Arthur C – London: E. Stock, 1891 – 1mf – us A.T.L.A. [240]
TYPESCRIPT OF TRAVEL DIARY / Aiken, Joseph Daniel – 1849. Records trip through Europe. 1 fiche – 9 – us South Carolina Historical [910]
TYPESCRIPT SERVICE RECORDS / South Carolina. Milita. First, Second and Third Regiment – War of 1812. 5 fiches – 9 – us South Carolina Historical [975]
TYPHOON AND OTHER STORIES / Conrad, Joseph – London: William Heinemann, 1903 – 1 roll – 1 – 1-55879-910-9 – uk Libr Preservation [830]
TYPICAL CHRISTIAN LEADERS / Clifford, John – London: H.Marshall, 1898 – 1mf – us A.T.L.A. [240]
TYPICAL ENGLISH CHURCHMEN FROM PARKER TO MAURICE : A SERIES OF LECTURES / ed by Collins, William Edward – London: Society for Promoting Christian Knowledge; New York: E.& J.B. Young, 1902. (The Church Historical Society; 65) – 1mf – us A.T.L.A. [240]
A TYPICAL MISSION IN CHINA / Soothill, William Edward – New York: Fleming H Revell, [1906?] – 1mf – 9 – 0-8370-6522-4 – 1986-0522 – us A.T.L.A. [240]
TYPICAL MODERN CONCEPTIONS OF GOD : OR, THE ABSOLUTE OF GERMAN ROMANTIC IDEALISM AND OF ENGLISH EVOLUTIONARY AGNOSTICISM: WITH A CONSTRUCTIVE ESSAY / Leighton, Joseph Alexander – NY: Longmans, Green, 1901 – 1mf – 9 – 0-8370-4087-6 – 1985-2087 – us A.T.L.A. [210]
TYPIST AND TYPEWRITING TRADES JOURNAL – London, UK. Mar 1906. -irr. 7 feet – 1 – uk British Libr Newspaper [650]
TYPOGRAPHIC MESSENGER – New York. v. 1-10. Nov 1865-1875 – 1 – us NY Public [070]
TYPOGRAPHICAL JOURNAL : 1889-1955 – (Coll title: Labor Union Periodicals, Pt 2) – 53r – 1 – $7,155.00 – 1-55655-313-7 – us UPA [680]
TYPOGRAPHICAL NEWS : MONTHLY NEWSLETTER OF THE CLEVELAND TYPOGRAPHICAL UNION – Cleveland, Oh. Jan 1928-Feb 1983 – 4r – 1 – us Western Res [071]
Typographical Union No 6. New York City *see*
- EXECUTIVE COMMITTEE MINUTES
- REGULAR MEETINGS MINUTES

O TYPOGRAPHO : ORGAM LITTERARIO, NOTICIOSO E BIOGRAPHICO DEDICADO A TYPOGRAPHICA PENEDENSE – Penedo, Alagoas. 16 Maio-Jul 1897 – 1,5,6 – bl Biblioteca [072]
LA TYPOLOGIE BAPTISMALE DANS L'ANCIENNE EGLISE / Lundberg, P – Leipzig/Upsala, 1942 – 5mf – 8 – Dfl22.00 – ne Slangenburg [240]
THE TYPOLOGY OF SCRIPTURE VIEWED IN CONNECTION WITH THE WHOLE SERIES OF THE DIVINE DISPENSATIONS / Fairbairn, Patrick – Funk & Wagnalls, 1900. 2v – 9 – $33.00 – us I.R.C. [240]
Typotius, J *see*
- SYMBOLA DIVINA ET HUMANA PONTIFICUM IMPERATORUM REGUM
- SYMBOLA VARIA DIVERSORUM PRINCIPUM, ARCHIDUCUM, DUCUM, COMITUM ET MARCHIONUM TOTIUS ITALIAE

TYPUS MUNDI IN QUO EIUS CALAMITATES ET PERICULA NEC NON DIVINI, HUMANIQUE AMORIS ANTIPATHIA, EMBLEMATICE PROPONUNTUR A RR.C.S.I.A – O 781. 1627 – 9 – ne IDC [999]
LE TYRAN DOMESTIQUE OU L'INTERIEUR D'UNE FAMILLE / Duval – (French Theatre Series). Paris. Vente, an XIII. 1805 – 9 – fr Hachette [820]
THE TYRANNY OF POLITICS / Freeman, John – 1fiche (29x) – 9 – 1.00f – at Libertarian Micro [320]
TYRAWLY HERALD – Ballina, Ireland. 25 Jan 1844-1 Sep 1870 – 9r – 1 – uk British Libr Newspaper [072]
Tyrensis, Willelmus *see* CHRONICON
TYRINGHAM 1759-1898 – (mf ed 1988) – 22mf – 9 – 0-87623-075-3 – us Holbrook [920]
THE TYRO – Woodstock, Ont: Adelphian Literary Society, [1872-18– or 19–] – 9 – cn C.I.H.M. [420]
Tyrol, Fritz *see* LESSINGS SPRACHLICHE REVISION SEINER JUGENDDRAMEN
TYRONE CONSTITUTION – Omagh, Ireland. Nov 1844- – 143+ r – 1 – uk British Libr Newspaper [072]
TYRONE DAILY HERALD – Tyrone, PA. -d 1887-1989. 137 rolls – 13 – $25.00r – us I.M.R. [071]
THE TYRONE HERALD – Tyrone, PA. -w 1858-1918 – 13 – $25.00r – us I.M.R. [071]
Tyrrell, George *see*
- CHRISTIANITY AT THE CROSS-ROADS
- HARD SAYINGS
- LEX CREDENDI
- LEX ORANDI
- OIL AND WINE
- THE OLD FAITH AND THE NEW WOMAN
- THROUGH SCYLLA AND CHARYBDIS

Tyrrell, J B *see*
- AN EXPEDITION THROUGH THE BARREN LANDS OF NORTHERN CANADA
- A SECOND EXPEDITION THROUGH THE BARREN LANDS OF NORTHERN CANADA

Tyrwhitt, Richard St John *see* THE NATURAL THEOLOGY OF NATURAL BEAUTY
TYSIACHA MATERIALY I DOKUMENTY, 1905-1907 – v1-8. 1925-28 – 1r – 1 – us Ross [947]
Tyson, E *see* ORANG-OUTANG
Tyssot de Patot, Simon *see*
- LA VIE, LES AVENTURES ET LE VOYAGE DE GROENLAND DU R. P. CORDELIER PIERRE DE MESANGE, AVEC UNE RELATION BIEN CIRCONSTANCIEE DE L'ORIGINE, DE L'HISTOIRE, DES MOEURS ET DU PARADIS DES HABITANTS DU POLE ARCTIQUE
- VOYAGES ET AVENTURES DE JACQUES MASSE

TYSYACHA – 1905 g.; Materialy i Dokumenty. Moscow Leningrad. v. 1-8 1925-1928 – 1 – us NY Public [999]
Tyszkiewicz, Alexandra *see* LA VILLE DE QUEBEC VUE PAR LE VOYAGEUR, 1776-1960
Tytler, Alexander F *see* AN ESSAY ON MILITARY LAW AND THE PRACTICE OF COURTS-MARTIAL
Tytler, Patrick Fraser *see* LIFE OF SIR WALTER RALEIGH: FOUNDED ON AUTHENTIC AND ORIGINAL DOCUMENTS, SOME OF THEM NEVER BEFORE PUBLISHED:.
TZ – Muenchen, DE. 1976- – ca 11r per yr – 1 – gw Mikrofilm [072]
EIN TZEYTLANG GESCHWIGNER CHRISTLICHER BRUEDER AUCH UM DIE WARHEIT WILLEN VERYAGT / Storch, N et al – Zwickau, J. Gastel. 1523. BME-17 1 – 9 – ne IDC [240]
TZU-LO-LAN – (Violet; A Literary Magazine). 1925 26-1931. Lacking: 1931. BCH-976 2 – 8 – ne IDC [480]
U AND LC – (1985-. 1,5,6) – 1982- – 9 – us UMI [073]
U NONGSAIN HIMA = THE NATION BUILDER – Shillong, India: Walter Roy Maring. [v2 n42-v6] aug 1961-64; [v8 n50-v10] jun 22 1966-68 – 2r – 1 – us Res Libr [072]

U SERIES. RELEASE U1-441, SEPT. 18, 1940-APR. 2, 1973 / U.S. Securities and Exchange Commission – 9 – us UMI [336]

U SERIES RELEASES – (Lacking: no U196) – nosU1-U441. 26 Sep 1940-2 Apr 1973 6mf – 9 – $9.00 – LLMC 89-003 – us L.L.M.C. [340]

UAR AGRICULTURE / Egypt. Ministry of Agriculture – Abdallah, H. 1965. BNE-4601 1 – 9 – ne IDC [630]

UAR DESERT DEVELOPMENT AND LAND RECLAMATION PROJECTS / Egypt. General Desert Development Organisation – 1961. BNE-4631 1 – 9 – ne IDC [333]

UAR ECONOMIC INDICATORS, 1961-1970 / Egypt. U.A.R. Central Agency for Public Mobilisation and Statistics – Cairo. 1971. BNE-4614 1 – 9 – ne IDC [310]

Ubald, Frere *see* BIO-BIBLIOGRAPHIE DU T.R.P. GEORGES-HENRI LEVESQUE, O.P., DOYEN DE LA FACULTE DES SCIENCES SOCIALES DE L'UNIVERSITE LAVAL

Ubangi-Shari. Assemblee territoriale *see* DEBATS

Ubbelohde, Wilh. *see* BEMERKUNGEN UEBER DEN EVANGELISCHEN RELIGIONSUNTERRICHT AN HOEHEREN LEHRANSTALTEN

Ubeda Sanchez, Jose *see* NORMAS Y PRECEPTOS DEL JUEGO DE DOMINO. LEXICOGRAFIA, ETIMOLOGIA

Ubertinus de Casali *see* ARBOR VITAE CRUCIFIXAE JESU

UBIISTVO TSARSKOI SEMII CHLENOV DOMA ROMANOVYKH NA URALIE / Dieterichs, Mikhail Konstantinovich – Vladivostok: Tip. Voen. akademii, 1922. 2v in 1 – 1 – CSUX88-B564 – us Hoover Inst Photo [947]

Ubud, Indonesia *see* PURI LUKISAN

THE UBYSSEY – Student newspaper of the University of British Columbia. 1918-79 – 1 – cn Commonwealth Micro [072]

UC DAVIS JOURNAL OF INTERNATIONAL LAW AND POLICY – v1. 1995 – 9 – $13.00set – us Hein [340]

UC DAVIS LAW REVIEW – v1-28. 1969-95 – 1,5,6 – $540.00 – us Hein [073]

THE U.C. LAND, MERCANTILE AND GENERAL ADVERTISER – Toronto: J Talbot, [1834-1835] – 9 – cn C.I.H.M. [330]

UCAPAWA NEWS *see* CANNERY AND FIELD UNION NEWS, 1937 : CIO NEWS CANNERY WORKERS EDITION, 1938-1939 : UCAPAWA NEWS, 1939-1944 : FTA NEWS, 1945-1950

UCHASTIE BIELGORODSKIKH ULAN V GRAZHDANSKOI VOINIE : 1917-1920 / Baidak, Andrei Artemevich – Bielgrad: Izd. sht.-rotmistra 12-go Ulanskago Bielgorodskago polka I.L. Sarnavskago, 1931 – 1 – CSUX89-B6824 – us Hoover Inst Photo [355]

UCHASTIE I PRIBYLI I RABOCHEE AKTSIONERSTVO (KOPARTNERSHIP) / Totomiants, V F – Ed 2. M., 1919 – 4mf – 9 – COR-125/1 – ne IDC [334]

UCHASTIE V PRIBYLI I KOPARTNERSHIP / Totomiants, V F – Pg., 1915 – 4mf – 9 – COR-124/1 – ne IDC [334]

UCHASTNIKI RUSSKOGO REVOLIUTSIONNOGO DVIZHENIIA EPOKHI BOR'BY S TSARIZMOM : BIOGR. UKAZATEL' CHLENOV VSESOIUZ – M., 1927. 288p – 4mf – 9 – ne IDC [320]

UCHEBNAIA KNIGA ROSSIISKOI SLOVESNOSTOSTI / Grech, N I – Ed. 3. v. 1-4. Spb. 1844. BR-6038 2 – 8 – ne IDC [460]

UCHEBNIK UGOLOVNOGO PRAVA / Poznyshev, S V – 2v. M. 1923. BR-9120 1 – 9 – ne IDC [360]

UCHENIE O GOSUDARSTVE I KONSTITUTSI RSFSR / Stuchka, Petr Ivanovich – M., 1922 – 4mf – 9 – ne IDC [320]

UCHENIE O LITSAKH IURIDICHESKIKH, PO NACHALAM NAUKI / Aleksandrovich, V – Moscow, 1865. 152p. BR-9026 1 – 9 – ne IDC [947]

UCHENYE ZAPISKI / Saratov Iuridicheskii Institut – Available: v. 12-1965. BR-8612 1 – 9 – ne IDC [340]

UCHENYE ZAPISKI / Vsesoiuznyi Institut Iuridicheskikh nauk. Moscow – Moscow, 1940-63. Continued as: yuchenye zapiski of the Inst. of Soviet Legislation. First series: vol. 5 available. Second series: vol. 1-17 available. BR-8619 1 – 9 – ne IDC [340]

UCHENYE ZAPISKI I. KAZANSKOGO UNIVERSITETA PO OTDELENIIU ISTORIKO-FILOLOGICHESKIKH I POLITIKO-IURIDICHESKIKH NAUK / Kazan Universitet. Russia – Kazan, 1862-65. Learned papers published by Kazan University, including materials on legal history and international law. B-1942/2 – 8 – ne IDC [340]

UCHENYE ZAPISKI IMPERATORSKOGO IUR'EVSKOGO UNIVERSITETA – (Missing: 1916(11-12)) – Iur'ev. v1-25. 1893-1917 – 978mf – 9 – ne IDC [370]

UCHENYE ZAPISKI INSTITUTA VOSTOKOVEDENIIA AN SSSR – Moscow, Leningrad. v6 (1953), v9 (1954), v16 (1958). BR-10,973/1 – 9 – ne IDC [025]

UCHENYE ZAPISKI KAZANSKOGO GOSUDARSTVENNOGO UNIVERSITETA / Kazan Universitet. Russia – n.1-, 1834-. Publication suspended 1917-24 – 1 – us U.W. Library [947]

Uchida, Naosaku *see* THE OVERSEAS CHINESE

Uchida, Takeo *see* POLITICAL SCIENCE IN ASIA AND THE PACIFIC

UCHITEL'SKAIA – 1924- – 1 – sz Infoprint [947]

UCHITEL'SKAIA GAZETA – (Backfile through 1998 $85r) – Russia, 1999- – 1r per y – 1 – $80.00 standing order – us Ross [072]

UCHITELSKAIA GAZETA – Moscow. U.S.S.R. 1946-1970 – 1 – us UMI [072]

UCHITELSKO DELO – Sofia, Bulgaria. 1951-59; 1981-86 – 6r – 1 – us L of C Photodup [949]

UCHITES' REVIZII! : KRAT. RUKOVODSTVO DLIA REVIZ. KOMIS. KOOP. TOVARISHCHESTV. / Khizhniakov, V V – M., L., 1925 – 1mf – 9 – COR-282/1 – ne IDC [334]

UCHREZHDENIE VOSPITATEL'NOGO DOMA DLIA PRINOSNYKH DETEI, DOMA I GOSPITALIA DLIA BEDNIKH RODITEL'NITS V STOLICHNOM GORODE MOSKVE – Moscow: The Imperial Academy of Sciences, 1767 – 3mf – 9 – $30.00 – us Ross [500]

UCHWALA KRAJOWEJ RADY NARODOWEJ Z DNIA 21.9.1946 R. W SPRAWIE PLANU ODBUDOWY GOSPODARCZEJ / Poland. Centralny Urzad Planowania – Warszawa. 1946. BD-740 1 – 9 – ne IDC [947]

UCI JOURNAL – Irvine, CA. UC Irvine: 1981-1989 – 1r – 1 – $50.00 – R04157 – us Library Micro [370]

UCITELKA – 1914 – 1 – us I.U. Libraries [073]

UCLA DAILY BRUIN / California. University. Los Angeles – Los Angeles. Calif. 1945-58 – 1 – us UMI [370]

UCLA DAILY BRUIN – Los Angeles, CA: UCLA, 1945-58; Mar-May 1972 – 12r – 1 – $600.00 – C02403A – us Library Micro [370]

UCLA EDUCATOR – v1-23 1957-81 1; 1977-81 5,6,9 – us UMI [370]

UCLA JOURNAL OF ENVIRONMENTAL LAW AND POLICY – v1-13. 1980-95 – 9 – $146.00 set – us Hein [340]

UCLA LAW REVIEW – v1-43. 1953-96 – 1,5,6,9 – $1,575.00 – us Hein [073]

UCLA PACIFIC BASIN LAW JOURNAL – (None publ 1987-88) – v1-13. 1982-95 – 9 – $134.00 set – us Hein [340]

UCLA WOMEN'S LAW JOURNAL – v1-4. 1991-94 – 9 – $50.00 set – us Hein [340]

UCUNCU BES YILLIK KALKINMA PLANI (1973-1977) BUYUME MODELI VE COZUMLERI / Turkey. Basbakanlik Devlet Planlama Teskilati – (Third Five Year Development Plan 1973-1977. Growth Model and Solutions). Ankara. 1971. BD-1771 – 9 – ne IDC [330]

L'UD – Bratislava, Czechoslovakia. Apr 1948-1980 – 43r – 1 – us L of C Photodup [072]

UDA CONGRESSIONAL NEWSLETTER *see* ADA WORLD

Udall, Nicholas *see* FLOURES FOR LATINE SPEKYNAE SELECTED AND GATHERED OUTE OF TERENCE, AND THE SAME TRANSLATED IN TO ENGLYSSHE

UDALRICUS. CONSTITUTIONES CLUNIACENSES. TROIS LIVRES / Ulrich de Ratisbonne, St – 12th c. – fr Armell [240]

UDANAVARGA – A collection of verses from the Buddhist canon. Compiled by Dharmatrata. Being the northern Buddhist version of Dhammapada. Trans. from the Tibetan of the Bkah-hgyur.London: Truebner, 1883. xvi,224p – 1 – us U.W. Library [280]

UDARNITSA URALA – Sverdlovsk, 1932-37 – 37mf – 9 – $240.00 – us Ross [305]

Udd, Edward *see* PSYCHOLOGICAL DESCRIPTORS OF PREDICTED ROS EXPERIENCES

UDDEVALLA TIDNING – Uddevalla, Sweden. 1853-54 – 1 reel – 1 – sw Kungliga [072]

UDDEVALLA VECKOBLAD – Uddevalla, 1903 – 9 – sw Kungliga [072]

UDDEVALLA WECKOBLAD – Uddevalla, Sweden. 1826-37 – 1 reel – 1 – sw Kungliga [072]

UDDEVALLABLADET – Uddevalla, Sweden. 1917-20 – 1 reel – 1 – sw Kungliga [072]

UDDEVALLAPOSTEN – Uddevalla, Sweden. 1979- – 1 – sw Kungliga [072]

UDDEVALLATIDNINGEN – Uddevalla, Sweden. 1902-17 – 11r – 1 – sw Kungliga [072]

UDDINGSTON STANDARD – Scotland, Jan 1905-Jan 1916 – 4r – 1 – uk British Libr Newspaper [072]

Uden, Horst *see*
- GOLD UND REIHERFEDERN
- DER UNSTERBLICHKEITS-KONZERN

UDFORLIG BESKRIVELSE OVER DE GRONLANDSKE SAELE 1/2 / Fabricius, O – Kjobenhavn. 1790-91. BH-474 2 – 8 – ne IDC [430]

UDGORN CYMRU – Merthyr Tydfil, Wales. 9 Apr-22 Oct 1842 – 20ft – 1 – uk British Libr Newspaper [072]

UDGORN HERALD – Pwllheli, Wales, UK. Jul 1898-1912; 1921. -w – 1 – uk British Libr Newspaper [072]

UDGORN Y BOBL – Denbigh, Wales. -w. March 1858-June 1865. 2 1 2 reels – 1 – uk British Libr Newspaper [072]

Udina Martorell, F *see* BARCELONA. ARCHIVO DE LA CORONA DE ARAGON GUIA HISTORICA Y DESCRIPTIVA...

UDINJI (CHEZ LES RIVERAINS DE LA BUSCHIMAIE) : ROMAN DE MOEURS CONGOLAISES / Cudell, C A – Bruxelles: P Lacomblez, 1905 – us Res Libr [390]

Udintsev, B *see* D. N. MAMIN-SIBIRIAK. RUKOPISI I PEREPISKA

UDOKA – (Backfiles and standing orders available) – Nigeria, 1990- – 5 – inquire – us Ross [960]

UDVIKLINGSPLAN FOR TIARET, 1966-1975 / Greenland – Copenhagen. 1964. (In Denmark. Betaenkning Fra Gronlandsudvalget af 1960). BD-732 1 – 9 – ne IDC [330]

UE NEWS : 1939-1955 / United Electrical Radio and Machine Workers of America – (Coll title: Labor Union Periodicals, Pt 1) – 5r – 1 – $675.00 – 1-55655-251-3 – us UPA [331]

Uebe, Auguste *see* MANUSCRIPTS ON THE HISTORY AND LEGENDS OF MANGAREVA IN HIS POSSESSION

Uebel, Otto *see* GRAYS EINFLUSS AUF DIE DEUTSCHE LYRIK IM ACHTZEHNTEN JAHRHUNDERT

UEBER 1,2-METHYL-PHENYLGLYCOLE / Zahn, Karl – Marburg, 1909 – 1mf – 9 – DM48.00 – 3-89349-653-X – gw Hänsel [540]

UEBER ANARCHIE UND ANARCHISMUS / Beckerath, Ulrich von – p316-319. 3 fiches (29x) – 9 – 1.00f – at Libertarian Micro [320]

UEBER AUFGABE UND METHODE DER SOGENANNTEN NEUTESTAMENTLICHEN THEOLOGIE / Wrede, William – (Includes bibliographical references) – Goettingen: Vandenhoeck und Ruprecht, 1897 – 1mf – 9 – 0-8370-6547-X – 1986-0547 – us A.T.L.A. [220]

UEBER BERECHTIGUNG DER KRITIK DES ALTEN TESTAMENTS / Koehler, August – Erlangen: A. Deichert, 1895. 1 fiche – 9 – us A.T.L.A. [240]

UEBER C. HOFMANN VON HOFMANNSWALDAU UND DIE UMARBEITUNG SEINES GETREUEN SCHAEFERS / Friebe, Karl – (Includes bibliographical references) – [S.l.: s.n.], 1886 (Greifswald: Druck von J Abel) – 1r – 1 – us U.W. Library [430]

UEBER CHR. D. GRABBES TRAGOEDIE "DON JUAN UND FAUST" / Nieten, Otto – (Includes bibliographical references) – Duisburg: J Ewich, 1906 – 1r – 1 – us U.W. Library [430]

UEBER DAS ALTER DER OSTJAKISCHEN UND WOGULISCHEN RENNTIERZUCHT / Donner, K – 1927. BU-577 2 – 8 – ne IDC [590]

UEBER DAS BETENDE ICH IN DEN PSALMEN : EIN BEITRAG ZUR ERKLAERUNG DES PSALTERS / Coblenz, Felix – Frankfurt a.M: J Kauffmann, 1897 – 1mf – 9 – 0-8370-2695-4 – 1985-0695 – us A.T.L.A. [220]

UEBER DAS BLEIBENDE IM GLAUBEN AN CHRISTUS : EINE CHRISTOLOGISCHE STUDIE / Haering, Theodor – Stuttgart: J F Steinkopf, 1880 – 1mf – 9 – 0-8370-5066-9 – 1985-3066 – us A.T.L.A. [240]

UEBER DAS DURCH DIE FRANZOESISCHE REVOLUTION HERBEIGEFUEHRTE BEDUERFNISS EINER NEUERN UND INNIGERN VERBINDUNG DER RELIGION MIT DER POLITIK / Baader, Franz von – Nuernberg, 1815 – 28p – 9 – DM48.00 – 3-89349-082-5 – gw Hänsel [320]

UEBER DAS GELDPRINZIP DER MODERNEN, TOTALITAEREN STAATEN / Beckerath, Ulrich von – 9 – 1.00f – at Libertarian Micro [335]

UEBER DAS GESPRAECH / Goes, Albrecht – Berlin: Furche, 1938. 46p – 1 – us U.W. Library [400]

UEBER DAS GNOSTISCHE BUCH PISTIS-SOPHIA; BROD UND WASSER, DIE EUCHARISTISCHEN ELEMENTE BEI JUSTIN : ZWEI UNTERSUCHUNGEN / Harnack, Adolf von – Leipzig: J.C. Hinrichs, 1891. (Texte und Untersuchungen zur Geschichte der altchristlichen Literatur, 7. Bd., Heft 2) – 1mf – us A.T.L.A. [240]

UEBER DAS GNOSTISCHE BUCH PISTIS-SOPHIA. BROT UND WASSER : DIE EUCHARISTISCHEN ELEMENTE BEI JUSTIN (T.U.U. 1-7/2) / Harnack, Adolf von – Leipzig, 1891 – 3mf – 9 – ne Slangenburg [240]

UEBER DAS "LEBEN JESU" VON RENAN : VORTRAG GEHALTEN ZU HALLE A S. DEN 13. JANUAR 1864 / Beyschlag, Willibald – Berlin: Ludwig Rauh, [1864] – 1mf – 9 – 0-8370-2329-7 – 1985-0329 – us A.T.L.A. [240]

UEBER DAS NATIONGEFUEHL; FRIEDRICH 2 UND JEAN-JACQUES ROUSSEAU : ZWEI FESTREDEN IN OEFFENTLICHEN SITZUNGEN DER KOENIGL. AKADEMIE DER WISSENSCHAFTEN ZU BERLIN / Du Bois-Reymond, Emil Heinrich – (Includes bibliographical references) – Berlin: F Duemmlers, 1879 – 1r – 1 – us U.W. Library [943]

UEBER DAS PATHOLOGISCHE BEI GOETHE / Moebius, Paul Julius – Leipzig: J A Barth, 1898 – 1r – 1 – us U.W. Library [430]

UEBER DAS POLITISCHE BEWUSSTSEIN VON FRAUEN IN DER BUNDESREPUBLIK : EINE SEKUNDAERANALYSE EMPIRISCHER MATERIALIEN / Heinz, Margarete – Frankfurt a.M., 1969 – 3mf – 9 – DM76.00 – 3-89349-363-8 – gw Hänsel [320]

UEBER DAS RECHT DEN STAAT ZU IGNORIEREN / Spencer, Herbert – From Social Statics, Ch. 19,21. 3 fiches (29x) – 9 – 1.00f – at Libertarian Micro [320]

UEBER DAS SYSTEM UND DIE CHARAKTERISTIK DER NATUERLICHEN FAMILIEN DER VOEGEL / Fitzinger, L J F J – Wien, 1856-65. 3pts. Z/1752/2 – 8 – ne IDC [590]

UEBER DAS VERHAELTNIS DER WICLIFITISCHEN...BIBELUEBERSETZUNG / Carr, Joseph – Leipzig: Universitaet, (189?). 1 fiche – 9 – us A.T.L.A. [240]

UEBER DAS VERHAELTNIS DES TEXTES DER DREI SYRISCHEN BRIEFE DES IGNATIOS ZU DEN UEBRIGEN RECENSIONEN DER IGNATIANISCHEN LITERATUR / Lipsius, Richard Adelbert – Leipzig: In Commission bei F.A. Brockhaus, 1859 – 1mf – us A.T.L.A. [240]

UEBER DAS VERHAELTNIS HEINRICH VON KLEISTS ZU C.M. WIELAND / Bheme, Herman – 1995 – 1mf – 9 – DM48.00 – 3-8267-3110-7 – gw Hänsel [430]

UEBER DAS VERHAELTNIS HEINRICH VON KLEISTS ZU C.M. WIELAND / Fehme, Hermann – (Includes bibliographical references) – Heidelberg: C Winter, 1914 – 1r – 1 – us U.W. Library [430]

UEBER DAS VERHAELTNIS VON DRAMA UND GESCHICHTE BEI FRIEDRICH HEBBEL / Koch, Herbert – (Includes bibliographical references) – Leipzig: W Wigand, 1904 – 1r – 1 – us U.W. Library [430]

UEBER DAS VERHAELTNIS VON MARTIN OPITZ ZU DANIEL HEINSIUS / Muth, Julius Bernhard – (Includes bibliographical references) – Leipzig: C G Naumann, 1872 – 1r – us U.W. Library [920]

UEBER DAS VERHAELTNISS DER ALTEN PHILOSOPHIE ZUM CHRISTENTHUM / Kahnis, Karl Friedrich August – Leipzig: Doerffling & Franke, 1884. 1 fiche – 9 – us A.T.L.A. [240]

UEBER DAS VERHAELTNISS DER PSALMEN ZU JEREMIA / Thayer, Charles Snow – Goettingen: Dieterich, 1901. 1 fiche – 9 – us A.T.L.A. [240]

UEBER DAS VERHALTNIS DER GRIECHISCHEN ZUR MODERN MUSIK / Schleicher, K – Cothen: P Schettlers Verlag, [1878] – 2mf – 9 – us Sibley [780]

UEBER DAS VOLKSTUM DER KOMANEN / Marquart, J – Abhandlungen der Koeniglichen Gesellschaft der Wissenschaften zu Goettingen, Philosophisch-Historische Klasse, ns v13 no 1 1912-14. BU-665 2 – 8 – ne IDC [306]

UEBER DAS WESEN DER GLETSCHER: UND, WINTERREISE IN DAS EISMEER / Hugi, Franz Joseph – Stuttgart: J.G. Cotta, 1842. xii,135p – 1 – us U.W. Library [550]

UEBER DEFLATION / Beckerath, Ulrich von – 9 – 1.00f – at Libertarian Micro [335]

UEBER DEN ALTDEUTSCHEN MINNESANG : VORTRAG GEHALTEN IN DER LITTERARISCHEN GESELLSCHAFT ZU ZERBST / Zuborg, Hermann – (Includes bibliographical references) – Jena: E Frommann, 1877 – 1r – 1 – us U.W. Library [780]

UEBER DEN BEGRIFF DER PRAESUPPOSITION / Keller, Rudi – Heidelberg, 1974 – 2mf – 9 – DM62.00 – 3-89349-399-9 – gw Hänsel [110]

UEBER DEN DRITTEN JOHANNESBRIEF (T.U.U. 1-15/3B) / Harnack, Adolf von – Leipzig, 1897 – 1mf – 9 – ne Slangenburg [240]

UEBER DEN EINFLUSS DER PALAESTINISCHEN EXEGESE AUF. DIE ALEXANDRINISCHE HERMENEUTIK / Frankel, Zacharias – Leipzig. 1851. BJ-32-26 1 – 9 – ne IDC [900]

UEBER DEN EINFLUSS DER WELTZUSTAENDE AUF DIE RICHTUNGEN DER KUNST : UND UEBER DIE WERKE FRIEDRICH HEBBEL'S / Bamberg, Felix – Hamburg: Hoffmann und Campe, 1846 – 1r – 1 – us U.W. Library [430]

UEBER DEN EINFLUSS DES HOLLAENDISCHEN DRAMAS AUF ANDREAS GRYPHIUS / Kollewijn, Roeland A – (Includes bibliographical references) – Amersfoort: A M Slothouwer, [18-?] – 1r – 1 – us U.W. Library [430]

UEBER DEN EINFLUSS DES ZEITUNGSWESENS AUF LITTERATUR UND LEBEN / Bulthaupt, H et al – Kiel: Lipsius und Tischer, 1891 – 1r – 1 – us U.W. Library [070]

UEBER DEN EINFLUSS IONISIERENDER STRAHLEN AUF DIE ERBSTRUKTUR / Schultz, G O – Summary in English, German, and Indonesian. SE 6901 1. 1958 – 9 – ne IDC [530]

UEBER DEN INDIVIDUELLEN BEWEIS FUER DIE FREIHEIT DES WILLENS : EIN KRITISCHER BEITRAG ZUR SELBSTERKENNTNISS / Liebmann, Otto – (Includes bibliographical references) – Stuttgart: Carl Schober, 1866 – 1mf – 9 – 0-8370-4305-0 – 1985-2305 – us A.T.L.A. [230]

UEBER DEN NAMEN ANARCHISMUS / Beckerath, Ulrich von – 9 – 1.00f – at Libertarian Micro [335]

UEBER DEN PSEUDOJUSTINISCHEN BRIEF AN DIOGNET : PROGRAMM FUER DIE RECTORATSFEIER DER UNIVERSITAET BASEL / Overbeck, Franz – Basel: Universitaetsdruckerei von C. Schultze, 1872 – 1mf – us A.T.L.A. [240]

UEBER DEN RELIGIOESEN GEHALT VON LESSINGS NATHAN DEM WEISEN / Kettner, Gustav – (Includes bibliographical references) – Naumburg a.S.: J Domrich, 1898 – 1r – 1 – us U.W. Library [430]

UEBER DEN TAG HINAUS : KRITISCHE BETRACHTUNGEN / Bab, Julius; ed by Bergholz, Harry – (Includes bibliographical references and index) – Heidelberg: L Schneider, 1960 – 1 – us U.W. Library [880]

UEBER DEN TOD DER SOEHNE ZEBEDAEI: EIN BEITRAG ZUR GESCHICHTE DES JOHANNESEVANGELIUMS / Schwartz, Eduard – Berlin: Weidmann, 1904. 1 fiche – 9 – us A.T.L.A. [240]

UEBER DEN UMGANG MIT WIENERN / Poetzl, Eduard – Berlin: Carl Stephenson, [1941] – 1r – 1 – us U.W. Library [830]

UEBER DEN UNTERSCHIED ZWISCHEN DER POSITIVEN UND DER LIBERALEN RICHTUNG IN DER MODERNEN THEOLOGIE / Kuebel, Robert – Noerdlingen: C H Beck, 1881 – 1mf – 9 – 0-8370-8584-5 – 1986-2584 – us A.T.L.A. [240]

UEBER DEN URSPRUNG DES EPISCOPATS IN DER CHRISTLICHEN KIRCHE : PRUEFUNG DER NEUESTENS VON HRN. DR. ROTHE AUFGESTELLTEN ANSICHT / Baur, Ferdinand Christian – Tuebingen: L.F. Fues, 1838 – 1mf – us A.T.L.A. [240]

UEBER DEN "ZAUBERBERG" VON THOMAS MANN / Graefe, Johanna – Berlin: Herbig, c1947 – 1r – 1 – us U.W. Library [430]

UEBER DEN ZUFALL : PHILOSOPHISCHE VORTRAEGE / Lasson, Adolf; ed by Roser, Andreas – 1918 repr 1994 – 1mf – 9 – DM60.00 – 3-89349-857-5 – gw Hänsel [190]

UEBER DES DIDYMUS VON ALEXANDRIEN IN EPISTOLAS CANONICAS ENARRATIO (T.U.U. 2-28/2C) / Klostermann, Erich – Leipzig, 1905 – 1mf – 9 – ne Slangenburg [240]

UEBER DEUTSCHE ORTSNAMEN / Hruschka, Alois – Prag: Verlag des deutschen Vereines zur Verbreitung gemeinnuetziger Kenntnisse, 1880 – 1r – 1 – us U.W. Library [910]

UEBER DIE ABFASSUNGSZEIT DES TRITOJESAIA / Littmann, Enno – Freiburg i.B.: J.C.B. Mohr, 1899. 1 fiche – 9 – us A.T.L.A. [240]

UEBER DIE ALLGEMEINEN KIRCHENVERSAMMLUNGEN = SUR LES CONCILES GENERAUX : ANLAESSLICH DES VON SR. H. DEM PAPSTE PIUS 9. AUF DEN 8. DEZEMBER 1869 EINBERUFENEN OEKUMENISCHEN CONCILS / Plantier, Claude Henri Augustin – (In German. Includes bibliographical references) – Freiburg i.B.: Herder, 1869 – 1mf – 9 – 0-8370-8370-2 – 1986-2370 – us A.T.L.A. [240]

UEBER DIE ART UND ZEIT DER ZAEHMUNG DES RENNTIERS / Sirelius, U T – (Journal Soc. Finno-Ougrienne, 1916-20). BU-576 2 – 8 – ne IDC [590]

UEBER DIE ART UND ZEIT DER ZAEHMUNG DES RENNTIERS / Sirelius, U T – (JSFOu. XXXIII, 1916-20. 2, 35p) – 8 – ne IDC [639]

UEBER DIE BEDEUTUNG DER)) 660, 661 DER DEUTSCHEN C P O... / Heidecker, H – Strassburg, 1892 – 2mf – 1 – ILM-2039/1 – ne IDC [327]

UEBER DIE BEFRUECHTUNG UND KEIMUNG DER ALGEN UND DAS WESEN DES ZEUGUNGSACTES / Pringsheim, N – Berlin. 1855. B-6395 2 – 8 – ne IDC [580]

UEBER DIE BEGABTENAUSLESE BEIM UEBERGANG VON DER GRUNDSCHULE ZUR HOEHEREN SCHULE (AN HAND DER ACH'SCHEN SUCHMETHODE) / Otto, Heinrich – Goettingen, 1931 – 2mf – DM62.00 – 3-8267-3047-X – gw Hänsel [370]

UEBER DIE BEIDEN ERSTEN PHASEN DES SPINOZISCHEN PANTHEISMUS : UND DAS VERHAELTNIS DER ZWEITEN ZUR DRITTEN PHASE: NEBST EINEM ANHANG, UEBER REIHENFOLGE... / Avenarius, Richard – Leipzig: E. Avenarius, 1868 – 1mf – us A.T.L.A. [140]

UEBER DIE BETEUERUNGEN IN SHAKESPEARE'S DRAMEN / Hoffmann, Heinrich – 1995 – 1mf – 9 – DM48.00 – 3-8267-3143-3 – gw Hänsel [420]

UEBER DIE BETONUNGSWEISE IN DER DEUTSCHEN LYRIK : DER NATURFORSCHENDEN GESELLSCHAFT ZU FREIBURG IM BREISGAU BEI GELEGENHEIT IHRES 50 JAEHRIGEN JUBILAEUMS DEN 12. AUGUST 1871 / Brambach, Wilhelm – Leipzig: B G Teubner, 1871 – 1r – 1 – us U.W. Library [780]

UEBER DIE BIBLIOTHEKEN DER METEORISCHEN UND OSSA-OLYMPISCHEN KLOESTER (T.U.U. 2-26/3B) / Berendts, Alexander – Leipzig, 1904 – 1mf – 9 – ne Slangenburg [240]

UEBER DIE BUERGERLICHE VERBESSERUNG DER JUDEN / Davidson, W – Berlin. 1789. BJ-23-108 1 – 9 – ne IDC [360]

UEBER DIE BUERGERLICHE VERBESSERUNG DER JUDEN / Dohm, CW – 2v. Berlin. Stettin. 1781-83. BJ-23-109 1 – 9 – ne IDC [956]

UEBER DIE CHRISTLICHKEIT UNSERER HEUTIGEN THEOLOGIE : STREIT- UND FRIEDENSSCHRIFT / Overbeck, Franz – Leipzig: E W Fritzsch, 1873 – 1mf – 9 – 0-8370-8700-7 – 1986-2700 – us A.T.L.A. [240]

UEBER DIE COUPONSPROCESSE ... / Bekker, E I – Weimar, 1881 – 3mf – 9 – ILM-3192/1 – ne IDC [327]

UEBER DIE DEUTSCHE COSMISCHE OPER / Reichardt, Johann F – 1774 – 9 – us Sibley [780]

UEBER DIE FORMEN DER GEBUNDENE REDE BEI DEN ALTAISCHEN TARTAREN / [Radlov, V V] – (Zeitschrift fuer Voelkerpsychologie und Sprachwissenschaft, 1866) – v4, p 85-114 – 8 – ne IDC [490]

UEBER DIE FORSCHUNGSERGEBNISSE DER SCHWEDISCHEN GROENLAND-EXPEDITION, 1899 / Stolpe, H J – BN 407 2. 1906 – 8 – ne IDC [910]

UEBER DIE FRUCHTENTWICKLUNG DER ASCOMYCETEN / Bary, H A de – Leipzig. 1863. B-6240 2 – 8 – ne IDC [580]

UEBER DIE GALGENLIEDER / Morgenstern, Christian – Berlin: B Cassirer, 1921 – 1r – 1 – us U.W. Library [780]

UEBER DIE GRENZEN / ed by Zentralleitung der Arbeitslager in der Schweiz – Affoltern und Wallisellen, nov 15 1944-45 n1-14 – 1 – Dist. gw Mikrofilm – gw Misc Inst [360]

UEBER DIE GRENZEN DER IMITATION DER ABENDLAENDISCHEN KULTUR UND IHRE PROBLEMATIK IM PROZESS DER KULTURDIFFUSION IN KOREA / Won, Moo Hurh – Heidelberg, 1965 – 2mf – DM62.00 – 3-89349-965-2 – gw Hänsel [303]

UEBER DIE GRIECHISCHE UEBERSETZUNG DES QOHELETH / Dillmann, August – (Includes bibliographical references) – [s.l: s.n, 1892?] – 1mf – 9 – 0-8370-2919-8 – 1985-0919 – us A.T.L.A. [220]

UEBER DIE HAMBURGER DRAMATURGIE UND CORNEILLES DISCOURS / Kurzreiter, Heinrich – [S.l.: s.n.], 1888 – 1r – 1 – us U.W. Library [430]

UEBER DIE IDEE EINER METAPHYSIK IM SINNE DES KRITISCHEN REALISMUS / Klamp, Gerhard – Gießen, 1925 – 1mf – DM48.00 – 3-8267-3031-3 – gw Hänsel [110]

UEBER DIE IN JESUS CHRIST 56-66 VORAUSGESETZTEN ZEITGESCHICHTLICHEN VERHAELTNISSE / Gressmann, Hugo – Goettingen: Dieterich (Kaestner), 1898. 1 fiche – 9 – us A.T.L.A. [240]

UEBER DIE INSEKTEN UND SPINNENFAUNA ISLANDS UND DER FAEROEER / Klinckowsstroem, A von – (Arkiv fuer Zool., v. 8 (12)). BZ-2178 2 – 8 – ne IDC [590]

UEBER DIE KIRCHLICHE BEDEUTUNG DER THEOLOGIE R. RITSCHL: CONFERENZVORTRAG / Frank, Franz H R – 1888 – 9 – us A.T.L.A. [240]

UEBER DIE MAAS, UEBER SCHELDE UND RHEIN! : GEDICHTE VOM FELDZUG IM WESTEN / Anacker, Heinrich – Muenchen: Zentralverlag der NSDAP, F Eher, 1942 – 1r – 1 – us U.W. Library [810]

UEBER DIE MUENZEN DER ILEKE ODER EHEMALIGEN CHANE VON TURKISTAN / Dorn, B – (Melanges Asiatiques, VIII. 1881). BU-653 2 – 8 – ne IDC [730]

UEBER DIE MUSIK DER ALTEN HEBRAER.. / Pfeiffer, A – 1779 – 9 – us Sibley [780]

UEBER DIE MUSIK DES RITTERS CHRISTOPH VON GLUCK; VERSCHEIDENE SCHRIFTEN GESAMMELT UND HERAUSGEGEBEN / Riedel, F J – Wien. 1775. BP-751 1 – 9 – ne IDC [780]

UEBER DIE MUSIK UND DEREN WIRKUNGEN, MIT ANMERKUNGEN. HERAUSGEGEBEN VON JOHANN HILLER / Chabanon, M P S de; ed by Hiller, Johann Adam – Leipzig. 1781. BP-665 1 – 9 – ne IDC [780]

UEBER DIE MUSIKALISCHE COMPOSITION / Scheibe, Johann Adolph – Erster Theil. Die Theorie. Der Melodie und Harmonie. 1773 – 9 – us Sibley [780]

UEBER DIE NEUTRALITAET BEY DEM GEGENWAERTIGEN KRIEGE / Hegewisch, D H – Kiel, 1793 – 1mf – 1 – ILM-2794/1 – ne IDC [327]

UEBER DIE NOTWENDIGKEIT UND MOEGLICHKEIT: EINER NEUEN AUSGABE DER HEBRAEISCHEN BIBEL / Kittel, Rudolf – Leipzig: A. Deichert, 1902. 1 fiche – 9 – us A.T.L.A. [220]

UEBER DIE PROTHALLIEN UND DIE KEIMPFLANZEN MEHRERER EUROPAEISCHER LYCOPODIEN / Bruchmann, H – Gotha. 1898. B-7168 1 – 9 – ne IDC [580]

UEBER DIE REISE UND ENTDECKUNGEN DES LIEUTENANT. IM RUSSISCHEN AMERIKA / Sagoskin, L – BN 380 2. 1848-49 – 8 – ne IDC [910]

UEBER DIE SAPINDACEEN HOLLAENDISCH-INDIENS... / Radlkofer, LA T – Amsterdam, [1879] – 2mf – 9 – 11,520/1 – ne IDC [950]

UEBER DIE SCHEERENSPINNEN, CHERNETIDAE. NEUESTE SCHRIFTEN NATURF / Menge, A – Z-2185 2. 1856 – 8 – ne IDC [590]

UEBER DIE SCHRIFTSTELLERISCHE THAETIGKEIT THOMAS ABBT'S / Geisler – Breslau: Druck von C H Storch – 1r – 1 – us U.W. Library [430]

UEBER DIE SCHULBILDUNG ZUR BESTIALITAET / Evers, Ernst August – Aarau, 1807 – 1 – DM30.00 – gw Mikro Press [150]

UEBER DIE SPRACHE DER GOTTSCHEDIN IN IHREN BRIEFEN / Lange, Adolf – (Includes bibliographical references) – Upsala: Almqvist & Wiksell. 2v. 1896-1901 – 1r – 1 – us U.W. Library [430]

UEBER DIE SPRACHE IN DEN DEUTSCHEN BRIEFEN DER HERZOGIN ELISABETH CHARLOTTE VON ORLEANS / Urbach, Adolf – (Includes bibliographical references) – Greifswald: F W Kunike, 1899 – 1r – 1 – us U.W. Library [430]

UEBER DIE THEORIE DER MUSIK / Forkel, JN – 1777 – 9 – us Sibley [780]

UEBER DIE THEORIE DER MUSIK, INSOFERN SIE LIEBHABERN UND KENNERN NOTHWENDIG UND NUESSLICH IST / Forkel, JN – Goettingen. 1777. BP-675 1 – 9 – ne IDC [780]

UEBER DIE UEBERLIEFERUNG UND DEN TEXTKRITISCHEN WERT DES DRITTEN ESRABUCHS / Moulton, Warren J – 1899-1900 – 1 – us A.T.L.A. [240]

UEBER DIE UMLAGERUNG VON ARYLSULFONSAEUREARYLESTERN IN ORTHO- UND PARA-OXYDIARYLSULFONE / Staehler, Gerhard – Marburg, 1951 – 1mf – 9 – DM48.00 – 3-89349-651-3 – gw Hänsel [540]

UEBER DIE VATERLANDSLIEBE : REDE AM GEBURTSFESTE SEINER MAJESTAET DES KOENIGS UND KAISERS, BEN 22. MAERZ 1879 / Wiencke, Otto – 2. Aufl. Ploen: W Hahn, [1879?] – 1r – 1 – us U.W. Library [943]

UEBER DIE VERNEHMUNG DER PARTEIEN ALS ZEUGEN IM CIVILPROZESS. / Affolter, Ludwig – Bern, Staempfli'sche buchdruckerei, 1879. 30 p. LL-4060 – 1 – us L of C Photodup [340]

UEBER DIE VIER GESETZENTWUERFE / Best, Dr – 9 – 1.00f – at Libertarian Micro [335]

UEBER DIE VON LESSING IN DEN ERSTEN DREI ABSCHNITEN SEINES LAOKOON AUSGESPROCHENEN ANSICHTEN / UEberegger, Jakob – Olmuetz: Verlag des k.k. deutschen Staats-Gymnasiums, 1893 – 1r – 1 – us U.W. Library [430]

UEBER DIE VON SEBASTIAN MUENSTER UND JEAN DU TILLET...EVANGELIUMS MATTHAEI / Herbst, Adolf – Goettingen: Dieterichs, 1879 – 1mf – 9 – 0-8370-3565-1 – 1985-1565 – us A.T.L.A. [220]

UEBER DIE WIEDERVEREINIGUNG DER CHRISTLICHEN KIRCHEN / Doellinger, Ignaz von – 1888 – 9 – us A.T.L.A. [240]

UEBER EINE SCHECKBANK (VERRECHUNGSBANK) / Beckerath, Ulrich von et al – 9 – $1.00f – at Libertarian Micro [335]

UEBER EINEN ALTBABYLONISCHEN KOENIGSCYLINDER DES KOENIGL. MUSEUMS UND EINIGE ANDERE CYLINDER UND GEMMEN / Schrader, Eberhard – [S.l.: s.n., 1879?] – 1mf – 9 – 0-8370-8619-1 – 1986-2619 – us A.T.L.A. [470]

UEBER EINIGE FARNE IN O.P. SWARTZ' HERBARIUM / Christensen, C F A – v. 9. (Arkiv fuer Botanik). 1910 – 9 – ne IDC [580]

UEBER EINIGE FARNGATTUNGEN / Mettenius, G H – Frankfurt a. M; 1856-1858. 6 pts. B-1251 2 – 8 – ne IDC [580]

UEBER EINIGE KUENSTLICHE GESCHLECHTER DER MALVENFAMILIE, DER KLASSE DER MONADELPHIEN / Medikus, F K – Mannheim, 1787. 158 pp. B-840 prSF 12,00 IDC 8 – ne IDC [580]

UEBER EINIGE PHOENIZISCHE INSCHRIFTEN / Hoffmann, Georg – (In German and Phoenician. Includes bibliographical references) – Goettingen: Dieterich, 1889 – 1mf – 9 – 0-8370-7221-2 – 1986-1221 – us A.T.L.A. [470]
UEBER FRIEDRICH UND DOROTHEA SCHLEGEL / Finke, Heinrich – Koeln, 1918 – 9 – DM48.00 – 3-89349-267-4 – gw Hänsel [920]
UEBER GENESIS UND COMPOSITION DER HALACHA-SAMMLUNG EDUJOT / Klueger, Hermann – Breslau: Th. Schatzky, 1895. 1 fiche – 9 – us A.T.L.A. [240]
UEBER GOETHE UND SPENGLER : APHORISTISCH / Dueren, Wilhelm – (Includes bibliographical references) – Bonn a.Rh.: Scheur, 1929 – 1r – 1 – us U.W. Library [430]
UEBER GOETHE'S NATURWISSENSCHAFTLICHE ARBEITEN : VORTRAG GEHALTEN IN DER DEUTSCHEN GESELLSCHAFT ZU KOENIGSBERG / Helmholtz, Hermann Ludwig Ferdinand von – New York: H Holt, 1889 – 1r – 1 – us U.W. Library [430]
UEBER GOETHE'S SPINOZISMUS : EIN BEITRAG ZUR TIEFEREN WUERDIGUNG DES DICHTERS UND FORSCHERS / Danzel, Theodor Wilhelm – Hamburg: J A Meissner, 1843 – 1r – 1 – us U.W. Library [430]
UEBER INTERNATIONALE EHESCHLIESSUNG... / Donle, L – Freiburg i B, 1892 – 1mf – 1 – ILM-3070/1 – ne IDC [327]
UEBER JOHANN GEORG JACOBIS JUGENDWERKE / Ransohoff, Georg – (Includes bibliographical references) – Berlin: Buchdruckerei von Gustav Schade (Otto Francke), 1892 – 1r – 1 – us U.W. Library [430]
UEBER JOSEPH GOERRES' SPRACHE UND STIL / Wagner, Ludwig – Strassburg i.E.: C & J Goeller, 1914 – 1r – 1 – us U.W. Library [430]
UEBER JUSTIN DEN MAERTYRER UND SEIN VERHAELTNIS ZU UNSERN EVANGELIEN : EIN PROGRAMM / Volkmar, Gustav – Zuerich, Kiesling, 1853 – 1mf – us A.T.L.A. [240]
UEBER KANADISCHES GELDWESEN / Beckerath, Ulrich von et al – 9 – $1.00f – at Libertarian Micro [335]
UEBER KIRCHENSTRAFEN / Schulte, Johann Friedrich von – Berlin: C.G. Luederitz, 1872 – 1mf – us A.T.L.A. [240]
UEBER KLOPSTOCKS NATURBETRACHTUNG / Roesiger, Ferdinand – (Includes bibliographical references) – Leipzig: B G Teubner, 1894 – 1r – 1 – us U.W. Library [430]
UEBER LAND AND MEER – Stuttgart, Germany. -w. 1858-1916. 57 reels – 1 – uk British Libr Newspaper [072]
UEBER LESSING'S EMILIA GALOTTI / Heidemann – Strassburg: R Schultz, 1881 – 1r – 1 – us U.W. Library [430]
UEBER LESSINGS EMILIA GALOTTI / Kettner, Gustav – (Includes bibliographical references) – Naumburg a.d. Saale: Lippert, [1893] – 1r – 1 – us U.W. Library [430]
UEBER LESSINGS MINNA VON BARNHELM / Kettner, Gustav – Berlin: Weidmann, 1896 – 1r – 1 – us U.W. Library [430]
UEBER LUEFTUNG UND BEFEUCHTUNG VON SCHULRAEUMEN / Peth, Wilhelm – 1995 – 1mf – 9 – DM48.00 – 3-8267-3210-3 – gw Hänsel [360]
UEBER MAHLEREI UND BILDHAUERARBEIT IN ROM / Rahmdohr, FW B von – O 1201 1. 3 v. 1787 – 9 – ne IDC [700]
UEBER MOSES MENDELSSOHNS TOD / Hoechheimer, S – Wien. 1786. BJ-23-113 1 – 9 – ne IDC [920]
UEBER NAMENSPHILOSOPHISCHE INTUITIONEN UND EIN GEFUEHL SCHLECHTHINNIGER NOTWENDIGKEIT / Schroeder, Severin – 1992 – iii/154p – 9 – DM98.00 – 3-89349-620-3 – gw Hänsel [190]
UEBER NEUE UND UNGENUEGEND BEKANNTE VOEGEL VON NEU-CHINA / Meyer, A B – (Sitzungsber. K. Akad. Wissensch. Wien. Abth. 1, 1874). 6 pts., index. Vienna. 1874-75. BZ-1853 2 – 8 – ne IDC [590]
UEBER NORDAMERIKANISCHE BAEUME UND STRAEUCHER / Medikus, F K – Mannheim. 1792. B-8140 1 – 9 – ne IDC [580]
UEBER OTWAY'S UND SCHILLER'S DON CARLOS / Loewenberg, Jakob – Lippstadt: A Staats, 1886 – 1r – 1 – us U.W. Library [430]
UEBER POPES EINFLUSS AUF HAGEDORN / Frick, Alfons – Wien: Verlag des Vereines zur Gruendung einer Mittelschule, [1900?] – 1r – 1 – us U.W. Library [430]
UEBER RICHARD JOHNSONS SEVEN CHAMPIONS OF CHRISTENDOM (1596) / Willkomm, Hans Werner – Berlin, 1911 – 2mf – DM62.00 – 3-8267-3070-4 – gw Hänsel [420]
UEBER ROBERT HAMERLINGS LYRIK : EINE LITERARISCHE STUDIE / Gnad, Ernst – (Includes bibliographical references) – Graz: Leuschner & Lubensky, 1891 – 1r – 1 – us U.W. Library [430]
UEBER SCHEFFELS KRANKHEIT : MIT EINEM ANHANG: KRITISCHE BEMERKUNGEN UEBER PATHOGRAPHIE / Moebius, Paul Julius – (Includes bibliographical references) – Halle: C Marhold, 1907 – 1r – 1 – us U.W. Library [920]
UEBER SCHILLERS UNTERSCHEIDUNG VON NAIVER UND SENTIMENTALISCHER DICHTUNG / Kraner, Christian Friedrich – 1995 – 1mf – 9 – DM48.00 – 3-8267-3126-3 – gw Hänsel [430]
UEBER SELENO UND VERWYANDTES / Roscher, Wilhelm Heinrich – 1890 – 1 – us I.U. Libraries [390]
UEBER SOPHOKLES' "KOENIG OEDIPUS" UND SCHILLERS "BRAUT VON MESSINA" / Wittich, Wilhelm – (Includes bibliographical references) – Cassel: J Has, 1887 – 1 – 1 – us U.W. Library [410]
UEBER STEUERFUNDATION / Beckerath, Ulrich von et al – 9 – $1.00f – at Libertarian Micro [335]
UEBER VERLORENE BRIEFE UND ACTENSTUECKE DIE SICH AUS DER CYPRIANISCHEN BRIEFSAMMLUNG ERMITTELN LASSEN (T.U.U. 2-23/2A) / Harnack, Adolf von – Leipzig, 1902 – 1mf – 9 – ne Slangenburg [240]
UEBER VERSCHIEDENE EINTHEILUNGEN DER HEILIGEN SCHRIFT : INSBESONDERE UEBER DIE CAPITEL-EINTHEILUNG STEPHAN LANGTONS IM 13. JARHUNDERTE [SIC] / Schmid, Otto – Graz:Leuschner & Lubensky, 1892 – 1mf – 9 – 0-8370-5104-5 – 1985-3104 – us A.T.L.A. [220]
UEBER WAHRHEIT UND GERECHTIGKEIT : ANTWORT AUF DEN IM OKTOBER 1875 VON DEN BISCHOEFEN BAYERNS BEI SR. MAJESTAET DEM KOENIG EINGEREICHTE VORSTELLUNG / Friedrich, Johann – Muenchen: T. Ackermann, 1876 – 1mf – us A.T.L.A. [240]
UEBER WIELANDS CLASSICITAET, SPRACHE UND STIL / Thalmayr, Franz – (Includes bibliographical references) – [Pilsen?]: Im Selbstverlage des Verfassers, [188-?] – 1r – 1 – us U.W. Library [430]
UEBER WOLFRAMS VON ESCHENBACH RELIGIOSITAET / Fritzsch, Robert – Leipzig, 1892 – 9 – DM48.00 – 3-89349-277-1 – gw Hänsel [240]
UEBER ZACHARIAS WERNERS "SOEHNE DES TALS" : EIN BEITRAG ZUR GESCHICHTE DER ROMANTIK / Palgen, Rudolf – (Includes bibliographical references (3rd prelim. leaf)) – Marburg a.L.: N G Elwert, 1917 – 1r – 1 – us U.W. Library [430]
UEBER ZEIT UND DICHTUNG : AUFSAETZE Z. LITERATUR / Busse, Carl – Konstanz a.B.: Reuss & Itta, c1915 – 1r – 1 – us U.W. Library [430]
UEBER ZOLA'S SPRACHGEBRAUCH / Lotsch, Fritz – 1995 – 1mf – 9 – DM48.00 – 3-8267-3128-X – gw Hänsel [440]
UEBER ZWEI RELIGIOESE PARAPHRASEN PIERRE CORNEILLE'S: L'IMITATION DE JESUS-CHRIST UND DIE LOUANGES DE LA SAINTE VIERGE / Koerting, Heinrich – Oppeln, 1882 – 1mf – 9 – DM38.00 – 3-89349-327-1 – gw Hänsel [440]
UEBERALL – Berlin, 1904/05, 1906/07 n27-52 – 1 – Inquire at Mikrofilmarchiv for details – gw Misc Inst [072]
UEBERBLICK UEBER DES GEBIET DER EV.-LUTHER. MISSION IM TAMULENLANDE / Handmann – 1898 – 1 – us A.T.L.A. [240]
UEberegger, Jakob *see* UEBER DIE VON LESSING IN DEN ERSTEN DREI ABSCHNITEN SEINES LAOKOON AUSGESPROCHENEN ANSICHTEN
UEBEREXPRESSION UND ANWENDUNG DER PHOSPHOMANNOMUTASE UND GDP-ALPHA-D-MANNOSE-PYROPHOSPHORYLASE AUS SALMONELLA ENTERICA, GRUPPE B ZUR PRAEPARATIVEN SYNTHESE VON GDP-ALPHA-D-MANNOSE / Ritter, Joerg Eberhard – 1995 – 2mf – 9 – DM80.00 – 3-8267-2162-4 – gw Hänsel [574]
DIE UEBERLIEFERUNG DER GRIECHISCHEN APOLOGETEN (T.U.U. 1-1/1.2.) / Harnack, Adolf von – Leipzig, 1882 – 5mf – 9 – ne Slangenburg [240]
DIE UEBERLIEFERUNG DER GRIECHISCHEN CHRISTL. LIT. / Siegmund, A – 1949 – 5mf – 9 – ne Slangenburg [240]
DIE UEBERLIEFERUNG DER JEREMIA-HOMILIEN DES ORIGENES (T.U.U. 2-16/3) / Klostermann, Erich – Leipzig, 1897 – 2mf – 9 – ne Slangenburg [240]
UEBERLIEFERUNG UND BESTAND DER HAGIOGRAPHISCHEN UND HOMILIETISCHEN LITERATUR DER GRIECHISCHEN KIRCHE VON DEN ANFAENGEN BIS ZUM ENDE DES 16. JAHRHUNDERTS : 1. TEIL: DIE UEBERLIEFERUNG / Ehrhardt, Albert – (1. Band (T.u.U. 4-50/1-5) Leipzig 1937. 2. Band (T.u.U. 4-51/1-5) Leipzig 1938. 3. Band, 1. Haelfte (T.u.U. 4-52/1-5) Leipzig 1943. 3. Band, 2. Haelfte (T.u.U. 4-52.2/1.2.) Leipzig 1943) – 45mf – 9 – ne Slangenburg [240]
UEBERLIEFERUNG UND TEXTGESCHICHTE DER LATEINISCHEN ORIGENESHOMILIEN ZUM ALTEN TESTAMENT (T.U.U. 3-42/1) / Baehrens, WA – Leipzig, 1916 – 4mf – 9 – ne Slangenburg [240]
DIE UEBERLIEFERUNGSGESCHICHTE DER BERGPREDIGT : EINE SYNOPTISCHE STUDIE ZU MT 4,23-7,29 UND LK 6,17-49 / Kraemer, Michael – Egelsbach, Koeln, New York, 1992 – 9 – DM48.00 – 3-89349-333-6 – gw Hänsel [240]
UEBERPRUEFUNG EINES SOFTWAREPROGRAMMES IM HINBLICK AUF SEINEN EINSATZ ALS PLANUNGS- UND STEUERUNGSINSTRUMENT / Maerz, Lothar – 1995 – 2mf – 9 – DM80.00 – 3-8267-2165-9 – gw Hänsel [000]
UEBER'S OHR GEHAUEN : HISTORISCHER SCHWANK IN 1 AKT / Theobald, A – Berlin: A W Hayn's Erben, 1873 – 1 – us U.W. Library [820]
DIE UEBERSECISCHE OESTERREICHISCHE WANDERUNG IN DEN JAHREN 1896-1898 FROM STATISTISCHE MONATSSCHRIFT / Buzek, Jozef – 1900 – 1r – 1 – us I.H.R.C. [304]
UEBERSETZUNGEN UND DEUTSCHE ABHANDLUNGEN WELCHE BEY DER CHURFURSTLICHE MAINZISCHEN. / Akademie Gemeinnuetziger Wissenschaften zu Erfurt – Erfurt, 1762-63. v.1-2 – 3 – us Readex [500]
UEBERSICHT DER ARBEITEN UND VERAENDERUNGEN DER SCHLESISCHEN GESELLSCHAFT FUER VATERLAENDISCHE CULTUR, 1824-1849 – (Cont. as: Jahresbericht der schlesischen Gesellschaft fuer vaterlaendische Cultur, 1850-1933. Register fuer 1804-1876. Bibliographie fuer 1900-1903. Breslau, 1851-1934. v28-106. Missing: 1824-1825, v1-2; 1877, v54) – Breslau. v1-27. (1825)-1850 – 475mf – 9 – 8613/1 – ne IDC [943]
UEBERSICHT DER GATTUNG ACONITUM / Reichenbach, Heinrich G L – Regensburg. 1819. B-5660 2 – 8 – ne IDC [580]
UEBERSICHT DER LEPIDOPTEREN-FAUNA DES GROSSHERZOGTUMS BADEN / ed by Spuler, A – Verh. Naturw. Vereins Karlsruhe, Berlin. v12, 1898. XII, 361p, 1tab – 8 – ne IDC [590]
UEBERSICHT DER NUTZBARSTEN UND SCHAEDLICHSTEN GEWAECHSE,... / Chamisso, LA von – Berlin, 1827 – 6mf – 9 – ne IDC [615]
UEBERSICHT UEBER DIE IM ARAMAEISCHEN, ARABISCHEN UND HEBRAEISCHEN UEBLICHE BILDUNG DER NOMINA / Lagarde, Paul de – Goettingen: Dieterich, 1889 – 1mf – 9 – 0-8370-8526-8 – 1986-2526 – us A.T.L.A. [470]
UEC GAZETE [METIN, FEYZ-I HUERRIYET, TASVIR-I HAYAL] – (Cikaranlar Movis, Vicdani, Yani; Idare Memuru: Mehmed Resad Efendi. No. 5 (37) (15 Eyluel 1908)) – Istanbul: Matbaa-i Sirket-i Sahafiyye-i Osmaniyye, 1908 – 1mf – 9 – $12.00 – us MEDOC [949]
UED PUBLICATIONS / University of Missouri. University Extension Division – No.1-71.1970-82 – 1,5 – us Spaulding [630]
UEHLING MESSENGER – Uehling, NE. -w. Jan 1926-Jan 1940 – 1 – us NE Hist [071]
UEHLING PRESS – Uehling, NE. -w. Jan-Dec 1925 – 1 – us NE Hist [071]
UEHLING PRESS – Uehling, NE. -w. Mar 1908-Aug 1917 – 1 – us NE Hist [071]
UEHLING TIMES – Uehling, NE. -w. Feb 1907-Feb 1908, scattered issues missing; Mar 1908-Dec 1909; Feb-Mar 1910, scattered issues missing – 1 – us NE Hist [071]
UELIOPILASLETH EESTI UELIOPILASKONNAA HAEAELEKANDJA – Tartus, 1920-1939 – 218mf – 9 – ne IDC [947]
UELKE – Ankara. Sahibi: Osman Enc, Yazi Isleri Mueduerue: Muzaffer Erdost. No. 1 (30 Agustos 1960) – 9 – $20.00 – us MEDOC [956]
UEMRAN – Istanbul: Mahmud Bey Matbaasi, 1887-1888 – 9 – $137.00 – us MEDOC [956]
Uenaydin, Rusen Esref *see* GECMIS GUENLER
UErfi [Betin], Saffet *see* ZIYA GOEKALP VE MEFKURE ARASINDAKI MUENASEBET VESILESIYLE BIR TETKIK TECRUEBESI
UES DE LOS ESTUDIANTES PARA LOS ESTUDIANTES – (Includes c.1: v.1:no.3 1954:July- v.1:no.4 (1954:Sept.); v.2:no.5 1955:Feb) – 1 – CSUXAJA8087-S – us Hoover Inst Photo [370]
UESKUB TARIHI VE CIVARI / Asim, Salih – Ueskub: Halil Kazim Matbaasi, 1923 – $25.00 – us MEDOC [956]
UESS-I INKILAB / Mithat, Ahmet – Istanbul: 1294-95 [1877-78] – $90.00 – us MEDOC [956]
Uestemir, Nahit *see* NUHUN GEMISI
UFA FEUILLETONS – (Gedruckte Manuskripte zur Weitergabe an die Feuilletonredaktionen der Zeitungen) – Berlin, n.d. – 1 – gw Mikrofilm [790]
UFAK MECMU'A-'I SI'IR / Tevfik – Istanbul, 1329 – 1mf – 9 – $6.00 – us MEDOC [949]
DAS UFFENBACHSCHE WAPPENBUCH / ed by Paravicini, Werner – 1990 – 60p + 3 color mf – DM420.00 – 3-89219-300-2 – gw Lengenfelder [920]
UFQ – Karachi: Ufq. -w. Begun in 1978 – 1 – us U.W. Library [073]
UFV INFORMA – Vicosa, 22 Dec 1977-31 May 1979 – 1,5,6 – bl Biblioteca [072]
UGANDA : STATISTICAL ABSTRACT 1957-1973 / Uganda. Statistics Division – (Coll title: African Official Statistical Serials, 1867-1982) – 32mf – 9 – £270.00 – uk Chadwyck [960]
Uganda *see*
- ANNUAL DEPARTMENTAL REPORTS
- BLUE BOOKS
- BUDGET PLANS
- THE FIRST FIVE-YEAR DEVELOPMENT PLAN 1961/62-1965/66
- A FIVE-YEAR CAPITAL DEVELOPMENT PLAN, 1955-1960
- GOVERNMENT PUBLICATIONS
- THE OFFICIAL GAZETTE OF THE UGANDA PROTECTORATE
- THE SECOND FIVE-YEAR PLAN, 1966-1971
- WHITE PAPER ON THE REPORT OF THE COMMITTEE OF INQUIRY INTO THE AFFAIRS OF ALL CO-OPERATIVE UNIONS IN UGANDA

UGANDA AND ITS PEOPLES / Cunningham, J F – London. 1905. BA-300 2 – 8 – ne IDC [301]
UGANDA ARGUS – Kampala, Uganda. -d. 17 Jan 1955-Dec 1961. 22 reels – 1 – uk British Libr Newspaper [072]
THE UGANDA COMPANY, LIMITED : THE FIRST FIFTY YEARS / Ehrlich, Cyril – Kampala: Uganda Co, 1953 – us Res Libr [380]
THE UGANDA DEVELOPMENT PLAN, 1961-1966 / Uganda. General Agreement on Tariffs and Trade – Geneva. 1966 – 9 – ne IDC [338]
Uganda. General Agreement on Tariffs and Trade *see* THE UGANDA DEVELOPMENT PLAN, 1961-1966
UGANDA HERALD – Kampala, Uganda. -tw. July 1912-Dec 1921; Jan 1941-May 1955. 38 reels – 1 – uk British Libr Newspaper [072]
UGANDA HUMAN RIGHTS ACTIVISTS – Kampala. 42 docs. 1986-1991 – 19mf – 9 – ne IDC [320]
Uganda Institute of Public Administration *see* ADMINISTRATION PAPERS
UGANDA JOURNAL – Kampala. v1-28. 1934-64; v1-20. Index – 156mf – 9 – A-477/2 – ne IDC [073]
UGANDA LAND REPORTS, 1914, 1926, 1932 / Great Britain. Commonwealth Office Library – 1 – uk Microform Academic [960]
UGANDA MISSION / Church Missionary Society – 1915-34 – 14r – 1 – uk Microform Academic [240]

THE UGANDA PROTECTORATE / Johnston, H H – 2v. London. 1902. BA-321 2 – 8 – ne IDC [960]

Uganda. Statistics Division *see* UGANDA

UGANDAN MATERIALS – Collection of notes, reports, documents, etc., on various topics – 1 – us Res Libr [960]

UGARITICA / Schaeffer, F-A, Cl. – Paris, 1939 – 13mf – 8 – Dfl46.00 – ne Slangenburg [270]

UGARITICA 2 / Schaeffer, F-A, Cl. – Paris, 1949 – 14mf – 8 – Dfl49.00 – ne Slangenburg [270]

UGARITICA 3 / Schaeffer, F-A, Cl. – Paris, 1956 – 11mf – 8 – Dfl39.00 – ne Slangenburg [270]

UGAV RACHEL / Morpurgo, R – Tel-Aviv. 1943. BJ-422-63 1 – 9 – ne IDC [470]

Ughelli, Ferd. *see* ITALIA SACRA SIVE DE EPISCOPIS ITALIAE

UGOL – (Library has: Nov. 1948) – Moskva: Ugletekhizdat, 193u – 1 – CSUX89-S767 – us Hoover Inst Photo [073]

UGOL', ZHELEZO I ZHIVOTNYE LIUDI / Reisner, L – M. 1925. BR-1231 2 – 8 – ne IDC [947]

UGOLOVNOE PRAVO RSFSR / Piontkovskii, A A – Obshchaia chast'. M. 1925. BR-9657 1 – 9 – ne IDC [300]

UGOLOVNOE ZAKONODATEL'STVO SSSR O SOIUZNYKH RESPUBLIK: SBORNIK / ed by Karev, D S – Moscow, 1957. 531p. BR-8690/2 – 8 – ne IDC [340]

UGOLOVNONPROTSESSUAL'NOE ZAKONODATEL'STVO SSSR I SOIUZNYKH RESPUBLIKI SBORNIK / ed by Karev, D S – Moscow, 1957. 507p. Texts of all-union and union republic legislation and codes governing criminal procedure. Subject index. BR-8642/2 – 8 – ne IDC [340]

UGOLOVNO-PROT SESSUALNYI KODEKS ARMIANSKOI SOVETSKOI SOTSIALISTICHESKOI RESPUBLIKI : S IZMENENIIAMI I DOPOLNENIIAMI NA 1 OKT. 1965 G., S PRILOZHENIEM POSTATE INO-SISTEMATIZIROVANNYKH MATERIALOV / Armenian SSR – Erevan: Aiastan, 1965 – 1 – CSUX91-B2393 – us Hoover Inst Photo [947]

UGOLOVNO-PROTSESSUALNYI KODEKS GRUZINSKOI SSR : VVODITSI A V DE ISTVIE S 1 MARTA 1961 G – Tbilisi: T SK KP Gruzii, 1961 – 1 – CSUX91-B1816 – us Hoover Inst Photo [947]

UGOLOVNY I KODEKS ESTONSKO I SSR : KOMMENTIROVANNOE IZDANIE – Tallin: E esti Raamat, 1968 – 1 – CSUX91-B2154 – us Hoover Inst Photo [340]

UGOLOVNY I KODEKS ESTONSKO I SSR – Tallin: Estonskoe gos. izd-vo, 1961 – 1 – CSUX91-B2160 – us Hoover Inst Photo [340]

UGOLOVNY I KODEKS GRUZINSKO I SSR : OFITSIALNY I TEKST S IZMENENII AMI NA 1 MAI A 1958 G. I S PRILOZHENIEM POSTATE INO SISTEMATIZIROVANNYKH MATERIALOV – Tbilisi: Gos. izd-vo "Sabchota Sakartvelo", 1958 – 1 – CSUX91-B1812 – us Hoover Inst Photo [340]

UGOLOVNYI KODEKS ARMIANSKOI SOVETSKOI SOTSIALISTICHESKOI RESPUBLIKI : S IZMENENIIAMI I DOPOLNENIIAMI NA 1 OKTIABRIA 1965 GODA I S PRILOZHENIEM POSTATE INO-SISTEMATIZIROVANNYKH MATERIALOV / Armenian SSR – Erevan: Aiastan, 1965 – 1 – CSUX91-B2690 – us Hoover Inst Photo [947]

UGOLOVNYI KODEKS AZERBAIDZHANSKOI SSR / Azerbaijan S.S.R. – Baku: Verkhovny i Sovet Azerba idzhansko i SSR, 1961 – 1 – CSUX91-B1806 – us Hoover Inst Photo [947]

UGOLOVNYI KODEKS GRUZINSKOI SOVETSKOI SOTSIALISTICHESKOI RESPUBLIKI : VVODITSIA V DEISTVIE S 1 MARTA 1961 GODA – [Tbilisi]: Sabchota Sakartvelo, 1961 – 1 – CSUX91-B1810 – us Hoover Inst Photo [947]

UGOLOVNYI KODEKS SOVETSKIKH RESPUBLIK / ed by Kanarskii, S M – 3rd ed. Kharkov, 1928. 588p. Comparative commentary on the RSFSR and Ukrainian criminal codes. BR-9613/1 – 9 – ne IDC [340]

UGROZHAET LI NASHEI PROMYSHLENNOSTI KRAKH? / Goldstein, Joseph M – Moskva: [s.n.], 1918 (Moskva: Tip. T-va I.D. Sytina) – 1 – CSUX88-B8773 – us Hoover Inst Photo [947]

Uhagon, Francisco R de *see* SEVILLA INTELECTUAL. SUS ESCRITORES Y ARTISTAS CONTEMPORANEOS POR D. JOSE CASCALES Y MUNOZ (INFORME)

Uhde-Bernays, Hermann *see*
- AUSGEWAEHLTE BRIEFE
- JOHANN JOACHIM WINCKELMANN
- WINCKELMANNS KLEINE SCHRIFTEN ZUR GESCHICHTE DER KUNST DES ALTERTUMS

Uhden, H F *see* THE NEW ENGLAND THEOCRACY

Uhland, Emilie Vischer *see* LUDWIG UHLANDS LEBEN

Uhland, Ludwig *see*
- ALTE HOCH- UND NIEDERDEUTSCHE VOLKSLIEDER
- DRAMATISCHE DICHTUNGEN
- THE POEMS
- THE SONGS UND BALLADS OF UHLAND
- UHLANDS GEDICHTE UND DRAMEN
- UHLANDS GESAMMELTE WERKE IN SECHS BAENDEN
- UHLANDS TAGEBUCH 1810-1820

UHLANDS DRAMATISCHE ARBEITSWEISE IN SEINEN HISTORISCHEN DRAMEN UND DRAMENENTWUERFEN / Lang, Ludwig – 1995 – 1mf – 9 – DM48.00 – 3-8267-3114-X – gw Hänsel [430]

UHLANDS DRAMEN UND DRAMENENTWUERFE / Duentzer, Heinrich – (Includes bibliographical references) – Leipzig: E Wartig, 1892 – 1r – 1 – us U.W. Library [430]

UHLANDS GEDICHTE UND DRAMEN / Uhland, Ludwig; ed by Holland, Wilhelm Ludwig – Stuttgart: J.G. Cotta, 1863 – 1r – 1 – us U.W. Library [800]

UHLANDS GEDICHTE UND DRAMEN / Uhland, Ludwig – Stuttgart: J G Cotta, 1889 – 1 – us U.W. Library [800]

UHLANDS GESAMMELTE WERKE IN SECHS BAENDEN / Uhland, Ludwig – (Includes bibliographical references) – Stuttgart: J G Cotta, [1892?] – 1r – 1 – us U.W. Library [800]

UHLANDS NORDISCHE STUDIEN / Moestue, Wilhelm – (Includes bibliographical references) – Berlin: W Suesserott, [1902?] – 1r – 1 – us U.W. Library [430]

UHLANDS TAGEBUCH 1810-1820 : AUS DES DICHTERS HANDSCHRIFTLICHEM NACHLASS / Uhland, Ludwig; ed by Hartmann, J – (Includes bibliographical references) – 2. Aufl. Stuttgart: J G Cotta, 1898 – 1r – 1 – us U.W. Library [430]

Uhlenbeck, C C *see*
- ESKIMO EN OER-INDOGERMAANSCH
- HET IDENTIFICEEREND KARAKTER DER POSSESSIEVE FLEXIE IN TALEN VAN NOORD-AMERIKA
- URALISCHE ANKLAENGE IN DEN ESKIMOSPRACHEN

Uhlenbusch, Hugo Paul *see* DER SCHATZ AUF GOTLAND

Uhlendorf, Bernhard A *see* CHARLES SEALSFIELD

Uhlendorf, Karen J *see* AN INVESTIGATION OF OUTDOOR ADVENTURE LEADERSHIP AND PROGRAMMING PREPARATION IN PHYSICAL EDUCATION BACCALAUREATE DEGREE PROGRAMS

Uhlhorn, Gerhard *see*
- ANTONIUS CORVINUS, EIN MAERTYRER DES EVANGELISCH-LUTHERISCHEN BEKENNTNISSES
- DAS BASILIDIANISCHE SYSTEM
- CHRISTIAN CHARITY IN THE ANCIENT CHURCH
- DIE CHRISTLICHE LIEBESTHAETIGKEIT
- KATHOLICISMUS UND PROTESTANTISMUS GEGENUEBER DER SOCIALEN FRAGE
- LUTHER AND THE SWISS
- THE MODERN REPRESENTATIONS OF THE LIFE OF JESUS
- DIE MODERNEN DARSTELLUNGEN DES LEBENS JESU
- DAS ROEMISCHE CONCIL
- URBANUS RHEGIUS
- VERMISCHTE VORTRAEGE

Uhlich, Rudolph *see* VERGLEICHENDE DARSTELLUNGEN DER GOTTESLEHREN VON SPINOZA UND MALEBRANCHE

Uhse, Bodo *see* DIE ERSTE SCHLACHT, VOM WERDEN UND VON DEN ERSTEN KAEMPFEN DES BATAILLONS EDGAR ANDRE

UHURU – Black Community News Service. Montreal – 1 – 65.00 – cn McLaren [072]

Ui Chathasaigh, Thomais *see* OCHT SGEALTA O CHOILLTE MAGHACH

UIDA REPORTER – 1972-79. (American Indian Periodicals in the Princeton University Library). 5 fiches – 9 – $45.00 – us UPA [305]

UIGURISCHE SPRACHDENKMAELER / [Radlov, V V] – (S. Malev, Ed.). Leningrad, 1928 – 305p – 8 – ne IDC [490]

UIGURSKORUSSKII SLOVAR' / Baskakov, N A & Nasilov, V M – M., 1939 – 7mf – 9 – U-318/2 – ne IDC [460]

UINTA COUNTY – ITS PLACE IN HISTORY / Stone, Elizabeth A – Laramie: Laramie Printing Co., 1924. Wyoming reel 3. (Cox Library Collection) – 5 – us Americana [978]

Uit de Bos, T *see* PLANTKUNDE VOOR HET VOORTGEZET ONDERWIJS IN INDONESIE

UIT DE GESCHIEDENIS VAN HET OUDE WIJHE : HISTORISCHE OPSTELLEN OVER HET KERSPEL WIJHE EN DE BOERHAAR MET EENIGE AANTEEKENINGEN OVER DE ADELIJKE HUIZEN IN DE OMGEVING – Zwolle, 1931 – Dfl9.00 – ne Slangenburg [240]

UIT DE GESCHIEDENIS VAN ONZE MIDDELEEUWSE LETTERKUNDE / Mierlo, J van – Dietsche Warende: Belfort, 1921 – 2mf – 8 – ne Slangenburg [290]

UIT HET WOORD : STICHTELIJKE BIJBELSTUDIEN / Kuyper, Abraham – Amsterdam: J A Wormser, [188-?] – 6mf – 9 – 0-8370-6269-1 – 1986-0269 – us A.T.L.A. [240]

THE UITENHAGE TIMES – (Title varies: Times 1944-61. Express. Times-Chronicle Express. Times. Uitenhage Times-Chronicle. Times for Uitenhage and Despatch, Mar 1961-68) – Uitenhage, South Africa. 3 Jun 1865-25 Dec 1874 – 5r – 1, 16 diazo available at reduced price – sa SA Libr [072]

UITENHAGE TIMES-CHRONICLE *see* THE UITENHAGE TIMES

UITERSTE WILLE VAN EEN MOEDER AAN HAAR TOEKOMENDE KIND : TOEGEEIGENT AAN DE VOLMAAKTSTE HUISMOEDER / Jocelyn Brook, E – Amsterdam, 1748 – 3mf – 9 – O-3095/1 – ne IDC [760]

UITGEZOGTE VERHANDELINGEN UIT DE NIEUWSTE WERKEN VAN DE SOCIETEITEN DER WETENSCHAPPEN IN EUROPA EN VAN ANDERE GELEERDE MANNEN – Amsterdam, 1756-65 – 3 – us Readex [500]

DE UITVINDING DER VERREKIJKERS / Waard, C de – H 655 2. 1906 – 8 – ne IDC [520]

UJ DONTVENYTAR. / Hungary. Courts – Budapest. On film: v1-35; 1911-43. LL-0246 – 1 – us L of C Photodup [340]

UJ DUNANTULI NAPLO *see* DUNANTULI NAPLO

UJ ELET – Budapest. v. 1-8 no. 11. Nov 13 1945-Mar 13 1952. Incomplete – 1 – us NY Public [072]

UJ ELOERE – New York: [SBS Pub Co], 1922-oct 19 1937 (national ed) – us Res Libr [071]

UJ EMBER – 1999- – 2r per y – 1 – us Ross [072]

UJ EMBER – Ungarn, 1976-1993ff – 18r – 1 – DM1,350.00 – gw Mikro Press [949]

UJ IGAZSAG – A francia orszagi es belgiumi magyar dolgozok egyetlen forradalmi lapja. Titre francais: La Nouvelle verite. no. 1-46. Paris. janv-nov 1935. mq no. 3, 6, 10, 18, 23, 26-28, 41 – 1 – fr A.C.R.P.P. [073]

UJ NEPBIROSAGI TORVENY *see* AZ UJ NEPBIROSAGI TORVENY (1947: 34. T.-C.) EGYSEGES SZERKEZETBEN A HATALYOS NEPBIROSAGI RENDELETEKKEL

UJ SZO – Bratislava, Czechoslovakia. Feb 1955-Jul 1956; Jul 1959-1983; 1984; 1988-1991 – 64r – 1 – us L of C Photodup [072]

UJ SZO – Toronto.v1-20, 1968-87 – 1 – 685.00 – cn McLaren [073]

UK COMPANIES ANNUAL REPORTS AND ACCOUNTS, 3RD SERIES INSURANCE AND FINANCIAL INSTITUTIONS – 251mf – 9 – uk Microform Academic [336]

UK PATENTS FOR INVENTION / British Library. Humanities and Social Sciences – (1617-1980. £345.00 (+ VAT UK); 1617-1899. £92.00 (+VAT UK); 1900-1980. £276.00 (+ VAT UK); 1930-1980. £230.00 (+ VAT UK)) – Index to names of applicants – 284mf – 9 – uk British Libr Humanities [020]

UKAZANIIA PRAVLENIIAM KREDITNYKH KOOPERATIVOV DLIA SAMOPROVERKI / Kil'chevskii, V A – Ed.2. M., 1918 – 1mf – 9 – COR-387/1 – ne IDC [334]

UKAZATEL' CHERTEZHEI MOSKOVSKIM TSERKVAM I SOSTOIAVSHIM V IKH PRIKHODAKH DVORAM I LAVKAM ZA 1775-1782 GG / Nikolaev, IN – pt. 1. M. 1884. BR-10,812 1 – 9 – ne IDC [025]

UKAZATEL' DELAM I RUKOPISIAM, OTNOSIASHCHIMSIA DO SIBIRI I PRINADLEZHASHIKH MOSKOVSKOMU GLAVNOMU ARKHIVU MINISTERSTVA INOSTRANNYKH DEL / Putsillo, M P – Moscow, 1879. 123p. BR-7228/2 – 8 – ne IDC [947]

UKAZATEL' DLIA OBOZRENIIA MOSKOVSKOI PATRIARSHEI RIZNITSY: BIBLIOTEKI / Savva, Arkhimandrit – 3rd ed. Moscow, 1858. 478p. BR-7324/2 – 8 – ne IDC [240]

UKAZATEL' IMMENOI I PREDMETNYI K TRUDU A.V. GORSKOGO I K.I. NEVOSTRUEVA: OPISANIE SLAVIANSKIKH RUKOPISEI MOSKOVSKOI SINODAL'NOI BIBLIOTEKI / Vitoshinskii, E M – Warsaw. 1915. PKG-E-49.21 BR-11,195 1 – 9 – ne IDC [010]

UKAZATEL' ISTORICHESKIKH ROMANOV ORIGINAL'NYKH PEREVODNYKH, RASZPOLOZHENNYKH PO STRANAM I EPOKHAM / Mezier, A V – Spb. 1902. BR-7151 2 – 8 – ne IDC [947]

UKAZATEL' IURIDICHESKIKH I DRUGIKH KNIG KNIZHNAGO MAGAZINA F.V. BUSYGINA – Moscow, 1915. 80p. BR-5664/2 – 8 – ne IDC [070]

UKAZATEL' IZDANII BYVSHAGO MINISTERSTVA ZEMLEDELIIA I GOSUDARSTVENNYKH IMUSHCHESTV PO SEL'SKOKHOZIAISTENNOI I LESNOI CHASTI VYSHEDSHIKH ZA 1903 GOD / Mamontov, I I – Spb. 1906. BR-7143 2 – 8 – ne IDC [460]

UKAZATEL' IZDANII MINISTERSTVA ZEMLEDELIIA I GOSUDARSTVENNYKH IMUSHCHESTV PO SEL'SKOKHOZIAISTVENNOI I LESNOI CHASTI VYSHEDSIKH SO VREMENINUCHREZHDENIIA ETOGO VEDOMSTVA (1894-1900) / Mamontov, I I – Ed. 2. Spb. 1900. BR-7141 2 – 8 – ne IDC [460]

UKAZATEL' IZDANII MINISTERSTVA ZEMLEDELIIA I GOSUDARSTVENNYKH IMUSHCHESTV PO SEL'SKOKHOZIAISTVENNOI I LESNOI CHASTI VYSHEDSKIKH ZA 1901 GOD / Mamontov, I I – Spb. 1903. BR-7142 2 – 8 – ne IDC [460]

UKAZATEL' K 1-20 VYPUSKAM "SBORNIKA MATERIALOV DLIA OPISANIIA MESTNOSTEI I IMEN KAVKAZA". 1881-1894 G / Kozubskii, E – Tiflis. 1895. BR-7126/2 – 4mf – 8 – ne IDC [460]

UKAZATEL' K IZDANIIAM IMP. KAVKAZSKAGO MEDITSINSKAGO OBSHCHESTVA ZA DVADTSAT' PIAT LET EGO SUSHCHESTVOVANIIA / Gadomskii, A – (s 1864 5 po 1888 9 g). Tiflis, 1893 – 8 – BR-7102 2 – ne IDC [947]

UKAZATEL' K KATALOGU KHRANIASHCHAGOSIA V IMP. PUBLICHNOI BIBLIOTEKE SOBRANIIA SLAVIANO-RUSSKIKH RUKOPISEI P. D. BOGDANOVA / Martinson, F A – Petrograd. 1916. BR-7301 2 – 8 – ne IDC [460]

UKAZATEL' K OPYTU ROSSIISKOI BIBLIOGRAFII V.S. SOPIKOVA / Rogozhin, V N – Spb. 1908. BR-7239 2 – 8 – ne IDC [460]

UKAZATEL' K RUSSKIM IZDANIIAM GRECHESKIKH I LATINSKIKH KLASSIKOV, AZBUK, RAZGOVOROV, GRAMMATIK I SLOVAREI OT NACHALA PO 1871 / Lebedev, V – M. 1878. BR-7129 – 8 – ne IDC [460]

UKAZATEL' KNIG, BROSHIUR, ZHURNAL'NYKH I GAZETNYKH STATEI I ZAMETOK NA RUSSKOM IAZYKE O CHUVASHAKH, V SVIAZI S DRUGIMI INORODTSAMI, SREDNIAGO POVOLZH'IA, S 1756 PO 1906 G. KAZAN', 1907 / Ivanov, A – BR-7110 2 – 8 – ne IDC [460]

UKAZATEL' KNIG DLIA CHTENIIA PO VOPROSAM KOOPERATSII / Portugalov, A V – Nizhnii Novgorod, 1913 – 1mf – 9 – COR-539/1 – ne IDC [334]

UKAZATEL' KNIG DLIA DETSKAGO CHTENIIA / Flerov, A E – (v vozraste 7-14 let). M. 1905. BR-7101 2 – 8 – ne IDC [947]

UKAZATEL' KNIG I STATEI O KOOPERATSII I MELKOM NARODNOM KREDITE – St Petersburg, 1903 – 3mf – 9 – COR-542/1 – ne IDC [334]

UKAZATEL' KNIG I STATEI OKHOTNICH'-IAGO I ZOOLOGICHESKAGO SODERZHANIIA / Sabaneev, L P – M. 1883. BR-7244 2 – 8 – ne IDC [590]

UKAZATEL' KNIG PO SEL'SKOMU KHOZIAISTVU ZA 1923-25 GG – Leningrad, 1928 – 3mf – 9 – COR-543/1 – ne IDC [334]

UKAZATEL' KNIG PO VOPROSAM VOSPITANIIA I OBUCHENIIA / Flerov, A E – Kritcheskii obzor pedagogicheskoi literatury. v. 1-2. M. 1905-06. BR-7100 2 – 8 – ne IDC [370]

UKAZATEL' KNIG, ZHURNAL'NYKH I GAZETNYKH STATEI I ZAMETOK O KIRGIZAKH / Alektorov, A E – kazan', 1900. 991p. BR-7052 2 – 8 – ne IDC [030]

UKAZATEL' KNIG, ZHURNAL'NYKH I GAZETNYKH STATEI PO SEL' SKOMU KHOZIAISTVU ZA 1890-1911 GG / Pedashenko, A D – Spb. 1891-1915. BR-7204 2 – 8 – ne IDC [380]

UKAZATEL' LITERATURY O SIONIZME – Spb. 1903. BR-7009 2 – 8 – ne IDC [470]

UKAZATEL' LITERATURY PO BUROVYM NA VODU SKVAZHINAM V ROSSII / Nikitin, S N – Ed. 2. L. 1924. BR-7177 2 – 8 – ne IDC [460]

UKAZATEL' LITERATURY PO ESTESTVENNO-ISTORICHESKOMU IZUCHENIIU TUL'SKOI GUBERNII / Kozmenko, A S – M. 1914. BR-7125 2 – 8 – ne IDC [460]

UKAZATEL' LITERATURY PO LESNOI TORGOVLE I PROMYSHLENNOSTI / Faas, V V – Petrograd. 1915. BR-7099 2 – 8 – ne IDC [460]

UKAZATEL' LITERATURY PO TELESNOMU VOSPITANIIA, RAZVITIIU I OBRAZOVANIIU / Arkhangel'skh, S K – St. Petersburg, n.d. 78p. BR-7056 2 – 8 – ne IDC [460]

UKAZATEL' LITERATURY PO TRAVOSEIANIIU I LUGOVODSTVY NA RUSSKOM IAZYKE / Dmitriev, A M – 1763-1904. gg. Spb. 1906. BR-7094 2 – 8 – ne IDC [460]

UKAZATEL' LITERATURY TSERKOVNAGO PRAVA PO 1910 G / Krasnozhen, M – Iur'ev. 1911. BR-5956 2 – 8 – ne IDC [460]

UKAZATEL' LUCHSHIKH, PO OTZYVAM PECHATI, UCHEBNIKOV, NAGLIADNYKH UCHEBNYKH POSOBII I METODICHESKIKH RUKOVODSTV NA RUSSKOM I UKRAINSKOM IAZYKAKH / Sollogub, B & Simonovskii, V – Spb, 1909 – 8 – BR-7273 2 – ne IDC [460]

UKAZATEL' MATERIALOV DLIA ISTORII TORGOVLI, PROMYSHLENNOSTI I FINANSOV Y PREDELAKH ROSSIISKOI IMPERII / Chernevskii, P O – Ot drevneishkikh vremen do kontsa XVIII stoletiia. Spb. 1883. BR-7091 2, 141p – 8 – COR-544/1 – ne IDC [947]

UKAZATEL' PERIODICHESKIKH IZDANII EMIGRATSII IZ ROSSII I SSSR ZA 1919-1952 GG / Institut po izucheniiu istorii i kul'tury S SS R – Munich, 1952 – 1 – 35.00r – us Hoover Inst Photo [010]

UKAZATEL' RUSSKOI EKONOMICHESKOI LITERATURY – Spb., 1903 – 2mf – 9 – R-7029/2 – ne IDC [334]

UKAZATEL' RUSSKOI MEDITSINSKOI LITERATURY / Rikker, K L – Izd. 13oe, dopolnennoe po le Ianvaria 1905 goda. Spb. 1905. BR-7236 2 – 8 – ne IDC [610]

UKAZATEL' SOCHINENII O KORENNYKH ZHITELIAKH PRIBALTIISKOGO KRAIA – Spb. 1868 – 2mf – 9 – ne IDC [947]

UKAZATEL' SOOBSHCHENII, SDELANNYKH NA OBSHCHIKH SOBRANIIAKH RUSSKAGO ENTOMOLOGICHESKAGO OBSHCHESTVA ZA 35 LET EGO SUSHCHESTVOVANIIA (1859-1894) / Mazarakii, V V – Spb. 1899. BR-7148 2 – 8 – ne IDC [590]

UKAZATEL' SOTSIOLOGICHESKOI LITERATURY / Kareev, N – Spb. 1897. BR-7116 2 – 8 – ne IDC [300]

UKAZATEL' STATEI PO PTSELOVODSTVU S 1741 PO 1890 GOD / Shavrov, I E – Spb. 1890. BR-7251 2 – 8 – ne IDC [947]

UKAZATEL TARIFOV ZHEL.-DOR. I VODNOGO TRANSPORTA R.S.F.S.R. – (Library has: no.21/31 Aug., 1921) – Moskva: Fin. ekon. upr. NKPS., 1920-1922 – 1 – CSUX89-S537 – us Hoover Inst Photo [380]

UKAZATEL TARIFOV ZHELEZNODOR-OZHNOGO I VODNOGO TRANSPORTA R.S.F.S.R. *see* UKAZATEL TARIFOV ZHEL.-DOR. I VODNOGO TRANSPORTA R.S.F.S.R.

UKAZATEL' TEKUSHCHEI PEDAGOGICHESKOI LITERATURY ZA 1897 GOD / Sliusarenko, O V – (Prodolzhenie i okonchanie). 1900 god. 6 v. M. 1897-1900. BR-7269 2 – 8 – ne IDC [490]

UKAZATEL' VOSPOMINANII, DNEVNIKOV I PUTEVYKH ZAPISOK 17-19 VV – Moscow, 1951. 224p. BR-11,008/1 – 9 – ne IDC [025]

UKAZATEL'K IZDANIIAM VREMENNOI KOMMISSII DLIA RAZBORA DREVNIKH AKTOV. 1-2 / Novitskii, I P – Kiev. 1878-82. BR-7180 2 – 8 – ne IDC [460]

UKAZATEL'K RUSSKIM POVREMENNYM IZDANIIAM I SBORNIKAM ZA 1703-1802 GG. I K ISTORICHESKOMU ROZYSKANIIU O NIKH / Neustroev, A N – St. Petersburg, 1898. xvi, 805,(1)p. B-1154 2 – 8 – ne IDC [947]

UKAZATEL'MATERIALOV PO ISTORII POCHT V ROSSII / Levinskii, V D & Tokmanov, I F – M. 1881. BR-7132 2 – 8 – ne IDC [947]

UKAZATEL'-SPRAVOCHNIK PROMYSLOVOI KOOPERATSII MOSKOVSKOI OBLASTI / Grinberg, B la. – M., L., 1934 – 2mf – 9 – COR-451/1 – ne IDC [334]

UKAZETS STARINNYKH RUKOPISEI / Strumenskii, M – Katalog otdela biblioteki. Vologda. 1919. PKG-E-7.7 BR-11,147 1 – 9 – ne IDC [025]

UKIAH CITY PRESS – Ukiah, CA. 1878-79 – 1r – 1 – $50.00 – B03045 – us Library Micro [071]

UKIAH DAILY JOURNAL – (Also known as: Redwood Journal Press Dispatch) – Ukiah, 1949-51; 1966-84 – 161r – 1 BC03046 – $8,050.00 – us Library Micro [071]

UKIAH NEWS – Ukiah, CA. 1953 – 1r – 1 – $50.00 – B03052 – us Library Micro [071]

UKIAH SENTINEL – Ukiah OR. Aug 9 1900 – 1 – us U.O. Library [071]

UKIAH TIMES – Ukiah, CA. 1914-17 – 1r – 1 – $50.00 – B03053 – us Library Micro [071]

UKIAH TIMES AND MENDOCINO DAILY TIMES – Ukiah, CA. 1912-13 – 1r – 1 – $50.00 – B03054 – us Library Micro [071]

UKRAIENSKA TRIBUNA – Munich. Germany. -w. 7 Jan 1947-29 May 1949. (3 reels) – 1 – uk British Libr Newspaper [947]

UKRAIENSKY SAMOSTIINIK – Munich. Germany. 7 Jan 1950-4 Aug 1957. (Imperfect). (4 reels) – 1 – uk British Libr Newspaper [947]

UKRAINA – Kiev, 1907 – 1 – us Ross [073]

UKRAINA – Kiev. v. 1-4. 1907 – 1 – us NY Public [073]

UKRAINA *see* KIEVSKAIA STARINA. EZHEMESIACHNYI ISTORICHESKII ZHURNAL

L'UKRAINE – Kiev, 1924-32 – 7r – 1 – us Ross [073]

Ukraine, Narodnyi komisariat iustytsii *see*
- BIULETEN NARODNOGO KOMISARIIATU IUSTYTSII
- OTCHET NARODNOGO KOMISSARIATA IUSTITSII ZA...
- SBORNIK TSIRKULIAROV N.K. IU. POLIKVIDATSIONNOMU OTDELU I OTCHETOV LIKV. OTDELA POOTDELENIIU TSERKVI OT GOSUDARSTVA
- SVODKA PO NARODNOMU KOMISSARIATU IUSTITSII U.S.S.R.

Ukraine, Tsentralne statystychne upravlinniaT Sentralnoe statistichesko upravlenie *see* OTCHET O DEIATELNOSTI TSENTRALNOGO STATISTICHESKOGO UPRAVLENIIA ZA... OPERATSIONNYI GOD

UKRAINETS U FRANTSII – (Ukrainets Ukrainets-chas). Paris. France. -w. 21 Mar-11 Jul, 14 Nov 1948-27 Nov 1960. (Imperfect). (8 reels) – 1 – uk British Libr Newspaper [947]

THE UKRAINIAN CANADIAN – Toronto. v. 1-22. 1947-68 – 1 – 685.00 – cn McLaren [073]

UKRAINIAN MATHEMATICAL JOURNAL – (v41-45 1989-93 $160.00v) – v19-40 1967-88 – 1,5 – $80.00v – us UMI [510]

Ukrainian Orthodox Church of America *see* DNIPRO

UKRAINIAN SERIALS – 195 titles – 9 – ne IDC [947]

UKRAINS'KA KHATA – Kyiv, Ukraine, 1909-1914 – 4r – 1 – us I.H.R.C. [947]

UKRAINSKE SLOVO – Uzhgorod, U.S.S.R. -f. 1 Sept 1932-14 Oct 1938. Imperfect. 1 reel – 1 – uk British Libr Newspaper [947]

UKRAINS'KI VISTI – Neu-Elm, Germany. Nov 1945-1978 – 12r – 1 – us L of C Photodup [072]

UKRAINSKI VISTI – Edmonton, Canada. -w. 1 Jan 1936-26 Dec 1939; 15 Dec 1946-5 July 1949; 29 Dec 1952-24 May 1954; 10 Jan 1955-Dec 1975. Imperfect. 26 reels – 1 – uk British Libr Newspaper [072]

UKRAINSKII FRONT (KRATKII OBZOR FONDA NO. 103) / U.S.S.R. Army – M. 1939. TsARKKA. BR-11,078 1 – 9 – ne IDC [355]

UKRAINSKII NAUKOVII INSTITUT – Warsaw. v1-48. 1931-39 – 5r – 1 – us Ross [943]

UKRAINSKY HOLOS – Winnipeg, Canada. -w. April 1920-Oct 1973. 54 1 2 reels – 1 – uk British Libr Newspaper [072]

UKRAINSKY KHLIBOROB – Sao Paulo. Brazil. -w. Oct 1931-Dec 1932, Jan 1936-Dec 1939. (2 reels) – 1 – uk British Libr Newspaper [072]

UKRAINSKY ROBITNIK – Toronto, Canada. Ukrainsky khristiansky robitnik Kanadiisky horozhanian. -w. 19 Nov 1948-7 July 1955. 7 reels – 1 – uk British Libr Newspaper [072]

UKRAJINA A RUSKO / Hrushevskyi, Mykhailo – Kyjiv: "Cas", 1919 – 1 – CSUX88-B1260 – us Hoover Inst Photo [947]

UKRAJINS'KI PYS'MENNYKY / Makhnovets, L E; ed by Bilets'kyi, O I – Bio-bibliohrafichnyi slovnyk. v. 1: Davnia ukrajins'ka literatura (XI-XVII st.). Kyiv. 1960. PKG-A-15.3 BR-11,294 1 – 9 – ne IDC [460]

UKRAYINETZ'-CHAS – Paris, July 10 1949-Dec 23 1951; 1953-1958 (incomplete) – 1 – us NY Public [947]

Ukrayin'skyi Naukovyi Instyutut *see* PRATZI

UKREPA. SLOVO K RUSSKOI ZEMLE O ZEMLE RODNOI, TAINOSTIAKH ZEMNYKH SUD'BE / Remizov, A – Petrograd, 1916. BR-852 2 – 8 – ne IDC [460]

Ukur, Fridolin *see*
- DARAH DAN PELUH: KUMPULAN SADJAK
- MALAM SUNJI; KUMPULAN SADJAK

UL (UNDERWRITERS LABORATORIES, INC.) – Standards. Printed index. Updated every 60 days – 6,9 – us Info Handling [621]

ULAM QUARTERLY / ed by Blass, Piotr – 1,5,9 – us Gordon [510]

ULAMA'S CONTRIBUTION TO THE STATE / Saifuddin, Zuhri – Address on 38th anniversary of Nahdlatul 'Ulama Party. SE 5615 1. 1965? – 9 – ne IDC [321]

ULAN ZALAT – (Kalmuck.) Prague, 1927-1930. 3 vols. in 1 – 1 – $35.00r – us Hoover Inst Photo [999]

ULANENPATROUILLE / Lange, Horst – Hamburg: H Goverts, 1940 – 1r – 1 – us U.W. Library [830]

Ulanowicz, R E *see* MATHEMATICAL MODELS IN BIOLOGICAL OCEANOGRAPHY

Ular, Alexander *see* DIE ZWERGENSCHLACHT

ULAR; DUA DRAMA DAN DUA TJERITA PENDEK / Suradji, D – SE 4072 1. 1963 – 9 – ne IDC [950]

Ulbricht, Walter *see* DAS NEUE OKONOMISCHE SYSTEM DER PLANUNG UND LEITUNG DER VOLKSWIRTSCHAFT IN DER PRAXIS: DISKUSSION ZUM REFERAT UND ZU DEN VORGELEGTEN ENTWURFEN DER DOKUMENTS..

Ulderic, Frere *see* NOTES BIO-BIBLIOGRAPHIE DU REVEREND FRERE PATRICE, S.C.

Ulfeldt, Grevinde Leonora Christina *see* MEMOIRS OF LEONORA CHRISTINA, DAUGHTER OF CHRISTIAN 4 OF DENMARK

ULFILAS, APOSTLE OF THE GOTHS : TOGETHER WITH AN ACCOUNT OF THE GOTHIC CHURCHES AND THEIR DECLINE / Scott, Charles A Anderson – Cambridge: Macmillan and Bowes, 1885 – 1mf – us A.T.L.A. [240]

ULI DER PAECHTER / Gotthelf, Jeremias; ed by Bloesch, Hans – (Includes bibliographical references) – Erlenbach, Zuerich: E Rentsch, 1921 – 1 – us U.W. Library [830]

ULI DER PAECHTER / Gotthelf, Jeremias – Braunschweig: G Westermann, 1921 – 1 – us U.W. Library [830]

ULI DER PAECHTER : EIN VOLKSBUCH / Gotthelf, Jeremias; ed by Vetter, Ferdinand – Bern: Schmid & Francke, 1899 – 1 – us U.W. Library [830]

Ul'ianitskii, V A *see* MEZHDUNARODNOE PRAVO PO LEKTSIIAM

Ulianov, Ivan *see* SOVETSKAI A RESPUBLIKA I KAZAKI

Ulinski, John A *see* SOME ASPECTS OF LOCAL GOVERNMENT IN INDONESIA

Ulitz, Arnold *see*
- ARARAT
- DER GROSSE JANJA
- DER VERLORENE RING

DER ULK : ILLUSTRIERTES WOCHENBLATT FUER HUMOR UND SATIRE – Berlin, Germany. 8 May 1872-8 Sep 1932 (incomplete) – 14r – 1 – gw Mikrofilm [073]

DER ULK : ILLUSTRIERTES WOCHENBLATT FUER HUMOR UND SATIRE – (Cont by: Ulk, 1875? Since 1873 suppl of Berliner Tageblatt) – Berlin, may 8 1872-sep 8 1899, jan 5 1906-sep 8 1932 – 1 – Inquire at Mikrofilmarchiv for details – gw Misc Inst [870]

DER ULK : ILLUSTRIERTES WOCHENBLATT FUER HUMOR UND SATIRE – (Mit Luecken, die zur Zeit noch ergaenzt werden) – Berlin, Mai 1872-Sep 1932 – 14r – 1 – DM1,050.00 – gw Mikro Press [790]

ULK *see* DER ULK

Ullathorne, William Bernard *see*
- CHARACTERISTICS FROM THE WRITINGS OF ARCHBISHOP ULLATHORNE
- CHRISTIAN PATIENCE

Ullery, Jacob G *see* MEN OF VERMONT

Ullman, W *see* LIBER REGIS CAPELLE

Ullmann, C *see*
- HISTORISCH ODER MYTHISCH?
- REFORMATOREN VOR DER REFORMATION VORNEHMLICH IN DEUTSCHLAND UND DEN NIEDERLAENDEN

Ullmann, Daniel *see* NON-SECTARIAN AND UNIVERSAL EDUCATION

Ullmann, Julius Frederick *see* EXPOSURE OF POPERY

Ullmann, Karl *see*
- THE SINLESSNESS OF JESUS; AN EVIDENCE FOR CHRISTIANITY
- THE SINLESSNESS OF JESUS: AN EVIDENCE FOR CHRISTIANITY
- DIE SUENDLOSIGKEIT JESU: EINE APOLOGETISCHE BETRACHTUNG

Ullmann, S *see* GESCHICHTE DER SPANISCH-PORTUGIESISCHEN JUDEN IN AMSTERDAM IM 17. JAHRHUNDERT

Ulloa, Antonio de *see*
- LA HISTORIA DELL' IMPRESA DI TRIPOLI DI BARBARIA, ...
- NOTICIAS AMERICANAS
- VITA DELL' INVITTISSIMO, E SACRATISSIMO IMPERATOR CARLO 5. ...

Ulloa Gofin, Alvaro F *see* MEMORIAL

Ulloa y Florez, Francisco, Ma *see* INFORME...PROPIEDAD...JUAN DE HINOJOSA Y..

ULLSTEINS BLATT DER HAUSFRAU *see*
- DIES BLATT GEHOERT DER HAUSFRAU

Ulman, Leon *see* OPINIONS OF THE OFFICE OF LEGAL COUNSEL OF THE UNITED STATES DEPARTMENT OF JUSTICE

Ulmann, Heinrich *see*
- FRANZ VON SICKINGEN
- DAS LEBEN DES DEUTSCHEN VOLKS BEI BEGINN DER NEUZEIT

Ulmer, Friedrich *see* DIE SEMITISCHEN EIGENNAMEN IM ALTEN TESTAMENT. 1. TEIL

Ulmer, G von *see*
- TRICHOPTERA
- DIE TRICHOPTEREN DES BALTISCHEN BERNSTEINS

ULRICEHAMNS TIDNING – Ulricehamn, Sweden, 1869-1900 – 10r – 1 – sw Kungliga [072]

ULRICEHAMNS TIDNING – Ulricehamn, Sweden. 1979- – 1 – sw Kungliga [072]

Ulrich, Christoffel *see* DEUTSCHE INNERLICHKEIT

Ulrich, Dale A *see* SPORT PROGRAM EFFECTS ON PARTICIPANTS WITH MENTAL RETARDATION

Ulrich de Ratisbonne, St *see* UDALRICUS. CONSTITUTIONES CLUNIACENSES. TROIS LIVRES

Ulrich, Paul *see* GUSTAV FREYTAGS ROMANTECHNIK

ULRICH VON HUTTEN / Nissel, Carl – Trauerspiel in 5 Acten. Leipzig, 1861 – 1 – DM30.00 – gw Mikro Press [820]

ULRICH ZASIUS : EIN BEITRAG ZUR GESCHICHTE DER RECHTSWISSENSCHAFT IM ZEITALTER DER REFORMATION / Stintzing, R – Basel: Schweighauser, 1857 – 1mf – us A.T.L.A. [240]

ULRICH ZWINGLI : EIN MARTIN LUTHER EBENBUERTIGER ZEUGE DES EVANGELISCHEN GLAUBENS: FESTSCHRIFT AUF DIE 400JAEHRIGEN GEBURTSTAGE DER REFORMATOREN ZUR BEFOERDERUNG WAHRER UNION AUF DEM BODEN DER FREIHEIT / Usteri, Johann Martin – Zuerich: S. Hoehr, 1883 – 1mf – us A.T.L.A. [240]

ULRICH ZWINGLI NACH DEN URKUNDLICHEN QUELLEN / Moerikofer, JC – Leipzig: S. Hirzel, 1867-1869 – 3mf – us A.T.L.A. [240]

Ulrichs, Christian *see* ZUR EMPFINDLICHKEIT DES TABAKKAEFERS LASIODERMA SERRICORNE (FABRICIUS) (COLEOPTERA: ANOBIIDAE) GEGENUEBER BEHANDLUNG MIT KOHLENSTOFFDIOXID UNTER HOCHDRUCK

ULRICH'S MICROFICHE – 1988. Quarterly: Oct, Jan, Apr, Jul. Complete eds. of Ulrich's International Periodicals Directory (now including Irregular Serials and Annuals) plus Ulrich's Update (formerly Bowker International Serials Update/Ulrich's Quarterly) – 9 – $350.00y – us Bowker [073]

ULRICH'S ON MICROFICHE / Bowker, Richard Rogers – (Quarterly $990.00) – 1997 – $680.00 – us Bowker [020]

Ulrici, Hermann *see* STRAUSS AS A PHILOSOPHICAL THINKER

ULRIKE WOYTICH : ROMAN / Wassermann, Jakob – Berlin: S Fischer, 1923 – 1r – 1 – us U.W. Library [830]

ULSTER COMMENTARY – v1- 1946- 1; v362- 5,6,9 – us UMI [073]

ULSTER EXAMINER – (Daily Examiner, 1871-72) – Belfast, Ireland. 14 Mar-31 Dec 1868; 1870-22 Jul 1882 – 21r – 1 – uk British Libr Newspaper [072]

ULSTER GENERAL ADVERTISER – Belfast, Ireland. 1851-53; 1858-70; 1872-Mar 1873. -w – 6r – 1 – uk British Libr Newspaper [072]

Ulster. General Synod. Ireland *see* RECORDS, 1691-1820

ULSTER OBSERVER – Belfast, Ireland. -w. 1 July 1862-16 Jan 1868. 5 1 2 reels – 1 – uk British Libr Newspaper [072]

ULSTER TIMES – Belfast. Ireland. -w. 31 Mar 1836-26 Aug 1843. (8 reels) – 1 – uk British Libr Newspaper [072]

THE ULSTERMAN – Belfast, Ireland. -w. 17 Nov 1852-31 Jan 1859. 6 reels – 1 – uk British Libr Newspaper [072]

ULTIMA AND CHILLINGOLLAH STAR – 1911-1951 – 7r – 1 – at Corangamite [980]

LA ULTIMA CIGUENA / Urabeyen, Felix – Madrid: Calpe, 1921 – 1 – sp Bibl Santa Ana [946]

ULTIMA LECCION DEL..."ABEJAS Y FLORES" / Rodriguez Rosillo, Abilio – Caceres: Instituto Nacional de Ensenanza Media "El Brocense", 1961 – 1 – sp Bibl Santa Ana [946]

LAS ULTIMAS DISPOSICIONES DEL ULTIMO PIZARRO DE LA CONQUISTA / Munoz de San Pedro, Miguel – Madrid: Imp. y Ed. Maestre, 1950 – 1 – sp Bibl Santa Ana [946]

THE ULTIMATE PROBLEMS OF CHRISTIANITY : EIGHT LECTURES / Clifford, John – (Includes indexes) – London: Kingsgate Press, [c1906] – 1mf – 9 – 0-8370-2689-X – 1985-0689 – us A.T.L.A. [240]

ULTIMATUM / Sanchez Bendito, Maria Jose – Madrid: Graf. DO-MO, 1971 – sp Bibl Santa Ana [946]

EL ULTIMO ANO DE PERON / Godio, Julio – [Bogota]: Universidad Simon Bolivar, 1st ed 1981 – 1 – CSUXADJ7563-B – us Hoover Inst Photo [320]

EL ULTIMO BRIDIS. ROMANCERO A LA MUERTE DE MANOLETE / Ramos Aparicio, Juan – Caceres: Imprenta La Moderna, (1949) – sp Bibl Santa Ana [780]

EL ULTIMO FILIBUSTERO. NOVELA HISTORICA. MANAGUA, 1933 / Chamorro, Pedro Joaquin – Madrid: Razon y Fe, 1934 – 1 – sp Bibl Santa Ana [830]

EL ULTIMO GALLINERO DE CON CANCIONES ESPIRITUALES DE JESUS DELGADO VALHOMDO, EN FESTIVAL DE TEATRO DE SITGES / Martinez Mediero, Manuel – Barcelona: AGPOgraf, 1971 – 1 – sp Bibl Santa Ana [240]

LOS ULTIMOS...!HASTA AHORA! / Sanchez-Arjona, Vicente – Sevilla: Graficas Tirvia, Tomo 5. 1959 – 1 – sp Bibl Santa Ana [810]

LOS ULTIMOS...!HASTA AHORA! / Sanchez-Arjona, Vicente – Sevilla: Imp. Alvarez, Tomos 1-4. 1959 – 1 – sp Bibl Santa Ana [810]

ULTRA : SECRET GERMAN MESSAGES FROM WORLD WAR 2 – (Military Signals: 143 reels. $15,785.00; Naval Signals: 173 reels. $14,280.00) – 200,000 secret German military messages intercepted by the British during World War 2. 316 reels – 1 – $25,555.00 – us UPA [940]

ULTRAMICROSCOPY – v1-15. 1975-84 – 1,5,6,13 – sz Elsevier [073]

ULTRAMONTANISM, OR, THE ROMAN CHURCH AND MODERN SOCIETY / Quinet, E – London: J. Chapman, 1845 – 1mf – us A.T.L.A. [240]

DER ULTRAMONTANISMUS ALS WELTANSCHAUUNG : AUF GRUND DES SYLLABUS / Goetz, Leopold Karl – Bonn: C. Georgi, 1905 – 1mf – us A.T.L.A. [240]

ULTRASONICS – (1982-. 1,5,6,9) – v1-. 1963- – 1 – us UMI [073]

ULTRASOUND IN MEDICINE AND BIOLOGY – v1- 1974- – 5,6,9 – us UMI [616]

ULTRIUSQUE COSMI MALORIS SCILICET ET MINORIS METAPHYSICA ATQUE TECHNICA HISTORIA / Flud, R – Oppenhemil: dere Johan-Theodi, 1617-1618 – 1 – us Sibley [780]

THE ULU, OR WOMAN'S KNIFE OF THE ESKIMO / Mason, Otis Tufton – BN 311 2. 1890 – 8 – ne IDC [306]

Uludong, F T *see* ANALYSIS OF THE DRAFT COMPACT OF ASSOCIATION

ULUM – Paris: Imprime Viktor Goupy. Cikaran: Ali Suavi, 1871-1872 – 9 – $25.00 – us MEDOC [956]

ULUM-I IKTISADIYYE VE ICTIMAIYYE MECMUASI – (Mueessisleri: Ahmed Suayb, Riza Tevfik, Mehmed Cavid. No. 1 (15 Kanuniewel 1324[1908])) – Istanbul: Hilal Matbaasi, Tanin Matbaasi, 1908-1911 – 2mf – 9 – $35.00 – us MEDOC [949]

Ulving, T *see* CONSONANT GRADATION IN ESKIMO

ULYSSES DISPATCH – Ulysses, NE. -w. May 1880; May 1882-May 1894; Oct 1895; Dec 1895-Jul 1904; Nov 1904; Jun 1908-May 1955 – 1 – us NE Hist [071]

ULYSSES REDUX: TRAGOEDIA NOVA / Gager, William – 1592. York Minster Library – 1 – uk Microform Academic [810]

ULYSSES S. GRANT PAPERS – (With guide) – 32r – 1 – $1,120.00 – Dist. us Scholarly Res – us L of C Photodup [975]

UM DEN KAISERSTUHL : EIN ROMAN AUS DEM DREISSIGJAEHRIGEN KRIEGE / Jensen, Wilhelm – Berlin: C Habel, 1878 – 1r – 1 – us U.W. Library [830]

UM DEN WEGZOLL / Kroeger, Timm – Hamburg: A Janssen, 1905 – 1r – 1 – us U.W. Library [830]

UM DIE WELTHERRSCHAFT : HISTORISCH-POLITISCHER ROMAN AUS DER GEGENWART / Retcliffe, John – Berlin: C Sigism, 1876 – us Res Libr [830]

UM GOETHE / Bahr, Hermann – (Includes bibliographical references) – Wien: Verlag des Volksbildungshauses Wiener Urania, 1917 – 1r – 1 – us U.W. Library [430]

UMAFRIKA – 17 Oct 1910-80. Continues: Izindaba Zabantu Bantu Topics. Zulu and Eng. 34 reels – 1 – 23.00r – us L of C Photodup [073]

UMAFRIKA – Mariannhill, South Africa. 1910-61 – 1 – sa State Libr [072]

L'UMANITA – 1987- – 2r per y – 5 – inquire – us Ross [072]

L'UMANITA – 1987-1995 – 2r per y – 5,6 – Sfr775.00 – sz Infoprint [072]

UMANITA – 1987-1995 – 2 times per yr – 6 – F2,900.00 – sz Infoprint [072]

UMANITA NOVA – Roma. 1963-66, 1968-. Incomplete. -w – 1 – us U.W. Library [073]

DIE UMARBEITUNG DER GOETHISCHEN GEDICHTE FUER DIE ERSTE GESAMTAUSGABE VON GOETHES WERKEN VOM JAHRE 1787-90 : BAND 8. WIEN UND LEIPZIG BEY J. STAHEL UND G.I. GOESCHEN. 1789 – (Includes bibliographical references) – Darmstadt: G Otto, 1901 – 1r – 1 – us U.W. Library [430]

UMAR-FALKE COLLECTION OF HAUSA MANUSCRIPTS IN ARABIC SCRIPT / Northwestern University. Library – 1 – us Res Libr [090]

Umasvati *see* TATTVARTHADHIGAMASU-TRA.ENGLISH AND SANSKRIT

UMATILLA COUNTY RECORD – Helix OR. Dec 21 28 1939 – 1 – us U.O. Library [071]

UMATILLA COUNTY SPECTATOR – Pendleton OR. Sep 7 1923 – 1 – us U.O. Library [071]

UMATILLA SPOKESMAN – Umatilla, OR. -w. 30 Oct 1925-8 Dec 1927. 1 roll – 1 – us U.O. Library [071]

UMATILLA SUN – Umatilla, OR. -w. 6 Oct 1949-31 Jan 1974. 6 rolls – 1 – us U.O. Library [071]

UMATILLA WARRIOR – Umatilla OR. Apr 26 May 24 1935 – 1 – us U.O. Library [071]

UMBERTO AND BRESCI – New York, NY, July 29, 1903 – 2mf or 1r – 1,9 – us I.H.R.C. [978]

UMBRAL DE ARMONIA, DE ALFONSO ALBALA / Sanchez Marin, Venancio – Madrid: Arbor, 1953 – 1 – sp Bibl Santa Ana [946]

Umbreit, Robert *see* BEITRAEGE ZUR GESCHICHTE DER ARBEITERBEWEGUNG IM RHEINISCH-WESTFAELISCHEN INDUSTRIEGEBIET

UMEA NYA TIDNING – Umea, Sweden. 1896-1928 – 18r – 1 – sw Kungliga [072]

UMEBLADET – (Nordsvenska Dagbladet, 1951-58) – Umea, Sweden. 1847-1951 – 241r – 1 – sw Kungliga [072]

UMENI A REMESLA / ed by Fabel, Karel – (1958-93 166mf) – 1994- – 4mf per y – 9 – inquire – us Ross [700]

UMER BLOK / Maiakovskii, Vladimir – Polnoe sobranie sochinenii. Tom 12. M., Goslitizdat. 1959. BR-3274 2 – 8 – ne IDC [460]

UMID – (Sal-i 1, shumarah-i 1-18 (15 Ramazan 1324-1 Safar 1325[6 November 1906-16 March 1907]); Purchase with Anjuman) – Tabriz – 1 – us MEDOC [950]

UMID-I IRAN – (New series 1-29 (8 Bahman 1357-29 Murdad 1358[27 January 1979-20 August 1979]). Missing issues: 2, 12, 15-18, 20-26) – Tihran: Ali Akbar Safi'pur – 1 reel – 1 – $95.00 – us MEDOC [950]

UMKC LAW REVIEW – (v1-53 1932-85 on reel $470.00. v54-63 1985-95 on mf $196.00. Title varies: v1-6 1932-38 as Kansas City Law Review. v7-31 1939-63 as University of Kansas City Law Review. v32-38 1964-70 as University of Missouri at Kansas City Law Review) – v1-63. 1932-95 – 5,6,9 – $666.00 set – us Hein [340]

Umlauf, Konrad *see* BERLINER ADRESSBUCH

UMLINDI WE NYANGA – East London, jan 15 1936-jan 16 1941 – us Res Libr [960]

UMM AL-QURA / Saudi Arabia – (1980-. ca 20.00y) – 1974-79 – 5r – 1 – $100.00; outside North America add $1.25r – us L of C Photodup [324]

UMMAT – (Sal-i 1, shumarah-'i 1–sal-i 2, shumarah-'i 99 (29 Farvardin 1358-18 Isfand 1359[Apr 18 1979-9 Mar 1981]). Missing issues: 24, 26, 72, 85, 101, 107, 108, 127) – Tehran: Junbish-i Musalmanan-i Mubariz, 1979- – 1 reel – 1 – $80.00 – us MEDOC [950]

UMPIRE/EMPIRE NEWS – 1884-1960 – 1 – uk Manchester Libr [072]

UMPQUA ENSIGN – (Set incl. Roseburg Ensign) – Roseburg, OR. 4 Feb 1872 – 2r – 1 – us U.O. Library [071]

UMPQUA FREE PRESS – Myrtle Creek OR. July 1 1982 + – 1 – us U.O. Library [071]

UMPQUA HERALD – Roseburg OR. May 10 1888 – 1 – us U.O. Library [071]

UMPQUA VALLEY TIMES – Roseburg, OR. 4 Dec 1905-1 Apr 1920. 8 rolls – 1 – us U.O. Library [071]

UMPQUA WEEKLY GAZETTE – Scottsburg, OR. 28 Apr 1854-3 Oct 1855. 1 roll – 1 – us U.O. Library [071]

UMSEBENZI / Communist Party. South Africa – Johannesburg-Cape Town. South Africa. July 1926-Mar. 1938. Missing Apr. 1-17, 1930; Apr. 1931; and June 1935 – 1 – 35.00r – us Hoover Inst Photo [072]

UMSEBENZI = THE SOUTH AFRICAN WORKER – Cape Town: Communist Party of South Africa, [1935-jun 6 1936] – 1r – 1 – us Res Libr [331]

UMSHUMAYELI WENDABA – Peddie, South Africa. 1 Jul 1837-30 Apr 1841. 1 reel – 1, 16 diazo available at reduced price – sa SA Libr [072]

DER UMSTURZ – Berlin, sep 1931-jan 1933 – 1 – Inquire at Mikrofilmarchiv for details – gw Misc Inst [072]

UMTALI POST *see* MANICA POST

UMTATA HERALD – Umtata, South Africa: Territorial Printers, 6 Feb 1884-25 Jun 1904 – 12r – 1 (diazo also available at reduced price) – sa SA Libr [072]

UMTATA HERALD *see* TERRITORIAL NEWS

UMTRI RESEARCH REVIEW – v13- 1982- – 1,5,6,9 – us UMI [620]

UMVIKELI-THEBE = THE AFRICAN DEFENDER – Cape Town: Moses M Kotane. n7-12 mar-oct/nov 1937 – us Res Libr [073]

UNA – v1-3. no. 10 (monthly: all publ). 1853-1855 – 1 reel – 1 – $65.00 – us UPA [360]

Una Sarton, Juan *see* MEMORIA...FERROCARRIL MERIDA-SEVILLA

DER UNABHAENGIGE – Bremen, Germany. 6 Oct 1892-30 Nov 1894 – 1r – 1 – gw Mikrofilm [072]

DER UNABHAENGIGE – (Cont by: Deutsches Volksblatt, nov 5 1893) – Bremen, sep 8, sep 22, oct 6 1892-sep 30 1894 – 1r – 1 – Inquire at Mikrofilmarchiv for details – gw Misc Inst [943]

UNAECHTER ACACIEN-BAUM. ZUR ERMUNTERUNG DES ALLGEMEINEN ANBAUES DIESER IN IHREN ART / Medikus, F K – Leipzig. 1794-97. B-8142 1 – 9 – ne IDC [580]

UNAMUNO / Barea, Arturo – Buenos Aires: Editorial Sur S.R.L., 1959 – 1 – sp Bibl Santa Ana [972]

UNAMUNO EN ALEMANIA / Sanchez Morales, Narciso – Pamplona: Ediciones Universidad de Navarra, 1969. Sep. de Nuestro Tiempo, pp. 411-432 – sp Bibl Santa Ana [946]

Unamuno, Miguel *see* PARA EVITAR EL VACIAMIENTO DEL PERONISMO

Unanue, H *see* HISTORIA DE LAS MISIONES

UNARMED DEFENSE FOR THE AMERICAN SOLDIER / U.S. Department of Defense – In Indonesian. SE 10,740 1. 1962 – 9 – ne IDC [324]

Unat, Faik Resit *see* KITAB-I CIHAN-NUEMA [NESRI TARIHI]

DAS UNAUSLOESCHLICHE SIEGEL : ROMAN / Langgaesser, Elisabeth – 3. Aufl. Hamburg: Claassen & Goverts, 1949, c1946 – 1r – 1 – us U.W. Library [830]

UNBEDEUTENDE REIMWOERTER UND ENJAMBEMENT BEI RILKE UND IN DER NEUEREN LYRIK / Wagner, Annemarie – (Includes bibliographical references) – Bonn a. Rh.: L Roehrscheid, 1930 – 1r – 1 – us U.W. Library [780]

Unbegaun, B O *see*
- CATALOGUE DES PERIODIQUES SLAVES ET RELATIFS AUX ETUDES SLAVES DES BIBLIOTHEQUES DE PARIS
- RUSSIAN VERSIFICATION

DER UNBEKANNTE GAST / Wassermann, Jakob – Berlin: S Fischer, 1923 – 1r – 1 – us U.W. Library [830]

DIE UNBEKANNTE H : NOVELLE / Muschler, Reinhold Conrad – Duesseldorf: W Plaut, c1934 – 1r – 1 – us U.W. Library [830]

UNBELIEF IN THE EIGHTEENTH CENTURY / Cairns, John – Edinburgh: Adam & Charles Black, 1881. 1 fiche – 9 – us A.T.L.A. [240]

UNBELIEF IN THE NINETEENTH CENTURY: A CRITICAL HISTORY / Sheldon, Henry Clay – New York: Eaton & Mains, 1907. 1 fiche – 9 – us A.T.L.A. [240]

UNBOUND RECORDS OF THE GENERAL LAND OFFICE RELATING TO PRIVATE LAND CLAIMS IN LOUISIANA, 1805-1896 – 2r – 1 – M1385 – us Nat'l Archives [324]

UNBOUND RECORDS OF THE U.S. HOUSE OF REPRESENTATIVES, 8TH CONGRESS, 1803-1805 – 1 – us Nat'l Archives [324]

UNBOUND RECORDS OF THE U.S. SENATE, 8TH CONGRESS, 1803-1805 / U.S. Senate – 5r – 1 – M1403 – us Nat'l Archives [324]

UNCALENDARED STATE PAPERS FOREIGN OF ELIZABETH 1 (MAY 1592-MAR 1603) / Great Britain. Public Record Office – (PRO Class SP75, 77, 78, 80, 81, 82, 84, 85, 94, 99). Denmark; Flanders; France; German Empire and Hungary; German States; Hamburg and Hanse Towns; Holland; Italian States and Rome; and Venice – 1 – us Primary [941]

THE UNCHANGING EAST / Barr, Robert – (v2. 03357) – v1. Boston: L. Page, 1900. 03356. (Pre-1900 Canadiana) – 9 – cn C.I.H.M. [950]

UNCIVILIZED: A POEM ON TITLE DEEDS / Cooke, Edmund Vance – 1p – 9 – 1.00f – at Libertarian Micro [320]

THE UNCIVILIZED RACES OF MEN IN ALL COUNTRIES OF THE WORLD : BEING A COMPREHENSIVE ACCOUNT OF THEIR MANNERS AND CUSTOMS, AND OF THEIR PHYSICAL, SOCIAL, MENTAL, MORAL AND RELIGIOUS CHARACTERISTICS / Wood, John G – 2v. 1879 – 1r – 1 – us Ross [306]

THE UNCLASSED / Gissing, George Robert – London: Lawrence and Bullen, 1895 – 1 roll – 1 – 1-55879-696-7 – uk Libr Preservation [890]

UNCLASSIFIED AND DECLASSIFIED REPORTS / Great Britain. Atomic Energy Authority – 1947-69 – 7 – uk Microform Academic [324]

UNCLE JOHN VASSAR : OR, THE FIGHT OF FAITH / Vassar, Thomas Edwin – New York: American Tract Society, c1879 – 1mf – 9 – 0-8370-6709-X – 1986-0709 – us A.T.L.A. [920]

Uncle Josephus *see* THRILLING FACTS FROM MISSIONARY FIELDS

UNCLE SILAS : A TALE OF BERTRAM-HAUGH / Le Fanu, Joseph Sheridan – London: Richard Bentley, 1864 – 2 rolls – 1 – 1-55879-221-X – uk Libr Preservation [830]

UNCOLLECTED ESSAYS / Pater, Walter – Portland, Me.: T.B. Mosher, 1903 – 1 roll – 1 – 1-55879-900-1 – uk Libr Preservation [840]

THE UNCONSCIOUS; AN INTRODUCTION TO FREUDIAN PSYCHOLOGY / Levine, Israel – London: L. Parsons, (1923). 215p – 1 – us U.W. Library [150]

UNCONSCIOUS TESTIMONY : OR, THE SILENT WITNESS OF THE HEBREW TO THE TRUTH OF THE HISTORICAL SCRIPTURES / Hutton, Charles F – (Includes indexes) – London: Kegan Paul, Trench, 1882 – 1mf – 9 – 0-8370-3710-7 – 1985-1710 – us A.T.L.A. [220]

UNCTAD OFFICIAL RECORDS : ANNEXES: 1ST-32ND SESSIONS / United Nations – 1965-1986 – E.71 F.81 S.71 – 9 – us U.N. Pubs [324]

UNCTAD OFFICIAL RECORDS : COMMITTEE ON COMMODITIES: 1ST-13TH SESSIONS / United Nations – 1965-1988 – E.19 F.21 R.11 S.15 – 9 – us U.N. Pubs [324]

UNCTAD OFFICIAL RECORDS : COMMITTEE ON ECONOMIC CO-OPERATION AMONG DEVELOPING COUNTRIES: 1ST-4TH AND 1ST SPEC. SESS / United Nations – 1977-1986 – E/F.5 E.6 F.1 R.3 – 9 – us U.N. Pubs [324]

UNCTAD OFFICIAL RECORDS : COMMITTEE ON INVISIBLES AND FINANCING RELATED TO TRADE: 1ST-12TH SESSIONS / United Nations – 1965-1987 – E.21 F.23 R.14 S.17 – 9 – us U.N. Pubs [324]

UNCTAD OFFICIAL RECORDS : COMMITTEE ON MANUFACTURES: 1ST-11TH SESSIONS / United Nations – 1965-1986 – E.15 F.16 R.11 S.14 – 9 – us U.N. Pubs [324]

UNCTAD OFFICIAL RECORDS : COMMITTEE ON PREFERENCES: 1ST-14TH SESSIONS / United Nations – 1968-1986 – E.20 F.12 R.13 S.16 – 9 – us U.N. Pubs [324]

UNCTAD OFFICIAL RECORDS : COMMITTEE ON SHIPPING: 1ST-13TH SESSION / United Nations – 1965-1988 – E/F.20 E.22 F.17 R.18 – 9 – us U.N. Pubs [324]

UNCTAD OFFICIAL RECORDS : COMMITTEE ON TRANSFER OF TECHNOLOGY: 1ST-6TH SESSIONS / United Nations – 1975-1988 – E.8 F.8 R.2 S.3 – 9 – us U.N. Pubs [324]

UNCTAD OFFICIAL RECORDS : INTERGOVERNMENTAL GROUP ON SUPPLEMENTARY FINANCING: 5TH SESSION / United Nations – 1969 – E.1 F.1 S.1 – 9 – us U.N. Pubs [324]

UNCTAD OFFICIAL RECORDS : OFFICIAL RECORDS. 1ST-29TH SESSIONS / United Nations – 1965-1985 – E.142 F.149 S.144 – 9 – us U.N. Pubs [324]

UNCTAD OFFICIAL RECORDS : PERMANENT GROUP ON SYNTHETICS AND SUBSTITUTES: 1ST-5TH SESSION / United Nations – 1965-1971 – E.5 F.5 R.5 S.5 – 9 – us U.N. Pubs [324]

UNCTAD OFFICIAL RECORDS : REPORT ON THE TRADE AND DEVELOPMENT BOARD TO THE GENERAL ASSEMBLY / United Nations – 1965-1988 – E/F.104 E.100 F.98 – 9 – us U.N. Pubs [324]

UNCTAD OFFICIAL RECORDS : RESOLUTIONS: 1ST-35TH SESSIONS / United Nations – 1965-1988 – E.69 F.76 R.33 S.44 – 9 – us U.N. Pubs [324]

UNCTAD OFFICIAL RECORDS : WORKING PARTY ON THE MEDIUM-TERM PLAN AND THE PROGRAMME BUDGET: 1ST-16TH SESSIONS / United Nations – 1980-1988 – E/F.16 E.18 F.6 R.6 – 9 – us U.N. Pubs [324]

"UND ALLES IST ZERSTOBEN" : ERINNERUNGEN AUS DER JAHRHUNDERTWENDE / Weisbach, Werner – Wien: H Reichner, c1937 – 1 – us U.W. Library [890]

UND DEINE WAELDER RAUSCHEN FORT : KINDHEIT IN UNTERSTEIER / Weinhandl, Margrete – 2. Aufl. Graz: Leykam-Verlag, 1943 – 1r – 1 – us U.W. Library [890]

UND DENNOCH BLUEHT DIE ERDE : ROMAN / Planner-Petelin, Rose – 3. Aufl. Hamburg: Hanseatische Verlagsanstalt, c1942 – 1r – 1 – us U.W. Library [830]

UND HATTET DER LIEBE NICHT : EIN ZYKLUS NEUER GEDICHTE / Wildgans, Anton – 5. Aufl. Berlin: A Juncker, 1917 – 1r – 1 – us U.W. Library [810]

EIN UND ZWANZIG SINAITISCHE INSCHRIFTEN : VERSUCH EINER ERKLAERUNG / Tuch, Friedrich – (In German and Aramaic) – Leipzig: Wilh Vogel, 1849 – 1mf – 9 – 0-8370-8392-3 – 1986-2392 – us A.T.L.A. [470]

UNDANG-UNDANG DASAR 1945 DAN PENDJELASAN / Indonesia. Constitution – SE-4274 1. 1962 – 9 – ne IDC [323]

Undank, J *see* EST-IL BON? EST-IL MECHANT?

UNDECIMA CONFERENCIA: INFLUENCIA DE LA MUJER EN LA SOCIEDAD / Moreno Nieto, Jose – 1869 – 9 – $1.50f – sp Bibl Santa Ana [305]

UNDER HIS BANNER : PAPERS ON THE MISSIONARY WORK OF MODERN TIMES / Tucker, Henry William – (Includes index) – 5th ed. London: S P C K, [ca 1876] – 2mf – 9 – 0-8370-6431-7 – 1986-0431 – us A.T.L.A. [240]

UNDER LOVE'S RULE / Braddon, Mary Elizabeth – British Fiction Archive: Unit 5 – 9 – uk Bell [830]

UNDER MARCHING ORDERS: A STORY OF MARY PORTER GAMEWELL / Hubbard, Ethel Daniels – New York: Presb. Board of For. Miss., 1909. xii,222p. 1 fiche – 9 – us A.T.L.A. [240]

UNDER ONE ROOF / Cholmondeley, Mary – British Fiction Archive: Unit 3 – 9 – uk Bell [830]

UNDER OUR FLAG: A STUDY OF NATIONAL CONDITIONS IN AMERICA FROM THE STANDPOINT OF WOMAN'S HOME MISSION WORK / Guernsey, Alice M – 1903 – 9 – us A.T.L.A. [240]

UNDER THE CROWN – v1, no.1-6. Jan-Jun 1869. -m. London: Groombridge, 1869. 1 reel. 1184 – 1 – us U.W. Library [800]

UNDER THE GRIDIRON: A SUMMER IN THE UNITED STATES AND THE FAR WEST, INCLUDING A RUN THROUGH CANADA / Davenport, Montague – London: Tinsley, 1876. 03644. (Pre-1900 Canadiana) – 9 – cn C.I.H.M. [910]

UNDER THE RED CROSS FLAG; WITH THE MEDICALS IN ACTION / Westerdale, T L Barlow – 2nd ed. London: C.H. Kelly, 1916 – 1 – us U.W. Library [355]

UNDER THE RED FLAG; AND OTHER TALES / Braddon, Mary Elizabeth – British Fiction Archive: Unit 5 – 9 – uk Bell [830]

UNDER THE STARS AND BARS: MEMORIES OF FOUR YEARS SERVICE WITH THE OGLETHORPES, OF AUGUSTA, GEORGIA / Clark, Walter A – 4 fiches. F-0732 – 9 – us A.G.L.L. [978]

UNDER THREE TSARS : LIBERTY OF CONSCIENCE IN RUSSIA, 1856-1909 / Latimer, Robert Sloan – New York: F.H. Revell, [1900?] – 1mf – us A.T.L.A. [947]

UNDER TWO FLAGS / Ouida – British Fiction Archive: Unit 3 – 9 – uk Bell [830]

UNDERGRADUATE STUDENTS' PERCEIVED REASONS FOR SELECTION OF HEALTH PROMOTION AS A MAJOR / Landers, Susan K A – Purdue University, 1996 – 1mf – 9 – HE 567 – us Microform Publ [613]

THE UNDERGROUND AND ALTERNATIVE PRESS IN BRITAIN – (1973-86. Available by the year) – Basic Set: 1961-72. Publs and docs of 83 groups and papers. Series: Harvester-Primary Social Sources. Includes bibliographical guides – 1,9 – us Primary [941]

THE UNDERGROUND AND ALTERNATIVE PRESS IN BRITAIN – Annual updates: 1973-1992 – 1 – us Primary [941]

THE UNDERGROUND AND ALTERNATIVE PRESS IN BRITAIN – Special supplement. Oz Magazine, 1967-73 – 1 – us Primary [941]

UNDERGROUND LITERATURE IN POLAND FROM WORLD WAR 2 – 1941?-1944 – 1 reel – 1 – CSUXANL3685-B – us Hoover Inst Photo [355]

UNDERGROUND MOVEMENTS IN BULGARIA DURING WORLD WAR 2 PAMPHLET COLLECTION – 1944 – 1 – CSUXANL3657-B – us Hoover Inst Photo [355]

UNDERGROUND MOVEMENTS IN ITALY DURING WORLD WAR 2 PAMPHLET COLLECTION – 1943-1984 – 1 reel – 1 – CSUXANM9884-B – us Hoover Inst Photo [355]

UNDERGROUND MOVEMENTS IN MACEDONIA DURING WORLD WAR 2 PAMPHLET COLLECTION – 1968 – 1 reel – 1 – CSUXANL3504-B – us Hoover Inst Photo [355]

UNDERGROUND MOVEMENTS IN NORWAY DURING WORLD WAR 2 PAMPHLET COLLECTION – 1943-1963 – 1 reel – 1 – CSUXANN0288-B – us Hoover Inst Photo [355]

UNDERGROUND MOVEMENTS IN OCCUPIED FRANCE DURING WORLD WAR 2 PAMPHLET COLLECTION – 1943-1987? – 2r – 1 – CSUXANM9882-B – us Hoover Inst Photo [355]

UNDERGROUND MOVEMENTS IN POLAND DURING WORLD WAR 2 PAMPHLET COLLECTION – 1944-1988 – 1 reel – 1 – CSUXANL3678-B – us Hoover Inst Photo [355]

UNDERGROUND MOVEMENTS IN SLOVAKIA PAMPHLET COLLECTION – 1969 – 1 – CSUXANL5648-B – us Hoover Inst Photo [355]

UNDERGROUND MOVEMENTS IN SLOVENIA DURING WORLD WAR 2 PAMPHLET COLLECTION – 1968-1971 – 1 reel – 1 – CSUXANL3515-B – us Hoover Inst Photo [355]

UNDERGROUND MOVEMENTS IN THE BALKANS DURING WORLD WAR 2 PAMPHLET COLLECTION – 1947 – 1 – CSUXANL3661-B – us Hoover Inst Photo [355]

UNDERGROUND MOVEMENTS IN THE NETHERLANDS DURING WORLD WAR 2 PAMPHLET COLLECTION – 1942-1982 – 1 reel – 1 – CSUXANN0287-B – us Hoover Inst Photo [355]

UNDERGROUND MOVEMENTS IN THE SOVIET UNION DURING WORLD WAR 2 PAMPHLET COLLECTION – 1943-1979 – 1 reel – 1 – CSUXANR3103-B – us Hoover Inst Photo [355]

UNDERGROUND MOVEMENTS IN YUGOSLAVIA PAMPHLET COLLECTION – 1945-1969? – 1 reel – 1 – CSUXANQ9810-B – us Hoover Inst Photo [947]

THE UNDERGROUND PRESS COLLECTIONS, 1965-1985 – (550 underground newspapers 1963-85. Hoover Supplement 266 titles $1295; University of Missouri-Columbia Supplement 123 titles $695) – 501r – 1 – $36,295.00 complete collection – us UMI [071]

UNDERGROUND SPACE – v.1- 1977- – 5,6,9 – us UMI [073]

UNDERGROUND SPACE *see* ADVANCES IN TUNNELLING TECHNOLOGY AND SURFACE USE

Underhill, Edward B *see*
- CONFESSIONS OF FAITH
- A MARTYROLOGY OF THE CHURCHES OF CHRIST, 1524-52

Underhill, Evelyn *see* RUYSBROECK

Underhill, Harry Clay *see* A TREATISE ON THE LAW OF LANDLORD AND TENANT.

UNDERRICHT DER NEWEN IRSALN VND SECT HALBEN, SO VETZT AN VIL ORTEN IM HEYLIGEN REICH ENTSTEEN – BME-105 1 – 9 – ne IDC [240]

UNDERRICHTUNG VON DEM WIDERTAUFF / Oecolampad, J & Ecolampadius, J – Basel, A. Cratandrus. 1527. BME-90 1 – 9 – ne IDC [240]

UNDERSCHEIT. TUSSCHEN RECHTE LEER VNDE VALSCHE LEER DER TWISTIGEN ARTICULEN / Adam, Pastor – BME-321 1 – 9 – ne IDC [240]

UNDERSEA BIOMEDICAL RESEARCH – (v.6-. 1979- 5,6,9) – v.1-. 1974- – 1 – us UMI [550]

UNDERSOGELSES-REISE TIL OSTKYSTEN AF GRONLAND / Graah, WA – Kjobenhavn. 1832. Illus. BN-229 2 – 8 – ne IDC [910]

UNDERSTANDING CHINA – Pasadena, CA. 1971-1976 – 1r – 1 – $50.00 – R03389 – us Library Micro [071]

UNDERSTANDING THE BIBLE (CCC159) / Hollister, G W – (In Chinese) – 1st ed. Hong Kong: Council on Christian Literature for Overseas Chinese, 1955 – 1r – 1 – 1984-B500 – us A.T.L.A. [220]

UNDERTAKER'S RECORDS / Smith, C.W., Mortuary, Douglas County, KS – 1890-1907 – 1 – us KS Hist [920]

UNDERTAKERS REGISTER / Lamb-Roberts Funeral Home, Ottawa, KS – 1912-1919 – 1 – us KS Hist [920]

UNDERTAKER'S REGISTER AND ACCOUNT BOOK[S] / Penwell, L.M. Undertaking Company, Topeka, KS – 1894-1947 – 1 – us KS Hist [920]

UNDERWEYSUNG DER MESSUMG MIT DEM ZIRKEL UND RICHTSCHEYT IN LINIEN EBNEN UND GANTZEN CORPOREN ZU SAMEN GEZOGE UND ZU NUTZ ALLE KUNST-LIEBHABENDEN MIT ZU GEHOERIGEN FIGUREN IN TRUCK GEBRACHT / Duerer, Albrecht – O 240. 1525 – 9 – ne IDC [760]

UNDERWEYSUNG DER PROPORTION UND STELLUNG DER POSSEN / Schoen, E – O 427 1. 1542 – 9 – ne IDC [760]

Underwood, Horace Grant *see*
- THE CALL OF KOREA
- HYMNS OF PRAISE

Underwood, L H *see* WITH TOMMY TOMPKINS IN KOREA

Underwood, Lillias Horton *see* FIFTEEN YEARS AMONG THE TOP-KNOTS, OR, LIFE IN KOREA

Underwood, Lisa S *see* ASSESSMENT OF THE PLANNING AND IMPLEMENTATION PROCESS OF WORKSITE HEALTH PROMOTION PROGRAMS

THE UNDERWORLD OF INDIA / MacMunn, George Fletcher – London: Jarrolds, 1933. 284p. ill – 1 – us U.W. Library [950]

UNDERWRITERS' REPORT OF CALIFORNIA – v.2-. 1906-. Continues Life Insurance Report – 1 – us UMI [073]

UNDERWRITERS SURVEY BUREAU *see* PLANS D'ASSURANCES DE VILLES DU QUEBEC

Underwriters Survey Bureau *see* INSURANCE PLAN OF THE CITY OF MONTREAL

UNDINE : AND SINTRAM AND HIS COMPANIONS / La Motte-Fouque, Friedrich Heinrich Karl – New ed. New York: G P Putnam, 1852 – 1r – 1 – us U.W. Library [830]

UNDINE: EINE ERZAHLUNG VON FRIEDRICH BARON DE LA MOTTE FOUQUE / La Motte-Fouque, Friedrich Heinrich Karl – Leipzig: G. Fock, 1889. 110p. illus. cover in colors – 1 – us U.W. Library [830]

UNDOGMATISCHES CHRISTENTUM : BETRACHTUNGEN EINES DEUTSCHEN IDEALISTEN / Dreyer, Otto – Braunschweig: C A Schwetschke, 1888 – 1mf – 9 – 0-8370-2962-7 – 1985-0962 – us A.T.L.A. [240]

Undolskii, V M *see* SLAVIANO-RUKOPISI V.M. UNDOLSHOGO.

UNDZER GEDANK = OUR THOUGHT – (In Yiddish) – Berlin, DE. no1. Mar 1931 – 1r – 1 – $25.00 – cn Can Microfilming [072]

UNDZER MOMENT = OUR MOMENT – (In Yiddish) – Regensburg, DE. no17(35). 25 Sep 1947 – 1r – 1 – $25.00 – cn Can Microfilming [072]

UNDZER MOMENT = OUR MOMENT – (In Yiddish) – Tel Aviv, IS. no29. 31 Aug 1950 – 1r – 1 – $25.00 – cn Can Microfilming [072]

UNDZER SHTIME = OUR VOICE – (In Yiddish) – Bergen-Belsen (British Zone), DE. no1 12 Jul 1945-no24 30 Oct 1947 – 1r – 1 – $50.00 – cn Can Microfilming [072]

UNDZER STIME – Paris. avr 1938-juin 1940. Titre francais: Notre Voix.En Yiddish – 1 – fr A.C.R.P.P. [073]

UNDZER VORT = OUR WORD – (In Yiddish) – Bamberg, DE. Mar 1946-v2 no47(no85) 5 Dec 1947 [Bamberg Edition of "Our Moment"] – 1r – 1 – $60.00 – cn Can Microfilming [072]

UNDZERE KINDER = OUR CHILDREN – (In Yiddish) – Brussels, BE. Mar 1947 – 1r – 1 – $20.00 – cn Can Microfilming [072]

UNE. CONSIGNAS APROBADAS POR EL PRIMER CONGRESO NACIONAL UNCISTA REUNIDO EN CARACAS... / Bayle, Constantino – Madrid: Razon y Fe, 1939 – 1 – sp Bibl Santa Ana [946]

D'UNE REFORME INTERNATIONALE DU DROIT MARITIME / Courcy, A de – Paris, 1863 – 3mf – 1 – ILM-3423/1 – ne IDC [327]

UNEMPLOYMENT COMPENSATION AND INTERPRETATION SERVICE BENEFIT SERIES / U.S. Dept of Health and Human Services – Social Security Board. v1-10. 1937-47 (all publ) – 340mf – 9 – $510.00 – LLMC 81-240 – us L.L.M.C. [360]

UNEMPLOYMENT IN STATES AND LOCAL AREAS / U.S. Department of Labor – Monthly – 9 – $41.00y in US $51.25 outside – S-N 829-002-00000-1. Sub-list ID-LAUS – us Gov't Printing [324]

UNEMPLOYMENT INSURANCE REVIEW / U.S. Department of Labor – Unemploy Insur Service, Manpower Admin. v1-5. 1964-68 (all publ) – 22mf – 9 – $33.00 – LLMC 81-244 – us L.L.M.C. [073]

UNEMPLOYMENT PROBLEM IN IMO STATE : A STUDY OF 1978 PRIMARY AND SECONDARY SCHOOL-LEAVERS / Nigeria. Imo State. Imo State Manpower Committee – 2mf – 9 – DE-104/1 – ne IDC [331]

DAS UNENDLICHE IN DER MITTELALTERLICHEN METAPHYSIK UND IN DER KANTISHEN DIALEKTIK / Dempf, A – Muenster, 1926 – 2mf – 8 – ne Slangenburg [110]

DIE UNENTWEGTEN : ROMAN / Achleitner, Richard – Graz: L Stocker, [1943] – 1r – 1 – us U.W. Library [830]

UNEQUAL OPPORTUNITIES : THE CASE OF WOMEN AND THE MEDIA / Gallagher, Margaret – 1981 repr 1983 – 9 – 92-3-101897-3 – fr UNESCO [305]

UNERFUELLTE GESCHICHTEN / Bartsch, Rudolf Hans – Leipzig: L Staackmann, c1916 – 1r – 1 – us U.W. Library [830]

UNESCO : IBE EDUCATION THESAURUS – 5th rev enl ed 1991 – xii/139p – 9 – 92-3-102723-9 – fr UNESCO [370]

UNESCO – (Regional Advisory Team for Education Planning in Asia. Long-term projections for education in Indonesia: report. SE 6050; 1. 1965. SF 12.00; 9. Science Cooperation Office for South East Asia. Proceedings of symposium on humid tropics vegetation, Tjiawi, Indonesia. SE 6967; 1. 1958. SF 16.00; IDC; 9) – ne IDC [324]

UNESCO : UNIVERSALITY AND INTERNATIONAL INTELLECTUAL CO-OPERATION / M'Bow, Amadou-Mahtar – 1986 – 9 – 92-3-102450-7 – fr UNESCO [340]

UNESCO *see*
- CUARTA CONFERENCIA INTERNACIONAL SOBRE LA EDUCACION DE ADULTOS, PARIS, 19-29 DE MARZO DE 1985
- FOURTH INTERNATIONAL CONFERENCE ON ADULT EDUCATION, PARIS, 19-29 MARCH 1985
- JOURNAL OF INFORMATION SCIENCE, LIBRARIANSHIP AND ARCHIVES ADMINISTRATION
- QUATRIEME CONFERENCE INTERNATIONAL SUR L'EDUCATION DES ADULTES, PARIS, 19-29 MARS 1985
- RECORDS OF THE GENERAL CONFERENCES
- RECORDS OF THE INTERGOVERNMENTAL COPYRIGHT CONFERENCE, GENEVA 1952
- STUDIES ON SELECTED DEVELOPMENT PROBLEMS IN VARIOUS COUNTRIES IN THE MIDDLE EAST
- UNESCO AND EDUCATION THROUGHOUT THE WORLD
- UNIVERSITY TEACHING OF SOCIAL SCIENCES INTERNATIONAL RELATIONS
- WORLD EDUCATION REPORT 1991

UNESCO ACTIVITIES IN THE FIELD OF SCIENCE AND TECHNOLOGY IN THE ARAB REGION – 1987 – 9 – 92-3-102423-X – fr UNESCO [340]

UNESCO AND EDUCATION THROUGHOUT THE WORLD / UNESCO – Paris, 1985 – 1mf – 9 – DE-133/1 – ne IDC [370]

UNESCO CHRONICLE / United Nations – v1-25. 1955-79 – 130mf – 9 – $195.00 – LLMC 81-910 – us L.L.M.C. [370]

UNESCO COURIER / United Nations – v1- . 1948- – 9 – LLMC 81-911 – us L.L.M.C. [370]

UNESCO COURIER – (v23- 1970- 5,6; v24- 1971- 9) – v1- 1948- – 1 – us UMI [370]

UNESCO Educational Planning Mission *see* THE DEVELOPMENT PROGRAMME IN EDUCATION FOR THE GAMBIA, 1965-1975

UNESCO et al *see* TROPICAL GRAZING LAND ECOSYSTEMS

UNESCO HANDBOOK FOR BIOLOGY TEACHERS IN AFRICA – 1986 – 329p – 9 – 92-3-102210-5 – fr UNESCO [370]

UNESCO. International Study of the Conceptualization and Methodology of Population Education (ISCOMPE) *see*
- POPULATION EDUCATION
- STUDY OF THE CONTRIBUTION OF POPULATION EDUCATION TO EDUCATIONAL RENEWAL AND INNOVATION IN EL SALVADOR, THE REPUBLIC OF KOREA, PHILIPPINES AND TUNISIA
- SURVEY AND ANALYSIS OF TEACHER-TRAINING ACTIVITIES IN POPULATION EDUCATION, FAMILY LIFE EDUCATION AND SEX EDUCATION
- TEACHER'S STUDY GUIDE ON THE BIOLOGY OF HUMAN POPULATIONS: ASIA

UNESCO LIST OF DOCUMENTS AND PUBLICATIONS : ANNOTATED LISTS AND INDEXES – 9 – fr UNESCO [020]

UNESCO LIST OF DOCUMENTS AND PUBLICATIONS 1987-1989 – (Trilingual: English/French/Spanish; volumes are not sold separately) – 1993 – 9 – 92-3-002840-1 – fr UNESCO [020]

UNESCO. Paris *see* CUMULATIVE INDEX TO ENGLISH TRANSLATIONS, 1948-1968, UNESCO

UNESCO SCIENCE AND TECHNOLOGY ACTIVITIES IN ASIA AND THE PACIFIC – 1983 – 9 – 92-3-102066-8 – fr UNESCO [500]

UNESCO. Social Science Documentation Centre *see* WORLD LIST OF SOCIAL SCIENCE PERIODICALS

UNESCO SOURCEBOOK FOR OUT-OF-SCHOOL SCIENCE AND TECHNOLOGY EDUCATION – 1986 – 202p – 9 – 92-3-102386-1 – fr UNESCO [370]

UNESCO SOURCEBOOK FOR SCIENCE IN THE PRIMARY SCHOOL : A WORKSHOP APPROACH TO TEACHER EDUCATION / Harlen, Wynne & Elstgeest, Jos – 1993 – 271p – 9 – 92-3-102721-2 – fr UNESCO [370]

UNESCO SOURCEBOOK IN CLIMATOLOGY FOR HYDROLOGISTS AND WATER RESOURCE ENGINEERS / ed by Sanderson, M – 1990 – xvi/109p – 9 – 92-3-102712-3 – fr UNESCO [550]

UNESCO STANDARD-SETTING INSTRUMENTS : INCORPORATING SUPPLEMENT 3 – 1994 – 9 – 92-3-102942-8 – fr UNESCO [620]

UNESCO STATISTICAL YEARBOOK – 9 – fr UNESCO [340]

UNESCO STATISTICAL YEARBOOK 1992 = ANNUAIRE STATISTIQUE DE L'UNESCO 1992 – (Trilingual: English/French/Spanish; Introductory texts are also in Russian and Arabic) – 1992 – 9 – 92-3-002801-0 – fr UNESCO [340]

UNESCO STATISTICAL YEARBOOK 1994 – (Trilingual: English/French/Spanish) – 1994 – 9 – 92-3-003032-5 – fr UNESCO [340]

UNESCO THESAURUS : A STRUCTURED LIST OF DESCRIPTORS FOR INDEXING AND RETRIEVING LITERATURE IN THE FIELDS OF EDUCATION, SCIENCE, SOCIAL AND HUMAN SCIENCES, CULTURE, COMMUNICATION AND INFORMATION – (English/French/Spanish) – new ed 1995 – 706 p – 9 – 92-3-003100-3 – fr UNESCO [020]

UNESCO THROUGH ITS POSTERS – (Trilingual: English/French/Spanish) – 1989 – 96p – 9 – fr UNESCO [060]

UNESCO (United Nations Educational, Scientific and Cultural Organization) *see* CHRONICLE

UNESCO YEARBOOK ON PEACE AND CONFLICT STUDIES – 9 – fr UNESCO [320]

UNESCO'S ACTIVITIES IN SCIENCE AND TECHNOLOGY IN THE EUROPEAN AND NORTH AMERICAN REGION – 1979 – 9 – 92-3-101727-6 – fr UNESCO [340]

UNESCO'S STANDARD-SETTING INSTRUMENTS – 9 – fr UNESCO [620]

UNFALLHEILKUNDE – v. 52-83. 1949-80 – 1,5,9 – 3264.00 – us UMI [617]

UNFALLSTATISTISCHES ZUR UNFALL VERSICHERUNG / Dehn, Paul – Leipzig, 1881. 52p – 1 – us U.W. Library [360]

UNFEHLBAR : SCHAUSPIEL IN FUENF AUFZUEGEN / Voss, Richard – Cassel: T Kay, 1874 – 1r – 1 – us U.W. Library [820]

DAS UNFEHLBARE LEHRAMT DES PAPSTES NACH DER ENTSCHEIDUNG DES VATICANISCHEN CONCILS / Ketteler, Wilhelm Emmanuel, Freiherr von – (Includes bibliographical references) – Mainz: Franz Kirchheim, 1871 – 1mf – 9 – 0-8370-8523-3 – 1986-2523 – us A.T.L.A. [240]

DER UNFEHLBARE PAPST. ERSTER VORTRAG / Elvenich, Peter Joseph – Breslau: Fiedler & Hentschel, 1874/75 [i.e. 1875] – 1mf – 9 – 0-8370-8420-2 – 1986-2420 – us A.T.L.A. [240]

DIE UNFEHLBARKEIT DES PAPSTES ALS LEHRER DER KIRCHE : UND DESSEN BEZIEHUNG ZU EINEM ALLGEMEINEN CONCILIUM / Weninger, Francis Xavier – (Earlier ed issued under title: Die apostolische Vollmacht des Papstes in Glaubens-Entscheidungen and On the apostolical and infallible authority of the Pope, when teaching the faithful) – Cincinnati: Benziger, 1869 – 1mf – 9 – 0-8370-6873-8 – 1986-0873 – us A.T.L.A. [240]

UNFILED PAPERS AND SLIPS BELONGING IN CONFEDERATE COMPILED SERVICE RECORDS / U.S. War Department. Confederate Records – (Includes printed guide) – M347 – 442r – 5 – us Nat'l Archives [324]

AN UNFINISHED LETTER TO THE RIGHT HONOURABLE WILLIAM PITT / Croft, Herbert – 1788. 59p. (English Linguistics Series 1500-1800) – 9 – us UMI [320]

THE UNFINISHED TASK OF THE CHRISTIAN CHURCH : INTRODUCTORY STUDIES IN THE PROBLEM OF THE WORLD'S EVANGELIZATION / Barton, James Levi – (Includes index) – New York: Student Volunteer Movt, 1908 – 1mf – 9 – 0-8370-6009-5 – 1986-0009 – us A.T.L.A. [240]

UNFORESEEN TENDENCIES OF DEMOCRACY / Godkin, Edwin L – (Constitutional and governmental issues in England, the U.S. and Australia) – Westminster: Archibald Constable & Co, 1903 – 3mf – 9 – $4.50 – LLMC 95-081 – us L.L.M.C. [323]

DIE UNFREIE UND DIE FREIE KIRCHE : IN IHREN BEZIEHUNGEN ZUR SKLAVEREI, ZUR GLAUBENS- UND GEWISSENSTYRANNEI UND ZUM DAEMONISMUS / Buchmann, J – Breslau: A. Gosohorsky, 1873 – 1mf – us A.T.L.A. [240]

DER UNGAR – (Buda-) Pest, jan 1-jun 29 1847 – 1 – Inquire at Mikrofilmarchiv for details – gw Misc Inst [072]

UNGARISCHE BIBLIOGRAPHIE DER TURKOLOGIE UND DER ORIENTALISCH-UNGARISCHEN BEZIEHUNGEN / Rasonyi, L – 1926-1934, 1935 – p 1-68 – 8 – ne IDC [940]

UNGARISCHE BIBLIOGRAPHIE DER TURKOLOGIE UND DER ORIENTALISCH-UNGARISCHEN BEZIEHUNGEN 1914-1925 / Moravcsik, J – KCsAII: 1926 – 1mf – 9 – ne IDC [956]

UNGARISCHE BIBLIOGRAPHIE DER TURKOLOGIE UND DER ORIENTALISCH-UNGARISCHEN BEZIEHUNGEN 1926-1934 / Rasonyi, L – Budapest, Leipzig, 1935 – 2mf – 9 – ne IDC [947]

UNGARISCHE BOTANISCHE BLAETTER : MAGYAR BOTANIKAI LAPOK – Budapest. v1-33. 1902-34 – 111mf – 9 – 7477/1 – ne IDC [580]

UNGARISCHE NACHRICHTEN – (Buda-) Pest, apr 1-dec 31 1862, jan 1-jun 29 1864, jan 1-sep 30 1865 – 1 – Inquire at Mikrofilmarchiv for details – gw Misc Inst [943]

DIE UNGARISCHE SPRACHE / Simonyi, S – Strassburg. 1907. BR-5340 2 – 8 – ne IDC [460]

UNGARISCHE VERFASSUNGSGESCHICHTE / Marczali, H – Tuebingen. 1910. BR-5325 2 – 8 – ne IDC [340]

UNGARISCHES STATISTISCHES JAHRBUCH / Hungary. Kozponti Statisztikai Hivatal – v. 1-24 26. 1893-1916 18. Budapest. (Lacking v. 9, 14, 22-23) – 1 – 85.00 – us L of C Photodup [943]

UNGARISCHES VERFASSUNGSRECHT / Marczali, H – Tuebingen. 1911. BR-5326 2 – 8 – ne IDC [340]

UNGARLAENDISCHE JUEDISCHE ZEITUNG – Budapest-Pozsony (Pressburg). v1-8? 1908-15? Complete. B371 (Leo Baeck Institute. German-Jewish Periodicals, Pt 1) – 2r – 1 – $135.00 – us UPA [270]

UNGAVA, A TALE OF ESQUIMAUX-LANDS / Ballantyne, Robert Michael – London: T. Nelson, 1858.07480.(Pre-1900 Canadiana) – 9 – cn C.I.H.M. [830]

UNGDOM – (Lacks some pgs and issues. Cont by: Lutheran Tidings) – Omaha, NE. v1-38 no 7. 1907-44 – 10r – 1 – ATLA S0228 – us A.T.L.A. [073]

UNGDOMS-VAENNEN : ILLUSTRERAD TIDSKRIFT FOER FROMSJANDE AF SANN GUDSFRUKTAN – (Some original pgs damaged) – Chicago, IL. v1-9. 1879-Jun 1887 – 3r – 1 – ATLA S0150 – us A.T.L.A. [073]

UNGDOMS-VAENNEN : ILLUSTRERAD TIDSKRIFT FOER HEMMET – (Lacks: v4 p139-140. Title varies) – St Paul, MN. v1-23. Nov 1895-Dec 1918 – 7r – 1 – ATLA S0151 – us A.T.L.A. [073]

UNGDOMS-VAENNEN: ILLUSTRERAD TIDSKRIFT FOER UNGDOM *see* UNGDOMS-VAENNEN

DEN UNGE LUTHER : STUDIER OVER HANS THEOLOGI / Ammundsen, Valdemar – Kobenhavn: V. Pios, 1907 – 1mf – us A.T.L.A. [240]

UNGEDRUCKTES AUS DEM GEOTHE-KREISE : MIT VIELEN FACSIMILES / ed by Mueller, Gustav Adolf – Muenchen: Seitz & Schauer, 1896 – 1r – 1 – us U.W. Library [920]

Unger, F J A N *see* SYNOPSIS PLANTARUM FOSSILIUM

Unger, Friedrich Wilhelm *see* QUELLEN DER BYZANTINISCHEN KUNSTGESCHICHTE

Unger, J F *see* ENTWURF MASCHINE WODURCH ALLES WAS AUF DEM CLAVIER GESPIELET WIRD, SICH VON SELBER IN NOTEN SETZT

Unger, Rudolf *see*
- HERDER, NOVALIS UND KLEIST
- SIBYLLINISCHE BLAETTER DES MAGUS

Ungern-Sternberg, F *see* VERSUCH EINER SYSTEMATIK DER SALICORNIEEN

DER UNGLUECKSEELIGE TODES-FALL CAROLI 12. : EIN DRAMA DES 18. JAHRHUNDERTS / ed by Heine, Carl – (Authorship attributed to Johann Joseph Kohlard) – Halle a.S: M Niemeyer, 1888 – 1r – 1 – us U.W. Library [820]

Ungnad, A *see*
- HAMMURABI'S GESETZ

Ungnad, Arthur *see* DIE RELIGION DER BABYLONIER UND ASSYRER..

UNG.-WEISSKIRCHNER VOLKSBLATT – Bela Crkva, Yugoslavia. Jul 1899-Oct 1902 – 1r – 1 – us L of C Photodup [949]

UNHCR – Geneva. United Nations High Commissioner for Refugees. 1972-81. 6 issues per year. Issued also in French. Continued by: Refugees – 1 – us U.W. Library [073]

UNHELDENHAFTE UND HELDENHAFTE MENSCHEN : BEI DEN WIENER DICHTERN UM 1900 / Mertens, Heinz – (Includes bibliographical references and index) – Bonn: L Roehrscheid, 1929 – 1r – 1 – us U.W. Library [430]

UNHOIB = BEGINNING – (In German) – Vienna, AU. v1 no1. 20 Jun 1923 – 1r – 1 – $25.00 – cn Can Microfilming [072]

THE UNHOLY WISH / Wood, Ellen – British Fiction Archive: Unit 1 – 9 – uk Bell [830]

UNIA RECORDS, MS 4038 – 1921-1986 – 16r – 1 – us Western Res [360]

A UNIAO – Campo Belo, 10 Jan, Aug-Sept 1895; Oct 1896; 24 Jun 1897 – 1,5,6 – bl Biblioteca [072]

A UNIAO : JORNAL POPULAR – Manaos, Amazonas. 26 Set-27 Out 1914 – 1,5,6 – bl Biblioteca [072]

A UNIAO – Manhumirim, Brazil. Aug 1956 – 1 – bl Biblioteca [072]

A UNIAO : ORGAO ABOLICIONISTA – Maceio, Alagoas. 8 Dez 1887; Mar, Jun-Jul, Set-20 Out 1888 – 1,5,6 – bl Biblioteca [072]

A UNIAO : ORGAO CONSAGRADO AO SPIRITISMO E AS QUESTOES SOCIAES – Penedo, Alagoas. 15 Jan 1897 – 1,5,6 – bl Biblioteca [072]

A UNIAO : ORGAO DO PARTIDO CONSERVADOR – Ouro Preto, 7 Sept 1886-Dec 1888; Jan-Jun, 2-16 Nov 1889 – 1,5,6 – bl Biblioteca [072]

A UNIAO : ORGAO DO "SYNDICATO DA UNIAO DOS LAVRADORES DE MANHUASSU" – Manhuassu, 30 Jan, Mar, 20 May 1937 – 1,5,6 – bl Biblioteca [072]

A UNIAO : PERIODICO EVOLUCIONISTA: ORGAO DA SOCIEDADES. FRANCISCO DE PAULA – Penedo, Alagoas. 30 Set 1896 – 1,5,6 – bl Biblioteca [072]

A UNIAO : REVISTA MENSAL DA SOCIEDADE PERSEVERANCA E AUXILIO DOS CAIXEIROS DE MACEIO – Maceio, Alagoas. 30 Abr, Jun, Ago-Out 1883; Mar, Jun, 30 Set 1884 – 1,5,6 – bl Biblioteca [072]

UNIAO : PERIODICO INDEPENDENTE, POPULAR, LITTERARIO, MERCANTIL E NOTICIOSO – Cidade de Uniao, Alagoas. 2-30 Ago 1899 – 1,5,6 – bl Bibliotoca [072]

UNIAO LIBERAL : COMMERCIAL, NOTICIOSA E AGRICOLA – (Cont as: Unaio Republicana) – Propria, 13 Mar-Apr, Aug, Nov 1886 – 1,5,6 – bl Biblioteca [072]

UNIAO LIBERAL : JORNAL POLITICO, COMMERCIAL E NOTICIOSO – Maceio, Alagoas. 12 Out 1869; Out 1870; Jul, 15 Dez 1871 – 1,5,6 – bl Biblioteca [072]
A UNIAO PORTUGUEZA – San Francisco, CA. May 1888-Aug 1906 – 3r – 1 – $150.00 – C02790 – us Library Micro [071]
UNIAO PORTUGUEZA – Oakland, CA. Apr 1910-Dec 1932 (broken file) – 1r – 1 – $50.00 – C02553 – us Library Micro [071]
A UNIAO POSTAL : ORGAO PHILATELICO E NOTICIOSO – '(s.l.') Sao Luiz, Brazil. 5 Aug 1893 – 1,5,6 – bl Biblioteca [072]
UNIAO POSTAL : PERIODICO LITTERARIO E NOTICIOSO – Ouro Preto, 19 Jun-31 Dec 1887 – 1,5,6 – bl Biblioteca [072]
UNIAO REPUBLICANA *see* UNIAO LIBERAL
UNIAO SPIRITA : ORGAM DA DELEGACIA DA UNIAO ESPIRITA DE PROPAGANDA NO BRAZIL – Penedo, Alagoas. 17 Jul 1896 – 1,5,6 – bl Biblioteca [072]
UNICAT / South Africa. State Library. Pretoria – National bibliographic tools on microfiche. Up to 1991 only – 9 – sa State Libr [020]
UNIDAD DE COMBATE Y VICTORIA / Mije, Antonio – Toulouse? 194? Fiche W 1050. (Blodgett Collection of Spanish Civil War Pamphlets) – 9 – us H.U. College Libr [946]
UNIDAD DE DESTINO / Falange Espanola Tradicionalista y de las Juntas Ofensivas Nacional-Sindicalistas – Madrid?, 1939. Fiche W 1236. (Blodgett Collection of Spanish Civil War Pamphlets) – 9 – us H.U. College Libr [946]
LA UNIDAD ESTRUCTURAL DE LOS LAIS DE MARIE DE FRANCE / Aragon Fernandez, Antonio – 2mf – 9 – Pta1,500.00 – 84-85422-13-9 – sp Pentalfa [140]
UNIDAD NACIONAL O LUCHA DE FACCIONES / Frigerio, Rogelio – Buenos Aires, 1961 – 1 – CSUXADN3751-B – us Hoover Inst Photo [320]
UNIDAD Y DIVERSIDAD DE LAS LETRAS HISPANICAS / Diez Canedo, Enrique – Madrid: Tipografia de Archivos, 1935 – 1 – sp Bibl Santa Ana [370]
UNIDAD Y LUCHA / Carrillo, Santiago – Toulouse? 1944. Fiche W 778. (Blodgett Collection of Spanish Civil War Pamphlets) – 9 – us H.U. College Libr [946]
UNIDO / United Nations – 8500mf – 9 – $16,000.00; $1.90f – uk UNIMICRO [338]
UNIDROIT PROCEEDINGS AND PAPERS / International Institute for the Unification of Private Law – 1928-81 – 43r – 1 – $2000.00 – us Trans-Media [340]
UNIFICACAO : ACAO E CORAGEM A SERVICO DA MACONARIA E DA HUMANIDADE – Manaus, Amazonas. Nov-Dez 1956 – 1,5,6 – bl Biblioteca [072]
UNIFICACION / Miquelarena, Jacinto – Tolosa, 193? Fiche W 1052. (Blodgett Collection of Spanish Civil War Pamphlets) – 9 – us H.U. College Libr [946]
UNIFICATION DEL DERECHO COMERCIAL / Canale, F – Buenos Aires, 1887 – 2mf – 9 – ILM-3546/1 – ne IDC [327]
L'UNIFICATION DU DROIT DU CHANGE / Bayalovitch, L – Lyon, 1934 – 6mf – 9 – ILM-3283/1 – ne IDC [327]
L'UNIFICATION DU DROIT MARITIME / Arriu, J – Toulouse, 1913 – 2mf – 9 – ILM-3225/1 – ne IDC [340]
THE UNIFIED DEVELOPMENT OF THE WATER RESOURCES OF THE JORDAN VALLEY REGION / United Nations – Prepared at the request of the United Nations under direction of Tennessee Valley Authority by Chas. T. Main, Inc. Boston, Mass. 1953. BNE-9813 1 – 9 – ne IDC [338]
UNIFORM CONSUMER CREDIT CODE – Working drafts for the 1968 and 1974 Acts. Ed. for filming by J. Myron Jacobstein, Stanford University. 1 reel – 1 – $50.00 – us Trans-Media [340]
UNIFORM CRIME REPORTS : CRIME IN THE UNITED STATES / U.S. Department of Justice – (Preapred annually. Add vols planned) – Federal Bureau of Investigation, 1930-93 – 178mf – 9 – $267.00 – LLMC 80-524 – us L.L.M.C. [340]
UNIFORM LAW CASES – 1959-71. 2 reels – 1 – $100.00 – us Trans-Media [340]
UNIFORM PUBLIC UTILITIES ACT / National Conference of Commissioners on Uniform State Laws – Chicago? 1928?. 40p. LL-551 – 1 – us L of C Photodup [340]
UNIFORM SOCIAL LAWS; A LECTURE / Smith, Walter George – Philadelphia: McVey, 1913. 27p. LL-1209 – 1 – us L of C Photodup [340]
UNIFORMEN-MARKT – Berlin, 1934-42 – 3r – 1 – Inquire at Mikrofilmarchiv for details – gw Misc Inst [390]
L'UNION – Bulletin puis Bulletin mensuel des ouvriers redige et publie par eux-memes. Dir. Vincard. Paris. dec 1843-sept 1846 – 1 – fr A.C.R.P.P. [073]
L'UNION : EDITION HEBDOMADAIRE – St-Hyacinthe, Canada. 9 oct 1873-29 dec 1911 – 9r – 1 – Can$50.00r – cn Can Microfilming [072]
L'UNION – Edmonton, Alberta. v2 n12. 30 jan 1919-v7 n2. 15 nov 1923 – 1r – 1 – Can$30.00 – cn Can Microfilming [072]
L'UNION – French Guiana. 1902-1903 – 1 – us UMI [072]
L'UNION – Lowell, MA. 8 mar 1889-v2 n3. 21 mar 1890 – 1r – 1 – Can$45.00 – cn Can Microfilming [071]
L'UNION – Montreal, Canada. 27 jul-10 sep 1858 – 1r – 1 – Can$30.00 – cn Can Microfilming [072]
L'UNION – Montreal, Canada. v1 n1. 10 nov 1941-22 avr 1944 – 1r – 1 – Can$50.00 – cn Can Microfilming [072]
L'UNION – Ogdensburgh, NY. v1 n14. 31 dec 1860-v1 n34. 16 jul 1861 – 1r – 1 – Can$30.00 – cn Can Microfilming [071]
L'UNION – Paris. Quotidienne. Ed. de midi. 14 janv-15 mai 1852 – 1 – fr A.C.R.P.P. [944]
L'UNION – Providence. R.I. 1912-1942 – 1 – us UMI [071]
L'UNION – Quebec, Canada. 24 jun 1885 – 1r – 1 – Can$25.00 – cn Can Microfilming [072]
L'UNION – Woonsocket, RI. v16 n4. avr 1916-v71 n1. jan a avr 1971 – 2r – 1 – Can$50.00 – cn Can Microfilming [071]
DIE UNION – (1954-78 38r DM2,850.00) – Dresden, DE. 1947 – 1r – 1 – DM80.00 – gw Mikro Press [072]
DIE UNION – Bremen, mar 15 1842-oct 6 1849 – 3r – 1 – Inquire at Mikrofilmarchiv for details – gw Misc Inst [072]
DIE UNION – Dresden, DE. Seit 1958 Halle/S. DE. 1947; Aug 1954-1990 – 53r – 1 – gw Mikrofilm [072]
DIE UNION – Hamburg, DE. 1874-25 May 1876 – 1r – 1 – gw Mikrofilm [072]
DIE UNION – Highland, IL: Aktien-Gesellschaft, oct 24 1863-oct 15 1868 – 2r – 1 – us Res Libr [071]
DIE UNION – Leipzig, DE. 1958-Oct 1971; Jul 1977-Jun 1990 – 35r – 1 – gw Mikrofilm [072]
LA UNION – Manaus, Amazonas. 20 Set 1909-1 Abr 1910 – 1,5,6 – bl Biblioteca [072]
THE UNION – (Also known as: Daily Morning Union; Morning Union; Morning Daily Union and Herald) – Grass Valley, CA. 1865-66 (broken file); 1867-89; 1890- – 442+ r – 1 – $22,100.00 ($350.00y) – B02277 – us Library Micro [071]
THE UNION – Arcata, CA. 1886- – 86+ r – 1 – $4,300.00 ($90.00y) – B02022 – us Library Micro [071]
THE UNION – Quebec: [s.n, 1841] (Quebec: W and H Cowan) – 9 – cn C.I.H.M. [331]
UNION – Alma. Kansas. 1871-1872 – 1 – us UMI [071]
UNION – Ashland. Ohio. 1861-1862 – 1 – us UMI [071]
UNION – Atlantic City. N.J. 1905-53 – 1 – us UMI [071]
UNION : BLAETTER DER EMIGRATION – Johannesburg, SA. 27 Oct 1939-Sep 1948 – 1r – 1 – gw Mikrofilm [072]
UNION – Bremen, DE. 1842-49 – 3r – 1 – gw Mikrofilm [072]
UNION – Darlington, SC. Baptist Educational and Missionary Convention of South Carolina. 1936-53. Single reels available – 1 – 48.00 – us A.B.H.S. [073]
UNION – Findlay, Ohio. 1890-1904 – 5r – 1 – $32.50r – us Archival [071]
UNION – Grass Morning Valley. Calif. 1890-1905; 1906-1917; 1918-1936; 1937- – 1 – us UMI [071]
UNION – Humbolt. Kan. 1867-1954 – 1 – us UMI [071]
UNION – Junction City. Kan. -w. 1865-1901 – 1 – us UMI [071]
UNION – La Porte, CA. 1868; 7, 24 Oct 1869 – 1r – 1 – $50.00 – B02338 – us Library Micro [071]
UNION – Miller. Neb. 1892-1895 – 1 – us UMI [071]
UNION : A MONTHLY RECORD OF MORAL, SOCIAL, AND EDUCATIONAL PROGRESS – 1-10 (all publ). 1842-1843 – 5mf – 9 – $55.00 – us UPA [335]
UNION – Rensselaer. Ind. 1868-1897 – 1 – us UMI [071]
UNION – Sacramento. Calif. 1966- – 1 – us UMI [071]
UNION – San Bruno, CA. 1938-41 – 2r – 1 – $100.00 – B02775 – us Library Micro [071]
UNION – San Diego. Calif. 1871- – 1 – us UMI [071]
UNION – San Diego. Calif. -w. 1868-77, 1889-1923 – 1 – us UMI [071]
UNION – Walla Walla. Wash. -w. 1869-89 – 1 – us UMI [071]
UNION – Warsaw. Ind. -w. 1904-41, 1946 – 1 – us UMI [071]
UNION *see*
– DEUTSCHES MONATSBLATT
UNION ADVOCATE – Auburn, CA. 1862-63 – 1r – 1 – $50.00 – B02032 – us Library Micro [071]
UNION ADVOCATE – Newcastle, Canada. 1868-73 – 2r – 1 – $136.00 – cn Library Assoc [971]
L'UNION AGRICOLE / ed by Leger, J O – Montreal, Canada. 1 nov 1919-v1 n3. 1 jan 1920 – 1r – 1 – Can$30.00 – cn Can Microfilming [072]
L'UNION ALSACIENNE – no. 4. Strasbourg. fevr 1848 – 1 – fr A.C.R.P.P. [073]
UNION BAND BAPTIST CHURCH. HOWARDSTOWN, KENTUCKY : CHURCH RECORDS – 1856-68.116p – 1 – 5.22 – us Baptist [978]
UNION BAPTIST CHURCH. ANDERSON COUNTY. SOUTH CAROLINA : CHURCH RECORDS – 1888-1967 – 1 – 33.12 – us Baptist [240]
UNION BAPTIST CHURCH. CHESTERFIELD, TENNESSEE : CHURCH RECORDS – 1842-1978 – 1 – 45.14 – us Baptist [240]
UNION BAPTIST CHURCH. MALTA BEND, MISSOURI : CHURCH RECORDS – 1860-Aug 1965 – 1 – 24.30 – us Baptist [240]
UNION BAPTIST CHURCH. PUTNAM, SOUTH CAROLINA : CHURCH RECORDS – 1804-1905 – 1 – 16.92 – us Baptist [240]
UNION BIBLE COMPANION: CONTAINING THE EVIDENCES...OF THE HOLY SCRIPTURES / Allibone, Samuel A – Philadelphia: Amer. Sun.-Sch. Un., 1871.1 fiche – 9 – us A.T.L.A. [240]
UNION BULLETIN – Walla Walla, WA. 1994 – 4+ r – 1 – $200.00 ($200.00y) – R04156 – us Library Micro [071]
UNION BULLETIN – Walla Walla. Wash. 1945- – 1 – us UMI [071]
L'UNION CANADIENNE – Levis, Canada. 9 jul-10 oct 1891 – 1r – 1 – Can$40.00 – cn Can Microfilming [072]
A UNION CARD IS A DEATH WARRANT IN FRANCO SPAIN – N.Y., 193? Fiche W1237. (Blodgett Collection of Spanish Civil War Pamphlets) – 9 – us H.U. College Libr [946]
UNION CATALOGUE OF FOREIGN LITERATURE IN SWEDISH RESEARCH LIBRARIES / Kungliga Biblioteket-Royal Library. Stockholm – Stockholm, 1975-1991 – 1 – sw Kungliga [025]
UNION CATALOGUE OF SCIENTIFIC LIBRARIES IN THE UNIVERSITY OF CAMBRIDGE: BOOKS PUBLISHED BEFORE 1801 / Cambridge University. Library – 9 fiches – 9 – £55.00 – uk Mansell Publ [500]
UNION CEMETERY RECORD / Hancock County, Ohio. Biglick Township. Board of Trustees – 1908-1990 – 1r – 1 – $32.50r – us Archival [324]
UNION CHRETIENNE DE JEUNES GENS – France. Correspondance fraternelle. devenu: Bulletin de l'Union chretienne de jeunes gens. no. 11-48. Paris. dec 1855-59 – 1 – fr A.C.R.P.P. [240]
UNION CITY FIRST BAPTIST CHURCH. UNION CITY, TENNESSEE : CHURCH RECORDS – 1901-02, 1927-85 – 1 – 139.82 – us Baptist [240]
UNION CITY FIRST BAPTIST CHURCH. UNION CITY, TENNESSEE : CHURCH RECORDS AND BULLETINS – 1946-53 – 1 – $70.92 – us Baptist [240]
Union Civica Radical *see* EL DEBATE SOBRE EL SEGUNDO PLAN QUINQUENAL EN LA CAMERA DE DIPUTADOS DE LA NACION
Union coloniale francaise. Paris *see* LA QUINZAINE COLONIALE
LA UNION CONSERVADORA – Badajoz, 1900. 2 numeros – 5 – sp Bibl Santa Ana [073]
UNION COUNTY FARMER – LaGrande OR. Nov 29 1894, Jan 14 21 28 1897 – 1 – us U.O. Library [071]
UNION COUNTY FIRST BAPTIST CHURCH. UNION COUNTY. SOUTH CAROLINA : CHURCH RECORDS – 1952-70 – 1 – 20.16 – us Baptist [240]
UNION COUNTY JOURNAL – Lewisburg, PA. -w 1972-84 – 13 – $25.00r – us I.M.R. [071]
UNION COUNTY RECORDER – LaGrande OR. Sep 17 1980-Dec 24 1981 – 1 – us U.O. Library [071]
UNION COUNTY REVIEW RECORDER – LaGrande OR. Sep 17 1980-Dec 24 1981 – 1 – us U.O. Library [071]
Union County. South Carolina *see* BAPTIST SUNDAY SCHOOL CONVENTION
UNION COUNTY STANDARD JOURNAL – Lewisburg. Pa. -w. 1952- – 1 – us UMI [071]
UNION COUNTY TIMES – Lake Butler. Fl. -w. 1935-Aug 1936, 1946- – 1 – us P.K. Yonge [071]
Union d'Algerie *see* LE CHEMINOT ALGERIEN
Union de Conductores de Automoviles de la Provincia de Caceres *see* MEMORIA DEL ANO 1945
Union de Conductores Deautomoviles de la Provincia de Caceres *see* MEMORIA, ANO 1946
Union de la Jeunesse Socialiste Congolaise *see* JEUNESSE ET REVOLUTION
L'UNION DE MAISONNEUVE – Maisonneuve, Canada. v1 n12. 8 jul 1916 – 1r – 1 – Can$25.00 – cn Can Microfilming [072]
L'UNION DE SAINT-ROCH ET SAINT-SAUVEUR – Quebec, Canada. 12 jun-10 jul 1875 – 1r – 1 – Can$25.00 – cn Can Microfilming [072]
UNION DEMOCRAT – (Also known as: Tuolumne Independent) – Sonora, CA. 1870-77; 1890- – 214+ r – 1 BC03001 – $10,700.00 ($400.00y) – us Library Micro [071]
UNION DEMOCRAT – Sonora. Calif. 1944- – 1 – us UMI [071]
L'UNION DEMOCRATIQUE – London, 25 Mar-3 Oct 1872 – 1r – 1 – uk British Libr Newspaper [072]
L'UNION DES CANTONS DE L'EST – (5 jan 1900-31 dec 1992 98r) – Arthabaska, Canada. 14 dec 1866-28 dec 1899 – 6r – 1 – Can$50.00r – cn Can Microfilming [072]
L'UNION DES CANTONS DE L'EST – Arthabaska, Canada. 1866-1900 – 12r – 1 – $780.00 – cn Library Assoc [971]
L'UNION DES DEUX CANADAS, 1841-1867 / David, Laurent Olivier – Montreal: Senecal, 1898. 02519. (Pre-1900 Canadiana) – 9 – cn C.I.H.M. [971]
Union des Industries Metallurgiques et Minieres *see* REVUE MENSUELLE DES QUESTIONS SOCIALES, OUVRIERES ET FISCALES
L'UNION DES METALLURGISTES / La Federation des travailleurs de la metallurgie – C.G.T. Paris. oct 1945-64 – 1 – fr A.C.R.P.P. [073]
L'UNION DES METAUX / La Federation des Ouvriers des Metaux et Similaires de France – Paris. aout 1914-janv 1940. devenu: L' Union des metallurgistes voir a ce titre – 1 – fr A.C.R.P.P. [331]
Union des Producteurs Agricoles *see* LA TERRE DE CHEZ-NOUS
Union des syndicats confederes des Chemins de Fer de l'Etat francais *see* LE CHEMINOT DE L'ETAT
Union deutscher Sozialisten und Gewerkschafter in der Schweiz *see* NEUES DEUTSCHLAND IM NEUEN EUROPA
Union Douaniere et Economique de l'Afrique Centrale *see* ANNUAIRES OFFICIELS, 1973 AND 1974
UNION FARMER *see* SHARECROPPER'S VOICE, 1935-1937 : SOUTHERN FARM LEADER, 1936 : STFU NEWS, 1938-1939 : TENANT FARMER, 1941-1942 : FARM WORKER, 1943-1944 : FARM LABOR NEWS, 1946-1951 : THE UNION FARMER, 1952-1953 : AGRICULTURAL UNIONIST, 1952-1954
L'Union federale des Ouvriers metallurgistes de France *see* L'OUVRIER METALLURGISTE
Union Federative du Centre *see* LA LUTTE SOCIALE
UNION FOR CIVIL LIBERTY (UCL) – Bangkok. 19 docs. 1984-1990 – 8mf – 9 – ne IDC [320]

UNION FOR DEMOCRATIC ACTION *see* ADA WORLD
L'UNION FRANCO-AMERICAINE – Lake Linden, MI. v2 n6. 5 fev 1891-v2 n28. 9 jul 1891 – 1r – 1 – Can$25.00 – cn Can Microfilming [071]
Union General de Trabajadores de Espana *see* PROGRAMA DE UNIDAD DE ACCION ENTRE LA U.G.T. Y LA C.N.T
Union Girls' School (Hangchow, China) *see* TWENTIETH ANNIVERSARY PUBLICATION OF THE UNION GIRLS' SCHOOL, HANGCHOW (CCC139)
UNION GROVE BC *see* ROCKY POINT BAPTIST CHURCH. RUSSELLVILLE, HAMBLEN COUNTY, TENNESSEE
Union Historical Co *see*
- THE HISTORY OF BOONE COUNTY AND ITS CITIES AND TOWNS
- HISTORY OF BUCHANAN COUNTY
- HISTORY OF IOWA COUNTY
- HISTORY OF JACKSON COUNTY
- HISTORY OF MADISON COUNTY
- HISTORY OF MAHASKA COUNTY
- HISTORY OF MARION COUNTY
- HISTORY OF POLK COUNTY
- HISTORY OF POWESHIEK COUNTY
- HISTORY OF WASHINGTON COUNTY

UNION HYMNAL / Society of American Cantors – Central Conference American Rabbis, 1897. 1 fiche – 9 – us A.T.L.A. [270]
UNION IM WAHLKAMPF : SONDERAUSGABE DES DEUTSCHLAND-UNION-DIENSTES – (Title change Sept 1949: Union in Deutschland) – Frankfurt, DE. 20 Mai 1949-Feb 1951 (incomplete) – 1 – gw Mikro Press [072]
UNION IM WAHLKAMPF *see* CDU-INFORMATIONSDIENST
UNION IN DEUTSCHLAND : INFORMATIONSDIENST DES ZONENAUSSCHUSSES DER CDU – (Cont by: Informationsdienst der CDU Deutschlands from 17 May 1950) – Frankfurt, DE. 12 Aug 1948-1952 (incomplete) – 1 – gw Mikro Press [072]
UNION IN DEUTSCHLAND *see*
- CDU-INFORMATIONSDIENST
- UNION IM WAHLKAMPF

UNION JOURNAL OR THE HALIFAX ADVERTISER – Feb 1759-Sep 1760 – 1 – uk Microform Academic [072]
UNION LABOR BULLETIN – Sacramento, CA. 1938-46 – 4r – 1 – $200.00 – C02747 – us Library Micro [331]
UNION LABOR BULLETIN – Sacramento. Calif. -w. 1938-46 – 1 – us UMI [071]
UNION LABOR BULLETIN – Salem OR. June 15 1938 – 1 – us U.O. Library [071]
UNION LABOR JOURNAL – Bakersfield, CA. 1943-49 – 6r – 1 – $300.00 – C02042 – us Library Micro [073]
UNION LABOR JOURNAL – Bakersfield. Calif. 1943-49 – 1 – us UMI [071]
UNION LABOR NEWS – (Library has: v.15, no.7,10; v.16, no.1-2,5,9; v.17, no.9; v.18, no.2-4,7; v.19, no.1 (July 1935-Jan. 1939)) – Indianapolis, Ind.: Wm. R. Bassett, 1922 – 1 – CSUX89-S79 – us Hoover Inst Photo [331]
UNION LABOR NEWS – Santa Barbara. Calif. 1952-1967 – 1 – us UMI [071]
UNION LEADER – Toledo. OH. 1907-54 – 1 – us UMI [071]
UNION LEDGER – Union, NE. -w. Aug-Sept 1910; Nov 1910-Feb 1911; Mar-Apr 1912 – 1 – us NE Hist [071]
L'UNION LIBERALE : AUTONOMISTE – Quebec, Canada. 3 mai 1888-28 nov 1896 – 1r – 1 – Can$40.00 – cn Can Microfilming [072]
UNION LIBERTY JOURNAL – Hamilton. Ohio. -w. 1973- – 1 – us UMI [071]
UNION LIST OF ARKANSAS NEWSPAPERS / Arkansas – 1819-1942. Partial inventory of AK newspaper files available in offices of publishers, libraries and private collections. 6 fiches. F-0015 – 9 – us A.G.L.L. [071]
UNION LIST OF CANADIAN NEWSPAPERS / National Library of Canada – Nov 1988. 17,000 entries. Register, 2 indexes. Updated annually – 9 – cn Nat'l Library [072]
UNION LIST OF SERIALS IN THE SOCIAL SCIENCES AND HUMANITIES (CANUC:S) / National Library of Canada – 1989- . 100,00 serials. Register, index. Updated annually – 9 – cn Nat'l Library [025]
THE UNION MAGAZINE – v1-3. 1901-03 (complete) – 1r – 1 – ATLA 1994-S510 – us A.T.L.A. [073]
UNION MAGAZINE / National Union of Ships' Stewards, Cooks, Butchers and Bakers – Liverpool, England. Marine Caterer. -m. July 1909-Dec 1921. 2 1 2 reels – 1 – uk British Libr Newspaper [331]
THE UNION MESSENGER – Basseterre. St. Kitts. Feb. 12, 23; Aug. 1, 9, 28, 1934; Feb. 10-12, 1942 – 1 – us NY Public [072]
UNION MESSENGER – Basseterre, St Kitts-Nevis. 1 Jan 1930-30 Jul 1938; 3 Jan 1939-23 Jun 1944; 12 Sep 1944-28 Nov 1951; 2 Jan 1958-27 Apr 1961 (imperfect).-tw. 25 reels – 1 – uk British Libr Newspaper [072]
UNION MISIONAL FRANCISCANA. SU NATURALEZA Y ORGANIZACION / Castro y Castro, Manuel – Madrid: Archivo Ibero Americano, 1960 – 1 – sp Bibl Santa Ana [240]
Union Missionary Convention *see* PROCEEDINGS OF THE UNION MISSIONARY CONVENTION: HELD IN NEW YORK, MAY 4TH & 5TH, 1854
L'UNION NATIONALE : QUOTIDIEN / ed by Lanctot, Mederic – (Bi-hebdomadaire: 3 sep 1864-7 nov 1867 1r Can$40.00) – Montreal, Canada. 8 sep 1864-v3 n98. 28 fev 1867 – 2r – 1 – Can$40.00r – cn Can Microfilming [072]
UNION NATIONALE – Montreal, Canada. 1864-67 – 5r – 1 – $325.00 – cn Library Assoc [971]
UNION NEWS / Oil, Chemical and Atomic Workers International Union – 1970$ – 1 – us UMI [073]
UNION NEWS – Towson, Maryland. 1900-1917 – 1 – us MD Archives [071]
L'UNION NOUVELLE – Los Angeles, CA. v53. n34. 27 jan 1934 – 1r – 1 – Can$25.00 – cn Can Microfilming [071]
Union of British Columbia Indian Chiefs *see* NESIKA
THE UNION OF CHRISTIAN FORCES IN AMERICA / Ashworth, Robert A – Philadelphia: American Sunday-School Union, c1915. (Green fund book : no. 19) – 1mf – us A.T.L.A. [240]
UNION OF EPISCOPAL METHODISMS / Foster, R S – New York: Hunt and Eaton; Cincinnati: Cranston and Stowe, 1892 – 1mf – us A.T.L.A. [240]
Union of German Socialist Organizations in Great Britain *see* NEWSLETTER
Union of Poles in America *see* RECORDS, MS P.P.
UNION OUVRIERE / Tristan, Flore Celestine – Paris, 1844. xliii,136p. 2 fiches. (Les Femmes Collection) – 9 – 6.00 – fr Bibl Nationale [830]
Union. Presbytery (Cum. Pres. Ch.) *see* MINUTES
Union. Presbytery (Pres. Ch. in the U.S.A.) *see* MINUTES, 1799-1948
Union Progressiste Senegalaise *see* L'UNITE AFRICAINE
UNION PROVOST MARSHAL'S FILE OF PAPERS RELATING TO INDIVIDUAL CIVILIANS / U.S. War Department. Confederate Records – 300 rolls. M345. Printed guide – 5 – us Nat'l Archives [324]
UNION PROVOST MARSHAL'S FILE OF PAPERS RELATING TO TWO OR MORE CIVILIANS / U.S. War Department. Confederate Records – 94 rolls. M416. Printed guide – 1 – us Nat'l Archives [324]
THE UNION RECORD – 1902-04 (complete) – 1r – 1 – ATLA R0120 – us A.T.L.A. [073]
UNION RECORD – Seattle. Wash. -w. 1900-20 – 1 – us UMI [071]
UNION RECORD – Seattle.WA. 1918-28 – 1 – us UMI [071]
UNION REGISTER – Portland OR. Oct 3 1952, Dec 25 1964 – 1 – us U.O. Library [071]
THE UNION REPORTER *see* GBU REPORTER
UNION REPUBLIC – Union, OR. -w. 17 Dec 1948-11 Aug 1972. 7 rolls – 1 – us U.O. Library [071]
L'UNION REPUBLICAINE DE SAONE-ET-LOIRE ET DE L'AIN – Macon, Sept. 1848 – June 1849 – 1r – fr Armell [944]
L'UNION REPUBLICAINE DU DOUBS – mars 1890-fevr 1892. devenu: Le Petit travailleur franc-comtois. mars 1892-sept 1893. Besancon – 1 – fr A.C.R.P.P. [331]
UNION REPUBLICAN – Albia. Iowa. -w. 1955-56. 1958 – 1 – us UMI [071]
UNION REVIEW – v.1-6. 1939-45. Continued by Union seminary quarterly review – 1,5,6,9 – us UMI [073]
UNION SEMINARY REVIEW : A PRESBYTERIAN QUARTERLY – v1-57. Oct 1889-Aug 1946 (complete) – 18r – 1 – ATLA S0222 – us A.T.L.A. [073]
UNION SIGNAL – Jan 1883-Dec 1933 – 1 – us Ohio Hist [360]
Union Signal *see* NATIONAL PROHIBITIONIST PERIODICAL
UNION, SOUTH CAROLINA : EARLY QUAKER CHURCH RECORDS – 1750-1815 – 1 – 5.00 – us Baptist [240]
UNION STAR – Brookneal. Va. 1916- – 1 – us UMI [071]
UNION TABLOID – (See also: Graphic Arts Unionist) – v1- 1978- – 1,5,6,9 – us UMI [331]
THE UNION THEOLOGICAL SEMINARY IN THE CITY OF NEW YORK : HISTORICAL AND BIOGRAPHICAL SKETCHES OF ITS FIRST FIFTY YEARS / Prentiss, George Lewis – New York: Anson D.F. Randolph, 1889 – 1mf – us A.T.L.A. [240]
THE UNION THEOLOGICAL SEMINARY IN THE CITY OF NEW YORK : ITS DESIGN AND ANOTHER DECADE OF ITS HISTORY / Prentiss, George Lewis – Asbury Park, N.J.: M., W. & C. Pennypacker, 1899 – 2mf – us A.T.L.A. [240]
Union Theological Seminary Library *see*
- THE SHELF LIST OF THE LIBRARY
- THE SHELF LIST OF THE UNION THEOLOGICAL SEMINARY LIBRARY

UNION TRIBUNE – Clarksburg. West Virginia. 1962-1965 – 1 – us UMI [071]
UNION UNIVERSITY, ITS HISTORY, INFLUENCE, CHARACTERISTICS AND EQUIPMENT. / Raymond, Andrew Van Vranken – New York: Lewis Publishing, 1907. 3v. illus. plates – 1 – us U.W. Library [370]
Union Veteran Publishing Co *see* SOLDIERS' AND PATRIOTS' BIOGRAPHICAL ALBUM
UNION W.A.G.E – Women's Alliance to Gain Equality. 1971-82 – 1 – us UMI [073]
UNION WITH GOD : A SERIES OF ADDRESSES / Harris, J Rendel – New York: A.D.F. Randolph, 1895 – 1mf – us A.T.L.A. [240]
UNION WITH GOD IN THOUGHT AND FAITH : REFLECTIONS ON THE ENLARGEMENT OF RELIGIOUS LIFE THROUGH MODERN KNOWLEDGE / Scull, David – Philadelphia: John C Winston, 1908 – 1mf – 9 – 0-8370-8943-3 – 1986-2943 – us A.T.L.A. [240]
UNION WORKER – (New York). 1925-27 – 1 – us A.J.P.C. [071]
UNION WORLD – New York. N.Y. 1959-1963 – 1 – us UMI [071]
L'UNIONE – Pueblo, CO, 1897-1900, 1916-1917, 1921-1927, 1931-1934 – 4r – 1 – us I.H.R.C. [978]
L'UNIONE – San Francisco, CA. 1927-44 – 4r – 1 BO2938 – $200.00 – us Library Micro [071]
THE UNIONIST – Ireland.7-24 May 1921 – 1 – ie Microforms [072]
UNIONIST AND HALIFAX JOURNAL – (Also: Morning Journal) – Halifax, Canada. 1854-59; 1862-69 – 13r – 1 – $845.00 – cn Library Assoc [971]
DER UNIONSBERUF DES EVANGELISCHEN PROTESTANTISMUS : AUS DER PRINCIPIELLEN EINHEIT, DER CONFESSIONELLEN SONDERUNG UND DER UNIONSGESCHICHTLICHEN ENTWICKLUNG DESSELBEN / Schenkel, Daniel – Heidelberg: K. Winter, 1855 – 2mf – us A.T.L.A. [240]
DIE UNIONSTAETIGKEIT JOHN DURIES UNTER DEM PROTEKTORAT CROMWELLS : EIN BEITRAG ZUR KIRCHENGESCHICHTE DES SIEBZEHNTEN JAHRHUNDERTS / Brauer, Karl – Marburg: N.G. Elwert, 1907 – 1mf – us A.T.L.A. [240]
UNION-SUN – Lockport. N.Y. and Journal. 1913- – 1 – us UMI [071]
UNIONSVERHANDLUNGEN ZWISCHEN KATHOLIKEN UND PROTESTANTEN IN DEN JAHREN 1530-1540 / Stupperich, Robert – Graefenhainichen, 1936 – 2mf – 9 – DM62.00 – 3-89349-337-9 – gw Hänsel [240]
UNION-THEATER-ZEITUNG – Berlin. mar 16, 1912 – 1 – gw Mikrofilm [790]
THE UNIQUE WEEKLY – Risingsun, Ohio. 1907-48 – 16r – 1 – $32.50r – us Archival [071]
UNIQUE-DERRICK – Risingsun, Ohio. 1948-58 – 5r – 1 – $32.50r – us Archival [071]
UNIQUEST – v1-9. 1974-78 (complete) – 1r – 1 – ATLA S0396 – us A.T.L.A. [073]
UNIR : LE JOURNAL OU TOUS LES PATRIOTES PEUVENT S'EXPRIMER LIBREMENT – Quebec, Canada. aut 1964-v1 n3. oct 1964 – 1r – 1 – Can$25.00 – cn Can Microfilming [971]
UNIT – Orland, CA. 1911-30; 1934-36; 1954-56; 1960-61 – 16r – 1 – $800.00 – B02564 – us Library Micro [071]
L'UNITA – 1945-1978 – 3r per y – 5,6 – Sfr1,123.00 – sz Infoprint [072]
L'UNITA – 1979-1995 – 4r per y – 5,6 – Sfr1,176.00 – sz Infoprint [945]
L'UNITA – Milan, Turin, and Rome. 1927-61. 34 reels – 1 – $2,575.00 – us UPA [335]
L'UNITA – Rome, Jan 1963-Dec 1967 – 51r – 1 – uk British Libr Newspaper [072]
L'UNITA – (Standing orders available) – Milano, 1962- – 1 – inquire – us Ross [945]
UNITARIAN CHRISTIANITY / Channing, William E – In works of William E. Channing.1896 – 9 – us A.T.L.A. [240]
THE UNITARIAN CHURCH : A STATEMENT / Crooker, Joseph Henry – Boston: Published for free distribution [by] American Unitarian Association, [1901?] – 1mf – us A.T.L.A. [240]
Unitarian Domestic Mission to the Poor. Manchester *see* ANNUAL REPORTS
UNITARIAN REVIEW – (Superseded by: New World). v. 1-36. 1874-1891 – 1,5,6 – us Princeton Micro [240]
UNITARIAN THOUGHT / Emerton, Ephraim – New York: Macmillan, 1911 – 1mf – us A.T.L.A. [240]
UNITARIAN UNIVERSALIST ACTION – 1965-66 (complete) – 1r – 1 – ATLA S0405 – us A.T.L.A. [073]
UNITARIAN UNIVERSALIST SERVICE COMMITTEE – Boston. 40 docs. 1981-1991 – 33mf – 9 – ne IDC [320]
UNITARIAN UNIVERSALIST WORLD : THE JOURNAL OF THE UNITARIAN UNIVERSALIST ASSOCIATION – v1-16. 1970-86 (complete) – 5r – 1 – ATLA S0367 – us A.T.L.A. [073]
UNITARIANISM: A DEVOTIONAL FAITH / Porter, John Scott – 18– – 9 – us A.T.L.A. [240]
UNITARIANISM IN AMERICA : A HISTORY OF ITS ORIGIN AND DEVELOPMENT / Cooke, Willis – Boston: American Unitarian Association, 1902 – 2mf – us A.T.L.A. [240]
UNITARIANISM: THE DOCTRINE OF OUR LORD JESUS CHRIST / Porter, John Scott – 1843 – 9 – us A.T.L.A. [240]
UNITARIANISM: THE FAITH OF THE APOSTLES / Porter, John Scott – 1844 – 9 – us A.T.L.A. [240]
THE UNITARIAN'S ANSWER / Dewey, Orville – 1826 – 9 – us A.T.L.A. [240]
L'UNITE – (Cont by: L'Unite Nationale 12 mai 1938. Cont by: L'Unite Nationale-L'Homme Libre 24 mai 1938-29 oct 1938) – Montreal, Canada. 24 jun 1935-5 mai 1938 – 1r – 1 – Can$60.00 – cn Can Microfilming [072]
L'UNITE – Hebdomadaire socialiste.Paris.1972-83. Fait suite a: Bulletin socialiste. Voir a ce titre – 1 – fr A.C.R.P.P. [335]
L'UNITE : PUBLIEE DURANT LA GREVE DES EMPLOYES DU "SOLEIL" – Quebec, 2 mars 1978-13 avr 1978 – 1r – 1 – Can$25.00 – cn Can Microfilming [072]
L'UNITE *see* LE TEMPS
L'UNITE AFRICAINE / Union Progressiste Senegalaise – (Lacks three issues) – 1956-Aug 1968 – 8r – 1 – $396.00 – us African Imprint [072]
L'UNITE LENINISTE – Organe des bolcheviks-leninistes francais. (Opposition). no. 1-17. Paris. dec 1927-mai 1928 – 1 – fr A.C.R.P.P. [335]
L'UNITE MORALE DES RELIGIONS / Bonet-Maury, Gaston – Paris: Felix Alcan, 1913 – 1mf – us A.T.L.A. [200]
L'UNITE NATIONALE – Montreal, dec 1953-aut-sep 1958f – 1r – 1 – Can$50.00 – cn Can Microfilming [072]
L'UNITE NATIONALE *see* L'UNITE
L'UNITE NATIONALE-L'HOMME LIBRE *see* L'UNITE
L'UNITE PAYSANNE – 1945-61. devenu: Democrate et paysan. oct-dec 1965. Paris – 1 – fr A.C.R.P.P. [330]
UNITED ACTION FOR A FREE INDONESIA – New York, 1947 – 5mf – 9 – SE-991/1 – ne IDC [950]
UNITED ALBION CIRCULAR – (Camden and Kentish Towns Gazette Camden and Kentish Towns, Hampstead, Highgate and St. Pancras Gazette St. Pancras Gazette). London. -w. 1866-1939. (55 reels) – 1 – uk British Libr Newspaper [072]

UNITED ALBION GAZETTE – London, UK. 1866-1939. -w. 55 reels – 1 – uk British Libr Newspaper [072]

United American Spanish Aid Committee *see* THE NEW SPANISH INQUISITION

United Arab Emirates *see* AL-JARIDAH AL-RASMIYAH

UNITED ARAB REPUBLIC : STATISTICAL HANDBOOK OF THE UNITED ARAB REPUBLIC, 1952-1971 / United Arab Republic. Central Agency for Public Mobilisation and Statistics – (Coll title: African Official Statistical Serials, 1867-1982) – 32mf – 9 – £270.00 – uk Chadwyck [960]

United Arab Republic *see*
- JOURNAL OFFICIAL
- JOURNAL OFFICIEL
- LE PLAN QUINQUENNAL POUR LE DEVELOPPEMENT ECONOMIQUE ET SOCIAL, 1960-1965 RESUME

UNITED ARAB REPUBLIC: CASE STUDY OF AID THROUGH TRADE AND REPAYMENT OF DEBT IN GOODS OR LOCAL CURRENCIES / Kardouche, GK – (United Nations conference on trade and development). 1966. BNE-4640 1 – 9 – ne IDC [336]

United Arab Republic. Central Agency for Public Mobilisation and Statistics *see*
- BASIC STATISTICS, 1964
- POPULATION AND DEVELOPMENT: A STUDY ON THE POPULATION INCREASE AND ITS CHALLENGE TO DEVELOPMENT IN EGYPT
- UNITED ARAB REPUBLIC

United Arab Republic. Ministry of Planning *see* DETAILED PLAN FOR ECONOMIC AND SOCIAL DEVELOPMENT FOR THE FIFTH YEAR 1964/65, OF THE FIVE YEAR PLAN

United Arab Republic. Ministry of Treasury *see* THE BUDGET REPORT

United Arab Republic. National Planning Committee *see*
- COMPREHENSIVE FIVE YEAR PLAN FOR ECONOMIC AND SOCIAL DEVELOPMENT, 1960-1965
- GENERAL FRAME OF THE 5-YEAR PLAN FOR ECONOMIC AND SOCIAL DEVELOPMENT, JUL 1960-JUN 1965

United Arab Republic. Southern Region. Ministry of Education. Department of Statistics *see* COMPARATIVE STATISTICS OF EDUCATION 1953/54-1960/61

UNITED ASIA – v1- 1948- 1; v27- 5,6,9 – us UMI [950]

United Automobile, Aircraft and Agricultural Implement Workers of America International Union *see* UNITED AUTOMOBILE WORKER

UNITED AUTOMOBILE WORKER : 1936-1955 / United Automobile, Aircraft and Agricultural Implement Workers of America International Union – (Coll title: Labor Union Periodicals, Pt 1) – 4r – 1 – $540.00 – 1-55655-252-1 – us UPA [331]

UNITED BAPTIST CHURCH. MURFREESBORO, TENNESSEE : CHURCH RECORDS – 1835-97 – 1 – 8.64 – us Baptist [240]

United Bible Societies *see* BULLETIN

THE UNITED BRETHREN – (Cont: The Christian Conservator) – v1-81. Jul 1885-Aug 1967 (complete) – 71r – 1 – ATLA S0144 – us A.T.L.A. [073]

UNITED BRETHREN REVIEW – (Cont: Quarterly Review) – v1-19. 1890-1908 (complete) – 6r – 1 – ATLA S0769 – us A.T.L.A. [073]

UNITED CANADA – Ottawa, 24 nov 1888-v15 n7. 20 dec 1902 – 6r – 1 – Can$75.00r – cn Can Microfilming [072]

United Cannery, Agricultural, Packing and Allied Workers of AmericaFood, Tobacco, and Agricultural and Allied Workers Union of America *see* CANNERY AND FIELD UNION NEWS, 1937 : CIO NEWS CANNERY WORKERS EDITION, 1938-1939 : UCAPAWA NEWS, 1939-1944 : FTA NEWS, 1945-1950

United Church Board for Homeland Ministries. Race Relations Department *see* ARCHIVES, 1942-76

THE UNITED CHURCH HOME MISSIONS / Norlie, Olaf Morgan – Minneapolis: Augsburg Publ. House, 1909.200p. 1 fiche – 9 – us A.T.L.A. [240]

UNITED CHURCH OF CANADA : YEARBOOK – 1926-91 (complete) – Inquire – 1 – ATLA S0614 – us A.T.L.A. [240]

UNITED CHURCH OF CHRI PENSION BOARD : REPORT – 1967-83 (complete) – 1r – 1 – ATLA S0577 – us A.T.L.A. [240]

UNITED CHURCH OF CHRI VERMONT CONFERENCE : MINUTES – 1966-92 (complete) – Inquire – 1 – ATLA S0603 – us A.T.L.A. [240]

UNITED CHURCH OF CHRIST : ANNUAL REPORT OF THE HAWAII CONFERENCE – 1963-91 (complete) – 2r – 1 – ATLA S0904 – us A.T.L.A. [240]

UNITED CHURCH OF CHRIST : MINUTES, REPORTS AND STATISTICS FOR THE YEAR... – 1976-90 (complete) – Inquire – 1 – ATLA S0889 – us A.T.L.A. [240]

United Church of Christ (Columbus Grove, Ohio) *see* RECORDS

United Church of Christ. Kansas. Oklahoma Conference *see* RECORDS

THE UNITED CHURCH OF THE UNITED STATES / Shields, Charles Woodruff – New York: Scribner, 1895 – 1mf – us A.T.L.A. [240]

UNITED DAILY NEWS – Taipei, Taiwan. 1973-83. 44 reels – 1 – 2200.00 – ch Transmission [072]

UNITED DAIRY FARMER *see* AFL CANNERY REPORTER, 1949-1954 : UNITED DAIRY FARMER, 1941, 1944-1945

United Electrical Radio and Machine Workers of America *see* UE NEWS

United Emmanuel Lutheran Church (ALC), Milberger, KS *see* CHURCH RECORDS

UNITED EMPIRE – v1-34. 1909-1943. Missing 1930-31, 1936-41 – 1 – cn Precision [971]

UNITED EMPIRE LOYALIST – Toronto, Canada. 1827 (supp. to Upper Canada Gazette, Welland Canal. 1835) – 1r – 1 – $68.00 – cn Library Assoc [971]

UNITED EMPIRE LOYALISTS / Harris, Edward – Jubilee ed. Toronto: W. Briggs, 1897. 05583. (Pre-1900 Canadiana) – 9 – cn C.I.H.M. [971]

THE UNITED EMPIRE LOYALISTS: AND THE MEMORIAL CHURCH, ADOLPNUSTOWN, ONTARIO: A SKETCH / Forneri, R S – s.l.: s.n., 1888 (Belleville, Ont.: Intelligencer). 03152. (Pre-1900 Canadiana) – 9 – cn C.I.H.M. [971]

UNITED EVANGELICAL ACTION – (1985-. 5,6,9) – 1942- – 1 – us UMI [240]

UNITED EVANGELICAL LUTHERAN CHURCH : LUTHERAN ALMANAC / United Evangelical Lutheran Church – 1918-59 (complete) – 4r – 1 – ATLA S0669 – us A.T.L.A. [240]

United Evangelical Lutheran Church *see* UNITED EVANGELICAL LUTHERAN CHURCH

United Farm Equipment and Metal Workers of America *see*
- CIO NEWS
- FE NEWS

UNITED FARMER – v1-14. Mar. 1922-Dec. 1935 – 1 – cn Precision [630]

UNITED FREE CHURCH OF SCOTLAND : HANDBOOK – 1961-91 (complete) – 1r – 1 – ATLA S0912 – us A.T.L.A. [240]

UNITED IRELAND – Ireland.13 Aug 1881-18 Feb 1882; 8 Apr-30 Dec 1882; 1883-10 Sept 1898. -w. 17 reels – 1 – uk British Libr Newspaper [072]

UNITED IRELAND – Ireland.16 Sept 1933-1936 – 1 – ie Microforms [072]

UNITED IRISHMAN – Dublin. Ireland. -w. 12 Feb-27 May 1848; 16 Sept 1876-17 Feb 1877. (mqn reel) – 1 – uk British Libr Newspaper [072]

UNITED IRISHMAN – Dublin, Ireland.1848 – 1 – Ir£16.00 – ie Microforms [072]

UNITED IRISHMAN – Ireland.1899-1906 – 1 – ie Microforms [072]

UNITED IRISHMAN – Ireland.1923 – 1 – ie Microforms [072]

UNITED IRISHMAN – Ireland.May 1932-9 Sept 1933 – 1 – ie Microforms [072]

UNITED IRISHMAN : A NATIONAL WEEKLY REVIEW – Dublin, 1900-06 – 2r – 1 – us Ross [072]

UNITED IRISHMAN – New York. 3 Jan 1885-28 May 1910 (imperfect).-w. 6 reels – 1 – uk British Libr Newspaper [071]

UNITED IRISHMAN AND GALWAY AMERICAN – Dublin. Ireland. -w. 25 Jul 1863-2 Apr 1864. (1 reel) – 1 – uk British Libr Newspaper [072]

United Kingdom *see* TREATY SERIES: 1892-1985

UNITED KINGDOM BALANCE OF PAYMENTS 1946/47-1967/77 – (Coll title: British Government Publications...1801-1977, Finance) – 45mf – 9 (£2,260.00 finance set of 93mf + 30r) – uk Chadwyck [339]

UNITED KINGDOM COMPANIES ANNUAL REPORTS... *see* UK COMPANIES ANNUAL REPORTS AND ACCOUNTS, 3RD SERIES INSURANCE AND FINANCIAL INSTITUTIONS

United Kingdom Department of the Environment. London *see* CATALOGUES OF THE UNITED KINGDOM DEPARTMENT OF THE ENVIRONMENT LIBRARY

UNITED KINGDOM LEADING FINANCIAL INSTITUTIONS ANNUAL REPORTS AND ACCOUNTS – 404mf – 9 – uk Microform Academic [380]

UNITED KINGDOM LEADING INDUSTRIAL COMPANIES' ANNUAL REPORTS AND ACCOUNTS – From 1933 – 744mf – 9 – uk Microform Academic [380]

United Kingdom. National Economic Development Council *see* THE GROWTH OF THE ECONOMY (1961-1966)

United Kingdom. Organization for European Economic Cooperation *see*
- GENERAL MEMORANDUM ON THE 1950/51 AND 1951/52 PROGRAMMES. UNITED KINGDOM
- INTERIM-REPORT ON THE EUROPEAN RECOVERY PROGRAMME. VOL. 2. THE LONG-TERM PROGRAMME FOR THE UNITED KINGDOM

UNITED KINGDOM WRECK REGISTERS, 1855-98 / Great Britain – Mss from National Maritime Museum, London – 1 – uk Microform Academic [941]

United Libertarian Organizations *see* SPANISH REVOLUTION

UNITED LUTHERAN – Pittsburgh, PA: United Lutheran Society. v1-13. jun 1962-75 – 2r – 1 – us Res Libr [071]

UNITED LUTHERAN CHURCH OF AMERICA : UNITED LUTHERAN – v1-10. 8 Jan 1908-29 Jun 1917 (complete) – 8r – 1 – ATLA S0245 – us A.T.L.A. [073]

United Metal Workers' International Union of AmericaUnited Brotherhood of Weldors, Cutters and Helpers of America *see* INTERNATIONAL METAL WORKER, 1902-1905 : UNITED WELDORS' NEWS, 1941-1945

UNITED METHODIST BOARD OF HIGHER EDUCATION AND MINISTRY QUARTERLY *see* RELIGION IN LIFE

United Methodist Church *see*
- A LIST OF OUR CHURCHES CLASSFIED IN ALPHABETICAL ORDER IN CIRCUITS
- PARISH RECORDS

United Methodist Church. Kansas West Conference *see* MINISTER AND CHURCH LISTS

United Methodist Women (U.S.). Toledo District *see* RECORDS

United Mine Workers *see*
- AFL CANNERY REPORTER, 1949-1954 : UNITED DAIRY FARMER, 1941, 1944-1945
- JOURNAL

THE UNITED MINE WORKER'S JOURNAL – v. 11-39. 19 Apr 1900-15 Dec 1928. Scattered issues wanting – 1 – 242.00 – us L of C Photodup [331]

UNITED MINE WORKER'S JOURNAL – Silver Springs. Md. 1954-1966 – 1 – us UMI [331]

UN *see*
- ANNEXES
- COMMITTEE ON THE PEACEFUL USES OF OUTER SPACE
- COMPENDIUM OF HUMAN SETTLEMENT STATISTICS
- COMPENDIUM OF SOCIAL STATISTICS
- CONFERENCE OF THE EIGHTEEN-NATION COMMITTEE ON DISARMAMENT
- CONFERENCE ON THE DISCONTINUANCE OF NUCLEAR WEAPON TESTS
- DEVELOPMENT FORUM
- DOCUMENTS OF THE U.N. CONFERENCE ON INTERNATIONAL ORGANIZATION, SAN FRANCISCO 1945
- DOCUMENTS OF THE U.N. ENVIRONMENT PROGRAMME
- RESOLUTIONS AND DECISIONS
- SUMMARY RECORDS OF PLENARY MEETINGS

United Nations *see*
- BIBLIOGRAPHY ON ECONOMIC AND SOCIAL PLANNING AND PROJECTIONS IN ECE COUNTRIES
- CEPAL REVIEW
- CEPAL REVIEW. 1983-86
- CHECKLIST OF DOCUMENTS, 1946-75
- CONFERENCE ON THE LAW OF THE SEA
- DOCUMENTS AND OFFICIAL RECORDS
- ECONOMIC AND SOCIAL COUNCIL OFFICIAL RECORDS
- ECONOMIC AND SOCIAL SURVEY FOR ASIA AND THE PACIFIC
- ECONOMIC BULLETIN FOR AFRICA
- ECONOMIC SURVEY FOR ASIA AND THE FAR EAST
- ECONOMIC SURVEY OF LATIN AMERICA
- ECONOMIC SURVEY OF LATIN AMERICA AND THE CARIBBEAN
- ECOSOC ECONOMIC AND SOCIAL COUNCIL
- ENERGY BALANCES AND ELECTRICITY PROFILES
- ENERGY STATISTICS YEARBOOK
- FLOOD CONTROL SERIES
- FOREIGN TRADE STATISTICS OF ASIA AND THE FAR EA SERIES A
- FOREIGN TRADE STATISTICS OF ASIA AND THE FAR EA SERIES B
- FOREIGN TRADE STATISTICS OF ASIA AND THE PACIFIC
- FOREIGN TRADE STATISTICS OF ASIA AND THE PACIFIC. SERIES A
- FOREIGN TRADE STATISTICS OF ASIA AND THE PACIFIC. SERIES B
- GENERAL ASSEMBLY
- GENERAL ASSEMBLY OFFICIAL RECORDS
- GENERAL ASSEMBLY PROVISIONAL RECORDS
- GENERAL SERIES DOCUMENTS
- THE GROWTH OF WORLD INDUSTRY
- HABITAT
- INDEX TO PROCEEDINGS OF THE ECONOMIC AND SOCIAL COUNCIL
- INDEX TO PROCEEDINGS OF THE GENERAL ASSEMBLY
- INDEX TO PROCEEDINGS OF THE SECURITY COUNCIL
- INDEX TO PROCEEDINGS OF THE TRUSTEESHIP COUNCIL
- INDUSTRIAL STATISTICS YEARBOOK
- INFORMATION CIRCULARS AND VARIOUS SALES CODES (ONUG)
- INTERNATIONAL COCOA COUNCIL U.N. COCOA CONFERENCES
- INTERNATIONAL COURT OF JUSTICE
- INTERNATIONAL LAW COMMISSION
- INTERNATIONAL REVIEW OF CRIMINAL POLICY
- INTERNATIONAL SEA-BORNE TRADE STATISTICS YEARBOOK (MARINE TRANSPORT)
- INTERNATIONAL TRADE CENTER
- JUDGMENTS OF THE U.N. ADMINISTRATIVE TRIBUNAL
- JUDGMENTS OF THE UNITED NATIONS ADMINISTRATIVE TRIBUNAL
- LAW LIBRARY COLLECTION
- MINERAL RESOURCES DEVELOPMENT SERIES
- MISCELLANEOUS DOCUMENTS
- MISCELLANEOUS STATISTICAL PAPERS
- A MORE EFFECTIVE ROLE FOR SOCIAL WELFARE IN ECONOMIC AND SOCIAL DEVELOPMENT IN JORDAN
- NARCOTIC DRUGS
- NATIONAL ACCOUNTS STATISTICS
- PEACEFUL USES OF ATOMIC ENERGY
- POPULATION STUDIES
- PREPARATION OF THE DRAFT HANDBOOK ON THE PEACEFUL SETTLEMENT OF DISPUTES BETWEEN STATES
- PROCEEDINGS OF THE INTERNATIONAL CONFERENCE ON PEACEFUL USES OF ATOMIC EENERGY
- PROCEEDINGS OF THE UNITED NATIONS CONFERENCE ON NEW SOURCES OF ENERGY
- PROCEEDINGS UN CONFERENCE ON NEW SOURCES OF ENERGY
- REPERTORY OF PRACTICE OF U.N. ORGANS
- REPERTORY OF PRACTICE OF UNITED NATIONS ORGANS
- REPORT OF THE PREPARATORY COMMITTEE FOR THE U.N. CONFERENCE ON ENVIRONMENT AND DEVELOPMENT
- REPORT ON THE U.N. CONFERENCE ON NEW SOURCES OF ENERGY
- REPORTS OF INTERNATIONAL ARBITRAL AWARDS
- REPORTS OF THE INTERNATIONAL ARBITRAL AWARDS
- SAMPLE SURVEYS OF CURRENT INTEREST
- SECURITY COUNCIL OFFICIAL RECORDS
- SECURITY COUNCIL. OFFICIAL RECORDS
- SECURITY COUNCIL OFFICIAL RECORDS
- SMALL INDUSTRY BULLETIN FOR ASIA AND THE FAR EAST
- SMALL INDUSTRY BULLETIN FOR ASIA AND THE PACIFIC
- STATISTICAL PAPERS SERIES ON YOUTH AND THE DISABLED
- STATISTICAL YEARBOOK FOR ASIA AND THE FAR EAST
- STATISTICAL YEARBOOK FOR ASIA AND THE PACIFIC
- STATISTICAL YEARBOOK FOR LATIN AMERICA
- STATISTICAL YEARBOOK FOR LATIN AMERICA AND THE CARIBBEAN

United Nations. Economic Commission for Asia and the Far East *see* REGIONAL HOUSING CENTRE, BANDUNG, DIRECTORY OF BUILDING RESEARCH AND DEVELOPMENT ORGANIZATIONS IN ECAFE-REGION

UN Economic Commission for Europe (ECE) *see*
- AGRICULTURAL COMMITTEE
- AUTOMATION COMMITTEE
- CHEMICAL INDUSTRY COMMITTEE
- COAL COMMITTEE
- COMMISSION
- CONFERENCE OF EUROPEAN STATISTICIANS COMMITTEE
- ELECTRIC POWER COMMITTEE
- ENERGY COMMITTEE
- ENGINEERING INDUSTRIES COMMITTEE
- ENVIRONMENT COMMITTEE
- GAS COMMITTEE
- HOUSING, BUILDING AND PLANNING COMMITTEE
- MISCELLANEOUS
- SCIENCE AND TECHNOLOGY COMMITTEE
- SENIOR ECONOMIC ADVISERS TO ECE GOVERNMENTS COMMITTEE
- STANDARDIZATION COMMITTEE
- STATISTICAL INDICATORS
- STEEL COMMITTEE
- TIMBER COMMITTEE
- TRADE COMMITTEE
- TRANSPORT COMMITTEE
- WATER COMMITTEE

UNITED NATIONS ESTADO MISIONERO / Bayle, Constantino – Madrid: Razon y Fe, 1934 – 1 – sp Bibl Santa Ana [946]

United Nations. Food and Agriculture Organization *see*
- AGRICULTURE IN THE NEAR EAST
- CROP AGRONOMY AND IMPROVEMENT IN CYRENAICA
- NUSA TENGGARA SURVEY REPORT. SE 4792/1. 1960
- PRELIMINARY REPORTS ON THE ECOLOGICAL SURVEY OF THE VEGETATION TYPES IN FOREST AND GRAZING LANDS OF JORDAN

United Nations. Food and Agriculture Organization. Development Center on Land Policy and Settlement for the Near East *see* THE ROLE OF LAND POLICY IN AGRICULTURAL PRODUCTION AND INCOME DISTRIBUTION IN THE NEAR EAST

United Nations. Food and Agriculture Organization. The Development of the Tribal Lands and Settlement Project *see* REPORT ON THE FARMING PROSPECTS IN THE PILOT AREA OF THE FAO-TRIBAL LANDS AND SETTLEMENT PROJECTS TEAM ON THE EASTERN REGION (CYRENAICA) OF LIBYA

United Nations. Food and Agriculture Organization. The Development of the Tribal Lands and Settlement Project. Libya Mission *see* A NOTE ON ORGANIZATION AND EXECUTION OF THE RECLAMATION CONTRACT BY NASA

United Nations. Food and Agriculture Organization. The Development of Tribal Lands and Settlement Project *see* FARM BUSINESS ANALYSIS OF 36 HOLDINGS IN EL USETA AREA OF JEBEL AL AKHDAR IN THE EASTERN REGION OF LIBYA

United Nations. Food and Agriculture Organization. The Development of Tribal Lands and Settlements Team Project *see* FARM PLAN FOR THE BU TRABA SETTLEMENT IN THE EASTERN REGION OF LIBYA

United Nations. General Assembly *see* REPORT

UNITED NATIONS INDUSTRIAL DEVELOPMENT ORGANIZATION : UNIDO / United Nations – 1965-1987 – E/F.3 E.9989 F.917 R.169 S.671 – 9 – us U.N. Pubs [338]

United Nations. International Court of Justice *see*
- ICJ PLEADINGS, BARCELONA TRACTION
- ICJ PLEADINGS/MEMOIRES
- ICJ YEARBOOK
- REPORTS OF JUDGMENTS, ADVISORY OPINIONS AND ORDERS

United Nations. International Law Commission *see* GENERAL SERIES DOCUMENTS

UNITED NATIONS JURIDICAL YEARBOOK / United Nations – 118mf – 9 – $220.00; $1.90f – uk UNIMICRO [340]

UNITED NATIONS JURIDICAL YEARBOOK / United Nations – (1982 and 1983 are not yet available in French and Spanish) – 1963-1983 – E.130 F.128 S.126 – 9 (ST/LEG/Ser.C/1-20) – us U.N. Pubs [340]

UNITED NATIONS LAWMAKING : CULTURAL AND IDEOLOGICAL RELATIVISM AND INTERNATIONAL LAWMAKING FOR AN ERA OF TRANSITION / McWhinny, Edward – 1984 – 200p – 9 – 92-3-102147-8 – fr UNESCO [340]

UNITED NATIONS LEGISLATIVE SERIES / United Nations – Includes compilations of legal texts submitted by governments on selected topics – 128mf – 9 – $240.00; $1.90f – uk UNIMICRO [340]

UNITED NATIONS LEGISLATIVE SERIES / United Nations – (Nos. 1-6. ST/LEG/Ser.B/1-6. E.45; Nos. 7-21. ST/LEG/Ser.B/7-21. E/F/S.145) – 9 – us U.N. Pubs [340]

U.N. LIST OF TREATY COLLECTIONS / United Nations. Office of Legal Affairs. Codification Division – Office of Legal Affairs, Codification Div, 1956 (all publ) – 2mf – 9 – $3.00 – LLMC 82-977 – us L.L.M.C. [340]

THE UNITED NATIONS MICROFILM UNIT : PANAMA – (Seccion Juridica. Primeria Noteria, 1825-1885. 74r.$4,400.00; Catalogo de Cedulas Reales, 1573-1648. 3r.$180.00; Treaty of 1826 Between Panama and the United States, Notes of the Foreign Minister of Panama. 1r.$65.00; Gazeta de Panama, 1878, 1881. 1r.$65.00; Gazeta de Panama, 1889-1899. 9r.$550.00; Mendoza Collection, Coleccion de Documentos Ineditos. 1r.$65.00; Gazeta de Panama: 1881 Enero 27. Parnaso Panameno and a collection of literary and political pamphlets .1r.$65.00; Coleccion de Documentos de Siglos 15 a 20 (and) Sosa: Indice de los documentos relativos a la conquista y colonizacion del Istmo de Panama, 1513-1700. 1r.$65.00; Continuation of the Index to 1826 and the Colon Fire Disaster, 1885. 1r.$65.00; The Arce Collection of historical and literary pamphlets. 8r.$480.00) – 100r – 1 – $6,000.00 set – us Universal [950]

UNITED NATIONS MONTHLY BULLETIN OF STATISTICS / United Nations – (Vols 1-26, 1947-1972. E/F.1330; Vols 27-44, 1973-1990. ST/ESA/STAT/Ser.Q/1-216. E/F.1298) – 9 – us U.N. Pubs [310]

UNITED NATIONS MONTHLY BULLETIN OF STATISTICS, 1946-86 / United Nations – Bilingual, French/English. -m. World statistics on 74 subjects from over 200 countries and territories. 2292 fiches – 9 – $4500.00; $1.90f – uk UNIMICRO [310]

U.N. MONTHLY CHRONICLE *see* U.N. CHRONICLE

D'UN NOUVEAU COMPLOT CONTRE LES INDUSTRIELS / Stendhal, Marie-Henri Beyle – Paris, Sautelet, 1825, 24 p. Les Saint-Simoniens, 1825-1834. 6977 – 9 – fr Hachette [305]

United Nations. Office of Legal Affairs *see* REPORTS OF INTERNATIONAL ARBITRAL AWARDS

United Nations. Office of Legal Affairs. Codification Division *see* U.N. LIST OF TREATY COLLECTIONS

United Nations. Preparatory Commission of the United Nations, 1945-46. London *see* DOCUMENTS AND OFFICIAL RECORDS

UNITED NATIONS QUESTIONNAIRE EC 121 (16) JANUARY 1964, ON INFLATION AND ECONOMIC DEVELOPMENT / United Nations. Dept. of Economic and Social Affairs – BNE-601 1 – 9 – ne IDC [330]

UNITED NATIONS REVIEW / United Nations – (Cont by: U.N. Chronicle) – v1-11. 1954-64 (all publ) – 128mf – 9 – $192.00 – LLMC 81-908 – us L.L.M.C. [340]

UNITED NATIONS REVIEW *see* UNITED NATIONS BULLETIN

United Nations. Security Council. Representative from the Netherlands *see*
- DOCUMENTS SUBMITTED TO THE COMMITTEE OF GOOD OFFICES BY THE NETHERLANDS DELEGATION IN THE PERIOD FROM THE BEGINNING OF THE NEGOTIATIONS UP TO JAN., 1948
- THREE MONTHS OF TRUCE ON JAVA AND SUMATRA

United Nations. Special Committee on Palestine *see*
- SUMMARY OF RECOMMENDATIONS
- SURVEY OF PALESTINE

United Nations. Statistical Office *see* POPULATION AND VITAL STATISTICS REPORT

UNITED NATIONS STATISTICAL YEARBOOK / United Nations – (1948-1972. E/F.307; 1973-1985/6. ST/ESA/STAT/Ser.S/1-11. E/F.197) – 9 – us U.N. Pubs [310]

UNITED NATIONS STATISTICAL YEARBOOK / United Nations – 467 fiches – 9 – $890.00; $1.90f – uk UNIMICRO [330]

UNITED NATIONS SUGAR CONFERENCES / United Nations – 1968, 1973, 1977-1986 – E/F.17 E.155 F.148 R.41 S.60 – 9 – us U.N. Pubs [320]

United Nations. Technical Assistance Administration *see* OUTLINE PLAN FOR THE CITY OF DJAKARTA

United Nations. Technical Assistance Mission to Indonesia *see* BRIEF REPORT ON THE WORK BEING DONE UNDER THE MINISTRY OF SOCIAL AFFAIRS, THE BUREAU OF NATIONAL RECONSTRUCTION, THE MINISTRY OF EDUCATION, AND THE MINISTRY OF LABOUR

UNITED NATIONS TIN CONFERENCES / United Nations – 1965, 1970, 1975, 1980-1986 – E/F.10 E.80 F.81 R.18 S.40 – 9 – us U.N. Pubs [320]

UNITED NATIONS TREATY SERIES / United Nations – (Cumulative Indexes, Nos. 1-14. (covering Vols 1-900). E.93 F.93; Volumes 1-1280. E/F.9,172; The following volumes are not yet available: 1099-1102, 1112, 1121, 1124, 1133-34, 1168, 1170, 1179, 1183, 1189, 1196, 1198-1200, 1203-05, 1208, 1211-13, 1216-18, 1220-1225, 1227-31, 1233-34, 1236-39, 1241-43, 1245-1248, 1250-1279) – 9 – us U.N. Pubs [340]

UNITED NATIONS TREATY SERIES / United Nations – (With index vols 1-17 1945-88. Updates available. Cont: League of Nations Treaty Series) – v1-1633. 1946-91 – 6759mf – 9 – $10,138.00 – LLMC 79-456 – us L.L.M.C. [340]

UNITED NATIONS TREATY SERIES *see* LEAGUE OF NATIONS TREATY SERIES

U.N. Trusteeship *see* TEXT OF THE TRUSTEESHIP AGREEMENT

THE U.N. TRUSTEESHIP MANDATE *see* ANNUAL REPORTS OF THE UNITED STATES TO THE TRUSTEESHIP COUNCIL OF THE U.N.

U.N. Visiting Mission to Observe the Referendum in Palau, may-jun 1979 *see* REPORT

United Nations. World Food Conference *see* WORKS

UNITED NEGRO COLLEGE FUND ARCHIVES, 1944-1971 (UNCF) – 3525mf – 9 – $9590.00 – us UMI [370]

United Packinghouse Workers of America *see* CIO NEWS

United Packinghouse Workers of AmericaPan-American Committee of Meat Workers *see* MEAT OF IT, 1945-1966 : INTERNATIONAL MEAT WORKER, 1946-1948

United Presbyterian Church in the U.S.A *see* CONSTITUTION, 1958-1983

United Presbyterian Church in the U.S.A. Board of National Missions *see* ANNUAL REPORTS, 1958-1973

United Presbyterian Church in the U.S.A. General Assembly *see* MINUTES AND REPORTS

United Presbyterian Church of North America *see* DIGEST OF THE PRINCIPAL ACTS AND DELIVERANCES

United Presbyterian Church of North America. Board of Christian Education *see* ANNUAL REPORTS, 1946-1958

United Presbyterian Church of North America. Board of Education *see* ANNUAL REPORTS, 1914-1946

United Presbyterian Church of North America. General Assembly *see* MINUTES AND REPORTS

UNITED PRESBYTERIAN HISTORICAL DIRECTORY / Clemmer, Myrtle M – 1968 – 1 – $50.00 – us Presbyterian [240]

THE UNITED PRESBYTERIAN MAGAZINE – v1-10. ns: v1-12. 1847-68 (complete) – 7r – 1 – ATLA S0221 – us A.T.L.A. [073]

UNITED PROGRESSIVE NEWS – Los Angeles, CA. 1935 – 1r – 1 – $50.00 – C03325 – us Library Micro [071]

United Provinces Historical Society *see* JOURNAL OF THE UNITED PROVINCES HISTORICAL SOCIETY

United Provinces. India. Legislative Council *see* PROCEEDINGS OF THE LEGISLATIVE COUNCIL OF THE UNITED PROVINCES

UNITED PUEBLOS QUARTERLY BULLETIN – 1940. (American Indian Periodicals in the Princeton University Library). 2 fiches – 9 – $45.00 – us UPA [305]

United Reformed Church History Society *see* JOURNAL

UNITED REFORMED CHURCH IN ENGLAND AND WALES : YEARBOOK – 1973-93 (complete) – Inquire – 1 – ATLA S0513 – us A.T.L.A. [240]

THE UNITED SECESSION MAGAZINE – (Lacks: v2 p749-756) – v1-11. ns: v1-3. 1833-46 – 5r – 1 – ATLA S0223 – us A.T.L.A. [073]

THE UNITED SERVICE GAZETTE – [Ottawa?: s.n, 1868?-18–?] – 9 – cn C.I.H.M. [355]

UNITED SERVICE GAZETTE – London, UK. Feb-Dec 1833; 1864.-irr. 1 reel – 1 – uk British Libr Newspaper [072]

UNITED SOCIETY FOR CHRISTIAN LITERATURE ARCHIVES 1799-1960 / School of Oriental and African Studies, London – (Includes printed guide) – 3,675mf – 9 – ne IDC [240]

United Society for the Propagation of the Gospel *see*
- AFRICAN ARCHIVES INDEX
- AMERICAN MATERIAL. PLUS INDEX
- "C" SERIES RECORDS RELATING TO CANADA (NOVA SCOTIA)
- "C" SERIES RECORDS RELATING TO THE WEST INDIES AND "X" SERIES RELATING TO CODRINGTON COLLEGE, BARBADOS
- GOLD COAST RECORDS
- INDIAN CALENDARS
- INDIAN RECORDS
- MISSIONARY ARCHIVES FOR SOUTH AFRICA
- SINHALESE MATERIAL
- SOUTH AFRICAN ARCHIVES: INDEX AND FINDING LISTS
- USPG NETWORK

United Society for the Propagation of the Gospel. Archives *see*
- CAPETOWN (SOUTH AFRICA) DIOCESAN RECORDS
- GRAHAMSTOWN (SOUTH AFRICA) DIOCESAN RECORDS
- MATERIAL RELATING TO CANADA
- NATAL (SOUTH AFRICA) DIOCESAN RECORDS
- ST. JOHN'S (SOUTH AFRICA) DIOCESAN RECORDS
- ZULULAND (SOUTH AFRICA) DIOCESAN RECORDS

United Society for the Propagation of the Gospel in Foreign Parts *see*
- ANNUAL REPORTS AND SERMONS, 1701-1845
- CALENDAR OF AFRICAN LETTERS
- MADAGASCAR RECORDS, 1866-1900

The United Society of Believers in Christ's Second Appearing *see* RECORDS

U. S. *see*
- ADMINISTRATIVE HISTORIES OF U.S. CIVILIAN AGENCIES
- AMERICAN STATE PAPERS
- CHECKLIST OF UNITED STATES PUBLIC DOCUMENTS
- CODE
- CODE OF FEDERAL REGULATIONS ON MICROFICHE
- THE FEDERAL CASES
- FEDERAL REGISTER
- FEDERAL REGISTER: INDEXES
- FEDERAL REGISTER ON MICROFICHE
- GOVERNMENT MANUAL
- RATIFIED INDIAN TREATIES, 1722-1869
- RECORDS OF THE U.S. NUERNBERG WAR CRIMES TRIALS: NG SERIES, 1933-48
- RECORDS RELATING TO CLAIMS AGAINST BRAZIL UNDER THE CONVENTION OF 1849
- RECORDS RELATING TO THE FIRST NORTHWEST BOUNDARY SURVEY COMMISSION, 1853-69
- STATE CONSTITUTIONAL CONVENTIONS ON MICROFICHE
- STATE DOCUMENTS
- TERRITORIAL PAPERS, INDEXED

U.S. *see*
- ANNUAL REPORTS (A-G)
- FEDERAL REGISTER
- WAR OF THE REBELLION

US – (1977. 1. 1978-80. 1,9) – 1977 – us UMI [073]

THE U.S. A CHRISTIAN NATION / Brewer, David J – Philadelphia: J.C. Winston, 1905. (Haverford Library lectures) – 1mf – us A.T.L.A. [240]

United States Adjutant-General's Office *see* GENERAL AND SPECIAL ORDERS, DEPARTMENT OF TEXAS, 1878-93

THE U.S. ADMINISTRATION OF THE RYUKYU ISLANDS, 1946-72 – 7r – 1 – $595.00 – S1664 – us Scholarly Res [980]

U.S. Administrative Conference of the United States *see* ACUS RECOMMENDATIONS AND REPORTS

U.S. Advisory Committee on Intergovernmental Relations *see* SIGNIFICANT FEATURES OF STATE AND LOCAL TAXES

U.S. Agency for International Development *see*
- THE AKADEMI ILMU PELAJARAN; PAST, PRESENT AND FUTURE
- THE AKADEMI ILMU PELAJARAN; PAST, PRESENT AND FUTURE. INDONESIAN MARITIME TRANSPORTATION
- CURRENCY EXCHANGE SURVEY; SURVEY REPORT
- FACT SHEETS ON MAJOR U.S. A.I.D. AND OTHER U.S. ASSISTED PROJECTS IN INDONESIA
- INDONESIAN-UNITED STATES COOPERATION FOR INDONESIAN ECONOMIC DEVELOPMENT
- LAND REFORM IN ALGERIA, TUNISIA, THE UNITED ARAB REPUBLIC
- MARINE TERMINAL OPERATIONS; ORGANIZATION, METHODS, FACILITIES,BY C. L. SAUERBIER. SE 11,627/1. 1964
- PARTICIPANT NEWSLETTER
- PROGRAM OPERATIONS STATUS REPORT AS OF JUNE 10, 1964
- PROJECT AUDIT REPORT: MALARIA ERADICATION, DEC. 20, 1957 THROUGH DEC. 31, 1961
- PUBLICATIONS
- REPORT ON U.S. ASSISTANCE TO MOROCCO, 1957-1963
- TECHNICAL EDUCATION SURVEY TEAM. REPORT,BY. R. L. BARLOGA. SE 11,630/1. 1955
- TERMINAL AND TRAFFIC OPERATIONS TRAINING PROGRAM (FOR INDONESIAN CARGO PERSONNEL)
- UNITED STATES ECONOMIC ASSISTANCE TO INDONESIA

U.S. Agency for international Development *see* LAND REFORM IN ALGERIA

U.S. AID Mission to Indonesia *see* DEVELOPING A MERCHANT MARINE OFFICER CORPS FOR INDONESIA

U.S. AID Mission to Indonesia. Employment and Manpower Advisor *see* HUMAN RESOURCE DEVELOPMENT IN INDONESIA; PROBLEMS, POLICIES, PROGRAMS

U.S. AIR FORCE JAG BULLETIN *see* AIR FORCE LAW REVIEW

UNITED STATES AIR FORCE JAG LAW REVIEW *see* AIR FORCE LAW REVIEW

U.S. AIR SERVICE – Feb 1919-Dec 1956 – 1 – 388.00 – us L of C Photodup [355]

THE U.S. AND ARGENTINA / Whitaker, Arthur Preston – Cambridge: Harvard University Press, 1954 – 1 – CSUXAGP8616-B – us Hoover Inst Photo [327]

THE UNITED STATES AND FRANCE : CORRESPONDENCE DEALING WITH ECONOMIC RELATIONS, 1811-1930 / ed by Howell, Williamson S – 1972 – 7r – 1 – $595.00 – S1873 – us Scholarly Res [337]

U.S. Anthracite Coal Strike Commission 1902-1903 *see* PROCEEDINGS

U.S. ARCHIVES WORLD WAR 2 : MSB458 NATIONAL REDOUBT GAULEITER FRANZ HOFER, CHIEF GERMAN GENERAL OF LOWER ALPINE ZONE – 1r – $50.00 – B50561 – us Library Micro [900]

U.S. ARMED FORCES IN VIETNAM, 1954-1975 – (Pt 1: Indochina Studies. ISBN 0-89093-444-4. $440.00; Pt 2: Vietnam – Lessons Learned. ISBN: 0-89093-445-2. $880.00; Pt 3: Vietnam – Reports of U.S. Army Operations. ISBN: 0-89093-446-0. $550.00; Pt 4: Vietnam – U.S. Army Senior Officer Debriefing Reports. ISBN: 0-89093-447-9. $440.00. With printed guides) – 1983 – 1 – $2,195.00 set – us UPA [950]

U.S. Army *see*
- AFTER-ACTION REPORT, THIRD U.S. ARMY. 1 AUGUST 1944-9 MAY 1945
- AIR SERVICE AND AIR CORPS NEWS LETTER, 1918-1935
- AMMISCA FILE: THE MAGRUDER MISSION TO CHINA
- BRIEF HISTORIES OF U.S. ARMY COMMANDS (ARMY POSTS) AND DESCRIPTIONS OF THEIR RECORDS
- DESCRIPTIVE COMMENTARIES FROM THE MEDICAL HISTORIES OF POSTS
- DIARY OF OPERATIONS DIVISION, WAR DEPARTMENT GENERAL STAFF, 1942-1946
- DOCUMENTS AND STUDIES ON THE JAPANESE FREE BALLOONS OF WORLD WAR 2
- FINAL REPORTS OF THE U.S. STRATEGIC BOMBING SURVEY
- HISTORICAL FILES OF THE AMERICAN EXPEDITIONARY FORCES IN SIBERIA
- HISTORICAL FILES OF THE AMERICAN EXPEDITIONARY FORCES, NORTH RUSSIA
- THE HISTORY OF ALLIED FORCE HEADQUARTERS, 1942-1945
- HISTORY OF THE MILITARY INTELLIGENCE DIVISION, DEPARTMENT OF THE ARMY GENERAL STAFF
- LETTERS SENT BY THE HEADQUARTERS OF THE ARMY
- LETTERS SENT BY THE POST COMMANDER AT FORT BAYARD, NEW MEXICO, 1888-97
- LETTERS SENT, FORT MOJAVE, ARIZONA TERRITORY, 1859-90
- MILITARY LAW REVIEW
- THE NEGRO IN THE MILITARY SERVICE OF THE UNITED STATES
- OFFICIAL RECORDS OF THE UNION AND CONFEDERATE ARMIES, 1861-65
- PUBLICATIONS
- RECORDS OF THE TENTH MILITARY DEPARTMENT, 1846-51
- REPORTS AND CORRESPONDENCE RELATING TO THE ARMY INVESTIGATIONS OF THE BATTLE OF WOUNDED KNEE AND TO THE SIOUX CAMPAIGN OF 1890-91
- REPORTS OF THE U.S. MILITARY GOVERNMENT FOR GERMANY, U.S. ZONE, 1945-1953
- RETURNS FROM REGULAR ARMY CAVALRY REQUIREMENTS
- RETURNS FROM REGULAR ARMY FIELD ARTILLERY BATTERIES AND REGIMENTS
- THE U.S. ARMY IN THE WORLD WAR, 1917-1919
- U.S. ARMY REGULATIONS
- THE WARTIME CONFERENCES OF THE COMBINED CHIEFS OF STAFF

U.S. Army. 2nd Cavalry Regiment. Company C *see* LETTERS

U.S. Army. 5th Cavalry, Missouri. Company F *see* ORDER BOOK OF CAPTAIN JOHN B. VANSANT

U.S. Army. A. E. F., 1917-1920 *see* EXPEDITION IN NORTH RUSSIA, 1918-1919

U.S. Army. Adjutant General's Office *see*
- COMPILED MILITARY SERVICE RECORD, COMPANY F, 15TH KANSAS CAVALRY, RELATING TO ORREN A. CURTIS
- GENERAL ORDERS AND CIRCULARS OF THE WAR DEPARTMENT AND HEADQUARTERS OF THE ARMY, 1809-1860
- NAME AND SUBJECT INDEX TO THE LETTERS RECEIVED BY THE APPOINTMENT, COMMISSION, AND PERSONAL BRANCH OF THE ADJUTANT GENERAL'S OFFICE, 1871-1894
- RECORDS RELATING TO THE 1811 AND 1815 COURTS-MARTIAL OF MAJOR GENERAL JAMES WILKINSON
- U.S. ARMY GENERALS' REPORTS OF CIVIL WAR SERVICE, 1864-1887

U.S. Army. A.E.F., 1917-1920. Fort Leavenworth, Kansas *see* ROSTERS OF STATION HOSPITAL, FORT LEAVENWORTH, KANSAS. SEPT 1918-DEC 1919. ALSO, MONTHLY STRENGTH RETURNS OF STATION HOSPITAL...JUL 1918-JUL 1919

U.S. Army. A.E.F. 1917-23 *see* RECORDS OF THE 27TH DIVISION OF THE A.E.F. (WORLD WAR I), 1917-19

U.S. Army. Air Force *see*
- AIR FORCE LAW REVIEW
- AIR UNIVERSITY REVIEW
- ANNUAL REPORTS
- GORRELL'S HISTORY OF THE AMERICAN EXPEDITIONARY FORCES AIR SERVICE
- MISSION AND COMBAT REPORTS OF THE FIFTH FIGHTER COMMAND
- PUBLICATIONS

U.S. Army. Air Force. Office of the Judge Advocate General *see* COURT MARTIAL REPORTS OF THE JUDGE ADVOCATE GENERAL (JAG) OF THE AIR FORCE...THE JUDICIAL COUNCIL, AND BOARDS OF REVIEW

U.S. Army Air Forces *see* AVIATION PSYCHOLOGY PROGRAM RESEARCH REPORTS

U.S. Army Air Forces. Eastern Command, Europe *see* EASCOM HISTORY, 1 OCTOBER 1944-1 APRIL 1945

U.S. Army. Army Commands *see*
- RECORDS OF THE U.S. ARMY WAR CRIMES TRIALS
- RECORDS OF THE U.S. ARMY WAR CRIMES TRIALS: UNITED STATES OF AMERICA V. ERNEST ANGERER ET AL
- RECORDS OF THE U.S. ARMY WAR CRIMES TRIALS: UNITED STATES OF AMERICA V. FRIEDRICH BECKER ET.AL
- RECORDS OF THE U.S. NUERNBERG WAR CRIMES TRIALS
- U.S. ARMY INVESTIGATION AND TRIAL RECORDS OF WAR CRIMINALS

U.S. Army. Army of the West *see* ORDERS ISSUED BY BRIGADE GENERAL STEPHEN W. KEARNEY AND BRIGADE GENERAL STERLING PRICE TO THE ARMY OF THE WEST, 1846-48

U.S. Army. Army, Pacific *see* THE HANDLING OF PRISONERS OF WAR DURING THE KOREAN WAR

U.S. Army. Army Service Forces. Special Services Division *see* HISTORY OF THE ENTERTAINMENT BRANCH, SPECIAL SERVICES DIVISION

U.S. Army. Brigade, 1st Division, 3rd Band *see* CIVIL WAR BAND BOOKS

U.S. ARMY BUILD-UP AND ACTIVITIES IN SOUTH VIETNAM, 1965-72 – $3,290.00 – 1-55655-156-8 – us UPA [355]

U.S. Army. Caribbean Army. Caribbean Defense Command. Historical Section *see* TEN STUDIES ON ASPECTS AND PROBLEMS OF THE CARIBBEAN DEFENSE COMMAND DURING THE EARLY AND MID 1940'S

U.S. Army. Caribbean Defense Command *see*
- FRENCH-AMERICAN MILITARY RELATIONS IN THE CARIBBEAN THEATRE IN WORLD WAR 2
- PANAMA CANAL STUDIES

U.S. Army. Caribbean Defense Command. Historical Section *see*
- BILATERAL STAFF CONVERSATIONS WITH LATIN AMERICAN REPUBLICS
- HISTORY OF THE TRINIDAD SECTOR AND BASE COMMAND
- LENDLEASE ACTIVITIES IN THE CARIBBEAN DEFENSE COMMAND
- WAR PLANS AND DEFENSE STUDIES: 1940-1949

U.S. Army. Cavalry, Kansas. 11th Regiment. Company K *see* ROSTER AND HISTORY OF CO. K

U.S. Army. Cavalry, Kansas Volunteer. 15th Regiment *see* SURGEON'S ORDER AND LETTER BOOK

U.S. Army Center of Military History *see* THE WAR AGAINST JAPAN

U. S. ARMY CENTER OF MILITARY HISTORY HISTORICAL MANUSCRIPTS COLLECTION : THE WAR AGAINST JAPAN – (China-Burma-India Theater, 1942-1944. 7reels; India-Burma Theater, 1944-1945. 6reels; China Theater, 1944-1945. 1reel; Southwest Pacific Area Theater. 14reels; Central Pacific/Pacific Ocean Areas Theater. 18reels; South Pacific Theater. 2reels; Internment, Security, and Prisoner of War Camps Reports. 1reel; Translations of Japanese Documents. 5reels; Guide also sold separately: $15.00) – 1991 – 54 rolls – 9 – $4,320.00 – Dist. us Scholarly Res – Published in cooperation with the Center of Military History – us L of C Photodup [355]

U.S. ARMY CENTER OF MILITARY HISTORY HISTORICAL MANUSCRIPTS COLLECTION : THE KOREAN WAR – (Guide also separately $20.00 S3334.G) – 1996 – 15r – 1 – $1,275.00 – S3334 – Co-publ with the U.S. Army Center of Military History – us Scholarly Res [950]

U.S. ARMY CENTER OF MILITARY HISTORY HISTORICAL MANUSCRIPTS COLLECTION : THE KOREANUPR – (Guide sold separately, ca $20.00) – ca 21r – 1 – ca $1,785.00 – D4154 – Co-publ with the U.S.Army Center of Military History 1995 – us Scholarly Res [950]

U.S. Army. Chemical Corps *see* SMOKE GENERATOR OPERATIONS IN THE MEDITERRANEAN AND EUROPEAN THEATERS OF OPERATIONS

U.S. Army, China Theater *see* HISTORY OF THE CHINA THEATER

U.S. Army. Commands *see*
- GERMAN DOCUMENTS AMONG THE WAR CRIMES RECORDS OF THE JUDGE ADVOCATE DIVISION, HEADQUARTERS, U.S. ARMY, EUROPE
- RECORDS OF THE U.S. NUERNBERG WAR CRIMES TRIALS

U.S. Army. Continental Commands *see*
- LETTERS SENT BY HEADQUARTERS, DEPARTMENT OF TEXAS, 1870-1898
- LETTERS SENT BY THE DEPARTMENT OF FLORIDA AND SUCCESSOR COMMANDS, APRIL 18, 1861-JANUARY 1869
- LETTERS SENT BY THE DEPARTMENT OF TEXAS AND THE FIFTH MILITARY DISTRICT, 1856-58 AND 1865-1870
- REGISTER OF LETTERS RECEIVED, AND LETTERS RECEIVED BY HEADQUARTERS, 9TH MILITARY DEPARTMENT, 1849-1853
- REGISTERS OF LETTERS RECEIVED, AND LETTERS RECEIVED BY HEADQUARTERS, DEPARTMENT OF NEW MEXICO, 1854-1865
- REGISTERS OF LETTERS RECEIVED BY HEADQUARTERS, DISTRICT OF NEW MEXICO, SEPTEMBER 1865-AUGUST 1890

U.S. Army. Corps of Engineers *see*
- MANHATTAN ENGINEER DISTRICT HISTORY
- PROFESSIONAL MEMOIRS
- PUBLICATIONS
- RETURNS OF THE CORPS OF ENGINEERS
- RETURNS OF THE CORPS OF TOPOGRAPHICAL ENGINEERS

U.S. Army Court of Military Appeals *see* INDEX AND LEGISLATIVE HISTORY

United States Army Dept of MIssouri and Mississippi *see* GENERAL ORDERS, GENERAL FIELD ORDERS AND CIRCULARS, 1861-62

U.S. Army. European Theater of Operations *see*
- THE FRENCH FORCES OF THE INTERIOR; THEIR ORGANIZATION AND PARTICIPATION IN THE LIBERATION OF FRANCE, 1944
- REPORTS OF THE GENERAL BOARD, U.S. FORCES, EUROPEAN THEATER

U.S. ARMY FAR EAST COMMAND : INTELLIGENCE SERIES – Introduction: A Brief History of the G-2 Section, GHQ, SWPA & Affiliated Units, 1948 1r L9400001. Vol 1: The Guerrilla Resistance Movement in the Philippines,...Tokyo, Japan, Mar 20 1948 1r L9400002. Vol 2: Intelligence Activities in the Philippines during the Japanese Occupation,...Tokyo, Japan, Jun 10 1948 1r L9400003. Vol 3: Operations of the Military Intelligence Section, GHQ, SWPA/FEC/SCAP,...Tokyo, Japan, Apr 1 1951 2r L9400004. Vol 4: Operations of the Allied Intelligence Bureau, GHQ, SWPA,...Tokyo, Japan, Aug 19 1948 1r L9400005. Vol 5: Operations of the Allied Translator and Interpreter Section, GHQ, SWPA,...Tokyo, Japan, Jul 12 1948 1r L9400006. Vol 6: Operations of the Allied Geographical Section, GHQ, SWPA,...Tokyo, Japan, Jun 10 1948 1r L9400007. Vol 7: Operations of the Technical Intelligence Unit in the SWPA,...Tokyo, Japan, Mar 20 1948 1r L9400008. Vol 8: Operations of the Counter Intelligence Corps in the SWPA,...Tokyo, Japan, Jul 29 1948 1r L9400009. Vol 9: Operations of the Civil Intelligence Section, GHQ, FEC & SCAP,...Tokyo, Japan, Dec 31 1949 1r L9400010. In English – 11r – 1 – $385.00 in US $40.00r – L9400001-L9400010 – Dist. us Scholarly Res – us L of C Photodup [350]

U.S. Army. Far East Command *see*
- ADMINISTRATIVE HISTORY, GENERAL HEADQUARTERS, UNITED STATES ARMY FORCES, PACIFIC
- A BRIEF HISTORY OF THE G-2 SECTION, GHQ, SWPA AND AFFILIATED UNITS
- THE GUERRILLA RESISTANCE MOVEMENT IN THE PHILIPPINES
- INTELLIGENCE ACTIVITIES IN THE PHILIPPINES DURING THE JAPANESE OCCUPATION
- INTELLIGENCE SERIES
- OPERATIONS OF THE ALLIED INTELLIGENCE BUREAU, GHQ, SWPA
- OPERATIONS OF THE ALLIED TRANSLATOR AND INTERPRETER SECTION, GHQ, SWPA
- OPERATIONS OF THE CIVIL INTELLIGENCE SECTION, GHQ, FEC AND SCAP
- OPERATIONS OF THE COUNTER INTELLIGENCE CORPS IN THE SWPA
- OPERATIONS OF THE MILITARY INTELLIGENCE SECTION, GHA, SWPA/FEC/SCAP
- OPERATIONS OF THE TECHNICAL INTELLIGENCE UNIT IN THE SWPA

U.S. Army. Fifth Army *see* THE FIFTH ARMY HISTORY, 1943-1945

U.S. Army. First Army *see* FIRST U.S. ARMY REPORT OF OPERATIONS, 1943-1945

U.S. Army. Forces in Korea *see* REPUBLIC OF KOREA ECONOMIC SUMMATION

U.S. Army. Forces in the Far East *see*
- LOGISTICAL SUPPORT TO PRISONERS OF WAR, JUL 1951-JUL 1953
- OPERATION LITTLE SWITCH

- ABSTRACTS OF WASHINGTON DONATION LAND CLAIMS, 1855-1902
- JOURNAL AND REPORT OF JAMES L. CATHCART AND JAMES HUTTON, AGENTS APPOINTED BY THE SECTY. OF THE NAVY TO SURVEY TIMBER RESOURCES BETWEEN THE MERMENTAU AND MOBILE RIVERS, 1818-19
- LETTERS RECEIVED BY THE SECTY. OF THE TREASURY AND THE COMM. OF THE GENERAL LAND OFFICE FROM THE SURVEYOR GENERAL OF THE TERRITORY NORTHWEST OF THE RIVER OHIO, 1797-1849
- LETTERS RECEIVED BY THE SURVEYOR GENERAL OF THE TERRITORY NORTHWEST OF THE RIVER OHIO, 1796-1856
- LETTERS SENT BY THE GENERAL LAND OFFICE TO THE SURVEYOR GENERAL, 1796-1901
- LETTERS SENT BY THE SURVEYOR GENERAL OF THE TERRITORY NORTHWEST OF THE RIVER OHIO, 1797-1854
- LIST OF NORTH CAROLINA LAND GRANTS IN TENNESSEE, 1778-91
- MISCELLANEOUS LETTERS SENT BY THE GENERAL LAND OFFICE, 1796-1889
- OREGON AND WASHINGTON DONATION LAND FILES
- REGISTER OF ARMY LAND WARRANTS ISSUED UNDER THE ACT OF 1788, FOR SERVICE IN THE REVOLUTIONARY WAR: MILITARY DISTRICT OF OHIO
- U.S. REVOLUTIONARY WAR BOUNTY LAND WARRANTS USED IN THE U.S. MILITARY DISTRICT OF OHIO AND RELATED PAPERS
- WAR OF 1812 MILITARY BOUNTY LAND WARRANTS

U.S. Bureau of Marine Inspection and Navigation *see* CERTIFICATES OF REGISTRY, ENROLLMENT, AND LICENSE ISSUED AT EDGARTOWN, MASSACHUSETTS, 1815-1913

U.S. Bureau of Medicine and Surgery (Navy) *see* PUBLICATIONS

U.S. Bureau of Mines *see*
- BULLETINS
- COLLECTION, 1985
- COLLECTION, 1986 UPDATE
- COLLECTION, 1987 UPDATE
- COLLECTION, 1988 UPDATE
- COLLECTION, 1989 UPDATE
- COLLECTION, 1990 UPDATE
- COLLECTION, 1910-69
- COLLECTION, 1910-87
- COLLECTION, 1970-75
- COLLECTION, 1976-80
- COLLECTION, 1981-84
- COLLECTION INDEX
- INFORMATION CIRCULARS
- MINERALS YEARBOOK
- OPEN FILE REPORTS COLLECTION
- PRELIMINARY CLASSIFIED INDEX OF TECHNICAL OIL MISSION REPORTS
- PUBLICATIONS
- REPORTS OF INVESTIGATIONS
- TECHNICAL PAPERS

U.S. Bureau of Mines *see* COLLECTION, 1991 UPDATE

U.S. Bureau of Narcotics and Dangerous Drugs *see*
- BNDD BULLETIN
- DRUG ENFORCEMENT

U.S. Bureau of Naval Weapons *see* PUBLICATIONS

U.S. Bureau of Plant Industry *see* BULLETIN

U.S. Bureau of Public Debt *see* RECORDS OF THE DELAWARE AND MARYLAND CONTINENTAL LOAN OFFICE, 1777-1790

U.S. Bureau of Reclamation *see*
- PROJECT HISTORIES AND REPORTS OF RECLAMATION BUREAU PROJECTS, 1905-25
- REPORT TO THE DIRECTOR GENERAL, CENTRAL WATER AUTHORITY OF JORDAN

U.S. Bureau of Refugees, Freedmen, and Abandoned Lands *see*
- RECORDS OF THE ASSISTANT COMMISSIONER, BUREAU OF REFUGEES, FREEDMEN, AND ABANDONED LANDS
- RECORDS OF THE ASSISTANT COMMISSIONER FOR THE DISTRICT OF COLUMBIA
- RECORDS OF THE ASSISTANT COMMISSIONER FOR THE STATE OF ARKANSAS
- RECORDS OF THE ASSISTANT COMMISSIONER FOR THE STATE OF GEORGIA..
- RECORDS OF THE ASSISTANT COMMISSIONER FOR THE STATE OF LOUISIANA
- RECORDS OF THE ASSISTANT COMMISSIONER FOR THE STATE OF MISSISSIPPI
- RECORDS OF THE ASSISTANT COMMISSIONER FOR THE STATE OF NORTH CAROLINA
- RECORDS OF THE ASSISTANT COMMISSIONER FOR THE STATE OF SOUTH CAROLINA
- RECORDS OF THE ASSISTANT COMMISSIONER FOR THE STATE OF TENNESSEE
- RECORDS OF THE ASSISTANT COMMISSIONER FOR THE STATE OF TEXAS
- RECORDS OF THE ASSISTANT COMMISSIONER FOR THE STATE OF VIRGINIA
- RECORDS OF THE SUPERINTENDENT OF EDUCATION FOR THE DISTRICT OF COLUMBIA
- RECORDS OF THE SUPERINTENDENT OF EDUCATION FOR THE STATE OF ALABAMA
- RECORDS OF THE SUPERINTENDENT OF EDUCATION FOR THE STATE OF ARKANSAS
- RECORDS OF THE SUPERINTENDENT OF EDUCATION FOR THE STATE OF LOUISIANA
- RECORDS OF THE SUPERINTENDENT OF EDUCATION FOR THE STATE OF NORTH CAROLINA
- RECORDS OF THE SUPERINTENDENT OF EDUCATION FOR THE STATE OF TENNESSEE
- RECORDS OF THE SUPERINTENDENT OF EDUCATION FOR THE STATE OF TEXAS
- RECORDS OF THE SUPERINTENDENT OF EDUCATION FOR THE STATE OF VIRGINIA
- RECORDS OF THE SUPT. OF EDUCATION FOR THE STATE OF GEORGIA..., 1865-70
- REGISTERS AND LETTERS RECEIVED BY THE COMMISSIONER..., 1865-72
- SELECTED RECORDS OF THE TENNESSEE FIELD OFFICE OF THE BUREAU.
- SELECTED SERIES OF RECORDS ISSUED BY THE COMMISSIONER..., 1865-72

U.S. Bureau of the Budget *see*
- BUDGET OF THE UNITED STATES GOVERNMENT
- GOVERNMENT CONTRACTS DIGEST

U.S. Bureau of the Census *see*
- 1900 CENSUS SCHEDULES
- 1910 CENSUS SCHEDULES
- 1970 DECENNIAL CENSUS GUIDE AND MICROFICHE
- 1980 DECENNIAL CENSUS GUIDE AND MICROFICHE
- 1990 DECENNIAL CENSUS GUIDE AND MICROFICHE
- AGRICULTURE SCHEDULES, PENNSYLVANIA FEDERAL DECENNIAL CENSUSES
- CATALOG OF PUBLICATIONS
- DECENNIAL CENSUS 1980
- DECENNIAL CENSUS PUBLICATIONS: POPULATION
- DESCRIPTION OF CENSUS ENUMERATION DISTRICTS, 1900
- DESCRIPTIONS OF CENSUS ENUMERATION DISTRICTS, 1830-90 AND 1910-50
- EIGHTH CENSUS OF THE UNITED STATES
- ELEVENTH CENSUS (1890): SPECIAL SCHEDULES ENUMERATING UNION VETERANS AND WIDOWS OF UNION VETERANS OF THE CIVIL WAR
- ELEVENTH CENSUS OF THE UNITED STATES
- FEDERAL MORTALITY CENSUS SCHEDULES, 1850-80, AND RELATED INDEXES IN THE CUSTODY OF THE DAUGHTERS OF THE AMERICAN REVOLUTION
- FEDERAL NONPOPULATION CENSUS SCHEDULES IN THE CUSTODY OF THE PENNSYLVANIA STATE LIBRARY, 1850-80
- FEDERAL NONPOPULATION DECENNIAL CENSUS SCHEDULES FOR NEBRASKA, 1860-80
- FIFTH CENSUS OF THE UNITED STATES
- FIRST CENSUS OF THE UNITED STATES
- FOURTH CENSUS OF THE UNITED STATES
- INDEX (SOUNDEX) TO 1880 POPULATION SCHEDULES:
- INDEX (SOUNDEX) TO 1900 FEDERAL POPULATION CENSUS SCHEDULES
- INDEX (SOUNDEX) TO 1910 FEDERAL POPULATION CENSUS SCHEDULES
- INDEX TO THE ELEVENTH CENSUS OF THE UNITED STATES
  MINNESOTA CENSUS SCHEDULES FOR 1870
- NINTH CENSUS OF THE UNITED STATES
- NON-DECENNIAL CENSUS PUBLICATIONS IN MICROFORM, 1820-1945
- NON-DECENNIAL CENSUS PUBLICATIONS IN MICROFORM, 1946-1967
- NONPOPULATION CENSUS SCHEDULES
- NONPOPULATION CENSUS SCHEDULES, 1850-60
- NONPOPULATION CENSUS SCHEDULES, 1850-80
- PENNSYLVANIA. RECORDS
- PUBLICATIONS
- PUBLICATIONS...: 1790 CENSUS, PRINTED SCHEDULES
- PUBLICATIONS, 1790-1916
- RECORDS OF THE 1820 CENSUS OF MANUFACTURES
- SCHEDULES OF THE COLORADO STATE CENSUS OF 1885
- SCHEDULES OF THE FLORIDA STATE CENSUS OF 1885
- SCHEDULES OF THE NEBRASKA STATE CENSUS OF 1885
- SCHEDULES OF THE NEW MEXICO TERRITORY CENSUS OF 1885
- SECOND CENSUS OF THE UNITED STATES
- SEVENTH CENSUS OF THE UNITED STATES
- SIXTH CENSUS OF THE UNITED STATES
- STATISTICAL ABSTRACT OF THE UNITED STATES
- TENTH CENSUS OF THE UNITED STATES
- THIRD CENSUS OF THE UNITED STATES

U.S. Bureau of the Census. South Carolina *see* U.S. CENSUS. ORIGINAL AGRICULTURE, INDUSTRY, SOCIAL STATISTICS AND MORTALITY SCHEDULES, 1850-80

U.S. Bureau of the Customs *see*
- COMPUTER-PROCESSED TABULATIONS OF DATA FROM SEAMEN'S PROTECTIVE CERTIFICATE APPLICATIONS TO THE COLLECTOR OF CUSTOMS FOR THE PORT OF PHILADELPHIA
- COPIES OF LISTS OF PASSENGERS ARRIVING AT MISCELLANEOUS PORTS ON THE ATLANTIC AND GULF COASTS AND AT PORTS ON THE GREAT LAKES, 1820-73
- IMPOST BOOKS OF THE COLLECTOR OF CUSTOMS AT PHILADELPHIA, 1789-1804
- INDEX TO PASSENGER LISTS OF VESSELS ARRIVING AT BALTIMORE, 1820-97 (FEDERAL PASSENGER LISTS)
- INDEX TO PASSENGER LISTS OF VESSELS ARRIVING AT BALTIMORE, 1833-66
- INDEX TO PASSENGER LISTS OF VESSELS ARRIVING AT BALTIMORE, MARYLAND
- INDEX TO PASSENGER LISTS OF VESSELS ARRIVING AT BOSTON, 1848-91
- INDEX TO PASSENGER LISTS OF VESSELS ARRIVING AT BOSTON, MASSACHUSETTS
- INDEX TO PASSENGER LISTS OF VESSELS ARRIVING AT NEW ORLEANS BEFORE 1900
- INDEX TO PASSENGER LISTS OF VESSELS ARRIVING AT NEW YORK, 1820-46
- INDEX TO PASSENGER LISTS OF VESSELS ARRIVING AT PHILADELPHIA, 1800-1906
- INDEX TO PASSENGERS OF VESSELS ARRIVING AT PORTS IN ALABAMA, FLORIDA, GEORGIA, AND SOUTH CAROLINA
- LETTERS RECEIVED BY THE SECRETARY OF THE TREASURY FROM SPECIAL AGENTS, 1854-61
- PASSENGER LISTS OF VESSELS ARRIVING AT BALTIMORE, 1820-91
- PASSENGER LISTS OF VESSELS ARRIVING AT BOSTON, 1820-91
- PASSENGER LISTS OF VESSELS ARRIVING AT NEW ORLEANS, LOUISIANA
- PASSENGER LISTS OF VESSELS ARRIVING AT NEW YORK, 1820-97
- PASSENGER LISTS OF VESSELS ARRIVING AT PHILADELPHIA, 1800-82
- PASSENGER LISTS OF VESSELS ARRIVING AT PORTLAND, MAINE
- PASSENGER LISTS OF VESSELS ARRIVING AT PROVIDENCE, RHODE ISLAND
- QUARTERLY ABSTRACTS OF PASSENGER LISTS OF VESSELS ARRIVING AT BALTIMORE, 1820-69
- QUARTERLY ABSTRACTS OF PASSENGER LISTS OF VESSELS ARRIVING AT NEW ORLEANS, 1820-75
- REGISTERS OF VESSELS ARRIVING AT THE PORT OF NEW YORK, NEW YORK FROM FOREIGN PORTS
- A SUPPLEMENT INDEX TO PASSENGER LISTS OF VESSELS ARRIVING AT ATLANTIC AND GULF COAST PORTS (EXCLUDING NEW YORK), 1820-74
- U.S. IMPORTS FOR CONSUMPTION

U.S. Bureau of the Mint *see*
- BULLION LEDGERS OF THE U.S. MINT AT PHILADELPHIA, 1794-1802
- CORRESPONDENCE...WITH THE BRANCH MINT AT DAHLONEGA, GEORGIA, 1835-61
- LETTERS SENT BY THE DIRECTOR OF THE U.S. MINT AT PHILADELPHIA, 1795-1817

U.S. Business and Defense Services Administration *see* PUBLICATIONS

THE U.S. CATHOLIC ALMANAC : OR, LAITY'S DIRECTORY FOR THE YEAR OF OUR LORD... – James Myres: Baltimore, 1833-37 – 1r – 1 – $40.00r – us U.N.D. Archives [240]

U.S. CATHOLIC PRESS – Hartford. Conn. -w. 1829-32 – 1 – us UMI [071]

U.S. CENSUS : WISCONSIN – (1850, 9r; Index: 1850.-36r; 1860, 27r; Index: 1860.-94r; 1870.-33r; Index: 1870.-130r) – 1 – us Historical Soc [304]

U.S. CENSUS AGRICULTURE, INDUSTRY, SOCIAL STATISTICS, AND MORTALITY SCHEDULES FOR SOUTH CAROLINA, 1850-1880 – South Carolina: Dept of Archives and History, 1995 – 17r – 1 – $1,445.00 – us Scholarly Res [630]

UNITED STATES CENSUS AND BUSINESS MANUAL : CONTAINING THE OFFICIAL CENSUS RETURNS FOR 1880 AND 1870 – 7th ed. Cincinnati: Benson Bros, 1882 – 3mf – 9 – $4.50 – LLMC 91-073 – us L.L.M.C. [340]

U.S. CENSUS. ORIGINAL AGRICULTURE, INDUSTRY, SOCIAL STATISTICS AND MORTALITY SCHEDULES, 1850-80 / U.S. Bureau of the Census. South Carolina – Printed introd. 22r M-2 – 1 – $75.00r – out-of-state orders: us Scholarly Res – us SC Archives [978]

U.S. Central Intelligence Agency *see*
- AFRICA, 1946-76
- CHIEFS OF STATE AND CABINET MEMBERS OF FOREIGN GOVERNMENTS
- CHINA, 1946-76
- CIA RESEARCH REPORTS
- COLLECTION WITH MAPS
- CONSOLIDATED TRANSLATION SURVEYS
- ECONOMIC AND ENERGY INDICATORS
- EUROPE, 1946-76
- INTERNATIONAL ECONOMIC AND ENERGY STATISTICAL REVIEW
- JAPAN, KOREA AND THE SECURITY OF ASIA, 1946-76
- LATIN AMERICA, 1946-76
- MAPS
- THE MIDDLE EAST, 1946-76
- NATIONAL BASIC INTELLIGENCE FACTBOOK/ WORLD FACTBOOK
- RESEARCH AIDS ON THE PEOPLE'S REPUBLIC OF CHINA
- THE SOVIET UNION, 1946-76
- VIETNAM AND SOUTHEAST ASIA, 1946-76

U.S. Central Intelligence Agency. U.S.S.R *see* REFERENCE AND RESEARCH MATERIALS

U.S. Chief Counsel for War Crimes. Nuremberg Military Tribunals *see* RECORDS...RELATING TO NAZI INDUSTRIALISTS

U.S. Chief of Counsel for Prosecution of Axis Criminality *see* NAZI CONSPIRACY AND AGGRESSION

U.S. Children's Bureau. Dept. of Health, Education and Welfare *see* PUBLICATIONS

U.S. CHRONICLE – Providence. R.I. 1784-1804 – 1,3 – us Readex [071]

U.S. CIRCUIT AND DISTRICT COURT REPORTS *see*
- CASES ADJUDGED IN THE U.S. CIRCUIT COURTS OF APPEAL
- THE FEDERAL CASES
- FEDERAL DECISIONS

U.S. Circuit and District Courts *see*
- ACT OF 1800 BANKRUPTCY CASE FILES OF THE U.S. DISTRICT COURT OF MARYLAND
- THE FEDERAL CASES: COMPRISING CASES ARGUED AND DETERMINED IN THE CIRCUIT AND DISTRICT COURTS OF THE UNITED STATES FROM THE EARLIEST TIMES TO THE BEGINNING OF THE FEDERAL REPORTER, 1789-1880.
- RECORDS OF THE U.S. DISTRICT COURT FOR THE EASTERN DISTRICT OF LOUISIANA
- WAR OF 1812 PRIZE CASE FILES OF THE U.S. DISTRICT COURT FOR THE EASTERN DISTRICT OF PENNSYLVANIA

U.S. Circuit and District Courts. California. Northern District *see* SELECTED INDEXES TO NATURALIZATION RECORDS

U.S. Circuit and District Courts. District of Columbia *see* MINUTES OF THE U.S. CIRCUIT COURT FOR THE DISTRICT OF COLUMBIA

U.S. Circuit and District Courts. Maryland *see*
- CRIMINAL CASE FILES OF THE U.S. CIRCUIT COURT FOR THE DISTRICT OF MARYLAND
- INDEX TO NATURALIZATION PETITIONS... 1797-1956

U.S. Department of Agriculture. Economic Research Service *see* THE AGRICULTURE OF MOROCCO: PROGRAMS, PROGRESS, PROSPECTS

U.S. Department of Agriculture. Library. Washington, D.C. *see* PLANT SCIENCE CATALOG

U.S. Department of Agriculture. Office of Experiment Stations *see* EXPERIMENT STATION RECORD

U.S. Department of Agriculture. Office of the Secretary *see*
- LETTERS SENT..., 1893-1929
- LETTERS SENT BY THE AS SECTY. OF AGRICULTURE, 1889-94

U.S. Department of Agriculture. Office of the Solicitor *see* FEDERAL FOOD AND DRUG ACT DECISIONS

UNITED STATES DEPARTMENT OF AGRICULTURE POMOLOGICAL WATERCOLORS – (Families and genera can be purchased separately. With index £84.00) – 70mf – 9 – £2,010.00 – uk Chadwyck [580]

U.S. Department of Commerce *see*
- OVERSEAS BUSINESS REPORTS
- PUBLICATIONS CATALOG AND INDEXES
- STATISTICAL ABSTRACTS

U.S. Department of Commerce. Bureau of International Commerce *see* OVERSEAS BUSINESS REPORTS

U.S. Department of Commerce. General Records *see* MINUTES OF THE INDUSTRIAL COMMISSION, 1898-1902

U.S. Department of Defense *see*
- PUBLICATIONS
- UNARMED DEFENSE FOR THE AMERICAN SOLDIER

US. Department of Defense *see* PUBLIC STATEMENTS BY THE SECRETARIES OF DEFENSE

U.S. Department of Energy *see* TECHNICAL BOOKS AND MONOGRAPHS

U.S. Department of Health and Human Services *see*
- DEPARTMENT OF HEALTH, EDUCATION AND WELFARE ANNUAL REPORTS
- HEALTH SCIENCES SERIALS
- WELFARE IN REVIEW

U.S. Department of Health, Education and Welfare *see*
- AN ANALYTICAL HISTORY OF THE PATENT POLICY OF THE DEPARTMENT OF HEALTH, EDUCATION, AND WELFARE
- DEPARTMENT OF HEALTH, EDUCATION AND WELFARE (1963-1969)
- LETTERS SENT BY THE COMMISSIONER OF EDUCATION, 1870-1909
- PUBLICATIONS

U.S. Department of Health, Education and Welfare. Library *see* SUBJECT CATALOG OF THE DEPARTMENT LIBRARY

U.S. Department of Health, Education and Welfare. Library. Washington D.C. *see* AUTHOR-TITLE CATALOG OF THE DEPARTMENT LIBRARY

U.S. Department of Housing and Urban Development *see*
- DEPARTMENT OF HOUSING AND URBAN DEVELOPMENT ANNUAL REPORTS
- ROSEBUD

U.S. Department of Housing and Urban Development. Library and Information Division *see* DICTIONARY CATALOG OF THE DEPARTMENT LIBRARY

U.S. Department of Housing and Urban Development. Library and Information Division. Washington, D.C. *see* THE DICTIONARY CATALOG OF THE UNITED STATES DEPARTMENT OF HOUSING AND URBAN DEVELOPMENT LIBRARY AND INFORMATION DIVISION

U.S. Department of Internal Revenue *see*
- APPOINTMENT PAPERS: TERRITORY OF COLOARDO
- ASSESSMENT LISTS FOR IOWA
- ASSESSMENT LISTS FOR KANSAS
- ASSESSMENT LISTS FOR KENTUCKY
- ASSESSMENT LISTS FOR LOUISIANA
- ASSESSMENT LISTS FOR MAINE
- ASSESSMENT LISTS FOR MARYLAND
- ASSESSMENT LISTS FOR MICHIGAN
- ASSESSMENT LISTS FOR MISSISSIPPI
- ASSESSMENT LISTS FOR MONTANA
- ASSESSMENT LISTS FOR NEVADA
- ASSESSMENT LISTS FOR NEW HAMPSHIRE
- ASSESSMENT LISTS FOR NORTH CAROLINA
- ASSESSMENT LISTS FOR PENNSYLVANIA
- ASSESSMENT LISTS FOR RHODE ISLAND
- ASSESSMENT LISTS FOR SOUTH CAROLINA
- ASSESSMENT LISTS FOR TEXAS
- ASSESSMENT LISTS FOR THE TERRITORY OF NEW MEXICO
- ASSESSMENT LISTS FOR VERMONT
- ASSESSMENT LISTS FOR VIRGINIA
- ASSESSMENT LISTS FOR WEST VIRGINIA

U.S. Department of Justice *see*
- ANNUAL REPORTS OF THE ATTORNEY GENERAL
- THE ATTORNEY GENERAL'S COMMITTEE ON ADMINISTRATIVE PROCEDURE
- THE ATTORNEY GENERAL'S SURVEY ON RELEASE PROCEDURES
- THE ATTTORNEY GENERAL'S INVESTIGATION OF GOVERNMENT PATENT PRACTICES AND POLICIES
- HISTORY OF THE DEPARTMENT OF JUSTICE (1963-69)
- IN THE CIRCUIT COURT OF APPEALS FOR THE EIGHTH CIRCUIT. DECEMBER TERM, 1909. NO.3150-NO.3163 UNITED STATES APPELLANT V. JAMES P. ALLEN ET AL.
- IN THE CIRCUIT COURT OF APPEALS FOR THE EIGHTH CIRCUIT. DECEMBER TERM, 1909. NO.3161-3163; 3150-3160 UNITED STATES, APPELLANT V. WALTER P. NICHOLS.
- INDEX TO NAMES OF U.S. MARSHALS, 1789-1960
- JAPANESE-AMERICAN EVACUATION CLAIMS ACT
- LETTERS RECEIVED BY THE DEPARTMENT OF JUSTICE FROM MISSISSIPPI
- LETTERS RECEIVED BY THE DEPARTMENT OF JUSTICE FROM SOUTH CAROLINA
- LETTERS RECEIVED BY THE DEPARTMENT OF JUSTICE FROM THE STATE OF GEORGIA
- LETTERS RECEIVED BY THE DEPARTMENT OF JUSTICE FROM THE STATE OF LOUISIANA
- LETTERS SENT BY THE DEPT. OF JUSTICE TO EXECUTIVE OFFICERS AND MEMBERS OF CONGRESS, 1871-1904
- LETTERS SENT...: GENERAL AND MISCELLANEOUS, 1818-1904
- LETTERS SENT...CONCERNING JUDICIARY EXPENSES, 1849-84
- LETTERS SENT...:INSTRUCTIONS TO U.S. ATTORNEYS AND MARSHALS, 1867-1904
- LETTERS SENT...TO JUDGES AND CLERKS, 1874-1904
- OFFICE OF LEGAL COUNSEL OPINIONS
- OPINIONS OF THE ATTORNEY GENERAL OF THE U.S.
- ORIGINAL OPINIONS OF THE JUSTICES OF THE U.S. SUPREME COURT DELIVERED AT THE JANUARY TERM 1832
- PEONAGE FILES, 1901-45
- PUBLICATIONS OF THE UNITED STATES DEPARTMENT OF JUSTICE
- RECORDS RELATING TO THE APPOINTMENT OF FEDERAL JUDGES, ATTORNEYS, AND MARSHALS FOR:
- RECORDS RELATING TO THE APPOINTMENT OF FEDERAL JUDGES, ATTORNEYS AND MARSHALS FOR OREGON
- UNIFORM CRIME REPORTS

U.S. DEPARTMENT OF JUSTICE : CURRENT DOCUMENTS ON MICROFICHE – 1985- – 9 – Apply for price – us CIS [340]

U.S. Department of Justice *see* ART GUIDES

U.S. Department of Justice. Bureau of Prisons *see* FEDERAL PROBATION

U.S. Department of Labor *see*
- ASSISTANT SECRETARY FOR LABOR-MANAGEMENT RELATIONS DECISIONS
- DEPARTMENT OF LABOR ANNUAL REPORTS
- LABOUR LAW AND PRACTICE IN THE KINGDOM OF LIBYA
- MINE SAFETY AND HEALTH ADMINISTRATION PUBLICATIONS
- MONTHLY LABOR REVIEW
- OCCUPATIONAL SAFETY AND HEALTH ADMINISTRATION REPORTS
- PUBLICATIONS
- REPORT ON CONDITION OF WOMAN AND CHILD WAGE-EARNERS IN THE UNITED STATES
- UNEMPLOYMENT IN STATES AND LOCAL AREAS
- UNEMPLOYMENT INSURANCE REVIEW
- WAGE DATA ON WAGE AND HOUR CASES, REGION 5, 1938-44

U.S. Department of Labor. Bureau of Labor Statistics *see*
- LABOR LAW AND PRACTICE IN LEBANON
- LABOR LAW AND PRACTICE IN MOROCCO

U.S. Department of Labor. Commission on Industrial Relations *see* REPORTS, 1912-15

U.S. Department of Labor. Pension Benefit Guaranty Corporation *see* ERISA UPDATE

U.S. Department of Labor. Women's Bureau *see*
- BULLETIN AND SPECIAL BULLETIN
- RECORDS...1918-65, PART 1
- RECORDS...1918-65, PART 2
- SPECIAL BULLETINS

U.S. Department of Navy. Naval Security Group. Command Headquarters *see* INTELLIGENCE REPORTS ON THE WAR IN THE ATLANTIC, 1942-45

U. S. Department of State *see*
- CONSULAR INSTRUCTIONS OF THE DEPARTMENT OF STATE, 1801-1834
- DESPATCHES FROM U.S. CONSULS IN GUAM, 1854-1856
- DESPATCHES FROM U.S. CONSULS IN NUERNBERG, 1846-1906
- DESPATCHES FROM U.S. CONSULS IN TRIPOLI, LIBYA, 1796-1885
- DESPATCHES FROM U.S. CONSULS TO ZITTAU, 1897-1906
- FOREIGN LETTERS OF THE CONTINENTAL CONGRESS AND THE DEPARTMENT OF STATE, 1785-1790

U.S. Department of State *see*
- ACCEPTANCES AND ORDER FOR COMMISSIONS IN THE RECORDS OF THE DEPARTMENT OF STATE
- THE ALASKA TREATY
- AMERICAN FOREIGN POLICY SERIES
- ARMS CONTROL AND DISARMAMENT
- BEVAN'S TREATIES
- BIOGRAPHIC REGISTER
- BULLETIN
- CASHBOOK OF THE DEPT. OF STATE, 1785-95
- CENTRAL AMERICA AND THE CARIBBEAN, 1930-45
- CODEBOOKS
- CONFIDENTIAL U.S. STATE DEPARTMENT CENTRAL FILES: ARGENTINA
- CONFIDENTIAL U.S. STATE DEPARTMENT CENTRAL FILES: GERMANY
- CONFIDENTIAL...CENTRAL FILES
- CONFIDENTIAL...SPECIAL FILES
- CONSULAR INSTRUCTIONS...1801-34
- CONSULTATION AMONG THE AMERICAN REPUBLICS WITH RESPECT TO THE ARGENTINE SITUATION
- COPYBOOKS OF GEORGE WASHINGTON'S CORRESPONDENCE WITH SECRETARIES OF STATE, 1789-96
- CORRESPONDENCE OF SECRETARY OF STATE BRYAN WITH PRESIDENT WILSON, 1913-15
- CORRESPONDENCE RELATING TO THE FILIBUSTERING EXPEDITION AGAINST THE SPANISH GOVERNMENT OF MEXICO, 1811-16
- CUBA, 1930-45
- DAMAGES IN INTERNATIONAL LAW
- DAYBOOK OF THE DEPARTMENT OF STATE FOR MISCELLANEOUS AND CONTINGENT EXPENSES
- DEPARTMENT OF STATE BULLETIN
- DESPATCHES FROM U.S. CONSULAR REPRESENTATIVES IN PUERTO RICO, 1821-99
- DESPATCHES FROM U.S. CONSULS IN AARAU, SWITZERLAND, 1898-1902
- DESPATCHES FROM U.S. CONSULS IN ACAPULCO, MEXICO, 1823-1906
- DESPATCHES FROM U.S. CONSULS IN ADEN, 1880-1906
- DESPATCHES FROM U.S. CONSULS IN AGUASCALIENTES, MEXICO, 1901-1906
- DESPATCHES FROM U.S. CONSULS IN AIX-LA-CHAPELLE GERMANY, 1849-1906
- DESPATCHES FROM U.S. CONSULS IN ALEPPO, SYRIA, 1835-1840
- DESPATCHES FROM U.S. CONSULS IN ALEXANDRETTA, TURKEY, 1896-1906
- DESPATCHES FROM U.S. CONSULS IN ALEXANDRIA, EGYPT, 1835-73
- DESPATCHES FROM U.S. CONSULS IN ALGIERS, ALGERIA, 1785-1906
- DESPATCHES FROM U.S. CONSULS IN ALICANTE, SPAIN, 1788-1905
- DESPATCHES FROM U.S. CONSULS IN ALTONA GERMANY, 1838-1869
- DESPATCHES FROM U.S. CONSULS IN AMAPALA, HONDURAS, 1873-1886
- DESPATCHES FROM U.S. CONSULS IN AMHERSTBURG, CANADA, 1882-1906
- DESPATCHES FROM U.S. CONSULS IN AMOOR RIVER, RUSSIA, 1856-74
- DESPATCHES FROM U.S. CONSULS IN AMOY, CHINA, 1844-1906
- DESPATCHES FROM U.S. CONSULS IN AMSTERDAM, NETHERLANDS, 1790-1906
- DESPATCHES FROM U.S. CONSULS IN ANCONA, ITALY, 1840-74
- DESPATCHES FROM U.S. CONSULS IN ANNABERG GERMANY, 1882-1906
- DESPATCHES FROM U.S. CONSULS IN ANTIGUA, LEEWARD ISLANDS, BRITISH WEST INDIES, 1794-1906
- DESPATCHES FROM U.S. CONSULS IN ANTOFAGASTA, CHILE, 1893-1906
- DESPATCHES FROM U.S. CONSULS IN ANTUNG, MANCHURIA, CHINA
- DESPATCHES FROM U.S. CONSULS IN ANTWERP, BELGIUM, 1802-1906
- DESPATCHES FROM U.S. CONSULS IN APIA, SAMOA, 1843-1906
- DESPATCHES FROM U.S. CONSULS IN ARCHANGEL, RUSSIA, 1833-61
- DESPATCHES FROM U.S. CONSULS IN ARICA, CHILE, 1849-1906
- DESPATCHES FROM U.S. CONSULS IN ASUNCION, PARAGUAY, 1844-1906
- DESPATCHES FROM U.S. CONSULS IN ATHENS, GREECE, 1837-1906
- DESPATCHES FROM U.S. CONSULS IN AUGSBURG GERMANY, 1846-1873
- DESPATCHES FROM U.S. CONSULS IN AUX CAYES, HAITI, 1797-1874
- DESPATCHES FROM U.S. CONSULS IN BAGHDAD, IRAQ, 1888-1906
- DESPATCHES FROM U.S. CONSULS IN BAHIA, BRAZIL, 1850-1906
- DESPATCHES FROM U.S. CONSULS IN BAMBERG GERMANY, 1892-1906
- DESPATCHES FROM U.S. CONSULS IN BANGKOK, SIAM
- DESPATCHES FROM U.S. CONSULS IN BARACOA, CUBA, 1827-46; 1878-99
- DESPATCHES FROM U.S. CONSULS IN BARBADOS, BRITISH WEST INDIES, 1823-1906
- DESPATCHES FROM U.S. CONSULS IN BARCELONA, SPAIN, 1797-1906
- DESPATCHES FROM U.S. CONSULS IN BARRANQUILLA, COLOMBIA, 1883-1906
- DESPATCHES FROM U.S. CONSULS IN BASLE, SWITZERLAND, 1830-1906
- DESPATCHES FROM U.S. CONSULS IN BATAVIA, JAVA, NETHERLANDS, EAST INDIES
- DESPATCHES FROM U.S. CONSULS IN BATHURST, GAMBIA, BRITISH AFRICA, 1857-89
- DESPATCHES FROM U.S. CONSULS IN BATUM, U.S.S.R., 1890-1906 (SIC)
- DESPATCHES FROM U.S. CONSULS IN BAY OF ISLANDS AND AUCKLAND, NEW ZEALAND, 1839-1906
- DESPATCHES FROM U.S. CONSULS IN BAYONNE, FRANCE, 1835-65
- DESPATCHES FROM U.S. CONSULS IN BEIRUT, LEBANON, 1836-1906
- DESPATCHES FROM U.S. CONSULS IN BELFAST, UNITED KINGDOM, 1796-1906
- DESPATCHES FROM U.S. CONSULS IN BELGRADE, SERBIA, 1883-1906
- DESPATCHES FROM U.S. CONSULS IN BELIZE, BRITISH HONDURAS, 1847-1906
- DESPATCHES FROM U.S. CONSULS IN BELLEVILLE, CANADA, 1878-1906
- DESPATCHES FROM U.S. CONSULS IN BERGEN, NORWAY, 1821-1906
- DESPATCHES FROM U.S. CONSULS IN BERLIN GERMANY, 1865-1906
- DESPATCHES FROM U.S. CONSULS IN BERMUDA, BRITISH WEST INDIES, 1818-1906
- DESPATCHES FROM U.S. CONSULS IN BERNE, SWITZERLAND, 1882-1906
- DESPATCHES FROM U.S. CONSULS IN BILBAO, SPAIN, 1791-1875
- DESPATCHES FROM U.S. CONSULS IN BIRMINGHAM, UNITED KINGDOM, 1869-1906
- DESPATCHES FROM U.S. CONSULS IN BOGOTA, COLOMBIA, 1851-1906
- DESPATCHES FROM U.S. CONSULS IN BOMA, CONGO, 1888-95
- DESPATCHES FROM U.S. CONSULS IN BOMBAY, INDIA, 1838-1906
- DESPATCHES FROM U.S. CONSULS IN BORDEAUX, FRANCE, 1783-1906
- DESPATCHES FROM U.S. CONSULS IN BOULOGNE, FRANCE, 1866-74
- DESPATCHES FROM U.S. CONSULS IN BRADFORD, UNITED KINGDOM, 1865-1906
- DESPATCHES FROM U.S. CONSULS IN BREMEN GERMANY, 1794-1906
- DESPATCHES FROM U.S. CONSULS IN BREMEN GERMANY, 1868-1906
- DESPATCHES FROM U.S. CONSULS IN BRESLAU, POLAND, 1878-1906 (SIC)
- DESPATCHES FROM U.S. CONSULS IN BRINDISI, ITALY, 1864-76
- DESPATCHES FROM U.S. CONSULS IN BRISTOL, UNITED KINGDOM, 1792-1906
- DESPATCHES FROM U.S. CONSULS IN BROCKVILLE, CANADA, 1885-1906
- DESPATCHES FROM U.S. CONSULS IN BRUNEI, BORNEO, 1862-68

- DESPATCHES FROM U.S. CONSULS IN BRUNSWICK (BRAUNSCHWEIG) GERMANY, 1858-1906
- DESPATCHES FROM U.S. CONSULS IN BRUSA (BROUSA), TURKEY, 1837-40
- DESPATCHES FROM U.S. CONSULS IN BRUSSELS, BELGIUM, 1863-1906
- DESPATCHES FROM U.S. CONSULS IN BUCHAREST, RUMANIA, 1866-85; 1892-1906
- DESPATCHES FROM U.S. CONSULS IN BUDAPEST HUNGARY, 1876-1906
- DESPATCHES FROM U.S. CONSULS IN BUENAVENTURA, COLOMBIA, 1867-85
- DESPATCHES FROM U.S. CONSULS IN BUENOS AIRES, ARGENTINA, 1811-1906
- DESPATCHES FROM U.S. CONSULS IN BURSLEM, UNITED KINGDOM, 1905-6
- DESPATCHES FROM U.S. CONSULS IN BUTARITARI, GILBERT ISLANDS, 1888-92
- DESPATCHES FROM U.S. CONSULS IN CADIZ, SPAIN, 1791-1904
- DESPATCHES FROM U.S. CONSULS IN CAGLIARI, ITALY, 1802-25
- DESPATCHES FROM U.S. CONSULS IN CAIRO, EGYPT, 1864-1906
- DESPATCHES FROM U.S. CONSULS IN CALAIS, FRANCE, 1804-1906
- DESPATCHES FROM U.S. CONSULS IN CALCUTTA, INDIA
- DESPATCHES FROM U.S. CONSULS IN CALLAO, PERU, 1854-1906
- DESPATCHES FROM U.S. CONSULS IN CAMARGO, MEXICO, 1870-80
- DESPATCHES FROM U.S. CONSULS IN CAMPBELLTON, CANADA, 1897-1906
- DESPATCHES FROM U.S. CONSULS IN CAMPECHE, MEXICO, 1820-80
- DESPATCHES FROM U.S. CONSULS IN CANDIA, CRETE, GREECE, 1836-41
- DESPATCHES FROM U.S. CONSULS IN CANEA, CRETE, GREECE, 1832-74
- DESPATCHES FROM U.S. CONSULS IN CANNES, FRANCE, 1891
- DESPATCHES FROM U.S. CONSULS IN CANTON, CHINA, 1790-1906
- DESPATCHES FROM U.S. CONSULS IN CAP HAITIEN, HAITI, 1797-1906
- DESPATCHES FROM U.S. CONSULS IN CAPE GRACIAS A DIOS, NICARAGUA, 1903-6
- DESPATCHES FROM U.S. CONSULS IN CAPE TOWN, UNION OF SOUTH AFRICA, 1800-1906
- DESPATCHES FROM U.S. CONSULS IN CARACAS, VENEZUELA, 1868-85
- DESPATCHES FROM U.S. CONSULS IN CARDENAS, CUBA, 1843-45; 1879-98
- DESPATCHES FROM U.S. CONSULS IN CARDIFF, UNITED KINGDOM, 1861-1906
- DESPATCHES FROM U.S. CONSULS IN CARLISLE, UNITED KINGDOM, 1867-69
- DESPATCHES FROM U.S. CONSULS IN CARLSBAD CZECHOSLOVAKIA, 1902-1906
- DESPATCHES FROM U.S. CONSULS IN CARLSRUHE (KARLSRUHE) GERMANY, 1854-74
- DESPATCHES FROM U.S. CONSULS IN CARRARA, ITALY, 1852-81
- DESPATCHES FROM U.S. CONSULS IN CARTAGENA, COLOMBIA, 1822-1906
- DESPATCHES FROM U.S. CONSULS IN CARTAGENA, SPAIN
- DESPATCHES FROM U.S. CONSULS IN CASTELLAMARE DI STABIA, ITALY, 1878-1906
- DESPATCHES FROM U.S. CONSULS IN CATANIA, ITALY, 1883-1906
- DESPATCHES FROM U.S. CONSULS IN CAYENNE, FRENCH GUIANA, 1801-97
- DESPATCHES FROM U.S. CONSULS IN CETTE, FRANCE, 1802-40
- DESPATCHES FROM U.S. CONSULS IN CHARLOTTETOWN, CANADA, 1857-1906
- DESPATCHES FROM U.S. CONSULS IN CHATHAM, CANADA, 1879-1906
- DESPATCHES FROM U.S. CONSULS IN CHAUDIERE JUNCTION, CANADA, 1898-1905
- DESPATCHES FROM U.S. CONSULS IN CHEFOO, CHINA, 1863-1906
- DESPATCHES FROM U.S. CONSULS IN CHEMNITZ GERMANY, 1867-1906
- DESPATCHES FROM U.S. CONSULS IN CHIHUAHUA, MEXICO, 1830-1906
- DESPATCHES FROM U.S. CONSULS IN CHINKIANG, CHINA, 1864-1902
- DESPATCHES FROM U.S. CONSULS IN CHIOS, GREECE, 1862-71
- DESPATCHES FROM U.S. CONSULS IN CHRISTIANIA, NORWAY, 1869-1906 (SIC)
- DESPATCHES FROM U.S. CONSULS IN CHRISTIANSUND, NORWAY, 1810-91
- DESPATCHES FROM U.S. CONSULS IN CHUNGKING, CHINA, 1896-1906
- DESPATCHES FROM U.S. CONSULS IN CIENFUEGOS, CUBA, 1876-1906
- DESPATCHES FROM U.S. CONSULS IN CIUDAD BOLIVAR, VENEZUELA, 1850-93
- DESPATCHES FROM U.S. CONSULS IN CIUDAD DEL CARMEN, MEXICO, 1830-72
- DESPATCHES FROM U.S. CONSULS IN CIUDAD JUAREZ (PASO DEL NORTE), MEXICO, 1850-1906
- DESPATCHES FROM U.S. CONSULS IN CLIFTON, CANADA, 1864-1906
- DESPATCHES FROM U.S. CONSULS IN COATICOOK, CANADA, 1864-1906
- DESPATCHES FROM U.S. CONSULS IN COBIJA, BOLIVIA, 1854-74
- DESPATCHES FROM U.S. CONSULS IN COBURG GERMANY, 1898-1906
- DESPATCHES FROM U.S. CONSULS IN COGNAC, FRANCE, 1883-98
- DESPATCHES FROM U.S. CONSULS IN COLLINGWOOD, CANADA, 1879-1906
- DESPATCHES FROM U.S. CONSULS IN COLOGNE (KOELN) GERMANY, 1876-1906
- DESPATCHES FROM U.S. CONSULS IN COLOMBO, CEYLON
- DESPATCHES FROM U.S. CONSULS IN COLON, PANAMA, 1852-1906
- DESPATCHES FROM U.S. CONSULS IN COLONIA, URUGUAY, 1870-1906
- DESPATCHES FROM U.S. CONSULS IN CONSTANTINOPLE, TURKEY, 1820-1906
- DESPATCHES FROM U.S. CONSULS IN COPENHAGEN, DENMARK, 1792-1906
- DESPATCHES FROM U.S. CONSULS IN COQUIMBO, CHILE, 1850-98
- DESPATCHES FROM U.S. CONSULS IN CORDOBA, ARGENTINA, 1870-1906
- DESPATCHES FROM U.S. CONSULS IN CORK, IRELAND, 1800-1906
- DESPATCHES FROM U.S. CONSULS IN CORNWALL, CANADA, 1901-6
- DESPATCHES FROM U.S. CONSULS IN CORUNNA, SPAIN, 1867-1906
- DESPATCHES FROM U.S. CONSULS IN CREFELD (KREFELD) GERMANY, 1878-1906
- DESPATCHES FROM U.S. CONSULS IN CURACAO, NETHERLANDS WEST INDIES, 1793-1906
- DESPATCHES FROM U.S. CONSULS IN CYPRUS, 1835-78
- DESPATCHES FROM U.S. CONSULS IN DAWSON CITY, CANADA, 1898-1906
- DESPATCHES FROM U.S. CONSULS IN DENIA, SPAIN, 1852-98
- DESPATCHES FROM U.S. CONSULS IN DRESDEN GERMANY, 1837-1906
- DESPATCHES FROM U.S. CONSULS IN DUBLIN, IRELAND, 1790-1906
- DESPATCHES FROM U.S. CONSULS IN DUCHY OF NASSAU GERMANY, 1854-69
- DESPATCHES FROM U.S. CONSULS IN DUESSELDORF GERMANY, 1881-1906
- DESPATCHES FROM U.S. CONSULS IN DUNDEE, UNITED KINGDOM, 1834-1906
- DESPATCHES FROM U.S. CONSULS IN DUNFERMLINE, UNITED KINGDOM, 1877-1906
- DESPATCHES FROM U.S. CONSULS IN DURANGO, MEXICO, 1886-1906
- DESPATCHES FROM U.S. CONSULS IN EDINBURGH, UNITED KINGDOM, 1893-1906
- DESPATCHES FROM U.S. CONSULS IN EIBENSTOCK GERMANY, 1902-6
- DESPATCHES FROM U.S. CONSULS IN ELBERFELD, LUBECK, AND ROSTOCK GERMANY, 1804-49; 1883-89
- DESPATCHES FROM U.S. CONSULS IN ELSINORE, DENMARK, 1792-1874
- DESPATCHES FROM U.S. CONSULS IN ENSENADA, MEXICO, 1888-1906
- DESPATCHES FROM U.S. CONSULS IN ERFURT GERMANY, 1892-94
- DESPATCHES FROM U.S. CONSULS IN ERZERUM, TURKEY, 1895-1904
- DESPATCHES FROM U.S. CONSULS IN FALMOUTH, BRITISH WEST INDIES, 1790-1905
- DESPATCHES FROM U.S. CONSULS IN FAYAL, AZORES, 1795-1897
- DESPATCHES FROM U.S. CONSULS IN FLORENCE, ITALY, 1824-1906
- DESPATCHES FROM U.S. CONSULS IN FOOCHOW, CHINA, 1849-1906
- DESPATCHES FROM U.S. CONSULS IN FORT ERIE, CANADA, 1865-1906
- DESPATCHES FROM U.S. CONSULS IN FRANKFURT ON THE MAIN GERMANY, 1829-1906
- DESPATCHES FROM U.S. CONSULS IN FREIBURG GERMANY, 1892-1906
- DESPATCHES FROM U.S. CONSULS IN FUERTH GERMANY, 1890-98
- DESPATCHES FROM U.S. CONSULS IN FUNCHAL, MADEIRA, PORTUGAL, 1793-1906
- DESPATCHES FROM U.S. CONSULS IN GABOON, 1856-88
- DESPATCHES FROM U.S. CONSULS IN GALATZ, RUMANIA, 1858-69
- DESPATCHES FROM U.S. CONSULS IN GALVESTON, TEXAS, 1832-46
- DESPATCHES FROM U.S. CONSULS IN GALWAY, IRELAND, 1834-63
- DESPATCHES FROM U.S. CONSULS IN GARRUCHA, SPAIN, 1877-97
- DESPATCHES FROM U.S. CONSULS IN GASPE BASIN, CANADA
- DESPATCHES FROM U.S. CONSULS IN GEESTEMUENDE GERMANY, 1867-82
- DESPATCHES FROM U.S. CONSULS IN GENEVA, SWITZERLAND, 1855-1906
- DESPATCHES FROM U.S. CONSULS IN GENOA, ITALY, 1799-1906
- DESPATCHES FROM U.S. CONSULS IN GEORGETOWN, DEMERARA, BRITISH GUIANA, 1827-1906
- DESPATCHES FROM U.S. CONSULS IN GHENT, BELGIUM, 1860-1906
- DESPATCHES FROM U.S. CONSULS IN GIBRALTAR, SPAIN, 1791-1906
- DESPATCHES FROM U.S. CONSULS IN GLASGOW, UNITED KINGDOM, 1801-1906
- DESPATCHES FROM U.S. CONSULS IN GLAUCHAU GERMANY, 1891-1906
- DESPATCHES FROM U.S. CONSULS IN GLOUCESTER, UNITED KINGDOM, 1879-86
- DESPATCHES FROM U.S. CONSULS IN GODERICH, CANADA,1865-1906
- DESPATCHES FROM U.S. CONSULS IN GOREE DAKAR, FRENCH AFRICA, 1883-1906
- DESPATCHES FROM U.S. CONSULS IN GOTHENBURG, SWEDEN, 1800-1906
- DESPATCHES FROM U.S. CONSULS IN GRAND BASSA, LIBERIA, 1868-82
- DESPATCHES FROM U.S. CONSULS IN GRENOBLE, FRANCE, 1893-1906
- DESPATCHES FROM U.S. CONSULS IN GRENVILLE, CANADA, 1904-6
- DESPATCHES FROM U.S. CONSULS IN GUADELOUPE, FRENCH WEST INDIES, 1802-1906
- DESPATCHES FROM U.S. CONSULS IN GUATEMALA CITY, GUATEMALA, 1824-1906
- DESPATCHES FROM U.S. CONSULS IN GUAYAQUIL, ECUADOR, 1826-1906
- DESPATCHES FROM U.S. CONSULS IN GUAYMAS, MEXICO, 1832-96
- DESPATCHES FROM U.S. CONSULS IN GUELPH, CANADA, 1883-1906
- DESPATCHES FROM U.S. CONSULS IN GUERRERO, MEXICO, 1871-88
- DESPATCHES FROM U.S. CONSULS IN HAKODATE, JAPAN
- DESPATCHES FROM U.S. CONSULS IN HALIFAX, CANADA, 1833-1906
- DESPATCHES FROM U.S. CONSULS IN HAMBURG GERMANY, 1790-1906
- DESPATCHES FROM U.S. CONSULS IN HAMILTON, CANADA, 1867-1906
- DESPATCHES FROM U.S. CONSULS IN HANGCHOW, CHINA, 1904-6
- DESPATCHES FROM U.S. CONSULS IN HANKOW, CHINA, 1861-1906
- DESPATCHES FROM U.S. CONSULS IN HANOVER GERMANY, 1854-67; 1893-1906
- DESPATCHES FROM U.S. CONSULS IN HARPUT, TURKEY, 1895-1906
- DESPATCHES FROM U.S. CONSULS IN HAVANA, CUBA, 1783-1906
- DESPATCHES FROM U.S. CONSULS IN HELSINGFORS, FINLAND, 1851-1906
- DESPATCHES FROM U.S. CONSULS IN HERMOSILLO, MEXICO, 1905-6
- DESPATCHES FROM U.S. CONSULS IN HESSE-CASSEL GERMANY, 1835-69
- DESPATCHES FROM U.S. CONSULS IN HESSE-DARMSTADT GERMANY, 1854-71
- DESPATCHES FROM U.S. CONSULS IN HESSE-HOMBURG GERMANY, 1854-66
- DESPATCHES FROM U.S. CONSULS IN HILO, HAWAII, 1853-72
- DESPATCHES FROM U.S. CONSULS IN HOBART, AUSTRALIA, 1842-1906
- DESPATCHES FROM U.S. CONSULS IN HONG KONG, 1844-1906
- DESPATCHES FROM U.S. CONSULS IN HONOLULU, HAWAII, 1820-1903
- DESPATCHES FROM U.S. CONSULS IN HORGEN, SWITZERLAND, 1882-98
- DESPATCHES FROM U.S. CONSULS IN HUDDERSFIELD, UNITED KINGDOM, 1890-1906
- DESPATCHES FROM U.S. CONSULS IN HULL, UNITED KINGDOM, 1879-1906
- DESPATCHES FROM U.S. CONSULS IN ILOILO, PHILIPPINE ISLANDS, 1878-86
- DESPATCHES FROM U.S. CONSULS IN IQUIQUE, CHILE, 1877-1906
- DESPATCHES FROM U.S. CONSULS IN JALAPA ENRIQUEZ, MEXICO, 1905-6
- DESPATCHES FROM U.S. CONSULS IN JEREZ DE LA FRONTERA, SPAIN, 1903-6
- DESPATCHES FROM U.S. CONSULS IN JERUSALEM, PALESTINE
- DESPATCHES FROM U.S. CONSULS IN KANAGAWA, JAPAN, 1861-97
- DESPATCHES FROM U.S. CONSULS IN KEHL GERMANY, 1882-1906
- DESPATCHES FROM U.S. CONSULS IN KINGSTON, CANADA, 1864-1906
- DESPATCHES FROM U.S. CONSULS IN KINGSTON, JAMAICA, BRITISH WEST INDIES, 1796-1906
- DESPATCHES FROM U.S. CONSULS IN KOENIGSBERG (FORMERLY EAST PRUSSIA GERMANY, NOW KALININGRAD U.S.S.R.), 1879-81
- DESPATCHES FROM U.S. CONSULS IN LA CEIBA, HONDURAS, 1902-6
- DESPATCHES FROM U.S. CONSULS IN LA GUAIRA, VENEZUELA, 1810-1906
- DESPATCHES FROM U.S. CONSULS IN LA PAZ, BOLIVIA, 1869-1901
- DESPATCHES FROM U.S. CONSULS IN LA PAZ, MEXICO
- DESPATCHES FROM U.S. CONSULS IN LA ROCHELLE, FRANCE, 1794-1906
- DESPATCHES FROM U.S. CONSULS IN LA UNION, EL SALVADOR, 1854-87
- DESPATCHES FROM U.S. CONSULS IN LAHAINA, HAWAII, 1850-71
- DESPATCHES FROM U.S. CONSULS IN LAMBAYEQUE, PERU, 1860-88
- DESPATCHES FROM U.S. CONSULS IN LAUTHALA, FIJI ISLANDS, 1844-90
- DESPATCHES FROM U.S. CONSULS IN LE HAVRE, FRANCE, 1789-1906
- DESPATCHES FROM U.S. CONSULS IN LEEDS UPON HULL, UNITED KINGDOM, 1797-1906
- DESPATCHES FROM U.S. CONSULS IN LEGHORN, ITALY, 1793-1906
- DESPATCHES FROM U.S. CONSULS IN LEIPZIG GERMANY, 1826-1906
- DESPATCHES FROM U.S. CONSULS IN LEITH, UNITED KINGDOM, 1798-1893
- DESPATCHES FROM U.S. CONSULS IN LEVUKA AND SUVA, FIJI ISLANDS, 1891-1906
- DESPATCHES FROM U.S. CONSULS IN LIBEREC CZECHOSLOVAKIA, 1886-1906
- DESPATCHES FROM U.S. CONSULS IN LIEGE, BELGIUM, 1863-1906
- DESPATCHES FROM U.S. CONSULS IN LIMA, PERU, 1823-54
- DESPATCHES FROM U.S. CONSULS IN LIMOGES, FRANCE, 1887-1906
- DESPATCHES FROM U.S. CONSULS IN LINDSAY, CANADA, 1891-92
- DESPATCHES FROM U.S. CONSULS IN LISBON, PORTUGAL, 1791-1906
- DESPATCHES FROM U.S. CONSULS IN LIVERPOOL, UNITED KINGDOM, 1790-1906
- DESPATCHES FROM U.S. CONSULS IN LONDON, ONTARIO, 1885-1906
- DESPATCHES FROM U.S. CONSULS IN LONDON, UNITED KINGDOM, 1790-1906
- DESPATCHES FROM U.S. CONSULS IN LONDONDERRY, UNITED KINGDOM, 1835-76
- DESPATCHES FROM U.S. CONSULS IN LOURENCO MARQUES, MOZAMBIQUE, PORTUGUESE AFRICA, 1854-1906
- DESPATCHES FROM U.S. CONSULS IN LUCERNE, SWITZERLAND, 1902-6
- DESPATCHES FROM U.S. CONSULS IN LUDWIGSHAFEN AM RHEIN GERMANY, 1858-74
- DESPATCHES FROM U.S. CONSULS IN LUXEMBOURG CITY, LUXEMBOURG, 1893-96
- DESPATCHES FROM U.S. CONSULS IN LYON, FRANCE, 1829-1906
- DESPATCHES FROM U.S. CONSULS IN MACAO, CHINA, 1849-69
- DESPATCHES FROM U.S. CONSULS IN MAGDEBURG GERMANY, 1890-1906
- DESPATCHES FROM U.S. CONSULS IN MAHE, SEYCHELLES ISLANDS, INDIAN OCEAN
- DESPATCHES FROM U.S. CONSULS IN MALAGA, SPAIN, 1793-1906
- DESPATCHES FROM U.S. CONSULS IN MALTA, 1801-1906
- DESPATCHES FROM U.S. CONSULS IN MANAGUA, NICARAGUA, 1884-1906
- DESPATCHES FROM U.S. CONSULS IN MANCHESTER, UNITED KINGDOM, 1847-1906
- DESPATCHES FROM U.S. CONSULS IN MANILA, PHILIPPINE ISLANDS
- DESPATCHES FROM U.S. CONSULS IN MANNHEIM GERMANY, 1874-1906
- DESPATCHES FROM U.S. CONSULS IN MANZANILLO, CUBA, 1844-46
- DESPATCHES FROM U.S. CONSULS IN MANZANILLO, MEXICO, 1855-1906

- DESPATCHES FROM U.S. CONSULS IN MAORIO, SPAIN, 1882-84; 1891-1906
- DESPATCHES FROM U.S. CONSULS IN MARACAIBO, VENEZUELA, 1824-1906
- DESPATCHES FROM U.S. CONSULS IN MARANHAM (MARANHAO), BRAZIL, 1817-76
- DESPATCHES FROM U.S. CONSULS IN MARSEILLES, FRANCE, 1790-1906
- DESPATCHES FROM U.S. CONSULS IN MATAMORAS, MEXICO, 1826-1906
- DESPATCHES FROM U.S. CONSULS IN MATANZAS, CUBA, 1820-99
- DESPATCHES FROM U.S. CONSULS IN MAYENCE (MAINZ) GERMANY, 1871-1906
- DESPATCHES FROM U.S. CONSULS IN MAZATLAN, MEXICO, 1826-1906
- DESPATCHES FROM U.S. CONSULS IN MEDAN-PADANG, SUMATRA, NETHERLANDS EAST INDIES, 1853-98
- DESPATCHES FROM U.S. CONSULS IN MEDELLIN, COLOMBIA, 1859-1902
- DESPATCHES FROM U.S. CONSULS IN MELBOURNE, AUSTRALIA, 1852-1906
- DESPATCHES FROM U.S. CONSULS IN MERIDA, 1843-97, AND PROGRESO, MEXICO, 1897-1906
- DESPATCHES FROM U.S. CONSULS IN MESSINA, ITALY, 1822-1906
- DESPATCHES FROM U.S. CONSULS IN MEXICO CITY, MEXICO, 1822-1906
- DESPATCHES FROM U.S. CONSULS IN MIER, MEXICO, 1870-78
- DESPATCHES FROM U.S. CONSULS IN MILAN, ITALY, 1874-1906
- DESPATCHES FROM U.S. CONSULS IN MINATITLAN, MEXICO, 1853-81
- DESPATCHES FROM U.S. CONSULS IN MONCTON, CANADA, 1885-1905
- DESPATCHES FROM U.S. CONSULS IN MONROVIA, LIBERIA, 1852-1906
- DESPATCHES FROM U.S. CONSULS IN MONTEREY, UPPER CALIFORNIA, 1834-48
- DESPATCHES FROM U.S. CONSULS IN MONTERREY, MEXICO, 1849-1906
- DESPATCHES FROM U.S. CONSULS IN MONTEVIDEO, URUGUAY, 1821-1906
- DESPATCHES FROM U.S. CONSULS IN MONTREAL, CANADA, 1850-1906
- DESPATCHES FROM U.S. CONSULS IN MORRISBURG, CANADA, 1882-1901
- DESPATCHES FROM U.S. CONSULS IN MOSCOW, U.S.S.R., 1857-1906 (SIC)
- DESPATCHES FROM U.S. CONSULS IN MUKDEN, MANCHURIA, CHINA
- DESPATCHES FROM U.S. CONSULS IN MUNICH (MUENCHEN) GERMANY, 1833-1906
- DESPATCHES FROM U.S. CONSULS IN MUSCAT, OMAN, 1880-1906
- DESPATCHES FROM U.S. CONSULS IN NAGASAKI, JAPAN, 1860-1906
- DESPATCHES FROM U.S. CONSULS IN NANKING, CHINA, 1902-6
- DESPATCHES FROM U.S. CONSULS IN NANTES, FRANCE, 1790-1906
- DESPATCHES FROM U.S. CONSULS IN NAPLES, ITALY, 1796-1906
- DESPATCHES FROM U.S. CONSULS IN NAPOLEON-VENDEE, FRANCE, 1800-70
- DESPATCHES FROM U.S. CONSULS IN NASSAU, BRITISH WEST INDIES, 1821-1906
- DESPATCHES FROM U.S. CONSULS IN NEW ORLEANS, LOUISIANA, 1798-1807
- DESPATCHES FROM U.S. CONSULS IN NEWCASTLE, AUSTRALIA, 1887-1906
- DESPATCHES FROM U.S. CONSULS IN NEWCASTLE UPON TYNE, UNITED KINGDOM, 1854-1906
- DESPATCHES FROM U.S. CONSULS IN NEWCHWANG, MANCHURIA, CHINA, 1865-1906
- DESPATCHES FROM U.S. CONSULS IN NICE, FRANCE, 1819-1906
- DESPATCHES FROM U.S. CONSULS IN NINGPO, CHINA, 1853-96
- DESPATCHES FROM U.S. CONSULS IN NOGALES, MEXICO, 1889-1906
- DESPATCHES FROM U.S. CONSULS IN NOTTINGHAM, UNITED KINGDOM, 1877-1906
- DESPATCHES FROM U.S. CONSULS IN NOUMEA, NEW CALEDONIA ISLAND, 1887-1905
- DESPATCHES FROM U.S. CONSULS IN NOVOROSSISK, U.S.S.R., 1883-84 (SIC)
- DESPATCHES FROM U.S. CONSULS IN NUEVITAS, CUBA, 1842-47; 1892-98
- DESPATCHES FROM U.S. CONSULS IN NUEVO LAREDO, MEXICO, 1871-1906
- DESPATCHES FROM U.S. CONSULS IN NUREMBERG, GERMANY, 1846-1906
- DESPATCHES FROM U.S. CONSULS IN OAXACA, MEXICO, 1869-78
- DESPATCHES FROM U.S. CONSULS IN ODESSA, U.S.S.R., 1831-1906 (SIC)
- DESPATCHES FROM U.S. CONSULS IN OLDENBURG GERMANY, 1856-69
- DESPATCHES FROM U.S. CONSULS IN OMOA, TRUJILLO, AND RUATAN, HONDURAS, 1831-93
- DESPATCHES FROM U.S. CONSULS IN OPORTO, PORTUGAL, 1821-77
- DESPATCHES FROM U.S. CONSULS IN ORILLIA, CANADA, 1893-1906
- DESPATCHES FROM U.S. CONSULS IN OSAKA AND HIOGO (KOBE), JAPAN
- DESPATCHES FROM U.S. CONSULS IN OTRANTO, ITALY, 1861-67
- DESPATCHES FROM U.S. CONSULS IN OTTAWA, CANADA, 1877-1906
- DESPATCHES FROM U.S. CONSULS IN PADANG, SUMATRA, NETHERLANDS, EAST INDIES
- DESPATCHES FROM U.S. CONSULS IN PAITA, PERU, 1833-74
- DESPATCHES FROM U.S. CONSULS IN PALERMO, ITALY, 1803-1906
- DESPATCHES FROM U.S. CONSULS IN PALMERSTON, CANADA, 1892-1900
- DESPATCHES FROM U.S. CONSULS IN PANAMA CITY, PANAMA,1823-1906
- DESPATCHES FROM U.S. CONSULS IN PARA, BRAZIL, 1831-1906
- DESPATCHES FROM U.S. CONSULS IN PARAMARIBO, BRAZIL, 1799-1897
- DESPATCHES FROM U.S. CONSULS IN PARIS, FRANCE, 1790-1906
- DESPATCHES FROM U.S. CONSULS IN PATRAS, GREECE, 1874-1906
- DESPATCHES FROM U.S. CONSULS IN PERNAMBUCO, BRAZIL, 1817-1906
- DESPATCHES FROM U.S. CONSULS IN PETERBOROUGH, CANADA, 1905-6
- DESPATCHES FROM U.S. CONSULS IN PETROPAVLOVSK, RUSSIA, 1875-78
- DESPATCHES FROM U.S. CONSULS IN PICTOU, CANADA, 1837-97
- DESPATCHES FROM U.S. CONSULS IN PIEDRAS NEGRAS, MEXICO, 1868-1906
- DESPATCHES FROM U.S. CONSULS IN PIRAEUS, GREECE, 1864-74
- DESPATCHES FROM U.S. CONSULS IN PLAUEN GERMANY, 1887-1906
- DESPATCHES FROM U.S. CONSULS IN PLYMOUTH, UNITED KINGDOM, 1793-1906
- DESPATCHES FROM U.S. CONSULS IN PONAPE, CAROLINE ISLANDS, 1890-92
- DESPATCHES FROM U.S. CONSULS IN PORSGRUND (PORSGRUNN), NORWAY, 1861-69
- DESPATCHES FROM U.S. CONSULS IN PORT ANTONIO, BRITISH WEST INDIES, 1895-1906
- DESPATCHES FROM U.S. CONSULS IN PORT AU PRINCE, HAITI, 1835-1906
- DESPATCHES FROM U.S. CONSULS IN PORT HOPE, CANADA, 1882-1906
- DESPATCHES FROM U.S. CONSULS IN PORT LIMON, COSTA RICA, 1902-06
- DESPATCHES FROM U.S. CONSULS IN PORT LOUIS, MAURITIUS, MASCARENE ISLANDS, INDIAN OCEAN
- DESPATCHES FROM U.S. CONSULS IN PORT MAHON, SPAIN, 1803-76
- DESPATCHES FROM U.S. CONSULS IN PORT ROWAN, CANADA, 1882-1906
- DESPATCHES FROM U.S. CONSULS IN PORT SAID, EGYPT, 1870-76
- DESPATCHES FROM U.S. CONSULS IN PORT STANLEY, CANADA, AND ST THOMAS, CANADA
- DESPATCHES FROM U.S. CONSULS IN PORT STANLEY, FALKLAND ISLANDS, 1851-1906
- DESPATCHES FROM U.S. CONSULS IN PORTO PRINCIPE AND XIBARA, CUBA, 1828-43
- DESPATCHES FROM U.S. CONSULS IN PRAGUE CZECHOSLOVAKIA, 1869-1906
- DESPATCHES FROM U.S. CONSULS IN PRESCOTT, CANADA, 1864-1906
- DESPATCHES FROM U.S. CONSULS IN PRETORIA, UNION OF SOUTH AFRICA, 1898-1906
- DESPATCHES FROM U.S. CONSULS IN PUERTO CABELLO, VENEZUELA, 1823-1906
- DESPATCHES FROM U.S. CONSULS IN PUERTO CORTER, HONDURAS, 1902-6
- DESPATCHES FROM U.S. CONSULS IN PUERTO PLATA, DOMINICAN REPUBLIC, 1875-1906
- DESPATCHES FROM U.S. CONSULS IN QUEBEC, CANADA, 1861-1906
- DESPATCHES FROM U.S. CONSULS IN REVAL, ESTONIA, 1859-70
- DESPATCHES FROM U.S. CONSULS IN RHEIMS, FRANCE, 1867-1906
- DESPATCHES FROM U.S. CONSULS IN RIGA, LATVIA, 1811-72; 1890-1906
- DESPATCHES FROM U.S. CONSULS IN RIMOUSKI, CANADA, 1897-1906
- DESPATCHES FROM U.S. CONSULS IN RIO DE JANEIRO, BRAZIL, 1811-1906
- DESPATCHES FROM U.S. CONSULS IN RIO GRANDE DO SUL, BRAZIL, 1829-97
- DESPATCHES FROM U.S. CONSULS IN RIO MACHA, COLOMBIA, 1835-83
- DESPATCHES FROM U.S. CONSULS IN ROME, ITALY, 1801-1906
- DESPATCHES FROM U.S. CONSULS IN ROSARIO, ARGENTINA, 1858-1906
- DESPATCHES FROM U.S. CONSULS IN ROTTERDAM, NETHERLANDS, 1802-1906
- DESPATCHES FROM U.S. CONSULS IN ROUBAIX, FRANCE, 1890-1906
- DESPATCHES FROM U.S. CONSULS IN ROUEN, FRANCE, 1790; 1878-1906
- DESPATCHES FROM U.S. CONSULS IN SABANILLA, COLOMBIA, 1856-84
- DESPATCHES FROM U.S. CONSULS IN SAGUA LA GRANDE, CUBA, 1878-1900
- DESPATCHES FROM U.S. CONSULS IN SAIGON, VIETNAM, 1889-1906
- DESPATCHES FROM U.S. CONSULS IN SALONICA, GREECE, 1832-40
- DESPATCHES FROM U.S. CONSULS IN SALTILLO, MEXICO, 1876-1906
- DESPATCHES FROM U.S. CONSULS IN SAMANA, DOMINICAN REPUBLIC, 1873-1905
- DESPATCHES FROM U.S. CONSULS IN SAN ANDRES, COLOMBIA, 1870-78
- DESPATCHES FROM U.S. CONSULS IN SAN BLAS, MEXICO, 1837-92
- DESPATCHES FROM U.S. CONSULS IN SAN DIMAS, MEXICO, 1871-73
- DESPATCHES FROM U.S. CONSULS IN SAN JOSE, COSTA RICA, 1852-1906
- DESPATCHES FROM U.S. CONSULS IN SAN JUAN DE LOS REMEDIOS, CUBA, 1844-46; 1879-98
- DESPATCHES FROM U.S. CONSULS IN SAN JUAN DEL NORTE, NICARAGUA, 1851-1906
- DESPATCHES FROM U.S. CONSULS IN SAN JUAN DEL SUR, NICARAGUA, 1847-81
- DESPATCHES FROM U.S. CONSULS IN SAN LUIS POTOSI, MEXICO, 1869-86
- DESPATCHES FROM U.S. CONSULS IN SAN SALVADOR, EL SALVADOR, 1868-1906
- DESPATCHES FROM U.S. CONSULS IN SANTA CATARINA, BRAZIL, 1831-74
- DESPATCHES FROM U.S. CONSULS IN SANTA FE, NEW MEXICO, 1830-46
- DESPATCHES FROM U.S. CONSULS IN SANTA MARTA, COLOMBIA, 1823-83
- DESPATCHES FROM U.S. CONSULS IN SANTANDER, SPAIN, 1862-92
- DESPATCHES FROM U.S. CONSULS IN SANTIAGO, CAPE VERDE ISLANDS, 1818-98
- DESPATCHES FROM U.S. CONSULS IN SANTIAGO DE CUBA, CUBA, 1799-1906
- DESPATCHES FROM U.S. CONSULS IN SANTO DOMINGO, DOMINICAN REPUBLIC, 1837-1906
- DESPATCHES FROM U.S. CONSULS IN SANTOS, BRAZIL, 1831-1906
- DESPATCHES FROM U.S. CONSULS IN SARNIA, CANADA, 1864-1906
- DESPATCHES FROM U.S. CONSULS IN SAULT STE. MARIE, CANADA, 1891-1906
- DESPATCHES FROM U.S. CONSULS IN SCHWERIN GERMANY, 1862-69
- DESPATCHES FROM U.S. CONSULS IN SEOUL, KOREA, 1886-1906
- DESPATCHES FROM U.S. CONSULS IN SEVILLE, SPAIN, 1859-1906
- DESPATCHES FROM U.S. CONSULS IN SHANGHAI, CHINA, 1847-1906
- DESPATCHES FROM U.S. CONSULS IN SHEFFIELD, UNITED KINGDOM, 1864-1906
- DESPATCHES FROM U.S. CONSULS IN SHERBROOKE, CANADA, 1879-1906
- DESPATCHES FROM U.S. CONSULS IN SIERRA LEONE, BRITISH AFRICA, 1858-1906
- DESPATCHES FROM U.S. CONSULS IN SINGAPORE, STRAITS SETTLEMENTS
- DESPATCHES FROM U.S. CONSULS IN SIVAS, TURKEY, 1886-1906
- DESPATCHES FROM U.S. CONSULS IN SMYRNA, TURKEY, 1802-1906
- DESPATCHES FROM U.S. CONSULS IN SOFIA, BULGARIA, 1901-4
- DESPATCHES FROM U.S. CONSULS IN SOLINGEN GERMANY, 1898-1905
- DESPATCHES FROM U.S. CONSULS IN SONNEBERG GERMANY, 1851-98
- DESPATCHES FROM U.S. CONSULS IN SONSONATE, EL SALVADOR, 1868-87
- DESPATCHES FROM U.S. CONSULS IN SOREL, CANADA, 1882-98
- DESPATCHES FROM U.S. CONSULS IN SOUTHAMPTON, UNITED KINGDOM, 1790-1906
- DESPATCHES FROM U.S. CONSULS IN SPEZIA, ITALY, 1856-69
- DESPATCHES FROM U.S. CONSULS IN ST BARTHOLOMEW, FRENCH WEST INDIES, 1799-1899
- DESPATCHES FROM U.S. CONSULS IN ST CHRISTOPHER, WEST INDIES FEDERATION, 1800-1906
- DESPATCHES FROM U.S. CONSULS IN ST CROIX, VIRGIN ISLANDS, 1791-1876
- DESPATCHES FROM U.S. CONSULS IN ST DENIS, REUNION ISLAND, MASCARENE ISLANDS, AND INDIAN OCEAN
- DESPATCHES FROM U.S. CONSULS IN ST ETIENNE, FRANCE, 1877-1906
- DESPATCHES FROM U.S. CONSULS IN ST EUSTATIUS, NETHERLANDS WEST INDIES, 1793-1838
- DESPATCHES FROM U.S. CONSULS IN ST GALL, SWITZERLAND, 1878-1906
- DESPATCHES FROM U.S. CONSULS IN ST GEORGE, BRITISH WEST INDIES, 1878-1906
- DESPATCHES FROM U.S. CONSULS IN ST HELENA, BRITISH WEST AFRICA, 1831-1906
- DESPATCHES FROM U.S. CONSULS IN ST HYACINTHE, CANADA, 1882-1906
- DESPATCHES FROM U.S. CONSULS IN ST JOHN, NEW BRUNSWICK, CANADA, 1835-1906
- DESPATCHES FROM U.S. CONSULS IN ST JOHN'S, NEWFOUNDLAND, CANADA, 1852-1906
- DESPATCHES FROM U.S. CONSULS IN ST JOHNS, QUEBEC, CANADA, 1864-1906
- DESPATCHES FROM U.S. CONSULS IN ST MARC, HAITI, 1861-91
- DESPATCHES FROM U.S. CONSULS IN ST MARTIN, NETHERLANDS WEST INDIES, 1848-1906
- DESPATCHES FROM U.S. CONSULS IN ST MICHAEL ISLAND, AZORES, 1897-1906
- DESPATCHES FROM U.S. CONSULS IN ST PAUL DE LOANDA, PORTUGUESE AFRICA, 1854-93
- DESPATCHES FROM U.S. CONSULS IN ST PETERSBURG, RUSSIA, 1803-1906
- DESPATCHES FROM U.S. CONSULS IN ST PIERRE AND MIQUELON, 1850-1906
- DESPATCHES FROM U.S. CONSULS IN ST PIERRE, MARTINIQUE, FRENCH WEST INDIES, 1790-1906
- DESPATCHES FROM U.S. CONSULS IN ST SALVADOR, BRAZIL, 1808-49
- DESPATCHES FROM U.S. CONSULS IN ST STEPHEN, CANADA, 1882-1906
- DESPATCHES FROM U.S. CONSULS IN ST THOMAS, VIRGIN ISLANDS, 1804-1906
- DESPATCHES FROM U.S. CONSULS IN ST UBEC, PORTUGAL, 1835-42
- DESPATCHES FROM U.S. CONSULS IN STANBRIDGE STATION, CANADA, 1878-1906
- DESPATCHES FROM U.S. CONSULS IN STAVANGER, NORWAY, 1905-6
- DESPATCHES FROM U.S. CONSULS IN STETTIN GERMANY, 1830-1906
- DESPATCHES FROM U.S. CONSULS IN STOCKHOLM, SWEDEN, 1810-1906
- DESPATCHES FROM U.S. CONSULS IN STRASBOURG, FRANCE, 1866-72
- DESPATCHES FROM U.S. CONSULS IN STRATFORD, CANADA, 1887-1906
- DESPATCHES FROM U.S. CONSULS IN STUTTGART GERMANY, 1830-1906
- DESPATCHES FROM U.S. CONSULS IN SWANSEA, UNITED KINGDOM, 1892-1906
- DESPATCHES FROM U.S. CONSULS IN SWATOW, CHINA, 1860-81
- DESPATCHES FROM U.S. CONSULS IN SYDNEY, AUSTRALIA, 1836-1906
- DESPATCHES FROM U.S. CONSULS IN SYDNEY, CANADA, 1838-1906
- DESPATCHES FROM U.S. CONSULS IN TABASCO, MEXICO, 1832-74
- DESPATCHES FROM U.S. CONSULS IN TAHITI, SOCIETY ISLANDS, FRENCH OCEANIA
- DESPATCHES FROM U.S. CONSULS IN TALCAHUANO, CHILE, 1836-95
- DESPATCHES FROM U.S. CONSULS IN TAMATAVE, MADAGASCAR, 1853-1906
- DESPATCHES FROM U.S. CONSULS IN TAMPICO, MEXICO, 1824-1906
- DESPATCHES FROM U.S. CONSULS IN TAMSUI, FORMOSA, 1898-1906
- DESPATCHES FROM U.S. CONSULS IN TANGIER, MOROCCO, 1797-1906
- DESPATCHES FROM U.S. CONSULS IN TARANTO, ITALY, 1861-76
- DESPATCHES FROM U.S. CONSULS IN TEGUCIGALPA, HONDURAS, 1860-1906
- DESPATCHES FROM U.S. CONSULS IN TEHERAN, IRAN, 1883-1906
- DESPATCHES FROM U.S. CONSULS IN TEHUANTEPEC, MEXICO, 1850-67

- DESPATCHES FROM U.S. CONSULS IN TENERIFFE, CANARY ISLANDS, 1795-1906
- DESPATCHES FROM U.S. CONSULS IN TETUAN, MOROCCO
- DESPATCHES FROM U.S. CONSULS IN TEXAS, 1825-44
- DESPATCHES FROM U.S. CONSULS IN THREE RIVERS, CANADA, 1881-1906
- DESPATCHES FROM U.S. CONSULS IN TIENTSIN, CHINA, 1868-1906
- DESPATCHES FROM U.S. CONSULS IN TORONTO, CANADA, 1864-1906
- DESPATCHES FROM U.S. CONSULS IN TREBIZOND, TURKEY, 1904-6
- DESPATCHES FROM U.S. CONSULS IN TRIESTE, ITALY, 1800-1906
- DESPATCHES FROM U.S. CONSULS IN TRINIDAD, CUBA, 1824-76
- DESPATCHES FROM U.S. CONSULS IN TRINIDAD, WEST INDIES FEDERATION, 1824-1906
- DESPATCHES FROM U.S. CONSULS IN TUMBES, PERU, 1852-74
- DESPATCHES FROM U.S. CONSULS IN TUNIS, TUNISIA, 1797-1906
- DESPATCHES FROM U.S. CONSULS IN TUNSTALL, UNITED KINGDOM, 1869-1905
- DESPATCHES FROM U.S. CONSULS IN TURIN, ITALY, 1877-1906
- DESPATCHES FROM U.S. CONSULS IN TURKS ISLAND, BRITISH WEST INDIES, 1818-1906
- DESPATCHES FROM U.S. CONSULS IN TUXPAN, MEXICO, 1879-1906
- DESPATCHES FROM U.S. CONSULS IN UTILA, HONDURAS, 1894-1906
- DESPATCHES FROM U.S. CONSULS IN VALENCIA, SPAIN, 1816-1906
- DESPATCHES FROM U.S. CONSULS IN VALPARAISO, CHILE, 1812-1906
- DESPATCHES FROM U.S. CONSULS IN VANCOUVER, CANADA, 1890-1906
- DESPATCHES FROM U.S. CONSULS IN VENICE, ITALY, 1830-1906
- DESPATCHES FROM U.S. CONSULS IN VERACRUZ, MEXICO, 1822-1906
- DESPATCHES FROM U.S. CONSULS IN VICTORIA, CANADA, 1862-1906
- DESPATCHES FROM U.S. CONSULS IN VIENNA, AUSTRIA, 1830-1906
- DESPATCHES FROM U.S. CONSULS IN VIGOR, SPAIN, 1852-62
- DESPATCHES FROM U.S. CONSULS IN VLADIVOSTOK, RUSSIA, 1898-1906
- DESPATCHES FROM U.S. CONSULS IN WALLACEBURG, CANADA, 1888-1905
- DESPATCHES FROM U.S. CONSULS IN WARSAW, POLAND, 1871-1906
- DESPATCHES FROM U.S. CONSULS IN WAUBAUSHENE, CANADA, 1890-93
- DESPATCHES FROM U.S. CONSULS IN WEIMAR GERMANY, 1893-1906
- DESPATCHES FROM U.S. CONSULS IN WINDSOR, NOVA SCOTIA, CANADA, 1872-1906
- DESPATCHES FROM U.S. CONSULS IN WINDSOR, ONTARIO, CANADA, 1864-1906
- DESPATCHES FROM U.S. CONSULS IN WINNIPEG, CANADA, 1869-1906
- DESPATCHES FROM U.S. CONSULS IN WOODSTOCK, CANADA, 1882-1906
- DESPATCHES FROM U.S. CONSULS IN YARMOUTH, CANADA, 1886-1906
- DESPATCHES FROM U.S. CONSULS IN YOKOHAMA, JAPAN, 1897-1906
- DESPATCHES FROM U.S. CONSULS IN ZACATECAS, MEXICO, 1860-84
- DESPATCHES FROM U.S. CONSULS IN ZANTE, GREECE, 1853-62
- DESPATCHES FROM U.S. CONSULS IN ZANZIBAR, BRITISH AFRICA
- DESPATCHES FROM U.S. CONSULS IN ZITTAU, GERMANY, 1897-1906
- DESPATCHES FROM U.S. CONSULS IN ZURICH, SWITZERLAND, 1852-1906
- DESPATCHES FROM U.S. MINISTERS TO ARGENTINA, 1817-1906
- DESPATCHES FROM U.S. MINISTERS TO AUSTRIA, 1838-1906
- DESPATCHES FROM U.S. MINISTERS TO BELGIUM, 1832-1906
- DESPATCHES FROM U.S. MINISTERS TO BOLIVIA, 1848-1906
- DESPATCHES FROM U.S. MINISTERS TO BRAZIL, 1809-1906
- DESPATCHES FROM U.S. MINISTERS TO CENTRAL AMERICA, 1824-1906
- DESPATCHES FROM U.S. MINISTERS TO CHILE, 1823-1906
- DESPATCHES FROM U.S. MINISTERS TO CHINA, 1843-1906
- DESPATCHES FROM U.S. MINISTERS TO COLOMBIA, 1820-1906
- DESPATCHES FROM U.S. MINISTERS TO CUBA, 1902-6
- DESPATCHES FROM U.S. MINISTERS TO DENMARK, 1811-1906
- DESPATCHES FROM U.S. MINISTERS TO ECUADOR
- DESPATCHES FROM U.S. MINISTERS TO FRANCE, 1789-1906
- DESPATCHES FROM U.S. MINISTERS TO GREAT BRITAIN, 1791-1906
- DESPATCHES FROM U.S. MINISTERS TO GREECE, 1868-1906
- DESPATCHES FROM U.S. MINISTERS TO HAITI, 1862-1906
- DESPATCHES FROM U.S. MINISTERS TO HAWAII, 1843-1900
- DESPATCHES FROM U.S. MINISTERS TO JAPAN, 1855-1906
- DESPATCHES FROM U.S. MINISTERS TO KOREA, 1883-1905
- DESPATCHES FROM U.S. MINISTERS TO LIBERIA, 1863-1906
- DESPATCHES FROM U.S. MINISTERS TO MEXICO, 1823-1906
- DESPATCHES FROM U.S. MINISTERS TO MONTENEGRO, 12 MAR 1905-14 JUN 1906
- DESPATCHES FROM U.S. MINISTERS TO MOROCCO, 1905-6
- DESPATCHES FROM U.S. MINISTERS TO PANAMA, 1903-06
- DESPATCHES FROM U.S. MINISTERS TO PARAGUAY AND URUGUAY, 1858-1906
- DESPATCHES FROM U.S. MINISTERS TO PERSIA, 1883-1906
- DESPATCHES FROM U.S. MINISTERS TO PERU, 1826-1906
- DESPATCHES FROM U.S. MINISTERS TO PORTUGAL, 1790-1906
- DESPATCHES FROM U.S. MINISTERS TO RUMANIA, 1880-1906
- DESPATCHES FROM U.S. MINISTERS TO RUSSIA, 1808-1906
- DESPATCHES FROM U.S. MINISTERS TO SERBIA, 5 JUL 1900-31 JUL 1906
- DESPATCHES FROM U.S. MINISTERS TO SIAM, 1882-1906
- DESPATCHES FROM U.S. MINISTERS TO SPAIN, 1792-1906
- DESPATCHES FROM U.S. MINISTERS TO SWEDEN AND NORWAY, 1813-1906
- DESPATCHES FROM U.S. MINISTERS TO SWITZERLAND, 1853-1906
- DESPATCHES FROM U.S. MINISTERS TO TEXAS, 1836-45
- DESPATCHES FROM U.S. MINISTERS TO THE DOMINICAN REPUBLIC, 1883-1906
- DESPATCHES FROM U.S. MINISTERS TO THE GERMAN STATES AND GERMANY, 1799-1801; 1835-1906
- DESPATCHES FROM U.S. MINISTERS TO THE ITALIAN STATES, 1832-1906
- DESPATCHES FROM U.S. MINISTERS TO THE NETHERLANDS, 1794-1906
- DESPATCHES FROM U.S. MINISTERS TO TURKEY, 1818-1906
- DESPATCHES FROM U.S. MINISTERS TO VENEZUELA, 1835-1906
- DESPATCHES RECEIVED BY THE DEPT. OF STATE FROM THE U.S. COMMISSION TO CENTRAL AND SOUTH AMERICA, 14 JULY 1884-26 DEC 1885
- DIPLOMATIC AND CONSULAR INSTRUCTIONS...1791-1801
- DIPLOMATIC HISTORY OF THE AMERICAN REVOLUTION
- DIPLOMATIC INSTRUCTIONS...1801-1906
- DIPLOMATIC LIST
- DOCUMENTS OF THE INTERDIVISIONAL COUNTRY AND AREA COMMITTEE
- DOCUMENTS OF THE POST WAR PROGRAMS COMMITTEE, 1944
- DOCUMENTS ON DISARMAMENT, 1945-1959
- DOMESTIC LETTERS OF THE DEPT. OF STATE, 1784-1906
- THE EXECUTIVE AGREEMENT SERIES
- FEDERAL REPUBLIC OF GERMANY
- FEDERAL REPUBLIC OF GERMANY: INTERNAL AFFAIRS, 1950-1954
- FOREIGN RELATIONS PAPERS OF THE UNITED STATES
- FOREIGN SERVICE LISTS
- GENERAL CORRESPONDENCE OF THE ALASKAN TERRITORIAL GOVERNOR
- GERMANY
- HONDURAS, 1930-45
- INTERNATIONAL ARBITRATIONS
- INVESTIGATION AND TRIAL PAPERS RELATING TO THE ASSASSINATION OF PRESIDENT LINCOLN
- JAPAN, 1914-1918
- JAPAN, 1919-1929
- JAPAN, 1930-1941
- THE JORDAN OLIVE OIL INDUSTRY
- JOURNAL OF CHARLES MASON KEPT DURING THE SURVEY OF THE MASON AND DIXON LINE, 1763-68
- JOURNAL OF THE VOYAGE OF THE USS NONSUCH UP THE ORINOCO, 1819
- LETTERS OF APPLICATION AND RECOMMENDATION DURING THE ADMINISTRATION OF ANDREW JACKSON, 1829-37
- LETTERS OF APPLICATION AND RECOMMENDATION DURING THE ADMINISTRATION OF JAMES MADISON, 1809-17
- LETTERS OF APPLICATION AND RECOMMENDATION DURING THE ADMINISTRATION OF JAMES MONROE, 1817-25
- LETTERS OF APPLICATION AND RECOMMENDATION DURING THE ADMINISTRATION OF JAMES POLK, ZACHARY TAYLOR, AND MILLARD FILLMORE
- LETTERS OF APPLICATION AND RECOMMENDATION DURING THE ADMINISTRATION OF JOHN ADAMS, 1797-1801
- LETTERS OF APPLICATION AND RECOMMENDATION DURING THE ADMINISTRATION OF JOHN QUINCY ADAMS, 1825-29
- LETTERS OF APPLICATION AND RECOMMENDATION DURING THE ADMINISTRATION OF THOMAS JEFFERSON, 1801-09
- LETTERS OF APPLICATION AND RECOMMENDATION DURING THE ADMINISTRATIONS OF ABRAHAM LINCOLN AND ANDREW JOHNSON, 1861-69
- LETTERS OF APPLICATION AND RECOMMENDATION DURING THE ADMINISTRATIONS OF FRANKLIN PIERCE AND JAMES BUCHANAN
- LETTERS OF APPLICATION AND RECOMMENDATION DURING THE ADMINISTRATIONS OF MARTIN VAN BUREN, WILLIAM HENRY HARRISON, AND JOHN TYLER, 1837-45
- LETTERS OF APPLICATION AND RECOMMENDATION DURING THE ADMINISTRATIONS OF ULYSSES S. GRANT
- LETTERS RECEIVED BY THE SECRETARY OF THE NAVY FROM THE ATTORNEY GENERAL OF THE UNITED STATES CONTAINING LEGAL OPINIONS AND ADVICE
- LETTERS RECEIVED...FROM THE AGENT FOR RED RIVER AFFAIRS, CANADA, 1867-1870
- LISTS OF U.S. CONSULAR OFFICERS, 1789-1939
- LISTS OF U.S. DIPLOMATIC OFFICERS, 1789-1939
- MALLOY'S TREATIES
- MANUAL FOR CLASSIFICATION OF CORRESPONDENCE, DEPT. OF STATE (4TH ED., 1938)
- MARSHALL/LOVETT MEMORANDUMS TO PRESIDENT TRUMAN, 1947-1948
- THE MIDDLE EAST, 1942-44
- MILLER'S TREATIES
- MINUTES OF TREATY CONFERENCES BETWEEN THE U.S. AND JAPANESE REPRESENTATIVES AND TREATY DRAFTS, 1872
- MISCELLANEOUS DOCUMENTS RELATING TO THE RECIPROCITY NEGOTIATIONS OF THE DEPT. OF STATE, 1848-54; 1884-85; 1891-92
- MISCELLANEOUS LETTERS OF THE DEPT. OF STATE, 1789-1906
- NICARAGUA, 1930-45
- NOTES FROM CENTRAL AMERICAN LEGATIONS IN THE U.S. TO THE DEPT. OF STATE, 1823-1906
- NOTES FROM FOREIGN CONSULS IN THE U.S. TO THE DEPT. OF STATE, 1789-1906
- NOTES FROM MISCELLANEOUS FOREIGN STATES TO THE DEPT. OF STATE, 1817-1906
- NOTES FROM THE ARGENTINE LEGATION IN THE U.S. TO THE DEPT. OF STATE, 1811-1906
- NOTES FROM THE AUSTRIAN LEGATION IN THE U.S. TO THE DEPARTMENT OF STATE, 1820-1906
- NOTES FROM THE BELGIAN LEGATION IN THE U.S. TO THE DEPT. OF STATE, 1832-1906
- NOTES FROM THE BOLIVIAN LEGATION IN THE U.S. TO THE DEPT. OF STATE, 1837-1906
- NOTES FROM THE BRAZILIAN LEGATION IN THE U.S. TO THE DEPT. OF STATE, 1824-1906
- NOTES FROM THE BRITISH LEGATION IN THE U.S. TO THE DEPT. OF STATE, 1791-1906
- NOTES FROM THE CHILEAN LEGATION IN THE U.S. TO THE DEPT. OF STATE, 1811-1906
- NOTES FROM THE CHINESE LEGATION IN THE U.S. TO THE DEPT. OF STATE, 1868-1906
- NOTES FROM THE COLOMBIAN LEGATION IN THE U.S. TO THE DEPT. OF STATE, 1810-1906
- NOTES FROM THE COSTA RICAN LEGATION IN THE U.S. TO THE DEPT. OF STATE, 1878-1906
- NOTES FROM THE CUBAN LEGATION IN THE U.S. TO THE DEPT. OF STATE, 1844-1906
- NOTES FROM THE DANISH LEGATION IN THE U.S. TO THE DEPT. OF STATE, 1801-1906
- NOTES FROM THE DEPT. OF STATE TO FOREIGN MINISTERS AND CONSULS IN THE U.S., 1793-1834
- NOTES FROM THE ECUADOREAN LEGATION IN THE UNITED STATES TO THE DEPARTMENT OF STATE
- NOTES FROM THE ECUADOREAN LEGATION IN THE U.S. TO THE DEPT. OF STATE, 1839-1906
- NOTES FROM THE FRENCH LEGATION IN THE U.S. TO THE DEPT. OF STATE, 1789-1906
- NOTES FROM THE GREEK LEGATION IN THE U.S. TO THE DEPT. OF STATE, 1823-1892
- NOTES FROM THE HAITIAN LEGATION IN THE U.S. TO THE DEPT. OF STATE, 1861-1906
- NOTES FROM THE HAWAIIAN LEGATION IN THE U.S. TO THE DEPT. OF STATE, 1841-1899
- NOTES FROM THE HONDURAN LEGATION IN THE U.S. TO THE DEPT. OF STATE, 1878-1906
- NOTES FROM THE ITALIAN LEGATION IN THE U.S. TO THE DEPT. OF STATE, 1861-1906
- NOTES FROM THE JAPANESE LEGATION IN THE U.S. TO THE DEPT. OF STATE. 1858-1906
- NOTES FROM THE KOREAN LEGATION IN THE U.S. TO THE DEPT. OF STATE, 1883-1906
- NOTES FROM THE LEGATION OF EL SALVADOR IN THE U.S. TO THE DEPT. OF STATE, 1879-1906
- NOTES FROM THE LEGATION OF THE DOMINICAN REPUBLIC IN THE U.S. TO THE DEPT. OF STATE, 1844-1906
- NOTES FROM THE LEGATION OF THE KINGDOM OF THE TWO SICILIES TO THE DEPT. OF STATE, 1826-1860
- NOTES FROM THE LEGATIONS OF THE GERMAN STATES AND GERMANY IN THE U.S. TO THE DEPT. OF STATE, 1817-1906
- NOTES FROM THE LIBERIAN LEGATION IN THE U.S. TO THE DEPARTMENT OF STATE, 1862-1898
- NOTES FROM THE LUXEMBOURG LEGATION IN THE U.S. TO THE DEPT. OF STATE, 1876-1903
- NOTES FROM THE MADAGASCAN LEGATION IN THE U.S. TO THE DEPT. OF STATE, 1883-1894
- NOTES FROM THE MEXICAN LEGATION IN THE U.S. TO THE DEPT. OF STATE, 1821-1906
- NOTES FROM THE MONTENEGRAN LEGATION IN THE U.S. TO THE DEPT. OF STATE, 1896-1905
- NOTES FROM THE NETHERLANDS LEGATION IN THE U.S. TO THE DEPT. OF STATE, 1784-1906
- NOTES FROM THE NICARAGUAN LEGATION IN THE U.S. TO THE DEPT. OF STATE, 1862-1906
- NOTES FROM THE NORWEGIAN LEGATION IN THE U.S. TO THE DEPT. OF STATE, 1905-6
- NOTES FROM THE PANAMANIAN LEGATION IN THE U.S. TO THE DEPT. OF STATE, 1903-6
- NOTES FROM THE PARAGUAYAN LEGATION IN THE U.S. TO THE DEPT. OF STATE, 1853-1906
- NOTES FROM THE PERSIAN LEGATION IN THE UNITED STATES TO THE DEPARTMENT OF STATE, 1887-1906
- NOTES FROM THE PERUVIAN LEGATION IN THE U.S. TO THE DEPT. OF STATE, 1827-1906
- NOTES FROM THE PORTUGUESE LEGATION IN THE U.S. TO THE DEPT. OF STATE, 1796-1906

- NOTES FROM THE RUSSIAN LEGATION IN THE U.S. TO THE DEPT. OF STATE, 1809-1906
- NOTES FROM THE SAMOAN LEGATION IN THE U.S. TO THE DEPT. OF STATE, 1856-1894
- NOTES FROM THE SARDINIAN LEGATION IN THE U.S. TO THE DEPT. OF STATE, 1838-61
- NOTES FROM THE SIAMESE LEGATION IN THE UNITED STATES TO THE DEPARTMENT OF STATE, 1876-1906
- NOTES FROM THE SPANISH LEGATION IN THE U.S. TO THE DEPT. OF STATE, 1790-1906
- NOTES FROM THE SWEDISH LEGATION IN THE U.S. TO THE DEPT. OF STATE, 1813-1906
- NOTES FROM THE SWISS LEGATION IN THE U.S. TO THE DEPT. OF STATE, 1882-1906
- NOTES FROM THE TEXAN LEGATION IN THE U.S. TO THE DEPT. OF STATE, 1836-1845
- NOTES FROM THE TUNISIAN LEGATION IN THE U.S. TO THE DEPT. OF STATE, 1805-6
- NOTES FROM THE TURKISH LEGATION IN THE U.S. TO THE DEPT. OF STATE, 1867-1906
- NOTES FROM THE URUGUAYAN LEGATION IN THE U.S. TO THE DEPT. OF STATE, 1834-1906
- NOTES FROM THE VENEZUELAN LEGATION IN THE U.S. TO THE DEPT. OF STATE, 1835-1906
- NOTES TO FOREIGN CONSULS IN THE U.S. FROM THE DEPT. OF STATE, 1853-1906
- NOTES TO THE LEGATIONS OF THE GERMAN STATES, 1834-1906
- NUMERICAL AND MINOR FILES OF THE DEPARTMENT OF STATE
- PALESTINE REFERENCE FILES OF DEAN RUSK AND ROBERT MCCLINTOCK, 1947-1949
- PAPERS AND MINUTES OF MEETINGS OF PRINCIPAL WORLD WAR 2 ALLIED MILITARY CONFERENCES
- PAPERS RELATING TO THE FOREIGN RELATIONS OF THE UNITED STATES
- PARDON PETITIONS AND RELATED PAPERS SUBMITTED IN RESPONSE TO PRESIDENT ANDREW JACKSON'S AMNESTY PROCLAMATION OF MAY 29, 1865
- PERSONAL AND CONFIDENTIAL LETTERS FROM SECRETARY OF STATE LANSING TO PRESIDENT WILSON, 1915-18
- POLICY PLANNING STAFF NUMBERED PAPERS, 1-63, 1947-49
- POLITICAL RELATIONS BETWEEN THE UNITED STATES AND EGYPT
- PUBLICATIONS
- PUBLICATIONS LIST
- PURPORT LISTS FOR THE DEPARTMENT OF STATE DECIMAL FILE, 1910-1944
- RECORDS OF DEPARTMENT OF STATE RELATING TO INTERNAL AFFAIRS OF YUGOSLAVIA, 1930-1944
- RECORDS OF NEGOTIATIONS CONNECTED WITH THE TREATY OF GHENT, 1813-15
- RECORDS OF THE ALASKAN TERRITORIAL LEGISLATURE
- RECORDS OF THE CONSTITUTIONAL CONVENTION OF 1787
- RECORDS OF THE DEPARTMENT OF STATE
- RECORDS OF THE DEPARTMENT OF STATE RELATING TO GUANO ISLANDS
- RECORDS OF THE DEPARTMENT OF STATE RELATING TO INTERNAL AFFAIRS OF AFGHANISTAN, 1930-1944
- RECORDS OF THE DEPARTMENT OF STATE RELATING TO INTERNAL AFFAIRS OF AUSTRIA, 1930-1944
- RECORDS OF THE DEPARTMENT OF STATE RELATING TO INTERNAL AFFAIRS OF CZECHOSLOVAKIA, 1010-1944
- RECORDS OF THE DEPARTMENT OF STATE RELATING TO INTERNAL AFFAIRS OF HUNGARY, 1930-1944
- RECORDS OF THE DEPARTMENT OF STATE RELATING TO INTERNAL AFFAIRS OF PALESTINE, 1930-1944
- RECORDS OF THE DEPARTMENT OF STATE RELATING TO INTERNAL AFFAIRS OF POLAND, 1916-1944
- RECORDS OF THE DEPARTMENT OF STATE RELATING TO INTERNAL AFFAIRS OF ROMANIA, 1910-1944
- RECORDS OF THE DEPARTMENT OF STATE RELATING TO INTERNAL AFFAIRS OF THE BALKAN STATES, 1940-1944
- RECORDS OF THE DEPARTMENT OF STATE RELATING TO INTERNAL AFFAIRS OF TURKEY, 1930-1944
- RECORDS OF THE DEPARTMENT OF STATE RELATING TO POLITICAL RELATIONS BETWEEN BOLIVIA AND OTHER STATES, 1910-1929
- RECORDS OF THE DEPARTMENT OF STATE RELATING TO POLITICAL RELATIONS BETWEEN CHINA AND JAPAN
- RECORDS OF THE DEPARTMENT OF STATE RELATING TO POLITICAL RELATIONS BETWEEN THE UNITED STATES AND SIAM
- RECORDS OF THE DEPARTMENT OF STATE RELATING TO POLITICAL RELATIONS BETWEEN THE UNITED STATES AND TURKEY
- RECORDS OF THE DEPARTMENT OF STATE RELATING TO PROPERTY CLAIMS OF U.S. CITIZENS AGAINST POLAND
- RECORDS OF THE DEPARTMENT OF STATE RELATING TO THE INTERNAL AFFAIRS OF ALBANIA, 1910-1944
- RECORDS OF THE DEPARTMENT OF STATE RELATING TO U.S. CLAIMS AGAINST RUSSIA
- RECORDS OF THE DEPARTMENT OF STATE RELATING TO WORLD WAR 2
- RECORDS OF THE GERMAN FOREIGN OFFICER RECEIVED BY THE DEPARTMENT OF STATE FROM THE BRITISH MUSEUM
- RECORDS OF THE OFFICE OF CHINESE AFFAIRS, 1945-55
- RECORDS OF THE U.S. CONSULATE IN JERUSALEM, PALESTINE: CONFIDENTIAL CORRESPONDENCE, 1920-35
- RECORDS OF THE U.S. CONSULATE AT CALLAO-LIMA, PERU, 1825-1912
- RECORDS OF THE U.S. CONSULATE IN BANGKOK, 1856-1912
- RECORDS OF THE U.S. CONSULATE IN BOMBAY, 1894-1912
- RECORDS OF THE U.S. CONSULATE IN KUNMING, 1922-28
- RECORDS OF THE U.S. CONSULATE IN MADRAS, 1908-12
- RECORDS OF THE U.S. LEGATION IN CHILE, 1893-1905
- RECORDS OF THE U.S. LEGATION IN CHINA, 1849-1931
- RECORDS OF THE U.S. LEGATION IN JAPAN, 1855-1912
- RECORDS OF THE U.S. LEGATION IN PARIS, 1836-42
- RECORDS OF THE U.S. LEGATION IN PERU
- RECORDS... RELATING TO COMMERCIAL RELATIONS BETWEEN THE UNITED STATES AND JAPAN, 1910-1949
- RECORDS... RELATING TO COMMERCIAL RELATIONS BETWEEN THE UNITED STATES AND RUSSIA/THE SOVIET UNION, 1910-1949
- RECORDS... RELATING TO INTERNAL AFFAIRS OF ALBANIA, 1910-1954
- RECORDS RELATING TO INTERNAL AFFAIRS OF AUSTRIA-HUNGARY AND AUSTRIA
- RECORDS RELATING TO INTERNAL AFFAIRS OF BULGARIA, 1910-1954
- RECORDS RELATING TO INTERNAL AFFAIRS OF CHINA, 1910-49
- RECORDS RELATING TO INTERNAL AFFAIRS OF CZECHOSLOVAKIA, 1910-1959
- RECORDS RELATING TO INTERNAL AFFAIRS OF EAST GERMANY, 1950-54
- RECORDS RELATING TO INTERNAL AFFAIRS OF FINLAND, 1910-1954
- RECORDS RELATING TO INTERNAL AFFAIRS OF GREECE, 1910-1954
- RECORDS RELATING TO INTERNAL AFFAIRS OF HUNGARY, 1912-1959
- RECORDS RELATING TO INTERNAL AFFAIRS OF JAPAN, 1910-1959
- RECORDS RELATING TO INTERNAL AFFAIRS OF KOREA, 1910-1959
- RECORDS RELATING TO INTERNAL AFFAIRS OF PALESTINE (ISRAEL), 1910-1949
- RECORDS RELATING TO INTERNAL AFFAIRS OF POLAND, 1916-1959
- RECORDS RELATING TO INTERNAL AFFAIRS OF ROMANIA, 1910-1959
- RECORDS RELATING TO INTERNAL AFFAIRS OF RUSSIA/THE SOVIET UNION, 1910-1944
- RECORDS RELATING TO INTERNAL AFFAIRS OF YUGOSLAVIA, 1910-1959
- RECORDS.... RELATING TO POLITICAL RELATIONS BETWEEN AUSTRIA-HUNGARY AND AUSTRIA AND OTHER STATES, 1910-1929
- RECORDS RELATING TO POLITICAL RELATIONS BETWEEN GERMANY AND OTHER STATES, 1910-29
- RECORDS RELATING TO POLITICAL RELATIONS BETWEEN RUSSIA/THE SOVIET UNION AND OTHER STATES, 1910-1944
- RECORDS RELATING TO POLITICAL RELATIONS BETWEEN THE AUSTRIA AND THE U.S., 1910-29
- RECORDS RELATING TO POLITICAL RELATIONS BETWEEN THE UNITED STATES AND JAPAN, 1910-1959
- RECORDS RELATING TO POLITICAL RELATIONS BETWEEN THE UNITED STATES AND KOREA, 1955-1959
- RECORDS RELATING TO POLITICAL RELATIONS BETWEEN THE UNITED STATES AND LATIN AMERICAN AND CARIBBEAN STATES, 1930-1944
- RECORDS RELATING TO POLITICAL RELATIONS BETWEEN THE UNITED STATES AND RUSSIA/THE SOVIET UNION, 1910-1944
- RECORDS RELATING TO POLITICAL RELATIONS BETWEEN THE U.S. AND GERMANY, 1930-39
- RECORDS RELATING TO POLITICAL RELATIONS OF LATIN AMERICAN AND CARIBBEAN STATES, 1930-1944
- RECORDS...OF THE SPECIAL INTERROGATION MISSION TO GERMANY, 1945-46
- RECORDS...RELATING TO INTERNAL AFFAIRS OF ARGENTINA, 1910-29
- RECORDS...RELATING TO INTERNAL AFFAIRS OF ARMENIA, 1910-29
- RECORDS...RELATING TO INTERNAL AFFAIRS OF ASIA, 1910-29
- RECORDS...RELATING TO INTERNAL AFFAIRS OF AUSTRALIA, 1910-1944
- RECORDS...RELATING TO INTERNAL AFFAIRS OF AUSTRIA-HUNGARY AND AUSTRIA, 1910-29
- RECORDS...RELATING TO INTERNAL AFFAIRS OF AUSTRIA-HUNGARY AND HUNGARY, 1912-29
- RECORDS...RELATING TO INTERNAL AFFAIRS OF BELGIUM, 1910-29
- RECORDS...RELATING TO INTERNAL AFFAIRS OF BOLIVIA, 1910-29
- RECORDS...RELATING TO INTERNAL AFFAIRS OF BRAZIL, 1910-29
- RECORDS...RELATING TO INTERNAL AFFAIRS OF BRITISH AFRICA, 1910-29
- RECORDS...RELATING TO INTERNAL AFFAIRS OF BRITISH ASIA, 1910-29
- RECORDS...RELATING TO INTERNAL AFFAIRS OF CENTRAL AMERICA, 1910-29
- RECORDS...RELATING TO INTERNAL AFFAIRS OF CHILE, 1910-29
- RECORDS...RELATING TO INTERNAL AFFAIRS OF CHINA, 1910-29
- RECORDS...RELATING TO INTERNAL AFFAIRS OF COSTA RICA, 1910-29
- RECORDS...RELATING TO INTERNAL AFFAIRS OF CUBA, 1910-29
- RECORDS...RELATING TO INTERNAL AFFAIRS OF EGYPT, 1910-29
- RECORDS...RELATING TO INTERNAL AFFAIRS OF EGYPT, 1930-39
- RECORDS...RELATING TO INTERNAL AFFAIRS OF EL SALVADOR, 1910-29
- RECORDS...RELATING TO INTERNAL AFFAIRS OF ESTONIA, 1910-44
- RECORDS...RELATING TO INTERNAL AFFAIRS OF ETHIOPIA, 1910-29
- RECORDS...RELATING TO INTERNAL AFFAIRS OF FINLAND, 1910-44
- RECORDS...RELATING TO INTERNAL AFFAIRS OF FRANCE, 1910-29
- RECORDS...RELATING TO INTERNAL AFFAIRS OF GERMANY, 1910-29
- RECORDS...RELATING TO INTERNAL AFFAIRS OF GREAT BRITAIN, 1910-29
- RECORDS...RELATING TO INTERNAL AFFAIRS OF GREECE, 1910-29
- RECORDS...RELATING TO INTERNAL AFFAIRS OF GREECE, 1930-39
- RECORDS...RELATING TO INTERNAL AFFAIRS OF GUATEMALA, 1910-29
- RECORDS...RELATING TO INTERNAL AFFAIRS OF HAITI, 1910-29
- RECORDS...RELATING TO INTERNAL AFFAIRS OF HONDURAS, 1910-29
- RECORDS...RELATING TO INTERNAL AFFAIRS OF INDIA AND BURMA, 1910-29
- RECORDS...RELATING TO INTERNAL AFFAIRS OF IRAN, 1930-39
- RECORDS...RELATING TO INTERNAL AFFAIRS OF IRAQ, 1930-44
- RECORDS...RELATING TO INTERNAL AFFAIRS OF ITALY, 1910-1929
- RECORDS...RELATING TO INTERNAL AFFAIRS OF JAPAN, 1910-29
- RECORDS...RELATING TO INTERNAL AFFAIRS OF KOREA, 1910-1929
- RECORDS...RELATING TO INTERNAL AFFAIRS OF LATVIA, 1910-1944
- RECORDS...RELATING TO INTERNAL AFFAIRS OF LEBANON, 1930-44
- RECORDS...RELATING TO INTERNAL AFFAIRS OF LIBERIA, 1910-29
- RECORDS...RELATING TO INTERNAL AFFAIRS OF LITHUANIA, 1910-44
- RECORDS...RELATING TO INTERNAL AFFAIRS OF MEXICO, 1910-29
- RECORDS...RELATING TO INTERNAL AFFAIRS OF MONTENEGRO AND TO POLITICAL RELATIONS BETWEEN THE U.S. AND MONTENEGRO, 1910-29
- RECORDS...RELATING TO INTERNAL AFFAIRS OF MOROCCO, 1910-29
- RECORDS...RELATING TO INTERNAL AFFAIRS OF NICARAGUA, 1910-29
- RECORDS...RELATING TO INTERNAL AFFAIRS OF PANAMA, 1910-1929
- RECORDS...RELATING TO INTERNAL AFFAIRS OF PERSIA, 1910-29
- RECORDS...RELATING TO INTERNAL AFFAIRS OF PERU, 1910-29
- RECORDS...RELATING TO INTERNAL AFFAIRS OF PORTUGAL, 1910-29
- RECORDS...RELATING TO INTERNAL AFFAIRS OF RUSSIA AND THE SOVIET UNION, 1910-29
- RECORDS...RELATING TO INTERNAL AFFAIRS OF SERBIA AND TO POLITICAL RELATIONS BETWEEN THE U.S. AND SERBIA, 1910-29
- RECORDS...RELATING TO INTERNAL AFFAIRS OF SIAM, 1910-29
- RECORDS...RELATING TO INTERNAL AFFAIRS OF SYRIA, 1930-44
- RECORDS...RELATING TO INTERNAL AFFAIRS OF THE BALTIC STATES, 1910-1944
- RECORDS...RELATING TO INTERNAL AFFAIRS OF THE DOMINICAN REPUBLIC, 1910-29
- RECORDS...RELATING TO INTERNAL AFFAIRS OF THE NETHERLANDS, 1910-29
- RECORDS...RELATING TO INTERNAL AFFAIRS OF THE PAPAL STATES (HOLY SEE), 1910-29
- RECORDS...RELATING TO INTERNAL AFFAIRS OF THE SOVIET UNION, 1930-39
- RECORDS...RELATING TO INTERNAL AFFAIRS OF TURKEY, 1910-29
- RECORDS...RELATING TO INTERNAL AFFAIRS OF VENEZUELA, 1910-29
- RECORDS...RELATING TO INTERNAL AFFAIRS OF YUGOSLAVIA, 1910-29
- RECORDS...RELATING TO POLITICAL RELATIONS BETWEEN ARGENTINA AND OTHER STATES, 1910-29
- RECORDS...RELATING TO POLITICAL RELATIONS BETWEEN ARMENIA AND OTHER STATES, 1910-29
- RECORDS...RELATING TO POLITICAL RELATIONS BETWEEN ASIA AND OTHER STATES (SIC), 1910-1929
- RECORDS...RELATING TO POLITICAL RELATIONS BETWEEN AUSTRIA-HUNGARY AND HUNGARY AND OTHER STATES, 1920-1929
- RECORDS...RELATING TO POLITICAL RELATIONS BETWEEN BELGIUM AND OTHER STATES, 1910-29
- RECORDS...RELATING TO POLITICAL RELATIONS BETWEEN BOLIVIA AND OTHER STATES, 1910-29
- RECORDS...RELATING TO POLITICAL RELATIONS BETWEEN BRAZIL AND OTHER STATES, 1910-29
- RECORDS...RELATING TO POLITICAL RELATIONS BETWEEN BRITISH AFRICA AND OTHER STATES, 1910-29
- RECORDS...RELATING TO POLITICAL RELATIONS BETWEEN BRITISH ASIA AND OTHER STATES, INCLUDING THE U.S., 1910-1929
- RECORDS...RELATING TO POLITICAL RELATIONS BETWEEN CENTRAL AMERICA AND OTHER STATES, 1910-29
- RECORDS...RELATING TO POLITICAL RELATIONS BETWEEN CHILE AND OTHER STATES, 1910-29
- RECORDS...RELATING TO POLITICAL RELATIONS BETWEEN CHINA AND OTHER STATES, 1910-29
- RECORDS...RELATING TO POLITICAL RELATIONS BETWEEN COSTA RICA AND OTHER STATES, 1910-29
- RECORDS...RELATING TO POLITICAL RELATIONS BETWEEN CUBA AND OTHER STATES, 1910-29
- RECORDS...RELATING TO POLITICAL RELATIONS BETWEEN EGYPT AND OTHER STATES, 1910-29
- RECORDS...RELATING TO POLITICAL RELATIONS BETWEEN EL SALVADOR AND OTHER STATES, 1910-29
- RECORDS...RELATING TO POLITICAL RELATIONS BETWEEN FINLAND AND OTHER STATES, 1910-44
- RECORDS...RELATING TO POLITICAL RELATIONS BETWEEN FRANCE AND OTHER STATES, 1910-29
- RECORDS...RELATING TO POLITICAL RELATIONS BETWEEN GREAT BRITAIN AND OTHER STATES, 1910-29

- RECORDS...RELATING TO POLITICAL RELATIONS BETWEEN GREECE AND OTHER STATES, 1910-29
- RECORDS...RELATING TO POLITICAL RELATIONS BETWEEN GUATEMALA AND OTHER STATES, 1910-29
- RECORDS...RELATING TO POLITICAL RELATIONS BETWEEN HAITI AND OTHER STATES, 1910-29
- RECORDS...RELATING TO POLITICAL RELATIONS BETWEEN INDIA AND BURMA AND OTHER STATES, 1910-29
- RECORDS...RELATING TO POLITICAL RELATIONS BETWEEN ITALY AND OTHER STATES, 1910-29
- RECORDS...RELATING TO POLITICAL RELATIONS BETWEEN JAPAN AND OTHER STATES, 1910-29
- RECORDS...RELATING TO POLITICAL RELATIONS BETWEEN LIBERIA AND OTHER STATES, INCLUDING THE U.S., 1919-29
- RECORDS...RELATING TO POLITICAL RELATIONS BETWEEN MEXICO AND OTHER STATES, 1910-29
- RECORDS...RELATING TO POLITICAL RELATIONS BETWEEN MOROCCO AND OTHER STATES, 1910-29
- RECORDS...RELATING TO POLITICAL RELATIONS BETWEEN NICARAGUA AND OTHER STATES, 1910-29
- RECORDS...RELATING TO POLITICAL RELATIONS BETWEEN PANAMA AND OTHER STATES, 1910-29
- RECORDS...RELATING TO POLITICAL RELATIONS BETWEEN PERSIA AND OTHER STATES, 1921-29
- RECORDS...RELATING TO POLITICAL RELATIONS BETWEEN PERU AND OTHER STATES, 1911-29
- RECORDS...RELATING TO POLITICAL RELATIONS BETWEEN RUSSIA AND THE SOVIET UNION AND OTHER STATES, 1910-29
- RECORDS...RELATING TO POLITICAL RELATIONS BETWEEN SIAM AND OTHER STATES, 1910-29
- RECORDS...RELATING TO POLITICAL RELATIONS BETWEEN THE NETHERLANDS AND OTHER STATES, 1910-29
- RECORDS...RELATING TO POLITICAL RELATIONS BETWEEN THE PAPAL STATES (HOLY SEE) AND OTHER STATES, 1910-29
- RECORDS...RELATING TO POLITICAL RELATIONS BETWEEN THE SOVIET UNION AND OTHER STATES, 1930-39
- RECORDS...RELATING TO POLITICAL RELATIONS BETWEEN THE UNITED STATES AND ASIA, 1920-1929
- RECORDS...RELATING TO POLITICAL RELATIONS BETWEEN THE UNITED STATES AND AUSTRALIA, 1910-1944
- RECORDS...RELATING TO POLITICAL RELATIONS BETWEEN THE UNITED STATES AND AUSTRIA-HUNGARY AND HUNGARY, 1921-1929
- RECORDS...RELATING TO POLITICAL RELATIONS BETWEEN THE UNITED STATES AND BELGIUM, 1910-29
- RECORDS...RELATING TO POLITICAL RELATIONS BETWEEN THE U.S. AND ARGENTINA, 1910-29
- RECORDS...RELATING TO POLITICAL RELATIONS BETWEEN THE U.S. AND BRAZIL, 1910-29
- RECORDS...RELATING TO POLITICAL RELATIONS BETWEEN THE U.S. AND BRITISH AFRICA, 1910-29
- RECORDS...RELATING TO POLITICAL RELATIONS BETWEEN THE U.S. AND CENTRAL AMERICA, 1911-29
- RECORDS...RELATING TO POLITICAL RELATIONS BETWEEN THE U.S. AND CHILE, 1910-29
- RECORDS...RELATING TO POLITICAL RELATIONS BETWEEN THE U.S. AND CHINA, 1910-29
- RECORDS...RELATING TO POLITICAL RELATIONS BETWEEN THE U.S. AND COSTA RICA, 1910-29
- RECORDS...RELATING TO POLITICAL RELATIONS BETWEEN THE U.S. AND CUBA, 1910-29
- RECORDS...RELATING TO POLITICAL RELATIONS BETWEEN THE U.S. AND EGYPT, 1910-29
- RECORDS...RELATING TO POLITICAL RELATIONS BETWEEN THE U.S. AND EL SALVADOR, 1910-29
- RECORDS...RELATING TO POLITICAL RELATIONS BETWEEN THE U.S. AND ETHIOPIA, 1910-29
- RECORDS...RELATING TO POLITICAL RELATIONS BETWEEN THE U.S. AND FINLAND, 1910-44
- RECORDS...RELATING TO POLITICAL RELATIONS BETWEEN THE U.S. AND FRANCE, 1910-29
- RECORDS...RELATING TO POLITICAL RELATIONS BETWEEN THE U.S. AND GREAT BRITAIN, 1910-29
- RECORDS...RELATING TO POLITICAL RELATIONS BETWEEN THE U.S. AND GREAT BRITAIN, 1930-39
- RECORDS...RELATING TO POLITICAL RELATIONS BETWEEN THE U.S. AND GREECE, 1910-29
- RECORDS...RELATING TO POLITICAL RELATIONS BETWEEN THE U.S. AND GUATEMALA, 1910-29
- RECORDS...RELATING TO POLITICAL RELATIONS BETWEEN THE U.S. AND HAITI, 1910-29
- RECORDS...RELATING TO POLITICAL RELATIONS BETWEEN THE U.S. AND HONDURAS, 1910-29
- RECORDS...RELATING TO POLITICAL RELATIONS BETWEEN THE U.S. AND INDIA AND BURMA, 1910-29
- RECORDS...RELATING TO POLITICAL RELATIONS BETWEEN THE U.S. AND ITALY, 1910-29
- RECORDS...RELATING TO POLITICAL RELATIONS BETWEEN THE U.S. AND JAPAN, 1910-29
- RECORDS...RELATING TO POLITICAL RELATIONS BETWEEN THE U.S. AND MEXICO, 1910-29
- RECORDS...RELATING TO POLITICAL RELATIONS BETWEEN THE U.S. AND MOROCCO, 1910-29
- RECORDS...RELATING TO POLITICAL RELATIONS BETWEEN THE U.S. AND NICARAGUA, 1910-29
- RECORDS...RELATING TO POLITICAL RELATIONS BETWEEN THE U.S. AND PANAMA, 1910-29
- RECORDS...RELATING TO POLITICAL RELATIONS BETWEEN THE U.S. AND PERSIA, 1921-29
- RECORDS...RELATING TO POLITICAL RELATIONS BETWEEN THE U.S. AND RUSSIA AND THE SOVIET UNION, 1910-29
- RECORDS...RELATING TO POLITICAL RELATIONS BETWEEN THE U.S. AND SIAM, 1909-29
- RECORDS...RELATING TO POLITICAL RELATIONS BETWEEN THE U.S. AND THE NETHERLANDS, 1910-29
- RECORDS...RELATING TO POLITICAL RELATIONS BETWEEN THE U.S. AND THE PAPAL STATES (HOLY SEE), 1910-29
- RECORDS...RELATING TO POLITICAL RELATIONS BETWEEN THE U.S. AND THE SOVIET UNION, 1930-39
- RECORDS...RELATING TO POLITICAL RELATIONS BETWEEN THE U.S. AND TURKEY, 1910-29
- RECORDS...RELATING TO POLITICAL RELATIONS BETWEEN THE U.S. AND VENEZUELA, 1910-29
- RECORDS...RELATING TO POLITICAL RELATIONS BETWEEN THE U.S. AND YUGOSLAVIA, 1910-29
- RECORDS...RELATING TO POLITICAL RELATIONS BETWEEN TURKEY AND OTHER STATES, 1910-29
- RECORDS...RELATING TO POLITICAL RELATIONS BETWEEN VENEZUELA AND OTHER STATES, 1910-29
- RECORDS...RELATING TO POLITICAL RELATIONS BETWEEN YUGOSLAVIA AND OTHER STATES, 1910-29 (SIC)
- RECORDS...RELATING TO POLITICAL RELATIONS OF EASTERN EUROPE
- RECORDS...RELATING TO POLITICAL RELATIONS OF TURKEY, GREECE, AND THE BALKAN STATES
- RECORDS...RELATING TO THE FIRST PANAMA CONGRESS, 1825-27
- RECORDS...RELATING TO THE INTERNAL AFFAIRS OF SAUDI ARABIA
- RECORDS...RELATING TO THE INTERNAL AFFAIRS OF TRANS-JORDAN
- RECORDS...RELATING TO THE PARIS PEACE COMMISSION, 1898
- RECORDS...RELATING TO WORLD WAR I AND ITS TERMINATION, 1914-29
- REPORTS OF CLERKS AND BUREAU OFFICERS OF THE DEPARTMENT OF STATE
- RESIGNATIONS AND DECLINATIONS AMONG THE RECORDS OF THE DEPT. OF STATE, 1789-1827
- RUSSIA
- RUSSIA AND THE SOVIET UNION, 1914-1941
- EL SALVADOR, 1930-45
- THE SOVIET UNION, 1919-1933
- THE SOVIET UNION, 1934-1941
- STATE DEPARTMENT REGISTERS OF CORRESPONDENCE, 1870-1906
- STATE DEPARTMENT TERRITORIAL PAPERS: MISSOURI, 1812-1820
- STATE DEPT. TERRITORIAL PAPERS
- THE TERRITORIAL PAPERS OF THE UNITED STATES
- THE TERRITORIAL PAPERS OF THE UNITED STATES: IOWA, 1838-1846
- THE TERRITORIAL PAPERS OF THE UNITED STATES: THE TERRITORY OF MINNESOTA, 1849-1858
- THE TERRITORIAL PAPERS OF THE UNITED STATES: THE TERRITORY OF OREGON, 1848-1859
- TRANSCRIPTS AND FILES OF THE PARIS PEACE TALKS ON VIETNAM, 1968-73
- TREATIES AND CONVENTIONS CONCLUDED BETWEEN THE U.S. AND OTHER POWERS SINCE JULY 4 1776
- TREATIES AND OTHER INTERNATIONAL ACTS OF THE UNITED STATES
- TREATIES IN FORCE
- TREATY INFORMATION BULLETIN
- THE TREATY SERIES
- UNITED STATES TREATIES AND OTHER INTERNATIONAL AGREEMENTS
- "WAR OF 1812 PAPERS" OF THE DEPT. OF STATE, 1789-1815
- WEEKLY REPORT ON MATTERS RELATING TO LATIN AMERICA

U.S.. Department of State *see* RECORDS OF THE DEPARTMENT OF STATE RELATING TO INTERNAL AFFAIRS OF BULGARIA, 1910-1944

U.S. DEPARTMENT OF STATE DECIMAL FILES : THE SOVIET UNION AND EASTERN EUROPE – (See also Records...Relating to...) – us Scholarly Res [947]

U.S. Department of State. Division of Mexican Affairs *see* WEEKLY REPORT

U.S. Department of State. International Business Practices Division *see* PATENT AND TECHNICAL INFORMATION AGREEMENTS.

U.S. DEPARTMENT OF STATE RECORDS. *see*

- POLITICAL RELATIONS BETWEEN THE UNITED STATES AND URUGUAY
- RECORDS RELATING TO INTERNAL AFFAIRS OF BRAZIL

U.S. Department of State Records *see*

- RECORDS RELATING TO INTERNAL AFFAIRS OF CENTRAL AMERICA, 1810-1959
- RECORDS RELATING TO INTERNAL AFFAIRS OF CHILE, 1910-1929
- RECORDS RELATING TO INTERNAL AFFAIRS OF COLOMBIA, 1810-1959
- RECORDS RELATING TO INTERNAL AFFAIRS OF COSTA RICA, 1810-1959
- RECORDS RELATING TO INTERNAL AFFAIRS OF CUBA, 1810-1959
- RECORDS RELATING TO INTERNAL AFFAIRS OF ECUADOR, 1810-1959
- RECORDS RELATING TO INTERNAL AFFAIRS OF GUATEMALA, 1810-1959
- RECORDS RELATING TO INTERNAL AFFAIRS OF HAITI, 1810-1959
- RECORDS RELATING TO INTERNAL AFFAIRS OF HONDURAS, 1810-1959
- RECORDS RELATING TO INTERNAL AFFAIRS OF MEXICO, 1810-1959
- RECORDS RELATING TO INTERNAL AFFAIRS OF NICARAGUA, 1810-1959
- RECORDS RELATING TO INTERNAL AFFAIRS OF PANAMA, 1810-1959
- RECORDS RELATING TO INTERNAL AFFAIRS OF PARAGUAY, 1810-1959
- RECORDS RELATING TO INTERNAL AFFAIRS OF PERU, 1810-1959
- RECORDS RELATING TO INTERNAL AFFAIRS OF THE DOMINICAN REPUBLIC, 1810-1959
- RECORDS RELATING TO INTERNAL AFFAIRS OF VENEZUELA, 1910-1944
- RECORDS RELATING TO POLITICAL RELATIONS BETWEEN SOUTH AMERICA AND OTHER STATES, 1810-1959
- RECORDS RELATING TO POLITICAL RELATIONS BETWEEN THE UNITED STATES AND THE AMERICAN STATES (THE MONROE DOCTRINE)
- RECORDS RELATING TO THE INTERNAL AFFAIRS OF ARGENTINA
- RECORDS RELATING TO THE INTERNAL AFFAIRS OF BOLIVIA, 1810-1959

U.S. Department of State. U.S. Mission to the United Nations *see* PRESS RELEASES

U.S. Department of the Interior *see*

- ABSTRACTS OF NORTH AMERICAN GEOLOGY (WASHINGTON)
- ALASKA NATIVE CLAIMS APPEALS BOARD DECISIONS AND ORDERS
- APPOINTMENT PAPERS: FLORIDA, 1849-1907
- APPOINTMENT PAPERS: MISSOURI
- APPOINTMENT PAPERS: NEVADA
- APPOINTMENT PAPERS: TERRITORY OF ARIZONA
- APPOINTMENT PAPERS: WYOMING
- BIOGRAPHICAL AND HISTORICAL INDEX OF AMERICAN INDIANS AND PERSONS INVOLVED IN INDIAN AFFAIRS
- BITUMINOUS COAL DIVISION, DECISIONS AND ORDERS
- BOARD OF CONTRACT APPEALS DECISIONS
- BOARD OF INDIAN APPEALS DECISIONS AND ORDERS
- BOARD OF INDIAN COMMISSIONERS' ANNUAL REPORTS
- BOARD OF LAND APPEALS DECISIONS AND ORDERS
- BOARD OF MINE OPERATIONS APPEALS DECISIONS AND ORDERS
- COMMISSIONER OF INDIAN AFFAIRS ANNUAL REPORTS
- DECISIONS
- DECISIONS OF THE DEPARTMENT OF THE INTERIOR
- DICTIONARY CATALOG OF THE DEPARTMENT LIBRARY
- DIGEST OF DECISIONS OF THE DEPARTMENT OF THE INTERIOR IN CASES RELATING TO THE PUBLIC LANDS (INDIAN MATTERS INCLUDED)
- DIGEST OF THE DECISIONS...IN CASES RELATED TO PUBLIC LANDS
- INDEX TO INDIAN DECISIONS
- INDEX/DIGESTS OF DECISIONS OF THE DEPARTMENT OF THE INTERIOR
- INDIAN CLAIMS COMMISSION ANNUAL REPORTS
- INTERIOR DEPARTMENT APPOINTMENT PAPERS: MISSISSIPPI
- INTERIOR DEPARTMENT APPOINTMENT PAPERS: NEW YORK
- INTERIOR DEPARTMENT APPOINTMENT PAPERS: NORTH CAROLINA
- KAPPLER'S INDIAN AFFAIRS
- LETTERS RECEIVED BY THE PATENTS AND MISCELLANEOUS DIVISION OF THE OFFICE OF THE SECRETARY OF THE INTERIOR RELATING TO CUBA, THE PHILIPPINE ISLANDS, AND PUERTO RICO
- PENSION AND BOUNTY-LAND CLAIMS DECISIONS
- PUBLICATIONS
- RECLAMATION AND RELATED LAWS ANNOTATED, 1866-1988
- SOLICTOR'S UNPUBLISHED OPINIONS, 1955-1974
- SURFACE MINING AND RECLAMATION APPEALS BOARD DECISIONS
- TERRITORIAL PAPERS: HAWAII
- TERRITORIAL PAPERS: OKLAHOMA

U.S. Department of the Interior *see* ORDER N3027

U.S. Department of the Interior. General Land Office *see* CIRCULARS AND REGULATIONS..

U.S. Department of the Interior Law Library *see* SECRETARY'S ORDERS

U.S. Department of the Interior. Office of Hearings and Appeals *see* DRAFTING OF INDIAN WILLS COVERING TRUST AND RESTRICTED PROPERTY

U.S. Department of the Interior. Office of the Secretary *see*

- FINAL ROLLS OF CITIZENS AND FREEDMEN OF THE FIVE CIVILIZED TRIBES IN INDIAN TERRITORY (AS APPROVED BY THE SECTY. OF THE INT. ON OR BEFORE MAR. 4, 1907, WITH SUPPLEMENTS DATED SEPT. 25, 1914)
- INTERIOR DEPARTMENT APPOINTMENT PAPERS:
- INTERIOR DEPARTMENT TERRITORIAL PAPERS:
- LETTERS SENT BY THE INDIAN DIVISION..., 1849-1903
- LETTERS SENT BY THE LANDS AND RAILROADS DIVISION..., 1849-1904
- RECORDS...RELATING TO THE YELLOWSTONE NATIONAL PARK, 1872-86
- RECORDS...RELATING TO WAGON ROADS, 1857-87

U.S. Department of the Interior. United States Geological Survey. Washington, D.C. *see* CATALOG OF THE UNITED STATES GEOLOGICAL SURVEY LIBRARY

U.S. Department of the Treasury *see*

- ALASKA FILE OF THE SPECIAL AGENTS DIVISION OF THE DEPARTMENT OF THE TREASURY
- SYNOPSIS OF SUNDRY DECISIONS OF THE TREASURY DEPARTMENT, 1868-1898
- TAXATION OF INCOME FLOWING THROUGH LIFE INSURANCE COMPANIES

– THE U.S. NATIONAL ECONOMY

U.S. Department of the Treasury. Commission on Private Philanthropy and Public Needs *see* RESEARCH PAPERS

U.S. Department of Transportation *see* TYPE CERTIFICATE DATA SHEETS AND SPECIFICATIONS

U.S. Department of War *see* RECORDS OF THE AMERICAN SECTION OF THE SUPREME WAR COUNCIL

US Dept of Agriculture. Office of the Solicitor *see* LAWS APPLICABLE TO THE U.S. DEPARTMENT OF AGRICULTURE

U. S. Dept of Commerce *see*
- FEDERAL MARITIME ADMINISTRATION AND MARITIME SUBSIDY BOARD ANNUAL REPORTS
- FEDERAL MARITIME BOARD AND MARITIME ADMINISTRATION ANNUAL REPORTS
- MARITIME SUBSIDY BOARD, MARITIME ADMINISTRATION AND DEPARTMENT OF COMMERCE DECISIONS

U.S. Dept of Commerce *see* U.S. MARITIME COMMISSION, MARITIME ADMINISTRATION, FEDERAL MARITIME BOARD, FEDERAL MARITIME COMMISSION DECISIONS

U. S. Dept of Health and Human Services *see* SOCIAL SECURITY BULLETIN

U.S. Dept of Health and Human Services *see*
- CRIME AND DELINQUENCY ABSTRACTS
- SOCIAL SECURITY ADMINISTRATION, FEDERAL SECURITY AGENCY ANNUAL REPORTS
- SOCIAL SECURITY BOARD ANNUAL REPORTS
- UNEMPLOYMENT COMPENSATION AND INTERPRETATION SERVICE BENEFIT SERIES

U.S. Dept of Immigration. Senate Committee on the Judiciary *see* COMPARATIVE PRINT OF THE TEXTS OF THE IMMIGRATION AND NATURALIZATION ACT AND THE IMMIGRATION AND NATURALIZATION LAWS EXISTING PRIOR TO THE ENACTMENT OF P.L. 414, JUNE 27, 1952, 66 STAT. 163

U.S. Dept of Labor *see*
- ADMINISTRATIVE LAW JUDGES DECISIONS
- GROWTH OF LABOR LAW IN THE UNITED STATES

US Dept of State *see* TWO ASPECTS OF TRUSTEESHIP

U. S. Dept of Veterans' Affairs *see* VETERANS' ADMINISTRATION ANNUAL REPORTS

U.S. DIRECT TAX OF 1798: TAX LISTS FOR THE STATE OF PENNSYLVANIA / U.S. Internal Revenue Service – 24 rolls. M372. Printed guide – 1 – us Nat'l Archives [324]

U.S. District Court. California. Northern District *see* INDEX TO PRIVATE LAND GRANT CASES

U.S. District Court. California. Southern District *see* INDEX TO PRIVATE LAND GRANT CASES

U.S. District Court for the District of Columbia *see*
- U.S. VS GEORGE GORDON LIDDY, EVERETT HOWARD HUNT, JAMES W. MCCORD, BERNARD L. BARKER, EUGENIO R. MARTINEZ, FRANK A. STURGIS, VIRGILIO R. GONZALEZ
- U.S. VS JOHN B. CONNALLY AND JAKE JACOBSEN
- U.S. VS JOHN D. EHRLICHMAN, CHARLES W. COLSON, G. GORDON LIDDY, BERNARD L. BARKER, FELIPE DEDIEGO, EUGENIO R. MARTINEZ
- U.S. VS JOHN N. MITCHELL, HARRY R. HALDEMAN, JOHN D. EHRLICHMAN, ROBERT C. MARDIAN, KENNETH W. PARKINSON

U.S. District Court. Massachusetts *see* WHAT IS TREASON?

U.S. District Court. New Jersey *see* A CHARGE TO THE GRAND JURY IN THE DISTRICT COURT OF THE UNITED STATES FOR THE DISTRICT OF NEW JERSEY, APRIL 21, 1863

U.S. District Court of Ohio *see* OHIO FEDERAL DECISIONS

U.S. District Courts *see* TRIAL OF AARON BURR AND HERMAN BLENNERHASSET, 1808

U.S. District Courts. California. Northern and Southern Districts *see* INDEX BY COUNTY TO PRIVATE LAND GRANT CASES

U.S. District Courts, California, Northern District *see* RECORDS OF THE U.S. DISTRICT COURT...AND PREDECESSOR COURTS, 1851-1950

U.S. District Courts. District of Columbia *see*
- HABEAS CORPUS CASE RECORDS,1820-63, OF THE CIRCUIT COURT FOR THE DISTRICT OF COLUMBIA
- RECORDS...RELATING TO SLAVES,1851-63

U.S. District Courts. Eastern District of Louisiana *see* LAND CLAIMS CASE FILE

U.S. District Courts. Georgia *see* MINUTES..., 1790-1842, AND INDEX TO PLAINTIFFS AND DEFENDANTS..., 1790-1860

U.S. District Courts. New Jersey *see* RECORDS OF THE U.S. DISTRICT COURT...AND PREDECESSOR COURTS, 1790-1950

U.S. District Courts. North Carolina, Eastern District *see* CONFEDERATE PAPERS...1861-65

U.S. District Courts. Pennsylvania, Eastern District *see* RECORDS...CONTAINING STATEMENTS OF FACTS IN FORFEITURE CASES, 1792-1918

U.S. District Courts. South Carolina *see*
- ADMIRALTY FINAL RECORD BOOKS AND MINUTES..., 1790-1857
- MINUTES, CIRCUIT AND DISTRICT COURT..., 1789-1842, AND INDEX TO JUDGMENTS, CIRCUIT AND DISTRICT COURTS, 1792-1874
- PRE-FEDERAL ADMIRALTY COURT REPORTS, PROVINCE AND STATE OF SOUTH CAROLINA, 1716-89
- RECORD OF ADMISSIONS TO CITIZENSHIP. 1790-1906

U.S. District Courts. Southern District of Georgia *see* INDEX BOOKS, 1789-1928, AND MINUTES AND BENCH DOCKETS, 1789-1870

U.S. District Courts. Virginia, Eastern District *see* CASE PAPERS...1863-65, RELATING TO THE CONFISCATION OF PROPERTY

U.S. District of Columbia *see*
- MACARTHUR AND MACKEY'S REPORTS OF CASES IN THE DISTRICT OF COLUMBIA, 1879-1880
- MACARTHUR'S REPORTS OF CASES IN THE DISTRICT OF COLUMBIA, 1873-1879

UNITED STATES ECONOMIC ASSISTANCE TO INDONESIA / U.S. Agency for International Development – SE 6143 1. 1966 – 9 – ne IDC [324]

U.S. Economic Survey Team to Indonesia *see* INDONESIA: PERSPEKTIP DAN SARAN2 UNTUK BANTUAN EKONOMI AMERIKA SERIKAT KEPADA PRESIDEN

U.S. Embassy. Indonesia *see*
- BRIEFING ON INDONESIA. 'PREPARED FOR VISIT OF CONGRESSIONAL DELEGATIONS TO INDONESIA IN 1959'
- INDONESIAN EXPORTS' TRENDS; GEOGRAPHIC ORIGIN
- INDONESIAN PRESS REVIEW

U.S. Embassy. Tokyo, Japan *see*
- DAILY SUMMARY OF THE JAPANESE PRESS
- SUMMARIES OF SELECTED JAPANESE MAGAZINES

U.S. Embassy. United Arab Republic *see* DAILY REVIEW OF THE ARABIC PRESS

U.S. Emergency Court of Appeals *see* RECORDS AND BRIEFS.

U.S. Employee's Compensation Appeals Board *see* DECISIONS

U.S. Energy Research and Development Administration *see* ERDA ENERGY RESEARCH ABSTRACTS

U.S. Environmental Protection Agency *see*
- EPA JOURNAL
- LEGAL COMPILATION

U. S. Environmental Science Services Administration *see* PUBLICATIONS

U.S. ESPIONAGE AND INTELLIGENCE, 1947-1995 – (Printed guide £630) – £2,940.00 – uk Chadwyck [327]

US ET COUSTUMES DE LA MER / Cleirac, Estienne – Bourdeaux: Jacques Mongiron Millanges, 1661. SEM105P293 – 8mf – 9 – Can$18.00 – cn Bibl Nat [623]

LES US ET COUTUMES DE LA MER / Cleirac, Estienne – Rouen: Chez Jean Viret, 1671. SEM105P294 – 8mf – 9 – Can$18.00 – cn Bibl Nat [623]

U.S. European Theater. Office of the Judge Advocate General *see* HISTORY BRANCH OFFICE OF JUDGE ADVOCATE GENERAL WITH THE U.S. FORCES EUROPEAN THEATER, 18 JULY, 1942-1 NOVEMBER, 1945

UNITED STATES EXPLORING EXPEDITION DURING THE YEARS 1838-1842 UNDER THE COMMAND OF CHARLES WILKES – (V10: Geology, by J.D. Dana. B2835; 2. 1849. Sfr76.00; 8. v15: Botany. Phanerogams, by Asa Gray. B5938; 2. 1854. Sfr100.00; 8. v16: Botany. Cryptogamia. Filices incl. Lycopodiaceae and Hydropterides, by W. D. Brackenridge. B6514; 2. 1854. Sfr39.00; 8. v17: Algae, by J.W. Bailey and W.H. Harvey. B5466; 2. 1862. Sfr12.00; 0) – ne IDC [910]

U.S. Farm Credit Administration *see* RECORDS OF FARMERS' MARKETING AND PURCHASING COOPERATIVES

U.S. Federal Aviation Administration *see* SUMMARY OF AIRWORTHINESS DIRECTIVES, VOLS 1 AND 2

U.S. Federal Aviation Agency *see* PUBLICATIONS

U.S. Federal Bureau of Investigation *see*
- COINTELPRO
- COMMUNIST INFILTRATION OF THE SOUTHERN CHRISTIAN LEADERSHIP CONFERENCE
- FBI AMERICAN LEGION CONTACT PROGRAM
- FBI FILE: MIBURN (MISSISSIPPI BURNING)
- FBI FILE ON A. PHILIP RANDOLPH
- FBI FILE ON ALBERT EINSTEIN
- FBI FILE ON MALCOLM X
- FBI FILE ON OSAGE INDIAN MURDERS
- FBI FILE ON PAUL ROBESON
- FBI FILE ON ROY WILKINS
- FBI FILE ON THE AMERICAN CHURCHWOMEN KILLED IN EL SALVADOR, DECEMBER 1980
- FBI FILE ON THE ATLANTA CHILD MURDERS (ATKID)
- FBI FILE ON THE BLACK PANTHER PARTY, NORTH CAROLINA
- FBI FILE ON THE COMMITTEE FOR PUBLIC JUSTICE
- FBI FILE ON THE FIRE BOMBING AND SHOOTING AT KENT STATE UNIVERSITY
- FBI FILE ON THE HIGHLANDER FOLK SCHOOL
- FBI FILE ON THE HOUSE COMMITTEE ON UN-AMERICAN ACTIVITIES (HUAC)
- FBI FILE ON THE KU KLUX KLAN MURDER OF VIOLA LIUZZO
- FBI FILE ON THE NATIONAL ASSOCIATION FOR THE ADVANCEMENT OF COLORED PEOPLE (NAACP)
- FBI FILE ON THE NATIONAL NEGRO CONGRESS
- FBI FILE ON THE STUDENT NONVIOLENT COORDINATING COMMITTEE (SNCC)
- FBI FILE ON THE STUDENTS FOR A DEMOCRATIC SOCIETY AND THE WEATHERMAN UNDERGROUND ORGANIZATION
- FBI FILES ON THE REVEREND JESSE JACKSON
- FBI FILING AND RECORDS PROCEDURES
- FBI MANUALS OF INSTRUCTION, INVESTIGATIVE PROCEDURES, AND GUIDELINES, 1927-1978
- FEDERAL SURVEILLANCE OF AFRO-AMERICANS (1917-25)
- J. ROBERT OPPENHEIMER
- LAW ENFORCEMENT BULLETIN
- MARCUS GARVEY
- MARTIN LUTHER KING, JR.
- THE MARTIN LUTHER KING, JR. FBI FILE
- THE OFFICIAL AND CONFIDENTIAL FILES OF FBI DIRECTOR JOHN EDGAR HOOVER
- WATERGATE FBI INVESTIGATION FILE

U.S. Federal Communications Commission *see*
- ANNUAL REPORTS OF THE FEDERAL COMMUNICATIONS COMMISSION
- FCC RECORD
- FEDERAL COMMUNICATIONS COMMISSION REPORTS
- PUBLICATIONS
- REPORTS

U.S. Federal Court *see* FEDERAL CASES 1789-1879

U.S. Federal Extension Service *see* ANNUAL REPORTS OF EXTENSION SERVICE FIELD REPRESENTATIVES

U.S. Federal Field Committee for Development Planning in Alaska *see* ALASKA NATIVES AND THE LAND

U.S. Federal Mine Safety and Health Review Commission *see* FEDERAL MINE SAFETY AND HEALTH REVIEW COMMISSION DECISIONS AND ORDERS

U.S. Federal Power Commission *see*
- FEDERAL POWER COMMISSION ANNUAL REPORTS
- FEDERAL POWER COMMISSION OPINIONS AND DECISIONS

U. S. Federal Register Division *see* THE UNITED STATES GOVERNMENT MANUAL

U.S. Federal Reserve Board *see* FEDERAL RESERVE BULLETIN

U. S. Federal Reserve System *see*
- LEGISLATION, MAJOR SPEECHES AND ESSAYS, AND SPECIAL REPORTS, 1913-1960
- MINUTES OF MEETINGS OF THE FEDERAL OPEN MARKET COMMITTEE, 1923-1975
- MINUTES OF THE FEDERAL OPEN MARKET COMMITTEE, 1936-61, AND OF ITS EXECUTIVE COMMITTEE, 1936-55

U.S. Federal Reserve System *see* PAPERS OF THE FEDERAL RESERVE SYSTEM

U. S. Federal Services Impasses Panel *see* RELEASES

U.S. Federal Supply Service *see* PUBLICATIONS

U.S. Federal Trade Commission *see*
- ECONOMIC INVESTIGATIONS
- FEDERAL TRADE COMMISSION ANNUAL REPORTS
- FEDERAL TRADE COMMISSION DECISIONS, FINDINGS, ORDERS AND STIPULATIONS
- FEDERAL TRADE COMMISSION, STATUTES AND COURT DECISIONS
- HISTORY OF THE FEDERAL TRADE COMMISSION (1963-69)
- IN THE MATTER OF EXXON CORPORATION ET AL
- MINUTES OF MEETINGS OF THE COMMISSION, 1915-49
- PUBLICATIONS
- RECORDS
- REPORTS

U.S. Federal Works Agency *see* CHECKLIST OF HISTORICAL RECORDS SURVEY PUBLICATIONS, APRIL 1943

U.S. Federal Writers' Project and Library of Congress *see*
- SLAVE NARRATIVES
- SLAVE NARRATIVES: APPRAISAL SHEETS

U.S. Fish and Wildlife Service *see*
- "ALASKA FILE" OF THE OFFICE OF THE SECRETARY OF THE TREASURY, 1868-1903
- FISHERY BULLETINS
- INDEXES
- PUBLICATIONS

U.S. Food and Drug Administration *see*
- FDA HANDBOOK OF TOTAL DRUG QUALITY
- FOOD AND DRUG REVIEW
- REQUIREMENTS OF THE UNITED STATES FOOD, DRUG, AND COSMETIC ACT. REVISION

U.S. Foreign Broadcast Information Service *see*
- AREA EDITIONS: ASIA AND PACIFIC
- AREA EDITIONS: COMMUNIST CHINA
- AREA EDITIONS: EASTERN EUROPE
- AREA EDITIONS: LATIN AMERICA
- AREA EDITIONS: MIDDLE EAST AND AFRICA
- AREA EDITIONS: SOVIET UNION
- AREA EDITIONS: WESTERN EUROPE
- CYBERNETICS IN THE U.S.S.R
- DAILY REPORT: SUPPLEMENT
- DAILY REPORTS

U.S. FOREIGN POLICY AND THE EXPORT OF NUCLEAR TECHNOLOGY TO THE MIDDLE EAST: HEARINGS. / U.S. Congress. House. Committee on Foreign Affairs. Subcommitee on International Organizations and Movements – Washington, Govt. Print. Off., 1974. 333 p. LL-2360 – 1 – us L of C Photodup [340]

U.S. Forest Service *see*
- MINUTES OF THE SERVICE COMMITTEE OF THE FOREST SERVICE
- PUBLICATIONS

U.S. General Accounting Office *see*
- COMPTROLLER GENERAL DECISIONS
- PUBLICATIONS
- REPORTS ON U.S. DISBURSEMENTS TO THE INDIANS
- SELECTED RECORDS OF THE GENERAL ACCOUNTING OFFICE RELATING TO THE FREMONT EXPEDITIONS AND THE CALIFORNIA BATTALION, 1818-90
- SUMMARY OF UNITED STATES ASSISTANCE TO JORDAN

U.S. General Land Office *see*
- FIELD NOTES FROM SELECTED...TOWNSHIP SURVEYS
- FOREST LIEU SELECTION DOCKET REGISTERS
- TOWNSHIP PLATS OF SELECTED STATES

U. S. Geological Survey *see*
- CATALOG OF THE LIBRARY
- GEOLOGICAL SURVEY AND MARINE CORPS SURVEYS AND MAPS OF THE DOMINICAN REPUBLIC, 1919-23

- HISTORIC AMERICAN BUILDINGS SURVEY
- INFORMATION BULLETIN
- LIBRARY OF CONGRESS ANNUAL REPORTS
- LIBRARY OF CONGRESS CLASSIFICATION SCHEDULES
- LIBRARY OF CONGRESS CLASSIFICATION SCHEDULES, COMBINED WITH ADDITIONS AND CHANGES THROUGH 1989
- LIBRARY OF CONGRESS SUBJECT HEADINGS IN MICROFORM
- MONTHLY CHECKLIST OF STATE PUBLICATIONS
- THE MUSIC CATALOG
- NAME AUTHORITIES CUMULATIVE MICROFORM ED
- NATIONAL REGISTER OF MICROFORM MASTERS
- NATIONAL UNION CATALOG
- NATIONAL UNION CATALOG. AUDIOVISUAL MATERIALS: INDEXES AND REGISTERS
- NATIONAL UNION CATALOG: BOOKS. INDEXES AND REGISTERS
- NATIONAL UNION CATALOG: CARTOGRAPHIC MATERIALS. INDEXES AND REGISTER
- NATIONAL UNION CATALOG: PRE-1956 IMPRINTS
- NATIONAL UNION CATALOG: REGISTER OF ADDITIONAL LOCATIONS
- PUBLICATIONS
- SHELFLIST
- SHELFLIST OF SELECTED CLASSES OF PJ AND PL (AFRICAN LINGUISTICS AND LITERATURE) AS OF 2/82
- SUBJECT CATALOG
- U.S. POSTERS FROM WORLD WAR 2
- U.S. POSTERS FROM WORLD WAR I

U.S. Library of Congress *see* CHARLES FENDERICH

US Library of Congress *see*
- LIBRARY OF CONGRESS CLASSIFICATION SCHEDULES THROUGH 1993
- LIBRARY OF CONGRESS CLASSIFICATION SCHEDULES WITH ADDITIONS AND CHANGES THROUGH 1992

U.S. Library of Congress. European Division *see* RUSSIAN IMPERIAL GOVERNMENT PUBLICATIONS: COLLECTION..

U.S. Library of Congress. General Reference and Bibliography Division *see* NIGERIAN OFFICIAL PUBLICATIONS, 1869-1959

U.S. Library of Congress. Geography and Map Division *see*
- THE BIBLIOGRAPHY OF CARTOGRAPHY
- LAND OWNERSHIP MAPS

U.S. Library of Congress. Law Library *see*
- COLONIAL-HISPANIC LEGAL DOCUMENTS (18TH-19TH CENTURIES)
- INDEX TO LATIN AMERICAN LEGISLATION, 1950-1961
- SPANISH LEGAL DOCUMENTS (15TH-19TH CENTURIES)

U.S. Library of Congress. Legislative Reference Service *see*
- COMPULSORY LICENSING OF PATENTS: A LEGISLATIVE HISTORY
- EXPEDITING PATENT OFFICE PROCEDURE; LEGISLATIVE HISTORY
- PATENT OFFICE FEES: A LEGISLATIVE HISTORY
- SINGLE COURT OF PATENT OF PATENT APPEALS: A LEGISLATIVE HISTORY

U.S. Library of Congress. Legislative Reference Service Congressional Research Service *see* MAJOR STUDIES AND ISSUE BRIEFS OF THE LEGISLATIVE REFERENCE SERVICE/RESEARCH SERVICE: 1916-74

U.S. Library of Congress. Music Division *see*
- BOOKS CONCERNING MUSIC PRINTED BEFORE 1800
- BOOKS ON MUSIC AND SOUND RECORDINGS
- WOODWIND INSTRUCTION BOOKS (PRE-1830)

U.S. Library of Congress. Orientalia Division *see* SOUTHEAST ASIA SUBJECT CATALOG

U.S. Library of Congress. Prints and Photographs Division *see*
- ALFRED CHENEY JOHNSTON STUDIO PORTRAITS
- BRADY STUDIO CARTE-DE-VISITE PORTRAITS
- BRADY STUDIO CIVIL WAR VIEWS
- BRITISH POLITICAL AND SOCIAL CARTOONS
- CIVIL WAR DRAWINGS BY EDWIN FORBES
- CIVIL WAR RAILROAD ALBUM
- FAR EAST VIEWS
- FARM SECURITY ADMINISTRATION-OFFICE OF WAR INFORMATION COLLECTION
- GILBERT H. GROSVENOR COLLECTION OF PHOTOGRAPHS OF THE ALEXANDER GRAHAM BELL FAMILY
- "GROSSDEUTSCHLAND IM WELTGESCHEHEN."
- HERMANN GOERING ALBUMS
- "IM KAMPF UM DAS DRITTE REICH"
- KERN COUNTY SURVEY
- LAWRENCE AND HOUSEWORTH STEREO VIEWS
- MEXICAN CARTE-DE-VISITE ALBUM
- NATIONAL CHILD LABOR COMMITTEE COLLECTION
- P.H. EMERSON'S "LIFE AND LANDSCAPE ON THE NORFOLK BROADS."
- P.H. EMERSON'S "PICTURES ON EAST ANGLIAN LIFE."
- REICHSMINISTERIUM FUER VOLKSAUFKLAERUNG UND PROPAGANDA ALBUM
- TREASURY DEPARTMENT EMPLOYEE CARICATURES
- "TURKESTANSKII AL'BOM."
- U.S. POSTERS
- W. FRANK CLARK GLASS NEGATIVES
- W.E.B. DUBOIS ALBUMS
- WHEELER SURVEY STEREOSCOPIC VIEWS
- YUDIN COLLECTION DRAWINGS OF CHINESE SUBJECTS

U.S. Library of Congress. Rare Book and Special Collections Division *see* FRANCIS LONGE COLLECTION OF THEATRICAL WORKS

U.S. Life-Saving Service. Point Betsie Life Saving Station. Frankfort, Michigan *see* RECORDS

U.S. LOCAL HISTORY CATALOG / New York Public Library. Research Libraries – 1974. 20,600 cards on 2 reels – 1 – $165.00 export $200.00 – 0-8161-1285-1 – uk Hall [978]

U.S. LOCAL HISTORY CATALOG / New York Public Library. Research Libraries. Local History and Genealogy Division – 1974. 20,600 cards. 2 reels. ISBN 0-8161-1285-1 – 1 – $180.00 – uk Hall [978]

U.S. Marine Corps. Historical Division *see* HISTORY OF THE UNITED STATES MARINE CORPS

U.S. Marine Corps (Navy) *see*
- MUSTER ROLLS
- PUBLICATIONS

U.S. MARITIME COMMISSION, MARITIME ADMINISTRATION, FEDERAL MARITIME BOARD, FEDERAL MARITIME COMMISSION DECISIONS / U.S. Dept of Commerce – (Set listed under: Federal Maritime Commission) – v1-20. 1919-78 (all publ) – 9 – us L.L.M.C. [324]

U.S. MARITIME COMMISSION, MARITIME ADMINISTRATION, FEDERAL MARITIME BOARD, FEDERAL MARITIME COMMISSION DECISIONS *see*
- FEDERAL MARITIME ADMINISTRATION AND MARITIME SUBSIDY BOARD ANNUAL REPORTS
- FEDERAL MARITIME BOARD AND MARITIME ADMINISTRATION ANNUAL REPORTS

U.S. Military Academy *see* SELECTED DOCUMENTS RELATING TO BLACKS NOMINATED FOR APPOINTMENT TO THE U.S. MILITARY ACADEMY DURING THE 19TH CENTURY

U.S. MILITARY ACADEMY CADET APPLICATION PAPERS, 1805-66 / U.S. War Department. Adjutant General's Office – 242 rolls. M688. Printed guide – 1 – us Nat'l Archives [324]

U.S. Military Assistance Command. Vietnam *see*
- CHRONOLOGY OF EVENTS PERTAINING TO U.S. INVOLVEMENT IN THE WAR IN VIETNAM AND SOUTHEAST ASIA
- THE OBSERVER
- VIET CONG AND NORTH VIETNAMESE ARMY TACTICAL STUDIES AND DOCTRINE

U.S. Military Intelligence *see*
- ARGENTINA, 1918-41
- BIWEEKLY INTELLIGENCE SUMMARIES, 1928-38
- CHINA, 1911-41
- COMBAT ESTIMATES
- FRANCE, 1919-41
- GERMANY, 1919-41
- GERMANY, 1941-44
- ITALY, 1918-41
- JAPAN, 1918-41
- MEXICO, 1919-41
- THE SOVIET UNION, 1919-44
- SURVEILLANCE OF RADICALS IN THE UNITED STATES, 1917-41

U.S. MILITARY INTELLIGENCE REPORTS *see*
- GERMANY, 1919-41
- GERMANY, 1941-44

U.S. MILITARY USES OF SPACE, 1945-1991 – (With 2-vol printed guide & index £630.00) – 239mf – 9 – £2,940.00 – uk Chadwyck [327]

U.S. Mine Safety and Health Administration *see* UPDATA INDEX

U.S. MINERAL LANDS : LAWS GOVERNING THEIR OCCUPANCY AND DISPOSITION, WITH COURT DECISION / Copp, Henry N – Publ. by the compiler. 1v. 1881 – 6mf – 9 – $9.00 – LLMC 82-101-5 – us L.L.M.C. [340]

UNITED STATES MINERAL LANDS. / Copp, Henry Norris – Washington, DC 1881. 560p. LL-510 – 1 – us L of C Photodup [340]

UNITED STATES MINT : DIRECTOR'S ANNUAL REPORTS – 1909-80 – 9 – LLMC 90-374 – us L.L.M.C. [336]

U.S. MONTHLY INDEX OF RUSSIAN ACCESSIONS – v. 1-22, n. 5. 1948-1969 – 1,5,6 – us Princeton Micro [324]

THE UNITED STATES MONTHLY LAW MAGAZINE – (Lacking: v6) – v1-6. 1850-53 (all publ) – 11mf – 9 – $49.50 – LLMC 82-968 – us L.L.M.C. [073]

UNITED STATES MUSICAL REVIEW – v1-14. Sept 1867-1874 – 1 – 675.00 – us Opus [073]

U.S. National Advisory Committee on Aeronautics *see*
- ANNUAL REPORTS
- BIBLIOGRAPHY
- COMPLETE COLLECTION
- INDEXES
- TECHNICAL MEMORANDUMS

U.S. National Aeronautics and Space Administration *see*
- COLLECTION
- PUBLICATIONS
- TECHNICAL BRIEFS

U.S. National Agricultural Library *see* BIBLIOGRAPHY OF AGRICULTURE

UNITED STATES NATIONAL ARBORETUM VASCULAR PLANT TYPE AND CULTIVAR COLLECTION – (Includes index £73.00) – 38mf – 9 – £360.00 – uk Chadwyck [580]

U.S. National Archives *see*
- RECORDS OF THE CHILDREN'S BUREAU, 1912-1969
- RECORDS OF THE WAR RELOCATION AUTHORITY

U.S. National Archives and Library of Congress *see* ARMENIAN GENOCIDE IN THE U.S. ARCHIVES, 1915-1918

U. S. National Archives and Records Administration, Office of the Federal Register *see* CODE OF FEDERAL REGULATIONS

U.S. National Archives and Records Service *see*
- THE ARCHIVES OF THE U.S. GOVERNMENT: A DOCUMENTARY HISTORY, 1774-1934
- CODE OF FEDERAL REGULATIONS
- DISPOSAL REGISTERS
- EXAMPLES OF RECORDS IN THE NATIONAL ARCHIVES FREQUENTLY USED IN GENEALOGICAL RESEARCH
- THE FEDERAL REGISTER
- FINDING AIDS TO NATIONAL ARCHIVES PHOTOGRAPHS RELATING TO THE THIRD GERMAN REICH
- GUIDES TO GERMAN RECORDS MICROFILMED AT ALEXANDRIA
- GUIDES TO RECORDS OF THE ITALIAN ARMED FORCES
- HISTORICAL SKETCHES FOR JURISDICTIONAL AND SUBJECT HEADINGS USED FOR THE LETTERS RECEIVED BY THE OFFICE OF INDIAN AFFAIRS, 1824-80
- INDEX TO THE JOURNALS OF THE CONTINENTAL CONGRESS, 1774-1789
- INDEX TO THE PAPERS OF THE CONTINENTAL CONGRESS, 1774-1789
- A MICROFILM SUPPLEMENT TO THE TERRITORIAL PAPERS OF THE U.S.: WISCONSIN, 1836-48
- NATIONAL ARCHIVES PROCEDURE: A GENERAL SERVICES ADMINISTRATION HANDBOOK (1960)
- PUBLICATIONS
- RECORDS OF SPECIAL AGENTS FOR SECURING THE FLORIDA ARCHIVES, 1819-35
- SELECTED PHOTOGRAPHS OF CALVIN COOLIDGE, 1917-1943
- SELECTED PHOTOGRAPHS OF DWIGHT D. EISENHOWER, 1943-1961
- SELECTED PHOTOGRAPHS OF FRANKLIN D. ROOSEVELT, 1913-45
- SELECTED PHOTOGRAPHS OF HARRY S. TRUMAN, 1885-1953
- THE TERRITORIAL PAPERS OF THE U.S
- WEEKLY COMPILATIONS OF PRESIDENTIAL DOCUMENTS, 1965-69

U.S. National Board of Health *see* LETTERS RECEIVED BY THE NATIONAL BOARD OF HEALTH

U.S. National Bureau of Standards *see*
- JOURNAL OF RESEARCH
- PUBLICATIONS
- PUBLICATIONS INDEX
- SCIENTIFIC PAPERS
- TECHNOLOGIC PAPERS
- TECHNOLOGICAL PAPERS

U.S. National Commission on Law Observance and Enforcement *see* NATIONAL COMMISSION ON LAW OBSERVANCE AND ENFORCEMENT

THE U.S. NATIONAL ECONOMY / U.S. Department of the Treasury – (Pt 1: Wilson Administration-Hoover Administration (1916-33) ISBN 0-89093-666-8. $965.00; Pt 2: Roosevelt Administration-Truman Administration (1933-53) ISBN 0-89093-667-6. $3,660.00; Pt 3: Eisenhower Administration (1953-61) ISBN 0-89093-668-4. $1,250.00; Pt 4: Kennedy Administration-Johnson Administration (1961-69) ISBN 0-89093-669-2. $2,510.00; Pt 5: Nixon Administration-Ford Administration (1969-77) ISBN 0-89093-670-6. $3,660.00; Pt 6: Carter Administration (1977-81) ISBN 0-89093-671-4. $1,830.00. All with printed guides) – 1916-81. Unpublished documentary collections from the U.S. Department of the Treasury – 1 – $13,180.00 set – us UPA [336]

UNITED STATES NATIONAL HERBARIUM, SMITHSONIAN INSTITUTION VASCULAR PLANT TYPES / Smithsonian Institution – (Families can be purchased separately. Index £245.00) – 1,082mf – 9 – £5,040.00 – uk Chadwyck [580]

U.S. National Institute of Justice *see*
- AMERICAN BAR ASSOCIATION MODEL PROCUREMENT CODE SLIM
- DISPUTE RESOLUTION SLIM
- FAMILY VIOLENCE SLIM
- ISSUES IN CORRECTIONS SLIM

U.S. National Institute of Justice NCJRS *see*
- COMMISSION REPORTS (SLIM)
- CUMULATIVE DOCUMENT RETRIEVAL INDEX (DRI)
- CUMULATIVE INDEX TO THE NCJRS MICROFICHE COLLECTION
- NCJRS MICROFICHE COLLECTION
- POLICE RESEARCH (SLIM)
- PUBLICATIONS SLIM
- SEXUAL EXPLOITATION OF CHILDREN SLIM
- TERRORISM SLIM

U.S. National Institutes of Health *see* PUBLICATIONS

U. S. National Labor Relations Board *see*
- LABOR-MANAGEMENT RELATIONS ACT (TAFT-HARTLEY), 1947
- LABOR-MANAGEMENT REPORTING AND DISCLOSURE ACT, 1959 (LANDUM-GRIFFIN)
- NATIONAL LABOR RELATIONS ACT (WAGNER ACT), 1935

U.S. National Labor Relations Board *see*
- ANNUAL REPORTS OF THE NATIONAL LABOR RELATIONS BOARD
- DECISIONS AND ORDERS
- INDEX OF DECISIONS OF THE NLRB – CLASSIFIED INDEX OF THE NLRB DECISIONS AND RELATED COURT CASES
- NATIONAL LABOR BOARD DECISIONS
- NATIONAL LABOR RELATIONS BOARD
- NATIONAL LABOR RELATIONS BOARD DECISIONS
- PUBLICATIONS
- TABLE OF CASES DECIDED BY THE N.L.R.B

U.S. National Labor Relations Board *see*
- CLASSIFICATION OUTLINE WITH TOPICAL INDEX FOR DECISIONS OF THE N.L.R.B. AND RELATED COURT DECISIONS
- CLASSIFIED INDEX, REGIONAL DIRECTORS' DECISIONS IN REPRESENTATION PROCEEDINGS

U.S. National Library of Medicine *see* PUBLICATIONS

U.S. National Marine Fisheries Service (NOAA) *see*
- CIRCULARS
- FISHERY LEAFLETS
- FISHERY STATISTICS OF THE UNITED STATES
- INDEXES
- MARINE FISHERIES REVIEW
- PUBLICATIONS
- TECHNICAL REPORTS

U.S. National Mediation Board *see* NATIONAL MEDIATION BOARD ANNUAL REPORTS

U.S. National Monetary Commission *see*
- NATIONAL MONETARY COMMISSION PUBLICATIONS
- PUBLICATIONS

U.S. National Museum *see* PROCEEDINGS

U.S. National Ocean Survey *see* PUBLICATIONS

U.S. National Oceanic and Atmospheric Administration *see*
- COM CATALOG TO NOAA REPORTS
- NOAA
- PUBLICATIONS
- SPECIAL SCIENTIFIC REPORTS FISHERIES

U.S. National Railroad Adjustment Board *see*
- NATIONAL RAILROAD ADJUSTMENT BOARD, 1ST DIVISION AWARDS
- NATIONAL RAILROAD ADJUSTMENT BOARD, 2ND DIVISION AWARDS
- NATIONAL RAILROAD ADJUSTMENT BOARD, 3RD DIVISION AWARDS
- NATIONAL RAILROAD ADJUSTMENT BOARD, 4TH DIVISION AWARDS

U.S. National Recovery Administration *see*
- DOCUMENT SERIES..., 1933-36
- NRA'S "BLUE EAGLE," A WEEKLY NEWSPAPER, JUNE 11, 1934-MAY 17, 1935

U.S. National Resources Planning Board *see* REPORTS..., 1933-43

U.S. National Science Foundation *see* PUBLICATIONS

U.S. National Security Council *see*
- MINUTES OF MEETINGS OF THE NATIONAL SECURITY COUNCIL
- THE WAR IN VIETNAM

US. National Security Council *see* DOCUMENTS OF THE NATIONAL SECURITY COUNCIL, 1947-1977

U.S. National Technical Information Service *see*
- AM ENGINEERING DATA BASE IN ORDER BY COUNTY AND STATE
- AM ENGINEERING DATA BASE IN ORDER BY STATE
- AMATEUR MASTER FILE
- AMATEUR MASTER FILE SUPPLEMENT
- ARMY MANUALS & REGULATIONS INDEX (CONSOLIDATED INDEX OF ARMY PUBLICATIONS AND BLANK FORMS)
- CABLE TV STATION DISTRIBUTION FILE
- CALLSIGN INDEX TO NON-GOVERNMENT MASTER FREQUENCY DATA BASE
- COMMERCIAL MASTER FILE-RESTRICTED
- COMMON CARRIER LAND MOBILE BASE STATION CUMULATIVE STAFF STUDY LISTING
- COMMON CARRIER LAND MOBILE BASE STATIONS DATA BASE (SUPPLIERS)
- COMMON CARRIER MICROWAVE CONSTRUCTION PERMIT FILE
- COMMON CARRIER MICROWAVE PENDING APPLICATION DUMP
- COMMUNITY UNIT CABLE FULL RECORD
- DIRECTORY OF COMPUTER SOFTWARE
- DIRECTORY OF COMPUTERIZED DATAFILES
- DIRECTORY OF JAPANESE TECHNICAL RESOURCES
- EPA PESTICIDE LABEL FILE
- FCC TELEPHONE EQUIPMENT REGISTRATION LIST
- FM ENGINEERING DATA BASE IN ORDER BY CHANNEL AND LOCATION
- FM ENGINEERING DATA BASE IN ORDER BY LOCATION
- MANAGEMENT DATA LIST (ML), ML-MARINE CORPS
- MANAGEMENT DATA LIST (ML), ML-NAVY
- MASTER FREQUENCY DATA BASE (SERVICE GROUP CODE SEQUENCE)
- MICROWAVE LICENSES ISSUED
- RESTRICTED/COMMERCIAL OPERATOR HISTORY FILE
- STATE INDEX TO NON-GOVERNMENT MASTER FREQUENCY DATA BASE
- TOXIC SUBSTANCES CONTROL ACT TEST SUBMISSIONS DATABASE (TSCATS)
- TV TRANSLATORS ENGINEERING DATA BASE IN ORDER BY STATE, CHANNEL, CALL
- TV TRANSLATORS ENGINEERING DATA BASE IN ORDER BY STATE, CITY, CHANNEL

U.S. National Transportation Safety Board *see* NATIONAL TRANSPORTATION SAFETY BOARD DECISIONS

U.S. National War Labor Board *see* PAPERS

U.S. Naval Academy *see*
- LETTERS RECEIVED BY THE SUPERINTENDENT OF THE U.S. NAVAL ACADEMY
- LETTERS SENT BY THE SUPERINTENDENT OF THE U.S. NAVAL ACADEMY
- REGISTERS OF LETTERS RECEIVED AND LETTERS RECEIVED BY THE SUPERINTENDENT OF THE U.S. NAVAL ACADEMY
- U.S. NAVAL ACADEMY REGISTERS OF DELINQUENCIES

U.S. NAVAL ACADEMY REGISTERS OF DELINQUENCIES / U.S. Naval Academy – 1846-50, 1853-82. Academic and Conduct Records of Cadets, 1881-1908. M991 – 45r – 1 – us Nat'l Archives [355]

UNITED STATES NAVAL ADMINISTRATION OF THE TTPI / Richard, Dorothy E – Washington: Off of Chief of Naval Operations. 3v. 1957 – 29mf – 9 – $43.50 – LLMC 82-100F Title 15 – us L.L.M.C. [324]

U.S. Naval Department *see* COMPILATION OF COURT MARTIAL ORDERS, 1916-1937

U.S. Naval Institute *see*
- PROCEEDINGS

U. S. Naval Intelligence *see* GEOGRAPHICAL HANDBOOK: PALESTINE AND TRANSJORDAN

U. S. Naval Material Command *see* PUBLICATIONS

U. S. Naval Observatory *see* CORRESPONDENCE OF THE U.S. NAVAL ASTRONOMICAL EXPEDITION TO THE SOUTHERN HEMISPHERE, 1846-61

U. S. Naval Observatory. Washington, DC *see* CATALOG OF THE LIBRARY

U.S. Naval Oceanographic Office *see* PUBLICATIONS

U.S. Navy *see*
- ANNUAL REPORTS..., 1822-66
- ANNUAL REPORTS OF FLEETS AND TASK FORCES OF THE U.S. NAVY
- COMMANDER IN CHIEF, U.S. FLEET, BATTLE EXPERIENCES, DEC. 1941-AUG. 1945
- INDEXES AND REGISTER TO THE CORRESPONDENCE OF THE OFFICE OF THE CHIEF OF NAVAL OPERATIONS AND THE OFFICE OF THE SECRETARY OF THE NAVY
- INTELLIGENCE DIVISION, OPNAV, COMBAT NARRATIVES
- NAVAL ADMINISTRATIVE HISTORIES OF WORLD WAR 2
- NAVAL WAR COLLEGE, BATTLE ANALYSIS SERIES
- NAVY DEPARTMENT GENERAL ORDERS AND CIRCULARS
- OFFICIAL RECORDS OF THE UNION AND CONFEDERATE NAVIES, 1861-65
- PUBLICATIONS
- RECORDS RELATING TO U.S. NAVY FLEET PROBLEMS, 1-22
- REPORTS OF THE U.S. NAVAL TECHNICAL MISSION TO JAPAN, 1945-46
- SELECTED NAVAL ATTACHE REPORTS RELATING TO THE WORLD CRISIS
- U.S. SUBMARINE WAR PATROL REPORTS AND RELATED DOCUMENTS, 1941-1945
- THE WAVES

U.S. NAVY ACTION AND OPERATIONAL REPORTS FROM WORLD WAR 2, PACIFIC THEATER – (Pt 1, CINCPAC: Commander-in-Chief Pacific Area: 16r. $1,760.00. ISBN 1-55655-190-8; Pt 2, Third Fleet and Third Fleet Carrier Task Forces: 16r. $1,760.00. ISBN 1-55655-191-6; Pt 3, Fifth Fleet and Fifth Fleet Carrier Task Forces: 12r. $1,320.00. ISBN 1-55655-192-4; Include printed guides) – 1 – us UPA [355]

U.S. Navy. Bureau of Naval Personnel *see*
- ABSTRACTS OF SERVICE RECORDS OF NAVAL OFFICERS ("RECORDS OF OFFICERS"), 1798-1893
- INDEX TO OFFICERS' JACKETS, 1913-25 (OFFICERS DIRECTORY)
- INDEX TO RENDEZVOUS REPORTS, ARMED GUARD PERSONNEL, 1917-20
- INDEX TO RENDEZVOUS REPORTS, BEFORE AND AFTER THE CIVIL WAR (1846-61; 1865-84)
- INDEX TO RENDEZVOUS REPORTS, CIVIL WAR, 1861-65
- INDEX TO RENDEZVOUS REPORTS, NAVAL AUXILIARY SERVICE, 1846-84

U.S. Navy. Chief of Naval OperationsOffice of the Secretary *see* SECRET AND CONFIDENTIAL CORRESPONDENCE..., 1919-27

U.S. Navy. Eastern Sea Frontier. Office of the Commander *see* WAR DIARY, EASTERN SEA FRONTIER

U.S. Navy. General Board *see* HEARINGS OF THE GENERAL BOARD OF THE U.S. NAVY, 1917-50

U.S. Navy. Gulf Sea Frontier. Office of the Commander *see* WAR DIARY, GULF SEA FRONTIER

U.S. Navy. Historical Center. Operational Archives Branch *see* ADMIRAL NIMITZ COMMAND SUMMARY

U.S. Navy. Judge Advocate General *see* RECORDS OF GENERAL COURTS-MARTIAL AND COURTS OF INQUIRY OF THE NAVY DEPT., 1799-1867

U.S. NAVY MEDICINE – (1979- 5,6,9) – 1970- – 1 – us UMI [610]

U.S. Navy. Office of Naval Records and Library *see*
- ANNUAL REPORTS OF THE GOVERNORS OF GUAM, 1901-41
- AREA FILE OF THE NAVAL RECORDS COLLECTION, 1775-1910
- CORRESPONDENCE OF THE SECRETARY OF THE NAVY RELATING TO AFRICAN COLONIZATION, 1819-1844
- HISTORY OF THE BOSTON NAVY YARD, 1797-1874
- JOURNAL OF JOHN LANDRETH ON AN EXPEDITION TO THE GULF COAST, NOV. 15, 1818-MAY 19, 1819
- JOURNAL OF LT. CHARLES GAUNTT (U.S.S. MACEDONIAN), JULY 29, 1818-JUNE 18, 1821
- JOURNAL OF LT. COMMANDER WILLIAM B. CUSHING, MAY 1961-FEB 1965
- JOURNAL OF LT. THOMAS A. DORIN (U.S.S. BRANDYWINE AND U.S.S. FALMOUTH), 1826-34
- LETTERS RECEIVED BY THE SECRETARY OF THE NAVY: CAPTAINS' LETTERS, 1805-61; 1866-85
- LETTERS RECEIVED BY THE SECRETARY OF THE NAVY FROM:
- LETTERS RECEIVED BY THE SECRETARY OF THE NAVY: MISCELLANEOUS LETTERS, 1801-84
- LETTERS SENT BY THE SECRETARY OF THE NAVY TO:
- LOG OF ARCTIC STEAMER JEANETTE
- LOG OF THE U.S.S. NAUTILUS, AUG. 1-31, 1958
- MISCELLANEOUS LETTERS SENT BY THE SECRETARY OF THE NAVY, 1798-1886
- PAPERS OF STEPHEN C. ROWAN, 1826-90
- PRIVATE JOURNALS OF COMMODORE M.C. PERRY, 1853-54
- RECORDS RELATING TO THE U.S. SURVEYING EXPEDITION TO THE NORTH PACIFIC OCEAN, 1852-63

U.S. Navy. Office of the Secretary *see*
- ANNUAL REPORTS OF THE SECRETARY OF THE NAVY, 1821-1901
- INDEXES AND SUBJECT CARDS TO THE SECRET AND CONFIDENTIAL CORRESPONDENCE OF THE SECRETARY..., MAR 1917-JUL 1919
- NAME AND SUBJECT INDEX TO THE GENERAL CORRESPONDENCE OF THE OFFICE OF THE SECRETARY OF THE NAVY

U.S. Navy. Pacific Ocean Area. Intelligence Center *see* MILITARY INTELLIGENCE IN THE PACIFIC, 1942-46

U.S. NEWS AND WORLD REPORT – (v62- 1967- 5,6; v68- 1970- 9) – v1- 1933- – 1 – us UMI [073]

U.S. NEWS AND WORLD REPORT. INDEX – v. 83-. 1977- – 9 – us UMI [073]

U.S. NUCLEAR HISTORY : NUCLEAR ARMS AND POLITICS IN THE MISSILE AGE, 1955-1968 – (With guide £630) – £2,940.00 – uk Chadwyck [327]

U.S. NUCLEAR NON-PROLIFERATION, 1945-1991 – (With 2-vol printed guide & index £630.00) – 448mf – 9 – £2,940.00 – uk Chadwyck [327]

U.S. Nuclear Regulatory Commission *see*
- ATOMIC ENERGY COMMISSION ANNUAL REPORTS
- HEARINGS
- NUCLEAR REGULATORY COMMISSION OPINIONS AND DECISIONS
- PUBLICATIONS

U.S. Nuclear Regulatory Commission *see* ATOMIC ENERGY COMMISSION REPORTS

U.S. Nuclear Regulatory Commission, et al *see* NUCLEAR ENERGY

THE U.S. OCCUPATION OF GERMANY : EDUCATIONAL REFORM, 1945-49 – (Guide only: $215.00. ISBN 1-55655-384-6) – 360mf – 9 – $2,190.00 – 1-55655-383-8 – us UPA [350]

U.S. Occupational Safety and Health Administration *see* PUBLICATIONS

U.S. Occupational Safety and Health Review Commission *see* OCCUPATIONAL SAFETY AND HEALTH REVIEW COMMISSION DECISIONS AND REPORTS

THE UNITED STATES OF AMERICA : A STUDY IN INTERNATIONAL ORGANIZATION / Scott, James Brown – New York: Oxford UP, American Branch, 1920 – 7mf – 9 – $10.50 – LLMC 95-005 – us L.L.M.C. [323]

UNITED STATES OF AMERICA : INDEX OF BOOKS AND ARTICLES IN THE RUSSIAN LANGUAGE ON CONTEMPORARY POLITICAL SITUATION, ECONOMY, CULTURE, GEOGRAPHY, AND HISTORY OF THE USA, 1968-84 – $220.00 – 1-55655-285-8 – us UPA [300]

UNITED STATES OF AMERICA TODAY *see* USA TODAY

U.S. Office of Censorship *see* HISTORY OF THE OFFICE OF CENSORSHIP

U.S. Office of Civil Affairs *see* CORRESPONDENCE OF THE OFFICE OF CIVIL AFAIRS IN THE DEPARTMENT OF TEXAS

U.S. Office of Education *see* PUBLICATIONS

U.S. Office of Explorations and Surveys *see* CORRESPONDENCE...CONCERNING ISSAC STEVENS' SURVEY OF A NORTHERN ROUTE FOR THE PACIFIC R.R., 1853-61

U.S. Office of Government Reports *see*
- MINUTES OF THE EXECUTIVE COUNCIL, JULY 11, 1933-NOV. 13, 1934
- PROCEEDINGS OF THE NATIONAL EMERGENCY COUNCIL, DEC. 19, 1933-APRIL 28, 1936

U.S. Office of International Regional Economics *see* OVERSEAS BUSINESS REPORTS

U.S. Office of Management and Budget *see*
- BUDGET OF THE UNITED STATES GOVERNMENT
- BUDGET OF THE UNITED STATES GOVERNMENT. APPENDIX

U.S. Office of Price Administration *see* STUDIES AND REPORTS..., 1941-46

U.S. Office of Price Stabilization *see* DEFENSE HISTORY PROGRAM STUDIES PREPARED DURING THE KOREAN WAR PERIOD

U.S. Office of Public Buildings and Grounds *see* RECORDS OF THE DI OF COLUMBIA COMMISSIONERS AND OF THE OFFICES CONCERNED WITH PUBLIC BUILDINGS, 1791-1867

U.S. Office of Scientific Research and Development *see* REPORTS

U.S. Office of Strategic Services *see*
- AFRICA: 1941-61
- CHINA AND INDIA
- EUROPE, 1950-61
- FOREIGN NATIONALITIES BRANCH FILES, 1942-45
- GERMANY AND ITS OCCUPIED TERRITORIES DURING WORLD WAR 2
- JAPAN AND ITS OCCUPIED TERRITORIES DURING WORLD WAR 2
- JAPAN, KOREA, SOUTHEAST ASIA AND THE FAR EAST GENERALLY
- LATIN AMERICAN: 1941-61
- THE MIDDLE EAST
- OSS/LONDON
- POSTWAR EUROPE
- POSTWAR JAPAN, KOREA AND SOUTHEAST ASIA
- SERIES: OSS/STATE DEPT. INTELLIGENCE AND RESEARCH REPORTS
- SOVIET UNION

U.S. Office of the Chief of Engineers *see*
- CORRESPONDENCE ("TOP SECRET") OF THE MANHATTAN ENGINEER DISTRICT, 1942-1946
- HARRISON-BUNDY FILES RELATING TO THE DEVELOPMENT OF THE ATOMIC BOMB, 1942-1946
- LETTERS SENT BY THE CHIEF OF ENGINEERS, 1812-1869

U.S. Office of the Chief of Military History *see*
- BIOGRAPHICAL SKETCHES OF CHINESE COMMUNIST MILITARY LEADERS
- A BRIEF HISTORY OF THE REPUBLIC OF CHINA ARMED FORCES
- A CHRONOLOGY OF IMPORTANT MILITARY EVENTS IN REPUBLICAN CHINA, 1924-1950, PART 1, 1924-1928
- CIVIL WAR IN CHINA, 1945-1950
- HISTORY OF SINO-JAPANESE WAR
- MILITARY CAMPAIGNS OF CHINA: 1924-1950
- ORGANIZATIONAL CHANGES IN THE CHINESE ARMY, 1895-1950
- PLA UNIT HISTORY
- THE POLITICAL DYNAMICS OF THE CHINESE MILITARY ELITE, PART 2, THE ROLE OF THE MILITARY ELITE IN THE CULTURAL REVOLUTION (1966-1968)
- STUDENT DIRECTORY OF THE FIRST AND SECOND INFANTRY BATTALIONS OF THE TWENTY-FIRST CLASS OF THE (NATIONALIST) CHINESE MILITARY ACADEMY

U.S. Office of the Federal Register *see* PUBLICATIONS

U.S. Office of the Inspector General *see* INSPECTION REPORTS OF THE OFFICE OF THE INSPECTOR GENERAL

U.S. Office of the Provost Marshal General *see* HISTORY OF MILITARY GOVERNMENT TRAINING

U.S. Office of the Quartermaster General *see*
- LETTERS, ORDERS FOR PAY, ACCOUNTS, RECEIPTS, AND OTHER SUPPLY RECORDS CONCERNING WEAPONS AND MILITARY STORES
- LETTERS SENT BY THE OFFICE OF THE QUARTERMASTER GENERAL, MAIN SERIES

U.S. Office of War Information.Overseas Picture Division. Washington Section *see* WRITTEN RECORDS

THE UNITED STATES OLYMPIC ACADEMY – (Individual titles also listed separately) – 1977-89 – Pts 1-15 incl Pt 10 selections 1 + 2 – 9 – $200.00 coll – us Microform Publ [790]

UNITED STATES OLYMPIC ACADEMY *see*
- COMPENDIUM OF THE SPEECHES PRESENTED BY EDUCATORS, OLYMPIC CHAMPIONS, ADMINISTRATORS, AND AVERY BRUNDAGE AT THE INTERNATIONAL OLYMPIC ACADEMY 1961-1985
- EDUCATING FOR A BETTER WORLD
- EXPANDING OLYMPIC HORIZONS
- GOLD OR LAUREL
- OLYMPIC EDUCATION
- THE OLYMPIC IDEAL
- OLYMPIC USA
- THE OLYMPICS
- OLYMPISM
- OLYMPISM, THE OLYMPIC GAMES AND THE WORLDWIDE OLYMPIC MOVEMENT
- PERSPECTIVES OF THE OLYMPIC GAMES
- PROCEEDINGS, UNITED STATES OLYMPIC ACADEMY 12
- PURPOSES, PRINCIPLES AND CONTRADICTIONS OF THE OLYMPIC MOVEMENT
- THE SPIRIT OF SPORT
- SPORT AND OLYMPISM
- UNITED STATES OLYMPIC COMMITTEE, UNITED STATES OLYMPIC ACADEMY

UNITED STATES OLYMPIC COMMITTEE, UNITED STATES OLYMPIC ACADEMY : A COLLECTION OF 23 REPRESENTATIVE PRESENTATIONS AT USOAS 1-9: A SOUVENIR PREPARED FOR THE CELEBRATION OF USOA 10 AT COLORADO SPRINGS, JUNE 10-14, 1986 – (Series: United States Olympic Academy, 10 Selections 1) – Colorado Springs, 1986 – 2mf – 9 – $8.00 – us Microform Publ [790]

U.S. Operations Mission to Indonesia *see*
- AGRICULTURAL EXTENSION AND AGRICULTURAL RESEARCH, INDONESIA; REPORT FOR YEARS 1951-1956
- GOOD HEALTH TO INDONESIA; REPORT OF JOINT REVIEW OF NEEDS OF THE PHARMACEUTICAL INDUSTRY OF INDONESIA
- HIGHER EDUCATION IN INDONESIA
- THE ICA AGRICULTURAL ASSISTANCE PROGRAM IN INDONESIA,BY LAWRENCE A. BEERY. SE 5340/1. 1959
- ICA ASSISTED PROJECTS WITHIN TRAVELING DISTANCE OF DJAKARTA
- INDONESIA AGRICULTURAL PROGRAM, 1951-1956
- PARTIAL REPORT ON JOINT ICA AGRICULTURAL PROGRAMS IN INDONESIA, 1957-1959
- PORT INFORMATION
- REPORT OF A JOINT REVIEW OF NEEDS OF THE MARITIME INDUSTRY OF INDONESIA
- REPORT ON INDUSTRIAL DEVELOPMENT FOR INDONESIA,BY RALF W. DUNKLE. SE 11,599/1. 1959
- SUMMARY OF AGRICULTURE ACTIVITIES

U.S. Operations Mission to Indonesia. Agriculture Division *see* REPORTS AND DOCUMENTS, DJAKARTA

U. S. Operations Mission to Morocco *see* THREE YEARS OF ECONOMIC AND TECHNICAL COOPERATION

U.S. Operations Mission to the Philippines *see* PHILIPPINES AGRICULTURAL LAND TENURE STUDY

UNITED STATES PATENT CLASSIFICATION DEFINITIONS / U. S. Patent Office – (Formerly: Classification Definitions (Patents)) – Dec 1994. Basic full set of definitions and quarterly sets of updated definitions for an indeterminate periods – 9 – $167.00y in US $208.75 outside – S-N 903-004-00000-2. Sub-list ID-CLDF – us Gov't Printing [324]

U. S. Patent Office *see* UNITED STATES PATENT CLASSIFICATION DEFINITIONS

U.S. Patent Office *see*
- INDEX OF PATENTS
- INDEX OF TRADEMARKS. 1927-1971
- OFFICIAL GAZETTE
- OFFICIAL GAZETTE: TRADEMARKS
- OFFICIAL GAZETTE-TRADEMARKS
- PATENT DRAWINGS, 1792-1833
- PUBLICATIONS

U.S. Patent Office. Commissioner *see* DECISIONS

UNITED STATES PATENTS, TRADE MARKS, DESIGNS AND COPYRIGHTS / Richards & Company. New York – 2nd ed. New York: Richards, 1896. 145p. LL-1560 – 1 – us L of C Photodup [340]

THE U.S. PLAYS OSTRICH – N.Y., 193? Fiche W1327. (Blodgett Collection of Spanish Civil War Pamphlets) – 9 – us H.U. College Libr [946]

U.S. Post Office *see*
- LISTS OF U.S. POST OFFICES
- RECORD OF APPOINTMENT OF POSTMASTERS, OCTOBER 1789-1832

U.S. Post Office Department. Records *see* LETTERS SENT BY THE POSTMASTER GENERAL, 1789-1836

U.S. Postal Service *see* SOLICITOR OF THE POST OFFICE OPINIONS

U.S. POSTERS / U.S. Library of Congress. Prints and Photographs Division – 7500 posters by U.S. artists, the Library's catalogued holdings as of 1976. 12 reels. P&P31, 34, and 35 – 1 – 23.00r – us L of C Photodup [080]

U.S. POSTERS FROM WORLD WAR 2 / U.S. Library of Congress – 1 – $12.00 – us L of C Photodup [977]

U.S. POSTERS FROM WORLD WAR I / U.S. Library of Congress – 1 – 15.00 – us L of C Photodup [977]

U. S. President *see*
- EXECUTIVE ORDER
- EXECUTIVE ORDERS
- MESSAGES BETWEEN FRANKLIN D. ROOSEVELT AND WINSTON S. CHURCHILL
- PRESIDENTIAL EXECUTIVE ORDERS
- PRESIDENTIAL PROCLAMATIONS
- PRESS CONFERENCES OF FRANKLIN D. ROOSEVELT
- PRESS RELEASES

U.S. President *see* PAPERS OF THE PRESIDENT'S MEDIATION COMMISSION, 1917-19

U.S. President *see*
- MESSAGE TRANSMITTING DRAFT OF PROPOSED LEGISLATION TO APPROVE THE "COMPACT OF FREE ASSOCIATION"
- MESSAGE TRANSMITTING HIS CERTIFICATION OF APPROVAL OF THE COMPACT OF FREE ASSOCIATION BETWEEN THE U.S. AND PALAU
- MESSAGE TRANSMITTING PROPOSED LEGISLATION TO APPROVE THE COMPACT OF FREE ASSOCIATION WITH THE FEDERATED STATES OF MICRONESIA AND THE MARSHALL ISLANDS
- PROCLAMATION OF THE U.S. PRESIDENT PLACING INTO FULL FORCE AND EFFECT THE COVENANT WITH THE COMMONWEALTH OF THE NORTHERN MARIANA ISLANDS, AND THE COMPACTS OF FREE ASSOCIATION WITH THE FEDERATED STATES OF MICRONESIA AND THE REPUBLIC OF THE MARSHALL ISLANDS

U.S. President. Commission on the Assassination of President Kennedy *see* NUMBERED DOCUMENTS.

U.S. President. Commission on the Assassination of President Kennedy (Warren Commission) *see* HEARINGS

U.S. President's Commission on the Assassination of President Kennedy *see* HEARINGS AND REPORTS

U.S. Prisoner of War Operations Division *see* HISTORICAL MONOGRAPH: PRISONER OF WAR OPERATIONS DIVISION, OFFICE OF THE PROVOST MARSHAL GENERAL

U.S. Provost Marshal General's Bureau *see* HISTORICAL REPORTS OF THE STATE ACTING ASSISTANT PROVOST MARSHALS GENERAL AND DISTRICT PROVOST MARSHALS, 1865

U.S. Public Health Service *see*
- NATIONAL NEGRO HEALTH NEWS
- PUBLICATIONS
- SUICIDE AMONG THE AMERICAN INDIANS
- TO THE FIRST AMERICANS

U.S. Public Health Service. Surgeon General *see* HIGH SCHOOLS AND SEX EDUCATION

U.S. Public Land Law Review Commission *see* ONE THIRD OF THE NATION'S LAND: A REPORT TO THE PRESIDENT AND TO THE CONGRESS

U.S. Railroad Labor Board *see* RAILROAD LABOR BOARD DECISIONS

U.S. Register of the Treasury *see* DAY BOOK OF THE REGISTER'S OFFICE OF THE TREASURY, 1789-91

UNITED STATES REPORTS – v1- 1754- 1; v375- 5,6; v423- 9 – us UMI [324]

U.S. REPORTS ON MICROFICHE : RETROSPECTIVE COLLECTION / U.S. Supreme Court – (Official compilation of supreme court decisions and orders. Coll is also available in multiyear subsets) – v1-501. 1790-1990 – 9 – $8,280.00 set – us CIS [340]

U.S. REVOLUTIONARY WAR BOUNTY LAND WARRANTS USED IN THE U.S. MILITARY DISTRICT OF OHIO AND RELATED PAPERS / U.S. Bureau of Land Management – Acts of 1788, 1803, and 1806. 16 rolls. M829 – 1 – us Nat'l Archives [324]

U.S. Sanitary Commission *see* U.S. SANITARY COMMISSION DOCUMENTS AND BULLETINS, 1861-1865

U.S. SANITARY COMMISSION DOCUMENTS AND BULLETINS, 1861-1865 / U.S. Sanitary Commission – From the British Library of Political and Economic Science (London) – 4r – 1 – £130.00 – uk Altair [360]

UNITED STATES SANITARY COMMISSION RECORDS. SERIES 1: MEDICAL COMMITTEE ARCHIVES, 1861-1865, AND SERIES 7: STATISTICAL BUREAU ARCHIVES, CAMP INSPECTION RECORDS, 1861-1865 : FROM THE HOLDINGS OF THE RARE BOOKS AND MANUSCRIPTS DIVISION CENTER FOR THE HUMANITIES, THE NEW YORK PUBLIC LIBRARY, ASTOR, LENOX, AND TILDEN FOUNDATIONS – (With Guide) – 1997 – ca 31r – 1 – ca $2,635.00 – S3357 – us Scholarly Res [350]

U.S. Secretary of State *see* RECORDS OF THE SECRETARY OF STATE'S STAFF COMMITTEE

U.S. Secretary of the Navy *see* GENERAL AND SPECIAL INDEXES TO THE GENERAL CORRESPONDENCE OF THE OFFICE OF THE SECRETARY OF THE NAVY

U.S. Secretary of War *see* TELEGRAMS COLLECTED BY THE OFFICE OF THE SECRETARY OF WAR

U.S. Securities and Excahnge Commission *see* SECURITIES ACT OF 1933 RELEASES

U. S. Securities and Exchange Commission *see* THE SEC RELEASE SERIES PRECEDING THE SEC DOCKET

U.S. Securities and Exchange Commission *see*
- ACCOUNTING SERIES
- ACCOUNTING SERIES RELEASES
- ANNUAL AND QUARTERLY CORPORATE REPORTS
- ASIAN DEVELOPMENT BANK ACT. RELEASE NO. 1, DEC. 18, 1967
- BRETTON WOODS AGREEMENT ACT. RELEASE NUMBER 1-2, JAN. 9, 1950-JAN. 19, 1955
- CORPORATE REORGANIZATION. 1-312, AUG. 11, 1938-JULY 12, 1972
- CORPORATE REORGANIZATION RELEASES
- HOLDING COMPANIES ACT OF 1935 RELEASES
- HOLDING COMPANY ACT OF 1935. SEP 1935-JAN 1973
- INTER-AMERICAN DEVELOPMENT BANK ACT. RELEASE NUMBER 1, OCT. 25, 1960
- INVESTMENT ADVISERS ACT OF 1940 RELEASES
- INVESTMENT AND ADVISORS ACT OF 1940. RELEASE NUMBER 1-358, OCT. 7, 1940-JAN. 22, 1973
- INVESTMENT COMPANY ACT OF 1940. RELEASE NUMBER 1-7639, SEPT. 23, 1940-JAN. 26, 1973
- INVESTMENT COMPANY ACT OF 1940 RELEASES
- LITIGATION. RELEASE NUMBER 1-5713, AUG. 5, 1942-JAN. 24, 1973
- LITIGATION RELEASES
- MONOPOLY STUDY RELEASES
- NO-ACTION AND INTERPRETATIVE LETTERS
- OFFICIAL SUMMARY OF STOCK TRANSACTIONS AND HOLDINGS
- PROTECTIVE AND REORGANIZATION COMMITTEES REPORTS
- PUBLICATIONS
- RELEASES ISSUED BY THE U.S. SECURITIES AND EXCHANGE COMMISSION, APRIL 2, 1973-DECEMBER 31, 1973
- RELEASES ISSUED IN SERIES BY THE U.S. SECURITIES AND EXCHANGE COMMISSION, 1933-1976
- REPORTS
- SEC DOCKET
- THE SEC DOCKET
- SECURITIES ACT OF 1933. RELEASE NUMBER 1-5359, MAY 27, 1933-JAN. 26, 1973
- SECURITIES AND EXCHANGE COMMISSION ANNUAL REPORTS
- SECURITIES AND EXCHANGE COMMISSION DECISIONS AND REPORTS
- SECURITIES EXCHANGE ACT OF 1934. RELEASE NUMBER 1-9984, AUG. 13, 1934-FEB. 2, 1973
- SECURITIES EXCHANGE ACT OF 1934 RELEASES
- SECURITIES INVESTOR PROTECTION ACT OF 1970. RELEASE NUMBER 1-2, DEC. 22, 1971-JUN. 24, 1973
- SPECIAL MARKET STUDY. RELEASE NUMBER 1-41, DEC. 19, 1961-NOV. 8, 1963
- STATISTICAL SERIES. RELEASE NUMBER 1-2635, AUG. 12, 1937-JAN. 31, 1973
- SURVEY SERIES. RELEASE NUMBER 1-161, JULY 31, 1940-AUG. 3, 1949
- TRUST INDENTURE ACT OF 1939. RELEASE NUMBER 1-336, JAN. 23, 1940-JAN. 19, 1973
- TRUST INDENTURE ACT OF 1939 RELEASES
- U SERIES. RELEASE U1-441, SEPT. 18, 1940-APR. 2, 1973

U.S. Securities and Exchange Commission. Office of the General Counsel *see* SECURITY AND EXCHANGE COMMISSION JUDICIAL DECISIONS

UNITED STATES SECURITIES AND EXCHANGE COMMISSION RELEASES – 1933-1973 – 9 – $3,200.00 set – us Hein [332]

U.S. Select Commission on Immigration and Refugee Policy *see* PAPERS

U.S. Selective Service System *see*
- MONOGRAPH SERIES; HISTORICAL AND OPERATIONAL BACKGROUND OF THE SELEC. SERV. SYS. IN THE U.S
- SEMIANNUAL REPORT OF THE DIRECTOR OF THE SELECTIVE SERVICE SYSTEM

U.S. Senate *see*
- BILL BOOKS OF THE U.S. SENATE, 1795-1845
- CIS U.S. SENATE EXECUTIVE DOCUMENTS AND REPORTS ON MICROFICHE
- ENGROSSED BILLS AND RESOLUTIONS OF THE U.S. SENATE, 1789-1817
- JOURNAL OF THE EXECUTIVE PROCEEDINGS OF THE U.S. SENATE, 1789-1823
- JOURNAL OF THE IMPEACHMENT PROCEEDINGS BEFORE THE U.S. SENATE, 1798-1805
- JOURNAL OF THE LEGISLATIVE PROCEEDINGS OF THE U.S. SENATE, 1789-1817
- JOURNAL OF THE SECRETARY OF THE SENATE, 1789-1845
- RECORDS OF THE SENATE SELECT COMMITTEE THAT INVESTIGATED JOHN BROWN'S RAID AT HARPER'S FERRY
- REGISTER OF CREDENTIALS OF U.S. SENATORS, 1789-1821
- REGISTERS OF DOCUMENTS PRESENTED TO THE U.S. SENATE, 1814-1828
- REPORTS OF THE IMMIGRATION COMMISSION, 1907-1910
- TRANSCRIBED REPORTS AND COMMUNICATIONS TRANSMITTED BY THE EXECUTIVE BRANCH TO THE U.S. SENATE, 1789-1819, AND TRANSCRIBED REPORTS OF SENATE COMMITTEES, 1798-1817
- TRANSCRIBED REPORTS OF COMMITTEES OF THE U.S. SENATE, 1817-1827
- TRANSCRIBED TREATIES AND CONVENTIONS APPROVED BY THE U.S. SENATE, 1789-1836
- UNBOUND RECORDS OF THE U.S. SENATE, 8TH CONGRESS, 1803-1805

U.S. Senate Committee on Foreign Relations *see* COMPILATION OF REPORTS OF THE FOREIGN RELATIONS COMMITTEE; 1789-1901

U.S. Senate Committee on Governmental Operations *see* STUDY ON FEDERAL REGULATIONS

U.S. Senate. Committee on Labor and Public Welfare *see* JOINT LABOR-MANAGEMENT TRUST FUNDS AND HISTORY OF THE COVERAGE OF NON-PROFIT HOSPITALS

THE U.S. SENATE HISTORICAL OFFICE ORAL HISTORY COLLECTION : INTERVIEWS WITH SENATE STAFF – (Records experiences of Senate staff members after the Legislative Reorganization Act of 1946. 24 interviews listed and may be purchased individually. Index sold separately on 3mf $15.00 S1874.I1) – 76mf – 9 – $380.00 set – S1874.1-24 – us Scholarly Res [320]

U.S. SENATE HISTORICAL OFFICE ORAL HISTORY COLLECTION *see*
- CARL M. MARCY, SENATE SERVICE 1950-1973
- DARRELL ST CLAIRE, SENATE SERVICE 1933-1939, 1949-1977
- DONALD J. DETWILER, SENATE SERVICE 1917-18
- DOROTHYE G. SCOTT, SENATE SERVICE 1945-1977
- F. NORDY HOFFMANN, SENATE SERVICE 1975-1981
- FLOYD M. RIDDICK, SENATE SERVICE 1947-1974
- FRANCIS J. ATTIG, SENATE SERVICE 1952-1974
- FRANCIS O. WILCOX, SENATE SERVICE 1947-1955
- GEORGE A. SMATHERS, U.S. SENATOR FROM FLORIDA 1951-1969
- GEORGE TAMES
- GROVER W. ENSLEY, SENATE SERVICE 1949-1957
- HOWARD SHUMAN, SENATE SERVICE 1955-1982
- J. FRANKLIN LITTLE, SENATE SERVICE 1910-1912
- JERRY T. VERKLER, SENATE SERVICE 1963-1974
- LEONHARD H. BALLARD, SENATE SERVICE 1947-1984
- PAT M. HOLT, SENATE SERVICE 1950-1977
- REIN J. VANDER ZEE, SENATE SERVICE 1961-1964
- ROY L. ELSON, SENATE SERVICE 1955-1969
- RUTH YOUNG WATT, SENATE SERVICE 1949-1979
- SCOTT I. PEEK, SENATE SERVICE 1952-1963
- STEWART E. MCCLURE, SENATE SERVICE 1949-1973
- WARREN FEATHERSTONE REID, SENATE SERVICE 1949-50, 1964-1981
- WILLIAM A. RIDGELY, SENATE SERVICE 1949-1977
- WILLIAM HILDENBRAND, SENATE SERVICE 1961-1984

U. S. SENATE JOURNAL OF THE EXECUTIVE PROCEEDINGS – 70r – 1 – $2,450.00 – Dist. us Scholarly Res – us L of C Photodup [323]

U.S. SENATE STUDY MISSION TO EASTERN (AMERICAN) SAMOA : REPORT OF SENATORS OREN LONG AND ERNEST GRUENING TO THE COMMITTEE ON INTERIOR AND INSULAR AFFAIRS / American Samoa. US Senate – 87th Congress 1st sess. Washington: GPO, 1961 – 3mf – 9 – $4.50 – LLMC 82-100C Title 36 – us L.L.M.C. [327]

UNITED STATES SERVICE MAGAZINE – v. 1-5. 1864-1866 – 1 – us UMI [355]

U.S. Social Security Administration *see* BULLETIN

U.S. Soil Conservation Service *see* PUBLICATIONS

U.S. State Bar Association *see* PROCEEDINGS

U. S. State Department *see*
- FEDERAL REPUBLIC OF GERMANY
- GERMANY

U.S. STATE DEPARTMENT INTELLIGENCE AND RESEARCH REPORTS *see* THE MIDDLE EAST

UNITED STATES STATUTES AT LARGE. / U. S. Laws, Statutes, etc – Washington, DC. On film: 1-76A; 1789-1962. LL-034 – 1 – us L of C Photodup [340]

THE UNITED STATES STATUTES AT LARGE OF THE UNITED STATES, FROM THE ORGANIZATION OF THE GOVERNMENT IN 1789 TO THE 102ND CONGRESS, 2ND SESSION, 1992 / U. S. Laws, Statutes, etc – v1-106 pt 6 – 2611mf – 9 – $3,916.00 – LLMC 80-030 – us L.L.M.C. [324]

U.S. STATUTES AT LARGE ON MICROFICHE : RETROSPECTIVE COLLECTION / U. S. Congress – (Available as a complete coll or in multivolume groups) – v1-108. 1789-1994 – 9 – $5,160.00 complete set – us CIS [340]

U. S. Strategic Bombing Survey *see*
- JOINT ARMY-NAVY INTELLIGENCE STUDIES (JANIS), 1944-1945
- TACTICAL MISSION REPORTS OF THE 20TH AND 21ST BOMBER COMMANDS, 1945

U.S. SUBMARINE WAR PATROL REPORTS AND RELATED DOCUMENTS, 1941-1945 : REFERENCE DOCUMENTS ON SUBMARINE OPERATIONS AND SUBMARINES / U.S. Navy – (With printed guide) – 1989 – 9r – 1 – $765.00 – S3177 – us Scholarly Res [355]

U.S. Subversive Activities Control Board *see* SUBVERSIVE ACTIVITIES CONTROL BOARD REPORTS

U.S. Superintendent for the Five Civilized Tribes *see* REPORT

U.S. Superintendent of Documents *see*
- CATALOG OF THE PUBLIC DOCUMENTS OF CONGRESS AND ALL DEPARTMENTS OF THE GOVERNMENT OF THE UNITED STATES
- MONTHLY CATALOG OF U.S. GOVERNMENT PUBLICATIONS

U. S. Supreme Court *see* FEDERAL DECISIONS

U.S. Supreme Court *see*
- ANTITRUST LAW
- APPELLATE CASE FILES. 1792-1831
- ATTORNEY ROLLS, 1790-1951
- CURRENT DECISIONS...WITH NOTES AND DIGEST
- DECISIONS ON THE LAW OF PATENTS FOR INVENTIONS RENDERED BY ENGLISH COURTS (V.1-3) AND BY THE U.S. SUPREME COURT (V.4-20)
- DOCKETS, 1791-1950
- THE GREAT STANDARD OIL MONOPOLY CASE
- INDEX TO APPELLATE CASE FILES, 1792-1909
- THE INSULAR CASES, COMPRISING THE RECORDS, BRIEFS, AND ARGUMENTS OF COUNSEL IN THE INSULAR CASES OF THE OCTOBER TERM, 1900
- THE LEGAL TENDER CASES OF 1871
- MINUTES. 1790-1950
- MORRISON'S TRANSCRIPT OF THE DECISIONS OF THE SUPREME COURT
- PATENT CASES DETERMINED IN THE SUP. CT., INCLUDING COPYRIGHT AND TRADEMARK
- PETERS' CONDENSED REPORTS OF DECISIONS IN THE SUPREME COURT OF THE U.S.
- PUBLICATIONS
- RECORDS AND BRIEFS
- RULES OF THE SUPREME COURT OF THE UNITED STATES, 1790-1984
- SUPREME COURT OF THE UNITED STATES
- UNITED STATES SUPREME COURT JOURNAL
- UNITED STATES SUPREME COURT REPORTS
- U.S. REPORTS ON MICROFICHE
- U.S. SUPREME COURT RECORDS AND BRIEFS ON MICROFICHE

U.S. SUPREME COURT AND FEDERAL JUDGES SUBJECT FILES / ed by Charns, Alexander – With printed guide – 8r – 1 – $880.00 – 1-55655-413-3 – us UPA [324]

UNITED STATES SUPREME COURT JOURNAL / U.S. Supreme Court – (The official daily record of all transactions affecting cases coming to or being considered by the Supreme Court. Add vols planned) – 1892-1991 – 825mf – 9 – $1,087-00 – LLMC 81-425 – us L.L.M.C. [340]

U.S. SUPREME COURT RECORDS AND BRIEFS ON MICROFICHE : COMPREHENSIVE COLLECTION, INCLUDES ALL FULL OPINIONS, PER CURIAMS, CERTIORARI DENIED, AND SUMMARY DISPOSITIONS – 1975/76- – 9 – Apply for prices – us CIS [340]

U.S. SUPREME COURT RECORDS AND BRIEFS ON MICROFICHE : FULL OPINIONS, OR ARGUED CASES, ALSO INCLUDING PER CURIAMS FROM 1975 ONWARD / U.S. Supreme Court – 1897/98- – 9 – Apply for price – us CIS [340]

UNITED STATES SUPREME COURT REPORTS : OFFICIAL EDITION – (Add vols planned) – v1-496. 1790-1989 – 4391mf – 9 – $6,586.00 – LLMC 78-050 – us L.L.M.C. [340]

UNITED STATES SUPREME COURT REPORTS / U.S. Supreme Court – Official ed. Washington: GPO. v1-105. 1790-1881 – 9 – $1,167.00 – LLMC 78-050 – us L.L.M.C. [340]

UNITED STATES SUPREME COURT REPORTS *see* ENCYCLOPEDIA OF THE U.S. SUPREME COURT REPORTS

UNITED STATES SUPREME COURT TAX CASES, 1944-1948 : REPORT TO THE JOINT COMMITTEE ON TAXATION – (Includes suppl vol 1949-53) – Washington: GPO. 1v. 1949, 1955 (all publ) – 9 – LLMC 95-136 – us L.L.M.C. [340]

U. S. Surgeon General *see*
- HEALTH CONSEQUENCES OF SMOKING: CUMULATIVE INDEX
- INDEX CATALOG OF THE ARMY MEDICAL LIBRARY, 1880-1961
- INDEX CATALOG OF THE LIBRARY OF THE SURGEON GENERAL'S OFFICE

U.S. Tariff Commission *see*
- ECONOMIC CONTROLS AND COMMERCIAL POLICY IN ARGENTINA
- PUBLICATIONS

U.S. Tax Court *see*
- BOARD OF TAX APPEALS, REPORTS
- DECISIONS
- PUBLICATIONS
- TAX COURT REPORTS
- U.S. TAX COURT REPORTS

U.S. TAX COURT REPORTS / U.S. Tax Court – (Add vols planned) – v1-94. 1942-89 – 1210mf – 9 – $1,815.00 – LLMC 79-418 – us L.L.M.C. [340]

U.S. TAXATION : MICRO-MINI PRINTS – 53 titles – 9 – $1,150.00 set – 0-89941-236-X – us Hein [323]

UNITED STATES TOBACCO JOURNAL – v1 no 13-v32 May 2 1876-Jan 30 1892. (Scattered issues lacking) – 1 – $160.00 – us L of C Photodup [380]

U.S. Treasury Department *see*
- BULLETIN
- CENTRAL TREASURY RECORDS OF THE CONTINENTAL AND CONFEDERATION GOVERNMENTS RELATING TO FOREIGN AFFAIRS
- CIRCULAR LETTERS OF THE SECRETARY OF THE TREASURY (T SERIES), 1789-1878
- CORRESPONDENCE OF THE SECRETARY OF THE TREASURY WITH COLLECTORS OF CUSTOMS, 1789-1833
- CORRESPONDENCE...RELATING TO THE ADMINSITRATION OF TRUST FUNDS FOR THE CHICKASAW AND OTHER TRIBES (S SERIES), 1834-72
- CUMULATIVE BULLETIN, INCOME TAX RULINGS
- DIGEST OF INCOME TAX RULINGS
- IRS CUMULATIVE BULLETIN
- LETTERS RECEIVED BY THE SECRETARY... FROM COLLECTORS OF CUSTOMS, 1833-69
- LETTERS RECEIVED BY THE SECRETARY... FROM COLLECTORS OF CUSTOMS AT PORT TOWNSEND, WASHINGTON, RELATING TO NOMINATIONS FOR OFFICE, 1865-1910
- LETTERS RECEIVED BY THE SECRETARY... RELATING TO PUBLIC LANDS, (N SERIES) 1831-49
- LETTERS RECEIVED BY THE SECRETARY... RELATING TO THE SUBTREASURY SYSTEM (U SERIES), 1846-60
- LETTERS RECEIVED IN THE OFFICE OF THE SECRETARY...RELATING TO CLAIMS, 1864-87
- LETTERS SENT BY THE SECRETARY... RELATING TO PUBLIC LANDS (N SERIES), 1801-78
- LETTERS SENT BY THE SECRETARY... RELATING TO RESTRICTED COMMERCIAL INTERCOURSE, 1861-87
- LETTERS SENT BY THE SECRETARY... RELATING TO THE SUBTREASURY SYSTEM (U SERIES), 1840-78
- LETTERS SENT BY THE SECRETARY...TO COLLECTORS AT PACIFIC PORTS, 1850-78
- LETTERS SENT TO THE PRESIDENT BY THE SECRETARY OF THE TREASURY, 1833-78
- LETTERS...TO COLLECTORS OF CUSTOMS AT ALL PORTS (1789-1847) AND AT SMALL PORTS (1847-78)
- MISCELLANEOUS LETTERS SENT BY THE SECRETARY..., 1870-87. AND BY THE ASSISTANT SECRETARY, 1876-93
- RECORDS OF THE COMMISSIONERS OF CLAIMS (SOUTHERN CLAIMS COMMISSION), 1871-80
- REGISTER OF MONTHLY REPORTS BY U.S. SECRET SERVICE AGENTS, DEC. 1864-FEB. 1871
- REGISTERS OF LETTERS RELATING TO CLAIMS RECEIVED IN THE OFFICE OF THE SECRETARY OF THE TREASURY, 1864-87
- TELEGRAMS SENT BY THE SECRETARY OF THE TREASURY (XA SERIES), 1850-74
- TREASURY BULLETIN
- TREASURY DECISIONS, 1899-1966
- TREASURY DECISIONS, INTERNAL REVENUE

U.S. Treasury Department *see*
- ANNUAL REPORTS OF THE SECRETARY OF THE TREASURY ON THE STATE OF THE FINANCES, 1790-1974
- PUBLICATIONS
- TAX DEPRECIATION AND THE NEED FOR THE RESERVE RATIO TEST

U.S. Treasury Department. Advisory Commission on Intergovernmental Relations *see* OVERLAPPING TAXES IN THE UNITED STATES

U.S. Treasury Department. Bureau of Accounts *see* BLOTTERS OF THE OFFICE OF THE REGISTER OF THE TREASURY, 1782-1810

U.S. Treasury Department. Bureau of Customs *see* BULLETIN

U.S. Treasury Department. Bureau of the Public Debt *see*
- CARD INDEX TO 'OLD LOAN' LEDGERS..., 1790-1836
- RECORDS...: CENTRAL TREASURY RECORDS RELATING TO THE LOAN OF 1790
- RECORDS...: CONNECTICUT LOAN OFFICE RECORDS RELATING TO THE LOAN OF 1790
- RECORDS...: DELAWARE LOAN OFFICE RECORDS RELATING TO THE LOAN OF 1790
- RECORDS...: GEORGIA LOAN OFFICE RECORDS RELATING TO THE LOAN OF 1790
- RECORDS...: GEORGIA LOAN OFFICE RECORDS RELATING TO VARIOUS LOANS, 1804-18
- RECORDS...: MARYLAND LOAN OFFICE RECORDS RELATING TO THE LOAN OF 1790
- RECORDS...: MARYLAND LOAN OFFICE RECORDS RELATING TO VARIOUS LOANS OF 1798 AND 1800
- RECORDS...: MASSACHUSETTS LOAN OFFICE RECORDS RELATING TO THE LOAN OF 1790
- RECORDS...: NEW HAMPSHIRE LOAN OFFICE RECORDS RELATING TO THE LOAN OF 1790
- RECORDS...: NEW JERSEY LOAN OFFICE RECORDS RELATING TO THE LOAN OF 1790
- RECORDS...: NORTH CAROLINA LOAN OFFICE RECORDS RELATING TO THE LOAN OF 1790
- RECORDS...: OLD LOANS RECORDS RELATING TO SELECTED LOANS OF THE PERIOD 1795-1807
- RECORDS...: PENNSYLVANIA LOAN OFFICE RECORDS RELATING TO THE LOAN OF 1790
- RECORDS...: RHODE ISLAND LOAN OFFICE RECORDS RELATING TO THE LOAN OF 1790
- RECORDS...: SOUTH CAROLINA LOAN OFFICE RECORDS RELATING TO THE LOAN OF 1790
- RECORDS...: VIRGINIA LOAN OFFICE RECORDS RELATING TO THE LOAN OF 1790

U.S. Treasury Department. Comptroller *see*
- COMPTROLLER OF THE TREASURY DECISIONS
- FIRST COMPTROLLER, DEPARTMENT OF THE TREASURY, DECISIONS

U.S. Treasury Department. Division of Customs *see* DIGEST OF DECISIONS UNDER THE CUSTOMS REVENUE LAWS

U.S. Treasury Department. First Auditor's Office *see*
- MISCELLANEOUS TREASURY ACCOUNTS OF THE FIRST AUDITOR (FORMERLY THE AUDITOR). OF THE TREASURY DEPARTMENT, SEPT. 6, 1790-JULY 15, 1840
- REGISTER OF AUDITS OF "MISCELLANEOUS TREASURY ACCOUNTS"

U.S. Treasury Department. General Accounting Office *see* INDEX TO THE PUBLISHED DECISIONS OF THE U.S. ACCOUNTING OFFICERS

U.S. Treasury Department. Office of Tax Analysis *see* TAX REFORM STUDIES AND PROPOSALS

U.S. Treasury Department. Office of the Comptroller of the Currency *see* REGISTERS OF SIGNATURES OF DEPOSITORS IN BRANCHES OF THE FREEDMEN'S SAVINGS AND TRUST COMPANY, 1865-74

U.S. Treasury Department. Office of the Secretary *see*
- LETTERS SENT...TO THE COLLECTORS OF CUSTOMS AT BALTIMORE, BOSTON, NEW ORLEANS, AND PHILADELPHIA ("I" SERIES), 1847-78
- LETTERS SENT...TO THE COLLECTORS OF CUSTOMS AT NEW YORK ("H" SERIES), 1847-78

U.S. Treasury Department. Third Auditor's Office *see* LEDGERS OF PAYMENTS, 1818-72, TO U.S. PENSIONERS UNDER ACTS OF 1818 THROUGH 1858

UNITED STATES TREATIES AND OTHER INTERNATIONAL AGREEMENTS / U. S. Treaties, etc – v1-30 1950-1979 – 1,5,6 – us Princeton Micro [977]

UNITED STATES TREATIES AND OTHER INTERNATIONAL AGREEMENTS / U.S. Department of State – v1-34 pt 1. 1950-82/83 – 1484mf – 9 – $2,226.00 – LLMC 79-442 – us L.L.M.C. [975]

UNITED STATES TREATIES AND OTHER INTERNATIONAL AGREEMENTS – Washington: Department of State. v1-35 pt 3. 1950-83 in 113bks – 9 – $2,035.00 set – us Hein [977]

UNITED STATES TREATIES AND OTHER INTERNATIONAL AGREEMENTS *see*
- TREATIES IN FORCE
- TREATY INFORMATION BULLETIN

U. S. Treaties, etc *see* UNITED STATES TREATIES AND OTHER INTERNATIONAL AGREEMENTS

U. S. TRIAL BRIEFS AND DOCUMENT BOOKS OF THE INTERNATIONAL MILITARY TRIBUNAL, 1945-1946 – T991 – 1r – $23.00 – us Nat'l Archives [340]

U. S. Veterans Administration *see*
- GENERAL INDEX TO PENSION FILES, 1861-1934
- INDEX TO INDIAN WARS PENSION FILES, 1892-1926
- INDEX TO MEXICAN WAR PENSION FILES, 1887-1926
- INDEX TO WAR OF 1812 PENSION APPLICATION FILES
- OLD WAR INDEX TO PENSION FILES, 1815-1926
- REVOLUTIONARY WAR PENSION AND BOUNTY-LAND WARRANT APPLICATION FILES, 1800-1900
- SCHEDULES ENUMERATING UNION VETERANS AND WIDOWS OF UNION VETERANS OF THE CIVIL WAR, 1890
- SELECTED RECORDS FROM REVOLUTIONARY WAR PENSION AND BOUNTY-LAND WARRANT APPLICATION FILES, 1800-1900
- VETERANS' ADMINISTRATION DECISIONS
- VETERAN'S ADMINISTRATION PENSION PAYMENT CARDS

U.S. Veteran's Education Appeals Board *see* SELECTED REPORTS OF CASES

U.S. Volleyball Association *see* ARCHIVES, HISTORY, RECORDS, ANNUAL GUIDES

U.S. Volleyball Association *see*
- VOLLEYBALL REVIEW, 1940-1973 – USA VOLLEYBALL REVIEW, 1973-1980 – VOLLEYBALL OFFICIAL GUIDE, 1976-1980
- VOLLEYBALL REVIEW, 1980-1981 – U.S.A. VOLLEYBALL REVIEW, 1981-1986 – VOLLEYBALL OFFICIAL GUIDE, 1981-1986

UNITED STATES VOLLEYBALL ASSOCIATION : ARCHIVES ETC., ADDITIONS NO 1 AND 2 – (Individual titles also listed separately) – 236mf complete coll – 9 – $400.00 set – us Microform Publ [790]

UNITED STATES VOLLEYBALL ASSOCIATION : ARCHIVES, HISTORY, RECORDS, ANNUAL GUIDES 1916-1975 – 126mf – 9 – $252.00 – us Microform Publ [790]

U.S. VS AT&T : COURT DOCUMENTS – 1974-84. With printed guide – 1 – $2,890.00 – 0-89093-680-3 – us UPA [340]

U.S. VS GEORGE GORDON LIDDY, EVERETT HOWARD HUNT, JAMES W. MCCORD, BERNARD L. BARKER, EUGENIO R. MARTINEZ, FRANK A. STURGIS, VIRGILIO R. GONZALEZ / U.S. District Court for the District of Columbia – The official transcript of the initial trial of the Watergate burglars. 1973 – 1 – $200.00 – 0-89093-039-2 – us UPA [324]

U.S. VS JOHN B. CONNALLY AND JAKE JACOBSEN / U.S. District Court for the District of Columbia – v1-11. 1975 – 1 – $100.00 – 0-89093-042-2 – us UPA [324]

U.S. VS JOHN D. EHRLICHMAN, CHARLES W. COLSON, G. GORDON LIDDY, BERNARD L. BARKER, FELIPE DEDIEGO, EUGENIO R. MARTINEZ / U.S. District Court for the District of Columbia – The official transcript of the White House "plumbers" case, focusing on the break-in at the office of Daniel Ellsberg's psychiatrist. 1974 – 1 – $200.00 – 0-89093-040-6 – us UPA [324]

U.S. VS JOHN N. MITCHELL, HARRY R. HALDEMAN, JOHN D. EHRLICHMAN, ROBERT C. MARDIAN, KENNETH W. PARKINSON / U.S. District Court for the District of Columbia – The official transcript of the major Watergate cover-up trial, containing transcripts of previously unreleased White House tapes. 1974-75 – 1 – $770.00 – 0-89093-041-4 – us UPA [324]

U.S. War Department *see*
- ANNUAL REPORTS OF THE WAR DEPARTMENT
- CORRESPONDENCE OF THE WAR DEPARTMENT RELATING TO INDIAN AFFAIRS, MILITARY PENSIONS, AND FORTIFICATIONS
- LETTERS SENT BY THE WAR DEPARTMENT RELATING TO NAVAL MATTERS
- MILITARY OPERATIONS OF THE CIVIL WAR: A GUIDE INDEX TO THE OFFICIAL RECORDS OF THE UNION AND CONFEDERATE ARMIES, 1861-1865, VOL. 1
- MINUTES OF MEETINGS OF THE STATE-WAR-NAVY COORDINATING COMMITTEE (SWNCC), 1944-47
- PAPERS PERTAINING TO VESSELS OF OR INVOLVED WITH THE CONFEDERATE STATES OF AMERICA: "VESSEL PAPERS"
- RECORDS OF THE VIRGINIA FORCES

U. S. War Department Adjutant General's Office *see* COMPILED SERVICE RECORDS OF SOLDIERS WHO SERVED IN THE AMERICAN ARMY DURING THE REVOLUTIONARY WAR

U. S. War Department. Adjutant General's Office *see*
- COMPILED SERVICE RECORDS OF VOLUNTEER SOLDIERS WHO SERVED DURING THE MEXICAN WAR IN ORGANIZATIONS FROM THE STATE OF PENNSYLVANIA
- RECORD CARDS TO THE CORRESPONDENCE OF THE WAR COLLEGE DIVISION, RELATED GENERAL STAFF, AND ADJUTANT GENERAL OFFICES

U.S. War Department. Adjutant General's Office *see*
- ARTILLERY FOR THE U.S. LAND SERVICE WITH PLATES, BY BREVET MAJOR ALFRED MORDECAI (WASHINGTON 1848-49)
- CABLEGRAMS EXCHANGED BETWEEN GENERAL HEADQUARTERS, AMERICAN EXPEDITIONARY FORCES, AND THE WAR DEPARTMENT
- CASE FILES OF INVESTIGATIONS BY LEVI C. TURNER AND LAFAYETTE C. BAKER, 1861-66
- CAVALRY TACTICS, U.S. ARMY, ASSIMILATED TO THE TACTICS OF INFANTRY AND ARTILLERY (NEW YORK, 1874)
- COMPILED RECORDS SHOWING SERVICE OF MILITARY UNITS IN VOLUNTEER UNION ORGANIZATIONS
- COMPILED SERVICE RECORDS OF VOLUNTEER SOLDIERS WHO SERVED DURING THE MEXICAN WAR IN MORMON ORGANIZATIONS
- COMPILED SERVICE RECORDS OF VOLUNTEER SOLDIERS WHO SERVED DURING THE MEXICAN WAR IN ORGANIZATIONS FROM THE STATE OF:
- COMPILED SERVICE RECORDS OF VOLUNTEER SOLDIERS WHO SERVED DURING THE MEXICAN WAR IN ORGANIZATIONS FROM THE STATE OF MISSISSIPPI
- COMPILED SERVICE RECORDS OF VOLUNTEER SOLDIERS WHO SERVED DURING THE WAR OF 1812 IN ORGANIZATIONS FROM THE TERRITORY OF MISSISSIPPI
- COMPILED SERVICE RECORDS OF VOLUNTEER SOLDIERS WHO SERVED FROM 1784 TO 1811
- COMPILED SERVICE RECORDS OF VOLUNTEER SOLDIERS WHO SERVED IN ORGANIZATIONS FROM THE STATE OF FLORIDA DURING THE FLORIDA INDIAN WARS
- COMPILED SERVICE RECORDS OF VOLUNTEER SOLDIERS WHO SERVED IN THE FLORIDA INFANTRY DURING THE WAR WITH SPAIN
- COMPILED SERVICE RECORDS OF VOLUNTEER UNION SOLDIERS WHO SERVED DURING THE CIVIL WAR IN ORGANIZATIONS FROM THE STATE OF:
- CROSS INDEX TO THE CENTRAL FILES OF THE ADJUTANT GENERAL'S OFFICE
- GENERAL INDEX TO COMPILED SERVICE RECORDS OF VOLUNTEER SOLDIERS WHO SERVED DURING THE WAR WITH SPAIN
- GENERAL JAMES WILKINSON'S ORDER BOOK, DECEMBER 31, 1796-MARCH 8, 1808
- HISTORICAL INFORMATION RELATING TO MILITARY POSTS AND OTHER INSTALLATIONS. CA. 1700-1900
- HISTORY OF THE PHILIPPINE INSURRECTION AGAINST THE U.S., 1899-1903, AND DOCUMENTS RELATING TO THE WAR DEPT. PROJECT FOR PUBLISHING THE HISTORY
- INDEX TO COMPILED SERVICE RECORDS OF REVOLUTIONARY WAR SOLDIERS WHO SERVED WITH THE AMERICAN ARMY IN GEORGIA MILITARY ORGANIZATIONS
- INDEX TO COMPILED SERVICE RECORDS OF VOLUNTEER SOLDIERS WHO SERVED DURING INDIAN WARS AND DISTURBANCES, 1815-58
- INDEX TO COMPILED SERVICE RECORDS OF VOLUNTEER SOLDIERS WHO SERVED DURING THE CHEROKEE DISTURBANCES AND REMOVAL IN ORGANIZATIONS FROM THE STATE OF GEORGIA
- INDEX TO COMPILED SERVICE RECORDS OF VOLUNTEER SOLDIERS WHO SERVED DURING THE CHEROKEE DISTURBANCES AND REMOVAL IN ORGANIZATIONS FROM THE STATE OF TENNESSEE AND THE FIELD AND STAFF OF THE ARMY OF THE CHEROKEE NATION
- INDEX TO COMPILED SERVICE RECORDS OF VOLUNTEER SOLDIERS WHO SERVED DURING THE CHEROKEE DISTURBANCES AND REMOVALS IN ORGANIZATIONS FROM THE STATE OF NORTH CAROLINA
- INDEX TO COMPILED SERVICE RECORDS OF VOLUNTEER SOLDIERS WHO SERVED DURING THE CHEROKEE REMOVAL IN ORGANIZATIONS FROM THE STATE OF ALABAMA
- INDEX TO COMPILED SERVICE RECORDS OF VOLUNTEER SOLDIERS WHO SERVED DURING THE CREEK WAR IN ORGANIZATIONS FROM THE STATE OF ALABAMA
- INDEX TO COMPILED SERVICE RECORDS OF VOLUNTEER SOLDIERS WHO SERVED DURING THE FLORIDA WAR IN ORGANIZATIONS FROM THE STATE OF ALABAMA
- INDEX TO COMPILED SERVICE RECORDS OF VOLUNTEER SOLDIERS WHO SERVED DURING THE MEXICAN WAR
- INDEX TO COMPILED SERVICE RECORDS OF VOLUNTEER SOLDIERS WHO SERVED DURING THE PATRIOT WAR, 1838-39
- INDEX TO COMPILED SERVICE RECORDS OF VOLUNTEER SOLDIERS WHO SERVED DURING THE PHILLIPPINE INSURRECTION
- INDEX TO COMPILED SERVICE RECORDS OF VOLUNTEER SOLDIERS WHO SERVED DURING THE WAR OF 1812
- INDEX TO COMPILED SERVICE RECORDS OF VOLUNTEER SOLDIERS WHO SERVED DURING THE WAR OF 1812 IN ORGANIZATIONS FROM THE STATE OF:
- INDEX TO COMPILED SERVICE RECORDS OF VOLUNTEER SOLDIERS WHO SERVED DURING THE WAR OF 1837-38 IN ORGANIZATIONS FROM THE STATE OF LOUISIANA
- INDEX TO COMPILED SERVICE RECORDS OF VOLUNTEER SOLDIERS WHO SERVED DURING THE WAR WITH SPAIN IN ORGANIZATIONS FROM THE STATE OF:
- INDEX TO COMPILED SERVICE RECORDS OF VOLUNTEER SOLDIERS WHO SERVED FROM 1784-1811
- INDEX TO COMPILED SERVICE RECORDS OF VOLUNTEER UNION SOLDIERS WHO SERVED DURING THE CIVIL WAR IN ORGANIZATIONS FROM THE STATE OF:
- INDEX TO COMPILED SERVICE RECORDS OF VOLUNTEER UNION SOLDIERS WHO SERVED DURING THE CIVIL WAR IN THE VETERAN RESERVE CORPS
- INDEX TO COMPILED SERVICE RECORDS OF VOLUNTEER UNION SOLDIERS WHO SERVED DURING THE CIVIL WAR WITH U.S. COLORED TROOPS
- INDEX TO GENERAL CORRESPONDENCE..., 1890-1917
- INDEX TO GENERAL CORRESPONDENCE OF THE RECORD AND PENSION OFFICE, 1889-1920
- INDEX TO THE WAR PRODUCTION BOARD POLICY DOCUMENTATION FILE
- INDEXES TO LETTERS RECEIVED...(MAIN SERIES), 1846, 1861-89
- INDEXES TO RECORDS OF THE WAR COLLEGE DIVISION AND RELATED GENERAL STAFF OFFICES
- LETTERS RECEIVED..., 1805-21
- LETTERS RECEIVED BY THE COMMISSION BRANCH OF THE ADJUTANT GENERAL'S OFFICE
- LETTERS RECEIVED BY THE OFFICE...(MAIN SERIES)
- LETTERS SENT BY THE GOVERNORS AND THE SECRETARY OF STATE OF CALIFORNIA, 1847-48
- LETTERS SENT...(MAIN SERIES), 1800-90
- LIEUT. ZEBULON PIKE'S NOTEBOOK OF MAPS, TRAVERSE TABLES, AND METEOROLOGICAL OBSERVATIONS, 1805-7
- MUSTER ROLLS AND PAYROLLS OF MILITIA AND REGULAR ARMY ORGANIZATIONS IN THE BATTLE OF TIPPECANOE, NOV. 1811
- OFFICIAL BATTLE LISTS OF THE CIVIL WAR
- ORDERS AND CIRCULARS ISSUED BY THE ARMY OF THE POTOMAC AND THE ARMY AND DEPARTMENT OF NORTHERN VIRGINIA, C.S.A
- ORDERS AND SPECIAL ORDERS BY MAJOR GENERAL WILLIAM O. BUTLER AND MAJOR GENERAL W.J. WORTH TO THE ARMY IN MEXICO, 1848
- ORDERS OF GENERAL ZACHARY TAYLOR TO THE ARMY OF OCCUPATION IN THE MEXICAN WAR, 1845-47
- THE ORDNANCE MANUAL FOR THE OFFICERS OF THE U.S. ARMY (3RD ED., PHILADELPHIA, 1862)
- RECORDS RELATING TO THE U.S. MILITARY ACADEMY, 1812-67
- REGISTER OF ENLISTMENTS IN THE U.S. ARMY, 1798-1914
- REGISTERS OF LETTERS RECEIVED, 1812-89
- RETURNS FROM REGULAR ARMY ARTILLERY REGIMENTS, JUNE 1821-JAN 1901
- RETURNS FROM REGULAR ARMY COAST ARTILLERY CORPS COMPANIES, FEB 1901-JUNE 1916
- RETURNS FROM REGULAR ARMY ENGINEER BATTALIONS, SEP 1846-JUNE 1916
- RETURNS FROM REGULAR ARMY INFANTRY REGIMENTS, JUNE 1821-DECEMBER 1916
- RETURNS FROM U.S. MILITARY POSTS, 1800-1916
- U.S. MILITARY ACADEMY CADET APPLICATION PAPERS, 1805-66

U.S. War Department. Collection of Revolutionary War Records *see*
- COMPILED SERVICE RECORDS OF AMERICAN NAVAL PERSONNEL AND MEMBERS OF THE DEPARTMENTS OF THE QUARTERMASTER GENERAL AND THE COMMISSARY GENERAL OF MILITARY STORES WHO SERVED DURING THE REVOLUTIONARY WAR
- GENERAL INDEX TO COMPILED MILITARY SERVICE RECORDS OF REVOLUTIONARY WAR SOLIDERS
- GENERAL ORDERS KEPT BY GENERAL WILLIAM HEATH, MAY 23, 1777-OCT 20, 1778
- INDEX TO COMPILED SERVICE RECORDS OF REVOLUTIONARY WAR PERSONNEL
- INDEX TO COMPILED SERVICE RECORDS OF REVOLUTIONARY WAR SOLDIERS WHO SERVED WITH THE AMERICAN ARMY IN CONNECTICUT MILITARY ORGANIZATIONS
- INDEX TO COMPILED SERVICE RECORDS OF VOLUNTEER SOLDIERS WHO SERVED DURING THE REVOLUTIONARY WAR IN ORGANIZATIONS FROM THE STATE OF NORTH CAROLINA
- MISCELLANEOUS NUMBERED RECORDS (THE MANUSCRIPT FILE) IN THE WAR DEPARTMENT COLLECTION OF REVOLUTIONARY WAR RECORDS
- NUMBERED RECORD BOOKS CONCERNING MILITARY OPERATIONS AND SERVICE, PAY AND SETTLEMENT OF ACCOUNTS, AND SUPPLIES IN THE WAR DEPARTMENT COLLECTION OF REVOLUTIONARY WAR RECORDS
- ORDERS, RETURNS, MORNING REPORTS, AND ACCOUNTS OF BRITISH TROOPS
- PERSONNEL RETURNS OF THE 6TH MASSACHUSETTS BATTALION
- REVOLUTIONARY WAR ROLLS, 1775-83
- SPECIAL INDEX TO NUMBERED RECORDS IN THE WAR DEPARTMENT COLLECTION OF REVOLUTIONARY WAR RECORDS
- VIRGINIA HALF PAY AND OTHER RELATED REVOLUTIONARY WAR PENSION APPLILCATION FILES
- WAR DEPARTMENT COLLECTION OF POST-REVOLUTIONARY WAR MANUSCRIPTS

U.S. War Department. Confederate Records *see*
- COMPILED RECORDS SHOWING SERVICE OF MILITARY UNITS IN CONFEDERATE ORGANIZATIONS

- COMPILED SERVICE RECORDS OF CONFEDERATE GENERALS AND STAFF OFFICERS, AND NONREGIMENTAL ENLISTED MEN
- COMPILED SERVICE RECORDS OF CONFEDERATE SOLDIERS WHO SERVED IN ORGANIZATIONS FROM THE STATE OF:
- COMPILED SERVICE RECORDS OF CONFEDERATE SOLDIERS WHO SERVED IN ORGANIZATIONS RAISED DIRECTLY BY THE CONFEDERATE GOVERNMENT
- COMPILED SERVICE RECORDS OF FORMER CONFEDERATE SOLDIERS WHO SERVED IN THE 1ST THROUGH 6TH U.S. VOLUNTEER INFANTRY REGIMENTS
- CONFEDERATE PAPERS RELATING TO CITIZENS OR BUSINESS FIRMS
- CONFEDERATE STATES ARMY CASUALTIES: LISTS AND NARRATIVE REPORTS, 1861-65
- CONSOLIDATED INDEX TO COMPILED SERVICE RECORDS OF CONFEDERATE SOLDIERS
- COPIES OF LETTERS AND TELEGRAMS RECEIVED AND SENT BY GOVERNOR ZEBULON B. VANCE OF NORTH CAROLINA, 1862-65
- CORRESPONDENCE AND REPORTS OF THE CONFEDERATE TREASURY DEPT., 1861-65
- INDEX TO COMPILED SERVICE RECORDS OF CONFEDERATE SOLDIERS WHO SERVED IN ORGANIZATIONS FROM THE STATE OF:
- INDEX TO COMPILED SERVICE RECORDS OF CONFEDERATE SOLDIERS WHO SERVED IN ORGANIZATIONS RAISED DIRECTLY BY THE CONFEDERATE GOV'T. AND OF CONFEDERATE GENERAL AND STAFF OFFICERS AND NON-REGIMENTAL ENLISTED MEN
- INDEX TO THE LETTERS RECEIVED BY THE CONFEDERATE ADJUTANT AND INSPECTOR GENERAL AND BY THE CONFEDERATE QUARTERMASTER GENERAL, 1861-65
- INDEX TO THE LETTERS RECEIVED BY THE CONFEDERATE SECRETARY OF WAR, 1861-65
- LETTERS AND TELEGRAMS SENT BY THE CONFEDERATE ADJUTANT AND INSPECTOR GENERAL, 1861-65
- LETTERS AND TELEGRAMS SENT BY THE ENGINEER BUREAU OF THE CONFEDERATE WAR DEPT., 1861-64
- LETTERS RECEIVED BY THE CONFEDERATE ADJUTANT AND INSPECTOR GENERAL, 1861-65
- LETTERS RECEIVED BY THE CONFEDERATE QUARTERMASTER GENERAL, 1861-65
- LETTERS RECEIVED BY THE CONFEDERATE SECRETARY OF WAR, 1861-65
- LETTERS SENT BY LIEUT. COLONEL G.H. HILL, COMMANDER OF THE CONFEDERATE ORDNANCE WORKS AT TYLER, TEXAS, 1864-65
- LETTERS SENT BY THE CONFEDERATE SECRETARY OF WAR, 1861-65
- LETTERS SENT BY THE CONFEDERATE SECRETARY OF WAR TO THE PRESIDENT, 1861-65
- RECORDS OF THE LOUISIANA STATE GOVT., 1850-88.
- RECORDS RELATING TO CONFEDERATE NAVAL AND MARINE PERSONNEL
- REGISTER OF CONFEDERATE SOLDIERS, SAILORS, AND CITIZENS WHO DIED IN FEDERAL PRISONS AND MILITARY HOSPITALS IN THE NORTH
- SELECTED RECORDS...RELATING TO CONFEDERATE PRISONERS OF WAR, 1861-65
- TELEGRAMS RECEIVED BY THE CONFEDERATE SECRETARY OF WAR, 1861-65
- TELEGRAMS SENT BY THE CONFEDERATE SECRETARY OF WAR, 1861-65
- UNFILED PAPERS AND SLIPS BELONGING IN CONFEDERATE COMPILED SERVICE RECORDS
- UNION PROVOST MARSHAL'S FILE OF PAPERS RELATING TO INDIVIDUAL CIVILIANS
- UNION PROVOST MARSHAL'S FILE OF PAPERS RELATING TO TWO OR MORE CIVILIANS

U.S. War Department. Cuban Census Office *see* INFORME SOBRE EL CENSO DE CUBA, 1899

U.S. War Department. General and Special Staffs *see* LIST OF THE PHOTOGRAPHS AND PHOTOG. NEGATIVES RELATING TO THE WAR FOR THE UNION

U.S. War Department. General Staff *see* MILITARY MONOGRAPH ON SIBERIA

U.S. War Department. General Staff. G-2 Division *see*
- HISTORY OF THE MILITARY INTELLIGENCE DIVISION, 7 DECEMBER 1941-2 SEPTEMBER 1945
- JAPANESE LANGUAGE PROGRAM AT THE UNIVERSITY OF MICHIGAN
- MISLS: THE TRAINING HISTORY OF THE MILITARY INTELLIGENCE SERVICE LANGUAGE SCHOOLS

U.S. War Department. Office of the Administrative Assistant *see*
- HISTORY OF THE U.S. STRATEGIC BOMBING SURVEY(EUROPEAN). 1944-45. V. 1-2. 1946
- HISTORY OF THE U.S. STRATEGIC BOMBING SURVEY(PACIFIC). 1945-46. V. 1-2. 1946

U.S. War Department. Office of the Chief of Engineers *see*
- BUELL COLLECTION OF HISTORICAL DOCUMENTS RELATING TO THE CORPS OF ENGINEERS, 1801-19
- LETTERS RECEIVED BY THE TOPOGRAPHICAL BUREAU..., 1824-65
- LETTERS SENT..., 1829-70
- LETTERS SENT BY THE OFFICE...RELATING TO INTERNAL IMPROVEMENTS, 1824-30
- REGISTERS OF LETTERS RECEIVED BY THE TOPOGRAPHICAL BUREAU OF THE WAR DEPT., 1824-66

U.S. War Department. Office of the Secretary *see*
- CONFIDENTIAL AND UNOFFICIAL LETTERS SENT BY THE SECRETARY..., 1814-47
- COPIES OF WAR DEPT. CORRESPONDENCE AND REPORTS, 1791-96
- INDEX TO TELEGRAMS COLLECTED BY THE OFFICE OF THE SECRETARY...(UNBOUND), 1860-70
- INDEXES TO LETTERS RECEIVED BY THE SECRETARY..., 1861-70
- INDEXES TO LETTERS SENT BY THE SECRETARY...RELATING TO MILITARY AFFAIRS, 1871-89
- LETTERS RECEIVED BY THE SECRETARY..., IRREGULAR SERIES, 1861-66
- LETTERS RECEIVED BY THE SECRETARY..., REGISTERED SERIES, 1801-70
- LETTERS RECEIVED BY THE SECRETARY..., UNREGISTERED SERIES, 1789-1861
- LETTERS RECEIVED BY THE SECRETARY...FROM THE PRESIDENT, EXECUTIVE DEPARTMENTS, AND WAR DEPARTMENT BUREAUS, 1862-70
- LETTERS SENT BY THE SECRETARY... RELATING TO MILITARY AFFAIRS, 1800-89
- LETTERS SENT BY THE SECRETARY...TO THE PRESIDENT AND EXECUTIVE DEPARTMENTS, 1863-70
- LETTERS SENT TO THE PRESIDENT BY THE SECRETARY..., 1800-63
- MISCELLANEOUS LETTERS SENT BY THE SECRETARY..., 1800-09
- ORDERS AND ENDORSEMENTS SENT BY THE SECRETARY..., 1846-70
- REGISTERS OF LETTERS RECEIVED BY THE SECRETARY..., IRREGULAR SERIES, 1861-66
- REGISTERS OF LETTERS RECEIVED BY THE SECRETARY..., MAIN SERIES, 1800-70
- REGISTERS OF LETTERS RECEIVED BY THE SECRETARY...FROM THE PRESIDENT, EXECUTIVE DEPARTMENTS, AND WAR DEPARTMENT BUREAUS, 1862-70
- REPORTS TO CONGRESS FROM THE SECRETARY OF WAR, 1803-70
- TELEGRAMS COLLECTED BY THE OFFICE OF THE SECRETARY...(UNBOUND), 1860-70

U.S. War Department. War Plans Division *see* NAME AND SUBJECT INDEX TO THE GENERAL CORRESPONDENCE OF THE WAR PLANS DIVISION

U.S. War Production Board *see*
- NUMBERED DOCUMENT FILE OF THE ADVISORY COMMISSION TO THE COUNCIL OF NATIONAL DEFENSE, 1940-41
- NUMBERED DOCUMENT FILE OF THE COUNCIL OF THE OFFICE OF PRODUCTION MANAGEMENT, 1940-42
- NUMBERED DOCUMENT FILE OF THE SUPPLY PRIORITIES AND ALLOCATIONS BOARD, SEPT. 2, 1941-JAN. 15, 1942
- PRESS RELEASES OF THE ADVISORY COMMISSION TO THE COUNCIL OF NATIONAL DEFENSE, JUNE 3, 1940-JAN. 15, 1941
- PROGRESS REPORTS OF THE ADVISORY COMMISSION TO THE COUNCIL OF NATIONAL DEFENSE, JULY 24, 1940-MAY 28, 1941

U.S. Weather Bureau *see*
- CLIMATOLOGICAL RECORDS OF THE WEATHER BUREAU, 1819-92
- RECORDS

U.S. Weather Bureau. Station 85, Alpena, Michigan *see* DAILY JOURNALS

U.S. WEEK – 1-2 no. 1 (all publ). 1941-1942 – 11mf – 9 – $65.00 – us UPA [071]

U. S. Work Projects Administration *see* INDEX TO REFERENCE CARDS FOR WORK PROJECTS ADMINISTRATION PROJECT FILES

U.S. Work Projects Administration. Connecticut *see* SHIP REGISTERS AND ENROLLMENTS

U.S. Work Projects Administration. Ohio *see* ANNALS OF CLEVELAND

U. S. Works Progress Administration. Federal Writers' Project *see* IDAHO ENCYCLOPEDIA

U.S. Works Progress Administration. San Francisco Office *see* CALIFORNIA ART RESEARCH

U. S. Works Projects Administration *see* ARCHIVES OF THE WORKS PROJECTS ADMINISTRATION AND PREDECESSORS, 1933-43

U.S. Works Projects Administration. South Carolina Historical Records Survey *see*
- CHURCH RECORDS
- INDEX TO TOMBSTONE INSCRIPTIONS

U. S. World War Two Crimes Records *see* DIARY OF HANS FRANK

U. S. World War Two War Crimes Records *see* MAUTHAUSEN DEATH BOOKS

U.S. World War Two War Crimes Records *see* TRIAL BRIEF AND DOCUMENT BOOKS

UNITED STATES-PANAMANIAN CRISIS – Panama City, Panama. 11-22 Jan 1964 – 1r – 1 – us L of C Photodup [072]

UNITED STATES-VIETNAM RELATIONS, 1945-67 : STUDY PREPARED BY THE DEPARTMENT OF DEFENSE ("THE PENTAGON PAPERS") – (Guide also sold separately for $10.00) – 1991 – 6r – 1 – $510.00 – S3276 – us Scholarly Res [327]

United Steel Workers of America *see* STEEL LABOR

United Suffragists *see* VOTES FOR WOMEN

United Transkeian Territories. General Council *see* PROCEEDINGS AND REPORTS OF SELECT COMMITTEES

United Workers Party *see* NEW ESSAYS

United World College of the Atlantic *see* PROJECT. THE SCIENCE JOURNAL

UNIT-REGISTER – (Cont by: Press-Register) – Orland, CA. 1962-82 – 40r – 1 – $2,000.00 – B02565 – us Library Micro [071]

UNITY – v. 6-29. 1895-1908 – 1 – us UMI [240]

UNITY AND CONTINUITY IN GOETHE / Willoughby, Leonard Ashley – Oxford: The Clarendon Press, 1947 – 1r – 1 – us U.W. Library [430]

UNITY AND MISSIONS : CAN A DIVIDED CHURCH SAVE THE WORLD? / Brown, Arthur Judson – New York: Fleming H. Revell, c1915 – 1mf – us A.T.L.A. [240]

THE UNITY AND SYMMETRY OF THE BIBLE / Gibson, John Monro – New York: Hodder & Stoughton, 189-?. 1 fiche – 9 – us A.T.L.A. [240]

UNITY BAPTIST CHURCH. SOUTH CAROLINA : CHURCH RECORDS – 1818-1904 – 1 – 12.00 – us Baptist [240]

UNITY BAPTIST CHURCH. SPARTANBURG COUNTY. SOUTH CAROLINA : CHURCH RECORDS – 1915-66 – 1 – 51.39 – us Baptist [240]

UNITY FOR SPAIN; CORRESPONDENCE BETWEEN THE COMMUNIST INTERNATIONAL AND THE LABOR AND SOCIALIST INTERNATIONAL, JUN-JULY, 1937 / Communist International – NY, 1937. Fiche W 1238. (Blodgett Collection of Spanish Civil War Pamphlets) – 9 – us H.U. College Libr [946]

UNITY, FREEDOM, FELLOWSHIP AND CHARACTER IN RELIGION – (Lacking some pgs) – v1-151. 1 Mar 1878-1965 – 43r – 1 – ATLA S0195 – us A.T.L.A. [073]

UNITY IN VARIETY:...ARGUMENTS BASED ON... DIVINE WORKMANSHIP IN OUR PLANET / Weldon, George Warburton – New-York, T. Whittaker, 1872...PR.-apply; ATL; 9 – us A.T.L.A. [240]

Unity, New Hampshire. Unity Baptist Church *see* RECORDS

THE UNITY OF GOVERNMENT IN THE CHURCH OF CHRIST : CONSIDERED IN REFERENCE TO THE GORHAM CONTROVERSY: A SERMON / Sumner, Robert – London: Burns and Lambert; Liverpool: Rockliff, 1850 – 1mf – 9 – 0-8370-7511-4 – 1986-1511 – us A.T.L.A. [240]

THE UNITY OF THE CHURCH / Boegner, Marc – [1914?] – 1mf – us A.T.L.A. [240]

THE UNITY OF THE EPISCOPATE : CONSIDERED IN REPLY TO THE WORK OF THE REV. T.W. ALLIES, M.A. ENTITLED 'THE CHURCH OF ENGLAND CLEARED FROM THE CHARGE OF SCHISM, UPON TESTIMONIES AND COUNCILS OF FATHERS OF THE FIRST SIX CENTURIES' / Thompson, Edward Healy – (Includes bibliographical references) – Philadelphia: Henry M'Grath, 1848 – 1mf – 9 – 0-8370-7029-5 – 1986-1029 – us A.T.L.A. [230]

UNITY OF TRUTH IN CHRISTIANITY AND EVOLUTION / Hark, Joseph Maximillian – New York: John A. Berry, 1888. 1 fiche – 9 – us A.T.L.A. [240]

UNITY (OR BROWN'S CREEK) BAPTIST CHURCH. UNION, SOUTH CAROLINA : CHURCH RECORDS – 1845-1943 – 1 – 6.89 – us Baptist [240]

UNIVERALISM AND ORTHODOXY: A COURSE OF EIGHT SERMONS / Forsey, G – Ottawa: Citizen, 1879. 04343. (Pre-1900 Canadiana) – 9 – cn C.I.H.M. [971]

UNIVERCOELUM : AND SPIRITUAL PHILOSOPHER – New York. v1-4. 1847-49 – 1r – 1 – us Ross [100]

L'UNIVERS – Nantes, 1 oct-19 dec 1870 – 1r – 1 – Can$30.00 – cn Can Microfilming [072]

L'UNIVERS – Paris. n497. 2 jan 1870-n626. 16 sep 1870 – 1r – 1 – Can$40.00 – cn Can Microfilming [072]

L'UNIVERS – Paris. Religieux, politique, philosophique, scientifique et litteraire. 3 nov 1833-janv 1860, avr 1867-2 aout 1914, janv-aout 1919. En janv 1860 fusionne avec: La Voix de la Verite pour former Le Quotidien: Le Monde.A partir de 1867 reparait parallelement au Monde – 1 – fr A.C.R.P.P. [073]

L'UNIVERS – Paris. v12 n512. 2 jan 1844-v14. n1358. 30 sep 1846 – 2r – 1 – Can$40.00 – cn Can Microfilming [072]

L'UNIVERS – Paris. v26 n68. 16 mai 1858-v28 n14. 23 jan 1860 – 1r – 1 – Can$40.00 – cn Can Microfilming [072]

L'UNIVERS ISRAEA1LITE – Paris. v. 1-94. Apr 1844-May 12 1939. Incomplete – 1 – us NY Public [270]

L'UNIVERS ISRAELITE – Paris. Journal des principes conservateurs du judaisme.Fond., S. Bloch.1844/45-sept 1928, 1933-39 – 1 – fr A.C.R.P.P. [270]

UNIVERS ISRAELITE : JOURNAL DES PRINCIPES CONSERVATEURS DU JUDAISME – Paris. v1-94. 1844-1939 – 24r – 1 – us Ross [270]

L'UNIVERS MACONNIQUE,... – Paris, 1835-36 – 5mf – 9 – VR-32.5/1 – ne IDC [944]

L'UNIVERS, OU HISTOIRE ET DESCRIPTION DE TOUS LES PEUPLES,... / Pauthier, PG – N.p., n.d. – 1mf – 9 – ne IDC [950]

L'UNIVERS POETIQUE D'ALEXANDRE BLOK / Bonneau, S – Paris, 1946 – 9mf – 9 – ne IDC [460]

L'UNIVERS POLITIQUE DES PAYSANS DANS LA FRANCE CONTEMPORAINE / Tavernier, Y et al – 11mf – 9 – Fr180.00 – fr Ethnologie [320]

UNIVERSA PHILOSOPHIA DE MORIBUS / Piccolomineus, F – N.p., 1596 – 11mf – 9 – CA-31/1 – ne IDC [100]

UNIVERSAE AQUATILIUM HISTORIAE PARS ALTERA / Rondelet, G – 2590 2. 1555 – 8 – ne IDC [574]

UNIVERSAE GEOMETRIAE MIXATEQUE MATHEMATICAE SYNOPSIS, ET BINI REFRACTIONUM DEMONSTRATARUM TRACTATUS / Mersenne, Marin – Avec une introduction de A. Beaulieu, Paris, A. Bertier, 1644, pieces liminaires et 589 p. Histoire des Sciences XVIIe-XIXe Siecles. 7965 – 9 – fr Hachette [510]

EL UNIVERSAL – Mexico. -d. 9 Oct 1916-23 June 1917. Imperfect. 2 reels – 1 – uk British Libr Newspaper [072]

EL UNIVERSAL – Mexico: s.n., 1916- [1930-33]; [1938-86] – us Res Libr [072]

O UNIVERSAL – Ouro Preto, 18 Jul 1825-30 May 1842 – 1,5,6 – bl Biblioteca [072]

UNIVERSAL – Bucharest, Romania. 1939-53 – 45r – 1 – us L of C Photodup [072]

UNIVERSAL BIOGRAPHY: CONTAINING A COPIOUS ACCOUNT, CRITICAL AND HISTORICAL, OF THE LIFE AND CHARACTER, LABORS AND ACTIONS OF EMINENT PERSONS, IN ALL AGES AND COUNTRIES, CONDITIONS AND PROFESSIONS. / Lempriere, John – New

York: E. Sargeant, 1810. 2v – 1 – us U.W. Library [920]

UNIVERSAL BRITISH DIRECTORY – 1794-1799 – 3r – 1 – uk Microform Academic [941]

UNIVERSAL CHURCH RECORD AND CLERK'S BOOKS / Bethany Baptist Church, Hunter, KS – 1878-1983 – 1 – us KS Hist [240]

UNIVERSAL CHURCH RECORD BOOK / Louisville. Kentucky. Davis Memorial Baptist Church – 1959-79 – 1 – 21.60 – us Baptist [240]

AN UNIVERSAL DICTIONARY OF THE MARINE: OR, A COPIOUS EXPLANATION OF THE TECHNICAL TERMS EMPLOYED IN THE CONSTRUCTION OF A SHIP. TO WHICH IS ANNEXED A TRANSLATION OF FRENCH SEA-TERMS / Falconer, William & Burney, W – 2 pts. 1830 – 9 – $20.00 – uk Libr Preservation [623]

THE UNIVERSAL ELEMENTS OF THE CHRISTIAN RELIGION : AN ATTEMPT TO INTERPRET CONTEMPORARY RELIGIOUS CONDITIONS: THE COLE LECTURES FOR 1905 / Hall, Charles Cuthbert – 4th ed. New York: Young People's Missionary Movement of the US and Canada, 1908, c1905 – 1mf – 9 – 0-8370-4732-3 – 1985-2732 – us A.T.L.A. [240]

Universal Ethiopian Students' Association *see* AFRICAN

UNIVERSAL EVENING POST *see* THE LONDON CHRONICLE OR UNIVERSAL EVENING POST

UNIVERSAL GAZETTE – Philadelphia, PA. 1797-1800 – 1,3 – us Readex [071]

UNIVERSAL GEOGRAPHY : BEING A DESCRIPTION OF ALL PARTS OF THE WORLD, WITH ANALYTICAL, SYNOPTICAL, AND ELEMENTARY TABLES / Malte-Brun, Conrad – Boston. 3v. 1865 – 2r – 1 – us Ross [900]

THE UNIVERSAL HERBAL / Green, T – ed. 2. 2 v. London. 1824. B-6220 2 – 8 – ne IDC [616]

UNIVERSAL HISTORY IN PERSPECTIVE: DIVIDED INTO THREE PARTS, ANCIENT, MIDDLE, AND MODERN / Willard, Emma Hart – Rev. ed.New York: A.S. Barnes, 1855. 526p. plates, ill., maps – 1 – us U.W. Library [900]

UNIVERSAL HUMAN RIGHTS – v. 1-. 1979- – 1,5,6,9 – us UMI [300]

UNIVERSAL JOURNAL – Dublin, Ireland. -sw. 14 17 Feb 1746. 2 ft – 1 – uk British Libr Newspaper [072]

UNIVERSAL NEGRO IMPROVEMENT ASSOCIATION *see* UNIA RECORDS, MS 4038

UNIVERSAL NEGRO IMPROVEMENT ASSOCIATION: RECORDS OF THE CENTRAL DIVISION, NEW YORK, 1918-1959 : FROM THE HOLDINGS OF THE SCHOMBURG CENTER FOR RESEARCH IN BLACK CULTURE, MANUSCRIPTS, ARCHIVES AND RARE BOOKS DIVISION: THE NEW YORK PUBLIC LIBRARY, ASTOR, LENOX AND TILDEN FOUNDATIONS – (Guide which covers all coll under "African-American Organizations" sold separately for $20.00 D3305.G1) – 1995 – 6r – 1 – $510.00 – D3305P01 – Dist. us Scholarly Res – us L of C Photodup [060]

THE UNIVERSAL PASSION / Young, Edward – Dublin: Printed by S. Powell, for G. Ewing, 1726-1727 v.1, 1727; v.6, 1726 – 1 – us U.W. Library [810]

UNIVERSAL PRIMARY EDUCATION : SPECIAL SURVEY IN OYO STATE 1975-1979 / Nigeria. Oyo State. Statistics Division – Ibadan, [198?] – 1mf – 9 – DE-625/1 – ne IDC [370]

Universal Serials and Book Exchange *see* USBE MICROFICHE LIST OF 10,000 TOP TITLES

UNIVERSALE RELIGION – (Some pgs lacking) – 1985-91 – Inquire – 1 – ATLA S0874 – us A.T.L.A. [073]

UNIVERSAL-HALBMONATSSCHRIFT – Berlin, 1913-14 – 1r – 1 – gw Mikrofilm [073]

UNIVERSALISM EXAMINED AND REFUTED / Lee, Luther – 1836 – 9 – us A.T.L.A. [240]

UNIVERSALIST ADVOCATE *see* GOSPEL MESSENGER, OR, UNIVERSALIST ADVOCATE

UNIVERSALIST LEADER : A JOURNAL OF LIBERAL CHRISTIANITY – v1-119. 1897-1961 (complete) – 61r – 1 – ATLA S0203 – us A.T.L.A. [073]

UNIVERSALITA E TERRITORIALITA DEL FALLIMENTO... / Enriques, G – Roma, 1934 – 2mf – 1 – ILM-2047/1 – ne IDC [327]

UNIVERSAL-LEXIKON DER GEGENWART UND VERGANGENHEIT ODER NEUESTES ENCYCLOPAEDISCHES WOERTERBUCH DER WISSENSCHAFTEN, KUENSTE UND GEWERBE (AEL, ABT.1;6.3) – 3rd ed. Altenburg, 1849-52 (mf ed 1993) – 90mf – 9 – DM1,490.00 – 3-89131-146-X – gw Fischer [030]

UNIVERSAL-LEXIKON DER GEGENWART UND VERGANGENHEIT ODER NEUESTES ENCYCLOPAEDISCHES WOERTERBUCH DER WISSENSCHAFTEN, KUENSTE UND GEWERBE BEARBEITET VON 220 GELEHRTEN (AEL, ABT.1;6.6) – (incl. 6 Supplementbaende, Altenburg 1851-54; "Neueste Ergaenzungen...". 2 Baende Altenburg 1855, 1856. Tafelband Altenburg 1848. "Erlaeuternder Atlas..." Stuttgart 1844) – 2nd rev ed. Altenburg, Stuttgart, 1840-54 (mf ed 1992) – 175mf – 9 – DM1,850.00 – 3-89131-080-3 – gw Fischer [030]

THE UNIVERSE – London. -w. 8 Dec 1860-Dec 1870. (10 reels) – 1 – uk British Libr Newspaper [072]

UNIVERSE *see* THE CATHOLIC TIMES

THE UNIVERSE. THE CATHOLIC HERALD AND VISITOR – (Lacking: v30. v33-34. Title varies) – v1-36,39. 1833-28 Sep 1867 – 12r – 1 – ATLA S0265 – us A.T.L.A. [073]

L'UNIVERSEL – Illustrations contemporaines puis Journal illustre. no. 1-176. Paris. avr 1862-aout 1865 – 1 – fr A.C.R.P.P. [073]

LA UNIVERSIDAD AL SERVICIO DE LA DEMOCRACIA, UNA EXPERIENCIA EN POLITICA UNIVERSITARIA / Gollan, Josue – [Santa Fe, Republica Argentina]: Editorial Rosario, 1945 – 1 – CSUXADJ9196-B – us Hoover Inst Photo [320]

Universidad Catolica de Chile, Biblioteca Central *see* BIBLIOGRAFIA ECLESIASTICA CHILENA

LA UNIVERSIDAD DE EXTREMADURA (RAZONES QUE ABANDONAN SU ESTABLECIMIENTO) / Diaz Bustamante y Quijano, Alfonso – Caceres: Imp. T. Rodriguez, 1968 – sp Bibl Santa Ana [370]

Universidad Laboral Hispanoamericana *see* RONDALLAS V PRUEBA MUSICAL DE UNIVERSIDADES LABORALES

Universidad Nacional de Litoral. Instituto de Estudio de la Realidad Nacional y del Tercer Mundo *see* JUAN PERON Y EL TERCER MUNDO

UNIVERSIDAD Y ESTUDIANTES : UNIVERSIDAD Y PERONISMO / Osvaldo Inglese, Juan et al – Buenos Aires: Ediciones Libera, [1965] – 1 – CSUXADJ1044-B – us Hoover Inst Photo [370]

UNIVERSIDAD Y PUEBLO : PLANTEOS Y TEXTOS / Cirigliano, Gustavo F J – Buenos Aires: Libreria del Colegio, [1973] – 1 – CSUXADH9238-B – us Hoover Inst Photo [370]

UNIVERSIDADE : INFORMATIVO DA UNIVERSIDADE FEDERAL DO ACRE – Rio Branco, Acre. Out-Nov 1985; Mar-Abr 1986 – 1 – bl Biblioteca [370]

UNIVERSIDADE DO POVO, SERIES – Sao Paulo, BL. 1963-1964 – 1r – $50.00 – R04187 – us Library Micro [072]

Universita di Firenze. Facolta di Lettere e Filosofia *see* PUBLICAZIONI

DIE UNIVERSITAET ERFURT IN IHREM VERHAELTNISSE ZU DEM HUMANISMUS UND DER REFORMATION / Kampschulte, FW – Trier: Fr. Lintz, 1858-1860 – 2mf – us A.T.L.A. [370]

DIE UNIVERSITAETEN DES MITTELALTERS BIS 1400 / Denifle, Heinrich – Berlin: Weidmann, 1885 – 2mf – us A.T.L.A. [370]

DIE UNIVERSITAETEN UND DAS OEFFENTLICHE LEBEN : UEBER DIE AUFGABE DES AKADEMISCHEN UNTERRICHTES UND SEINE ZWECKMAESSIGERE GESTALTUNG / Kaehler, Martin – Erlangen: A. Deichert, 1891 – 1mf – us A.T.L.A. [370]

UNIVERSITAETSBIBLIOTHEK DER FREIEN UNIVERSITAET BERLIN = UNIVERSITY LIBRARY OF THE FREE UNIVERSITY OF BERLIN : ALPHABETISCHER KATALOG/ MONOGRAPHIEN – 1982 – 846 fiches (1:42) – 9 – diazo DM2,800.00 – 3-598-30340-8 – gw Saur [020]

UNIVERSITAETSPROFESSOR DR. JOSEF NADLER ZUM 75. GEBURTSTAG – (Includes bibliographical references) – Wien: OEsterreichischer Bundesverlag, 1959 – 1r – 1 – us U.W. Library [370]

L'UNIVERSITAIRE – Quebec, Canada. 10 nov 1916-v1 n23. 11 mai 1917 – 1r – 1 – Can$35.00 – cn Can Microfilming [072]

UNIVERSITAS – v7-21. 1954-68 (complete) – 1r – 1 – ATLA S0539 – us A.T.L.A. [073]

UNIVERSITAS PADJADJARAN. BALAI PENELITIAN PENDIDIKAN. WARTA BHALAI / Bandung, Indonesia – (Irregular) – Bandung, 1968 – 2mf – 9 – SE-1331/1 – ne IDC [370]

Universite Buddhique Preah Sihanouk Raj *see* CULTURE ET CIVILISATION KHMERES

L'Universite d'Alger *see* ANNALES DE L'INSTITUT D'ETUDES ORIENTALES

Universite de DOUAI *see* RECUEIL FACTICE DE MEMOIRES DE MEDECINE SOUTENUS A L'UNIVERSITE DE DOUAI, ET DE QUELQUES ACTES ADMINISTRATIFS CONCERNANT CETTE UNIVERSITE

l'Universite de Lille *see* REVUE DU NORD

Universite de Louvain *see* REVUE D'HISTOIRE ECCLESIASTIQUE

Universite de Montreal *see* LE JOURNAL DES ETUDIANTS

Universite de Nantes *see* CREATION, INSTITUTION, FONDATION ET PRIVILEGES DE L'UNIVERSITE DE NANTES

Universite de Paris *see* LA VIE UNIVERSITAIRE A PARIS

UNIVERSITE IMPERIALE : ARRETE SUR LES LIVRES CLASSIQUES QUI SONT MIS A L'USAGE DES LYCEES ET DES COLLEGES / Fontanes, Louis J-P de – [S.l.]: Fain, [1809?] – 1 – F50.00 – fr Armell [370]

L'UNIVERSITE LAVAL ET LES FETES DU CINQUANTENAIRE / Roy, Camille – Quebec: Dussault and Proulx, 1903. SEM16P201 – 1r – 5 – Can$9.00 – cn Bibl Nat [370]

Universite Laval. Quebec, Canada *see*
- LES BIBLIOGRAPHIES DU COURS DE BIBLIOTHECONOMIE
- LES BIBLIOGRAPHIES DU COURS DE BIBLIOTHECONOMIE DE L'UNIVERSITE LAVAL, 1947-1966

L'UNIVERSITE SYNDICALISTE – Editee par la Section des professeurs et assimiles de la Federation de l'enseignement laic, affiliee a la Confederation Generale du Travail unitaire et a l'Internationale des travailleurs de l'enseignement. Paris. 1928-juin juil 1936 avec un suppl au no. du 15 mai 1938 – 1 – fr A.C.R.P.P. [073]

LES UNIVERSITES FRANCAISES AU MOYEN-AGE : AVIS A M. MARCEL FOURNIER, EDITEUR DES STATUTS ET PRIVILEGES DES UNIVERSITES FRANCAISES / Denifle, Heinrich – Paris: E. Bouillon, 1892 – 1mf – us A.T.L.A. [370]

UNIVERSITETSKII VOPROS / Gilarov-Platonov, N P – Sovremennyia izvestiia 1868-1884 gg). Spb. 1903. BR-15,003 2 – 8 – ne IDC [370]

UNIVERSITETY I NAUCHNYE UCHREZHDENII A / Narkompros RSFSR – i dop. izd. Moskva, Leningrad: Obedinennoe nauchnotekh. izdvo, 2-oe perer 1935 – 1 – CSUX90-B6774 – us Hoover Inst Photo [947]

UNIVERSITIES AND ENVIRONMENTAL EDUCATION – 1986 – 9 – 92-3-102364-0 – fr UNESCO [370]

Universities' Mission to Central Africa *see*
- CENTRAL AFRICA
- DOCUMENTS
- REPORTS

UNIVERSITIES QUARTERLY – 1-29 1946-75 1; v25-29 5,6 – us UMI [370]

UNIVERSITY ADDRESSES : BEING ADDRESSES ON SUBJECTS OF ACADEMIC STUDY, DELIVERED TO THE UNIVERSITY OF GLASGOW / Caird, John – Glasgow: J. MacLehose; New York: Macmillan, 1898 – 1mf – us A.T.L.A. [370]

UNIVERSITY ADMINISTRATION – v1- 1974- 1; v4- 5,6,9 – us UMI [073]

UNIVERSITY AFFAIRS = AFFAIRES UNIVERSITAIRES – (v1-16 1959/60-1975. v17-18 1976-77 Can$100.00 per block) – Ottawa. v1-36. 1959/60-1995- – 5 – Can$50.00y – cn Micromedia [370]

UNIVERSITY AND HISTORICAL ADDRESSES : DELIVERED DURING A RESIDENCE IN THE UNITED STATES AS AMBASSADOR OF GREAT BRITAIN / Bryce, James – New York: Macmillan, 1913 – 1mf – us A.T.L.A. [900]

UNIVERSITY AND HISTORICAL ADDRESSES : DELIVERED DURING A RESIDENCE IN THE UNITED STATES AS AMBASSADOR OF GREAT BRITAIN / Bryce, James – New York: The Macmillan Co, 1913 – 5mf – 9 – $7.50 – LLMC 92-220 – us L.L.M.C. [323]

UNIVERSITY AND OTHER SERMONS / Creighton, Louise & Creighton, Mandell – London, New York: Longmans, Green, 1903 – 1mf – us A.T.L.A. [240]

UNIVERSITY AS AN INSTITUTION TODAY / Cabal, Alfonso Borrero – 1994 – 238p – 9 – 92-3-102939-8 – fr UNESCO [370]

University Berkeley. Institute for the Study of Social Change *see* EMMA GOLDMAN PAPERS

University College of Dar es Salaam. History Dept. *see* AGRICULTURE AND POLITICS IN MERU-ARUSHA

UNIVERSITY DAILY – Morgantown. West Virginia. 1880-98 – 1 – us UMI [071]

UNIVERSITY DAILY KANSAN – Lawrence. Kan. 1956- – 1 – us UMI [370]

UNIVERSITY EDUCATION: INAUGURAL ADDRESS DELIVERED IN CONVOCATION HALL, MANITOBA COLLEGE, WINNIPEG, NOVEMBER 10TH, 1899 / Bryce, George – Winnipeg?, 1899? 02848. (Pre-1900 Canadiana) – 9 – cn C.I.H.M. [370]

University Film Association *see* JOURNAL

UNIVERSITY GAZETTE – [Montreal?: Undergraduates of McGill University, 1873-189- or 19–] – 9 – cn C.I.H.M. [370]

UNIVERSITY HERALD – Ada, Ohio. 1885-96 – 3r – 1 – $32.50r – us Archival [071]

THE UNIVERSITY IN RELATION TO PROFESSIONAL EDUCATION: BEING THE ANNUAL UNIVERSITY LECTURE OF MCGILL UNIVERSITY, MONTREAL, IN THE SESSION OF 1887-8 / Dawson, John William – Montreal?: s.n., 1887 (Montreal: Gazette). 02611. (Pre-1900 Canadiana) – 9 – cn C.I.H.M. [971]

THE UNIVERSITY LAW REVIEW – (Cont: The Intercollegiate Law Journal) – University of the City of NY. v1-3. 1893-97 (all publ) – 12mf – 9 – $18.00 – LLMC 82-969 – us L.L.M.C. [073]

UNIVERSITY LAW REVIEW *see* THE INTERCOLLEGIATE LAW JOURNAL

UNIVERSITY MAGAZINE – Free Review Series. 1897-1900 – 1 – uk Microform Academic [073]

UNIVERSITY MAGAZINE – (v1-6 1901/02-1907. v7-10 1908-11. v11-14 1912-15. v15-19 1916-20 Can$100.00 per block) – Toronto. v1-19. 1901/02-1920 – 5 – cn Micromedia [370]

University of Abidjan *see* VOCABULAIRE ESSENTIEL DE L'ENSEIGNEMENT PRIMAIRE

UNIVERSITY OF AKRON BUSINESS REVIEW *see* AKRON BUSINESS AND ECONOMIC REVIEW

UNIVERSITY OF ARKANSAS AT LITTLE ROCK LAW JOURNAL – v1-17. 1978-95 – 9 – $267.00 set – us Hein [340]

THE UNIVERSITY OF ARKANSAS LAW SCHOOL BULLETIN – (Cont by: Arkansas Law Review) – v1-11. 1929-46 (all publ) – 11mf – 9 – $16.50 – LLMC 84-405 – us L.L.M.C. [073]

UNIVERSITY OF BALTIMORE INTELLECTUAL PROPERTY LAW JOURNAL – v1-2. 1992-94 – 9 – $28.00 set – us Hein [340]

UNIVERSITY OF BALTIMORE JOURNAL OF ENVIRONMENTAL LAW – (v1-3 1991-93 $37.50v. v4 1994 $12.00v) – v1-4. 1991-94 – 5,6,9 – $50.00 set – us Hein [340]

UNIVERSITY OF BALTIMORE LAW REVIEW – v1- 1971- 1; v8- 5,6,9 – us UMI [340]

UNIVERSITY OF BALTIMORE LAW REVIEW – (v1-14 1971-85 on reel $152.00. v15-24 1985-95 mf $161.00) – v1-24. 1971-95 – 5,9,6 – $313.00 set – us Hein [340]

University of Birmingham *see* HISTORICAL JOURNAL

UNIVERSITY OF BRIDGEPORT LAW REVIEW *see* QUINNIPAC LAW REVIEW

UNIVERSITY OF BRISTOL THEATRE COLLECTION – (Pt 1: Sets, mModels & costume designs 1987 $699. Pt 2: Beerbohm Tree Collection 1988 $6,400. Pt 3: Card catalogue 1990 $579. Pt 4: Old Vic archives 1989 $5,016. Pt 5: Picture collection 1990 $1,444. Pt 6: Miscellaneous material 1990 $1,060. Printed catalogue and indexes included) – 30 colour, 3055 b/w mf – 15,9 – $12,160.00 set – 1-869934-08-3 – uk Emmett [790]

UNIVERSITY OF BRITISH COLUMBIA LAW REVIEW – v1-29. 1959-95 – 9 – $424.00 set – us Hein [340]

University of California at Berkeley *see*
- THE BANCROFT LIBRARY, UNIVERSITY OF CALIFORNIA, BERKELEY
- EAST ASIATIC LIBRARY. AUTHOR-TITLE AND SUBJECT CATALOGS. 1968

University of California at Berkeley. Giannini Foundation of Agricultural Economics *see* DICTIONARY CATALOG OF THE GIANNINI FOUNDATION OF AGRICULTURAL ECONOMICS LIBRARY

University of California at Berkeley. The Bancroft Library *see* THE BANCROFT LIBRARY, UNIVERSITY OF CALIFORNIA, BERKELEY

University of California at Berkeley. Water Resources Center *see*
- DICTIONARY CATALOG OF THE ARCHIVES
- DICTIONARY CATALOG OF THE WATER RESOURCES CENTER ARCHIVES

University of California at San Diego. Scripps Institution of Oceanography *see*
- CATALOGS OF THE SCRIPPS INSTITUTION OF OCEANOGRAPHY LIBRARY

University of Chicago *see*
- CATALOG OF THE ORIENTAL INSTITUTE LIBRARY
- CATALOGS OF THE FAR EASTERN LIBRARY. 1973

University of Chicago. Far Eastern Library *see*
- AUTHOR-TITLE CHINESE CATALOG
- AUTHOR-TITLE JAPANESE CATALOG
- CLASSIFIED CATALOG AND SUBJECT INDEX

UNIVERSITY OF CHICAGO LAW REVIEW – v1-61. 1933-94 – 1,5,6,9 – $1,485.00 – us Hein [073]

UNIVERSITY OF CHICAGO LAW SCHOOL RECORD – (v1-30 1951-84 on reel $82.00. v31-41 1985-95 on mf $108.00) – v1-41. 1951-95 – 5,6,9 – $190.00 set – us Hein [340]

UNIVERSITY OF CHICAGO LEGAL FORUM – 1986-1995 – 9 – $116.00set – us Hein [340]

UNIVERSITY OF CHICAGO OCCASIONAL PAPERS – v1-32. 1971-95 1610 $10.00set – 9 – us Hein [340]

University of Chicago. Oriental Institute *see* CATALOG OF THE LIBRARY

University of Cincinnati *see* CATALOG OF THE MODERN GREEK COLLECTION

UNIVERSITY OF CINCINNATI LAW REVIEW – (With index v1-45) – v1-64. 1927-96 – 1,5,6 – $1,305.00 – us Hein [073]

UNIVERSITY OF COLORADO LAW REVIEW – v1-66. 1928-95 – 1,5,6 – $810.00 – us Hein [073]

UNIVERSITY OF DAYTON LAW REVIEW – (v1-10 1976-85 on reel $145.00. v11-20 1985-95 on mf $164.00) – v1-20. 1976-95 – 5,6,9 – $309.00 set – us Hein [340]

UNIVERSITY OF DETROIT JOURNAL OF URBAN LAW *see* UNIVERSITY OF DETROIT MERCY LAW REVIEW

UNIVERSITY OF DETROIT LAW JOURNAL *see* UNIVERSITY OF DETROIT MERCY LAW REVIEW

UNIVERSITY OF DETROIT LAW REVIEW *see* UNIVERSITY OF DETROIT MERCY LAW REVIEW

UNIVERSITY OF DETROIT MERCY INTERNATIONAL LAW FORUM – (Title varies: v1-2. 1991, as University of Detroit Mercy International Newsletter) – v1-4. 1991-1994 – 9 – $16.00set – us Hein [340]

UNIVERSITY OF DETROIT MERCY INTERNATIONAL NEWSLETTER *see* UNIVERSITY OF DETROIT MERCY INTERNATIONAL LAW FORUM

UNIVERSITY OF DETROIT MERCY LAW REVIEW – (v1-62 1931-85 on reel $620.00. v63-72 1985-95 on mf $184.00. Title varies: v1-43 1931-66 as University of Detroit Law Journal. v44-53 1967-76 as Journal of Urban Law. v54-61 1977-84 as University of Detroit Journal of Urban Law. v62-68 1985-90 as University of Detroit Law Review. Supersedes University of Detroit Bi-Monthly Law Review. Publication suspended 1933-39. v19-32 skipped in numbering) – v1-18, 33-72. 1931-95 – 5,6,9 – $804.00 set – us Hein [340]

University of Florida. Agricultural Experiment Station *see*
- AGRONOMY DEPARTMENT RESEARCH REPORT
- BULLETIN
- CIRCULAR
- SUNSHINE STATE AGRICULTURAL RESEARCH REPORT

University of Florida. Agricultural Experiment Station.Food and Resource Economics Department *see*
- ECONOMICS INFORMATION REPORT
- ECONOMICS REPORT
- STAFF PAPER SERIES
- STAFF REPORT EXECUTIVE SUMMARY

University of Florida at Gainesville *see*
- CATALOG OF THE LATIN AMERICAN COLLECTION, UNIVERSITY OF FLORIDA LIBRARIES
- CATALOG OF THE P.K. YONGE LIBRARY OF FLORIDA HISTORY

University of Florida. Cooperative Extension Service *see*
- ANNUAL REPORT
- BULLETIN
- CIRCULAR

University of Florida. Florida Cooperative Extension Service. Florida Sea Grant *see* SEA GRANT REPORT

University of Florida. Florida Sea Grant Program *see* TECHNICAL PAPER

University of Florida. Institute of Food and Agricultural Science *see* ANNUAL RESEARCH REPORT

UNIVERSITY OF FLORIDA LAW REVIEW *see* FLORIDA LAW REVIEW

University of Georgia. Agricultural Experiment Station *see*
- GEORGIA AGRICULTURAL RESEARCH
- RESEARCH BULLETIN
- RESEARCH REPORT
- SERVING GEORGIA THROUGH RESEARCH: BIENNIAL REPORT
- SOUTHERN COOPERATIVE SERIES: BULLETIN
- SPECIAL PUBLICATION

University of Georgia. Agricultural Extension Service *see*
- BULLETIN
- CIRCULAR
- LEAFLET

UNIVERSITY OF HAWAII LAW REVIEW – (Hein Co has later vols) – v1-6 no 2. 1979-84 (all offered) – 33mf – 9 – $49.50 – LLMC 83-400 – us L.L.M.C. [073]

UNIVERSITY OF HAWAII LAW REVIEW – v1-17. 1979-95 – 9 – $257.00 set – us Hein [340]

University of Illinois at Urbana-Champaign, Communications Library *see* CATALOG OF THE COMMUNICATIONS LIBRARY

UNIVERSITY OF ILLINOIS LAW BULLETIN *see* ILLINOIS LAW QUARTERLY

UNIVERSITY OF ILLINOIS LAW FORUM – 1949- 1; 1975- 5,6,9 – us UMI [340]

UNIVERSITY OF JUDAISM DIRECTION – Los Angeles, CA. 1973-85 – 1 – us A.J.P.C. [071]

UNIVERSITY OF KANSAS CITY LAW REVIEW *see* UMKC LAW REVIEW

UNIVERSITY OF KANSAS LAW REVIEW – (v1-33 1952-85 on reel $400.00. v34-43 1985-95 on mf $205.00) – v1-43. 1952-95 – 5,6,9 – $605.00 set – us Hein [340]

University of Keele *see* THE TAMWORTH COURT ROLLS

University of Kentucky. Agricultural Experiment Station *see*
- ANNUAL REPORT
- BULLETIN
- PROGRESS REPORT
- REGULATORY BULLETIN

University of Kentucky. Cooperative Extension Service *see*
- AGRICULTURAL ECONOMICS EXTENSION SERIES AND INFORMATION SERIES
- DEV
- ID
- KENTUCKY FARM BUSINESS ANALYSIS PROGRAM; ANNUAL SUMMARY

University of Kentucky. Department of Agricultural Economics *see*
- AEC
- KENTUCKY AGRI-BUSINESS QUARTERLY
- KENTUCKY AGRI-BUSINESS SPOTLIGHT
- RESEARCH REPORT
- STAFF PAPERS

University of Kentucky. Department of Agricultural Engineering *see*
- AEES
- AEN

University of Kentucky. Department of Agronomy *see* AGR

University of Kentucky. Department of Animal Sciences *see* ASC

University of Kentucky. Department of Entomology *see* ENT

University of Kentucky. Department of Forestry *see* FOR

University of Kentucky. Department of Horticulture *see* HO

University of Kentucky. Department of Plant Pathology *see* PPA

University of Kentucky. Department of Rural Sociology *see* RS

University of Kentucky. Department of Veterinary Science *see* VET

UNIVERSITY OF KUWAIT IN YEARS 18 / Kuwait. Kuwait University – (In Arabic and English) – Safat, 1985 – 9mf – 9 – DE-618/1 – ne IDC [370]

University of London. Institute of Education *see* CATALOGUE OF THE COMPARATIVE EDUCATION LIBRARY

University of London. Library *see* THE PALEOGRAPHY COLLECTION

University of London. London School of Hygiene and Tropical Medicine *see* LONDON SCHOOL OF HYGIENE AND TROPICAL MEDICINE LIBRARY

University of London. School of Oriental and African Studies *see*
- LIBRARY CATALOGUE
- LIBRARY CATALOGUE OF THE SCHOOL OF ORIENTAL AND AFRICAN STUDIES

University of London. Warburg Institute. Library *see*
- CATALOG OF THE LIBRARY. SECOND EDITION REVISED AND ENLARGED
- CATALOG OF THE WARBURG INSTITUTE LIBRARY

UNIVERSITY OF LOS ANGELES LAW REVIEW *see* LOYOLA OF LOS ANGELES LAW REVIEW

UNIVERSITY OF MANITOBA MEDICAL JOURNAL – (v1-45 1929/30-1975 Can$300.00. Cont by: Manitoba Medicine at v57 1987) – Winnipeg. v1-56. 1929/30-1986 – 5 – Can$50.00y – cn Micromedia [610]

UNIVERSITY OF MANITOBA MEDICAL JOURNAL *see* MANITOBA MEDICINE

UNIVERSITY OF MIAMI ENTERTAINMENT AND SPORTS LAW REVIEW – (Title varies: v1-5 1984-1988 as Entertainment and Sports Law Journal) – v1-12. 1984-1995 – 9 – $143.00 set – us Hein [340]

UNIVERSITY OF MIAMI INTERAMERICAN LAW REVIEW – (v1-16 1969-85 on reel $206.00. v17-26 1985-95 on mf $180.00. Title varies: v1-15 1969-84 as Lawyer of the Americas) – v1-26. 1969-95 – 5,6,9 – $386.00 set – us Hein [340]

UNIVERSITY OF MIAMI LAW REVIEW – (v1-39 1947-85 on reel $580.00. v40-49 1985-95 on mf $217.00) – v1-49. 1947-95 – 5,6,9 – $797.00 set – us Hein [340]

UNIVERSITY OF MIAMI YEARBOOK OF INTERNATIONAL LAW – v1-2. 1991-93 – 9 – $20.00 set – us Hein [340]

UNIVERSITY OF MICHIGAN BUSINESS REVIEW – (See also: Michigan Business Review) – v26- 1974- 1,5,6; v28- 9 – us UMI [380]

UNIVERSITY OF MICHIGAN JOURNAL OF LAW REFORM – (v1-18 1968-85 on reel or mf $240.00. v19-28 1985-95 on mf $253.00. Title varies: v1-3 1968-70 as Prospectus) – v1-28. 1968-95 – 5,6,9 – $493.00 set – us Hein [340]

University of Michigan. William L. Clements Library *see* RESEARCH CATALOG OF MAPS OF AMERICA TO 1860 IN THE WILLIAM L. CLEMENTS LIBRARY

University of Missouri. Agricultural Experiment Station *see*
- BULLETIN
- CIRCULARS
- PROJECT ANNOUNCEMENT
- RESEARCH BULLETIN
- SPECIAL REPORTS

University of Missouri. Agricultural Extension Service *see*
- EXTENSION CIRCULAR
- EXTENSION MANUALS
- MISCELLANEOUS PUBLICATIONS

UNIVERSITY OF MISSOURI AT KANSAS CITY LAW REVIEW *see* UMKC LAW REVIEW

UNIVERSITY OF MISSOURI BULLETIN : LAW SERIES – nos 1-40. 1913-28 (all publ) – 38mf – 9 – $57.00 – LLMC 84-613 – us L.L.M.C. [073]

University of Missouri. Freedom of Information Center *see* REPORT

University of Missouri. University Extension Division *see* UED PUBLICATIONS

University of Montreal *see* GALAS D'INAUGURATION

THE UNIVERSITY OF NALANDA / Sankalia, Hasmukhlal Dhirajlal – Preface by H. Heras. Madras: B.G. Paul, 1934. 259p. illus. Includes bibliography. (Studies in Indian History, Indian Historical Research Institute, v12) – 1 – us U.W. Library [950]

University of Nebraska *see* CAPTURED GERMAN RECORDS FILMED AT BERLIN

University of Nebraska. State Museum *see* BULLETIN

UNIVERSITY OF NEW BRUNSWICK LAW JOURNAL – 1947- 1; 1978- 5,6,9 – us UMI [340]

UNIVERSITY OF NEW BRUNSWICK LAW JOURNAL – (v1-33 1947-84 on reel $180.00. v34-44 1985-95 on mf $177.00. Index v1-36 1947-87. Title varies: v1-4 1947-51 as University of New Brunswick Law School Journal) – v1-44. 1947-95 – 5,6,9 – $357.00 set – us Hein [340]

UNIVERSITY OF NEW BRUNSWICK LAW SCHOOL JOURNAL *see* UNIVERSITY OF NEW BRUNSWICK LAW JOURNAL

UNIVERSITY OF NEW SOUTH WALES JOURNAL – v1-15. 1975-92 – 1,5,6 – $180.00 – us Hein [073]

UNIVERSITY OF NEWARK LAW REVIEW *see* RUTGERS LAW REVIEW

THE UNIVERSITY OF OTTAWA REVIEW *see* THE OWL

UNIVERSITY OF OTTAWA REVIEW – (Cont: The Owl) – [Ottawa?]: The students, [1898-1915] – 9 – cn C.I.H.M. [370]

University of Pennsylvania *see* MUSEUM JOURNAL

UNIVERSITY OF PENNSYLVANIA JOURNAL OF INTERNATIONAL BUSINESS LAW – (Title varies: v1-4 1977-1982 as Journal of Comparative Corporate Law and Securities Regulation. v5-8 1983-1986 as Journal of Comparative Business and Capital Market Review) – v1-16. 1987-95 – 9 – $375.00 set – us Hein [340]

UNIVERSITY OF PENNSYLVANIA LAW REVIEW – (Add vols as copyright expires) – v1-68. 1852-1919/20 – 592mf – $888.00 – LLMC 95-142 – us L.L.M.C. [073]

UNIVERSITY OF PENNSYLVANIA LAW REVIEW – v1-144. 1852-1996 – 1,5,6,9 – $3,555.00 – us Hein [073]

UNIVERSITY OF PENNSYLVANIA LAW REVIEW *see* THE AMERICAN LAW REGISTER AND REVIEW

University of Pennsylvania. Library *see*
- CATALOG OF THE EDGAR FAHS SMITH MEMORIAL COLLECTION IN THE HISTORY OF CHEMISTRY
- INDIC MANUSCRIPT COLLECTION

University of Pennsylvania. Wharton School. Industrial Research Department *see* RESEARCH STUDIES

UNIVERSITY OF PITTSBURGH LAW REVIEW – (Suspended Fall 1942-Oct 1947) – v1-56. 1935-95 – 9 – $910.00 set – us Hein [340]

UNIVERSITY OF PITTSBURGH LAW REVIEW – v1-57. 1935-96 – 1,5,6 – $1,170.00 – us Hein [073]

UNIVERSITY OF PUGET SOUND LAW REVIEW – v1-17. 1977-94 – 1,5,6 – $270.00 – us Hein [073]

UNIVERSITY OF QUEENSLAND LAW JOURNAL – v1-18. 1948-1995 – 9 – $316.00 set – us Hein [340]

UNIVERSITY OF RICHMOND LAW NOTES *see* UNIVERSITY OF RICHMOND LAW REVIEW

UNIVERSITY OF RICHMOND LAW REVIEW – (v1-19 1958-85 on reel $268.00. v20-29 1985-95 on mf $247.00. Title varies: v1-2 1958-65 as University of Richmond Law Notes) – v1-29. 1958-95 – 9 – $515.00 set – us Hein [340]

UNIVERSITY OF SAN FRANCISCO MARITIME LAW JOURNAL – v1-7. 1989-95 – 9 – $109.00 set – us Hein [340]

UNIVERSITY OF TASMANIA LAW REVIEW – (v1-7 1958-83 on reel $100.00. v8-12 1984-93 on mf $128.00) – v1-14. 1958-95 – 5,6,9 – $228.00 set – us Hein [340]

UNIVERSITY OF TASMANIA LAW REVIEW – (v.5- 1978- 5,6,9) – v.2-. 1964- – 1 – us UMI [340]

University of Tennessee. Agricultural Experiment Station *see* BULLETIN

University of Tennessee.Agricultural Experiment Station *see*
- ANNUAL REPORT
- TENNESSEE FARM AND HOME SCIENCE PROGRESS REPORT

University of Tennessee.Agricultural Extension Service *see*
- PUBLICATIONS
- RESOURCE DEVELOPMENT NEWSLETTER
- TENNESSEE EXTENSION REVIEW

University of Tennessee.Institute of Agriculture *see*
- AG INSTITUTE NEWS
- AG INSTITUTE REPORT
- THE NEWS
- REPORTER
- THIRD THURSDAY

University of Texas at Austin *see*
- CATALOG OF THE LATIN AMERICAN COLLECTION OF THE UNIVERSITY OF TEXAS LIBRARY

University of the West Indies. Imperial College of Tropical Agriculture. Trinidad *see* CATALOGUE OF THE IMPERIAL COLLEGE OF TROPICAL AGRICULTURE

UNIVERSITY OF TOLEDO LAW REVIEW – (v1-16 1969-85 on reel $240.00. v17-26 1986-95 on mf $176.00) – v1-26. 1969-95 – 5,6,9 – $416.00 set – us Hein [340]

UNIVERSITY OF TORONTO FACULTY OF LAW REVIEW – v1-53. 1942-95 – 9 – $452.00 set – us Hein [340]

UNIVERSITY OF TORONTO. INSTITUTE OF AEROSPACE STUDIES *see* COLLECTION

UNIVERSITY OF TORONTO LAW JOURNAL – Downsview. v144. 1951-94 – 9 – Can$28.00y – cn Micromedia [340]

UNIVERSITY OF TORONTO MEDICAL JOURNAL – (v1-46 1923/24-1969/70 Can$880.00 5) – Toronto. v1-71. 1923/24-1993/94 – 5,9 – Can$20.00y – cn Micromedia [610]

UNIVERSITY OF TORONTO QUARTERLY – Downsview. v1-63. 1931-1993/94 – 9 – Can$28.00y – cn Micromedia [370]

UNIVERSITY OF VIRGINIA LAW REVIEW – (Add vols as copyright expires) – v1-6. 1913-1919/20 – 42mf – $63.00 – LLMC 90-334 – us L.L.M.C. [073]

University of Virginia Library *see* THE CARTER FAMILY PAPERS, 1659-1797, IN THE SABINE HALL COLLECTION

UNIVERSITY OF WEST LOS ANGELES LAW REVIEW – v1- 1969- 1; v10- 5,6,9 – us UMI [340]

UNIVERSITY OF WEST LOS ANGELES LAW REVIEW *see* UWLA LAW REVIEW

UNIVERSITY OF WESTERN AUSTRALIA ANNUAL LAW REVIEW *see* UNIVERSITY OF WESTERN AUSTRALIA LAW REVIEW

UNIVERSITY OF WESTERN AUSTRALIA LAW REVIEW – (Title varies: v1-4 1948-59 as University of Western Australia Annual Law Review) – v1-25. 1948-95 – 9 – $378.00 set – us Hein [340]

UNIVERSITY OF WESTERN ONTARIO LAW REVIEW – (Title varies: v1-5 1961-66 as Western Law Review. v6-14 1967-75 as Western Ontario Law Review. Superseded by Canadian Journal of Law and Jurisprudence) – v1-24. 1961-87 – 9 – $183.00 set – us Hein [340]

UNIVERSITY OF WESTERN ONTARIO LAW REVIEW *see* CANADIAN JOURNAL OF LAW AND JURISPRUDENCE

UNIVERSITY OF WINDSOR REVIEW – (No issues publ in 1980/81. Cont by: Windsor Review at v26 1993) – Windsor. v1-25. 1965-92 – 9 – Can$20.00y – cn Micromedia [370]

UNIVERSITY OF WINDSOR REVIEW *see* WINDSOR REVIEW

University of Wisconsin *see* BADGER HERALD

University of Wisconsin. Conference on World Land Tenure Problem *see* LAND TENURE: PROCEEDINGS OF THE INTERNATIONAL CONFERENCE ON LAND TENURE AND RELATED PROBLEMS IN WORLD AGRICULTURE, HELD AT MADISON, WISCONSIN, 1951

UNIVERSITY OF WISCONSIN-LA CROSSE ADULT FITNESS/CARDIAC REHABILITATION GRADUATE PROGRAM ASSESSMENT / Anderson, Paula – University of Wisconsin-La Crosse, 1995 – 1mf – 9 – HE 562 – us Microform Publ [613]

UNIVERSITY PARK BAPTIST CHURCH (FORMERLY: TEMPLE). EUGENE, OREGON : CHURCH RECORDS – 1948-73 – 1 – $23.67 – us Baptist [240]

UNIVERSITY PLACE GAZETTE – University Place, NE. -w. May 1894; Oct 1895-Aug 1896; Oct 1896-Sept 1898 – 1 – us NE Hist [071]

UNIVERSITY PLACE NEWS – University Place, NE. -w. Nov 1905-Jan 1956 – 1 – us NE Hist [071]

UNIVERSITY PRESS – Irvine, CA. 1979 – 1r – 1 – $50.00 – R04040 – us Library Micro [071]

UNIVERSITY PUBLISHING – (1981-. 5,6,9) – 1976- – 1 – us UMI [070]

UNIVERSITY QUARTERLY REVIEW – Toronto: [s.n, 1890] – 9 – cn C.I.H.M. [370]

UNIVERSITY QUESTION / Ryerson, Adolphus Egerton – Quebec: Thompson and Co. SEM105P335 – 1mf – 9 – Can$2.25 – cn Bibl Nat [370]

UNIVERSITY SERMONS / Caird, John – Glasgow: J. MacLehose, 1898 – 1mf – us A.T.L.A. [240]

UNIVERSITY TEACHING OF SOCIAL SCIENCES INTERNATIONAL RELATIONS / UNESCO – 4mf – 7 – uk Microform Academic [327]

O UNIVERSO – Manaos, Amazonas. 9 Jan, Maio, Jul-Set 1915; 29 Jun 1917 – 1,5,6 – bl Biblioteca [072]

UNIVERSUL – Bucharest, Romania. 1939-May 1953 – 44r – 1 – us L of C Photodup [949]

UNIVERSUL – Bucharest. Rumania. -d. 16 Jan-4 Dec 1916, 30 Jan-23 May 1920, 1 Jan 1938-22 Nov 1949, 5 Apr 1951-20 Jul 1953. (79 reels) – 1 – uk British Libr Newspaper [949]

UNIX REVIEW – (1986- . 5,6,9) – v1- . 1983- – 1 – us UMI [073]

UNIYA – (Formerly Asian Bureau Australia) – Sydney. 59 docs. 1980-1991 – 19mf – 9 – ne IDC [320]

THE UNJUST JUDGE : OR, THE EVILS OF INTEMPERANCE ON JUDGES, LAWYERS, AND POLITICIANS, BY A MEMBER OF THE OHIO BAR / Stevens, William – Mansfield, OH: no publisher, 1854 – 1r – 1 – us Western Res [340]

UNJUST JUDGE : OR, THE EVILS OF INTEMPERANCE ON JUDGES, LAWYERS, AND POLITICIANS, BY A MEMBER OF THE OHIO BAR / Stevens, William – Mansfield, Ohio: n.p., 1854 – 1r – 1 – us Western Res [340]

THE UNKNOWN / Bech, Birger – Toronto: Queen City Publ. Co., 1887. 03534. (Pre-1900 Canadiana) – 9 – cn C.I.H.M. [830]

THE UNKNOWN EROS AND OTHER ODES : ODES I.-XXXI / Patmore, Coventry Kersey Dighton – London: George Bell and Sons, 1877 – 1 roll – 1 – 1-55879-176-0 – uk Libr Preservation [810]

THE UNKNOWN GOD, OR, INSPIRATION AMONG PRE-CHRISTIAN RACES / Brace, Charles Loring – New York: A.C. Armstrong, 1890 – 1mf – us A.T.L.A. [210]

UNKNOWN LIBERIA / Greenwall, Harry James & Wild, Roland – London: Hutchinson, 1936. 47 illus. 283p – 1 – us U.W. Library [960]

UNLV GABBS GABB – Las Vegas, CA. 1943-1944 – 2r – 1 – $100.00 – B06073 – us Library Micro [370]

Unna, G *see* KOVEZ LE-ZIKHRO SHEL GEDALYAH UNNA

Unnik, W C van *see* NESTORIAN QUESTIONS ON THE ADMINISTRATION OF THE EUCHARIST, BY ISHO'YABH 4

THE UNNOTICED THINGS OF SCRIPTURE / Kip, William Ingraham – New York: Thomas Whittaker, 1868. 1 fiche – 9 – us A.T.L.A. [240]

UNNUMBERED GENERAL PUBLICATIONS / Connecticut. Agricultural Experiment Station. New Haven – 1925-73 – 1,5,6 – us Spaulding [630]

UNNUMBERED PUBLICATIONS / Connecticut. Agricultural Experiment Station. Storrs – 1958-63 – 1,5,6 – us Spaulding [630]

UNNUMBERED PUBLICATIONS / North Carolina. State University. Raleigh. Agricultural Policy Institute – 1,5 – us Spaulding [630]

THE UNOCCUPIED MISSION FIELDS OF AFRICA AND ASIA / Zwemer, Samuel Marinus – New York: Laymen's Missionary Movement, 1911 – 1mf – us A.T.L.A. [240]

Unold, Joh. *see* DIE ETHNOLOGISCHEN UND ANTHROPOGEOGRAPHISCHEN ANSCHAUUNGEN BEI J KANT UND J REINHARD FORSTER

DER UNPARTHEYISCHE BIBLIOTHECARIUS – Leipzig. v1-13. 1713-16 (mf ed 1991) – 15mf – 9 – DM98.00 – 3-89131-046-3 – gw Fischer [430]

UNPRINTED SESSIONAL PAPERS / Canada. Parliament – 12th-32nd Parliaments. 1916-84 – 5 – cn Micromedia [324]

UNPUBLISHED DISPOSITIONS : PROBLEMS OF ACCESS AND USE IN THE COURTS OF APPEALS / Steinstra, Donna – Washington: FJC, 1985 – 1mf – 9 – $1.50 – LLMC 95-327 – us L.L.M.C. [340]

UNPUBLISHED DRAMA DEPOSITS, 1900-1906 / U.S. Copyright Office – 214 reels of unpublished drama deposits now in public domain. Further reels as deposits enter the public domain. 214 reels – 1 – 4762.00 – us L of C Photodup [790]

UNPUBLISHED FINDING AIDS FOR GENEALOGICAL RESEARCH, SERIES 1 – Parts 1 and 2. The calendars and indexes of allegations for marriage licences issued by the Vicar General for the Province of Canterbury and by the faculty office for the Archbishop of Canterbury, 1534-1850 – 1 – us Primary [025]

UNPUBLISHED FINDING AIDS FOR GENEALOGICAL RESEARCH, SERIES 2 – The Society of Genealogists' Apprenticeship Index – 9 – us Primary [920]

UNPUBLISHED HISTORY / Wallace, David Duncan – 1946. Title: A Hundred Years of William Gregg and Graniteville. Typescript. 7 fiches – 9 – us South Carolina Historical [978]

UNPUBLISHED LETTERS TO ELLEN KEY / Rilke, Rainer Maria – 294 2. (Mss.: 73 dated, 3 updated, 1 fragment). Sept. 6, 1902-Apr. 21, 1914 – 8 – ne IDC [860]

UNPUBLISHED MANUSCRIPTS / British Architectural Library – With printed index – 1 – £690.00 – uk World [720]

UNPUBLISHED RECORDS OF THE ESTABLISHED CHURCH OF ENGLAND, 1540-1720 – The Gibson Papers, Fairhurst Papers and Henry VIII divorce papers from the Lambeth Palace Library, London – 1 – us Primary [240]

UNPUBLISHED RECORDS...DIVISION OF RESEARCH AND INVESTIGATION, 1912-15 / U.S. Commission on Industrial Relations – Reports, staff studies and background research materials. With printed guide – 16r – 1 – $1,540.00 – 0-89093-744-3 – us UPA [330]

UNPUBLISHED REPORTS / U.S. Commission on the Organization of the Executive Branch of the Government (Hoover Commission) – 1 – $161.00 – us L of C Photodup [977]

UNPUBLISHED STATE PAPERS OF THE ENGLISH CIVIL WAR AND INTERREGNUM – (Part One: Parliamentary Committees. Part Two: Parliamentary Surreys of Crown Lands. Part Three: Certificates as to Sales of Crown Lands and Particulars for the Sale of the Estates of Charles I. Part Four: Particulars for the Sale of Free-farm Rents. Part Five: Documents relating to various Parliamentary accounts and to Ecclesiastical Affairs) – 1 – us Primary [944]

UNRAST : ROMAN DES MALERS KAI JANSEN / Lorenz, Gerhard – Muenchen: Deutscher Volksverlag, c1943 – 1r – 1 – us U.W. Library [830]

UNREGISTERED LETTERS RECEIVED AND RELATED RECORDS / Northern Pacific Railway Company. Secretary's Department – 1864-76 – 36r – 1 – $1260.00 $40.00r – us M.H.S. [380]

UNREPORTED DECISIONS / Virginia. Supreme Court – (A Pre-NRS title) – v1-2. 1730-1799 (all publ) – 19mf – 9 – $28.50 – LLMC 90-314 – us L.L.M.C. [340]

Unruh, Friedrich Franz von *see* FRIEDRICH HOELDERLIN

Unruh, Fritz von *see*
- EIN GESCHLECHT
- HEINRICH AUS ANDERNACH
- VOR DER ENTSCHEIDUNG

UNRUHIGE GAESTE : EIN ROMAN AUS DEM SAEKULUM / Raabe, Wilhelm Karl – Berlin: G Grote, 1886 – 1r – 1 – us U.W. Library [830]

UNS EEKBOOM – (Also known as: De Eekboom) – Berlin, jul 1893-1900 – 1 – Inquire at Mikrofilmarchiv for details – gw Misc Inst [072]

Unsain, Alejandro M *see* LAWS, ETC

UNSCHEDULED EVENTS – v1-3. 1967-69 – 3mf – 9 – $5.00f – us Ross [300]

THE UNSEEN WORLD : COMMUNICATIONS WITH IT, REAL OR IMAGINARY, INCLUDING APPARITIONS, WARNINGS, HAUNTED PLACES, PROPHECIES, AERIAL VISIONS, ASTROLOGY, ETC / Neale, John Mason – London: J. Masters, 1853 – 1mf – us A.T.L.A. [130]

UNSER FOLK – New York, NY. 1931-32 – 1 – us A.J.P.C. [071]

UNSER GOTTESGLAUBE = THE FAITH OF A MODERN PROTESTANT / Bousset, Wilhelm – (In English) – New York: Scribner's, 1909 – 1mf – 9 – 0-8370-2433-1 – 1985-0433 – us A.T.L.A. [240]

UNSER HEER – v. 1-3. Jan 1942-Oct 1944. (v. 3, nos. 1, 7, 11, 13, 16-18 wanting) – 1 – 19.00 – us L of C Photodup [943]

UNSER HEILIGER VATER PAPST LEO 13 : IN SEINEM LEBEN UND WIRKEN / Kuehne, Benno – New York: Benziger, 1883 – 1mf – 9 – 0-8370-8524-1 – 1986-2524 – us A.T.L.A. [920]

UNSER JOURNAL – (Bronx). 1920 – 1 – us A.J.P.C. [073]

UNSER LEBEN – (Missing: 1907(78,120,124,158)) – Warsaw, Odessa, 1907 – 1r – 1 – J-92-22/3 – ne IDC [072]

Unser, Matthias *see* DIE WIRTSCHAFTLICHKEIT DER INFORMATIONSVERARBEITUNG UNTER BESONDERER BERUECKSICHTIGUNG DES TRANSAKTIONSKOSTENANSATZES

UNSER RUNDFUNK *see* DER RUNDFUNK

UNSER SENDER : BEILAGE: EUROPAEISCHE VORTRAGSFOLGEN – (Cont by: Arbeitersender, 1930 n2) – Berlin, mar 9, 1930-jan 3, 1931 – 1r – 1 – gw Mikrofilm [073]

UNSER SENDER – (Cont by: Arbeitersender, 1930 n2) – Berlin. feb 1929-feb 24, 1933 – 6r – 1 – gw Mikrofilm [073]

UNSER SENDER – (Cont by: Arbeitersender, 1930 n2. Also suppl available: Europaeische Vortragsfolgen, mar 9 1930-jan 3 1931, 1r) – Berlin, feb 1929-feb 24 1933 – 1 – Inquire at Mikrofilmarchiv for details – gw Misc Inst [790]

UNSER STANDPUNKT – Kiel, Germany. Jun 1952-Aug 1959; 10 Oct 1960-1962; 17 Jan 1964-Jun 1966 (incomplete) – 1 – gw Mikrofilm [072]

UNSER WEG – Berlin, 1919-21 (incomplete), 1928-31 (incomplete) – 1 – Inquire at Mikrofilmarchiv for details – gw Misc Inst [072]

UNSER WERK – Bremen, Germany. 1941-Apr 1943 – 1r – 1 – gw Mikrofilm [072]

UNSER WERK – (Incl spec issue, concerning the 25th jubilee) – Bremen, 1941-apr 1943 – 1r – 1 – Inquire at Mikrofilmarchiv for details – gw Misc Inst [072]

UNSER WINKEL – (Newark). 1925 – 1 – us A.J.P.C. [073]

UNSER WORT – (Chicago). 1915-18 – 1 – us A.J.P.C. [335]

UNSER WORT : HALBMONATS-/ MONATZEITSCHRIFT DER INTERNATIONALEN LINKEN OPPOSITION BZW. DER INTERNATIONALEN KOMMUNISTEN DEUTSCHLANDS – Prag-Paris-Antwerpen-New York. Mar 1933-Jul 1941 – 1r – 1 – gw Mikrofilm [072]

UNSERE EVANGELIEN: IHRE QUELLEN UND IHR QUELLENWERT VOM STANDPUNKT DES HISTORIKERS / Soltau, Wilhelm – Leipzig: Dieterich, 1901. 1 fiche – 9 – us A.T.L.A. [240]

UNSERE KLEINE ZEITUNG – Berlin. -m – 1 – us U.W. Library [073]

UNSERE LITERATURGESELLSCHAFT : KRITIK UND POLEMIK / Koch, Hans – (Includes bibliographical references and index) – 1. Aufl. Berlin: Dietz Verlag, 1965 – 1r – 1 – us U.W. Library [430]

UNSERE MEINUNG (FDP) – Muenchen, DE. 20 Mar 1951-Mar 1956 – 1 – gw Mikrofilm [072]

UNSERE NACHBARN : NEUE SKIZZEN / Christen, Ada – Dresden: H Minden, 1884 – 1 – us U.W. Library [830]

UNSERE NIBELUNGENFAHRT / Wislicenus, Konrad – Berlin-Wilmersdorf: H Paetel, [1912] – 1r – 1 – us U.W. Library [890]

UNSERE RELIGIOESEN ERZIEHER : EINE GESCHICHTE DES CHRISTENTUMS IN LEBENSBILDERN / Baumgarten, O et al; ed by Bess, B – Leipzig: Quelle & Meyer, 1908 – 2mf – us A.T.L.A. [240]

UNSERE SCLAVEN : EIN SOCIALES SCHAUSPIEL IN 5 ACTEN / Sacher-Masoch, Leopold, Ritter von – Wien: Wallishauser (Josef Klemm), 1873 – 1r – 1 – us U.W. Library [820]

UNSERE TAKTIK BEIM GENERALSTREIK / Hue, Otto – Bochum, 1905 – 1 – DM30.00 – gw Mikro Press [330]

UNSERE WIRKLICHKEIT / Hauptmann, Carl – Muenchen: G D W Callwey, 1902 – 1r – 1 – us U.W. Library [840]

UNSERE ZEIT : HALBMONATS-/MONATSSCHRIFT FUER POLITIK, LITERATUR, WIRTSCHAFT, SOZIALPOLITIK UND ARBEITERBEWEGUNG – (Formerly publ in Berlin) – Basel-Paris-Prag-Strassburg. apr 1 1933-jul 1935 – 1 – Dist. gw Mikrofilm – gw Misc Inst [072]
UNSERE ZEIT, LEIPZIG 1857-1891 : JAHRBUCH ZUM CONVERSATIONS-LEXICON 1857-64; DEUTSCHE REVUE DER GEGENWART 1865-91 – 1994 – 440 fiches (1:24) – 9 – silver DM6,900.00 (Diazo DM5,900.00. ISBN: 3-598-32292-5) – 3-598-32293-3 – gw Saur [943]
UNSERER FORDERUNGEN ALS INDIVIDUALISTISCHE ANARCHISTEN / Armand, E – Our Demands as Individualist Anarchists.1945 – 9 – 1.00f – at Libertarian Micro [335]
UNSETTLED QUESTIONS TOUCHING THE FOUNDATIONS OF CHRISTIANITY : A BOOK FOR THOUGHTFUL YOUNG MEN / Otts, John Martin Philip – New York: Fleming H Revell, c1893 – 1mf – 9 – 0-8370-4652-1 – 1985-2652 – us A.T.L.A. [230]
UNSOUNDNESS OF MIND / Clouston, Thomas Smith – New York: E.P. Dutton, 1911. xxxi,360p.illus – 1 – us U.W. Library [612]
THE UNSPECIFIC SCANDAL: AN ORIGINAL, POLITICAL, CRITICAL AND GRITTICAL EXTRAVAGANZA, PERFORMED AT THE GREAT DOMINION THEATRE, OTTAWA, IN THE YEAR OF GRACE, 1873 / Fuller, William Henry – Ottawa: s.n., 1874 (Ottawa: A. Woodburn). 03271. (Pre-1900 Canadiana) – 9 – cn C.I.H.M. [820]
UNSTERBLICHE : NOVELLEN / Hohlbaum, Robert – Leipzig: L Staackmann, 1919 – 1r – 1 – us U.W. Library [830]
DER UNSTERBLICHKEITS-KONZERN : EIN ZEITBILD / Uden, Horst – Salzburg: Verlag "Das Bergland-Buch", 1943 – 1r – 1 – us U.W. Library [830]
DIE UNSUENDLICHKEIT CHRISTI / Atzberger, Leonhard – Muenchen: Ernst Stahl, 1883 – 1mf – us A.T.L.A. [240]
UNTER DEM BANNER DES MARXISMUS – Berlin. Mar. 1925-June 1930; Feb. 1931-Sept. 1932; Mar. Apr. 1933-Nov. 1935. Missing: no. 2, 1935 – 1 – 35.00r – us Hoover Inst Photo [073]
UNTER DER LINDE : ZWOELF NOVELLEN / Heimburg, W – 2. Aufl. Stuttgart: Union Deutsche Verlagsgesellschaft, 1890 – 1 – us U.W. Library [830]
UNTER DEUTSCHEN PALMEN / Benkard, Christian – Stuttgart: Deutsche Verlags-Anstalt. 2v. 1889 – 1 – us U.W. Library [830]
UNTER DREI GOUVERNEUREN : 16 JAHRE DIENST IN DEUTSCHEN TROPEN / Methner, Wilhelm – Breslau: W G Korn, [1938] – us Res Libr [920]
DIE UNTER HIPPOLYTS NAMEN UEBERLIEFERTE SCHRIFT UEBER DEN GLAUBEN : NACH EINER UEBERSETZUNG DER GEORGISCHEN VERSION / ed by Bonwetsch, Nathanael – Leipzig: J.C. Hinrichs, 1907. (Texte und Untersuchungen zur Geschichte der altchristlichen Litratur; der ganzen Reihe 31. Bd., Heft 2: 3. Reihe, 1. Bd., Heft 2) – 1mf – us A.T.L.A. [240]
DIE UNTER HIPPOLYTS NAMEN UEBERLIEFERTE SCHRIFT UEBER DEN GLAUBEN (T.U.U. 3-31/2A) / Bonwetsch, G N – Leipzig, 1907 – 1mf – 9 – ne Slangenburg [240]
UNTER MARIA THERESIA : ZEITBILD IN 5 AKTEN / Schwarz, Adolf – Berlin: Druck von Marschner & Stephan, 1874 – 1r – 1 – us U.W. Library [820]
UNTER WESTLICHEN STERNEN : GEDICHTE / Ilgen, Pedro – Leipzig, Berlin: C Wigand, 1905 – 1r – 1 – us U.W. Library [810]
DER UNTERGANG DES SONNENREICHES : DER SCHICHSALSWEG DES ALTEN PERU: EIN ROMAN / Zedtwitz, Franz Xaver, Graf – Berlin: Buchmeister-Verlag, 1942 – 1r – 1 – us U.W. Library [830]
DER UNTERGANG KARTHAGOS : EIN DRAMA IN DREI AKTEN / Moeller, Eberhard Wolfgang – Berlin: A Langen, G Mueller, 1941 – 1r – 1 – us U.W. Library [820]
UNTERHALTUNGEN, BAND 1-3, JANUAR 1766-JUNIUS 1767 – Hamburg: M C Book, 1766-70 – 1 – us Sibley [780]
UNTERLAENDER KURIER – Hagueneau, France. 1904-18. In German – 1 – fr A.C.R.P.P. [072]
UNTERNEHEMENSZUSAMMENSCHLUSSE NACH 23 GWB UND ART 66 MUV / Luebbing, Wendel – Gottingen, 1965. 155 p. LL-401 – 1 – us L of C Photodup [340]
UNTERNEHMERISCHE ZUSAMMENARBEIT MIT DEM SUEDLICHEN AFRIKA : FALLSTUDIE "JOINT VENTURE IN SUEDAFRIKA". FALLBEISPIEL "JOINT VENTURE MIT PARTNERN AUS NAMIBIA" / Wiesner, Knut – 1994 – 1mf – 9 – DM48.00 – 3-89349-870-2 – gw Hänsel [338]
DIE UNTERNEHMUNG IM MARKT. FESTSCHRIFT FUER WILHELM RIEGER, ZU SEINEM 75 GEBURTSTAG / Rieger, Wilhelm – Koeln, 1953 – 1 – DM30.00 – gw Mikro Press [920]
DIE UNTERORDNUNG DER SAETZE BEI CHAUCER / Eitle, Hermann – Tuebingen, 1913 – 2mf – DM62.00 – 3-8267-3054-2 – gw Hänsel [420]
UNTERRICHT (EIN KURTZE), DEN PFARHERRN VND PREDIGERN, INN MEINER GNEDIGEN HERRN DER MARGGRAFFEN ZU BRANNDENBURG. WES SIE DAS VOLCK WIDER ETLICHE VERFUERISCHE LERE, VERMANEN VND VNTERRICHTEN SOLLEN – 1528. BME-145 1 – 9 – ne IDC [240]
UNTERRICHT FUER SPAETAUSGESIEDELTE KINDER UND JUGENDLICHE / Kostrzewa, Frank – 1992 – 51p – 9 – DM48.00 – 3-89349-554-1 – gw Hänsel [370]
UNTERRICHT IM GENERALBASSE ZUM GEBRAUCHE FUER LEHRER UND LERNENDE.. / Kessel, Johann C – Neue verbesserte und vermehrte Auflage. 1791 – 9 – us Sibley [780]
UNTERRICHT IM GENERALBASS-SPIELEN AUF. DER ORGEL ODER SONST EINEM CLAVIER-INSTRUMENTE / Telemann, G M – Hamburg. 1773. BP-766 1 – 9 – ne IDC [780]
UNTERRICHT VON DER TEUTSCHEN SPRACHE UND POESIE, DEREN URSPRUNG, FORTGANG UND LEHR-SAETZEN... / Morhofen, D G – Ed3. Luebeck, Leipzig, 1718 – 14mf – 9 – ne IDC [430]
UNTERRICHTSPRAXIS – (v.14-. 1981-. 5,6,9) – v.1-. 1968- – 1 – us UMI [370]
UNTERRICHTUNG (GRUNDTLICHE) DAS VOLCK WIDER ETLICHE VERFUERISCHE LERE DER WIDERTAUFFER – BME-15 1 – 9 – ne IDC [240]
DIE UNTERSCHEIDUNGSLEHREN DER VERSCHIEDENEN CHRISTLICHEN BEKENNTNISSE IM LICHTE GOETTLICHEN WORTS / Graul, Karl – Leipzig: Doerffling und Franke, 1865. xii,142p – 1 – us U.W. Library [240]
UNTERSUCHUNG DER REAKTIVITAET-MECHANISMUS-BEZIEHUNG BEI SUBSTITUTIONSREAKTIONEN VON PLATIN(II)-KOMPLEXEN : ANWENDUNG VON HOCHDRUCKKINETISCHEN METHODEN / Schmuelling, Michael – 1995 – 2mf – 9 – DM80.00 – 3-8267-2136-5 – gw Hänsel [540]
UNTERSUCHUNG DER VERKERNUNG DER JAHRRINGSTRUKTUR SOWIE DER ROHDICHTE AN DOUGLASIEN [PSEUDOTSUGA MENZIESII (MIRB.) FRANCO] UNTERSCHIEDLICHER KRONENKLASSEN / Krischer, Volker – 1995 – 2mf – 9 – DM80.00 – 3-8267-2123-3 – gw Hänsel [634]
UNTERSUCHUNG DES BEI DER VERFORMUNG VON METALLTRAEGERN ENTSTEHENDEN KOERPERSCHALL / Fricke, Heiko – 1994 – 1mf – DM60.00 – 3-8267-2075-X – gw Hänsel [620]
UNTERSUCHUNG SYNTAKTISCHER STRUKTUREN IN RECHTSSPRACHLICHEN EINZELTEXTEN AUS ZWICKAUER STADTBUECHERN DER 1. HAELFTE DES 16. JAHRHUNDERTS / Broemme, Simone – 1992 – 182p – 9 – DM98.00 – 3-89349-588-6 – gw Hänsel [430]
UNTERSUCHUNG UEBER ALTER, URSPRUNG, ZWECK DER DEKRETALEN DES FALSCHEN ISIDORUS / Gfoerer, AF – Freiburg: Friedrich Wagner, 1848 – 1mf – us A.T.L.A. [240]
UNTERSUCHUNG UEBER DIE ENTWICKLUNG UND DEN STAND DER BETRIEBSVERHAELTNISSE EINES SCHLESISCHEN RITTERGUTES / Himmel, Paul – Kiel, 1908 – 1 – DM30.00 – gw Mikro Press [943]
EINE UNTERSUCHUNG UEBER WIRKUNGSUNTERSCHIEDE ZWISCHEN FERMENTIERTEN UND UNFERMENTIERTEM ISCADOR BEI HIV-POSITIVEN UND GESUNDEN PROBANDEN / Arif, Nail – 1995 – 2mf – 9 – DM80.00 – 3-8267-2090-3 – gw Hänsel [616]
UNTERSUCHUNG UND OPTIMIERUNG ALTERNATIVER ZAHNFUELLUNGS-COMPOSITE-MATERIALIEN AUF DER BASIS VON POLYBUTADIENEPOXID / Koch, Stefan – 1995 – 2mf – 9 – DM80.00 – 3-8267-2225-6 – gw Hänsel [617]
UNTERSUCHUNG VON ALGORITHMEN ZUR NULLSTELLENBESTIMMUNG (INSBESONDERE VON POLYNOMEN) HINSICHTLICH IHRES FEHLERVERHALTENS / Woerle, Regine – 1994 – 1mf – DM60.00 – 3-89349-892-3 – gw Hänsel [510]
UNTERSUCHUNG VON SCHALTNETZTEILEN MIT KONTINUIERLICHEN RESONANZSCHWINGUNGEN / Luedeke, Hans-Peter – 1994 – 2mf – 9 – DM80.00 – 3-89349-872-9 – gw Hänsel [621]
UNTERSUCHUNG ZUM SPRACHLICHEN MODEVERHALTEN / Kirchner, Rita – 1995 – 1mf – 9 – DM60.00 – 3-8267-2230-2 – gw Hänsel [150]
UNTERSUCHUNG ZUR RAEUMLICHEN UND SOZIALEN STRUKTUR UND DEREN ENTWICKLUNG BEI TAMMAR-WALLABIES, MACROPUS EUGENII (DESMAREST, 1817) / Volger, Katrin – 1993 – 3mf – 9 – DM98.00 – 3-89349-662-9 – gw Hänsel [574]
UNTERSUCHUNGEN UBER DIE VERWANDTSCHAFT DER UBERLIEFERUNGEN VON BARBOUR'S BRUCE / Muehleisen, Wilhelm – Bremen, 1912 – 1 – DM30.00 – gw Mikro Press [420]
UNTERSUCHUNGEN UEBER DEN BAU DER CYANOPHYCEEN UND BAKTERIEN / Fischer, A – Jena. 1897. B-6360 2 – 8 – ne IDC [580]
UNTERSUCHUNGEN UEBER DEN EINFLUSS DER FERTIGUNGSBEDINGUNGEN BEIM SPRITZGIESSEN AUF DIE FESTIGKEITSEIGENSCHAFTEN VON PROBESTAEBEN AUS POLYAETHYLEN / Maier, Georg – Rosenheim, 1969 – 4mf – DM90.00 – 3-89349-888-5 – gw Hänsel [660]
UNTERSUCHUNGEN UEBER DEN ENTWICKLUNGSGANG UND DIE FUNKTION DES DIALOGS IN DER ISLAENDISCHEN SAGA / Ludwig, Werner – Graefenhainichen, 1934 – 2mf – 9 – DM62.00 – 3-89349-343-3 – gw Hänsel [490]
UNTERSUCHUNGEN UEBER DEN FLECHTENTHALLUS / Schwendener, S – (C.W. Naegeli, Beitraege zur wissenschaftlichen Botanik, heft 2). Leipzig. 1858. B-5385 2 – 8 – ne IDC [580]
UNTERSUCHUNGEN UEBER DEN URSPRUNG DER HARMONIE UND IHRE ALLMAEHLIGE AUSBILDUNG / Dalberg, Johann F H von – P-668. 8 v. 1800 – 9 – ne IDC [780]
UNTERSUCHUNGEN UEBER DIE AETIOLOGIE DER WUNDINFECTIONSKRANKHEITEN / Koch, R – Leipzig, 1878 – 2mf – 9 – ne IDC [616]
UNTERSUCHUNGEN UEBER DIE AEUSSERE ENTWICKLUNG DER AFRIKANISCHEN KIRCHE : MIT BESONDERER VERWERTUNG DER ARCHAEOLOGISCHEN FUNDE / Schwarze, Alexis – Goettingen: Vandenhoeck & Ruprecht, 1892 – 1mf – us A.T.L.A. [240]
UNTERSUCHUNGEN UEBER DIE ALTTESTAMENTLICHEN ZITATE BEI LUKAS (T.U.U. 5-104) / Holtz, T – Berlin, 1968 – 4mf – 9 – ne Slangenburg [240]
UNTERSUCHUNGEN UEBER DIE DEUTSCHE UEBERSETZUNG DES ALTEN TESTAMENTS / Matthias, Adolf – Greifswald, 1902. 1 fiche – 9 – us A.T.L.A. [240]
UNTERSUCHUNGEN UEBER DIE EDESSENISCHE CHRONIK (T.U.U. 1-9/1A) / Hallier, L – Leipzig, 1892 – 3mf – 9 – ne Slangenburg [240]
UNTERSUCHUNGEN UEBER DIE HALACHISCHEN MIDRASCHIM / Albeck, H – Berlin. 1927. BJ-32-25 1 – 9 – ne IDC [900]
UNTERSUCHUNGEN UEBER DIE LEPIDOPTERENFAUNA DER BUCOVINA / Hormuzaki, C von – Czernowitz, 1894. 183p.Z/1355/2 – 8 – ne IDC [590]
UNTERSUCHUNGEN UEBER DIE MOTIVE DER ROBIN-HOOD-BALLADEN / Kiessmann, Rudolf – 1995 – 1mf – 9 – DM48.00 – 3-8267-3124-7 – gw Hänsel [420]
UNTERSUCHUNGEN UEBER DIE REDAKTION DER MISCHNA / Albeck, H – Berlin. 1923. BJ-32-1 1 – 9 – ne IDC [900]
UNTERSUCHUNGEN UEBER DIE RESTE EINES HEBRAEISCHEN TEXTES VOM ERSTEN MAKKABAEERBUCH / Schweizer, Abraham – (In German, Hebrew, and Greek. Includes bibliographical references) – Berlin: M Poppelauer, 1901 – 1mf – 9 – 0-8370-9743-6 – 1986-3743 – us A.T.L.A. [220]
UNTERSUCHUNGEN UEBER DIE SOGEN. CLEMENTINISCHE LITURGIE IM 8. BUCH DER APOSTOLISCHEN KONSTITUTIONEN / Drews, Paul – Tuebingen: J.C.B. Mohr, 1906. (Studien zur Geschichte des Gottesdienstes und des gottesdienstlichen Lebens / von Paul Drews; 2-3) – 1mf – us A.T.L.A. [240]
UNTERSUCHUNGEN UEBER DIE TEXTGESTALT UND DIE ECHTHEIT DES BUCHES MICHA : EIN KRITISCHER COMMENTAR ZU MICHA / Ryssel, Victor – (Includes bibliographical references) – Leipzig: S Hirzel, 1887 – 1mf – 9 – 0-8370-5010-3 – 1985-3010 – us A.T.L.A. [220]
UNTERSUCHUNGEN UEBER DIE VERMEHRUNG DER LAUBMOOSE DURCH BRUTORGANE UND STECKLINGE / Correns, C E – Jena. 1899. B-1188 2 – 8 – ne IDC [580]
UNTERSUCHUNGEN UEBER DIE WIRKUNG VON ALUMINIUM- UND H-IONEN AUF DIE SPROSSZELLEN CALCICOLER UND CALCIFUGER ARTEN / Gerdes, Gerriet – 1993 – 1mf – 9 – DM60.00 – 3-89349-844-3 – gw Hänsel [574]
UNTERSUCHUNGEN UEBER FARNPROTHALLIEN / Heim, C – (Flora. v. 82.) Marburg. 1896. B-7193 2 – 8 – ne IDC [580]
UNTERSUCHUNGEN UEBER JOSEPHUS / Druener, Hans – Marburg: Joh. Hamel, 1896. 1 fiche – 9 – us A.T.L.A. [240]
UNTERSUCHUNGEN UEBER NORMATIVES UND NICHT-NORMATIVES DENKEN / Feldkeller, Paul – Tuebingen, 1913 – 2mf – DM62.00 – 3-8267-3040-2 – gw Hänsel [120]
UNTERSUCHUNGEN UEBER RAMLERS UND LESSINGS BEARBEITUNG VON SINNGEDICHTEN LOGANS / Heuschkel, Walter – (Includes bibliographical references) – Jena: A Kaempfe, 1901 – 1r – 1 – us U.W. Library [430]
UNTERSUCHUNGEN UEBER SELAGINELLA SPINULOSA A. BR / Bruchmann, H – Gotha. 1897. B-7167 1 – 9 – ne IDC [580]
UNTERSUCHUNGEN UEBER SPRACHE UND STIL DES JUNGEN HERDER / Haussmann, Johannes – (Includes bibliographical references (p. ix-x)) – Borna-Leipzig: R Noske, 1906 – 1r – 1 – us U.W. Library [430]
UNTERSUCHUNGEN UEBER VERSCHIEDENE SYSTEME DES WASSERREISANBAUS MIT DEM ALGENFARN AZOLLA UND DESSEN WIRKUNGEN AUF UNKRAUTFLORA UND ERTRAGSPARAMETER / Gerdes, Gerriet – 1993 – 2mf – 9 – DM80.00 – 3-89349-846-X – gw Hänsel [631]
UNTERSUCHUNGEN UEBER WIELAND'S DON SYLVIO : MIT BERUECKSICHTIGUNG DER UEBRIGEN DICHTUNGEN DER BIBERACHER ZEIT / Martens, Alfred – (Includes bibliographical references) – Halle a.S: E Karras, 1901 – 1r – 1 – us U.W. Library [430]
UNTERSUCHUNGEN ZU CLAUDIO MONTEVERDIS MESSKOMPOSITIONEN / Hust, Gerhard – Heidelberg, 1970 – 3mf – DM76.00 – 3-89349-835-4 – gw Hänsel [780]
UNTERSUCHUNGEN ZU DEN HOMER-APORIEN DES ARISTOTELES / Hintenlang, Hubert – Heidelberg, 1961 – 2mf – DM62.00 – 3-89349-839-7 – gw Hänsel [180]
UNTERSUCHUNGEN ZU EINER TYPIK DES SELBST IN DER ERFAHRUNG / Scheer, Brigitte – Frankfurt a.M., 1969 – 3mf – 9 – DM76.00 – 3-89349-383-2 – gw Hänsel [120]
UNTERSUCHUNGEN ZU HEINRICH VON VELDEKE / Jungbluth, Guenther – (Includes bibliographical references) – Frankfurt am Main: M Diesterweg, 1937 – 1r – 1 – us U.W. Library [943]
UNTERSUCHUNGEN ZU NILUS DEM ASKETEN (T.U.U. 3-42/2) / Heussi, Karl – Leipzig, 1917 – 3mf – 9 – ne Slangenburg [240]
UNTERSUCHUNGEN ZUM AUFBAU VON HISTON-GEN-GRUPPEN DES MENSCHEN / Runge, Dorothee Monika – 1995 – 1mf – 9 – DM60.00 – 3-8267-2108-X – gw Hänsel [574]

UNTERSUCHUNGEN ZUM BUCH AMOS / Loehr, Max – (Includes bibliographical references) – Giessen: J Ricker (Alfred Toepelmann), 1901 – 1mf – 9 – 0-8370-4167-8 – 1985-2167 – us A.T.L.A. [220]

UNTERSUCHUNGEN ZUM DIALOG BEI CHRISTOPHER FRY / Kohn-Zwilling, Isolde – Frankfurt a.M., 1972 – 3mf – 9 – DM76.00 – 3-89349-751-X – gw Hänsel [410]

UNTERSUCHUNGEN ZUM EXZITONENTRANSFER IN ASYMMETRISCHEN CDTE/(CD,MN)TE-DOPPELGRABENSTRUKTUREN / Hiecke, Katharina – 1995 – 1mf – 9 – DM60.00 – 3-8267-2261-2 – gw Hänsel [530]

UNTERSUCHUNGEN ZUM GRIECHISCHEN SCHMUCK AN BEISPIELEN DES 7. UND 6. JAHRHUNDERTS V. CHR / Gesenhoff, Georgia – 1994 – 3mf – 9 – DM98.00 – 3-89349-859-1 – gw Hänsel [930]

UNTERSUCHUNGEN ZUM PROBLEM DER NORMVORSTELLUNG / Deusinger, Ingrid M – Frankfurt a.M., 1969 – 3mf – 9 – DM76.00 – 3-89349-388-3 – gw Hänsel [110]

UNTERSUCHUNGEN ZUM WACHSTUM UND ZUR DOTIERUNG VON EPITAKTISCHEN ZNTE-SCHICHTEN / Woerle, Klaus – 1994 – 1mf – DM60.00 – 3-89349-893-1 – gw Hänsel [530]

UNTERSUCHUNGEN ZUR ANTHOCYANBIOSYNTHESE AN GENETISCH DEFINIERTEN BLUETEN UND ZELLKULTUREN DER DAHLIE UND DER SOMMERASTER / Gallus, Heidrun – 1994 – 2mf – DM80.00 – 3-8267-2004-0 – gw Hänsel [580]

UNTERSUCHUNGEN ZUR BEDEUTUNG DER EHESCHLIESSUNG FUER DEN VERLAUF SCHIZOPHRENER ERKRANKUNGEN / Stahl, Andreas – 1994 – 1mf – DM60.00 – 3-8267-2056-3 – gw Hänsel [616]

UNTERSUCHUNGEN ZUR BIOGRAPHIE PHILIPP ZESENS / Gebhardt, Max – (Includes bibliographical references) – Berlin: C Rehm, 1888 – 1 – us U.W. Library [430]

UNTERSUCHUNGEN ZUR "EINKLEIDUNG" EINIGER PLATONISCHER DIALOGE / Muthmann, Fritz – Bonn 1961 – 1 – DM30.00 – gw Mikro Press [180]

UNTERSUCHUNGEN ZUR ENTWICKLUNGSGESCHICHTE DER ARISTOTELISCHEN METEOROLOGIE / Strohm, Hans – Leipzig, 1935 – 84p – 9 – DM48.00 – 3-89349-007-8 – gw Hänsel [550]

UNTERSUCHUNGEN ZUR FUNKTION UND BETEILIGUNG EINES GTP-BINDENDEN PROTEINS AM INTRAZELLULAEREN TRANSPORT IN NEURONALEM GEWEBE / Lindenblatt, Joerg – 1991 – 2mf – 9 – DM98.00 – 3-89349-446-4 – gw Hänsel [574]

UNTERSUCHUNGEN ZUR GESCHICHTE DER GRIECHISCHEN SPRACHE : VON DER HELLENISTISCHEN ZEIT BIS ZUM 10. JAHRHUNDERT N. CHRISTI / Dieterich, Karl – (Includes index) – Leipzig: B G Teubner, 1898 – 1mf – 9 – 0-8370-9284-1 – 1986-3284 – us A.T.L.A. [450]

UNTERSUCHUNGEN ZUR GESCHICHTE DER GRIECHISCHEN VATERUNSER-EXEGESE (T.U.U. 3-40/3) / Walther, G – Leipzig, 1914 – 2mf – 9 – ne Slangenburg [240]

UNTERSUCHUNGEN ZUR KENNTNIS VON ORDNUNGSVORGAENGEN IN FLUORIT-UEBERSTRUKTUR-PHASEN IM SYSTEM SRF$_2$-YBF$_3$: MOEGLICHKEITEN UND GRENZEN DER ELEKTRONENMIKROSKOPIE BEI DER AUFKLAERUNG ATOMARER STRUKTUREN / Ziel, Rainer – 1995 – 2mf – 9 – DM80.00 – 3-8267-2133-0 – gw Hänsel [530]

UNTERSUCHUNGEN ZUR KOSMOLOGIE DES HELLENISTISCHEN UND PALAESTINISCHEN JUDENTUMS (T.U.U. 5-97) / Weiss, H F – Berlin, 1966 – 7mf – 9 – ne Slangenburg [240]

UNTERSUCHUNGEN ZUR KRITIK DES ALTEN TESTAMENTS / Noeldeke, Theodor – (Includes bibliographical references) – Kiel: Schwers, 1869 – 1mf – 9 – 0-8370-4596-7 – 1985-2596 – us A.T.L.A. [220]

UNTERSUCHUNGEN ZUR PRAKTISCHEN ANWENDBARKEIT WAESSRIGER ZWEIPHASENSYSTEME AUF DER BASIS NICHTIONISCHER TENSIDE ALS TECHNISCHE REINIGUNGSMETHODE FUER AMPHIPHILE PROTEINE / Minuth, Mark Torsten – 1995 – 2mf – 9 – DM80.00 – 3-8267-2245-0 – gw Hänsel [574]

UNTERSUCHUNGEN ZUR PROBLEMATIK BEI DER FESTSETZUNG VON MAXIMALEN IMMISSIONSKONZENTRATIONEN FUER OZON / Kleinschmidt, Juergen – 1994 – 3mf – 9 – DM98.00 – 3-89349-861-3 – gw Hänsel [360]

UNTERSUCHUNGEN ZUR REPRODUZIERBARKEIT VON LAKTAT-SCHWELLEN, RESPIRATORISCHEN SCHWELLEN UND KATECHOLAMINSCHWELLEN UND ZU IHREM VERHAELTNIS UNTEREINANDER / Li, Yin – 1995 – 1mf – 9 – DM60.00 – 3-8267-2238-8 – gw Hänsel [612]

UNTERSUCHUNGEN ZUR REVALGISIERUNG UND ZUM ANTETORSIONSREZIDIV NACH INTERTROCHANTEREN OSTEOTOMIEN BEI KINDERN UND JUGENDLICHEN / Steffen, Hans-Michael – 1994 – 2mf – DM80.00 – 3-8267-2011-3 – gw Hänsel [618]

UNTERSUCHUNGEN ZUR RUSSISCHEN HISTORISCHEN WORTBILDUNG AM BEISPIEL DER WORTBILDUNGSKATEGORIEN "NOMINA AGENTIS" UND "NOMINA INSTRUMENTI" IN DER PERIODE VOM 11.-17. JAHRHUNDERT / Totzke, Steffen – 1991 – 283p – 9 – DM98.00 – 3-89349-416-2 – gw Hänsel [460]

UNTERSUCHUNGEN ZUR SEMANTISCHEN KONGRUENZ SUBSTANTIVISCH-VERBALER LEXEMVERBINDUNGEN IM RUSSISCHEN UND DEUTSCHEN (MANUSKRIPT 1984) / Jaehnert, Katrin – 1993 – 2mf – 9 – DM80.00 – 3-89349-778-1 – gw Hänsel [430]

UNTERSUCHUNGEN ZUR STEIGERUNG DER INTERPRETATIONSSICHERHEIT AKUSTO-MIKROSKOPISCHER BILDER / Laun, Uwe – 1995 – 3mf – 9 – DM98.00 – 3-8267-2247-7 – gw Hänsel [530]

UNTERSUCHUNGEN ZUR TRISTANSAGE / Kelemina, Jakob – 1910 – 1 – us I.U. Libraries [410]

UNTERSUCHUNGEN ZUR UEBERLIERFERUNGSGESCHICHTE DER AELTESTEN LATEINISCHEN MOENCHSREGELN / Plenkers, H – Muenchen, 1906 – 3mf – 8 – Dfl13.00 – ne Slangenburg [240]

UNTERSUCHUNGEN ZUR VERAENDERUNG DER INFORMATIONSVERARBEITUNGSFAEHIGKEIT VON 9 BIS 12JAEHRIGEN KINDERN IM VERLAUF VON LERNPROZESSEN UNTERSCHIEDLICHER MODALITAETSPRAEFERENZEN / Becker, Werner – 1992 – 305p – 9 – DM98.00 – 3-89349-592-4 – gw Hänsel [370]

UNTERTHAENIGE REDEN : VIER VORLESUNGEN, OEFFENTLICH GEHALTEN ZU KOENIGSBERG IM WINTER 1843,... / Walesrode, Ludwig Reinhold – Zuerich: Verlag des literarischen Comptoirs, 1843 – 1r – 1 – us U.W. Library [850]

UNTERVEGS = THE TRANSIENT – (In Yiddish) – Frankfurt-Zeilsheim, DE. no2 Apr 1946-no3 May 1946 – 1r – 1 – $25.00 – cn Can Microfilming [072]

UNTERWEGS ZUR SACHE / Jungel, Eberhard – Muenchen, 1972 – 5mf – 8 – ne Slangenburg [290]

THE UNTILLED FIELD / Moore, George – London: T. Fisher Unwinn, 1903 – 1 roll – 1 – 1-55879-605-3 – uk Libr Preservation [890]

"UNTO THIS LAST" : FOUR ESSAYS ON THE FIRST PRINCIPLES OF POLITICAL ECONOMY / Ruskin, John – London: Smith, Elder, 1862 – 1 roll – 1 – 1-55879-494-8 – uk Libr Preservation [320]

THE UNTOUCHABLES OF INDIA / Ouwerkerk, Louise – London, New York: Oxford University Press, 1945.47p. illus. map, diagr – 1 – us U.W. Library [950]

UNTUK DEMOKRASI, PERSATUAN DAN MOBILISASI / Aidit, Dipa Nusantara – SE-4505 1. CC PKI 25 Apr. 1962 – 9 – ne IDC [335]

UNUM CORPUS – nos 1-21. 1933-54 (complete) – 1r – 1 – ATLA S0665C – us A.T.L.A. [073]

DER UNVERBLUEMTE AMOR : NOVELLE / Hotzel, Curt – [Bayreuth]: Gauverlag Bayreuth, 1944 – 1r – 1 – us U.W. Library [830]

DIE UNVEREINBARKEIT DER NEUEN PAEPSTLICHEN GLAUBENSDEKRETE MIT DER BAYERISCHEN STAATSVERFASSUNG / Berchtold, Joseph – (Includes bibliographical references) – Muenchen: Rieger, 1871 – 1mf – 9 – 0-8370-8481-4 – 1986-2481 – us A.T.L.A. [240]

DAS UNVERLIERBARE / Weiss, Ernst – Berlin: E Rowohlt, c1928 – 1r – 1 – us U.W. Library [830]

UNVERRUECKBARE GRENZSTEINE: EIN OFFENES WORT AN HERRN D. RADE UND SEINE FREUNDE / Ecke, Gustav – Berlin: Positiven Union, 1907. 1 fiche – 9 – us A.T.L.A. [240]

DIE UNVERZEIHLICHE TORHEIT : ROMAN AUS DER GEGENWART / Voigtel, Otto – 3. Aufl. Muenchen: F Eher, 1943 – 1r – 1 – us U.W. Library [830]

DIE UNVOELKOMMENHEIT DES VOELKERRECHTS / Burckhardt, W – Bern, 1923 – 1mf – 1 – ILM-3133/1 – ne IDC [327]

Unwerth, Wolf von *see* GESCHICHTE DER DEUTSCHEN LITERATUR BIS ZUR MITTE DES ELFTEN JAHRHUNDERTS

UNWISE LAWS (ON PROTECTING TARIFFS) / Blair, Lewis H – 1886. 1 fiche (29x) – 9 – 1.00f – at Libertarian Micro [320]

DIE UNWISSENSCHAFTLICHKEIT IM GEBIETE DER ALTTESTAMENTLICHEN KRITIK : BELEGT AUS DEN SCHRIFTEN NEUERER KRITIKER BESONDERS DER HERREN VON BOHLEN UND VATKE / Drechsler, Moritz – (Includes bibliographical references) – Leipzig: Karl Tauchnitz, 1837 – 1mf – 9 – 0-8370-9378-3 – 1986-3378 – us A.T.L.A. [220]

UNZER BULLETIN = OUR BULLETIN – (In Yiddish) – Warsaw, PL. no6 no26 Jun 1949 – 1r – 1 – $25.00 – cn Can Microfilming [072]

UNZER CHAVER = OUR COMRADE – (In Yiddish) – New York City, NY. v1 no1 Mar 1927-Jun 1927 – 1r – 1 – $25.00 – cn Can Microfilming [071]

UNZER EXSPRES = OUR EXPRESS – (Yiddish daily) – Warsaw, PL. v6 no241a 19 Oct 1932-v12 no? 30 Sep 1938 – 1r – 1 – $30.00 – cn Can Microfilming [072]

UNZER FRAYHAYT = OUR FREEDOM – (Yiddish bi-monthly. Includes Kinderland suppl) – Warsaw, PL. v5 no7 Mar 1934-v10 no4(no157) May 1939 – 1r – 1 – $25.00 – cn Can Microfilming [072]

UNZER FRAYND = OUR FRIEND – (In Yiddish) – Vilnius, LT. no107. 6 Mar 1923 – 1r – 1 – $25.00 – cn Can Microfilming [072]

UNZER GEZUNT – New York. N.Y. 1910-16 – 1 – us A.J.P.C. [071]

UNZER GEZUNT = OUR HEALTH – (Yiddish monthly) – New York City, NY. v1 no1 Aug 1932-Dec 1932 – 1r – 1 – $25.00 – cn Can Microfilming [071]

UNZER GRODNER EKSPRES = OUR GRODNO EXPRESS – (In Yiddish) – Grodno, PL. no202 31 Aug 1930-no207 5 Sep 1930 – 1r – 1 – $30.00 – cn Can Microfilming [072]

UNZER HAYNT = OUR DAY – (In Yiddish) – Munich, DE. v1 no1-2 Feb 1951-v1 no6 23 Mar 1951 – 1r – 1 – $25.00 – cn Can Microfilming [072]

UNZER HILF = OUR HELP – (In Yiddish) – Vilnius, LT. v1 no1/2 Jun 1921-v2 no5/12 31 Dec 1923 – 1r – 1 – $25.00 – cn Can Microfilming [072]

UNZER KAMF – New York, NY. 1932 – 1 – us A.J.P.C. [071]

UNZER LEBEN = OUR LIFE – (In Yiddish) – Warsaw, PL. v2 no286. 24 Dec 1908 – 1r – 1 – $25.00 – cn Can Microfilming [072]

UNZER LEBN = OUR LIFE – (In Russian – Yiddish) – Shanghai, CC. no13 25 Jul 1941; (no14) 1 Aug 1941 – 1r – 1 – $25.00 – cn Can Microfilming [072]

UNZER LEBN = OUR LIFE – (In Yiddish) – Wlodzimierz, PL. v3 no15 12 Apr 1929; v4 no9(no9) 8 Feb 1930 – 1r – 1 – $25.00 – cn Can Microfilming [072]

UNZER MEZRITSHER VOKHNBLAT = OUR WEEKLY – (In Yiddish) – Miedzyrzec, PL. Jun 1930 – 1r – 1 – $25.00 – cn Can Microfilming [072]

UNZER SHRIFT – New York, NY. 1912 – 1 – us A.J.P.C. [071]

UNZER SHTIME = OUR VOICE – (In Yiddish and English) – Montreal, CN. no 1. 1943-1944 – 1r – 1 – Can$30.00 – cn Can Microfilming [072]

UNZER TSAYT [NUESTRA ERA] = NEW ERA – (In Yiddish) – Buenos Aires, AG. v13 no386 26 Jul 1946-no429 3 Oct 1947 – 1r – 1 – $30.00 – cn Can Microfilming [072]

UNZER TSAYTUNG = OUR NEWS – (In Yiddish) – Piotrkow, PL. v3 no45 12 Nov 1926-v7 no7 14 Feb 1930 – 1r – 1 – $25.00 – cn Can Microfilming [072]

UNZER TSAYTUNG = OUR TIMES – (In Yiddish. Daily) – Bialystok, PL. v2 no302. 30 Dec 1935 – 1r – 1 – $25.00 – cn Can Microfilming [072]

UNZER TSIL = OUR GOAL – (In Yiddish) – Linz, AU. v1 no7 30 May 1947-9 Jan 1948 – 1r – 1 – $30.00 – cn Can Microfilming [072]

UNZER VEG = THE JEWISH TRIBUNE – (In Yiddish and English) – Montreal, CN, 1935 – 1r – 1 – Can$25.00 – cn Can Microfilming [072]

UNZER VEG = OUR WAY – (In Yiddish) – Siedlce, PL. v5 no32 24 Aug 1928 (no193) – 1r – 1 – $25.00 – cn Can Microfilming [072]

UNZER VEG = OUR WAY – (In Yiddish) – Stockholm, SW. v- no- 24 Jan 1947 – 1r – 1 – $25.00 – cn Can Microfilming [072]

UNZER VELT = OUR WORLD – NOTRE MONDE – (In Yiddish) – Munich, DE. v2 no42 24 Oct 1947-no221 7 Jul 1950 – 1r – 1 – $35.00 – cn Can Microfilming [072]

UNZER VORT = THE LABOUR VOICE – Montreal, CN. v1 no 3, v3 no 33. 1927-1934 – 1r – 1 – Can$60.00 – cn Can Microfilming [072]

UNZER VORT – New York, NY. 1945-50 – 1 – us A.J.P.C. [071]

UNZER VORT = NOTRE PAROLE – (In Yiddish) – Brussels, BE. v1 no49 7 Jul 1945-v3 no21 17 Mar 1948 – 1r – 1 – $35.00 – cn Can Microfilming [072]

UNZER VORT = OUR WORD – (In Yiddish) – New York City, NY. v2 no10 Dec 1946-v3 no7 Oct 1947 – 1r – 1 – $25.00 – cn Can Microfilming [071]

UNZER WEG – Munich. n1-252. 1945-49 – 2r – 1 – us Ross [072]

UNZER WEG = OUR WAY – (In Yiddish) – Munich, DE. v1 n10. 7 Dec 1945-n290. 28 Dec 1950 – 1r – 1 – $50.00 – cn Can Microfilming [072]

UNZER WELT = OUR WORLD – (In Yiddish) – Warsaw, PL. v1 no10 21 Jun 1935-v5 no29(no219) 21 Jul 1939 – 1r – 1 – $60.00 – cn Can Microfilming [072]

UNZER ZEIT – Kishineff, Rumania. v2-5. 1923-26 – 1r – 1 – us Ross [072]

UNZER ZHURNAL = OUR JOURNAL – (In Yiddish) – Slonim, PL. no2 May 1921; no9 Dec 1921 – 1r – 1 – $25.00 – cn Can Microfilming [072]

L'UOMO BIANCO E L'UOMO DE COLORE: LETTURE SU L'ORIGINE E LA VARIETA DELLA RAZZE UMANE / Lombroso, Cesare – Turin: Fratelli Bocca, 1892. 395p. 5 fiches. (Miscellaneous Selections) – 9 – 12.00 – fr Bibl Nationale [306]

L'UOMO NUOVO – New York, NY, 1916-1917 – 2mf or 1r – 1,9 – us I.H.R.C. [978]

L'UOMO QUALUNQUE – 1945-1960 – L100,000 – sz Infoprint [072]

L'UOMO QUALUNQUE – Italy, 1945-60 – 13 – inquire – us Ross [072]

UP AND DOWN THE IRRAWADDI : OR THE GOLDEN DAGON / Palmer, J W – New York, 1859 – 4mf – 9 – ne IDC [950]

UP HERE, LIFE IN CANADA'S NORTH – Yellowknife. v1-9. 1984/85-1993/94 – 9 – Can$20.00y – cn Micromedia [910]

THE UPANISHADS : PART 1: THE KHANDOGYA-UPANISHAD, THE TALAVAKARA-UPANISHAD, THE AITAREYA-ARANYAKA, THE KAUSHITAKI-BRAHMANA-UPANISHAD, AND THE VAGASANEYISAMHITA-UPANISHAD / ed by Mueller, Friedrich Max – (Translated by F.Max Mueller) – 1879 – 8mf – 8 – ne Slangenburg [280]

THE UPANISHADS : PART 2 THE KATHA-UPANISHAD, THE MUNDAKA-UPANISHAD, THE TAITTRIYAKA-UPANISHAD, THE BRIHADARANYAKA-UPANISHAD, THE SVETASVATARA-UPANISHAD, THE PRASNA-UPANISHAD, AND THE MAITRAYANA-BRAHMANA-UPANISHAD / ed by Mueller, Friedrich Max – (Translated by F. Max Mueller) – 1884 – 7mf – 8 – ne Slangenburg [280]

UPANISHADS. MANDUKYA-UPANISHAD – With Gaudapada's Karikas and the Bhashya of S'ankara. Manilal N. Dvivedi, trans. Bombay: Bombay Theosophical Publication Fund, 1894. 137p – 1 – us U.W. Library [280]

UPCOTT COLLECTION OF LITERARY AUTOGRAPHS, 1765-1830 – (With printed index) – 6r – 1 – £415.00 – uk Chadwyck [070]
UPDATA GOVERNMENT DOCUMENTS COLLECTIONS ON MICROFICHE *see*
- UPDATA GOVERNMENT DOCUMENTS – RESEARCH AND DEVELOPMENT DOCUMENTS

UPDATA GOVERNMENT DOCUMENTS – RESEARCH AND DEVELOPMENT DOCUMENTS : CENTRAL INTELLIGENCE AGENCY (CIA) – (Index available) – 1960-86 – 1230mf – 9 – $4,900.00 coll – us Ross [327]
UPDATA GOVERNMENT DOCUMENTS – RESEARCH AND DEVELOPMENT DOCUMENTS : COAL GASIFICATION AND LIQUEFACTION – (Index available) – 1910-75 – 1195mf – 9 – $4,800.00 coll – us Ross [660]
UPDATA GOVERNMENT DOCUMENTS – RESEARCH AND DEVELOPMENT DOCUMENTS : CRANFIELD COLLEGE OF AERONAUTICS – (Index available) – 1976-77 – 475mf – 9 – $2,400.00 coll – us Ross [629]
UPDATA GOVERNMENT DOCUMENTS – RESEARCH AND DEVELOPMENT DOCUMENTS : DEFENSE METALS INFORMATION CENTER – (Index available) – 1952-71 – 662mf – 9 – $3,300.00 coll – us Ross [660]
UPDATA GOVERNMENT DOCUMENTS – RESEARCH AND DEVELOPMENT DOCUMENTS : INSTITUTE OF AEROSPACE STUDIES (IAS) – (Index available) – 1948-86 – 881mf – 9 – $4,400.00 coll – us Ross [629]
UPDATA GOVERNMENT DOCUMENTS – RESEARCH AND DEVELOPMENT DOCUMENTS : MINE SAFTEY AND HEALTH – (Index available) – 1973-79 – 460mf – 9 – $2,300.00 coll – us Ross [360]
UPDATA GOVERNMENT DOCUMENTS – RESEARCH AND DEVELOPMENT DOCUMENTS : NATIONAL ADVISORY COMMITTEE FOR AERONAUTICS (NACA) – (Index available) – 1915-58 – 13,909mf – 9 – $41,700.00 coll – us Ross [629]
UPDATA GOVERNMENT DOCUMENTS – RESEARCH AND DEVELOPMENT DOCUMENTS : NATIONAL AERONAUTICS AND SPACE ADMINISTRATION (NASA) – (Index available) – 1958-74 – 126,831mf – 9 – $295,000.00 coll – us Ross [629]
UPDATA GOVERNMENT DOCUMENTS – RESEARCH AND DEVELOPMENT DOCUMENTS : UNITED STATES ARMY HANDBOOKS – (Index available) – 1960-77 – 528mf – 9 – $2,600.00 coll – us Ross [355]
UPDATA GOVERNMENT DOCUMENTS – RESEARCH AND DEVELOPMENT DOCUMENTS : UNITED STATES BUREAU OF MINES – (Index available) – 1910-91 – 17,753mf – 9 – $53,300.00 coll – us Ross [622]
UPDATA GOVERNMENT DOCUMENTS – RESEARCH AND DEVELOPMENT DOCUMENTS : UNITED STATES DEPARTMENT OF AGRICULTURE (USDA) – (Index available) – 1862-1986 – 14,086mf – 9 – $42,300.00 coll – us Ross [630]
UPDATA GOVERNMENT DOCUMENTS – RESEARCH AND DEVELOPMENT DOCUMENTS : UNITED STATES NATIONAL MARINE FISHERIES SERVICE (NOAA) – (Index available) – 1871-1986 – 4210mf – 9 – $16,800.00 coll – us Ross [639]
UPDATA GOVERNMENT DOCUMENTS – RESEARCH AND DEVELOPMENT DOCUMENTS : USGS WATER SUPPLY PAPERS – (Index available) – 1896-1978 – 8079mf – 9 – $32,000.00 coll – us Ross [550]
UPDATA INDEX / U.S. Mine Safety and Health Administration – Updata number, subj. and title on all publications issued. 1 fiche – 9 – 10.00 – us Updata [324]
UPDATE – v1-10. 1977-86 (complete) – 3r – 1 – ATLA S0773 – us A.T.L.A. [073]
UPDATE: A QUARTERLY JOURNAL ON NEW RELIGIOUS MOVEMENTS – (1985-. 5,6,9) – v6-. 1982- – 1 – us UMI [200]
UPDATE ON LAW-RELATED EDUCATION (ABA) – v1-16. 1977-92 – 9 – 105.00 set – us Hein [370]
UPDATED WORLD REVIEW OF INTERACTIONS BETWEEN MARINE MAMMALS AND FISHERIES – 1991 – 64p – it F.A.O. [639]
Upham, Charles W *see* LETTERS ON THE LOGOS
Upham, Francis Bourne *see* SIMON PETER, FISHERMAN
Upham, Francis William *see*
- SAINT MATTHEW'S WITNESS TO WORDS AND WORKS OF THE LORD
- STAR OF OUR LORD
- THOUGHTS ON THE HOLY GOSPELS
- THE WISE MEN

Upham, Thomas Cogswell *see* ABSOLUTE RELIGION
Uphoff, Carl Emil *see* DER EWIGE JAN
UPHOLSTERER *see* INTERIORS
UPHOLSTERER AND INTERIOR DECORATOR *see* INTERIORS
UPHOLSTERING TODAY – 1985-. -m – 1 – us UMI [670]
UPLAND COURIER – Upland, CA. 1965-83 – 16r – 1 – $800.00 – B03055 – us Library Micro [071]
UPLAND EAGLE – Upland, NE. -w. May 1901; Aug-Sept 1902; Nov-Dec 1902; Apr-Jun 1908; Aug 1908-Aug 1932; May 1940 – 1 – us NE Hist [071]
UPLAND NEWS – Upland, CA. 1912-90 – 91r – 1 – $4,550.00 – R03056 – us Library Micro [071]
UPLAND TODAY – San Bernardino, CA. 1983 – 1r – 1 – $50.00 – R04101 – us Library Micro [071]
THE UPLIFT OF CHINA / Smith, Arthur Henderson – (Includes index) – New York: Educational Dept of the Domestic and Foreign Missionary Society of the Protestant Episcopal Church, c1907 – 1mf – 9 – 0-8370-6381-7 – 1986-0381 – us A.T.L.A. [950]
UPLNY MISTOPISNY SLOVNIK KRALOVSTFI CESKEHO. / Kotyska, Vaclav – 1895. Czechoslovakia-Gazetteers – 1 – us U.W. Library [030]
UPPER CALIFORNIA DIRECTORY – State of California. 1886 – 1r – 1 – $50.00 – D112 – us Library Micro [978]
UPPER CANADA CHAMBERS / Ontario. Canada – v1-2. 1848-53 (all publ) – 7mf – 9 – $11.50 – LLMC 81-053 – us L.L.M.C. [340]
UPPER CANADA COMMON PLEAS / Ontario. Canada – v1-32. 1850-82 (all publ) – 218mf – 9 – $327.00 – LLMC 81-054 – us L.L.M.C. [340]
UPPER CANADA COURT RECORDS : REPORT OF THE ONTARIO BUREAU OF COURT RECORDS / Ontario. Canada – 1v. 1789-94 (all publ) – 5mf – 9 – $7.50 – LLMC 81-055 – us L.L.M.C. [340]
UPPER CANADA GAZETTE OR AMERICAN ORACLE – (Also: York Weekly Post, 1821. Missing: 1846-47) – Ontario, 1793-1848 – 15r – 1 – $975.00 – cn Library Assoc [971]
UPPER CANADA HERALD – Kingston, Ontario. v4 n194. 19 nov 1822 – 1r – 1 – Can$25.00 – cn Can Microfilming [072]
UPPER CANADA HOUSE OF ASSEMBLY : JOURNALS AND APPENDICES – 1st sess 9th Parl 13 Jan 1825-5th sess 13th Parl 10 Feb 1840 – 9r – 1 – Can$65.00r – cn Commonwealth Micro [324]
UPPER CANADA JURIST / Ontario. Canada – (Title became v1+ 2 of Upper Canada Queen's Bench Reports, Old series) – v1-2. 1830-48 (all publ) – 17mf – 9 – $25.00 – us L.L.M.C. [340]
UPPER CANADA JURIST *see* UPPER CANADA QUEEN'S BENCH REPORTS
UPPER CANADA LAW JOURNAL / Canada. Ontario – (Cont by: Canada Law Journal) – v1-10. 1855-64; ns: v1-3. 1865-87 (all publ) – 49mf – 9 – $73.00 – LLMC 81-014 – us L.L.M.C. [340]
UPPER CANADA LAW JOURNAL *see*
- CANADA LAW JOURNAL
- THE LOCAL COURTS' AND MUNICIPAL GAZETTE

THE UPPER CANADA LAW JOURNAL AND LOCAL COURTS GAZETTE *see* THE CANADA LAW JOURNAL
THE UPPER CANADA LAW JOURNAL AND LOCAL COURTS' GAZETTE – (Cont by: The Canada Law Journal) – Barrie [Ont.]: "Barrie Herald", 1855-[1867] – 9 – cn C.I.H.M. [340]
UPPER CANADA LAW JOURNAL, NEW SERIES *see* CANADA LAW JOURNAL
UPPER CANADA QUEEN'S BENCH / Ontario. Canada – 2nd series: v1-46. 1844-82 (all publ) – 340mf – 9 – $510.00 – LLMC 81-058 – us L.L.M.C. [340]
UPPER CANADA QUEEN'S BENCH REPORTS / Ontario. Canada – (Cont: Upper Canada Jurist) – os: v3-6. 1833-46 (all publ) – 29mf – 9 – $43.50 – LLMC 81-057 – us L.L.M.C. [340]
UPPER CANADA QUEEN'S BENCH REPORTS, OLD SERIES *see* UPPER CANADA JURIST
UPPER CANADA REPORTS / Canada – Law reports covering the 1823-1900 period of what is now Ontario. 206v – 9 – Can$1,125.00 – cn Carswell [340]
UPPER CANADA SKETCHES / Conant, Thomas – Toronto: W. Briggs, 1898. 00740. (Pre-1900 Canadiana) – 9 – cn C.I.H.M. [971]
UPPER DES MOINES – Algona. Iowa. -w. 1951- – 1 – us UMI [071]
UPPER FAIRFOREST BAPTIST CHURCH. UNION COUNTY. SOUTH CAROLINA : CHURCH RECORDS – 1820-73, 1971-73 – 1 – 12.60 – us Baptist [240]
Upper Gilmanton, New Hampshire. Upper Gilmanton Free Will Baptist Church *see* RECORDS
UPPER ISLANDER – Campbell River, British Columbia, CN. Feb 1943-1972 – 9r – 1 – cn Commonwealth Micro [072]
UPPER LAKE REGION / J.H. Beers and Co – Biographical sketches illustrated. Chicago, 1905. Minnesota Reel 2. The Cox Library Collection – 5 – us Americana [978]
UPPER MAUMEE RIVER VALLEY / Brant, Fuller and Co – History of Allen County and Fort Wayne. Madison: 1889. Vols. 1-2. Indiana Reel 4. (The Cox Library Collection) – 5 – us Americana [978]
UPPER MOUNTAINS NEWS – Katoomba, Dec 17 1968-Jun 31 1969 – 1 – at Pascoe [072]
UPPER MURRAY AND MITTA HERALD – 1921-1974 – 15r – 1 – at Corangamite [980]
Upper Sandusky. Ohio. First Universalist Church *see* CHURCH RECORDS, MS 1559
Upper Sandusky. Ohio. John Stewart United Methodist Church *see* RECORDS
Upper Sandusky. Ohio. St. Paul's Lutheran Church *see* RECORDS
UPPER SANDY NEWS – Portland OR. July 11 1947-Mar 8 1956 – 1 – us U.O. Library [071]
UPPER SHIRE VALLEY DEPARTMENT PROJECT (KASUPE MWANZA) / Israel. Ministry of Foreign Affairs. International Cooperation Division – A prefeasibility study. Report on a survey mission by a Dutch-Israeli team, Dec 1975-Jan 1976. Apr 1976. 154 p. Maps. In cooperation with the Royal Netherlands Government. International Technical Assistance Dept., Ministry of Foreign Affairs, The Hague – 9 – $3.00 – is I.T.T.I. [956]
Upper Volta *see*
- ECONOMIE ET PLAN DE DEVELOPPEMENT
- JOURNAL OFFICIEL DE LA HAUTE-VOLTA
- JOURNAL OFFICIEL DE LA REPUBLIQUE DE HAUTE-VOLTA
- PLAN INTERIMAIRE, 1963-1964
- LE PLAN QUINQUENNAL 1972-1976
- PLAN-CADRE DE DEVELOPPEMENT, 1967-1970
- PLAN-CADRE DE HAUTE-VOLTA. ANNEE INTERIMAIRE 1971
- PROJET DE PLAN QUINQUENNAL, 1963-67

Upper Volta. Assemblee Nationale *see* PLAN QUINQUENNAL DE DEVELOPPEMENT ECONOMIQUE ET SOCIAL 1972-1976
Upper Volta. Ministere du Plan *see* PLAN QUINQUENNAL DE DEVELOPPEMENT ECONOMIQUE ET SOCIAL 1972-1976
UPPLANDS NYHETER – Borlange, Sweden. 1979- – 1 – sw Kungliga [072]
UPPLANDS-BRO *see* LOKALTIDNINGEN JARFALLA/UPPLANDS-BRO
Uppsala University Library, Stockholm *see* THUNBERG CORRESPONDENCE
UPPSALADEMOKRATEN – Gavle, Sweden. 1980- – 1 – sw Kungliga [072]
Upravleniia Upolnomochennogo Narodnogo komissariata vneshne i torgovli R.S.F.S.R. pri Sovnarkome USSR *see* VESTNIK VNESHNE I TORGOVLI UKRAINY
Upravlinii a narodno-hospodarskoho obliku USSR *see* HROMADSKE KHARCHUVANNIA UKRAINY 1933 R
UPSALA – Uppsala, Sweden. 1845-1958 – 269r – 1 – sw Kungliga [072]
UPSALA NYA TIDNING – Uppsala, Sweden. 1890-1978 – 500r – 1 – sw Kungliga [072]
UPSALA NYA TIDNING – Uppsala, Sweden. 1979- – 1 – sw Kungliga [072]
UPSALAPOSTEN – Uppsala, Sweden. 1857-96 – 38r – 1 – sw Kungliga [072]
THE UP-TO-DATE PRIMER: A FIRST BOOK OF LESSONS FOR LITTLE POLITICAL ECONOMISTS: IN WORDS OF ONE SYLLABLE WITH PICTURES / Bengough, John Wilson – New York, Toronto: Funk & Wagnalls, 1896. c1894. 00132. (Pre-1900 Canadiana) – 9 – cn C.I.H.M. [320]
UPTON BAPTIST CHURCH. UPTON, KENTUCKY : CHURCH RECORDS – 1870-1986 – 1 – 84.29 – us Baptist [240]
Upton, Harriet Taylor *see*
- 20TH CENTURY HISTORY OF TRUMBUL COUNTY
- HISTORY OF THE WESTERN RESERVE
- PAPERS, MS 1746

Upton, S Jill *see* A COMPARISON OF CARDIORESPIRATORY FITNESS OF TRAINED AND UNTRAINED MIDDLE-AGED WOMEN
UPTON SINCLAIR'S : A MONTHLY MAGAZINE FOR A CLEAN PEACE AND THE INTERNATION – 1-10 (all publ). 1918-1919 – 2mf – 9 – $35.00 – us UPA [335]
UPTON SINCLAIR'S EPIC NEWS – (Also known as: End Poverty Paper) – Los Angeles, CA. May 1934-Sept 1947 – 3r – 1 – $150.00 – C02402 – us Library Micro [071]
UPWARD – 6Apr 1941-61 – 1 – 402.99 – us Baptist [240]
UQYANUS / ed by Allah, Hajji Sayyid Farraj – (Sal-i 1, shumarah-'i 1-17. (17 Rabi II 1326-1 Jumada 1326[18 May 1908-1 June 1908])) – Tehran: Mirza Abd al Rahim Illahi – 1 reel – 1 – $65.00 – us MEDOC [950]
UR EXCAVATION TEXTS. (ROYAL INSCRIPTIONS, 5. 8) / Sollberger – 9 – ne IDC [930]
UR EXCAVATIONS, 3: ARCHAIC SEAL-IMPRESSIONS / Legrain, L – 1936 – 9 – $10.00 – us I.R.C. [930]
UR RELIGIONENS HISTORIA / Soederblom, Nathan – Stockholm, P.A. Norstedt, [1915] – 1mf – us A.T.L.A. [240]
Urabeyen, Felix *see* LA ULTIMA CIGUENA
Uragon, F de *see* INDICE DE LAS PRUEBAJ DE CABALLEROS DE LA ORDEN DE SANTIAGO
Uragon, Marques de Laurencin *see* LA OVANDINA, DE PEDRO MEXIA DE OVANDO
URAIAN MANIPOL (GARISGARIS BESAR HALUAN NEGARA) JOGJAKARTA, MADJELIS LUHUR TAMAN SISWA / Djadji Darmowijono, R – SE-4877 1. 1964 – 9 – ne IDC [950]
URALISCHE ANKLAENGE IN DEN ESKIMOSPRACHEN / Uhlenbeck, C C – (Zeitschr. der Deutsch. morgenlaend. Gesellschaft. Bd. 59). Berlin. 1905. BN-435 2 – 8 – ne IDC [490]
URALOBLSOVNARKHOZA : V.S.N.KH. R.S.F.S.R., URALSKI I OBLASTNO I SOVET NARODNOGO KHOZI A ISTVA – (Includes c.1: 1924/1925:no.1) – Sverdlovsk: Sovet, 1925- – 1 – CSUXAKZ6757-S – us Hoover Inst Photo [947]
URALSKIE PARTIZANY : POKHOD OTRIADOV BLIUKHERA-KASHIRINA V 1918 GODU / Golubykh, M – Ekaterinburg: Uralkniga, 1924 – 1 – CSUX88-B7717 – us Hoover Inst Photo [355]
URAL'SKII KOOPERATOR : IZD EKATERINBURG, O-VA POTREBITELEI – (Missing: 1915 n4-5; 1917 n3-1918 n2, 5-6, 8-19) – Ekaterinburg, 1910-18 n21 – 40mf – 9 – COR-700/1 – ne IDC [334]
URAL'SKII KOOPERATOR : IZD ORG BIURO TSENTROSOIUZA, ETC – (Missing: 1926 n26-27; 1930 n4-8, 10-11, 15) – Ekaterinburg, (Sverdlovsk), 1924-30 n17/18 – 174mf – 9 – COR-701/1 – ne IDC [334]
URAL'SKII OKHOTNIK – (Missing: 1932 n8-12) – Ekaterinburg, (Sverdlovsk), 1924-33 n6 – 109mf – 9 – COR-702/1 – ne IDC [334]
URAL'SKOE KHOZIAISTVO – (Missing: 1917 n5-...; 1917 n3-4; 1918 n23-24) – Ekaterinburg, 1910-18 n36 – 81mf – 9 – COR-703/1 – ne IDC [334]
URANA SHIRE ADVOCATE – Jan 2 1947-Dec 18 1947 – 1 – at Pascoe [072]
URANIA – 1970-1989 – 493mf – 1 – DM2,810.10 – gw Mikro Press [600]
URANIA : MUSIKZEITSCHRIFT FUER ORGELBAU, ORGEL- UND HARMONIUMSPIEL – Erfurt. v1-37. 1844-80 – 65mf – 9 – DM300.00 – gw Mikro Press [073]
URANIA, OR A CHOICE COLLECTION OF PSALM TUNES, ANTHEMS, AND HYMNS / Lyon, James – Philadelphia, 1761. MUSIC 1123 – 1 – us L of C Photodup [780]

URANIA, OR A CHOICE COLLECTION OF PSALM TUNES, ANTHEMS, AND HYMNS: TO WHICH ARE PREFIX'D THE PLAINEST, AND MOST NECESSARY RULES OF PSALMODY... / Lyon, James – Philadelphia: H Dawkins, 1761 – 1 – us Sibley [780]

L' URANIE *see* VOYAGE AUTOUR DU MONDE EXECUTE SUR LES CORVETTES DE S.M. L'URANIE ET LA PHYSICIENNE, 1817-1820

L'URANIE *see*
- VOYAGE AUTOUR DU MONDE. EXECUTE SUR LES CORVETTES DE S.M. L'URANIE ET LA PHYSICIENNE, 1817-1820
- VOYAGE AUTOUR DU MONDE EXECUTE SUR LES CORVETTES DE S.M. L'URANIE ET LA PHYSICIENNE, 1817-1820
- VOYAGE AUTOUR DU MONDE. EXECUTE SUR LES CORVETTES DE S.M. L'URANIE ET LA PHYSICIENNE, 1817-1820

Urbach, Adolf *see* UEBER DIE SPRACHE IN DEN DEUTSCHEN BRIEFEN DER HERZOGIN ELISABETH CHARLOTTE VON ORLEANS

Urbain, A *see* EIN MARTYROLOGIUM DER CHRISTLICHEN GEMEINDE ZU ROM (T.U.U. 2-21/3)

URBAN ANALYSIS – 1982 – 1,5,9 – us Gordon [310]

URBAN AND RURAL SOCIAL CONDITIONS IN INDUSTRIAL BRITAIN, SERIES 2 : THE REPORTS TO THE LOCAL GOVERNMENT BOARD, 1869-1908 / Great Britain. Local Government Board – 9 – us Primary [941]

URBAN AND RURAL SOCIAL CONDITIONS IN INDUSTRIAL BRITAIN, SERIES 3 : PUBLIC HEALTH-THE JOURNAL OF THE SOCIETY OF MEDICAL OFFICERS OF HEALTH, 1888-1920 / Great Britain. Medical Officers of Health – 9 – us Primary [941]

URBAN AND RURAL SOCIAL CONDITIONS IN INDUSTRIAL GREAT BRITAIN, SERIES ONE : THE LOCAL REPORTS TO THE GENERAL BOARD OF HEALTH, 1848-1857 / Great Britain. General Board of Health – 9 – us Primary [941]

URBAN CONDITIONS IN AFRICA / Comhaire, J – A select reading list on urban problems in Africa. New and rev. ed. London. 1952. BA-244 2 – 8 – ne IDC [960]

URBAN DESIGN – v. 7-. 1976- – 1,5,6,9 – us UMI [360]

URBAN DOCUMENTS MICROFICHE COLLECTION – (Printed index available $425.00 ea) – v1- 1972/73- – 4800mf per yr – 9 – Apply for prices – us CIS [324]

URBAN ECOLOGY – v1-8. 1975-84 – 1,5,6,13 – sz Elsevier [574]

URBAN EDGE – (v.3-. 1979- 5,6,9) – v.1-. 1977- – 1 – us UMI [073]

URBAN EDUCATION – v1- 1964- 1; v10- 5,6,9 – us UMI [073]

URBAN EDUCATION – 1964- – 1 – us UMI [370]

URBAN FOCUS – (Ceased v12 1983/84) – Kingston. v1-12. 1972/73-1983/84 – 9 – Can$20.00y – cn Micromedia [307]

URBAN FORUM = COLLOQUE URBAIN – (Ceased v4 no 6 1980) – Ottawa. v1-4. 1975/76-1978/80 – 9 – Can$20.00y – cn Micromedia [073]

URBAN HEALTH – (v.8-. 1979- 5,6,9) – v.1-. 1972- – 1 – us UMI [073]

Urban, I *see* SYMBOLAE ANTILLANAE, SEU FUNDAMENTA FLORAE INDIAE OCCIDENTALIS

URBAN LAW AND POLICY – v1-5. 1979-84 – 1,5,6,13 – sz Elsevier [073]

URBAN LAW ANNUAL *see* WASHINGTON UNIVERSITY JOURNAL OF URBAN AND CONTEMPORARY LAW

URBAN LAW REVIEW – University of Texas. v1-3. 1975-80 (all publ) – 5,6 – $47.00 set – us Hein [340]

URBAN LAWYER (ABA) – (v1-16 1969-84 on reel $226.00. v17-27 1985-95 on mf $297.00) – v1-27. 1969-95 – 5,6,9 – $523.00 set – us Hein [340]

Urban League *see* REVIEW

URBAN LEAGUE REVIEW – 1985-. -q – 1 – us UMI [073]

URBAN LIFE – (v.9- 1980- 5,6,9) – v.4- 1975- – 1 – us UMI [307]

URBAN LIFE AND CULTURE – v.1-3. 1972-75. Continued by Urban Life – 1 – us UMI [307]

URBAN LIFE UNDER THE OLD REGIME / ed by Mousnier, Roland – 1974. 18 titles in French – 9 – fr Hachette [944]

URBAN MISSION – Sept 1983-May 1987 (complete) – 1r – 1 – ATLA S0854 – us A.T.L.A. [240]

URBAN RESEARCH BULLETIN – Ottawa. v1-6. 1969-1974/75 – 9 – Can$20.00 – cn Micromedia [307]

URBAN RESEARCH NEWS – v1-11 1966-77 1; v10-11 5,6,9 – us UMI [300]

URBAN STUDIES – (1984-. 1,5,6,9) – v1-. 1964- – 1 – us UMI [073]

URBAN STUDIES – 30v – 9 – £198.00 – 0042-0980 – uk Carfax [307]

URBAN SYSTEMS *see* COMPUTERS, ENVIRONMENT AND URBAN SYSTEMS

URBANISM PAST AND PRESENT – (v.9-. 1979- 5,6,9) – v.1-. 1975- – 1 – us UMI [073]

Urbano, L *see* SCHOLASTICA COMMENTARIA IN PRIMAM PARTEM SUMMAE THEOLOGICAE S. THOMAE AQUINATIS. Q1-Q26

Urbano Octavo. Papa *see* BREVE...UNIVERSI

URBANUS RHEGIUS : LEBEN UND AUSGWAEHLTE SCHRIFTEN / Uhlhorn, Gerhard – Elberfeld: R.L. Friderichs, 1861 – 1mf – us A.T.L.A. [240]

Urbigerus, Baro *see* APHORISMI URBIGERANI, OR CERTAIN RULES, CLEARLY DEMONSTRATING THE THREE INFALLIBLE WAYS OF PREPARING THE GRAND ELIXIR..

Urbina, Antonio *see* LA LUCHA DE CLASES Y EL SENTIDO NACIONAL Y SOCIAL DEL NUEVO ESTADO

URCHRISTENTUM IN KORINTH: EINE RELIGIONS- UND KULTURGESCHICHTLICHE STUDIE / Hollmann, Georg – Leipzig: J.C. Hinrichs, 1903. 1 fiche – 9 – us A.T.L.A. [240]

URCHRISTLICHE LITERATURGESCHICHTE: DIE SCHRIFTEN DES NEUEN TESTAMENTS / Soden, Hermann – Berlin: Alexander Duncker, 1905.1 fiche – 9 – us A.T.L.A. [240]

DIE URCHRISTLICHE UND DIE HEUTIGE MISSION : EIN VERGLEICH / Weinel, Heinrich – Tuebingen: J.C.B. Mohr, 1907 – 1mf – us A.T.L.A. [240]

Urcullu, Jose de Moctezuma *see* TRAGEDIA

Urdaneta, Ramon *see* REALIDAD DE UN CUATRICENTENARIO

Urechi, Gregoire *see* CHRONIQUE DE MOLDAVIE

UREDNI LIST REPUBLIKY CESKOSLOVENSKE – (Includes index 1957-60) – Prague, Czechoslovakia. v33-42. 1952-61 – 4r – 1 – us Ross [324]

UREMIA INVESTIGATION – v8-. 1984- – 1,5,6,9 – us UMI [073]

Urena y Semenjaud, Rafael *see* FUERO DE USAGRE (SIGLO 18)

Urfe, Honore d' *see* ASTREE

Uriarte, Jose E *see* CATALOGO RAZONADO DE OBRAS ANONIMAS Y SENDONIMAS DE AUTORES DE LA COMPANIA DE JESUS

Uriarte, Jose Eugenio de *see* VIDA DEL P. BERNARDO FRANCISCO DE HOYOS DE LA COMPANIA DE JESUS

Uriarte, Roberto F *see* LOS AMORES DE PERON

Uribe, Angel *see*
- CUARTERO, BALTASAR Y VARGAS ZUNIGA, ANTONIO. INDICE DE LA COLECCION SALAZAR. TOMOS 23-27. MADRID, 1959-1960
- FR. ALONSO GUERRO EN LA INMACULADA EN LA LITERATURA FRANCISCANO-ESPANOLA
- GIL BECERRA, BENITO, EN LA INMACULADA EN LA LITERATURA FRANCISCANO-ESPANOLA
- INDICE DE LA COLECCION SALAZAR, TOMOS 20, 8-37. MADRID, 1961-1966
- JIMENEZ DE SAMANIEGO, JOSE, GENERAL DE LA ORDEN Y OBISPO DE PLASENCIA, EN LA INMACULADA EN LA LITERATURA FRANCISCANO-ESPANOLA
- JUAN DE LOS ANGELES...EN LA INMACULADA EN LA LITERATURA FRANCISCANO-ESPANOLA
- TREJO PANIAGUA, ANTONIO (VICARIO DE LA ORDEN Y OBISPO DE CARTAGENA) EN LA INMACULADA EN LA LITERATURA FRANCISCANO-ESPANOLA

Uribe, Vicente *see*
- LOS CAMPESINOS Y LA REPUBLICA
- NUESTROS HERMANOS, LOS CAMPESINOS
- LA POLITICA AGRARIA DEL PARTIDO COMUNISTA
- EL PROBLEMA DE LAS NACIONALIDADES EN ESPANA A LA LUZ DE LA GUERRA POPULAR POR LA INDEPENDENCIA DE LA REPUBLICA ESPANOLA
- QUE ES Y QUE REPRESENTA LA UNION NACIONAL DE LOS ESPANOLES

Urio, F *see* TE DEUM...ALS QUELLEN ZU HANDEL'S SAUL, ALLEGRO...

DIE URKUNDEN ARNOLFS (MGH DIPLOMATA 3: 3.BD) – 1940 – Dfl39.00 – ne Slangenburg [240]

URKUNDEN AUS DEM ANTIMONTANISTISCHEN KAMPFE DES ABENDLANDES : EINE QUELLENKRITISCHE UNTERSUCHUNG / Rolffs, Ernst – Leipzig: J C Hinrichs, 1895 – 1mf – us A.T.L.A. [240]

URKUNDEN AUS DEM ANTIMONTANISTISCHEN KAMPFE DES ABENDLANDES (T.U.U. 1-12/4A) / Rolffs, Ernst – Leipzig, 1895 – 3mf – 9 – ne Slangenburg [240]

URKUNDEN DER 18. DYNASTIE / Sethe, K – Leipzig. 5v. 1906-1909 – 25mf – 9 – ne IDC [956]

URKUNDEN DER FAMILIE VON SALDERN / ed by Grotefend, Otto – Hildesheim: A. Lax, 1932. illus. Bibliog – 1 – us U.W. Library [920]

URKUNDEN DES ALTBABYLONISCHEN ZIVIL- UND PROZESSRECHTS / Schorr, M – (Text in German and Akkadian; introduction and notes in German) – Leipzig: J C Hinrichs, 1913 – 2mf – 9 – 0-8370-7334-0 – 1986-1334 – us A.T.L.A. [340]

URKUNDEN DES ALTEN REICHS / Sethe, K – 4v. Leipzig. 1903-33 – 9 – ne IDC [390]

DIE URKUNDEN DES DEUTSCH-ORDENS-CENTRALARCHIVES ZU WIEN / ed by Pettenegg, E G von – Prag, Leipzig, 1887 – 9mf – 9 – ne IDC [943]

URKUNDEN DES KLOSTERS RAITENHASLACH 1034-1350 / ed by Krausen, Edgar – Muenchen, 1959 – 14mf – 8 – Dfl49.00 – ne Slangenburg [240]

DIE URKUNDEN HEINRICHS 2. UND ARDUINS (MGH DIPLOMATA 4: 3.BD) – 1900-1903 – Dfl81.00 – ne Slangenburg [240]

DIE URKUNDEN HEINRICHS 3 (MGH DIPLOMATA 4: 5.BD) – 1931 – Dfl70.00 – ne Slangenburg [240]

DIE URKUNDEN HEINRICHS 4 (MGH DIPLOMATA 4: 6.BD. 1.TEIL) : 1056-1076 – 1941 – Dfl35.00 – ne Slangenburg [240]

DIE URKUNDEN HEINRICHS 4 (MGH DIPLOMATA 4: 6.BD. 2.TEIL) : 1077-1106 – 1959 – Dfl49.00 – ne Slangenburg [240]

DIE URKUNDEN HEINRICHS DES LOEWEN (MGH DIPLOMATA 5: 1.BD) : HERZOGS VON SACHSEN UND BAYERN – (1. Teil: Texte 1941 Dfl39.00. 2. Teil: Einleitung, Nachtraege Und Register 1949) – Dfl19.00 – ne Slangenburg [240]

DIE URKUNDEN KARLS 3. (MGH DIPLOMATA 3: 2.BD) – 1936-1937 – Dfl46.00 – ne Slangenburg [240]

DIE URKUNDEN KONRAD 1., HEINRICH 1. UND OTTO 1 (MGH DIPLOMATA 4: 1.BD) – 1879-1884 – Dfl70.00 – ne Slangenburg [240]

DIE URKUNDEN KONRADS 2 (MGH DIPLOMATA 4: 4.BD) : MIT NACHTRAEGEN ZU DEN URKUNDEN HEINRICHS 2 – 1909 – Dfl53.00 – ne Slangenburg [240]

DIE URKUNDEN KONRADS 3. UND SEINES SOHNES HEINRICH (MGH DIPLOMATA 4: 9.BD) – 1969 – Dfl95.00 – ne Slangenburg [240]

DIE URKUNDEN LOTHARS 1. UND LOTHARS 2. (MGH DIPLOMATA 2: 3.BD) – 1966 – Dfl70.00 – ne Slangenburg [240]

DIE URKUNDEN LOTHARS 3. UND DER KAISERIN RICHENZA (MGH DIPLOMATA 4: 8.BD) – 1927 – Dfl32.00 – ne Slangenburg [240]

DIE URKUNDEN LUDWIGS DES DEUTSCHEN, KARLMANNS UND LUDWIGS DES JUENGEREN (MGH DIPLOMATA 3: 1.BD) – 1934 – Dfl49.00 – ne Slangenburg [240]

DIE URKUNDEN OTTO DES 2 (MGH DIPLOMATA 4: 2.BD. 1.TEIL) – 1888 – Dfl35.00 – ne Slangenburg [240]

DIE URKUNDEN OTTO DES 3 (MGH DIPLOMATA 4: 2.BD. 2.TEIL) – 1893 – Dfl56.00 – ne Slangenburg [240]

DIE URKUNDEN PIPPINS, KARLMANNS UND KARLS D. GROSSEN (MGH DIPLOMATA 2: 1.BD) – 1906 – Dfl53.00 – ne Slangenburg [240]

URKUNDEN UEBER LANDVERGABE AUS DER FATIMIDEN- UND BUJIDENZEIT / Lohlker, Ruediger – 1992 – 96p – 9 – DM75.00 – 3-89349-578-9 – gw Hänsel [943]

DIE URKUNDEN UEBER REMBRANDT (1575-1721) / Hofstede de Groot, Cornelius – Haag. v3. 1906 – 7mf – ne IDC [750]

DAS URKUNDEN- UND KANZLEIWESEN DES BOEHMISCHEN UND ROEMISCHEN KOENIGS WENZEL (4.) 1376-1419 (MGH SCHRIFTEN..: 23.BD) : EIN BEITRAG ZUR SPAETMITTELALTERLICHEN DIPLOMATIK / Hlavaek, I – 1970 – Dfl39.00 – ne Slangenburg [240]

URKUNDEN ZUR ERSTEHUNGSGESCHICHTE DES DONATISMUS / ed by Soden, H von – KIT 122. Bonn, 1913 – Dfl6.00 – ne Slangenburg [240]

DIE URKUNDEN ZWENTIBOLDS UND LUDWIGS DES KINDES (MGH DIPLOMATA 3: 4.BD) – 1960 – Dfl39.00 – ne Slangenburg [240]

URKUNDENBUCH DER EVANGELISCHEN UNION : MIT ERLAEUTERUNGEN / ed by Nitzsch, Carl Immanuel – Bonn: A. Marcus, 1853 – 1mf – us A.T.L.A. [240]

URKUNDENBUCH DES ABTEI ALTENBERG / ed by Mosler, Hans – Bonn. Bd 1, 1138-1400. 1912; Duesseldorf. Bd 2, 1400-1803. 1955 – 15mf – 8 – Dfl11.00 – ne Slangenburg [240]

URKUNDENBUCH DES KLOSTERS HELIGENKREUZTAL / ed by Hauber, A – Stuttgart. Bd 1-2. 1910-13 – Bd1 18mf; bd2 12mf – 8 – Dfl105.00 – ne Slangenburg [240]

URKUNDENBUCH FUER DIE GESCHICHTE DES NIEDERRHEINS – Duesseldorf. bd1-2. 1840-1846 – Dfl105.00 – ne Slangenburg [240]

URKUNDENFUNDE ZUR GESCHICHTE DES CHRISTLICHEN ALTERTUMS / Lechler, Gotthard Victor – Leipzig: A. Edelmann, 1886 – 1mf – us A.T.L.A. [240]

DER URLAUB / Zillich, Heinrich – Muenchen: A Langen, G Mueller, 1933 – 1r – 1 – us U.W. Library [830]

Urmanskii, Ivan *see* DOLO I POLITIKU!

UR-MARCUS : VERSUCH EINER WIEDERHERSTELLUNG DER AELTESTEN MITTEILUNGEN UEBER DAS LEBEN JESU / Wendling, Emil – Tuebingen: J C B Mohr, 1905 – 1mf – 9 – 0-8370-5780-9 – 1985-3780 – us A.T.L.A. [220]

UROKI GRAZHDANKSOI VOINY / Gusev, Sergiei Ivanovich – Izd. 2-e, perer. i dop. Moskva: Gos. izdvo, 1921 – 1 – CSUX89-B701 – us Hoover Inst Photo [947]

UROKI PERVYKH SHAGOV REVOLIUTSII / Bogdanov, Aleksandr I – [S.l.: s.n.], 1917 (Moskva: Tip. I A.G. Sazonova) – 1 – CSUX88-B4439 – us Hoover Inst Photo [947]

DER UROLOGE A – v. 1-19. 1962-80 – 1,5,9 – 1810.00 – us UMI [616]

DER UROLOGE B – v. 10-20. 1970-80 – 1,5,9 – 1048.00 – us UMI [616]

UROLOGIA INTERNATIONALIS – v30-. 1975- – 1,5,9 – us UMI [616]

UROLOGIC CLINICS OF NORTH AMERICA – v1- 1974- 1; v3- 5,6,9 – us UMI [616]

UROLOGIC NURSING *see* AUAA JOURNAL

UROLOGIC RADIOLOGY – v.1-3, 1979-81. ISSN:0171-1091 – 1,5,6,9,13 – 67.00v – us UMI [616]

UROLOGIC RADIOLOGY *see* ABDOMINAL IMAGING

UROLOGICAL RESEARCH – v. 1-8. 1973-80 – 1,5,9 – 708.00 – us UMI [616]

UROLOGY – v1- 1973- 1; v11- 5,6,9 – us UMI [616]

UROZHAI TRAV V SAMARSKOI GUBERNII V...GODU / Samarskoe gubernskoe statisticheskoe biuro – (Includes c.1: 1919) – [Samara: Biuro'), 19uu – 1 – CSUXAKY6250-S – us Hoover Inst Photo [320]

Urquhart, John *see* DIE NEUEREN ENTDECKUNGEN UND DIE BIBEL. ERSTER BAND, VON DER SCHOEPFUNG BIS ZU ABRAHAM

Urquhart, Thomas *see* LOGOPANDECTEISION, OR AN INTRODUCTION TO THE UNIVERSAL LANGUAGE

Urquijo, Julio de La Cruz de Sangre *see* EL CURA DE SANTA CRUZ. SAN SEBASTIAN, 1928

Ursinus, Zach *see*
- OPERA THEOLOGICA
- TRACTATIONES THEOLOGICAE

DER URSPRUNG DER BISCHOEFLICHEN INSIGNIEN UND EHRENRECHTE / Klauser, T – Krefeld, 1948 – 1mf – 8 – Dfl6.00 – ne Slangenburg [240]

URSPRUNG DER SAGEN VON ABRAHAM, ISAAC UND JACOB : KRITISCHE UNTERSUCHUNG / Bernstein, Aaron David – Berlin:Franz Duncker, 1871 – 1mf – 9 – 0-8370-2297-5 – 1985-0297 – us A.T.L.A. [220]

DER URSPRUNG DES DONATISMUS / Voelter, Daniel – Freiburg i.B.: J.C.B. Mohr, 1883 – 1mf – us A.T.L.A. [240]

DER URSPRUNG DES HEILIGEN ABENDMAHLS / Clemen, Carl – Leipzig: J.C.B. Mohr, 1898. (Hefte zur "Christlichen Welt"; Nr. 37) – 1mf – us A.T.L.A. [240]

DER URSPRUNG DES MOENCHTUMS / Heussi, Karl – Tuebingen, 1936 – 9mf – 8 – Dfl32.00 – ne Slangenburg [240]
DER URSPRUNG DES MOENCHTUMS IM NACHCONSTANTINISCHEN ZEITALTER / Weingarten, Hermann – Gotha: F.A. Perthes, 1877 – 1mf – us A.T.L.A. [240]
DER URSPRUNG DES SONNTAGS : MIT BESONDERER BERUECKSICHTIGUNG DER LEHREN DER SAMSTAGS-ADVENTISTEN / Rauschenbusch, August – Hamburg: J.G. Oncken Nachfolger, 1887 – 1mf – us A.T.L.A. [240]
URSPRUNG, UMFANG, HEMMNISSE, UND AUSSICHTEN DER ALTKATHOLISCHEN BEWEGUNG : VORTRAG IM BERNER GROSSRATHSSAALE AM 7. JANUAR 1873 GEHALTEN UND MIT LITERARISCHEN ANMERKUNGEN VERMEHRT / Nippold, Friedrich – Berlin: C.G. Luederitz, 1873 – 1mf – us A.T.L.A. [240]
URSPRUNG UND GESCHICHTE DER BEZEICHNUNGEN "REFORMIERTE" UND "LUTHERISCHE" KIRCHE / Heppe, Heinrich – (Includes bibliographical references) – Gotha: Friedrich Andreas Perthes, 1859 – 1mf – 9 – 0-8370-8825-9 – 1986-2825 – us A.T.L.A. [240]
URSPRUNG UND GESCHICHTE DES FRUEHCHRISTLICHEN OSTERKALENDERS (T.U.U. 5-121) / Strobel, A – 1977 – 9mf – 9 – Dfl32.00 – ne Slangenburg [240]
URSPRUNG UND VERBREITUNG DER DREIFALTIGKEITSMESSE / Klaus, A – Werl i. West., 1938 – 3mf – 8 – Dfl13.00 – ne Slangenburg [240]
DER URSPRUNG UNSERER EVANGELIEN NACH DEN URKUNDEN, LAUT DEN NEUERN ENTDECKUNGEN UND VERHANDLUNGEN / Volkmar, Gustav – Zuerich, 1866 – Dfl13.00 – ne Slangenburg [240]
DIE URSRPUNG DES MYTHOSBEGRIFFES IN DER MODERNEN BIBELWISSENSCHAFT / Hartlich, C & Sachs, W – Tuebingen, 1952 – 4mf – 8 – ne Slangenburg [220]
URSULA SCHREIBT INS FELD : ECHTE BRIEFE AUS DEN JAHREN 1914-1919 / ed by Hase-Koehler, Else von – Leipzig: Koehler & Amelang, c1931 – 1r – 1 – us U.W. Library [943]
Urteaga, H H *see* FUNDACION ESPANOLA...POR EL VIRREY DEL PERU, DON FRANCISCO DE TOLEDO. LIMA, 1926
DIE URTEILSFREIHEIT ALS GRUNDLAGE DER RECHTFERTIGUNG DES RELIGIOESEN GLAUBENS / Stettheimer, Ettie – Wittenberg: Herrose & Ziemsen, 1903. 1 fiche – 9 – us A.T.L.A. [240]
URTEXT UND UEBERSETZUNGEN DER BIBEL : IN UEBERSICHTLICHER DARSTELLUNG – Leipzig: J C Hinrichs, 1897 – 1mf – 9 – 0-8370-9304-X – 1986-3304 – us A.T.L.A. [220]
A URTIGA – Estancia, Brazil. 7 Jul 1852 – 1 – bl Biblioteca [072]
L'URTO DI NAVI ... / Benfante, G – Torino, Firenze, Roma, 1887 – 3mf – 9 – ILM-3360/1 – ne IDC [327]
L'URTO DI NAVI IN MARE / Buzzati, G C – Padova, Verona, 1889 – 2mf – 1 – ILM-3250/1 – ne IDC [327]
Uruguary *see* DIARIO OFICIAL. 1890-
URUGUAY : ANUARIO ESTADISTICO 1884-1967/69 / Uruguay. Direccion General de Estadistica y Censos – (1941 not available. Coll title: Latin American and Caribbean Official Statistical Serials, 1821-1982) – 466mf – 9 – £2,450.00 – uk Chadwyck [972]
Uruguay *see* DIARIO OFICIAL. SECCION AVISOS
Uruguay. Comision de Inversiones y Desarrollo Economico *see* PLAN NACIONAL DE DESARROLLO ECONOMICO Y SOCIAL, 1965-1974
Uruguay. Direccion General de Estadistica y Censos *see* URUGUAY
Uruguay. Laws, Statutes, etc *see* RECOPILACION DE LEYES, DECRETOS Y CONVENIOS VIGENTES EN MATERIA PESQUERA
Uruguay. Ministerio de defense nacional.. *see* MEMORIA
Uruguay.Laws, Statutes, etc *see* CODIGO CIVIL DE LA REPUBLICA ORIENTAL DEL URUGUAY
Urunuela Ortiz, Juan *see* CANCION DE CUNA
Urvoy, Y *see*
– LES BASSINS DU NIGER
– HISTOIRE DES POPULATIONS DU SOUDAN CENTRAL
– HISTOIRE DES POPULATIONS DU SOUDAN CENTRAL (COLONIE DU NIGER)
URWA AL WUTQA *see* AL-'URWA AL-WUTQA
URWAEHLER-ZEITUNG – Berlin, Germany.1849-53 – 1 – gw Mikrofilm [072]
URWAEHLER-ZEITUNG *see* VOLKS-ZEITUNG
URWALD-DOCUMENTE : VIER JAHRE UNTER DEN CROSSFLUSSNEGERN KAMERUNS / Mansfeld, Alfred – Berlin: D Reimer, 1908 – us Res Libr [920]
DIE URWELT DER SCHWEIZ / Heer, Oswald – 5239 2. 1865 – 9 – ne IDC [949]
Urwick, William *see* THE SERVANT OF JEHOVAH
USA : ECONOMICS, POLITICS, IDEOLOGY, 1970-09 – $2,645.00 – 1-55655-274-2 – us UPA [330]
USA – Issue Nos. 1-5 Aug 1941-Summer 1942 – 5mf – 15 – $31,95 – us Comics [760]
USA – Issue Nos. 6-10 Dec 1942-Sept 1943 – 5mf – 15 – $31,95 – us Comics [760]
USA TODAY – 1989 – 1mf – 1 – $25.00 – B06060 – us Library Micro [071]
USA TODAY – v107- 1978- – 1,5,6,9 – us UMI [073]
U.S.A. VOLLEYBALL REVIEW *see* VOLLEYBALL REVIEW, 1980-1981 – U.S.A. VOLLEYBALL REVIEW, 1981-1986 – VOLLEYBALL OFFICIAL GUIDE, 1981-1986
USA VOLLEYBALL REVIEW *see* VOLLEYBALL REVIEW, 1940-1973 – USA VOLLEYBALL REVIEW, 1973-1980 – VOLLEYBALL OFFICIAL GUIDE, 1976-1980
USA WEEKEND *see* FAMILY WEEKLY
Usagre. Ayuntamiento *see* ORDENANZAS MUNICIPALES
USAGRICULTURE *see* FARMER
USAHA GOTONG ROJONG MASJARAKAT DESA BODJONEGORO; LAPORAN / Sumarsidik – SE 4574 1. 1962 – 9 – ne IDC [950]
USAHA Industri Indonesia *see* A LOAN APPLICATION FOR THE PURCHASE OF ROLLING STOCK
Usakligil, Halit Ziya *see* MENSUR SIIRLER
USATAGES DE BARCELONA I COMMEMORACIONS DE PERE ALBERT, A CURA DE JOSEP ROVIRA I ERMENGOL / Barcelona – Barcelona: Editorial Barcino, 1933. 307, (1)p. (Els nostres classics. Collecio A, v.43-44) – 1 – us U.W. Library [340]
USBE MICROFICHE LIST OF 10,000 TOP TITLES / Universal Serials and Book Exchange – Periodical titles available. Main entry, ISSN, OCLC number. Bibliog. information from CONSER – 9 – 10.00; 25.00 – us Universal [020]
USCHAWA BAPTIST CHURCH, DRAUDSES 50 G. JUBILEJA = THE 50TH ANNIVERSARY OF THE CHURCH – Riga, 1911. Publ. No. 6346,no. 1. One of six items on reel. Total Pages 152 – 1 – us Baptist [240]
THE USE AND NEED OF THE LIFE OF CARRY A. NATION / Nation, Carry Amelia Moore – 1905 – 9 – us A.T.L.A. [920]
USE OF AIRCRAFT IN AGRICULTURE – 1972 – 166p – it F.A.O. [631]
USE OF AIRCRAFT IN AGRICULTURE / Akesson, N B & Yates, W E – 1974 – 217p – it F.A.O. [631]
USE OF F.A.O. SPECIFICATIONS FOR PLANT PROTECTION PRODUCTS – 2nd rev ed 1979 – 92p – it F.A.O. [660]
THE USE OF FERTILIZERS IN 1966 / Libya. Ministry of Agriculture and Animal Wealth. Department of Planning and Agricultural Economics. Statistics Division – Bulletin nr. 4. BNE-1017 1 – 9 – ne IDC [631]
THE USE OF HEART RATE AND PERCEIVED EXERTION TO PREDICT AEROBIC AND ANAEROBIC RESPONSES DURING WEIGHT LIFTING IN MALE AND FEMALE COLLEGE STUDENTS / Song, Qilai – University of Mississippi, 1995 – 1mf – 9 – $4.00 – PH1478 – us Microform Publ [612]
USE OF HOUSEHOLD SURVEYS FOR COLLECTION OF FOOD AND AGRICULTURAL STATISTICS (PROVISIONAL) – 1983 – 46p – it F.A.O. [300]
THE USE OF HUMAN REASON IN RELIGION, IN ANSWER TO THE METHODISTS; THE DOCTRINE OF FREE-GRACE BEING EXPLAINED IN THE MEDIUM, ACCORDING TO THE CHURCH OF ENGLAND / Nelson, G – London, 1741 – 5mf – 9 – MP-292/1 – ne IDC [240]
THE USE OF INDIGENOUS CULTURE AS A MEDIUM FOR DEVELOPMENT : THE INDONESIAN CASE / Colletta, N J – 1975 – 1mf – 9 – DE-557/1 – ne IDC [370]
THE USE OF LABANOTATION SCORE ANALYSIS IN THE DEVELOPMENT OF THE EXPRESSIVE PERFORMER / Williams, Valerie L – Texas Woman's University, 1994 – 1mf – 9 – PE 3680 – us Microform Publ [790]
THE USE OF LIGHTS IN CHRISTIAN WORSHIP / Dendy DR – London, 1959 – 4mf – 8 – Dfl19.00 – ne Slangenburg [240]
THE USE OF NOYE IN THE AUTHENTICALLY PAULINE EPISTLES / Blythe, Wayne T – 1981 – 1 – 6.00 – us Baptist [240]
THE USE OF OCLC IN ACADEMIC LIBRARIES IN NEW YORK STATE. A REPORT OF A SURVEY. ED 244-637 / Horenstein, Bonnie – 9 – us EDRS [020]
THE USE OF OXYGEN CONSUMPTION AND BLOOD LACTATE MEASURES IN TRAINING FOR PEAK CHAMPIONSHIP SWIMMING PERFORMANCE / Hannah, J M – 1990 – 2mf – 9 – $8.00 – us Microform Publ [612]
THE USE OF PROGRAMME EVALUATION IN ONTARIO OLDER ADULT CENTRES / Wong, L – 1991 – 2mf – 9 – $8.00 – us Microform Publ [360]
THE USE OF PROXY REPORTS AS PREDICTORS OF MAXIMAL AEROBIC POWER IN CHILDREN / Parrish, Valerie D & McMurray, Robert G – 1993 – 1mf – $4.00 – us Microform Publ [150]
USE OF RATING OF PERCEIVED EXERTION FOR PHYSICAL CONDITIONING : A THREE MONTH VALIDATION STUDY IN THE FIELD / Smith, Brian A – Indiana University, 1994 – 2mf – 9 – $8.00 – PSY1865 – us Microform Publ [150]
USE OF RULE 12(B)(6) IN TWO FEDERAL DISTRICT COURTS / Willging, Thomas E – Washington: FJC, 1989 – 1mf – 9 – $1.50 – LLMC 95-347 – us L.L.M.C. [340]
USE OF SALINE WATERS FOR CROP PRODUCTION – 1992 – 147p – it F.A.O. [631]
THE USE OF SARUM / ed by Frere, Walter H – (Vol 1: The Sarum Customs. Cambridge, 1898; Vol 2: The Ordinal and Tonal. Cambridge, 1901) – 14mf – 8 – Dfl39.00 – ne Slangenburg [240]
THE USE OF SCRIPTURES IN THEOLOGY / Clarke, William Newton – 1905 – 9 – us A.T.L.A. [240]
USE OF SOCIO-ECONOMIC INDICATORS IN DEVELOPMENT PLANNING – 2nd ed 1979 – 282p – 9 – 92-3-101329-7 – fr UNESCO [338]
USE OF SPACE SYSTEMS FOR PLANETARY GEOLOGY AND GEOPHYSICS – (Suppl to v17, Space and Technology) – 1968 – 6mf – 9 – $15.00 – 0-87703-135-5 – us Univelt [629]
USE OF STANDARD PRETRIAL PROCEDURES : ASSESSMENT OF LOCAL RULE 235 OF THE NORTHERN DISTRICT OF GEORGIA / Seron, Carroll – Washington: FJC, 1986 – 2mf – 9 – $3.00 – LLMC 95-333 – us L.L.M.C. [340]
THE USE OF SYSTEMS THEORY OF ORGANIZATION IN ANALYZING, PLANNING AND ADMINISTERING THE WORK OF FIRST BAPTIST CHURCH, COLUMBIA, TENNESSEE / Brown, Ronald Keith – 1982 – 1 – 6.64 – us Baptist [240]
THE USE OF THE APOCRYPHA IN THE CHRISTIAN CHURCH / Daubney, William Heaford – 1900 – 1 – us A.T.L.A. [240]
USE OF THE APOCRYPHA IN THE CHRISTIAN CHURCH / Daubney, William Heaford – London: C.J. Clay, 1900.1 fiche – 9 – us A.T.L.A. [240]
USE OF THE EXERCISE BENEFITS/BARRIERS SCALE IN NORTH CAROLINA DEPARTMENT OF CORRECTION EMPLOYEES / Poole, Karen L & Ainsworth, Barbare E – 1992 – 2mf – 9 – $8.00 – us Microform Publ [150]
USE OF THE HEALTH BELIEF MODEL IN DETERMINING MAMMOGRAPHY SCREENING PRACTICE IN OLDER WOMEN / Dickason, Elizabeth L & Legos, Patricia M – 1991 – 2mf – 9 – $8.00 – us Microform Publ [613]
USE OF THE SCRIPTURES IN THEOLOGY / Clarke, William Newton – New York: Charles Scribner, 1905. 1 fiche – 9 – us A.T.L.A. [240]
USE OF VARIABLE BODY WEIGHT RESISTANCE IN DEVELOPING UPPER BODY STRENGTH / Noie, Dennis R – 1981 – 2mf – 9 – $8.00 – us Microform Publ [790]
USEBELARUSKI ZEZD SAVETA U RABOCHYKH, SI ALI ANSKIKH I CHYRVONA-ARME ISKIKH DEPUTATA U *see* STENAHRAFICHNAI A SPRAVAZDACHA
USED EQUIPMENT DIRECTORY – 1984- – 1,5,6,9 – us UMI [600]
USEFUL ENGLISH / Bondan, Molly – SE-10,750 1. 1951 – 9 – ne IDC [420]
THE USEFUL INSTRUCTOR – Halifax, NS: [s.n, 1887] (Halifax, NS: Nova Scotia Print. Co.) – 9 – cn C.I.H.M. [760]
THE USEFUL NATIVE PLANTS OF AUSTRALIA (INCLUDING TASMANIA) / Maiden, J H – London, Sydney, 1889. 696 pp. B-5139 2 – 8 – ne IDC [580]
THE USEFUL PLANTS OF INDIA / Drury, H – Madras. 1858. B-7311 1 – 9 – ne IDC [580]
Usener, Hermann *see*
– GOETTERNAMEN
– VORTRAEGE UND AUFSAETZE
– DAS WEIHNACHTSFEST
Ushakov, I I *see* O PROEKTE OBSHCHEGO KOOPERATIVNOGO ZAKONA
Usher, F Linder *see* REMINISCENCES OF THE EARLY BENCH AND BAR OF ILLINOIS
Usher, John Palmer *see* PAPERS
Usher, Roland G *see*
– A CRITICAL STUDY OF THE HISTORICAL METHOD OF SAMUEL RAWSON GARDINER
– THE RECONSTRUCTION OF THE ENGLISH CHURCH
– THE RISE OF THE AMERICAN PEOPLE
LES USILES SIC D'ALIENES DE LA PROVINCE DE QUEBEC: REPONSE A "QUELQUES CONSIDERATION SUR LE LOI DE 1885", (48 VICTORIA, CHAPITRE 34) – 1885? 02208. (Pre-1900 Canadiana) – 9 – cn C.I.H.M. [971]
L'USINE – Journal de l'industrie et de la metallurgie. Paris. 1919-6 juin 1940 – 1 – fr A.C.R.P.P. [660]
L'USINE NOUVELLE – (Also available on CD-ROM) – France. 1988-1995 – 3r per y – 5,6 – Sfr989.00 – sz Infoprint [944]
USINE NOUVELLE – 1988-1995 – 3 times per yr – 6 – F4,000.00 – sz Infoprint [072]
USING AND MISUSING LEGISLATIVE HISTORY : A RE-EVALUATION OF THE STATUS OF LEGISLATIVE HISTORY IN STATUTORY INTERPRETATION, 5 JAN 1989 – n.p., n.d. – 2mf – 9 – $3.00 – LLMC 94-368 – us L.L.M.C. [340]
USING DATA PROCESSING TOOLS FOR PREPARING AGRICULTURAL DEVELOPMENT PROJECTS – it F.A.O. [338]
USING FOLK ENTERTAINMENTS TO PROMOTE NATIONAL DEVELOPMENT / Ranganath, H K – 1980 – 9 – 92-3-101773-X – fr UNESCO [350]
Usinger, Fritz *see* GESICHTER UND GESICHTE
USLOVII A I KHOD PROIZROSTANII A KHLEBOV UROZHAI A 1918-1919 S.-KH. G. V KIEVSKO I GUB = VEGETATION ET RECOLTE DES CEREALES AU GOUVERNEMENT DE KIEFF 1918-1919 / Dubenetskii, N O; ed by Volkova & A M – Kiev: [Kievskoe gubernskoe statisticheskoe bi uro], 1920 – 1 – CSUX91-B1467 – us Hoover Inst Photo [630]
USLOVNOSTI / Kuzmin, M – Stat'i ob iskusstve. Petrograd. 1923. BR-1355 2 – 8 – ne IDC [460]
USMAN : PELADJARAN BAHASA INDONESIA OENTOEK SEKOLAH RENDAH. OLEH OESMAN. DJILID I. – (Microfiche No 177) – Djakarta, Balai Poestaka, 2602 – 1mf – 9 – SE-2002/1 – ne IDC [950]
Usman el Muhammady, T. M *see*
– IMAN DAN ISLAM. (SERIE ISLAMOLOGIE)
– MENTJIPTAKAN UHUWWAH ISLAMIJAH
Usman, Sjarif *see* DEMOKRASI POLITIK DALAM ISLAM
Usol'tev, I F *see* INFRARED SYSTEMS: FOR DETECTION, DIRECTION-FINDING AND AUTOMATIC TRACKING OF MOVING OBJECTS
Uson, C *see* LERIDA. ARCHIVO HISTORICO PROVINCIAL INVENTARIO DE PROTOCOLOS NOTARIALES
USPEKHI MATEMATISCHESKIKH NAUK – Progess in Mathematical Sciences. v1-10. 1946-55 – 1,5,6 – us Princeton Micro [073]
USPEKHI POTREBITEL'SKOI KOOPERATSII / Fishgendler, A M – M., 1923 – 1mf – 9 – COR-366/1 – ne IDC [334]
Uspenskii, A I *see* ZAPISNYE KNIGI I BUMAGI STARINNYKH DVORTSOVYKH PRIKAZOV. DOKUMENTY 18-19 VV. BYVSHEGO ARKHIVA ORUZHEINOI PALATY

USPG NETWORK / United Society for the Propagation of the Gospel – nos.29-ns no.6. 1967-77 – 1 – us UMI [240]

U.S.S. Constitution *see* LOGBOOKS AND JOURNALS

USS SAN FRANCISCO MISCELLANEOUS FILES : A HISTORY OF THE HEAVY CRUISER SAN FRANCISCO, AND DATA ON MEMORIAL SHRINE AT PT. LOBOS – 1r – 1 – $50.00 – B40323 – us Library Micro [355]

USSBS TRANSCRIPTS OF INTERROGATIONS AND INTERRROGATION REPORTS OF JAPANESE INDUSTRIAL, MILITARY, AND POLITICAL LEADERS, 1945-46 – 1993 – 9r – 1 – $207.00 set in US $30.00r outside – M1654 – us Nat'l Archives [355]

USSEL ET SON PAYS : 1680-1789 / Lemaitre, N – F160.00 – fr Ethnologie [944]

Usser, J *see* CHRONOLOGIA SACRA

Ussher, George Neville *see* THE ELEMENTS OF ENGLISH GRAMMAR

Ussher, J *see* BUSINESS CORRESPONDENCE

Ussher, James *see* IMMANUEL

Ussishkin, A M M *see* SEFER USSISHKIN

Ussishkin, M *see* OUR PROGRAMME

U.S.S.R. *see*
- DIRECTIVES FOR THE FIVE YEAR PLAN FOR ECONOMIC DEVELOPMENT OF THE USSR FOR 1966-1970
- DIRECTIVES OF THE FIVE YEAR ECONOMIC DEVELOPMENT PLAN OF THE USSR FOR 1971-1975
- DIREKTIVY 23 S'EZDA KPSS PO PIATILETNEMU PLANU RAZVITIIA NARODNOGO KHOZIAISTVA SSSR NA 1966-1970 GODY
- KONTROLNYE TSIFRY RAZVITIIA NARODNOGO KHOZIAISTVA SSSR NA 1959-1965 GG
- PLANOVOYE KHOZYAIUNIONSTVO
- S'EZD SOVETOV SOIUZA SOVETSHIKH SOTSIALISTICHESKIKH RESPUBLIK: STENOGRAFICHESKII OTCHET
- S'EZD ZASEDANIIA VERKHNOVNOVO SOVETA SSSR: STENOGRAFICHESKII OTCHET
- SOTSIALISTICHESKAIA ZAKONNOST'. ORGAN PROKURATURY SSSR
- STATE FIVE-YEAR PLAN. FOR THE PERIOD 1971-1975, PT. 1-2
- TSENTRAL'NOE STATISTICHESKOE UPRAVLENIE, VESTNIK STATISTKI
- TSENTRAL'NYI ISPOLNITEL'NYI KOMITET SOIUZA SOVETSKIKH SOTSIALISTICHESKIKH RESPUBLIK (TSIK): STENOGRAFICHESKII OTCHET
- VEDOMOSTI VERKHOV NOVO SOVETA RSFSR
- VEDOMOSTI VERKHOVNOVO SOVETA SSSR
- ZAKON O PIATILETNEM PLANE VOSSTANOVLENIA I RAZVITIIA NARODNOGO KHOZIAISTVA SSSR NA 1946-1950 GG

USSR : NARODNOE KHOZIAISTVO SSSR 19956-1965 / USSR. Tsentral'noe Statisticheskoe Upravlenie SSSR – (Coll title: European Official Statistical Serials, 1841-1984) – 79mf – 9 – £6.00f (set £685.00 93mf) – uk Chadwyck [947]

USSR : PROMYSHLENNOST SSSR 1957, 1964 / USSR. Tsentral'noe Statistichesko Upravlenie SSSR – (Coll title: European Official Statistical Serials, 1841-1984) – 11mf – 9 – £7.00f (set £685.00 93mf) – uk Chadwyck [947]

USSR : VZESHNAYA TORGOVLYA SSSR 1918-1966 / USSR. Mezhdunarodnye Otnoshenlya – (Coll title: European Official Statistical Serials, 1841-1984) – 3mf – 9 – £7.00f (set £685.00 93mf) – uk Chadwyck [947]

U.S.S.R. Arkhivnogo Stoitel'stva v SSSR *see* VOPROSY ARKHIVOVEDENIIA I ISTOCHNIKOVEDENIIA V BSSR

U.S.S.R. Army *see*
- ARKHIV KRASNOI ARMII
- IUGO-ZAPADNYI FRONT (OBZOR FONDA NO. 102)
- IUZHNYI FRONT (PROTIV VRANGELIA) 27 SENTIABRIA-10 DEKABRIA 1920 G. ORGANIZATSIIA, SOSTAV I BOEVYE DEISTVIIA
- UKRAINSKII FRONT (KRATKII OBZOR FONDA NO. 103)
- ZAPADNYI FRONT (19 FEVRALIA 1919 G.-8 APRELIA 1924 G.). KRATKII OBZOR FONDA NO. 104

U.S.S.R. Army. Tsentral'nyi Arkhiv RKKA *see* 13 IA ARMIZ

U.S.S.R. Biblioteki SSSR *see* SPRAVOCHNIK. ESTESTVENNYE I FIZIKOMATEMATICHESKIE NAUKI

U.S.S.R. COMPUTATIONAL MATHEMATICS AND MATHEMATICAL PHYSICS *see* COMPUTATIONAL MATHEMATICS AND MATHEMATICAL PHYSICS

USSR. Gosplan *see* GOSUDARSTVENNYI PIATILETNII PLAN RAZVITIIA NARODNOGO KHOZIAISTVA SSSR NA 1971-1975 GG

U.S.S.R. Gosudarstvennaia Planovaia Komisiia *see* PROEKT VTOROGO PIATILETNEGO PLANA RAZVITIIA NARODNOGO KHOZIAISTVA SSSR, 1933-1937 GG

U.S.S.R. Gosudarstvennaia Planovaia Komissiia *see*
- LE BILAN DE L'EXECUTION DU PREMIER PLAN QUINQUENNAL DE L'ECONOMIE NATIONAL DE L'U.R.S.S
- ITOGI VYPOLNENIIA VTOROGO PIATILETNEGO PLANA RAZVITIIA NARODNA-KHOZIAISTVENNYI SOIUZA SSR
- NARODNO-KHOZIAISTVENNYI PLAN NA 1935 G
- NARODNO-KHOZIAISTVENNYI PLAN NA 1935 GOD
- NARODNO-KHOZIAISTVENNYI PLAN NA 1936 G
- NARODNO-KHOZIAISTVENNYI PLAN SOIUZA SSSR NA 1937 G
- PIATILETNII PLAN NARODNO-KHOZIAISTVENNOGO STROITELSTVA SSSR
- THE SECOND FIVE-YEAR PLAN FOR THE DEVELOPMENT OF THE NATIONAL ECONOMY OF THE USSR (1933-1937)
- SUMMARY OF THE FULFILMENT OF THE FIRST FIVE-YEAR PLAN FOR THE DEVELOPMENT OF THE NATIONAL ECONOMY OF THE USSR
- VTOROI PIATILETNII PLAN RAZVITIIA NARODNOGO KOZIAISTVA SSSR, 1933-1937 GG
- VYPOLNEMIE PLANA PERVOGO GODA PIATILEKTI

U.S.S.R. Gosudarstvennaia Publichnaia biblioteka im. M.E. Saltykova-Shchedrina *see* SBORNIK

U.S.S.R. Istoriia Leningrada *see* KATALOG RUKOPISEI

U.S.S.R. Komissiia po izdaniia dokumentov epokhi imperializma *see* MEZHDUNARODNYE OTNOSHENIIA V EPOKHU IMPERIALIZMA

U.S.S.R. Komitet Flotskoi Biblioteki.. *see* PREDUVEDOMLENIE

U.S.S.R. Kommunisticheskaia Partiia Sovetskogo Soiuza *see* DIREKTIVYPO SHESTOMU PIATILETNEMU PLANU 1956-1960 GG

U.S.S.R. Krasnyi Arkhiv *see* RED ARCHIVES

USSR. Mezhdunarodnye Otnoshenlya *see* USSR

U.S.S.R. Ministerstva Kultury. RSFSR *see* SPISOK GOSUDARSTVENNYKH MUZEEV SSSR (PO SOSTOIANIIU NA 1 IANVARIA 1968 GODS)

U.S.S.R. Moscow *see*
- INDUSTRIA
- POPOLNENIE FONDOV TSENTRAL'NOGO PARTIINOGO ARKHIVA IML PRI TSK KPSS

U.S.S.R. S'Ezd Sovietov Soiuza Sovietskikh Sotsialisticheskikh Respublik *see* STENOGRAFICHESKII OTCHET

USSR. Tsentral'noe Statistichesko Upravlenie SSSR *see* USSR

U.S.S.R. Tsentral'noe statisticheskoe upravlenie *see* TRUDY

U.S.S.R. Tsentralnoe Statisticheskoe Upravlenie *see*
- ITOGI VYPOLNENIIA NARODNOKHOZI-AISTVENNOGO PLANA SSSR I SOIUZNYKH RESPUBLIK V 1964 G
- OB ITOGAKH VYPOLNENIIA GOS. PLANA RAZVITIIA NARODNOGO KHOZIAISTVA SSSR NA 1960 G. ZA PERVOE POLUGODIE
- OB ITOGAKH VYPOLNENIIA GOSUDARSTVENNOGO PLANA RAZVITIIA NARODNOGO KHOZIAISTVA SSSR V 1955 G
- OB ITOGAKH VYPOLNENIIA GOSUDARSTVENNOGO PLANA RAZVITIIA NARODNOGO KHOZIAISTVA SSSR V 1956 G
- OB ITOGAKH VYPOLNENIIA GOSUDARSTVENNOGO PLANA RAZVITIIA NARODNOGO KHOZIAISTVA SSSR V 1957 G
- OB ITOGAKH VYPOLNENIIA GOSUDARSTVENNOGO PLANA RAZVITIIA NARODNOGO KHOZIAISTVA SSSR V 1958 G
- OB ITOGAKH VYPOLNENIIA GOSUDARSTVENNOGO PLANA RAZVITIIA NARODNOGO KHOZIASISTVA SSSR V 1959 G
- OB ITOGAKH VYPOLNENIIA PIATOGO PIATILETNEGO PLANA RAZVITIIA SSSR I SOIUZNYKH RESPUBLIK NA 1951-1955 GG

USSR. Tsentral'noe Statisticheskoe Upravlenie SSSR *see* USSR

U.S.S.R. Tsentral'nykh Gosudarstvennykh Arkhivakh SSSR *see* TEMATIKA ISSLEDOVANII PO DOKUMENTAL'NYM MATERIALAM

U.S.S.R. Tzentral'noye Statisticheskoye Upravleniye *see* SEKTZIYA STATISTIKI SOTZIAL'NOVE SOSTAVA I DVIZHENIYA NASELENIYA. YESTESTVENNOE DVIZHENIE NACELENIYA SSSR

U.S.S.R. Zasedaniia Verkhovnogo Sovieta SSSR *see* STENOGRAFICHESKII OTCHET

Ustal', A T *see* MEZHDUNARODNO-PRAVOVOI REZHIM TERRITORIAL'NYKH VOD

USTAV I BRACNO PRAVO / Tomac, Dragutin – Zagreb, "Linotip," 1925. 187 p. LL-4050 – 1 – us L of C Photodup [340]

USTAV POTREBITEL'SKOGO OBSHCHESTVA, UPRAVLIAEMOGO OBSHCHIM SOBRANIEM EGO CHLENOV : PRAKT. RAZ"IASNENIIA / Bat', A G & Baranov, A A – M., 1926 – 2mf – 9 – COR-322/1 – ne IDC [334]

USTAV VSEROSSIISKOGO KOOPERATIVNOGO BANKA – M., 1923 – 1mf – 9 – COR-407/1 – ne IDC [334]

Usteri, Johann Martin *see*
- ULRICH ZWINGLI
- WISSENSCHAFTLICHER UND PRAKTISCHER COMMENTAR UEBER DEN ERSTEN PETRUSBRIEF
- ZWINGLI UND ERASMUS

Usteri, P *see*
- DELECTUS OPUSCULORUM BOTANICORUM
- MAGAZIN FUER DIE BOTANIK

USTROISTVO I UPRAVLENIE GORODOV ROSSII / Ditiatin, I – v. 1. Goroda Rossii v XVIII stoletii. Spb. 1875. BR-6138 2 – 8 – ne IDC [947]

UST'-TSILEMSKIE RUKOPISNYE SBORNIKI 16-20 VV / Malyshev, VI – Syktyvkar, 1960. 215p BR-10,967/1 – 9 – ne IDC [025]

UT BROCHDOERP / Trede, Paul – Garding: H Luhr & Dircks, 1920 – 1r – 1 – us U.W. Library [800]

UT, MI, SOL, RE, FA, LA, TOTA MUSICA ET HARMONIA AETERNA / Buttstett, J H – c1717. Erfurt – 9 – us Sibley [780]

UT MINEN LUETTEN GORDEN : PLATTDUETSCHE LYRIK / Schroeder, Helmuth – Ribnitz in Mecklenburg: Suelfstverlag, 1909 – 1r – 1 – us U.W. Library [810]

UTAH : CODE ANNOTATED – Charlottesville: Michie Co, 1953-Jun 1996 update – 9 – $2,178.00 set – us Hein [340]

UTAH : SESSION LAWS OF AMERICAN STATES AND TERRITORIES – 1851-1995 – 9 – $786.00 set – us Hein [340]

Utah *see*
- REPORTS AND OPINIONS (A-G)
- REPORTS, PRE-NRS

UTAH AND THE MORMONS – 1 – us Primary [240]

UTAH AS IT IS / Kenner, S A – Salt Lake City: Deseret News, 1904. Utah reel 1. (Cox Library Collection) – 5 – us Americana [978]

UTAH ATTORNEY GENERAL REPORTS AND OPINIONS – (6 1896-1970 $140.00. 9 1985 n11-1996 n16 $603.00. 1971-1985m n10 not available) – 1896-1996 no 6 – 6,9 – $743.00 set – us Hein [340]

UTAH BAR JOURNAL – 1st series: v1-14. 1970-87; 2nd series: v1-8. 1988-95 – 9 – $70.00; $155.00 – us Hein [340]

UTAH BAR JOURNAL – (Missing: v1-2) – v1-9. 1975-81 – 6mf – 9 – $27.00 – LLMC 84-683 – us L.L.M.C. [073]

THE UTAH BATTERIES: A HISTORY / Mabey, Charles R – Salt Lake City: Daily Reporter Co., 1900. Utah reel 4. (Cox Library Collection) – 5 – us Americana [978]

UTAH FARMER – v1-91. 1880-1971 – 1 – us UMI [630]

UTAH FARMER-STOCKMAN – (1985- . 5,6,9) – v92- . 1972- – 1 – us UMI [636]

UTAH GAZETTEER AND DIRECTORY OF LOGAN, OGDEN, PROVO, AND SALT LAKE CITY FOR 1884 / Sloan, Robert W – Salt Lake City: Herald Printing and Publ. Co., 1884. Utah reel 5. (Cox Library Collection) – 5 – us Americana [978]

UTAH LAW REVIEW – (v1-9 1949-84 on reel $400.00. 1985-95 on mf $226.00. Vol numbering discontinued after v9) – v1-9 + 1966-95; 1949-95 – 5,6,9 – $626.00 set – us Hein [340]

UTAH MAPS 1 : CITIES AND TOWNS – 1884-1904. 290 maps. 23 towns. Sanborn Company Fire Insurance Maps – 1 – $48.00r – us Shkurkin [910]

UTAH MAPS 2 : URBAN SALT LAKE COUNTY – 1884-1916. 650 maps, mostly Salt Lake City. Sanborn Company Fire Insurance Maps – 1 – $78.00r – us Shkurkin [910]

Utah. Presbytery (Pres. Ch. in the U.S.A.) *see* MINUTES, 1871-1908

UTAH SINCE STATEHOOD / Warrum, Noble – (v3-4. Utah reel 2) – Salt Lake City: S.J. Clarke Publ. Co., 1919. v1-2. Utah reel 1. (Cox Library Collection) – 5 – us Americana [978]

Utah. State Bar Association *see* PROCEEDINGS

UTAH STATE BAR ASSOCIATION BULLETIN – 1896-1930 (all publ) – 9 – LLMC 84-682 – us L.L.M.C. [073]

UTAH STATE GAZETTEER 1922-1923 / Polk – Utah reel 5. (Cox Library Collection) – 5 – us Americana [978]

UTAH STATE GAZETTEER 1930-1931 / Polk – Utah reel 5. (Cox Library Collection) – 5 – us Americana [978]

Utah. Supreme Court *see* UTAH SUPREME COURT REPORTS

UTAH SUPREME COURT REPORTS / Utah. Supreme Court – (Pre-NRS run: v1-2 1851-79 5mf $22.50. Vols after 1918 to be filmed after copyright expires) – v1-52. 1851-1918 – 84mf (1:42) 98mf (1:24) – 9 – $525.00 – LLMC 84-210 – us L.L.M.C. [340]

Utah. Synod. (Pres. Ch. in the U.S.A.) *see* MINUTES, 1900-1911

UTAH TERRITORIAL BAR ASSOCIATION REPORTS – v1-5. 1894-1898 (all publ) – 6mf – $9.00 – LLMC 84-681 – us L.L.M.C. [073]

UTAH-IDAHO WITNESS – Sandy, UT. 1986-1991. 371p – 1 – $20.60 – us Baptist [071]

UTAQ-I TIJARAT – Tehran: Sal-i 4, shumarah-'i 49-72 (1 Aban 1311-2 Mihr 1312 (23 October 1932-24 September 1933]) – 2r – 1 – $275.00 – us MEDOC [950]

UTARID – Titre francais: Mercure. Journal universel. no. 1-5. Paris. juil 1859 – 1 – fr A.C.R.P.P. [073]

Utbi *see* KITAB-I-YAMANI

UTBYGGINGSPROGRAMMET FOR NORD-NORGE, 1952-1960 / Norway – Bergen. 1961 – 9 – ne IDC [338]

Utermann, Wilhelm *see*
- DAS LIED VOM ALTEN EISENHUTH
- NEUN GESCHICHTEN

Uthman ibn Umar, called Ibn al-Hajib *see* KAFIYA LI IBN AL-HAJIB

THE UTICA SLATE FORMATION: WITH SPECIAL REFERENCE TO THE EXPOSURES OF THAT FORMATION AT AND NEAR OTTAWA CITY / Ami, Henry Marc – Ottawa: Citizen, 1882. 02398. (Pre-1900 Canadiana) – 9 – cn C.I.H.M. [550]

UTICA SUN – Utica, NE. -w. Nov 1892; Oct 1895-Oct 1898; Feb 1899-Oct 1902, scattered issues missing; Mar 1908-Jul 1919; Sept 1921-Dec 1923; Jan-Jul 1925; Feb-Jul 1926; Jan 1927-Nov 1955 – 1 – us NE Hist [071]

L'UTILE ET LE FUTILE / Morin, Victor – Montreal: Editions Bernard Valiquette, 1943. SEM105P765 – 4mf – 9 – Can$9.00 – cn Bibl Nat [971]

UTILIDADES DEL AGUA I DE LA NIEVE, DEL BEVER FRIO I CALIENTE... / Cardoso, F – Madrid, 1637 – 4mf – 9 – sp Cultura [615]

UTILISSIM, PROMT...Y FACIL REMEY E MEMORIAL PARA PRESERVARSE Y CURAR DE LA PESTE / Girauld de Montpellier, A – Perpinan, 1587 – 3mf – 9 – sp Cultura [614]

UTILITY MODEL PUBLICATIONS IN NUMERICAL ORDER, 1990 / Japan. Patent Office – 1950- . Full set as published after examination for opposition, under annually arranged serial numbers, all classes. 78 reels containing over 49,760 applications examined and published for opposition during 1990 – 5,6,9 – Y546,000.00 – ja Nippon Tech [324]

UTILIZACION DE LA RIQUEZA NACIONAL EN BENEFICIO DE PUEBLO / Spain. Ministerio de Hacienda y Economia – Barcelona, 19?? Fiche W1244. (Blodgett Collection of Spanish Civil War Pamphlets) – 9 – us H.U. College Libr [946]

UTILIZATION OF GENETIC RESOURCES : SUITABLE APPROACHES, AGRONOMICAL EVALUATION AND USE – 1989 – 126p – it F.A.O. [630]
UTILIZATION OF HEALTH CARE PROFESSIONALS IN SELECTED INDUSTRIAL SETTINGS / Hawkins, Margaret C – 1988 – 139p 2mf – 9 – $8.00 – us Microform Publ [613]
UTILIZATION OF KRILL – 1977 – 67p – it F.A.O. [639]
UTILIZATION OF RENEWABLE ENERGY SOURCES AND ENERGY-SAVING TECHNOLOGIES BY SMALL-SCALE MILK PLANTS AND COLLECTION CENTRES – 1992 – 120p – it F.A.O. [660]
THE UTILIZATION OF THE 225-TEST T PREDICT ONE REPETITION MAXIMUM BENCH PRESS WITH COLLEGE FOOTBALL PLAYERS / Slovak, John P – East Texas State University, 1996 – 1mf – 9 – PH 1509 – us Microform Publ [612]
UTILIZATION OF TROPICAL FOODS – it F.A.O. [630]
UTILIZATION OF VISUAL CUES BY SKILLED AND UNSKILLED BASKETBALL PLAYERS / Helmly, Ruth C – 1989 – 66p 1mf – 9 – $4.00 – us Microform Publ [790]
UTILIZING EDUCATION AND HUMAN RESOURCE SECTOR ANALYSES / Kemmerer, Frances – 1994 – 97p – 9 – 92-803-1151-4 – fr UNESCO [370]
Utin, Ia. *see* SOBRANIE VAZHNEISHIKH PAMIATNIKOV PO ISTORII DREVNIAGO RUSSKAGO PRAVA
Utitz, Emil *see* J.J. WILHELM HEINSE UND DIE AESTHETIK ZUR ZEIT DER DEUTSCHEN AUFKLAERUNG
Utley, Robert M *see* CUSTER BATTLEFIELD NATIONAL MONUMENT, MONTANA
UT'N KNICK : PLATTDEUTSCHES / Stinde, Julius – Berlin: Freund & Jeckel, 1894 – 1 – us U.W. Library [800]
UTOPIAN CLASSROOM – v.9- 1981- – 1,5,6,9 – us UMI [073]
UTOPIAN LITERATURE, PRE-1900 IMPRINTS – (Titles from holdings of Rare Books Room, William R. Perkins Library, Duke University, and Rare Books and Special Collections Dept of Lewis Pattee Library at Pennsylvania State University. Cataloging available) – 1993mf – 9 – $5455.00 – us UMI [190]
UTOPIAS AU SIECLE DES LUMIERES – (Following authors from this series are also listed separately in this Directory:. Andre de Ligneville, Jean-Francois. Berington, Simon. Brancas-Villeneuve, Abbe Andre Francois de. Castilhon, Jean-Louis. Coyer, Abbe Gabriel-Francois. Desfontaines, Abbe Pierre-Francois Guyot. Foigny, Gabriel de. Gueudeville, Nicolas. Jaunez-Sponville, Pierre-Ignace and Nicolas Bugnet. La Dixmerie, Nicolas B. de. Lassay (Armand-Leon de Madaillon de Lesparre, Mis de). Leczinski, Stanislas, roi de Pologne. Legrand, Marc-Antoine. Le Mercier de la Riviere. Lesconvel, Pierre de. Luchet (Jean-Pierre-Louis de la Roche Du Maine, Mis de). Marivaux, Pierre Carlet de Chamberlain de. Martigny, Comte de. Mercier, Louis-Sebastien. More, Thomas and Nicolas Gueudeville. Morelly. Moutonnet de Clairfons, Julien-Jacques. Pechmeja, Jean de Retif de la Bretonne, Nicolas Edme. Rustaing de Saint-Jory, Louis. Saige, Joseph. Say, Jean-Baptiste. Serane, Abbe Philippe. Tiphaigne de la Roche, Charles-Francois. Tyssot de Patot, Simon. Vairasse D'Allais, Denis. Varennes de Mondasse. Villeneuve, N. de) – Series. Rare 18th Century works covering a broad range of subjects representing varied social, political and philosophical points of view. In French. 41 titles also available individually – 9 – fr Hachette [190]
UTOPIAS OF THE ENLIGHTENMENT / ed by Soboul, Albert – 40 titles in French. 1677-1815 – 9 – fr Hachette [321]
UTRAQUISTEN UND TABORITEN : EIN BEITRAG ZUR GESCHICHTE DER BOEHMISCHEN REFORMATION IM 15. JAHRHUNDERT / Krummel, Leopold – (Includes bibliographical references) – Gotha: Friedrich Andreas Perthes, 1871 – 1mf – 9 – 0-8370-9397-X – 1986-3397 – us A.T.L.A. [943]
UTRO – Sofia, Bulgaria. Apr 1939-Sept 1944 (scattered issues) – 4r – 1 – us L of C Photodup [949]
UTRO ROSSII – 1912, 1917-18 – 1r – 1 – us Ross [947]
Utsch, Juergen *see* FLEXIBLE ARBEITSZEIT
Utsch, Sabine *see* DIE HEPATISCHE DURCHBLUTUNG BEI HYPERTHERMIE
Utsumi, Toshio *see* THE EFFECT OF SHORT-TERM SLIDE BOARD TRAINING ON LOWER EXTREMITY LATERAL MOVEMENT
THE UTTERANCES OF AMOS : ARRANGED STROPHICALLY / Harper, William Rainey – [S.l.: s.n., 190-?] – 1mf – 9 – 0-8370-9787-8 – 1986-3787 – us A.T.L.A. [220]
UTTOXETER ADVERTISER – England.1890-1911; 1913-83. -w. 59 reels – 1 – uk British Libr Newspaper [072]
UTUNK – Cluj, Romania. -w. Jan 1965-Dec 1970. 6 reels – 1 – uk British Libr Newspaper [949]
UTUSAN KATOLIK – Semarang. Incomplete. SE 435 1. 1951-1968 – 9 – ne IDC [240]
UTUSAN MELAYU – Kuala Lumpur, Malaysia. 1958-1965 – 26r – 1 – us L of C Photodup [072]
UTUSAN ZAMAN – Singapore, 1961 – 1r – 1 – us L of C Photodup [072]
Utuy Tatang Sontani *see*
– SANG KURIANG; OPERA DUA BABAK
– SI KABAIAN. RASSKAZ-STSENKA V DVUK CHASTIAKH
– SI KAMPENG
UUD 1945 DAN MANIFESTO POLITIK REPUBLIK INDONESIA / Indonesia. Constitution – SE-2824 1. 1959 – 9 – ne IDC [323]
UUS ILM – New York, NY. 1912, 1919-1927, 1930 – us I.H.R.C. [071]
UUWF JOURNAL *see* KYRIOKOS. UUWF JOURNAL
UWLA LAW REVIEW – (v1-16 1969-84 on reel $105.00. v17-26 1985-95 on mf $175.00. Index v1-13 1968-81. Title varies: v1-13 1969-81 as University of West Los Angeles Law Review) – v1-26. 1969-95 – 5,6,9 – $280.00 set – us Hein [340]
UXBRIDGE 1702-1900 – (Mf 1-8: Births & Deaths 1702-1846. Mf 9-14: Marriages, Intenionss 1717-1844. Mf 15-22: Vital Records 1702-1845. Mf 23-26: Church Records 1727-1833. Mf 27: Stray Animals 1727-75. Mf 28-31: Military Records 1739-98. Mf 32-43: Town Records 1727-83. Mf 44-52: Town Records 1782-97. Mf 53-64: Town Records 1794-1830. Mf 65-71: Town Records 1828-48. Mf 72-79: Town Records 1848-90. Mf 80-90: Town Accounts 1767-1855. Mf 91-103: Mortgages 1835-58. Mf 104-105: Voters 1884-1903. Mf 106-107: Vitals 1815-44. Mf 108-112: Intentions, Marriages 1834-94. Mf 113-115: Intentions Index 1835-94. Mf 116-118: Vital Records 1843-55. Mf 119-120: Birth Index 1843-92. Mf 121-122: Marriage Index 1844-92. Mf 123-124: Death Index 1844-92. Mf 125-134: Vital Records 1855-92. Mf 135-137: Birth Index 1893-1928. Mf 138-139: Marriage Index 1893-1928. Mf 140-141: Death Index 1893-1928. Mf 142-144: Vital Records 1893-1900) – (mf ed 1993) – 144mf – 0-87623-169-5 – us Holbrook [920]
UXBRIDGE TIMES JOURNAL – Uxbridge, 1931-1984 – 45r – 1 – cn Preston [971]
DE UYT-SPRAECKE VAN ANNA VYTDENHOE. WAER IN GHEHANDELT WORDET VAN DEN SPAENSCHEN VREDE / Viverus, Iac – Leyden, Chr. Guyot. 1598. BME-210 1 – 9 – ne IDC [240]
UZ : UNSERE ZEIT – (Later publ in Essen) – Neuss, Duisburg. 1990-96 – 9r – 1 – gw Mikrofilm [360]
Uz, Johann Peter *see* BRIEFE VON JOHANN PETER UZ AN EINEN FREUND
UZ UND CRONEGK : ZWEI FRAENKISCHE DICHTER AUS DEM VORIGEN JAHRHUNDERT: EIN BIOGRAPHISCHER VERSUCH / Feuerbach, Henriette – Leipzig: W Engelmann, 1866 – 1r – 1 – us U.W. Library [430]
UZBEK TEXTS FROM AFGHAN TURKESTAN – 1938 – 1 – us I.U. Libraries [490]
UZBEKISTON ADABIYOT VA SANATI – Tashkent, USSR. Nov 9, 16, Dec 7, 28 1990; Feb-Dec 13 1991; Mar 20-Dec 25 1992 – 1r – 1 – us L of C Photodup [072]
Uzkov, Ivan *see* PROTIV RELIGII ZA VOINSVUYUSHCHEE BEZBOZHIE
Uzoaga, W Okefie *see* THE IMPACT OF FOREIGN LOANS ON THE LIBERIAN FISCAL SYSTEM
UZ/UNSERE ZEIT – Neuss-Duisburg, Germany. 8 Jun 1977-1989 – 35r – 1 – gw Mikrofilm [072]
V BORBIE S BOLSHEVIKAMI I NIEMTSAMI : STATI I GAZETY "OBSHCHEE DI ELO" (1917 G.) / Burtsev, Vladimir Lvovich – Parizh: "Union", 1919. 2v – 1 – CSUX89-B6304 – us Hoover Inst Photo [947]
V BORBIE S BOLSHEVIZMOM : VOSPOMINANIIA / Avalov, Pavel Mikhailovich – Gliukshtadt: Izd-vo i tip. I.I. Augustina, 1925 – 1 – CSUX88-B5542 – us Hoover Inst Photo [947]
V DYMU. VTORAIA KNIGA STIKHOV / Otsup, N – Paris. 1926. BR-1219 2 – 8 – ne IDC [460]
V KHAOSIE SOBYTII / Gefshtetter, Ippolit – [S.l.]: Kn-vo "Druze i svobody i pori adka", 1905 (S.-Peterburg: Tip. I.V. Leonteva) – 1 – CSUX89-B3365 – us Hoover Inst Photo [947]
V KOGTIAKH U BOLSHEVIKOV : V TIURMIEI NA VOLIE / Badrin, N – Gelsingfors: "Fundament", 1919 – 1 – CSUX88-B7121 – us Hoover Inst Photo [947]
V LABORATORII PISATELIA / Medvedev, P – Sovetskii pisatel', L. 1960. BR-1421 2 – 8 – ne IDC [460]
V MAGAZINE – Magazine illustre du M.L.N. Paris, Bruxelles ?. sept 1944-sept 1945 – 1 – fr A.C.R.P.P. [073]
V MIRE KNIG – (Includes c.1: 1965-1969) – Moskva: [s.n.], 1961-. 18v – 1 – CSUXAKZ0047-S – us Hoover Inst Photo [070]
V NASHI DNI / Dikgof-Derental, Aleksandr Arkadevich – Praga: Slavi anskoe izd-vo, 1922 – 1 – CSUX88-B7202 – us Hoover Inst Photo [943]
V OSENNIKH SADAKH, LITERATURA SEGODNIASHNIAGO DNIA / Abramovich, N Ia – M. 1909. BR-3246 2 – 8 – ne IDC [460]
V POISKAKH PUTI ISKUSSTVA / Polianin, A – Severnye zapiski. v5-6. 1913 – 8 – BR-3694 2 – ne IDC [700]
V POMOSHCH' RABOTNIKAM V POTREBITEL'NYKH OBSHCHESTVAKH : SBORNIK INSTRUKTSII, USTAVOV I PR / ed by Kheisin, M L – Pg., 1818 – 2mf – 9 – COR-323/1 – ne IDC [334]
V POMOSHCH' SEL'SKOMU KOOPERATORU : PRAKTICHESKOE POSOBIE SOST. GRUPPOI SPETSIALISTOV PRI SEL'SKOSOIUZE – Moscow, Leningrad, 1925 – 3mf – 9 – COR-466/1 – ne IDC [334]
V POMOSHCH' UCHITELIU – STROITELIU DEREVENSKOI KOOPERATSII / Chetyrkina, VI; ed by Kantor, M – M., 1926 – 2mf – 9 – COR-525/1 – ne IDC [334]
V POMOSHCH ZEMLEDEL'TSU – (Missing: 1923 n10-12; 1924 n6; 1927 n1) – Omsk, Novo Nikolaevsk, Novo Sibirsk, 1922-29 n14 – 60mf – 9 – COR-552/1 – ne IDC [334]
V POVESTKU DNIA / Maiakovskii, Vladimir – Stikhi 1926-30. M. 1936. BR-1007 2 – 8 – ne IDC [460]
V PROSNUVSHEMSIIA KITAE / Korsakov, V V – Moscow, 1911 – 1 – $35.00r – us Hoover Inst Photo [947]
V RAZDVINUTOI DALI. POEMA O ROSSII / Bal'mont, K D – Belgrad. 1930. BR-546 2 – 8 – ne IDC [460]
V ROZOVOM BLESKE / Remizov, A – Izd. Imeni Chekhova: New York, 1952. 419, (3)p. BR-853 2 – 8 – ne IDC [460]
V STRANE GINDENBURGA. OCHERKI SOVREMENNOI GERMANII / Reisner, L – M. 1926. BR-1232 2 – 8 – ne IDC [320]
V ULIKU VREMENI / Meshcherskii, Vladimir P – Ed. 2. Spb. 1879. BR-10.604 2 – 8 – ne IDC [460]
V ZASCHITU MIRA – Moscow, 1951-56.Lacking: 1951-52 (1-19). BR-10,462/1 – 9 – ne IDC [947]
V ZASHCHITU SLOVA – Sbornik. Stat'i, stikhotvoreniia i zametki: Mikhailovskago, Arsen'eva, Korolenko i dr. Spb. 1905. – 9 – BR-10 100 1 – ne IDC [460]
v2 (1971) *see* CHISLENNYE METODY MEKHANIKI SPLOSHNOI SREDY
v3 n1,4-5 1972) *see* CHISLENNYE METODY MEKHANIKI SPLOSHNOI SREDY
V1-23, 1843-83 – v. 1-23. 1848-83 – 1 – us A.T.L.A. [073]
VAABEN – 1943 – 1 – us I.U. Libraries [390]
VAAD HAIR BULLETIN – (In Yiddish and English) – Montreal, CN, 1934 – 1r – 1 – Can$25.00 – cn Can Microfilming [072]
VA'AD KOL HA-KOLELIM HA-PEKIDUT VE-HA-AMARKALUT DE-EREZ HA-KODESH BE-I(R)T(EHILLAH) AMSTERDAM – (vah Yerushalayim). v. 9. 1911. BJ-27-236 1 – 9 – ne IDC [900]
Vaad Leumi General Council *see* LOCAL GOVERNMENT IN PALESTINE
VAAL ADVERTISER *see* THE DIAMOND NEWS
VABA EESTI SONA (ESTONIA) – (Backfile through 1998 $85r) – New York, 1999- – 1r per y standing order – 1 – us Ross [071]
VABA ESTLANE – (In Estonian. Some issues missing) – Canada, 1952-76 – 26r – 1 – cn Commonwealth Micro [072]
Vaca de Guzman, Jose Maria *see*
– OBRAS QUE DEDICA A LA REINA. TOMO 1
– OBRAS QUE DEDICA A LA REINA. TOMO 2
– OBRAS QUE DEDICA A LA REINA. TOMO 3
Vaca de Guzman, O *see* DICTAMEN SOBRE LA UTILIDAD...DE LA EXCAVACION DEL POZO-AIRON...PARA EVITAR TERREMOTOS
Vaca Morales, Francisco *see*
– AL LADO DEL GUADIANA
– EL ARTE Y LA PINTURA DE ADELARDO COVARSI
LES VACANCES – Roxton Falls [Quebec]: J Tarte, [1894] – 9 – cn C.I.H.M. [440]
Vacandard, E *see* THE INQUISITION
VACATION BIBLE SCHOOL MATERIALS: BEGINNER, PRIMARY, JUNIOR, INTERMEDIATE AND BULLETINS JOINT SERVICE – 1938-53. 7008p – 1 – 245.28 – us Baptist [240]
VACATION BIBLE SCHOOL MATERIALS, NURSERY INTERMEDIATE – 1958-62 – 1 – 70.00 – us Baptist [240]
VACATION TOURISTS AND NOTES OF TRAVEL IN 1860 1861, 1862-3 / ed by Galton, Francis – Cambridge: Macmillan, 1861-1864.3v. illus – 1 – us U.W. Library [910]
Vacca, Roberto *see*
– EVA PERON
– LA VIDA DE EVA PERON
VACHER'S EUROPEAN COMPANION – (1979- 5,6,9) – 1972- – 1 – us UMI [073]
VACHER'S PARLIAMENTARY COMPANION – (1979- 5,6,9) – 1832- – 1 – us UMI [073]
Vachon, Gaston *see* LE PROGRES-DIMANCHE
Vachon, Madeleine E *see* BIBLIOGRAPHIE ANALYTIQUE DE JACQUES DE MONLEON
Vachon, Seraphin *see* LE TRAVAILLEUR DU LAC MEGANTIC
VACUUM. SURFACE SCIENCE AND THIN FILMS – v1- 1951- – 5,6,9 – us UMI [530]
VAD AR EVANGELIUM? / Arbman, Per Theodor – (In Swedish) – Upsala: Almquist & Wiksell, 1907 – 1mf – 9 – 0-8370-2110-3 – 1985-0110 – us A.T.L.A. [220]
VADEMECUM ECONOMICO PER L'AOI / Banco di Roma – Verona: Mondadori, 1937 – us Res Libr [330]
VADEMECUM FUER ANGEHENDE THEOLOGEN / Frank, Franz H R – 1892 – 9 – us A.T.L.A. [240]
DIE VADERLAND – Johannesburg, South Africa. 1915-64 – 1 – sa State Libr [072]
VADERLAND – Johannesburg, South Africa. 3 Jan 1965 – 1 – sa Microfile [960]
VADERLANDSCHE CLUB : STATUTEN EN HUISHOUDELIJK REGLEMENT – Batavia, 1933 – 1mf – 9 – SE-816/1 – ne IDC [060]
Vaderlandsche Club *see* STATUTEN EN HUISHOUDELIKJ REGLEMENT
O VADIO : ORGAM POPULAR – Penedo, Alagoas. 3 Out 1910; Fev-Jun, Out-5 Nov 1911 – 1,5,6 – bl Biblioteca [072]
VADSTENA TIDNING *see* MOTALA TIDNING
Vaenius, O *see*
– L'AME AMANTE DE SON DIEU, REPRESENTEE DANS LES EMBLEMES DE HERMANNUS HUGO SUR SES PIEUX DESIRS
– AMORUM EMBLEMATA, FIGURIS AENEIS INCISA STUDIO OTHONIS VAENI BATAVO-LUGDUNENSIS
– EMBLEMATA HORATIANA, IMAGINIBUS IN AES INCISIS ATQUE LATINO, GERMANICO, GALLICO ET BELGICO CARMINE ILLUSTRATA
VAER LOESEN – v1-72. 1910-81 – 1 – us A.T.L.A. [073]
VAERMLANDSBERG – Kristinehamn, Filipstad. 1886-1901 – 9 – sw Kungliga [072]
VAESTERBOTTENS LANTMANNABLAD – Skellefteå, 1919-20 – 9 – sw Kungliga [072]
VAESTERNORRLANDS DAGBLAD – Sundsvall, 1902-03 – 9 – sw Kungliga [072]
VAEXJOE STIFTS HEMBYGDSKALENDER – (Lacking: v56 1965) – v1-71. 1909-80 – 8r – 1 – ATLA S0504 – us A.T.L.A. [073]

VAEXJOEBLADET KRONOBERGAREN – Vaexjoe, 1995- – 9 – sw Kungliga [072]

Vaez, P *see* APOLOGIA MEDICINALIS ACEDUNT EGREGIAE CENSURAE DE VENAE SEXTIONE IN FEBRIBUS...

VAFA – (Sal-i 1, shumarah-'i 1-12 (Hamal 1302-Dalv va Hut 1302[March 1923-January and February 1924]). Sal-i 2-3, shumarah-i 1-8 (Hamal 1303-Aqrab 1304[March 1924-October 1924])) – Tehran – 1r – 1 – $140.00 – us MEDOC [950]

VAGABOND – (1974 iss 18-19 were not available for filming) – Ellensburg. v6-15 1966-72. v14-17 1972-73. v20-30 1975-spr 1979 1; v20-22 1975. v23-26 1976-77*. v27-30 spr 1978-spr 1979 5; v20-28 1975-fal 1978*. v29-30 win-spr 1979 9 – 1,5,9 – D6816 – us UMI [073]

VAGABOND – v1-9. 1970 – 9 – $5.00f – us Ross [073]

VAGABONDS ALL / Parry, Edward A – New York: Charles Scribner's Sons, 1926 – 4mf – 9 – $6.00 – LLMC 92-185 – us L.L.M.C. [340]

Vaganay, L *see* L'EVANGILE DE PIERRE

Vagner, Nicolas *see* EXAMEN CRITIQUE DE LA DOCTRINE DITE RELIGION SAINT-SIMONIENNE

Vagner, Y et al *see* DETSKAIA ENTSIKLOPEDIIA

LA VAGUE – Hebdomadaire de combat, socialiste, feministe. Dir. Pierre Brizon. no. 1-278. 1918-mai 1923. devenu: Le Bloc des rouges. De Jaures a Lenine. Journal d'union entre les petits, de combat contre les gros. no. 1-69. mai 1923-sept oct 1924. mq no. 67. devenu: La Vague ouvriere et paysanne. Organe du Bloc des rouges. 3e s., no. 1-56. oct 1924-juin 1926. mq no. 14-15. puis La Vague. Organe de rassemblement revolutionnaire. n.s., no. 1-21. 15 nov 1936-15 nov 1937. mq no. 14-18, 20. Paris – 1 – fr A.C.R.P.P. [335]

VAHDET – Halep, Iskenderun. Sahibi ve Mes'ul Mueduerue: Nuri Genc. Nos. 52 (25 Kanuniewel 1928), 522 (31 Kanunisani 1937) – 9 – $25.00 – us MEDOC [956]

VAHDETNAME / Efendi, Ahmedi – Istanbul, 1302 – 6mf – 9 – $12.00 – us MEDOC [949]

Vahl, M *see*
- ECLOGAE AMERICANAE
- ENUMERATIO PLANTARUM
- HERBARIUM
- ICONES ILLUSTRATIONI PLANTARUM AMERICANARUM
- SYMBOLAE BOTANICAE

DI VAHRHEIT – New York. v. 1-14. Nov 11 1905-Feb 28 1919 – 1 – us NY Public [305]

Vaideanu, G *see* CONTENTS OF EDUCATION

Vaihinger, Hans *see* NIETZSCHE ALS PHILOSOPH

VAIHINGER KREISZEITUNG – Vaihingen, Germany. 1983- – 1 – gw Mikrofilm [072]

Vail, A L *see* A MEMORIAL OF JAMES M. HAWORTH

Vail, Albert L *see*
- MARY WEBB AND THE MOTHER SOCIETY
- THE MORNING HOUR OF THE AMERICAN BAPTIST MISSIONS
- STEWARDSHIP AMONG BAPTISTS

Vail, Thomas H *see* THE COMPREHENSIVE CHURCH,OR, CHRISTIAN UNITY AND ECCLESIASTICAL UNION

Vailas, Arthur C *see* THE EFFECT OF EXOGENOUS RECOMBINANT PORCINE SOMATOTROPIN ON PIG COMMON CALCANEAN TENDON BIOCHEMISTRY

VAILIMA LETTERS... / Stevenson, Robert Louis – London: Methuen, 2nd ed 1895 – 1 roll – 1 – 1-55879-701-7 – uk Libr Preservation [860]

Vaillancourt, Cyrille *see* ALPHONSE DESJARDINS

Vaillancourt, Emilienne *see* BIO-BIBLIOGRAPHIE ANALYTIQUE DE EDDY BOUDREAU, MEMBRE DE LA SOCIETE DES ECRIVAINS CANADIENS ET DE LA SOCIETE DES POETES

Vaillancourt, Gerard *see* ENQUETE SUR LA LOI DE LA CONVENTION COLLECTIVE ET SON EXPLICATION

Vaillant, A *see* LE TRAITE CONTRE LES BOGOMILES

Vaillant, M L *see* EXPEDITIONS SCIENTIFIQUES DU "TRAVAILLEUR" ET DU "TALISMAN" PENDANT LES ANNEES 1880, 1881, 1882, 1883

Vaillant, S *see*
- BOTANICON PARISIENSE
- DISCOURS SUR LA STRUCTURE DES FLEURS

Vairasse D'Allais, Denis *see* HISTOIRE DES SEVARAMBES, PEUPLES QUI HABITENT UNE PARTIE DU TROISIEME CONTINENT COMMUNEMENT APPELE LA TERRE AUSTRALE: CONTENANT UN COMPTE EXACT DU GOUVERNEMENT DES MOEURS, DE LA RELIGION ET DU LANGAGE DE CETTE NATION

Vaisesika Dasapadartha Sastra *see* THE VAISESIKA PHILOSOPHY, ACCORDING TO THE D.-S. CHINESE TEXT

THE VAISESIKA PHILOSOPHY, ACCORDING TO THE D.-S. CHINESE TEXT / Vaisesika Dasapadartha Sastra – 1917 – 1 reel – 5 – uk Microform Academic [180]

VAITANA SUTRA / Garbe, R – Strassburg. 1878. BI-504 2 – 8 – ne IDC [280]

Vajirevudh, King of Siam *see* BAEPRIAN KHONG KRASUANG SUKSATHIKAN NANGSU AN PHASA THAI RUANG

VAJRACCHEDIKA. ENGLISH – The Diamond Sutra: or Prajnaparamita. Trans. and introd. and notes by William Gemmell. New York: E.P. Dutton; London: K. Paul Trench, Truebner & Co., 1913. xxxii,117p – 1 – us U.W. Library [280]

Vakhtin, V V *see* OB IASNITEL'NYI MORSKOI SLOVAR'

VAKTARAN – Omaha, NE. -w. 20 Aug 1868. In Swedish – 1 – us NE Hist [071]

VAKYAVALI : OR, EXERCISES IN IDIOMS, ENGLISH AND TELUGU / Brown, Charles Philip – Madras, 1852 – us Res Libr [410]

Val, Andr. du *see*
- DE SUPREMA ROMANI PONTIFICIS IN ECCLESIAM POTESTATE DISPUTATIO QUADRIPARTITA

VAL BELAIR – Val St-Michel, Canada. 28 jan 1966 – 1r – 1 – Can$25.00 – cn Can Microfilming [072]

THE VAL D'OR STAR – Val d'Or. v2 n23. 14 fev 1947; v2 n24. 28 fev 1947 – 1r – 1 – Can$25.00 – cn Can Microfilming [072]

LE VAL LORETTE – Loretteville, Canada. 1 jun 1974; v1 n5. 15 aut 1974 – 1r – 1 – Can$25.00 – cn Can Microfilming [072]

Valcarcel, Joaquin, Ma *see* DEFENSA ORAL... MANUEL BLANCO

Valckenaer, L C *see* OBSERVATIONES ACADEMICAE, QUIBUS VIA MUNITUR AD ORIGINES GRAECAS INVESTIGANDAS, LEXICORUMQUE DEFECTUS RESARCIENDOS

Valdemorales. Ayuntamiento *see* FIESTAS Y FESTEJOS EN HONOR DE SU PATRONA LA SANTISIMA VIRGEN DEL ROSARIO 1977

Valdeobispo. Ayuntamiento *see* ORDENANZAS MUNICIPALES...

Valder, Barbara *see* DIE SCHULE FUER DAS VIOLONCELLO

Valdes, F *see* DISPUTA...Y AVERIGUACIONES DE LA ENFERMEDAD PESTILENTE...

Valdes Gomez, J A *see* ETUDE DE GROUPES D'HABITATIONS DU CENTRE CEREMONIAL MAYA DU MUNDO PERDIDO, TIKAL, GUATEMALA

Valdes, Juan de *see*
- 17 OPUSCULES
- COMMENTARY UPON THE GOSPEL OF ST MATTHEW
- SPIRITUAL MILK, OR, CHRISTIAN INSTRUCTION FOR CHILDREN

Valdes, Octavio *see* EL PADRE TEMBLEQUE. MEXICO, 1945

Valdes Vergara, Francisco *see* PROBLEMAS ECONOMICOS DE CHILE

VALDIBAS VESTNESIS – Riga, 1918-41 – 41r – 1 – $2,800.00 coll – us Ross [072]

VALDIBAS VESTNESIS – Riga, De 1918 a 1941 – 41r – 1 – Sfr4,920.00 – sz Infoprint [947]

LOS VALDIVIA / Rugula, Jose de & Solar y Taboada, Antonio – Badajoz: Arqueros, 1929 – 1 – sp Bibl Santa Ana [946]

Valdivia, A *see* TRACTADO EN EL QUE SE EXPLICA LA ESENCIA Y NATURALEZA DE LA ENFERMEDAD (QUE LLAMAN IANDRES)

Valdivia, Pedro de *see*
- CARTAS DE D...QUE TRATAN DEL DESCUBRIMIENTO Y CONQUISTA DE CHILE
- PEDRO DE VALDIVIA
- RETRATO DE...

Valdivieso, Joseph *see* VIDA, EXCELENCIAS Y MUERTE DE...SAN JOSEPH...COMENTADA... DON DIEGO SUAREZ DE FIGUEROS...

Valdor, Jean *see* LES TRIOMPHES DE LOUIS LE JUSTE, 13E DU NOM, ROY DE FRANCE...

Valdour, Jacques *see*
- ATELIERS ET TAUDIS DE LA BANLIEU DE PARIS
- LES MINEURS, OBSERVATIONS VECUES
- OUVRIERS PARISIENS D'APRES-GUERRE

VALE DO PARAOPEBA – Brumadinho, Brazil. Aug-Dec 1974; Jan, Mar-Apr, June, Aug, Oct, Dec 1975; Jan-Feb, Jun, Sept, Nov-Dec 1976; Jun 1977 – 1 – bl Biblioteca [072]

O VALE DO RIO DOCE : HEBDOMADARIO DA DEFESA DOS INTERESSES GERAIS DA REGIAO – Governador Valadares, 3-17 Jun 1945 – 1,5,6 – bl Biblioteca [072]

VALE QUIEN SIRVE / OJE – Caceres: Imp. Sanguino, 1963 – 1 – sp Bibl Santa Ana [946]

VALE UN PERU / Garcia Calderon, Ventura – Madrid: Razon y Fe, 1940 – 1 – sp Bibl Santa Ana [972]

Valence, Pierre *see* INTRODUCTIONS IN FRENSSHE FOR HENRY THE YONGE ERLE OF LYNCOLN

Valencia de Alcantara. Ayuntamiento *see*
- FERIA Y FIESTAS 1977
- FERIA Y FIESTAS. PROGRAMA OFICIAL 1972
- PROGRAMA OFICIAL DE FERIA Y FIESTAS. AGOSTO, 1960

VALENCIA DE ALCANTARA EN EL CONCEPTO PROTOHISTORICO / Vilanova y Piera, Juan – Madrid: Tip. Fortanet, 1889 – 1 – sp Bibl Santa Ana [946]

Valencia de Alcantara. Estacion de Renfe *see*
- FESTIVIDAD DE SAN FERNANDO 30 DE MAYO 1959, VALENCIA DE ALCANTARA
- GRANDES FIESTAS EN HONOR DE SAN FERNANDO. ESTACION DE LA RENFE...JULIO, 1959

VALENCIA DEL REY / Duarte Insua, Lino – Badajoz: Dip. Prov, 1944 – 1 – sp Bibl Santa Ana [946]

Valencia, Melchor de *see* ILLUSTRIUM JURIS TRACTATUUM

VALENCIA VALLEY NEWS *see* NEWHALL SIGNAL

Valencia y Bravo, Alonso *see* DEFENSA... ORDEN DE ALCANTARA

Valenciennes, A *see* HISTOIRE NATURELLE DES POISSONS

Valenciennes, M *see* POISSONS, CATALOGUE DES PRINCIPALES ESPECES DE POISSONS

Valente, Waldemar *see* SINCRETISMO RELIGIOSO AFRO-BRASILEIRO

Valentia, Greg. De *see*
- COMMENTARIORUM THEOLOGICORUM TOMI QUATUOR
- DE REBUS FIDEI HOC TEMPORE...

Valentijn, F *see* OUD EN NIEUW OOST-INDIEN

VALENTIN / Kingsley, Henry – British Fiction Archive: Unit 2 – 9 – uk Bell [830]

Valentin, G *see* DEUTSCHE DICHTUNG

VALENTIN OU LE PAYSAN ROMANESQUE. OPERA COMIQUE EN DEUX ACTES / Berton, H – Paris: LeDuc, 1814 – 1 – us Sibley [780]

Valentin, Veit *see* DER NATURALISMUS UND SEINE STELLUNG IN DER KUNSTENTWICKLUNG

VALENTINE CARD COLLECTION: A SELECTION / Metropolitan Toronto Central Library – 1 – 35.00 – cn McLaren [760]

Valentine, J *see* MARCHES AND MINUETTS, 16 IN EIGHT PARTS FOR 2 VIOLINS, 2 HAUTBOYS OR GERMAN FLUTES, 2 FRENCH HORNS, TENOR, AND BASS. OP. 8

Valentine, Milton *see* NATURAL THEOLOGY

VALENTINE NEWSPAPER – Valentine, NE. -w. Apr 1888-Feb 1919; Jul 1919 to date – 1 – us NE Hist [071]

VALENTINE OU LA NINA CANADIENNE COMEDIE EN UN ACTE / Leblanc de Marconnay, Hyacinthe – Montreal: Impr. de l'Ami du peuple, 1836. SEM16P162 – 1r – 5 – Can$9.00 – cn Bibl Nat [820]

Valentinov, N *see* NOVAIA EKONOMICHESKAIA POLITIKA I KRIZIS PARTI I POSLE SMERTI LENINA

Valenton, T *see*
- ATLAS DER BAUMARTEN VON JAVA...
- BIJDRAGEN TOT DE KENNIS DER BOOMSOORTEN VAN JAVA

Valenzuela, Jesus Z *see* HISTORY OF JOURNALISM IN THE PHILIPPINE ISLANDS

Valera, Fernando *see* LA REPUBLICA ES LA REVOLUCION ESPANOLA

Valera, Juan *see* PEPITA JIMENEZ

VALERIA, THE MARTYR OF THE CATACOMBS : A TALE OF EARLY CHRISTIAN LIFE IN ROME / Withrow, W H – Toronto: William Briggs, [18..?] – 1mf – us A.T.L.A. [240]

THE VALERIAN – Valier. Mont. 1947-1948 – 1 – us UMI [071]

VALERIAN, A NARRATIVE POEM / Linn, John Blair – 1805 – 1 – $50.00 – us Presbyterian [810]

THE VALERIAN PERSECUTION : A STUDY OF THE RELATIONS BETWEEN CHURCH AND STATE IN THE THIRD CENTURY A.D. / Healy, Patrick J – London: A. Constable; Boston: Houghton, Mifflin, 1905 – 1mf – us A.T.L.A. [240]

Valerien, Jean *see* INNOVATIONS FOR LARGE CLASSES

VALERII BRIUSOV / Aikhenvald, Iu – 1910. BR-1963 2 – 8 – ne IDC [920]

VALERII BRIUSOV I NASLEDIE PUSHKINA / Zhirmunskii, V M – "El' zevir". Spb. 1922. BR-2239 2 – 8 – ne IDC [460]

VALERII BRIUSOV V AUTOBIOGRAFICHESKIKH ZAPISIAKH, PIS'MAKH, VOSPOMINANIIAKH SOVREMENNIKOV I OTZYVAKH KRITIKI / Ashukin, N – 1929. BR-1978 2 – 8 – ne IDC [920]

Valero de Bernabe, Antonio et al *see* LA PATRIA DEL ALMIRANTE...

Valero Silva, Jose *see* EL LEGALISMO DE HERNAN CORTES COMO INSTRUMENTO DE SU CONQUISTA

Valero y Lossa, Francisco *see* CARTA PASTORAL

Valesii, Notae H *see* EXCERPTA DE LEGATIONIBUS (CBH 1,2)

Valeton, Josue Jean Philippe *see* AMOS UND HOSEA

Valeton, Jozua J P *see* AMOS UND HOSEA: EIN KAPITEL AUS DER GESCHICHTE DER ISRAELITISCHEN RELIGION

Valette *see* LA JOURNEE DE LA PETITE MENAGERE

VALEUR INTERNATIONALE DES... / Grapin, P – Paris, 1934 – 3mf – 1 – ILM-1710/1 – ne IDC [327]

LES VALEURS MORALES ET LA THEOLOGIE JOHANNIQUE (EVANGILE ET EPITRES) / Lazure, N – 1935 – 7mf – 8 – ne Slangenburg [220]

Valgoma Dalmiro y Finestrat, Ramon *see* REAL COMPANIA DE GUARDIAS MARINAS Y COLEGIO NAVAL. CATALOGO DE PRUEBAS DE CABALLEROS ASPIRANTES. VOL. 2. MADRID, 1944

Valgoma y Diaz-Varela, Dalmiro de la *see*
- ASCENDIENTES Y DESCENDIENTES DE HERNANDO CORTES
- CARTAS DE GODOY A FERRER DEL RIO
- EL CONDE DE CANILLEROS
- RODRIGUEZ-MONINO Y LA REAL ACADEMIA DE LA HISTORIA

THE VALIANT WOMAN = FEMME FORTE : CONFERENCES ADDRESSED TO LADIES LIVING IN THE WORLD / Landriot, Monseigneur, Archbishop of Rheims – (In English) – Dublin: M H Gill, 1886 – 1mf – 9 – 0-8370-7077-5 – 1986-1077 – us A.T.L.A. [305]

A VALID AND RELIABLE INSTRUMENT FOR THE DIRECT MEASURE OF PERCEIVED BODY SIZE IN CHILDREN / Stevens, Deborah A – 1989 – 178p 2mf – 9 – $8.00 – us Microform Publ [150]

A VALIDATION AND COMPARATIVE EVALUATION OF FOUR PREDICTIVE DEVICES FOR CLASSIFYING FEDERAL PROBATION CASELOADS / Eaglin, James B & Lombard, Patricia A – Washington: FJC, Feb 1982 – 2mf – 9 – $3.00 – LLMC 95-827 – us L.L.M.C. [340]

VALIDATION OF A CARDIORESPIRATORY FITNESS TEST FOR MEN WITH MENTAL RETARDATION / Rintala, P – 1990 – 2mf – 9 – $8.00 – us Microform Publ [612]

VALIDATION OF A CONCEPTUAL MODEL CHARACTERIZING COLLEGE STUDENT-ATHLETES' READINESS TO RETIRE FROM COMPETITIVE SPORT PARTICIPATION / Lantz, Christopher D – West Virginia University, 1995 – 1mf – 9 – PSY 1893 – us Microform Publ [150]

VALIDATION OF A CYCLE ERGOMETER VO2MAX PREDICTION EQUATION FOR NONSEDENTARY COLLEGE-AGE WOMEN / McNamara, Michael J & Terry, Lawrence A – 1992 – 1mf – $4.00 – us Microform Publ [612]

VALIDATION OF A MODIFIED CLOSED CIRCUIT, OXYGEN DILUTION RESIDUAL VOLUME METHOD / Johnson, Brenda M – 1993 – 1mf – $4.00 – us Microform Publ [612]

VALIDATION OF EQUATIONS TO PREDICT LACTATE THRESHOLD, FIXED BLOOD LACTATE CONCENTRATIONS, AND PEAK VALUES FROM A 3200 METER PERFORMANCE TIME / La Mere, Vern J & Butts, Nancy Kay – 1991 – 2mf – $8.00 – us Microform Publ [612]

VALIDATION OF FITNESSGRAM ONE-MILE RUN/ WALK CRITERION-REFERENCED STANDARDS IN MEN AND WOMEN 18 TO 25 YEARS OF AGE / O'Bannon, Jane P & Cureton, Kirk J – 1992 – 1mf – 9 – $4.00 – us Microform Publ [612]

VALIDATION OF THE DELTA T MODE OF THE OMNISOUND 3000(TM) / Billings, Carolyn – Brigham Young University, 1995 – 1mf – 9 – PE 3630 – us Microform Publ [617]

VALIDATION OF THE MAXIMAL MET PREDICTION EQUATIONS ON THE SCHWINN AIR-DYNE / Johnson, Jana A & Kaufman, Wayne S – 1992 – 1mf – $4.00 – us Microform Publ [617]

A VALIDATION STUDY OF THE Q-PLEX 1 CARDIOP-ULMONARY EXERCISE SYSTEM / Davey, William G & Butts, Nancy Kay – 1991 – 1mf – $4.00 – us Microform Publ [617]

VALIDIERUNG FLUOROMETRISCHER BESTIMMUNGEN VON ENZYMAKTIVITAETEN UND BIOMASSEPARAMETERN UNTER BESONDERER BERUECKSICHTIGUNG MINIATURISIERTER TESTANSAETZE / Friedrichs, Heinz Michael – 1993 – 2mf – 9 – DM80.00 – 3-89349-750-1 – gw Hänsel [574]

THE VALIDITY AND BEARING OF THE TESTIMONY OF CHRIST AND HIS APOSTLES / Hemphill, Charles Robert – NY: Funk & Wagnalls, 1888 – 1mf – 9 – 0-8370-20875 – 1985-0087 – us A.T.L.A. [220]

VALIDITY AND OBJECTIVITY OF A RATING SCALE FOR THE OVERHEAD AND FOREARM VOLLEYBALL PASS / Higgins, Kathleen L – 1994 – 2mf – $8.00 – us Microform Publ [790]

THE VALIDITY AND RELIABILITY OF HEART RATE AS A MEASURE OF DAILY ENERGY EXPENDITURE / Washburn, Richard A – 1981 – 2mf – 9 – $8.00 – us Microform Publ [790]

VALIDITY AND RELIABILITY OF THE 20-METER SHUTTLE TEST IN AMERICAN FEMALES 19-34 / LaMontagna, R – 1991 – 1mf – 9 – $4.00 – us Microform Publ [613]

VALIDITY CONCERNS IN PREVIOUS STUDIES EXAMINING THE FREQUENCY OF ANOREXIA NERVOSA IN FEMALE BALLET DANCERS / Nelson, Dave Paul – University of Oregon, 1995 – 2mf – 9 – $8.00 – PSY1856 – us Microform Publ [150]

THE VALIDITY OF ANGLICAN ORDINATIONS AND ANGLICAN CLAIMS TO APOSTOLICAL SUCCESSION EXAMINED / Kenrick, Peter Richard – Philadelphia: Eugene Cummiskey, 1848 – 1mf – us A.T.L.A. [240]

THE VALIDITY OF CONGREGATIONAL ORDINATION : DUDLEIAN LECTURE AT HARVARD UNIVERSITY / Walker, Williston – Hartford, Conn.: Case, Lockwood & Brainard, 1898 – 1mf – us A.T.L.A. [240]

THE VALIDITY OF ENGLISH ORDINATIONS FROM AN ORTHODOX CATHOLIC POINT OF VIEW / Androutsos, Chrestos – London: Grant Richards, 1909 – 1mf – us A.T.L.A. [240]

THE VALIDITY OF RATE REGULATIONS, STATE AND FEDERAL / Reeder, Robert Patterson – Philadelphia, Johnson, 1914. 440 p. LL-1043 – 1 – us L of C Photodup [340]

VALIDITY OF TECHNIQUES FOR MEASURING BLOOD CHOLESTEROL WITH THE REFLOTRON / O'Mara, C M – 1990 – 1mf – 9 – $4.00 – us Microform Publ [612]

VALIDITY OF THE ASTRAND-RHYMING NOMOGRAM FOR MODERATELY ACTIVE ADULT FEMALES / Eberhart, Jean M – 1977 – 1mf – 9 – $4.00 – us Microform Publ [790]

VALIDITY OF THE SIT-AND-REACH TEST FOR MALE AND FEMALE ADOLESCENTS / Garcia, Susan C – 1994 – 1mf – $4.00 – us Microform Publ [612]

THE VALIDITY OF THE TECUMSEH SELF-ADMINISTERED OCCUPATIONAL ACTIVITY QUESTIONNAIRE / Chriscoe, Stephen B – University of North Carolina a Chapel Hill, 1995 – 2mf – 9 – $8.00 – PH1454 – us Microform Publ [612]

THE VALIDITY OF THE TEEM 100 METABOLIC ANALYSIS SYSTEM / Logerstedt, David S – University of North Carolina at Chapel Hill, 1995 – 2mf – 9 – $8.00 – PH1468 – us Microform Publ [612]

VALIDITY OF WHOLE-BODY BIOELECTRICAL IMPEDANCE ANALYSIS IN THE PREDICTION OF PERCENT BODY FAT IN WOMEN / Askim, Karen L – 1988 – 158p 2mf – 9 – $8.00 – us Microform Publ [617]

Valiquette, John E *see* A STUDY OF UPPER EXTREMITY STRENGTH AND ENDURANCE OF EDUCABLE MENTALLY RETARDED AND NON-RETARDED BOYS IN SELECTED ONTARIO SEPARATE SCHOOLS

Valisinha, Devapriya *see* BUDDHIST SHRINES IN INDIA

Valk, M.H. van der *see* AN OUTLINE OF MODERN CHINESE FAMILY LAW

Valk, S N *see* SOVETSKAIA ARKHEOGRAFIIA

Valkenburgh, Sallie van *see* GRAN QUIVIRA

Valla, G *see* GEORGII VALLAE PLACENTINI VIRI CLARISS..

Valladares Sotomayor, Antonio *see*
- SEMANARIO ERUDITO. TOMOS 1 Y 2
- SEMANARIO ERUDITO. TOMOS 3 Y 4
- SEMANARIO ERUDITO. TOMOS 5 Y 6
- SEMANARIO ERUDITO. TOMOS 7 Y 8
- SEMANARIO ERUDITO. TOMOS 9 Y 10
- SEMANARIO ERUDITO. TOMOS 11 Y 12
- SEMANARIO ERUDITO. TOMOS 13 Y 14
- SEMANARIO ERUDITO. TOMOS 15 Y 16
- SEMANARIO ERUDITO. TOMOS 17 Y 18
- SEMANARIO ERUDITO. TOMOS 19 Y 20
- SEMANARIO ERUDITO. TOMOS 21 Y 22
- SEMANARIO ERUDITO. TOMOS 23 Y 24
- SEMANARIO ERUDITO. TOMOS 25 Y 26
- SEMANARIO ERUDITO. TOMOS 27 Y 28
- SEMANARIO ERUDITO. TOMOS 29 Y 30
- SEMANARIO ERUDITO. TOMOS 31 Y 32
- SEMANARIO ERUDITO. TOMOS 33 Y 34

VALLADOLID. ARCHIVO GENERAL DE SEMANCAS. SECRETARIA DE ESTADO. CAPITULACIONES CON INGLATERRA ... / Paz, J – Madrid, 1947 – 11mf – 9 – sp Cultura [320]

VALLADOLID. ARCHIVO GENERAL DE SIMANCAS DIVERSOS DE CASTILLA. CAMARA DE CATILLA / Paz, J – Madrid, 1904 – 9 – sp Cultura [025]

VALLADOLID. ARCHIVO GENERAL DE SIMANCAS GUIA DEL INVESTIGADOR / Plaza, A de la – Valladolid, 1962 – 9 – sp Cultura [025]

VALLADOLID. ARCHIVO GENERAL DE SIMANCAS. SECRETARIA DE ESTADO. CAPITULACIONES CON FRANCIA Y NEGOCICACIONES... / Paz, J – Madrid; 1914 – 16mf – 9 – sp Cultura [320]

VALLADOLID. ARCHIVO GENERAL DE SIMANCAS. SECRETARIA DE ESTADO. CAPITULACIONES CON LA CASA DE AUSTRIA... / Paz, J – Madrid, 1942 – 8mf – 9 – sp Cultura [320]

VALLADOLID. ARCHIVO GENERAL DE SIMANCAS. SECRETARIA DE GUERRA (S. 18)...HOJAS DE SERVICIOS DE AMERICA / Alvarez, C – Valladolid, 1958 – 6mf – 9 – sp Cultura [324]

VALLADOLID. ARCHIVO GENERAL DESIMANCAS. DIRECCION GENERAL DEL TESORO. TITULOS DE INDIAS / Magdaleno, R – Valladolid, 1954 – 9 – sp Cultura [025]

Vallance, Aymer *see* WILLIAM MORRIS, HIS ART, HIS WRITINGS, AND HIS PUBLIC LIFE

Vallancey, Charles *see* COLLECTANEA DE REBUS HIBERNICIS

Vallandigham, Clement Laird *see* LETTERS AND FAMILY PAPERS, MS 1381

Vallandigham, Edward N *see* DELAWARE AND THE EASTERN SHORE

Vallange, de *see* GRAMMAIRE FRANCOISE RAISONNEE

Vallara, F M *see* PRIMIZIE DI CANTO FERMO DEL PADRE FRANCESCO MARIA VALLARA DA PARMA

Vallart, J *see* GRAMMAIRE FRANCOISE

Valle, A *see* SANTA MARIA EN INDIAS

Valle, A Cascales *see* HISTORIA DE LA "CUERDA GRANADINA", CONTADA POR ALGUNOS DE SUS...MADRID, 1926

DER VALLE A LA SIERA (EXTREMAURA) / Sansinena Araguete, Enrique – Badajoz: Tip. Vda. de Argueros, 1949 – sp Bibl Santa Ana [946]

DER VALLE A LA SIERRA / Sansinena Araguete, Enrique – (Extremanza) – Badajoz: Tip. A.Arqueros, 1949 – 1 – sp Bibl Santa Ana [946]

Valle, Antonio *see* CARTAS INEDITAS Y SEMI-INEDITAS DE DONOSO CORTES

VALLE DE LAGRIMAS Y DIVERSAS RIMAS / Mesa, Cristobal – 1607 – 9 – 1.50f – sp Bibl Santa Ana [810]

EL VALLE DE RUISENADA, POR MIGUEL DE ASUA Y CAMPOS / T'Serclaes, Duque de – Madrid: Fortanet, 1916. B.R.A.H. 69, pp. 16-18 – sp Bibl Santa Ana [946]

VALLE DEL JERTE / Centro de Iniciativas Turisticas de Plasencia – Plasencia: Imp. Sanchez Rodrigo. S.A., 1977 – 1 – sp Bibl Santa Ana [910]

EL VALLE DEL JERTE, SUS REALIDADES Y ESPERANZAS / Alias Pozas, Isabel Margarita – Plasencia: Graf. Sandoval, 1970 – 1 – sp Bibl Santa Ana [946]

Valle, G della *see*
- STORIA DEL DUOMO DI ORVIETO
- VITE DEI PITTORI ANTICHI GRECI E LATINI

Valle, Rafael Heliodoro *see* SANTIAGO EN AMERICA. MEXICO, 1946

Valle-Arizpe, Artemio del *see*
- ANDANZAS DE HERNAN CORTES
- VIRREYES Y VIRREINAS DE LA NUEVA ESPANA...PRIMERA Y SEGUNDA SERIE. 2 VOL...

Vallee, Camille *see* BIBLIOGRAPHIE DE JOSEPH BELLEAU

LA VALLEE DE DARROR; VOYAGES ET PAYS SOMALIS (AFRIQUE ORIENTALE) TYPES, SCENES, PAYSAGES. / Revoil, Georges – Paris. 1882 – 1 – us Res Libr [960]

LA VALLEE DE LA CHAUDIERE – Ste-Marie de Beauce, Canada. 29 jan 1891 – 1r – 1 – Can$25.00 – cn Can Microfilming [072]

LA VALLEE DE LA DIABLE / ed by Lefebvre, Elois – St-Jovite, Canada. 19 oct 1950-18 jul 1979 – 11r – 1 – Can$65.00r – cn Can Microfilming [072]

VALLEE DE LA LIEVRE, REGION DE L'OTTAWA: RAPPORT SOUMIS PAR P.B. BENOIT, PRESIDENT...LE 10 JANVIER 1884 / Societe de Colonisation Montarville – Montreal, 1884. 02189. (Pre-1900 Canadiana) – 9 – cn C.I.H.M. [971]

LA VALLEE DE LA MATAPEDIA / Buies, Arthur – Quebec: Leger Brousseau, imp.-ed. 1896. SEM105P27 – 1mf – 9 – Can$2.25 – cn Bibl Nat [910]

LA VALLEE DE LA MATAPEDIA: OUVRAGE HISTORIQUE ET DESCRIPTIF / Buies, Arthur – Quebec: L. Brousseau, 1895. 00366. (Pre-1900 Canadiana) – 9 – cn C.I.H.M. [971]

LA VALLEE DE LA PETITE NATION – Buckingham. v1-11. 1961-72. SEM35P231 – 5r – 1 – Can$312.00 – cn Bibl Nat [072]

LA VALLEE DE L'OTTAWA – Hull, Canada. 16 aut 1884-3 jul 1888; hebdo 8 nov 1890 – 3r – 1 – Can$50.00r – cn Can Microfilming [072]

LA VALLEE D'OTTAWA : SEMI-QUOTIDIENNE – Hull, Canada. 21 mai 1890 – 1r – 1 – Can$25.00 – cn Can Microfilming [072]

VALLEE-POUSIN, LOUIS DE LA NIRVANA... / ed by Bayle, Constantino – Madrid: Razon y Fe, 1927 – 1 – sp Bibl Santa Ana [946]

VALLEJO CITY DIRECTORIES INCLUDING BENICIA, FAIRFIELD AND SURROUNDING AREAS – Solano Co, CA. 1870-1979 – 34r – 1 – $1,700.00 – D098 – us Library Micro [978]

VALLEJO EVENING NEWS-CHRONICLE – Vallejo, CA. 1945-72 – 315r – 1 BC03063 – $15,750.00 – us Library Micro [071]

Vallejo Seco, Guillermo *see* MEMORIA A LARGO PLAZO

VALLEJO TIMES-HERALD AND NEWS CHRONICLE – Vallejo, CA. 1943-50; 1956; 1959-60; 1963-65; 1966-73 – 258r – 1 BC03067 – $12,900.00 – us Library Micro [071]

VALLEJO-BENICIA – 1921-31; 1933-45; 1992- – 13+ r – 1 – $650.00 – P00139 – us Library Micro [910]

Vallentin, Berthold *see* WINCKELMANN

Vallentin, E F *see* ILLUSTRATIONS OF THE FLOWERING PLANTS AND FERNS OF THE FALKLAND ISLANDS

Valles de Covarrubias, F *see*
- IN APHORISMO ET LIBELLUM DE ALIMENTO HIPOCRATIS, COMMENTARIA
- METHODUS MEDENDI...

VALLE-SAPUCAHY : SEMANARIO POPULAR – Pouso Alegre, 13 Feb 1886 – 1,5,6 – bl Biblioteca [072]

Vallet *see* [LE SECRET DES MUSES, LIV. 1] PARADISUS MUSICUS TESTUDINIS, IN QUO, MULTAE INSIGNES ET ANTE HUNC DIEM INAUDITE, GALLICAE, GERMANICAE, ANGLICAE, HYSPANICAE...

Valleton, Henri *see* LES EMEUTIERS

Vallette, Marguerite Eymery *see*
- MADAME ADONIS
- LA MARQUISE DE SADE
- POURQUOI JE NE SUIS PAS FEMINISTE

VALLEY ADVANCE – Vicennes. Ind. 1965- – 1 – us UMI [071]

VALLEY COLLEGE SCRAP BOOK – San Bernardino, CA. 1929-91 – 3r – 1 – $150.00 – R02770 – us Library Micro [370]

VALLEY COUNTY GAZETTE – Glendive. Mont. 1894-1899 – 1 – us UMI [071]

VALLEY COUNTY JOURNAL – Ord. Neb. 1881-1886 – 1 – us UMI [071]

VALLEY COUNTY NEWS – Glendive. Mont. -w. 1904-16, 1920-23 – 1 – us UMI [071]

VALLEY COUNTY NEWS – Glendive. MT. -sw. 1917-19 – 1 – us UMI [071]

VALLEY COUNTY TIMES – Ord, NE. -w. May 1897-Aug 1901; Nov 1901 – 1 – us NE Hist [071]

VALLEY DAILY NEWS – Tarentum. Pa. 1904-1970 – 1 – us UMI [071]

VALLEY ECHO – Tower City, PA. 1882-1901. 3 rolls – 13 – $25.00r – us I.M.R. [071]

VALLEY ENTERPRISE – Valley, NE. -w. Dec 1892; Oct 1895-Feb 1898, scattered issues missing; Jun 1906-Oct 1911; Sept 1914; Jan 1918-Aug 1920; Jun 1921-Feb 1926; Apr 1926-Sept 1927, scattered issues missing; Nov 1927-Jun 1932; Mar 1937-Dec 1947 – 1 – us NE Hist [071]

Valley Falls. Kansas. St. Paul's Evangelical Lutheran Church *see* RECORDS

VALLEY FORGE LIFE – King of Prussia. Pa. 1963- – 1 – us UMI [071]

VALLEY HERALD – Milton-Freewater, OR. -w. 5 Jan 1961-. – 10r – 1 – us U.O. Library [071]

VALLEY HERALD – Yuba City, CA. Apr 1979-Oct 1985 – 13r – 1 – $650.00 – B03129 – us Library Micro [071]

VALLEY HERALD *see* INDEPENDENT HERALD

VALLEY INDEPENDENT – Monessen. Pa. 1902- – 1 – us UMI [071]

VALLEY JOURNAL – (1973-1978.-6r) – Dundas, 1979 – 2r – 1 – cn Preston [971]

VALLEY JOURNAL – Cupertino, CA. Jul 1970-79 – 24r – 1 – $1,200.00 – B02156 – us Library Micro [073]

VALLEY JOURNAL – Mountain View, CA. 1970-79 – 24r – 1 CB02504 – $1,200.00 – us Library Micro [071]

VALLEY JOURNAL – Sunnyvale, CA. 1970-81 – 27r – 1 – $1,350.00 – B03024 – us Library Micro [073]

VALLEY JOURNAL – Sunnyvale. Calif. 1970- – 1 – us UMI [071]

VALLEY LEAVES, THE TENNESSEE VALLEY GENEALOGICAL SOCIETY QUARTERLY – v1 1967. Indexed. F-0158 – 3mf – 9 – us A.G.L.L. [920]

VALLEY MIRROR – Chelan. Wash. -w. 1925-59 – 1 – us UMI [071]

THE VALLEY NEWS – Sayre, PA., 1905-1952 – 13 – $25.00r – us I.M.R. [071]

VALLEY NEWS – Anderson, CA. 1910-68 – 24r – 1 – $1,200.00 – B02016 – us Library Micro [071]

VALLEY NEWS – Anderson. Calif. -w. 1945- – 1 – us UMI [071]

VALLEY NEWS – El Cajon, CA. 1927-61; 1964-65 – 40r – 1 – $2,000.00 – C02195 – us Library Micro [071]

VALLEY NEWS – El Cajon. Calif. 1944-1964 – 1 – us UMI [072]

VALLEY NEWS – Eugene, OR. -w. 29 Jul 1971-9 Apr 1979. – 5r – 1 – us U.O. Library [071]

VALLEY NEWS – Lebanon. N.H. 1952- – 1 – us UMI [071]

VALLEY NEWS – Santa Ynez, CA. 1925 – 69+ r – 1 – $3,450.00 ($50.00y) – H04068 – us Library Micro [071]

VALLEY NEWS – White River Junction. Vt. 1952- – 1 – us UMI [071]

VALLEY NEWS *see* DAILY CALIFORNIAN

VALLEY NEWS DISPATCH – Tarentum. Pa. 1971- – 1 – us UMI [071]

VALLEY NEWS TRIBUNE – Eugene OR. Oct 4 1977-Apr 9 1979 – 1 – us U.O. Library [071]

VALLEY OF THE UPPER MAUMEE RIVER, V2 – Historical account of Allen County and the City of Fort Wayne, IN. Includes biog. sketches. Indexed. 9 fiches. F-0294 – 9 – us A.G.L.L. [920]

THE VALLEY PEOPLE / Day, John – Napa Co, 1935 – 1r – 1 – $50.00 – B40244 – us Library Micro [978]

THE VALLEY PIONEER – Danville, CA. 1961-81; 1982-87 – 60r – 1 – $3,000.00 – B02162 – us Library Micro [071]
VALLEY PRESS – Anderson. Calif. 1968- – 1 – us UMI [071]
VALLEY PRESS – Box Elder. Mont. 1912-1927 – 1 – us UMI [071]
VALLEY PRESS – Felton, CA. 1989-1994 – 5r – 1 – $250.00 – B06025 – us Library Micro [071]
VALLEY PRESS – Gerlach, NV. 1961-1962 – 1r – 1 – $50.00 – U04540 – us Library Micro [071]
VALLEY RECORD – Ashland. Or. 1890-1911 – 1 – us UMI [071]
VALLEY RECORD – Ashland, OR. -w. 1893-1911 – 1 – 120.00 – us Oregon Hist [071]
VALLEY RECORD – Ashland, OR. -w. 31 May 1888-19 Oct. 1899. – 1r – 1 – us U.O. Library [071]
VALLEY REGISTER – Middletown. Md. -w. 1858-1930, 1932-37, 1958- – 1 – us UMI [071]
THE VALLEY REVIEW – Lodi, CA. 1881-1884; 1888-1893 – 2r – 1 – $100.00 – C03277 – us Library Micro [071]
VALLEY SENTINEL – Carlisle. Pa. -w. 1874-82 – 1 – us UMI [071]
VALLEY SENTINEL – Coquille. Or. 1960-1963 – 1 – us UMI [071]
VALLEY STANDARD – Sunnyvale, CA. 1964-65 – 5r – 1 – $250.00 – B03025 – us Library Micro [071]
THE VALLEY STAR – Newville, PA. -w 1838-1864; 1859-1907. 3 rolls – 13 – $25.00r – us I.M.R. [071]
VALLEY SUN AND BREEZE – San Fernando, CA. 1970-71 – 3r – 1 – $150.00 – C02784 – us Library Micro [071]
THE VALLEY TIMES – Newville, PA., 1907-1910 – 13 – $25.00r – us I.M.R. [071]
THE VALLEY TIMES *see* PLEASANTON TIMES
VALLEY TIMES – Amity, OR. -w. 6 Jun 1901-26 May 1904. 1 roll – 1 – us U.O. Library [071]
VALLEY TIMES – Battle Mountain, NV. 1981 – 1r – 1 – $50.00 – N03700 – us Library Micro [071]
VALLEY TIMES – Belt. Mont. -w. 1894-1918, 1922-47, 1966-67 – 1 – us UMI [071]
VALLEY TIMES – (Cont by: Times, Livermore) – Dublin, CA. Aug 1971-Feb 1978 – 79r – 1 – $3,950.00 – B02183 – us Library Micro [071]
VALLEY TIMES – Hollywood, CA. 1955-1961 – 73r – 1 – $3,650.00 – R04032 – us Library Micro [071]
VALLEY TIMES – North Hollywood. Calif. 1944-57 – 1 – us UMI [071]
VALLEY TIMES – San Fernando, CA. 1938-58; Feb-Mar 1970 – 149r – 1 – $7,450.00 – C02785 – us Library Micro [071]
VALLEY TIMES – (Set Incl. Valley News (Beaverton)) – Beaverton, OR. -w. 2 Feb 1951-6 Aug 1977+. – 37r – 1 – us U.O. Library [071]
VALLEY TIMES BULLETIN – Lake Elsinore, CA. 1972-1976 – 3r – 1 – $150.00 – R04046 – us Library Micro [071]
THE VALLEY TIMES STAR – Newville, PA., 1858-1988 – 13 – $25.00r – us I.M.R. [071]
VALLEY TIMES-NEWS – North Las Vegas. Nev. -w. 1959- – 1 – us UMI [071]
VALLEY TIMES/SAN RAMON VALLEY TIMES – Pleasanton, CA. 1975 – 340+ r – 1 – $17,000.00 ($700.00y) – B03196 – us Library Micro [071]
THE VALLEY TRIBUNE – Bainville. Mont. 1911-1932 – 1 – us UMI [071]
VALLEY TRIBUNE – Kettle Falls. Wash. 1907-1908 – 1 – us UMI [071]
VALLEY VIEW BAPTIST CHURCH. VINE GROVE, KENTUCKY : CHURCH RECORDS – 1977-1985 – 1 – $27.00 – us Baptist [240]
VALLEY VIRGINIAN – Staunton. Va. 1870-1890 – 1 – us UMI [071]
VALLEY VIRGINIAN – Waynesboro. Va. 1919-29 – 1 – us UMI [071]
THE VALLEY VOICE – Penn Valley, CA. 1989 – 6+ r – 1 – $300.00 ($50.00y) – B05044 – us Library Micro [071]
Vallings, James Frederick *see* JESUS CHRIST THE DIVINE MAN
Vallisnieri, A *see* DE' CORPI MARINI, CHE SU' MONTI SI TROVANO
Vally, Georges *see* MALARIA
Valmiki *see* RAMAYAN
Valmiki, Ramayana *see* DITJERITAKAN KEMBALI
Valmont de Bomare, J C *see* DICTIONNAIRE RAISONNE UNIVERSEL D'HISTOIRE NATURELLE
Valois, Noel *see*
– GUILLAUME D'AUVERGNE, EVEQUE DE PARIS (1228-1249)
– HISTOIRE DE LA PRAGMATIQUE SANCTION DE BOURGES SOUS CHARLES 7
VALOR MILITAR DE LA "ZONA DE DEFENSA DEL NOROESTE PENINSULAR" / Chamorro Martinez, Manuel – Badajoz: Imp. de la Dip. Provincial, 1970 – sp Bibl Santa Ana [350]
VALOR NO TIENE EDAD Y SANSON DE EXTREMADURA. EL / Diamante, Juan Bautista – Madrid: Rivadeneyra, 1859 – 1 – sp Bibl Santa Ana [946]
Valoris, Maxime *see* LE COURRIER DE LYON
Valous, G de *see*
– LE MONACHISME CLUNISIEN DES ORIGINES AU 15E SIECLE
– LE TEMPOREL DE LA SITUATION FINANCIERE DES ETABLISSEMENTS DE L'ORDRE DE CLUNY DU 12E AU 14E SIECLE
VALPARAISO HI-LITES – Valparaiso, Saunders County, NE: Nov 1, 1972-June 3, 1976 – us NE Hist [978]
VALPARAISO MESSENGER – Valparaiso. Ind. -d. 1874-75 – 1 – us UMI [071]
VALPARAISO UNIVERSITY LAW REVIEW – (v1-19 1966-85 on reel $220.00. v20-29 1985-95 on mf $201.00) – v1-29. 1966-95 – 5,6,9 – $421.00 set – us Hein [340]
VALPARAISO VISITOR – Valparaiso, NE. -w. May 1892; Oct 1895-Jan 1901; Apr 1901-Dec 1952 – 1 – us NE Hist [071]
Valsalva, A M *see* DE AURE HUMANA TRACTATUS
VALSE CARNAVALESQUE POUR DEUX PIANOS A 4 MAINS, OP. 73 / Chaminade, C – (2 parts) – Paris: Enoch, c 1894 – 1 – us Sibley [780]
VALSE, OP. 46, NO. 1 / Moszkowski, M – Breslau: Hainauer, 188- – 1 – us Sibley [780]
VALSE PENSIVE, OP. 20 / Liapunov, S – [19–] – 1 – us Sibley [780]
VALSTIECIU LAIKRASTIS – (Backfile through 1998 $85r) – Lithuania, 1999- – 1r per y – 1 – $80.00 standing order – us Ross [072]
Valton, J *see* JOURNALS, 1765-1794
VALUATION OF PUBLIC SERVICE CORPORATIONS. / Whitten, Robert Harvey – (Supplement. New York, 1914. 799, 1443 p) – New York, Banks, 1912. 798 p. LL-1504 – 1 – us L of C Photodup [340]
VALUATION REPORTS / U.S. Interstate Commerce Commission – v22-57. Jul 1929-64 (all publ) – 361mf – 9 – $541.00 – LLMC 78-228 – us L.L.M.C. [324]
THE VALUE AND DESTINY OF THE INDIVIDUAL : THE GIFFORD LECTURES FOR 1912 / Bosanquet, Bernard – London, New York: Macmillan, 1913 – 1mf – us A.T.L.A. [120]
VALUE LINE INVESTMENT SURVEY – (1969-79. Ratings, reports and index 38r 5) – 1980-. -q. Ratings and Reports; Selection and Opinion; Summary and Index. Ca 28mf per quarter. Available to printed version subscribers – 9 – us Value [332]
VALUE LINE INVESTMENT SURVEY : EXPANDED EDITION – (Publ quarterly) – 1997 – 26mf per quarter – 9 – us Value [332]
THE VALUE OF RELIGIOUS FACTS : A STUDY OF SOME ASPECTS OF THE SCIENCE OF RELIGION / Woods, James Haughton – New York: E P Dutton, 1899 – 1mf – 9 – 0-8370-5904-6 – 1985-3904 – us A.T.L.A. [200]
VALUE OF THE STUDY OF CHURCH HISTORY IN MINISTERIAL EDUCATION : LA LECTURE / Smyth, Egbert Coffin – Andover: Warren F. Draper, 1874 – 1mf – us A.T.L.A. [240]
VALUE ORIENTATIONS OF PRESERVICE PHYSICAL EDUCATION TEACHERS / Smith, Geoffrey C & Jewett, Ann E – 1992 – 1mf – 9 – $4.00 – us Microform Publ [150]
VALUES EDUCATION : THEORY, PRACTICE, PROBLEMS, PROSPECTS / ed by Meyer, John R & Burnham, Brian & Cholvat, John – 1975 – viii/167p+fiche – $15.00 – 0-88920-048-3 – cn W.L.U. Press [370]
Valuev, D A et al *see*
– SIMBIRSKII SBORNIK
Valverde de Hamusco, J *see* HISTORIA DE LA COMPOSICION DEL CUERPO HUMANO
Valverde de Leganes. Ayuntamiento *see* ORDENANZAS MUNICIPALES
Valverde del Fresno *see* FIESTAS DE AGOSTO DE 1971 EN HONOR DE NTRA. SRA. DE LA ASUNCION
Valverde Grimaldi, Felix *see* FELIX PANORAMAS INTIMOS
Valverde Horosco, D *see*
– PROTECCION DE LA DOCTRINA DE HIPOCRATES Y GALENO, ACERCA DEL METHODO DE CURAR...
– RESPUESTA AL PARECER QUE DIO CIERTO MEDICO
Valverde Tellez, E *see* BIO-BIBLIOGRAFIA ECLESIASTICA MEXICANA (1821-1943)
VALVOJA – Helsingissa. v22-42. 1902-22 – 1 – 207.00 – us L of C Photodup [073]
VAM TORN VNDE DER GUEDICHEIT GADES / Huberinus, Caspar – [Magdeburg: Michael Lotther, 1535]. [G.F.: 1.20] – 5mf – 9 – HUB-89/1 – ne IDC [240]
Vambery, Armin *see* CENTRAL ASIA AND THE ANGLO-RUSSIAN FRONTIER QUESTION; A SERIES OF POLITICAL PAPERS
Vambery, H *see* ETYMOLOGISCHES WOERTERBUCH DER TURKO-TATARISCHEN SPRACHEN
O VAMPYRO : JORNAL HUMORISTICO – Maceio, Alagoas. 10 Jun, Ago, 17-24 Nov 1877 – 1,5,6 – bl Biblioteca [072]
VAN 13 MOMENTEN UIT EEN 13-JARIG BESTAAN / Beretty, D W – Aneta-Batavia, 1931 – 6mf – 9 – ne IDC [950]
VAN BIBEL NAAR JERUZALEM: DE GODSPRAKEN VAN SIONS LIJDEN EN HEERLIJKHEID (JESAJA 40-66) / Gunning, J H – Rotterdam: J.M. Bredee, 1898. 1 fiche – 9 – us A.T.L.A. [240]
Van Braght, T J *see* A MARTYROLOGY OF THE CHURCHES OF CHRIST
Van Brunt, Walter *see* DULUTH AND THE COUNTY OF ST LOUIS
Van Buren, Martin *see* PAPERS
Van Cleaf, Aaron R *see* HISTORY OF PICKAWAY COUNTY AND REPRESENTATIVE CITIZENS
Van Cott, Maggie Newton *see* MRS. VAN COTT'S PRAISE BOOK
Van Cuyck, J W *see* SOMMIGE BELIJDINGHEN, SCHRIFTLIJCKE SENTBRIEUEN, ENDE TESTAMENTEN
VAN DE GEESTELIJCKE RESTITUTION, DAT IS, HOE DAT, ALWAT VANDEN BEGHINNE GHESCHIET IS, IN CHRISTO JESU GHEESTELIJCK VERUULT / Philips, Dirk – BME-301 1 – 9 – ne IDC [240]
VAN DE MENSCHWERDINGHE ONSES HEEREN JESU CHRISTI, DES EENGHEBOOREN SOONS SYNES EEWIGHEN ENDE ALMACHTIGHEN VADERS / Philips, Dirk – BME-309 1 – 9 – ne IDC [240]
Van Delden, M *see* ENGLISH IDIOM FOR HIGH SCHOOLS
Van den Berg *see* CONSTRAINED BY JESUS' LOVE
Van den Eikhof, Victoria E *see* THE EFFECTS OF ANKLE SPRAINS AND EXTERNAL SUPPORT ON MUSCLE ONSET LATENCIES
Van Der Sterre, Ioann. *see* CHRYSOST O. PRAEM. VITA S. NORBERTI
Van Der Zee, Jacob *see* THE BRITISH IN IOWA
VAN DIE AART, BLINDTHEYT, DWALINGHE VNDE DUYSTERNISSE DESER ARGE BOOSE WERLT / Joris, David – 1556. BME-371 1 – 9 – ne IDC [240]
VAN DIE ECHT DER CHRISTENEN, HOE SY VAN GODT BEUOLEN / Philips, Dirk – 1569. BME-313 1 – 9 – ne IDC [240]
VAN DIE GHEMEYNTE GODTS, HOE DIE VANDEN BEGINNE GHEWEEST IS. EEN CORTE BEKENTENISSE / Philips, Dirk – BME-302 1 – 9 – ne IDC [240]
VAN DIE KINDERDOOP, HET DERDE BOECK. VERCLARENDE DATMEN DIE KINDEREN MOET DOOPEN / Duncanus, M – Antwerpen, M. de Roy. 1591. BME-194 1 – 9 – ne IDC [240]
VAN DIE RECHTE KENNISSE JESU CHRISTI, DES EENIGHEN GHEBOOREN SOONS DES ALMACHTIGEN ENDE LEUENDIGHEN GODS / Philips, Dirk – BME-310 1 – 9 – ne IDC [240]
VAN DIE RECHTE WARE KENTENISSE CHRISTI VNDE KRAFT DES ALDERHEYLICHSTEN GHELOOFS / Joris, David – Wtghegaen in 't Jaer. 1554. BME-369 1 – 9 – ne IDC [240]
VAN DIE VREEMDE TONGHEN OF TALEN DER MENSCHEN, AEN V MYNE KINDEREN VERSCHREUEN / Joris, David – 1545. BME-365 1 – 9 – ne IDC [240]
Van Donkelaar, Paul *see* PREPROGRAMMING VS. ON-LINE PREPARATION IN SIMPLE MOVEMENT SEQUENCES
Van Dun, Frank *see* AUTHORITARIAN AND LIBERTARIAN VIEWS OF SOCIETY
Van Duser, Bruce L *see* THE EFFECT OF ORAL SMOKELESS TOBACCO ON THE CARDIOVASCULAR AND METABOLIC RESPONSES IN HUMANS DURING REST AND EXERCISE
Van Dyke, Henry *see*
– THE GOSPEL FOR A WORLD OF SIN
– THE REALITY OF RELIGION
– THE STORY OF THE PSALMS
Van Dyke, Henry J *see* THE VARIATIONS OF CALVINISM
Van Gennep, Arnold *see* L'ETAT ACTUEL DU PROBLEME TOTEMIQUE
VAN GHEBODEN, OFTE INSETTINGHEN ENDE LEERINGHE DER MENSCHEN – Hierachter is noch by ghevoecht een Liedeken van ij. Vrienden opgeoffert te Lonnen in Enghelant. Int iaer. M.D.LXXV. 1579. BME-241 1 – 9 – ne IDC [240]
VAN GULIK COLLECTION : CHINESE BOOKS ON MICROFICHE / ed by Ma, John & Wu, Joyce – (Pt 1: Folk novels 822mf. Pt 2: Literature and fine arts 670mf. Pt 3: Music scores and music books 200mf) – 9 – ne IDC [480]
VAN HET RECHT CHRISTEN GHELOOUE, DAT DES MENSCHEN HARTE OMKEERT, VERANDERT. ENDE SALICH MAECKET / Simons, Menno – Anno. 1556. 8, Julij. M.S. BME-283 1 – 9 – ne IDC [240]
VAN HOC – Hanoi, Vietnam. 1961-April 1963 – 1 – us Res Libr [072]
Van Hook, Larue *see* GREEK LIFE AND THOUGHT; A PORTRAYAL OF GREEK CIVILIZATION
Van Horne, D *see* RELIGION AND REVELATION
Van Marum, Martinus *see* PAPERS
Van Metre, Isaian *see* HISTORY OF BLACK HAWK COUNTY AND REPRESENTATIVE CITIZENS
Van Ness, IJ *see* PAPERS OF I.J. VAN NESS
VAN NESS' REPORTS OF TWO CASES IN THE PRIZE COURT OF THE NEW YORK DISTRICT / Van Ness, W P – New York: Banks Gould. 1v. 1814 (all publ) – 1mf – 9 – $1.50 – LLMC 81-473 – us L.L.M.C. [340]
Van Ness, W P *see* VAN NESS' REPORTS OF TWO CASES IN THE PRIZE COURT OF THE NEW YORK DISTRICT
Van Norden, Charles *see*
– JESUS: AN UNFINISHED PORTRAIT
– THE OUTERMOST RIM AND BEYOND
VAN NOSTRAND'S ECLECTIC ENGINEERING MAGAZINE *see* VAN NOSTRAND'S ENGINEERING MAGAZINE
VAN NOSTRAND'S ENGINEERING MAGAZINE – (Merged into: American Engineer and Railroad Journal. Former title: Van Nostrand's Eclectic Engineering Magazine) – New York. v1-35. jan 1869-dec 1886 – 1 – D2791 – us UMI [625]
Van Overbergh, Cyrille *see* LES BANGALA... AVEC LA COLLAB. DE ED. DE JONGHE...
VAN SU DIA – no. 22, 24-31, 33, 35, 37-38, 41-43, 48. Hanoi. oct 1956-janv 1959 – 1 – fr A.C.R.P.P. [073]
Van Swieten *see* DESCRIPCION...DE LAS ENFERMEDADES MAS COMUNES DEL EXERCITO CON UN NUEVO METODO DE CURAR EL MAL VENEREO
Van Tassel, Charles S *see* STORY OF THE MAUMEE VALLEY AND TOLEDO AND THE SANDUSKY REGION
Van Valin, W B *see* ESKIMOLAND SPEAKS
VAN VERBORGENHEIT DER SCHRIFFT DES RYKES CHRISTI, VNDE VAN DEM DAGHE DES HEREN, DURCH DE GEMEINTE CHRISTI THO MUENSTER / Rothmann, B – Muenster. 1535. BME-182 1 – 9 – ne IDC [240]
Van Vollenhoven Institute, University of Leiden *see* DISSERTATIONS ON NETHERLANDS INDIES LAW 1850-1945
Van Voorhis, John S *see* THE OLD AND NEW MONONGAHELA
Van Wert County. Ohio. Auditor *see*
– DEED RECORDS
– ENUMERATIONS OF SOLDIERS
– REAPPRAISMENTS
– SCHOOL LAND RECORD
– TRANSFER RECORDS
Van Wert County, Ohio. Board of County Commissioners *see* BLIND RELIEF RECORDS

Van Wert County. Ohio. Board of County Commissioners *see*
- ADMISSIONS TO COUNTY HOSPITAL
- COMMISSIONERS' JOURNALS
- INDEX TO JOURNALS, BILLS
- INDEX TO JOURNALS, INFIRMARY
- JOURNALS, BRIDGES, ROADS, DITCHES
- MINUTES

Van Wert County. Ohio. Common Pleas. Civil Division *see*
- CHANCERY RECORDS
- COMPLETE RECORDS
- JOURNALS
- JUDGMENT INDEXES, DIRECT
- JUDGMENT INDEXES, REVERSE
- NATURALIZATION FILES
- NATURALIZATION RECORDS
- NATURALIZATIONS, DECLARATIONS

Van Wert County, Ohio. Common Pleas. Criminal Div. *see* CORONERS' INQUESTS

Van Wert County. Ohio. Common Pleas. Criminal Div *see*
- COMPLETE RECORDS
- CORONERS' INQUESTS

Van Wert County. Ohio. Common Pleas. Domestic *see* COMPLETE RECORDS, DIVORCE

Van Wert County. Ohio. Common Pleas. Juvenile Court *see* MOTHERS' PENSION RECORDS

Van Wert County. Ohio. County Home *see*
- MINUTES
- PATIENT ACCOUNT RECORD
- PAYROLL RECORD
- RECEIPTS AND EXPENDITURES RECORD
- REGISTER
- SEMI-ANNUAL REPORTS

Van Wert County. Ohio. District Court *see*
- COMPLETE RECORDS
- JOURNALS

Van Wert County. Ohio. Pleasant Township. Board of Education *see* MINUTES

Van Wert County. Ohio. Pleasant Township. Board of Trustees *see*
- CEMETERY RECORDS
- MINUTES AND ACCOUNT BOOKS
- RECORD OF EARMARKS AND BRANDS
- STATE CHARITIES REPORT

Van Wert County. Ohio. Pleasant Township. Township Clerk *see*
- CIVIL WAR BOUNTY RECORD
- LIQUOR BLACKLISTS
- PAUPER REGISTERS

Van Wert County. Ohio. Probate Court *see*
- ADMINISTRATION DOCKETS
- BIRTH RECORDS
- DEATH RECORDS
- GENERAL INDEX TO BIRTHS
- GENERAL INDEX TO DEATHS
- INDEX TO ESTATES
- JOURNALS
- LAND SALES RECORDS
- MARRIAGE RECORDS
- STATEMENTS OF BIRTHS AND DEATHS
- WILL RECORDS

Van Wert County. Ohio. Recorder *see* ENTRY RECORD

Van Wert County. Ohio. Sheriff *see* JAIL REGISTER

Van Wert County. Ohio. Soldiers' Relief Commission *see* BURIAL RECORDS

Van Wert County. Ohio. Supreme Court *see*
- CHANCERY RECORDS
- COMPLETE RECORD

Van Wert County. Ohio Treasurer *see* TAX DUPLICATES

Van Wert County. Ohio. Treasurer *see* RECORDS OF OFFICIALS' BONDS

Van Wert County, Ohio. Van Wert, City. City Council *see* INDENTURES

Van Wert County.Ohio. Middlepoint Methodist Charge *see* RECORDS

Van Wert. Ohio. First United Methodist Church *see* RECORDS

Van Winkle, Daniel *see* HISTORY OF THE MUNICIPALITIES OF HUDSON COUNTY

Van Zandt, Nicholas B *see* A FULL DESCRIPTION OF THE SOIL, WATER, TIMBER, AND PRAIRIES OF EACH LOT, OR QUARTER SECTION OF THE MILITARY LAND BETWEEN THE MISSISSIPPI AND ILLINOIS RIVERS

Van Zile, Philip Taylor *see* ELEMENTS OF THE LAW OF BAILMENTS AND CARRIERS, INCLUDING PLEDGE AND PAWN AND INNKEEPERS

EL VANADIO EN ESPANA / Munoz del Castillo, Jose – Madrid: Imprenta Velasco, 1900 – sp Bibl Santa Ana [946]

Vance, James Isaac *see*
- THE COLLEGE OF APOSTLES: A STUDY OF THE TWELVE
- THE ETERNAL IN MAN

Vance, William Reynolds *see* CASES ON THE LAW OF INSURANCE...2ND ED

VanClief, Elizabeth W *see* INFLUENTIAL PHYSICAL EDUCATION BOOKS OF THE TWENTIETH CENTURY

THE VANCOUVER AND BRITISH COLUMBIA GUIDE – Vancouver: H P Judd, 1889-[18– or 19–] – 9 – cn C.I.H.M. [910]

VANCOUVER BI-WEEKLY WORLD – Vancouver, British Columbia, CN. Dec 1895-Sept 1903 – 5r – 1 – cn Commonwealth Micro [072]

THE VANCOUVER CHESNUT – [Vancouver?: s.n, 18–?-19–?] – 9 – cn C.I.H.M. [072]

VANCOUVER DAILY COLUMBIAN – Vancouver, WA. 1910-20 – 1 – 322.00 – us Oregon Hist [071]

VANCOUVER DAILY EVENING POST – Victoria, Canada. 1864-66 – 3r – 1 – $204.00 – cn Library Assoc [971]

VANCOUVER DAILY NEWS ADVERTISER – (Some issues missing) – Vancouver, British Columbia, CN. May 1886-Jun 1917 – 78r – 1 – cn Commonwealth Micro [072]

THE VANCOUVER DAILY WORLD – Vancouver, British Columbia. v16 n68. 20 jun 1896 – 1r – 1 – Can$25.00 – cn Can Microfilming [072]

VANCOUVER DAILY WORLD – Vancouver, British Columbia, CN. Sept 1888-Mar 1924 – 144r – 1 – cn Commonwealth Micro [072]

VANCOUVER EXPRESS – Vancouver, British Columbia, CN. Nov. 1978-May 1979; Apr-May 1984 – 1 – cn Commonwealth Micro [072]

Vancouver, G A *see* A VOYAGE OF DISCOVERY TO THE NORTH PACIFIC OCEAN, AND ROUND THE WORLD

VANCOUVER MAGAZINE – (v1-22 1967-89 Can$46.00y. v23-28 1990-95 Can$37.00y) – Vancouver. v1-28. 1967-95 – 9 – cn Micromedia [910]

VANCOUVER NEWS HERALD – Vancouver, British Columbia, CN. Apr 1933-Sept 1957 – 114r – 1 – cn Commonwealth Micro [072]

Vancouver. Planning Department *see* QUARTERLY REVIEW

VANCOUVER PLANNING DEPT QUARTERLY REVIEW – (Index 1979-81 Can$20.00. Cease v14 no 3 1987) – Vancouver. v1-14. 1974-1987 – 9 – Can$20.00y – cn Micromedia [350]

VANCOUVER REGISTER – Vancouver, WA. And pred. 1881-1902. Incomplete – 1 – 120.00 – us Oregon Hist [071]

VANCOUVER SATURDAY SUNSET – Vancouver, British Columbia, CN. Jun 1907-May 1915 – 5r – 1 – cn Commonwealth Micro [072]

VANCOUVER SOCIAL REGISTER AND CLUB DIRECTORY – Vancouver: Welch and Gibbs, 1914 – 1r – 1 – cn U.B.C. Preserve [910]

VANCOUVER STOCK EXCHANGE REVIEW – Vancouver, 1964-94 – 9 – Can$28.00y – cn Micromedia [332]

THE VANCOUVER SUN – Vancouver, Feb 1912- – 36r per yr – 1 – Can$53.00r – cn Commonwealth Micro [072]

VANCOUVER TIMES – Vancouver, British Columbia, CN. Sept 1964-Aug 1965 – 12r – 1 – cn Commonwealth Micro [072]

THE VANCOUVER TYPOGRAPHER – Vancouver: Union Printers of Vancouver, [1892-189- or 19–] – 9 – cn C.I.H.M. [680]

VANCOUVER WEEKLY NEWS ADVERTISER – Vancouver, British Columbia, CN. Sept 1888-Dec 1910 – 9r – 1 – cn Commonwealth Micro [072]

VANCOUVER WEEKLY PROVINCE – Vancouver, British Columbia, CN. Mar 1894-Apr 1897 – 2r – 1 – cn Commonwealth Micro [072]

VANCOUVER WEEKLY WORLD – Canada. -w. Jan 1895-March 1896. 1 reel – 1 – uk British Libr Newspaper [072]

VANCOUVER WEEKLY WORLD – Vancouver, British Columbia, CN. Sept 1888-Dec 1910 – 2r – 1 – cn Commonwealth Micro [072]

VANCOUVER WORLD – Canada. -d. July-Aug 1915. 1 reel – 1 – uk British Libr Newspaper [072]

Vancsa, Kurt *see* FRANZ GRILLPARZER

THE VANDAMM COLLECTION *see*
- EXPRESSIONIST THEATER
- GREAT AMERICAN DRAMA
- LANDMARKS IN AMERICAN STAGE DESIGN
- MODERN EUROPEAN DRAMA
- MUSICALS
- O'NEILL
- SHAKESPEARE

VANDE BEIAERDEN DOOPE: CORTE ENDE GETROUWE WAERSCHOUWINGHE / Coornhert, D V – 1575. BME-212 1 – 9 – ne IDC [240]

VANDE VREMDE ENDE ONSCHRIFTMATIGHE MANIERE DER WEDER-DOOPSCHER LEERAREN HEYMELIJCKE GHEBEDEN / Lansbergivs, F – Rotterdam, J. van Waesberghe. 1596. BME-251 1 – 9 – ne IDC [240]

VANDE WEDERGEBOORTE ENDE NIEUWE CREATURE EEN CORTE VERMANINGHE ENDE AENWIJSINGHE WT DE HEYLIGHE SCHRIFT / Philips, Dirk – BME-306 1 – 9 – ne IDC [240]

Vandelli, D *see*
- FASCICULUS PLANTARUM CUM NOVIS GENERIBUS ET SPECIEBUS
- FLORAE LUSITANICAE ET BRASILIENSIS SPECIMEN

Vandenbuclke, J *see* HANS-GEORG GADAMER

VANDER DOOPE ONSES HEEREN JESU CHRISTI, BEKENTNISSE DOOR DIERICK PHILIPS / Philips, Dirk & Kimedoncius, J – Middelburgh, J. Wullebrechts. 1589. BME-304 1 – 9 – ne IDC [240]

Vander Linde, Darl W *see* EFFECT OF MUSCLE LENGTH ON MOTOR UNIT FIRING BEHAVIOR IN HUMAN TIBIALIS ANTERIOR MUSCLE

VANDER SENDINGE DER PREDICANTEN OFT LEERAERS / Philips, Dirk – 1559. BME-311 1 – 9 – ne IDC [240]

VANDERBILT INTERNATIONAL *see*
- VANDERBILT JOURNAL OF TRANSNATIONAL LAW

VANDERBILT JOURNAL OF TRANSNATIONAL LAW – (v1-17 1967-84 on reel or mf $235.00. v18-28 1985-95 on mf $228.00. Title varies: v1-4 1967-71 as Vanderbilt International) – v1-28. 1967-95 – 5,6,9 – $465.00 set – us Hein [340]

VANDERBILT JOURNAL OF TRANSNATIONAL LAW – (With cum index 1-4 (1967-71). Former title: Vanderbilt International) – Nashville. v1-30. win 1967-nov 1997+ 1; v9-10 win 1976-fal 1977*. v 11 win-fal 1978. v12-13 win 1979-fal 1980*. v 14 win-fal 1981. v15-27 win 1982-nov 1994*. v28-30 jan 1995-nov 1997+ 5; v9-30 win 1976-nov 1997+ 9 – 1,5,9 – D6809 – us UMI [340]

VANDERBILT LAW REVIEW – (v1-37 1947-84 on reel or mf $876.00. v38-48 1985-95 on mf $295.00) – v1-48. 1947-95 – 5,6,9 – $1,175.00 set – us Hein [340]

VANDERBILT LAW REVIEW – (With cum index 1-10 1947-aug 1957, 11-20 1957-67) – Nashville. v25-50. jan 1972-nov 1997+ 1; v1-10 dec 1947-aug 1957. v11-50+ 5; v27-50. jan 1972-nov 1997+ 9 – 1,5,9 – D6513 – us UMI [340]

Vanderburgh, Henry *see* HENRY VANDERBURGH PAPERS, MS 132

Vanderheyden, J F *see* HULDE ALBUM

Vanderhorst, Elias *see* ESTATE RECEIPT BOOK

Vanderveer, Beth *see* MANAGEMENT BEHAVIORS OF WOMEN DIRECTORS IN LEISURE SERVICES AGENCIES IN THE UNITED STATES

Vane, C W *see* MEMOIRS AND CORRESPONDENCE [DESPATCHES, AND OTHER PAPERS,] OF VISCOUNT CASTLEREAGH, SECOND MARQUESS OF LONDONDERRY

Vangroenweghe, D *see*
- ESSAI D'ETUDE D'UN NSAMBO
- LA GRANDE FETE BOBONGO CHEZ LES EKONDA, ZAIRE

THE VANGUARD – Bathurst, Gambia. -w. 15 March 1958-31 Dec 1960. 1 reel – 1 – uk British Libr Newspaper [072]

THE VANGUARD – Manila, Philippines. Ceased in 1940? illus – 1 – us U.W. Library [073]

THE VANGUARD – Rangoon, Burma. Apr-Dec 1961 – 3r – 1 – us L of C Photodup [072]

THE VANGUARD : A TALE OF KOREA / Gale, James Scarth – New York: Fleming H Revell, c1904 – 1mf – 9 – 0-8370-6496-1 – 1986-0496 – us A.T.L.A. [950]

THE VANGUARD – Toronto: [s.n, 1893-1895?] – 9 – cn C.I.H.M. [170]

VANGUARD : AN ANARCHIST COMMUNIST JOURNAL – 1-4 2+9. 1932-1939 – 8mf – 9 – $55.00 – us UPA [335]

VANGUARD – Milwaukee. v24-28. jan 1977-dec 1981 – 1 – D11481 – us UMI [073]

VANGUARD – Portland OR. Nov 26 1958, Feb 11 1959 – 1 – us U.O. Library [071]

VANGUARD – v1-6 (all publ). 1902-1908 – 1 reel – 1 – $115.00 – us UPA [335]

A VANGUARDA – Cassia, 16 Jan-Mar 1927; Jul-Dec 1933; Jun 1935 -Dec 1937; Jan-Jul, Oct-Nov 1938; Apr-May, Sep-Oct 1939; Feb, May 1940; Jan-Mar, Jul-31 Aug 1941 – 1,5,6 – bl Biblioteca [072]

A VANGUARDA – Espinosa, Brazil. May, Jul-Aug, Oct 1928 – 1 – bl Biblioteca [072]

A VANGUARDA – Lisbon, 23 Jan 1917-31 Dec 1918 – 4r – 1 – uk British Libr Newspaper [072]

A VANGUARDA : ORGAM DO CENTRO DA MOCIDADE LIVRE PENSADORA – Curitiba, 22 Jan 1905-22 Jan 1906 – 1,5,6 – bl Biblioteca [072]

A VANGUARDA : ORGAM INDEPENDENTE – ORIENTACAO CATHOLICA – Curvello, 5 Nov 1936-27 May 1937 – 1,5,6 – bl Biblioteca [072]

A VANGUARDA – Santos, Brazil. 16 Jan-Mar 1909; Feb-Sept 1912. Incomplete – 1 – bl Biblioteca [072]

A VANGUARDA CARNAVALESCA – Penedo, Alagoas. 24 Fev 1935 – 1,5,6 – bl Biblioteca [072]

LA VANGUARDIA : ORGANO DEL PARTIDO SOCIALISTA / Socialist Party. Argentine Republic – Buenos Aires, Argentina. 1944-78 – 1 – $35.00r – us Hoover Inst Photo [972]

LA VANGUARDIA ESPANOLA – Barcelona: [s.n.], [jan 28 1939-1955]; 1956-jul 1970; 1974-aug 15 1978 – us Res Libr [072]

Vanheest, Jaci L *see* THE EFFECTS OF HAND COOLING DURING STRENUOUS EXERCISE ON METABOLIC AND CARDIORESPIRATORY FUNCTION

Vanicek, Alois *see* FREMDWOERTER IM GRIECHISCHEN UND LATEINISCHEN

VANIDADES CONTINENTAL – Virginia Gardens. v14-32 jan 1974-dec 1992. v34 jan-dec 1994*. v35-37 jan 1995-dec 1997+ 1; v16-20 jan 1976-dec 1980. v21-25 jan 1981-dec 1985*. v26-32 jan 1986-dec 1992. v34 jan-dec 1994*. v35-37 jan 1995-dec 1997+ 5; v16-19 jan 1976-dec 1979*. v20-32 jan 1980-dec 1992. v34 jan-dec 1994*. v35-37 jan 1995-dec 1997+ 9 – 1,5,9 – D8947 – us UMI [073]

Vanier, Ignace *see* DISCOURS SUR L'EDUCATION

VANITY FAIR – Lincoln, NE. -w. Apr 1891-Feb 1893 – 1 – us NE Hist [071]

VANITY FAIR – New York. v1-7. dec 1859-jul 1863 – 1 – D6019 – us UMI [073]

VANITY FAIR : A NOVEL WITHOUT A HERO / Thackeray, William Makepeace – London: Smith, Elder and Co., 1867 – 1 roll – 1 – 1-55879-241-4 – uk Libr Preservation [830]

VANITY FAIR – Toronto: C W Parker, [1886-18– or 19–] – 9 – cn C.I.H.M. [971]

VANITY FAIR – (with cum Index 1-45. Absorbed by: Vogue, mar 1936; resumed publication mar 1983. Former title: Dress & Vanity Fair sept-dec 1913) – New York. v1-45. sep 1913-feb 1936 1; v 46-58 mar 1983-dec 1995, 1996, 1997+ 1,5,9 – 1,5,9 – D5347 – us UMI [390]

VANITY FAIR *see* VOGUE

THE VANITY OF A LIFE OF FASHIONABLE PLEASURE / Boardman, Henry Augustus – 1839 – 1 – $50.00 – us Presbyterian [240]

VanLaer, C *see*
- MAGNIFICAT AND NUNC DIMITTIS [SATB ORGAN]
- SPRINGTIME PLEASURES. FOR PIANO

LA VANNERIE DU PAYS NDUT, REPUBLIQUE DU SENEGAL / Porcell, M – 9 – F50.00 – fr Ethnologie [306]

Van-Praet, M *see* ABSORPTION ET DIGESTION CHEZ ACTINIA EQUINA L., NUTRITION DES ACTINIAIRES

Vanselow, Karl et al *see*
- GESCHLECHT UND GESELLSCHAFT (HQ 3)
- SEXUALREFORM (HQ 4)

Vansina, Jan *see*
- L'EVOLUTION DU ROYAUME RWANDA DES ORIGINES A 1900
- IBITEEKEREZO: HISTORICAL NARRATIVES FROM RWANDA
- KUBA FIELD NOTES

Vansleb, J M *see* HISTOIRE DE L'EGLISE D'ALEXANDRIE

Vansteenberghe, E *see* LE CARDINAL NICOLAS DE CUES (1401-1464)

VANUA SCOPE / ed by Delcoitre, Patrick Antoine – Port Vila, Vanuatu, mar 1993-jan 1994 – PMB Doc427 – at Pacific Mss [072]

Vanuatu Chamber of Commerce see BULLETIN OF THE NEW HEBRIDES CHAMBER OF COMMERCE, INDUSTRY AND AGRICULTURE / BULLETIN OF THE VANUATU CHAMBER OF COMMERCE
Vanuatu. National Library see MISCELLANEOUS PAPERS
VAOVAO – Frantsay malagasy. no. 1-262. Antananarivo. 1897-1901; no. 313. 19 dec 1902; no. 321-323. 20 fevr-6 mars 1903; no. 352. 25 sept 1903; no. 363. 11 dec 1903; no. 730-940. 1911-15 janv 1915. mq no. 886-911 – 1 – fr A.C.R.P.P. [073]
VAPAAKIRKOLLINEN LIIKE SUOMESSA (THE FREE CHURCH MOVEMENT IN FINLAND) / Makinen, Antti – Helsinki: Vapaan Lahetyksen, 1911. 348p – 1 – 13.92 – us Baptist [240]
VAPAUS – Sudbury. 1958-74 – 1 – 1785.00 – cn McLaren [073]
VAPAUS SANA – (In Finnish) – Canada, 1932-77 – 44r – 1 – cn Commonwealth Micro [072]
VAPROSY LITERATURY – Moscow. U.S.S.R. 1967- – 1 – us UMI [072]
Vaquero Mayor, Agustin see REGISTRO DE MATRICULA
VAR INDUSTRI – 1972-76 1; 1976- 5,6,9 – us UMI [338]
VAR KYRKA – (Lacking: nos 47-52 1978) – 1969-82 – 13r – 1 – ATLA S0790 – us A.T.L.A. [073]
VAR LOESEN – (Some pgs lacking) – v1-82. 1910-91 – 29r – 1 – ATLA S0503 – us A.T.L.A. [073]
VAR MATIN – 1993-1995 – 6r per y – 5,6 – Sfr1,176.00 – sz Infoprint [073]
LA VARA – New York, NY. 1922-48 – 1 – us A.J.P.C. [071]
LA VARA – New York. v. 2 no. 67-v. 26 no. 24. Dec 7 1923-Feb 13 1948. Incomplete – 1 – us NY Public [305]
LA VARA = THE TRUTH – (In Ladino) – New York City, NY. v26 no1 5 Sep 1947-16 Jan 1948 – 1r – 1 – $30.00 – cn Can Microfilming [071]
VARA HEM see ORESUNDSPOSTEN
VARADOURO : UM JORNAL DAS SELVAS – Rio Branco, Acre. Maio 1977-Dez 1981 – 1,5,6 – bl Biblioteca [072]
Varagnac, Andre see DEFINITION DU FOLKLORE
Varallyay, G see REVIEW OF RESEARCH ON SALT-AFFECTED SOILS
Vararuci, Bhagavan see SARA-SAMUCCAYA
VARBERGS TIDNING – Varberg, Sweden. 1953-62 – 21r – 1 – sw Kungliga [072]
VARBERGSPOSTEN – Varberg, Sweden. 1894-1903 – 10r – 1 – sw Kungliga [072]
Varchi, Benedetto see DUE LEZIONI, NELLA PRIMA DELLE QUALI SI DICHIARA UN SONETTO DI M. MICHELAGNOLO BUONAROTTI. NELLA SECONDA SI DISPUTA QUALE SIA PIU NOBILE ARTE LA SCULTURA, O LA PITTURA
VARDAMAN'S – Jackson. Miss. -w. 1908-23 – 1 – us UMI [071]
Vardon, Harry see HOW TO PLAY GOLF
Vare, Daniele see DIE STROMSCHNELLEN DES YANGTZE
Varela, Cipriano see
- EXORTACION PASTORAL
- INSTRUCCIONES IMPORTANTES QUE... SR.D....COMUNICA A TODOS...
- INSTRUCIONES..
- NOVENA-MARIA SANTISIMA MADRE DE DIOS Y SENORA NUESTRA QUE CON EL TITULO DEL PUERTO VENERA Y TIENE POR PATRONA LA CIUDAD DE PLASENCIA...
- NOVENA...NTRA. SRA. PUERTO..

Varela, Pedro see REFLEXIONES SOBRE LA HUMANIDAD DE LOS ESPANOLES EN LAS INDIAS
Varela, R see PROCESSUS POLITIQUES A TLAYACAPAN, MORELOS, MEXIQUE
VARENFLORA VOOR JAVA... / Backer, C A & Posthumus, O – Buitenzorg, 1939 – 5mf – 9 – ne IDC [580]
Varennes de Mondasse see LA DECOUVERTE DE L'EMPIRE DE CANTAHAR
Varennes, Kathleen M de see BIBLIOGRAPHIE ANNOTEE D'OUVRAGES GENEALOGIQUES A LA BIBLIOTHEQUE DU PARLEMENT
Varennes, Marguerite-de see BIBLIOGRAPHIE ANALYTIQUE DES ECRITS PUBLIES PAR LES SOEURS DE LA CHARITE DE QUEBEC, 1942-1961
Varennes, Raymond de see IDEES PATRIOTIQUES, SUR LA METHODE ET L'IMPORTANCE D'UNE EDUCATION NATIONALE POUR ASSURER LE REGENERATION DE LA FRANCE
Varga, E see SSSR V SISTEME MIROVOGO KHOZIAISTVA
Varga, T see TEACHING SCHOOL MATHEMATICS
Vargas, Adolfo de see
- FLORES Y ABROJOS
- EL GORRO DE DORMIR
- REAL HOSPICIO DE BADAJOZ. FUNDACION

Vargas Ponce, Jose see DESCRIPCION DE LAS ISLAS BALEARES
Vargas Ugarte, Ruben see DON BENITO MARIA DE MOXO Y DE FRANCOLI, ARZOBISPO DE CHARCAS
Vargas Zuniga, Antonio see INDICE DE LA COLECCION SALAZAR, TOMOS 20, 8-37. MADRID, 1961-1966
Vargas Zuniga, Rodrigo see
- EN EL PUEBLO DORMIDO
- REGALO DE BODAS

DI VARHAYT – (Irregular publication. Missing: nos 1-3,6,8-13,18-End) – Moscow. 1918 – 1r – 1 – J-92-32/3 – ne IDC [072]
VARIA RHETORICA / Fortunatianus, Severianus, Julius, etc – 15th century. Holkham Ms 510 – 1 – uk Microform Academic [760]
VARIABLES RELATED TO KNOWLEDGE LEVELS OF AGING AND PLANNING FOR FUTURE AGING OF TEXAS HIGH SCHOOL GRADUATES / Ellerd, Andria & Kaplan, Leah E – 1991 – 1mf 1610 $4.00 – 9 – us Microform Publ [150]
VARIAN, ALEXANDER, JR., LETTERS, MS 3141 – 1861-1864 – 1 reel – 1 – us Western Res [976]
VARIANT USES OF ALEPH IN IQISA / Finnan, Alan Pierson – 1982 – 1 – 5.00 – us Baptist [240]
DIE VARIANZ PHRASEOLOGISCHER WENDUNGEN UNTER BESONDERER BERUECKSICHTIGUNG DER LEXIKALISCHQUANTITAVEN VARIANTEN VON PHRASEOLOGISMEN IM RUSSISCHEN / Mueller, Renate – Leipzig, 1978 – 2mf – DM62.00 – 3-89349-912-1 – gw Hänsel [460]
VARIAS MATERIAS DE DIVERSAS FACULTADES Y CIENCIAS : POLITICA CONTRA LA PESTE... / Salado Garces y Ribera, F – Utrera, 1655 – 9mf – 9 – sp Cultura [616]
VARIAS NOTAS Y APUNTES SOBRE TEMAS DE LETRAS CLASICAS / Gonzales de la Calle, Pedro Urbano – Madrid: Libreria general de Victoriano Suarez, 1916 – 1 – sp Bibl Santa Ana [946]
VARIATION GEOGRAPHIQUE ET TAXONOMIE DES PLACOSTYLUS (GASTEROPODES PULMONES STYLOMMATOPHORES) EN NOUVELLE-CALEDONIE / Cherel-Mora, C – 9 – F40.00 – fr Ethnologie [590]
VARIATIONEN UEBER EIN FRANZOESISCHES LIED IN E FUER KLAVIER ZU 4 HAENDEN, OP.10 / Schubert, Franz – (Holograph of mm. 35-69[end of var. 2, var. 3 and beg. of var. 4] for piano 4 hands) – Ms score, [1818, September] – 1 – us Sibley [780]
VARIATIONEN UEBER EIN THEMA VON HAENDEL FUR PIANOFORTE...OP. 26... / Volkmann, Richard von – Pest: Gust. Heckenast, [18–] – 1 – us Sibley [780]
VARIATIONS, 7, SUR L'AIR BEGLUECKT DURCH DICH POUR LE PIANOFORTE / Zapf, J N – Vienne: Eder, 180- – 1 – us Sibley [780]
VARIATIONS BRILLANTES SUR LA MARCHE BOHEMIENNE...POUR LE PIANOFORTE A QUATRE MAINS.. / Moscheles, Ignaz – 184-? – 9 – us Sibley [780]
VARIATIONS DE LA PERSONNALITE PAR LES DOCTEURS H. BOURRU ET P. BUROT / Bourru, Henri et Ferdinand Burot – (French Precursors of Psychiatry Series). Paris. J. B. Bailliere. 1888 – 9 – fr Hachette [150]
DES VARIATIONS DU LANGAGE FRANCAIS DEPUIS LE 12E SIECLE / Genin, F – 1845 – 9 – fr I.C.S. [440]
VARIATIONS ET RONDEAUX POUR LE PIANOFORTE / Pollini, F – Zuric: J G Naigueli, 1805 – 1 – us Sibley [780]
THE VARIATIONS OF CALVINISM / Van Dyke, Henry J – New York: Anson D.F. Randolph, [1890?] – 1mf – us A.T.L.A. [240]
VARIATIONS POUR 2 PIANOS, OP. 5 / Enesco, G – (2 pts) – Paris: Enoch & Co, ca 1899 – 1 – us Sibley [780]
VARIATIONS POUR LE PIANOFORTE SUR UNE WALZE FAVORITE DE MOZART / Gelinek, J – Paris: Janet et Cotelle, 181- – 1 – us Sibley [780]
VARIED TYPES / Chesterton, GK – New York: Dodd, Mead, 1903 – 1 roll – 1 – 1-55879-947-8 – uk Libr Preservation [840]
VARIEDADES : ESPANA HALLO SU HOMBRE (PIO 12) / Bayle, Constantino – Madrid: Razon y Fe, 1940 – 1 – sp Bibl Santa Ana [240]
VARIETES – Brussels. v. 1-2. May 15 1928-Apr 15 1930 – 1 – us NY Public [073]
VARIETES – Revue mensuelle illustree de l'esprit contemporain. Dir. P.G. Van Hecke. Bruxelles. 15 mai 1928-15 avr 1930 – 1 – fr A.C.R.P.P. [073]
VARIETES ORIENTALES HISTORIQUES, GEOGRAPHIQUES, SCIENTIFIQUES, BIBLIOGRAPHIQUES ET LITTERAIRES / Rosny, Leon de – Troisieme ed. revue et corrigee. Paris: Maisonneuve et Cie. 1872 – 9 – 10.00 – fr Orientalistes [950]
VARIETY – New York. v. 1-255. Dec 16 1905-Aug 31 1969 – 1 – us NY Public [790]
VARIETY – New York. v1-341. dec 1905-jan 1991 1; v342-369. jan 1991-feb 1998+ 1,5,9 – 1,5,9 – D18402 – us UMI [073]
VARIETY – NY City, NY. 1967-1975 – 26r – 1 – $1,300.00 – R04930 – us Library Micro [071]
VARIETY – v1- 1905- – 1 – inquire – us Ross [073]
VARIETY THEATRE – London, UK. Jan 1906. -irr. 9 feet – 1 – uk British Libr Newspaper [790]
LA VARIOLE ET LA VACCINATION COMPULSOIRE / Gariepy, Romuald – s.l.: s.n., 1874?. 04322. (Pre-1900 Canadiana) – 9 – cn C.I.H.M. [971]
Varios see CUADERNOS DE LA CATEDRA FEIJOO (1 A 24) (CATEDRA FEIJOO-CENTRO DE ESTU DIOS DEL SIGLO XVIII)
VARIOS JUICIOS... / Torre Isunza de Hita, Pedro – 2nd ed. corregida y aumentada. Cabra: Imp. Manuel Cordon, 1929 – sp Bibl Santa Ana [946]
VARIOS JUICIOS CRITICOS EMITIDOS POR LA PRENSA DE GRAN CIRCULACION Y PRIVADAMENTE SOBRE LA LABOR CIENTIFICA Y LITERARIA DE RAMON DE TORRE ISUNZA CON ANOTACIONES DE SU HERMANO D. PEDRO Y APENDICE / Torre Isunza de Hita, Pedro – Cabra: Imp. Manuel Cordon, 1927 – sp Bibl Santa Ana [440]
VARIOUS DOCUMENTS ADDRESSED TO THE HONORABLE LOUIS JOSEPH PAPINEAU, SPEAKER OF THE HOUSE OF ASSEMBLY / Viger, Denis Benjamin – [s.l: s.n, 1834 ?]. SEM105P1378 – 1mf – 9 – Can$2.25 – cn Bibl Nat [971]
THE VARIOUS EFFECTS OF CRYOGENIC MODALITIES WITH REGARDS TO RESTRICTION OF BLOOD VOLUME IN THE MALE FOREARM / Jenkins, Barry – 1982 – 1mf – 9 – $4.00 – us Microform Publ [790]
VARIOUS FRAGMENTS, TOGETHER WITH TWO ESSAYS FROM VOL. 1 OF HIS "ESSAYS" / Spencer, Herbert – 1897. 253p. 1 fiche (24x) – 9 – 1.00f – at Libertarian Micro [320]
VARIOUS KINDS OF FLOOR DECORATIONS / Carwitham, J – O-1193 1. 1739 – 9 – ne IDC [740]
VARIOUS MANUSCRIPTS AND PAPERS, 188?-19-?; AND PRESS COPY BOOK : SERMONS, ARTICLES AND LETTERS, 1867-1873 / Fison, Lorimer – 1r – 1 – at Pacific Mss [920]
VARIOUS MINISTERS AND OFFICIALS, 1824-1949 / Great Britain. Foreign Office – FO 800: 115-146 Landsdowne Papers, 1898-1926 – 15r – 1 – us Ross [324]
VARIOUS MSS / Pliny, Virgil, etc – From Holkham mss. 395, 433, 399.Holkham Hall, Norfolk, England – 1 – uk Microform Academic [025]
VARIOUS TRACTS / Penn, J – London, [1762] – 5mf – 9 – MP-416/1 – ne IDC [240]
Varis, Tapio see
- INTERNATIONAL FLOW OF TELEVISION PROGRAMMES
- TRANSNATIONAL COMMUNICATION AND CULTURAL INDUSTRIES

VARLDEN I DAG – (Varlden Runt, 1937 1-3) – Stockholm, Sweden. 1937-42 – 4r – 1 – sw Kungliga [073]
VARLDEN RUNT see VARLDEN I DAG
Varley, Allen see RED SEA, GULD OF ADEN AND SUEZ CANAL
Varley, Henry see FAITH AND FORM
LA VARLOPPE – St-Hyacinthe, Canada. 2 mar-27 avr 1935 – 1r – 1 – Can$35.00 – cn Can Microfilming [072]
Varma, S see CRITICAL STUDIES IN THE PHONETIC OBSERVATIONS OF INDIAN GRAMMARIANS
VARMLANDS FOLKBLAD – Karlstad, 1918- – 1 – sw Kungliga [072]
VARMLANDS FOLKBLAD – Karlstad, Sweden. 1903, 1906-10. 3 reels. 1918-47. 97 reels – 1 – sw Kungliga [072]
VARMLANDSBERG – Molkom, Filipstad, Sweden. 1906-63 – 1 – sw Kungliga [072]
VARMLANDSBERG see FILIPSTADS TIDNING
VARMLANDSBYGDEN – Karlstad, Sweden. 1972 – 1 reel – 1 – sw Kungliga [072]
VARMLANDSBYGDEN – Karlstad, Sweden. 1979- – 1 – sw Kungliga [072]
VARNAMO NYHETER – Varnamo, Sweden. 1930-78 – 200r – 1 – sw Kungliga [072]
VARNAMO NYHETER – Varnamo, Sweden. 1979- – 1 – sw Kungliga [072]
VARNAMOTIDNINGEN see JONKOPINGSPOSTEN
Varnes, David J see LANDSLIDE HAZARD ZONATION
Varnhagen von Ense, Karl August see
- BIOGRAPHISCHE DENKMALE
- BRIEFWECHSEL ZWISCHEN VARNHAGEN UND RAHEL
- DENKWUERDIGKEITEN DES EIGENEN LEBENS
- DENKWUERDIGKEITEN UND VERMISCHTE SCHRIFTEN
- DEUTSCHE ERZAEHLUNGEN
- TAGEBUECHER

VARONES HEROYCOS...SAN GABRIEL / Trujillo, Antonio de – 1693 – 9 – 1.50f – sp Bibl Santa Ana [240]
Varoqui, J F see ETUDE MONOGRAPHIQUE DE LA COMMUNE DE BAUBIGNY (COTE D'OR)
VART LAND – Stockholm, Sweden. 1885-1908 – 57r – 1 – sw Kungliga [072]
VARTIJA – 1956-92 (complete) – Inquire – 1 – ATLA S0753 – us A.T.L.A. [073]
VAS NEPE – Szombathely, Hungary. 1962-81 – 49r – 1 – us L of C Photodup [072]
Vasak, Karel see INTERNATIONAL DIMENSIONS OF HUMAN RIGHTS
Vasari, Giorgio see
- VITE DE' PIU ECCELLENT PITTORI, SCULTORI E' ARCHITETTI
- LE VITE DE' PIU ECCELLENTI ARCHITETTI, PITTORI ET SCULTORI ITALIANI, DA CIMABUE INSINO A' TEMPI NOSTRI...
- VITE DE' PIU ECCELLENTI PITTORI SCULTORI E ARCHITETTI
- VITE DE' PIU ECCELLENTI PITTORI, SCULTORI E ARCHITETTI
- LE VITE DE' PIU ECCELLENTI PITTORI, SCULTORI, E ARCHITETTORI
- LE VITE DE PIU ECCELLENTI PITTORI, SCULTORI ED ARCHITETTORI

VASARISTUDIEN VON WOLFGANG KALLAB / Schlosser, Julius von – Wien. v15. 1908. N.S. – 7mf – ne IDC [700]
VASAVAKANYAKAPURANAMU : SAMSKRUTANU, ANDHRA ANUVDAMU – (In Telugu or Sanskrit) – 1900? – 1 – us U.W. Library [490]
VASBYNYTT see NORRORT
Vascellini, G see STATUE E GRUPPI, IN BRONZO E IN MARMO, CHE SONO IN FIRENZE ALLA VISTA DEL PUBBLICO...
VASCO NUNEZ DE BALBOA / Nunez de Balboa, Vasco – Madrid: Ediciones de la Vicesecretaria de Educacion Popular, 1945 – 1 – sp Bibl Santa Ana [910]
VASCO NUNEZ DE BALBOA / (Sanchez) Larragoiti, Antonio de – Madrid: Talleres Graficos Victoria, 1958 – sp Bibl Santa Ana [910]
VASCO NUNEZ DE BALBOA. ADELANTADO DE LA COSTA DEL MAR DEL SUR / Alvarado Garaicoa, Toedoro – Guayaquil: Imp. de la Universidad, 1950 – sp Bibl Santa Ana [910]
VASCO NUNEZ DE BALBOA. DESCUBRIDOR DEL PACIFICO / Romoli, Cathleen – Madrid: Espasa Calpe S.A., 1955 – sp Bibl Santa Ana [910]
Vasconcellos-Abreu, Guilherme de see PASSOS DOS LUSIADAS ESTUDADOS A LUZ DA MITOLOJIA..
Vasconcelos, Jose see BREVE HISTORIA DE MEXICO
Vasif, Ahmed see MEHASIN UEL-AS-AR VE HAKA'IK UEL-AHBAR (VASIF TARIHI)
Vasil'chenko, V E see OCHERK ISTORII BIBLIOTECHNOGO DELA V ROSSII 11-18 VV
Vasil'chikov, A I see
- MELKII ZEMEL'NYI KREDIT V ROSSII
- SEL'SKII BYT I SEL'SKOE KHOZIAISTVO V ROSSII

Vasil'ev, I I *see* BIBLIOGRAFICHESKII UKAZATEL' STATEI, OTNOSIASHCHIKHSIA K PSKOVSKOI GUBERNII, 1517-1887 G
Vasil'ev, N P *see* "OPPOZITSIIA"
Vasilevich, G M *see* SBORNIK MATERIALOV PO EVENSKIISKOMU (TUNGUSSKOMU) FOL'KLORU
Vasil'evskii, L G *see* ORGANIZATSIIA I PRAKTIKA PROMYSLOVOI KOOPERATSII
Vasilevskii, N M *see* KAK KREST'IANINU OBZAVESTIS' MASHINOI
Vasnetsov, N M *see* MATERIALY DLIA OB IASNITEL'-NOGO OBLASTNOGO SLOVARIA VIATSKOGO GOVORA
Vasnetsov, Viktor Mikhailovich *see* OPIS' DOKUMENTAL'NYKH MATERIALOV LICHNOGO FONDA.NO.716
Vasquez, Juan *see* RECOPILACION DE SONETOS Y VILLANCICOS A QUATRO Y CINCO
Vasquez Nunez, Guillermo *see* OBRAS COMPLETAS 1. MERCEDARIOS ILUSTRES INTRODUCCION Y NOTAS DE RICARDO SANLES MARTINEZ. MADRID, 1966
Vassaevs, L *see* IN ANATOMEN CORPORIS HUMANI...
VASSAL LETTER BOOKS, 1769-1800 / Sheffield. Central Library – BRRAM – 1 – uk Microform Academic [920]
Vassar, T E *see* CHARACTER STUDIES
Vassar, Thomas Edwin *see* UNCLE JOHN VASSAR
Vasseur, Andre *see*
– BIBLIOGRAPHIE DES REVUES ET JOURNAUX LITTERAIRES DES 19E ET 20E SIECLES
Vasseur, Dom L Le *see* EPHERMERIDES ORDINIS CARTUSIENSIS
Vasseur, P *see* RECHERCHES SUR LES PEUPLEMENTS SCIAPHILES DES RECIFS CORALLIENS DE LA REGION DE TULEAR (S.W. DE MADAGASCAR)
Vassiere, P de la *see* VINGT ANS A MADAGASCAR
A VAST PUBLIC UTILITY: THE STATE IN AUSTRALIANS' EXPERIENCE AND EXPECTATIONS / Collins, Hugh – 11p., 1986 – 9 – 1.00f – at Libertarian Micro [335]
VASTERBOTTENS FOLKBLAD – Umea, Sweden. 1917-78 – 407r – 1 – sw Kungliga [072]
VASTERBOTTENS FOLKBLAD – Umea, Sweden. 1979- – 1 – sw Kungliga [072]
VASTERBOTTENSKURIREN – Umea, Sweden. 1900-78 – 456r – 1 – sw Kungliga [072]
VASTERBOTTENSKURIREN – Umea, Sweden. 1979- – 1 – sw Kungliga [072]
VASTERBOTTNINGEN – Burtrask, Sweden. 1979- – 1 – sw Kungliga [072]
VASTERBYGDEN – Uddevalla, Sweden. 1972 – 1 reel – 1 – sw Kungliga [072]
VASTERBYGDEN – Uddevalla, Sweden. 1979- – 1 – sw Kungliga [072]
VASTERNORRLANDS ALLEHANDA – Harnosand, Sweden. 1873- – 1 – sw Kungliga [072]
VASTERORT – (Jarfalla Nyheter, 1979-82; Jarva Nyheter, 1979-82; Malaroarnas Nyheter, 1979-82) – Stockholm, Sweden. 1979-87 – 1 – sw Kungliga [072]
VASTERVIKS VECKOBLAD – Vastervik, Sweden. 1834-1919 – 51r – 1 – sw Kungliga [072]
VASTERVIKSDEMOKRATEN – Kalmar, Sweden. 1984-85 – 1 – sw Kungliga [072]
VASTERVIKSDEMOKRATEN *see* OSTRA SMALAND
VASTERVIKSTIDNINGEN – Vastervik, Sweden. 1919-78 – 258r – 1 – sw Kungliga [072]
VASTERVIKSTIDNINGEN – Vastervik, Sweden. 1979- – 1 – sw Kungliga [072]
VASTGOTABLADET – Tidaholm, Sweden. 1979-81 – 1 – sw Kungliga [072]
VASTGOTABLADET *see* FALKOPINGS TIDNING
VASTGOTADEMOKRATEN – Boras, Sweden. 1926-78 – 350r – 1 – sw Kungliga [072]
VASTGOTADEMOKRATEN – Boras, Sweden. 1979-86 – 1 – sw Kungliga [072]
VASTMANLANDS FOLKBLAD – (Folkbladet for Vastmanland, 1959-66; Folket, 1966-70) – Vasteras, Sweden. 1918-59 – 268r – 1 – sw Kungliga [072]
VASTMANLANDS FOLKBLAD – Vasteras, Sweden. 1971-78 – 11r – 1 – sw Kungliga [072]
VASTMANLANDS FOLKBLAD – Vasteras, Sweden. 1979- – 1 – sw Kungliga [072]
VASTMANLANDS NYHETER – (Suppl: Kvallsstunden 1938-78) – Vasteras, Sweden. 1917- – 1 – sw Kungliga [072]
Vasys', I M *see* BANKOVYE KOMISSIONNYE OPERATSII V SEL'SKO-KHOZIAISTVENNYKH KREDITNYKH TOVARISHCHESTVAKH
Vasys', IM *see* IZUCHENIE RAIONA I POSTROENIE GODOVOGO OPERATIVNO-KHOZIAISTVENNOGO PLANA SEL'SKOKHOZIAISTVENNOGO KREDITNOGO TOVARISHCHESTVA
VATAN – Edirne: Vilayet Matbaasi, 1910-19? – 9 – $10.00 – us MEDOC [956]
VATAN YAHUT SILISTRE – 1307 [1890] – $38.00 – us MEDOC [470]
VATANDAS – Selanik: Selanik Ittihad ve Terakki Cemiyeti. Mueduer: A. Ismet. No. 41 (10 Temmuz 1326 [1910]) – 9 – $25.00 – us MEDOC [956]
DER VATER / Bauernfeld, Eduard von – Wien: A Mausberger; Leipzig: P Baumgaertner, 1840 – 1 – us U.W. Library [820]
DER VATER : DREI ERZAEHLUNGEN / Wiechert, Ernst Emil – Muenchen: K Desch, 1945 – 1r – 1 – us U.W. Library [830]
VATER BRAHM : EIN TRAUERSPIEL AUS DEM VIERTEN STAND / Schaufert, Hippolyt August – Mainz: F Kirchheim, 1871 – 1r – 1 – us U.W. Library [820]
DER VATER DER MEDEA : LUSTSPIEL IN DREI AUFZUEGEN / Reitler, Marzellin Adalbert – [Wien: J N Vernay, 188-?] – 1r – 1 – us U.W. Library [820]
Vater, Fritz *see* HERR HEINRICH
VATER, SOHN UND GEIST : UNTER DEN HEILIGEN DREIHEITEN UND VOR DER RELIGIOESEN DENKWEISE DER GEGENWART / Soederblom, Nathan – Tuebingen: J.C.B. Mohr, 1909 – 1mf – us A.T.L.A. [240]
VATER UND SOHN : EIN DRAMA AUS DER JUGEND FRIEDRICHS DES GROSSEN / Goltz, Joachim, Freiherr von der – Muenchen: G Mueller, 1922 – 1r – 1 – us U.W. Library [820]
VATERLAENDISCHE BALLADEN UND GESAENGE / Lingg, Hermann – Muenchen: J J Lentner, 1869 – 1r – 1 – us U.W. Library [810]
VATERLAENDISCHE BLAETTER FUER BADEN – Karlsruhe, Germany. 16 Jan-12 Mai 1849 – 1 – gw Mikrofilm [072]
VATERLAENDISCHES MAGAZIN FUER BELEHRUNG, NUTZEN UND UNTERHALTUNG – Erlangen, Germany. 1837 – 1 – gw Mikrofilm [072]
DAS VATERLAND – Berlin, 1808/09 – 1r – 1 – Inquire at Mikrofilmarchiv for details – gw Misc Inst [943]
VATERLAND : DRAMA / Strauss, Emil – 2. Aufl. Muenchen: A Langen, G Mueller, 1936 – 1r – 1 – us U.W. Library [820]
DES VATERS FLUCH : HISTORISCHES DRAMA IN DREI ACTEN, AUS DER ZEIT DES LETZTEN HOHENSTAUFEN / Bieleck, Rudolph – Wien: Im Selbstverlage des Verfassers, 1874 – 1 – us U.W. Library [820]
DAS VATER-SOHN-MOTIV IN DER DICHTUNG / Wais, Kurt – (Includes bibliographical references) – Berlin: W de Gruyter & Co. 2v. 1931 – 1 – us U.W. Library [430]
DIE VATERUNSER-ERKLAERUNG DES THEOPHILUS VON ANTIOCHIEN : EINE QUELLENUNTERSUCHUNG ZU DEN VATERUNSER-ERKLAERUNG DES TERTULLIAN, CYPRIAN, CHROMATIUS UND HIERONYMUS / Loeschke, Gerhard – Berlin: Trowitzsch, 1908 – 1mf – us A.T.L.A. [240]
Vatican Council. 1st *see* AKTENSTUECKE ZUM CONCIL
THE VATICAN COUNCIL AND ITS DEFINITIONS : A PASTORAL LETTER TO THE CLERGY / Manning, Henry Edward – (Some of the appendixes in Latin. Includes bibliographical references) – New York: Sadlier, 1871 – 1mf – 9 – 0-8370-8450-4 – 1986-2450 – us A.T.L.A. [240]
THE VATICAN DECREES IN THEIR BEARING ON CIVIL ALLEGIANCE; A POLITICAL EXPOSTULATION. TO WHICH ARE ADDED: A HISTORY OF THE VATICAN COUNCIL; TOGETHER WITH THE LATIN AND ENGLISH TEXT OF THE PAPAL SYLLABUS AND THE VATICAN DECREES / Gladstone, William Ewart – 1875 – 1 – us A.T.L.A. [240]
DAS VATICANISCHE CONCIL = CONCILE DU VATICAN : SEINE GESCHICHTE UND SEINE POLITISCHEN UND RELIGIOESEN FOLGEN / Pressense, Edmond de – Noerdlingen: C H Beck, 1872 – 1mf – 9 – 0-8370-8934-4 – 1986-2934 – us A.T.L.A. [240]
IL VATICANO REGIO : TARLO SUPERSTITE DELLA CHIESA CATTOLICA: STUDII DEDICATI AL GIOVANE CLERO ED AL LAICATO CREDENTE USCENTE IL 1883 / Curci, Carlo Maria – (Includes bibliographical references) – Firenze: Fratelli Bencini, 1883 – 1mf – 9 – 0-8370-8893-3 – 1986-2893 – us A.T.L.A. [240]
VATICINIUM JESIAIAE: CAP. 24-27 / Boehl, Eduard – Lipziae: J.E. Hinrichs, 1861. 1 fiche – 9 – us A.T.L.A. [240]
Vatland, Howard W *see* A PILOT ASSESSMENT OF NONNEUTRAL POSTURES AND WORKER DISCOMFORT IN VDT OPERATORS
[Vatrantsev..., B D et al] *see* DMITRI I LEONIDOVICH KHORVAT
Vattaso, Marcus *see*
– INITIA PATRUM, CONLEGIT AC LITTERARUM ORDINE DISPOSUIT
Vattel, Emer de *see* LE DROIT DES GENS OU PRINCIPES DE LA LOI NATURELLE APPLIQUES A LA CONDUITE ET AUX AFFAIRES DES NATIONS ET DES SOUVERAINS
Vauban, Sebastien Le Prestre de *see* TRAITE DE LA DEFENSE DES PLACES
Vaucanson, J de *see* LE MECANISME DU FLUTEUR AUTOMATE
Vaucher, Edouard *see* ESSAI DE METHODOLOGIE DES SCIENCES THEOLOGIQUES
Vaucher, J P *see* HISTOIRE DES CONFERVES D'EAU DOUCE
Vaudelin, le P G *see*
– INSTRUCTIONS CRETIENNES
– NOUVELLE MANIERE D'ECRIRE COMME ON PARLE EN FRANCE
Vaugelas, Cl. Favre de *see*
– NOUVELLES REMARQUES SUR LA LANGUE FRANCOISE
– OBSERVATIONS DE L'ACADEMIE FRANCOISE SUR LES REMARQUES DE M. DE VAUGELAS
– REMARQUES SUR LA LANGUE FRANCAISE
Vaughan, Charles John *see*
– E PROS ROMAIOUS EPISTOLE
– HEROES OF FAITH
– HEROES OF FAITH: LECTURES ON THE 11TH CHAPTER...EPISTLES TO THE HEBREWS
– LECTURES ON ST PAUL'S EPISTLE TO THE PHILIPPIANS
Vaughan, Herbert Millingchamp *see* THE MEDICI POPES
Vaughan, John Gaines *see* THE WONDERFUL BOOK
Vaughan, John Stephen *see*
– DANGERS OF THE DAY
– THE PURPOSE OF THE PAPACY
Vaughan, N R *see* A COMPARISON BETWEEN STAIRCLIMBING AND GRADED WALKING IN PERIPHERAL VASCULAR OCCLUSIVE DISEASE
Vaughan, Robert *see*
– ENGLISH NONCONFORMITY
– ESSAYS ON HISTORY, PHILOSOPHY, AND THEOLOGY
– JOHN DE WYCLIFFE, D.D.
– REVOLUTIONS IN ENGLISH HISTORY
– THE WAY TO REST
Vaughan, Roger William Bede *see*
– LECTURES ON THE REASONABLENESS OF CHRISTIANITY AND THE SHALLOWNESS OF UNBELIEF
– THE LIFE AND LABOURS OF SAINT THOMAS OF AQUIN
Vaughan, Thomas *see* A GRAMMAR OF THE TURKISH LANGUAGE
Vaughan, William *see* COMPUTERS AND THE HISTORY OF ART
Vaughn, Robert *see* TRACTS AND TREATISES OF JOHN DE WYCLIFFE
Vaught, L A *see* VAUGHT'S PRACTICAL CHARACTER READER
VAUGHT'S PRACTICAL CHARACTER READER / Vaught, L A – Chicago: Vaught-Rocine Pub Co, 1907 – 3mf – 9 – $3.00 – LLMC 92-114 – us L.L.M.C. [340]
Vauquelin de la Fresnaye, J *see* ART POETIQUE FRANCOIS
Vaussard, M-M *see* LE CARMEL. PARIS, 1929
Vaux *see* A LETTER FROM THE RIGHT HON. LORD BROUGHAM TO THE RIGHT HON. SIR JAMES GRAHAM, BT., M.P., ON THE MAKING AND DIGESTING OF THE LAW
VAUXHALL GARDENS : THEATRICAL ENTERTAINMENT IN VICTORIAN ENGLAND – Garrick Club Collections – 1 reel – 1 – $75.00 – us UMI [790]
VAUXHALL GARDENS ARCHIVE – (Records 200 yrs of public displays, theatrical and musical performances and reproduces 150 songbooks. With printed guide) – 78 b/w 1 colour mf – 9,15 – $454.00 – 1-869934-19-9 – uk Emmett [790]
Vawter Family *see* PAPERS OF THE VAWTER FAMILY
VAX PROFESSIONAL – (1986-. 1,5,6) – 1979- – 9 – us UMI [073]
VAXHOLMS TIDNING – Vaxholm, Stockholm. 1923-63 – 9 – sw Kungliga [072]
VAXHOLMS TIDNING *see* NORRORT
VAXJOBLADET – Vaxjo, 1979-93 – 1 – sw Kungliga [072]
VAXJOBLADET *see* BLEKINGE LANS TIDNING
Vay, Peter *see* EMPIRES AND EMPERORS OF RUSSIA, CHINA, KOREA, AND JAPAN.NOTES AND RECOLLECTIONS
DER VAYTER MIZROKH = THE FAR EAST – (In Yiddish – Russian) – Harbin, CC. v2 no30(35). 22 Apr 1922 – 1r – 1 – $25.00 – cn Can Microfilming [072]
Vaz Dias, A M *see*
– DE DEELNAME DER MARRANEN IN HET OPRICHTINGSKAPITAAL DER OOST-INDISCHE COMPAGNIE
– EEN VERZOEK OM DE JODEN IN AMSTERDAM EEN BEPAALDE WOONPLAATS AAN TE WIJZEN
VAZA – St Petersburg, 1848-74 – 328mf – 9 – $1,890.00 coll – us Ross [640]
VAZHNEISHIE PRAVITEL'STVENNYE POSTANOVLENIIA O KUSTARNO-REMESLENNOI PROMYSHLENNOSTI I PROMYSLOVOI KOOPERATSII – (1. Postanovlenie SNK SSSR ot 21 maia 1928 g. 2. Postanovlenie SNK SSSR ot 3-10 maia 1927 g. 3. Postanovlenie EKOSO RSFSR ot 5 aprelia 1928 g. 4. Postanovlenie EKOSO RSFSR ot 7 iiunia 1928 g. 5. Postanovlenie EKOSO RSFSR ot 23 tevralia 1928 g. 6. Postanovlenie VTsIK i SNK RSFSR ot 16 ianvaria 1928 g. 7. Postanovlenie VTsIK i SNK RSFSR ot 20 avgusta 1928 g. 8. Instruktsiia VSNKh RSFSR po primeneniiu VISIK i SNK RSFSR ot 20 avgusta 1928 g.) – Ed 2. M., 1929 – 1mf – 9 – COR-290/1 – ne IDC [334]
VAZNIKNOVENIE RAZVITIIA SOVETSKOGO ZAKONODATEL'STVA O ZAKLIUCHENIE I RASTORZHENII BRAKA V UZBEKISTANE / Atakhodshaev, F M – Tashkent, 1963. 131p. BR-9106 1 – 9 – ne IDC [640]
Vazquez Camarasa, Enrique *see* LA AUTORIDAD DOCTRINAL DE LA IGLESIA CATOLICA Y LA LIBERTAD DE PENSAMIENTO
Vazquez de Cilleros, Francisco *see* EL MAESTRO...ORACION FUNEBRE
Vazquez, Gabr. S J *see*
– DE CULTU ADORATIONIS LIBRI TRES
Vazquez Garcia, Juan Antonio *see* APORTACIONES AL ESTUDIO DEL PROCESO DE INDUSTRIALIZACION EN ASTURIAS
Vazquez, Isaac *see* FR. JUAN DE CARTAGENA
Vazquez, J *see* IUZIO SO LA ENFERMEDAD QUE...AFLIGE A TOLEDO...
Vazquez, Jose Andr'es *see* ARIAS MONTANO
VBER DOCTOR BALTHAZARS TOUFFBUECHLIN / Zwingli, H – Zuericn, Chr. Froschouer. 1525. BME-85 1 – 9 – ne IDC [240]
VCHERA I DNES – Sofia, Bulgaria. -d. 27 Nov 1939-9 April 1940. 1 reel – 1 – uk British Libr Newspaper [949]
VCHERA I SEGODNIA / Chulkov, G I – "Severnye dni". M. 1916. BR-2041 2 – 8 – ne IDC [460]
VD (VENEREAL DISEASE) NEWS – v. 1-. 1976- – 1,5,6,9 – us UMI [616]
VDE (VERBAND DEUTSCHER ELEKTROTECHNIKER) – Printed index. Updated every 60 days – 6,9 – us Info Handling [621]
VEAC NOU – Bucharest, Romania. -sw. 6 April 1951-7 Aug 1959. 4 reels – 1 – uk British Libr Newspaper [949]
VEASE FORNER Y SEGARRA, JUAN PABLO / Fox Novel, M – 9 – $1.50f – sp Bibl Santa Ana [920]
Vecchi, Bernardo Valentino *see*
– MIGUIRTINIA
– NEL SUD DELL'IMPERO
– SOMALIA
Vecellio, C *see*
– CORONA DELLE NOBILI, ET VIRTUOSE DONNE
– HABITI ANTICHI, ET MODERNI DI TUTTO IL MONDO

VECER – Maribor, Yugoslavia. 1962; May 1967-1970 – 17r – 1 – us L of C Photodup [949]

VECERNI CESKE SLOVO – Prague. 1934-1939. Incomplete. Not collated – 1 – us NY Public [999]

VECERNI CESKE SLOVO – Prague, Czechoslovakia. Feb, Apr 1926; Sept-Oct 1938; 20 Jul 1940 – 2r – 1 – us L of C Photodup [072]

VECERNI PRAHA – Prague, Czechoslovakia. 1962-64; Jan-Jun 1968; 1969; Jan-Jun 1970 – 8r – 1 – us L of C Photodup [072]

VECERNIK – Bratislava, Czechoslovakia. Nov 1956-1959; 1961 – 5r – 1 – us L of C Photodup [072]

VECERNJI LIST – Zagreb, Yugoslavia. Jul 1959-1970 – 38r – 1 – us L of C Photodup [949]

VECHERNA MOSKVA – Moscow, USSR. 1969-1981 – 13r – $650.00 – B63593 – us Library Micro [072]

VECHERNAIA MOSKVA – Moscow. U.S.S.R. 1929-1930; 1933-1962; 1964- – 1 – us UMI [072]

VECHERNAYA MOSKVA – Moscow. 21 Jan 1931-13 Feb 1937; 20 May-13 Sep 1939; 19 Aug-30 Dec 1942; 1 Jul 1943-30 Nov 1945; 1 Jan 1946-14 Jul 1948; 2 Jan 1959-Dec 1964; Jul-Dec 1965.-d. 29 reels – 1 – uk British Libr Newspaper [072]

VECHERNEE VREMIA – (Library has: no. 1-649 (Nov. 26, 1911-Dec. 31, 1913); scattered holdings from between July 21, 1914-June 30, 1915 and in 1917) – S.-Peterburg: A.S Suvorin, 1911- – 1 – CSUX87-S435 – us Hoover Inst Photo [947]

VECHERNEE VREMIA – Petrograd. 1917. Gaps – 1 – 35.00r – us Hoover Inst Photo [072]

VECHERNI NOVINI – Sofia, Bulgaria. Aug 1951-1987 – 50r – 1 – us L of C Photodup [949]

VECHERNI NOVINI – Sofia, Bulgaria. -d. June 1959-Dec 1970. 30 reels – 1 – uk British Libr Newspaper [949]

VECHERNI NOVINI *see* IZGREV

VECHERNIE IZVESTIIA MOSKOVSKOGO SOVETA RABOCHIKH I KRASNOARMEISKIKH DEPUTATOV I OBLASTNOGO ISPOLNITEL'NOGO KOMITETA SOVETOV – Moscow, USSR. Nov 9 1918-Feb 14 1920 – 1r – 1 – us L of C Photodup [072]

VECHERNII MINSK – (Backfile through 1998 $85r) – Belarus, 1999- – 6r per y standing order – 1 – us Ross [072]

VECHERNII PETERBURG – (Backfile through 1998 $85r) – Russia, 1999- – 2r per y – 1 – $160.00 standing order – us Ross [072]

VECHERNII PETERSBURG – 1993-1995 – 1 – F2,095.00 – sz Infoprint [072]

VECHERNII PETERSBURG – (Standing order available from De 1994 +. 3r per year. Sfr338.00y) – Avant 1993 – 3r – 1 – Sfr360.00 – sz Infoprint [947]

VECHERNJE NOVOSTI – Belgrade, Yugoslavia. May-Dec 1954; 1957-Oct 1961 – 13r – 1 – us L of C Photodup [949]

VECHNYE SPUTNIKI / Merezhkovskii, Dimitrii – Ed. 3. 7 v. Spb. 1906-08. BR-799 2 – 8 – ne IDC [460]

VECHNYE SPUTNIKI / Merezhkovskii, Dimitrii – Tom III: Portrety iz vsemirnoi literatury. Ed. 2. Spb. 1899. BR-798 2 – 8 – ne IDC [460]

VECHNYE SPUTNIKI / Merezhkovskii, Dimitrii – Tom III: portrety iz vsemirnoi literatury. Spb. 1897. BR-797 2 – 8 – ne IDC [460]

VECKOPOSTEN – Stockholm, Sweden. 1868-1962 – 1 – sw Kungliga [072]

VECKOTIDNINGEN TIDEN – Stockholm, Sweden. 1884-85 – 1 reel – 1 – sw Kungliga [072]

VECKOTIDNINGEN VD – Boras, Sweden. 1987-90 – 1 – sw Kungliga [072]

VECTOR – Vancouver. v28-35. 1986/87-1993/94 – 9 – Can$20.00y – cn Micromedia [510]

THE VEDANTA-SUTRAS : PART 2 / ed by Mueller, Friedrich Max – (With full Index to both Parts) – 1896 – 9mf – 8 – ne Slangenburg [280]

THE VEDANTA-SUTRAS, WITH RAMANUGA'S SRIBHASHYA / ed by Mueller, Friedrich Max – (Translated by G. Thibaut) – 1904 – 14mf – 8 – ne Slangenburg [280]

THE VEDANTA-SUTRAS, WITH THE COMMENTARY BY SANKARAKARYA : PART 1 / ed by Mueller, Friedrich Max – (Translated by G. Thibaut) – 1890 – 10mf – 8 – ne Slangenburg [280]

THE VEDAS, OR THE RELIGIOUS BOOKS OF THE HINDOOS; A LECTURE DELIVERED IN CENTRAL HALL, BROOKLYN, NEW YORK, NOV. 11TH, 1884 / Schmidt, H C – Brooklyn, NY: Evang. Lutheran Church, 1884. 23p – 1 – us U.W. Library [280]

VEDAS. RIG-VEDA SANHITA – v.1. 1838 – 1 – uk Microform Academic [280]

VEDAS. SAMA-VEDA. (THE SANHITA OF THE "SAMAN-VEDA") – 1842-43 – 1 – uk Microform Academic [280]

Vedder, Henry Clay *see*
- AMERICAN WRITERS OF TO-DAY
- BALTHASAR HUEBMAIER
- CHRISTIAN EPOCH-MAKERS
- THE DAWN OF CHRISTIANITY, OR, STUDIES OF THE APOSTOLIC CHURCH
- A HISTORY OF THE BAPTISTS IN THE MIDDLE STATES
- OUR NEW TESTAMENT
- THE RECENT MOVEMENT TOWARD CHRISTIAN UNITY
- THE REFORMATION IN GERMANY

THE VEDDER LECTURES *see* THE SCIENCE OF REVEALED TRUTH IMPREGNABLE

THE VEDDER LECTURES, 1875 *see* "THE LIGHT BY WHICH WE SEE LIGHT"

Vedel, Waldemar *see* IDEALES CULTURALES DE LA EDAD MEDIA. TOMO 4. LA VIDA MONASTICA

Veder, W R *see* THE SCALIGER PATERIKON

Veder, William R *see* EARLY SLAVIC TEXTS

VEDIC CHRONOLOGY AND VEDANGA JYOTISHA: CONTAINING ALSO CHALDEAN AND INDIAN VEDAS AND OTHER MISCELLANEOUS ESSAYS / Tilak, Bal Gangadhar – Poona: Tilak Bros., 1925. 174p.illus – 1 – us U.W. Library [520]

VEDIC HYMNS : PART 1 / ed by Mueller, Friedrich Max – (Translated by F. Max Mueller) – 1891 – 12mf – 8 – ne Slangenburg [280]

VEDIC HYMNS : PART 2 / ed by Mueller, Friedrich Max – (Translated by F. Max Mueller) – 1897 – 9mf – 8 – ne Slangenburg [280]

VEDOMOSTI FEDERAL'NOGO SOBRANIIA ROSSISKOI FEDERATSII – Moscow: Izd. Federal'noe Sobraniia Rossiiskoi Federatsii, 1990- – 50mf – 9 – $95.00y – us East View [320]

VEDOMOSTI VERKHOV NOVO SOVETA RSFSR / U.S.S.R. – Bulletin of Russian Republic Supreme Soviet. Moscow. -irr. 1961- – 1 – us UMI [073]

VEDOMOSTI VERKHOVNOGO SOVETA I PRAVITEL'STVA ESTONSKOI SOVETSKOI SOTSIALISTICHESKOI RESPUBLIKI – (Missing: 1987(p1-108); 1989) – Tallin, 1968-1990(2) – 270mf – 9 – ne IDC [320]

VEDOMOSTI VERKHOVNOGO SOVETA I PRAVITEL'STVA LATVIISKOI SOVETSKOI SOTSIALISITICHESKOI RESPUBLIKI – (Missing: 1968 v26(p1-20)) – Riga, 1960(23-48); 1961-1971 – 186mf – 9 – ne IDC [320]

VEDOMOSTI VERKHOVNOGO SOVETA I PRAVITEL'STVA LITOVSKOI SOVETSKOI SOTSIALISTICHESKOI RESPUBLIKI – (Many issues missing) – Vilnius, 1959-1989 – 217mf – 9 – ne IDC [320]

VEDOMOSTI VERKHOVNOGO SOVETA RSFSR – (3 issues appeared in 1957; 20 in 1958; 48 in 1959; 50 in 1960; 49 in 1961; and 52 annually since 1962. Annual subject indexes; Supplemented: 1989. 13mf) – M., 1958-1989 – 9 – R-8349/1 – ne IDC [320]

VEDOMOSTI VERKHOVNOGO SOVETA SSSR / Russia. (1923-U.S.S.R.). Laws, Statutes, etc – 1 – $220.00 – us L of C Photodup [947]

VEDOMOSTI VERKHOVNOGO SOVETA UKRAINSKOI SSR – (In Ukrainian and Russian; 15 consecutively numbered issues published from 1941-1945; monthly in 1946-1947; 3 issues in 1948 and 1953; 6 issues in 1949, 1954-1955; 5 issues in 1950 and 1951; 11 issues in 1956 and 1957; 15 issues in 1958; 36 issues in 1959; 49 issues in 1960; 51 issues in 1969. Annual indexes; Supplemented: 1969-1973. 92 mf) – Kiev, 1959, 1965-1973 – 9 – R-8615/1 – ne IDC [320]

VEDOMOSTI VERKHOVNOVO SOVETA SSSR / U.S.S.R. – Bulletin of U.S.S.R. Supreme Soviet. Moscow. -irr. 1961- – 1 – us UMI [073]

Veeder, Van Vechten *see*
- LEGAL MASTERPIECES, SPECIMENS OF ARGUMENTATION AND EXPOSITION

VEEL SCHOONE GRONDIGE LEERINGEN WT DES HEEREN WOORT / Henrick Alewijnsz – 1577. BME-185 1 – 9 – ne IDC [240]

VEEL SCHOONE GRONDIGE LEERINGEN WT DES HEEREN WOORT / Henrick Alewijnsz – 1581. BME-186 1 – 9 – ne IDC [240]

Veen, E van *see* KROONE DER VIER HOOFT-DEUGHDEN, TOE-GHE-EYGENT AEN DE H. MAGHET ENDE MOEDER GODS MARIA

Veen, J van der *see*
- ZINNE-BEELDEN, OFT ADAMS APPEL
- ZINNE-BEELDEN, OFT ADAMS APPEL, VERCIERT MET SEER AARDIGE KONST-PLATEN

Veen, J. van der *see* ZINNE-BEELDEN, OFT ADAMS APPEL

Veen, O van *see*
- AMORIS DIVINI EMBLEMATA
- AMORUM EMBLEMATA
- LES EMBLEMES DE L'AMOUR HUMAIN
- DE GODLIEVENDE ZIEL VERTOONT IN ZINNEBEELDEN
- DE LEERMEESTER DER ZEDEN, VERTOOND IN HORATIUS ZINNEBEELDEN, LIERZANGEN, ENZ. LOF VAN'T LANDLEVEN, EN BEISPIEGELING OP 'T LEVEN DER MENSCHEN, VERBEELD IN DE VIER GETYDEN DES JAARS
- Q. HORATII FLACCI EMBLEMATA
- ZINNEBEELDEN DER GODDELYKE LIEFDE
- ZINNEBEELDEN. UIT HORATIUS FLACCUS

Veen, S D Van *see* ACTA DER PROVINCIALE EN PARTICULIERE SYNODEN

VEER SAVARKAR'S "WHIRL-WIND PROPAGANDA": STATEMENTS, MESSAGES & EXTRACTS FROM THE PRESIDENT'S DIARY OF HIS PROPAGANDISTIC TOURS. / Savarkar, Vinayak Damodar – Bombay. 1941 – 1 – us Res Libr [320]

DAT VEERTE GEBOTT : ERZAEHLUNG IN MUENSTERLAENDER MUNDART / Wibbelt, Augustin – Essen (Ruhr): Fredebeul und Koenen, 1920 – 1r – 1 – us U.W. Library [390]

DER VEG = THE ROAD – Toronto, CN. v15 no 807 and 813. 1940 – 1r – 1 – Can$35.00 – cn Can Microfilming [072]

Vega, Andr. de *see* DE IUSTIFICATIONE DOCTRINA UNIVERSA

Vega Carpio, Lope de *see* EL CUERDO EN SU CASA

Vega de Hoz, Baron de *see* T'SERCLAES FIRMA LA CANDIDATURA DEL MARQUES DE SAN JUAN DE PIEDRAS ALTAS

Vega des Jesus, Ramon *see* THE EFFECT OF LACTIC ACID ON FAT MOBILIZATION AND UTILIZATION IN TRAINED SUBJECTS

Vega, Fernando de la *see* LETRADOS Y POLITICOS

Vega, Lope de *see* HOLOGRAPH, COPY AND PRINTED PLAYS.

Vega Mateos, Celestino *see*
- EL JUGUETE CAIDO
- EL JUGUETE CAIDO. NOTAS BIBLIOGRAFICAS DE PEREZ COMENDADOR

Vega y Relea, Juvenal de *see* LA PRENSA COMO AGENTE DE EDUCACION

Vegas Fabian, Gonzalo *see* TRES FARMACEUTICOS EXTREMENOS

VEGAS FAERD KRING ASIEN OCH EUROPA / Nordenskiold, A E – BN 328 2. 2 v. 1880-81 – 8 – ne IDC [950]

VEGAS GAY TIMES – Las Vegas, NV. 1978-1981 – 1r – 1 – $50.00 – U04864 – us Library Micro [305]

Las Vegas, New Mexico *see* MISCELLANEOUS EARLY NEWSPAPERS

VEGAS VISITOR – Las Vegas. Nev. 1969- – 1 – us UMI [071]

VEGAS VISITOR – Las Vegas, NV. 1969-1983; 1993 – 14+ r – 1 – $700.00 ($50.00y) – N04616 – us Library Micro [071]

THE VEGAS VOICE – Las Vegas, NV. 1972-1975; 1976-1980; 1981-1982 – 7r – 1 – $350.00 – N03707 – us Library Micro [071]

Vegesack, Siegfried von *see*
- DIE BALTISCHE TRAGOEDIE
- BLUMBERGSHOF...
- DIE GESTOHLENE SEELE
- HERREN OHNE HEER
- KLEINE HAUSAPOTHEKE
- DER LEBENSSTROM
- TOTENTANZ IM LIVLAND

VEGESACKER WOCHENBLATT – Bremen, Germany.1849-51 – 1 – gw Mikrofilm [073]

VEGESACKER WOCHENBLATT *see* NORDDEUTSCHE VOLKSZEITUNG

VEGESACKER WOCHENSCHRIFT *see* NORDDEUTSCHE VOLKSZEITUNG

VEGETABLE GROWERS NEWS / Virginia. Truck Experiment Station. Norfolk – v. 1-24, no. 6. 1946-69 – 1,5,6 – us Spaulding [630]

THE VEGETABLE KINGDOM / Lindley, J – London. 1846. B-6030 2 – 8 – ne IDC [580]

VEGETABLE MATERIA MEDICA OF THE UNITED STATES OR, MEDICAL BOTANY / Barton, W P C – Philadelphia, 1817-18. 2v. B-5834-2 – 8 – ne IDC [580]

VEGETABLE PRODUCTION UNDER ARID AND SEMI-ARID CONDITIONS IN TROPICAL AFRICA – 1988 – 449p – it F.A.O. [338]

THE VEGETABLE SYSTEM / Hill, J – 26 v. London. 1761-75. B-5953 2 – 165mf – 8 – ne IDC [630]

VEGETABLE TERATOLOGY / Masters, M T – London, 1869. 534 pp. B-7379 1 – 9 – ne IDC [580]

VEGETABLE TERATOLOGY AN ACCOUNT OF THE PRINCIPAL DEVIATIONS FROM THE USUAL STRUCTURE OF PLANTS / Masters, M T – Ray Society. 1869 – 1 reel or 13mf – 1 – uk Microform Academic [580]

VEGETARIAN TIMES – (Absorbed: Well-being) – Harrisburg. v1-34 1974-dec 1979*. v35-244 jan 1980-dec 1997+ 1; v35-42 jan-dec 1980. v43-172 jan 1981-dec 1991*. v173-244 jan 1992-dec 1997+ 5; v35-244 jan 1980-dec 1997+ 9 – 1,5,9 – D11713 – us UMI [613]

VEGETARIANISM IN THE LIGHT OF THEOSOPHY: A LECTURE / Besant, Anne Wood – London: Theosophical Publishing Society, 1894. 22p – 1 – us U.W. Library [140]

DI VEGETARISHE VELT = THE VEGETARIAN WORLD – Brooklyn, NY. v1 no 1. 1921 – 1r – Can$25.00 – cn Can Microfilming [071]

DER VEGETARISHER GEDANK = VEGETARIAN THOUGHT – Los Angeles, CA. v1 no 4. 1930 – 1r – Can$25.00 – cn Can Microfilming [071]

VEGETATIO – Den Haag. v80-97 jul 1948-jan 1991*. v98-133 feb 1991-dec 1997+ 1; v92-115 feb 1991-dec 1994*. v116-133 jan 1995-dec 1997+ 5; v92-133. feb 1991-dec 1997+ 9 – 1,5,9 – D16846 – us UMI [580]

Veghel, Optat de *see* BENOIT DE CANFIELD (1562-1610)

Vehbi *see* LUETFIYE-I VEHBI

Vehbi, Suembulzade *see* TUHFE-I VEHBI

VEHICLE SYSTEM DYNAMICS – Lisse. v1-19. 1972-90 – 5,9 – Dfl2,280.00; Dfl120.00v – ne Swets [629]

Vehse, Eduard *see* ILLUSTRIERTE GESCHICHTE DES PREUSSISCHEN HOFES, DES ADELS UND DER DIPLOMATIE VOM GROSSEN KURFUERSTEN BIS ZUM TODE KAISER WILHELMS 1

Veidle, V *see* O POSLEDNIKH STIKHAKH MANDEL'SHTAMA

Veiga, Estacio *see* GIBRALTAR E OLIVENOA

THE VEIL OF GOD / Robinson, H Wheeler – 1936 – 1 – 5.00 – us Baptist [240]

VEIL PARTLY LIFTED AND JESUS BECOMING VISIBLE / Furness, William H – Boston: Ticknor & Fields, 1864. 1 fiche – 9 – us A.T.L.A. [240]

Veil, Wolfgang Heinrich *see* GOETHE ALS PATIENT

LA VEILLE DE LA LOI DE L'AN 10, 1763-1802 : ETUDE SUR L'EGLISE REFORMEE A LA FIN DU 18E SIECLE D'APRES DES DOCUMENTS INEDITS / Doumergue, Emile – Paris: Grassart, 1879 – 1mf – us A.T.L.A. [944]

Veillecheze, Alfred de *see* 7 BROCHURES MICROFILMEES ENSEMBLE, DONT 6 EXTRAITES DU "BULLETIN DE LA SOCIETE ARCHEOLOGIQUE DE NANTES ET DE LA LOIRE-INFERIEURE"

LA VEILLEE PITTORESQUE – Musee encyclopedique. no. 1. Paris. 1850 – 1 – fr A.C.R.P.P. [073]

LES VEILLEES CANADIENNES – Montreal, Canada. jul 1853 (5 issues) – 1r – 1 – Can$25.00 – cn Can Microfilming [072]

LES VEILLEES DES CHAUMIERES – Montreal: A Roussin, [1895-189-?] – 9 – cn C.I.H.M. [971]

LES VEILLEES DU PERE BON SENS – Montreal, Canada. 27 dec 1865-dec 1873 – 1r – 1 – Can$45.00 – cn Can Microfilming [072]

VEINTE Y SEIS CARTAS AL...VALDEGAMAS... ENSAYO SOBRE EL LIBERALISMO / Martin Mateos, N – 1851 – 9 – 1.50f – sp Bibl Santa Ana [320]

VEINTE Y SEIS CARTAS...VALDEGAMAS... ENSAYO...LIBERALISMO / Mateos, Nicomedes – 1851 – 9 – 1.50f – sp Bibl Santa Ana [320]
VEINTI UN DIAS EN EL ASILO SAN MIGUEL / Fenix, Victoria – [Buenos Aires], 1955 – 1 – CSUXAJL9775-B – us Hoover Inst Photo [360]
Veitch, John *see* SKETCHES IN HISTORY AND POETRY
VEJA – Sao Paulo. 1968-77* 1; v487-799 1978-83. v800-903 1984-85*. v 904-1008 1986-87 1,9; v487-538 1978. v539-590 1979*. v591-643 1980. v644-695 1981*. v696-747 1982. v748-1008 1987* 5; v20-25 1988-92. v26-27 1993-94*. v28-30 1995-97+ 1,5,9 – 1,5,9 – D10265 – us UMI [073]
VEJECES, (RECUERDOS AUTOBIOGRAFICOS) / Nieto y Serrano, M – Madrid, 1901 – 5mf – 9 – sp Cultura [946]
VEK – (Backfile through 1998 $85r) – 1999- – 1r per y – 1 – $80.00 standing order – us Ross [072]
Vekeman, G *see*
- LA CLOCHE DU DIMANCHE
- LE JOURNAL DU PEUPLE

Vekeman, Gustave *see* LA PROVINCE DE QUEBEC: DOCUMENTS EMPRUNTES A LA BROCHURE OFFICIELLE..
DER VEKER = AWAKENING – (In Yiddish) – Vilnius, LT. v1 no11. 19 Jan 1906 – 1r – 1 – $25.00 – cn Can Microfilming [072]
DER VEKER = AWAKENING – (Yiddish daily) – Minsk, RU. no1029 26 Oct 1921; no1030 27 Oct 1921 – 1r – 1 – $25.00 – cn Can Microfilming [072]
DER VEKER – (Irregular publication) – Vilna, 25 Dec 1905-Feb 14 1906 – 1r – 1 – J-92-15/3 – ne IDC [072]
DER VEKER – Vilna, Russia. v1. 1906 – 1r – 1 – us Ross [072]
DER VEKER – Wilna. v. 1 no. 1-33. Jan 7-Feb 16 1906 – 1 – us NY Public [305]
VEKHI – Sbornik statei o russkoi intelligentsii. (Berdiaev. Gershenson, P. Struve i dr.). Izd. Kushnereva. Ed. 5. M. 1910. B-1373 2 – 8 – ne IDC [190]
Vela Hidalgo y Burriel, Angel *see* LA CAZA DEL PERDIGON
La Velada *see* FIESTAS EN HONOR DE NUESTRA EXCELSA PATRONA LA SANTISIMA VIRGEN DE FUENTE SANTA. 1974
LA VELADA, 1973, 15, 16 Y 17 DE AGOSTO – Zorita: Imprenta Carrasco, 1973 – 1 – sp Bibl Santa Ana [946]
VELADA EN HONOR / Moreno Nieto, Jose – 1882 – 9 – 1.50f – sp Bibl Santa Ana [440]
LA VELADA. FIESTAS 1971 EN ZORITA / Zorita. Ayuntamiento – S.l., s.i., s.a. – 1 – sp Bibl Santa Ana [390]
VELAND : TRAGOEDIE / Hauptmann, Gerhart – 1. bis 5. Aufl. Berlin: S Fischer, 1925 – 1r – 1 – us U.W. Library [820]
Velankar, Hari Damodar *see* JINARATNAKOSA: AN ALPHABETICAL REGISTER OF JAIN WORKS AND AUTHORS
Velarde Lombrana, Julian *see* GNOSEOLOGIA DE LA GRAMATICA GENERATIVA
Velasco, A *see* TEORIA Y PRACTICA DE LA PINTURA
Velasco, Matias *see* DEMOSTRA-CION...ENGANO...FRAY MARCOS DE ALCALA. FUNDACION DESCALZAS
Velasco y Jaraquemada, M de *see* VERSOS O BERZAS
Velasco y Rodriguez, Antonio *see* NOTA EXPLICATIVA DE LOS PRODUCTOS QUE EXHIBE...
Velazquez, A *see* LIBRO DE LA MELANCOLIA...
Velazquez de Mena *see* TRATADO DEL... LINAJE DE VERA...SIERRA BRAVA
Velazquez de Velasco, Luis J *see*
- NOTICIA DEL VIAJE DE ESPANA
- ORIGENES DE LA POESIA CASTELLANA

Velazquez, P *see* TRATADO DE LAS VIRTUDES Y EXCELENCIAS DE LOS BANOS DE TIERMAS
Velazquez, Sebastian *see* EXAMEN DE LA VIOLENCIA ARGENTINA
Veldeke, Heinrich von *see* ENEAS ROMAN
Veldhuis, Robert J *see* A FIVE-MILE MOUNTAIN BICYCLE TEST TO PREDICT VO2MAX
Velds, G J *see* DE ONDERWERPING VAN DJAMBI, 1901-1907. BEKNOPTE GESCHIEDENIS, NAAR OFFICIEELE GEGEVENS SAMENTGESTELD
Velenovski, J *see* FLORA CRETACAE BOHEMIAE NEUE BEITRAEGE
Veley, Margaret *see* A MARRIAGE OF SHADOWS AND OTHER POEMS. WITH BIOGRAPHICAL PREFACE BY LESLIE STEPHEN
Velez, Pedro M *see* OBSERVACIONES AL LIBRO DE AUBSEY F.C. BELL SOBRE FRAY LUIS DE LEON. EL ESCORIAL, 1931
VELHA SERRANA – Pitanguy, 13 Oct, Dec 1912; 28 Jun 1914 – 1,5,6 – bl Biblioteca [072]
O VELHO LINO : ORGAO DE PROPAGANDA – Manoas, Amazonas. 1 Jan 1915 – 1,5,6 – bl Biblioteca [072]
Velho Sobrinho, J F *see* DICIONARIO BIO-BIBLIOGRAFICO BRASILEIRO
Veliaminof-Zernof, V de *see* DICTIONNAIRE DJAGHATAI-TURC
Velichko, K et al *see* THE MILITARY ENCYCLOPEDIA
VELIKAIA KNIAGINIA EKATERINA ALEKSEEVNA 1729-1761 G. ISTORICHESKII OCHERK / Dirin, P – Spb. 1894. BR-10,519 2 – 8 – ne IDC [947]
VELIKAIA ROSSIIA – Rostov, Sevastopol, Novorossisk. June 1919-Oct. 1920. Gaps – 1 – 35.00r – us Hoover Inst Photo [072]
VELIKI OKTIABR'I NEPROLETARSKIE PARTII : MATERIALY KONF. (MAI 1981 V KALININE) / ed by Mintz, I I – M., 1982. 255p – 3mf – 9 – ne IDC [320]
VELIKIE I UDEL'NYE KNIAZI SEVERNOI RUSI V TATARSKOI PERIODE / Ekzempliarskii, A – St. Petersburg, 1889-91.2v. BR/10,369/1 – 9 – ne IDC [947]
VELIKII OKEAN : [PRIAMURSKII KOOPERATOR] – (Missing: 1917 n3-8, 12-1918 n1-2) – Vladivostok, 1917 n1-18 n4 – 6mf – 9 – COR-553/1 – ne IDC [334]
DEN VELIKO I REVOLI UT SII : ODNODNEVNAI A GAZETA, IZDAVAEMAI A OBEDINENNYMI REDAKT SII AMI: PRAVDA – KRASNAI A GAZETA – MAKHOVIK V POLZU GOLODAI ASHCHIKH KRESTI AN. PRAVDA (MOSCOV, R.S.F.S.R.: 1917) KRASNAI A GAZETA. MAKHOVIK – (Includes c.1: 1921:Nov. 7) – Petrograd: Petr. gub. komitet. Rossi isko i kommunistich. partii (bolshevikov), 19uu – 1 – CSUXANR1849-S – us Hoover Inst Photo [947]
VELIKORUSSKIIA BYLINY KIEVSKOGO TSIKLA : RUSSKII FILOLOGICHESKII VESTNIK / Khalanskii, MG – v12(p136-159, 218-250). 1884; v13(p71-139, 350-410), v14(p113-155). 1885 – 7mf – 9 – R-2298/2 – ne IDC [947]
Velis, Jean-Pierre *see* THROUGH A GLASS, DARKLY
VELKD-INFORMATIONEN – (Lacking: v16 nos 3-4 Sep 1973) – 1969-86 – 2r – 1 – ATLA S0850 – us A.T.L.A. [073]
Vellard, J *see* UNE MISSION D'UN ANTHROPOLOGUE FRANCAIS EN AMERIQUE DU SUD
Vellard, Jet al *see* LES POUPEES KARAJA DU MUSEE DE L'HOMME
VELLENAUX: A NOVEL / Forest, Edmund William – Saint John, N.B.: s.n., 1874 (Saint John, N.B.: Daily News). 03154. (Pre-1900 Canadiana) – 9 – cn C.I.H.M. [830]
VELLOSIA : CONTRIBUICOES DO MUSEU BOTANICO DO AMAZONAS – Manaos, Amazonas. 1887; 1885-1888 – 1,5,6 – bl Biblioteca [072]
Vellozo, J M da Conceicao *see*
- FLORAE FLUMINENSIS
- FLORAE FLUMINENSIS, SEU DESCRIPTIONUM PLANTARUM PRAEFECTURA FLUMINENSI SPONTE NASCENTIUM

Velmede, August Friedrich *see* KRIEGSDICHTER ERZAEHLEN
LE VELO – Journal quot. de la velocipedie.Paris.Dir., Paul Rousseau. Dec 1892-20 nov 1904. Devenu: Journal de l'Automobile, du Cyclisme et de tous les Sports. 1894-juil 1906. Mq: mars 1906 – 1 – fr A.C.R.P.P. [944]
Velo Nieto, Gervasio *see*
- CABALLEROS CLERIGOS EXTREMENOS DEL ORDEN Y CABALLERIA DE ALCANTARA
- CASTILLO DE GUADAMUZ
- CASTILLO DE LA ALTA EXTREMADURA
- EL CASTILLO DE SANTIBANEZ EL ALTO
- EL CASTILLO Y PLAZA FUERTE DE ALCANTARA
- CASTILLOS DE LA ALTA EXTREMADURA
- ESCARAMUZAS EN LA FRONTERA CACERENA, CON OCASION DE LAS GUERRAS POR LA INDEPENDENCIA DE PORTUGAL
- FRAY D. ALONSO DE VALENCIA Y BRAVO, DEL ORDEN Y CABALLERIA DE ALCANTARA (1723-1778)
- HERNAN CENTENO. EL TRAVIESO, SENOR DEL CASTILLO DE RAPAPELO EN SIERRA DE GATA
- HIJOS ILUSTRES DE EXTREMADURA
- SENORES DE PASARON
- TORRES DE HIDALGOS CACERENOS

Velsen, Wilhelm von *see* BEITRAEGE ZUR GESCHICHTE DER ARBEITERBEWEGUNG DES NIEDERRHEINISCH-WESTFAELISCHEN BERGBAUES
DI VELT = THE WORLD – (In Yiddish) – St-Petersburg, RU. v? no1/2 1920 – 1r – 1 – $25.00 – cn Can Microfilming [072]
Velten, Carl *see* SAFARI ZA WASUAHELI
Velter, Joseph M *see* DAS DORF IN DER TAIGA
Veltman, A F *see*
- PRIKLIUCHENIIA POCHERPNUTYIA IZ MORIA ZHITEISKAGO
- SERDTSE DUMKA. PRIKLIUCHENIE
- STRANNIK
- SVATOSLAVICH. VRAZHII PITOMETS

IL VELTRO – New York, NY. 1924-1925(?) – us I.H.R.C. [073]
VELT-SHPIGEL = WORLD MIRROR – (Yiddish weekly) – Warsaw, PL. v1 no1 16 Jan 1927-v3 no52 26 Dec 1929 – 1r – 1 – $50.00 – cn Can Microfilming [072]
VELVET LIGHT TRAP – Austin. v1-40. jun 1971-fal 1997+ 1; v1-8 jun 1971-spr 1973. v13-20 fal 1974-sum1983*. v21 sum 1985. v22 1986*. v23-40 spr 1989-fal 1997+ 5; v15-40 fal 1975-fal 1997+ 9 – 1,5,9 – D7503 – us UMI [073]
Venable, Francis Preston *see* A SHORT HISTORY OF CHEMISTRY
Venable, Richard Morton *see* THE LAW OF REAL PROPERTY AND LEASEHOLD ESTATES IN MARYLAND, ABRIDGED FROM LECTURES DELIVERED TO THE LAW SCHOOL OF THE UNIVERSITY OF MARYLAND
VENANGO ARGUS – Venango, NE. -w. Aug 1889-Feb 1890 – 1 – us NE Hist [071]
VENANGO COUNTY-HER PIONEERS AND PEOPLE / Babcock, Charles A – Genealogical and biographical. Chicago, J. H. Beers and Co., 1919. Vols. 1-2. Pennsylvania Reel 40. (The Cox Library Collection) – 5 – us Americana [978]
VENANGO SPECTATOR – Franklin. Pa. 1862-1871 – 1 – us UMI [071]
VENANTI HONORI CLEMENTIANI FORTUNATI PRESBYTERI ITALICI OPERA PEDESTRIA (MGH 1: 4. 2.TEIL) / ed by Krusch, B – 1885 – Dfl22.00 – ne Slangenburg [240]
VENANTI HONORI CLEMENTIANI FORTUNATI PRESBYTERI ITALICI OPERA POETICA (MGH 1: 4.BD. 1. TEIL) / ed by Leo, F – 1881 – Dfl42.00 – ne Slangenburg [240]
Venatier, Hans *see* VOGT BARTOLD
Venatorius, Th *see* PRO BAPTISMO ET FIDE PARVULORUM ADUERSUS ANABAPTISTAS. ITEM. EPIPHANIA CRUCIS THEOPHILI
O VENCEDOR – Manaos, Amazonas. Jul 1914; Jan 1915 – 1,5,6 – bl Biblioteca [072]
VENCESLAI PHILOMANTHIS DE NOVA DOMO MUSICORUM LIVRI QUATUOR / Philomathes, V – [Colophone], Impressum Vienne Pannonie per Hieronymus Vietorem et Joannem Singrenium, anno millesimo quigentesimo. Septimo Kalendas Augusti – 1 – us Sibley [780]
VENCESLAI PHILOMATHIS DE NOVA DOMO MVSICORVM LIBRI QVATVOR COMPENDIOSO CARMINE ELVOVBRATI / Philomathes, V – Vitebergae. 1534. BP-428 1 – 9 – ne IDC [780]
VEND – (Absorbed by: Vending Times) – Cincinnati. v1-25 1946-71*. v26-28 jan 1972-jan 1974 – 1 – D6340 – us UMI [073]
VEND *see* VENDING TIMES
VENDAVAL / Soriano Diaz, Antonio – Badajoz: Tip. clasica, 1946 – sp Bibl Santa Ana [946]
VENDETTA / Corelli, Marie – British Fiction Archive: Unit 1 – 9 – uk Bell [830]
Vendiere, Louise *see* COCCINELLE
VENDING TIMES – (Absorbed: Vend, 1974) – New York. v1-15 1961-75*. v16-37 1976-jan 1998+ 1; v16 1976*. v19-37 1979-jan 1998+ 5; v16 1976. v19-37 1979-jan 1998+ 9 – 1,5,9 – D11242 – us UMI [073]
VENDING TIMES *see* VEND
VENDREDI – Hebdomadaire litteraire, politique et satirique. no. 1-158. nov 1935-nov 1938. devenu: Reflets de la semaine. no. 159-163. nov-dec 1938. Paris – 1 – fr A.C.R.P.P. [073]
Vendryes, A *see* MONOGRAPHIE DES ISOETEAE
Venegas de Henestrosa *see* LIBRO DE CIFRA NUEVA PARA TECLA, ARPA Y VIHUELA
Venegas, Francisco Javier *see*
- DOCUMENTO INEDITO...MANUEL GOMEZ
- DOCUMENTOS AUTOGRAFOS E INEDITOS

EL VENERABLE BARRANTES / Correal y Frente de Andrade, Narciso – La Coruna, 1915 – 1 – sp Bibl Santa Ana [946]
LE VENERABLE FRANCOIS DE LAVAL, PREMIER EVEQUE DE QUEBEC ET APOTRE DU CANADA: SA VIE ET SES VIRTUS / Gosselin, Auguste – Quebec: L.J. Demers, 1890. 03483. (Pre-1900 Canadiana) – 9 – cn C.I.H.M. [920]
LE VENERABLE GERONIMO.. / Burlaton, Louis – 1931 – 1 – us A.T.L.A. [240]
VENERDI (SUPPLE. REPUBB.) – 1987 – 1r – 5,6 – Sfr214.00 – sz Infoprint [072]
VENERDI (SUPPLE. REPUBB.) – 1988-1989 – 2r per y – 5,6 – Sfr374.00 – sz Infoprint [072]
VENETIA TRIONFANTE / Marostica, V – Venetia, 1572 – 1mf – 9 – H-8331/1 – ne IDC [945]
VENETIAN BALLADS COMPOS'D BY SIGR. HASSE AND ALL THE CELEBRATED ITALIAN MASTERS / Hasse, J A – 3v. c.1750 – 9 – us Sibley [780]
VENETIAN OPERA LIBRETTI – Part One: Venetian Opera Libretti Collection of the University of California at Los Angeles, 1635-1769 – 50r – 1 – us Primary [780]
Venetianer, Ludwig *see* EZEKIELS VISION UND DIE SALOMONISCHEN WASSERBECKEN
THE VENETIANS / Braddon, Mary Elizabeth – British Fiction Archive: Unit 5 – 9 – uk Bell [830]
Venezky, Richard L *see*
- A MICROFICHE CONCORDANCE TO OLD ENGLISH

VENEZUELA : ANUARIO ESTADISTICO 1877-1969 / Venezuela. Direccion General de Estadistica y Censos Nacionales – (Some issues between 1879-1937 not publ. 1878, 1884, 1887, 1889, 1891, 1941 not available. Coll title: Latin American and Caribbean Official Statistical Serials, 1821-1982) – 228mf – 9 – £1,440.00 – uk Chadwyck [972]
Venezuela *see*
- GACETA OFICIAL
- PLAN CUATRIENAL, 1960-1964

Venezuela. Comision Presidencial para el Estudio del Proyecto Educativo Nacional *see* EDUCACION EN VENEZUELA
Venezuela. Coordination and Economic Planning Office *see* PLAN DE LA NACION, 1960-1964
Venezuela. Direccion General de Estadistica y Censos Nacionales *see* VENEZUELA
Venezuela. Inter-American Economic and Social Council *see* EVALUACION DEL PLAN DE LA NACION 1963-1966 DE VENEZUELA
Venezuela. Ministerio de educacion nacional *see* MEMORIA Y CUENTA
Venezuela. Ministerio de Hacienda *see* CUENTA GENERAL DE RENTAS Y GASTOS Y CUENTA DE GASTOS DEL DEPARTMENTO DE HACIENDA
Venezuela. Oficina Central de Coordinacion y Planificacion *see* PLAN DE LA NACION, 1965-1968
Venezuela. Oficina Centrale de Coordinacion y Planificacion *see* PLAN DE LA NACION, 1963-1966
Venezuela. Presidente *see* PLAN DE OBRAS PUBLICAS NACIONALES PARA EL PERIODO PRESIDENCIAL, 1941 A 1946
Venezuela. Universidad Central. Caracas *see* ANALES
VENEZUELEN HERALD – Caracas. 15 Aug 1898-5 Nov 1904 – 1 – us NY Public [072]
VENGANZA CUMPLIDA / Sanchez Arjona y Sanchez Arjona, Jose – 1882 – 9 – 1.50f – sp Bibl Santa Ana [810]
LA VENGEANCE DE PLUTON, OU SUITE DES MUSES RIVALES / Cubieres-Palmezeaux, M de – Paris. 19 mai 1778 – 9 – fr Hachette [820]
VENGEANCE OF OUR LORD : MEDIEVAL DRAMATIZATIONS OF THE DESTRUCTION OF JERUSALEM / Wright, Stephen K – 1989 3mf – Can$29.00 – 0-88844-089-8 – cn Pontif [790]
Vengerov, S A *see*
- EPOKHA BIELINSKAGO
- GEROICHESKII KHARAKTER RUSSKOI LITERATURY

- OSNOVNYE CHERTY ISTORII NOVEISEI RUSSKOI LITERATURY
- RUSSKAIA LITERATURA 20 VEKA
- RUSSKAIA POEZIIA
- RUSSKIIA KNIGI. S BIOGRAFICHESKIMI DANNYMI OB AVTORAKH I PEREVODCHIKAKH, (1708-1893)

Vengerova, Z *see*
- LITERATURNYIA KHARAKTERISTIKI
- POETY-SIMVOLISTY VO FRANTSII "VESTNIK EVROPY"

LE VENGEUR – Dir. politique Felix Pyat. no. 1-35; 2e s., no. 1-56. Paris. 3 fevr-24 mai 1871 – 1 – fr A.C.R.P.P. [073]

LE VENGEUR / La Federation Revolutionnaire de la Region du Nord – Organe de la Federation revolutionnaire de la region du Nord. no. 2-3, 7. Lille. aout-sept 1883 – 1 – fr A.C.R.P.P. [073]

LE VENGEUR DE MONTCALM / Durandal, Pierre – Paris: H. Lecene et H. Oudin, 1887. 02272. (Pre-1900 Canadiana) – 9 – cn C.I.H.M. [971]

VENICE – 1994 – 9 – 92-3-102974-6 – fr UNESCO [910]

Venice. Biennale D'Arte *see* PUBLICATIONS OF THE VENICE BIENNALE, 1895-1977 (PVB)

VENICE EVENING VANGUARD – Venice, CA. 1911-69 – 217r – 1 – $10,850.00 – C03070 – us Library Micro [071]

VENICE FIRST BAPTIST CHURCH. VENICE, FLORIDA : CHURCH RECORDS – 1934-1984 – 6r – 1 – $171.86 – us Baptist [240]

VENICE GONDOLIER – Venice, Florida. 1968- – 1 – us P.K. Yonge [071]

VENICE MARINA NEWS AND VANGUARD – Santa Monica, CA. 1957 – 269+ r – 1 – $13,450.00 ($135.00y) – R03526 – us Library Micro [071]

LA VENIDA DE CRISTINA / Donoso Cortes, Juan Francisco – 1829 – 9 – 1.50f – sp Bibl Santa Ana [830]

Venkatarama Aiyar, K *see* A MANUAL OF TRANSLATION FROM TAMIL INTO ENGLISH

Venn, Arthur *see* DIE POLEMISCHEN SCHRIFTEN DES GEORG NIGRINUS GEGEN JOHANN NAS

VENNOR'S WEATHER BULLETIN – Montreal: H G Vennor, [1882?-18– or 19–] – 9 – cn C.I.H.M. [350]

Venok, M Iu *see* LERMONTOVU

LA VENTANA – 1931-37.668p – 1 – 23.38 – us Baptist [240]

LA VENTE DE L'ASSURANCE-VIE SELON LES BESOINS : PROGRAMMES D'ASSURANCE-VIE ET EXPERTISES DE SUCCESSION: BIBLIOGRAPHIE ANALYTIQUE / Lavallee, Irene – [1955]. SEM105P4 – 1mf – 9 – cn Bibl Nat [360]

VENTE ET AFFERMAGE DE CHEVAUX PERCHERONS, ARABES, ET CAROSSIERS NORMANDS: CATALOGUE POUR 1889-1890 / La compagnie du haras national – (Montreal: Gebhardt-Berthiaume), 1889. 04235. (Pre-1900 Canadiana) – 9 – cn C.I.H.M. [636]

Ventenat, E P *see*
- DECAS GENERUM NOVORUM
- DESCRIPTION DES PLANTES NOUVELLES ET PEU CONNUES. DANS LE JARDIN DE J. M. CELS
- JARDIN DE LA MALMAISON
- TABLEAU DU REGNE VEGETAL SELON LA METHODE DE JUSSIEU

VENTICINQUE ANNI DI MISSIONE FRA GLI IMMIGRATI DI BOSTON, MASS – 1883-1913 – 1r – 1 – us I.H.R.C. [240]

LA VENTILATION LIBRE DES EGOUTS EN RAPPORT AVEC L'HYGIENE DE L'HABITATION / Baillairge, Charles – 1892. 00069. (Pre-1900 Canadiana) – 9 – cn C.I.H.M. [628]

Vento, M *see* SIX SONATAS FOR THE HARPSICHORD WITH AN ACCOMPANIMENT FOR A VIOLIN OR GERMAN FLUTE

VENTURA COUNTY INCLUDING VENTURA, OXNARD, SANTA PAULA, FILLMORE AND OJAI – Ventura Co, CA. 1918-1919; 1926-1949 – 11r – 1 – $550.00 – D106 – us Library Micro [978]

VENTURA COUNTY LABOR NEWS – Ventura, CA. 1937-1948 – 3r – 1 – $150.00 – B03686 – us Library Micro [071]

VENTURA COUNTY NEWS – Ventura, CA. 1943-1950; 1957-1962 – 6r – 1 – $300.00 – B03685 – us Library Micro [071]

VENTURA FREE PRESS – Ventura, CA. 1875-1918; 1920-1927 – 33r – 1 – $1,650.00 – B03562 – us Library Micro [071]

VENTURA FREE PRESS – Ventura, CA. 1890-1891; 1904-1910; 1915-1930; 1932-1934; 1935 – 48r – 1 – $2,400.00 – BC03563 – us Library Micro [071]

VENTURA INDEPENDENT – Ventura, CA. 1896-1903 – 3r – 1 – $150.00 – B03687 – us Library Micro [071]

VENTURA REPUBLICAN – Ventura, CA. 1904-1905 – 1r – 1 – $50.00 – B03688 – us Library Micro [071]

VENTURA SIGNAL – Ventura, CA. 1871-1885 – 3r – 1 – $150.00 – B03686 – us Library Micro [071]

VENTURA VIDETTE – Ventura, CA. 1889-1890 – 2r – 1 – $100.00 – B03564 – us Library Micro [071]

VENTURA WEEKLY DEMOCRAT – Ventura, CA. 1891-1894; 1896-1901 – 3r – 1 – $150.00 – B03687 – us Library Micro [071]

VENTURA WEEKLY POST – Ventura, CA. 1925-1930; 1932; 1936-1938 – 6r – 1 – $300.00 – B03688 – us Library Micro [071]

VENTURA-OXNARD – 1909-33; 1992- – 29+ r – 1 – $1,450.00 – P00140 – us Library Micro [910]

THE VENTURE – London, 1903, 1905 – 1r – 1 – £60.00 – uk Chadwyck [760]

VENTURE : AN ANNUAL OF ART AND LITERATURE – London. v1-2. 1903-05 – 1 – D5180 – us UMI [073]

VENTURE – Forest Grove OR. Aug 31 Sept 21 1887 – 1 – us U.O. Library [071]

VENTURE – Kalida, Ohio. 1845-54 – 1r – 1 – $32.50r – us Archival [071]

Venture Development Management Resources Inc *see* A REASSESSMENT OF GUAM'S POLITICAL RELATIONSHIP WITH THE UNITED STATES

VENTURE OF RATIONAL FAITH / Benson, Margaret – London: Macmillan, 1908.1 fiche – 9 – us A.T.L.A. [240]

Venturi, Adolfo *see*
- I MICETI DELL' AGRO BRESCIANO
- STORIA DELL ARTE ITALIANA
- STUDI MICOLOGICI

VENUS PHYSIQUE / Maupertuis, Pierre-Louis M de – 1re ed., s.l., 1745, viii-194 p. Histoire des Sciences XVIIe-XIXe Siecles. 7931 – 9 – fr Hachette [580]

Veo, Ettore *see* ROMA POPOLARESCA

Vera, Augusto *see* STRAUSS: L'ANCIENNE ET LA NOUVELLE FOI

Vera Camacho, Juan Pedro *see* COMO NOS VEN LOS DE FUERA

Vera Cruz. Mexico (State) *see* GACETA OFICIAL

Vera, E de *see* LA CARIDAD MISIONAL Y LA EPISTOLA DE SAN PABLO A LOS FILIPENSES. BADAJOZ

Vera e Isla Fernandez, Fernando de la *see*
- TRADUCION EN VERSO DEL SALMO L. DE DAVID. MISERERE MEI DEUS
- VERSOS

Vera, Emilio *see* LA MARCHA DE LA CARRONA

Vera, Francisco *see*
- LA CULTURA ESPANOLA MEDIEVAL
- LA INAPRESABLE

VERA, FRANCISCO. SENECA. MADRID, 1934 / Iriarte-A G, Joaquin – Razon y Fe, 1935 – 1 – sp Bibl Santa Ana [946]

Vera Mendoza, Fernando de *see* PANEGIRICO POR LA POESIA

LA VERA REDENZIONE – Bridgeport, CT, 1917 – 2mf or 1r – 1,9 – us I.H.R.C. [978]

Vera y Figueroa, Juan Antonio *see*
- CENTON EPISTOLARIO DEL BACHILLER FERNAN GOMEZ DE CIBDADREAL. GENERACIONES...
- EPITOME DE LA VIDA Y HECHOS DEL INVICTO EMPERADOR CARLOS 5
- EPITOME...CARLOS V
- EL FERNANDO DO SEVILLA RESTAURADA
- EL REY D. PEDRO DEFENDIDO

Vera y Mendoza, Fernando de *see* PANEGYRICO POR LA POESIA

Veracini, F *see* ADRIANO, SONGS IN THE OPERA

VERAENDERUNG STRUKTURELLER UND SOZIALETHISCHER GRUNDLAGEN DES DEUTSCHEN GESUNDHEITSWESENS DURCH DAS GESUNDHEITSREFORMGESETZ UND DAS GESUNDHEITSSTRUKTURGESETZ : (AUF DEM WEG ZUM SOZIALSTAAT DER POSTMODERNE?) / Rothfuss, Joerg – 1995 – 1mf – 9 – DM60.00 – 3-8267-2174-8 – gw Hänsel [340]

VERAENDERUNGEN VON PLASMAFAKTOREN WAEHREND DER LAGERUNG VON THROMBOZYTEN UND IHR EINFLUSS AUF DEREN FUNTKIONSFAEHIGKEIT / Schroeter, Astrid – 1995 – 2mf – 9 – DM80.00 – 3-8267-2149-7 – gw Hänsel [616]

DIE VERANLASSUNG UND DIE QUELLEN VON JOHANN ELIAS SCHLEGELS "CANUT" / Paul, Gustav – (Includes bibliographical references) – Darmstadt: C F Winter, 1915 – 1r – 1 – us U.W. Library [430]

VERANTWOORDINGE EENDER REQUESTE. DAER IN GETRACKTEERT WORDE, OFT OORLOCH. GHEOORLOFT SY – Door I.P. 1597. BME-220 1 – 9 – ne IDC [240]

VERANTWORTUNG CASPAR TAUBERS, DER ZU WIEN VERPRANT IST WORDEN / Guttmann, L – 1524. BME-8 1 – 9 – ne IDC [240]

Verany, J B *see* MOLLUSQUES MEDITERRANEENS

Verard, A *see* THE ART OF GOOD LIVING AND GOOD DYING

THE VERB AND THE SENTENCE IN CHRONICLES, EZRA, AND NEHEMIAH / Corwin, Rebecca – (Includes bibliographical references) – Borna near Leipzig: [s.n.], 1909 (Robert Noske) – 1mf – 9 – 0-8370-9216-7 – 1986-3216 – us A.T.L.A. [220]

Verba, Daniel *see* ENQUETE CINEMATOGRAPHIQUE SUR LES STEELBANDS DE TRINIDAD

VERBAAL GEHOUDEN BY DEN COMMISSARIS VAN DE CAAP DE GOEDE HOOP, A J SLUYSKEN, ZEEDERT HET ARRIVEMENT DER ENGELSCHE VLOOT, ONDER DEN ADMIRAAL S G KEIT ELPHINSTONE : DEN 10 JUNY 1795, EN DE OVERGAAVE VAN DIE KOLONIE AAN DE WAPENEN VAN GROOT-BRITTANNIEN, DEN 16 SEPTEMBER DAAR AAN VOLGENDE – Den Hage: Isaac van Cleef, 1797 – us Res Libr [960]

Verband der Baecker, Konditoren und verwandten Berufsgenossen Deutschlands *see* JAHRBUCH

Verband der Bergarbeiter Deutschlands *see*
- GESCHAEFTSBERICHT
- JAHRBUCH
- JAHRESBERICHT

Verband der Bergbauindustriearbeiter Deutschlands *see*
- JAHRBUCH
- PROTOKOLL DER GENERALVERSAMMLUNG

Verband der Bergbauindustriearbeiter Deutschlands. Bezirk Saarbruecken *see* JAHRESBERICHT

Verband der Brauerei- und Muehlenarbeiter und verwandter Berufsgenossen *see* JAHRBUCH

Verband der Buchbinder und Papierverarbeiter Deutschlands *see*
- GESCHAEFTSBERICHT
- PROTOKOLL DER VERHANDLUNGEN

Verband der deutschen Buchdrucker *see*
- JAHRESBERICHT
- PROTOKOLL DER GENERALVERSAMMLUNG
- RECHENSCHAFTSBERICHTE

Verband der deutschen Gewerkvereine (Hirsch-Duncker) *see* DIE VERHANDLUNGEN DES ORDENTLICHEN..

Verband der deutschen Hutarbeiter *see* JAHRESBERICHT UND ABRECHNUNG

Verband der deutschen Juden *see*
- DIE LEHREN DES JUDENTUMS NACH DEN QUELLEN

Verband der Fabrik-, Land-, Hilfsarbeiter und Arbeiterinnen Deutschlands *see* BERICHT...AN DEN ORDENTLICHEN VERBANDSTAG

Verband der Fabrikarbeiter Deutschlands *see*
- JAHRBUCH
- PROTOKOLL DER ERSTEN KONFERENZ..
- PROTOKOLL UEBER DIE VERHANDLUNGEN DES ERSTEN AUSSERORDENTLICHEN VERBANDSTAGES

Verband der Gaertner und Gaertnereiarbeiter *see* GESCHAEFTSBERICHT

Verband der Gaswirtsgehilfen *see* PROTOKOLL UEBER DIE VERHANDLUNGEN DES VERBANDSTAGES

Verband der Gemeinde- und Staatsarbeiter *see*
- GESCHAEFTSBERICHT
- JAHRESBERICHT
- PROTOKOLL UEBER DIE VERHANDLUNGEN DES VERBANDSTAGES

Verband der Gemeinde- und Staatsarbeiter. Reichssektion Kammereibetriebe. Reichskonferenz *see* PROTOKOLL...

Verband der Graphischen Hilfsarbeiter und -arbeiterinnen Deutschlands *see* GESCHAEFTSBERICHT

Verband der Hut- und Filzwarenarbeiter und arbieterinnen Deutschlands *see* PROTOKOLL

VERBAND DER JUEDISCHEN JUGENDVEREINE DEUTSCHLANDS – Berlin. v1-13. 1910-1922. Lacking misc. issues. B378 (Leo Baeck Institute. German-Jewish Periodicals, Pt 1) – 1r – 1 – $75.00 – us UPA [270]

Verband der landwirtschaftlichen Genossenschaften im Koenigreiche Sachsen *see* BERICHT UEBER DAS GESCHAFTSJAHR..

Verband der Lithographen, Steindrucker und verwandten Berufe *see* BERICHTE UND PROTOKOLL..

Verband der Maler, Lackierer, Anstreicher, Tuencher und Weissbinder Deutschlands *see*
- JAHRBUCH
- JAHRESBUCH
- NIEDERSCHRIFT DER VERHANDLUNGEN DER ERSTEN REICHSKONFERENZ..
- PROTOKOLL

Verband der Nahrungsmittel- und Getraenkearbeiter *see*
- JAHRBUCH
- PROTOKOLL DES ORDENTLICHEN VERBANDSTAGES

Verband der Schneider, Schneiderinnen und Waeschearbeiter Deutschlands *see* PROTOKOLL..

Verband der Steinsetzer, Pflasterer und Berufsgenossen Deutschlands. Berlin *see*
- DENKSCHRIFT
- JAHRESBERICHT
- PROTOKOLL DER VERHANDLUNGEN DES VERBANDSTAGES

Verband der Tapezierer und verwandten Berufsgenossen Deutschlands *see* PROTOKOLL DES ORDENTLICHEN VERBANDSTAGES

Verband der weiblichen Handels- und Bueroangestellten *see* ARBEITSBERICHT

Verband deutscher Arbeitsnachweise *see* GESCHAEFTSBERICHT

Verband deutscher Berufsfeuerwehrmaenner *see* JAHRESBERICHT

DER VERBAND DEUTSCHER JOURNALISTEN- UND SCHRIFTSTELLERVEREINE UND DIE BESCHLUESSE SEINER DELEGIERTENTAGE, 1895 BIS 1904 / Thiess, Karl – Hamburg: Im Selbstverlag des Verbandes, 1905 – 1r – 1 – us U.W. Library [360]

Verband Deutscher Schriftsteller *see* PHANTASIE UND VERANTWORTUNG

VERBAND DEUTSCHER SCHRIFTSTELLER. PHANTASIE UND VERANTWORTUNG : DOKUMENTATION DES DRITTEN SCHRIFTSTELLERKONGRESSES DES VERBANDES DEUTSCHER SCHRIFTSTELLER (VS) IN DER IG DRUCK UND PAPIER / ed by Bingel, Horst – (Includes bibliographical references) – Frankfurt (Main): Fischer-Taschenbuch-Verlag, 1975 – 1 – us U.W. Library [430]

Verband deutscher Textilarbeiter *see* GESCHAEFTSBERICHT

VERBATIM REPORT OF PROCEEDINGS / South Africa. Natives Representative Council – (Lacks: 2nd sessions 1938 and 1942) – Pretoria, 1937-46 – us Res Libr [324]

VERBE – Revue mensuelle. no. 60-126. Paris. avr 1954-61 – 1 – fr A.C.R.P.P. [073]

LE VERBE SUMERIEN / Jestin, R – v1: Determinatives, verbales et infixes.1943. (Etudes Orientales 7). BNE-452/1 – 9 – ne IDC [490]

VERBECK OF JAPAN : A CITIZEN OF NO COUNTRY: A LIFE STORY OF FOUNDATION WORK INAUGURATED BY GUIDO FRIDOLIN VERBECK / Griffis, William Elliot – New York: Fleming H Revell, c1900 – 1mf – 9 – 0-8370-6573-9 – 1986-0573 – us A.T.L.A. [920]

Verbin, Andrei *see* SERIKATBURUH SOVJET

Verbist, P J *see* LES BELGES AU CANADA

O VERBO – Cidade do Recreio, 16. 31 Apr 1939; Feb-Jun 1940; Mar-Apr, Jun, Aug, Oct-Dec 1941; Jan-Feb, May, Jul 1942; Feb 1943-24 Dec 1944 – 1,5,6 – bl Biblioteca [072]

O VERBO : ORGAO DA MUNICIPALIDADE – Villa Nepomuceno, 5 Jun 1916 – 1,5,6 – bl Biblioteca [072]

VERBO *see* ANZEIGER VOM OBERLAND

VERBO SEEBLATT *see* WUERTTEMBERGISCHES SEEBLATT

DAS VERBOT DER QUINTEN-PARALLELEN : EINE MONOGRAPHISCHE STUDIE... / Tappert, W – Leipzig: H Matthes, 1869 – 1 – us Sibley [780]

DER VERBOTE, POLITISCHE UND SOZIAL-OEKONOMISCHE MONATSCHRIFT – 1866-71. Organ of Sektionsgruppe deutscher Sprache of IWA. (Serial publications of German trade unions in the Memorial Library, University of Wisconsin-Madison.) – 1 – us U.W. Library [073]

VERBPRAEFIGIERUNG DES DEUTSCHEN : SKALIERUNGSVERBEN MIT UEBER- UND UNTER- / Risch, Gabriela – 1995 – 2mf – 9 – DM80.00 – 3-8267-2114-4 – gw Hänsel [430]

DIE VERBREITUNG OBERLAENDISCHER MYSTIKERWERKE IM NIEDERLAENDISCHEN / Dolch, A – 1919 – 2mf – 8 – ne Slangenburg [290]

VERBUM DOMINI – 1(1921)-24(1944) – 117mf – 9 – Dfl410.00 – ne Slangenburg [073]

VERBUM DOMINI – Rome. v1-24. 1921-1944 – 117mf – 9 – ne IDC [240]

VERCLARINGE (EEN CORTE EENUULDIGHE) WT DER HEYLIGER SCHRIFT. DER EERLIJCKER ENDE REYNDER ECHTE. DOOR CORN. I – Middelb., R. Schilders. 1591. BME-225 1 – 9 – ne IDC [240]

VERCLARINGHE VANT VADER ONSE. OP EEN NIEUW WEDER MET ALDER NEERSTICHEYT DEURSIEN / Joris, David – BME-378 1 – 9 – ne IDC [240]

Vercruysse, Bruno *see* THE IMMACULATE CONCEPTION

Vercruysse, Jeroom *see*
- HOLBACH AND HIS FRIENDS ANTICLERICAL THOUGHT IN FRANCE: 1760-1789
- OUVRAGES SUR VOLTAIRE, 1788-1826
- VOLTAIRE ET LA HOLLANDE

LA VERDAD – Almendralejo. 1884 – 9 – 1.50f – sp Bibl Santa Ana [072]

LA VERDAD – Almendralejo, 1884 – 5 – sp Bibl Santa Ana [073]

LA VERDAD ACRISOLADA EN LAS LETRAS DIVINAS Y HUMANAS...RESPONDIENDO AL AUTO... / Aldrete y Soto, L – Valencia, 1682 – 2mf – 9 – sp Cultura [600]

VERDAD DE POLITICA / Estrella Estralla, Jose Emilio – Madrid: Graficas Menor, 1965 – sp Bibl Santa Ana [320]

VERDAD DEL MOVIMIENTO (CONFERENCIA... DISCURSO DE LA FUNDACION / Romero Carvajal, Jose Ignacio – Caceres: Tip. de El Noticiero, 1964 – 1 – sp Bibl Santa Ana [320]

VERDAD ILUSTRADA CONTRA LAS IMPOSTURAS QUE HA ESCRITO EL R.P. FR. MARCOS DE ALCALA / Camberos de Yegros, Fernando – 1737 – 9 – 1.50f – sp Bibl Santa Ana [946]

LA VERDAD SOBRE ESPANA / Goebbels, Joseph – Berlin, 1937? Fiche W924. (Blodgett Collection of Spanish Civil War Pamphlets) – 9 – us H.U. College Libr [946]

LA VERDAD SOBRE LA TRAGEDIA DE CASAS VIEJAS, POR EL COMITE NACIONALE. / Confederacion Nacional de Trabajo. Spain – Barcelona, n.d. Fiche W 1326. (Blodgett Collection of Spanish Civil War Pamphlets) – 9 – us H.U. College Libr [946]

LA VERDAD SOBRE LOS SUCECOS EN LA RETAGUARDIA LEAL, LOS ACONTECIMIENTOS DE CATALUNA / Souchy, Agustin – Buenos Aires, 1937. Fiche W1168. (Blodgett Collection of Spanish Civil War Pamphlets) – 9 – us H.U. College Libr [946]

LA VERDAD SOCIAL – Badajoz, 1922. 1 numero – 5 – sp Bibl Santa Ana [073]

A VERDADE : HEBDOMADARIO NEUTRO – Pao d'Assucar, Alagoas. 3 Set-24 Dez 1893 – 1,5,6 – bl Biblioteca [072]

A VERDADE : ORGAM IMPARCIAL E NOTICIOSO – Maceio, Alagoas. 30 Out, 18 Nov 1878 – 1,5,6 – bl Biblioteca [072]

A VERDADE : ORGAO SPIRITA – Cuiaba, 27 Jul-Sep, Nov 1894; Jan-Mar, May, Jul-Dec 1895; Jan-26 Mar 1896 – 1,5,6 – bl Biblioteca [072]

A VERDADE – Raul Soares, 29 Mar 1931 – 1,5,6 – bl Biblioteca [072]

A VERDADE : SEMANARIO IMPARCIAL E POPULAR – Itajuba, 4 Mar 1886-Mar 1889; Jan 1893; Sep 1894; Aug, Oct-Nov 1895; Jan-9 May 1896 – 1,5,6 – bl Biblioteca [072]

A VERDADE CONSTITUCIONAL – Rio de Janeiro, 16 Mar 1822 – 1,5,6 – bl Biblioteca [072]

A VERDADE E NADA MAIS / Botto, Antonio – Coimbra, 1935 – 1 – us Res Libr [440]

A VERDADE HISTORICA SOBRE O 15 DE NOVEMBRO / Correia, Leoncio – Rio de Janeiro: Imprensa nacional, 1939. 312p. Plates, facsims., music. Music by Deodora da Fonseca, 1827-92. Also: Historia de las misiones...en el estade de Chile. By Jose Sallusti. Santiago: Lourdes, 1906 – 1 – us U.W. Library [972]

A VERDADE SEM REBUCO – Rio de Janeiro, 18 May-31 Aug 1829 – 1,5,6 – bl Biblioteca [072]

O VERDADEIRO LIBERAL : PERIODICO POLITICO LITTERARIO – Rio de Janeiro, 2 Mar-6 Apr 1826 – 1,5,6 – bl Biblioteca [072]

O VERDADEIRO PATRIOTA – Rio de Janeiro, 23 Sep 1830-17 Jun 1831 – 1,5,6 – bl Biblioteca [072]

VERDADERA APOLOGIA EN DEFENSA DE LA MEDICINA RACIONAL PHILOSOPHICA... / Zapata, D – Madrid, 1691 – 2mf – 9 – sp Cultura [610]

VERDADERA HISTORIA DE LOS SUCESOS DE LA CONQUISTA DE LA NUEVA ESPANA / Diaz del Castillo, Bernal – Guatemala: Urbe-Giron, fotografos, 1892 – 1 – sp Bibl Santa Ana [946]

LA VERDADERA PATRIA DE CRISTOBAL COLON / Paramos, Jose G – Madrid: Razon y Fe, 1926 – 1 – sp Bibl Santa Ana [946]

VERDADERA RELACION DE LO SUSSEDIDO EN LOS REYNOS...DEL PERU...INTRODUCCION DE JOSE TORIBIO MEDINA. PARIS 1930 / Albenino, Nicolas de – Madrid: Razon y Fe, 1935 – 1 – sp Bibl Santa Ana [972]

VERDADERA RELACION DELO SUSSEDIDO ENLOS REYNOS E PROVINCIAS DEL PERU DESDE LA YDA DEELLOS DEL VIREY BLASCO NUNES VELA...Y MUERTE DE GONCALO PICARRO. SEVILLA. 1549 / Albenino, Nicolao de – Reproduction fac-simile avec une introduction de Jose Toribio Medina. Paris. Institut d'Ethnologie. 1930 – 1 – sp Bibl Santa Ana [946]

VERDADERA RELACION...LAS BATUECAS / Gonzalez de Manuel, Thomas – 1693 – 9 – 1.50f – sp Bibl Santa Ana [946]

VERDADERA Y NOTABLE RELACION DEL DESCUBRIMIENTO Y CONQUISTA DE GUATEMALA / Diaz del Castillo, Bernal – Guatemala: Centro America, 1933.-v1 – sp Bibl Santa Ana [972]

VERDADERA Y NOTABLE RELACION DEL DESCUBRIMIENTO Y CONQUISTA DE LA NUEVA ESPANA Y GUATEMALA / Diaz del Castillo, Bernal – (Tomo 2: Bibliografia Guatemala, Centro America) – 1934 – 1 – sp Bibl Santa Ana [972]

VERDADERA...CONQUISTA DE MEJICO / Jerez, Francisco de – 1891 – 9 – 1.50f – sp Bibl Santa Ana [972]

VERDADERA...NUEVA ESPANA / Diaz del Castillo, Bernal – (1892 ed.1.50f; 9) – 1862-63.3v – 9 – 1.50f – sp Bibl Santa Ana [972]

EL VERDADERO CONOCIMIENTO DE LA PESTE, SUS CAUSAS, SENALES Y PRESERVACION... / Rosell, J F – Barcelona, 1632 – 3mf – 9 – sp Cultura [616]

VERDADEROS INTERESES DE LA PATRIA / Caracciolo, Luis Antonio – 1785 – 1mf – 9 – Pta1,000.00 – 84-7848-169-9 – sp Pentalfa [946]

VERDAGUER / Serra Boldu, Valerio – Barcelona, 1932; Madrid: Razon y Fe, 1932 – 1 – sp Bibl Santa Ana [999]

Verdaguer, Jose A *see* HISTORIA ECLESIASTICA DE CUYO. TOMO 1. MILANO, 1931

VERDANDISTEN – Stockholm, Sweden. 1897-1903 – 1 – sw Kungliga [072]

VERDE : REVISTA MENSAL DE ARTE E CULTURA – Cataguazes, Sep 1927-Jan 1928; May 1929 – 1,5,6 – bl Biblioteca [072]

Verde, Josefina *see* CANTO A LA VERA

VERDE OLIVO / Cuban Revolutionary Armed Forces – Havana. Mar 1960-Dec 1978 – 1 – 35.00r – us Hoover Inst Photo [073]

VERDE OLIVO – Havana, CU. 1981-1986 – 16r – $800.00 – R04209 – us Library Micro [072]

VERDENER ALLER-ZEITUNG – Verden, Germany.1978- – 1 – gw Mikrofilm [072]

VERDENER NACHRICHTEN – Bremen, Germany.28 Feb 1980- – 1 – gw Mikrofilm [072]

VERDENER-ALLER-ZEITUNG *see* KREISZEITUNG

Verdi, Giuseppe *see* MACBETH: DRAMMA LIRICO IN QUATTRO ATTI..

Verdi, Tullio Suzzara *see* MATERNITY

VERDICT – Gainesville. v7. sep 1973-aug 1974 – 1 – D9513 – us UMI [073]

Verdier, Cardinal et al *see* L'HOMME DE COULEUR

Verdier, James Robert *see* PAPERS OF JOHN AND JAMES VERDIER

Verdier, John Mark *see*
- ACCOUNT BOOK
- PAPERS OF JOHN AND JAMES VERDIER

VERDIGRE CITIZEN – Verdigre, NE. -w. Jun 1965-Jul 1966 – 1 – us NE Hist [071]

VERDIGRE EAGLE – Verdigre, NE. -w. Apr-May 1900; Nov 1900; Jan 1908-May 1964 – 1 – us NE Hist [071]

VERDIGRE EAGLE – Verdigre, NE. -w. Aug 1966 to date – 1 – us NE Hist [071]

VERDON DELPHIC – Verdon, NE. -w. Mar 1920-May 1921 – 1 – us NE Hist [071]

VERDON VIDETTE – Verdon, NE. -w. Nov 1884-Nov 1887; Nov 1888-Jun 1900; Aug 1900-Jan 1901; Apr 1901-Jul 1902; Sept 1902; Nov 1904; Jul 1907; May 1914-Jul 1916 – 1 – us NE Hist [071]

VERDON VISITOR AND THE SALEM STANDARD – Verdon, NE. -w. Feb 1925-Aug 1928 – 1 – us NE Hist [071]

DIE VERDREHTE GEDANKENMUEHLE.. / Wilsmann, Aloys Christof – Nuernberg, Willmy Verlag, 1944. 127p. illus – 1 – us U.W. Library [790]

Verdugo, J *see* RESPUESTA A LA APROBACION DEL LIBRO DE...LUIS ALDRETE EN QUE SE TRATA DEL AGUA DE LA VIDA

VERDUN, ARGONNE-METZ (1914-1918) / France. Ministere de l'Education nationale – Clermont-Ferrand, c1925. 192p. (Guides illustres Michelin des Champs de Bataille) – 1 – us U.W. Library [910]

VERDUN FREE PRESS / ed by McBride, ArcH – Verdun, Canada. v2 n28. 13 fev 1919; v3 n17. 27 nov 1919 – 1r – 1 – Can$25.00 – cn Can Microfilming [072]

LE VERE IMAGINI ET DESCRITIONI DELLE PIV NOBILLI CITTA DEL MONDO – Ventijs, 1569 – 1mf – 9 – H-8168/1 – ne IDC [956]

Vereeniging ter beoefening der Joodsche Wetenschappen *see* TIJDSCHRIFT

VEREENIGN DERKBLAD DER NEDERDUITSCHE GEREFORMEERDE KERKEN : DIE KERKEBODE – 1853-1992 (incomplete) – 136r – 1 – ATLA S0125 – us A.T.L.A. [240]

VEREENINGE (BROEDERLICKE) VAN SOMMIGHE KINDEREN GODS / Satler, Michiel – 1565. BME-68 1 – 9 – ne IDC [240]

VEREENINGE (BROEDERLICKE) VAN SOMMIGHE KINDEREN GODS, AENGAENDE SEUEN ARTICULEN. ITEM EENEN SENDBRIEF VAN MIECHIEL SATLER – 1560. BME-67 1 – 9 – ne IDC [240]

DIE VEREHRUNG DER HEILIGEN UND IHRER RELIQUIEN IN DEUTSCHLAND BIS ZUM BEGINNE DES 13. JAHRHUNDERTS / Beissel, Stephan – Freiburg im Breisgau, St. Louis, Mo.: Herder, 1890 – 1mf – us A.T.L.A. [240]

DIE VEREHRUNG DER HEILIGEN UND IHRER RELIQUIEN IN DEUTSCHLAND WAEHREND DER ZWEITEN HAELFTE DES MITTELALTERS / Beissel, Stephan – Freiburg im Breisgau, St. Louis, Mo.: Herder, 1892 – 1mf – us A.T.L.A. [240]

Verein Deutscher Ingenieure. Berlin *see* ZEITSCHRIFT

Verein fuer Geschichte der Deutschen in Boehmen. Prague *see* JAHRBUCH

Verein fuer Geschichte der Duetschen in Boehmen *see* MITTEILUNGEN

Verein fuer Geschichte der Stadt Nuernberg *see*
- JAHRESBERICHT
- MITTEILUNGEN

Verein fuer Geschichte und Altertum Schlesien *see* CODEX DIPLOMATICUS SILESIAE

Verein fuer hansische Geschichte *see*
- HANSERECESSE

Verein fuer Hessische Geschichte und Landeskunde *see* ZEITSCHRIFT DES VEREINES FUER HESSISCHE GESCHICHTE UND LANDESKUNDE

Verein fuer Naturkunde in OEsterreich, Ob der Enns, Linz *see* JAHRESBERICHT

Verein fuer Niederdeutsche Sprachforschung *see* KORRESPONDENZBLATT DES VEREINS FUER NIEDERDEUTSCHE SPRACHFORSCHUNG

Verein fuer Thueringische Geschichte und Altertumskunde *see* ZEITSCHRIFT

Verein ostdeutscher Holzhaendler und Saegewerke. Berlin *see* BERICHT UEBER DIE 32. ORDENTLICHE HAUPTVERSAMMLUNG....MITTWOCH. 6 OCT 1926. 68P. ILLUS. (SERIAL PUBLICATIONS OF GERMAN TRADE UNIONS IN THE MEMORIAL LIBRARY, UNIVERSITY OF WISCONSIN-MADISON.)

Verein zur Abwehr des Antisemitismus *see* ABWEHR-BLAETTER

Verein zur Gruendung und Erhaltung einer Akademie fuer die Wissenschaft des Judenthums *see* KORRESPONDENZBLATT

VEREINBARUNGEN UEBER DEN GERICHTSSTAND IM INTERNATIONALEN RECHTSVERKEHR / Berliner, M W – Muenchen, 1936 – 2mf – 9 – ILM-2233/1 – ne IDC [327]

VEREINBARUNGEN UEBER DEN GERICHTSSTAND IM INTERNATIONALEN RECHTSVERKEHR / Berliner, M W – Muenchen, 1936 – 2mf – 9 – ILM-2013/1 – ne IDC [327]

VEREINIGTER DEUTSCHER REDNER UND RHEINISCH-WESTPHAELISCHER COURIER – Bochum, 1850 (incomplete) – 1 – Inquire at Mikrofilmarchiv for details – gw Misc Inst [943]

DIE VEREINIGUNG CHRISTLICHER KIRCHEN : EINE VON DER HAAGER GESELLSCHAFT ZUR VERTHEIDIGUNG DER CHRISTLICHEN RELIGION GEKROENTE PREISSCHRIFT / Joss, Gottlieb – Leiden: E.J. Brill, 1877 – 1mf – us A.T.L.A. [240]

Vereinigung der deutschen Arbeitgeberverbaende *see* GESCHAEFTSBERICHT

Vereinigung deutscher Auslandsbeamten *see* NACHRICHTENBLATT

VEREINSAMTES HERZ / Weinheber, Josef – Leipzig: P List, 1935 – 1 – us U.W. Library [810]

Vereiskii, N G *see* O RUKOPISIAKH PO GEOLOGII I GEOMORFOLOGII, KHRANIASHCHIKHSIA V ARKHIVE GOSUDARSTVENNOGO GEOGRAFICHESKOGO OBSHCHESTVA

Verekha, P *see* LITERATURA RUSSKAGO LESOVODSTVA

Verelius, O *see* INDEX LINGUAE VETERIS SCYTHO-SCANDICAE SIVE GOTHICAE...

Vereshchagin, V A *see*
- RUSSKAIA I INOSTRANNAIA KNIGA 15-19 VEKA
- RUSSKII KNIZHNYI ZNAK
- RUSSKIIA ILLIUSTRIROVANNYIA IZDANIIA 18 I 19 STOLETII (1720-1870)

VERESK / Ivanov, G – Vtoraia kniga stikhov. Ed. 2. Berlin. 1923. BR-1188 2 – 8 – ne IDC [460]

VERESK / Ivanov, G – Vtoraia kniga stikhov. Petrograd. 1916. BR-1187 2 – 8 – ne IDC [460]

Veret, Jeanne-Desiree *see* LETTRE AU ROI, ECRITE SOUS L'IMPRESSION DES EVENEMENTS DES 5 ET 6 JUIN 1832

DIE VERFASSUNG DER HESSEN-DARMSTAEDTISCHEN LANDSTAENDE AM AUSGANG DES 18. JAHRHUNDERTS / Hermann, Fritz H – 1995 – 1mf – 9 – DM48.00 – 3-8267-3166-2 – gw Hänsel [340]

DIE VERFASSUNG UND VERWALTUNG DES ROEMISCHEN STAATES / Madvlg, Johan Nicolai – Dargestellt von dr. J. N. Madvig. Leipzig, B. G. Teubner, 1881-82. 2 v. Film Mas 9121 – 1 – us H.U. Library [930]

VERFASSUNGSGESCHICHTE DER DEUTSCHEN KIRCHE IM MITTELALTER / Werminghoff, Albert – Leipzig: B.G. Teubner, 1913 – 1mf – us A.T.L.A. [240]

DAS VERFASSUNGSRECHT DER BENEDIKTINISCHEN MOENKSKONGREGATION / Dammertz, V – St. Ottilien, 1963 – 4mf – 8 – Dfl19.00 – ne Slangenburg [240]

DIE VERFASSUNGSTHEORIE KARL V. ROTTECKS / Herdt, Ursula – Heidelberg, 1967 – 4mf – 9 – DM90.00 – 3-89349-398-0 – gw Hänsel [320]

EIN VERFEHLTES LEBEN : PREIS-NOVELLE / Siemering, A – San Antonio: Freie Presse, 1876 – 1r – 1 – us U.W. Library [830]

DIE VERFLUCHUNGEN UND BESCHIMPFUNGEN DES HERRN CHRISTUS UND DER CHRISTEN DURCH DIE PAEPSTE, BISCHOEFE UND PRIESTER DER ROEMISCHEN KRICHE UND DIE PFLICHT JEDES CHRISTEN DIESEN VERSUCHUNGEN GEGENUEBER / Grassmann, Robert – Stettin, 1895 – 2mf –

9 – DM62.00 – 3-89349-321-2 – gw Hänsel [240]

VERFOLGER DER BOSHEIT – Koeln, Germany. 1848-16 Mar 1850 – 1 – gw Mikrofilm [072]

VERFOLGER DES BOSHEIT – Koeln. nos 31-45. 1849-1850 – 1r – 1 – DM80.00 – gw Mikro Press [072]

VERGANGENHEIT UND GEGENWART IN EINS : FESTWORT ZUR FEIER VON GOETHES GEBURTSTAG AM 27. AUGUST 1938 IM ROEMER ZU FRANKFURT AM MAIN / Koch, Franz – Halle a. d. Saale: M Niemeyer, 1939 – 1r – 1 – us U.W. Library [430]

Vergara Cabezas, F *see* APOLOGIA DE LOS BANOS DE LA MUY NOBLE Y LEAL CIUDAD DE ALHAMA

Vergara y Velasco, Francisco J *see* NUEVA GEOGRAFICA DE COLOMBIA

Verge, Ch. *see* DIPLOMATES ET PUBLICISTES

VERGEBLICHER FISCHZUG : ERLEBNISSE UND BEGEGNUNGEN / Alverdes, Paul – Muenchen: A Langen, G Mueller, 1942, c1937 – 1r – 1 – us U.W. Library [943]

Verger, Francois-J *see* ARCHIVES CURIEUSES DE LA VILLE DE NANTES ET DES DEPARTEMENTS DE L'OUE..

LE VERGER, LE POTAGER ET LE PARTERRE DANS LA PROVINCE DE QUEBEC OU CULTURE RAISONNEE DES FRUITS. / Provancher, Leon A – 3rd ed. Quebec: C Darveau, 1885. SEM105P88 – 4mf – 9 – Can$9.00 – cn Bibl Nat [631]

Verger, Pierre *see* FIESTAS Y DANZAS EN EL CUZCO Y EN LOS ANDES

Vergerii, P P et al *see* OPUSCULA 36/SONETTI E POESIE ITALIANE DI VARI AUTORI

Vergerio, Pietro Paolo *see*
- LE CONSEIL DE TROIS EVESQUES SUR LA DETERMINATION DU CONCILE GENERAL DE TRENTE
- CONSILIUM QUORUNDAM EPISCOPORUM BONONIAE CONGREGATORUM

EIN VERGESSENER FUEHRER AUS DER RHEINISCHEN GEISTESGESCHICHTE DES NEUNZEHNTEN JAHRHUNDERTS, JOHANN WILHELM JOSEPH BRAUN (1801-1863) : PROFESSOR DER THEOLOGIE IN BONN / Schroers, Heinrich – Bonn, Leipzig, 1925 – xvi/614p – 9 – DM98.00 – 3-89349-108-2 – gw Hänsel [240]

Vergil *see*
- BUCOLICA ET GEORGICA
- OPERA

VERGILBTE BLAETTER AUS DER GRAUEN STADT / Storm, Gertrud – Regensburg: Habbel & Naumann, 1922 – 1r – 1 – us U.W. Library [910]

VERGISSMEINNICHT / Schreiber, F – St. Louis, MO: "Amerika", 1902 – 1r – 1 – us U.W. Library [810]

DER VERGLEICH BEI GOETHE UNTER BESONDERER BERUECKSICHTIGUNG DER VERGLEICHENDEN LITERATURKRITIK / Cornu, Charles – Bern, 1952 – 2mf – DM62.00 – 3-8267-3055-0 – gw Hänsel [430]

EIN VERGLEICH DER BUCH- UND FILMFASSUNGEN VON SHAFFERS EQUUS UND AMADEUS / Drobnitzky, Bettina – 1991 – 80p – 9 – DM98.00 – 3-89349-428-6 – gw Hänsel [430]

VERGLEICH DER GASTRALEN SAEURESEKRETION BEI DIABETIKERN MIT UND OHNE AUTONOME NEUROPATHIE / Butzlaff, Martin E – 1995 – 1mf – 9 – DM60.00 – 3-8267-2134-9 – gw Hänsel [616]

VERGLEICH DEUTSCHER SONDERSTRAFNORMEN MIT DEN ENTSPRECHENDEN OESTERREICHISCHEN BESTIMMUNGEN / Griesheimer, Friedrich – 1995 – 1mf – 9 – DM48.00 – 3-8267-3181-6 – gw Hänsel [340]

VERGLEICH ZWISCHEN DEM ENGLISCHEN UND DEUTSCHEN WECHSELRECHT...1927 / Goeringer, H – N.p., n.d. – 1mf – 1 – ILM-3464/1 – ne IDC [327]

VERGLEICHENDE ANALYSE DER FERNSEHSPORTBERICHTERSTATTUNG DER ARD AUS DER SICHT VON KOMMUNIKATOREN UND REZIPIENTEN / Boll, Stefan – 1994 – 2mf – DM80.00 – 3-8267-2051-2 – gw Hänsel [302]

VERGLEICHENDE ANALYTISCHE STUDIE ZWISCHEN DER NATUERLICHEN UND DER EINGESTELLTEN KOPFHALTUNG NACH AESTHETISCH-METRISCHEN FAKTOREN ZUR BESTIMMUNG EINES HARMONISCHEN PROFILS / Schmidt, Ambrosius – 1995 – 2mf – 9 – DM80.00 – 3-8267-2257-4 – gw Hänsel [611]

VERGLEICHENDE ANATOMIE UND PHYSIOLOGIE DER INSECTEN IN MONOGRAPHIEN BEARBEITET : ERSTE MONOGRAPHIE. DIE WEIBLICHEN GESCHLECHTSORGANE DER KAEFER / Stein, S F N von – Berlin, 1847 – VIII, 139p, 9pls – 8 – ne IDC [590]

VERGLEICHENDE DARSTELLUNGEN DER GOTTESLEHREN VON SPINOZA UND MALEBRANCHE / Uhlich, Rudolph – Doebeln, 1903 – 9 – DM48.00 – 3-89349-273-9 – gw Hänsel [190]

VERGLEICHENDE GRAMMATIK DER SLAVISCHEN SPRACHEN / Miklosich, F – 2nd ed. 4v. Vienna, 1875-83. BR-4987 2 – 8 – ne IDC [460]

VERGLEICHENDE MORPHOLOGIE DER PILZE / Tavel, F von – Jena, 1892. 208 pp., pls. B-6320 1 – 9 – ne IDC [580]

VERGLEICHENDE RELIGIONSWISSENSCHAFT UND INSPIRATION DER HEILIGEN SCHRIFT / Kessler, Lina – (Includes bibliographical references) – Goettingen: Vandenhoeck & Ruprecht, 1905 – 1mf – 9 – 0-8370-3894-4 – 1985-1894 – us A.T.L.A. [220]

VERGLEICHENDE STUDIE ZWEIER UNTERSCHIEDLICHER LAKTATMESSMETHODEN / Mutschler, Harry – 1994 – 1mf – DM60.00 – 3-8267-2069-5 – gw Hänsel [790]

VERGLEICHENDE UNTERSUCHUNGEN DER EXTRAZELLULAEREN KOHLEHYDRAT-KOMPONENTEN VON NOSTOC PUNCITFORME UND NOSTOC MUSCORUM / Meyer, Timothy A – 1995 – 1mf – 9 – DM60.00 – 3-8267-2195-0 – gw Hänsel [574]

VERGLEICHENDE UNTERSUCHUNGEN DER KEIMUNG, ENTFALTUNG UND FRUCHTBILDUNG HOEHEREN KRYPTOGAMEN / Hofmeister, W F B – Leipzig. 1851. B-7100 2 – 8 – ne IDC [580]

VERGLEICHENDE UNTERSUCHUNGEN UEBER STABILITAET UND SUBSTITUTIONSVERHALTEN TUMORHEMMENDER RUTHENIUM(III)KOMPLEXE IN PHYSIOLOGISCHEM BLUTPUFFER / Hartmann, Markus – 1995 – 1mf – 9 – DM60.00 – 3-8267-2271-X – gw Hänsel [540]

VERGLEICHENDES INDOGERMANISCH-SEMITISCHES WOERTERBUCH / Moeller, Hermann – Goettingen: Vandenhoeck & Ruprecht, 1911 – 1mf – 9 – 0-8370-8460-1 – 1986-2460 – us A.T.L.A. [040]

Vergnes, Jacques P *see* MEMOIRE SUR LA STATISTIQUE DU DEPARTEMENT DE LA HAUTE-SAONE

Vergote, J *see* JOSEPH EN EGYPTE

DAS VERHAELTNIS AESTHETIK ZUR ETHIK BEI SCHILLER / Heine, Gerhard – 1995 – 1mf – 9 – DM48.00 – 3-8267-3125-5 – gw Hänsel [110]

DAS VERHAELTNIS DER CHRISTLICHEN GLAUBENSLEHRE ZU...AKADEMISCHER WISSENSCHAFT / Schmidt, Hermann – Gotha: F.A. Perthes, 1881. 1 fiche – 9 – us A.T.L.A. [240]

DAS VERHAELTNIS DER ETHIK THOMAS HILL GREENS ZU DERJENIGEN KANTS / Guenther, Oskar – Dresden, 1915 – 1mf – 9 – DM48.00 – 3-89349-298-4 – gw Hänsel [170]

DAS VERHAELTNIS DER ROEMISCHEN KIRCHE ZU DEN KLEINASIATISCHEN VOR DEM NICAENISCHEN KONZIL / Berendts, Alexander – Leipzig: A. Deichert, 1898. (Studien zur Geschichte der Theologie und der Kirche; 1. Bd., Heft 3) – 1mf – us A.T.L.A. [240]

DAS VERHAELTNIS DES DEUTERONOMIUMS ZU 2. KOEN: 22., 23., UND ZU PROPHETIE JEREMIA / Boetticher, Otto – 1906 – 1 – us A.T.L.A. [240]

DAS VERHAELTNIS DES EVANGELISCHEN GLAUBENS ZUR LOGOSLEHRE : VORTRAG / Kaftan, Julius – Freiburg i. B: J C B Mohr (Paul Siebeck), 1896 – 1mf – 9 – 0-8370-4613-0 – 1985-2613 – us A.T.L.A. [240]

DAS VERHAELTNIS DES STAATES ZUR KIRCHE NACH HUMANISTISCHER ANSCHAUUNG VERNEHMLICH BEI ERASMUS / Maurer, Wilhelm – 1930. 32p – 1 – us U.W. Library [320]

DAS VERHAELTNIS VON RELIGION UND SITTLICHKEIT IN DER AUFFASSUNG DES JUENGEREN SCHLEIERMACHER / Simon, Karl-Theodor – 1993 – 1mf – 9 – DM48.00 – 3-89349-272-0 – gw Hänsel [200]

DAS VERHAELTNIS VON THEOLOGIE UND ERKENNTNISTHEORIE / Steinbeck, Johannes – Leipzig: Doerffling & Franke, 1898. 1 fiche – 9 – us A.T.L.A. [240]

VERHAELTNISS ALBERT DES GROSSEN ZU MOSES MAIMONIDES / Joel, M – Breslau. 1863. BJ-33-35 1 – 9 – ne IDC [180]

DAS VERHAELTNISS DER MASSORA ZUR SEPTUAGINTA IM JEREMIA / Kuehl, Ernst – (Includes bibliographical references) – Halle: [s.n.], 1882 – 1mf – 9 – 0-8370-7472-X – 1986-1472 – us A.T.L.A. [220]

DAS VERHAELTNISS DES CHRISTENTHUMS ZU CULTUR- UND LEBENSFRAGEN DER GEGENWART / Harless, Adolf von – Erlangen: Theodor Blaesing, 1866. 1 fiche – 9 – us A.T.L.A. [240]

DAS VERHAELTNISS DES JAKOBUS, BRUDER DES HERRN, ZU JAKOBUS ALPHAEI / Schaf, Philipp – Berlin: A. Wohlgemuth, 1842 – 1mf – us A.T.L.A. [240]

DAS VERHAELTNISS DES THOMAS VON AQUINO ZUM JUDENTHUM UND ZUR JUEDISCHEN LITTERATUR / Guttmann, J – Goettingen. 1891. BJ-33-36 1 – 9 – ne IDC [240]

DIE VERHAENGNISVOLLE FASCHINGSNACHT : POSSE MIT GESANG IN DREI AUFZUEGEN / Nestroy, Johann – Wien: C Daberkow, [1895?] – 1r – 1 – us U.W. Library [790]

DAS VERHALTEN DER TELISCHEN VERBEN IN DEN ROMANISCHEN SPRACHEN EROERTERT AN DER INTERFERENZ VON ASPEKT UND AKTIONSART / Klein, Horst G – 1994 – 3mf – DM76.00 – 3-89349-995-4 – gw Hänsel [440]

VERHANDELING OVER DE BROEDERSCHAP VAN G. GROOTE EN OVER DEN INVLOED DER FRATERHUIZEN / Delprat, G H M – Arnhem, 1856 – 7mf – 8 – Dfl28.00 – ne Slangenburg [240]

VERHANDELINGEN / Bataafsch Genootschap der Proefondervindelijke Wijsbegeerte. Rotterdam – 1774-98 – 3 – us Readex [100]

VERHANDELINGEN / Teyler's tweede genootschap, Haarlem – Haarlem, 1781-1866 – 3 – us Readex [949]

VERHANDELINGEN OVER DE NATUURLIJKE GESCHIEDENIS DER NEDERLANDSCHE OVERZEESCHE BEZITTINGEN,... / Korthals, PW & Temminck, C J – Leiden, 1839-1842[-1844] – 23mf – 9 – ne IDC [943]

VERHANDELINGEN UITG. DOOR HET ZEEUWSCH GENOOTSCHAP DER WETENSCHAPPEN TE VLISSINGEN / Zeeuwsch genootschap der wetenschappen, Middelburg – Middelburg. 1769-92 – 3 – us Readex [500]

VERHANDELINGEN VAN HET BATAVIAASCH GENOOTSCHAP DER KONSTEN EN WEETENSCHAPPEN – Ed 2. 1781-1825. v1-9 – 73mf – 9 – SE-17A/2 – ne IDC [950]

VERHANDELINGEN VAN HET BATAVIAASCH GENOOTSCHAP DER KONSTEN EN WETENSCHAPPEN – Batavia, 1779-1950.- v1-79. Index 1779-1940 – 1,041mf – 9 – SE-17/2 – ne IDC [950]

VERHANDELINGEN VAN HET BATAVIAASCH GENOOTSCHAP VAN KUNSTEN EN WETENSCHAPPEN – Ed3: v3. 1824 – 7mf – 9 – SE-17B/2 – ne IDC [700]

VERHANDELINGEN VAN HET KONINKLIJK INSTITUUT VOOR TAAL-, LAND- EN VOLKENKUNDE / Netherlands – (All other volumes available in print) – v1-64. Leiden. 1938-73. Available: 1940-48, v3-7; 1952, 11, 14, 24, 26, 38. 1963, v40. BSE-12,104/P – 38mf – 9 – ne IDC [949]

VERHANDELINGEN VAN HET PROVINCIAAL UTRECHTSCH GENOOTSCHAP VAN KUNSTEN EN WETENSCHAPPEN / Provinciaal Utrechts genootschap van kunsten en wetenschappen – Utrecht, 1781-1821 – 3 – us Readex [500]

VERHANDLUNGEN / Evangelische Kirche von Westfalen – 1946-78.Lacks a few scattered pages. 8 reels – 1 – us A.T.L.A. [073]

VERHANDLUNGEN / Historischer Verein. Niederbayern – Landshut. Bd. 15-74; 1870-1941. Film Mas C 322 – 1 – us H.U. Library [073]

VERHANDLUNGEN / Historischer Verein. Oberpfalz and Regensburg – Regensburg. v27-76 1871-1926. Film Mas C 360 – 1 – us H.U. Library [943]

VERHANDLUNGEN / Salzburg. Landtag – 1864-1936 37. Few scattered issues wanting – 1 – 900.00 – us L of C Photodup [943]

VERHANDLUNGEN / Sozialdemokratische Arbeiterpartei Deutschoesterreichs – Protokoll des Parteitages. Vienna. 1888 1889-1926. Incomplete – 1 – us NY Public [335]

VERHANDLUNGEN DER KAISERLICH-KOENIGLICHEN ZOOLOGISCH-BOTANISCHEN GESELLSCHAFT WIEN *see* VERHANDLUNGEN DES ZOOLOGISCH-BOTANISCHEN VEREINS IN WIEN

VERHANDLUNGEN DER KAMMER DER ABGEORDNETEN DES BAYERISCHEN LANDTAGES : STENOGRAPHISCHE BERICHTE – no1 May 1866-no86 Feb 1871 – 4r – DM300.00 – gw Mikro Press [324]

VERHANDLUNGEN DER KAMMER DER REICHSRAETHE DES KOENIGREICHES BAYERN – no1 23 May 1866-no23 17 Feb 1871 – 3r – DM225.00 – gw Mikro Press [324]

VERHANDLUNGEN DER KONFERENZ.. / Deutscher Holzarbeiter-Verband. Berlin – v1. 1914. Only 1st conference proceedings published. (Serial publications of German trade unions in the Memorial Library, University of Wisconsin-Madison.) – 1 – us U.W. Library [330]

VERHANDLUNGEN DER LANDESSYNODE DER EVANGELISCHEN LANDESKIRCHE IN BADEN / Evangelische Landeskirche in Baden – 1948-92 (complete) – Inquire – 1 – ATLA S0389 – us A.T.L.A. [073]

VERHANDLUNGEN DER VERFASSUNGGEBENDEN LANDESVERSAMMLUNG...BELIAGEN – Stuttgart. 1919-33. 7 reels – 1 – 23.00r – us L of C Photodup [943]

VERHANDLUNGEN DER VERFASSUNGGEBENDEN LANDESVERSAMMLUNG...PROTOKOLLE / Wuerttemberg. Landtag – Stuttgart. 1919-33. 11 reels – 1 – 23.00r – us L of C Photodup [943]

VERHANDLUNGEN DER VERFASSUNGGEBENDEN LANDESVERSAMMLUNG...REGISTER / Wuerttemberg. Landtag – Stuttgart. 1919-33. 1 reel – 1 – 23.00r – us L of C Photodup [943]

VERHANDLUNGEN DER ZOOLOGISCH-BOTANISCHEN GESELLSCHAFT IN WIEN *see* VERHANDLUNGEN DES ZOOLOGISCH-BOTANISCHEN VEREINS IN WIEN

VERHANDLUNGEN DES BOTANISCHEN VEREINS FUER DIE PROVINZ BRANDENBURG UND DIE ANGRENZENDEN LAENDER – Hannover, Berlin. v1-81. 1859-1941 – 400mf – 9 – 5599c/2 – ne IDC [580]

VERHANDLUNGEN DES DEUTSCHEN BUNDESRATES, 1949-1995 / Germany. Federal Republic. Bundesrat – (1st Session: 1949-53 128mf diazo DM3,500 silver DM3,850. 2nd Session: 1954-57 111mf diazo DM3,050 silver DM3,360. 3rd Session: 1958-61 91mf diazo DM2,550 silver DM2,810. 4th Session: 1962-65 100mf diazo DM2,750 silver DM3,030. 5th Session: 1966-69 120mf diazo DM3,250 silver DM3,575. 6th Session: 1970-72 122mf diazo DM3,350 silver DM3,685. 7th Session: 1973-76 187 mf diazo DM2,900 silver DM3,190. 8th Session: 1977- 1980 177mf diazo DM3,000 silver DM3,300. 9th Session: 1981-82 97mf DM1,988.50 silver DM2,190; 10th Session: 1983-86 185mf and Konkordanzliste diazo DM4,161.50 silver DM4,600; 11th Session: 1987-1990 250mf and Konkordanzliste diazo DM5,375 silver DM5,800. 12th Session: 1991-1994 334mf diazo DM6,630 ISBN 3-598-31949-5 silver DM7,300 ISBN 3-598-30873-6) – 1st-12th Sessions. 1949-95. Printed indexes. Available by Session – 9 – Co-publ with C.H. Beck, Munich – gw Saur [943]

VERHANDLUNGEN DES DEUTSCHEN BUNDESTAGES, 1949-1995 / Germany. Federal Republic. Bundestag – (1st Session: 1949-53 91mf diazo DM2,450 silver DM2,700. 2nd Session: 1953-57 113mf diazo DM2,950 silver DM3,250. 3rd Session: 1957-61 96 mf diazo DM2,550 silver DM2,810. 4th Session: 1961-65 112mf diazo DM2,950 silver DM3,250. 5th Session: 1965-69 153mf diazo DM3,900 silver DM4,290. 6th Session: 1969-72 148mf diazo DM3,800 silver DM4,180. 7th Session: 1972- 76 248 mf diazo DM3,750 silver DM4,840. 8th Session: 1976-80 196mf diazo DM3,450 silver DM3,850. 9th Session: 1980-83 115mf diazo DM2,357.50 silver

DM2,600. 10th Session 1983-87 240mf and Konkordanzliste diazo DM5,289 silver DM5,850. 11th Session: 1987-91 316mf and Konkordanzliste diazo DM6,794 silver DM7,200. 12th Session 1991-94 385mf diazo DM7,624.50 ISBN 3-598-31929-0 silver DM8,800 ISBN 3-598-30872-8) – 1st-12th Sessions. 1949-95. Printed indexes. Available by Session – 9 – Co-publ with C.H. Beck, Munich – gw Saur [943]

VERHANDLUNGEN DES NATURHISTORISCHEN VEREINES DER PREUSSISCHEN RHEINLANDE – Bonn. v1-88. 1844-1932 – 434mf – 9 – 8632/1 – ne IDC [500]

DIE VERHANDLUNGEN DES ORDENTLICHEN.. / Verband der deutschen Gewerkvereine (Hirsch-Duncker) – Berlin. v1,13,15. 1871-1904. (Serial publications of German trade unions in the Memorial Library, University of Wisconsin-Madison.) – 1 – us U.W. Library [330]

VERHANDLUNGEN DES VEREINS ZUR BEFOERDERUNG DES GARTENBAUES... – Berlin. 21v. 1824-53. Register – 100mf – 9 – 8594/1 – ne IDC [630]

VERHANDLUNGEN DES VEREINS ZUR BEFOERDERUNG DES GARTENBAUES... – N.S. Berlin. 7v. 1853-59 – 34mf – 9 – 8595/1 – ne IDC [630]

VERHANDLUNGEN DES ZOOLOGISCH-BOTANISCHEN VEREINS IN WIEN – (Cont. as: Verhandlungen der kaiserlich-koeniglichen zoologisch-botanischen Gesellschaft in Wien. Wien, 1858-1915. v8-67. Cont. as: Verhandlungen der zoologisch-botanischen Gesellschaft in Wien. Wien, 1918-1941. v68-91. Index 1851-1890) – Wien. v1-7. 1852-57 – 1153mf – 9 – Z-304c/2 – ne IDC [590]

VERHANDLUNGEN. LEGISLATURPERIODE / Germany. Reichstag – 1871-1918 – 1 – $3,455.00 – us L of C Photodup [943]

DIE VERHANDLUNGEN PIUS 4. MIT DEN KATHOLISCHEN MAECHTEN UEBER DIE NEUBERUFUNG DES TRIDENTINER CONCILS IM JAHRE 1560 BIS ZUM ERLASS DER INDIKTIONSBULLE VOM 29. NOV. DESSELBEN JAHRES : HISTORISCHE ABHANDLUNG / Voss, Wilhelm – (Includes bibliographical references) – Leipzig: Hesse & Becker, 1887 – 1mf – 9 – 0-8370-8630-2 – 1986-2630 – us A.T.L.A. [240]

DIE VERHANDLUNGEN PIUS 4. MIT DEN KATHOLISCHEN MAECHTEN UEBER DIE NEUBERUFUNG DES TRIDENTINER CONCILS IM JAHRE 1560 BIS ZUM ERLASS DER JURISDIKTIONSBULLE VOM 29. NOV. DESSELBEN JAHRES : HISTORISCHE ABHANDLUNG / Voss, Wilhelm – Leipzig, 1887 – 2mf – 9 – DM62.00 – 3-89349-344-1 – gw Hänsel [240]

DIE VERHANDLUNGEN SCHWEDENS UND SEINER VERBUENDETEN MIT WALLENSTEIN UND DEM KAISER VON 1631 BIS 1634 / Irmer, G – Leipzig. 3v. 1888-1891 – 18mf – 9 – ne IDC [943]

VERHANDLUNGEN. STENOGRAPHISCHE / Germany. Reichstag – 1-13. 1871-1918 – 1 – $4,301.00 – us L of C Photodup [324]

VERHANDLUNGEN, STENOGRAPHISCHE BERICHTE / Germany. Federal Republic. Bundestag – Anlagen zu den Stenographischen Berichten. 1949-70 – 1 – 1932.00 – us L of C Photodup [943]

VERHANDLUNGEN ZWISCHEN SENAT UND BURGERSCHAFT / Hamburg – Hamburg.1860-1933. Indexes, 1859-1920. 53 reels – 1 – 23.00r – us L of C Photodup [943]

VERHANDLUNGEN...AM 6 UND 7 OCTOBER 1872 / Eisenacher Versammlung zur Besprechung der Socialen Frage, (1872) – Leipzig, 1873. 267p – 1 – us U.W. Library [943]

VERHANDLUNGEN...BEILAGEN / Wuerttemberg. Landstande. Kammer des abgeordneten – Stuttgart. 1856-1918. 50 reels – 1 – 23.00r – us L of C Photodup [943]

VERHANDLUNGEN...PROTOKOLLE / Wuerttemberg. Landstande. Kammer der Abgeordneten – Stuttgart. 1856-1918. 42 reels – 1 – 23.00r – us L of C Photodup [943]

VERHANDLUNGSBERICHT DER KONFERENZ.. / Deutscher Textilarbeiter-Verband – Berlin. v2. 1918. (Serial publications of German trade unions in the Memorial Library, University of Wisconsin-Madison.) – 1 – us U.W. Library [330]

VERHANDLUNGSBERICHT UEBER DEN VERBANDSTAG / Zentralverband der Landarbeiter – v3. 1926. Berlin. (Serial publications of German trade unions in the Memorial Library, University of Wisconsin-Madison.) – 1 – us U.W. Library [330]

VERHANDLUNGSBERICHT UEBER DIE REICHSKONFERENZ DER BURSTEN- UND PINSELMACHER / Deutscher Holzarbeiter-Verband. Berlin – 1913. (Serial publications of German trade unions in the Memorial Library, University of Wisconsin-Madison.) – 1 – us U.W. Library [330]

VERHEIRATHET AUS RACHE : LUSTSPIEL IN 3 AKTEN – Berlin: A W Hayn's Erben, 1874 – 1r – 1 – us U.W. Library [820]

VERIDICUS CHRISTIANUS / David, J – Antwerpen, 1601 – 7mf – 9 – ne IDC [700]

VERIDIQUE...NOUVELLE HISTOIRE / Diaz del Castillo, Bernal – (1879 ed.1.50f; 9) – 1877 – 9 – 1.50f – sp Bibl Santa Ana [972]

Verill, D *see* MALTBY GENEALOGY MSS

Verino, U *see* DE ILLUSTRATIONE URBIS FLORENTIAE

Verissimo de Mattos, Jose *see* PARA E AMAZONAS; QUESTAO DE LIMITES

Verissimo Serano, Joaquin *see* ITINERARIOS DE EL REI D. SEBASTIAO...

LE VERITABLE AMI DES LOIS OU LES REPUBLICAINS A L'EPREUVE / Cizos, Duplessis De. (La Citoyenne Villeneuve) – (French Theatre Series). Paris. Barba. s.d – 9 – fr Hachette [820]

LA VERITABLE AUTEUR DE LA PEREGRINATIO SOLVIAE, LA VIERGE ESPAGNOLE ETHERIA / Ferotin, M – H-213 2. 1903 – 8 – ne IDC [450]

LA VERITABLE DEVOTION ENVERS LA SAINTE VIERGE / Crasset, J S J – Paris, 1679 – 13mf – 8 – ne Slangenburg [240]

VERITABLE DISCOVRS DE MEMORABLE VICTOIRE OBTENVE CONTRE LE TURCQ PAR LES CHRESTIENS LE 22. DE IUIN L'AN 1593 – Anvers, 1593 – 1mf – 9 – H-8209/1 – ne IDC [956]

LE VERITABLE GOUVERNEMENT DE L'ORDRE DE CISTEAUX / Meschet, D Louis – Paris, 1678 – 19mf – 8 – Dfl67.00 – ne Slangenburg [240]

LE VERITABLE PHILANTHROPE, OU L'ISLE DE LA PHILANTHROPIE, SUIVIE DE LA BONNE MERE, DE LA PROMENADE SOLITAIRE, DU SOMMEIL ET DE LA TOILETTE DE VENUS. PRECEDE D'ANECDOTES ET DE DETAILS PEU CONNUS SUR J. J. ROUSSEAU : AVEC UNE REFUTATION DE SON PRETENDU SUICIDE / Moutonnet de Clairfons, Julien-Jacques – (Utopias in the Enlightenment series). 1790 – 9 – fr Hachette [830]

VERITABLE RELATION DE L'EFFROYABLE MORT DE TROIS SORCIERS ET MAGICIENS, EXECUTES DANS LA VILLE DE BAZAS – Paris. 1637 – 9 – fr Hachette [360]

VERITABLE RELATION DES IUSTES PROCEDURES OBSERVEES AU FAICT DE LA POSSESSION DES URSULINES DE LOUDUN / Saint-Remi, Tranquille de – 1634 – 9 – fr Hachette [360]

LE VERITABLE VAUBAN, SE MONTRANT AU LIEU DU FAUX VAUBAN / Sturm, L – La Haya, 1709 – 5mf – 9 – sp Cultura [946]

LES VERITABLES MOTIFS DE LA CONVERSION DE L'ABBE DE LA TRAPPE... – 1685 – 4mf – 8 – Dfl19.00 – ne Slangenburg [240]

VERITABLES PRINCIPES DE LA GRAMMAIRE / Chesneau du Marsais, C – (Linguistics series). 1729 – 9 – fr Hachette [440]

LES VERITABLES REGLES DE L'ORTHOGRAPHE FRANCEZE / Lesclache, L de – 1668 – 9 – fr I.C.S. [440]

VERITAS – (Includes c.1: 1942-1949:March) – Buenos Aires: Departamento de Prensa Panamericana, 19uu – 1 – CSUXAJM0181-S – us Hoover Inst Photo [972]

VERITAS – (Includes c.1: v.29:no.269 1959:Feb., v.29:no.275 (1959:Aug.); v.32:no.305 1962:Feb., v.32:no.307 (1962:Apr.); v.33:no.323 1963:Aug.; v.34:no.334 1964:July-v.4) – Edicion argentina. Buenos Aires: Veritas Editorial, 1959- – 1 – CSUXADQ5674-S – us Hoover Inst Photo [972]

VERITAS – (Includes c.1: v.8:no.88 1963:Apr.30, v.8:no.92 (1963:Aug.30); v.9:no.99 1964:Mar.30; v.9:no.103 1964:July-v.9:no.107 (1964:Nov.)) – Edicion continental. Buenos Aires: Veritas Editorial, 195u – 1 – CSUXADQ5634-S – us Hoover Inst Photo [972]

VERITAS – (Includes c.1: v.9:no.100/101 1939:May; v.10:no.111/113 1940:Apr./May; v.10:no.119 1940:Nov.-v.11:no.124/125 (1941:May/June); v.11:no.129 1941:Sept.; v.11:no.13) – Buenos Aires: [s.n.], 1931 – 1 – CSUXADQ5681-S – us Hoover Inst Photo [073]

VERITAS – Manila. No.1-.20-26 Nov 1983-. -w.Chiefly in English – 1 – us U.W. Library [073]

VERITAS ARGENTINA – (Includes c.1: v.26:no.235 1956:Apr., v.27:no.249 (1957:June); v.28:no.262 1958:June-v.28:no.264 (1958:Sept.)) – Buenos Aires: [Veritas Editorial, 1956-1959?] – 1 – CSUXADQ5656-S – us Hoover Inst Photo [972]

Veritas, Armand *see* LE LUTIN

VERITAS. LA VIE CHRETIENNE RAISONNEE ET MEDITEE 4. LA MAISON PATERNELLE 1933 / Gerest, Regis – Madrid: Razon y Fe, 2v. 1934 – 1 – sp Bibl Santa Ana [920]

LA VERITE : BULLETIN D'ETUDE MENSUEL A L'USAGE DES PRESIDENTS, DIRECTEURS ET MEMBRES DE L'ASSOCIATION "LES JEUNES LAURENTIENS" – Montreal: l'Association, 1944-46. SEM16P340 – 1r – 5 – Can$9.00 – cn Bibl Nat [360]

LA VERITE – Guadeloupe. French West Indies.1890-1906 – 1 – us UMI [072]

LA VERITE – (Includes c.1: no.513(1958:Nov.15) – no.560(1973:Apr.)) – Paris: La Verite, 1958- – 4r – 1 – CSUXAMK7464-S – us Hoover Inst Photo [944]

LA VERITE – (Includes c.1: no.79(1945:Jan.21)-no.512(1958:Oct.2)) – Paris: La Verite, 1940- – 2r – 1 – CSUXAMK7442-S – us Hoover Inst Photo [944]

LA VERITE – Magog, Canada. 16 fev 1966-14 jun 1967 – 1r – 1 – Can$40.00 – cn Can Microfilming [072]

LA VERITE – Montreal, Canada. 1 aut-26 aut 1867 – 1r – 1 – Can$25.00 – cn Can Microfilming [072]

LA VERITE – Organe de l'opposition communiste. no. 1. aout 1929; no. 1-255. sept 1929-janv 1936. Le sous-titre varie. Elements repris par: La Verite. Organe theorique pour la construction de la 4e Internationale. Paris – 1 – fr A.C.R.P.P. [335]

LA VERITE – Organe de l'opposition communiste. Paris. France. -w. 15 Aug, 13 Sep 1929-29 Jan 1936; Jun 1938; 15 Mar, 5 May, 1 Jul, Aug 1939. (Imperfect). (3 reels) – 1 – uk British Libr Newspaper [072]

LA VERITE – Organe independant d'union franco-musulmane. Par la France, pour la France. Bougie. no. 1-2. dec 1934-janv 1935 – 1 – fr A.C.R.P.P. [073]

LA VERITE – Organe theorique communiste internationaliste (Bolchevik-Leniniste, pour la construction de la IVe Internationale). no. 1, 4-6. Suresnes. dec 1937-39 – 1 – fr A.C.R.P.P. [335]

LA VERITE – Ottawa, Ontario. 14 sep 1878 – 1r – 1 – Can$25.00 – cn Can Microfilming [072]

LA VERITE – Paris, France. Journal politique et quotidien. Red. en chef Ed. Portalis. 7 oct 1870-2 sept 1871 – 1 – fr A.C.R.P.P. [944]

LA VERITE – Paris, France. Journal quotidien democrate. Dir. Paul Meunier. no. 1-697. 11 dec 1917-10 nov 1919 – 1 – fr A.C.R.P.P. [944]

LA VERITE – Politique, religieuse, sociale. Dir. M. Balitout. Paris. 16 mai-dec 1893 – 1 – fr A.C.R.P.P. [073]

LA VERITE – puis MENSUEL TROTSKYSTE. no. 19-560. Paris. 1945-avr 1973 – 1 – fr A.C.R.P.P. [335]

LA VERITE : ULTRAMONTAIN / ed by Tardivel, Jules-Paul – Quebec, Canada. 14 jul 1881-16 jun 1923 – 11r – 1 – Can$55.00r – cn Can Microfilming [072]

LA VERITE – Woonsocket, RI. 31 mai 1928-v1 n26. 22 nov 1928 – 1r – 1 – Can$25.00 – cn Can Microfilming [071]

VERITE – Ottawa, mai 1963-jun 1963 – 1r – 1 – Can$25.00 – cn Can Microfilming [072]

LA VERITE DES TRAVAILLEURS – Mensuel. n.s. aout 1952. devenu: L' Internationale. n.s., no. 1. juin 1962. devenu: Quatrieme Internationale. no. 1. nov. 1965. Paris. aout 1952-juin 1968, juin 1970 (no. special) – 1 – fr A.C.R.P.P. [335]

LA VERITE SUR LA RUSSIE / Dolgoroukov – (Russia 19th Century series). 1860 – 9 – fr Hachette [947]

LA VERITE SUR L'EMPEREUR NICOLAS. HISTORIE INTIME DE SA VIE ET DE SON REGNE, PAR UN RUSSE / Sazonov, Nicolas Ivanovitch – (Russia 19th C. series). 1854 – 9 – fr Hachette [920]

LA VERITE SUR LES ENFANTS TROUVES / Brochard, Andre Theodore – Paris, E. Plon, 1876. 5 fiches. (Statistics Series: Medical Studies) – 9 – 12.00 – fr Bibl Nationale [310]

LA VERITE TOGOLAISE – Lome. Sep 1957-Feb 1966 gaps – 1 – 35.00r – us Hoover Inst Photo [072]

VERITES D'HIER? : LA THEOLOGIE TRADITIONELLE ET LES CRITIQUES CATHOLIQUES / Le Morin, Jean – (Includes bibliographical references and index) – Paris: E Nourry, 1906 – 1mf – 9 – 0-8370-8690-6 – 1986-2690 – us A.T.L.A. [240]

VERITY AND VALUE OF THE MIRACLES OF CHRIST / Cooper, Thomas – London: Hodder & Stoughton, 1882. 1 fiche – 9 – us A.T.L.A. [240]

DIE VERJAEHRUNGSEINREDE... / Treutler, A – Borna, Leipzig, 1909 – 1mf – 9 – ILM-3485/1 – ne IDC [327]

DE VERJARING IN HET INTERNATIONAAL PRIVAATRECHT / Asscher, B E – Amsterdam, 1884 – 1mf – 9 – ILM-2970/1 – ne IDC [340]

Verjus, A *see* LA VIE DE MONSIEUR LE NOBLETZ, PRESTRE ET MISSIONNAIRE DE BRETAGNE

VERKAUFSORGANISATIONEN VON UNTERNEHMUNGEN DER WESTDEUTSCHEN MASCHINENINDUSTRIE / Schmidt, Karl – Koeln, 1926 – 2mf – DM 62.00 – 3-8267-3065-8 – gw Hänsel [650]

VERKETTUNG VON DICHTER UND WERK BEI THOMAS HARDY / Bliemel, B – H-335 2. 1936 – 8 – ne IDC [420]

Verkindert, J *see* SOMMIGE BRIEUEN, TESTAMENTEN, ENDE BELIJDINGEN

DIE VERKLAERUNG JESU CHRISTI IN DER SEELE / Arnold, Gottfried – Aus den gewoehnlichen Sonn- und Festtags-Episteln auf dem Fuerstlichen Schlosse zu Allstedt gezeiget, nebst dessenkurtzen Anmerckungenueber die Passion.... 1721 – 1 – us A.T.L.A. [240]

VERKLAREND WOORDENBOEK DER WETENSCHAPPELIJKE NAMEN VAN DE IN NEDERLAND EN NEDERLANDSCH INDIE IN HET WILD GROEIENDE EN IN TUINEN EN PARKEN GEKWEEKTE VARENS EN HOGERE PLANTEN / Backer, C A – Groningen, Batavia, 1936 – 8mf – 9 – ne IDC [580]

VERKLARINGHE DER SCHEPPENISSEN AN V MIJN BEMINDE KINDEREN VNDE GHEBROEDERS / Joris, David – 1553. BME-368 1 – 9 – ne IDC [240]

DIE VERKNOECHERUNG DES OS INCISIVUM IM MENSCHLICHEN FETUS / Wallesch-Gladzinski, Doris – 1995 – 1mf – 9 – DM60.00 – 3-8267-2131-4 – gw Hänsel [618]

DIE VERKOMMENEN : BERLINER SITTEN-ROMAN / Kretzer, Max – 3. durchgesehene Aufl. Leipzig: F Luckhardt, 1900 – 1r – 1 – us U.W. Library [830]

DER VERKUENDIGER – (Title changes: Solinger Wochenblatt, 1 Jan 1822; Solinger Kreis-Intelligenz blatt, 9 Jan 1835; Solinger Tageblatt, 1 Oct 1912) – Solingen, Germany. 1992- – 8r per yr – 1 – gw Mikrofilm [072]

VERKUENDIGUNGS-BLATT – Freiburg, Germany. 1849 – 1 – gw Mikrofilm [072]

Verkuyl, Johannes *see*
- AKU PERTJAJA; SEBUAH URAIAN TENTANG INDJIL DAM SERUAN UNTUK PERTJAJA
- EENIGE MEDEDEELINGEN OVER DE KERKELIJKE ARBEID EN DE GEESTELIJKE STROOMINGEN IN DE BURGER-INTERNEERINGSKAMPEN IN INDIE
- ETIKA SEKSUIL
- FRAGMENTA APOLOGETIKA; KRITIK DAN DJAWAB
- TAFSIRAN-TAFSIRAN ALKITAB INDJIL JAHJA

Verlac, Bertrand *see* NOUVEAU PLAN D'EDUCATION POUR LES CLASSES DE CITOYENS

DER VERLAG VON MOHR UND ZIMMER IN HEIDELBERG UND DIE HEIDELBERGER ROMANTIK / Reichel, Otto – Muenchen, 1913 – 2mf – DM62.00 – 3-8267-3084-4 – gw Hänsel [430]

Verlaguet, P A *see*
- CARTULAIRE DE L'ABBAYE DE BONNEVAL EN ROUERGUE
- CARTULAIRE DE L'ABBAYE DE SILVANES

DIE VERLASSENEN / Bauernfeld, Eduard von – Wien: L Rosner, 1878 – 1 – us U.W. Library [820]

VERLEGUNG ETLICHER VNCHRISTLICHER ARTIKEL WELCHE DIE WIDERTEUFFER FURGEBEN / Melanchthon, Phil – Wittemberg, G. Rhaw. n.d. BME-100 1 – 9 – ne IDC [240]

VERLEGUNG ETLICHER VNCHRISTLICHER ARTIKEL WELCHE DIE WIDERTEUFFER FURGEBEN / Melanchthon, Phil – Wittemberg, G. Rhaw. n.d. BME-99 1 – 9 – ne IDC [240]

VERLEGUNG ETLICHER VNCHRISTLICHER ARTIKEL WELCHE DIE WIDERTEUFFER FURGEBEN / Melanchthon, Philip – Zwickaw, W. Meyerpeck. 1536. BME-101 1 – 9 – ne IDC [240]

VERLIEBTE ODERFAHRT / Sturm, Stefan – Breslau: Schlesien-Verlag, [194-?] – 1r – 1 – us U.W. Library [830]

VERLOBUNG UND HOCHZEIT : NACH DEN NORDGERMANISCHEN RECHTEN DES FRUEHEREN MITTELALTERS / Lehmann, Karl – (Includes bibliographical references) – Muenchen: C. Kaiser, 1882 – 1r – 1 – us U.W. Library [340]

DER VERLORENE KLANG : EINES GEIGENBAUERS GLUECK UND NOT / Schupp, Johannes Martin – 6. Aufl. Muenchen: F Eher, c1934 – 1r – 1 – us U.W. Library [830]

DER VERLORENE RING : NOVELLEN / Ulitz, Arnold – Breslau: Gauverlag-NS-Schlesien, 1941 – 1r – 1 – us U.W. Library [830]

Verlot, J B *see* CATALOGUE RAISONNE DES PLANTES VASCULAIRES DU DAUPHINE

VERMAAKLYK LUSTHOF VAN ZEDE – EN ZINNEBEELDEN WAAR IN VOORKOMEN LEERZAAME... / Berkenkamp, F – 1st ed. Amsterdam, 1768 – 3mf – 9 – ne IDC [700]

Vermeer, B *see*
- ARCHIVE OF THE FOURTH RUSSELL TRIBUNAL
- ON THE RIGHTS OF THE INDIANS OF THE AMERICAS

VERMEERDERDE ZEDE EN HARPGEZANGEN / Alewyn, A – (together with: Muncq, A. de. Eenzaame bezigheden) – Amsterdam, 1711 – 4mf – 9 – ne IDC [700]

Vermeersch, Arthur *see* LES DESTINEES DU CONGO BELGE

DIE VERMEIDBARKEIT DES VERBOTSIRRTUMS / Schneider, Werner – Bonn 1964 – 1 – DM30.00 – gw Mikro Press [943]

Vermeil, E *see* L'ALLEMAGNE CONTEMPORAINE 1919-1924. SA STRUCTURE ET SON EVOLUTION POLITIQUES

Vermeil, Edmond *see* JEAN-ADAM MOEHLER ET L'ECOLE CATHOLIQUE DE TUBINGUE, 1815-1840

VERMERCKT AIN VNNDERWEYSUNG. WIDER DIE SECT DER ZWYTAUFFER / Parfusser, A – 1535. BME-130 1 – 9 – ne IDC [240]

Vermeren, M F *see* DE LISTIGE ONSTANTVASTIGHEYT DES WERELTS

VERMERSCH-JOURNAL – London, UK. 17/18 Dec 1871-23 Mar 1872 – 1 – uk British Libr Newspaper [072]

VERMERSCH-JOURNAL – no. 1-82. Londres. 17 dec 1871-22 mars 1872 – 1 – fr A.C.R.P.P. [073]

VERMILION NEWS – Vermilion, CO. 1897-1964 – 25r – 1 – $32.50r – us Archival [071]

VERMILION PHOTOJOURNAL – Vermilion, Ohio.1961- – 19r – 1 – $32.50r – us Archival [071]

VERMILLION RIVER COUNTRY STAR – Alberta, CN. 1974-77 – 1r – 1 – cn Commonwealth Micro [072]

VERMILLION RIVER NEWS – Alberta, CN. 1961-63 – 1r – 1 – cn Commonwealth Micro [072]

VERMILLION SIGNAL – Alberta, CN. 1907-10 – 1r – 1 – cn Commonwealth Micro [072]

VERMILLION STANDARD – Alberta, CN. 1909-94 – 49r – 1 – cn Commonwealth Micro [072]

Vermilye, Elizabeth B *see* THE LIFE OF ALEXANDER DUFF

...VERMISCHTE MUSICALISHE CHORAL GEDANCKEN, NACH ANLEITUNG DERER GEWOEHNLICHSTEN EVANGELISCHEN KIRCHEN-GESAENGE AUF VERSCHEIDENTLICHE ART GOTT ZU EHREN UND ALLEN MUSIQUE-LIEBENDEN...ERSTE PROBE / Vogler, J K – Vinar: Excudit Jon. Martin Jauch, 1737 – 1 – us Sibley [780]

VERMISCHTE SCHRIFTEN / Maltitz, Gotthilf August, Freiherr von – Hamburg: Schuberth, [18–] – 1 – us U.W. Library [880]

VERMISCHTE SCHRIFTEN, UND, AMERIKANISCHE GEDICHTE / Spielhagen, Friedrich – Leipzig: L Staackmann, 1872 – 1 – us U.W. Library [800]

VERMISCHTE VORTRAEGE : UEBER KIRCHLICHES LEBEN DER VERGANGENHEIT UND DER GEGENWART / Uhlhorn, Gerhard – Stuttgart: Meyer & Zeller, 1875 – 1mf – us A.T.L.A. [240]

DIE VERMOEGENSRECHTLICHEN BEZIEHUNGEN DER EHEGATTEN NACH DEM RECHTE DES BAYERISCHEN STAMMES IN NEUERER ZEIT / Hofmann, Hans-Otto – 1994 – 2mf – 9 – DM62.00 – 3-8267-3007-0 – gw Hänsel [340]

VERMONT : SESSION LAWS OF AMERICAN STATES AND TERRITORIES – 1778-1995 – 9 – $997.50 – us Hein [340]

VERMONT : STATUTES ANNOTATED – (Includes latest pocket parts suppl) – Oxford: Equity Pub Co, 1958-Jun 1996 update – 9 – $698.00 set – us Hein [340]

Vermont *see*
- REPORTS AND OPINIONS (A-G)
- REPORTS, PRE-NRS

Vermont. Agricultural Experiment Station *see*
- AGRICULTURAL ECONOMIC RESEARCH MONOGRAPH
- ANNUAL REPORT AND BULLETIN
- PAMPHLET
- RESEARCH REPORT. 5. 1-69. 1951-69 (MISCELLANEOUS PUBLICATION)
- VERMONT FARM AND HOME SCIENCE

Vermont. Agricultural Extension Service *see*
- AGRICULTURAL TRENDS
- ANNUAL REPORT
- BRIEFLETS
- CIRCULAR
- DOLLARS AND DECISIONS
- GREEN MOUNTAIN DAIRYING
- GREEN MOUNTAIN GROWER
- THIS MONTH IN VERMONT EXTENSION
- VERMONT NATURAL RESOURCES FORUM

VERMONT ATTORNEY GENERAL REPORTS AND OPINIONS – (1975 not available) – 1904-1974 – 6 – $140.00set – us Hein [340]

Vermont Baptist Historical Society *see* PAPERS

VERMONT BAPTIST INFORMANT – Burlington, VT. Vermont Baptist Convention. 1916, 1925-32, 1934-64. Single reels available – 1 – 77.50 – us A.B.H.S. [073]

Vermont Baptist Ministers Conference and Aid Society *see* RECORDS

VERMONT BAPTIST MISSIONARY MAGAZINE – (Publication is believed to have ceased with v1 n6 apr 1812) – Rutland. v1. jan 1811-apr 1812 – 1 – D4100 – us UMI [210]

VERMONT BAR ASSOCIATION PROCEEDINGS – v1-58. 1878-1964 – 67mf – 9 – $301.00 – LLMC 84-684 – us L.L.M.C. [073]

VERMONT BAR JOURNAL AND LAW DIGEST – (Title varies: v1 as the Newsletter (Vermont Bar Association). v2-5 as Vermont Bar Newsletter) – v1-21. 1976-95 – 9 – $230.00 set – us Hein [340]

VERMONT BAR NEWSLETTER *see* VERMONT BAR JOURNAL AND LAW DIGEST

VERMONT BUSINESS – (Cont: Vermont Business World. Cont by: Vermont Business Magazine) – Bellows Falls. sep 1983-dec 1987* – 1 – D17914.01 – us UMI [338]

VERMONT BUSINESS *see*
- VERMONT BUSINESS MAGAZINE
- VERMONT BUSINESS WORLD

VERMONT BUSINESS DIRECTORY 1879/80 – Vermont Reel 5. (The Cox Library Collection) – 5 – us Americana [978]

VERMONT BUSINESS MAGAZINE – (Cont: Vermont Business) – Brattleboro. jan 1988-92* 1; 1993-94*. 1995-97+ 1,5,9 – 1,5,9 – D17914.02 – us UMI [338]

VERMONT BUSINESS MAGAZINE *see* VERMONT BUSINESS

VERMONT BUSINESS WORLD – (Cont by: Vermont Business) – Springfield. 1979-aug 1983* – 1 – D17914 – us UMI [338]

VERMONT BUSINESS WORLD *see* VERMONT BUSINESS

Vermont. College of Agriculture *see* ANNUAL REPORT

VERMONT CONGREGATIONAL CONFERENCE : MINUTES – 1908-26 (complete) – 2r – 1 – ATLA S0601 – us A.T.L.A. [240]

VERMONT CONGREGATIONAL CONFERENCE AND DOMESTIC MISSIONARY SOCIETY – 1927-65 (complete) – 2r – 1 – ATLA S0602 – us A.T.L.A. [240]

VERMONT FARM AND HOME SCIENCE / Vermont. Agricultural Experiment Station – v. 1, no. 1-V. 13, no. 3. 1955-71 – 1,5,6 – us Spaulding [630]

VERMONT GAZETTE – Bennington, Vt. 1783-1807; 1816-20 – 3 – us Readex [071]

VERMONT HISTORICAL GAZETTEER / Hemenway, Abbie M – Vol. 1: History of Addison, Bennington, Caledonia, Chittenden and Essex Counties. Burlington, 1868. Vermont Reel 2. (The Cox Library Collection) – 5 – us Americana [978]

VERMONT HISTORICAL GAZETTEER / Hemenway, Abbie M – Vol. 2: History of Franklin, Grand Isle, Lamoille and Orange Counties. Burlington, 1871. Vermont Reel 2. (The Cox Library Collection) – 5 – us Americana [978]

VERMONT HISTORICAL GAZETTEER / Hemenway, Abbie M – Vol. 3: History of Orleans and Rutland Counties. Claremont, Claremont Manufacturing Co., 1877. Vermont Reel 3. (The Cox Library Collection) – 5 – us Americana [978]

VERMONT HISTORICAL GAZETTEER / Hemenway, Abbie M – Vol. 4: Local History of all the towns in the state, civil, educational, biographical, religious and military; towns of Washington County with histories of Swanton in Franklin and Hubbarton in Rutland County. Montpelier, Vermont Watchman and State Journal Press, 1882. Vermont Reel 3. (The Cox Library Collection) – 5 – us Americana [978]

VERMONT HISTORICAL GAZETTEER / Hemenway, Abbie M – Vol. 5: Local history of all the towns in the state, civil, educational, biographical, religious, and military. Brandon, Mrs. Carrie E. H. Page, 1891. Vermont Reel 3. (The Cox Library Collection) – 5 – us Americana [978]

VERMONT IN THE CIVIL WAR / Benedict, G G – Burlington, The Free Press Association, 1886. Vols. 1-2. Vermont Reel 4. (The Cox Library Collection) – 5 – us Americana [978]

VERMONT INTELLIGENCER – Bellows Falls. Vt. 1817-20 – 1,3 – us Readex [071]

THE VERMONT ISSUE – Burlington, VT. v8 n12. nov 1909 – 1r – 1 – Can$25.00 – cn Can Microfilming [071]

VERMONT LAND GRANTEES 1749-1803 – (Arranges in alphabetical order nearly 14,000 recipients of the New Hampshire Land Grants and the Vermont Charters. Includes annotated bibliography of the boundary disputes between New Hampshire and Vermont) – (mf ed 1986) – 1mf – 9 – 0-87623-029-X – us Holbrook [978]

VERMONT LEGAL CATECHISM : THE REVISED STATUTES OF VERMONT REDUCED TO QUESTIONS AND ANSWERS FOR THE USE OF SCHOOLS AND FAMILYS / Wedgewood, William B – Brattleboro, VT: Joseph Steen, 1844 – 2mf – 9 – $3.00 – LLMC 91-093 – us L.L.M.C. [340]

VERMONT LIFE – v1- 1946- v33- 5,6,9 – us UMI [073]

VERMONT MIRROR – Middlebury, VT. 1812-16 – 3 – us Readex [071]

VERMONT NATURAL RESOURCES FORUM / Vermont. Agricultural Extension Service – v. 1-3. 1966-69 – 1,5,6 – us Spaulding [333]

Vermont. New England Cooperative Extension *see* PUBLICATION NEC

THE VERMONT OF TODAY / Stone, Arthur F – New York, Lewis Historical Publishing Co., 1929. Vols. 1-2. Vermont Reel 5; Vols. 3-4. Vermont Reel 6. (The Cox Library Collection) – 5 – us Americana [978]

VERMONT PATRIOT – Montpelier, VT. v25 n36. 29 aug 1850 – 1r – 1 – Can$25.00 – cn Can Microfilming [071]

Vermont. Resources Research Center *see* REPORT

Vermont. State Bar Association *see* PROCEEDINGS

VERMONT STATESMAN – Castelton, VT. v2 n1. 25 aug 1841-v3 n26. 15 feb 1843 – 1r – 1 – Can$50.00 – cn Can Microfilming [071]

Vermont. Supreme Court *see*
- AIKEN'S REPORTS
- BRAYTON'S REPORTS
- D. CHIPMAN'S REPORTS
- N. CHIPMAN'S REPORTS
- TYLER'S REPORTS
- VERMONT SUPREME COURT REPORTS

VERMONT SUPREME COURT REPORTS / Vermont. Supreme Court – (Pre-NRS: v1-57 1826-85 452mf $678.00. Vols after v127 in copyright. No updates planned) – v1 127. 1826-1970 – 940mf – 9 – $1,410.00 – LLMC 82-992 – us L.L.M.C. [340]

VERMONT SUPREME COURT REPORTS *see*
- AIKEN'S REPORTS
- BRAYTON'S REPORTS
- D. CHIPMAN'S REPORTS
- N. CHIPMAN'S REPORTS
- TYLER'S REPORTS

VERMONT TELEGRAPH – Brandon. v5. nov 1832-mar 1838* – 1 – D11602 – us UMI [073]

VERMONT TELEGRAPH – Brandon, VT. 1831-33 – 1 – 19.25 – us A.B.H.S. [073]

VERMONT WATCHMAN AND STATE JOURNAL – Montpelier, VT. v41 n22. 15 apr 1847; v42 n19. 23 mar 1848 – 1r – 1 – Can$25.00 – cn Can Microfilming [071]

VERMONTERS / Kent, Dorman B E – The Vermont Historical Society, 1937. Vermont Reel 12. (The Cox Library Collection) – 5 – us Americana [978]

A VERNACULAR BIBLIOGRAPHY FOR THE LANGUAGES OF NIGERIA / East, R M – Zaria, 1941 – 1mf – ne IDC [470]

A VERNACULAR BIBLIOGRAPHY FOR THE LANGUAGES OF NIGERIA / East, R M – Zaria. 1941. BA-486 2 – 8 – ne IDC [014]

Vernay, Joseph *see* ESSAI SUR LA PEDAGOGIE DE LEIBNIZ

Verne, Jules *see*
- L'ARCHIPEL EN FEU
- BOURSES DE VOYAGE
- LE CHEMIN DE FRANCE: GILBRALTER
- LES CINQ CENTS MILLIONS DE LA BEGUM
- DEUX ANS DE VACANCES
- L'ETONNANTE AVENTURE DE LA MISSION BARSAC
- FAMILLE SANS NOM
- L'ILE MYSTERIEUSE: LE SECRET DE L'ILE
- L'INVASION DE LA MER
- LES NAUFRAGES DU JONATHAN
- NORD CONTRE SUD
- LE PHARE DU BOUT DU MONDE
- LE PILOTE DU DANUBE
- LES TRIBULATIONS D'UN CHINOIS EN CHINE

Verneil-Puyraseau, Jean J *see*
- MEMOIRE SUR LE DEPARTEMENT DE LA CORREZE
- STATISTIQUE GENERALE DE LA FRANCE. DEPARTEMENT DU MONT-BLANC

VERNER'S PRIDE / Wood, Ellen – British Fiction Archive: Unit 1 – 9 – uk Bell [830]

Vernes, Jacob *see* DIALOGUES PAR UN MINISTRE SUISSE

Vernes, Maurice *see*
- DE NATURA FIDEI APUD PAULUM APOSTOLUM: MYSTICANE IN EA CONTINEANTUR ELEMENTA, NECNE
- ESSAIS BIBLIQUES
- HISTOIRE DES IDEES MESSIANIQUES
- MELANGES DE CRITIQUE RELIGIEUSE
- LE PEUPLE D'ISRAEL ET SES ESPERANCES RELATIVES A SON AVENIR
- LA REDEMPTION D'APRES JESUS-CHRIST
- LES RESULTATS DE L'EXEGESE BIBLIQUE: L'HISTOIRE, LA RELIGION, LA LITTERATURE

Verneuil, E de *see* THE GEOLOGY OF RUSSIA IN EUROPE AND THE URAL MOUNTAINS

Verneuil, Victor *see* MES AVENTURES AU SENEGAL. SOUVENIRS DE VOYAGE

VERNEY'S MONTHLY BANKERS' LIST – Toronto: T H Chesnut, [1884?-189- or 19–] – 9 – cn C.I.H.M. [332]

Vernier, L *see* ETUDE SUR VOLTAIRE GRAMMAIRIEN

DE VERNIEUWDE GULDEN WINCKEL DER KUNSTLIEVENDE NEDERLANDERS : WAER IN DEN MENSCHE DOOR POETISCHE, HISTORISCHE EN MORALE LEERINGEN, VERTOONT WORT, HOEDANIGH HY ZIJN LEVEN, HANDEL ENDE WANDEL, ZEDIGHLIJCK, EERBAERLIJCK EN VERMAKELIJCK SAL OVERBRENGEN / Vondel, J van den – Amsterdam, 1622 – 2mf – 9 – O-3194/1 – ne IDC [760]

Verninac de Saint-Maur, Raymond de *see* DESCRIPTION PHYSIQUE ET POLITIQUE DU DEPARTEMENT DU RHONE

VERNON / Baptist Association. Louisiana – 1955-87 – 1 – 62.72 – us Baptist [240]

Vernon, Ambrose White *see* THE RELIGIOUS VALUE OF THE OLD TESTAMENT IN THE LIGHT OF MODERN SCHOLARSHIP

VERNON DAILY NEWS – (1993.-12r; 1892-1975.-106r) – Vernon, 1976-1992 – 154r – 1 – cn Preston [971]

Vernon, Edward *see* PAPERS OF EDWARD VERNON AND SIR CHARLES WAGER

Vernon, Leroy M *see* SOUTH-WESTERN METHODISM

VERNON MINER – Vernon, NV. 1 Mar 1907 – 1r – 1 – $50.00 – U04778 – us Library Micro [071]

VERNON NEWS – British Columbia, CN. May 1891-Dec 1970 – 66r – 1 – cn Commonwealth Micro [072]

VERNON, OHIO, TAXES, MS V.F. O – (List of persons and personal property in the township subject to the county levy agreeable to an Act of the Legislature) – 1799 – 1r – 1 – us Western Res [978]

VERNON, OHIO, TAXES, MS V.F.O. – (Return of all lands of the resident proprietors for the 8th district according to the original lists) – 1801 – 1r – 1 – us Western Res [978]

Vernon, R (Mrs) *see* JAMES CALVERT

Vernon, William *see* READINGS ON THE INFERNO OF DANTE

VERNONIA EAGLE – Vernonia, OR. -w. 11 Aug 1922-19 Sept 1974. 17 rolls – 1 – us U.O. Library [071]

THE VERNON-WAGER PAPERS – 6r – 1 – $210.00 – Dist. us Scholarly Res – us L of C Photodup [355]

VERNUNFT UND SCHOENHEIT : ZEUGNISSE SEINES GLAUBENS / Schiller, Friedrich von; ed by Neuwinger, Rudolf – (Includes bibliographical references and index) – 1. Aufl. Berlin: Nordland-Verlag, 1940 – 1r – 1 – us U.W. Library [430]

IL VERO E, MIRABILISSIMO APPARATO OVER CONCIERO CON IL GLORIOSO TRIONFO NELL' INCLITA CITTA DI VENETIA – N.p., n.d. – 1mf – 9 – H-8187/1 – ne IDC [945]

IL VERO ET SVPERBO APPARATO...PER LA GRANDE ALLEGREZZA HAUUTA, PER LA VITORIA DE' CHRISTIANI IN ONOR DE LA SANTISSIMA LEGA / Toscano, R – N.p., [1571] – 1mf – 9 – H-8322/1 – ne IDC [945]

VEROCHENIE EVANGEL'SKIKH KHRISTIAN = CONFESSION OF FAITH OF THE EVANGELICAL CHRISTIANS – St. Petersburg, 1914. Publ. by All-Russian Union of Evangelical Christians. Includes Union's Constitution – 1 – 5.00 – us Baptist [240]

VEROEFFENTLICHUNGEN / Cologne. Museum fuer Ostasiatische Kunst – Berlin. v1-2 1922-1923 – 1 – us NY Public [700]

VEROIATNOSTNYE AVTOMATY / Bukharev, Rais Gatich – Kazan: Izd-vo Kazan skogo universiteta, 1970. On reel with Samarskii, AA. Vredenie v teoriiu raznostnykh skhem. Moskva, 1971 – 1 – us U.W. Library [621]

Veron, Eugene *see* LES INSTITUTIONS OUVRIERES DE MULHOUSE ET DES ENVIRONS

Veron, F *see*
- ABBREGE DES METHODES DE TRAICTER DES CONTROVERSES
- REGLE GENERALE DE LA FOY CATHOLIQUE

Veron, Pierre *see* EN 1900

VERORDENINGEN VOOR HET NEDERLANDS-ISRAELIETISCH KERKGENOOTSCHAP – Amsterdam, 1871-1925 – 13mf – 9 – J-261-115/1 – ne IDC [949]

VERORDNUNGSBLATT / Austria.Bundesministerium fuer Unterricht – Wien. 1869-1938 – 1 – 414.00 – us L of C Photodup [370]

VERORDNUNGSBLATT DES MILITAERBEFEHLSHABERS IN BELGIEN UND NORDFRANKREICH FUER DIE BESETZTEN GEBIETE BELGIENS UND NORDFRANKREICHS – Bruessel, 1940-44 (incomplete) – 1 – Inquire at Mikrofilmarchiv for details – gw Misc Inst [350]

VERORDNUNGSBLATT DES MILITAERBEFEHLSHABERS IN SERBIEN – Belgrad, 1941 n4,8,16 – 1 – Dist. gw Mikrofilm – gw Misc Inst [949]

VERORDNUNGSBLATT DES REICHSMINISTERS FUER DIE BESETZTEN OSTGEBIETE – Berlin, 1942 (incomplete) – 1 – Inquire at Mikrofilmarchiv for details – gw Misc Inst [350]

VERORDNUNGSBLATT FUER DAS K. U. K. HEER / Austro-Hungarian Monarchy. Reichskriegsministerium – v. 46-68. 1896-1918. V. 46, no. 37, 46; V. 47-53 WANTING – 1 – 523.00 – us L of C Photodup [355]

VERORDNUNGSBLATT FUER DIE BESETZTEN GEBIETE IN POLEN – Berlin, 1939 n1 – 1 – Inquire at Mikrofilmarchiv for details – gw Misc Inst [350]

VERORDNUNGSBLATT FUER GROSS-BERLIN – 1945-1976 – 544mf – 1 – DM3,100.80 – gw Mikro Press [320]

VEROUCHENIE RUSSKIKH "EVANGEL'SKIKH" KHRISTIAN-BAPTISTOV = CONFESSION OF FAITH OF THE RUSSIAN EVANGELICAL CHRISTIANS-BAPTISTS – Rostov-on-Don: F.P. Pavlov, 1906. 24p – 1 – $5.00 – us Baptist [240]

DIE VERPACKUNGSVERORDNUNG : EIN WISSENSCHAFTLICHER DISKUSSIONSBEITRAG / Kranz, Michael & Vogl, Reiner – 1993 – 1mf – 9 – DM60.00 – 3-89349-758-7 – gw Hänsel [338]

DE VERPLICHTINGEN VAN DEN WERKGEVER, KRACHTENS DE VERSCHILLENDE SOCIALE VERZEKERINGSWETTEN EN DE BESLUITEN, VEREVENINGSHEFFING, LOONBELASTING EN COMMISSARISSENBELASTING / Grinten, Willem Christiaan Leonard van der – 4druk. Alphen aan den Rijn, Samsom, 1943. 98p. LL-4103 – 1 – us L of C Photodup [340]

DE VERPLICHTINGEN VAN NEDERLAND ALS NEUTRALE MOGENDHEID... / Crommelin, H A – Leiden, 1880 – 1mf – 1 – ILM-1888/1 – ne IDC [327]

VERPONDINGSQUOHIER ZUTPHEN 1640-1650 / ed by Krenck – Dfl77.00 – ne Slangenburg [240]

Verrall, G H *see* A LIST OF BRITISH DIPTERA

DER VERRAT DES SCHWARZGELBEN GEWERKVEREINS DER BERGARBEITER – Bochum 1912 – 1 – DM30.00 – gw Mikro Press [331]

VERRAZANO THE EXPLORER: BEING A VINDICATION OF HIS LETTER AND VOYAGE: WITH AN EXAMINATION OF THE MAP OF HIERONIMO DE VERRAZANO: AND A DISSERATION UPON THE GLOBE OF VLPIUS: TO WHICH IS PREFIXED A BIBLIOGRAPHY OF THE SUBJECT / De Costa, Benjamin Franklin – New York: A. S. Barnes, 1880. 02698. (Pre-1900 Canadiana) – 9 – cn C.I.H.M. [910]

VERRERIES ET VERRIERS DANS LE DEPARTEMENT DE LA HAUTE-MARNE 1500 A 1830 / Euvrard, Paul – St. Dizier. 1933. (La Condition Ouvriere. Part Two.) – 9 – 2.50 – fr Bibl Nationale [360]

Verres, J *see* LUTHER

Verret, Madeleine *see* BIBLIOGRAPHIE DE JOSEPH-EDMOND ROY

DIE VERRUFENE INSEL : EINE ERZAEHLUNG AUS DEUTSCHEM GRENZLAND / Pirich, Hermann – Berlin: Verlag Die Heimatbuecherei, [1942] – 1r – 1 – us U.W. Library [830]

Verryke, E *see*
- ZEDERRYKE ZINNEBEELDEN
- ZEDERYKE ZINNEBEELDEN
- ZEDERYKE ZINNEBEELDEN, VERTOONT IN KONSTPLATEN...

LES VERS DE LA MORT / Helinadus of Froidmont – (Translated into modern french by J. Coppin) – Paris, 1930 – 3mf – 8 – ne Slangenburg [290]

LES VERS DE LA MORT / Helinant, Moine de Froidmont – Paris: Fr. Wulff and Em. Walberg, 1905 – 4mf – 8 – Dfl19.00 – ne Slangenburg [240]

VERS DEMAIN / ed by Even, Louis & Cote-Mercier, G – Montreal, Canada. 1 nov 1939-dec 1975 – 5r – 1 – cn Can Microfilming [072]

VERS ET PROSE – Dir. Paul Fort. Paris. mars 1905-07 (I-VII) – 1 – fr A.C.R.P.P. [073]

LE VERS FRANCAIS ANCIEN ET MODERNE / Tobler, A – 1885 – 9 – fr I.C.S. [810]

VERS LA RELIGION ETERNELLE : MEDITATIONS D'UN LIBRE PENSEUR RELIGIEUX / Genouy, Oswald – Paris: Librairie Fischbacher, 1909 – 1mf – 9 – 0-8370-4938-5 – 1985-2938 – us A.T.L.A. [210]

VERS LE CHRIST PAR LE VEDANTA / Johanns, P – (Tome 1, Louvain, 1932. 5mf; Tome 2, Louvain, 1933. 5mf) – 8 – ne Slangenburg [240]

VERS ODER PROSA IM HOHEN DRAMA DES ACHTZEHNTEN JAHRHUNDERTS / Grohmann, Willy – 1995 – 1mf – 9 – DM48.00 – 3-8267-3115-8 – gw Hänsel [400]

VERS UNE JUSTICE UNIVERSELLE – 1993 – sz I.C.J. [320]

VERSACLIMBER EXERCISE ELICITS HIGHER MAXIMAL OXYGEN UPTAKE IN WOMEN ROWERS THAN DOES TREADMILL EXERCISE OR ROWING ERGOMETRY / Brahler, C Jayne & Blank, Sally E – 1993 – 2mf – 9 – $8.00 – us Microform Publ [613]

VERSAILLES AND THE COURT UNDER LOUIS XIV / Farmer, James Eugene – New York: The Century Co., 1905.xii,447p. front., plates, ports., fold. plans – 1 – us U.W. Library [944]

VERSAILLES ET PARIS – ou Rapport des seances de l'Assemblee nationale et des communes de Paris. devenu: Assemblee nationale et commune de Paris, etc., par continuation du journal intitule: Versailles et Paris. no. 1-360. Paris. aout 1789-juil 1790 – 1 – fr A.C.R.P.P. [073]

Versailles. France *see* BULLETIN MUNICIPAL OFFICIEL

EIN VERSAMLUNG ODER ZAMENFUEGUNG, ETLICHER EINHEILIGER SPRUECH. NACH DER ORTHNUNG DES A. B. C. BETREFFENDE / Guelich van Berch, Heindrik – 1592. BME-262 1 – 9 – ne IDC [240]

DIE VERSCHIEDENEN EIDESARTEN NACH MOSAISCH-TALMUDISCHEN RECHTE / Blumenstein, J – Frankfurt a.M.: J. Kauffmann, 1883. 1 fiche – 9 – us A.T.L.A. [270]

DER VERSCHLOSSENE GARTEN : GEDICHTE AUS DEN JAHREN 1901-1909 / Weigand, Wilhelm – Leipzig: Insel Verlag, 1909 – 1r – 1 – us U.W. Library [810]

VERSCHOLLENES UND NEUES : EIN DICHTERBUCH AUS DEUTSCHLAND UND OESTERREICH / ed by Bodenstedt, Friedrich – 4. Aufl. Hannover: Helwing, 1877 – 1 – us U.W. Library [800]

Verschuere Reynvaan, J *see*
- MUZIJAKAL KUNST-WOORDENBOEK
- MUZIJKAAL KUNST-WOORDENBOEK

DIE VERSCHWOERUNG DER 47 SAMURAI : EINE JAPANISCHE HELDENGESCHICHTE / Lux, Hanns Maria – Leipzig: P Reclam, 1942 – 1r – 1 – us U.W. Library [830]

VERSES AND TRANSLATION / Calverley, Charles Stuart – Cambridge: Deighton, Bell; London: Bell and Daldy, 1862 – 1 roll – 1 – 1-55879-886-2 – uk Libr Preservation [810]

VERSES FOR CHILDREN / Ewing, Juliana Horatia – British Fiction Archive: Unit 1 – 9 – uk Bell [830]

VERSES ON VARIOUS OCCASIONS / Newman, John Henry – London: Burns Oates, & Co., 1868 – 1 roll – 1 – 1-55879-825-0 – uk Libr Preservation [240]

VERSES WRITTEN IN INDIA / Lyall, Alfred Comyn – London: Kegan Paul, Trench, 1889 – 1 roll – 1 – 1-55879-805-6 – uk Libr Preservation [810]

VERSHINY / Ivanov-Razumnik, R I – O Bloke i Belom. Izd. "Kolos". Petrograd. 1923. BR-1315 2 – 8 – ne IDC [460]

VERSHINY – Zhurnal literaturno-khudozhestvennyi. St. Petersburg, 1914-15. v1-32. Lacking: 1915 (6, 24-25). B-1959/2 – 8 – ne IDC [073]

Vershofen, Wilhelm *see* HEILIGES FEUER

VERSICULI / Haultain, Theodore Arnold – Toronto, 1893. 05516. (Pre-1900 Canadiana) – 9 – cn C.I.H.M. [810]

LA VERSIFICATION FRANCOISE / Richelet, P – 1671 – 9 – fr I.C.S. [440]

LA VERSION METRICA DEL SALTERIO DE BENITO ARIAS MONTANO / Diego, Sandalio – Malaga: Revista Espanola de Estudios Biblicos, 1928 – 1 – sp Bibl Santa Ana [780]

VERSION PARAFRASEADA DE LA ORACION ANGELICA, QUE CANTA LA IGLESIA EN EL SABADO SANTO DEL CIRIO PASCUAL / Salas, Francisco Gregorio de – Madrid: Imp. Andres Ramirez, 1775 – 1 – sp Bibl Santa Ana [946]

VERSION...LAMENTACIONES DE JEREMIAS / Salas, Francisco Gregorio de – 1778 – 9 – 1.50f – sp Bibl Santa Ana [220]

VERSION...ORACION ANGELICAL...PASCUAL / Salas, Francisco Gregorio de – 1775 – 9 – 1.50f – sp Bibl Santa Ana [810]

VERSION...TE DEUM LAUDAMUS...MAGNIFICAT ANIMA MEA / Salas, Francisco Gregorio de – 1776 – 9 – 1.50f – sp Bibl Santa Ana [810]

VERSLAG / Asian and Australian Trade Union Conference. Peking, 1949 (16 Nov-1 Dec) – 9 – SE-11,757/1 – ne IDC [331]

VERSLAG AFD. SEMARANG EN OMSTREKEN DER VEREENIGING TOT OPRICHTING VAN JONGEVROUWEN SCHOLEN IN NEDERLANDSCH-INDIE OVER DE JAREN 1918-1919 – Semarang, 1920 – 1mf – 9 – SE-1601/1 – ne IDC [950]

VERSLAG DER WERKZAAMHEDEN VAN DE VEREENIGING "PRO-JUVENTUTE" TE MEDAN – Medan, 1924-1933 – 5mf – 9 – SE-20,129/1 – ne IDC [950]

VERSLAG EENER BOTANISCHE DIENSTREIS DOOR DE MINAHASA / Koorders, SH – Batavia, 's-Gravenhage, 1898 – 9mf – 9 – ne IDC [580]

VERSLAG VAN DE HANDELMAATSCHAPPIJ GUENTZEL UND SCHUMACHER – Medan, 1911-1959. Nos 6-54 – 10mf – 9 – SE-20,126/1 – ne IDC [950]

VERSLAG VAN DE N.V. DELI COURANT – (Lacking: 1940-1946) – 1919-1952 – 4mf – 9 – SE-20,123/1 – ne IDC [950]

VERSLAG VAN DE POSTSPAARBANK IN NEDERLANDSCH-INDIE OVER DE JAREN 1937-1939, 1941-1946 – (Continued as: Bank Tabungan Pos.-Annual report 1955.-Djakarta, 1957) – Batavia, 1938-1947 – 7mf – 9 – SE-271/1 – ne IDC [332]

VERSLAG VAN DE TOESTAND DER GEMEENTE SEMARANG OVER 1914-1932 – Semarang, [1915-1933] – 130mf – 9 – SE-1588/1 – ne IDC [304]

VERSLAG VAN DE VERRICHTINGEN VAN DEN GEMEENTERAAD VAN MEDAN – Medan, 1918-1929 – 39mf – 9 – SE-20,131/1 – ne IDC [950]

VERSLAG VAN DIE KOMMISSIE VIR DIE SOSIO-EKONOMIESE ONTWIKKELING VAN DIE BANTOGEBIEDE BINNE DIE UNIE VAN SUID-AFRIKA / South Africa. Commission for the Socio-Economic Development of the Bantu Areas – (Filmed with: Summary of the Report...) – [s.l: s.n.,] 1954-55 – us Res Libr [330]

VERSLAG VAN HET ALGEMEEN DELISCH EMIGRATIE KANTOOR – Medan, 1919-1931 – 4mf – 9 – SE-20,130/1 – ne IDC [950]

VERSLAG VAN HET PROEFSTATION VOOR DE JAVA-SUIKERINDUSTRIE OVER DE JAREN 1941-1956 – (Continues as: Laporan dari Balai Penjelidikan Perusahaan 2 Gula) – 1957-1969. Soerabaja – 16mf – 9 – SE-837/1 – ne IDC [338]

VERSLAGEN DER JAVASCHE BANK / Javasche Bank. Batavia – (Continued as: Reports of the Bank Indonesia. Jarkarta, 1952-67. v40-54. Lacking: 1854-63, v2; 1961, v48.) – Batavia, 1828-1952. v1-39 – 247mf – 9 – ne IDC [950]

VERSLAGEN EN MEDEDEELINGEN VAN DE NEDERLANDSCHE ORNITHOLOGISCHE VEREENIGING – (Cont. as: Jaarboekje der Nederlandsche Ornithologische Vereeniging. Wageningen, 1910-1911. v7-8. Cont. as: Ardea. Tijdschrift der Nederlandsche Ornithologische Vereeniging. (Unie). Leiden, 1912-1942. v1-31) – Wageningen. v1-6. 1904-09. Index – 138mf – 9 – Z-2041c/2 – ne IDC [590]

Versluis, W *see* HOE WIJ MOGELIJK ZULLEN SLAGEN IN DE NIEUWE NEDERLANDSCHE VOLKSPLANTING IN NIEUW-GUINEA

VERSO L'UNIFICAZIONE DEL DIRITTO DEL MARE / Berlingieri, F – Roma, 1918 – 5mf – 9 – ILM-3761/1 – ne IDC [327]

DIE VERSOEHNUNGSLEHRE : AUF GRUND DES CHRISTLICHEN BEWUSSTSEINS / Kreibig, Gustav – (Includes bibliographical references) – Berlin:Wiegandt u. Grieben, 1878 – 1mf – 9 – 0-8370-4420-0 – 1985-2420 – us A.T.L.A. [240]

VERSOS / Vera e Isla Fernandez, Fernando de la – 1883 – 9 – 1.50f – sp Bibl Santa Ana [810]

VERSOS DE JUVENTUDY...VEJEZ / Sanchez-Arjona, Vicente – Sevilla: Imp. Carlos Acuna, 1951 – 1 – sp Bibl Santa Ana [810]

VERSOS O BERZAS / Velasco y Jaraquemada, M de – Fregenal de la Sierra: Imprenta de Cristobal Navarro, 1871 – 1 – sp Bibl Santa Ana [240]

VERSTAENDIGUNG – Bruenn, Czechoslovakia. 6 Mai-28 Okt 1922, 29 Jan 1924-13 Jan 1925 – 1 – gw Mikrofilm [072]

VERSTAENDIGUNG – Bruenn, may 6-oct 28 1922, jan 29 1924-jan 13 1925 – 2r – 1 – Inquire at Mikrofilmarchiv for details – gw Misc Inst [943]

DAS VERSTAENDNIS DER SUENDE IN ROEMER 7 / Maemecke, Thomas – 1995 – 1mf – 9 – DM60.00 – 3-8267-2169-1 – gw Hänsel [240]

Verstappen, Herman Theodoor *see* THE PHYSIOGRAPHIC BASIS OF PIONEER SETTLEMENT IN SOUTHERN SUMATRA

DAS VERSTEIGERERGEWERBE IN GEWERBEPOLITISCH-RECHTLICHER ENTWICKLUNGSBETRACHTUNG / Rohrscheidt, Joachim von – Leipzig, 1937 – 1mf – DM48.00 – 3-8267-3005-4 – gw Hänsel [340]

Verstralen, H *see* TWEE SCHONE BRIEUEN. WT DER GHEVANCKENISSE

VERSUCH EINER ALLEGORIE, BESONDERS FUER DIE KUNST / Winckelmann, Johann Joachim – O 465. 1766 – 9 – ne IDC [700]

VERSUCH EINER ANLEITUNG ZUM PRAELUDIREN FUER UNGEUEBTERE MIT BEYSPIELEN ERLAUTERT / Vierling, J G – Leipzig. BP-499 1 – 9 – ne IDC [780]

VERSUCH EINER ANLEITUNG ZUR COMPOSITION / Koch, Heinrich C – P 350. 3 v. 1782-1793 – 9 – ne IDC [780]

VERSUCH EINER ANLEITUNG ZUR COMPOSITION / Koch, Heinrich C – (v. 1. 8.90; 9. v. 2. 10.20; R; 9. v. 3. 11.50; R; 9) – 1782-93.3v – 9 – us Sibley [780]

VERSUCH EINER ANWEISUNG DIE FLOTE TRAVERSIERE ZU SPIELEN / Quantz, Johann Joachim – 1752 – 9 – us Sibley [780]

VERSUCH EINER AVIFAUNA VON PREUSSISCH-SCHLESIEN / Floericke, C E – Marburg, 1892. 157p. Z/1754/2 – 8 – ne IDC [590]

VERSUCH EINER BESCHREIBUNG DER RECKANSCHEN SCHULEINRICHTUNG / Riemanns, Carl Friedrich – Berlin u. Stettin, 1781 – 1 – DM30.00 – gw Mikro Press [370]

VERSUCH EINER BURJAETISCHEN SPRACHLEHRE NEBST KURZEM WOERTERVERZEICHNISS / Castren, M A; ed by Schiefner, A – St. Petersburg, 1857.224p. BU-379/2 – 8 – ne IDC [430]

VERSUCH EINER DARSTELLUNG DER CHRISTOLOGIE DES KORAN / Gerock, C F – Hamburg und Gotha, 1839 – 3mf – 8 – ne Slangenburg [260]

VERSUCH EINER DARSTELLUNG DER ETHIK JOSEPH BUTLERS / Ayer, Joseph Cullen – Leipzig: G.Kreysing, 1893 – 1mf – us A.T.L.A. [170]

VERSUCH EINER EINFUEHRUNG IN DAS STUDIUM DER KOLEOPTERN / Imhoff, L – Basel, 1856. Z/1369/2 – 8 – ne IDC [590]

VERSUCH EINER ERKLAERUNG VON EPHESER 5:31 / Menzel, G – Leipzig: W. Mertens, 1884. 1 fiche – 9 – us A.T.L.A. [240]

VERSUCH EINER GESCHICHTE DER MAHLERISCHEN HARMONIE UEBERHAUPT UND DER FARBENHARMONIE INSBESONDERE / Hoffman, J L – Halle. 1786. BP-324 1 – 9 – ne IDC [780]

VERSUCH EINER GESCHICHTE DES MARIEN- UND ANNEN-CULTUS IN DER KATHOLISCHEN KIRCHE / Frantz, Clamor – (Includes hymns to Mary and Anne) – Halberstadt: Robert Frantz, 1854 – 1mf – 9 – 0-8370-8340-0 – 1986-2340 – us A.T.L.A. [240]

VERSUCH EINER GRAMMATIK DER DAJACKSCHEN SPRACHE / Hardeland, A – SE-1620 1. 1858 – 9 – ne IDC [490]

VERSUCH EINER GRUENDLICHEN VIOLINSCHULE / Mozart, Leopold – 1756 – 9 – us Sibley [780]

VERSUCH EINER GRUENDLICHEN VIOLINSCHULE, ENTWORFEN UND MIT 4 KUPFERTAFELN SAMMT EINER TABELLE VERSEHEN VON LEOPOLD MOZART / Mozart, Leopold – P 730. 1756 – 9 – ne IDC [780]

VERSUCH EINER KOIBALISCHEN UND KARAGASSISCHEN SPRACHLEHRE, NEBST WOERTERVERZEICHNISSEN AUS DEN TATARISCHEN MINDARTEN DES MINNUSINSCHEN KREISES / Castren, M A – (A. Schiefner, Ed.). Spb. 1857. xix, 210pp. BU-324 2 – 8 – ne IDC [490]

VERSUCH EINER KRITISCHEN LITERATUR DER RUSSISCHEN GESCHICHTE : ERSTER TEIL ENTHALTEND DIE LITERATUR DER AELTEREN ALLGEMEINEN NORDISCHEN GESCHICHTE / Buhle, J G – Moskva, 1810 – 7mf – 9 – ne IDC [947]

VERSUCH EINER NEUEN LEHRART DIE PFLANZEN NACH ZWEI METHODEN ZUGLEICH / Medikus, F K – Vorlesungen der Kurpfaelzich-physikalisch-oekonomischen Gesellschaft. v. 2. 1787. B-8136 1 – 9 – ne IDC [580]

VERSUCH EINER RECONSTELLATION DES DEBORALIEDES / Niebuhr, Carl – (Song of Deborah in Hebrew and German. Includes bibliographical references) – Berlin: George Nauck (Fritz Ruehe), 1894 – 1mf – 9 – 0-8370-4007-8 – 1985-2007 – us A.T.L.A. [220]

VERSUCH EINER SCHRIFTGEMAESSEN...DEM HERRN JESU UND SEINER MUTTER / Koelling, Heinrich – Gotha: F.A. Perthes, 1875. 1 fiche – 9 – us A.T.L.A. [240]

VERSUCH EINER SYSTEMATIK DER SALICORNIEEN / Ungern-Sternberg, F – Dorpat. 1866. B-5578 2 – 8 – ne IDC [580]

VERSUCH EINER TECHNOLOGIE UND TERMINOLOGIE DER HANDWERKE IN DER MISNAH : 1. TEIL: SPINNEN, FAERBEN, WEBEN, WALKEN / Rieger, Paul – (No more published. Includes bibliographical references and Hebrew index) – Berlin: Mayer & Mueller, 1894 – 1mf – 9 – 0-8370-6347-7 – 1986-0347 – us A.T.L.A. [930]

VERSUCH EINES LEHRBUCHS DER PRAKTISCHEN MUSIK IN SYSTEMATISCHER ORDNUNG ENTWORFEN / Klein, J J – 1783 – 9 – us Sibley [780]

VERSUCH EINES MOEGICHST VOLLSTAENDIGEN WOERTERBUCHS DER BOTANISCHEN TERMINOLOGIE / Roemer, J J – Zuerich, 1816 – 9mf – ne IDC [580]

VERSUCH EINES VOLLSTAENDIGEN GRAMMATISCH-KRITISCHEN WORTERBUCHES DER HOCHDEUTSCHEN MUNDART... / Adelung, J C – Leipzig. 4v. 1774-80 – 40mf – 9 – HL-1/1 – ne IDC [054]

VERSUCH IN FIGURIRTEN CHORAELEN: SOWOHL FUER DIE ORGEL, ALS FUER DAS CLAVICHORD... / Marpurg, Friedrich Wilhelm – Berlin und Amsterdam: bey J J Hummel, [1790?] – 1 – us Sibley [780]

VERSUCH UEBER DAS SCHOENE, DA MAN UNTERSUCHT...UND IN DER MUSIK BESTEHE.. / Andre, Yves-Marie – 1757 – 2 – us Sibley [780]

VERSUCH UEBER DEN MUSIKALISCHEN AUSDRUCK / Avison, K – Aus dem Englischen uebersetzt. Leipzig. 1775. BP-632 1 – 9 – ne IDC [780]

VERSUCH UEBER DIE MUSIKALISCHE INTERVALLEN.. / Riedt, Friedrich W – 1753 – 2 – us Sibley [780]

VERSUCH UEBER DIE MUSIKALISCHE TEMPERATUR NEBST EINEM ANHANG / Marpurg, Friedrich Wilhelm – P 715. 1776 – 9 – ne IDC [780]

VERSUCH UEBER DIE MUSIKALISCHE TEMPERATUR, NEBST EINEM ANHANG UEBER DEN RAMEAU- UND KIRNBERGERSCHEN GRUNDBASZ / Marpurg, Friedrich Wilhelm – 1776 – 9 – us Sibley [780]

VERSUCH UEBER DIE WAHRTE ART DAS CLAVIER ZU SPIELEN MIT EXEMPELN / Bach, C P E – P-141. 1753 – 9 – ne IDC [780]

VERSUCH UEBER SIE WAHRE ART DAS CLAVIER ZU SPIELEN... / Bach, C P B – Berlin: George Ledewig Winter, 1759 – 1 – us Sibley [780]

DIE VERSUCHE, MELANCHTHON ZUR KATHOLISCHEN KIRCHE ZURUECKZUFUEHREN / Kawerau, Gustav – Halle, Verein fuer Reformationsgeschichte, 1902. (Schriften des Vereins fuer Reformationsgeschichte; 19. Jahrg., Schrift 73) – 1mf – us A.T.L.A. [240]

VERSUCHE UND ABHANDLUNGEN. / Naturforschende Gesellschaft. Danzig – 1747-56. v. 1-3 – 3 – us Readex [530]

VERSUCHE ZUR ERKLAERUNG SCHWIERIGER STELLEN IN GOETHES DRAMEN / Willenbuecher, Heinrich – (Includes bibliographical references) – [S.l.]: [s.n.], 1906 – 1r – 1 – us U.W. Library [430]

DIE VERSUCHUNG DES PESCARA : NOVELLE / Meyer, Conrad Ferdinand – 13. Aufl. Leipzig: H Haessel, 1899 – 1 – us U.W. Library [830]

LE VERT ET OR *see* LE JOURNAL DES ETUDIANTS DE L'UNIVERSITE DE SHERBROOKE

Vertegenwoordigend en Intermediair Wetgevend Lichaam des Bataffschen volks *see* DAGVERHAAL DER HANDELINGEN

VERTHEIDIGUNG DES HERRN WIELAND GEGEN DIE WOLKEN / Lenz, Jakob Michael Reinhold; ed by Schmidt, Erich – Berlin: B Behr, 1902 – 1r – 1 – us U.W. Library [430]

VERTICA – Oxford. v1-14. 1976-90 – 1,5,9 – D49279 – us UMI [073]

VERTICAL FILE COLLECTION ON CANADIAN ARTISTS / Art Gallery of Ontario – 9 – in prep – cn McLaren [700]

VERTICAL LAND / Janze, Comte de – London: Duckworth, [1928] – us Res Libr [960]

VERTICE: REVISTA LITERARIA – v. 1-5, nos. 1-27. 1937-42. (LC lacks vol. 2, nos. 13-18. December 1938-May 1939) – 1 – 20.00 – us L of C Photodup [800]

Vertot, R A de *see* HISTOIRE DES CHEVALLIERS HOSPITALIERS DE S JEAN DE JERUZALEM

VERTRAULICHE BRIEFE DES FREIHERRN VON THUGUT, OESTERR. MINISTERS DES AEUSSERN / ed by Vivenot, A von – Wien. 2v. 1872 – 11mf – 9 – ne IDC [943]

VERTRAUTE BRIEFE UEBER FRANKREICH / Reichardt, Johann F – 1792-93.2v – 2 – us Sibley [780]

VERTREES BAPTIST CHURCH. VERTREES, KENTUCKY : CHURCH RECORDS – 1888-1974. Known as New Union Baptist Church until 20 Jan 1900 – 1 – 35.73 – us Baptist [240]

VERTRIEB ANARCHISTISCHER LITERATUR / Dermassen, Bern – 2p – 9 – 1.00f – at Libertarian Micro [335]

LES VERTUS DU VRAI PRELAT REPRESENTEES EN LA VIE DE MGR. L'EMINENTISSIME CARDINAL DE LA ROCHEFOUCAULT / La Moiriniere, M M de – Paris, 1646 – 9mf – 9 – CA-171/1 – ne IDC [240]

VERT-VERT – Paris. 5 sept 1832-31 aout 1837. Mq: no.216, 1833; no.197, 1837 – 1 – fr A.C.R.P.P. [073]

DER VERUNTREUTE HIMMEL : DIE GESCHICHTE EINER MAGD / Werfel, Franz – Stockholm: Bermann-Fisher, 1939 – 1 – us U.W. Library [830]

Vervaeke, Monique *see* LE FONCTIONNEMENT DU MARCHE DU LOGEMENT ET LE PEUPLEMENT RESIDENTIEL

VERVE – Revue artistique et litteraire. Dir. E. Teriade. no. 1-4. Paris. dec 1937-oct 1938 – 1 – fr A.C.R.P.P. [073]

VERVENA. POEZY 1918-1919 GG / Severianin, I – Jur'ev. 1920. BR-1040 2 – 8 – ne IDC [460]

VERVOLG DER LEERZAAME ZINNEBEELDEN, SPIEGEL DER BOETVAARDIGHEID... / Spinniker, A – Haarlem, 1758 – 3mf – 9 – ne IDC [700]

DIE VERWALTUNG DER STADT MUENSTER VON DEN LETZTEN ZEITEN DER FUERSTBISCHOEFLICHEN BIS ZUM AUSGANG DER FRANZOESISCHEN HERRSCHAFT 1802-1813 / Engler, Bruno – Hildesheim, 1905 – 93p – 9 – DM48.00 – 3-89349-035-3 – gw Hänsel [350]

VERWALTUNGSABKOMMEN ZWISCHEN BUND UND LANDERN IN DER BUNDESREPUBLIK DEUTSCHLAND. EINE KRITISCHE UNTERSUCHUNG DER GEGENWARTIGEN STAATSPRAXIS MIT EINE-ZUSAMMENSTELLUNG DER ZWISCHEN BUND UND LANDERN ABGESCHLOSSENEN ABKOMREN / Grawert, Rolf – Berlin: Duncker u. Humblot (1967) – 1 – us U.W. Library [943]

DIE VERWALTUNGS-AKADEMIE. EIN HANDBUCH FUER DEN BEAMTEN IM NATIONALSOZIALISTISCHEN STAAT.. / Lammers, Hans Heinrich – Berlin: Industrieverlag Spaeth & Linde, (1934-36?). 3v.Includes bibliographies – 1 – us U.W. Library [340]

VERWALTUNGSBERICHT DES VORSTANDES / Zentralverband der Toepfer und Berufsgenossen Deutschlands – 1914-15. Berlin. (Serial publications of German trade unions in the Memorial Library, University of Wisconsin-Madison.) – 1 – us U.W. Library [330]

VERWALTUNGSBLATT DES PREUSSISCHEN LANDESVERBANDES JUEDISCHER GEMEINDEN – Berlin. v1-16. 1923-1938. Lacking misc. issues. B465 (Leo Baeck Institute. German-Jewish Periodicals, Pt 1) – 1r – 1 – $75.00 – us UPA [270]

VERWALTUNGSBLATT DES PREUSSISCHEN LANDESVERBANDES JUEDISCHER GEMEINDEN – (Cont by: Gemeindeblatt fuer die juedischen Gemeinden Preussens, may 1934; Juedisches Gemeindeblatt fuer die Synagogen-Gemeinden in Preussen und Norddeutschland, aug 1937) – Berlin, sep 25 1923-nov 1 1938 (incomplete) – 1r – 1 – Inquire at Mikrofilmarchiv for details – gw Misc Inst [270]

DIE VERWANDELTEN / Alverdes, Paul – Muenchen: A Langen, G Mueller, 1938 – 1r – 1 – us U.W. Library [943]

DIE VERWANDELTEN WEIBER, ODER DER TEUFEL IST LOS, ERSTER THEIL / Hiller, Johann Adam – Eine comische Oper in drey Aufzuegen with Sinfonia and 4 compositions by Hiller and 12 compositions by J.C. Standfuss. 1770 – 9 – us Sibley [780]

VERWANDLUNG DER HERZEN : ROMAN / Ziesel, Kurt – Wien: Wiener Verlag, 1943 – 1r – 1 – us U.W. Library [830]

DES VERWEGENEN CHIRURGUS WELTBERUEHMBT WUNDER-DOKTOR JOHANN ANDREAS EISENBART : TUGENDEN UND LASTER GETREULICH MITGETEILT UND VORGESTELLT / Winckler, Josef – Berlin: Deutsche Buch-Gemeinschaft, 1933 – 1 – us U.W. Library [920]

VERWEGENES SPIEL : KRIMINAL-ROMAN / Mueller, K (Kurt) – Leipzig: Lipsia-Verlag Friedrich, 1944 – 1r – 1 – us U.W. Library [830]

VERWENDUNG VON EINSTELLUNGSKONZEPTEN IN DER MARKTFORSCHUNG / Leipelt, Detlef – 1992 – 1mf – 9 – DM75.00 – 3-89349-602-5 – gw Hänsel [650]

DIE VERWENDUNGSPOTENZEN DER AUSDRUCKSMITTEL FUNKTIONAL-SEMANTISCHER FELDER BEI DER SPRACHLICHEN REALISIERUNG VON HANDLUNGSTYPEN/ KOMMUNIKATIONSVERFAHREN / Lohde, Michael – 1994 – 2mf – 9 – DM80.00 – 3-89349-874-5 – gw Hänsel [460]

VERWORRENES LEBEN = SHORT STORIES. SELECTIONS : NOVELLEN UND SKIZZEN / Raabe, Wilhelm Karl – Glogau [Glogow, Poland]: Carl Flemming, 1862 – 1r – 1 – us U.W. Library [830]

THE VERY JOYOUS, PLEASANT AND REFRESHING HISTORY OF THE FEATS, EXPLOITS, TRIUMPHS AND ACHIEVEMENTS OF THE GOOD KNIGHT WITHOUT FEAR AND WITHOUT REPROACH, THE GENTLE LORD DE BAYARD / Mailles, Jacques de – London: Longman, Brown, Green, and Longmans, 1848. xii,252p. illus – 1 – us U.W. Library [830]

A VERY NECESSARY BOKE BOTHE IN ENGLYSHE AND IN FRENCHE – Anon. 1550. 36p. (English Linguistics Series 1500-1800) – 9 – us UMI [420]

A VERY PROFITABLE BOKE TO LERNE THE MANNER OF REDYNG, WRITYNG, AND SPEAKYNG ENGLISH AND SPANISH – Anon. 1554. 135p. (English Linguistics Series 1500-1800) – 9 – us UMI [420]

VERY WELL / Hurtado, Antonio – 1870 – 9 – 1.50f – sp Bibl Santa Ana [830]

VERZAMELAAR, DE – Cape Town, South Africa. 7 Jan 1826-19 Dec 48. 3 reels. Suspended: 1829-39 – 1, 16 diazo available at reduced price – sa SA Libr [072]

VERZAMELING VAN ALLE MEEST BEKENDE NEGERENGELSCHE SPREEKWOORDEN MET UITGEZOCHT HOLLANDSCH, ENGELSCH EN DUITSCH MORAAL / Halfhide, J J – Coronie. 3v. 1886 – 5mf – ne IDC [390]

VERZAMELING VAN UITGEKORENE ZIN-SPREUKEN / Burg, H van den – O 184. 1743 – 9 – ne IDC [430]

VERZAMELING VAN ZINSPREUKEN, ZINNEBEELDEN, EN ZINNEBEELDIGE VERCIERINGEN ENZ. – Amsterdam, 1741 – 4mf – 9 – ne IDC [700]

VERZEICHNIS DER ARMENISCHEN HANDSCHRIFTEN DER KOENIGLICHEN UNIVERSITAETSBIBLIOTHEK ZU TUEBINGEN / Finck, FN & Gjandschezian, L – Tuebingen, 1907 – 3mf – 9 – ne IDC [460]

VERZEICHNIS DER CHINESISCHEN UND MANDSCHUISCHEN BUECHER UND HANDSCHRIFTEN DER KOENIGLICHEN BIBLIOTHEK ZU BERLIN,... / Klaproth, J H – Paris, 1822 – 5mf – 9 – ne IDC [480]

VERZEICHNIS DER CHINESISCHEN UND MANDSCHU-TUNGUSISCHEN BUECHER UND HANDSCHRIFTEN DER KOENIGLICHEN BIBLIOTHEK ZU BERLIN / Schott, W – Berlin, 1840 – 2mf – 9 – ne IDC [480]

VERZEICHNIS DER ERSTDRUCKE HOFMANNSTHALS / Steiner, Herbert – Zuerich: s.n., 1937? – 1r – 1 – us U.W. Library [018]

VERZEICHNIS DER MITGLIEDER DES VEREINS FUER REFORMATIONS-GESCHICHTE : NEBST BERICHT UEBER DIE TAETIGKEIT DES VEREINS IN DEN 25 JAHREN VON 1883-1908 – Halle a.S.: Wischan & Burkhardt, [1908?] – 1mf – us A.T.L.A. [240]

VERZEICHNIS DER PFLANZEN, WELCHE WAEHREND DER 1829-1830 UNTERN. REISE IM CAUCASUS GEFUNDEN WORDEN SIND / Meyer, C A – Spb., 1831. 241 pp. B-723 2 – 8 – ne IDC [580]

VERZEICHNIS DER ZU BADEN IM BADEN-BADISCHEN ANWESENDEN KURGAESTE IM SOMMER 1807 – Baden-Baden, 1807 – 1 – Dist. gw Mikrofilm – gw Misc Inst [790]

VERZEICHNISS DER ABHANDLUNGEN DER KOENIGLICH PREUSSISCHEN AKADEMIE DER WISSENSCHAFTEN VON 1710-1870 IN ALPHABETISCHER FOLGE DER VERFASSER – Berlin, 1871. Nach den Klassen..., 1822-1872. Berlin, 1873 – 6mf – 9 – H-410/2 – ne IDC [500]

VERZEICHNISS DER AUF DER TAURISCHEN HALBINSEL WILDWACHSENDEN PFLANZEN / Steven, C von – (Bull. Soc. Imp. Naturalistes de Moscou, v. 29-30, 1856-57). B-1048 2 – 8 – ne IDC [580]

VERZEICHNISS DER BOTANISCHEN AUTOREN... ERLANGEN, 1870 : NACHTRAG ZUM VERZEICHNISS DER BOTANISCHEN AUTOREN... ERLANGEN, 1873 / Salomon, C – Erlangen, 1873 – 2mf – ne IDC [580]

VERZEICHNISS DER IM JAHRE 1832 IM OESTLICHEN THEILE DES ALTAI-GEBIRGES GESAMMELTEN PFLANZEN / Bunge, A A von – (Mem. Ac. Imp. Sc. Spb.). v. 2. 1835. B-5866 2 – 8 – ne IDC [580]

VERZEICHNISS DER IM JAHRE 1904-1922 ERSCHIENENEN MUSIKALIEN, AUCH MUSIKALISCHEN SCHRIFTEN UND ABBILDUNGEN MIT ANZEIGE DER VERLEGER UND PREISE / ed by Hofmeister, F D – (Missing: 1908. v57) – Leipzig. v53-72. 1904-1923 – 79mf – ne IDC [780]

VERZEICHNISS DER PFLANZENKULTUREN IN DEN GRAEFL. HOFFMANNSEGGISCHEN GAERTEN ZU DRESDEN UND RAMMENAU / Hoffmannsegg, J C von – Dresden. 1824. B-856 2 – 8 – ne IDC [580]

VERZEICHNISS DER VON FRIEDRICH PHILIPPI AUF DER HOCHEBENE DER PROVINZEN ANTOFAGASTA UND TARAPACA. PFLANZEN / Philippi, R A – Leipzig. 1891. B-5637 2 – 8 – ne IDC [580]

VERZEICHNISS DERJENIGEN PFLANZEN, WELCHE NACH DER ANZAHL UND DER BESCHAFFENHEIT / Roth, A W – Altenburg. 1781. B-5689 2 – 8 – ne IDC [580]

VERZEICHNISS SCHLESINGER SPINNEN / Lebert, H – Z-2179 2. 1875 – 8 – ne IDC [590]

Verzhbitskii, N *see* VSTRECHI S ESENINYM

EEN VERZOEK OM DE JODEN IN AMSTERDAM EEN BEPAALDE WOONPLAATS AAN TE WIJZEN / Vaz Dias, A M – Jaarboek Amstelodamum. 1938 39. BJ-262-64 1 – 9 – ne IDC [949]

VES' LENINGRAD – 1894-1934. 1895, 1900, 1909, 1916-17 Wanting – 1 – 613.00 – us L of C Photodup [947]

VESAIK-I TARIHIYE VE SIYASIYE TETEBBUATI – Istanbul: Ahmet Ihsan ve Suerekasi, 1326 [1910] 5v – 9 – $90.00 – us MEDOC [956]

Vesalius, A *see*
- DE HUMANI CORPORIS FABRICA
- FABRICA DE CORPORIS HUMANI, LIBRI SEPTEM

VESELCHAK – Zhurnal vsiakiky raznykh strannostei svetskikh literaturnykh i inykh. St. Petersburg, 1858-59. BR-4021/2 – 8 – ne IDC [073]

Veseli, F *see* AROSLAVSKI I SBORNIK, POSVI ASHCHENNY I GODOVSHCHINI E VELIKO I OKTI ABRSKO I REVOLIUTSII I II ULSKIM SOBYTII AM V I AROSLAVLI E

Veselovskii, A *see*
- SLAVIANSKIA SKAZANIIA O SOLOMONE I KITOVRASE I ZAPADNYIA LEGENDY O MOROLFE I MERLINE
- SLAVIANSKIE SKAZANIIA O SOLOMONE I KITOVRASE I ZAPADNYE LEGENDY O MOROL'FE I MERLINE

Veselovskii, A A *see* LIUBOVNAIA LIRIKA 18 VEKA

Veselovskii, A N *see*
- PROSVETITELNYI VEK I ALEKSANDROVSKAIA PORA
- ZAPADNOE VLIIANIE V NOVOI RUSSKOI LITERATURE

VESENNEE KONTRAGENSTVO MUZ – Sbornik. M. 1915. BR-1937 2 – 8 – ne IDC [460]

VESENNEE POROSH'E / Remizov, A – St. Petersburg, 1915. 328p. BR-854 2 – 8 – ne IDC [460]

VESENNII POTOK – Ezhemesiachnyi zhurnal. St. Petersburg, 1906. No.1, xxiii,304p. BR-4183/2 – 8 – ne IDC [073]

Vesey, Francis, Sr *see* VESEY'S SENIOR'S REPORTS

VESEY'S SENIOR'S REPORTS / Vesey, Francis, Sr – (With notes and suppl vol by Robert Belt "comprising corrections of statement and extracts of the decrees and order from the registrar's books, references to cases cited, subsequent determinations on the several points, some manuscript cases, new marginal notes, and a copious index". London: Pheney & Sweet, 1818-25) – v1-3. 1746-55 (all publ) – 20mf – 9 – $30.00 – LLMC 84-791 – us L.L.M.C. [324]

VESHNIIA VODY – Nauchno-literaturno-khudozhest-Vennyi zhurnal. St. Petersburg, Petrograd, 1914-17. Lacking some issues. B-1961/2 – 8 – ne IDC [947]

Vesin, L *see* ISTORICHESKII OBZOR UCHEBNIKOV OBSHCHEI I RUSSKOI GEOGRAFII, IZDANNYKH SO VREMENI PETRA VELIKAGO PO 1876 GOD. (1710-1876 G.)

VESNA – Velke Mezirici, Czechoslovakia. v7-10. 1888-1891 – 1 – us I.U. Libraries [073]

VESNIK – Belgrade, Yugoslavia. -w. 1958-70. 2 reels – 1 – uk British Libr Newspaper [949]

A VESPA – Maroim, Brazil. 27 Apr 1892 – 1 – bl Biblioteca [072]

Vesper, Will *see*
- BILD DES FUEHRERS
- DER ENTFESSELTE SAEUGLING
- DAS HARTE GESCHLECHT
- RUFE IN DIE ZEIT
- DER SELTSAME SPRINGINSFELD
- DIE WANDERUNG DES HERRN ULRICH VON HUTTEN

LE VESPERAL ROMAIN A L'USAGE DU DIOCESE DE QUEBEC – Quebec: John Neilson, 1802. SEM16P36 – 1r – 5 – Can$12.00 – cn Bibl Nat [240]

VESPERAL ROMAIN A L'USAGE DU DIOCESE DE QUEBEC – 2nd ed. Quebec: Neilson and Cowan, 1828. SEM16P137 – 1r – 5 – Can$9.00 – cn Bibl Nat [240]

Vesque, J *see* LE CIRQUE EN FRANCE DE LA BELLE EPOQUE A LA FIN DE LA DEUXIEME GUERRE MONDIALE

Vesque, M *see* LE CIRQUE EN FRANCE DE LA BELLE EPOQUE A LA FIN DE LA DEUXIEME GUERRE MONDIALE

THE VESSEL, THE DEED AND THE IDEA: ANARCHISM IN PATERSON / Carey, George W – 1895-1908, 1980 – 9 – 1.00f – at Libertarian Micro [335]

IL VESSILLO ISRAELITICO – Casale. v. 1-70. 1853-Oct 1922 – 1 – us NY Public [305]

VEST' – Ezhenedel'nyi obshchestvenno politicheskii i literaturnyi zhurnal. St. Petersburg, 1906. v1-12. B-1962/2 – 8 – ne IDC [947]

LA VESTALE / Jouy & Spontini – French Theatre Series. Paris. Roullet, 4th ed. 1810 – 9 – fr Hachette [820]

VESTERNS SVENSKA TRIBUN – Omaha, NE. -w. 10 Apr 1901-16 Mar 1904. In Swedish. Title varies – 1 – us NE Hist [071]

DET VESTGRONLANDSKE SPROG / Schultz-Lorentzen, C W – 1934 – 8 – BN-384 2 – ne IDC [490]

VESTIARIUM CHRISTIANUM : THE ORIGIN AND GRADUAL DEVELOPMENT OF THE DRESS OF HOLY MINISTRY IN THE CHURCH / Marriott, Wharton B – London: Rivingtons, 1868 – 1mf – us A.T.L.A. [240]

VESTIBULUM LINGUAE LATINAE / Willis, Thomas – 1651. 316p. (English Linguistics Series 1500-1800) – 9 – us UMI [450]

EL VESTIDO LARGO / Garcia Jimeno, Fernando y Jesus – Madrid: R. Velasco, imp., 1903 – 1 – sp Bibl Santa Ana [946]

VESTIGES OF THE NATURAL HISTORY OF CREATION / Chambers, Robert – London: John Churchill, 1845 – 1 roll – 1 – 1-55879-719-X – uk Libr Preservation [210]

VESTIGES OF THE SPIRIT-HISTORY OF MAN / Dunlap, Samuel Fales – New York: D. Appleton, 1858. 404p – 1 – us U.W. Library [306]

VESTKUSTEN – San Francisco & Oakland, California. 1887-1967 – 72r – 1 – sw Kungliga [071]

VESTMANLANDS LANS TIDNING – (Suppl: VLT-extra, 1975-78 3r) – Vasteras, Sweden. 1831-1978 – 532r – 1 – sw Kungliga [072]

VESTMANLANDS LANS TIDNING – Vasteras, Sweden. 1979- – 1 – sw Kungliga [072]

THE VESTMENTS CONTROVERSY / Primus, J H – Kampen, 1960 – 5mf – 8 – ne Slangenburg [240]

VESTNIK / Kommunisticheskaya Akademiya. Moscow – Moscow. 1922-1935 no 8 – 1 – us NY Public [947]

VESTNIK – Milwaukee, WI, 1925, 1928 – 6mf or 1 reel – 9,1 – us I.H.R.C. [975]

VESTNIK / Moscow. Universitet – (Moscow University Magazine). 1966- – 1 – us UMI [073]

VESTNIK – New York, NY, 1909 – 1mf or 1 reel – 1,9 – us I.H.R.C. [975]

VESTNIK – Organ tserkovno-obshchestvennoi zhizni. Paris, 1937-39.BR-5730/2 – 8 – ne IDC [073]

VESTNIK – Pueblo, CO, 1932 – 1mf or 1 reel – 1,9 – us I.H.R.C. [975]

VESTNIK – Toronto. 1941-60; 1971- – 1 – 120.00y – cn McLaren [073]

VESTNIK AKADEMII NAUK SSSR – Moscow, 1931-72.Lacking: 1931-39 (1-3); 1941 (4); 1942 (1,4-6); 1943 (1-5, 7-12). BR-10,470/1 – 9 – ne IDC [947]

VESTNIK ARKHEOLOGII I ISTORII – v. 1-23. Spb. 1885-1918. B-1435 2 – 8 – ne IDC [930]

VESTNIK ARTEL'NOGO TRUDA – (Missing: 1922 n1-2) – M., 1921-22 n12 – 4mf – 9 – COR-554/1 – ne IDC [334]

VESTNIK AZII – v. 11-17. Harbin. 1912-13. B-1230 2 – 8 – ne IDC [460]

VESTNIK BLAGOTVORITEL'NOSTI – St. Petersburg, 1897-1902. Lacking some issues.BR-9271/2 – 8 – ne IDC [947]

VESTNIK BUNDA – Izdanie zagranichnago komiteta. Geneva, 1904. v1-5. BR-3462/2 – 8 – ne IDC [073]

VESTNIK EVREISKOGO OTDELA NARODNOGO KOMISSARIATA PO DELAM NATSIONAL'NOSTEI – v. 1-2. M. 1920. BR-3508 2 – 8 – ne IDC [460]

VESTNIK EVREISKOI OBSHCHINY – Zhurnal. Spb. 1913-14. BR-4189 2 – 8 – ne IDC [073]

VESTNIK FINANSOV PROMYSHLENNOSTI I TORGOVLI / Russia. Ministerstvo Finansov – St Petersburg. 1867-1917. Incomplete – 1 – us NY Public [336]

VESTNIK FINANSOV, PROMYSHLENNOSTI I TORGOVLI – Spb. 1885-1917. Lacking: 1885-99; (nr. 1, pt. 2, 6) (nr. 3, pt. 27, 33, 35, 36, 38) (nr. 4, pt. 41, 50) 1906. BR-11.031 2 – 8 – ne IDC [073]

VESTNIK GOSUDARSTVENNOGO STRAKHOVANIIA : DVUKHNEDELNY I ORGAN GLAVNOGO PRAVLENIIA GOSUDARSTVENNOGO STRAKHOVANIIA – (Library has: 1926, no. 1-24; missing no. 17-18) – Moskva: Izdvo Gosstrakha SSSR, 1922-1930. 9v – 1 – CSUX90-S40 – us Hoover Inst Photo [650]

VESTNIK GRUZII – Tiflis, 1907. v1. BR-4198/2 – 8 – ne IDC [947]

VESTNIK I BIBLIOTEKA SAMOOBRAZOVANIIA – Nauchno-populiarnyi zhurnal po vsem otrasliam znaniia. St. Petersburg, 1903-04. Lacking some issues.BR-4197/2 – 8 – ne IDC [947]

VESTNIK IMPERATORSKOGO RUSSKOGO GEOGRAFICHESKOGO OBSHCHESTVA – v. 1-30. Spb. 1851-60. B-1964 2 – 8 – ne IDC [910]

VESTNIK INOSTRANNOI LITERATURY – Ezhemesiachnyi literaturno-istoricheskii zhurnal. Spb. 1891-1916. Lacking: 1908, v. 18 (8-12); 1909, v. 19 (1-12); 1916, v. 26 (9-12). B-1965 2 – 8 – ne IDC [073]

VESTNIK IRRIGATSII : EZHEMESIACHNYI ZHURNAL UPRAVLENIIA VODNOGO KHOZIAISTVA SREDNE I AZII – (Includes c.1: 1925:Jan.-Mar., May, July-Oct., Dec.,; 1926:July, Nov.; 1927:Jan.-Mar., July-Oct., Dec.; 1928:Apr.-June; 1929:Mar.-Aug.) – Tashkent: Izd. Vodkhoza Sr. Az., 1923-1930. 8v – 1 – CSUXAKY5572-S – us Hoover Inst Photo [627]

VESTNIK IUGO-ZAPADNOI I ZAPADNOI ROSSII – Istoriko-literaturnyi zhurnal. Kiev, 1862-71. Lacking some issues. B-1967/2 – 8 – ne IDC [073]

VESTNIK IZIASHCHNYKH ISKUSSTV, IZDAVAEMYI PRI IMPERATORSKOI AKADEMII KHUDOZHESTV – St. Petersburg, 1883-90.v1-8. B-1966/2 – 8 – ne IDC [947]

VESTNIK KALUZHSKOI KOOPERATSII – (Cont as: Kaluzhskii Vestnik Kooperatsii I Sel'skogo Khoziaistva. Kaluga, 1919 n8/9. Missing: 1917-18 n5; 1918 n12-end) – Kaluga, 1917-18 n12 – 6mf – 9 – COR-597/1 – ne IDC [334]

VESTNIK KARELO-MURMANSKOGO KRAIA – (Includes c1: 1924 n5-6,8,12-13. 1925 n1/2-3, 5-11,14-31/32. 1926 n8,12-15,17,19/20) – Leningrad: Pravlenie Murmansko i zh.d., 1924 – 1 – CSUXAKZ2867-S – us Hoover Inst Photo [073]

VESTNIK KHAR'KOVSKOGO ISTORIKO-FILOLOGICHESKOGO OBSHCHESTVA – Khar'kov, v1-5. 1911-1914 – 10mf – 9 – R-4188/2 – ne IDC [947]

VESTNIK KHAR'KOVSKOGO ISTORIKO-FILOLOGICHESKOGO OBSHCHESTVA – Khar'kov. v1-5. 1911-1914 – 10mf – 9 – ne IDC [460]

VESTNIK KNIGOPRODAVTSEV – Ezhenedel'noe izdanie. Moscow, 1900-01. BR-4306/2 – 8 – ne IDC [947]

VESTNIK KOMISSII ISPOLZOVANIIA : ORGAN KOMISSII ISPOLZOVANIIA PRI SOVETE TRUDA I OBORONY – (Library has: Oct. 1921) – Moskva: Komispolz, 1920-1921. 2v – 1 – CSUX89-S771 – us Hoover Inst Photo [331]

VESTNIK KOMITETA PO DELAM IZOBRETENII – (Library has: Jan.-June, Aug.-Nov./Dec. 1925; Mar., Oct. 1926; Feb.-Apr., June 1931) – Leningrad: Izd. Komiteta po delam izobretenii, 1924-1931. 8v – 1 – CSUX90-S34 – us Hoover Inst Photo [600]

VESTNIK KOMITETA PO IZOBRETATELSTVU / Komitet po izobretatelstvu pri STO – (Library has: July, Sept. 1931; Feb.-Mar./Apr. 1932; Sept.-Dec. 1934; 1935) – Leningrad: Izd. Komt po izobretatelstvu, 1931-1936 – 1 – CSUX90-S642 – us Hoover Inst Photo [600]

VESTNIK KOMMUNISTICHESKOI AKADEMII – 1922-35 – 1 – 148.00 – us L of C Photodup [947]

VESTNIK KOOPERATIVNOGO KREDITA : IZD MOSKOVSKOGO NARODNOGO BANKA – M., 1918 n1-16 – 7mf – 9 – COR-555/1 – ne IDC [334]

VESTNIK KOOPERATIVNYKH SLUZHASHCHIKH – M., 1916 – 2mf – 9 – COR-556/1 – ne IDC [334]

VESTNIK KOOPERATIVNYKH SOIUZOV – (Missing: 1915; 1917 n2) – M., 1915-17 n8 – 13mf – 9 – COR-557/1 – ne IDC [334]

VESTNIK KOOPERATSII – (Missing: 1918 n7-8) – Spb., 1909-18 n12 – 102mf – 9 – COR-559/1 – ne IDC [334]

VESTNIK KOOPERATSII – (Missing: 1922 n1-1923 n16) – Vitebsk, 1922-23 n17 – 1mf – 9 – COR-558/1 – ne IDC [334]

VESTNIK KUSTARNOI PROMYSHLENNOSTI – (Missing: 1921 n1-3, 6; 1922 n1-2) – M., 1921-22 n10 – 7mf – 9 – COR-560/1 – ne IDC [334]

VESTNIK KUSTARNOI PROMYSHLENNOSTI *see* VESTNIK VSEROSSIISKIKH S'EZDOV DEATELEI PO KUSTARNOI PROMYSHLENNOSTI

VESTNIK LENINGRADSKOGO UNIVERSITETA : SERIIA EKONOMIKI, FILOSOFII I PRAVA / Leningrad. Universitet – (Suppl.: 1973-90(4). 115mf. Dfl699.00) – 1956-90(4). BR-10,472/1 – 241mf – 9 – ne IDC [330]

VESTNIK LENINGRADSKOGO UNIVERSITETA : SERIIA ISTORII, IAZYKA I LITERATURY / Leningrad. Universitet – L. 1956-72; 1973-75. BR-10,471 1 – 9 – ne IDC [370]

VESTNIK LITERATURY – Illiustrirovannyi dvukhnedel'nyi zhurnal slovesnosti nauki i bibliografii. St. Petersburg, 1905. v1-24. B-1969/2 – 8 – ne IDC [073]

VESTNIK MAN'CHZHURII – Harbin. 1923, 1924 has title: Ekonomicheskii vestnik Man'chzhurii. 1923-1932. 1926, nos. 1-7; 1927, nos. 1-6; 1928, nos. 1-7; 1929, nos. 1-11; 1931, nos. 1-6; 1932, nos. 1-12 – 1 – 35.00r – us Hoover Inst Photo [330]

VESTNIK MELKOGO KREDITA – Spb., 1912-17 n9 – 126mf – 9 – COR-562/1 – ne IDC [334]

VESTNIK METALLISTA – Petrograd. 1917-1918; nos. 1-6 – 1 – 35.00r – us Hoover Inst Photo [072]

VESTNIK MOSKOVSKOGO UNIVERSITETA – (Available: 1946(1); 1950(2, 4, 7); 1951(1, 4, 7); 1952(4, 7, 11); 1953-1989; Supplemented: 1971-1989. 123mf) – S.12. Pravo. M., 1946-1989 – 9 – R-8617/1 – ne IDC [340]

VESTNIK MURMANA – (Includes c.1: no.40 1923:Oct.6-no.42 (1923:Oct.20); no.48 1923:Dec.1; no.50 1923:Dec.15-no.51 (1923:Dec.22); no.75 1924:June 9) – Petrograd: Pravlenie Murmansko i zh.d., 1923 – 1 – CSUXAKZ1832-S – us Hoover Inst Photo [320]

VESTNIK NARODNOGO KOMISSARIATA INOSTRANNYKH DEL – Moskva: Narkominodel, 1919-1922. 4v – 1 – CSUX90-S572 – us Hoover Inst Photo [320]

VESTNIK NARODNOGO KOMISSARIATA PROSVESHCHENIIA – (Includes c.1: no.1 1921:Oct.-no.2 (1921:Nov.)) – Minsk: Gos izdvo S.S.R.B., 1921 – 1 – CSUXAKY9901-S – us Hoover Inst Photo [370]

VESTNIK NARODNOGO KOMISSARIATA VNESHNE I TORGOVLI – Moskva: Narkomvneshtorg, 1921-1922. 2v – 1 – CSUX90-S125 – us Hoover Inst Photo [380]

VESTNIK N.K.I.D. *see* VESTNIK NARODNOGO KOMISSARIATA INOSTRANNYKH DEL

VESTNIK OBRAZOVANIIA I VOSPITANIIA – Nauchno-Pedagogicheskii zhurnal.Kazan', 1914-16. 9v. BR-8185/2 – 8 – ne IDC [073]

VESTNIK OBSHCHESTVA RASPROSTRANENIIA PROSVESHCHENIIA MEZHDU EVREIAMI V ROSSII – St. Petersburg, 1910-13.v1-22.BR-8186/2 – 8 – ne IDC [947]

VESTNIK OBSHCHESTVA REVNITELEI ISTORII – St. Petersburg, 1914. v1. Continued as: Vestnik Imperatorskogo Obshchestva Revnitelei Istorii. v2-3, 1915-16. B-1444/2 – 8 – ne IDC [947]

VESTNIK ODESSKOGO GUB. OTDELA NARODNOGO OBRAZOVANIIA = VISTNIK ODESKOHO HUB. VIDDILU NARODNOI OSVITY – Odessa: Otdel, 1920-1922. 3v – 1 – CSUX89-S901 – us Hoover Inst Photo [370]

VESTNIK OPYTNOGO DELA / N.K.Z. Upravlenie po opytnomu delu Sredne-chernozemnoi oblasti – (Library has: July/Aug. 1921) – Voronezh: Red.-izdatelskii komitet Narkomzema Sredne-chernozemno i oblasti, 1921-1929 – 1 – CSUX89-S787 – us Hoover Inst Photo [600]

VESTNIK OPYTNOGO DELA SR.-CHERN. OBL. – (Library has: 1929) – Voronezh: Izdvo "Kommuna", 1926-1929. 4v – 1 – CSUX89-S793 – us Hoover Inst Photo [600]

VESTNIK OPYTNOGO DELA SREDNE-CHERNOZEMNOI OBLASTI *see* VESTNIK OPYTNOGO DELA SR.-CHERN. OBL.

VESTNIK PARIZHKIKH MOD – Moscow, 1836-50.Lacking: 1946-47. BR-8187/2 – 8 – ne IDC [947]

VESTNIK PARTII NARODNOI SVOBODY – St. Petersburg. Feb.-May, 1906, nos. 1-12; 1917, nos. 1-5, 17-18 – 1 – 35.00r – us Hoover Inst Photo [335]

VESTNIK PECHATNOGO DELA I IZVESTIIA OBSHCHESTVA VLADELTSEV PECHATNYKH ZAVEDENII V S. PETERBURGE – (Lacking: n1 1909) – Spb, 1908-10 – 8 – BR-4308 2 – ne IDC [947]

VESTNIK PETROGRADSKOGO TSENTRAL'NOGO SEL'SKOKHOZIAISTVENNOGO OBSHCHESTVA – Pg., 1915-16 n10 – 6mf – 9 – COR-563/1 – ne IDC [334]

VESTNIK POPECHITEL'STV O NARODNOI TREZVOSTI – Ezhenedel'nyi zhurnal. St. Petersburg, 1903-05. Lacking some issues. BR-9273/2 – 8 – ne IDC [073]

VESTNIK PRAVA I NOTARIATA – Organ advokatury, notariata, suda. Ezhenedel'nyi zhurnal. M. 1908-17. Lacking: 1908-09. BR-9573 1 – 9 – ne IDC [073]

VESTNIK PROMYSHLENNOSTI, TORGOVLI I TRANSPORTA / Sovet sezdov promyshlennosti i transporta – Moskva: Izd. Torgovo-promyshlenno i gazety, 1923-1926. 4v – 1 – CSUX90-S195 – us Hoover Inst Photo [380]

VESTNIK PROMYSHLENNOSTII TORGOVLI – (Library has: no.1-9, 1922) – Moskva: Vysshii sovet narodnogo khoziaistva, 1922. 1v – 1 – CSUX89-S812 – us Hoover Inst Photo [338]

VESTNIK PROMYSLOVOI KOOPERATSII – (Missing: 1920 n1-2) – M., 1919-20 n4 – 5mf – 9 – COR-564/1 – ne IDC [334]

VESTNIK PROSVESHCHENIIA – (Library has: Jan./March 1919) – Petrograd: Izd. Narodnogo Komissariata po prosveshcheniiu, 1918-1919. 2v – 1 – CSUX90-S111 – us Hoover Inst Photo [370]

VESTNIK PROTIVOVOZDUSHNOI OBORONY – (Library has: Jan.-Apr., July-Sept., Nov. 1936; Apr., June-July 1937; Jan. 1966-Dec. 1971) – Moskva: Gos. voen. izdvo, 1931- – 1 – CSUX90-S557 – us Hoover Inst Photo [355]

VESTNIK PSIKHOLOGII, KRIMINAL'NOI ANTROPOLOGII I GIPNOTIZMA – Spb. 1904-16. Lacking: v. 6, 1906; v. 4, 1913; v.?, 1915. BR-10,496 2 – 9 – ne IDC [150]

VESTNIK PSKOVSKOI KOOPERATSII *see* IZVESTIIA PSKOVSKOGO GUBSOIUZA

VESTNIK PUTE I SOOBSHCHENIIA POLITICHESKOI I EKONOMICHESKOI ZHIZNI, LITERATURY I ISKUSSTVA *see* VIESTNIK PUTE I SOOBSHCHENIIA

VESTNIK RABOCH. I KREST. PRAVITELSTVA SOIUZA SSR. PRILOZHENIE *see* VESTNIK TSENTRALNOGO ISPOLNITELNOGO KOMITETA, SOVETA NARODNYKH KOMISSAROV I SOVETA TRUDA I OBORONY SOIUZA SOVETSKIKH SOTSIALISTICHESKIKH RESPUBLIK. PRILOZHENIE

VESTNIK SAMARSKOGO GUBERNSKOGO STATISTICHESKOGO BIURO / Samarskoe gubernskoe statisticheskoe biuro – (Includes c.1: no.1 1920:Nov./Dec.-no.2 (1921:Jan./Mar.)) – Samara: [Biuro], 1921. 2no – 1 – CSUXAKZ2561-S – us Hoover Inst Photo [304]

VESTNIK SEL'SKOKHOZIAISTVENNOI KOOPERATSII – M., 1919 n1-2 – 1mf – 9 – COR-566/1 – ne IDC [334]

VESTNIK SHKOLY – Obshchestvenno-pedagogicheskii literaturno-nauchnyi zhurnal. nr. 1-103. Petrograd. 1914-16. Lacking: 1914 (35, 46); 1915, (71); 1916, (103). BR-8188 2 – 8 – ne IDC [370]

VESTNIK SIBIRSKOI SEL'SKOKHOZIAISTVENNOI KOOPERATSII – (Cont as: Sibirskaia Sel'skokhoziaistvennaia Kooperatsiia. Novosibirsk, 1928-29 n10/11) – Novosibirsk, 1925-27 n18 – 48mf – 9 – COR-567/1+COR-688/1 – ne IDC [334]

VESTNIK SLAVIANSTVA – Kazan', 1888-96. v1-11. Lacking some issues. B-1972/2 – 8 – ne IDC [947]

VESTNIK SOTSIALISTICHESKOI AKADEMII – v. 1-6. M. 1922-23. Cont. as: Vestnik Kommunisticheskoi akademii. v. 7-42. M. 1924-30. BR-164 2 – 8 – ne IDC [300]

VESTNIK SOVETSKOI IUSTITSII : DVUKHNEDELNYI ZHURNAL NARKOMIUSTA I IURIDICHESKOGO OBSHCHESTVA USSR – (Library has: 1927, no. 1-24) – Kharkov: I Urid. izdvo NKIU USSR, 1922-1928. 7v – 1 – CSUX89-S800 – us Hoover Inst Photo [340]

VESTNIK SOVETSKOI IUSTITSII NA UKRAINE – (Library has: 1922, no.1) – Kharkov: Izd. Narodnogo komissariata iustitsii, 1922. 1v – 1 – CSUX89-S880 – us Hoover Inst Photo [340]

VESTNIK SPB-AGO VRACHEBNAGO OBSHCHESTVA VZAIMNOI POMOSHCHI – St. Petersburg, 1902-15.Lacking some issues. BR-9274/2 – 8 – ne IDC [947]

VESTNIK SREDNEGO POVOLZHIA : ORGAN SAMARSKOGO GUBISPOLKOMA I SREDNE-VOLZHSKOI PLANOVOI KOMISSII – Samara: Samarski i Gubispolkom i SR.-Volzhsk. planov. kom., 1925-1926. 2v – 1 – CSUX89-S815 – us Hoover Inst Photo [320]

VESTNIK STATISTIKI – (Journal of statistics). 1919-30 – 3 – us Readex [310]

VESTNIK STATISTIKI – Journal of Statistics. Moscow. U.S.S.R. 1961- – 1 – us UMI [073]

VESTNIK STATISTIKI – Moscow. 1919-1929; Jan.-Feb. 1949; 1951-1955 – 1 – 35.00r – us Hoover Inst Photo [073]

VESTNIK STATISTIKI – Moscow. 1919-25 – 1 – 92.00 – us L of C Photodup [310]

VESTNIK STATISTIKI / Russia. (1919-). Tsentral'noe Statisticheskoe Upravlenie – (Central Statistical Administration: Journal of statistics). 34 v. 1919-30 – 3 – us Readex [310]

VESTNIK STRAKHOVOGO SOVETA / Russian S.F.S.R. Strakhovoi sovet – (Includes c.1: no.1 1918:May) – Moskva: Komissariat, 1918 – 1 – CSUXAKZ3078-S – us Hoover Inst Photo [650]

VESTNIK STUDENCHESKOI KOOPERATSII – M., 1916 n1-5 – 2mf – 9 – COR-568/1 – ne IDC [334]

VESTNIK TEATRA = THEATER NEWS – Moscow. n1-94 + 3 suppls. feb 2 1919-aug 15 1921 – 29mf – 9 – $230.00 – us Ross [790]

VESTNIK TEATRA *see* ERMITAZH

VESTNIK TEKHNICHESKOI LITERATURY KNIZHNAGO MAGAZINA G. V. GOL'STENA – Spb. 1908-14. Available: 1908, 2-20; 1909, 1-6; 1910, 2-12; 1913, 3-7; 1914, 1-6, 10 12. BR-4309 2 – 8 – ne IDC [073]

VESTNIK TSENTRALNOGO ISPOLNITELNOGO KOMITETA, SOVETA NARODNYKH KOMISSAROV I SOVETA TRUDA I OBORONY SOIUZA SOVETSKIKH SOTSIALISTICHESKIKH RESPUBLIK. PRILOZHENIE – (Includes c.1: 1924:no.1) – [Moskva: T SIK], 1923 – 1 – CSUXAKZ0114-S – us Hoover Inst Photo [320]

VESTNIK TVERSKOI KOOPERATSII – (Missing: 1919 n1) – Tver, 1919 n1-2 – 2mf – 9 – COR-569/1 – ne IDC [334]

VESTNIK VNESHNE I TORGOVLI UKRAINY / Upravleniia Upolnomochennogo Narodnogo komissariata vneshne i torgovli R.S.F.S.R. pri Sovnarkome USSR – (Library has: Aug. 8, Aug. 22, Oct. 27, Dec. 22, 1923; Jan. 17, Apr. 12, 1924) – Kharkov: Izd. Redizdata Ukrvneshtorga, 1922-1924. 3v – 1 – CSUX89-S932 – us Hoover Inst Photo [380]

VESTNIK VOENNYKH ZNANII – Saraevo, 1929-31. v1-10. BR-5732/2 – 8 – ne IDC [947]

VESTNIK VOZDUSHNOGO FLOTA – (Library has: March-Aug., Oct. 1933) – Moskva: Gos. voen. izdvo, 1918-1961. 43v – 1 – CSUX90-S117 – us Hoover Inst Photo [355]

VESTNIK VREMENNAGO PRAVITEL'STVA – Petrograd. Continuation of Pravitel'stvennyi vestnik. Mar. 5-Oct. 26, 1917, nos. 1(46)-186(232). Missing: nos. 9, 14-16, 25, 26, 29, 30, 35, 36 – 1 – 35.00r – us Hoover Inst Photo [072]

VESTNIK VREMENNAGO PRAVITELSTVA – Petrograd. no. 1-187. Mar 5-Oct 27 1917. Incomplete – 1 – us NY Public [072]

VESTNIK VREMENNAGO PRAVITELSTVA – Russia. n1-187. 1917 – 2r – 1 – us Ross [947]

VESTNIK VREMENNAGO PRIAMURSKAGO PRAVITEL'STVA – Vladivostok. June 30-July 21, Aug. 9-17, 1921 – 1 – 35.00r – us Hoover Inst Photo [072]

VESTNIK VSEROSSIISKIKH S'EZDOV DEATELEI PO KUSTARNOI PROMYSHLENNOSTI – (Cont as: Vestnik Kustarnoi Promyshlennosti. Spb., 1914-18 n9. Missing: 1915 n9-10; 1916 n10; 1917 n1, 6-10) – Spb., 1912-13 – 51mf – 9 – COR-561/1 – ne IDC [334]

VESTNIK VYSSHEI SHKOLY – Journal of Higher Education. Moscow. U.S.S.R. 1961- – 1 – us UMI [073]

VESTNIK VYSSHEI SHKOLY – Moscow, 1940-71.Lacking issues. BR-10,476/1 – 9 – ne IDC [073]

VESTNIK ZHIZNI – Ezhenedel'nyi nauchnyi, literaturnyi i politicheskii zhurnal. St. Petersburg, 1906-07. BR-4865/2 – 8 – ne IDC [947]

VESTOVOI – Zhurnal voenno-bibliograficheskii. Spb. 1902-05. Lacking: 1906 (115-116); 1909 (153-154, 156-157); 1910 (159-164); 1911 (176, 181-182); 1912 (184-192, 194); 1913 (196-198, 200-205); 1914 (208-213, 215); 1915 (220-224). BR-4310 2 – 8 – ne IDC [073]

VESTRY BOOKS, 1830-1912/NEATH, MINUTE BOOK / Neath. England – 1792 – 1 – uk Microform Academic [941]

VESTRY MINUTES / Bradford Springs. South Carolina. St. Philip's (Episcopal) Church – 1846-54.1 fiche – 9 – us South Carolina Historical [978]

VESTRY MINUTES / Charleston. South Carolina. St. Luke's (Episcopal) Church – 1866-1905. 9 fiches – 9 – us South Carolina Historical [978]

VESTRY MINUTES / Fort Motte. South Carolina. St. Matthew's (Episcopal) Church – 1767-78, 1785-1838. 4 fiches – 9 – us South Carolina Historical [978]

IL VESUVIO – Philadelphia, PA, 1896 – 2mf or 1r – 1,9 – us I.H.R.C. [978]

O VESUVIO : SEMANARIO LITTERARIO E NOTICIOSO – Manoas, Amazonas. 4-25 Abr 1909 – 1,5,6 – bl Biblioteca [072]

VESY – Moscow. year 1. no. 1-year 6. no. 12. Jan 1904-Dec 1909 – 1 – us NY Public [073]

VESY – Nauchno-literaturnyi i kritiko-bibliograficheskii ezhemesiachnik. (Red. S.A. Poliakov). 12 v. M. 1904-09. B-1111 2 – 8 – ne IDC [460]

VET / University of Kentucky. Department of Veterinary Science – No.1-24.1973-79. 1 fiche – 9 – us Spaulding [630]

VET. TE CONCORDANTIAE HEBR / Mandelkern, S – 1937 – 50mf – 8 – ne Slangenburg [220]

Vetancourt, Agustin de *see* TEATRO MEXICANO

LE VETEMENT DES LAPONS DE KAUTOKEINO / Roue-Delaporte, M – 9 – F70.00 – fr Ethnologie [306]

VETEMENT, PARURE, PARFUMS ET COIFFURE CHEZ LES TEDDA DU TIBESTI / Lopatinsky, O – 9 – F30.00 – fr Ethnologie [306]

Vetenskaps-Societeten i Upsala *see*
- ACTA SOCIETATIS REGIAE SCIENTIARUM UPSALIENSIS
- NOVA ACTA REGIAE SOCIETATIS SCIENTIARUM UPSALIENSIS. UPSALIAE, 1773-1850

VETER S KAVKAZA / Belyi, A – (Vpechatleniia). M. 1928. BR-605 2 – 8 – ne IDC [460]

VETERAN GUERILLA – (Includes v.1: no. 2-20, 22-37; v.2: no. 38-46, 48, 50-54; v.3: no. 58-59, 70-72, 74-76; v.5: no. 106, 108) – Sacramento, Calif.: Fernando V. Dulay, 1945- – 1 – CSUX87-S78 – us Hoover Inst Photo [355]

A VETERAN OF 1812: THE LIFE OF JAMES FITZGIBBON / FitzGibbon, Mary Agnes – Toronto: William Briggs; Montreal: C. Coates; Halifax: S. Huestis, 1894. 03110. (Pre-1900 Canadiana) – 9 – cn C.I.H.M. [971]

VETERANS' ADMINISTRATION ANNUAL REPORTS / U. S. Dept of Veterans' Affairs – (Offered as part of: LLMC's Military Law Collection) – 1934-79 – 141mf – 9 – $211.00 – LLMC 81-245 – us L.L.M.C. [324]

VETERANS' ADMINISTRATION DECISIONS / U. S. Veterans Administration – (Includes separate index vol and 4 suppl for v1. Apparently publ between 1946-55) – Washington: GPO. v1-2 in 7bks. 1931-55 decisions nos 1-715 – 41mf – 9 – $61.00 – LLMC 80-522 – us L.L.M.C. [324]

VETERAN'S ADMINISTRATION PENSION PAYMENT CARDS / U. S. Veterans Administration – 1907-33. 2539 rolls. M850 – 1 – us Nat'l Archives [331]

VETERANS REVIEW – Los Angeles, CA.Nov/Dec 1974-May/Jun 1984. English – 1 – us A.J.P.C. [071]

VETERES ARCUS AUGUSTORUM TRIUMPHIS INSIGNES / Bellori, Giovanni Pietro – Romae. 1690. BO-144 1 – 9 – ne IDC [410]

VETERINARY CLINICAL PATHOLOGY – v6-1977- 1; v8- 1979- 5,6,9 – us UMI [636]

VETERINARY CLINICS OF NORTH AMERICA *see*
- VETERINARY CLINICS OF NORTH AMERICA – LARGE ANIMAL PRACTICE
- VETERINARY CLINICS OF NORTH AMERICA – SMALL ANIMAL PRACTICE

VETERINARY CLINICS OF NORTH AMERICA. EQUINE PRACTICE – v1-. 1985- – 1,5,6,9 – us UMI [636]

VETERINARY CLINICS OF NORTH AMERICA. FOOD ANIMAL PRACTICE – v1-. 1985- – 1,5,6,9 – us UMI [636]

VETERINARY CLINICS OF NORTH AMERICA – LARGE ANIMAL PRACTICE – (Cont in part: Veterinary Clinics of North America) – Philadelphia. v1-6. 1979-84* – 1 – D14738 – us UMI [636]

VETERINARY CLINICS OF NORTH AMERICA – LARGE ANIMAL PRACTICE *see* VETERINARY CLINICS OF NORTH AMERICA – SMALL ANIMAL PRACTICE

VETERINARY CLINICS OF NORTH AMERICA – SMALL ANIMAL PRACTICE – (Cont in part, in 1979, by: Veterinary Clinics of North America – Large Animal Practice. Former title: Veterinary Clinics of North America) – Philadelphia. v1-20 jan 1971-nov 1990. v21-23 jan 1991-nov 1993*. v24-27 jan 1994-nov 1997+ 1; v1-18 jan 1971-nov 1988. v19-23 jan 1989-nov 1993*. v24-27 jan 1994-nov 1997+ 5; v5-20 feb 1975-nov 1990. v21-23 jan 1991-nov 1993*. v24-27 jan 1994-nov 1997+ 9 – 1,5,9 – D6470 – us UMI [636]

VETERINARY CONTRIBUTION TO PUBLIC HEALTH PRACTICE – 1975 – 79p – it F.A.O. [636]

VETERINARY DERMATOLOGY – Elmsford. v1-8. aut 1989-1997+ 1,5,9; v2 1991* 5; v3 1993* 1,5,9 – 1,5,9 – D49605 – us UMI [636]
VETERINARY DIAGNOSTIC BACTERIOLOGY : A MANUAL OF LABORATORY PROCEDURES FOR SELECTED DISEASES OF LIVESTOCK – 1990 – 210p – it F.A.O. [636]
VETERINARY ECONOMICS – Lenexa. v1-15 1960-74*. v16-38 1975-1997+ 1; v16-18 1975-77*. v19-22 1978-81. v23-35 1982-94*. v36-38 1995-97+ 5; v16-38. 1975-97+ 9 – 1,5,9 – D10366 – us UMI [636]
VETERINARY EPIDEMIOLOGY AND ECONOMICS IN AFRICA = EPIDEMIOLOGIE ET ECONOMIE VETERINAIRES EN AFRIQUE. MANUEL A L'USAGE DES PLANIFICATEURS DE LA SANTE ANIMALE : A MANUAL FOR USE IN THE DESIGN AND APPRAISAL OF LIVESTOCK HEALTH POLICY / Putt, SN H et al – 1987 – 9 – $22.00 – 92-9053-147-9 – et ILRI [636]
VETERINARY IMMUNOLOGY AND IMMUNOPATHOLOGY – Amsterdam. v1-17. 1980-87 1,5; v18-29 feb 1988-sep 1991. v30-42 nov 1991-1994*. v43-60 1995-97+ 1,5,9 – 1,5,9 – D42339 – us UMI [636]
VETERINARY IMMUNOLOGY AND IMMUNOPATHOLOGY – v1-7. 1980-84 – 1,5,6,13 – sz Elsevier [073]
VETERINARY MEDICINE – (Cont: VM/SAC Veterinary Medicine/Small Animal Clinician) – Lenaxa. v80-92. 1985-97+ – 1 – D2413.01 – us UMI [636]
VETERINARY MICROBIOLOGY – Amsterdam. v1-21. 1976-feb 1990 1,5; v16-21. jan 1988-feb 1990 9; v22-57. mar 1990-nov 1997+ 1,5,9 – 1,5,9 – D42062 – us UMI [636]
VETERINARY MICROBIOLOGY – v1-9. 1976-84 – 1,5,6,13 – sz Elsevier [073]
VETERINARY NEWSLETTER / Georgia. University. Agricultural Extension Service – v. 1-58. 1962-69 – 1,5,6 – us Spaulding [636]
VETERINARY PARASITOLOGY – Amsterdam. v1-37. 1975-90 1,5; v26-37. dec 1987-1990 9; v38-69. 1991-97+ 1,5,9 – 1,5,9 – D42063 – us UMI [636]
VETERINARY PARASITOLOGY – v1-15. 1975-84 – 1,5,6,13 – sz Elsevier [636]
VETERINARY PATHOLOGY – (Former title: Pathologia Veterinaria) – Basel. v3-11. 1966-74 1; v7-9 1970-72. v11 1974 5 – 1,5 – D2072 – us UMI [636]
VETERINARY PRACTICE – 1965- 1; 1975- 5,6,9 – us UMI [636]
VETERINARY RADIOLOGY – 1980- – 1,5,6,9 – us UMI [636]
VETERINARY RECORD – (Incl v2 1980- of its suppl: In Practice) – London. v1-141. 1888-1997+ 1; v82-85 fal 1968-dec 1969. v88-141 1971-97+ 5; v96-141. 1975-97+ 9 – 1,5,9 – D2146 – us UMI [636]
VETERINARY RECORD – v58-82. 1946-68 – 1,5,6 – us Princeton Micro [073]
VETERINARY RESEARCH – (Cont: Annales de Recherches Veterinaires – Annals of Veterinary Research) – Paris. v24-25 1993-94*. v26-28 1995-97+ – 1 – D42463.01 – us UMI [636]
VETERINARY RESEARCH COMMUNICATIONS – v1-8. 1977-84 – 1,5,6,13 – sz Elsevier [073]
VETERIS HOMINIS PER EXPENSA QUATUOR NOVISSIMA METAMORPHOSIS, ET NOVI GENESIS / Stanihursto, Guillermo – Antwerpen, 1661 – 4mf – 9 – ne IDC [700]
VETERIS TESTAMENTI CONCORDANTIAE HEBRAICAE / Mandelkern, S – Ed. 2a – Dfl175.00 – ne Slangenburg [220]
VETERIS TESTAMENTI GRAECI : CODICES VATICANUS ET SINAITICUS CUM TEXTU RECEPTO / Nestle, Eberhard – Lipsiae: F A Brockhaus, 1880 – 1mf – 9 – 0-8370-9493-3 – 1986-3493 – us A.T.L.A. [220]
VETERUM ALIQUOT SCRIPTORUM. SPICILEGIUM / Achery, D'Dom Luc – Ed 2a. Parisiis. Tom. 1-2. 1661-1687; Ed 1a. Parisiis. Tom 3-13. 1665-1681 – 15mf – 8 – Dfl735.00 – ne Slangenburg [240]
VETERUM SCRIPTORUM ET MONUMENTORUM HISTORICORUM, DOGMATICORUM, MORALIUM AMPLISSIMA COLLECTIO / Martene, Edmond & Durand, U – Parisiis. v1-9. 1724-33 – 320mf – 9 – Dfl1,124.00 – ne Slangenburg [220]
VETLANDAPOSTEN – Eksjo, Sweden. 1893-1960 – 85r – 1 – sw Kungliga [072]
VETLANDAPOSTEN *see* SMALANDSTIDNINGEN
Vetro, VL *see* THE EFFECTS OF AEROBIC DANCE EXERCISE AND NUTRITION INTERVENTION IN CHOLESTEROL LEVELS
Vetter, Ferdinand *see*
– DIE ARMENNOT; EIN SYLVESTERTRAUM; EINES SCHWEIZERS WORT
– DER BAUERN-SPIEGEL, ODER, LEBENSGESCHICHTE DES JEREMIAS GOTTHELF
– DER JUNGE HALLER
– KAETHI, DIE GROSSMUTTER, ODER, DER WAHRE WEG DURCH JEDE NOT
– LEIDEN UND FREUDEN EINES SCHULMEISTERS
– DIE PREDIGTEN TAULERS
– SCHILLERS FLUCHT AUS STUTTGART
– ULI DER PAECHTER
– WIE ANNE BAEBI JOWAEGER HAUSHALTET UND WIE ES IHM MIT DEM DOKTERN GEHT
– WIE ULI DER KNECHT, GLUECKLICH WIRD
VETTER GABRIEL : NOVELLE / Heyse, Paul; ed by Corwin, Robert N – (German text with an introduction and notes in English. Includes bibliographical references) – New York: H Holt, 1911 – 1 – us U.W. Library [830]
Vetter, Heinrich *see* OESTERREICHISCHES GEFALLS-STRAFRECHT VON HEINRICH VETTER
Vetter, Paul *see*
– DIE METRIK DES BUCHES JOB
– DIE RELIGIONSVERHANDLUNGEN AUF DEM REICHSTAGE ZU REGENSBURG 1541
LA VETTONIA / Rodriguez Ordonez, Joaquin – 1879 – 9 – 1.50f – sp Bibl Santa Ana [830]
VETTUORIA INCONTRA EL TURCO, DE MENON / Menon (pseud. Agostino Rava) – Venetia, 1571 – 1mf – 9 – H-8317/1 – ne IDC [956]
VETUS DISCIPLINA CANONICORUM REGULARIUM ET SAECULARIUM / Amort, E – Venetiis. v1-2. 1747 – Dfl81.00 – ne Slangenburg [240]
VETUS DISCIPLINA MONASTICA / Herrgott, M – Parisiis, 1726 – 15mf – 8 – Dfl32.00 – ne Slangenburg [240]
VETUS LITURGIA ALEMANICA / ed by Gerbertus, M – San Blasii. v1-3. 1776 – 24mf – 8 – Dfl84.00 – ne Slangenburg [240]
VETUS REGISTRUM SARISBERIENSE = REGISTER OF ST OSMUND : ALIAS DICTUM REGISTRUM S. OSMUNDI EPISCOPI (RS78) / Salisbury (Diocese); ed by Rich-Jones, W – v1 1883 v2 1884 – Dfl30.00v – ne Slangenburg [240]
VETUS TESTAMENTUM – Leiden. v1-40. 1951-90 – 5,9 – Dfl4,000.00; Dfl100.00v – ne Swets [240]
VETUS TESTAMENTUM HEBRAICUM / ed by Kennicott, Benjaminus – 2 v. 1776-1780 – 1 – us A.T.L.A. [220]
Vetvenitskii, Konstantin *see* VNEBOGOSLUZHEBNAYA BESEDA O POCHITANII SVYATYKH IKON. OTVET POSLEDOVATELYAM PASHKOVA
LA VEUVE EN DROIT CANONIQUE / Rosambert, Andre – Paris: Jouve, 1923. xviii,248p. (Les Femmes Collection) – 3mf – 9 – $8.00 – fr Bibl Nationale [240]
VI – (Konsumentbladet 1930-36) – Stockholm, Sweden. 1937-67 – 33r – 1 – sw Kungliga [073]
VI DIRO SENTITE BENE / Cimarosa, D – (Full score) – London: Skillern, Goulding, 179- – 1 – us Sibley [780]
V.I. LENIN I ISTORIIA KLASSOV I POLITICHESKIKH PARTII V. ROSSII / AON PRI TSK KPSS / ed by Kim, M P – L., 1970. 519p – 6mf – 9 – ne IDC [320]
V.I. LUKIN, 1737-1794 / Berkov, P N – M, L 1950. BR-6095 2 – 8 – ne IDC [920]
VI – VOLKS-ILLUSTRIERTE *see* SOWJETRUSSLAND IM BILD
VIA – Cambridge. v1-7. 1968-83* – 1 – D12327 – us UMI [073]
VIA BRIUSOV / Lelevich, G – 1926 – 8 – BR-1361 2 – ne IDC [947]
VIA CHRISTI : AN INTRODUCTION TO THE STUDY OF MISSIONS / Hodgkins, Louise Manning – (Includes index) – New York: Macmillan, 1901 – 1mf – 9 – 0-8370-6503-8 – 1986-0503 – us A.T.L.A. [240]
VIA LACTEA : ORGAM DO GREMIO LITTERARIO "JOSE DO PATROCINIO" – Diamantina, May 1914 – 1,5,6 – bl Biblioteca [072]
THE VIA MEDIA OF THE ANGLICAN CHURCH / Newman, John Henry Cardinal – London: Longmans, Green, 1885 – 3mf – us A.T.L.A. [240]
THE VIA MEDIA OF THE ANGLICAN CHURCH. ILLUSTRATED IN LECTURES, LETTERS AND TRACTS WRITTEN BETWEEN 1830 AND 1841, WITH PREFACE AND NOTES / Newman, John Henry – London: B.M. Pickering, 1877 – 1 roll – 1 – 1-55879-488-3 – uk Libr Preservation [240]
VIA ROMANA DE MERIDA A SALAMANCA / Blazquez, Antonio – Madrid: Fortanet, 1912. B.R.A.H. 61, pp. 101-116 – sp Bibl Santa Ana [920]
VIA ROMANA DE MERIDA A VILLAFRANCA DE LOS BARROS / Monsalud, Marques de – Madrid: Fortanet, 1896. pp. 533-534. Boletin de la Real Academia de la Historia 28, 1896 – 1 – sp Bibl Santa Ana [946]
THE VIA VITAE OF ST BENEDICT / Hayes, Dom B – London, 1908 – 5mf – 8 – Dfl22.00 – ne Slangenburg [240]
VIA Y VIRTUDES DEL VENERABLE...PADRE CHRISTOBAL DE SANTA CATHALINA / Poffadas, Francisco de – Cordoba: Oficina de Diego y Juan Rodriguez – 1 – sp Bibl Santa Ana [240]
VIACHESLAV IVANOV / Stepun, F A – "Sovremennye zapiski". v. 62. Paris. 1936. BR-3297 2 – 8 – ne IDC [920]
VIACHESLAV IVANOV. RUSSKAIA MYSL' / Shestov, L – v10 1916. BR-3299 2 – 8 – ne IDC [190]
Viader, J *see* REFLEXIONES SOBRE LAS ENFERMEDADES QUE AFLIGEN A LAS TROPAS...DEL ROSELLON
VIAGE ESTATICO AL MUNDO PLANETARIO. TOMO 1 / Hervas y Panduro, Lorenzo – 1793 – 1mf – 9 – Pta1,000.00 – 84-85422-91-0 – sp Pentalfa [520]
VIAGE ESTATICO AL MUNDO PLANETARIO. TOMO 2 / Hervas y Panduro, Lorenzo – 1793 – 1mf – 9 – Pta1,000.00 – 84-85422-92-9 – sp Pentalfa [520]
VIAGE ESTATICO AL MUNDO PLANETARIO. TOMO 3 / Hervas y Panduro, Lorenzo – 1794 – 2mf – 9 – Pta1,500.00 – 84-85422-93-7 – sp Pentalfa [520]
VIAGE ESTATICO AL MUNDO PLANETARIO. TOMO 4 / Hervas y Panduro, Lorenzo – 1794 – 1mf – 9 – Pta1,000.00 – 84-85422-94-5 – sp Pentalfa [520]
VIAGEM AO ARAGUAYA / Magalhaes, Couto de – Sao Paulo, 3.a ed 1934 – 6mf – 8 – ne Slangenburg [910]
VIAGEM AO TAPAJOS / Coudreau, Henri – Sao Paulo, 1944 – 6mf – 8 – ne Slangenburg [910]
VIAGENS AO NORDESTE DO BRASIL : "TRAVELS IN BRAZIL" / Koster, Henry – Sao Paulo, 1942 – 11mf – 8 – ne Slangenburg [910]
VIAGENS NO BRASIL / Gardner, George – Sao Paulo, 1942 – 8mf – 8 – ne Slangenburg [910]
VIAGGI FATTI DA VINETIA, ALLA TANA, IN PERSIA, IN INDIA, ET IN CONSTANTINOPOLI / ed by Manuzio, Aldo – Vinegia, 1545 – 4mf – 9 – H-8152/1 – ne IDC [956]
VIAGGIO DA VENETIA, A COSTANTINOPOLI PER MARE, E PER TERRA, ET INSIEME QUELLO DI TERRA SANTA / Rosaccio, G – Venetia, 1598 – 4mf – 9 – H-8399/1 – ne IDC [956]
VIAGGIO DA VENETIA AL SANTO SEPOLCRO, ET AL MONTE SINAI : CON IL DISSEGNO DELLE CITTA CASTELLI, VILLE, CHIESE, MONASTERIJ, ISOLE, PORTI, ET FIUMI, ... / Noe, B – Venetia, 1598 – 3mf – 9 – H-8218/1 – ne IDC [956]
VIAGGIO E MISSIONE CATTOLICA FRA I MENSA I BOGOS E GLI HABAB : CON UN CENNO GEOGRAFICO E STORICO DELL'ABISSINIA / Sapeto, Giuseppe – Roma: Propaganda Fide, 1857 – us Res Libr [240]
VIAIE DE LA TIERRA SANTA, Y DESCRIPCION DE IERUSALEN, Y DEL SANTO MONTE LIBANO, CON SON RELACION DE COSAS MARAUILLOSAS, ... / Ceuerio de Vera, J – Madrid, 1597 – 4mf – 9 – H-8393/1 – ne IDC [956]
O VIAJANTE – Uba, 15 Oct, Dec 1957; Mar, May, Sep-Nov 1958; Jan, Apr-May, Jul-Dec 1959; Jan-May, Jul, Oct-Dec 1960; Jan-Jun, Oct-Dec 1961; Jan, Mar, May-Aug, Oct-Nov 1962; Jan-Dec 1963; Jan, Nov 1964; Jul, Sep, Dec 1965; Dec 1967; Sep 1968; Jun, Sep, Nov-Dec 1969; Jul-Aug 1970; Jan 1973-Dec 1977; Feb, Sep, Nov-Dec 1979; Jan, Oct, Dec 1980 – 1,5,6 – bl Biblioteca [072]
VIAJANTE – Sobral-CE, Brazil. 13 Out 1886 – 1 – bl Biblioteca [072]
VIAJE DE CAMPOMANES A EXTREMADURA / Rodriguez Amaya, Esteban – Badajoz: Imp. de la Dip. Provincial, 1948 – sp Bibl Santa Ana [946]
VIAJE DE ESPANA. TOMO 1 / Ponz, Antonio – "nd ed 1776 – 1mf – 9 – Pta1,000.00 – 84-7848-370-5 – sp Pentalfa [946]
VIAJE DE ESPANA. TOMO 2 / Ponz, Antonio – 2nd ed 1777 – 1mf – 9 – Pta1,000.00 – 84-7848-371-3 – sp Pentalfa [946]
VIAJE DE ESPANA. TOMO 3 / Ponz, Antonio – 1774 – 1mf – 9 – Pta1,000.00 – 84-7848-372-1 – sp Pentalfa [946]
VIAJE DE ESPANA. TOMO 4 / Ponz, Antonio – 1779, 2nd ed – 1mf – 9 – Pta1,000.00 – 84-7848-373-X – sp Pentalfa [946]
VIAJE DE ESPANA. TOMO 5 / Ponz, Antonio – 2nd ed 1782 – 1mf – 9 – Pta1,000.00 – 84-7848-374-8 – sp Pentalfa [910]
VIAJE DE ESPANA. TOMO 6 / Ponz, Antonio – 1776 – 1mf – 9 – Pta1,000.00 – 84-7848-375-6 – sp Pentalfa [910]
VIAJE DE ESPANA. TOMO 7 / Ponz, Antonio – 1778 – 1mf – 9 – Pta1,000.00 – 84-7848-376-4 – sp Pentalfa [910]
VIAJE DE ESPANA. TOMO 8 / Ponz, Antonio – 1778 – 1mf – 9 – Pta1,000.00 – 84-7848-377-2 – sp Pentalfa [910]
VIAJE DE ESPANA. TOMO 9 / Ponz, Antonio – 1780 – 1mf – 9 – Pta1,000.00 – 84-7848-378-0 – sp Pentalfa [910]
VIAJE DE ESPANA. TOMO 10 / Ponz, Antonio – 1781 – 1mf – 9 – Pta1,000.00 – 84-7848-379-9 – sp Pentalfa [946]
VIAJE DE ESPANA. TOMO 11 / Ponz, Antonio – 1783 – 1mf – 9 – Pta1,000.00 – 84-7848-380-2 – sp Pentalfa [946]
VIAJE DE ESPANA. TOMO 12 / Ponz, Antonio – 1783 – 1mf – 9 – Pta1,000.00 – 84-7848-381-0 – sp Pentalfa [946]
VIAJE DE LOS DUQUES DE BEJAR AL... BATUECAS – 1900 – 9 – 1.50f – sp Bibl Santa Ana [920]
VIAJE DE LOS RIOS DE ESPANA / Lorenzo, Pedro de – Madrid: Editora Nacional, 1968 – 1 – sp Bibl Santa Ana [946]
VIAJE DE SS.MM.Y A.A. A PORTUGAL EN DICIEMBRE DE 1866 – Madrid: Imp. y Estreotipia de M. Rivadeneyra, 1867 – 1 – sp Bibl Santa Ana [946]
VIAJE DE UN MONJE JERONIMO AL VIRREINATO DEL PERU EN EL SIGLO 17 / Silva, J Francisco – Madrid: Tip. Archivos, Bibliotecas y Museos, 1922. B.R.A.H. 81, pp. 433-460 y 82, pp. 132-164 y 201-214 – sp Bibl Santa Ana [946]
VIAJE ELECTORAL HECHO CON LA BOLSA A CUESTAS Y EL CUERPO MOLIDA A PALOS POR A LOS INFIERNOS DEL SUFRAGIO UNIVERSAL / Barrantes Moreno, Vicente – Madrid: Imp. Vda. e Hijos de Galiano, s.a. – 1 – sp Bibl Santa Ana [320]
UN VIAJE FASCINANTE POR LA AMERICA HISPANA DEL SIGLO 16. MADRID, 1969 / OC ANA D IEGO DE-A L V A REZ, A RTURO; ed by Ronco Tovar, O F M – Madrid: Graf. Calleja, 1969 – 1 – sp Bibl Santa Ana [970]
VIAJE LITERARIO AL NORTE CACERENO / Cortes Vazquez, Luis – Salamanca: Graf. Cervantes, 1973 – 1 – sp Bibl Santa Ana [440]
VIAJE POR ESPANA / Ponz, Antonio – v7-8. 1734 – 9 – 1.50f – sp Bibl Santa Ana [946]
VIAJE POR ESPANA Y PORTUGAL EN LOS ANOS 1494 Y 1495... / Muenzer, Jeronimo – Madrid: Tip. Arch. Bibl. y Mus., 1924. B.R.A.H. 84, pp. 32-119 y 197-279 – sp Bibl Santa Ana [306]
VIAJE Y PEREGRINACION DE JERUSALEN / Juan del Santisimo Sacramento, Fray – Lisboa: Imprenta de Domingo Gonzales, 1744 – 1 – sp Bibl Santa Ana [946]
VIAJE...CACERES / Ortega Munilla, Jose – 1881 – 9 – 1.50f – sp Bibl Santa Ana [910]
VIAJES DE BENJAMIN DE TUDELA. 1160-1173 / Gonzales Llubera, Ignacio – Madrid: V.H. Sanz Calleja Editores e impresores, 1918 – 1 – sp Bibl Santa Ana [910]
LOS VIAJES DE JOHN HAWKINS A AMERICA (1562-1595) / Rumen de Armas, Antonio – Madrid: Missionalia Hispanica, V. 1948 – 1 – sp Bibl Santa Ana [240]
VIAJES POR LA AMERICA MERIDIONAL / Azara, Felix – Madrid: Razon y Fe, 2v. 1934 – 1 – sp Bibl Santa Ana [970]

Vial Solar, Javier *see* EL CABALLERO DE LA GLORIA
Viana, Luiz *see* O NEGRO NA BAHAI
Viance, Georges *see* FORCE ET MISERE DU SOCIALISME
VIANDE / Morocco. Division du Plan et des Statistiques – 1965. BNE-3048 1 – 9 – ne IDC [310]
VIANGCHAN MAI : LAO-LANGUAGE DAILY NEWSPAPER – (Jan 1983-Jun 1983 $50.00v) – Vientiane, Laos. Jan 1976-Dec 1982, Jan 1984-Dec 1986 – 1 – $100.00v – us Asia Libr [072]
Viard, Edouard *see* AU BAS-NIGER
Viardot, Louis *see* REASONS FOR UNBELIEF
VIAS FERREAS. ASIENTO Y CONSERVACION... / Alonso, Julio – Caceres: Imp. Moderna, 1930 – 1 – sp Bibl Santa Ana [946]
VIAS FERREAS. ASIENTO Y CONSERVACION. ATLAS / Alonso, Julio – Caceres: Imp. Moderna, 1930 – 1 – sp Bibl Santa Ana [946]
VIAS ROMANAS DE LA BETURIA DE LOS TURDULOS, POR DON ANGEL DELGADO / Blazquez, Antonio – Madrid: Fortanet, 1912. B.R.A.H. 61, pp. 359-370 – sp Bibl Santa Ana [920]
LAS VIAS ROMANAS DEL NORDESTE DE MERIDA / Roso de Luna, Mario – Madrid: Fortanet, 1912. B.R.A.H. 60, pp. 373-379 – sp Bibl Santa Ana [306]
VIAS ROMANAS ENTRE TOLEDO Y MERIDA. INFORMES / Coello, Francisco – Madrid: Fortanet, 1889. B.R.A.H. XV, pp. 5-43 – sp Bibl Santa Ana [946]
VIATA CAPITALEI – Bucharest, Romania. May 1949-Mar 1954 – 9r – 1 – us L of C Photodup [949]
VIATA CAPITALEI – Bucharest. Rumania. -w. 5 May 1949-26 Mar 1954. (11 reels) – 1 – uk British Libr Newspaper [949]
VIATA ECONOMICA – Bucharest, Romania. -w. 23 Aug 1963-Dec 1970. 7 reels – 1 – uk British Libr Newspaper [949]
VIATA NOUA – Galati, Romania. 1962-81 – 26r – 1 – us L of C Photodup [949]
VIATA SINDICALA – Bucharest, Romania. 1945-Mar 1953 – 13r – 1 – us L of C Photodup [949]
VIATA SINDICALA – Bucharest. Rumania. -d. 5 Apr 1951-12 Mar 1953. (Imperfect). (4 reels) – 1 – uk British Libr Newspaper [949]
VIATICUM NOVUM / Gessner, C (Jacques Houllier) – Tiguri: Apud Christophorum Frosch[overum], 1565 – 1mf – ne IDC [610]
VIATOR – Berkeley. v1-19 1970-88*. v20-21 1989-90. v22-25 1991-94*. v26-28 1995-97+ – 1 – D15685 – us UMI [073]
VIATSKAIA GUB – Sel'sko-khoziaistvennyi obzor Viatskoi gubernii za 1893 god, Vyp. 2. Leto i osen'za 1903 god, Vyp. 1. Viatka. 1894, 1903. BRZ-228 2 – 8 – ne IDC [947]
VIATSKAIA GUB – Statisticheskoe opisanie Urzhumskago uezda Viatskoi gubernii (sostavil N. Romanov). Viatka. 1879. BRZ-227 2 – 8 – ne IDC [947]
VIATSKII KOOPERATOR – (Missing: 1918 n1, 5-7, 10-12, 14-18; 1919 n12-17) – Viatka, 1918-20 n4 – 20mf – 9 – COR-575/1 – ne IDC [334]
Viazemskii, T K *see* BIBLIOGRAFIIA PO VOPROSU OB ALKOGOLIZME
Vibbert, William H *see* A GUIDE TO READING THE HEBREW TEXT
VIBRACIONES DE UNA LIRA / Moreno Torrado, Luis – 1887 – 9 – 1.50f – sp Bibl Santa Ana [810]
VIBRANT LIFE – (Cont: Your Life and Health) – Hagerstown. v 1-13. 1985-97+ 1,5,9; v10. 1994* 5 – 1,5,9 – D14894 – us UMI [613]
VIBRATION ENGINEERING = VIBROTEKHNIKA – Washington. v1-4. 1987-90* – 1 – D16664 – us UMI [620]
VIBRATIONAL SPECTROSCOPY – (Material for 1990- also included in the micro-edition of: Analytica Chimica Acta) – Amsterdam. v1-9 dec 1990-sep 1995*. v10-13 nov 1995-1998+ – 1,5,9 – D42630 – us UMI [530]
VICARIA DE LA SOLIDARIDAD DEL ARZOBISPADO DE SANTIAGO = VICARIATE OF SOLIDARITY OF THE ARCHBISHOP OF SANTIAGO – Santiago. 296 docs. 1980-1990 – 189mf – 9 – ne IDC [320]
THE VICARIOUS SACRIFICE, GROUNDED IN PRINCIPLES OF UNIVERSAL OBLIGATION / Bushnell, Horace – New York: Charles Scribner, 1866, c1865 – 2mf – 9 – 0-8370-9449-6 – 1986-3449 – us A.T.L.A. [240]
Vicary, T *see* THE ENGLISHMAN'S TREASURE
VICE-MAMA : EINE ERZAEHLUNG / Wildenbruch, Ernst von – Berlin: G Grote, 1903 – 1r – 1 – us U.W. Library [830]
VICENTE BARRANTES / Blanco Garcia, Francisco – Madrid: Saenz de Jubera, 1909 – sp Bibl Santa Ana [440]
Vicente Yanez, Juan *see* COMPENDIO... ANTIGUEDAD...NTR. SRA. GUADALUPE
Vicentino, N *see* L'ANTICA MUSICA RIDOTTA ALLA MODERNA PRATTICA
Vicesecretaria provincial de obras sindicales *see* 5TH EXPOSICION REGIONAL FILATELICA CACERENA
Vicetia, A M *see* LEXICON BONAVENTURIANUM
Vickers, John *see* THE REAL JESUS: A REVIEW OF HIS LIFE, CHARACTER, AND DEATH, FROM A JEWISH STANDPOINT
Vickers, K H *see* HUMPHREY DUKE OF GLOUCESTER. A BIOGRAPHY
Vickery, D J *see* SCHOOL BUILDINGS AND NATURAL DISASTERS
Vico, Giambattista *see* PRINCIPI DI SCIENZA NUOVA D'INTORNO ALLA COMUNE NATURA DELLE NAZIONI
VICOSENSE : PERIODICO DE LITTERATURA, INDUSTRIA E NOTICIAS – Vicosa, Alagoas. 30 Set 1893 – 1,5,6 – bl Biblioteca [072]
O VICOSO : PERIODICO DESTINADO A PROMOVER OS INTERESSES CATHOLICOS SEM SE DESCUIDAR DOS OUTROS INTERESSES DA PATRIA E DO POVO – Marianna, 31 Oct 1893; Feb-Jun, Aug-Dec 1894; Jun, Apr-May, Jul-Dec 1895; Jan-Mar, May-Aug, Oct-Dec 1896; Jan 1897-31 Dec 1899 – 1,5,6 – bl Biblioteca [072]
UNA VICTIMA DE AMOR DIVINO : VIDA EXTRAORDINARIA DE LA M.R. SOR FILOMENA... / ed by Bayle, Constantino – Madrid: Razon y Fe, 1926 – 1 – sp Bibl Santa Ana [240]
VICTIMAS Y VERDUGOS / Tejado, Gabino – Tomo I-II. 1896 – 9 – 1.50f – sp Bibl Santa Ana [946]
LES VICTIMES CLOITREES / Boutet, Monvel De – (French Theatre Series). Bordeaux, et Paris. Lepetit. 1792 – 9 – fr Hachette [820]
LA VICTOIRE – Montreal, Canada. 2 aut 1941-8 dec 1944 – 1r – 1 – Can$50.00 – cn Can Microfilming [072]
LA VICTOIRE – Paris. -d 2 jan 1916-12 Aug 1919. Not complete. 7 reels – 1 – uk British Libr Newspaper [072]
LA VICTOIRE / ed by Pascal, Joseph et al – St-Eustache, Canada. 16 jul 1948-24 jul 1958 – 6r – 1 – Can$70.00r – cn Can Microfilming [072]
LA VICTOIRE / La Republique Autoritaire – Quotidien socialiste national. Dir. Gustave Herve. Red. en chef, Marcel Bucard.Paris.1916-20 juin 1940 – 1 – fr A.C.R.P.P. [072]
VICTOIRE : ORGANE OFFICIEL DU FRONT DE LIBERATION DU QUEBEC / Front de liberation du Quebec – [Quebec]: FLQ. v1 no 1- 1967-. SEM35P183 – 1r – 1 – Can$15.00 – cn Bibl Nat [320]
VICTOIRES ET CHANSONS / Hugolin, Pere – Quebec: [s.n], 1913 ([Quebec: Imp. de l'Evenement]). SEM105P1665 – 1mf – 9 – Can$2.25 – cn Bibl Nat [780]
THE VICTOR BERGER PAPERS / ed by Stevens, Michael E – (Includes guide) – 1994 – 55r – 1 – $4,400.00 – D3302 – us L of C Photodup [320]
VICTOR COUSIN / Simon, Jules – Trans. by Melville B. Anderson and Edward Playfair Anderson. Chicago: A.C. McClurg, 1888. 220p – 1 – us U.W. Library [830]
Victor, H *see* THRESOR DES TROIS LANGUES, FRANCOISE, ITALIENNE, ET ESPAGNOLLE
VICTOR HEHN : EIN BILD SEINES LEBENS UND SEINER WERKE / Schrader, Otto – (Includes bibliographical references) – Berlin: S Calvary, 1891 – 1r – 1 – us U.W. Library [920]
VICTOR HUGO / Gautier, Theophile – Paris: E. Fasquelle, 1902. 292p. 4 fiches. (Literature Collection) – 9 – $10.00 – fr Bibl Nationale [440]
VICTOR OU L'ENFANT DE LA FORET / Guilbert de Pixerecourt – (French Theatre Series). Paris. Barba, an XI. 1803 – 9 – fr Hachette [820]
Victor, Walther *see* HEINE
Victore, Andreas de Sancto *see*
- EXPOSITIO SUPER DANIELEM
- EXPOSITIONES HISTORICAE IN LIBROS SALOMONIS

Victore, Hugo de St. *see* CANONICI REGULARIS SCTI VICTORIS PARISIENSIS OPERA OMNIA
VICTORIA – (Cont: Good Housekeeping's Victoria) – New York. v2 aug-dec 1988*. v3-11 feb 1989-dec 1997+ – 1 – D16495.01 – us UMI [073]
VICTORIA. 1899 FEDERAL REFERENDUM. ROLL OF ELECTORS WHO VOTED – 12v – 50mf and hard copy contents list – 9 – A$65.00 – at State Libr Vic [320]
VICTORIA AND ALBERT MUSEUM CATALOGUE – (Individual titles not listed separately) – London, 1862-1974 – 152 catalogues on 216mf – 9 – £1,360.00 – uk Chadwyck [700]
THE VICTORIA AND ALBERT MUSEUM LIBRARY SUBJECT CATALOGUE / Victoria and Albert Museum. London – (Over 1,500,000 entries, cross-references. All titles up to the end of 1979 as well as many received in 1980 and 1981. Published in 4 sections, each available and also listed separately) – 879mf – 9 – $4,800.00 complete series – 1-900853-20-5 – uk Mindata [700]
THE VICTORIA AND ALBERT MUSEUM LIBRARY SUBJECT CATALOGUE *see*
- APPLIED AND MINOR ARTS
- BOOK ART
- FINE ART AND ARCHAEOLOGY
- GENERAL ALPHABETICAL SEQUENCE

Victoria and Albert Museum. London *see*
- ARCHITECTURE AND SCULPTURE COLLECTION
- ART OF INDIA
- THE ART PRESS
- BRITISH POSTERS TO 1988
- CATALOGUE OF BOOKS IN THE PIOT COLLECTION
- CATALOGUES OF THE COLLECTION OF PRINTS, DRAWINGS AND PAINTINGS IN THE VICTORIA AND ALBERT MUSEUM
- CERAMICS COLLECTION
- DECORATIVE ART IN THE VICTORIA AND ALBERT MUSEUM
- DESIGN
- ENGLISH ARCHITECTURAL DRAWINGS
- FINE ART
- FINE ART AND DESIGN IN THE VICTORIA AND ALBERT MUSEUM
- FURNITURE AND WOODWORK COLLECTION
- GARRICK PAPERS
- GRAPHIC ART
- THE HOUSE OF WORTH FASHION DESIGNS
- THE JEWELLERY GALLERY
- LOCAL AND TRADITIONAL COSTUME
- METALWORK
- THE MUSLIM WORLD
- THE NATIONAL COLLECTION OF WATERCOLOURS
- NETSUKE
- PAQUIN WORTH FASHION DRAWINGS 1865-1956
- STUART MONARCHS: CORRESPONDENCE
- TEXTILE DESIGNS 1840-1985
- TEXTILES
- THEATRE COSTUME DESIGNS
- THEATRE SET DESIGNS
- TRADE CATALOGUES IN THE VICTORIA AND ALBERT MUSEUM
- THE VICTORIA AND ALBERT MUSEUM LIBRARY SUBJECT CATALOGUE
- VISUAL CATALOGUE OF FASHION AND COSTUME
- VISUAL CATALOGUE OF MINIATURE PAINTINGS
- WOMEN ARTISTS

Victoria and Albert Museum. London. Archive of Art and Design *see* HEAL'S CATALOGUES 1850-1950
Victoria and Albert Museum. London. Theatre Museum *see* THE RUSSIAN BALLET OF SERGE DIAGHILEV
Victoria and Albert Museum. National Art Library. London *see*
- THE MUSLIM WORLD
- NATIONAL ART LIBRARY CATALOGUE, VICTORIA AND ALBERT MUSEUM. AUTHOR CATALOGUE

Victoria. Australia *see* GOVERNMENT GAZETTE
Victoria. Australia. Parliament *see*
- LEGISLATIVE ASSEMBLY
- LEGISLATIVE COUNCIL
- PARLIAMENTARY DEBATES

VICTORIA CITY DIRECTORY 1901 – Victoria, BC: O B Ormond and P C MacGregor, 1901 – 1r – 1 – cn U.B.C. Preserve [910]
VICTORIA DAILY CHRONICLE – Canada. -d. July 1864-June 1866. Very imperfect. 32 ft – 1 – uk British Libr Newspaper [072]
VICTORIA DAILY CHRONICLE – Victoria, British Columbia, CN. May 1863-Jun 1866 – 7r – 1 – cn Commonwealth Micro [072]
VICTORIA DAILY COLONIST – Victoria, British Columbia, CN. 1967-80 – 240r – 1 – cn Commonwealth Micro [072]
VICTORIA DAILY EVENING POST – Victoria, British Columbia, CN. Apr-Nov 1909 – 3r – 1 – cn Commonwealth Micro [072]
VICTORIA DAILY GLOBE – Victoria, British Columbia, CN. Feb-Aug 1899 – 1r – 1 – cn Commonwealth Micro [072]
VICTORIA DAILY PRESS – Victoria, British Columbia, CN. Mar 1861-Oct 1862 – 2r – 1 – cn Commonwealth Micro [072]
VICTORIA DAILY STANDARD – Victoria, British Columbia, CN. Jul 1870-Dec 1886 – 5r – 1 – cn Commonwealth Micro [072]
VICTORIA DAILY STANDARD – Victoria, Canada. 1870-73 – 8r – 1 – $520.00 – cn Library Assoc [971]
VICTORIA DAILY WEEKLY TIMES – Victoria, British Columbia, CN. 1886-1913 – 19r – 1 – cn Commonwealth Micro [072]
VICTORIA ELECTORAL ROLL – 1949 – 355mf – 9 – A$360.00 – at State Libr Vic [920]
LA VICTORIA EXIJE EL PARTIDO UNICO DEL PROLETARIADO: CARTA DEL BURO / Partido Comunista de Espana. Comite Central – n.p. 193? Fiche W1246. (Blodgett Collection of Spanish Civil War Pamphlets) – 9 – us H.U. College Libr [946]
VICTORIA MAGAZINE – London. v1-36. may 1863-dec 1880* – 1 – D2840 – us UMI [073]
THE VICTORIA MAIL – Victoria, BC: E K Sargison, [1883?-18– or 19–] – 9 – cn C.I.H.M. [072]
Victoria, Maximio S *see* LAS DISCORDANCIAS ENTRE ALBERDI Y SUS ADVERSARIOS, SOBRE LA CULTURA PUBLICA
VICTORIA POLICE GAZETTE – 1853-1870 – 117mf – 9 – A$170.00 – at State Libr Vic [072]
VICTORIA PRICES CURRENT AND SHIPPING LIST – [Victoria, BC?]: A Stenhouse, [1860-18– or 19–] – 9 – cn C.I.H.M. [380]
VICTORIA TIMES – Victoria, Canada. Jun 1884-Sept 1980 – 1 – cn Commonwealth Micro [072]
VICTORIA TIMES-COLONIST – Victoria, Canada. Sept 1980- – 1 – cn Commonwealth Micro [072]
VICTORIA UNIVERSITY OF WELLINGTON LAW REVIEW – v.1-10, 1953-80 – 1,5 – 77.25 – us Gaunt [340]
THE VICTORIA WEEKLY BUDGET AND TOWN MAJOR'S JOURNAL – Victoria, BC: R McManus, [1889-18– or 19–] – 9 – cn C.I.H.M. [072]
VICTORIA WEEKLY CHRONICLE – Canada. -w. Jan 1864-June 1866. 2 reels – 1 – uk British Libr Newspaper [072]
VICTORIA WEEKLY TIMES – Canada. Victoria Times. April 1893-Dec 1911. 36 1 2 reels – 1 – uk British Libr Newspaper [072]
THE VICTORIAN – Melbourne, Australia. 5 Jul 1862-2 Apr 1864.-w. 1mqn reels – 1 – uk British Libr Newspaper [072]
VICTORIAN ART : SUBJECT COLLECTIONS – (Individual titles not listed separately) – 75 catalogues on 100mf – 9 – £630.00 – uk Chadwyck [700]
VICTORIAN BOOKBINDINGS : A PICTORIAL SURVEY / Allen, Sue – rev ed 1972 – 3mf – 15 – $34.00f – 0-226-68787-2 – us Chicago [760]
THE VICTORIAN CITY, INDUSTRIALISATION AND SOCIAL REFORM – (Part 2: Correspondence, Section B) – The papers of Sir Edwin Chadwick, 1800-90. Part 1: The Correspondence, Section A – 1 – us Primary [941]
THE VICTORIAN ERA SERIES *see* BRITISH FOREIGN MISSIONS, 1837-97
VICTORIAN EXPRESS – Garaldton, Australia. Geraldton Express. -w. Jan 1885-March 1916. 21 reels – 1 – uk British Libr Newspaper [072]
VICTORIAN FICTION AND OTHER NINETEENTH CENTURY FICTION – 549r – 1 – $34,200.00 – us OmniSys [420]
VICTORIAN HIGHLAND PIPE BAND ASSOCATION MINUTES – 1924-1955 – 14mf – 9 – at Corangamite [780]
VICTORIAN HIGHLAND PIPE BAND ASSOCIATION DELEGATES – 1946-1950 – 4mf – 9 – at Corangamite [780]

VICTORIAN LITERATURE : SIXTY YEARS OF BOOKS AND BOOKMEN / Shorter, Clement King – London: J. Bowden, 1897 – 1 roll – 1 – 1-55879-414-X – uk Libr Preservation [420]

VICTORIAN NATURALIST : THE JOURNAL AND MAGAZINE OF THE FIELD NATURALISTS' CLUB OF VICTORIA – (Missing: v19(p.52-69, 93-103); v39(p.77-96); v40(p.209-234); v45(p. 89-120)) – Melbourne. v19-48. 1902/1903-1932 – 90mf – 9 – 8549/1 – ne IDC [500]

VICTORIAN NEWSLETTER – Bowling Green. v1-92. apr 1952-fal 1997+ 1; v41-92. spr 1972-fal 1997+ 5; v49-92 spr 1976-fal 1997+ 9 – 1,5,9 – D7001 – us UMI [941]

VICTORIAN PAINTINGS WATERCOLOURS AND DRAWINGS : INCLUDING TOPOGRAPHICAL, MARINE AND SCOTTISH PICTURES – (73,000 reproductions, 7,500 artists) – $4,100.00 – 1-900853-95-7 – uk Mindata [750]

VICTORIAN PERIODICALS NEWSLETTER – (Cont by: Victorian Periodicals Review) – Toronto. v1-11. jan 1968-win 1978 1; v1-6 jan 1968-dec 1973*. v8-11 mar 1975-win 1978 5,9 – 1,5,9 – D10063 – us UMI [941]

VICTORIAN PERIODICALS NEWSLETTER *see* VICTORIAN PERIODICALS REVIEW

VICTORIAN PERIODICALS REVIEW – (Cont: Victorian Periodicals Newsletter) – Toronto. v12-30. spr 1979-win 1997+ – 1,5,9 – D10063.01 – us UMI [941]

VICTORIAN PERIODICALS REVIEW *see* VICTORIAN PERIODICALS NEWSLETTER

VICTORIAN PHILANTHROPY AND SOCIAL PROBLEMS. SERIES ONE: ARCHIVES OF THE RAGGED SCHOOL UNION AND THE SHAFTESBURY SOCIETY / Shaftesbury Society. Great Britain. Archives – (Part 1: Minutes of the Ragged School Union and Shaftesbury Society, 1844-1944. Part 2: The Ragged School Union Magazine, 1849-1975. Part 3: The Ragged School Union Magazine and continuations, 1876-1907) – 1844-1944. Series: Victorian Philanthropy and Social Problems – 1,9 – us Primary [025]

VICTORIAN PHILANTHROPY AND SOCIAL PROBLEMS. SERIES TWO: ARCHIVES OF THE CHARITY ORGANISATION SOCIETY, 1869-1938 – Includes: Charity Organisation Society, 1872-84; Charity Organisation Review, 1885-1921; Charity Organisation Quarterly, 1921-38 – 1 – us Primary [025]

VICTORIAN PHOTOGRAPHIC COLLECTION / Windsor Castle. Royal Archives – With printed index – 14 – £1,100.00 – uk World [700]

VICTORIAN POETRY – Morgantown. v1-35. 1963-97+ 1; v14-35. 1976-97+ 5,9 – 1,5,9 – D10365 – us UMI [420]

VICTORIAN POLICE GAZETTE CONSOLIDATED INDEX – 1859-1863 – 17mf – 9 – A$40.00 – at State Libr Vic [360]

VICTORIAN RAILWAYS WEEKLY NOTICES 1894-95 – 1v – 10mf – 9 – A$25.00 – at State Libr Vic [380]

THE VICTORIAN STATUTES : IN FOUR VOLUMES – (V1-3 contain public acts. v4 contains private acts. Suppl vol v5 publ in 1868 contains "A Selection of Imperial Statutes Apparently in Force in Australia") – John Ferres. v1-5. 1866 – 49mf – 9 – $73.00 – LLMC 96-008 – us L.L.M.C. [323]

VICTORIAN STUDIES – Bloomington. v1-41. sep 1957-sum 1998+ 1; v14-41. sep 1970-sum 1998+ 5; v20-41. aut 1976-sum 1998+ 9 – 1,5,9 – D1135 – us UMI [941]

VICTORIA-REGIA – Manaos, Amazonas. Jun 1933 – 1,5,6 – bl Biblioteca [072]

VICTORIOUS LIVING (CCC177) / Hsieh, Shou-ling – (In Chinese) – Shanghai: Association Press of China, 1941 – 1r – 1 – 1984-B500 – us A.T.L.A. [240]

VICTORIS VITENSIS HISTORIA PERSECUTIONIS AFRICANAE PROVINCIAE (MGH 1: 3. BD. 1. TEIL) / ed by Halm, C – 1879 – Dfl13.00 – ne Slangenburg [240]

Victoroff-Toporoff, V *see* ROSSICA ET SOVIETICA

THE VICTORY – St-Eustache, Canada. 28 jan 1954-v16 n17. 27 jul 1967 – 1r – 1 – Can$30.00 – cn Can Microfilming [072]

VICTORY *see* VICTORY BULLETIN

THE VICTORY: A NEW COLLECTION OF SACRED AND SECULAR MUSIC, COMPRISING A GREAT VARIETY OF TUNES, ANTHEMS, GLEES, ELEMENTARY EXERCISES AND SOCIAL SONGS... / Bradbury, William Batchelder – Ed. by Chester G. Allen and William F. Sherman. New York: Biglow & Main (Successors to William B. Bradbury), 1869. MUSIC 897 – 1 – us L of C Photodup [780]

VICTORY BULLETIN – (Former titles: Defense 1940-dec 9, 1941; Victory dec 16, 1941-mar 3, 1943) – Washington. 1940-44* – 1 – D5787 – us UMI [977]

Victory, Messack *see*
- THE STATE VS. MESSACK VICTORY AND OTHERS, IN THE SUPREME COURT OF SOUTH AFRICA (APPELLATE DIVISION)
- THE STATE VS. MESSACK VICTORY AND OTHERS, IN THE SUPREME COURT OF SOUTH AFRICA (SOUTH WEST AFRICA DIVISION)

THE VICTORY OF FAITH / Hare, Julius Charles – London: Macmillan, 1874 – 1mf – us A.T.L.A. [240]

VICTORY OF LOVE (CCC148) / Ho, David Chi-hsing – (In Chinese) – 1st ed. Hong Kong: Council on Christian Literature for Overseas Chinese, 1954 – 1r – 1 – 1984-B500 – us A.T.L.A. [240]

THE VICTORY OF THE GOSPEL : A SURVEY OF WORLD-WIDE EVANGELISM / Lilley, James Philip – (Includes bibliographical references and index) – London: Morgan & Scott, 1910 – 1mf – 9 – 0-8370-6140-7 – 1986-0140 – us A.T.L.A. [230]

VICTRIX – Curitiba, 1902-03. Incomplete – 1,5,6 – bl Biblioteca [072]

LA VID Y EL VINO EN LA TIERRA DE BARROS / Vidal Aragon, Pedro – Madrid: Ministerio de agricultura, 1964 – 1 – sp Bibl Santa Ana [630]

VIDA : REVISTA UNIVERSITARIA – Rio de Janeiro, Apr 1934-Dec 1936 – 1,5,6 – bl Biblioteca [072]

VIDA CIVIL Y MILITAR DE DON HERMENEGILDO GALEANA / Castro, Justino M – Mexico, 1931; Madrid: Razon y Fe, 1932 – 1 – sp Bibl Santa Ana [355]

A VIDA CONTRADICTORIA DE MACHADO DE ASSIS / Pontes, Eloy – Rio de Janeiro. 1939 – 1 – us Res Libr [972]

LA VIDA DE EVA PERON / Borroni, Otelo & Vacca, Roberto – [Buenos Aires]: Editorial Galerna, [1971-, c1970] – 1 – CSUXADQ5201-B – us Hoover Inst Photo [320]

VIDA DE FEDERICO 2 REY DE PRUSIA / Calzada, Bernardo Maria de – 1788 – 1mf – 9 – Pta1,000.00 – 84-7848-224-5 – sp Pentalfa [920]

VIDA DE GONZALO PIZARRO / Cardenal Iracheta, Manuel – Madrid: Ediciones Cultura Hispanica, 1953 – sp Bibl Santa Ana [920]

VIDA DE HERNANDO CORTES HECHA PEDAZOS.. / Morales, Adolfo de – 1795 – 9 – $1.50f – sp Bibl Santa Ana [946]

VIDA DE JUAN DUNS SCOTO / Jimenez Samaniego, Jose – (1741.$1.50f) – 1677 – 9 – $1.50f – sp Bibl Santa Ana [240]

VIDA DE LA SIERVA DE DIOS SOR ASUNCION GALAN DE SAN CAYETANO / Farina, P Jose Agustin – Barcelona: Luis Gili, 1924 – 1 – sp Bibl Santa Ana [240]

VIDA DE LA SIERVA DE DIOS SOR MARIA DE LOS DOLORES Y PATROCINIO, POR LA R.M. SOR MARIA ISABEL DE JESUS... / Bayle, Constantino – Madrid: Razon y Fe, 1926 – 1 – sp Bibl Santa Ana [240]

VIDA DE LA VENERABLE MARIA DE JESUS / Arcos, Francisco de – 1671 – 9 – $1.50f – sp Bibl Santa Ana [240]

VIDA DE LA VENERABLE SIERRA DE DIOS MARIA DE S. FRANCISCO, LLAMADA COMUNMENTE LA ROZAS... / Aluin, Juan – Tortosa: Imp. de Jose L. Foquet Sales, 1905. Reimpreso de Madrid, Eugenio Rodriguez, 1682. Andres Vazquez Jose – sp Bibl Santa Ana [240]

VIDA DE PIZARRO / Montolin, Manuel de – Segunda edicion. Barcelona. I.G. Seix Barral Hnos. S.A. Editores, 1934 – sp Bibl Santa Ana [350]

VIDA DE SAN ALBERTO MAGNO. DOCTOR DE LA IGLESIA / Menendez Reigada, A G – Almagro, Madrid: Razon y Fe, 1933 – 1 – sp Bibl Santa Ana [240]

VIDA DE SAN BERNARDO ABAD DE CLARAVAL / Bayle, Constantino & Pons, Jaime – Barcelona, Madrid: Razon y Fe, 1944 – 1 – sp Bibl Santa Ana [240]

VIDA DE SAN PEDRO DE ALCANTARA / Religioso de la Orden de San Francisco, Un – Madrid: Apostolado de la Prensa S.A., 1947 – 1 – sp Bibl Santa Ana [240]

VIDA DE SAN PEDRO DE ALCANTARA / Rivadeneira, Pedro de – 1880 – 9 – $1.50f – sp Bibl Santa Ana [240]

VIDA DE SCALABRINI ORTIZ / Galasso, Norberto – [Buenos Aires]: Ediciones del Mar Dulce, [1970] – 1 – CSUXAHZ2554-B – us Hoover Inst Photo [920]

VIDA DEL BEATO JUAN DE AVILA, POR UN SACERDOTE. MADRID, 1928 / Bayle, Constantino – Madrid: Razon y Fe, 1929 – 9 – sp Bibl Santa Ana [240]

VIDA DEL CONQUISTADOR DEL PERU DON FRANCISCO PIZARRO Y DE SUS HERMANOS HERNANDO, JUAN Y GONZALO PIZARRO Y FRANCISCO MARTIN DE ALCANTARA / Cuneo-Vidal, Romulo – Barcelona: Casa Editorial M.s.a. – sp Bibl Santa Ana [350]

VIDA DEL CURA DE ARS BARCELONA, 1929 / Trochu, Francisco – Madrid: Razon y Fe, 1930 – 1 – sp Bibl Santa Ana [946]

VIDA DEL JOVEN DON FRANCISCO ROMERO Y FERNANDEZ DE CORDOBA / Reyes, Rafael de los – Jerez: Tip. de Francisco Salido, 1905 – 1 – sp Bibl Santa Ana [920]

VIDA DEL P. BERNARDO FRANCISCO DE HOYOS DE LA COMPANIA DE JESUS / Uriarte, Jose Eugenio de – Barcelona: Francisco Rosal, 1896 – 1mf – 9 – 1986-1111 – us A.T.L.A. [920]

VIDA DEL PADRE CRISTOBAL DE SANTA CATALINA / Posadas, Francisco de – Cordoba: Diego de Valverde, 1699 – 1 – sp Bibl Santa Ana [240]

VIDA DEL SEGOVIANO RODRIGO DE CONTRERAS, DEL MARQUES DE LOZOYA Y COLECCION DE LAS MEMORIAS...DE LOS VIRREYES DEL PERU DE RICARDO BELTRAN ROZPIDE / Bayle, Constantino – Madrid: Razon y Fe, 1923 – 1 – sp Bibl Santa Ana [920]

A VIDA DO VISCONDE DO URUGUAI (1807-1866) / Souza, Jose Antonio Soares de – Sao Paulo, 1944 – 12mf – 8 – ne Slangenburg [972]

A VIDA DRAMATICA DE EUCLYDES DA CUNHA / Pontes, Eloy – Rio de Janeiro. 1938 – 1 – us Res Libr [972]

LA VIDA ECONOMICA SOCIAL DE NUEVA ESPANA AL FINALIZAR EL SIGLO 16. PROLOGO Y NOTAS DE ALBERTO MA CARRENO. MEXICO, 1944 / Gomez de Cervantes, Gonzalo – Madrid: Razon y Fe, 1947 – 1 – sp Bibl Santa Ana [330]

VIDA EJEMPLAR FR. PEDRO DE LA PURIFICACION / Estrada, Antonio – 1833 – 9 – $1.50f – sp Bibl Santa Ana [240]

LA VIDA EN CACERES EN LOS SIGLOS 12 Y 16 AL 18 / Orti Belmonte, Miguel Angel – Caceres: Dip. Prov., 1949 – 1 – sp Bibl Santa Ana [946]

LA VIDA EN LA AMAZONIA PERUANA. OBSERVACION DE UN MEDICO. LIMA, 1944 / Kuczynski Godard, Maximo H – Madrid: Razon y Fe, 1947 – 1 – sp Bibl Santa Ana [306]

LA VIDA EN MEXICO DURANTE UNA RESIDENCIA DE DOS ANOS EN ESE PAIS(...) / Calderon de la Barca, Francisco E I de – Mexico: Porrua, 1959. 2v – fr Armell [972]

LA VIDA EN SONETOS. SONETOS DE JUVENTED / Sanchez-Arjona, Vicente – Sevilla: Imp. Carlos Acuna, Tomo 1. 1941 – 1 – sp Bibl Santa Ana [810]

LA VIDA EN SONETOS. SONETOS DE JUVENTUD / Sanchez-Arjona, Vicente – Sevilla: Imp. Carlos Acuna, Tomo 2. 1943 – 1 – sp Bibl Santa Ana [810]

LA VIDA EN SONETOS. SONETOS DE JUVENTUD / Sanchez-Arjona, Vicente – Sevilla: Imp. Carlos Acuna, Tomo 3. 1944 – 1 – sp Bibl Santa Ana [810]

VIDA ESCOLAR : BOLEITIM QUINZENAL DO GRUPO ESCOLAR DE LAVRAS – Lavras, 1 May 1907-15 Nov 1908 – 1,5,6 – bl Biblioteca [072]

VIDA ESCOLAR : ORGAO DOS ESTUDANTES DE CAMPO GRANDE – Campo Grande, 20 May-Oct 1934; May-Aug, Out-Nov 1935; Jun 1936; Jun 1937 – 1,5,6 – bl Biblioteca [072]

VIDA, EXCELENCIAS Y MUERTE DE...SAN JOSEPH...COMENTADA...DON DIEGO SUAREZ DE FIGUEROS... / Valdivieso, Joseph – Madrid: Francisco del Hierro, Tomo 1. 1727 – 1 – sp Bibl Santa Ana [240]

VIDA GRAFICA DE SANTA TERESA DE JESUS / Jesus, Gabriel de – Madrid, 1933; Madrid: Razon y Fe, 1934 – 1 – sp Bibl Santa Ana [240]

VIDA GRAFICA DE SANTA TERESA DE JESUS. LA SANTA DE LA RAZA. VOLUMEN 1 / Jesus, Gabriel de – Madrid: Razon y Fe, 1929 – 1 – sp Bibl Santa Ana [240]

VIDA GRAFICA DE SANTA TERESA DE JESUS. TOMO 4. MADRID, 1935 / Jesus, Gabriel de – Madrid: Razon y Fe, 1935 – 1 – sp Bibl Santa Ana [240]

LA VIDA INTENSA. VENCIDO / Trevillano, Salvador – Madrid: Rafael C. Reggio. editor, s.a. – 1 – sp Bibl Santa Ana [946]

A VIDA LITERARIA – Curityba, 20 Jul-30 Oct 1887 – 1,5,6 – bl Biblioteca [072]

VIDA LITERARIA : CRITICA, INFORMACION, BIBLIOGRAFIA – v1-5. 1928-32 – 1r – 1 – us Ross [440]

LA VIDA MILITAR EN ESDANA / Barado, Francisco – 1888 – 9 – $1.50f – sp Bibl Santa Ana [355]

VIDA MODERNA – Rio de Janeiro, 1 Jul 1886-25 Jun 1887 – 1,5,6 – bl Biblioteca [072]

VIDA NUEVA – Las Vegas, NV. 1979-1981 – 1r – 1 – $50.00 – U04912 – us Library Micro [071]

VIDA OPERARIA : ORGAO DE DEFEZA DAS CLASSES LABORIOSAS DE MANAOS – Manaos, Amazonas. 8 Fev-26 Set 1920 – 1,5,6 – bl Biblioteca [072]

VIDA, PASION Y MUERTE DE VASCO NUNEZ DE BALBOA (DESCUBRIDOR DEL OCEANO PACIFICO) Y FRANCISCO DE ORELLANA (DESCUBRIDOR DEL RIO AMAZONAS) / Alvarado Garaicoa, Toedoro – Guayaquil: Universidad de Guayaquil, 1972 – sp Bibl Santa Ana [946]

VIDA POLITICA – (Suppl of: A Manha) – Rio de Janeiro, 23 Nov 1947-4 Feb 1951 – 1,5,6 – bl Biblioteca [072]

VIDA PROFESIONAL Y ACADEMICA DE FRANCISCO DE SANCHEZ DE LAS BROZAS / Gonzalez de la Calle, Pedro Urbano – Madrid, 1922 – 1 – sp Bibl Santa Ana [920]

LA VIDA SOCIAL EN LA COLONIA SEGUN LOS "LIBROS DEL CABILDO DE QUITO" / Bayle, Constantino – Madrid: Razon y Fe, 1936 – 1 – sp Bibl Santa Ana [306]

VIDA Y COSTUMBRES DE LOS INDIGENAS ARAUCANOS... / Moesbach, Ernesto W de – Santiago de Chile: Cervantes, 1930 – 1 – F236.25 – fr Armell [306]

VIDA Y ENSUENO / Cordero, Juan Luis – Caceres: Tip. La Minerva de Serafin Rodas, s.a. – sp Bibl Santa Ana [920]

VIDA Y HAZANAS DE ALVAR NUNEZ CABEZA DE VACA. MADRID, 1928 / Bellogin Garcia, Andres – Madrid: Razon y Fe, 1930 – 1 – sp Bibl Santa Ana [920]

VIDA Y HECHOS DEL CONQUISTADOR DEL PERU : DON FRANCISCO PIZARRO / Bermejo, Vladimiro – Arrequipa: Talleres Graficos Portugal, 1942 – sp Bibl Santa Ana [972]

VIDA Y OBRAS DE DON JUAN PABLO FORNER Y SEGARRA, MADRID, 1944 / Jimenez Salas, Maria; ed by Errandonea, Ignacio – Madrid: Razon y Fe, 1945 – 1 – sp Bibl Santa Ana [920]

VIDA Y OBRAS DE SANTA MARIA MARGARITA DE ALOCOQUE, 3 TOMOS. EXAMEN DE LIBROS / Bayle, Constantino – Madrid: Razon y Fe, 1922 – 1 – sp Bibl Santa Ana [240]

VIDA Y TRABAJOS DE UN LIBRO VIEJO / Campos, Jorge – Valencia: Editorial Castalia, 1949 – sp Bibl Santa Ana [920]

VIDA Y VIRTUDES DEL VENERABLE SIERVO DE DIOS EL PADRE / Posadas, Francisco de – Cristobal de Santa Catalina. Cordoba. Imp. F. Colorado Calvo. 1933 – 1 – sp Bibl Santa Ana [240]

VIDA Y...CRISTOBAL DE SANTA CATALINA / Posadas, Francisco de – (1690 edition is also available) – 1691 – 9 – $1.50f – sp Bibl Santa Ana [920]

VIDA Y...D. JUAN DE RIBERA...OBISPO DE BADAJOZ / Jimenez, Juan – 1734 – 9 – $1.50f – sp Bibl Santa Ana [240]

VIDA Y...DON DIEGO DE ARCE REYNOSO / Giraldo, Juan Manuel – 1695 – 9 – $1.50f – sp Bibl Santa Ana [920]

VIDA...DE SANTA TERESA DE JESUS... / Jesus, Gabriel de – Madrid, 1930; Madrid: Razon y Fe, 1931 – 1 – sp Bibl Santa Ana [240]

VIDA...DE...SAN PEDRO DE ALCANTARA...SACADA A LA LUZ JUAN DE LA CALZADA...TOMO 4... / Diego de Madrid – Madrid: Manuel Martin, 1765 – 1 – sp Bibl Santa Ana [946]

VIDA...DONA LUISA DE CARVAJAL / Munoz, Luis – 1897 – 9 – 1.50f – sp Bibl Santa Ana [920]

VIDA...FRANCISCO VALERO Y LOSA / Reyes, Fr. Antonio de los – 1792 – 9 – 1.50f – sp Bibl Santa Ana [920]

VIDA...FRAY SEBASTIAN DE APARICIO. MEXICO. 1965 / Sanchez Parejo, Bartolome – Madrid: Graf. Callejo, 1966 – 1 – sp Bibl Santa Ana [240]

VIDA...JUAN DUNSIO ESCOTO / Jimenez Samaniego, Jose – 1867 – 9 – 1.50f – sp Bibl Santa Ana [240]

VIDAL, APOTRE COMPAGNON DE LA FEMME EN PRISON / Vidal, Edmond – Ibid., 27 p. Les Saint-Simoniens, 1825-1834. 6917 – 9 – fr Hachette [335]

Vidal Aragon, Pedro *see* LA VID Y EL VINO EN LA TIERRA DE BARROS

Vidal, Ceferino G *see* MES DE MAYO PARA NINOS

Vidal, Edmond *see*
- AU PEUPLE
- VIDAL, APOTRE COMPAGNON DE LA FEMME EN PRISON

Vidal, Fabian *see*
- EL EJERCITO DE LA MONARQUIA Y EL EJERCITO DE LA REPUBLICA
- OBSERVACION SOBRE EL VOMITO PERIODICO...

Vidal, J M Moscou *see* DURANT LE PREMIER...SOVIETIQUE (1917-1920). PARIS

Vidal y Soler, S *see*
- PHANEROGAMAE CUMINGIANAE PHILIPPINARUM
- SINOPSIS DE FAMILIAS Y GENEROS DE PLANTAS LENOSAS DE FILIPINAS

VIDA...MADRE ISABEL DE LA CRUZ / Solano de Figueroa y Altamirano, Juan – 1703 – 9 – 1.50f – sp Bibl Santa Ana [240]

VIDA...MARIA DE CRISTO / San Antonio Capilla, Fr. Fernando – 1716 – 9 – 1.50f – sp Bibl Santa Ana [240]

Vidart Schuch, Luis *see* LA FILOSOFIA ESPANOLA

VIDAS DE DONA FRANCISCA FERNANDEZ DE CORDOBA DE ROMERO Y DE SOR REGLA ROMERO Y FERNANDEZ DE CORDOBA / Religiosa Concepcionista – Sevilla: Tip. de El Correo e Andalucia, 1904? – 1 – sp Bibl Santa Ana [920]

LAS VIDAS DE LOS PINTORES Y ESTATUARIOS EMINENTES ESPANOLES / Palomino, A A – Londres. 1744. BO-1066 1 – 9 – ne IDC [700]

LAS VIDAS DE LOS PINTORES Y ESTATUARIOS EMINENTES ESPANOLES... / Palomino, A A – Londres, 1744 – 2mf – ne IDC [700]

VIDAS PARALELAS (GRIEGO) (SIECLE 14) / Plutarco – Madrid – 1r – 5,6 – sp Cultura [090]

VIDA...SAN PEDRO DE ALCANTARA / Diego de Madrid – 3v. 1765 – 9 – $1.50f – sp Bibl Santa Ana [240]

VIDA...SAN PEDRO DE ALCANTARA / San Bernardo, Alonso de – 1783 – 9 – $1.50f – sp Bibl Santa Ana [240]

VIDENSKABELIGE MEDDELELSER FRA DEN NATURHISTORISKE FORENING I KJOBENHAVN – Kjøbenhavn, 1849-1928 – 514mf – 9 – 7330/2 – ne IDC [500]

VIDEO *see* VIDEO MAGAZINE

VIDEO BUSINESS – Radnor. 1981-94* 1; 1995-97+ 1,5,9 – 1,5,9 – D21953 – us UMI [330]

VIDEO DEMOCRACY: THE VOTE-FROM-HOME REVOLUTION / Hollander, Richard – 1985. 161p. ISBN:0-912338-52-0 – 9 – 9.95 – us Lomond [320]

VIDEO MAGAZINE – (Former title: Video 1978-87) – Armonk. v1-10 win 1978-1987*. v11-21 apr 1987-mar 1998+ 1; v11 apr1987-mar 1988*. v12-21 apr 1988-mar 1998+ 5; v11-21. apr 1987-mar 1998+ 9 – 1,5,9 – D16709 – us UMI [073]

VIDEO REVIEW – New York. v1-5. apr 1980-1984* 1; v6-14 apr 1985-win 1993. v15 1994*. v16 1995 1,9; v6-8 apr 1985-mar 1988*. v9-14 apr 1988-win 1993. v15 1994*. v16 1995 5 – 1,5,9 – D15426 – us UMI [073]

VIDEO SOFTWARE MAGAZINE – New York. 1985-94* 1; 1995-97+ 1,5,9 – 1,5,9 – D21398 – us UMI [073]

VIDEO SYSTEMS – Overland Park. v1-17. nov 1975-1991* 1; v18-20 1992-94*. v21-23 1995-97+ 1,5,9 – 1,5,9 – D14286 – us UMI [073]

VIDEO WORLD-WIDE : AN INTERNATIONAL STUDY / ed by Alvarado, Manuel – 1988 – xiii/328p – 9 – 92-3-102521-X – Co-published with John Libbey, London – fr UNESCO [380]

VIDEODISC AND OPTICAL DISK – (Cont: Videodisc, videotex. Cont by: Optical Information Systems) – Westport. v4-5. mar 1984-dec 1985 – 1,5,9 – D13007.02 – us UMI [073]

VIDEODISC AND OPTICAL DISK *see* VIDEODISC, VIDEOTEX

VIDEODISC, VIDEOTEX – (Cont: Videodisc/teletext. Cont by: Videodisc and Optical Disk) – Westport. v1-4. sum 1981-feb 1984 – 1,5,9 – D13007.01 – us UMI [073]

VIDEODISC, VIDEOTEX *see*
- VIDEODISC AND OPTICAL DISK
- VIDEODISC/TELETEXT

VIDEODISC/TELETEXT – (Cont by: Videodisc, videotex) – Westport. v1. win-spr 1981 – 1,5,9 – D13007 – us UMI [073]

VIDEODISC/TELETEXT *see* VIDEODISC, VIDEOTEX

VIDEOGRAPHY – New York. v1-22. apr 1976-dec 1997+ 1,5,9; v1-2 apr 1976-dec 1977* 5 – 1,5,9 – D11702 – us UMI [073]

VIDEONEWS – (v.10- 1980- 5,6,9) – v.6-1976- – 1 – us UMI [380]

VIDEOPEDIA MICROFICHE SERVICE – Ingram's weekly fiche with the most current video product information – 9 – 125.00y – us Ingram [380]

THE VIDETTE – Iuka. Miss. 1902-1903; 1915-1920; 1946-1960 – 1 – us UMI [071]

VIDETTE – Montesano. Wash. -w. 1883-1959 – 1 – us UMI [071]

VIDETTE – Wichita. Kan. 1870-71 – 1 – us UMI [071]

VIDETTE-MESSENGER – Valparaiso. Ind. 1927- – 1 – us UMI [071]

VIDICI – Belgrade, Serbia: 1938. v1-2. 1938-1939 – 1 – us I.U. Libraries [073]

VIDNESBRYDET – Portland OR. Jan 2 1901-Dec 25 1912 – 1 – us U.O. Library [071]

VIDNESBYRDET – Seattle, WA. 1901-12 – 1 – 48.00 – us Oregon Hist [071]

VIDNESBYRDET – Seattle WA. Nov 27 1912-Dec 29 1915 – 1 – us U.O. Library [071]

VIDNEWS – v.1-6. 1971-76. Continued by Videonews – 1 – us UMI [380]

Vidocq *see*
- MEMOIRES DE VIDOCQ
- LES VOLEURS

VIDY I ZADACHI KOOPERATSII / Lozovyi, A – Khar'kov, 1926 – 1mf – 9 – COR-263/1 – ne IDC [334]

Vidyanatha *see* PRATAPARUDRIYAMU: ANU ALANKARASASTRAMU; RATNAPANA MANEDU VYAKHYANAMUTONGUDA..

LA VIE – Charlesbourg, Canada. v1 n1. 6 mai 1959 – 1r – 1 – Can$25.00 – cn Can Microfilming [072]

LA VIE ADMIRABLE DE SOEUR MARIE DE L'INCARNATION / Duval, A – Douay, 1621 – 8mf – 9 – CA-165/1 – ne IDC [240]

VIE AERIENNE ET SPORTIVE – Paris. v1-19. 1916-33 – 4r – 1 – us Ross [073]

LA VIE ARTISTIQUE – Montreal, Canada. 25 nov 1905-v1 n5. dec 1905 – 1r – 1 – Can$35.00 – cn Can Microfilming [700]

LA VIE AUTOMOBILE – 1948-56 – 1,5,6 – us Princeton Micro [073]

LA VIE BRUYANTE DE JULES VALLES / Rouchon, Ulysse – Paris (I-III). 1935-39 – 1 – fr A.C.R.P.P. [920]

VIE DE BARBEROUSSE, GENERAL DES ARMEES NAVALES DE SOLIMAN 2... / Richer, Adrien – Avignon: Joly, 1811 – 1 – F78.75 – fr Armell [355]

VIE DE CALVIN / Puaux, Francois – Strasbourg: Bergez-Levrault, 1864 – 1mf – us A.T.L.A. [240]

VIE DE CATHERINE TEKAKWITHA, VIERGE IROQUOISE: DECEDEE EN ODEUR DE SAINTETE A L'ANCIEN VILLAGE DU SAULT ST LOUIS, LE 17 AVRIL, 1680 / Burtin, Nicholas Victor – Quebec: L. Brousseau, 1894. 02007. (Pre-1900 Canadiana) – 9 – cn C.I.H.M. [920]

LA VIE DE CLAUDE BERNARD, DIT LE PAUVRE PRESTRE / Le Gauffre, T – Paris, 1642 – 7mf – 9 – CA-173/1 – ne IDC [240]

VIE DE DJELAL-EDDIN MANKOBIRTI / El-Nesawi – Texte arabe et traduction par O. Houdas. 1891, 1895 – 9 – fr Orientalistes [920]

VIE DE J.-J. ROUSSEAU, PRECEDEE DE QUELQUES LETTRES RELATIVES AU MEME SUJET / Barruel-Beauvert, Antoine-Joseph Comte de – London, Paris. 1789 – 9 – fr Hachette [190]

LA VIE DE JOSEPH-FRANCOIS PERRAULT: SURNOMME LE PERE DE L'EDUCATION DU PEUPLE CANADIEN / Casgrain, Philippe Baby – Quebec: C. Darveau, 1898. 00540. (Pre-1900 Canadiana) – 9 – cn C.I.H.M. [370]

LA VIE DE LA SOEUR MARGUERITE BOURGEOIS / Ransonet, Michel F – Avignon: chez Barnabe, 1728. SEM16P79 – 1r – 5 – Can$9.00 – cn Bibl Nat [240]

LA VIE DE LA VENERABLE LOUISE DE MARILLAC, VEUVE DE M. LEGRAS / Gobillon, N – Paris, 1769 – 5mf – 9 – CA-167/1 – ne IDC [240]

LA VIE DE LA VENERABLE MERE JEANNE DE LESTONAC / Beaufils, G – Toulouse, 1742 – 5mf – 9 – CA-157/1 – ne IDC [240]

LA VIE DE LA VENERABLE MERE JEANNE FRANCOISE FREMIOT / Maupas du Tour, H de – Ed 3. Paris, 1645 – 7mf – 9 – CA-177/1 – ne IDC [240]

LA VIE DE LA VENERABLE MERE MARIE DE L'INCARNATION / Martin, Charles – Paris, 1677 – 9mf – 9 – CA-176/1 – ne IDC [240]

LA VIE DE LA VENERABLE MERE MARIE DE L'INCARNATION, PREMIERE SUPERIEURE DES URSULINES DE LA NOUVELLE-FRANCE / Marie de l'Incarnation, Mere – Paris, 1677. SEM105P810 – 9mf – 9 – Can$20.25 – cn Bibl Nat [240]

VIE DE LA VENEREE ANNE-ELISABETH GOTTRAU, ABBESE DES BERNARDINES DE LA MAIGRAUGE : OEUVRE POSTHUME DE DOM MARCEL MOREAU, DIRECTEUR DU MONAST ERE (1803) / Moreau, Marcel; ed by Ruedin, Charles – Fribourg: Saint-Paul, 1884 – 1mf – 9 – 0-8370-7491-6 – 1986-1491 – us A.T.L.A. [920]

LA VIE DE M. DE RENTY OU L'IDEE D'UN CHRETIEN PARFAIT / Saint-Jure, J -B – Paris, 1651 – 3mf – 9 – CA-178/1 – ne IDC [240]

LA VIE DE M. JEAN-JACQUES OLIER / Giry, F – N.p., 1687 – 2mf – 9 – CA-166/1 – ne IDC [240]

VIE DE M. LE PREMIER PRESIDENT DE LAMOIGNON, ECRITE D'APRES LES MEMOIRES DU TEMPS ET LES PAPIERS DE LA FAMILLE... – Paris: Nyon l'aine, 1781 – fr Armell [920]

LA VIE DE MESSIRE CHRISTOPHLE D'AUTHIER DE SISGAU, EVEQUE DE BETHLEEM / Borely, N – Lyon, 1703 – 5mf – 9 – CA-159/1 – ne IDC [240]

LA VIE DE MESSIRE JEAN D'ARANTHON D'ALEX, EVEQUE ET PRINCE DE GENEVE / Le Masson, Dom Inn. O Cart. – Lyon, 1697 – 7mf – 9 – CA-174/1 – ne IDC [240]

LA VIE DE MGR. ALAIN DE SOLMINIHAC, EVEQUE... DE CAORS / Chastenet, L – Caors, 1662 – 9mf – 9 – CA-164/1 – ne IDC [240]

VIE DE MGR. D'HULST / Baudrillart, Alfred – Paris: Poussielgue, 1912-1914 – 3mf – us A.T.L.A. [240]

LA VIE DE MONSIEUR LE NOBLETZ, PRESTRE ET MISSIONNAIRE DE BRETAGNE / Verjus, A – Paris, 1666 – 7mf – 9 – CA-179/1 – ne IDC [240]

VIE DE QUELQUES-UNES DE NOS GRANDES SAINTES AU PAYS DE LIEGE / Nimal, H – Liege, 1898 – Dfl25.00 – ne Slangenburg [240]

LE VIE DE RENE VAILLIE, VAINQUEUR DE TOMBOUCTOU. / Lamande, Andre – Paris. 1928 – 1 – us Res Libr [920]

LA VIE DE S. NORBERT, ARCHEVEQUE DE MAGDEBOURG ET FONDATEUR DE L'ORDRE DES CHANOINES PREMONTREZ / Hugo, L C – Luxembourg, 1704 – 11mf – 8 – Dfl39.00 – ne Slangenburg [240]

VIE DE SAINT ANTOINE DE PADOUE / Ghyvelde, Frederic de – Montreal, 1931. SEM105P534 – 3mf – 9 – Can$6.75 – cn Bibl Nat [240]

VIE DE SAINT CAMILLE DE LELLIS...PARIS, 1932 / Debout – Madrid: Razon y Fe, 1934 – 1 – sp Bibl Santa Ana [240]

VIE DE SAINT VIATEUR: CONFESSEUR ET LECTEUR DE L'EGLISE DE LYON / Bourget, Ignace – Montreal: Institution de sourds-muets, 1897. 00214. (Pre-1900 Canadiana) – 9 – cn C.I.H.M. [240]

VIE DE SAINTE MARIE MADELEINE. BARCELONA / Jean, B – Madrid: Razon y Fe, 1934 – 1 – sp Bibl Santa Ana [240]

VIE DE SCHILLER / Regnier, Adolphe – (Includes bibliographical references) – Paris: Hachette, 1859 – 1r – 1 – us U.W. Library [920]

LA VIE DE TRAVAIL ET SES PROBLEMES / Naville, P – F30.00 – fr Ethnologie [331]

LA VIE DE VOLTAIRE / Duvernet, T I – Geneve. 1786 – 9 – fr Hachette [920]

VIE DE VOLTAIRE / Mazure, F A J – Paris: A. Emery, 1821 – 9 – fr Hachette [920]

LA VIE DELL'ARIA – Rome. Italy. -w. 18 Nov 1934-4 Sep 1937, 16 Mar-25 May, 29 Dec 1940, 12 Jan 1941-25 Jan 1942. (2 reels) – 1 – uk British Llbr Newspaper [072]

LA VIE D'EMIGRANT EN AMERIQUE (REPUBLIQUE ARGENTINE, ETATS-UNIS ET CANADA) / Foubert, Auguste – Paris: s.n., 1875 (Paris: P. Dupont). 05599. (Pre-1900 Canadiana) – 9 – cn C.I.H.M. [971]

VIE DES ARTS / Societe la Vie des Arts – Montreal: la Societe. no 1- 1956-. SEM105P2 – 9 – cn Bibl Nat [700]

LA VIE DES JUSTES / Martene, Dom E – (Ed. Heurtebize). Tome 1. 1924 – Dfl19.00 – ne Slangenburg [240]

LA VIE DES JUSTES / Martene, Dom E – (Ed. Heurtebize). Tome 2. 1925 – Dfl19.00 – ne Slangenburg [240]

LA VIE DES JUSTES / Martene, Dom E – (Ed. Heurtebize). Tome 3. 1926 – Dfl22.00 – ne Slangenburg [240]

LA VIE DES LETTRES – puis et des arts. Collection anthologique et critique de poemes et de proses. Paris. juil 1920-avr 1924, n.s – 1 – fr A.C.R.P.P. [073]

LA VIE DES PEINTRES FLAMANDS, ALLEMANDS ET HOLLANDOIS... / Descamps, Jean Baptiste – Paris. 4v. 1753-1764 – 30mf – ne IDC [750]

VIE DES SAINTS / Blemur, R M J de – Lyon. Tom. 1-4. 1689 – Dfl361.00 – ne Slangenburg [240]

LA VIE DU CARDINAL DE BERULLE / Habert, G – Paris, 1646 – 11mf – 9 – CA-169/1 – ne IDC [240]

LA VIE DU PERE CHARLES DE CONDREN / Amelotte, D – Paris, 1643 – 8mf – 9 – CA-156/1 – ne IDC [240]

LA VIE DU PERE J. RIGOLEUC / Champion, P – Paris, 1686 – 6mf – 9 – CA-162/1 – ne IDC [240]

VIE DU PERE ROMILLION, PRETRE DEL'ORATOIRE DE JESUS. VIE DU PERE ROMILLION, PRETRE DEL'ORATOIRE DE JESUS / Bourguignon, C – Marseille, 1669 – 5mf – 9 – CA-161/1 – ne IDC [240]

LA VIE DU RAIL – (Also available on CD-ROM) – France. 1989-1995 – 2r per y – 5,6 – Sfr642.00 – sz Infoprint [380]

VIE DU RAIL – 1989-1995 – 2 times per yr – 6 – F2,400.00 – sz Infoprint [072]

LA VIE DU R.P. CESAR DE BUS / Marcel, J – Lyon, 1619 – 5mf – 9 – CA-175/1 – ne IDC [240]

LA VIE DU R.P. JEAN-FRANCOIS REGIS / La Brouee, C – Puy, 1650 – 4mf – 9 – CA-170/1 – ne IDC [240]

LA VIE DU R.P. PIERE FOURIER / Bedel, J – Paris, 1645 – 6mf – 9 – CA-158/1 – ne IDC [240]

VIE DU R.P. PIERRE FOURNIER / Blemur, R M J de – Paris, 1678 – Dfl9.00 – ne Slangenburg [240]

LA VIE DU SULTAN RABAH; LES FRANCAIS AU TCHAD / Dujarric, Gaston – Paris, 1902 – 1 – us Res Libr [920]

VIE DU VENERABLE JOSEPH ANCHIETA : DE LA COMPAGNIE DE JESUS: PRECEDEE DE LA VIE DU P. EMMAN. DE NOBREGA, DE LA MEME COMPAGNIE / Sainte-Foy, Charles – Paris: H Casterman, 1858 – 1mf – 9 – 0-8370-6944-0 – 1986-0944 – us A.T.L.A. [920]

LA VIE DU VENERABLE PERE DOM CLAUDE MARTIN, RELIGIEUX BENEDICTIN DE LA CONGREGATION DE S. MAUR... / Martene, Edmond – Tours: P Masson, 1697. SEM105P1500 – 5mf – 9 – Can$11.25 – cn Bibl Nat [240]

LA VIE DU VENERABLE SERVITEUR DE DIEU VINCENT DE PAUL / Abelly, L – Paris, 1664 – 13mf – 9 – CA-155/1 – ne IDC [240]

LA VIE D'UN ARTISTE / Lepage, Auguste – Paris: P. Ollendorff, 1882. 299p. 4 fiches. (Art) – 9 – 10.00 – fr Bibl Nationale [920]

LA VIE ECOLIERE – v1-57. 1911-67. SEM16P355 – 1r – 5 – Can$15.00 – cn Bibl Nat [370]

LA VIE ECONOMIQUE – v1- 1928- 1; v49-5,6,9 – us UMI [330]

LA VIE EN AEROPLANE DE LOUIS BLERIOT / Rol Press Agency. France – 100 candid shots taken between 1905 and 25 July 1909. 1 reel. (Collections of the Department of Prints and Photographs) – 1 – $50.00 – fr Bibl Nationale [770]

LA VIE EN AFRIQUE OU TROIS ANS DANS L'AFRIQUE CENTRALE / Becker, Jerome – (African Library). Paris, Bruxelles: Lebegue, 1887 – 9 – fr Hachotte [960]

LA VIE ET LA DOCTRINE SPIRITUELLE DU PERE LOUIS LALLEMANT / Champion. P – Paris, 1694 – 6mf – 9 – CA-163/1 – ne IDC [240]

LA VIE ET LA TECHNIQUE DES P.T.T. : ORGANE MENSUEL DU COMMISSARIAT DES POSTES AND TELEGRAPHES DE L'URSS – (Includes c.1: no.8 1925:Aug) – Moscou: Commissariat, 192u – 1 – CSUXAKZ0025-S – us Hoover Inst Photo [944]

LA VIE ET L'OEUVRE DE L'ABBE PROVANCHER / Huard, Victor Amedee – 1926 – 1 – us A.T.L.A. [920]

VIE ET TECHNIQUES DE CHASSE DES INDIENS DE MISTASSINI / Chambaron, D – 9 – F100.00 – fr Ethnologie [306]

LA VIE ETERNELLE : SEPT DISCOURS / Naville, Ernest – (Includes bibliographical references) – 5e ed. Geneve. A Cherbuliez, 1872 – 1mf – 9 – 0-8370-3877-4 – 1985-1877 – us A.T.L.A. [210]

LA VIE FINANCIERE – Economique, industrielle, commerciale. Dir. Raoul Charbonnel. Paris. 1920-24 – 1 – fr A.C.R.P.P. [380]

LA VIE FRANCAISE – La semaine economique et financiere. Paris. Devenu par fusion: La Vie francaise l'Opinion. 1955-63, juil 1973-1993 – 1 – fr A.C.R.P.P. [380]

LA VIE FUTURE D'APRES LE MAZDEISME : A LA LUMIERE DES CROYANCES PARALLELES DANS LES AUTRES RELIGIONS: ETUDE D'ESCHATOLOGIE COMPAREE / Soederblom, Nathan – Paris: E. Leroux, 1901 – 2mf – us A.T.L.A. [200]

LA VIE FUTURE D'APRES SAINT PAUL / Bruston, Charles – Paris: Fischbacher, 1895 – 1mf – 9 – 0-8370-2501-X – 1985-0501 – us A.T.L.A. [220]

LA VIE HEUREUSE – Revue feminine universelle illustree. Paris. oct 1902-juil 1914 – 1 – fr A.C.R.P.P. [073]

LA VIE ILLUSTREE / ed by Berthelot, Hector et al – Montreal, Canada. 1 fev-1 jun 1889 – 1r – 1 – Can$35.00 – cn Can Microfilming [073]

LA VIE INDUSTRIELLE, COMMERCIALE, AGRICOLE, FINANCIERE – Quotidien economique du soir. Paris. 20 nov 1940-16 aout 1944 – 1 – fr A.C.R.P.P. [073]

LA VIE INTELLECTUELLE DANS UNE ABBAYE LORAINE AU 17E ET 18E SIECLES / Jerome, A – Nancy, 1911 – Dfl6.00 – ne Slangenburg [240]

VIE (LA) ET DOCTRINE DE DAVID GEORGE, HOLANDOIS ET CHEF DES HERETIQUES – Basle. 1560. BME-267 1 – 9 – ne IDC [240]

LA VIE, LES AVENTURES ET LE VOYAGE DE GROENLAND DU R. P. CORDELIER PIERRE DE MESANGE, AVEC UNE RELATION BIEN CIRCONSTANCIEE DE L'ORIGINE, DE L'HISTOIRE, DES MOEURS ET DU PARADIS DES HABITANTS DU POLE ARCTIQUE / Tyssot de Patot, Simon – (Utopias in the Enlightenment Series). 1720 – 9 – fr Hachette [800]

LA VIE, L'EVOLUTION, LE MATERIALISME: MEMOIRE LU...DEVANT LA SOCIETE ROYALE DU CANADA...23 MAI 1899 / Baillairge, Charles – 1899?. 02504. (Pre-1900 Canadiana) – 9 – cn C.I.H.M. [500]

LA VIE LITTERAIRE – Revue mensuelle d'information litteraire et artistique. no. 1-3, no. special. Neuilly, Paris. janv-juil 1931 – 1 – fr A.C.R.P.P. [073]

VIE MEDICALE AU CANADA FRANCAIS – (Cont: Laval Medical) – Montreal. v1-11. 1972-82 1; v1 1972. v5-8 1976-79*. v9 1980. v10-11 1981-82* 5; v5 1976*. v7-9 1978-80* v10-11 1981-82 9 – 1,5,9 – D6418 – us UMI [610]

LA VIE MODERNE – Journal hebdomadaire illustre, litteraire et artistique. Le sous-titre varie. Paris. avr 1879-nov 1902, nov-dec 1917 – 1 – fr A.C.R.P.P. [073]

VIE MUSICALE : SERVICE DE LA MUSIQUE DE LA DIRECTION DES ARTS ET DES LETTRES.... / Quebec. (Province). Ministere des Affaires Culturelles – Quebec: le Service. nos 1-19. 1965-71. SEM16P286 – 1r – 5 – Can$9.00 – cn Bibl Nat [780]

LA VIE MUSICALE: REVUE BIMENSUELLE DE LA MUSIQUE SUISSE ET ETRANGERE – v. 1-8. 1907-14 – 1 – 67.00 – us L of C Photodup [780]

LA VIE MYSTIQUE D'UN MONASTERE DE DOMINICAINES AU MOYEN AGE D'APRES LA CHRONIQUE DE TOESS / Ancelet-Hustache, J – Paris, 1928 – Dfl19.00 – ne Slangenburg [240]

Vie, N -S de *see* JESUS-CHRIST PAR L. CL. FILLION

LA VIE NOUVELLE – Revue protestante hebdomadaire. Red. en chef Louis Lafon. Montauban. mai 1925-juin 1940 – 1 – fr A.C.R.P.P. [240]

LA VIE OUVRIERE – Paris. Oct 1909-juil 1914, avr 1919-sept 1939, 8 sept 1944-1993. Pour le Supplement voir I.S.R – 1 – fr A.C.R.P.P. [073]

LA VIE OUVRIERE : POUR LES OUVRIERS ET LES CULTIVATEURS – Montreal, Canada. v1 n6. oct 1933-v2 n19. 10 nov 1934 – 1r – 1 – Can$25.00 – cn Can Microfilming [331]

LA VIE OUVRIERE EN FRANCE / Pelloutier, Fernand L E – Paris. 1900. (La Condition Ouvriere. Part Two.) – 9 – 10.00 – fr Bibl Nationale [360]

LA VIE PAROISSIALE – Mont-Joli. v9 n48. 5 fev 1937; n51. 26 fev 1937; v10 n42. 24 dec 1937 – 1r – 1 – Can$25.00 – cn Can Microfilming [072]

VIE POLITIQUE, LITTERAIRE ET MORALE DE VOLTAIRE / Lepan, E M J – Ou l'on refute Condorcet et ses autres historiens, en citant et rapprochant un grand nombre de faits inconnus et tres curieux. Paris. Imp. de Cordier. 1817. XV – 9 – fr Hachette [190]

LA VIE POPULAIRE – Montreal: F X Lessard, [1888?-18– our 19–] – 9 – cn C.I.H.M. [971]

LA VIE PRIVEE DU ROI DE PRUSSE / Voltaire, Francois Marie Arouet de – Ou memoires pour servir a la vie de M. de Voltaire, ecrits par lui-meme. Amsterdam. les Heritiers de MM. Rey. 1784 – 9 – fr Hachette [920]

VIE QUAKER – 1971-84 (complete) – 1r – 1 – ATLA S0861 – us A.T.L.A. [073]

LA VIE QUOTIDIENNE D'UNE COOPERATIVE DE TRAVAIL AGRICOLE FAMILIALE VENDEE / Hutin, P – 9 – F110.00 – fr Ethnologie [306]

VIE SIMPLE = THE SIMPLE LIFE / Wagner, Charles – (In English) – Popular ed. New York: McClure, Phillips, 1904, c1901 – 1mf – 9 – 0-8370-6955-6 – 1986-0955 – us A.T.L.A. [240]

LA VIE SOCIALE ET ECONOMIQUE DES LAPONS DE KAUTOKEINO / Delaporte, Y – 9 – F100.00 – fr Ethnologie [305]

LA VIE SOCIALISTE – Hebdomadaire de documentation edite par le groupe d'etudes et d'entente: La Vie socialiste puis Hebdomadaire de documentation internationale et d'education socialiste. Paris. juil 1920-nov 1923, mars 1926-juil 1935 – 1 – fr A.C.R.P.P. [335]

LA VIE SOCIALISTE – Revue bi-mensuelle internationale. Red. en chef, Francis de Pressense. no.1-19. 5 nov 1904-aout 1905 – 1 – fr A.C.R.P.P. [335]

VIE SPIRITUELLE : BIBLIOGRAPHIE ANALYTIQUE DES ARTICLES DU "SUPPLEMENT DE LA VIE SPIRITUELLE", 1951-1954 INCLUSIVEMENT / Sainte-Theresita, Marie-de – 1962. SEM105P4 – 1mf – 9 – Can$2.25 – cn Bibl Nat [240]

VIE SPIRITUELLE : BIBLIOGRAPHIE ANALYTIQUE DES ARTICLES DU "SUPPLEMENT DE LA VIE SPIRITUELLE", 1955-1958 INCL / Marie de St-Thomas d'Aquin – 1962. SEM105P4 – 1mf – 9 – Can$2.25 – cn Bibl Nat [240]

LA VIE SYNDICALE / Confederation Generale du Travail Unitaire – no. 1-30. Paris. oct 1922-janv fevr 1928 – 1 – fr A.C.R.P.P. [331]

LA VIE SYNDICALE (C.S.N.) – (Becomes: Le Travail jan 1942-jan 1975) – Montreal, Canada. nov 1924-dec 1941 – 6r – 1 – Can$65.00r – cn Can Microfilming [072]

VIE, TRAVAUX ET DOCTRINE SCIENTIFIQUE D'ETIENNE GEOFFROY SAINT-HILAIRE / Geoffroy Saint-Hilaire, Isidore – Paris, P. Bertrand, 1847, 479 p. Histoire des Sciences XVIIe-XIXe Siecles. 7928 – 9 – fr Hachette [920]

LA VIE UNIVERSITAIRE A PARIS / Universite de Paris – Pub. sous les auspices du Conseil de l'Universite par Paul Boyer... Maurice Caullery. 92 photos. Paris: A. Colin, 1918. 231p – 1 – us U.W. Library [370]

VIEDOMOSTI ODESSKAGO GRADONACHALSTVA – (Library has holdings (incomplete) from betwenn July 25, 1878 and May 28, 1881) – Odessa: S.L. Isokovich, 1868- – 1 – CSUX88-S163 – us Hoover Inst Photo [360]

LES VIEILLES FAMILLES D'YAMACHICHE / Desaulniers, Francois Lesieur – Montreal: C O Beauchemin et Fils; A P Pigeon, 4v. 1898-1908. SEM105P6 – 12mf – 9 – Can$27.00 – cn Bibl Nat [920]

Vieillot, L J P *see*
- ANALYSE D'UNE NOUVELLE ORNITHOLOGIE ELEMENTAIRE
- LA GALERIE DES OISEAUX

VIEJA BIOGRAFIA DE D. PEDRO DE ALVARADO. LUGARTENIENTE DE HERNAN CORTES Y CONQUISTADOR DE GUATEMALA / Munoz de San Pedro, Miguel – Badajoz: Dipt. Provincial de Badajoz, 1947 – 1 – sp Bibl Santa Ana [910]

EL VIEJO Y LA NINA / Fernandez de Moratin, Leandro – 1795 – 1mf – 9 – Pta1,000.00 – 84-7848-185-0 – sp Pentalfa [946]

Viel-Castel, Louis de *see* HISTOIRE DE LA RESTAURATION

Viellard, Gilbert Pierre *see* NOTES SUR LES COUTUMES DES PEULS AU FOUTA DJALLON

LES VIELLES FAMILLES D'YAMACHICHE, TOME PREMIER: DIX GENEALOGIES COMPRENANT LES BLAIS, LACERTE, LAMY.. / Desaulniers, Francois Lesieur – avec preface par Raphael Bellemare et une poesie de Neree Beauchemin. Montreal: Beauchemin, 1898. 03751. (Pre-1900 Canadiana) – 9 – cn C.I.H.M. [971]

LES VIELLES FAMILLES D'YAMACHICHE, TOME QUATRIEME: VINGT-TROIS GENEALOPES COMPRENANT LES AUCOIN, BETTEZ, BOISVERT.. / Desaulniers, Francois Lesieur – Montreal?: s.n., 1908 (Montreal: Pigeon). 03754. (Pre-1900 Canadiana) – 9 – cn C.I.H.M. [971]

LES VIELLES FAMILLES D'YAMACHICHE, TOME TROISIEME: VINGT-CINQ GENEALOGIES COMPRENANT LES LESIEUR, HEROUX, MILETTE.. / Desaulniers, Francois Lesieur – preface par Omer Heroux. Montreal?: s.n., 1900 (Montreal: Pigeon). 03753. (Pre-1900 Canadiana) – 9 – cn C.I.H.M. [971]

LA VIELLEUSE DU BOULEVARD / Hector Chaussier – (French Theatre Series). Paris. M. Cavanagh, an XI. 1803 – 9 – fr Hachette [820]

Vienna. Naturhistorisches Museum *see* ANNALEN

Vienna. Universitaet *see* DISSERTATIONES PHILOLOGAE VINDOBONENSES

VIENNE SUR LE RHONE : LA VILLE ET LES HABITANTS. SITUATION ET ATTITUDES. SOCIOLOGIE D'UNE CITE FRANCAISE / Clement, P & Xydias, N – F50.00 – fr Ethnologie [307]

VIENNESE POPULAR SONG : TRANSCRIBED FOR VIOLIN AND PIANO – New York: C Fisher, ca 1915 – 1 – us Sibley [780]

Viennot, Jean-Pierre *see* CONTRIBUTION A L'ETUDE DE LA SOCIOLOGIE ET DE L'HISTOIRE DU MOUVEMENT NATIONAL KURDE

VIENTO AMARRADO / Canal Rosado, Jose – Caceres: Imp. Moderna, 1954. Cuad. Alcantara, no 9 – sp Bibl Santa Ana [946]

VIENTOS ALEGRES, VIENTOS DESOLADOS / Calvo Flores, Josquin – Barcelona: Editorial Campos, 1972 – 1 – sp Bibl Santa Ana [946]

VIENYBE LIETUVNIKU. (VIENYBE) – Plymouth, Pennsylvania & New York. 1 Jan 1890-Dec 1932. (42 reels) – 1 – uk British Libr Newspaper [071]

VIER AKADEMISCHE VORTRAEGE UND FUENFZIG APHORISMEN / Oosterzee, Johannes Jacobus van – Gotha: Andreas Perthes, 1868. 1 fiche – 9 – us A.T.L.A. [240]

VIER BUECHER VON DER KIRCHE : SEITENSTUECK ZU LOEHE'S DREI BUECHERN VON DER KIRCHE / Delitzsch, Franz – Dresden: J. Naumann, 1847 – 1mf – us A.T.L.A. [240]

VIER BUECHER VON MENSCHLICHER PROPORTION / Duerer, Albrecht – O-241. 1528 – 9 – ne IDC [760]

VIER BUECHER VON WAHREM CHRISTENTHUMB... / Arndt, Johann – Magdeburg, 1610-1615. 4v – 20mf – 9 – ne IDC [240]

VIER CHRISTLICHE PREDIGTEN VOM WUCHER, DARINNEN NEBEN DER SUMMARISCHEN AUSSLEGUNG ETTLICHER EUANGELIEN IM ADUENT... / Andreae d.A E, J – Tuebingen, 1589 – 3mf – 9 – ne IDC [240]

VIER GESPRAECHE UEBER DIE MALEREI, GEFUEHRT ZU ROM / Joaquim de Vasconcellos, Francesco de Hollanda – O 517x. 1538 – 9 – ne IDC [760]

VIER MAEDCHENLEBEN, ODER, DEUTSCH UND AMERIKANISCH : ERZAEHLUNG FUER DEUTSCHLANDS TOECHTER / Laddey, Emma – Stuttgart: A Bonz, 1879 – 1r – 1 – us U.W. Library [830]

Viera Clavijo, Jose *see*
- NOTICIAS DE LA HISTORIA GENERAL DE CANARIAS. TOMO 1
- NOTICIAS DE LA HISTORIA GENERAL DE CANARIAS. TOMO 2
- NOTICIAS DE LA HISTORIA GENERAL DE CANARIAS. TOMO 3
- NOTICIAS DE LA HISTORIA GENERAL DE CANARIAS. TOMO 4

Viera, Josef *see* DEUTSCH-OSTAFRIKA UNVERLOREN!

Vierbach, A *see* DIE LITURGISCHEN ANSCHAUUNGEN DES VITUS ANTON WINTER

DER VIER-CAPITEL-BRIEF DES PAULUS AN DIE KORINTHER / Hausrath, Adolf – Heidelberg: Fr Bassermann, 1870 – 1mf – 9 – 0-8370-3534-1 – 1985-1534 – us A.T.L.A. [220]

Viereck, George Sylvester *see* GEDICHTE

Viereck, Paulus *see* SERMO GRAECUS QUO SENATUS POPULUSQUE ROMANUS MAGISTRATUSQUE POPULI ROMANI USQUE AD TIBERII CAESARIS AETATEM IN SCRIPTIS PUBLICIS USI SUNT EXAMINATUR

VIERGE / Orsini, Mathieu – (In English. Includes bibliographical references) – Dublin: M H Gill, 1886 – 1mf – 9 – 0-8370-3527-9 – 1985-1527 – us A.T.L.A. [920]

LA VIERGE IMMACULEE / Ghyvelde, Frederic de – Quebec, 1904. SEM105P538 – 4mf – 9 – Can$9.00 – cn Bibl Nat [240]

LA VIERGE INMACULEE ET LE PROBLEME DE L'APOSTOLAT MUSULMAN... / Bassetti-Sani, Julio – Madrid: Archivo Ibero-Americano, 1959 – 1 – sp Bibl Santa Ana [240]

LES VIERGES FOLLES / Esquiros, Alphonse – Paris: Le Gallois, 1840. 128p. (Les Femmes Collection) – 2mf – 9 – $6.00 – fr Bibl Nationale [830]

LES VIERGES MERES ET LES NAISSANCES MIRACULEUSES / Saintyves, Pierre – 1908 – 1 – us I.U. Libraries [390]

Vierhapper, F *see* MONOGRAPHIE DER ALPINEN ERIGERON-ARTEN EUROPAS UND VORDERASIENS

VIER-HONDERD-JAERIG JUBILE VAN HET HOOG-WEERDIG EN ALDERHEYLIGSTE SACRAMENT VAN MIRAKEL... / Boeck, F J de – Brussel, 1770 – 9mf – 9 – ne IDC [700]

DER VIERJAEHRIGE POLNISCHE REICHSTAG, 1788 BIS 1791 / Kalinka, V – 2v. Berlin. 1896-98. BR-5475 2 – 8 – ne IDC [940]

DER VIERJAHRESPLAN – Berlin. 1937-38. jul 1939-mar 1944. may-aug 15, 1944 – 6r – 1 – gw Mikrofilm [330]

DER VIERJAHRESPLAN – Berlin, 1937-38, jul 1939-mar 1944, may-aug 15 1944 – 6r – 1 – Inquire at Mikrofilmarchiv for details – gw Misc Inst [330]

Vierling, J G *see* VERSUCH EINER ANLEITUNG ZUM PRAELUDIREN FUER UNGEUEBTERE MIT BEYSPIELEN ERLAUTERT

Vierordt, Heinrich *see*
- AUSGEWAEHLTE DICHTUNGEN
- DEUTSCHE HOBELSPAENE
- FRESKEN

DAS VIERTE BUCH ESRA : AUF SEINE QUELLEN / Kabisch, Richard – (Includes bibliographical references and index) – Goettingen: Vandenhoeck & Ruprecht, 1889 – 1mf – 9 – 0-8370-3823-5 – 1985-1823 – us A.T.L.A. [220]

DAS VIERTE BUCH ESRA UND APOKALYPTISCHE GEHEIMNISSE UEBERHAUPT / Volkmar, Gustav – Zuerich, 1858 – 2mf – 8 – ne Slangenburg [220]
VIERTE BUCH MOSIS = NUMBERS, OR, THE FOURTH BOOK OF MOSES / Lange, Johann Peter – (In English) – New York: Charles Scribner, 1900, c1879 – 1mf – 9 – 0-8370-3065-X – 1985-1065 – us A.T.L.A. [220]
DAS VIERTE GEBOT : VOLKSSTUECK IN VIER AKTEN / Anzengruber, Ludwig – Stuttgart: J G Cotta, 1912 – 1r – 1 – us U.W. Library [820]
VIERTEL JAHRESHEFTE DER BERLINER GEWERKSCHAFTSSCHULE – 1925-27, 1931. 1928-30, 1932 incomplete. (Serial publications of German trade unions in the Memorial Library, University of Wisconsin-Madison.) – 1 – us U.W. Library [331]
VIERTELJAHRESHEFTE ZUR ZEITGESCHICHTE – Ed. by H. Rothfels, Th. Eschenberg, et al. Stuttgart. v1-8. 1953-60. H-191/2 – 8 – ne IDC [073]
VIERTELJAHRESSCHRIFT FUER BIBELKUNDE, TALMUDISCHE UND PATRISTISCHE STUDIEN – Berlin. v1-3. 1903-1905; 1907-1909. B383 (Leo Baeck Institute. German-Jewish Periodicals, Pt 1) – 1r – 1 – $75.00 – us UPA [270]
VIERTELJAHRSCHRIFT FUER VOLKSWIRTSCHAFT, POLITIK UND KULTURGESCHICHTE – v. 1-120. 1863-93 – 1 – 240.00 – us L of C Photodup [300]
VIERTELJAHRSSCHRIFT DER NATURFORSCHENDEN GESELLSCHAFT IN ZUERICH – (Missing: 1898. v43(p.1-253)) – Zuerich. v39-77. 1894-1932. Beiblatt. nos 1-20. 1923-32 – 277mf – 9 – 8704/1 – ne IDC [500]
VIERTELJAHRSSCHRIFT FUER DERMATOLOGIE UND SYPHILIS – (Cont: Archiv fuer Dermatologie und Syphilis. Cont by: Archiv fuer Dermatologie und Syphilis) – Heidelberg. v6-20. 1874-88* – 1 – D13135.01 – us UMI [616]
VIERTELJAHRSSCHRIFT FUER LITTERATURGESCHICHTE – Weimar. v1-6. 1888-93 – 67mf – 9 – H-422/2 – ne IDC [400]
VIERTELJAHRSSCHRIFT FUER MUSIKWISSENSCHAFT / ed by Chrysander, Friedrich et al – P 624. Leipzig v.1-10. 1885-1894 – 73mf – 9 – ne IDC [073]
VIERTELJAHRSSCHRIFT FUER WISSENSCHAFTLICHE PHILOSOPHIE 1.1877-25.1901 : VIERTELJAHRSSCHRIFT FUER WISSENSCHAFTLICHE PHILOSOPHIE UND SOZIOLOGIE 26.1902-40.1916 – Leipzig, 1877-1916 (mf ed 1993) – 162mf – 9 – DM1,890.00 – 3-89131-165-6 – gw Fischer [100]
VIERTZIG KURTZE PREDIG VBER DEN GANTZEN CATECHISMUM / Huberinus, Caspar – Nuernberg: J. vom Berg & U. Neuber, 1561. [G.F.: 21.5] – 4mf – 9 – HUB-79/1 – ne IDC [240]
VIERTZIG KURTZE PREDIG VBER DEN GANTZEN CATECHISMUM... / Huberinus, Caspar – Nuernberg: Johann Daubmann, 1550. [GF-21.1] – 9mf – 9 – HUB-49/1 – ne IDC [240]
DIE VIERZIG TAGE DES MUSA DAGH : ROMAN / Werfel, Franz – Berlin: P Zsolnay. 2v. 1933 – 1 – us U.W. Library [830]
Vies, A et al *see* CONNECTIVE TISSUE RESEARCH
VIES DES FAMEUX ARCHITECTES [ET SCULPTEURS] DEPUIS LA RENAISSANCE DES ARTS... / Dezallier d'Argenville, AN – Paris. 2v. 1787 – 14mf – ne IDC [700]
VIES DES PREMIERS-PEINTRES DU ROI, DEPUIS M. LE BRUN, JUSQU'A PRESENT / Lepicie, B – Paris. 2v. 1752 – 5mf – ne IDC [750]
VIES IMAGINAIRES / Schwob, Marcel – Mayenne: E. Soudee, c1896. 276p. 3 fiches. (Literature Collection) – 9 – 8.00 – fr Bibl Nationale [830]
VIESTNIK – Moscow, 1922-35 – 7r – 1 – us Ross [335]
VIESTNIK FINANSOV, PROMYSHLENNOSTI I TORGOVLI / Russia. Ministerstvo Finansov – 1877-87 – 5r – 1 – us Ross [336]
VIESTNIK IUGOZAPADNOI I ZAPADNOI ROSSII – Kiev-Vilnius. 1862-71 – 1 – 184.00 – us L of C Photodup [073]
VIESTNIK NARODNOGO KOMISSARIATA TORGOVLI I PROMYSHLENNOSTI – Moskva: Komissariat, 1918-1919. 2v – 1 – CSUX90-S473 – us Hoover Inst Photo [338]
VIESTNIK. ORGAN TSERKOVNO-OBSHCHESTVENNOI ZHIZN' – Paris, 1937 – 1 reel – 1 – us I.H.R.C. [944]
VIESTNIK PUTE I SOOBSHCHENIIA – (Library has: 1918: nos. 1-31/32, 1919: nos. 1-14/15) – Moskva: Izd. Narodnogo komissariata pute i soobshcheniia, 1918-1919. 2v – 1 – CSUX89-S882 – us Hoover Inst Photo [380]
VIESTNIK RUSSKAGO STUDENCHESKAGO KHRYSTIANSKAGO DVIZHENIIA – Paris, 1926-1936 – 1 reel – 1 – us I.H.R.C. [944]
VIESTNIK VREMENNAGO PRAVITEL'STVA / Russia. (1917-Provisional Government) – St. Petersburg. 5 Mar-26 Oct 1917. (Wanting four issues) – 1 – $23.00 – us L of C Photodup [324]
VIESY – Moscow. v1-6. 1904-09 – 3r – 1 – us Ross [460]
VIESY – v. 1-6. 1904-09 – 1 – 65.00 – us L of C Photodup [460]
VIET CONG AND NORTH VIETNAMESE ARMY TACTICAL STUDIES AND DOCTRINE / U.S. Military Assistance Command. Vietnam – 18 v. 1965-70 – 1 – 26.00 – us L of C Photodup [950]
VIET NAM – Hanoi. v197-228. 1975-77 1; v205-228. jan 1976-1977* 5,9 – 1,5,9 – D10497 – us UMI [073]
VIET REPORT – (Superseded by: Leviathan) – New York. v1-3. jul 1965-sum 1968 – 1 – D2419 – us UMI [073]
VIET-DAN – Bao xuat ban moi ngay. Saigon. 18 mars 1933-13 janv 1938 – 1 – fr A.C.R.P.P. [073]
VIETNAM – Leesburg. v1-10. sum 1988-apr 1998+ 1,5,9; v1-7. sum 1988-apr 1995* 5 – 1,5,9 – D17197 – us UMI [073]
Vietnam *see*
– CONG BAO VIET-NAM
– CONG-BAO VIET-NAM CONG-HOA
– MISCELLANEOUS PUBLICATIONS
VIETNAM – A DOCUMENTARY COLLECTION : RECORDS OF THE WESTMORELAND V. CBS CASE – (Printed guide only, $100.00) – 1,010mf – 9 – $4,485.00 – us UPA [977]
VIETNAM AND SOUTHEAST ASIA : SPECIAL STUDIES 1960-80 / ed by Kesaris, Paul – 1982. 13r. With printed guide – 1 – $1,430.00 – 0-89093-383-9 – us UPA [320]
VIETNAM AND SOUTHEAST ASIA, 1946-76 / U.S. Central Intelligence Agency – (Supplement: $580.00 ISBN 0-89093-628-5) – 1982. Series: CIA Research Reports – 1 – $690.00 – 0-89093-451-7 – us UPA [950]
VIETNAM COURIER – Hanoi. North Vietnam. 1964- – 1 – us UMI [072]
VIETNAM COURIER – Hanoi, VM. 1966-1972 – 1r – $50.00 – R042233 – us Library Micro [072]
Vietnam. Directorate General of Planning *see* FOUR-YEAR NATIONAL ECONOMIC DEVELOPMENT PLAN. 1972-1975
VIETNAM DOCUMENTS AND RESEARCH NOTES SERIES : TRANSLATION AND ANALYSIS OF SIGNIFICANT VIET CONG/ NORTH VIETNAMESE DOCUMENTS – 6r – 1 – $660.00 – 1-55655-416-8 – us UPA [324]
VIETNAM HON – Tribune libre des etudiants et des travailleurs annamites. no. 1-7. Paris. janv-juil 1926. mq no. 3 – 1 – fr A.C.R.P.P. [073]
VIETNAM ILLUSTRATED – Apr-Dec 1973 – 9 – us UMI [073]
VIETNAM MAGAZINE – Saigon. 1968-75* – 1 – D8430 – us UMI [073]
VIETNAM PERSPECTIVES – New York. v1-3. aug 1965-nov 1967 – 1 – D7391 – us UMI [073]
VIETNAM POLICY PROPOSALS: HEARINGS. / U.S. Congress. Senate. Committee on Foreign Relations – Washington, Govt. Print. Off., 1970. 405 p. LL-2347 – 1 – us L of C Photodup [340]
VIETNAM PRESS – Saigon. South Vietnam. 1955-1967 – 1 – us UMI [072]
VIETNAM REPORT – Saigon. v1-2. 1972-73 1; v1. 1972 5 – 1,5 – D7927 – us UMI [073]
Vietnam. South. Direction Generale du Plan *see*
– DEUXIEME PLAN QUINQUENNAL, 1962-1966
– PROJET DU PLAN QUINQUENNAL (1957-1961)
VIETNAM THANH NIEN TAP CHI – no. 1-5 6. Hanoi. 1er juil 1923-mars juin 1924 – 1 – fr A.C.R.P.P. [073]
VIETNAM, THE MEDIA, AND PUBLIC SUPPORT FOR THE WAR – 11 reels with printed guide – 1 – $1,060.00 – 0-89093-496-7 – us UPA [977]
VIETNAMESE COLLECTION OF THE ANU LIBRARY / ed by Mai Than-trong & Hiep Nguyen Duc – 1983 – A$10.00 – 0-86758-145-X – at BISA [010]
VIETNAMESE LAW – (Titles also listed separately) – 100mf – 9 – ne IDC [340]
VIETNAMESE LAW COLLECTION – (Titles listed separately) – 100mf – 9 – ne IDC [340]
Vietnamese Lawyer's association *see* NHA NUOC VA PHAP LUAT
Vietor, Karl *see*
– GEIST UND FORM
– DER JUNGE GOETHE
– DIE LYRIK HOELDERLINS
LE VIEUX CELIBATAIRE / Collin d'Harleville, Jean Francois – (French Theatre Series). Paris. Maradan, an II. 1792 – 9 – fr Hachette [820]
LES VIEUX CHANTS POPULAIRES SCANDINAVES / Pineau, Leon – 1901 – 1 – us I.U. Libraries [390]
LE VIEUX HONFLEUR ET SES MARINS: BIOGRAPHIES ET RECITS MARITIMES / Breard, Charles – Rouen: Impr. Cagniard, 1897. 00258. (Pre-1900 Canadiana) – 9 – cn C.I.H.M. [920]
LE VIEUX LACHINE: ET LE MASSACRE DU 5 AOUT 1689: CONFERENCE DONNEE DEVANT LA PAROISSE DE LACHINE, LE 6 AOUT 1889 / Girouard, Desire – (Montreal: Gebhardt-Berthiaume, 1889. 03442. (Pre-1900 Canadiana) – 9 – cn C.I.H.M. [971]
VIEUX MANOIRS, VIEILLES MAISONS – Quebec: Ls-A Proulx, 1927. SEM105P1408 – 5mf – 9 – Can$11.25 – cn Bibl Nat [720]
LE VIEUX MONTREAL : FONDATION, DEVELOPPEMENT, VISITE / Morin, Victor – Montreal, 1942. SEM105P755 – 1mf – 9 – Can$2.25 – cn Bibl Nat [971]
LE VIEUX MONTREAL, 1611-1803 – Montreal: H. Beaugrand, 1884. 03526. (Pre-1900 Canadiana) – 9 – cn C.I.H.M. [971]
LE VIEUX MONTREALAIS = THE OLD MONTREALER / ed by Fitzpatrick, Liam – Montreal. v1 n1. 15 mai 1992-v1 n3. 15 aut 1992 – 1r – 1 – Can$25.00 – cn Can Microfilming [072]
LE VIEUX TEMPS / Grignon, Joseph-Jerome – Saint-Jerome: Librairie Prevost, 1921. SEM105P1746 – 1mf – 9 – Can$2.25 – cn Bibl Nat [971]
LE VIEUX TRIBUN DU PEUPLE – (Annee 1789). Paris. Imprimerie du Cercle Social, An 4. Redacteur: Nicolas de Bonneville – 9 – fr Hachette [321]
LE VIEUX TRIBUN DU PEUPLE ET SA BOUCHE DE FER – Paris: Imprimerie-Librairie du Cercle social, 1796-97. Redacteur: Nicolas de Bonneville – 9 – fr Hachette [321]
Vievento, A *see* QUELLEN ZUR GESCHICHTE DER DEUTSCHEN KAISERPOLITIK OESTERREICHS WAEHREND DER FRANZOESISCHEN REVOLUTIONSKRIEGE 1790-1801
VIEW – Reno, NV. 1966-1967 – 1r – 1 – $50.00 – B06068 – us Library Micro [071]
VIEW – v.1-. 1980- – 1,5,6,9 – us UMI [073]
VIEW BART KENNEDY'S PAPER – London, UK. 12 Jan-25 Apr 1911.-w. 1/4 reel – 1 – uk British Libr Newspaper [072]
A VIEW OF ALL THE RIGHT HONOURABLE LORD MAYORS OF THIS HONOURABLE CITY OF LONDON, 1558-1601 / Jaggard, W – 1 – uk Microform Academic [941]
A VIEW OF CONGREGATIONALISM : ITS PRINCIPLES AND DOCTRINES, THE TESTIMONY OF ECCLESIASTICAL HISTORY IN ITS FAVOR, ITS PRACTICE AND ITS ADVANTAGES / Punchard, G – Boston: Congregational Board of Publication, 1856 – 1mf – us A.T.L.A. [240]
THE VIEW OF INDIA EXTRA GANGEM, CHINA; AND, JAPAN / Pennant, T – (Index) – London, 1800 – 6mf – 9 – ne IDC [950]
A VIEW OF SOUTH CAROLINA / Drayton, John – ca.1802. 7 fiches – 9 – us South Carolina Historical [975]
A VIEW OF THE CAUSES AND CONSEQUENCES OF THE PRESENT WAR WITH FRANCE / Erskine, T – London, 1797 – 2mf – 1 – ILM-2580/1 – ne IDC [327]
A VIEW OF THE ENGLISH STAGE : OR, A SERIES OF DRAMATIC CRITICISMS / Hazlitt, William – London: Printed for Robert Stodart, Anderson and Chase; Edinburgh: Bell and Bradfute, 1818 – 1 roll – 1 – 1-55879-343-7 – uk Libr Preservation [790]
VIEW OF THE HISTORICAL AND ACTUAL STATE OF THE MILITARY FORCE OF GREAT BRITAIN / Dupin, Charles – London: John Murray. 2v. 1822 – 8mf – 9 – $12.00 – LLMC 90-034 – us L.L.M.C. [340]
VIEW OF THE STATE OF EUROPE DURING THE MIDDLE AGES / Hallam, Henry – 3v. 1870 – 1 – us A.T.L.A. [900]
VIEW OF THE STATE OF EUROPE DURING THE MIDDLE AGES / Hallam, Henry – London: John Murray, 7th ed 1837 – 3 rolls – 1 – 1-55879-255-4 – uk Libr Preservation [940]
Vieweg, Rudolf *see* VP
VIEWPOINTS – (Cont by: Viewpoints in Teaching and Learning. Former title: Indiana University. School of Education. Bulletin of the School of Education 1924-69) – Bloomington. v1-53. sep 1924- nov 1977 1; v49-53. jan 1973-nov 1977 5; v52-53. jan 1976-nov 1977 9 – 1,5,9 – D9801 – us UMI [370]
VIEWPOINTS – (Cont by: Viewpoints, the Journal for Data Collection) – Rocky Hill. v1-9 1960-68*. v10-15 jan 1969-spr 1975 1; v13-14. sum 1972-spr 1974 5 – 1,5 – D5095 – us UMI [073]
VIEWPOINTS *see*
– VIEWPOINTS IN TEACHING AND LEARNING
– VIEWPOINTS, THE JOURNAL FOR DATA COLLECTION
VIEWPOINTS IN TEACHING AND LEARNING – (Cont: Viewpoints) – Bloomington. v54-59. jan 1978-spr 1983 – 1,5,9 – D9801.01 – us UMI [370]
VIEWPOINTS IN TEACHING AND LEARNING *see* VIEWPOINTS
VIEWPOINTS, THE JOURNAL FOR DATA COLLECTION – (Cont: Viewpoints. Cont by: Journal of Data Collection) – Rocky Hill. v16-21. may 1976-jul 1981 1,5,9; v18-19. jan 1978-jul 1979* 5,9 – 1,5,9 – D5095.01 – us UMI [073]
VIEWPOINTS, THE JOURNAL FOR DATA COLLECTION *see* VIEWPOINTS
VIEWS AND OPINIONS / Ouida – British Fiction Archive: Unit 3 – 9 – uk Bell [830]
VIEWS AND REVIEWS : ESSAYS IN APPRECIATION / Henley, William Ernest – London: David Nutt, 1890 – 1 roll – 1 – 1-55879-500-6 – uk Libr Preservation [840]
VIEWS IN REFERENCE TO THE SIMPLIFICATION OF CIVIL PRACTICE IN THE COURTS OF NEW YORK STATE / Cuvillier, Louis Andrew – New York, 1916. 4 p. LL-1387 – 1 – us L of C Photodup [340]
VIEWS OF SANCTIFICATION / Finney, Charles G – Oberlin: James Steele, 1840 – 1mf – us A.T.L.A. [240]
VIEWS OF THE UNITED STATES' COMMISSIONERS ON THE ALASKA BOUNDARY.. / U.S. Commissioners on the Alaska Boundary – 1898?. 05597. (Pre-1900 Canadiana) – 9 – cn C.I.H.M. [971]
VIEWS OF THEOLOGY : AS DEVELOPED IN THREE SERMONS : AND ON HIS TRIALS BEFORE THE PRESBYTERY AND SYNOD OF CINCINNATI, JUNE, 1835 : WITH REMARKS ON THE PRINCETON REVIEW / Beecher, Lyman – Boston: J.P. Jewett; Cleveland, Ohio: Jewett, Proctor & Worthington, 1853. (Beecher's works; v3) – 2mf – 9 – us A.T.L.A. [240]
VIEWS ON THE SYNOD / Central Conference of American Rabbis – Baltimore: Lord Baltimore Press, 1905 – 1mf – 9 – 0-8370-2617-2 – 1985-0617 – us A.T.L.A. [270]
VIGA-GLUMS SAGA – Story of Viga-Glum. Trans. from the Icelandic, with notes and introd. by Sir Edmund Head. London, Edinburgh: Williams and Norgate, 1866. xvi,124p. 2 geneal. tab – 1 – us U.W. Library [430]
Vigee *see* LA MATINEE D'UNE JOLIE FEMME
VIGENCIA DEL FRENTE E JUVENTUDES EN EL PRESENTE Y EN EL FUTURO DE ESPANA / Diaz Moreno, Juan – Caceres: Imp. Sergio Dorado, 1973 – 1 – sp Bibl Santa Ana [946]
Viger, Denis Benjamin *see*
– ANALYSE D'UN ENTRETIEN SUR LA CONSERVATION DES ETABLISSEMENS DU BAS-CANADA
– CONSIDERATIONS SUR LES EFFETS QU'ONT PRODUIT EN CANADA
– COPY OF A COMMUNICATION AND OTHER PAPERS...FROM THE HONORABLE DENIS BENJAMIN VIGER

- DIVERS DOCUMENTS ADDRESSED TO THE HONORABLE LOUIS JOSEPH PAPINEAU...
- DIVERS DOCUMENTS ADRESSES A L'HONORABLE LOUIS JOSEPH PAPINEAU...
- DOCUMENT FROM THE HONORABLE DENIS BENJAMIN VIGER, DATED 25TH OCTOBER, 1832
- A LETTER TO THE RIGHT HON. LORD VISCOUNT GODERICH
- MEMOIRES RELATIFS A L'EMPRISONNEMENT DE L'HONORABLE D. B. VIGER
- OBSERVATIONS ON A LETTER FROM JAMES STUART,...TO THE RIGHT HONORABLE LORD VISCOUNT GODERICH RELATING TO ANIMADVERSIONS AND IMPUTATIONS ON HIS CONDUCT AND CHARACTER IN CERTAIN PROCEEDINGS OF THE ASSEMBLY OF LOWER CANADA
- VARIOUS DOCUMENTS ADDRESSED TO THE HONORABLE LOUIS JOSEPH PAPINEAU, SPEAKER OF THE HOUSE OF ASSEMBLY

Viger, Jacques *see* ARCHEOLOGIE RELIGIEUSE DU DIOCESE DE MONTREAL, 1850

Vigfusson, G *see* ICELANDIC SAGAS AND OTHER HISTORICAL DOCUMENTS RELATING TO THE SETTLEMENTS AND DESCENTS OF THE NORTHMEN ON THE BRITISH ISLES (RS88)

LA VIGIE : DU DISTRICT DE BEAUHARNOIS P.Q. – Valleyfield, Canada. v1 n7. 14 fev 1931-v2 n47. 24 nov 1932 – 1r – 1 – Can$25.00 – cn Can Microfilming [072]

LA VIGIE : HEBDO / ed by Barthe, Ulrich – Quebec Canada. 30 jun 1906-31 mai 1913 – 4r – 1 – Can$45.00 – cn Can Microfilming [072]

LA VIGIE – Journal republicain, politique, hebdomadaire. Red. en chef E. Le Blond. no. 1-27. Cayenne. juil 1890-janv 1891. mq no. 24 – 1 – fr A.C.R.P.P. [073]

LA VIGIE – La Baie, 12 jun 1963-18 jan 1967f – 1r – 1 – Can$75.00 – cn Can Microfilming [072]

LA VIGIE – Montreal, Canada. 28 mar 1935 – 1r – 1 – Can$25.00 – cn Can Microfilming [072]

LA VIGIE DE ROYAN – Bordeaux. 3 juil 1859-30 sept 1860 – 1 – fr A.C.R.P.P. [073]

LA VIGIE MAROCAINE – Casablanca, Morocco: [s.n.,] 1957-oct 1971 – 50r – 1 – us Res Libr [072]

VIGIL – Charleston. v1-6. feb-apr 1798 – 1 – D3672 – us UMI [978]

VIGILANCE / Comite d'Action Antifasciste et de Vigilance – Bulletin bimensuel. puis Bulletin du Comite de vigilance des intellectuels antifascistes. no. 1-59, 61. Paris. avr 1934-janv 1938 – 1 – fr A.C.R.P.P. [073]

VIGILANCE RECORD – London, UK. 15 Jan-15 Feb, 15 Sept-15 Nov 1894.-m. 1 foot – 1 – uk British Libr Newspaper [072]

VIGILANCE RECORD : ORGAN OF THE NATIONAL VIGILANCE ASSOCIATION – London, 1887-1930 – 85mf – 9 – W-34/1 – ne IDC [360]

VIGILANT – Goldfield, NV. 30 Jan 1905 – 1r – 1 – $50.00 – U04563 – us Library Micro [071]

VIGILANT PRESS : A COLLECTION OF CASE STUDIES – 1989 – 9 – 92-3-102623-2 – fr UNESCO [070]

VIGILANT REPORTER – Reno, NV. Aug-Sep 1957 – 1r – 1 – $50.00 – U04722 – us Library Micro [071]

O VIGILANTE : CRITICO E NOTICIOSO – Pilar, Alagoas. 22-29 Jan, Mar, Maio, Jul, Set 1888; Jul, Set, Dez 1889; Mar, Nov 1890; Out, Nov 1891; Jun-Jul 1898; Maio, 18 Nov 1900 – 1,5,6 – bl Biblioteca [072]

O VIGILANTE : ORGAM HUMORISTICO, LITFRARIO E NOTICIOSO – Maceio, Alagoas. 27 Jan 1923 – 1,5,6 – bl Biblioteca [072]

O VIGILANTE : PERIODICO CRITICO, SATYRICO E NOTICIOSO – Maceio, Alagoas. 2 Set-10 Nov 1878 – 1,5,6 – bl Biblioteca [072]

THE VIGILANTE – San Francisco, CA. SF State University: 1922 – 1r – 1 – $50.00 – B03675 – us Library Micro [071]

VIGILANTE – Manaus, Amazonas. 3 Mar 1986 – 1,5,6 – bl Biblioteca [072]

VIGILANTE *see* GOLDEN GATOR

Vigilante, Florence *see* JOURNAL OF TEACHING IN SOCIAL WORK

VIGILIAE CHRISTIANAE – Leiden. v1-44. 1947-90 – 5,9 – Dfl5,280.00; Dfl120.00v – ne Swets [240]

VIGILIAE CHRISTIANAE – v1-38. 1947-84 – 1,5,6,13 – sz Elsevier [073]

VIGNA, LUIS. BREVIARIO DE DOCTRINA CATOLICA. BARCELONA, 1943 / Marquez, Gabino – Madrid: Razon y Fe, 1945 – 1 – sp Bibl Santa Ana [240]

Vignau, V *see* INDICE DE LAS PRUEBAJ DE CABALLEROS DE LA ORDEN DE SANTIAGO

Vigne d'Octon, Paul *see*
- AU PAYS DES FETICHES
- TERRE DE MORT

Vigne, Paul *see* LES RIVIERES DU SUD DE LA SENEGAMBIE

LA VIGNE: SA CULTURE ET SA TAILLE / Chapais, Jean Charles – Montreal: E. Senecal, 1881. 02098. (Pre-1900 Canadiana) – 9 – cn C.I.H.M. [631]

Vigneault-Page, Celine *see* FRERE ROBERT SYLVAIN, E.C., DOCTEUR ES LETTRES

VIGNETTES FROM NATURE / Allen, Grant – London: Chatto & Windus, 1881. 05090. (Pre-1900 Canadiana) – 9 – cn C.I.H.M. [574]

Vignet-Zunz, J *see* HOMMES DE L'OUARSENIS

Vignola, Giacomo Barozzi *see* REGLES DES CINQ ORDRES D'ARCHITECTURE DE VIGNOLE

Vignola, J *see*
- ARCHITECTURA
- DE LAS CINCO ORDENES DE ARCHITECTURA
- LE DUE REGOLE DELLA PROSPETTIVA PRATICA
- REGLA DE LAS CINCO ORDENES DE ARCHITECTURA

Vignole, Barozzio de *see* LIVRE NOUVEAU... D'ARCHITECTURE

Vignoli, Tito *see* MYTH AND SCIENCE

Vignon, Louis Valery *see* LA FRANCE DANS L'AFRIQUE DU NORD

Vigny, Alfred de *see* CINQ-MARS: OR, A CONSPIRACY UNDER LOUIS 13

VIGO AND PARKE COUNTIES / Beckwith, H W – Chicago: H.H. Hill and N. Iddings, Publs., 1880.Indiana Reel 28. (The Cox Library Collection) – 5 – us Americana [978]

Vigo, J de *see*
- THE MOST EXCELLENT WORCKES OF CHIRURGERY
- THE MOST EXCELLENT WORKES OF CHIRURGERY...
- THE MOST EXCELLENT WORKES OF CHIRURGERY
- THE WHOLE WORKE OF THAT FAMOUS CHIRURGION

Viguie, Christine A *see* BLOOD GLUTATHIONE OXIDATION DURING HUMAN EXERCISE

VIIKOSANOMAT – (In Finnish) – Canada, May 1975-86 – 6r – 1 – cn Commonwealth Micro [072]

VIISKUMMEND AASTAT APOSTLITE RADADEL, 1884-1934 / Kaups, Richard – Fifty Years in the Paths of the Apostles, 1884-1934. Tallinn: Publishing House of the Union of the Estonian Baptist Churches, 1934. 242p – 1 – 9.68 – us Baptist [240]

VIJFJARIG OVERZICHT VAN DE STERFTE NAAR DEN LEEFTIJD EN DE OORZAKEN VAN DEN DOOD IN ELKE GEMEENTE VAN NEDERLAND / Netherlands. (Kingdom, 1815-). Department van Binnenlandsche Zaken – v. 1-5. 1875 80-1895 99 – 1 – 87.00 – us L of C Photodup [949]

THE VIKING – (Incl Golden Anniversary issue) – Long Beach, CA: Long Beach City College, Sept 1927-May 1987 – 12r – 1 – $600.00 – B02365 – us Library Micro [370]

VIKING SETTLERS IN GREENLAND AND THEIR DESCENDANTS DURING FIVE HUNDRED YEARS / Norlund, Poul – London: Cambridge University Press, 1936. 160p.illus.maps, plans. Trans. from the Danish by W.E. Calvert. Bibliography – 1 – us U.W. Library [970]

VIKING TALES OF THE NORTH / ed by Anderson, Rasmus Bjorn – Sagas of Thorstein, Viking's son, and Fridthjof the Bold. Chicago: S. C. Griggs and Co., 1877. xviii,370p – 1 – us U.W. Library [390]

VIKINGEN – Stockholm, 1882-89 – 9 – sw Kungliga [072]

THE VIKINGS IN WESTERN CHRISTENDOM, A.D. 789 TO A.D. 888 / Keary, Charles Francis – New York: G.P. Putnam; London: T.F. Unwin, 1891.xi,571p. double map – 1 – us U.W. Library [940]

VIKRAM AND THE VAMPIRE, OR, TALES OF HINDU DEVILRY / Burton, Richard Francis – 1870 – 1 – us I.U. Libraries [390]

VIKTORIA : EINE ERZAEHLUNG VON JUNGEN MENSCHEN / Thomas, Adrienne – Basel: Atrium-Verlag, 1937 – 1r – 1 – us U.W. Library [430]

Viktorov, A E *see*
- SOBRANIE RUKOPISEI I.D. BELIAEVA
- SOBRANIE RUKOPISEI P.I. SEVAST'IANOVA
- SOBRANIE RUKOPISEI V.I. GROGOROVICHA

VILAG – Budapest. Hungary. -d. 14 May 1945-31 Oct 1948. (Very imperfect). (6 reels) – 1 – uk British Libr Newspaper [072]

LES VILAINS DANS LES OEUVRES DES TROUVERES / Ledieu, Alcius – Paris: J. Maisonneuve, 1890. 114p. 2 fiches. (Literature Collection) – 9 – 6.00 – fr Bibl Nationale [440]

Vilakazi, B W *see* CONCEPTION AND DEVELOPMENT OF POETRY IN ZULU

Vilanova y Piera, Juan *see* VALENCIA DE ALCANTARA EN EL CONCEPTO PROTOHISTORICO

VILAYET SALNAMES : ADANA SALNAMESI – (1287[1870], def'a 1. – 2mf. $225.00; 1312[1894]. – 4mf. $150.00) – 9 – us MEDOC [949]

VILAYET SALNAMES : AMARI-I KISHVAR SALNAMESI – 1358 [1979-1980], sal-i 1 – 22mf – 9 – $50.00 – us MEDOC [949]

VILAYET SALNAMES : ANKARA SALNAMESI – (1307 M[1891]. – 5mf. $39.00; 1311[1893]. – 6mf. $42.00; 1318[1890]. – 5mf. $39.00; 1325[1907]. – 7mf. $42.00) – 9 – us MEDOC [949]

VILAYET SALNAMES : AYDIN SALNAMESI – (1300[1883]. – 4mf. $36.75; 1308[1891]. – 18mf. $50.00; 1312[1894]. – 11mf. $50.00; 1316[1898]. – 8mf. $44.00; 1317[1889]. – 8mf. $44.00; 1326[1908]. – 12mf. $50.00) – 9 – us MEDOC [949]

VILAYET SALNAMES : BAGHDAD SALNAMESI – (1309[1892], def'a 8. – 6mf. $42.00; 1313-14K[1897], def'a 12. – 6mf. $42.00; 1316K[1898], def'a 14. – 5mf. $42.00; 1317K[1899], def'a 15. – 5mf. $39.00; 1318K[1900]. – 9mf. $45.00; 1325[1907]. – 6mf. $42.00) – 9 – us MEDOC [949]

VILAYET SALNAMES : BASRA SALNAMESI – (1308[1891], def'a 1. – 3mf. $50.00; 1318[1900]. – 5mf. $39.00) – 9 – us MEDOC [949]

VILAYET SALNAMES : BEIRUT SALNAMESI – (1318[1900], def'a 2. – 5mf. $65.00; 1332-33[1917]. – 11mf. $50.00; 1333-35[1917]. – 9mf. $47.25) – 9 – us MEDOC [949]

VILAYET SALNAMES : BITLIS SALNAMESI – 1310 [1892] – 5mf – 9 – $39.00 – us MEDOC [949]

VILAYET SALNAMES : BOLU SALNAMESI – (1334[1918]. – 6mf. $39.00; 1337-38M[1921-1922]. – 12mf. $50.00) – 9 – us MEDOC [949]

VILAYET SALNAMES : BOSNA SALNAMESI – 1291 [1874] – 3mf – 9 – $32.50 – us MEDOC [949]

VILAYET SALNAMES : CEBEL-I LUEBNAN SALNAMESI – (1304[1887]. – 2mf. $26.25; 1309[1892], def'a 6. – 2mf. $75.00) – 9 – us MEDOC [949]

VILAYET SALNAMES : CEZAIR-I BAHRI-I SEFID SALNAMESI – (1292[1875], def'a 6. – 2mf. $275.00; 1301[1894], def'a 8. – 5mf. $39.00; 1311[1893], def'a 11. – 5mf. $39.00; 1312[1894], def'a 12. – 3mf. $26.25; 1313[1895], def'a 13. – 5mf. $39.00; 1321[1903], def'a 20. – 5mf. $39.00) – 9 – us MEDOC [949]

VILAYET SALNAMES : DIYARBAKR SALNAMESI – (1286[1869]. – 2mf. $75.00; 1300[1883]. – 2mf. $75.00; 1302[1885]. – 6mf. $42.00; 1308[1891]. – 2mf. $75.00; 1312[1894]. – 4mf. $36.75; 1316[1898], def'a 15. – 3mf. $75.00; 1317[1899]. – 4mf. $36.75; 1319[1901], def'a 18. – 4mf. $40.00; 1321[1903]. – 4mf. $36.75; 1323[1905]. 4mf. – $36.75) – 9 – us MEDOC [949]

VILAYET SALNAMES : EDIRNE SALNAMESI – (1300[1883], def'a 9. – 4mf. $36.75; 1305[1888], def'a 14. – 4mf. $325.00; 1309[1892], def'a 18. 11mf. $50.00; 1310[1893], def'a 19. – 12mf. $50.00; 1313M[1897], def'a 23. – 5mf. $39.00; 1314M[1898], def'a 24. – 5mf. $36.75; 1319M[1903], def'a 28. – 20mf. $52.50) – 9 – us MEDOC [949]

VILAYET SALNAMES : GIRID SALNAMESI – 1310 [1892] – 4mf – 9 – $50.00 – us MEDOC [949]

VILAYET SALNAMES : HALEP SALNAMESI – (1288[1871], def'a 5. – 2mf. $325.00; 1291[1874], def'a 8. – 2mf. $95.00; 1302[1885]. – 4mf. $36.75; 1305[1888], def'a 16. – 3mf. $65.00; 1307[1890], def'a 18. – 3mf. $75.00; 1309[1892], def'a 20. – 3mf. $95.00; 1310[1893], def'a 21. – 4mf. $75.00; 1313[1895], def'a 23. – 4mf. $80.00; 1314[1896], def'a 24. – 4mf. $90.00; 1315[1897], def'a 25. – 4mf. $80.00; 1316[1898], def'a 26. – 4mf. $80.00; 1317[1899], def'a 27. – 6mf. $42.00; 1318[1900], def'a 28. – 5mf. $90.00; 1319[1901], def'a 29. – 5mf. $90.00; 1320[1902], def'a 30. – 7mf. $42.00; 1321[1903], def'a 31. – 8mf. $44.00; 1322[1904], def'a 32. – 6mf. $100.00; 1323[1905], def'a 33. – 7mf. $120.00; 1324[1906], def'a 34. – 8mf. $44.00; 1326[1908], def'a[35]. – 7mf. $120.00) – 9 – us MEDOC [949]

VILAYET SALNAMES : HICAZ SALNAMESI – (1301[1884].-4mf. $36.75; 1305[1888].-4mf. $36.75; 1306[1889] 5mf. $39.00; 1309[1892].-5mf. $39.00) – 9 – us MEDOC [949]

VILAYET SALNAMES : HUDAVENDIGAR SALNAMESI – (1302[1885].-8mf. $44.00; 1307M[1891].-7mf. $42.00; 1310[1892].-8mf. $44.00; 1313[1895].-7mf. $42.00; 1315[1897].-5mf. $39.00; 1316[1898].-6mf. $42.00; 1318[1900].-4mf. $47.00; 1321[1903].-6mf. $42.00; 1323[1905].-5mf. $39.00; 1324[1906].-12mf. $50.00; 1325[1907].-11mf. $50.00;[1927].-9mf. $47.25) – 9 – us MEDOC [949]

VILAYET SALNAMES : ISKODRA SALNAMESI – 1312 [1894] – 3mf – 9 – $32.50 – us MEDOC [949]

VILAYET SALNAMES : KARESI SALNAMESI – 1305 [1888] – 3mf – 9 – $26.25 – us MEDOC [949]

VILAYET SALNAMES : KASTAMONU SALNAMESI – (1310[1892].-10mf. $47.25; 1311[1893].-6mf. $42.00; 1312[1894], def'a 18.-5mf. $450.00; 1314[1896], def'a 19.-7mf. $50.00; 1317[1899].-6mf. $39.00) – 9 – us MEDOC [949]

VILAYET SALNAMES : KONYA SALNAMESI – (1298[1881].-3mf. $26.25; 1310[1892].-7mf. $42.00; 1317[1899].-6mf. $42.00; 1322M[1906].-5mf. $39.00) – 9 – us MEDOC [949]

VILAYET SALNAMES : KOSOVA SALNAMESI – (1300[1883], def'a 2.-3mf. $45.00; 1311[1893].-5mf. $39.00; 1314[1896].-12mf. $50.00; 1318[1900].-16mf. $52.50) – 9 – us MEDOC [949]

VILAYET SALNAMES : MA'MURET UEL-AZIZ SALNAMESI – 1310 [1892] – 4mf – 9 – $36.75 – us MEDOC [949]

VILAYET SALNAMES : MANASTIR SALNAMESI – 1305 [1888] – 10mf – 9 – $47.25 – us MEDOC [949]

VILAYET SALNAMES : MOSUL SALNAMESI – (1308[1891].-5mf. $39.00; 1310[1892].-7mf. $42.00; 1325[1907].-4mf. $36.75) – 9 – us MEDOC [949]

VILAYET SALNAMES : SELANIK SALNAMESI – (1307[1890].-5mf. $39.00; 1315[1897].-10mf. $50.00) – 9 – us MEDOC [949]

Vil'do, Iu et al *see* OCHERKI DEREVENSKOI KOOPERATSII

Vilenskogo, V et al *see* DEVIATY I VAL

Vilia Franca de Los Barros. Ayuntamiento *see* FIESTAS DEL CARMEN, JULIO 1963

Viliamsa, V R *see* OTCHET EKSPEDITSII KOMZETA 1927 GODA PO OBSLEDOVANIIU BIROBIDZHANSKOGO RAIONA DALNEVOSTOCHNOGO KRAIA (BIROBIDZHANA)

VILIEMARIE: PETITES FLEURS RELIGIEUSES DE VIEUX MONTREAL / Dupuy, Paul – Avec une introduction par H. A. Verreau. Montreal: Cadieux & Derome, 1885. 02805. (Pre-1900 Canadiana) – 9 – cn C.I.H.M. [971]

VILLA BORGHESE FUORI DI PORTA PINCIANA / Manilli, J – O-959 1. 1650 – 9 – ne IDC [700]

VILLA BURGHESIA VULGO PINCIANA POETICE DESCRIPTA AB A. B. PATAVINO / Brigentius, A – Roma. 1716. BO-1047 1 – 9 – ne IDC [700]

LA VILLA DE CACERES Y LA REINA CATOLICA: 2. ORDENANZAS SOBRE LAS LABRANZAS Y PASTOS DE ZAFRA Y ZAFRILLA, DE LA "PENAS DE GANADOS" Y ADMINISTRACION DE LOS BIENES PROPIOS DEL CONCEJO DE CACERES...LOS JURAMENTOS DE LOS REYES CATOLICOS /

Floriano Cumbreno, Antonio C – Caceres, 1917 – 1 – sp Bibl Santa Ana [350]

LA VILLA DE SANTA CRUZ DE PANIAGUA Y SAN PEDRO DE ALCANTARA / Santa Cruz de Paniagua. Ayuntamiento – Plasencia: Graficas Sandoval, 1962 – sp Bibl Santa Ana [240]

Villa, E de *see*
- EXAMEN DE BOTICARIOS
- LIBRO DE LAS VIDAS DE DOZE PRINCIPES DE LA MEDICINA
- NOUVEAUX GASCONISMES CORRIGES, AN 10

Villa, Jose *see* ENGLISH-TAGALOG VOCABULARY

VILLA PAMPHILIA, EIUSQUE PALATIUM – Romae, Iacobi de Rubeis, s.a. O 416 – 9 – ne IDC [930]

VILLA SCHOENOW : EINE ERZAEHLUNG / Raabe, Wilhelm Karl – Braunschweig: G Westermann, 1884 – 1r – 1 – us U.W. Library [830]

Villaamil y Castro, J *see* CATALOGO MANUSCRITO DE LA BIBLIOTECA DE LA UNIVERSIDAD CENTRAL DE MADRID

Villacorta, Carlos A *see* CODICES MAYAS...

Villacorta, J Antonio *see* ESTUDIOS BIBLIOGRAFICOS SOBRE RAFAEL LANDIVAR. GUATEMALA, 1931

Villacorte, J Antonio *see* CODICES MAYAS...

Villaescusa, Julian de *see* MONOGRAFIA... ALANGE

Villafranca de los Barros *see*
- COMUNIDAD DE LABRADORES. ORDENANZAS DE LA COMUNIDAD DE LABRADORES DE VILLAFRANCA DE LOS BARROS
- EL CREDITO EXTREMENO. ESTATUTOS Y REGLAMENTO DE EL CREDITO EXTREMENO (CAJA RURAL) SOCIEDAD DE SOCORROS MUTUOS Y CAJA DE AHORROS...ESTABLECIDO EN...
- DISCURSOS LEIDOS EN EL ACTO DE REPARTO DE PREMIOS...ORGANIZADO POR EL EXCMO. AYUNTAMIENTO
- FIESTAS DEL CARMEN
- FIESTAS DEL CARMEN, 1964
- FIESTAS DEL CARMEN 1976
- PRESUPUESTO MUNICIPAL ORDINARIO DE INGRESOS Y GASTOS (CON UN APENDICE CONTENIENDO LAS ORDENANZAS MUNICIPALES. ANO 1930
- REVISTA DE FERIAS Y FIESTAS 1966

Villafranca de los Barros. Ayuntamiento *see* MEMORIA DEL EJERCICIO DE 1927 LERIDA... PRESUPUESTO ORDINARIO PARA 1928

Villafranca de los Barros. Cofradia del Stmo.C. de la Fe *see* REGLAS PARA LA COFRADIA DEL STMO. CRISTO DE LA FE Y DE LA STMA. VIRGEN DE LOS DOLORES

Villafranca de los Barros. Comunidad de Labradores *see*
- MEMORIA Y BALANCE PRESENTADO POR EL SINDICATO EN LA JUANTA GENERAL ORDINARIA DE 8 DE DICIEMBRE COMPLEMENTADA CON DATOS HASTA EL 31 DE DICIEMBRE DE 1918
- ORDENANZAS

Villafranca de los Barros. Sociedad. Cooperativa de Panificacion de San Jose *see* REGLAMENTO

Villafranca de los Barros. Sociedad Coral e instrumental Santa Cecilia *see* REGLAMENTO REFORMADO DE LA SOCIEDAD CORAL E INSTRUMENTAL SANTA CECILIA

Villafranca de los Barros. Sociedad Cultural Recreativa. La Pena *see* REGLAMENTO

Villafranca de los BarrosEl Credito Extremeno *see*
- ESTATUTOS DE SOCIEDAD DE SOCORROS MUTUOS Y CAJA DE AHORROS, CONSTITUIDA EN VILLAFRANCA DE LOS BARROS EN 7 DE MAYO DE 1905, S.L.,S.I.,S.A.
- MEMORIA Y BALANCE DEL PRIMER EJERCICIO PARA DAR CUENTA EN LA JUNTA GENERAL QUE HA DE CELEBRARSE EL DIA 28 DE JULIO DE 1907

VILLAGE AID FIVE YEAR PLAN, 1955/56-1959/60 / Pakistan. Ministry of Economic Affairs. Village Aid Administration – Karachi. 1956. BD-443 1 – 9 – ne IDC [338]

THE VILLAGE CHURCH / Ditchfield, P H – London: Methuen, 1915 – 1mf – us A.T.L.A. [240]

A VILLAGE COMMUNE / Ouida – British Fiction Archive: Unit 3 – 9 – uk Bell [830]

VILLAGE FOLK-TALES OF CEYLON; COLLECTED AND TRANSLATED / Parker, H – London, 1910-1914. 3 vols. BI-989 2 – 8 – ne IDC [390]

VILLAGE HERALD – Woodbury. N.J. and Advertiser. 1824-29 – 1 – us UMI [071]

VILLAGE HYMNS – Hartford. Connecticut. 1824. Suppl. to Dr. Watt's Psalm and Hymns – 1 – 17.50 – us Baptist [240]

VILLAGE IRRIGATION PROGRAMMES : A NEW APPROACH IN WATER ECONOMY – 1976 – 26p – it F.A.O. [333]

THE VILLAGE LABOURER, 1760-1832 : A STUDY IN THE GOVERNMENT OF ENGLAND BEFORE THE REFORM BILL / Hammond, John Lawrence & Hammond, Barbara – London, New York: Longmans, Green, 1912 – 1mf – us A.T.L.A. [305]

VILLAGE LIFE IN CHINA / Smith, A H – New York. 1900. BCH-862 2 – 8 – ne IDC [307]

VILLAGE LIFE IN PALESTINE : A DESCRIPTION OF THE RELIGION, HOME LIFE, MANNERS, CUSTOMS, CHARACTERISTICS AND SUPERSTITIONS OF THE PEASANTS OF THE HOLY LAND, WITH REFERENCE TO THE BIBLE / Lees, George Robinson – (Includes index) – New rev ed. London; New York: Longmans, Green, 1907 – 1mf – 9 – 0-8370-7230-1 – 1986-1230 – us A.T.L.A. [956]

VILLAGE LIST OF DISTRICT NO 9, KARIMNAGAR : ACCORDING TO POPULATION CENSUS / Hyderabad. India. Department of Statistics and Census – (Also available: District 7 Nalgonda. District 8 Warangal. District 10 Adilabad. District 11 Aurangabad. District 13 Nanded. District 16 Raechur) – Hyderabad: Govt Press, 1941 – us Res Libr [310]

VILLAGE MILK PROCESSING – 1988 – 75p – it F.A.O. [338]

VILLAGE MUSEUM – (Publication is believed to have ceased with v1 n6 nov 20, 1820) – Cortland Village. v1. oct-nov 1820 – 1 – D4101 – us UMI [978]

THE VILLAGE ON THE CLIFF / Thackeray, Anne – British Fiction Archive: Unit 3 – 9 – uk Bell [830]

THE VILLAGE PIONEER – Danville, CA. 1960-1963 – 1r – 1 – $50.00 – B02163 – us Library Micro [071]

VILLAGE PIONEER – (Cont by: Tri-Valley News) – Livermore, CA. 1971-73 – 18r – 1 – $900.00 – B02358 – us Library Micro [071]

VILLAGE PIONEER – (See: Tri-Valley News, Livermore) – San Ramon, CA. 1971-73 – 18r – 1 – $900.00 – B02933 – us Library Micro [071]

THE VILLAGE RECORD – Chester, PA., 1895-1911 – 13 – $25.00r – us I.M.R. [071]

VILLAGE SCENES: A CANADIAN POEM / Coughlin, Dennis – s.l.: s.n., 1889 (Ottawa: A. Woodburn). 00251. (Pre-1900 Canadiana) – 9 – cn C.I.H.M. [810]

VILLAGE SERMONS : SECOND SERIES / Hort, Fenton John Anthony – London; New York: Macmillan, 1905 – 1mf – 9 – 0-8370-9792-4 – 1986-3792 – us A.T.L.A. [240]

VILLAGE SERMONS IN OUTLINE / Hort, Fenton John Anthony – London; New York: Macmillan, 1900 – 1mf – 9 – 0-8370-9793-2 – 1986-3793 – us A.T.L.A. [240]

UN VILLAGE SOUS L'EQUATEUR / Benigno-Boriko, L – 9 – F90.00 – fr Ethnologie [305]

VILLAGE STATISTICS / Madras. India. Census Office – (For the districts: Anantapur, Bellary, Chingleput, Chitoor, Coimbatore, Cuddapah, East Godavari Agency, East Godavari (Plains), Ganjam, Guntur, Kurnool, Madura, Malabar, Nellore, North Arcot, Ramnad, Salem, South Arcot, South Coorg, South Kanara, Tanjore, Tinnevelly, Trichinopoly and Vizagapatam) – 1931 – us Res Libr [310]

THE VILLAGE VOICE – New York. N.Y. 1957- – 1 – us UMI [071]

VILLAGE VOICE – New York. v1-42. oct 1955-dec 1997+ 1; v24-42. 1979-97+ 5,9 – 1,5,9 – D5921 – us UMI [073]

VILLAGE WORK IN INDIA : PEN PICTURES FROM A MISSIONARY'S EXPERIENCE / Russell, Norman – New York: Fleming H Revell, 1902 – 1mf – 9 – 0-8370-6611-5 – 1986-0611 – us A.T.L.A. [950]

VILLAGE-COMMUNITIES IN THE EAST AND WEST / Maine, Henry James Sumner – New ed. London: Murray, 1890. xii/413p – 1 – us U.W. Library [360]

THE VILLAGER – Crystal Bay. NV. 1961-1962; 1963 – 1r – 1 – $50.00 – UN04483 – us Library Micro [071]

THE VILLAGER – Penn Valley, Western Nevada Co, Eastern Yuba Co, CA. 1984-1989 – 4r – 1 – $200.00 – B03630 – us Library Micro [071]

VILLAGER – Crystal Bay. Nev. 1961-1962 – 1 – us UMI [071]

VILLAGER : A LITERARY PAPER – Greenwich Village. v1. apr-jun 1819 – 1 – D4102 – us UMI [073]

VILLAGER – Richland. Wash. -w. 1945-50 – 1 – us UMI [071]

VILLAGER – Toronto, 1988-1990 – 3r – 1 – cn Preston [971]

VILLAGES IN INDONESIA / Kuntjaraningrat – SE-5844 1. 1967 – 9 – ne IDC [305]

THE VILLAGES OF THE BIBLE / Hood, Edwin Paxton – w index. London. 1874 – 9 – us A.T.L.A. [240]

VILLAGE-SAVANE EN PAYS ADIOUKROU / Pairault, Claude – (Africa series). 1969 – 9 – fr Hachette [960]

Villagutierre Soto-Mayor, Juan de *see* HISTORIA DE LA CONQUISTA DE LA PROVINCIA DE ITZA...

Villain, Etienne Francois *see* HISTOIRE CRITIQUE DE NICOLAS FLAMEL ET DE PERENELLE SA FEMME; ON Y A JOINT LE TESTAMENT DE PERENELLE & PLUSIEURS AUTRES PIECES INTERESSANTES

VILLAINAGE IN ENGLAND / Vinogradoff, Paul – H 1165 2. 1892 – 8 – ne IDC [941]

Villalba Dieguez, Fernando *see* CUENTOS REALISTAS

Villalba, Joaquin *see*
- EPIDEMIOLOGIA ESPANOLA. TOMO 1
- EPIDEMIOLOGIA ESPANOLA. TOMO 2

Villalobos Bote, Rufino *see*
- AURAS DE ARGEME
- RECUERDOS DE AYER

Villalobos R, Sergio *see* INDICE DE LA COLECCION DE HISTORIADORES Y DE DOCUMENTOS RELATIVOS A LA INDEPENDENCIA DE CHILE

Villalon, R Aunony *see* CONGRESO INTERNACIONAL DE BRUSELAS (1888)

Villamont, Jacques de *see* LES VOYAGES DU SEIGNEUR DE VILLAMONT, CHEVALIER DE L'ORDRE DE HIERUSALEM. DIVISEZ EN TROIS LIVRES

Villamor Angulo, Hilario *see* FINES Y UTILIDAD DE LA SINDICACION GANADERA POR...

Villamor, Ignacio *see* INDUSTRIOUS MEN

Villamur, Roger *see* NOTRE COLONIE DE LA COTE D'IVOIRE

Villani, Arnaud *see* PHILOSOPHIE CRITIQUE DE LA COMMUNICATION

Villani, Giovanni *see*
- LA CRONICA DI GIOVANNI VILLANI: ANNOTATA AD USO DELLA GIOVENTU
- HISTORY

Villani, Matteo *see* HISTORY

VILLANOVA ENVIRONMENTAL LAW JOURNAL – v1-6. 1990-95 – 9 – $86.00 set – us Hein [340]

VILLANOVA LAW REVIEW – (v1-29 1956-84 on reel $588.00. v30-39 1985-94 on mf $267.00) – v1-39. 1956-94 – 5,6,9 – $855.00 set – us Hein [340]

VILLANOVA SPORTS AND ENTERTAINMENT LAW FORUM – v1-2. 1994-95 – 9 – $20.00set – us Hein [340]

VILLANUEVA DE LA VERA. FIESTAS DE PERO PALO, 1965 / Gutierrez Macias, Valeriano – Plasencia: Imprenta Padilla, 1965 – 1 – sp Bibl Santa Ana [390]

Villanueva, Joaquin Lorenzo *see* MI DESPEDIDA DE LA CURIA ROMANA

Villanueva y Canedo, Luis *see*
- ELEMENTOS DE HISTORIA UNIVERSAL
- ESTUDIO BIOGRAFICO HERNANDO DE SOTO
- EXPLORADORES Y CONQUISTADORES EXTREMENOS EN AMERICA
- HERNANDO DE SOTO
- MEMORIAS...ACADEMIA...LEGISLACION
- RESUMEN...HISTORIA UNIVERSAL

Villar del Rey *see* FESTEJOS Y ROMERIA EN HONOR DEL SANTO PATRON DE LAS HERMANDADES. "SAN ISIDRO LABRADOR"

Villar del Rey. Ayuntamiento *see* ORDENANZAS MUNICIPALES

VILLARD EXCURSION FILE / Northern Pacific Railway Company – (Records celebrating the opening in 1883 of the Northern Pacific main line from Lake Superior, MN to Puget Sound, WA) – 1r with filmed inventory – 1 – $30.00 – us M.H.S. [380]

Villarejo, Avencio *see* ASI ES LA SELVA. ESTUDIO GEOGRAFICO Y ETNOLOGIA DE LA PROVINCIA DE BAJO AMAZONAS. LIMA, 1943

Villaret, E de *see*
- DAI NIPPON
- NUMISMATIQUE JAPONAISE

Villari, Luigi *see* FIRE AND SWORD IN THE CAUCASUS

Villari, Pasquale *see*
- THE BARBARIAN INVASIONS OF ITALY
- MEDIAEVAL ITALY FROM CHARLEMAGNE TO HENRY 7

Villarreal, J *see* DE SIGNIS...MORBI SUFFOCANTIS...

Villarreal, Jose *see* THE EFFECT OF TWO TYPES OF PLYOMETRIC TRAINING IN IMPROVING VERTICAL JUMP ABILITY IN FEMALE COLLEGE SOCCER PLAYERS

Villars, D *see*
- HISTOIRE DES PLANTES DE DAUPHINE
- PROSPECTUS DE L'HISTOIRE DES PLANTES DE DAUPHINE

Villas, Gaspar do Couto Ribeiro *see* OS PORTUGUESES NA COLONICAO...LISBOA, 1929

Villault, Nicolas *see* RELATION DES COTES D'AFRIQUE APPELEES GUINEE: AVEC LA DESCRIPTION DU PAYS, MOEURS ET FACONS DE VIVRE DES HABITANTS, DES PRODUCTIONS DE LA TERRE ET DES MARCHANDISES QU'ON EN APPORTE, AVEC LES REMARQUES HISTORIQUES SUR LES COTES

Villault, Sieur de Bellefond N *see* RELATIONS DES COSTES D'AFRIQUE APPELEES GUINEE

Villaurrutia, W R *see*
- LA EMBAJADA DEL MARQUES DE COGOLLUDO A ROMA EN 1687 Y EL DUQUE DE MEDINACELI Y LA GIORGINA. MADRID, 1929
- ESPANA EN EL CONGRESO DE VIENA SEGUN LA CORRESPONDENCIA OFICIAL DE D. PEDRO GOMEZ LABRADOR
- EL REY JOSE NAPOLEON. LA MISION DEL BARON DE AGRA. ALGUNOS CUADROS DEL MUSEO DEL PRADO. EL PAPA DE VELAZQUEZ. MADRID, 1929

Ville, Antoine de *see* LES FORTIFICATIONS.

LA VILLE AUX CLOCHERS DANS LA VERDURE = THE CITY OF SPIRES IN THE GREEN / Morin, Victor – Montreal, 1923. SEM105P753 – 1mf – 9 – Can$2.25 – cn Bibl Nat [910]

LA VILLE DE NANTES ET LA LOIRE-INFERIEURE / Nantes, Loire-Inferieure – Nantes: Grimaud, 1898 – 3r – 1 – F765.68 – fr Armell [910]

LA VILLE DE QUEBEC VUE PAR LE VOYAGEUR, 1776-1960 : BIBLIOGRAPHIE ANALYTIQUE DES IMPRIMES / Tyszkiewicz, Alexandra – 1964. SEM105P4 – 1mf – 9 – cn Bibl Nat [910]

UNE VILLE FRANCAISE MODERNE : AUXERRE EN 1950. ETUDE DE STRUCTURE SOCIALE ET URBAINE / Bettelheim, Ch. & Frere, S – F50.00 – fr Ethnologie [910]

VILLE MYSTIQUE / Morin, Victor – Hull, 1943. SEM105P777 – 1mf – 9 – Can$2.25 – cn Bibl Nat [830]

LA VILLE NOUVELLE OU LE PARIS DES SAINT-SIMONIENS / Duveyrier, Charles – Paris, F. Didot, 1832, p. 315-314 (extrait de "Paris ou le livre des cent et un"). Les Saint-Simoniens, 1825-1834. 6095 – 9 – fr Hachette [335]

Villecourt, L *see* LA PROTECTION DES MINORITES DANS LES PAYS BALTIQUES...

Villecourt, R *see* L'ARGUS

Villedieu, Marie C H des Jardins *see* LES DESORDRES DE L'AMOUR

Villegas, Alfredo *see* NUEVO LIBRO DE YERBAS DE CACERES O SEA DESCRIPCION DE TODAS LAS DEHESAS SOTOS...

Villehardouin, Geoffroy de *see*
- HISTOIRE DE L'EMPIRE DE CONSTANTINOPLE SOUS LES EMPEREURS FRANCOIS (CBH 26)
- MEMOIRS OF THE CRUSADES

Villela de Aldana, Fr. Juan *see* EXPEDICION DEL MAESTRE DE CAMPO BERNARDO DE ALDANA A HUNGRIA

Villelune, E de *see* AU COEUR DE L'AFRIQUE

Villemandy, Leusdende *see* OPERA OMNIA

LA VILLEMARQUE, COLLECTEUR DE CHANTS POPULAIRES / Laurent, D – Etude des sources du premier Barzaz-Breiz a partir des originaux de collecte (1833-40) – 9 – F250.00 – fr Ethnologie [780]

Villeneuve, Josse de *see* LETTRE SUR LE MECHANISME DE L'OPERA ITALIEN..

Villeneuve, N de *see* LE VOYAGEUR PHILOSOPHE DANS UN PAIS INCONNU AUX HABITANTS DE LA TERRE

Villeneuve-Bargemont, Alban de *see* ECONOMIE POLITIQUE CHRETIENNE, OU RECHERCHES SUR LA NATURE ET LES CAUSES DU PAUPERISME EN FRANCE ET EN EUROPE, ET SUR LES MOYENS DE LE SOULAGER ET DE LE PREVENIR

Villerme, Louis Rene *see*
- DES ASSOCIATIONS OUVRIERES
- DES ASSOCIATIONS OUVRIERES DE LA COLLECTION DES 'PETITS TRAITES PUBLIES PAR L'ACADEMIE DES SCIENCES MORALES ET POLITIQUES.' (CONDITION OF 19TH C. FRENCH
- DE LA MORTALITE DANS LES DIVERS QUARTIERS DE LA VILLE DE PARIS ET DES CAUSES QUI LA RENDENT TRES DIFFERENTE DANS PLUSIEURS D'ENTRE EUX
- DE LA MORTALITE D'ENFANS-TROUVES CONSIDEREE DANS SES RAPPORTS AVEC LE MODE D'ALLAITEMENT, ET SUR L'ACCROISSEMENT DE LEUR NOMBRE EN FRANCE
- DE LA SANTE DES OUVRIERS EMPLOYES DANS LES FABRIQUES DE SOIE, DE COTON ET DE LAINE
- DES PRISONS, TELLES QU'ELLES SONT ET TELLES QU'ELLES DEVRAIENT ETRE PAR RAPPORT A L'HYGIENE, A LA MORALE ET A L'ECONOMIE
- DES SOCIETES DE PREVOYANCES OU DE SECOURS MUTUELS: RECHERCHES SUR L'ORGANISATION DE CES INSTITUTIONS
- DES EPIDEMIES SOUS LES RAPPORTS DE L'HYGIENE PUBLIQUE, DE LA STATISTIQUE MEDICALE ET DE L'ECONOMIE POLITIQUE
- MEMOIRE SUR LA DISTRIBUTION DE LA POPULATION FRANCAISE PAR SEXE ET PAR ETAT ET SUR LA NECESSITE DE PERFECTIONNER NOS TABLEAUX DE POPULATION ET DE MORTALITE
- MEMOIRE SUR LA TAILLE DE L'HOMME EN FRANCE
- NOTE SUR LA MORTALITE PARMI LES FORCATS DU BAGNE DE ROCHEFORT, SUR LA FREQUENCE DE LEURS MALADIES
- NOTE SUR LES RAVAGES DU CHOLERA-MORBUS EN MAISONS GARNIES DE PARIS DEPUIS LE 19 MARS JUSQU'AU LE 1ER AOUT 1832
- SUR LA DUREE MOYENNE DES MALADIES AUX DIFFERENS AGES
- SUR LES CITES OUVRIERES
- TABLEAU COMPARATIF POUR CHACUN DES DEPARTEMENTS DE LA FRANCE CONTINENTALE ET DES RESULTATS STATISTIQUES RELATIFS A LEUR POPULATION.
- TABLEAU DE L'ETAT PHYSIQUE ET MORAL DES OUVRIERS EMPLOYES DANS LES MANUFACTURES DE COTON, DE LAINE ET DE SOIE

Villers, Alexander von *see* BREVIER DER LEBENSKUNST

Villers, C de *see* DIALOGUES SUR LA MUSIQUE

LES VILLES DISPARUES DE LA LOIRE-INFERIEURE / Maitre, Leon – (Les Villes disparues des Namnetes: geographie historique et descriptive de la Loire-Inferieure, T.1. Nantes: Grimaud, 1893; T.2. Rennes: Oberthur, 1895) – 1 – F657.52 – fr Armell [944]

Villette, Ch. de *see* MEMOIRES ET ANECDOTES, POUR SERVIR A L'HISTOIRE DE M. DE VOLTAIRE

Villien, A *see* L'ABBE EUSEBE RENAUDOT

Villier, Joseph *see* NOUVEAU PLAN D'EDUCATION ET D'INSTRUCTION PUBLIQUE DEDIE A L'ASSEMBLEE NATIONALE

VILLIERS AND HEYTESBURY AGRIC. ASSOC. – 1853-1911. Minutes. VHAA1 – 1r – 5 – at Corangamite [630]

Villiers de L'Isle Adam, Auguste de *see* LE NOUVEAU MONDE: DRAME EN 5 ACTES, EN PROSE

Villiers du Terrage, Marc de *see* UN EXPLORATEUR DE LA LOUISIANE

Villiers et Gouffe *see* CANGE OU LE COMMISSIONNAIRE BIENFAISANT

Villiers, F de *see* TABLEAUX SYNOPTIQUES DES LEPIDOPTERES D'EUROPE

Villiers, George William Frederick *see* THE CLARENDON PAPERS, 1867-1870

Villiers, L *see* CONTRIBUTION A L'ETUDE DE LA NUTRITION ET DE SES ASPECTS ENERGETIQUES CHEZ DES FORMES JUVENILES DE DELTENTOSTEUS QUADRIMACULATUS (VALENCIENNES) (PISCES: GOBIIDAE)

Villot, E-C-E *see* MOEURS, COUTUMES ET INSTITUTIONS DES INDIGENES DE L'ALGERIE

Villot, Frederic *see* TABLEAU COMPARATIF POUR CHACUN DES DEPARTEMENTS DE LA FRANCE CONTINENTALE ET DES RESULTATS STATISTIQUES RELATIFS A LEUR POPULATION.

Villot, Marie Joseph Frederic *see* NOTICES DES TABLEAUX EXPOSES DANS LES GALERIES DU MUSEE NATIONAL DE LOUVRE

Villoteau, G *see* MEMOIRE SUR LA POSSIBILITE ET L'UTILITE D'UNE THEORIE EXACTE DES PRINCIPES NATURELS DA LA MUSIQUE...

Villotte, J *see* DICTONARIUM NOVUM LATINO-ARMENIUM...

Vilmar, August Friedrich Christian *see* VORLESUNGEN UEBER DIE GESCHICHTE DER DEUTSCHEN NATIONAL-LITERATUR

Vil'na. Public Library *see* SISTEMATICHESKII KATALOG RUSSKAGO OTDELENIIA VILENSKOI PUBLICHNOI BIBLIOTEKI

VILNE SLOVO – (In Ukranian) – Canada, 1934-77 – 36r – 1 – cn Commonwealth Micro [072]

DER VILNER EXSPRES – (In Yiddish) – Vilnius, LT. v4 no185 (no980). 10 Aug 1937 – 1r – 1 – $25.00 – cn Can Microfilming [072]

VILNER RADIO – (In Yiddish) – Vilnius, LT. v8 no185. Aug 1937 – 1r – 1 – $25.00 – cn Can Microfilming [072]

VILNER RADIO – Vilnius, 1930-39 – 16r – 1 – $1,200.00 – us Ross [072]

VILNER TOG = VIRNER DAY – (In Yiddish) – Vilnius, LT. no94. 25 Apr 1926 – 1r – 1 – $25.00 – cn Can Microfilming [072]

VILONIA, ARKANSAS. BERYL BAPTIST CHURCH – Church Records, 1889-May 1988. 1,756p – 1 – $79.02 – us Baptist [240]

VILTIS – Denver. v1-31 1954-73*. v32-52 may 1973-apr 1994. v54-57 may 1994-apr 1998 1; v35-37 may 1976-apr 1979*. v38 may 1979-apr 1980. v39-52 may 1980-apr 1994*. v54 may-oct 1994*. v55-57 mar 1995-apr 1998+ 5; v32-52 may 1976-apr 1994. v54-57 may 1994-apr 1998+ 9 – 1,5,9 – D9296 – us UMI [073]

VIMMERBY TIDNING – Vimmerby, Sweden. 1979- – 1 – sw Kungliga [072]

LE VIMONTAIS – Ville de Laval (Vimont), Canada. 5 sep 1964; v1 n2. 3 oct 1964 – 1r – 1 – Can$25.00 – cn Can Microfilming [072]

LA VINA DESTRUIDE. A HUNGRIA, EN SU MARTIRIO / Frutos Cortes, Eugenio – Zaragoza: Imprenta Libreria General, 1957 – sp Bibl Santa Ana [100]

Vinajeras, Antonio *see* EL CONGRESO DE GUINEA

VINAYA TEXTS : PART 1: THE PATIMOKHA. THE MAHAVAGGA, 1-4 / ed by Mueller, Friedrich Max – (Translated from the Pali by T.W. Rhys Davids and Hermann Oldenberg) – 1881 – 7mf – 8 – ne Slangenburg [280]

VINAYA TEXTS : PART 2: THE MAHAVAGGA, 5-10. THE KULLAVAGGA 1-3 / ed by Mueller, Friedrich Max – (Translated from the Pali by T.W. Thys Davids and Hermann Oldenberg) – 1882 – 8mf – 8 – ne Slangenburg [280]

VINAYA TEXTS : PART 3: THE KULLAVAGGA, 4-12 / ed by Mueller, Friedrich Max – (Translated from the Pali by T.W. Rhys Davids and Hermann Oldenberg) – 1885 – 8mf – 8 – ne Slangenburg [280]

Vinburg, A I *see* KRIMINALISTIKA

Vincard, Pierre *see* LES OUVRIERS DE PARIS. ALIMENTATION

Vincens-Planchut, Jean Cesar *see* TOPOGRAPHIE DE LA VILLE DE NISMES ET DE SA BANLIEUE

Vincent, Alexander *see* LEX MUNDI

Vincent, Barbara S *see* THE CONSEQUENCES OF MANDATORY MINIMUM PRISON TERMS

Vincent, Charles Edward Howard *see* A POLICE CODE, AND MANUAL OF THE CRIMINAL LAW. 3D ED

Vincent, Elizabeth Carter *see* THE MADONNA IN LEGEND AND HISTORY

Vincent, Ernst *see*
- TAG UND DAEMMERUNG
- ZWEI GOETHE-STUDIEN

Vincent, Francis *see* LE TRAVAILLE DU STYLE CHEZ SAINT FRANCOIS DE SALES

Vincent G *see* LES LYCEENS, CONTRIBUTION A L'ETUDE DU MILIEU SCOLAIRE

Vincent, John H *see* THE CHAUTAUQUA MOVEMENT

Vincent, John Martin *see* HISTORICAL RESEARCH

Vincent, Marvin Richardson *see*
- THE AGE OF HILDEBRAND
- BIBLICAL INSPIRATION AND CHRIST
- A CRITICAL AND EXEGETICAL COMMENTARY ON...PHILIPPIANS AND...PHILEMON
- GATES INTO THE PSALM-COUNTRY
- A HISTORY OF THE TEXTUAL CRITICISM OF THE NEW TESTAMENT
- STRANGER AND GUEST
- THE TWO PRODIGALS

Vincente Cascante, Ignacio *see* HERALDICA GENERAL Y FUENTES DE LAS ARMAS DE ESPANA

Vincenti, Leonello *see* SAGGI DI LETTERATURA TEDESCA

VINCENZ VON LERIN UND GENNADIUS (T.U.U. 3-31/2B) / Koch, H – Leipzig, 1907 – 1mf – 9 – ne Slangenburg [240]

Vinci, L *see*
- L'ARTASERSE
- TWELVE SOLOS FOR A GERMAN FLUTE OR VIOLIN, WITH A THOROUGH BASS FOR THE HARPSICHORD OR VIOLONCELLE...

Vinciguerra, Barbara A *see* MOOD STATES AND INJURY IN INTERCOLLEGIATE FIELD HOCKEY PLAYERS

EL VINCULO DEL MATRIMONIO... / Garcia Cantero, Gabriel – Madrid: Arch. Ibero Americano, 1960 – 1 – sp Bibl Santa Ana [240]

Vindel, Francisco *see* LA CULTURA Y LA IMPRENTA EUROPEAS EN EL JAPON DURANTE LOS SIGLOS 16 Y 17. LA INICIATIVA ESPANOLA BASE DE LA IMPORTANTE GESTA (1548-1616)

VINDEX OR THE DOCTRINES OF THE STRICTURES VINDICATED / Campbell, John P – 1806 – 1 – $50.00 – us Presbyterian [240]

VINDICAE GROTIANI DOGMATIS DE PRAESCRIPTIONE INTER GENTES LIBERAS... / Buchholtz, H F – Helmstadi, 1696 – 1mf – 1 – ILM-2563/1 – ne IDC [327]

A VINDICATION OF COMMENTS ON THE TRANSLATION OF EPHESIANS I IN THE DELEGATES' VERSION OF THE NEW TESTAMENT / Boone, William J, Bp – 1852 – 1 – us A.T.L.A. [240]

A VINDICATION OF DOCTRINAL STANDARDS: WITH SPECIAL REFERENCE TO THE STANDARDS OF THE PRESBYTERIAN CHURCH / Caven, William – Toronto: J. Campbell, 1875. 00523. (Pre-1900 Canadiana) – 9 – cn C.I.H.M. [240]

VINDICATION OF LUTHER AGAINST HIS RECENT ENGLISH ASSAILANTS / Hare, Julius Charles – London: J.W. Parker, 1855 – 1mf – us A.T.L.A. [240]

VINDICATION OF LUTHER AGAINST HIS RECENT ENGLISH ASSAILANTS... / Hare, Julius Charles – London: John W. Parker and Son, 1855 – 1 roll – 1 – 1-55879-444-1 – uk Libr Preservation [240]

A VINDICATION OF NATURAL SOCIETY: OR, A VIEW OF THE MISERIES AND EVILS ARISING TO MANKIND FROM EVERY SPECIES OF ARTIFICIAL SOCIETY / Burke, Edmund – 1756. 54p – 9 – 1.00f – at Libertarian Micro [335]

A VINDICATION OF THE AUTHOR'S APOLOGY, WITH REFLECTIONS ON THE REPLY.. / O'Kelly, James – 1801 – 1 – us A.T.L.A. [240]

A VINDICATION OF THE BAPTISTS FROM THE CRIMINALITY OF A CHARGE EXHIBITED AGAINST THEM BY THE REV. MR. WESLEY / Kingsford, W – Canterbury, 5th ed 1789 – 1mf – 9 – MP-554/1 – ne IDC [240]

A VINDICATION OF THE CAPACITY OF THE NEGRO RACE FOR SELF-GOVERNMENT, AND CIVILIZED PROGRESS, AS DEMONSTRATED BY HISTORICAL EVENTS OF THE HAYTIAN REVOLUTION : AND THE SUBSEQUENT ACTS OF THAT PEOPLE SINCE THEIR NATIONAL INDEPENDENCE / Holly, James Theodore – New Haven, 1857 – 1r – 1 – us Ross [972]

A VINDICATION OF THE FREE CHURCH CLAIM OF RIGHT / Moncreiff, Henry Wellwood – Edinburgh: Maclaren & Macniven, 1877 – 1mf – us A.T.L.A. [240]

VINDICATION OF THE GOVERNMENT OF NEW-ENGLAND CHURCHES / Wise, John – 1717 – 9 – 10.00 – us Scholars' Facs [240]

A VINDICATION OF THE 'METHODIST DISSECTED' : OR, THE METHODISTS' WRITINGS BRIEFLY EXAMINED / Fletcher, N – Halifax, 1750 – 1mf – 9 – MP-339/1 – ne IDC [240]

A VINDICATION OF THE METHODIST EPISCOPACY / Bangs, Nathan – 1820 – 9 – us A.T.L.A. [240]

A VINDICATION OF THE MOSAIC AUTHORSHIP OF THE PENTATEUCH / Elliott, Charles – (Includes subject index) – Cincinnati:Walden and Stowe, 1884 – 1mf – 9 – 0-8370-3058-7 – 1985-1058 – us A.T.L.A. [220]

VINDICATION OF THE MOSAIC AUTHORSHIP OF THE PENTATEUCH / Elliott, Charles – Cincinnati: Walden & Stowe, 1884. 1 fiche – 9 – us A.T.L.A. [220]

A VINDICATION OF THE PROCEEDINGS AGAINST THE SIX MEMBERS OF E— HALL, OXFORD – London, 1768 – 1mf – 9 – MP-451/1 – ne IDC [240]

A VINDICATION OF THE REV. MR. MAXFIELD'S CONDUCT IN NOT CONTINUING WITH THE REV. MR. JOHN WESLEY, AND OF HIS BEHAVIOUR SINCE THAT TIME;... / Maxfield, T – London, 1767 – 1mf – 9 – MP-445/1 – ne IDC [240]

A VINDICATION OF THE RIGHTS OF MEN : IN A LETTER TO THE RIGHT HONOURABLE EDMUND BURKE OCCASIONED BY HIS REFLECTIONS ON THE REVOLUTION IN FRANCE / Wollstonecraft, Mary – London: J. Johnson, 1790 – 1 roll – 1 – 1-55879-866-8 – uk Libr Preservation [320]

A VINDICATION OF THE RIGHTS OF MEN / Wollstonecraft, Mary – 1790 – 9 – $10.00 – us Scholars' Facs [360]

A VINDICATION OF THE RIGHTS OF WOMAN / Wollstonecraft, Mary – London, 1792 – 5mf – 9 – ne IDC [320]

A VINDICATION OF THE SEVENTEENTH ARTICLE OF THE CHURCH OF ENGLAND FROM THE ASPERSIONS CAST ON IT IN A SERMON LATELY PUBLISHED BY MR. JOHN WESLEY / Oulton, J – London, 1760 – 1mf – 9 – MP-392/1 – ne IDC [240]

THE VINDICATOR – Belfast, Ireland. -w. 1 May 1839-5 Feb 1848. 8 reels – 1 – uk British Libr Newspaper [072]

THE VINDICATOR – (Cont by: The Vindicator and Commercial News v2 n38 13 mar 1858-29 sep 1863) – Quebec, Canada. v1 n2. 12 dec 1857-v2 n37. 11 mar 1858 – 1r – 1 – Can$40.00 – cn Can Microfilming [072]

THE VINDICATOR *see* THE IRISH VINDICATOR AND CANADA GENERAL ADVERTISER

VINDICATOR – Charlottetown, Canada. 1862-64 – 1 reel – 1 – $68.00 – cn Library Assoc [971]

VINDICATOR – Decatur, NE. -w. Apr. 1877-Apr. 1878 – 1 – us NE Hist [071]

VINDICATOR – Estherville. Iowa. And Republican. 1902-44 – 1 – us UMI [071]

VINDICATOR – Montreal, Canada. 1828-37 – 6r – 1 – $390.00 – cn Library Assoc [971]

VINDICATOR – Valley Falls. Kan. 1925-1954 – 1 – us UMI [071]

VINDICATOR – Youngstown. Ohio. 1887- – 1 – us UMI [071]

VINDICATOR – Youngstown. Ohio. -w. 1876-89, 1949- – 1 – us UMI [071]

THE VINDICATOR AND CANADIAN ADVERTISER *see* THE IRISH VINDICATOR AND CANADA GENERAL ADVERTISER

THE VINDICATOR AND COMMERCIAL NEWS *see* THE VINDICATOR

VINDICIAE IGNATIANAE, OR, THE GENUINE WRITINGS OF ST IGNATIUS : AS EXHIBITED IN THE ANTIENT [SIC] SYRIAC VERSION, VINDICATED FROM THE CHARGE OF HERESY / Cureton, William – London: Rivingtons, 1846 – 1mf – us A.T.L.A. [240]

VINDT MOLLE OG DENS EJERE / Kristensen, Evald Tang – 1887 – 1 – us I.U. Libraries [390]

Viner, Charles *see*
- A GENERAL ABRIDGEMENT OF LAW AND EQUITY
- A GENERAL ABRIDGEMENT OF LAW AND EQUITY; ALPHABETICALLY DIGESTED UNDER PROPER TITLES, WITH NOTES AND REFERENCES TO THE WHOLE

VINER GENERAL ABRIDGEMENT OF LAW AND EQUITY – 6 reels – 1 – $250.00 – us Trans-Media [340]

VINER GEZEYRE – Cracow. 1609. BJ-43-135 1 – 9 – ne IDC [956]

VINETA / Werner, E – 2. Aufl. Leipzig: E Keil. 2v in 1. 1877 – 1 – us U.W. Library [830]

VINETAS CASTUERANAS / Mena, Vicente – Villanueva de la Serena: Imp. de Nicolas Diestro, 1929 – 1 – sp Bibl Santa Ana [946]

Viney, N M *see* A BIBLIOGRAPHY OF BRITISH SOMALILAND

THE VINEYARD / Jones, Idwal – Napa Co, 1942 – 1r – 1 – $50.00 – B40245 – us Library Micro [978]

THE VINEYARD – v3-15. 21 Jul 1937-1 Jun 1949 (complete) – 6r – 1 – ATLA S0537 – us A.T.L.A. [073]

VINGT ANS A MADAGASCAR : COLONIALISATION – TRADITIONS HISTORIQUES / Vassiere, P de la – Paris: V Lecoffre, 1885 – us Res Libr [960]

VINGT ANS APRES, 1884-1904: RECIT VERIDIQUE, HISTORIQUE, ANECDOTIQUE, EPIQUE ET TYPIQUE D'UN CONVENTUM D'ANCIENS COLLEGIENS / Morin, Victor – Montreal, 1909. SEM105P780 – 1mf – 9 – Can$2.25 – cn Bibl Nat [830]

VINGT ANS APRES: LE CLUB DES 21 EN 1879: COURTE BIOGRAPHIE DE CHACUN DE SES MEMBRES / Baillairge, Charles – 1899?. 00964. (Pre-1900 Canadiana) – 9 – cn C.I.H.M. [971]

VINGT QUATRE VARIATIONS : AMUSEMENT POUR UN VIOLON SEUL / Debar, C C – Paris: L'Auteur, ca 1800 – 1 – us Sibley [780]

VINGT-CINQ ANS A PARIS (1826-1850) : JOURNAL DU COMTE RODOLPHE APPONYI, ATTACHE DE L'AMBASSADE D'AUTRICHE-HONGRIE A PARIS / ed by Daudet, E – Paris. v1-3. 1913-1914 – 18mf – 9 – ne IDC [943]

LE VINGT-QUATRE JUIN : COLLABORATION DE CINQ JOURNAUX DE LA VILLE DE QUEBEC – Quebec, Canada. 24 jun 1880 – 1r – 1 – Can$25.00 – cn Can Microfilming [072]

Vinicchayakoul, Serm *see* L'ORGANISATION DE LA FAMILLE D'APRES LE NOUVEAU CODE CIVIL ET COMMERCIAL SIAMOIS

Viniegra de Vera, Virgilio *see*
- UN NOTABLE MOSAICO EN SANTA MARTA (BADAJOZ). EL ARTE ANTIGUO EN LOS CAMPOS
- PAGINAS DE SANTA MARTA

Viniegra, Salvador *see* CATALOGO OFICIAL ILUSTRADO DE LA EXPOSICION DE LAS OBRAS DE FRANCISCO DE ZURBARAN

VINIEGRA VERA, VIRGILIO. CORRESPONDIENTE DE LA REAL ACAD. DE LA HISTORIA EN SANTA MARTA / Castaneda, Vicente – Madrid: Tip. Arch., Bibl. y Mus, 1928. B.R.A.H. 92, p. 444 – sp Bibl Santa Ana [946]

Vink, Marc P *see* THE EFFECT OF REGULARLY SCHEDULED DAILY SUPERVISOR VERBAL FEEDBACK ON USE OF PERSONAL PROTECTIVE EQUIPMENT

Vinogradoff, Paul *see*
- ENGLISH SOCIETY IN THE ELEVENTH CENTURY
- ESSAYS IN LEGAL HISTORY
- OUTLINES OF HISTORICAL JURISPURDENCE
- ROMAN LAW IN MEDIAEVAL EUROPE
- VILLAINAGE IN ENGLAND

Vinogradov, I A *see* ARKHIVY AKADEMII NAUK SOTSIALISTICHESKIKH STRAN. BIBLIOGRAFIIA

Vinogradov, P P *see* MORSKOE PRAVO

Vinogradov, V V *see* IAZYK PUSHKINA

Vinson, Auguste *see* VOYAGE A MADAGASCAR AU COURONNEMENT DE RADAMA 2

Vinson, J *see* LES FRANCAIS DANS L'INDE

VINTE DE AGOSTO : ORGAO DO PARTIDO CONSERVADOR – Ouro Preto, 14 Sept 1885-3 Sept 1886 – 1,5,6 – bl Biblioteca [072]

VINTE DE JANEIRO – Manaos, Amazonas. 20 Jan 1901; 20 Jan 1903; Manaos, Amazonas. 22 Jan 1903 – 1,5,6 – bl Biblioteca [072]

VINTE DE JULHO : REVISTA LITTERARIA, INSTRUCTIVA E NOTICIOSA – Pilar, Alagoas. 22 Set, Nov 1892; Dez 1895; Jun 1897; Dez 1899; Jul 1900; Fev, Abr 1902; Jun 1904; Out-Dez 1909; Jan-25 Jul 1909 – 1,5,6 – bl Biblioteca [072]

VINTE E DOIS DE ABRIL – Vicosa, Alagoas. 22 Abr 1900; Abr 1901; 15 Jul 1904 – 1,5,6 – bl Biblioteca [072]

VINTE E OITO DE JULHO : JORNAL PARA TENTAMENS LITTERARIOS – Sao Luiz, 31 Mar-18 Apr 1870. 28 Jul 1892 – 1,5,6 – bl Biblioteca [072]

VINTE OITO DE SETEMBRO : DEDICADO AOS ASSIGNANTES DO ESTADO DO AMAZONAS – Manaos, Amazonas. Sem Data – 1,5,6 – bl Biblioteca [072]

Vinton, Alexander Hamilton *see* FOUR LECTURES

Vinuela Angulo, Urbano *see* EL PENSAMIENTO POLITICO Y SOCIAL DE JAMES FENIMORE COOPER

Vinzani del Aguila, F *see* NATURALEZA DE LA AGUA TERMAL AZIDA DE PUERTOLLANO

VIOLA E. GARFIELD ALBUMS ON TOTEM ART / Garfield, Viola E – (1794 photographs and Garfield's notes. Well documented as to location, cultural group, date, and provenance) – 60mf – 9 – $60.00 set – us U.W. Libraries [306]

VIOLATIONS OF HUMAN RIGHTS : POSSIBLE RIGHTS OF RECOURSE AND FORMS OF RESISTANCE – 1984 – 236p – 9 – 92-3-102114-1 – fr UNESCO [320]

VIOLENCE AGAINST WOMEN – Thousand Oaks. v1-3. 1995-97+ – 1,5,9 – D21507 – us UMI [360]

VIOLENCE AND ABUSE ABSTRACTS – Thousand Oaks. v1-3. 1995-97+ – 1,5,9 – D21511 – us UMI [360]

VIOLENCE AND ITS CAUSES : METHODOLOGICAL AND THEORETICAL ASPECTS OF RECENT RESEARCH ON VIOLENCE – 1980 – 269p – 9 – 92-3-101809-4 – fr UNESCO [360]

VIOLENCE AND TERROR IN THE MASS MEDIA / Gerbner, George – 1989 – 9 – 92-3-102603-8 – fr UNESCO [380]

VIOLENT FORCES OF NATURE / ed by Maybury, Robert – 1986. 377p. ISBN:0-912338-38-5 – 9 – 15.50 – us Lomond [574]

Violet, B *see* DIE PALAESTINISCHEN MAERTYRER DES EUSEBIUS VON CAESAREA (T.U.U. 1-14/4)

A VIOLETA : PERIODICO EXCLUSIVAMENTE LITTERARIO – Maceio, Alagoas. Maio-Jun 1900 – 1,5,6 – bl Biblioteca [072]

Violette, E M *see* HISTORY OF ADAIR COUNTY

VIOLIN ICONOGRAPHY : ILLUSTRATIONS OF FINE VIOLINS INDEXED... / Goodkind, Herbert S – 19– – 1r – 1 – $32.50r – us Archival [780]

VIOLIN TIMES : A MONTHLY JOURNAL FOR PROFESSIONAL AND AMATEUR VIOLINISTS AND QUARTET PLAYERS – London. v1-14. nov 1893-dec 1907 – 1 – D5349 – us UMI [780]

THE VIOLIN WORLD – New York, 1892-1928 – 1 – £115.00 – uk Chadwyck [780]

Viollet, Paul *see* L'INFAILLIBILITE DU PAPE ET LE SYLLABUS

Viollet-Le-Duc, Eugene Emmanuel *see*
- DE LA DECORATION APPLIQUEE AUX EDIFICES.
- DICTIONNAIRE RAISONNE DE L'ARCHITECTURE FRANCAISE DU 11 AU 16 SIECLE
- DICTIONNAIRE RAISONNE DE L'ARCHITECTURE FRANCAISE DU XIE AU XVIE SIECLES
- HISTOIRE D'UN DESSINATEUR: COMMENT ON APPREND A DESSINER

Viollet-le-Duc, Eugene Emmanuel *see* DU STYLE GOTHIQUE AU DIX-NEUVIEME SIECLE

LE VIOLON : HUMORISTIQUE / ed by Berthelot, Hector – Montreal, Canada. 25 sep 1886-28 jan 1888 – 1r – 1 – Can$50.00 – cn Can Microfilming [073]

VIONVILLE : EIN HELDENLIED IN DREI GESAENGEN / Wildenbruch, Ernst von – 5. Aufl. Berlin: Freund & Jeckel, 1892 – 1r – 1 – us U.W. Library [780]

Viotti, Giovanni B *see*
- CONCERTO QUATRIEME POUR PIANO
- [POLACCA] ARIA CONSOLA AMATI BENE. CAVATA NEL 'OPERA LA COSA RARA
- SINFONIA CONCERTANTE NO. 1, G. 76; ARRANGED FOR PIANOFORTE BY D. STEIBEL
- THREE QUARTETTS FOR FLUTE, VIOLIN, TENOR, AND VIOLINCELLO
- TROIS QUATUORS POUR FLUTE, VIOLON, VIOLA ET VIOLONCELLE

Viperanus, J A *see* DE BELLO MELITENSI HISTORIA

Vipper, S *see* DVE INTELLIGENTSII (I DRUGIE OCHERKI)

VIRAVINODA, MEWARAKA ITIHASA / Shyamaladasa, Kaviraja – Udaipur: Rajayantralaya, 1886 – us Res Libr [950]

Virchow, R LK *see* DIE CELLULARPATHOLOGIE IN IHRER BEGRUENDUNG AUF PHYSIOLOGISCHE UND PATHOLOGISCHE GEWEBELEHRE

Virchow, Rudolf *see* GOETHE ALS NATURFORSCHER UND IN BESONDERER BEZIEHUNG AUF SCHILLER

VIRCHOW-PIRQUET MEDICAL SOCIETY : PROCEEDINGS OF THE VIRCHOW-PIRQUET MEDICAL SOCIETY – (Publication is believed to have ceased with v34 1980. Formed by the union of: Rudolf Virchow Medical Society in the City of New York. Proceedings; and: Pirquet Bulletin of Clinical Medicine) – New York. v30-34. 1976-1980* – 1 – D12716.01 – us UMI [610]

Virchow-Pirquet Medical Society *see* PROCEEDINGS

VIRCHOWS ARCHIV – (Formed by the union of: Virchows Archiv. A, Pathological Anatomy and Histopathology; and: Virchows Archiv. B, Cell Pathology including Molecular Pathology) – Berlin. v424-425 1994*. v426-431 1995-97+ – 1 – D20710 – us UMI [611]

VIRCHOWS ARCHIV *see*
- VIRCHOWS ARCHIV. A
- VIRCHOWS ARCHIV. B

VIRCHOWS ARCHIV. A : PATHOLOGICAL ANATOMY AND HISTOLOGY – (Cont: Virchows Archiv. Abteilung A. Pathologische Anatomie. Pathology. Cont by: Virchows Archiv. A, Pathological Anatomy and Histopathology) – Berlin. v362-397. 1974-nov 1982* – 1 – D13239.03 – us UMI [611]

VIRCHOWS ARCHIV. A : PATHOLOGICAL ANATOMY AND HISTOPATHOLOGY – (Merged with: Virchows Archiv. B, Cell Pathology including Molecular Pathology; to form: Virchows Archiv. Cont: Virchows Archiv. A: Pathological Anatomy and Histology) – Berlin. v398-413 dec 1982-oct 1988*. v414-423 dec 1988-dec 1993 – 1 – D13239.04 – us UMI [611]

VIRCHOWS ARCHIV. A: PATHOLOGICAL ANATOMY AND HISTOLOGY *see*
- VIRCHOWS ARCHIV. A
- VIRCHOWS ARCHIV. ABTEILUNG A

VIRCHOWS ARCHIV. A, PATHOLOGICAL ANATOMY AND HISTOPATHOLOGY *see*
- VIRCHOWS ARCHIV
- VIRCHOWS ARCHIV. A
- VIRCHOWS ARCHIV. B

VIRCHOWS ARCHIV. ABTEILUNG A : PATHOLOGISCHE ANATOMIE. PATHOLOGY – (Cont: Virchows Archiv fuer pathologische Anatomie und Physiologie und fuer klinische Medizin; cont by: Virchows Archiv. A: Pathological Anatomy and Histology) – Berlin. v344-361. mar 1968-mar 1973* – 1 – D13239.02 – us UMI [611]

VIRCHOWS ARCHIV. ABTEILUNG A. PATHOLOGISCHE ANATOMIE. PATHOLOGY *see*
- VIRCHOWS ARCHIV. A
- VIRCHOWS ARCHIV FUER PATHOLOGISCHE ANATOMIE UND PHYSIOLOGIE UND FUER KLINISCHE MEDIZIN

VIRCHOWS ARCHIV. B : CELL PATHOLOGY INCLUDING MOLECULAR PATHOLOGY – (Merged with: Virchows Archiv. A, Pathological Anatomy and Histopathology; to form: Virchows Archiv. Cont: Virchows Archiv. B, Cell Pathology = Zellpathologie) – Berlin. v30-64. 1980-dec1993* – 1 – D13240.01 – us UMI [611]

VIRCHOWS ARCHIV. B = ZELLPATHOLOGIE : CELL PATHOLOGY – (Cont by: Virchows Archiv. B, Cell Pathology including Molecular Pathology) – Berlin. v1-15 mar 1968-mar 1974*. v16-22 1974-76. v23-29 1977-79* – 1 – D13240 – us UMI [611]

VIRCHOWS ARCHIV. B, CELL PATHOLOGY INCLUDING MOLECULAR PATHOLOGY *see*
- VIRCHOWS ARCHIV
- VIRCHOWS ARCHIV. A
- VIRCHOWS ARCHIV. B

VIRCHOWS ARCHIV. B, CELL PATHOLOGY = ZELLPATHOLOGIE *see* VIRCHOWS ARCHIV. B

VIRCHOW'S ARCHIV FUER PATHOLOGISCHE ANATOMIE UND KLINISCHE MEDIZIN – v. 1-158. 1847-1899 – 1,5,6 – us Princeton Micro [611]

VIRCHOWS ARCHIV FUER PATHOLOGISCHE ANATOMIE UND PHYSIOLOGIE UND FUER KLINISCHE MEDIZIN – (Cont: Archiv fuer pathologische Anatomie und Physiologie und fuer klinische Medizin; cont by: Virchows Archiv. Abteilung A. Pathologische Anatomie. Pathology) – Berlin. v171-343. 1903-68* – 1 – D13239.01 – us UMI [611]

VIRCHOWS ARCHIV FUER PATHOLOGISCHE ANATOMIE UND PHYSIOLOGIE UND FUER KLINISCHE MEDIZIN *see* VIRCHOWS ARCHIV. ABTEILUNG A

Virdung, S *see* MVSICA GETUTSCHT VND AUSSGEZOGE DURCH SEBASTIANU VIRDUG PRIESTERS VO AMBERG VN ALLES GESANG AUS DEN NOTE IN DIE

Virey, P H *see* LE TOMBEAU DE REKHMARA, PREFET DE THEBES SOUS LA 17E

VIRGEN DE GUADALUPE – 1859 – 9 – 1.50f – sp Bibl Santa Ana [240]

LA VIRGEN DE GUADALUPE EN MEJICO / Cuevas, Mariano – Madrid: Fortanet, 1919. B.R.A.H. 75. pp. 185-199 – 1 – sp Bibl Santa Ana [240]

LA VIRGEN DE LA MONTANA / Hurtado, Antonio – 1895 – 9 – 1.50f – sp Bibl Santa Ana [830]

LA VIRGEN DE LAS LAGRIMAS DE SIRACUSA. RELATO HISTORICO / Corredor Garcia, Antonio – Caceres: Edic. Cruzada Mariana, 2nd ed 1954 – 1 – sp Bibl Santa Ana [946]

LA VIRGEN DE LOS REMEDIOS / Sanchez-Arjona, Vicente – Sevilla: Imp. Zambrano, 1956 – 1 – sp Bibl Santa Ana [810]

LA VIRGEN DEL PILAR Y AMERICA / Bayle, Constantino – Madrid: Razon y Fe, 1941 – sp Bibl Santa Ana [240]

Virgen, Juan de la *see*
- ADDICION AL PARECER DEL R.P. FR... ACERCA DE UNA ELECCION QUE DIO EN DOCE DE DICIEMBRE DE 1639 POR EL MISMO PADRE A PETICION DEL PADRE FR. SEBASTIAN DE MORATILLA VICARIO DE LA SANTA CASA DE GUADALUPE Y PROFESSO DELLA
- PARECER QUE DIO EL R.P...ACERCA SI ERA VALIDA UNA ELECCION. VICARIO DE GUADALUPE

LA VIRGEN MARIA EN LA DIOCESIS DE LA CONCEPCION DURANTE LA DOMINACION ESPANOLA (1550-1810) / Munoz Olave, Reinaldo – Santiago de Chile, 1929; Madrid: Razon y Fe, 1932 – 1 – sp Bibl Santa Ana [240]

LA VIRGEN MARIA EN LA VIDA Y EN LA OBRA DE BENITO ARIAS MONTANO / Bengoechea, I(OC D) – Salamanca, 1979 – 1 – sp Bibl Santa Ana [240]

VIRGEN Y MARTIR...GUADALUPE... ANORANZAS – 1895 – 9 – 1.50f – sp Bibl Santa Ana [240]

VIRGIL / Sellar, W Y – 1897 – 1 – uk Microform Academic [450]

Virgilio *see* LA ENEIDA DE...

VIRGILIO MARON. PUBLIO. LAS OBRAS / Lopez, Diego – Lisboa: Antonia Alvarez, 1627 – 1 – sp Bibl Santa Ana [946]

THE VIRGIN BIRTH / Gruetzmacher, Richard H – New York: Eaton & Mains, 1907. 1 fiche – 9 – us A.T.L.A. [240]

VIRGIN BIRTH / Hoben, Allan – Chicago: University of Chicago, 1903. 1 fiche – 9 – us A.T.L.A. [240]

THE VIRGIN BIRTH OF CHRIST / Orr, James – New York: Charles Scribner, 1907. 1 fiche – 9 – us A.T.L.A. [240]

THE VIRGIN BIRTH OF CHRIST: AN HISTORICAL AND CRITICAL ESSAY / Lobstein, Paul – New York: G.P. Putnam, 1903. 1 fiche – 9 – us A.T.L.A. [240]

VIRGIN ISLAND : CODE ANNOTATED – Oxford, Equity Publishing Comp. Superseded vols. Includes latest Pocket Parts supplement – 9 – Inquire – us Hein [340]

VIRGIN ISLANDS : ATTORNEY GENERAL OPINIONS – (Includes Hein's Attorney General Reports and Opinions Microfiche Project) – v1-10. 1935-86 – 9 – $138.00 set – us Hein [340]

VIRGIN ISLANDS : SESSION LAWS OF AMERICAN STATES AND TERRITORIES – 1925-93 – 9 – $484.00 set – us Hein [340]

Virgin Islands *see* REPORTS AND OPINIONS (A-G)

VIRGIN ISLANDS BAR JOURNAL – (Publication is believed to have ceased with v5 n1 sum 1974) – Christiansted. v1-5 jan 1967-sum 1974 1; v4-5. jan 1973-sum 1974 1,5,9 – 1,5,9 – D9867 – us UMI [073]

Virgin Islands. Danish Government *see* CUSTOMS JOURNALS.

Virgin Islands. Economic Development Board *see* THE OVERALL ECONOMIC DEVELOPMENT PROGRAM

THE VIRGIN OF THE WORLD OF HERMES MERCURIUS TRISMEGISTUS / Kingsford, Anna Bonus – London: George Redway, 1885. xxx,154p. 1 fiche – 9 – us A.T.L.A. [240]

VIRGINEI OU LES DECEMVIRS. TRAGEDIE LYRIQUE EN TROIS ACTES / Berton, H – Paris: Dufaut et DuBois, 1823 – 1 – us Sibley [780]

VIRGINES CHRISTI (T.U.U. 3-31/2C) / Koch, H – Leipzig, 1907 – 1mf – 9 – ne Slangenburg [240]

VIRGINES SUBINTRODUCTAE : EIN BEITRAG ZUM 7. KAPITEL DES 1. KORINTHERBRIEFS / Achelis, Hans – Leipzig: J.C. Hinrichs, 1902 – 1mf – 9 – 0-8370-2036-0 – 1985-0036 – us A.T.L.A. [240]

VIRGINIA – 17r – 1 – $1,360.00 – us Scholarly Res [370]

VIRGINIA : CODE OF VIRGINIA – Charlottesville: Michie Co, 1950-Jun 1996 update – 9 – $3,303.00 set – us Hein [340]

VIRGINIA : SESSION LAWS OF AMERICAN STATES AND TERRITORIES – 1776-1995 – 9 – $1,967.00 set – us Hein [340]

Virginia *see*
- CALENDAR OF VIRGINIA STATE PAPERS AND OTHER MANUSCRIPTS
- MISCELLANEOUS NEWSPAPERS
- REPORTS AND OPINIONS (A-G)
- REPORTS, POST-NRS
- REPORTS, PRE-NRS
- THE STATE OF VIRGINIA IN ACCOUNT WITH OFFICERS OF THE ARMY OF THE REVOLUTION. PRIVATE ACCOUNTS OF GENERAL CHARLES SCOTT
- VIRGINIA REPORTS ANNOTATED

VIRGINIA AGRICULTURAL ECONOMICS / Virginia. Polytechnic Institute. Extension Division – v. 1-214. 1931-69 – 1,5,6 – us Spaulding [338]

Virginia. Agricultural Experiment Station. Blacksburg *see*
- AGRICULTURAL ECONOMICS SPECIAL REPORT N.2
- AGRONOMY MIMEOGRAPHED CIRCULAR
- ANALYTICAL INDEX AND LIST OF PUBLICATIONS
- ANIMAL HUSBANDRY RESEARCH SUMMARY
- ANNOUNCEMENT
- ANNUAL REPORT
- BULLETIN
- CIRCULAR
- A FARM BUSINESS SURVEY OF THE EARLY POTATO SEASON OF VIRGINIA
- LEAFLET
- RESEARCH REPORT
- RURAL SOCIOLOGY REPORT
- SPECIAL REPORT: ENTOMOLOGY
- TECHNICAL BULLETIN
- THE VIRGINIA FRUIT SIZER

VIRGINIA AGRICULTURAL INSTRUCTOR / Virginia. Polytechnic Institute. College of Agriculture – 12 fiches – 9 – us Spaulding [630]

VIRGINIA AND TRUCKEE RAILROAD DIRECTORY – Placer Co, CA. 1873-1874 – 1r – 1 – $50.00 – D075 – us Library Micro [380]

VIRGINIA ARGUS – Richmond. Va. -w. 1797-1816 – 1 – us UMI [071]

VIRGINIA ATTORNEY GENERAL REPORTS AND OPINIONS – (6 1837-1979 $315.00. 9 1979-1994 $367.50) – 1837-1994 – 6,9 – $682.00 set – us Hein [340]

VIRGINIA BAPTIST PREACHER – Richmond. Va. Ed. by Elder Henry Keeling. 1842-57 – 1 – 137.58 – us Baptist [240]

VIRGINIA BAPTISTS, STRUGGLES AND TRIUMPHS / Curry, J LM – 1873 – 1 – 5.00 – us Baptist [240]

VIRGINIA BAR ASSOCIATION JOURNAL – v1-21. 1975-95 – 9 – $172.00 set – us Hein [340]

VIRGINIA BAR ASSOCIATION REPORTS – (Includes 1st-11th mid-winter meetings) – Proceedings, 1st-84th annual meetings. 1889-1973 – 134mf – 9 – $603.00 – LLMC 84-686 – us L.L.M.C. [340]

VIRGINIA BAR ASSOCIATION REPORTS AND PROCEEDINGS – 1st-84th Annual Meetings. 1889- – 134mf – $603.00 – LLMC 84-686 – us L.L.M.C. [073]

VIRGINIA BAR EXAMINATIONS / Boyd, Thomas Munford – Richmond, Appeals Press 1925 289 p. LL-721 – 1 – us L of C Photodup [340]

VIRGINIA BAR NEWS *see* VIRGINIA LAWYER

Virginia. Bureau of Financial Institutions. State Corporation Commission *see* REPORTS SHOWING THE CONDITION OF BANKS, SAVINGS AND LOAN ASSOCIATIONS, INDUSTRIAL LOAN ASSOCIATIONS, CREDIT UNIONS

Virginia. Bureau of Insurance *see* REPORTS OF THE COMMISSIONER OF INSURANCE

Virginia. Bureau of Labor and Industry *see* STATE LABOR REPORTS

VIRGINIA CAVALCADE – Richmond. v1-47 sum 1951-spr 1998+ 1; v21-37 sum 1971-spr 1988. v38-44 sum 1988-spr 1995*. v45-47 sum 1995-spr 1998+ 5; v25-47. sum 1975-spr 1998+ 9 – 1,5,9 – D3440 – us UMI [073]

VIRGINIA CITY CHRONICLE – Virginia City, NV. 1962 – 1r – 1 – $50.00 – N04783 – us Library Micro [071]

VIRGINIA CITY TIMES – Virginia City, NV. 1959 – 1r – 1 – $50.00 – U03714 – us Library Micro [071]

Virginia. Commission on Constitutional Government *see* THE "FULL FAITH AND CREDIT CLAUSE" OF THE UNITED STATES CONSTITUTION; AN INSTRUMENT OF FEDERALISM

VIRGINIA DAILY UNION – Virginia City, NV. 1863; 1864-65 – 2r – 1 – $100.00 – U04787 – us Library Micro [071]

VIRGINIA DAILY UNION – Virginia City, NV. 1864-1865 – 1r – 1 – $50.00 – U04799 – us Library Micro [071]

THE VIRGINIA DAIRY INDUSTRY / Virginia. Polytechnic Institute. Extension Division – 1fiche – 9 – us Spaulding [636]

Virginia. Dept. of Labor and Industry *see* REPORTS

Virginia. Dept. of Taxation *see* REPORTS

VIRGINIA EVENING CHRONICLE – Virginia City, NV. 1874-1927 – 49r – 1 – $2,450.00 – NC04800 – us Library Micro [071]

Virginia. Fairfax County *see*
- CIRCUIT SUPERIOR COURT
- COURT RECORDS
- FAIRFAX COUNTY, VIRGINIA COURT RECORDS ABSTRACTS OF CHANCERY PAPERS 1748-1870 INCLUDING SURNAME AND SUBJECT INDEXES
- FAIRFAX COUNTY, VIRGNIA RECORD OF ROADS

Virginia Feed Convention and Nutrition Conference *see* PROCEEDINGS AND RESEARCH SUMMARIES

VIRGINIA FREE PRESS – Charles Town. West Virginia. 1856-1861; 1865-96 – 1 – us UMI [071]

VIRGINIA FREE PRESS – Charleston. West Virginia. 1853-1866 – 1 – us UMI [071]

THE VIRGINIA FRUIT SIZER / Virginia. Agricultural Experiment Station. Blacksburg – 1910. 1 fiche – 9 – us Spaulding [630]

VIRGINIA GAZETTE – 1736-80 – 6r – 1 – $135.00 – us I.E.A.H.C. [071]

VIRGINIA GAZETTE – Norfolk.VA. (Norfolk Intelligencer). -w. 1774-76 – 1 – us UMI [071]

VIRGINIA GAZETTE – Richmond. VA. Also: Richmond and Manchester Advertiser. (The Argus). -w. 1793-1803 – 1 – us UMI [071]

VIRGINIA GAZETTE – Richmond. Va. and General Advertiser. 1790-1809 – 1 – us UMI [071]

VIRGINIA GAZETTE – Richmond. Va. and Weekly Advertiser. -W. 1787-89 – 1 – us UMI [071]

VIRGINIA GAZETTE – Richmond. Va. or The American Advtr. -W. 1782-86 – 1 – us UMI [071]

VIRGINIA GAZETTE – Williamsburg. Va. -w. 1853-1926, 1930- – 1 – us UMI [071]

THE VIRGINIA GAZETTE DAYBOOKS, 1750-52 AND 1764-66 – (With printed guide) – 1r – 1 – $85.00 – D3184 – us Scholarly Res [978]

VIRGINIA GAZETTE, PETERSBURG INTELLIGENCER – Petersburg. VA.Also: Commercial Advertiser. -w. 1795-1804; 1926-28 – 1 – us UMI [071]

VIRGINIA HALF PAY AND OTHER RELATED REVOLUTIONARY WAR PENSION APPLILCATION FILES / U.S. War Department. Collection of Revolutionary War Records – 18 rolls. M910 – 1 – us Nat'l Archives [324]

VIRGINIA HISTORICAL REGISTER AND LITERARY COMPANION – Richmond. v1-6. jan 1848-oct 1853 – 1 – D4618 – us UMI [978]

VIRGINIA HISTORICAL SOCIETY, AN OCCASIONAL BULLETIN *see* VIRGINIA MAGAZINE OF HISTORY AND BIOGRAPHY

Virginia. House of Burgesses *see* JOURNALS OF THE HOUSE OF BURGESSES OF VIRGINIA, 1619-1776

[VIRGINIA] IDOL MIO QUEST'ALMA AMANT... / Tarchi, A – (Full score) – London: Longman & Broderip, 1786 – 1 – us Sibley [780]

VIRGINIA INDEPENDENT CHRONICLE – Richmond. Va. -w. 1786-90 – 1 – us UMI [071]

Virginia. Industrial commission *see* OPINIONS

VIRGINIA JOURNAL AND ALEXANDRIA ADVERTISER – Alexandria. Va. 1785-88 – 1 – us UMI [071]

VIRGINIA JOURNAL OF EDUCATION – (Cont: Journal of Virginia Education) – Richmond. v74-91. sep 1980-jun 1998+ – 1,5,9 – D1899.02 – us UMI [370]

VIRGINIA JOURNAL OF EDUCATION – (v43 was not available for filming; cont by: Journal of Virginia Education) – Richmond. v1-72. oct 1907-may 1979 1; v63-72. sep 1969-may 1979 5; v69-72. sep 1975-may 1979 9 – 1,5,9 – D1899 – us UMI [370]

VIRGINIA JOURNAL OF INTERNATIONAL LAW – v1-33. 1960-93 – 1,5,6 – $540.00 – us Hein [073]

VIRGINIA JOURNAL OF SCIENCE – Lancaster. v1-48 1950-97+ 1; v27-32 spr 1976-win 1981. v33-45 spr 1982-win 1994*. v46-48 1995-97+ 5; v27-48. 1976-97+ 9 – 1,5,9 – D10414 – us UMI [500]

VIRGINIA JOURNAL OF SOCIAL POLICY AND THE LAW – v1-3. 1993-96 – 9 – $32.00 set – us Hein [340]

[VIRGINIA] LA MIA SPOSA. OVERTURE / Albertini, G – London: Longman & Broderip, 1786 – 1 – us Sibley [780]

VIRGINIA LAW JOURNAL – (Began as monthly, became a weekly after 1888) – Richmond. v1-17. Jan 1877-Sept 1893 (all publ) – 149mf – 9 – $223.00 – LLMC 88-012 – us L.L.M.C. [073]

VIRGINIA LAW REGISTER – os: Lynchburg. v1-20. May 1895-1915. ns: Charlottesville: Michie Co. v1-13. 1916-28 – 369mf – 9 – $553.00 – LLMC 88-013 – us L.L.M.C. [073]

VIRGINIA LAW REGISTER *see* VIRGINIA LAWYER

VIRGINIA LAW REVIEW – v1-80. 1913-94 – 1,5,6,9 – $2,520.00 – us Hein [073]

VIRGINIA LAW WEEKLY – Charlottesville. On film: v6-9; 1953-57. LL-016 – 1 – us L of C Photodup [340]

VIRGINIA LAWYER – (Title varies: v1-35, 1952-87, as Virginia Bar News. One issue in volume designated Virginia Law Register) – v1-43. 1952-94 – 9 – $575.00 set – us Hein [340]

VIRGINIA LIBRARIAN – (Cont: Virginia Librarian Newsletter. Cont by: Virginia Libraries) – Alexandria. v32-41. 1986-95 1,9; v32-40 1986-94*. v41 1995 5 – 1,5,9 – D10053.01 – us UMI [020]

VIRGINIA LIBRARIAN *see*
- VIRGINIA LIBRARIAN NEWSLETTER
- VIRGINIA LIBRARIES

VIRGINIA LIBRARIAN NEWSLETTER – (Cont by: Virginia Librarian; former title: Virginia Librarian apr 1954-1973) – Richmond. v1-19 1953-73*. v20-31 1974-85 1; v21-24 feb 1975-dec 1978*. v25 1979. v26-31 1980-85* 5; v21-24 feb 1975-dec1978*. v25-29 1979-83. v30-31 1984-85* 9 – 1,5,9 – D10053 – us UMI [020]

VIRGINIA LIBRARIAN NEWSLETTER *see* VIRGINIA LIBRARIAN

VIRGINIA LIBRARIES – (Cont: Virginia Librarian) – Alexandria. v42-43 1996-97+ – 1,5,9 – D10053.02 – us UMI [020]

VIRGINIA LIBRARIES *see* VIRGINIA LIBRARIAN

VIRGINIA LITERARY MUSEUM AND JOURNAL OF BELLES LETTRES, ARTS, SCIENCES, ETC – Charlottesville. v1. jun 1829-jun 1830 – 1 – D5350 – us UMI [978]

VIRGINIA MAGAZINE OF HISTORY AND BIOGRAPHY – (For 1980-90, the micro-edition includes: Virginia Historical Society, An Occasional Bulletin; for 1991- , History Notes) – Richmond. v1-105. jul 1893-oct 1997+ 1; v77-105. jan 1969-oct 1997+ 5; v85-105. jan 1977-oct 1997+ 9 – 1,5,9 – D908 – us UMI [975]

VIRGINIA MAGAZINE OF HISTORY AND BIOGRAPHY – v. 2-54. 1894-1946 – 1,5,6 – us Princeton Micro [920]

VIRGINIA MEDICAL – (Cont: Virginia Medical Monthly; Cont by: Virginia Medical Quarterly) – Richmond. v103-117. aug 1976-jun 1990 – 1,5,9 – D909.01 – us UMI [610]

VIRGINIA MEDICAL *see*
- VIRGINIA MEDICAL MONTHLY
- VIRGINIA MEDICAL QUARTERLY

VIRGINIA MEDICAL MONTHLY – (Cont by: Virginia Medical. Former titles: Virginia Medical Monthly apr 1874-mar 1896; Virginia Medical Semi-monthly apr 10, 1896-dec 21, 1917) – Richmond. v1-45 1871-1917*. v45-103 apr 1918-jul 1976 1; v98-103. jan 1971-jul 1976 5; v101-103. jan 1974-jul 1976 9 – 1,5,9 – D909 – us UMI [610]

VIRGINIA MEDICAL MONTHLY *see*
- VIRGINIA MEDICAL
- VIRGINIA MEDICAL MONTHLY

VIRGINIA MEDICAL QUARTERLY : VMQ – (Cont: Virginia Medical) – Richmond. v117-124. sum 1990-1997+ 1,9; v117-120 sum 1990-fal 1993. v121 1994*. v122-124 1995-97+ 5 – 1,5,9 – D909.02 – us UMI [610]

VIRGINIA MEDICAL QUARTERLY *see* VIRGINIA MEDICAL

VIRGINIA MEDICAL SEMI-MONTHLY *see* VIRGINIA MEDICAL MONTHLY

[VIRGINIA] NON LAGRIMAR BEN MIO / Tarchi, A – (Full score) – London: Longman & Broderip, 1786 – 1 – us Sibley [780]

Virginia. Polytechnic Institute *see* VIRGINIA TECH FORESTER

VIRGINIA POLYTECHNIC INSTITUTE AND STATE UNIVERSITY. WATER RESOURCES RESEARCH CENTER. BULLETIN *see* VIRGINIA WATER RESOURCES RESEARCH CENTER. BULLETIN

Virginia. Polytechnic Institute. College of Agriculture *see*
- THE AGREVIEW
- THE ECONOMIC ANALYST
- VIRGINIA AGRICULTURAL INSTRUCTOR
- VIRGINIA SOIL SURVEY NEWSLETTER
- VPI AGRICULTURAL JOURNAL

Virginia. Polytechnic Institute. College of Agriculture. Wood Research Laboratory *see* BULLETIN

Virginia. Polytechnic Institute. Extension Division *see*
- BULLETIN
- CIRCULAR
- CONFERENCE PROCEEDINGS
- DAIRY PROFITS BY BETTER FEEDING
- EXTENSION DIVISION NEWS
- EXTENSION SERVICE NEWS
- FIVE-YEAR PROGRAM FOR AGRICULTURAL DEVELOPMENT
- FIVE-YEAR PROGRAM FOR THE DEVELOPMENT OF VIRGINIA AGRICULTURE
- HEAD, HEART, HEALTH AND HANDS IN VIRGINIA
- HINTS FOR TOMORROW'S POULTRYMEN
- LEAFLET
- MA
- MARKET REVIEW OF PEEP AND MOO
- MB
- ME
- MISCELLANEOUS PUBLICATIONS
- NURSERYMEN'S NOTEBOOKS: DISEASES OF ORNAMENTALS
- POULTRY PELLETS
- PUBLICATION
- THREE YEARS OF EXTENSION WORK IN AGRICULTURE AND HOME ECONOMICS IN VIRGINIA
- VIRGINIA AGRICULTURAL ECONOMICS
- THE VIRGINIA DAIRY INDUSTRY
- VIRGINIA PROCESSOR
- VIRGINIA'S OPPORTUNITY IN AGRICULTURE

Virginia. Polytechnic Institute. Research Division. Blacksburg *see*
- BULLETIN
- RESEARCH REPORT

VIRGINIA POLYTECHNIC INSTITUTE. WATER RESOURCES RESEARCH CENTER. BULLETIN *see* VIRGINIA WATER RESOURCES RESEARCH CENTER. BULLETIN

VIRGINIA PRESBYTERIANISM AND RELIGIOUS LIBERTY IN COLONIAL AND REVOLUTIONARY TIMES / Johnson, Thomas Cary – Richmond, Va.: Presbyterian Committee of Publication, 1907 – 1mf – us A.T.L.A. [240]

VIRGINIA PROCESSOR / Virginia. Polytechnic Institute. Extension Division – v. 1-10. 1959-67 – 1,5,6 – us Spaulding [630]

VIRGINIA QUARTERLY REVIEW – (A national Journal of literature and discussion.) v. 1-18. 1925-1942 – 1,5,6 – us Princeton Micro [073]

VIRGINIA QUARTERLY REVIEW – (Cum Index for v1-20 1925-44) – Charlottesville. v1-73. 1925-97+ 1; v45-73. 1969-97+ 5; v52-73. 1976-97+ 9 – 1,5,9 – D851 – us UMI [420]

Virginia. Railroad Commissioner *see* REPORTS
VIRGINIA RELIGIOUS MAGAZINE – Lexington. v1-3. 1805-07 – 1 – D3673 – us UMI [210]
VIRGINIA REPORTS ANNOTATED / Virginia – v1-26. 1730-1880 (all publ) – 272mf – 9 – $408.00 – LLMC 90-314 – us L.L.M.C. [340]
VIRGINIA REVIEW – Virginia, NE. -w. Mar-Jul 1922 – 1 – us NE Hist [071]
VIRGINIA SELECTION OF PSALMS, HYMNS AND SPIRITUAL SONGS – 3rd ed. 1842 – 1 – 18.41 – us Baptist [240]
VIRGINIA SOIL SURVEY NEWSLETTER / Virginia. Polytechnic Institute. College of Agriculture – v. 1-26. 1938-72 – 1,5,6 – us Spaulding [631]
VIRGINIA STATE BAR ANNUAL REPORTS – (Lacking: no 28) – nos 1-34. 1938-72 – 33mf – 9 – $49.50 – LLMC 84-685 – us L.L.M.C. [073]
Virginia. State Bar Association *see* PROCEEDINGS
VIRGINIA STATE COLLEGE GAZETTE – v38-53. 1933-47 – 1r – 1 – us Ross [370]
Virginia. State Corporation Commission *see* REPORTS
Virginia. State Tax Commission *see* REPORTS
VIRGINIA STATESMAN – Wheeling. West Virginia. 1828-1829 – 1 – us UMI [071]
Virginia. Supreme Court *see*
- UNREPORTED DECISIONS
- VIRGINIA SUPREME COURT RECORDS AND BRIEFS
- VIRGINIA SUPREME COURT REPORTS
- WYTHE'S CHANCERY REPORTS

Virginia. Supreme Court. Colonial Court *see* RANDOLF AND BARRADALL'S REPORTS
Virginia. Supreme Court. General Court *see* JEFFERSON'S REPORTS
VIRGINIA SUPREME COURT RECORDS AND BRIEFS / Virginia. Supreme Court – (No updates) – documents for v222 only – 538mf – 9 – $538.00 – LLMC 84-900 – us L.L.M.C. [340]
VIRGINIA SUPREME COURT REPORTS – v1-238. 1730-1989 – 9 – $3,577.00 – us Hein [340]
VIRGINIA SUPREME COURT REPORTS / Virginia. Supreme Court – (Pre-NRS: v1-82 1730-87 699mf $1,048.00. Updates planned) – v1-238. 1730-1989 – 2385mf – 9 – $3,578.00 – LLMC 80-819 – us L.L.M.C. [340]
VIRGINIA SUPREME COURT REPORTS *see*
- JEFFERSON'S REPORTS
- PATTON, JR. AND HEATH'S REPORTS
- RANDOLF AND BARRADALL'S REPORTS
- UNREPORTED DECISIONS
- VIRGINIA REPORTS ANNOTATED
- VIRGINIA SUPREME COURT RECORDS AND BRIEFS
- WYTHE'S CHANCERY REPORTS

Virginia. Supreme Court. Special Court of Appeals *see* PATTON, JR. AND HEATH'S REPORTS
THE VIRGINIA TECH – Blacksburg. Va. 1961-1971 – 1 – us UMI [071]
VIRGINIA TECH FORESTER / Virginia. Polytechnic Institute – 1945-69. 15 fiches – 9 – us Spaulding [634]
Virginia. Truck Experiment Station. Norfolk *see*
- BULLETIN
- CIRCULAR
- VEGETABLE GROWERS NEWS

Virginia. University. Phelps-Stokes Fellowship Fund *see* PHELPS-STOKES FELLOWSHIP FUND
VIRGINIA VALLEY RECORDS / Wayland, John W – Genealogical and historical material of Rockingham County and Related Regions. Strasburg, Shenandoah Publishing House, 1930. Virginia Reel 4. (The Cox Library Collection) – 5 – us Americana [978]
VIRGINIA WATER RESOURCES RESEARCH CENTER. BULLETIN – (No vol indicated for 1965-93. Former titles: Virginia Polytechnic Institute. Water Resources Research Center. Bulletin 1965-69; Virginia Polytechnic Institute and State University. Water Resources Research Center. Bulletin 1970-sep 1972) – Blacksburg. 1965-93. v183-185 1994*. v186-197 1995-97+ – 1 – D9657 – us UMI [600]
THE VIRGINIA WOOLF MANUSCRIPTS – From the Henry W. and Albert A. Berg Collection of the New York Public Library – 21r – 1 – us Primary [420]
THE VIRGINIA WOOLF MANUSCRIPTS FROM THE MONKS HOUSE PAPERS AT THE UNIVERSITY OF SUSSEX – 1 – us Primary [420]
VIRGINIAN – Covington. Va. 1946- – 1 – us UMI [071]
VIRGINIAN – Lynchburg. Va. 1822-93 – 1 – us UMI [071]
VIRGINIAN – Lynchburg. Va. -tw. 1857-59 – 1 – us UMI [071]
VIRGINIAN – Richmond. Va. 1910-20 – 1 – us UMI [071]
THE VIRGINIAN CHURCHMAN – Richmond. Va. 1966-1969 – 1 – us UMI [071]
VIRGINIAN-PILOT – (Missing: oct-dec 1903. Former titles: Norfolk Virginian 1865-98; Virginian-pilot 1898-1911; Virginian-pilot and Norfolk landmark 1912-38) – Norfolk, VA. 1899-1997 – 1 – D60607 – us UMI [073]
VIRGINIAN-PILOT *see* VIRGINIAN-PILOT
VIRGINIAN-PILOT AND NORFOLK LANDMARK *see* VIRGINIAN-PILOT
THE VIRGINIANS : A TALE OF THE LAST CENTURY / Thackeray, William Makepeace – Boston: Fields, Osgood, 1870 – 1 roll – 1 – 1-55879-751-3 – uk Libr Preservation [830]
VIRGINIA'S COLONIAL SCHOOLMASTERS – (Documented account of all known schoolmasters from 1660-1776. Over 300 identified) – (mf ed 1990) – 1mf – 9 – 0-87623-118-0 – us Holbrook [370]
VIRGINIA'S OPPORTUNITY IN AGRICULTURE / Virginia. Polytechnic Institute. Extension Division – 8fiches – 9 – us Spaulding [630]
VIRGINIA-TENNESSEAN – Bristol, VA. 1950-85 – 1 – us UMI [071]
VIRGINIBUS PUERISQUE : AND OTHER PAPERS / Stevenson, Robert Louis – London: C. Kegan Paul, 1881 – 1 roll – 1 – 1-55879-702-5 – uk Libr Preservation [420]
Virginie Marie, Soeur *see* BOIGRAPHIE [I.E. BIOGRAPHIE] DE MONSIEUR L'ABBE HERMANN PLANTE, BACHELIER ES ARTS DE L'UNIVERSITE LAVAL, LICENCIE ES LETTRES DE L'UNIVERSITE DE MONTREAL, LICENCIE EN DICTION DE L'ECOLE CLASSIQUE DE MONTREAL
VIRGINISCHE-ZEITUNG – Richmond. Va. 1915-1926 – 1 – us UMI [071]
VIRGO MARIA MYSTICA SOLIS IMAGINE EMBLEMATICE EXPRESSA / Leenheer, J de – O 339. 2 v. 1681 – 9 – ne IDC [240]
Virgouroux et al *see* DICTIONNAIRE DE LA BIBLE
UNA VIRIAO TORQUES, EXTREMENA DE ORELLANA DE LA SIERRA / Rada Delgado, Juan de Dios de la – Madrid: Fortanet, 1888. B.R.A.H. XII, pp. 237-238 – sp Bibl Santa Ana [946]
VIRIATO / Sanchez Loro, Domingo – (Suplemento del Boletin Informativo de la Asociacion de Amigos de Guadalupe) – Caceres: Garcia Floriano, 1947 – 1 – sp Bibl Santa Ana [946]
VIRIATO / Schulken, Adolf – Porto: Renascenca, 1927 – 1 – sp Bibl Santa Ana [946]
VIRIDARIUM HUMILITATIS / Dumas, Petrus – Friburgi Helvetiorum, 1685 – 6mf – 8 – Dfl25.00 – ne Slangenburg [240]
VIRITTAJA – Helsinki. v54-58. 1950-54 – 1 – D639 – us UMI [073]
Virmontois, Petrus *see* QUAESTIO MEDICA DE MUSICES UTILITATE IN MORBIS CURANDIS..
Virolleaud, Ch. *see*
- LA DEESSE ANAT.
- LA LEGENDE DE KERET
- LA LEGENDE PHENICIENNE DE DANEL
- LE PALAIS ROYAL D'UGARIT 2

VIROLOGY ABSTRACTS – 9 – us C.S.A. [576]
LOS VIRREINATOS EN EL SIGLO 18. MADRID, 1945 / Alcazar Molina, Cayetano – Madrid: Razon y Fe, 1948 – 1 – sp Bibl Santa Ana [946]
VIRREYES Y VIRREINAS DE LA NUEVA ESPANA...PRIMERA Y SEGUNDA SERIE. 2 VOL... / Valle-Arizpe, Artemio del – Madrid, 1934 – 1 – sp Bibl Santa Ana [946]
DOS VIRTSHAFTLEKHE LEBN = THE ECONOMIC LIFE – (In Yiddish) – Warsaw, PL. v1 no6-7 Sep/Oct 1934; v1 no8-9 Nov/Dec 1934 – 1r – 1 – $25.00 – cn Can Microfilming [072]
VIRTUD Y CIENCIA / Diaz Maciaz, Jose – 1892 – 9 – 1.50f – sp Bibl Santa Ana [830]
THE VIRTUES AND THEIR REASONS : A SYSTEM OF ETHICS FOR SOCIETY AND SCHOOLS / Bierbower, Austin – 3rd ed. Chicago: George Sherwood, 1888 – 1mf – 9 – 0-8370-6017-6 – 1986-0017 – us A.T.L.A. [170]
VIRUS GENES – Boston. v1-15. nov 1987-nov 1997+ – 1,5,9 – D16847 – us UMI [575]
VIRUS RESEARCH : AN INTERNATIONAL JOURNAL OF MOLECULAR AND CELLULAR VIROLOGY – Amsterdam. v1-49. 1984-97+ 1,5; v9-49 1988-97+ 9 – 1,5,9 – D42427 – us UMI [616]
Viry, Joseph M F J *see* MEMOIRE STATISTIQUE DU DEPARTEMENT DE LA LYS
VISALAANDHRA – (Telugu language) – Vijayawada, India. Jul-Sept 1966 – 1r – 1 – us L of C Photodup [072]
VISALIA SUN – Visalia, CA. Sep-Dec 1860 – 1r – 1 CB03079 – $50.00 – us Library Micro [071]
VISALIA TIMES-DELTA – Visalia, CA. 1902-08; 1928- – 507+ r – 1 CB03081 – $25,350.00 ($480.00y) – us Library Micro [071]
VISALIA WEEKLY DELTA – Visalia, CA. 1859-89; 1901-02 – 16r – 1 CB03080 – $800.00 – us Library Micro [071]
VISAO – Sao Paulo, BL. 1972-1989 – 48r – $2,400.00 – R04188 – us Library Micro [072]
VISBY TIDNING – Visby, 1811 – 9 – sw Kungliga [072]
Visch, C de *see*
- AUCTARIUM D.C. DE VISCH AD BIBLIOTHECAM SCRIPTORUM S.O. CISTERCIENSIS
- BIBLIOTHECA SACRI ORDINIS CISTERCIENSIS

Vischer, Eberhard *see*
- DIE OFFENBARUNG JOHANNIS (T.U.U. 1-2/3)
- DIE PAULUSBRIEFE

Vischer, Friedrich Theodor *see*
- AUSGEWAEHLTE WERKE
- DER DEUTSCHE KRIEG 1870-71
- KRITISCHE GAENGE

VISCONDE DO RIO BRANCO – Visconde do Rio Branco, 27 Dec 1953; Dec 1977-20 May 1979 – 1,5,6 – bl Biblioteca [072]
Vishnevskii, D *see* KIEVSKAIA AKADEMIIA V PERVOI POLOVINE 18 STOLETIIA
THE VISHNU PURANA / Wilson, H H – A system of Hindu mythology and tradition. London. 1840. Bl-1072 1 – 9 – ne IDC [290]
VISHNU PURANA / Puranas – 1840 – 1 – uk Microform Academic [280]
VISHVAVALNI – Hubli, India. Jul-Sept 1966 – 1r – 1 – us L of C Photodup [072]
VISHWAMITRA – Calcutta, India. 1960-Aug 1966 – 20r – 1 – us L of C Photodup [072]
VISHWAMITRA – New Delhi, India. 1944-53 – 20r – 1 – us L of C Photodup [072]
Visiani, R de *see*
- FLORA DALMATICA
- ILLUSTRAZIONE DI ALCUNE PIANTE DELLA GRECIA E DELLA ASIA MINORE

VISIBLE LANGUAGE – (Former title: Journal of Typographic Research 1967-70) – Providence. v1-8 1967-jan 1974*. v9-31 1975-97+ 1; v9-31. 1975-97+ 5,9 – 1,5,9 – D10277 – us UMI [760]
THE VISIGOTHIC CODE = FORUM JUDICUM / ed by Scott, S P – Boston: The Boston Book Co, 1910 – 6mf – 9 – $9.00 – LLMC 95-194 – us L.L.M.C. [340]
THE VISION : OR HELL, PURGATORY, AND PARADISE OF DANTE ALIGHIERI / Dante, Alighieri – London: Printed for Taylor and Hessey, 2nd ed 1819 – 2 rolls – 1 – 1-55879-262-7 – uk Libr Preservation [810]
VISION – Mexico City, MX. 1974- – 34+ r – $1,700.00 ($90.00y) – R60713 – us Library Micro [072]
LA VISION DE LA FEMME A TRAVERS LES CONTES BETI. ETUDE ETHNOLINGUISTIQUE / Mbah-Onana, J – 9 – F150.00 – fr Ethnologie [305]
LA VISION DE SAN ALONSO RODRIGUEZ PINTADA POR FRANCISCO DE ZURBARAN EN 1630 / Escobar, Francisco – Madrid: Fortanet, 1917. B.R.A.H. lxxi/pp. 523-533 – 1 – sp Bibl Santa Ana [946]
VISION DEL MUNDO DESDE YUSTE / Sanchez Morales, Narciso – Plasencia: Imp. La Victoria, 1978 – 1 – sp Bibl Santa Ana [946]
VISION HISTORICA DE ESPANA DESDE LA ABDICACION DE CARLOS 5TH EN BRUSELAS / Manzanares, Luis Angel – Caceres: Tip. Extremadura, 1978 – 1 – sp Bibl Santa Ana [946]
THE VISION OF A SHORT LIFE : A MEMORIAL OF WARREN BARTLETT SEABURY: ONE OF THE FOUNDERS OF THE YALE MISSION COLLEGE IN CHINA / Seabury, Joseph Bartlett – Cambridge: Riverside Press, 1909 – 1mf – 9 – 0-8370-6372-8 – 1986-0372 – us A.T.L.A. [920]
A VISION OF JUDGEMENT / Southey, Robert – London: Longman, Hurst, Rees, Orme, and Brown, 1821 – 1 roll – 1 – 1-55879-431-X – uk Libr Preservation [810]
THE VISION OF THE EVENING AND THE MORNING : A STUDY OF THE PROPHECY OF DANIEL 8 / Kolvoord, John & Kellogg, Moses Eastman – Battle Creek, MI: [s.n., c1907] – 1mf – 9 – 0-8370-3983-5 – 1985-1983 – us A.T.L.A. [220]
VISION OF THE EVENING AND THE MORNING: A STUDY OF THE PROPHECY OF DANIEL VIII / Kolvoord, John – Battle Creek, MI, 1907. 1 fiche – 9 – us A.T.L.A. [240]
LA VISION PUBLIQUE, D'UN HORRIBLE ET TRES ESPOUVANTABLE DEMON, SUR L'EGLISE CATHEDRALE DE QUIMPER, CORENTIN – Rennes. 1620 – 9 – fr Hachette [360]
VISION RESEARCH – (Absorbed: Clinical Vision Sciences jan 1994) – Oxford. v1-37. 1961-97+ 1,5; v10-37. 1970-97+ 9 – 1,5,9 – D49244 – us UMI [612]
VISIONS / Montgomery, H H – Westminster: Society for the Propagation of the Gospel in Foreign Parts, 1909 – 1mf – us A.T.L.A. [240]
VISIONS AFRICAINES – Bruxelles. v1(1-6). 1961-62 – 3mf – 9 – A-696/2 – ne IDC [960]
VISIONS AND NARRATIVES OF THE OLD TESTAMENT / Hare, George Emlen – New York: E P Dutton, 1889 – 1mf – 9 – 0-8370-3471-X – 1985-1471 – us A.T.L.A. [220]
VISIONS OF GOD: THE APOCALYPSES OF OUR SAVIOR, JESUS CHRIST, GIVEN TO JOHN, THE LAST OF THE TWELVE APOSTLES : A PRACTICAL INTERPRETATION OF THE VISIONS OF THE SEER OF PATMOS / Rafferty, A C – Kansas City, MO: Word and Way, [1898?] – 1mf – 9 – 0-8370-4823-0 – 1985-2823 – us A.T.L.A. [220]
VISIONS OF SIR HEISTER RYLEY – London. aug 1710-feb 1711 – 1 – D5352 – us UMI [210]
THE VISIONS OF THE APOCALYPSE AND THEIR LESSONS / Scott, Thomas Lucas – London: Skeffington, 1893. 1 fiche – 9 – us A.T.L.A. [240]
VISIONS. THIRD SERIES : FOR MISSIONARIES AND OTHERS / Montgomery, H H – Westminster: Society for the Propagation of the Gospel in Foreign Parts, 1915 – 1mf – us A.T.L.A. [240]
A VISIT OF JAPHETH TO SHEM AND HAM / Mutchmore, Samuel Alexander – 2nd ed. Philadelphia: Pres. Publ. Co., 1890 – 1 – us U.W. Library [910]
A VISIT TO ABYSSINIA; AN ACCOUNT OF TRAVEL IN MODERN ETHIOPIA / Winstanley, William – 2v. 1881 – 1 – us A.T.L.A. [910]
A VISIT TO CANADA AND THE UNITED STATES OF AMERICA: ALSO A SECOND VISIT TO SPAIN / Gadsby, John – London: Gadsby, 1873. 04158. (Pre-1900 Canadiana) – 9 – cn C.I.H.M. [910]
A VISIT TO CAPE COLONY AND NATAL IN 1879 / Derham, Walter – Bristol: Privately printed by H Mardon, 1879 – us Res Libr [910]
VISIT TO FIVE SOCIALIST STATES / Aidit, Dipa Nusantara – (speech). 3 pts. in 1 v. SE-4397 1. 1958? – 9 – ne IDC [335]
A VISIT TO FREELAND OR THE NEW PARADISE REGAINED / Hertzka, Theodor – With the German text: Eine Reise nach Freiland. 1 fiche (29x) – 9 – 1.00f – at Libertarian Micro [320]
A VISIT TO PEKING / Happer, Andrew P – 1879 – 9 – $50.00 – us Presbyterian [240]
A VISIT TO THE PHILIPPINE ISLANDS / Bowring, J – London, 1859 – 5mf – 9 – ne IDC [950]
UNA VISITA AL MONASTERIO DE YUSTE / Alarcon, Pedro Antonio de – Madrid: Imprenta Casado, 1944 – 1 – sp Bibl Santa Ana [350]
VISITA DEL REY D. ALFONSO 13 A BADAJOZ – Badajoz: Tip. La Economica, 1906 – 1 – sp Bibl Santa Ana [350]

LA VISITA DEL SOL / Diez Canedo, Enrique – Madrid: Imp. Gutemberg Castro, 1907 – 1 – sp Bibl Santa Ana [946]
VISITATION CHARGES DELIVERED TO THE CLERGY AND CHURCHWARDENS OF THE DIOCESES OF CHESTER AND OXFORD / Stubbs, William & Holmes, E E – London, New York: Longmans, Green, 1904 – 1mf – us A.T.L.A. [240]
THE VISITATION OF YORKSHIRE, MADE IN THE YEARS 1584-85, BY ROBERT GLOVER, SOMERSET HERALD.. / Glover, Robert; ed by Foster, Joseph – London, privately printed for the ed., 1875. xix,734p. illus., facsim., geneal. tables – 1 – us U.W. Library [920]
VISITATION RETURNS 1766-1815 / Lambeth Palace. Library – (including the Canterbury Peculiars). With printed index – 1 – £1,795.00 – uk World [240]
UNE VISITE AUX COLONIES DE LA REPUBLIQUE ARGENTINE / Peyret, Alexis – Paris. 1889. ii, 372p. (Travel series) – 9 – 12.00 – fr Bibl Nationale [910]
UNE VISITE CHEZ LE CAPITAINE B.. / Bellevue, Jean – Montreal: G.E. Desbarats, 1874. 00116. (Pre-1900 Canadiana) – 9 – cn C.I.H.M. [830]
UNE VISITE DANS LES ECOLES DU MANITOBA / Lacasse, Zacharie – Montreal: Librairie Saint Joseph: Cadieux & Derome, 1897. SEM105P455 – 1mf – 9 – Can$2.25 – cn Bibl Nat [370]
VISITE PASTORALE DU DIOCESE DE DIE PAR CHARLES-JACQUES DE LEBERON / Chevalier, Jules – 1644. Reprod. du "Bulletin de la Societe d'archeologie et de statistique de la Drome", 1912-13. c.200p. (Religion series) – 9 – 9.00 – fr Bibl Nationale [240]
LE VISITEUR DU PAUVRE / Gerando, J M de – (Condition of 19th C. French working class series). 1820 – 9 – fr Hachette [360]
VISITING JUDGES IN FEDERAL DISTRICT COURTS / Steinstra, Donna – Washington: FJC, 1985 – 1mf – 9 – $1.50 – LLMC 95-328 – us L.L.M.C. [340]
VISITING LECTURE SERIES / Texas A & M University. Department of Recreation and Parks – No.1-7. 1968-71. 2 fiches – 9 – us Spaulding [630]
THE VISITOR – Baltimore. Md. 1925 – 1 – us A.J.P.C. [071]
VISITOR – Central Falls. R.I. -w. 1869-91 – 1 – us UMI [071]
VISITOR – Providence. RI.1875-84 – 1 – us UMI [071]
VISITOR – Richmond. v1-2. feb 1809-aug 1810 – 1 – D4103 – us UMI [073]
VISITOR'S LESSON LEAFLETS – 1939-61 – 1 – 169.68 – us Baptist [240]
VISITOR'S REGISTER / Defiance County, Ohio. County Home – 1880-1951 – 1r – 1 – $32.50r – us Archival [324]
VISITORS REGISTERS / Williams County. Ohio. County Home – 1874-1953 – 1r – 1 – $32.50r – us Archival [324]
Viskovatov, A *see* KRATKAIA ISTORIIA PERVOGO KADETSKOGO KORPUSA
VISNIK AKADEMII NAUK URSR – Kiev, 1928-70. Lacking many issues. BR-10,479/1 – 9 – ne IDC [500]
VISOES DE HOJE : PERIODICO LITTERARIO – Manaos, Amazonas. 15 Nov 1908; Ago, 5 Nov 1910 – 1,5,6 – bl Biblioteca [072]
Visscher, L G *see* CHRONOLOGISCHE TAFEL VOOR DE GESCHIEDENIS DER ISRAELIETEN IN NEDERLAND
Visscher, R *see*
- SINNEPOPPEN
- SINNEPOPPEN VAN ROEMER VISSCHER
- ZINNE-POPPEN

Visschers, P *see* ONUITGE GEVEN BRIEVEN VAN EENIGE PATERS DER SOCIETEIT VAN JESUS, MISSIONARISSEN IN CHINA VAN DE 17 EN 18 EEUW
Visseq, Alexandre *see* GRAMMAIRE FIOTE
Visser, G *see* HENDRIK MANDE, BIJDRAGE TOT DE KENNIS DER NOORD-NEDERLANDSCHE MYSTIEK
Vissiere, A *see* SOUMISSION DES TRIBUS MUSULMANES DU TURKESTAN PAR LA CHINE (1757-1759) (APPENDICE TROIS LETTRES DE L'EMPEREUR K'IEN-LONG AU KHAN DE BADAKCHAN)
VISTA – New York. v1-9. jul 1965-dec 1973 1; v8-9 jul 1972-dec 1973 1,5 – 1,5 – D6884 – us UMI [073]
VISTA – (v1 1988 v3 1990 Can$20.00y. v2 1989 Can$28.00y. Ceased v3 no 3 1990) – Toronto. v1-3. 1988-1990 – 9 – cn Micromedia [338]
VISTA GENERAL DEL BARRIO JUDIO DE HERVAS – 1 – sp Bibl Santa Ana [946]
VISTA VOICE – Vista, CA. 1990-1991 – 2r – 1 – $100.00 – H04076 – us Library Micro [071]
VISTAS IN ASTRONOMY – (Absorbed: Astronomy Quarterly 1992) – London. v1-41. 1955-97+ 1,5,9; v24 1980* 9; v30-32 1987-89* 9 – 1,5,9 – D49245 – us UMI [520]
VISTI – Kiev, USSR. Feb 29-Dec 13 1940; Jan 15-Feb 28 Apr 5-6 1941 – 1r – 1 – us L of C Photodup [072]
VISTI Z UKRAINY – (Backfile through 1998 $85r) – Ukraine, 1999- – 2r per y – 1 – $160.00 standing order – us Ross [072]
VISTNIK – Lvov. 1933-1934, year 1, vol. 1, no. 1-year 2, vol. 4, no. 12; 1935-1936, year 3, vol. 1, no. 1-year 4, vol. 4, no. 12; 1937-1938, year 5, vol. 1, no. 1-year 6, vol. 3, no. 9 – 1 – 35.00r – us Hoover Inst Photo [072]
VISTNIK = MESSENER – Pittsburgh, PA, 1941-1955 – 1r – 1 – us I.H.R.C. [071]
VISTO – 1989-1995 – 1r per y – 5,6 – Sfr428.00 – sz Infoprint [072]
VISUAL ANTHROPOLOGY / ed by Hockings, Paul – 9,5,1 – us Harwood [302]
VISUAL ARTS AND ARCHITECTURE SPECIALIST COLLECTION / ed by Fawcett, Trevor – 2 units per yr – ca 500mf per unit – 15 – uk Chadwyck [700]
VISUAL CATALOGUE OF FASHION AND COSTUME / Victoria and Albert Museum. London – (A chronological record of 4 centuries of Western fashion as illustrated in 4,500 engravings, drawings and designs. Includes b/w mf index) – 57 colour mf – 15 – $1,027.00 – 0-907696-02-3 – uk Emmett [740]
VISUAL CATALOGUE OF MINIATURE PAINTINGS / Victoria and Albert Museum. London – (V & A Museum's entire coll of miniatures, providing a source of 2,300 portraits. Accompanying catalogue lists details of artists and sitters) – 40 colour 2 b/w mf – 15,9 – $1,054.00 – 0-907696-00-7 – uk Emmett [750]
VISUAL COMMUNICATION PRODUCTS: (ARTIFICIAL) LIGHT – P/MS, University Park, PA. 1979 – 195p 8mf – 9 – $0.50f – us Lawrence Pub [720]
VISUAL COMMUNICATION PRODUCTS: BLACK, GRAY AND WHITE DRAWING MEDIA – Management Services, University Park, PA. 1975 – 40p 36 illus 1mf – 9 – $0.50f – us Lawrence Pub [720]
VISUAL COMMUNICATION PRODUCTS: FUNCTION – Pattee, University Park, PA. 1975 – 105p 5mf – 9 – $0.50f – us Lawrence Pub [720]
VISUAL COMMUNICATION PRODUCTS: FUNCTION 2 – P/MS, University Park, PA. 1976 – 186p 8mf – 9 – $0.50f – us Lawrence Pub [720]
VISUAL COMMUNICATION PRODUCTS: FUNCTION 2M – P/MS, University Park, PA. 1976 – 377p 16mf – 9 – $0.50f – us Lawrence Pub [720]
VISUAL COMMUNICATION PRODUCTS: LIGHT – P/MS, University Park, PA. 1976 – 500p 20mf – 9 – $0.50f – us Lawrence Pub [720]
VISUAL COMMUNICATION PRODUCTS: MOVEMENT – Pattee, University Park, PA. 1975 – 172p 7mf – 9 – $0.50f – us Lawrence Pub [720]
VISUAL COMMUNICATION PRODUCTS: MOVEMENT 2 – P/MS, University Park, PA. 1977 – 276p 12mf – 9 – $0.50f – us Lawrence Pub [720]
VISUAL COMMUNICATION PRODUCTS: SPACE – Pattee, University Park, PA. 1975 – 147p 6mf – 9 – $0.50f – us Lawrence Pub [720]
VISUAL COMMUNICATION PRODUCTS: SPACE 2 – P/MS, University Park, PA. 1976 – 205p 9mf – 9 – $0.50f – us Lawrence Pub [720]
VISUAL COMMUNICATION PRODUCTS: SPACE 2D – M.S., University Park, PA. 1976 – 61p 2mf – 9 – $0.50f – us Lawrence Pub [720]
VISUAL COMMUNICATION PRODUCTS: SPACE 4 – Pattee, University Park, PA. 1983. Space 3 is unpublished – 58p 3mf – 9 – $0.50f – us Lawrence Pub [720]
VISUAL COMMUNICATION PRODUCTS: SPACE 5 – Pattee, University Park, PA. 1983 – 119p 17mf – 9 – $0.50f – us Lawrence Pub [720]
VISUAL COMMUNICATION PRODUCTS: STRUCTURES – Pattee, University Park, PA. 1975 – 290p 6mf – 9 – $0.50f – us Lawrence Pub [720]
VISUAL COMMUNICATION PRODUCTS: STRUCTURES 2 – P/MS, University Park, PA. 1977 – 114p 5mf – 9 – $0.50f – us Lawrence Pub [720]
VISUAL COMMUNICATION PRODUCTS: STRUCTURES 3 – P/MS, University Park, PA. 1980 – 49p 2mf – 9 – $0.50f – us Lawrence Pub [720]
VISUAL COMMUNICATION PRODUCTS: STRUCTURES 4 – Pattee, University Park, PA. 1983 – 37p 2mf – 9 – $0.50f – us Lawrence Pub [720]
VISUAL COMMUNICATION PRODUCTS: STRUCTURES 5 – Pattee, University Park, PA. 1989 – 112p 4mf – 9 – $0.50f – us Lawrence Pub [720]
VISUAL COMMUNICATION PRODUCTS: SYSTEMS – Pattee, University Park, PA. 1975 – 135p 6mf – 9 – $0.50f – us Lawrence Pub [720]
VISUAL COMMUNICATION PRODUCTS: SYSTEMS 2 – P/MS, University Park, PA. 1977 – 106p 5mf – 9 – $0.50f – us Lawrence Pub [720]
VISUAL COMMUNICATION PRODUCTS: SYSTEMS 3 – Pattee, University Park, PA. 1985 – 81p 4mf – 9 – $0.50f – us Lawrence Pub [720]
VISUAL COMMUNICATION PRODUCTS: SYSTEMS 4 – Pattee, University Park, PA. 1985 – 120p 5mf – 9 – $0.50f – us Lawrence Pub [720]
VISUAL COMPUTER – Berlin. v1-10 jun 1985-sep 1994*. v11-13 1995-97+ 1; v5-10 1989-sep 1994*. v11-13 1995-97+ 1,5,9 – 1,5,9 – D16976 – us UMI [000]
VISUAL CUE UTILIZATION IN SKILLED SOFTBALL PLAYERS / Nevole, George J, Jr. – 1988 – 158p 2mf – 9 – $8.00 – us Microform Publ [790]
VISUAL EDUCATION – (Publication is believed to have ceased with apr 1980) – London. 1950-75* 1; 1976-apr 1980 1,5,9 – 1,5,9 – D11321 – us UMI [370]
VISUAL MEDIA = MEDIAS VISUELS – Etobicoke. v1-6. 1988/89-1993/94 – 9 – Can$20.00y – cn Micromedia [380]
VISUAL MERCHANDISING – (Cont: Display World. Cont by: Visual Merchandising & Store Design) – Cincinnati. v102-113. jun 1973-dec 1982 1,5; v105-113 1975-82 9 – 1,5,9 – D244.01 – us UMI [330]
VISUAL MERCHANDISING *see* VISUAL MERCHANDISING AND STORE DESIGN
VISUAL MERCHANDISING AND STORE DESIGN – (Cont: Visual Merchandising) – Cincinnati. v114-128. 1983-97+ – 1,5,9 – D244.02 – us UMI [330]
VISUAL MERCHANDISING & STORE DESIGN *see* VISUAL MERCHANDISING
VISUAL NEUROSCIENCE – New York. v1-13 1988-94*. v14-19 1995-97+ – 1 – D17121 – us UMI [574]
VISUAL PRETRAINING EFFECTS ON COINCIDENT TIMING SKILL ACQUISITION AND RETENTION / Pellett, Tracy L – 1990 – 2mf – 9 – $8.00 – us Microform Publ [150]
VISUAL RESOURCES : AN INTERNATIONAL JOURNAL OF DOCUMENTATION / ed by Roberts, Helene E & Sundt, Christine L – 9,5,1 – us Gordon [020]
VISVA-BHARATI QUARTERLY – 1923- 1; 1975-5,6,9 – us UMI [073]
VISVA-BHARATI QUARTERLY – v. 1-29. Santiniketan. 1923-64. BI-120 2 – 310mf – 8 – ne IDC [073]
VISWAKERALAM – Trivandrum, India. Jul-Sept 1966 – 1r – 1 – us L of C Photodup [072]
Vita, A de *see* BATTAGLIONE GARIBALDI, OTTOBRE 1936-APRILE 1937
VITA ADAE ET EVAE / ed by Meyer, Wilhelm – Abaw PP 14. Bd. 3. Abt. – 2mf – 8 – ne Slangenburg [220]
VITA ANSKARII AUCTORE RIMBERTO (MGH 7: 55.BD) : ACCEDIT VITA RIMBERTI – 1884 – Dfl9.00 – ne Slangenburg [240]
DIE VITA ANTONII ALS GESCHICHTSQUELLE NACHRICHTEN D. AKADEMIE D. WISSENSCHAFTEN IN GOETTINGEN / Doerries, H – 1949 – 4mf – 8 – ne Slangenburg [240]
VITA BENEDICTI IMAGINIBUS EXPRESSA CUM VERSIBUS – ca 30p + c 2 color mf – ca DM380.00 – 3-89219-021-6 – gw Lengenfelder [090]
VITA BENNONIS 2 (MGH 7: 56.BD) : EPISCOPI OSNABRUGENSIS AUCTORE NORTBERTO ABBATE IBURGENSI – 1902 – Dfl6.00 – ne Slangenburg [240]
VITA BULGARA – Sofia, Bulgaria. Aug 1940-Aug 1941 – 1r – 1 – us L of C Photodup [949]
VITA. DA LUI MEDESIMO SCRITTA / Cellini, B – O-975 1. 1728 – 9 – ne IDC [920]
LE VITA DE' PITTORI, SCULTORI ET ARCHITETTI MODERNI / Bellori, Giovanni Pietro – O-978 1. 1728 – 9 – ne IDC [700]
VITA DEL BEATO CLEMENTE MA. HOFBAUER : SACERDOTE E PROPAGATORE INSIGNE DELLA CONGREGAZIONE DEL SS. REDENTORE / Haringer, Michael – (Includes bibliographical references) – Roma: Monaldi, 1887 – 1mf – 9 – 0-8370-7704-4 – 1986-1704 – us A.T.L.A. [920]
VITA DEL BEATO GIOVANNI GRANDE DETTO IL PECADOR : RELIGIOSO PROFESSO DELL'ORDINE OSPITALIERO DI SAN GIOVANNI DI DIO – Roma: G A Bertinelli, 1853 – 1mf – 9 – 0-8370-7503-3 – 1986-1503 – us A.T.L.A. [920]
VITA DEL CAVALIERE GIO. LORENZO BERNINO / Baldinucci, Filippo – Firenze. 1682. BO-136 1 – 9 – ne IDC [920]
VITA DEL CAVALIERE GIO. LORENZO BERNINO / Baldinucci, Filippo – O 974. 1682 – 9 – ne IDC [920]
VITA DEL GRAZIOSISSIMO PITTORE FRANCESCO MAZZOLA, DETTO IL PARMIGIANINO / Affo, I – O-1064. 1784 – 9 – ne IDC [750]
VITA DELL' INVITTISSIMO, E SACRATISSIMO IMPERATOR CARLO 5. ... / Ulloa, Antonio de – Venetia, 1574 – 8mf – 9 – H-8345/1 – ne IDC [956]
VITA DELLA B. GIOVANNA DI LESTONNAC : BARONESSA DI MONTFERRANT-LANDIRAS: FONDATRICE DELL'ORDINE DELLE FIGLIE DI NOSTRA SIGNORA / Sardi, Vincenzo – Roma: Tipografia Vaticana, 1900 – 1mf – 9 – 0-8370-6698-0 – 1986-0698 – us A.T.L.A. [920]
VITA DI GIACOPE ROBUSTI DETTO IL TINTERETTO... / Ridolfi, C – Venetia, 1642 – 9 – ne IDC [750]
VITA DI GIACOPO ROBUSTI DETTO IL TINTORETTO / Ridolfi, C – O 1077 1. 1642 – 9 – ne IDC [920]
VITA DI SANCTI PADRI – 1468. Holkham ms. 130. Holkham Hall, Norfolk, England – 1 – uk Microform Academic [025]
VITA, ELOGIO E MEMORIE DELL' EGREGIO PITTORE PIETRO PERUGINO F. DEGLI SCOLARI DI ESSO / Orsini, B – BO 967 1804 – 9 – ne IDC [920]
VITA GALENI PERGAMENI EX GALENOPSO / Laguna, A de – Venecia, 1548 – 7mf – 9 – sp Cultura [610]
VITA HEINRICI 4 IMPERATORIS (MGH 7: 58.BD) – Ed 3a. 1899 – Dfl6.00 – ne Slangenburg [240]
LA VITA INTERNATIONALE – Milan. Anno: 9-17; 1906-1914. Missing: nos. 18-24, 1914 – 1 – 35.00r – us Hoover Inst Photo [073]
LA VITA ITALIANA – San Francisco, CA. May 1910-1912 – 5r – 1 – $250.00 – B02832 – us Library Micro [071]
VITA MEINWERCI EPISCOPI PATHERBRUNNENSIS (MGH 7: 59.BD) – 1921 – Dfl19.00 – ne Slangenburg [240]
VITA NUOVO – Rock Springs, WY. Feb 1908-Oct 1909 – 1r – 1 – us I.H.R.C. [071]
VITA NUOVO – Rock Springs, Wyoming. -w. 7 Feb 1908-23 Oct 1909. 1 reel – 1 – us I.H.R.C. [071]
VITA, PASSIO ET RESURRECTIO IESU CHRISTI, VARIJS ICONIBUS A CELEBERRIMO PICTORE M. D. V. EXPRESSA, AB ADRINO COLLART NUNC PRIMUM IN AES INCISIS / Vos, M de – s.l., s.a. BO-1087 1 – 9 – ne IDC [240]
VITA SACKVILLE WEST AND HAROLD NICOLSON : MSS., LETTERS AND DIARIES / Sackville West, Vita & Nicolson, Harold – From Sissinghurst Castle, Kent; the Huntington Library, California; and other Libraries – 1 – us Primary [420]
VITA SANCTAE HILDEGARDIS – 1993 – 3mf – 9 – Bf1,300.00 – 2-503-64262-4 – be Brepols [450]
VITA SANCTI PAVLI APOSTOLI,... / Major, G – VVittembergae, 1556 – 1mf – ne IDC [240]
VITA...CONRADI GESNERI TIGURINI, CONSCRIPTA A IOSIA SIMLERO TIGURINO / Simmler, J – Tiguri: Froschoverus, 1566 – 2mf – ne IDC [580]

VITAE AC GESTA ABBATUM ADWERDENSIUM / Koppius, F – Groningae, 1850 – Dfl9.00 – ne Slangenburg [240]
VITAE ALIAEQUE HISTORIAE MINORES (SUPPL. TOM. 1-12, PARS 3) (MGH 5: 15.BD) : SUPPL. TOMI 13 – 1887-1888 – Dfl126.00 – ne Slangenburg [240]
VITAE ET ICONES SVLTANORVM TVRCICORVM, PRINCIPVM PERSORVM... / Boissard, J J – Francforti ad Moenum, 1596 – 4mf – 9 – H-8385/1 – ne IDC [956]
VITAE ILLUSTRIUM MEDICORUM... / Castellano, P – Amberes, 1617 – 5mf – 9 – sp Cultura [610]
VITAE PAPARUM AVENIONENSIUM / Baluzius, Stephanus; ed by Mollat, G – New ed par G. Paris. Tome 1-4. 1916-1922 – 47mf – 8 – Dfl165.00 – ne Slangenburg [240]
VITAE PATRUM : UNTERSUCHUNGEN UEBER TEXT, SYNTAX UND WORTSCHATZ DER SPAETLATEINISCHEN VITAE PATRUM / Salonius, A H – 1920 – 12mf – 9 – ne Slangenburg [240]
VITAE PATRVM, IN VSUM MINISTRORUM VERBI, QUO AD EIUS FIERI POTUIT REPURGATAE / Major, G – VVittembergae, 1544 – 8mf – ne IDC [240]
VITAE SANCTAE KATHARINAE – 1992 – 14mf – 9 – Bf2,875.00 – 2-503-64192-X – be Brepols [240]
VITAE SANCTI BONIFATII ARCHIEPISCOPI MOGUNTINI (MGH 7: 57.BD) – 1905 – Dfl25.00 – ne Slangenburg [240]
VITAE SANCTORUM HIBERNIAE / Plummer, Ch – Oxford. Tom 1-2. 1910 – Dfl63.00 – ne Slangenburg [240]
VITAL AND SOCIAL STATISTICS / Putnam County. Ohio. Probate Court – 1873-1908 – 1r – 1 – $32.50r – us Archival [324]
Vital, Antonio Alonso *see* SOLIDARIDAD HUMANA
VITAL CHRISTIANITY – (Title varies: Gospel Trumpet) – 1881-1992 – 93r – 1 – ATLA S0051 – us A.T.L.A. [073]
VITAL HISTORICAL RECORDS OF JACKSON COUNTY / Daughters of American Revolution. Kansas City Chapter – 1826-76.Kansas City, 1933-34. Missouri Reel 20. (The Cox Library Collection) – 5 – us Americana [978]
VITAL ISSUES – Washington. v1-33. 1951-84 1; v21-33 1971-84 5; v27-33 1977-84 9 – 1,5,9 – D6774 – us UMI [073]
VITAL NOTES ON MEDICAL PERIODICALS – Chicago. 1952-72* – 1 – D8053 – us UMI [610]
VITAL QUESTIONS: THE DISCUSSIONS OF THE GENERAL CHRISTIAN CONFERENCE...OCTOBER 22ND TO 25TH / Christian Conference. 1888. Montreal, Quebec – Under the auspices and direction of the Montreal branch of the Evangelical Alliance. Montreal: W. Drsydale, 1889. 00635. (Pre-1900 Canadiana) – 9 – cn C.I.H.M. [240]
VITAL RECORDS OF ABINGTON MASSACHUSETTS TO 1850 – (mf ed 1912) – 2mf – 9 – us Holbrook [920]
VITAL RECORDS OF ACTON MASSACHUSETTS TO 1850 – (mf ed 1923) – 1mf – 9 – us Holbrook [920]
VITAL RECORDS OF ALFORD MASSACHUSETTS TO 1850 – (mf ed 1902) – 1mf – 9 – us Holbrook [920]
VITAL RECORDS OF AMESBURY MASSACHUSETTS TO 1850 – (mf ed 1913) – 2mf – 9 – us Holbrook [920]
VITAL RECORDS OF ANDOVER MASSACHUSETTS TO 1850 – Topsfield: Topsfield Historical Society, 1912 – 3mf – 9 – us Holbrook [920]
VITAL RECORDS OF ARLINGTON MASSACHUSETTS TO 1850 – Boston: New England Historic Genealogical Society, 1904 – 1mf – 9 – us Holbrook [920]
VITAL RECORDS OF ASHBURNHAM MASSACHUSETTS TO 1850 – Worcester: Franklin P. Rice, 1909 – 1mf – 9 – us Holbrook [920]
VITAL RECORDS OF ASHFIELD MASSACHUSETTS TO 1850 – Boston: New England Genealogical Society, 1942 – 1mf – 9 – us Holbrook [920]
VITAL RECORDS OF ATHOL MASSACHUSETTS TO 1850 – Worcester: Franklin P. Rice, 1910 – 1mf – 9 – us Holbrook [920]
VITAL RECORDS OF ATTLEBOROUGH MASSACHUSETTS TO 1850 – Salem: The Essex Institute, 1934 – 2mf – 9 – us Holbrook [920]
VITAL RECORDS OF AUBURN MASSACHUSETTS TO 1850 – Worcester: Franklin P. Rice, 1900 – 1mf – 9 – us Holbrook [920]
VITAL RECORDS OF BARRE MASSACHUSETTS TO 1850 – Worcester; Franklin P. Rice, 1903 – 1mf – 9 – us Holbrook [920]
VITAL RECORDS OF BECKETT MASSACHUSETTS TO 1850 – Boston: New England Historic Genealogical Society, 1903 – 1mf – 9 – us Holbrook [920]
VITAL RECORDS OF BEDFORD MASSACHUSETTS TO 1850 – Boston: New England Historic Genealogical Society, 1903 – 1mf – 9 – us Holbrook [920]
VITAL RECORDS OF BELLINGHAM MASSACHUSETTS TO 1850 – Boston: New England Historic Genealogical Society, 1904 – 1mf – 9 – us Holbrook [920]
VITAL RECORDS OF BEVERLY MASSACHUSETTS TO 1850 – Topsfield: Topsfield Historical Society, 1906 – 3mf – 9 – us Holbrook [920]
VITAL RECORDS OF BILLERICA MASSACHUSETTS TO 1850 – Boston: New England Historic Genealogical Society, 1908 – 1mf – 9 – us Holbrook [920]
VITAL RECORDS OF BOLTON MASSACHUSETTS TO 1850 – Worcester: Franklin P. Rice, 1910 – 1mf – 9 – us Holbrook [920]
VITAL RECORDS OF BRAINTREE MASSACHUSETTS TO 1850 – Braintree: Town, 1886 – 3mf – 9 – us Holbrook [920]
VITAL RECORDS OF BREWSTER MASSACHUSETTS TO 1850 – Boston: Massachusetts Society of Mayflower Descendants, 1904 – 1mf – 9 – us Holbrook [920]
VITAL RECORDS OF BRIDGEWATER MASSACHUSETTS TO 1850 – Boston: New England Historic Genealogical Society, 1916 – 3mf – 9 – us Holbrook [920]
VITAL RECORDS OF BRIMFIELD MASSACHUSETTS TO 1850 – Boston: New England Historic Genealogical Society, 1931 – 1mf – 9 – us Holbrook [920]
VITAL RECORDS OF BROCKTON MASSACHUSETTS TO 1850 – Boston: New England Historic Genealogical Society, 1911 – 1mf – 9 – us Holbrook [920]
VITAL RECORDS OF BROOKFIELD MASSACHUSETTS TO 1850 – Worcester: Franklin P. Rice, 1909 – 2mf – 9 – us Holbrook [920]
VITAL RECORDS OF BROOKLINE MASSACHUSETTS TO 1850 – Salem: The Essex Institute, 1929 – 1mf – 9 – us Holbrook [920]
VITAL RECORDS OF BUCKLAND MASSACHUSETTS TO 1850 – Salem: The Essex Institute, 1934 – 1mf – 9 – us Holbrook [920]
VITAL RECORDS OF BURLINGTON MASSACHUSETTS TO 1850 – Boston: Thomas W. Baldwin, 1915 – 1mf – 9 – us Holbrook [920]
VITAL RECORDS OF CAMBRIDGE MASSACHUSETTS TO 1850 – Boston: Thomas W. Baldwin, 1914 – 5mf – 9 – us Holbrook [920]
VITAL RECORDS OF CANTON AND STOUGHTON MASSACHUSETTS TO 1850 – Canton: Town of Canton, 1896 – 1mf – 9 – us Holbrook [920]
VITAL RECORDS OF CARLISLE MASSACHUSETTS TO 1850 – Salem: The Essex Institute, 1918 – 1mf – 9 – us Holbrook [920]
VITAL RECORDS OF CARVER MASSACHUSETTS TO 1850 – Boston: New England Historic & Genealogical Society, 1911 – 1mf – 9 – us Holbrook [920]
VITAL RECORDS OF CHARLEMONT MASSACHUSETTS TO 1850 – Boston: New England Historic & Genealogical Society, 1917 – 1mf – 9 – us Holbrook [920]
VITAL RECORDS OF CHARLTON MASSACHUSETTS TO 1850 – Worcester: Franklin P. Rice, 1905 – 1mf – 9 – us Holbrook [920]
VITAL RECORDS OF CHELMSFORD MASSACHUSETTS TO 1850 – Salem: The Essex Institute, 1914 – 2mf – 9 – us Holbrook [920]
VITAL RECORDS OF CHELSEA MASSACHUSETTS TO 1850 – Boston: Thomas W. Baldwin, 1916 – 2mf – 9 – us Holbrook [920]
VITAL RECORDS OF CHESTER MASSACHUSETTS TO 1850 – Boston: New England Historic & Genealogical Society, 1911 – 1mf – 9 – us Holbrook [920]
VITAL RECORDS OF CHILMARK MASSACHUSETTS TO 1850 – Boston: New England Historic & Genealogical Society, 1904 – 1mf – 9 – us Holbrook [920]
VITAL RECORDS OF COHASSET MASSACHUSETTS TO 1850 – Boston: Thomas W. Baldwin, 1916 – 1mf – 9 – us Holbrook [920]
VITAL RECORDS OF COLRAIN MASSACHUSETTS TO 1850 – Salem: The Essex Institute, 1934 – 1mf – 9 – us Holbrook [920]
VITAL RECORDS OF CONCORD MASSACHUSETTS TO 1850 – Concord: Town of Concord, 1891 – 2mf – 9 – us Holbrook [920]
VITAL RECORDS OF CONWAY MASSACHUSETTS TO 1850 – Boston: New England Historic & Genealogical Society, 1943 – 1mf – 9 – us Holbrook [920]
VITAL RECORDS OF DALTON MASSACHUSETTS TO 1850 – Boston: New England Historic & Genealogical Society, 1906 – 1mf – 9 – us Holbrook [920]
VITAL RECORDS OF DANA MASSACHUSETTS TO 1850 – Boston: Thomas W. Baldwin, 1925 – 1mf – 9 – us Holbrook [920]
VITAL RECORDS OF DANVERS MASSACHUSETTS TO 1850 – Salem: The Essex Institute, 1909 – 3mf – 9 – us Holbrook [920]
VITAL RECORDS OF DARTMOUTH MASSACHUSETTS TO 1850 – Boston: New England Historic & Genealogical Society, 1929 – 3mf – 9 – us Holbrook [920]
VITAL RECORDS OF DEERFIELD MASSACHUSETTS TO 1850 – Boston: Thomas W. Baldwin, 1920 – 1mf – 9 – us Holbrook [920]
VITAL RECORDS OF DOUGLAS MASSACHUSETTS TO 1850 – Worcester: Franklin P. Rice, 1906 – 1mf – 9 – us Holbrook [920]
VITAL RECORDS OF DOVER MASSACHUSETTS TO 1850 – Boston: New England Historic & Genealogical Society, 1908 – 1mf – 9 – us Holbrook [920]
VITAL RECORDS OF DRACUT MASSACHUSETTS TO 1850 – Boston: New England Historic & Genealogical Society, 1907 – 1mf – 9 – us Holbrook [920]
VITAL RECORDS OF DUDLEY MASSACHUSETTS TO 1850 – Worcester: Franklin P. Rice, 1908 – 1mf – 9 – us Holbrook [920]
VITAL RECORDS OF DUNSTABLE MASSACHUSETTS TO 1850 – Salem: The Essex Institute, 1913 – 1mf – 9 – us Holbrook [920]
VITAL RECORDS OF DUXBURY MASSACHUSETTS TO 1850 – Boston: New England Historic & Genealogical Society, 1911 – 2mf – 9 – us Holbrook [920]
VITAL RECORDS OF EAST BRIDGEWATER MASSACHUSETTS TO 1850 – Boston: New England Historic & Genealogical Society, 1917 – 1mf – 9 – us Holbrook [920]
VITAL RECORDS OF EDGARTOWN MASSACHUSETTS TO 1850 – Boston: New England Historic & Genealogical Society, 1906 – 1mf – 9 – us Holbrook [920]
VITAL RECORDS OF ESSEX MASSACHUSETTS TO 1850 – Salem: The Essex Institute, 1908 – 1mf – 9 – us Holbrook [920]
VITAL RECORDS OF FITCHBURG MASSACHUSETTS TO 1850 – Fitchburg: Fitchburg Historical Society, 1899 – 3mf – 9 – us Holbrook [920]
VITAL RECORDS OF FOXBOROUGH MASSACHUSETTS TO 1850 – Boston: New England Historic & Genealogical Society, 1911 – 1mf – 9 – us Holbrook [920]
VITAL RECORDS OF FRAMINGHAM MASSACHUSETTS TO 1850 – Boston: Thomas W. Baldwin, 1911 – 2mf – 9 – us Holbrook [920]
VITAL RECORDS OF GARDNER MASSACHUSETTS TO 1850 – Worcester: Franklin P. Rice, 1907 – 1mf – 9 – us Holbrook [920]
VITAL RECORDS OF GEORGETOWN MASSACHUSETTS TO 1850 – Salem: The Essex Institute, 1928 – 1mf – 9 – us Holbrook [920]
VITAL RECORDS OF GILL MASSACHUSETTS TO 1850 – Boston: New England Historic & Genealogical Society, 1904 – 1mf – us Holbrook [920]
VITAL RECORDS OF GILL, MASSACHUSETTS TO THE YEAR 1850 – Boston, 1904. Massachusetts Reel 8. (The Cox Library Collection) – 5 – us Americana [978]
VITAL RECORDS OF GLOUCESTER MASSACHUSETTS TO 1850 – Topsfield: Topsfield Historical Society, 1917 – 5mf – 9 – us Holbrook [920]
VITAL RECORDS OF GRAFTON MASSACHUSETTS TO 1850 – Worcester: Franklin P. Rice, 1906 – 1mf – 9 – us Holbrook [920]
VITAL RECORDS OF GRANVILLE MASSACHUSETTS TO 1850 – Boston: New England Historic Genealogical Society, 1914 – 1mf – 9 – us Holbrook [920]
VITAL RECORDS OF GREAT BARRINGTON MASSACHUSETTS TO 1850 – Boston: New England Historic Genealogical Society, 1904 – 1mf – 9 – us Holbrook [920]
VITAL RECORDS OF GREENFIELD MASSACHUSETTS TO 1850 – Boston: New England Historic Genealogical Society, 1915 – 1mf – 9 – us Holbrook [920]
VITAL RECORDS OF GROTON MASSACHUSETTS TO 1850 – Salem: The Essex Institute, 1926 – 2mf – 9 – us Holbrook [920]
VITAL RECORDS OF HALIFAX MASSACHUSETTS TO 1850 – Boston: Massachusetts Society of Mayflower Descendants, 1905 – 1mf – 9 – us Holbrook [920]
VITAL RECORDS OF HAMILTON MASSACHUSETTS TO 1850 – Salem: The Essex Institute, 1908 – 1mf – 9 – us Holbrook [920]
VITAL RECORDS OF HANSON MASSACHUSETTS TO 1850 – Boston: New England Historic Genealogical Society, 1911 – 1mf – 9 – us Holbrook [920]
VITAL RECORDS OF HARDWICK MASSACHUSETTS TO 1850 – Boston: Thomas W. Baldwin, 1917 – 1mf – 9 – us Holbrook [920]
VITAL RECORDS OF HARVARD MASSACHUSETTS TO 1850 – Boston: Thomas W. Baldwin, 1917 – 1mf – 9 – us Holbrook [920]
VITAL RECORDS OF HAVERHILL MASSACHUSETTS TO 1850 – Topsfield: Topsfield Historical Society, 1910 – 2mf – 9 – us Holbrook [920]
VITAL RECORDS OF HEATH MASSACHUSETTS TO 1850 – Boston: New England Historic Genealogical Society, 1915 – 1mf – 9 – us Holbrook [920]
VITAL RECORDS OF HINSDALE MASSACHUSETTS TO 1850 – Boston: New England Historic Genealogical Society, 1902 – 1mf – 9 – us Holbrook [920]
VITAL RECORDS OF HOLDEN MASSACHUSETTS TO 1850 – Worcester: Franklin P. Rice, 1904 – 1mf – 9 – us Holbrook [920]
VITAL RECORDS OF HOLLISTON MASSACHUSETTS TO 1850 – Boston: New England Historic Genealogical Society, 1908 – 1mf – 9 – us Holbrook [920]
VITAL RECORDS OF HOPKINTON MASSACHUSETTS TO 1850 – Boston: New England Historic Genealogical Society, 1911 – 2mf – 9 – us Holbrook [920]
VITAL RECORDS OF HUBBARDSTON MASSACHUSETTS TO 1850 – Worcester: Franklin P. Rice, 1907 – 1mf – 9 – us Holbrook [920]
VITAL RECORDS OF HULL MASSACHUSETTS TO 1850 – Boston: Thomas W. Baldwin, 1911 – 1mf – 9 – us Holbrook [920]
VITAL RECORDS OF IPSWICH MASSACHUSETTS TO 1850 – Salem: The Essex Institute, 1910 – 3mf – 9 – us Holbrook [920]
VITAL RECORDS OF KINGSTON MASSACHUSETTS TO 1850 – Boston: New England Historic Genealogical Society, 1911 – 1mf – 9 – us Holbrook [920]
VITAL RECORDS OF LANCASTER MASSACHUSETTS TO 1850 – Lancaster: Town of Lancaster, 1890 – 2mf – 9 – us Holbrook [920]
VITAL RECORDS OF LAWRENCE MASSACHUSETTS TO 1850 – Salem: The Essex Institute, 1926 – 1mf – 9 – us Holbrook [920]
VITAL RECORDS OF LEE MASSACHUSETTS TO 1850 – Boston: New England Historic Genealogical Society, 1903 – 1mf – 9 – us Holbrook [920]

VITAL RECORDS OF LEICESTER MASSACHUSETTS TO 1850 – Worcester: Franklin P. Rice, 1903 – 1mf – 9 – us Holbrook [920]

VITAL RECORDS OF LONDONDERRY / Annis, Daniel G – Births, marriage intentions, marriages, and deaths from earliest date to 1910. Manchester Historic Asso., 1914. New Hampshire Reel 7. (The Cox Library Collection) – 5 – us Americana [920]

VITAL RECORDS OF MALDEN MASSACHUSETTS TO 1850 – Malden: City of Malden, 1903 – 1mf – 9 – us Holbrook [920]

VITAL RECORDS OF MANCHESTER MASSACHUSETTS TO 1850 – Salem: The Essex Institute, 1903 – 1mf – 9 – us Holbrook [920]

VITAL RECORDS OF MANSFIELD MASSACHUSETTS TO 1850 – Salem: The Essex Institute, 1933 – 1mf – 9 – us Holbrook [920]

VITAL RECORDS OF MARBLEHEAD MASSACHUSETTS TO 1850 – Salem: The Essex Institute, 1903 – 4mf – 9 – us Holbrook [920]

VITAL RECORDS OF MARLBOROUGH MASSACHUSETTS TO 1850 – Worcester: Franklin P. Rice, 1908 – 1mf – 9 – us Holbrook [920]

VITAL RECORDS OF MEDFIELD MASSACHUSETTS TO 1850 – Boston: New England Historic Genealogical Society, 1903 – 1mf – 9 – us Holbrook [920]

VITAL RECORDS OF MEDFORD MASSACHUSETTS TO 1850 – Boston: New England Historic Genealogical Society, 1907 – 2mf – 9 – us Holbrook [920]

VITAL RECORDS OF MEDWAY MASSACHUSETTS TO 1850 – Salem: The Essex Institute, 1905 – 1mf – 9 – us Holbrook [920]

VITAL RECORDS OF MENDON MASSACHUSETTS TO 1850 – Boston: Thomas W. Baldwin, 1920 – 2mf – 9 – us Holbrook [920]

VITAL RECORDS OF METHUEN MASSACHUSETTS TO 1850 – Topsfield: Topsfield Historical Society, 1909 – 1mf – 9 – us Holbrook [920]

VITAL RECORDS OF MIDDLEFIELD MASSACHUSETTS TO 1850 – Boston: New England Historic Genealogical Society, 1907 – 1mf – 9 – us Holbrook [920]

VITAL RECORDS OF MIDDLETON MASSACHUSETTS TO 1850 – Topsfield: Topsfield Historical Society, 1904 – 1mf – 9 – us Holbrook [920]

VITAL RECORDS OF MILFORD MASSACHUSETTS TO 1850 – Boston: Thomas W. Baldwin, 1917 – 1mf – 9 – us Holbrook [920]

VITAL RECORDS OF MILLBURY MASSACHUSETTS TO 1850 – Worcester: Franklin P. Rice, 1903 – 1mf – 9 – us Holbrook [920]

VITAL RECORDS OF MILTON MASSACHUSETTS TO 1850 – Milton: Town of Milton, 1900 – 1mf – 9 – us Holbrook [920]

VITAL RECORDS OF MONTAGUE MASSACHUSETTS TO 1850 – Salem: The Essex Institute, 1934 – 1mf – 9 – us Holbrook [920]

VITAL RECORDS OF MONTGOMERY MASSACHUSETTS TO 1850 – Boston: New England Historic Genealogical Society, 1902 – 1mf – 9 – us Holbrook [920]

VITAL RECORDS OF NANTUCKET MASSACHUSETTS TO 1850 – Boston: New England Historic Genealogical Society, 1925 – 7mf – 9 – $42.00 – us Holbrook [920]

VITAL RECORDS OF NATICK MASSACHUSETTS TO 1850 – Boston: Thomas W Baldwin, 1910 – 1mf – 9 – $6.00 – us Holbrook [920]

VITAL RECORDS OF NEW ASHFORD MASSACHUSETTS TO 1850 – Boston: New England Historic Genealogical Society, 1916 – 1mf – 9 – $6.00 – us Holbrook [920]

VITAL RECORDS OF NEW BEDFORD MASSACHUSETTS TO 1850 – Boston: New England Historic Genealogical Society, 1932 – 4mf – 9 – $24.00 – us Holbrook [920]

VITAL RECORDS OF NEW BRAINTREE MASSACHUSETTS TO 1850 – Boston: New England Historic Genealogical Society, 1904 – 1mf – 9 – $6.00 – us Holbrook [920]

VITAL RECORDS OF NEW BRAINTREE MASSACHUSETTS TO 1850 – Salem: Essex Institute, 1911 – 4mf – 9 – $24.00 – us Holbrook [920]

VITAL RECORDS OF NEW SALEM MASSACHUSETTS TO 1850 – Salem: Essex Institute, 1927 – 1mf – 9 – $6.00 – us Holbrook [920]

VITAL RECORDS OF NEWBURYPORT MASSACHUSETTS TO 1850 – Salem: Essex Institute, 1911 – 4mf – 9 – $24.00 – us Holbrook [920]

VITAL RECORDS OF NEWTON MASSACHUSETTS TO 1850 – Boston: New England Historic Genealogical Society, 1905 – 2mf – 9 – $12.00 – us Holbrook [920]

VITAL RECORDS OF NORTHBRIDGE MASSACHUSETTS TO 1850 – Boston: Thomas W Baldwin, 1916 – 1mf – 9 – $6.00 – us Holbrook [920]

VITAL RECORDS OF NORTON MASSACHUSETTS TO 1850 – Boston: New England Historic Genealogical Society, 1906 – 1mf – 9 – $6.00 – us Holbrook [920]

VITAL RECORDS OF OAKHAM MASSACHUSETTS TO 1850 – Worcester: Franklin P Rice, 1905 – 1mf – 9 – $6.00 – us Holbrook [920]

VITAL RECORDS OF OTIS MASSACHUSETTS TO 1850 – Boston: New England Historic Genealogical Society, 1941 – 1mf – 9 – $6.00 – us Holbrook [920]

VITAL RECORDS OF OXFORD MASSACHUSETTS TO 1850 – Worcester: Franklin P Rice, 1905 – 1mf – 9 – $6.00 – us Holbrook [920]

VITAL RECORDS OF PALMER MASSACHUSETTS TO 1850 – Boston: New England Historic Genealogical Society, 1941 – 1mf – 9 – us Holbrook [920]

VITAL RECORDS OF PELHAM MASSACHUSETTS TO 1850 – Boston: New England Historic Genealogical Society, 1902 – 1mf – 9 – us Holbrook [920]

VITAL RECORDS OF PEMBROKE MASSACHUSETTS TO 1850 – Boston: New England Historic Genealogical Society, 1911 – 1mf – 9 – $6.00 – us Holbrook [920]

VITAL RECORDS OF PERU MASSACHUSETTS TO 1850 – Boston: New England Historic Genealogical Society, 1902 – 1mf – 1 – $6.00 – us Holbrook [920]

VITAL RECORDS OF PETERSHAM MASSACHUSETTS TO 1850 – Worcester: Frank Rice, 1904 – 1mf – 9 – $6.00 – us Holbrook [920]

VITAL RECORDS OF PHILLIPSTON MASSACHUSETTS TO 1850 – Worcester: Frank Rice, 1906 – 1mf – 9 – $6.00 – us Holbrook [920]

VITAL RECORDS OF PLYMOUTH MASSACHUSETTS 1662-1839 – Boston: Massachusetts Society of Mayflower Descendant, 1899-1937 – 2mf – 9 – $12.00 – us Holbrook [920]

VITAL RECORDS OF PLYMPTON MASSACHUSETTS TO 1850 – Boston: New England Historic Genealogical Society, 1923 – 2mf – 9 – $12.00 – us Holbrook [920]

VITAL RECORDS OF PRINCETON MASSACHUSETTS TO 1850 – Worcester: Frank Rice, 1902 – 1mf – 9 – $6.00 – us Holbrook [920]

VITAL RECORDS OF READING MASSACHUSETTS TO 1850 – Boston: Thomas W Baldwin, 1912 – 2mf – 9 – us Holbrook [920]

VITAL RECORDS OF REHOBOTH MASSACHUSETTS TO 1850 / Arnold, James N – Providence: Narragansett Publ Co, 1897 – 3mf – 9 – us Holbrook [920]

VITAL RECORDS OF RICHMOND MASSACHUSETTS TO 1850 – Boston: New England Historic Genealogical Society, 1913 – 1mf – 9 – us Holbrook [920]

VITAL RECORDS OF ROCHESTER MASSACHUSETTS TO 1850 – Boston: New England Historic Genealogical Society, 1914 – 2mf – 9 – us Holbrook [920]

VITAL RECORDS OF ROCKPORT MASSACHUSETTS TO 1850 – Salem: Essex Institute, 1924 – 1mf – 9 – us Holbrook [920]

VITAL RECORDS OF ROWLEY MASSACHUSETTS TO 1850 – Boston: Thomas W Baldwin, 1928 – 2mf – 9 – us Holbrook [920]

VITAL RECORDS OF ROXBURY MASSACHUSETTS TO 1850 – Salem: Essex Institute, 1925 – 3mf – 9 – us Holbrook [920]

VITAL RECORDS OF ROYALSTON MASSACHUSETTS TO 1850 – Worcester: Frank P Rice, 1906 – 1mf – 9 – us Holbrook [920]

VITAL RECORDS OF RUTLAND MASSACHUSETTS TO 1850 – Worcester: Frank P Rice, 1905 – 1mf – 9 – us Holbrook [920]

VITAL RECORDS OF SALEM MASSACHUSETTS TO 1850 – Salem: Essex Institute, 1916-25 – 7mf – 9 – us Holbrook [920]

VITAL RECORDS OF SALISBURY MASSACHUSETTS TO 1850 – Topsfield Historical Society, 1915 – 2mf – 9 – us Holbrook [920]

VITAL RECORDS OF SANDISFIELD MASSACHUSETTS TO 1850 / Smith, Elizur Yale – Rutland, VT: The Tuttle Publ Co, 1936 – 1mf – 9 – us Holbrook [920]

VITAL RECORDS OF SAUGUS MASSACHUSETTS TO 1850 – Salem: Essex Institute, 1907 – 1mf – 9 – us Holbrook [920]

VITAL RECORDS OF SCITUATE MASSACHUSETTS TO 1850 – Boston: New England Historic Genealogical Society, 1909 – 3mf – 9 – us Holbrook [920]

VITAL RECORDS OF SHARON MASSACHUSETTS TO 1850 – Boston: Thomas W Baldwin, 1909 – 1mf – 9 – us Holbrook [920]

VITAL RECORDS OF SHELBURNE MASSACHUSETTS TO 1850 – Boston: New England Historic Genealogical Society, 1931 – 1mf – 9 – us Holbrook [920]

VITAL RECORDS OF SHERBORN MASSACHUSETTS TO 1850 – Boston: Thomas W Baldwin, 1911 – 1mf – 9 – us Holbrook [920]

VITAL RECORDS OF SHIRLEY MASSACHUSETTS TO 1850 – Boston: New England Historic Genealogical Society, 1918 – 1mf – 9 – us Holbrook [920]

VITAL RECORDS OF SHREWSBURY MASSACHUSETTS TO 1850 – Worcester: Franklin P Rice, 1904 – 1mf – 9 – us Holbrook [920]

VITAL RECORDS OF SOUTHBOROUGH MASSACHUSETTS TO 1850 – Worcester: Franklin P Rice, 1903 – 1mf – 9 – us Holbrook [920]

VITAL RECORDS OF SPENCER MASSACHUSETTS TO 1850 – Worcester: Franklin P Rice, 1909 – 1mf – 9 – us Holbrook [920]

VITAL RECORDS OF STONEHAM MASSACHUSETTS TO 1850 – Salem: Essex Institute, 1918 – 1mf – 9 – us Holbrook [920]

VITAL RECORDS OF STOW MASSACHUSETTS TO 1850 – Boston: New England Historic Genealogical Society, 1911 – 1mf – 9 – us Holbrook [920]

VITAL RECORDS OF STURBRIDGE MASSACHUSETTS TO 1850 – Boston: New England Historic Genealogical Society, 1906 – 1mf – 9 – us Holbrook [920]

VITAL RECORDS OF SUDBURY MASSACHUSETTS TO 1850 – Boston: New England Historic Genealogical Society, 1903 – 1mf – 9 – us Holbrook [920]

VITAL RECORDS OF SUTTON MASSACHUSETTS TO 1850 – Worcester: Franklin P Rice, 1907 – 2mf – 9 – us Holbrook [920]

VITAL RECORDS OF TAUNTON MASSACHUSETTS TO 1850 – Boston: New England Historic Genealogical Society, 1929 – 3mf – 9 – us Holbrook [920]

VITAL RECORDS OF TEMPLETON MASSACHUSETTS TO 1850 – Worcester: Franklin P Rice, 1907 – 1mf – 9 – us Holbrook [920]

VITAL RECORDS OF TEWKSBURY MASSACHUSETTS TO 1850 – Salem: Essex Institute, 1912 – 1mf – 9 – us Holbrook [920]

VITAL RECORDS OF TISBURY MASSACHUSETTS TO 1850 – Boston: New England Historic Genealogical Society, 1910 – 9 – us Holbrook [920]

VITAL RECORDS OF TOPSFIELD MASSACHUSETTS TO 1850 – Topsfield: Topsfield Historical Society, 1903 – 1mf – 9 – us Holbrook [920]

VITAL RECORDS OF TRURO MASSACHUSETTS TO 1850 / Bowman, George Ernest Bowman – Boston: Mayflower Society, 1933 – 2mf – 9 – us Holbrook [920]

VITAL RECORDS OF TYNGSBOROUGH MASSACHUSETTS TO 1850 – Salem: Essex Institute, 1913 – 1mf – 9 – us Holbrook [920]

VITAL RECORDS OF TYRINGHAM MASSACHUSETTS TO 1850 – Boston: New England Historic Genealogical Society, 1903 – 9 – us Holbrook [920]

VITAL RECORDS OF UPTON MASSACHUSETTS TO 1850 – Worcester: Franklin P Rice, 1904 – 1mf – 9 – us Holbrook [920]

VITAL RECORDS OF UXBRIDGE MASSACHUSETTS TO 1850 – Boston: Thomas W Baldwin, 1916 – 1mf – 9 – us Holbrook [920]

VITAL RECORDS OF WAKEFIELD MASSACHUSETTS TO 1850 – Boston: Thomas W Baldwin, 1912 – 1mf – 9 – us Holbrook [920]

VITAL RECORDS OF WALPOLE MASSACHUSETTS TO 1850 – Boston: New England Historic Genealogical Society, 1902 – 1mf – 9 – us Holbrook [920]

VITAL RECORDS OF WALTHAM MASSACHUSETTS TO 1850 – Boston: New England Historic Genealogical Society, 1904 – 1mf – 9 – us Holbrook [920]

VITAL RECORDS OF WARREN MASSACHUSETTS TO 1850 – Worcester: Franklin P Rice, 1910 – 1mf – 9 – us Holbrook [920]

VITAL RECORDS OF WASHINGTON MASSACHUSETTS TO 1850 – Boston: New England Historic Genealogical Society, 1904 – 1mf – 9 – us Holbrook [920]

VITAL RECORDS OF WAYLAND MASSACHUSETTS TO 1850 – Boston: New England Historic Genealogical Society, 1910 – 1mf – 9 – us Holbrook [920]

VITAL RECORDS OF WENHAM MASSACHUSETTS TO 1850 – Salem: Essex Institute, 1904 – 1mf – 9 – us Holbrook [920]

VITAL RECORDS OF WEST BOYLSTON MASSACHUSETTS TO 1850 – Worcester: Franklin P Rice, 1911 – 1mf – 9 – us Holbrook [920]

VITAL RECORDS OF WEST BRIDGEWATER MASSACHUSETTS TO 1850 – Boston: New England Historic Genealogical Society, 1911 – 1mf – 9 – us Holbrook [920]

VITAL RECORDS OF WEST NEWBURY MASSACHUSETTS TO 1850 – Salem: Essex Institute, 1910 – 1mf – 9 – us Holbrook [920]

VITAL RECORDS OF WEST SPRINGFIELD MASSACHUSETTS TO 1850 – Boston: New England Historic Genealogical Society, 1944 – 2mf – 9 – us Holbrook [920]

VITAL RECORDS OF WEST STOCKBRIDGE MASSACHUSETTS TO 1850 – Boston: New England Historic Genealogical Society, 1907 – 1mf – 9 – us Holbrook [920]

VITAL RECORDS OF WESTBOROUGH MASSACHUSETTS TO 1850 – Worcester: Franklin P Rice, 1903 – 1mf – 9 – us Holbrook [920]

VITAL RECORDS OF WESTFORD MASSACHUSETTS TO 1850 – Salem: Essex Institute, 1915 – 1mf – 9 – us Holbrook [920]

VITAL RECORDS OF WESTMINSTER MASSACHUSETTS TO 1850 – Worcester: Franklin P Rice, 1908 – 1mf – 9 – us Holbrook [920]

VITAL RECORDS OF WESTPORT MASSACHUSETTS TO 1850 – Boston: New England Historic Genealogical Society, 1918 – 1mf – 9 – us Holbrook [920]

VITAL RECORDS OF WEYMOUTH MASSACHUSETTS TO 1850 – Boston: New England Historic Genealogical Society, 1910 – 2mf – 9 – us Holbrook [920]

VITAL RECORDS OF WILLIAMSTOWN MASSACHUSETTS TO 1850 – Boston: New England Historic Genealogical Society, 1907 – 1mf – 9 – us Holbrook [920]

VITAL RECORDS OF WINCHENDON MASSACHUSETTS TO 1850 – Boston: New England Historic Genealogical Society, 1909 – 1mf – 9 – us Holbrook [920]

VITAL RECORDS OF WINDSOR MASSACHUSETTS TO 1850 – Boston: New England Historic Genealogical Society, 1917 – 1mf – 9 – us Holbrook [920]

VITAL RECORDS OF WORTHINGTON MASSACHUSETTS TO 1850 – Boston: New England Historic Genealogical Society, 1911 – 1mf – 9 – us Holbrook [920]
VITAL RECORDS OF WRENTHAM MASSACHUSETTS TO 1850 – Boston: Thomas W Baldwin, 1910 – 2mf – 9 – us Holbrook [920]
VITAL SPEECHES OF THE DAY – New York. v1-64. oct 1934-oct1998 1; v50 oct 1983-oct 1984*. v51-64 oct 1984-oct 1998+ 9 – 1,9 – D173 – us UMI [320]
VITAL SPEECHES OF THE DAY – v. 1-31. 1934-1965 – 1 – us Princeton Micro [850]
VITAL STATISTICS TABLES / Palestine. Department of Statistics – Jerusalem. 1922-45. BJ-28-120 1 – 9 – ne IDC [956]
THE VITALITY OF PLATONISM, AND OTHER ESSAYS / Adam, James; ed by Adam, Adele Marion – Cambridge: University Press; New York: Putnam, 1911 – 1mf – us A.T.L.A. [180]
VITAMIN E SUPPLEMENTATION, DELAYED-ONSET MUSCULAR SORENESS, MUSCLE TISSUE DAMAGE AND LIPID PEROXIDATION / Harris, Michael B – University of North Carolina at Chapel Hill, 1995 – 2mf – 9 – $8.00 – PH1462 – us Microform Publ [612]
VITAS SANCTORUM PATRUM EMERETENSIUM – 1992 – 2mf – 9 – Bf1,050.00 – 2-503-61162-1 – be Brepols [240]
VITCHIZNA – Kiev, 1941-72. Lacking many issues. BR-10,480/1 – 9 – ne IDC [947]
VITE DE PITTORI ANTICHI... / Dati, C R – Firenze, 1667 – 3mf – ne IDC [750]
LE VITE DE' PITTORI, DEGLI SCULTORI ET ARCHITETTI VERONESI / Pozzo, FB Dal. – Verona, 1718 – 7mf – ne IDC [700]
VITE DE' PITTORI E SCULTORI FERRARESE... / Baruffaldi, G – Ferrara. 2v. 1844-1846 – 22mf – ne IDC [700]
LE VITE DE' PITTORI, SCULTORI, ARCHITETTI, ED INTAGLIATORI 1572-1642 / Baglione, G – Napoli, 1733 – 4mf – ne IDC [700]
VITE DE' PITTORI, SCULTORI ED ARCHITETTI MODERNI... / Pascoli, L – Roma. 2v. 1730-1736 – 13mf – ne IDC [700]
VITE DE' PITTORI, SCULTORI ED ARCHITETTI PERUGINI / Pascoli, L – Roma, 1732 – 3mf – ne IDC [700]
LE VITE DE' PITTORI, SCULTORI ET ARCHITETTI 1572-1642 / Baglione, G – Roma, 1652 – 4mf – ne IDC [700]
LE VITE DE' PITTORI, SCULTORI ET ARCHITETTI MODERNI... / Bellori, Giovanni Pietro – Roma, 1728 – 6mf – ne IDC [700]
LE VITE DE' PITTORI, SCULTORI, ET ARCHITETTI MODERNI / Bellori, Giovanni Pietro – Roma, 1672 – 6mf – ne IDC [700]
LE VITE DE PITTORI, SCVLTORI ET ARCHITETTI MODERNI, SCRITTE DA GIO : PIETRO BELLORI. PARTE PRIMA... / Bellori, Giovanni Pietro – Roma, 1675 – 5mf – ne IDC [700]
VITE DE' PIU ECCELLENT PITTORI, SCULTORI E' ARCHITETTI / Vasari, Giorgio – Firenze. O 1062 1. 7 v. 1767-1772 – 9 – ne IDC [920]
LE VITE DE' PIU ECCELLENTI ARCHITETTI, PITTORI ET SCULTORI ITALIANI, DA CIMABUE INSINO A' TEMPI NOSTRI... / Vasari, Giorgio – Firenze. 2v. 1550 – 12mf – ne IDC [700]
VITE DE' PIU ECCELLENTI PITTORI SCULTORI E ARCHITETTI / Vasari, Giorgio; ed by Bottari, G – Roma, 1759-1760 – 35mf – ne IDC [700]
VITE DE' PIU ECCELLENTI PITTORI, SCULTORI E ARCHITETTI / Vasari, Giorgio – Firenze. 7v. 1767-1772 – 51mf – ne IDC [700]
LE VITE DE' PIU ECCELLENTI PITTORI, SCULTORI, E ARCHITETTORI / Vasari, Giorgio – Fiorenza. 3v. 1568 – 23mf – ne IDC [700]
LE VITE DE PIU ECCELLENTI PITTORI, SCULTORI ED ARCHITETTORI / Vasari, Giorgio; ed by Milanesi, G M – (Index) – Firenze. 8v. 1878-1885 – 74mf – ne IDC [700]
VITE DEGL' IMPERATORI DE TVRCHI... / Bertelle, P – Vicenza, 1599 – 2mf – 9 – H-8404/1 – ne IDC [945]
LE VITE DEGLI ARCADI ILLUSTRI-SCRITTE DA DIVERSI AUTORI / ed by Crescimbeni, Giovanni Mario – Pubblicate d'ordine della Generale adunanza...Roma: Antonio de'Rossi, 17? – 1 – us U.W. Library [920]
VITE DEI PITTORI ANTICHI GRECI E LATINI / Valle, G della – Siena, 1795 – 5mf – ne IDC [750]
VITE DEI PITTORI VECELLI DI CADORE / Ticozzi, S – O 1073 1. 1817 – 9 – ne IDC [920]
VITE DE'PITTORI, SCULTORI ED ARCHITETTI MODERNI / Pascoli, L – O-1070 1. 2 v. 1730-1736 – 9 – ne IDC [920]
VITE DE'PITTORI, SCULTORI ED ARCHITETTI PERUGINI / Pascoli, L – O-1071 1. 1732 – 9 – ne IDC [920]
Viteau, Joseph *see*
– ETUDE SUR LE GREC DU NOUVEAU TESTAMENT
– ETUDE SUR LE GREC DU NOUVEAU TESTAMENT COMPARE AVEC CELUI DES SEPTANTE
Viterbo, Sousa *see* TRABALHOS NAUTICOS DOS PORTUGUEZES NOS SECULOS 16 E 17
Viteri, Jacqueline E *see* THE EFFECTS OF TELEVISION VIEWING ON THE SELF-REGULATION OF EXERCISE INTENSITY
VITJAZ' – NR. 1-2. Belgrad. 1922. BR-3480 2 – 8 – ne IDC [460]
Vitman, F *see* SUMMA PLANTARUM
Vito, L de *see* VOCABOLARIO DELLA LINGUA TIGRIGNA
Vitoria. Spain (Diocese) *see* EL CLERO VASCO, FIEL AL GOBIERNO DE LA REPUBLICA, SE DIRIGE AL SUMO PONTIFICE
VITORIA Y CARLOS 5TH EN LA SOBERANIA HISPANOAMERICANA. SALAMANCA, 1937 / Andres Marcos, Teodoro – Burgos: Razon y Fe, 1938 – 1 – sp Bibl Santa Ana [970]
Vitorino, Maria R *see* PARTICIPANTS BENEFITS ASSESSMENT AT A CAMPUS RECREATIONAL FACILITY
Vitoshinskii, E M *see* UKAZATEL' IMMENOI I PREDMETNYI K TRUDU A.V. GORSKOGO I K.I. NEVOSTRUEVA: OPISANIE SLAVIANSKIKH RUKOPISEI MOSKOVSKOI SINODAL'NOI BIBLIOTEKI
Vitruve, Marc *see*
– ARCHITECTURE OU ART DE BIEN BASTIR
– LES DIX LIVRES D'ARCHITECTURE DE VITRUVE
Vitruvio, M *see*
– DE ARCHITECTURA
– DE ARCHITECTURA, ALCALA DE HENARES, 1582
VITRUVIUS BRITANNICUS / Campbell, Colin – O-189. 5 v. 1715-1771 – 9 – ne IDC [720]
Vittadini, C *see*
– DESCRIZIONE DEI FUNGHI MANGERECCI PIU COMUNI DELL' ITALIA E DE VELENOSI CHE POSSONO CO' MEDESIMI CONFONDERSI
– MONOGRAPHIA LYCOPERDINEORUM AUGUSTAE TAURINORUM, 1842
– MONOGRAPHIA TUBERACEARUM
– TENTAMEN MYCOLOGIUM SEU AMANITARUM ILLUSTRATIO
LA VITTORIA – New York, NY. 1940 – us I.H.R.C. [071]
LA VITTORIA – Toronto. 1942-43 – 1 – 65.00 – cn McLaren [072]
VITTORIA ACCOROMBONA : EIN ROMAN / Tieck, Ludwig – Stuttgart: J G Cotta, Kroener, [18–?] – 1r – 1 – us U.W. Library [830]
Vitvits'ka, O *see* VODIANI ZNAKY NA PAPERI UKRAJINS'KIKH DOKUMENTIV XVI I XVII VV. (1566-1651)
Viu, Jose de *see*
– ANTIGUEDADES DE EXTREMADURA
– COLECCION...ANTIGUEDADES DE ESTREMADURA (SIC)
– EXTREMADURA...INSCRIPCIONES Y DOCUMENTOS
– TRATADO RELIGIOSO...ANTIGUEDADES DE ESTREMADURA
Viunova, N M et al *see* DIREKTIVY GLAVNOGO KOMANDOVANIIA KRASNOI ARMII, 1917-1920
Vivaldi, A *see* [ESTRO ARMONICO, N 3] VIVALDI'S 3D CONCERTO, CON VIOLINO SOLO OBLIGATO
Vivaldi, Antonio *see*
– [ESTRO ARMONICO, N 12] VIVALDI'S 5TH CONCERTO
– L'ESTRO ARMONICO, OP. 3, NO. 5
VIVE LA PROTECTION: BROCHURE CONTRE LE LIBRE ECHANGE OU LA RECIPROCITE ILLIMITEE D'APRES M.C. BEAUSOLEIL – Montreal, 1891. 03180. (Pre-1900 Canadiana) – 9 – cn C.I.H.M. [971]
VIVE LAURIER : MARCHE BRILLANTE POUR PIANO / Contant, Alexis – Montreal: J G Yon, 1897. SEM105P905 – 1mf – 9 – Can$2.25 – cn Bibl Nat [780]
VIVE TU VIDA / Marquez, Gabino & Arami, M M – Barcelona, 1943; Madrid: Razon y Fe, 1944 – 1 – sp Bibl Santa Ana [946]
Vivenot, A von *see*
– VERTRAULICHE BRIEFE DES FREIHERRN VON THUGUT, OESTERR. MINISTERS DES AEUSSERN
– ZUR GESCHICHTE DES RASTADTER CONGRESSES
Viverus, Iac *see* DE UYT-SPRAECKE VAN ANNA VYTDENHOE. WAER IN GHEHANDELT WORDET VAN DEN SPAENSCHEN VREDE
Vives, D Jose *see* ANTIFONARIO VISIGOTICO...
VIVIAN: A TALE OF CHATEAU RICHER / Gahan, James Joseph – s.l.: s.n., 1880 (Toronto: P. Boyle). 03280. (Pre-1900 Canadiana) – 9 – cn C.I.H.M. [830]
Vivian, R Gordon *see* GRAN QUIVIRA
Viviani, D *see*
– ELENCHUS PLANTARUM HORTI BOTANICI J. CAR. DINEGRO
– FLORAE LIBYCAE SPECIMEN
– PLANTARUM AEGYPTIARUM DECADES 4
LA VIVIENDA PROPIA, REALIDAD ARGENTINA / Argentina. Direccion General de Relaciones Culturales y Difusion – [Buenos Aires?], 1953. 1v – 1 – CSUXADJ0160-B – us Hoover Inst Photo [306]
Vivier, G du *see*
– BRIEFVE INSTITUTION DE LA LANGUE FRANCOISE, EXPLIQUEE EN ALEMAN
– SYNONYMES
VIVIR EN CRISTIANO / Cotallo Sanchez, Jose Luis – Caceres: Seminario Mayor (Tip. Extremadura), 1962 – 1 – sp Bibl Santa Ana [240]
VIVRE / ed by Gagnon, Jean-Louis & Chalout, Pierre – Quebec, Canada. 15 mai 1934-v2 n5. 15 mai 1935 – 1r – 1 – Can$40.00 – cn Can Microfilming [073]
VIXEN. 1879 / Braddon, Mary Elizabeth – British Fiction Archive: Unit 5 – 9 – uk Bell [830]
VIZANTIISKII VREMENNIK, IZDAVAEMYI PRI IMPERATORSKOI AKADEMII NAUK – St. Petersburg, 1894-1928. v1-25. B-1975/2 – 8 – ne IDC [500]
VIZANTIISKOE OBOZRENIE – Yuryev. v. 1-3. no. 2. 1915-1917 – 1 – us NY Public [073]
VIZANTIISKOI OBOZRENIE-REVUE BYZANTINE – Iur'ev, 1915-16. v1-2. Incomplete. BR-3481/2 – 8 – ne IDC [949]
VJESNIK – (Cont as: Novi Vjesnik 1992) – Jugoslawien, 1976-1992ff – 102r – 1 – DM7,650.00 – gw Mikro Press [949]
VJESNIK – (Some issues lacking) – Zagreb, Yugoslavia. Jun 1945-Sept 1946; 1948-76 – 106r – 1 – us L of C Photodup [949]
VJESNIK *see* NOVI VJESNIK
VJESNIK TAGESZEITUNG FUER JUGOSLAWEN IN EUROPA – Frankfurt, Germany. 1 Sept 1978- – 1 – gw Mikrofilm [072]
VKLAD / Bednyi, Demian – Moskva: Gosfinizdat, 1934 – 1 – CSUX88-B5409 – us Hoover Inst Photo [999]
VKLAD PRAVITEL' STVA, UCHENYKH I DRUGIKH OBSHCHESTV NA POL'ZU RUSSKAGO PROSVESHCHENIIA / Mezhov, VI – Bibliograficheskii ukazatel'. Spb. 1886. BR-5936 2 – 8 – ne IDC [010]
VKLADNYE OPERATSII KREDITNYKH KOOPERATIVOV : PRAKTICHESKOE RUKOVODSTVO / Ivanov, VI – M., 1928 – 2mf – 9 – COR-379/1 – ne IDC [334]
VLAAMS JAARBOEK VOOR MUZIEKGESCHIEDENIS – (v1,2/3,4-5. Dfl60.00v. v5. 1959 as: Vereniging voor Muzeikgeschiedenis. Jaarboek) – Antwerp. v1-5. 1939-59. All published – 5,9 – Dfl240.00 – ne Swets [780]
VLAD. SOLOV'EV I MY. SOVREMENNYE ZAPISKI / Berdiaev, N A – 1937. BR-3252 2 – 8 – ne IDC [190]
Vladilenkina, E *see* 15 S"EZD VKP(B) I KOOPERATSIIA
Vladimir, Arkhimandrit *see* SISTEMATICHESKOE OPISANIE RUKOPISEI MOSKOVSKOI SINODAL'NOI (PATRIARSHEI) BIBLIOTEKI
VLADIMIR IL'ICH LENIN / Maiakovskii, Vladimir – Poema. M. 1934. BR-1008 2 – 8 – ne IDC [920]
VLADIMIR MAIAKOVSKII / Grigorian, R – Erevan'. 1952. BR-1281 2 – 8 – ne IDC [920]
VLADIMIR MAIAKOVSKII / Maiakovskii, Vladimir – Sbornik I pod red. A. L. Dymshitsa i O. V. Tsekhovitsera. Akad. nauk SSSR, institut literatury. M., L. 1940. BR-3575 1 – 9 – ne IDC [920]
VLADIMIR MAIAKOVSKII / Maslin, N – M. 1949. BR-1416 2 – 8 – ne IDC [920]
VLADIMIR SLOV'EV. SOVREMENNYE ZAPISKI / Shestov, L – v33. Paris. 1928. BR-3300 2 – 8 – ne IDC [190]
Vladimirov, M *see* DREVNE RUSSKAIA MINIATIURA
Vladimirov, M K *see* OCHEREDNYE ZADACHI KHOZIAISTVENNOGO STROITEL'STVA
Vladimirov, P V *see* OBZOR IUZHNO-RUSSKIKH I ZAPADNO-RUSSKIKH PAMIATNIKOV PISMENNOSTI OT 11 DO 17 ST
Vladimirov, S *see* OB ESTETIKAKH I VZGLIADAKH MAIAKOVSKOGO
Vladimirova, V *see* GOD SLUZHBY "SOTSIALISTOV" KAPITALISTAM
VLADIMIRSKIE GUBERNSKIE VEDOMOSTI – (Complete run with index) – 1838-1917 – 123r – 1 – $10,500.00 set – us Ross [072]
Vladislavlev, I V *see*
– BIBLIOGRAFICHESKII EZHEGODNIK, VYPUSK 4
– LITERATURA VELIKOGO DESIATILETIIA (1917-1927)
– RUSSKIE PISATELI
– ZHIZN' ZAMECHATEL'NYKH LIUDEI
DEN VLADIVOSTOKA – (Includes c.1 1918:Mar.21, May 17, 27-28, July 15, Aug.28) – Vladivostok: "Dalnevostochnai a pechat", 1918 – 1 – CSUXANR2182-S – us Hoover Inst Photo [947]
Vladykov, D I *see* RUKOVODSTVO DLYA BESED S ADVENTISTAMI, BAPTISTAMI, PASHKOVSTAMI, I DRUG
VLAJKA – Prague, Czechoslovakia. Sept 1941-Jul 1942 – 1r – 1 – us L of C Photodup [072]
Vlasov, M E *see* KLASSY I KOOPERATSIIA V DEREVNE SSSR
Vlasov, P A *see*
– 10 LET RABOTY ARTELI "METALLIST"
– 20 LET RABOTY NAZAR'EVSKOI ARTELI
Vlasova, M N *see* PROLETARIAT FINLIANDII V GODY PERVOI RUSSKOI REVOLIUTSII
VLAST' NARODA – Moscow, v1-199, 1917. Lacking parts. BR-3478/2 – 8 – ne IDC [025]
VLAST' SOVETOV – 1917-38 – 1 – 222.00 – us L of C Photodup [947]
VLAST' SOVETOV – Moscow. Jan. 1919-Dec. 1927; May 1932-Aug. 1938 gaps – 1 – 35.00r – us Hoover Inst Photo [947]
VLAST' VSEROSSIISKAGO IMPERATORA / Kazanskii, P E – Odessa, 1913. 960p. Treatise on the authority of the Russian Tsardom by a jurist opposed to liberal constitutional reforms.BR-9722/1 – 9 – ne IDC [340]
Vlavonou, A *see* TENDANCES ET PERSPECTIVES DE L'AGRICULTURE ET DE L'ELEVAGE EN AFRIQUE SUB-SAHARIENNE
DE VLINDERS VAN NEDERLAND. MACROLEPIDOPTERA, SYSTEMATISCH BESCHREVEN / ed by Snellen, P C T – 's-Gravenhage, 1867 – XI, [I], 763p, 4pls – 8 – ne IDC [590]
DE VLINDERS VAN NEDERLAND. MICROLEPIDOPTERA, SYSTEMATISCH BESCHREVEN / ed by Snellen, P C T – Leiden, 1882 – XIII, 1196p, 14pls – 8 – ne IDC [590]
VLKSM I KOOPERATSIIA / Levitas, I – M., 1929 – 4mf – 9 – COR-150/1 – ne IDC [334]
VLSI DESIGN : AN INTERNATIONAL JOURNAL OF CUSTOM-CHIP DESIGN, SIMULATION, AND TESTING / ed by Zobrist, George W – 9,5,1 – us Gordon [621]
VLT-EXTRA *see* VESTMANLANDS LANS TIDNING
Vltimi Auisi di Venetia *see* NARRATIONE DELLA GUERRA PRINCIPIATA CONTRA IL GRAN TURCO, ...
VM/SAC VETERINARY MEDICINE/SMALL ANIMAL CLINICIAN *see* VETERINARY MEDICINE
EIN VND FUENFFTZIG GOTTSELIGE, CHRISTLICHE EVANGELISCHE ANDACHTEN ODER GEISTREICHE BETRACHTUNGEN... / Gerhard, J – Jehna, 1608 – 7mf – ne IDC [240]

VNDERRICHT WIDER DIE LERE DER WIDERTEUFFER AUSZ DEM LATEIN VERDEUTSCHET DURCH JU JONAS / Melanchthon, Philip – Wittemberg. 1528. BME-102 1 – 9 – ne IDC [240]

VNEBOGOSLUZHEBNAYA BESEDA O POCHITANII SVYATYKH IKON *see* PASHKOVITES

VNEBOGOSLUZHEBNAYA BESEDA O POCHITANII SVYATYKH IKON. OTVET POSLEDOVATELYAM PASHKOVA / Vetvenitskii, Konstantin – St. Petersburg, 1891 – 1 – 9.96 – us Baptist [240]

VNESHKOLNOE OBRAZOVANIE : ORGAN VNESHKOLNOGO OTDELA TSENTRALNOGO NARODNOGO KOMISSARIATA PO PROSVESHCHENIIU – Moskva: Otdel, 1919. 1v – 1 – CSUX90-S149 – us Hoover Inst Photo [370]

VNESHNIAIA POLITIKA ROSSII V NACHALE TSARSTVOVANIIA E KATERINY II 1762-1774 / Chechulin, N D – Spb, 1896 – 6mf – 1 – ILM-2517/1 – ne IDC [327]

VNESHNIAIA POLITIKA SSSR; SBORNIK DOKUMENTOV. SOSTAVITEL' A.S. TISMINETS – Moscow, 1944-1946. 4 vols – 1 – 35.00r – us Hoover Inst Photo [335]

VNESHNIAIA TORGOVLIA : EZHENEDELNIK NARKOMVNESHTORGA – (Library has: May 15, July 15, Nov. 18, 1923; Feb. 21, 1925; Jan. 10, Feb. 7, Feb. 14, Mar. 7, Apr. 6, Apr. 20, 1926) – Moskva: Izdat. N.K.V.T., 1922-1926 – 1 – CSUX89-S866 – us Hoover Inst Photo [380]

VNESHNIAIA TORGOVLIA – (Library has: 1933-1935, 1937, 1939-1988) – Moskva: "Vneshtorgizdat", 1931- – 1 – CSUX89-S761 – us Hoover Inst Photo [380]

VNESHNIAIA TORGOVLIA – (Missing: 1931(1-14); 1933(25-36); 1940; 1941(4-11); 1942-1944; 1952-1959; Supplemented: 1960-1989(12). 264mf) – Organ Narodnogo komissariata torgovli. M., 1931(4)-1989(12) – 9 – R-9311/1 – ne IDC [947]

VNESHNIAIA TORGOVLIA *see* VNESHNIAIA TORGOVLIA SSSR V...G

VNESHNIAIA TORGOVLIA PO EVROPEISKO I GRANITSE : STATISTICHESKI I OBZOR / N.K.V.T., Glavnoe tamozhennoe upravlenie S.S.S.R. – Moskva: Glav. tamozhennoe upr., 192u – 1 – CSUX89-S721 – us Hoover Inst Photo [380]

VNESHNIAIA TORGOVLIA ROSSII I GLAVNEISHIKH EVROPEISKIKH GOSUDARSTV V DIAGRAMMAKH I TABLITSAKH / Parmenov, IS – Odessa, 1916 – 1 – $35.00r – us Hoover Inst Photo [380]

VNESHNIAIA TORGOVLIA SOIUZA SSR – (Library has: 1956-1968) – Moskva: Vneshtorg, 1956. 13v – 1 – CSUX90-S552 – us Hoover Inst Photo [380]

VNESHNIAIA TORGOVLIA SOIUZA SSR : STATISTICHESKII OBZOR / Narodnyi komissariat vneshnei torgovli, Otdel tam. statistiki – (Library has: Apr.-May, Sept., Dec. 1931; Dec. 1932; Jan.-Dec. 1934; Jan.-Dec. 1935) – Moskva: Vneshtorgizdat, 1929-1935 – 1 – CSUX89-S589 – us Hoover Inst Photo [380]

VNESHNIAIA TORGOVLIA SSSR – (Library has: 1969-1974) – Moskva: Statistika, 1969. 6v – 1 – CSUX90-S616 – us Hoover Inst Photo [380]

VNESHNIAIA TORGOVLIA SSSR *see*
- VNESHNIAIA TORGOVLIA
- VNESHNIAIA TORGOVLIA SOIUZA SSR

VNESHNIAIA TORGOVLIA SSSR V...G / Ministerstvo vneshne i torgovli, Glavnoe planovo- ekonomicheskoe upravlenie – (Library has: 1975-1987) – Moskva: "Statistika", 1976-1988. 13v – 1 – CSUX90-S619 – us Hoover Inst Photo [330]

VNESHNIE EKONOMICHESKIE SVIAZI SSSR V... G / Ministerstvo vneshnikh ekonomicheskikh sviaze i SSSR, Glavnoe ekonomicheskoe upravlenie – Moskva: Finansy i Statistika, 1989- – 1 – CSUX90-S623 – us Hoover Inst Photo [330]

VNESHNYAYA TORGOVLYA – Foreign Trade. Moscow. U.S.S.R. 1961- – 1 – us UMI [330]

VNESIAIA POLITIKA ROSSII V NACHALE TSARSTVOVANIIA EKATERINY 2 / Chechulin, N D – 1762-74. Spb. 1896. BR-4109 2 – 8 – ne IDC [947]

VNI ESHKOLNIKI I NAROD / Evdokimov, Andrei Andreevich – Izd. 2-e. Moskva: Trud, 1917 – 1 – CSUX89-B3795 – us Hoover Inst Photo [947]

VNUTRENNIAIA TORGOVLIA / Shreter, Viktor Nikolaevich – Moskva, Izdatel'stvo "Ekonomicheskaia ahizn", 1926. 226p. LL-4005 – 1 – us L of C Photodup [340]

VO IMIA SOTSIALIZMA : RI ECH K TOVARISHCHAM RABOCHIM / Aleksinskii, Grigorii Alekseevich – Petrograd: Izd. Mar-ii Malykh, [1917] – 1 – CSUX88-B9667 – us Hoover Inst Photo [335]

VOBIF – Verordnungsblatt fuer die franzoesischen besetzten Gebiete. Paris. juil 1940-juil 1944 – 1 – fr A.C.R.P.P. [073]

Voblyi, KG *see* K AGRARNOMU VOPROSU V ROSSII

VOCA – Portland OR. July 17 1947, Aug 6 13 20 1953 – 1 – us U.O. Library [071]

VOCABOLARIO DELLA LINGUA TIGRIGNA : INTRODUZIONE E INDICE ITALIANO-TIGRIGNA DEL DOTT / Vito, L de – Roma, 1896 – 2mf – ne IDC [440]

VOCABOLARIO TIGRAY-ITALIANO E REPERTORIO ITALIANO-TIGRAY / Bassano, F da. – Roma, 1918 – 7mf – NE-20178/1 – ne IDC [054]

VOCABOLARIO TOSCANO DELL'ARTE DEL DISEGNO... / Baldinucci, Filippo – Firenze, 1681 – 6mf – ne IDC [700]

VOCABOLARIO TOSCANO DELL'ARTE DEL DISEGNO...CON LA NOTIZIA DE'NOMI E QUAL TA DELLE GIOIE, METALLI, PIETRE DURE.. / Baldinucci, Filippo – Firenze, Santi Franchi, 1681. With his cominciamento, e progresso dell'arte dell'intagliare in rame... Firenze, 1686 – 1 – us U.W. Library [440]

VOCABULAIRE D'ACCESSION A L'INFORMATION / Tachdijian. A – (Africa series). 1970 – 9 – fr Hachette [960]

VOCABULAIRE D'ENVIRON 1500 MOTS FRANCAIS AVEC LEURS CORRESPONDANTS EN OUOLOF DE SAINT-LOUIS, EN POULAR (TOUCOULEUR) DU FOUTA, EN SONINKE (SARAKHOLLE) DE BAKEL / Faidherbe, Louis Leon Cesar – St. Louis (Senegal), Imprimerie du gouvernement. 1864 – 9 – $5.00 – fr Orientalistes [490]

VOCABULAIRE DES FRANCS-MACONS – Paris, 1808 – 3mf – ne IDC [944]

VOCABULAIRE DES HOMONYMES SIMPLES DE LA LANGUE FRANCAISE / Baillairge, Charles – 1891. 00806. (Pre-1900 Canadiana) – 9 – cn C.I.H.M. [440]

VOCABULAIRE DES PRINCIPALES RACINES MALAISES ET JAVANAISES DE LA LANGUE MALGACHE / Marre, Aristide – Paris, Ernest Leroux. 1896 – 9 – $5.00 – fr Orientalistes [490]

VOCABULAIRE DU BAS LANGAGE REMOIS / Saubinet, E – 1845 – 9 – fr I.C.S. [440]

VOCABULAIRE ESSENTIEL DE L'ENSEIGNEMENT PRIMAIRE / University of Abidjan – (Africa series). 2 v. 1970 – 9 – fr Hachette [370]

VOCABULAIRE ET GRAMMAIRE POUR LES LANGUES MALGACHES, SAKALAVE ET BETSIMITSARA / Dalmond – Ile Bourbon, Imprimerie de Lahuppe. 1842 – 9 – $5.00 – fr Orientalistes [490]

LE VOCABULAIRE ET LA SOCIETE DE ROBERT BRASILLACH ET P. LA ROCHELLE / Franco Arias, Froilan – 3mf – 9 – Pta2,000.00 – 84-85422-26-0 – sp Pentalfa [440]

VOCABULAIRE LANGROIS / Mulson – 1822 – 9 – fr I.C.S. [440]

VOCABULAIRE LATIN-FRANCAIS / Garbini – 1487 – 9 – fr I.C.S. [450]

VOCABULAIRES COMPARATIFS DE PLUS DE 60 LANGUES OU DIALECTES PARLES A LA COTE D'IVOIRE ET DANS LES REGIONS LIMITROPHES : AVEC DES NOTES LINGUISTIQUES ET ETHNOLOGIQUES / Delafosse, Maurice – Paris: E Leroux, 1904 – us Res Libr [470]

VOCABULAIRES GUIOLOF, MANDINGUE, FOULE, SARACOLE, SERAIRE, BAGNON ET FLOUPE, RECUEILLIS A LA COTE D'AFRIQUE / Avezac-Macaya, Armand d'; ed by Avezac, d' – La preface est datee de 1844 – 9 – $5.00 – fr Orientalistes [490]

VOCABULARIO AMARICO-ITALIANO / Guidi, Ignazio – Roma: Casa editrice italiana, 1901 – us Res Libr [440]

VOCABULARIO DEGLI ACCADEMICI DELLA CRUSCA, QUARTA IMPRESSIONE – 5v. Firenze. 1729-38. BO-101 1 – 106mf – 9 – ne IDC [400]

VOCABULARIO DESCRIPTIVO...DICCIONARIO / Garces y Gonzales, Valeriano – 1875 – 9 – 1.50f – sp Bibl Santa Ana [440]

VOCABULARIOS BREVIOLOQUUS CUM ARTE DIPHTHONGANDI, PUNCTUANDI ET ACCENTUANDI / Reuchlin, J – Estrasburgo, 1504 – 13mf – 9 – sp Cultura [450]

VOCABULARIOS INDIGENAS DE VENEZUELA. / Raimundo, Jacques – Rio de Janeiro. 1934 – 1 – us Res Libr [490]

VOCABULARIUM, DAS IST : WOERTERBUCH, TEUTSCH-ITALIENISCH / Messerschmid, Georg Friedrich – Durlach, 1625 – 9 – 3-89131-085-4 – gw Fischer [040]

VOCABULARIUM LATINO-SINICUM / Goncalves, J A – Macao, 1836 – 3mf – ne IDC [450]

VOCABULARIUM VAN VREEMDE WOORDEN, VOORKOMENDE IN HET AMBONSCH-MALEISCH, BENEVENS KORTE OPMERKINGEN OVER DIT LOCAAL-MALEISCH EN VERDER EENIGE AMBONSCHE SPREEKWOORDEN, EIGENAARDIGE UITDRUKKINGEN EN GEZEGDEN TE AMBON GEBRUIKELIJK / Hoevell, G W W C van – Dordrecht, 1876. 58p – 1mf – 9 – ne IDC [490]

VOCABULARY : SANSKRIT-TIBETAN-ENGLISH – Calcutta. v4[1-2]. 1910, 1916 – 6mf – ne IDC [054]

A VOCABULARY AND OUTLINES OF GRAMMAR OF THE NITLAKAPAMUK OR THOMPSON TONGUE...TOGETHER WITH A PHONETIC CHINOOK DICTIONARY.. / Good, John Booth – Victoria, B.C.: St. Paul's Mission Press, 1880. 02276. (Pre-1900 Canadiana) – 9 – cn C.I.H.M. [490]

VOCABULARY OF ENGLISH HOMONYMS / Baillairge, Charles – Quebec: C. Darveau, 1891. 00071. (Pre-1900 Canadiana) – 9 – cn C.I.H.M. [420]

VOCABULARY OF NEW TESTAMENT WORDS : CLASSIFIED ACCORDING TO ROOTS WITH STATISTICS OF USAGE BY AUTHORS / Davis, Ozora Stearns – 2nd rev ed. Hartford, CT: Hartford Seminary Press, 1895, c1893 – 1mf – 9 – 0-8370-9224-8 – 1986-3224 – us A.T.L.A. [450]

A VOCABULARY OF SUCH WORDS IN THE ENGLISH LANGUAGE AS ARE OF DUBIOUS OR UNSETTLED ACCENTUATION – Anon. 1797. 192p. (English Linguistics Series 1500-1800) – 9 – us UMI [420]

VOCABULARY OF THE CANTON DIALECT / Morrison, R – Macao. 3pts. 1828 – 8mf – ne IDC [480]

A VOCABULARY OF THE HOK-KEEN DIALECT... – N.p., 1838 – 2mf – ne IDC [480]

A VOCABULARY OF THE SGAU KAREN LANGUAGE / Wade, Johathan – Tavoy [Burma]: Karen Mission Press, 1849 – us Res Libr [480]

VOCABULARY OF THE TIGRE LANGUAGE / Beurmann, M von – Halle, London. 1868 – 1mf – ne IDC [440]

A VOCABULARY OF THE YORUBA LANGUAGE, ETC ETC / Crowther, Samuel Adjai – [London: W M Watts, 1870] – us Res Libr [470]

VOCABULARY TO THE TELUGU BIBLE : CONTAINING THE VOCABLES TO THE PRESCRIBED BIBLICAL TEXT FOR BOTH THE VERNACULAR EXAMINATIONS OF MISSIONARIES / Holler, P – (Filmed with: A Small English-Telugu Dictionary) – Rajahmundry, 1900 – us Res Libr [220]

VOCAL AND INSTRUMENTAL TUTORS – 1998 – 600mf – 9 – ne MMF Publ [780]

VOCAL MIMICRY IN THE SUPERB LYREBIRD / Thorburn, Lyndal – microfiche – A$15.00 – at R.A.O.U. [590]

VOCAL MUSIC BEFORE 1820 – 1999 – 600mf – 9 – ne MMF Publ [780]

THE VOCAL ORGAN, OR A NEW ART OF TEACHING THE ENGLISH ORTHOGRAPHIE / Price, Owen – 1665. 95p. (English Linguistics Series 1500-1800) – 9 – us UMI [420]

THE VOCAL PRECEPTOR OR KEY TO SACRED MUSIC FROM CELEBRATED AUTHORS / Stevenson, A – Montreal, 1811. SEM105P15 – 1mf – 9 – Can$2.25 – cn Bibl Nat [780]

VOCAL SOUNDS / Tucker, Abraham – 1773. 159p. (English Linguistics Series 1500-1800) – 9 – us UMI [400]

VOCATIONAL EDUCATION – Peoria. v1-3. sep 1911-may 1914 – 1 – D5703 – us UMI [370]

VOCATIONAL EDUCATION IN AGRICULTURE RESEARCH SERIES: BULLETIN / Georgia. University. Department of Agriculture Education – n.1-6.1963-65 – 1,5 – us Spaulding [630]

VOCATIONAL EDUCATION JOURNAL – (Cont: VocEd. Cont by: Techniques) – Alexandria. v60-71. aug 1985-may 1996 – 1,5,9 – D2203.02 – us UMI [370]

VOCATIONAL EDUCATION JOURNAL *see* VOCED

VOCATIONAL GUIDANCE QUARTERLY – (Cont by: Career Development Quarterly) – Washington. v1-34. aut 1952-jun 1986 1; v20-34. sep1971-jun 1986 5; v24-34. sep 1975-jun 1986 9 – 1,5,9 – D3178 – us UMI [073]

VOCATIONAL GUIDE *see* ANNUAL GUIDANCE INDEX

VOCATIONAL TRAINING AND JOB CREATION SCHEMES IN BELGIUM : STUDY UNDERTAKEN ON BEHALF OF THE EUROPEAN CENTRE FOR DEVELOPMENT OF VOCATIONAL TRAINING / Volz, J – Berlin, 1983 – 2mf – 9 – DE-142/1 – ne IDC [370]

VOCATIONALIZATION OF EDUCATION: PROFILE AND DIRECTIONS : REPORT OF THE NATIONAL SEMINAR ON VOCATIONALIZATION OF EDUCATION 24-26 APRIL 1984 / India. National Council of Educational Research and Training. Publication Department – New Delhi, 1985 – 3mf – 9 – DE-697/1 – ne IDC [370]

VOCATIONS : CONDITIONS OF ADMISSION, ETC., INTO THE MONASTERIES, CONGREGATIONS, SOCIETIES, RELIGIOUS INSTITUTES ETC.: ACCORDING TO AUTHENTICAL INFORMATION AND THE LATEST REGULATIONS / Hohn, Hermann – London: R & T Washbourne; New York: Benziger, 1910 – 1mf – 9 – 0-8370-6982-3 – 1986-0982 – us A.T.L.A. [240]

LA VOCE COLONIALE = THE COLONIAL VOICE – New Orleans, LA: P Montelepre, dec 8 1917-1930 – us Res Libr [071]

LA VOCE DALMATICA – Zadar, Yugoslavia. Nov 1918-May 1919 – 1r – 1 – us L of C Photodup [949]

LA VOCE DEGLI ITALO-CANADESE – Toronto. 1938-40 – 1 – 65.00 – cn McLaren [072]

LA VOCE DEL POPOLO – Philadelphia, PA. Apr 1909-1909 – 1r – 1 – us I.H.R.C. [071]

LA VOCE DEL POPOLO – San Francisco, CA, 1868-1905 – 1r – 1 – us I.H.R.C. [978]

LA VOCE DEL POPOLO – (Some issues lacking) – Rijeka, Yugoslavia. 1950-53; 1956-Jun 1979; Jan 1980-Jan 1987 – 78r – 1 – us L of C Photodup [949]

LA VOCE DEL POPOLO *see* LA VOIX DU PEUPLE

LA VOCE DEL POPOLO ITALIANO – Cleveland. Ohio. 1909-1922 – 1 – us UMI [071]

LA VOCE DEL POPULO – (First Italian newspaper in California) – San Francisco, CA. 1868-1905 – 1r – 1 – $50.00 – B02830 – us Library Micro [071]

LA VOCE DELA COLONIA – Philadelphia, PA, 1896 – 1mf or 1r – 1,9 – us I.H.R.C. [978]

LA VOCE DELLA COLONIA *see* LA VOCE DEL POPOLO

LA VOCE DELLO SCHIAVO – Tampa, FL, 1900-1901 – 6mf or 1r – 1,9 – us I.H.R.C. [978]

LA VOCE D'ITALIA – New York, NY. May 4 1946-1949 – us I.H.R.C. [071]

LA VOCE D'ITALIA = THE VOICE OF ITALY – Montreal, 20 jun 1968 – 1r – 1 – Can$25.00 – cn Can Microfilming [072]

VOCE EVANGELICA – 1968; 1972-91 (complete) – Inquire – 1 – ATLA S0477 – us A.T.L.A. [073]

VOCE REPUBBLICANA – 1987-1995 – 2r per y – 5,6 – Sfr775.00 – sz Infoprint [072]

VOCED – (Cont: American Vocational Journal. Cont by: Vocational Education Journal) – Arlington. v53-60. sep 1978-may 1985 – 1,5,9 – D2203.01 – us UMI [370]

VOCED *see* VOCATIONAL EDUCATION JOURNAL

VOCES LLENAS DE AMOR A FERNANDO 6 / Nipho, Francisco Mariano – 1759 – 1mf – 9 – Pta1,000.00 – 84-7848-168-0 – sp Pentalfa [920]

VOCHENBLAT = JEWISH WEEKLY – (In Yiddish) – Bergen-Belsen (British Zone), DE. no11(60) 1 Jul 1949-no21(no70) 9 Dec 1949 – 1r – 1 – $30.00 – cn Can Microfilming [072]

VOCHENZAITUNG (THE JEWISH WEEKLY) – (Yidishe Post (Jewish Post) 10 Nov 1950-20 Oct 1961) – London, UK. 31 Jan 1936-31 Mar 1950 – 1 – uk British Libr Newspaper [072]

Vocht, H de *see* MATERIALS FOR THE STUDY OF OLD ENGLISH DRAMA
Vockrodt-Scholz, Viola *see* ASSOZIATIONSVERSUCHE MIT JUGENDLICHEN RAUCHERN UND NICHTRAUCHERN
VOCUBULAIRE FRANCAIS-ESQUIMAU : DIALECTE DES TCHIGLIT / Petitot, E – Paris, 1876 – 5mf – ne IDC [440]
VOCUBULAIRE FRANCAIS-ESQUIMAU. DIALECTE DES TCHIGLIT. 64, 75 P / Petitot, E – BN 341 2. 1876 – 8 – ne IDC [040]
VODIANI ZNAKY NA PAPERI UKRAJINS'KIKH DOKUMENTIV XVI I XVII VV. (1566-1651) / Kamanin, I M & Vitvits'ka, O – Kiev, 1923. BR-10,331/1 – 9 – ne IDC [460]
VODNOE DELO – Zhurnal, posiashchennyi Tekhnicheskim, promyshlennym i ekonomicheskim interesam volopol' zovaniia v Rossii. St. Petersburg, 1907-10. BR-2309/2 – 8 – ne IDC [460]
VODNY I TRANSPORT – (Library has: 1918, no.6) – Moskva: Upravlenie, 1918. 1v – 1 – CSUX90-S332 – us Hoover Inst Photo [380]
VODNY I TRANSPORT – (Library has: Jan. 1925) – Moskva: NKPS Transpechat, 1923-1940. 18v – 1 – CSUX89-S928 – us Hoover Inst Photo [380]
VODNYI TRANSPORT – Moscow, USSR. 1972-1980 – 7r – $350.00 – B63594 – us Library Micro [072]
VODOLAZ – Ezhenedel'nyi khudozhestvennyi i politiko-satiricheskii zhurnal. St. Petersburg, 1906. v1-5. BR-3477/2 – 8 – ne IDC [460]
DIE VOEGEL DER PALAEARKTISCHEN FAUNA / Hartert, E J O – 3v. Berlin. 1903-22. BZ-1792 2 – 8 – ne IDC [590]
DIE VOEGEL DES KREISES UMAN / Goebel, H – St. Petersburg, 1879. 283p. (Beitraege zur Kenntnis des Russischen Reiches). v2.BZ/1767/2 – 8 – ne IDC [590]
DIE VOEGEL EUROPAS / Selliers von Moranville, L – Wien. 1844. Z-1928 2 – 8 – ne IDC [590]
DIE VOEGEL EUROPAS / Susemihl, J C & Susemihl, E – Z 1942. 1851 – 9 – ne IDC [590]
DIE VOEGEL GRIECHENLANDS / Lindermayer, A – Z 1840. 1860 – 9 – ne IDC [590]
Voegler, Gudrun *see* DAS 9. BUCH INNERHALB DER PHARSALIA DES LUCAN UND DIE FRAGE DER VOLLENDUNG DES EPOS
VOELE GOEDE VND CHRISTELYCKE LERINGHEN OP DEN 25. PSALM IN EEN MANIERE VAN BIDDEN GESCREUEN. ANNO 1539 / Simons, Menno – BME-272 1 – 9 – ne IDC [240]
Voelker, Johannes *see* DIE LETZTEN TAGE VON KOLBERG
Voelker, Karl *see*
- DER PROTESTANTISMUS IN POLEN AUF GRUND DER EINHEIMISCHEN GESCHICHTSSCHREIBUNG
- DER PROTESTANTISMUS IN POLEN AUF GRUND DER EINHEIMISCHEN GESCHICHTSSCHREIBUNG DARGESTELLT
- TOLERANZ UND INTOLERANZ IM ZEITALTER DER REFORMATION

Voelker, Monika *see* DIE AUSEINANDERSETZUNG MIT DER FRANZOESISCHEN REVOLUTION IN DER GESCHICHTSSCHREIBUNG DER "KLEINDEUTSCHEN" SCHULE
DIE VOELKER UND DAS MEER ... / Boehtlingk, A – Berlin, 1915 – 1mf – 9 – ILM-2186/1 – ne IDC [327]
Voelker, W *see*
- FORTSCHRIFT UND VOLLENDUNG BEI PHILO VON ALEXANDRIEN (T.U.U. 4-49/1)
- SCALA PARADISI
- DAS VOLLKOMMENHEITSIDEAL DES ORIGENES
- DER WAHRE GNOSTIKER NACH CLEMENS ALEXANDRINUS (T.U.U. 5-57)

DER VOELKERBUND... / Guggenheim, P – Leipzig, Berlin, 1932 – 4mf – 1 – ILM-4024/1 – ne IDC [327]
VOELKERBUND UND VOELKERRECHT – Berlin, 1934/35-1937/38 – 1 – Inquire at Mikrofilmarchiv for details – gw Misc Inst [327]
DAS VOELKERRECHT... / Bulmerincq, A von – Freiburg, 1889 – 3mf – 1 – ILM-146/1 – ne IDC [327]
DAS VOELKERRECHT DER ZUKUNFT / Bekker, E I – Heidelberg, 1915 – 1mf – 9 – ILM-1703/1 – ne IDC [327]
VOELKERRECHT UND VOELKERPOLITIK / Bernstein, E – Berlin, 1919 – 2mf – 9 – ILM-1708/1 – ne IDC [327]
DIE VOELKERRECHTLICHE ANERKENNUNG DER STAATEN / Hartmann, G – Weimar, 1932 – 1mf – 1 – ILM-1519/1 – ne IDC [327]
DIE VOELKERRECHTLICHE ANERKENNUNG VON MANDSCHUKUO / Behr, H – Würzburg, 1936 – 1mf – 9 – ILM-1551/1 – ne IDC [327]
VOELKERRECHTLICHE GRENZEN... / Glatzel, W – Tuebingen, 1936 – 2mf – 1 – ILM-2088/1 – ne IDC [327]
DAS VOELKERRECHTLICHE MANDAT / Fricko, A – N.p., n.d. – 1mf – 1 – ILM-2387/1 – ne IDC [327]
DAS VOELKERRECHTLICHE PROTEKTORAT / Heilborn, P – Berlin, 1891 – 2mf – 1 – ILM-2127/1 – ne IDC [327]
DIE VOELKERRECHTLICHE REPATRIATIONSPFLICHT... / Claparede, A R – Wuerzburg, 1911 – 2mf – 1 – ILM-3199/1 – ne IDC [327]
DER VOELKERRECHTLICHE SCHUTZ...AUF HOHER SEE / Becker, P – Wuerzburg, 1919 – 9 – 1mf – ILM-3459/1 – ne IDC [327]
DIE VOELKERRECHTLICHE STELLUNG DES PAPSTES / Geffcken, F Heinrich – Berlin: C. Habel, 1885 – 1mf – us A.T.L.A. [240]
VOELKERRECHTLICHE UND STATSRECHTLICHE STUDIEN / Dahn, F – Berlin, 1884 – 5mf – 1 – ILM-3450/1 – ne IDC [327]
DIE VOELKERRECHTLICHEN GRUNDSAETZE DER KRIEGFUEHRUNG ZU LANDE UND ZUR SEE / Endres, K – Berlin, 1909 – 2mf – 1 – ILM-921/1 – ne IDC [327]
VOELKERRECHTSPOLITIK ALS WISSENSCHAFT / [Feilchenfeld, E H] – Berlin, 1922 – 3mf – 1 – ILM-1733/1 – ne IDC [327]
VOELKERWOHLSTAND UND WELTWIRTSCHAFT / Schulze, Georg – Leipzig: W. Goldmann, 1942. 320p – 1 – us U.W. Library [337]
VOELKISCHER BEOBACHTER – Berlin, Germany.1920-28 Apr 1945; Munich, Germany. 1932-1944 (Ausgabe Sueddeutschland); 1932-1945 (Ausgabe Muenchen) – 1 – gw Mikrofilm [072]
VOELKISCHER BEOBACHTER : BERLINER AUSGABE – Berlin, jan-aug 1940, 1943-apr 20 1945 – 1 – Inquire at Mikrofilmarchiv for details – gw Misc Inst [320]
VOELKISCHER BEOBACHTER : KAMPFBLATT DER NATIONAL-SOZIALISTISCHEN BEWEGUNG GROSSDEUTSCHLANDS – Berlin, Muenchen. 1920-1945 – 52r – 1 – DM4,680.00 – gw Mikro Press [072]
VOELKISCHER BEOBACHTER : NORDDEUTSCHE AUSGABE – Berlin, 1920-apr 28 1945 – 1 – Inquire at Mikrofilmarchiv for details – gw Misc Inst [320]
VOELKISCHER BEOBACHTER : NORDDEUTSCHE AUSGABE – Munich: F Eher Nachf., [1933-44] jul-aug 1940; jan-feb, apr-dec 1941; apr-dec 1944 – us Res Libr [072]
VOELKISCHER BEOBACHTER *see*
- MUENCHENER BEOBACHTER

Voelkl, Judith E *see* THE DAILY EXPERIENCES OF OLDER ADULTS RESIDING IN INSTITUTIONAL ENVIRONMENTS
Voelter, Daniel *see*
- AEGYPTEN UND DIE BIBEL
- DIE ENTSTEHUNG DER APOKALYPSE
- DER ERSTE PETRUSBRIEF
- DIE OFFENBARUNG JOHANNIS
- PAULUS UND SEINE BRIEFE
- DER URSPRUNG DES DONATISMUS

Voeltzkow, A *see* REISE IN OSTAFRIKA IN DEN JAHREN 1903-1905
Voemel, Alexander *see* JOH. CASPAR LAVATER 1741-1801
VOENNAIA MYSL' I REVOLIUTSIIA – Moscow, 1923-24.v1-5; v1-8. BR-3476/2 – 8 – ne IDC [335]
VOENNAIA MYSL' I REVOLIUTSIIA – Moscow. v1-2 1921-22. v1-6 1923. v1-8 1924 – 1 – D2668 – us UMI [073]
VOENNAIA NAUKA I REVOLIUTSIIA – Moscow, 1922. v1-2. BR-3475/2 – 8 – ne IDC [335]
VOENNAIA PODGOTOVKA OKTIABRIA / Buiskii, A – 2-e izd. Moskva: Gos. izd-vo, Otdel voen. lit-ry, 1930 – 1 – CSUX88-B3935 – us Hoover Inst Photo [947]
VOENNAIA RABOTA RS-DRP BOLSHEVIKOV / Aroslavskii, Emelian – Leningrad: Rabochee izdvo "Pribo i", 1927 – 1 – CSUX88-B1189 – us Hoover Inst Photo [355]
VOENNI IZVESTIYA – Sofia, Bulgaria. -d. 5 March 1917-21 May, 4-19 Dec 1918; 2 Jan, 21 Feb-5 March 1919. Very imperfect. 1 reel – 1 – uk British Libr Newspaper [949]
VOENNO-BIBLIOGRAFICHESKII SPRAVOCHNIK – (Library has: Oct. 1927; Feb., Apr., July 1928) – Moskva: Gos. izdvo, 1927-1929. 3v – 1 – CSUX89-S848 – us Hoover Inst Photo [355]
VOENNOE DELO – (Library has: 1918, nos. 1, 4-10, 12, 14-28; 1919, nos. 1-34/25; 1920, nos. 1-11, 15) – Moskva: [s.n.] 1918- – 1 – CSUX90-S453 – us Hoover Inst Photo [355]
VOENNOE DELO ZA GRANITSEI – Voenno-nanchnyi illiustrirovannyi zhurnal. Warsaw, 1911-14. v25-41. BR-2308/2 – 8 – ne IDC [947]
VOENNOE MINISTERSTVO – Stoletie voennago ministerstva, 1802-1902. Istoricheskii ocherk. St. Petersburg, 1902-14. 13v. index 1909-10, 2v.BR-4264/2 – 8 – ne IDC [947]
VOENNO-ISTORICHESKII SBORNIK – Moscow. 1919-1921, nos. 1-4 – 1 – 35.00r – us Hoover Inst Photo [947]
VOENNO-ISTORICHESKII SBORNIK – Prilozhenie k zhurnalu Voennyi sbornik. St. Petersburg, 1911-16. BR-1436/2 – 8 – ne IDC [947]
VOENNO-ISTORICHESKII VESTNIK – Kiev, 1909-14. Lacking some issues. B-1437/2 – 8 – ne IDC [947]
VOENNO-ISTORICHESKII ZHURNAL – Moscow. Jan.-Dec. 1960; index. Missing: no. 4 – 1 – 35.00r – us Hoover Inst Photo [947]
VOENNO-MEDITSINSKO AKADEMII LIBRARY *see* SISTEMATICHESKII KNIZHNYI KATALOG BIBLIOTEKI IMP. VOENNO-MEDITSINSKOI AKADEMII
VOENNO-PEDAGOGICHESKII ZHURNAL – Moscow, 1920. v1-4. Lacking: v1-2. BR-3474/2 – 8 – ne IDC [370]
VOENNO-REVOLIUTSIONNAIA MYSL' – Petrograd, 1919.No.1-2. BR-3473/2 – 8 – ne IDC [335]
VOENNYE ZNANIIA – (Includes 1956, no.1-1957, no.12; 1962, no.6-. For latest issues contact publisher) – Moskva: Izd.-vo DOSAAF SSSR, 1948- – 1 – CSUX90-S463 – us Hoover Inst Photo [355]
VOENNYI LETCHIK – Sevastopol'. 1917. No.1-3 available. BR-8380/1 – 9 – ne IDC [947]
VOENNYI MIR – Illiustrirovannyi voenno-obshchestvennyi zhurnal. Moscow, 1911-14. BR-4174/2 – 8 – ne IDC [947]
VOENNYI SBORNIK – Obshchestva revnitelei voennykh znanii. Belgrad, 1921-30. v1-11. BR-4023/2 – 8 – ne IDC [947]
VOENNYI SBORNIK – Sistematicheskii Ukazatel'za 1858-1890 gg. Sistematicheskii Ukazatel' za 1891-1897 gg. St Petersburg. 1891, 1898 – 1 – us NY Public [355]
VOENNYI SBORNIK – St. Petersburg, 1858-1917. B-1231/2 – 8 – ne IDC [947]
VOENNYI SBORNIK OBSHCHESTVA REVNITELEI VOENNYKH ZNANII I KRUZHKOV VYSSHAGO VOENNAGO SAMOOBRAZOVANIIA – Belgrade. 1921-1929, v. 1-10 – 1 – 35.00r – us Hoover Inst Photo [947]
VOENNYI VESTNIK – Ezhemesiachnyi zhurnal. Sevastopol, 1920. BR-3472/2 – 8 – ne IDC [947]
Voenskii, K *see* OTECHESTVENNAIA VOINA V RUSSKOI ZHURNALISTIKE
Voet, J E *see* CATALOGUS SYSTEMATICUS COLEOPTERORUM
Voeta, David *see* DIARY
VOETIUS OVER HET GEZAG DER SYNODEN / Bouwman, M – Amsterdam, 1937 – 7mf – 8 – Dfl30.00 – ne Slangenburg [240]
Vogel, C *see*
- LA DISCIPLINE PENITENTIELLE EN GAULE DES ORIGINES A LA FIN DU 7TH SIECLE
- INTRODUCTION AUX SOURCES DE L'HISTOIRE DU CULTE CHRETIEN AU MOYEN AGE

Vogel, F *see* MAGNI FELICIS ENNODI OPERA (MGH 1: 7.BD)
Vogel, Hermann *see* CHRISTIAN FRIEDRICH HUNOLD (MENANTES)
Vogel, Julius *see*
- KAETCHEN SCHOENKOPF
- THE OFFICIAL HANDBOOK OF NEW ZEALAND

Vogel, M *see* DIE GRIECHISCHEN SCHREIBER DES MITTELALTERS UND DER RENAISSANCE
Vogel, Theodor *see* ZUR CHARAKTERISTIK DES LUKAS
VOGELBILDER AUS FERNEN ZONEN / Reichenow, A – Kassel. 1878-83. Z-1885 2 – 8 – ne IDC [590]
Vogelpohl, Wilhelm *see* DEUTSCHE DICHTUNG
Vogels, H J *see* DIE HARMONISTIK IM EVANGELIENTEXT IN CODEX CANTABRIGIENSIS (T.U.U. 3-36/1A)
DE VOGELS VAN NEDERLANDSCH-INDIE... / Schlegel, H – Leiden, Amsterdam, n.d – 10mf – 9 – Z-1911/2 – ne IDC [590]
Vogl, Johann Nepomuk *see* LYRISCHE GEDICHTE, BALLADEN UND ERZAEHLUNGEN
Vogl, Reiner *see* DIE VERPACKUNGSVERORDNUNG
Vogler, E Williams *see* THE EFFECTS OF A GROUP-ORIENTED CONTINGENCY MANAGEMENT SYSTEM ON BEHAVIORALLY DISORDERED STUDENTS IN PHYSICAL EDUCATION
Vogler, Georg Joseph *see*
- CHORAL-SYSTEM
- [HERMANN VON UNNA] OVERTURE; ARRANGED FOR PIANO
- KUHRPFAELZISCHE TONSCHULE
- TONWISSENSCHAFT UND TONSETZKUNST

Vogler, J K *see* ...VERMISCHTE MUSICALISHE CHORAL GEDANCKEN, NACH ANLEITUNG DERER GEWOEHNLICHSTEN EVANGELISCHEN KIRCHEN-GESAENGE AUF VERSCHEIDENTLICHE ART GOTT ZU EHREN UND ALLEN MUSIQUE-LIEBENDEN...ERSTE PROBE
Vogler, Martin *see* QUALITAETSSICHERUNG IN DER KRANKENPFLEGE
VOGNI E ZASHCHITY : IZ VPECHATLIENII POLITICHESKAGO ZASHCHITNIKA / Berenshtam, Vladimir – Berlin: Izd. G. Shte init sa, 1909 – 1 – CSUX89-B7295 – us Hoover Inst Photo [947]
DI VOGSHOL = ANTHOLOGY : ZAMLBUKH – (In Yiddish) – Warsaw, PL. 1930? – 1r – 1 – $25.00 – cn Can Microfilming [072]
Vogt *see* POISONS DE FLECHES ET POISONS D'EPREUVE
VOGT BARTOLD : DER GROSSE ZUG NACH DEM OSTEN / Venatier, Hans – Leipzig: Schwarzhaeupter-Verlag, 1943 – 1r – 1 – us U.W. Library [830]
Vogt, Friedrich Hermann Traugott *see*
- GESCHICHTE DER DEUTSCHEN LITTERATUR VON DEN AELTESTEN ZEITEN BIS ZUR GEGENWART
- GESCHICHTE DER MITTELHOCHDEUTSCHEN LITERATUR

Vogt, Helmut *see* DER KOENIGSTRAUM
Vogt, J *see* CATALOGUS HISTORICO-CIRTICUS LIBRORUM RARIORUM
Vogt, Mauritius *see* CONCLAVE THESAURI MAGNAE ARTIS MUSICAE..
Vogt, Paul *see* DER GRUNDTON IN GOETHES LEBENSANSCHAUUNG
Vogt, Wilhelm *see* DIE VORGESCHICHTE DES BAUERNKRIEGES
Vogtherr, H *see* EYN SCHOENE UND GOTSELIGE KURTZWEIL EINES CHRISTLICHEN LOSSBUCHS, NACH ORDNUNG EINES ALPHABETS
LA VOGUE – puis Revue mensuelle de litterature, d'art et d'actualite. Paris. avr-dec 1886, juil-aout 1889, 1899-1901 – 1 – fr A.C.R.P.P. [073]
VOGUE – (Absorbed: Vanity Fair mar 1936) – New York. v1-187. dec 1892-dec 1997+ 1; v153-158 1969-71. v161-187 1973-97+ 5; v135-187. 1960-97+ 9 – 1,5,9 – D696 – us UMI [073]
VOGUE – New York, 1892-1906 – 10r – 1 – us Ross [073]
VOGUE – (v. 157- 1971- 5,6. v. 166- 1976-9) – v. 1- 1892- – 1 – us UMI [073]
VOGUE/FRANCE – 1988-1995 – 3r per y – 5,6 – Sfr695.00 – sz Infoprint [073]
VOIAGE DE LEVANT FAIT PAR LE COMMANDEMENT DU ROY EN L'ANNEE 1621 / Deshayes de Courmenin, Louis – Paris, A. Taupinart, 1624, vi-404-20 p. French Voyagers in the Mediterranean 16th to 18th Centuries. 5961 – 9 – fr Hachette [944]
THE VOICE – Castries. St. Lucia. -w. 30 Aug 1879-14 May 1881, 16 Jul 1881-14 Jan 1882. (Imperfect). (1 reel) – 1 – uk British Libr Newspaper [072]
THE VOICE – Chelsea, Quebec: J Brown, [1876?-18– or 19–] – 9 – cn C.I.H.M. [240]
THE VOICE – Montreal, Canada. v5 n1. jan-v5 n4. oct 1880 – 1r – 1 – Can$25.00 – cn Can Microfilming [072]
THE VOICE – New York City. v1-13. 1879-91 – 3r – 1 – £165.00 – uk Chadwyck [780]
THE VOICE – New York, dec 19 1889-95 – us Res Libr [071]

THE VOICE – New York, NY. Nov 1966-Winter 1970. Ceased publication – 1 – us A.J.P.C. [071]
VOICE – 1927-Oct 1976 (complete) – 10r – 1 – ATLA S0291 – us A.T.L.A. [073]
VOICE – (Also known as: California Voice) – Berkeley, CA. 1984-1987; 1989-1991; 1993 – 4r – 1 – $200.00 – B06014 – us Library Micro [071]
VOICE – Atlanta. Ga. 1968- – 1 – us UMI [071]
VOICE – Camden. N.J. 1955-67 – 1 – us A.J.P.C. [071]
VOICE – (Former title: Voice of the Negro jan 1904-oct 1906) – Chicago. v1-4. jan 1904-oct 1907 – 1 – D3352 – us UMI [073]
VOICE – Kenesaw-Adams Co. Neb. 1939-1942 – 1 – us UMI [071]
VOICE – Las Vegas. Nev. 1964- – 1 – us UMI [071]
VOICE – Lincoln, NE. -w. Oct 1946-May 1953 – 1 – us NE Hist [071]
VOICE – Milan, Ohio. 1969-71 – 1r – 1 – $32.50r – us Archival [071]
VOICE – Phoenix, AZ. 1972-90 – 7r – 1 – $350.00 – R01503 – us Library Micro [071]
VOICE 660 – Los Angeles, CA. 1977-1984 – 2r – 1 – $100.00 – R03326 – us Library Micro [071]
THE VOICE, 1917-1954 – 94mf – 9 – Dfl1,590.00 – M393 – ne MMF Publ [780]
VOICE FOR HUMAN RIGHTS – (Library has: v.1, no.2, 4-5 (Sept. 1939; Jan., April 1940) – New York: Committee of Catholics for Human Rights, 1939-1940. 2v – 1 – CSUX89-S114 – us Hoover Inst Photo [320]
A VOICE FROM THE FIELD – Montreal, Canada. v2 n5. aut 1890 – 1r – 1 – Can$25.00 – cn Can Microfilming [790]
A VOICE FROM THE FIELD – Montreal: [s.n, 1889?-18– or 19–] ([Montreal]: City Print and Pub.) – 9 – cn C.I.H.M. [240]
A VOICE FROM THE KAHLAMBA: NO. 2, THE NATAL KAFIRS. / Moodie, Donald – Pietermaritzburg. 1857 – 1 – us Res Libr [306]
A VOICE FROM THE KAHLAMBA: ORIGIN OF THE BUSHMAN / Moodie, Donald – Cape Town. 1855 – 1 – us Res Libr [306]
A VOICE FROM THE NILE : AND OTHER POEMS. WITH A MEMOIR OF THE AUTHOR BY BERTRAM DOBELL / Thomson, James – London: Reeves and Turner, 1884 – 1 roll – 1 – 1-55879-889-7 – uk Libr Preservation [810]
VOICE, JULY 1939 *see* VOICE FOR HUMAN RIGHTS
VOICE NEWS – San Diego. Calif. 1965- – 1 – us UMI [071]
VOICE OF CHINA *see* HUASHENG BAO
VOICE OF FREE INDONESIA – (Lacking: 1947, V.2(p. 109-230, no. 66-67)) – Djakarta, 1945-1947 – 40mf – 9 – SE-978/1 – ne IDC [950]
VOICE OF INDIA – Bombay, India. -m. 1883-1889. 6 reels – 1 – uk British Libr Newspaper [072]
VOICE OF INDIA – (Missing: 1885. v3) – Bombay. v1-7. 1883-89. v10-26. 1890-1908 – 1093mf – 9 – I-114/2 – ne IDC [380]
VOICE OF INDIA, INDIAN SPECTATOR AND CHAMPION – Bombay, India. -w. 1903-1904. 6 reels – 1 – uk British Libr Newspaper [072]
VOICE OF INDONESIA : BROADCASTING SERVICE, MINISTRY OF INFORMATION – (Missing: Several issues) – Djakarta, 1950(Sept)-1962(Jan) – 22mf – 9 – SE-1984/1 – ne IDC [380]
VOICE OF IOWA – Cedar Rapids. v1-3. jan 1857-oct 1858 – 1 – D5022 – us UMI [073]
VOICE OF ISRAEL – San Francisco. Calif. 1870-74 – 1 – us A.J.P.C. [071]
VOICE OF LABOR : A WEEKLY PERIODICAL FOR THOSE WHO WORK AND THINK – no1-36 (all publ). 1907 – 1 reel – 1 – $65.00 – us UPA [335]
THE VOICE OF LABOUR – Johannesburg, South Africa. 31 Jul 1909-31 May 1912. 5 reels – 1, 16 diazo available at reduced price – sa SA Libr [072]
VOICE OF LABOUR – London, England. -w. 18 Jan-21 Sept 1907. 29 ft – 1 – uk British Libr Newspaper [072]
THE VOICE OF LABOUR (IRISH OPINION) – Dublin, Ireland.1 Dec 1917-20 Sept 1919; 22 Oct 1921-7 May 1927 – 1 – ie Microforms [072]
VOICE OF MALTA – Valletta, Malta. -w. 1 Feb 1959-11 Sept 1964. Lacking 1963. 3 reels – 1 – uk British Libr Newspaper [072]
VOICE OF NEW INDONESIA – 1958/1959 – 5mf – 9 – SE-731/1 – ne IDC [380]
THE VOICE OF PERON / Peron, Juan Domingo – [Buenos Aires], 1950 – 1 – CSUXAHZ5006-B – us Hoover Inst Photo [320]
THE VOICE OF SACRED TRIPLES / Applegate, Thomas – Boston: E P Dutton, 1866 – 1mf – 9 – 0-8370-2109-X – 1985-0109 – us A.T.L.A. [220]
VOICE OF SPAIN; A MONTHLY JOURNAL OF FACTS AND PICTURES – London, 1-3. Fiche W1249. (Blodgett Collection of Spanish Civil War Pamphlets) – 9 – us H.U. College Libr [946]
VOICE OF ST LUCIA – Castries. St. Lucia. 1885-1961, 1967 – 1 – us UMI [072]
VOICE OF ST LUCIA – Castries, St. Lucia. Jan 1889-30 Jun 1926; 2 Oct 1926-Dec 1932. (imperfect). -sw. 32mqn reels – 1 – uk British Libr Newspaper [072]
THE VOICE OF THE BONDSMAN – Stratford [Ont]: J J E Linton, [1856-18–] – 9 – cn C.I.H.M. [240]
THE VOICE OF THE CHURCH IN SPAIN – London, 1937. Fiche W1250. (Blodgett Collection of Spanish Civil War Pamphlets) – 9 – us H.U. College Libr [946]
VOICE OF THE FUGITIVE – Sandwich and Windsor, Canada. 1851-52 – 1 reel – 1 – $68.00 – cn Library Assoc [971]
VOICE OF THE LEAGUE – Cleveland. Ohio. 1938-1941 – 1 – us UMI [071]
VOICE OF THE NATION : ENGLISH-LANGUAGE DAILY NEWSPAPER – (Continued as Nation Review) – Bangkok, Thailand. Jan 1975-Dec 1975 – 1 – $250.00v – us Asia Libr [072]
VOICE OF THE NEGRO – 1-4 2+10 (all publ). 1904-1907 – 32mf – 9 – $90.00 – us UPA [975]
VOICE OF THE NEGRO – Atlanta. v. 1-4. no. 2. 1904-1907 – 1 – us NY Public [305]
VOICE OF THE NEGRO : AN ILLUSTRATED MONTHLY MAGAZINE – v1-4. 1904-07 – 1r – 1 – us Ross [073]
VOICE OF THE NEGRO *see* VOICE
VOICE OF THE NEGROIDS IN THE PACIFIC TO THE NEGROIDS THROUGHOUT THE WORLD / Papuan National Committee – SE-10,369 1. 1962? – 9 – ne IDC [980]
THE VOICE OF THE PEOPLE – Kingston [Ont]: W Kelly, v1 no 1(Dec 1889)- – 9 – cn C.I.H.M. [320]
VOICE OF THE PEOPLE – London, UK. 1883. -irr. 9 feet – 1 – uk British Libr Newspaper [072]
VOICE OF THE PEOPLE – Manchester. England. -w. Jan-Sep 1831. (1 reel) – 1 – uk British Libr Newspaper [072]
VOICE OF THE PEOPLE – Reno, NV. 1910-11 – 1r – 1 – $50.00 – U04723 – us Library Micro [071]
VOICE OF THE PEOPLE – Toronto: [s.n. 1877?] – 9 – cn C.I.H.M. [320]
VOICE OF THE PEOPLE-SUPPLEMENT TO ALL NEWSPAPERS – London, UK. 1848. -w. 5 feet – 1 – uk British Libr Newspaper [072]
THE VOICE OF THE PRECIOUS BLOOD – St.-Hyacinthe [Quebec]: Monastery of the Precious Blood, [1895-1898] – 9 – cn C.I.H.M. [210]
THE VOICE OF THE SEVEN THUNDERS, OR, LECTURES ON THE APOCALYPSE / Martin, J Lemuel – Cincinnati: Central Book Con., 1879. 1 fiche – 9 – us A.T.L.A. [240]
VOICE OF THE SHEPHERD – Utica. v1. mar-sep 1845* – 1 – D11603 – us UMI [240]
VOICE OF THE TRUTH – Providence. RI.1867-72 – 1 – us UMI [071]
VOICE OF THE VAAD – (In English and ?) – Montreal, CN. v23 no 24. 1961-1984 – 1r – 1 – Can$50.00 – cn Can Microfilming [072]
VOICE OF THE VAAD – (many missing) – (Montreal, Quebec) v2, no. 2/3 (Dec. 1962)-v26, no. 1 (Oct. 1986) – us A.J.P.C. [270]
VOICE OF THE WEST RIDING – Yorkshire. England. 1833-34 – 1 – uk Microform Academic [072]
THE VOICE OF TRUTH / Cates, J M D – 1887 – 1 – 11.20 – us Baptist [240]
VOICE OF WARNING – Boston. v1. oct 1842* – 1 – D11604 – us UMI [073]
VOICE OF WOMEN = LA VOIX DES FEMMES – 1960-74 – 1 – $75.00 – cn McLaren [305]
THE VOICE OF ZION – (New York). 1907 – 1 – us A.J.P.C. [270]
VOICE SYNTHESIS AND RECOGNITION DIRECTORY – 1985- – 1 – us UMI [073]
VOICES – New York. v1-33. fal 1965-win 1997+ 1; v12 spr 1976-win 1977*. v13-15 spr 1977-win 1980. v16 spr 1980-win 1981*. v17-25 spr 1981-win 1989. v26-30 spr 1990-win 1994*. v31-33 spr 1995-win 1997+ 5; v12-33. spr 1976-win 1997+ 9 – 1,5,9 – D3385 – us UMI [073]
VOICES FROM BABYLON : OR, THE RECORDS OF DANIEL THE PROPHET / Seiss, Joseph Augustus – (Includes index) – Philadelphia: Porter & Coates, c1879 – 1mf – 9 – 0-8370-5223-8 – 1985-3223 – us A.T.L.A. [220]
VOICES FROM ELLIS ISLAND : AN ORAL HISTORY OF AMERICAN IMMIGRATION – (Also available on 185mf for $950.00 under ISBN: 1-55655-041-3) – 8r – 1 – $950.00 – 1-55655-071-5 – us UPA [304]
VOICES FROM THE ORIENT, OR, THE TESTIMONY OF THE MONUMENTS: OF THE RECENT HISTORICAL AND TOPOGRAPHICAL DISCOVERIES: AND OF THE CUSTOMS AND TRADITIONS OF THE PEOPLE IN THE ORIENT TO THE VERACITY OF THE SACRED RECORD / Burnfield, George – Toronto: C. Robinson, 1884. 00341. (Pre-1900 Canadiana) – 9 – cn C.I.H.M. [950]
VOICES FROM THE VINEYARD – Oct 1920-Winter 1971 (complete) – 2r – 1 – ATLA S0491 – us A.T.L.A. [073]
VOICES OF THE PROPHETS: TWELVE LECTURES / Gifford, Edwin Hamilton – Edinburgh: T. & T. Clark, 1874. 1 fiche – 9 – us A.T.L.A. [240]
THE VOICES OF THE PSALMS / Walsh, William Pakenham – New York: Thomas Whittaker, 1890. 1 fiche – 9 – us A.T.L.A. [240]
VOICES OF THE SOUL ANSWERED IN GOD / Reid, John – (Includes bibliographical references) – 3rd ed. New York: Robert Carter, 1871, c1865 – 1mf – 9 – 0-8370-5151-7 – 1985-3151 – us A.T.L.A. [210]
VOICES OF THE SPIRIT / Matheson, George – New York: A C Armstrong, 1903 – 1mf – 9 – 0-8370-6276-4 – 1986-0276 – us A.T.L.A. [240]
VOICES OF THE WOMEN'S MOVEMENT – (Pt 1: Pamphlets on Women's Suffrage, The International Women's Movement and related issues. Pt 2: Pamphlets on the Employment of Women, Women's Industries, and Related Issues) – 1 – us Primary [320]
VOID JUDICIAL AND EXECUTION SALES, AND THE RIGHTS, REMEDIES AND LIABILITIES OF PURCHASERS THEREAT. / Kleber, John Christopher – New York, Banks Law Publishing Co., 1899. 489 p. LL-793 – 1 – us L of C Photodup [340]
VOIE DE LENINE – Revue marxiste de discussion. no. 1-3. Paris. avr-juin 1939 – 1 – fr A.C.R.P.P. [335]
LA VOIE DU NORD *see* DOLBEAU JOURNAL
LA VOIE DU PEUPLE – no. 1-35. Paris. 2 fevr-17 mars 1887 – 1 – fr A.C.R.P.P. [073]
VOIE LIBRE A LA VERITE / Gonzalez, Ceferino – Paris, 1938? Fiche W927. (Blodgett Collection of Spanish Civil War Pamphlets) – 9 – us H.U. College Libr [946]
Voigt, Bernhard *see*
– DIE DEUTSCHE LANDNAHME
Voigt, Edmund *see* SHAKESPEARES NATURSCHILDERUNGEN
Voigt, Felix Alfred *see*
– ANTIKE UND ANTIKES LEBENSGEFUEHL IM WERKE GERHART HAUPTMANNS
– HAUPTMANN-STUDIEN; UNTERSUCHUNGEN UEBER LEBEN UND SCHAFFEN GERHART HAUPTMANNS
Voigt, Georg *see* ENEA SILVIO DE' PICCOLOMINI, ALS PAPST PIUS DER ZWEITE: UND SEIN ZEITALTER
Voigt, J C *see* GESPRAECH VON DER MUSIK, ZWISCHEN EINEM ORGANISTEN UND ADJUVATEN
Voigt, J O *see* HORTUS SUBURBANUS CALCUTTENSIS
Voigt, Julius *see* DIE SOGENANNTE ILMENAUISCHE EMPOERUNG VON 1768
Voigtel, Otto *see* DIE UNVERZEIHLICHE TORHEIT
VOILA MONTREAL : JOURNAL BILINGUE – Montreal, nov 1980 – 1r – 1 – Can$25.00 – cn Can Microfilming [072]
LE VOILE D'ISIS – Revue mensuelle d'etudes esoteriques, psychiques et divinatoires. Fondee par le Dr. Papus. Paris. 1896-nov 1898, 1910, 1920-juin 1922 – 1 – fr A.C.R.P.P. [150]
LE VOILIN, BAROQUET – New Brunswick, aut 1965-16 aut 1972 – 1r – 1 – cn Can Microfilming [072]
VOINA – St. Petersburg. 1914-1915, nos. 2, 4-12 – 1 – 35.00r – us Hoover Inst Photo [947]
VOINA I EVREI – Moscow, 1914-16.Nos.1-14. BR-4182/2 – 8 – ne IDC [947]
VOINA I KRASNOE ZNAMIA / Dalnii, V – Petrograd: "Narodnoe di elo", 1917 – 1 – CSUX88-B8392 – us Hoover Inst Photo [947]
VOINA I MIR – Ezhemesiachnyi illiustrirovannyi voenno-obshchestvennyi zhurnal. Moscow, 1906-07. Lacking: 1907 (10-12). BR-4175/2 – 8 – ne IDC [073]
VOINA I MIR / Maiakovskii, Vladimir – Petrograd. 1917. BR-1009 2 – 8 – ne IDC [460]
VOINA I MIR – Vestnik voennoi nauki i tekhniki. Berlin, 1922-25. v1-18. BR-4181/2 – 8 – ne IDC [500]
VOINA I REVOLIUTSIIA / Aleksinskii, Grigorii Alekseevich – Petrograd: Izd. knizhn. magazina M.A. I Asnago (byv. M. Popova.), 1917 – 1 – CSUX88-B6731 – us Hoover Inst Photo [947]
VOINA I REVOLIUTSIIA – Voenno-politicheskii zhurnal. Moscow, 1925-36. v1-12:6. Lacking issues. BR-8266/2 – 8 – ne IDC [073]
VOINA I RUSSKOE SAMOSOZNANIE : PUBLICHNAI A LEKTSII A / Bulgakov, Sergei Nikolaevich – Moskva: Tip. T-va I.D. Sytina, 1915 – 1 – CSUX88-B9649 – us Hoover Inst Photo [947]
VOINA I ZEMEL'NAIA KOOPERATSIIA / Oganovskii, N P – Pg., M., 1917 – 1mf – 9 – COR-81/1 – ne IDC [334]
VOINATA MEZHDU VIZANTIIA I BULGARIIA V 986 GODINA I OBSADATA NA SOFIIA OT IMPERATORA VASILII 2 BULGAROUBIETS / Avramov, Vasil – Sofia: Pechatnitsa na Voenno-izdatelski fond, 1936 – us Res Libr [949]
VOINSTVUIUSHCHII ATEIZM – Ezhemesiachnyi nauchno politicheskii zhurnal. Moscow, Leningrad, 1931. Nos.1-12. BR-4874/2 – 8 – ne IDC [073]
VOIR : HEBDO. ARTS ET SPECTACLES – Montreal. v1 n1. 27 nov 1986-v2 n5. 24. dec 1987 – 1r – 1 – cn Can Microfilming [072]
VOIR – Montreal: Communicatins Voir inc. v4 no 1(23/29 nov 1989)-. SEM35P360 – 7r – 1 – Can$385.00 – cn Bibl Nat [073]
THE VOIR DIRE EXAMINATION, JUROR CHALLENGES, AND ADVERSARY ADVOCACY / Bermant, Gordon & Shapard, John – Washington: FJC, Nov 1978 – 1mf – 9 – $1.50 – LLMC 95-826 – us L.L.M.C. [340]
Voisin-Bey, Francois Philippe *see* LE CANAL DE SUEZ
Voission, Louis P *see* LES ISLES SAMOA ET L'ARRANGEMENT ANGLO-ALLEMAND
Voit, J G W *see* HISTORIA MUSCORUM FRONDOSORUM
VOIT TOUT – Montreal. n37. 5 oct 1954 – 1r – 1 – Can$25.00 – cn Can Microfilming [072]
Voitinskii, I S *see* TRUDOVOE PRAVO. CHAST'L
VOITLEJA – Ettlingen. Germany. -m. Jul 1952-Dec 1975. (2 reel) – 1 – uk British Libr Newspaper [947]
Voitsekhovskii, S F *see* KOOPERATIVNOE ZAKONODATEL'STVO
LA VOIX – Hebdomadaire de gauche, politique, economique et social. Red. en chef Jean Luchaire, b. de Jouvenel. Paris. fevr 1928-29 juin 1930 – 1 – fr A.C.R.P.P. [073]
LA VOIX – Montreal, Canada. aut 1880 – 1r – 1 – Can$25.00 – cn Can Microfilming [072]
LA VOIX ANTIFASCISTE – Paris. Organe quotidien pour la lutte mondiale contre le fascisme. 29 dec 1927-4 fevr 1928 – 1 – fr A.C.R.P.P. [944]
LA VOIX COMMERCIALE *see* LE SPORT
LA VOIX DE DRUMMOND / ed by McKenzie, Charles – Drummondville, Canada. 24 jun 1931-20 aut 1931 – 1r – 1 – Can$30.00 – cn Can Microfilming [072]

LA VOIX DE FRANCE – Dir. R. Coffin, H. Torres, E. Bure. New York. nov 1941-mars 1943 – 1 – fr A.C.R.P.P. [944]
LA VOIX DE FRANCE – New York City, NY. ns: 15 jan 1942; v2 n1. 1 oct 1942 – 1r – 1 – Can$25.00 – cn Can Microfilming [071]
LA VOIX DE GASPE – Gaspe, Canada. 13 sep 1928-v2 n41. 26 dec 1930 – 1r – 1 – Can$45.00 – cn Can Microfilming [072]
LA VOIX DE GUILLAUME : COUTURE – Levis, 31 jan 1947 – 1r – 1 – Can$25.00 – cn Can Microfilming [072]
LA VOIX DE JACQUES-CARTIER – Longueuil, Ville de Jacques Cartier, Canada. v1 n1. 3 jul 1958; v1 n2. 11 jul 1858 – 1r – 1 – Can$25.00 – cn Can Microfilming [072]
LA VOIX DE LA BAIE – Bagotville, Canada. 24 jun 1948-v6 n52. 16 jul 1954 – 2r – 1 – Can$60.00r – cn Can Microfilming [072]
LA VOIX DE LA JEUNESSE TRIFLUVIENNE – Trois-Rivieres, Canada. v11 n524. 15 dec 1923-v11 n527. 15 mar 1924 – 1r – 1 – Can$25.00 – cn Can Microfilming [072]
LA VOIX DE LA RIVE-SUD – Boucherville. v2 n36. 10 sep 1959 – 1r – 1 – Can$25.00 – cn Can Microfilming [072]
LA VOIX DE LA TERRE / Parti Agraire et Paysan Francais – Paris. dec 1928-aout 1939 – 1 – fr A.C.R.P.P. [073]
LA VOIX DE LA VALLEE – (Cont by and filmed with: L'Avant-Poste Gaspesien 17 nov 1944-29 dec 1991) – Amqui, Canada. 14 nov 1941-10 nov 1944 – 39r – 1 – Can$75.00r – cn Can Microfilming [072]
LA VOIX DE L'ANCIENNE-LORETTE – Ancienne Lorette, Canada. v1 n2. jun 1962; v1 n4. aut 1962 – 1r – 1 – Can$25.00 – cn Can Microfilming [072]
LA VOIX DE LAVAL – Ville de Laval. v1 n14. 26 sep 1979 – 1r – 1 – Can$25.00 – cn Can Microfilming [072]
LA VOIX DE L'ECOLIER – Joliette, Canada. 2 oct 1876-v3 n20. 24 jul 1879 – 1r – 1 – Can$30.00 – cn Can Microfilming [072]
LA VOIX DE L'EST / ed by Gagne, Rolland – Granby, Canada. 20 jun 1935-28 fev 1984 – 182r – 1 – cn Can Microfilming [072]
LA VOIX DE L'EST – Organe regional. Nancy. 1936-38 – 1 – fr A.C.R.P.P. [073]
LA VOIX DE L'OUTAOUAIS – Hull et Bryson, Canada. 16 jul 1902 – 1r – 1 – Can$25.00 – cn Can Microfilming [072]
LA VOIX DE MATANE – (Cont by: La Voix Gaspesienne) – Matane, Canada. v1 n2. 27 dec 1945-v11 n27. 25 jul 1957 – 3r – 1 – Can$60.00r – cn Can Microfilming [072]
LA VOIX DE MATANE *see* LA VOIX GASPESIENNE
LA VOIX DE SHAWINIGAN *see* LE SPORT
LA VOIX DE WOLFE – (Cont by: Le Mini-Journal, Disraeli 11 dec 1969-v2 n30. 2 dec 1970) – Victoriaville, Canada. 23 aut 1969-4 dec 1969 – 1r – 1 – Can$35.00 – cn Can Microfilming [072]
LA VOIX DES ARTISTES / Comite Central des Artistes – Peinture, sculpture. no. 1-15. Paris. aout 1849-50 – 1 – fr A.C.R.P.P. [073]
LE VOIX DES BOIS-FRANCS / ed by Camille, M & Duguay, M – Victoriaville, Canada. 25 aut 1928-27 oct 1966 – 11r – 1 – Can$60.00r – cn Can Microfilming [072]
LA VOIX DES CLUBS – Paris. Journal quotidien des Assemblees populaires. 8-26 mars 1848. devenu: La Sentinelle des clubs. Journal special des Societes republicaines. 2-7 avr 1848 – 1 – fr A.C.R.P.P. [944]
VOIX DES FEMMES – Journal puis Journal quotidien SOCIALISTE ET POLITIQUE. Organe des interets de toutes. no. 1-45. Paris. mars-juin 1848 – 1 – fr A.C.R.P.P. [073]
LA VOIX DES MILLE-ILES – Sainte-Therese de Blainville, v1 no 1- 1937-. SEM35P178 – 43r – 1 – cn Bibl Nat [073]
LA VOIX DES TRAVAILLEURS / Communist Party. France – Organe des ouvriers et paysans de la region, sous la direction du Parti communiste. devenu: La Voix du Midi. Toulouse. 1933-37 – 1 – fr A.C.R.P.P. [073]
LA VOIX D'OUTREMONT – Outremont, Canada. 1 avr 1963 – 1r – 1 – Can$25.00 – cn Can Microfilming [072]
VOIX DU BASUTOLAND – Roma, Basutoland: Vicariat apostolique du Bastutoland. [v7-26] n26-100. apr/jun 1945-64 – us Res Libr [240]
LA VOIX DU CHEF-LIEU – (Bilingual: French/ English) – Ste-Rose, Ville de Laval, Canada. v1 n8. nov 1964 – 1r – 1 – Can$20.00 – cn Can Microfilming [072]
LA VOIX DU CONGOLAISL – Leopoldville. Africa. Mar. 1945-Dec. 1959. Missing 73, 123 – 1 – 35.00r – us Hoover Inst Photo [072]
LA VOIX DU GOLFE – Rimouski, Canada. 25 jun 1867-14 jul 1871 – 2r – 1 – Can$40.00r – cn Can Microfilming [072]
LA VOIX DU LAC ST-JEAN – St-Felicien, 24 jan 1962-15 aut 1973f – 6r – 1 – Can$65.00 – cn Can Microfilming [072]
LA VOIX DU MINEUR – Organe du syndicat unitaire des mineurs et similaires du bassin d'Anzin-Denain. Denain. dec 1934-juin 1939 – 1 – fr A.C.R.P.P. [331]
LA VOIX DU MINEUR 1935 – no. 28-29. Lens. sept oct 1935 – 1 – fr A.C.R.P.P. [331]
LA VOIX DU MINEUR 1907-1914 / Federation des Mineurs du Nord et du Pas-de-Calais – Lens. sept 1907-aout 1914 – 1 – fr A.C.R.P.P. [622]
LA VOIX DU MINEUR 1933-1939 – Organe du syndicat unitaire des mineurs du Nord. Douai. nov 1933-sept 1939 – 1 – fr A.C.R.P.P. [331]
LA VOIX DU NORD – (Ed. Lille-ville. 1969-1990. 1) – Lille. Toutes eds. 1958-juin 1990 – 1 – fr A.C.R.P.P. [072]
LA VOIX DU PAYSAN – Organe des Comites et ligues d'action et de defense paysannes. Dir. Henri Dorgeres. avr 1933-avr 1937. devenu: Le Cri du paysan. mai 1937-janv 1940. Paris – 1 – fr A.C.R.P.P. [073]
LA VOIX DU PEUPLE / ed by Bechard, Auguste – Louiseville, Canada. v1 n6. 29 mai 1890 – 1r – 1 – Can$25.00 – cn Can Microfilming [072]
LA VOIX DU PEUPLE / C G T – no. 1-729; 2e s.-4e s., no. 1-224. Paris. 9 dec 1900-juin 1939 – 1 – fr A.C.R.P.P. [073]
LA VOIX DU PEUPLE / Communist Party. France – no. 1-81. Clermont-Ferrand. 13 sept 1944-45. mq no. 49 – 1 – fr A.C.R.P.P. [073]
LA VOIX DU PEUPLE – Hull, Canada. 14 jan 1905 – 1r – 1 – Can$25.00 – cn Can Microfilming [072]
LA VOIX DU PEUPLE – (Includes: La Voce del popolo. The People's Voice) – Ville St-Leonard. v2 n2. fev 1970-mai 1973 – 1r – 1 – Can$25.00 – cn Can Microfilming [072]
LA VOIX DU PEUPLE : JOURNAL DES OUVRIERS ET DES FAMILLES – Quebec, Canada. 21 dec 1907 – 1r – 1 – Can$20.00 – cn Can Microfilming [072]
LA VOIX DU PEUPLE – Longueil, Canada. 30 oct 1900 – 1r – 1 – Can$25.00 – cn Can Microfilming [072]
LA VOIX DU PEUPLE – Montmagny, Canada. v5 n1. 24 dec 1937-27 dec 1963 – 4r – 1 – Can$50.00r – cn Can Microfilming [072]
LA VOIX DU PEUPLE – Montreal, Canada. v1 n2. 19 avr 1941-v1 n6. 14 jun 1941 – 1r – 1 – Can$25.00 – cn Can Microfilming [072]
LA VOIX DU PEUPLE – Organe de defense morale et materielle des musulmans algeriens. Alger. sept 1933-mai 1935 – 1 – fr A.C.R.P.P. [073]
LA VOIX DU PEUPLE – Quebec, Canada. v1 n2. 2 jan 1852-v1 n18. 27 avr 1852 – 1r – 1 – Can$25.00 – cn Can Microfilming [072]
LA VOIX DU PEUPLE – St-Jean, Canada. v2 n37. 13 aut 1880-v2 n38. 19 aut 1881 – 1r – 1 – Can$25.00 – cn Can Microfilming [072]
LA VOIX DU PEUPLE – St-Roch Canada. n2,4,10. n.d. 1879(?) – 1r – 1 – Can$25.00 – cn Can Microfilming [072]
LA VOIX DU PEUPLE – Tribune de la democratie et du travail. Journal politique hebdomadaire. No.1, 6-25. Paris. 6 fevr, 13 avr-28 aout 1869 – 1 – fr A.C.R.P.P. [073]
LA VOIX DU PEUPLE DE LA GUADELOUPE – Pointe-a-Pitre. Guadeloupe. Jan. 19, 26, 1935 – 1 – us NY Public [072]
LA VOIX DU PRECIEUX SANG = THE VOICE OF THE PRECIOUS BLOOD – St-Hyacinthe, Quebec: Soeurs du precieux sang, [1894-1898] – 9 – cn C.I.H.M. [210]
LA VOIX DU PRECIEUX SANG *see* THE VOICE OF THE PRECIOUS BLOOD
VOIX DU PRINTEMPS / Jaell, Marie – Six morceaux pour piano a 4 mains. 1886? – 9 – us Sibley [780]
LA VOIX DU PROPRIETAIRE – Montreal, Canada. 1 jan 1950 – 1r – 1 – Can$25.00 – cn Can Microfilming [072]
LA VOIX DU SUD – Lac Etchemin, Canada. dec 1961-v1 n14. 4 oct 1962 – 1r – 1 – Can$30.00 – cn Can Microfilming [072]
LA VOIX DU SUD : PERIODIQUE COUVRANT TOUTES LES FAMILLES DE DORCHESTER ENTIEREMENT DEVOUE AU COMTE – Lac Etchemin: '(s.n.)' v1 no 2 (fev 1961)-. SEM35P130 – 41r – 1 – cn Bibl Nat [920]
LA VOIX D'UN EXILE / Frechette, Louis-Honore – 1mf – 9 – Can$2.25 – SEM105P23 – cn Bibl Nat [920]
LA VOIX GASPESIENNE – (Cont: La Voix de Matane) – Matane, Canada. v26 n1. 2 mar 1956-18 dec 1991 – 50r – 1 – Can$75.00r – cn Can Microfilming [072]
LA VOIX GASPESIENNE *see* LA VOIX DE MATANE
LA VOIX INDIGENE – puis libre. Journal d'union francomusulmane et de defense des interets indigenes. Constantine. 1932-40, 1946-52 – 1 – fr A.C.R.P.P. [073]
LES VOIX INTIMES / Caouette, Jean Baptiste – Avec une preface de Benjamin Suite. Quebec: L. J. Demers, 1892. 00474. (Pre-1900 Canadiana) – 9 – cn C.I.H.M. [830]
LA VOIX LIBRE – Organe de defense de tout Francais contre l'arbitraire et le favoritisme. Dir. E. Ganofsky. Saigon. sept 1921-fevr 1932 – 1 – fr A.C.R.P.P. [073]
LA VOIX METROPOLITAINE / ed by Jean-Yvon & Houle, Hector – Sorel, Canada. v4 n27. 7 jul 1964; 3 aut 1965-30 aut 1972 – 5r – 1 – Can$65.00r – cn Can Microfilming [072]
LA VOIX NATIONALE : REVUE MENSUELLE – Montreal. jun 1927-v39 n11. mai 1966 – 6r – 1 – Can$60.00r – cn Can Microfilming [073]
LA VOIX OUVRIERE – Organe des groupes legionnaires d'entreprises. no. 1-51. Lyon. 1er juin 1942-15 aout 1944. mq no. 12, 48 – 1 – fr A.C.R.P.P. [073]
LA VOIX PAYSANNE / G LP – Lyon. no. 1-22. 20 sept 1943-5 aout 1944. mq no. 15-19 – 1 – fr A.C.R.P.P. [073]
LA VOIX POPULAIRE / ed by Mercier, Jean-Jacques – Montreal, Canada. 17 avr 1946-22 dec 1991 – 68r – 1 – Can$70.00r – cn Can Microfilming [072]
LA VOIX REGIONALE – Granby, Canada. 15 jun 1971-v3 n16. 2 oct 1973 – 1r – 1 – Can$25.00 – cn Can Microfilming [072]
LA VOIX SEFARAD – Montreal, Quebec, Canada. 1977-81 – 1 – us A.J.P.C. [072]
Voizard, E *see* ETUDE SUR LA LANGUE DE MONTAIGNE
Vojvodina. Yugoslavia *see* SLUZBENI LIST
DER VOKALISMUS DER MUNDART DES ZUERCHER OBERLANDES / Weber, Albert – Zuerich, 1918 – 2mf – DM62.00 – 3-8267-3048-8 – gw Hänsel [390]
DI VOKH = THE WEEK – (In Yiddish) – Paris, FR. no6. 22 Jan 1947 – 1r – 1 – $25.00 – cn Can Microfilming [072]
VOKHNBLAT = WEEKLY / ed by Trepman, Paul – Bergen-Belsen, DE. v1 no1 5 Dec 1947-v4 no80 18 Aug 1950 – 1r – 1 – $50.00 – cn Can Microfilming [072]
VOKIECIU LITERATUROS ISTORIJA / Ehret, Joseph – Kaunas: V.D. Univ. Teol.-Filosofijos Fakulteto Leidinys, 1931- – 1r – 1 – us U.W. Library [430]
VOKRUG SVETA – Zhurnal zemlivedeniia, estestvennykh nauk, noveishikh, otkrytii, izobretenii i nabliudenii. St. Petersburg, 1861-68. v1-8. Lacking: 1864,v4, no.8,p225-260. BR-4200/2 – 8 – ne IDC [947]
Vokrus Dostoevskogo i Gor'kogo *see* BIULLETENI LITERATURY I ZHIZNI
VOL 54 A 57 *see* LE JOURNAL DES ETUDIANTS
O VOLANTE – Manaus, Amazonas. 16 Maio 1976 – 1,5,6 – bl Biblioteca [072]
O VOLANTIM – Rio de Janeiro, 1 Sep-31 Oct 1822 – 1,5,6 – bl Biblioteca [072]
VOLATAS : ORGAM LITTERARIO – Manaos, Amazonas. 15 Ago-4 Out 1895 – 1,5,6 – bl Biblioteca [072]
Volbeding, Joh. Ernst *see* CONSTANTIN TISCHENDORF IN SEINER FUENFUNDZWANZIGJAEHRIGEN SCHRIFTSTELLERISCHEN WIRKSAMKEIT
VOLCANOLOGY AND SEISMOLOGY / ed by Rykunov, L N – 9,5,1 – us Gordon [550]
VOLCANOLOGY-ARCHAELOGY COLLECTION *see*
– THE ARCHAEOLOGY OF THE NAPA, CALIFORNIA REGION
– ILIAMNA VOLCANO AND ITS BASEMENT
VOLCANOLOGY-ARCHAEOLOGY – (Titles listed individually) – 1 – $50.00r – us Library Micro [550]
O VOLCAO – '(s.l.')-Sao Luis, Brazil. 10 Apr, Jun, 1 Aug 1849 – 1,5,6 – bl Biblioteca [072]
VOLCHII SMEKH / Gallch, Iurii – Riga: Gramatu dragus, 1929. 217p. In Cyrillic characters – 1 – us U.W. Library [830]
Volck, Herbert *see* DIE WOELFE
Volck, Wilhelm *see*
– DIE BIBEL ALS KANON: DREI VORTRAEGE
– HEILIGE SCHRIFT UND KRITIK
LE VOLEUR : HEBDO LITTERAIRE – Quebec, Canada. 2,9 jun 1881 – 1r – 1 – Can$25.00 – cn Can Microfilming [072]
LES VOLEURS / Vidocq – 1837 – 9 – fr I.C.S. [830]
Vol'f, M O *see*
– SISTEMATICHESKII KATALOG KNIZHNYKH MAGAZINOV T-VA M.O. VOL'F
– SISTEMATICHESKII KATALOG NOVEISHIKH KNIG IZD. M.O. VOL'F
– SISTEMATICHESKII KATALOG (NOVYI) RUSSKAGO OTDELENIIA KNIZHNAGO MAGAZINA M. O. VOL'FA. 1830-1880
Vol'fing, Emil' Medtner *see* MODERNIZM V MUZYKE
Volger, Katrin *see* UNTERSUCHUNG ZUR RAEUMLICHEN UND SOZIALEN STRUKTUR UND DEREN ENTWICKLUNG BEI TAMMAR-WALLABIES, MACROPUS EUGENII (DESMAREST, 1817)
VOLGO-DONSKOI KOOPERATOR – Tsaritsin, 1923-24 n1 – 21 mf – 9 – COR-571/1 – ne IDC [334]
VOLGO-KASPIISKII KOOPERATOR – (Missing: 1918-19 n1-5) – Astrakhan', 1918-19 n6/10 – 2mf – 9 – COR-570/1 – ne IDC [334]
Volhardt, R *see* BIBLIOGRAPHIE DER MUSIK-WERKE IN DER RATSSCHULBIBLIOTHEK ZU ZWICKAU
VOLIA – Ezhemesiachnik Soiuza byvshikh politicheskii zakliuchennykh iz SSSR. Munich, 1952-54 (2). BR-8343/2 – 8 – ne IDC [947]
VOLIA – Plovdiv, Bulgaria. Mar-Sept 1943 – 1r – 1 – us L of C Photodup [949]
VOLIA ROSSII – Prague. 1930, nos. 2-12; 1931, nos. 1-12; 1932, nos. 1-6 – 1 – $35.00r – us Hoover Inst Photo [947]
VOLIA ROSSII – Prague, Czechoslovakia. Sept 1920-Oct 1921 – 1r – 1 – us L of C Photodup [072]
VOLIA ROSSII – Zhurnal politiki i kul'tury. Prague, 1922-32. V1-28 published as Ezhenedel'nik. BR-3469/2 – 8 – ne IDC [947]
VOLIA TRUDA / Revoliutsionnogo Kommunizma Partii. Tsentral'nogo komiteta – Moscow. 1918, nos. 31-64. Missing: nos. 39-42, 47 – 1 – 35.00r – us Hoover Inst Photo [335]
Volin, A *see* MOLODAIA ROSSIIA
VOLINER GEDANK = VOLINER THOUGHT – (In Yiddish) – New Wolin, PL. v1 no7 5 Aug 1927 – 1r – 1 – $25.00 – cn Can Microfilming [072]
VOLINER LEBEN = LIFE – (In Yiddish) – Rowne, PL. v4 no278 10 May 1927-v6 no532 20 Dec 1929 – 1r – 1 – $25.00 – cn Can Microfilming [072]
VOLINER SHTIME = VOLINER VOICE – (In Yiddish) – Rowne, PL. v2 no2 Jan 1928-v3 no14 (no107) 5 Apr 1929 – 1r – 1 – $25.00 – cn Can Microfilming [072]
VOLINER VOKH = VOLINER WEEK – (Yiddish weekly) – Rowne, PL. v3 no43 12 Oct 1926; v3 no50 10 Dec 1925 – 1r – 1 – $25.00 – cn Can Microfilming [072]
O VOLITIVO – Uberaba, 21 Sep 1884 – 1,5,6 – bl Biblioteca [072]
DAS VOLK – Berlin, 1945-1946 – 1r – 1 – DM80.00 – gw Mikro Press [943]
DAS VOLK – Berlin, jul 7 1945-apr 21 1946 – 1r – 1 – Inquire at Mikrofilmarchiv for details – gw Misc Inst [072]
DAS VOLK – East Berlin, Germany. 7 Jul 1945-21 Apr 1946 – 1 – gw Mikrofilm [072]
DAS VOLK – Erfurt, East Germany. Aug 1954-Jun 1981 – 1 – gw Mikrofilm [072]
DAS VOLK – London. -w. 7 May-20 Aug 1859. (12 feet) – 1 – uk British Libr Newspaper [072]
DAS VOLK – New York, NY. 1907-08. The People – 1 – us A.J.P.C. [071]
HET VOLK / Sociaal-Democratische Arbeiderspartij – Amsterdam, 1900-27 – 1 – us Hoover Inst Photo [331]
VOLK – London, UK. 7 May-20 Aug 1859 – 1 – uk British Libr Newspaper [072]

EIN VOLK - EIN REICH - EIN FUEHRER! : GEDICHTE UM OESTERREICHS HEIMKEHR / Anacker, Heinrich – Muenchen: F Eher Nachf., 1938 – 1r – 1 – us U.W. Library [810]
Volk, Georg *see* SUNNDAG UN WERDAG
VOLK, ICH BRECHE DEINE KOHLE! : ERZAEHLUNGEN EINES DEUTSCHEN BERGMANNS / Wohlgemuth, Otto – Berlin: Junge Generation Verlag, 1936 – 1 – us U.W. Library [890]
Volk, P *see* DER LIBER ORDINARIUS DES LUETTICHER ST JAKOBSKLOSTERS
VOLK UND LAND – (Lacking: 1920) – Berlin. 1919-20. BJ-23-58 1 – 26mf – 9 – ne IDC [470]
VOLK UND REICH – Politische Monatshefte. Berlin.1933 – 1 – fr A.C.R.P.P. [073]
VOLK UND ZEIT – Berlin, Germany.1926-32 – 1 – gw Mikrofilm [072]
VOLK UND ZEIT : BILDER ZUM VORWAERTS – Berlin, 1919-1933 – 4r – 1 – DM300.00 – gw Mikro Press [943]
VOLK UND ZEIT – Hamburg, Germany. Mai 1923-No.3, 1932 – 1 – gw Mikrofilm [072]
VOLK UND ZEIT – (Used as a suppl, eg of Volkszeitung, Duesseldorf) – Berlin, 1924 n29-1932 n3 – 3r – 1 – Inquire at Mikrofilmarchiv for details – gw Misc Inst [072]
Volkaersbeke, P K de *see* JOYEUSE ENTREE DE L'EMPEREUR MAXIMILIEN I A GAND, EN 1508
VOLKAN – (1992 Iz Yayinciliik reprint edition) – Istanbul: Ahmed Saki Bey Matbaasi, Nos. 1-110 (1908-1909) – 12mf – 9 – $200.00 – us MEDOC [949]
Volkel, Lowell M *see* 1820 FEDERAL CENSUS OF ILLINOIS
VOLKENRECHT / Fabius, D P D – Amsterdam, 1907 – 2mf – 1 – ILM-3576/1 – ne IDC [327]
VOLKISCHER BEOBACHTER – (Some issues lacking) – Munich, Germany. 1920-Jun 1938; 1942-43 – 53r – 1 – us L of C Photodup [072]
Volkmann, Erich Otto *see* DIE ROTEN STREIFEN
Volkmann, Richard von *see*
- AU COIN DU FEU
- VARIATIONEN UEBER EIN THEMA VON HAENDEL FUR PIANOFORTE...OP. 26...

Volkmar, Gustav *see*
- HIPPOLYTUS UND DIE ROEMISCHEN ZEITGENOSSEN, ODER, DIE PHILOSOPHUMENA UND DIE VERWANDTEN SCHRIFTEN NACH URSPRUNG, COMPOSITION UND QUELLEN
- JESUS NAZARENUS UND DIE ERSTE CHRISTLICHE ZEIT
- DIE NEUENTDECKTE URCHRISTLICHE SCHRIFT
- EINE NEU-TESTAMENTLICHE ENTDECKUNG UND DEREN BESTREITUNG, ODER DIE GESCHICHTS-VISION DES BUCHES HENOCH IM ZUSAMMENHANG
- UEBER JUSTIN DEN MAERTYRER UND SEIN VERHAELTNIS ZU UNSERN EVANGELIEN
- DER URSPRUNG UNSERER EVANGELIEN NACH DEN URKUNDEN, LAUT DEN NEUERN ENTDECKUNGEN UND VERHANDLUNGEN
- DAS VIERTE BUCH ESRA UND APOKALYPTISCHE GEHEIMNISSE UEBERHAUPT

Volkov, A *see*
- IZMENENIE POLOZHENIIA ZHENSHCHINY I DEMOGRAFICHESKOE RAZVITIE SEMI
- OCHERKI RUSSKOI LITERATURY KONTSA 19NACHALA 20 VEKOV
- POEZIIA BURZHUAZNOGO UPADKA
- POEZIIA RUSSKOGO IMPERIALIZMA

Volkova *see* USLOVII A I KHOD PROIZROSTANII A KHLEBOV UROZHAI A 1918-1919 S.-KH. G. V KIEVSKO I GUB
Volkova, M P *see* OPISANIE MAN'CHZHURSKIKH RUKOPISEI INSTITUTA NARODOV AZII AN SSSR
VOLKOVISKER LEBN = WOLKOWYSK LIFE – (Yiddish weekly) – Wolkowysk, PL. v1 no8 29 Sep 1926; v7 no275 14 Jan 1932 – 1r – 1 – $25.00 – cn Can Microfilming [072]
VOLKOVISKER VOKHNBLAT = WOLKOWYSK WEEKLY – (In Yiddish) – Wolkowysk, PL. v2 no78 13 Oct 1929; v2 no79 25 Oct 1929 – 1r – 1 – $25.00 – cn Can Microfilming [072]
VOLKSANZEIGER – Novy Bor, Czechoslovakia. Mar-Apr 1941; 8 Jan 1943 – 1r – 1 – us L of C Photodup [072]
VOLKSARMEE – Berlin, 1957-sep 30 1990 – 30r – 1 – Inquire at Mikrofilmarchiv for details – gw Misc Inst [355]
VOLKSARMEE – East Berlin, Germany. 1957-85 – 1 – gw Mikrofilm [072]
VOLKSAUSGABE SEINER WERKE IM URTEXT / Gotthelf, Jeremias – Bern: Schmid & Francke. 10v. 1898-1900 – 1 – us U.W. Library [800]
VOLKSBAETIN – Muenchen, Germany. 4 Mai 1849-Okt 1852 – 1 – gw Mikrofilm [072]
DER VOLKSBEGRIFF DER DEUTSCHEN VOLKSKUNDE IN SEINER GESCHICHTLICHEN ENTWICKLUNG / Ihme, Heinrich – 1995 – 1mf – 9 – DM48.00 – 3-8267-3204-9 – gw Hänsel [943]
HET VOLKSBLAD – Cape Town, South Africa. 3 Jan 1856-29 Mar 1886. 26 reels. Absorbed by: Evening Express – 1, 16 diazo available at reduced price – sa SA Libr [072]
DIE VOLKSBLAD – Bloemfontein, South Africa. 1916-1981 – 1 – sa State Libr [072]
DIE VOLKSBLAD – Bloemfontein, South Africa. 3 Jan 1933-31 Dec 1948. 48 reels – 1, 16 diazo available at reduced price – sa SA Libr [072]
VOLKSBLATT – Bochum, Jan-Jun 1899; Jan 1900-Jul 1901; Jul-Sept 1902; Aug 1914-Dec 1919; Oct 1920-27 Feb 1933 – 47r – 1 – DM3,525.00 – gw Mikro Press [072]
VOLKSBLATT – Braunschweig, 1917-1918 – 3r – 1 – DM225.00 – gw Mikro Press [072]
VOLKSBLATT – Braunschweig, Germany. 27 Apr 1917-9 Nov 1918 – 1 – gw Mikrofilm [072]
VOLKSBLATT – Buenos Aires, Argentina. Nov. 1941-1 Aug 1943 – 1 – gw Mikrofilm [072]
VOLKSBLATT – Buenos Aires, nov 1 1941-aug 1 1943 – 1r – 1 – Inquire at Mikrofilmarchiv for details – gw Misc Inst [972]
VOLKSBLATT – Goettingen. apr 1, 1921-nov 30, 1923. jan 2-feb 28, 1933 – 4r – 1 – gw Mikrofilm [943]
VOLKSBLATT – Halle Saale, Germany. 1917-20. (incompl.) – 1 – gw Mikrofilm [072]
VOLKSBLATT – Pittsburgh. Pa. 1859-1877; 1885-1900 – 1 – us UMI [071]
VOLKSBLATT – Pittsburgh. PA.Also: Freiheits Freund. 1859-77, 1885-1942 – 1 – us UMI [071]
VOLKSBLATT – Wien: "Herold", Druck- und Verlags-GmbH, may 1-2 1964-nov 15 1970 – 27r – 1 – us Res Libr [072]
VOLKSBLATT AN DER NORDSEE *see* DER MITTHEILER AN DER UNTERWESER
VOLKSBLATT AN DER WESER *see* DER MITTHEILER AN DER UNTERWESER
VOLKSBLATT BERLIN *see*
- SPANDAUER VOLKSBLATT

VOLKSBLATT FUER BERGISCH GLADBACH UND UMGEBUNG – (Suppl available from other sources, inquire: Mikrofilmarchiv Dortmund. Cont by: Bergisch-Gladbacher Volkszeitung, oct 1 1906. Rheinisch-Bergische Zeitung, jan 2 1930) – Bergisch-Gladbach, oct 4 1890-mar 15 1945 – 1 – Dist. gw Mikrofilm – gw Misc Inst [943]
VOLKSBLATT FUER DEN WAHLKREIS BOCHUM UND UMGEBUNG – (1899-sep 1902: Bereichsausgabe der Rheinisch-Westfaelischen Arbeiter-Zeitung, Dortmund, since oct 1902 independent) – Bochum, 1899-1902, oct 1 1907-jun 30 1908, dec 16 1913, aug 1914-19, oct 1920-feb 27 1933 – 1 – Inquire at Mikrofilmarchiv for details – gw Misc Inst [943]
VOLKSBLATT FUER DEN WAHLKREIS BOCHUM UND UMGEBUNG – (Cont: Bereichsausgabe der Rheinisch-Westfaelischen Arbeiter-Zeitung, Dortmund, oct 1, 1902) – Bochum. oct 1, 1907-jun 30, 1908 – 2r – 1 – gw Mikrofilm [072]
VOLKSBLATT FUER DIE KREISE BONN UND SIEG – Bonn, apr 24-dec 29 1849 – 1 – Inquire at Mikrofilmarchiv for details – gw Misc Inst [943]
VOLKSBLATT FUER HARBURG, WILHELMSBURG UND UMGEBUNG – (Cont by: Volksblatt fuer Harburg-Wilhelmsburg und Umgebung, dec 10, 1927) – Hamburg-Harburg. 1904. 1913 (incomplete). jun 1, 1914-apr 30, 1915 – 3r – 1 – gw Mikrofilm [943]
VOLKSBLATT FUER HARBURG-WILHELMSBURG UND UMGEBUNG *see* VOLKSBLATT FUER HARBURG, WILHELMSBURG UND UMGEBUNG
VOLKSBLATT FUER LUENEBURG UND UMGEBUNG – Lueneburg, Germany. 25 Jul 1914-30 Jun 1917; 2 Jan-30 Mar 1918; Jul 1918-5 Mai 1922; 1923; Aug-Dez 1924; 1925 – 1 – gw Mikrofilm [072]
VOLKSBLATT FUER LUENEBURG UND UMGEBUNG – Lueneburg, Jul 1914-Jun 1917; Jan- Mar, Jul-Dec 1918; 1919-21; Jan, Jun- 1922; 1923; Aug-Dec 1924; Jan-Dec 1925; Jan-Dec 1926 – 17r – 1 – DM1,275.00 – gw Mikro Press [072]
VOLKSBLATT FUER RHEINE UND UMGEBUNG *see*
- VOLKS-ZEITUNG FUER RHEINE UND UMGEBUNG

VOLKSBODE – Cape Town, South Africa. 18 Feb 1887-29 Apr 1896. 6 reels – 1, 16 diazo available at reduced price – sa SA Libr [072]
DER VOLKSBOTE – Bozen, 1931-37, 1986- – 1 – Inquire at Mikrofilmarchiv for details – gw Misc Inst [945]
DER VOLKSBOTE – Muenchen, DE. 1848-49 – 1 – gw Mikrofilm [072]
DER VOLKSBOTE – Osijek, Yugoslavia. Mar 1927-Apr 1928 – 1r – 1 – us L of C Photodup [949]
DER VOLKSBOTE *see* LUEBECKER BUERGERFREUND
VOLKSBOTE *see* DEUTSCHER VOLKSFREUND
VOLKSDEUTSCHE ZEITUNG – Brno, Czechoslovakia. Feb-Apr 1939; 31 May 1939-Nov 1940 – 7r – 1 – us L of C Photodup [072]
VOLKSDEUTSCHE ZEITUNG – Bruenn, sep 2 1939-nov 30 1940 – 1 – Inquire at Mikrofilmarchiv for details – gw Misc Inst [943]
VOLKSDEUTSCHES ABENDBLATT – Brno, Czechoslovakia. Mar 1939-Nov 1940 – 2r – 1 – us L of C Photodup [072]
VOLKS-ECHO : (AUSGABE A) – (Publ started in Detmold) – Bielefeld, jul 16 1946-50 – 1 – Inquire at Mikrofilmarchiv for details – gw Misc Inst [072]
DER VOLKSFREUND – Ansbach, jan-mar, may 1798, jul 1798-jun 1799 – 1r – 1 – Dist. gw Mikrofilm – gw Misc Inst [943]
DER VOLKSFREUND – Bielefeld, Germany. Jun 1848-Jul 1850 – 1 – gw Mikrofilm [072]
DER VOLKSFREUND – Bielefeld, Lemgo, Wiedenbrueck. Jun 10 1848-jul 12 1850 – 1r – 1 – Inquire at Mikrofilmarchiv for details – gw Misc Inst [943]
DER VOLKSFREUND – (Cont: Woechentliches Amts- und Intelligenzblatt fuer das Oberamt Balingen, -1840; Der Albbote, -1849; Amts- und Intelligenzblatt fuer das Oberamt Balingen, -1866. Cont by: Der Wille, jun 1 1933; Der Albbote, apr 1 1935; Balinger Heimatblatt, may 2 1935; Der Albbote Talgang-Zeitung, aug 30 1939; Der Wille, feb 2 1942; Schwaebisches Tagblatt, Bereichsausgabe, 1946; Der Volksfreund, sep 1 1949) – Balingen, Ebingen. feb 7 1835-apr 19 1945, jan 4 1946-50 – 1 – Dist. gw Mikrofilm – gw Misc Inst [943]
DER VOLKSFREUND – Duisburg, Germany. 13 Jun 1849-30 Jun 1850, inc – 1 – gw Mikrofilm [072]
DER VOLKSFREUND – Jena, Germany. Jan-Sept 1818 – 1 – gw Mikrofilm [072]
DER VOLKSFREUND – Karlsruhe, Germany. 1881-99; Jul 1905-18 Mar 1933 – 1 – gw Mikrofilm [072]
DER VOLKSFREUND : TAGESZEITUNG FUER DAS WERKTAETIGE VOLKS BADEN – (Vorgaenger: Der Rheinbote) – Offenburg/ Karlsruhe, 1881-99; 1905-33 – 78r – 1 – DM5,850.00 – gw Mikro Press [072]
DER VOLKSFREUND – (Title changes: Konstanzisches Intelligenzblatt, 1810; Konstanzer politische Zeitung, 2 Jul 1821; Konstanzer Zeitung, 2 Jan 1829) – Konstanz, Germany. 1848-1849 – 2r – 1 – gw Mikrofilm [072]
VOLKSFREUND – Braunschweig, 1871-1933 – 93r – 1 – DM6,975.00 – gw Mikro Press [072]
VOLKSFREUND – Braunschweig, Germany. Also as: Braunschweiger Volksfreund. (15 May 1871-31 Dec 1906). 15 May 1871-2 Mar 1933 – 1 – gw Mikrofilm [072]
VOLKSFREUND – Karlsruhe, Germany. -d. 1 Sept 1916-6 Aug 1919. 4 reels – 1 – uk British Libr Newspaper [072]
VOLKSFREUND *see* BRAUNSCHWEIGER VOLKSFREUND
VOLKSFREUND FUER DAS MITTLERE DEUTSCHLAND – Frankfurt, Germany. 29 Mar 1857-1863, 1865-15 Jul 1866 – 1 – gw Mikrofilm [072]
VOLKSFREUND FUER DAS MITTLERE DEUTSCHLAND – Frankfurt M., Mar 1857-63; 1865-Jul 1866 – 5r – 1 – DM375.00 – gw Mikro Press [072]
DER VOLKSFREUND FUER STADT UND LAND BRESLAU – Breslau (Wroclaw), Poland. 1881-84 – 1 – gw Mikrofilm [943]
DER VOLKSFUEHRER – Heidelberg, Germany. 12 Jan-22 Jun 1849 – 1 – gw Mikrofilm [072]
VOLKSFUNK – Berlin, Germany.1932-33 – 1 – gw Mikrofilm [072]
VOLKSFUNK *see* DER NEUE RUNDFUNK
DE VOLKSGAZET – Antwerp, 1914, 1919, 1945 (all incompl) – 1 – us Hoover Inst Photo [072]
VOLKSGESETZBUCH. GRUNDREGEL UND BUCH I / Hedemann, Justus W & Lehmann, Heinrich & Siebert, Wolfgang – Muenchen Berlin, 1942 – 1 – DM30.00 – gw Mikro Press [943]
VOLKSGLAUBE UND VOLKSBRAUCH DER SIEBENBUERGER SACHSEN. 1893 / Wlislocki, Heinrich von – 1 – us I.U. Libraries [390]
VOLKSKAMMER.. / Germany. Democratic Republic. Volkskammer – 8 Nov 1950-2 Nov 1951. Issued in 2 pts: Sitzungs-Protokolle; and Drucksachen-Sammlung – 1 – us U.W. Library [324]
VOLKSKAMMER DER DDR – 1950-1989 – 242mf – 1 – DM1,379.40 – gw Mikro Press [320]
VOLKSKUNDE – Ghent, Belgium. v6-10. 1893-98 – 1 – us I.U. Libraries [390]
VOLKSKUNDLICHES AUS ALTTURKESTAN. IN: ASIA MAJOR / Brockelmann, C – Leipzig, 1925. v2, p 110-124 – 8 – ne IDC [950]
VOLKSLIED, VOLKSTANZ, VOLKSMUSIK – Vienna. v.5-41. 1903-39 – 1 – 92.00 – us L of C Photodup [780]
VOLKSMAEHRCHEN UND EPISCHE DICHTUNG / Bernhardi, Theodor von – 1871 – 1 – us I.U. Libraries [390]
VOLKSRAAD – Jaargang 1. Weltevreden. Jaarboekje. 1922-23. BSE-1445 1 – 2mf – 9 – ne IDC [950]
DE VOLKSRAAD ALS KRISTALLISATOR VAN HET "INDISCHE BEWUSTZIJN" / Hart, G H C – 's-Gravenhage, 1938 – 1mf – 9 – ne IDC [320]
VOLKSRECHT – Zuerich, 1944 (incompl) – 1 – us Hoover Inst Photo [331]
VOLKSRECHT (USPD) – Frankfurt, Germany. Feb 1919-Sept 1922 – 1 – gw Mikrofilm [072]
VOLKSRECHT (USPD) – Frankfurt M., Feb 1919-Sept 1922 – 5r – 1 – DM375.00 – gw Mikro Press [072]
VOLKSRUF – Pancevo, Yugoslavia. 1936-37 – 1r – 1 – us L of C Photodup [949]
VOLKSSCHAUSPIELE AUS DEM BOEHMERWALDE / ed by Ammann, Johann Josef – v1 only. 1898. Folk-drama – 1 – us I.U. Libraries [390]
VOLKSSCHULE UND KIRCHE : AUCH EINE SOZIALE FRAGE: EIN BEITRAG ZUR DIESTERWEG-FEIER / Baumgarten, Otto – Leipzig: Fr Wilh Grunow, 1890 – 1mf – 9 – 0-8370-7525-4 – 1986-1525 – us A.T.L.A. [370]
VOLKSSPIEGEL *see* BRESLAUER VOLKSSPIEGEL
DER VOLKSSTAAT – Leipzig, Germany. Okt. 1869-Sept. 1876 – 1 – gw Mikrofilm [072]
DER VOLKSSTAAT – Leipzig, Oct 1869-Oct 1876 – 4r – 1 – DM400.00 – gw Mikro Press [072]
DER VOLKSSTAAT *see* DEMOKRATISCHES WOCHENBLATT
DIE VOLKSSTIMME – Duesseldorf, Germany. Jun-17 Dez 1848 – 1 – gw Mikrofilm [072]
DIE VOLKSSTIMME – Hermannstadt, Rumaenien.10 Aug 1934-3 Mai 1935 – 1 – gw Mikrofilm [949]
VOLKSSTIMME – Bielitz, Poland.Aug-Dez 1925, Jan-Okt 1926, 1927-30 – 1 – gw Mikrofilm [943]
VOLKSSTIMME – Bielitz-Biala, aug-dec 1925, jan-oct 1926, 1927-30 – 1 – Inquire at Mikrofilmarchiv for details – gw Misc Inst [947]
VOLKSSTIMME – Budapest, 1877-80 (incomplete), 1894-96 (incomplete), 1898-1924 – 23r – 1 – Inquire at Mikrofilmarchiv for details – gw Misc Inst [943]
VOLKSSTIMME – Budapest, 1906, 1914, 1915 (all incompl) – us Hoover Inst Photo [072]
VOLKSSTIMME – Chemnitz, 1915-17 – 7r – 1 – DM525.00 – gw Mikro Press [072]
VOLKSSTIMME – Chemnitz, East Germany. 1915-17, 11 Sept 1945-17 Jan 1949 – 1 – gw Mikrofilm [072]

VOLKSSTIMME – Chemnitz, Germany. -d. 31 Aug 1916-8 Aug 1919. 7 reels – 1 – uk British Libr Newspaper [072]

VOLKSSTIMME – Cologne. Germany. -w. 4 Mar 1946-1 Sep 1949. (5 reels) – 1 – uk British Libr Newspaper [072]

VOLKSSTIMME – (Cont by: Magdeburger Volksstimme. Also Bereichsausgaben available (nur Kreisseiten): BURG/Magdeburg, apr 3 1958-oct 31 1961; GARDELEGEN, apr 3 1958-83 (incomplete), sep 19 1985-90; GENTHIN, apr 3 1958-oct 31 1961; HALBERSTADT, apr 2 1958-oct 31 1961, jan 20-dec 30 1967, jul 3 1984-90; HALDENSLEBEN, apr 1 1958-oct 31 1961, dec 7 1963-90 (incomplete); HAVELBERG, apr 1 1958-oct 31 1961; KALBE, apr 2 1958-87 (incomplete); KLOETZE, apr 2 1958-90 (incomplete); OSCHERSLEBEN, apr 3 1958-oct 31 1961; OSTERBURG, apr 1 1958-90 (incomplete); SALZWEDEL, apr 2 1958-90 (incomplete); SCHNEEBERG, apr 1-nov 29 1958; SCHOENEBECK, apr 30 1958-dec 21 1967 (incomplete); SEEHAUSEN, apr 1 1958-oct 31 1961, 1963, 1965 (incomplete); STASSFURT, apr 1 1958-oct 30 1961, mar 6 1963-dec 16 1966 (incomplete), sep 19 1985-90; STENDAL, apr 1 1948-sep 29 1990 (incomplete), 1992- ; TANGERHUETTE, apr 1 1958-87 (incomplete); WANZLEBEN, apr 2 1958-oct 31 1961, feb 14-dec 6 1963, apr 13-may 14 1966, sep 19 1985-90; WERNIGERODE, apr 2 1958-sep 17 1966 (incomplete), jul 9 1983-90; WOLMIRSTEDT, apr 3 1958-oct 31 1961, sep 19 1985-90; ZERBST, apr 2 1958-nov 4 1967 (incomplete)) – Magdeburg, 1895-mar 15 1933, aug 22-dec 31 1947, aug 1954- – 1 – Inquire at Mikrofilmarchiv for details – gw Misc Inst [072]

VOLKSSTIMME – Franfurt M., Nov 1905-08; Mar 1909-Sept 1910; 1913-Mar 1933 – 60r – 1 – DM4,500.00 – gw Mikro Press [072]

VOLKSSTIMME – Frankfurt, Germany. Nov 1905-1908; Mar 1909-Sept 1910; 1913-33 – 1 – gw Mikrofilm [072]

VOLKSSTIMME – Karl-Marx-Stadt, East Germany. 1945-62 – 1 – gw Mikrofilm [072]

VOLKSSTIMME : LANDESZEITUNG DER SPD LANDESVERBAND SACHSEN – (Cont as: Volksstimme: Tribuene der Einheit Feb-Mar 1946. Saechsische Zeitung: Organ der SED Apr-May 1946. Volksstimme: Organ der SED May 1946- 1949) – Chemnitz, Oct 1945-Apr 1946 – 3r – 1 – DM225.00 – gw Mikro Press [072]

VOLKSSTIMME – Luedenscheid, Germany. 1911-Okt 1917; Jan-23 Dez 1919; Jul-Dez 1920; Jan-Mar, Jul-Dez 1921; Jul 1922-1932 – 1 – gw Mikrofilm [072]

VOLKSSTIMME – Magdeburg, Aug-Dec 1947 – 1r – 1 – DM80.00 – gw Mikro Press [072]

VOLKSSTIMME – Magdeburg, East Germany. 22 Aug-Dec 1947; Aug 1954-Jun 1981 – 1 – gw Mikrofilm [072]

VOLKSSTIMME : ORGAN DER SOZIALDEMOKRATIE DES SAUERLANDES – (Cont as: Neue Freie Presse Jan-Dec 1919; Jul-Dec 1920; Jan-Mar, Jul-Dec 1921; Jul-Dec 1922. Volksstimme 1923-32) – Luedenscheid, Hagen. 1911-1917 – 38r – 1 – DM2,850.00 – gw Mikro Press [072]

VOLKSSTIMME – Stuttgart, Germany. 1947-10 Aug 1950 – 1 – gw Mikrofilm [072]

VOLKSSTIMME : ZENTRALORGAN DES SOZIALDEMOKRATISCHE PARTEI UNGARNS – Budapest, 1877-80 (incompl), 1894-96 (incompl), 1898-1924 – 1 – gw Mikrofilm [335]

VOLKSSTIMME *see*
- VOLKSSTIMME
- VOLKSSTIMME FUER WESTFALEN UND LIPPE

VOLKSSTIMME FUER WESTFALEN UND LIPPE – (Cont as: Mitteilungsblatt Jan 1920. Volksstimme Feb-Jun 1920; Apr-Jun 192l) – Hagen, Apr-Sept 1919; Jan 1920 – 2r – 1 – DM150.00 – gw Mikro Press [072]

VOLKSSTIMME FUER WESTFALEN UND LIPPE – Hagen, Germany. Apr-Sept 1919; Jan-Jun 1920; Apr-Jun 1921 – 1 – gw Mikrofilm [072]

VOLKSTELLING 1930 – (In Dutch and English) – Batavia, 1933-1936 – 112mf – 9 – SE-27/2 – ne IDC [950]

DIE VOLKSTEM – Pretoria, South Africa. -d. 1914-50 – 1 – sa State Libr [072]

VOLKSTEM – Pretoria, South Africa. 1873-1951. -w – 1 – sa State Libr [072]

VOLKSTRIBUENE – La Tribune du peuple. Strasbourg. janv-avr 1926. Absorbe par: L' Humanite de Strasbourg voir a ce titre – 1 – fr A.C.R.P.P. [073]

DER VOLKSVEREIN – Moenchengladbach, Germany. 1891-1932 – 1 – gw Mikrofilm [072]

VOLKSVEREIN : ZEITSCHRIFT DES VOLKSVEREINS FUER DAS KATHOLISCHE DEUTSCHLAND – Moenchengladbach, 1891-1932 – 2r – 1 – DM250.00 – gw Mikro Press [072]

DER VOLKSVERTRETER – Berlin, sep 1845-jun 1847 – 1 – Inquire at Mikrofilmarchiv for details – gw Misc Inst [943]

VOLKSVERTRETER – Berlin, Germany.Sept 1845-Jun 1847 – 1 – gw Mikrofilm [072]

DE VOLKSVRIEND *see* DE ZUID-AFRIKAAN

VOLKSVRIEND – (Absorbed by: De Zuid Afrikaan) – Cape Town, South Africa. 8 Jan 1862-30 Aug 1871 – 5r – 1, 16 diazo available at reduced price – sa SA Libr [072]

VOLKSWACHT – Bernburg, 1919-33 – 1 – Inquire at Mikrofilmarchiv for details – gw Misc Inst [072]

VOLKSWACHT – Bielefeld, jul 1 1890-feb 27 1933 – 1 – Inquire at Mikrofilmarchiv for details – gw Misc Inst [072]

VOLKSWACHT – Gera, East Germany. Aug 1954-Jun 1981 – 1 – gw Mikrofilm [072]

VOLKSWACHT *see* DIE ARBEITER-ZEITUNG

VOLKSWACHT FUER OBERPFALZ UND NIEDERBAYERN : SOZIALDEMOKRATISCHE TAGESZEITUNG – Regensburg, 1920-33 – 23r – 1 – DM1,725.00 – gw Mikro Press [072]

VOLKSWACHT FUER SCHLESIEN – Breslau, nov 15 1930 – 1 – Inquire at Mikrofilmarchiv for details – gw Misc Inst [072]

DER VOLKSWART – Bruenn, Czechoslovakia. 18 Okt 1933-21 Mar 1934, inc – 1 – gw Mikrofilm [072]

DER VOLKSWART – Bruenn, oct 18 1933-mar 21 1934 (incomplete) – 1r – 1 – Inquire at Mikrofilmarchiv for details – gw Misc Inst [943]

VOLKSWARTE – Goettingen. feb 10 (n1), oct 27 (n36), 1849 – 1 – gw Mikrofilm [943]

VOLKSWEHR – Bruenn, 1927-33 – 1 – Inquire at Mikrofilmarchiv for details – gw Misc Inst [943]

VOLKSWEHR – Gablonz, Czechoslovakia.12 Feb 1927-14 Okt 1933 – 1 – gw Mikrofilm [072]

VOLKSWEHR – (Missing: 1923) – Jablonec nad Nisou, Czechoslovakia. Oct 1919-1932 – 5r – 1 – us L of C Photodup [072]

DER VOLKSWILLE – (Cont by: Augsburger Volkszeitung, oct 25 1878) – Augsburg, 1876-apr 30 1879 – 1 – Dist. gw Mikrofilm – gw Misc Inst [072]

VOLKSWILLE – Budapest, Hungary. 21 Jun-18 Okt 1895 – 1 – gw Mikrofilm [072]

VOLKSWILLE – Budapest, jun 21-oct 18 1895 – 1r – 1 – Inquire at Mikrofilmarchiv for details – gw Misc Inst [943]

VOLKSWILLE – Hannover, 1914-Feb 1933 – 53r – 1 – DM3,975.00 – gw Mikro Press [072]

VOLKSWILLE – Hannover, Germany. 1914-Feb 1933 – 1 – gw Mikrofilm [072]

VOLKSWILLE – Kattowitz (Katowice), Poland. Okt 1925-33 – 1 – gw Mikrofilm [943]

VOLKSWILLE – (Some issues lacking) – Karlovy Vary, Czechoslovakia. July 1933; Sept 1938. – 1r – 1 – us L of C Photodup [072]

VOLKSWILLE (DER KAMPF) – Augsburg, sep 1 1919-jan 13 1921 (incomplete) – 1 – Dist. gw Mikrofilm – gw Misc Inst [072]

DER VOLKSWIRTSCHAFTSPLAN, 1950 / Germany. Democratic Republic. Amt fuer Information – Berlin. 1950. BD-735 1 – 9 – ne IDC [338]

DER VOLKSWIRTSCHAFTSPLAN, 1951 DAS ERSTE JAHR DES FUENFJAHRPLANES DER DEUTSCHEN DEMOKRATISCHEN REPUBLIK / Germany. Democratic Republic. Amt fuer Information – Berlin. 1951. BD-737 1 – 9 – ne IDC [338]

DIE VOLKSZEITUNG : LABOUR WEEKLY – Montreal. v1 n3. 3 mai 1912-v1 n26. 11 oct 1912 – 1r – 1 – Can$50.00 – cn Can Microfilming [072]

DIE VOLKSZEITUNG – Wilna. v. 1-2 no. 1-434. Mar 4 1906-Sept 1 1907 and supplements – 1 – us NY Public [072]

VOLKS-ZEITUNG – Berlin, Germany. -d. 9 April 1853-31 Dec 1897. 101 reels – 1 – uk British Libr Newspaper [072]

VOLKS-ZEITUNG – (Cont: Urwaehler-Zeitung, -apr 8 1853. Cont by: Berliner Volks-Zeitung, jul 1 1904; Berliner Volkszeitung, nov 27 1930) – Berlin, mar 29-dec 30 1849, 1850-59, apr 1 1860-jun 29 1873, 1874-76, apr 1 1877-jun 30 1878, oct 1 1878-80, apr 4-dec 31 1882, jan 1-jun 29 1884, oct 1 1884-sep 30 1886, 1887-aug 31 1889, oct 1-dec 31 1889, apr 1 1890-mar 29 1891, jul 1-sep 30 1891, jan 1-dec 13 1892, 1893, apr 2 1894-sep 30 1895, jan 1-sep 30 1896, jan 1-mar 31 1897, jul 1 1897-1943 (incomplete) – 167r – 1 – Inquire at Mikrofilmarchiv for details – gw Misc Inst [943]

VOLKS-ZEITUNG – (Missing: nos 11,14,16-19,32,34,36,201) – Vilna, Feb 19-Dec 31 1906 – 1r – 1 – J-92-16/3 – ne IDC [072]

VOLKS-ZEITUNG – Prigrevica, Yugoslavia. May 1941-1942 – 1r – 1 – us L of C Photodup [949]

VOLKSZEITUNG – Bayreuth, jul 1796-jun 1797 – 1r – 1 – Dist. gw Mikrofilm – gw Misc Inst [943]

VOLKSZEITUNG – Bismarck, ND; Winona, MN. oct 26 1927-sep 19 1928 (incomplete) – 1r – 1 – Inquire at Mikrofilmarchiv for details – gw Misc Inst [072]

VOLKSZEITUNG – (Cont by: Deutsche Volkszeitung in Polen, oct 1 1936) – Bromberg, sep 1922-jun 17 1937 – 1 – Inquire at Mikrofilmarchiv for details – gw Misc Inst [943]

VOLKSZEITUNG – Duesseldorf, Germany. Okt-Dez 1890; 1892-4 Jul 1896; 1898-26 Jan 1899; Sept 1899-Jul 1902; 1903-27 Mar 1933 – 1 – gw Mikrofilm [072]

VOLKSZEITUNG – Halle Saale, Germany. 1921-22. Incompl – 1 – gw Mikrofilm [072]

VOLKSZEITUNG – Vilna, Russia. n1-434. 1906-07 – 3r – 1 – us Ross [072]

VOLKSZEITUNG *see* SCHWAEBISCHE VOLKSZEITUNG

VOLKS-ZEITUNG FUER RHEINE UND UMGEBUNG – (Cont by: Volksblatt fuer Rheine und Umgebung. Muensterlaendische Volkszeitung. Zeno-Zeitung. Westfaelische Tageszeitung) – Rheine, mar 23 1878-1944 (very incomplete), sep 1949-76 – 1 – gw Mikrofilm [943]

VOLKS-ZEITUNG FUER RHEINE UND UMGEBUNG – (Title changes: Volksblatt fuer Rheine und Umgebung; Muensterlaendische Volkszeitung; Zeno-Zeitung; Westfaelische Tageszeitung) – Rheine/Westf., West Germany. 1992- – 7r per yr – 1 – gw Mikrofilm [072]

VOLKS-ZEITUNG (URWAEHLER-ZEITUNG) – (29 Mar 1849-1859. Apr 1860-Jun 1873. Jan-Jun 1880. Jul-Dez 1882. 1887-Aug 1889. Sept 1890-Mar 1891. 1892-93. Jan-Jun 1896. Jul-Dez 1897. Okt-Dez 1904. Okt-Dez 1911. Jan-Mar, Jul-Sept 1913. Jan-Mar 1914. Okt-Dez 1916. Okt-Dez 1919. Apr-Jun 1920) – Berlin, Germany – 1 – gw Mikrofilm [072]

VOLKSZEITUNG/FREIE PRESSE : ORGAN DER SPD – Duesseldorf, Oct-Dec 1890; 1892-Jul 1896; 1898-Jan 1899; Sept 1899-Jul 1902; 1903-Feb 1933 – 79r – 1 – DM5,925.00 – gw Mikro Press [072]

VOLKSZEITUNG-TRIBUNE – Omaha, NE. -w. (-d 1912-59). Oct 1912-Sep 1913; Mar 1914-Aug 1916; Nov 1916 to date – 1 – us NE Hist [071]

Vollbeding, J C *see* KURZGEFASSTE GESCHICHTE DER ORGEL AUS DEM FRANZOESISCHEN DES DOM BEDOS DE CELLES

DIE VOLLENDUNG DES ARISCHEN MYSTERIUMS IN BAYREUTH / Schroeder, Leopold von – (Includes bibliographical references and index) – Muenchen: J F Lehmann, 1911 – 1r – 1 – us U.W. Library [790]

Vollenhoven, M W R van *see* THE TRAGEDY OF SPAIN

Vollenhoven, S C S van *see* ESSAI D'UNE FAUNE ENTOMOLOGIQUE DE L'ARCHIPEL INDO-NEERLANDAIS

Vollering, Andre *see*
- MANUEL D'UTILISATION DU SYSTEME BIP
- RAPPORT DE PROGRAMMATION DU SYSTEME BIP

Vollers, Karl *see*
- SEMITISCHE MISZELLEN
- DIE SOLARE SEITE DES ALTTESTAMENTLICHEN GOTTESBEGRIFFES

Vollert, Wilhelm *see*
- GEDANKENGANG DES V. FRANK'SCHEN SYSTEMS DER CHRISTLICHEN WAHRHEIT
- TABELLEN ZUR NEUTESTAMENTLICHEN ZEITGESCHICHTE

VOLLEYBALL OFFICIAL GUIDE *see*
- VOLLEYBALL REVIEW, 1940-1973 – USA VOLLEYBALL REVIEW, 1973-1980 – VOLLEYBALL OFFICIAL GUIDE, 1976-1980
- VOLLEYBALL REVIEW, 1980-1981 – U.S.A. VOLLEYBALL REVIEW, 1981-1986 – VOLLEYBALL OFFICIAL GUIDE, 1981-1986

VOLLEYBALL REVIEW, 1940-1973 – USA VOLLEYBALL REVIEW, 1973-1980 – VOLLEYBALL OFFICIAL GUIDE, 1976-1980 / U.S. Volleyball Association – 67mf – 9 – $134.00 – us Microform Publ [790]

VOLLEYBALL REVIEW, 1980-1981 – U.S.A. VOLLEYBALL REVIEW, 1981-1986 – VOLLEYBALL OFFICIAL GUIDE, 1981-1986 / U.S. Volleyball Association – 43mf – 9 – $86.00 – us Microform Publ [790]

DER VOLLKOMMENE CAPELLMEISTER / Mattheson, J – P 399. 1739 – 9 – ne IDC [780]

VOLLKOMMENE CAPELLMEISTER, DAS IST GRUNDLICHE ANZEIGE ALLER DERJENIGEN SACHEN DIE EINER WISSEN, KONNEN, UND VOLLKOMMEN INNE HABEN MUSS, DER EINER CAPELLE MIT EHREN UND NUTZEN VORSTEHEN WILL; ZUM VERSUCH VON MATTHESON – Hamburg: Christian Herold, 1739 – 28mf – 9 – us Sibley [780]

DAS VOLLKOMMENE VERBRECHEN / Andreas, Fred – Berlin-Grunewald: H Hillger, c1944 – 1r – 1 – us U.W. Library [943]

DAS VOLLKOMMENHEITSIDEAL DES ORIGENES / Voelker, W – 1931 – 4mf – 9 – ne Slangenburg [240]

Vollmer, F *see* FL. MEROBAUDIS RELIQUIAE (MGH 1: 14.BD)

Vollmer, Hans *see* DIE ALTTESTAMENTLICHEN CITATE BEI PAULUS

Vollrath, Wilhelm *see* GOETHE UND GROSSBRITANNIEN

VOLLSTAENDIGE BESCHREIBUNG DES SCHWEIZERLANDES ODER GEOGRAPHISCH-STATISTISCHES HAND-LEXIKON UEBER ALLE IN GESAMMTER EIDSGENOSSENSCHAFT BEFINDLICHER KANTONE, BEZIRKE, KREISE, AEMTER (AEL, ABT 1;30) / ed by Lutz, Markus – 2nd ed Aarau. 4 bde. 1827-1828 (mf ed 1995) – 8mf – 9 – DM240.00 – 3-89131-208-3 – gw Fischer [059]

VOLLSTAENDIGE NATURGESCHICHTE DER FORSTLICHEN CULTURPFLANZEN DEUTSCHLANDS / Hartig, T – Berlin. 1851. B-5476 2 – 8 – ne IDC [580]

VOLLSTAENDIGE SAMMLUNG ALLER AELTEREN UND NEUEREN KONKORDATE NEBST EINER GESCHICHTE IHRES ENTSTEHENS UND IHRER SCHICKSALE VON ERNST MUENCH / Muench, Ernst – Leipzig, 1830-1831. 2 Bde. 1,316p – DM300.00 – 3-89349-221-6 – gw Hänsel [240]

VOLLSTAENDIGES BUECHER-LEXIKON, ENTHALTEND ALLE VON 1750 IN DEUTSCHLAND UND DEN ANGRENZENDEN LAENDERN GEDRUCKTEN BUECHER / Kayser, Christian Gottlob – Leipzig. 36v. 1834-1911 – 9 – subsc: DM2,400 diazo DM2,780.00 silver – gw Olms [010]

EIN VOLLSTAENDIGES LEBEN JESU, SEINER HEILIGEN MUTTER MARIA, UND DER UEBRIGEN HEILIGEN SEINER ZEIT / Bayerle, Bernard Gustav – (Includes index of saints) – New York: S Zickel [distributor], 1862 – 2mf – 9 – 0-8370-6884-3 – 1986-0884 – us A.T.L.A. [240]

DIE VOLLSTRECKUNG AUSLAENDISCHER CIVILURTEILE IN DER SCHWEIZ / Gruebler, R – Basel, 1906 – 2mf – 1 – ILM-2239/1 – ne IDC [327]

DIE VOLLSTRECKUNG VON URTEILEN UND SCHIEDSSPRUECHEN... / Haeger, W – Berlin, 1910 – 4mf – 1 – ILM-2253/1 – ne IDC [327]

VOLNAIA SIBIR – Obshchestvenno-ekonomicheskii sbornik. Prague, 1927-30.v1-9. Lacking: some pages of v3, v6-7. BR-3471/2 – 8 – ne IDC [330]

VOLNE SLOVO – Kulturni List Proletarskych Bezvercu. Moravska Ostravska. v1,no.1-v9, no.8. 8 Jan 1931-1 Aug 1939. Incomplete – 1 – us NY Public [073]

VOLNENII A V VOISKAKH I VOENNYIA TIURMY : PREDISLOVIIA: VSTUPITELNAIA STATIA "SOLDATCHINA" / Bonch-Bruevich, Vladimir Dmitrievich – 2-e izd. Moskva: "Kommunist", 1919 – 1 – CSUX89-B1844 – us Hoover Inst Photo [947]

VOL'NITSA – Literaturno-khudozhestvennyi zhurnal. v. 1-2. Spb. 1906. BR-5734 2 – 8 – ne IDC [073]

VOL'NOE EKONOMICHESKOE OBSHCHESTVO – (1901 has not been publ. Missing: 1835, v1 p1-54; 1887 v1 p482-484; 1890 v6 p78-81; 1898 v5-6; 1899 v3; 1915 v3-6) – Trudy. Spb., 1765-1821; 1833; 1835; 1842-1915 – 2466 mf – 9 – R-4168/2 – ne IDC [334]
VOL'NYI DISKUSSIONYI LISTOK – Izdanie gruppy sotsial-revoliutsionerov.Paris, 1905. Nos.1-2. BR-3470/2 – 8 – ne IDC [073]
VOL'NYI UNIVERSITET – Zhurnal nauchnyi i obshestvennyi. St. Petersburg, 1914.v1-16. BR-4176/2 – 8 – ne IDC [500]
VOLOGODSKII SBORNIK, IZDAVAEMYI VOLOGODSKIM GUBERNSKIM STATISTICHESKIM KOMITETOM, POD RED. F.A. ARSEN'EVA – (Missing: 1879 v1) – Vologda. v1-5. 1879-1887 – 18mf – 9 – ne IDC [947]
VOLOGODSKII SBORNIK, IZDAVAEMYI VOLOGODSKIM GUBERNSKIM STATISTICHESKIM KOMITETOM, POD RED. F.A. ARSEN'EVA – (Missing: 1879 v1) – Vologda. v1-5. 1879-1887 – 18mf – 9 – RET-27/1 – ne IDC [947]
VOLONTAIRE – London, UK. Pour la cite chretienne. Organe du Glaive de l'Esprit. Oct 1941-Jul 1944 – 1 – uk British Libr Newspaper [072]
VOLONTAIRE *see* DOBROVOLET S
LE VOLONTAIRE JOSEPH-LOUIS GUERIN DU CORPS DES ZOUAVES PONTIFICAUX FRANCO-BELGES – Nantes: Mazeau, 1860 – 1 – F56.93 – fr Armell [240]
LA VOLONTE – Paris. Journal quotidien. Dir. Dubarry. 8 oct 1925-26, juil 1928-juin 1929, janv-juin 1932 – 1 – fr A.C.R.P.P. [072]
LA VOLONTE – Quebec, Canada. 1 mar 1876-23 jan 1877 – 1r – 1 – Can$30.00 – cn Can Microfilming [072]
VOLONTES – Revue mensuelle. no. 1-20. Paris. 1938-aout 1939 – 1 – fr A.C.R.P.P. [073]
VOLONTES DE CEUX DE LA RESISTANCE – Paris: CDLR. v1-2 n54. nov 29 1944-dec 5 1945 – us Res Libr [944]
Voloshin, M *see*
- ANNO MUNDI ARDENTIS 1915
- CHAIKA I SOLOMEIA
- STICHOTVORENIIA
- STIKHI I PEREVODY

Vol'pe, Ts. *see* SUD'BA BLOKA
Volpert, P A *see* TSCH'ONG HUANG, DER SCHUTZGOTT DER STADTE IN CHINA
Vol'pin, M E *see* CHEMISTRY REVIEWS
VOLTA REVIEW – (Former title: Association Review 1899-1909) – Washington. v1-99. oct 1899-nov 1997+ 1; v71-99. jan 1969-nov 1997+ 5; v78-99. jan 1976-nov 1997+ 9 – 1,5,9 – D906 – us UMI [073]
LE VOLTAIRE – Paris. Dir., Jules Laffitte. 5 juil 1878-aout 1908, 15 sept-31 dec 1909, 7 fevr-29 dec 1910, janv-24 juil 1911, 1913-aout 1914, 5 aout 1916-11 oct 1925, 12 avr 1930 – 1 – fr A.C.R.P.P. [073]
LE VOLTAIRE – Paris. -w 5 Jul 1878-31 Dec 1897. 43 reels – 1 – uk British Libr Newspaper [072]
VOLTAIRE / Harel, M M – Recueil des particularites curieuses de sa vie et de sa mort. Porrentruy. Goetschy. 1781. IV – 9 – fr Hachette [920]
VOLTAIRE : SERMON DES CINQUANTE / Voltaire, Francois-Marie Arouet de – 1763 – fr Armell [440]
VOLTAIRE APPRECIE. COMEDIE / Billard-Duminceau, E – s.l – 9 – fr Hachette [820]
VOLTAIRE AUX FRANCAIS, SUR LEUR CONSTITUTION / Laya, Jean H – Paris. Maradan. 1789 – 9 – fr Hachette [944]
VOLTAIRE ET LA HOLLANDE / Vercruysse, Jeroom – (Studies on Voltaire and the eighteenth century, v46) – Oxford. 1966 – 9 – $27.00 – 0-7294-0132-4 – uk Voltaire [920]
VOLTAIRE ET SON GENIE / Bros – Paris. 1817 – 9 – fr Hachette [920]
Voltaire, Francois Marie Arouet de *see*
- LETTRE PHILOSOPHIQUE, MORALE ET LITTERAIRE DE VOLTAIRE AUX FRANCAIS
- LETTRES DE M. DE VOLTAIRE ET DE SA CELEBRE AMIE
- LA VIE PRIVEE DU ROI DE PRUSSE

Voltaire, Francois-Marie Arouet de *see*
- L'EVANGILE DU JOUR
- LE FANATISME, OU MAHOMET LE PROPHETE
- VOLTAIRE

VOLTAIRE, JUGE PAR LES FAITS / Lebrun-Tossa – Paris. Plancher. 1817 – 9 – fr Hachette [920]
VOLTAIRE: LITERARY CRITIC / Williams, David – (Studies on Voltaire and the eighteenth century, v48) – Oxford. 1966 – 9 – $45.00 – 0-7294-0133-2 – uk Voltaire [920]
VOLTAIRE, MADAME DE POMPADOUR ET QUELQUES ARPENTS DE NEIGE / Tasse, Joseph – Levis: Pierre Georges Roy, 1898. SEM105P394 – 2mf – 9 – Can$4.50 – cn Bibl Nat [830]
VOLTAIRE ON SHAKESPEARE / Besterman, Theodore – (Studies on Voltaire and the eighteenth century, v54) – Oxford. 1967 – 9 – $27.00 – 0-7294-0152-9 – uk Voltaire [440]
VOLTAIRE OU LE TRIOMPHE DE LA PHILOSOPHIE MODERNE / Berchoux, J de – Paris. Lyon. 1814. XV – 9 – fr Hachette [190]
VOLTAIRE OU UNE JOURNEE DE FERNEY / Piis et al – French Theatre Series. Paris. Barba, an X. 1802 – 9 – fr Hachette [820]
VOLTAIRE UND DIE FRANZOSISCHE STRAFRECHTSPFLEGE IM ACHTZEHNTEN JAHRHUNDERT / Hertz, Eduard – Stuttgart: Enke, 1887. 530p. LL-4105 – 1 – us L of C Photodup [340]
VOLTAIRE'S BRITISH VISITORS / Beer, Sir Gavin de & Rousseau, Andre Michel – (Studies on Voltaire and the eighteenth century, v49) – Oxford. 1967 – 9 – $54.00 – 0-7294-0255-X – uk Voltaire [920]
VOLTAIRE'S CANDIDE: ANALYSIS OF A CLASSIC / Bottiglia, William F – (Studies on Voltaire and the eighteenth century, v7) – Oxford. 1964 – 9 – $36.00 – 0-7294-0064-6 – uk Voltaire [440]
VOLTAIRE'S 'CANDIDE': THE PROTEAN GARDENER, 1755-1762 / Murray, Geoffrey – (Studies on Voltaire and the eighteenth century, v69) – Oxford. 1970 – 9 – $45.00 – 0-7294-0162-6 – uk Voltaire [440]
VOLTAIRE'S CATALOGUE OF HIS LIBRARY AT FERNEY / ed by Havers, G R & Torrey, N L – (Studies on Voltaire and the eighteenth century, v9) – Oxford. 1959 – 9 – $27.00 – 0-7294-0065-4 – uk Voltaire [010]
VOLTAIRE'S CONCEPT OF INTERNATIONAL ORDER / Perkins, Merle L – (Studies on Voltaire and the eighteenth century, v36) – Oxford. 1965 – 9 – $36.00 – 0-7294-0129-4 – uk Voltaire [440]
VOLTAIRE'S GHOST TO THE APOSTLE OF THE SINLESS FOUNDERY : A FAMILIAR EPISTLE FROM THE SHADES / Combe, W – London, 1779 – 1mf – 9 – MP-537/1 – ne IDC [240]
VOLTAIRE'S LITERARY CAREER FROM 1728 TO 1750 / Conlon, P M – (Studies on Voltaire and the eighteenth century, v14) – Oxford. 1960 – 9 – $45.00 – 0-7294-0068-9 – uk Voltaire [920]
LA VOLTAIRIADE / Grambert, Joseph – ou Aventures de Voltaire dans l'autre monde, occasionnees par un evenement arrive dans celui-ci. Paris. Patris. 1815 – 9 – fr Hachette [830]
VOLTAIRIANA / Cousin d'Avallon – ou Recueil des bons mots. Plaisanteries, pensees ingenieuses et saillies spirituelles de Voltaire, suivi des anecdotes peu connues. Paris. Pillot. 1801. VIII – 9 – fr Hachette [920]
VOLTAIRIMEROS / Baston, G A H – ou Premiere journee de M. de V. dans l'autre monde. Bruxelles. 1779 – 9 – fr Hachette [830]
Volter, Daniel *see* DAS MESSIANISCHE BEWUSSTSEIN JESU
VOL'TER I EGO KNIGA O PETRE VELIKOM / Shmurlo, E G – Prague. 1929. BR-7887 2 – 8 – ne IDC [460]
Volterra, Edoardo *see* LA CONCEPTION DU MARIAGE D'APRES LES JURISTES ROMAINES
A VOLUME OF MEMOIRS AND GENEALOGY OF REPRESENTATIVE CITIZENS OF THE CITY OF SEATTLE AND THE COUNTY OF KING – Chicago, 1903. Washington reel 2. (Cox Library Collection) – 5 – us Americana [978]
VOLUMES OF DUPLICATE CERTIFICATES OF NATURALIZATION, 1904-1917 / Department of External Affairs 1, Melbourne – 36r – 1 – CRS A40 – at Archives [920]
VOLUMES OF ENROLLED LETTERS OF NATURALIZATION, 1863-1903 / Chief Secretary's Office – 14r – 1 – CRS A727 – at Archives [920]
VOLUMES OF ENROLLED LETTERS OF NATURALIZATION, 1865-1903 / General Registry Office – 8r – 1 – CRS A733 – at Archives [920]
VOLUMES OF SUPPLEMENTS TO THE QUEENSLAND GOVERNMENT GAZETTE RELATING TO CONTINGENTS FOR SOUTH AFRICA, 1900-1903 / Chief Secretary's Office, Queensland – 4r – 1 – CRS B5171 – at Archives [920]
VOLUNTAD: COMEDIA EN TRES ACTOS Y EN PROSA / Perez Galdos, Benito – Madrid: Libreria de los Sucesores de Hernando, 1907. 77p – 1 – us U.W. Library [820]
LA VOLUNTAD POPULAR HACE SOBERANAS A LAS NACIONES / Argentina. Direccion General de Relaciones Culturales y Difusion – [Buenos Aires?, 1952?] – 1 – CSUXAJA7453-B – us Hoover Inst Photo [972]
LA VOLUNTAD Y EL LIBRE ALBEDRIO EN LOS AUTOS SACRAMENTALES DE CALDERON / Frutos Cortes, Eugenio – Zaragoza: Tip. La Academica, 1948. Rev. Universidad (no 1 de 1948) – sp Bibl Santa Ana [440]
VOLUNTARY ASSOCIATION THEIR USE AND ABUSE / Stow, Baron – (A discourse). 1837 – 1 – 5.00 – us Baptist [240]
VOLUNTARYIST – Grambling. 1982-94* 1; 1995-97+ 1,5,9 – 1,5,9 – D22589 – us UMI [073]
VOLUNTEER – Rochester and New York, 1841-42 – 1r – 1 – $68.00 – cn Library Assoc [971]
VOLUNTEER : WEEKLY DEMOCRATIC NEWSPAPER – Hamilton, OH. 5 Sept-3 Oct 1821 – 1r – 1 – us Western Res [071]
VOLUNTEER ENLISTMENT PAPERS / Wood County. Ohio. Probate Court – 1862 – 1r – 1 – $32.50r – us Archival [324]
THE VOLUNTEER FOR LIBERTY – Madrid. May 24 1937-Nov 7 1938. Incomplete – 1 – us NY Public [946]
VOLUNTEER JOURNAL – Manchester. England. -w. 7 Sep 1860-14 Mar 1862. (1 reel) – 1 – uk British Libr Newspaper [072]
VOLUNTEER LEADER – (Former title: Auxiliary Leader 1960-68) – Chicago. v1-38. 1960-97+ 1; v15 1974. v16 1975*. v17 1976. v18-21 1977-80*. v22 1981. v23-34 1982-93* v35-38 1994-97+ 5; v15-38. 1974-97+ 9 – 1,5,9 – D7523 – us UMI [370]
THE VOLUNTEER REVIEW AND MILITARY AND NAVAL GAZETTE – Ottawa: Moss and O'Brien, [1867-1876] – 9 – cn C.I.H.M. [355]
VOLUNTEER SERVICE GAZETTE AND MILITARY DISPATCH – London. -w. 26 Oct 1859-Dec 1863. (4 reels) – 1 – uk British Libr Newspaper [072]
THE VOLUNTEER'S ACTIVE SERVICE MANUAL, OR, INTERNAL ECONOMY AND STANDING ORDERS FOR VOLUNTEERS WHEN ON ACTIVE SERVICE:.. – Comp. by Maj. F.E. Dixon. Toronto: G. Adam, 1867. 02725. (Pre-1900 Canadiana) – 9 – cn C.I.H.M. [971]
VOLUNTEERS FOR CLEVELANDERS IN ISRAEL – (Cleveland, Ohio) no. 12 (Feb. 1981-Sept. 1984) – us A.J.P.C. [270]
VOLVOCINEAE / Korsikov, O A – (Vyznacnyk prisnovodnych vodorostej URSR. v. 4). Ky'iv. 1938. B-6133 2 – 8 – ne IDC [999]
Volynskii, A L *see*
- BOR'BA ZA IDEALIZM
- KNIGA VELIKAGO GNEVA

Volz, G B *see* PREUSSISCHE UND OESTERREICHISCHE ACTEN ZUR VORGESCHICHTE DES SIEBENJAEHRIGEN KRIEGES
Volz, J *see* VOCATIONAL TRAINING AND JOB CREATION SCHEMES IN BELGIUM
Volz, Paul *see*
- DER GEIST GOTTES UND DIE VERWANDTEN ERSCHEINUNGEN IM ALTEN TESTAMENT UND IN ANSCHLIESSENDEN JUDENTUM
- JUEDISCHE ESCHATOLOGIE VON DANIEL BIS AKIBA
- MOSE
- DER PROPHET JEREMIA
- DIE VOREXILISCHE JAHWEPROPHETIE UND DER MESSIAS

VOM BUERGERKRIEG – Berlin, 1923-25 (incomplete) – 1r – 1 – Inquire at Mikrofilmarchiv for details – gw Misc Inst [072]
VOM BUERGERKRIEG – Berlin Vienna. 1923-25. Incompl – 1 – gw Mikrofilm [073]
VOM CHRISTLICHEN RITTER / Huberinus, Caspar – Neueburg a.d. Donau: [Hans Kilian], 1545. [G.F.: 19.1] – 2mf – 9 – HUB-44/1 – ne IDC [240]
VOM DEM TOUFF. VOM WIDERTAUFF. VNND VOM KINDERTOUFF / Zwingli, H – Zuerich, J. Hager. 1525. BME-84 1 – 9 – ne IDC [240]
VOM DEUTSCHEN WESEN / Boerger, Willi – Wuerzburg: K. Triltsch, 1943. 160p – 1 – us U.W. Library [330]
VOM EWIGEN KAMPF : GEDICHTE / Huenefeld, Guenther, Freiherr von – Berlin: Pontos Verlag, 1929 – 1r – 1 – us U.W. Library [810]
VOM EXPRESSIONISMUS ZUM "SOZIALISTISCHEN REALISMUS" : DER WEG JOHANNES R. BECHERS ALS KUENSTLER UND MENSCH. EIN BEITRAG ZUR PHAENOMENOLOGIE DER MARXISTISCHEN AESTHETIK / Herden, Editha Martina – Heidelberg, 1962 – 2mf – 9 – DM62.00 – 3-89349-689-0 – gw Hänsel [700]
VOM GEGENSGANG DER BIBEL DURCH DIE HEIDENWELT / Hesse, Johannes – Calw: Verlag der Vereinsbuchhandlung, 1910 – 2mf – 9 – 0-8370-6741-3 – 1986-0741 – us A.T.L.A. [220]
VOM GEIST DER HEBRAEISCHEN POESIE / Herder, Johann Gottfried – H-269 2. 2 v. 1782-1783 – 9 – ne IDC [470]
VOM GHETTO ZUR MACHT: DIE GESCHICHTE DES AUFSTIEGS DER JUDEN AUF DEUTSCHEN BODEN / Kernholt, Otto – Leipzig: T. Weicher, 1921. x,319p – 1 – us U.W. Library [305]
VOM HEILIGEN REICH DER DEUTSCHEN / Hoelderlin, Friedrich – Jena: E Diederichs, c1935 – 1r – 1 – us U.W. Library [800]
VOM HEILIGEN SACRAMENT DES LEIBS VND BLUTS VNSERS HERREN IESV CHRISTI. UNTERRICHT VND BEKENTNIS... / Eber, P – Witteberg, 1562 – 6mf – 9 – ne IDC [240]
VOM JUEDISCHEN KRIEGE / Flavius, Josephus; ed by Berendts Alexander & Grass, K – Dorpart. 1-4. 1924-1927 – 12mf – 8 – ne Slangenburg [220]
VOM KREIGE; OF WARFARE / More, Thomas, Sir – German and English extracts from "Utopia". 1 fiche (29x) – 9 – $1.00f – at Libertarian Micro [320]
VOM KRIEGSSCHAUPLATZE DER ISRAELITISCHEN RELIGIONSWISSENSCHAFT : EINE GEMEINVERSTAENDLICHE SCHILDERUNG DER KAEMPFE AUF DEM GEBIETE DER MODERNEN BIBELWISSENSCHAFT / Jampel, Sigmund – Frankfurt a. Main: J Kauffmann, 1909 – 1mf – 9 – 0-8370-3768-9 – 1985-1768 – us A.T.L.A. [270]
DIE VOM MISSALE ROMANUM ABWEICHENDEN LESETEXTE FUER DIE MESZFEIERN NACH DEN NOTIERUNGEN DES AUS MONTE-CASINO STAMMENDEN CODEX VAT. LAT. 6082 / Dold, A – Muenster, 1947 – 1mf – 8 – Dfl6.00 – ne Slangenburg [240]
VOM NIGER-BENUE : BRIEFE AUS AFRIKA / ed by Flegel, Eduard – Leipzig: W Friedrich, 1890 – us Res Libr [860]
VOM NULLPUNKT ZUR WENDE : ANMERKUNGEN ZUR DEUTSCHEN LITERATUR ZWISCHEN 1945 UND 1989 / Jung, Werner – 1995 – 2mf – 9 – DM80.00 – 3-8267-2179-9 – gw Hänsel [430]
VOM PAPSTE / Maistre, Joseph de; ed by Bernhart, Joseph – Muenchen, 1923 – 2v 337/337p – 9 – DM98.00 – 3-89349-117-1 – gw Hänsel [240]
VOM RECHTE DES WIDERSTANDES / Dahlmann, FC – 7p – 9 – 1.00f – at Libertarian Micro [335]
VOM SACRAMENT DER DANCKSAGUNG. VERTEUETSCHT D. L. HAETZER / Oecolampad, J & Ecolampadius, J – Zuerich, Chr. Froschouer. 1526. BME-53 1 – 9 – ne IDC [240]
VOM SINN DER GOETHESCHEN NATURFORSCHUNG / Jablonski, Walter – (Includes bibliographical references) – Berlin: Reuss & Pollack, 1927 – 1r – 1 – us U.W. Library [430]
VOM SINN DES JUDENTUMS, SAMMELBAND / Birnbaum, N – Frankfort on the Main. 1924. BJ-100-24 1 – 9 – ne IDC [270]
VOM TAETIGEN LEBEN : GOETHES BRIEFE AUS DER ZWEITEN HAELFTE SEINES LEBENS / ed by Hartung, Ernst – Ebenhausen bei Muenchen: W Langewiesche-Brandt, 1911 – 1r – 1 – us U.W. Library [920]

VOM UEBEN UND SPIELEN ZUMN GESTALTEN MIT DEM BALL : RHYTHMISCHE GYMNASTIK IN EINER 6. KLASSE / Ettinger-Hengstebeck, Irmlind – 1995 – 1mf – 9 – DM60.00 – 3-8267-2246-9 – gw Hänsel [790]

LOS VOM ULTRAMONTANISMUS : AN HERRN DR. ALBERT FRITSCH AUF SEINE SCHRIFT, 56 PREIS-AUFGABEN FUER PROTESTANTEN IN OEFFENTLICHEN BRIEFEN AN MEINEN FREUND MAX, PROTESTANTISCHEN PFARRER ZU X: EINE OFFENE ANTWORT / Boetticher, Wilhelm – Wetter a.d. Ruhr: Carl Edelhoff, 1899 – 1mf – 9 – 0-8370-8406-7 – 1986-2406 – us A.T.L.A. [230]

VOM URSPRUNG DES GEISTES AUS DER GESCHLECHTLICHKEIT : ZUR CHRONOLOGISCHEN UND SYSTEMATISCHEN ENTWICKLUNG DER AESTHETIK WILHELM VON HUMBOLDTS / Koenig, Irina – 1992 – vii/203p – 9 – DM48.00 – 3-89349-413-8 – gw Hänsel [190]

VOM WAREN ERKENDTNUSS GOTTES. VON NEWEM UEBERLESEN, FLEISSIG CORRIGIERT VNND GEBESSERT / Huberinus, Caspar – [Augsburg: Philipp Ulhart], 1541. [G.F.: 14.5] – 5mf – 9 – HUB-77/1 – ne IDC [240]

VOM WARHAFFTIGEN TAUFF JOANNIS, CHRISTI / Eleutherobion, Saint – 1550. BME-82 1 – 9 – ne IDC [240]

VOM WERT DER TRADITION / Tavel, Rudolf von – Bern: Schweizer Bibliophilen-Gesellschaft, 1935 – 1r – 1 – us U.W. Library [949]

VOM WORT UND GEDANKEN DER ARBEIT BEI GOETHE / Weinrich, Rainer – (Includes bibliographical references) – Berlin: Junker und Duennhaupt, 1939 – 1 – us U.W. Library [430]

VOM ZORN VND DER GUETE GOTTES / Huberinus, Caspar – Wittenberg: [Georg Rhau, 1534]. [G.F.: 1.9] – 3mf – 9 – HUB-3/1 – ne IDC [240]

VOM ZORN VND DER GUETTE GOTTES / Huberinus, Caspar – [Augsburg: Philipp Ulhart], 1540. [G.F.: 1.6] – 3mf – 9 – HUB-70/1 – ne IDC [240]

VOM ZORN VND DER GUETTE GOTTES / Huberinus, Caspar – [Augsburg: Philipp Ulhart], 1542. [G.F.: 1.7] – 3mf – 9 – HUB-2/1 – ne IDC [240]

IL VOMERO – Philadelphia, PA. 1940-1941 – us I.H.R.C. [073]

VON BILDERN VND ALTARN JN DEN EUANGELISCHEN KIRCHEN AUGSPURGISCHER CONFESSION / Gedik, S – Magdeburgk, 1597 – 2mf – ne IDC [240]

VON BOESEN FALSCHEN ZUNGEN / Huberinus, Caspar – [Augsburg: Philipp Ulhart, um 1534]. [G.F.: 12.2] – 1mf – 9 – HUB-68/1 – ne IDC [240]

VON BOESEN FALSCHEN ZUNGEN / Huberinus, Caspar – [Augsburg: Philipp Ulhart, um 1542-1547]. [G.F.: 12.4] – 1mf – 9 – HUB-83/1 – ne IDC [240]

VON DEM ANFANG UND WESEN DER HAILIGEN STATT JERUSALEM / Brant, S – O-1010. 1518 – 9 – ne IDC [956]

VON DEM AYD SCHWOEREN / Fabri von Hailbrunn, J – Auch von der Widertauffer Marter. Vnd von der gemainschafft der Widertauffer. Augspurg. 1550. BME-134 1 – 9 – ne IDC [240]

VON DEM BAUE DER SUESEN POMERANZANSTAUDE / Medikus, F K – Bemerkungen der Kurpfaelzischen physikalisch-oekonomischen Gesellschaft. 1776. B-8129 1 – 9 – ne IDC [580]

VON DEM GEIST DER WIDERTEUFFER. M. VORREDE (V.) M. LUTHER / Menius, J – Wittemberg, N. Schirlentz. 1544. BME-129 1 – 9 – ne IDC [240]

VON DEM GSATZ GOTTES / Denck, H – BME-60 1 – 9 – ne IDC [240]

VON DEM KONIGREYCH VND PRIESTERTHUM CHRISTI DER HUNDERT VND ZEHENDE PSALM DAUIDS / Bugenhagen, J – Wittemberg, 1526 – 1mf – 9 – ne IDC [240]

VON DEM PREDIG AMPT / Zwingli, H – Zuerich, Chr. Froschouer. 1525. BME-87 1 – 9 – ne IDC [240]

VON DEM VNUERSCHAMPTEN FRAEFEL, ERGERLICHEM VERWYRREN VNND VNWARHAFFTEM LEEREN, DER SELBSGESANDTEN WIDERTOEUFFERN / Bullinger, Heinrich – Zuerich, Chr. Froschouer. 1531. BME-116 1 – 9 – ne IDC [240]

VON DEM ZWECKE JESU UND SEINER JUENGER / Reimarus, Hermann Samuel – 2mf – 8 – ne Slangenburg [290]

VON DEN CEREMONIEN BEY DEM HEILIGEN ABENDMAHL / Gedik, S – Berlin, 1615 – 1mf – ne IDC [240]

VON DEN EUENGELISCHEN ZECHEN, VND VON DER CHRISTEN RED. AUSZ HAILIGER GESCHRIFFT / Haetzer, L – 1525. BME-52 1 – 9 – ne IDC [240]

VON DEN MANIGFALTIGEN IM GLAUBENN ZERSPALTUNGENN / Entfelder, Chr – Straszpurg. 1530. BME-71 1 – 9 – ne IDC [240]

VON DEN VNGEBORN KINDERN, VND VON DEN KINDERN, DIE WIR NICHT TEUFFEN KOENNEN / Bugenhagen, J – Wittemberg, J. Klug. 1552. BME-135 1 – 9 – ne IDC [240]

VON DEN WICHTIGSTEN PFLICHTEN EINES ORGANISTEN / Tuerk, Daniel G – Halle. Hemmerdeschen Buchhandlung. 1787. BP-494 1 – 9 – ne IDC [780]

VON DER CALUINISCHEN PREDICANTEN SCHWINDELGEIST VNND DEM GERECHTEN GERICHT GOTTES VBER DISE SECT / Huber, S – Tuebingen, 1591 – 1mf – ne IDC [240]

VON DER CAPSTADT INS LAND DER MASCHUKULUMBE / Holub, E – 2v. Wien. 1890-91. BA-171 2 – 8 – ne IDC [960]

VON DER CLOSTER KEUESCHEYT VNND CHRISTENLICHER BEICHT... / Bugenhagen, J – [Hagenau], 1529 – 1mf – 9 – ne IDC [240]

VON DER FALLSTRICKEN ETLICHERR NEWER SACRAMENTSCHWERMER ZU WITTENBERG / Wigand, Johann – 1572 – 1 – us A.T.L.A. [240]

VON DER HERMETISCHENN PHILOSOPHIA. ITEM, DICTA ALANI. EXLIBRIS HENRICI VUOLFFIJ. IETZ VON NEWEN WIDERUMB MIT FLEISS CORRIGIRT, VND VBERSEHEN / Bernard of Trevisano – Strassburg, 1586 – 1 – us U.W. Library [190]

VON DER HEXE DIE EINE HEILIGE WAR / Guenther, Agnes – Marburg an der Lahn: Verlag der Christlichen Welt, [pref. 1913] – 1r – 1 – us U.W. Library [830]

VON DER MESS, VND WER DER RECHT PRIESTER SEY / Kretz, M – Freiburg i.B., J. Woerlin. 1525. BME-31 1 – 9 – ne IDC [240]

VON DER MODERATION UND MESSIGUNG HERRN PHILLIPI MELANTHONIS IN DEM BETRUEBTEM LANGWIRIGEM STREITE VOM HEILIGEN ABENDMAHL / Hoffmann, David – Helmstadt, 1592 – 2mf – ne IDC [240]

VON DER MUSICA ALTEN UND NEUEN LIEDERN/SENDE-SCHREIBEN/NEBST EINER/ ANNO 1675. VOR SEHL – Johan Kruegers Gesang-Buch. Greiffswald. ca.1690. BP-442 1 – 9 – ne IDC [780]

VON DER MUSICALISCHEN DECLAMATION / Schuback, Jacob – 1775 – 9 – us Sibley [780]

VON DER NACHFOLGE JESU CHRISTI.. / Blumhardt, Christoph – 1924 – 1 – us A.T.L.A. [240]

VON DER NEIGUNG DER PFLANZEN ZICH ZU BEGATTEN / Medikus, F K – (Historia et Commentationes Academiae. v. 3. Theodoro-Palatinae. 1775). B-8127 1 – 9 – ne IDC [580]

VON DER NOTHWENDIGKEIT EINER THEOLOGISCHEN GRUNDLAGE DER GESAMMTEN STAATSWISSENSCHAFTEN UND DER STAATSWIRTHSCHAFT INSBESONDRE / Mueller, Adam – Leipzig, 1819 – 70p – 9 – DM48.00 – 3-89349-083-3 – gw Hänsel [240]

Von der Osten, Hans Henning *see*
- DISCOVERIES IN ANATOLIA
- EXPLORATIONS IN HITTITE ASIA MINOR

VON DER REINSTEN GLUECKSELIGKEIT DES MENSCHEN / Werfel, Franz – Stockholm: Bermann-Fischer, 1938 – 1r – 1 – us U.W. Library [850]

VON DER RENAISSANCE ZU JESUS: BEKENNTNISSE EINES MODERNEN STUDENTEN / Spemann, Franz – Stuttgart: J.F. Steinkopf, 1903.1 fiche – 9 – us A.T.L.A. [240]

VON DER SENDUNG DES DICHTERS : AUFSAETZE / Lissauer, Ernst – Jena: E Diederichs, 1922 – 1r – 1 – us U.W. Library [840]

VON DER WAREN LIEB / Denck, H – 1527. BME-61 1 – 9 – ne IDC [999]

VON DER WAREN NYESSUNG BEYD LEIBS UND BLUTS CHRISTI / Zyegler, C – Strassburg, W. Kapfel. 1524. BME-20 1 – 9 – ne IDC [240]

VON DER WELT ZUM HIMMELREICH, ODER, DIE JOHANNEISCHE DARSTELLUNG DES WERKES JESU CHRISTI / Koehler, H – Halle: Max Niemeyer, 1892. 1 fiche – 9 – us A.T.L.A. [240]

VON DER WIDERGEBURT VNND HERKUMMEN EYNES CHRISTEN MENSCHENS / Crauthwaldt, S von – 1538. BME-75 1 – 9 – ne IDC [240]

VON DER WIDERTAUFFE AN ZWEN PFARHERRN EIN BRIEF / Luther, Martin – Wittemberg. 1528; Nuermberg, G. Wachter. 1528. BME-93 1 – 9 – ne IDC [240]

VON DEUTSCHER REDE / Jens, Walter – Muenchen: R Piper & Co Verlag, 1969 – 1 – us U.W. Library [430]

VON EINEM, DER SEINE AHNEN SUCHEN GING : VATERLAENDISCHE ERZAEHLUNG AUS HARTER NOTZEIT / Torrund, Jassy – Goerlitz: C A Starke, 1937, c1936 – 1r – 1 – us U.W. Library [943]

VON ER LERNHARD KEISER DES EUANGELI WILLEN VERBRANDT / Luther, Martin – Wittemberg, H. Lufft. 1528. BME-10 1 – 9 – ne IDC [240]

VON FUERSTEN UND ANDEREN STERBLICHEN ERINNERUNGEN EINES KRIMINALKOMISSARS / Tresckow, Hans von – Berlin: F. Fontane & Co., 1922. 240p – 1 – us U.W. Library [943]

VON GOETHES SPRACHE UND STIL IM ALTER / Knauth, Paul – (Includes bibliographical references) – Leipzig: G Fock, 1894 – 1r – 1 – us U.W. Library [430]

VON GOTTES VNND CHRISTI JESU VNNSERS HERREN ERKANDTNUSZ, AIN BEDACHT / Entfelder, Chr – BME-73 1 – 9 – ne IDC [240]

VON H. SCHRIFFT. 2. VON DER CHRISTLICHEN KIRCHEN. 3. VON DER BAEPTISCHEN KIRCHEN. 4. VON D. LUTHERS PERSON. 5. VON HANS PISTORIJ PERSON VND SEINEM SCHRECKLICHEM ANBLJCK / Huber, S – N.p., 1596 – 3mf – ne IDC [240]

VON JUNGER LIEBE, LUST UND LEID : DREI VARIATIONEN UEBER EIN THEMA / Storm, Theodor; ed by Langenbucher, Hellmuth – Bayreuth: Der Gauverlag, 1944 – 1r – 1 – us U.W. Library [430]

VON KETZERN UND IREN VERBRENNEN ETC / Fridberger, B – 1524. BME-36 1 – 9 – ne IDC [240]

V-on, L *see* VSEROSSIISKI KOOPERATIVNYI S"EZD V S-PETERBURGE

VON LUDWIG TIECK ZU E.T.A. HOFFMANN : STUDIEN ZUR ENTWICKLUNGSGESCHICHTE DES ROMANTISCHEN SUBJEKTIVISMUS / Jost, Walter – (Includes bibliographical references) – Frankfurt am Main: M Diesterweg, 1921 – 1r – 1 – us U.W. Library [430]

VON LUEBECKS THUERMEN – Luebeck, 1891-apr 11 1933 – 10r – 1 – gw Mikrofilm [072]

VON MANCHERLEI HOELLE UND SELIGKEIT : ERZAEHLUNGEN / Goltz, Joachim, Freiherr von der – Muenchen: A Langen, G Mueller, 1936 – 1r – 1 – us U.W. Library [830]

VON NAH UND FERN – Berlin, 1912-15 – 1 – Inquire at Mikrofilmarchiv for details – gw Misc Inst [072]

VON NAZARETH NACH GOLGATHA / Maurenbrecher, Max – Berlin-Schoeneberg: Hilfe, 1909.1 fiche – 9 – us A.T.L.A. [240]

VON NEUEN FREIHEITEN DES GEISTES : EINE AUSWAHL / Nietzsche, Friedrich Wilhelm – [Muenchen]: Muenchner Buchverlag, 1943 – 1r – 1 – us U.W. Library [190]

VON NEWEN SCHWERMEREYEN SECHS CAPITEL. DER SEELEN SELIGKEIT BETREFFENDE / Cochleus, J – Leipzig, M. Blum. 1534. BME-127 1 – 9 – ne IDC [240]

VON REIMARUS ZU WREDE : EINE GESCHICHTE DER LEBEN-JESU-FORSCHUNG / Schweitzer, Albert – (Includes author & title index) – Tuebingen: J C B Mohr, 1906 – 1mf – 9 – 0-8370-5185-1 – 1985-3185 – us A.T.L.A. [240]

THE VON RHODEN COLLECTION OF RESEARCH MATERIALS ON THE ROLE OF THE GERMAN AIR FORCE IN WORLD WAR 2, 1911-47 – 73r – $1,679.00 – T971 – us Nat'l Archives [355]

VON SIEBOLD COLLECTION / National Museum of Ethnology, Leiden – (Most of the rare books in this collection are in Japanese) – 411mf – 9 – ne IDC [480]

VON WARER GOTSELIGKAYT, WIE DER MENSCH ALLHIE IN DISER ZEYT DARTZU KOMMEN MAG / Entfelder, Chr – 1530. BME-72 1 – 9 – ne IDC [240]

VON WEIMAR ZU HITLER / Braun, Otto – New York: Europa Verlag, c1940. 458p With: Hume: With Helps to the Study of Berkeley by T.H. Huxley. 1 reel. 1290 – 1 – us U.W. Library [943]

VONCKEN DER LIEFDE JESU, VAN HET GODTBEGERENDE ZIELENVIER : BLOEMITJES DER SALIGE HOOPE, TOT VERHEUGELYKHEID DER WANDELAARS, LANGS DEN WEG, NA VREDEN RYK / Luyken, J – 1st ed. Amsterdam, 1687 – 3f – 9 – O-3114/1 – ne IDC [760]

VONCKEN DER LIEFDE JESU, VAN HET GODT-BEGERENDE ZIELEN-VUUR / Luiken, J – O 677. 1696 – 9 – ne IDC [240]

Vondel, J van den *see*
- DEN GULDEN WINCKEL DER KONSTLIEVENDE NEDERLANDERS GESTOFFEERT MET VEEL TREFFELYCKE HISTORISCHE, PHILOSOPHISCHE, POEETISCHE MORALE ENDE SCHRIFTUERLIJCKE LEERINGEN
- TOONEEL DES MENSCHELIKKEN LEVENS
- TOONEEL DES MENSCHELIKKEN LEVENS, OF DE VERNIEUWDE GULDEN WINKEL
- TOONEEL DES MENSCHELYKEN LEVENS
- DE VERNIEUWDE GULDEN WINCKEL DER KUNSTLIEVENDE NEDERLANDERS
- VORSTELIICKE WARANDE DER DIEREN

Vondenvelden, William *see* EXTRAITS DES TITRES DES ANCIENNES CONCESSIONS DE TERRE EN FIEF ET SEIGNEURIE

VONKEN DER LIEFDE JEZUS, VAN HET GOD-BEGEERENDE ZIELEN-VUUR / Luiken, J – O 676. 1717 – 9 – ne IDC [240]

VOORBEELDELYKE ZEEDE-LESSEN, GENOOMEN UYT DEN EERSTEN TOESTAND DES WERELDS, DES MENSCHEN LEVEN, AMPTEN, STAATEN, KONSTEN, EN NEYGINGEN DES GEMOEDS : TOT VORDERING TER GODVRUGTIGHEID: ALS EEN VERVOLG OP DE LEERZAAME ZINNEBEELDEN / Graauwhart, Hendrik – 1st ed. Amsterdam, 1709 – 4mf – 9 – O-3074/1 – ne IDC [760]

VOOR-BEELDT DER WAERE DEUGHT, NAMENTLIJCK VAN DE MAEGHDELIJCKE REYNIGHEYDT... / Nerrincq, F – Mechelen, 1692 – 3mf – 9 – ne IDC [700]

VOORDRACHTEN GEHOUDEN VOOR HET KONINKLIJK INSTITUT VAN INGENIEURS – Hague. v1-71 1951 – 1 – D649 – us UMI [620]

Voorhees, Donald S *see*
- MANUAL ON RECURRING PROBLEMS IN CRIMINAL TRIALS
- RECURRING PROBLEMS IN THE TRIAL OF A CRIMINAL ACTION

Voorhelm Schneevoogt, G *see* ICONES PLANTARUM RARIORUM

HET VOORHOF DER ZIELE / Hoogstraten, Francois van – O 299. 1668 – 9 – ne IDC [760]

DIE VOORLIGTER – (Lacks: Dec 1975. 1977-78) – Johannesburg, 1937-76; 1979-84 – 15r – 1 – ATLA S0585 – us A.T.L.A. [073]

VOORSPELLINGEN VAN DE H. HILDEGARDE OMTRENT DE BELGISCHE OMWENTELING / Hildegarde, H – Dfl6.00 – ne Slangenburg [240]

DE VOORTREKKER – Krugersdorp, South Africa. 1898-99 – 1 – sa State Libr [072]

VOORUIT / Belgische WerkliedenpartijParti ouvrier belge – Ghent, 1914-17 (few issues), 1918 (incompl) – 1 – us Hoover Inst Photo [331]

VOORUZHENNOE VOSSTANIE V DEKABRE 1905 GODA / Aroslavskii, Emelian – Moskva: Gos. izdvo, 1926 – 1 – CSUX88-B828 – us Hoover Inst Photo [947]

O VOORUZHENNOM MORSKOM NEITRALITETE – Spb. 1859. On Catherine the Great's celebrated Armed Neutrality, taken from Russian archives. Bibliography. BR-9505 1 – 9 – ne IDC [321]

VOORWAARTS – Paarl, South Africa. 15 Apr 1902-29 Dec 1904. 3 reels – 1, 16 diazo available at reduced price – sa SA Libr [072]

VOOR-WINCKEL VAN PATIENTIE IN DEN DROEVEN TEGENSPOEDT : VERSIEN MET POETSCHE LEERINGE ENDE SENTENTIEN VAN AUGUSTINUS / Lijftocht, F – Emmerich, Koeln, Utrecht, 1679; 1681 – 6mf – 9 – O-3119/1 – ne IDC [760]

Voorzanger, J L *see* HET JOODSCH IN NEDERLAND

Vopenka, Petr *see* MATHEMATICS IN THE ALTERNATIVE SET THEORY

"VOPLOSHCHENIE." / Avraamov, A – Esenin-Mariengof, Moscow, 1921. 44p. BR-1979 2 – 8 – ne IDC [460]

VOPROS O MEZHDUNARODNOI ORGANIZATSII SOEDINENNYE SHTATY EVROPY : APPRAISAL OF PROPOSALS FOR AN INTERNATIONAL ORGANIZATION UNITING THE EUROPEAN STATES / Kamarovskii, L A – Moscow, 1905 – 9 – BR-9152/1 – ne IDC [320]

VOPROS O RUNAKH U SLAVIAN. GRECHESKOE PIS'MO IX-X STOLETII. / Iagich, V & Gardthausen, V – Moscow, 1911. v3. BR-10,321/1 – 9 – ne IDC [450]

VOPROSY ARKHIVOVEDENIIA – Nauchno-informatsionnyi biulletin'. M. 1956-65; index. 1966. BR-10,786 1 – 9 – ne IDC [025]

VOPROSY ARKHIVOVEDENIIA I ISTOCHNIKOVEDENIIA V BSSR / U.S.S.R. Arkhivnogo Stoitel'stva v SSSR – Materialy nauchnoi knoferentsii arkhivistov i istorikov, posviashchennoi 50 letiiu Ed. by V.N. Zhigalov. Minsk. 1971. BR-11.291 1 – 9 – ne IDC [025]

VOPROSY DNIA I ZHIZNI / Gol'tsev, V A – M. 1892. BR-10.579 2 – 8 – ne IDC [460]

VOPROSY EKONOMIKI – 1948-52 – 1 – 74.00 – us L of C Photodup [947]

VOPROSY EKONOMIKI – Moscow. 1948-1970 – 1 – 35.00r – us Hoover Inst Photo [330]

VOPROSY EKONOMIKI – Problems of Economics. Moscow. U.S.S.R. 1961- – 1 – us UMI [073]

VOPROSY FILOSOFII – Problems of Philosophy. Moscow. U.S.S.R. 1961- – 1 – us UMI [100]

VOPROSY ISTORII – Moscow. Jan. 1945-Dec. 1960. Missing July-Dec. 1945 – 1 – 35.00r – us Hoover Inst Photo [947]

VOPROSY ISTORII – Problems of History. Moscow. U.S.S.R. 1961- – 1 – us UMI [947]

VOPROSY ISTORII = QUESTIONS / PROBLEMS OF HISTORY – (1986-93 backfile available 182mf $900) – 24mf per y – 9 – $150.00y – Norman Ross Publishing – us Ross [900]

VOPROSY ISTORII GOSUDARSTVA I PRAVA ESTONSKOI SSR DO OKTIABR'SKOI REVOLIUTSII / Egorov, Iu. – Tartu, 1966 – 2mf – 9 – ne IDC [320]

VOPROSY ISTORII KPSS – 1957-60. Missing no. 1, 1957 – 1 – 35.00r – us Hoover Inst Photo [947]

VOPROSY ISTORII KPSS – Moscow, 1957-72.BR-10,482/1 – 9 – ne IDC [947]

VOPROSY ISTORII KPSS – Problems of History of Communist Party of the Soviet Union. Moscow. U.S.S.R. 1961- – 1 – us UMI [073]

VOPROSY KOOPERATIVNOGO DVIZHENIA V ROSSII / Merkulov, A V – Pg., 1918 – 3mf – 9 – COR-72/1 – ne IDC [334]

VOPROSY LITERATURNYI I ESTETIKI / Meilakii, B – Sbornik statei. Izd. Sovetskii pisatel'. L. 1958. BR-1426 2 – 8 – ne IDC [460]

VOPROSY LITERATURY = QUESTIONS / PROBLEMS OF LITERATURE : JOURNAL OF LITERARY CRITICISM AND SCHOLARSHIP – (1957-90 2115mf $5,000. Individual issues $25 ea. Printed index 1957-87 $50) – 1991- – 60mf per y – 9 – $240.00y – us Ross [410]

VOPROSY METODOLOGII PLANIROVANIIA PROSVETITELNOI RABOTY / Narodnyi komissariat prosveshcheniia RSFSR – (Library has v.3 (1929)) – Moskva, Leningrad: Gos. izdvo, 1929 – 1 – CSUX90-S658 – us Hoover Inst Photo [370]

VOPROSY NASHEGO VREMENI / Bers, E – Spb., 1906. 155p – 2mf – 9 – ne IDC [320]

VOPROSY POETIKI – Leningrad: Gosudarstvennyi Institut Istorii Iskusstv. v1-13. 1923-29 – 2r – 1 – us Ross [460]

VOPROSY POETIKI – St Petersburg, 1923-1929. v. 1-13 – 1 – us NY Public [410]

VOPROSY PRAKTICHESKOI RABOTY RABOCHEI KOOPERATSII : SBORNIK DLIA KOOP. AKTIVA I RABOTNIKOV TSRK I GORPO – M., 1929 – 2mf – 9 – COR-245/1 – ne IDC [334]

VOPROSY PROIZVODITELNOI KOOPERATSII – Ekaterinodar, 1920 n1 – 1mf – 9 – COR-572/1 – ne IDC [334]

VOPROSY SOVETSKOGO STROITEL'STVA: SBORNIK STATEI / ed by Alymov, A A & Cheliapov, N I – Moscow, 1934. 222p. BR-9645 1 – 9 – ne IDC [947]

VOPROSY SOVETSKOI TORGOVLI / Narkomtorga SSSR i Tsentrosoiuza – (Library has: 1938-1940; missing Dec. 1939, Jan. 1940) – Moskva: Gostorgizdat, 1938-1940. 3v – 1 – CSUX90-S544 – us Hoover Inst Photo [380]

VOPROSY STANDARTIZATSII I KACHESTVA PRODUKTSII / Emel'ianova, M B – Tallin, 1967 – 4mf – 9 – ne IDC [350]

VOPROSY TEORII I PSIKHOLOGII TVORCHESTVA – Kharkov. v. 1-6. no. 1; v. 7. 1909-1916 – 1 – us NY Public [150]

VOPROSY TEORII I PSIKHOLOGII TVORCHESTVA / ed by Lezin, B A – Khar'kov. pt1-8. 1907-1923 – 39mf – 9 – RET-28/1 – ne IDC [947]

VOPROSY TEORII I PSIKHOLOGII TVORCHESTVA / ed by Lezin, B A – Khar'kov. pt1-8. 1907-1923 – 39mf – 9 – ne IDC [947]

VOPROSY TEORII LITERATURY / Zhirmunskii, V M – L. 1928. BR-2240 2 – 8 – ne IDC [460]

VOPROSY TRANSPORTNOGO PRAVA / I Uridicheski i otdel Vestnika pute i soobshcheniia – (Library has: June/July, Oct./Nov. 1925) – Moskva: Izd. NKPS, 1925. 1v – 1 – CSUX89-S936 – us Hoover Inst Photo [380]

VOR DER ENTSCHEIDUNG : EIN GEDICHT / Unruh, Fritz von – 2.-5. Aufl. Berlin: E Reiss, 1919 – 1r – 1 – us U.W. Library [810]

VORANSCHLAG / Austro-Hungarian Monarchy – 1869-1915 – 1 – 758.00 – us L of C Photodup [943]

DIE VORBEREITUNG DES PIETISMUS : IN DER REFORMIERTEN KIRCHE DER NIEDERLANDE BIS ZUR LABADISTISCHEN KRISIS 1670 / Goeters, Wilhelm – Leipzig: J.C. Hinrichs; Utrecht: A. Oosthoek, 1911 – 1mf – us A.T.L.A. [240]

DIE VORBEREITUNG DES PIETISMUS IN DER REFORMIERTER KIRCHE DER NIEDERLAENDE / Goeters, Wilhelm – Leipzig, 1911 – Dfl25.00 – ne Slangenburg [240]

VORBEREITUNG ZUR WAARENKUNDE ODER ZUR KENNTNIS DE VORNEHMSTEN AUSLAENDISCHEN WAAREN / Beckmann, Johann – 2. Band. Goettingen, 1796 – 1 – DM30.00 – gw Mikro Press [380]

Vorberg, Axel *see* DIE EINFUEHRUNG DER REFORMATION IN ROSTOCK

DER VORBOTE – Politische und Sozial-oekonomische Monatsschrift. Geneva. v. 1-6. 1866-1871 – 1 – us NY Public [335]

VORBOTE – Bern. Internationale marxistische Rundschau. Herausgeber: Anton Pannekoek und Henriette Roland-Holst. Complete file; rare. Nos. 1 2, Jan.-Apr. 1916 – 1 – 35.00r – us Hoover Inst Photo [073]

VORBOTE – Chicago.1874-1907 – 1 – gw Mikrofilm [071]

VORBOTE – Unabhaengiges Organ fuer die wahren Interessen des Proletariats. Wochenblatt der "Chicagoer Arbeiter-Zeitung" Chicago. v. 1-34. Feb 14 1874-Dec 1907. Incomplete – 1 – us NY Public [335]

VORBOTE : (WOCHENBLATT DER "CHICAGOER ARBEITERZEITUNG") – Chicago. v1-34. 1874-1907 – 16r – 1 – us Ross [071]

Vorbrodt, Walther *see* GOTTHOLD EPHRAIM LESSING

DER VORCHRISTLICHE JESUS: NEBST WEITEREN VORSTUDIEN ZUR ENTSTEHUNGSGESCHICHTE / Smith, William Benjamin – Giessen: Alfred Toepelmann, 1906. 1 fiche – 9 – us A.T.L.A. [240]

DIE VOREXILISCHE JAHWEPROPHETIE UND DER MESSIAS : IN IHREM VERHAELTNIS / Volz, Paul – (Includes bibliographical references and index) – Goettingen: Vandenhoeck und Ruprecht, 1897 – 1mf – 9 – 0-8370-6442-2 – 1986-0442 – us A.T.L.A. [220]

VORGEMACH DER MUSICALISCHEN COMPOSITION / Sorge, G A – 1745-47.3v – 9 – us Sibley [780]

DIE VORGESCHICHTE DER ERBFOERSTER- : TRAGOEDIE VON OTTO LUDWIG / Sieburg, Erich – (Includes bibliographical references) – Berlin: E Ebering, 1903 – 1r – 1 – us U.W. Library [430]

DIE VORGESCHICHTE DES BAUERNKRIEGES / Vogt, Wilhelm – Halle: Verein fuer Reformationsgeschichte, 1887. ([Schriften des Vereins fuer Reformationsgeschichte; Bd. 20]) – 1mf – us A.T.L.A. [940]

DIE VORHERRSCHAFT BERLINS : LITTERARISCHE ANREGUNGEN / Lienhard, Friedrich – Berlin: Meyer & Wunder, 1902 – 1r – 1 – us U.W. Library [840]

VORHERSAGE DER SCHWINGFESTIGKEIT VON SCHWEISSVERBINDUNGEN AUF DER BASIS DES STATISTISCHEN GROESSENEINFLUSSES / Kreuzer, Wolfgang – 1995 – 2mf – 9 – DM80.00 – 3-8267-2212-4 – gw Hänsel [620]

Vorhis, Phillip E *see* THE EFFECT OF RAPID WEIGHT LOSS/WEIGHT GAIN ON MUSCULAR POWER OF INTERCOLLEGIATE WRESTLERS

EINE VORKANONISCHE UEBERLIEFERUNG DES LUKAS IN EVANGELIUM UND APOSTELGESCHICHTE / Feine, Paul – Gotha, 1891 – 5mf – 8 – ne Slangenburg [220]

EINE VORKANONISCHE UEBERLIEFERUNG DES LUKAS IN EVANGELIUM UND APOSTELGESCHICHTE / Feine, Paul – Gotha: F.A. Perthes, 1891. 1 fiche – 9 – us A.T.L.A. [240]

VORLAEUFER DES ANTICHRIST / Mueller-Gangiaff, Erich – Berlin, Wedding-Verlag, c 1948. 343 p. (Buchreihe der Berliner Hefte) Film Mas 8915 – 1 – us H.U. Library [240]

VORLAEUFIGE BEOBACHTUNGEN DER SCHWAEMME UM REGENSBURG / Schaeffer, J C – Regensburg. 1759. B-6310 2 – 8 – ne IDC [580]

VORLAEUFIGER PROSPEKT EINER SCHULBIBEL : NEBST AUSGEWAEHLTEN PROBESTUECKEN / Schuetz, A von – Glueckstadt: J J Augustin, 1888 – 1mf – 9 – 0-8370-7586-6 – 1986-1586 – us A.T.L.A. [370]

VORLAGE DER ESKIMO-SAMMLUNG DES FORSCHUNGSREISENDEN BERNARD HANTZSCH / Preuss, K Th – BN 353. 2. 1913 – 8 – ne IDC [305]

VORLAGEN...AM 27 MAI 1867 / Mansfeld'sche Kupferschieferbauende Gewerkschaft – 24p. (Serial publications of German trade unions in the Memorial Library, University of Wisconsin-Madison.) – 1 – us U.W. Library [331]

VORLESUNGEN UEBER BIBLISCHE THEOLOGIE UND MESSIANISCHE WEISSAGUNGEN DES ALTEN TESTAMENTS : MIT DEM BRUSTBILDE HITZIG'S UND EINER LEBENS- UND CHARAKTER-SKIZZE / Hitzig, Ferdinand; ed by Kneucker, J J – (Includes biographical sketch of the author, bibliographical references and indexes) – Karlsruhe: H Reuther, 1880 – 1mf – 9 – 0-8370-3598-8 – 1985-1598 – us A.T.L.A. [220]

VORLESUNGEN UEBER CHRISTLICHE GLAUBENSLEHRE / Beck, Johann Tobias; ed by Lindenmeyer, Julius – Guetersloh: C. Bertelsmann, 1886-1887 – 4mf – us A.T.L.A. [240]

VORLESUNGEN UEBER DIE APOKALYPSE / Bleek, Friedrich; ed by Hossbach, Th – Berlin: George Reimer, 1862 – 1mf – 9 – 0-8370-2373-4 – 1985-0373 – us A.T.L.A. [220]

VORLESUNGEN UEBER DIE APOKALYPSE = LECTURES ON THE APOCALYPSE / Bleek, Friedrich; ed by Davidson, Samuel – (In English) – London: Williams & Norgate, 1875 – 1mf – 9 – 0-8370-2372-6 – 1985-0372 – us A.T.L.A. [220]

VORLESUNGEN UEBER DIE GESCHICHTE DER DEUTSCHEN LITERATUR / Brederlow, CG F; ed by Garber, Klaus – Leipzig, 1844 – 5mf – 9 – subsc: DM45.00 diazo DM50.00 silver – gw Olms [430]

VORLESUNGEN UEBER DIE GESCHICHTE DER DEUTSCHEN NATIONAL-LITERATUR / Vilmar, August Friedrich Christian; ed by Garber, Klaus – 2nd ed. Marburg, 1847 – 8mf – 9 – subsc: DM58.00 – gw Olms [430]

VORLESUNGEN UEBER DIE GESCHICHTE DER MESSIANISCHEN IDEE / Anger, Rudolf; ed by Krenkel, Max – Berlin: F. Henschel, 1873 – 1mf – 9 – 0-8370-2104-9 – 1985-0104 – us A.T.L.A. [240]

VORLESUNGEN UEBER DIE GESCHICHTE DER TEUTSCHEN NATIONAL-LITERATUR / Wachler, Ludwig; ed by Garber, Klaus – Frankfurt, 1818-19 – 6mf – 9 – subsc: DM46.00 – gw Olms [430]

VORLESUNGEN UEBER DIE THEOLOGIE DES ALTEN TESTAMENTS / Haevernick, Heinrich Andreas Christoph; ed by Hahn, Heinrich August – (Includes supplemental essays on special Old Testament subjects) – 2. Aufl. Frankfurt a. M.; Erlangen: Heyder & Zimmer, 1863 – 1mf – 9 – 0-8370-3446-9 – 1985-1446 – us A.T.L.A. [220]

VORLESUNGEN UEBER NEUTESTAMENTLICHE THEOLOGIE / Baur, Ferdinand Christian – Leipzig: Fues (L.W. Reisland), 1864. 1 fiche – 9 – us A.T.L.A. [240]

VORLESUNGEN UEBER NEUTESTAMENTLICHE ZEITGESCHICHTE / Schneckenburger, Matthias – Frankfurt a.M.: H.L. Broenner, 1862. 1 fiche – 9 – us A.T.L.A. [240]

VORLESUNGEN UND ABHANDLUNGEN / Traube, L; ed by Boll, F – (1. Zur Palaeographie und Handschriftenkunde. Muenchen 1909 9mf; 2. Einleitung in die lateinische Philologie des Mittelalters. Muenchen 1911 5mf; 3. Kleine Schriften. Muenchen 1920 10mf) – 8 – ne Slangenburg [450]

Vormbaum, R *see* EVANGELISCHE SCHULORDNUNGEN

VORMORGEN / Toller, Ernst – Potsdam: Kiepenheuer, [c1924] – 1r – 1 – us U.W. Library [810]

Vorms, A E *see* ZAKONY O CHAST NOI PROMYSHLENNOSTI

Vorob'eva-Desiatovskaia, M I et al *see* OPISANIE KITAISKIKH RUKOPISEI DUN'KHUAUNSKOGO FONDA INSTITUTA NARODOV AZII

Vorob'ev-Nabatov, N A *see*
- RATSIONALIZATSIIA KOOPERATIVNOI RABOTY
- REZHIM EKONOMII I KOOPERATSIIA

VOROLD – (In Icelandic) – Canada, Sept 1918-1920 – 1r – 1 – cn Commonwealth Micro [072]

VORONEZHKII KOOPERATOR I ZEMLEDELETS – (Missing: 1918 n1-4, 7-16, 20-end) – Voronezh, 1918-19 n5 – 5mf – 9 – COR-574/1 – ne IDC [334]

VORONEZHSKAIA KOOPERATIVNAIA NIVA – Voronezh, 1916-17 n1 – 3mf – 9 – COR-573/1 – ne IDC [334]

VORONEZHSKII LITERATURNYI SBORNIK : POVREMENNOE IZDANIE / ed by Malykhih, P – Voronezh. v1. 1861 – 7mf – 9 – RET-29/1 – ne IDC [947]

VORONEZHSKII LITERATURNYI SBORNIK : POVREMENNOE IZDANIE / ed by Malykhih, P – Voronezh. v1. 1861 – 7mf – 9 – ne IDC [947]

Voronich, K I *see* PREDSTAVITELI PECHATI V KOMMISII

Voronov, A D *see* SHTUNDIZM. OCHERK RELIGIOZNOGO-BYTOVOI ZHIZNI V MALOROSSII

Voronov, A S *see* ISTORIKO-STATICHESKOE OBOZRENIE UCHEBNOGO ZAVEDENII S. PETERBURGSKOGO UCHEBNOGO OKRUGA S 1715 PO 1828 VKLIUCHITEL'NO

Voronova, T P *see* FRANTSUZSKIE SREDNEVEKOVYE RUKOPISNYE KNIGI V SOBRANII GOSUDARSTVENNOI PUBLICHNOI BIBLIOTEKI IM. M.E. SALTYKOVA-SHCHEDRINA

Voronskii, A K *see* LITERATURNYE PORTRETY

Vorontsov, V P *see*
- NASHI NAPRAVLENIIA
- SUD'BY KAPITALIZMA V. ROSSII

VOROS ZASZLO – Tirgu-Mures, Romania. 1968-71; 1973; Jul 1975-76; 1978-81 – 11r – 1 – us L of C Photodup [949]

Vorosmartym, Mihaly *see* OSSZES MUNKAI

Vorovskii, V *see* MASLODEL'NYE ARTELI V VOLOGODSKOI GUBERNII

VORSTADTGESCHICHTEN / Seidel, Heinrich – 5. Aufl. Leipzig: A G Liebeskind, 1890 – 1 – us U.W. Library [830]

VORSTAEDTISCHE BLAETTER – (Incl table of contents 1896-1927) – Luebeck, 1896-1933 – 9r – 1 – gw Mikrofilm [943]

VORSTELIICKE WARANDE DER DIEREN : WAER IN DE ZEDEN-RIJCKE PHILOSOPHIE, POETISCH, MORAEL, EN HISTORIAEL, VERMAKELIJCK EN TREFFELIJCK WORT VOORGHESTELT: MET EXEMPLEN UYT DE OUDE HISTORIEN, IN PROSE;... / Vondel, J van den – 1st ed. Amsterdam, 1617 – 3mf – 9 – O-3199/1 – ne IDC [760]

DIE VORSTELLUNG VOM SCHOEPFUNGSMITTLER IM HELLENISTISCHEN JUDENTUM UND URCHRISTENTUM (T.U.U. 5-82) / Hegermann, H – Berlin, 1961 – 4mf – 9 – ne Slangenburg [240]

DIE VORSTELLUNGEN VON DEUTSCHLAND IM ALTFRANZOESISCHEN HELDENEPOS / Remppis, Max – Tuebingen, 1911 – 2mf – DM62.00 – 3-8267-3060-7 – gw Hänsel [440]

Vorstius, Joris *see* ZENTRALBLATT FUER BIBLIOTHEKSWESEN

DOS VORT = THE WORD – (In Yiddish) – Munich, DE. v2 no41 12 Mar 1948-v3 no44 11 Nov 1949 – 1r – 1 – $35.00 – cn Can Microfilming [072]

VORT = WORD – (In Yiddish) – Munich, DE. no27 9 May 1947-no42 22 Aug 1947 – 1r – 1 – $30.00 – cn Can Microfilming [072]

Vortisch, Hermann *see* DIE RELATIVITAETSTHEORIE UND IHRE BEZIEHUNG ZUR CHRISTLICHEN WELTANSCHAUUNG

VORTRAEGE : GEHALTEN AUF DER 6. GENERALVERSAMMLUNG DES VEREINS FUER REFORMATIONSGESCHICHTE AM 11. APRIL 1901 IN BRESLAU VON ERICH BRANDENBURG UND GERHARD EBERLEIN / Brandenburg, Erich – Halle: Verein fuer Reformationsgeschichte, 1901. (Schriften des Vereins fuer Reformationsgeschichte; 19. Jahrg., Schrift 70) – 1mf – us A.T.L.A. [240]

VORTRAEGE DER THEOLOGISCHEN KONFERENZ ZU GIESSEN / Eibach, R., et al – Giessen: J. Ricker, 1889. 1 fiche – 9 – us A.T.L.A. [240]

VORTRAEGE UND AUFSAETZE / Usener, Hermann – Leipzig: B.G. Teubner, 1907 – 1mf – us A.T.L.A. [240]

VORTRAGE DES HESSISCHEN THEOLOGISCHEN FERIENKURSES, HEFT 1 *see* DER DEKALOG ALS KATECHETISCHES LEHRSTUCK

VORWAERTS – (1972-1991 37r DM2,590.00. From 1992 1r per yr DM70.00. Cont as: Sozialdemokratisches Magazin/Vorwaerts 1989) – Hannover-Bonn, 1948-1971 – 22r – 1 – DM1,540.00 – gw Mikro Press [072]

VORWAERTS – Berlin, 1884-1933 – 158r – 1 – DM11,850.00 – gw Mikro Press [072]

VORWAERTS – Berlin, Germany. 1891-Feb 1933 – 104r – 1 – us L of C Photodup [072]

VORWAERTS – (Cont as monday-issue of Neues Deutschland) – Berlin, 1946-47, apr-sep 1949 – 11r – 1 – Inquire at Mikrofilmarchiv for details – gw Misc Inst [072]

VORWAERTS – Jimbolia, Romania. Jan-May 1923 – 1r – 1 – us L of C Photodup [949]

VORWAERTS – Leipzig, Oct 1876-Oct 1878 – 2r – 1 – DM150.00 – gw Mikro Press [072]

VORWAERTS – Muenchen, DE. 6 Aug 1848-14 May 1849 – 1 – gw Mikrofilm [072]

VORWAERTS – New York: Sozialistische Arbeiter-Partei von Nord-Amerika. v1-2. 1892-94 – 1r – 1 – us Ross [071]

VORWAERTS – Paris, 1844-45 – 1r – 1 – DM80.00 – gw Mikro Press [072]

VORWAERTS : PARISER DEUTSCHE ZEITSCHRIFT – (Cont: Vorwaerts. Pariser Signale. Other titles: Der Sozial-Demokrat, Leipzig, Zuerich, Berlin) – Paris, FR. 1844 – 1 – gw Mikrofilm [072]

VORWAERTS – Pariser deutsche Zeitschrift. no. 1-104. Paris. 1844 – 1 – fr A.C.R.P.P. [073]

VORWAERTS – Potsdam, DE. 1844 – 1r – 1 – gw Mikrofilm [072]

VORWAERTS – (Some issues lacking) – Liberec, Czechoslovakia. 12 May 1920; 18 Oct 1927; 1930; Aug 1931-Aug 1934 – 7r – us L of C Photodup [072]

VORWAERTS / Sozialdemokratische Partei Deutschlands – Berlin, 1891-1933 – 1 – gw Mikrofilm [335]

VORWAERTS : SOZIALDEMOKRATISCHE WOCHENZEITUNG – (Began as a weekly in Hannover under the title: Neuer Vorwaerts. Since Mar 1986 a magazine) – Bonn. 1966-79 – 1 – gw Mikrofilm [072]

VORWAERTS : SOZIALDEMOKRATISCHE WOCHENZEITUNG – (Publ started in Hannover as Neuer Vorwaerts. Since mar 1986 publ as a magazine) – Bonn, sep 11 1948- – Inquire at Mikrofilmarchiv for details – gw Misc Inst [320]

VORWAERTS : VOLKSTASCHENBUCH – Leipzig, DE. 1843-45 – 1r – 1 – gw Mikrofilm [072]

VORWAERTS : WOCHENBLATT DER NEW YORKER VOLKSZEITUNG – New York, 1894-96 – 1r – 1 – us Ross [071]

VORWAERTS : ZENTRALORGAN DER SOZIALDEMOKRATISCHEN PARTEI DEUTSCHLANDS – Berlin, 1891-Feb 1933 – 1 – gw Mikrofilm [335]

VORWAERTS *see*
- BERLINER VOLKSBLATT
- DEMOKRATISCHES WOCHENBLATT
- NEUER VORWAERTS

VORWAERTS. PARISER SIGNALE *see* VORWAERTS

VORWARTS – 1948- – 1r per y – 1 – us Ross [072]

VORWARTS – Bonn, DE. 1976-1986 – 22r – $1,100.00 – R04234 – us Library Micro [072]

DER VORWURF DES ATHEISMUS IN DEN DREI ERSTEN JAHRHUNDERTEN (T.U.U. 2-28/4A) / Harnack, Adolf von – Leipzig, 1905 – 1mf – 9 – ne Slangenburg [240]

VOS DO EVANGELHO – v19-26. 1964-71 (complete) – Inquire – 1 – ATLA S0895 – us A.T.L.A. [073]

Vos, Geerhardus *see*
- THE MOSAIC ORIGIN OF THE PENTATEUCHAL CODES
- THE PAULINE ESCHATOLOGY
- THE TEACHING OF JESUS CONCERNING THE KINGDOM OF GOD AND THE CHURCH

Vos, M de *see* VITA, PASSIO ET RESURRECTIO IESU CHRISTI, VARIJS ICONIBUS A CELEBERRIMO PICTORE M. D. V. EXPRESSA, AB ADRINO COLLART NUNC PRIMUM IN AES INCISIS

Vos, Willem Hermanus *see* DIE BALLADE IN AFRIKAANS

VOSDUKHOPLAVITEL – Spb. 1903-17. Lacking: 1903 (1); 1905 (7-12); 1906 (1-5); 1912 (3). BR-9272 2 – 8 – ne IDC [073]

Vosen, Christian Hermann *see* DAS CHRISTENTHUM UND DIE EINSPRUECHE SEINER GEGNER

VOSKHOD – Leningrad. v1-26. 1881-1906 – 24r – 1 – us Ross [072]

VOSKHOD – Leningrad. v1-26. 1882-1906 – 24r – 1 – us Ross [072]

VOSKHOD – St Petersburg. Monthly v. 1-26 no. 3. Jan 1881-Mar 1906. Incomplete – 1 – us NY Public [073]

VOSKHOD – St Petersburg. (Russian) Weekly v. 1-26 no. 26. 1882-1906 – 1 – us NY Public [073]

VOSKRESNAYA BESEDA – St. Petersburg. Nos.1-52, 1895.540p – 1 – 21.60 – us Baptist [240]

VOSKRESNOE CHTENIE – (Missing: 1849/1850(43); 1860/1861(3, p. 29-32); 1862/1863(3); 1864/1865(27-55); 1872(11, 12, 16, 18, 21, 23, 24, 26, 36, 37, 43, 45, 47); 1873(14-50); 1875(1-50); 1877-1879; 1880(15, 40); 1881-1882; 1883(19, p. 175-176; 22, 23, 32, 33, 42, 50); Supplemented: 1840-1883(52). 305mf) – Ed.2. Kiev, 1837-1883(52) – 9 – R-18411/1 – ne IDC [947]

VOSKRESNYI LISTOK MUZYKI I OB'IAVLENII – St Petersburg, 1878-80 – 9mf – 9 – us Ross [780]

VOSKRESSHIE BOGI / Merezhkovskii, Dimitrii – Leonardo da Vinchi. 2 v. Berlin. 1922. BR-801 2 – 8 – ne IDC [700]

VOSPITANIE I OBUCHENIE – v. 1. Spb. 1881-1917. Lacking: 1882 (3-12), 1883 (1-12), 1884 (4-12), 1885 (4-12), 1886 (2, 5), 1896 (8), 1898 (12), 1899 (4-7), 1900 (1, 5, 12), 1901 (1-2, 5, 9-11), 1902 (2, 4-5, 10-11), 1903 (10), 1905 (1), 1906 (5, 11), 1907 (8, 10-11), 1912 (2-4, 8), 1913 (6, 9), 1914 (1-2, 5-12), 1915 (9), 1916 (11-12). B-1978 2 – 8 – ne IDC [073]

VOSPOMANINIIA KAVKAZKAGO GRENADERA, 1914-1920 / Popov, K – Bielgrad: [Russkaia tip.], 1925 – us Res Libr [947]

VOSPOMINANII A : T SARSTVOVANIE NIKOLAI A 2 / Witte, Sergei I Ulevich – Berlin: Knvo "Slovo", 1922. 2v – 1 – CSUX89-B4688 – us Hoover Inst Photo [947]

VOSPOMINANII A O SOVI ETSKIKH TI URMAKH / Chernova-Kolbasina, Olga E – [Parizh]: Izd. Parizhsko i gruppy sodi e istvii a Partii sotsialistov-revoliut sionerov, 1921 – 1 – CSUX88-B7627 – us Hoover Inst Photo [320]

VOSPOMINANIIA / Arnol'd, Iu. K – Moscow, 1892-93. v1-3. BR-9054 2 – 8 – ne IDC [780]

VOSPOMINANIIA, (1763-1819) / Labzina, A E – Spk, 1903 – 8 – BR-7640 2 – ne IDC [920]

VOSPOMINANIIA, 1777-1834 / Lubianovskii, F P – M. 1872. BR-7665 2 – 8 – ne IDC [460]

VOSPOMINANIIA O BLOKE / Gorodetskii, S – Pechat' i revoliutsiia. v. 1. 1922. BR-3266 2 – 8 – ne IDC [335]

VOSPOMINANIIA O BLOKE : KOMMENTARII Z.G. MINTS – n4, 290-378p. 1981 – 2mf – 9 – ne IDC [947]

Vospominaniia o Bloke *see* KOMMENTARII Z. G. MINTS

VOSPOMINANIIA O PEREZHITOM I VIDENNOM V 1864-1909 GG / Ianzhul, I I – v. 1-2. Spb. 1911. Lacking: v. 1. BR-9211 1 – 9 – ne IDC [338]

VOSPOMINANIIA OB ALEKSANDRE BLOKE / Annenkov, I – Novyi Zhurnal. New York. 1956. BR-3247 2 – 8 – ne IDC [460]

VOSPOMINANIIA OB ALEKSANDRE BLOKE / Piast, V – Pis'ma Bloka. Petrograd. 1923. BR-1495 2 – 8 – ne IDC [460]

VOSPOMINANIIA ZA 50 LET / Elpat'evskii, S la – L. 1929. BR-10,080 1 – 9 – ne IDC [305]

VOSPOMINANIIA ZHIZNI F. G. TERNERA / Terner, F G – v. 1-2. Spb. 1910-11. BR-9207 1 – 9 – ne IDC [947]

DIE VOSS – Berlin, feb 5 1921-22 – 2r – 1 – Inquire at Mikrofilmarchiv for details – gw Misc Inst [072]

Voss, Abraham *see*
- BRIEFE VON JOHANN HEINRICH VOSS
- SAEMMTLICHE POETISCHE WERKE

Voss, Hans *see* JULIUS PINCAS DIT PASCIN

Voss, Heinrich *see* GOETHE VON SCHILLER IN BRIEFEN

Voss, Johann Heinrich *see*
- BRIEFE VON JOHANN HEINRICH VOSS
- POETISCHE WERKE
- SAEMMTLICHE POETISCHE WERKE

Voss, Richard *see*
- DAHIEL, DER KONVERTIT
- DER HEILIGE HASS
- UNFEHLBAR

Voss, Wilhelm *see*
- DIE VERHANDLUNGEN PIUS 4. MIT DEN KATHOLISCHEN MAECHTEN UEBER DIE NEUBERUFUNG DES TRIDENTINER CONCILS IM JAHRE 1560 BIS ZUM ERLASS DER INDIKTIONSBULLE VOM 29. NOV. DESSELBEN JAHRES
- DIE VERHANDLUNGEN PIUS 4. MIT DEN KATHOLISCHEN MAECHTEN UEBER DIE NEUBERUFUNG DES TRIDENTINER CONCILS IM JAHRE 1560 BIS ZUM ERLASS DER JURISDIKTIONSBULLE VOM 29. NOV. DESSELBEN JAHRES

VOSSA SENHORIA – Abaete, Brazil. Sept, Nov-Dec 1948; Jan-Mar 1949 – 1 – bl Biblioteca [072]

VOSSA SENHORIA : SEMANARIO INDEPENDENTE E NOTICIOSO, DE TUDO UM POUCO – Pitangui, 10 Feb 1952-16 Sep 1956 – 1,5,6 – bl Biblioteca [072]

Vosseler, Edward Adolph *see* CASES ON THE LAW OF EXECUTORS AND ADMINISTRATORS

Vossenholivs, A *see* DIALOGVS. EIN GOETTLICH VND CHRISTLICH GESPRECK, MIT DEN WEDDERDOEPEREN, SACRAMENTERENEN, VND ANDEREN SECTEN MEHR IM NEDDERLANDE

VOSSISCHE ZEITUNG – (1918-33 86r DM6,450.00) – Berlin, 1812-15 – 3r – 1 – DM225.00 – gw Mikro Press [072]

VOSSISCHE ZEITUNG : BEILAGE: ZEITBILDER – (Cont: Koeniglich Berlinische privilegirte Staats- und gelehrte Zeitung, 1779-1911) – Berlin. aug 2, 1914-16. 1918-mar 25, 1934 – 7r – 1 – gw Mikrofilm [072]

VOSSISCHE ZEITUNG – Berlin, 1850-1919 – 1161r – 1 – uk British Libr Newspaper [072]

VOSSISCHE ZEITUNG – Berlin, Germany. Jul 1900-Mar 1934 – 168r – 1 – us L of C Photodup [072]

VOSSISCHE ZEITUNG – Berlin, Germany.1725, 1735-43, 1745, 1758, 1766, 1812-15, 1847-Mar 1934 – 1 – gw Mikrofilm [072]

VOSSISCHE ZEITUNG – (Cont: Koeniglich Berlinische privilegirte Staats- und gelehrte Zeitung, 1779-1911) – Berlin. jul 2-dec 31, 1816. jul 2, 1818-27. apr 1, 1828-30. jan 30, 1843-dec 24, 1846 – 19r – 1 – gw Mikrofilm [072]

VOSSISCHE ZEITUNG – (Cont: Koeniglich Berlinische privilegirte Staats- und gelehrte Zeitung (1779-1911). Suppl available: Zeitbilder, 1914-22; Fuer Reise und Wanderung, 1924; Literarische Umschau, 1924; Musik-Blatt, sep 6-dec 20 1924; Recht und Leben, 1924-dec 25 1925; Umschau in Technik, n.d.) – Berlin, 1912-mar 31 1934 – 1 – Inquire at Mikrofilmarchiv for details – gw Misc Inst [943]

VOSSISCHE ZEITUNG : SONNTAGSBEILAGE – (Cont: Koeniglich Berlinische privilegirte Staats- und gelehrte Zeitung, 1779-1911) – Berlin. 1867-71. 1875. 1877. mar 11-18, 1888. 1894. 1896 n1-51. 1897-98. 1899-1905. 1910 – 6r – 1 – gw Mikrofilm [072]

VOSSISCHE ZEITUNG *see* KOENIGLICH BERLINISCHE PRIVILEGIRTE STAATS- UND GELEHRTE ZEITUNG

Vossius, G J *see*
- DE QUATTUTOR ARTIBUS POPULARIBUS: GRAMMATICA. MUSICA
- DE THEOLOGIA GENTILI ET PHYSIOLOGIA CHRISTIANA

Vossius, I *see* DE POEMATUM CANTU ET VIRIBUS RYTHMI

VOSSTANOVLENIE KHOZIA ISTVA I RAZVITIE PROIZVODITELNYKH SIL I UGO-VOSTOKA R.S.F.S.R., POSTRADAVSHEGO OT NEUROZHAIA 1921 G : ZAPISKA GOSUDARSTVENNOI OBSHCHEPLANOVOI KOMISSII SOVETA TRUDA I OBORONY R.S.F.S.R. – Moskva: [Tip. III Kommunistich. internatsion.], 1921 – 1 – CSUX89-B2401 – us Hoover Inst Photo [947]

VOSSTANOVLENIE KREST'IANSKOGO KHOZIAISTVA V ROSSII I NASHI ZADACHI / Osinskii, N – M., 1922 – 1mf – 9 – COR-498/1 – ne IDC [334]

VOSTOCHNOE OTDIELENIE : ZAPISKI / Russkoe Arkheologicheskoe Obshchestvo. Leningrad – v1-25. 1886-1921 – 5r – 1 – us Ross [930]

VOSTOCHNYE RUKOPISI INSTITUTA VOSTOKOVEDENIIA AKADEMII NAUK SSSR / Tikhonov, D I – (Uchenye zapiski Instituta vostokovedeniia AN SSSR, v6, 1953). BR-10,970 1 – 9 – ne IDC [025]

VOSTOK = THE EAST – Perth Amboy, NJ, 1940-1950 – 1r – 1 – us I.H.R.C. [071]

VOSTOK – Perth Amboy, NJ: Greek Catholic Carpatho-Russian Benevolent Assoc Liberty, 1920-50. 1927; 1930-33; 1935-42; 1945-47; 1950 – us Res Libr [073]

Vostokov, A K *see* SLOVAR' TSERKOVNO-SLAVIANSKOGO IAZYKA

Vostokov, AKh. *see* SOBRANIE SLAVIANSKIKH PAMIATNIKOV

VOSTOKOVEDENIE V IZDANIIAKH AKADEMII NAUK 1726-1917. BIBLIOGRAFIIA / Livotova, O E et al – Moscow, 1966. 143p. BR-10,972/1 – 9 – ne IDC [010]

THE VOTE *see* WOMEN'S FREEDOM LEAGUE

VOTE – The organ of the Women's Freedom League. London. -w. 30 Oct 1909-10 Nov 1933. (11 reels) – 1 – uk British Libr Newspaper [360]

VOTER REGISTRATION RECORDS / Monroe County. Mich, Bedford Township. Board of Elections – 1906-1946 – 2r – 1 – $32.50r – us Archival [324]

THE VOTERS AND TAXPAYERS OF BUREAU COUNTY, ILLINOIS / H.F. Kett and Co – Chicago, 1877. Illinois Reel 12. The Cox Library Collection – 5 – us Americana [978]

VOTERS ARGUMENT : AMENDMENTS TO THE CONSTITUTION AND PROPOSED STATUTES WITH ARGUMENTS RESPECTING THE SAME – (Yrly update subsc $50.00y B50522) – 1883-1993 – 9 – $250.00 – B50521 – us Library Micro [340]

VOTERS DIGEST – Portland OR. May June Sep 1935, Oct 1939, Dec 1948-Jan 1949, Aug-Sep 1950 – 1 – us U.O. Library [071]

VOTERS NEWS DIGEST – Portland OR. July 1934 – 1 – us U.O. Library [071]

THE VOTER'S TEXT BOOK : COMPRISING A COLLECTION OF THE MOST IMPORTANT DOCUMENTS AND STATISTICS CONNECTED WITH THE POLITICAL HISTORY OF THE U.S. / Hiatt, James M – Indianapolis: Asher, Adams & Higgins, 1868 – 5mf – 9 – $7.50 – LLMC 92-161 – us L.L.M.C. [340]

VOTES AND PROCEEDINGS / Southwest Africa. Legislative Assembly – 1st-8th Assembly. 1926-62 – 1 – 209.00 – us L of C Photodup [960]

VOTES FOR WOMEN / United Suffragists – London. Oct 1907-Feb 1918.-m,-w. 8 reels – 1 – uk British Libr Newspaper [320]

VOTES FOR WOMEN – v. 1-9. Oct 1907-Feb 1918 – 1 – $160.00 – us L of C Photodup [320]
VOTING REGISTERS / Illinois – v1-78, 1818-1847. V149-0008 to 0030 – 1 – us A.G.L.L. [920]
EL VOTO PERONISTA / Mora y Araujo, Manuel & Llorente, Ignacio – Buenos Aires: Editorial Sudamericana, c1980 – 1 – CSUXADL7497-B – us Hoover Inst Photo [320]
VOTRE COTTAGE – Quebec. v1 n2. 1947-1951/52 – 1r – 1 – Can$30.00 – cn Can Microfilming [072]
VOTSARENIE IMPERATRITSY ANNY IOANNANOVNY / Korsakov, D A – Istoricheskii etiud. Kazan'. 1880. BR-6059 2 – 8 – ne IDC [947]
VOUCHER RECORD / Monroe County. Mich, Bedford Township. Township Treasurer – 1878-1898 – 1r – 1 – $32.50r – us Archival [324]
DE VOV ET CONSVETVDINE ET DE STILO CVRIAE REGALIS / Salazar, Petrus – Granada, 1579 – 1 – us U.W. Library [240]
Vowinckel, Ernst *see*
– GESCHICHTE UND DOGMATIK
– RELIGION UND RELIGIONEN
Vowinckel, Hans August *see*
– HANS AUGUST VOWINCKEL, DER DICHTER UND SOLDAT
– SCHILLER DER DICHTER DER GESCHICHTE
Vowinckel, Renate *see* HANS AUGUST VOWINCKEL, DER DICHTER UND SOLDAT
VOX – Gibraltar. -w. 1958-69. 7 reels – 1 – uk British Libr Newspaper [072]
VOX DEI: THE DOCTRINE OF THE SPIRIT AS...SET FORTH IN THE...TESTAMENTS / Redford, Robert Ainslie – London: James Nisbet, 1889. 1 fiche – 9 – us A.T.L.A. [240]
VOX ECCLESIAE ANGLICANAE ON THE CHURCH, MINISTRY, AND SACRAMENTS : A SELECTION OF PASSAGES FROM THE WRITINGS OF THE CHIEF DIVINES OF THE CHURCH OF ENGLAND / Perry, George G – London: Rivingtons, 1868 – 1mf – us A.T.L.A. [240]
VOX EVANGELICA – London. v1-12 1962-83*. v13-27 1983-97+ 1; v13-24 1983-jun 1994*. v25-27 1995-97+ 5; v13-27. 1983-97+ 9 – 1,5,9 – D13920 – us UMI [240]
THE VOX HUMANA – Cambridge, 1872-79 – 1 – £115.00 – uk Chadwyck [780]
THE VOX POPULI – Accra. Ghana. -w. Jan 1930-Feb 1939. (18 reels) – 1 – uk British Libr Newspaper [072]
VOX POPULI / Indonesia. Kementerian Penerangan – 1950. SE-3062-1 – 9 – ne IDC [324]
VOX REFORMATA – (No vol indicated for issues 1962-88) – Geelong. dec 1962-1988*. v52-58 may 1989-1993. v59 aug-aug 1994*. v60-62 1995-97+ – 1 – D15384 – us UMI [240]
VOX SANGUINIS – (Former title: Bulletin van het Centraal Laboratorium van de Bloedtransfusiedienst van het Nederlandse Rode Kruis 1951-52) – Basel. v12-27. 1967-74 1,5; 1994*. v68-69 1995. 1996-97+ 1,5,9 – 1,5,9 – D2079 – us UMI [610]
VOX SANGUINIS – v28-. 1975- – 1,5,9 – us UMI [616]
VOX SUPREMA OLORIS PARTHENII... / Biechteler, B – (3 parts: vox cantans, organo, violino solo) – Augustae-Vindelicorum: J J Lotter, 1731 – us Sibley [780]
VOX WESLEYANA – Winnipeg: Free Press Company, [1897?-19–] – 9 – cn C.I.H.M. [370]
VOYA. VOICE OF YOUTH ADVOCATES – (1982- 1,5,6,9) – v1- 1978- – 1 – us UMI [305]
VOYAGE A CONSTANTINOPLE FAIT A L'OCCASION DE L'AMBASSADE DE M. LE COMTE DE CHOISEUL-GOUFFIER A LA PORTE OTTOMANE / Martin, Guillaume – Paris, F. Plee, 1821, viii-256 p., grav. French Voyagers in the Mediterranean 16th to 18th Centuries. 6003 – 9 – fr Hachette [944]
VOYAGE A ERMENONVILLE / Thiery, Avocat – Ou Lettre sur la Translation de J.J. Rousseau au Pantheon. Paris: Meurant, 1794 – 9 – fr Hachette [190]
VOYAGE A LA COTE DE GUINEE / Labarthe, Pierre – Paris. 1903. BA-326 2 – 8 – ne IDC [910]
VOYAGE A LA COTE DE GUINEE / Labarthe, Pierre – Paris, Debray. 1803 – 9 – 10.00 – fr Orientalistes [910]
VOYAGE A LA COTE DE GUINEE, DANS LE GOLFE DE BIAFRA, A L'ILE DE FERNANDO-PO, L'ILE DE STE HELENE ET AUTRES ILES DANS LE PASSAGE / Boudyck Bastiaanse, J H van – (African Library). La Haye. Belinfante. 1853 – 9 – fr Hachette [960]
VOYAGE A LA COTE OCCIDENTALE D'AFRIQUE / Grandpre, Louis de – Paris, Dentu. 1801 – 9 – 20.00 – fr Orientalistes [910]
VOYAGE A LA COTE OCCIDENTALE D'AFRIQUE DANS LES ANNEES 1786 ET 1787 CONTENANT LA DESCRIPTION DES MOEURS, USAGES, LOIS, GOUVERNEMENT ET COMMERCE DES ETATS DU CONGO, FREQUENTES PAR LES EUROPEENS, ET UN PRECIS DE LA TRAITE DES NOIRS / Grandpre, Louis de – 2v. 1801. (Africa Library) – 9 – fr Hachette [306]
VOYAGE A LA COTE ORIENTALE D'AFRIQUE : EXECUTE PAR LE BRICK LE DUCOUEDIC...ALBUM / Guillain, Charles – Paris: A Bertrand, [1875] – us Res Libr [910]
UN VOYAGE A LA GUADELOUPE : ETUDE SUR LES ANTILLES / Alexis, R P – Quebec: Impr. de l'Evenement, 1908. SEM105P732 – 1mf – 9 – Can$2.25 – cn Bibl Nat [910]
VOYAGE A LA NOUVELLE GUINEE / Sonnerat, P – Paris, 1776. xii/206p. 120pls. 5743/2 – 9mf – 8 – ne IDC [980]
VOYAGE A LA NOUVELLE PHILADELPHIE / Saige, Joseph – (Utopias in the Enlightenment series). 1803 – 9 – fr Hachette [830]
VOYAGE A LA RIVIERE DE SIERRA-LEONE, SUR LA COTE D'AFRIQUE / Matthews, John – Traduction de l'anglais. Paris, Hautbout l'Aine. 1797 – 9 – 5.00 – fr Orientalistes [910]
VOYAGE A L'ILE D'UTOPIE / More, Thomas, Sir & Saint-Pierre, Jacques Henri de – Paris: Delagrave, 1888. 317p. 4 fiches. (Philosophy Collection) – 9 – 10.00 – fr Bibl Nationale [320]
VOYAGE A MADAGASCAR AU COURONNEMENT DE RADAMA 2 / Vinson, Auguste – Paris: Roret, 1865 – us Res Libr [910]
VOYAGE A MADAGASCAR ET AUX ILES COMORES / Leguevel de Lacombe, B F – Paris, L. Dessessart. 1840 – 9 – 22.50 – fr Orientalistes [910]
VOYAGE A MEROE, AU FLEUVE BLANC AU-DELA DE FAZOQL DANS LE MIDI DU ROYAUME DE SENNAR, A SYOUAH ET DANS CINQ AUTRES OASIS; FAIT DANS LES ANNEES 1819, 1820, 1821 ET 1822 / Cailliaud, F – 4v. Paris. 1826-27. B-5499 2 – 8 – ne IDC [910]
VOYAGE A MONTBAR CONTENANT DES DETAILS TRES INTERESSANTS SUR LE CARACTERE, LA PERSONNE ET LES ECRITS DE BUFFON... / Herault de Sechelles, Marie-Jean – Paris: Sovet, an IX – fr Armell [910]
VOYAGE A SAMOA : LETTRES A MARGUERITTE MORENO / Schwob, Marcel – (13 lettres ecrites d'octobre 1901 a mars 1902 et publ. ensuits sous ce titre) – fr Armell [910]
VOYAGE A SEGOU, 1878-1879 : REGIGE D'APRES LES NOTES ET JOURNAUX DE VOYAGE DE SOLEILLET / Gravier, Gabriel – Paris: Challamel aine, 1887 – us Res Libr [910]
VOYAGE AGRONOMIQUE DANS LE SENATORERIE DE DIJON / Francois de Neufchateau, Nicolas-Louis – 1806 – 9 – fr Hachette [944]
VOYAGE AGRONOMIQUE EN AUVERGNE / Pradt, D G F de – 1828 – 9 – fr Hachette [630]
THE VOYAGE AND SHIPWRECK OF ST. PAUL : WITH DISSERTATIONS ON THE LIFE AND WRITINGS OF ST. LUKE AND THE SHIPS AND NAVIGATION OF THE ANCIENTS / Smith, James – (Includes bibliographical references) – 3rd ed. London: Longmans, Green, 1866 – 1mf – 9 – 0-8370-6384-1 – 1986-0384 – us A.T.L.A. [910]
A VOYAGE AROUND THE WORLD IN THE YEARS 1800-04; IN WHICH THE AUTHOR VISITED MADEIRA, THE BRAZILS, CAPE OF GOOD HOPE. / Turnbull, John – 2nd ed. 1813 – 9 – uk Libr Preservation [910]
VOYAGE AU CANADA DANS LE NORD DE L'AMERIQUE SEPTENTRIONALE FAIT DEPUIS L'AN 1751 A 1761 – Quebec: Leger Brousseau, 1887. 00853. (Pre-1900 Canadiana) – 9 – cn C.I.H.M. [971]
VOYAGE AU CANADA PENDANT LES ANNEES 1795, 1796 ET 1797 / Weld, Isaac – Paris: chez Gerard, an XI. 3v. 1803? SEM35P82 – 1r – 1 – Can$23.00 – cn Bibl Nat [910]
VOYAGE AU CONGO / Lemaire, Charles Francois Alexandre – [Bruxelles?: n.d.] – us Res Libr [910]
VOYAGE AU CONGO ET DANS L'INTERIEUR DE L'AFRIQUE EQUINOXALE / Douville, Jean-Baptiste – Paris, Jules Renouard. 1832 – 9 – 30.00 – fr Orientalistes [910]
VOYAGE AU CONGO ET DANS L'INTERIEUR DE L'AFRIQUE EQUINOXIALE : FAIT DANS LES ANNEES 1828, 1829 ET 1830 / Douville, Jean-Baptiste – Paris: Renouard, 1832 – us Res Libr [910]
VOYAGE AU DARFOUR OU L'AIGUISEMENT DE L'ESPRIT, PAR LE VOYAGE AU SOUDAN ET PARMI LES ARABES DU CENTRE DE L'AFRIQUE / Mohammad ibn Omar al Tounisi ibn Solaiman – (African Library). Paris. B. Duprat. 1850 – 9 – fr Hachette [960]
VOYAGE AU DARFOUR PAR LE CHEYKH MOHAMMED EBN-OMAR EL-TOUNSY / Mohammad ibn Omar al Tounisi ibn Solaiman – (African Library). Paris. B. Duprat. 1845 – 9 – fr Hachette [960]
VOYAGE AU LEVANT, C'EST A DIRE DANS LES PRINCIPAUX ENDROITS DE L'ASIE MINEURE DE MEME QUE DANS LES PLUS CONSIDERABLES VILLES D'EGYPTE, DE SYRIE, DE LA TERRE SAINTE; ENRICHI DE PLUS DE DEUX CENS TAILLES DOUCES / Bruin, Cornelis de – Delft, H. de Kroonevelt, 1700, x-408-6 p. French Voyagers in the Mediterranean 16th to 18th Centuries. 5978 – 9 – fr Hachette [956]
VOYAGE AU OUADAY / Ibn-Omar El-Tounsy, Cheyky M – Traduction de l'arabe. Paris, Benjamin Duprat, Arthus Bertrand. 1851 – 9 – 22.50 – fr Orientalistes [910]
VOYAGE AU PAYS DE BAMBOUC SUIVI D'OBSERVATIONS INTERESSANTES SUR LES CASTES INDIENNES, SUR LA HOLLANDE ET SUR L'ANGLETERRE / Coste d'Arnobat, Pierre-Nicolas – (African Library series). 1789 – 9 – fr Hachette [910]
VOYAGE AU PAYS DES SENOUSSIA A TRAVERS LA TRIPOLITAINE ET LES PAYS TOUAREG / Otsmane el-Hachaichi, Mohammed ben – 2. ed. Paris: A Challamel, 1912 – us Res Libr [910]
VOYAGE AU POLE BOREAL, FAIT EN 1773 PAR ORDRE DU ROI D'ANGLETERRE, TRAD. DE L'ANGLAIS / Phipps, C J – ii, 239 p., app., 19 pls., maps. BH 490 2. 1775 – 8 – ne IDC [910]
VOYAGE AU POLE SUD ET DANS L'OCEANIE SUR L'ASTROLABE ET LA ZELEE, 1837-1840 – 23v. 1842-1854. Also Atlas of voyage. 7v. in 5. Botanique. 2 v. 5909 2. 1845, 1853 – 8 – ne IDC [910]
VOYAGE AU SENEGAL / Durand, Jean-Baptiste-Leonard – 2v. Paris. 1802. BA-305 2 – 8 – ne IDC [900]
VOYAGE AU SENEGAL / Durand, Jean-Baptiste-Leonard – Paris, H. Agasse. 1802 – 9 – 22.50 – fr Orientalistes [910]
VOYAGE AU SENEGAL PENDANT LES ANNEES 1784 ET 1785, D'APRES LES MEMOIRES DE LAJAILLE / Labarthe, Pierre – Paris. 1802. BA-327 2 – 8 – ne IDC [910]
VOYAGE AU SENEGAL PENDANT LES ANNEES 1784 ET 1785 PUBLIE D'APRES LES MEMOIRES DE LAJAILLE / Lajaille, Andre C – (African Library). Paris. Dentu, an X-XII – 9 – fr Hachette [960]
VOYAGE AUTOUR DU MONDE 1836 ET 1837 – Geologie Et Mineralogie par Chevalier, 1844 – 8 – ne IDC [550]
VOYAGE AUTOUR DU MONDE 1836 ET 1837 – Physique par Darondeau. 4v. 1840-1846 – 8 – ne IDC [550]
VOYAGE AUTOUR DU MONDE 1836 ET 1837 – Relation du Voyage par A. de la Salle. 3v. plus atlas. 1845-1852 – 8 – ne IDC [910]
VOYAGE AUTOUR DU MONDE 1836 ET 1837 – Zoologie par Eydoux et Souleyet. 2v. plus atlas. 1841-1852 – 8 – ne IDC [590]
VOYAGE AUTOUR DU MONDE 1836 ET 1837 – Zoophytologie par Laurent. 1844 – 8 – ne IDC [590]
VOYAGE AUTOUR DU MONDE 1836 ET 1837 SUR LA CORVETTE LA BONITE – 3v. 1844-1866 – 8 – ne IDC [910]
VOYAGE AUTOUR DU MONDE EXECUTE SUR LA CORVETTE LA COQUILLE 1822-1825 – par L.I. Duperrey. Zoologie, par Lesson et Garnot. 2842 2. 2v. 1826-1830 – 8 – ne IDC [910]
VOYAGE AUTOUR DU MONDE EXECUTE SUR LES CORVETTES DE S.M. L'URANIE ET LA PHYSICIENNE, 1817-1820 / ed by Freycinet, Louis de – 9v. 1824-1844 – 8 – ne IDC [530]
VOYAGE AUTOUR DU MONDE EXECUTE SUR LES CORVETTES DE S.M. L'URANIE ET LA PHYSICIENNE, 1817-1820 : MAGNETISME TERRESTRE – 1842 – 8 – ne IDC [520]
VOYAGE AUTOUR DU MONDE EXECUTE SUR LES CORVETTES DE S.M. L'URANIE ET LA PHYSICIENNE, 1817-1820 : METEOROLOGIE – 1844 – 8 – ne IDC [550]
VOYAGE AUTOUR DU MONDE EXECUTE SUR LES CORVETTES DE S.M. L'URANIE ET LA PHYSICIENNE, 1817-1820 : NAVIGATION ET HYDROGRAPHIE – 2 pts. 1826 – 8 – ne IDC [520]
VOYAGE AUTOUR DU MONDE EXECUTE SUR LES CORVETTES DE S.M. L'URANIE ET LA PHYSICIENNE, 1817-1820 : OBSERVATIONS DU PENDULE – 1826 – 8 – ne IDC [910]
VOYAGE AUTOUR DU MONDE. EXECUTE SUR LES CORVETTES DE S.M. L'URANIE ET LA PHYSICIENNE, 1817-1820 : BOTANIQUE / Gaudichaud, C – 1826 – 8 – ne IDC [580]
VOYAGE AUTOUR DU MONDE. EXECUTE SUR LES CORVETTES DE S.M. L'URANIE ET LA PHYSICIENNE, 1817-1820 : ZOOLOGIE / Quoy & Gaimard – Z 2149/2. 1v, with atlas. 1824 – 8 – ne IDC [590]
VOYAGE AUTOUR DU MONDE. LES ANNEES 1830, 1831, 1832 / Eydoux, J F T & Gervais, F L P – 2614 2. 1836-1839 – 8 – ne IDC [910]
VOYAGE AUTOUR DU MONDE, PAR LA FREGATE DU ROI LA BOUDEUSE, ET LA FLUTE L'ETOILE; EN 1766, 1767, ET 1769 / Bougainville, L A de – Paris, 2v. 1771 – 9 – ne IDC [520]
VOYAGE AUTOUR DU MONDE SUR LA COQUILLE PENDANT 1822-1825 – By L. I. Duperrey. Histoire du Voyage. Paris. 1826. Atlas. BH-1822 1 – 9 – ne IDC [910]
VOYAGE AUTOUR DU MONDE SUR LA COQUILLE PENDANT 1822-1825 – Par L. I. Duperrey. Hydrographie et Physique. 2 v. Paris. 1827-29. Atlas. BH-1823 1 – 9 – ne IDC [910]
VOYAGE AUTOUR DU MONDE SUR LA CORVETTE "LA COQUILLE" 1822-25 / Duperrey, M L I – 1 – uk Microform Academic [910]
VOYAGE AUX DEUX NILS EXECUTE DE 1860 A 1864 PAR ORDRE DE L'EMPEREUR / Lejean, Guillaume M – (African Library). Paris. Hachette. 1865 – 9 – fr Hachette [960]
VOYAGE AUX GRANDS LACS D'AFRIQUE ORIENTALE / Burton, Richard Francis – Traduction de l'anglais. Paris, Librairie de L. Hachette & Cie. 1862 – 9 – 20.00 – fr Orientalistes [910]
VOYAGE AUX GRANDS LACS DE L'AFRIQUE ORIENTALE / Burton, Richard Francis – (African Library). Paris. Hachette. 1862 – 9 – fr Hachette [960]
VOYAGE AUX INDES ORIENTALES PENDANT LES ANNEES 1825-1829 / Belanger, C & Bory de Saint-Vincent, J B G M – Botanique. Cryptogamie. Paris. 1833-37. B-5842 2 – 7mf – 8 – ne IDC [910]
VOYAGE AUX MERS POLAIRES A LA RECHERCHE DE SIR JOHN FRANKLIN / Bellot, Joseph Rene – Nouv. ed. Paris: Garnier Freres, 1880. 06265. (Pre-1900 Canadiana) – 9 – cn C.I.H.M. [910]
VOYAGE AUX REGIONS EQUINOCTIALES DU NOUVEAU CONTINENT / Humboldt, Alexander von & Bonpland, A J A – Pt. 6, Botanique, Sect. 1. Plantae aequinoctiales. 2 v. Paris. 1805, 1808-17. B-2263 2 – 8 – ne IDC [910]
VOYAGE AUX REGIONS EQUINOCTIALES DU NOUVEAU CONTINENT, FAIT EN 1799-1804 / Humboldt, Alexander von et al – Pt. 6, Sect. 3, Nova genera et species plantarum. 7 V. Paris. 1815-23, 1825. B-214 2 – 8 – ne IDC [910]

VOYAGE AUX REGIONS EQUINOXIALES DU NOUVEAU CONTINENT / Humboldt, Alexander von & Bonpland, A J A – 6r – 1 – $450.00 – us OmniSys [970]

VOYAGE AUX REGIONS EQUINOXIALES DU NOUVEAU CONTINENT, FAIT DANS LES ANNEES 1799-1804 / Humboldt, Alexander von & Bonpland, A J A – B-2656 2. 6 v. 1805-35 – 8 – ne IDC [910]

VOYAGE AUX SOURCES DU NIL, EN NUBIE ET EN ABYSSINIE / Bruce, James – Paris, Hotel de Thou. 1790-91 – 9 – 165.00 – fr Orientalistes [910]

VOYAGE BOTANIQUE DANS LE MIDDE DE L'ESPAGNE / Boissier, E P – 1839-45 – 2r – 5 – uk Microform Academic [910]

VOYAGE BOTANIQUE DANS LE MIDI DE L'ESPAGNE / Boissier, E P – 2v. Paris. 1839-45. B-5181 2 – 8 – ne IDC [580]

VOYAGE CURIEUX DU R. P. LOUIS HENNEPIN / Hennepin, Louis – Leide: Pierre Vander Aa, 1704. SEM16P49 – 1r – 5 – Can$12.00 – cn Bibl Nat [910]

VOYAGE D'ALCIMEDON, OU NAUFRAGE QUI CONDUIT AU PORT. HISTOIRE PLUS VRAIE QUE VRAISEMBLABLE MAIS QUI PEUT ENCOURAGER A LA RECHERCHE DE TERRES INCONNUES / Martigny – (Utopias in the Enlightenment series). 1751 – 9 – fr Hachette [830]

VOYAGE DANS DAHOMEY / Guillevin, M – Paris, Arthur Bertrand. 1862 – 9 – 5.00 – fr Orientalistes [910]

VOYAGE DANS LA HAUTE ET BASSE EGYPTE: FAIT PAR ORDRE DE L'ANCIEN GOUVERNEMENT ET CONTENANT DES OBSERVATIONS DE TOUS GENRES, AVEC UNE COLLECTION DE 40 PLANCHES GRAVEES PAR J.P.B. TARDIEU DESSINEES SUR LES LIEUX / Sonnini de Manoncourt, Charles N S – Paris, F. Buisson, an VII 1799, 3 v., vii-425 plus 417 plus 424 p. plus illus. French Voyagers in the Mediterranean 16th to 18th Centuries. 5990-92 bis – 9 – fr Hachette [956]

VOYAGE DANS LA PARTIE MERIDIONALE DE L'AFRIQUE / Barrow, John – Traduction de l'anglais. Paris, Dentu. 1801 – 9 – 22.50 – fr Orientalistes [910]

VOYAGE DANS L'AFRIQUE AUSTRALE / Delegorgue, Adolphe – Paris, A. Rene et Cie. 1847 – 9 – 35.00 – fr Orientalistes [910]

VOYAGE DANS L'AFRIQUE OCCIDENTALE / Raffenel, Jean-Baptiste A – Paris, Arthus Bertrand. 1846 – 9 – 17.50 – fr Orientalistes [910]

VOYAGE DANS L'AFRIQUE OCCIDENTALE EN 1843 ET 1844 / Raffenel, Anne – Paris. 1846. BA-156 2 – 8 – ne IDC [910]

VOYAGE DANS L'AFRIQUE OCCIDENTALE, PENDANT LES ANEES 1818, 1819, 1820 ET 1821, DEPUIS LA RIVIERE GAMBIE JUSQU'AU NIGER. V. V. V / Gray, William & Gray, Cochard – African Library. Paris. Avril de Gastel. 1826 – 9 – fr Hachette [960]

VOYAGE DANS L'AFRIQUE SEPTENTRIONALE, DEPUIS LE CAIRE JUSQU'A MOURZOUK, CAPITALE DU ROYAUME DE FEZZAN / Hornemann, Friedrich K – (African Library). Paris. Dentu, an XI. 1803 – 9 – fr Hachette [960]

VOYAGE DANS LE JURA / Lequinio de Kerblay, Joseph M – an IX – 9 – fr Hachette [944]

VOYAGE DANS LE PAYS D'ASCHANTIE, OU RELATION DE L'AMBASSADE ENVOYEE DANS CE ROYAUME PAR LES ANGLAIS / Bowdich, Thomas Edward – (African Library). Paris. Lib. de Gide fils. 1819 – 9 – fr Hachette [960]

VOYAGE DANS LE SOUDAN OCCIDENTAL / Mage, Abdon Eugene – Paris: L Hatchette, 1872 – us Res Libr [910]

VOYAGE DANS LE SOUDAN OCCIDENTAL. 1863-1866 / Mage, M E – Paris. 1868. BA-163 2 – 8 – ne IDC [910]

VOYAGE DANS LE SOUDAN OCCIDENTAL (SENEGAMBIE, NIGER) 1863-1866 / Mage, M E – Paris. 1868 – 9 – 20.00 – fr Orientalistes [910]

VOYAGE DANS LE SOUDAN OCCIDENTAL (SENEGAMBIE-NIGER) 1863-1866 / Mage, Abdon Eugene – Paris: L Hatchette, 1868 – us Res Libr [910]

VOYAGE DANS LE SUD-OUEST DE L'AFRIQUE ON RECITS D'EXPLORATIONS FAITES EN 1861 ET 1862 DEPUIS LA BAIE DE VALFICH JUSQU'AUX CHUTES VICTORIA / Baine, Thomas – (African Library). Paris. Hachette. 1868 – 9 – fr Hachette [960]

VOYAGE DANS LE TIMANNI, LE KOURANKO ET LE SOULIMANA, CONTREES DE L'AFRIQUE OCCIDENTALE / Laing, Alexander G – (African Library). Paris. Delaforest. 1826 – 9 – fr Hachette [960]

VOYAGE DANS LES QUATRE PRINCIPALES ILES DES MERS D'AFRIQUE / Bory de Saint-Vincent, J B C M – 3v. atlas. Paris. 1804. B-537 2 – 8 – ne IDC [910]

VOYAGE DANS LES QUATRE PRINCIPALES ILES DES MERS D'AFRIQUE / Bory de Saint-Vincent, J B C M – Paris, F. Buisson. 1804 – 9 – 42.00 – fr Orientalistes [910]

VOYAGE DANS L'INDE PENDANT LES ANNEES 1828 A 1832 / Jacquemont, V – 4v. text, 2 v. atlas. Paris. 1841-44. B-5222 2 – 8 – ne IDC [910]

VOYAGE DANS L'INTERIEUR DE L'AFRIQUE / Damberger, Christian F – Paris et Strasbourg, A. Koenig – 9 – 20.00 – fr Orientalistes [910]

VOYAGE DANS L'INTERIEUR DE L'AFRIQUE / Park, Mungo – Traduction de l'anglais. Paris, Tavernier, Dentu, Carteret. 1800 – 9 – 22.50 – fr Orientalistes [910]

VOYAGE DANS L'INTERIEUR DE L'AFRIQUE AUX SOURCES DU SENEGAL ET DE LA GAMBIE / Mollien, Gaspard T – 2ed. Paris, Arthus Bertrand. 1822 – 9 – 22.50 – fr Orientalistes [910]

VOYAGE DANS L'INTERIEUR DE L'AFRIQUE DEPUIS LE CAP DE BONNE ESPERANCE, A TRAVERS LA CAFRERIE, LES ROYAUMES DE MATAMAM, D'ANGOLA, DE MASSI, DE MONOEMUGI, DE MUSCHAKO, ETC. EN CONTINUANT PAR LE DESERT DU SAHARA ET LA PARTIE SEPTENTRIONALE DE LA BARBARIE / Damberger, Christian F – (African Library series). 2 v. 1801 – 9 – fr Hachette [910]

VOYAGE DANS L'INTERIEUR DE L'AFRIQUE DEPUIS LE CAP DE BONNE-ESPERANCE, A TRAVERS LA CAFRERIE, LES ROYAUMES DE MATAMAN, DE MASSI, DE MONOEMUGI, DE MUSCHAKO, ETC. / Taurinius, Zacharias – Paris, 1801 – 1 – us Res Libr [960]

VOYAGE DANS L'INTERIEUR DE L'AFRIQUE PAR LE CAP DE BONNE ESPERANCE / Le Vaillant, Francois – Bruxelles, Benoit Le Francq. 1791 – 9 – 20.00 – fr Orientalistes [910]

VOYAGE DE DALMATIE, DE GRECE, ET DU LEVANT / Wheler, George – Anvers; Paris, D. Horthmels, 1689, 2 v., xii-607-8 p. et gravures h.-t. French Voyagers in the Mediterranean 16th to 18th Centuries. 5977 – 9 – fr Hachette [949]

VOYAGE DE DECOUVERTE AUX TERRES AUSTRALES / Peron, F & Freycinet, Louis de – Paris, Imprimerie Imperiale. 1807-16 – 9 – $30.00 – fr Orientalistes [910]

VOYAGE DE DECOUVERTES DE L'ASTROLABE EXECUTE – 1826-1829. Botanique. (2 pts. by A. Lesson and A. Richard). 5908 2. 1832 – 8 – ne IDC [910]

VOYAGE DE DIMO ET NICOLO STEPHANOPOLI EN GRECE PENDANT LES ANNEES 5 ET 6 REDIGE PAR UN PROFESSEUR DU PRYTANEE SERIEYS / Stephanopoli de Comnene, Dimo et Nicolaos – Paris, Guillement, an VIII, 1799-1800. 2v. xvi/303 plus 319p illustrations, plans. French Voyagers in the Mediterranean 16th to 18th Centuries. 6004-05 – 9 – fr Hachette [949]

VOYAGE DE GUINEE / Bosman, Willem – Autrecht, Antoine Shouten. 1705 – 9 – 17.50 – fr Orientalistes [910]

VOYAGE DE GUINEE CONTENANT UNE DESCRIPTION NOUVELLE ET TRES EXACTE DE CETTE COTE OU L'ON TROUVE ET OU L'ON TRAFIQUE L'OR, LES DENTS D'ELEPHANT, ET LES ESCLAVES: DE CES PAYS ROYAUMES, ET REPUBLIQUE, DES MOEURS DES HABITANTS / Bosman, Willem – (African Library series). 1705 – 9 – fr Hachette [305]

VOYAGE DE LYBIE AU SENEGAL, LE LONG DU NIGER AVEC LE DESCRIPTION DES HABITANTS QUI SONT LE LONG DE CE FLEUVE, LEURS COUTUMES ET FACONS DE VIVRE, LES PARTICULARITES LES PLUS REMARQUABLES DE'CES PAYS / Jannequin, Claude – (African Library). 1643 – 9 – fr Hachette [306]

UN VOYAGE DE NOCES A CHICAGO / Cannart d'Hamale, Arthur de – Bruxelles: J. Lebegue, 1895? 00466. (Pre-1900 Canadiana) – 9 – cn C.I.H.M. [910]

VOYAGE D'ETUDE AU CANADA / Bareel, Louis – 1900. 02574. (Pre-1900 Canadiana) – 9 – cn C.I.H.M. [910]

VOYAGE D'EXPLORATION AUX MONTAGNES BLEUES; DECOUVERTE DU MONT-AUX-SOURCES, MARS-MAI 1836....1932 / Arbousset, Jean Thomas – 1 – us A.T.L.A. [240]

VOYAGE D'ITALIE, DE DALMATIE, DE GRECE ET DU LEVANT, FAIT AUX ANNEES 1675 ET 1676 / Spon, Jacob & Wheler, George – Lyon: A. Cellier, 1678. 3v xxii/405 plus 413-17 plus 204-228p. illustr. French Voyagers in the Mediterranean 16th to 18th Centuries. 5969 – 9 – fr Hachette [949]

A VOYAGE DOWN THE AMOOR: WITH A LAND JOURNEY THROUGH SIBERIA, AND INCIDENTAL NOTICES OF MANCHOORIA, KAMSCHATKA, AND JAPAN / Collins, Perry McDonough – New York: D. Appleton and Company, 1860.390p. 4 pl – 1 – us U.W. Library [910]

VOYAGE DU CHEVALIER DES MARCHAIS EN GUINEE / Labat, Jean-Baptiste – Paris, C. Osmot. 1730 – 9 – 45.00 – fr Orientalistes [910]

VOYAGE DU SIEUR DE DIEREVILLE EN ACADIE: PRECEDE D'UNE INTRODUCTION ET SUIVI DE NOTES ET D'EXTRAITS / Diereville, N – par L. U. Fontaine. Quebec?: s.n., 1885 (Quebec: A. Cote). 02707. (Pre-1900 Canadiana) – 9 – cn C.I.H.M. [910]

VOYAGE DU SIEUR PAUL LUCAS EN LEVANT: ON Y TROUVERA ENTR'AUTRE UNE DESCRIPTION DE LA HAUTE EGYPTE, SUIVANT LE COURS DU NIL. (TOME SECOND): ON Y VERRA LE RECIT DE L'ENTREPRISE VIOLENTE DU PACHAT DE BABYLONE : L'ETABLISSEMENT DES MISSIONNAIRES. ET L'HISTOIRE DU JEUNE PALEOLOGUE / Lucas, Paul – Paris, G. Vandive, 1704, 2 v., xxvii-372 plus 416-8 p. French Voyagers in the Mediterranean 16th to 18th Centuries. 5983-84 – 9 – fr Hachette [956]

VOYAGE DU S.Y. BELGICA EN 1897-1898-1899 – Expedition Antarctique Belge. Oceanographie-Geologie. 2834 2. 1902-1912 – 8 – ne IDC [910]

VOYAGE D'UN OFFICIER FRANCAIS, PRISONNIER EN RUSSIE, SUR LES FRONTIERES DE CET EMPIRE, DU COTE DE L'ASIE... – Paris, Plancher: Delaunay, 1817 – 1 – F129.04 – fr Armell [355]

VOYAGE EN ABYSSINIE / Salt, Henry – Traduction de l'anglais. Paris, Magimel. 1816 – 9 – 27.00 – fr Orientalistes [910]

VOYAGE EN ABYSSINIE, DANS LE PAYS DES GALLA, DE CHOA ET D'IFAT / Combes, EdmondTamisier, M. – Paris, Louis Dessessart. 1883 – 9 – $40.00 – fr Orientalistes [910]

VOYAGE EN ABYSSINIE DANS LES PROVINCES DU TIGRE : DU SAMEN ET DE L'AMHARA / Ferret, Pierre Victoire & Galinier – Paris: Paulin. 3v. 1847-48 – us Res Libr [910]

VOYAGE EN ABYSSINIE, DANS LES PROVINCES DU TIGRE, DU SAMEN ET DE L'AMHARA / FerretGalinier – Paris, Paulin. 1847 – 9 – $45.00 – fr Orientalistes [910]

VOYAGE EN ABYSSINIE EXECUTE DE 1862 A 1864 / Lejean, Guillaume M – (African Library). Paris. Hachette. 1873 – 9 – fr Hachette [960]

VOYAGE EN ABYSSINIE, EXECUTE PENDANT LES ANNEES / Richard, Achille – 595. 2 V. 1847 PLUS ATLAS. 1839-1843 – 9 – ne IDC [910]

VOYAGE EN AFRIQUE AU ROYAUME DE BARCAH ET DANS LE CYRENAIQUE A TRAVERS DE DESERT / Cella, Paolo della – (African Library). Paris. Armand-Aubree. 1840 – 9 – fr Hachette [960]

VOYAGE EN AFRIQUE ET EN ASIE, PRINCIPALEMENT AU JAPON, PENDANT LES ANNEES 1770-1779 / Thunberg, Charles-Pierre – Traduction du suedois. Paris: Fuchs. 1794 – 9 – 15.00 – fr Orientalistes [910]

VOYAGE EN AFRIQUE OU CINQ ANNEES DE SEJOUR / Cowper – Traduction de l'anglais. Paris, 1833 – 9 – 10.00 – fr Orientalistes [910]

VOYAGE EN BARBARIE / Iret, J L M – ou Lettres ecrites de l'ancienne Numidie pendant 1785 et 1786. Avec en Essai sur l'Histoire Naturelle de ce pays. 2 v. Paris. 1789. B-5570 2 – 8 – ne IDC [910]

VOYAGE EN BARBARIE, OU LETTRES ECRITES DE L'ANCIENNE NUMIDIE PENDANT 1785 ET 1786 / Poiret, J L M – Avec un Essai sur l'Histoire Naturelle de ce pays. 5570. 2 v. 1789 – 9 – ne IDC [910]

VOYAGE EN BIRMANIE....TRADUIT DE L'ANGLAIS ET AUGM. D'UNE INTROD. PAR ADRIEN LAUNAY. 1891 / Bigandet, Paul Ambrose, Bp – 1 – us A.T.L.A. [240]

VOYAGE EN ECOSSE ET AUX ILES HEBRIDES / Necker de Saussure, Louis Albert – Geneve: J.J. Paschoud, 1821. 3v. illus – 1 – us U.W. Library [910]

VOYAGE EN GRECE DE XAVIER SCROFANI, SICILIEN: FAIT EN 1794 ET 1795; TRAD. DE L'ITALIEN PAR J. F. C. BLANVILLE : AVEC UNE CARTE GENERALE DE LA GRECE ANCIENNE ET MODERNE, ET DIX TABLEAUX DU COMMERCE DES ILES DITES VENITIENNES, DE LA MOREE, ET DE LA ROMELIE MERIDIONALE / Scrofani, Saverio – Paris et Strasbourg, Trenttel et Wurtz, an IX 1801, 2 v., xii-167 plus 168 p. French Voyagers in the Mediterranean 16th to 18th Centuries. 6000-01 – 9 – fr Hachette [930]

VOYAGE EN GRECE ET EN TURQUIE FAIT PAR ORDRE DE LOUIS XVI ET AVEC L'AUTORISATION DE LA COUR OTTOMANE AVEC UN VOLUME GRAND IN 40, CONTENANT UNE TRES BELLE CARTE COLORIEE ET DES PLANCHES GRAVEES EN TAILLE DOUCE / Sonnini de Manoncourt, Charles N S – Paris, F. Buisson,an IX 1801, 2 v., 460 plus 460 p. et Atlas. French Voyagers in the Mediterranean 16th to 18th Centuries. 5998-99 bis – 9 – fr Hachette [949]

VOYAGE EN GUINEE ET DANS LES ILES CARAIBES, EN AMERIQUE / Isert, Paul Erdmann – (African Library). 1793 – 9 – fr Hachette [910]

VOYAGE EN ORIENT / Clercq, Louis de – Four of six collections of photographs, 1858-60.1 reel. (Collections of the Department of Prints and Photographs) – 1 – $50.00 – fr Bibl Nationale [770]

VOYAGE EN SENEGAMBIE : HAUT NIGER, BAMBOUCK, FOUTA-DJALLON ET GRAND-BELEDOUGOU, 1880-1885 / Bayol, Jean – Paris: L Baudoin, 1888 – us Res Libr [910]

VOYAGE EN TERRE SAINTE / Goesbriand, Louis de – Montreal: Cadieux & Derome, 1884. 03457. (Pre-1900 Canadiana) – 9 – cn C.I.H.M. [910]

UN VOYAGE EN YACHT: LETTRES DE HAUTES LATITUDES: RECIT D'UN VOYAGE FAIT EN 1856, SUR LE YACHT LE "FOAM", EN ISLANDE, A JAN-MAYEN ET AU SPITZBERG / Dufferin, Lord – Par Lord Dufferin, gouverneur-general du Canada: Traduit, avec la permission de Son Excellence par T. P. Bedard. Montreal: s.n., 1876 (Montreal: Burland-Desbarats). 02789. (Pre-1900 Canadiana) – 9 – cn C.I.H.M. [971]

VOYAGE ET AVENTURES DE FR. LEGUAT EN DEUX ISLES DESERTES DES INDES ORIENTALES / Leguat, Francois – (African Library series). 2v. 1708 – 9 – fr Hachette [910]

VOYAGE FAIT PAR ORDRE DU ROY LOUIS 14TH DANS LA PALESTINE AVEC LA DESCRIPTION GENERALE DE L'ARABIE FAITE PAR LE SULTAN ISMAEL ABULFEDA, TRADUITE EN FRANCAIS SUR LES MEILLEURS MANUSCRITS PAR M.D.L.R. (DE LA ROQUE) / Arvieux, Laurent d' – Paris, A. Cailleau, 1717, 444 p., illustr. French Voyagers in the Mediterranean 16th to 18th Centuries. 5981 – 9 – fr Hachette [944]

VOYAGE HISTORIQUE, LITTERAIRE ET PITTORESQUE DANS LES ISLES ET POSSESSIONS CI-DEVANT VENITIENNES DU LEVANT; SAVOIR: CORFOU, PAXO, BUCINTRO, PARGA, PREVESA, VONIZZA, SAINTE-MAURE, THIAQUI, CEPHALONIE, ZANTE... : CONTENANT LA DESCRIPTION DE CHACUNE DE CES FLES ET POSSESSIONS, L'HISTOIRE ET LES MONUMENTS ANCIENS, L'INDUSTRIE, LA NAVIGATION, LE COMMERCE / Grasset-Saint-Sauveur, Andre – Paris, Tavernie, an VIII 1800, 3 v., xvi-407 plus 358 plus 383 p. plus Atlas. French Voyagers in the Mediterranean 16th to 18th Centuries. 5995-97 bis – 9 – fr Hachette [949]

THE VOYAGE OF CADAMOSTO – Trans. Crone, G.; Crone, R. A 354. 1937 – 9 – ne IDC [910]

A VOYAGE OF CONSOLATION: BEING IN THE NATURE OF A SEQUEL TO THE EXPERIENCES OF "AN AMERICAN GIRL IN LONDON" / Duncan, Sara Jeannette – By Mrs. Everard Cotes. New York: D. Appleton, 1898. 05299. (Pre-1900 Canadiana) – 9 – cn C.I.H.M. [910]

A VOYAGE OF DISCOVERY AND RESEARCH IN THE SOUTHERN AND ANTARCTIC REGIONS, DURING THE YEARS 1839-43 / Ross, James Clark – London, 1847 – 2v 2mf – 9 – 1-55879-124-8 – uk Libr Preservation [910]

A VOYAGE OF DISCOVERY. FOR THE PURPOSE OF EXPLORING BAFFIN'S BAY / Ross, James Clark – BN 376 2. 1819 – 8 – ne IDC [910]

A VOYAGE OF DISCOVERY, MADE UNDER THE ORDERS OF THE ADMIRALTY, IN HIS MAJESTY'S SHIPS ISABELLA AND ALEXANDER FOR THE PURPOSE OF EXPLORING BAFFIN'S BAY, AND ENQUIRING INTO THE POSSIBILITY OF A NORTH-WEST PASSAGE / Ross, John – 2nd ed. 2v. 1819 – 9 – $60.00 – uk Libr Preservation [910]

A VOYAGE OF DISCOVERY TO THE NORTH PACIFIC OCEAN, AND ROUND THE WORLD / Vancouver, G A – BN 439 2. 3v. 1798 – 8 – ne IDC [910]

A VOYAGE OF DISCOVERY TOWARDS THE NORTH POLE...IN HIS MAJESTY'S SHIPS DOROTHEA AND TRENT, UNDER THE COMMAND OF CAPTAIN DAVID BUCHAN, R.N., 1818.. / Beechey, Frederick William – 1843 – 9 – 20.00 – uk Libr Preservation [910]

VOYAGE OF H.M.S. BLONDE TO THE SANDWICH ISLANDS 1824-25 / Byron, George Anson – 1826 – 9 – 20.00 – uk Libr Preservation [910]

VOYAGE OF H.M.S. HERALD DURING 1848-1851. ZOOLOGY. VERTEBRATES INCLUDING FOSSIL MAMMALS / Richardson, J – 1852-54 – 8 – G-146 2 – ne IDC [590]

THE VOYAGE OF ITALY / Lassels, R – O-955 1. 1670 – 9 – ne IDC [945]

THE VOYAGE OF PIERRE ANGIBAUT: KNOWN AS CHAMPDORE: CAPTAIN IN THE MARINE OF NEW FRANCE: MADE TO THE COAST OF MAINE, 1608 / De Costa, Benjamin Franklin – Albany N.Y.: J. Munsell, 1891. 04216. (Pre-1900 Canadiana) – 9 – cn C.I.H.M. [910]

THE VOYAGE OF THE 'FOX' IN THE ARCTIC SEAS : A NARRATIVE OF THE DISCOVERY OF THE FATE OF SIR JOHN FRANKLIN / McClintock – BN 301 2. 1859 – 8 – ne IDC [910]

VOYAGE OF THE PAPER CANOE: A GEOGRAPHICAL JOURNEY OF 2500 MILES, FROM QUEBEC TO THE GULF OF MEXICO, DURING THE YEARS 1874-5 / Bishop, Nathaniel Holmes – Boston: Lee and Shepard, 1878. 00142. (Pre-1900 Canadiana) – 9 – cn C.I.H.M. [910]

VOYAGE PENDANT LES ANNEES 1822-1825. BOTANIQUE / Brongniart, A T – 5861 2. 1829 – 8 – ne IDC [910]

VOYAGE PITTORESQUE DANS LE BOCAGE DE LA VENDEE OU VUES DE CLISSON [...] DESSINEES [...] / Thienon, C – Paris: Didot, 1817 – fr Armell [910]

VOYAGE PLUS : REVUE – Montreal, hiver 1987-mai 1990f – 1r – 1 – Can$75.00 – cn Can Microfilming [072]

VOYAGE ROUND THE WORLD : INCLUDING TRAVELS IN AFRICA, ASIA, AUSTRALASIA, AMERICA, ETC FROM 1827 TO 1832 / Holman, James – London: Smith, Elder, 1834-35 – us Res Libr [910]

VOYAGE SUR LA COTE ET DANS L'INTERIEUR DE L'AFRIQUE OCCIDENTALE / Hecquard, Hyacinthe – Paris: Benard, 1855 – us Res Libr [910]

VOYAGE SUR LA COTE ET DANS L'INTERIEUR DE L'AFRIQUE OCCIDENTALE / Hecquard, Louis Hyacinthe – Paris, Imprimerie du Benard et Cie. 1855 – 9 – 12.50 – fr Orientalistes [910]

VOYAGE SUR LA COTE ORIENTALE DE LA MER ROUGE, DANS LE PAYS D'ADEL ET LE ROYAUME DE CHOA / Rochet d'Hericourt, C E X – Paris, Arthus Bertrand. 1841 – 9 – 15.00 – fr Orientalistes [910]

A VOYAGE TO AFRICA / Hutton, W – 1821 – 12mf – 7 – uk Microform Academic [910]

A VOYAGE TO AFRICA; INCLUDING A NARRATIVE OF AN EMBASSY TO ONE OF THE INTERIOR KINGDOMS. / Hutton, William – London. 1821 – 1 – us Res Libr [960]

A VOYAGE TO COCHINCHINA, IN THE YEARS 1792 AND 1793 : TO WHICH IS ANNEXED AN ACCOUNT OF A JOURNEY, MADE IN THE YEARS 1801 AND 1802,... / Barrow, J – London, 1806 – 6mf – 9 – ne IDC [910]

A VOYAGE TO GUINEA, BRASIL AND THE WEST-INDIES / Atkins, James – 2ND ED. A 113. 1737 – 9 – ne IDC [910]

A VOYAGE TO NEW GUINEA, AND THE MOLUCCAS, FROM BALAMBANGAN / Forrest, T – London, 1780 – 6mf – ne IDC [910]

A VOYAGE TO NORTH-AMERICA, UNDERTAKEN BY COMMAND OF THE PRESENT KING OF FRANCE, CONTAINING THE GEOGRAPHICAL DESCRIPTION AND NATURAL HISTORY OF CANADA AND LOUISIANA.... : ILLUSTRATED WITH A NUMBER OF CURIOUS PRINTS AND MAPS NOT IN ANY OTHER EDITION / Charlevoix, Francois Xavier de – Dublin. John Exshaw and James Potts. 2v. 1766 SEM16P14 – 1r – 5 – Can$14.00 – cn Bibl Nat [910]

VOYAGE TO OCEANIC ISLANDS, 1873-1876. REPORT ON ROCK SPECIMENS / Renard, A – 2819 2. 1889 – 8 – ne IDC [550]

A VOYAGE TO THE CAPE OF GOOD HOPE, TOWARDS THE ANTARCTIC POLAR CIRCLE AND AROUND THE WORLD FROM THE YEAR 1772 TO 1776 / Sparmann, A – Trans. Ed. 2. 2 v. London. 1786. BA-137 2 – 8 – ne IDC [910]

A VOYAGE TO THE CAPE OF GOOD HOPE, TOWARDS THE ANTARCTIC POLAR CIRCLE, AND ROUND THE WORLD...1772, TO 1776 / Sparmann, A – Pretoria, State Library, 1979. Orig. publ., London: Printed for G.G.J. and J. Robinson, Paternoster Row, 1786. (Microfiche Reprint Series, State Library, no.5). 9 fiche. Printed booklet. Accounts of Sparrman's travels through Southern Africa – 9 – sa State Libr [910]

A VOYAGE TO THE EAST INDIES IN 1747 AND 1748 / Noble, CF – London, 1762 – 5mf – 9 – ne IDC [910]

A VOYAGE TO THE ISLANDS MADERA, BARBADOS, NIEVES, ST CHRISTOPHERS AND JAMAICA / Sloane, H – 5328. 2 V. 1707-1725 – 9 – ne IDC [910]

A VOYAGE TO THE PACIFIC OCEAN / Cook, James & King, J – 2nd ed. BN-169 2. 3 v. 1784 – 8 – ne IDC [910]

VOYAGE TO THE RIVER SIERRA LEONE / Matthews, John – London. 1788. BA-118 2 – 8 – ne IDC [910]

A VOYAGE TO THE SOUTH ATLANTIC AND ROUND CAPE HORN INTO THE PACIFIC OCEAN, FOR THE PURPOSE OF EXTENDING THE SPERMACETI WHALE FISHERIES / Colnett, James – 1798 – 9 – uk Libr Preservation [910]

A VOYAGE TO THE SOUTH SEA, UNDERTAKEN BY COMMAND OF HIS MAJESTY, FOR THE PURPOSE OF CONVEYING THE BREAD-FRUIT TREE TO THE WEST INDIES, IN HIS MAJESTY'S SHIP THE BOUNTY / Bligh, William – 1792 – 9 – uk Libr Preservation [910]

A VOYAGE TOWARDS THE SOUTH POLE IN 1822-24. / Weddell, James – 2nd ed....with an account of a second voyage performed by the Beaufoy, Captain Brisbane, to the Same Seas. 1827 – 9 – uk Libr Preservation [910]

VOYAGES – (All "voyages" are listed under the name of the vessel, when given, with cross-reference entries under the names of the authors and or the editors) – ne IDC [910]

VOYAGES – Washington. v1-5. 1967-73 – 1 – D5965 – us UMI [073]

THE VOYAGES AND ADVENTURES OF F. MENDEZ PINTO / Mendes Pinto, F – London, 1653 – 4mf – 9 – ne IDC [910]

VOYAGES AND TRAVELS TO INDIA / Annesley, G – 3v. London. 1809. B-6451 2 – 8 – ne IDC [910]

THE VOYAGES AND WORKS OF / Davis, J – BN 190 1880 – 8 – ne IDC [910]

VOYAGES AU JAPON / Thunberg, C P – 530. 4v. 1796 – 9 – ne IDC [910]

VOYAGES DANS L'AMERIQUE MERIDIONALE... EXECUTE PENDANT LES ANNEES 1826-1833 / Orbigny, Alcide d' – Paris. 1835-1847. 7 v; 2 v. atlas. B-6100 1; Z 310 2 – 8 – ne IDC [910]

VOYAGES DANS LES DESERTS DU SAHARA PAR M. FOLLIE, OFFICIER D'ADMINISTRATION DANS LES COLONIES. CONTENANT: 1)LA RELATION DE SON NAUFRAGE ET DE SES AVENTURES PENDANT SON ESCLAVAGE. 2)UN PRECIS EXACT DES MOEURS DES UAGES ET DES OPINIONS DES HABITANTS / Follie, M – (African Library series). 1792 – 9 – fr Hachette [960]

VOYAGES DANS L'INTERIEUR DE L'AFRIQUE PENDANT LES ANNEES 1797, 1798 / Hornemann, Friedrich K – Traduction de l'anglais. Paris, Andre. 1802 – 9 – 10.00 – fr Orientalistes [910]

VOYAGES DE CYRUS. DISCOURS SUR LA MYTHOLOGIE / Ramsay, Andrew Michael – Paris: Ferra jeune, 1826. x,406p. 5 fiches. (Literature Collection) – 9 – 12.00 – fr Bibl Nationale [910]

VOYAGES DE LA CORVETTE "L'ASTROLABE" / Lesson, A & Richard, A – 1826-29 – 1 – uk Microform Academic [910]

LES VOYAGES DE LA NOUVELLE-FRANCE OCCIDENTALE, DICTE CANADA, FAITS PAR LE SR DE CHAMPLAIN,.... / Champlain, Samuel de – Paris: chez Pierre-le-Mur, 1632. SEM35P4 – 1r – 1 – Can$15.00 – cn Bibl Nat [910]

LES VOYAGES DE LA NOUVELLE-FRANCE OCCIDENTALE, DICTE CANADA, FAITS PAR LE SR. DE CHAMPLAIN (1603-1629) – Paris, France. 1632 – 1r – 1 – cn Can Microfilming [910]

LES VOYAGES DE LA NOUVELLE-FRANCE OCCIDENTALE, DICTE CANADA, FAITS PAR LE SR DE CHAMPLAIN, XAINCTONGEOIS,... / Champlain, Samuel de – Paris: de l'imprimerie de Pierre-Le-Mur, 1640. SEM16P233 – 1r – 5 – Can$14.00 – cn Bibl Nat [910]

VOYAGES DES FRANCAIS AU CANADA, DANS L'AMERIQUE CENTRALE ET AU BRESIL DANS LES PREMIERES ANNEES DU 16E SIECLE / Gaffarel, Paul – s.l.: s.n., 1890? (Dijon France: Darantiere). 04327. (Pre-1900 Candiana) – 9 – cn C.I.H.M. [910]

VOYAGES DU CAPITAINE ROBERT LADE EN DIFFERENTES PARTIES DE L'AFRIQUE, DE L'ASIE ET DE L'AMERIQUE / Prevost, Antoine F – Paris: Didot. 2v. 1744. SEM16P251 – 1r – 5 – Can$19.00 – cn Bibl Nat [910]

LES VOYAGES DU SEIGNEUR DE VILLAMONT, CHEVALIER DE L'ORDRE DE HIERUSALEM. DIVISEZ EN TROIS LIVRES / Villamont, Jacques de – Derniere edition. Revue, corrigee et cottee par l'autheur. Paris, C. de Montreuil et I. Richer, 1600, xiv, p.-347 ff.-43 p. French Voyagers in the Mediterranean 16th to 18th Centuries. 5958 – 9 – fr Hachette [944]

LES VOYAGES DU SIEUR DE CHAMPLAIN XAINTONGEOIS, CAPITAINE ORDINAIRE POUR LE ROY EN LA MARINE, DIVISEZ EN DEUX LIVRES / Champlain, Samuel de – Paris: Jean Berjon, 1613. SEM35P3 – 1r – 1 – Can$15.00 – cn Bibl Nat [910]

LES VOYAGES DU SIEUR DU LOIR CONTENUS EN PLUSIEURS LETTRES ECRITES DU LEVANT, AVEC PLUSIEURS PARTICULARITEZ QUI N'ONT POINT ENCORE ESTE REMARQUEES TOUCHANT LA GRECE, ET LA DOMINATION DU GRAND SEIGNEUR...EN 1639 – Paris, G. Clouzier, 1654, xiv-358-23 p. French Voyagers in the Mediterranean 16th to 18th Centuries. 5962 – 9 – fr Hachette [949]

LES VOYAGES DU SIEUR LE MAIRE AUX ILES CANARIES, CAP-VERD, SENEGAL ET GAMBIE / Le Maire, Jacques – Paris, J. Collombat. 1695 – 9 – 7.50 – fr Orientalistes [910]

LES VOYAGES DU SIEUR LE MAIRE AUX ILES CANARIES, CAP-VERT, SENEGAL ET GAMBIE SOUS M. DANCOURT, DIRECTEUR GENERAL DE LA COMPAGNIE ROYALE D'AFRIQUE / Le Maire, Jacques – (African Library). 1695 – 9 – fr Hachette [910]

VOYAGES EN AFRIQUE / Ledyard, John – Paris, Xhrouet et Deterville. 1804 – 9 – 17.50 – fr Orientalistes [910]

VOYAGES EN AFRIQUE, ASIE, INDES ORIENTALES ET OCCIDENTALES FAITS PAR JEAN MOCQUET, GARDE DU CABINET DES SINGULARITES DU ROI, AUX TUILERIES / Mocquet, Jean – (African Library series). 1617 – 9 – fr Hachette [910]

VOYAGES EN AFRIQUE, ASIE, INDES ORIENTALES & OCCIDENTALES / Mocquet, Jean – Paris. 1617 – 1 – us Res Libr [910]

VOYAGES EN EGYPTE ET EN NUBIE, CONTENANT LE RECIT DES RECHERCHES ET DECOUVERTES ARCHEOLOGIQUES FAITES DANS LES PYRAMIDES, TEMPLES, RUINES ET TOMBES DE CES PAYS / Belzoni, Giovanni Battista – (African Library). Paris. Librairie francaise et etrangere Galignani. 1821 – 9 – fr Hachette [960]

VOYAGES EN GUINEE ET DANS LES ILES CARAIBES EN AMERIQUE. / Isert, Paul Erdmann – Paris. 1793 – 1 – us Res Libr [910]

VOYAGES ET AVENTURES DANS L'AFRIQUE EQUATORIALE / Du Chaillu, Paul Belloni – Paris, M. Levy. 1863 – 9 – 17.50 – fr Orientalistes [910]

VOYAGES ET AVENTURES DE JACQUES MASSE / Tyssot de Patot, Simon – (Utopias in the Enlightenment series). 1710 – 9 – fr Hachette [800]

VOYAGES ET DECOUVERTES DANS L'AFRIQUE SEPTENTRIONALE ET CENTRALE PENDANT LES ANNEES 1849 A 1855 / Barth, Heinrich – (African Library). Paris. A. Bohne. 1860 – 9 – fr Hachette [960]

VOYAGES ET DECOUVERTES DANS LE NORD ET LES PARTIES CENTRALES DE L'AFRIQUE / Denham, D & Clapperton & Denham, Oudney – Traduction de l'anglais. Paris, Arthus Bertrand. 1826 – 9 – $35.00 – fr Orientalistes [910]

LES VOYAGES ET DECOUVERTES DE PAUL SOLEILLET DANS LE SAHARA ET DANS LE SOUDAN. / Soleillet, Paul – Paris. n.d – 1 – us Res Libr [910]

VOYAGES ET MEMOIRES SUR LE CANADA / Franquet, Louis – Quebec?: s.n., 1889 (Quebec: A. Cote). 02085. (Pre-1900 Canadiana) – 9 – cn C.I.H.M. [910]

VOYAGES, EXPLORATIONS, AVENTURES / Noir, Louis Salmon – Paris: Fayard, 1899. 27v. (Literature Collection) – 54mf – 9 – $134.00 – fr Bibl Nationale [910]

LES VOYAGES FAMEUX DU SIEUR VINCENT LE BLANC MARSEILLAIS, QU'IL A FAIT DEPUIS L'AGE DE DOUZE ANS JUSQU'A SOIXANTE AUX QUATRE PARTIES DU MONDE / Bergeron, Pierre – (African Library series). 1649 – 9 – fr Hachette [910]

VOYAGES FROM CHINA TO THE NORTHWEST COAST OF AMERICA, 1788 AND 1789, AND FROM BENGAL 1786 / Meares, J – 1 – uk Microform Academic [910]

VOYAGES FROM MONTREAL TO THE PACIFIC, 1789-1793 / MacKenzie, Alexander – London: Printed for T Cadell jr et al. 2v. 1802. SEM35P73 – 1r – 1 – Can$20.00 – cn Bibl Nat [910]

VOYAGES IMAGINAIRES, ROMANESQUES, MARVEILLEUX, ALLEGOREQUES AMUSANS, COMIQUES ET CRITIQUES SUIVIS DES SONGES ET VISIONS ET DES ROMANS CABALISTIQUES – Amsterdam, Paris, 1787-89. 201 fiches. (Literature Collection) – 9 – 497.00 – fr Bibl Nationale [830]

THE VOYAGES OF. 1612-1622 / Baffin, W – BN-111 2. 1881 – 8 – ne IDC [910]

THE VOYAGES OF CADAMOSTO / ed by Crone, G R – London. 1937. BA-354 2 – 8 – ne IDC [910]

THE VOYAGES OF THE CABOTS IN 1497 AND 1498: WITH AN ATTEMPT TO DETERMINE THEIR LANDFALL AND TO IDENTIFY THEIR ISLAND OF ST JOHN / Dawson, Samuel Edward – Montreal: W. Brown, 1894. 03777. (Pre-1900 Canadiana) – 9 – cn C.I.H.M. [971]

VOYAGES PITTORESQUES DE LA FLANDRE ET DU BRABANT / Descamps, Jean Baptiste – Amsterdam. 1772. BO-987 1 – 9 – ne IDC [910]

VOYAGES TOWARDS THE NORTH WEST / ed by Rundall, Thomas – Hakluyt Society. 1496-1631 – 5mf – 7 – uk Microform Academic [910]

LE VOYAGEUR – Sudbury, 1968-1988 – 27r – 1 – cn Preston [971]

LE VOYAGEUR – Sudbury, Ontario. 12 jun 1968-v2 n1. 11 jun 1869 – 1r – 1 – cn Can Microfilming [072]

LE VOYAGEUR *see* LE PHARILLON

LE VOYAGEUR PHILOSOPHE DANS UN PAIS INCONNU AUX HABITANTS DE LA TERRE / Villeneuve, N de – Par M. de Listonai. (Utopias of the Enlightenment series). 1761 – 9 – fr Hachette [320]

VOYAGEURS CHINOIS CHEZ LES KHITAN ET LES JOUTCHEN / Chavannes, E – (Journal Asiatique, S. 9, v. 9. 1897; S. 9, v. 11. 1898). Paris. BU-611 2 – 8 – ne IDC [910]

Voysey, Charles *see* RELIGION FOR ALL MANKIND: BASED ON FACTS WHICH ARE NEVER IN DISPUTE

Voyt, J *see* EYN SERMONN VOM NEWEN JARE

A VOZ – Lisbon, 18 Mar 1941-25 May 1945; 1 Jan-31 Aug 1946 – 18r – 1 – uk British Libr Newspaper [072]

VOZ ARGENTINA – (Includes c.1: v.1:no.1 1944:Oct.-v.1:no.14 (1945:Feb.); v.1:no.20 1945:Apr.-v.1:no.22 (1945:Apr.); v.1:no.25 1945:May-v.1:no.29 (1945:June); v.1:no.31 1945:July) – 1944 – 1 – CSUXAJB7773-S – us Hoover Inst Photo [972]

VOZ CENTRAL – Uberlandia, Brazil. Feb 1940 – 1 – bl Biblioteca [072]

A VOZ DA CIDADE – Paraguassu, 3 Nov 1963; Dec 1977; Jan-Dec 1979; Jan-24 Dec 1982 – 1,5,6 – bl Biblioteca [072]

VOZ DA COLONIA – Bristol. R.I. 1926-1939 – 1 – us UMI [071]

A VOZ DA RELIGIAO NO CARIRI – Crato, 10 Dec 1868-11 Dec 1870 – 1,5,6 – bl Biblioteca [072]

VOZ DE CAMPESTRE : ORGAO INDEPENDENTE – Campestre, 24 Mar 1963 – 1,5,6 – bl Biblioteca [072]

VOZ DE CAMPESTRE : ORGAO MUNICIPAL DE PROPAGANDA E DIFUSAO DO REGIMEN DE 10 DE NOVEMBRO – Campestre, 30 Mar-Apr, Jun, Oct, 31 Dec 1941 – 1,5,6 – bl Biblioteca [072]

VOZ DE CANDEIAS : JORNAL APOLITICO CATOLICO A SERVICO DO MUNICIPIO – Candeias, 15 Aug-Dec 1974; Jan-Oct, Nov-Dec 1975; Feb 1976-Jan 1977 – 1,5,6 – bl Biblioteca [072]

LA VOZ DE DIOS / Cuadrado Ceballos, Juan – Caceres: Tip. Jomarun, 1st ed 1955 – 1 – sp Bibl Santa Ana [240]

LA VOZ DE ESPANA : SEMANARIO DEFENSOR DE LOS INTERESSES DE SU COLONIA EN EL NORTE DEL BRASIL – Manaos, Amazonas. 6 Jan-Mar 1901; Out, Dez 1905; Set 1906; Jan, Jul-30 Nov 1907 – 1,5,6 – bl Biblioteca [072]

LA VOZ DE EXTREMADURA – Madrid, 1893 – 5 – sp Bibl Santa Ana [073]

LA VOZ DE EXTREMADURA – Spain. 1893-94, no. sueltos – 9 – 1.50f – sp Bibl Santa Ana [072]

LA VOZ DE LA FRONTERA – Baja, CA. 1886-88 – 1r – 1 – $50.00 – C02039 – us Library Micro [071]

LA VOZ DE LA FRONTERA – Baja. Calif. 1887-1888 – 1 – us UMI [071]

LA VOZ DE LA FRONTERA – Mexicali (Baja California), MX. 1886-1888; 1964- – 440+ r – $22,000.00 ($925.00y) – R02039 – us Library Micro [072]

LA VOZ DE LA FRONTERA – Mexicali (Mexico), CA. 1886-1888; 1964 – 375+ r – 1 – $18,750.00 ($960.00y) – RC03337 – us Library Micro [071]

A VOZ DE LORIGA : ORGAO DA COLONIA LORIGUENSE EM MANAOS – Loriga, Amazonas. 1 Ago 1909 – 1,5,6 – bl Biblioteca [072]

LA VOZ DE LOS BARROS – Almendralejo, 1908-1909 – 5 – sp Bibl Santa Ana [073]

VOZ DE LUZIANIA – Luziania-GO, Brazil. Jan 1982-Dez 1985 – 1 – bl Biblioteca [072]

LA VOZ DE MEXICO – Mexico City, Mexico. Mar 23 1939-Feb 27 1944. Incomplete – 1 – us NY Public [072]

LA VOZ DE MUNICIPIO – Caceres.1899, no. sueltos – 9 – 1.50f – sp Bibl Santa Ana [072]

VOZ DE S. JOAO – S. Joao Nepomuceno, 8 Mar 1975-Dec 1978; Jan-Dec 1981; Jan-31 Dec 1983 – 1,5,6 – bl Biblioteca [072]

A VOZ DE THEBAS – Thebas de Leopoldina, 14 Jul 1895; Sept 1896; 17 Jun 1897 – 1,5,6 – bl Biblioteca [072]

LA VOZ DEL CORAZON / Hurtado, Antonio – 1867 – 9 – 1.50f – sp Bibl Santa Ana [830]

LA VOZ DEL MUNICIPIO – Plasencia, 1899 – 5 – sp Bibl Santa Ana [073]

LA VOZ DEL PUEBLO – Merida, 1892. Un solo numero – 5 – sp Bibl Santa Ana [073]

LA VOZ DEMOCRATICA – Merida, 1923. 1 numero – 5 – sp Bibl Santa Ana [073]

VOZ DIAMANTINA – Diamantina, 27 Mar 1966-Dec 1967; Feb-30 Dec 1979 – 1,5,6 – bl Biblioteca [072]

VOZ DIOCESANA : ORGAO OFFICIAL DA DIOCESE DE CAMPANHA – Campanha, 25 Dec 1953; Jan 1979-15 Dec 1980 – 1,5,6 – bl Biblioteca [072]

A VOZ DO AMAZONAS – Manaos, Amazonas. 17 Out 1866-31 Mar 1867 – 1,5,6 – bl Biblioteca [072]

VOZ DO COLEGIO – Conselheiro Lafaiete, Brazil. Sep 1934; Mar-Apr, Jun-Jul 1935 – 1 – bl Biblioteca [072]

A VOZ DO GINASIO D. BOSCO – Cachoeira do Campo, Brazil. Sept.-Nov. 1945 – 1 – bl Biblioteca [072]

A VOZ DO NORTE : ORGAM POLITICO – LITTERARIO – NOTICIOSO – Diamantina, 22 Jul 1917; 27 Jan 1918 – 1,5,6 – bl Biblioteca [072]

A VOZ DO NORTE : ORGAO DE INTERESSES GERAES – Villa de Sao Joao Evange-Lista, 1 Feb-16 Mar 1923 – 1,5,6 – bl Biblioteca [072]

A VOZ DO POVO – Pocos de Caldas, 28 Dec 1905 – 1,5,6 – bl Biblioteca [072]

VOZ DO POVO : ORGAO-NEUTRAL-DOS INTERESSES MORAES E MATERIAES DA PROVINCIA – (Cont by: Echo dos Andes) – Manaos, Amazonas. 29 Jan 1882 – 1,5,6 – bl Biblioteca [072]

VOZ DO POVO – Sao Joao Nepomuceno, 22 Mar-Apr 1908; Jul 1933-24 Mar 1935 – 1,5,6 – bl Biblioteca [072]

A VOZ DO SERRO – Serro, 31 Jul-20 Nov 1912 – 1,5,6 – bl Biblioteca [072]

VOZ DO SERTAO : SEMANARIO INDEPENDENTE – Bom Despacho, 11 Jul-Dec 1937; Mar-19 Jun 1938 – 1,5,6 – bl Biblioteca [072]

A VOZ DOS TRABALHADORES : JORNAL DO PT – Rio Branco, Acre. Abr 1983 – 1,5,6 – bl Biblioteca [072]

A VOZ ESTUDANTIL : ORGAO DO ESTUDANTE ACREANO – Rio Branco, Acre. 5-23 Abr 1960 – 1,5,6 – bl Biblioteca [072]

VOZ FLUMINENSE – Rio de Janeiro, 22 Oct 1829-27 Apr 1831 – 1,5,6 – bl Biblioteca [072]

LA VOZ MESTINZA – Irvine, CA. 1979-1989 – 1r – 1 – $50.00 – R04035 – us Library Micro [071]

A VOZ NACIONALISTA : ORGAO DE CONSOLIDACAO DE UMA CONSCIENCIA POLITICA – Rio Branco, Acre. 13 Mar 1960 – 1 – bl Biblioteca [320]

VOZ NACIONALISTA – (Includes c.1: v.1:no.5 1954:May 20) – 1 – CSUXADN3459-S – us Hoover Inst Photo [972]

VOZ PROLETARIA – (Includes c.1: v.17:no.341-343 1964:June 12-26; v.17:no.348-394 1964:July 31-1965:June 16; v.18:no.396-408 1965:June 30-Sept.22; v.18:no.410-411 1965:Sept.29-0) – 1 – CSUXADP3529-S – us Hoover Inst Photo [972]

VOZDUKHOPLAVATEL' – Russia, 1903-17 – 259mf – 9 – $1,490.00 set – us Ross [330]

VOZDUSHNYI PUT'. RAZSKAZY / Bal'mont, K D – Berlin. 1923. BR-547 2 – 8 – ne IDC [460]

Voznesenskh, S *see* RUSSKAIA LITERATURA O SLAVIANSTVE

Voznesenskii, S *see* SLAVIANSTVO V RUSSKOI ZHURNALISTIKE 1896-1914 GG

Vozniak, M *see* ISTORIIA UKRAJINS'KOJI LITERATURY

VOZROJDENIE – Titre francais: La Renaissance. Paris. juin 1925-juin 1940 – 1 – fr A.C.R.P.P. [073]

VOZROZHDENIE – La Renaissance Quotidien russe. Paris. France. -d. 25 May 1925-23 Sep, 8, 13, 30 Dec 1926, 15 Jan 1927-30 May, 8, 16 Jul-2 Sep, 13 Oct, 9 Dec 1928, 1 Jan-30 Jul, 31 Oct 1929-29 Jun 1930, 18-21 Jan, 19 Feb-12 Apr 1935, 5 Mar-20 Jun, 18 Jul-22 Aug, 17 Oct 1936-30 Jun 1939, 1 Sep 1939-7 Jun 1940. (22 reels) – 1 – uk British Libr Newspaper [947]

VOZROZHDENIE – Literaturno-politicheskie tetradi. v. 1-216. Paris. 1949-69. BR-5736 2 – 8 – ne IDC [320]

VOZROZHDENIE – Paris, 1926-1939 (incomplete) – 1 – us NY Public [947]

VOZROZHDENIE – Paris, 1926-39 – 31r – 1 – us Ross [072]

VOZROZHDENIE – Zhurnal obshchestvennoi-politicheskii, kul'turno-filosofskii, populiarno-nauchnyi, literaturno-khudozhestvennyi. M. 1908-10. B-1438 2 – 8 – ne IDC [320]

VOZROZHDENIE AZII – (Library has holdings (incomplete) from between Feb. 15, 1933 and Oct. 11, 1942) – Tiantszin: "Vozrozhdenie Azii", 1933- – 1 – CSUX86-S488 – us Hoover Inst Photo [950]

VOZROZHDENIE SELA I KOOPERATSIIA / Evdokimov, Andrei Aandreevich – M., 1914 – 1mf – 9 – COR-21/1 – ne IDC [334]

VOZROZHDENIE SIEVERA – Arkhangel'sk, USSR. Aug 1918-Dec 1919 – 3r – 1 – us L of C Photodup [072]

O VOZROZHDENII KRESHCHENIEM": V" ZASHCHITU KRESHCHENIYA MLADENTSEV" PROTIV" BAPTISTOV" = ON REBIRTH BY BAPTISM: IN DEFENSE OF BAPTISM OF INFANTS AGAINST THE BAPTISTS / Aleksii – Vladimir, 1916 – 1r – 1 – $7.32 – us Baptist [240]

VOZVRASHCHENIE NA RODINU / Belyi, A – M. 1922. BR-608 2 – 8 – ne IDC [460]

VOZVRAT. TRET'IA SIMFONIIA. POVEST' / Belyi, A – Berlin. 1922. BR-607 2 – 8 – ne IDC [460]

VP : EIN HEIMKEHRER ERZAEHLT / Vieweg, Rudolf – Berlin: Verlag Kultur und Fortschritt, 1952 – 1r – 1 – us U.W. Library [943]

V.P. JOURNAL *see* KOSMOS

VP JOURNAL – (Cont by: Kosmos) – [Cobourg, Ont.: Science Association of Victoria University, 1883-1885] – 9 – cn C.I.H.M. [500]

V.P. JUAN DE JESUS MARIA (ARAVALLES), CARMELITA DESCALZO, 1... – Madrid: Razon y Fe, 1926 – 1 – sp Bibl Santa Ana [240]

VPERED – Dvukhnedel'noe obozrenie. God 1-2, v. 1-49. London. 1876-77. BR-3452 2 – 8 – ne IDC [460]

VPERED – En avant. Geneva and Moscow. Switzerland. -w. 4 Jan-18 May 1905, 11, 24 Dec 1906, 7 Feb, 1 May 1907. (24 ft) – 1 – uk British Libr Newspaper [072]

VPERED – Izdanie ideinoi gruppy "Vpered". nr. 1-6. Geneva. 1915-17. BR-3453 2 – 8 – ne IDC [321]

VPERED – London. Forward. (In Russian.) 15 Jan 1875-31 Dec 1876.-f. 1 reel – 1 – uk British Libr Newspaper [072]

VPERED – Paris. n1-3. July 1910-May 1911 – 1 – us NY Public [947]

VPERED / Social Democratic Labor Party. Russia – Geneva. Jan. 4-May 18, 1905, nos. 1-18 – 1 – 35.00r – us Hoover Inst Photo [335]

VPERED I PROLETARII – Pervye Bol'chevistskie Gazety 1905 g. Moscow. v. 1-6. 1924-1925 – 1 – us NY Public [335]

VPI AGRICULTURAL JOURNAL / Virginia. Polytechnic Institute. College of Agriculture – v.1-2. 4 fiches – 9 – us Spaulding [073]

VRAGILI TRUDOVOMU NARODU EVREI / Abramova – Tiflis: Tip. "Kartli", 1917 – 1 – CSUX89-B5465 – us Hoover Inst Photo [947]

VRAI / ed by Hebert, Jacques et al – Montreal, Canada. 2 oct 1954-16 mai 1959 – 2r – 1 – Can$55.00r – cn Can Microfilming [072]

LE VRAI BAVARD *see* LE BAVARD

LE VRAI CANADIEN – Montreal, Canada. v1 n2. 27 nov 1840-26 mar 1841 – 1r – 1 – Can$35.00 – cn Can Microfilming [072]

LE VRAI CANADIEN – Ottawa, Ontario. jun 1896 – 1r – 1 – Can$25.00 – cn Can Microfilming [072]

LE VRAI CANADIEN – Quebec, Canada. 1810-11 – 1 reel – 1 – $68.00 – cn Library Assoc [971]

LE VRAI CANADIEN – Quebec, Canada. 28 fev 1810; 10 mar 1810-6 mar 1811 – 1r – 1 – Can$25.00 – cn Can Microfilming [072]

LE VRAI CANARD / ed by Berthelot, Hector – Montreal, Canada. 23 aut 1879-5 nov 1881 – 1r – 1 – Can$35.00 – cn Can Microfilming [072]

LE VRAI LOUP-GAROU / ed by Corbeil, F – Montreal, Canada. 14 mai 1892; 2 oct 1897; v7 n2. 9 oct 1897 – 1r – 1 – Can$30.00 – cn Can Microfilming [072]

LE VRAI PATRIOTE – Montreal, Canada. 28 nov-12 dec 1917 – 1r – 1 – Can$30.00 – cn Can Microfilming [072]

LE VRAI SENS DU SYSTEME DE LA NATURE / Helvetius, Claude-Adrien – (D'Holbach series). 1774 – 9 – fr Hachette [190]

LA VRAIE ITALIE – Organe de liaison intellectuelle entre l'Italie et les autres pays dirige par Giovanni Papini. no. 1-10 12. Florence. fevr 1919-mai 1920 – 1 – fr A.C.R.P.P. [073]

LA VRAIE REPUBLIQUE – Red. en chef Thore. Paris. 26 mars-21 aout 1848 – 1 – fr A.C.R.P.P. [073]

LES VRAIS DEBATS – (Filmed with: L'Avenir, Montreal. 21 oct 1900-10 fev 1901) – Montreal, Canada. 14 oct 1900 – 1r – 1 – Can$35.00 – cn Can Microfilming [072]

LES VRAIS POURTRAITS DES HOMMES ILLUSTRES... / Beze, Th. de – Geneve: Jean de Laon, 1581 – 4mf – 9 – ne IDC [240]

LES VRAIS PRINCIPES CONSTITUTIONNELS / Thiery, Avocat – Precedes d'une lettre a MM. les Deputes aux Etats-Generaux, sur la distinction des deux Pouvoirs. 1789 – 9 – fr Hachette [321]

LES VRAIS PRINCIPES DE LA LANGUE FRANCOISE / Girard – 1747 – 9 – fr I.C.S. [440]

LE VRAY ET PARFAIT GUIDON DE LA LANGUE FRANCOISE / Duez, N – 1669 – 9 – fr I.C.S. [440]

LA VRAYE ET ANCIENNE ORTHOGRAPHE FRANCOISE / Simon, E – 1609 – 9 – fr I.C.S. [440]

LA VRAYE INTRODUCTION A LA LANGUE FRANCOISE / La Grue, Th. – 1669 – 9 – fr I.C.S. [440]

VRBASKE NOVINY – Banja Luka, Yugoslavia. 1937-Mar 1938 – 1r – 1 – us L of C Photodup [949]

Vrcevic, Vuk *see* NARODNE PRIPOVIJESTI I PRESUDE

Vreeland, H *see* HUGO GROTIUS...

VREEMDELINGEN TE AMSTERDAM IN DE EERSTE HELFT DER ZEVENTIENDE EEUW / Dillen, J G van – Tijdschrift voor Geschiedenis. v. 50. 1935. BJ-262-15 1 – 9 – ne IDC [949]

Vreese, W de *see* BESCHRIJVING DER HANDSCHRIFTEN VAN JAN VAN RUUSBROEC'S WERKEN

VREME – Belgrade. Yugoslavia. -d. 2 Sep 1939-17 Mar 1941. (19 reels) – 1 – uk British Libr Newspaper [949]

VREME – Plovdiv, Bulgaria. May-Dec 1945 (scattered issues) – 1r – 1 – us L of C Photodup [949]

VREME – Sofia, Bulgaria. Jun 1948-Mar 1949 – 1r – 1 – us L of C Photodup [949]

VREMENNIK – Izd. Severnago kruzhka liubitelei iziashchnykh iskusstv. v. 1. 1916. BR-4870 2 – 8 – ne IDC [460]

VREMENNIK / Russia. (1923-U.S.S.R.). Glavnaia Palata Mer i Vesov – 1894-1930 – 1 – $46.00 – us L of C Photodup [324]

VREMENNIK IMPERATORSKOGO MOSKOVSKOGO OBSHCHESTVA ISTORII I DREVNOSTEI ROSSIISKIKH – v. 1-25. M. 1849-57. B-1980 2 – 8 – ne IDC [947]

VREMENNIK OBSHCHESTVA DRUZEI RUSSKOI KNIGI – v. 1-4. Paris. 1925-38. BR-3454 2 – 8 – ne IDC [010]

VREMENNIK PUSHKINSKOI KOMISSI / Pushkin, Alexander Sergevich – S. 1. 6v. L. 1936-41. PKG-C-34.6 BR-11,218 1 – 9 – ne IDC [460]

VREMENNOE SOGLASHCHENIE [SIC] MEZHDU ROSSIE I I FINLANDIE I O SPLAVE LESNYKH MATERIALOV PO REKAM MINALANIOKI I TULEMANIOKI – Gelsingfors: [s.n.], 1921 – 1 – CSUX91-B219 – us Hoover Inst Photo [340]

VREMIA – Zhurnal literaturnyi i politicheskii. Spb. 1861-63. B-1054 2 – 8 – ne IDC [320]

VREMIA PAVLA I EGO SMERT' – Zapiski sovremennikov i uchastnikov. M. 1908. BR-244 2 – 8 – ne IDC [460]

VRI MAGAZINE – [Montreal?]: VRI Club, [1894-1897?] (Montreal: J Lovell) – 9 – cn C.I.H.M. [355]

EEN VRIENDELICKE TSAMENSPRECKINGHE, VAN TWEE PERSOONEN VAN DER DOOPE DER IONGHER ONMONDIGHER KINDEREN / Buwo, B – 1564. BME-197 1 – 9 – ne IDC [240]

EEN VRIENDELICKE TSAMENSPREKINGHE, VAN TWEE PERSOONEN, VAN DER DOOPE DER IONGHER ONMONDIGHER KINDEREN / Buwo, B – Ghendt, Ferd. Sampsons. 1580. BME-198 1 – 9 – ne IDC [240]

DE VRIENDENKRING – v32-61. 1961-90 (complete) – 6r – 1 – ATLA S0375 – us A.T.L.A. [073]

Vries, A G C de *see* NEDERLANDSCHE EMBLEMATA

Vriese, de *see* TIJDSCHRIFT VOOR NATUURLIJKE GESCHIEDENIS EN PHYSIOLOGIE

Vriese, W H de *see*

- DESCRIPTIONS ET FIGURES DES PLANTES NOUVELLES ET RARES DU JARDIN BOTANIQUE DE L'UNIVERSITE DE LEIDE
- ILLUSTRATIONS D'ORCHIDEES DES INDES ORIENTALES NEERLANDAISES...
- MONOGRAPHIE DES MARATTIACEES
- PLANTAE INDIAE BATAVAE ORIENTALIS...

VRIJ SPANJE – Amsterdam, 1946. Fiche W1496. (Blodgett Collection of Spanish Civil War Pamphlets) – 9 – us H.U. College Libr [946]

VRIJ SPANJE – Volledig verslag van wat er voorviel en gesproken werd op de grote betoging in de Markthallen te Amsterdam op 5 januari 1946. Amsterdam, 1946. Fiche W1494. (Blodgett Collection of Spanish Civil War Pamphlets) – 9 – us H.U. College Libr [946]

DE VRIJDAGAVOND – Amsterdam. v1-9. 1924-32 – 200mf – 9 – J-262-117/1 – ne IDC [073]

VRIJE OPMERKER – Pretoria. South Africa. 1905-07 – 1 – sa State Libr [072]

HET VRIJE WOORD – Amsterdam. nos 1-16. 1895-96 – 2mf – 9 – J-261-118/1 – ne IDC [073]

Vrijman, L C *see* SLAVENHALERS IN SLAVENHANDEL

Vring, Georg von der *see*
- DER FERNE SOHN
- DIE SPUR IM HAFEN

Vromant, G *see* DE BONIS ECCLESIAE TEMPORALIBUS

DE VROUW EN DE OPBOUW – (1940(May)-1949(April) has not been published) – Amersfoort, 1934-50(1) – 6mf – 9 – J-261-116/1 – ne IDC [073]

VROUWEN ZENDINGSBLAD – (Title varies) – v1-9. 1934-46 (complete) – 1r – 1 – ATLA S0697 – us A.T.L.A. [073]

Vroye, Theodore J de *see* DE LA MUSIQUE RELIGIEUSE.

VRSPRUNG DES TURKISCHEN REICHS BIS AUFF DENITZIGEN SOLYMAN / Giovio, P – N.p., [1538] – 2mf – 9 – H-8256/1 – ne IDC [956]

AIN VRTAYL GOTTES VNSERS EEGEMAHELS, WIE MAN SICH MIT ALLEN GOETZEN UND BILDNUSSEN HALTEN SOLL / Haetzer, L – Zuerich. 1523. BME-48 1 – 9 – ne IDC [240]

DE VRUCHT DER ASSYRIOLOGIE VOOR DE VERGELIJKENDE GESCHIEDENIS DER GODSDIENSTEN / Tiele, Cornelis Petrus – Amsterdam: P N van Kampen, 1877 – 1mf – 9 – 0-8370-7347-2 – 1986-1347 – us A.T.L.A. [230]

VSE NOVOSTI LITERATURY, ISKUSSTVA, TEATRA, TEKHNIKI I PROMYSHLENNOSTI – NR. 1-4. Spb. 1910. BR-4871 2 – 8 – ne IDC [460]

VSELENSKOE CHUVSTVO / Lapshin, I I – Spb. 1911. BR-5810 2 – 8 – ne IDC [999]

VSEMIRNAIA NOV' – Ezhenedel'nyi illiustrirovannyi zhurnal. Spb. 1910-16. Lacking: v. 1-52, 1910; v. 1-52, 1911; v. 1-21, 23, 27-28, 30, 32, 35-36, 38-52, 1912; v. 2, 4, 5, 7, 26, 44, 48, 50, 52, 1914; v. 1, 5-9, 15-17, 19-22, 32-52, 1915; v. 146, 48-52, 1916. B-1981 2 – 8 – ne IDC [073]

VSEMIRNYI KONGRESS" BAPTISTOV" V" LONDONE V" 1905 GODU = WORLD CONGRESS OF BAPTISTS IN LONDON IN 1905 / Ivanov, V V & Mazaev D I – Rostov-on-Don, 1907-1909, parts 1, 2, 4 of 4 parts – 1r – 1 – $27.68 – us Baptist [240]

VSEMIRNYI PUTESHESTVENNIK – v. 1-9. Spb. 1867-71. BR-4178 2 – 8 – ne IDC [073]

VSEMIRNYI TRUD – Ucheno-literaturnyi zhurnal. Spb. 1867-72. Lacking: 1868 (11-12); 1872 (6-12). B-1983 2 – 8 – ne IDC [073]

VSEMIRNYI VESTNIK – Spb. 1903-08. Lacking: 1908 (11-12). B-1984 2 – 8 – ne IDC [073]

VSEOBSHCHAIA BIBLIOTEKA – Dvukhnedel'nyi illiustrirovannyi literaturno-politicheskii zhurnal. Spb. 1906-07. B-1985 2 – 8 – ne IDC [320]

VSEOBSHCHAIA BIBLIOTEKA ROSSII ILI KATALOG KNIG DLIA IZUCHENIIA NASHEGO OTECHESTVA V VSEKH OTNOSHENIIAKH I PODROBNOSTIAKH – Pribavlenie vtoroe. (Katalog knig biblioteki A.D. Chertkova). M. 1845. BR-7018 2 – 8 – ne IDC [020]

VSEOBSHCHEE OBIAZATEL'NOE OBUCHENIE NARODA V ROSSII I ZA GRANITSEI / Arkad'ev, E I – Material dlia bibliograficheskago ukazatelia literatury etogo voprosa. Moscow, 1905. 48p. BR-5874 2 – 8 – ne IDC [460]

VSEOBSHCHIE ADMINISTRATIVNYE SOIUZY GOSUDARSTV / Kazanskii, P E – Odessa, 1897. 3v. Tsarist work on international organizations. BR-9689/1 – 9 – ne IDC [947]

VSEOBSHCHII GEOGRAFICHESKII I STATISTICHESKII SLOVAR' / Gagarin, S P – M., 1843. v1-3 – 32mf – 9 – R-8387/2 – ne IDC [304]

VSEOBSHCHII ZHURNAL LITERATURY, ISKUSSTVA, NAUKI I OBSHCHESTVENNOI ZHIZNI – Ezhemesiachnyi illiustrirovannyi. Spb. 1910-12. Lacking: 1910 (1-12), 1911 (1-6), 1912 (3-12). B-1986 2 – 8 – ne IDC [073]

VSEPODDANNEISHII OTCHET O DEISTVIAKH VOENNAGO MINISTERSTVA – Leningrad, 1858-1912 – 19r – 1 – us Ross [947]

VSEPODDANNEISHII OTCHET O DEISTVIAKH VOENNAGO MINISTERSTVA / Russia. Voennoe Ministerstvo – St Petersburg. 1858-1861; 1863-1867; 1869; 1872-1892; 1895; 1899-1903; 1905-1912 – 1 – us NY Public [947]

VSEPODDANNEISHII OTCHET OBER-PROKURORA SVYATEISHAGO SINODA – The Humble Report of the Chief Procurator of the Holy Synod. Orthodox Eastern Church, Russian, Holy Synod. 1884, 1898, 1914 – 1 – 52.16 – us Baptist [073]

VSEPODDANNEISHII OTCHET PREDSEDATELIA / Russia. Gosudarstvennyi sovet – Petrograd, 1892-1916. 25 vols – 1 – 35.00r – us Hoover Inst Photo [324]

VSEPODDANNISHII OTCHET OBER-PROKURORA / Eastern Orthodox Church. Russian Synod – St Petersburg. 1883-1894 95 – 1 – us NY Public [240]

VSEROSSIISKI KOOPERATIVNYI S"EZD V S-PETERBURGE / V-on, L – Kiev, 1912 – 1mf – 9 – COR-17/1 – ne IDC [334]

VSEROSSIISKII KOOPERATIVNYI BANK – M., 1925 – 1mf – 9 – COR-374/1 – ne IDC [334]

VSEROSSIISKII KOOPERATIVNYI BANK : OTCHET ZA 1928-1929 OPERATSIONNYI GOD – M., 1930 – 1mf – 9 – COR-375/1 – ne IDC [334]

VSEROSSIISKII KOOPERATIVNYI BANK (VSEKOBANK) : DLIA CHEGO ON OBRAZOVAN, KTO IAVLIAETSIA EGO PAISHCHIKAMI, KAKIE SREDSTVA IM SOBRANY, KAK ON KREDITUET KOOPERATSIIU, CHTO IM DELANO... – M., 1925 – 1mf – 9 – COR-376/1 – ne IDC [334]

Vserossiiskii kooperativnyi lesnoi soiuz *see* OTCHET ZA...G

Vserossiiskii pochtovo-telegrafnyi soiuzTsentralny i komitet *see* PROTOKOLY TSENTRALNAGO ISPOLNITELAGO KOMITETA VSEROSSIISKAGO

Vserossiiskii tsentralnyi sovet professionalnykh soiuzov *see* BIULLETEN VSEROSSIISKOGO TSENTRALNOGO SOVETA PROFESSIONALNYKH SOIUZOV

Vserossiiskoe soveshchanie sovetov rabochikh i soldatskikh deputatov. Leningrad *see* STENOGRAFICHESKII OTCHET

Vsesoiuznaia Knizhnaia Palata *see* LETOPIS RETSENZII

VSESOIUZNAIA KOMMUNISTICHESKAIA PARTIIA – 15 s"ezd, 1927. Stenograficheskii otchet. v. 2. M. 1962. B-1351 2 – 8 – ne IDC [335]

VSESOIUZNAIA KOMMUNISTICHESKAIA PARTIIA – 16 s"ezd. 1930. Stenograficheskii otchet. M. 1931. B-1299 2 – 8 – ne IDC [335]

VSESOIUZNAIA KOMMUNISTICHESKAIA PARTIIA / Communist Party Congress. 1917. (Sixth) – (Stenographic reports of the Communist Party Congresses from the 6th Congress, August, 1917). 1923-1939 – 3 – us Readex [335]

VSESOIUZNAIA KOMMUNISTICHESKAIA PARTIIA BOLSHEVIKOV *see* PARTII A V BORBE S BIUROKRATIZMOM

Vsesoiuznaia Kommunisticheskaia Partiia... S'ezd *see* STENOGRAFICHESKII OTCHET

Vsesoiuznaia Kommunisticheskaya Partiia Bol'shevikov. S'ezd Rossiiskoi Kommunisticheskoi Partii (b) *see* STENOGRAFICHESKI OTCHET

VSESOIUZNAIA PEREPIS' NASELENIIA 1926 GODA / Russia. (1923-U.S.S.R.). Tsentral'noe statisticheskoe upravlenie. Otdel perepisi – (Russian census, 1926). v. 1-56. 1928-33. Plus 2 v. on questionnaires and 1 v. summary – 1 – $215.00 – us L of C Photodup [947]

VSESOIUZNOE OBSHCHESTVO POLITICHESKIKH KATORZHAN I SSYL'NO-POSELENTSEV – Kruzhok Narodovol'tsev: Trudy, 1928-31 – 1r – 1 – us Ross [335]

Vsesoiuznoie Obshchestvo Polikatorzhan in Ssyl'no-Poselentzev. Kruzhok Narodovol'tzev *see* TRUDY

Vsesoiuzny i kozhevennyi sindikat *see* SINDITSIROVANNAIA KOZHEVENNAIA PROMYSHLENNOST ZA...

Vsesoiuznyi Institut Iuridicheskikh nauk. Moscow *see* UCHENYE ZAPISKI

VSESOIUZNYI IURIDICHESKII ZAOCHNYI INSTITUT – (Missing: 1964, V.3; 1966, V.5-6; 1967, V.9-10; 1969, V.13; 1971, V.17-18, 23; 1975, V.25; 1977, V.52; 1979; 1982; Supplemented: 1963, V.2; 1967-1969, V.11-12; 1970, V.14-16(2); 1971, V.19-22(2); 1972, V.24; 1972, V.26-1977, V.51; 1977, V.53-1978, V.62; 1980(1-5)-1981(1-4); 1983-1987(1). 176mf) – M., 1961-1987 – 9 – R-8639/1 – ne IDC [340]

Vsesoiuznyi Iuridicheskii Zaochnyi Institut. Moscow *see* TRUDY

Vsevolodskii-Gerngross, V N *see* ISTORIIA TEATRAL'NOGO OBRAZOVANIIA V ROSSII (17-18 VV.)

VSIA KOOPERATSIIA SSSR : SPRAVOCHNIK-EZHEGODNIK DLIA KOOPERATOROV I KHOZIAISTVENNIKOV – M., 1928 – 13mf – 9 – COR-711/1 – ne IDC [334]

VSIA MOSKVA – 1896-1936. Moskva: A.S. Suvorin. annual – 1 – us U.W. Library [947]

VSIA MOSKVA (ALL MOSCOW) ADDRESS AND REFERENCE BOOK : 1875-1917 FROM THE RUSSIAN STATE LIBRARY – Moscow: Suvorin Publ, 1917 – 867mf – 9 – $3,700.00 – us Ross [947]

VSIA ROSSIIA (ALL RUSSIA) AND VES' SSSR (ALL USSR) BUSINESS DIRECTORIES, 1895-1931 – (1: St Petersburg 1895, 1897, 1899, 1900, 1902 219mf $1,050. 2: Kiev 1911-13 1923 83mf $400. 3: Moscow-Leningrad 1923-26, 1929-31 (Leningrad in 1926 only) 155mf $750) – 457mf – 9 – $1,950.00 set – us Ross [030]

VSTRECHA / Otsup, N – Poema. Paris. 1928. BR-1220 2 – 8 – ne IDC [460]

VSTRECHI / Piast, V – Izd. Federatsiia. M. 1929. BR-1496 2 – 8 – ne IDC [999]

VSTRECHI S ESENINYM / Verzhbitskii, N – Vospominaniia. Tbilisi. 1961. BR-2193 2 – 8 – ne IDC [460]

VSTRECHI S MANDEL'SHTAMOM / Chukovskii, N – M. 1964. BR-3650 2 – 8 – ne IDC [460]

VTORAIA GOSUDARSTVENNAIA DUMA / Kaminka, A I & Nabokov, V D – St. Petersburg, 1907. viii, 308p. Account of the activities of the Second State Duma based on weekly press surveys, with emphasis on concerns of the People's Freedom Party, to which authors adhered. BR-260/2 – 8 – ne IDC [947]

VTOROE SOBRANIE UPOLNOMOCHENNYKH VSEROSSIISKOGO SOIUZA SEL'SKOKHOZIAISTVENNOI KOOPERATSII 22-27 FEVRALIA 1924 GODA – Moscow, 1924 – 1mf – 9 – COR-470/1 – ne IDC [334]

VTOROI MISSIONERSKII SVEZD V MOSKVE = THE SECOND MISSIONARY CONGRESS IN MOSCOW / ed by Skvortsov, Vasilii M – European Baptist materials. Moscow, 1891, 56p – 1 – us Baptist [240]

VTOROI PIATILETNII PLAN RAZVITIIA NARODNOGO KOZIAISTVA SSSR, 1933-1937 GG / U.S.S.R. Gosudarstvennaia Planovaia Komissiia – 2v. M. 1934. BD-213 1 – 9 – ne IDC [330]

VTOROI VSEROSSIISKOI S"EZD PO KOOPERATSII V G. KIEVE, 1-7 AVG. 1913 G : TRUDY. VYP. 1. OBSHCHIE SOBRANIIA S"EZDA – Kiev, 1915 – 4mf – 9 – COR-18/1 – ne IDC [334]

VTR WORKSHOP : SMALL FORMAT VIDEO / Atienza, Loretta J – 2nd ed 1979 – 114p – 9 – 92-3-101467-6 – fr UNESCO [380]

VU – Journal de la semaine. Paris. mars 1928-mai 1940. En mai 1937 absorbe Vu et Lu et parait jusqu'en mars 1938 sous le titre de: Vu et Lu – 1 – fr A.C.R.P.P. [073]

VU AN NGUYEN QUANG ICH VA DONG BON CAN TOI LOI DUNG DANH NGHIA TAP DOAN MIEN NAM THAP MUOI DE AN CAP CMA CONG = THE CASE OF NGUYEN QUANG ICH ET AL GUILTY OF EMBEZZLEMENT OF PUBLIC PROPERTY / The People's Court of Nam Dinh Province – 1970 – 1mf – 9 SEL-115/1 – ne IDC [340]

VU DUC CHIEU. PHAP CHE LA GI? = WHAT IS LAW? – Hanoi: Pho Thong Publishing House, 1974 – 3mf – 9 SEL-118/1 – ne IDC [340]

VUE : NEWS MAGAZINE OF CATV AND PAY-CABLE – (Cont: CATV. Absorbed by: TVC) – Denver. v10-12. oct 1976-sep 1978 1,5; v10 oct-dec 1976*. v11-12 jan 1977-sep 1978 9 – 1,5,9 – D8073.01 – us UMI [073]

EL VUELO DE ISIS A LASMIL Y UNA NOCHES OCULTISTAS / Roso de Luna, Mario – Madrid: Editorial Pueyo, 1923 – 1 – sp Bibl Santa Ana [130]

Vuelta Ciclista *see* 1ST VUELTA CICLISTA A CACERES 1970. ORGANIZA CLUB POLIDEPORTIVO UNION. COLABROA FEDERACION EXTREMENA DE CICLISMO. CACERES, FERIA DE 1970

VUES PATRIOTIQUES SUR L'EDUCATION DU PEUPLE, TANT DES VILLES QUE DES CAMPAGNES / Philipon de la Madelaine, Louis – Lyon. P. Bruyset-Ponthus. 1783. 6781 – 9 – fr Hachette [360]

Vuilleumier, Henri *see* ETUDE SUR LE MONOTHEISME DES HEBREUX: SON CARACTERE, SES ORIGINES

Vuillot, Paul *see* L'EXPLORATION DU SAHARA

VUKALA-YI MURAFA'AH – Muqaddimah az Jinab Mawlavi Hafiz Jalal al-Din Ahmad Ja'fari Zaynabi. Landan: Matba'i Anvar Ahmadi – 1 reel – 1 – $42.00 – us MEDOC [950]

VUKOVA PREPISKA / Karadzic, Vuk Stefanovic – Beograd: Stamp. u Drz. Stamp. Kralj. Srbije. 1907-13. 7v. In Cyrillic – 1 – us U.W. Library [460]

VULCAN ADVOCATE – Alberta, CN. Mar 1912-Dec 1985 – 26r – 1 – cn Commonwealth Micro [072]

Vulcanii, B *see* DE IMPERIO ET REBUS GESTIS IUSTINIANI (CBH 4)

DER VULGAERE RATIONALISMUS, ODER, DAS MODERNE HEIDENTHUM...CHRISTLICHEN KIRCHE / Lichtenstein, J – Cincinnati: H.M. Moos, 1868. 1 fiche – 9 – us A.T.L.A. [240]

VULGARIZACIONES HISTORICAS. / Perez Galdos, Benito – Madrid, 1909. 267p – 1 – us U.W. Library [972]

THE VULGATE : THE SOURCE OF FALSE DOCTRINES / Henslow, George – (Includes bibliographical references & index) – London: Williams & Norgate, 1909 – 1mf – 9 – 0-8370-3564-3 – 1985-1564 – us A.T.L.A. [220]

Vulliod, Amedee *see* PIERRE ROSEGGER

Vulson, Marc de, Sieur de la Colombiere *see* LA SCIENCE HEROIQVE, TRAITANT DE LA NOBLESSE, DE L'ORIGINE DES ARMES, DE LEURS BLASONS, & SYMBOLES

Vuorio, Anelma Kaarina Kojonen *see* DIE KARAS

VUOSIKIRJA-TURUN ARKKIHIIPPAKUNTA – v26-40. 1976-91 – 1r – 1 – ATLA S0898 – us A.T.L.A. [073]

Vu-van-Hien *see* LA PROPRIETE COMMUNALE AU TONKIN (CONTRIBUTION A L'ETUDE HISTORIQUE, JURIDIQUE ET ECONOMIQUE DES CONG-DIEN ET CONG-THO EN PAYS D'ANNAM)

VUZRAZHDANIE NA BALGARSKIIA NAROD TSARKOVNO-NATSIONALNI BORNI I POSTIZHENIIA / Nikov, P – Sofiia. 1929. BR-3835 2 – 8 – ne IDC [947]

V.V. KAPNIST (1757-1823) / Berkov, P N – M., L. 1950. BR-6096 2 – 8 – ne IDC [920]

V.V. MAIAKOVSKII / Novikov, V – M. 1952. BR-1464 2 – 8 – ne IDC [920]

V.V. MAIAKOVSKII / Zubov, Iu. S – Kratkii rekomendatel'nyi ukazatel' literatury. M. 1955. BR-2244 2 – 8 – ne IDC [460]

VVEDENIE K KURSE MEZHDUNARODNOGO PRAVA / Kazanskii, P E – Odessa, 1901. 386p. Introductory text on public international law with the author's general views on the subject. BR-9486/1 – 9 – ne IDC [340]

VVEDENIE V METRIKU: TEORIIA STIKHA / Zhirmunskii, V M – M. 1925. B-973 2 – 8 – ne IDC [460]

VVEDENIE V TEORIIU RAZNOSTNYKH SKHEM / Samarskii, Aleksandr Andreevich – Moskva: Nauka, 1971 – 1 – us U.W. Library [510]

Vvedenskii, A I *see*
- FILOSOFSKIE OCHERKI
- PSIKHOLOGIIA BEZ VSIAKOI METAFIZIKI

VVV – New York. v. 1-4. June 1942-Feb 1944 – 1 – us NY Public [999]

VY OCH REVY *see* GOTEBORGS MORGONPOST

VYBORY V SOVETY V SOIUZE SSR / T Sentralny i ispolnitelnyi komitet Soiuza SSRTsentralnaia izbiratelnaia komissiia T SIK Soiuza SSSR – (Includes: c.1: 1934/1935) – Moskva: Vlastsovetov, 19uu – 1 – CSUXAKZ0192-S – us Hoover Inst Photo [320]

VYCHODOSLOVENSKE NOVINY – Kosice, Czechoslovakia. 1958-63; 1965-Jun 1966 – 6r – 1 – us L of C Photodup [072]

Vygodskii, D *see* POEZIIA I POETIKA

VYNER MANUSCRIPTS : MEDIEVAL DOCUMENTS FROM 1100-1600 / Leeds. City Archives – (Documents relating to Yorkshire Estates of Fountains Abbey) – 2r – 1 – uk Microform Academic [240]

Vynnychenko, Volodymyr *see* NOVA ZAPOVID

VYPOLNEMIE PLANA PERVOGO GODA PIATILEKTI / U.S.S.R. Gosudarstvennaia Planovaia Komissiia – M. 1930. BD-247 1 – 9 – ne IDC [330]

VYPOVED OBVINENEHO A SVEDKA V KONANI PRED SUDOM / Mathern, V – Praha. 1968. BR-8767 1 – 9 – ne IDC [460]

vyrabotannyi gruppoi chlenov "Soiuza osvobozhdeniia *see* OSNOVOI GOSUDARSTVENNYI ZAKON ROSSISSKOI IMPERII

VYSHKA – Baku (Azerbaijan), USSR. 1971-1981 – 11r – $550.00 – B63587 – us Library Micro [072]

Vysshii Sovet Narodnogo Khoziaistva *see* NARODNOE KHOZIAISTVO

Vysshii soviet narodnago khoziaistva *see* TRUDY...VSEROSSIISKAGO SIEZDA SOVIETOV NARODNAGO KHOZIAISTVA

VYSTAVKA LERMONTOVSKIKH FONDOV MOSKOVSKIKH MUZEEV / Moscow. Literaturnogo Muzeia – M. 1940. PKG-B-66 BR-10,704 1 – 9 – ne IDC [460]

VYSTAVKA PROIZVEDENII PECHATI ZA 1908 GOD – Spb, 1909 – 8 – BR-4563 2 – ne IDC [947]

VYSTAVKA PROIZVEDENII PECHATI ZA 1909 GOD – Spb, 1911 – 8 – BR-5609 2 – ne IDC [947]

VYSTAVKA PROIZVEDENII PECHATI ZA 1910 GOD – Spb, 1912 – 8 – BR-5610 2 – ne IDC [947]

VYVOZ SVINE I – S.-Peterburg: Tip. V. F. Kirshbauma, 1913 – 1 – CSUX89-B6607 – us Hoover Inst Photo [947]

VZVIKHRENNAIA. RUS' / Remizov, A – Izd. Tair: Paris, 1927. 533p. BR-855 2 – 8 – ne IDC [460]

W – New York, 1972- – 1 – $175.00y – us Fairchild Micro [390]

W Arndt, W *see* GREGORII TURONENSIS OPERA (MGH 2: 1.BD)

W. FRANK CLARK GLASS NEGATIVES / U.S. Library of Congress. Prints and Photographs Division – 321 glass negatives from early 1900's. 2 reels. P&P5201 – 1 – 23.00r – us L of C Photodup [080]

W R Carpenter & Ltd. Tulagi Branch *see* BRANCH MANAGER'S CORRESPONDENCE AND RELATED PAPERS

W. ROBERTSON NICOLL, LL.D. : EDITOR AND PREACHER / Stoddart, Jane T – London: S.W. Partridge, 1903 – 1mf – us A.T.L.A. [240]

W.A. and C.L. Goodspeed, Publishers *see* HISTORY OF THE COUNTY OF MIDDLESEX, CANADA

W.A. JEFFRIES AND CO.'S KAMLOOPS AND DISTRICT DIRECTORY, 1914-15 : CONTAINING A COMPLETE STREET LIST, ALPHABETICAL LIST OF ALL FIRMS, CORPORATIONS, AND PRIVATE CITIZENS OF THE CITY OF KAMLOOPS,... – Kamloops, B.C.: W.A. Jeffries and Co, 1915 – 1r – 1 – cn U.B.C. Preserve [910]

W.A. JEFFRIES AND CO.'S KAMLOOPS CITY DIRECTORY, 1913 : CONTAINING A COMPLETE STREET LIST, ALPHABETICAL LIST OF ALL FIRMS, CORPORATIONS, AND PRIVATE CITIZENS OF THE CITY OF KAMLOOPS,... – Vancouver: W.A. Jeffries & Co, 1913 – 1r – 1 – cn U.B.C. Preserve [910]

W.A. JEFFRIES AND CO.'S SOUTHEAST KOOTENAY DIRECTORY, 1914 : CONTAINING A COMPLETE STREET LIST, ALPHABETICAL LIST OF ALL FIRMS, CORPORATIONS AND PRIVATE CITIZENS OF CRANBROOK AND FERNIE;... – Nelson, B.C.: W.A. Jeffries & Co, 1914 – 1r – 1 – cn U.B.C. Preserve [910]

W.A. JEFFRIES' VERNON CITY AND OKANAGAN VALLEY DIRECTORY, 1913 : CONTAINING A COMPLETE STREET LIST OF THE CITY OF VERNON, ALSO ALPHABETICAL LIST OF ALL FIRMS, CORPORATIONS AND PRIVATE CITIZENS OF THE TOWNS IN THE OKANAGAN VALLEY – Vernon, BC: W A Jeffries, 1913 – 1r – 1 – cn U.B.C. Preserve [910]

Wa, K M *see* A COMPARISON OF THREE HYDROSTATIC WEIGHING TECHNIQUES

DIE WAAGE – v13-19. 1974-80 – 1,5,6,9 – us UMI [073]

WAAGE – (Former title: Gruenenthal Waage 1959-69) – Stolberg. v19. 1980 1,5; v19. 1980 9* – 1,5,9 – D9307 – us UMI [073]

WAAK – Amsterdam. nos 1-31. 1933 – 5mf – 9 – J-261-119/1 – ne IDC [073]

Waard, C de *see* DE UITVINDING DER VERREKIJKERS

DEWAARDE DER SYRISCHE EVANGELIEN / Wildeboer, Gerrit – Leiden: E J Brill, 1880 – 1mf – 9 – 0-8370-5847-3 – 1985-3847 – us A.T.L.A. [220]

WAAREN-PREISE – Bremen, 1846-47 – 1 – Inquire at Mikrofilmarchiv for details – gw Misc Inst [380]

DE WAARHEID – (Set includes a 1975-1990 index) – 1945-1990 – 2,420mf – 9 – Dfl12,110.00 silver Dfl11,000.00 diazo – ne MMF Publ [320]

WAARHEID – South African Gentile National Socialist Movement. 23 Feb 1934-29 Jul 1938 – 1 – us Res Libr [960]

DE WAARHEIDSVRIEND – v61 nos 17-80. 1973-92 (incomplete) – 11r – 1 – ATLA S0479 – us A.T.L.A. [073]

WABAUNSEE COUNTY HERALD – Alma. Kansas. 1869-1871; 1880-1881 – 1 – us UMI [071]

Wabaunsee County. Kansas. School District 2 *see* TEACHERS' REGISTER

Wabaunsee County. Kansas. Wabaunsee Township *see* RECORDS

Wabaunsee County, KS. School District No. 1 *see* RECORDS

WABAUNSEE COUNTY NEWS – Alma. KS. 1872-94 – 1 – us UMI [071]

Wabaunsee. Kansas *see* SCRAPBOOK

Wabaunsee. Kansas. Congregational Christian Community Church *see* RECORDS

Wabaunsee. Kansas. First Church of Christ *see* RECORDS

Waccamaw. South Carolina. All Saints Episcopal Church *see* RECORDS

Wace, Alan *see* MYCENAE: AN ARCHAEOLOGICAL HISTORY AND GUIDE

Wace, Henry *see*
- THE BIBLE AND MODERN INVESTIGATION: THREE LECTURES DELIVERED TO CLERGY AT THE REQUEST OF THE BISHOP; WITH AN ADDRESS ON THE AUTHORITY OF HOLY SCRIPTURES
- CHRISTIANITY AND AGNOSTICISM: REVIEWS OF SOME RECENT ATTACKS ON THE CHRISTIAN FAITH
- THE GOSPEL AND ITS WITNESSES
- THE SACRIFICE OF CHRIST

Wace, Henry et al *see* CHRISTIANITY AND AGNOSTICISM

DIE WACHENDE KIRCHE – v1-41. Sep 1866-1907 (complete) – 6r – 1 – ATLA S0174 – us A.T.L.A. [073]

Wachenhusen, Hans *see* KEJSARDOEMETS QVINNOR

Wachler, Ludwig *see* VORLESUNGEN UEBER DIE GESCHICHTE DER TEUTSCHEN NATIONAL-LITERATUR

Wachob, I S *see* CHICAGO LAW JOURNAL

Wachsmann, Konrad *see* ASPEKTE

Wachsmuth, C *see* THE NORTH AMERICAN CRINOIDEA CAMERATA

Wachsmuth, Wilhelm *see* HERZOG KARL AUGUST UND GOETHE

Wachstein, B *see*
- GEOGRAPHISCHES REGISTER ZU "KATALOG DER SALO COHN'SCHEN SCHENKUNGEN", WIEN, 1911, 1914
- KATALOG DER SALO COHN'SCHEN SCHENKUNGEN
- ZUR BIBLIOGRAPHIE DER GEDAECHTNIS- UND TRAUERVORTRAEGE IN DER HEBRAEISCHEN LITERATUR

DIE WACHT – Backa Palanka, Yugoslavia. Oct 1925-1935; Oct 1937-Feb 1938 – 3r – 1 – us L of C Photodup [949]

DIE WACHT – Deutsch Palanka, Jugoslawien. 5 Jan 1936-17 Dez 1939 – 1 – gw Mikrofilm [949]

WACHTER AM ERIE – (Semi-weekly, later daily German language Republican newspaper) – Cleveland, Cuyahoga, OH. 9 Aug 1852-30 Sept 1893 – 47r – 1 – us Western Res [071]

WACHTER AM ERIE – (Weekly edition of this German language Republican newspaper) – Cleveland, Cuyahoga, OH. 4 Jan 1866-5 Aug 1886 – 7r – 1 – us Western Res [071]

Wachter, J G *see* GLOSSARIUM GERMANICUM CONTINENS ORIGINES ET ANTIQUITATES TOTIUS LINGUAE GERMANICAE...

WACHTER UND ANZEIGER : DAILY GERMAN LANGUAGE NEWSPAPER – Cleveland, OH. 2 Jan 1894-31 Dec 1898 – 9r – 1 – us Western Res [071]

WACHTER UND ANZEIGER : SUNDAY GERMAN LANGUAGE NEWSPAPER – Cleveland, OH. 7 Jan 1894-14 Aug 1898 – 5r – 1 – us Western Res [071]

WACHTER UND ANZEIGER : WEEKLY GERMAN LANGUAGE NEWSPAPER – Cleveland, Oh. 13 Aug 1971-30 Dec. 1982 – 7r – 1 – us Western Res [071]

WACHTER UND ANZEIGER : WEEKLY GERMAN LANGUAGE NEWSPAPER – Cleveland, OH. 4 July 1894-28 Dec 1898 – 4r – 1 – us Western Res [071]

WACHUSETT STAR – Barre, MA. 1847-48 – 1 – us Readex [071]

WACKENRODER E IL MISTICISMO ESTETICO / Santoli, Vittorio – (Includes bibliographical references) – Rieti: Bibliotheca editrice, 1929 – 1r – 1 – us U.W. Library [430]

WACKENRODER UND SEIN EINFLUSS AUF TIECK : EIN BEITRAG ZUR QUELLENGESCHICHTE DER ROMANTIK / Koldewey, Paul – (Includes bibliographical references) – Leipzig: Dieterich, 1904 – 1r – 1 – us U.W. Library [430]

Wackenroder, Wilhelm Heinrich *see*
- HERZENSERGIESSUNGEN EINES KUNSTLIEBENDEN KLOSTERBRUDERS
- OPERE E LETTERE
- WERKE UND BRIEFE

Wacker, Emil *see* DIE KOESTLICHE PERLE UND DIE INNERE MISSION

Wackernagel, Wilhelm *see* ALTHOCHDEUTSCHE LESESTUECKE

WACO BAPTIST CHURCH. NORTH CAROLINA : CHURCH RECORDS – 1842-1958 – 1 – 42.12 – us Baptist [240]

WACO MESSENGER – Waco. Tex. oct. 10, Nov. 28, 1941 – 1 – us NY Public [071]

WACO STAR – Waco, NE. -w. Apr 1916-Dec 1918 – 1 – us NE Hist [071]

WACO, TEXAS. GHOLSON BAPTIST CHURCH – Church Records, 1886-October 1986. Lacking 1899-August 1916, 1929-1939, July 1981-September 1983. 1,292p – 1 – $58.14 – us Baptist [240]

Wad, Atul *see* TECHNOLOGY ASSESSMENT

Waddell, Joseph A *see* ANNALS OF AUGUSTA COUNTY 1726-1871

Waddington, Alfred *see* CANADA PACIFIC RAILWAY: ELEMENTS FOR A PROSPECTUS

Wade *see* AN EARLY HISTORY OF FAYETTE COUNTY

Wade, Benjamin Franklin *see* PAPERS

Wade, Johathan *see* A VOCABULARY OF THE SGAU KAREN LANGUAGE

Wade, Magatte *see* UN EPISODE DE L'EPOPEE DU KAJOOR

Wad-el-Ward, Gamahliel *see* PALESTINE THROUGH THE EYES OF A NATIVE

Wadepuhl, Walter *see* GOETHES STELLUNG ZUR FRANZOESISCHEN ROMANTIK

WADI HADRAMAWT AND THE WALLED CITY OF SHIBAM / Lewcock, Ronald – 1986 – 9 – 92-3-102338-1 – fr UNESCO [956]

WADI HALFA SOCIAL AND ECONOMIC SURVEY: REPORT ON THE INCOME AND EXPENDITURE SURVEY, INCLUDING RESULTS OF A LIVESTOCK SURVEY / Sudan. Dept. of Statistics – 1963. BNE-7627 1 – 9 – ne IDC [310]

Wadia, P A *see* THE PHILOSOPHERS AND THE FRENCH REVOLUTION

WADJAH SEMANGAT / Ozu, S – Bandung, Perpoestakaan Tjahaja, 2602. 106p – 123-124mf – 9 – ne IDC [950]

WADLEY BAPTIST CHURCH. WADLEY, GEORGIA : CHURCH RECORDS – 1869-1928; 1934-69 – 1 – 51.75 – us Baptist [240]

WADSTENA LANS TIDNING – Vadstena, Sweden. 1857-1933. Ostgotakuriren 1932-33 – 1 – sw Kungliga [072]

Wadstrom, Carl Bernhard *see*
- ESSAY ON COLONIZATION
- AN ESSAY ON COLONIZATION, PARTICULARLY APPLIED TO THE WESTERN COAST OF AFRICA.

DER WAECHTER – Bielefeld, 1864-jun 30 1902 – 1 – Inquire at Mikrofilmarchiv for details – gw Misc Inst [072]

DER WAECHTER AM RHEIN – Koeln, Germany. Jun-Nov 1848 – 1 – gw Mikrofilm [072]

WAECHTER DER HEIMAT : ROMAN AUS DER LEIDENS- UND KAMPFZEIT DES OST-SUDETENLANDES / Kunz, Grete – 3. Aufl. Muenchen: F Eher, 1943 – 1r – 1 – us U.W. Library [830]

WAECHTER UND ANZEIGER – Cleveland, Chicago. 1972-84 – 1 – gw Mikrofilm [071]

WAECHTERSTIMME NIC. GALLI. WO VND IN WAS STUECKEN VNTER DEM NAMEN LUTHERI DER AUGSPURGISCHEN CONFESSION VND H. SCHRIFT... / Gallus, N – Regensburg, [1560] – 1mf – ne IDC [240]

WAEHRUNGS-BIBLIOTHEK – 1895- – 1 – us U.W. Library [073]

WAEHRUNGSFRAGEN / Best, Dr – 9 – 1.00f – at Libertarian Micro [335]

DIE WAEHRUNGSPOLITISCHE KOOPERATION IN DER EUROPAEISCHEN GEMEINSCHAFT : VON DER HAAGER GIPFELKONFERENZ 1969 BIS ZUM EUROPAEISCHEN WAEHRUNGSSYSTEM 12.03.1979 / Bozkurt, Mahmut – 1995 – 2mf – 9 – DM80.00 – 3-8267-2082-2 – gw Hänsel [332]

WAELDER UND LATERNENSCHEIN / Zillich, Heinrich – Leipzig: L Staackmann, 1944 – 1r – 1 – us U.W. Library [830]

WAELDER UND MENSCHEN : EINE JUGEND / Wiechert, Ernst Emil – Muenchen: A Langen/G Mueller, c1936 – 1r – 1 – us U.W. Library [943]

Waelti, C *see*
- ALPENKLAENGE UND LAWINENDONNER
- STURMVOGEL UND NACHTIGALL

WAERACHTIGE AENWYSINGHE VNDE CLAER VERHAEL VAN DIE WEDERBRENGHINGHE DES MENSCHEN / Joris, David – BME-374 1 – 9 – ne IDC [240]

EEN WAERACHTIGH VERHAAL DER T'ZAMENSPREKINGHEN TUSSCHEN MENNO SIMONS ENDE MARTINUS MIKRON VAN DER MENSCHWERDINGHE JESU CHRISTI / Micron, M – Embden, G. Ctematius. 1556. BME-187 1 – 9 – ne IDC [240]

EEN WAERACHTIGH VERHAAL DER T'ZAMENSPREKINGHEN TUSSHEN MENNO SIMONS ENDE MARTINUS MIKRON VAN DER MENSCHWERDINGHE JESU CHRISTI / Micron, M – t'Hantwerpen, J. Troyens. 1582. BME-188 1 – 9 – ne IDC [240]

WAERME- UND STOFFUEBERTRAGUNG – v. 1-14. 1968-80 – 1,5,9 – 1397.00 – us UMI [073]

WAERSCHOUWINGHE (EEN CHRISTELIJCKE) VOOR DE EENVOUDIGHE CHRISTENEN – .Teghen verscheyden valsche Leeringhen ende Heresien,. Door L. G. P. Delff, Aelbr. Hendricxz. 1584. BME-246B 1 – 9 – ne IDC [240]

WAERSCHOUWINGHE (EEN CHRISTELIJCKE) VOOR DE EENVOUDIGHE CHRISTENEN – Teghen verscheyden valsche Leeringhen ende Heresien. Door L.G.P. Delff, Aelbr. Hendricxz. 1585. BME-246 1 – 9 – ne IDC [240]

WAERSCHOUWINGHE VOOR DEN DACH DES HEEREN / Joris, David – Maio, int Jaer. 1551. BME-367 1 – 9 – ne IDC [240]

Waescher, Aribert *see* GEDANKEN NACH ZWEI UHR NACHTS

Waetzoldt, Stephan *see* ZWEI GOETHEVORTRAEGE

Waetzoldt, Wilhelm *see* HEBBEL UND DIE PHILOSOPHIE SEINER ZEIT

Waffelaert, Gustave Joseph *see* DE DUBIO SOLVENDO IN RE MORALI

DIE WAFFEN NIEDER : EINE LEBENSGESCHICHTE / Suttner, Bertha von – Dresden: E Pierson, 1892 – 1r – 1 – us U.W. Library [920]

DER WAFFENSCHMIED – Berlin, 1941-44 (incomplete) – 1 – Inquire at Mikrofilmarchiv for details – gw Misc Inst [355]

WAFFEN-SS DURING WORLD WAR 2 PAMPHLET COLLECTION – 194?-1943 – 1 reel – 1 – CSUXANM8194-B – us Hoover Inst Photo [355]

Waffle, Albert Edward *see* THE INTERPRETER WITH HIS BIBLE

DIE WAGE – Lemgo, Germany. 1848-52 – 1 – gw Mikrofilm [072]

WAGE AND PRICE CONTROL / ed by Shenoy, Sudha – 2fiches (29x) – 9 – 1.00f – at Libertarian Micro [320]
WAGE DATA ON WAGE AND HOUR CASES, REGION 5, 1938-44 / U.S. Department of Labor – 9 rolls. T950 – 1 – us Nat'l Archives [331]
WAGE RATES IN SHANGHAI / Shanghai. Bureau of Social Affairs – Shanghai. 1935. BCH-840 2 – 8 – ne IDC [331]
Wagenaar, Chr. *see* THESAURUS GRAECITATIS MONASTICAE
Wagenaar, K T et al *see* PRODUCTIVITY OF TRANSHUMANT FULANI CATTLE IN THE INNER NIGER DELTA OF MALI
WAGENER FIRST BAPTIST CHURCH. WAGENER, SOUTH CAROLINA : CHURCH RECORDS – 1887-1972 – 1 – 25.60 – us Baptist [240]
Wagener, Herrmann *see* STAATS- UND GESELLSCHAFTS-LEXIKON (AEL, ABT 1;14)
Wagenfeld, Karl *see*
- UN BUTEN SINGT DE NACHTIGALL
- HATT GIEGEN HATT
- NE GOEPPS VULL
- WELTBRAND

WAGENSEIL COLLECTION / ed by Sueß, Hermann & Bobzin, Hartmut – mf ed 1996 – 1700mf – 9 – DM21,500.00 – 3-89131-227-X – gw Fischer [260]
Wagenseil, Johann C *see*
- DE SACRI ROM. IMPERII LIBERA CIVITATE NORIBERGENSI COMMENTATIO
- ...DE SACRI ROMANI IMPERII LIBERA CIVITATE NORIBERGENSI COMMENTATIO..

Wagenseller *see* SNYDER COUNTY ANNALS
Wagenseller, George W *see*
- SNYDER COUNTY MARRIAGES 1835-1899
- TOMBSTONE INSCRIPTIONS OF SNYDER COUNTY

Wager, Daniel E *see* OUR COUNTY AND ITS PEOPLE-ONEIDA
WAGGA WAGGA EXPRESS – 1858. 1929-38 – 27r – 9 – at Pascoe [072]
WAGGA WAGGA EXPRESS – Australia. Sep 1892-Jan 1898.-d. (7 reels) – 1 – uk British Libr Newspaper [072]
Waggerl, Karl Heinrich *see*
- BROT
- MUETTER

Waggett, Philip Napier *see* RELIGION AND SCIENCE: SOME SUGGESTIONS...OF THE RELATIONS BETWEEN THEM
Waggone, Clark *see* HISTORY OF THE CITY OF TOLEDO AND LUCAS COUNTY
WAGHORN'S GUIDE – Winnipeg: [s.n. 1884-19–] – 9 – cn C.I.H.M. [910]
Wagler, J G *see* SYSTEMA AVIUM
WAGNER : EINE BIOGRAPHIE / Kapp, Julius – (Includes index) – 16. bis 19. Aufl. Berlin: Schuster & Loeffler, 1910 – 1r – 1 – us U.W. Library [780]
Wagner, A *see* DIE FAMILIE DER HELICINIDAE
Wagner, Albert *see*
- AKZEPTANZPROBLEME BEIM EINSATZ INNOVATIVER INFORMATIONSTECHNOLOGIE IM BUERO- UND VERWALTUNGSBEREICH ANALYSIERT AM BEISPIEL EINES INDUSTRIEBETRIEBES
- ERHEBUNGSINSTRUMENTARIUM ZU AKZEPTANZPROBLEMEN BEIM EINSATZ INNOVATIVER INFORMATIONSTECHNOLOGIE IM BUERO- UND VERWALTUNGSBEREICH ANALYSIERT AM BEISPIEL EINES INDUSTRIEBETRIEBES
- MATERIALIEN ZU AKZEPTANZPROBLEMEN BEIM EINSATZ INNOVATIVER INFORMATIONSTECHNOLOGIE IM BUERO- UND VERWALTUNGSBEREICH ANALYSIERT AM BEISPIEL EINES INDUSTRIEBETRIEBES
- SCHULUNGSPROGRAMME ZU AKZEPTANZPROBLEMEN BEIM EINSATZ INNOVATIVER INFORMATIONSTECHNOLOGIE IM BUERO- UND VERWALTUNGSBEREICH ANALYSIERT AM BEISPIEL EINES INDUSTRIEBETRIEBES

Wagner, Albert Malte *see*
- FRIEDRICH HEBBELS DRAMATISCHER STIL
- LESSING

Wagner, Annemarie *see* UNBEDEUTENDE REIMWOERTER UND ENJAMBEMENT BEI RILKE UND IN DER NEUEREN LYRIK
Wagner, Charles *see* VIE SIMPLE
Wagner, Christian *see*
- GESAMMELTE DICHTUNGEN
- NEUE DICHTUNGEN
- NEUER GLAUBE
- SONNTAGSGAENGE

Wagner, Dale R *see* PHYSIOLOGICAL RESPONSE OF TRAINED CYCLISTS TO VARIOUS CYCLING HANDLEBAR POSTURES
Wagner, Donald Blackmore *see* SCANDINAVIAN UNION CATALOGUE OF EAST ASIAN MATERIALS
Wagner, Henry R *see* THE RISE OF FERNANDO CORTES
Wagner, Horst *see* DER ZENTRALE GEGENSTAND IM DRAMA LESSINGS, KLEISTS UND GRILLPARZERS
Wagner, J *see* DEUTSCH-OSTAFRIKA
Wagner, K E *see* OVERCORRECTION AND TIMEOUT TECHNIQUES TO DECREASE TIME OFF-TASK DURING A GROSS MOTOR PERFORMANCE OF EMOTIONALLY DISTURBED MALES
Wagner, Karl *see* BRIEFE AN UND VON JOHANN HEINRICH MERCK
Wagner, Ludwig *see* UEBER JOSEPH GOERRES' SPRACHE UND STIL
Wagner, Marianne *see* ZEITMORPHOLOGISCHE VERGLEICH VON HERMANN HESSES "DEMINAN," "SIDDHARTA," "NARZISS UND GOLDMUND" ZUR AUGWEISUNG TYPISCHER GESTALTZUEGE
WAGNER, MITOLOGO Y OCULTISTA (EL DRAMA MUSICAL DE WAGNER Y LOS MISTERIOS DE LA ANTIGUEDAD), PROLOGO DE ADOLFO BONILLA Y SAN MARTIN / Roso de Luna, Mario – Madrid: Vda. de Pueyo, 1917 – 1 – sp Bibl Santa Ana [780]
Wagner, Norman E et al *see* MOYER SITE
Wagner, P *see* DIE MESSE IM MITTELALTER UND IHRE GESANGLICHE AUSSTATTUNG
Wagner, Pat *see* THE NETWORKING GAME
Wagner, Philipp *see*
- EIN ACHTUNDVIERZIGER
- KLAENGE AUS VERGANGENEN ZEITEN

Wagner Printing Co *see* KNOX COUNTY HONOR ROLL 1917-18-19
Wagner, R *see* [TRISTAN UND ISOLDE]. EINLEITUNG, ARRANGED FOR ORGAN BY E. LEMARE
Wagner, Richard *see*
- THE DUSK OF THE GODS
- DER FLIEGENDE HOLLAENDER
- DER GEBRAUCH DES IMPERATIVISCHEN INFINITIVS IM GRIECHISCHEN
- LOHENGRIN
- THE MASTER-SINGERS OF NUREMBERG
- DIE MEISTERSINGER VON NUERNBERG
- NACHGELASSENE SCHRIFTEN UND DICHTUNGEN
- PARSIFAL
- PROSE WORKS
- RICHARD WAGNER JAHRBUCH
- RICHARD WAGNERS TONDRAMEN
- SKIZZEN UND ENTWUERFE ZUR RING-DICHTUNG
- TANNHAEUSER
- TANNHAEUSER UND DER SAENGERKRIEG AUF WARTBURG
- TRISTAN UND ISOLDE

WAGNER UND NIETZSCHE : IHR KAMPF GEGEN DAS NEUNZEHNTE JAHRHUNDERT / Hildebrandt, Kurt – (Includes index) – In Breslau: F Hirt, 1924 – 1 – us U.W. Library [943]
Wagner, W *see*
- L'INDUSTRIE DES ARANEINA
- NABLYUDENIYA NAD ARANEINA

Wagner, Warren Herbert *see* A LEGISLATIVE HISTORY OF THE MOTOR CARRIER ACT, 1935.
WAGNER'S DIE MEISTERSINGER / Dry, Wakeling – Philadelphia: G W Jacobs, [19–?] – 1r – 1 – us U.W. Library [790]
WAGNERS SAGOR / Baath, Albert Ulrik – Stockholm: P A Norstedt, 1903-1908 – 1r – 1 – us U.W. Library [790]
Wagniere, J L *see* MEMOIRES SUR VOLTAIRE ET SUR SES OUVRAGES PAR LONGCHAMP ET WAGNIERE SES SECRETAIRES
Wahab *see* BEBERAPA HAL TENTANG KESUSILAAN DALAM PRAKTEK KEDOKTERAN
Wahid Hasjim, Abdul *see* THE MINISTRY OF RELIGIOUS AFFAIRS
Wahjo, P *see* EPISTOLA DAN INDJIL HARI MINGGU DAN HARI RAYA
Wahjudi *see* BRIGADE MAUT
Wahl, Georg *see* HANS SACHS UND GOETHE
Wahl, Hans *see*
- TIEFURT
- WIELAND UND NAPOLEON

Wahl, J A et al *see*
- LE CHOIX, LE MONDE, L'EXISTENCE

DIE WAHL PIUS' 5 ZUM PAPSTE / Hilliger, Benno – (Includes bibliographical references) – Leipzig: Gustav Fock, 1891 – 1mf – 9 – 0-8370-8520-9 – 1986-2520 – us A.T.L.A. [240]
Wahle, Julius *see* GOETHES BRIEFE AN FRAU VON STEIN
Wahlenberg, G *see*
- FLORA CARPATORUM PRINCIPALIUM
- FLORA LAPPONICA, EXHIBENS PLANTAS GEOGRAPHICE

Wahlstedt, L J *see*
- MONOGRAFI OEFVER SVERIGES OCH NORGES CHARACEER
- OM CHARACEERNAS KNOPPAR OCH OEFVERINTRING

WAHN UND WIRKLICHKEIT IM DRAMA DER GOETHEZEIT : EINE DICHTUNGSGESCHICHTLICHE STUDIE UEBER DIE FORMEN DER WIRKLICHKEITSERFASSUNG / Kaestner, Erhart – (Includes bibliographical references) – Leipzig: J J Weber, 1929 – 1r – 1 – us U.W. Library [430]
WAHOO NEWSPAPER – Wahoo, NE. -w. Apr 1893; May 1896-Sept 1902; Jan 1908 to date – 1 – us NE Hist [071]
WAHOO WASP – Wahoo, NE. -w. Sept 1875-Nov 1879; Jan 1880-Aug 1885; Nov 1885-Nov 1886; Jun-Dec 1892, scattered issues missing; Oct 1895-Feb 1896, scattered issues missing; Apr 1896-May 1917; Oct 1917-Mar 1949 – 1 – us NE Hist [071]
WAHPETON HIGHLIGHTS – 1953-79. (American Indian Periodicals in the Princeton University Library). 34 fiches – 9 – $120.00 – us UPA [305]
DER WAHRE AMERIKANER – Lancaster. Pa. 1804-1811 – 1,3 – us Readex [071]
DAS WAHRE DEUTSCHLAND – Berlin, 1938-40 – 1 – Inquire at Mikrofilmarchiv for details – gw Misc Inst [072]
DAS WAHRE DEUTSCHLAND – Berlin, Germany.1938-40 – 1 – gw Mikrofilm [072]
DAS WAHRE DEUTSCHLAND / Deutschen Freiheitspartei – London. Jan. 1938-Nov. Dec. 1940 (complete) – 1 – 35.00r – us Hoover Inst Photo [073]
DAS WAHRE DEUTSCHLAND – London, England.1938-40 – 1 – gw Mikrofilm [072]
DIE WAHRE GESCHICHTE VOM WIEDERHERGESTELLTEN KREUZ / Werfel, Franz – Los Angeles: Privatdruck der Pazifischen Presse, c1942 – 1 – us U.W. Library [830]
DAS WAHRE GESICHT DES BERGARBEITERSTREIKS IM NIEDERRHEINISCH-WESTFALISCHEN INDUSTRIEGEBIET JANUAR-FEBRUAR 1905 – Ein Mahnwort fuer Arbeiter und Berger. Dortmund 1905 – 1 – DM30.00 – gw Mikro Press [331]
DER WAHRE GNOSTIKER NACH CLEMENS ALEXANDRINUS (T.U.U. 5-57) / Voelker, W – Berlin, 1952 – 12mf – 9 – ne Slangenburg [240]
DER WAHRE INWENDIGE UND AUSWENDIGE CHRIST, VORGESTELLET IN ZWEYEN THEILEN / Dieterici, Wilhelm – 1739 – 1 – us A.T.L.A. [240]
DER WAHRE JACOB : ILLUSTRIERTE HUMORISTISCH-SATIRISCHE ZEITSCHRIFT MIT EINEM BEIBLATT FUER UNTERHALTUNG UND BELEHRUNG – Stuttgart, 1888-Feb 1933 – 7r – 1 – DM700.00 – gw Mikro Press [073]
DER WAHRE JAKOB – Stuttgart u. Berlin, Germany. Illustrierte Humoristisch-satirische Zeitschrift mit einem Beiblatt fuer Unterhaltung und Belehrung. 1890-Feb 1933 – 1 – gw Mikrofilm [072]
DIE WAHRE SEPARATION = THE TRUE SEPARATION / Bimeler, Joseph Michael – (In German) – Zoar, Tuscarawas, OH – 1r – 1 – us Western Res [240]
DIE WAHREN GRUNDSAETZE ZUM GEBRAUCH DER HARMONIE / Kirnberger, Johann P – 1773 – 9 – us Sibley [780]
DIE WAHREN GRUNDZAETZE ZUM GEBRAUCH DER HARMONIE ALS EIN ZUSATZ ZU DER KUNST DES REINEN SATZES IN DER MUSIK / Kirnberger, Johann P – Berlin. 1773. BP-346 1 – 9 – ne IDC [780]
DIE WAHREN HINDERNISSE UND DIE GRUNDBEDINGUNGEN EINER DURCHGREIFENDEN REFORM DER KATHOLISCHEN KIRCHE ZUNAECHST IN DEUTSCHLAND / Pichler, Aloys – (Includes bibliographical references) – Leipzig: Fues, 1870 – 2mf – 9 – 0-8370-8931-X – 1986-2931 – us A.T.L.A. [240]
DIE WAHREN LEHREN JESU / Thudichum, Friedrich – Leipzig: Max Saengewald, 1901. 1 fiche – 9 – us A.T.L.A. [240]
DIE WAHREN MITTEL, LAENDER UND STAATEN GLUECKLICH, IHRE BEHERRSCHER MAECHTIG UND DIE UNTERTHANEN REICH ZU MACHEN; ODER GROSSES UND VOLLSTAENDIGES OECONOMISCH- UND PHYSICALISCHES LEXIKON (AEL, ABT. 1; 36) – Leipzig. 8 Theile. 1750-57 (mf ed 1997) – 68mf – 9 – DM760.00 – 3-89131-275-X – gw Fischer [943]
DIE WAHRHEIT – Berlin, DE. 1977-Nov 1989 – 39r – 1 – gw Mikrofilm [072]
DIE WAHRHEIT – (Cont by: Neue Niedersaechsische Volksstimme, feb 1, 1956) – Hannover. nov 12, 1949-aug 17, 1956 – 13r – 1 – gw Mikrofilm [072]
DIE WAHRHEIT – (Cont by: NZ – Neue Zeitung, dec 1-7 1989) – Berlin, 1955-dec 7 1989 – 1 – Inquire at Mikrofilmarchiv for details – gw Misc Inst [072]
DIE WAHRHEIT – (St. Louis). 1871 – 1 – us A.J.P.C. [073]
DIE WAHRHEIT – Unabhaengige Zeitschrift fuer juedische Interessen. Vienna. v1-54. 1885-1938. Lacking: 1885-1903. B388 (Leo Baeck Institute. German-Jewish Periodicals, Pt 1) – 3r – 1 – $205.00 – us UPA [270]
DIE WAHRHEIT – Wochenschrift fuer Leben und Lehre im Judenthum. Prague. v1-2. 1871-72. Complete. B387 (Leo Baeck Institute. German-Jewish Periodicals, Pt 2) – 1r – 1 – $75.00 – us UPA [270]
DIE WAHRHEIT DES CHRISTENTHUMS = EVIDENCES OF CHRISTIANITY : AUS DER GESCHICHTLICHEN BEDEUTUNG UND WIRKUNG DESSELBEN ERWIESEN / McIlvaine, Charles Pettit – Philadelphia: Leighton Publications Behoerde, 1874 – 1mf – 9 – 0-8370-7486-X – 1986-1486 – us A.T.L.A. [230]
DIE WAHRHEIT UBER ANNA BLUME; KRITIK DER KUNST, KRITIK DER KRITIK; KRITIK DER ZEIT / Spengemann, Christof – Hannover: Zweemann, 1920 – 1 – us U.W. Library [830]
DIE WAHRHEIT UEBER SPANIEN / Goebbels, Joseph – Berlin, 1937. Fiche W925. (Blodgett Collection of Spanish Civil War Pamphlets) – 9 – us H.U. College Libr [946]
WAHRHEIT UND DICHTUNG IN UNSERER RELIGION / Lobstein, Paul – Tuebingen: J.C.B. Mohr, 1905. 1 fiche – 9 – us A.T.L.A. [240]
DER WAHRHEITSFREUND – v1-33. 1915-47 (gaps) – 20r – 1 – ATLA 1994-S029 – us A.T.L.A. [073]
DER WAHRHEITSZEUGA – German Baptist. 1879-1941 – 1 – 1089.09 – us Baptist [240]
Wahrmund, Ludwig *see* KATHOLISCHE WELTANSCHAUUNG UND FREIE WISSENSCHAFT
WAI CHIAO KUNG PAO / China – Diplomatic Gazette. Peking Jul 1921-Apr 1928. nos 1-82 – 13r – 1 – $220.00 – us Chinese Res [950]
WAI CHIAO KUNG PAO / China. Ministry of Foreign Affairs – Peking. July 1, 1921-Apr. 30, 1928. (4715.5 2084) – 1 – 35.00r – us Hoover Inst Photo [324]
WAI CHIAO P'ING LUN – Nanking. (Diplomatic Review). June 1932-July 1937 (4820.1 2000) – 1 – 35.00r – us Hoover Inst Photo [950]
WAI CHIAO PU KUNG PAO / China. Ministry of Foreign Affairs – Gazette.Nanking, Loyang and Chunking. v.1-v.15, n.12. May 1928-Feb 1943. Missing: v.10, n.3-6; v.11, n.7-12; v.13, n.5-12; v.14, n.1-8; v.15, n.1-6. 20 reels – 1 – 360.80 – us Chinese Res [324]
WAI CHIAO PU KUNG PAO – (Some issues were not available for filming) – Nanking. 1955-56. – 1 – D2657 – us UMI [073]
Waibel, Leo *see* BEITRAEGE ZUR LANDESKUNDE VON SUEDWESTAFRIKA
WAIBLINGER : EIN TRAUERSPIEL UNSERER ZEIT IN FUENF AUFZUEGEN / Kirchbach, Wolfgang – 2. verb. Aufl. Muenchen: O Heinrichs, 1887 – 1r – 1 – us U.W. Library [820]
WAI-CHIAO P'ING-LUN – Review of Foreign Affairs. Nanking, 1932-37. 9v. -m. BCH-360/1 – 9 – ne IDC [950]
WAI-CHIAO PU CH'ING-PAO – Newsletter of the Ministry of Foreign Affairs. 1938-1939 (1 vol.). (2991.52 2009) – 1 – 35.00r – us Hoover Inst Photo [950]
WAI-CHIAO PU KUNG PAO – Nanking. (Ministry of Foreign Affairs Gazette). May 1928-June 1935. (4715.5 2084.1) – 1 – 35.00r – us Hoover Inst Photo [950]

WAI-CHIAO VEN-CHIU – Foreign Affairs Research. Chungking, 1939-42. v1-4. -m, -bi-m. Lacking: 1939, v1 (1,6); 1940, v2 (5,6); 1940, v3 (2-6); 1942, v4 (1-4). BCH-361/1 – 9 – ne IDC [950]
WAI-CHIAO YUEH PAO – Peiping. (Foreign Affairs Monthly). July 30, 1932-July 1937. (4820.1 2074) – 1 – $35.00r – us Hoover Inst Photo [950]
WAI-CHIAO YUEH-PAO – Foreign Affairs.Peiping, 1932-37. 11v. BCH-362/2 – 8 – ne IDC [950]
WAI-CHIAO-KUNG-PAO = OFFICIAL GAZETTE OF THE FOREIGN AFFAIRS, CHINA – In Chinese. No1-82, 1921-1928. Lacks: No. 14 – 14r – 1 – Y120,000.00 – ja Yushodo [327]
A WAIF'S PROGRESS / Broughton, Rhoda – British Fiction Archive: Unit 4 – 9 – uk Bell [830]
Waigandt, Alex *see* A COMPARATIVE ANALYSIS OF THE LEADERSHIP STYLES OF HEAD FOOTBALL COACHES FROM TADITIONALLY BLACK AND WHITE UNIVERSITIES AND COLLEGES
Wailes, G H *see*
– THE BRITISH FRESHWATER RHIZOPODA AND HELIOZA
– THE BRITISH FRESHWATER RHIZOPODA AND HELIOZOA
Wailly, N F *see* DICTIONNAIRE DES RIMES DE RICHELET. AN 7
WAIMATE TIMES – New Zealand. -w. 22 Mar 1899-18 Mar 1922. (Imperfect). (25 reels) – 1 – uk British Libr Newspaper [072]
Wainewright, Thomas Griffiths *see* ESSAYS AND CRITICISMS
Wainio, E A *see*
– ETUDE SUR LA CLASSIFICATION NATURELLE ET LA MORPHOLOGIE DES LICHENS DU BRESIL
– LICHENES INSULARUM PHILIPPINARUM 2
– MONOGRAPHIA CLADONIARUM UNIVERSALIS
– REVISIO LICHENUM HOFFMANNIANORUM
– REVISIO LICHENUM IN HERBARIO LINNAEI OSSERVATORUM
Wainright, G A *see* BALABISH (MEES VOL 37)
WAIRARAPA TIMES-AGE – Masterton, New Zealand. -d. 7 May 1962-Aug 1972. 74 reels – 1 – uk British Libr Newspaper [072]
WAIROA BELL – Aratapu. New Zealand. -w. 11 Nov-16 Dec 1892, 24 Mar-1 Sep 1893. (Imperfect). (19 ft) – 1 – uk British Libr Newspaper [072]
Wais, Kurt *see* DAS VATER-SOHN-MOTIV IN DER DICHTUNG
Wait, Frederick Scott *see* A TREATISE ON FRAUDULENT CONVEYANCES AND CREDITORS' BILLS.
Wait, William *see*
– A TREATISE UPON SOME OF THE GENERAL PRINCIPLES OF THE LAW.
– WAIT'S TABLE OF NEW YORK CASES
Waite, Terence M *see* THE EFFECTS OF A HEALTH RELATED PHYSICAL FITNESS CURRICULUM ON SELECTED FITNESS VARIABLES
WAITEMATA POST – (Waitemata News). Auckland. New Zealand. -w. 19 May 1910-5 Mar 1917. (Imperfect). (3 reels) – 1 – uk British Libr Newspaper [072]
WAIT'S TABLE OF NEW YORK CASES : AFFIRMED, REVERSED OR CITED...IN ALL NEW YORK COURTS FROM 1794-1880 / Wait, William – (v2 by R E Andrews) – Albany: Gould & Son, 1836; 1880 (all publ) – 14mf – 9 – $21.00 – LLMC 79-524 – us L.L.M.C. [340]
Waitz, G et al *see* MONUMENTA GERMANIAE HISTORICA 3 (MGH 3: 1 BD)
Waitz, Hans *see*
– DIE PSEUDOKLEMENTINEN
– DIE PSEUDOKLEMENTINEN HOMILIEN UND REKOGNITIONEN
– DAS PSEUDOTERTULLIANISCHE GEDICHT ADVERSUS MARCIONEM
Waizenegger, Joachim *see* KRANKENPFLEGE IM KRANKENHAUS
WAJ W. FETLERS IR BAPTISTS? = IS W. FETLER A BAPTIST? / Lauberts, Peter – Riga: Union of Latvian Baptist Churches, 1926. Publ. No. 6299 d. One of five items on a reel – 1 – us Baptist [240]
Wajong, J *see*
– ORGANISASI DAN ADMINISTRASI; PENUNTUN UNTUK MEMPELADJARI ORANISASI DALAM DINAS ADMINISTRASI SERTA TANGGUNGDJAWAB DAN KEWADJIBAN PEMIMPIN
– PERIMBANGAN KEUANGAN ANTARA NEGARA DAN DAERAH2
Wajs, C *see* ESSAI DE MISE EN RELATION DU SYSTEME DE PARENTE ET DE LA TENURE FONCIERE DANS LE VILLAGE DE ST-CYR-SUR-MORIN (SEINE ET MARNE)
Wake (Archbishop) *see* CORRESPONDENCE, 1697-1725
WAKE FOREST BAPTIST CHURCH. WAKE FOREST, NORTH CAROLINA : CHURCH RECORDS – 1835-1939 – 1 – 65.34 – us Baptist [240]
WAKE FOREST LAW REVIEW – v1-29. 1965-94 – 1,5,6 – $630.00 – us Hein [073]
WAKE UNION BAPTIST CHURCH. WAKE FOREST, NORTH CAROLINA : CHURCH RECORDS – 1789-1922 – 1 – 22.23 – us Baptist [240]
WAKE UP! MONTREAL! : COMMERCIALIZED VICE AND ITS CONTRIBUTORIES / Hart, E I – [Montreal]: the Witness press, 1919. SEM105P1494 – 1mf – 9 – Can$2.25 – cn Bibl Nat [306]
WAKEFIELD ADVERTISER AND GAZETTE – England. 4 Sep 1906-1 Sep 1925.-w. 6mqn reels – 1 – uk British Libr Newspaper [072]
Wakefield, Amor William *see* CIVIL WAR LETTERS
WAKEFIELD AND DEWSBURY JOURNAL – England. -w. 4 Oct 1833-13 June 1834. 24 ft – 1 – uk British Libr Newspaper [072]
WAKEFIELD AND WEST RIDING EXAMINER. (WAKEFIELD JOURNAL AND EXAMINER) – England. Jan 1849-Dec 1852. -w. 3 reels – 1 – uk British Libr Newspaper [072]
WAKEFIELD EXPRESS – Yorkshire. 1852 to date – 1 – uk Microform Academic [072]
WAKEFIELD FREE PRESS, AND WEST RIDING ADVERTISER – England. 24 Nov 1860-15 Feb 1902 (missing 1892).-w. 31mqn reels – 1 – uk British Libr Newspaper [072]
WAKEFIELD JOURNAL – Wakefield, NE. -w. Jan-Feb 1896; Apr 1896-Mar 1898; Jul 1899-Jan 1900 – 1 – us NE Hist [071]
The Wakefield Opera House. Yorkshire *see* TWO LETTER BOOKS
Wakefield, Priscilla Bell *see*
– THE TRAVELLER IN AFRICA: CONTAINING SOME ACCOUNT OF THE ANTIQUITIES, NATURAL CURIOSITIES, AND INHABITANTS OF SUCH PARTS OF THAT CONTINENT AND ITS ISLANDS...EXPLORED BY EUROPEANS
– THE TRAVELLER IN ASIA:...
WAKEFIELD REPUBLICAN – Wakefield, NE. -w. Dec 1892; Oct 1895-May 1898; Feb 1899-May 1901; Mar-Oct 1902, scattered issues missing; Jan 1903-Aug 1906; Oct 1906-Mar 1907; Jan 1908 to date – 1 – us NE Hist [071]
Wakefield. Yorkshire *see* POLL BOOK OF THE BOROUGH ELECTION 1868
Wakeham, W *see* REPORT OF THE EXPEDITION TO HUDSON BAY AND CUMBERLAND GULF IN THE STEAMSHIP 'DIANA.' BN 443/2. 1898
Wakeley, Arthur C *see* OMAHA: THE GATE CITY AND DOUGLAS COUNTY
Wakeley, Joseph Beaumont *see* ANECDOTES OF THE WESLEYS: ILLUSTRATIVE OF THEIR CHARACTER AND PERSONAL HISTORY
Wakeman, Henry Offley *see* THE CHURCH AND THE PURITANS, 1570-1660
DIE WAKETTING – Johannesburg: Ossewabrandwag. n1-5 [n.d.] – us Res Libr [072]
LE "WAKF" DE FAMILLE; ETUDE CRITIQUE / Saad, Ahmed Zaki – Paris, 1928. 128p. LL-12034 – 1 – us L of C Photodup [340]
WAKTAREN – Stockholm, Sweden. 1853-88 – 20r – 1 – sw Kungliga [072]
WAKULLA COUNTY NEWS – Crawfordville. Fl. -w. 1955- – 1 – us P.K. Yonge [071]
Wal, H van der *see* WATER FOR FRESHWATER FISH CULTURE
Walbe, Ute *see* PHRASEOLOGISCHE EINHEITEN IN PUBLIZISTISCHEN TEXTEN DES ENGLISCHEN UND RUSSISCHEN
Walbridge, Arthur Dewey *see* STATE OF NEW YORK. FOURTH JUDICIAL DEPARTMENT. ATTORNEYS' DIRECTORY FOR 1872
WALBRIDGE NEWS – Walbridge, Ohio. 1936-39 – 1r – 1 – $32.50r – us Archival [071]
Walch, J G *see* NEUER BUECHER-SAAL DER GELEHRTEN WELT ODER AUSFUEHRLICHE NACHRICHTEN VON ALLERHAND NEUEN BUECHERN UND ANDERN ZUR HEUTIGEN HISTORIE DER GELEHRSAMKEIT GEHOERIGEN SACHEN
WALCHA NEWS – Oct 8 1904-Dec 28 1907 – 1 – at Pascoe [072]
WALCHA WITNESS – Jan 1 1898-Dec 29 1906 – 1 – at Pascoe [072]
Walckenaer, C A *see*
– HISTOIRE NATURELLE DES ARANEIDES
– RECHERCHES GEOGRAPHIQUES SUR L'INTERIEUR DE L'AFRIQUE SEPTENTRIONALE
– TABLEAU DES ARANEIDES
Walcker, Karl *see* ZUR VERSOEHNUNG DES BESITZES UND DER ARBEIT
DER WALD : ROMAN / Wiechert, Ernst Emil – Berlin: G Grote, 1936 – 1r – 1 – us U.W. Library [830]
DER WALD IN DER DEUTSCHEN DICHTUNG / Baumgart, Wolfgang – Berlin: W de Gruyter & Co, 1936 – 1 – us U.W. Library [430]
DER WALD UND SEINE KINDER : EINE AUSWAHL / Linke, Johannes – Leipzig: L Staackmann, 1937 – 1r – 1 – us U.W. Library [810]
DIE WALDBAUERN : GESCHICHTEN AUS DER BERGHEIMAT / Rosegger, Peter – Berlin: Paul Franke, [193-?] – 1 – us U.W. Library [830]
Waldberg, Maximilian R von *see*
– STUDIEN ZU LESSINGS STIL IN DER HAMBURGISCHEN DRAMATURGIE
– DER WALDBRUDER
Waldboro, Maine.South Waldboro Baptist Church *see* RECORDS
DER WALDBRUDER : EIN PENDANT ZU WERTHERS LEIDEN / Lenz, Jakob Michael Reinhold; ed by Waldberg, Maximilian R von – Berlin: W H Kuehl, 1882 – 1r – 1 – us U.W. Library [820]
WALDECKISCHE LANDESZEITUNG – Korbach, West Germany. 1976$ – 1 – gw Mikrofilm [072]
Waldeck-Rousseau, Rene *see* LE PERE
DER WALDECK'SCHE VOLKSBOTE – Arolsen, may 2 1848-sep 25 1850 – 1r – 1 – Dist. gw Mikrofilm – gw Misc Inst [943]
WALDECKSCHER ANZEIGER – Arolsen, 1932-deb 28 1934 – 3r – 1 – Dist. gw Mikrofilm – gw Misc Inst [943]
WALDECKSCHER ANZEIGER – (Incl suppl) – Brilon, oct 13 1851-feb 28 1934 – 27r – 1 – Inquire at Mikrofilmarchiv for details – gw Misc Inst [943]
Walden, Paul *see* GOETHE UND DIE NATURWISSENSCHAFTEN
Walden, Treadwell *see* THE GREAT MEANING OF METANOIA
DIE WALDENSER IM MITTELALTER : ZWEI HISTORISCHE UNTERSUCHUNGEN / Dieckhoff, A W – Goettingen: Vandenhoeck und Ruprecht, 1851 – 1mf – us A.T.L.A. [940]
DIE WALDENSER UND DIE DEUTSCHEN BIBELUEBERSETZUNGEN / Keller, Ludwig – Leipzig: S. Hirzel, 1886. 1 fiche – 9 – us A.T.L.A. [240]
DIE WALDENSER UND DIE VORLUTHERISCHE DEUTSCHE BIBELUEBERSETZUNG : EINE KRITIK DER NEUESTEN HYPOTHESE / Jostes, Franz – (Includes bibliographical references) – Munster I/W: Heinrich Schoningh, 1885 – 1mf – 9 – 0-8370-3806-5 – 1985-1806 – us A.T.L.A. [220]
WALDENSES, OR PROTESTANT VALLEYS OF PIEDMONT AND DAUPHINY / Beattie, William – London: George Virtue, 1836 – 1 reel – 1 – $20.40 – us Baptist [240]
DER WALDENSISCHE URSPRUNG DES CODEX TEPLENSIS UND DER VORLUTHERISCHEN DEUTSCHEN BIBELDRUCKE : GEGEN DIE ANGRIFFE VON FRANZ JOSTES / Haupt, Herman – (Includes bibliographical references & appendixes) – Wuerzburg: Stahel, 1886 – 1mf – 9 – 0-8370-3529-5 – 1985-1529 – us A.T.L.A. [220]
Walder, J *see* THE AX LAID TO THE ROOT
WALDHEIMAT : ERZAEHLUNGEN AUS DER JUGENDZEIT / Rosegger, Peter – Leipzig: L Staackmann, [1919] – 1 – us U.W. Library [430]
WALDIES LITERARY OMNIBUS – Philadelphia, PA., 1837 – 13 – $25.00r – us I.M.R. [071]
WALDLEUTE : SCHAUSPIEL IN VIER AKTEN / Hauptmann, Carl – Stuttgart: J G Cotta, 1896 – 1r – 1 – us U.W. Library [820]
Waldman, Marilyn R *see* ISLAM-FICHE
Waldmann, Peter *see* EL PERONISMO 1943-1955
Waldmann, S *see* LES ESQUIMAUX DU NORD DU LABRADOR
WALDO / Bagwell, N D – Toronto: W. Briggs, Montreal: C. Coates; Halifax: S. Huestis, 1890. 02376. (Pre-1900 Canadiana) – 9 – cn C.I.H.M. [971]
WALDO AND THE WALDENSIANS BEFORE THE REFORMATION / Comba, Emilio – New York: R. Carter: Dodd, Mead, 1880 – 1mf – us A.T.L.A. [240]
Waldo, Dwight *see* THE STUDY OF PUBLIC ADMINISTRATION
WALDPORT RECORD – Waldport, OR. -w. 31 Mar 1948-30 Nov 1950. 2 rolls – 1 – us U.O. Library [071]
WALDPORT TRIBUNE – Waldport, OR. -w. 5 Jun 1926-27 Nov 1941. 3 rolls – 1 – us U.O. Library [071]
WALDPORT WATCHMAN – Waldport, OR. -w. 15 Apr 1915-27 Sept 1917. 1 roll – 1 – us U.O. Library [071]
WALDSHUTER KREISZEITUNG : BA DES SUEDKURIER – Waldshut-Konstanz, Germany. 1 Sept 1978- – ca 9r per yr – 1 – gw Mikrofilm [072]
Waldstein, F de et al *see* DESCRIPTIONES ET ICONES PLANTARUM RARIORUM HUNGARIAE
Waldstein, Louis *see* THE SUBCONSCIOUS SELF AND ITS RELATION TO EDUCATION AND HEALTH
WALDVEILCHEN / Joerger, M J – Baltimore: J und C Kreuzer, 1872 – 1r – 1 – us U.W. Library [810]
WALES : AN INVENTORY OF THE HISTORICAL MONUMENTS / Great Britain. Royal Commissions on Ancient and Historical Monuments and Constructions – (Anglesey 1937 7mf £44; Caernarvonshire 15mf £126; Carmarthen 1917 5mf £42; Denbigh 1914 4mf £34; Flint 1912 3mf £25; Merioneth 1921 4mf £34; Montgomery 1911 3mf £25; Pembroke 1925 8mf £67; Radnor 1913 3mf £25) – 52mf – 9 – uk Chadwyck [930]
WALES, 1822 : BRITISH ISLES CENSUS DIRECTORIES PROJECT, WALES – (In prep) – at Vine [941]
WALES BAPTIST CHURCH (FORMERLY: SOUTH BRIMFIELD). WALES, MASSACHUSETTS : CHURCH RECORDS – Original MS. 1825-44; Copy MS 1736-1954 – 1 – 15.57 – us Baptist [240]
Wales. National Library *see* AMERICAN MATERIAL IN THE NATIONAL LIBRARY OF WALES
Walesrode, Ludwig Reinhold *see* UNTERTHAENIGE REDEN
Waley, Muhammad Isa *see* PHOTOGRAPH ALBUMS OF SULTAN 'ABDULHAMID 2 IN THE BRITISH LIBRARY
Walford, William *see* THE MANNER OF PRAYER
WALFORD'S ANTIQUARIAN: A MAGAZINE AND BIBLIOGRAPHICAL REVIEW *see* WALFORD'S ANTIQUARIAN MAGAZINE & BIBLIOGRAPHICAL REVIEW
WALFORD'S ANTIQUARIAN MAGAZINE & BIBLIOGRAPHICAL REVIEW – (Former titles: Antiquarian magazine & Bibliographer jan 1882-jun 1885. Walford's Antiquarian: a Magazine and Bibliographical Review jul 1885-dec 1886) – London. v1-12. jan 1882-nov 1887 – 1 – D2964 – us UMI [010]
WALGETT NEWS – Jan 3-Dec 24 1885; Jan 1 1898-May 4 1901 – 1 – at Pascoe [072]
WALHALLA – Philadelphia. v1-4. jul 1845-jun 1847 – 1 – D5355 – us UMI [073]
WALHALLA CHRONICLE – 1871-1881 – 1 reel – 1 – at Corangamite [980]
Walicki, A *see* BLEDY NASZE
Waline, P *see* LES SYNDICATS AUX ETATS-UNIS
THE WALK, CONVERSATION, AND CHARACTER OF JESUS CHRIST OUR LORD / Whyte, Alexander – New York: Fleming H Revell, 1905 – 1mf – 9 – 0-8370-9436-4 – 1986-3436 – us A.T.L.A. [240]
WALKA KLAS = LA LUTTE DES CLASSES / Miedzynarodowej Socyjalno-Rewolucyjnej Partyi – Geneve, mai 1884-juin 1887 – 1 – fr A.C.R.P.P. [073]
Walkenshaw, Lewis C *see* ANNALS OF SOUTHWESTERN PENNSYLVANIA
Walker, A *see* A COLLECTION OF LESSONS AND SONGS ADAPTED TO THE CELESTINA
Walker, Ben *see* FRESNO COUNTY "BLUE BOOK"
Walker, Charles M *see* HISTORY OF ATHENS COUNTY
Walker, Cornelius *see* OUTLINES OF CHRISTIAN THEOLOGY
Walker, Craven H *see* AN ELEMENTARY AND PRACTICAL GRAMMAR OF THE GALLA OR OROMO LANGUAGE

Walker, George Leon *see*
- HISTORY OF THE FIRST CHURCH IN HARTFORD, 1633-1883
- SOME ASPECTS OF THE RELIGIOUS LIFE OF NEW ENGLAND
- THOMAS HOOKER

Walker, J A *see* THE EFFECT OF BROMELAIN ON RECOVERY FROM EXERCISE-INDUCED SKELETAL MUSCLE INJURY

Walker, John *see*
- A CRITICAL PRONOUNCING DICTIONARY AND EXPOSITOR OF THE ENGLISH LANGUAGE
- ELEMENTS OF ELOCUTION
- THE MELODY OF SPEAKING DELINEATED; OR, ELOCUTION TAUGHT LIKE MUSIC
- A RHETORICAL GRAMMAR

Walker, John Q. *see* JOURNAL OF CHROMATOGRAPHIC SCIENCE

WALKER LAKE BULLETIN – Hawthorne, NV. 1883-1905; 1911-12; 1914-16; 1918-19; 1922; Jan-Oct 1924 – 33r – 1 – $1,650.00 – U04585 – us Library Micro [071]

Walker, Norman Lockhart *see*
- CHAPTERS FROM THE HISTORY OF THE FREE CHURCH OF SCOTLAND
- LIFE IN THE SPIRIT
- OUR CHURCH HERITAGE, OR, THE SCOTTISH CHURCHES VIEWED IN THE LIGHT OF THEIR HISTORY
- SCOTTISH CHURCH HISTORY
- THOMAS CHALMERS
- WILLIAM GARDEN BLAIKIE

Walker, Obadiah *see* OF EDUCATION ESPECIALLY OF YOUNG GENTLEMEN

Walker, Patrick *see* SIX SAINTS OF THE CONVENANT

Walker, Robert H *see* LETTERS AND LETTER BOOKS, 1887-1903

Walker, Sheila *see* A SURVEY OF CORPORATE FITNESS PROGRAMS

Walker, Thomas *see*
- BEBBLY
- PAPERS

Walker, Timothy *see* INTRODUCTION TO AMERICAN LAW...11TH ED

Walker, William *see*
- JOURNAL
- JOURNALS
- THE LIFE AND TIMES OF THE REV. JOHN SKINNER
- THE LIFE OF THE RIGHT REVEREND ALEXANDER JOLLY, D.D.
- MUSIC BOOK MADE BY WILLIAM WALKER FOR MISS ELIZABETH R. ADAMS
- SOME IMPROVEMENTS TO THE ART OF TEACHING
- THE SOUTHERN HARMONY AND MUSICAL COMPANION
- A TREATISE OF ENGLISH PARTICLES

Walker, William Lowe *see*
- THE CROSS AND THE KINGDOM
- THE GOSPEL OF RECONCILIATION, OR, AT-ONE-MENT
- THE SPIRIT AND THE INCARNATION
- WHAT ABOUT THE NEW THEOLOGY?

Walker, William Slee *see* ERRORS IN CRIMINAL PROCEEDINGS IN ALL STATES AND TERRITORIES AND FEDERAL COURTS WHERE JUDGMENTS HAVE BEEN AFFIRMED.

Walker, Williston *see*
- THE CREEDS AND PLATFORMS OF CONGREGATIONALISM
- GREAT MEN OF THE CHRISTIAN CHURCH
- A HISTORY OF THE CONGREGATIONAL CHURCHES IN THE UNITED STATES
- JOHN CALVIN
- PROFESSOR GEORGE BARKER STEVENS, D.D., LL.D.
- THE REFORMATION
- THE VALIDITY OF CONGREGATIONAL ORDINATION

Walker-Arnott, G A *see*
- THE BOTANY OF CAPTAIN BEECHEY'S VOYAGE
- THE BRITISH FLORA COMPRISING THE PHAENOGAMOUS OR FLOWERING PLANTS AND THE FERNS
- DISPOSITION METHODIQUE DES ESPECES DE MOUSSES
- PRODROMUS FLORAE PENINSULAE INDIAE ORIENTALIS
- PUGILLUS PLANTARUM INDIAE ORIENTALIS
- TENTAMEN METHODI MUSCORUM

WALKER'S HIBERNIAN MAGAZINE : OR, COMPENDIUM OF ENTERTAINING KNOWLEDGE – (Former title: Hibernian Magazine, or, Compendium of Entertaining Knowledge jan 1771-apr 1785) – Dublin. v1-8 1771-78. jan 1779-dec 1811 – 1 – D4351 – us UMI [941]

WALKER'S REPORTS / Pennsylvania. Superior Court – (A Pre-NRS title) – v1-4. 1855-85 (all publ) – 8mf – 9 – $36.00 – LLMC 84-203 – us L.L.M.C. [340]

WALKERTON WEEKLY – Walkerton, Se1989-1992 – 4r – 1 – cn Preston [971]

WALKING – (Cont: Walking Magazine) – Boston. 1994* 1; 1995-97+ 1,5,9 – 1,5,9 – D19364.01 – us UMI [790]

WALKING *see* WALKING MAGAZINE

WALKING MAGAZINE – (Cont by: Walking) – Boston. 1986-94* – 1 – D19364 – us UMI [790]

WALKING MAGAZINE *see* WALKING

WALKING TEACHER FUNCTIONAL LITERACY PROGRAM FOR HILL TRIBE GROUPS 1976-1981 / Thailand. Ministry of Education – 1976 – 1mf – 9 – DE-296/1 – ne IDC [370]

WALKING WITH GOD : THE LIFE HID WITH CHRIST / Prime, Samuel Irenaeus – New York: A.D.F. Randolph, c1872 – 1mf – us A.T.L.A. [240]

Walkley, Arthur Bingham *see*
- FRAMES OF MIND
- PLAYHOUSE IMPRESSIONS

WALKS IN A FOREST : AND OTHER POEMS. TO WHICH ARE ADDED, SOME POEMS NOT BEFORE PUBLISHED / Gisborne, Thomas – London: Printed for T. Cadell and W. Davies, 8th ed 1813 – 1 roll – 1 – 1-55879-640-1 – uk Libr Preservation [810]

Wall *see* HISTORY OF MIDDLESEX COUNTY 1664-1920

Wall, A J *see* INDIAN SNAKE POISONS, THEIR NATURE AND EFFECTS

WALL DRAWINGS AND MONUMENTS OF EL KAB / Tylor, J J – London, 1896. BNE-395 1 – 9 – ne IDC [740]

Wall, G *see* A CATALOGUE OF THE FERNS INDIGENOUS TO CEYLON

Wall, Otto Augustus *see* THE PRESCRIPTION: THERAPEUTICALLY, PHARMACEUTICALLY, GRAMMATICALLY AND HISTORICALLY CONSIDERED

WALL STREET AND TECHNOLOGY – (Cont: Wall Street Computer Review) – New York. v9 oct 1991-aug 1992*. v10-11 sep 1992-jun 1994. v12 jul-dec 1994*. v13-15 jan 1995-jan 1998+ 1,9; v9-12 oct 1991-dec 1994*. v13-15 jan 1995-jan 1998 5 – 1,5,9 – D15851.01 – us UMI [000]

WALL STREET AND U.S. BUSINESS NEWS – 1973- – 1,5,6,9 – us UMI [073]

WALL STREET COMPUTER REVIEW – (Cont by: Wall street & Technology) – New York. v1-8. jul 1983-aug 1991* 1; v9. sep 1991-jan 1992* 1,5,9 – 1,5,9 – D15851 – us UMI [000]

WALL STREET COMPUTER REVIEW *see* WALL STREET AND TECHNOLOGY

THE WALL STREET JOURNAL – Los Angeles. Calif. Pacific ed. 1937- – 1 – us UMI [071]

WALL STREET JOURNAL – Chicago.IL. 1957-69. Midwest ed – 1 – us UMI [071]

WALL STREET JOURNAL : EASTERN EDITION – (Silver format. This newspaper is indexed, available in hard copy on a monthly basis) – New York. jul 1889-1891. jul 1892-1997 1; 1979-96+ 9 – 1,9 – D60541 – us UMI [071]

WALL STREET JOURNAL : EASTERN EDITION – (Vesicular format. This newspaper is indexed, available in hard copy on a monthly basis) – New York. jul 1889-1891. jul 1892-1997 1; 1979-97 9 – 1,9 – D60621 – us UMI [071]

WALL STREET JOURNAL : EUROPE – Brussels. 1983-97 – 1 – D60627 – us UMI [071]

WALL STREET JOURNAL : MIDWEST EDITION – Naperville. jul 1951-1997 – 1 – D60640 – us UMI [071]

WALL STREET JOURNAL : SOUTHWEST EDITION – Dallas. may 1948-1997 – 1 – D60641 – us UMI [071]

WALL STREET JOURNAL : WESTERN EDITION – Los Angeles. 1937-96+ – 1 – D60642 – us UMI [071]

WALL STREET JOURNAL CLIPPING FILE : CORPORATE NEWS – New York. 1968-87 – 9 – D60626 – us UMI [071]

WALL STREET JOURNAL CLIPPING FILE : GENERAL NEWS – New York. 1968-87 – 9 – D60625 – us UMI [071]

WALL STREET JOURNAL CLIPPING FILE : STOCK, BOND & COMMODITY QUOTATIONS – New York. oct 1968-1996+ – 9 – D60624 – us UMI [071]

WALL STREET JOURNAL INDEX – (Index to the Eastern Edition. Available in 12 sb monthly iss and an annual hb cumulation. Beginning with 1981, the annual vol incl the index to: Barron's) – New York. New York. 1955-96+ – 1 – D60639 – us UMI [071]

WALL STREET LETTER – New York. v1-26. 1969-94* 1,5; v27-29. 1995-97+ 1,5,9 – 1,5,9 – D17775 – us UMI [073]

WALL STREET REVIEW OF BOOKS – v1-1973- 1; v6- 5,6,9 – us UMI [330]

WALL STREET & TECHNOLOGY *see* WALL STREET COMPUTER REVIEW

WALL STREET TRANSCRIPT – (Cum indexes for v1-6 available) – New York. v1-125 jun 1963-sep 1994. v126 oct-dec 1994*. v127-138 1995-97+ – 1 – D1746 – us UMI [073]

Wall, W D *see*
- CONSTRUCTIVE EDUCATION FOR ADOLESCENTS
- CONSTRUCTIVE EDUCATION FOR SPECIAL GROUPS

WALLA WALLA STATESMAN – Walla Walla, WA. And pred. – w. 1861-69, 1872-73 – 1 – 72.00 – us Oregon Hist [071]

Wallace *see* EARLY NEW ZEALAND

Wallace, Alexander *see* THE CLOUDS OF THE BIBLE

Wallace, Alfred Russel *see*
- ON MIRACLES AND MODERN SPIRITUALISM: THREE ESSAYS
- LA SELECTION NATURELLE, ESSAIS

Wallace, Charles J *see* THE ANALOGY OF EXISTENCES AND CHRISTIANITY

THE WALLACE COLLECTION / London Gallery – (Over 4,000 reproductions, including many details, fully-captioned. With printed index of artists) – 74mf – 9 – $400.00 – 0-907006-28-0 – uk Mindata [700]

Wallace, David A *see* THE THEOLOGY OF NEW ENGLAND

Wallace, David Duncan *see*
- COLLECTION
- THE LONG LABRADOR TRAIL
- PAPERS OF DAVID DUNCAN WALLACE
- SCRIPT AND PHOTOS
- UNPUBLISHED HISTORY

Wallace, George S *see* ANNALS AND FAMILIES OF CABELL COUNTY

Wallace, H B *see* SMITH'S LEADING CASES

Wallace, Henry *see* REPRESENTATIVE RESPONSIBILITY:...THE DIVINE PROCEDURE IN PROVIDENCE AND REDEMPTION

Wallace, Henry Agard *see*
- HENRY A. WALLACE PAPERS
- THE PAPERS OF HENRY A. WALLACE AS VICE-PRESIDENT
- THE PRICE OF VISION

WALLACE HERALD – Wallace, NE. -w. Jan-Nov 1892, scattered issues missing; Jan-Jul 1893, scattered issues missing; Oct-Dec 1895 – 1 – us NE Hist [071]

Wallace, J B *see* WALLACE SENIOR'S REPORTS OF CASES IN THE THIRD CIRCUIT

Wallace, J W *see* WALLACE JUNIOR'S REPORTS OF CASES IN THE THIRD CIRCUIT, 1842-1862

Wallace, Janet P *see* THE POST-EXERCISE BLOOD PRESSURE RESPONSE TO ACUTE EXERCISE IN BORDERLINE HYPERTENSIVE WOMEN

Wallace, Janet P, *see* GLYCOSYLATED HEMOGLOBIN AND THE OXYGEN KINETICS IN INDIVIDUALS WITH TYPE 2 DIABETES

Wallace, Joseph *see* PAST AND PRESENT OF THE CITY OF SPRINGFIELD AND COUNTY OF SANGAMON

WALLACE JUNIOR'S REPORTS OF CASES IN THE THIRD CIRCUIT, 1842-1862 / Wallace, J W – Philadelphia: Walker/T & J W Johnson. v1-3. 1849-71 (all publ) – 18mf – 9 – $27.00 – LLMC 81-474 – us L.L.M.C. [340]

Wallace, Neil *see* A SHRED OF EVIDENCE ON PUBLIC ACCEPTANCE OF PRIVATELY ISSUED CURRENCY

Wallace, O C S *see* WHAT BAPTISTS BELIEVE; THE NEW HAMPSHIRE CONFESSION, AN EXPOSITION

Wallace, Robert *see* GEORGE BUCHANAN

WALLACE SENIOR'S REPORTS OF CASES IN THE THIRD CIRCUIT / Wallace, J B – Philadelphia: Asbury Dickins. 1v. 1801 (all publ) – 3mf – 9 – $4.50 – LLMC 81-475 – us L.L.M.C. [340]

WALLACE STAR – Wallace, NE. -w. Jul 1891-Jul 1893, scattered issues missing – 1 – us NE Hist [071]

WALLACE STEVENS – CUMMINGTON PRESS CORRESPONDENCE, 1941-1951 – 1 reel – 1 – uk Microform Academic [975]

WALLACE TUG – Wallace, NE. -w. Apr 1896; Jun 1896-Apr 1898 – 1 – us NE Hist [071]

Wallace, W F *see* HISTORY OF NAPA COUNTY

WALLACE WINNER – Wallace, NE. -w. Jun-Oct 1914; Feb 1915; Mar 1945; Mar 1948-Sept 1950; Mar 1951-Aug 1954; Dec 1955 – 1 – us NE Hist [071]

WALLACE'S FARM AND DAIRY *see* WALLACES FARMER

WALLACES FARMER – (Vols 1-22 1855-97 were not available for filming. Former titles: Farm and Dairy 1874-93. Wallace's Farm and Dairy 1894-sep 13, 1895) – Des Moines. v23-122. 1898-1997+ 1; v104-113 1979-88. v114-119 1989-94*. v120-122 1995-97+ 5; v104-122 1979-1997 9 – 1,5,9 – D912 – us UMI [630]

Wallbridge, Edwin Angel *see* THE DEMERARA MARTYR

Wallen, W *see* TWO ESSAYS ELUCIDATING THE GEOMETRICAL PRINCIPLES OF GOTHIC ARCHITECTURE

Wallenborn, Franz *see* 1000 TAGE WESTFRONT

WALLENSTEIN : A DRAMA IN TWO PARTS / Schiller, Friedrich von – London: Printed for T.N. Longman and O. Rees, by G. Woodfall, 1800 – 1 roll – 1 – 1-55879-316-X – uk Libr Preservation [820]

WALLENSTEIN : EIN DRAMATISCHES GEDICHT / Schiller, Friedrich von – (Includes bibliographical references) – Leipzig: Max Hesse, [1903?] – 1r – 1 – us U.W. Library [820]

WALLENSTEIN / Kugler, Bernhard – Berlin: Luederitz, 1873 – 1 – 1 – us U.W. Library [943]

WALLENSTEIN UND SEINE VERBINDUNGEN MIT DEN SCHWEDEN / ed by Hildebrand, E – Frankfurt am Main, 1885 – 1mf – 9 – ne IDC [943]

DIE WALLENSTEIN-LITERATUR, 1626-1878 / Schmid, Guenther – Prag etc, 1878 – 2mf – 9 – H-562/2 – ne IDC [019]

WALLENSTEIN'S ENDE / ed by Hallwich, H – Leipzig. 2v. 1879 – 16mf – 9 – ne IDC [943]

Waller, Charles B *see* THE APOCALYPSE: VIEWED UNDER THE LIGHT OF THE DOCTRINES OF THE UNFOLDING AGES

Waller, Charles Henry *see* THE NAMES ON THE GATES OF PEARL: AND OTHER STUDIES

Waller, D J *see*
- AN ALPHABETICAL AND CHRONOLOGICAL ARRANGEMENT OF THE WESLEYAN METHODIST MINISTERS AND PREACHERS ON TRIAL IN CONNEXION WITH THE BRITISH AND IRISH CONFERENCES; ...FROM THE COMMENCEMENT OF THEIR ITINERANCY TO...1900; ...
- AN ALPHABETICAL ARRANGEMENT OF ALL THE WESLEYAN METHODIST MINISTERS AND PREACHERS ON TRIAL IN CONNEXION WITH THE BRITISH AND IRISH CONFERENCES; ...FROM THE COMMENCEMENT OF THEIR ITINERANCY TO...1892; ...
- AN ALPHABETICAL ARRANGEMENT OF ALL THE WESLEYAN METHODIST MINISTERS AND PREACHERS ON TRIAL IN CONNEXION WITH THE BRITISH AND IRISH CONFERENCES; ...FROM THE COMMENCEMENT OF THEIR ITINERANCY TO...1896; ...

Waller, Jocelyn *see* THE CANADIAN SPECTATOR

Waller, John L *see* LETTERS TO A REFORMER, ALIAS CAMPBELLITE

Wallerand, G *see* HENRI BATE DE MALINES

Wallerius, Johan Gottschalk *see* D.D. BREVIS INTRODUCTIO IN HISTORIAM..

Wallerstein, Immanuel Maurice *see* LIBERATION MOVEMENTS IN LUSOPHONE AFRICA

Wallesch-Gladzinski, Doris *see* DIE VERKNOECHERUNG DES OS INCISIVUM IM MENSCHLICHEN FETUS

DIE WALLFAHRT NACH LOURDES : EIN HUMORISTISCH-SATYRISCHES EPOS / Rose, Moritz – Leipzig: A H Payne, 1875 – 1r – 1 – us U.W. Library [870]

WALLFAHRTEN ZU UNSERER LIEBEN FRAU IN LEGENDE UND GESCHICHTE / Beissel, Stephan – Freiburg im Breisgau, St. Louis, Mo.: Herder, 1913 – 2mf – us A.T.L.A. [240]

Wallhausen, J J von *see* L'ART MILITAIRE POUR L'INFANTERIE
Wallich, N *see*
- DESCRIPTIONS OF SOME RARE AND CURIOUS PLANTS
- HERBARIUM
- A NUMERICAL LIST OF DRIED SPECIMENS OF PLANTS IN THE EAST INDIA COMPANY'S MUSEUM
- PLANTAE ASIATICAE RARIORES
- TENTAMEN FLORAE NEPALENSIS

Wallick, Mark E *see* THE PHYSIOLOGIC RESPONSES TO IN-LINE ROLLER SKATING COMPARED TO TREADMILL RUNNING
Walling, Hermine *see* ENTWURZELT
WALLINGFORD CHRONICLE – England. -w. 7 Feb 1868-21 Jan 1870. 1 reel – 1 – uk British Libr Newspaper [072]
WALLINGFORD TIMES – England. 10 Feb 1882-22 Jun 1888 (1882 imperfect).-w. 5mqn reels – 1 – uk British Libr Newspaper [072]
WALLINGTON AND CARSHALTON HERALD – London, England. -w. 1881-97. 15 reels – 1 – uk British Libr Newspaper [072]
WALLINGTON AND CARSHALTON TIMES – London, England. -w. 27 March 1919-Dec 1956. 38 reels – 1 – uk British Libr Newspaper [072]
WALLINGTON AND CARSHALTON WEEKLY RECORD – London, England. -w. 4 April 1907-4 Nov 1915. 6 reels – 1 – uk British Libr Newspaper [072]
Wallis, Alfred *see* THE POETICAL WORKS OF ROBERT STEPHEN HAWKER...
Wallis, Henry Richard *see* THE HANDBOOK OF UGANDA
Wallis, Jason D *see* ACUTE EFFECTS OF STRENGTH TRAINING ON CARDIORESPIRATORY PARAMETERS DURING SUBSEQUENT AEROBIC EXERCISE
Wallis, John *see* GRAMMATICA LINGUAE ANGLICANAE
Wallis John E P *see* ENGLISH STATE TRIALS, 1163-1858
Wallner, Franz *see* PROVISOR'S LEIDEN
Walloaep, O *see* DAGBOAGER FRA HANS REJSER I GROANLAND 1739-1753
LA WALLONIE – Revue mensuelle de litterature et d'art. Liege. juin 1886-1892 (I-VII) – 1 – fr A.C.R.P.P. [073]
WALLONISMES / Dory, I – 1877-1878 – 9 – fr I.C.S. [440]
WALLOWA CHIEFTAIN – Enterprise, OR. 7 Jan 1909-29 Dec 1910. 1 roll – 1 – us U.O. Library [071]
WALLOWA CHIEFTAIN – Joseph OR. May 15 1884 – 1 – us U.O. Library [071]
WALLOWA COUNTY CHIEFTAIN – Enterprise, OR. -w. 1 Apr 1943-. – 17r – 1 – us U.O. Library [071]
WALLOWA COUNTY REPORTER – Enterprise, OR. -w. 2 Aug 1917-10 Feb 1921. 1 roll – 1 – us U.O. Library [071]
WALLOWA NEWS – Wallowa, OR. 25 Jul 1902-19 Apr 1907. 1 roll – 1 – us U.O. Library [071]
WALLOWA RECORD – Wallowa, OR. -w. 2 Dec 1948-6 Dec 1962. 4 rolls – 1 – us U.O. Library [071]
WALLOWA SUN – Wallowa, OR. 13 Aug 1907-28 Jan 1915. 3 rolls – 1 – us U.O. Library [071]
WALLOWA SUN – Wallowa OR. Jan 15 Mar 19 Apr 2-Dec 31 1909, Jan 7-Dec 30 1910, Aug 30 1912, Dec 20 27 1917, Jan 3 10 1918, Sep 11 1919, July 25 1924 + – 1 – us U.O. Library [071]
WALLOWA SUN – Wallowa, OR. -w. 1915-42 – 1 – 257.00 – us Oregon Hist [071]
Wallraf-Richartz-Museum. Cologne *see* 100 JAHRE WALLRAF-RICHARTZ MUSEUM 1861-1961
Wallroth, C F W *see*
- ANNUS BOTANICUS
- FLORA CRYPTOGAMICA GERMANIAE
- NATURGESCHICHTE DER FLECHTEN

Walls, Alfred *see* THE OLDEST DRAMA IN THE WORLD: THE BOOK OF JOB: ARRANGED IN DRAMATIC FORM
WALLSEND AND PLATTSBURG SUN – Feb 22 1886-Aug 8 1896 – 1 – at Pascoe [072]
WALLSEND HERALD. (THE HERALD AND ADVERTISER) – England. 4 Oct 1901-14 Feb 1913.-w. 10 reels – 1 – uk British Libr Newspaper [072]
WALNUT CREEK SUN – Walnut Creek, CA. 1955-1965 – 16r – 1 – $800.00 – B03689 – us Library Micro [071]
WALNUT GROVE BAPTIST CHURCH. GREENWOOD COUNTY. SOUTH CAROLINA : CHURCH RECORDS – 1926-54 – 1 – 24.03 – us Baptist [240]
WALNUT GROVE BAPTIST CHURCH. STEWART COUNTY. TENNESSEE : CHURCH RECORDS – 1892-Feb 1904 – 1 – 9.09 – us Baptist [240]
WALNUT KERNEL – Walnut Creek, CA. 1967-1972 – 32r – 1 – $1,600.00 – B03690 – us Library Micro [071]
WALNUT STREET BAPTIST CHURCH. LOUISVILLE, KENTUCKY : CHURCH RECORDS – (Deacons' Minutes, 1907-July 1984) – 1844-Jan 1990 – 8r – 1 – $627.30 – us Baptist [240]
WALNUT VALLEY TIMES – El Dorado. Kan. 1870-1918 – 1 – us UMI [071]
Walpers, W G *see*
- ANNALES BOTANICES SYSTEMATICAE
- REPERTORIUM BOTANICES SYSTEMATICAE

Walpole, Frederick *see* FOUR YEARS IN THE PACIFIC: IN HER MAJESTY'S SHIP COLLINGWOOD, FROM 1844 TO 1848
Walpole, George Henry Somerset *see* THE KINGDOM OF HEAVEN: WHAT IT IS AND HOW WE ENTER IT
Walpole, H *see*
- AEDES WALPOLIANAE
- ANECDOTES OF PAINTING IN ENGLAND. STRAWBERRY HILL

Walpole, Horace *see* THE CASTLE OF OTRANTO
WALPOLE SOCIETY – London. v1-28. 1912-1939/40 – 221mf – 9 – O-524c/1 – ne IDC [360]
Walpole Society. London *see* PUBLICATIONS
Walpole, Spencer *see* THE LIFE OF THE RT. HON. SPENCER PERCEVAL, INCLUDING HIS CORRESPONDENCE WITH NUMEROUS DISTINGUISHED PERSONS
Walraet, M *see*
- ACTES DE PHILIPPE IER, DIT LE NOBLE, COMTE ET MARQUIS DE NAMUR (1196-1212)

Walras, L *see* LES ASSOCIATIONS POPULAIRES DE CONSOMMATION, DE PRODUCTION ET DE CREDIT
WALSALL ADVERTISER – England. -w. 22 Nov 1862-25 Dec 1915. Lacking Jan-May 1896. 52 reels – 1 – uk British Libr Newspaper [072]
WALSALL FOOTBALL NEWS – England.1920-2 Sept 1939. -w.8 reels – 1 – uk British Libr Newspaper [072]
WALSALL FREE PRESS AND GENERAL ADVERTISER – England. -w. 8 Nov 1856-2 May 1903. Lacking 1896-97. 31 1 2 reels – 1 – uk British Libr Newspaper [072]
WALSALL OBSERVER – England, 1868- – 194+ r – 1 – uk British Libr Newspaper [072]
WALSALL PIONEER ETC – England, 1916-Mar 1922 – 6r – 1 – uk British Libr Newspaper [072]
Walser, H *see* GEOGRAFIA DE SUIZA. BARCELONA, 1929
Walsh, Correa M *see* THE POLITICAL SCIENCE OF JOHN ADAMS
Walsh, James *see* AMERICAN JESUITS. NEW YORK 1934
Walsh, James Joseph *see* CATHOLIC CHURCHMEN IN SCIENCE. FIRST SERIES
Walsh, John Johnston *see* A MEMORIAL OF THE FUTTEHGURH MISSION
Walsh, Rodolfo J *see*
- OPERACION MASACRE
- QUIEN MATO A ROSENDO

Walsh, Walter *see*
- THE JESUITS IN GREAT BRITAIN
- THE RELIGIOUS LIFE AND INFLUENCE OF QUEEN VICTORIA
- THE RITUALISTS
- THE SECRET HISTORY OF THE OXFORD MOVEMENT

Walsh, William Francis *see*
- SELECT CASES ON THE LAW OF REAL PROPERTY
- A TREATISE ON THE LAW OF REAL PROPERTY

Walsh, William Pakenham *see*
- HEROES OF THE MISSION FIELD
- THE MOABITE STONE
- MODERN HEROES OF THE MISSION FIELD
- THE VOICES OF THE PSALMS

Walshe, Peter *see* BLACK NATIONALISM IN SOUTH AFRICA
WALSH'S ILLUSTRATED MONTHLY MAGAZINE *see* WALSH'S MAGAZINE
WALSH'S MAGAZINE – (Cont: Walsh's Illustrated Monthly Magazine) – Toronto: J.C. Walsh, v1 no 2(Nov 1895)- – 9 – cn C.I.H.M. [073]
Walster, G W *see* PITHY BIT ARITHMETIC APPLIED TO THE COMPUTATION OF SOME ELEMENTARY TRANSCENDENTAL AND SPECIAL FUNCTIONS
Walston, Ben B, Jr *see* SKETCH OF ELDER DANIEL PARKER AND THE PILGRIM BAPTIST CHURCH
WALT WHITMAN / Bucke, Richard Maurice – Philadelphia: D. McKay, 1883. 00326. (Pre-1900 Canadiana) – 9 – cn C.I.H.M. [920]
WALT WHITMAN NEWSLETTER *see* WALT WHITMAN REVIEW
WALT WHITMAN QUARTERLY REVIEW – (Cont: Walt Whitman Review) – Iowa City. v1-14. jun 1983-spr 1998+ 1,9; v1-12 jun 1983-spr 1995*. v13-14 sum 1996-spr 1998 5 – 1,5,9 – D14588 – us UMI [420]
WALT WHITMAN QUARTERLY REVIEW *see* WALT WHITMAN REVIEW
WALT WHITMAN REVIEW – (Cum Indexes for vols 1-15 1955-69 available. Cont by: Walt Whitman Quarterly Review. Former title: Walt Whitman Newsletter 1955-58) – Detroit. v1-28. 1955-82 1; v17-28. mar 1971-1982 5; v22-28 mar 1976-1982 9 – 1,5,9 – D2540 – us UMI [420]
WALT WHITMAN REVIEW *see* WALT WHITMAN QUARTERLY REVIEW
Walter, Beate *see* ELIZABETH 1 AND THE ENGLISH PARLIAMENT
Walter, C *see* PRET BAPTISTU SEKTI
Walter, Carroll Gibson *see* BRIEF-WRITING AND ADVOCACY
Walter, E *see* SERMONS FOR THE YEAR (CCC303)
Walter, Emil *see* DIE SPRACHLICHE BEHANDLUNG DES TEXTES IN DER PROBEBIBEL
Walter, Erich *see* ADOLF FRIEDRICH GRAF VON SCHACK ALS UEBERSETZER
WALTER FLEX, EIN DEUTER DES WELTKRIEGES : EIN BEITRAG ZUR LITERATURGESCHICHTLICHEN WERTUNG DEUTSCHER KRIEGSDICHTUNG / Klein, Johannes – (Includes bibliographical references) – Marburg a.L.: N G Elwert, 1929 – 1r – 1 – us U.W. Library [430]
WALTER FOLGER BROWN PAPERS / Brown, Walter Folger – 1907-50. 2 reels – 1 – us Ohio Hist [920]
Walter, Franz *see* DIE PROPHETEN IN IHREM SOZIALEN BERUF UND DAS WIRTSCHAFTSLEBEN IHRER ZEIT
Walter, G A *see* TROIS QUATUORS CONCERTANS
WALTER HAGEMANN PAMPHLET COLLECTION – 1959 – 1 – CSUXANR9533-B – us Hoover Inst Photo [320]
Walter, Hans *see* DIE SOCIALISTEN
Walter, J E C *see* NORDISK ORNITHOLOGIE
Walter, Johann *see* DER RELIGIOESE GEHALT DES GALATERBRIEFES
Walter, Johannes von *see*
- FRANZ VON ASSISI UND DIE NACHAHMUNG CHRISTI
- FRAUENLOS UND FRAUENARBEIT IN DER GESCHICHTE DES CHRISTENTUMS
- DIE NEUESTE BEURTEILUNG DES ERASMUS
- DAS WESEN DER RELIGION NACH ERASMUS UND LUTHER

WALTER K. BAILEY PAPERS *see* BAILEY, WALTER K., PAPERS, MS 4665
Walter, Margot *see* STRUKTURANALYSEN VON ROMANEN VIRGINIA WOOLFS
Walter, N *see* DER THORA-AUSLEGE ARISTOBULOS (T.U.U. 5-86)
Walter Of Colveltry *see* MEMORIALE FRATRIS WALTERI DE COVENTRIA (RS58)
WALTER OGILBY: A NOVEL / Kinzie, Juliette Augusta – Philadelphia: Lippincott, 1869. 2v in 1 – 1 – us U.W. Library [830]
WALTER PATER / Greenslet, Ferris – New York: McClure, Phillips, 1903 – 1 roll – 1 – 1-55879-882-X – uk Libr Preservation [720]
Walter, Patrick *see* THE ACUTE PHYSIOLOGICAL RESPONSES TO WALKING WITH AND WITHOUT POWER POLES IN PATIENTS WITH CARDIAC DISEASE
Walter, Richard J *see* STUDENT POLITICS IN ARGENTINA
WALTER SAVAGE LANDOR : A CRITICAL STUDY / Evans, Edward Waterman – New York, London: The Knickerbocker Press, G.P. Putnam's Sons, 1892 – 1 roll – 1 – 1-55879-298-8 – uk Libr Preservation [720]
Walter, T *see* FLORA CAROLINIANA
WALTER ULBRICHT: PAMPHLET COLLECTION – 1951-1967 – 2r – 1 – CSUXANS5593-B – us Hoover Inst Photo [320]
WALTER WHARTON'S LAND SURVEY REGISTER 1675-1679 / Myers, A C – Wilmington, Hist. Soc. of Delaware, 1955. Delaware Reel 2. (The Cox Library Collection) – 5 – us Americana [978]
Walterboro. South Carolina. St. Jude's Episcopal Church *see* REGISTERS
Walters, H B *see* CHURCH BELLS OF ENGLAND
Walters, Thomas *see* ROBERT RAIKES: FOUNDER OF SUNDAY SCHOOLS
WALTHAM ABBEY AND CHESHUNT WEEKLY TELEGRAPH *see* CHESHUNT AND WALTHAM WEEKLY TELEGRAPH
WALTHAM CROSS AND CHESHUNT TELEGRAPH *see*
- CHESHUNT AND WALTHAM WEEKLY TELEGRAPH
- WALTHAM TELEGRAPH

WALTHAM FOREST EXTRA – London, UK. 1984 – 1r – 1 – uk British Libr Newspaper [072]
WALTHAM TELEGRAPH – England, Sep 1974-Dec 1981 – 8r – 1 – uk British Libr Newspaper [072]
WALTHAMSTOW AND LEYTON GUARDIAN – London, 1889; 1921- – 119+ r – 1 – uk British Libr Newspaper [072]
Walther, Ernst *see* BIBELWORT UND BIBELWISSENSCHAFT
Walther, G *see* UNTERSUCHUNGEN ZUR GESCHICHTE DER GRIECHISCHEN VATERUNSER-EXEGESE (T.U.U. 3-40/3)
Walther, J *see* DAS CHRISTLICH KINDERLIED
Walther, J G *see*
- MUSICALISCHES LEXICON
- MUSICALISCHES LEXICON ODER MUSICALISCHE BIBLIOTHEC...

Walther, Johann J *see* HORTULUS CHELICUS
Walther, Michael *see*
- HARMONIA BIBLICA
- OFFICINA BIBLICA

Walther, Wilhelm *see*
- LUTHER IM NEUESTEN ROEMISCHEN GERICHT
- LUTHERS BERUF
- LUTHERS GLAUBENSGEWISSHEIT
- LUTHERS WAFFEN

WALTHILL CITIZEN – Walthill, NE. -w. Jan 1918 to date – 1 – us NE Hist [071]
WALTHILL TIMES – Walthill, NE. -w. Nov 1906-Dec 1917; Feb 1918-Jun 1920, scattered issues missing; Feb 1921-Nov 1926; Mar 1927-Jun 1933, scattered issues missing; Aug 1933-Nov 1937; May 1938-Jun 1939 – 1 – us NE Hist [071]
Walthoffen, Hippolyt Walter von *see* DIE GOTTESIDEE IN RELIGIOESER UND SPEKULATIVER RICHTUNG
Waltmann, Frank *see* FORMEN DER REGIONALEN ZUSAMMENARBEIT AM SCHWARZEN MEER UND IN ZENTRALASIEN VOR DEM HINTERGRUND EUROPAEISCHER INTEGRATIONSERFAHRUNGEN
Walton, Peter T *see* THE EFFECTS OF SOLID AND LIQUID CARBOHYDRATE FEEDINGS ON HIGH INTENSITY INTERMITTENT EXERCISE PERFORMANCE
WALTRAMI UT VIDETUR LIBER DE UNITATE ECCLESIAE CONSERVANDA (MGH 7: 39.BD) – 1883 – Dfl13.00 – ne Slangenburg [240]
Waltson, R B *see* HMS "CHALLENGER" EXPEDITION, 1878-1883. MOLLUSCABY
Waltz, George B *see*
- DIRECTORY OF THE CITY OF FAIRFIELD AND JEFFERSON COUNTY FOR 1899

Walworth, Clarence A *see* THE OXFORD MOVEMENT IN AMERICA, OR, GLIMPSES OF LIFE IN AN ANGLICAN SEMINARY
WALWORTH FAMILY PAPERS, MS 1901 / John Walworth Family – 1774-1867. 2 reels. Includes 9 page guide – 1 – us Western Res [920]
Walz, K *see* DIE LEHRE DER KIRCHE VON DER H. SCHRIFT NACH DER SCHRIFT SELBST GEPRUEFT
Walzel, Oskar *see*
- GESCHICHTE DER DEUTSCHEN LITERATUR
- HEINRICH HEINES SAEMTLICHE WERKE

Walzel, Oskar Franz *see*
- FRIEDRICH HEBBEL UND SEINE DRAMEN
- HEBBELPROBLEME
- HEINRICH VON KLEISTS KUNST
- MNEMOSYNE
- NEUERE DEUTSCHE DICHTUNG UND DIE SCHULE
- RICHARD WAGNER IN SEINER ZEIT UND NACH SEINER ZEIT
- ROMANTISCHES

WALZER FUR DAS PIANOFORTE ZU VIER HAENDEN...OP. 44 / Scharwenka, X – Leipzig: C F Peters, [188-] – 1 – us Sibley [780]
WALZER FUR PIANO. LES ADIEUX, OP. 185 : CONTAINS ALSO: AURORA...OP. 156, PRIGINAL OBEROESTERICHHER LANDLER, OP. 186, GEISTES-SCHWINGEN, OP. 191, DIE PETERSBURGER, MAYLANDER KROUNGSWALZER, OP. 133 / Lanner, Josef – (Set of 6) – Wien: Haslinger, 1841 – 1 – us Sibley [780]
Wambaugh, Eugene *see*
– A SELECTION OF CASES ON AGENCY
– A SELECTION OF CASES ON INSURANCE
– THE STUDY OF CASES
Wamble, Hugh *see* BAPTIST HISTORY
WAN SALEH KEHILANGAN DJANGGUT / Ali, Is. – SE-4908 1 – 9 – ne IDC [950]
Wanamaker, George W *see* HISTORY OF HARRISON COUNTY
WAN-CHOU CHIH – 1828, 10. BCH-642 2 – 8 – ne IDC [950]
WANDA / Ouida – British Fiction Archive: Unit 3 – 9 – uk Bell [830]
WANDALIA / Krantz, A – Frankofurti. 1575. Index. BH-101 2 – 8 – ne IDC [240]
WANDEL DER KLINISCHEN PAEDIATRIE, DARGESTELLT AM STATIONAEREN KRANKENGUT DER LANDESKINDERKLINIK KOHLHOF IN DEN JAHREN 1963-1977 / Ommer, Beduja – Saarland, 1983 – 3mf – DM76.00 – 3-89349-885-0 – gw Hänsel [618]
WANDEL DES GRIECHENBILDES IM ACHTZEHNTEN JAHRHUNDERT : WINCKELMANN, LESSING, HERDER / Ephraim, Charlotte – (Includes bibliographical references) – 1r – 1 – us U.W. Library [430]
Wandelaincourt, Hubert *see* PLAN D'EDUCATION PUBLIQUE PAR LE MOYEN DUQUEL ON REDUIT A CINQ ANNEES LE COURS DES ETUDES ORDINAIRES
Wandell, Samuel Henry *see* THE LAW OF INNS, HOTELS AND BOARDING HOUSES.
DER WANDERER : MITTEILUNGSBLATT DER NATURFREUNDE-ORTSGRUPPE AUE I E – (Since 1926 publ in Dresden) – Bannewitz, 1922-33 – 3r – 1 – Dist. gw Mikrofilm – gw Misc Inst [790]
WANDERER – v1-13. Apr 1884-96. Potsdam etc. -m. Title varies: 1. 13. Jahrg., Arbieter Kolonie. (Serial publications of German trade unions in the Memorial Library, University of Wisconsin-Madison.) – 1 – us U.W. Library [331]
WANDERING JEW: A STATEMENT...OF THE JEWISH VIEW OF JUDAISM / Felsenthal, Bernhard – Chicago: Carpenter & Sheldon, 1872. 1 fiche – 9 – us A.T.L.A. [270]
A WANDERING JEW IN BRAZIL / Ginsburg, S L – 1922 – 1 – 10.22 – us Baptist [910]
WANDERING RECOLLECTIONS OF A SOMEWHAT BUSY LIFE / Neal, John – An autobiography. Boston: Roberts Bros., 1869. 431p – 1 – us U.W. Library [920]
WANDERINGS AND EXCURSIONS IN SOUTH WALES, WITH THE SCENERY OF THE RIVER WYE / Roscoe, Thomas – London: Bohn, 1854. 336p. illus – 1 – us U.W. Library [910]
WANDERINGS BY THE LOIRE...WITH TWENTY-ONE ENGRAVINGS BY J.M.W. TURNER... / Ritchie, Leitch – (Microf. avec Thienon, C. – Voyage pittoresque dans le bocage de la Vendee ou Vues de Clisson...dessinees... par C. Thienon... – Paris: Didot, 1817) – London: Longman, 1833 – 1 – F306.46 – fr Armell [760]
WANDERINGS IN BURMA / Bird, George W – London: Simpkin, Marshall, Hamilton, Kent & Co. Ltd., 1897. 410p. Plates, maps, plans – 1 – us U.W. Library [910]
WANDERINGS IN WEST AFRICA FROM LIVERPOOL TO FERNANDO PO / Burton, Richard Francis – 2v. London. 1863. BA-287 2 – 8 – ne IDC [910]
WANDERINGS OF A PILGRIM / Harsha, David A – pref. 1854 – 9 – us A.T.L.A. [240]
THE WANDERINGS OF PLANTS AND ANIMALS FROM THEIR FIRST HOME / Hehn, Victor – London: S. Sonnenschein, 1888. xiii,523p – 1 – us U.W. Library [574]
WANDERUNG : AUFZEICHNUNGEN VON HERMANN HESSE / Hesse, Hermann – 14. bis 23. Aufl. Berlin: Suhrkamp, 1949 – 1r – 1 – us U.W. Library [910]
DIE WANDERUNG DES HERRN ULRICH VON HUTTEN : EIN TAGEBUCH-ROMAN / Vesper, Will – 5. Aufl. Guetersloh: C Bertelsmann, 1943, c1922 – 1 – us U.W. Library [830]
WANDERUNG UND HEIMKUNFT : HOELDERLINS ELEGIE "DER WANDERER" / Ruprecht, Erich – (Includes bibliographical references) – Stuttgart: R Schmiedel, 1947 – 1 – us U.W. Library [430]
WANDERUNGEN DURCH DEN THIERKREIS / Wienbarg, Ludolf – Hamburg: Hoffmann und Campe, 1835 – 1r – 1 – us U.W. Library [890]
WANDER-VORTRAEGE AUS KUNST UND GESCHICHTE / Eckardt, Ludwig – Stuttgart: Rieger, 1868 – 1 – us U.W. Library [700]
Wandle, H B *see* AMERICAN LEADING CASES
DIE WANDLUNG : ERZAEHLUNG / Heuschele, Otto – Stuttgart: J F Steinkopf, 1945 – 1r – 1 – us U.W. Library [830]
WANDLUNGEN DER GEDICHTE CONRAD FERDINAND MEYERS : MIT ZAHLREICHEN ERSTABDRUECKEN UND ZWISCHENFASSUNGEN UND ZUM ERSTENMAL GESAMMELTEN GELEGENHEITSGEDICHTEN / Moser, Heinrich – (Includes bibliographical references) – Leipzig: H Haessel, 1900 – 1r – 1 – us U.W. Library [430]
DER WANDSBECKER BOTE : AUSWAHL AUS SEINEN WERKEN / Claudius, Matthias; ed by Gerok, Karl – 2. Aufl. Gotha: F A Perthes, 1889 – 1 – us U.W. Library [800]
DER WANDSBECKER BOTE – Hamburg, Germany. 1771-75 – 1 – gw Mikrofilm [072]
DER WANDSBECKER BOTHE / ed by Bode, Johann Joachim Christoph & Claudius Matthias – (Forts. ab 1773: Der deutsche, sonst Wandsbecker Bothe) – Hamburg, 1771-75. Hildesheim, 1978 – 47mf – 9 – DM430.00 – gw Olms [430]
Wane, Animata *see* GUELADIO HAM BODEDIO
Wang, Chang-Chih *see* THREE-SELF MOVEMENT (CCC304)
Wang, Chao-Ming *see* CHINA'S PROBLEMS AND THEIR SOLUTION
Wang, Chih-hsin *see*
– CHINESE CLASSICAL STORIES (CCC308)
– A CHRISTIAN STUDY OF BUDDHISM (CCC305)
– CHUNG-KUO LI SHIH TI SHANG TI KUAN (CCC306)
– CHUNG-KUO TSUNG CHIAO SZU SHIH TA KANG (CCC309)
– HISTORY OF CHRISTIANITY IN CHINA (CCC307)
Wang, Chung-min *see* CHINESE CHRISTIAN MONOGRAPH (CCC310)
Wang, Hsiang-hsien *see* CHRISTIANS AND WARTIME SERVICE (CCC311)
Wang, Jen-shu *see* ON THE INDONESIAN STRUGGLE AGAINST IMPERIALISM
Wang, K'uei-sheng *see* THE JESUS I KNOW (CCC313)
Wang, Ming-tao *see*
– CHINESE CHRISTIAN MONOGRAPH (CCC316)
– TALKS TO YOUNG CHRISTIANS (CCC315)
– THE WORDS OF MY MOUTH (CCC314)
Wang, P C *see* AN INQUIRY INTO THE PERCEIVED IDEALS HELD BY EXPERTS FOR REGIONAL TOURISM DEVELOPMENT IN THE STATE OF PENNSYLVANIA FOR THE YEAR 2000
Wang, Richard L C *see* THE GAUSS-JORDAN INVERSION FOR A SYMMETRIC NON-NEGATIVE DEFINITE MATRIX
Wang, Stephen *see* GREAT HYMNS AND HYMN WRITERS (CCC317)
Wang, Tzu-chung *see* THE LIFE AND TEACHINGS OF JESUS (CCC318)
Wang, Yuan-te *see* MODEL PERSONAL WORK (CCC319)
Wangemann, Hermann Theodor *see*
– GESCHICHTE DER BERLINER MISSIONGESELLSCHAFT UND IHRER ARBEITEN IN SUEDAFRICA
– GESCHICHTE DER BERLINER MISSIONGESELLSHAFT UND IHRER ARBEITEN IN SUDAFRICA, MIT EINER UEBERSICHTSKARTE UND VIELEN BILDERN
Wanger, W *see* THE NTU GOD-NAMES
Wanhal, J B *see*
– QUARTETS, TWO
– QUINTETS, TWO CAPITAL, FOR VIOLIN, VIOLA, 2 HORNS [AD LIB], AND BASS
– SIX PRELUDES FACILES POUR L'ORGUE OU LE PIANO-FORTE...
– SIX SONATAS FOR 2 VIOLINS AND VIOLONCELLO, OP. 12
– THREE FACILES SONATINAS POUR LE CLAVECIN AVEC VIOLON AD LIB
– TREIZE PIECES POUR PIANOFORTE A QUATRE MAINS...
Waniek, Gustav *see*
– GRILLPARZER UNTER GOETHE'S EINFLUSS
– KOENIG OTTOKARS GLUECK UND ENDE
WAN-KUO-KUNG-PAO – Invaluable material for the student of modern China, the Sino-Japanese War and the Reform movement. 1868-1882; 1889-1906 – 1 – 35.00r – us Hoover Inst Photo [950]
Wanless, William James *see* THE MEDICAL MISSION
WANLI CHENZHOU ZHI, 1576 / Hunan Province. China – Records of Chenzhou in the reign of Wanli. 20 vols. Comp. by Hu Han. (Rare Local Records in Chinese...1420-1507). F A88 – 9 – $40.50 – cc Microforms [950]
WANLI CILI XIAN ZHI, 1573 / Hunan Province. China – Records of Cili County in the reign of Wanli. 18 vols. Comp. by Chen Guangqian. (Rare Local Records in Chinese...1420-1507). F A90 – 9 – $18.00 – cc Microforms [950]
WANLI HUANGYAN XIAN ZHI, 1579 / Zhejiang Province. China – Records of Huangyan County in the reign of Wanli. 7 vols. Comp. by Yuan Yingqi. F A23. (Rare Local Records in Chinese...1420-1507) – 9 – $31.50 – cc Microforms [950]
WANLI TONGZHOU ZHI, APPROX. 1579 / Jiangsu Province. China – Records of Tongzhou in the reign of Wanli. 8 vols. Comp. by Shen Mingchen. F A12. (Rare Local Records in Chinese...1420-1507) – 9 – $49.50 – cc Microforms [950]
WANN WURDEN UNSERE EVANGELIEN VERFASST / Tischendorf, Constantin von – (In English) – Leipzig: J C Hinrichs, 1865 – 1mf – 9 – 0-8370-5538-5 – 1985-3538 – us A.T.L.A. [220]
Wanner, R J *see* PALAEONTOLOGIE VON TIMOR, NEBST KLEINEREN BEITRAEGEN ZUR PALAEONTOLOGIE EINIGER ANDERN INSELN DES OSTINDISCHEN ARCHIPELS
Wansbrough, C E *see* HANDBOOK AND INDEX TO THE MINUTES OF THE CONFERENCE
Wanta, Daniel *see* METABOLIC RESPONSES TO GRADED DOWNHILL WALKING
WANTAGE CHRONICLE – England, May 1876-Dec 1879 – 3r – 1 – uk British Libr Newspaper [072]
WANTAGE FREE PRESS – England, Oct 1902-Dec 1904 – 1r – 1 – uk British Libr Newspaper [072]
Wantner *see* A HISTORY OF GLOUCESTERSHIRE
Wappler, Paul *see*
– DIE TAEUFERBEWEGUNG IN THUERINGEN VON 1526-1584
– THOMAS MUENZER IN ZWICKAU UND DIE "ZWICKAUER PROPHETEN"
WAQAI AL-MISRIYAH *see* AL-WAQA'I' AL-MISRIYAH
THE WAR AGAINST JAPAN / U.S. Army Center of Military History – (China-Burma-India Theater: 1942-44 r1-7. India-Burma Theater: 1944-45 r8-13. China Theater: 1944-45 r14. Southwest Pacific Area Theater: r15-27 and 54. Central Pacific/ Pacific Ocean Areas Theater: r28-45. South Pacific Theater: r46-47. Internment, Security, and Prisoner of War Camps Reports: r48. Translations of Japanese Documents: r49-53. With guide) – Historical Manuscripts Collection, 1991 – 54r – 1 – $4,590.00 – S3199 – us Scholarly Res [950]
WAR AGAINST WAR : A CHRONICLE OF THE INTERNATIONAL CRUSADE OF PEACE – London, England. 13 Jan-31 Mar 1899 – 30ft – 1 – uk British Libr Newspaper [320]
WAR AGAINST WAR : A CHRONICLE OF THE INTERNATIONAL CRUSADE OF PEACE – London. n1-12. 1899 – 1r – 1 – us Ross [327]
WAR AGAINST WAR – London. Nos 1-12 Jan 13 – Mar 31 1899 – 1 – us NY Public [320]
WAR AND DECOLONIZATION IN INDONESIA, 1940-1950 : PART 1: THE ARCHIVE OF DR. H.J. VAN MOOK, 1942-1948 / General State Archives of the Netherlands – 1997 – 406mf – 9 – Dfl3,450.00 – ne MMF Publ [950]
WAR AND DECOLONIZATION IN INDONESIA, 1940-1950 : PART 2: THE ARCHIVE OF DR. P.J. KOETS, 1946-1949 / General State Archives of the Netherlands – 1997 – 351mf – 9 – Dfl2,985.00 – ne MMF Publ [950]
THE WAR AND ELIZABETH (ELIZABETH'S CAMPAIGN) / Ward, Mary Augusta – British Fiction Archive: Unit 2 – 9 – uk Bell [830]
WAR COMMENTARY – v2,no9. Jul 1941. London: Freedom Press. -m. Continues: Revolt. Continued by: War Commentary for Anarchism – 1 – us U.W. Library [073]
WAR COMMENTARY FOR ANARCHISM – v2,no10-v6,no21.Aug 1941-11 Aug 1945. London: Freedom Press. illus. Continued by: Freedom through Anarchism – 1 – us U.W. Library [073]
WAR CRY / Salvation Army – 1879-1939 – 42r – 1 – uk Microform Academic [240]
WAR CRY, 1881-1981 / Salvation Army – (U.S. editions) – Salvation Army Archives and Research Center, New York – 54r – 1 – $3995.00 – us UMI [240]
WAR DEPARTMENT COLLECTION OF POST-REVOLUTIONARY WAR MANUSCRIPTS / U.S. War Department. Collection of Revolutionary War Records – 4rolls. M904 – 1 – us Nat'l Archives [324]
WAR DIARIES AND CORRESPONDENCE / Jodl, Alfred – 2 rolls.T989 – 1 – us Nat'l Archives [940]
WAR DIARIES AND CORRESPONDENCE OF GEN. ALFRED JODL, 1937-1945 – T989 – 2r – $46.00 – us Nat'l Archives [355]
WAR DIARIES OF THE GERMAN SUBMARINE COMMAND, AUGUST 1938-JANUARY 1945 – 1984 – 5r – 1 – $425.00 – S1671 – Co-publ with the U.S. Naval Historical Center – us Scholarly Res [355]
WAR DIARY, EASTERN SEA FRONTIER / U.S. Navy. Eastern Sea Frontier. Office of the Commander – Dec 1941-Aug 1945 – 13r – 1 – $1,105.00 – S1672 – us Scholarly Res [355]
WAR DIARY, GULF SEA FRONTIER / U.S. Navy. Gulf Sea Frontier. Office of the Commander – (With printed guide) – Apr 1942-Jul 1945 – 17r – 1 – $1,445.00 – S1674 – us Scholarly Res [355]
WAR DIARY, OPERATIONS DIVISION, GERMAN NAVAL STAFF, 1939-45 / Germany. Navy. Operations Division. Staff – (Includes printed guide) – 1984 – 17r – 1 – $1,445.00 – S1673 – Co-publ in cooperation with the U.S. Naval Historical Center – us Scholarly Res [355]
WAR FOOD SERIES / South Dakota. Agricultural Extension Service. State College of Agriculture and Mechanic Arts – Nos 1-7 1944-45 – 1,5,6 – us Spaulding [350]
THE WAR IN SPAIN / Fischer, Louis – NY, 1937. Fiche W 885. (Blodgett Collection of Spanish Civil War Pamphlets) – 9 – us H.U. College Libr [946]
THE WAR IN THE AIR : AND PARTICULARLY HOW MR. BERT SMALLWAYS FARED WHILE IT LASTED / Wells, H G – London: G. Bell and Sons, 1908 – 1 roll – 1 – 1-55879-929-X – uk Libr Preservation [830]
THE WAR IN THE SOUDAN: AND THE CAUSES WHICH LEAD TO IT: WITH SHORT BIOGRAPHICAL SKETCHES OF THE PRINCIPAL PERSONAGES ENGAGED / Haultain, Theodore Arnold – Toronto: Grip Print. and Pub. Co., 1885.05517.(Pre-1900 Canadiana) – 9 – cn C.I.H.M. [960]
THE WAR IN VIETNAM : CLASSIFIED HISTORIES BY THE NATIONAL SECURITY COUNCIL / U.S. National Security Council – 1981 – 1 – $810.00 – 0-89093-243-3 – us UPA [950]
THE WAR IN VIETNAM : PAPERS OF WILLIAM C. WESTMORELAND, PART 1: HISTORY, STATEMENTS, AND CLIPPINGS FILES – 1993 – 25r – 1 – $3,125.00 – 1-55655-468-0 – us UPA [355]
THE WAR IN WEXFORD; AN ACCOUNT OF THE REBELLION IN THE SOUTH OF IRELAND IN 1798 TOLD FROM ORIGINAL DOCUMENTS / Wheeler, Harold Felix Baker – London: J. Lane; New York: John Lane, 1910. xvi,343p. plates, maps – 1 – us U.W. Library [941]
WAR INCONSISTENT WITH THE RELIGION OF JESUS CHRIST / Dodge, David Low – Boston, 1905 – 2mf – 1 – ILM-4094/1 – ne IDC [327]
WAR INCONSISTENT WITH THE RELIGION OF JESUS CHRIST / Dodge, David Low – Boston: Published for the International Union [by] Ginn, 1905 – 1mf – us A.T.L.A. [240]
WAR JESUS EKSTATIKER?: EINE UNTERSUCHUNG ZUM LEBEN JESU / Holtzmann, Oskar – Tuebingen: J.C.B. Mohr, 1903. 1 fiche – 9 – us A.T.L.A. [240]
WAR JOURNAL – (A rare pro-American account of the 1812-14 war) – 12 Mar-10 Dec 1813 – 1r – 1 – Can$68.00r – cn Commonwealth Micro [975]

WAR MEDICINE – v. 1-8. 1941-1945 – 1,5,6 – us Princeton Micro [616]

WAR MEMORIALS IN THE SOVIET UNION PAMPHLET COLLECTION – 1969-1974 – 1 reel – 1 – CSUXANR3159-B – us Hoover Inst Photo [355]

WAR MEMORIES OF AN ARMY CHAPLAIN / Trumbull, Henry Clay – New York: Scribner, 1898 – 2mf – us A.T.L.A. [350]

THE WAR NEXT DOOR / Albert, Carlos L – SE-5172 1. 1965 – 9 – ne IDC [950]

WAR NOTES – Montreal. J Dougall, [1884?-1885?] – 9 – cn C.I.H.M. [170]

WAR OF 1812 : FIRST SERIES: CONTAINING A FULL AND DETAILED NARRATIVE OF THE OPERATIONS OF THE RIGHT DIVISION, ON THE CANADIAN ARMY / Richardson, John – Brockville: s.n, 1842. SEM105P437 – 2mf – 9 – Can$4.50 – cn Bibl Nat [355]

WAR OF 1812 MILITARY BOUNTY LAND WARRANTS / U.S. Bureau of Land Management – 1815-58. 14 rolls. M848 – 1 – us Nat'l Archives [324]

"WAR OF 1812 PAPERS" OF THE DEPT. OF STATE, 1789-1815 / U.S. Department of State – 7rolls. M588. Printed guide – 1 – us Nat'l Archives [324]

WAR OF 1812 PRIZE CASE FILES OF THE U.S. DISTRICT COURT FOR THE EASTERN DISTRICT OF PENNSYLVANIA / U.S. Circuit and District Courts – 1812-15. 2 rolls – 1 – M966 – us Nat'l Archives [324]

THE WAR OF 1812-13-14 BETWEEN GREAT BRITAIN AND THE UNITED STATES: A LECTURE DELIVERED AT THE MONTREAL MILITARY INSTITUTE AND BEFORE THE NUMISMATIC AND ANTIQUARIAN SOCIETY OF MONTREAL IN FEBRUARY 1899 / Campbell, Francis Wayland – Montreal: A. Pelletier, 1899. 02017. (Pre-1900 Canadiana) – 9 – cn C.I.H.M. [971]

WAR OF 1914-1918 – ARAB BUREAU PAPERS, 1911-1920 / Great Britain. Foreign Office – FO 882 – 16r – 1 – us Ross [941]

WAR OF 1914-1918 – JEDDA AGENCY PAPERS, 1913-1925 / Great Britain. Foreign Office – FO 686 – 25r – 1 – us Ross [941]

WAR OF THE GAEDHIL WITH THE GAIL (RS48) : OR THE INVASIONS OF IRELAND BY THE DANES AND OTHER NORSEMEN. IRISH TEXT, WITH TRANSLATION / ed by Todd, J H – 1867 – Dfl35.00 – ne Slangenburg [941]

WAR OF THE REBELLION – 1880-1901 – 1 – us UMI [976]

WAR OF THE REBELLION – Comp. by Richard H. Orton. 1890. Item J. Records of California men in the War of the Rebellion, 1861-1867. 887p. SW16-0045 – 5 – us A.G.L.L. [976]

WAR OF THE REBELLION : OFFICIAL RECORDS OF THE UNION AND CONFEDERATE ARMIES – Series 1: v36; v53. Govt Printing Off, 1891; 1898 – 2r – 1 – $100.00 – B40144 – us Library Micro [976]

WAR OF THE REBELLION / U.S. – 1891-1913 – 9 – 1500.00 – us Opus [976]

THE WAR ON POVERTY, 1964-68 / ed by Gelfand, Mark I – Part 1: White House Central Files. 16r. $1,540.00. ISBN: 0-89093-495-9; Part 2: Records of the President's National Advisory Commission on Rural Poverty, 1966-67. 25r. $2,975.00. ISBN: 1-55655-465-6 – 1 – us UPA [323]

WAR OVER THE FALKLAND ISLANDS? / Zube, John – 1fiche (29x) – 9 – 1.00f – at Libertarian Micro [320]

WAR, PEACE AND THE STATE / Rothbard, Murray N – 1fiche (29x) – 9 – 1.00f – at Libertarian Micro [320]

WAR PLANS AND DEFENSE STUDIES: 1940-1949 / U.S. Army. Caribbean Defense Command. Historical Section – 1 reel – 1 – 20.00 – us L of C Photodup [355]

WAR RESISTERS LEAGUE : WRL NEWS – New York. v1-140 1945-66*. v141-244 1967-oct 1984 1; v163-179 1971-73. v198-244 1977-oct 1984* 5; v198-227 1977-81*. v228-244 1982-oct 1984 9 – 1,5,9 – D2347 – us UMI [360]

THE WAR REVENUE LAW OF 1898 / Heydecker, Edward Le Moyne – Albany, NY: Bender: 1898. 167p. LL-174 – 1 – us L of C Photodup [340]

War Veterans Torch Commando. (South Africa) *see* MISCELLANEOUS DOCUMENTS

WAR WHOOP – San Bernardino, CA. 1927-1973 – 4r – 1 – $200.00 – R03465 – us Library Micro [071]

THE WAR WITH SPAIN. II.THE VENEZUELAN DISPUTE / Marburg, Theodore – Reprinted from Baltimore American. Baltimore: J. Murphy & Co., 1898. 50p – 1 – us U.W. Library [972]

WAR WORK DURING WORLD WAR 2 PAMPHLET COLLECTION – 1941-1943 – 1 reel – 1 – CSUXANN3604-B – us Hoover Inst Photo [355]

WARA RESEARCH – Djakarta. Incomplete. SE 702 1. 1960-1969 – 9 – ne IDC [073]

WARBERGS NYA TIDNING *see* WARBERGS TIDNING

WARBERGS TIDNING – Varberg, Sweden. 1857-63 – 1 – sw Kungliga [072]

WARBERGS TIDNING – (Warbergs Nya Tidning 1885-87) – Varberg, Sweden. 1884-85 – 3r – 1 – sw Kungliga [072]

Warburg Institute *see* JOURNAL

Warburton, Eliot *see* THE CRESCENT AND THE CROSS

Warburton, W *see* THE DOCTRINE OF GRACE

Warburton, William *see* A CRITICAL AND PHILOSOPHICAL ENQUIRY INTO THE CAUSES OF PRODIGIES AND MIRACLES, AS RELATED BY HISTORIANS

Ward, Allen T *see* FAMILY CORRESPONDENCE

Ward, Artemas *see* ARTEMAS WARD PAPERS, 1721-1953

Ward, Bernard *see*
- CATHOLIC LONDON A CENTURY AGO
- THE DAWN OF THE CATHOLIC REVIVAL IN ENGLAND, 1781-1803
- THE EVE OF CATHOLIC EMANCIPATION
- HISTORY OF ST. EDMUNDS COLLEGE, OLD HALL
- THE SEQUEL TO CATHOLIC EMANCIPATION

Ward, Bernardo *see* PROYECTO ECONOMICO Y OBRA PIA

Ward, Christopher L *see* THE DELAWARE CONTINENTALS 1776-1783

Ward Family *see* LETTERS

Ward, Harriet *see* FIVE YEARS IN KAFFIRLAND

Ward, Harry F *see* SPAIN'S DEMOCRACY TALKS TO AMERICA

Ward, Ida Carolina *see* THE PHONETIC AND TONAL STRUCTURE OF EFIK

Ward, J *see* THE BOROUGH OF STOKE ON TRENT, STAFFORDSHIRE

Ward, Jeffrey J *see* EVALUATION OF THE SET-POINT AND PROPORTIONAL CONTROL MODELS OF HUMAN THERMOREGULATION DURING EXERCISE

Ward, John *see*
- EXPERIENCES OF A DIPLOMATIST, BEING RECOLLECTIONS OF GERMANY, FOUNDED ON DIARIES KEPT DURING THE YEARS 1840-1870
- FOUR ESSAYS UPON THE ENGLISH LANGUAGE

Ward, Julius H *see* PHILLIPS BROOKS' ADDRESSES

WARD LISTS AND OTHER RECORDS OF THE CITY OF GLOUCESTER / Gloucester. England – 1843-86 – 8r – 1 – uk Microform Academic [941]

Ward, Mary Augusta *see*
- CANADIAN BORN (LADY MERTON, COLONIST)
- THE CASE OF RICHARD MEYNELL
- THE CORYSTON FAMILY
- COUSIN PHILIP (HELENA)
- DAPHNE, OR, MARRIAGE A LA MODE
- DELIA BLANCHFLOWER
- DIANA MALLORY
- ELEANOR
- ELTHAM HOUSE
- FENWICK'S CAREER
- A GREAT SUCCESS
- HARVEST
- HELBECK OF BANNISDALE
- THE HISTORY OF DAVID GRIEVE
- LADY CONNIE
- LADY ROSE'S DAUGHTER
- MARCELLA
- THE MARRIAGE OF WILLIAM ASHE
- THE MATING OF LYDIA
- MILLY AND OLLY
- MISS BRETHERTON
- MISSING
- ROBERT ELSMERE
- SIR GEORGE TRESSADY
- THE STORY OF BESSIE COSTRELL
- THE WAR AND ELIZABETH (ELIZABETH'S CAMPAIGN)

Ward, Nathaniel *see* THE SIMPLE COBBLER OF AGGAWAM IN AMERICA

Ward, Wilfrid Philip *see*
- THE LIFE AND TIMES OF CARDINAL WISEMAN
- THE LIFE OF JOHN HENRY, CARDINAL NEWMAN
- PROBLEMS AND PERSONS
- TEN PERSONAL STUDIES
- WILLIAM GEORGE WARD AND THE OXFORD MOVEMENT
- THE WISH TO BELIEVE

Ward, William *see* AN ESSAY ON GRAMMAR, AS IT MAY BE APPLIED TO THE ENGLISH LANGUAGE

Wardell, John Wilford *see* A STUDY OF WESTERN RESERVE ARCHITECTURE AS TYPIFIED BY CHURCHES IN OHIO DURING THE PERIOD 1800-1860

THE WARDEN OF GALWAY – Galway, Ireland. 1 Feb-17 Aug 1853 – 20ft – 1 – uk British Libr Newspaper [072]

Warden, Robert Bruce *see*
- ASPECTS OF ADJUDICATION
- AN ESSAY ON THE LAW OF ART

Warder Family *see* PAPERS: CORRESPONDENCE, CLIPPINGS, MANUSCRIPTS AND BOOK OF THE FAMILY

Wardin, Albert *see* AN INDEX IN TWO PARTS TO EVANGELICAL SECTARIANS IN MISSIONERSKOE OBZRENIE, 1896-1916

Wardlaw J S *see* LECTURES ON THE PROPHECIES OF ZECHARIAH

Wardlaw, Ralph *see* LECTURES ON THE PROPHECIES OF ZECHARIAH

Wardlow, Ralph *see* LECTURE ON THE EPISTLE OF JAMES

Ward-Perkins, John Bryan *see* POMPEII A.D. 79

Ward-Price, Henry Lewis *see* LAND TENURE IN THE YORUBA PROVINCES

WARD'S AUTO WORLD – (Cont: Ward's Quarterly) – Detroit. v5-24. feb 1969-1988* 1; v25-33 1989-97+ 1,9; v25-30 1989-94*. v31-33 1995-97+ 5 – 1,5,9 – D17555.01 – us UMI [620]

WARD'S AUTO WORLD *see* WARD'S QUARTERLY

WARD'S DEALER BUSINESS – (Cont: Auto Age Dealer Business) – Overland Park. v30-32. nov 1995-aug 1998+ – 1,5,9 – D18406.03 – us UMI [380]

WARD'S QUARTERLY – (Cont by: Ward's Auto World) – Detroit. v1-4. win 1965-1968* – 1 – D17555 – us UMI [620]

WARD'S QUARTERLY *see* WARD'S AUTO WORLD

WARDSHIP IN INTERNATIONAL LAW / Fenwick, C G – Washington, 1919 – 1mf – 1 – ILM-1921/1 – ne IDC [327]

WARE 1735-1890 – 50mf – 9 – us Holbrook [920]

Ware, A *see* WARE'S REPORTS OF CASES IN THE DISTRICT COURTS FOR MAINE AND MASSACHUSETTS, 1822-1874

Ware, John Fothergill Waterhouse *see* SELF-CONSECRATION

DE WARE PATRIOT – Ladysmith, South Africa. 1856-57 – 1 – sa State Libr [072]

WARE PATRIOT – (Hertford & Ware Patriot, 1834-) – England, 1833-35 – 1r – 1 – uk British Libr Newspaper [072]

WARE REPUBLIKEIN – Johannesburg, South Africa. 1940-43 – 1 – sa State Libr [960]

WARE SHOALS FIRST BAPTIST CHURCH. WARE SHOALS, SOUTH CAROLINA : CHURCH RECORDS – 1925-72 – 1 – 13.73 – us Baptist [240]

Ware, William *see* JULIAN, OR, SCENES IN JUDEA

WAREHAM 1719-1892 – (Mf 1-3: Town & Vital Records 1719-1828. Mf 4-11: Town & Vital Records 1697-1854. Mf 12-14: Births 1719-1847. Mf 14-17: Marriage Intentions 1739-1854. Mf 17-19: Marriages 1697-1845. Mf 19: Deaths 1740-1855. Mf 20-24: Births 1859-92. Mf 25-27: Marriage Intentions 1846-91. Mf 26: Tax Assessments 1871-73. Mf 28-31: Marriages 1854-92. Mf 32-35: Deaths 1856-92. Mf 36-37: Birth Index 1859-92. Mf 38-39: Marriage Index 1697-1892. Mf 40-41: Death Index 1856-92) – (mf ed 1984) – 41mf – 0-931248-65-5 – us Holbrook [920]

Wareham, J M *see* CHILDREN OF CENTRAL AFRICA

WAREHOUSING MANAGEMENT – (Cont in part: Distribution) – Radnor. 1994* 1; 1995-97+ 1,5,9 – 1,5,9 – D24842 – us UMI [380]

DAS WAREN KERLE / Killinger, Manfred, Freiherr von – 1. Aufl. Muenchen: F Eher, 1944 – 1r – 1 – us U.W. Library [830]

WAREN-PREISE – Bremen, Germany.1846-47 – 1 – gw Mikrofilm [073]

WARE'S REPORTS OF CASES IN THE DISTRICT COURTS FOR MAINE AND MASSACHUSETTS, 1822-1874 / Ware, A – v1-3. 2nd ed of vl. Boston: Little Brown, 1856; 1st + 2nd eds of v2. Portland: Thurston, 1849, Loring, Short & Harmon, 1873. 1st ed of v3. Portland: Loring, Short & Harmon, 1874 (all publ) – 21mf – 9 – $31.50 – LLMC 81-476 – us L.L.M.C. [340]

Warfel, Harry R *see* STUDIES IN WALT WHITMAN'S LEAVES OF GRASS

Warfield, Benjamin Breckinridge *see*
- AN INTRODUCTION TO THE TEXTUAL CRITICISM OF THE NEW TESTAMENT
- THE LORD OF GLORY
- THE RIGHT OF SYSTEMATIC THEOLOGY

Warfield, Ethelbert, D *see* THE KENTUCKY RESOLUTIONS OF 1798

WARFIELD'S – (Cont by: Warfield's Business Record) – Baltimore. v1-6 mar 1986-91* – 1 – D18192 – us UMI [380]

WARFIELD'S *see* WARFIELD'S BUSINESS RECORD

WARFIELD'S BUSINESS RECORD – (Cont: Warfield's) – Baltimore. v7-9 1992-94*. v10-12 1995-97+ – 1,5,9 – D18192.01 – us UMI [380]

WARFIELD'S BUSINESS RECORD *see* WARFIELD'S

Wargosupono, S *see* ILMU BERUSAHA PRAKTIS UNTUK SEKOLAH TEHNIK 3 TAHUN

WARHAFFTER GRUENDTLICHER BERICHT VON RECHTER ORDENLICHER WAHL VNND BERUFF DER EUANGELISCHEN PREDIGER... / Hunnius, A – N.p., 1589 – 1mf – ne IDC [240]

WARHAFFTIGE HISTORIE, WIE DAS EUANGELIUM ZU MUENSTER ANGEFANGEN, VND DARNACH DURCH DIE WIDDERTEUFFER, WIDDER AUFFGEHOERT HAT / Dorpius, H – 1536. BME-162 1 – 9 – ne IDC [240]

WARHEIT = TRUTH – New York. v1-14. 1905-19 – 37r – 1 – us Ross [071]

WARHEYT = TRUTH – (In Yiddish) – New York City, NY. v6 n1548. 6 May 1910-v14 n3245. 28 Feb 1919 – 1r – 1 – $30.00 – cn Can Microfilming [071]

Waring, E J *see* BIBLIOTHECA THERAPEUTICA,...

Waring, Luther Hess *see*
- THE LAW AND THE GOSPEL OF LABOR
- THE POLITICAL THEORIES OF MARTIN LUTHER

Warington, George *see*
- CAN WE BELIEVE IN MIRACLES?
- WHEN WAS THE PENTATEUCH WRITTEN?

Warkentin, Roderich *see* HEINRICH VON KLEIST IN SEINEN BRIEFEN

WARLEIGH / Bray, Anna Eliza – British Fiction Archive: Unit 2 – 9 – uk Bell [830]

Warming, Eugenius *see* LEHRBUCH DER OEKOLOGISCHEN PFLANZENGEOGRAPHIE.

WARMINSTER AND WEST WILTS HERALD *see* WARMINSTER HERALD

WARMINSTER AND WESTBURY JOURNAL – (Warminster Journal 1929-) – England, 19 Nov 1881-12 Apr 1918; 15 Aug 1919-1962 – 69r – 1 – uk British Libr Newspaper [072]

WARMINSTER HERALD – (Warminster & West Wilts Herald, 26 Jun 1866-93) – Warminster, England. 7 Mar 1857-1893 – 37r – 1 – uk British Libr Newspaper [072]

WARMINSTER JOURNAL *see* WARMINSTER AND WESTBURY JOURNAL

WARMINSTER MISCELLANY AND LOCAL ADVERTISER – England.1855; Sept 1836-Jan 1858; Apr 1858-1863. -w. 1/2 reel – 1 – uk British Libr Newspaper [072]

WARMLANDSBERG – Kristinehamn, Filipstad, Sweden.1886-1901 – 1 – sw Kungliga [072]

Warmoth, Henry C *see* PAPERS

Warmus, William *see*
- CZECHOSLOVAKIAN DIARY: 1980
- EMILE GALLE: DREAMS INTO GLASS

Warne, J *see*
- THE BISHOP OF LONDON'S DOCTRINE OF JUSTIFICATION, IN HIS LATE PASTORAL LETTER,...
- THE SPIRIT OF THE MARTYRS REVIVED IN THE DOCTRINES OF THE REVEREND MR. GEORGE WHITEFIELD AND THE JUDICIOUS AND FAITHFUL METHODISTS,...

Warneck, Gustav *see*
- ABRISS EINER GESCHICHTE DER PROTESTANTISCHEN MISSIONEN
- GEGENSEITIGEN BEZIEHUNGEN ZWISCHEN DER MODERNEN MISSION UND CULTUR
- DIE MISSION IN DER SCHULE
- OUTLINES OF A HISTORY OF PROTESTANT MISSIONS

Warnefridi, Pauli *see* DIACONI CASINENSIS IN SANCTAM REGULAM COMMENTARIUM
Warner, Beers and Co *see* HISTORY OF CUMBERLAND AND ADAMS COUNTIES
Warner, Beverley Ellison *see* THE FACTS AND THE FAITH
Warner, G F *see*
- GIRALDI CAMBRENSIS OPERA, VOLS 8 (RS21)
- THE STOWE MISSAL

Warner, George H *see* MILITARY RECORDS OF SCHOHARIE COUNTY VETERANS OF FOUR WARS
WARNER M. BATEMAN PAPERS *see* BATEMAN, WARNER M., PAPERS, MS 2900
Warner, M M *see* WARNER'S HISTORY OF DAKOTA COUNTY
Warner, Sarah Gildersleeve *see* JOURNAL
Warner, Warren *see* THE EXPERIENCES OF A BARRISTER
WARNER'S HISTORY OF DAKOTA COUNTY / Warner, M M – Dakota City: Lyons Mirror Job Office, 1893. Nebraska Reel 7. (The Cox Library Collection) – 5 – us Americana [978]
A WARNING AGAINST COUNTENANCING THE MINISTRATIONS OF MR. GEORGE WHITEFIELD PUBLISHED IN THE NEW CHURCH AT BRISTOW UPON SABBATH, JUNE 6, 1742,... / Gib, A – Edinburgh, 1742 – 1mf – 9 – MP-295/1 – ne IDC [240]
WARNUNG AN ALLE / Bethmann, Johann Philipp – 1p. 1986 – 9 – 1.00f – at Libertarian Micro [335]
WARNUNG ETLICHER OEBRIGKAIT *see* WARNUNG GETREWE CHRISTENLICHE VND NUTZLICHE, ETLICHER OEBRIGKAIT
WARNUNG GETREWE CHRISTENLICHE VND NUTZLICHE, ETLICHER OEBRIGKAIT – 1525 – 9 – BME-30 1 – ne IDC [240]
WARNUNG (GETREWE) DER PREDIGER ZU STRASZBURG VBER DIE ARTICKEL SO J. KAUTZ HAT LASSEN AUSZGOHN – Straszburg. 1527. BME-106 1 – 9 – ne IDC [240]
EIN WARNUNG VOR DEM TEUEFFEL / Greyffenberger, H – 1524. BME-22 1 – 9 – ne IDC [240]
THE WARPATH – San Francisco, CA. 1968-73 – 1r – 1 – $50.00 – R02862 – us Library Micro [071]
WARPATH – 1968- . (American Indian Periodicals in the Princeton University Library). 4 fiches – 9 – $45.00 – us UPA [305]
WAR/PEACE REPORT – New York. v1-13. apr 1961-dec 1974 1; v10-13. 1970-74 5; v13 jun-dec 1974* 9 – 1,5,9 – D2330 – us UMI [360]
WARRACKNABEAL HERALD – 1921-1930. WH1-17 – 17r – 1 – at Corangamite [072]
WARRACKNABEAL HERALD – 1937-1967 – 30r – 1 – at Corangamite [072]
Warrell, Theresa *see* THE IDENTIFICATION OF THE MINIMUM QUALIFICATIONS FOR TENNIS TEACHING PROFESSIONALS TO BE HIRED AT MANAGED TENNES FACILITIES IN THE UNITED STATES
WARREN 1727-1893 – (Mf 1-23: Town & Vital Records 1727-1844. Mf 24-25: Vital Records 1817-49. Mf 26-27: Rebellion Record 1861-66. Mf 28-29: Index to Marriage Intentions 1850-88. Mf 30-37: Marriage Intentions 1850-1904. Mf 38-39: Index to Births 1844-88. Mf 40-41: Index to Marriages 1844-1907. Mf 42-44: Index to Deaths 1844-94. Mf 45-46: Births, Marriages, Deaths 1844-53. Mf 47-51: Births 1854-88. Mf 52-56: Marriages 1854-1907. Mf 57-63: Deaths 1854-94; Deaths 1795-1877. Mf 64-65: Western Library Records 1802-32. Mf 66-68: Births 1889-98 & Index 1889-1910) – (mf ed 1990) – 67mf – 0-87623-105-9 – us Holbrook [920]
WARREN 1791-1869 – (Mf 1: Church & Vital Records 1791-1837. Mf 2: Church Records & Deaths 1791-1836. Mf 3: Church Records 1836-55. Mf 4: Church Records 1856-68. Mf 5: Church & Vital Records 1836-69) – (mf ed 1991) – 5mf – 9 – us Holbrook [920]
WARREN AND BARRINGTON GAZETTE – Warren. R.I. -w. 1866-1908, 1909-63 – 1 – us UMI [071]
WARREN COMMISSION : REPORT OF THE PRESIDENT'S COMMISSION ON THE ASSASINATION OF PRESIDENT JOHN F. KENNEDY – Law Library Microform Consortium. Hearings v1-26 and Report – 9 – $312.00 set – us Hein [320]
WARREN COMMISSION HEARINGS AND REPORT ON THE ASSASSINATION OF PRESIDENT KENNEDY – 27v published 1964-65 – 7r – 1 – $525.00 – us UMI [977]
WARREN CONSTITUTION : WEEKLY DEMOCRATIC NEWSPAPER – Warren, Trumbull, OH. 9 Aug 1870 – 1r – 1 – us Western Res [071]
WARREN COUNTY, GEORGIA. NEW PROVIDENCE BAPTIST CHURCH – Church Records, 1835-February 1930. 916p – 1 – $41.22 – us Baptist [240]
Warren County. Ohio. Providence Baptist Church *see* CHURCH RECORDS, MS 1512
WARREN DAILY CHRONICLE : DAILY INDEPENDENT NEWSPAPER – (1895-July 1903, 1904-1911, 1914-1922 lacking 1912-1913, scattered issues) – Warren, OH. 2 Jul 1894-26 Apr 1924 – 13r – 1 – us Western Res [071]
WARREN DEMOCRATIC CITIZEN : WEEKLY DEMOCRATIC NEWSPAPER – Lebanon, OH. 20 nov 1862-2 may 1863 – 1r – 1 – us Western Res [071]
Warren, Denise M *see*
- AKAN (TWI-FANTE) LANGUAGE COLLECTION
- COLLECTION OF AKAN (TWI-FANTE) MATERIALS

Warren, Edward Henry *see*
- CORPORATE ADVANTAGES WITHOUT INCORPORATION.
- SELECT CASES AND OTHER AUTHORITIES ON THE LAW OF PRIVATE CORPORATIONS

Warren, Elizabeth *see* BUSINESS BANKRUPTCY
Warren, F E *see*
- THE ANTIPHONARY OF BANGOR
- THE LEOFRIC MISSAL
- THE LITURGY AND RITUAL OF THE ANTE-NICENE CHURCH
- THE LITURGY AND RITUAL OF THE CELTIC CHURCH

WARREN FEATHERSTONE REID, SENATE SERVICE 1949-50, 1964-1981 : CHIEF AIDE TO SENATOR WARREN MAGNUSON – 3mf – 9 – $15.00 – us Scholarly Res [320]
WARREN FIRST BAPTIST CHURCH. WARREN, ARKANSAS : CHURCH RECORDS – 13 Jul 1919-24 Jan 1973 – 1 – 23.13 – us Baptist [240]
Warren, G *see* THE ANTIPHONARY OF BANGOR: PART 2
THE WARREN G. HARDING PAPERS / Harding, Warren G; ed by Lentz, Andrea D – (With printed guide. Sections available: Senatorial Papers 1915-21 8r $600. Presidential Election Papers 1918-21 102r $7,650. Presidential Papers 1921-23 108r $8,100) – 263r – 1 – $19,725.00 – D3167 – Dist. us Scholarly Res – us Ohio Hist [977]
Warren, Henry White *see* THE BIBLE IN THE WORLD'S EDUCATION
Warren, Israel Perkins *see*
- THE BOOK OF REVELATION
- THE BOOK OF REVELATION: AN EXPOSITION: BASED ON...PROF. STUART'S COMMENTARY

Warren, J A *see* DOES VITAMIN E SUPPLEMENTATION ATTENUATE EXERCISE-INDUCED SKELETAL MUSCLE INJURY
Warren, J C *see* THE MASTODEN GIGANTEUS OF NORTH AMERICA
Warren, John R *see* EFFECTS OF NUTRITIONAL INTERVENTION ON BLOOD GLUCOSE LEVELS IN WOMEN (AGE 73-85)
Warren, Joseph *see* A GLANCE BACKWARD AT FIFTEEN YEARS OF MISSIONARY LIFE IN NORTH INDIA
Warren, Josiah *see*
- EQUITABLE COMMERCE
- TRUE CIVILIZATION, AN IMMEDIATE NECESSITY AND THE LAST GROUND FOR HOPE FOR MANKIND

Warren, Mercy *see* MERCY WARREN PAPERS, 1709-1841
WARREN MIRROR – Warren, PA. -sw 1897-1910; 1912-1913 – 13 – $25.00r – us I.M.R. [071]
WARREN NEWSLETTER AND TRUMBULL COUNTY REPUBLICAN – (Weekly Democratic-Republican newspaper) – Warren, OH, 24 aug 1830-12 feb 1839 – 2R – 1 – us Western Res [071]
WARREN, OHIO, TAXES, MS V.F. O – (List of all the lands in the northwestern territory claimed by the residents of the district, subject to territorial taxation for the year 1801) – 1801 – 1r – 1 – us Western Res [978]
WARREN, OHIO, TAXES, MS V.F.O. – (True Copy of the list of residents land in the township) – 1805 – 1r – 1 – us Western Res [978]
Warren, Richard *see* FAMILIES OF THE PILGRIMS
Warren, S *see* CHRONICLES OF WESLEYAN METHODISM, FIRST DEPARTMENT
Warren, Samuel *see*
- ADVENTURES OF AN ATTORNEY IN SEARCH OF PRACTICE
- THE EXPERIENCES OF A BARRISTER AND CONFESSIONS OF AN ATTORNEY

WARREN SENTINEL – Front Royal. Va. 1919-1922; 1935-1945; 1950- – 1 – us UMI [071]
WARREN STREET EXPOSITION – Warren, OH, 5-7 oct. 1898 – 1 reel – 1 – us Western Res [338]
WARREN TRIBUNE : WEEKLY REPUBLICAN NEWSPAPER – Warren, Trumbull, OH. 23 Apr 1889-22 Apr 1890 – 1r – 1 – us Western Res [071]
WARREN UNION BAPTIST CHURCH. CULLOM ASSOCIATION. NORTH CAROLINA : CHURCH RECORDS – Cullom Association. Warrenton. North Carolina.Warren Union Baptist Church – 1 – 5.00 – us Baptist [240]
WARREN WEEKLY TRIBUNE : WEEKLY REPUBLICAN NEWSPAPER – Warren, OH. 1 Sept 1893-25 May 1916 – 4r – 1 – us Western Res [071]
WARREN WEEKLY TRIBUNE – (Weekly Republican newspaper) – Warren, OH. jan 3-dec 26, 1918 – 1r – 1 – us Western Res [071]
Warren, William Fairfield *see*
- CONSTITUTIONAL LAW QUESTIONS NOW PENDING IN THE METHODIST EPISCOPAL CHURCH
- SYSTEMATISCHE THEOLOGIE
- THAT PSEUDO-JUDICIAL DECLARATION OF 1888

WARREN-ADAMS PAPERS, 1767-1822 – (Letters of John, Abigail, and Samuel Adams and James and Mercy Warren) – Massachusetts Historical Society – 1r – 1 – $85.00 – us UMI [920]
WARRENPOINT WEEKLY AND COUNTY DOWN ADVERTISER – Ireland. Down Examiner. -w. 18 April-21 Nov 1953. 25 ft – 1 – uk British Libr Newspaper [072]
WARRENSBURG BAPTIST CHURCH. GREENS COUNTY. TENNESSEE : CHURCH RECORDS – 1793, 1874-91 – 1 – 8.64 – us Baptist [240]
WARRENTON, COLUMBIA PRESS *see* COLUMBIA PRESS
WARRENTON NEWS AND CLATSOP COUNTY ARGUS – Warrenton, OR. -w. 6 Mar 1925-8 Dec 1932. 1 roll – 1 – us U.O. Library [071]
Warriner, Solomon *see* MUSICA SACRE
Warring, Charles Bartlett *see*
- GENESIS I AND MODERN SCIENCE
- THE MOSAIC ACCOUNT OF CREATION...THE ONENESS OF GENESIS AND SCIENCE

WARRIOR CREEK BAPTIST CHURCH. LOURENS ASSOCIATION. GRAY COURT, SOUTH CAROLINA : CHURCH RECORDS – 1843-1911; 1917-32. Typescript – 1 – 28.08 – us Baptist [240]
WARRNAMBOOL AGRICULTURAL SOCIETY – 1911-1990. Minutes. WAS1-2 – 2r – 5 – at Corangamite [630]
WARRNAMBOOL AND DISTRICT HISTORICAL VEHICLE CLUB MINUTES – 1973-1993 – 1r – 5 – at Corangamite [980]
WARRNAMBOOL AND DISTRICT HISTORICAL VEHICLE CLUB NEWSLETTER – 1973-1994 – 2r – 5 – at Corangamite [980]
WARRNAMBOOL AND DISTRICT PHOTOS – 1886. WDP1 – 12mf – 9 – at Corangamite [910]
WARRNAMBOOL BASE HOSPITAL – 1878-1987. Annual Reports. WBHAR1-2 – 2r – 1 – at Corangamite [910]
WARRNAMBOOL BASE HOSPITAL – 1926-1965. News Clippings. WBH1 – 1r – 1 – at Corangamite [910]
WARRNAMBOOL CEMETARY REGISTER – 1974-2/1994 – 21r – 9 – at Corangamite [920]
WARRNAMBOOL CEMETERY GRAVE PLANS – 1854-1988 – 5r – 5 – at Corangamite [910]
WARRNAMBOOL CEMETERY REGISTER – 1856-1984. WCT1 – 1r – 1 – at Corangamite [920]
WARRNAMBOOL CITY COUNCIL MINUTES – 1856-1993 Incls. 2A-F – 68r – 1 – at Corangamite [910]
WARRNAMBOOL CITY COUNCIL RATES – 1864-1975 – 70r – 1,5 – at Corangamite [910]
WARRNAMBOOL DEATH NOTICES – 1982-1992 – 6r – 9 – at Corangamite [920]
WARRNAMBOOL ECHO – 1891-1899. WE1-8 – 8r – 1 – at Corangamite [072]
WARRNAMBOOL EXAMINER – 1853-1857. WEX1 – 1r – 1 – at Corangamite [072]
WARRNAMBOOL FIRE BRIGADE AUXILIARY – 1955-1989. Minutes. WFBA1 – 1r – 1 – at Corangamite [910]
WARRNAMBOOL FIRE BRIGADE MINUTES – 1863-1980. WFB1-3 – 3r – 1 – at Corangamite [910]
WARRNAMBOOL HARBOUR MASTERS JOURNAL – 1861-1868 – 7mf – 9 – at Corangamite [980]
WARRNAMBOOL HARBOUR MASTERS JOURNAL TRANSCRIPT – 1861-1868 – 2r – 9 – at Corangamite [980]
WARRNAMBOOL INDEPENDENT – 1883-1886. WI1-4 – 4r – 1 – at Corangamite [072]
WARRNAMBOOL INDEPENDENT – Australia. Jun 1883-Sep 1886.-w. 3mqn reels – 1 – uk British Libr Newspaper [072]
WARRNAMBOOL LIGHTHOUSE JOURNAL – 1859-1872 – 6mf – 9 – at Corangamite [980]
WARRNAMBOOL SHIRE MINUTE BOOKS – 1862-1992. SOW1-19 – 22r – 1; 5 – at Corangamite [910]
WARRNAMBOOL SHIRE RATE BOOKS – 1874-1981. SOWR1-28 – 40r – 1; 5 – at Corangamite [910]
WARRNAMBOOL STANDARD – 1931-8/1995 – 345r – 1 – at Corangamite [072]
WARRNAMBOOL STANDARD – Australia. Sep 1877-Aug 1896 (missing Jul 1893-Dec 1895).-w. 23mqn reels – 1 – uk British Libr Newspaper [072]
WARRNAMBOOL THEATRE COMPANY PROGRAMMES – 1955-1985. WTC1 – 1r – 1 – at Corangamite [910]
Warrum, Noble *see* UTAH SINCE STATEHOOD
WARS AND REVOLUTIONS / Sutton, Anthony – A comprehensive list of conflicts, including fatalities. Pt. 2:1900-72. Special Project 1973. 206p – 1 – 35.00r – us Hoover Inst Photo [900]
THE WARS OF RELIGION IN FRANCE, 1559-1576 : THE HUGUENOTS, CATHERINE DE MEDICI AND PHILIP 2 / Thompson, James – Chicago: University of Chicago Press, 1909 – 2mf – us A.T.L.A. [944]
THE WARS OF THE HUGUENOTS / Hanna, William – 1872 – 9 – us A.T.L.A. [240]
THE WARSAV VOICE – (Comes in English) – 1988 – 1 – sz Infoprint [947]
WARSAW BULLETIN – Warsaw, IL. v3-22. 1856-87 – 5r – 1 – us Ross [071]
WARSAW BULLETIN – Warsaw, Ill. Apr 4 1856-July 1 1887. Incomplete – 1 – us NY Public [071]
WARSAW SIGNAL – Warsaw, IL. 1840-53 – 5r – 1 – us Ross [071]
WARSAW SIGNAL – Warsaw, Ill. 1st series v. 2-3; n.s. v. 1-8. May 1841-Oct 1842; Feb 1844-Mar 1853. Incomplete – 1 – us NY Public [071]
Warsaw. University *see* ZAPISKI OBSHCHESTVA ISTORII FILOLOGII I PRAVA PRI VARSHAVSKOM UNIVERSITETE
THE WARSAW VOICE – (Backfile 1988-98 $85r) – 1999- – 2r per y – 1 – $160.00 standing order – us Ross [072]
THE WARSAW WEEKLY – Warsaw, Poland. Aug 1937-Feb 1938 – 1r – 1 – us L of C Photodup [943]
Warschauer, Joseph *see*
- JESUS: SEVEN QUESTIONS
- PROBLEMS OF IMMANENCE

WARSCHAUER ZEITUNG – Warsaw, Poland. Nov 1939-1940 – 4r – 1 – us L of C Photodup [943]
WARSCHAUER ZEITUNG – Warschau (Warszawa), Poland. 12 Nov 1939-1940 – 1 – gw Mikrofilm [072]
WARSHIP INTERNATIONAL – Toledo. v1-12. 1964-75* 1; v13-34 1976-97+ 1,5,9; v29-31. 1992-94* 5 – 1,5,9 – D9866 – us UMI [623]
WART NYA HEM – Kearney, NE. -w. 4 Jan 1877-17 May 1877. In Swedish – 1 – us NE Hist [071]
WARTA BANDUNG – Bandung. Indonesia. 1964-1965 – 1 – us UMI [072]

WARTA EKONOMI MARITIM – (English Summary Edition. Missing: 1968, v1-2(1-16), v2(18-49, 51-55, 57-87); 1969, v3(89, 92, 123); 1971, v4(285-286, 292-296), v5(319-332, 336-338, 343-344)) – Tandjung Priok: Jajasan Maritim Press. v1-6(1-499). 1968-73 – 304mf – 9 – SE-1987/1 – ne IDC [330]

WARTA EKONOMI MARITIM REVIEW – (Missing: 1971, v3(23); 1972, v4(33)) – Tandjung Priok: Jajasan Maritim Press. v1-3(1-41). 1969-72 – 64mf – 9 – SE-1988/1 – ne IDC [330]

WARTA EKONOMI UNTUK INDONESIA – Djakarta. Incomplete. SE 306 1. 1952-1963 – 9 – ne IDC [338]

WARTA INDUSTRI – Djakarta. Incomplete. SE 307 1. 1955-1966 – 9 – ne IDC [380]

WARTA NEGARA – Penang, Malaysia. 1958-Oct 1960 – 6r – 1 – us L of C Photodup [072]

WARTA SARBUPRI. DJAKARTA, DPP SARBUPRI – SE 437 1. Lacking: v. 1-3; 1948-1952. 1948-1957 – 9 – ne IDC [073]

WARTABHAKTI – Djakarta. Indonesia. 1960-1965 – 1 – us UMI [072]

DIE WARTBURG – Braunschweig, Germany. Jan.-June, 1851 – 1 – gw Mikrofilm [072]

DIE WARTBURG : DEUTSCH-EVANGELISCHES WOCHENSCHRIFT – (Lacking: v22 1923 p92-100) – v14-33; v37-39. 1915-34; 1938-40 – Inquire – 1 – ATLA S0063 – us A.T.L.A. [073]

Wartenegg, Wilhelm von *see* ERINNERUNGEN AN FRANZ GRILLPARZER

THE WARTIME CONFERENCES OF THE COMBINED CHIEFS OF STAFF / U.S. Army – 1941-45 – 3r – 1 – $255.00 – S1675 – Co-publ with the Center for Military History – us Scholarly Res [355]

WAR-TIME SERMONS / Henson, H Hensley – London, New York: Macmillan, 1915 – 1mf – us A.T.L.A. [240]

WARTIME TRANSLATIONS OF SEIZED JAPANESE DOCUMENTS : ALLIED TRANSLATOR AND INTERPRETER SECTION RECORDS, 1942-45 – (Guide only, $455.00) – 9 – $9,485.00 – us UPA [950]

Wartluft, Elizabeth M *see* THE FUNCTIONS OF DANCE IN SOCIAL GATHERINGS IN SEATTLE'S ARAB-AMERICAN COMMUNITY

WARUM KOENNEN WIR DAS APOSTOLISCHE GLAUBENSBEKENNTNIS NICHT AUFGEBEN? : ZWEITE STREITSCHRIFT ZUM KAMPF UM DAS APOSTOLIKUM / Cremer, Hermann – Berlin: Wiegandt & Grieben, 1893 – 1mf – us A.T.L.A. [240]

WARUM UND WOFUER WIR KAEMPFEN / Haller, Johannes – Tuebingen: Kloeres, 1914. 28p – 1 – us U.W. Library [940]

Warvelle, George William *see*
- A COMPENDIUM OF FREEMASONRY IN ILLINOIS
- PRINCIPLES OF THE LAW OF REAL PROPERTY.
- A TREATISE ON THE PRINCIPLES AND PRACTICE OF THE ACTION OF EJECTMENT AND STATUTORY SUBSTITUTES

WARWICK 1739-1890 – 33mf – 9 – us Holbrook [920]

WARWICK COURIER *see* COURIER WARWICK

WARWICKSHIRE, 1822 : BRITISH ISLES CENSUS DIRECTORIES PROJECT, ENGLAND – (In prep) – at Vine [941]

WARWICKSHIRE, 1830 : BRITISH ISLES CENSUS DIRECTORIES PROJECT, ENGLAND. VOL 260 – 9mf – 9 – A$57.00 – at Vine [941]

WARWICKSHIRE, 1842 : BRITISH ISLES CENSUS DIRECTORIES PROJECT, ENGLAND – (In prep) – at Vine [941]

WARWICKSHIRE, 1850 : BRITISH ISLES CENSUS DIRECTORIES PROJECT, ENGLAND – at Vine [941]

WARWICKSHIRE, 1854 : BRITISH ISLES CENSUS DIRECTORIES PROJECT, ENGLAND. VOL 7 – 8mf – 9 – A$51.00 – at Vine [941]

WARWICKSHIRE, 1862 : BRITISH ISLES CENSUS DIRECTORIES PROJECT, ENGLAND. VOL 131 – 3mf – 9 – A$21.00 – at Vine [941]

WARWICKSHIRE, 1874 : BRITISH ISLES CENSUS DIRECTORIES PROJECT, ENGLAND. VOL 56 – 8mf – 9 – A$51.00 – at Vine [941]

WARWICKSHIRE, 1888 : BRITISH ISLES CENSUS DIRECTORIES PROJECT, ENGLAND – (In prep) – at Vine [941]

WARWICKSHIRE, 1924 : BRITISH ISLES CENSUS DIRECTORIES PROJECT, ENGLAND. VOL 203 – 7mf – 9 – A$45.00 – at Vine [941]

WARWICKSHIRE (BIRMINGHAM), 1777 : BRITISH ISLES CENSUS DIRECTORIES PROJECT, ENGLAND. VOL 242 – 2mf – 9 – A$15.00 – at Vine [941]

WARWICKSHIRE (BIRMINGHAM), 1816 : BRITISH ISLES CENSUS DIRECTORIES PROJECT, ENGLAND – (In prep) – at Vine [941]

WARWICKSHIRE (BIRMINGHAM), 1823 : BRITISH ISLES CENSUS DIRECTORIES PROJECT, ENGLAND. VOL 97 – 4mf – 9 – A$27.00 – at Vine [941]

WARWICKSHIRE (BIRMINGHAM), 1824 : BRITISH ISLES CENSUS DIRECTORIES PROJECT, ENGLAND – (In prep) – at Vine [941]

WARWICKSHIRE (BIRMINGHAM), 1829 : BRITISH ISLES CENSUS DIRECTORIES PROJECT, ENGLAND. VOL 61 – 1mf – 9 – A$9.00 – at Vine [941]

WARWICKSHIRE (BIRMINGHAM), 1837 : BRITISH ISLES CENSUS DIRECTORIES PROJECT, ENGLAND. VOL 196 – 1mf – 9 – A$9.00 – at Vine [941]

WARWICKSHIRE (BIRMINGHAM), 1852 : BRITISH ISLES CENSUS DIRECTORIES PROJECT, ENGLAND – at Vine [941]

WARWICKSHIRE (BIRMINGHAM), 1870 : BRITISH ISLES CENSUS DIRECTORIES PROJECT, ENGLAND – at Vine [941]

WARWICKSHIRE (BIRMINGHAM), 1919 : BRITISH ISLES CENSUS DIRECTORIES PROJECT, ENGLAND – (In prep) – at Vine [941]

WARWICKSHIRE (BRIMINGHAM AND COVENTRY), 1805 : BRITISH ISLES CENSUS DIRECTORIES PROJECT, ENGLAND. VOL 164 – 1mf – 9 – A$9.00 – at Vine [941]

WARWICKSHIRE CHRONICLE – Warwick, England. -w. 19 April 1826-19 Dec 1827. 50 ft – 1 – uk British Libr Newspaper [072]

WARZU DAS HAILIGE CREUETZ NUTZ VNND GUT SEY / Huberinus, Caspar – [Augsburg: Philipp Ulhart], 1533. [G.F.: 11.3] – 1mf – 9 – HUB-31/1 – ne IDC [240]

WARZU DAS HAYLIGE CREUETZ NUTZ VND GUT SEY / Huberinus, Caspar – [Augsburg: Philipp Ulhart], 1542. [G.F.: 11.6] – 1mf – 9 – HUB-67/1 – ne IDC [240]

WAS CHRIST BORN AT BETHLEHEM? : A STUDY ON THE CREDIBILITY OF ST. LUKE / Ramsay, William Mitchell – (Includes bibliographical references and appendix) – New York: G P Putnam; London: Hodder & Stoughton, 1898 – 1mf – 9 – 0-8370-4838-9 – 1985-2838 – us A.T.L.A. [220]

WAS CHRIST IN ADAM? / Miller, John – 3rd ed. Princeton, NJ: Evangelical Reform Publ Co, 1887, c1877 – 1mf – 9 – 0-8370-4103-1 – 1985-2103 – us A.T.L.A. [240]

WAS DER GOTTLOSE UND FALSCHE PROPHET MAHOMET FUER EIN FALSCHE VERFUEHRISCHE KETZEREY VND LEHR ERDACHT DURCH WELCHE ER IN GROSSES ANSEHEN BEY ALLERLEY VOELCKER KOMMEN VND JHM EIN GEWALTIGEN ANHANG GEMACHT... / Loew, C – Coelln, 1596 – 2mf – 9 – H-8389/1 – ne IDC [260]

WAS DER TAG MIR ZUTRAEGT : FUENFUNDSECHZIG NEUE STUDIEN / Altenberg, Peter – 9. bis 11. Aufl. Berlin: S Fischer, 1921 – 1r – 1 – us U.W. Library [430]

WAS DER WIND ERZAEHLT : POESIEN IN NIEDERDEUTSCHER MUNDART / Wette, Hermann – (Includes glossary) – Koeln: A Ahn, 1884 – 1r – 1 – us U.W. Library [390]

WAS DIE SCHWALBE SANG : ROMAN / Spielhagen, Friedrich – Leipzig: P Reclam, jun., [19–?] – 1r – 1 – us U.W. Library [830]

WAS GEREDT SEY, DAS DIE SCHRIFFT SAGT, GOTT THUE VND MACHE GUTS VND BOESES / Denck, H – 1526. BME-59 1 – 9 – ne IDC [240]

WAS HABEN WIR HEUTE AN PAULUS? / Wernle, Paul – Basel: Helbing & Lichtenhahn, 1904. 1 fiche. 8370-5798-1 – 9 – us A.T.L.A. [240]

WAS HALTET IHR VON JESUS? : BEITRAEGE ZUM GESPRAECH UEBER JESUS VON NAZARETH / ed by Trilling, W & Berndt, Inge – Leipzig, 1975 – 6mf – 8 – ne Slangenburg [240]

WAS HEISST UND ZU WELCHEN ENDE STUDIERT MAN DOGMENGESCHICHTE? / Krueger, Gustav – 1895 – 1 – us A.T.L.A. [240]

WAS ICH IM BERLINER REICHSTAG SAGTE / Liebknecht, Wilhelm – Leipzig, 1867 – 1 – DM30.00 – gw Mikro Press [943]

WAS IST DIE WAHRHEIT VON JESU?: ZEITFRAGE UND BEKENNTINISS / Koenig, Heinrich – Leipzig: F.A. Brockhaus, 1867. 1 fiche – 9 – us A.T.L.A. [240]

WAS IST SCHRIFTGEMAESS?: VORTRAG / Stange, Carl – Leipzig: Dieterich, 1904. 1 fiche – 9 – us A.T.L.A. [240]

WAS IT A PISTOL : A NUT FOR LAWYERS – Washington: Rufus H Darby, 1890 – 2mf – 9 – $3.00 – LLMC 91-002 – us L.L.M.C. [810]

WAS JEDERMANN HEUTE VON DER MISSION WISSEN MUSS / Struempfel, Emil – Berlin: Martin Warneck, 1901 – 1mf – 9 – 0-8370-6706-5 – 1986-0706 – us A.T.L.A. [240]

WAS JESUS INFLUENCED BY BUDDHISM. A COMPARATIVE STUDY OF THE LIVES AND THOUGHTS OF GAUTAMA AND JESUS / Goddard, Dwight – Thetford, VT, (c1927). 249p – 1 – us U.W. Library [230]

WAS MACHEN WIR CHRISTEN MIT UNSERN JUDEN!? / Plath, Karl Heinrich Christian – Noerdlingen: C.H. Beck, 1881 – 1mf – us A.T.L.A. [230]

WAS MUSS AN DEN STAATSVERFASSUNGEN GEAENDERT WERDEN DAMIT EIN ANDAUERNDER FRIEDE MOEGLICH WIRD, UND WIE KOENNEN DIESE REFORMEN DURCHGESETZT WERDEN? / Zube, John – 3fiches (29x) – 9 – 1.00f – at Libertarian Micro [320]

WAS TUN, SIBYLLE / Schieker-Ebe, Sofie – Stuttgart: K Thienemann, 1943 – 1r – 1 – us U.W. Library [830]

WAS WISSEN WIR VON JESUS? : EINE ABRECHNUNG MIT PROFESSOR D BOUSSET IN GOETTINGEN / Kalthoff, Albert – Schmargendorf-Berlin: "Renaissance", 1904 – 1mf – 9 – 0-8370-3840-5 – 1985-1840 – us A.T.L.A. [240]

WASCANA REVIEW – Regina. v1-29. 1966-94 – 9 – Can$20.00y – cn Micromedia [073]

WASCO COUNTY SUN – The Dalles OR. Mar 21 28 Apr 11 1883 + – 1 – us U.O. Library [071]

WASCO NEWS – Wasco, OR. -w. 28 Oct 1897-17 Jan 1908. 2 rolls – 1 – us U.O. Library [071]

Wase, Christopher *see* METHODI PRACTICAE SPECIMEN: AN ESSAY OF A PARCTICAL GRAMMAR

Wasersztrum, Serge *see* FRENCH PRECURSORS OF PSYCHIATRY AND PSYCHOANALYSIS, 1750-1900

Washburn College. Topeka, Kansas *see*
- RECORDS, 1865-89
- RECORDS, 1881-1926

Washburn, Emory *see*
- A MANUAL OF CRIMINAL LAW, INCLUDING THE MODE OF PROCEDURE BY WHICH IT IS ENFORCED
- A TREATISE ON THE AMERICAN LAW OF REAL PROPERTY

Washburn, George *see* WOMAN: HER WORK IN THE CHURCH

Washburn, George P *see* PAPERS

WASHBURN LAW JOURNAL – (v1-24 1960-85 on reel $330.00. v25-34 1985-95 on mf $179.00) – v1-34. 1960-95 – 5,6,9 – $509.00 set – us Hein [340]

Washburn, Pat *see* SCRAPBOOKS, LETTERS, AND CLIPPINGS

Washburn, Richard A *see* THE VALIDITY AND RELIABILITY OF HEART RATE AS A MEASURE OF DAILY ENERGY EXPENDITURE

Washburn, W Wyan *see* BROTHER JOHN'S CANAAN IN CAROLINA, 1872-1956

WASHINGTON : REVISED CODE OF WASHINGTON ANNOTATED – St Paul: West Pub Co, 1961-Jan 1996 update – 9 – $1,705.00 set – us Hein [340]

WASHINGTON : SESSION LAWS OF AMERICAN STATES AND TERRITORIES – 1854-1995 – 9 – $1,562.00 set – us Hein [340]

Washington *see*
- REPORTS AND OPINIONS (A-G)
- REPORTS, POST-NRS
- REPORTS, PRE-NRS

WASHINGTON 1755-1907 – (Mf 1: Town Records 1778-84. Mf 2: Town Records 1784-89. Mf 3: Town Records 1789-95. Mf 4: Town Records 1795-1801. Mf 5: Town Records 1801-06. Mf 6: Town Records 1807-1812. Mf 7: Town Records 1812-18. Mf 8: Town & Vital Records 1771-1819. Mf 9: Vital Records 1755-1859. Mf 10: Town & Vital Records 1804-77. Mf 11: Town Records 1832-77. Mf 12: Town Records 1798-1875. Mf 13: Births 1842-66; Marriages 1842-50. Mf 14: Marriages 1851-62; Deaths 1842-63. Mf 15: Deaths 1864-1930. Mf 16: Deaths 1931-87. Mf 17: Marriages 1862-1906. Mf 18: Births 1864-1907) – (mf ed 1988) – 18mf – 9 – 0-87623-082-6 – us Holbrook [920]

WASHINGTON ACADEMY OF SCIENCES : JOURNAL OF THE WASHINGTON ACADEMY OF SCIENCES – Washington. v1-85. jul 1911-dec 1997+ 1; v62-74 mar 1972-dec 1984 v75-82 mar 1985-dec 1992*. v83-85 mar 1993-dec 1997+ 5; v67-85. mar 1977-dec 1997+ 9 – 1,5,9 – D7669 – us UMI [500]

Washington Academy of Sciences *see* – JOURNAL

WASHINGTON ACADEMY OF SCIENCES: JOURNAL – v. 1-69. 1911-79 – 1, 5, 6 – 350.00 – us Princeton Micro [500]

Washington. Agricultural College Experiment Station *see* DAIRYING INSTITUTE PROCEEDINGS

Washington. Agricultural College Experiment Station. Dep't. of Animal Science *see* BEEF CATTLE DAY (PROCEEDINGS)

Washington. Agricultural Experiment Station *see*
- BULLETIN
- BULLETIN, SPECIAL SERIES
- CIRCULAR
- POPULAR BULLETIN
- REPORT
- TECHNICAL BULLETIN

Washington. Agricultural Extension Service *see*
- EXTENSION BULLETIN
- EXTENSION CIRCULAR
- EXTENSION MIMEO
- FARM WAR NEWS
- MISCELLANEOUS PUBLICATION
- WASHINGTON'S RESEARCH PROGRESS

Washington. Agricultural Extension Service, Pullman *see* POULTRY POINTERS

WASHINGTON ALLSTON PAPERS, 1800-1843 – Massachusetts Historical Society – 2r – 1 – $155.00 – us UMI [760]

WASHINGTON AND LEE LAW REVIEW – Lexington. v1-47 fal 1939-fal 1990* 1; v48-54 win 1991-fal 1997+ 1,5,9 – 1,5,9 – D14890 – us UMI [340]

WASHINGTON AND LEE LAW REVIEW – v1-51. 1939-94 – 1,5,6 – $1,035.00 – us Hein [073]

WASHINGTON ATTORNEY GENERAL REPORTS AND OPINIONS – (6 1888-1980 $280.00. 9 1981-1995 $170.00) – 1888-1995 – 6,9 – $450.00 set – us Hein [340]

Washington, B *see* WASHINGTON'S REPORTS OF CASES IN THE THIRD CIRCUIT, 1803-1827

WASHINGTON BAPTIST CHURCH. PELZER, SOUTH CAROLINA : CHURCH RECORDS – 1821-1952. Treasurer's report. 1953-71 – 1 – 44.80 – us Baptist [240]

A WASHINGTON BIBLE-CLASS / Hamilton, Gail – NY: D Appleton, 1891, c1890 – 1mf – 9 – 0-8370-3574-0 – 1985-1574 – us A.T.L.A. [220]

Washington, Booker T *see*
- THE STORY OF THE NEGRO
- WASHINGTON, BOOKER T, SELECTED WORKS

Washington, Booker T. *see* PAPERS

WASHINGTON, BOOKER T, SELECTED WORKS : AND MISCELLANEOUS WORKS ON THE AMERICAN NEGRO BY OTHER AUTHORS / Washington, Booker T – 1867-1937 – 1r – 1 – us Ross [975]

WASHINGTON BULLETIN – (Cont by: Washington Social Legislation Bulletin. Former titles: Child Welfare Information Service, Bulletin jan 2, 1945-aug 1946. Social Legislation Information Service, Bulletin 1946-60) – Washington. v22-24 jan 1971-apr 1976 1; v22-23 jan 1971-dec 1974*. v24 jan 1975-apr 1976 5,9 – 1,5,9 – D7096 – us UMI [360]

WASHINGTON BUSINESS JOURNAL – McLean. v1-13 may 1982-1994*. v14-16 1995-97+ – 1 – D16693 – us UMI [380]

WASHINGTON CHURCH BOOK / Beaufort County. North Carolina. First Baptist Church – 1821-37, 1852-56, 1859-61, 1865-83 – 1 – 5.00 – us Baptist [240]

WASHINGTON COUNTY HATCHET – (Set incl. Washington County Hatchet and Forest Grove Times) – Forest Grove, OR. -w. 12 Apr 1895-3 Aug 1899. – 1r – 1 – us U.O. Library [071]

WASHINGTON COUNTY HATCHET AND FOREST GROVE TIMES – Forest Grove OR. June 4 1896-Aug 26 1897 – 1 – us U.O. Library [071]
WASHINGTON COUNTY NEWS – Chipley. Fl. -w. 1946- – 1 – us P.K. Yonge [071]
WASHINGTON COUNTY NEWS – Forest Grove OR. May 22 1903-Mar 2 1911 – 1 – us U.O. Library [071]
WASHINGTON COUNTY NEWS – Forest Grove. Or. -w. 1909-11 – 1 – us UMI [071]
WASHINGTON COUNTY NEWS-TIMES – Forest Grove, OR. and yWashington County News. -w. 1909-52 – 1 – 504.00 – us Oregon Hist [071]
WASHINGTON COUNTY NEWS-TIMES – Forest Grove, OR. -w. 1 Jan 1953-. – 29r – 1 – us U.O. Library [071]
WASHINGTON COUNTY NEWS-TIMES – Forest Grove. Or. -w. 1909-52 – 1 – us UMI [071]
WASHINGTON COUNTY REGISTER – Washington. Kan. 1926-1951 – 1 – us UMI [071]
WASHINGTON COUNTY REVIEW-HERALD – Arlington, NE. -w. May 1901-Sep. 1902; Mar. 1908-Jan. 1951 – 1 – us NE Hist [071]
WASHINGTON CRIME NEWS SERVICES' CORPORATE SECURITY DIGEST – (Formed by the merger of: Computer Crime Digest; and: Security Systems Digest. Cont by: Washington Crime News Services' Security Director's Digest) – Springfield. v1-8. sep 1987-dec 1994 1,9; v1 sep-dec 1987*. v2 1988. v3-8 1989-94* 5 – 1,5,9 – D16288 – us UMI [360]
WASHINGTON CRIME NEWS SERVICES' CORPORATE SECURITY DIGEST *see* WASHINGTON CRIME NEWS SERVICES' SECURITY DIRECTOR'S DIGEST
WASHINGTON CRIME NEWS SERVICES' NARCOTICS DEMAND REDUCTION DIGEST – (Merged with: Narcotics Control Digest; to form: Narcotics Enforcement & Prevention Digest) – Fairfax. v1-6. may 1989-dec 1994* – 1,5,9 – D17145 – us UMI [360]
WASHINGTON CRIME NEWS SERVICE'S SECURITY DIRECTOR'S DIGEST *see* WASHINGTON CRIME NEWS SERVICES' CORPORATE SECURITY DIGEST
WASHINGTON CRIME NEWS SERVICES' SECURITY DIRECTOR'S DIGEST – (Cont: Washington Crime News Services' Corporate Security Digest) – Fairfax. v1-3. 1995-97+ – 1,5,9 – D21158 – us UMI [360]
WASHINGTON CRIMINAL JUSTICE REPORT'S CRIME VICTIMS DIGEST – (Cont by: Crime Victims Digest) – Springfield. v1-5. oct 1973-dec 1988*. v6-8 jan 1989-jul 1991 – 1 – D15224 – us UMI [360]
THE WASHINGTON DAILY NEWS – Washington. D.C. 30 Mar 1940; 14 Jun 1941 – 1 – us NY Public [071]
WASHINGTON DAILY RECORD – Washington, DC. On film: 15 Jul 1932-13 Jan 1936. LL-012 – 1 – us L of C Photodup [340]
WASHINGTON, DC. E STREET BAPTIST CHURCH : AND OTHER BAPTIST CHURCHES OF THE DC VICINITY – (Index included. 210p) – 1 reel – 1 – $9.45 – us Baptist [240]
Washington, DC. Library of Congress. Prints and Photographs Division *see* HISTORIC AMERICAN BUILDINGS SURVEY
Washington, DC. National Gallery of Art *see* THE INDEX OF AMERICAN DESIGN (TIAM)
WASHINGTON DEMOCRAT – Colfax. Wash. -w. 1881-82 – 1 – us UMI [071]
WASHINGTON DEMOCRAT – Hillsboro OR. Feb 15 May 17 24 Aug 23 1889, June 20 July 25 Aug 1-29 1890, Sep 5 12 19 1890, Feb 6 1891 – 1 – us U.O. Library [071]
WASHINGTON DEMOCRAT – Olympia. Wash. 1864-1865 – 1 – us UMI [071]
WASHINGTON DOSSIER – 1986- – 1,5,6,9 – us UMI [073]
THE WASHINGTON EXAMINER – Seattle. Wash. 1960 – 1 – us A.J.P.C. [071]
WASHINGTON FARMER – v35,no.12-v96,no.12. 15 Jun 1914-Jun 1971 – 1 – us UMI [630]
WASHINGTON FARMER-STOCKMAN – v96,no.13-v104. 1 Jul 1971-1979 – 1 – us UMI [636]
WASHINGTON FARMER-STOCKMAN. INLAND EDITION – (1985- . 5,6,9) – v105- . 1980- – 1 – us UMI [636]
WASHINGTON FARMER-STOCKMAN. PACIFIC EDITION – (1985- . 5,6,9) – v105- . 1980- – 1 – us UMI [636]
WASHINGTON FIRST BAPTIST CHURCH. WASHINGTON, DISTRICT OF COLUMBIA : CHURCH RECORDS – v. 1-8. 1802-1952. (Complete) – 1 – 166.50 – us Baptist [240]
WASHINGTON FIRST BAPTIST CHURCH. WILKES COUNTY. GEORGIA : CHURCH RECORDS – 1827-1905 – 1 – 40.14 – us Baptist [240]
Washington, George *see*
- THE JOURNAL OF MAJOR GEO. WASHINGTON
- LETTERS
- PAPERS
- THE WRITINGS OF GEORGE WASHINGTON

THE WASHINGTON GLADDEN COLLECTION / ed by Arnold, Gary J – (With printed guide) – 52r – 1 – $4,420.00 – D3174 – Dist. us Scholarly Res – us Ohio Hist [920]
WASHINGTON HEALTH RECORD – Washington. 1978-93* 1; 1994-97+ 1,5,9 – 1,5,9 – D21689 – us UMI [613]
WASHINGTON INDEPENDENT – Hillsboro, OR. -w. 28 Dec 1874-14 Oct 1875 – 1r – 1 – us U.O. Library [071]
WASHINGTON JEWISH DIGEST – Washington, D.C. 1959-60 – 1 – us A.J.P.C. [071]
WASHINGTON JOURNAL – Washington, DC. 1972-77 – 1 – gw Mikrofilm [071]
WASHINGTON JOURNALISM REVIEW *see*
- WJR
- AMERICAN JOURNALISM REVIEW

THE WASHINGTON LAW REPORTER – (This title covers the municipal and other lower courts in Washington, DC) – v1- 1874-end of copyright – 9 – LLMC 82-971 – us L.L.M.C. [073]
WASHINGTON LAW REVIEW – v1-71. 1925-96 – 1,5,6,9 – $1,080.00 – us Hein [073]
WASHINGTON LAWYER – (Supersedes District Lawyer) – v1-9. 1986-95 – 9 – $216.00 set – us Hein [340]
WASHINGTON LAWYER *see* DISTRICT LAWYER
WASHINGTON MONTHLY – v1- 1969- 1; v3-5,6; v7- 9 – us UMI [073]
WASHINGTON OBSERVER – Washington, DC. 1968-76 – 1r – 1 – $50.00 – R05504 – us Library Micro [071]
WASHINGTON OFFICE ON AFRICA – Washington DC. 112 docs. 1980-1991 – 14mf – 9 – ne IDC [320]
WASHINGTON OFFICE ON HAITI – Washington D.C. 15 docs. 1985-1988 – 3mf – 9 – ne IDC [320]
WASHINGTON OFFICE ON LATIN AMERICA (WOLA) – Washington DC. 289 docs. 1980-1991 – 71mf – 9 – ne IDC [320]
THE WASHINGTON POST INDEX – 1 – us UMI [071]
Washington. Presbytery (Pres. Ch. in the U.S.A.) *see* MINUTES, 1799-1821
WASHINGTON PRESS – Fremont, CA. 1909-1910 – 1r – 1 – $50.00 – B02253 – us Library Micro [071]
WASHINGTON PRESS – Niles, Fremont, CA. 1909-10 – 1r – 1 – $50.00 – B02527 – us Library Micro [071]
WASHINGTON QUARTERLY MAGAZINE OF ARTS, SCIENCE AND LITERATURE – v. 1. July 1823-April 1824 – 1 – us UMI [073]
WASHINGTON REGISTER – Salem, NY: John M Looker, 1809-11 – 1r – 1 – us Res Libr [071]
WASHINGTON REPORT – v.1-. 1979- – 1,5,6,9 – us UMI [073]
WASHINGTON REPORT ON HEALTH LEGISLATION *see* HEALTH LEGISLATION AND REGULATION
WASHINGTON REPORT ON HEALTH LEGISLATION AND REGULATION *see* HEALTH LEGISLATION AND REGULATION
WASHINGTON REPORT ON THE MEDICAL SCIENCES *see* FAULKNER AND GRAY'S MEDICINE AND HEALTH
WASHINGTON REPORTER – Washington. PA.1808-1967 – 1 – us UMI [071]
WASHINGTON REVIEW OF STRATEGIC AND INTERNATIONAL STUDIES – v1 1978 – 1,5,6,9 – us UMI [320]
WASHINGTON SOCIAL LEGISLATION BULLETIN *see* WASHINGTON BULLETIN
WASHINGTON SPECTATOR – v. 1-2. 1975-76 – 1 – us UMI [320]
WASHINGTON SPECTATOR AND BETWEEN THE LINES – v. 2-. 1976- – 1,5,6,9 – us UMI [320]
WASHINGTON STANDARD – Olympia. Wash. -w, sw. 1860-1921 – 1 – us UMI [071]
WASHINGTON STAR – Washington, D.C. 1852- – 1 – us UMI [071]
Washington (State) *see* STATE LABOR REPORTS
Washington. (State) *see* MISCELLANEOUS NEWSPAPERS
Washington. State Bar Association *see* PROCEEDINGS
WASHINGTON STATE BAR ASSOCIATION REPORTS – (Missing: 1st-5th meetings) – 1st-39th annual meetings 1894-1927 + 1933-34 (all publ) – 34mf – 9 – $153.00 – LLMC 84-687 – us L.L.M.C. [340]
WASHINGTON STATE BAR NEWS – v1-49. 1947-95 – 9 – $557.00 set – us Hein [340]
WASHINGTON STATE BAR REVIEW – v1-2. 1934-36 (all publ) – 2mf – 9 – $9.00 – LLMC 84-688 – us L.L.M.C. [073]
Washington State Historical Society *see* PUBLICATIONS 1907-1914
Washington State Potato Conference *see* PROCEEDINGS
WASHINGTON SUPREME COURT REPORTS, 1ST SERIES – (No Pre-NRS vols) – v1-200. 1890-1939 (all publ) – 1793mf – 9 – $2,689.00 – LLMC 82-993 – us L.L.M.C. [340]
WASHINGTON SUPREME COURT REPORTS, NEW SERIES – (Vols after 1975 still in copyright) – v1-84. 1939-75 (complete) – 893mf – 9 – $1,339.00 – LLMC 92-994 – us L.L.M.C. [340]
WASHINGTON TERRITORY REPORTS – v1-3. 1854-88 (all publ) – 20mf – 9 – $30.00 – LLMC 91-301 – us L.L.M.C. [324]
THE WASHINGTON TRIBUNE – Washington. D.C. Oct. 22, 1926; May 11, Oct. 29, Dec. 14, 21, 1940; Jan. 18, 1941; June 17, 1944 – 1 – us NY Public [071]
Washington. University *see* THE METROPOLITAN TRACT OF THE UNIVERSITY OF WASHINGTON
WASHINGTON UNIVERSITY JOURNAL OF URBAN AND CONTEMPORARY LAW – (v1-27 1968-84 on reel $267.00. v28-49 1985-96 on mf $309.00. Title varies: v1-23 1968-82 as Urban Law Annual. Vols covering 1968-73 unnumbered. 1974-77, 1979-80 2v per yr) – v1-49. 1968-96 – 5,6,9 – $576.00 – us Hein [340]
WASHINGTON UNIVERSITY LAW QUARTERLY – v1-28 (1915-43, 1949-79). v58-72 (1980-94) 74v – 1,5,6 – $1,170.00 – us Hein [073]
WASHINGTON UNIVERSITY LAW QUARTERLY – (v1-62 1915-85 on reel $680.00. v63-73 1985-95 on mf $225.00. Title varies: v1-21 1915-36 as St. Louis Law Review. Vol numbering discontinued after v28 1943. Resumed with v58 1988. Suspended 1943-49) – v1-73. 1915-95 – 5,6,9 – $905.00 set – us Hein [340]
WASHINGTON WATCH – 1976- – 9 – us UMI [073]
WASHINGTON WEST OF THE CASCADES / Hunt, Herbert & Taylor – Seattle: S.J. Clarke Publ. Co., 1917. v1-3. Washington reel 2.(Cox Library Collection) – 5 – us Americana [978]
Washington. Western Washington Research and Extension Center. Puyallup. Agricultural Experiment Station *see*
- MONTHLY BULLETIN
- POPULAR BULLETIN

WASHINGTON WOMEN'S REPRESENTATIVE – v3-. 1978- – 1,5,6,9 – us UMI [305]
WASHINGTONIAN – 1976- – 9 – us UMI [073]
WASHINGTON'S GRAND MARCH, COMPOSED AND ARRANGED FOR THE PIANO FORTE – n.p. after 1820.Music-3082, Item 13 – 1 – us L of C Photodup [780]
WASHINGTON'S MARCH AS PERFORMED AT THE NEW THEATRE – Philadelphia: G. Willig, n.d. Music-3082, Item 14 – 1 – us L of C Photodup [780]
WASHINGTON'S REPORTS OF CASES IN THE THIRD CIRCUIT, 1803-1827 / Washington, B – Philadelphia: Nicklin. v1-4. 1826-29 (all publ) – 30mf – 9 – $45.00 – LLMC 81-477 – us L.L.M.C. [340]
WASHINGTON'S RESEARCH PROGRESS / Washington. Agricultural Extension Service – 1956-72 – 1,5,6 – us Spaulding [630]
WASHOE COUNTY CITIZEN – Reno, NV. 1960-66 – 1r – 1 – $50.00 – U04724 – us Library Micro [071]
WASHOE RAMBLER – Reno, NV. 1978; 1985-1986 – 1r – 1 – $50.00 – U04894 – us Library Micro [071]
WASHOE RAMBLER – Washoe City, NV. v1 1977-v9 1985 – 1r – 1 – $50.00 – U04902 – us Library Micro [071]
WASHOE TIMES – Washoe City, NV. 1863 (scattered issues) – 1r – 1 – $50.00 – U04805 – us Library Micro [071]
WASHOE WEEKLY STAR – Washoe City, NV. Aug-Dec 1864 – 1r – 1 – $50.00 – U04806 – us Library Micro [071]
Wasielewski, Waldemar von *see* GOETHE UND DIE DESCENDENZLEHRE
Wasilewski, Leon *see* JOZEF PILSUDSKI, JAKIM GO ZNALEM
WASIR REKSAWARDAJA : NGGEDEKAKE ASIL BOEMI – (Microfiche No 178) – Djakarta, Gunseikanbu Kokumin Tosyokyoku, 2604 – 1mf – 9 – SE-2002/1 – ne IDC [950]
Waskiewicz, Becky A *see* THE EFFECTS OF A LEISURE ACTIVITY VISITATION TRAINING PROGRAM ON THE VISITOR'S PERCEIVED SATISFACTION OF VISITS WITH INDIVIDUALS WITH DEMENTIA RELATED DISEASES INCLUDING ALZHEIMER'S DISEASE
THE WASP – (Illustrated political weekly) – San Francisco, CA. 1876-94 – 7r – 1 – $350.00 – B02863 – us Library Micro [320]
THE WASP – Montreal, 10 nov 1878 – 1r – 1 – Can$25.00 – cn Can Microfilming [072]
THE WASP – Nauvoo, Ill. v. 1, no. 12. July 2 1842 – 1 – us NY Public [071]
THE WASP – (Title varies: Critic, Oct 13-30 1888) – Kimberley, South Africa. 13 Oct-17 Nov 1888 – 1r – 1, 16 diazo available at reduced price – sa SA Libr [072]
WASP – Gering, NE. -w. Nov 1912-Oct 1913 – 1 – us NE Hist [071]
WASP – v. 1. July 7, 1802-January 1803 – 1 – us UMI [073]
WASP – Wahoo. Neb. 1880-1949 – 1 – us UMI [071]
WASSAJA : NATIONAL NEWSPAPER OF INDIAN AMERICA – San Francisco. v1-9. 1973-82 – 82mf – 9 – $5.00f – us Ross [071]
WASSAJA – San Francisco, CA. 1973-79 – 4r – 1 – $200.00 – R02864 – us Library Micro [071]
Wassell *see* HISTORY OF DWIGHT
DAS WASSER DES LEBENS : EIN MAERCHEN DER BRUEDER GRIMM IN REDE, REIM UND REIGEN DER BUEHNE UEBERMITTELT / Guembel-Seiling, Max – Leipzig: Breitkopf & Haertel, 1921 – 1r – 1 – us U.W. Library [820]
DAS WASSERGEBIET FINNLANDS ... / Bjoerksten, S R – Helsingfors, 1925 – 3mf – 9 – ILM-2342/1 – ne IDC [327]
WASSERMANN : SEIN KAMPF UM WAHRHEIT / Goldstein, Walter Benjamin – Leipzig: Grethlein, c1929 – 1r – 1 – us U.W. Library [430]
Wassermann, Jakob *see*
- DER AUFRUHR UM DEN JUNKER ERNST
- CASPAR HAUSER
- CHRISTIAN WAHNSCHAFFE
- CHRISTOPH COLUMBUS, DER DON QUICHOTE DES OZEANS
- COLUMBUS, DON QUIXOTE OF THE SEAS
- DOCTOR KERKHOVEN
- FABER, ODER, DIE VERLORENEN JAHRE
- DER FALL MAURIZIUS
- DIE KUNST DER ERZAEHLUNG
- LEBENSDIENST
- LUKARDIS
- DIE MASKEN ERWIN REINERS
- MEIN WEG ALS DEUTSCHER UND JUDE
- DER NIEGEKUESSTE MUND
- OBERLINS DREI STUFEN
- SELBSTBETRACHTUNGEN
- ULRIKE WOYTICH
- DER UNBEKANNTE GAST
- THE WORLD'S ILLUSION

Wassermann-Speyer, Julie *see* JAKOB WASSERMANN UND SEIN WERK
DIE WASSERNOT IM EMMENTAL; DIE ARMENNOT; EINES SCHWEIZERS WORT / Gotthelf, Jeremias; ed by Hunziker, Rudolf – (Includes bibliographical references) – Erlenbach, Zuerich: E Rentsch, 1925 – 1 – us U.W. Library [830]
DIE WASSERNOT IM EMMENTHAL; FUENF MAEDCHEN; DURSLI DER BRANNTWEINLAEUTER / Gotthelf, Jeremias; ed by Kronauer, Fr – Bern: Schmid & Francke, 1898 – 1 – us U.W. Library [830]
Wasserschleben, H *see* DIE IRISCHE KANONENSAMMLUNG
DIE WASSERSNOT IM EMMENTAL AM 13. AUGUST 1837 / Gotthelf, Jeremias; ed by Duerer-Bund – Muenchen: G D W Callwey, [19-?] – 1 – us U.W. Library [830]

WASSERSTOFFPEROXID ALS MITTEL ZUR KONTINUIERLICHEN DEKONTAMINATION DENTALER BEHANDLUNGSEINHEITEN / Weihe, Stephan – 1995 – 2mf – 9 – DM80.00 – 3-8267-2219-1 – gw Hänsel [617]
Wast, Hugo *see* TIERRA DE JAGUARES
WASTE AGE – (v.10-. 1979- 5,6,9) – v1-. 1970- – 1 – us UMI [360]
WASTE MANAGEMENT – v1- 1980- – 5,6,9 – us UMI [660]
WASTE MANAGEMENT AND RESOURCES RECOVERY: INFORMATION DATABASE – (Annual Update. $495.00y; 9) – 1949-79. Ed. by R. Voight – 9 – $3500.00; $225.00t – us I.R.E. [628]
WASTEWATER TREATMENT AND USE IN AGRICULTURE – 1992 – 139p – it F.A.O. [631]
WASTRA VARMLAND – Saffle, Sweden. 1910-15, 1921-25 – 9r – 1 – sw Kungliga [072]
WASU MAGAZINE / West African Students' Union of Great Britain and Ireland – n.s.vol. 12, nos. 1-3. Mar 1945-Summer 1947 – 1 – us Res Libr [960]
WAT GELOOFDEN DE JODEN IN DEN TIJD VAN JEZUS? / Oort, Henricus – Assen: L. Hansma, 1906. 1 fiche – 9 – us A.T.L.A. [270]
WAT SEI ALLES MAKET! : SCHWAENKE UND GESCHICHTEN / Henze, Wilhelm – Hannover: F Gersbach, 1921 – 1r – 1 – us U.W. Library [830]
WATAN – Delhi, India. 30 Aug 1946-1953 (scattered issues) – 8r – 1 – us L of C Photodup [072]
THE WATCH ADJUSTER'S MANUAL: BEING A PRACTICAL GUIDE FOR THE WATCH AND CHRONOMETER ADJUSTER FOR ISOCHRONISM, POSITIONS AND TEMPERATURES / Fritts, Charles Edgar – ("Excelsior"). Toronto: P. Ellis, 1894. 03260. (Pre-1900 Canadiana) – 9 – cn C.I.H.M. [971]
WATCH AND CLOCK REVIEW *see* AMERICAN HOROLOGIST AND JEWELER
THE WATCH COMMITTEES *see* HUMAN RIGHTS WATCH
WATCHDOG OF LABOUR – Ireland.11-29 Nov 1919 – 1 – ie Microforms [072]
THE WATCHFUL PILGRIM – nos 1, 3-4, 11, 41, 56, 67, 92, 96, 98-101, 106, 120, 130-132 (complete) – 1r – 1 – ATLA 1994-S017 – us A.T.L.A. [073]
THE WATCHMAN – 1835-84. Methodist newspaper – 1 – £950.00 – uk World [240]
THE WATCHMAN – Nassau, Bahamas. -w. 5 Nov 1901-29 June 1907. Imperfect. 3 reels – 1 – uk British Libr Newspaper [072]
THE WATCHMAN : OBITUARIES TAKEN FROM THE WATCHMAN AND THE METHODIST TIMES UP TO 1931 / ed by Leary, William – N.p., n.d. – 1mf – 9 – ne IDC [240]
WATCHMAN – Boston. Mass. 1897-1912. (Complete) – 1 – 431.76 – us Baptist [240]
WATCHMAN – (Monthly Liberal-Free Thinker newspaper) – Ravenna, OH. nov, 1834-jan, 1835 – 1r – 1 – us Western Res [071]
WATCHMAN – v. 1. 1819 – 1 – us UMI [240]
WATCHMAN AND COUNTY OF WEXFORD ADVERTISER – Ireland.17 Jul 1869-4 Sept 1886. -w. 7 reels – 1 – uk British Libr Newspaper [072]
WATCHMAN AND EXAMINER – 1913-70 – 1 – 2,738.54 – us Baptist [240]
THE WATCHMAN AND WESLEYAN ADVERTISER – London, England. -w. 1857-66. 10 reels – 1 – uk British Libr Newspaper [072]
THE WATCHMAN AND WEST AFRICAN RECORD – Freetown. Sierra Leone. -m. Apr 1876-Dec 1886. (Imperfect). (1 reel) – 1 – uk British Libr Newspaper [072]
WATCHMAN EXAMINER AND WATCHMAN – Boston. Mass. 1819-96 – 1 – 1645.00 – us Baptist [240]
WATCHMAN OF THE PRAIRIE – Illinois. 1847-53 – 1 – 30.62 – us Baptist [240]
THE WATCHMAN / THE LACHUTE WATCHMAN – Lachute, Canada. v1 n16. 21 dec 1877-28 dec 1992 – 40r – 1 – Can$70.00r – cn Can Microfilming [072]
WATCHMAN WARDER – Lindsay, 1901-1920 – 20r – 1 – cn Preston [971]
WATCH-TOWER – Cooperstown, N.Y. 1814-20 – 3 – us Readex [071]
THE WATCHWORD / ed by Gordon, Saint A J & Cameron, Saint Robert – (Merged with: Truth to become Watchword and Truth) – 1878-1897 – 46mf – 9 – $240.00 – us Schnappsburg [240]
THE WATCHWORD – Ireland.1 Nov 1930-24 Dec 1932 – 1 – ie Microforms [072]
WATCHWORD *see* TRUTH, 1875-1897
WATCHWORD AND TRUTH *see*
– THE RECORD OF CHRISTIAN WORK
– THE WATCHWORD
WATCHWORD AND TRUTH, 1897-1921 / ed by Cameron, Robert – 2nd ed – 83mf – 9 – $250.00 – us Schnappsburg [200]
WATCHWORD OF LABOUR – Ireland.27 Sept 1919-4 Dec 1920 – 1 – ie Microforms [072]
Watelet, Claude H de *see*
– DICTIONNAIRE DES ARTS DE PEINTURE, SCULPTURE ET GRAVURE
WATER, AIR, AND SOIL POLLUTION – (v21-. 1984-. 5,6,9) – v1-. Nov 1971- – 1 – us UMI [360]
WATER AND ENERGY : DEMAND AND EFFECTS / Davis, George H – 1985 – 129p – 9 – 92-3-102328-4 – fr UNESCO [333]
WATER AND POLLUTION CONTROL – (v108-119 1970-81 Can$28.00y. Absorbed by and filmed with: Process Industrie Canada for v123-125 1985-87. Incorporates: Process Industries Canada at v130 no 2 1992) – Unionville. v108-133. 1970-95 – 9 – Can$20.00y – cn Micromedia [628]
WATER AND POLLUTION CONTROL *see* PROCESS INDUSTRIES CANADA
WATER AND SEWAGE WORKS – (See also: Industrial Water and Wastes) – v1- 1890- 1; v115- 5,6; v123- 9 – us UMI [628]
WATER AND WASTE TREATMENT – 1948- 1; 1975- 5,6,9 – us UMI [628]
WATER AND WASTES ENGINEERING – v1- 1964- 1; v8- 5,6; v12- 9 – us UMI [628]
WATER AND WASTES ENGINEERING – 1973- – 9 – us UMI [628]
THE WATER BIRDS OF NORTH AMERICA / Baird, Spencer Fullerton – 2v. Boston: Little, Brown, 1884. 05652, 05653.(Pre-1900 Canadiana) – 9 – cn C.I.H.M. [590]
WATER BUFFALO – 1977 – 283p – it F.A.O. [636]
WATER COMMITTEE / UN Economic Commission for Europe (ECE) – 1966-87 – E/F.11 E.332 F.260 R.243 – 9 – us U.N. Pubs [340]
WATER FOR FRESHWATER FISH CULTURE : SIMPLE METHODS FOR AQUACULTURE / Coche, A G & Wal, H van der – 1981 – 111p – it F.A.O. [639]
WATER INTERNATIONAL – v1-9. 1975-84 – 1,5,6,13 – sz Elsevier [550]
WATER LAW IN SELECTED AFRICAN COUNTRIES : BENIN, BURUNDI, ETHIOPIA, GABON, KENYA, MAURITIUS, SIERRA LEONE, SWAZILAND, UPPER VOLTA, ZAMBIA – 1980 – 273p – it F.A.O. [640]
WATER LAW IN SELECTED EUROPEAN COUNTRIES, VOL 1 : BELGIUM, ENGLAND, WALES, FRANCE, ISRAEL, ITALY, SPAIN AND TURKEY – 1979 – 263p – it F.A.O. [640]
WATER LAW IN SELECTED EUROPEAN COUNTRIES, VOL 2 : CYPRUS, FINLAND, THE NETHERLANDS, UNION OF SOVIET SOCIALIST REPUBLICS, YUGOSLAVIA – 1983 – 162p – it F.A.O. [340]
WATER LAWS IN MOSLEM COUNTRIES, VOL 1 – 1976 – 229p – it F.A.O. [340]
WATER LAWS IN MOSLEM COUNTRIES, VOL 2 – 1978 – 314p – it F.A.O. [340]
WATER LEGISLATION IN SOUTH AMERICAN COUNTRIES – 1983 – 181p – it F.A.O. [340]
WATER LIFTING DEVICES – 1986 – 308p – it F.A.O. [627]
THE WATER OF THE WONDROUS ISLES / Morris, William – [Hammersmith: Kelmscott Press, 1897] – 1 roll – 1 – 1-55879-591-X – uk Libr Preservation [830]
WATER POLLUTION CONTROL – 1901- 1; 1975- 5,6,9 – us UMI [628]
Water Pollution Control Federation *see*
– JOURNAL
WATER POLLUTION RESEARCH IN CANADA – 1980- – 5,6,9 – us UMI [360]
WATER POWER – (See now: Water Power and Dam Construction) – v1-26 1949-74 1; v23-26 5,6 – us UMI [550]
WATER QUALITY CRITERIA FOR EUROPEAN FRESHWATER FISH – 1987 – 87p – it F.A.O. [639]
WATER QUALITY CRITERIA FOR EUROPEAN FRESHWATER FISH : REPORT ON NICKEL AND FRESHWATER FISH – 1984 – 29p – it F.A.O. [639]
WATER QUALITY CRITERIA FOR EUROPEAN FRESHWATER FISH : REPORT ON NITRITE AND FRESHWATER FISH – 1984 – 29p – it F.A.O. [639]
WATER QUALITY FOR AGRICULTURE – rev ed 1985 – 186p – it F.A.O. [631]
WATER QUALITY IN WARMWATER FISH PONDS / Auburn University. Agricultural Experiment Station – 1970. 1 reel – 1, 5 – us Spaulding [639]
WATER QUALITY INTERNATIONAL – 1,5,69 – us UMI [360]
WATER RESEARCH – (Combined with Water Science and Technology. 36 issues/y. £1,823.00y. Back issues of journal available from UMI) – 12 issues/y. v27. 1993 – 9 – £840.00y – uk Elsevier Sci [550]
WATER RESEARCH – v1- 1967- – 5,6,9 – us UMI [550]
WATER RESEARCH *see* AIR AND WATER POLLUTION
THE WATER RESOURCE IN TROPICAL AFRICA AND ITS EXPLOITATION = L'EXPLOITATION DES RESSOURCES HYDAULIQUES EN AFRIQUE TROPICALE / Edwards, K A et al – 1983 – 9 – $26.00 – 92-9053-110-X – et ILRI [333]
WATER RESOURCES – v1-20. 1974-93 – 1,5 – $80.00v – us UMI [333]
WATER RESOURCES DEVELOPMENT SERIES / United Nations – (Nos. 23-44. ST/ECAFE/ Ser.F/23-44. E.99; Nos. 45-63. ST/ESCAP/ Ser.F/45-66. E.74) – 9 – us U.N. Pubs [333]
WATER RESOURCES DEVELOPMENT SERIES (ESCAP) / United Nations – 231mf – 9 – $440.00; $1.90f – uk UNIMICRO [333]
WATER RESOURCES RESEARCH, MONTHLY SINCE 1983 – (v1-10 1965-74 $30.00y 1,5,6,13. v7-10 1971-74 $25.00y 9. v11-12 1975-76 $30.00y 1,5,6,13 $35.00y 9. v13 1977 $35.00 1,5,6,13 $75.00 9. v14 1978 $35.00 1,5,6,13 $85.00 9. v15 1979 $35.00 1,5,6,13 $105.00 9. v16 1980 $45.00 1,5,6,13 $125.00 9. v17 1981 $55.00 1,5,6,13 $145.00 9. v18 1982 $55.00 1,5,6,13 $145.00 9. v28 1992 $505.00. v29 1993 $530.00. v30 1994 $660.00. v31 1995 $675.00) – v1-18 1965-82 Quarterly 1965-67 bi-monthly 1968-82. – us A.G.U. [550]
WATER RIGHTS IN THE WESTERN STATES. / Weil, Samuel Charles – 3d ed. San Francisco, Bancroft-Whitney, 1911. 2 v. LL-851 – 1 – us L of C Photodup [340]
WATER SCIENCE AND TECHNOLOGY – (Formerly: Progress in Water Technology) – v1- 1972- – 5,6,9 – us UMI [550]
WATER SUPPLY AND MANAGEMENT – v. 1-. 1977- – 5,6,9 – us UMI [628]
WATER SUPPLY OF GREATER LONDON / Dickinson, H W – 6mf – 7 – uk Microform Academic [628]
WATER SUPPLY PAPERS / U. S. Geological Survey – Nos 10-2176. 1898-1976 – 1,5,6 – us Princeton Micro [550]
WATER SUPPLY PAPERS / U. S. Geological Survey – Nos 1-2250. 1896-1983. 50 states and Canada – Ca 7800mf – 9 – $12,900.00 – us Updata [550]
WATER SUPPLY PAPERS, ALABAMA / U. S. Geological Survey – 767mf – 9 – $1550.00 – us Updata [550]
WATER SUPPLY PAPERS, ALASKA / U. S. Geological Survey – 131mf – 9 – $260.00 – us Updata [550]
WATER SUPPLY PAPERS, ARIZONA / U. S. Geological Survey – 782mf – 9 – $1580.00 – us Updata [550]
WATER SUPPLY PAPERS, ARKANSAS / U. S. Geological Survey – 643mf – 9 – $1280.00 – us Updata [550]
WATER SUPPLY PAPERS, CALIFORNIA / U. S. Geological Survey – 1378mf – 9 – $2750.00 – us Updata [550]
WATER SUPPLY PAPERS, CANADA / U. S. Geological Survey – 563mf – 9 – $1120.00 – us Updata [550]
WATER SUPPLY PAPERS, COLORADO / U. S. Geological Survey – 1538mf – 9 – $3070.00 – us Updata [550]
WATER SUPPLY PAPERS, CONNECTICUT / U. S. Geological Survey – 704mf – 9 – $1400.00 – us Updata [550]
WATER SUPPLY PAPERS, DELAWARE / U. S. Geological Survey – 599mf – 9 – $1200.00 – us Updata [550]
WATER SUPPLY PAPERS, DISTRICT OF COLUMBIA / U. S. Geological Survey – 381mf – 9 – $760.00 – us Updata [550]
WATER SUPPLY PAPERS, FLORIDA / U. S. Geological Survey – 612mf – 9 – $1200.00 – us Updata [550]
WATER SUPPLY PAPERS, GEORGIA / U. S. Geological Survey – 908mf – 9 – $1820.00 – us Updata [550]
WATER SUPPLY PAPERS, HAWAII / U. S. Geological Survey – 320mf – 9 – $650.00 – us Updata [550]
WATER SUPPLY PAPERS, IDAHO / U. S. Geological Survey – 1029mf – 9 – $2050.00 – us Updata [550]
WATER SUPPLY PAPERS, ILLINOIS / U. S. Geological Survey – 1007mf – 9 – $2000.00 – us Updata [550]
WATER SUPPLY PAPERS, INDIANA / U. S. Geological Survey – 869mf – 9 – $1750.00 – us Updata [550]
WATER SUPPLY PAPERS, IOWA / U. S. Geological Survey – 959mf – 9 – $1900.00 – us Updata [550]
WATER SUPPLY PAPERS, KANSAS / U. S. Geological Survey – 866mf – 9 – $1750.00 – us Updata [550]
WATER SUPPLY PAPERS, KENTUCKY / U. S. Geological Survey – 826mf – 9 – $1650.00 – us Updata [550]
WATER SUPPLY PAPERS, LOUISIANA / U. S. Geological Survey – 741mf – 9 – $1500.00 – us Updata [550]
WATER SUPPLY PAPERS, MAINE / U. S. Geological Survey – 819mf – 9 – $1650.00 – us Updata [550]
WATER SUPPLY PAPERS, MARYLAND / U. S. Geological Survey – 670mf – 9 – $1350.00 – us Updata [550]
WATER SUPPLY PAPERS, MASSACHUSETTS / U. S. Geological Survey – 646mf – 9 – $1300.00 – us Updata [550]
WATER SUPPLY PAPERS, MICHIGAN / U. S. Geological Survey – 581mf – 9 – $1160.00 – us Updata [550]
WATER SUPPLY PAPERS, MINNESOTA / U. S. Geological Survey – 871mf – 9 – $1750.00 – us Updata [550]
WATER SUPPLY PAPERS, MISCELLANEOUS / U. S. Geological Survey – 207mf – 9 – $400.00 – us Updata [550]
WATER SUPPLY PAPERS, MISSISSIPPI / U. S. Geological Survey – 791mf – 9 – $1600.00 – us Updata [550]
WATER SUPPLY PAPERS, MISSOURI / U. S. Geological Survey – 1104mf – 9 – $2200.00 – us Updata [550]
WATER SUPPLY PAPERS, MONTANA / U. S. Geological Survey – 1301mf – 9 – $2600.00 – us Updata [550]
WATER SUPPLY PAPERS, NEBRASKA / U. S. Geological Survey – 863mf – 9 – 1750.00 – us Updata [550]
WATER SUPPLY PAPERS, NEVADA / U. S. Geological Survey – 783mf – 9 – $1560.00 – us Updata [550]
WATER SUPPLY PAPERS, NEW HAMPSHIRE / U. S. Geological Survey – 571mf – 9 – $1150.00 – us Updata [550]
WATER SUPPLY PAPERS, NEW JERSEY / U. S. Geological Survey – 740mf – 9 – $1500.00 – us Updata [550]
WATER SUPPLY PAPERS, NEW MEXICO / U. S. Geological Survey – 1277mf – 9 – $2550.00 – us Updata [550]
WATER SUPPLY PAPERS, NEW YORK / U. S. Geological Survey – 1316mf – 9 – $2650.00 – us Updata [550]
WATER SUPPLY PAPERS, NORTH CAROLINA / U. S. Geological Survey – 977mf – 9 – $1950.00 – us Updata [550]
WATER SUPPLY PAPERS, NORTH DAKOTA / U. S. Geological Survey – 927mf – 9 – $1850.00 – us Updata [550]
WATER SUPPLY PAPERS, OHIO / U. S. Geological Survey – 917mf – 9 – $1800.00 – us Updata [550]
WATER SUPPLY PAPERS, OKLAHOMA / U. S. Geological Survey – 596mf – 9 – $1200.00 – us Updata [550]
WATER SUPPLY PAPERS, OREGON / U. S. Geological Survey – 1427mf – 9 – $2850.00 – us Updata [550]
WATER SUPPLY PAPERS, PENNSYLVANIA / U. S. Geological Survey – 1081mf – 9 – $2160.00 – us Updata [550]
WATER SUPPLY PAPERS, RHODE ISLAND / U. S. Geological Survey – 513mf – 9 – $1020.00 – us Updata [550]
WATER SUPPLY PAPERS, SOUTH CAROLINA / U. S. Geological Survey – 584mf – 9 – $1170.00 – us Updata [550]

WATER SUPPLY PAPERS, SOUTH DAKOTA / U. S. Geological Survey – 729mf – 9 – $1450.00 – us Updata [550]
WATER SUPPLY PAPERS, TENNESSEE / U. S. Geological Survey – 794mf – 9 – $1580.00 – us Updata [550]
WATER SUPPLY PAPERS, TEXAS / U. S. Geological Survey – 1030mf – 9 – $2060.00 – us Updata [550]
WATER SUPPLY PAPERS, UTAH / U. S. Geological Survey – 985mf – 9 – $1970.00 – us Updata [550]
WATER SUPPLY PAPERS, VERMONT / U. S. Geological Survey – 757mf – 9 – $1500.00 – us Updata [550]
WATER SUPPLY PAPERS, VIRGINIA / U. S. Geological Survey – 1217mf – 9 – $2450.00 – us Updata [550]
WATER SUPPLY PAPERS, WASHINGTON / U. S. Geological Survey – 1010mf – 9 – $2020.00 – us Updata [324]
WATER SUPPLY PAPERS, WEST VIRGINIA / U. S. Geological Survey – 970mf – 9 – $1940.00 – us Updata [550]
WATER SUPPLY PAPERS, WISCONSIN / U. S. Geological Survey – 788mf – 9 – $1570.00 – us Updata [550]
WATER SUPPLY PAPERS, WYOMING / U. S. Geological Survey – 1409mf – 9 – $2800.00 – us Updata [550]
WATER USE SEMINAR (1972, DAMASCUS) – 1976 – 318p – it F.A.O. [631]
THE WATER WHEEL OF LOVE / Megally, S & Heath-Stubbs, J – (Popular poetry of modern Egypt). NE-293 1 – 9 – ne IDC [810]
THE WATER-BABIES : A FAIRY TALE FOR A LANDBABY / Kingsley, Charles – London: Macmillan, 1863 – 1 roll – 1 – 1-55879-371-2 – uk Libr Preservation [830]
WATER-BASED RECREATIONISTS' PREFERENCES FOR DIRECT/INDIRECT MANAGEMENT STRATEGIES BY VISITOR CHARACTERISTICS, PAST EXPERIENCES, AND PERCEIVED SITE PROBLEMS / Tsao, E-Shu – 1993 – 2mf – $8.00 – us Microform Publ [650]
WATERCOLOR *see* AMERICAN ARTIST
WATERCOLOURS : SUBJECT COLLECTIONS – (Individual titles not listed separately) – 89 catalogues on 97mf – 9 – £710.00 – uk Chadwyck [750]
WATER-CURE JOURNAL *see* HEALTH
WATER-CURE JOURNAL – A GUIDE TO HEALTH *see* HEALTH
WATER-CURE JOURNAL AND HERALD OF HEALTH – DEVOTED TO PHYSIOLOGY, HYDROPATHY AND THE LAWS OF LIFE *see* HEALTH
WATER-CURE JOURNAL AND HERALD OF REFORMS *see* HEALTH
WATERFORD ADVERTISER – Ireland. -w. 10 Jul-11 Dec 1848. (7 ft) – 1 – uk British Libr Newspaper [072]
WATERFORD CHRONICLE – Ireland. -sw. 1 Jan-31 Dec 1771. (1 reel) – 1 – uk British Libr Newspaper [072]
WATERFORD EVENING NEWS – Ireland.1827-40; 22 Sept 1848-1868; 1875-95. -w. 31 reels – 1 – uk British Libr Newspaper [072]
WATERFORD FREEMAN – Ireland. -w. 12 Jul 1845-24 Apr 1847. (2 reels) – 1 – uk British Libr Newspaper [072]
WATERFORD MIRROR – Ireland. -tw. 1 Aug 1808-31 Jul 1809, 29 May 1813, 1 Jan 1827-Dec 1840. (15 reels) – 1 – uk British Libr Newspaper [072]
WATERFORD STAR – Waterford, 1897-1934 – 19r – 1 – cn Preston [971]
WATERFORD (WATERFORD), 1805 : BRITISH ISLES CENSUS DIRECTORIES PROJECT, IRELAND. VOL 11 – 1mf – 9 – A$9.00 – at Vine [941]
WATERGATE FBI INVESTIGATION FILE / U.S. Federal Bureau of Investigation – 1984 – 9r – 1 – $765.00 – S1762 – us Scholarly Res [360]
WATERGATE TRIAL *see* OFFICIAL TRANSCRIPT OF THE WATERGATE TRIAL, 1974-75
Waterhouse, G A *see* THE BUTTERFLIES OF AUSTRALIA; A MONOGRAPH OF THE AUSTRALIAN RHOPALOCERA
Waterhouse, Gilbert *see* A SHORT HISTORY OF GERMAN LITERATURE
THE WATERHUSTLERS / Boyle, Robert H et al – 1r – 5,9 – $50.00 – B70012 – us Library Micro [360]
Waterland, D *see* REGENERATION STATED AND EXPLAINED ACCORDING TO SCRIPTURE AND ANTIQUITY;...
WATERLOO ADVERTISER – Waterloo, Canada. 1856-75 – 6r – 1 – $390.00 – cn Library Assoc [971]
WATERLOO ADVERTISER *see* THE ADVERTISER AND EASTERN TOWNSHIPS SENTINEL
WATERLOO ADVERTISER AND DISTRICT OF BEDFORD TIMES *see* THE ADVERTISER AND EASTERN TOWNSHIPS SENTINEL
WATERLOO ADVERTISER AND EASTERN TOWNSHIPS ADVOCATES *see* THE ADVERTISER AND EASTERN TOWNSHIPS SENTINEL
WATERLOO AND CROSBY HERALD – Merseyside. 1895 to 1974 – 79r – 1 – uk Microform Academic [072]
WATERLOO DOCK REGISTERS FROM 1827 TO 1850 – Plus printed finding list – ca 35r – 1 – £1,300.00 – uk Altair [380]
WATERLOO: THE CAMPAIGN AND BATTLE / DePeyster, John Watts – New York: C.H. Ludwig, 1893. 32p. illus. maps – 1 – us U.W. Library [941]
WATERLOO WEEKLY GAZETTE – Waterloo, NE. Jul 1881-Jun 1882 – 1 – us NE Hist [071]
Waterlot, E G *see* LES BAS-RELIEFS DES BATIMENTS ROYAUX D'ABOMEY (DAHOMEY)
Waterman, A N *see* HISTORICAL REVIEW OF CHICAGO AND COOK COUNTY
Waterman, Harrison L *see* HISTORY OF WAPELLO COUNTY
Waterman, John H *see* GENERAL HISTORY OF SEWARD COUNTY, NEBRASKA
Waterman, Lucius *see*
- GOD'S BALANCE OF FAITH AND FREEDOM
- THE POST-APOSTOLIC AGE

Waterman, P *see* NIGERIAN LABOUR STUDIES
Waterman, Thomas Whitney *see* A DIGEST OF DECISIONS IN CRIMINAL CASES, CONTAINED IN THE REPORTS OF THE FEDERAL COURTS.
THE WATERS OF EDEIRA / Ouida – British Fiction Archive: Unit 3 – 9 – uk Bell [830]
Waters, Richard L *see* PUBLIC LIBRARY QUARTERLY
WATERSHED DEVELOPMENT WITH SPECIAL REFERENCE TO SOIL AND WATER CONSERVATION – 1979 – 266p – it F.A.O. [333]
WATERSHED MANAGEMENT FIELD MANUAL : SLOPE TREATMENT MEASURES AND PRACTICES – 1988 – 153p – it F.A.O. [631]
Waterson, A *see* PLANNING IN MOROCCO: ORGANIZATION AND IMPLEMENTATION
WATERSPORT – v1-4. 1966-70 – 13mf – 9 – $5.00f – us Ross [790]
Waterton, Charles *see* PAPERS
Waterville, Maine. Baptist Sabbath School Society of Waterville *see* RECORDS
THE WATERWAYS JOURNAL – St. Louis. Mo. 1937-1953; 1959- – 1 – us UMI [628]
Waterworth, William *see*
- ORIGIN AND DEVELOPMENTS OF ANGLICANISM
- ORIGIN AND DEVELOPMENTS OF ANGLICANISM; OR A HISTORY OF THE LITURGIES, HOMILIES, ARTICLES, BIBLES, PRINCIPLES AND GOVERNMENTAL SYSTEM OF THE CHURCH OF ENGLAND

WATFORD AND WEST HERTS REVIEW – (Also known as: Review (Watford Edn)) – May 12-Dec 29 1983; 1984-Jun, Jul 5-Sep 27, Oct 1990-Dec 19 1996 – 45r – 1 – uk British Libr Newspaper [072]
WATFORD OBSERVER – England. West Herts & Watford Observer. -w. Jan 1863-Dec 1978; 1981. 155 1 2 reels – 1 – uk British Libr Newspaper [072]
Watin, Jean Felix *see* L'ART DU PEINTRE, DOREUR ET VERNISSEUR
Watkins, Arthur Charles *see* PILGRIM SONGS: BEING A RENDERING INTO ENGLISH OF FIFTEEN HEBREW LYRICS
Watkins, Francis N *see* A CATALOG OF THE DESCENDANTS OF THOMAS WATKINS
Watkins, John *see* LIFE, POETRY, AND LETTERS OF EBENEZER ELLIOTT, THE CORN-LAW RHYMER
Watkins, Robin G *see*
- HISTORY OF MONTEREY AND SANTA CRUZ COUNTIES

Watkins, Vernon Phillips *see* SELECTED POEMS
Watkins, W *see* LINEAR AND MULTILINEAR ALGEBRA
Watkinson, F *see* ONE HUNDRED YEARS IN THE PAJARO VALLEY
Watkinson, William Lonsdale *see* THE INFLUENCE OF SCEPTICISM ON CHARACTER
Watner, Carl *see* COLLECTED WORKS OF LYSANDER SPOONER
Watrons, Ansil *see* HISTORY OF LARIMER COUNTY
Watrous, Jerome A *see* MEMOIRS OF MILWAUKEE
Watson, Andrew *see* THE AMERICAN MISSION IN EGYPT, 1854 TO 1896
Watson, Charles Roger *see*
- EGYPT AND THE CHRISTIAN CRUSADE
- FAR NORTH IN INDIA
- GOD'S PLAN FOR WORLD REDEMPTION
- IN THE KING'S SERVICE
- IN THE VALLEY OF THE NILE
- THE SORROW AND HOPE OF THE EGYPTIAN SUDAN

Watson, E Y *see* HESPERIIDAE INDICAE
Watson, Edward William *see*
- THE CHURCH OF ENGLAND
- LIFE OF BISHOP JOHN WORDSWORTH

Watson, Frederick *see* THE LAW AND THE PROPHETS
Watson, Henry *see* THE MUSIC LIBRARY..
Watson, John *see* CHRISTIANITY AND IDEALISM
Watson, John F *see* ANNALS OF PHILADELPHIA, AND PENNSYLVANIA IN THE OLDEN TIME
Watson, Richard *see* THE LIFE OF REV. JOHN WESLEY,...FOUNDER OF THE METHODIST SOCIETIES
Watson, Robert Alexander *see*
- THE BOOK OF JOB
- BOOK OF NUMBERS
- GOSPELS OF YESTERDAY
- JUDGES AND RUTH

Watson, S *see*
- BIBLIOGRAPHICAL INDEX TO NORTH AMERICAN BOTANY;...
- BOTANY OF THE FORTIETH PARALLEL (U.S.A.)

Watson, Seth B *see* HINTS TOWARDS THE FORMATION OF A MORE COMPREHENSIVE THEORY OF LIFE
Watson, Sidney O *see* DIARY
Watson, Thomas *see* THE HEKATOMPATHIA, OR PASSIONATE CENTURIE OF LOVE
Watson, William *see*
- THE COLLECTED POEMS OF WILLIAM WATSON
- ENGLISH LYRICS
- EPIGRAMS OF ART, LIFE, AND NATURE
- EXCURSIONS IN CRITICISM
- THE ISOKO MSS

Watson, William H *see* THE SUNDAY SCHOOL UNION, ITS HISTORY AND WORK
Watson-Bitar, M *see* THE RELATIONSHIP BETWEEN BONE MINERAL DENSITY AND SELECTED VARIABLES
WATSON'S WEEKLY ART JOURNAL – New York City. v1-87. 1864-1905 – 38r – 1 – £1,940.00 – uk Chadwyck [780]
WATSON'S WEEKLY ART JOURNAL – v1-87. Apr 1864-Oct 1905 – 1 – 2100.00 – us Opus [073]
WATSONVILLE : THE FIRST 100 YEARS – Santa Cruz Co, 1852-1952 – 1r – 1 – $50.00 – B40268 – us Library Micro [978]
Watt, Francis *see* THE LAW'S LUMBER ROOM
Watt, G *see*
- A DICTIONARY OF THE ECONOMIC PRODUCTS OF INDIA
- THE WILD AND CULTIVATED COTTON PLANTS OF THE WORLD; REVISION OF THE GENUS GOSSYPIUM

Watt, Morris W *see* NEW ZEALAND REGISTERED SHIPS 1840-1950
Watt, Thomas *see* GRAMMAR MADE EASIE
Wattenbach, W *see*
- ANLEITUNG ZUR GRIECHISCHEN PALAEOGRAPHIE
- DEUTSCHLANDS GESCHICHTSQUELLEN IM MITTELALTER
- DAS SCHRIFTWESEN IM MITTELALTER

WATTENSCHEIDER ZEITUNG *see* WESTDEUTSCHE ALLGEMEINE ZEITUNG (WAZ)
Watters, Mary *see* A HISTORY OF THE CHURCH IN VENEZUELA. CHAPEL HILL, 1933
Watts, Alan *see* ZEN
WATTS AND SERGEANT'S REPORTS / Pennsylvania. Superior Court – (A Pre-NRS title) – v1-9. 1841-45 (all publ) – 18mf – 9 – $81.00 – LLMC 84-201 – us L.L.M.C. [340]
Watts, Isaac *see* THE ART OF READING AND WRITING ENGLISH
Watts, Parris *see* DEVELOPMENT AND VALIDATION OF THE WELLNESS KNOWLEDGE, ATTITUDE, AND BEHAVIOR INSTRUMENT
WATTS' REPORTS / Pennsylvania. Superior Court – (A Pre-NRS title) – v1-10. 1832-40 (all publ) – 20mf – 9 – $90.00 – LLMC 84-200 – us L.L.M.C. [340]
Watts, Robert *see*
- ATOMISM: DR. TYNDALL'S ATOMIC THEORY OF THE UNIVERSE
- THE NEWER CRITICISM AND THE ANALOGY OF THE FAITH: A REPLY TO...W. ROBERTSON SMITH
- THE RULE OF FAITH AND THE DOCTRINE OF INSPIRATION

Watts, William Lord *see* ACROSS THE VATNA JOKULL; OR, SCENES IN ICELAND; BEING A DESCRIPTION OF HITHERTO UNKNOWN REGIONS
Watts-Dunton, Theodore *see* THE COMING OF LOVE: RHONA BOSWELL'S STORY
Watzinger, Carl Hans *see* DER LAEUFER VON MARATHON
Watzlik, Hans *see*
- O BOEHMEN!
- HILLEBIEGEL
- DIE KROENUNGSOPFER
- DER RUECKZUG DER DREIHUNDERT

Waugh, D C *see* SLAVIANSKIE RUKOPISI SOBRANIIA GRAFA F.A. TOLSTOGO. MATERIALY K ISTORII SOBRANIIA I UKAZATELI STARYKH I NOVYKH SHIFROV
WAUNETA BREEZE – Wauneta, NE. -w. May 1887; Nov 1892; Oct 1895-Mar 1899; Aug 1902 to date – 1 – us NE Hist [071]
WAUSA ENTERPRISE-HERALD – Wausa, NE. -w. Jun 1892; Oct 1895-Feb 1896; May 1896-May 1898; Feb 1899-Jan 1901; May 1901-Jan 1902; Mar-May 1902 – 1 – us NE Hist [071]
WAUSA GAZETTE – Wausa, NE. -w. Dec 1898 to date – 1 – us NE Hist [071]
Wauseon Ministerial Association (Wauseon, Ohio) *see* MINUTES
WAUSEON REPUBLICAN – Wauseon, Ohio. 1876-1972 – 59r – 1 – $32.50r – us Archival [071]
Wauters, Alphonse Jules *see*
- BIBLIOGRAPHIE DU CONGO, 1880-1895
- BIBLIOGRAPHIE DU CONGO, 1880-1895..

WAVE – Enid. Okl. 1894-1908 – 1 – us UMI [071]
WAVE MOTION – v1-6. 1979-84 – 1,5,6,13 – sz Elsevier [550]
THE WAVERLY ADVOCATE – Waverly, PA., 1870-1879 – 13 – $25.00r – us I.M.R. [071]
WAVERLY FREE PRESS – Towanda, PA., 1897-1906 – 13 – $25.00r – us I.M.R. [071]
THE WAVERLY REVIEW – Waverly, PA., 1880-1881 – 13 – $25.00r – us I.M.R. [071]
THE WAVERLY SUN – Waverly, PA., 1945-1949 – 13 – $25.00r – us I.M.R. [071]
WAVERLY WATCHMAN – Waverly, NE. -w. Dec 1892; Oct 1895-Feb 1898; Apr 1898-Jun 1899; Dec 1901-Jan 1903; Mar 1908-Apr 1934 – 1 – us NE Hist [071]
THE WAVES : RECORDS OF THE ASSISTANT CHIEF OF NAVAL PERSONNEL FOR WOMEN, 1942-1972 / U.S. Navy – (With printed guide) – 1991 – 20r – 1 – $1,700.00 – S3211 – us Scholarly Res [355]
WAVES – (Ceased: v15 1986/87) – Richmond Hill. v1-15. 1972-87 – 9 – Can$20.00y – cn Micromedia [073]
WAVES IN RANDOM MEDIA – v1. 1991 – 1,5,6,9 – £143.00 – uk I.O.P. [530]
WAWAS ENDE : EIN DOKUMENT / Heiseler, Henry von – Muenchen: A Langen/G Mueller, 1933 – 1r – 1 – us U.W. Library [830]
Wawra, H *see* SERTUM BENGUELENSE
WAX BAPTIST CHURCH. SILVER CREEK, GEORGIA : CHURCH RECORDS – 1936-82 – 1 – 40.50 – us Baptist [240]
Waxman, M *see* THE PHILOSOPHY OF DON HASDAI CRESCAS
THE WAY / Albany. Georgia. First Baptist Church – 1955-Sept 1987. Church bulletins – 1 – 269.64 – us Baptist [240]
WAY – (1985-. 5,6,9) – v1-. 1961- – 1 – us UMI [073]
THE WAY INTO THE HOLIEST : EXPOSITIONS OF THE EPISTLE TO THE HEBREWS / Meyer, Frederick Brotherton – New York:Fleming H. Revell, c1893 – 1mf – 9 – 0-8370-4414-6 – 1985-2414 – us A.T.L.A. [220]
THE WAY OF HOLINESS MADE PLAIN – [Richmond Hill, Ont?: s.n.], 1879-1881 – 9 – cn C.I.H.M. [240]

THE WAY OF HOLINESS: WITH NOTES BY THE WAY, BEING A NARRATIVE OF RELIGIOUS EXPERIENCE RESULTING FROM A DETERMINATION TO BE A BIBLE CHRISTIAN / Palmer, Phoebe Worrell – 1867 – 9 – us A.T.L.A. [240]

THE WAY OF MARTHA AND THE WAY OF MARY / Graham, Stephen – London: Macmillan, 1915 – 1mf – us A.T.L.A. [240]

THE WAY OF SALVATION: A SERMON DELIVERED AT MORRISTOWN, NEW JERSEY, 8 FEB 1829 / Barnes, Albert – 7th ed., 1836 – 9 – us A.T.L.A. [240]

THE WAY OUT FROM THE DOOM OF THE WELFARE SOCIETY / Hardy, George – 1fiche. (24x) – 9 – 1.00f – at Libertarian Micro [320]

THE WAY OUT OF AGNOSTICISM : OR, THE PHILOSOPHY OF FREE RELIGION / Abbot, Francis Ellingwood – Boston: Little, Brown, 1890 – 1mf – 9 – 0-8370-2010-7 – 1985-0010 – us A.T.L.A. [210]

THE WAY, THE TRUTH, AND THE LIFE : LECTURES TO EDUCATED HINDUS / Seelye, Julius Hawley – Boston:Congregational Publishing Society, 1873 – 1mf – 9 – 0-8370-5215-7 – 1985-3215 – us A.T.L.A. [240]

THE WAY THINGS ARE AND OTHER STORIES / Maltz, Albert – Introd. by Michael Gold.New York: International Publishers, (c1938). ix,11+218p. 1 reel. 1295 – 1 – us U.W. Library [830]

THE WAY TO GOD AND HOW TO FIND IT / Moody, Dwight Lyman – Chicago: F H Revell, c1884 – 1mf – 9 – 0-8370-9805-X – 1986-3805 – us A.T.L.A. [240]

THE WAY TO REST : RESULTS OF A LIFE-SEARCH AFTER RELIGIOUS TRUTH / Vaughan, Robert – London: Longmans, Green, 1866 – 1mf – 9 – 0-8370-5671-3 – 1985-3671 – us A.T.L.A. [240]

THE WAY TO THINGS BY WORDS / Cleland, John – 1766. 140p. (English Linguistics Series 1500-1800) – 9 – us UMI [400]

THE WAYANG OR SHADOW PLAY AS GIVEN IN JAVA / Hinloopen Labberton, C van – SE-821 1 – 9 – ne IDC [390]

THE WAYFARER – (Cont by and filmed with: Quaker Monthly) – v19-43. 1940-1964 (complete) – 3r – 1 – ATLA S0374 – us A.T.L.A. [073]

WAYFARER *see* QUAKER MONTHLY

WAYLAND 1638-1905 – (Mf 1-4: Births 1650-1784. Mf 4-5: Marriages 1677-1784. Mf 6,10,12: Deaths 1642-1844. Mf 7-8,11: Births 1724-1844. Mf 8-9,13: Intentions 1788-1852. Mf 9-10,13: Marriages 1690-1843. Mf 12-14:Miscellaneous 1789-1857. Mf 15-16: Vital Registers 1843-59. Mf 17-22: Vital Registers 1860-92. Mf 23-24: Birth Index [1753-1892]. Mf 24-25: Marriage Index [1677-1882]. Mf 26: Intentions Index 1843-52. Mf 27-28: Death Index [1796-1892]. Mf 29-71: Town Records 1638-1853. Mf 72-79,81: Mortgages 1840-75. Mf 80: Military 1861-64, 1874-78. Mf 81: Voters 1877-86. Mf 82-83: Death Index 1892-1905. Mf 84-85: Marriage Index 1892-1905. Mf 86-87: Birth Index 1892-1905. Mf 88-89: Births 1892-1905. Mf 90-91: Marriages/Deaths 1892-1905) – (mf ed 1996) – 91mf – 0-87623-389-2 – us Holbrook [920]

Wayland, Francis *see*
- A MEMOIR OF THE LIFE AND LABORS OF THE REV. ADONIRAM JUDSON, D.D.
- SALVATION BY CHRIST

Wayland, John W *see*
- HISTORY OF ROCKINGHAM COUNTY
- HISTORY OF SHENANDOAH COUNTY
- HOPEWELL FRIENDS HISTORY OF FREDERICK COUNTY
- MEN OF MARK OF HARRISON AND ROCKINGHAM COUNTY
- VIRGINIA VALLEY RECORDS

THE WAYLAND NEWS – Iowa City. Iowa. 1920-1932; 1935-1937; 1940; 1942; 1944-1951; 1953 – 1 – us UMI [071]

WAYMARKS IN CHURCH HISTORY / Bright, William – London; New York: Longmans, 1894 – 2mf – us A.T.L.A. [240]

WAYMARKS, OR COUNSEL AND ENCOURAGEMENT FOR PENITENT SEEKERS OF SALVATION / Dewart, Edward Hartley – Toronto?: s.n., 1867 (Toronto: Wesleyan Methodist). 04281. (Pre-1900 Canadiana) – 9 – cn C.I.H.M. [971]

Wayne, Anthony *see* PAPERS, 1793-1794

WAYNE COUNTY DEMOCRAT – Wooster. Ohio. 1850-1861; 1873-1913 – 1 – us UMI [071]

WAYNE COUNTY ENQUINER – Bethany, PA., 1830-1832 – 13 – $25.00r – us I.M.R. [071]

THE WAYNE COUNTY HERALD – Honesdale, PA. -w 1830-1844; 1848-1912 – 13 – $25.00r – us I.M.R. [071]

WAYNE COUNTY HERALD BETHANY – Honesdale, PA., 1840-1859 – 13 – $25.00r – us I.M.R. [071]

THE WAYNE COUNTY MEDIATION PROGRAM IN THE EASTERN DISTRICT OF MICHIGAN / Shuart, Kathy L – Washington: FJC, Oct 1984 – 1mf – 9 – $1.50 – LLMC 95-370 – us L.L.M.C. [340]

WAYNE COUNTY NEWS – Wayne. West Virginia. -w. 1932-68 – 1 – us UMI [071]

WAYNE DEMOCRAT : SEPTEMBER 28 1894-NOVEMBER 25 1937 – 1995 – us NE Hist [977]

WAYNE DEMOCRATIC PRESS – Lyons. N.Y. 1872-1903; 1912-1938 – 1 – us UMI [071]

WAYNE HERALD – Wayne, NE. -w. (-sw 1967 to date). Aug 1876; Jan 1884-Dec 1885; Jan 1888-Dec 1891; Jul 1892; Jan 1893-Dec 1894; Aug 1895-Oct 1918; Jan 1919 to date – 1 – us NE Hist [071]

WAYNE LAW REVIEW – (v1-31 1954-85 on reel $675.00. v32-41 1985-95 on mf $280.00) – v1-41. 1954-95 – 5,6,9 – $955.00 set – us Hein [340]

WAYNE NEWS – Wayne, NE. -w. (-sw 1887; 1897-98). Dec 1885-Aug 1887; Jan-Dec 1889; May 1892-Feb 1896, scattered issues missing; Apr 1896-Apr 1897; Nov 1898-Mar 1932; Jan-Dec 1933; Nov-Dec 1934; Jul 1935-Mar 1943 – 1 – us NE Hist [071]

WAYNE OBSERVER – Wayne, Co. 1898-1954 – 18r – 1 – $32.50r – us Archival [071]

Wayne. Ohio. Wayne United Methodist Church *see* RECORDS

Wayne, Pennsylvania. Central Baptist Church *see* MINUTES

WAYNE REPUBLICAN – Wayne, NE. -w. Nov 1892; Aug 1895-Jul 1904 – 1 – us NE Hist [071]

Wayne State College *see* THE GOLDENROD

WAYNE STATER – Xenia. Ohio. 1961-1968 – 1 – us UMI [370]

WAYNESVILLE NEWS – Lebanon. Ohio. 1884-1887; 1895 – 1 – us UMI [071]

THE WAYS OF GOD WITH MAN : AS REVEALED IN THE SCRIPTURES, FROM CREATION TO THE END OF TIME / Sibthorpe, W M – London: Elliot Stock, 1899 – 1mf – 9 – 0-8370-6376-0 – 1986-0376 – us A.T.L.A. [220]

WAYS OF THE SPIRIT : AND OTHER ESSAYS / Hedge, Frederic Henry – (Includes bibliographical references) – Boston: Roberts, 1877 – 1mf – 9 – 0-8370-4904-0 – 1985-2904 – us A.T.L.A. [240]

WAYS TO WIN : THOUGHTS AND SUGGESTIONS WITH REGARD TO PERSONAL WORK FOR CHRIST / Hague, Dyson – 2nd ed. London: Marshall Bros, 1890 – 1mf – 9 – 0-8370-6189-X – 1986-0189 – us A.T.L.A. [240]

WAYSIDE SKETCHES IN ECCLESIASTICAL HISTORY : NINE LECTURES WITH NOTES AND PREFACE / Bigg, Charles – London; New York: Longmans, Green, 1906 – 1mf – us A.T.L.A. [240]

W.B. Rogers Printing Co *see* ROGER'S SOUVENIR HISTORY OF MERCER COUNTY

WBA REVIEW / Ladies of the Maccabees of the World & Woman's Benefit Association of the Maccabees – Port Huron, MI. 1897-1907 – 2r – 1 – us Ross [360]

WBMU TIDINGS – Amherst, N.S.: [s.n. 1894?-19–] – 9 – cn C.I.H.M. [240]

WE ALL ARE LUMUMBA – League of People's Culture. SE 10,777 1. 1961? – 9 – ne IDC [360]

WE AND THE WORLD / Ewing, Juliana Horatia – British Fiction Archive: Unit 1 – 9 – uk Bell [830]

WE MUST MEET OUR DUTY AND CONVINCE THE WORLD THAT WE ARE JUST FRIENDS AND BRAVE ENEMIES / Kennedy, Robert Francis – In Indonesian. SE-4948 1 – 9 – ne IDC [320]

WE SHAKE HANDS / Association of American Indian Affairs – 1958. (American Indian Periodicals in the Princeton University Library). 1 fiche – 9 – $45.00 – us UPA [305]

WE THE PEOPLE – Portland OR. Sep 18 1945 – 1 – us U.O. Library [071]

WE WARNED YOU, GENTLEMEN / Weizmann, C – (Testimony before the Anglo-American Committee of Inquiry on Palestine). Jerusalem. 1946. BJ-28-23 1 – 9 – ne IDC [956]

WEALDSTONE HARROW AND WEMBLEY OBSERVER – (Also known as: Harrow Observer) – Apr 26-Dec 27 1895; 1896-98; 1906-21; 1945-47; 1949-Nov 9 1973; 1974-78; Feb 16 1979-86; Jan 8 1987-Jun 1997 – 213 1/2r – 1 – uk British Libr Newspaper [072]

WEAPON SYSTEMS ACQUISITION PROCESS: HEARINGS...MAY 12, 1972 / U.S. Congress. Senate. Committee on Armed Services – Washington, Govt. Print. Off., 1972. 43 p. LL-2274 – 1 – us L of C Photodup [340]

WEAR – (v.36-64. 1976-80. 1,5,6,9) – v1-100. 1958-84 – 1,5,6,13 – sz Elsevier [073]

Weare, Meshech *see* MESHECH WEARE PAPERS, 1776-1786

THE WEATHERLY HERALD – Weatherly, PA. 1888-1894. Also incl. The Record (Mauch Chunk), 1890-92. 1 roll – 13 – $25.00r – us I.M.R. [071]

WEATHERVANE – Martinsburg. West Virginia. 1927-1946 – 1 – us UMI [071]

WEATHERWISE – (v.23-35. 1970-82. 5,6,9) – v.1-35. 1948-82 – 1 – us UMI [073]

Weaver, George Sumner *see* AIMS AND AIDS FOR GIRLS AND YOUNG WOMEN, ON THE VARIOUS DUTIES OF LIFE, INCLUDING PHYSICAL, INTELLECTUAL, AND MORAL DEVELOPMENT

Weaver, J Calvin *see* ONE HUNDRED YEARS OF MEDICINE IN DEKALB COUNTY

Weaver, James B *see* PAST AND PRESENT OF JASPER COUNTY

Weaver, Jonathan *see* CHRISTIAN THEOLOGY

Weaver, Joseph Myrtle *see* A PREACHER'S AND A BANKER'S VIEWS ON IMPORTANT SUBJECTS

THE WEAVERS; A DRAMA OF THE FORTIES / Hauptmann, Gerhart – Mary Morison, trans. New York: B.W. Huebsch, 1911. viii,148p – 1 – us U.W. Library [820]

WEAVERS AND WEFT; AND OTHER TALES / Braddon, Mary Elizabeth – British Fiction Archive: Unit 5 – 9 – uk Bell [830]

W.E.B. DUBOIS ALBUMS / U.S. Library of Congress. Prints and Photographs Division – Photographs, charts, and legal materials compiled by DuBois for the Negro Exhibit in the American section of the 1900 Exposition Universelle in Paris. 3 reels. P&P11930-11932 – 1 – 23.00r – us L of C Photodup [080]

W.E.B. DUBOIS PAPERS – 1877-1965 – 89r – 1 – us UMI [920]

WEB FOOT – Salem OR. Dec 23 1905 – 1 – us U.O. Library [071]

Webb, Beatrice *see* DIARY OF BEATRICE WEBB 1873-1943

Webb, C C J *see* JOANNIS SARESBERIENSIS EPISCOPI CARNOTENSIS POLICRATICI

Webb, Catherine *see* INDUSTRIAL COOPERATION: THE STORY OF A PEACEFUL REVOLUTION

Webb, Daniel *see* FACTORS INFLUENCING AFRICAN-AMERICAN STUDENTS AT HISTORICALLY BLACK COLLEGES AND UNIVERSITIES TO ENTER THE ADAPTED PHYSICAL EDUCATION PROFESSION

Webb, Frank J *see* THE GARIES AND THEIR FRIENDS

Webb, G J *see* NORA MCCARTY

Webb, George Franklin *see* MISSISSIPPI MANUAL OF LEGAL AND BUSINESS FORMS.

Webb, P B *see*
- FRAGMENTA FLORULAE AETHIOPICOAEGYPTIACAE EX PLANTIS PRAECIPUE
- HISTOIRE NATURELLE DES ILES CANARIES
- OTIA HISPANICA

Webb, Ralph L *see* JOURNAL OF ENHANCED HEAT TRANSFER

Webb, Sidney *see* THE PROGRESS OF SOCIALISM

Webbe, Joseph *see*
- AN APPEALE TO TRUTH
- THE FIRST COMEDY OF PUB. TERENTIUS, CALLED ANDRIA
- LESSONS AND EXERCISES OUT OF CICERO AD ATTICUM
- PUERILES CONFABULATIUNCULAE, OR CHILDRENS TALKE
- THE SECOND COMEDIE OF PUB. TERENTIUS, CALLED EUNUCHUS

Webber, Henry William *see* THE HISTORY OF A COLORADO REAL ESTATE MORTGAGE.

Webber, R P *see* ALPHABET MALGACHE POUR SERVIR D'INTRODUCTION A UNE GRAMMAIRE

WEBBIA : RACOLTA DI SCRITTI BOTANICI – Firence. v1-5. 1905-23 – 27mf – 9 – 8577/1 – ne IDC [580]

Weber, A *see* INDISCHE STUDIEN

Weber, Albert *see* DER VOKALISMUS DER MUNDART DES ZUERCHER OBERLANDES

Weber, Alfred *see*
- DE L'ECONOMIE DU SALUT
- DIE RELIGION ALS WILLE ZUM EWIGEN LEBEN: EINE VORTRAG

Weber, Emil *see* DER EINFLUSS DER PROTESTANTISCHEN SCHULPHILOSOPHIE AUF DIE ORTHODOX-LUTHERISCHE DOGMATIK

Weber, F *see*
- BOTANISCHES TASCHENBUCH AUF DAS JAHR 1807
- GROSSBRITANNIENS CONFERVEN
- HISTORIAE MUSCORUM HEPATICORUM PRODROMUS

Weber, Ferdinand *see* JUEDISCHE THEOLOGIE: AUF GRUND DES TALMUD UND VERWANDTER SCHRIFTEN

Weber, Friedrich Wilhelm *see* DREIZEHNLINDEN

Weber, Georg *see* ALLGEMEINE WELTGESCHICHTE MIT BESONDERER BERUECKSICHITIGUNG DES GEISTES$ UND CULTURLEBENS DER VOELKER UND MIT BENUTZUNG DER NEUEREN GESCHICHTLICHEN FORSCHUNGEN

Weber, Gottfried *see*
- CAECILIA
- WOLFRAM VON ESCHENBACH

Weber, Jaroy *see* MISC. SCRAPBOOKS

Weber, Jules *see* LA METHODE D'EDUCATION SUIVIE PAR JESUS D'APRES LES SYNOPTIQUES

Weber, Karl Friedrich *see* SPRACHFEHLER, WORTSPIELE, ETC.

Weber, Robert *see* POEMS

Weber, Rolf *see* DIE BEDEUTUNG VON GRUPPEN- UND MINDERHEITENRECHTEN FUER DIE SUEDAFRIKANISCHE VERFASSUNGSENTWICKLUNG

Weber, S *see* DIE KATHOLISCHE KIRCHE IN ARMENIEN

Weber, Th *see* JOHANNES DER TAEUFER UND DIE PARTEIEN SEINER ZEIT: EIN ZEITSPIEGEL

Weber, Werner *see* TAGEBUCH EINES LESERS

Weber-Van Bosse, A *see* MONOGRAPHIE DES CAULERPES

WEBFOOT SCOUT – Portland OR. Dec 1935, Apr 1936 – 1 – us U.O. Library [071]

WEBSTER 1832-1905 – (Mf 1: Births 1799-1844. Mf 1-2: Marriages 1832-44. Mf 2: Deaths 1803-44. Mf 3-4: Births 1844-60. Mf 4: Marriages 1844-52. Mf 4-5: Deaths 1844-59. Mf 6-10: Births 1860-89. Mf 11-16: Birth Index 1844-1908. Mf 17-23,36-39: Marriages 1853-1903. Mf 24-27: Marriage Index 1844-1908. Mf 28-31,40-43: Deaths 1860-1910. Mf 32-35: Death Index 1844-1908) – (mf ed 1986) – 43mf – 0-87623-003-6 – us Holbrook [920]

Webster, Carl David *see* JOURNAL OF APPLIED AQUACULTURE

WEBSTER COUNTY ARGUS – Red Cloud, NE. -w. (-sw 1912-13). Mar 1881; Aug 1881-Dec 1887; Jan 1889-Aug 1930 – 1 – us NE Hist [071]

WEBSTER COUNTY ARGUS – Red Cloud. Neb. 1881-1930 – 1 – us UMI [071]

Webster, Daniel *see*
- PAPERS
- PAPERS OF DANIEL WEBSTER, 1798-1852

WEBSTER ECHO – Webster Springs. West Virginia. 1896-1903; 1909-1912; 1917-1928; 1945-1953; 1962-1963 – 1 – us UMI [071]

Webster, J J *see* TO THE ELECTORS OF THE COUNTY OF STANSTEAD

Webster, James B *see* CHRISTIAN EDUCATION AND THE NATIONAL CONSCIOUSNESS IN CHINA (CCC320)

Webster, New York. Webster Baptist Church *see* RECORDS

Webster, Noah *see*
- DISSERTATIONS ON THE ENGLISH LANGUAGE
- A GRAMMATICAL INSTITUTE OF THE ENGLISH LANGUAGE
- HISTORY OF ANIMALS
- SKETCHES OF AMERICAN POLICY

Webster, Prentiss *see* A TREATISE ON THE LAW OF CITIZENSHIP IN THE UNITED STATES

WEBSTER PROGRESS – Europa. Miss. 1951-60 – 1 – us UMI [071]
WEBSTER REPUBLICAN – Webster Springs. West Virginia. 1934-1968 – 1 – us UMI [071]
Webster, Thomas *see*
- HISTORY OF THE METHODIST EPISCOPAL CHURCH IN CANADA
- LIFE OF REV. JAMES RICHARDSON
- WEBSTER'S PATENT REPORTS

WEBSTER V. REPRODUCTIVE HEALTH SERVICES : BRIEFS AND RELATED DOCUMENTS / Protti, Maria – (With mf binder 1990) – 1v – 9 – $195.00 set – 0-89941-741-8 – us Hein [360]
Webster, William *see* THE SYNTAX AND SYNONYMS OF THE GREEK TESTAMENT
Webster, William Henry Bayley *see* NARRATIVE OF A VOYAGE TO THE SOUTHERN ATLANTIC OCEAN IN 1828, 29, 30, PERFORMED IN H.M. SLOOP CHANTICLEER
WEBSTER'S – Reidsville. N.C. -w. 1897-98 – 1 – us UMI [071]
WEBSTER'S PATENT REPORTS / Webster, Thomas – (Reports and notes of cases on Letters Patent for inventions) – London: Thomas Blenkarn. v1-2. 1884 (all publ) – 13mf – 9 – $19.50 – LLMC 84-330 – us L.L.M.C. [340]
W.E.C.A.F.C. *see*
- NATIONAL REPORTS AND SELECTED PAPERS PRESENTED AT THE 1ST SESSION OF THE WORKING PARTY ON FISHERIES ECONOMICS AND PLANNING
- NATIONAL REPORTS AND SELECTED PAPERS PRESENTED AT THE 5TH SESSION OF THE WORKING PARTY ON ASSESSMENT OF MARINE FISHERY RESOURCE. SAINT GEORGE, BERMUDA, NOV 1986
- NATIONAL REPORTS AND SELECTED PAPERS PRESENTED AT THE 6TH SESSION OF THE WORKING PARTY ON ASSESSMENT OF MARINE FISHERY RESOURCES; SUPPLEMENT
- REPORT OF THE 1ST SESSION OF THE WORKING PARTY ON FISHERY ECONOMICS AND PLANNING
- REPORT OF THE 2ND SESSION OF THE COMMITTEE FOR THE DEVELOPMENT AND MANAGEMENT OF FISHERIES IN THE LESSER ANTILLES. CASTRIES, SAINT LUCIA, 1985
- REPORT OF THE 2ND WORKSHOP ON THE BIOLOGICAL AND ECONOMICAL MODELLING OF THE SHRIMP RESOURCES ON THE GUYANA-BRAZIL SHELF
- REPORT OF THE 3RD SESSION OF THE COMMITTEE FOR THE DEVELOPMENT AND MANAGEMENT OF FISHERIES IN THE LESSER ANTILLES. FORT-DE-FRANCE, MARTINIQUE, JULY 1987
- REPORT OF THE 3RD SESSION OF THE WORKING PARTY ON FISHERY STATISTICS
- REPORT OF THE 4TH SESSION OF THE COMMITTEE FOR THE DEVELOPMENT AND MANAGEMENT OF FISHERIES IN THE LESSER ANTILLES
- REPORT OF THE 4TH SESSION OF THE WORKING PARTY ON ASSESSMENT OF MARINE FISHERY RESOURCES. PAIPA, COLOMBIA, 1984
- REPORT OF THE 5TH SESSION OF THE WORKING PARTY ON ASSESSMENT OF MARINE FISHERY RESOURCES. SAINT GEORGE, BERMUDA, 1986
- REPORT OF THE 6TH SESSION OF THE WORKING PARTY ON ASSESSMENT OF MARINE FISHERY RESOURCES
- REPORT OF THE 7TH SESSION OF THE WESTERN CENTRAL ATLANTIC FISHERY COMMISSION
- REPORT OF THE EXPERT CONSULTATION ON THE USE OF MICROCOMPUTERS FOR PROCESSING STATISTICAL AND BIOLOGICAL DATA. CHAGUARAMAS, TRINIDAD AND TOBAGO, 1986
- REPORT OF THE WORKSHOP ON THE USE OF LENGTH-FREQUENCY DATA FOR THE ASSESSMENT OF FISHERY RESOURCES OF THE CARIBBEAN ISLANDS

DEN WECH DES EEUWICH LEVENS BESCHREVEN INT LATIJN... / Sucquet, A – Antwerpen, 1622 – 11mf – 9 – ne IDC [700]
DAS WECHSELINDOSSAMENT... / Aronowsky, S S – Zuerich, 1917 – 2mf – 9 – ILM-3458/1 – ne IDC [340]
WECHSELKURSRISIKO UND EXPORTENTSCHEIDUNG : DIREKTES UND INDIREKTES HEDGING / Kratzenberg, Andree – 1995 – 1mf – 9 – DM60.00 – 3-8267-2203-5 – gw Hänsel [332]
DIE WECHSELWIRKUNG ORGANISCHER MOLEKUELE MIT SUPRA-MOLEKULAREN VERBINDUNGEN : ADSORPTIONS-/DESORPTIONS-UNTERSUCHUNGEN UND VERGLEICHENDE KRAFTFELDRECHNUNGEN AN CALIXARENEN / Gerlach, Andreas – 1993 – 2mf – 9 – DM80.00 – 3-89349-804-4 – gw Hänsel [540]
WECHSLER UND HAENDLER : KOMOEDIE / Johst, Hanns – Muenchen: A Langen, 1923 – 1r – 1 – us U.W. Library [820]
DER WECKER – New York. 1924; 1939-43; 1946-56; 1959-66 – 1 – us A.J.P.C. [073]
Weckerlin, Jean Baptiste *see* CHANSONS ET RONDES ENFANTINES DES PROVINCES DE LA FRANCE
Weckherlin, Georg Rodolf *see* GEDICHTE
Weckherlin, Georg Rudolf *see* GEDICHTE
WECKHERLIN'S ECLOGUES OF THE SEASONS... / Johnson, Elizabeth Frienćh – 1922 – 1r – 1 – us U.W. Library [430]
WECKOBLADET – Motala, 1887-90 – 9 – sw Kungliga [072]
Wedde, Johannes *see* THEODOR STORM
Weddell Family *see* CIVIL WAR LETTERS
Weddell, H A *see*
- CHLORIS ANDINA. ESSAI D'UNE FLORE DE LA REGION ALPINE DES CORDILLERES DE L'AMERIQUE DU SUD
- MONOGRAPHIE DE LA FAMILLE DES URTICEES

Weddell, James *see* A VOYAGE TOWARDS THE SOUTH POLE IN 1822-24.
Wedderburn, David *see* A SHORT INTRODUCTION TO GRAMMAR
WEDDERBURN EXPRESS – 1921-1957. WEX1-16 – 16r – 1 – at Corangamite [072]
WEDDING BELLS – London, UK. 15 Dec 1893. -w. 1 foot – 1 – uk British Libr Newspaper [073]
WEDDING CEREMONIALS / Indonesia – SE-3666 1 – 9 – ne IDC [390]
Wedekind, Frank *see*
- THE AWAKENING OF SPRING, A TRAGEDY OF CHILDHOOD
- ERDGEIST
- DER KAMMERSAENGER
- KOENIG NICOLO, ODER, SO IST DAS LEBEN
- PANDORA'S BOX; A TRAGEDY IN THREE ACTS
- SUCH IS LIFE

Wedemeyer, Dan J *see* METHODS OF COMMUNICATION PLANNING
WEDERANTWOORT OP ZEKEREN BRIEF BY GELLIUM ONDERTEECKENT WAER IN HY SIJNE MEYNINGE VNDE OORDEEL STELT. IN 'T JAER 1545 / Blesdijk, Nicolaas M van – 1607. BME-386 1 – 9 – ne IDC [240]
WEDERLEGGHINGHE (EEN GRONDELICKE ENDE SEER SCHOONE) TEGHEN DE PRINCIPAELSTE POINCTEN ENDE ARGUMENTEN DER WEDER-DOOPEREN – Ghendt, Corn. de Rekenaere. 1581. BME-213-1 – 9 – ne IDC [240]
WEDERLEGGINGE EENS TRACTAETS, GHEMAECKT DOOR TWEE WATERLANTSCHE WEDERDOOPERSSCHE BISSCHOPPEN, NAMELIJCK: HANS DE RIES, ENDE JACOB JANSZ / Boeckaert, C – Amstelredam, Jan Willemsz. 1597. BME-340 1 – 9 – ne IDC [240]
WEDEROPBOUW : MAANDBLAD GEWIJD AAN DE JONG-JAVANEN-BEWEGING EN HET JAVAANSE GEESTESLEVEN – (Lacking: 1918, V.1(2); 1919, V.2(1-4, 6-11)) – Weltevreden, 1918-1923. v1-6 – 14mf – 9 – SE-20,013/1 – ne IDC [072]
Wedge *see* HISTORY OF BARRON COUNTY
Wedgewood, William B *see* VERMONT LEGAL CATECHISM
Wedgwood, Julia *see* THE MORAL IDEAL
Wedgwood Museum *see* WEDGWOOD PAPERS 1765-1906
WEDGWOOD PAPERS 1765-1906 / Wedgwood Museum – American papers from the Wedgwood Museum. BRRAM – 1 – uk Microform Academic [970]
WEDJANGAN REVOLUSI; KARYA BUNG KARNO. SEBUAH KAMUS ILMU PERDJUANGAN UNTUK RAKJAT / Sukarno, Pres. Indonesia – SE 6680 1. 1965 – 9 – ne IDC [025]
Wedmore Parish. England *see* PARISH REGISTERS
WEDNESBURY BOROUGH NEWS – England. -w. 1970-74. 10 reels – 1 – uk British Libr Newspaper [072]
WEDNESBURY, WEST BROMWICH AND DARLASTON EXAMINER – (Midland Examiner and Times). Wednesbury. England. -w. 19 Sep 1874-6 Oct 1877. (3 reels) – 1 – uk British Libr Newspaper [072]
WEDNESDAY SENTINEL – LeMars. Iowa. -w. 1953-57 – 1 – us UMI [071]
WEDNESDAY THE TENTH: A TALE OF THE SOUTH PACIFIC / Allen, Grant – Boston: D. Lothrop, 1890. 05091. (Pre-1900 Canadiana) – 9 – cn C.I.H.M. [830]
Weech, Friedrich von *see* ROEMISCHE PRAELATEN AM DEUTSCHEN RHEIN 1761-1764
Weed, George Ludington *see* A LIFE OF ST PETER: FOR THE YOUNG
WEED LOG – Weed, CA. 1939-1943 – 2r – 1 – $100.00 – B03692 – us Library Micro [071]
WEED NEWS – Weed, CA. 1977 – 1r – 1 – $50.00 – B05068 – us Library Micro [071]
WEED PRESS – Weed, CA. 1926-39; 1983- – 10+ r – 1 – $500.00 ($90.00y) – B03090 – us Library Micro [071]
WEED SCIENCE – (Formerly: WEEDS). v. 3-22. 1959-1974 – 1,5,6 – us Princeton Micro [630]
WEED SCIENCE – v3-22. 1959-74 – 1,5,6 – us Princeton Micro [631]
WEED SCIENCE AND WEED CONTROL IN SOUTHEAST ASIA – 1987 – 208p – it F.A.O. [631]
Weeden, William Babcock *see* THE MORALITY OF PROHIBITORY LIQUOR LAWS
WEEDS AND TURF – 1962-Nov 1964 – 1 – us UMI [631]
WEEDS IN TROPICAL CROPS : SELECTED ABSTRACTS ON CONSTRAINTS ON PRODUCTION CAUSED BY WEEDS IN MAIZE, RICE, SORGHUM-MILLET, GROUNDNUTS AND CASSAVA, 1952-1980 – 1981 – 94p – it F.A.O. [630]
WEEDS IN TROPICAL CROPS. SUPPLEMENT : REVIEW OF ABSTRACTS – 1982 – 62p – it F.A.O. [630]
WEEDS TREES AND TURF – (v.20-. 1981-. 5,6,9) – Dec 1964- – 1 – us UMI [631]
THE WEEK – London. -w. 29 Mar 1933-15 Jan 1941, 23 Oct 1942-18 Dec 1946. (3 reels) – 1 – uk British Libr Newspaper [072]
THE WEEK – Toronto, 1883-96 – 6r – 1 – $390.00 – cn Library Assoc [971]
A WEEK IN THE NEIGHBOURHOOD OF LAKE ETCHEMIN AND QUEBEC / Bulger, George Ernest – Secunderabad, India: Regimental Press, 1869. 02015. (Pre-1900 Canadiana) – 9 – cn C.I.H.M. [971]
THE WEEK SANCTIFIED BY THE DEVOTION TO THE SACRED HEART OF JESUS / Desjardins, E – Translated from the French of the 41st edition by Ferdinand Belanger. Quebec: L. Brosseau, 1874. 04284. (Pre-1900 Canadiana) – 9 – cn C.I.H.M. [971]
WEEKBLAD VAN HET RECHT – 's-Gravenhage. On film: v1-32, 34-93, 96-97; 1839-70, 1872-1931, 1934-35. LL-0231 – 1 – us L of C Photodup [340]
WEEKBLAD VOOR INDIE – Soerabaja, 1904-1920. v1-17 – 354mf – 9 – SE-20,016/1 – ne IDC [072]
WEEKBLAD VOOR ISRAELIETISCHE HUISGEZINNEN – (Missing: 1872/1873, v3(1-52); 1875/1876, v6(1-52); 1882, v13(1-52); 1895, v26(1-52); 1906, v37(1)) – Rotterdam. v1-71. 1870-1940 – 661mf – 9 – J-261-132/1 – ne IDC [270]
WEEKBULLETIN / Nederlandse Hervormde Kerk – 1982-83.1 reel – 1 – us A.T.L.A. [073]
WEEKBULLETIN VAN HET PERSBUREAU / Nederlandse Hervormde Kerk – 1969-85.7 reels – 1 – us A.T.L.A. [073]
WEEK-DAY RELIGION / Miller, James Russell – Philadelphia: Presbyterian Board of Publ and Sabbath-School Work, c1880 – 1mf – 9 – 0-8370-7247-6 – 1986-1247 – us A.T.L.A. [240]
WEEKEND CHRONICLE – Valletta, Malta. Nov 1981-Juni 18 1988 – 8r – 1 – us L of C Photodup [072]
WEEKEND MAGAZINE INDEX – Montreal, 1952-1975 – 13r – 1 – cn Preston [971]
WEEK-END STAR – (1988-1992.-6r) – Toronto, 1993 – 1r – 1 – cn Preston [971]
THE WEEKENDER – Wyandotte. Mich. 1964-1965 – 1 – us UMI [071]
THE WEEKENDERS / Gunther, Max – With drawings by Susan Perl. Philadelphia: Lippincott 1964 – 1 – us U.W. Library [978]
THE WEEKLY – Carson City, NV. 1891-1918 – 19r – 1 – $950.00 – U04475 – us Library Micro [071]
WEEKLY – Orvada, NV. 1924-25 – 1r – 1 – $50.00 – U04635 – us Library Micro [071]
WEEKLY ABSTRACT – Salem OR. Jan 29 Mar 19 1914 – 1 – us U.O. Library [071]
WEEKLY ADVOCATE – Belleville. Ill. 1840-1910 – 1 – us UMI [071]
WEEKLY ADVOCATE – Dorris, CA. 1911-12 – 1r – 1 – $50.00 – B02176 – us Library Micro [071]
WEEKLY AGE – Clinton. Iowa. 1869-1901 – 1 – us UMI [071]
WEEKLY AGE – Melbourne, 1865-68 – 2r – 1 – A$62.00 silver A$54.00 vesicular – at Pascoe [072]
THE WEEKLY AGRICOLE – Davis, CA. 1915-22 – 3r – 1 – $150.00 – B02165 – us Library Micro [071]
WEEKLY AGRICULTURAL REVIEW ETC – Dublin, Ireland.15 Apr 1859-Jun 1867. -w. 7 1/2 reels – 1 – uk British Libr Newspaper [072]
WEEKLY ALBERTAN – Alberta, CN. 1904-06 – 1r – 1 – cn Commonwealth Micro [072]
WEEKLY ALLIANCE – LaGrande OR. May 7 1913 – 1 – us U.O. Library [071]
WEEKLY AND MONTHLY ORTHODOX – London. -w. 27 Jan-28 Jul 1849. (31 ft) – 1 – uk British Libr Newspaper [072]
THE WEEKLY ARGUS – Montreal, Canada. v2 n52. 31 oct 1856; v4 n15. 12 fev 1858 – 1r – 1 – Can$25.00 – cn Can Microfilming [072]
WEEKLY ARGUS – Beloit. Wis. 1885-1888 – 1 – us UMI [071]
WEEKLY ARGUS – Dover. Ohio. 1880-1882; 1885-1888; 1892-1920; 1921-1922; 1924- – 1 – us UMI [071]
WEEKLY ARGUS – Petaluma. Calif. 1873-1879 – 1 – us UMI [071]
WEEKLY ASTORIAN – Astoria, OR. 5 Mar 1874-20 Sept 1901. 8 rolls; 21 Oct 1949-29 Oct 1965. 3 rolls – 1 – us U.O. Library [071]
WEEKLY BEACON – North Baltimore, Ohio. 1884-88 – 1r – 1 – $32.50r – us Archival [071]
THE WEEKLY BEE – Sacramento, CA. 1877-1900 – 10r – 1 – $500.00 – R03443 – us Library Micro [071]
WEEKLY BEE – Portland OR. June 15 July 6 1876, May 24 1877 – 1 – us U.O. Library [071]
THE WEEKLY BLADE – Santa Ana, CA. 1888-1905 – 2r – 1 – $100.00 – R02937 – us Library Micro [071]
WEEKLY BOND BUYER – v126-168. 1953-67 – 1,5,6 – us Princeton Micro [332]
WEEKLY BRIEFINGS / Royal Institution of Chartered Surveyors – 1966-88. Continued annually – 1 – uk World [520]
WEEKLY BRITISH COLONIST – Canada. Victoria Weekly Colonist Semi-weekly Colonist. Jan 1864-April 1912. Imperfect. 55 reels – 1 – uk British Libr Newspaper [072]
WEEKLY BRITISH COLONIST – Victoria, British Columbia, CN. Dec 1861-Jun 1865 – 1r – 1 – cn Commonwealth Micro [072]
THE WEEKLY BUDGET *see* THE BUDGET
WEEKLY BUDGET – Lancaster. Pa. 1911-1929 – 1 – us UMI [071]
THE WEEKLY BULLETIN – Dillsburg, PA. -w 1916-73. 16 rolls – 13 – $25.00r – us I.M.R. [071]
THE WEEKLY BULLETIN – Freetown, Sierra Leone: [s.n.], 1957-58; 1960-jan 17 1961 – 1r – 1 – us Res Libr [072]
WEEKLY BULLETIN / Russian Soviet Government Bureau – New York. v. 1. no. 1-13. Mar 3 1919-May 26 1919 – 1 – us NY Public [073]
WEEKLY BULLETIN / Russian Soviet Government Bureau – New York. v1. 1919. – 1r – 1 – us Ross [947]
WEEKLY BURTONIAN – Tekamah. Neb. 1874-1901 – 1 – us UMI [071]
WEEKLY BUTTE RECORD – Oroville, CA. 1853-58; 1861-87 – 16r – 1 – $800.00 – B02578 – us Library Micro [071]
WEEKLY CALIFORNIAN – Berkeley, CA. 1926-1927 – 1r – 1 – $50.00 – C03160 – us Library Micro [071]
THE WEEKLY CALISTOGIAN – Calistoga, CA. 1896-1961; 1974-77; 1989- – 42+ r – 1 – $2,100.00 ($50.00y) – B02090 – us Library Micro [071]
WEEKLY CALL – Battle Creek. Mich. 1885-1886 – 1 – us UMI [071]

WEEKLY CALL – Lincoln. Neb. 1889-1898 – 1 – us UMI [071]
THE WEEKLY CHRONICLE : COMMERCIAL AND SHIPPING GAZETTE – Quebec, Canada. v35 n1225. 12 aut 1881; v39 n3432. 9 avr 1885 – 1r – 1 – Can$25.00 – cn Can Microfilming [072]
WEEKLY CHRONICLE – Bozeman. Mont. 1891-1900; 1902-1912; 1913-1916; 1919 – 1 – us UMI [071]
WEEKLY CHRONICLE – Tralee, Ireland. -w. 8 Feb-28 June 1875. 15 ft – 1 – uk British Libr Newspaper [072]
WEEKLY CITIZEN – Eugene OR. May 7 Apr 11 25 May 2 1900 – 1 – us U.O. Library [071]
WEEKLY CLARION – Jackson. Miss. 1869-1890 – 1 – us UMI [071]
WEEKLY COAST MAIL – Marshfield, OR. 29 Nov 1902-30 Jun 1906. – 3r – 1 – us U.O. Library [071]
THE WEEKLY COLONIST – Quebec, Canada. v1 n8. 22 jul 1854 – 1r – 1 – Can$25.00 – cn Can Microfilming [072]
WEEKLY COLUMBIAN – (The Columbian. Weekly ed. British Columbian). New Westminster. Canada. -w. Feb 1890-1922. (39mqn reels) – 1 – uk British Libr Newspaper [072]
WEEKLY COLUSA SUN – Colusa. Calif. 1862-1864; 1869-1872; 1877-1878; 1883-1892 – 1 – us UMI [071]
WEEKLY COMET – Denver. Col. 1922-23 – 1 – us A.J.P.C. [071]
WEEKLY COMPILATION OF PRESIDENTIAL DOCUMENTS – v1- 1965- 1; v6- 5,6; v12- 9 – us UMI [324]
WEEKLY COMPILATION OF PRESIDENTIAL DOCUMENTS – Law Library Microfilm Consortium. v1-25. 1965-89 – 9 – $795.00 set – us Hein [350]
WEEKLY COMPILATION OF PRESIDENTIAL DOCUMENTS – v26-31. 1990-95 – 9 – $295.00 run – us Hein [350]
WEEKLY COMPILATION OF THE PRESIDENTIAL DOCUMENTS – v1-30 no 49. 1965-94 – 1082mf – 9 – $1,623.00 – LLMC 79-424 – us L.L.M.C. [324]
WEEKLY COMPILATIONS OF PRESIDENTIAL DOCUMENTS, 1965-69 / U.S. National Archives and Records Service – 5rolls. M839 – 1 – us Nat'l Archives [324]
WEEKLY COURIER – Lafayette. Ind. 1878; 1886-1887; 1893-1897; 1901-1903; 1905-06; 1908; 1910; 1913-1914; 1916-1918 – 1 – us UMI [071]
WEEKLY COURIER – Launceston, Australia. 6 Jul 1901-13 Sep 1917; 26 Jun 1919-22 Jun 1922.-w. 53 reels – 1 – uk British Libr Newspaper [072]
WEEKLY COURIER – McCook, NE. Apr 1890; Jun 1890-Jan 1891; Aug 1895-Dec 1901 – 1 – us NE Hist [071]
WEEKLY COURIER – Ottumwa. Iowa. 1879-1885 – 1 – us UMI [071]
WEEKLY COURIER – Saginaw. Mich. 1876-1878; 1881-1889 – 1 – us UMI [071]
WEEKLY COURIER – San Bernardino, CA. 1891-94 – 3r – 1 RC02771 – $150.00 – us Library Micro [071]
WEEKLY COURIER – San Bernardino. Calif. 1891-1894 – 1 – us UMI [071]
WEEKLY COURIER *see* COURIER
WEEKLY CRITICAL REVIEW – Paris, France. -w. 22 Jan 1903-25 March 1904. 3 reels – 1 – uk British Libr Newspaper [072]
WEEKLY DEMOCRAT – Huntington. Ind. 1879-1893 – 1 – us UMI [071]
WEEKLY DEMOCRAT – Ottumwa. Iowa. 1871-1878; 1881-1885; 1890-1904 – 1 – us UMI [071]
WEEKLY DEMOCRAT Poplarville. Miss. 1940-1954 – 1 – us UMI [071]
WEEKLY DEMOCRAT – Seymour. Ind. 1881-1901 – 1 – us UMI [071]
WEEKLY DEMOCRAT – Vale, OR. 29 Jun 1901-15 Mar 1902. 1 roll – 1 – us U.O. Library [071]
WEEKLY DEMOCRATIC PRESS – Salem OR. Apr 24 1869, Sep 4 11 18 Nov 6 20 1869, Jan 8 June 11 1870 + – 1 – us U.O. Library [071]
WEEKLY DEMOCRATIC REVIEW – Salem OR. Oct 9 1865-Aug 17 1867 + – 1 – us U.O. Library [071]
WEEKLY DETROIT FREE PRESS – Detroit, MI. Detroit Free Press. British edition. -w. 16 July 1881-1 April 1899. 17 reels – 1 – uk British Libr Newspaper [071]
WEEKLY DIGEST OF NON-ENGLISH PRESS / Singapore. Public Relations Office – 1952-59 – 1 – 175.00 – us L of C Photodup [900]
THE WEEKLY DISPATCH – Hull, Canada. v1 n19. 15 avr 1881; v10. 22 mar 1890 – 1r – 1 – Can$25.00 – cn Can Microfilming [072]
WEEKLY DISPATCH – Columbus. Miss. 1903-1910 – 1 – us UMI [071]
WEEKLY DISPATCH – London, England. Sunday Dispatch. -w. 27 Sept 1801-20 Dec 1804; 5 Oct 1806; 5 July, 6 Sept 1807; 9 Jan 1814; 5 Jan 1817-Dec 1819; Jan 1870-11 June 1961. 159 reels – 1 – uk British Libr Newspaper [072]
WEEKLY DISPATCH – Michigan City. Ind. 1881-1886; 1891-1913 – 1 – us UMI [071]
WEEKLY DISPATCH – New Martinsville. West Virginia. 1901-1909 – 1 – us UMI [071]
WEEKLY DISPATCH – San Antonio. Tex. 1901-1931; 1932-1937; 1943-1950 – 1 – us UMI [071]
WEEKLY DISPATCH – St. Thomas, Canada. 1853-76 – 9r – 1 – $585.00 – cn Library Assoc [971]
WEEKLY EAGLE – Grand Rapids. Mich. 1864-1868 – 1 – us UMI [071]
WEEKLY ECONOMIC REVIEW – (Cont. as: Indonesian news and economic bulletin. The Hague, 1956-1957) – The Hague, 1951-56 – 98mf – 9 – Se-573/1 – ne IDC [330]
WEEKLY ELKO INDEPENDENT – (Also known as: Daily Independent) – Elko, NV. 1869-71; 1975-79; 1887-99; 1908-18; 1924; 1927-79; 1982- – 78+ r – 1 – $3,900.00 ($60.00y) – U04496 – us Library Micro [071]
WEEKLY ENTOMOLOGIST – Altrincham. v1-3. (1862)-1863 – 11mf – 9 – Z-1009/2 – ne IDC [590]
THE WEEKLY EXAMINER – (Cont by: Examiner-Courier 24 fev 1933-28 dec 1934. Cont by: The Westmount Examiner v7 n1. 1 fev 1935-28 dec 1967) – Outremont, Canada. v1 n11. 30 nov 1929-16 fev 1933 – 10r – 1 – Can$75.00r – cn Can Microfilming [072]
THE WEEKLY EXAMINER – (Cont by: The Sherbrooke Examiner 17 aut 1888-11 jul 1904) – Sherbrooke Canada. v2 n71. 27 feb 1880-7 oct 1887 – 9r – 1 – Can$75.00r – cn Can Microfilming [072]
WEEKLY EXAMINER – Calcutta, India. -w. 14 March 1840-31 July 1841. 1 reel – 1 – uk British Libr Newspaper [072]
WEEKLY EXPOSITOR – Fresno, CA. 1872-98 – 12r – 1 BC02259 – $600.00 – us Library Micro [071]
THE WEEKLY EXPOSITOR, OR, REFORMER OF PUBLIC ABUSES, AND RAILWAY AND MINING INTELLIGENCE – Montreal: J Tennyson, [1846-1847] – 9 – cn C.I.H.M. [971]
WEEKLY FOCUS *see* FOCUS
THE WEEKLY FREE PRESS – (Title varies: Kimberley Free Press, Feb 1904-1907) – Kimberley, South Africa. 24 Jul 1897-28 Dec 1907 – 7r – 1,16 diazo available at reduced price – sa SA Libr [072]
WEEKLY FREE PRESS – Friend, NE. Sep. 1887-Apr. 1889 – 1 – us NE Hist [071]
WEEKLY FREE PRESS – Redding, CA. 1893-94; 1899-1991 – 1r – 1 – $50.00 – B02677 – us Library Micro [071]
WEEKLY FREE PRESS – Redding. Calif. 1888-1891; 1895-1897; 1899-1903 – 1 – us UMI [071]
WEEKLY FREEMAN'S JOURNAL – Dublin. Ireland. -w. 1841-44. (4 reels) – 1 – uk British Libr Newspaper [072]
WEEKLY GAZETTE – (Cont by: The Gazette, Montreal 1884) – Montreal, Canada. v99 n35. 3 sep 1875; v102 n11. 18 mar 1878; v108 n41. 3 oct 1884 – 1r – 1 – Can$35.00 – cn Can Microfilming [072]
WEEKLY GAZETTE – Lima. Ohio. 1856-1858 – 1 – us UMI [071]
WEEKLY GAZETTE – Missoula. Mont. 1890-1892 – 1 – us UMI [071]
WEEKLY GAZETTE – Reno, NV. 1879-80; 1883-1900 – 10r – 1 – $500.00 – U04725 – us Library Micro [071]
WEEKLY GAZETTE – Waukegan. Ill. 1850-86 – 1 – us UMI [071]
WEEKLY GAZETTE OF THE REPUBLIC OF IRAQ – Baghdad, 1948-55; 1958-70 – 16r – 1 – us Ross [324]
WEEKLY GAZETTE-TIMES – Corvallis, OR. 2 Jul 1909-1 Sep 1921. 5 rolls – 1 – us U.O. Library [071]
THE WEEKLY GLEANER *see* THE GLEANER
WEEKLY GLEANER – (An American-Jewish publ) – San Francisco, CA. Jan-Dec 1857 – 1r – 1 – $50.00 – B02865 – us Library Micro [071]
WEEKLY GLEANER – San Francisco. Calif. 1857-61 – 1 – us A.J.P.C. [071]
WEEKLY GLOBE – Adams. Neb. 1896-1959 – 1 – us UMI [071]
WEEKLY GLOBE – Lincoln. Neb. 1877-1881 – 1 – us UMI [071]
WEEKLY GLOBE AND CANADA FARMER – Toronto, 1878-1883 – 4r – 1 – cn Preston [971]
WEEKLY GUERNSEY TIMES – Cambridge. Ohio. 1860-1909; 1917-1919 – 1 – us UMI [071]
WEEKLY HAMILTON TELEGRAPH : WEEKLY DEMOCRATIC NEWSPAPER – Hamilton, OH. 17 Jan 1858-6 Jun 1861 – 2r – 1 – us Western Res [071]
WEEKLY HAMPSHIRE INDEPENDENT *see* HAMPSHIRE INDEPENDENT
THE WEEKLY HERALD – Hampstead, 14 apr 1989-30 jan 1991 – 1r – 1 – Can$75.00 – cn Can Microfilming [072]
WEEKLY HERALD – Canada. Calgary Weekly Herald Alberta Farmer. March 1907-Dec 1921. 16 reels – 1 – uk British Libr Newspaper [072]
WEEKLY HERALD – (Cork Weekly Herald, 1875-81) – Cork, Ireland. 1874-84; 1887-96. -w – 20r – 1 – uk British Libr Newspaper [072]
WEEKLY HERALD – Delphos. Ohio. 1872-1897 – 1 – us UMI [071]
WEEKLY HERALD – Delphos, Ohio. 1872-1910 – 13r – 1 – $32.50r – us Archival [071]
WEEKLY HERALD – Huntington. Ind. 1901-1905 – 1 – us UMI [071]
WEEKLY HERALD – Newman Grove, NE. Dec 1896-Feb 1897; Jun 1897-Feb 1898; Apr 1898-Mar 1899, scattered issues missing; Feb-Jun 1900 – 1 – us NE Hist [071]
WEEKLY HERALD – Oskaloosa. Iowa. 1852-1857 – 1 – us UMI [071]
WEEKLY HERALD – St. Mary's Kersey, PA. -w 1889-1904 – 13 – $25.00r – us I.M.R. [071]
WEEKLY HERALD AND ALGOMAMIN LAKESUP MINJNL – (1885-1890.-1r) – Thunder Bay, 1896-1901No – 2r – 1 – cn Preston [971]
WEEKLY HERALD-DISSEMINATOR – (Incl. Albany Herald and Weekly Herald) – Albany, OR. 5 Nov 1886-15 Sep 1904 – 1 – us U.O. Library [071]
WEEKLY ILLUSTRATED PAPER – Bridgetown, Barbados. -w. 10 May-27 Dec 1919; 1 May 1920-13 Aug, 24, 31 Dec 1921. Imperfect. 1 reel – 1 – uk British Libr Newspaper [072]
WEEKLY INDEPENDENT – Jacksonville OR. May 28 1912 – 1 – us U.O. Library [071]
WEEKLY INDEPENDENT – Johnstown. OH. And: Independent. 1884-98; 1902-19; 1940-49 – 1 – us UMI [071]
WEEKLY INDEX – Forest Grove OR. May 1 1906 – 1 – us U.O. Library [071]
WEEKLY INDEX – Salinas, CA. 1873-1906 – 34r – 1 – $1,700.00 – B02756 – us Library Micro [071]
WEEKLY INDUSTRIAL WORKER – Seattle etc. Apr 14 1917-1964 – 1 – us NY Public [331]
WEEKLY INTELLIGENCER – Belleville, 1902-1922 – 21r – 1 – cn Preston [971]
Weekly Irish Times *see* SINN FEIN REBELLION HANDBOOK
THE WEEKLY ITEM – Mount Carmel. Pa. -w. 1886-96 – 1 – us UMI [071]
WEEKLY ITEM – Mount Carmel, PA. -w 1888-1896 – 13 – $25.00r – us I.M.R. [071]
WEEKLY JEFFERSONIAN – Findlay, Ohio. 1911-21 – 5r – 1 – $32.50r – us Archival [071]
WEEKLY JOURNAL – Antigo. Wis. 1898-1906 – 1 – us UMI [071]
WEEKLY JOURNAL – Dunkirk. N.Y. 1863-1866; 1869-1870; 1874-1883 – 1 – us UMI [071]
WEEKLY JOURNAL – Lawrence. Kan. 1886-1889 – 1 – us UMI [071]
WEEKLY JOURNAL – Logansport. Ind. 1870-1876 – 1 – us UMI [071]
WEEKLY JOURNAL – Napa, CA. 1905-1914 – 5r – 1 – $250.00 – B02513 – us Library Micro [073]
WEEKLY JOURNAL – Weston, Ohio. 1957-58 – 1r – 1 – $32.50r – us Archival [071]
WEEKLY JOURNAL *see* SALINAS DEMOCRAT
WEEKLY JOURNAL OF COMMERCE – New York, 1828-68 – 11r – 1 – us Ross [380]
THE WEEKLY JURIST *see* MONTHLY JURIST
WEEKLY KANSAS CHIEF – Troy. Kan. 1873-1899 – 1 – us UMI [071]
WEEKLY KLAMATH RECORD – Klamath Falls, OR. 29 Sept 1916-28 Feb 1922. 1 roll – 1 – us U.O. Library [071]
WEEKLY LAW BULLETIN / Ohio – (Title varies: v1-2 Cincinnati Weekly Law Bulletin. v3-7, 11-12 Weekly Law Bulletin. v8-10, 13-46 Weekly Law Bulletin and Ohio Law Journal. v47-66 The Ohio Law Bulletin) – v1-66. 1876-1921 (all publ) – 331mf – 9 – $496.00 – LLMC 86-100 – us L.L.M.C. [340]
WEEKLY LEADER – Blair, NE. Nov. 1895-Feb. 1896; May 1896-Jan. 1897 – 1 – us NE Hist [071]
WEEKLY LEADER – Grand Rapids. Mich. 1879-1890 – 1 – us UMI [071]
WEEKLY LEADER-TRIBUNE – Marion. Ind. 1913-1914 – 1 – us UMI [071]
WEEKLY LEDGER – Fairfield. Iowa. 1852-1854 – 1 – us UMI [071]
WEEKLY LEDGER *see* LEDGER DISPATCH
WEEKLY LEDGER-JOURNAL – Fairfield. IA. 1921-28 – 1 – us UMI [071]
THE WEEKLY MAIL – Johannesburg, South Africa. Feb 1989-Jan 18 1990 – 2r – 1 – us L of C Photodup [072]
WEEKLY MAIL – Canada. Toronto Weekly Mail. 21 Feb 1873-July 1884. Lacking Sept 1874-March 1876; July 1881-June 1883. 6 reels – 1 – uk British Libr Newspaper [072]
WEEKLY MAIL – (To be continued) – Johannesburg, South Africa. 14 Jun 1985- – 6r – 1 – sa Microfile [072]
WEEKLY MANITOBA LIBERAL – Manitoba, CN. July 1912-Dec 1945 – 17r – 1 – cn Commonwealth Micro [072]
WEEKLY MANITOBAN – Winnipeg, Canada. 1870-74 – 2r – 1 – $136.00 – cn Library Assoc [971]
WEEKLY MARKET LETTER – Goldfield, NV. 1909 – 1r – 1 – $50.00 – U04564 – us Library Micro [071]
WEEKLY MERCED HERALD – Merced, CA. 1865-69 – 1r – 1 – $50.00 – B02455 – us Library Micro [071]
WEEKLY MERCURY – Constantine. Mich. 1855-1858; 1860-71 – 1 – us UMI [071]
WEEKLY MERCURY – Oroville, CA. 1875-87 – 5r – 1 – $250.00 – C02579 – us Library Micro [071]
WEEKLY MERCURY – (Set incl. Willamette Valley Mercury (Corvallis); Willamette Mercury (Corvallis); Weekly Oregon Mercury (Salem); Weekly Salem Mercury (Salem)) – Salem, OR. 13 Apr 1872-19 Mar 1978. – 2r – 1 – us U.O. Library [071]
WEEKLY MESSENGER – Boston. Mass. 1811-1820 – 3 – us Readex [071]
WEEKLY MINE REVIEW – Lovelock, NV. Aug-Dec 1915 – 1r – 1 – $50.00 – U04626 – us Library Micro [071]
WEEKLY MINER – Butte. Mont. 1891-1893 – 1 – us UMI [071]
WEEKLY MINING EXPOSITOR – Ely, NV. 1907-15 – 8r – 1 – $400.00 – U04506 – us Library Micro [071]
THE WEEKLY MIRROR – Halifax: J Bowes, [1835-1837] – 9 – cn C.I.H.M. [971]
WEEKLY MIRROR – Lyons. Iowa. 1854-1858; 1870-1892 – 1 – us UMI [071]
WEEKLY MISCELLANY – Dublin. Ireland. -w. 10 Jan 1734-4 Jan 1735. (10 ft) – 1 – uk British Libr Newspaper [072]
WEEKLY MISCELLANY – Halifax, N.S.: W Cunnabell, [1863-1864?] – 9 – cn C.I.H.M. [971]
WEEKLY MISSOULIAN – Missoula. Mont. 1893-1894; 1906 – 1 – us UMI [071]
WEEKLY MONEY DESPATCH – 1843-1844 – 1r – 9 – A$29.00 silver A$25.00 vesicular – at Pascoe [072]
WEEKLY MOON – Battle Creek. Mich. 1884-1885 – 1 – us UMI [071]
WEEKLY MOUNTAINEER – The Dalles OR. Feb 6 1861-May 28 1862, May 22 1879-Feb 22 1881 + – 1 – us U.O. Library [071]
WEEKLY MUSICAL TRANSCRIPT – (Musical Transcript). London. -w. 10 Oct 1853-23 Dec 1854. (1 reel) – 1 – uk British Libr Newspaper [073]
WEEKLY NATIONAL INTELLIGENCER – Washington. -w. 30 April 1859-29 Dec 1864. Imperfect. 3 reels – 1 – uk British Libr Newspaper [071]
WEEKLY NEW ERA – Lancaster. Pa. 1877-1919 – 1 – us UMI [071]

WEEKLY NEWS – Beatrice, NE. Jan. 1900-Nov. 1900 – 1 – us NE Hist [071]

WEEKLY NEWS – Caliente, NV. 1920-25 – 1r – 1 – $50.00 – U04433 – us Library Micro [071]

WEEKLY NEWS – Colwyn Bay, Scotland. Colwyn Bay Weekly News North Wales Weekly News. -w. Feb 1889-Dec 1955. 56 1 2 reels – 1 – uk British Libr Newspaper [072]

WEEKLY NEWS – Colwyn Bay, Wales. Colwyn Bay Weekly News North Wales Weekly News. -w. Feb 1889-Dec 1932. Lacking 1897, 1910. 55 reels – 1 – uk British Libr Newspaper [072]

WEEKLY NEWS – Goldfield, NV. 1905-1910; 1929; 1931 – 7r – 1 – $350.00 – U04565 – us Library Micro [071]

WEEKLY NEWS – Hastings. Neb. 1897-1902 – 1 – us UMI [071]

WEEKLY NEWS – Huntingdon, PA. – 13 – $25.00r – us I.M.R. [071]

WEEKLY NEWS – Lincoln, NE. (-sw 1895-97). Oct 1885-Oct 1889; Jan 1890-Dec 1891; Mar-May 1892; Jan 1893-Dec 1896; May-Sep 1897, scattered issues missing – 1 – us NE Hist [071]

WEEKLY NEWS – Mansfield. Ohio. 1901-1911 – 1 – us UMI [071]

WEEKLY NEWS – Nelson, Canada. -w. April 1902-July 1913. Imperfect. 4 reels – 1 – uk British Libr Newspaper [072]

WEEKLY NEWS – Norfolk. Neb. 1889-1900 – 1 – us UMI [071]

WEEKLY NEWS – Portland. Or. 1883-1887 – 1 – us UMI [071]

WEEKLY NEWS – Providence. R.I. 1892-1902 – 1 – us UMI [071]

WEEKLY NEWS AND CHRONICLE – London, UK. 1895. -w. 1 reel – 1 – uk British Libr Newspaper [072]

WEEKLY NEWS BULLETIN – (Missing: 1974(Oct 26)-1975(July 1)) – Jerusalem: Government Press Office. v1-16. 1961-76. Ceased after 1976 – 467mf – 9 – J-81-2/1 – ne IDC [073]

WEEKLY NEWS FOR WEST BROMWICH, OLDBURY, SMETHWICK, ETC – England. -w. 1907-16. Lacking 1912. 9 reels – 1 – uk British Libr Newspaper [072]

WEEKLY NEWS JOURNAL – Norfolk. Neb. 1884-1917 – 1 – us UMI [071]

WEEKLY NEWS SUN – Newport, PA., 1929-1945 – 13 – $25.00r – us I.M.R. [071]

WEEKLY NEWS-DEMOCRAT – Huntington. Ind. 1903-1910 – 1 – us UMI [071]

WEEKLY NONPARIEL – Council Bluffs. Iowa. 1857-65; 1868-74 – 1 – us UMI [071]

WEEKLY NORTHERN WHIG – Belfast, Ireland. 6 Feb 1858-27 Apr 1940.-w. 75 reels – 1 – uk British Libr Newspaper [072]

WEEKLY NORTHWEST – (Weekly Democratic newspaper) – Napoleon, OH. apr 12, 1866-apr 22, 1869 – 1r – 1 – us Western Res [071]

THE WEEKLY NOTES : BEING NOTES OF CASES HEARD AND DETERMINED BY THE HOUSE OF LORDS, THE SUPERIOR COURTS OF EQUITY AND THE COMMON LAW, THE COURTS OF PROBATE AND DIVORCE, AND THE ADMIRALTY COURT / Great Britain. England – (Missing: 1867 pt2. 1875 pt1. 1876 pt2. Updates planned) – London: Incorporated Council on Law Reporting for England and Wales, 1866-1925 – 524mf – 9 – $786.00 – LLMC 95-228 – us L.L.M.C. [324]

WEEKLY NOTES FOR SPEAKERS / Independent Labour Party. Great Britain – 1926-31 – 1 – uk Microform Academic [360]

WEEKLY NUGGET – Placerville, CA. 1901-09 (broken series) – 9r – 1 – $450.00 – B02631 – us Library Micro [071]

WEEKLY OBSERVER – Belfast. Ireland. -w. 25 Jan 1868-25 Nov 1872. (5 reels) – 1 – uk British Libr Newspaper [072]

WEEKLY OBSERVER – LaGrande. Or. 1906-1913 – 1 – us UMI [071]

WEEKLY OBSERVER – Newcastle West, Ireland. 21 Aug 1915-20 Dec 1919.-w. 2men reels – 1 – uk British Libr Newspaper [072]

WEEKLY OIL REVIEW – Sistersville. West Virginia. 1903-24 – 1 – us UMI [071]

WEEKLY ONTARIO – Belleville, 1910-1925 – 15r – 1 – cn Preston [971]

WEEKLY ONTARIO AND BAY OF QUINTE CHRONICLE – Belleville, Ontario, Canada. -w. Nov 1913-Dec 1921. Lacking May-Sept 1919. 12 1 2 reels – 1 – uk British Libr Newspaper [072]

WEEKLY ORACLE – (Reilly's Weekly Oracle). Dublin. Ireland. -w. 3 May 1735-31 Aug 1736. (34 ft) – 1 – uk British Libr Newspaper [072]

WEEKLY OREGON DEMOCRAT – Salem OR. Mar 22 1894 – 1 – us U.O. Library [071]

WEEKLY OREGON MERCURY – Salem OR. Oct 15 1870-Nov 12 1870 – 1 – us U.O. Library [071]

WEEKLY OREGON UNIONIST – Salem OR. Aug 7-Sep 10 1869 – 1 – us U.O. Library [071]

WEEKLY OREGONIAN – Portland OR. Dec 4 1850-Dec 27 1856 + – 1 – us U.O. Library [071]

WEEKLY OROVILLE UNION – Oroville, CA. Aug 1862-1864 – 2r – 1 CB02580 – $100.00 – us Library Micro [071]

WEEKLY OUTLOOK – Beloit. Wis. 1880-1884 – 1 – us UMI [071]

WEEKLY PANOLIAN – Batesville. Miss. 1902-1913; 1950-1960 – 1 – us UMI [071]

WEEKLY PANTAGRAPH – Bloomington. Ill. 1857; 1860; 1861; 1913 – 1 – us UMI [071]

WEEKLY PATRIOT – Iowa Hill, CA. 1859-1860 – 1r – 1 – $50.00 – C03254 – us Library Micro [071]

WEEKLY PATRIOT – Woonsocket. R.I. 1833-1840; 1843-1904 – 1 – us UMI [071]

WEEKLY PENINSULA HERALD – Monterey, CA. Apr 1978-80 – 3r – 1 – $150.00 – B02485 – us Library Micro [071]

WEEKLY PENSACOLIAN – Pensacola. Fl. Dec. 1883-Aug. 1889 – 1 – us P.K. Yonge [071]

WEEKLY PEOPLE – 1890- – 1 – us UMI [073]

WEEKLY PEOPLE – New York, Apr 5 1891-1966 – 1 – us NY Public [071]

WEEKLY PEOPLE – New York. v1-84. 1891-1975 – 37r – 1 – us Ross [071]

WEEKLY PEOPLES CAUSE – Red Bluff, CA. 1881-83; 1886-87; Jun-Dec 1891; 1893-1909; 1914 – 13r – 1 – $650.00 – B02668 – us Library Micro [071]

WEEKLY PEOPLES CAUSE *see* DAILY PEOPLES CAUSE

WEEKLY PICAYUNE – New Orleans. La. Indexed. 1841-1846 – 1 – us UMI [071]

WEEKLY PIONEER – Bemidji. Minn. 1906-1912 – 1 – us UMI [071]

WEEKLY PIONEER – Big Rapids. Mich. 1874-1884 – 1 – us UMI [071]

WEEKLY PLACER HERALD – (See: Placer Herald-Rocklin) – Auburn, CA. 1852-1947 – 53r – 1 BC02034 – $2,650.00 – us Library Micro [071]

WEEKLY POST – Elko, NV. 1876-77 – 1r – 1 – $50.00 – U04501 – us Library Micro [071]

WEEKLY PRESS – Adrian. Mich. 1874-1904 – 1 – us UMI [071]

WEEKLY PRESS – Belfast, Ireland. May-Dec 1858; Jun 1859-1866; 1868-69.-w. 5 reels – 1 – uk British Libr Newspaper [072]

WEEKLY PRESS – Owosso. Mich. 1862-1893 – 1 – us UMI [071]

WEEKLY RANGOON TIMES AND OVERLAND SUMMARY – Burma. 24 Nov 1906-24 Jun 1922. 39 reels – 1 – uk British Libr Newspaper [072]

WEEKLY READER FUNDAY – v.1-. 1980- – 1,5,6,9 – us UMI [800]

WEEKLY READER NEWS HUNT – (See also: My Weekly Reader 2) – v46- 1976- 1; v46-5,6,9 – us UMI [370]

WEEKLY READER WHIZ – (See also: My Weekly Reader 3) – v46-47. 1976-78 – 1,5,6,9 – us UMI [370]

WEEKLY RECORD – Eugene, OR. 26 Jan 1898-18. Jan 1899. – 1r – 1 – us U.O. Library [071]

WEEKLY RECORD – Eustis, NE. Dec. 1892; Oct. 1895-Oct. 1896; Dec. 1896-Jul. 1897; Sep. 1897-Jun. 1901 – 1 – us NE Hist [071]

WEEKLY RECORD – (Inglewood Record and Waitara Age). Inglewood. New Zealand. -w. 12 Jan 1901-1 Oct 1920. (1918 very imperfect). (20 reels) – 1 – uk British Libr Newspaper [072]

WEEKLY RECORD – Pioche, NV. 1876-99; 1906-25 – 39r – 1 – $1,950.00 – U04649 – us Library Micro [071]

WEEKLY RECORD – Salem, OR. 7 Oct 1867-13 Jul 1868. 1 roll – 1 – us U.O. Library [071]

WEEKLY RECORDER – Bridgetown, Barbados. 20 Nov 1897-13 Aug 1910 (imperfect).-w. 10 reels – 1 – uk British Libr Newspaper [072]

WEEKLY RECORDER – Brockville, 1830-1957 – 40r – 1 – cn Preston [971]

WEEKLY RECORDER – Chillicothe. Ohio. 1814-20 – 1,3 – us Readex [071]

WEEKLY REGISTER – Friendship. N.Y. 1872-1893 – 1 – us UMI [071]

WEEKLY REGISTER – Sydney, 1843-45 – 2r – 1 – A$58.00 silver A$50.00 vesicular – at Pascoe [072]

WEEKLY REPORT / U.S. Department of State. Division of Mexican Affairs – Nos 1-30 Sep 24 1919 – Apr 17 1920 – 1 – $23.00 – us L of C Photodup [972]

WEEKLY REPORT ON MATTERS RELATING TO LATIN AMERICA / U.S. Department of State – Nos 1-108 Jan 12 1918 – Jan 29, 1920 – 1 – $26.00 – us L of C Photodup [972]

THE WEEKLY REPORTER / Great Britain. Superior Courts of Equity and Law – (1st vol describes coverage as "Cases decided in the Superior Courts of Equity and Law". By the last vol coverage was described as "Cases decided in the Supreme Court of Judicature with Appeals to the House of Lords and the Privy Council") – London: Wildy & Sons. v1-54. 1852/53-1905/06 (all publ) – 597mf – 9 – $895.00 – LLMC 95-229 – us L.L.M.C. [324]

WEEKLY REPORTER – Coldwater. Mich. 1896-1898 – 1 – us UMI [071]

WEEKLY REPORTER. APPELLATE HIGH COURT – By D. Sutherland. Special issue. Reports of decisions. v. 1-25. Calcutta. 1862-85. BI-665 2 – 343mf – 8 – ne IDC [073]

WEEKLY REPORTS *see* ITOGI 7-MI DNE I

WEEKLY REPORTS ON MARKET PRICES IN TRIPOLI – 1957. BNE-616 1 – 9 – ne IDC [338]

WEEKLY REPUBLICAN – Emporia. Kan. 1882-1905 – 1 – us UMI [071]

WEEKLY REPUBLICAN – Junction City OR. Nov 26 1879 – 1 – us U.O. Library [071]

WEEKLY REPUBLICAN – Lansing. Mich. 1855-1885 – 1 – us UMI [071]

WEEKLY REPUBLICAN – Warsaw. Ind. 1880-1882 – 1 – us UMI [071]

WEEKLY REVIEW – 1-8 2+27 (all publ). 1936-1943 – 2r – 1 – $230.00 – us UPA [335]

WEEKLY REVIEW – Augusta, GA. 1965-67 – 1r – 1 – us Ross [071]

WEEKLY REVIEW – Flint. Mich. 1923-1933 – 1 – us UMI [071]

WEEKLY REVIEW – Montreal, Canada. v1 n8. 27 jul 1866 – 1r – 1 – Can$25.00 – cn Can Microfilming [072]

WEEKLY REVIEW – Pacific Grove, CA. 1906-12 – 2r – 1 – $100.00 – B02588 – us Library Micro [071]

WEEKLY REVIEW – v. 1-45. 21 Mar 1925-5 Jun 1947 – 1 – 176.00 – us L of C Photodup [073]

WEEKLY REVIEW *see* PORTERVILLE PAPERS

WEEKLY REVIEW OF THE FAR EAST – (China Weekly Review). Shanghai. China. -w. 4 Jun 1921-28 Aug 1926, 2 Jan-25 Dec 1937. (13 reels) – 1 – uk British Libr Newspaper [072]

WEEKLY SCIOTO GAZETTE – (Weekly edition of this Republican newspaper) – Chillicothe, OH. mar 23, 1858-apr 26, 1859 – 2r – 1 – us Western Res [071]

WEEKLY SCOTT VALLEY NEWS – Fort Jones, CA. 1881-86 – 1r – 1 – $50.00 – B02244 – us Library Micro [071]

WEEKLY SENTINEL – Blue Springs, NE. Mar. 1892-May 1892; Sep. 1895-Sep. 1918 – 1 – us NE Hist [071]

WEEKLY SENTINEL – Parkersburg. West Virginia. 1875-1895 – 1 – us UMI [071]

WEEKLY SENTINEL – Red Bluff, CA. Mar-Jul 1883; 1887-88; 1891-92; 1904-05; 1912-15; 1921-27 – 9r – 1 – $450.00 – B02669 – us Library Micro [071]

WEEKLY SENTINEL – Santa Cruz, CA. 1905-08 – 5r – 1 – $250.00 – R04112 – us Library Micro [071]

WEEKLY SENTINEL – Thunder Bay, 1875-1894 – 4r – 1 – cn Preston [971]

WEEKLY SIGNAL – Holton. Kan. 1886-1905 – 1 – us UMI [071]

WEEKLY SOLANO HERALD – Fairfield, CA. 1863-69 – 2r – 1 – $100.00 – C02230 – us Library Micro [071]

WEEKLY SOLANO HERALD – Suisun, CA. 1866-1869 – 1r – 1 – $50.00 – B03019 – us Library Micro [071]

WEEKLY SOLANO REPUBLICAN – Fairfield, CA. 1866-71; 1878-81; 1891-1905; 1916-61 – 63r – 1 BC02231 – $3,150.00 – us Library Micro [071]

WEEKLY SPECTATOR – Accra, Ghana. Aug 17 1974-Oct 17 1981; 1982-1991 – 7r – 1 – us L of C Photodup [072]

WEEKLY STANDARD – Buenos Aires. Argentina. -w. 5 Jan 1870-17 Jun 1874. (5 reels) – 1 – uk British Libr Newspaper [072]

WEEKLY STANDARD – Friend, NE. Feb. 1890-Dec. 1892. Incomplete; Apr. 1893-Apr. 1895; Jul. 1895-Mar. 1900 – 1 – us NE Hist [071]

WEEKLY STANDARD – Portland OR. Nov 7 1879, Oct 15 1880 – 1 – us U.O. Library [071]

WEEKLY STANDARD – San Angelo. Tex. 1938- – 1 – us UMI [071]

WEEKLY STATE DEMOCRAT – Lincoln, NE. Oct 1879-Feb 1882; Sep 1887 – 1 – us NE Hist [071]

WEEKLY STATE JOURNAL – Lincoln, NE. (-sw 1891-1903). Sep 1867-Dec 1870; Jun 1871; Jan 1874-Dec 1906; Oct 1919-Jan 1924 – 1 – us NE Hist [071]

WEEKLY STATE JOURNAL – Lincoln. Neb. 1867-1924 – 1 – us UMI [071]

WEEKLY STOCKTON DEMOCRAT – Stockton, CA. 1857-1862 – 2r – 1 – $100.00 – C03657 – us Library Micro [071]

WEEKLY SUGAR REPORT / Czarnikow-Rionda Company, New York – 1911-Apr. 1939 – 1 – us NY Public [330]

THE WEEKLY SUN – San Bernardino, CA. 1895-1905 – 4r – 1 – $200.00 – R02772 – us Library Micro [071]

WEEKLY SUN – Canada. St. John Weekly Sun The News. -w. Jan 1886-March 1910. 29 1 2 reels – 1 – uk British Libr Newspaper [072]

WEEKLY SUN – Portland, OR. 15 Feb 1895-19 Apr 1895. 1 roll – 1 – us U.O. Library [071]

WEEKLY SUN – Seymour. Ind. 1871-1872 – 1 – us UMI [071]

WEEKLY SYDNEY DESPATCH – Sydney, 1843-44 – 1r – 1 – at Pascoe [072]

WEEKLY TALK – Salem OR. Sep 23 1881 – 1 – us U.O. Library [071]

WEEKLY TELEGRAM – Blair, NE. Dec. 1894-Mar. 1895; Jul. 1895-Oct. 1895 – 1 – us NE Hist [071]

WEEKLY TELEGRAM – Richmond. Ind. 1862-1889 – 1 – us UMI [071]

WEEKLY TELEGRAM – Winfield. KS. 1887-91 – 1 – us UMI [071]

THE WEEKLY TELEGRAPH – Port Elizabeth, South Africa. 1 May 1909-27 Dec 1919. 11 reels – 1, 16 diazo available at reduced price – sa SA Libr [072]

WEEKLY TELEGRAPH – Airdrie, Scotland, UK. 4 Oct 1879-30 Apr 1880. -w. – 1/4r – 1 – uk British Libr Newspaper [072]

WEEKLY TELEGRAPH – London, UK. 1860. -w. 2 feet – 1 – uk British Libr Newspaper [072]

WEEKLY TELEGRAPH – North Platte, NE. -w. Nov 1903; Jan 1904-Jan 1909; Jun 1909-Jun 1918, scattered issues missing; Aug 1918-Dec 1924 – 1 – us NE Hist [071]

WEEKLY TELEGRAPH – North Platte. Neb. 1904-1924 – 1 – us UMI [071]

WEEKLY TELEGRAPH *see*
– FOOTHILL WEEKLY TIDINGS
– SHEFFIELD WEEKLY TELEGRAPH

WEEKLY TELEPHONE *see* DAILY EVENING TELEPHONE

WEEKLY TEXAS STATE GAZETTE – Austin, TX. 1849-51 – 1r – 1 – us Ross [071]

THE WEEKLY TIDINGS – Elko, NV. 1898 – 1r – 1 – $50.00 – U04502 – us Library Micro [071]

WEEKLY TIDINGS *see* FOOTHILL WEEKLY TIDINGS

THE WEEKLY TIMES / ed by Yamaska Printing Co. – St-Hyacinthe, Canada. v22. 10 jul 1908-5 nov 1909; ns: v4. 13 sep 1940-v4 n55. 15 nov 1940 – 1r – 1 – Can$25.00 – cn Can Microfilming [072]

WEEKLY TIMES – Beatrice. Neb. 1893-1908 – 1 – us UMI [071]

WEEKLY TIMES – London, UK. 1835-36 – 1r – 1 – uk British Libr Newspaper [072]

WEEKLY TIMES – Los Gatos, CA. 1982 – 25+ r – 1 – $1,250.00 ($120.00y) – B02410 – us Library Micro [071]

WEEKLY TIMES – Metropolis. Ill. 1867-1872 – 1 – us UMI [071]

WEEKLY TIMES – Olean. N.Y. 1884-1900 – 1 – us UMI [071]
WEEKLY TIMES – Portland. Or. 1855-1859 – 1 – us UMI [071]
WEEKLY TIMES – Seymour. Ind. 1874-1877 – 1 – us UMI [071]
WEEKLY TIMES ADVOCATE – Escondido, CA. 1909-1960 – 30r – 1 – $1,500.00 – R03213 – us Library Micro [071]
WEEKLY TIMES (MELBOURNE) – 1869-1895. WT1-65 – 65r – 1 – at Corangamite [072]
WEEKLY TIMES (MELBOURNE) – 1910-1935. WT66-168 – 103r – 1 – at Corangamite [072]
THE WEEKLY TRANSCRIPT – v1 nos1-11. 1861 (all publ) – 2mf – $3.00 – LLMC 90-336 – us L.L.M.C. [073]
WEEKLY TRANSCRIPT – Peoria. Ill. 1867-1873; 1876-1877; 1879-1880; 1882-1890; 1892 – 1 – us UMI [071]
WEEKLY TRIBUNE – Callaway, NE. Dec.1892; Feb.1896-Apr. 1898. Incomplete; Mar. 1899-Feb. 1905 – 1 – us NE Hist [071]
WEEKLY TRIBUNE – Hornellsville. N.Y. 1880-1899 – 1 – us UMI [071]
WEEKLY TRIBUNE – Oak, NE. -w. Jul 1911-Sept 1913 – 1 – us NE Hist [071]
WEEKLY TRIBUNE – South Haven. Mich. 1899-1902 – 1 – us UMI [071]
WEEKLY TRIBUNE – Yreka, CA. 1880-82 – 1r – 1 – $50.00 – B03123 – us Library Micro [071]
WEEKLY TRIBUNE AND EDUCATIONAL JOURNAL – St John, N.B.: G.W. Day, [1860-18–?] – 9 – cn C.I.H.M. [073]
WEEKLY TRUE SUN – London, UK. 1833-39. -w. 6 reels – 1 – uk British Libr Newspaper [072]
WEEKLY UNION – Rock Island. Ill. 1896-1904; 1908-1910 – 1 – us UMI [071]
WEEKLY UNION – Yreka, CA. 1865-97 – 7r – 1 – $350.00 – B03124 – us Library Micro [071]
WEEKLY VINDICATOR – Belfast, Ireland. 1848-52. -w.1 1/2 reels – 1 – uk British Libr Newspaper [072]
THE WEEKLY VISITOR – Toronto: P.H. Stewart, [1857?-18–?] – 9 – cn C.I.H.M. [971]
WEEKLY VISITOR – Independence, OR. -w. 25 Apr 1913-26 Dec 1915. 1 roll – 1 – us U.O. Library [071]
WEEKLY VISITOR – Lafayette, OR. 25 Apr 1913-26 Dec 1915. 1 roll – 1 – us U.O. Library [071]
WEEKLY VISITOR – New York, NY. 1817-20. Also: New York Chronicle, 1769-70; Constitutional Gazette, 1775-76. Sold as one unit – 3 – us Readex [071]
WEEKLY WAVE – Odell, NE. Oct 1895-Jul 1919 – 1 – us NE Hist [071]
WEEKLY WHIG – Vicksburg. Miss. 1859-1861 – 1 – us UMI [071]
WEEKLY WITNESS AND CANADIAN HOMESTEAD *see* THE MONTREAL WITNESS
WEEKLY WONDER – Parsons. Kan. 1879-80 – 1 – us UMI [071]
THE WEEKLY WORLD – San Diego, CA. 1872-1875 – 1r – 1 – $50.00 – C03662 – us Library Micro [071]
WEEKLY WORLD – Pascoag. R.I. 1932-1933 – 1 – us UMI [071]
WEEKLY WORLD – Portland. Or. 1886-1891 – 1 – us UMI [071]
WEEKLY WORLD-HERALD – Omaha, NE. Jul 1889-Dec 1891; Mar 1892-Oct 1894, scattered issues missing; Mar 1895-Feb 1896; Apr 1896-Apr 1898; Nov 1898; Feb 1899 – 1 – us NE Hist [071]
WEEKLY WYMOREAN – Wymore, NE. Oct 1884; Nov 1888-Nov 1894; Jan 1895-Jan 1901; Apr 1901-Oct 1903; Dec 1903-Mar 1942 – 1 – us NE Hist [071]
Weeks, Edward P *see* A COMMENTARY ON THE MINING LEGISLATION OF CONGRESS WITH A PRELIMINARY REVIEW OF THE REPEALED SECTIONS OF THE MINING ACT OF 1866...2ND ED
Weeks, John H *see* AMONG THE PRIMITIVE-BAKONGO
Weeks, Nancy *see*
- ATTORNEY FEE PETITIONS
- DISTRICT COURT IMPLEMENTATION OF AMENDED CIVIL RULE 16

WEEK'S NEWS – London, UK. 1871-12 Jul 1879. -w. 17 reels – 1 – uk British Libr Newspaper [072]
WEEKS NEWS *see* BRIEF
Weeks, Robert Dodd *see* JEHOVAH-JESUS
Weeks, Rufus W *see* THEY MUST, OR, GOD AND THE SOCIAL DEMOCRACY
Weeks, Stephen Beauregard *see*
- CHURCH AND STATE IN NORTH CAROLINA
- SOUTHERN QUAKERS AND SLAVERY

Weeland, Horst *see* BRIEFE DEUTSCHER PHILOSOPHEN (1750-1850)
WEEPING WATER REPUBLICAN – Weeping Water, NE. -w. Apr 1882-Apr 1883; Apr 1886-Jul 1887; Sep 1887-Mar 1890; May 1892-Jul 1894; Nov 1894; Sep 1895-Oct 1941; Jun 1949 to date – 1 – us NE Hist [071]
Weeramantry, C G *see* HUMAN HIGHTS AND SCIENTIFIC AND TECHNOLOGICAL DEVELOPMENT
Weerth, Georg *see*
- AUSGEWAEHLTE WERKE
- LEBEN UND THATEN DES BERUEHMTEN RITTERS SCHNAPPHAHNSKI

DER WEG – Berlin, 1946-50 (incomplete) – 1 – Inquire at Mikrofilmarchiv for details – gw Misc Inst [072]
DER WEG = THE WAY – (In Yiddish) – Montreal, Canada. 15 oct 1915-v2 n211. 21 jun 1916 – 2r – 1 – Can$52.00r – cn Can Microfilming [072]
DER WEG = THE WAY – (In Yiddish) – Warsaw, PL. v2 no9 23 Jan 1906 – 1r – 1 – $25.00 – cn Can Microfilming [072]
DER WEG = THE WAY : JUDISCHE MONATSSCHRIFT – (In German) – Vienna, AU. v1 no1-2. 20 Aug 1903 – 1r – 1 – $25.00 – cn Can Microfilming [072]
DER WEG = THE WAY – Montreal, CN. no 211. 1915-1916 – 2r – 1 – Can$60.00 – cn Can Microfilming [072]
DER WEG DER FRAU – Berlin, 1931-33 – 1r – 1 – Inquire at Mikrofilmarchiv for details – gw Misc Inst [072]
DER WEG DER FRAU – Berlin, DE. 1931-33 – 1r – 1 – gw Mikrofilm [305]
DER WEG HINAUF : ROMAN / Zahn, Ernst – Guetersloh: C Bertelsmann, c1935 – 1r – 1 – us U.W. Library [830]
DER WEG INS LEBEN – Yxtaholm u. Orrhammar, Flen, Sweden. Kameradschaftsbriefe junger Deutscher in Schweden.Aug 1944-May 1945 – 1 – gw Mikrofilm [073]
DER WEG INS LICHT : ROMAN / Wenz-Hartmann, Gisela – Leipzig: E Huyke, [1944?] – 1r – 1 – us U.W. Library [830]
DER WEG NACH ROM : EIN WINCKELMANN-ROMAN / Back, Claus – (Includes bibliographical references) – 1. Aufl. Berlin: Buchverlag Der Morgen, 1964 – 1r – 1 – us U.W. Library [830]
DER WEG UEBER DEN VULKAN / Grupe-Loercher, Erica – Dresden: F Mueller, 1944 – 1r – 1 – us U.W. Library [830]
WEG UND WAHRHEIT – (Lacks some pgs and issues) – v5-46. 1950-92 – Inquire – 1 – ATLA S0397 – us A.T.L.A. [073]
WEG UND ZIEL – Blaetter fuer Theorie und Praxis der Arbeiterbewegung. Prag u. Wien. Aug 1936-Sept 1938 – 1 – gw Mikrofilm [073]
DER WEG ZU GOTT UNSERM VATER : EINE EINFUEHRUNG INS VATERUNSER ALS EINLEITUNG IN DIE CHRISTLICHE LEHRE / Jaeger, Samuel – Halle a. S: Verlag der Buchh. des Waisenhauses, 1902 – 1mf – 9 – 0-8370-4610-6 – 1985-2610 – us A.T.L.A. [240]
DER WEG ZUM FRIEDEN: EIN NACHTRAG ZU DEM BUCHE, IM KAMPF UM DIE WELTANSCHAUUNG / Wimmer, Richard – Freiburg i.B.: J.C.B. Mohr, 1893. 1 fiche – 9 – us A.T.L.A. [240]
DER WEG ZUM GLUECK / Bayer, Robert von – Stuttgart: Deutsche Verlags-Anstalt. 3v. 1889 – 1 – us U.W. Library [830]
DER WEG ZUM GRAL : RICHARD WAGNERS KAEMPFERLEBEN: ROMAN / Andreevsky, Alexander von – Berlin: Bong, [c1941] – 1r – 1 – us U.W. Library [830]
DER WEG ZUM MYTHOS : ZUR WIEDERGEBURT DER KUNST AUS DEM GEISTE DER RELIGION / Michel, Ernst – Jena: E Diederichs, 1919 – 1r – 1 – us U.W. Library [700]
WEGE UND ZIELE DER CULTURENTWICKLUNG : ESSAYS / Lasker, Eduard – Leipzig: Brockhaus, 1881 – 1r – 1 – us U.W. Library [840]
Wegener, Georg *see* ZUR KRIEGEZEIT DURCH CHINA, 1900-1901
Wegener, Leo *see* DER WIRTSCHAFTLICHE KAMPF DER DEUTSCHEN UM DIE PROVINZ POSEN
WEGERECHT : EINZIEHUNG EINES FUSSWEGES / Albrecht, Erwin – 1992 – 60p – 9 – DM48.00 – 3-89349-600-9 – gw Hänsel [340]
Wegg, Jervis *see* ANTWERP, 1477-1559, FROM THE BATTLE OF NANCY TO THE TREATY OF CATEAU CAMBRESIS
Weghorn, Hans *see* HOCHAUFLOESENDE INTERFEROMETRISCHE MESSUNGEN IN DER ASTONOMIE MIT CCD-DETEKTOREN
Wegner, Max *see* BORIUS WICHART
Wegner, Michael S *see* THE ACCURACY OF VARIOUS INDIRECT DETERMINATIONS OF BODY COMPOSITION
WEGRAYSZ KEYSERLICHER MAIESTAT LEGATION MIT 32. JAR ZU DEM TURCKEN GESCHICKT WIE VND WAS GESTALT SIE HINEIN VND WIDERUMB HERAUSZ KOMEN I.. / Curipeschitz, B – N.p., 1532 – 1mf – 9 – H-8142/1 – ne IDC [956]
Wegrich, Arno *see* ZIGEUNER CHRISTL
WEGWEISER FUER DIE JUGENDLITERATUR – Berlin, 1905-14 – 1r – 1 – Inquire at Mikrofilmarchiv for details – gw Misc Inst [410]
WEGWEISER FUER DIE JUGENDLITERATUR – Berlin. v1-10. 1905-14. Complete. B391 (Leo Baeck Institute. German-Jewish Periodicals, Pt 2) – 1r – 1 – $60.00 – us UPA [270]
WEGWEISER IN DIE MARIANISCHE LITERATUR : ZUNAECHST FUER MAIVORTRAEGE UND VEREINSANSPRACHEN / Kolb, Georg – (Includes bibliographical references and index) – Freiburg i.B.; St Louis, MO: Herder, 1888 – 1mf – 9 – 0-8370-8439-3 – 1986-2439 – us A.T.L.A. [240]
WEGWEISER ZUR QUELLEN- UND LITTERATURKUNDE DER KIRCHENGESCHICHTE : EINE ANLEITUNG ZUR PLANMAESSIGEN AUFFINDUNG DER LITTERARISCHEN UND MONUMENTALEN QUELLEN DER KIRCHENGESCHICHTE UND IHRER BEARBEITUNGEN / Bratke, Eduard – Gotha: F.A. Perthes, 1890 – 1mf – us A.T.L.A. [240]
Wehage, Joseph *see* DIE RECHTLICHE STELLUNG DER KATHOLISCHEN KIRCHE IM LANDESTEIL OLDENBURG UNTER BESONDERER BERUECKSICHTIGUNG DER GESCHICHTLICHEN ENTWICKLUNG
Wehl, Feodor von *see* THEODOR STORM
Wehner, Josef Magnus *see*
- ERSTE LIEBE
- HEBBEL
- MEIN LEBEN
- SIEBEN VOR VERDUN
- STADT UND FESTUNG BELGERAD

Wehnert, Bruno *see* GOETHES REIM
WEHR- UND AUSSENPOLITIK IM GESPALTENEN DEUTSCHLAND. REFERAT AUF DEM SPD-PARTEITAG 1958 IN STUTTGART / Erler, Fritz – Bonn, 1958 – 1 – DM30.00 – gw Mikro Press [943]
Wehrli, Max *see* DAS BAROCKE GESCHICHTSBILD IN LOHENSTEINS ARMINIUS
Wei, Bing *see* A COMPARISON OF PERCEPTIONS OF THE IMPORTANCE BETWEEN PHYSICAL EDUCATION GRADUATE TEACHING ASSISTANTS AND GRADUATE PROGRAM COORDINATORS ON SELECTION OF GRADUATE TEACHING ASSISTANTS AND THEIR TEACHING PERFORMANCE CRITERIA
Wei, Chuo-ming *see*
- BASIC ELEMENTS OF THE CHRISTIAN FAITH (CCC321)
- TEN TALKS ON THE APOSTLES' CREED (CCC322)

WEI LI PAO *see* GUARDIAN OF TRUTH
WEI LIAO HSIEN CH'IH CHIU KUO KEI AI KUO P'ENG YU TI (CCC127) : 14 FENG HSIN / Feng, Yu-hsiang – (In Chinese) – [s.l: s.n, 1945] – 1r – 1 – 1984-B500 – us A.T.L.A. [240]
WEI SHENG KUNG PAO / China. Ministry of Public Health – Health gazette. Nanking, 1929-Aug 1930. v.1-v.2, n.8. 4 reels – 1 – 75.00 – us Chinese Res [324]
WEI SHENG KUNG PAO / China. Ministry of Public Health – (Official Gazette). 2 v. Nanking. 1929-30. Lacking: v. 2 (12) 1930. BCH-1093 1 – 9 – ne IDC [324]
DIE WEIBER VON WEISBER / Andre, J – Offenbach: J Andre, 1802 – 1 – us Sibley [780]
Weichberger, Alexander *see* DAS GOETHEHAUS AM FRAUENPLAN
Weichenmayr, Franz *see* DRAMATISCHE HANDLUNG UND AUFBAU IN HEBBELS HERODES UND MARIAMNE
WEICHSEL-POST – Graudenz (Grudziadz), Poland. Sept 1922-Mar 1926 – 1 – gw Mikrofilm [943]
Weidauer, Jens *see* SELBSTTAETIGE IDENTIFIKATION UND ADAPTION VON PARAMETERN EINER FELDORIENTIERT GEREGELTEN ASYNCHRONMASCHINE
Weidenmann, Alfred *see* JAKKO
WEIDIANZIXUE YU JISUANJI – Microelectronics & Computer. 1984-85. F/P 297 – 9 – $4.50f – cc Microforms [073]
Weidig, Friedrich Ludwig *see* RELIQUIEN FRIEDRICH LUDWIG WEIDIG'S
Weidkuhn, Wilmar *see*
- KATHARSIS ZWISCHEN DIESSEITS UND JENSEITS
- PSYCHOANALYTISCHE SOZIALTHERAPIE PSYCHOGENER ERKRANKUNGEN
- REZIPROKE FORSCHUNG, IM PSYCHOSOZIALEN PRAXISFELD, EINER KREBSSTATION – UNTER DER BERUECKSICHTIGUNG DES, HERRSCHENDEN, BIOMEDIZINISCHEN PARADIGMAS

Weidlein, Johann *see* SCHICKSALSJAHRE DER UNGARNDEUTSCHEN
Weidner, E F *see* STUDIEN ZUR HETHITISCHEN SPRACHWISSENSCHAFT
Weidner, Revere Franklin *see* AN INTRODUCTION TO DOGMATIC THEOLOGY: BASED ON LUTHARDT
Weiffenbach, Wilhelm *see*
- DER WIEDERKUNFTSGEDANKE JESU
- ZUR AUSLEGUNG DER STELLE PHILIPPER 2, 5-11...PAULINISCHEN CHRISTOLOGIE

Weigand, Georg *see* J.G. SCHUMMEL
Weigand, Wilhelm *see* DER VERSCHLOSSENE GARTEN
Weigel, Chr *see* ETHICA NATURALIS
Weigel, Erhard *see* ERHARDI WEIGELII SACRAE CAESAR
WEIGHT AND BODY COMPOSITION CHANGES AS A FUNCTION OF DIET DURING A MOUNTAINEERING EXPEDITION / Tanner, David A – Indiana University, 1995 – 3mf – 9 – $12.00 – PE3622 – us Microform Publ [612]
Weight, Brita N *see* THE RELATIONSHIP BETWEEN SPIRITUALITY AND LEISURE FUNCTIONING IN ADULTS, AS MEASURED BY SPIRITUAL WELL-BEING AND PERCEIVED FREEDOM IN LEISURE
WEIGHT TRAINING ECONOMY AS A FUNCTION OF INTENSITY OF THE SQUAT AND OVERHEAD PRESS EXERCISE / Kalb, J S – 1987 – 1mf – 9 – $4.00 – us Microform Publ [613]
WEIGHT WATCHERS MAGAZINE – (1983-. 1,5,6,9) – v1-. 1968- – 1 – us UMI [073]
WEIGHT WATCHERS MAGAZINE – New York. v1-3. 1968-71 – 72mf – 9 – $5.00f – us Ross [613]
Weihe, Stephan *see* WASSERSTOFFPEROXID ALS MITTEL ZUR KONTINUIERLICHEN DEKONTAMINATION DENTALER BEHANDLUNGSEINHEITEN
WEIHE UND KROENUNG DES PAPSTES IM MITTELALTER / Eichmann, E – Muenchen, 1951 – 2mf – 8 – Dfl9.00 – ne Slangenburg [240]
WEIHNACHLS LIE – [s.l.] 1907 – 1,5,6 – bl Biblioteca [072]
DAS WEIHNACHTSFEST : SEINE ENTSTEHUNG UND ENTWICKLUNG / Meyer, Arnold – Tuebingen: J.C.B. Mohr, 1913 – 1mf – us A.T.L.A. [390]
DAS WEIHNACHTSFEST / Usener, Hermann – Bonn: F. Cohen, 1911 – 1mf – us A.T.L.A. [306]
WEIHNACHTSGESCHICHTEN / Kolbenheyer, Erwin Guido – Muenchen: A Langen/G Mueller, 1933 – 1r – 1 – us U.W. Library [390]
WEIHNACHTSKRIPPENSPIEL : AUS SCHLESISCHEN SPIELEN ZUSAMMENGESTELLT – Halle: M Niemeyer, 1921 – 1r – 1 – us U.W. Library [820]
Weijers, Henrico E *see* DIVERSORUM...LOCOS DE REGIA..
Weil, C *see* LA FONCTION GONADOTROPE DE L'HYPOPHYSE AU COURS DU CYCLE SEXUEL DE DEUX POISSONS TELEOSTEENS, LA CARPE (CYPRINUS CARPIO) ET LA TRUITE (SALMO GAIRDNERI) SON CONTROLE PAR L'HYPOTHALAMUS, LES GONADES ET LES FACTEURES EXTERNES
Weil, D S W Marie *see* JOURNAL OF COMMUNITY PRACTICE
Weil, Felix Jose *see* ARGENTINE RIDDLE
Weil, I *see* PHILOSOPHIE RELIGIEUSE DE LEVI-BEN-GERSON

Weil, Julien *see* NOTE SUR UNE ANCIENNE TRADUCTION FRANCAISE MANUSCRITE DE L'ITINERAIRE DE BENJAMIN DE TUDELE

Weil, M H *see* LES DESSOUS DU CONGRES DE VIENNE

Weil, Samuel Charles *see* WATER RIGHTS IN THE WESTERN STATES.

Weil, Thomas *see*
- GESUNDHEITSFOERDERUNG ALS ARBEITSFELD SOZIALER THERAPIE
- EINE INSTITUTION ZIEHT UM

Weil, Thomas E et al *see* AREA HANDBOOK FOR ARGENTINA

WEILBURGER TAGEBLATT – Weilburg, jul 1 1933-mar 8 1945 – 20r – 1 – gw Mikrofilm [943]

WEILBURGER TAGEBLATT – Wetzlar, Germany. 1 Jun 1983- – 1 – gw Mikrofilm [072]

Weilenmann, Alexander *see* EVALUATION RESEARCH AND SOCIAL CHANGE

Weiler, A G *see* NECROLOGIE, KRONIEK EN CARTULARIUM C.A. VAN HET FRATERHUIS TE DOESBURG (1432-1559)

Weill, Raymond *see* LE SEJOUR DES ISRAELITES AU DESERT ET LE SINAI DANS LA RELATION PRIMITIVE

WEIMARS FESTGRUESSE ZUM 28. AUGUST 1899 : GOETHES VATERSTADT UND DEM FREIEN DEUTSCHEN HOCHSTIFT DARGEBRACHT VON DER GROSSHERZOGLICHEN BIBLIOTHEK, DEM GOETHE-NATIONAL-MUSEUM, DEM GOETHE-SCHILLER-ARCHIV – Weimar: H Boehlau, 1899 – 1r – 1 – us U.W. Library [430]

Weinand, Heinz Gerd *see* TRAENEN

Weinand, Maria *see* DAS BERUFSIDEAL DER VOLKSSCHULLEHRERIN UNTER BESONDERER BERUECKSICHTIGUNG DES BERUFSMOTIVES UND DES BERUFSVORBILDES

Weinberger, Andreas *see*
- DAS HANDGRANATENKOEPFL

Weinel, Heinrich *see*
- DIE BERGPREDIGT
- JESUS IM NEUNZEHNTEN JAHRHUNDERT
- DIE NICHTKIRCHLICHEN UND DIE FREIE THEOLOGIE
- PAULUS
- PAULUS: DER MENSCH UND SEIN WERK: DIE ANFAENGE DES CHRISTENTUMS
- ST. PAUL: THE MAN AND HIS WORK
- DIE STELLUNG DES URCHRISTENTUMS ZUM STAAT
- DIE URCHRISTLICHE UND DIE HEUTIGE MISSION
- DIE WIRKUNGEN DES GEISTES UND DIE GEISTER IM NACHAPOSTOLISCHEN ZEITALTER BIS AUF IRENAEUS

Weingarten, Hermann *see*
- DIE REVOLUTIONSKIRCHEN ENGLANDS
- DER URSPRUNG DES MOENCHTUMS IM NACHCONSTANTINISCHEN ZEITALTER

Weinhandl, Margrete *see* UND DEINE WAELDER RAUSCHEN FORT

Weinheber, Josef *see*
- ADEL UND UNTERGANG
- SPAETE KRONE
- VEREINSAMTES HERZ

DIE WEINHEILIGEN : EINE FROEHLICHE LEGENDE / Winckler, Josef – (Publ in 1942 under title: Die froehliche Weinreise) – Koeln: Staufen-Verlag, 1934 – 1r – 1 – us U.W. Library [390]

WEINHEIMER NACHRICHTEN – Weinheim, Germany. 1 Jun 1983- – 1 – gw Mikrofilm [072]

Weinhold, Karl *see* MARTIN OPITZ VON BOBERFELD

Weinmann, J A *see* ENUMERATIO STIRPIUM IN AGRO PETROPOLITANO

Weinrich, A K H *see* WOMEN AND RACIAL DISCRIMINATION IN RHODESIA

Weinrich, Rainer *see* VOM WORT UND GEDANKEN DER ARBEIT BEI GOETHE

Weinstein, Art T *see* JOURNAL OF SEGMENTATION IN MARKETING

Weinstein, S *see* INTERNATIONAL JOURNAL OF NEUROSCIENCE

Weinstein, Stephen *see* THE NIXON ADMINISTRATION

Weinstock, Harris *see* JESUS THE JEW: AND OTHER ADDRESSES

Weintraub, Stanley *see* BERNARD SHAW: THE DIARIES, 1885-1897

WEIR OF HERMISTON : AN UNFINISHED ROMANCE / Stevenson, Robert Louis – London: Chatto and Windus, 1896 – 1 roll – 1 – 1-55879-603-7 – uk Libr Preservation [830]

Weir, Thomas Hunter *see* A SHORT HISTORY OF THE HEBREW TEXT OF THE OLD TESTAMENT

Weis, Frederick Lewis *see* ANCESTRAL ROOTS OF SIXTY COLONISTS WHO CAME TO NEW ENGLAND BETWEEN 1623 AND 1650

Weis, Ludwig *see* DER ALTE UND DER NEUE GLAUBE

Weisbach, Werner *see* "UND ALLES IST ZERSTOBEN"

Weisbrem, I *see*
- BEIN HA-ZEMANIM
- HA-GORAL VE-HA-YERUSHAH
- HAY AGOROT

Weise, Christian *see* CHRISTIAN WEISE'S BAUERN-KOMOEDIE VON TOBIAS UND DER SCHWALBE

Weisenboehler, Oskar *see* GESCHICHTE DES RELIGIONSUNTERRICHTS IN DER EVANGELISCHEN VOLKSSCHULE WUERTTEMBERGS

Weishaar, Friedrich *see* C.F. MEYERS "ANGELA BORGIA"

Weishampel, John F, Jr *see* THE PRAYER MEETING HYMN BOOK

DIE WEISHEIT DES JESUS SIRACH / Smend, Rudolf – Berlin, 1906 – 12mf – 8 – ne Slangenburg [220]

WEISHENGWU XUEBAO – Acta Microbiologica Sinica. In Chinese but English abstracts to the main articles. F p46 – 9 – $3.50f – cc Microforms [073]

WEISHENGWUXUE TONGBAO – Microbiology. In prep. F/P 307 – 9 – 4.00f – cc Microforms [073]

Weiskopf, Franz Carl *see* ELEND UND GROESSE UNSERER TAGE

Weismantel, Leo *see*
- DIE GESCHICHTE DES RICHTERS VON ORB
- DIE HOELLISCHE TRINITAET
- MEIN LEBEN

Weiss, Albert Maria *see* HUMANITAET UND HUMANISMUS. ERSTER THEIL

Weiss, Bernhard *see*
- DIE APOSTELGESCHICHTE (T.U.U. 1-9/3.4.)
- DER CODEX D IN DER APOSTELGESCHICHTE (T.U.U. 2-17/1)
- A COMMENTARY ON THE NEW TESTAMENT. VOLUME 2, LUKE-THE ACTS
- A COMMENTARY ON THE NEW TESTAMENT. VOLUME 3, ROMANS-COLOSSIANS
- A COMMENTARY ON THE NEW TESTAMENT. VOLUME 4, THESSALONIANS-REVELATION
- DIE DREI BRIEFE DES APOSTEL JOHANNES
- DER HEBRAEERBRIEF IN ZEITGESCHICHTLICHER BELEUCHTUNG (T.U.U. 3-35/3)
- DER JAKOBUSBRIEF UND DIE NEUERE KRITIK
- DIE JOHANNES-APOKALYPSE (T.U.U. 1.7/1)
- DIE KATHOLISCHEN BRIEFE (T.U.U. 1-8/3)
- KRITISCH EXEGETISCHES HANDBUCH UEBER DIE BRIEFE PAULI AN TIMOTHEUS UND TITUS
- LEHRBUCH DER BIBLISCHEN THEOLOGIE DES NEUEN TESTAMENTS
- LEHRBUCH DER EINLEITUNG IN DAS NEUE TESTAMENT
- DAS MATTHAEUSEVANGELIUM UND SEINE LUCAS-PARALLELEN
- DER PHILIPPER-BRIEF AUSGELEGT UND DIE GESCHICHTE SEINER AUSLEGUNG
- THE PRESENT STATUS OF THE INQUIRY CONCERNING THE GENUINENESS OF THE PAULINE EPISTLES
- DIE QUELLEN DER SYNOPTISCHEN UEBERLIEFERUNG (T.U.U. 3-32/3)
- DIE QUELLEN DES LUKASEVANGELIUMS
- DIE RELIGION DES NEUEN TESTAMENTS
- TEXTKRITIK DER PAULINISCHEN BRIEFE (T.U.U. 1-14/3)
- TEXTKRITIK DER VIER EVANGELIEN (T.U.U. 2-19/2)

WEISS COLLECTION ON THE BELGIAN CONGO / Weiss, Herbert F, collector – 1947-62 – 1 – us Res Libr [960]

Weiss, Ernst *see* DAS UNVERLIERBARE

Weiss, H F *see* UNTERSUCHUNGEN ZUR KOSMOLOGIE DES HELLENISTISCHEN UND PALAESTINISCHEN JUDENTUMS (T.U.U. 5-97)

Weiss, Herbert F, collector *see* WEISS COLLECTION ON THE BELGIAN CONGO

Weiss, Jean Jacques *see* COMBAT CONSTITUTIONNEL: 1868-1886

Weiss, Johannes *see*
- DIE AUFGABEN DER NEUTESTAMENTLICHEN WISSENSCHAFT IN DER GEGENWART
- PAUL AND JESUS
- DIE PREDIGT JESU VOM REICHE GOTTES

Weiss, Karl Fr. *see* STUDIEN ZUR ALLGEMEINEN THEORIE DES WERTS

Weiss, Maureen R *see*
- AN EXAMINATION OF THE SOURCES AND LEVELS OF PERCEIVED COMPETENCE IN MALE AND FEMALE INTERSCHOLASTIC COACHES
- THE ROLE OF COGNITIVE APPRAISAL AND FRIENDSHIP PROVISIONS IN CHILDREN'S EXPERIENCE OF AFFECT IN PHYSICAL ACTIVITY

Weiss, Steven M *see* A COMPARISON OF MALADAPTIVE BEHAVIORS OF ATHLETES AND NON-ATHLETES

DIE WEISSAGUNGEN JESU CHRISTI : VON SEINEM TODE, SIENER AUFERSTEHUNG UND WIEDERKUNFT UND IHRE ERFUELLUNG / Schwartzkopff, Paul – (Includes bibliographical references) – Goettingen:Vandenhoeck und Ruprecht, 1895 – 1mf – 9 – 0-8370-5181-9 – 1985-3181 – us A.T.L.A. [240]

WEISSAGUNGEN JESU VON SEINEM TODE, SEINER AUFERSTEHUNG UND WIEDERKUNFT UND IHRE ERFUELLUNG = THE PROPHECIES OF JESUS CHRIST RELATING TO HIS DEATH, RESURRECTION, AND SECOND COMING, AND THEIR FULFILMENT / Schwartzkopff, Paul – (In English. Includes bibliographical references and index) – Edinburgh: T & T Clark, 1897 – 1mf – 9 – 0-8370-5179-7 – 1985-3179 – us A.T.L.A. [240]

Weissbach, Franz Heinrich *see* DIE SUMERISCHE FRAGE

Weissbart, Gertrud *see* BUERGERLICHES LEBENSGEFUEHL IN GRILLPARZERS DRAMEN

Weissblueth, Eyal *see* THE EFFECT OF ALTERING SPEED OF BACKWARD MOVEMENT OF THE TRUNK ON ANTICIPATORY POSTURAL ADJUSTMENTS

Weisse, Christian Hermann *see* KRITIK UND ERLAEUTERUNG DES GOETHE'SCHEN FAUST

DER WEISSE FAECHER : EIN ZWISCHENSPIEL / Hofmannsthal, Hugo von – Leipzig: Insel-Verlag, 1907 – 1r – 1 – us U.W. Library [820]

DER WEISSE MANTEL FAELLT : AUS DEN SCHICKSALSJAHREN DES DEUTSCHEN RITTERORDENS / Hirsch, Hermann – 2. Aufl. Stuttgart: G Truckenmueller, 1940 – 1r – 1 – us U.W. Library [830]

Weissenberg, S *see* BEITRAEGE ZUR FRAUENBIOLOGIE

WEISSENBURGER TAGBLATT – Weissenburg, West Germany. 1977- – 1 – gw Mikrofilm [072]

Weiss-Ferdl *see* ICH BIN KEIN INTELLEKTUELLER

Weissflog, Gotthard *see* LANDNUTZUNG UND WALDMERKMALE IN OSTTHUERINGEN

Weisslovits, N *see* PRINZ UND DERWISCH

Weisz, Heinrich *see* DIE PESCHITTA ZU DEUTEROJESAIA

Weitbrecht, Mrs *see* FOUR YEARS IN ASHANTEE BY THE MISSIONARIES RAMSEYER AND KUEHNE.

DAS WEITE LAND : ROMAN / Ahlers, Rudolf – Braunschweig: G Westermann, c1940 – 1r – 1 – us U.W. Library [830]

DER WEITE WEG : ALLES DEUTSCHE MEINT DAS REICH / Winnig, August – Hamburg: Hanseatische Verlagsanstalt, c1932 – 1 – us U.W. Library [130]

Weitenberg, J J S *see* ARMENIAN SOURCES

Weitenkampf, Frank *see*
- SOCIAL HISTORY OF THE UNITED STATES
- SOCIAL HISTORY OF THE UNITED STATES: HOW THE COMIC ARTISTS SAW US

DER WEITER MISROCH – Harbin, China. v1-2. 1921-22 – 1r – 1 – us Ross [072]

Weitnauer, Alfred *see* LACHENDES ALLGAEU

Weitzenegger, Karsten *see* TALLERES PUBLICOS IN COSTA RICA

DER WEIZENSTRAUSS : ROMAN / Zillich, Heinrich – Muenchen: A Lange/G Mueller, c1938 – 1r – 1 – us U.W. Library [830]

Weizmann, C *see*
- THE JEWISH PEOPLE AND PALESTINE
- WE WARNED YOU, GENTLEMEN

Weizsaecker, Carl von *see* THE APOSTOLIC AGE OF THE CHRISTIAN CHURCH

Weizsaecker, Karl Heinrich von *see*
- DAS APOSTOLISCHE ZEITALTER DER CHRISTILCHEN KIRCHE
- FERDINAND CHRISTIAN BAUR

Weizsaecker, Paul *see* DIE BILDNISSE WIELANDS

WEKELIJKSE KRONIEK VAN DE REGEERINGS VOORLICHTINGS DIENST – (Lacking: 1946(1-25); 1947(28-29, 43, 46, 72-74); 1948 (91, 101, 105, 109-119, 121-122, 124-125)) – Batavia, 1946-1949 – 51mf – 9 – SE-531/1 – ne IDC [350]

WEKELIJKSE KRONIEK VAN DE REGEERINGS VOORLICHTINGS DIENST – (Missing: 1946(1-25); 1947(28-29, 42, 46, 72-74); 1948(91, 101, 105, 109-119, 121-122, 124-125)) – Batavia, 1946-49 – 51mf – 9 – SE-531/1 – ne IDC [073]

Welborn, David M *see* REGULATORY AGENCY CHAIRMEN AND THE REGULATORY PROCESS

Welch, A C *see* JEREMIAH. HIS TIME AND HIS WORK

Welch, Alice Kemp *see* OF SIX MEDIAEVAL WOMEN; TO WHICH IS ADDED A NOTE ON MEDIAEVAL GARDENS

Welch, Claude Emerson *see* CAMEROUN POLITICAL EPHEMERA, 1954-1963

Welch, James E *see* DIARY

Welch, Ransom Bethune *see* FAITH AND MODERN THOUGHT

WELCHE BEDEUTUNG HAT DIE KONNEKTORREGION IN TRYPTOPHAN SYNTHASE AUS SACCHAROMYCES CEREVISIAE? REINIGUNG DES BIFUNKTIONELLEN ENZYMS UEBER EINEN GENTECHNISCHEN ANSATZ UND CHARAKTERISIERUNG DURCH PROTEOLYSE / Reckmann, Birgit – 1995 – 2mf – 9 – DM80.00 – 3-8267-2143-8 – gw Hänsel [540]

WELCHE REFORMEN ERSCHEINEN BEI DER JETZIGEN STELLUNG UND AUFGABE DES EVANGELISCHEN RELIGIONSUNTERRICHTS AUF GYMNASIEN NOTWENDIG? / Meyer, K W – Meldorf: P Bundies, 1873 – 1mf – 9 – 0-8370-7566-1 – 1986-1566 – us A.T.L.A. [370]

WELCHE VRSACH GEBIND ZE UFRUREN / Zwingli, H – Zuerich, Chr. Froschouer. 1525. BME-86 1 – 9 – ne IDC [240]

Welcker, Karl *see* DAS STAATS-LEXIKON

WELCOME – Portland OR. May 7 1882 – 1 – us U.O. Library [071]

WELCOME BAPTIST CHURCH. ANDERSON COUNTY. SOUTH CAROLINA : CHURCH RECORDS – 1894-1972 – 1 – 21.60 – us Baptist [240]

WELCOME BAPTIST CHURCH. GREENVILLE, SOUTH CAROLINA : CHURCH RECORDS – 25 Apr 1875-11 Oct 1961 – 1 – 25.16 – us Baptist [240]

WELCOME TIDINGS – (Lacks: 211, 300, 302-304, 309) – nos 1-311. 1887-94 – 1r – 1 – ATLA 1994-S012 – us A.T.L.A. [073]

WELCOME TO THE RANSOMED, OR, DUTIES OF THE COLORED INHABITANTS OF THE DISTRICT OF COLUMBIA / Payne, Daniel A – 1862 – 1 – $50.00 – us Presbyterian [976]

WELCOMING AMERICA'S NEWEST COMMONWEALTH : THE 2ND INTERIM REPORT TO THE CONGRESS OF THE U.S. OF THE NORTHERN MARIANA ISLANDS COMMISSION ON FEDERAL LAWS, PARTS 1 AND 2 WITH DOCUMENTARY SUPPLEMENT / Northern Mariana Islands (Commonwealth) – Washington: The Commission, Aug 1985 – 18mf – 9 – $27.00 – LLMC 82-100J Title 25 – us L.L.M.C. [324]

Weld, Isaac *see* VOYAGE AU CANADA PENDANT LES ANNEES 1795, 1796 ET 1797

WELD PAPERS 1839-1889 – BRRAM – 1 – uk Microform Academic [025]

WELDALERT (AN SDI SERVICE) – 1,5,69 – us UMI [670]

WELDER – 1977- – 1,5,6,9 – us UMI [670]

WELDING ABSTRACTS – 1,5,69 – us UMI [670]

WELDING AND FABRICATING DATA BOOK – 1984- – 1,5,6,9 – us UMI [670]

WELDING AND SURFACING REVIEWS / ed by Paton, B E – 9,5,1 – us Harwood [670]

WELDING DESIGN AND FABRICATION – (See now: Welding Design and Fabrication Including Welding Engineer) – ns v1-47 1930-74 1; v44-47 5,6 – us UMI [670]

WELDING DESIGN AND FABRICATION INCLUDING WELDING ENGINEER – v48-1975- – 1,5,6,9 – us UMI [670]

WELDING DISTRIBUTOR – 1984- – 1,5,6,9 – us UMI [670]

WELDING ENGINEER – v1-25 1915-40 – 1 – us Princeton Micro [670]

WELDING ENGINEER – v1-25 1915-40 – 1 – us Princeton Micro [670]

WELDING IN THE WORLD – v1- 1962- – 5,6,9 – us UMI [670]

WELDING JOURNAL – v1- 1922- 1; v45- 5,6; v55- 9 – us UMI [670]

WELDING JOURNAL – v1-25 1922-46 – 1,5,6 – us Princeton Micro [670]

WELDING JOURNAL – v15-34 1936-55 – 1,5,6 – us Princeton Micro [670]
Weldler-Steinberg, A *see* THEODOR KOERNERS BRIEFWECHSEL MIT DEN SEINEN
Weldon, George Warburton *see* UNITY IN VARIETY:...ARGUMENTS BASED ON...DIVINE WORKMANSHIP IN OUR PLANET
Weldon, J *see* DIVINE HARMONY
WELDON PAPERS: BENEDICTINE RECORDS FROM DOUAI ABBEY / Douai Abbey – Ms. 17th Century – 3r – 1 – uk Microform Academic [240]
WELFARE IN REVIEW / U.S. Department of Health and Human Services – HEW, Social and Rehabilitation Service. v1-10. 1963-72 (all publ) – 49mf – 9 – $73.00 – LLMC 81-209 – us L.L.M.C. [360]
WELFARE WORK – 1920-31 – 1 – us UMI [073]
Welk, Ehm *see*
- DIE FANFARE IM PARISER EINZUGSMARSCH
- DIE GERECHTEN VON KUMMEROW
- DIE HEIDEN VON KUMMEROW
- DER HOHE BEFEHL
- DIE LEBENSUHR DES GOTTLIEB GRAMBAUER

Welke, Martin *see*
- HAMBURGISCHER UNPARTHEYISCHER CORRESPONDENT
- ZEITUNG AUS DEM FELDLAGER

THE WELL AT THE WORLD'S END / Morris, William – [Hammersmith: Kelmscott Press, 1896] – 1 roll – 1 – 1-55879-592-8 – uk Libr Preservation [830]
Wellamn, Francis L *see* DAY IN COURT
Wellan, J W I *see*
- PALEMBANG IN 1934
- DE STAD PALEMBANG IN 1935

WELLAND AND PORT COLBORNE EVENING TRIBUNE – Welland, Ju1929-1929De – 1r – 1 – cn Preston [971]
WELLAND CANAL HISTORY – Port Colborne, 1824-1923 – 1r – 1 – cn Preston [971]
WELLAND TELEGRAPH – Welland, 1871-1918 – 24r – 1 – cn Preston [971]
WELLAND TRIBUNE – Welland, 1872-1909 – 17r – 1 – cn Preston [971]
WELLAND TRIBUNE AND PEOPLES PRESS – Welland, 1903-1920 – 9r – 1 – cn Preston [971]
WELLAND TRIBUNE AND TELEGRAPH – Welland, 1921-1925 – 6r – 1 – cn Preston [971]
WELL-BEING – 1975- 1; 1978- 5,6,9 – us UMI [610]
WELL-BEING *see* VEGETARIAN TIMES
WELLDOER – Liverpool, England. Feb 1912-Jan 1913. -w. 1/4 reel – 1 – uk British Libr Newspaper [072]
DIE WELLE : GEDICHTE / Hoerner, Herbert von – Stuttgart: Engelhornverlag A Spemann, 1942 – 1r – 1 – us U.W. Library [810]
Wellek, Rene *see* IMMANUEL KANT IN ENGLAND, 1793-1838
Wellems, Hugo *see* CHRISTOPH PANKRATIUS MIESERICH UNTER DEN SELIGEN
Wellens, J *see* GENERALIS COLLECTIONIS, OMNIUM OPERUM ILLUSTRISSIMI AC REVERENDISSIMI DOMINI...
Weller, Anton Friedrich Tuedel *see*
- AB DAFUER, NACH AFRIKA
- BONZEN UND REBELLEN

Weller, PT *see* THE EASTER SERMONS OF ST AUGUSTINE
Weller, S *see* THE TRIAL OF MR. WHITEFIELD'S SPIRIT; IN SOME REMARKS UPON HIS FOURTH JOURNAL,...
Weller, Tuedel *see*
- PETER MOENKEMANN, FREIKORPSKAEMPFER AN DER RUHR
- RABAUKEN!

WELLFLEET 1723-1890 – 23mf – 9 – us Holbrook [920]
Wellhausen, Julius *see*
- ANALYSE DER OFFENBARUNG JOHANNIS
- DIE COMPOSITION DES HEXATEUCHS UND DER HISTORISCHEN BUECHER DES ALTEN TESTAMENTS
- ERWEITERUNGEN UND AENDERUNGEN IM VIERTEN EVANGELIUM
- DAS EVANGELIUM JOHANNIS
- DAS EVANGELIUM LUCAE
- DAS EVANGELIUM MARCI
- DAS EVANGELIUM MATTHAEI
- DIE PHARISAEER UND DIE SADDUCAEER
- PROLEGOMENA TO THE HISTORY OF ANCIENT ISRAEL
- DER TEXT DER BUECHER SAMUELIS

WELLHAUSEN'S METHODE / Naumann, O – Leipzig: J.C. Hinrichs, 1886. 1 fiche – 9 – us A.T.L.A. [240]
Wellington, Arthur Wellesley *see* MAXIMS AND OPINIONS
WELLINGTON DEANERY MAGAZINE – Guelph [Ont]: Advocate Pub. Co, v1 no 1(July 1900)- – 9 – cn C.I.H.M. [971]
WELLINGTON JOURNAL – New Zealand. -w. 13 Apr-22 Jul 1868. (1 reel) – 1 – uk British Libr Newspaper [072]
WELLINGTON ST METHODIST MONTHLY – London, Ont: [Printed] under the auspices of the Epworth League of Christian Endeavor, [1893?-189- or 19–] – 9 – cn C.I.H.M. [240]
WELLINGTONIAN – Wellington. Kansas. 1881-1885 – 1 – us UMI [071]
Wellisch, Hans H *see*
- CONRAD GESSNER

Wellman, Francis Lewis *see*
- THE ART OF CROSS-EXAMINATION
- DAY IN COURT; OR, THE SUBTLE ARTS OF GREAT ADVOCATES

Wells, Amos Russell *see*
- BIBLE MINIATURES: CHARACTER SKETCHES OF...HEROES AND HEROINES OF HOLY WRIT
- THE MISSIONARY MANUAL

WELLS CHAPEL BAPTIST CHURCH. WALLACE, NORTH CAROLINA : CHURCH RECORDS – 1803-1934, 1949-66 – 1 – 64.62 – us Baptist [240]
WELLS CHAPEL BAPTIST CHURCH. WILMINGTON ASSOCIATION. WALLACE, NORTH CAROLINA : CHURCH RECORDS – 1803-1934; 1949-66 – 1 – 64.62 – us Baptist [240]
Wells, Charles Luke *see*
- THE AGE OF CHARLEMAGNE (CHARLES THE GREAT)
- MANUAL OF EARLY ECCLESIASTICAL HISTORY TO 476 A.D.

Wells, Christine L *see* THE BODY COMPOSITION OF MASTERS WOMEN ENDURANCE ATHLETES FROM 35 TO 74 YEARS OF AGE
Wells, D B [et al] *see* CONSERVATION OF NATIONAL IDEALS
Wells, David Ames *see* PAPERS OF DAVID AMES WELLS
Wells, Edward L *see* CORRESPONDENCE
Wells, Edwin P *see* THE COMMEMORATIVE SERVICES OF THE FIRST BAPTIST CHURCH OF BOSTON, MASSACHUSETTS (250TH ANNIVERSARY)
WELLS' EVERY MAN HIS OWN LAWYER AND BUSINESS FORM BOOK / Wells, John G – New rev. ed. New York, 1879. 612 p. L.C. copy imperfect: portrait wanting. LL-1549 – 1 – us L of C Photodup [340]
WELLS FARGO AND CO. DIRECTORY OF PRINCIPAL CHINESE BUSINESS IN SAN FRANCISCO AND OTHER CITIES – San Francisco, 1882 – 1r – 1 – $50.00 – B40324 – us Library Micro [978]
Wells, Frederic P *see* HISTORY OF NEWBURY
Wells, H G *see*
- ANTICIPATIONS OF THE REACTION OF MECHANICAL AND SCIENTIFIC PROGRESS UPON HUMAN LIFE AND THOUGHT
- THE FIRST MEN IN THE MOON
- THE FOOD OF THE GODS
- IN THE DAYS OF THE COMET
- LOVE AND MR. LEWISHAM
- A MODERN UTOPIA
- NON-FICTIONAL WORKS OF H.G. WELLS
- THE SEA LADY
- THE STOLEN BACILLUS
- TALES OF SPACE AND TIME
- THIRTY STRANGE STORIES
- THE WAR IN THE AIR
- WHEN THE SLEEPER WAKES

Wells, H T *see* LAWYER AND UNITED STATES FORM-BOOK
Wells, Harry L *see* HISTORY OF BUTTE COUNTY
Wells, James *see*
- STEWART OF LOVEDALE
- STEWART OF LOVEDALE; THE LIFE OF JAMES STEWART.

Wells, John C *see*
- LAWYER AND UNITED STATES FORM-BOOK

Wells, John Cleland *see* A TREATISE ON THE DOCTRINES OF RES ADJUDICATA AND STARE DECISIS
Wells, John G *see* WELLS' EVERY MAN HIS OWN LAWYER AND BUSINESS FORM BOOK
WELLS JOURNAL ETC – Somerset, England. 2 Aug 1851-25 Sept 1869; 19 Feb 1870-6 Jun 1872; 1873-1980. -w. 134 reels – 1 – uk British Libr Newspaper [072]
Wells, William Harvey *see* THE GRADED SCHOOL. A GRADED COURSE OF INSTRUCTION FOR PUBLIC SCHOOLS
WELLSBORO AGITATOR – Wellsboro, PA. -w 1955-1963 – 13 – $25.00r – us I.M.R. [071]
WELLSBORO GAZETTE – Wellsboro, PA. -w 1889-1990 (Combined with Mansfield) – 13 – $25.00r – us I.M.R. [071]
WELLSVILLE UNION – (Weekly Republican newspaper) – Salem, OH. Aug 27 1863-20 Aug 1868 – 2r – 1 – us Western Res [071]
THE WELL-TUNED ORGAN...WHETHER OR NO INSTRUMENTAL AND ORGANICAL MUSIC BE LAWFUL IN HOLY PUBLICK ASSEMBLIES / Brookbank, Joseph – 1660 – 9 – us Sibley [780]
Welman, C W *see* THE NATIVE STATES OF THE GOLD COAST
Welsby, WN *see* MEESON AND WELSBY'S REPORTS
Welsh, Charles *see* ON COLOURED BOOKS FOR CHILDREN
WELSH HISTORY REVIEW – v1- 1960- 1; v8- 5,6,9 – us UMI [941]
WELSH INDUSTRIAL TIMES AND MONMOUTHSHIRE LABOUR CHRONICLE – Swansea, Wales, Aug 1888-Dec 1891 – 1r – 1 – uk British Libr Newspaper [072]
Welsh, James William *see* ISOKO CLANS OF THE NIGER DELTA
Welsh, Janet *see* CORRESPONDENCE
WELSH NECK BAPTIST CHURCH. DARLINGTON COUNTY. SOCIETY HILL. SOUTH CAROLINA : CHURCH RECORDS – 1737-1991. (Complete) – 1 – $42.84 – us Baptist [240]
Welsh, Robert Ethol *see*
- THE CHALLENGE TO CHRISTIAN MISSIONS
- IN RELIEF OF DOUBT

WELSH TRACT BAPTIST MEETING. PENCADER HUNDRED. NEW CASTLE COUNTY. DELAWARE : CHURCH RECORDS – 1701-1828 (in two parts) – 1 – 10.98 – us Baptist [240]
WELSH WESLEYAN METHODISM, 1800-1858 : ITS ORIGINS, GROWTH AND SECESSIONS / Williams, A H – Bangor, 1935. 378p – 4mf – 9 – ne IDC [240]
Welsh, William *see* WOMEN HELPERS IN THE CHURCH: THEIR SAYINGS AND DOINGS
WELSHMAN – Carmarthen, Wales, UK. 13 Jan 1832-1847. -w. 7 1/2 reels – 1 – uk British Libr Newspaper [072]
DE WELSPREKENDHEID : EENE LEZING / Bavinck, Herman – Derde Druk. Kampen: G Ph Zalsman, 1909 – 1mf – 9 – 0-8370-7364-2 – 1986-1364 – us A.T.L.A. [080]
DI WELT = THE WORLD – (In Yiddish) – Warsaw, PL. v2 no7 2 Mar 1934-v2 no36 12 Oct 1934 – 1r – 1 – $35.00 – cn Can Microfilming [072]
DIE WELT : AUSGABE BERLIN – Berlin. 1996- – 11r a year – 1 – gw Mikrofilm [072]
DIE WELT : AUSGABE BERLIN – Berlin, apr 2-may 15 1951, jul 2-aug 15 1951, nov-dec 1955, 1996- – 1 – Inquire at Mikrofilmarchiv for details – gw Misc Inst [072]
DIE WELT – Bonn, Germany. 3 Jan 1983- – 1 – gw Mikrofilm [072]
DIE WELT – Hamburg. 1979- – 370.00y; CPC; 9 – gw Alpha Com [072]
DIE WELT – Hamburg, Germany. -d. 2 April-9 Aug, 12 Oct 1946-Dec 1952. 24 reels – 1 – uk British Libr Newspaper [072]
DIE WELT – Hamburg. mar 26, 1946-1961. 1975-79. feb 10, 1981-95 – 1 – gw Mikrofilm [072]
DIE WELT – Hamburg: Verlag Die Welt, 1953-feb 1978; apr 1978-dec 31 1981/jan 1 1982 – us Res Libr [072]
DIE WELT – (Lacking: 1913. v17(36,37). 1907, v11 has not been published.) – v. 1-18. Vienna. Cologne. Berlin. 1897-1914. BJ-23-59 1 – 531mf – 9 – ne IDC [290]
DIE WELT – Stockholm, Sweden. Zeitschrift fuer Politik, Wirtschaft und Arbeiterbewegung. 18 Sept 1939-28 May 1943. Continued by: Politische Information. Stockholm – 1 – gw Mikrofilm [072]
DIE WELT – Vienna etc. v. 1-18 no. 31. June 1897-July 1914 – 1 – us NY Public [305]
DIE WELT – (Yrly reel count varies. 1979- on fiche. Inquire for price) – 1946- – 1 – inquire – us Ross [072]
DIE WELT *see* RUNDSCHAU UEBER POLITIK, WIRTSCHAFT UND ARBEITERBEWEGUNG
WELT – Vienna. v1-18. 1897-1914 – 9r – 1 – us Ross [072]
DIE WELT AM ABEND – Berlin, 1924-33 (incomplete) – 30r – 1 – Inquire at Mikrofilmarchiv for details – gw Misc Inst [943]
DIE WELT AM MONTAG – Berlin, 1904-mar 6 1933, mar 7-jun 1933 (incomplete) – 18r – 1 – Inquire at Mikrofilmarchiv for details – gw Misc Inst [943]
DIE WELT AM MONTAG – Berlin, 1905-1933 – 17r – 1 – DM1,190.00 – gw Mikro Press [072]
DIE WELT AM MONTAG – Berlin, Germany.1905-Feb 1933 – 1 – gw Mikrofilm [072]
WELT AM MONTAG – (Herausgegeben vom franzoesischen Informationsdienst). Austria. -w. 18 Feb 1946-9 Feb 1948. (3 reels) – 1 – uk British Libr Newspaper [072]
DIE WELT AM MORGEN *see* BERLIN AM MORGEN
WELT AM SONNTAG – 1979- – 9 – inquire – us Ross [072]
WELT AM SONNTAG – Hamburg. 1979- – 22150.00y; CPC; 9 – gw Alpha Com [072]
WELT AM SONNTAG – Hamburg: Die Welt Verlags-GmbH, 1967-dec 21 1980 – us Res Libr [072]
WELT DER ARBEIT – Cologne. Germany. -w. 27 Jan 1950-20 Dec 1957. (23 reels) – 1 – uk British Libr Newspaper [072]
WELT DER ARBEIT – Koeln, 1958-1988 – 30r – 1 – DM2,250.00 – gw Mikro Press [072]
WELT DER ARBEIT – Koeln, West Germany. 1968- – 1 – gw Mikrofilm [360]
WELT DER ARBEIT (COLOGNE) – 1968-1995 – 3 times per yr – 1 – F371.00 – sz Infoprint [072]
WELT DES ISLAMS – Leiden. v1-30. 1951-90 – 5,9 – Dfl2,400.00; Dfl80.00v – ne Swets [260]
WELT IM FILM – Zuerich, nov 5-dec 3 1913 – 1 – gw Mikrofilm [790]
WELT (MICROFICHES) – 1979-1995 – 1 – F2,572.00 – sz Infoprint [072]
DIE WELT OHNE TRANSZENDENZ : EINE STUDIE ZU THOMAS MANNS "DR. FAUSTUS" UND SEINEN NEBENSCHRIFTEN / Holthusen, Hans Egon – Hamburg: H Ellermann, 1949 – 1r – us U.W. Library [430]
WELT- UND GOTTESREICHSKLAENGE : GEMISCHTE GEDICHTE / Ilgen, Pedro – Highland, IL: P Ilgen, 1892 – 1r – 1 – us U.W. Library [810]
DIE WELT VON HEUTE – Prague, Czechoslovakia. Mar-Apr 1934 – 1r – 1 – us L of C Photodup [072]
DIE WELTANSCHAUUNG DES JUNGEN WIELAND : EIN BEITRAG ZUR GESCHICHTE DER AUFKLAERUNG / Ermatinger, Emil – (Includes bibliographical references and index) – Frauenfeld: Huber, 1907 – 1r – 1 – us U.W. Library [190]
DIE WELTANSCHAUUNG GERHART HAUPTMANNS IN SEINEN WERKEN / Herrmann, Christian – Berlin: Paetel, 1926 – 1r – 1 – us U.W. Library [430]
WELTANSCHAUUNG UND NATURDEUTUNG : VORLESUNGEN UEBER GOETHES NATURANSCHAUUNG / Michel, Ernst – Jena: Diederichs, 1920 – 1r – 1 – us U.W. Library [430]
WELTANSCHAUUNGEN IN VERGANGENHEIT UND GEGENWART / Hofer, Hans – Wernigerode: Zeitbuecher-Verlag, 1921. 3v – 1 – us U.W. Library [100]
DES WELTBERUEHMTEN MEDICI, PHYSICI UND POLYHISTORIS CONRADI GESNERI LEBEN UND SCHRIFTEN – Leipzig, etc, 1711 – 2mf – ne IDC [610]
DAS WELTBILD ERNST JUENGERS : DARSTELLUNG UND DEUTUNG / Brock, Erich – (Includes bibliographical references) – Zuerich: Leemann, c1945 – 1r – 1 – us U.W. Library [430]
DAS WELTBILD GABIROLS / Simon, H – 1957 – 1mf – 8 – ne Slangenburg [100]
DAS WELTBILD IN GELLERTS DICHTUNG / May, Kurt – (Includes bibliographical references) – Frankfurt am Main: M Diesterweg, 1928 – 1r – 1 – us U.W. Library [430]
DAS WELTBILD IN KLOPSTOCKS MESSIAS / Woehlert, Hans – (Includes bibliographical references) – Halle a.S.: M Niemeyer, 1915 – 1r – 1 – us U.W. Library [430]
WELTBOTHE – Lebanon, PA, 1809-10; Reading, PA, 1810-20. Also: Amerikanischer Beobachter, Philadelphia, PA, 1808-11.Sold as one unit – 1,3 – us Readex [071]

WELTBRAND : NEUE FOLGE: KRIEGSGEDICHTE IN MUENSTERLAENDISCHER MUNDART / Wagenfeld, Karl – Bocholt: J & A Temming, 1915 – 1r – 1 – us U.W. Library [390]
WELTBUCH: SPIEGEL VND BILDTNISZ DES GANTZEN ERDTBODENS / Franck von Woerd, S – Tuebingen, U. Morhart. 1534. BME-78 1 – 9 – ne IDC [240]
DIE WELTBUEHNE – 1947-1950, 1953-1955, 1969-1989 – 1,468mf – 1 – DM8,367.60 – gw Mikro Press [073]
WELTBUERGERTUM IN DER DEUTSCHEN LITERATUR VON HERDER BIS NIETZSCHE / Francke, Kuno – (Includes bibliographical references and index) – Berlin: Weidmannsche Buchhandlung, 1928 – 1 – us U.W. Library [430]
WELTCHRONIK / Ems, Rudolf von – 27p + 7 color mf – Dm620.00 – 3-89219-012-7 – gw Lengenfelder [900]
WELT-DIENST – (Beilage: Informationen zur Judenfrage, oct 1, 1943-feb 1, 1945 (incomplete)) – Erfurt/Frankfurt. dec 1, 1933-jan 1/2, 1945 – 1 – gw Mikrofilm [073]
Welte, B *see* DIE POSTBAPTISMALE SALBUNG
Welter, W L *see*
- LIJST DER NEDERLANDSCHE HANDSCHRIFTEN IN DE KEIZERLIJKE BIBLIOTHEEK TE ST PETERSBURG
Welters, A *see* KLUIZENAARS IN LIMBURG
DER WELTFREUND : ERSTE GEDICHTE / Werfel, Franz – Muenchen: K Wolff, 1920 – 1r – 1 – us U.W. Library [810]
WELTFRONT GEGEN IMPERIALISTISCHEN KRIEG UND FASCHISMUS – no. 1, 3-4. oct-nov 1933. devenu: Front mondial. Halbmonatsorgan des Weltkomitees zum Kampf gegen imperialistischen Krieg und Faschismus. juin 1934-janv 1935. devenu: Volksfront gegen imperialistischen Krieg und Faschismus. no. 1. aout 1935. Paris – 1 – fr A.C.R.P.P. [073]
DER WELTHEILAND: EINE JENAER ROSENVORLESUNG MIT ANMERKUNGEN / Lietzmann, Hans – Bonn: A. Marcus & E. Weber, 1909. 1 fiche – 9 – us A.T.L.A. [240]
Welti, Heinrich *see*
- GESCHICHTE DES SONETTES IN DER DEUTSCHEN DICHTUNG
- SONN- UND FEIERTAGS-SONETTE
WELT-IBERBLIK = WORLD REVIEW – (In Yiddish. Bi-weekly) – Warsaw, PL. no8. Dec 1935 – 1r – 1 – $25.00 – cn Can Microfilming [072]
WELTINNIGKEIT : NEUE GEDICHTE / Seidel, Ina – 5 verm. Aufl. Stuttgart: Deutsche Verlags-Anstalt, 1921, c1918 – 1r – 1 – us U.W. Library [810]
DER WELTKAMPF – (Incl index for 1942) – Muenchen, 1943 – 5r – 1 – gw Mikrofilm [943]
WELTKAMPF – Zwickau, DE. 1920; 1922-23 (all incomplete) – 1r – 1 – gw Mikrofilm [072]
DER WELTKRIEG / Baer, A – Berlin 1915 – 1mf – 9 – ILM-332/1 – ne IDC [340]
DER WELTKRIEG / Helfferich, Karl Theodor – Berlin: Ullstein, 1919. 3v – 1 – us U.W. Library [940]
DER WELTKRIEG – Windhoek, South West Africa. 1916-19 – 1 – sa State Libr [072]
DAS WELTLICHE OBERKEITT DEN WIDERTAUFFEREN MIT LEIBLICHER STRAFF / Luther, Martin – Wittemberg. 1536. BME-95 1 – 9 – ne IDC [240]
DER WELTMARKT – Hannover, Germany. 1918 – 1 – gw Mikrofilm [072]
DER WELTMARKT : MITTEILUNGEN DER GESELLSCHAFT FUER WARENKUNDE E.V. – Hannover, 1918 – 1r – 1 – DM80.00 – gw Mikro Press [072]
DER WELTMARKT – Mitteilungen fuer Gesellschaft fuer Warenkunde e.v. Hamburg, Germany. 1918 – 1 – gw Mikrofilm [073]
DIE WELTMISSION – (Cont: Das Wort in der Welt) – 1958-86 (complete) – 5r – 1 – ATLA S0818 – us A.T.L.A. [073]
WELTMISSION UND THEOLOGISCHE ARBEIT / Richter, Julius – Guetersloh: C. Bertelsmann, 1913 – 1mf – us A.T.L.A. [240]
Welton, D M *see* THE BOOK OF GENESIS
DIE WELT-POST – Omaha, Lincoln, NE. 13 Apr 1916-20 Oct 1972. Title varies – 1 – us NE Hist [071]
DIE WELTPOST UND DER STAATSANZEIGER – (Cont by: Amerika-Woche, Chicago) – Omaha, NE. 1973 (no.17)-1982 – 1 – gw Mikrofilm [071]
WELTPRESSE – (Herausgegeben vom britischen Weltnachrichtendienst). Vienna. Austria. -d. 18 Sep 1945-31 Aug 1950. (Imperfect). (18 reels) – 1 – uk British Libr Newspaper [072]
Weltrich, Richard *see* RICHARD WAGNERS TRISTAN UND ISOLDE ALS DICHTUNG
WELTSPIEGEL – Berlin, 1904-39 – 26r – 1 – Inquire at Mikrofilmarchiv for details – gw Misc Inst [900]
DER WELTVERBAND DER STAATENLOSEN UND DU / Solneman, K H Z – 1fiche (29x) – 9 – 1.00f – at Libertarian Micro [320]
DIE WELTWOCHE – 1980-1994 – 1 – sz Infoprint [072]
Welty, E O *see* GEMEINSCHAFT UND EINZELMENSCH
DE WELVOORZIENE WYNKELDER... / Abraham a Sancta Clara – 1st ed. Amsterdam, 1737 – 6mf – 9 – ne IDC [700]
Welwitsch, F M J *see*
- CATALOGUE OF THE AFRICAN PLANTS COLLECTED BY F. WELWITSCH IN 1853-1861
- SERTUM ANGOLENSE
Welwitsch, R *see* APONTAMENTOS PHYTOGEOGRAPHICOS. ANGOLA
WELWYN AND HATFIELD TIMES – England, Jul-Dec 1958; Aug-Dec 1959; 1961; 1973; Jan-Apr 1978; 1980- – 69+ r – 1 – uk British Libr Newspaper [072]
WELWYN AND WELWYN GARDEN CITY HERALD (HATFIELD) *see* WELWYN GARDEN CITY HERALD AND POST
WELWYN GARDEN CITY HERALD AND POST – (Also known as: Herald; Welwyn and Welwyn Garden City Herald (Hatfield)) – Nov 23-Dec 1990; Jul 4-Sep 26 1991; Jul 15-Sep 30, Oct 7 1993-Mar 1994; Apr 7-Jun 23, Jul 7-Dec 15 1994; Jan 5-Feb 23, Mar-Jun, Jul 6-Nov 16 1995; Jan 18-Jun 28, Jul-Dec 1996 – 10 1/2r – 1 – uk British Libr Newspaper [072]
Welzel, Barbara *see* KENNEN UND SAMMELN
Wembridge, Eleanor Rowland *see* THE RIGHT TO BELIEVE
Wemmer, Dagmar *see* DIE DOLDENBLUETLER ALS HEILPFLANZEN IM MITTELALTER
WEN HUI BAO – (1979-90, 1r/y; 1991- , 2r/y) – Wenhui Daily. China. In Chinese. Current subscription. Annual delivery. Backfiles supplied on request. M D14 – 1 – $55.00r – cc Microforms [072]
WEN WU – (1955 $3.50f; 1950-54, 1956- $4.50f) – Cultural Relics. In Chinese but Table of Contents in English in each issue. F p20 – 9 – cc Microforms [073]
WEN WU – Academic Magazine, 1950-52. Original title: Information. In 1957 named changed to Historical Property. Not published 1966-70. 689 ill. HG11f – 9 – 2295.00 – cc Globe [073]
WEN-CHAI – (Literary Digest). v. 1-14. 1937-48. Available: v. 1 (1, 3) 1937; v. 2 (1-2), v. 10-14, 1946-48. BCH-961 2 – 8 – ne IDC [480]
WEN-CH'ANG HSIEN-CHIH – 1858, 16. BCH-638 2 – 8 – ne IDC [950]
WEN-CH'AO – (Literary Tide). v. 1-7. 1946. BCH-962 2 – 8 – ne IDC [480]
WENCHI, WENCHI CONGKAN = THE ARTICLES DIGEST – Oct 1945-Jun 1947. 2 reels. M-C64 – 1 – $68.00 – cc Microforms [073]
WEN-CHIAO-YUEH-PAO = FOREIGN AFFAIRS MONTHLY – v1-9, 1932-36. In Chinese – 10r – 1 – Y99,000.00 – ja Yushodo [327]
Wendebourg, W *see* LOUIS HARMS ALS MISSIONSMANN
Wendel, Friedrich *see* DAS NEUNZEHNTE JAHRHUNDERT IN DER KARIKATUR
Wendel, Hermann *see* HEINRICH HEINE
WENDELL 1763-1893 – (Mf 1: Birth & Marriage Indexes 1763-1844. Mf 1-2: Births & Marriages 1763-1844. Mf 3: Marriage Intentions 1787-1850. Mf 4: Marriage Intentions 1850-90. Mf 4: Deaths 1780-1844; Town Records 1823. Mf 5: Births & Marriages 1844-62. Mf 6: Deaths 1844-62. Mf 7: Births 1862-92. Mf 8: Marriages 1859-92. Mf 9: Deaths 1862-92) – (mf ed 1983) – 9mf – 0-931248-49-3 – us Holbrook [920]
WENDELL PHILLIPS : THE AGITATOR / Martyn, Carlos – London; New York: Funk & Wagnalls, 1890 – 2mf – us A.T.L.A. [240]
WENDINGEN – Amsterdam, 1918-31 – 4r b/w 1r col – 1,14 – £325.00 – uk Chadwyck [720]
WENDISCHES VOLKSTHUM IN SAGE, BRAUCH UND SITTE / Schulenburg, Wilibald von – 1882 – 1 – us I.U. Libraries [390]
Wendland, H L *see* BEITRAEGE ZUR BOTANIK
Wendland, J C *see*
- BOTANISCHE BEOBACHTUNGEN NEBST EINIGEN NEUEN GATTUNGEN UND ARTEN
- COLLECTIO PLANTARUM
- ERICARUM ICONES ET DESCRIPTIONES
- HORTUS HERRENHUSANUS, SEU PLANTAE RARIORES QUAE IN HORTO REGIO HERRENHUSANO
- SERTUM HANNOVERANUM
Wendland, Johannes *see* DIE RELIGIOESE ENTWICKLUNG SCHLEIERMACHERS
Wendland, Paul *see* EIN WORT DES HERAKLIT IM NEUEN TESTAMENT
Wendler, Otto Bernhard *see* SPUK UM MITTERNACHT
Wendling, Emil *see*
- GOETHES BUEHNENBEARBEITUNG VON "ROMEO UND JULIA"
- UR-MARCUS
Wendriner, Karl Georg *see* DER EINFLUSS VON GOETHES WILHELM MEISTER AUF DAS DRAMA DER ROMANTIKER
Wendt, Hans *see* STUBE 118
Wendt, Hans Hinrich *see*
- DER ERFAHRUNGSBEWEIS FUER DIE WAHRHEIT DES CHRISTENTHUMS
- THE IDEA AND REALITY OF REVELATION AND TYPICAL FORMS OF CHRISTIANITY
- KRITISCH EXEGETISCHES HANDBUCH UEBER DIE APOSTELGESCHICHTE
Wendt, Herbert *see* DER SCHWARZ-WEISS-ROTE KONTINENT
Wendte, Charles William *see* FREEDOM AND THE CHURCHES
Wendte, CW *see* THE YORKE-WENDTE CONTROVERSY
Wenger, Leopold *see* DER HEUTIGE STAND DER ROEMISCHEN RECHTSWISSENSCHAFT; ERREICHTES UND ERSTREBTES
WENG-YUAN HSIEN HSIN-CHIH – 1820, 12, 3. BCH-603 2 – 8 – ne IDC [950]
WENHAM 1642-1900 – (Mf 1-5: Vital Records & Index 1695-1743. Mf 6-7: Vital Records 1700-1810. Mf 8-9: Vital Records 1791-1844. Mf 10-13: Church Records 1644-83. Mf 14-15: Vital Records 1654-1799. Mf 16-23: Town Records 1642-1731. Mf 24-28: Town Records 1731-96. Mf 29-35: Tax Payers 1731-77. Mf 36-37: Rebellion Record 1861-66. Mf 38: Vital Records 1843-50. Mf 39-41: Index Vital Records 1851-1900. Mf 42-48: Vital Records 1851-1900) – (mf ed 1990) – 48mf – 0-87623-110-5 – us Holbrook [920]
WEN-HSUEH – Literature. v. 1-9 (14). Shanghai. 1934-37. monthly. Lacking: v. 9 (3-4) 1937. BCH-363 2 – 8 – ne IDC [480]
WEN-HSUEH CHI-K'AN – Literary Quarterly. 2 v. Peiping. 1934-35. BCH-364 2 – 8 – ne IDC [480]
WEN-HSUEH TSA-CHIH – Literary Magazine. Shanghai. (1-4). 1937, 1947-48. BCH-366 2 – 8 – ne IDC [480]
WEN-HSUEH YUEH-PAO – (Literature Monthly). 1940. Lacking: pt. 2. BCH-968 2 – 8 – ne IDC [480]
WEN-HUA T'U-SHU-KUAN CHUAN-K'O-HSUEH-HSIAO CHI-K'AN / Boone Library School – Quarterly. v. 1-9. Wuchang. 1929-37. Lacking: v. 1-3, 1929-31. BCH-368 2 – 8 – ne IDC [370]
WEN-HURA CHIEN-SHE – (Cultural construction). 3 v. Shanghai. 1934-36. monthly. Lacking: v. 1 (4-11) 1935; v. 2 (1-6, 8-12) 1935 36; v. 3 (1-12) 1937. BCH-367 1 – 9 – ne IDC [000]
WEN-I CHAN-HSIEN – (Literary Front). v. 1 (1-2). 1939. Lacking: v. 1 (2) 1939. BCH-967 2 – 8 – ne IDC [480]
WEN-I CHEN'TI – (Literary Battleground). v. 1-4. Hankow. 1938-39. BCH-963 2 – 8 – ne IDC [480]
WEN-I HSIN-CH'AO – (New Literary Tide). v. 1-2. Shanghai. 1938. Lacking: v. 2 – 8 – ne IDC [480]
WEN-I HSIN-CHI – (New Literary Collections). 1948. BCH-965 2 – 8 – ne IDC [480]
WEN-I HSIN-WEN – (Literary News). v. 1-6. 1939. Lacking: v. 1-5. BCH-966 2 – 8 – ne IDC [480]
Wenig, Richard *see* IN MONSUN UND PORI
Weninger, Alexander *see* DIE WUNDER VON LOURDES
Weninger, Francis Xavier *see*
- ANDACHTS-BUECHLEIN ZU EHREN DER ELF MARTYRER-SCHAAREN AUS DER GESELLSCHAFT JESU
- ANDACHTSBUECHLEIN ZU EHREN DER SECHSUNDZWANZIG [SIC] JAPANESISCHEN MARTYRER
- ANDACHTSBUECHLEIN ZU EHREN DER SELIGEN VIERZIG MARTIRER DER GESELLSCHAFT JESU, IGNATIUS AZEVEDO UND SEINER GEFAEHRTEN
- ANDACHTSBUECHLEIN ZU EHREN DER ZWEI SELIGEN, JOHANNES UND ANDREAS
- ANDACHTSBUECHLEIN ZU EHREN DES SELIGEN PETER CLAVER
- DIE APOSTOLISCHE VOLLMACHT DES PAPSTES IN GLAUBENS-ENTSCHEIDUNGEN
- CATECHISMI TRES SYSTEMATICE COORDINATI PRO PLENA JUVENTUTIS CHRISTIANAE INSTRUCTIONE
- CATHOLICITY, PROTESTANTISM AND INFIDELITY
- EASTER IN HEAVEN
- EPITOME PASTORALIS AD USUM CLERI IN STATIBUS FOEDERATIS AMERICAE
- ERNEUERUNG DER HEILIGEN MISSION IN ZWEI ABTHEILUNGEN
- DIE HEILIGE MISSION
- KATHOLICISMUS, PROTESTANTISMUS UND UNGLAUBE
- KLEINER KATECHISMUS DER CHRISTLICHEN LEHRE
- KLEINSTER KATECHISMUS ZUM NOTHWENDIGSTEN UNTERRICHT FUER DIE ERSTE KOMMUNION
- A MANUAL OF THE CATHOLIC RELIGION FOR CATECHISTS, TEACHERS AND SELFINSTRUCTION
- MODERN OBJECTIONS AGAINST THE CATHOLIC CHURCH, THE POPE AND THE JESUITS ANSWERED
- DER MONAT MARIAE
- ON PAPAL INFALLIBILITY
- ON THE APOSTOLICAL AND INFALLIBLE AUTHORITY OF THE POPE, WHEN TEACHING THE FAITHFUL
- ORIGINAL, SHORT AND PRACTICAL SERMONS FOR EVERY FEAST OF THE ECCLESIASTICAL YEAR
- ORIGINAL, SHORT AND PRACTICAL SERMONS FOR EVERY SUNDAY OF THE ECCLESIASTICAL YEAR
- ORIGINELLE, KURZ-GEFASSTE, PRAKTISCHE FASTEN-PREDIGTEN
- ORIGINELLE, KURZ-GEFASSTE, PRAKTISCHE FEST-PREDIGTEN ZU EHREN DER HL. APOSTEL, ORDENSSTIFTER, LANDES-PATRONE UND SCHUTZHEILIGEN
- ORIGINELLE, KURZ-GEFASSTE, PRAKTISCHE MARIANISCHE FEST-REDEN
- ORIGINELLE, KURZ-GEFASSTE, PRAKTISCHE PREDIGTEN ZU EHREN DES ALLERHEILIGSTEN SAKRAMENTES
- ORIGINELLE, KURZ-GEFASSTE, PRAKTISCHE SONNTAGS-PREDIGTEN FUER DAS GANZE KIRCHENJAHR
- ORIGINELLE, KURZ-GEFASSTE, PRAKTISCHE STANDESPREDIGTEN FUER EHEMAENNER, EHEFRAUEN, JUENGLINGE UND JUNGFRAUEN
- ORIGINELLE, KURZ-GEFASSTE, PRAKTISCHE STANDES-PREDIGTEN FUER EHEMAENNER, EHEFRAUEN, JUENGLINGE UND JUNG-FRAUEN
- OSTERN IM HIMMEL
- DIE PHARISAEER UND VERFOLGER DER KIRCHE IN UNSEREN TAGEN
- PHOTOGRAPHIC VIEWS
- PRAKTISCHE WINKE FUER MISSIONAERE
- SUMMA DOCTRINAE CHRISTIANAE IN USUM DOCENTIUM
- DIE UNFEHLBARKEIT DES PAPSTES ALS LEHRER DER KIRCHE
- WER IST DER PAPST, UND WER IST PIUS 9. UNTER DEN PAEPSTEN?
- ZUR SELIGSPRECHUNGS-FEIER DES SELIGEN PETER CANISIUS
WENJAMINOW UEBER DIE ALEUTISCHEN INSELN UND DEREN BEWOHNER / Lowe, F – BN 442 2. 1842 – 8 – ne IDC [306]
WENJI YUEKAN = LITERARY MONTHLY – 1936. 1 reel. M-C56 – 1 – $40.00 – cc Microforms [800]
Wenley, Robert Mark *see*
- MODERN THOUGHT AND THE CRISIS IN BELIEF
- SOCRATES AND CHRIST
WENLI PARTICLES / Brandt, J J – Peiping. 1929. BCH-935 2 – 8 – ne IDC [530]
"WENN DEIN ICH DENK". LISD FUER EINE SINGSTIMME MIT BEGLEITUNG DES PIANO / Schenk, L – (Original manuscript) – New York, 1881 – 1 – us Sibley [780]
Wenner, George Unangst *see* RELIGIOUS EDUCATION AND THE PUBLIC SCHOOL
Wennerberg, D K *see* THE EFFECT OF ADHESIVE ANKLE STRAPPING UPON ISOKINETIC STRENGTH AS MEASURED BY USE OF THE BIODEX DYNAMOMETER

WENO – Lincoln, NE. -w. Sep 1938-Feb 1940 – 1 – us NE Hist [071]

WEN-SHIH – (Literature and History). v. 1 (1-4). Peiping. 1934. Bi-monthly. BCH-369 1 – 9 – ne IDC [480]

WEN-SHI-ZHE – (1981-84 $3.50f; 1978-80, 1986- $4.50f) – Journal of Literature, History & Philosophy. Journal of Shandong University. In Chinese but Table of Contents in English in each issue. F p207 – 9 – cc Microforms [073]

Wensinck, A J *see* MYSTIC TREATISES BY ISAAC OF NINEVEH

Wensley. Yorkshire *see* PARISH REGISTERS

WENSLEYDALE ADVERTISER – Hawes, England. 2 Jan 1844-19 Dec 1848 – 1r – 1 – uk British Libr Newspaper [072]

Wente, Edward F *see* AN X-RAY ATLAS OF THE ROYAL MUMMIES

WENTWORTH ADVOCATE – Jun 2 1888-Jul 5 1888 – 1 – at Pascoe [072]

Wentworth and Co *see* GARDEN OF THE WORLD

Wentworth Historical Society *see* PAPERS AND RECORDS

Wentworth, W C *see* COLONIAL MICROFICHE

Wentzeke, P *see* MINERVA-HANDBUECHER

Wentzel, G *see* DIE GRIECHISCHE UEBERSETZUNG DER VIRI INLUSTRES DES HIERONYMUS (T.U.U. 1-13/3)

Wentzlaff-Eggebert, Friedrich-Wilhelm *see* LATEINISCHE UND DEUTSCHE JUGENDDICHTUNGEN

WENXUE = LITERATURE – Jul 1933-Nov 1937. 1 reel. M/C45 – 1 – $45.00 – cc Microforms [800]

WENXUE CONGBAO = LITERARY GAZETTE – Apr-Aug 1936. 6 fiches.F-C54 – 9 – $27.00 – cc Microforms [800]

WENXUE PINGLUN – (1978-81 $3.50f; 1982 $4.50f) – Literary Criticisms. In Chinese but Table of Contents in English in each issue. F p25 – 9 – cc Microforms [480]

WENXUE YICHAN – (1983-84 $3.50f; 1982, 1990- $4.50f) – Literature Heritage Quarterly. In Chinese but Table of Contents in English in each issue. F p26 – 9 – cc Microforms [480]

WENXUE YUEBAO = THE LITERARY MONTHLY – Jun-Dec 1932. 9 fiches.F-C44 – 9 – $40.50 – cc Microforms [800]

WENXUEBAO – Literature Press. China. In Chinese. Current subscription. Annual delivery. 1981- . 1r per yr. M D10 – 1 – $28.00r – cc Microforms [072]

WENYI = LITERATURE AND ART – Oct-Dec 1933. -m. 6 fiches. F-C46 – 9 – $27.00 – cc Microforms [800]

WENYI BAO – China. Journal of Literature. -w. 1986-. M-D109 – 1 – $28.00r – cc Microforms [480]

WENYI LILUN YANJIU – Theoretical Studies of Literature and Art. In Chinese but Table of Contents in English in each issue. F p28 – 9 – $3.50f – cc Microforms [480]

WENYI ZHANXIAN = THE ART AND LITERARY FRONT – Feb-Nov 1939. 3 fiches.F-C60 – 9 – $13.50 – cc Microforms [800]

WENYI ZHENDI = LITERATURE AND ART TRIBUNE – v1-5, no.2. Apr 1938-Aug 1940. 1 reel.M-C75 – 5 – $40.00 – cc Microforms [800]

Wenyon, C M *see* PROTOZOOLOGY, A MANUAL FOR MEDICAL MEN

WENYUANGE SIKU QUANSHU – Complete four-part Encyclopaedia of Wenyuan Studio. 573 reels. M/G 3 – 5 – $20,055.00 – cc Microforms [030]

Wenzel, Guido *see* FRIEDRICH HOELDERLIN UND JOHN KEATS ALS GEISTESVERWANDTE DICHTER

Wenzel, Gusztav *see* AZ EGYETEMES EUROPAI JOGTORTENETNEK ROVID VAZLATA

Wenzel, Natalja *see* RUSSISCHE FACHWORTSCHAETZE UND IHRE SEMANTIK

WENZHAI BAO = WEEKLY DIGEST – China. 1983-. M-D32 – 1 reel/y – 1 – $23.00r – cc Microforms [072]

Wenz-Hartmann, Gisela *see* DER WEG INS LICHT

WENZHOU RIBAO – China. Wenzhou Daily. 1985-. M-D96 – 1 reel/y – 1 – $55.00r – cc Microforms [072]

WEP RESEARCH WORKING PAPERS / International Labour Organisation – (1981. 55v. Sfr400.00; 1982. 36v. Sfr375.00; 1983. 47v. Sfr400.00; 1984. 18v. Sfr275.00; 1985. 21v. Sfr275.00; 1986. 27v. Sfr325.00; 1987. 39v. Sfr475.00; 1988. 23v. Sfr225.00; 1989. 37v. Sfr400.00; 1990. 38v. Sfr400.00 ; 1991. 32v. Sfr325.00; 1992. 27v. Sfr300.00; 1993. Sfr180.00) – 1974-80. 314v – 9 – Sfr2000.00 – sz I.L.O. [330]

Wepf, Louis *see* DIE OFFENBARUNG JOHANNIS INS LICHT GESTELLT

WER DIE WARHAIT WARLICH LIEB HAT, MAG SICH HIERINNE BRUFEN IM ERKANDTNUSZ SEYNES GLAUBENS / Denck, H – BME-62 1 – 9 – ne IDC [240]

WER HAT DAS CHRISTENTUM BEGRUENDET, JESUS ODER PAULUS / Meyer, Arnold – (In English) – London, New York:Harper & Brothers, 1909 – 1mf – 9 – 0-8370-4400-6 – 1985-2400 – us A.T.L.A. [240]

WER HAT DAS CHRISTENTUM BEGRUENDET, JESUS ODER PAULUS? / Meyer, Arnold – Tuebingen:(Paul Siebeck), 1907 – 1mf – 9 – 0-8370-4402-2 – 1985-2402l – us A.T.L.A. [240]

WER HAT DIE FUENF BUECHER MOSES VERFAS EINE HISTORISCH-KRITISCHE STUDIE / Finke, G – Leipzig: A. Deichert, 1900. 1 fiche – 9 – us A.T.L.A. [240]

WER IST DER PAPST, UND WER IST PIUS 9. UNTER DEN PAEPSTEN? : EINE FESTREDE / Weninger, Francis Xavier – Baltimore: Gebrueder Kreuzer, 1871 – 1mf – 9 – 0-8370-6874-6 – 1986-0874 – us A.T.L.A. [240]

WER WAR'S? : SCHWANK IN VIER AUFZUEGEN / Reitler, Marzellin Adalbert – Wien: Im Selbstverlage des Verfassers, 1881 – 1r – 1 – us U.W. Library [820]

WERAG/WESTFUNK – Koeln, dec 3 1920-may 26 1941 – 23r – 1 – gw Mikrofilm [790]

WERBEN UND VERKAUFEN – Muenchen, jan 11-jun 28, oct 4-dec 20 1985 – 1 – gw Mikrofilm [380]

WERBUNG IM RUNDFUNK – (Cont by: Media-Perspektiven, 1970) – Frankfurt/Main. 1963-93 – 12r – 1 – gw Mikrofilm [380]

WERBUNG IM RUNDFUNK *see* MEDIA-PERSPEKTIVEN

Werckmeister, A *see*
- CRIBRUM MUSICUM ODER MUSICALISCHES SIEB
- CRIBRVM MVSICVM ODER MUSICALISCHES SIEB
- ERWEITERTE UND VERBESSERTE ORGELPROBE
- ...ERWEITERTE UND VERBESSERTE ORGEL-PROBE.
- HARMONOLOGIA MUSICA, ODER KURTZE ANLEITUNG ZUR MUSICALISCHEN COMPOSITION
- HARMONOLOGIA MUSICA ODER KURTZE ANLEITUNG ZUR MUSICALISCHEN COMPOSITION
- HYPOMNEMATA MUSICA, ODER MUSIKALISCHES MEMORIAL/WELCHES BESTEHT IN KURTZER ERINNERUNG DESSEN
- MUSICAE MATHEMATICAE
- MUSICAE MATHEMATICAE HODEGUS CURIOSUS, ODER RICHTIGER MUSICALISCHER WEG-WEISER
- MUSICALISCHE PARODOXALDISCOURSE, ODER UNGEMEINE VORSTELLUNGEN
- DIE NOTHWENDIGSTEN ANMERCKUNGEN UND REGELN WIE DER BASSUS CONTINUUS ODER GENERAL-BASS WOL KOENNE TRACTIRET WERDEN
- ORGANUM GRUNINGENSE REDIVIVUM
- ORGEL-PROEF OF NAAUWKEURIGE BESCHRYVING VAN 'T GEENE DAT ER VOOR HET AANBESTEEDEN VAN NIEUWE EN TE RENOVEERENE OUDE ORGELS NODIG DIENE IN ACHT GENOMEN
- WERCKMEISTERS ERWEITERTE UND VERBESSERTE ORGELPROBE

WERCKMEISTERS ERWEITERTE UND VERBESSERTE ORGELPROBE / Werckmeister, A – Leipzig. 1754. BP-513 1 – 9 – ne IDC [780]

Werdelin, Ingvar *see* SCIENCE AND TECHNOLOGY IN THE PRIMARY SCHOOL OF TOMORROW

DAS WERDEN DES GRIMMELSHAUSENBILDES IM 19. UND 20. JAHRHUNDERT / Salditt, Barbara – (Includes bibliographical references) – Chicago: Distributed by the University of Chicago Libraries, 1933 – 1r – 1 – us U.W. Library [430]

Werfel, Franz *see*
- DER ABITURIENTENTAG
- EINE BLASSBLAUE FRAUENSCHRIFT
- BOCKSGESANG
- EINANDER
- GEDICHTE
- GEDICHTE AUS DREISSIG JAHREN
- DER GERICHTSTAG
- GESAENGE AUS DEN DREI REICHEN
- PAULUS UNTER DEN JUDEN
- POEMS
- DAS REICH GOTTES IN BOEHMEN
- DER VERUNTREUTE HIMMEL
- DIE VIERZIG TAGE DES MUSA DAGH
- VON DER REINSTEN GLUECKSELIGKEIT DES MENSCHEN
- DIE WAHRE GESCHICHTE VOM WIEDERHERGESTELLTEN KREUZ
- DER WELTFREUND
- WIR SIND

DAS WERK CONRAD FERDINAND MEYERS : RENAISSANCE-EMPFINDEN UND STILKUNST / Baumgarten, Franz Ferdinand – (Includes bibliographical references) – 2. durchges. Aufl. Muenchen: Georg Mueller, 1920. – 1r – 1 – us U.W. Library [430]

WERKE / Bach, Johann Sebastian – v. 1-46. 1851-1899 – 1 – 260.00 – us L of C Photodup [780]

WERKE / Beethoven, Ludwig van – v. 1-44. 1888 – 1 – 148.00 – us L of C Photodup [780]

WERKE / Berlioz, Hector – v. 1-20. 1900-07 – 1 – 74.00 – us L of C Photodup [780]

WERKE / Brentano, Clemens; ed by Preitz, Max – Leipzig: Bibliographisches Institut. 3v. 1914 – 1 – us U.W. Library [800]

WERKE / Chamisso, Adelbert von – 2. Aufl. Leipzig: Weidmann. 6v. 1842 – 1 – us U.W. Library [800]

WERKE / Handel, George Frederic – v. 1-100. 1858-92 – 1 – 260.00 – us L of C Photodup [780]

WERKE / Hoelderlin, Friedrich; ed by Schneider, Manfred – Stuttgart: Walter Haedecke. 4v. 1921 – 1 – us U.W. Library [800]

WERKE / Kleist, Heinrich von – Berlin: Gustav Hempel, [18–] – 1 – us U.W. Library [800]

WERKE / Lessing, Gotthold Ephraim – Hrsg. von G. Witkowski. Kritisch durchgesehene und erlaeuterte Ausg. Leipzig, Bibliographisches Instit, 1911. 7 v. (Meyers Klassiker-Ausgaben) Film Mas C 714 – 1 – us H.U. Library [800]

WERKE / Mendelssohn, Felix – Fritisch durchgesehene Ausgabe von Julius Reitz. Mit genehmigung der Originalverlager. Leipzig. 1874-77. 42 v – 1 – 125.00 – us L of C Photodup [780]

WERKE : MIT VIELEN HOLZSCHNITTEN UND BILDERN NACH KUPFERSTICHEN VON CHODOWIECKI / Claudius, Matthias – Dresden: O Guenther. 2v. [1938] – 1 – us U.W. Library [800]

WERKE / Scheffel, Joseph Viktor von – Hrsg. von Friedrrich Panzer. Kritisch durchgesehene und erlaeuterte Ausg. Leipzig, Bibliographisches Institut, 1919. 4v. (Meyers Klassiker-Ausgaben) Film Mas 8593 – 1 – us H.U. Library [800]

WERKE / Storm, Theodor – Bremen-Horn: Walter Dorn, 1948-1950 – 1 – us U.W. Library [800]

WERKE = WORKS / Jean Paul – Berlin: G Hempel, [1879?] – 1 – us U.W. Library [430]

WERKE = WORKS / Wildermuth, Ottilie – 1. Gesammt-Ausg. Stuttgart: Adolf Krabbe. 8v. 1862 – 1 – us U.W. Library [800]

DIE WERKE DER HADEWIJCH AUS DEM ALTFLAEMISCHEN – (UEbersetzt von J.O. Plassman) – Hannover, 1923 – 4mf – 8 – ne Slangenburg [290]

DIE WERKE DES KONRAD VON MEGENBERG (MGH 10: 2.BD) : 1. STUECK: PLANCTUS ECCLESIAE IN GERMANIAM – 1941 – Dfl19.00 – ne Slangenburg [240]

WERKE UND BRIEFE / Wackenroder, Wilhelm Heinrich; ed by Leyen, Friedrich von der – Jena: E Diederich, 1910 – 1 – us U.W. Library [430]

WERKEN / Obrecht, Jacob – 24v. 1908-21 – 1 – 46.00 – us L of C Photodup [780]

DE WERKEN DER MARNIX-VEREENIGING – (Titles also listed individually) – Serie 1-3. 11 Dln. Utrecht, 1870-1889 – Dfl242.00 set – ne Slangenburg [240]

DE WERKEN DER MARNIX-VEREENIGING *see*
- ACTA VAN DE NEDERLANDSCHE SYNODEN DER ZESTIENDE EEUW (DE WERKEN..2,3)
- ACTEN VAN DE CLASSICALE EN SYNODALE VERGADERINGEN DER VERSCHILLENDEN GEMEENTEN IN HET LAND VAN CLEEF, STICHT VAN KEULEN EN AKEN 1571-1589 (DE WERKEN..2,2)
- ACTEN VAN DE COLLOQUIA DER NEDERLANSCHE GEMEENTEN IN ENGELAND 1575-1624 (DE WERKEN..2,1)
- BESCHEIDEN AANGAANDE DE KERKHERVORMING IN VLAANDEREN (DE WERKEN..3,3)
- BRIEVEN UIT ONDERSCHEIDENE KERKELIJKE ARCHIEVEN (DE WERKEN..3,2)
- BRIEVEN UIT ONDERSCHEIDENE KERKELIJKE ARCHIEVEN (DE WERKEN..3,4)
- GESCHIEDENISSEN ENDE HANDELINGEN.DER NEDERDUYTSCHE NATIE IN ENGELANT (DE WERKEN..3,1)
- HANDELINGEN VAN DE KERKERAAD DER NEDERL. GEMEENTE TE KEULEN, 1571-1591 (DE WERKEN..1,3)
- KERKERAADS-PROTOCOLLEN DER HOLLANDSCHE GEMEENTE TE LONDEN 1569-1571 (DE WERKEN..1,1)
- STUKKEN BETR. DE DIACONIE DER VREEMDELINGEN TE EMDEN 1560-1576 (DE WERKEN..1,2)

Werkheiser, Don *see*
- IS IT POSSIBLE TO SURVIVE?
- ON NEW HUMAN RELATIONS

WERKINTERPRETATIONEN ZUR DEUTSCHEN LITERATUR / Hartmann, Horst et al – (Includes bibliographical references) – Berlin: Volk und Wissen, 1986 – 1r – 1 – us U.W. Library [430]

WERKMEISTER-ZEITUNG – Duesseldorf, Germany. 1904-June, 1934 – 1 – gw Mikrofilm [072]

WERKSMEISTER-ZEITUNG – Duesseldorf, 1904-Jun 1934 – 1 – DM1,710.00 – gw Mikro Press [072]

WERKSTATTSTECHNIK – v39-70 1949-80 – 1,5,9 – $2304.00 – us UMI [740]

WERKSTOFFE UND KORROSION *see* MATERIALS AND CORROSION

DER WERKVEREIN – Essen-Ruhr, 1914-18 – 2r – 1 – DM150.00 – gw Mikro Press [072]

DER WERKVEREIN – Essen-Ruhr, Germany. 1914-18 – 1 – gw Mikrofilm [073]

Werminghoff, Albert *see*
- GESCHICHTE DER KIRCHENVERFASSUNG DEUTSCHLANDS IM MITTELALTER
- VERFASSUNGSGESCHICHTE DER DEUTSCHEN KIRCHE IM MITTELALTER

WERMLANDS LAENS TIDNING – Karlstad, 1871-79 – 9 – sw Kungliga [072]

WERMLANDS LANS ANNONSBLAD – Filipstad, Sweden. 1895-99 – 2r – 1 – sw Kungliga [072]

WERMLANDS TIDNING *see* NYA WERMLANDSTIDNINGEN

WERMLANDSTIDNINGEN *see* NYA WERMLANDSTIDNINGEN

Werne, Ferdinand *see* EXPEDITION TO DISCOVER THE SOURCES OF THE WHITE NILE, IN THE YEARS 1840, 1841

Werner, A *see* INTRODUCTORY SKETCH OF THE BANTU LANGUAGES

Werner, A G *see* NEW THEORY OF THE FORMATION OF VEINS; WITH ITS APPLICATION TO THE ART OF WORKING MINES

Werner, E *see*
- GEBANNT UND ERLOEST
- GLUECK AUF!
- SANKT MICHAEL
- SIEGWART
- VINETA

Werner, Eugene *see* MEDITATIONS SUR LA VIE DE L'APOTRE SAINT-PIERRE

Werner, J *see* DER PAULINISMUS DES IRENAEUS (T.U.U. 1-6/2)

Werner, K *see*
- DIE SCHOLASTIK DES SPAETEREN MITTELALTERS

Werner, Karl *see* ALCUIN UND SEIN JAHRHUNDERT

[WERNER MAIHOFER: PAMPHLET COLLECTION] – 1974? – 1 – CSUXANS3220-B – us Hoover Inst Photo [320]

Werner, Max *see* DAS CHRISTENTUM UND DIE MONISTISCHE RELIGION

[WERNER NAUMANN PAMPHLET COLLECTION] – 1953 – 1 – CSUXANR9553-B – us Hoover Inst Photo [320]

Werner, R M *see* LUSTIGE REYSS-BESCHREIBUNG AUS SALTZBURG IN VERSCHIEDENE LAENDER

Werner, Richard Maria *see* LESSINGS EMILIA GALOTTI
Werner-Ferrel, Sally D *see* A COMPARISON OF THE RATIO OF SHOULDER CONCENTRIC INTERNAL ROTATION TO ECCENTRIC EXTERNAL ROTATION OF MALE SWIMMERS VS. NONSWIMMERS
Wernerian Natural History Society. Edinburgh *see* MEMOIRS
Wernischeck, J J *see* GENERA PLANTARUM
Wernle, Paul *see*
- DIE ANFAENGE UNSERER RELIGION
- CALVIN UND BASEL BIS ZUM TODE DES MYCONIUS, 1535-1552
- DER CHRIST UND DIE SUENDE BEI PAULUS
- EINFUEHRUNG IN DAS THEOLOGISCHE STUDIUM
- EVANGELISCHES CHRISTENTUM IN DER GEGENWART
- QUELLEN DES LEBENS JESU
- DIE REICHSGOTTESHOFFNUNG IN DEN AELTESTEN CHRISTLICHEN DOKUMENTEN UND BEI JESUS
- RENAISSANCE UND REFORMATION
- THE SOURCES OF OUR KNOWLEDGE OF THE LIFE OF JESUS
- DIE SYNOPTISCHE FRAGE
- WAS HABEN WIR HEUTE AN PAULUS?

WERRA-RUNDSCHAU – Eschwege, West Germany. 1 Jun 1969- – 1 – gw Mikrofilm [072]
Werrekoren, H M *see* DIE SCHLACHT VOR PAVIA LA BATTAGLIA TALIANA A QUATRO VOCI, COMPOSTA DA M. MATHIAS FIAMENGO, MAESTRO DI CAPELLA DEL DOMO DI MILANO, CON ALCUNE VILLOTTE PIACEVOLE NOVAMENTE CON OGNI DILIGENTIA STAMPATE, E CORRETTE
Wertheimer, E von *see* GRAF JULIUS ANDRASSY. SEIN LEBEN UND SEINE ZEIT
Werther, C Waldemar *see* ZUM VICTORIA NYANZA; EINE ANTISKLAVEREI-EXPEDITION UND FORSCHUNGSREISE
Werther, Richard *see* DAS APOSTOLICUM
WERTSYSTEME VON ENGLISCHLEHRERN : EINE KRITISCHE ANALYSE ALLTAEGLICHEN ENGLISCHUNTERRICHTS / Hart, Hans-Ulrich – 1992 – 225p – DM98.00 – 3-89349-472-3 – gw Hänsel [370]
WERTURTEILE UND GLAUBENSURTEILE: EINE UENTERSUCHUNG / Reischle, Max – Halle a.S.: Max Niemeyer, 1900. 1 fiche – 9 – us A.T.L.A. [240]
WESCOLITE – Dillon. Mont. 1928- – 1 – us UMI [071]
DAS WESEN DER FARRENKRAEUTER / Kaulfuss, G F – Leipzig. 1827. B-7207 1 – 9 – ne IDC [580]
DAS WESEN DER RELIGION / Bousset, Wilhelm – 3. Aufl, Volksausg. 6. Halle a. S: Gebauer-Schwetschke, 1906 – 1mf – 9 – 0-8370-2426-9 – 1985-0426 – us A.T.L.A. [200]
WESEN DER RELIGION = WHAT IS RELIGION? / Bousset, Wilhelm – (In English. Includes index) – 1mf – 9 – 0-8370-2427-7 – 1985-0427 – us A.T.L.A. [200]
DAS WESEN DER RELIGION NACH ERASMUS UND LUTHER : VORTRAG / Walter, Johannes von – Leipzig: A. Deichert, 1906 – 1mf – us A.T.L.A. [240]
DAS WESEN DES CHRISTENTUMS / Harnack, Adolf von – Leipzig: J.C. Hinrichs, 1905. 1 fiche – 9 – us A.T.L.A. [240]
DAS WESEN DES PROTESTANTISMUS : AUS DEN QUELLEN DES REFORMATIONSZEITALTERS / Schenkel, Daniel – (Includes bibliographical references) – 2. Aufl. Schaffhausen: Brodtmann, 1862 – 2mf – 9 – 0-8370-8864-X – 1986-2864 – us A.T.L.A. [240]
DAS WESEN DES SACHENRECHTS IN GEGENUEBERSTELLUNG ZUM SCHULDRECHT UNTER DEM BESONDEREN ASPEKT EINER ERFASSUNG DES ABSTRAKTIONSPRINZIPS / Moellers, Martin – 1992 – viii/208p – 9 – DM98.00 – gw Hänsel [340]
DAS WESEN DES VOELKERRECHTLICHEN MANDATS... / Fulda, U – Marburg, 1934 – 1mf – 1 – ILM-1959/1 – ne IDC [327]
WESEN UND URSPRUNG DER STATUS CONSTRUCTUS IM HEBRAEISCHEN : EIN BEITRAG ZUR NOMINALFLEXION IM SEMITISCHEN / Philippi, Friedrich Wilhelm Martin – (Includes bibliographical references and index) – Weimar: Hermann Boehlau, 1871 – 1mf – 9 – 0-8370-9262-0 – 1986-3262 – us A.T.L.A. [470]
WESEN UND URSPRUNG DES KATHOLIZISMUS / Sohm, Rudolf – Leipzig: B.G. Teubner, 1912 – 2mf – us A.T.L.A. [240]
WESER BOTE – Bremen, Germany.23 Jun-15 Sept 1945 – 1 – gw Mikrofilm [072]
WESER BOTE – Bremen, jun 23-sep 15 1945 – 1r – 1 – Inquire at Mikrofilmarchiv for details – gw Misc Inst [943]
WESER ZEITUNG – (Cont: Weser-Zeitung, 1844-48. Bremer Weser-Zeitung, -mar 4 1849. Cont by: Weser-Zeitung mit Bremer Nachrichten, oct 1 1934. oct 1 1934-aug 31 1944 publ as a weekly. Suppl available: Sonntagsblatt, feb 18 1844-feb 27 1848, jan-nov 1851; Bunte Truhe, 1919-42. Ausgabe fuer Ausland und Uebersee: 1866-70, 1934-36, 1938-42) – Bremen, 1844-1936, 1938-42 – 1 – Inquire at Mikrofilmarchiv for details – gw Misc Inst [943]
WESER ZEITUNG *see* WESER-ZEITUNG
WESER-DAMPFBOOT – Minden, Germany. 1844 – 1 – gw Mikrofilm [072]
WESERDAMPFBOOT – Bielefeld, 1844 – 1 – Inquire at Mikrofilmarchiv for details – gw Misc Inst [072]
WESER-KURIER – (Also suppl available: Stadtteil-Umschau, oct 1 1981- . Also Bereichsausgaben available. ACHIM, Achimer Kurier, fe 8 1972-) – Bremen, sep 19 1945- – 1 – Inquire at Mikrofilmarchiv for details – gw Misc Inst [072]
WESER-KURIER – Bremen, Germany. Sept 1945-Oct 1949; Jul 1967-Apr 1968; Nov 1973-Jul 1991 – 220r – 1 – us L of C Photodup [072]
WESER-KURIER – Bremen, West Germany. 1945- – 1 – gw Mikrofilm [072]
WESERMUENDER NEUESTE NACHRICHTEN *see* PROVINZIALZEITUNG
WESER-SONNTAGSBLATT – Bremen, Germany.1844-Feb 1848 – 1 – gw Mikrofilm [072]
WESER-WARTE – Bremen, aug 6 1929-aug 2 1930 – 1r – 1 – Inquire at Mikrofilmarchiv for details – gw Misc Inst [072]
WESER-WARTE – Bremen, Germany.6 Aug 1929-2 Aug 1930 – 1 – gw Mikrofilm [072]
WESER-ZEITUNG – (Cont by: Bremer Weser-Zeitung, jan 1, 1849. Weser Zeitung, mar 5, 1849. Weser-Zeitung mit Bremer Nachrichten, oct 1, 1934. Since oct 1, 1934 as a weekly) – Bremen. 1844-jun 30, 1846. jul 1, 1847-mar 31, 1848. jul 1, 1848-1936. jan 5, 1938-42 – 258r – 1 – gw Mikrofilm [072]
WESER-ZEITUNG *see* WESER ZEITUNG
WESER-ZEITUNG MIT BREMER NACHRICHTEN – Bremen, Germany.1934-36; 1938-42 – 1 – gw Mikrofilm [072]
WESER-ZEITUNG MIT BREMER NACHRICHTEN *see*
- WESER ZEITUNG
- WESER-ZEITUNG

WESLEY AND GOETHE / Bashford, James Whitford – Cincinnati: Jennings and Pye; New York: Eaton and Mains, c1903 – 1mf – us A.T.L.A. [200]
WESLEY AND HIS COLABORERS / Larrabee, William Clark – 1851 – 9 – us A.T.L.A. [240]
WESLEY AND HIS WORK, OR, METHODISM AND MISSIONS : A VOLUME OF ADDRESSES / Candler, Warren A – Nashville, Tenn.: Publishing House of the M.E. Church, South: Smith & Lamar [distributor], 1912 – 1mf – us A.T.L.A. [240]
WESLEY, AND METHODISM / Taylor, Isaac – London: Longman, Brown, Green, and Longmans, 1851 – 1mf – us A.T.L.A. [240]
THE WESLEY BANNER AND REVIVAL RECORD – (Missing: 1852, V.4(p. 233-240)) – London, 1849-1852. V.1-4 – 22mf – 9 – MP-354/1 – ne IDC [240]
WESLEY BIBLIOGRAPHY / Green, Richard – 1733-91 – 1 – 11.93 – us Baptist [240]
Wesley, Charles *see*
- DIARIES AND POCKET-BOOKS, 1772, 1805, 1809-1810, 1815, 1817, 1822
- IN-LETTERS, 1735-1787
- IN-LETTERS, 1737-1786
- IN-LETTERS, 1742-1788
- IN-LETTERS, 1752-1783
- IN-LETTERS, 1789-1828
- IN-LETTERS FROM METHODIST PREACHERS ON RELIGIOUS EXPERIENCE, 1738-1788
- OUT-LETTERS, 1728-1787
- OUT-LETTERS, 1733-1787
- OUT-LETTERS, 1739-1766
- OUT-LETTERS, 1740-1783
- OUT-LETTERS, 1748-1787
- OUT-LETTERS, 1788-1830
- OUT-LETTERS, 1795-1833
- THE POETICAL WORKS OF JOHN AND CHARLES WESLEY
- STRICTURES ON THE SUBSTANCE OF A SERMON PREACHED AT BALTIMORE...

Wesley, John *see*
- EXPLANATORY NOTES UPON THE OLD TESTAMENT
- THE POETICAL WORKS OF JOHN AND CHARLES WESLEY

Wesley, Martha *see* DIARY AND MEMORANDA BOOK, 1730-1759
Wesley, S *see* A MORNING AND EVENING CHURCH SERVICE IN F
Wesley, Sally *see*
- IN- AND OUT-LETTERS, 1776-1826
- IN- AND OUT-LETTERS, 1780-1823
- IN-LETTERS, 1775-1820
- IN-LETTERS, 1780-1827
- OUT-LETTERS, 1788-1826
- OUT-LETTERS AND POEMS, 1775-1828

Wesley, Samuel *see*
- ANTHEMS
- MANUSCRIPT SERMONS, 1710-1723, 1730-1734
- OUT-LETTERS AND MISCELLANEOUS PAPERS, 1772-1835
- OUT-LETTERS AND MISCELLANEOUS PAPERS, 1785-1835

Wesley, Sarah *see*
- IN- AND OUT-LETTERS, 1750-1815
- IN-LETTERS, 1749-1789
- IN-LETTERS, 1749-1810
- IN-LETTERS, 1756-1812
- IN-LETTERS, 1776-1816
- OUT-LETTERS, 1789-1797
- OUT-LETTERS AND MISCELLANEOUS PAPERS, 1754-1816

THE WESLEYAN – Montreal: Printed for the Committee... by J.E.L. Miller, v1 no 1 (Aug 6 1840)- – 9 – cn C.I.H.M. [240]
WESLEYAN – Halifax, Canada. 1838-84 – 15r – 1 – $975.00 – cn Library Assoc [971]
WESLEYAN ADVOCATE – (Lacking: v21-23; v30-33. 1863-65; 1972-75. Title varies) – v1-109. 1843-1976 – 72r – 1 – ATLA S0241 – us A.T.L.A. [073]
WESLEYAN AND TRACTARIAN WORSHIP / Dearing, F – London, 1966 – 3mf – 8 – Dfl13.00 – ne Slangenburg [240]
WESLEYAN CHRISTIAN ADVOCATE – Macon, GA. v41-119. Jul 1878-Mar 1957 (complete) – 80r – 1 – ATLA S0034 – us A.T.L.A. [073]
WESLEYAN CHRONICLE – Melbourne, Australia. 1 Jan 1861-20 Apr 1875 – 4 1/2r – 1 – uk British Libr Newspaper [072]
THE WESLEYAN DAILY RECORDER / Wesleyan Methodist Church in Canada. Conference – (Cont by: The Daily Recorder) – Toronto: [s.n. 1869-1870] – 9 – cn C.I.H.M. [240]
THE WESLEYAN DAILY RECORDER *see* THE DAILY RECORDER
Wesleyan Education Committee. Great Britain *see* ANNUAL REPORTS
WESLEYAN LOCAL PREACHERS : BIOGRAPHICAL ILLUSTRATIONS OF THEIR POSITION IN THE CONNEXION, UTILITY IN THE CHURCH, AND INFLUENCE IN THE WORLD / Lawson, W D – Newcastle-upon-Tyne, 1874. xvi/334p – 4mf – 9 – ne IDC [240]
WESLEYAN LOCAL PREACHERS : BIOGRAPHICAL ILLUSTRATIONS OF THEIR POSITION IN THE CONNEXION, UTILITY IN THE CHURCH, AND INFLUENCE IN THE WORLD – Newcastle-upon-Tyne, 1874 – 4mf – 9 – ne IDC [240]
WESLEYAN MANUAL / Lee, Luther – 1862 – 9 – us A.T.L.A. [240]
WESLEYAN METHODISM REGARDED AS THE SYSTEM OF A CHRISTIAN CHURCH / Rule, William Harris – London: Aylott and Jones, 1846 – 1mf – us A.T.L.A. [240]
THE WESLEYAN METHODIST – (Cont: Toronto Periodical Journal, or, Wesleyan Methodist) – Toronto: [s.n. 1845-18–?] – 9 – cn C.I.H.M. [240]
THE WESLEYAN METHODIST *see*
- TORONTO PERIODICAL JOURNAL, OR, WESLEYAN METHODIST
- WESLEYAN ADVOCATE

Wesleyan Methodist Association *see* ASSEMBLY. MINUTES...
WESLEYAN METHODIST ASSOCIATION MAGAZINE – (Coll title: The People Called Methodists, Phase 3: Primary Sources, 1801-1850) – London. v1-20. 1838-1857 – 132mf – 9 – MP-352/1 – ne IDC [240]
WESLEYAN METHODIST CHURCH : CONFERENCE. MINUTES... – (Missing: 1812; 1815; 1819; 1836; 1840; 1844) – London, Bristol, 1791-1850 – 88mf – 9 – MP-345/1 – ne IDC [240]
Wesleyan Methodist Church *see* CONFERENCE. MINUTES...
Wesleyan Methodist Church in Canada. Conference *see* THE WESLEYAN DAILY RECORDER
Wesleyan Methodist Church in Canada. Missionary Society *see* WESLEYAN MISSIONARY NOTICES, CANADA CONFERENCE
WESLEYAN METHODIST CHURCH IN CANADA. MISSIONARY SOCIETY. WESLEYAN MISSIONARY NOTICES, CANADA CONFERENCE *see* MISSIONARY NOTICES OF THE METHODIST CHURCH OF CANADA
WESLEYAN METHODIST CONNEXION : A CHRONOLOGICAL AND ALPHABETICAL LIST OF ALL THE ITINERANT METHODIST PREACHERS IN THE CONNEXION OF THE LATE REV. JOHN WESLEY, AND WITH THE METHODIST CONFERENCE IN THE YEAR 1814 – Exeter, [1814] – 1mf – 9 – ne IDC [240]
WESLEYAN METHODIST MAGAZINE : AN INDEX TO THE MEMOIRS, OBITUARIES AND BIOGRAPHIES AS CONTAINED IN THE WESLEYAN METHODIST MAGAZINES, 1840 TO 1932 / ed by Leary, William – Chester, 1984 – 2mf – 9 – ne IDC [240]
WESLEYAN METHODIST MAGAZINE : AN INDEX TO THE MEMOIRS, OBITUARY NOTICES AND RECENT DEATHS, TOGETHER WITH THE REFERENCES TO THE LOCAL HISTORIES OF METHODISM ,... / Jackson, Francis Marris – 2mf – 9 – ne IDC [240]
WESLEYAN METHODIST MAGAZINE : AN INDEX TO THE MEMOIRS, OBITUARY NOTICES AND RECENT DEATHS, TOGETHER WITH THE REFERENCES TO THE LOCAL HISTORIES OF METHODISM,... / Jackson, Francis Marris – (Supplement) – v7. 1909-1910 – 2mf – 9 – ne IDC [240]
THE WESLEYAN METHODIST MAGAZINE OF CANADA – Toronto: A Green, 1862 – 9 – cn C.I.H.M. [240]
WESLEYAN MISSIONARY NOTICES *see* MISSIONARY NOTICES, RELATING PRINCIPALLY TO THE FOREIGN MISSIONS, ESTABLISHED BY WESLEY AND COKE...THE METHODIST CONFERENCE
WESLEYAN MISSIONARY NOTICES, CANADA CONFERENCE / Wesleyan Methodist Church in Canada. Missionary Society – (Cont by: Missionary Notices of the Methodist Church of Canada) – Toronto: Wesleyan Conference Office, [1854-1874] – 9 – cn C.I.H.M. [240]
Wesleyan Reform Union *see* ORIGIN AND HISTORY OF THE WESLEYAN REFORM UNION, WITH A BRIEF SUMMARY OF METHODIST SECESSIONS
WESLEYAN REPOSITORY – v1-3. 15 Feb 1821-Apr 1824 (complete) – 1r – 1 – ATLA S0171 – us A.T.L.A. [073]
THE WESLEYAN REPOSITORY AND LITERARY RECORD – Toronto: A Green, [1860-18–?] – 9 – cn C.I.H.M. [240]
WESLEYAN TAKINGS; OR, CENTENARY SKETCHES OF MINISTERIAL CHARACTER, AS EXHIBITED IN THE WESLEYAN CONNEXION DURING THE FIRST HUNDRED YEARS OF ITS EXISTENCE / [Everett, J] – London. 2v. 1840-1851 – 11mf – 9 – ne IDC [240]
Wesleyan Theological Institution *see* A CATALOGUE OF BOOKS AND MANUSCRIPTS PRESENTED TO THE WESLEYAN THEOLOGICAL INSTITUTION, IN THE YEAR MDCCCLIX, BY J. HEALD, ESQ.
WESLEYAN THEOLOGICAL JOURNAL – (v.16-. 1981-. 5,6,9) – v.1-. 1966- – 1 – us UMI [240]
THE WESLEYAN-METHODIST MISSIONS IN JAMAICA AND HONDURAS DELINEATED : CONTAINING A DESCRIPTION OF THE PRINCIPAL STATIONS, TOGETHER WITH A CONSECUTIVE ACCOUNT OF THE RISE AND PROGRESS OF THE WORK OF GOD AT EACH / Samuel, Peter – London: Partridge & Oakey, 1850 – 1mf – us A.T.L.A. [240]
WESLEY'S WORLD PARISH : A SKETCH OF THE HUNDRED YEARS' WORK OF THE WESLEYAN METHODIST MISSIONARY SOCIETY / Findlay, George G & Findlay, Mary Grace – New York: Hodder and Stoughton, [1913?] – 1mf – us A.T.L.A. [240]
WESMORE COMPANY HISTORICAL SOCIETY NEWS – Greensburg, PA., 1818-1866 – 13 – $25.00r – us I.M.R. [071]
Wesselski, Albert *see* DER HODSCHA NASREDDIN

Wessely, N H *see*
- DIVREI SHALOM VE-EMET
- SHIREI TIFERET

Wessen, Marta *see*
- REVELATIONES S. BIRGITTAE

Wessenberg, I *see* RITUAL NACH DEM GEISTE UND DEN ANORDNUNGEN DER KATHOLISCHEN KIRCHE

Wessenberg, Ignaz Heinrich, Freiherr von *see* BETRACHTUNGEN UEBER DIE VERHAELTNISSE DER KATHOLISCHEN KIRCHE IM UMFANGE DES DEUTSCHEN BUNDES

WESSEX POEMS AND OTHER VERSES / Hardy, Thomas – [London, New York: Harper, 1898] – 1 roll – 1 – 1-55879-758-0 – uk Libr Preservation [810]

DE WEST – Surinam. 1909-1961 also 1967-1968 – 1 – us UMI [072]

THE WEST – Florence. Or. -w. 1893-96, 1901-21 – 1 – us UMI [071]

THE WEST – Florence, OR. -w. 1893-96, 1902-21 – 1 – 113.00 – us Oregon Hist [071]

THE WEST – Regina, Canada. 19 Dec 1906-28 Dec 1910 – 3 1/2r – 1 – uk British Libr Newspaper [072]

WEST – Florence, OR. -w. 2 rolls. 9 Oct 1891-24 Mar 1893; 17 Jul 1896-27 Dec 1901 – 1 – us U.O. Library [071]

West, Aaron *see* PAPERS

WEST AFRICA – London, 1917- – 2r per y – 1 – inquire – us Ross [072]

WEST AFRICA – London, England, 1932-67 – 38r – 1 – us Ross [072]

WEST AFRICA – London, Jan 1943-Dec 1964 – 30r – 1 – uk British Libr Newspaper [072]

WEST AFRICA – London, UK. 1970-1993 – 42r – $2,100.00 – R63566 – us Library Micro [072]

WEST AFRICA – (Missing: 1917(1-26)) – London. v1-50. 1917-66 – 2461mf – 9 – A-238/2 – ne IDC [960]

WEST AFRICA – (Stm available to date) – 1917-to date – to 1990 112r – 1 – uk Microform Academic [073]

WEST AFRICA AND TRADER'S REVIEW – London. -w. May 1900-Dec 1906. (9 reels) – 1 – uk British Libr Newspaper [072]

WEST AFRICA AND TRADERS' REVIEW – London. v1-4 n1-106 may 1900-02; v6 n133-158 jul-dec 1903 – us Res Libr [380]

West Africa Mission. (Pres. Ch. in the U.S.A.) *see* SELECTED DOCUMENTS

WEST AFRICA TIMES – (Times of West Africa). Accra. Ghana. -d. Mar 1931-Mar 1935. (5 reels) – 1 – uk British Libr Newspaper [072]

WEST AFRICAN GAZETTE – Accra. Ghana. -w. 8 Feb-7 Mar 1896. (5 ft) – 1 – uk British Libr Newspaper [072]

West African Institute of Social and Economic Research. Ibadan *see* CONFERENCE PROCEEDINGS

WEST AFRICAN JOURNAL OF EDUCATION – v1- 1957- 1; v21- 5,6,9 – us UMI [370]

WEST AFRICAN MAIL – (African Mail). Liverpool. England. -w. Apr 1903-Jan 1917. (19 reels) – 1 – uk British Libr Newspaper [072]

THE WEST AFRICAN MONITOR – (Library has 38 no. issued between Feb. 10, 1948 and Jan. 24, 1951) – Cape Coast, Ghana: Monitor, 194u – 1 – CSUX86-S88 – us Hoover Inst Photo [960]

WEST AFRICAN POLITICAL EPHEMERA: MISCELLANEOUS POLITICAL PUBLICATIONS – 1948-62 – 1 – us Res Libr [960]

WEST AFRICAN REPORTER – Freetown. Sierra Leone. -w. Jul 1876-Dec 1877, Jan 1879-Dec 1884. (3 reels) – 1 – uk British Libr Newspaper [072]

West African Students' Union of Great Britain and Ireland *see* WASU MAGAZINE

WEST AMERICAN SHELLS / Keep, J – Z-595 2. 1904 – 8 – ne IDC [590]

West, Anson *see* THE OLD AND THE NEW MAN, OR, SIN AND SALVATION

WEST AUSTRALIAN – Perth, Australia. Nov 1879-May 1940; 14 Jan-15 Mar 1941; 1 Oct 1957-29 Jun 1963; 30 Mar-20 Jul, 21 Dec 1964-8 Apr 1965; Nov 1965-Jun 1975 (missing 1889-95).-w,d. 628 reels – 1 – uk British Libr Newspaper [072]

WEST AUSTRALIAN MINING, BUILDING AND ENGINEERING JOURNAL – Perth, Australia. 11 Apr 1903-8 Dec 1917 (1913-17 very imperfect). -w – 12r – 1 – uk British Libr Newspaper [622]

WEST AUSTRALIAN TIMES – Perth, Australia. -w. 14 Jan-29 Sept 1864. 30 ft – 1 – uk British Libr Newspaper [072]

THE WEST BANK AND THE RULE OF LAW / Shehadeh, Kuttab – 1980 – sz I.C.J. [320]

West Bengal. India. Development Department *see*
- SECOND FIVE YEAR PLAN OF WEST BENGAL ANNUAL PLAN, 1958-59
- SECOND FIVE-YEAR PLAN OF WEST BENGAL PROGRAMME FOR 1956-57

WEST BOYLSTON 1843-1899 – (Mf 1-4: Birth Index 1843-99+. Mf 5-7: Marriage Index 1843-99+. Mf 8-10: Death Index 1843-99+. Mf 11: Births 1843-50. Mf 11: Marriages 1843-50. Mf 11-12: Deaths 1843-50. Mf 13-19: Births 1851-99. Mf 20-23: Marriages 1851-99. Mf 24-28: Deaths 1851-99) – (mf ed 1993) – 28mf – 0-87623-179-2 – us Holbrook [920]

WEST BRANCH BEOBACHTER – Williamsport, PA., 1873-1893 – 13 – $25.00r – us I.M.R. [071]

WEST BRANCH DEMOCRAT – Williamsport, PA., 1860-1865 – 13 – $25.00r – us I.M.R. [071]

WEST BRIDGEWATER 1762-1900 – (Mf 1-3: Births & Deaths 1762-1882. Mf 4-9: Town Records 1822-49. Mf 10-17: Town Records 1850-78. Mf 18-23: Town Accounts 1822-69. Mf 24-26: Tax Valuation 1824-26. Mf 27-31: Tax Valuation 1828-32. Mf 32-33: Tax Valuation 1834. Mf 34-35: Military 1861-65. Mf 36-38: Marriages 1822-55. Mf 36-41: Intentions 1822-86+. Mf 41: Births & Deaths 1801-35. Mf 42-43: Birth Index 1843-1908. Mf 43-44: Death Index 1843-1908. Mf 44-45: Marriage Index 1843-1908. Mf 46: Births 1843-53. Mf 47: Marriages 1843-48. Mf 47: Deaths 1843-51. Mf 48-49: Births 1854-1900. Mf 50-51: Deaths 1852-1900. Mf 52-54: Marriages 1848-1900) – (mf ed 1995) – 54mf – 0-87623-377-9 – us Holbrook [920]

WEST BRIDGFORD ADVERTISER – Nottingham, England. Apr 1915-May 1930.-w. 12mqn reels – 1 – uk British Libr Newspaper [072]

WEST BROMWICH MIDLAND CHRONICLE – England. Midland Chronicle. -w. 1970-80. 23 1 2 reels – 1 – uk British Libr Newspaper [072]

WEST BROMWICH PARLIAMENTARY DIVISION CHALLENGE – West Bromwich. England. -m. Jun, Jul 1939. (3 ft) – 1 – uk British Libr Newspaper [072]

WEST BROMWICH REPORTER – West Bromwich. England. -w. 5 Jul-27 Sep 1869. (9 ft) – 1 – uk British Libr Newspaper [072]

WEST BROMWICH WESLEYAN RECORD – West Bromwich, England. Apr 1871-May 1873 – 32ft – 1 – uk British Libr Newspaper [072]

WEST BROOKFIELD 1848-1891 – (Mf 1: Births 1848-69. Mf 2: Births 1870-87. Mf 3: Births 1887-91; Deaths 1848-71. Mf 4: Deaths 1872-87. Mf 5: Deaths 1888-91; Marriages 1848-70. Mf 6: Marriages 1870-91. Mf 7-8: Birth Index 1848-91+. Mf 8-10: Marriage Index 1848-91+. Mf 10-12: Death Index 1848-91) – (mf ed 1986) – 12mf – 9 – 0-87623-022-2 – us Holbrook [920]

West Cameroon *see* WEST CAMEROON GAZETTE

WEST CAMEROON GAZETTE / West Cameroon – Oct. 1961-1971. Buea – 1 – us NY Public [324]

WEST CARLETON BANNER – West Carleton, 1979-1981 – 3r – 1 – cn Preston [971]

West Centre Harbor, New Hampshire. West Centre Harbor Sunday School *see* RECORDS

West Centre Harbor, New Hampshire. West Centre Harbor Union Meeting House Society *see* RECORDS

West, Charlotte *see* MEDIA COVERAGE OF WOMEN'S NCAA VARSITY SPORTS AS A FUNCTION OF THE STRUCTURE OF THE SPORTS INFORMATION OFFICE

WEST CHESTER EVERETT PRESS – Everett, PA., 1902-1912 – 13 – $25.00r – us I.M.R. [071]

WEST CHINA MISSIONARY CONFERENCE – Chentu: Canadian Methodist Mission Press, 1908 – 1mf – us A.T.L.A. [240]

WEST CHINA MISSIONARY NEWS – v1-45, no. 5-12 (?) (all publ ?). 1899-Dec 1943 (?) – 7r – 1 – $820.00 – us UPA [240]

THE WEST COAST LEADER – (Issues for 1919-20 filmed consecutively with: Courrier du pacifique jun 21 1919-jun 10 1920) – Lima, Peru: The West Coast Pub Co, [1912-32] – 15r – 1 – us Res Libr [072]

WEST COAST REPORTER. – (Covers the US and State Supreme Courts for AZ, CA, CO, NV and OR. And the State Supreme Courts for ID, MT, NM, UT, WA and WY.) – San Francisco: Bancroft-Whitney. v1-10 + digest for v1-4 (all publ) – 95mf – 9 – $142.00 – LLMC 81-417 – us L.L.M.C. [073]

WEST COAST SAILOR – San Francisco, CA. Oct 1943-1951 – 2r – 1 – $100.00 – C02866 – us Library Micro [071]

WEST COAST SAILORS – San Francisco. Calif. -w. 1943-51 – 1 – us UMI [071]

WEST COAST SIGNAL – Eureka, CA. 1871-79 – 2r – 1 – $100.00 – B02225 – us Library Micro [071]

WEST COUNTY NEWS – Sebastopol, CA. 1984-1986 – 2r – 1 – $100.00 – B03652 – us Library Micro [071]

WEST COUNTY TIMES – Pinole, CA. 1984-1989 – 125r – 1 – $6,250.00 – B03396 – us Library Micro [071]

WEST COUNTY TIMES – Richmond, CA. 1989 – 100+ r – 1 – $5,000.00 ($580.00y) – B05048 – us Library Micro [071]

WEST COVINA TRIBUNE – West Covina, CA. 1980 – 22+ r – 1 – $1,100.00 ($135.00y) – R03572 – us Library Micro [071]

WEST COVINA VALLEY HERALD – West Covina, CA. 1956-1957 – 1r – 1 – $50.00 – H04039 – us Library Micro [071]

WEST CUMBERLAND TIMES – Cockermouth, England. 1918-39 – 37r – 1 – uk British Libr Newspaper [072]

WEST CUMBERLAND TIMES AND STAR – Cockermouth, England. 1982-83; 1986- – 39+ r – 1 – uk British Libr Newspaper [072]

WEST END ADVOCATE – Valley, NE. -w. Jul 1919-Jul 1920 – 1 – us NE Hist [071]

WEST END INDEPENDENT – Los Angeles, CA. 1990 – 1r – 1 – $50.00 – R04066 – us Library Micro [071]

WEST FIFE ECHO – Dunfermline, Scotland. 1921 – 1r – 1 – uk British Libr Newspaper [072]

West, Fleming *see* ALCUIN AND THE RISE OF THE CHRISTIAN SCHOOLS

WEST FORK MEETING HOUSE. CHRISTIAN COUNTY. KENTUCKY : CHURCH RECORDS – 1803-22 – 1 – 5.58 – us Baptist [240]

West, G M *see* REMINISCENCES AND LETTERS

West, G S *see*
- A MONOGRAPH OF BRITISH DESMIDACEAE
- A MONOGRAPH OF THE BRITISH DESMIDIACEAE
- A TREATISE ON THE BRITISH FRESHWATER ALGAE

WEST GEMANY'S POLITICAL RELATIONS WITH EAST GERMANY PAMPHLET COLLECTION – 1958-1987 – 1 reel – 1 – CSUXANS1112-B – us Hoover Inst Photo [327]

[WEST GERMAN CIVILIZATION AND CULTURE PAMPHLET COLLECTION] – 1951-1988 – 1 reel – 1 – CSUXANS2478-B – us Hoover Inst Photo [306]

[WEST GERMAN FOREIGN RELATIONS PAMPHLET COLLECTION] – 1950-1986 – 1 reel – 1 – CSUXANS1101-B – us Hoover Inst Photo [327]

[WEST GERMAN POLITICS AND GOVERNMENT PAMPHLET COLLECTION] – 1949-1980 – 4r – 1 – CSUXANS1087-B – us Hoover Inst Photo [320]

WEST GERMAN POLITICS AND GOVERNMENT–1982 TO THE PRESENT–PAMPHLET COLLECTION – 1987-1989 – 1 reel – 1 – CSUXANS2513-B – us Hoover Inst Photo [320]

WEST GERMAN RADICALISM PAMPHLET COLLECTION – 1967-1977 – 1 reel – 1 – CSUXANS2487-B – us Hoover Inst Photo [320]

WEST GERMANY'S POLITICAL RELATIONS WITH FRANCE PAMPHLET COLLECTION – 1985 – 1 – CSUXANS1107-B – us Hoover Inst Photo [327]

WEST GERMANY'S POLITICAL RELATIONS WITH ISRAEL PAMPHLET COLLECTION – 19??-1987 – 1 reel – 1 – CSUXANS1121-B – us Hoover Inst Photo [327]

WEST GERMANY'S POLITICAL RELATIONS WITH POLAND PAMPHLET COLLECTION – 1961-1971 – 1 reel – 1 – CSUXANS1126-B – us Hoover Inst Photo [327]

WEST GERMANY'S POLITICAL RELATIONS WITH SOUTH AFRICA PAMPHLET COLLECTION – 1975? – 1 – CSUXANS1133-B – us Hoover Inst Photo [327]

WEST GERMANY'S POLITICAL RELATIONS WITH THE UNITED STATES PAMPHLET COLLECTION – 1953-1962 – 1 reel – 1 – CSUXANS1136-B – us Hoover Inst Photo [327]

West, H *see* BIDRAG TIL BESKRIVELSE OVER ST CROIX MED EN KORT UDSIGT OVER ST THOMAS, ST JEAN, TORTOLA, SPANISHTOWN OG CRABENEILAND

WEST HAM GUARDIAN ETC – London, UK. 6 Oct 1888-28 Sep 1889; Nov 1889-3 Nov 1894; Apr-Dec 1897; 1898-1902 – 10r – 1 – uk British Libr Newspaper [072]

WEST HIGHLAND FREE PRESS – 1 – £42.00r – uk Scot News [072]

West India Committee *see* SLAVERY TRACTS AND PAMPHLETS

THE WEST INDIAN – Grenada.1951-61 – 1 – us UMI [072]

WEST INDIAN – Grenada. Aug. 1950-71, 1973 (incomplete) – 1 – us UMI [072]

WEST INDIAN – St. George's, Grenada. -d. 1 Jan-25 Nov 1915; 16 June 1916-18 March 1917; 7 Jan 1930-31 July 1938; 7 Jan 1939-29 Dec 1951; 1 Jan-24 Nov 1957; 1 April 1962-30 Dec 1970. 87 reels. Mail edition, 14 April 1917-3 Dec 1920. 53 ft – 1 – uk British Libr Newspaper [072]

WEST INDIAN (HAITI) COLLECTION : FROM THE HOLDINGS OF THE SCHOMBURG CENTER FOR RESEARCH IN BLACK CULTURE, MANUSCRIPTS, ARCHIVES AND RARE BOOKS DIVISION: THE NEW YORK PUBLIC LIBRARY, ASTOR, LENOX AND TILDEN FOUNDATIONS – (Guide which covers all colls under "International Affairs" sold separately for $20.00 D3305.G5) – 1995 – 1r – 1 – $85.00 – D3305P16 – us Scholarly Res [972]

WEST INDIAN MEDICAL JOURNAL – (v.28-. 1979- 5,6,9) – v.1-. 1951- – 1 – us UMI [073]

WEST INDIAN NEWS OBSERVER – Toronto. 1967-69 – 1 – 60.00 – cn McLaren [971]

WEST INDIAN REVIEW – Kingston, Jamaica. v1-6. 1934-55 – 11r – 1 – us Ross [072]

THE WEST INDIAN-AMERICAN – New York. v. 1. no. 1-v. 3. no. 8. Jan Feb. 1959-July Aug. 1961 – 1 – us NY Public [071]

WEST INDIER – Surinam. 1871-1898 – 1 – us UMI [072]

THE WEST INDIES AND THE SPANISH MAIN / Trollope, Anthony – London: Chapman & Hall, 1859 – 1 roll – 1 – 1-55879-452-2 – uk Libr Preservation [972]

WEST INDIES GAZETTE – Trinidad. (Associated States). 1958-60 – 1 – us NY Public [071]

WEST INDIES MISSION RECORDS / Church Missionary Society – 1819-61 – 19r – 1 – uk Microform Academic [972]

West Indies University. Institute of Social and Economic Research. (Eastern Caribbean) *see* CARIBBEAN – GENERAL

WEST IRIAN EXCERPTS FROM INDONESIAN NATIONAL NEWS AGENCY / Antara. (Indonesian National News Agency) – SE-10,301 1. 1960 – 9 – ne IDC [950]

WEST IRIAN IMPLEMENTATION OF THE ACT OF FREE CHOICE, JULY 14-AUGUST 2, 1969 / Indonesia. Departemen Dalam Negeri – SE-8518 1. Sec. Ed. 1969 – 9 – ne IDC [324]

WEST IRIAN LIBERATION CAMPAIGN / Indonesia. Kementerian Penerangan – SE-3156 1. v. 4-5 only. 1957- – 9 – ne IDC [324]

West, James Columbus *see* A COMPENDIUM OF ALL THE INSTRUCTIONS AND INDICTMENTS WHICH ARE APPROVED AND CRITICISED IN THE MISSOURI SUPREME AND APPELLATE COURT REPORTS

WEST JERSEY EVANGELIST – 1828 – 1 – $50.00 – us Presbyterian [240]

WEST JERSEY MAIL – Camden. N.J. 1845-1847 – 1 – us UMI [071]

WEST JERSEY PRESS – Camden. N.J. 1861-1940 – 1 – us UMI [071]

WEST JERSEYMAN – Camden. N.J. 1847-1854 – 1 – us UMI [071]

West, Mrs. Jessie C *see* A PIONEER HISTORY OF BECKER COUNTY

WEST KENT ARGUS – London. -w. 1894-1931. (30 reels) – 1 – uk British Libr Newspaper [072]
WEST KENT GUARDIAN AND GRAVESEND AND MILTON EXPRESS, ETC *see* GREENWICH, WOOLWICH, DEPTFORD AND WEST KENT GUARDIAN
WEST KENT MERCURY *see* BROMLEY MERCURY
WEST LAKE COUNTY NEWS-HERALD – Willoughby. Ohio. 1933- – 1 – us UMI [071]
WEST LANCASHIRE EVENING GAZETTE – 1 – uk Microform Academic [072]
WEST LANE NEWS – Veneta, OR. -w. 29 Jun 1961-. – 11r – 1 – us U.O. Library [071]
WEST LONDON AND FULHAM TIMES – London. -w. 1904-15. (6 reels) – 1 – uk British Libr Newspaper [072]
WEST LONDON OBSERVER – London. -w. 1916-79. (99 reels) – 1 – uk British Libr Newspaper [072]
WEST LONDON REPORTER *see* KENSINGTON AND HAMMERSMITH REPORTER
WEST LONDON TIMES – London. -w. Jun 1860-Dec 1867. (6 reels) – 1 – uk British Libr Newspaper [072]
WEST LOS ANGELES INDEPENDENT – Santa Monica, CA. 1929-1994 – 303r – 1 – $15,150.00 – R04113 – us Library Micro [071]
WEST LOTHIAN COURIER – Bathgate, Scotland. Jun 1873-Dec 1903.-w. 20 reels – 1 – uk British Libr Newspaper [072]
West, Lucy Fisher *see* PAPERS OF MARTIN VAN BUREN
WEST MANSFIELD ENTERPRISE – West Mansfield, Ohio. 1893-1916 – 2r – 1 – $32.50r – us Archival [071]
WEST MARIN STAR – Point Reyes, CA. 1927-47 – 7r – 1 – $350.00 – B02640 – us Library Micro [071]
West, Mary *see* PAPERS
WEST MIDDLESEX GAZETTE: EALING EDITION *see* MIDDLESEX COUNTY TIMES
West Millgrove, Ohio. Congregational Church of West Millgrove *see* RECORDS
WEST MONROE FIRST BAPTIST CHURCH. WEST MONROE, LOUISIANA : CHURCH RECORDS – 1848-1953 – 1 – 20.88 – us Baptist [240]
West, Nathaniel *see* DANIEL'S GREAT PROPHECY: THE EASTERN QUESTION: THE KINGDOM
WEST NEBRASKA BEACON – Oshkosh, NE. -w. Feb 1929-Jul 1936 – 1 – us NE Hist [071]
WEST NEWBURY 1804-1905 – (Mf 1-5: Town Records 1819-34. Mf 6-7: Births 1804-44. Mf 8-9: Marriages & Deaths 1819-44. Mf 10: Births 1844-53. Mf 10: Marriages & Deaths 1844-49. Mf 11-13: Births 1848-1905. Mf 13-15: Marriages 1848-1905. Mf 15-18: Deaths 1848-1905. Mf 19: Soldiers & Seamen 1914-19. Mf 20-21: Pauper Register 1917-43) – (mf ed 1990) – 21mf – 0-87623-107-5 – us Holbrook [920]
WEST OF ENGLAND ADVERTISER – (Bristol and West of England Advertiser. 1875) – Plymouth, England. 3 Jan 1874-2 Mar 1876. -w – 2r – 1 – uk British Libr Newspaper [072]
WEST OF ENGLAND EXAMINER – Bristol. England. -w. 30 May-12 Dec 1874. (33 ft) – 1 – uk British Libr Newspaper [072]
THE WEST OF ENGLAND JOURNAL OF SCIENCE AND LITERATURE – Bristol, 1836 – 3 – us Readex [500]
West of Scotland Iron and Steel Institute *see* JOURNAL
WEST OMAHA STAR – Omaha, NE. -w. Jun 1933-Jul 1940 – 1 – us NE Hist [071]
WEST OMAHA SUN – Omaha, NE. -w. Jun 1894-Aug 1895, scattered issues missing; Oct 1895-Feb 1901; Dec 1959 to date – 1 – us NE Hist [071]
WEST OREGONIAN – Myrtle Point OR. Jan 27-Feb 24 1894 – 1 – us U.O. Library [071]
WEST PARISH BAPTIST CHURCH. PARTRIDGEFIELD, MASSACHUSETTS : CHURCH RECORDS – 1797-1903 – 1 – 14.64 – us Baptist [240]
WEST PARK BAPTIST CHURCH. PECOS, TEXAS : CHURCH RECORDS – 1945-70 – 1 – 43.29 – us Baptist [240]
West Point Alumni Foundation Inc *see* REGISTER OF GRADUATES AND FORMER CADETS, UNITED STATES MILITARY ACADEMY, WEST POINT, NEW YORK 1802-1946
WEST POINT BAPTIST CHURCH. HANCOCK COUNTY. HAWESVILLE, KENTUCKY : CHURCH RECORDS – 1841-86, Jul 1921-Sept 1982 – 1 – 44.10 – us Baptist [240]
WEST POINT NEWS – West Point, NE. -w. 18 Nov 1870- . Scattered issues missing – 1 – us NE Hist [071]
WEST PYMBLE GAZETTE – Oct 1957-Nov 1969 – 1 – at Pascoe [072]
THE WEST QUEBEC POST – Buckingham: N/A Publications. v89-96. 1983-1991. SEM35P269 – 12r – 1 – Can$455.00 – cn Bibl Nat [072]
West, R A *see* SKETCHES OF WESLEYAN PREACHERS
WEST RAND REVIEW KOERANT – Krugersdorp, South Africa. 1898-1958 – 1 – sa State Libr [072]
West, Robert A *see* RECORDS OF THE PROCEEDINGS AND DEBATES AT THE SIXTY-FIRST ANNUAL CONVENTION OF THE PROTESTANT EPISCOPAL CHURCH IN THE DIOCESE OF NEW YORK..
WEST ROXBURY 1712-1873 – 38mf – 9 – us Holbrook [920]
WEST ROXBURY SERMONS : 1837-1848 / Parker, Theodore – Boston: Roberts, 1892 – 1mf – us A.T.L.A. [240]
WEST SALEM CITIZEN – Salem OR. Oct 4-Nov 15 1962 – 1 – us U.O. Library [071]
WEST SALEM CLARION – Salem OR. Mar 5-July 30 1931 – 1 – us U.O. Library [071]
WEST SALEM CLARION NEWS CRIER – Salem OR. Aug 7-Sep 4 1931 – 1 – us U.O. Library [071]
WEST SALEM MAIL – Independence, OR. -w. 8 Dec 1938-28 Dec 1939. 1 roll – 1 – us U.O. Library [071]
WEST SCHUYLKILL HERALD – Tower City, PA. -w 1898-1985 – 13 – $25.00r – us I.M.R. [071]
WEST SCHUYLKILL PRESS – Tremont, PA., 1877-1937 – 13 – $25.00r – us I.M.R. [071]
WEST SCHUYLKILL PRESS-PINE GROVE HERALD – Tremont, PA. 1937-1976 – 13 – $25.00r – us I.M.R. [071]
WEST SHORE – Portland. Or. 1875-1891 – 1 – us UMI [071]
WEST SHORE – Portland, OR. Aug 1875-2 May 1891. 6 rolls – 1 – us U.O. Library [071]
WEST SHORE TIMES – Lemoyne. Pa. 1962-1969 – 1 – us UMI [071]
WEST SHORE TIMES – Lemoyne, PA. -w 1962-1973 – 13 – $25.00r – us I.M.R. [071]
WEST SIDE – Independence, OR. -w. 17 Jan 1890-12 Sept 1901. 2 rolls – 1 – us U.O. Library [071]
WEST SIDE ADVOCATE – West Linn, OR. -w. 11 May 1939-26 Oct 1939. 1 roll – 1 – us U.O. Library [071]
West Side Baptist Church, Topeka, KS *see* RECORDS
WEST SIDE HERALD – Oakland, NE. -m. Nov 1915-Apr 1933; Jun 1933-Mar 1937; Jun 1937-Jun 1941; Aug 1941 – 1 – us NE Hist [071]
WEST SIDE NEWS – Grand Rapids. Mich. -w. 1914-29, 1935-50 – 1 – us UMI [071]
WEST SIDE REMINDER – Multnomah, OR. -w. 21 Dec 1939-26 Feb 1942. – 1r – 1 – us U.O. Library [071]
WEST SIDE STUDIES, CARRIED ON UNDER THE DIRECTION OF PAULINE GOLDMARK – New York: Survey Associates, 1914. 2v. 1 illus., plates, diagrs. Russell Sage Foundation publications – 1 – us U.W. Library [360]
WEST SIDE TELEPHONE – McMinnville OR. June 15 1886-Jan 31 1889 – 1 – us U.O. Library [071]
WEST SPRINGS BAPTIST CHURCH. UNION COUNTY. SOUTH CAROLINA : CHURCH RECORDS – (344p) – 1939-1987 – 1 reel – 1 – $15.48 – us Baptist [240]
WEST STOCKBRIDGE 1774-1902 – (mf ed 1988) – 21mf – 9 – 0-87623-080-X – us Holbrook [920]
West Sumner, Maine. West Sumner Baptist Church *see* RECORDS
WEST SUSSEX GAZETTE – Arundel. England. -w. 1860-1958. (Wanting 1896, 1911). (77 reels) – 1 – uk British Libr Newspaper [072]
West Sussex Record Office, Chichester *see* RICHARD COBDEN PAPERS
WEST TEXAS BAPTIST – Abilene. Texas. 5 Mar 1925-Apr 1942 – 1 – 99.89 – us Baptist [240]
WEST TOLEDO HERALD – Toledo, Ohio. 1949- – 16r – 1 – $32.50r – us Archival [071]
WEST UMATILLA NEWS – (Set incl. Stanfield Standard) – Stanfield, OR. -w. 13 Dec 1927-27 Dec 1928. – 1r – 1 – us U.O. Library [071]
WEST UNION GAZETTE – West Union, NE. -w. May 1892; Jun 1892; Oct 1895-Aug 1896 – 1 – us NE Hist [071]
West Union. Ohio. Mt. Leigh Presbyterian Church *see* CHURCH RECORDS, MS 477
WEST VALLEY TIMES – San Jose. Calif. 1966- – 1 – us UMI [071]
WEST VALLEY TIMES – Sunnyvale, CA. 1963-65 – 3r – 1 – $150.00 – B03026 – us Library Micro [071]
WEST VANCOUVER NEWS – Vancouver, British Columbia, CN. Mar 1931-Jul 1957 – 8r – 1 – cn Commonwealth Micro [072]
WEST VIRGINIA – 3r – 1 – $240.00 – us Scholarly Res [370]
WEST VIRGINIA : CODE ANNOTATED – Charlottesville: Michie Co, 1966-Jan 1996 update – 9 – $2,315.00 set – us Hein [340]
WEST VIRGINIA : SESSION LAWS OF AMERICAN STATES AND TERRITORIES – 1861-1995 – 9 – $1,229.00 set – us Hein [340]
West Virginia *see*
– REPORTS AND OPINIONS (A-G)
– REPORTS, POST-NRS
– REPORTS, PRE-NRS
WEST VIRGINIA AND ITS PEOPLE / Miller & Maxwell – New York, Lewis Historical Publishing Co., 1913. Vols. 1-3. West Virginia Reel 1. (The Cox Library Collection) – 5 – us Americana [978]
WEST VIRGINIA ARGUS – Kingwood. West Virginia. 1878-1916 – 1 – us UMI [071]
WEST VIRGINIA ATTORNEY GENERAL REPORTS AND OPINIONS – (6 1893-1968 $245.00 9 1968-1993 + indexes $130.00) – 1893-1993 and Indexes – 6,9 – $375.00 set – us Hein [340]
WEST VIRGINIA BAPTIST – Oct 1934-Apr 1950 – 1 – 105.00 – us Baptist [240]
WEST VIRGINIA BAR *see*
– WEST VIRGINIA LAW REVIEW
West Virginia. Bureau of Labor Statistics *see* STATE LABOR REPORTS
WEST VIRGINIA DEMOCRAT – Charleston. West Virginia. 1887-88 – 1 – us UMI [071]
WEST VIRGINIA EDUCATION ASSOCIATION. WVEA SCHOOL JOURNAL *see* WV SCHOOL JOURNAL
WEST VIRGINIA FOURTH ESTATESMAN – Morgantown. West Virginia. 1941-1959 – 1 – us UMI [071]
WEST VIRGINIA FREEMAN – Parkersburg. West Virginia. 1881-1888 – 1 – us UMI [071]
WEST VIRGINIA HILLBILLY – Richmond. West Virginia. 1956-1968 – 1 – us UMI [071]
WEST VIRGINIA LAW QUARTERLY *see* WEST VIRGINIA LAW REVIEW
WEST VIRGINIA LAW QUARTERLY AND THE BAR *see* WEST VIRGINIA LAW REVIEW
WEST VIRGINIA LAW REVIEW – 1894- – 1,5,6,9 – us UMI [340]
WEST VIRGINIA LAW REVIEW – (v1-2 of this title are called the "West Virginia Bar"; v3-24 are called "The Bar"; v25-51 are called "West Virginia Law Quarterly and The Bar." With v52 1949/50, the publication was taken over by the College of Law of West Virginia University and acquired its present title Add vols as copyright expires) – v1-26. 1894-1920 – 193mf – $289.00 – LLMC 95-143 – us L.L.M.C. [073]
WEST VIRGINIA LAW REVIEW – (v1-87 1894-1984 on reel $870.00. v88-97 1985-95 on mf $247.00. Title varies: v1-2 1894-95 as West Virginia Bar. v3-24 1896-1917 as the Bar. v25-51 1917-49 as West Virginia Law Quarterly) – v1-97. 1894-1995 – 5,6,9 – $1,117.00 set – us Hein [340]
WEST VIRGINIA LAWYER – (Supersedes West Virginia State Bar Journal) – v1-9. 1985-96 – 9 – $175.00 set – us Hein [340]
WEST VIRGINIA LAWYER *see* WEST VIRGINIA STATE BAR JOURNAL
WEST VIRGINIA LEGISLATIVE HANDBOOK AND MANUAL AND OFFICIAL REGISTER / Harris, John T – Charleston, Jarrett Printing Co., 1923. West Virginia Reel 6. The Cox Library Collection – 5 – us Americana [340]
WEST VIRGINIA SCHOOL JOURNAL *see* WV SCHOOL JOURNAL
WEST VIRGINIA SOUTHERN BAPTIST – St. Albans, WV. 1986-1991. 600p – 1 – $28.48 – us Baptist [071]
West Virginia. State Bar Association *see* PROCEEDINGS
WEST VIRGINIA STATE BAR ASSOCIATION REPORTS – (Lacking: 9th meeting pp1-24. 11th-15th meetings) – 1st-75th annual meetings 1887-1959 (all publ) – 77mf – 9 – $346.00 – LLMC 84-689 – us L.L.M.C. [340]
WEST VIRGINIA STATE BAR JOURNAL – (Superseded by West Virginia Lawyer) – v1-9. 1975-84 – 9 – $42.00 – us Hein [340]
WEST VIRGINIA STATE BAR JOURNAL *see* WEST VIRGINIA LAWYER
WEST VIRGINIA SUPREME COURT REPORTS – (Pre-NRS run: v1-45 1853-78 356mf $534.00. Vols after 1920 to be filmed after copyright expires) – v1-171. 1852-1920 – 1368mf – 9 – $2,052.00 – LLMC 80-820 – us L.L.M.C. [340]
WEST VIRGINIA TODAY / Clarke, Walter E – A Work for Newpaper and Library Reference; contains biographical records. New Orleans, West Virginia Editors Association, James O. Jones Co., 1941. West Virginia Reel 7. (The Cox Library Collection) – 5 – us Americana [920]
WEST VIRGINIAN – Fairmont. West Virginia. 1904-1970 – 1 – us UMI [071]
WEST VIRGINIANS OF 1934-35 / Wheeling Intelligencer – Wheeling. West Virginia Reel 7. (The Cox Library Collection) – 5 – us Americana [920]
West, W *see*
– A CONTRIBUTION TO THE FRESHWATER ALGAE OF THE NORTH OF IRELAND
– A MONOGRAPH OF BRITISH DESMIDACEAE
– A MONOGRAPH OF THE BRITISH DESMIDIACEAE
WEST WASHINGTON COUNTY NEWS – (Set incl. Cornelius News) – Cornelius, OR. -w 12 Oct 1928-7 Dec 1928. – 1r – 1 – us U.O. Library [071]
WEST WIMMERA MAIL – 1887-1941. WWM1-24 – 24r – 1 – at Corangamite [072]
Westarp, Graf von *see* KONSERVATIVE POLITIK IM LETZTEN JAHRZEHNT DES KAISERREICHES BAND I
WESTBOROUGH 1717-1900 – (Mf 1-14: Vital Records 1717-1842. Mf 15-20: Vital Records 1720-1864. Mf 21: Inhabitants, 1776-77. Mf 22-26: Tax Lists 1756-99. Mf 27-35: Town Records 1717-81. Mf 36-43: Town Records 1782-1809. Mf 44-52: Town Records 1810-43. Mf 53-60: Town Records 1839-57. Mf 61-69: Town Records 1857-75. Mf 70-77: Town Records 1875-90. Mf 78-85: Town Records 1890-1900. Mf 86-90: Town Accounts 1806-48. Mf 91-92: Military 1861-65. Mf 93: Pauper Records 1824-1991. Mf 94-96: Church Record 1724-1874. Mf 97-99: Church Record 1808-35. Mf 100-103: Church Records 1835-56. Mf 104-109: Church Records 1856-89. Mf 110: Vital Records 1843-50. Mf 111-115: Births 1851-91. Mf 116-117: Births 1892-1900. Mf 118-120: Marriages 1719-1861. Mf 121-125: Marriages 1851-1900. Mf 126-133: Deaths 1851-1901) – (mf ed 1993) – 133mf – 0-87623-161-X – us Holbrook [920]
Westbrook, Richard Brodhead *see*
– THE BIBLE-WHENCE AND WHAT?
– MAN-WHENCE AND WHITHER?
WESTCHESTER – Peekskill. N.Y. and Putnam Republican. 1835-55 – 1 – us UMI [071]
WESTCHESTER AND BRONX COUNTIES – 1929. New York Reel 39. (The Cox Library Collection) – 5 – us Americana [978]
WESTCHESTER BAPTIST CHURCH. VALHALLA, NEW YORK : CHURCH RECORDS – 1966-Nov 1967 – 1 – 5.00 – us Baptist [240]
WESTCHESTER COUNTY / Spooner, W W – Biographical. New York, New York History Co., 1900. New York Reel 38. (The Cox Library Collection) – 5 – us Americana [978]
WESTCHESTER HERALD – Mount Pleasant, NY. 1818-20 – 1 – us Readex [071]

WESTCHESTER LADERA OBSERVER – Santa Monica, CA. 1957 – 269+ r – 1 – $13,450.00 ($135.00y) – R03527 – us Library Micro [071]

Westcott, Brooke Foss *see*
- THE BIBLE IN THE CHURCH
- CHARACTERISTICS OF THE GOSPEL MIRACLES
- CHRISTUS CONSUMMATOR: SOME ASPECTS OF THE WORK AND PERSON OF CHRIST IN RELATION TO MODERN THOUGHT
- CHRISTUS CONSUMMATOR: CHRIST IN RELATION TO MODERN THOUGHT
- THE EPISTLES OF ST. JOHN
- THE EPISTLES OF ST JOHN: THE GREEK TEXT, WITH NOTES AND ESSAYS
- ESSAYS IN THE HISTORY OF RELIGIOUS THOUGHT IN THE WEST
- A GENERAL VIEW OF THE HISTORY OF THE ENGLISH BIBLE
- THE GOSPEL OF LIFE
- INTRODUCTION TO THE STUDY OF THE GOSPELS
- THE REVELATION OF THE RISEN LORD
- SAINT PAUL'S EPISTLE TO THE EPHESIANS: THE GREEK TEXT WITH NOTES AND ADDENDA
- SOME LESSONS OF THE REVISED VERSION OF THE NEW TESTAMENT
- THE TWO EMPIRES

Westcott, Frank Nash *see* CATHOLIC PRINCIPLES

WESTDEUTSCHE ALLGEMEINE ZEITUNG – Essen. 1979-80 – 9 – 22370.00y – gw Alpha Com [072]

WESTDEUTSCHE ALLGEMEINE ZEITUNG (WAZ) – (Also Bereichsausgaben available: BOCHUM, jul 1 1967- ; BOCHUM-WATTENSCHEID, Wattenscheider Zeitung, oct 1 1957-59, 1991- ; BOTTROP, sep 1 1978- ; CASTROP-RAUXEL, 1991- ; DORTMUND, apr 3 1948- ; DUISBURG, nov 1-30 1966, 1977- ; GELSENKIRCHEN, sep 1 1978- ; GELSENKIRCHEN-BUER, 1991- ; GLADBECK, 1991- ; HALTERN, 1991- ; HERNE, sep 1 1978- ; HERNE-WANNE-EICKEL, 1991- ; LUENEN, 1991- ; MUELHEIM/Ruhr, Muelheimer Zeitung, sep 1 1978- ; OBERHAUSEN, 1977- ; RECKLINGHAUSEN, 1991- ; WITTEN, jan 2-jun 29 1957, 1991-) – Essen, 1950- – 1 – Inquire at Mikrofilmarchiv for details – gw Misc Inst [072]

WESTDEUTSCHE ALLGEMEINE ZEITUNG (WAZ) – Bochum, West Germany. 1977- – 1 – gw Mikrofilm [072]

WESTDEUTSCHE ALLGEMEINE ZEITUNG (WAZ) – Bottrop, West Germany. 1 Sept 1978- – 1 – gw Mikrofilm [072]

WESTDEUTSCHE ALLGEMEINE ZEITUNG (WAZ) – Duisburg, West Germany. 1977- – 1 – gw Mikrofilm [072]

WESTDEUTSCHE ALLGEMEINE ZEITUNG (WAZ) – Essen. jul 1972 – 1r – 1 – gw Mikrofilm [072]

WESTDEUTSCHE ALLGEMEINE ZEITUNG (WAZ) – Gelsenkirchen, West Germany. 1 Sept 1978- – 1 – gw Mikrofilm [072]

WESTDEUTSCHE ALLGEMEINE ZEITUNG (WAZ) – Herne, West Germany. 1 Sept 1978- – 1 – gw Mikrofilm [072]

WESTDEUTSCHE ALLGEMEINE ZEITUNG (WAZ) – Muelheim-Ruhr, West Germany. Muelheimer Zeitung. 1 Sept 1978- – 1 – gw Mikrofilm [072]

WESTDEUTSCHE ALLGEMEINE ZEITUNG (WAZ) – Oberhausen, West Germany. 1977- – 1 – gw Mikrofilm [072]

WESTDEUTSCHE ARBEITERZEITUNG – Moenchengladbach, 1899-1917; 1919-32 – 9r – 1 – DM720.00 – gw Mikro Press [072]

WESTDEUTSCHE ARBEITERZEITUNG – Moenchengladbach, Germany. 1899-1917, 1919-32 – 1 – gw Mikrofilm [072]

WESTDEUTSCHE ILLUSTRIERTE ZEITUNG *see* ILLUSTRIERTE WESTDEUTSCHE WOCHENSCHAU

WESTDEUTSCHE RUNDSCHAU – Duesseldorf, Wuppertal. 1946-49 – 4r – 1 – DM320.00 – gw Mikro Press [072]

WESTDEUTSCHE RUNDSCHAU – Wuppertal u. Duesseldorf, West Germany. 8 May 1946-49 – 1 – gw Mikrofilm [072]

WESTDEUTSCHE UNTERHALTUNGSBEILAGE – Moenchengladbach, Germany. 1899-1904 – 1 – gw Mikrofilm [072]

WESTDEUTSCHE ZEITUNG – Koeln, Germany. 25 May 1849-21 Jul 1850 – 1 – gw Mikrofilm [072]

WESTDEUTSCHE ZEITUNG (WZ) – Duesseldorf, West Germany. Duesseldorfer Nachrichten. 1978- – 1 – gw Mikrofilm [072]

WESTDEUTSCHE ZEITUNG (WZ) – Krefeld, West Germany. Krefelder Zeitung. 1977- – 1 – gw Mikrofilm [072]

WESTDEUTSCHER ALLGEMEINE – Essen: J Funke, 1953-80 – us Res Libr [072]

WESTDEUTSCHER BEOBACHTER – Bonn, Germany. 1 Jul 1931-Mar 1945 – 1 – gw Mikrofilm [072]

WESTDEUTSCHER BEOBACHTER – Bonn, jul 1 1931-mar 2 1945 – 19r – 1 – Inquire at Mikrofilmarchiv for details – gw Misc Inst [320]

WESTDEUTSCHER BEOBACHTER – Koeln, 1925-Feb 1945 – 61r – 1 – DM4,575.00 – gw Mikro Press [072]

WESTDEUTSCHER BEOBACHTER – Koeln, Germany. Title change: Die Neue Front (Dec 1928-Mar 1929). 1925-Feb 1945.Incompl – 1 – gw Mikrofilm [072]

WESTDEUTSCHES TAGEBLATT – Dortmund. Germany. -d. 28 Aug 1946-7 Dec 1949, 6 Feb 1950-29 Nov 1952. (Imperfect). (14 reels) – 1 – uk British Libr Newspaper [072]

WESTDEUTSCHES TAGEBLATT – Dortmund, West Germany. 24 Aug 1946-28 Sept 1949 – 1 – gw Mikrofilm [072]

WESTDEUTSCHES VOLKS-ECHO – Dortmund, West Germany. Die Zeitung der Werktaetigen fuer Ruhrgebiet-Westfalen. 7 May 1946-4 May 1948 – 1 – gw Mikrofilm [072]

WESTELIKE STEM – Potchefstroom. South Africa. 1915-55 – 1 – sa State Libr [072]

DER WESTEN *see* BERLIN-WILMERSDORFER ZEITUNG

HET WESTEN – Potchefstroom, South Africa. 1905-15 – 1 – sa State Libr [072]

WEST-END JOURNAL : JOURNAL DE L'OUEST – Montreal. v7 n32. 23 nov 1960-v9 n37. 28 nov 1962 – 1r – 1 – Can$35.00 – cn Can Microfilming [072]

WESTER- OCH NORRBOTTENS LANS NYA TIDNING – Umea, Sweden. 1841-42 – 1 reel – 1 – sw Kungliga [072]

WESTER- OCH NORRBOTTENS LANS TIDNING – Umea, Sweden. 1841 – 1 reel – 1 – sw Kungliga [072]

WESTER ROSS PART 2 1851 CENSUS INDEX : ARGYLL AND WEST SCOTLAND CENSUS INDEX, PART 6 / Gibson, Peter & Macinnes, John – 1994 – 2mf – 9 – A$19.95 – 0-646-19935-8 – at Seanachas [920]

Wester, Ursula *see* DIE AKROTERFIGUREN DES TEMPELS DER ATHENER AUF DELOS

WESTERBOTTEN – Umea, Sweden. 1869-1912 – 29r – 1 – sw Kungliga [072]

Westerburg, Hans *see* PREUSSEN UND ROM AN DER WENDE DES 18. JAHRHUNDERTS

Westerdale, T L Barlow *see* UNDER THE RED CROSS FLAG; WITH THE MEDICALS IN ACTION

Westerfield, R Carl *see* THE EFFECTS OF EXERCISE ON LOW-DENSITY-LIPOPROTEIN-RECEPTOR MEDIATED CLEARANCE AND ATHEROSCLEROTIC LESIONS IN DIETARY INDUCED HYPERLIPIDEMIC NZW RABBITS

Westergaard, Harald *see* CONTRIBUTIONS TO THE HISTORY OF STATISTICS

Westergaard, N L *see* BUNDEHESH, LIBER PEHLVICUS E VETUSTISSIMO CODICE HAVNIENSI DESCRIPSIT

WESTERHAM HERALD – England.Jun 1882-Sept 1935. -w. 41 reels. Jan-Jun 1892-1894 not available – 1 – uk British Libr Newspaper [072]

Westerlund, C A *see*
- FAUNA DER IN DER PALAEARCTISCHEN REGION. LEBENDEN BINNENCONCHYLIEN
- FAUNA EUROPAEA MOLLUSCORUM EXTRAMARINORUM
- FAUNULA MOLLUSCORUM HISPALENSIS
- KATALOG DER IN DER PALAEARCTISCHEN REGION LEBENDEN BINNECONCHYLIEN
- SYNOPSIS MOLLUSCORUM EXTRAMARINORUM REGIONIS PALAEARCTICAE
- SYNOPSIS MOLLUSCORUM EXTRAMARINORUM SCANDINAVIAE
- SYNOPSIS MOLLUSCORUM IN REGIONE PALAEARCTICA

Westermaier, M *see* ZUR ENTWICKLUNG UND STRUKTUR EINIGER PTERIDOPHYTEN AUS JAVA

Westermann, Diedrich *see*
- EVEFIALA
- THE KPELLE LANGUAGE IN LIBERIA: GRAMATICAL OUTLINE, COLLOQUIAL SENTENCES AND VOCABULARY

WESTERMANN'S ILLUSTRIRTE DEUTSCHE MONATSHEFTE – Braunschweig, 1856-57 (incomplete), 1870 (incomplete), 1871-mar 1875 – 1 – Inquire at Mikrofilmarchiv for details – gw Misc Inst [072]

WESTERN AMERICAN – Portland OR. Nov 30 1922-Sep 28 1923 – 1 – us U.O. Library [071]

WESTERN AMERICANA – (1138v. Individual subject collections available: Agriculture $430; Conservation and Use of Resources $390; Culture, Religion, Education $410; Directories and Guidebooks $405; Earlier Wests $940; Extractive Industries $1185; Frontier Thesis $125; Fur Trade and Early Exploration $545; Government and Politics $805; Government and Scientific Exploration $780; Indians $1755; Land and Water Questions of the Public Domain $580; Livestock Industry $545; Mormon Utah $625; Other Ethnic Influences $335; Politics and Diplomacy of Expansion $380; Regional, State, and Local Histories $735; The Trails West $415; Transportation $830; Travel Accounts, Memoirs, Reminiscences $1125; Urban Development $700; Women of the West $535) – 5222mf – 9 – $14,575.00 complete collection – us UMI [975]

WESTERN AMERICANA : FRONTIER HISTORY OF THE TRANS-MISSISSIPPI WEST, 1550-1900 – Based primarily on the collection of the Yale University and the Newberry Libraries – 1 – us Primary [978]

WESTERN AMERICANA : TRANS-MISSISSIPPI WEST, TRAVELS IN THE WEST AND SOUTHWEST – (From the end of the Civil War until the 1920s) – 9 – us Primary [975]

WESTERN ARGUS – Ballinasloe. Ireland. -w. Apr 1828-Oct 1829, Feb-Apr, Jul 1830-Jan 1833. (4 reels) – 1 – uk British Libr Newspaper [072]

WESTERN ARGUS – Kansas City. Kan. 1858-61 – 1 – us UMI [071]

Western Australia. Australia. Parliament *see* LEGISLATIVE COUNCIL

WESTERN AUSTRALIA PROVINCIAL MAGAZINE – v4-9. 1934-39 (complete) – 1r – 1 – ATLA S0716C – us A.T.L.A. [073]

WESTERN AUSTRALIAN GOLDFIELDS COURIER – Coolgardie, Australia. Nov 1894-Oct 1895; Mar 1896-Oct 1898.-w. 5men reels – 1 – uk British Libr Newspaper [072]

WESTERN AUSTRALIAN INDUSTRIAL GAZETTE – Perth, Australia. -m. March 1925-March 1930. 2 reels – 1 – uk British Libr Newspaper [072]

WESTERN AUSTRALIAN TIMES – Perth, Australia. Jan 1875-Nov 1879.-w. 3 reels – 1 – uk British Libr Newspaper [072]

THE WESTERN AVERNUS : OR, TOIL AND TRAVEL IN FURTHER NORTH AMERICA / Roberts, Morley – London: Smith, Elder, 1887 – 1 roll – 1 – 1-55879-413-1 – uk Libr Preservation [910]

Western Bakery. Lawrence, Kansas *see* DAYBOOK

WESTERN BAPTIST REVIEW – Frankfort, KY. Sep 1845-Aug 1849. 1948p – 1 – 68.18 – us Baptist [240]

WESTERN BAPTIST REVIEW – v. 5, no. 5. 1851; Proceedings, 33rd Annual Session, Bethel Baptist Assn., Ky., 1857; Bracken Assn., Ky., 1864; Minutes, 28th Annual, Bethel Baptist Assn., Ky., 1852; Minutes, 54th Annual Session, Union Assn. of United Baptists, Ky., 1867; Proceedings, 1st Anniversary, Southern Bapt. Sabbath School Union, 1860 – 1 – 5.00 – us Baptist [240]

Western Biographical Publishing Co *see*
- AMERICAN BIOGRAPHICAL HISTORY OF EMINENT AND SELF-MADE MEN OF THE STATE OF MICHIGAN
- THE BIOGRAPHICAL CYCLOPEDIA AND PORTRAIT GALLERY WITH AN HISTORICAL SKETCH OF THE STATE OF OHIO
- EMINENT AND SELF-MADE MEN
- A HISTORY OF AND BIOGRAPHICAL CYCLOPEDIA OF BUTLER COUNTY

WESTERN BOOKS ON ASIA : JAPAN – (Pt 1: 300-vol units of ca 1000mf) – ca 10,000mf – 9 – us Primary [950]

WESTERN BOOKS ON ASIA : MIDDLE EAST AND ISLAM – 300-vol units – 10,000mf – 9 – us Primary [956]

WESTERN BOOKS ON CHINA PUBLISHED UP TO 1850 / ed by Lust, John – (Includes printed bibliography by John Lust: Western Books on China published up to 1850 in the Library of the SOAS. Individual titles available) – 4682mf – 9 – ne IDC [950]

WESTERN BREEZE – Cut Bank. Mont. 1966- – 1 – us UMI [071]

WESTERN BUSINESS AND INDUSTRY – v18-41. Mar. 1944-Dec. 1967. Missing v35 – 1 – cn Precision [380]

[WESTERN CAMPAIGNS DURING WORLD WAR 2 PAMPHLET COLLECTION] – 1942-1944 – 1 rool – 1 – CSUXANM8164-B – us Hoover Inst Photo [355]

[WESTERN CAMPAIGNS IN WORLD WAR 1 PAMPHLET COLLECTION] – 1914-19?? – 2r – 1 – CSUXAML7892-B – us Hoover Inst Photo [355]

WESTERN CHAMPION – Parkes, Jan 7 1898-Dec 31 1914 – 1 – at Pascoe [072]

WESTERN CHRISTIAN – Elgin, IL. 1845-46. Northwestern Baptist Anti-Slavery Convention – 1 – us A.B.H.S. [073]

WESTERN CHRISTIAN ADVOCATE : WESTERN EDITION – Cincinnati, OH. v1-100. May 1834-1934 (complete) – 83r – 1 – ATLA S0046 – us A.T.L.A. [073]

WESTERN CHRONICLE – Three Rivers. Mich. 1849-51; 57-64 – 1 – us UMI [071]

THE WESTERN CHURCHMAN – Winnipeg: [s.n. 1896-1900?] – 9 – cn C.I.H.M. [240]

WESTERN CITIZEN URBANA GAZETTE – Urbana. Ohio. 1838-1845 – 1 – us UMI [071]

WESTERN CIVILIZATION AND THE NATIVES OF SOUTH AFRICA / Schapera, I – London. 1934. Index. BA-397 2 – 8 – ne IDC [960]

WESTERN CLACKAMAS REVIEW – Lake Oswego OR. Dec 11 1925, May 26 1927, Apr 18 19 1929, Jan 5 1928-Sep 5 1929 – 1 – us U.O. Library [071]

WESTERN COLORADO MAPS : CITIES AND TOWNS – 1883-1904. 270 maps. 24 towns. Sanborn Company Fire Insurance Maps – 1 – $47.00r – us Shkurkin [910]

WESTERN COMMERCE AND INDUSTRY MAGAZINE – (v1-21 1949-69 Can$420.00) – Winnipeg. v1-46. 1949-94 – 9 – Can$20.00y – cn Micromedia [380]

WESTERN COMRADE – Los Angeles. Calif. 1913-18 – 1 – us UMI [071]

WESTERN COMRADE – v1-6, no. 2 (all publ). 1913-1918 – 1 reel – 1 – $115.00 – us UPA [335]

WESTERN COUNTY NEWS – Kalida, Ohio. 1931-47 – 3r – 1 – $32.50r – us Archival [071]

WESTERN DAKOTA SHEEP DAY / North Dakota. University. Agricultural Experiment Station – 1961-75 – 1,5,6 – us Spaulding [636]

WESTERN DIVISION *see*
- MONTHLY LETTER LEAFLET
- WFM SOCIETY
- WOMAN'S FOREIGN MISSIONARY SOCIETY

WESTERN ECHO – Cape Coast. Ghana. -irr. Nov 1885-Dec 1887. (1 reel) – 1 – uk British Libr Newspaper [072]

WESTERN ECHO – St. Ives, England. Feb 1903-Jan 1957.-w. 16mqn reels – 1 – uk British Libr Newspaper [072]

WESTERN ECONOMIC JOURNAL – v. 1-11. 1962-73 – 1,5,6,9 – us UMI [330]

WESTERN ELECTRIC NEWS – v1-21. 1912-32 – 1,5,6 – us Princeton Micro [073]

WESTERN ELECTRICIAN – v1-43. 1887-1908 – 1,5,6 – us Princeton Micro [073]

WESTERN EUROPE IN THE FIFTH CENTURY: AN AFTERMATH / Freeman, Edward A – London, New York: Macmillan, 1904. vi,386p. Includes index – 1 – us U.W. Library [900]

WESTERN EUROPEAN CENSUS REPORTS : 1960 CENSUS PERIOD (1959-1969) – (A collection of 73 titles for 22 countries. Together with: Blake, Judith and Jerry J Donovan: Western European Censuses, 1960, an English-language guide) – 1085mf – 9 – $5.00f – us Ross [310]

WESTERN EUROPEAN EDUCATION – (1982-. 1,5,6,9) – v1-. 1969- – 1 – us UMI [073]

WESTERN FARMER – Leoti. Kansas. 1888-1890 – 1 – us UMI [071]

WESTERN FARMER – Portland, OR. -m,-sm. Jan 1906-15 Jul 1926 – 7r – 1 – us U.O. Library [071]

WESTERN FEED – v18-20. Sept 1963-Apr 1965 – 1 – us UMI [636]

WESTERN FEED AND SEED – v1-18. 1945-Aug 1963 – 1 – us UMI [636]

WESTERN FIELD : FOR THE HUNTER, THE ANGLER, THE YACHTSMAN, THE CAMPER AND THE LOVER OF OUT-DOOR LIFE – v1-23 (all publ). Aug 1902-Jun 1914; frequency varies; numbering irregular; subtitle varies – 8r – 1 – $830.00 – us UPA [970]
WESTERN FOLKLORE – v1- 1942- 1; v30- 5,6; v35- 9 – us UMI [390]
WESTERN FREEMEN'S BULLETIN *see* AMERICAN FREEDMEN'S BULLETIN
WESTERN FRUIT GROWER – v1- 1954- 1; v95- 5,6,9 – us UMI [634]
WESTERN GAZETTE – Bloomfield. Iowa. -w. 1854-55 – 1 – us UMI [071]
WESTERN GAZETTE – Lima. OH. 1854-59 – 1 – us UMI [071]
WESTERN GAZETTE (NORTH AND EAST SOMERSET ED.) – Yeovil, England.1910. -w. 1 reel – 1 – uk British Libr Newspaper [072]
WESTERN GAZETTE (NORTH, MID AND EAST SOMERSET ED.) – Yeovil, England.1901. -w. 1 reel – 1 – uk British Libr Newspaper [072]
WESTERN GAZETTE (YEOVIL AND SOUTH SOMERSET ED.) – Yeovil, England.1902-03; 1906-09; 1912-71; 1974-76; 1983. -w.123 1/2 reels – 1 – uk British Libr Newspaper [072]
WESTERN GEM – Ballina. Ireland. -w. 1 Apr-9 Dec 1843. (9 ft) – 1 – uk British Libr Newspaper [072]
WESTERN HERALD – Sandwich, Canada. 1838-42 – 1 reel – 1 – $68.00 – cn Library Assoc [971]
WESTERN HERALD (BOURKE) – Jan 1 1896-Dec 30 1903. Jan 3 1906-Dec 30 1914 – 9 – at Pascoe [072]
Western Historical Co *see*
– HISTORY OF DANE COUNTY
– HISTORY OF MILWAUKEE
– AN ILLUSTRATED HISTORY OF CENTRAL OREGON
WESTERN HOME BUILDER – Carlin, NV. 1914-19 (scats) – 2r – 1 – $100.00 – U04437 – us Library Micro [071]
WESTERN HOME JOURNAL – Lawrence. Kan. -w. 1869-85 – 1 – us UMI [071]
WESTERN HOME MONTHLY *see* NATIONAL HOME MONTHLY
WESTERN HOME VISITOR – (General weekly newspaper; 6 issues in the run; aug 5, 1852; jan 22, apr 16, june 25, nov 26 & dec 31, 1853) – Mount Vernon, OH. aug 5, 1852-dec 31, 1853 – 1r – 1 – us Western Res [071]
WESTERN HUMANITIES REVIEW – v1- 1947- 1; v25- 5,6; v30- 9 – us UMI [420]
THE WESTERN IDEAL – Pueblo. Colo. Feb. 13, 20, 1942 – 1 – us NY Public [071]
WESTERN INDEPENDENT – Calgary, Alberta. Canada. Oct 1919-Apr 1920 – 1 – cn Commonwealth Micro [072]
WESTERN INTELLIGENCER – Hudson. Ohio. 1827-1830 – 1 – us UMI [071]
WESTERN INTELLIGENCER – (Weekly Presbyterian newspaper, publ in Cleveland to june 4, 1828, and in Hudson thereafter) – Hudson, OH. july 20, 1827-feb 9, 1830 – 1r – 1 – us Western Res [071]
WESTERN INVERNESS 1851 CENSUS INDEX : ARGYLL AND WEST SCOTLAND CENSUS INDEX, PART 9 / Gibson, Peter & Macinnes, John – 1995 – 2mf – 9 – A$19.95 – 0-646-24543-0 – at Seanachas [920]
THE WESTERN JEWISH NEWS – (In Yiddish) – Winnipeg. v1 n5. 4 nov 1926; v24 n1. 6 jan 1949-6 mar 1978 – 8r – 1 – Can$65.00 – cn Can Microfilming [072]
WESTERN JEWISH WORLD – Denver. Col. 1923 – 1 – us A.J.P.C. [071]
WESTERN JOURNAL OF BLACK STUDIES – (v.4-. 1980- 5,6,9) – v.1-. 1977- – 1 – us UMI [073]
WESTERN JURIST – v1-17. 1867-83 (all publ) – 127mf – 9 – $190.00 – LLMC 82-972 – us L.L.M.C. [073]
WESTERN KANSAS – Leoti. Kan. 1891-1896 – 1 – us UMI [071]
WESTERN KANSAS ENSIGN – Bellefont. Kan. 1889-91 – 1 – us UMI [071]
WESTERN KANSAS JOURNAL – Salina. Kans. and predecessors. 1871-1920 – 1 – us UMI [071]
WESTERN KANSAS LIVESTOCK JOURNAL – Dodge City. Kan. 1899-1903 – 1 – us UMI [636]
WESTERN KANSAS PRESS – Great Bend. Kan. 1962- – 1 – us UMI [071]
WESTERN KANSAS WORLD – Wakeeney. Kansas. 1879-1930 – 1 – us UMI [071]
WESTERN LABOR NEWS – Winnipeg, Canada. v28 n29. 11 fev 1921 – 1r – 1 – Can$30.00 – cn Can Microfilming [072]
WESTERN LANDOWNER *see* COPP'S LAND OWNER
WESTERN LANE NEWS ADVERTISER – Florence OR. Oct 27 1955 – 1 – us U.O. Library [071]
THE WESTERN LAW JOURNAL – Cincinnati. v1-10. 1843-53 (all publ) – 9 – LLMC 82-973 – us L.L.M.C. [073]
THE WESTERN LAW MONTHLY – Cleveland. v1-5. 1859-63 (all publ) – 30mf – 9 – $45.00 – LLMC 82-974 – us L.L.M.C. [073]
WESTERN LAW REPORTER / Canada. General – v1-34. 1905-16 (all publ) – 323mf – 9 – $484.00 – LLMC 81-005 – us L.L.M.C. [340]
WESTERN LAW REVIEW *see* UNIVERSITY OF WESTERN ONTARIO LAW REVIEW
WESTERN LAW TIMES AND REPORTS / Manitoba. Canada – v1-6. 1890-95 (all publ) – 28mf – 9 – $42.00 – LLMC 81-025 – us L.L.M.C. [340]
WESTERN LIFE (WHITE CLIFFS) – Nov 13 1897-Jun 25 1898. Jun 16 1900- Feb 21 1903 – at Pascoe [072]
WESTERN LIVESTOCK REPORTER – Billings. Mont. -w. 1954-59, 1966 – 1 – us UMI [636]
WESTERN LIVING – (v1-3 1971-74 Can$20.00y.v4-5 1974-75 Can$28.00y. v6-12 1976-82 Can$37.00y. v13-25 1983-95 Can$46.00y) – Vancouver. v1-25. 1971/72-1995 – 9 – Price varies – cn Micromedia [790]
WESTERN LUMBERMAN – Vancouver, Canada. -w. Oct 1919-Dec 1921. 3 reels – 1 – uk British Libr Newspaper [073]
WESTERN MAIL – Cardiff, England. -d. Feb-June 1874; Jan-July 1888; July-Dec 1892; Jan-June 1897; Sept-Dec 1898; May-Aug 1899; Jan-April 1900. 13 reels – 1 – uk British Libr Newspaper [072]
WESTERN MAIL – Cardiff, Wales. -d. Jan 1873-June 1874; 1878; 1883; 1888; 1892; Jan-June 1897; Sept-Dec 1898; May-Aug 1899; Jan-April 1900. 22 1 2 reels – 1 – uk British Libr Newspaper [072]
WESTERN MAIL – Perth, Australia. Dec 1885-Nov 1930.-w,d. 10mqn reels – 1 – uk British Libr Newspaper [072]
WESTERN MAIL FROM 1955-1969 – Cardiff.1960-69 – 56r – £35.00r – uk Microform Academic [072]
WESTERN MARYLAND: A PROFILE / Hattery, Thomas H – 1980. Economics and politics of six Western Maryland counties – 9 – us Lomond [320]
WESTERN MESSAGE – Warsaw, Ill. v. 1. no. 1-48. Jan 7 1843-Feb 7 1844 – 1 – us NY Public [071]
WESTERN MESSENGER – Macon, MO. Baptist State Convention of Missouri. Oct 1901-Mar 1904 – 1 – us A.B.H.S. [071]
WESTERN METHODIST RECORDER – (Cont: Methodist Recorder. Cont by: Western Recorder) – Victoria, B.C.: British Columbia Conference of the Methodist Church, [1899-1925] – 9 – cn C.I.H.M. [240]
WESTERN METHODIST RECORDER *see* METHODIST RECORDER
WESTERN MIDNIGHT CRY *see* DAY STAR
WESTERN MINER – Reno, NV. 1915-16; 1919; Mar-May 1927 – 1r – 1 – $50.00 – U04726 – us Library Micro [071]
WESTERN MINERVA / Rafinesque-Schmaltz, Constantine S – or American annals of knowledge and literature. n.p. 1821. B-8118 1 – 9 – ne IDC [000]
WESTERN MINING NEWS – Spokane, WA. 1972-1981 – 10r – 1 – $500.00 – N05408 – us Library Micro [622]
THE WESTERN MISSIONARY – Winnipeg: [s.n. 1890-189- or 19–] – 9 – cn C.I.H.M. [240]
THE WESTERN MONITOR – 2 Jan-28 Dec 1819 – 1 – $60.00 – us OmniSys [071]
WESTERN MONITOR – Fayette. Mo. 1829-1830 – 1 – us UMI [071]
WESTERN MONITOR – Lexington. KY. 1814-16 – 1 – us UMI [071]
WESTERN MUSICAL WORLD – Cleveland. v4-25. 1864-88 – r2-11 – 1 – £550.00 – uk Chadwyck [780]
WESTERN NATIONALIST – Boyle, Ireland. -w. 9 March 1907-21 April 1920. 5 reels – 1 – uk British Libr Newspaper [072]
WESTERN NEBRASKA OBSERVER – Kimball, NE. -w. May 1885-May 1891, scattered issues missing; May 1892; Jan-Dec 1893; Nov-Dec 1895; Feb 1896; Apr 1896 to date – 1 – us NE Hist [071]
WESTERN NEVADA MINER – Mina, NV. 19 Nov 1918; 1908-30 – 3r – 1 – $150.00 – U04627 – us Library Micro [071]
WESTERN NEW ENGLAND LAW REVIEW – (v1-7 1978-85 on reel $120.00. v8-16 1985-94 on mf $115.00) – v1-16. 1978-9 – 5,6,9 – $235.00 set – us Hein [340]
WESTERN NEW YORK BAPTIST MAGAZINE – v1-4. May 1814-Nov 1825 (complete) – 1r – 1 – ATLA R0114 – us A.T.L.A. [073]
Western New York. Synod (Pres. Ch. in the U.S.A.) *see* MINUTES, 1870-1881
THE WESTERN NEWS – Hamilton. Mont. 1950-1954; 1966- – 1 – us UMI [071]
THE WESTERN NEWS – Libby. Mont. 1902-1954; 1966- – 1 – us UMI [071]
WESTERN NEWS – Ballinasloe. Ireland. -w. 9 Nov 1878-5 Nov, 3 Dec 1887, 28 Jan, 25 Feb 1888-2 Jan 1892, 1 Oct, 31 Dec 1898, 16 Dec 1899-27 Dec 1902, 25 Apr-4 Jul 1903, 18 Nov 1905-4 Dec 1926. (18 reels) – 1 – uk British Libr Newspaper [072]
WESTERN NEWS – University of Western Ontario student newspaper. 1980-81 – 1 – cn Commonwealth Micro [072]
WESTERN NIGERIA DEVELOPMENT PLAN, 1962-68 / Nigeria. Western – Sessional Paper No. 8 of 1962. Ibadan. 1962 – 9 – ne IDC [338]
WESTERN NIGERIA DEVELOPMENT PLAN, 1962-68, FIRST PROGRESS REPORT / Nigeria. Western. Ministry of Planning and Community Development – Official Document No. 2 of 1964. Ibadan. 1964. BD-427 1 – 9 – ne IDC [338]
WESTERN NORTH CAROLINA-A HISTORY 1730-1913 / Arthur, John P – Asheville: Edward Buncombe Chapter of the D.A.R., 1914. North Carolina Reel 1. (The Cox Library Collection) – 5 – us Americana [978]
WESTERN OBSERVER – Jacksonville. Ill. 1830-31 – 1 – us UMI [071]
WESTERN OBSERVER – South Shields, England. -w. May-Oct 1911. 1 2 reel – 1 – uk British Libr Newspaper [072]
WESTERN OIL REPORTER – v41-42. 1984-85 – 1,5,6,9 – us UMI [660]
WESTERN OIL WORLD – v42-. 1985- – 1,5,6,9 – us UMI [660]
WESTERN ONTARIO BUSINESS – Ontario Prov., Canada. 1975-79 – 1 – cn Commonwealth Micro [072]
WESTERN ONTARIO LAW REVIEW *see* UNIVERSITY OF WESTERN ONTARIO LAW REVIEW
THE WESTERN OR WAILING WALL IN JERUSALEM / Great Britain. Colonial Office – Memorandum by the Secretary of State for the Colonies. London. 1928. BJ-28-71 1 – 9 – ne IDC [956]
WESTERN OREGON – Cottage Grove, OR. -w. 2 Nov 1905-24 Sep 1909. 1 roll – 1 – us U.O. Library [071]
Western Pacific Archives *see* LIST OF ARCHIVES OF THE NEW HEBRIDES BRITISH SERVICE AND RELATED RECORDS
WESTERN PALLADIUM – (Weekly National Republican, Whig, and Republican newspaper) – New Lisbon, OH. Jul 4 1829-Jan 25 1855 – 1r – 1 – us Western Res [071]
WESTERN PEOPLE – Ballina, Ireland. 4 May 1889-Dec 1976.-w. 109 reels – 1 – uk British Libr Newspaper [072]
WESTERN PEOPLE – Ballina, Ireland. -d. 1889-1986. 200 reels – 1 – PS27.50r – ie European Micro [072]
THE WESTERN PIONEERS, OR, MEMORIALS OF THE LIVES AND LABOURS OF THE REV. RICHARD BOARDMAN AND THE REV. JOSEPH PILMOOR : THE FIRST PREACHERS APPOINTED BY JOHN WESLEY TO LABOUR IN NORTH AMERICA / Lockwood, John P – London: Wesleyan Conference Office, 1881 – 1mf – us A.T.L.A. [240]
WESTERN PLAINS ADVERTISER – 1961-1993 – 14r – 1 – at Corangamite [072]
WESTERN POLITICAL QUARTERLY – v1- 1948- 1; v23- 5,6; v29- 9 – us UMI [320]
WESTERN PRESS – 1866-1870. 1868/9 lost. WP1 – 1r – 1 – at Corangamite [072]
WESTERN PRODUCER – Saskatchewan, CN. 1924- – 4r per yr – 1 – cn Commonwealth Micro [073]
WESTERN PROGRESSIVE – Eugene OR. May June 1930 – 1 – us U.O. Library [071]
WESTERN PROVINCE ADVERTISER – Paarl, South Africa. 17 Jan 1880-24 Dec 1883. 2 reels – 1, 16 diazo available at reduced price – sa SA Libr [072]
THE WESTERN QUEBEC REPORTER – Aylmer, Canada. 19 dec 1962-v10 n36. 10 sep 1972 – 1r – 1 – Can$30.00 – cn Can Microfilming [072]
WESTERN RANGER – Valparaiso. Ind. w. 1847-49 – 1 – us UMI [071]
WESTERN REAL ESTATE BULLETIN – Salem OR. Aug 15-Nov 1928 – 1 – us U.O. Library [071]
WESTERN RECORDER – Kentucky. 1835-1991. Baptist Banner, 1835-51 – 1 – $4,421.20 – us Baptist [240]
WESTERN RECORDER *see* WESTERN METHODIST RECORDER
WESTERN RECREATION – Victoria [B.C.]: Recreation Pub. Co, [1897-189-] – 9 – cn C.I.H.M. [790]
WESTERN REGION DEVELOPMENT PLAN, 1960-65 / Nigeria. Western – (Sessional Paper no. 17 of 1959). Ibadan. 1959 – 9 – ne IDC [338]
WESTERN REGULAR BAPTIST – British Columbia. Jun 1948-Nov 1957 – 1 – 25.55 – us Baptist [240]
WESTERN REPORT – (v5,6 1990-92 Can$82.00y) – Edmonton. v1-9. 1986/87-1994/95 – 9 – Can$73.00y – cn Micromedia [073]
THE WESTERN REPORTER. – (Covers Supreme Courts of IN, IL, MI, MO, OH and NY) – New York: Lawyers' Co-op. v1-14. 1885-88 (all publ) – 9 – LLMC 81-418 – us L.L.M.C. [073]
WESTERN RESERVE CHRONICLE – Warren. Ohio. -w. 1873-1904, 1911 – 1 – us UMI [071]
WESTERN RESERVE CHRONICLE : WEEKLY NATIONAL REPUBLICAN AND WHIG NEWSPAPER – Warren, OH. 11 Oct 1816-29 Dec 1840 – 7r – 1 – us Western Res [071]
WESTERN RESERVE CHRONICLE : WEEKLY NATIONAL REPUBLICAN, WHIG, FREE SOIL AND REPUBLICAN NEWSPAPER – (1852, 1855-1864, 1866-1869, 1872-1879, 1887-1905, 1907-1911 lacking) – Warren, OH. 5 Jan 1841-28 July 1921 – 10r – 1 – us Western Res [071]
WESTERN RESERVE DEMOCRAT : WEEKLY DEMOCRATIC NEWSPAPER – (April 1885-1918, 1920-1933 lacking) – Warren, OH. 30 Mar 1883-27 Dec 1934 – 2r – 1 – us Western Res [071]
WESTERN RESERVE DEMOCRAT – (Weekly Democratic newspaper) – Warren, OH. jan 6-dec 29, 1938 – 1r – 1 – us Western Res [071]
Western Reserve Historical Society *see* INDEX OF NAMES CONTAINED ON CENSUS RETURNS OF PORTAGE CO., OHIO FOR 1850
WESTERN RESERVE HISTORICAL SOCIETY TRACTS – (Monographs concerning the early history of Cleveland, the Connecticut Western Reserve, and the Northwest Territory) – Western Reserve Historical Society of Cleveland, OH – 4r – 1 – us Western Res [978]
THE WESTERN RESERVE LAW JOURNAL – v1-7. 1894-1901 (all publ) – 21mf – 9 – $31.50 – LLMC 82-975 – us L.L.M.C. [073]
WESTERN RESERVE LAW NOTES – v1-2. 1941-1942 (all publ) – 2mf – $3.00 – LLMC 90-339 – us L.L.M.C. [073]
WESTERN RESERVE MANUSCRIPTS, MS 1 – (Records relating to the operation of the Connecticut Land Company, the survey and settlement of the Connecticut Western Reserve, and writings and memoranda of early settlers of the region) – 1795-1869 – 6r – 1 – us Western Res [978]
WESTERN RESERVE MIRROR : WEEKLY REPUBLICAN NEWSPAPER – West Farmington, OH. 23 Jul 1896 – 1r – 1 – us Western Res [071]
Western Reserve Normal School. Milan, Ohio *see* RECORDS
Western Reserve. Ohio. Presbytery *see* CHURCH RECORDS, MS 482
WESTERN RESOURCES – Lincoln. Lancaster County, Nebraska. Jan 1887-Nov 21, 1894 – 1 – us NE Hist [071]
WESTERN RURAL – Chicago. Ill. and American Stockman. 1881-95 – 1 – us UMI [071]
WESTERN SAMOA : SEVENTH DEVELOPMENT PLAN 1992-1994 / National Planning Office – Apia, 1992 – 2mf – 9 – ne IDC [338]
Western Samoa. Department of Economic Development *see* SECOND FIVE YEAR DEVELOPMENT PLAN 1971-1975

WESTERN SAMOA GAZETTE – v3-4. 1958-64 – 2r – 1 – us Ross [324]
WESTERN SAMOAS ECONOMIC DEVELOPMENT PROGRAMME, 1966-1970 / Samoa. Western. Economic Development Board – 1v. Apia. 1966 – 9 – ne IDC [338]
WESTERN SENTINEL – Etna Mills, CA. 1918; 1920-52 – 13r – 1 – $650.00 – B02207 – us Library Micro [071]
WESTERN SHORE GAZETTEER AND COMMERCIAL DIRECTORY FOR CALIFORNIA / Sprague, C P & Atwell, H W – Woodland, 1870. Calif. reel 36.(Cox Library Collection) – 5 – us Americana [978]
WESTERN SKIES: A NARRATIVE OF AMERICAN TRAVEL IN 1868 / Bell, John H – 1870. 02331. (Pre-1900 Canadiana) – 9 – cn C.I.H.M. [910]
WESTERN SLOPES CONNECTION – Nevada City, CA. 1975-79 – 3r – 1 – $150.00 – B02524 – us Library Micro [071]
WESTERN SOCIALIST – (Library has: v.1, no.1, 3-6, 10-11, 13, 30-31; Jan. 2-July 31, 1919) – Portland, Ore.: Western Socialist Pub. Co., 1919- – 1 – CSUX87-S374 – us Hoover Inst Photo [320]
WESTERN SPIRIT – Paola. Kansas. 1873-1876; 1877-1931 – 1 – us UMI [071]
WESTERN STAMP COLLECTOR – Albany, OR. -sw. 9 Feb 1933-. – 1 – us U.O. Library [760]
WESTERN STANDARD : WEEKLY DEMOCRATIC NEWSPAPER – Celina, OH. 1852-70 – 5r – 1 – us Western Res [071]
WESTERN STANDARD ILLUSTRATED WEEKLY – Calgary, Canada. Western Standard Sunday Calgary Sunday Standard Calgary Western Standard Illustrated Weekly. -w. April 1913-July 1918. 7 reels – 1 – uk British Libr Newspaper [072]
THE WESTERN STAR – (Cont by: Western Star and Evening Post 5 sep-3 oct 1830 1r Can$40.00) – Montreal, Canada. 23 mar 1819-v1 n53. 24 sep 1819 – 1r – 1 – Can$40.00 – cn Can Microfilming [072]
WESTERN STAR – (1907-1992.-293r) – Cornerbrook, 1993 – 16r – 1 – cn Preston [971]
WESTERN STAR – Ballinasloe. Ireland. -w. Oct 1845-Aug 1869, Dec 1888-May 1902. (19 reels) – 1 – uk British Libr Newspaper [072]
WESTERN STAR – Bath and London, England. -w. 3 Oct-5 Dec 1840. 6 ft – 1 – uk British Libr Newspaper [072]
WESTERN STAR – Curling, Canada. -f. July 1911-Dec 1921. 4 reels – 1 – uk British Libr Newspaper [072]
WESTERN STAR – Dallas, TX. Afro-American. 1902-03, 1915-17 – 1 – 23.25 – us A.B.H.S. [071]
WESTERN STAR – Lebanon. Ohio. 1816-1853; 1964- – 1 – us UMI [071]
WESTERN STAR – Roseburg, OR. 14 Dec 1877-24 Dec 1880. 1 roll – 1 – us U.O. Library [071]
WESTERN STAR AND EVENING POST *see* THE WESTERN STAR
WESTERN STAR OREGON WEEKLY – Portland. Or. 1851-1859 – 1 – us UMI [071]
WESTERN STATE UNIVERSITY LAW REVIEW – v1-19. 1972-92 – 1,5,6 – $315.00 – us Hein [073]
WESTERN SUBURBS ADVERTISER – 1966-6/68. WSA1-4 – 4r – 1 – at Corangamite [072]
WESTERN SUN – Birmingham. Ala. -w. 1959-62 – 1 – us UMI [071]
WESTERN SUN – Lynnwood. Wash. 1966- – 1 – us UMI [071]
THE WESTERN SUNBEAM – Winnipeg: Western Sunbeam, v1 no 1(Apr 1891)- – 9 – cn C.I.H.M. [073]
WESTERN TAX COLLECTOR – Crescent City, CA. 16 Dec 1939 – 1r – 1 – $50.00 – B02150 – us Library Micro [071]
WESTERN TELEGRAPH – Rossville, OH, 28 Nov 1834 and 26 Aug 1836 – 1 reel – 1 – us Western Res [320]
WESTERN TELEGRAPH – Rossville. Ohio. 1838-1839 – 1 – us UMI [071]
WESTERN TELEGRAPH – Washington. Pa. and Washington Advertiser. 1795-97 – 1 – us UMI [071]
WESTERN TELEGRAPH : WEEKLY DEMOCRATIC NEWSPAPER – Hamilton, OH, 9 Dec 1836-20 Aug 1846 – 2r – 1 – us Western Res [071]
WESTERN TELEGRAPH AND BUTLER COUNTY, OHIO ADVERTISER – (Weekly Democratic newspaper) – Rossville, OH. Nov 28 1834, Aug 26 1836 – 1r – 1 – us Western Res [071]
WESTERN TIMBER INDUSTRY – (Set incl. Western Equipment and Timber News (Portland); National Timber Industry (Portland)) – Portland, OR. -m. Dec 1957-Apr 1975+. – 2r – 1 – us U.O. Library [071]
WESTERN TIMES – Ahmedabad, India. Jul 1967-1980 – 46r – 1 – us L of C Photodup [072]
WESTERN TRANSVAAL RECORD – Klerksdorp, South Africa. 1888-1981 – 1 – sa State Libr [072]
WESTERN VOICE, FEB 1968-MAY 1970 *see* WESTERN VOICE FROM OUT OF THE ROCKIES
WESTERN VOICE FROM OUT OF THE ROCKIES – (Library has: v6 n38-v35 n[16?]; Oct 15 1942-Apr 23 1970. Scattered issues missing) – Englewood, CO: Western Voice, 1935 – 1 – CSUX87-S427 – us Hoover Inst Photo [978]
WESTERN WANDERINGS: RECORD OF TRAVEL IN THE EVENING LAND / Boddam-Whetham, John W – London: R. Bentley, 1874. 00157. (Pre-1900 Canadiana) – 9 – cn C.I.H.M. [910]
WESTERN WATCHMAN – Eureka, CA. 1886-98 – 4r – 1 – $200.00 – C02226 – us Library Micro [071]
WESTERN WATCHMAN – Eureka. Calif. 1886-1898 – 1 – us UMI [071]
WESTERN WAVE – Western, NE. -w. Mar 1885-Apr 1889; Aug 1889-Jan 1894, scattered issues missing; Mar 1894-Apr 1895; Jul 1895-Jul 1956 – 1 – us NE Hist [071]
WESTERN WHIG STANDARD – Tiffin, Ohio. 1849-50 – 1r – 1 – $32.50r – us Archival [071]
WESTERN WOMAN VOTER – v1-3. no. 1 (monthly: all publ). 1911-13 – 1 reel – 1 – $55.00 – us UPA [320]
WESTERN WOMEN IN EASTERN LANDS : AN OUTLINE STUDY OF FIFTY YEARS OF WOMAN'S WORK IN FOREIGN MISSIONS / Montgomery, Helen Barrett – (Includes statistical table, bibliographies, and index) – New York: Publ for the Central Committee on the United Study of Missions [by] Macmillan, 1910 – 1mf – 9 – 0-8370-6685-9 – 1986-0685 – us A.T.L.A. [305]
WESTERN WORKER / Communist Party.U.S.A – v1-6 (all publ). 1932-37 – 3r – 1 – $345.00 – us UPA [073]
THE WESTERN WORLD *see* THE RAILWAY AND SHIPPING WORLD
WESTERN WORLD – Bandon, OR. -w. 25 Mar 1915-29 Dec 1975+. – 24r – 1 – us U.O. Library [071]
WESTERN WORLD – Portland OR. July Aug 1933 – 1 – us U.O. Library [071]
WESTERN WORLD – South Bend. Wash. -w. 1889-1890 – 1 – us UMI [071]
WESTERN WORLD – Warsaw, Ill. v. 1. May 13 1840-May 5 1841. Incomplete – 1 – us NY Public [071]
WESTERN WORLD REVIEW – Non-partison review and opinion journal. quarterly. Essentially Libertarian, also Conservative and 'classical' Liberal opinion. Covers all subjects – 9 – 1.00f – at Libertarian Micro [073]
WESTERN WORLD REVIEW – Winter 1976 77. Special issue on Henry Meulen's free banking ideas. 5 fiches (24x) – 9 – 1.00f – at Libertarian Micro [320]
WESTERN YOUTH – Independence, OR. -w. 9 Apr 1918-12 Jun 1918. 1 roll – 1 – us U.O. Library [071]
Westervelt, Frances A *see* HISTORY OF BERGEN COUNTY 1630-1923
WESTERWAELDER ZEITUNG – Koblenz, Germany. 1 Sept 1978- – 1 – gw Mikrofilm [072]
WESTERWAELDER ZEITUNG – Montabaur, West Germany.1 Sept 1978- – 1 – gw Mikrofilm [072]
WESTFAELISCHE ALLGEMEINE VOLKSZEITUNG *see* WESTFAELISCHE ARBEITER ZEITUNG
WESTFAELISCHE ARBEITER ZEITUNG – (Westfaelische Freie Presse. Oct 1890-Sept 1892. Rheinisch-Westfaelische Arbeiter-Zeitung. Oct 1892-4 Oct 1902. Westfaelische Allgemeine Volkszeitung. 5 Oct 1917-Feb 1933. Westfaelische Post. Apr 1933) – Dortmund, Germany. Oct 1890-Apr 1903; 1905-May 1917; Jul 1917-19; Oct 1921-Jun 1922; Jul 1924-Mar 1925; 1926-Feb 1933; 4-24 Apr 1933 – 104r – 1 – gw Mikrofilm [072]
WESTFAELISCHE ARBEITER-ZEITUNG – Dortmund, Germany. Sept 1888-24 Aug 1889. Continued by: Arbeiter-Zeitung – 1 – gw Mikrofilm [072]
DER WESTFAELISCHE BUERGER- UND BAUERNFREUND – Soest, Germany. Jul 1848-49 – 1 – gw Mikrofilm [072]
WESTFAELISCHE FREIE PRESSE *see* WESTFAELISCHE ARBEITER ZEITUNG
WESTFAELISCHE LANDESZEITUNG – Dortmund, Germany. s. yGeneral-Anzeiger, Dortmund – 1 – gw Mikrofilm [072]
WESTFAELISCHE LANDESZEITUNG, AUSGABE B *see* ROTE ERDE
WESTFAELISCHE LANDESZEITUNG/ROTE ERDE *see* GENERAL-ANZEIGER
WESTFAELISCHE NACHRICHTEN – Muenster, West Germany. 1958- – 1 – gw Mikrofilm [072]
WESTFAELISCHE NEUESTE NACHRICHTEN *see* BIELEFELDER GENERALANZEIGER
WESTFAELISCHE POST *see*
– HAGENER VOLKSZEITUNG
– WESTFAELISCHE ARBEITER ZEITUNG
WESTFAELISCHE REFORM – Dortmund, Germany. 1886; 1888-1893; 1895; Jan.-Maerz 1900 – 1 – gw Mikrofilm [072]
WESTFAELISCHE RUNDSCHAU – (Also available: Ausgabe 5 DW, 1991- (12r per yr); Ausgabe 1 SN, 1991- (12r per yr). Also Bereichsausgaben available: ALTENA, 1961-62, 1990- ; ARNSBERG, 1961-62, 1977- ; ARNSBERG, AUSGABE NEHEIM-HUESTEN, 1961-62; BECKUM, 1961-62; BAD BERLEBURG, 1961-62, 1991- ; BETZDORF, 1991- ; BOCHOLT, 1961-62; BOCHUM, 1961-62; BOCHUM, AUSGABE WATTENSCHEID, 1961-62; CASTROP-RAUXEL, 1961-62, 1990- ;COESFELD, 1961-62; GELSENKIRCHEN, 1961-62; GLADBECK, 1961-62; HAGEN, mar 20 1946-62, 1990- ; HAGEN, AUSGABE HAGEN-HOHENLIMBURG, 1991- ; HAMM, 1961-62; HATTINGEN, 1991- ; HERNE, 1961-62; HERNE, AUSGABE WANNE-EICKEL, 1961-62; ISERLOHN, 1961-62, 1990- ; KAMEN, 1961-62, 1991- ; LUEDENSCHEID, 1961-62, 1990- ; LUENEN, 1961-62, 1990- ; MEINERZHAGEN, 1990- ; MESCHEDE, 1961-62, 1990- ; MUENSTER, 1961-62; OLPE, 1990- ; PLETTENBERG, 1990- ; RECKLINGHAUSEN, 1961-62; SCHWELM, 1990- ; SCHWERTE, 1961-62, 1990- ; SIEGEN, 1961-62, 1990- ; SOEST, 1961-62; SPROCKHOEVEL, 1990- ; TECKLENBURG, 1961-62; UNNA, 1961-62, 1990- ; WARSTEIN, 1991- ; WETTER, 1990- ; WITTEN, mar 20 1946-76, 1991-) – Dortmund, mar 20 1946- – 1 – Inquire at Mikrofilmarchiv for details – gw Misc Inst [072]
WESTFAELISCHE RUNDSCHAU – Dortmund, Germany. -w. 20 March 1946-24 May 1949. 3 reels – 1 – uk British Libr Newspaper [072]
WESTFAELISCHE RUNDSCHAU – Dortmund, West Germany. 20 Mar 1946-49, 1954-60, 1963- – 1 – gw Mikrofilm [072]
WESTFAELISCHE TAGESZEITUNG *see*
– VOLKS-ZEITUNG FUER RHEINE UND UMGEBUNG
WESTFAELISCHE VOLKSZEITUNG – Bochum, 1872-1941 – 1 – Inquire at Mikrofilmarchiv for details – gw Misc Inst [943]
WESTFAELISCHE ZEITUNG – Bielefeld, West Germany.Title change: Neue Westfaelische (3 Jul 1967).1958- – 1 – gw Mikrofilm [072]
WESTFAELISCHE ZEITUNG – (Cont: Oeffentliche Anzeigen des Districtes [...], -1812; Oeffentliche Anzeigen der Grafschaft Ravensberg, -1857; Bielefelder Kreisblatt, -1864; Bielefelder Wochenblatt, -1876; Bielefelder Tageblatt, -nov 1883. Cont by: Neue Westfaelische, Bielefeld, jul 3 1967) – Bielefeld, 1811-aug 31 1944, oct 23 1949- – 1 – Inquire at Mikrofilmarchiv for details – gw Misc Inst [943]
WESTFAELISCHE ZEITUNG *see* FREIE PRESSE
DIE WESTFAELISCHEN MUSENALMANACHE UND POETISCHEN TASCHENBUECHER : EIN BEITRAG ZUR GESCHICHTE DER LITERARISCHEN KULTUR WESTFALENS IN DER ERSTEN HAELFTE DES 19. JAHRHUNDERTS / Casser, Paul – Muenster, 1928 – 186p – 9 – DM48.00 – 3-89349-060-4 – gw Hänsel [430]
WESTFAELISCHER ANZEIGER – Hamm, West Germany. 1958- – 1 – gw Mikrofilm [072]
WESTFAELISCHER ANZEIGER *see* KREIS HAMMSCHES WOCHENBLATT
WESTFAELISCHER ANZEIGER UND KURIER *see* KREIS HAMMSCHES WOCHENBLATT
WESTFAELISCHER BEOBACHTER – Bottrop, 1930-34 – 1 – Inquire at Mikrofilmarchiv for details – gw Misc Inst [943]
WESTFAELISCHER KAEMPFER – (Cont by: Der Kaempfer, apr 1, 1932) – Dortmund/Hamm. feb 1, 1925-jan 31, 1933 (incomplete). feb 15-20, 1933 – 1 – gw Mikrofilm [072]
WESTFAELISCHER MERKUR – Muenster, Germany. 1848-5 May 1849; 30 Jul 1914-16 (incompl.); 1917-18 – 1 – gw Mikrofilm [072]
WESTFAELISCHES TAGEBLATT *see* HAGENER VOLKSZEITUNG
WESTFAELISCHES VOLKSBLATT – Paderborn, West Germany.1977- – 1 – gw Mikrofilm [072]
WESTFAELISCH-LIPPISCHE VOLKSZEITUNG – Bielefeld, aug 1914-jun 1915 – 1 – Inquire at Mikrofilmarchiv for details – gw Misc Inst [943]
WESTFALEN ZEITUNG – Bielefeld, Germany. Westfalen-Blatt. -d. 15 March 1946-31 Dec 1953. 29 reels – 1 – uk British Libr Newspaper [072]
WESTFALEN-BLATT – Bielefeld, West Germany. 1976$ – 1 – gw Mikrofilm [072]
WESTFALEN-BLATT – (Cont: Westfalen-Zeitung, -jun 1950) – Bielefeld, mar 15 1946- – 1 – Inquire at Mikrofilmarchiv for details – gw Misc Inst [072]
WESTFALENPOST – Hagen, Germany. 1977- – 1 – gw Mikrofilm [072]
WESTFALENPOST-WP – Hagen, West Germany. 1977- – 1 – gw Mikrofilm [072]
WESTFALEN-ZEITUNG *see* WESTFALEN-BLATT
WESTFALISCHE LANDESZEITUNG : ROTE ERDE – (Library has: v.50,no.174-v.54,no.310; v.56-v.57,no.97; Jul. 1937-Apr. 1944; many missing issues) – Dortmund: Nationalsozialistische Deutsche Arbeiter-Partei, 19uu- – 1 – CSUX89-S41 – us Hoover Inst Photo [320]
WESTFALISCHE RUNDSCHAU – Dortmund, Germany. 1962-Apr 1971 – 80r – 1 – us L of C Photodup [072]
Westfall Thompson, J *see* THE MEDIEVAL LIBRARY
WESTFIELD 1669-1895 – 114mf – 9 – 0-87623-014-1 – us Holbrook [920]
WESTFORD 1726-1902 – (Mf 1-63,67: Town Records 1726-1862. Mf 9-10: Vital Records 1701-65. Mf 13-14,17,19: Marriages 1772-88. Mf 20: Intentions 1765-90. Mf 29,39: Marriages 1787-1815. Mf 40: Births 1821-27. Mf 46,54: Marriages 1813-35. Mf 64-93: Accounts 1760-1863. Mf 94-97: Mortgages 1838-59. Mf 98-105:Town Records 1794-1846. Mf 104: Fence Disputes 1846-95. Mf 105,123:Strays/Dogs 1847-74. Mf 106-112: School Records 1801-69. Mf 113-127: Tax/Misc 1840-96. Mf 128-136: Militia 1840-77. Mf 131-33,137-39: Voters 1877-1911. Mf 140-155: Church Records 1727-1896. Mf 156-167: Births, Deaths 1701-1874. Mf 168-176: Marriages 1681-1902. Mf 177-184,191: Burials 1849-60. Mf 185-187:Death Index 1844-1902. Mf 88-191: Deaths 1844-1902. Mf 192-197: Marriage Index 1844-1902. Mf 198-199,191: Marriages 1844-1902. Mf 200-205:Birth Index 1842-1902. Mf 206-209,176: Births 1842-1902) – (mf ed 1996) – 209mf – 0-87623-387-6 – us Holbrook [920]
WESTFUNK – (Also called: Funk-Spiegel; Radio Illustrierte. Cont by: Hoeren und Fernsehen, aug 31, 1952. Hoeren und Sehen, nov 2, 1952. TV Fernseh-Woche, may 19, 1957. TV Hoeren und Sehen, feb 4, 1962) – Hamburg, Bremen, Koeln. apr 17, 1949-jan 7, 1994 (incomplete) – 180r – 1 – gw Mikrofilm [790]
WESTHAMPTON 1778-1893 – 10mf – 9 – us Holbrook [920]
Westhoff, Franz *see* E.G. KOLBENHEYERS PARACELSUS-TRILOGIE
Westhovius, W W W *see* CIMBRI, EMBLEMATA. CHRISTIANO 4. DICATA

WESTKUSTEN – Kungsbacka, Sweden. 1874-76 – 1 – sw Kungliga [072]

Westlake, H F *see* THE PARISH GUILDS OF MEDIEVAL ENGLAND

WESTLAND – Saarbruecken, Germany. Unabhaengige Deutsche Wochenzeitung. 18 Nov 1933-1 Dec 1934. Continued by: Grenzland. Saarbruecken. (MA) – 1 – gw Mikrofilm [072]

WESTLAND : UNABHAENGIGE DEUTSCHE WOCHENZEITUNG (Title change: Grenzland, 2 Dec 1934) – Saarbruecken, Germany. 18 Nov 1933-13 Jan 1935 – 2r – 1 – gw Mikrofilm [072]

WESTLAND – Unabhaengige deutsche Wochenzeitung. Saarbruecken. nov 1933-34. devenu: Grenzland. Voir a ce titre – 1 – fr A.C.R.P.P. [073]

Westley, S *see* LOW LEVEL AERIAL SURVEY TECHNIQUES

Westley, S B *see* EAST AFRICAN PASTORALISM

Westman, Knut B *see*
- BIRGITTA-STUDIER
- DEN SVENSKA KYRKANS UTVECKLING

WESTMEATH GUARDIAN – Mullingar, Ireland. 1851-60; 1862-87; 1889-92. -w. 15 reels – 1 – uk British Libr Newspaper [072]

WESTMEATH INDEPENDENT – Athlone, Ireland. Jun 1846-1853; 1855-83; 1886-96. -w.22 reels – 1 – uk British Libr Newspaper [072]

WESTMINISTER DAILY PILOT – Westminister, CA. 1966 – 9r – 1 – $450.00 – R04040 – us Library Micro [071]

Westminister. Presbytery (Pres. Ch. in the U.S.A.) *see* MINUTES, 1870-1924

WESTMINISTER REVIEW – v1-181. 1824-1914 – 1 – us Princeton Micro [073]

WESTMINISTER TRIBUNE – Westminister, CA. 1891-1892 – 1r – 1 – $50.00 – R04132 – us Library Micro [071]

WESTMINSTER 1728-1905 – (Mf 1-12: Vital Records 1738-1852. Mf 5,12: Intentions 1764-94. Mf 13-63: Town Records 1759-1851. Mf 4-75: Selectmen Records 1791-1850. Mf 75-85: Proprietors 1728-57. Mf 86-92: Misc Records 1790-1894. Mf 93-99: Pews, Mortgages 1827-57. Mf 99-105: Court Records 1786-1805. Mf 99,106-108: Military 1840-74. Mf 109-130: Taxes 1810-49. Mf 131-136: Poor 1817-67,1905-41. Mf 137-141,146: School 1803-69. Mf 142-144: Marriages 1774-1853. Mf 144-146: Intentions 1794-1853. Mf 147: Births, Deaths 1825-45. Mf 147-152: Intentions 1854-1914. Mf 150-152: Boundaries 1888-1953. Mf 153-154: Vitals Index 1754-1853. Mf 153: Marriages 1754-99. Mf 154-155: Vital Records 1832-53. Mf 156-157,160: Birth Index 1816-1905. Mf 158-160: Death Index 1853-1912. Mf 161-162: Marriage Index 1853-1910. Mf 163-166: Deaths 1853-1912. Mf 167-169: Marriages 1853-1910. Mf 170-172: Births 1816-1905) – (mf ed 1997) – 172mf – 0-87623-391-4 – us Holbrook [920]

Westminster Abbey. Library *see*
- THE EARLY MANUSCRIPT COLLECTION
- EARLY PRINTED AND MANUSCRIPT MUSIC

WESTMINSTER AND PIMLICO NEWS – London, 1887- – 125+ r – 1 – uk British Libr Newspaper [072]

WESTMINSTER BAPTIST CHURCH. OCONEE COUNTY. WESTMINSTER, SOUTH CAROLINA : CHURCH RECORDS – 1844-92; 1901-41; 1942-47; 1954-72 – 1 – 60.75 – us Baptist [240]

Westminster Cathedral *see* CATHOLIC COLONIAL MISSIONS

Westminster Cathedral. Archives *see*
- GRADWELL LETTERS, 1777-1833, FROM THE ARCHIVES OF THE ARCHBISHOP OF WESTMINSTER
- INDEX OF TITLE PAGES TO PAMPHLET LITERATURE IN THE ARCHIVES OF THE ARCHBISHOP OF WESTMINSTER
- THE LETTERS OF ARCHBISHOP ALLEN
- REGISTERS OF BIRTHS, MARRIAGES AND DEATHS
- SERIES A
- SERIES A: INDICES TO THE ARCHIVES

THE WESTMINSTER CONFESSION OF FAITH / Carruthers, SW – 1937 – 1 – $50.00 – us Presbyterian [240]

WESTMINSTER CONFESSION OF FAITH : WITH INTRODUCTION AND NOTES / Macpherson, John – (Includes index) – 2nd ed. Edinburgh: T & T Clark, [1882?] – 1mf – 9 – 0-8370-8764-3 – 1986-2764 – us A.T.L.A. [240]

THE WESTMINSTER CONFESSION OF FAITH AND THE THIRTY-NINE ARTICLES OF THE CHURCH OF ENGLAND : THE LEGAL, MORAL, AND RELIGIOUS ASPECTS OF SUBSCRIPTION TO THEM / Donaldson, James – London; New York: Longmans, Green, 1905 – 1mf – us A.T.L.A. [240]

THE WESTMINSTER CONFESSION OF FAITH CRITICALLY COMPARED WITH THE HOLY SCRIPTURES AND FOUND WANTING : OR, A NEW EXPOSITION OF THE DOCTRINES OF THE CHRISTIAN RELIGION, IN HARMONY WITH THE WORD OF GOD, AND NOT AT VARIANCE WITH MODERN SCIENCE / Stark, James – (Includes index) – London: Longman, Green, Longman, Roberts, & Green, 1863 – 1mf – 9 – 0-8370-8947-6 – 1986-2947 – us A.T.L.A. [240]

THE WESTMINSTER CONFESSION OF FAITH EXAMINED ON THE BASIS OF THE OTHER PROTESTANT CONFESSIONS / Goodsir, Joseph Taylor – London: Williams and Norgate, 1868 – 2mf – 9 – 0-8370-8903-4 – 1986-2903 – us A.T.L.A. [240]

WESTMINSTER FIRST BAPTIST CHURCH (FORMERLY: OLD WESTMINSTER). WESTMINSTER, SOUTH CAROLINA : CHURCH RECORDS – 1836-1904 – 1 – 17.01 – us Baptist [240]

WESTMINSTER GAZETTE – London, Jan 1893-Jan 1928 – 201r – 1 – uk British Libr Newspaper [072]

WESTMINSTER GAZETTE – Westminster, CA. 1931-1941 – 3r – 1 – $150.00 – R04133 – us Library Micro [071]

WESTMINSTER HALL : OR PROFESSIONAL RELICS AND ANECDOTES OF THE BAR, BENCH AND WOOLSACK – (Lacking: p68-69) – London: John Knight & Henry Lacey, 1825 – 4mf – 9 – $6.00 – LLMC 95-205 – us L.L.M.C. [870]

WESTMINSTER HALL CHRONICLE AND LEGAL EXAMINER – London. v1-2 pt 5 no 21. 7 Nov 1835-26 Mar 1836 (all publ) – 14mf – 9 – $21.00 – LLMC 87-400 – us L.L.M.C. [073]

WESTMINSTER HERALD – Westminster, CA. 1979 – 7+ r – 1 – $350.00 ($50.00y) – RR04134 – us Library Micro [071]

Westminster. London *see* SELECTED PLANS OF STREETS AND BUILDINGS

WESTMINSTER OBSERVER – Westminster, CA. 1976-1978 – 1r – 1 – $50.00 – R04135 – us Library Micro [071]

WESTMINSTER REVIEW – 1824-1866 – 32r – 1 – uk Microform Academic [073]

WESTMINSTER REVIEW – London. v1-181.1824-1914 – 1 – us Princeton Micro [800]

WESTMINSTER REVIEW – v. 1-181. 1824-1914 – 1 – us UMI [073]

WESTMINSTER SERMONS / Henson, H Hensley – London: James Clarke, 1910 – 1mf – us A.T.L.A. [240]

WESTMINSTER SERMONS / Kingsley, Charles – London: Macmillan, 1874 – 1mf – 9 – 0-8370-7471-1 – 1986-1471 – us A.T.L.A. [240]

WESTMINSTER STUDIES IN EDUCATION – 1978- 16v – 9 – £123.50 – 0140-6728 – uk Carfax [370]

WESTMORELAND AND IND. REGISTER – Greensburg, PA., 1812-1817 – 13 – $25.00r – us I.M.R. [071]

Westmoreland, New Hampshire. East Westmoreland Baptist Church *see* RECORDS

WESTMORELAND PILOT – Montross. Va. 1967 – 1 – us UMI [071]

WESTMORLAND, 1820 : BRITISH ISLES CENSUS DIRECTORIES PROJECT, ENGLAND – (In prep) – at Vine [941]

WESTMORLAND, 1828 : BRITISH ISLES CENSUS DIRECTORIES PROJECT, ENGLAND – at Vine [941]

WESTMORLAND, 1829 : BRITISH ISLES CENSUS DIRECTORIES PROJECT, ENGLAND. VOL 122 – 2mf – 9 – A$15.00 – at Vine [941]

WESTMORLAND, 1834 : BRITISH ISLES CENSUS DIRECTORIES PROJECT, ENGLAND – (In prep) – at Vine [941]

WESTMORLAND, 1849 : BRITISH ISLES CENSUS DIRECTORIES PROJECT, ENGLAND – at Vine [941]

WESTMORLAND, 1851 : BRITISH ISLES CENSUS DIRECTORIES PROJECT, ENGLAND. VOL 134 – 3mf – 9 – A$21.00 – at Vine [941]

WESTMORLAND, 1855 : BRITISH ISLES CENSUS DIRECTORIES PROJECT, ENGLAND – at Vine [941]

WESTMORLAND, 1885 : BRITISH ISLES CENSUS DIRECTORIES PROJECT, ENGLAND – at Vine [941]

WESTMORLAND, 1905 : BRITISH ISLES CENSUS DIRECTORIES PROJECT, ENGLAND. VOL 75 – 4mf – 9 – A$27.00 – at Vine [941]

WESTMORLAND (KENDALL), 1805 : BRITISH ISLES CENSUS DIRECTORIES PROJECT, ENGLAND. VOL 181 – 1mf – 9 – A$9.00 – at Vine [941]

THE WESTMOUNT ADVERTISER – Westmount, Canada. 17 dec 1898 – 1r – 1 – Can$25.00 – cn Can Microfilming [072]

THE WESTMOUNT EXAMINER *see* THE WEEKLY EXAMINER

THE WESTMOUNT NEWS – Westmount, Canada. 5 oct 1907-14 oct 1921 – 3r – 1 – Can$75.00r – cn Can Microfilming [072]

WESTMOUNT WEEKLY NEWS AND WEST END ADVERTISER – Westmount, Canada. 16 nov 1895 – 1r – 1 – Can$25.00 – cn Can Microfilming [072]

WEST-OESTLICHER DIVAN / Goethe, Johann Wolfgang von – (Includes bibliographical references) – Berlin: Turm-Verlag, 1948 – 1r – 1 – us U.W. Library [830]

Weston, Agnes Elizabeth *see* MY LIFE AMONG THE BLUEJACKETS

Weston, David *see* THE BAPTISTS AND THE NATIONAL CENTENARY

WESTON FIRST BAPTIST CHURCH. WESTON, WEST VIRGINIA : CHURCH RECORDS – 1867-1903, 1914-72 – 1 – 59.58 – us Baptist [240]

Weston, Joan *see* A STUDY OF BIOMECHANICAL VARIABLES IN THE COUNTERMOVEMENT JUMP AND THE DROP JUMP PERFORMED BY FEMALE INTERCOLLEGIATE ATHLETES

WESTON LEADER – Weston, OR. -w. 13 Apr 1888-15 Nov 1946, – 1 – us U.O. Library [071]

WESTON MERCURY – Weston-super-Mare, England. 1855- – 204+ r – 1 – uk British Libr Newspaper [072]

Weston, Plowden Charles Jennett *see*
- METEOROLOGICAL RECORDS
- PLANTATION RECORDS

Weston, R *see* BOTANICUS UNIVERSALIS ET HORTULANUS

WESTON STAR – Weston-super-Mare, England. Jan-Sep 1900 – 1r – 1 – uk British Libr Newspaper [072]

WESTON TIMES – Weston, Ontario, CN. 1890-1973 – 34r – 1 – cn Commonwealth Micro [072]

THE WESTONIAN – Weston-super-Mare. England. -w. Jan 1844-Feb 1848. (1 reel) – 1 – uk British Libr Newspaper [072]

WESTON-SUPER-MARE ADVERTISER – England. -w. Nov 1928-May 1930. (1 reel) – 1 – uk British Libr Newspaper [072]

WESTON-SUPER-MARE CHRONICLE – England. -w. Apr 1860-Jan 1861. (1 reel) – 1 – uk British Libr Newspaper [072]

WESTON-SUPER-MARE DIRECTORY – England. -w. Apr-Jul 1858. (1 reel) – 1 – uk British Libr Newspaper [072]

WESTON-SUPER-MARE GAZETTE – England. -w and sw. 1845-1951. (95 reels) – 1 – uk British Libr Newspaper [072]

WESTPHAELISCHE BEMUEHUNGEN – Lemgo, Germany. 1753-1755 – 1 – gw Mikrofilm [072]

DAS WESTPHAELISCHE DAMPFBOOT – Bielefeld, Paderborn. 1845-may 17 1848 – 1 – Inquire at Mikrofilmarchiv for details – gw Misc Inst [943]

DAS WESTPHAELISCHE DAMPFBOOT – Bielefeld Paderborn, Germany. 1845-Mar 1848 – 1 – gw Mikrofilm [072]

WESTPHAELISCHE STADT= UND LANDCHRONIK [...] – Bueckeburg, 1793 – 1r – 1 – Inquire at Mikrofilmarchiv for details – gw Misc Inst [943]

WESTPHAELISCHER ANZEIGER – (Cont by: Rheinland-Westfaler Anzeiger, 1816. Rheinischer-Westfaelischer Anzeiger, apr 2, 1816. Der Sprecher, 1831. Publ in Hamm since oct 1818, in Wesel since 1841) – Dortmund. jul 3, 1798-1806. jul 3, 1807-1811. 1816-17. 1819-27. apr 5, 1829-sep 28, 1831. jan 4-sep 29, 1832. 1833-jun 30, 1841. oct 2, 1841-jun 30, 1847 – 25r – 1 – gw Mikrofilm [943]

WESTPHAELISCHER BEOBACHTER – Kleve, may 24 1755-jun 17 1757 – 1 – gw Mikrofilm [943]

WESTPHAELISCHER MONITEUR – Kassel, Germany.29 Dez 1807-08 – 1 – gw Mikrofilm [072]

WESTPHAELISCHES AMTSBLATT – Dortmund. 1814-15 – 1r – 1 – gw Mikrofilm [943]

Westphal, F *see* ZUR ERINNERUNG AN FUERST GEORG DEN GOTTSELIGEN ZU ANHALT

Westphal, Gustav *see* JAHWES WOHNSTAETTEN: NACH DEN ANSCHAUUNGEN DER ALTEN HEBRAEER

WESTPORT 1717-1900 – (Mf 1-5: Vital Records 1719-1829. Mf 5-6: Marriages 1788-1821. Mf 7-12: Town Records 1787-1943. Mf 13-14: Vital Records 1825-45. Mf 14-17: Town Records 1698-1896. Mf 17: Vital Records 1730-1846. Mf 18-21: Birth Index 1843-92. Mf 21-24: Marriage Index 1843-92. Mf 25-27: Death Index 1843-92. Mf 28-29: Intentions Index 1850-96. Mf 30-32: Intentions 1850-96. Mf 33-34: Births 1843-56. Mf 35: Marriages 1843-57. Mf 35-36: Deaths 1848-56. Mf 37-40: Births 1857-92. Mf 41-42: Marriages 1857-92. Mf 43-46: Deaths 1857-93. Mf 47: Births 1893-1900. Mf 48: Marriages 1893-1900. Mf 49: Deaths 1893-1904) – (mf ed 1992) – 49mf – 0-87623-149-0 – us Holbrook [920]

WEST-PREUSSISCHE ELBINGSCHE ZEITUNG VON STAATS- UND GELEHRTEN SACHEN – Elbing, Germany.1800, 1802, 1812-13, 1818, 1827 – 1 – gw Mikrofilm [072]

WESTPREUSSISCHE ZEITUNG – Elblag, Poland. Oct 1935-Jun 1936 – 2r – 1 – us L of C Photodup [943]

Westpreussischer Geschichtsverein *see* ZEITSCHRIFT

WESTRALIAN WORKER – Perth. Australia. -w. 31 Oct 1924-27 Dec 1946. (23mqn reels) – 1 – uk British Libr Newspaper [072]

Westring, N *see* ARANEAE SVECICAE DESCRIPTAE

WESTSIDE ENTERPRISE – Independence OR. Jan 21 1904-Apr 18 1905, Oct 27 1905, July 17-Aug 14 1906, Feb 21 1908-May 31 1913, Jan 5 1917-June 26 1969 – 1 – us U.O. Library [071]

Westside Presbyterian Church, Lawrence, KS *see* RECORDS

WESTVIEW BAPTIST CHURCH. SHELBY, NORTH CAROLINA : CHURCH RECORDS – 1961-63 – 1 – 24.39 – us Baptist [240]

WESTWARD COLLECTOR QUARTERLY – Nanaimo. v1. 1973-1974 – 9 – Can$20.00 – cn Micromedia [073]

WESTWOOD BAPTIST CHURCH. EDMONTON, ALBERTA. CANADA : CHURCH RECORDS – 1950-71 – 1 – 13.84 – us Baptist [240]

WESTWOOD HILLS NEWS – Westwood, CA. 1927-1937 – 5r – 1 – $250.00 – R03574 – us Library Micro [071]

WESTWOOD HILLS PRESS – Westwood, CA. 1934-1953 – 20r – 1 – $1,000.00 – R03575 – us Library Micro [071]

WESTWOOD INDEPENDENT; WESTWOOD SUGAR PINE – Westwood, CA. 1917-May 1921 – 1r – 1 – $50.00 – B03094 – us Library Micro [071]

Westwood, J O *see*
- ARCANA ENTOMOLOGICA; OR ILLUSTRATIONS OF NEW RARE, AND INTERESTING INSECTS
- THE GENERA OF DIURNAL LEPIDOPTERA

WESTWOOD SUGAR PINE *see* WESTWOOD INDEPENDENT; WESTWOOD SUGAR PINE

WETASKIWIN TIMES – Alberta, CN. 1928-33; 1963-88 – 40r – 1 – cn Commonwealth Micro [072]

WETMORE BAPTIST CHURCH. DELANO, TENNESSEE : CHURCH RECORDS – (Includes history, 1915-1986) – Sept 1915-Apr 1990, lacking Sept 1979-Jan 1982 – 1 reel – 1 – $40.50 – us Baptist [240]

Wette, Hermann *see*
- NEUE WESTFAELISCHE GEDICHTE
- WAS DER WIND ERZAEHLT

WETTERAUER ANZEIGENBLATT – Friedberg. mar 25, 1948-apr 29, 1949 – 1 – gw Mikrofilm [072]

WETTERAUER NACHRICHTEN – Bad Nauheim, dec 24 1948-apr 30 1950 – 1 – gw Mikrofilm [072]

WETTERAUER VOLKSBLATT – Friedberg. jun 28, 1848-jun 30, 1849 – 1r – 1 – gw Mikrofilm [072]

WETTERAUER ZEITUNG – Friedberg. may 3, 1950-77 – 1 – gw Mikrofilm [072]

WETTERLEUCHTEN UM BARBARA : ROMAN AUS DER STEIERMARK / Wurmbrand, Irmgard – Salzburg: Verlag "Das Bergland-buch", 1940 – 1r – 1 – us U.W. Library [830]

Wettstein, R von *see* MONOGRAPHIE DER GATTUNG EUPHRASIA

WETZEL DEMOCRAT – New Martinsville. West Virginia. -w. 1898-1958 – 1 – us UMI [071]

WETZEL REPUBLICAN – New Martinsville. West Virginia. -w. 1898-1912, 1916-1924, 1934-66 – 1 – us UMI [071]

Wetzel, T *see* ARCHIVES OF PHYTOPATHOLOGY AND PLANT PROTECTION

DER WETZLARER GOETHE / Gloel, Heinrich – Wetzlar: Wetzlarer Heimatverlag, 1932 – 1r – 1 – us U.W. Library [430]

WETZLARER NEUE ZEITUNG – Wetzlar, West Germany. 1969- – 1 – gw Mikrofilm [072]

WETZLARER NEUE ZEITUNG *see* HINTERLAENDER ANZEIGER

Wetzstein, O *see*
- DIE GESCHICHTLICHE ENTWICKLUNG DES DEUTSCHEN REALSCHULWESENS
- DIE GESCHICHTLICHE ENTWICKLUNG DES REALSCHULWESENS IN DEUTSCHLAND

Wevers, John W *see* SEPTUAGINTA

WEWNETRZNE DZIEJE POLSKI ZA STANISLAWA AUGUSTA, 1764-1794 / Korzon, T – v. 1-6. Warsaw. 1897-98. BR-5476 2 – 8 – ne IDC [947]

WEXFORD CONSERVATIVE – Ireland. -w. 19 Sep 1832-18 Apr 1846. (13 reels) – 1 – uk British Libr Newspaper [072]

WEXFORD CONSTITUTION – Ireland.1859-87. -d. 22 1/2 reels – 1 – uk British Libr Newspaper [072]

WEXFORD EVENING POST – Ireland. -sw. 7 Mar 1826-23 Mar 1830. (4 reels) – 1 – uk British Libr Newspaper [072]

WEXFORD FREEMAN – Ireland. -w. 30 May 1832-31 May 1837. (4 reels) – 1 – uk British Libr Newspaper [072]

WEXFORD HERALD – Ireland. -w. 2 Jan 1828-1 Aug 1832. (4 reels) – 1 – uk British Libr Newspaper [072]

WEXJOBLADET – Vaxjo, Sweden. 1810-55 – 6r – 1 – sw Kungliga [072]

Wey, Fr *see* REMARQUES SUR LA LANGUE FRANCAISE AU 19E SIECLE

Weyand *see* AN EARLY HISTORY OF FAYETTE COUNTY

Weyand, Peter G *see* PEAK OXYGEN DEFICIT AS A PREDICTOR OF SPRINT AND MIDDLE-DISTANCE TRACK PERFORMANCE

Weydt, Guenther *see* WILHELM MEISTERS THEATRALISCHE SENDUNG

Weyer, E M *see*
- AN ALEUTIAN BURIAL
- THE ESKIMOS; THEIR ENVIRONMENT AND FOLKWAYS

Weyerman, J C *see* DE LEVENSBESCHRYVINGEN DER NEDERLANDSCHE KONST-SCHILDERS EN KONST-SCHILDERESSEN...

Weyher, Charles-L *see* 4 OEUVRES MICROFILMEES ENSEMBLE

Weyland, Hans *see* DER BAUERNGENERAL

Weymayr, Christian *see* STRUKTURUNTERSUCHUNGEN AN SCHNECKENGALACTANEN MIT HILFE MONOKLONALER ANTIKOERPER UND SEQUENTIELLEM SMITH-ABBAU

WEYMOUTH 1633-1900 – (Mf 1-5: Births 1633-1844. Mf 6-8: Marriages 1656-1840. Mf 9-10: Deaths 1639-1844. Mf 11: Out-of-Town Marriages 1643-1799. Mf 12-13: Births 1633-1785. Mf 14-15: Marriages & Intentions 1655-1791. Mf 15-17: Deaths 1639-1844. Mf 18-21: Vital Records 1655-1790. Mf 22: Births 1784-1806; Deaths 1802-45. Mf 23-25: Births 1785-1844. Mf 26-34: Intentions & Marriages 1790-1851. Mf 35-51: Intentions 1851-89. Mf 52-58: Intentions Index 1849-1937. Mf 59: Proprietors 1644. Mf 60-82: Town Records 1642-1836. Mf 83-85: Militia Rolls 1840-57. Mf 86-90: Rebellion Records 1861-65. Mf 91-93: Military Records 1861-65. Mf 94-95: Civil War Bounty Payments. Mf 96-97: Civil War Burials 1869-1931. Mf 98-99: Vital Records 1840-49. Mf 100-102: Births 1843-60. Mf 102-103: Marriages 1844-53. Mf 103-104: Deaths 1844-60. Mf 105-108: Death Index 1861-1910. Mf 109-115: Deaths 1861-1900. Mf 116-119: Marriage Index 1853-1910. Mf 120-129: Marriages 1853-94. Mf 130-134: Birth Index 1849-1910. Mf 135-142: Births 1861-94) – (mf ed 1991) – 142mf – 0-87623-122-9 – us Holbrook [920]

WEYMOUTH POOLE AND DORCHESTER GAZETTE – England.16, 23 Aug 1821; 11 Jul 1822; 25 Sept 1823; 8 Apr 1824. -w. 11 feet – 1 – uk British Libr Newspaper [072]

Weyse, C E *see* ALLEGRIDI BRAVURA POUR LE PIANOFORTE

WEYSSAGUNG AUSZ HEILIGER GOTLICHER GESCHRIFFT / Hoffman, M – 1530. BME-177 1 – 9 – ne IDC [240]

Wezel, Johann Karl *see* HERRMANN UND ULRIKE

WFM SOCIETY / Presbyterian Church in Canada. Woman's Foreign Missionary Society – (Cont by: Presbyterian Church in Canada. Woman's Foreign Missionary Society. Western Division. Woman's Foreign Missionary Society) – [Toronto?: s.n. 1884?-1886] – 9 – cn C.I.H.M. [240]

WFSA LECTURES – (Cont by: Lectures in Anaesthesiology) – Oxford. v1-2. 1984 1,9; v1-2. 1984* 5 – 1,5,9 – D15568 – us UMI [617]

WHALEMEN: THE FRIEND, A MONTHLY JOURNAL – v1-34. 1844-85 – 9 – 385.00 – us Opus [073]

WHALEMEN'S SHIPPING LIST AND MERCHANTS TRANSCRIPT – v1-24. 1843-1904 – 9 – 500.00 – us Opus [073]

Whalen, Sean C *see* THE RELATIONSHIP BETWEEN PRECOMPETITIVE AFFECT AND COLLEGIATE BASEBALL PERFORMANCE

A WHALING CRUISE TO BAFFIN'S BAY AND THE GULF OF BOOTHIA / Markham, A H – BN 310 2. 1874 – 8 – ne IDC [910]

WHALING LOG BOOKS: EARLY 19TH / Hull. Central Library – century – 2r – 1 – uk Microform Academic [639]

WHARNCLIFFE MANUSCRIPTS RELATING TO AMERICAN CIVIL WAR / Sheffield. City Library – 1864-1872. BRRAM – 1 – uk Microform Academic [920]

Wharton, Clarence R *see* TEXAS UNDER MANY FLAGS

Wharton, Francis *see* THE SILENCE OF SCRIPTURE

Wharton, Francis A *see*
- A COMMENTARY ON THE LAW OF AGENCY AND AGENTS
- A COMMENTARY ON THE LAW OF EVIDENCE IN CIVIL ISSUES
- DIGEST OF THE INTERNATIONAL LAW OF THE UNITED STATES
- DIPLOMATIC HISTORY OF THE AMERICAN REVOLUTION
- A TREATISE ON CRIMINAL LAW
- A TREATISE ON CRIMINAL PLEADING AND PRACTICE. 8TH ED
- A TREATISE ON THE CRIMINAL LAW OF THE UNITED STATES

Wharton, George Mifflin *see* ANSWER TO MR. BINNEY'S REPLY TO "REMARKS" ON HIS TREATISE ON THE HABEAS CORPUS

Wharton, H T *see* A LIST OF BRITISH BIRDS

Wharton, Hy *see* ANGLIA SACRA

Wharton, Jeremiah *see* THE ENGLISH-GRAMMAR

Wharton, John Jane Smith *see* THE LAW LEXICON

WHARTON MAGAZINE – V. 1-. 1976- – 1,5,6,9 – us UMI [330]

Wharton, Morton Bryan *see*
- FAMOUS MEN OF THE OLD TESTAMENT
- FAMOUS WOMEN OF THE NEW TESTAMENT: A SERIES OF POPULAR LECTURES

Wharton, Richard *see* OBSERVATION ON THE AUTHENTICITY OF BRUCE'S TRAVELS IN ABYSSINIA

Wharton, T *see* ADENOGRAPHIA: SIVE, GLANDULARUM TOTIUS CORPORIS DESCRIPTIO

WHARTON'S LAW LEXICON *see* THE LAW LEXICON

WHARTON'S REPORTS / Pennsylvania. Superior Court – (A Pre-NRS title) – v1-6. 1836-41 (all publ) – 41mf – 9 – $61.00 – LLMC 84-202 – us L.L.M.C. [340]

WHAT ABOUT THE NEW THEOLOGY? / Walker, William Lowe – (Includes bibliographical references and index) – 2nd ed. Edinburgh: T & T Clark, 1907 – 1mf – 9 – 0-8370-5693-4 – 1985-3693 – us A.T.L.A. [240]

WHAT ARE HUMAN RIGHTS / Akeroyd, Ivy A – 1969 – 9 – 1.00f – at Libertarian Micro [320]

WHAT BAPTISTS BELIEVE; THE NEW HAMPSHIRE CONFESSION, AN EXPOSITION / Wallace, O C S – Nashville, TN: The Sunday School Board of the Southern Baptist Convention, 1934. By permission – 1 – 5.44 – us Baptist [240]

WHAT BUTTE COUNTY OFFERS THE HOME-SEEKER / Mansfield, George C & Smith, Walter – 1r – 1 – $50.00 – B40211 – us Library Micro [978]

WHAT CAN BE CERTAINLY KNOWN OF GOD AND OF JESUS OF NAZARETH? : AN INQUIRY / Capes, John Moore – London: J Bumpus, 1880 – 1mf – 9 – 0-8370-3180-X – 1985-1180 – us A.T.L.A. [210]

WHAT CATHOLICS BELIEVE AND DO : OR, SIMPLE INSTRUCTIONS CONCERNING THE CHURCH'S FAITH AND PRACTICE / Ritchie, Arthur – (Includes index) – New York: [s.n.], 1891 – 1mf – 9 – 0-8370-8783-X – 1986-2783 – us A.T.L.A. [240]

WHAT DOES CHRISTIANITY MEAN? / Faunce, William Herbert Perry – New York: Fleming H. Revell, c1912. The Cole lectures for 1912 / delivered before Vanderbilt University – 1mf – us A.T.L.A. [240]

WHAT DOES FREEDOM MEAN TO YOU? / Clinchy, Russell J – 1952. 1 riche (29x) – 9 – 1.00f – at Libertarian Micro [320]

WHAT DOES HISTORY TEACH? / Blackie, John Stuart – New York: Scribner, 1886. 1 fiche – 9 – us A.T.L.A. [240]

WHAT DOES IT COST?: STATISTICAL REPORT, &C, PRESENTED TO THE CONVENTION..., HELD IN TORONTO, SEPTEMBER 7TH, 8TH, AND 9TH, 1869 / Convention of the Canada Temperance Union – Napanee, Ont,: s.n., 1869 (Napanee, Ont.: Henry Bros.). 02031. (Pre-1900 Canadiana) – 9 – cn C.I.H.M. [971]

WHAT EVERY GOOD LIBERAL NEEDS TO KNOW: THE ECONOMICS OF FRIEDRICH VON HAYEK / Dunbar, Leo – 3p – 9 – 1.00f – at Libertarian Micro [320]

WHAT EVERYBODY SHOULD KNOW ABOUT THE LAWS OF MARRIAGE AND DIVORCE... ALSO THE DIVORCE LAWS OF MEXICO, CUBA, CANADA, ENGLAND, AND FRANCE / Hudgings, William Franklyn – New York: New Century Co., 1935. 68p. LL-753 – 1 – us L of C Photodup [340]

WHAT FRANCES E. WILLARD SAID / Willard, Frances Elizabeth; ed by Anna A – Gordon – 9 – us A.T.L.A. [240]

WHAT FUTURISTS BELIEVE / Coates, Joseph F & Jaratt, Jennifer – The views of 17 futurists on important issues. A World Future Society Book – 9 – us Lomond [300]

WHAT GUNPOWDER PLOT WAS / Gardiner, Samuel R – London: Longmans, Green, 1897 – 1mf – us A.T.L.A. [240]

WHAT HAS TO BE CHANGED IN THE CONSTITUTIONS OF ALL STATES AND HOW CAN THESE REFORMS BE REALIZED? / Zube, John – A comprehensive and radical peace programme interrelating most of the ideas expressed in the "Peace Plans" Series. 5 fiches. (24x) – 9 – 1.00f – at Libertarian Micro [320]

'WHAT HATH GOD WROUGHT!' : A CENTENARY MEMORIAL OF THE PRIMITIVE METHODIST CHURCH / Kendall, H B – London, [1907] – 1mf – 9 – ne IDC [240]

THE WHAT, HOW, AND WHY OF CHURCH BUILDING / Kramer, G W – New York: [s.n.], 1897 – 1mf – us A.T.L.A. [720]

WHAT I KNOW ABOUT COMMERCIAL TRAVELLING: WHO WE ARE, WHAT WE ARE, WHAT WE DO AND HOW WE DO IT / Belcher, Alexander Emerson – Toronto: Hunter, Rose, 1883. 06221. (Pre-1900 Canadiana) – 9 – cn C.I.H.M. [380]

"WHAT I REMEMBER OF THE BATTLE OF THE BLUE, AND INCIDENTS CONNECTED WITH IT" / Kemp, John – 1864 – 1 – us KS Hist [976]

WHAT IS AN ORTHODOX BAPTIST? / Grime, J H – Lebanon, Tennessee. 8 Jul 1935 – 1 – 5.00 – us Baptist [240]

WHAT IS CHRISTIANITY (CCC279) / Shen, Ts'ing-lai – (In Chinese) – Shanghai: Publication Dept., National Committee, YMCAs of China, 1923 – 1r – 1 – 1984-6618 – us A.T.L.A. [240]

WHAT IS CHRISTIANITY?: SIXTEEN LECTURES / Harnack, Adolf von – London: Williams & Norgate, 1901. 1 fiche – 9 – us A.T.L.A. [240]

WHAT IS CHURCH HISTORY? : A VINDICATION OF THE IDEA OF HISTORICAL DEVELOPMENT / Schaff, Philip – Philadelphia: J.B. Lippincott, 1846 – 1mf – us A.T.L.A. [240]

WHAT IS COMMUNISM? AND OTHER ANARCHIST ESSAYS / Andrews, J A; ed by James, Bob – On 1889 Melbourne, introd. by Bob James.190p – 9 – 1.00f – at Libertarian Micro [335]

WHAT IS FAITH? : A HERMIT'S EPISTLE TO SOME THAT ARE WITHOUT / Skrine, John Huntley – London, NY: Longmans, Green, 1907 – 1mf – 9 – 0-8370-5387-0 – 1985-3387 – us A.T.L.A. [240]

WHAT IS HAPPENING IN SPAIN? / Rios, Fernando de los – London, 1937. Fiche W1142. (Blodgett Collection of Spanish Civil War Pamphlets) – 9 – us H.U. College Libr [946]

WHAT IS INSPIRATION?: A FRESH STUDY OF THE QUESTION / De Witt, John – New York: Anson D.F. Randolph, 1893. 1 fiche – 9 – us A.T.L.A. [240]

WHAT IS JUDAISM? : OR, A FEW WORDS TO THE JEWS / Lewin, Raphael de Cordova – (Includes bibliographical references) – NY: D Appleton, 1870 – 1mf – 9 – 0-8370-4097-3 – 1985-2097 – us A.T.L.A. [270]

WHAT IS JUSTICIALISM? / Argentina. Direccion General de Relaciones Culturales y Difusion – [Buenos Aires?: General Department of Cultural Relations and Diffusion, 1950?] – 1 – CSUXAJA7408-B – us Hoover Inst Photo [360]

WHAT IS MAN'S DESTINY? / Labadie, Laurance – 1fiche (29x) – 9 – 1.00f – at Libertarian Micro [320]

WHAT IS MODERN ROMANISM? : A CONSIDERATION OF SUCH PORTIONS OF HOLY SCRIPTURE, AS HAVE ALLEGED BEARINGS ON THE CLAIMS OF MODERN ROME / Seymour, George Franklin – Milwaukee: Young Churchman, 1888 – 1mf – 9 – 0-8370-8471-7 – 1986-2471 – us A.T.L.A. [240]

WHAT IS MUTUALISM? / Swartz, Clarence B – 1927. 266p. 1 fiche (24x) – 9 – 1.00f – at Libertarian Micro [320]

WHAT IS NATURAL THEOLOGY? : AN ATTEMPT TO ESTIMATE THE CUMULATIVE EVIDENCES OF MANY WITNESSES TO GOD / Barry, Alfred – (Signatures of pgs are out of order: p305-320 follow p288 and p289-304 follow p320) – London: Society for Promoting Christian Knowledge, [1877] – 1mf – 9 – 0-8370-2193-6 – 1985-0193 – us A.T.L.A. [210]

WHAT IS POALE ZIONISM? / Locker, B – London. 1938. BJ-28-16 1 – 9 – ne IDC [956]

WHAT IS POLITICAL SCIENCE? / Ashley, William James – An inaugural lecture given in the Convocation Hall of the University of Toronto, 9th November 1888. Toronto: Rowsell & Hutchinson, 1888. 02460. (Pre-1900 Canadiana) – 9 – cn C.I.H.M. [320]

WHAT IS RELIGION / Bousset, Wilhelm – New York: G.P. Putnam, 1907. 1 fiche – 9 – us A.T.L.A. [240]

WHAT IS TECHNOCRACY? / Raymond, Allen – 1st ed. New York: Whittlesey House, McGraw-Hill, 1933. vii,180p. Expansion of four articles from New York Herald Tribune, Dec. 1932 – 1 – us U.W. Library [600]

WHAT IS THE CHRISTIAN CHURCH? (CCC85) / Ch'en, Chi-yun – (In Chinese) – Shanghai: Christian Literature Society, 1949 – 1r – 1 – 1984-B500 – us A.T.L.A. [240]

WHAT IS THE CHRISTIAN FAITH? (CCC206) = SHE MO SHIH CHI TU CHIAO HSIN YANG / Kiang, Wen-han – (In Chinese) – Shanghai: Association Press of China, 1949 – 1r – 1 – 1984-B500 – us A.T.L.A. [240]

WHAT IS THE CHURCH, OR, PLAIN INSTRUCTION ABOUT THE CHURCH, ESPECIALLY IN ENGLAND : HER DOCTRINE, HER DISCIPLINE, HER OFFICES / Woodhouse, Reginald Illingworth – (Includes index) – New York: D Appleton, 1887 – 1mf – 9 – 0-8370-8877-1 – 1986-2877 – us A.T.L.A. [240]

WHAT IS THE MORAL STATUS OF MATERIAL POSSESSIONS? A CHRISTIAN DEFENCE OF PROPERTY RIGHTS / Burke, T Patrick – 9 – $1.00f – at Libertarian Micro [170]

WHAT IS THE USE OF THE VICTORIAN ORDER OF NURSES FOR CANADA? / Aberdeen and Temair, Ishbel Gordon, Marchioness of – Ottawa: Mortimer, 1900. 07174. (Pre-1900 Canadiana) – 9 – cn C.I.H.M. [360]

WHAT IS TO BE DONE? LIFE / Tolstoy, Leo – New York: Crowell, c1899 – xiv/441p – 1 – us U.W. Library [460]

WHAT IS TREASON? / U.S. District Court. Massachusetts – Salem, Swasey, 1863. 17 p. LL-1232 – 1 – us L of C Photodup [340]

WHAT IS TRUTH? / Argyll, George Douglas Campbell – 1889? – 1 – us A.T.L.A. [240]

WHAT IS TRUTH? / Rawlence, E A – London: Elliot Stock, 1904 – 1mf – 9 – 0-8370-8703-1 – 1986-2703 – us A.T.L.A. [240]
WHAT JESUS SAYS : BEING AN ARRANGEMENT OF THE WORDS OF OUR SAVIOR UNDER APPROPRIATE HEADINGS / Russell, Frank – (Includes index) – Kalamazoo, MI: Kalamazoo Pub Co, 1875 – 1mf – 9 – 0-8370-9175-6 – 1986-3175 – us A.T.L.A. [220]
WHAT LIES BEHIND THE "PATRIOTISM" OF THE FASCIST EX-GENERALS: GERMANY AND ITALY AID THE REBELS IN ORDER TO TAKE POSSESSION OF SPAIN / North American Committee to Aid Spanish Democracy – Washington, DC. 1936? Fiche W1083. (Blodgett Collection of Spanish Civil War Pamphlets) – 9 – us H.U. College Libr [946]
WHAT METHODISM OWES TO WOMEN / Buckley, James Monroe; ed by Carroll, H K et aL – From Methodist Episcopal Church Centennial Conference, Baltimore, 1884. Proceedings, Sermon, Essays, and addresses...9-17 Dec 1884, with an historical statement – 9 – us A.T.L.A. [240]
WHAT MOSES SAW OR HEARD, OR, THE IDEA OF GOD IN THE OLD TESTAMENT / Butler, A O – Chicago: R.R. Donnelley, 1889. 1 fiche – 9 – us A.T.L.A. [220]
WHAT NIETZSCHE TAUGHT / Wright, Willard Huntington – New York: B.W. Huebsch, 1915 – 333p – 1 – us U.W. Library [190]
WHAT RELIGION DOES FOR PERSONALITY (CCC94) = TSUNG-CHIAO YU JEN-KE / Ch'en, W Y – (In Chinese) – 1st ed. Shanghai: Association Press of China, 1935 – 1r – 1 – 1984-B500 – us A.T.L.A. [200]
WHAT SHALL WE DO WITH OUR DAUGHTERS?; SUPERFLUOUS WOMEN, AND OTHER LECTURES / Livermore, Mary Ashton Rice – 1883 – 9 – us A.T.L.A. [240]
WHAT SHALL WE THINK OF CHRISTIANITY? : THE LEVERING LECTURES BEFORE THE JOHN HOPKINS UNIVERSITY, 1899 / Clarke, William Newton – 3rd ed. New York: Charles Scribner, 1899 – 1mf – 9 – 0-8370-2675-X – 1985-0675 – us A.T.L.A. [240]
WHAT SORT OF THING IS JESUS? (CCC107) = YEH SU SHI SHIH NO TUNG SI / Chu, Chih-hsin – (In Chinese) – [s.l: s.n, 1929 – 1r – 1 – 1984-B500 – us A.T.L.A. [240]
WHAT SPANISH DEMOCRACY IS FIGHTING FOR – London, 1938? Fiche W1252. (Blodgett Collection of Spanish Civil War Pamphlets) – 9 – us H.U. College Libr [946]
WHAT THE JAPANESE DID TO ISLAM IN JAVA / Nieuwenhuijze, Christoffel Anthonie Olivier Van – SE-12.024 1. 1947 – 9 – ne IDC [360]
WHAT TO BELIEVE : BEING A SERIES OF LECTURES TO ENGLISH SPEAKING NATIVES OF INDIA UPON IMPORTANT RELIGIOUS SUBJECTS / Jardine, Robert – Calcutta: C B Lewis, Baptist Mission Press, 1876 – 1mf – 9 – 0-8370-3772-7 – 1985-1772 – us A.T.L.A. [230]
WHAT WE KNOW ABOUT JESUS / Dole, Charles Fletcher – Chicago: Open Court, 1908 – 1mf – 9 – 0-8370-2948-1 – 1985-0948 – us A.T.L.A. [240]
WHAT WOMEN WROTE: SCENARIOS, 1912-29 – 2 reels with printed guide – 1 – $210.00 – 0-89093-988-4 – us UPA [760]
WHAT ZIONISM HAS GIVEN THE JEWS / Magnes, J L – Ed. 2. New York. 1911. BJ-28-18 1 9 – ne IDC [956]
WHATCOM REVEILLE – Bellingham. Wash. -w, sw. 1883-84 – 1 – us UMI [071]
WHATELY 1771-1895 – (mf ed 1987) – 37mf – 9 – 0-87623-045-1 – us Holbrook [920]
Whately, E J *see* THE LIFE AND WORK OF MARY LOUISA WHATELY
Whately, Elizabeth Jane *see* HOW TO ANSWER OBJECTIONS TO REVEALED RELIGION
Whately, Mary Louisa *see* AMONG THE HUTS IN EGYPT, SCENES FROM REAL LIFE
Whately, Richard *see*
- ELEMENTS OF RHETORIC
- ESSAYS ON SOME OF THE DIFFICULTIES IN THE WRITINGS OF THE APOSTLE PAUL
- A GENERAL VIEW OF THE RISE, PROGRESS, AND CORRUPTIONS OF CHRISTIANITY
- INTRODUCTORY LESSONS ON CHRISTIAN EVIDENCES

WHAT'S IT ABOUT IN INDONESIA? – SE-11,842 1. 2 pts. in 1 v. 1947 – 9 – ne IDC [950]
WHEAT CENTER NEWS – Dutton. Mont. 1969- – 1 – us UMI [071]
WHEAT FROM THE FIELDS OF BOAZ / Thomas, Arthur G – Philadelphia: Am. Bapt. Pub. Soc., 1878.1 fiche – 9 – us A.T.L.A. [240]
WHEATLAND GRAPHIC – Wheatland, CA. 1882-85 – 1r – 1 – $50.00 – B03098 – us Library Micro [071]
WHEATLAND HERALD – Marysville, CA. 1934-35 – 1r – 1 – $50.00 – B02435 – us Library Micro [071]
WHEATLAND NEWSPAPERS – (Consists of: Record 1877-78. Graphic 1883-89. Bear River News Nov-Dec 1881) – 1r – 1 – $50.00 – B06012 – us Library Micro [071]
WHEATLEY, BANNEKER AND HORTON / Allen, W G – Boston, 1895 – 1r – 1 – us Ross [975]
Wheatley, H B *see* DOMESDAY STUDIES
Wheatley, Leonard Abercromby *see* THE STORY OF THE IMITATIO CHRISTI
Wheatley, Phillis *see* SELECTED WORKS BY AND ABOUT PHILLIS WHEATLEY
Wheatly, C *see* ST. JOHN'S TEST OF KNOWING CHRIST, AND BEING BORN OF HIM
Whedon, Daniel Denison *see* THE FREEDOM OF THE WILL
WHEEL LIFE – London, England. -w. 7 Nov 1884-2 Oct 1885. 1 reel – 1 – uk British Libr Newspaper [072]
THE WHEEL OF THE LAW. BUDDHISM, ILLUSTRATED FROM SIAMESE SOURCES BY THE MODERN BUDDHIST, A LIFE OF BUDDHA, AND AN ACCOUNT OF THE PHRABAT / Alabaster, Henry – London: Truebner, 1871. lviii,323p – 1 – us U.W. Library [280]
WHEEL OUTINGS IN CANADA: AND C.W.A. HOTEL GUIDE – ed. by P.E. Doolittle. Toronto: Canadian Wheelmen's Association, 1895. 00457.(Pre-1900 Canadiana) – 9 – cn C.I.H.M. [910]
WHEELCHAIR BASKETBALL : AN ANALYSIS OF THE FACTORS LEADING TO TEAM SUCCESS / Fontaine, Pamela – Texas Woman's University, 1994 – 1mf – 9 – PE 3641 – us Microform Publ [790]
Wheeler, Benjamin Ide *see* DIONYSOS AND IMMORTALITY; THE GREEK FAITH IN IMMORTALITY AS AFFECTED BY THE RISE OF INDIVIDUALISM
Wheeler, C F *see* MICHIGAN FLORA
WHEELER COUNTY ADVERTISER – Bartlett. Neb. 1886-1888 – 1 – us UMI [071]
WHEELER COUNTY CHRONICLE – Mitchell OR. July 4 1929-July 21 1941, July 4 1929-Sep 5 1929 – 1 – us U.O. Library [071]
WHEELER COUNTY GAZETTE – Cumminsville, NE. -w. Sep. 1883-Apr. 1888. Incomplete – 1 – us NE Hist [071]
WHEELER COUNTY INDEPENDENT – Bartlett, NE. -w. Nov. 1892-Apr. 1911. Incomplete; Jun. 1911$ – 1 – us NE Hist [071]
WHEELER COUNTY INDEPENDENT – Bartlett. Neb. 1892-1964 – 1 – us UMI [071]
WHEELER COUNTY REPUBLICAN – Bartlett, NE. -w. Jun. 1886-Aug. 1888 – 1 – us NE Hist [071]
Wheeler, Edmund *see* THE HISTORY OF NEWPORT 1766-1878
Wheeler, H M *see* HEBREW FOR SELF-INSTRUCTION
Wheeler, Harold Felix Baker *see* THE WAR IN WEXFORD; AN ACCOUNT OF THE REBELLION IN THE SOUTH OF IRELAND IN 1798 TOLD FROM ORIGINAL DOCUMENTS
Wheeler, J T *see*
- MEMORANDUM ON THE RECORDS IN THE FOREIGN DEPARTMENT
- MEMORANDUM ON THE RECORDS OF THE HOME DEPARTMENT

Wheeler, John H *see*
- DIARIES
- SCRAPBOOKS

Wheeler, Mary Sparkes *see* FIRST DECADE OF THE WOMAN'S FOREIGN MISSIONARY SOCIETY OF THE METHODIST EPISCOPAL CHURCH, WITH SKETCHES ON ITS MISSIONARIES
WHEELER RECORDER – Wheeler, OR. -w. 17 Sept 1931-12 Jul 1934. 1 roll – 1 – us U.O. Library [071]
WHEELER REPORTER – Wheeler, OR. -w. 1 Jul 1915-22 Mar 1935. 2 rolls – 1 – us U.O. Library [071]
Wheeler Robinson, H *see* THE CROSS IN THE OLD TESTAMENT
Wheeler, Russel R *see* THE FEDERAL APPELLATE JUDICIARY IN THE 21ST CENTURY
Wheeler, Russell R *see*
- ADMINISTERING THE FEDERAL JUDICIAL CIRCUITS
- CREATING THE FEDERAL JUDICIAL SYSTEM
- DESK BOOK FOR CHIEF JUDGES OF U.S. DISTRICT COURTS
- JUDICIAL DISCIPLINE AND REMOVAL IN THE U.S.
- ORIGINS OF THE ELEMENTS OF FEDERAL COURT GOVERNANCE
- THE WRITING AND RATIFICATION OF THE U.S. CONSTITUTION

WHEELER SURVEY STEREOSCOPIC VIEWS / U.S. Library of Congress. Prints and Photographs Division – 252 stereo cards of Wheeler's mapping expedition west of the 100th meridian. 1871-74. 1 reel. P&P3427 – 1 – 23.00r – us L of C Photodup [080]
WHEELER'S MANCHESTER CHRONICLE – Manchester, Great Britain. 1781-1842 – 1 – uk Manchester Libr [072]
WHEELERS MANCHESTER CHRONICLE – 1781-1842 – 1 – uk Microform Academic [073]
Wheeling Intelligencer *see* WEST VIRGINIANS OF 1934-35
Wheelock, Eleazar *see*
- PAPERS OF ELEAZAR WHEELOCK
- THE PAPERS OF ELEAZAR WHEELOCK

WHEELS WITHIN WHEELS; HOW RUSSIA USES UNITED NATIONS AGAINST SPAIN / Jimenez Quilez, Manuel – Washington, DC. 1947. 2v. Fiche W972. (Blodgett Collection of Spanish Civil War Pamphlets) – 9 – us H.U. College Libr [946]
THE WHEELWOMAN – London, England. -w. 23 May 1896-28 Jan 1899. 5 reels – 1 – uk British Libr Newspaper [072]
Wheelwright, John *see* HIS WRITINGS
Wheler, George *see*
- VOYAGE DE DALMATIE, DE GRECE, ET DU LEVANT
- VOYAGE D'ITALIE, DE DALMATIE, DE GRECE ET DU LEVANT, FAIT AUX ANNEES 1675 ET 1676

WHELER'S SOUTHERN MONTHLY MAGAZINE – A Reflex of Literature and Art. Athens, Ga. n.s. v. 1-2. no. 1. July 1849-Jan 1850. Price includes The Mistletoe – 1 – us NY Public [800]
WHELER'S SOUTHERN MONTHLY MAGAZINE – Athens, GA. v1; ns: v1-2. 1849-50 – 1r – 1 – us Ross [073]
WHEN A MAN'S SINGLE : A TALE OF LITERARY LIFE / Barrie, James Matthew – London: Hodder and Stoughton, 1888 – 1 roll – 1 – 1-55879-599-5 – uk Libr Preservation [830]
WHEN CIVIL LAW FAILS: MARTIAL LAW AND ITS LEGAL BASIS IN THE UNITED STATES / Rankin, Robert Stanley – Durham, N.C., Duke, 1939, 224 p. LL-1559 – 1 – us L of C Photodup [340]
WHEN GOD WOKE UP FROM HIS ETERNAL SLUMBER / Arrigoni, Enrico – Biblical Fairy Tales, No.1 – 9 – 1.00f – at Libertarian Micro [335]
WHEN THE SLEEPER WAKES / Wells, H G – London, New York: Harper & Brothers, 1899 – 1 roll – 1 – 1-55879-415-8 – uk Libr Preservation [830]
WHEN THE SONG BEGINS / Miller, James Russell – New York: Thomas Y Crowell, c1905 – 1mf – 9 – 0-8370-7248-4 – 1986-1248 – us A.T.L.A. [240]
WHEN THOUGHTS WILL SOAR : A ROMANCE OF THE IMMEDIATE FUTURE / Suttner, Bertha von – Boston, New York: Houghton Mifflin, 1914 – 1r – 1 – us U.W. Library [830]
WHEN WAS THE PENTATEUCH WRITTEN? / Warington, George – London: SPCK; New York: Pott, Young, [1873] – 1mf – 9 – 0-8370-5713-2 – 1985-3713 – us A.T.L.A. [220]
WHENCE AND WHITHER : AN INQUIRY INTO THE NATURE OF THE SOUL, ITS ORIGIN AND ITS DESTINY / Carus, Paul – Chicago: Open Court, 1903 – 1mf – us A.T.L.A. [120]
WHERE AND HOW; A CORPORATION HAND BOOK CONTAINING THE LAWS OF DELAWARE, NEW JERSEY, NEW YORK AND PENNSYLVANIA. / Parker, John Scott – 7th ed. New York: Broun-Green, 1923. 335p. LL-1058 – 1 – us L of C Photodup [340]
WHERE AND HOW; A HAND BOOK OF INCORPORATION. BEING A DIGEST AND COMPARISON OF THE CORPORATION LAWS OF NEW YORK, NEW JERSEY, MAINE, DELAWARE, WEST VIRGINIA, SOUTH DAKOTA, MASSACHUSETTS. / Parker, John Scott – New York: Broun-Green, 1903. 176p. LL-1063 – 1 – us L of C Photodup [340]
WHERE DOES THE SKY BEGIN / Gladden, Washington – Boston: Houghton, Mifflin, 1904 – 1mf – 9 – 0-8370-4932-6 – 1985-2932 – us A.T.L.A. [240]
WHERE DWELLS "OUR LADY OF THE SUNSHINE" / Aberdeen and Temair, Ishbel Gordon – Toronto, G. Morang, 1898. 00768. (Pre-1900 Canadiana) – 9 – cn C.I.H.M. [971]
WHERE IS THE CONSCIENCE OF THE WORLD? / Medical Bureau and North American Committee to Aid Spanish Democracy – n.p., n.d. Fiche W 1040. (Blodgett Collection of Spanish Civil War Pamphlets) – 9 – us H.U. College Libr [946]
WHERE THE BIBLE SPEAKS, OR, MISSION STUDIES IN THE BIBLE / McLean, Archibald – New York: Fleming H. Revell, 1907. 241p. 1 fiche – 9 – us A.T.L.A. [240]
WHERE THE BOOK SPEAKS : OR, MISSION STUDIES IN THE BIBLE / McLean, Archibald – New York: Fleming H Revell, c1907 – 1mf – 9 – 0-8370-6219-5 – 1986-0219 – us A.T.L.A. [220]
WHERE THE FUTURE BEGINS / M'Bow, Amadou-Mahtar – 1982 – 118p – 9 – 92-3-102046-3 – fr UNESCO [303]
WHERE TO SPEND THE SUMMER: A DESCRIPTION OF SOME OF CANADA'S SUMMER RESORTS AND HOW TO GET TO THEM – Ottawa: E. King, 1892? 02486. (Pre-1900 Canadiana) – 9 – cn C.I.H.M. [910]
WHEREFORE, O GOD? : OR, A MODERN ESDRAS / Herbert, Charles – New York: Thomas Y Crowell, c1897 – 1mf – 9 – 0-8370-4884-2 – 1985-2884 – us A.T.L.A. [210]
WHERE'S WHAT: SOURCES OF INFORMATION FOR FEDERAL INVESTIGATORS – 1967 – 1. 9.00; ; 9 – 18.00 – us L of C Photodup [360]
Wherry, E M *see* ISLAM AND CHRISTIANITY IN INDIA AND THE FAR EAST
Wherry, Elwood Morris *see* MISSIONS AT HOME AND ABROAD
THE WHETSTONE OF WITTE / Recorde, Robert – British Library – 1 – uk Microform Academic [820]
Whewell, William *see* LECTURES ON THE HISTORY OF MORAL PHILOSOPHY IN ENGLAND
Whibley, Charles *see* LITERARY STUDIES
Whichcote, Benjamin *see* THE CAMBRIDGE PLATONISTS
Whidborne, G F *see* A MONOGRAPH OF THE DEVONIAN FAUNA OF THE SOUTH OF ENGLAND
WHIDBY NEWS-TIMES – Oak Harbor, WA. 1981- – 30+ r – 1 – $1,500.00 ($90.00y) – B05403 – us Library Micro [071]
WHIDBY TODAY – Oak Harbour, WA. 1980-90 – 10r – 1 – $500.00 – B05404 – us Library Micro [071]
WHIG – Angelica. N.Y. and Advocate. 1846-56 – 1 – us UMI [071]
WHIG – Oct. 15, 1807-Dec. 1810 – 1 – us NY Public [073]
WHIG – Richmond. Va. -d. 1860-65 – 1 – us UMI [071]
WHIG – Richmond. Va. -sw. 1835-61, 1865-74 – 1 – us UMI [071]
WHIG ALMANAC AND POLITICIAN'S REGISTER, 1834-1914/ THE DAILY NEWS ALMANAC AND POLITICAL REGISTER, 1885-1937 – 537mf – 9 – $1475.00 – us UMI [975]
WHIG PRESS – Middletown. N.Y. 1853; 1860-1865 – 1 – us UMI [071]
WHIG PRESS – Newburgh. N.Y. 1800-1865 – 1 – us UMI [071]
WHIG STANDARD – Hillsdale. Mich. 1846-1849 – 1 – us UMI [071]
WHIG STANDARD – Tiffin, Ohio. 1845-49 – 1r – 1 – $32.50r – us Archival [071]
THE WHIG-STANDARD – Kingston, Ontario, CN. 1834- – 24r per yr – 1 – Can$53.00r – cn Commonwealth Micro [072]
Whilden, R Furman *see* NOTEBOOK
WHILE SEWING SANDALS, OR, TALES OF A TELUGU PARIAH TRIBE / Clough, Emma – 1899 – 1 – us A.T.L.A. [830]

Whinery, Leo H *see* THE ROLE OF THE COURT EXPERT IN PATENT LITIGATION

Whinnom, Keith *see* SPANISH CONTACT VERNACULARS IN THE PHILIPPINE ISLANDS

Whipple, Phila M *see* NEGRO NEIGHBORS, BOND AND FREE

THE WHIRLPOOL / Gissing, George Robert – London: Lawrence and Bullen, 1897 – 1 roll – 1 – 1-55879-697-5 – uk Libr Preservation [890]

WHISPER = WEI YIN – (In Chinese) – v1-2. 1928-30 (complete) – 1r – 1 – ATLA S0319A – us A.T.L.A. [073]

WHISPER MONTHLY = WEI YIN YUEH K'AN – (In Chinese) – v1-2. 1931-32 (complete) – 1r – 1 – ATLA S0319B – us A.T.L.A. [073]

WHISTLEPUNK – Hood River, OR. -w. 26 Aug 1965-8 Aug 1968. 1 roll – 1 – us U.O. Library [071]

Whistler, James Abbott McNeill *see* THE GENTLE ART OF MAKING ENEMIES

Whistling, Carl Friedrich *see* HANDBUCH DER MUSIKALISCHEN LITERATUR ODER ALLGEMEINES SYSTEMATISCH-GEORDNETES VERZEICHNISS DER IN DEUTSCHLAND UND IN DEN ANGRENZENDEN LAENDERN GEDRUCKTEN MUSIKALIEN AUCH MUSIKALISCHEN SCHRIFTEN UND ABBILDUNGEN MIT ANZEIGE DER VERLEGER UND PREISE

Whiston, T *see* THE IMPORTANT DOCTRINES OF ORIGINAL SIN, JUSTIFICATION BY FAITH AND REGENERATION CLEARLY STATED FROM SCRIPTURE AND REASON, AND VINDICATED FROM THE MISREPRESENTATIONS OF THE METHODISTS;...

Whitaker, Alexander *see* GOOD NEWES FROM VIRGINIA

Whitaker, Arthur Preston *see*
- ARGENTINA
- ARGENTINE UPHEAVAL
- THE U.S. AND ARGENTINA

WHITAKER BOOKS OUT OF PRINT – Published annually in June – 17 – £115.00 – uk Whitaker [010]

Whitaker, Epher *see* NEW FRUITS FROM AN OLD FIELD

Whitaker, J I S *see* THE BIRDS OF TUNISIA

Whitaker, J. & Sons *see*
- WHITAKER'S BOOKS IN PRINT ON MICROFICHE
- WHITAKER'S NEW AND FORTHCOMING BOOKS

Whitaker, Leighton C *see* JOURNAL OF COLLEGE STUDENT PSYCHOTHERAPY

WHITAKER'S BOOK LIST – Publ annually in May – 9 – £58.00 – uk Whitaker [020]

WHITAKER'S BOOKS IN PRINT – Updated mthly or quarterly – 17 – Apply – uk Whitaker [010]

WHITAKER'S BOOKS IN PRINT ON MICROFICHE / Whitaker, J. & Sons – 1997 – uk Whitaker [020]

WHITAKER'S ISBN LISTING / J. Whitaker and Sons – 1997 – 140mf – 9 – uk Whitaker [020]

WHITAKER'S NEW AND FORTHCOMING BOOKS : WEEKLY FICHE / Whitaker, J. & Sons – 1997 – uk Whitaker [020]

Whitbey, John *see* BEAUTIES OF PRIESTERCRAFT

Whitbread, Samuel *see* PAPERS

WHITBY ARGOSY – Whitby, 1970-1971 – 1r – 1 – cn Preston [971]

Whitby, Daniel *see* EXAMEN VARIANTIUM LECTIONUM JOHANNIS MILLII

WHITBY FREE PRESS – (1993.-2r) – Whitby, 1971-1992 – 29r – 1 – cn Preston [971]

WHITBY GAZETTE – England. 20 Jul-28 Sep 1854; 20 Jul-21 Sep 1855; 3 Jul-25 Sep 1856; 20 Jun 1857-31 Dec 1859; 5 Jan 1861-22 Dec 1883 (imperfect).-w. 9 reels – 1 – uk British Libr Newspaper [072]

WHITBY WEEKLY NEWS – Whitby, 1955-1967 – 6r – 1 – cn Preston [971]

WHITBY WORLD – Whitby, 1970-1971 – 1r – 1 – cn Preston [971]

Whitby. Yorkshire *see* PARISH REGISTERS

WHITCHURCH HERALD – England.1898; 1911. -w. 2 reels – 1 – uk British Libr Newspaper [072]

White, Alma *see*
- MY TRIP TO THE ORIENT
- WHY I DO NOT EAT MEAT

THE WHITE AND BLACK BOOKS OF THE CINQUE PORTS / Brodhull & Guestlings – 1433- – 2r – 1 – uk Microform Academic [941]

THE WHITE AND BLUE – Toronto: University College Literary and Scientific Society, [1879-1880?] – 9 – cn C.I.H.M. [370]

WHITE AND BLUE – Toronto.7 Oct 1879-20 Mar 1880 – 1 – 40.00 – cn McLaren [073]

WHITE AND WILSON'S REPORTS / Texas. Civil Appeals Court – (A Pre-NRS title) – v1-4. 1883-1892 (all publ) – 31mf – 9 – $46.50 – LLMC 92-408 – us L.L.M.C. [340]

White, Andrew Dickson *see*
- ANDREW DICKSON WHITE PAPERS, 1832-1918
- SEVEN GREAT STATESMEN IN THE WARFARE OF HUMANITY WITH UNREASON

White, B F *see* THE SACRED HARP

White, C *see* THE INSERVICE NEEDS OF SOUTH CAROLINA PUBLIC SCHOOL PHYSICAL EDUCATORS PROVIDING INSTRUCTION TO HANDICAPPED STUDENTS

White, C M N *see*
- ELEMENTS IN LUVALE BELIEFS AND RITUALS
- AN OUTLINE OF LUVALE SOCIAL AND POLITICAL ORGANISATION
- A PRELIMINARY SURVEY OF LUVALE RURAL ECONOMY

White, Charles L *see* A CENTURY OF FAITH

THE WHITE CITY / Moses & Selby – Chicago: Chicago World Book Co., 1893. Illinois Reel 1. (The Cox Library Collection) – 5 – us Americana [978]

White Cloud. Kansas. Community Church *see* RECORDS

White, David McKelvy *see* FRANCO SPAIN... AMERICA'S ENEMY

THE WHITE DOE OF RYLSTONE : OR, THE FATE OF THE NORTONS, A POEM / Wordsworth, William – London: Longman, Hurst, Rees, Orme and Brown, 1815 – 1 roll – 1 – 1-55879-334-8 – uk Libr Preservation [810]

White, Edward *see* EVANSVILLE AND ITS MEN OF MARK

White, Edward Joseph *see*
- THE LAW OF MINES AND MINING INJURIES
- THE LAW OF PERSONAL INJURIES IN MINES.
- LEGAL ANTIQUITIES

White, Ellen Gould Harmon *see* CHRIST'S OBJECT LESSONS

White, Evelyn H G *see* THE MONASTERIES OF THE WADI'N NATRUN

White, Frank *see* WHITE'S MANUAL FOR BUSINESS CORPORATIONS.

White, Frank H *see* CHRIST IN THE TABERNACLE: WITH SOME REMARKS ON THE OFFERINGS

White, Frederick Thomas *see* A SELECTION OF LEADING CASES IN EQUITY, WITH NOTES

White, G F *see* ENVIRONMENTAL EFFECTS OF ARID LAND IRRIGATION IN DEVELOPING COUNTRIES

White, George *see*
- HISTORICAL COLLECTIONS OF GEORGIA:...FACTS, TRADITIONS, BIOGRAPHICAL SKETCHES, ANECDOTES, ETC
- A SERMON AGAINST THE METHODISTS, PREACH'D AT COLNE AND MARSDEN IN THE COUNTY OF LANCASTER TO A VERY NUMEROUS AUDIENCE, AT COLNE, JULY 24 AND AT MARSDEN, AUGUST 7, 1748

White, H J *see* A GRAMMAR OF THE VULGATE

White, H M *see* REVEREND WILLIAM S. WHITE, D.D., AND HIS TIMES (1800-1873)

WHITE HAT – London, UK. 1819. -irr. 7 feet – 1 – uk British Libr Newspaper [072]

WHITE HEATHER: A NOVEL / Black, William – British Fiction Archive: Unit 4 – 9 – uk Bell [830]

White, Henry Alexander *see* THE ORIGIN OF THE PENTATEUCH IN THE LIGHT OF THE ANCIENT MONUMENTS

White, Henry Kirke *see*
- THE POETICAL WORKS OF HENRY KIRKE WHITE AND JAMES GRAHAME
- THE REMAINS OF HENRY KIRKE WHITE OF NOTTINGHAM, LATE OF ST JOHN'S COLLEGE, CAMBRIDGE. WITH AN ACCOUNT OF HIS LIFE, BY ROBERT SOUTHEY

THE WHITE HOODS / Bray, Anna Eliza – British Fiction Archive: Unit 2 – 9 – uk Bell [830]

White, Horatio Stevens *see* LESSING

THE WHITE HOUSE / Braddon, Mary Elizabeth – British Fiction Archive: Unit 5 – 9 – uk Bell [830]

WHITE HOUSE CONFERENCE.. / White House Conference of Library and Information Services. 1979. Washington, DC – Washington: GPO, (1980).101p. 1 reel.1219 – 1 – us U.W. Library [020]

White House Conference of Library and Information Services. 1979. Washington, DC *see* WHITE HOUSE CONFERENCE..

White House Hotel. Ellsworth, Kansas *see* REGISTERS

White, James *see* THE ENGLISH VERB

White, John *see* POTTERY TECHNIQUES OF NATIVE NORTH AMERICA

White, John W *see* ARGENTINA, THE LIFE STORY OF A NATION

White, Joseph *see* SACRORUM EVANGELIORUM VERSIO SYRIACA PHILOXENIANA...

White, Lorenzo *see* THE DEMOCRACY OF CHRISTIANITY

White, M I *see* PROS AND CONS, A GUIDE TO THE CONTROVERSIES OF THE DAY

THE WHITE MAN'S BURDEN : A DISCUSSION OF THE INTERRACIAL QUESTION WITH SPECIAL REFERENCE TO THE RESPONSIBILITY OF THE WHITE RACE TO THE NEGRO PROBLEM / Riley, B F – Birmingham, Ala.: B.F. Riley, c1910 – 1mf – us A.T.L.A. [303]

THE WHITE MAN'S FOOT / Allen, Grant – London: Hatchards, 1888.05093.(Pre-1900 Canadiana) – 9 – cn C.I.H.M. [971]

THE WHITE MAN'S GRAVE : A VISIT TO SIERRA LEONE IN 1834 / Rankin, F Harrison – London: R Bentley, 1836 – us Res Libr [960]

THE WHITE MAN'S WORK IN ASIA AND AFRICA : A DISCUSSION OF THE MAIN DIFFICULTIES OF THE COLOUR QUESTION / Alston, Leonard – London; New York: Longmans, Green, 1907 – 1mf – us A.T.L.A. [240]

WHITE PAPER (DRAFT) OUTLINING THE EDUCATIONAL RECONSTRUCTION PROPOSED TO BE UNDERTAKEN DURING THE NEXT 15-20 YEARS, WITH SPECIAL REFERENCE TO THE NEW FOURTH FIVE YEAR PLAN (1969-1974) / India. Maharashtra. Ministry of Education – Bombay, 1968 – 1mf – 9 – DE-551/1 – ne IDC [370]

WHITE PAPER ON THE ESTABLISHMENT OF A UNIVERSITY IN WESTERN NIGERIA / Nigeria. Western Region – Ibadan, 1960 – 1mf – 9 – DE-126/1 – ne IDC [370]

WHITE PAPER ON THE NATIONALIZATION OF THE SUEZ MARITIME CANAL COMPANY / Egypt. Ministry of Foreign Affairs – Published by the Government of Egypt on 12 Aug 1956 – 9 – ne IDC [338]

WHITE PAPER ON THE REPORT OF THE COMMITTEE OF ENQUIRY INTO THE DISTURBANCES AT THE UNIVERSITY OF GHANA CAMPUS, LEGON, 17TH JANUARY 1975 / Ghana – Accra – 1mf – 9 – DE-431/1 – ne IDC [370]

WHITE PAPER ON THE REPORT OF THE COMMITTEE OF INQUIRY INTO THE AFFAIRS OF ALL CO-OPERATIVE UNIONS IN UGANDA / Uganda – A 734 1. 1968 – 9 – ne IDC [338]

WHITE PAPER ON THE REPORT OF THE EDUCATION REVIEW COMMITTEE : TOGETHER WITH THE RECOMMENDATIONS IN BRIEF OF THE ... COMMITTEE, AND THE REPORT OF THE SPECIAL COMMITTEE ON DELIMITATION OF FUNCTIONS OF UNIVERSITY INSTITUTIONS / Ghana – Accra, 1968 – 1mf – 9 – DE-432/1 – ne IDC [370]

White, Paul Hamilton Hume *see* DOCTOR OF TANGANYIKA

White, Peter G *see* THE EASTERN TOWNSHIPS ADVERTISER

WHITE PINE NEWS – Ely, NV. Feb 1867; May-Aug 1870; July-Sep 1872; 1881-1923 – 23r – 1 – $1,150.00 – U04507 – us Library Micro [071]

WHITE PINE NEWS – Hamilton, NV. 1870-76 – 1r – 1 – $50.00 – U04575 – us Library Micro [071]

WHITE PINE NEWS – Taylor, NV. 1886-88 – 1r – 1 – $50.00 – U04760 – us Library Micro [071]

WHITE PINE REFLEX – Taylor, NV. 1884-85 – 1r – 1 – $50.00 – U04761 – us Library Micro [071]

WHITE PINE SUFFRAGIST – Ely, NV. 31 Oct 1914 – 1r – 1 – $50.00 – U04508 – us Library Micro [320]

White, R *see* APPROACHES TO THE STUDY OF THE ENVIRONMENTAL IMPLICATIONS OF CONTEMPORARY URBANIZATION

WHITE RIBBON – Carson City, NV. Jul 1894 (scats) – 1r – 1 – $50.00 – U04476 – us Library Micro [071]

THE WHITE ROBE OF CHURCHES OF THE 11TH CENTURY : PAGES FROM THE STORY OF GLOUCESTER CATHEDRAL / Spence, H Donald M – London: J.M. Dent, 1899 – 1mf – us A.T.L.A. [240]

WHITE SPRINGS BAPTIST CHURCH. LAURENS COUNTY. GLENWOOD, GEORGIA : CHURCH RECORDS – 1881 – Aug 1982 – 1 – 30.42 – us Baptist [240]

WHITE SPRINGS BAPTIST CHURCH. LAURENS COUNTY. GLENWOOD, GEORGIA : CHURCH RECORDS – 1881-Aug 1982 – 1 – 30.42 – us Baptist [240]

THE WHITE STONE CANOE: A LEGEND OF THE OTTAWAS / Edgar, James David – Illustrations by W. D. Blatchly. Toronto: Toronto News Co., 1885. 02883. (Pre-1900 Canadiana) – 9 – cn C.I.H.M. [971]

White, Thomas *see* THE THEORY AND PRACTICE OF SHIP BUILDING

White, Truman C *see* OUR COUNTY AND ITS PEOPLE-ERIE

White, Wesley D *see* PAPERS

White, Wilbert Webster *see*
- INDUCTIVE STUDIES IN THE TWELVE MINOR PROPHETS
- THIRTY STUDIES IN THE REVELATION OF JESUS CHRIST TO JOHN

White, William Allen *see* LETTERS TO DAN CASEMENT

White, William Charles *see* A COMPENDIUM AND DIGEST OF THE LAWS OF MASSACHUSETTS

White, William Hale *see*
- THE AUTOBIOGRAPHY OF MARK RUTHERFORD
- CATHARINE FURZE. BY MARK RUTHERFORD. EDITED BY HIS FRIEND, REUBEN SHAPCOTT
- CLARA HOPGOOD. EDITED BY HIS FRIEND, REUBEN SHAPCOTT
- MIRIAM'S SCHOOLING AND OTHER PAPERS. EDITED BY [THE AUTHOR'S] FRIEND REUBEN SHAPCOTT
- PAGES FROM A JOURNAL, WITH OTHER PAPERS. BY MARK RUTHERFORD
- THE REVOLUTION IN TANNER'S LANE. EDITED BY [THE AUTHOR'S] FRIEND, REUBEN SHAPCOTT

White, William S *see* REVEREND WILLIAM S. WHITE, D.D., AND HIS TIMES (1800-1873)

WHITE WINGS : AND INDEXES TO PERSONS' AND SHIPS NAMED / Brett, Henry – (v1 publ 1914 contains information about the voyages of many ships that brought immigrants to NZ 1850-1900. v2 publ 1928 describes European settlement and has further info on ships. Alphabetical indexes listing name of every person and ship included. Index mf available separately 1mf NZ$3.00) – 6mf – 9 – NZ$22.00 – 0-908989-38-5 – nz BAB [980]

WHITE WINGS: A YACHTING ROMANCE / Black, William – British Fiction Archive: Unit 4 – 9 – uk Bell [830]

THE WHITECHAPEL MURDERS PAPERS. LETTERS RELATING TO JACK THE RIPPER / Corporation of London Record Office, London – 19thc – £100.00 – uk World [360]

WHITECOURT STAR – Whitecourt, Alberta, CN. 1980-89 – 20r – 1 – cn Commonwealth Micro [072]

Whitefield, Edwin *see* PAPERS

Whitefield, George *see*
- A BRIEF ACCOUNT OF THE OCCASION, PROCESS AND ISSUE OF A LATE TRIAL AT THE ASSIZE HELD AT GLOUCESTER, MARCH 3, 1743,...
- THE CHRISTIAN'S COMPANION
- A LETTER TO THE REVEREND DR. DURELL, VICE-CHANCELLOR OF THE UNIVERSITY OF OXFORD, OCCASIONED BY A LATE EXPULSION OF SIX STUDENTS FROM EDMUND HALL
- A LETTER TO THE REVEREND MR. JOHN WESLEY, IN ANSWER TO HIS SERMON ENTITULED 'FREE-GRACE'

Whitefield, Maine. Second Baptist Church at King's Mills *see* RECORDS

Whitefield, Wilfred J *see* PAPERS

WHITEHAVEN GAZETTE – England. -w. Apr 1819-Dec 1820. (1 reel) – 1 – uk British Libr Newspaper [072]

Whitehead, A W *see* GASPARD DE COLIGNY

Whitehead, Charles *see* THE SOLITARY

Whitehead, P J P et al *see* FISHES OF THE NORTH-EASTERN ATLANTIC AND THE MEDITERRANEAN

Whitehead, PG *see* DISPERSION AND SELF-PURIFICATION OF POLLUTANTS IN SURFACE WATER SYSTEMS

WHITEHORSE STAR – Whitehorse, Canada. 1901-16, 1963 – 10r – 1 – $650.00 – cn Library Assoc [971]

Whitehouse, David *see*
- GLASS
- GLASS OF THE ROMAN EMPIRE

Whitehouse. Ohio. Whitehouse Natural Gas and Oil Company *see* RECORDS

Whitehouse, Owen Charles *see* A PRIMER OF HEBREW ANTIQUITIES

Whitehouse, Robert Treat *see* EQUITY JURISDICTION, PLEADING AND PRACTICE IN MAINE

THE WHITEHOUSE SIFTINGS – [Sackville, N.B.]: Mt Allison Ladies' College Rhetoric Class, [1894?-189- or 19–] – 9 – cn C.I.H.M. [370]

Whitehouse, William Fitzhugh *see* THE REDEMPTION OF THE BODY

WHITELAW AVENUE BAPTIST CHURCH. WOOD RIVER, ILLINOIS : CHURCH RECORDS – 27 May 1934-Sep 1967 – 1 – 31.59 – us Baptist [240]

Whiteley, D *see*
- ILLUSTRIOUS LOCAL PREACHERS

Whiteley, W H *see* A LINGUISTIC BIBLIOGRAPHY OF EAST AFRICA

Whitelocke, John *see* TRIAL OF LIEUTENANT GENERAL JOHN WHITELOCKE, COMMANDER IN CHIEF OF THE EXPEDITION AGAINST BUENOS AYRES

WHITELOCKE PAPERS / Bath. Archives (Marquess). Longleat – 17th century. Parcels 1-9 plus 30 v. Longleat – 23r – 1 – uk Microform Academic [025]

Whitely, H C *see* BLINDED EAGLE: A SHORT LIFE OF EDWARD IRVING

Whitely, W T *see* A BAPTIST BIBLIOGRAPHY

Whiteman, Marjorie M *see* DAMAGES IN INTERNATIONAL LAW

Whiteman, Maxwell *see* THE AFRO-AMERICAN HISTORY SERIES

WHITE'S MANUAL FOR BUSINESS CORPORATIONS. / White, Frank – 2d ed. Albany, N.Y., White, 1899. 259 p. LL-1633 – 1 – us L of C Photodup [340]

WHITESBURG FIRST BAPTIST CHURCH. NOLACHUCKY ASSOCIATION. WHITESBURG, TENNESSEE : CHURCH RECORDS – Jun 1785-Oct 1892. Formerly Bent Creek – 1 – $16.38 – us Baptist [240]

Whiteside, Joseph *see* HISTORY OF THE WESLEYAN METHODIST CHURCH OF SOUTH AFRICA

WHITESVILLE BAPTIST CHURCH. KENTUCKY : CHURCH RECORDS – 1878-2 Aug 1961 – 1 – 77.22 – us Baptist [240]

White-Synder Family *see* GENEALOGICAL PAPERS

Whitfield County. Georgia *see* OFFICIAL HISTORY.

Whitfield, Davis *see* ATTITUDES OF OLYMPIC SPORT STUDENT-ATHLETES AND COACHES TOWARD NCAA RESTRICTIONS ON PRACTICE TIME-IN SEASON

Whitfield, E E *see* AN EXPOSITION OF THE GOSPEL OF MARK

Whitfield, R P *see* MOLLUSCA AND CRUSTACEA OF THE MIOCENE FORMATIONS OF NEW JERSEY

Whitfield, William *see* HISTORY OF SNOHOMISH COUNTY

WHITHER? A THEOLOGICAL QUESTION FOR THE TIMES / Briggs, Charles Augustus – 1890 – 9 – us A.T.L.A. [240]

WHITHER INDONESIA? PKI AND CCP / Cheng, Hsueh-chia – SE-2576 1. 1960 – 9 – ne IDC [305]

WHITHER THE NEW SPAIN; GENERAL FRANCO'S POLICY AS REFLECTED IN THE SPANISH NATIONALIST PRESS – London, 1939. Fiche W1253. (Blodgett Collection of Spanish Civil War Pamphlets) – 9 – us H.U. College Libr [946]

WHITLEY COUNTY COMMERCIAL – Columbia City. Ind. 1071-1879 – 1 – us UMI [071]

WHITLEY COUNTY REPUBLICAN – Columbia City. IN. Also: Whitley County Commercial. 1864-70 – 1 – us UMI [071]

Whitley, W T *see* CUTTINGS NOTEBOOKS RELATING TO ENGLISH ARTISTS

Whitlock, J H *see* SIXTY REASONS WHY THE CAMBELLITE CHURCH IS NOT AND CAN NOT BE THE CHURCH OF CHRIST

Whitman, Albery A *see* A SELECTION OF WORKS

Whitman, Benjamin *see* HISTORICAL REFERENCE BOOK

Whitman, Charles S *see*
- PATENT LAWS AND THE PRACTICE OF OBTAINING LETTERS PATENT FOR INVENTIONS IN THE UNITED STATES AND FOREIGN COUNTRIES
- WHITMAN'S PATENT CASES IN THE UNITED STATES SUPREME COURT

Whitman, Russell *see* LAW STUDENTS' REVIEW AND QUIZ BOOK.

WHITMAN SUN – Whitman, NE. -w. Apr 1897-Aug 1901, scattered issues missing – 1 – us NE Hist [071]

Whitman, Walt *see*
- DEMOCRATIC VISTAS AND OTHER PAPERS
- DRUM-TAPS (1865) AND SEQUEL TO DRUM-TAPS (1865-66)
- LEAVES OF GRASS

WHITMAN'S PATENT CASES IN THE UNITED STATES SUPREME COURT / Whitman, Charles S – (Patent laws and practice of obtaining Letters patent for inventions in the US and foreign countries. Includes copyright and trademark laws) – Washington: Morrison. v1-2. 1810-74 (all publ) – 22mf – 9 – $33.00 – LLMC 81-424 – us L.L.M.C. [340]

WHITMIRE FIRST BAPTIST CHURCH (CALLED LOWER DUNCAN'S CREEK, 1786-1903). WHITMIRE, SOUTH CAROLINA : CHURCH RECORDS – 1841-1955 – 1 – 25.65 – us Baptist [240]

Whitmore, F B *see* INFIDEL OBJECTIONS TO THE SCRIPTURES

Whitney *see*
- HISTORICAL AND BIOGRAPHICAL RECORD OF LENAWEE COUNTY
- KENNEBEC VALLEY, MAINE

Whitney, C *see* ON SNOW-SHOES TO THE BARREN GROUNDS

Whitney Museum of American Art. New York *see* CATALOG OF THE LIBRARY OF THE WHITNEY MUSEUM OF AMERICAN ART

Whitney Museum of American Art. New York. Library *see* CATALOG OF THE LIBRARY

Whiton, James Morris *see*
- THE DIVINE SATISFACTION:...WHAT SHOULD... BE THOUGHT ABOUT THE ATONEMENT
- EARLY PUPILS OF THE SPIRIT:...THE PROPHETS OF ISRAEL; AND, WHAT OF SAMUEL?
- GETTING TOGETHER:...FRIENDS...ON THE REGULATIVE IDEAS OF RELIGIOUS THOUGHT
- GLORIA PATRI
- THE GOSPEL ACCORDING TO MATTHEW... FOR BIBLE READERS & FOR SUNDAY SCHOOL TEACHERS
- MIRACLES AND SUPERNATURAL RELIGION

Whitrow, Magda *see* ISIS CUMULATIVE BIBLIOGRAPHY 1913-65: A BIBLIOGRAPHY OF THE HISTORY OF SCIENCE FORMED FROM ISIS CRITICAL BIBLIOGRAPHIES 1-90, 1913-65

Whitsett, James *see* MATERIALS (BIOGRAPHICAL AND GENEALOGICAL)

WHITSITT CONTROVERSY: BOTH SIDES – 1897 – 1 – 5.00 – us Baptist [240]

Whitsitt, William H *see*
- JOURNAL
- ORIGIN OF THE DISCIPLES OF CHRIST (CAMBELLITES)
- ORIGIN OF THE DISCIPLES OF CHRIST (CAMPBELLITIES)
- A QUESTION IN BAPTIST HISTORY

WHITSTABLE TIMES – England. -w. 1864-1975. Lacking 1896. 93 1 2 reels – 1 – uk British Libr Newspaper [072]

Whittaker, William Henry *see* THE OHIO JUSTICES' CODE

Whitteker, John Edwin *see* THE SEPARATED LIFE: A BIBLICAL DEFENCE OF THE DIVINITY OF CHRIST

Whitten, Bess E *see* BUSINESS LIBRARY REVIEW

Whitten, David O *see* BUSINESS LIBRARY REVIEW

Whitten, Indy *see* THE CRUSADE THAT LASSOED SPANISH HEARTS

Whitten, Robert Harvey *see* VALUATION OF PUBLIC SERVICE CORPORATIONS.

Whittier, John Greenleaf *see*
- LEGENDS OF NEW ENGLAND
- A SELECTION OF WORKS BY JOHN GREENLEAF WHITTIER

THE WHITTIER NEWS – Whittier, CA. 1913-1923 – 24r – 1 – $1,200.00 – C03579 – us Library Micro [071]

WHITTINGTON AND HIS CAT – 1885. The history of Sir Richard Whittington – 1 – us I.U. Libraries [390]

Whittle, R C *see* THE EFFECTS OF DEHYDRATION AND TEMPERATURE ON MOVEMENT AND REACTION TIME IN COLLEGE AGE MALES

WHITTLESEY, CHARLES, PAPERS, MS 3196 – 1783-1889 – 17r – 1 – us Western Res [978]

WHIZ COMICS – Issue Nos. 11-15 Dec 1940-Apr 1941 – 5mf – 15 – $31.95 – us Comics [760]

WHIZ COMICS – Issue Nos. 1-5 Feb 1940-Jun 1940 – 5mf – 15 – $31.95 – us Comics [760]

WHIZ COMICS – Issue Nos. 16-20 Apr 1941-Aug 1941 – 5mf – 15 – $31.95 – us Comics [760]

WHIZ COMICS – Issue Nos. 21-25 Sept 1941-Dec 1941 – 5mf – 15 – $31.95 – us Comics [760]

WHIZ COMICS – Issue Nos. 26-30 Jan 1942-May 1942 – 5mf – 15 – $31.95 – us Comics [760]

WHIZ COMICS – Issue Nos. 31-35 Jun 1942-Sept 1942 – 5mf – 15 – $31.95 – us Comics [760]

WHIZ COMICS – Issue Nos. 36-40 Oct 1942-Feb 1943 – 5mf – 15 – $31.95 – us Comics [760]

WHIZ COMICS – Issue Nos. 41-45 Apr 1943-Aug 1943 – 5mf – 15 – $31.95 – us Comics [760]

WHIZ COMICS – Issue Nos. 46-50 Sept 1943-Jan 1944 – 5mf – 15 – $31.95 – us Comics [760]

WHIZ COMICS – Issue Nos. 6-10 Jul 1940-Nov 1940 – 5mf – 15 – $31.95 – us Comics [760]

WHO CHRONICLE – (Former title: Chronicle of the World Health Organization 1947-58) – Geneva. v1-40. 1947-86 1; v25-40 1971-86 5; v30-40 1976-86 9 – 1,5,9 – D 1741 – us UMI [613]

WHO IS HE?: AN APPEAL TO THOSE WHO REGARD WITH ANY DOUBT THE NAME OF JESUS / Smiley, Sarah Frances – New York: A.D.F. Randolph, 1877.1 fiche – 9 – us A.T.L.A. [240]

WHO WERE THE LIBYANS? A 626. 1891 / Page Renouf, P Le – 9 – ne IDC [956]

WHO WROTE THE BIBLE? / Gladden, Washington – 1891 – 9 – us A.T.L.A. [240]

WHO WROTE THE BIBLE? A BOOK FOR THE PEOPLE / Gladden, Washington – Boston: Houghton, Mifflin, 1891 – 9 – us A.T.L.A. [240]

THE WHOLE DUTY OF MAN / Hammond, H – London: Eyres, Mount & Page, 1735 – 6mf – 9 – $9.00 – LLMC 91-503 – us L.L.M.C. [170]

WHOLE EARTH NEWSLETTER – v1-16. 1970-87 (complete) – 1r – 1 – ATLA S0860 – us A.T.L.A. [073]

WHOLE EARTH REVIEW – No.44-.1985- – 1,5,6,9 – us UMI [500]

THE WHOLE LAW RELATIVE TO THE DUTY AND OFFICE OF A JUSTICE OF THE PEACE / ed by Williams, Thomas Walter – London Robinson, 1793-95. 4 v. LL-153 – 1 – us L of C Photodup [340]

THE WHOLE SET OF BOOKS BY MR. CHEN-KUO-FU / Chen-kuo-fu – (v.1. Education and Culture. v.2. Political and Economics. v.3. Manners and custom.(1). v.4. Manners and custom.(2). v.5. Lifes Memory. v.6. Cure and Sanitation. (1). v.7. Cure and Sanitation. (2). v.8. Miscellany. (1). v.9. Miscellany. (2). v.10. Miscellany. (3)) – (Chen-kuo-fu hsien-sheng chuan-chi). 1952. 10v. 2864p. 2 reels – 1 – 97.50 – ch Transmission [000]

THE WHOLE SPEECH WHICH WAS DELIVERED TO THE REVEREND CLERGY OF THE GREAT CITY OF LONDON ON TUESDAY THE 8TH OF MAY 1759,... / Free, J – London, [1759] – 1mf – 9 – MP-382/1 – ne IDC [240]

THE WHOLE TRUTH Castle. Mont. 1897-1898 – 1 – us UMI [071]

THE WHOLE VOLUME OF CHRONICLES CONTAINING THE CHRONICLES OF ENGLAND, THE CHRONICLES OF SCOTLAND, THE CHRONICLES OF IRELAND / Holinshed, R – H-350 2 – 8 – ne IDC [880]

THE WHOLE WORKE OF THAT FAMOUS CHIRURGION / Vigo, J de – London, 1586 – 19mf – 9 – ne IDC [617]

WHOLESALE MARKETS : PLANNING AND DESIGN MANUAL – 1992 – 209p – it F.A.O. [650]

WHOLESALE PRICES IN TRIPOLI TOWN / Libya. Ministry of Planning and Development. Census and Statistical Department – 1966, 1969-72. BNE-617 1 – 9 – ne IDC [338]

WHOLESOMENESS OF IRRADIATED FOOD : REPORT OF THE JOINT F.A.O./W.H.O. EXPERT COMMITTEE, GENEVA, 1976 – 1977 – 44p – it F.A.O. [640]

WHO'S DRUNK, WHEN? – Sacramento, Calif., Rose, 1947 61 p. LL-1372 – 1 – us L of C Photodup [340]

WHO'S WHO AMONG WOMEN OF CALIFORNIA / Lyons, Louis S – San Francisco: Security Publ. Co., 1922. California reel 38. (Cox Library Collection) – 5 – us Americana [920]

WHO'S WHO IN ALABAMA 1939-1940 / Matlock, Guy E – Birmingham: Dubose Publ. Co., 1940. Alabama Reel 2. (The Cox Library Collection) – 5 – us Americana [978]

WHO'S WHO IN ARCHITECTURE – 1914, 1923, 1926. Printed text – 9 – £80.00 – uk World [720]

WHO'S WHO IN ARIZONA / Conners, Jo – Tucson: Arizona Daily Star, 1913. Arizona Reel 3. (The Cox Library Collection) – 5 – us Americana [978]

WHO'S WHO IN AUSTRALIA – International Press Service Association, 1922, 1927, 1929, 1935 – 48mf – 9 – A$80.00 – at State Libr Vic [920]

WHO'S WHO IN CALIFORNIA, 1928-1929 / Detwiler, Justice B – San Francisco: Who's Who Publ. Co., 1929. California reel 39. (Cox Library Collection) – 5 – us Americana [920]

WHO'S WHO IN CALIFORNIA, 1942-1943 / Fletcher, Russell H – Los Angeles: Who's Who Publ. Co., 1941. California reel 39. (Cox Library Collection) – 5 – us Americana [920]

WHO'S WHO IN CONNECTICUT / Duffy, Ward E – New York, Lewis Historical Publ. Co., 1933. Connecticut Reel 2. (The Cox Library Collection) – 5 – us Americana [978]

WHO'S WHO IN DENVER AND COLORADO, 1940, 1941 AND 1942 / Capital Publishing Co – Denver, 1940. Colorado reel 3. (Cox Library Collection) – 5 – us Americana [920]

WHO'S WHO IN INDIA, CONTAINING LIVES AND PORTRAITS OF RULING CHIEFS, NOTABLES, TITLED PERSONAGES, AND OTHER EMINENT INDIANS – Popular ed. Lucknow: Newul Kishore Press, 1911.1v – 1 – us U.W. Library [920]

WHO'S WHO IN LINCOLN COUNTY / Baldwin, Sara M – Lincoln: Robert M. Baldwin, 1928. Nebraska Reel 11. (The Cox Library Collection) – 5 – us Americana [978]

WHO'S WHO IN LOS ANGELES, 1924 / Lang, Charles J – Los Angeles, 1924. Calif. reel 39. (Cox Library Collection) – 5 – us Americana [920]

WHO'S WHO IN LOS ANGELES, 1925-1926 / Lang, Charles J – Los Angeles: Who's Who in Los Angeles Publ., 1926. Calif. reel 39. (Cox Library Collection) – 5 – us Americana [920]

WHO'S WHO IN LOS ANGELES, 1926-1927 / Lang, Charles J – Los Angeles, 1927. Calif. reel 39. (Cox Library Collection) – 5 – us Americana [920]

WHO'S WHO IN LOS ANGELES, 1927-1928 / Lang, Charles J – Los Angeles, 1928. Calif. reel 39. (Cox Library Collection) – 5 – us Americana [920]

WHO'S WHO IN LOS ANGELES, 1928-1929 / Lang, Charles J – Los Angeles, 1929. Calif. reel 39. (Cox Library Collection) – 5 – us Americana [920]

WHO'S WHO IN LOS ANGELES, 1930-1931 / Lang, Charles J – Los Angeles, 1931. Calif. reel 39. (Cox Library Collection) – 5 – us Americana [920]

WHO'S WHO IN LOUISIANA AND MISSISSIPPI / The Times-Picayune – 1918. Louisiana Reel 1.(The Cox Library Collection) – 5 – us Americana [978]

WHO'S WHO IN METHODISM, 1933 : AN ENCYCLOPAEDIA OF THE PERSONNEL AND DEPARTMENTS, MINISTERIAL AND LAY, IN THE UNITED CHURCH OF METHODISM – London, 1933 – 6mf – 9 – ne IDC [240]

WHO'S WHO IN MISSISSIPPI / Kelly, Thomas E – Jackson: Tucker Printing House, 1914. Mississippi Reel 1. (The Cox Library Collection) – 5 – us Americana [978]

WHO'S WHO IN NEBRASKA / Nebraska Press Association – Lincoln, 1940. Nebraska Reel 13. (The Cox Library Collection) – 5 – us Americana [978]
WHO'S WHO IN NEVADA / Bessie Beatty Home Printing Co – Los Angeles, 1907. Nevada reel 1. (Cox Library Collection) – 5 – us Americana [920]
WHO'S WHO IN NEW CHINA / Kwee, Kek Beng – In Indonesian. SE-3075 1. 1953 – 9 – ne IDC [920]
WHO'S WHO IN NORTH VIETNAM – [Washington, DC: Off of External Research, US Dept of State], 1972 – us Res Libr [324]
WHO'S WHO IN OMAHA 1928 / Baldwin, Sara M – Louisville, Omaha, Hebron: Robert M. Baldwin Corp. Nebraska Reel 13. (The Cox Library Collection) – 5 – us Americana [978]
WHO'S WHO IN RELIGIOUS, FRATERNAL, SOCIAL, CIVIC AND COMMERCIAL LIFE ON THE PACIFIC COAST, STATE OF WASHINGTON / Searchlight Publishing Co – Seattle, 1926-27. Washington reel 8. (Cox Library Collection) – 5 – us Americana [920]
WHO'S WHO IN SOUTH CAROLINA / Crawford, Geddings H; ed by Crawford, Geddings H – Columbia, McCaw Printers, 1921. South Carolina Reel 3. (The Cox Library Collection) – 5 – us Americana [978]
WHO'S WHO IN TEXAS / Bailey, Emory E – Dallas: Who's Who Publishing Co., 1931. Texas Reel 13. (The Cox Library Collection) – 5 – us Americana [978]
WHO'S WHO IN THE PHILIPPINES; A BIOGRAPHICAL DICTIONARY OF NOTABLE LIVING MEN OF THE PHILIPPINE ISLAND – v11, 1940-41. Manila: McCullough. Annual. Continued by: Philippines Who's who – 1 – us U.W. Library [920]
WHO'S WHO IN WASHINGTON STATE 1927 / Allen, Arthur H – Seattle, 1927. Washington reel 8. (Cox Library Collection) – 5 – us Americana [978]
WHO'S WHO IN WESTERN CANADA / ed by Parker, C W – Winnipeg and Portland: Canadian Press Assoc. Ltd., 1911.Canada reel 2. (Cox Library Collection) – 5 – us Americana [920]
WHO'S WHO OF CEYLON / Abeyesooriya, Samson – 3rd ed. [Colombo: "Morning Leader" Press, 1928] – us Res Libr [950]
WHO'S WHO ON THE OHIO RIVER AND ITS TRIBUTARIES / Leahy, Ethel C – Cincinnati: E.C. Leahy Publ. Co., 1931. Ohio Reel 11. (The Cox Library Collection) – 5 – us Americana [978]
WHY? – 1-2 2+7 (all publ). 1913-1914 – 4mf – 9 – $35.00 – us UPA [335]
WHY A TWO-THOUSAND DOLLAR CAR COSTS FIFTEEN THOUSAND DOLLARS / Barnett, John – 1986. 1p – 9 – 1.00f – at Libertarian Micro [335]
WHY AM I A BAPTIST? / Porter, J W – 1 – 5.00 – us Baptist [240]
THE WHY AND HOW OF FOREIGN MISSIONS / Brown, Arthur Judson – New York: Presbyterian Church U.S.A., 1908. xii/286p. 1 fiche – 9 – us A.T.L.A. [240]
WHY BISHOPS BACK FRANCO; REPORT OF VISIT OF INVESTIGATION TO SPAIN / McGovern, John – London, 1936? Fiche W1010. (Blodgett Collection of Spanish Civil War Pamphlets) – 9 – us H.U. College Libr [946]
WHY FEAR EVOLUTION? (CCC161) = WEI SHE MO P'A CHIN HUA LUN / Hollister, G W – (In Chinese) – Hong Kong: Council on Christian Literature for Overseas Chinese, 1955 – 1r – 1 – 1984-B500 – us A.T.L.A. [240]
WHY FOUR GOSPELS?, OR, THE GOSPEL FOR ALL THE WORLD / Gregory, Daniel Seeley – Cincinnati: Hitchcock & Walden, 1880 – 9 – us A.T.L.A. [240]
WHY FRAU FROHMANN RAISED HER PRICES : AND OTHER STORIES / Trollope, Anthony – London: W. Isbister, 1882 – 1 roll – 1 – 1-55879-372-0 – uk Libr Preservation [830]
WHY I AM NOT AN INFIDEL: A LECTURE / Nourse, Robert – New York: Fleming H. Revell, 1898. 1 fiche – 9 – us A.T.L.A. [240]
WHY I BECAME A CHRISTIAN (CCC164) = HSIEH, CHING-SHENG – (In Chinese) – Shanghai: Association Press of China, 1940 – 1r – 1 – 1984-B500 – us A.T.L.A. [240]
WHY I DO NOT EAT MEAT / White, Alma – Zarephath, N.J.: Pentecostal Union (Pillar of Fire), 1915 – 1mf – us A.T.L.A. [240]
WHY I FOLLOW JESUS (CCC296) / Tsao, Hsin-ming – (In Chinese) – 1st ed. Hong Kong: Council on Christian Literature for Overseas Chinese, 1956 – 1r – 1 – 1984-6635 – us A.T.L.A. [240]
WHY I STILL BELIEVE THAT MOSES WROTE DEUTERONOMY : SOME REFLECTIONS AFTER READING PROFESSOR ROBERTSON SMITH'S ADDITIONAL ANSWER TO THE LIBEL / Douglas, George Cunningham Monteath – Edinburgh: Maclaren & Macniven, 1878 – 1mf – 9 – 0-8370-2957-0 – 1985-0957 – us A.T.L.A. [220]
WHY INDONESIA OPPOSES BRITISH-MADE MALAYSIA / Indonesia – 1964. SE-5975-1 – 9 – ne IDC [950]
WHY MEN HATE / Tenenbaum, Samuel – New York: Jewish Book Guild of America, c1947. 368p. Bibliography – 1 – us U.W. Library [360]
WHY NOT?: A PLEA FOR THE ORDINATION OF THOSE WOMEN WHOM GOD HAS CALLED TO PREACH THE GOSPEL / Sellew, Walter Ashbel – 1894 – 9 – us A.T.L.A. [240]
WHY NOT TRY FREEDOM? / Read, Leonard E – 1958. 90p. Together with: Essays from "Essays On Liberty", v.III-V. 161p total. 1 fiche (24x) – 9 – 1.00f – at Libertarian Micro [320]
THE WHY OF METHODISM / Dorchester, Daniel – New York: Phillips & Hunt; Cincinnati: Cranston & Stowe, 1887 – 1mf – us A.T.L.A. [240]
WHY PAUL FERROLL KILLED HIS WIFE / Clive, Caroline – New York: Carleton, 1862 – 1 roll – 1 – 1-55879-953-2 – uk Libr Preservation [830]
WHY PEOPLE MOVE : COMPARATIVE PERSPECTIVES ON THE DYNAMICS OF INTERNAL MIGRATION / Balan, George – 1981 – 342p – 9 – 92-3-101909-0 – fr UNESCO [304]
WHY PERON CAME TO POWER : THE BACKGROUND TO PERONISM IN ARGENTINA / ed by Barager, Joseph R – New York: Knopf, [1968] – 1 – CSUXAHZ7179-B – us Hoover Inst Photo [320]
WHY SPAIN FIGHTS ON / Fischer, Louis – London, 1937? Fiche W 886. (Blodgett Collection of Spanish Civil War Pamphlets) – 9 – us H.U. College Libr [946]
WHY THE EMBARGO AGAINST THE SPANISH REPUBLIC SHOULD BE LIFTED NOW – N.Y., 1939? Fiche W1254. (Blodgett Collection of Spanish Civil War Pamphlets) – 9 – us H.U. College Libr [946]
WHY WAGES RISE / Harper, F A – 1957. Also: In Search of Peace. 1951. Together, 166p. 1 fiche (24x) – 9 – 1.00f – at Libertarian Micro [320]
WHY WAS LOUISBURG TWICE BESEIGED?: A PAPER READ BEFORE THE SOCIETY OF COLONIAL WARS IN THE COMMONWEALTH OF MASSACHUSETTS AT BOSTON, APRIL 30, 1895 / Bent, Samuel Arthur – Boston: The Society, 1895. 02313. (Pre-1900n Canadiana) – 9 – cn C.I.H.M. [971]
WHY WE ARE CHRISTIANS (CCC219) = NGO MEN SHEN MO TSO CHI TU T'U / Liao, An-jen – (In Chinese) – Shanghai: Christian Literature Society, 1933 – 1r – 1 – 1984-B500 – us A.T.L.A. [240]
WHY WE BELIEVE THE BIBLE / King, Henry Melville – New York: American Tract Society, 1902. 1 fiche – 9 – us A.T.L.A. [240]
Whymper, C *see* EGYPTIAN BIRDS
Whymper, Edward *see*
- THE ASCENT OF THE MATTERHORN
- SCRAMBLES AMONGST THE ALPS
- TRAVELS AMONGST THE GREAT ANDES OF THE EQUATOR

Whymper, F *see* TRAVEL AND ADVENTURE IN THE TERRITORY OF ALASKA
Whyte, Alexander *see*
- BIBLE CHARACTERS. AHITHOPHEL TO NEHEMIAH
- THE WALK, CONVERSATION, AND CHARACTER OF JESUS CHRIST OUR LORD

Whyte, Digby N B *see* KEY TRENDS AND ISSUES IMPACTING LOCAL GOVERNMENT RECREATION AND PARK ADMINISTRATION IN THE 1990S
Whyte, R O et al *see* GRASSES IN AGRICULTURE
Whytt, R *see*
- AN ESSAY ON THE VITAL AND OTHER INVOLUNTARY MOTIONS OF ANIMALS
- OBSERVATIONS ON THE DROPSY IN THE BRAIN

WIADOMOSCI – London, UK. Tygodnik. 14 Apr 1946- – 1 – uk British Libr Newspaper [072]
WIADOMOSCI CODZIENNE – Cleveland: S A Dangel, [1918-oct 15 1966] – us Res Libr [071]
WIADOMOSCI LITERACKIE – Warsaw. v. 1-16. Jan 6 1924-Sept 3 1939. Incomplete – 1 – us NY Public [460]
WIADOMOSCI LITERACKIE – Warsaw. v1-16. 1924-39 – 5r – 1 – us Ross [460]
WIADOMOSCI POLSKIE – 1939-44 – 1r – 1 – inquire – us Ross [072]
WIADOMOSCI POLSKIE – London, UK. 17 Mar 1940-13 Feb 1944 – 1 – uk British Libr Newspaper [072]
WIADOMOSCI POLSKIE – Sydney, Australia. -w. 17 March 1957-5 Dec 1965. Imperfect. 4 reels – 1 – uk British Libr Newspaper [072]
WIADOMOSCI STATYSTYCZNE O STOSUNKACH KRAJOWYCH – Lwow, 1911 – 1r – 1 – us I.H.R.C. [947]
WIARA I OJCZYZNA : URZEDOWY ORGAN ZJEDNOCZENIA POLSKIEGO RZYMSKO-KATOLICKIEGO W AMERYCE POD OPIEKA BSJ – Chicago: Spolka Wydaw. Pol. w Chicago, oct 9-dec 1891; jan-dec 24 1896 – 1r – 1 – us Res Libr [073]
WIARUS POLSKI – Bochum, dec 25 1890-97 (incomplete), 1900, apr 20-dec 31 1901, 1903-05, 1907, 1915-16 (incomplete), jan-sep 1924, 1925-28 (incomplete), jan-jul 12 1939 – 1 – Inquire at Mikrofilmarchiv for details – gw Misc Inst [943]
WIARUS POLSKI – Bochum, Germany.20 Apr-26 Nov 1901; 29 Mar 1903-5 Dez 1905; 1907 – 1 – gw Mikrofilm [072]
WIARUS POLSKI – (Inkl beilagen) – Bochum, Apr-Nov 1901; Mar 1903-Dec 1905; Jan-Dec 1907 – 4r – 1 – DM320.00 – gw Mikro Press [072]
Wibbelt, Augustin *see*
- DAS BUCH VON DEN VIER QUELLEN
- DE JAERFSCHOPP
- DE PASTOR VON DRIEBECK
- DE STRUNZ
- HUS DAHLEN
- JOSEPH VON GOERRES ALS LITTERARHISTORIKER
- MAETEN-GAITLINK
- DE PASTOR VON DRIEBECK
- SCHULTE WITTE
- DE STRUNZ
- DAT VEERTE GEBOTT
- WILDE BLUMEN
- WILDRUPS HOFF

Wibel, A W E C *see* PRIMITAIE FLORAE WERTHEMENSIS
Wiberg, Anders *see* DIARIES
WIBERG PAPERS, 1850-73 – ABMS. Germany. 2194p – 1 – $76.79 – us Baptist [240]
Wichern, Johann Hinrich *see* NOTHSTAENDE DER PROTESTANTISCHEN KIRCHE UND DIE INNERE MISSION
Wichert, Ernst *see*
- DIE FABRIK ZU NIEDERBRONN
- DIE GNAEDIGE FRAU VON PARETZ
- IM BANNE DES SCHICKSALS
- EIN KLEINES BILD

WICHITA COUNTY DEMOCRAT – Leoti. Kansas. -w. 1886-87 – 1 – us UMI [071]
WICHITA COUNTY HERALD – Coronado. Kansas. 1886-1887 – 1 – us UMI [071]
Wichita. Kansas *see* RECORDS
DAS WICHTIGSTE DER WOCHE *see* REICHSSENDER BRESLAU: NACHRICHTENDIENST
DER WICHTIGSTEN BEKENNTNISSCHRIFTEN DER EVANGELISCH-REFORMIRTEN KIRCHE : MIT GESCHICHTLICHEN EINLEITUNGEN UND ANMERKUNGEN / ed by Bodemann, Friedrich Wilhelm – 2. Aufl. Goettingen: Vandenhoeck und Ruprecht, 1867 – 1mf – 9 – 0-8370-8885-2 – 1986-2885 – us A.T.L.A. [240]
DIE WICHTIGSTEN FRAGEN IM LEBEN JESU: FERIENKURSVORTRAEGE / Soden, Hermann – Berlin: Arthur Glaue, 1909. 1 fiche – 9 – us A.T.L.A. [240]
DIE WICHTIGSTEN SAETZE DER NEUEREN ALTTESTAMENTLICHEN KRITIK : VOM STANDPUNKTE DER PROPHETEN AMOS UND HOSEA AUS BETRACHTET: EIN BEITRAG ZUM VERSTAENDNIS / Billeb, Hermann – Halle a.S: Eduard Anton, 1893 – 1mf – 9 – 0-8370-2342-4 – 1985-0342 – us A.T.L.A. [220]
WICI – Chicago: KON, 1916-17 – us Res Libr [071]
Wick, Gerald L et al *see* HARVESTING OCEAN ENERGY
Wickel, Marc *see* SM22, EIN ENIGMATISCHES PROTEIN DER GLATTEN MUSKULATUR
Wickersham, Cornelius Wendell *see* A TREATISE ON STOCK WITHOUT PAR VALUE OF ORDINARY BUSINESS CORPORATIONS
Wickersham, James *see* OLD YUKON TALES, TRAILS AND TRIALS
WICKETS IN THE WEST, OR, THE TWELVE IN AMERICA / Fitzgerald, Robert Allan – London: Tinsley Bros., 1873. 03109. (Pre-1900 Canadiana) – 9 – cn C.I.H.M. [971]
Wickham, Gertrude van Rensselaer *see* PAPERS, MS 1085
Wickham Legg, J *see*
- THE CLERC'S BOOK OF 1549
- CRAMMER'S LITURGICAL PROJECTS
- ENGLISH ORDERS FOR CONSECRATING CHURCHES IN THE 17TH CENTURY
- INVENTORIES OF CHRIST CHURCH CANTERBURY
- MISSALE AD USUM ECCLESIAE WESTMONASTERIENSIS: FAC. 3
- MISSALE AD USUM ECCLESIAE WESTMONASTERIENSIS: FACS. 2
- MISSALE AD USUM ECCLESIAE WESTMONASTERIENSIS. FASC. 1
- THE PROCESSIONAL OF THE NUNS OF CHESTER
- THE SECOND RECENSION OF THE QUIGNON BREVIARY, VOL. 1
- THE SECOND RECENSION OF THE QUIGNON BREVIARY, VOL. 2
- THREE CORONATION ORDERS
- TRACTS ON THE MASS

Wickings, H F *see*
- COVENANT PEOPLE OF GOD (CCC324)
- THE GOOD NEWS (CCC323)

WICKLOW NEWSLETTER – Ireland.1858-59; 1861-76; 1879-84; 1886-96. -w. 14 reels – 1 – uk British Libr Newspaper [072]
WICKLOW PEOPLE – Wicklow, Ireland. -d. 1898-1904, 1986.10 reels – 1 – PS27.50r – ie European Micro [072]
Wickmann, H *see* DIE ENTSTEHUNG DER FAERBUNG DER VOGELEIER
Wickremasinghe, M de Zilva *see* EPIGRAPHIA ZEYLANICA
Wicksteed, Philip Henry *see* DANTE AND AQUINAS
WICLIF AND HUS / Loserth, Johann – London: Hodder and Stoughton, 1884 – 1mf – us A.T.L.A. [240]
WICOMICO NEWS – Salisbury. Md. -w. 1899-1937 – 1 – us UMI [071]
WICTORIA REGIA. CHETVERTAIA KNIGA POEZ / Severianin, I – M. 1915. BR-1041 2 – 8 – ne IDC [920]
Widawan, Rosa *see* MODERN INDONESIAN DRAMA
DER WIDDERTEUFFER LERE VND GEHEIMNIS. AUS HEILIGER SCHRIFFT WIDDERLEGT. MART. LUTH. VON DER WIDDERTAUFFE AN ZWEEN PFARHER, EIN BRIEFF. PHILIP MELANCHTON. VNTERRICHT WIDDER DIE LERE DER WIDERTOUFFER... / Menius, J – 1534. BME-128/1 – 9 – ne IDC [240]
Widdicombe, John *see*
- FOURTEEN YEARS IN BASUTOLAND
- FOURTEEN YEARS IN BASUTOLAND; A SKETCH OF AFRICAN MISSION LIFE

WIDE ANGLE – (v.4-. 1980- 5,6,9) – v.1-. 1976- – 1 – us UMI [073]
A WIDE DOMINION / Bindloss, Harold – London: Fisher Unwin, 1899. 00831. (Pre-1900 Canadiana) – 9 – cn C.I.H.M. [971]
THE WIDE WEST – San Francisco, CA. Mar 1854-Jul 1858 – 2r – 1 – $100.00 – C02867 – us Library Micro [071]
Widekehr, J *see*
- 1ER QUINTETTO POUR 2 VIOLONS, 2 ALTOS ET BASSE
- TROIS QUATUORS. 2E LIVRE

WIDENER JOURNAL OF PUBLIC LAW – v1-4. 1992-95 – 9 – $76.00 set – us Hein [340]
THE WIDENESS OF GOD'S MERCY / Meyer, Frederick Brotherton – Cincinnati: Jennings and Graham; New York: Eaton and Mains, [1906?] – 1mf – 9 – 0-8370-7178-X – 1986-1178 – us A.T.L.A. [240]
Widengren, C *see* MUHAMMAD, THE APOSTLE OF GOD AND HIS ASCENSION
Widengren, George *see* LITERARY AND PSYCHOLOGICAL ASPECTS OF THE HEBREW PROPHETS
Widenmann, Pauline *see* LIEDER UND GEDICHTE

WIDER DEN NEWEN TAUFFORDEN, NOTWENDIGE WARNUNG AN ALLE CHRISTGLEUBIGEN / Rhegius, Urbanus – Augspurg. 1527. BME-108 1 – 9 – ne IDC [240]
WIDER DIE VERFLUCHTE LERE DER CARLSTADER, VND ALLE FUERNEMSTE HEUBTER DER SACRAMENTIRER, ROTTENGEISTER, WIDERTEUFFER / Alberus, E – Newenbrandenburg. 1565. BME-199 1 – 9 – ne IDC [240]
WIDER KLIEFOTH UND LUTHARDT : IN SACHEN DER LUTHERBIBEL / Schlottmann, Konstantin – (Includes bibliographical references) – Halle a. S:Eugen Strien, 1885 – 1mf – 9 – 0-8370-5102-9 – 1985-3102 – us A.T.L.A. [220]
WIDERLEGTE VORURTHEILE VOM URSPRUNGE DER KIRCHEN MUSIC / Ruetz, Caspar – 1750. WIDERLEGTE VORURTHEILE VON DER BESSCHAFFENHEIT DER HEUTIGEN KIRCHEMUSIC. 1752. WIDERLEGTE VORURTHEILE VON DER WIRKUNG DER KIRCHENMUSIC. 1753. 3v – 9 – us Sibley [780]
DER WIDERSCHEIN : EINE RUECKSCHAU, 1893-1943 / Leip, Hans; ed by Buchmann, Klaere – Stuttgart: Cotta, 1943 – 1r – 1 – us U.W. Library [840]
WIDERSTAND ALS "HOCHVERRAT" 1933-1945 : DIE VERFAHREN GEGEN DEUTSCHE REICHSANGEHOERIGE VOR DEM REICHSGERICHT, DEM VOLKSGERICHTSHOF UND DEM REICHSKRIEGSGERICHT / Zarusky, Juergen & Mehringer, Hartmut; ed by Institut fuer Zeitgeschichte Muenchen – (Registerband ca 760p ca DM248.00 ISBN: 3-598-33676-4. Free to subsc of the mf ed) – (mf ed 1994-97) – 754mf (1:24) – 9 – diazo DM8,900.00 silver DM9,800.00 – 3-598-33670-5 – silver ISBN: 3-598-33673-X – gw Saur [340]
DER WIDERTOEUFFEREN VRSPRUNG, FUERGANG, SECTEN, WAESEN, FUERNEMME VND GEMEINE JRER LEER ARTICKEL / Bullinger, Heinrich – Zuerych, CHr. Froschower. 1561. BME-118 1 – 9 – ne IDC [240]
DER WIDERTOUFFEREN URSPRUNG/FURGANG/ SECTION/WASEN/FURNEM ME UND GEMINE JRER LEER ARTICKLE / Bullinger, Heinrich – 1561 – 1 – 8.08 – us Baptist [240]
Widgery, Alban G *see* LIFE'S BASIS AND LIFE'S IDEAL
Widjajanto, M R *see* SILUMAN DJALUGIGIS
Widmann, Elisabeth *see* JOSEF VIKTOR WIDMANN
Widmann, Ines *see*
- DIE SCHWABENMARGRET
- DER SOHN

Widmann, Joseph Viktor *see*
- BUDDHA
- MODERNE ANTIKEN
- DIE MUSE DES ARETIN
- DIE PATRIZIERIN
- SOMMERWANDERUNGEN UND WINTERFAHRTEN

Widmann, Max *see*
- GOTTFRIED KELLER UND J V WIDMANN
- JOSEF VIKTOR WIDMANN

THE WIDOW MARRIED : A SEQUEL TO "THE WIDOW BARNABY" / Trollope, Frances Milton – London: H. Colburn, 1840 – 2 rolls – 1 – 1-55879-267-8 – uk Libr Preservation [830]
A WIDOWER INDEED / Broughton, Rhoda – With: Elizabeth Bisland.British Fiction Archive: Unit 4 – 9 – uk Bell [830]
WIDOWERS' HOUSES : A COMEDY: FIRST ACTED AT THE INDEPENDENT THEATRE IN LONDON / Shaw, Bernard – London: Henry & Co., 1893 – 1 roll – 1 – 1-55879-202-3 – uk Libr Preservation [820]
WIDUKINDI MONACHI CORBEIENSIS RERUM GESTARUM SAXONICARUM LIBRI 3 (MGH 7: 60.BD) – 1935 – Dfl22.00 – ne Slangenburg [240]
Widule, Carol J *see* DETERMINATION OF THE PRECISION, ACCURACY AND RESOLUTION OF A VIDEO-BASED MOTION ANALYSIS SYSTEM
Widule, Carole J *see* THE DEVELOPMENT OF A VIDEO-BASED MOTION ANALYSIS SYSTEM
WIE AIN BETRUEBTER MENSCH RUEFFT ZU GOTT VMB HILFF VND WIE DER GAYST GOTTES JN TROESTET / Huberinus, Caspar – [Augsburg: Philipp Ulhart], 1540. [G.F.: 7.12] – 1mf – 9 – HUB-88/1 – ne IDC [240]
WIE ANNE BAEBI JOWAEGER HAUSHALTET UND WIE ES IHM MIT DEM DOKTERN GEHT / Gotthelf, Jeremias; ed by Ineichen, Alfred – (Includes bibliographical references) – Erlenbach, Zuerich: E Rentsch, 1921 – 1 – us U.W. Library [830]
WIE ANNE BAEBI JOWAEGER HAUSHALTET UND WIE ES IHM MIT DEM DOKTERN GEHT / Gotthelf, Jeremias; ed by Vetter, Ferdinand – Bern: Schmid & Francke. 2v. 1899 – 1 – us U.W. Library [830]
WIE DENKT DAS VOLK UEBER DIE SPRACHE? / Polle, Friedrich – Leipzig: B.G. Teubner, 1898. 188p – 1 – us U.W. Library [400]
WIE DIE ALTEN DEN TOD GEBILDET / Lessing, Gotthold Ephraim – O 1041. 1769 – 9 – ne IDC [190]
WIE DIE GSCHRIFFT VERSTENDIGKLICH SOLL VNTERSCHIDEN UNDE ERKLAERT WERDEN / Sattler, M – BME-69 1 – 9 – ne IDC [240]
WIE DIE MENSCHEN KOCHEN LERNTEN / Lippert, Julius – Prag: Verlag des Deutschen Vereines zur Verbreitung gemeinnuetziger Kenntnisse, 1879 – 1r – 1 – us U.W. Library [640]
WIE ENTSTANDEN MEINE ANEKDOTEN / Schaefer, Wilhelm – Dortmund: F W Ruhfus, 1910 – 1r – 1 – us U.W. Library [430]
WIE GRETE AUFHOERTE EIN KIND ZU SEIN : EINE ERZAEHLUNG AUS SUEDAFRIKA / Grimm, Hans – Leipzig: P Reclam, 1944, c1939 – 1r – 1 – us U.W. Library [830]
WIE HABEN WIR ZAEHLEN UND RECHNEN GELERNT? : WIE ZAEHLTEN UND RECHNETEN DIE ALTEN? / Koch, M – Prag: Verlag des deutschen Vereines zur Verbreitung gemeinnuetziger Kenntnisse, 1878 – 1r – 1 – us U.W. Library [943]
WIE ICH ES SEHE / Altenberg, Peter – Berlin: S Fischer, 1896 – 1r – 1 – us U.W. Library [430]
WIE ICH ES SEHE / Altenberg, Peter – Berlin: S Fischer, 1918 – 1r – 1 – us U.W. Library [943]
WIE LUDWIG HETZER ZU CONSTANTZ MIT DEM SCHWERT GERICHT / Blaurer, Th – Constantz, J. Spitzenberg. 1529. BME-11 1 – 9 – ne IDC [240]
WIE MAN CHRISTLICHER WEYSZ BEICHTEN / Brysgawer, M – 1524. BME-21 1 – 9 – ne IDC [240]
WIE MAN DAS VOLCK ZUR BUSS VND ERNSTLICHEM GEBET WIDER DEN TUERCKEN AUFF DER CANTZEL VERMANEN SOL.. / Dietrich, Veit – 1542 – 1 – us A.T.L.A. [240]
WIE MAN DIE FALSCHEN PROPHETEN ERKENNEN IA GREIFFEN MAG / Rhegius, Urbanus – Brunswick, A. Goldbeck. 1539. BME-111 1 – 9 – ne IDC [240]
WIE MAN DIE KRANCKEN TROESTEN SOLL / Huberinus, Caspar – [Augsburg, Philipp Ulhart], 1542. [G.F.: 6.1] – 2mf – 9 – HUB-24/1 – ne IDC [240]
WIE MANN DAS KLAR HELL GOTS WORT PREDIGEN SOLL / Fritzhans, J – 1524. BME-19 1 – 9 – ne IDC [240]
WIE SOLLEN WIR HEINE VERSTEHEN : EINE PSYCHOLOGISCHE STUDIE / Poritzky, J E – (Includes bibliographical references) – Berlin: C Duncker, 1896 – 1r – 1 – us U.W. Library [430]
WIE STEHT GOETHE ZU DANTE? : ERICH SCHMIDT UND KARL VOSSLER IN DANKBARKEIT ZUGEEIGNET / Pochhammer, Paul – Berlin: Verlag fuer Fortbildung, [1910?] – 1r – 1 – us U.W. Library [410]
WIE ULI DER KNECHT GLUECKLICH WIRD : EINE GABE FUER DIENSTBOTEN UND MEISTERLEUTE / Gotthelf, Jeremias; ed by Hunziker, Rudolf – (Includes bibliographical references) – Erlenbach, Zuerich: E Rentsch, 1921 – 1 – us U.W. Library [830]
WIE ULI DER KNECHT, GLUECKLICH WIRD : EINE GABE FUER DIENSTBOTEN UND MEISTERLEUTE / Gotthelf, Jeremias; ed by Vetter, Ferdinand – Bern: Schmid & Francke, 1899 – 1 – us U.W. Library [830]
WIE WURDEN DIE BUECHER DES NEUEN TESTAMENTS HEILIGE SCHRIFT?: FUENF VORTRAEGE / Lietzmann, Hans – Tuebingen: J.C.B. Mohr, 1907. 1 fiche – 9 – us A.T.L.A. [240]
Wieber, Georg-Friedrich *see* DIE CHORFUGE IN HAENDELS WERKEN
Wiechert, Ernst Emil *see*
- DAS EINFACHE LEBEN
- DER EXOTE
- DIE FLUCHT
- DIE GEBAERDE; DER FREMDE
- GESCHICHTE EINES KNABEN
- HIRTENNOVELLE
- JAHRE UND ZEITEN
- JEDERMANN
- DIE JEROMIN-KINDER
- DIE KLEINE PASSION
- DER KNECHT GOTTES ANDREAS NYLAND
- REDE AN DIE DEUTSCHE JUGEND, 1945
- DER SILBERNE WAGEN
- DER TOTENWALD
- DER VATER
- WAELDER UND MENSCHEN
- DER WALD

WIECZOR – Katowice, Poland. 1957-68 – 24r – 1 – us L of C Photodup [943]
WIECZOR – Warsaw, Poland. Oct 1946-Aug 1948 – 2r – 1 – us L of C Photodup [943]
Wieczorek, Tadeusz *see* ELEMENTS OF THE STRUCTURE AND TERMINOLOGY OF AGRICULTURAL EDUCATION IN POLAND
Wiedeburg, Johann Ernst Basilius *see* NEUE MUTHMASUNGEN UEBER DIE SONNENFLECKEN..
Wiedeburg, Michael Johann Friedrich *see* DER SICH SELBST INFORMIRENDE CLAVIERSPIELER...
WIEDERGEBOREN / Kunzemann, Gertrud – Muenchen: C Roehrig, [1942] – 1r – 1 – us U.W. Library [830]
WIEDERGEBURT : LIEDER AUS DEM OSTEN / Luetzkendorf, Felix – Berlin: Suhrkamp, 1944 – 1r – 1 – us U.W. Library [810]
DIE WIEDERGEBURT DER DICHTUNG AUS DEM RELIGIOESEN ERLEBNIS : GEDANKEN ZUR PSYCHOLOGIE DES KATHOLISCHEN LITERATURSCHAFFENS / Muth, Karl – Kempten, Muenchen, 1909 – 172p – 9 – DM48.00 – 3-89349-113-9 – gw Hänsel [410]
DIE WIEDERHERSTELLUNG ISRAELS UNTER DEN ACHAEMENIDEN : KRITISCH-HISTORISCHE UNTERSUCHUNG MIT INSCHRIFTLICHER BELEUCHTUNG / Jampel, Sigmund – (Includes bibliographical references) – Breslau: Wilhelm Koebner, 1904 – 1mf – 9 – 0-8370-3769-7 – 1985-1769 – us A.T.L.A. [270]
DIE WIEDERKEHR DES NOVALIS : BERICHT DES RATSDIENERS JOHANN CHRISTOPH BOETTCHER AUS DEM JAHRE 1945 / Augustiny, Waldemar – Guetersloh: C Bertelsmann, c1948 – 1r – 1 – us U.W. Library [830]
DER WIEDERKUNFTSGEDANKE JESU : NACH DEN SYNOPTIKERN / Weiffenbach, Wilhelm – (Includes bibliographical references) – Leipzig: Breitkopf & Haertel, 1873 – 1mf – 9 – 0-8370-5739-6 – 1985-3739 – us A.T.L.A. [240]
DIE WIEDERKUNFTSWEISSAGUNG JESU CHRISTI / Mehlhorn, Paul – Jena, 1874. 1 fiche – 9 – us A.T.L.A. [240]
WIEDERSEHEN MIT DER JUGEND : ERZAEHLUNGEN / Meckel, Eberhard – Stuttgart: Cotta, 1944 – 1r – 1 – us U.W. Library [830]
DIE WIEDERTAEUFER ZU MUENSTER : EINE BIBLIOGRAPHISCHE ZUSAMMENSTELLUNG / Bahlmann, Paul – (Includes bibliographical references) – Muenster: Regensburg, 1894 – 1mf – 9 – 0-8370-8882-8 – 1986-2882 – us A.T.L.A. [240]
DIE WIEDERTAEUFER ZU MUENSTER IN DER DEUTSCHEN DICHTUNG / Hermsen, Hugo – (Includes bibliographical references) – Stuttgart: J B Metzler, 1913 – 1 – us U.W. Library [430]
DIE WIEDERVEREINIGUNG DER MORGEN- UND ABENDLAENDISCHEN KIRCHE : EIN RUECKBLICK AUF DEN MUENCHENER ALTKATHOLIKEN-CONGRESS, UND EIN VORBLICK AUF DIE ZU LOESENDE AUFGABE: OFFENER BRIEF AN DEN GRAFEN DMITRY TOLSTOY / Overbeck, J J – Halle: H.W. Schmidt, 1873 – 1mf us A.T.L.A. [240]
WIEDERVERHEIRATUNG... / Baerwald, M – Borna, Leipzig, 1906 – 1mf – 9 – ILM-3108/1 – ne IDC [340]
Wied-Neuwied, M A P zu *see* REISE NACH BRASILIEN IN DEN JAHREN 1815-1817
WIEDZA I ZYCIE – v19-22, 1952-55 – 1 – us I.U. Libraries [073]
Wiegand, F *see*
- DAS APOSTOLISCHE SYMBOL IM MITTELALTER
- DAS HOMILIARIUM KARLS DES GROSSEN AUF SEINE URSPRUENGLICHEN GESTALT HIN UNTERSUCHT
- DIE STELLUNG DES APOSTOLISCHEN SYMBOLS IM KIRCHLICHEN LEBEN DES MITTELALTERS 1

Wieger, Leon *see* BOUDDHISME CHINOIS. EXTRAITS DU TRIPITAKA, DES COMMENTAIRES, TRACTS, ETC
Wiegleb, Johann Christian *see* GESCHICHTE DES WACHSTUMS UND DER ERFINDUNGEN DER CHEMIE, IN DER NEUERN ZEIT
WIELAND – Berlin, 1915 n1-1917 n9, 1918 n10-1920 n6 – 2r – 1 – Inquire at Mikrofilmarchiv for details – gw Misc Inst [072]
WIELAND : ETUDE LITTERAIRE, SUIVIE D'ANALYSES ET DE MORCEAUX CHOISIS DE CET AUTEUR TRADUITS POUR LA PREMIERE FOIS EN FRANCAIS / Hallberg, L Eugene – (Includes bibliographical references) – Paris: E Thorin, 1869 – 1 – us U.W. Library [430]
WIELAND / Sengle, Friedrich – (Includes bibliographical references and index) – 1. Aufl. Stuttgart: J B Metzler, 1949 – 1 – us U.W. Library [430]
Wieland, Christoph Martin *see*
- BEITRAEGE ZUR WIELAND-BIOGRAPHIE
- DER DEUTSCHE MERKUR
- DER DEUTSCHE MERKUR, WEIMAR 1773-1789; DER NEUE TEUTSCHE MERKUR, WEIMAR 1790-1810
- GESCHICHTE DER GELEHRTHEIT
- GESCHICHTE DES PRINZEN BIRIBINKER
- THE GRACES
- NEUE BRIEFE CHR. MART. WIELANDS
- OBERON
- WIELANDS AUSGEWAEHLTE WERKE

WIELAND UND DIE ANTIKE : BEITRAG ZUR GESCHICHTE DER ENTWICKLUNG DER DEUTSCHEN LITERATUR IM 18. JAHRHUNDERT / Doell, M – (Includes bibliographical references) – Muenchen: J Gotteswinter, 1896 – 1 – us U.W. Library [430]
WIELAND UND DIE SCHWEIZ / Ermatinger, Emil – (Includes bibliographical references) – Leipzig: H Haessel, 1924 – 1 – us U.W. Library [943]
WIELAND UND MARTIN UND REGULA KUENZLI : UNGEDRUCKTE BRIEFE UND WIEDERAUFGEFUNDENE ACTENSTUECKE / ed by Hirzel, Ludwig – (Includes bibliographical references and index) – Leipzig: S Hirzel, 1891 – 1 – us U.W. Library [860]
WIELAND UND NAPOLEON / Wahl, Hans – Weimar: A Duncker, 1933 – 1 – us U.W. Library [430]
Wieland-Museum *see* HEINRICH V. KLEIST – KANT UND WIELAND
WIELANDS ABDERITEN : VORTRAG / Seuffert, Bernhard – (Includes bibliographical references) – Berlin: Weidmann, 1878 – 1r – 1 – us U.W. Library [430]
WIELANDS "AGATHON" UND DIE ANFAENGE DES MODERNEN BILDUNGSROMANS / Schroeder, Friedrich Wilhelm – (Includes bibliographical references) – Koenigsberg i.Pr: Hartung, 1904 – 1r – 1 – us U.W. Library [430]
WIELANDS AUFSAETZE UEBER DIE FRANZOESISCHE REVOLUTION : EINIGE BEITRAEGE ZU IHRER WISSENSCHAFTLICHEN ERFORSCHUNG / Koskull, Harald, Baron von – Riga: W F Haecker, 1901 – 1 – us U.W. Library [430]
WIELANDS AUSGEWAEHLTE WERKE / Wieland, Christoph Martin; ed by Boelsche, Wilhelm – Leipzig: M Hesse, [1902] – 1r – 1 – us U.W. Library [430]
WIELANDS BILDUNGSIDEAL / Hamann, Hermann Emil – Chemnitz: H Wilisch, 1907 – 1r – 1 – us U.W. Library [430]
WIELANDS DON SYLVIO UND OBERON AUF DER DEUTSCHEN SINGSPIELBUEHNE / Bobrik, Johannes Eduard Guenther – (Includes bibliographical references) – Koenigsberg i.Pr: O Kuemmel, 1909 – 1r – 1 – us U.W. Library [430]
WIELAND'S NEUER AMADIS / Harn, Edith Muriel – (Includes bibliographical references) – Goettingen: Vandenhoeck & Ruprecht; Baltimore: The Johns Hopkins Press, 1928 – 1r – 1 – us U.W. Library [430]
WIELANDS OBERON / Duentzer, Heinrich – (Title on added t.p: Erlaeuterungen zu Wielands Oberon) – 2. neu durchgesehene und verm. Aufl. Leipzig: Ed Wartig, 1880 – 1r – 1 – us U.W. Library [430]

WIELANDS "PERVONTE" / Muncker, Franz – Muenchen: Verlag der K Akademie, 1903 – 1 – us U.W. Library [430]

WIELANDS ROMANE : EIN BEITRAG ZUR GESCHICHTE UND THEORIE DER PROSADICHTUNG / Bobertag, Felix – (Includes bibliographical references) – Breslau: Grass, Barth, [1871?] – 1 – us U.W. Library [430]

WIELANDS VERHAELTNIS ZU LUCIAN / Kersten – (At head of title: Hoehere Staatsschule in Cuxhaven) – Cuxhaven: G Rauschenplat, 1900 – 1r – 1 – us U.W. Library [430]

WIELANDS WERKE / ed by Klee, Gotthold – (Includes bibliographical references) – Leipzig: Bibliographisches Institut, [1900?] – 1r – 1 – us U.W. Library [430]

Wieman, Henry Nelson *see* IS THERE A GOD?

Wiemer, Rudolf Otto *see* FRITZ UND DIE SOLDATENSTIEFEL

WIEN : EIN ROMAN / Anders, Artur – Wien: Wiener Literarische Anstalt; Leipzig: Wila, 1921 – 1r – 1 – us U.W. Library [830]

Wien, Wilhelm *see* GOETHE UND DIE PHYSIK

Wienbarg, Ludolf *see*
- AESTHETISCHE FELDZUEGE
- WANDERUNGEN DURCH DEN THIERKREIS

Wienberg, Dieter *see* EL CICLO DEL CERDO EN ESPANA. INVESTIGACIONES SOBRE LAS FLUCTUACIONES DE LA PRODUCCION Y DE LOS PRECIOS DESDE 1939 A 1956 POR...Y..., BAJO LA DIRECCION DE GASPAR GONZALEZ

Wiencke, Otto *see* UEBER DIE VATERLANDSLIEBE

WIENER ALLGEMEINE LITERATURZEITUNG – Wien, 1813-16 (mf ed 1991) – 48mf – 9 – DM420.00 – 3-89131-037-4 – gw Fischer [430]

(WIENER) ALLGEMEINE MUSIKALISCHE ZEITUNG / ed by Seyfried, Joseph von & Kanne, Friedrich August – Wien, 1817-24. Hildesheim, 1990 – 37mf – 9 – DM250.00 diazo DM290.00 silver – gw Olms [780]

WIENER ALLGEMEINE MUSIKZEITUNG – Vienna. 1841-48. 4 reels – 1 – 71.00 – us L of C Photodup [780]

WIENER ALLGEMEINE ZEITUNG – Vienna, AU. 2 April 1917-5 Aug 1919 (incomplete) – 5r – 1 – uk British Libr Newspaper [072]

WIENER AUSGABE *see* DIES BLATT GEHOERT DER HAUSFRAU

WIENER BAUINDUSTRIE-ZEITUNG – Vienna, 1883-1920. 32 reels – 1 – $2,660.00 – us UPA [720]

WIENER BEITRAEGE ZUR KUNST UND KULTURGESCHICHTE ASIENS – v. 1-11. Wien. 1926-37. BCH-875 2 – 38mf – 8 – ne IDC [950]

WIENER ELEGIEN / Saar, Ferdinand von – Heidelberg: Georg Weiss, 1893 – 1r – 1 – us U.W. Library [810]

WIENER ENTOMOLOGISCHE MONATSCHRIFT – Wien. v1-8. 1857-1864 – 62mf – 9 – Z-1010/2 – ne IDC [590]

WIENER ENTOMOLOGISCHE ZEITUNG – Wien. v1-38. 1882-1921 – 231mf – 9 – Z-1011/2 – ne IDC [590]

Wiener Goethe-Verein *see* FESTSCHRIFT FUER EDUARD CASTLE ZUM ACHTZIGSTEN GEBURTSTAG

Wiener, Harold Marcus *see*
- ESSAYS IN PENTATEUCHAL CRITICISM
- STUDIES IN BIBLICAL LAW

WIENER JAHRBUCH FUER KUNSTGESCHICHTE *see* KUNSTGESCHICHTLICHES JAHRBUCH DER K.K. ZENTRAL-KOMMISSION...

WIENER KLINIK 1. 1875-33. 1907 – Wien, 1875-1907 (mf ed 1994) – 119mf – 9 – DM1,480.00 – 3-89131-187-7 – gw Fischer [610]

WIENER KLINISCHE WOCHENSCHRIFT – v.37-38, 1924-25; v.40, 1927; v.42-53, 1929-40; v.59-69, 1947-57; v.72-93, 1960-81. ISSN:0043-5325 – 1,5,6,9,13 – 102.00v – us UMI [616]

WIENER KURIER – Vienna, Austria. -w. 27 Aug 1945-14 Feb 1948. 9 reels – 1 – uk British Libr Newspaper [072]

Wiener, Leo *see* THE HISTORY OF YIDDISH LITERATURE IN THE NINETEENTH CENTURY

WIENER LITERATURZEITSCHRIFTEN DER ERSTEN HAELFTE DES 19. JAHRHUNDERTS – (Annalen der oesterreichischen Literatur. Regensburg 1802; Annalen der Literatur und Kunst in den oesterreichischen Staaten. Wien 1803-1805; Neue Annalen der Literatur des oesterreichischen Kaiserthumes. Wien 1807-1808; Annalen der Literatur und Kunst in dem oesterreichischen Kaiserthume. Wien 1809; Annalen der Literatur und Kunst des In- und Auslandes. Wien 1810; Annalen der Literatur und Kunst in dem oesterreichischen Kaiserthume. Wien 1811-1812) – mf ed 1991 – 169mf – 9 – DM980.00 – 3-89131-036-6 – gw Fischer [430]

WIENER LITERATURZEITSCHRIFTEN DER ERSTEN HAELFTE DES 19. JAHRHUNDERTS *see*
- JAHRBUECHER DER LITERATUR
- WIENER ALLGEMEINE LITERATURZEITUNG

WIENER LUFTSCHIFFER-ZEITUNG 1. 1902-13. 1914 / ed by Silberer, Victor – Wien, 1902-1914 (mf ed 1994) – 52mf – 9 – DM540.00 – 3-89131-167-2 – gw Fischer [073]

Wiener, Max *see* DIE ANSCHAUUNGEN DER PROPHETEN VON DER SITTLICHKEIT

WIENER MEDIZINISCHE WOCHENSHRIFT – v.96-129. 1946-79 – 1,5,6 – us Princeton Micro [610]

WIENER MORGENZEITUNG = MORNING DAILY – (In Yiddish) – Vienna, AU. no154. Jul 1915 – 1r – 1 – $25.00 – cn Can Microfilming [072]

WIENER PRAEHISTORISCHE ZEITSCHRIFT – Wien. v1-17. 1914-1930 – 35mf – 9 – HA-2/1 – ne IDC [930]

WIENER STUDIEN – Wien. v1-58. 1879-1940 – 329mf – 9 – 1104c/2 – ne IDC [943]

WIENER TAGESZEITUNG – (Neue Wiener Tageszeitung). Vienna. Austria. -d. 22 Jun 1947-30 Jun 1950. (9 reels) – 1 – uk British Libr Newspaper [072]

WIENER ZEITSCHRIFT 1792-1793 / ed by Hoffmann, Leopold Alois – Wien, 1792-1793 (mf ed 1993) – 12mf – 9 – DM280.00 – 3-89131-159-1 – gw Fischer [100]

WIENER ZEITUNG – Vienna. Austria. 1846-50 – 1 – gw Mikrofilm [072]

WIENER ZEITUNG – Vienna, Austria. -d. 13 Feb-24 Sept 1916; 21 Sept 1945-Dec 1960; April 1964-Dec 1970; Jan 1972-Dec 1976. 138 reels – 1 – uk British Libr Newspaper [072]

WIENER ZEITUNG – Vienna. Sept. 21, 1945-1969 – 1 – us NY Public [072]

Wieniawski, H *see* CAPRICE IN A MINOR, ARRANGED BY KREISLER

Wier, Johann *see* CINQ LIVRES DE L'IMPOSTURE ET TROMPERIE DES DIABLES, DES ENCHANTEMENTS ET SORCELLERIES

Wierer, K *see* FERTILIZER MARKETING

Wiermann, Heinrich (Hermann Robolsky) *see* DEUTSCHE POLITIK SEIT BISMARCKS ENTLASSUNG 1890-1892

Wieruszowski, Alfred *see* GOETHE ALS RECHTSANWALT

"WIES" / Duda-Dziewierz, Krystyna – Warszawa-Poznan, 1939 – 1r – 1 – us I.H.R.C. [947]

WIES MALOPOLSKA A EMIGRACJA AMERIKANSKA : STUDIUM WSI BABICA POWAITU RZESZOWSKIEGO / Duda-Dziewierz, Krystyna – Warszawa-Posnan, 1939 – 1r – 1 – us I.H.R.C. [304]

Wiesbaden. Regierungsbezirk *see* AMTSBLATT DER KOENIGLICHEN REGIERUNG ZU WIESBADEN

WIESBADENER KURIER – Wiesbaden, 1954-jan 1 1969 – 81r – 1 – gw Mikrofilm [072]

WIESBADENER KURIER – Wiesbaden, West Germany.1969- – 1 – gw Mikrofilm [072]

WIESBADENER TAGBLATT – Wiesbaden, West Germany.May-Jun 1964; 1 Sept 1978- – 1 – gw Mikrofilm [072]

WIESCI – London, UK. May 1956 – 1 – uk British Libr Newspaper [072]

WIESCI POLSKIE – Budapest. Hungary. -w. Jan 1941-Mar 1944. (Imperfect). (1 reel) – 1 – uk British Libr Newspaper [072]

Wiese, Benno von *see*
- FAUST ALS TRAGOEDIE
- SCHILLER

Wiese, Ernst August *see*
- 100 SILBERNE BLECHBESTECKE
- REIN ZU DOLLE

Wiese, Hugo von *see* DER KAMPF UM GLATZ

Wieseler, Karl *see*
- BEITRAEGE ZUR RICHTIGEN WUERDIGUNG DER EVANGELIEN UND DER EVANGELISCHEN GESCHICHTE
- COMMENTAR UEBER DEN BRIEF PAULI AN DIE GALATER
- ZUR GESCHICHTE DER NEUTESTAMENTLICHEN SCHRIFT UND DES URCHRISTENTHUMS

Wiesner, Iris *see* PROJEKTMANAGEMENT INTERNATIONALER KOOPERATIONSVORHABEN MITTLERER UNTERNEHMEN IN DER EUROPAEISCHEN GEMEINSCHAFT

Wiesner, Knut *see* UNTERNEHMERISCHE ZUSAMMENARBEIT MIT DEM SUEDLICHEN AFRIKA

Wiessalla, Josef *see* NIEMANDS LAND

Wiet, G *see* LES BIOGRAPHIES DU MANHAL SAFI

WIG AND GOWN : STORY OF THE TEMPLE, GRAY'S AND LINCOLN'S INNS / Blackham, Robert J – London: Low/Marston, 1932? – 4mf – 9 – $6.00 – LLMC 84-275 – us L.L.M.C. [340]

Wigan. -Independent Methodist Bookroom *see* INDEPENDENT METHODIST ARCHIVES

Wigand, Johann *see* VON DER FALLSTRICKEN ETLICHERR NEWER SACRAMENTSCHWERMER ZU WITTENBERG

WIGAND'S CONVERSATIONS-LEXIKON [UND] DIE NEUE ZEIT (ERSTER SUPPLEMENTBAND ZU WIGAND'S CONVERSATIONS-LEXIKON)(AEL, ABT 1;17) / ed by Otto, Wigand – Leipzig, 1846-1852; 1884 (mf ed 1993) – 101mf – 9 – DM1,420.00 – 3-89131-105-2 – gw Fischer [030]

Wigandus, J *see*
- DE ANABAPTISMO
- ETLICHER WIDERTEUFFERISCHER SCHWERMEREYEN, WELCHE SICH JETZT WIDER REGEN, WIDERLEGUNG

Wigard, F *see* STENOGRAPHISCHER BERICHT UEBER DIE VERHANDLUNGEN DER DEUTSCHEN CONSTITUIERENDEN NATIONALVERSAMMLUNG ZU FRANKFURT 1848-49

Wiget, Wilhelm *see* DIE LAUTE DER TOGGENBURGER MUNDARTEN

Wiggam, Albert Edward *see* SORRY BUT YOU'RE WRONG ABOUT IT

Wiggers, F H *see* PRIMITIAE FLORAE HOLSATICAE

Wiggers, G F *see* AN HISTORICAL PRESENTATION OF AUGUSTINISM AND PELAGIANISM

Wiggershaus, Rolf *see* ZUM BEGRIFF DER REGEL IN DER PHILOSOPHIE DER UMGANGSSPRACHE UEBER WITTGENSTEIN, AUSTIN UND SEARLE

Wigglesworth, Janet K et al *see* THE RELIABILITY OF TWO MEASURES OF CARDIAC OUTPUT USING CO2 REBREATHING

Wight, R *see*
- CATALOGUE OF DRIED SPECIMENS OF INDIAN PLANTS DISTRIBUTED BY DR. R. WRIGHT
- CONTRIBUTIONS TO THE BOTANY OF INDIA
- ICONES PLANTARUM INDIAE ORIENTALIS

Wiglesworth, L W *see* THE BIRDS OF CELEBES AND THE NEIGHBOURING ISLANDS

WIGMORE : CELEBRATION LEGAL ESSAYS, BY VARIOUS AUTHORS TO MARK THE TWENTY-FIFTH YEAR OF SERVICE OF JOHN H. WIGMORE AS PROFESSOR OF LAW IN NORTHWESTERN UNIVERSITY – Chicago: Northwestern University Press, 1919 – 7mf – 9 – $10.50 – LLMC 95-153 – us L.L.M.C. [340]

Wigmore, John H *see* FORMATIVE INFLUENCES OF LEGAL DEVELOPMENT

Wigmore, John Henry *see*
- A TREATISE ON THE ANGLO-AMERICAN SYSTEM OF EVIDENCE IN TRIALS AT COMMON LAW...2ND ED
- A TREATISE ON THE SYSTEM OF EVIDENCE IN TRIALS AT COMMON LAW.

Wignjoamidjojo, B *see* PENDIDIKAN MENGABDI MANIPOL

WIGTONSHIRE, 1837 : BRITISH ISLES CENSUS DIRECTORIES PROJECT, SCOTLAND. VOL 57 – 1mf – 9 – A$9.00 – at Vine [941]

WIGTONSHIRE, 1852 : BRITISH ISLES CENSUS DIRECTORIES PROJECT, SCOTLAND. VOL 15 – 1mf – 9 – A$9.00 – at Vine [941]

Wihan, Josef *see* LESSINGS "MINNA VON BARNHELM" UND GOLDONIS LUSTSPIEL "UN CURIOSO ACCIDENTE"

WIJ BOUWEN ZEEDIJKEN : DE GESCHIEDENIS VAN EEN ARBEIDSKAMERAADSCHAP / Grell, Guenther – (Translation of: Wir ziehen Deiche am Meeresstrand) – Amsterdam: Westland, 1943 – 1r – 1 – us U.W. Library [830]

Wijewardene, D R *see* MSS. LETTERS, 1912-50

Wijler, J S *see* ISAAC DE PINTO, SA VIE ET SES OEUVRES

Wijnaendts van Resandt, Willem *see* DE GEZAGHEBBERS DER OOST-INDISCHE COMPAGNIE OP HARE BUITEN-COMPTOIREN IN AZIE

DE WIJSBEGEERTE DER WETSIDEE / Dooyeweerd, H – Boek 1: De Wetsidee als Grondlegging der wijsbegeerte. – Amsterdam, 1935. – 17mf; Boek 2: De functionele Zin-structuur der tijdelijke werkelijkheid. – Amsterdam, 1935. – 17mf; Boek 3: De Individualiteits-structuren der tijdelijke werkelijkheid. – Amsterdam, 1936. – 21mf – 8 – ne Slangenburg [120]

Wiklund, Karl Bernhard *see* LAPPERNE

Wikstroem, J E *see* CONSPECTUS LITTERATURAE BOTANICAE IN SUECIA

WILBER REPUBLICAN – Wilber, NE. -w. Feb 1887-May 1889; Aug 1889-Mar 1896, scattered issues missing; May 1896-May 1898; Jul 1898 to date – 1 – us NE Hist [071]

WILBER UNION – Wilber, NE. -w. Apr 1886-Jan 1887 – 1 – us NE Hist [071]

Wilberforce, Robert Isaac *see* AN INQUIRY INTO THE PRINCIPLES OF CHURCH-AUTHORITY

Wilberforce, Samuel *see*
- ESSAYS
- HEROES OF HEBREW HISTORY

WILBERFORCE SLAVERY, RELIGION AND POLITICS : SERIES ONE: THE WILBERFORCE PAPERS FROM THE BODLEIAN LIBRARY, OXFORD – (Pt 1: Papers of William Wilberforce (1759-1833) und Robert Isaac Wilberforce (1802-1857) 17r $ 2,100.00. Pt 2: Papers of Samuel Wilberforce (1818-1873) 20r of 35 mm silber-halide positive microfilm $2,400.00. Pt 3: Papers of Samuel Wilberforce (1818-1873) 19r of 35 mm siver-halide positive microfilm $2,400.00. A single guide accompanies pts 1-3) – Marlborough: Adam Matthew Publications, 1996 – 1 – uk Matthew [320]

Wilberforce, Wilfred *see* CATHOLICISME EN ANGLETERRE AU 19E SIECLE

WILBERSKE LISTY – Wilber, NE. -w. 7 Jun 1905-27 May 1914. In Bohemian – 1 – us NE Hist [071]

WILBRAHAM 1762-1895 – 40mf – 9 – 0-87623-028-1 – us Holbrook [920]

Wilbrandt, Adolf von *see*
- ADAMS SOEHNE
- ARRIA UND MESSALINA
- ASSUNTA LEONI
- DER DORNENWEG
- FRIEDRICH HOELDERLIN – FRITZ REUTER
- GEDICHTE
- GIORDANO BRUNO
- LIEDER UND BILDER
- DIE MALER
- EIN MECKLENBURGER
- DER MEISTER VON PALMYRA
- NEUE GEDICHTE
- NOVELLEN AUS DER HEIMAT
- DIE REISE NACH RIVA
- ROBERT KERR
- DIE ROTHENBURGER
- TIMANDRA
- DIE TOCHTER DES HERREN FABRICIUS
- DIE TOCHTER DES HERRN FABRICIUS

Wilbur, Asa *see* BIBLICAL STANDPOINT

Wilbur, John *see* A NARRATIVE AND EXPOSITION OF THE LATE PROCEEDINGS OF NEW ENGLAND YEARLY MEETING

WILBURTON FIRST BAPTIST CHURCH. WILBURTON, OKLAHOMA : CHURCH RECORDS – 1907-Jan 1961 – 1 – 36.90 – us Baptist [240]

Wilcocke, Samuel Hill *see* THE SCRIBBLER

Wilcox, Alvin H *see* A PIONEER HISTORY OF BECKER COUNTY

WILCOX BANNER – Wilcox, NE. -w. Jul 1904-Jun 1907; Sept 1907 – 1 – us NE Hist [071]

WILCOX COUNTY CHRONICLE – Abbeville. Ga. 1955-1963 – 1 – us UMI [071]

WILCOX COUNTY CHRONICLE – Abbeville. Georgia. 1955-63 – 1 – us UMI [071]

Wilcox, Ella Wheeler *see* MAURINE

WILCOX HERALD – Wilcox, NE. -w. Apr 1895-Jul 1908; Sept 1911-Apr 1914; Nov 1918-Apr 1920, scattered issues missing; Jun 1920-Dec 1941 – 1 – us NE Hist [071]
Wilcox, John S *see* HISTORICAL ENCYCLOPEDIA OF ILLINOIS AND HISTORY OF KANE COUNTY
WILCOX POST – Wilcox, NE. -w. Jan 1893-Dec 1894 – 1 – us NE Hist [071]
Wilcox, Richard *see* GOETHES EINFLUSS AUF GEORGE MEREDITH
WILCOX WINNER – Wilcox, NE. -w. Jan-Dec 1928 – 1 – us NE Hist [071]
THE WILD AND CULTIVATED COTTON PLANTS OF THE WORLD; REVISION OF THE GENUS GOSSYPIUM / Watt, G – 7323. 1907 – 9 – ne IDC [580]
WILD EELIN, HER ESCAPADES, ADVENTURES AND BITTER SORROWS / Black, William – British Fiction Archive: Unit 4 – 9 – uk Bell [830]
WILD FLOWERS : OR, PASTORAL AND LOCAL POETRY / Bloomfield, Robert – London: Printed for Vernor, Hood, and Sharpe [etc.], 1806 – 1 roll – 1 – 1-55879-721-1 – uk Libr Preservation [810]
WILD FLOWERS OF CANADA – Montreal: The Montreal Star, s.d. SEM16P355 – 1r – 5 – Can$15.00 – cn Bibl Nat [580]
THE WILD FOWL OF THE UNITED STATES AND BRITISH POSSESSIONS, OR, THE SWAN, GEESE, DUCKS, AND MERGANSERS OF NORTH AMERICA: WITH ACCOUNTS OF THEIR HABITS, NESTING, MIGRATIONS, AND DISPERSIONS... : A BOOK FOR THE SPORTSMAN, AND FOR THOSE DESIROUS OF KNOWING HOW TO DISTINQUISH THESE WEB-FOOTED BIRDS AND TO LEARN THEIR WAYS IN THEIR NATIVE WILDS / Elliot, Daniel Giraud – New York: P. Harper, 1898. 02903. (Pre-1900 Canadiana) – 9 – cn C.I.H.M. [971]
Wild, Joseph *see* THE LOST TEN TRIBES, AND 1882
THE WILD PALMS – Concordance to the novel – 9mf – 9 – us UMI [420]
Wild, Roland *see* UNKNOWN LIBERIA
WILDBADER TAGBLATT : BA DER SUEDWEST-PRESSE – Wildbad-Ulm, Germany. 1 Jan 1980-30 Nov 1991 – 1 – gw Mikrofilm [072]
WILDE BLUMEN : GEDICHTE FUER DIE JUNGE WELT / Wibbelt, Augustin – Essen (Ruhr): Fredebeul & Koenen, [1911?] – 1 – us U.W. Library [810]
Wilde, E *see* GESCHICHTE DER OPTIK
DER WILDE JAEGER : EINE WAIDMANNSMAER / Wolff, Julius – 2. Aufl. Berlin: G Grote, 1891 – 1r – 1 – us U.W. Library [430]
DER WILDE JAEGER : EINE WAIDMANNSMAER / Wolff, Julius – Berlin: G Grote, 1902 – 1 – us U.W. Library [830]
Wilde, Norman *see* FRIEDRICH HEINRICH JACOBI
Wilde, Oscar *see*
- THE BALLAD OF READING GOAL
- DE PROFUNDIS
- THE IMPORTANCE OF BEING EARNEST
- INTENTIONS, THE DECAY OF LYING, PEN, PENCIL AND POISON, THE CRITIC AS ARTIST, THE TRUTH OF MASKS
- LADY WINDERMERE'S FAN
- THE PICTURE OF DORIAN GRAY
- POEMS
- A WOMAN OF NO IMPORTANCE
- THE WOMAN'S WORLD

Wildeboer, Gerrit *see*
- DIE LITTERATUR DES ALTEN TESTAMENTS NACH DER ZEITFOLGE IHRER ENTSTEHUNG
- DEWAARDE DER SYRISCHE EVANGELIEN

Wildeman, E de *see*
- LES ALGUES DE LA FLORE DE BUITENZORG...
- FLORE DES ALGUES DE BELGIQUE
- ICONES SELECTAE HORTI THENENSIS
- PRODROME DE LA FLORE ALGOLOGIQUE DES INDES NEERLANDAISES

WILDENBRUCH ALS DRAMATIKER : KRITISCHE UNTERSUCHUNGEN / Roehr, Julius – Berlin: C Duncker, [1908?] – 1r – 1 – us U.W. Library [430]
Wildenbruch, Ernst von *see*
- CHRISTOPH MARLOW
- GESAMMELTE WERKE
- KINDERTHRAENEN
- LETZTE GEDICHTE
- DIE LETZTE PARTIE
- LIEDER UND BALLADEN
- NEID
- DIE QUITZOWS
- VICE-MAMA
- VIONVILLE

WILDENGRUND : CHRONIK EINES DORFES IM GEBIRGE / Sturm, Stefan – Karlsbad: A Kraft, 1943 – 1r – 1 – us U.W. Library [830]
Wildenhahn, August *see* MARTIN LUTHER
Wildenow, Eugen *see* THEODOR KOERNER UND DIE SEINEN
Wilder, Martha L *see* MEMOIR OF ROBERT MOFFAT
Wilder, Robert Parmelee *see*
- AMONG INDIA'S STUDENTS
- SALVATION

Wildermann, Ferdinand *see* HEIMGEKEHRT
Wildermuth, Adelheid *see* OTTILIE WILDERMUTHS LEBEN
Wildermuth, Ottilie *see*
- BEIM LAMPENLICHT
- OTTILIE WILDERMUTHS LEBEN
- OTTILIE WILDERMUTH'S WERKE
- WERKE

WILDERNESS : AMERICA'S LIVING HERITAGE ANTHOLOGY / ed by Brower, David – 1r – 5,9 – $50.00 – B70015 – us Library Micro [574]
WILDERNESS : THE EDGE OF KNOWLEDGE-ANTHOLOGY / ed by McCloskey, Maxine E – 1r – 5,9 – $50.00 – B70014 – us Library Micro [574]
WILDERNESS – v46-. 1982- – 1,5,6,9 – us UMI [574]
WILDERNESS IN A CHANGING WORLD ANTHOLOGY / ed by Kilgore, Bruce M – 1r – 5,9 – $50.00 – B70013 – us Library Micro [574]
Wildgans, Anton *see*
- ARMUT
- INFANTERIE!
- KIRBISCH, ODER, DER GENDARM, DIE SCHANDE UND DAS GLUECK
- LEGENDE
- LIEBE
- DIE SONETTE AN EAD
- UND HATTET DER LIEBE NICHT

Wildgans, Lilly *see* ANTON WILDGANS
WILDLAND FIRE MANAGEMENT TERMINOLOGY – 1986 – 298p – it F.A.O. [360]
WILDLIFE – v16-20 1974-78 1,5,6; v18-20 9 – us UMI [590]
WILDLIFE RESEARCH SERIES / Auburn University. Agricultural Experiment Station. Zoology-Entomology Departmental Series – No.1. 1974. 1 reel – 1, 5 – us Spaulding [590]
WILDOMAR NEWS – Temecula, CA. 1990 – 1+ r – 1 – $50.00 ($50.00y) – R04130 – us Library Micro [071]
WILDRUPS HOFF : EINE ERZAEHLUNG IN MUENSTERLAENDER MUNDART: MIT DER FORTSETZUNG MARIECHEN WILDRUPS / Wibbelt, Augustin – 4. Aufl. Essen-Ruhr: Fredebeul und Koenen, 1906 – 1r – 1 – us U.W. Library [390]
WILEMAN'S BRAZILIAN REVIEW – Rio de Janeiro. Brazil. -w. 6 Sep 1928-26 Nov 1934. (7 reels) – 1 – uk British Libr Newspaper [072]
WILEMAN'S BRAZILIAN REVIEW – v.1-36, no.7.1915-41. Scattered issues lacking – 1 – 560.00 – us L of C Photodup [330]
Wiles, Joseph Pitt *see* HALF-HOURS WITH THE MINOR PROPHETS AND THE LAMENTATIONS
Wiley *see* BIOGRAPHICAL AND PORTRAIT CYCLOPEDIA OF NIAGARA COUNTY
WILEY AND PUTNAM'S LITERARY NEWSLETTER AND MONTHLY REGISTER OF NEW BOOKS, FOREIGN AND AMERICAN – 1841-47 – 1r – 1 – us Ross [410]
Wiley, Isaac William *see* WOMAN AND HOME MISSIONARY WORK
Wiley, Samuel T *see*
- BIOGRAPHICAL AND PORTRAIT CYCLOPEDIA OF CHESTER COUNTY
- BIOGRAPHICAL AND PORTRAIT CYCLOPEDIA OF FAYETTE COUNTY
- CYCLOPEDIA OF DELAWARE COUNTY
- CYCLOPEDIA OF INDIANA AND ARMSTRONG COUNTIES
- HISTORY OF MONONGALIA COUNTY

Wilgus, Horace La Fayette *see* SHOULD THERE BE A FEDERAL INCORPORATION LAW FOR COMMERCIAL CORPORATIONS?
[WILHELM 2 PAMPHLET COLLECTION] – 1913-1934 – 1 reel – 1 – CSUXANR3406-B – us Hoover Inst Photo [943]
Wilhelm 3, Friedrich *see* PAPERS
WILHELM CARDINAL ALLEN (1532-1594) UND DIE ENGLISCHEN SEMINARE AUF DEM FESTLANDE / Bellesheim, Alphons – Mainz: F. Kirchheim, 1885 – 1mf – us A.T.L.A. [240]
WILHELM GROENNING : MISSIONAR IM TELUGU-LANDE, IN INDIEN / ed by Wischan, Frederick – Philadelphia: A Hellwege, 1891 – 1mf – 9 – 0-8370-6633-6 – 1986-0633 – us A.T.L.A. [920]
Wilhelm, Gustav *see* DIE REPUBLIK DER THIERE
Wilhelm, Hans Hermann *see*
- DIE FRICKES
- ROBERT WANDELT

WILHELM HEINSE UND SEIN EINFLUSS AUF DIE ROMANTIK / Nehrkorn, Hans – (Includes bibliographical references) – Goslar: F A Lattmann, 1904 – 1r – 1 – us U.W. Library [430]
WILHELM HERBSTS HILFSBUCH FUER DIE DEUTSCHE LITTERATURGESCHIHTE / Herbst, Wilhelm; ed by Brenning, Emil – (Includes bibliographical references) – Gotha: F A Perthers, 1897 – 1 – us U.W. Library [430]
WILHELM HOFMEISTER: THE WORKS AND LIFE OF A NINETEENTH CENTURY BOTANIST / Goebel, K von – 1926 – 1 $24.00; 7 $50.00 – uk Microform Academic [580]
WILHELM JORDAN / Schiffner, K – Frankfurt a.M.: A Osterrieth, 1889 – 1r – 1 – us U.W. Library [920]
[WILHELM KAUFMANN PAMPHLET COLLECTION] – 1976 – 1 – CSUXANR2769-B – us Hoover Inst Photo [320]
WILHELM MEISTERS THEATRALISCHE SENDUNG / Goethe, Johann Wolfgang von; ed by Weydt, Guenther – Bonn: H Bouvier, 1949 – 1r – 1 – us U.W. Library [830]
WILHELM MEISTERS THEATRALISCHE SENDUNG : MITTEILUNGEN UEBER DIE WIEDERGEFUNDENE ERSTE FASSUNG VON WILHELM MEISTERS LEHRJAHREN / Goethe, Johann Wolfgang von; ed by Billeter, Gustav – Zuerich: Rascher, 1910 – 1r – 1 – us U.W. Library [830]
WILHELM MEISTERS WANDERJAHRE : ODER, DIE ENTSAGENDEN: EIN ROMAN VON GOETHE NACH DER ERSTEN FASSUNG DES JAHRES 1821 / Goethe, Johann Wolfgang von; ed by Hecker, Max – Berlin: Dom Verlag, 1921 – 1 – us U.W. Library [830]
WILHELM MUELLER AND THE GERMAN VOLKSLIED / Allen, Philip Schuyler – [Chicago?], 1901 – 1r – 1 – us U.W. Library [780]
WILHELM RAABES ROMAN "DIE AKTEN DES VOGELSANGS" / Boenneken, Margarete – (Includes bibliographical references and index) – Marburg a.L.: N G Elwert, 1918 – 1r – 1 – us U.W. Library [430]
WILHELM VON HUMBOLDT : CHARAKTERISTIK UND LEBENSBILD / Leitzmann, Albert – Halle a.d.S.: M Niemeyer, 1919 – 1r – 1 – us U.W. Library [920]
WILHELM VON HUMBOLDTS BRIEFE AN KARL GUSTAV BRINKMANN / ed by Leitzmann, Albert – (Includes bibliographical references and index) – Leipzig: Karl W Hiersemann, 1939 – 1 – us U.W. Library [860]
WILHELM VON HUMBOLDTS SONNETTDICHTUNG / Leitzmann, Albert – Bonn: Marcus & Weber, 1912 – 1r – 1 – us U.W. Library [430]
WILHELM VON OCKHAM ALS POLITISCHER DENKER UND SEIN BREVILOQUIUM DE PRINCIPATU TYRANNICO (MGH SCHRIFTEN..: 8.BD) / Scholz, R – 1944 – Dfl25.00 – ne Slangenburg [240]
WILHELM VON ORANIEN : DER BEFREIER DER NIEDERLANDE / Trauttwein von Belle, E – Berlin: Ludertitz, 1867 – 1r – 1 – us U.W. Library [949]
WILHELM VON POLENZ : EIN BEITRAG ZUR LITERATURGESCHICHTE DER GEGENWART / Ilgenstein, Heinrich – Berlin: F Fontane, 1904 – 1r – 1 – us U.W. Library [430]
WILHELM VON ST. THIERRY : EIN REPRAESENTANT DER MITTELALTERLICHEN FROEMMIGKEIT / Kutter, Hermann – Giessen: J. Ricker, 1898 – 1mf – us A.T.L.A. [240]
WILHELM WAIBLINGER IN SEINEN PROSAWERKEN / Ruland, Ilse – (Includes bibliographical references) – Stuttgart: W Kohlhammer, 1922 – 1r – 1 – us U.W. Library [430]
Wilhelm, Wolfgang *see* DAS BILD IN DIR
Wilhelmi, Adolph *see* DMITRI IWANOWITSCH
Wilhelmi Malmesbiriensis *see* DE GESTIS PONTIFICUM ANGLORUM LIBRI QUINQUE (RS52)
Wilhelmine, Margravine *see* MEMOIREN DER MARKGRAEFIN WILHELMINE VON BAYREUTH
WILHELMSHAVENER ZEITUNG – Wilhelmshaven, West Germany. 1969- – 1 – gw Mikrofilm [072]
Wilhelmsmeyer, Hans *see* CARL GUSTAV CARUS ALS ERBE UND DEUTER GOETHES
WILIBALD PIRKHEIMER : EIN LEBENSBILD AUS DEM ZEITALTER DES HUMANISMUS UND DER REFORMATION / Roth, Friedrich – Halle: Verein fuer Reformationsgeschichte, 1887. ([Schriften des Vereins fuer Reformationsgeschichte; Bd. 21]) – 1mf – us A.T.L.A. [240]
WILIBALD PIRKHEIMERS STELLUNG ZUR REFORMATION : EIN BEITRAG ZUR BEURTEILUNG DES VERHAELTNISSES ZWISCHEN HUMANISMUS UND REFORMATION / Drews, Paul – Leipzig: Fr. Wilh. Grunow, 1887 – 1mf – us A.T.L.A. [240]
Wilke, Fritz *see* JESAJA UND ASSUR...UNTERSUCHUNG ZUR POLITIK DES PROPHETEN JESAJA
Wilke, Karl *see*
- DAS HAUS DES DR. PRADE
- PRISONER HALM

Wilkens, C A *see*
- FRAY LUIS DE LEON
- GESCHICHTE DES SPANISCHEN PROTESTANTISMUS IM SECHSZEHNTEN JAHRHUNDERT
- SPANISH PROTESTANTS IN THE SIXTEENTH CENTURY
- TILEMANN HESSHUSIUS

Wilkerson, Bethany A *see* THE EFFECTS OF SIZE AND WEIGHT ON BASKETBALL FREE THROW PERFORMANCE
Wilkerson, Jerry D *see*
- A BIOMECHANICAL AND PHYSIOLOGICAL ANALYSIS OF EFFICIENCY DURING DIFFERENT RUNNING PACES
- OPTIMAL DROP HEIGHT PREDICTION FROM LOWER BODY STRENGTH FOR PLYOMETRIC JUMP TRAINING
- A STUDY OF BIOMECHANICAL VARIABLES IN THE COUNTERMOVEMENT JUMP AND THE DROP JUMP PERFORMED BY FEMALE INTERCOLLEGIATE ATHLETES

Wilkes, Charles *see* AUTOBIOGRAPHY
Wilkes-Barre: Draugas, 1909-1916 *see* DRAUGAS
Wilkie, D *see* THE STAR AND COMMERCIAL ADVERTISER
Wilkie, Franc Bangs *see*
- DAVENPORT PAST AND PRESENT
- SKETCHES AND NOTICES OF THE CHICAGO BAR.

Wilkin, G F *see* THE PROPHESYING OF WOMEN; A POPULAR AND PRACTICAL EXPOSITION OF THE BIBLE DOCTRINE
Wilkin, Terence J *see* AUTOIMMUNITY
Wilkins, A S *see* ROMAN EDUCATION
Wilkins, John *see*
- THE DISCOVERY OF A WORLD IN THE MOONE
- ESSAY TOWARDS A REAL CHARACTER AND A PHILOSOPHICAL LANGUAGE
- AN ESSAY TOWARDS A REAL CHARACTER, AND A PHILOSOPHICAL LANGUAGE

WILKINSON ADVERTISER – Woodville. Miss. 1854-1855 – 1 – us UMI [071]
Wilkinson, Henry Spenser *see* THE COMMAND OF THE SEA
Wilkinson, J H *see* FOUR LECTURES ON THE EARLY HISTORY OF THE GOSPELS DELIVERED AT MILBORNE PORT, SOMERSET, ADVENT, 1897
Wilkinson, James John Garth *see* THE NEW JERUSALEM AND THE OLD JERUSALEM
Wilkinson, John J *see* JAMES MARTINEAUS ETHIK
Wilkinson, Michael O *see* AN EXAMINATION OF EPINEPHRINE AND ATHLETIC PERFORMANCE: PSYCHOPHYSIOLOGICAL, COGNITIVE, AND BEHAVIORAL INDICES OF AROUSAL
Wilkinson, Richard James *see* LAW
Wilkinson, Samuel Hinds *see* THE LIFE OF JOHN WILKINSON
Wilkinson, Spenser *see* PAPERS
Wilks, Ivor *see* CATALOGUE OF ARABIC MANUSCRIPTS FROM GHANA AND ADJACENT TERRITORIES FROM INSTITUTE OF AFRICAN STUDIES
Wilks, Mark *see* HISTORICAL SKETCHES OF THE SOUTH OF INDIA, IN AN ATTEMPT TO TRACE THE HISTORY OF MYSOOR..

Will, Georg Andreas *see* NUERNBERGISCHES GELEHRTEN-LEXICON
THE WILL HAYS PAPERS – (Part 1: Dec 1921-Mar 1929. 43 reels. ISBN: 0-89093-935-7. $4,140.00; Part 2: Apr 1929-Sept 1945. 35 reels. ISBN: 0-89093-936-5. $3,370.00. With printed guides) – 1 – $7,135.00 – us UPA [920]
Will, Hubert L et al *see* THE ROLE OF THE JUDGE IN THE SETTLEMENT PROCESS
WILL NAMIBIA'S ELECTION BE FREE AND FAIR? – 1989 – sz I.C.J. [320]
THE WILL OF AETHELGIFU : A 10TH CENTURY ANGLO-SAXON MANUSCRIPT – Trans. & examined by Dorothy Whitelock, with a note on the document by Neil Ker. Oxford: Roxburghe Club, 1968 – 1 – us U.W. Library [941]
WILL RECORDS / Fulton County. Ohio. Probate Court – 1859-1970 – 14r – 1 – $32.50r – us Archival [324]
WILL RECORDS / Putnam County. Ohio. Probate Court – 1837-1941 – 12r – 1 – $32.50r – us Archival [324]
WILL RECORDS / Van Wert County. Ohio. Probate Court – 1840-1921 – 5r – 1 – $32.50r – us Archival [324]
WILL RECORDS / Wyandot County. Ohio. Probate Court – 1900-1908 – 2r – 1 – $32.50r – us Archival [324]
WILL WARBURTON : A ROMANCE OF REAL LIFE / Gissing, George Robert – London: A. Constable, 1905 – 1 roll – 1 – 1-55879-756-4 – uk Libr Preservation [830]
WILLAKENZIE WEEKLY – Eugene OR. Mar 7-June 20 1963 – 1 – us U.O. Library [071]
WILLAMETTE BRIDGE – Portland, OR. 7 Jun 1968-14 Jul 1971. 2 rolls – 1 – us U.O. Library [071]
WILLAMETTE CITIZEN – Salem OR. Aug 29 1928 – 1 – us U.O. Library [071]
WILLAMETTE FARMER – Salem, OR. -w. 28 Jun 1869-26 Aug 1887. 5 rolls – 1 – us U.O. Library [071]
WILLAMETTE LAW JORUNAL *see* WILLAMETTE LAW REVIEW
WILLAMETTE LAW REVIEW – (v1-20 1959-84 on reel $245.00. v21-30 1985-94 on mf $195.00. Title varies: v1-14 1959-78 as Willamette Law Journal) – v1-30. 1959-94 – 5,6,9 – $4,410.00 set – us Hein [340]
WILLAMETTE VALLEY OBSERVER – Eugene, OR. 10 Jan 1975-21 July 1982 – 1r – 1 – us U.O. Library [071]
WILLAMETTE WEEK – Portland, OR. -w. 16 Nov 1975-. – 1r – 1 – us U.O. Library [071]
WILLAMINA TIMES – Willamina, OR. -w. 17 Jul 1924-20 Mar 1974. 12 rolls – 1 – us U.O. Library [071]
Willard *see* HISTORY OF HERKIMER COUNTY
Willard, Ashton Rollins *see* A LEGISLATIVE HANDBOOK RELATING TO THE PREPARATION OF STATUTES.
Willard, Emma Hart *see* UNIVERSAL HISTORY IN PERSPECTIVE: DIVIDED INTO THREE PARTS, ANCIENT, MIDDLE, AND MODERN
Willard, Frances Elizabeth *see*
- OCCUPATIONS FOR WOMEN
- WHAT FRANCES E. WILLARD SAID
- WOMAN AND TEMPERANCE, OR, THE WORK AND WORKERS OF THE WOMAN'S CHRISTIAN TEMPERANCE UNION
- WOMAN IN THE PULPIT

Willard, John *see* A TREATISE ON EQUITY JURISPRUDENCE
Willard, Mary B *see* WOMAN'S WORK IN THE CHURCH: ANOTHER VERSION
WILLARD STRAIGHT PAPERS – 23 reels – 1 – us UMI [920]
WILLARD'S MUSICAL VISITOR – Indianopolis. v1-2. 1870-71 – 1r – 1 – £60.00 – uk Chadwyck [780]
WILLAURA FARMER – 1906-1916. WF1-3 – 3r – 1 – at Corangamite [072]
Willcox, Giles Buckingham *see* THE PRODIGAL SON
Willdenow, C L *see*
- ENUMERATIO PLANTARUM HORTI REGII BOTANICI BEROLINENSIS
- FLORAE BEROLINENSIS PRODROMUS
- GRUNDRISS DER KRAEUTERKUNDE ZU VORLESUNGEN ENTWORFEN
- HERBARIUM
- HISTORIA AMARANTHORUM
- HORTUS BEROLINENSIS SIVE ICONES ET DESCRIPTIONES PLANTARUM RARIORUM
- PHYTOGRAPHIA, SEU DESCRIPTIO RARIORUM MINUS COGNITARUM PLANTARUM

DER WILLE *see* DER VOLKSFREUND
Wille, Bruno *see*
- EINSIEDLER UND GENOSSE
- DAS GEFAENGNIS ZUM PREUSSISCHEN ADLER
- DER GLASBERG
- OFFENBARUNGEN DES WACHOLDERBAUMS

Wille, N *see* ALGOLOGISCHE NOTIZEN. 1-6
WILLE UND MACHT – Berlin, jul 1933-apr 1944 – 4r – 1 – Inquire at Mikrofilmarchiv for details – gw Misc Inst [072]
WILLE UND MACHT – Berlin. v. 1. nos. 12 13-v. 12. no. 3 4. July 1933-Mar Apr 1944. Incomplete – 1 – us NY Public [999]
WILLE UND MACHT : FUEHRERORGAN DER NATIONALSOZIALISTISCHEN JUGEND – Berlin. v1-12. 1933-44 – 4r – 1 – us Ross [320]
Willeke, Venencio *see* SAO FRANCISCO DAS CHAGAS...
Willelmi Malbesbiriensis *see* DE GESTIS REGUM ANGLORUM LIBRI QUINQUE
Willemenot, Luis G *see* EL DIVINO AMOR
Willemet, P R *see* MONOGRAPHIE POUR SERVIR A L'HISTOIRE NATURELLE ET BOTANIQUE DE LA FAMILLE DES PLANTES ETOILEES
DEN ,WILLEN ZUM IDEAL' INS LEBEN SELBST VERWANDELN / Heukenkamp, Marianne – 1991 – 205p – 9 – DM98.00 – 3-89349-432-4 – gw Hänsel [430]
Willenbuecher, Heinrich *see* VERSUCHE ZUR ERKLAERUNG SCHWIERIGER STELLEN IN GOETHES DRAMEN
WILLENHALL REPORTER ETC – Bilston, England. 21 Nov 1885-24 Dec 1886; Jan-Jul 1887. -w. 1 1/2 reels – 1 – uk British Libr Newspaper [072]
Willermoz, J B *see* DIVERSE PIECES
Willert, P F *see* HENRY OF NAVARRE AND THE HUGUENOTS IN FRANCE
Willet, Andrew *see* SYNOPSIS PAPISMI
Willett, Herbert Lockwood *see*
- STUDIES IN THE FIRST BOOK OF SAMUEL: FOR THE USE OF...SECONDARY SCHOOLS
- THE TEACHINGS OF THE BOOKS

Willey, H *see* A SYNOPSIS OF THE GENUS ARTHONIA
Willging, Thomas E *see*
- ASBESTOS CASE MANAGEMENT
- ATTORNEY FEE PETITIONS
- COURT-APPOINTED EXPERTS
- JUDICIAL REGULATION OF ATTORNEYS' FEES
- PARTIAL PAYMENT OF FILING FEES IN PRISONER IN FORMA PAUPERIS CASES IN FEDERAL COURTS
- THE RULE 11 SANCTIONING PROCESS
- TRENDS IN ASBESTOS LITIGATION
- USE OF RULE 12(B)(6) IN TWO FEDERAL DISTRICT COURTS

William 3, King *see* LETTERS OF WILLIAM 3 AND LOUIS 14 AND THEIR MINISTERS
WILLIAM A. RIDGELY, SENATE SERVICE 1949-1977 : SENATE DISBURSEMENT OFFICE – 2mf – 9 – $10.00 – us Scholarly Res [320]
WILLIAM ALEXANDER FOSTER SCRAPBOOK *see* CANADA'S FIRST MOVEMENT: WILLIAM ALEXANDER FOSTER SCRAPBOOK
WILLIAM ALLAIR / Wood, Ellen – British Fiction Archive: Unit 1 – 9 – uk Bell [830]
WILLIAM AND MARY: A TALE OF THE SIEGE OF LOUISBURG, 1745 / Hickey, David – Toronto: W. Briggs, 1884. 05562. (Pre-1900 Canadiana) – 9 – cn C.I.H.M. [971]
WILLIAM AND MARY BILL OF RIGHTS JOURNAL – (Supersedes Colonial Lawyer) – v1-5. 1992-95 – 9 – $45.00 set – us Hein [340]
WILLIAM AND MARY ENVIRONMENTAL LAW AND POLICY REVIEW – (Note: v7-10 never publ. Title varies: v1-6 1975-81 as Environmental Practice News. v11-14 1986-89 as Environmental Practice News. v15-18 1990-94 as William and Mary Journal of Environmental Law) – v1-20. 1975-96 – 9 – $103.00 set – us Hein [340]
WILLIAM AND MARY LAW REVIEW – (v1-25 1957-84 on reel $430.00. v26-36 1984-95 on mf $249.00. Supersedes William and Mary Review of Virginia Law) – v1-36. 1957-95 – 5,6,9 – $679.00 set – us Hein [340]
WILLIAM AND MARY QUARTERLY – v1- 1944-1; v26- 5,6; v33- 9 – us UMI [970]
WILLIAM AND MARY QUARTERLY – Williamsburg, VA. series 2: v1-23. 1921-43 – 7r – 1 – us Ross [370]
WILLIAM AND MARY REVIEW OF VIRGINIA LAW *see* WILLIAM AND MARY LAW REVIEW
William, Aneurin *see* CO – PARTNERSHIP AND PROFIT – SHARING
WILLIAM BEACH LAWRENCE VS. R.H. DANA, JR., ET AL / Lawrence, William Beach – Boston, Mudge, 1867. 563 p. LL-375 – 1 – us L of C Photodup [340]
WILLIAM BLAKE : A CRITICAL ESSAY / Swinburne, Algernon Charles – London: John Camden Hotten, 2nd ed 1868 – 1 roll – 1 – 1-55879-313-5 – uk Libr Preservation [420]
THE WILLIAM BLATHWAYT PAPERS AT COLONIAL WILLIAMSBURG, 1631-1722 – 9 – $1,105.00 – 1-55655-137-1 – us UPA [975]
WILLIAM CAREY : A BIBLIOGRAPHY / Belchor, Joseph – Philadelphia: American Baptist Publication Society, c1853 – 1mf – us A.T.L.A. [240]
WILLIAM CAREY : THE SHOEMAKER WHO BECAME "THE FATHER AND FOUNDER OF MODERN MISSIONS" / Myers, John Brown – New York: Fleming H Revell, [1887?] – 1mf – 9 – 0-8370-6230-6 – 1986-0230 – us A.T.L.A. [920]
William Carey College. Library *see* CATALOGUE OF EARLY INDIAN IMPRINTS
WILLIAM CHAPIN DEMING OF WYOMING / Spring, Agnes W – Arthur H. Clark Co., 1944. Wyoming reel 3. (Cox Library Collection) – 5 – us Americana [978]
WILLIAM CONGREVE / Congreve, William – With introd. by William Archer. New York: American Book Co., c1912 – 1 – us U.W. Library [920]
WILLIAM CONYNGHAM PLUNKET : FOURTH BARON PLUNKET AND SIXTY-FIRST ARCHBISHOP OF DUBLIN : A MEMOIR / How, Frederick Douglas – London: Isbister, 1900 – 1mf – us A.T.L.A. [240]
WILLIAM E. DODGE : THE CHRISTIAN MERCHANT / Martyn, Carlos – New York: Funk & Wagnalls, 1890 – 1mf – us A.T.L.A. [380]
WILLIAM EDWARD BURGHARDT DU BOIS: THE TRAIL OF HIS IDEAS / Broderick, Francis L – Unpub. doctoral dissertation, Harvard Univ., 1955. No. 81-2. 1 reel – 1 – $20.00 – us Partington [920]
WILLIAM ELLERY CHANNING : MINISTER OF RELIGION / Chadwick, John White – Boston: Houghton, Mifflin, 1903 – 2mf – us A.T.L.A. [240]
WILLIAM ELLERY CHANNING PAPERS, 1791-1892 / Channing, William E – Massachusetts Historical Society – 5r – 1 – $380.00 – us UMI [920]
WILLIAM G. MATHER PAPERS *see* MATHER, WILLIAM G., PAPERS, MS 4578
WILLIAM GARDEN BLAIKIE : AN AUTOBIOGRAPHY : RECOLLECTIONS OF A BUSY LIFE / Blaikie, William Garden; ed by Walker, Norman Lockhart – London: Hodder and Stoughton, 1901 – 1mf – us A.T.L.A. [240]
WILLIAM GASTON PAPERS / Gaston, William – 1744-1844. University of North Carolina Library. Guide – 1 – $144.00 – us U.N.C. Southern Hist [920]
WILLIAM GEORGE WARD AND THE OXFORD MOVEMENT / Ward, Wilfrid Philip – 2nd ed. London, New York: Macmillan, 1890. xxxi,481p – 1 – us U.W. Library [920]
WILLIAM GEORGE WARD AND THE OXFORD MOVEMENT / Ward, Wilfrid Philip – London, New York: Macmillan, 1889 – 2mf – us A.T.L.A. [240]
THE WILLIAM H. HASTIE PAPERS / Hastie, William H – (Pt 1, Judicial Activities: 65r. ISBN 0-89093-812-1. $7,155.00; Pt 2, Civil Rights, Organizational and Private Activities: 42r. ISBN 0-89093-813-X. $4,620.00; Guide only to both parts $150.00) – 1 – us UPA [920]
WILLIAM HEATH PAPERS, 1774-1872 / Heath, William – Massachusetts Historical Society – 46r – 1 – $3505.00 – us UMI [920]
WILLIAM HENRY SEWARD / Lothrop, Thortoin K – Boston & NY: Houghton, Mifflin & Co, 1899 – 5mf – 9 – $7.50 – LLMC 96-034 – us L.L.M.C. [975]
WILLIAM HICKLING PRESCOTT / Ogden, Rollo – New York, Boston: Houghton, Mifflin and Co., 1904. viii,239p – 1 – us U.W. Library [920]
WILLIAM HILDENBRAND, SENATE SERVICE 1961-1984 : SECRETARY OF THE SENATE – 4mf – 9 – $20.00 – us Scholarly Res [320]
WILLIAM J. JORDAN PAPERS, MS P.P. / Jordon, William J – 1861-64. 1 reel – 1 – us Western Res [920]
William J. Park and Co *see* HISTORY OF DANE COUNTY
William J. Sullivan Collection/21st Ohio Volunteer Infantry *see* RECORDS
William J. Sullivan Collection/Arnold McMahan *see* PAPERS
WILLIAM JAMES / Boutroux, Emile – New York: Longmans, Green, 1912 – 1mf – us A.T.L.A. [190]
WILLIAM JAMES ALS RELIGIONSPHILOSOPH / Busch, K A – Goettingen: Vandenhoeck & Ruprecht, 1911 – 1mf – us A.T.L.A. [240]
WILLIAM LAUD / Hutton, William Holden – London: Methuen, 1895. (Leaders of religion) – 1mf – us A.T.L.A. [240]
WILLIAM LAUD : SOMETIME ARCHBISHOP OF CANTERBURY: A STUDY / Benson, Arthur Christopher – London: Kegan Paul, Trench, 1887 – 1mf – us A.T.L.A. [240]
WILLIAM LAW, NONJUROR AND MYSTIC : AUTHOR OF A SERIOUS CALL TO A DEVOUT AND HOLY LIFE, & C., FORMERLY FELLOW OF EMMANUEL COLLEGE, CAMBRIDGE: A SKETCH OF HIS LIFE, CHARACTER, AND OPINIONS / Overton, John H – London: Longmans, Green, 1881 – 2mf – us A.T.L.A. [240]
WILLIAM LIVINGSTON PAPERS, 1695-1839 / Livingston, William – (Late 18th-c. letterbooks, MS, and law and case registers) – Massachusetts Historical Society – 25r – 1 – $1860.00 – us UMI [920]
WILLIAM LLOYD GARRISON PAPERS, 1833-1881 / Garrison, William Lloyd – Massachusetts Historical Society – 1r – 1 – $85.00 – us UMI [920]
WILLIAM LLOYD GARRISON, THE ABOLITIONIST / Grimke, Archibald H – New York: Funk & Wagnalls, 1891. (American reformers) – 1mf – us A.T.L.A. [240]
WILLIAM LOWNDES PAPERS / Lowndes, William Thomas – 1754-1918. University of North Carolina Library. Guide – 1 – $36.00 – us U.N.C. Southern Hist [920]
WILLIAM MATHER : A SKETCH OF HIS LIFE AND WORK / Mather, James S – Jaffna: M Nalliah, 1922 – us Res Libr [920]
WILLIAM MILNER OF HALIFAX – A PIONEER OF CHEAP LITERATURE / Eastwood, R – 1mf – 9 – uk Microform Academic [920]
WILLIAM MITCHELL LAW REVIEW – (v1-10 1985-84 on reel $160.00. v11-20 1985-94 on mf $230.00) – v1-20. 1974-94 – 5,6,9 – $390.00 set – us Hein [340]
WILLIAM MORRIS – Part 1: Manuscripts from the British Library, London Part 2: Manuscripts from the Huntington Library, San Marino, California. Part 3: Archives of the Socialist League, 1884-1891 from the International Institute for Social History, Amsterdam. Part 4: Art, Book Design, and Literary Papers from the National Art Library, Victoria and Albert Museum, London; the Society of Antiquaries, London; and the British Library Department of Printed Books – 1 – us Primary [090]
WILLIAM MORRIS : POET, CRAFTSMAN, SOCIALIST / Cary, Elisabeth Luther – New York, London: G.P. Putnam's Sons, The Knickerbocker Press, 1902 – 1 roll – 1 – 1-55879-522-7 – uk Libr Preservation [420]
WILLIAM MORRIS, HIS ART, HIS WRITINGS, AND HIS PUBLIC LIFE : A RECORD / Vallance, Aymer – London: G. Bell and Sons, 1897 – 1 roll – 1 – 1-55879-692-4 – uk Libr Preservation [740]
WILLIAM MOULTRIE: ARMS AND THE MAN / Thomas, Robert Gibbes – 1930. 9 fiches. Typescript – 9 – us South Carolina Historical [920]
WILLIAM OF GERMANY: A SUCCINCT BIOGRAPHY OF WILLIAM 1, GERMAN EMPEROR AND KING OF PRUSSIA / Forbes, Archibald – New York: Cassell & Co., 1888.viii,366p. illus – 1 – us U.W. Library [920]
William Of Newburg *see*
- HISTORIA RERUM ANGLICARUM, BK 5 (CHRONICLES..2)
- HISTORIA RERUM ANGLICARUM, BKS 1-4 (CHRONICLES..1)

WILLIAM P. PALMER COLLECTION *see*
- PALMER, WILLIAM P., COLLECTION, MS 3947
- PALMER, WILLIAM P., COLLECTION, MSS 3947

WILLIAM PENN PAPERS, 1644-1718 / Penn, William – (3000 documents from 60 institutions and individuals) – Historical Society of Pennsylvania – 14r – 1 – $945.00 – us UMI [240]

WILLIAM PEPPERRELL PAPERS, 1683-1769 / Pepperrell, William – (3v of letters related to Louisbourg Expedition of 1745-46) – Massachusetts Historical Society – 2r – 1 – $155.00 – us UMI [920]

WILLIAM PICKENS PAPERS : FROM THE HOLDINGS OF THE SCHOMBURG CENTER FOR RESEARCH IN BLACK CULTURE, MANUSCRIPTS, ARCHIVES AND RARE BOOKS DIVISION: THE NEW YORK PUBLIC LIBRARY, ASTOR, LENOX AND TILDEN FOUNDATIONS – (Guide which covers all coll under "Civil Rights Advocates" sold separately for $20.00 D3305.G3) – 1995 – 29r – 1 – $2,465.00 – D3305P08 – Dist. us Scholarly Res – us L of C Photodup [306]

WILLIAM PLUMER PAPERS, 1778-1854 / Plumer, William – 24r – 1 – $1775.00 – us UMI [920]

William Randolph Hearst Collection *see* PHOTOGRAPHS AND ACQUISITION RECORDS

William Rishanger *see* CHRONICA ET ANNALES 1259-1307 (CHRONIA..2)

WILLIAM S. GRAY RESEARCH COLLECTION IN READING / Svobodny, Dolly – (Also available on CD-ROM) – 25,000 titles. ca 7750mf. 1884-1980, 1982-85, 1986-1990, 1991-92 – 9 – us A.T.B.I. [370]

WILLIAM SMEAL COLLECTION / Glasgow. Public Library – 1 – £480.00 – uk World [025]

William, Watkin Wynn *see* AN INTRODUCTION TO THE ARTICLES OF THE CHURCH OF ENGLAND

WILLIAM WETMORE STORY AND HIS FRIENDS / James, Henry – Boston: Houghton-Mifflin. 2v. 1903 – 8mf – 9 – $12.00 – LLMC 91-076 – us L.L.M.C. [340]

WILLIAM WILBERFORCE / Stoughton, John – New York: A.C. Armstrong, 1880 – 1mf – us A.T.L.A. [240]

THE WILLIAM WIRT PAPERS / Wirt, William; ed by Boles, John B – (Guide sold separately $10.00) – 1972 – 24r – 1 – $1,800.00 – S1624 – Dist. us Scholarly Res – us L of C Photodup [340]

WILLIAM WORDSWORTH, HIS DOCTRINE AND ART IN THEIR HISTORICAL RELATIONS / Beaty, Arthur – Madison. 1927. 2nd ed. 310 p. 1 reel – 1 – us U.W. Library [420]

WILLIAMETE BULLETIN OF INTERNATIONAL LAW AND POLICY – v1-2. 1993-94 – 9 – $18.00set – us Hein [340]

Williams, A H *see* WELSH WESLEYAN METHODISM, 1800-1858

Williams, Aaron *see* THE HARMONY SOCIETY AT ECONOMY, PENNA

Williams ab Ithel, J W *see*
- THE PHYSICIANS OF MYDDVAI; MEDDYGON MYDDFAI
- THE PHYSICIANS OF MYDDVAL; MEDDYGON MIDDFAL

WILLIAMS, A.C., PAPERS, MS 593 – 1888-1903 – 1r – 1 – us Western Res [240]

Williams, Albert B *see* PAST AND PRESENT OF KNOX COUNTY

Williams, Albert Rhys *see* OCHERKI RUSSKO I REVOLIUTSII

Williams, Alice Tapp *see* DIARIES

Williams, B S *see*
- THE ORCHID-GROWER'S MANUAL
- SELECT FERNS AND LYCOPODS: BRITISH AND EXOTIC

Williams, Byron *see* HISTORY OF CLERMONT AND BROWN COUNTIES

Williams, C F A *see* THE ARISTOXENIAN THEORY OF MUSICAL RHYTHM

Williams, Charles *see*
- THE ALPS, SWITZERLAND, AND THE NORTH OF ITALY
- A BRIEF HISTORY OF THE BAPTIST CHURCH, HEBDEN BRIDGE, YORKSHIRE, ENGLAND
- HISTORY OF BAPTISTS IN NORTH CAROLINA

Williams, Chase and Co *see* HISTORY OF PENOBSCOT COUNTY

Williams, Cora May *see* A REVIEW OF THE SYSTEMS OF ETHICS

WILLIAMS COUNTY GAZETTE – Bryan, Ohio. 1857-59 – 1r – 1 – $32.50r – us Archival [071]

WILLIAMS COUNTY LEADER – Bryan, Ohio. 1859-62 – 2r – 1 – $32.50r – us Archival [071]

Williams County, Ohio. Auditor *see*
- ENUMERATIONS OF YOUTH
- TAX LIST

Williams County. Ohio. Auditor *see*
- CIVIL WAR BOUNTIES AND PAPERS
- MILITIA ROLLS AND ENUMERATIONS

Williams County. Ohio. Board of County Commissioners *see*
- COMMISSIONERS' JOURNALS
- INDEX TO JOURNALS

Williams. County, Ohio. Common Pleas. Criminal Div. *see* CORONER'S INQUESTS

Williams County. Ohio. County Home *see*
- MINUTES
- VISITORS REGISTERS

Williams. County, Ohio. Probate Court *see* GUARDIAN RECORD

Williams County, Ohio. Pulaski Township. Board of Education *see* RECORDS

Williams County, Ohio. Treasurer *see* TAX DUPLICATES

Williams County. Ohio. Treasurer *see* TAX DUPLICATES

Williams, D W *see* HISTORY OF JACKSON COUNTY, OHIO

Williams, Daniel Roderick *see* THE ODYSSEY OF THE PHILIPPINE COMMISSION

Williams, David *see* VOLTAIRE: LITERARY CRITIC

Williams, David J *see* REGULATING TAXI OPERATORS: SOME HISTORICAL INSIGHTS

Williams, Edward T *see* NIAGARA COUNTY-A CONCISE RECORD OF HER PROGRESS AND PEOPLE 1821-1921

Williams, Emyr W *see* EFFECTS OF A MULTIMEDIA PERFORMANCE PRINCIPLE TRAINING PROGRAM ON CORRECT ANALYSIS AND DIAGNOSIS OF THROWLIKE MOVEMENTS

Williams, Ernest E *see*
- ECONOMIC LIBERTY
- FREE TRADE VS PROTECTION

Williams, F E *see* PAPUANS OF THE TRANS-FLY

WILLIAMS FARMER – Williams, CA. Jan-Feb 1900; 1905-06; 1913; 1916-19; 1923-24; 1932-67 – 14r – 1 – $700.00 – B03101 – us Library Micro [630]

Williams, Franklin H *see* REPORT OF PRESIDENT'S PERSONAL REPRESENTATIVE ON THE STATUS NEGOTIATIONS [TTPI (U.S.)]

Williams, G *see* MEMORIALS OF THE REIGN OF KING HENRY 6 (RS56)

Williams, Gardner F *see* THE DIAMOND MINES OF SOUTH AFRICA

Williams, Gareth *see* TOWARDS LIFELONG EDUCATION

Williams, George *see*
- THE ORTHODOX CHURCH OF THE EAST IN THE EIGHTEENTH CENTURY
- THE PATRIARCHATE OF ANTIOCH

Williams, George W *see* A HISTORY OF THE NEGRO TROOPS IN THE WAR OF THE REBELLION, 1861-1865 109=PRECEDED BY A REVIEW OF THE MILITARY SERVICES OF NEGROES IN ANCIENT AND MODERN TIMES

Williams, George Washington *see* HISTORY OF NEGRO RACE IN AMERICA FROM 1619 TO 1880

Williams, Gorham Deane *see* THE MASSACHUSETTS PEACE OFFICER

Williams, Mrs H J *see* HISTORY OF SCHLEY COUNTY GEORGIA

WILLIAM'S HASTINGS NEWS – Hastings, NE. -w. Aug 1897-Dec 1900; Feb 1901-Nov 1902 – 1 – us NE Hist [071]

Williams, Henry Wilkinson *see* A MANUAL OF NATURAL AND REVEALED THEOLOGY

Williams, Holly *see* LOOKING AT AND EVALUATING DANCE

Williams, Howard Y *see* PAPERS

Williams, Hugh *see* CHRISTIANITY IN EARLY BRITAIN

WILLIAMS, H.Z. AND BROTHERS *see*
- HISTORY OF PREBLE COUNTY
- HISTORY OF TRUMBUL AND MAHONING COUNTIES
- HISTORY OF WASHINGTON COUNTY

Williams, Isaac *see*
- THE CHARACTERS OF THE OLD TESTAMENT
- FEMALE CHARACTERS OF HOLY SCRIPTURE

Williams, Israel *see* ISRAEL WILLIAMS PAPERS, 1730-1785

Williams, J Fletcher *see* A HISTORY OF THE CITY OF ST PAUL AND OF THE COUNTY OF RAMSEY

Williams, J W *see* THE SHELL-COLLECTOR'S HANDBOOK FOR THE FIELD

Williams, Jack M *see* HISTORY OF VERMILION COUNTY

Williams, Jay H *see* EXTRACELLULAR CALCIUM AND THE INOTROPIC EFFECT OF EPINEPHRINE ON ISOLATED SKELETAL MUSCLE

Williams, Jeffrey P *see* THE CUMULATIVE EFFECTS OF MULTIPLE EXERCISE BOUTS OF EQUAL CALORIC EXPENDITURE ON EXCESS POST-EXERCISE OXYGEN CONSUMPTION

Williams, John *see*
- THE LIFE AND ACTIONS OF ALEXANDER THE GREAT
- THOUGHTS ON THE ORIGIN AND ON THE MOST RATIONAL AND NATURAL METHOD OF TEACHING THE LANGUAGES

Williams, John K *see* CHAINING AUSTRALIA, CHURCH BUREAUCRACIES AND POLITICAL ECONOMY

Williams, John Monroe *see* SELECTED PAPERS

Williams, Kathleen *see* AGE DIFFERENCES IN PERFORMANCE OF A COINCIDENT ANTICIPATION TASK: APPLICATION OF A MODIFIED INFORMATION PROCESSING MODEL

WILLIAMS LAKE TRIBUNE – B.C. Canada. Dec 1965-67 – 1 – cn Commonwealth Micro [072]

Williams, Lavon *see* SITUATIONAL AND CONTEXTUAL INFLUENCES ON GOAL ORIENTATIONS

Williams, Leighton *see* SERAMPORE LETTERS

Williams, Martha A *see* PHYSICAL FITNESS OF DEAF AND HEARING ADOLESCENT FEMALES

Williams, Micajah T *see* PAPERS

Williams, Mornay *see* SERAMPORE LETTERS

Williams, Nathan Witter *see* THE LIVING GOD

Williams, Nathaniel Marshman *see* THE GOSPEL ACCORDING TO MATTHEW

Williams, Owen *see* ECONOMIC GEOGRAPHY OF THE TRANSVAAL

Williams, Peter A *see* JOURNAL OF COORDINATION CHEMISTRY

Williams Publishing Co *see* NOTABLE MEN OF WISCONSIN

Williams, Robert *see* SOVETSKAI A SISTEMA ZA RABOTO I

Williams, Robert Folkestone *see* LIVES OF THE ENGLISH CARDINALS; INCLUDING HISTORICAL NOTICES OF THE PAPAL COURT, FROM NICHOLAS BREAKSPEAR (POPE ADRIAN 4) TO THOMAS WOLSEY, CARDINAL LEGATE

Williams, Roger *see*
- A KEY INTO THE LANGUAGE OF AMERICA
- LETTERS AND PAPERS OF ROGER WILLIAMS

Williams, S W *see* AN ENGLISH AND CHINESE VOCABULARY, IN THE COURT DIALECT

Williams, Salena *see* EFFECTS OF A COMPETITIVE SEASON ON BODY COMPOSITION IN FEMALE INTERCOLLEGIATE ATHLETES

Williams, Samuel C *see* HISTORY OF THE LOST STATE OF FRANKLIN

Williams, T O *see*
- IMPACT DES POLITIQUES DES PRIX DU BETAIL SUR LA PRODUCTION DE VIANDE ET DE LAIT DANS CERTAINS PAYS DE L'AFRIQUE SUBSAHARIENNE
- IMPACT OF LIVESTOCK PRICING POLICIES ON MEAT AND MILK OUTPUT IN SELECTED SUB-SAHARAN AFRICAN COUNTRIES

Williams, Thomas Walter *see* THE WHOLE LAW RELATIVE TO THE DUTY AND OFFICE OF A JUSTICE OF THE PEACE

Williams, Valerie L *see* THE USE OF LABANOTATION SCORE ANALYSIS IN THE DEVELOPMENT OF THE EXPRESSIVE PERFORMER

Williams, W W *see* HISTORY OF THE FIRE LANDS

Williams, Walter *see*
- HISTORY OF NORTHEASTERN MISSOURI
- HISTORY OF NORTHWEST MISSOURI

Williams, William Harrison, Sr *see* PAPERS AND SERMONS OF WILLIAM HARRISON WILLIAMS, SR.

Williams, William R *see*
- CAUSES OF THE INCREASES OF THE CHURCHES
- CHRIST, A HOME MISSIONARY
- THE DOCTRINE OF SCRIPTURE CONCERNING THE HOLY GHOST, IN ITS RELATIONS TO MINISTERIAL EDUCATION
- GOD'S RESCUES

WILLIAMSBURG 1771-1899 – 25mf – 9 – 0-87623-070-2 – us Holbrook [920]

WILLIAMSBURG DAILY NEWS – Charleston. West Virginia. 1945-1954 – 1 – us UMI [071]

Williamsburgh. South Carolina. Board of Commissioners *see* JOURNAL

Williamson C W *see* THE HISTORY OF ADAMS COUNTY, ILLINOIS

Williamson, C W *see* HISTORY OF WESTERN OHIO AND AUGLAIZE COUNTY

Williamson, Edward Hand *see* A HANDBOOK OF THE LAW OF PROTE COMPILED FROM DECISIONS OF AMERICAN AND ENGLISH COURTS

Williamson, J *see* FERNS OF KENTUCKY

Williamson, Jean Bisset *see* LE PAYSAGE ITALIEN DANS LES ROMANS DE LAMARTINE

Williamson, John Rutter *see* THE HEALING OF THE NATIONS

Williamson Law Book Company *see* WILLIAMSON'S COMPLETE CODE OF PRACTICE IN BANKRUPTCY. NEW IN FORCE

Williamson, S G *see* AKAN RELIGION AND THE CHRISTIAN FAITH

Williamson, W C *see*
- THE BRITISH HYDRACARINA
- THE RECENT FORAMINIFERA OF GREAT BRITAIN

WILLIAMSON'S COMPLETE CODE OF PRACTICE IN BANKRUPTCY. NEW IN FORCE / Williamson Law Book Company – Rochester, N.Y., 1899. 1. p. I, 32, xxx 2 107, 27, 44 p. LL-1561 – 1 – us L of C Photodup [340]

WILLIAMSPORT EXAMINER – Williamsport, PA. -w 1955-1956 – 13 – $25.00r – us I.M.R. [071]

WILLIAMSPORT MORNING STANDARD – Williamsport, PA., 1868-1869 – 13 – $25.00r – us I.M.R. [071]

WILLIAMSPORT NEWS – Williamsport, PA. -d 1889-1912 – 13 – $25.00r – us I.M.R. [071]

WILLIAMSPORT PRESS – Williamsport, PA., 1859-1861 – 13 – $25.00r – us I.M.R. [071]

WILLIAMSPORT REPUBLICAN – Williamsport, PA., 1891 – 13 – $25.00r – us I.M.R. [071]

THE WILLIAMSPORT TIMES – Williamsport, PA., 1932 – 13 – $25.00r – us I.M.R. [071]

WILLIAMSTOWN 1757-1900 – (Mf 1-2: Births & Deaths by Family 1757-1843. Mf 3: Residents in 1830 – Births, Deaths 1761-1830. Mf 4-6: Births & Deaths 1757-1820. Mf 5: Marriages 1784-88. Mf 7: Marriages, Intentions, Births 1801-34. Mf 8-12: Proprietors Records 1753-1804. Mf 13-16: Birth & Marriage Indexes 1860-93. Mf 17,37-39: Death Index 1860-1987. Mf 18-22,77: Births 1860-98. Mf 23-26,40-41: Deaths 1860-1907. Mf 27-29,63: Marriages 1860-1902. Mf 30-32: Birth Index 1893-1987. Mf 33-36: Marriage Index 1894-1987. Mf 37-39: Index to Deaths 1893-1987) – (mf ed 1988) – 12v on Mf 1-41, 63, 77 – 0-87623-076-1 – us Holbrook [920]

WILLIAMSTOWN ADVERTISER – 1992-8/95 – 11mf – 9 – at Corangamite [980]

Willich, C *see* KRIEGSTAGE IN SUEDWEST

Willige, Wilhelm *see* KLASSISCHE GESTALTUNG UND ROMANTISCHER EINFLUSS IN DEN DRAMEN HEINRICHS VON KLEIST

Willimczik, Kurt *see* E.T.A. HOFFMANN

Willing, Jennie Fowler *see*
- HOW TO WIN SOULS
- WOMAN AND THE PENTECOST

Willink, D *see* BLOEMKRANS VAN CHRISTELYKE LIEFDE-EN ZEEDEDICHTEN

WILLIPA HARBOR PILOT – South Bend. Wash. 1902-1918 – 1 – us UMI [071]

Willis Bund, John William *see* THE CELTIC CHURCH OF WALES

Willis, John T *see* PRESIDENTIAL ELECTIONS IN MARYLAND

Willis, N P *see* CANADIAN SCENERY

Willis, Richard Storrs *see* OUR CHURCH MUSIC

Willis, Robert *see* SERVETUS AND CALVIN

Willis, Thomas *see*
- AFFECTIONUM QUAE DICUNTUR HYSTERICAE ET HYPOCHONDRIACAE PATHOLOGIA...
- CEREBRI ANATOME: CUI ACCESSIT NERVORUM DESCRIPTIO ET USUS
- DE ANIMA BRUTORUM
- DIATRIBAE DUAE MEDICOPHILOSOPHICAE,... DE FERMENTATIONE...DE FEBRIBUS, ...DE URINIS
- PHARMACEUTICE RATIONALIS
- PROTEUS VINCTUS
- VESTIBULUM LINGUAE LATINAE

Willis, William *see*
- HISTORY OF SACRAMENTO COUNTY
- A HISTORY OF THE LAW, THE COURTS, AND THE LAWYERS OF MAINE, FROM ITS FIRST COLONIZATION TO THE EARLY PART OF THE PRESENT CENTURY
- THE SOCIETY AND FELLOWSHIP OF THE INNER TEMPLE

Willisen, Karl Wilhelm von *see* THEORIE DES GROSSEN KRIEGE

WILLISON'S MONTHLY – v. 1-5. 1925-29 – 1 – 125.00 – cn McLaren [073]

Williston, Samuel *see* NEGOTIABLE INSTRUMENTS

Williston, Timothy *see* ORTHODOX PATHS RETRACED

THE WILLITS NEWS – Willits, CA. Mar 1892-1907 (broken series); 1908-44; 1946- – 69+ r – 1 – $3,450.00 ($180.00y) – B03103 – us Library Micro [071]

Willkomm, Ernst *see* SAGEN UND MAERCHEN AUS DER OBERLAUSITZ

Willkomm, H M *see*
- ICONES ET DESCRIPTIONES PLANTARUM NOVARUM CRITICARUM ET RARIORUM EUROPAE AUSTRO-OCCIDENTALIS PRAECIPUE HISPANIAE
- ILLUSTRATIONES FLORAE HISPANIAE INSULARUMQUE BALEARUM
- PRODROMUS FLORAE HISPANICAE
- DIE STRAND-UND STEPPENGEBIETE DER IBERISCHEN HALBINSEL UND DEREN VEGETATION

Willkomm, Hans Werner *see* UEBER RICHARD JOHNSONS SEVEN CHAMPIONS OF CHRISTENDOM (1596)

Willmarth, J W *see*
- DIARY
- DIARY OF JOHN COMER

Willmett Family *see* RECORDS

Willmott, Lesslie Earl et al *see* JESUS (CCC325)

Willms, Agnes *see*
- BEIM LAMPENLICHT
- OTTILIE WILDERMUTHS LEBEN

Willms, Jens-Peter *see* GESTALTUNGSMITTELANALYSE BEI DIENSTLEISTUNGEN

WILLOUGHBY INDEPENDENT : WEEKLY REPUBLICAN NEWSPAPER – Willoughby, OH. 18 Apr 1879-2 Mar 1911 – 11r – 1 – us Western Res [071]

Willoughby, Leonard Ashley *see*
- THE CLASSICAL AGE OF GERMAN LITERATURE, 1748-1805
- UNITY AND CONTINUITY IN GOETHE

WILLOUGHBY TOWNSHIP TRUSTEES RECORDS, MS 91 – (Minutes of trustee meetings, election results, school district records, indentures and land records) – 1815-74 – 1r – 1 – us Western Res [978]

WILLOUGHBY TWP. CEMETERY RECORDS, MS 430 – 1861-1888 – 1 reel – 1 – us Western Res [978]

Willoughby, W C *see* THE SOUL OF THE BANTU: A SYMPATHETIC STUDY OF THE MAGICO-RELIGIOUS PRACTICES AND BELIEFS

Willoughby, Westel Woodbury *see*
- THE AMERICAN CONSTITUTIONAL SYSTEM
- THE CONSTITUTIONAL LAW OF THE UNITED STATES
- PRINCIPLES OF THE CONSTITUTIONAL LAW OF THE UNITED STATES

WILLOW BAPTIST CHURCH. BROOKSVILLE, KENTUCKY : CHURCH RECORDS – 1818-Jan 1964 – 1 – 47.70 – us Baptist [240]

WILLOW REVIEW – Willows, CA. 1901-1915 – 4r – 1 – $200.00 – C03694 – us Library Micro [071]

WILLOW SWAMP BAPTIST CHURCH. ORANGEBURG COUNTY. SOUTH CAROLINA : CHURCH RECORDS – (282p) – 1805-1887, Nov 1924-Aug 1926, June 1940-1985 – 1 reel – 1 – $12.69 – us Baptist [240]

WILLOWS JOURNAL – Willows, CA. 1917-34 (broken series); 1935- – 140+ r – 1 BC03105 – $7,000.00 ($135.00y) – us Library Micro [073]

Willrich, Hugo *see* JUDAICA

Wills, Franz Hermann *see* AUSSAAT UND ERNTE

WILLS; OR, THE LAW OF SUCCESSION AFTER DEATH. / Chadman, Charles Erehart – Chicago: Drake 1903. 280p. LL-784 – 1 – us L of C Photodup [340]

WILLS, WHY MAKE THEM, HOW MAKE THEM; AN EFFORT TO BE OF SERVICE. / Federal Council of the Churches of Christ in America. Committee on Financial and Fiduciary Matters – New York, 1928. 23p. LL-313 – 1 – us L of C Photodup [336]

Wills, William *see* AN ESSAY ON THE PRINCIPLES OF CIRCUMSTANTIAL EVIDENCE, ILLUSTRATED BY NUMEROUS CASES...5TH ENGLISH ED. (1902) WITH AMERICAN NOTES BY GEORGE E. BEERS...AND ARTHUR L. CORBIN

Willson, Joseph *see* A FAVORITE SONATA FOR THE PIANO FORTE WITH AN ACCOMPANIMENT FOR THE VIOLIN

Willson, Thomas B *see* HISTORY OF THE CHURCH AND STATE IN NORWAY

WILLST DU DEIN RECHT, SO HILF DIR SELBST / Mielke, Manfred – Freiburg im Breisgau: Vereinigte Vertriebe fuer Wirtschafts und Steuerliteratur, 1954. 123p. LL-4110 – 1 – us L of C Photodup [340]

Willughby, F *see* HISTORIA PISCIUM LIBRI QUATUOR

[WILLY BRANDT: PAMPHLET COLLECTION] – 1962-1981 – 1 reel – 1 – CSUXANS3619-B – us Hoover Inst Photo [320]

Wilmart, Dom A et al *see* THE BOBBIO MISSAL

Wilmarth, James W *see* WOMAN'S WORK IN THE CHURCH

Wilmer, Lambert A *see* MERLIN (1827), TOGETHER WITH RECOLLECTIONS OF EDGAR A. POE

Wilmer, Ruediger *see* LEHREVALUATION ALS EINE MASSNAHME DER QUALITAETSSICHERUNG UND - VERBESSERUNG IN DER MEDIZINISCHEN AUSBILDUNG

Wilmers, Anne *see* KANTS DING AN SICH – EIN UNLOESBARES PROBLEM?

WILMERSDORFER ZEITUNG *see* BERLIN-WILMERSDORFER ZEITUNG

Wilmington. Delaware. Hanover Street Presbyterian Church. Sunday School *see* ONE HUNDREDTH ANNIVERSARY

WILMINGTON JOURNAL – Long Beach, CA. 1933-1936 – 16r – 1 – $800.00 – R04054 – us Library Micro [073]

WILMINGTON PRESS – Wilmington, CA. 1932-1945 – 29r – 1 – $1,450.00 – R04138 – us Library Micro [071]

WILMINGTON PRESS JOURNAL – Wilmington, CA. 1943-1959 – 54r – 1 – $2,700.00 – R04139 – us Library Micro [071]

WILMINGTON SHOPPING NEWS – Wilmington, CA. v1-13 – 8r – 1 – $400.00 – R04140 – us Library Micro [071]

Wilmot, Alexander *see* THE LIFE AND TIMES OF SIR RICHARD SOUTHEY

Wilmot, Arthur Parry Eardley *see* MANNING THE NAVY; A STATEMENT, IN WHICH THE EVILS AND LOSSES ARISING FROM THE PRESENT SYSTEM ARE SET FORTH, AND A REMEDY IS PROPOSED, WHEREBY A PERMANENT NAVY MAY BE ESTABLISHED, AND THE CONDITION OF THE BRITISH SEAMAN IMPROVED

Wilmot, Sydney Marow Eardley *see*
- THE DEVELOPMENT OF NAVIES DURING THE LAST HALF-CENTURY
- THE LIFE OF VICE-ADMIRAL EDMUND, LORD LYONS

Wilner, H *see* DES ADELARD VON BATH TRAKTAT DE EODEM ET DIVERSO

Wilpert, J *see*
- DIE KATAKOMBENGEMAELDE UND IHRE ALTEN COPIEN
- DIE MALEREIEN DER KATAKOMBEN ROMS

WILSHIRE PRESS – (Various titles include: Griffith Parks News, Hollywood Independent, Los Angeles City News, Los Angeles City Press, Los Feliz Hills News, Northwest Leader, Parkside Journal, Westlake Post, Wilshire Press) – Los Angeles, CA. 1940; 1942-1966; 1968-1986 – 130r – 1 – $6,500.00 – H03330 – us Library Micro [071]

WILSHIRE'S – 1-17 2+13 (all publ). 1900-1915 – 3r – 1 – $400.00 – us UPA [335]

WILSHIRE'S MAGAZINE – London. Jul 1912-Apr 1914.-m. 14 ft – 1 – uk British Libr Newspaper [072]

Wilsmann, Aloys Christof *see* DIE VERDREHTE GEDANKENMUEHLE..

Wilson *see*
- ABSTRACTS OF WILLS OF CHATHAM COUNTY, 1773-1817
- BIOGRAPHICAL SKETCHES OF THE LEADING MEN OF CHICAGO

Wilson, A *see*
- AMERICAN ORNITHOLOGY
- THE CHARTIST MOVEMENT IN SCOTLAND
- SCOTTISH CHARTIST BIOGRAPHIES

Wilson, A W *see* PAPERS, 1854-1916. (MIMEO.)

Wilson, Alexander *see* THE PROPHETS AND PROPHECY...IN ISRAEL TO THE CLOSE OF THE EIGHTH CENTURY B.C

WILSON BAPTIST CHURCH. SOUTH ROANOKE ASSOCIATION. NORTH CAROLINA : CHURCH RECORDS – 1860-1907 – 1 – 19.62 – us Baptist [240]

Wilson, Bird *see* MEMOIR OF THE LIFE OF THE RIGHT REVEREND WILLIAM WHITE, D.D.

Wilson, Brian *see* AUDIENCE REACTIONS TO THE PORTRAYAL OF BLACKS IN ATHLETIC APPAREL COMMERCIALS

WILSON BULLETIN – v1- 1889- 1; v83- 5,6; v88- 9 – us UMI [073]

Wilson, Charles Thomas *see* PEASANT LIFE IN THE HOLY LAND

Wilson, D *see* HIGH PERFORMANCE POLYMERS

Wilson, D B *see* AN EVALUATION OF NATURE CENTER MANAGERS'PERCEPTIONS OF THEIR JOB RESPONSIBILITIES WITH REGARD TO EDUCATIONAL BACKGROUND, SERVICES/RESOURCES OFFERED, NUMBER OF YEARS AS ADMINISTRATOR, AND BUDGET OF THE NATURE CENTER

Wilson, Erasmus *see* STANDARD HISTORY OF ALLEGHENY COUNTY AND CITY OF PITTSBURGH

WILSON FIRST BAPTIST CHURCH. WILSON, ARKANSAS : CHURCH RECORDS – Aug 1925-62 – 1 – 14.85 – us Baptist [240]

Wilson, G *see*
- THE CONSTITUTION OF NGONDE
- ESSAY ON THE ECONOMICS OF DETRIBALIZATION IN NORTHERN RHODESIA
- THE LAND RIGHTS OF INDIVIDUALS AMONG THE NYAKYUSA
- THE STUDY OF AFRICAN SOCIETY

Wilson, Gilbert B *see* BEITRAG ZUR VORGESCHICHTE DER AUFLOESUNG DER KLOESTER IN ENGLAND UND WALES SPECIELL UNTER DER REGIERUNG HEINRICHS 8

Wilson, Gilbert L *see* PAPERS: DIARIES, NOTEBOOKS AND REPORTS

Wilson, Grove *see* KERN COUNTY WHO'S WHO

Wilson, H Austin *see*
- THE BENEDICTIONAL OF ARCHBISHOP ROBERT
- THE CALENDAR OF ST WILLIBRORD
- EPISCOPACY AND UNITY
- THE GREGORIAN SACRAMENTARY UNDER CHARLES THE GREAT
- THE MISSAL OF ROBERT OF JUMIEGES
- OFFICIUM ECCLESIASTICUM ABBATUM SECUNDUM USUM EVESHAMENSIS MONASTERII
- THE ORDER OF THE COMMUNION 1548
- THE PONTIFICAL OF MAGDALEN COLLEGE, OXFORD

Wilson, H H *see*
- DOCUMENTS ILLUSTRATIVE OF THE BURMESE WAR
- THE VISHNU PURANA

Wilson, Harriet E *see* STREET AND INTERURBAN RAILWAY SYSTEMS IN OHIO, 1860-1946

Wilson, Henry *see*
- HISTORY OF THE RISE AND FALL OF THE SLAVE POWER IN AMERICA
- TESTIMONIES OF AMERICAN STATESMEN AND JURISTS TO THE TRUTHS OF CHRISTIANITY

Wilson, Herbert Wrigley *see* IRONCLADS IN ACTION

WILSON HIGH SCHOOL YEARBOOK – Campanile, Long Beach, CA. 1927-93 – 15r – 1 – $750.00 – R60016 – us Library Micro [370]

Wilson, J *see*
- CHEERFUL AYRES OR BALLADS, FIRST COMPOSED FOR ONE SINGLE VOICE AND SINCE SET FOR THREE VOICES
- MEDICAL NOTES ON CHINA

Wilson, J B *see* HANDING OVER NOTES

Wilson, J E *see* AN ANALYSIS OF VISUAL REACTION TIME, DYNAMIC REACTION ACTIVITY, AND DEPTH PERCEPTION OF MALES WEARING COLOR EYE SHIELDS

Wilson, J T *see* CONTINENTAL DRIFT EMPHASIZING THE HISTORY OF THE SOUTH ATLANTIC AREA

Wilson, Jacob *see* PHRASIS

Wilson, James *see* THE WORKS OF JAMES WILSON, ASSOCIATE JUSTICE OF THE SUPREME COURT OF THE UNITED STATES.

Wilson, James Maurice *see*
- ESSAYS AND ADDRESSES:...SOME RELIGIOUS QUESTIONS IN A SCIENTIFIC SPIRIT
- THE GOSPEL OF THE ATONEMENT

Wilson, Janice *see* ADAPTIVE NATURE OF AGONISTIC BEHAVIOUR IN WINTER FLOCKS OF THE GREY-BREASTED SILVEREYE

Wilson, John *see*
- THE BRIGHTS OF SUFFOLK, ENGLAND
- LECTURES ON FOREIGN CHURCHES, SECOND SERIES
- THE PARSI RELIGION

Wilson, Joseph M *see* PRESBYTERIAN HISTORICAL ALMANAC..

Wilson, Kirk *see* LANGUAGE, READING AND DEAFNESS

Wilson, L M *see* THE MONTREAL EVENING JOURNAL

Wilson, Laurie J *see* COMMUNICATION TECHNOLOGY AND DEVELOPMENT

WILSON LIBRARY BULLETIN – v. 1-23. 1914-1949 – 1,5,6 – us Princeton Micro [020]

WILSON LIBRARY BULLETIN – (v. 43- 1968-5,6. v. 45- 1970- 9) – v. 1- 1914- – 1 – us UMI [020]

Wilson, P *see* GOVERNMENT AND POLITICS OF INDIA AND PAKISTAN: 1885-1955

Wilson Palmer, Beverly *see* THE THADDEUS STEVENS PAPERS

Wilson, Philip K *see*
- CORONARY HEART DISEASE RISK FACTORS IN CHILDREN AGES 9 TO 11 YEARS
- THE PHYSIOLOGICAL RESPONSES OF THE ADDITION OF HAND HELD WEIGHTS TO STATIONARY BICYCLING
- THE RELATIONSHIP BETWEEN HEART RATE AND RATE OF PERCEIVED EXERTION AMONG PHASE 2 CARDIAC REHABILITATION PATIENTS WITH VARIOUS MODES OF EXERCISE

WILSON QUARTERLY – (1982-. 1,5,6,9) – v1-. 1976- – 1 – us UMI [073]

Wilson, R T *see*
- LIVESTOCK PRODUCTION IN CENTRAL MALI
- SMALL RUMINANTS IN AFRICAN AGRICULTURE

Wilson, R T et al *see* RECHERCHES SUR LES SYSTEMES DES ZONES ARIDES DU MALI

Wilson, Robert D *see*
- STUDIES IN DANIEL
- STUDIES IN THE BOOK OF DANIEL

Wilson, Robert Thomas *see* AN ENQUIRY INTO THE PRESENT STATE OF THE MILITARY FORCE OF THE BRITISH EMPIRE, WITH A VIEW TO ITS REORGANIZATION

Wilson, Roland I *see* ORANGE-BELLIED PARROT RECOVERY PLAN

Wilson, Roland K et al *see* INDIVIDUALISM AND THE LAND QUESTION

Wilson, Samuel Graham *see* PERSIA

Wilson, Thomas *see* THE ARTE OF RHETORIQUE

Wilson, W *see* BRYOLOGIA BRITTANICA

Wilson, Warren H *see*
- THE CHURCH AT THE CENTER
- THE CHURCH OF THE OPEN COUNTRY

Wilson, William *see* THE POPULAR PREACHERS OF THE ANCIENT CHURCH

Wilson, William Dexter *see* THE FOUNDATIONS OF RELIGIOUS BELIEF...NATURAL THEOLOGY VINDICATED

Wilson, William H *see* LAND OWNERSHIP IN MICRONESIA

Wilson, Woodrow *see*
- CONSTITUTIONAL GOVERNMENT IN THE UNITED STATES
- PAPERS

WILSON'S EXPERIMENT – Belleville, C.W. [Ont]: J Wilson, [1847-18–?] – 9 – cn C.I.H.M. [971]

WILSON'S MONTHLY MERCURY – Saint John, N.B.: J.N. Wilson, [1874?-1875?] – 9 – cn C.I.H.M. [073]

WILSON'S SUPERIOR COURT REPORTS / Indiana. Superior Court – 1v. 1871-74 (all publ) – 7mf – 9 – $10.50 – LLMC 84-134 – us L.L.M.C. [340]

WILSONVILLE REVIEW – Wilsonville, NE. -w. Feb 1893-Feb 1894; Mar-Dec 1895; Feb 1896-Jul 1907; Nov 1907-Sept 1966 – 1 – us NE Hist [071]

WILSONVILLE TIMES – Wilsonville, OR. -w. 29 Mar 1972-30 May 1984 – 1r – 1 – us U.O. Library [071]

WILTFEBER, DER EWIGE DEUTSCHE; DIE GESCHICHTE EINES HEIMATSUCHERS / Struebe, Hermann – Leipzig: G.K. Sarasin, 1921, c1912. 352p – 1 – us U.W. Library [830]

Wilton, Adam's Run. South Carolina. Christ (Episcopal) Church *see* CASHBOOK

WILTON PARISH, 1726-1800 / Fairfield County. Connecticut – By Marian Olmstead, 1900. Historical sketch. 1 fiche. F-0080 – 9 – us A.G.L.L. [920]

WILTON SANKAWULO : TWO NOVELS AND A COLLECTION OF KPELLE TALES – 1r – $49.50 – us African Imprint [800]
WILTS AND GLOUCESTERSHIRE STANDARD – Malmesbury & Cirencester, England. 1837-1976.-w. 140mqn reels – 1 – uk British Libr Newspaper [072]
WILTS RECORD SOCIETY – (Coll title: Publications of the English Record Societies, 1835-1972...) – v1-3. 1896-1902 – 15mf – 9 – £130.00 – uk Chadwyck [941]
WILTSHIRE, 1822 : BRITISH ISLES CENSUS DIRECTORIES PROJECT, ENGLAND – (In prep) – at Vine [941]
WILTSHIRE, 1830 : BRITISH ISLES CENSUS DIRECTORIES PROJECT, ENGLAND – at Vine [941]
WILTSHIRE, 1844 : BRITISH ISLES CENSUS DIRECTORIES PROJECT, ENGLAND – (In prep) – at Vine [941]
WILTSHIRE, 1852 : BRITISH ISLES CENSUS DIRECTORIES PROJECT, ENGLAND. VOL 195 – 2mf – 9 – A$15.00 – at Vine [941]
WILTSHIRE, 1867 : BRITISH ISLES CENSUS DIRECTORIES PROJECT, ENGLAND. VOL 91 – 5mf – 9 – A$33.00 – at Vine [941]
WILTSHIRE, 1875 : BRITISH ISLES CENSUS DIRECTORIES PROJECT, ENGLAND. VOL 103 – 5mf – 9 – A$33.00 – at Vine [941]
WILTSHIRE, 1889 : BRITISH ISLES CENSUS DIRECTORIES PROJECT, ENGLAND. VOL 127 – 5mf – 9 – A$33.00 – at Vine [941]
WILTSHIRE, 1899 : BRITISH ISLES CENSUS DIRECTORIES PROJECT, ENGLAND – at Vine [941]
WILTSHIRE, 1911 : BRITISH ISLES CENSUS DIRECTORIES PROJECT, ENGLAND – at Vine [941]
WILTSHIRE, 1923 : BRITISH ISLES CENSUS DIRECTORIES PROJECT, ENGLAND – (In prep) – at Vine [941]
WILTSHIRE, 1929 : BRITISH ISLES CENSUS DIRECTORIES PROJECT, ENGLAND – (In prep) – at Vine [941]
WILTSHIRE, 1939 : BRITISH ISLES CENSUS DIRECTORIES PROJECT, ENGLAND – (In prep) – at Vine [941]
WILTSHIRE ARCHAEOLOGICAL AND NATURAL HISTORY SOCIETY – Records Branch. H 846 2. v1-17 1939-1961 – 8 – ne IDC [930]
WILTSHIRE (BRADFORD, DEVIZES, SALISBURY AND TROWBRIDGE), 1805 : BRITISH ISLES CENSUS DIRECTORIES PROJECT, ENGLAND. VOL 168 – 1mf – 9 – A$9.00 – at Vine [941]
WILTSHIRE GAZETTE *see* DEVIZES AND WILTSHIRE GAZETTE
WILTSHIRE GAZETTE AND HERALD – Swindon. England. -w. 1950-81. (73 reels) – 1 – uk British Libr Newspaper [072]
WILTSHIRE TIMES *see* TROWBRIDGE ADVERTISER
WILTSHIRE TIMES AND NEWS (WEST WILTS ED.) *see* TROWBRIDGE ADVERTISER
WILTSHIRE TIMES AND TROWBRIDGE ADVERTISER *see* TROWBRIDGE ADVERTISER
THE WIMA-EDGAR LETTERS: A SERIES OF OPEN LETTERS BETWEEN MR. J. D. EDGAR, M.P., TORONTO AND MR. ERASTUS WIMAN, NEW YORK / Edgar, James David – Unrestricted reciprocity as distinguished from commercial union. s.l.: s.n., 1887?. 02884. (Pre-1900 Canadiana) – 9 – cn C.I.H.M. [971]
Wiman, Erasus *see* CONJURATION WIMAN-LAURIER CONTRE LE CANADA: LE CANADA POUR LES ETATS-UNIS, COMPLOT DEMASQUE
Wimberley, Lowry Charles *see* DEATH AND BURIAL LORE IN THE ENGLISH AND SCOTTISH POPULAR BALLADS
WIMBLEDON BORO' NEWS – London, 1906-17 – 11r – 1 – uk British Libr Newspaper [072]
WIMBLEDON BORO' NEWS AND MERTON DISTRICT ADVERTISER *see* WIMBLEDON NEWS AND DISTRICT ADVERTISER
WIMBLEDON COURIER AND DISTRICT ADVERTISER – London, 20 Mar 1880-25 Mar 1882 – 2r – 1 – uk British Libr Newspaper [072]
WIMBLEDON NEWS AND DISTRICT ADVERTISER – London, Oct 1894-Dec 1905 – 11r – 1 – uk British Libr Newspaper [072]
Wimmer, Richard *see*
- DIE BIBLISCHEN WUNDERGESCHICHTEN
- GEWISSENSFRAGEN: RELIGIOESE BRIEFE AUS DER GEGENWART FUER DIE GEGENWART
- IM KAMPF UM DIE WELTANSCHAUUNG
- DER WEG ZUM FRIEDEN: EIN NACHTRAG ZU DEM BUCHE, IM KAMPF UM DIE WELTANSCHAUUNG

WIMMERA STAR – 1882-1913 – 14mf – 1 – at Corangamite [980]
WIMMERBY TIDNING – Vimmerby, Sweden. 1844. 1 reel; 1884-1925. 22 reels – 1 – sw Kungliga [072]
WIMMERBY WECKOTIDNING – Vimmerby, Sweden. 1856-84 – 9r – 1 – sw Kungliga [072]
WIMPEL DER KURENKAEHNE : GESCHICHTE, BEDEUTUNG, BRAUCHTUM / Woede, Hans – (Includes bibliographical references and index) – Wuerzburg: Holzner, 1965 – 10r – 1 – us U.W. Library [943]
WIN NEWS – Lexington. v1-17. 1975-91* 1; v18 1992*. v19 1993. v20 1994*. v21-23 1995-97+ 1,9; v18-20 1992-94*. v21-23 1995-97+ 5 – 1,5,9 – D19278 – us UMI [073]
Winar, David L *see* PODER POLITICO Y EDUCACION
Winarti, Partaningrat *see* REPORT OF VISITS PAID BY DR. WALTER T. LORCH TO LIBRAIRIES OF UNIVERSITIES AND SCIENTIFIC INSTITUTES IN DJAKARTA, BOGOR AND BANDUNG, DURING HIS STAY IN INDONESIA
Winborne, Benjamin B *see* THE COLONIAL AND STATE POLITICAL HISTORY OF HERTFORD COUNTY
Winchell, Alexander *see* RECONCILIATION OF SCIENCE AND RELIGION
Winchell, James M *see* AN ARRANGEMENT OF THE PSALMS AND SPIRITUAL SONGS OF THE REV. ISAAC WATTS, D.D
Winchell, Lilbourne Alsip *see* HISTORY OF FRESNO COUNTY AND THE SAN JOAQUIN VALLEY
WINCHELSEA STAR – 1977-1984. WIS1-7 – 7r – 1 – at Corangamite [072]
Winchelsey, Robert *see* REGISTER, 1294-1313
WINCHENDON 1763-1891 – 46mf – 9 – us Holbrook [920]
THE WINCHESTER BIBLE – With printed index and catalogue – 14 – £575.00 – uk World [240]
Winchester, C T *see* THE LIFE OF JOHN WESLEY
Winchester Cathedral *see* MANUSCRIPT COLLECTION
Winchester College. Warden and Fellows' Library *see*
- THE COLLECTION OF 17TH AND 18TH CENTURY MANUSCRIPTS
- MEDIAEVAL MANUSCRIPT COLLECTION

WINCHESTER FIRST BAPTIST CHURCH. WINCHESTER, TENNESSEE : CHURCH RECORDS – 1842-1937 – 1 – 27.99 – us Baptist [240]
WINCHESTER GAZETTE EXTRA – Swindon, England. Mar 1981- – 35+ r – 1 – uk British Libr Newspaper [072]
WINCHESTER RECORDER – Winchester, CA. 1892-1893 – 1r – 1 – $50.00 – R04142 – us Library Micro [071]
THE WINCHESTER TROPER, FROM MANUSCRIPTS OF THE 10TH AND 11TH CENTURIES... / ed by Frere, Walter H – London: Harrison & Sons, 1894 – 1 – us Sibley [780]
THE WINCHESTER TROPER, FROM MSS OF THE 10TH AND 11TH CENTURIES, WITH OTHER DOC. ILL. THE HISTORY OF TROPES IN ENGLAND AND FRANCE / Frere, Walter H – 1894 – 6mf – 8 – Dfl25.00 – ne Slangenburg [240]
Winckel, Christiaan Philip Karel *see* ESSAI SUR LES PRINCIPES REGISSANT L'ADMINISTRATION DE LA JUSTICE AUX INDES ORIENTALES HOLLANDAISES SURTOUT DANS LES ILES DE JAVA ET DE MADOURA ET LEUR APPLICATION
WINCKELMANN / Vallentin, Berthold – (Includes bibliographical references) – Berlin: G Bondi, 1931 – 1r – 1 – us U.W. Library [700]
Winckelmann, Johann Joachim *see*
- AUSGEWAEHLTE BRIEFE
- AUSGEWAEHLTE SCHRIFTEN UND BRIEFE
- SAEMTLICHE WERKE
- VERSUCH EINER ALLEGORIE, BESONDERS FUER DIE KUNST
- WINCKELMANNS BRIEFE AN SEINE ZUERICHER FREUNDE
- WINCKELMANNS KLEINE SCHRIFTEN ZUR GESCHICHTE DER KUNST DES ALTERTUMS
- WORKS. 1825... 1825-1829

Winckelmann, Otto *see* DER SCHMALKALDISCHE BUND, 1530-1532, UND DER NUERNBERGER RELIGIONSFRIEDE
WINCKELMANN UND HOMER : MIT BENUTZUNG DER HAMBURGER HOMER-AUSSCHREIBUNGEN WINCKELMANNS / Kraus, Konrad – (Includes bibliographical references) – Berlin: Junker und Duennhaupt, 1935 – 1r – 1 – us U.W. Library [430]
WINCKELMANNS BRIEFE AN SEINE ZUERICHER FREUNDE : NACH DEN AUF DER ZUERICHER STADTBIBLIOTHEK AUFBEWAHRTEN ORIGINALEN IN VERMEHRTER UND VERBESSERTER GESTALT / Winckelmann, Johann Joachim; ed by Bluemner, Hugo – (Includes bibliographical references) – Freiburg i.B: J C B Mohr, 1882 – 1r – 1 – us U.W. Library [920]
WINCKELMANNS KLEINE SCHRIFTEN ZUR GESCHICHTE DER KUNST DES ALTERTUMS : MIT GOETHES SCHILDERUNG WINCKELMANNS / Winckelmann, Johann Joachim; ed by Uhde-Bernays, Hermann – Leipzig: Insel-Verlag, 1913 – 1 – us U.W. Library [720]
Winckler, Hugo *see*
- ALTBABYLONISCHE KEILSCHRIFTTEXTE
- KEILINSCHRIFTLICHES TEXTBUCH ZUM ALTEN TESTAMENT
- LISTE AUSGEWAEHLTER KEILSCHRIFTZEICHEN
- THE TELL-EL-AMARNA-LETTERS

Winckler, Josef *see*
- DER ALTE FRITZ
- DES VERWEGENEN CHIRURGUS WELTBERUEHMBT WUNDER-DOKTOR JOHANN ANDREAS EISENBART
- EISERNE SONETTE
- IRRGARTEN GOTTES
- MITTEN IM WELTKRIEG
- DER TOLLE BOMBERG
- DES VERWEGENEN CHIRURGUS WELTBERUEHMBT WUNDER-DOKTOR JOHANN ANDREAS EISENBART
- DIE WEINHEILIGEN

WINDAUSCHE ZEITUNG – Windau, Latvija (Ventspils, U.S.S.R.). 28 Oct 1924-22 Mar 1930. Incompl – 1 – gw Mikrofilm [943]
Windecker, W C *see* TREFFPUNKT WIESBADEN
Windegg, Eggert *see* MOERIKE-ALBUM
Windel, H *see* PRINZ FRIEDRICH VON HOMBURG
Windelband, Wilhelm *see* DIE PHILOSOPHIE IM DEUTSCHEN GEISTESLEBEN DES 19 JAHRHUNDERTS
Windelband-Heimsoeth *see* LEHRBUCH DER GESCHICHTE DER PHILOSOPHIE
Windham.Connecticut *see* HISTORY OF ANCIENT WINDHAM, CONNECTICUT
THE WINDHOEK ADVERTISER – Windhoek, Southwest Africa: J Meinert, feb 25 1922-1945. [1945-61] – us Res Libr [072]
WINDHOEK ADVERTISER – Windhoek, South West Africa. 1919-45 – 1 – sa State Libr [072]
WINDHOEK ADVERTISER – Windhoek, South West Africa. 29 Dec 1945-29 Dec 1961 end – 19 rolls – 1 – sa Microfile [960]
Windle, Henry E *see* LECTURES ON THE EPISTLES TO THE SEVEN CHURCHES OF ASIA
A WINDOW IN THRUMS / Barrie, James Matthew – London: Hodder and Stoughton, 1889 – 1 roll – 1 – 1-55879-464-6 – uk Libr Preservation [830]
WINDOWS ON CREATIVITY AND INVENTION / ed by Richardson, Jacques – 1988. 338p. ISBN: 0-912338-58-X – 9 – 15.75 – us Lomond [500]
WINDSOR 1778-1908 – (Mf 1-2: Vital Records to 1850. Mf 3: Births 1844-86. Mf 4: Marriages 1845-67. Mf 4: Deaths 1844-83. Mf 5: Marriage Intentions 1846-1920. Mf 6: Marriage Intentions 1920-86. Mf 7: Births 1886-1908. Mf 7: Marriages 1867-1909. Mf 8: Deaths 1883-1908) – (mf ed 1987) – 8mf – 0-87623-065-6 – us Holbrook [920]
WINDSOR AND ETON EXPRESS – England, Aug 1812-1928; 1832-38; 1840-1987; 1992- – 213+ r – 1 – uk British Libr Newspaper [072]
WINDSOR CASTLE : AN HISTORICAL ROMANCE / Ainsworth, William Harrison – London: Henry Colburn, 1843 – 2 rolls – 1 – 1-55879-106-X – uk Libr Preservation [830]
Windsor Castle. Royal Archives *see*
- CUMBERLAND MAPS
- CUMBERLAND MAPS: CATALOGUE AND INDEX
- CUMBERLAND PAPERS
- CUMBERLAND PAPERS, INDEX
- HISTORY AND ANTIQUITIES OF THE BOROUGH OF NEW WINDSOR
- STUART PAPERS
- VICTORIAN PHOTOGRAPHIC COLLECTION

Windsor Castle. Royal Library *see* THE ETCHINGS OF HOLLAR IN THE ROYAL LIBRARY
WINDSOR EVENING RECORD – Ontario, CN. 1893-1917 – 84r – 1 – cn Commonwealth Micro [072]
WINDSOR EXPRESS AND RICHMOND ADVERTISER – May 17 1843-May 9 1844 – 9 – at Pascoe [072]
WINDSOR GAZETTE – Windsor, VT. 3 mar 1801-v1 n52. 23 feb 1802 – 1r – 1 – Can$55.00 – cn Can Microfilming [071]
WINDSOR HERALD – Windsor, Canada. 1855-56 – 1 reel – 1 – $68.00 – cn Library Assoc [971]
WINDSOR HERALD *see* BERKSHIRE CHRONICLE, WINDSOR HERALD
WINDSOR REVIEW – (Cont: University of Windsor Review at v26 1993) – v26- 1993- – 9 – Can$20.00y – cn Micromedia [370]
WINDSOR REVIEW *see* UNIVERSITY OF WINDSOR REVIEW
THE WINDSOR STAR – Windsor, Ontario, CN. 1893- – 24r per yr – 1 – Can$53.00r – cn Commonwealth Micro [072]
WINDSOR YEARBOOK OF ACCESS TO JUSTICE – v1-14. 1981-94 – 9 – $177.00 set – us Hein [340]
Windsor.Connecticut *see* HISTORY OF ANCIENT WINDSOR, CONNECTICUT
WINDSPEAKER – (v1-7 1983/84-1989/90 Can$115.00y. v1-3 publ under the title AMMSA) – Edmonton. v1-13. 1983/84-1995/96 – 1 – Can$85.00y – cn Micromedia [073]
WINDY CITY TIMES – Chicago: Sentury Publications, v1, no1-, Sept 26, 1985- – 1 – Can$170.00y – cn McLaren [302]
WINE AND AGRICULTURAL COLLECTION *see* WOMEN ON THE LAND; THE WOMEN'S LAND ARMY
WINE AND AGRICULTURE COLLECTION *see*
- CALIFORNIA FARM OBSERVER
- CALIFORNIA FARMER
- THE FARM TRIBUNE
- IRRIGATION BULLETIN
- THE IRRIGATION BULLETIN
- PACIFIC RURAL PRESS
- POMOTROPICS
- REDLANDS CITROGRAPH
- RURAL REVIEW
- THE WEEKLY AGRICOLE

Wineklmann, E A *see* BIBLIOTHECA LIVONIAE HISTORICA: SYSTEMATISCHES VERZEICHNIS DER QUELLEN UND HILFSMITTEL ZUR GESCHICHTE ESTLANDS, LIVLANDS UND KURLANDS
Winer, Georg Benedikt *see* A GRAMMAR OF THE IDIOM OF THE NEW TESTAMENT, PREPARED AS A SOLID BASIS FOR THE INTERPRETATION OF THE NEW TESTAMENT
Wines, Francis *see* LEDGER
Winey *see* SNYDER COUNTY ANNALS
Winfield, Charles B *see* HISTORY OF THE COUNTY OF HUDSON
Wing, J van *see* RELIGION ET MAGIE
Wing, Kittridge A *see* BANDELIER NATIONAL MONUMENT, NEW MEXICO
Wing, R P van *see* ETUDES BAKONGO
Wing, Talcott E *see* HISTORY OF MONROE COUNTY
Wingate, Allison M *see* AN INVESTIGATION INTO THE STATE OF CRISIS MANAGEMENT PLANS AT NATIONAL COLLEGIATE ATHLETIC ASSOCIATION DIVISION 1-A ATHLETIC DEPARTMENTS
Wingate, Ashmore Kyle Paterson *see* LIFE OF JOHN RUSKIN
Wingate, Catherine F *see* EXPLORING THE KARATE WAY OF LIFE
THE WINGATE TEST : THE EFFECT OF LOAD ON THE POWER OUTPUTS OF COLLEGE-AGE FEMALE ATHLETES AND NONATHLETES / Bradley, A L – 1991 – 1mf – 9 – $4.00 – us Microform Publ [613]
WINGED BEAN PRODUCTION IN THE TROPICS – 1982 – 223p – it F.A.O. [338]
Wingfield, Marshall *see* HISTORY OF CAROLINE COUNTY
WINGHAM ADVANCE-TIMES – Ontario Prov., Canada. 1885-1967. Title varies – 1 – cn Commonwealth Micro [072]
WINGHAM CHRONICLE – Jan 1 1898-Dec 28 1907 – 9 – at Pascoe [072]

WINGOLF : KRITISCHE AUSGABE NEBST COMMENTAR / Klopstock, Friedrich Gottlieb – (Includes bibliographical references) – Wien: C Gerold, 1882 – 1r – 1 – us U.W. Library [430]

Wininger, S *see* GROSSE JUEDISCHE NATIONAL-BIOGRAPHIE

Winkelmann, F *see*
- ALBERT EHRHARD UND DIE ERFORSCHUNG DER GRIECHISCH-BYZANTINISCHEN HAGIOGRAPHIE (T.U.U. 5-111)
- DIE TEXTBEZEUGUNG DER VITA CONSTANTINI DES EUSEBIUS VON CAESAREA (T.U.U. 5-84)

Winkler A *see* TAGEBUECHER VON FRIEDRICH VON GENTZ (1829-1831)

Winkler, E T *see* BOOKS OF SERMONS

Winkler, Eugen Gottlob *see*
- DICHTERISCHE ARBEITEN
- GESTALTEN UND PROBLEME

Winkler, Joerg *see*
- MESSUNG VON MUSKELANTWORTEN AUF UNTERSCHIEDLICHE MODULATIONSFORMEN BEI FUNKTIONELLER NEUROMUSKULAERER STIMULATION AN GESUNDEN UND QUERSCHNITTGELAEHMTEN
- RUECKENSCHULE FUER ANGEHOERIGE IM PFLEGEDIENST

Winklhofer, Alois *see* HOELDERLIN UND CHRISTUS

Winks, Joseph F *see* THE BAPTIST JUBILEE MEMORIAL

Winkworth, Catherine *see*
- CHRISTIAN SINGERS OF GERMANY
- LYRA GERMANICA. SECOND SERIES, THE CHRISTIAN LIFE

Winlock, H E *see*
- MATERIALS USED AT THE EMBALMING OF KING TUT-ANKH-AMUN
- THE MONASTERY OF EPIPHANIUS AT THEBES
- THE TREASURE OF THREE EGYPTIAN PRINCESSES

WINNEBAGO CHIEFTAIN – Winnebago, NE. -w. Aug 1909-Sept 1914; May-Oct 1919, scattered issues missing; Jul 1921-Nov 1926; Aug 1929-Aug 1932 – 1 – us NE Hist [071]

Winnebago. Presbytery (Presbyterian Church in the USA) *see* MINUTES, 1851-1892

WINNEBAGO RECORDER – Winnebago, NE. -w. Oct 1940-Jan 1946 – 1 – us NE Hist [071]

WINNEMUCCA ARGENT – Winnemucca, NV. 24 Sep 1968 – 1r – 1 – $50.00 – U04811 – us Library Micro [071]

WINNEMUCCA REPUBLICAN *see* SILVER STATE

Winner, Septimus *see*
- WINNER'S BAND OF FOUR; BEING A CHOICE SELECTION OF POPULAR MELODIES, ARRANGED AS EASY QUARTETS FOR VIOLIN OR FLUTE, CORNET OR CLARIONET, 2ND VIOLIN AND VIOLONCELLO.
- WINNER'S EASY SYSTEM, FOR THE FLUTE
- WINNER'S MUSIC OF THE TIME

WINNER'S BAND OF FOUR; BEING A CHOICE SELECTION OF POPULAR MELODIES, ARRANGED AS EASY QUARTETS FOR VIOLIN OR FLUTE, CORNET OR CLARIONET, 2ND VIOLIN AND VIOLONCELLO. / Winner, Septimus – Boston: Oliver Ditson & Co., 1873. MUSIC 1987, Item 3 – 1 – us L of C Photodup [780]

WINNER'S EASY SYSTEM, FOR THE FLUTE / Winner, Septimus – Philadelphia: Sep. Winner & Co., 1866. Includes: "America," "Hail Columbia," "Johnny Smoker," "Santa Lucea " "Star Spangled Banner," "Wearing of the Green," and "Yankee Doodle." MUSIC 1987, Item 2 – 1 – us L of C Photodup [780]

WINNER'S MUSIC OF THE TIME / Winner, Septimus – Containing the most popular polkas, waltzes, cotillions, quadrilles, schottisches, etc., also, a large collection of ballad airs, opera melodies, fancy dances, marches, reels, jigs, etc., arranged in any easy manner as solos, duetts, trios & quartettes. New York: Firth, Pond & Co., 1857. Includes: "Hail Columbia," "Nelly Bly," "Star-Spangled Banner," and "Yankee Doodle." MUSIC 1987, Item 1 – 1 – us L of C Photodup [780]

WINNERS OF THE WEST – St. Joseph. MO.1923-44 – 1 – us UMI [071]

WINNI MINI MART – Winnemucca, NV. 1977; 1978 – 1r – 1 – $50.00 – U04904 – us Library Micro [071]

Winnig, August *see*
- DAS BUCH WANDERSCHAFT
- FRUEHROT
- DIE HAND GOTTES
- DER WEITE WEG

WINNING A PRIMITIVE PEOPLE : SIXTEEN YEARS' WORK AMONG THE WARLIKE TRIBE OF THE NGONI AND SENGA AND TUMBUKA PEOPLES OF CENTRAL AFRICA / Fraser, Donald – London: Seeley, Service,1914 – 1mf – us A.T.L.A. [240]

THE WINNING OF THE SUDAN / Crabites, Pierre – London: G Routledge, 1934 – us Res Libr [960]

'WINNING THROUGH' / Reddin, D Thomas – Typewritten manuscript of his autobiography written 1936/37 – 1r – 1 – at Pacific Mss [240]

Winnington Ingram, Arthur F *see*
- NEW TESTAMENT DIFFICULTIES. FIRST SERIES:...FOR WORKING MEN
- OLD TESTAMENT DIFFICULTIES:...PAPERS WRITTEN FOR WORKING MEN

WINNIPEG DAILY TIMES – Winnipeg, Canada. 1879-85 – 16r – 1 – $1,040.00 – cn Library Assoc [971]

WINNIPEG EVENING TRIBUNE – Canada, Oct 1920-Jun 1922 – 20 1/2r – 1 – uk British Libr Newspaper [072]

WINNIPEG FREE PRESS – Winnipeg, Manitoba, CN. 1874- – 36r per yr – 1 – Can$53.00r – cn Commonwealth Micro [072]

WINNIPEG GENERAL STRIKE CLIPPINGS / Canada. Department of Labour – 1 – cn Micromedia [331]

WINNIPEG ILLUSTRATED – Winnipeg: G Bishop, [18– 18- or 19–] – 9 – cn C.I.H.M. [910]

THE WINNIPEG REAL ESTATE REGISTER – Winnipeg: S.A. Rowbotham, [1885?-18– or 19–] – 9 – cn C.I.H.M. [333]

WINNIPEG SUN – Winnipeg, Manitoba, CN. 1980- – 24r per yr – 1 – Can$55.00r – cn Commonwealth Micro [072]

WINNIPEG TELEGRAM *see* MORNING TELEGRAM

THE WINNIPEG TRIBUNE – Winnipeg: Tribune Newspaper Co, jul 1938-44 – 77r – 1 – us Res Libr [072]

WINNIPEG TRIBUNE – Winnipeg, Manitoba, CN. 1890-1980 – 1226r – 1 – cn Commonwealth Micro [072]

WINONA / Bunnell, Lafayette H – And its environs on the Mississippi in ancient and modern days. Winona: Jones and Kroeger, 1897. Minnesota Reel 17. (The Cox Library Collection) – 5 – us Americana [978]

WINSFORD CHRONICLE – England, 27 Jun 1942-1980; 1987- – 110+ r – 1 – uk British Libr Newspaper [072]

WINSFORD GUARDIAN – Cheshire. 1967 to date – 1 – uk Microform Academic [072]

WINSFORD MIDDLEWICH GUARDIAN – Northwich, England. 1876-1926; 1986- – 115+ r – uk British Libr Newspaper [072]

WINSIDE TRIBUNE – Winside, NE. -w. Jan 1892; Oct 1895-Jan 1896; Mar 1896-Dec 1900; Apr 1901-Sept 1902; Mar 1908-Jul 1952; Jan 1954-Dec 1956 – 1 – us NE Hist [071]

Winskill, Peter T *see* TEMPERANCE STANDARD BEARERS OF THE NINETEENTH CENTURY: A BIOGRAPHICAL AND STATISTICAL TEMPERANCE DICTIONARY

Winslow, Hubbard *see* MORAL PHILOSOPHY

Winslow, Jan D *see* MEDIA COVERAGE OF WOMEN'S NCAA VARSITY SPORTS AS A FUNCTION OF THE STRUCTURE OF THE SPORTS INFORMATION OFFICE

Winslow, Octavius *see*
- THE GLORY OF THE REDEEMER IN HIS PERSON AND WORK
- PATRIARCHAL SHADOWS OF CHRIST AND HIS CHURCH...JOSEPH AND HIS BRETHREN

THE WINSLOW PAPERS – Private Collection of the American Revolutionary Period. 15 reels with printed guide – £650.00 – uk World [975]

Winsor, Justin *see* NARRATIVE AND CRITICAL HISTORY OF AMERICA

Winstanley, William *see*
- THE LIVES OF THE MOST FAMOUS ENGLISH POETS
- A VISIT TO ABYSSINIA; AN ACCOUNT OF TRAVEL IN MODERN ETHIOPIA

[WINSTON CHURCHILL PAMPHLET COLLECTION] – 19??-1965 – 1 reel – 1 – CSUXANP3025-B – us Hoover Inst Photo [320]

WINSTON COUNTY JOURNAL – Louisville. Miss. 1902-1903; 1915-1953 – 1 – us UMI [071]

Winston, William J *see*
- HEALTH MARKETING QUARTERLY
- JOURNAL OF CUSTOMER SERVICE IN MARKETING AND MANAGEMENT
- JOURNAL OF HOSPITAL MARKETING
- JOURNAL OF PROFESSIONAL SERVICES MARKETING

WINSTON-SALEM EVENING STAR – Winston-Salem. N.C. 1926-1927 – 1 – 50.00y – us UMI [071]

WINSTON-SALEM JOURNAL – Winston-Salem, NC. 1898- – 1 – us UMI [071]

WINSTON-SALEM WEEKLY SENTINEL – Winston-Salem, NC. 1897-1904 – 1 – us UMI [071]

WINSTON-SALEM WESTERN SENTINEL – Winston-Salem, NC. 1903-26 – 1 – us UMI [071]

Winter, Friedrich Gotthard *see* GOETHE'S DEUTSCHE GESINNUNG

Winter, Friedrich Julius *see* JOHANN ARNDT, DER VERFASSER DES "WAHREN CHRISTENTUMS"

Winter, J M *see* FIRST WORLD WAR: A DOCUMENTARY RECORD

Winter, Julius *see* DIE ETHIK DES CLEMENS VON ALEXANDRIEN

Winter, Nevin O *see* A HISTORY OF NORTHWEST OHIO

WINTER PARK BAPTIST CHURCH. WILMINGTON, NORTH CAROLINA : CHURCH RECORDS – Jun 1917-62. Newsletters. 1955-65. Bulletins. 1940-66 – 1 – 238.40 – us Baptist [240]

Winter, Peter van *see*
- ONDER KRUGERS' HOLLANDERS GESCHIEDENIS VAN DE NEDERLANDSCHE ZUID-AFRIKAANSCHE SPOORWEG-MAATSCHAPPIJ
- SEPTUOR POUR 2 CORS, ALRINETTE IN B, 2 VIOLONS, ALTO, ET BASSE, OP. 10
- STABAT MATER

Winter, Peter von *see* OTTETTO POUR VIOLON, VIOLA, VIOLONCELLE, FLUTE, CLARINETTE, BASSON ET DEUX CORS

Winter, Wilma G *see* PERCEPTIONS OF LEISURE, RELIGION AND WELL-BEING OF SELECTED WORKING AND NON-WORKING WOMEN AGED 25-45

Winter, Zikmund *see*
- MISTR KAMPANUS: HISTORICKY OBRAZ Z DOBY BELOHORSKE
- ZIVOT CIRKEVNI V CECHACH

Winterberg, Constantin *see* FRA LUCA PACIOLI DIVINA PROPORTIONE (DIE LEHRE VON GOLDENEN SCHMITT)

Winterbotham, W *see* AN HISTORICAL, GEOGRAPHICAL, AND PHILOSOPHICAL VIEW OF THE CHINESE EMPIRE;...

Winterbottom, T *see* AN ACCOUNT OF THE NATIVE AFRICANS IN THE NEIGHBOURHOOD OF SIERRA LEONE

WINTERBRAUTNACHT / Hohlbaum, Robert – Karlsbad: A Kraft, 1944 – 1r – 1 – us U.W. Library [830]

Winterfeld, Adolf Wilhelm Ernst von *see* DIE MEMOIREN DER FRAU V. KRILWITZ

Winterfeld, Ernst von *see* COMMENTAR UEBER DAS BUCH IOB ERSTER TEIL, UEBERSETZUNG UND SPRACHLICHE ANALYSE

Winterfeldt, Hans Karl von *see* PAPERS

EIN WINTER-IDYLL / Stieler, Karl – 32. Aufl. Stuttgart: Adolf Bonz, 1902 – 1r – 1 – us U.W. Library [810]

DAS WINTERLAGER / Alverdes, Paul – Muenchen: A Langen/G Mueller, 1935 – 1r – 1 – us U.W. Library [430]

THE WINTERS EXPRESS – Winters, CA. 1887- – 54+ r – 1 BC03108 – $2,700.00 ($50.00y) – us Library Micro [071]

Winters, W *see* AN ACCOUNT OF THE REMARKABLE MUSICAL TALENTS OF SEVERAL MEMBERS OF THE WESLEY FAMILY

WINTER'S WREATH – 1828-32 – 25mf – 9 – £210.00 – uk Chadwyck [800]

WINTERSAAT : LETZTE GEDICHTE / Mueller-Jahnke, Clara – Goslar: F A Lattmann, 1907 – 1r – 1 – us U.W. Library [810]

Winterscheidt, Heinrich *see* BEITRAEGE ZUR GESCHICHTE UND ZUM VERSTAENDNIS DES MASSBEGRIFFS

Winterswyl, L A *see* DIE GEMEINDEGESAENGE DER HEILIGEN MESSE

WINTERTHUR – (v16- 1981- 5,6,9) – v1-1964- – 1 – us UMI [700]

Winterthur Museum *see* TRADE CATALOGUES

Winterton, Paul *see* REPORT ON RUSSIA

WINTERTON REMEMBERED : THE RESTAGING OF FOUR DANCES BY DEE WINTERTON / Goodwin, Nolan W – Brigham Young University, 1994 – 1mf – 9 – $4.00 – PE3592 – us Microform Publ [790]

THE WINTHROP FLEET OF 1630 / Banks, Charles Edward – The vessels, the voyage, passengers & their English homes. From original authorities. Item P.119p. Indexed, SW16-0076 – 5 – us A.G.L.L. [920]

Winthrop, John *see* RELATION OF A VOYAGE FROM BOSTON TO NEWFOUNDLAND, FOR THE OBSERVATION OF THE TRANSIT OF VENUS, 6 JUN 1761

WINTHROP PAPERS, 1537-1905 – Massachusetts Historical Society – 53r – 1 – $4085.00 – us UMI [920]

WINTHROP SARGENT PAPERS, 1771-1948 / Sargent, Winthrop – Massachusetts Historical Society – 7r – 1 – $540.00 – us UMI [920]

Winthrop, W *see* AN ABRIDGEMENT OF MILITARY LAW

"WINTHROP'S DIGESTS" / U.S. Army. Judge Advocate General – Digest of opinions of the Judge Advocate General of the Army by William Winthrop. 1v.viii,136p. Washington: GPO, 1865; 3rd ed. xvi, 393p. Washington: GPO, 1868; another ed., "not properly a new ed.", xv,606p. Washington: GPO, 1880; another ed., "not properly a new ed.", 868p. Washington: GPO, 1895.84-228 – 9 – us L.L.M.C. [340]

Winton, George B *see*
- MEXICO TO-DAY
- A NEW ERA IN OLD MEXICO

Winton Jacob, S *see* JAIPUR PORTFOLIO OF ARCHITECTURAL DETAILS

WINTON TIMES – Winton, CA. 1979- – 10+ r – 1 – $500.00 ($90.00y) – B03109 – us Library Micro [071]

Wintzingeroda-Knorr, Levin Freiherr von *see* DIE KAEMPFE UND LEIDEN DER EVANGELISCHEN AUF DEM EICHSFELDE WAEHREND DREIER JAHRHUNDERTE

Winyaw. South Carolina. Prince Frederick Episcopal Church *see* RECORDS

Winyaw. South Carolina. Prince George Episcopal Church *see* REGISTER

WIPONIS OPERA (MGH 7: 61.BD) : ACCEDUNT EXCERPTA EX ANNAL. SANGALENS MAIOR., HERIMANNO AUGIENSI, CHRON. SUEV. UNIVERSALI ET DUO CARMINA – 1915 – Dfl9.00 – ne Slangenburg [240]

Wipper, Paul *see* MIT LEIB UND LEBEN

WIR ABER SIND DAS KORN : GEDICHTE / Schumann, Gerhard – Muenchen: A Langen/ G Mueller, 1943, c1936 – 1r – 1 – us U.W. Library [810]

WIR BRAUCHEN EINE NEUE AUSSENPOLITIK / Ollenhauer, Erich – Sozialdemokratische Vorschlage zur Wiedervereinigung Deutschlands. Bonn 1956 – 1 – DM30.00 – gw Mikro Press [943]

WIR IM FERNEN VATERLAND GEBOREN...DIE CENTURIA THAELMANN / Mohr, E – Paris, 1938. Fiche W 1053. (Blodgett Collection of Spanish Civil War Pamphlets) – 9 – us H.U. College Libr [946]

WIR KAEMPFEN UND SIEGEN FUER DICH FREIHEIT / Gruenberg, Gottfried – Berlin, 1956. Fiche W931. (Blodgett Collection of Spanish Civil War Pamphlets) – 9 – us H.U. College Libr [946]

WIR KATHOLIKEN UND DIE DEUTSCHE LITERATUR / Falkenberg, Heinrich – (Includes bibliographical references and index) – Bonn: C Georgi, 1909 – 1r – 1 – us U.W. Library [430]

WIR MENSCHEN DER INDONESISCHEN ERDE / Brandstetter, R – v. 1-11. SE-446 1. 1921-1937 – 9 – ne IDC [073]

WIR SIND / Werfel, Franz – Leipzig: K Wolff, c1914 – 1r – 1 – us U.W. Library [810]

WIR SIND UTOPIA : NOVELLE / Andres, Stefan Paul – Berlin: U Riemerschmidt, 1943 – 1r – 1 – us U.W. Library [830]

WIR TRAGEN DAS LEBEN / Goote, Thor – Berlin: W Kolk, 1932 – 1r – 1 – us U.W. Library [830]

WIR WACHSEN IN DAS REICH HINEIN / Anacker, Heinrich – Muenchen: F Eher Nachf., 1938 – 1r – 1 – us U.W. Library [943]

Wiramihardja, J *see* BUKU PELADJARAN SEDJARAH DUNIA UNTUK S.M.P. TJORAK BARU

Wirapustaka, N *see* TATATJARA. ANGGITANIPOEN KJAI TOEWIN NJAI PADMASOESASTRA; DIPOEN BIJANTOE DATENG BAGOES NGARPAH

WIRELESS WORLD – v. 7-64. 1919-1958 – 1,5,6 – us Princeton Micro [621]
Wirgman, A Theodore *see*
- THE CONSTITUTIONAL AUTHORITY OF BISHOPS IN THE CATHOLIC CHURCH
- FOREIGN PROTESTANTISM WITHIN THE CHURCH OF ENGLAND
- THE HISTORY OF THE ENGLISH CHURCH AND PEOPLE IN SOUTH AFRICA

WIRIT BUDI PEKERTI (IRAMA KEBATHINAN) / Prabhajasa, S – SE-5594 1. 1962 – 9 – ne IDC [950]
Wirjono, Prodjodikoro *see*
- ASAS-ASAS HUKUM PERDATA INTERNASIONAL
- HUKUM ATJARA PIDANA DI INDONESIA
- HUKUM LAUT BAGI INDONESIA
- HUKUM PERDATA TENTANG PERSETUDJUAN2 TERTENTU

WIRKENDES WORT – Duesseldorf. v1-12. 1950-62. H-366/2 – 8 – ne IDC [400]
DIE WIRKSAMKEIT WALTER KRUSES ALS DIREKTOR DES HYGIENINSTITUTES AN DER LEIPZIGER UNIVERSITAET VON 1913-1933/34 / Baumann, Simone – Leipzig, (ca.1980) – 1mf – DM48.00 – 3-8267-2005-9 – gw Hänsel [610]
DIE WIRKUNG DER AUFHEBUNG DER GOLDKLAUSELN / Behrend, C – Leipzig, 1936 – 1mf – 9 – ILM-3344/1 – ne IDC [327]
DIE WIRKUNG VON DEHYDRATION UND REHYDRATION AUF DIE HERZFUNKTION GESUNDER PROBANDEN / Rothfuss, Joerg – 1994 – 1mf – DM60.00 – 3-8267-2060-1 – gw Hänsel [611]
DIE WIRKUNGEN DES GEISTES UND DIE GEISTER IM NACHAPOSTOLISCHEN ZEITALTER BIS AUF IRENAEUS / Weinel, Heinrich – Freiburg i.B.: J.C.B. Mohr, 1899 – 1mf – us A.T.L.A. [240]
DIE WIRKUNGEN DES HEILIGEN GEISTES / Gunkel, Hermann – Goettingen: Vandenhoeck & Rup., 1899. 1 fiche – 9 – us A.T.L.A. [240]
WIRKUNGEN GOETHES IN DER GEGENWART / Carossa, Hans – Leipzig: Inselverlag, 1938 – 1r – 1 – us U.W. Library [430]
WIRKUNGS- UND ERINNERUNGSSTAETTEN DES DICHTERS HOFFMANN VON FALLERSLEBEN IN WORT UND BILD / ed by Andree, Fritz – (Includes bibliographical references) – Fallersleben: Druck, Just & Seiffert, 1960 – 1r – 1 – us U.W. Library [920]
WIRKUNGSKREIS DES STRAFGESETZES, ... / Berner, A F – Berlin, 1853 – 3mf – 9 – ILM-2421/1 – ne IDC [327]
WIRRWARR : A SCHWAEAEBISCHS ZEIDSCHBIAGALE, GSCHRIIBA WIAMR SCHWAEZZD / Anton, Ludwig – Esslingen am Neckar: E Koenig, [19–?] – 1r – 1 – us U.W. Library [430]
Wirt *see* REGISTER OF OHIO SOCIETY OF SONS OF THE AMERICAN REVOLUTION 1917-18-19-20-21
WIRT COUNTY JOURNAL – Elizabeth. West Virginia. -w. 1936-68 – 1 – us UMI [071]
Wirt, William *see* THE WILLIAM WIRT PAPERS
Wirth, Johann *see* MOSCHEROSCHS GESICHTE PHILANDERS VON SITTEWALT
DIE WIRTSCHAFT – 1976-1983 – 205mf – 1 – DM1,168.50 – gw Mikro Press [335]
DIE WIRTSCHAFT – Berlin, 1953-mar 10 1983 – 34r – 1 – Inquire at Mikrofilmarchiv for details – gw Misc Inst [330]
DIE WIRTSCHAFT – Berlin, DE. 1953-Mar 1983 – 34r – 1 – gw Mikrofilm [072]
DIE WIRTSCHAFT – v1-. Apr 1946-. illus. ports., maps. Frequency varies – 1 – us U.W. Library [073]
WIRTSCHAFT UND STATISTIK – Berlin, 1930-44 (incomplete) – 1 – Inquire at Mikrofilmarchiv for details – gw Misc Inst [310]
WIRTSCHAFT UND VERKEHR – Duesseldorf. Jahrg. 1-15, nr. 6; Jan. 1923-Mar. 1937. "Mitteilungen der Industrie- und Handelskammer zu Duesseldorf." Incomplete: v. 1, no. 3, 5 wanting. Film Mas C 744 – 1 – us H.U. Library [073]
WIRTSCHAFTBLATT / Berliner Industrie Und Handeskammer – Berlin. jahrg.37. May 1903-Jun. 1939. Incomplete – 1 – us NY Public [330]
DER WIRTSCHAFTLICHE KAMPF DER DEUTSCHEN UM DIE PROVINZ POSEN / Wegener, Leo – Posen 1903 – 1 – DM30.00 – gw Mikro Press [943]
WIRTSCHAFTLICHE SELBSTVERWALTUNG – Berlin, 1923-24 – 1 – Inquire at Mikrofilmarchiv for details – gw Misc Inst [072]
WIRTSCHAFTLICHE SELBSTVERWALTUNG – Berlin, Germany.1923-24 – 1 – gw Mikrofilm [072]
DIE WIRTSCHAFTLICHEN VERTRAEGE DEUTSCHLANDS / Boschinger, H von – Berlin, 1892 – 3mf – 9 – ILM-2373/1 – ne IDC [327]
DIE WIRTSCHAFTLICHKEIT DER INFORMATIONSVERARBEITUNG UNTER BESONDERER BERUECKSICHTIGUNG DES TRANSAKTIONSKOSTENANSATZES / Unser, Matthias – 1995 – 2mf – 9 – DM80.00 – 3-8267-2089-X – gw Hänsel [650]
DIE WIRTSCHAFTLICHKEIT VON ERSATZINVESTITIONEN. INVESTITIONSRECHNUNG IN DER BETRIEBSWIRTSCHAFTLICHEN PRAXIS / Goeßl, Manfred M – 1995 – 3mf – 9 – DM98.00 – 3-8267-2113-6 – gw Hänsel [332]
WIRTSCHAFTS- UND SOZIALGEOGRAPHISCHE UNTERSUCHUNGEN IN SAN CARLOS (NICARAGUA) UNTER BESONDERER BERUECKSICHTIGUNG DES INFORMELLEN SEKTORS / Bartsch, Gerhard N – 1994 – 2mf – 9 – DM80.00 – 3-89349-865-6 – gw Hänsel [550]
DIE WIRTSCHAFTSDEMOKRATIE IM SINNE DER FREIEN GEWERKSCHAFTEN / Hammon, Ulrich – 1995 – 1mf – 9 – DM48.00 – 3-8267-3163-8 – gw Hänsel [331]
WIRTSCHAFTSENGLISCH : KATEGORISIERUNG WIRTSCHAFTSENGLISCHER AEUSSERUNGEN / Thormann, Isabelle – 1994 – 3mf – 9 – DM98.00 – 3-89349-852-4 – gw Hänsel [420]
DIE WIRTSCHAFTSETHISCHEN LEHREN DER KIRCHENVAETER : THEOLOGISCHE STUDIEN DER LEO-GESELLSCHAFT 18 / Seipel, I – Wien, 1907 – 7mf – 9 – ne Slangenburg [240]
WIRTSCHAFTSWERBUNG – Berlin, 1934-42, mar 1943-44 – 3r – 1 – Inquire at Mikrofilmarchiv for details – gw Misc Inst [650]
WIRTSCHAFTSWERBUNG – Berlin. 1934-42. mar 1943-44 – 3r – 1 – gw Mikrofilm [380]
WIRTSCHAFTSWISSENSCHAFT – 1953-1989 – 1,410mf – 1 – DM8,037.00 – gw Mikro Press [335]
WIRTSCHAFTSWOCHE – Duesseldorf. 1979- – 9 – 22150.00y – gw Alpha Com [073]
WIRTSCHAFTSZEITUNG *see* DEUTSCHE ZEITUNG/CHRIST UND WELT
WIRTSCHAFTSZEITUNG DER ZENTRALMAECHTE – Berlin, Germany. 1 Sep 1916-25 Jul 1919 – 4r – 1 – uk British Libr Newspaper [072]
WIRTSCHAFTSZEITUNG DER ZENTRALMAECHTE – Berlin, sep 1916-jul 25 1919 – 4r – 1 – Inquire at Mikrofilmarchiv for details – gw Misc Inst [330]
Wirtzung, C *see* GENERAL PRACTISE OF PHYSICKE
WISA HANDBOOK : A SHORT INTRODUCTION TO THE WISA DIALECT OF NORTH-EAST RHODESIA / Madan, Arthur Cornwallis – Oxford: Clarendon Press, 1906 – us Res Libr [470]
WISBYPOSTEN – Visby, 1866-79 – 9 – sw Kungliga [072]
Wischan, Frederick *see* WILHELM GROENNING
WISCONSIN : SESSION LAWS OF AMERICAN STATES AND TERRITORIES – 1836-1993 – 9 – $1,654.00 set – us Hein [340]
WISCONSIN : WEST'S WISCONSIN STATUTES ANNOTATED – St Paul: West Pub Co, 1957-Jan 1995 update – 9 – $1,830.00 set – us Hein [340]
Wisconsin *see*
- REPORTS AND OPINIONS (A-G)
- REPORTS, POST-NRS
- REPORTS, PRE-NRS
- STATE LABOR REPORTS

WISCONSIN 4-H LEADER / Wisconsin. Agricultural Extension Service – 1948-Spring 1961 – 1,5 – us Spaulding [630]
Wisconsin. Agricultural Experiment Station *see*
- ANNUAL REPORT
- BULLETINS AND REVISIONS
- CIRCULAR AND REVISIONS
- EXPERIMENT STATION NOTES
- EXPERIMENTS IN AMBER CANE AND THE ENSILAGE OF FODDERS
- MISCELLANEOUS PUBLICATIONS
- RESEARCH BULLETIN
- RESEARCH REPORT
- SPECIAL BULLETIN
- STENCIL BULLETIN

Wisconsin. Agricultural Extension Service *see*
- ANNUAL REPORT
- CIRCULAR 4-H
- CIRCULAR AND REVISIONS
- ECONOMIC INFORMATION FOR WISCONSIN FARMERS
- EXTENSION BULLETIN
- EXTENSION NEWSLETTER
- FACT SHEET
- MISCELLANEOUS EXTENSION PUBLICATIONS
- RADIO CIRCULAR
- RECENT RESEARCH IN COOPERATIVE EXTENSION WORK
- SPECIAL CIRCULAR
- STENCIL BULLETIN AND REVISIONS
- STENCIL CIRCULAR AND REVISIONS
- TOWN AND COUNTRY CHURCH LEADERS CONFERENCE
- WISCONSIN 4-H LEADER

WISCONSIN AGRICULTURIST – Racine. Wis. Survey Editions. 1941-1964 – 1 – us UMI [071]
WISCONSIN ATTORNEY GENERAL REPORTS AND OPINIONS – (6 1852-1979 $595.00. 9 v68-83. 1979-1995 $150.00) – v68-83. 1852-1995 – 6,9 – $747.50set – us Hein [340]
Wisconsin. Bank Comptroller *see* REPORTS
WISCONSIN BAR BULLETIN *see* WISCONSIN LAWYER
WISCONSIN BLUE BOOK, 1921 / State Printing Board – 1921. Wisconsin Reel 23. The Cox Library Collection – 5 – us Americana [978]
Wisconsin. College of Agricultural and Life Sciences. Cooperative Extension Programs *see* RESOURCE REPORT
Wisconsin. College of Agricultural and Life Sciences. Dept. of Agricultural and Extension Education *see* TEACHING AGRICULTURE
Wisconsin. College of Agricultural and Life Sciences. Dept. of Agricultural Economics *see*
- AGRICULTURAL ECONOMICS
- FARM BUSINESS SUMMARY
- FARM RECORD SUMMARIES: REPORT
- MANAGING THE FARM
- STAFF PAPER: SERIES
- WISCONSIN FARM ENTERPRISE BUDGETS

Wisconsin. College of Agricultural and Life Sciences. Dept. of Agricultural Engineering *see* MISCELLANEOUS PUBLICATIONS
Wisconsin. College of Agricultural and Life Sciences. Dept. of Dairy Science *see*
- DAIRY REPORT
- WISCONSIN: USDA SIRE REPORT

Wisconsin. College of Agricultural and Life Sciences. Dept. of Forestry *see*
- ANNUAL REPORT
- FORESTRY RESEARCH NOTES
- MISCELLANEOUS PUBLICATIONS

Wisconsin. College of Agricultural and Life Sciences. Dept. of Rural Sociology *see*
- MISCELLANEOUS PUBLICATIONS
- POPULATION NOTE
- POPULATION SERIES: WISCONSIN'S POPULATION

Wisconsin. College of Agriculture. Conservation Education Programs *see* CONSERVATION CENTENNIAL SYMPOSIUM: THE QUEST FOR QUALITY IN WISCONSIN
Wisconsin. College of Agriculture. Dept. of Agricultural and Extension Education *see*
- MISCELLANEOUS PUBLICATIONS
- RESEARCH IN COOPERATIVE EXTENSION WORK

Wisconsin. College of Agriculture. Dept. of Agricultural Economics *see* MISCELLANEOUS PUBLICATIONS
Wisconsin. College of Agriculture. Dept. of Agricultural Journalism *see* BULLETIN
Wisconsin. College of Agriculture. Dept. of Dairy and Food Industries *see* MISCELLANEOUS PUBLICATIONS
Wisconsin. College of Agriculture. Dept. of Dairy Industry *see* MISCELLANEOUS PUBLICATION
Wisconsin. College of Agriculture. Dept. of Dairy Science *see* DEPARTMENTAL BULLETIN
Wisconsin. College of Agriculture. Dept. of Poultry Husbandry *see* CONSUMER EGG SURVEY
Wisconsin. College of Agriculture. Dept. of Poultry Science *see* HATCH
Wisconsin. College of Agriculture. Dept. of Rural Sociology *see* WORKSHOP FOR PROFESSIONAL COMMUNITY LEADERS
Wisconsin. College of Agriculture. Dept. of Soils *see*
- MISCELLANEOUS PUBLICATIONS
- SOILS BULLETIN

Wisconsin. College of Agriculture. School of Home Economics *see* MISCELLANEOUS PUBLICATIONS
Wisconsin Colony. Russell County, Kansas *see* RECORDS
Wisconsin. Commissioner of Banking *see* REPORTS
Wisconsin. Commissioner of Credit Unions *see* REPORTS
Wisconsin. Commissioner of Insurance *see* WISCONSIN INSURANCE REPORTS
Wisconsin. Commissioner of Savings and Loan *see* REPORTS
Wisconsin. Commissioner of Securities *see* REPORTS
WISCONSIN: COUNTY AND REGIONAL HISTORIES – 1 – us Primary [978]
Wisconsin. Dept. of Industry, Labor and Human Relations *see* REPORTS
Wisconsin. Dept. of Revenue *see*
- REPORTS
- TAXES, AIDS AND SHARED TAXES IN WISCONSIN MUNICIPALITIES

Wisconsin. Dept. of Revenue. Bureau of Local Financial Assistance *see* BULLETINS
Wisconsin. Division of Labor Standards *see* CHILD LABOR AND STREET TRADES PERMITS ISSUED IN WISCONSIN
Wisconsin. Employment Relations Board *see* DECISIONS
Wisconsin. Employment Relations Commission *see* REPORTS
WISCONSIN EVANGELICAL LUTHERAN CHURCH SYNOD : YEARBOOK AND DIRECTORY – 1939-91 (complete) – Inquire – 1 – ATLA S0613 – us A.T.L.A. [240]
WISCONSIN EVANGELICAL LUTHERAN SYNOD : YEARBOOK, REPORTS, MEMORIALS, PROCEEDINGS / Wisconsin Evangelical Lutheran Synod – v21-48. 1931-85 (complete) – 5r – 1 – ATLA S0823 – us A.T.L.A. [240]
Wisconsin Evangelical Lutheran Synod *see* WISCONSIN EVANGELICAL LUTHERAN SYNOD
WISCONSIN FARM ENTERPRISE BUDGETS / Wisconsin. College of Agricultural and Life Sciences. Dept. of Agricultural Economics – Nov. 1968-Jun 1971, n.1-8 – 1,5 – us Spaulding [332]
Wisconsin. Industrial Commission *see* WORKMEN'S COMPENSATION REPORTS
Wisconsin. Industrial Commission. Statistical Dept *see* STREET TRADES PERMITS
WISCONSIN INSURANCE REPORTS / Wisconsin. Commissioner of Insurance – 1869-1978. 879 fiches. (Harvard Law School Library Collection.) – 9 – $1.50f – us H.U. Law [336]
THE WISCONSIN JEWISH CHRONICLE – Milwaukee, WI. 1980-86 – 1 – us A.J.P.C. [071]
Wisconsin. Land Tenure Center *see*
- ANNUAL REPORTS 1964-68
- DISCUSSION PAPER
- NEWSLETTER
- PAPERS
- REPRINT
- RESEARCH PAPER
- TRAINING AND METHODS SERIES

WISCONSIN LAW REVIEW – v1- 1920- 1; 1974- 5,6; 1976- 4 x 6 in. 9 – us UMI [340]
WISCONSIN LAW REVIEW – (v1-1984, 1920-84 on reel or mf $1,150.00. 1985-95 on mf $285.00) – v1-12 + 1938-95; 1920-95 – 5,6,9 – $1,435.00 set – us Hein [340]
WISCONSIN LAWYER – (Title varies: v1-21 1927-1948, as Bulletin of the State Bar of Wisconsin v22-61 1949-1988 as Wisconsin Bar Bulletin) – v1-68. 1927-95 – 9 – $1,043.00 set – us Hein [340]
WISCONSIN LUTHERAN QUARTERLY – v1-91. 1904-94 (complete) – 19r – 1 – ATLA S0454 – us A.T.L.A. [073]
WISCONSIN NEWS – Milwaukee. Wis. -d. 1918-39 – 1 – us UMI [071]
WISCONSIN PROGRESSIVES : THE PAPERS OF RICHARD T. ELY, EDWARD A. ROSS, CHARLES MCCARTHY, CHARLES R. VAN HISE AND JOHN R. COMMONS – (Richard T. Ely Papers 191r £10,025.00. Edward A. Ross Papers 40r £2,100.00. Charles McCarthy Papers 32r £1,680.00. John R. Commons Papers 24r £1,260.00. Charles R. Van Hise Papers 63r £3,300.00. With printed guides £21.00) – 350r – 1 – £16,045.00 – uk Chadwyck [978]

Wisconsin. Public Service Commission *see*
- ORDERS
- REPORTS

Wisconsin. Railroad Commission *see*
- OPINIONS AND DECISIONS
- REPORTS

Wisconsin. Railroad Commissioner *see* REPORTS

Wisconsin. State Bar Association *see* PROCEEDINGS

WISCONSIN STATE BAR ASSOCIATION REPORTS – 1st-34th annual meetings 1878-1944 (all publ) – 51mf – 9 – $229.00 – LLMC 84-690 – us L.L.M.C. [340]

WISCONSIN STATE BAR BULLETIN – (Missing: v2 p51-52. v26. v52 p47-50) – v1-55. 1927-82 – 97mf – 9 – $436.00 – LLMC 84-691 – us L.L.M.C. [073]

WISCONSIN STATE CENSUS – (1855, 4r, 1875, 6r; 1855, 9r; Soldiers and Sailors: 1885, 1r; 1895, 11r; Soldiers and Sailors: 1895, 1r; 1905, 40r; 1905, Index) – 1 – us Historical Soc [304]

WISCONSIN. STATE CENSUS – (1855. 3r; 1875. 5r; 1885. 10r; 1895. 10r) – 1 – us Historical Soc [978]

Wisconsin. State Employment Service *see* REPORTS

Wisconsin. The State Historical Society, Madison. Library *see* AUTHOR-TITLE CATALOG

WISCONSIN STATE JOURNAL – Madison. Wis. 1853- – 1 – us UMI [071]

Wisconsin. Supreme Court *see*
- BURNETT'S REPORTS
- CHANDLER'S REPORTS
- PINNEY'S REPORTS
- WISCONSIN SUPREME COURT REPORTS

WISCONSIN SUPREME COURT REPORTS / Wisconsin. Supreme Court – (Pre-NRS: v1-45 1853-78 356mf $534.00. Updates planned) – v1-171. 1852-1920 – 1368mf – 9 – $2,052.00 – LLMC 80-820 – us L.L.M.C. [340]

WISCONSIN SUPREME COURT REPORTS *see*
- BURNETT'S REPORTS
- CHANDLER'S REPORTS
- PINNEY'S REPORTS

Wisconsin. Tax Commission *see* REPORT

WISCONSIN. TERRITORIAL CENSUS – (1836-1842. 1r; 1846. 1r; 1867. 1r) – 1 – us Historical Soc [978]

WISCONSIN: USDA SIRE REPORT / Wisconsin. College of Agricultural and Life Sciences. Dept. of Dairy Science – 1966-68 – 1,5 – us Spaulding [636]

WISCONSIN VALLEY LEADER – Wisconsin Rapids. Wis. 1902-17 – 1 – us UMI [071]

WISCONSIN VOCATIONAL EDUCATOR – (v.5-. 1980- 5,6,9) – v.1-. 1976- – 1 – us UMI [073]

WISCONSIN WOMEN'S LAW JOURNAL – v1-10. 1985-1995 – 9 – $87.00set – us Hein [340]

THE WISCONSIN/WARNER BROS. SCREENPLAY SERIES – (Part 2: Women's Films, Section A. Part 3: Social Drama. Part 4: The Musical Drama. Part 5: Crime. Part 6: Horror/Detective/Murder/Melodrama. Part 7: War Films. Part 8: Westerns. Part 9: Comedy. Part 10: Adventure/Biography/Classics) – Part 1: Gangster Films (synopses, story outlines, treatments, dialogues and shooting scripts of 34 movies from Little Caesar to White Heat) – 1 – us Primary [790]

THE WISDOM OF GANDHI / Gandhi, Mahatma – Introd. by Thomas Kiernan. New York: Philosophical Library, 1967. 112p – 1 – us U.W. Library [280]

WISDOM OF JAMES THE JUST / Carpenter, William Boyd – New York: T Whittaker, 1903 – 1mf – 9 – us A.T.L.A. [240]

THE WISDOM OF JESUS THE SON OF SIRACH : OR, ECCLESIASTICUS: IN THE REVISED VERSION: WITH INTRODUCTION AND NOTES / Oesterley, William Oscar Emil – (Includes indexes) – Cambridge: University Press; New York: G P Putnam [distributor], 1912 – 2mf – 9 – 0-8370-6828-2 – 1986-0828 – us A.T.L.A. [220]

THE WISDOM OF SOLOMON : IN THE REVISED VERSION / Gregg, John A F – (Includes index) – Cambridge:University Press, 1909 – 1mf – 9 – 0-8370-4336-0 – 1985-2336 – us A.T.L.A. [220]

THE WISDOM OF THE APOCALYPSE / McIlvaine, James Hall – New York: A.D.F. Randolph, 1886.1 fiche – 9 – us A.T.L.A. [240]

Wise, Daniel *see* BRIDAL GREETINGS

Wise, Edward *see* THE LAW RELATING TO RIOTS AND UNLAWFUL ASSEMBLIES, TOGETHER WITH A VIEW OF THE DUTIES, POWERS AND LIABILITIES OF MAGISTRATES, CONSTABLES.

Wise, Isaac Mayer *see*
- A DEFENSE OF JUDAISM VERSUS PROSELYTIZING CHRISTIANITY
- SELECTED WRITINGS OF ISAAC M. WISE

Wise, Ivan M *see*
- FOOTSTEPS OF THE FLOCK

Wise, John *see* VINDICATION OF THE GOVERNMENT OF NEW-ENGLAND CHURCHES

THE WISE MEN : WHO THEY WERE AND HOW THEY CAME TO JERUSALEM / Upham, Francis William – (Includes appendixes on the meaning of the terms East and Far East and on the relation of the Persian and Hebrew religions) – NY: Sheldon, 1869 – 1mf – 9 – 0-8370-5602-0 – 1985-3602 – us A.T.L.A. [220]

Wise, Michael et al *see* MUSIC MANUSCRIPTS

Wise, Thomas J *see*
- HELLAS
- LITERARY ANECDOTES OF THE NINETEENTH CENTURY

Wise, Thomas James *see* THE ASHLEY LIBRARY

THE WISE WOMAN OF INVERNESS: A TALE; AND OTHER MISCELLANIES / Black, William – British Fiction Archive: Unit 4 – 9 – uk Bell [830]

Wiseberg, Laurie *see* HUMAN RIGHTS INTERNET

Wiseman, C M *see* CENTENNIAL HISTORY OF LANCASTER, OHIO AND LANCASTER PEOPLE

Wiseman, M W *see* THE DYNAMICS OF RELIGION

Wiseman, Nicholas Patrick *see*
- ESSAYS ON VARIOUS SUBJECTS
- RECOLLECTIONS OF THE LAST FOUR POPES AND OF ROME IN THEIR TIMES

Wiseman, R *see* SEVERAL CHIRURGICALL TREATISES

WISE'S EVERY PLACE IN NEW ZEALAND *see* WISE'S NEW ZEALAND INDEX 1915

WISE'S EVRY PLACE IN NEW ZEALAND *see* WISE'S NEW ZEALAND INDEX 1939

WISE'S NEW ZEALAND INDEX 1915 – (Place names listed alphabetically, with description of each) – Dunedin: H Wise & Co, 1915 – 4mf – 9 – NZ$16.00 – 0-908989-11-3 – NZNB N2366 – nz BAB [980]

WISE'S NEW ZEALAND INDEX 1939 – (Place names listed alphabetically, with description of each) – Dunedin: H Wise & Co, 1939 – 4mf – 9 – NZ$16.00 – 0-908989-12-1 – NZNB N2372 – nz BAB [980]

WISE'S NZ DIRECTORY 1872-1873 – (Publ as NZ Commercial Directory) – 4mf – 9 – NZ$16.00 – 0-908797-46-X – nz BAB [980]

WISE'S NZ DIRECTORY 1875-1876 – 6mf – 9 – NZ$24.00 – 0-908797-44-3 – nz BAB [980]

WISE'S NZ DIRECTORY 1878-1879 – (Alphabetical lists of towns, country areas, streets, surnames, trades & advertisements etc) – 7mf – 9 – NZ$28.00 – 0-908797-33-8 – nz BAB [980]

WISE'S NZ DIRECTORY 1887-1888 – 11mf – 9 – NZ$43.00 – 0-908797-43-5 – nz BAB [980]

WISE'S NZPO DIRECTORY 1900 – 15mf – 9 – NZ$54.00 – 0-908797-75-3 – nz BAB [920]

WISE'S NZPO DIRECTORY 1901 – 15mf – 9 – NZ$54.00 – 0-908989-09-1 – nz BAB [920]

WISE'S NZPO DIRECTORY 1902 – 16mf – 9 – NZ$58.00 – 0-908797-72-9 – nz BAB [920]

WISE'S NZPO DIRECTORY 1903 – 17mf – 9 – NZ$61.00 – 0-908797-96-6 – nz BAB [920]

WISE'S NZPO DIRECTORY 1904 – 13mf – 9 – NZ$49.00 – 0-908797-92-3 – nz BAB [920]

WISE'S NZPO DIRECTORY 1905 – 12mf – 9 – NZ$46.00 – 0-908989-04-0 – nz BAB [920]

WISE'S NZPO DIRECTORY 1906 – 13mf – 9 – NZ$49.00 – 0-908797-42-7 – nz BAB [980]

WISE'S NZPO DIRECTORY 1907 – 14mf – 9 – NZ$52.00 – 0-908989-29-6 – nz BAB [980]

WISE'S NZPO DIRECTORY 1908 – 14mf – 9 – NZ$52.00 – 0-908797-73-7 – nz BAB [920]

WISE'S NZPO DIRECTORY 1909 – 13mf – 9 – NZ$49.00 – 0-908989-00-8 – nz BAB [920]

WISE'S NZPO DIRECTORY 1910 – 16mf – 9 – NZ$58.00 – 0-908989-10-5 – nz BAB [030]

WISE'S NZPO DIRECTORY 1911 – 17mf – 9 – NZ$61.00 – 0-908797-74-5 – nz BAB [920]

WISE'S NZPO DIRECTORY 1912 – 17mf – 9 – NZ$61.00 – 0-908989-05-9 – nz BAB [920]

WISE'S NZPO DIRECTORY 1913 – 16mf – 9 – NZ$58.00 – 0-908989-01-6 – nz BAB [920]

WISE'S NZPO DIRECTORY 1914 – 17mf – 9 – NZ$61.00 – 0-908797-91-5 – nz BAB [920]

WISE'S NZPO DIRECTORY 1915 – 17mf – 9 – NZ$61.00 – 0-908989-21-0 – nz BAB [030]

WISE'S NZPO DIRECTORY 1916 – 17mf – 9 – NZ$61.00 – 0-908797-93-1 – nz BAB [920]

WISE'S NZPO DIRECTORY 1917 – 17mf – 9 – NZ$61.00 – 0-908989-37-7 – nz BAB [980]

WISE'S NZPO DIRECTORY 1918 – 17mf – 9 – NZ$61.00 – 0-908797-48-6 – nz BAB [980]

WISE'S NZPO DIRECTORY 1919 – 17mf – 9 – NZ$61.00 – 0-908797-97-4 – nz BAB [920]

WISE'S NZPO DIRECTORY 1920 – 17mf – 9 – NZ$61.00 – 0-908989-19-9 – nz BAB [030]

WISE'S NZPO DIRECTORY 1921 – 18mf – 9 – NZ$64.00 – 0-908797-98-2 – nz BAB [920]

WISE'S NZPO DIRECTORY 1922 – 18mf – 9 – NZ$64.00 – 0-908797-76-1 – nz BAB [920]

WISE'S NZPO DIRECTORY 1923 – 18mf – 9 – NZ$64.00 – 0-908989-02-4 – nz BAB [920]

WISE'S NZPO DIRECTORY 1924 – 19mf – 9 – NZ$67.00 – 0-908989-20-2 – nz BAB [030]

WISE'S NZPO DIRECTORY 1925 – 19mf – 9 – NZ$67.00 – 0-908797-94-X – nz BAB [920]

WISE'S NZPO DIRECTORY 1926 – 19mf – 9 – NZ$67.00 – 0-908989-39-3 – nz BAB [920]

WISE'S NZPO DIRECTORY 1927 – 19mf – 9 – NZ$67.00 – 0-908797-70-2 – nz BAB [920]

WISE'S NZPO DIRECTORY 1928 – 20mf – 9 – NZ$70.00 – 0-908797-77-X – nz BAB [920]

WISE'S NZPO DIRECTORY 1930 – 18mf – 9 – NZ$64.00 – 0-908797-78-8 – nz BAB [920]

WISE'S NZPO DIRECTORY 1931 – 17mf – 9 – NZ$61.00 – 0-908797-79-6 – nz BAB [920]

WISES NZPO DIRECTORY 1933 – 17mf – 9 – NZ$61.00 – 0-908797-71-0 – nz BAB [920]

WISE'S NZPO DIRECTORY 1934 – 18mf – 9 – NZ$64.00 – 0-908989-06-7 – nz BAB [920]

WISE'S NZPO DIRECTORY 1936 – 18mf – 9 – NZ$64.00 – 0-908797-80-X – nz BAB [980]

WISE'S NZPO DIRECTORY 1938 – 19mf – 9 – NZ$67.00 – 0-908797-95-8 – nz BAB [920]

WISE'S NZPO DIRECTORY 1940 – 20mf – 9 – NZ$70.00 – 0-908797-40-0 – nz BAB [920]

WISE'S NZPO DIRECTORY 1942 – 21mf – 9 – NZ$73.00 – 0-908989-22-9 – nz BAB [030]

WISE'S NZPO DIRECTORY 1943 – 21mf – 9 – NZ$73.00 – 0-908797-99-0 – nz BAB [920]

WISE'S NZPO DIRECTORY 1946 – 23mf – 9 – NZ$79.00 – 0-908989-03-2 – nz BAB [920]

WISE'S NZPO DIRECTORY 1947 – 25mf – 9 – NZ$85.00 – 0-908989-17-2 – nz BAB [030]

WISE'S NZPO DIRECTORY 1955 – 25mf – 9 – NZ$85.00 – 0-908989-28-8 – nz BAB [030]

WISE'S NZPO DIRECTORY 1950-1 – 22mf – 9 – NZ$76.00 – 0-908989-07-5 – nz BAB [920]

WISE'S NZPO DIRECTORY 1953-4 – 24mf – 9 – NZ$82.00 – 0-908989-08-3 – nz BAB [920]

WISE'S NZPO DIRECTORY 1880-81 – 8mf – 9 – NZ$30.00 – 0-908797-49-4 – nz BAB [980]

WISE'S NZPO DIRECTORY 1883-84 – 10mf – 9 – NZ$40.00 – 0-908797-35-4 – nz BAB [980]

WISE'S NZPO DIRECTORY 1885-86 – 10mf – 9 – NZ$40.00 – 0-908797-34-6 – nz BAB [980]

WISE'S NZPO DIRECTORY 1890-91 – 12mf – 9 – NZ$46.00 – 0-908797-47-8 – nz BAB [980]

WISE'S NZPO DIRECTORY 1892-93 – 12mf – 9 – NZ$46.00 – 0-908797-50-8 – nz BAB [980]

WISE'S NZPO DIRECTORY 1894-95 – 13mf – 9 – NZ$49.00 – nz BAB [980]

WISE'S NZPO DIRECTORY 1896-97 – 15mf – 9 – NZ$54.00 – 0-908797-52-4 – nz BAB [980]

WISE'S NZPO DIRECTORY 1898-1899 – 15mf – 9 – NZ$54.00 – 0-908797-53-2 – nz BAB [980]

WISE'S VICTORIA POST OFFICE DIRECTORIES 1884-1900 – (Directories for 1884-85, 1888-89, 1891-92, 1893-94, 1895-96, 1897-98, 1899-1900) – 7v – 125mf and hard copy contents list – 9 – A$100.00 – at State Libr Vic [380]

THE WISH TO BELIEVE : A DISCUSSION CONCERNING THE TEMPER OF MIND IN WHICH A REASONABLE MAN SHOULD UNDERTAKE RELIGIOUS INQUIRY / Ward, Wilfrid Philip – London: Kegan Paul, Trench, 1885 – 1mf – 9 – 0-8370-6847-9 – 1986-0847 – us A.T.L.A. [230]

Wishard, Luther Deloraine *see*
- A NEW PROGRAMME OF MISSIONS
- THE STUDENTS' CHALLENGE TO THE CHURCHES

Wishard, Samuel Ellis *see* THE TESTIMONY OF THE BIBLE CONCERNING...DESTRUCTIVE CRITICISM

Wishart, Alfred Wesley *see* THE SOCIAL MISSION OF THE CHURCH

WISHAW PRESS – 1 – £42.00r – uk Scot News [072]

WISHAW PRESS – Scotland, UK. 1973-84 – 20r – 1 – uk British Libr Newspaper [072]

Wishek, Nina F *see* ALONG THE TRAILS OF YESTERDAY

WIS-KONSTIGE MUSYKA VERTOONENDE DE OORSAECKE VAN 'T GELUYT, DE REDENS DER ZANGH TOONEN TELKONSTIGH UYTGEREECKENT ENDE HET MAKEN EN STELLEN DER SPEELTUYGEN, ALSMEDE VAN DER OUDEN MUSIJCK / Nierop, D R van – Amsteldam. 1659. BP-415 1 – 9 – ne IDC [780]

WISKUNDIG GENOOTSCHAP ONDER DE ZINSPREUK : "EEN ONVERMOEIDE ARBEID KOMT ALLES TO BOVEN" – Amsterdam. Wiskundige verlustiging, in eene aaneenschakeling van uitgeleezene voorstellen, met derzelver. 1793-95. v1-2 – 3 – us Readex [500]

WISKUNDIG GENOOTSCHAP ONDER DE ZINSPREUK: "EEN ONVERMOEIDE ARBEID KOMT ALLES TO BOVEN" – Amsterdam. Kunstoeffeningen over verscheide nuttige onderwerpen der wiskunde...1782-88 – 3 – us Readex [500]

Wislicenus, Konrad *see* UNSERE NIBELUNGENFAHRT

Wismes, Gaetan de *see* UNE PAGE DE LA TERREUR A NANTES

Wisner, David M *see* DETERMINATION OF THE PRECISION, ACCURACY AND RESOLUTION OF A VIDEO-BASED MOTION ANALYSIS SYSTEM

WISNER FREE PRESS – Wisner, NE. -w. Mar-May 1898; Oct 1898-Oct 1906; Apr 1907-Feb 1910; Jun 1914-Sept 1916 – 1 – us NE Hist [071]

WISNER NEWS-CHRONICLE – Wisner, NE. -w. Mar-Dec 1892, scattered issues missing; Oct 1895-Apr 1896, scattered issues missing; May 1896-Aug 1898; Nov 1898-Sept 1901; Nov 1901-Apr 1906, scattered issues missing; May 1924 to date – 1 – us NE Hist [071]

WISSENSBASIERTES INFORMATIONSSYSTEM ZU PROBLEMSTELLUNGEN AUS EMPIRISCHEN LOGISTIK-UNTERSUCHUNGEN / Schoder, Detlef – 1993 – 2mf – 9 – DM80.00 – 3-89349-780-3 – gw Hänsel [000]

WISSENSCHAFT UND FORTSCHRITT – 1965-1989 – 325mf – 1 – DM1,852.50 – gw Mikro Press [500]

WISSENSCHAFT UND WEISHEIT – 1(1934)-31(1968) – 131mf – 9 – Dfl469.00 – ne Slangenburg [073]

WISSENSCHAFT UND WEISHEIT – (1944-1949 have not been publ) – Duesseldorf. v1-31. 1934-1968 – 131mf – 9 – ne IDC [200]

DIE WISSENSCHAFT VON DER GESELLSCHAFT / Andrews, Stephen Pearl – W. Russbueldt, 1904. 1 fiche (29x) – 9 – 1.00f – at Libertarian Micro [320]

DIE WISSENSCHAFTLICH GEORDNETE WELTANSICHT / Albrecht, Carl – Kiel: C. Albrecht, 1874.1 fiche – 9 – us A.T.L.A. [240]

WISSENSCHAFTLICHE ERGEBNISSE DER DEUTSCHEN ATLANTISCHEN EXPEDITION AUF DEM FORSCHUNGS- UND VERMESSUNGSSCHIFF "METEOR", 1925-1927 / Meteor Expedition – (Pt 3, v1-2, containing: Stocks, T. and G. Wuest. Morphologie des Atlantischen Ozeans. Pratje, O. Die Sedimente des Suedatlantischen Ozeans. 2821) – 1935 – 9 – ne IDC [910]

WISSENSCHAFTLICHE ERGEBNISSE DES SCHWEDISCHEN SUEDPOLAR-EXPEDITION 1901-1903 / Nordenskjoeld, O – v. 3: Geologie Und Palaeontologie. 2822 2. 1916 – 8 – ne IDC [910]

WISSENSCHAFTLICHE KRITIK DER EVANGELISCHEN GESCHICHTE / Ebrard, Johannes Heinrich August – Frankfurt a.M. 2 Theile 1842 – 20mf – 8 – ne Slangenburg [240]

WISSENSCHAFTLICHE STUDIEN UND MITTEILUNGEN : AUS DEM BENEDIKTINER ORDEN – 1(1881)-2(1882) – 685mf – 9 – Dfl123.00 – ne Slangenburg [073]

WISSENSCHAFTLICHE STUDIEN UND MITTHEILUNGEN AUS DEM BENEDICTINER-ORDEN... – Bruenn, etc. 2v. 1880-81 – 33mf – 9 – H-580/2 – ne IDC [240]

DIE WISSENSCHAFTLICHE UND DIE KIRCHLICHE METHODE IN DER THEOLOGIE : EIN ENCYKLOPAEDISCHER VERSUCH / Bernoulli, Carl Albrecht – Freiburg i. B:J C B Mohr (Paul Siebeck), 1897 – 1mf – 9 – 0-8370-2296-7 – 1985-0296 – us A.T.L.A. [210]

WISSENSCHAFTLICHE VEROEFFENTLICHUNGEN AUS DEN SIEMENS-WERKEN – v. 1-21. 1920-1943 – 1,5,6 – us Princeton Micro [500]

WISSENSCHAFTLICHE VEROEF-FENTLICHUNG(EN) DER DEUTSCHEN ORIENT - GESELLSCHAFT – (Missing: v3, 37, 38, 41) – Leipzig. v1-55. 1900-32 – 539mf – 9 – H-581/2 – ne IDC [943]

WISSENSCHAFTLICHE ZEITSCHRIFT FUER JUEDISCHE THEOLOGIE – Frankfurt am Main, etc. 5v. 1835-1844 – 49mf – 9 – H-614/2 – ne IDC [270]

WISSENSCHAFTLICHER UND PRAKTISCHER COMMENTAR UEBER DEN ERSTEN PETRUSBRIEF / Usteri, Johann Martin – (Includes bibliographical references) – Zuerich: S Hoehr, 1887 – 1mf – 9 – 0-8370-9324-4 – 1986-3324 – us A.T.L.A. [220]

WISSENSCHAFTLICH-POPULAERE NATURGESCHICHTE DER VOEGEL / Fitzinger, L J F J – Wien, 1862-63 (-1864). 2v. Z/1753/2 – 8 – ne IDC [590]

Wisser, Wilhelm *see*
- AUF DER MAERCHENSUCHE
- PLATTDEUTSCHE VOLKSMAERCHEN

Wissmann, H von *see* IM INNERN AFRIKAS

Wissmann, Paul *see* DIE GROESSEREN DICHTUNGEN VON JAMES MONTGOMERY

WIT AND HUMOR OF BENCH AND BAR / Brown, Marshall – Chicago: T H Flood & Co, 1899 – 7mf – 9 – $10.50 – LLMC 95-155 – us L.L.M.C. [870]

WIT AND HUMOR OF THE AGE / Landon, Melville D – Chicago: Star Publ Co, 1883 – 9mf – 9 – $13.50 – LLMC 91-053 – us L.L.M.C. [870]

WIT AND HUMOR OF THE BIBLE: A LITERARY STUDY / Shutter, Marion Daniel – Boston: Arena, 1893. 1 fiche – 9 – us A.T.L.A. [240]

Wit, Augusta de *see* FACTS AND FANCIES ABOUT JAVA

Wit, P de *see* ZEITSCHRIFT FUER INSTRUMENTENBAU

THE WITCH: A CANADIAN LEGEND / Casgrain, Henri-Raymond – Trans. from the French by A. W. L. Gompertz. Montreal: C. Beauchemin, 1895. 00534. (Pre-1900 Canadiana) – 9 – cn C.I.H.M. [390]

WITCHCRAFT AND QUAKERISM : A STUDY IN SOCIAL HISTORY / Gummere, Amelia Mott – (Includes bibliographical references) – Philadelphia: Biddle; London: Headley, c1908 – 1mf – 9 – 0-8370-8822-4 – 1986-2822 – us A.T.L.A. [230]

WITCHCRAFT IN EUROPE AND AMERICA – An extensive collection of pre-1900 material on the subject of witchcraft – 1 – us Primary [130]

WITCHCRAFT IN FRANCE – 16th-18th century. 99 titles – 9 – fr Hachette [944]

WITELO, EIN PHILOSOPH UND NATURFORSCHER DES 12. JAHRHUNDERTS / Baeumker, C – Muenster, 1908 – 12mf – 8 – ne Slangenburg [100]

WITELO, EIN PHILOSOPH UND NATURFORSCHER DES 12. JHT. : BGPHMA 3/2 / Baeumker, C – Muenster, 1908 – 12mf – 9 – ne Slangenburg [240]

WITH ESSEX IN IRELAND / Lawless, Emily – British Fiction Archive: Unit 4 – 9 – uk Bell [830]

WITH GOD IN PRAYER / Brent, Charles H – Philadelphia: G.W. Jacobs, 1907 – 1mf – us A.T.L.A. [240]

WITH GOD IN THE WORLD : A SERIES OF PAPERS / Brent, Charles H – New York: Longmans, Green, 1900, c1099 – 1mf – us A.T.L.A. [240]

WITH OPEN FACE: JESUS MIRRORED IN MATTHEW, MARK, AND LUKE / Bruce, Alexander Balmain – New York: Scribner, 1896. 1 fiche – 9 – us A.T.L.A. [240]

WITH POOR IMMIGRANTS TO AMERICA / Graham, Stephen – New York: Macmillan, 1914 – 1mf – us A.T.L.A. [240]

WITH THE ARABS IN TENT AND TOWN : AN ACCOUNT OF MISSIONARY WORK, LIFE AND EXPERIENCES IN MOAB AND EDOM / Forder, Archibald – 3rd ed. London: Marshall, [1902?] – 1mf – 9 – 0-8370-6185-7 – 1986-0185 – us A.T.L.A. [240]

WITH THE DUTCH IN THE EAST : AN OUTLINE OF THE MILITARY OPERATIONS IN LOMBOCK, 1894 / Cool, W – London, 1897 – 5mf – 9 – ne IDC [350]

WITH THE EYES OF YOUTH; AND OTHER SKETCHES / Black, William – British Fiction Archive: Unit 4 – 9 – uk Bell [830]

WITH THE ROYAL CANADIANS / Brown, Stanley McKeown – Toronto: Publishers' Syndicate, 1900. 02852. (Pre-1900 Canadiana) – 9 – cn C.I.H.M. [971]

WITH THE RUSSIAN PILGRIMS TO JERUSALEM / Graham, Stephen – London; New York: Macmillan, 1913 – 1mf – us A.T.L.A. [240]

WITH THE TIBETANS IN TENT AND TEMPLE : NARRATIVE OF FOUR YEAR'S RESIDENCE ON THE TIBETAN BORDER AND OF A JOURNEY INTO THE FAR INTERIOR / Rijnhart, Susie Carson – Chicago: Fleming H. Revell, 1901 – 1mf – us A.T.L.A. [240]

WITH TOMMY TOMPKINS IN KOREA / Underwood, L H – New York: F.H. Revell, c1905 – 1mf – us A.T.L.A. [240]

Wither, F *see* A COLLECTION OF EMBLEMS, ANCIENT AND MODERNE

Wither, George *see* THE HYMNES AND SONGS OF THE CHURCH, DIVIDED INTO TWO PARTS:...CANONICALL HYMNES...THE SECOND PART...SPIRITUALL SONGS..

Withering, W *see*
- AN ACCOUNT OF THE FOXGLOVE, AND SOME OF ITS MEDICAL USES
- AN ARRANGEMENT OF BRITISH PLANTS
- AN ARRANGEMENT OF BRITISH PLANTS; ACCORDING TO LATE IMPROVEMENTS OF THE LINNAEAN SYSTEM
- A BOTANICAL ARRANGEMENT OF ALL THE VEGETABLES NATURALLY GROWING IN GREAT BRITAIN
- A BOTANICAL ARRANGEMENT OF BRITISH PLANTS
- A SYSTEMATIC ARRANGEMENT OF BRITISH PLANTS

Witherow, Thomas *see* "THE NEW TESTAMENT ELDER"

WITHERSPOON : PROCEEDINGS AND ADDRESSES AT THE LAYING OF THE CORNER-STONE AND AT THE UNVEILING OF THE STATUE OF JOHN WITHERSPOON, IN FAIRMOUNT PARK, PHILADELPHIA / Breed, Wiliam P – Philadelphia: Presbyterian Board of Publication, c1877 – 1mf – us A.T.L.A. [240]

Witherspoon, Halliday *see* MEN OF ILLINOIS

Witherspoon, John *see* LECTURES ON ELOQUENCE AND MORAL PHILOSOPHY

WITHIN OUR LIMITS : ESSAYS ON QUESTIONS MORAL, RELIGIOUS, AND HISTORICAL / Gardner, Alice – London: T.F. Unwin, 1913 – 1mf – us A.T.L.A. [240]

WITHIN PRISON WALLS : BEING A NARRATIVE OF PERSONAL EXPERIENCE DURING A WEEK OF VOLUNTARY CONFINEMENT IN THE STATE PRISON AT AUBURN, N.Y. / Osborne, Thomas Mott – Osborne, New York/London: D Appleton, 1928 – 4mf – 9 – $6.00 – LLMC 92-143 – us L.L.M.C. [360]

WITHIN THE MAZE / Wood, Ellen – British Fiction Archive: Unit 1 – 9 – uk Bell [830]

Withington, Leonard *see* SOLOMON'S SONG

WITHOUT GOD: NEGATIVE SCIENCE AND NATURAL ETHICS / Greg, Percy – London: Hurst and Blackett, 1883 – 1mf – 9 – us A.T.L.A. [140]

Withrow, W H *see* VALERIA, THE MARTYR OF THE CATACOMBS

Witkowkski, Gustave Jules A *see* LES MEDECINS AU THEATRE DE L'ANTIQUITE AUX DIX-SEPTIEME SIECLE

Witkowski, Georg *see*
- DIEDERICH VON DEM WERDER
- LUDWIG TIECKS AUSGEWAEHLTE WERKE IN VIER BAENDEN
- MINIATUREN

THE WITNESS : FOR CHRIST AND HIS CHURCH – (Some pgs lacking) – v1-72. 1917-72; 1974-89 – 42r – 1 – ATLA S0192 – us A.T.L.A. [073]

THE WITNESS – (Is absorbed by: The Presbyterian Witness) – Halifax, N.S.: [s.n. 1856?-1905] – 9 – cn C.I.H.M. [240]

WITNESS (1985-. 5,6,9) – v1-. 1917- – 1 – us UMI [240]

WITNESS – Belfast, Ireland. 3 Jan, 20 Feb-24 Dec 1874; 23 Jul 1875-1881; 1883; 1885-86; 1888-96; Jan-26 Mar, 3-31 Dec 1926. -w. 20 reels – 1 – uk British Libr Newspaper [072]

WITNESS – Edinburgh, Scotland, UK.1846-47. -w. 2 reels – 1 – uk British Libr Newspaper [072]

THE WITNESS OF DENIAL / Scudder, Vida Dutton – New York: E P Dutton, 1895 – 1mf – 9 – 0-8370-5323-4 – 1985-3323 – us A.T.L.A. [230]

WITNESS OF HISTORY TO CHRIST: FIVE SERMONS / Farrar, Frederic William – London: Macmillan, 1892.1 fiche – 9 – us A.T.L.A. [240]

THE WITNESS OF LUKE TO CHRIST / Stonehouse, Ned B – 1951 – 9 – $10.00 – us I.R.C. [240]

THE WITNESS OF MATTHEW AND MARK TO CHRIST / Stonehouse, Ned B – 1944 – 9 – $10.00 – us I.R.C. [240]

THE WITNESS OF ST. JOHN TO CHRIST : BEING THE BOYLE LECTURES FOR 1870 / Leathes, Stanley – (Includes bibliographical references) – London: Rivingtons, 1870 – 1mf – 9 – 0-8370-5662-4 – 1985-3662 – us A.T.L.A. [220]

THE WITNESS OF ST. PAUL TO CHRIST : BEING THE BOYLE LECTURES FOR 1869: WITH AN APPENDIX ON THE CREDIBILITY OF THE ACTS IN REPLY TO THE RECENT STRICTURES OF DR. DAVIDSON / Leathes, Stanley – London: Rivingtons, 1869 – 1mf – 9 – 0-8370-9713-4 – 1986-3713 – us A.T.L.A. [220]

THE WITNESS OF THE GOSPELS / Barnes, Arthur Stapylton – (Includes appendix) – London: Sands; St Louis, MO: B Herder, 1906 – 1mf – 9 – 0-8370-6882-7 – 1986-0882 – us A.T.L.A. [220]

WITNESS OF THE HEART TO CHRIST / Carpenter, William Boyd – London: S.P.C.K., 1879. 1 fiche – 9 – us A.T.L.A. [240]

THE WITNESS OF THE OLD TESTAMENT TO CHRIST / Leathes, Stanley – London: Rivingtons, 1868. 1 fiche – 9 – us A.T.L.A. [240]

THE WITNESS OF THE PSALMS TO CHRIST AND CHRISTIANITY : EIGHT LECTURES... / Alexander, William – (Includes synopses of lectures. Includes appendix) – NY: E P Dutton, 1877 – 1mf – 9 – 0-8370-2067-0 – 1985-0067 – us A.T.L.A. [220]

THE WITNESS OF THE SPIRIT : A SERMON PREACHED BEFORE THE UNIVERSITY OF OXFORD / Randolph, T – Oxford, 1768 – 1mf – 9 – MP-455/1 – ne IDC [240]

THE WITNESS OF THE VULGATE, PESHITTA AND SEPTUAGINT TO THE TEXT OF ZEPHANIAH / Zandstra, Sidney – (In English, Latin and Greek. Includes bibliographical references) – New York: Columbia University Press, 1909 – 1mf – 9 – 0-8370-9355-4 – 1986-3355 – us A.T.L.A. [220]

THE WITNESS OF TRUTH – (Cont by: The Christian Banner) – Picton [Ont]: D Oliphant, [1845-1850] – 9 – cn C.I.H.M. [240]

WITNESS RECORD / Putnam County. Ohio. Probate Court – 1892-1897 – 1r – 1 – $32.50r – us Archival [324]

WITNESS TO THE INFLUENCE OF CHRIST / Carpenter, William Boyd – London: Archibald Constable, 1905. 1 fiche – 9 – us A.T.L.A. [240]

WITNESSES FOR CHRIST AND MEMORIALS OF CHURCH LIFE FROM THE FOURTH TO THE THIRTEENTH CENTURY / Tylor, Charles, Backhouse, Edward – London: Simpkin, Marshall, Hamilton, Kent, 1894 – 2mf – us A.T.L.A. [240]

WITNESSES TO CHRIST : A CONTRIBUTION TO CHRISTIAN APOLOGETICS / Clark, William – Chicago: A C McClurg, 1888 – 1mf – 9 – 0-8370-2670-9 – 1985-0670 – us A.T.L.A. [230]

THE WITNESSES TO THE HISTORICITY OF JESUS = ZEUGNISSE FUER DIE GESCHICHTLICHKEIT JESUS / Drews, Arthur – (Includes bibliographical references and index) – London: Watts, 1912 – 1mf – 9 – 0-8370-9695-2 – 1986-3695 – us A.T.L.A. [240]

WITNEY EXPRESS – England. -w. 15 July 1869-15 Nov 1888. 18 reels – 1 – uk British Libr Newspaper [072]

WITNEY GAZETTE. (WITNEY & WEST OXFORDSHIRE GAZETTE) – England. 30 Dec 1882-Dec 1967 (missing 1896, 1898, 1911).-w. 49 reels – 1 – uk British Libr Newspaper [072]

WITNEY TELEGRAPH – England. -w. 13 Oct-10 Nov 1866; 17 Oct 1868-20 Feb 1869. 25 ft – 1 – uk British Libr Newspaper [072]

WITS STUDENT – (Title varies: Witwatersrand Student, 1948-Apr 1949; Cont by: WITS: The Witwatersrand Student News Magazine, Aug-Oct 1953. All reels incomplete) – Johannesburg, South Africa. 25 Feb 1960-1 May 1987 – 7r – 1, 16 diazo available at reduced price – sa SA Libr [072]

THE WITT LIBRARY : 10 YEAR UPDATE 1981-1991 / Courtauld Institute of Art – (With printed contents list) – 1992 – 5719mf – 9 – $21,067.00 – 1-869934-29-6 – uk Emmett [700]

THE WITT LIBRARY / Courtauld Institute of Art – (Pt 1: American-Czech schools $12,464. Pt 2: French, German schools $13,300. Pt 3: Greek-Middle Eastern schools $9,500. Pt 4: Netherlands-Yugoslavian schools $12,920. With printed contents list) – 14,854mf – 9 – $38,000.00 set – 1-869934-28-8 – uk Emmett [700]

Witt, R de *see* TEXT ZU DEN ILLUSTRATIONEN AUS REUTER'S WERKEN

Witt, R E *see* ALBINUS AND THE HISTORY OF MIDDLE PLATONISM. CAMBRIDGE CLASSICAL STUDIES

WITTE LILJEN : UND ANDERE ERZAEHLUNGEN / Krueger, Ferdinand – Essen-Ruhr: Fredebeul & Koenen, [19–?] – 1r – 1 – us U.W. Library [830]

Witte, Sergei I Ulevich *see* VOSPOMINANII A

Wittek, Erhard *see*
- BEWAEHRUNG DER HERZEN
- DURCHBRUCH ANNO ACHTZEHN
- SCHNELLER FUSS UND PFEILMAEDCHEN
- DER SOHN DES MANITU
- TRAUM IM FEBRUAR

Wittekindt, Wilhelm *see* JOHANN CHRISTIAN KRUEGER ALS LUSTSPIELDICHTER

Witten, W *see* A KINEMATIC AND KINETIC ANALYSIS OF THE OVERGRIP GIANT SWING ON THE UNEVEN PARALLEL BARS

WITTENBERG UND ROM : KLOSTERNOVELLEN AUS LUTHER'S ZEIT / Kuehne, F Gustav – Berlin: O Janke, 1877 – 1r – 1 – us U.W. Library [830]

Wittenmyer, Annie Turner *see*
- HISTORY OF THE WOMAN'S TEMPERANCE CRUSADE
- THE WOMEN OF THE REFORMATION
- WOMEN'S WORK FOR JESUS

Witthaus, Rudolph August *see* MEDICAL JURISPRUDENCE, FORENSIC MEDICINE AND TOXICOLOGY

Witti, Francis X *see* DIARY DURING AN EXCURSION ACROSS NORTH BORNEO FROM MARUDA BAY TO SANDAKAN

Wittich, Manfred *see* GELEGENHEITSGEDICHTE UND PROLOGE FUER ARBEITERFESTE

Wittich, Wilhelm *see* UEBER SOPHOKLES' "KOENIG OEDIPUS" UND SCHILLERS "BRAUT VON MESSINA"

Wittichen, Carl *see* DAS LEBEN JESU IN URKUNDLICHER DARSTELLUNG...MARCUS, MATTHAEUS UND LUCAS

Wittichen, F C *see* BRIEFE VON UND AN FRIEDRICH VON GENTZ

Wittig, Hildja Yukino *see* MEGALITHGRAEBER IN YAMATO AUS DREI PERIODEN DER KOFUN-ZEIT

Wittig, Horst E *see*
- ADOLF REICHWEIN (1898-1944)
- KARL MARX
- KARL MARX UEBE DIE POLYTECHNISCHE BILDUNGSIDEE UND DER EINFLUSS SEINER ERZIEHUNGSIDEOLOGIE AUF DIE SOZIALISTISCHE PAEDAGOGIK UND VORSCHULERZIEHUNG IN DER EHEM. UDSSR

Wittmann, M *see*
- DIE STELLUNG DES THOMAS VON AQ. ZU AVENCEBROL
- ZUR STELLUNG AVENCEBROLS IM ENTWICKLUNGSGANGE D. ARAB. PHILOSOPHIE

Wittmer, Felix *see* SAENGE VON LIEBEN UND STERBEN

Wittrock, V B *see*
- FOERSOEK TILL EN MONOGRAPHI OEFVER ALGSLAEGTET MONOSTROMA
- ICONOTHECAE BOTANICAE. CATALOGUS ILLUSTRATUS HORTI BERGIANI STOCKHOLMIENSIS

Witts Family *see* PAPERS, C. 1883-1968

Wittstock, Erwin *see* STATION ONEFREIT

Witty, Frank *see* EYE-OPENER

WITWATERSRAND STUDENT *see* WITS STUDENT

THE WITWATERSRAND STUDENT NEWS MAGAZINE *see* WITS STUDENT

WITWER GENEALOGY OF AMERICA / Witwer, George, Witwer Ananias Cline – South Bend, Indiana: L.D. Hardy Company, 1909 – 1r – 1 – us Western Res [920]

Witwer, George, Witwer Ananias Cline *see* WITWER GENEALOGY OF AMERICA

Witzany, Rudolf *see* DIE HEIMLICHE NOT

Witzschel, B *see* ZEITSCHRIFT FUER MATHEMATIK UND PHYSIK MIT LITERATURZEITUNG DER ZEITSCHRIFT FUER MATHEMATIK UND PHYSIK

WIVES AS THEY WERE, AND MAIDS AS THEY ARE : A COMEDY, IN FIVE ACTS. PERFORMED AT THE THEATRE ROYAL, COVENT-GARDEN BY MRS. INCHBALD / Inchbald, Mrs. – London: Printed for G.G. and J. Robinson, 1797 – 1 roll – 1 – 1-55879-332-1 – uk Libr Preservation [820]

WIWAT : THAI-LANGUAGE WEEKLY NEWS MAGAZINE – (Continued as Khao Phiset) – Bangkok, Thailand. Jan 1985-Jun 1985 – 1 – $50.00v – us Asia Libr [073]

Wizemann, Karl *see* FAUST UND DER WEG ZUM LEBEN

W.J. AGAINST J.W. : OR, THREE LETTERS TO THE REV. MR. JOHN WESLEY, DESIGNED AS AN ANSWER TO A PAMPHLET OF HIS CALLED 'A CALM ADDRESS TO THE INHABITANTS OF ENGLAND' / Jordan, W – [?London], 1777 – 1mf – 9 – MP-522/1 – ne IDC [240]

W.J. Fenton & Co *see* REAL ESTATE CATALOGUE

WJR – (Cont: WJR. Washington Journalism Review. Cont by: Washington Journalism Review) – Washington. v3-4 dec 1981-dec 1982 – 1,5,9 – D12946.01 – us UMI [070]

WJR : WASHINGTON JOURNALISM REVIEW – (Cont by: WJR) – Washington. v1-2. oct 1977-dec 1980* 1; v3. jan-nov 1981 1,5,9 – 1,5,9 – D12946 – us UMI [070]

WJR *see* WJR

WJR. WASHINGTON JOURNALISM REVIEW *see* WJR

[WLADYSLAW GOMULKA PAMPHLET COLLECTION] – 1956 – 1 reel – 1 – CSUXANL7242-B – us Hoover Inst Photo [320]

[WLADYSLAW SIKORSKI PAMPHLET COLLECTION] – 1942-1951 – 1 reel – 1 – CSUXANL6758-B – us Hoover Inst Photo [320]

Wlislocki, Heinrich von *see* VOLKSGLAUBE UND VOLKSBRAUCH DER SIEBENBUERGER SACHSEN. 1893

WM. TURNER ELLIS (INDEX) : MEMORIES, MY 72 YEARS IN THE ROMANTIC COUNTY OF YUBA, CALIFORNIA – 1939 – 1r – 5,9 – $50.00 – B40151 – us Library Micro [920]

WM. W. RICHARDSON DIARIES *see* RICHARDSON, WM. W., DIARIES, MS 2136

WO LAG DAS PARADIES? : EINE BIBLISCH-ASSYRIOLOGISCHE STUDIE: MIT ZAHLREICHEN ASSYRIOLOGISCHEN BEITRAEGEN ZUR BIBLISCHEN LAENDER- UND VOELKERKUNDE UND EINER KARTE BABYLONIENS / Delitzsch, Friedrich – (Includes bibliographical references and indexes) – Leipzig: J C Hinrichs, 1881 – 1mf – 9 – 0-8370-9377-5 – 1986-3377 – us A.T.L.A. [220]

Wobbermin, G *see* ALTCHRISTLICHE LITURGISCHE STUECKE AUS DER KIRCHE AEGYPTENS (T.U.U. 2-17/3B1)

Wobbermin, Georg *see*
- DER CHRISTLICHE GOTTESGLAUBE
- THEOLOGIE UND METAPHYSIK
- ZWEI AKADEMISCHE VORLESUNGEN UEBER GRUNDPROBLEME DER SYSTEMISCHEN THEOLOGIE

Wobersin, Franz *see* DIE ECHTHEIT DER BILOAMSPRUECHE, NUM. 22-24

DIE WOCHE – Berlin, mar 18 1899-sep 6 1944 – 1 – Inquire at Mikrofilmarchiv for details – gw Misc Inst [072]

DIE WOCHE – Berlin. mar 18, 1899-sep 6, 1944 – 47r – 1 – gw Mikrofilm [072]

DIE WOCHE – (Cont as: Hermannstaedter Zeitung 1990) – Rumaenien, 1976-1992ff – 17r – 1 – DM1,275.00 – gw Mikro Press [949]

DIE WOCHE – Hamburg, 1993-1994 – 4r – 1 – DM300.00 (1995 subsc DM140.00) – gw Mikro Press [943]

DIE WOCHE – Hermannstadt (Sibiu), Romania. Hrsg.: Kreiskomitee der RKP und Kreisvolksrat fuer Sibiu. 1972- – 1 – gw Mikrofilm [949]

DIE WOCHE – Hodschag (Odzaci), Jugoslawien. 1936-17 Dez 1939 – 1 – gw Mikrofilm [949]

DIE WOCHE – Odzaci, Yugoslavia. Feb 1927-35 – 2r – 1 – us L of C Photodup [949]

DIE WOCHE IN AUSTRALIEN – Bankstown, Sydney, Australia. 1972-78. Incompl – 1 – gw Mikrofilm [072]

DIE WOCHE IN ISRAEL-NEUESTE NACHRICHTEN – Tel Aviv, Israel. 1972 – 1 – gw Mikrofilm [072]

WOCHEN KURIER – Das Blatt der Heimatfernen. fevr 1945-mai 1947. devenu: Neuer Kurier. mai-nov 1947. devenu: Deutsche Zeitung in Frankreich. nov 1947-48. Paris – 1 – fr A.C.R.P.P. [073]

DAS WOCHENBLATT – (1925 is missing?) – Austin, TX. 1924-mar 23 1933 (incomplete) – 3r – Dist. gw Mikrofilm – gw Misc Inst [072]

DAS WOCHENBLATT – Deutsche demokratische Wochenzeitung. Titre francais: La Semaine hebdomadaire. no. 1-2. Paris. fevr 1939 – 1 – fr A.C.R.P.P. [073]

WOCHENBLATT – Findlay, Ohio. 1892-96 – 1r – 1 – $32.50r – us Archival [071]

WOCHENBLATT – Kleve, Germany. 1848-49 – 1 – gw Mikrofilm [072]

WOCHENBLATT – Offenburg, Germany. 1848-1849 – 1 – gw Mikrofilm [072]

WOCHENBLATT – Recklinghausen, Germany. 1848-1849 – 1 – gw Mikrofilm [072]

WOCHENBLATT – (Title changes: Hanauer Wochenblatt, 6 Jan 1869; Hanauer Kreisblatt, 1 Jan 1870; Hanauer Anzeiger 1 May 1872) – Hanau, West Germany. 1976- – ca 8r per yr – 1 – gw Mikrofilm [072]

WOCHENBLATT DER KOENIGLICH BAIERISCHEN STADT BURGHAUSEN *see* OETTINGER UND BURGHAUSER ANZEIGER

WOCHENBLATT DER NEW YORKER VOLKSZEITUNG – New York: Socialistic Cooperative Pub Assoc, jun-sep 1888; jun 1891-jun 1892 – 1r – 1 – us Res Libr [071]

WOCHENBLATT DER STADT BURGHAUSEN *see* OETTINGER UND BURGHAUSER ANZEIGER

WOCHEN-BLATT DER STADT HOF *see* NEUES HOEFER INTELLIGENZ-BLATT

WOCHENBLATT DER STADT HOF – Hof Saale, Germany. 1848-1849 – 1 – gw Mikrofilm [072]

WOCHENBLATT DES BOENNISCHEN BEZIRKS – Bonn, Germany. Title changes: Feuilles d'Affiches... Bonner Nachrichts- und Anzeigeblatt (5 Jan 1812 zweisprachig); Boennisches Wochenblatt (22 Jan 1814); Bonner Wochenblatt (4 Feb 1816); Bonner Zeitung (Sept Oct 1850). 6 Feb 1808-12 Jan 1811; 5 Jan 1812-30 Sept 1891 – 1 – gw Mikrofilm [072]

WOCHENBLATT DES BOENNISCHEN BEZIRKS *see* BONNER WOCHENBLATT

WOCHENBLATT DES NATIONALVEREINS – Frankfurt-Heidelberg, Germany. 6 Apr 1865-30 Sept 1867 – 1 – gw Mikrofilm [072]

WOCHENBLATT FUER DEN KREIS ALTENA *see* ALTENAER KREISBLATT

WOCHENBLATT FUER DEN KREIS ALTENA UND DIE STADT ALTENA *see* ALTENAER KREISBLATT

WOCHENBLATT FUER DEN KREIS BRILON – Brilon, 1848 (incomplete), 1849 n6 – 1 – Inquire at Mikrofilmarchiv for details – gw Misc Inst [943]

WOCHENBLATT FUER DEN OBERAMTSBEZIRK BIBERACH *see* ANZEIGER VOM OBERLAND

WOCHENBLATT FUER DIE BEZIRKE DER KOENIGLICHEN LANDGERICHTE BURGHAUSEN, ALTOETTING, MUEHLDORF, NEUMARKT UND TITTMONING *see* OETTINGER UND BURGHAUSER ANZEIGER

WOCHENBLATT FUER DIE BEZIRKE DER KOENIGLICHEN LANDGERICHTE BURGHAUSEN, ALTOETTING UND MUEHLDORF *see* OETTINGER UND BURGHAUSER ANZEIGER

WOCHENBLATT FUER DIE KREISE NEUHALDENSLEBEN, GARDELEGEN UND WOLMIRSTEDT UND DEN AMTSBEZIRK CALVOERDE – Neuhaldensleben, Germany. 1892 (Nrn.75-152) – 1 – gw Mikrofilm [072]

WOCHENBLATT FUER DIE PROVINZ HANAU – Hanau, Germany. 1848, 1849 – 1 – gw Mikrofilm [072]

WOCHENBLATT FUER DIE PROVINZ NIEDERHESSEN – Kassel, Germany.1848-49 – 1 – gw Mikrofilm [072]

WOCHENBLATT FUER DIE STADT UND DEN KREIS CLEVE – Kleve, Niederrhein, Germany. 1848-49 – 1 – gw Mikrofilm [072]

WOCHENBLATT FUER DIE STADT UND DEN KREIS HAMM *see* KREIS HAMMSCHES WOCHENBLATT

WOCHENBLATT FUER FREUNDE DER WEISHEIT UND LITTERATUR – Berlin, 1783 – 1mf – 9 – VR-32.6/1 – ne IDC [073]

WOCHENBLATT FUER FRIEDBERG UND DIE GEGEND *see* ALLGEMEINES FRIEDBERGER WOCHENBLATT FUER STADT- UND LANDLEUTE

WOCHENPOST – Berlin, 1991-1994 – 8r – 1 – DM600.00 (1995 subsc DM140.00) – gw Mikro Press [943]

WOCHENPOST – Berlin, dec 24 1953, dec 24 1954, dec 24 1955, 1956- – 1 – Inquire at Mikrofilmarchiv for details – gw Misc Inst [072]

WOCHENPOST – East Berlin, Germany. 1956-79 – 1 – gw Mikrofilm [072]

WOCHENPOST – Kattowitz (Katowice), Poland. 3 Sept 1938-2 Sept 1939 – 1 – gw Mikrofilm [943]

WOCHENPOST – London, UK. Printed for the Prisoners of War Recreational Association. 3 Mar 1945 – 1 – uk British Libr Newspaper [072]

DIE WOCHENSCHAU *see* ILLUSTRIERTE WESTDEUTSCHE WOCHENSCHAU

WOCHENSCHRIFT DES NATIONALVEREINS – Coburg, Germany. May 1, 1860-1863 – 1 – gw Mikrofilm [072]

WOCHENSCHRIFT DES NATIONALVEREINS – Coburg, Germany. May 1860-63. 2967-68 – 1 – DM230.00 – gw Mikro Press [072]

WOCHENSCHRIFT DES NATIONALVEREINS – Coburg, Mai 1860-1863 – 2r – 1 – DM230.00 – gw Mikro Press [943]

WOCHENSCHRIFT DES TAUBSTUMMEN-PARTEI-BUNDES DEUTSCHLANDS – Berlin, dec 6 1919-20 – 1 – Inquire at Mikrofilmarchiv for details – gw Misc Inst [360]

WOCHENSCHRIFT FUER GAERTNEREI UND PFLANZENKUNDE – Berlin. 15v. 1858-72 – 75mf – 9 – 8596/1 – ne IDC [631]

WOCHENSCHRIFT FUER VEGESACK UND UMGEBUNG – Bremen, Germany.1866, 1868-71 – 1 – gw Mikrofilm [073]

WOCHENSCHRIFT FUER VEGESACK UND UMGEGEND *see* NORDDEUTSCHE VOLKSZEITUNG

WOCHENSCHRIFT [ILLUSTRIERTE] FUER ENTOMOLOGIE – (Cont. as: Zeitschrift Allgemeine) fuer Entomologie. Neudamm, 1898-1904. v3-9) – Neudamm. v1-2. 1896-97 – 126mf – 9 – Z-1012/2 – ne IDC [590]

WOCHENTLICHE PHILADELPHISCHE STAATSBOTE – Philadelphia. Pa. 1762-1779 – 3 – us Readex [071]

WOCHENZEITUNG FUER DEUTSCHE FLUECHTLINGE AUS DEM OSTGEBIETEN IN DAENEMARK *see* DEUTSCHE NACHRICHTEN

Wocke, Helmut *see*
- ARTHUR FITGER
- HOELDERLINS CHRISTLICHES ERBE

Wocke, M F *see* CATALOG DER LEPIDOPTEREN EUROPA'S UND DER ANGRENZENDEN LAENDER

Wodarski, John S *see* JOURNAL OF HUMAN BEHAVIOR IN THE SOCIAL ENVIRONMENT

WODROW-KENRICK CORRESPONDENCE – From Dr. Williams' Library, London. BRRAM – 2r – 1 – uk Microform Academic [025]

WOECHENTLICHE ANZEIGEN FUER LEHE, UMGEGEND UND LAND WURSTEN *see* DER MITTHEILER AN DER UNTERWESER

WOECHENTLICHE ANZEIGEN UND NACHRICHTEN VON JEVER *see* JEVERISCHE WOECHENTLICHE ANZEIGEN UND NACHRICHTEN

WOECHENTLICHE NACHRICHTEN UND ANMERKUNGEN DIE MUSIK BETREFFEND / Hiller, Johann Adam – Jahrgang 1-4. Erstes-Viertes Vierteljahr. v. 4 has title: "Musikalische Nachrichten und Anmerkungen. " Contains also: Anhang zu dem dritten jahrgange der nachrichten und anmerkungen die musik betreffend. (Vom 1. bis 26. Stueck). 1769. 1766-70 – 9 – us Sibley [780]

WOECHENTLICHE OSNABRUECKISCHE ANZEIGEN – (Cont by: Osnabrueckische Oeffentliche Anzeigen, 1815) – Osnabrueck, sep 3 1817, apr 1-dec 30 1818, 1827, 1829-31, 1833, 1835-36, 1838, 1840, 1843, jan 3-jul 29 1846, 1849-53, 1856-mar 31 1869, 1875, 1878, 1882, 1884-85 – 28r – 1 – gw Mikrofilm [943]

WOECHENTLICHE OSNABRUECKISCHE ANZEIGEN – Osnabrueck, Germany. 1768-70 (incompl.), 1773-74 – 1 – gw Mikrofilm [072]

WOECHENTLICHE RELATION – Halle, Germany. 1709-38 – 1 – gw Mikrofilm [072]

WOECHENTLICHE UNTERHALTUNGEN UEBER DIE ERDE UND IHRE BEWOHNER – (Only register and table of contents) – Berlin, 1784-88 – 1 – Inquire at Mikrofilmarchiv for details – gw Misc Inst [900]

WOECHENTLICHE ZEITUNG AUSS MEHRERLEY OERTHER – Hamburg, 1618-78 – 9 – gw Olms [072]

WOECHENTLICHES AMTS- UND INTELLIGENZBLATT FUER DAS OBERAMT BALINGEN *see* DER VOLKSFREUND

WOECHENTLICHES FRAG- UND KUNDSCHAFFTS-BLATH – (Title changes: Mannheimer Intelligenzblatt, 4 May 1790; Mannheimer Tageblaetter, 2 Jan 1819; Mannheimer Tageblatt, 1 Jan 1836; Mannheimer Journal, 1 Jul 1837; Badische Volks-Zeitung, 20 Jun 1885; General-Anzeiger, 2 Oct 1886; Badische Neueste Nachrichten, 1912, Mannheimer General-Anzeiger, 2 Oct 1916; Neue Mannhei mer Zeitung, 19 Sep 1924) – Mannheim, Germany. 1850-1871 – 23r – 1 – gw Mikrofilm [072]

Woede, Hans *see* WIMPEL DER KURENKAEHNE

Woehlert, Hans *see* DAS WELTBILD IN KLOPSTOCKS MESSIAS

DIE WOELFE : 33000 KILOMETER KRIEGSABENTEUER IN ASIEN / Volck, Herbert – Berlin: Ullstein, c1936 – 1 – us U.W. Library [950]

Woelffin, E *see* BENEDICTI REGULA MONACHORUM

Woelfflin, H *see* KUNSTGESCHICHTLICHE GRUNDBEGRIFFE

Woelfl, J *see* TROIS TRIOS POUR PIANO ET STRINGS, OP. 23

Woerfel, Laurie A *see* THE EFFECTS OF GENDER ON ALT-PE MOTOR IN JUNIOR HIGH PHYSICAL EDUCATION

Woerle, Klaus *see* UNTERSUCHUNGEN ZUM WACHSTUM UND ZUR DOTIERUNG VON EPITAKTISCHEN ZNTE-SCHICHTEN

Woerle, Regine *see* UNTERSUCHUNG VON ALGORITHMEN ZUR NULLSTELLENBESTIMMUNG (INSBESONDERE VON POLYNOMEN) HINSICHTLICH IHRES FEHLERVERHALTENS

Woerner, B *see* JOHANN ADAM MOEHLER

Woerner, Hans *see* BRIEFE NACH DEM WESTWALL

Woerner, Roman *see* NOVALIS' HYMNEN AN DIE NACHT UND GEISTLICHE LIEDER

Woerner, U C *see* GERHART HAUPTMANN

WOERTERBUCH BIBLISCHER EIGENNAMEN DES ALTEN UND NEUEN TESTAMENTES / Schuetze, J; ed by Schmidt, J – Konstanz, (ca. 1900) – 2mf – DM62.00 – 3-8267-3027-5 – gw Hänsel [220]

WOERTERBUCH DER BESCHREIBENDEN BOTANIK / Bischoff, G W – Stuttgart, 1839 – 5mf – ne IDC [580]

WOERTERBUCH DER BESCHREIBENDEN BOTANIK / Bischoff, G W – Stuttgart, 1857 – 3mf – ne IDC [580]

WOERTERBUCH DER DEUTSCHEN PLANZEN-NAMEN,... / Salomon, C – Stuttgart, 1903 – 3mf – ne IDC [580]

WOERTERBUCH DER DEUTSCHEN SPRACHE : MIT BELEGEN VON LUTHER BIS GEGENWART / Sanders, Daniel – Leipzig. 4v. 1876-1885 – 65mf – ne IDC [430]

WOERTERBUCH ZUR DEUTSCHEN LITERATUR / Roehl, Hans – Leipzig: B G Teubner, 1921 – 1 – us U.W. Library [430]

Wogue, L *see* HISTOIRE DE LA BIBLE ET DE L'EXEGESE BIBLIQUE JUSQU'A NOS JOURS

WOHIN MIT DEN RUSSISCHEN JUDEN? HAMBURG. 1891. BJ-72-503/1 / Bodenheimer, M J – 9 – ne IDC [270]

WOHLAU : GESCHICHTE DES FUERSTENTUMS UND DES KREISES / Juhnke, Richard – (Includes bibliographical references and index) – Wuerzburg: Holzner Verlag, 1965 – 10r – 1 – us U.W. Library [910]

Wohlenberg, Gustav *see* DER ERSTE UND ZWEITE PETRUSBRIEF UND DER JUDASBRIEF
WOHLFAHRTSPFLEGE – Berlin, 1887-1928 – 1r – 1 – DM80.00 – gw Mikro Press [072]
WOHLFAHRTSPFLEGE – Berlin, Germany. 1887-1928 (inc.) – 1 – gw Mikrofilm [072]
Wohlgemuth, J *see* JUEDISCHE STUDIEN
Wohlgemuth, Otto *see* VOLK, ICH BRECHE DEINE KOHLE!
DAS WOHLTEMPERIETE CLAVIER. 24 PRELUDES UND FUGUES / Bach, Johann Sebastian – Zuric, 1802 – 1 – us Sibley [780]
EINE WOHLTHAT : VOLKSDRAMA IN VIER ACTEN / Saar, Ferdinand von – Heidelberg: Georg Weiss, 1887 – 1r – 1 – us U.W. Library [820]
WOHNRAUMVERSORGUNG FUER JUNGE ERWACHSENE IM BEREICH DER JUGEND-/ SOZIALHILFE DURCH SELBSTHILFEINITIATIVEN : KONZEPTIONEN UND REALISIERUNGSBEDINGUNGEN / Kolhoff, Ludger – 1993 – 2mf – 9 – DM80.00 – 3-89349-830-3 – gw Hänsel [360]
WOHNUNGSWIRTSCHAFT – Berlin, 1924 – 1 – Inquire at Mikrofilmarchiv for details – gw Misc Inst [330]
WOHNUNGSWIRTSCHAFT – Berlin, Germany.1924 – 1 – gw Mikrofilm [072]
Woillez, Catherine *see* L'ORPHELINE DE MOSCOU OU LA JEUNE INSTITUTRICE
WOKHNSHRIFT – (Hebrew weekly) – Warsaw, PL. v1 n1. 23 Jan 1931-n206. 4 Jul 1935 – 2r – 1 – $65.00r – cn Can Microfilming [072]
WOLA LUDU – Warsaw. Poland. -w. 28 Nov 1949-30 May 1953. (Imperfect). (15 reels) – 1 – uk British Libr Newspaper [943]
WOLBACH MESSENGER – Wolbach, NE. -w. Nov-Dec 1908; Feb 1909; Jun 1909-Jun 1943; Aug 1946 to date – 1 – us NE Hist [071]
WOLCOTTVILLE REGISTER – Torrington. Conn. -w. 1874-81 – 1 – us UMI [071]
Woldemar, M *see* QUATUOR DIALOQUE
WOLF CREEK BAPTIST CHURCH (FORMERLY: PRIVETT SPRINGS). SPRING CITY, TENNESSEE : CHURCH RECORDS – 1869-1987 – 1 – 132.71 – us Baptist [240]
Wolf, Edmund Jacob *see* THE LUTHERANS IN AMERICA
Wolf, Friedrich *see*
- DAS BIST DU
- CYANKALI [PARAGRAPH SYMBOL] 218
- ELEMENTE
- FLORIDSDORF

Wolf, G F *see* KURZGEFASSTES MUSIKALISCHES LEXIKON, ZUSAMMENGETRAGEN VON GEORG FRIEDRICH WOLF
Wolf, Gerson *see* GRILLPARZER ALS ARCHIVDIRECTOR
Wolf, Gustav *see* ZUR GESCHICHTE DER DEUTSCHEN PROTESTANTEN, 1555-1559
A WOLF IN SHEEP'S CLOATHING : OR, AN OLD JESUIT UNMASKED, CONTAINING AND ACCOUNT OF THE WONDERFUL APPARITION OF FATHER PETRE'S GHOST IN THE FORM OF THE REV. JOHN WESLEY,... / Bull, P – (Originally published in Dublin) – London, [1777] – 1mf – 9 – MP-517/1 – ne IDC [240]
Wolf, J *see* TASCHENBUCH DER DEUTSCHEN VOEGELKUNDE
Wolf, Johann Theobald *see* GEDICHTE DER GEBRUEDER WOLF
Wolf, Manfred *see* GUIDO FISCHER (1877-1959)
Wolf, N M von *see* GENERA ET SPECIES PLANTARUM VOCABULIS CHARACTERISTICIS DEFINITA
Wolf, Otmar *see* DIE FUERSTIN AMALIE VON GALITZIN UND FRIEDRICH LEOPOLD GRAF ZU STOLBERG-STOLBERG
Wolf, Richard M *see* JUDGING EDUCATIONAL RESEARCH BASED ON EXPERIMENTS AND SURVEYS
Wolf, Rosalie S *see* JOURNAL OF ELDER ABUSE AND NEGLECT
Wolf, Simon *see* THE AMERICAN JEW AS PATRIOT, SOLDIER AND CITIZEN
WOLFE / Bradley, Arthur Granville – London: Macmillan and Co., 1895. 00979. (Pre-1900 Canadiana) – 9 – cn C.I.H.M. [971]
Wolfe, Bertram D *see* THE BRIDGE AND THE ABYSS
Wolfe, Charles *see* REMAINS OF THE LATE REV. CHARLES WOLFE. WITH A BRIEF MEMOIR OF HIS LIFE BY THE LATE REV. JOHN A. RUSSELL
Wolfe, Samuel Herbert *see* INHERITANCE TAX CALCULATIONS
WOLFE TONE WEEKLY – Ireland.4 Sept 1937-Sept 1938 – 1 – ie Microforms [072]
Wolfe, William G *see* STORIES OF GUERNSEY COUNTY
Wolfeborough, New Hampshire. Wolfeborough Baptist Church *see* RECORDS
WOLFENBERG / Black, William – British Fiction Archive: Unit 4 – 9 – uk Bell [830]
WOLFENBUETTELER ZEITUNG – Wolfenbuettel, Germany. 1981- – 1 – gw Mikrofilm [072]
Wolff, Albert *see* POESIE UND PROSA AUS DEM LITERARISCHEN NACHLASS
Wolff, C *see* JEREMIA IM FRUEHJUDENTUM UND URCHRISTENTUM (T.U.U. 5-118)
Wolff, Eugen *see*
- BLAETTER AUS DEM WERTHER-KREIS
- BRIEFE VON HEINRICH HEINE AN HEINRICH LAUBE
- ENTWICKLUNGSGESCHICHTLICHE GOETHE-KRITIK
- GESCHICHTE RUECKWAERTS?
- LEBENSERINNERUNGEN
- SARDOU, IBSEN, UND DIE ZUKUNFT DES DEUTSCHEN DRAMAS

Wolff, G A *see* PLATENS WERKE
Wolff, Gottfried August Benedikt *see* DER CANTOR
Wolff, Julius *see*
- AUS DEM FELDE
- DER FAHRENDE SCHUELER
- DIE PAPPENHEIMER
- DER RATTENFAENGER VON HAMELN
- DAS RECHT DER HAGESTOLZE
- SCHAUSPIELE
- SCHAUSPIELE; DICHTUNGEN AUS DEM NACHLASS
- DER SUELFMEISTER
- TANNHAEUSER
- DER WILDE JAEGER

Wolff, Ludwig *see*
- ALMANACH FUER FREUNDE DER SCHAUSPIELKUN JAHRGANG (1)-(6), JAHRGANG 7-10
- DAS DEUTSCHE SCHRIFTTUM BIS ZUM AUSGANG DES MITTELALTERS

Wolff, Max Josef *see* GOETHE
Wolff, Milton *see*
- FASCIST SPAIN, MENACE TO WORLD PEACE

Wolff, O *see* DAS BUCH JUDITH ALS GESCHICHTLICHE URKUNDE
Wolff, Oskar Ludwig Bernhard *see* ENCYCLOPAEDIE DER DEUTSCHEN NATIONAL-LITERATUR
Wolff, Theodor *see* THROUGH TWO DECADES
Wolff-Cassel, Louis *see* "ICH"
WOLFFGANG CASPAR PRINTZENS VON WALDTHURN PHRYNIS MITILENAEUS, ODER SATYRISCHER COMPONIST, WELCHER / Printz, Wolfgang C – 3v. in 1. Dresden und Leipzig. 1696. BP-738 1 – 9 – ne IDC [780]
Wolff-Kassel, Ludwig *see* RACHEGEISTER, ODER, DAEMON UNS'RER ZEIT
WOLFF'S ALMANACH FUER FREUNDE DER SCHAUSPIELKUNST *see* ALMANACH FUER FREUNDE DER SCHAUSPIELKUN JAHRGANG (1)-(6), JAHRGANG 7-10
WOLFF'S TELEGRAPHISCHES BUREAU – Berlin, jul 28 1914-jun 10 1923 (incomplete) – 1r – 1 – Inquire at Mikrofilmarchiv for details – gw Misc Inst [072]
Wolfram, Ludwig Hermann *see* FAUST
WOLFRAM VON ESCHENBACH : SEINE DICHTERISCHE UND GEISTESGESCHICHTLICHE BEDEUTUNG / Weber, Gottfried – (Includes bibliographical references) – Frankfurt am Main: M Diesterweg, 1928- – 1 – us U.W. Library [430]
Wolfrum, Renate *see* BAU EINER KALIBRIERSTATION FUER THERMOKOPPEL UND WAERMELEITFAEHIGKEIT VON KUNSTSTOFFEN
WOLFSBURGER NACHRICHTEN – Wolfsburg, West Germany.1977- – 1 – gw Mikrofilm [072]
Wolfskehl, Karl *see*
- DEUTSCHE DICHTUNG
- HIOB, ODER, DIE VIER SPIEGEL

Wolfson, Elliot R *see* THE JOURNAL OF JEWISH THOUGHT AND PHILOSOPHY
Wolfson, H A *see* THE PHILOSOPHY OF SPINOZA
DER WOLGADEUTSCHE – Berlin, jun 3 1922-jun 1 1924 – 1 – Inquire at Mikrofilmarchiv for details – gw Misc Inst [947]
WOLGEGRUENDETER BEWEISS VON DER VOLLSTAENDIGKEIT UND VOLLKOMMENHEIT DER HEILIGEN BIBEL:... / Cramer, D – Wittemberg, 1603 – 3mf – 9 – ne IDC [240]
Wolkenstein, Oswald von *see* LIEDERHANDSCHRIFT B
Wolle, F *see* FRESH-WATER ALGAE OF THE UNITED STATES EXCL. OF THE DIATOMACEAE
WOLLESTOOK GAZETTE – St John, N.B.: Published in connection with the St John Grammar School Debating Society, [1882-1884] – 9 – cn C.I.H.M. [370]
Wolley-Dod, A H *see* A LIST OF THE FLOWERING PLANTS AND FERNS OF THE CAPE PENINSULA
Wollheim da Fonseca *see* HERDER'S CID
Wollick (Wolquier), Nicolaus *see* OPUS AUREUM MUSICE CASTIGATISIIMU DE GREGORIANA ET FIGURATIVA
DER WOLLMARKT : LUSTSPIEL IN VIER AUFZUEGEN / Hauff, Wilhelm – Leipzig: P Reclam, [19–?] – 1 – us U.W. Library [820]
WOLLONDILLY PRESS (BOWRAL) – Mar 31 1906-Jun 20 1914 – 9 – at Pascoe [072]
WOLLSTEINER ZEITUNG – Lissa (Leszno), Poland. Jun 1926-32 – 1 – gw Mikrofilm [943]
Wollstonecraft, Mary *see*
- THE EMIGRANTS
- MARY
- ORIGINAL STORIES FROM REAL LIFE
- A VINDICATION OF THE RIGHTS OF MEN
- A VINDICATION OF THE RIGHTS OF WOMAN

WOLNA POLSKA – Moscow. 1943-1946. Not collated – 1 – us NY Public [943]
WOLNA POLSKA – Moscow. USSR. -w. 1 Mar 1943-15 Feb 1946. (1 reel) – 1 – uk British Libr Newspaper [943]
WOLNA POLSKA – Moscow: Zwiazek Patrjotow Polskich. v1-2. 1943-46 – 1r – 1 – us Ross [072]
WOLNA POLSKA – Organ Zwiazku Patriotow Pulskich. 1943-46. Moscow weekly. Issue missing – 1 – 35.00r – us Hoover Inst Photo [943]
WOLNOSC – Legnica, Poland. Mar 1947-1948; Mar 1950-1954 – 13r – 1 – us L of C Photodup [943]
WOLNOSC – Poznan. Poland. -d. 23 Jan 1952-31 Aug, 9 Sep-31 Dec 1953, 21 Mar-1 Nov 1954. (8 reels) – 1 – uk British Libr Newspaper [947]
WOLNOSC – Poznan, Poland. Feb 1945-Feb 1947 – 3r – 1 – us L of C Photodup [943]
Wolowski, Louis Francois M R *see* ETUDES D'ECONOMIE POLITIQUE ET DE STATISTIQUE
Wolpe, Harold *see* RACE, CLASS AND THE APARTHEID STATE
Wolseley, Field Marshal Viscount *see* PAPERS OF WOLSELEY
Wolter, Joseph *see* GUSTAV FRIEDRICH WILHELM GROSSMANN
Wolter, Udo *see* EVA PERON
Woltereck, C et al *see* AUSFUEHRLICHER BERICHT VON ALLERHAND NEUEN BUECHERN UND ANDEREN DINGEN SO ZUR HEUTIGEN HISTORIE DER BELEHRSAMKEIT GEHOERIG
Woltereck, Kaete A *see* GOETHES EINFLUSS AUF NOVALIS HEINRICH VON OFTERDINGEN
Wolvaardt, Pieter Jacobus *see* BOTSWANA
WOLVERHAMPTON CHRONICLE – England. -w. 1830-66. 21 reels – 1 – uk British Libr Newspaper [072]
WOLVERHAMPTON EXPRESS AND STAR *see* MIDLAND COUNTIES EVENING EXPRESS
WOLVERHAMPTON JOURNAL – England. 3 Sep 1853-25 Sep 1869.-w. 10mqn reels – 1 – uk British Libr Newspaper [072]
WOLVERHAMPTON SPIRIT OF THE TIMES – England. -w. 9 July 1859-Dec 1865. 6 1 2 reels – 1 – uk British Libr Newspaper [072]
WOLVERINE STATE BAPTIST HERALD – Flint, MI. Wolverine State Baptist Convention. Mar 1928-Mar 1931 – 1 – 16.20 – us A.B.H.S. [071]
WOLVERTON EXPRESS ETC – Wolverton, England. 17 Apr-26 Dec 1901; 1902-55. -w. 39 reels – 1 – uk British Libr Newspaper [072]
Wolzogen, Ernst von *see*
- DER ERZKETZER
- HEITERES UND WEITERES
- DIE KINDER DER EXCELLENZ
- KOENIG KARL
- DER KRAFT-MAYR
- MEIN ERSTES ABENTEUER

Wolzogen, Hans von *see*
- RAABENWEISHEIT
- RICHARD WAGNER
- DIE SPRACHE IN RICHARD WAGNERS DICHTUNGEN

WOMAN : HER POSITION AND INFLUENCE IN ANCIENT GREECE AND ROME, AND AMONG THE EARLY CHRISTIANS / Donaldson, James – London; New York: Longmans, Green, 1907 – 1mf – us A.T.L.A. [305]
WOMAN AND ARTIST / O'Rell, Max – Toronto: G.J. McLeod, c1900. 03705. (Pre-1900 Canadiana) – 9 – cn C.I.H.M. [305]
WOMAN AND HER SAVIOUR IN PERSIA / Laurie, Thomas – (Includes appendix and index) – Boston: Gould & Lincoln, 1863 – 1mf – 9 – 0-8370-6137-7 – 1986-0137 – us A.T.L.A. [305]
WOMAN AND HOME MISSIONARY WORK / Wiley, Isaac William – From the Ladies Repository, v29 (n.s.v4), Aug 1869, p85-89 – 9 – us A.T.L.A. [240]
WOMAN AND TEMPERANCE, OR, THE WORK AND WORKERS OF THE WOMAN'S CHRISTIAN TEMPERANCE UNION / Willard, Frances Elizabeth – 1886. c1883 – 9 – us A.T.L.A. [240]
WOMAN AND THE GOSPEL IN PERSIA / Laurie, Thomas – (Includes index) – 2nd ed. Chicago: Woman's Presbyterian Board of Missions of the Northwest, c1887 – 1mf – 9 – 0-8370-6506-2 – 1986-0506 – us A.T.L.A. [305]
WOMAN AND THE PENTECOST / Willing, Jennie Fowler – From Guide to holiness. v.68(NS), Jan 1898, pp21-23. Filmed with Willing's Woman in Gospel Evangelism, and Woman under Pentecostal Baptism – 9 – us A.T.L.A. [240]
WOMAN AS A MINISTER OF RELIGION / Safford, Mary Augusta – (The World's Congress of Representative Women, ed. by May Wright Sewall, 1894, p. 236-241) – 9 – us A.T.L.A. [240]
WOMAN AS CONGREGATIONAL VOTER / Pfatteicher, Ernst P H – Lutheran Church Review, 18, 1899 – 9 – us A.T.L.A. [240]
WOMAN BEFORE THE LAW / Proffatt, John – New York: Putnam's, 1874. 137p. LL-1108 – 1 – us L of C Photodup [340]
THE WOMAN BLESSED BY ALL GENERATIONS, OR, MARY : THE OBJECT OF VENERATION, CONFIDENCE, AND IMITATION TO ALL CHRISTIANS / Melia, Raphael – London: Longmans, Green, 1868 – 2mf – 9 – 0-8370-8361-3 – 1986-2361 – us A.T.L.A. [240]
WOMAN C P A – (v.43-. 1981-. 5,6,9) – v.1-. 1937- – 1 – us UMI [380]
WOMAN, CHURCH AND STATE / Gage, Matilda Joslyn – 1909 – 9 – us A.T.L.A. [240]
WOMAN COACH – (See also: Coaching: Women's Athletics) – v1-2. 1975-1976 – 1 – us UMI [790]
A WOMAN HATER / Reade, Charles L – British Fiction Archive: Unit 2 – 9 – uk Bell [830]
WOMAN: HER POSITION AND INFLUENCE IN ANCIENT GREECE AND ROME, AND AMONG THE EARLY CHRISTIANS / Donaldson, James – London, New York: Longmans, Green and Co., 1907.278p. Reprint of five articles from the Contemporary Review – 1 – us U.W. Library [930]
WOMAN: HER WORK IN THE CHURCH / Washburn, George – 1868 – 9 – us A.T.L.A. [240]
WOMAN IN MISSIONS: PAPERS AND ADDRESSES PRESENTED AT WOMAN'S CONGRESS OF MISSIONS, 2-4 OCT 1893 IN THE HALL OF COLUMBUS, CHICAGO – Comp. by E. M. Wherry. 1894 – 9 – us A.T.L.A. [240]
WOMAN IN THE MINISTRY / Bowles, Ada Chastina Burpee – (Woman's Work in America, ed. by Annie Nathan Meyer, 1891, p. 206-217) – 9 – us A.T.L.A. [240]
WOMAN IN THE PULPIT / Kollock, Florence E – (The World's Congress of Representative Women, ed. by May Wright Sewall, 1894, p. 22.-228) – 9 – us A.T.L.A. [240]
WOMAN IN THE PULPIT / Willard, Frances Elizabeth – c1888 – 9 – us A.T.L.A. [240]
A WOMAN INTERVENES / Barr, Robert – London: Chatto & Windus, 1896. 03358. (Pre-1900 Canadiana) – 9 – cn C.I.H.M. [830]

A WOMAN OF NO IMPORTANCE / Wilde, Oscar – London: J. Lane, 1894 – 1 roll – 1 – 1-55879-544-8 – uk Libr Preservation [820]

THE WOMAN PATRIOT – v1-16 no 12 (all publ) 1919-32 – 2r – 1 – $125.00 – us UPA [320]

THE WOMAN QUESTION / Stephenson, P D – Presbyterian Quarterly, 13, 1899 – 9 – us A.T.L.A. [240]

THE WOMAN QUESTION / Thompson, Helen Hills Strong – From: The Ladies Repository, XV, 29. Aug 1869, p147-148 – 9 – us A.T.L.A. [240]

WOMAN REBEL – v1 nos 1-6 (all publ) 1914 – 1r – 1 – $60.00 – us UPA [305]

WOMAN TODAY : WITH INDEX, APRIL 1937-OCTOBER 1939 – 1990 – 9mf – 9 – NZ$39.60 – nz Nat'l Libr [305]

WOMAN TO-DAY, WITH INDEX. APRIL 1937-OCTOBER 1939 – 1990 – 9mf – NZ$39.60 – nz Nat'l Libr [305]

WOMAN UNDER MONASTICISM : CHAPTERS ON SAINT-LORE AND CONVENT LIFE BETWEEN A.D. 500 AND A.D. 1500 / Eckenstein, Lina – Cambridge: University Press; New York: Macmillan [distributor], 1896 – 2mf – us A.T.L.A. [305]

THE WOMAN VOTER – Clarksdale. Miss. 1922-1924 – 1 – us UMI [071]

THE WOMAN VOTER – v1-8, no. 5 (monthly: all publ). 1910-17 – 2r – 1 – $185.00 – us UPA [320]

THE WOMAN WHO DID / Allen, Grant – London: J. Lane, 1895. 05094. (Pre-1900 Canadiana) – 9 – cn C.I.H.M. [830]

THE WOMAN WHO STOLE EVERYTHING. LEIPZIG, 1928 / Bennett, Arnold; ed by Bayle, Constantino – Madrid: Razon y Fe, 1928 – 9 – sp Bibl Santa Ana [830]

THE WOMAN WORKER – Ireland.1928 – 1 – ie Microforms [072]

THE WOMAN WORKER / National Federation of Women Workers – London. -m. Sep. 1907-Jan. 1910; Jan. 1916-Jul. 1921. 2 reels – 1 – uk British Libr Newspaper [331]

THE WOMAN WORKER – n.s. 1908-10 – 1 – uk World [305]

WOMAN WORKER – ns nos 1-64 (all publ) 1916-21 – 1r – 1 – $100.00 – us UPA [320]

WOMAN'S ART JOURNAL – (1985- . 5,6,9) – v1- . 1980- – 1 – us UMI [073]

Woman's Benefit Association of the Maccabees *see* WBA REVIEW

THE WOMAN'S BIBLE / Stanton, Elizabeth Cady et al – Parts 1 and 2. 1895-98 – 9 – us A.T.L.A. [240]

WOMAN'S CALL TO THE MINISTRY / Bartlett, Caroline J – (The World's Congress of Representative Women, May Wright Sewall, ed. 1894) – 9 – us A.T.L.A. [240]

WOMAN'S CENTURY – 1915-21 – 1 – $195.00 – cn McLaren [640]

Woman's Christian Temperance Union *see*
- MATERIALS
- PAPERS

THE WOMAN'S DREADNOUGHT – 1914-24 – 1 – uk World [320]

THE WOMAN'S DREADNOUGHT – (Workers' Dreadnought). Published by the East London Federation of the Suffragettes (by the Workers' Suffrage Federation). London. -w. Mar 1914-Jun 1924. (3 reels) – 1 – uk British Libr Newspaper [320]

WOMANS EQUITY ACTION LEDGER – Washington, DC. 1971-79 – 1r – 1 – $50.00 – R05505 – us Library Micro [071]

WOMAN'S FOREIGN MISSINARY SOCIETY *see* MONTHLY LETTER LEAFLET

WOMAN'S FOREIGN MISSIONARY SOCIETY / Presbyterian Church in Canada. Woman's Foreign Missionary Society. Western Division – (Cont: Presbyterian Church in Canada. Woman's Foreign Missionary Society. Western Division. W.F.M. Society) – [Mar 1886]-Sept 1886 – 9 – cn C.I.H.M. [240]

WOMAN'S FOREIGN MISSIONARY SOCIETY *see*
- MONTHLY LETTER LEAFLET
- WFM SOCIETY
- WOMAN'S FOREIGN MISSIONARY SOCIETY

WOMAN'S FOREIGN MISSIONARY SOCIETY. *see* FOREIGN MISSIONARY TIDINGS

WOMAN'S HERALD – London, UK. 1893. -w. 1 reel – 1 – uk British Libr Newspaper [072]

WOMAN'S HIGH CALLING / Gale, Martha Tyler – 1876 – 9 – us A.T.L.A. [240]

THE WOMAN'S JOURNAL – Ottawa, Canada. v2 n11. Jul 1886 – 1r – 1 – Can$25.00 – cn Can Microfilming [072]

A WOMAN'S LIFE-WORK: LABORS AND EXPERIENCES OF LAURA S. HAVILAND / Haviland, Laura Smith – 1889 – 9 – us A.T.L.A. [240]

THE WOMAN'S MANUAL OF PARLIAMENTARY LAW : WITH PRACTICAL ILLUSTRATIONS ESPECIALLY FOR WOMEN'S ORGANIZATIONS / Shattuck, Harriette R – Boston, Lee & Shepard, 1900 – 4mf – 9 – $6.00 – LLMC 92-165 – us L.L.M.C. [340]

Woman's Messenger Staff *see*
- THE ADVENTURES OF MISS KANG (CCC327)
- SHORT STORIES FOR YOUNG PEOPLE, VOL 1 (CCC328)
- TALES FOR CHILDREN, BK 1 (CCC326)

WOMAN'S MINISTRY: A SPIRITUAL EXPOSITION OF WOMAN'S PLACE IN THE CHURCH OF GOD / Needham, Elizabeth A – c1895 – 9 – us A.T.L.A. [240]

WOMAN'S MINISTRY, AS EXEMPLIFIED IN SOUTHERN SCHOOLS / Chaney, George Leonard – (The religious magazine and monthly review, v. 44, Sept. 1870, p. 331-342) – 9 – us A.T.L.A. [240]

WOMAN'S MISSIONARY FRIEND – v1-72. May 1869-Aug 1940 (complete) – 20r – 1 – ATLA S0876 – us A.T.L.A. [073]

WOMAN'S MISSIONARY RECORDER – Jan 1935-Mar 1938 (complete) – 1r – 1 – ATLA S0686 – us A.T.L.A. [240]

WOMAN'S PIETY AND ITS BEAUTY / Jones, Harry W – c1902 – 9 – us A.T.L.A. [240]

WOMAN'S PLACE IN ASSEMBLIES FOR PUBLIC WORSHIP / Stevenson, J M – (The Presbyterian Quarterly and Princeton Review, v. 2, Jan. 1873, p. 42-59) – 9 – us A.T.L.A. [240]

WOMAN'S PLACE IN CHURCH WORK / Butler, Josephine Elizabeth Grey – (The Magazine of Christian Literature, v. 5, April 1892, p. 31-37) – 9 – us A.T.L.A. [240]

WOMAN'S PLACE IN CHURCH WORK – The Review of Reviews, v. 5, April 1892, p. 343 – 9 – us A.T.L.A. [240]

WOMAN'S PLACE IN RELIGIOUS MEETINGS / Duren, Charles – The Congregational Review, v8, Jan 1868, p22-29 – 9 – us A.T.L.A. [240]

WOMAN'S PLACE TO-DAY / Blake, Lillie Devereux – 1883 – 9 – us A.T.L.A. [240]

WOMAN'S POSITION IN THE CHURCH / Harford, Mrs. Keister – From the Quarterly Review of the United Brethren in Christ, xv/5, Apr 1894, pp135-141 – 9 – us A.T.L.A. [240]

WOMAN'S PROTEST – v1-11, no. 8 (monthly: all publ). 1912-17 – 1 reel – 1 – $115.00 – us UPA [305]

A WOMAN'S PULPIT / Phelps, E S – Atlantic Monthly, 26, 1870 – 9 – us A.T.L.A. [240]

Woman's Relief Corps. Page Corps no. 60 (Sylvania, Ohio) *see* RECORDS

WOMAN'S RESOLVE, OR, ME, WOMAN VERSUS ME, MAN: A RALLYING SONG FOR WOMEN / Gates, Hartley Baxter – Stanstead, Quebec?: s.n., 1898. 03296. (Pre-1900 Canadiana) – 9 – cn C.I.H.M. [971]

WOMAN'S RIGHT TO PREACH THE GOSPEL / Lee, Luther – 1853 – 9 – us A.T.L.A. [240]

WOMAN'S RIGHTS / Todd, John – 1867 – 9 – us A.T.L.A. [240]

WOMAN'S RIGHTS AND DUTIES / Fairchild, James H – From the Oberlin quarterly review, v.4, 1849, pp 325-357 – 9 – us A.T.L.A. [240]

WOMAN'S RIGHTS AND DUTIES / Foote, C C – From the Oberlin Quarterly Review, v.3, Oct 1849, pp 381-408 – 9 – us A.T.L.A. [240]

WOMAN'S SHARE IN PRIMITIVE CULTURE / Mason, Otis Tufton – New York: Macmillan, 1895. xiii,295p. illus., plates – 1 – us U.W. Library [900]

WOMAN'S SPHERE AND INFLUENCE / Anderson, Samuel G – 1898 – 9 – us A.T.L.A. [240]

WOMAN'S SPHERE IN THE CHURCH / Torrey, Charles W – (The Congregational Quarterly, v. 9, April 1867, p. 163-171) – 9 – us A.T.L.A. [240]

WOMAN'S SUFFRAGE / ed by Scott, Anne Firor & Chafe, William H – (Pt A: National Leaders 18r ISBN 1-55655-126-6 $2,140.00. Pt B: New York 15r ISBN 1-55655-127-4 $1,785.00. Pt C: The South 8r ISBN 1-55655-128-2 $955.00. Pt D: New England 65r ISBN 1-55655-129-0 $7,745.00. Pt E: The Midwest and Far West 35r ISBN 1-55655-130-4 $4,170.00) – Series 1: Women's Studies Manuscript Collections from the Schlesinger Library, Radcliffe College – 1 – $16,795.00 – us UPA [305]

WOMAN'S SUFFRAGE: THE REFORM AGAINST NATURE / Bushnell, Horace – 1869 – 9 – us A.T.L.A. [240]

A WOMAN'S THOUGHTS ABOUT WOMEN / Craik, Dinah Maria – New York: Rudd & Carleton, 1858 – 1 – us U.W. Library [305]

THE WOMAN'S TRIBUNE – 26 v. 1883-1909. Four scattered issues missing – 1 – $62.00 – us L of C Photodup [305]

WOMAN'S TRIBUNE – Portland OR. July 8 1905 – 1 – us U.O. Library [071]

A WOMAN'S TRIP TO ALASKA: BEING AN ACCOUNT OF A VOYAGE THROUGH THE INLAND SEAS OF THE SITKAN ARCHIPELAGO IN 1890 / Collis, Septima Maria – New York: Cassell, 1890. 03388. (Pre-1900 Canadiana) – 9 – cn C.I.H.M. [910]

A WOMAN'S VIEW OF DRAMA, 1790-1830 : THE DIARIES OF ANNA MARGARETTA LARPENT FROM THE HUNTINGTON LIBRARY – (Includes guide) – Marlborough: Adam Matthew Publications, 1996 – 9r – 1 – $1,100.00 – uk Matthew [790]

WOMAN'S VOICE IN THE CHURCH / Goodenow, Smith B – (New Englander, v. 36, Jan. 1877, p. 115-131) – 9 – us A.T.L.A. [240]

WOMAN'S WORK : A FOREIGN MISSION'S MAGAZINE, 1885-1924 – 6r – 1 – $510.00 – D3327 – Co-publ with the Presbyterian Historical Society, Dept of History, Presbyterian Church (U.S.A.) 1995 – us Scholarly Res [240]

WOMAN'S WORK *see* LADIES' COMMITTEE FOR AMELIORATING THE CONDITION OF WOMEN IN HEATHEN COUNTRIES, FEMALE EDUCATION...

WOMAN'S WORK FOR WOMAN, 1871-1885 – 3r – 1 – $255.00 – D3326 – Co-publ with the Presbyterian Historical Society, Dept of History, Presbyterian Church (U.S.A.) 1995 – us Scholarly Res [200]

WOMAN'S WORK IN MODERN SOCIETY / Cusack, Mary – London?, 1874.xii,373p – 1 – us U.W. Library [305]

WOMAN'S WORK IN THE AMERICAN CHURCH / Twing, Mary A E – (The Church Review, v. 60, Jan. 1891, p. 182-192) – 9 – us A.T.L.A. [240]

WOMAN'S WORK IN THE CHURCH / Fry, Benjamin St. James – From Proceedings, Second Ecumenical Methodist Conference held in the Metropolitan Methodist Episcopal Church, Washington, Oct 1891, 1892. p290-314 – 9 – us A.T.L.A. [240]

WOMAN'S WORK IN THE CHURCH / Hargrove, R K – (The Methodist Review, v. 43, March-April 1896, p. 3-14) – 9 – us A.T.L.A. [240]

WOMAN'S WORK IN THE CHURCH / Humphreys, John F – (The Homiletic Review, v. 25 June 1893, p. 495-499) – 9 – us A.T.L.A. [240]

WOMAN'S WORK IN THE CHURCH / Wilmarth, James W – (The Baptist Quarterly Review, v. 10, Oct. 1888, p. 466-488) – 9 – us A.T.L.A. [240]

WOMAN'S WORK IN THE CHURCH: ANOTHER VERSION / Willard, Mary B – From: The Ladies Repository, v32, Apr 1872, p280-282 – 9 – us A.T.L.A. [240]

WOMAN'S WORK IN THE CHURCH: HISTORICAL NOTES ON DEACONESSES AND SISTERHOODS / Ludlow, J M – 1865 – 9 – us A.T.L.A. [240]

THE WOMAN'S WORLD / ed by Wilde, Oscar – 3v Nov 1887-Oct 1890. London: Cassel, 1888-90. (Literature Collection) – 20mf – 9 – $50.00 – fr Bibl Nationale [800]

WOMEN ADVISING WOMEN : PART 1: EARLY WOMEN'S JOURNALS, CA 1700-1832, FROM THE BODLEIAN LIBRARY, OXFORD – (Part 2: Advice Books, Manuals, Almanacs and Journals, ca 1625-1837, 20r. $2,400.00. Part 3: The Lady's Magazine, 1770-1800, 15r $1,800.00. Part 4: The Lady's Magazine, 1801-1832. 17r $2,000.00) – Marlborough Adam Matthew Publications, 1992 – 17r – 1 – $2,000.00 – uk Matthew [305]

WOMEN AND CITIZENSHIP IN INDONESIA / Asian-African Women's Conferences, 1958 – SE-4588 1 – 9 – ne IDC [320]

WOMEN AND CRIMINAL JUSTICE / ed by Hale, Donna C – v1- 1989- – 1,9 ($120.00 in US $168.00 outside hardcopy subsc) – us Haworth [340]

WOMEN AND ECONOMICS; A STUDY OF THE ECONOMIC RELATION BETWEEN MEN AND WOMEN AS A FACTOR IN SOCIAL EVOLUTION / Gilman, Charlotte Perkins – 2nd ed. Boston: Small, Maynard & Co., 1899. 358p – 1 – us U.W. Library [305]

WOMEN AND EDUCATION, 1849-1921 – The papers of Emily Davies and Barbara Bodichon from Girton College, Cambridge – 1 – us Primary [370]

WOMEN AND HEALTH : A MULTIDISCIPLINARY JOURNAL OF WOMEN'S HEALTH ISSUES / ed by Stellman, Jeanne Mager – v1- 1976- – 1,9 ($250.00 in US $350.00 outside hardcopy subsc) – us Haworth [613]

WOMEN AND HEALTH/MENTAL HEALTH – (Distributed for the National Women's History Project. Six main subjects and appendix. With printed guide) – 14r – 1 – $1,190.00 – D3278 – us Scholarly Res [305]

WOMEN AND LAW – (Distributed for the National Women's History Project. With printed guide. 6 sections) – 40r – 1 – $3,400.00 – S3278 – us Scholarly Res [305]

WOMEN AND LITERATURE – v. 3-. 1975- – 1,5,6,9 – us UMI [305]

WOMEN AND MEDIA DECISION-MAKING : THE INVISIBLE BARRIERS – 1987 – 9 – 92-3-102505-8 – fr UNESCO [305]

WOMEN AND MISSIONS – 1924-46 – 1 – $250.00 – us Presbyterian [240]

WOMEN AND MISSIONS, 1924-1946 – 4r – 1 – $340.00 – D3329 – Co-publ with the Presbyterian Historical Society, Dept of History, Presbyterian Church (U.S.A.) 1995 – us Scholarly Res [240]

WOMEN AND MONEY – 1mf – 9 – $0.50 – nz SROW [330]

WOMEN AND POLITICS : A QUARTERLY JOURNAL OF RESEARCH AND POLICY STUDIES / ed by Clark, Janet M – v1- 1980- – 1,9 ($250.00 in US $350.00 outside hardcopy subsc) – us Haworth [320]

WOMEN AND RACIAL DISCRIMINATION IN RHODESIA / Weinrich, A K H – 1979 – 143p – 9 – 92-3-101621-0 – fr UNESCO [305]

WOMEN AND SPORT IN VICTORIAN AMERICA / Powell, Roberta B – 1981 – 2mf – 9 – $8.00 – us Microform Publ [790]

WOMEN AND THE LABOUR MOVEMENT, 1906-1977 – Conference reports and publications of the Women's Labour League, 1906-18 and of the Labour Party Women's Group, 1918-77 – 1 – us Primary [331]

WOMEN AND THE SOCIAL CONTROL OF THEIR BODIES – Part 1: The Malthusian, 1879-1921; and Eugenics Review, 1909-1921 – 1 – us Primary [305]

WOMEN AND THERAPY : A FEMINIST QUARTERLY / ed by Rothblum, Esther D – v1- 1982- – 1,9 ($225.00 in US $315.00 outside hardcopy subsc) – us Haworth [615]

WOMEN AND VICTORIAN VALUES, 1837-1910 : ADVICE BOOKS, MANUALS AND JOURNALS FOR WOMEN – (Part 1: Sources from the Bodleian Library, Oxford) – Marlborough: Adam Matthew Publications, 1996 – 20r – 1 – $2,400.00 – uk Matthew [305]

WOMEN AND WOMEN'S RIGHTS *see* PERIODICALS ON WOMEN AND WOMEN'S RIGHTS

WOMEN AND WORK – (1979- 5,6,9) – 1972- – 1 – us UMI [305]

WOMEN AND WORK IN URUGUAY / Taglioretti, Graciela – 1984 – 9 – 92-3-102110-9 – fr UNESCO [331]

[WOMEN AND WORLD WAR 1 PAMPHLET COLLECTION] – 1914-1919 – 2r – 1 – CSUXANM5019-B – us Hoover Inst Photo [305]

[WOMEN AND WORLD WAR 2 PAMPHLET COLLECTION] – 1941-1945 – 1 reel – 1 – CSUXANP1459-B – us Hoover Inst Photo [305]

WOMEN ARTISTS : SUBJECT COLLECTIONS – (Individual titles not listed separately) – 49 catalogues on 54mf – 9 – £400.00 – uk Chadwyck [700]

WOMEN ARTISTS / Victoria and Albert Museum. London – (Printed catalogue included) – 20mf – 15 – $714.00 – 1-869934-57-1 – uk Emmett [700]

WOMEN AS PREACHERS / Cort, C – Reformed Quarterly (Church) Review29 (1882) – 9 – us A.T.L.A. [240]

WOMEN AT WORK – (1980- 5,6,9) – 1977- – 1 – us UMI [305]

WOMEN, EDUCATION AND LITERATURE : THE PAPERS OF MARIA EDGEWORTH, 1768-1849 – (Part 1: The Edgeworth Papers from the Bodleian Library, Oxford. Part 2: The Edgeworth Papers From the National Library of Ireland. ca 20r. $2,400.00) – Marlborough: Adam Matthew Publications, 1994 – 25r – 1 – $2,800.00 – uk Matthew [305]

WOMEN, EMANCIPATION AND LITERATURE : THE PAPERS OF HARRIET MARTINEAU, 1802-1876, FROM BIRMINGHAM UNIVERSITY LIBRARY – Marlborough: Adam Matthew Publications, 1991 – 17r – 1 – $2,100.00 – uk Matthew [410]

WOMEN, FASHION AND SOCIETY – Part 1: The Queen, 1861-1885 – 1 – us Primary [306]

THE WOMEN FRIENDS OF JESUS: A COURSE OF POPULAR LECTURES BASED UPON THE LIFE AND CHARACTERS OF THE HOLY WOMEN OF GOSPEL HISTORY / McCook, Henry Christopher – 1886 – 9 – us A.T.L.A. [240]

WOMEN – FROM WITCH-HUNT TO POLITICS : SELECTION OF ARTICLES REPRODUCED FROM CULTURES-DIALOGUE BETWEEN THE PEOPLES OF THE WORLD – 1985 – 9 – 92-3-102333-0 – fr UNESCO [305]

WOMEN HELPERS IN THE CHURCH: THEIR SAYINGS AND DOINGS / ed by Welsh, William – 1872 – 9 – us A.T.L.A. [240]

WOMEN, HOUSEHOLDS AND CHANGE / ed by Masini, Eleonora & Stratigos, Susan – 9 – $18.00 – ja U.N. Univ [305]

WOMEN IN AMERICA : CORE PRIMARY SOURCES FOR WOMEN'S STUDIES, SERIES 1 – Part One: Papers and Correspondence from Radcliffe College – 1 – us Primary [305]

WOMEN IN ARAB SOCIETY : WORK PATTERNS AND GENDER RELATIONS IN EGYPT, JORDAN AND SUDAN / Shami, S et al – 1991 – 9 – 92-3-102655-0 – Co-published with Berg – fr UNESCO [331]

WOMEN IN AUSTRALIA – 11mf – 9 – A$60.00 – at State Libr Vic [920]

WOMEN IN CHRISTIAN CIVILIZATION / Higginson, Thomas Wentworth – In: The Religious Aspects of the Age, 1858, pp79-88 – 9 – us A.T.L.A. [240]

WOMEN IN DEVELOPING ECONOMIES : MAKING VISIBLE THE INVISIBLE / ed by Massiah, Joycelin – 1993 – 300p – 9 – 92-3-102807-3 – Co-published with Berg Publishers Inc., which has exclusive sales rights in the UK – fr UNESCO [305]

WOMEN IN ENGINEERING EDUCATION / Michel, Jean – 1988 – 162p – 9 – 92-3-102490-6 – fr UNESCO [370]

WOMEN IN FISHING COMMUNITIES : GUIDELINES: A SPECIAL TARGET GROUP OF DEVELOPMENT PROJECTS – 1988 – 71p – it F.A.O. [305]

WOMEN IN FOOD PRODUCTION, FOOD HANDLING AND NUTRITION : WITH SPECIAL EMPHASIS ON AFRICA – 1979 – 232p – it F.A.O. [640]

WOMEN IN GERMAN – no.6, Feb. 1976-. Madison, Wis.: Women in German, 1976- – 1 – us U.W. Library [305]

[WOMEN IN GERMANY PAMPHLET COLLECTION] – 1914-1921 – 1 reel – 1 – CSUXANR9425-B – us Hoover Inst Photo [305]

WOMEN IN NATIONAL POLITICS / ed by Harrison, Cynthia – (Pt A: Democrats – Sue Shelton White, Mary Dewson, Emma Guffey Miller 14r ISBN 1-55655-423-0 $1,670.00. Pt B: Republicans – Jeannete Rankin 11r ISBN 1-55655-424-9 $1,430.00. Jessica Weis 20r ISBN 1-55655-438-9 $3,100.00. Katherine Graham Howard 17r ISBN 1-55655-439-7 $1,845.00) – Series 2: Women's Studies Manuscript Collections from the Schlesinger Library, Radcliffe College – 1 – us UPA [305]

WOMEN IN SACRED HISTORY: A SERIES OF SKETCHES DRAWN FROM SCRIPTURAL, HISTORICAL AND LEGENDARY SOURCES / Stowe, Harriet Beecher – 1874 – 9 – us A.T.L.A. [240]

WOMEN IN THE CHURCH / Bottome, Margaret McDonald – (The Homiletic Review, vol. 21, June 1891, p. 505-514) – 9 – us A.T.L.A. [240]

WOMEN IN THE CHURCH / Fink, R A – (The Quarterly Review of the Evangelical Lutheran Church, v. 4, April 1874, p. 220-233) – 9 – us A.T.L.A. [240]

WOMEN IN THE EARLY CHRISTIAN MINISTRY / Dietrick, Ellen Battelle – 1897 – 9 – us A.T.L.A. [240]

WOMEN IN THE MINISTRY / Shaw, Anna Howard – (The Chautauquan, v. 27, Aug. 1898, p. 489-496) – 9 – us A.T.L.A. [240]

WOMEN IN THE MISSION FIELD, PIONEERS AND MARTYRS / Buckland, Augustus R – 1895 – 9 – us A.T.L.A. [240]

WOMEN IN THE PULPIT / Dever, M – Lutheran Quarterly 34, 1904 – 9 – us A.T.L.A. [240]

WOMEN IN WHITE RAIMENT / Lemley, John – 1903-04 – 9 – us A.T.L.A. [240]

WOMEN, INDUSTRY AND TRADE UNIONISM – The Gertrude Tuckwell Collection, 1890-1920, from Congress House: London – 1 – us Primary [305]

WOMEN LAWYERS JOURNAL – 1911- 1; 1975- 5,6,9 – us UMI [340]

WOMEN LIVING UNDER MUSLIM LAWS = FEMMES SOUS LOIS MUSULMANES: RESEAU INTERNATIONALE DE SOLIDARITE : INTERNATIONAL SOLIDARITY NETWORK – Montpellier. 11 docs. 1986-1991 – 12mf – 9 – ne IDC [340]

WOMEN OF CHINA – 1979-1995 – 9 – F742.00 – sz Infoprint [072]

WOMEN OF CHINA – (1982 $14.00) – 1979-81. In English. -m. Annual delivery. F E6 – 9 – $4.50f – cc Microforms [920]

WOMEN OF CHRISTIANITY : EXEMPLARY FOR ACTS OF PIETY AND CHARITY / Kavanagh, Julia – (Includes index) – London: Smith, Elder, 1852 – 2mf – 9 – 0-8370-6988-2 – 1986-0988 – us A.T.L.A. [920]

THE WOMEN OF THE ARABS : WITH A CHAPTER FOR CHILDREN / Jessup, Henry Harris; ed by Robinson, C S & Riley, Isaac – New York: Dodd & Mead, c1873 – 1mf – us A.T.L.A. [305]

WOMEN OF THE BIBLE – New York: Harper, 1900 – 1mf – 9 – 0-8370-6407-4 – 1986-0407 – us A.T.L.A. [220]

WOMEN OF THE BIBLE : SKETCHES OF ALL THE PROMINENT FEMALE CHARACTERS IN THE OLD AND THE NEW TESTAMENT / Norval, Leigh – Nashville, TN: M E Church, South, 1890, c1889 – 1mf – 9 – 0-8370-9810-6 – 1986-3810 – us A.T.L.A. [220]

WOMEN OF THE FRENCH REVOLUTION / Stephens, Winifred – London. 1922 – 1 – us Res Libr [944]

WOMEN OF THE NEW TESTAMENT / Adeney, Walter Frederic – 1899 – 9 – us A.T.L.A. [240]

WOMEN OF THE OLD TESTAMENT : STUDIES IN WOMANHOOD / Horton, Robert Forman – New York: Thomas Whittaker, [c1897] – 1mf – 9 – 0-8370-3671-2 – 1985-1671 – us A.T.L.A. [305]

THE WOMEN OF THE REFORMATION / Wittenmyer, Annie Turner – New York: Phillips & Hunt; Cincinnati: Cranston & Stowe, 1885 – 2mf – us A.T.L.A. [940]

WOMEN OF THE REFORMED CHURCH / Good, James I – 1901 – 9 – us A.T.L.A. [240]

WOMEN OF WORTH: A BOOK FOR GIRLS – Ill. by W. Dickes. New York: W.A. Townsend, 1860. viii,302p. illus – 1 – us U.W. Library [920]

WOMEN ON THE LAND; THE WOMEN'S LAND ARMY / Kipp, Catherine G – California Northern Div, 1918-20 – 1r – 1 – $50.00 – C70081 – us Library Micro [331]

WOMEN ON THE MOVE : CONTEMPORARY CHANGES IN FAMILY AND SOCIETY – 1984 – 9 – 92-3-102157-5 – fr UNESCO [305]

WOMEN, POLITICS AND INDUSTRY, 1906-1918 / Women's Labour League. Minutes and Records, 1906-18 – 1 – us Primary [305]

WOMEN, POLITICS AND WELFARE : THE PAPERS OF NANCY ASTOR, 1879-1964 FROM READING UNIVERSITY LIBRARY – (Part 1: Political Diaries, Autobiography, Speeches and Papers on Prospective Legislation. Part 2: Subject Files – Children and the Family. ca 20 reels. $2,400.00. Part 3: Subject Files – Health, Birth Control and Social Insurance. ca 21r $2,400.00. Part 4: Subject Files – Women, The Franchise, Marriage Laws and Papers Regarding Pressure Groups. ca 19 reels. $2,400.00) – Marlborough: Adam Matthew Publications, 1994 – 20r – 1 – $2,400.00 – uk Matthew [305]

WOMEN PREACHERS / Brown, O E – From the evangelist, July 24, 1872, p 234. Filmed with Brown's "Women's Preaching." – 9 – us A.T.L.A. [240]

WOMEN PREACHERS / Hunter, Fannie McDowell – 1905 – 9 – us A.T.L.A. [240]

WOMEN: SHALL THEY PREACH? / Seebach, M R – Lutheran Quarterly, 33. 1903 – 9 – us A.T.L.A. [240]

WOMEN, SLAVES OF HISTORY OR HISTORY OF SLAVES / Hollander, Nancy – Buenos Aires: Editorial La Pleyade, 1974 – 1 – CSUXADH5691-B – us Hoover Inst Photo [305]

WOMEN, SUFFRAGE AND POLITICS – Part 1: The Papers of Sylvia Pankhurst, 1882-1960 from the International Instituut voor Sociale Geschiedenis, Amsterdam. 25r. $2,950.00; Part 2. 12r. $1,450.00. Marlborough: Adam Matthew Publications, 1991 – 1 – uk Matthew [320]

WOMEN, WAR AND SOCIETY, 1914-1918 – (Part 1: The Army, Belgium and Benevolent Organisations. Part 2: The British Red Cross, Colonies, Decorations and Honours, Education. Part 3: Employment. Part 4: Food, France, India, Italy, Romania, Switzerland, Land and Local Records. Boxes 113-145. Part 5: Munitions, Prisoners, Relief Funds, Russia, Serbia, Rebels, Suffrage Politics, United States Volunteer Corps, Welfare, WRAF, WRENS and Women's Work. Boxes 146-185) – The Women at Work Collection in the Imperial War Museum, London – 1 – us Primary [941]

Women's Art Library *see* CONTEMPORARY WOMEN ARTISTS

WOMEN'S CLUB NEWS – New Hebrides, mar 1971-jun 1980 – 1r – 1 – PMB Doc426 – at Pacific Mss [072]

WOMEN'S CONCERNS AND PLANNING : A METHODOLOGICAL APPROACH FOR THEIR INTEGRATION INTO LOCAL, REGIONAL AND NATIONAL PLANNING – 1986 – 166p – 9 – 92-3-102392-6 – fr UNESCO [305]

WOMEN'S DISABILITIES REMOVAL BILL / Bright, John – A speech of John Bright in the House of Commons, London, 26th April, 1876. Toronto: Blackett Robinson, 1889. 00270. (Pre-1900 Canadiana) – 9 – cn C.I.H.M. [323]

WOMEN'S FRANCHISE : A RECORD OF THE WOMEN'S SUFFRAGE MOVEMENT – London, 1907-09 – 26mf – 9 – W-32/1 – ne IDC [305]

WOMEN'S FREEDOM LEAGUE – (Cont. as: The Vote, Organ of the Women's Fredom League. London, 1909-1933. Cont. as: The Women's Freedom League Bulletin. London, 1934-1961. Missing: Many parts) – London, 1909 – 297mf – 9 – W-33/1 – ne IDC [305]

THE WOMEN'S FREEDOM LEAGUE BULLETIN *see* WOMEN'S FREEDOM LEAGUE

Women's History Research Center *see* THE THREE COLLECTIONS: HERSTORY; WOMEN AND HEALTH-MENTAL HEALTH; WOMEN AND LAW

WOMEN'S INDUSTRIAL NEWS – London, England. Organ of the Women's Industrial Council. -m. Oct 1895-Oct 1914. 2 reels – 1 – uk British Libr Newspaper [072]

Women's International League for Peace and Freedom *see* WOMEN'S INTERNATIONAL LEAGUE FOR PEACE AND FREEDOM PAPERS, 1915-1978

WOMEN'S INTERNATIONAL LEAGUE FOR PEACE AND FREEDOM PAPERS, 1915-1978 / Women's International League for Peace and Freedom – 115r – 1 – $7250.00 – us UMI [977]

WOMEN'S INTERNATIONAL NETWORK – Lexington. 49 docs. 1980-1991 – 54mf – 9 – ne IDC [320]

WOMEN'S JOURNALS OF THE INTER-WAR YEARS : PART 1 "EVE", 1919-1929 – Marlborough: Adam Matthew Publications, 1994 – ca 26r – 1 – $3,100.00 – uk Matthew [305]

WOMEN'S JOURNALS OF THE NINETEENTH CENTURY – (Part 1: The Women's Penny Paper and Women's Herald, 1888-1893) – Marlborough: Adam Matthew Publications, 1994 – 4r – 1 – $490.00 – uk Matthew [305]

Women's Labour League. Minutes and Records, 1906-18 *see* WOMEN, POLITICS AND INDUSTRY, 1906-1918

WOMEN'S LANGUAGE AND EXPERIENCE, 1500-1940 : WOMEN'S DIARIES AND RELATED SOURCES. PART 1: SOURCES FROM BEDFORDSHIRE AND HERTFORDSHIRE COUNTY RECORD OFFICES – (Guide included) – Marlborough: Adam Matthew Publications, 1993 – 16r – 1 – $1,950.00 – uk Matthew [305]

WOMEN'S LANGUAGE AND EXPERIENCE, 1500-1940 : WOMEN'S DIARIES AND RELATED SOURCES. PART 2: SOURCES FROM BIRMINGHAM CENTRAL LIBRARY AND BIRMINGHAM UNIVERSITY LIBRARY – (Guide included) – 1996 – 24r – 1 – $2,800.00 – uk Matthew [305]

WOMEN'S LANGUAGE AND EXPERIENCE, 1500-1940 : WOMEN'S DIARIES AND RELATED SOURCES. PART 3: SOURCES FROM SUFFOLK COUNTY RECORD OFFICE AND CAMBRIDGE UNIVERSITY LIBRARY – (Guide included) – ca 20r – 1 – $2,400.00 – uk Matthew [305]

WOMEN'S LEAGUE OUTLOOK – (Some issues are missing) – New York, NY. v4 n1 (Sept 1933)-v11 n2 (Dec 1940) – 1r – 1 – us A.J.P.C. [073]

WOMEN'S MINISTRY AND OTHER PAPERS / Miller, James R – 1875 – 9 – us A.T.L.A. [240]

WOMEN'S MISSIONARY SERVICE – (Cont as: Methodist Missionary Society Women's Work. London, 1935-1965. Missing: (1858)-1922) – London, (1858)-1934 – 79mf – 9 – H-2757/1 – ne IDC [305]

THE WOMEN'S MOVEMENT IN CUBA, 1898-1958 : THE STONER COLLECTION ON CUBAN FEMINISM / ed by Stoner, K Lynn – (With printed guide) – 1991 – 13r – 1 – $1,105.00 – D3248 – us Scholarly Res [305]

Women's National Anti-Suffrage League *see* THE ANTI-SUFFRAGE REVIEW

Women's National Indian Association *see*
– ANNUAL REPORTS
– THE INDIAN'S FRIEND

Women's Peace Union *see* THE RECORDS OF THE WOMEN'S PEACE UNION, U.S. BRANCH, 1921-1940

WOMEN'S PERIODICALS, 18TH CENTURY TO THE GREAT DEPRESSION – Comprehensive collection of 18th and 19th century women's periodicals – 1 – us Primary [305]

WOMEN'S POLITICAL TIMES – Rochester, NY. 1982-1983 – 1r – 1 – $50.00 – R04934 – us Library Micro [320]

WOMEN'S POSITION AND WORK IN THE CHURCH / Niccolls, Samuel J – Presbyterian Review, 10, 1889 – 9 – us A.T.L.A. [240]

WOMEN'S QUARTERLY – Irvine, CA. 1987-1989 – 1r – 1 – $50.00 – R04041 – us Library Micro [073]

THE WOMEN'S REVIEW OF BOOKS – v1-. 1983- – 1,5,6,9 – us UMI [410]

WOMEN'S RIGHTS, 1814-1912 – (From Cornell University's Olin Library Collection of Women's Rights Pamphlets) – 120mf – 1 – $345.00 – us UMI [305]

WOMEN'S RIGHTS LAW REPORTER – (v1-8 1971-85 on reel $120.00. v9-15 1986-94 on mf $154.00) – Rutgers University. v1-15. 1971-94 – 5,6,9 – $274.00 set – us Hein [340]

WOMEN'S RIGHTS LAW REPORTER – (v4-. 1977-. 5,6,9) – v. 1-. 1971- – 1 – us UMI [340]

WOMEN'S SOCIAL AND POLITICAL EMANCIPATION – The Suffragette Fellowship Collection in the Museum of London – 1 – us Primary [320]

Women's Social and Political Union *see*
– BRITANNIA. 1-7. 18 OCT 1912-20 DEC 1918
– THE SUFFRAGETTE

WOMEN'S SPORTS – (1983-. 1,5,6,9) – v1-. 1979- – 1 – us UMI [073]

WOMEN'S SPORTS AND FITNESS – 1985-. -m – 1 – us UMI [073]

WOMEN'S STUDIES / ed by Martin, W – 1972 – 1,5,9 – us Gordon [305]

WOMEN'S STUDIES INTERNATIONAL FORUM – (Formerly: Women's Studies International Quarterly) – v1- 1978- – 5,6,9 – us UMI [305]

WOMEN'S STUDIES INTERNATIONAL QUARTERLY *see* WOMEN'S STUDIES INTERNATIONAL FORUM

WOMEN'S STUDIES MANUSCRIPT COLLECTIONS FROM THE SCHLESINGER LIBRARY RADCLIFFE COLLEGE *see* SEXUALITY, SEX EDUCATION, AND REPRODUCTIVE RIGHTS

WOMEN'S STUDIES MANUSCRIPT COLLECTIONS FROM THE SCHLESINGER LIBRARY, RADCLIFFE COLLEGE *see*
- WOMAN'S SUFFRAGE
- WOMEN IN NATIONAL POLITICS

WOMEN'S SUFFRAGE COLLECTION FROM MANCHESTER CENTRAL LIBRARY, PART 1 : LYDIA BECKER AND THE PAPERS OF THE MANCHESTER SOCIETY FOR WOMEN'S SUFFRAGE – (Part 2: The Papers of Millicent Garrett Fawcett. Sections on Women's Suffrage, Education, Employment, Welfare, The First World War and Other Women's Issues. 18r $2,200.00) – Marlborough: Adam Matthew Publications, 1994 – 12r – 1 – $1,450.00 – uk Matthew [320]

WOMEN'S SUFFRAGE IN WISCONSIN, PARTS 1-2 – (Part 1: Records of the Wisconsin Woman Suffrage Association, 1892-1925. 18r. $1,980.00. ISBN 1-55655-119-3; Part 2: The Papers of Ada Lois James, 1816-1952. 24r. $2,640.00. ISBN 1-55655-120-7) – Grassroots Women's Organizations Series – $3,430.00 set – us UPA [320]

WOMEN'S SUFFRAGE RECORD – London, England. -irr. June 1903-Nov 1906. 10 ft – 1 – uk British Libr Newspaper [320]

Women's Trade Union League *see*
- PAPERS
- PAPERS OF THE WTUL AND ITS PRINCIPAL LEADERS

WOMEN'S WEAR DAILY – New York, 1910-41 – 178r – 1 – us Ross [640]

WOMEN'S WEAR DAILY – New York, 1911- – 1 – $330.00y – us Fairchild Micro [390]

WOMEN'S WEAR DAILY – New York. June 1910-1944. Lack Oct-Dec 1911 – 1 – us NY Public [380]

WOMEN'S WEAR DAILY *see* WWD

WOMEN'S WORK FOR JESUS / Wittenmyer, Annie Turner – 1873 – 9 – us A.T.L.A. [240]

WOMEN'S WORLD – Washington, DC. 1979-84 – 1 – us A.J.P.C. [071]

Womer, Parley Paul *see* THE CHURCH AND THE LABOR CONFLICT

Won, Moo Hurh *see* UEBER DIE GRENZEN DER IMITATION DER ABENDLAENDISCHEN KULTUR UND IHRE PROBLEMATIK IM PROZESS DER KULTURDIFFUSION IN KOREA

WONDER MINING NEWS – Wonder, NV. 1907-09; 1910-12 (scats); 1908-12 – 4r – 1 – $200.00 – U04823 – us Library Micro [071]

WONDER WOMAN – Issue Nos. 11-15 Winter 1944-Winter 1945 – 5mf – 15 – $31.95 – us Comics [760]

WONDER WOMAN – Issue Nos. 1-5 Summer 1942-Jun-Jul 1943 – 5mf – 15 – $31.95 – us Comics [760]

WONDER WOMAN – Issue Nos. 16-20 Mar-Apr 1946-Nov-Dec 1946 – 5mf – 15 – $31.95 – us Comics [760]

WONDER WOMAN – Issue Nos. 21-25 Jan-Feb 1947-Sept-Oct 1947 – 5mf – 15 – $31.95 – us Comics [760]

WONDER WOMAN – Issue Nos. 26-30 Nov-Dec 1947-Jul-Aug 1948 – 5mf – 15 – $31.95 – us Comics [760]

WONDER WOMAN – Issue Nos. 6-10 Fall 1943-Fall 1944 – 5mf – 15 – $31.95 – us Comics [760]

THE WONDERFUL BOOK / Vaughan, John Gaines – Boston: Cushman Press, 1906. 1 fiche – 9 – us A.T.L.A. [240]

WONDERLAND – Gardiner. Mont. 1902-1905 – 1 – us UMI [071]

Wong, Hwa Chieh *see* CHRISTIAN MORALITY AND TRADITIONAL CHINESE ETHICS (CCC329)

Wong, L *see* THE USE OF PROGRAMME EVALUATION IN ONTARIO OLDER ADULT CENTRES

Won-Yong, Kim *see* RECENT ARCHAEOLOGICAL DISCOVERIES IN THE REPUBLIC OF KOREA

Woo, Y K *see*
- CHRISTIANITY IN THE LIGHT OF TODAY (CCC200)
- THE LIFE OF H.L. ZIA (CCC176)
- TO THE YOUTH (CCC201)

Wood, Alley and Co *see*
- HISTORY OF GOODHUE COUNTY
- HISTORY OF SOLANO COUNTY

WOOD AND WOOD PRODUCTS – v54- 1949- – 1,5,6,9 – us UMI [338]

Wood, Anthony A *see* THE LIFE OF ANTHONY A WOOD, WRITTEN BY HIMSELF

Wood, C A *see* ESSEX COUNTY HISTORY AND DIRECTORY

WOOD CARVINGS AND WEATHERVANES (TIAM, PT 7) – (With printed catalogue ISBN: 0-914146-74-2 £30) – 25mf – 15 – £460.00 – uk Chadwyck [730]

WOOD CARVINGS IN ENGLISH CHURCHES / Bond, Francis – v. 1: Misericords; v. 2: Stalls and Tabernacle Work, Bishop's Thrones and Chairs. H-1247 2. 1910 – 8 – ne IDC [941]

Wood, Charles James *see* SURVIVALS IN CHRISTIANITY

Wood, Clement *see* A SELECTION OF NEGRO SONGS

WOOD COUNTY FREE PRESS – Bowling Green, Ohio. 1900-10 – 4r – 1 – $32.50r – us Archival [071]

WOOD COUNTY GAZETTE – Bowling Green, Ohio. 1886-89 – 3r – 1 – $32.50r – us Archival [071]

WOOD COUNTY HERALD – Weston, CO. 1891-1949 – 18r – 1 – $32.50r – us Archival [071]

WOOD COUNTY HERALD – Weston. Ohio. 1891-1919 – 1 – us UMI [071]

WOOD COUNTY INDEPENDENT – Perrysburg, Ohio. 1862-63 – 1r – 1 – $32.50r – us Archival [071]

WOOD COUNTY NEWS – Bowling Green, Ohio. 1878-1934 – 36r – 1 – $32.50r – us Archival [071]

Wood County. Ohio. Auditor *see*
- ABSTRACTS OF TAXES
- CIVIL WAR BOUNTIES
- ENUMERATION SAILORS AND SOLDIERS
- ENUMERATION SCHOOL AGE YOUTH
- MILITIA ROLL

Wood County. Ohio. Bloom Township. Board of Trustees *see*
- CEMETERY RECORDS
- MINUTES

Wood County. Ohio. Board of County Commissioners *see*
- BLIND RELIEF APPLICATIONS
- BLIND RELIEF PAPERS
- COMMISSIONERS' JOURNALS
- COURTHOUSE CONSTRUCTION RECORD
- JOURNALS, COUNTY HOME

Wood County. Ohio. Board of Education *see* MINUTES

Wood County. Ohio. Bowling Green City. Board of Education *see* MINUTES

Wood County. Ohio. Bowling Green, City. Board of Public Utilities *see* MINUTES

Wood County. Ohio. Bowling Green. City City Council *see*
- ORDINANCE BOOK
- ORDINANCES AND RESOLUTIONS

Wood County. Ohio. Bowling Green. City Council *see* MINUTES

Wood County. Ohio. Bowling Green. City Mayor *see*
- ANNUAL REPORTS
- REPORTS TO COUNCIL AND CITIZENS

Wood County. Ohio. Bowling Green, City. Safety/Service Director *see*
- CEMETERY DEED RECORD
- CEMETERY LOT OWNERS INDEX

Wood County. Ohio. Bradner, Village. Board of Education *see* MINUTES

Wood County. Ohio. Bradner. Village Council *see* MINUTES

Wood County. Ohio. Bradner, Village. Village Council *see* ACCOUNT RECORDS

Wood County. Ohio. Common Pleas. Civil Division *see*
- APPEARANCE DOCKETS
- COMPLETE RECORDS
- DIVORCE CASES
- ESTATE SETTLEMENTS
- JOURNALS
- PARTITION RECORDS / SETTLEMENTS
- RECORD OF INDENTURES

Wood County. Ohio. Common Pleas. Civil Divison *see* DEEDS AND LAND SALES

Wood County. Ohio. Common Pleas. Criminal Div. *see* CORONERS' INQUESTS

Wood County. Ohio. County Home *see*
- CENSUS OF IDIOTS
- INDENTURE RECORDS
- REGISTER
- TWP. TRUSTEES RELIEF RECORDS

Wood County. Ohio. Freedom Township. Board of Trustees *see*
- CEMETERY DEED RECORDS
- CEMETERY RECORDS
- MINUTES

Wood County. Ohio. Freedom Township. Justice of the Peace *see* CIVIL DOCKET

Wood County. Ohio. General Health District *see* BIRTH CERTIFICATES

Wood County. Ohio. Grand Rapids Twp Board of Trustees *see* BEAVER CREEK CEMETERY RECORD

Wood County. Ohio. Lake Township. Board of Education *see* CLASS REGISTERS

Wood County. Ohio. Lake Township. Township Clerk *see* DIRECTORY OF NAMES

Wood County. Ohio. Lake Township. Township Trustees *see* CEMETERY DEED RECORDS

Wood County. Ohio. Middletown Township. Township Clerk *see*
- BIRTH CERTIFICATES
- BURIAL REMOVAL PERMITS
- DEATH CERTIFICATES

Wood County. Ohio. Pemberville, Village. Board of Public Affairs *see*
- MINUTES
- RECORD OF RESOLUTIONS

Wood County. Ohio. Pemberville, Village. Cemetery Association *see* CEMETERY RECORDS

Wood County. Ohio. Pemberville. Village Cemetery Association *see*
- BURIAL RECORDS
- TRUSTEES MINUTES

Wood County. Ohio. Pemberville. Village Council *see*
- RECORD OF ORDINANCES
- RECORD OF RESOLUTIONS

Wood County. Ohio. Pemberville, Village. Village Council *see* MINUTES

Wood County. Ohio. Perrysburg Township. Board of Education *see* ENUMERATION: SCHOOL, AGE, YOUTH

Wood County. Ohio. Plain Township. Board of Education *see* RECORD OF SCHOOL EXPENDITURES

Wood County. Ohio. Portage Township. Board of Trustees *see* CEMETERY DEED RECORDS

Wood County. Ohio. Probate Court *see*
- BIRTH RECORDS
- BIRTH REGISTRATIONS
- DEATH RECORDS
- NATURALIZATION RECORDS
- NATURALIZATIONS, DECLARATIONS
- VOLUNTEER ENLISTMENT PAPERS

Wood County. Ohio. Recorder *see* ENTRY RECORD

Wood County. Ohio. Soldiers' Relief Commission *see* RELIEF RECORDS

Wood County. Ohio. Treasurer *see* TAX DUPLICATES

Wood County. Ohio. Weston. Village Council *see*
- CEMETERY RECORDS
- MINUTES
- ORDINANCE RECORDS

WOOD COUNTY REPUBLICAN – Bowling Green, Ohio. 1918-45 – 8r – 1 – $32.50r – us Archival [071]

WOOD COUNTY SENTINEL – Bowling Green. Ohio. 1867-1891 – 1 – us UMI [071]

WOOD COUNTY SENTINEL – Bowling Green, Ohio. 1891-1906 – 8r – 1 – $32.50r – us Archival [071]

WOOD COUNTY TRIBUNE – Bowling Green. Ohio. 1889-1890 – 1 – us UMI [071]

WOOD COUNTY TRIBUNE – Bowling Green, Ohio. 1889-1906 – 3r – 1 – $32.50r – us Archival [071]

WOOD COUNTY TRIBUNE – Wisconsin Rapids. Wis. 1920-22 – 1 – us UMI [071]

Wood, E M R *see* A MONOGRAPH OF BRITISH GRAPTOLITES

Wood, Edwin O *see* HISTORY OF GENESEE COUNTY

Wood, Ellen *see*
- ADAM GRAINGER
- ANNE HEREFORD
- ASHLEY
- BESSY RANE
- THE CHANNINGS
- COURT NETHERLEIGH
- DANESBURY HOUSE
- DENE HOLLOW
- EAST LYNNE
- EDINA
- ELSTER'S FOLLY
- GEORGE CANTERBURY'S WILL
- THE HOUSE OF HALLIWELL
- JOHNNY LUDLOW
- LADY ADELAIDE('S OATH)
- LADY GRACE
- A LIFE'S SECRET
- LORD OAKBURN'S DAUGHTERS
- THE MASTER OF GREYLANDS
- MILDRED ARKELL
- MRS. HALLIBURTON'S TROUBLES
- ORVILLE COLLEGE
- OSWALD CRAY
- POMEROY ABBEY
- THE RED COURT FARM
- ROLAND YORKE
- ST. MARTIN'S EVE
- THE SHADOW OF ASHLYDYAT
- THE STORY OF CHARLES STRANGE
- TOLD IN THE TWILIGHT
- TREVELYN HOLD
- THE UNHOLY WISH
- VERNER'S PRIDE
- WILLIAM ALLAIR
- WITHIN THE MAZE

WOOD EXTRACTION WITH OXEN AND AGRICULTURAL TRACTORS – 1986 – 107p – it F.A.O. [634]

Wood, Ezra Morgan *see* HOW THE BIBLE WAS MADE

WOOD GAS AS ENGINE FUEL – 1986 – 184p – it F.A.O. [621]

Wood, Henry *see* GOD'S IMAGE IN MAN

Wood, Horace Gay *see*
- A TREATISE ON THE LAW OF MASTER AND SERVANT
- A TREATISE ON THE LEGAL REMEDIES OF MANDAMUS AND PROHIBITION, HABEAS CORPUS, CERTIORARI AND QUO WARRANTO
- A TREATISE ON THE LIMITATION OF ACTIONS AT LAW AND IN EQUITY

Wood, Irving Francis *see*
- THE SPIRIT OF GOD IN BIBLICAL LITERATURE
- A TENABLE THEORY OF BIBLICAL INSPIRATION: AN ADDRESS

Wood, J F *see* ESSEX COUNTY HISTORY AND DIRECTORY

Wood, J G *see* MAN AND BEAST, HERE AND HEREAFTER

Wood, Jefri *see* GUIDELINE SENTENCING

Wood, John *see* THE STORY OF THE EVANGELIZATION SOCIETY

Wood, John G *see* THE UNCIVILIZED RACES OF MEN IN ALL COUNTRIES OF THE WORLD

Wood, Joseph *see* THE ANALOGIES OF BEING AS EMBODIED IN AND UPON THIS ORB

Wood, M Sandra *see* MEDICAL REFERENCE SERVICES QUARTERLY

Wood, Martin L *see* PRESCHOOL CHILDREN'S ASSESSMENT OF HEALTH VALUE RELATED TO SELECTED NONHEALTH VALUES

Wood, Nadine MS *see* EFFECTIVENESS OF SELECTED COMPONENTS IN BEHAVIORAL WEIGHT-LOSS INTERVENTIONS

Wood, Nancy *see* CLEAR CUT

WOOD PRESERVATION MANUAL – 1986 – 156p – it F.A.O. [670]

Wood, R F *see* PAST AND PRESENT OF DALLAS COUNTY

Wood, R H *see* MEMORANDUM ON A PROPOSED SUDAN INDUSTRIAL DEVELOPMENT BANK AND RELATED MATTERS

Wood, Ray O *see* PHYSICAL AGGRESSION AS A FUNCTION OF ANGER IN MEN AND WOMEN

WOOD RIVER SUNBEAM – Wood River, NE. -w. Mar 1906; Aug-Nov 1906; Feb 1908-Oct 1913 – 1 – us NE Hist [071]

WOOD RIVER SUNBEAM – Wood River, NE. -w. Nov 1895; Jan 1896; Apr 1896-May 1898; Oct 1898; Jan 1899-Dec 1900; Apr 1901-Dec 1904; Feb 1905-Dec 1923; Jan 1926-Nov 1942; Dec 1943 to date – 1 – us NE Hist [071]

Wood, S V *see*
- A MONOGRAPH OF THE EOCENE BIVALVES OF ENGLAND
- A MONOGRAPH OF THE EOCENE CEPHALOPODA AND UNIVALVES OF ENGLAND

Wood, Samuel George *see* THE REGISTRY ACT OF 1865

Wood, Samuel Newitt *see*
- LETTERS TO SALMON PORTLAND CHASE
- PAPERS

WOOD SCIENCE AND TECHNOLOGY – v1-14 1967-80 – 1,5,9 – $1281.00 – us UMI [670]

Wood, W *see*
- GENERAL CONCHOLOGY, OR A DESCRIPTION OF SHELLS ARRANGED ACCORDING TO THE LINNEAN SYSTEM
- INDEX ENTOMOLOGICUS
- INDEX TESTACEOLOGICUS

Wood, W M *see* HISTORY OF ALAMEDA COUNTY

Wood, Wallace A *see* REMINISCENCES

Wood, Will C *see*
- FIVE PROBLEMS OF STATE AND RELIGION
- SABBATH ESSAYS

Wood, William Page *see*
- THE CONTINUITY OF SCRIPTURE
- CONTINUITY OF SCRIPTURE

Wood, William Spicer *see* PROBLEMS IN THE NEW TESTAMENT: CRITICAL ESSAYS
Woodall, J *see* THE SURGEONS MATE OR MILITARY AND DOMESTIQUE SURGERY
WOODBINE BAPTIST CHURCH. ST JOSEPH, MISSOURI : CHURCH RECORDS – 1901-60 – 1 – 33.30 – us Baptist [240]
Woodbridge *see* HISTORY OF DULUTH AND ST LOUIS COUNTY PAST AND PRESENT
WOODBRIDGE AND VAUGHAN NEWS – Woodbridge, Ontario, CN. 1948-83 – 33r – 1 – cn Commonwealth Micro [072]
WOODBRIDGE MERCURY EXTRA (EAST ED.) – Ipswich, England. May-Dec 1985.-w. 1/2 reel – 1 – uk British Libr Newspaper [072]
WOODBRIDGE REPORTER – England. 1978-81.-w. 8 reels – 1 – uk British Libr Newspaper [072]
WOODBROOKE STUDIES : CHRISTIAN DOCUMENTS IN SYRIAC, ARABIC AND GARSHUNDI / ed by Mingana, A – 7v – 56mf – 9 – ne Slangenburg [240]
WOODBURN INDEPENDENT – Woodburn, OR. -w. 1 Dec 1888-. – 37r – 1 – us U.O. Library [071]
Woodburn, James A *see* THE AMERICAN REPUBLIC AND ITS GOVERNMENT
WOODBURN TRIBUNE – Woodburn, OR. -w. 21 Jul 1911-6 Mar 1914. 1 roll – 1 – us U.O. Library [071]
Woodbury, A M *see* THE ALTERNATIVE TO SOCIALISM AND SPURIOUS CAPITALISM: NATURAL CAPITALISM
WOODBURY AND MINOT'S REPORTS OF CASES IN THE FIRST CIRCUIT, 1845-1847 / Woodbury, C L & Minot, G – Boston: Little-Brown. v1-3. 1847-52 (all publ) – 18mf – 9 – $27.00 – LLMC 81-478 – us L.L.M.C. [340]
Woodbury, C L *see* WOODBURY AND MINOT'S REPORTS OF CASES IN THE FIRST CIRCUIT, 1845-1847
Woodbury, Levi *see* LEVI WOODBURY PAPERS
WOODCHIPS – v1-6. Dec 1972-Aug 1977. Continued by: Morris Arboretum Newsletter – 1 – us UMI [634]
Woodcock, I *see* DIARIES, 1825-1858
Woodhead, H G W *see* CHINA YEAR BOOK
Woodhead, N *see* FRESHWATER ALGAE OF SIERRA LEONE
Woodhouse, F C *see*
- THE MILITARY RELIGIOUS ORDERS OF THE MIDDLE AGES
- MONASTICISM, ANCIENT AND MODERN

Woodhouse, Reginald Illingworth *see* WHAT IS THE CHURCH, OR, PLAIN INSTRUCTION ABOUT THE CHURCH, ESPECIALLY IN ENGLAND
Woodkirk. Yorkshire *see* PARISH REGISTERS
WOODLAND BAPTIST CHURCH (FORMERLY: BROWN'S CREEK). HAYWOOD COUNTY. TENNESSEE : CHURCH RECORDS – 1835-81 – 1 – 10.89 – us Baptist [240]
WOODLAND DAILY DEMOCRAT : DAVIS EDITION – Davis, CA. 1972-1984 – 143r – 1 – $7,150.00 – B02166 – us Library Micro [071]
WOODLAND DAILY DEMOCRAT – Woodland, CA. Jan-Jun 1915; 1916; 1937-84 – 272r – 1 BC003111 – $13,600.00 – us Library Micro [071]
WOODLAND RECORD – Woodland, CA. 1943-56 – 27r – 1 – $1,350.00 – C03112 – us Library Micro [071]
WOODLAWN BOOSTER – Chicago. Ill. 1932-1959 – 1 – us UMI [071]
WOODLAWN COMMUNITY BOOSTER – Portland OR. June 15 Aug 10 1939, May 30 1940 – 1 – us U.O. Library [071]
WOODLAWN GAZETTE – Aliquippa. Pa. 1922-1928 – 1 – us UMI [071]
WOODLAWN NEWS – Aliquippa. Pa. 1921-1923 – 1 – us UMI [071]
WOODMEN OF THE WORLD – Omaha, Nebraska, 1984-1988 monthly – 1 – $35.00r – us NE Hist [073]
WOODMONT BAPTIST CHURCH. NASHVILLE, TENNESSEE : CHURCH RECORDS – 1941-77, Nov 1979-1989 – 1 – $212.12 – us Baptist [240]
WOODRIDGE BAPTIST CHURCH. AIKEN COUNTY. SOUTH CAROLINA : CHURCH RECORDS – 1961-Feb 1973 – 1 – 25.20 – us Baptist [240]
Woodrow, Peter J *see* RISING FROM THE ASHES
Woodruff, Edwin H *see* WOODRUFF'S CASES ON THE LAW OF INSURANCE
Woodruff, George E *see* FIFTEEN YEARS AGO: OR THE PATRIOTISM OF WILL COUNTY
Woodruff, George P *see* COMMODITY EXCHANGES
Woodruff, R W *see* NEW YORK MASONIC CODE...
Woodruff, William T *see* NEW YORK MASONIC CODE...
WOODRUFF'S CASES ON THE LAW OF INSURANCE / Woodruff, Edwin H – New York: Baker, Voorhis. 1900 (all publ) – 7mf – 9 – $10.50 – LLMC 95-050 – us L.L.M.C. [340]
Woods, Charlotte Elizabeth *see* THE GOSPEL OF RIGHTNESS: A STUDY IN PAULINE PHILOSOPHY
Woods, Francis Henry *see* A GUIDE TO THE STUDY OF THEOLOGY: ADAPTED...TO THE OXFORD HONOUR SCHOOL
Woods, H *see* A MONOGRAPH OF THE CRETACEOUS LAMELLIBRANCHIA OF ENGLAND
Woods, Henry *see* THE HISTORY OF THE PRESBYTERIAN CONTROVERSY, WITH EARLY SKETCHES OF PRESBYTERIANISM
Woods Hole Oceanographic Institution *see* OCEANOGRAPHIC INDEX
Woods Hole Oceanographic Institution. Marine Biological Laboratory *see* CATALOG OF THE LIBRARY
Woods Hole Oceanographic Institution. Marine Biological Laboratory. Woods Hole, Massachusetts *see* CATALOG OF THE LIBRARY OF THE MARINE BIOLOGICAL LABORATORY AND THE WOODS HOLE OCEANOGRAPHIC INSTITUTION
Woods Hole Oceanographic Institution. Woods Hole, Massachusetts *see* OCEANOGRAPHIC INDEX
Woods, James Haughton *see*
- THE VALUE OF RELIGIOUS FACTS
- THE YOGA-SYSTEM OF PATANJALI

Woods, Leonard *see* HISTORY OF THE ANDOVER THEOLOGICAL SEMINARY
Woods, Lydia A *see* DEVELOPMENT OF AN INVENTORY TO ASSESS MULTICULTURAL EDUCATION ATTITUDES, COMPETENCIES AND KNOWLEDGE OF PHYSICAL EDUCATION PROFESSIONALS
Woods, R E Broughall *see* A SHORT INTRODUCTORY DICTIONARY OF THE KAONDE LANGUAGE
WOODS' REPORTS OF CASES IN THE FIFTH CIRCUIT, 1870-1883 / Woods, W B – Chicago: Callaghan. v1-4. 1875-83 (all publ) – 33mf – 9 – $49.50 – LLMC 81-479 – us L.L.M.C. [340]
Woods, W B *see* WOODS' REPORTS OF CASES IN THE FIFTH CIRCUIT, 1870-1883
Woods, Walter Hastings *see* DIARY
Woodson, Carter Godwin *see*
- COLLECTION
- THE EDUCATION OF THE NEGRO PRIOR TO 1861

Woodson, W H *see* HISTORY OF CLAY COUNTY
WOODSTOCK BAPTIST CHURCH. SOMERSET, KENTUCKY : CHURCH RECORDS – 1869-1979. Formerly Pleasant Hill Baptist Church. Name changed 1963. 1414p – 1 – 63.63 – us Baptist [240]
THE WOODSTOCK COLLEGE MONTHLY – (Cont by: McmMaster University Monthly) – Woodstock, Ont: Philomathic Society of Woodstock College, [1890-1891?] – 9 – cn C.I.H.M. [370]
WOODSTOCK COLLEGE MONTHLY *see* THE MCMASTER UNIVERSITY MONTHLY
THE WOODSTOCK HERALD AND BROCK DISTRICT GENERAL ADVERTISER – 1846-47 – 1 – 35.00 – cn McLaren [072]
WOODSTOCK HERALD AND CHARLBURY MESSENGER – England.Sept 1875-Feb 1876. -m. 10 feet – 1 – uk British Libr Newspaper [072]
WOODSTOCK LETTERS : A HISTORICAL JOURNAL OF JESUIT EDUCATIONAL AND MISSIONARY ACTIVITIES – Full text of 320 issues published from 1872 to 1969 – 500mf – 9 – $2,230.00 – us UPA [240]
WOODVILLE LIMESTONE – Woodville, Ohio. 1967-1978 – 4r – 1 – $32.50r – us Archival [071]
Woodward *see* HISTORY OF BURLINGTON AND MERCER COUNTIES
Woodward, A S *see* THE FOSSIL FISHES OF THE ENGLISH CHALK
WOODWARD BAPTIST CHURCH. CHESTER, SOUTH CAROLINA : CHURCH RECORDS – 1874-1951 – 1 – 30.15 – us Baptist [240]
Woodward, H *see* DESCRIPTION OF A COLLECTION OF FOSSIL SHELLS, CORALS, ETC. FROM SUMATRA, OBTAINED BY R.D.M. VERBEEK
Woodward, S P *see* A MANUAL OF THE MOLLUSCA OR RUDIMENTARY TREATISE OF RECENT AND FOSSIL SHELLS
Woodward, Thomas *see* LETTERS ON ROMANISM
Woodward, William Harrison *see*
- DESIDERIUS ERASMUS
- STUDIES IN EDUCATION DURING THE AGE OF THE RENAISSANCE, 1400-1600

WOODWIND INSTRUCTION BOOKS (PRE-1830) / U.S. Library of Congress. Music Division – 1 – 354.00 – us L of C Photodup [780]
WOODWIND INSTRUCTIONAL BOOKS – 1600-1830 – 1 – 391.00 – us L of C Photodup [780]
WOODWINDS – New York. v. 1, no. 1-4, 6-2, no. 2. Dec 1947-Mar, May, Jul 1948 – 1 – us NY Public [780]
WOODWORKER PROJECTS AND TECHNIQUES – (1986- 1,5,6) – 1983- – 9 – us UMI [640]
Woodworth, R S *see*
- PSYCHOLOGIE

WOOL QUALITY / Barker, S G – 1931 – 11mf – 7 – uk Microform Academic [680]
WOOL, WOOLLENS AND SHEEP / Bischoff – 1842 – 22mf – 7 – uk Microform Academic [636]
Wooldridge, J W *see* HISTORY OF THE SACRAMENTO VALLEY
Wooldridge, S W *see* LONDON ESSAYS IN GEOGRAPHY
WOOLER'S BRITISH GAZETTE AND MANCHESTER OBSERVER – London. -w. 25 Aug 1821-14 Sep 1822. (34 ft) – 1 – uk British Libr Newspaper [072]
Woolf, Virginia *see*
- CONCORDANCES TO THE NOVELS OF VIRGINIA WOOLF
- ORLANDO

Woollacott, Marjorie H *see*
- EFFECTS OF AGE, VELOCITY, AND ADDED MASS ON POSTURAL ADJUSTMENTS ASSOCIATED WITH A RAPID ARMRAISING MOVEMENT
- SOFT NEUROLOGICAL SIGNS IN CLUMSY CHILDREN

Woollen, William Watson *see* INTOXICATING LIQUORS; THE LAW RELATING TO THE TRAFFIC IN INTOXICATING LIQUORS AND DRUNKENNESS
Woollen, William Wesley *see* BIOGRAPHICAL AND HISTORICAL SKETCHES OF EARLY INDIANA
Woolley, C L *see* THE CITY OF AKHENATEN (MEES VOL 38)
Woolley, Leonard *see*
- ABRAHAM: RECENT DISCOVERIES AND HEBREW ORIGINS
- AN ACCOUNT OF THE EXCAVATIONS AT TELL ATCHANA
- EXCAVATIONS AT UR: A RECORD OF TWELVE YEARS WORK

Woolley, R M *see*
- THE BENEDICTIONAL OF JOHN LONGLONDE
- THE CANTERBURY BENEDICTIONAL
- THE GILBERTINE RITE

Woolley, W *see* A CURE FOR CANTING
Woolley. Yorkshire *see* PARISH REGISTERS
Woolls, W *see*
- A CONTRIBUTION TO THE FLORA OF AUSTRALIA
- LECTURES ON THE VEGETABLE KINGDOM, WITH SPECIAL REFERENCE TO THE FLORA OF AUSTRALIA

Woolman, John *see* THE JOURNAL, WITH OTHER WRITINGS..
Woolridge, J W *see* THE HISTORY OF THE SACRAMENTO VALLEY
Woolsey, George *see* LETTERBOOK OF GEORGE WOOLSEY AND GEORGE SALMON
Woolson, Constance Fenimore *see* EAST ANGELS, A NOVEL
WOOLSTON INDEPENDENT – England. -w. 11 Feb 1905-8 April 1911. 5 reels – 1 – uk British Libr Newspaper [072]
Woolston, Thomas *see* DISCOURS SUR LES MIRACLES DE JESUS-CHRIST
Woolwich, Maine.Woolwich Baptist Church *see* RECORDS
WOOLWICH MERCURY – London, England. -w. April-Dec 1981. 1 1 2 reels – 1 – uk British Libr Newspaper [072]
Woolworth, J M *see* WOOLWORTH'S REPORTS OF CASES IN THE EIGHTH CIRCUIT, 1863-1869
WOOLWORTH'S REPORTS OF CASES IN THE EIGHTH CIRCUIT, 1863-1869 / Woolworth, J M – Chicago: Callaghan. 1v. 1870 (all publ) – 5mf – 9 – $7.50 – LLMC 81-480 – us L.L.M.C. [340]
WOOMELANG AND MALLEE GAZETTE – 1955-1960. WMG1 – 1r – 1 – at Corangamite [072]
WOOMELANG SUN – 1910-1955. WOS1-17 – 17r – 1 – at Corangamite [072]
EEN WOORD OVER HET GREGORIAANSCH / Janssen, N A – Amsterdam, 1860 – 1mf – 8 – Dfl6.00 – ne Slangenburg [240]
WOORD UND DIENST – v1-40. 1954-91 (complete) – 11r – 1 – ATLA S0464 – us A.T.L.A. [073]
WOORD VAN DEN VADER – Aan het hof van assises te Parij, 3 april 1833. Gravenhage, Bij M. de Lyon, 30 maart 1834, x-46 p. Les Saint-Simoniens, 1825-1834. 6902 – 9 – fr Hachette [335]
WOORDENBOEK VOOR VRIJMETSELAREN / Carpentier Alting, A S – Amsterdam, 1884 – 8mf – 8 – ne Slangenburg [013]
Woosley, Louisa M *see*
- SHALL WOMAN PREACH?
- SHALL WOMAN PREACH? OR, THE QUESTION ANSWERED

WOOSTER DEMOCRAT : WEEKLY WHIG NEWSPAPER – Wooster, OH. 16 Sept 1840-19 Jul 1849 – 3r – 1 – us Western Res [071]
WOOSTER JOURNAL AND DEMOCRATIC NEWS : WEEKLY NATIONAL REPUBLICAN, LATER WHIG, NEWSPAPER – Wooster, OH. 28 Apr 1836-26 Aug 1840 – 1r – 1 – us Western Res [071]
WOOSTER SPECTATOR – (Weekly general newspaper) – Wooster, OH. may 10, 1823-mar 26, 1825 – 1r – 1 – us Western Res [071]
WOOSTER & WAYNE SPECTATOR – (Weekly general newspaper) – Wooster, OH. apr 2, 1825-feb 25, 1826 – 1r – 1 – us Western Res [071]
Woosung *see* MITTEILUNGEN AUS DEN TECHNISCHEN INSTITUTEN DER STAATLICHEN TUNG-CHI-UNIVERSITAET
Wooten, Dudley G *see* COMPREHENSIVE HISTORY OF TEXAS
Wooton, E O *see* FLORA OF NEW MEXICO
Wopfner, H *see* QUELLEN ZUR GESCHICHTE DES BAUERNKRIEGS IN DEUTSCHTIROL 1525
WORCESTER 1719-1890 – 282mf – 9 – 0-931248-22-1 – us Holbrook [920]
Worcester Cathedral *see* THE REGISTRUM SEDE VACANTE
Worcester County. Massachusetts Bar *see* ADDRESSES BEFORE THE MEMBERS OF THE BAR, OF WORCESTER COUNTY, MASSACHUSETTS: BY JOSEPH WILLARD, OCTOBER 2, 1829; EMORY WASHBURN, FEBRUARY 7, 1856; DWIGHT FOSTER, OCTOBER 3, 1878
THE WORCESTER COURANT – (Title varies: De Worcestersche Courant, 1865-66) – Worcester, South Africa. 13 May 1865-30 Apr 1869 – 2r – 1, 16 diazo available at reduced price – sa SA Libr [072]
WORCESTER HERALD – England. -w. 1829-36. (3 reels) – 1 – uk British Libr Newspaper [072]
Worcester (Hereford and Worcester) *see* CHURCH CALENDAR, CLERGY LIST, AND GENERAL ALMANACK FOR THE DIOCESE OF WORCESTER
WORCESTER INTELLIGENCER – Brookfield, MA. 1794-95. Also: Moral and Political Telegraphe, 1795-96; Political Repository, 1798-1802. Sold as one unit – 3 – us Readex [071]
Worcester, John *see* MATTHEW'S GOSPEL
Worcester, John Hopkins (Mrs) *see* THE LIFE OF DAVID LIVINGSTONE
Worcester, Massachusetts. Baptist City Mission Board *see* RECORDS
Worcester Monastery *see* THE LIBER ALBUS OR WHITE BOOK, 1301-1446
Worcester, Samuel T *see* HISTORY OF THE TOWN OF HOLLIS
THE WORCESTER STANDARD – Worcester, South Africa. 4 Jul 1896-24 Dec 1931 – 18r – 1,16 diazo available – sa SA Libr [072]
WORCESTER WEEKLY NEWS – Worcester, South Africa.31 Jul 1880-17 Aug 1882. 1 reel – 1, 16 diazo available at reduced price – sa SA Libr [072]

DE WORCESTERSCHE COURANT *see* THE WORCESTER COURANT
WORCESTERSHIRE, 1830 : BRITISH ISLES CENSUS DIRECTORIES PROJECT, ENGLAND. VOL 143 – 1mf – 9 – A$9.00 – at Vine [941]
WORCESTERSHIRE, 1840 : BRITISH ISLES CENSUS DIRECTORIES PROJECT, ENGLAND – at Vine [941]
WORCESTERSHIRE, 1842 : BRITISH ISLES CENSUS DIRECTORIES PROJECT, ENGLAND – (In prep) – at Vine [941]
WORCESTERSHIRE, 1850 : BRITISH ISLES CENSUS DIRECTORIES PROJECT, ENGLAND – at Vine [941]
WORCESTERSHIRE, 1854 : BRITISH ISLES CENSUS DIRECTORIES PROJECT, ENGLAND. VOL 7 – 5mf – 9 – A$33.00 – at Vine [941]
WORCESTERSHIRE, 1862 : BRITISH ISLES CENSUS DIRECTORIES PROJECT, ENGLAND. VOL 132 – 2mf – 9 – A$15.00 – at Vine [941]
WORCESTERSHIRE, 1873 : BRITISH ISLES CENSUS DIRECTORIES PROJECT, ENGLAND – at Vine [941]
WORCESTERSHIRE, 1892 : BRITISH ISLES CENSUS DIRECTORIES PROJECT, ENGLAND – at Vine [941]
WORCESTERSHIRE, 1904 : BRITISH ISLES CENSUS DIRECTORIES PROJECT, ENGLAND. VOL 113 – 7mf – 9 – A$45.00 – at Vine [941]
WORCESTERSHIRE, 1924 : BRITISH ISLES CENSUS DIRECTORIES PROJECT, ENGLAND. VOL 204 – 7mf – 9 – A$45.00 – at Vine [941]
Worcestershire Archaeological Society *see* TRANSACTIONS
WORCESTERSHIRE (DUDLEY AND KIDDERMINSTER), 1805 : BRITISH ISLES CENSUS DIRECTORIES PROJECT, ENGLAND. VOL 176 – 1mf – 9 – A$9.00 – at Vine [941]
WORCESTERSHIRE HISTORICAL SOCIETY – (Coll title: Publications of the English Record Societies, 1835-1972...) – v1-43. 1893-1957 – 162mf – 9 – £1,020.00 – uk Chadwyck [941]
WORCESTERSHIRE (NORTH), 1823 : BRITISH ISLES CENSUS DIRECTORIES PROJECT, ENGLAND. VOL 99 – 1mf – 9 – A$9.00 – at Vine [941]
WORCESTERSHIRE (NORTH), 1829 : BRITISH ISLES CENSUS DIRECTORIES PROJECT, ENGLAND. VOL 63 – 1mf – 9 – A$9.00 – at Vine [941]
WORCESTERSHIRE (WORCESTER AND GREAT MALVERN), 1847 : BRITISH ISLES CENSUS DIRECTORIES PROJECT, ENGLAND – at Vine [941]
WORCH'S MUSICAL MONTHLY – Washington, 1886-97 – 1 – £60.00 – uk Chadwyck [780]
WORD AND SPIRIT – (1985-. 5,6,9) – v1-. 1979- – 1 – us UMI [240]
WORD AND WAY – Missouri. 1896-1991 – 1 – $2,998.60 – us Baptist [240]
THE WORD AND WORKS OF GOD : A COURSE OF ADDRESSES TO YOUNG MEN / Lothian, Maurice – 2nd rev ed. Edinburgh:Johnstone, Hunter, 1878 – 1mf – 9 – 0-8370-4181-3 – 1985-2181 – us A.T.L.A. [220]
THE WORD AND WORKS OF GOD: A COURSE OF ADDRESSES TO YOUNG MEN / Lothian, Maurice – Edinburgh: Johnstone, Hunter, 1878. 1 fiche – 9 – us A.T.L.A. [240]
WORD AND WORLD – (1985-. 5,6,9) – v1-. 1981- – 1 – us UMI [240]
WORD AND WORLD – v1-12. 1981-82 (complete) – Inquire – 1 – ATLA S0815 – us A.T.L.A. [073]
THE WORD IN THE SERVICE OF AN UNDERSTANDING BETWEEN ALL MANKIND = UN APPEL 'A LA RAISON HUMAINE – The Hague: [s.n.], 1919. 12nos – 1 – CSUX86-S11 – us Hoover Inst Photo [240]
THE WORD OF GOD OPENED: ITS INSPIRATION, CANON, AND INTERPRETATION / Peirce, Bradford Kinney – New York: Carlton & Porter, 1868. 1 fiche – 9 – us A.T.L.A. [240]
WORD PROCESSING AND INFORMATION SERVICES *see* ADMINISTRATIVE MANAGEMENT
WORD PROCESSING SYSTEMS – v. 6- 1979- – 1,5,6,9 – us UMI [510]
WORD PROCESSING WORLD – v1-6 1974-79 1; v5-6 5,6,9 – us UMI [510]
THE WORD PROTESTANT IN LITERATURE, HISTORY AND LEGISLATION : AND ITS INTRODUCTION INTO THE AMERICAN CHURCH / Cavanagh, William Henry – (Includes bibliographical references) – Philadelphia: George W Jacobs, 1899 – 1mf – 9 – 0-8370-8728-7 – 1986-2728 – us A.T.L.A. [240]
A WORD TO THE REV. MR. JOHN WESLEY, ON ACCOUNT OF HIS GREAT ENMITY TO BEHMEN AND CALLING HIM DEMONOSOPHER;... – [N.p.], 1783 – 1mf – 9 – MP-546/1 – ne IDC [240]
A WORD TO THE WISE : A COMEDY / Kelly, H – London, 1795 – 2mf – 9 – ne IDC [820]
Worden Methodist Episcopal Church *see* RECORDS
WORDS – 1985- – 1,5,6,9 – us UMI [073]
WORDS AND MUSIC – v1- 1994- – 9 – Can$20.00y – cn Micromedia [780]
WORDS AND PLACES : ETYMOLOGICAL ILLUSTRATIONS OF HISTORY, ETHNOLOGY AND GEOGRAPHY / Taylor, Isaac – (Includes bibliographies and indexes) – London; New York: Macmillan, 1873 – 1mf – 9 – 0-8370-8793-7 – 1986-2793 – us A.T.L.A. [900]
WORDS MADE VISIBLE / Shaw, Samuel – 1679. 202p. (English Linguistics Series 1500-1800) – 9 – us UMI [420]
WORDS OF A BELIEVER ON THE WAYS OF PROVIDENCE TOWARDS MAN HERE AND HEREAFTER / Melia, Pius – London: Dolman, 1879 – 1mf – 9 – 0-8370-7003-1 – 1986-1003 – us A.T.L.A. [210]
WORDS OF CHEER – v1-10. 1876-85; v33-75. 1908-50 (incomplete) – 8r – 1 – ATLA 1994-S011 – us A.T.L.A. [073]
THE WORDS OF CHRIST AS PRINCIPLES OF PERSONAL AND SOCIAL GROWTH / Bascom, John – London: G.P. Putnam's, 1884. vii,220p – 1 – us U.W. Library [240]
THE WORDS OF CHRIST AS PRINCIPLES OF PERSONAL AND SOCIAL GROWTH / Bascom, John – New York: G P Putnam's, 1884 – 1mf – 9 – 0-8370-2201-0 – 1985-0201 – us A.T.L.A. [230]
WORDS OF INDIGNATION AND OF TRUTH / Brouwer, Johannes – Valencia, 1936? Fiche W 768. (Blodgett Collection of Spanish Civil War Pamphlets) – 9 – us H.U. College Libr [946]
WORDS OF JESUS / Dalman, Gustaf – Edinburgh: T.& T. Clark, 1909. 1 fiche – 9 – us A.T.L.A. [240]
THE WORDS OF MY MOUTH (CCC314) = CHI TU T'U TI YEN YU / Wang, Ming-tao – (In Chinese) – 2nd ed. Singapore: Book Missionaries (Bible Christians), 1957 – 1r – 1 – 1984-6653 – us A.T.L.A. [240]
Wordsell, W C *see* THE PRINCIPLES OF PLANT TERATOLOGY
Wordsworth, Charles *see*
- CEREMONIES AND PROCESSIONS OF THE CATHEDRAL CHURCH OF SALISBURY
- NOTES ON MEDIAEVAL SERVICES IN ENGLAND
- THE OLD SERVICE-BOOKS OF THE ENGLISH CHURCH
- THE OUTLINES OF THE CHRISTIAN MINISTRY

Wordsworth, Charles Favell Forth *see* A SUMMARY OF THE LAW OF PATENTS AND OF EXTENSION OF PATENTS
Wordsworth, Christopher *see*
- IRENICUM WESLEYANUM, OR, PROPOSALS FOR UNION WITH WESLEYAN METHODISTS
- REMARKS ON M. BUNSEN'S WORK ON ST HIPPOLYTUS
- ST. HIPPOLYTUS AND THE CHURCH OF ROME IN THE EARLIER PART OF THE THIRD CENTURY

WORDSWORTH CIRCLE – v1- 1970- 1; v5-5,6; v7- 9 – us UMI [420]
Wordsworth, Dorothy *see* RECOLLECTIONS OF A TOUR MADE IN SCOTLAND A.D. 1803. EDITED BY J.C. SHAIRP
Wordsworth, John *see*
- THE MINISTRY OF GRACE
- THE NATIONAL CHURCH OF SWEDEN
- THE ONE RELIGION: TRUTH, HOLINESS, AND PEACE DESIRED BY THE NATIONS

Wordsworth, William *see*
- A DESCRIPTION OF THE SCENERY OF THE LAKES IN THE NORTH OF ENGLAND...
- THE EXCURSION
- MEMORIALS OF A TOUR ON THE CONTINENT, 1820
- POEMS, CHIEFLY OF EARLY AND LATE YEARS
- POEMS OF WORDSWORTH. CHOSEN AND EDITED BY MATTHEW ARNOLD
- THE PRELUDE
- PROSE WORKS.
- PROSE WORKS OF WILLIAM WORDSWORTH. EDITED BY WILLIAM KNIGHT
- THE RIVER DUDDON
- THE WHITE DOE OF RYLSTONE

WORDSWORTH'S FORMATIVE YEARS / Meyer, George Wilbur – Ann Arbor: University of Michigan Press, 1943. vii,265p. (University of Michigan publications. Language and literature, vol. XX) – 1 – us U.W. Library [920]
WORDSWORTH'S POLITISCHE ENTWICKLUNG / Guettler, Felix – (Includes bibliographical references) – Stuttgart: Metzler, 1914 – 1 – us U.W. Library [420]
Wordworth, C *see*
- THE MANNER OF CORONATION OF KING CHARLES 1 OF ENGLAND AT WESTMINISTER, 2 FEBR. 1626
- ORDINALE SARUM SIVE DIRECCTORIUM SACERDOTUM LIBER
- THE TRACTS OF CLEMENT MAYDESTON WITH THE REMAINS OF CAXTON'S ORDINALE

WORK – (Cont: M5V Magazine 1994) – 1994- – 9 – Can$20.00y – cn Micromedia [331]
WORK *see* M5V MAGAZINE
THE WORK ACCOMPLISHED BY THE HEALTH DEPARTMENT OF THE SPANISH GOVERNMENT – Washington, DC. 193? Fiche W1185. (Blodgett Collection of Spanish Civil War Pamphlets) – 9 – us H.U. College Libr [946]
WORK AND OCCUPATIONS – v.9-. 1982- – 1,5,6,9 – us UMI [300]
WORK AND PLAY; OR, LITERARY VARIETIES / Bushnell, Horace – New York: C. Scribner, 1864. vi,464p. Essays. 1 reel – 1 – us U.W. Library [840]
WORK AND WORKERS IN THE MISSION FIELD – (Cont as: The Foreign Field of the Wesleyan Methodist Church. London, 1904/1905-1931/1932. v1-28. Cont as: The Kingdom Overseas. London, 1933-1969. v1-37. Missing: 1943. v11) – London. v1-13. 1892-1904 – 355mf – 9 – H-2752/1 – ne IDC [240]
Work, Edgar Whitaker *see* THE HOUSE OF CHIMHAM
Work, John *see* COLLECTION OF NEGRO SPIRITUALS
Work, M N *see* BIBLIOGRAPHY OF THE NEGRO IN AFRICA AND AMERICA
THE WORK OF CHRIST IN THE COVENANT OF REDEMPTION / Graves, J R – 1883 – 1 – 19.91 – us Baptist [240]
THE WORK OF GOD IN GREAT BRITAIN : UNDER MESSRS. MOODY AND SANKEY, 1873 TO 1875 : WITH BIOGRAPHICAL SKETCHES / Clark, Rufus W – New York: Harper, 1875 – 1mf – us A.T.L.A. [240]
THE WORK OF THE DEFENDERS OF RELIGION AND CIVILIZATION: VICTIMS OF THE BOMBING OF BARCELONA ON JANUARY 30, 1938 – n.p., 1938? Fiche W1256. (Blodgett Collection of Spanish Civil War Pamphlets) – 9 – us H.U. College Libr [946]
THE WORK OF THE HOLY SPIRIT IN MAN = OEUVRE DU SAINT-ESPRIT DANS L'HOMME : DISCOURSES DELIVERED AT GENEVA / Tophel, Gustave – (In English) – 2nd rev ed. Chicago, IL: Chicago Foundlings' Home, 1883, c1880 – 1mf – 9 – 0-8370-5384-6 – 1985-3384 – us A.T.L.A. [240]
THE WORK OF THE REPUBLIC IN THE FIELD OF EDUCATION – Washington, DC, 193? Fiche W1186. (Blodgett Collection of Spanish Civil War Pamphlets) – 9 – us H.U. College Libr [946]
THE WORK OF W. DE BRAILES, AN ENGLISH ILLUMINATOR OF THE 13TH CENTURY / Cockerell, Sydney Carlyle – Cambridge. 1930 – 1 – us U.W. Library [760]
WORK PEOPLE'S COLLEGE : PAPERS – 1904-1911, 1916-1926, 1942-1962 – 1r – 1 – us I.H.R.C. [370]
WORK STUDY AND MANAGEMENT SERVICES – (See also: Management Services) – v1-ns 19. 1956-75 – 1 – us UMI [650]
WORKBENCH – v1- 1946- 1; v27- 5,6; v31- 9 – us UMI [740]
WORKBOOK FOR SECRETARIES AND TYPISTS IN ANY AGENCY OF THE GOVERNMENT / Indonesia – SE-5718 1. 1958 – 9 – ne IDC [370]
THE WORKER : 1958-1961 – 9 – $485.00 – us UPA [320]
THE WORKER – Bournemouth, England. Southern Worker. -m. May 1912-April 1916; May 1919-Oct Nov 1921. 1 2 reel – 1 – uk British Libr Newspaper [072]
THE WORKER – Brisbane, Australia. 8 Jun-28 Dec 1916; 20 Jan 1921-30 Dec 1946 (imperfect).-w. 31 reels – 1 – uk British Libr Newspaper [072]
THE WORKER – Huddersfield, England. The organ of the Huddersfield Socialist Party. -w. 21 July 1905-25 Nov 1922. 11 reels – 1 – uk British Libr Newspaper [072]
THE WORKER – Ireland.28 Dec 1914-30 Jan 1915 – 1 – ie Microforms [072]
THE WORKER – New York. v. 11. no. 4-v. 18. no. 38. Apr 28 1901-Dec 19 1908 – 1 – us NY Public [331]
THE WORKER – (The Weekly Worker). The organ successively of the Clyde Workers' Committee, the National Workers' Committees, the British Bureau of the Red International Labour Unions, and the National Minority Movement. Glasgow and London. -w. 14 Dec 1918-25 Feb 1933. (6 reels) – 1 – uk British Libr Newspaper [331]
THE WORKER – Toronto. 1948-50 – 1 – 60.00 – cn McLaren [971]
THE WORKER – Toronto. Jan 7 1928-Nov 4 1939. Incomplete – 1 – us NY Public [331]
THE WORKER = LE TRAVAILLEUR – Montreal, Canada. n1. 1 mai 1920 – 1r – 1 – Can$25.00 – cn Can Microfilming [072]
THE WORKER – Yorkshire. 1913-14, Jan-Oct 1915 – 1 – uk Microform Academic [072]
THE WORKER *see* THE OHIO SOCIALIST, 1919 : THE TOILER, 1919-1922 : THE WORKER, 1922
WORKER – Brisbane, 1890-93 – 1r – 1 – at Pascoe [072]
WORKER – no1-23 (all publ). 1910-1912 – 1 reel – 1 – $65.00 – us UPA [335]
THE WORKER, 1922 : THE DAILY WORKER, 1923-1924 – 9 – $100.00 – us UPA [320]
THE WORKER AND HIS BIBLE / Eiselen, Frederick Carl – New York: Methodist Book, 1909. 1 fiche – 9 – us A.T.L.A. [240]
WORKER AND TECHNOLOGICAL CHANGE, 1930-80 – (With printed guide and companion vol "Connecticut Workers and Technological Change") – 54mf – 9 – £130.00 – uk Chadwyck [331]
THE WORKER : THE MIDWEEK WORKER : 1961-1968 – 9 – $1,180.00 – us UPA [320]
WORKERS AGE / Independent Labor League of America – 1-9 2+42 (all publ). 1932-1941 – 3r – 1 – $345.00 – us UPA [331]
WORKERS' COUNCIL – 1-10 (all publ). 1921 – 2mf – 9 – $35.00 – us UPA [331]
Workers' Educational Institute *see* MARXIST
WORKER'S FRIEND – London, UK. 1912. -w. 1 reel – 1 – uk British Libr Newspaper [072]
THE WORKERS' HERALD – Johannesburg, South Africa. 27 Mar 1926-30 Nov 1928 – 1r – 1, 16 diazo available at reduced price – sa SA Libr [072]
WORKERS IN THE DAWN / Gissing, G – 1880 – 1 – uk Microform Academic [941]
Workers' International Industrial Union *see* INDUSTRIAL UNION NEWS
WORKERS' LEAGUE FOR A REVOLUTIONARY PARTY : BULLETIN – 1-13 2+1 (all publ). 1937-1950 – 25mf – 9 – $140.00 – us UPA [331]
Workers Library Publishers. New York *see* SPAIN DEFENDS DEMOCRACY
WORKER'S LIFE – London, England. -w. 28 Jan 1927-20 Dec 1929. 1 1 2 reels – 1 – uk British Libr Newspaper [072]
WORKERS' LIFE / Communist Party. Great Britain – 1927-29 – 1 – uk World [335]
WORKER'S MANAGEMENT IN ALGERIA / International Labour Organisation – Cooperative information. 1971. Koulytvhisky, S. BNE-8721 1 – 9 – ne IDC [331]
WORKERS OWN – Cardiff, Wales. -m. Sept 1912-Feb 1918. 1 2 reel – 1 – uk British Libr Newspaper [072]
WORKERS PARTY AND PROGRESS PARTY OF AUSTRALIA, 1975-79 – Platforms, leaflets, and newsletters. 2 fiches – 9 – 1.00f – at Libertarian Micro [320]
Workers' Party of Marxist Unification *see* SPANISH REVOLUTION
Workers Party. U.S.A *see*
- LABOR ACTION
- NEW MILITANT

WORKER'S POWER – Highland Park, MI. 1970-1975 – 2r – 1 – $100.00 – R04391 – us Library Micro [331]

WORKERS' REPUBLIC – Dublin, Ireland.1898-1903 – 1 – ie Microforms [072]
WORKERS' REPUBLIC – Dublin, Ireland.1915-16 – 1 – ie Microforms [072]
THE WORKERS' VANGUARD – Toronto: Workers Vanguard Pub. Association, 1955 – 1 – CSUXALM3312-S – us Hoover Inst Photo [331]
WORKERS VANGUARD – NY City, NY. no345-376. 1980-1985 – 3r – 1 – $150.00 – R04931 – us Library Micro [331]
THE WORKERS' VOICE – Dublin, Ireland.1930-36 – 1 – ie Microforms [072]
WORKER'S VOICE – St John's, Antigua, 1965-67 – 1r – 1 – $60.00r – us Ross [331]
THE WORKERS' WEEKLY / Communist Party. Great Britain – 1923-27 – 1 – uk World [335]
WORKER'S WEEKLY / Communist Party. Great Britain – London. Feb 1923-Jan 1927.-w. 2 reels – 1 – uk British Libr Newspaper [072]
WORKES / Pare, A – London, 1634 – 52mf – 9 – ne IDC [610]
WORKING AND WAITING FOR TIBET : A SKETCH OF THE MORAVIAN MISSION TO THE WESTERN HIMALAYAS / Schneider, Hermann – London: Morgan and Scott, [1891?] – 1mf – us A.T.L.A. [240]
WORKING FOR JESUS : OR, INDIVIDUAL EFFORT FOR THE SALVATION OF PRECIOUS SOULS / Dickson, James A R – New rev enl ed. New York: American Tract Society, c1896 – 1mf – 9 – 0-8370-7215-8 – 1986-1215 – us A.T.L.A. [240]
WORKING MAN – London, UK. 1 Jan-17 Aug 1867. -w. 3 feet – 1 – uk British Libr Newspaper [072]
THE WORKING MAN'S CHRIST / Thoms, Craig S – New York: Dodd, Mead, 1914 – 1mf – us A.T.L.A. [240]
WORKING MAN'S FRIEND AND POLITICAL MAGAZINE – London, UK. 1832-33. -irr. 15 feet – 1 – uk British Libr Newspaper [073]
THE WORKING MEN'S ADVOCATE – Sunbury, PA. -w 1833-38. 1 roll – 13 – $25.00r – us I.M.R. [071]
WORKING MOTHER – (1982- 1,5,6,9) – v4-1981- – 1 – us UMI [306]
WORKING NORTH FROM PATAGONIA: BEING THE NARRATIVE OF A JOURNEY, EARNED ON THE WAY, THROUGH SOUTHERN AND EASTERN SOUTH AMERICA / Franck, Harry Alverson – New York: The Century Co., 1921.xiv,650p. maps – 1 – us U.W. Library [910]
WORKING PAPERS / International Congress of European and Western Ethnology. Stockholm, Sweden. 1951 – 1951 – 1 – us I.U. Libraries [390]
WORKING PAPERS FOR A NEW SOCIETY – v1-8 1973-81 1; v4-8 5,6,9 – us UMI [300]
WORKING PAPERS FOR THE DEVELOPMENT PERSPECTIVE (1975-1980) / Pakistan. Planning Commission. – Karachi. 2v. 1975 – 8mf – 9 – DE-575/1 – ne IDC [370]
WORKING PAPERS FOR THE SECOND FIVE YEAR PLAN : EMPLOYMENT AND EARNINGS: TRENDS SINCE INDEPENDENCE WITH PROSPECTS FOR 1980-1985 AND BEYOND / Gambia. Ministry of Economic Planning and Industrial Development – Banjul, 1978 – 1mf – 9 – DE-425/1 – ne IDC [331]
WORKING PAPERS FOR THE SECOND FIVE YEAR PLAN : A REVIEW OF EDUCATION, YOUTH, SPORTS AND CULTURE, AND TENTATIVE PLAN 1981-1986 / Gambia. Ministry of Economic Planning and Industrial Development – Banjul, 1980 – 2mf – 9 – DE-423/1 – ne IDC [370]
WORKING PAPERS FOR THE SECOND FIVE YEAR PLAN : A REVIEW OF HEALTH, LABOUR AND SOCIAL WELFARE AND TENTATIVE PLAN 1981-1986 / Gambia. Ministry of Economic Planning and Industrial Development – Banjul, 1980 – 2mf – 9 – DE-424/1 – ne IDC [360]
WORKING PAPERS IN ECONOMICS – (Series 1 1985-87 $1995; Series 2 1985-87 $1390; Series 3 1985-87 $860. Ca 1500 reports added each year) – 486mf – 9 – us UMI [330]
WORKING PAPERS IN PHONETICS / California. University Los Angeles. Phonetics Laboratory – (1974- . 5,6. 1975- . 9) – 1964- – .1 – us UMI [400]
WORKING PAPERS MAGAZINE – v8-. 1981- – 1,5,6,9 – us UMI [300]
WORKING PAPERS ON BILINGUALISM – Toronto. v1-19. 1973-79 – 9 – Apply – cn Micromedia [400]
WORKING PEOPLE AND THEIR EMPLOYERS / Gladden, Washington – Boston: Lockwood, Brooks, 1876 – 1mf – us A.T.L.A. [240]
WORKING PEOPLE'S DAILY – Burma. Rangoon. 1964- – 1 – us UMI [072]
WORKING PEOPLE'S DAILY – Rangoon, Burma. Mar 1978-Feb 1993 – 54r – 1 – us L of C Photodup [072]
A WORKING THEOLOGY / MacColl, Alexander – (Includes bibliographical references) – New York: Charles Scribner, 1909 – 1mf – 9 – 0-8370-4261-5 – 1985-2261 – us A.T.L.A. [240]
WORKING THESES FOR DEVELOPING TECHNICAL EDUCATION IN INDONESIA / Indonesia. Dept. of Education – SE-3409 1. 1959 – 9 – ne IDC [324]
WORKING WITH BRAILLE : A STUDY OF BRAILLE AS A MEDIUM OF COMMUNICATION / Humpshire, Barry – 1981 – 177p – 9 – 92-3-101864-7 – fr UNESCO [370]
WORKING WITH STREET CHILDREN : SELECTED CASE-STUDIES FROM AFRICA, ASIA AND LATIN AMERICA – 1995 – 304p – 9 – 92-3-103096-5 – fr UNESCO [305]
THE WORKING WOMAN – New York. Dec. 1929-Dec. 1935: miscellaneous offerings. Missing: scattered issues – 1 – 35.00r – us Hoover Inst Photo [305]
WORKING WOMAN – v1- 1976- – 1,5,6,9 – us UMI [305]
WORKING WOMEN IN VICTORIAN BRITAIN, 1850-1910 : THE DIARIES AND LETTERS OF ARTHUR J. MUNBY (1898-1910) AND HANNAH CULWICK (1833-1909) FROM TRINITY COLLEGE, CAMBRIDGE – Marlborough: Adam Matthew Publications, 1993 – 32r – 1 – $3,800.00 – uk Matthew [331]
WORKING WOMEN OF THIS CENTURY; THE LESSON OF THEIR LIVES / Balfour, Clara Lucas Liddell – 3rd ed. London, New York: Cassell, Petter, and Galpin, 1868. 419p – 1 – us U.W. Library [920]
THE WORKINGMAN AND SOCIAL PROBLEMS / Stelzele, Charles – New York, F.H. Revell, 1903 – 1mf – us A.T.L.A. [303]
WORKINGMAN'S ADVOCATE – Chicago. v.1-12. 1864-77 – 1 – 51.00 – us L of C Photodup [331]
WORKINGMAN'S ADVOCATE – New York. N.Y. 1840; 1844-48 – 1 – us UMI [071]
WORKINGMAN'S JOURNAL – Columbus. Kan. 1869-72 – 1 – us UMI [071]
WORKINGMEN AND THE CHURCH / Coyle, Robert F – Chicago, Illinois: Winona Publ, 1903 – 1mf – us A.T.L.A. [240]
WORKLIFE – 1974- – 9 – us UMI [073]
WORKLIFE – v. 1-. 1976- – 1,5,6,9 – us UMI [650]
THE WORKMAN : A FAMILY JOURNAL OF CHRISTIAN ACTIVITY – (Lacking some pgs. Several mergers) – v1-16. 17 Feb 1881-8 Oct 1898 – 8r – 1 – ATLA S0102 – us A.T.L.A. [073]
THE WORKMAN : HIS FALSE FRIENDS AND HIS TRUE FRIENDS / Thompson, Joseph Parrish – New York: American Tract Society, c1879 – 1mf – us A.T.L.A. [240]
THE WORKMAN – Panama and Panama Canal Zone. 12 Apr 1919-24 Dec 1930. 5 reels – 1 – 23.00r – us L of C Photodup [073]
WORKMAN – Moline. Ill. -w. 1854-57, 1873-76 – 1 – us UMI [071]
Workman, Gayle J *see* SEX ROLE PERCEPTIONS AND DEFENSE MECHANISMS OF FEMALE ATHLETES
Workman, George Bell *see* THE DEVELOPMENT OF THE MOTIVE OF PROTESTANT MISSIONS TO CHINA, 1807-1928
Workman, George Coulson *see* THE SERVANT OF JEHOVAH, OR, THE PASSION-PROPHECY OF SCRIPTURE
Workman, Herbert Brook *see*
- CHRISTIAN THOUGHT TO THE REFORMATION
- THE EVOLUTION OF THE MONASTIC IDEAL
- THE LETTERS OF JOHN HUS
- THE MARTYRS OF THE EARLY CHURCH
- METHODISM
- PERSECUTION IN THE EARLY CHURCH

Workman, T *see* SPIDERS
WORKMAN'S TIMES – Huddersfield, London and Manchester. -w. Aug 1890-Mar 1894. (2 reels) – 1 – uk British Libr Newspaper [072]
THE WORKMANSHIP OF THE PRAYER BOOK IN ITS LITERARY AND LITURGICAL ASPECTS / Dowden, John – London: Methuen, 1902. (The Churchman's library) – 1mf – us A.T.L.A. [240]
THE WORKMEN'S CIRCLE CALL – New York. N.Y. 1956-1969 – 1 – us UMI [071]
Workmen's Club *see* JOURNAL AND OFFICIAL GAZETTE
THE WORKMEN'S COMPENSATION ACT OF QUEBEC & REPORTED DECISIONS (CASES REPORTED TO 1ST JANUARY, 1916) / Merrill, Walter Alfred – Montreal: Wilson & Lafleur, 1916. 69p. LL-2222 – 1 – us L of C Photodup [340]
WORKMEN'S COMPENSATION LAW JOURNAL : REPORTS OF ALL THE DECISIONS RENDERED IN COMPENSATION AND FEDERAL EMPLOYERS' LIABILITY CASES IN THE FEDERAL COURTS AND IN THE STATE APPELLATE COURTS – (Includes digest for v1-8) – NY: C C Hines's Sons. v1-10. 1918-1922 cases; 1917 cases in 2 suppl vols (all publ) – 9 – us L.L.M.C. [340]
WORKMEN'S COMPENSATION REPORTS / Wisconsin. Industrial Commission – n.1-33, 1911-66. 33 fiches. (Harvard Law School Library Collection.) – 9 – 1.50f – us H.U. Law [331]
THE WORKS / Berkeley, George; ed by Fraser, Alexander Campbell – Oxford: Clarendon Press, 1871. 4v – 1 – us U.W. Library [190]
THE WORKS... / Toplady, Augustus Montague – (New edition, with an enlarged memoir of the author) – London, 1825.-6v – 33mf – 9 – MP-490/1 – ne IDC [240]
WORKS / Aldred, Guy – 1888-1963. With printed index – 1 – £540.00 – uk World [941]
WORKS / Bancroft, Hubert Howe – San Francisco. 39v. 1882-90 – 23r – 1 – us Ross [830]
WORKS / Channing, William E – Boston. 6v. 1848 – 1r – 1 – us Ross [976]
WORKS / Chaundler, Thomas – 1457-61. Ms R. 14.5 Trinity College, Cambridge – 4mf – 14 – uk Microform Academic [760]
WORKS / Fletcher, John W – 2d ed. 9 v. 1815-18 – 1 – us A.T.L.A. [240]
WORKS / Fusslin, Johann C – Fusslin, Conrad Orell, Comp. 5 v. in 3. Zurich. Switzerland. 1741 – 1 – 52.50 – us Baptist [240]
WORKS / Hale, Edward Everett – Boston, 10v. 1898-1901 – 1 – 46.00 – us L of C Photodup [830]
WORKS / Irving, Washington – new ed. New York, 1849-51 – 3r – 1 – us Ross [830]
WORKS / Luther, Martin – Eng. tr. Wace. First principles of the Reformation; or, The ninety-five theses and the three primary works of Dr. Martin Luther trans. into English. 1885 – 1 – us A.T.L.A. [240]
WORKS / Newman, John Henry – London, New York: Longmans, Green, 1898-1903 – 20 rolls – 1 – 1-55879-977-X – uk Libr Preservation [240]
WORKS / Perkin – 1612-13 – 2r – 1 – uk Microform Academic [941]
WORKS / Poe, Edgar Allen – 6v. 1884 – 1 – 19.00 – us L of C Photodup [830]
WORKS / Reade, Charles L – London: Chatto & Windus, 1896-1903 – 9 rolls – 1 – 1-55879-226-0 – uk Libr Preservation [800]
WORKS / Smyth, John – 2V. 1915 – 1 – 32.55 – us Baptist [240]
WORKS / United Nations. World Food Conference – Rome, 1974 – 29mf – 9 – $5.00f – us Ross [340]
WORKS. 1805 / Novalis – Berlin, 1805. 2v – 1 – us U.W. Library [800]
WORKS. 1825... 1825-1829 / Winckelmann, Johann Joachim – 1 – us U.W. Library [720]
WORKS, 1883-1922 / Du Bois, W E B – The first four decades of his published writings A collected edition of his shorter works. Comp. by Paul G. Partington. Whittier, California. 1979. 3 rolls – 1 – 60.00 – us Partington [360]
WORKS BY AND ABOUT GEORGE W CABLE – 1883-1905 – 1r – 1 – us Ross [975]
WORKS BY CASPAR HUBERINUS / ed by Franz, G – 45 titles – 9 – ne IDC [240]
WORKS. FIRST AMERICAN EDITION OF THE WORKS OF THE REV. D.W. CAHILL, D.D. : THE HIGHLY DISTINGUISHED IRISH PRIEST, PATRIOT AND SCHOLAR: CONTAINING A BRIEF SKETCH OF HIS LIFE, THE MOST IMPORTANT ADDRESSES, SPEECHES, CONTROVERSIAL SERMONS ETC DELIVERED IN IRELAND, ENGLAND AND SCOTLAND / Cahill, Daniel William – New York: A Franchi, 1854 – 1mf – 9 – 0-8370-9688-X – 1986-3688 – us A.T.L.A. [240]
THE WORKS OF ANNA LAETITIA BARBAULD / Barbauld, Anna Letitia – London: Longman, Hurst, Rees, Orme, Brown, and Green, 1825 – 1 roll – 1 – 1-55879-238-4 – uk Libr Preservation [840]
THE WORKS OF ARTHUR B. DAVIES / ed by Czestochowski, Joseph S – 1979 – 5 color 2 b&w mf – 15,9 – $90.00f – 0-226-68946-8 – us Chicago [700]
THE WORKS OF CHARLES SUMNER – Boston. 5v. 1870-83 – 4r – 1 – us Ross [975]
WORKS OF EDMUND BURKE / Burke, Edmund – v. 1-12. 1899 – 1 – 59.00 – us L of C Photodup [190]
WORKS OF EPICTETUS / Epictetus – Discourses (in four books), Enchiridion, and fragments. Thomas Wentworth Higginson, trans. New and rev. ed. Boston: Little, Brown and Co., 1890. 2v – 1 – us U.W. Library [450]
THE WORKS OF GEORGE BORROW / Borrow, George Henry; ed by Shorter, Clement King – [London: Constable; New York: Gabriel Wells, Norwich ed 1923-24] – 9 rolls – 1 – 1-55879-204-X – uk Libr Preservation [800]
THE WORKS OF GEORGE MEREDITH / Meredith, George – [New York: C. Scribner's Sons, 1909-12] – 15 rolls – 1 – 1-55879-225-2 – uk Libr Preservation [820]
WORKS OF HENRY PURCELL / Purcell, Henry – v. 1-26. 1878-1928 – 9 – 55.00 – us L of C Photodup [780]
THE WORKS OF JAMES WILSON, ASSOCIATE JUSTICE OF THE SUPREME COURT OF THE UNITED STATES. / Wilson, James – Chicago, Callaghan, 1896. 2 v. LL-2421 – 1 – us L of C Photodup [340]
THE WORKS OF JOHN AND CHARLES WESLEY : A BIBLIOGRAPHY,... / Green, R – London, 2nd rev ed 1906 – 4mf – 9 – ne IDC [240]
THE WORKS OF JOHN HUNTER / Hunter, J – vols 1-4 plus atlas, 1835-1837 – 47mf – 9 – ne IDC [610]
THE WORKS OF JONATHAN SWIFT – 19v. 1814 – 3r – 1 – us Ross [420]
THE WORKS OF JOSEPH V. STALIN – 66mf – 9 – us UMI [320]
THE WORKS OF MR. ABRAHAM COWLEY / Cowley, Abraham – London, 1668 – 1 – us U.W. Library [920]
THE WORKS OF PERCY BYSSHE SHELLEY / Shelley, Percy Bysshe – London: E. Moxon, 1850 – 1 roll – 1 – 1-55879-674-6 – uk Libr Preservation [800]
THE WORKS OF ROBERT BURNS : WITH AN ACCOUNT OF HIS LIFE AND A CRITICISM ON HIS WRITINGS – London. 4v. 1813 – 1r – 1 – us Ross [420]
THE WORKS OF THE HIGHLY EXPERIENCED AND FAMOUS CHYMIS / Glauber, Johann – London, 1689 – 1 – us U.W. Library [540]
THE WORKS OF THE HON. JAMES WILSON – (James Wilson was a member of both the Federal and the Pennsylvania consitutional conventions, a signer of the Declaration of Independence, a justice of the U.S. Supreme Court and professor of law in the College of Pennsylvania. This first volume covers his lectures on law) – Philadelphia: Bronson & Chauncey. 1v. 1804 – 5mf – 9 – $7.50 – LLMC 95-070 – us L.L.M.C. [340]
THE WORKS OF THE LATE WILLIAM GADSBY / Gadsby, William – 2v. 1851 – 9 – us A.T.L.A. [240]
THE WORKS OF THE LEARNED T. BROWNE / Browne, T – 1686 – 28mf – 8 – ne IDC [610]
THE WORKS OF THE REV. GEORGE CRABBE / Crabbe, George – London: John Murray, 1823 – 3 rolls – 1 – 1-55879-249-X – uk Libr Preservation [810]
THE WORKS OF THE REV. WILLIAM JAY / Jay, William – 3v. 1852-55 – 1 – us A.T.L.A. [240]

THE WORKS OF THE REVEREND GEORGE CRABBE, LL. B. / Crabbe, George – London: Printed for J. Hatchard, 1816 – 2 rolls – 1 – 1-55879-248-1 – uk Libr Preservation [810]
THE WORKS OF WILLIAM H SEWARD / ed by Baker, George E – New York. v1-3. 1853 – 1r – 1 – us Ross [976]
WORKS PROGRESS ADMINISTRATION – San Francisco, 1935-38 – 1r – 1 – $50.00 – B40325 – us Library Micro [978]
WORKSHOP FOR PROFESSIONAL COMMUNITY LEADERS / Wisconsin. College of Agriculture. Dept. of Rural Sociology – 1959-65 – 1,5 – us Spaulding [630]
WORKSOP ADVERTISER – (Worksop and Retford Advertiser Bassetlaw and County Express). England. -w. 7 Jun 1873-30 May 1874. (Imperfect). (31 ft) – 1 – uk British Libr Newspaper [072]
THE WORLD – Calcutta, India. -w. 15 Oct 1791-Feb 1793. 1 reel – 1 – uk British Libr Newspaper [072]
THE WORLD – Charleston. S.C. and Sunday Budget. 1888-91 – 1 – us UMI [071]
THE WORLD – Dublin. Ireland. -w. 16 May 1840-27 Dec 1851. (12 reels) – 1 – uk British Libr Newspaper [072]
THE WORLD – London, England. -w. 4 May 1827-28 March 1832. 3 reels – 1 – uk British Libr Newspaper [072]
THE WORLD – New York. Morning ed. 1860-1931 – 517r – 1 – us Ross [071]
THE WORLD – New York. Morning ed. June 14 1860-Feb 27 1931 – 1 – us NY Public [071]
THE WORLD – Rio Linda, CA. 1983-1984 – 1r – 1 – $50.00 – B05050 – us Library Micro [071]
THE WORLD – Rohnert Park, CA. 1965-1969 – 7r – 1 – $350.00 – B05055 – us Library Micro [071]
THE WORLD *see* BRITAIN AND EUROPE SINCE 1945-1973 UPDATE
WORLD – Aberdeen. Wash. 1908-1968 – 1 – us UMI [071]
WORLD – Bangkok. Thailand. 1957- – 1 – us UMI [072]
WORLD – Birmingham. Ala. 1945- – 1 – us UMI [071]
WORLD – Indianapolis. Ind. 1887-1892 – 1 – us UMI [071]
WORLD – Lawrence. Kan. 1892-1911 – 1 – us UMI [071]
WORLD – New York, 1860-94 – 14r – 1 – us Ross [071]
WORLD – New York. Evening ed. Oct 10 1887-Feb 26 1931. Incomplete – 1 – us NY Public [071]
WORLD – Opelousas. La. 1940- – 1 – us UMI [071]
WORLD – Portland OR. Mar 6-27 1897 – 1 – us U.O. Library [071]
WORLD – Portland, OR. -w. 1885-87 – 1 – 24.00 – us Oregon Hist [071]
WORLD – Rainier OR. Mar 2 1972-July 25 1979 – 1 – us U.O. Library [071]
WORLD – (Set incl. Coos Bay Times) – Coos Bay, OR. -d. 4 Jul 1906-15 Aug 1978+. – 206r – 1 – us U.O. Library [071]
WORLD – Wenatchee. Wash. 1905- – 1 – us UMI [071]
WORLD – Weston. West Virginia. 1886-99 – 1 – us UMI [071]
WORLD *see* BANTU WORLD
WORLD AFFAIRS – (See: Canada and the World) – Oakville. v1-35. 1936-95 – 9 – cn Micromedia [327]
WORLD AFFAIRS *see*
– BRITAIN AND EUROPE SINCE 1945-1973 UPDATE
– CANADA AND THE WORLD
WORLD AFFAIRS REPORT – Stanford, CA. 1983 – 1r – 1 – $50.00 – R04124 – us Library Micro [071]
WORLD AGRICULTURAL STATISTICS 1986 : F.A.O. STATISTICAL POCKETBOOK – 1986 – 208p – it F.A.O. [310]
WORLD AGRICULTURE : THE LAST QUARTER CENTURY – 1970 – 42p – it F.A.O. [630]
WORLD ALMANAC – 1868-1876; 1885- – 1 – us UMI [030]
WORLD ALMANAC AND BOOK OF FACTS – (1985-. 1,5,6) – 1868- – 9 – us UMI [030]
WORLD AND HIS WIFE AND THE PLAYBOX – London, UK. Nov 1904-May 1910. -w. 5 1/4 reels – 1 – uk British Libr Newspaper [072]
THE WORLD AND ITS GOD / Mauro, Philip – London: Morgan & Scott, 1908. 1 fiche. 8370-4328-X – 9 – us A.T.L.A. [240]
THE WORLD AND THE INDIVIDUAL. FIRST SERIES, THE FOUR HISTORICAL CONCEPTIONS OF BEING : GIFFORD LECTURES / Royce, Josiah – New York: Macmillan, 1900, c1899 – 2mf – us A.T.L.A. [210]
THE WORLD AND THE KINGDOM / Thompson, Hugh Miller – New York: Thomas Whittaker, 1888 – 1mf – 9 – 0-8370-5596-2 – 1985-3596 – us A.T.L.A. [240]
THE WORLD AND THE LOGOS / Thompson, Hugh Miller – New York: G.P. Putnam, 1886. 1 fiche – 9 – us A.T.L.A. [240]
WORLD APPAREL FIBRE CONSUMPTION SURVEY 1983 – 1983 – 150p – it F.A.O. [310]
WORLD APPAREL FIBRE CONSUMPTION SURVEY 1985 – 1985 – 172p – it F.A.O. [310]
WORLD APPAREL FIBRE CONSUMPTION SURVEY 1987 – 1987 – 151p – it F.A.O. [338]
WORLD APPAREL FIBRE CONSUMPTION SURVEY 1989 – 1989 – 158p – it F.A.O. [339]
WORLD ARCHAEOLOGY – v1-2 n2. 1969-70 – 16mf – 9 – $5.00f – us Ross [930]
WORLD ART / ed by Edgar, Ray – 9,5,1 – us Gordon [700]
THE WORLD AS WILL AND IDEA / Schopenhauer, Arthur – Trans. from German by R.B. Haldane and J. Kemp. London: Routledge and Kegan Paul, 1883. 3v – 1 – us U.W. Library [190]
WORLD AT THE CROSS ROADS : RUSSIAN MIR NA PEREPUTI E / Brasol, Boris Leo – Bielgrad: Vseslavi anski i knizhny i magazin, 1922 – 1 – CSUX88-B1559 – us Hoover Inst Photo [947]
WORLD BANANA ECONOMY : STATISTICAL COMPENDIUM – 1983 – 36p – it F.A.O. [338]
WORLD BANANA ECONOMY 1970-1984 : STRUCTURE, PERFORMANCE AND PROSPECTS – 1986 – 91p – it F.A.O. [338]
World Bank. International Bank for Reconstruction and Development *see* REPORTS AND SUMMARY PROCEEDINGS
WORLD CARTOGRAPHY / United Nations – 43mf – 9. – $78.00; $1.90f – uk UNIMICRO [910]
WORLD CARTOGRAPHY / United Nations – (Vols 1-12. ST/SOA/Ser.L/1-12. E.28; Vols 13-29. ST/ESA/Ser.L/13-19. E.17) – 9 – us U.N. Pubs [910]
WORLD CEMENT – v13, no.2-. Mar 1982- – 1,5,6,9 – us UMI [073]
WORLD CEMENT TECHNOLOGY – v8-13, no.1. 1977-Jan-Feb 1982 – 1,5,6,9 – us UMI [073]
WORLD CENSUS OF AGRICULTURE 1980 : METHODOLOGICAL REVIEW – 1992 – 370p – it F.A.O. [630]
WORLD CHRISTIANITY – v1-3. 1937-39 (complete) – Inquire – 1 – ATLA 1993-S520 – us A.T.L.A. [073]
WORLD COAL – v1 1975- – 1,5,6,9 – us UMI [622]
WORLD COFFEE SURVEY – 1968 – 476p – it F.A.O. [338]
WORLD COIN NEWS – v1-10 1973-83 – 1,5,6 – us Princeton Micro [730]
WORLD COMMUNICATION REPORT – 1989 – 576p – 9 – 92-3-102628-3 – fr UNESCO [380]
WORLD COMPENDIUM OF FOREST AND FOREST PRODUCTS RESEARCH INSTITUTIONS – 1986 – 624p – it F.A.O. [060]
WORLD CONFERENCE ON EDUCATION FOR ALL : CATALOGUE OF DOCUMENTS – (Bilingual: English/French) – 1992 – 114p – 9 – 92-3-002817-7 – fr UNESCO [370]
World Conference on Faith and Order *see* SCRAPBOOKS, 1910-30
WORLD CONGREGATIONALISM – v1-7 no 19. 1959-Jan 1965 (complete) – 5r – 1 – ATLA B0063 – us A.T.L.A. [073]
WORLD COUNCIL OF CHURCHES = COMMISSION OF THE CHURCHES ON INTERNATIONAL AFFAIRS – Geneva. 70 docs. 1980-1990 – 63mf – 9 – ne IDC [320]
WORLD COUNCIL OF CHURCHES : COMMITTEE ON THE CHURCH AND THE JEWISH PEOPLE – 1963-80 (complete) – 1r – 1 – ATLA S0634 – us A.T.L.A. [240]
WORLD COUNCIL OF CHURCHES : DIVISION OF INTER-CHURCH AID – 1965-84 (complete) – 5r – 1 – ATLA S0552 – us A.T.L.A. [240]
WORLD COUNCIL OF CHURCHES. CENTRAL COMMITTEE : MINUTES – v30-36: 1977-84 (complete) – 1r – 1 – ATLA S0731 – us A.T.L.A. [240]
WORLD COUNCIL OF CHURCHES: CENTRAL COMMITTEE 1946 – (Meeting of the provisional Committe (Geneve 1946) 4mf; 1. Meeting of the Central Comm. (A'dam-Woudschoten 1948) 2mf; 4. Meeting of the Central Comm. (Rolle 1951) 3mf) – 8 – ne Slangenburg [240]
WORLD COUNCIL OF CHURCHES. FAITH AND ORDER COMMISSION : MINUTES – (Filmed with: Correspondence of Secretaries, R W Brown and R H Gardiner) – 1924-32 –)R – 1 – ATLA S0075 – us A.T.L.A. [240]
World Council of Churches, Geneva *see* INTERNATIONAL MISSIONARY COUNCIL ARCHIVES 1910-1961
World Council of Churches. Geneva *see* CLASSIFIED CATALOG OF THE ECUMENICAL MOVEMENT
THE WORLD COURT MAGAZINE – Aug 1915 – Jul 1919 – 36mf – 9 – $140.00 – us UPA [900]
WORLD CROPS *see* AGRICULTURE INTERNATIONAL
THE WORLD CRUISE OF R.I. DEWARUTJI : YALESVEVA JAYAMAHA: AT SEA IS OUR GREATNESS / Indonesia. Departemen Penerangan – SE-11,658 1. 1964? – 9 – ne IDC [910]
WORLD DEVELOPMENT – v1- 1973- – 5,6,9 – us UMI [338]
WORLD DIRECTORY OF HUMAN RIGHTS RESEARCH AND TRAINING INSTITUTIONS 1992 – (Trilingual: English/Franc£6ais and Espan£4ol) – 2nd ed 1992 – 9 – 92-3-002794-4 – fr UNESCO [320]
WORLD DIRECTORY OF NATIONAL SCIENCE AND TECHNOLOGY POLICY MAKING BODIES – (Trilingual: English, French, Spanish) – 2nd ed 1991 – 9 – 92-3-002711-1 – fr UNESCO [500]
WORLD DIRECTORY OF PEACE RESEARCH AND TRAINING INSTITUTIONS 1991 – (Available in English/French/Spanish) – 7th ed 1991 – 9 – 92-3-002752-9 – fr UNESCO [320]
WORLD DIRECTORY OF RESEARCH PROJECTS, STUDIES AND COURSES IN SCIENCE AND TECHNOLOGY POLICY – (Trilingual: English/French/Spanish) – 2nd ed 1990 – 9 – 92-3-002639-5 – fr UNESCO [500]
WORLD DIRECTORY OF TEACHER-TRAINING INSTITUTIONS – (Trilingual: English/French/ Spanish) – 1993 – 9 – 92-3-002800-2 – Co-published with the International Council for Education for Teaching (ICE) – fr UNESCO [370]
WORLD DIRECTORY OF TEACHING AND RESEARCH INSTITUTIONS IN INTERNATIONAL LAW – (Available in English/French/Spanish) – 2nd ed 1990 – 9 – 92-3-002644-1 – fr UNESCO [340]
WORLD DOMINION PRESS INFORMATION SERVICE – v2-3. 1937-38 (incomplete) – 1r – 1 – ATLA S0706C – us A.T.L.A. [073]
WORLD ECONOMIC OUTLOOK: A SURVEY BY THE STAFF OF THE INTERNATIONAL MONETARY FUND – (1984- . 5,6,9) – v1- . 1980- – 1 – us UMI [337]
WORLD ECONOMIC SURVEY / United Nations – 167mf – 9 – $300.00; $1.90f – uk UNIMICRO [330]
WORLD ECONOMIC SURVEY / United Nations – (1948-1972. ST/ECA/. E.115 F.129 S.199; 1973-1988. ST/ESA/. E.77 F.76 S.76; 1978 and 1988 are not yet available in French and Spanish) – 9 – us U.N. Pubs [330]
THE WORLD ECONOMY – (1982-. 1,5,6,9) – v1-. 1977- – 1 – us UMI [337]
WORLD EDUCATION REPORT 1991 / UNESCO – (Also published in French, Spanish and Arabic) – 1991 – 149p – 9 – 92-3-102751-4 – fr UNESCO [370]
WORLD EDUCATION REPORT 1993 – 1993 – 172p – 9 – 92-3-102935-5 – fr UNESCO [370]
WORLD EMPLOYMENT PROGRAMME : WEP RESEARCH WORKING PAPERS – (12v 1994 Sfr145.00 ISBN: 92-2-110004-9. 16v 1993 Sfr180.00 ISBN: 92-2-109579-7. 27v 1992 Sfr300.00 ISBN: 92-2-108973-8. 32v 1991 Sfr325.00 ISBN: 92-2-108589-9. 38v 1990 Sfr400.00 ISBN: 92-2-108173-7. 37v 1989 Sfr400.00 ISBN: 92-2-107592-3. 23v 1988 Sfr225.00 ISBN: 92-2-107176-6. 39v 1987 Sfr475.00 ISBN: 92-2-106762-9. 27v 1986 Sfr325.00 ISBN: 92-2-106167-1. 21v 1985 Sfr275.00 ISBN: 92-2-105596-5. 18v 1984 Sfr275.00 ISBN: 92-2-105113-7. 47v 1983 Sfr400.00 ISBN: 92-2-103868-8. 36v 1982 Sfr375.00 ISBN: 92-2-103519-0. 55v 1981 Sfr400.00 ISBN: 92-2-103158-6. 314v 1974-1980 Sfr2,000.00 ISBN: 92-2-102752-X) – 1981-94 – sz I.L.O. [331]
WORLD ENERGY SUPPLIES / United Nations – (1929-1954. ST/STAT/Ser.J/1-2. E/F.6; 1955-1972. ST/STAT/Ser.J/3-17. E.44; 1970-1973. ST/ESA/STAT/Ser.J/18-22. E.39) – 9 – us U.N. Pubs [333]
WORLD ENGLISHES – 1,5,69 – us UMI [420]
WORLD FAITHS – 1949-88 (complete) – Inquire – 1 – ATLA S0624 – us A.T.L.A. [073]
WORLD FAITHS INSIGHT – (1986- . 5,6,9) – 1980- – 1 – us UMI [200]
THE WORLD FEDERALIST MOVEMENT : A COLLECTION OF THE MOST IMPORTANT JOURNALS ON MICROFICHE / Baratta, Joseph Preston – (Union Now Bulletin – Washington, DC, New York City 1939-40. Federal Union World – New York City, Washington, DC, 1940-45. Student Federalist – Scarsdale, NY, Washington, DC 1943-49. Freedom and Union – Washington, DC 1946-78. World Government News – New York 1943-52. Documents 1-150 – Chicago 1945-48. Common Cause – Chicago 1947-51. The Federalist – New York, Washington, DC 1951-69. The Peace Lobby – Washington, DC 1969-71. Federalist Letter – Washington, DC 1971-73. World Citizen-Federalist Letter – Washington, DC 1973-75. World Federalist USA Report – Washington, DC 1975. World Federalist – Washington, DC 1976-88. UN Reform Campaigner – Wayne, NJ, Washington, DC 1976-88. One World – Chicago, 1953-73. World Federalist – Amsterdam, The Hague, Ottawa 1951-74. Transnational Perspectives – Geneva 1974-88) – 1989 – 1r + 252mf – 1,9 – $900.00 – us Ross [320]
WORLD FEDERALIST MOVEMENT / ed by Baratta, Joseph Preston – (With printed guide) – 252mf – 1 – $900.00 – us Ross [320]
WORLD FOOD CONFERENCE, ROME, ITALY : PRE, IN AND POST-SESSION DOCUMENTATION OF THE UNITED NATIONS CONFERENCE HELD IN ROME – 1974 – E.29 F.24 R.22 S.24 – 9 (E/CONF.65/) – us U.N. Pubs [640]
WORLD FOOD PROGRAMME : REPORTS OF THE U.N./FAO COMMITTEE ON FOOD AID POLICIES AND PROGRAMMES, ROME – it F.A.O. [338]
WORLD FOOD SECURITY : SELECTED THEMES AND ISSUES – 1988 – 108p – it F.A.O. [338]
THE WORLD FOR CHRIST / Behrends, Adolphus Julius Frederick – New York: Eaton & Mains; Cincinnati: Curts & Jennings, 1896 – 1mf – 9 – 0-8370-6015-X – 1986-0015 – us A.T.L.A. [240]
WORLD FOR PEACE AND DEMOCRACY – New York. v1-6. 1933-39 – 1r – 1 – us Ross [327]
WORLD FOREST PRODUCTS DEMAND AND SUPPLY 1990 AND 2000 – 1982 – 366p – it F.A.O. [338]
World Future Society *see* ...BULLETIN
WORLD FUTURES / ed by Laszlo, E – (Incorporating Philosophy Forum) – 1,5,9 – us Gordon [100]
WORLD HEALTH – 1948- 1; 1977- 5,6,9 – us UMI [610]
WORLD HEALTH FORUM – v.1-. 1980- – 1,5,6,9 – us UMI [073]
World Health Organization *see* BULLETIN
THE WORLD HERALD – Brooklyn, New York. v. 1. 1936 37 – 1 – us NY Public [071]
WORLD HOSPITALS – v1- 1964- 1; v12- 6; v11- 1975- 9 – us UMI [610]
WORLD INDEX – Wenatchee. Wash. 1880-1920 – 1 – us UMI [071]
WORLD INDUSTRIA – Johannesburg, 1965-67 – 2r – 1 – us Ross [072]
WORLD ISSUES – v1-4 1976-79 – 1,5,6,9 – us UMI [320]
WORLD JEWISH TRIBUNE – (V1, No2, (5 June 1979)-v1, No41, (14 Mar. 1980); Lacking: v1, No15, (4 Sept. 1979); v1, No20-38, (12 Oct. 1979-22 Feb. 1980)) – New York, N.Y. – 1 – us A.J.P.C. [071]
WORLD JOURNAL OF SURGERY / Societe Internationale de Chirurgie and Collegium International Chirurgiae Digestivae – v.1-6, 1977-81. ISSN:0364-2313 – 1,5,6,9,13 – 82.00v – us UMI [617]

WORLD: JOURNAL OF THE UNITARIAN UNIVERSALIST ASSOCIATION – v1- . 1987- – 1,5,6,9 – us UMI [073]

WORLD JOURNAL OF UROLOGY – v1-. 1983- – 1,5,6,9 – us UMI [073]

World League Against Alcoholism *see* PAPERS

THE WORLD LIGHTED: A STUDY OF THE APOCALYPSE / Smith, Charles Edward – New York: Funk & Wagnalls, 1890.1 fiche – 9 – us A.T.L.A. [240]

WORLD LIST OF FORESTRY SCHOOLS – 1981 – 118p – it F.A.O. [634]

WORLD LIST OF INSTITUTIONS ENGAGED IN FORESTRY AND FOREST PRODUCTS RESEARCH – 1985 – 171p – it F.A.O. [060]

WORLD LIST OF SEED SOURCES – 1986 – 438p – it F.A.O. [631]

WORLD LIST OF SOCIAL SCIENCE PERIODICALS / UNESCO. Social Science Documentation Centre – (English/Spanish/French) – 8th rev ed 1991 – xv/1264p – 9 – 92-3-002734-0 – fr UNESCO [300]

WORLD LITERATURE WRITTEN IN ENGLISH – v31- 1991- – 9 – Can$20.00y – cn Micromedia [400]

WORLD MARKET FOR TROPICAL HORTICULTURAL PRODUCTS – 1988 – 257p – it F.A.O. [650]

WORLD MARXIST REVIEW – v1- 1958- 1; v14- 5,6; v19- 9 – us UMI [335]

WORLD MEAT ECONOMY IN FIGURES – 1985 – 194p – it F.A.O. [339]

WORLD MINERAL STATISTICS 1882-1966 : INCLUDING ANNUAL GENERAL REPORTS UPON THE MINERAL INDUSTRY OF THE UNITED KINGDOM OF GREAT BRITAIN AND IRELAND 1894-1896 – (Coll title: British Government Publications...1801-1977, Minerals) – 13r – 1 (£1,890.00 minerals set 36r) – uk Chadwyck [550]

World Missionary Conference 1910 Edinburgh, Scotland *see* THE HISTORY AND RECORDS OF THE CONFERENCE

World Missionary Conference (1910 : Edinburgh, Scotland) Continuation Committee *see* THE CONTINUATION COMMITTEE CONFERENCES IN ASIA, 1912-1913

WORLD MODELS – 1976- – 1,5,6,9 – us UMI [790]

WORLD NEWS – London. 1954-62. C.P.G.B. Series One (Journals) – 1 – uk World [073]

WORLD NEWS AND VIEWS – 1922-53 – 16r – 1 – us Ross [900]

WORLD NEWS AND VIEWS – Berlin etc. v. 2. no. 17-v. 33. no. 50. Mar 3 1922-Dec 19 1953. Incomplete. Includes supplement Daylight – 1 – us NY Public [072]

WORLD NEWS AND VIEWS – Berlin. Vienna. London. Oct. 1921-Dec. 1953 gaps – 1 – 35.00r – us Hoover Inst Photo [073]

WORLD NEWS AND VIEWS – C.P.G.B. Series One (Journals). 1937-53 – 1 – uk World [073]

WORLD NUTRITION AND NUTRITION EDUCATION / Sinclair, H M & Howat, G R – 1980 – 272p – 9 – 92-3-101736-5 – fr UNESCO [640]

THE WORLD OF COMETS / Guillemin, Amedee – Trans. and ed. by James Glaisher. London: S. Low, Marston, Searle & Rivington, 1877. xxxviii,548p. illus., tables, diagrs – 1 – us U.W. Library [520]

THE WORLD OF INSECTS: A GUIDE TO ITS WONDERS / Douglas, J W – London, 1856. x,244p. Z/1197/2 – 8 – ne IDC [590]

WORLD OF JESUS (CCC133) / Gutzlaff, Karl Friedrich August – (In Chinese) – [s.l: s.n, 1837] – 1r – 1 – 1984-B500 – us A.T.L.A. [240]

THE WORLD OF PORT ROYAL : THE JANSENIST MOVEMENT IN THE CATHOLIC CHURCH, 17TH-18TH CENTURIES – (With printed guide) – (mf ed 1997) – 511mf – 9 – Dfl7,775.00 – ne MMF Publ [240]

WORLD OF SAVANNAS : ECONOMIC DRIVING FORCE, ECOLOGICAL CONSTRAINTS AND POLICY OPTIONS FOR SUSTAINABLE LAND USE – 9 – 92-3-102750-6 – fr UNESCO [333]

A WORLD OF WONDERS, OR, DIVERS DEVELOPMENTS, SHOWING THE THOROUGH TRIUMPH OF ANIMAL MAGNETISM IN NEW ENGLAND. / Peabody, Joel R – Boston, 1838 – 1 – us U.W. Library [150]

WORLD OIL – v1- 1916- 1; v160- 5,6; v182- 9 – us UMI [660]

THE WORLD, OR INSTABILITY / Rafinesque-Schmaltz, Constantine S – 1836 – 9 – 15.00 – us Scholars' Facs [810]

WORLD OVER; TEACHER'S EDITION – (v.42-. 1980- 5,6,9) – v.1-. 1940- – 1 – us UMI [073]

WORLD PATENT INFORMATION – v1- 1979- – 5,6,9 – us UMI [340]

WORLD PATENTS ABSTRACTS: BY SUBJECT – Annual Eng. lang. abstracts for new patents and applications from 15 major patent issuing authorities. Arranged by subject. General, mechanical, electrical. Available by year and subject – 5,6 – uk Derwent [600]

WORLD POLICY JOURNAL – v1-. 1983- – 1,5,6,9 – us UMI [073]

WORLD POLITICAL OPINION AND SOCIAL SURVEYS – Series One: British Opinion Polls 1945-1988 – 9 – us Primary [320]

WORLD POLITICS – v1- 1948- 1; v23- 5,6; v28- 9 – us UMI [327]

WORLD PROBLEMS IN THE CLASSROOM – 1981 – 59p – 9 – 92-3-101817-5 – fr UNESCO [370]

WORLD PULP AND PAPER DEMAND, SUPPLY AND TRADE, VOL 1 : SELECTED PAPERS OF AN EXPERT CONSULTATION, TUNIS, 1977 – 1977 – 336p – it F.A.O. [380]

WORLD PULP AND PAPER DEMAND, SUPPLY AND TRADE, VOL 2 : SELECTED PAPERS OF AN EXPERT CONSULTATION, TUNIS, 1977 – 1977 – 248p – it F.A.O. [380]

WORLD REVIEW – v2-nsv50. 1936-53 – 1 – us UMI [073]

WORLD REVIEW OF INTERACTIONS BETWEEN MARINE MAMMALS AND FISHERIES – 1984 – 197p – it F.A.O. [639]

WORLD REVIEW OF REVIEWS – v1-. 1936- – 1 – us UMI [073]

WORLD SCIENCE REPORT 1993 – 1994 – 278p – 9 – 92-3-102938-X – fr UNESCO [500]

WORLD SERIES CRICKET, TELEVISION AND AUSTRALIAN CULTURE / Quick, S P – 1990 – 3mf – 9 – $12.00 – us Microform Publ [790]

WORLD STATISTICAL COMPENDIUM FOR RAW HIDES AND SKINS, LEATHER AND LEATHER FOOTWEAR 1966-1985 – 1986 – 131p – it F.A.O. [310]

WORLD STATISTICS IN BRIEF / United Nations – E.20 – 9 (ST/ESA/STAT/Ser.V/1-4) – us U.N. Pubs [304]

WORLD STUDENT CHRISTIAN FEDERATION – Kowloon, Geneva. 24 docs. 1980-1991 – 17mf – 9 – ne IDC [240]

WORLD SURVEY – 1-7 (all publ). 1941-1942 – 6mf – 9 – $45.00 – us UPA [900]

WORLD TENNIS – New York. v17-18. 1970 – 25mf – 9 – $5.00f – us Ross [790]

WORLD TENNIS – (v. 22- 1974- 5,6. v. 23- 1975- 9) – v. 1- 1953- – 1 – us UMI [790]

WORLD TOBACCO – v.67-. 1980- – 1,5,6,9 – us UMI [073]

WORLD TODAY – v. 1-25. London. 1945-69 – 9 – 24225.00; 9.00v – uk Dawson [900]

THE WORLD TOMORROW – 1918-34 – 87mf – 9 – $355.00 – us UPA [320]

WORLD TRENDS AND ISSUES IN ADULT EDUCATION / Bhola, H S – 1988 – 177p – 9 – 92-3-102581-3 – Co-published with Jessica Kingsley Publishers, London – fr UNESCO [370]

WORLD UNITY MAGAZINE – v1-15. Oct 1927 – Mar 1935 – 76mf – 9 – $305.00 – us UPA [320]

[WORLD WAR 1 ALMANACS PAMPHLET COLLECTION] – 1914-1919 – 5r – 1 – CSUXAMK5705-B – us Hoover Inst Photo [940]

[WORLD WAR 1 AND ART PAMPHLET COLLECTION] – 1914-19?? – 2r – 1 – CSUXAML7874-B – us Hoover Inst Photo [700]

[WORLD WAR 1 AND THE CATHOLIC CHURCH PAMPHLET COLLECTION] – 1914-1927 – 2r – 1 – CSUXANL3043-B – us Hoover Inst Photo [240]

[WORLD WAR 1 ARMISTICE PAMPHLET COLLECTION] – 1918-1919 – 1 reel – 1 – CSUXANM5031-B – us Hoover Inst Photo [940]

WORLD WAR 1 BATTLEFIELD GUIDES PAMPHLET COLLECTION – 19??-1926 – 2r – 1 – CSUXAML7886-B – us Hoover Inst Photo [355]

WORLD WAR 1 CAMPAIGNS IN THE BALKAN PENINSULA PAMPHLET COLLECTION – 1916-1923 – 1 reel – 1 – CSUXANL2928-B – us Hoover Inst Photo [355]

WORLD WAR 1 CAMPAIGNS IN TURKEY AND THE NEAR EAST PAMPHLET COLLECTION – 1917-1918? – 1 reel – 1 – CSUXANL2933-B – us Hoover Inst Photo [355]

WORLD WAR 1 CHILDREN'S LITERATURE PAMPHLET COLLECTION – 1915-19?? – 2r – 1 – CSUXAML7851-B – us Hoover Inst Photo [410]

WORLD WAR 1 COOKBOOKS PAMPHLET COLLECTION – 1915-1919 – 2r – 1 – CSUXANL3623-B – us Hoover Inst Photo [640]

WORLD WAR 1 EXHIBITIONS AND MUSEUMS PAMPHLET COLLECTION – 1914-1938 – 2r – 1 – CSUXAMK5722-B – us Hoover Inst Photo [060]

WORLD WAR 1 HUMOR PAMPHLET COLLECTION – 1914-1919 – 2r – 1 – CSUXAML7870-B – us Hoover Inst Photo [870]

WORLD WAR 1 IN RUSSIA PAMPHLET COLLECTION – 1915-1924 – 1 reel – 1 – CSUXANR2572-B – us Hoover Inst Photo [355]

WORLD WAR 1 IN SERBIA PAMPHLET COLLECTION – 1915-1928? – 1 reel – 1 – CSUXANQ5691-B – us Hoover Inst Photo [355]

WORLD WAR 1 MEMORIALS AND MONUMENTS IN FRANCE PAMPHLET COLLECTION – 1916-1986 – 1 reel – 1 – CSUXANM5457-B – us Hoover Inst Photo [355]

WORLD WAR 1 MEMORIALS AND MONUMENTS IN GERMANY PAMPHLET COLLECTION – 1915-1917? – 1 reel – 1 – CSUXANM5465-B – us Hoover Inst Photo [355]

WORLD WAR 1 MEMORIALS AND MONUMENTS PAMPHLET COLLECTION – 1918-1926 – 1 reel – 1 – CSUXANM5451-B – us Hoover Inst Photo [355]

WORLD WAR 1 MISCELLANEA PAMPHLET COLLECTION – 1914-1939 – 4r – 1 – CSUXAML7862-B – us Hoover Inst Photo [355]

WORLD WAR 1 POSTERS PAMPHLET COLLECTION – 1914-1919 – 1 reel – 1 – CSUXAML7877-B – us Hoover Inst Photo [355]

WORLD WAR 1 REGISTERS AND BIOGRAPHIES OF THE DEAD AND WOUNDED PAMPHLET COLLECTION – 1915-1921 – 1 reel – 1 – CSUXANL2817-B – us Hoover Inst Photo [920]

WORLD WAR 1 REPARATIONS PAMPHLET COLLECTION – 1916-1932 – 2r – 1 – CSUXANM5039-B – us Hoover Inst Photo [320]

WORLD WAR 1 SERMONS PAMPHLET COLLECTION – 1913-1925 – 4r – 1 – CSUXAML7858-B – us Hoover Inst Photo [240]

WORLD WAR 1 SOURCES AND DOCUMENTS PAMPHLET COLLECTION – 1914 – 2r – 1 – CSUXAML2929-B – us Hoover Inst Photo [355]

THE WORLD WAR 1 SURVEY – 39 reels with printed guide – 1 – $3,755.00 – 0-89093-362-6 – us UPA [977]

WORLD WAR 2 CAMPAIGNS IN GREECE PAMPHLET COLLECTION – 1941 – 1 reel – 1 – CSUXANL3500-B – us Hoover Inst Photo [355]

WORLD WAR 2 CAMPAIGNS IN POLAND PAMPHLET COLLECTION – 1939-1985 – 1 reel – 1 – CSUXANL3487-B – us Hoover Inst Photo [355]

WORLD WAR 2 CAMPAIGNS IN THE SOVIET UNION PAMPHLET COLLECTION – 1941?-1987 – 1 reel – 1 – CSUXANR2623-B – us Hoover Inst Photo [355]

WORLD WAR 2 COMBAT INTERVIEWS – $3,465.00 – 1-55655-135-5 – us UPA [355]

WORLD WAR 2 IN POLAND PAMPHLET COLLECTION – 1939-1945 – 1 reel – 1 – CSUXANL2983-B – us Hoover Inst Photo [355]

WORLD WAR 2 IN ROMANIA PAMPHLET COLLECTION – 1939?-1975 – 1 reel – 1 – CSUXANQ4842-B – us Hoover Inst Photo [355]

WORLD WAR 2 IN THE SOVIET UNION – 1941-1989 – 1 reel – 1 – CSUXANR2636-B – us Hoover Inst Photo [355]

WORLD WAR 2 IN YUGOSLAVIA PAMPHLET COLLECTION – 1941-1942 – 1 reel – 1 – CSUXANL2996-B – us Hoover Inst Photo [355]

WORLD WAR 2 JUVENILE LITERATURE PAMPHLET COLLECTION – 1939?-1965 – 1 reel – 1 – CSUXANM8107-B – us Hoover Inst Photo [410]

WORLD WAR 2 MUSEUMS PAMPHLET COLLECTION – 1940?-1981 – 1 reel – 1 – CSUXANM5481-B – us Hoover Inst Photo [060]

WORLD WAR 2 PAMPHLET COLLECTION – 1939-1978 – 1 reel – 1 – CSUXANM6419-B – us Hoover Inst Photo [355]

WORLD WAR 2 SERMONS PAMPHLET COLLECTION – 1939-1945 – 1 reel – 1 – CSUXANM8109-B – us Hoover Inst Photo [240]

WORLD WAR II THROUGH THE AMERICAN NEWSREELS, 1942-1945 / ed by Short, Ken – 229mf – 9 – $745.00 – us UMI [977]

WORLD WAR ONE ARMISTICE – 1 – us Ross [940]

WORLD WAR TWO IN THE WEST – Papers Presented at the Conference. Sept 5-9 1950. Amsterdam – 1 – us NY Public [940]

WORLD WIDE / ed by McDougall, John R – Montreal, Canada. v4 n24. 11 jun 1904 – 1r – 1 – Can$25.00 – cn Can Microfilming [072]

WORLD WIDE FUND FOR NATURE : A SELECTION OF UNPUBLISHED WWF PROJECT REPORTS / ed by Scott, Anony – (Includes a printed guide) – 1993 2 installments – 164mf – 9 – ne IDC [500]

WORLD WIDE STUDY OF BAPTIST EVANGELISM / McClellan, Albert – 1963-65. 570p – 1 – 19.95 – us Baptist [240]

World Zionist Organization *see*
- CONSTITUTION
- REPORT OF THE REORGANIZATION COMMISSION OF THE EXECUTIVE OF THE ZIONIST ORGANIZATION ON THE WORK OF THE ZIONIST ORGANIZATION IN PALESTINE
- STATEMENT OF THE ZIONIST ORGANIZATION REGARDING PALESTINE
- STATEMENTS AND DOCUMENTS

WORLD-HEALERS; OR, THE LOTUS GOSPEL AND ITS BODHISATTVAS, COMPARED WITH EARLY CHRISTIANITY. / Gordon, Elizabeth Anna – rev. and enl. ed. Tokyo, 1913. 2v. plates. fold. map – 1 – us U.W. Library [210]

WORLD-JOURNAL-TRIBUNE – New York. N.Y. 1966-1967 – 1 – us UMI [071]

WORLDMISSION : FIDES SERVICE – 1956-64 (complete) – 1r – 1 – ATLA S0663 – us A.T.L.A. [073]

WORLD-NEWS – Roanoke. Va. 1911- – 1 – us UMI [071]

THE WORLD'S BEST ORATIONS / ed by Brewer, David J – St Louis, Chicago: Fred P Kaiser. v1-10. 1899 – 50mf – 9 – $75.00 – LLMC 94-267 – us L.L.M.C. [340]

WORLD'S CRISIS – (Lacks some pgs. Title varies) – 1871-1954 – Inquire – 1 – ATLA S0329 – us A.T.L.A. [073]

WORLD'S CRISIS – v. 1-32. 1854-1892 – 1 – us UMI [240]

THE WORLD'S EDITION OF THE GREAT PRESBYTERIAN CONFLICT, PATTON VS. SWING : BOTH SIDES OF THE QUESTION / Swing, David – Chicago: George Macdonald, 1874 – 1mf – us A.T.L.A. [240]

WORLD'S FINEST – Comics. Issue Nos. 1-5 Feb 1941-Spring 42 – 5mf – 15 – $31.95 – us Comics [760]

WORLD'S FINEST – Comics. Issue Nos. 6-10 Summer 42-Summer 43 – 5mf – 15 – $31.95 – us Comics [760]

THE WORLD'S ILLUSION / Wassermann, Jakob – New York: Harcourt, Brace, 1922, c1920 – 1r – 1 – us U.W. Library [430]

THE WORLD'S LEGAL PHILOSOPHIES / Berolzheimer, Fritz – N.Y.: Macmillan Co, 1912 (1924 reprint) – 6mf – 9 – $9.00 – LLMC 95-190 – us L.L.M.C. [340]

WORLD'S PAPER TRADE REVIEW *see* PAPER

WORLD'S WORK – New York, 1900-06 – 3r – 1 – us Ross [073]

WORLD'S WORK – v. 1-61. 1900-1932 – 1 – us Princeton Micro [073]

THE WORLD'S WORK AND THE CALENDAR; TELLING THE STORY OF THE EVOLUTION OF THE JULIAN-GREGORIAN CALENDAR, OF HOW IT FAILED TO ANTICIPATE THE NEEDS OF A CHANGED CIVILIZATION... INTERNATIONAL UNDERTAKING TO IMPROVE IT / Stiles, Meredith Newcomb – Boston: R. G. Badger, c1933. 181p. illus. diagrs – 1 – us U.W. Library [520]

WORLD-TELEGRAM – New York. N.Y. and Sun. 1950-66 – 1 – us UMI [071]
WORLD-TELEGRAM – New York. N.Y. and Sun. School pages. 1949-1965 – 1 – us UMI [071]
WORLD-TELEPHONE – Bloomington. Ind. 1901-1917; 1943-1947 – 1 – us UMI [071]
WORLDWIDE LIST OF TEXTILE RESEARCH INSTITUTES – 1974 – 47p – it F.A.O. [670]
WORLDWIDE MEETINGS AND INCENTIVES – v.1-. 1980- – 1,5,6,9 – us UMI [300]
WORLDWIDE NEWS SERVICE – New York, NY. Seven Arts Feature Syndicate News. 13 Sept 1935-1939?; 27 Dec 1968-4 Dec 1986. English. Ceased publication – 1 – us A.J.P.C. [071]
Wormald, F *see*
- ENGLISH BENEDICTINE CALENDARS AFTER A.D. 1100
- ENGLISH CALENDARS BEFORE A.D. 1100
- ORDINES OF HAYMO OF FAVERSHAM

Wormer, Oliver Gerd *see* CHEMISCHE GASPHASENABSCHEIDUNG VON VANADIUMOXIDEN
Worms, Carl *see*
- DEMETRIUS

Worms, E A *see* CAHIERS DE TERRAIN, KIMBERLEY, AUSTRALIE DU NORD-OUEST
Worms, M *see* DIE LEHRE VON DER ANFANGSLOSIGKEIT D. WELT BEI DEN MITTELALT. ARAB. PHILOSOPHEN
Wormser, C W *see* JOURNALISTIEK OP JAVA
DAS WORMSER KONKORDAT UND SEIN VORURKUNDEN : HINSICHTLICH ENTSTEHUNG, FORMULIERUNG, RECHTSGUELTIGKEIT / Bernheim, Ernst – Breslau: M. & H. Marcus, 1906 – 1mf – us A.T.L.A. [340]
WORMSER ZEITUNG – Worms, West Germany. 1848-49; 1978- – 1 – gw Mikrofilm [072]
WORMWOOD / Corelli, Marie – British Fiction Archive: Unit 1 – 9 – uk Bell [830]
Woroniecki, E *see* POLAND. HER PEOPLE, HISTORY, INDUSTRIES, FINANCE, SCIENCE
Woronow, G N *see* BEITRAEGE ZUR KENNTNIS DER LILIACEEN DER KAUKASUS-LAENDER. I. TRANSKAUKASISCHE BELLEVALIA ARTEN
WORRAL'S TEXTILE DIRECTORIES – 1913-1962 – 1 – uk Manchester Libr [670]
Worsaae, Jens Jakob Asmussen *see*
- AN ACCOUNT OF THE DANES AND NORWEGIANS IN ENGLAND..
- MINDER OM DANSKE OG NORDMAENDENE I ENGLAND, SKOTLAND OG IRLAND

Worsfold, Thomas Cato *see* STAPLE INN AND ITS STORY
WORSHIP – 26(1951)-52(1963) – 180mf – 9 – Dfl630.00 – ne Slangenburg [073]
WORSHIP IN SONG / Holbrook, Jos. P – 1 – 15.04 – us Baptist [240]
WORSHIP OF BAALIM IN ISRAEL: BASED UPON...R. DOZY, THE ISRAELITES AT MECCA / Oort, Henricus – London: Longmans, Green, 1865. 1 fiche – 9 – us A.T.L.A. [270]
THE WORSHIP OF THE ROMANS, VIEWED IN RELATION TO THE ROMAN TEMPERAMENT / Granger, Frank Stephen – London, 1895. 313p – 1 – us U.W. Library [250]
Worsley, Charles *see* MASTER WORSLEY'S BOOK ON THE HISTORY AND CONSTITUTION OF THE MIDDLE TEMPLE
Worsley, Frederick William *see* THE FOURTH GOSPEL AND THE SYNOPTISTS:...THE JOHANNINE PROBLEM
DOS WORT – New York, NY. 1921-25 – 1 – us A.J.P.C. [071]
DOS WORT – Warsaw. v1-2. 1933-1934 – 2v – 1 – J-92-29/3 – ne IDC [072]
DAS WORT – Literarische Monatsschrift. Moskau (Moskva, U.S.S.R.). Jul 1936-Mar 1939 – 1 – gw Mikrofilm [430]
DAS WORT – Stockholm, Sweden. 1937-40; Jun 1945-Aug 1946 – 1 – gw Mikrofilm [072]
EIN WORT DES HERAKLIT IM NEUEN TESTAMENT / Wendland, Paul – Berlin: Georg Reimer, 1898. 1 fiche – 9 – us A.T.L.A. [240]
DAS WORT IN DER WELT *see* DIE WELTMISSION
WORT UND GEIST / Gruetzmacher, Richard Heinrich – Leipzig: A. Deichert, 1902. 1 fiche – 9 – us A.T.L.A. [240]
WORTE DES SAMMLERS (KOHELITH)...IN DEUTSCHE REIME GEBRACHT / Rosenthal, Hermann – New York: International News, 1885. 1 fiche – 9 – us A.T.L.A. [240]
WORTE ZUR VERSTAENDIGUNG IM STREITE UEBER DIE PAEPSTLICHE UNFEHLBARKEIT / Mayr, Aloys – Wuerzburg: Julius Kellner, 1871 – 1mf – 9 – 0-8370-8456-3 – 1986-2456 – us A.T.L.A. [240]
DE WORTEL, DEN OORSPRONCK ENDE HET FONDAMENT DE WEDERDOOPEREN. ANNO 1565 / Bres, G de – Ouergheset door J. D. R. 1570. BME-230 1 – 9 – ne IDC [240]
DE WORTEL, DEN OORSPRONCK ENDE HET FONDAMENT DE WEDERDOOPEREN. ANNO 1565 / Bres, G de – Ouergheset door J. D. R. Amsterdam, J. E. Cloppenburgh. 1589. BME-231 1 – 9 – ne IDC [240]
Worters, Garance *see* AMERICAN BIOGRAPHICAL ARCHIVE (ABA 1)
DIE WORTHAEUFUNG IM BAROCK / Pliester, Hans – (Includes bibliographical references) – Bonn a. Rh.: L Roehrscheid, 1930 – 1r – 1 – us U.W. Library [430]
WORTHIES AND WORKERS OF THE ROCK RIVER CONFERENCE / Field, A D – Cincinnati: Cranston and Curts, 1896. Illinois Reel 51. (The Cox Library Collection) – 5 – us Americana [978]
WORTHING GAZETTE – England, 1889-1981 – 128r – 1 – uk British Libr Newspaper [072]
WORTHING GAZETTE AND HERALD *see* WORTHING GAZETTE
WORTHING HERALD – England, May 1920- – 149+ r – 1 – uk British Libr Newspaper [072]
WORTHINGTON 1763-1895 – (mf ed 1987) – 28mf – 9 – 0-87623-064-8 – us Holbrook [920]
Worthington, Thomas *see* PAPERS
DER WORTSCHATZ DES APOSTELS PAULUS : BEITRAG ZUR SPRACHGESCHICHTLICHEN ERFORSCHUNG DES NEUEN TESTAMENTS / Naegeli, Theodor – (Includes index) – Goettingen: Vandenhoeck & Ruprecht, 1905 – 1mf – 9 – 0-8370-9259-0 – 1986-3259 – us A.T.L.A. [450]
WORTSINN UND WORTSCHOEPFUNG BEI MEISTER ECKEHART / Fahrner, Rudolf – (Includes bibliographical references) – Marburg a.L.: N G Elwert, 1929 – 1r – 1 – us U.W. Library [430]
WORUEBER MAN IN DER BREMER GESELLSCHAFT SPRICHT – Bremen, Germany.Nov 1907-Mai 1908; Okt 1908-Okt 1909 – 1 – gw Mikrofilm [073]
WORUEBER MAN IN DER BREMER GESELLSCHAFT SPRICHT – Bremen, nov 1907, feb-may, oct-dec 1908, jan-jul, oct 1909 – 1r – 1 – Inquire at Mikrofilmarchiv for details – gw Misc Inst [390]
WOTANIN – 1970-76. (American Indian Periodicals in the Princeton University Library) – 9 – $90.00 – us UPA [305]
Wotschke, T *see* GESCHICHTE DER REFORMATION IN POLEN
Woude, Utig S v. d. *see* ACTA CAPITULI WINDESHEMENSIS
WOUDT VAN WONDERLICKE SINNE-FABULEN DER DIEREN... / Perret, E – Rotterdam, 1633 (1632) – 2mf – 9 – ne IDC [700]
WOULD CHRIST BELONG TO A LABOR UNION?, OR, HENRY FIELDING'S DREAM / Myers, Cortland – 1900 – 1 – us A.T.L.A. [240]
WOUNDS OF THE BRAIN PROVED CURABLE / Yonge, J – M 429. 1682 – 9 – ne IDC [617]
WOUNDS OF THE WORLD / Pearse, Mark Guy – 1912 – 9 – us A.T.L.A. [240]
Woyt, Johann Jacob *see* GAZOPHYLACIUM MEDICO-PHYSICUM ODER SCHATZKAMMER / MEDICINISCH- UND NATUERLICHER DINGE... (AEL, ABT.3;2)
Woytt, L W M *see* WYOTTENS EMBLEMATISCHER PARNASSUS
WP WITTGENSTEINER NACHRICHTEN – Berleburg, Germany. 1 Sept 1978- – 1 – gw Mikrofilm [072]
WPA, HILLSBORO GUIDE – Montgomery News, 1940. (Illinois Reel 46). (The Cox Library Collection) – 5 – us Americana [978]
WP-WITTGENSTEINER NACHRICHTEN – Bad Berleburg, West Germany. 1 Sept 1978- – 1 – gw Mikrofilm [072]
Wragg, R A *see* WRAGG'S IMPROVED FLUTE PRECEPTOR
WRAGG'S IMPROVED FLUTE PRECEPTOR / Wragg, R A – (Autographed) – London: Author, 1806 – 1 – us Sibley [780]
Wrangel, Wolf, Freiherr von *see* DER KREIS MOHRUNGEN
Wratislaw, A H *see* JOHN HUSS
WRBASER ZEITUNG – Vrbas, Yugoslavia. Aug 1920-1921; 1924; 1927-39 – 5r – 1 – us L of C Photodup [949]
A WREATH OF MALAYALAM PROVERBS AND THEIR CORRESPONDING ENGLISH PROVERBS – (On the same reel: One Thousand Malayalam Proverbs) – Mangalore: Basel Mission Book & Tract Depository, 1906 – 1 – us Res Libr [390]
WRECKAGE, SEVEN STUDIES / Crackanthorpe, Hubert – London: William Heinemann, 1893 – 1 roll – 1 – 1-55879-525-1 – uk Libr Preservation [890]
THE WRECKER / Stevenson, Robert Louis & Osbourne, Lloyd – London: Cassell & Company, 1892 – 1 roll – 1 – 1-55879-703-3 – uk Libr Preservation [830]
Wrede, Adolf *see* ERNST DER BEKENNER, HERZOG VON BRAUNSCHWEIG UND LUENEBURG
Wrede, Clemens, Freiherr von *see* ZUSAMMENHAENGE VON ALLGEMEINER WEHRPFLICHT UND VOLKSWIRTSCHAFT ALS GRUNDLAGE ZUR BEURTEILUNG DEUTSCHER WEHRPOLITIK
Wrede, William *see*
- DIE ECHTHEIT DES ZWEITEN THESSALONICHERBRIEFS (T.U.U. 2-24/2)
- THE ORIGIN OF THE NEW TESTAMENT
- PAUL
- PAULUS
- UEBER AUFGABE UND METHODE DER SOGENANNTEN NEUTESTAMENTLICHEN THEOLOGIE

Wren, Christopher *see* PARENTALIA
Wreszinski, W *see*
- DER LONDONER MEDIZISCHE PAPYRUS UND DER PAPYRUS HEARST
- DER PAPYRUS EBERS

WREXHAM ADVERTISER – (Lacking: Jul-Dec 1872) – Wales, 1869-80 – 11 1/2r – 1 – uk British Libr Newspaper [072]
WREXHAM GUARDIAN – Wales, 4 Sep 1869-Dec 1884 – 15r – 1 – uk British Libr Newspaper [072]
Wriede, Hinrich *see*
- LEEGE LUED

Wright, Alan N *see* THERAPEUTIC POTENTIAL OF THE OUTWARD BOUND PROCESS: AN EVALUATION OF A TREATMENT PROGRAM FOR JUVENILE DELINQUENTS
Wright, Allen *see* CHANTA LEKSIKON
Wright, Arthur *see* THE COMPOSITION OF THE FOUR GOSPELS
Wright, Beverly and Company. Dodge City, Kansas *see* RECORDS
Wright, C E *see* SURFACE WATER AND GROUNDWATER INTERACTION
Wright, Charles *see* A HISTORY OF LLOYD'S FROM THE FOUNDING OF LLOYD'S COFFEE HOUSE TO THE PRESENT DAY
Wright, Charles Henry Hamilton *see*
- THE BIBLE READERS' MANUAL, OR, AIDS TO BIBLICAL STUDY FOR STUDENTS OF THE HOLY SCRIPTURES
- BIBLICAL ESSAYS: EXEGETICAL STUDIES ON JOB, JONAH, EZEKIEL, PETER, APOCALYPSE
- DANIEL AND ITS CRITICS
- THE FATHERHOOD OF GOD
- AN INTRODUCTION TO THE OLD TESTAMENT
- A PRIMER OF ROMAN CATHOLICISM

WRIGHT COUNTY MONITOR – Clarion. Iowa. -w. 1951- – 1 – us UMI [071]
Wright, G Frederick *see*
- AMERICA'S PROMINENT FAMILIES
- STANDARD HISTORY OF LORAIN COUNTY

Wright, G J *see* MERCANTILE JOURNAL
Wright, George Frederick *see*
- THE DIVINE AUTHORITY OF THE BIBLE
- THE LOGIC OF CHRISTIAN EVIDENCES
- SCIENTIFIC ASPECTS OF CHRISTIAN EVIDENCES
- SCIENTIFIC CONFIRMATIONS OF OLD TESTAMENT HISTORY

Wright, Herbert Francis *see* MEMORANDUM IN SUPPORT OF THE RETENTION OF THE SPANISH EMBARGO
Wright, John W *see* CURIOUS FACTS, MYTHS, LEGENDS, AND SUPERSTITIONS CONCERNING CHRIST
Wright, Julia McNair *see* PRIEST AND NUN
WRIGHT, LEVI, DIARY, MS P.P. – 1864-1866 – 1 reel – 1 – us Western Res [976]
Wright, M von *see* FINLANDS FOGLAR, HUFVUDSAKLIGEN TILL DERAS DRAGTER BESKRIFNA
Wright, Orville *see* SCRAPBOOKS
Wright, R Glenn *see* CHRONOLOGICAL BIBLIOGRAPHY OF ENGLISH LANGUAGE FICTION IN THE LIBRARY OF CONGRESS THROUGH 1950
Wright, Robert *see* A MEMOIR OF GENERAL JAMES OGLETHORPE
Wright, Robert Samuel *see* THE LAW OF CRIMINAL CONSPIRACIES AND AGREEMENTS
Wright, Stephen K *see* VENGEANCE OF OUR LORD
Wright, Stevens *see* HISTORY OF THE SHAFTSBURY BAPTIST ASSOCIATION, VERMONT, 1781-1853
Wright, T *see*
- ALEXANDRI NECKAM DE NATURIS RERUM, LIBRI DUO (RS34)
- ANGLO-LATIN SATIRICAL POETS AND EPIGRAMMATISTS OF THE TWELFTH CENTURY (RS59)
- CHRONICLE OF PIERRE DE LANGTOFT (RS47)
- MONOGRAPH ON THE BRITISH FOSSIL ECHINODERMATA OF THE OOLITIC FORMATIONS
- MONOGRAPH ON THE LIAS AMMONITES OF THE BRITISH ISLANDS

Wright, Thomas *see*
- EARLY CHRISTIANITY IN ARABIA
- ESSAYS ON ARCHAEOLOGICAL SUBJECTS, AND ON VARIOUS QUESTIONS CONNECTED WITH THE HISTORY OF ART, SCIENCE AND LITERATURE IN THE MIDDLE AGES
- THE LIFE OF WALTER PATER
- QUEEN ELIZABETH AND HER TIMES

Wright, Vincent *see* SUPPRESSIO VERI, OR THE DANGERS OF THE PRESS
Wright, W *see*
- APOGRYPHAL ACTS OF THE APOSTLES EDITED FROM SYRIACS MSS
- CATALOGUE OF SYRIAC MANUSCRIPTS IN THE BRITISH MUSEUM
- CATALOGUE OF THE ETHIOPIC MSS IN THE BRITISH MUSEUM
- A SHORT HISTORY OF SYRIAC LITERATURE

Wright, W A *see* METRICAL CHRONICLE OF ROBERT OF GLOUCESTER (RS86)
Wright, Wilbur *see* SCRAPBOOKS
Wright, Willard Huntington *see* WHAT NIETZSCHE TAUGHT
Wright, William *see* LECTURES ON THE COMPARATIVE GRAMMAR OF THE SEMITIC LANGUAGES.
Wright, William Burnet *see* CITIES OF PAUL
WRIGHT'S CHANCERY APPEALS DECISIONS / Tennessee. Supreme Court – (A Pre-NRS title) – v1-2. 1901-1902 (all publ) – 18mf – 9 – $27.00 – LLMC 91-039 – us L.L.M.C. [340]
WRIGHT'S REPORTS / Ohio. Supreme Court – (A Pre-NRS title. 1st ed. Columbus: I N Whiting 1835. 2nd ed. Cincinnati: Clarke & Co 1884) – 1v. 1831-34 (all publ) – 3mf – 9 – $13.50 – LLMC 84-188 – us L.L.M.C. [340]
WRIGLEY'S BRITISH COLUMBIA DIRECTORY, 1918 – Vancouver, BC: Wrigley Directories, 1918 – 1r – 1 – cn U.B.C. Preserve [971]
WRIGLEY'S BRITISH COLUMBIA DIRECTORY, 1919 – Vancouver, BC: Wrigley Directories, 1919 – 1r – 1 – cn U.B.C. Preserve [971]
WRIGLEY'S BRITISH COLUMBIA DIRECTORY, 1930-1932 – Vancouver, BC: Wrigley Directories, 1930-32 – 6r – 1 – Can$70.00r – cn U.B.C. Preserve [971]
WRIGLEY'S GREATER VANCOUVER AND NEW WESTMINSTER (BRITISH COLUMBIA) DIRECTORY, 1933 – Vancouver, BC: Wrigley Directories, 1933 – 1r – 1 – Can$70.00 – cn U.B.C. Preserve [971]
Wrisberg, Craig *see* THE RELATIVE EFFECTS OF A LIVE AND VIDEOTAPED INSTRUCTOR O RATINGS OF PERCEIVED EXERTION AND SUBJECTIVE FEELINGS OF STUDENTS IN AN AEROBIC EXERCISE CLASS
THE WRIT – Detroit. 1v. 1901 (all publ) – 1mf – 9 – $1.50 – LLMC 82-976 – us L.L.M.C. [073]
WRIT – Ada, OH. 1958-96 – 1r – 1 – $32.50r – us Archival [978]
WRITER – Boston. v. 1-53. 1887-1940 – 1,5,6 – us Princeton Micro [410]
WRITER – (v. 82- 1969- 5,6. v. 83- 1970- 9) – v. 1- 1887- – 1 – us UMI [410]
WRITERS AND SCHOLARS EDUCATIONAL TRUST *see* INDEX ON CENSORSHIP/ WRITERS AND SCHOLARS EDUCATIONAL TRUST
THE WRITER'S BULLETIN AND LITERARY REPORTER – New York. v. 1-8. no. 7. Aug 1911-Aug 1917 – 1 – us NY Public [410]
WRITER'S DIGEST – (v. 49- 1969- 5,6. v. 50- 1970- 9) – v. 1- 1920- – 1 – us UMI [410]

WRITERS DIGEST – Cincinnati. vol. 1-29. December 1920-November 1949. (Scattered issues lacking) – 1 – 220.00 – us L of C Photodup [070]

WRITERS OF GENESIS: AND RELATED TOPICS, ILLUSTRATING DIVINE REVELATION / Cowley, Edward – New York: T. Whittaker, 1890. 1 fiche – 9 – us A.T.L.A. [220]

THE WRITERS OF THE NEW TESTAMENT: THEIR STYLE AND CHARACTERISTICS / Simcox, William Henry – London: Hodder & Stoughton, 1890. 1 fiche – 9 – us A.T.L.A. [240]

WRITERS' PROGRAM, NEW YORK CITY: NEGROES OF NEW YORK : FROM THE HOLDINGS OF THE SCHOMBURG CENTER FOR RESEARCH IN BLACK CULTURE, MANUSCRIPTS, ARCHIVES AND RARE BOOKS DIVISION: THE NEW YORK PUBLIC LIBRARY, ASTOR, LENOX AND TILDEN FOUNDATIONS – (Guide which covers all coll under "Literature and the Arts" sold separately for $20.00 D3305.G6) – 1995 – 5r – 1 – $425.00 – D3305P22 – Dist. us Scholarly Res – us L of C Photodup [305]

WRITING A SCIENTIFIC PAPER / Tripathi, Bansh R – 1992 – 9 – $6.00 – 92-9053-235-1 – et ILRI [500]

WRITING ABOUT EAKINS : THE MICROFICHE EDITION OF THE MANUSCRIPTS IN CHARLES BREGLER'S THOMAS EAKINS COLLECTION – us Penn Academy [760]

THE WRITING AND RATIFICATION OF THE U.S. CONSTITUTION : AN ABBREVIATED BIBLIOGRAPHY / Wheeler, Russell R – Washington: FJC, 1986 – 1mf – 9 – $1.50 – LLMC 95-803A – us L.L.M.C. [340]

THE WRITING AND RATIFICATION OF THE U.S. CONSTITUTION : A BIBLIOGRAPHY / Wheeler, Russell R – Washington: FJC, 1986 – 1mf – 9 – $1.50 – LLMC 95-903B – us L.L.M.C. [340]

THE WRITING OF HISTORY / Fortescue, John William – London: Williams and Norgate, 1926. 3,74p – 1 – us U.W. Library [900]

WRITINGS / Harley, Lee C – 20th century. 8 fiches – 9 – us South Carolina Historical [800]

WRITINGS / Homer, William Bradford – With a memoir by Edwards A. Park. 1842 – 1 – us A.T.L.A. [240]

WRITINGS / Hubmaier, Balthasar – v. 1-6. 1525-27. (English translation) – 1 – 24.11 – us Baptist [240]

WRITINGS / Hubmaier, Balthasar – v. 1-6. 1525-27. (German) – 1 – 23.80 – us Baptist [240]

WRITINGS, 1862?-1908 / Blyden, Edward Wilmot – 1 – us Res Libr [960]

WRITINGS AND DISPUTATIONS / Cranmer, Thomas – v. 1 The sacrament of the Lord's Supper. H-345 2. 1844 – 8 – ne IDC [240]

WRITINGS AND PAPERS OF FATIMA MASSAQUOI-FAHNBULLEH / Massaquoi-Fahnbulleh, Fatima – 1r – 1 – $49.50 – us African Imprint [960]

THE WRITINGS IN PROSE AND VERSE OF RUDYARD KIPLING – New York. 18v. 1898-1900 – 3r – 1 – us Ross [420]

WRITINGS, LETTERS AND HYMNS AND SPIRITUAL SONGS / Russell, Anna B & Russell, Cora – 1832 – 1 – 7.56 – us Baptist [240]

WRITINGS OF A. DORIS B. HENRIES / Henries, A Doris B – 1r – 1 – $49.50 – us African Imprint [960]

THE WRITINGS OF GEORGE WASHINGTON / Washington, George – 14 v. 1889-93 – 9 – 55.00 – us L of C Photodup [975]

"WRITINGS OF JESSIE KENNEDY SNELL" / Snell, Jessie Kennedy – 1 – us KS Hist [978]

WRITINGS OF PROFESSOR B.B. EDWARDS / Park, Edwards Amasa – Boston: J.P. Jewett, 1853 – 3mf – us A.T.L.A. [240]

WRITINGS OF S. JANGABA M. JOHNSON / Johnson, S Jangaba M – 2r – 1 – $49.50r – us African Imprint [960]

WRITINGS OF THOMAS JEFFERSON / Jefferson, Thomas – Thomas Jefferson Memorial Association – 5r – 1 – $370.00 – us UMI [920]

WRITINGS ON AMERICAN HISTORY *see* AMERICAN HISTORICAL ASSOCIATION ANNUAL REPORT

WRITINGS ON PIRATES / Trott, Nicholas – 1718. 1 fiche – 9 – us South Carolina Historical [900]

WRITINGS UPON THE CONSTITUTION BY JOHN MARSHALL – Boston: James Munroe & Co, 1839 – 8mf – 9 – $12.00 – LLMC 90-300 – us L.L.M.C. [320]

WRITTEN RECORDS / U.S. Office of War Information.Overseas Picture Division. Washington Section – 1935-46 – 1 – 529.00 – us L of C Photodup [977]

Wrobel, J *see* BERNARDI SILVESTRIS

THE WRONG BOX / Stevenson, Robert Louis & Osbourne, Lloyd – London: Longmans, Green, 1889 – 1 roll – 1 – 1-55879-704-1 – uk Libr Preservation [830]

Wrzos, Conrad *see* PILSUDSKI I PILSUDCZYCY

W.S. Dunbar and Co *see*
- BIOGRAPHICAL HISTORY OF CHEROKEE COUNTY
- BIOGRAPHICAL HISTORY OF SHELBY AND AUDUBON COUNTIES

W.S. Ferguson and Co *see* TIOGA COUNTY

WSBC HORIZONS – Casper, Wyoming: Wyoming Southern Baptist Convention, 1985-1991 – 1 reel – 1 – $15.12 – us Baptist [240]

WSCF DOSSIER – Geneva. v1-11. aug 1973-jul 1976* – 1 – D11300 – us UMI [240]

WSEOBECNY ROSTLINOPIS / Presl, J S – 2v. Praze. 1846. B-5148 2 – 8 – ne IDC [580]

WSPOLCZESNOSC – Warsaw, Poland. -w. March-Dec 1958; Jn 1965-Dec 1970. 4 reels – 1 – uk British Libr Newspaper [947]

WSPOLNOTA – (Backfile through 1998 $85r) – Poland, 1999- – 1r per y – 1 – $80.00 standing order – us Ross [072]

WSPOMNIENIA Z LAT NIEDOLI I NIEWOLI, 1914-1918 / Biaynia-Cho odecki, Jozef – Lwow: Nak. autora, 1919 (Lwow: Z druk. L. Wisniewskiego) – 1 – CSUX88-B9277 – us Hoover Inst Photo [940]

WSROD POLONII W AMERYCE : DRUGA SERYA: LISTOW Z AMERYKI / Dunikowski, Emil Habdank – Lwow, 1893 – 1r – 1 – us I.H.R.C. [947]

WU CHIA T'UNG CHI YUEH K'AN / China. Ministry of Industries – Monthly price statistics of the Ministry of Industries. 9 v. Nanking. 1929-37. Lacking: v. 1 (2) 1929; v. 3 (4, 5, 8, 9, 12) 1931; v. 4 (1-3, 5, 6) 1932; v. 6 (1) 1934; v. 7 (1) 1935; v. 9 (5-12) 1937. BCH-1094 1 – 9 – ne IDC [380]

Wu, Eugene *see* LEADERS OF 20TH CENTURY CHINA

Wu, Joyce *see* VAN GULIK COLLECTION

Wu, Lei-ch'uan *see*
- THE CHRISTIAN HOPE (CCC330)
- CHRISTIANITY AND CHINESE CULTURE (CCC331)
- MOTZE AND JESUS (CCC332)

WU NIEN LAI CHIH KUANG-TUNG CHIEN-SHE – Reconstruction in Kwangtung in the Past Five Years. 1 reel – 1 – 32.00 – us Chinese Res [950]

Wu Nuan-sen *see* KUANG-TUNG TAN-HSING FA-LING HUI-TSUAN

Wu, Shih-huang *see* YEH CH'ENG TA KUAN. DJAKARTA DAHULU DAN SEKARANG

Wu, Y *see* ROLE STRESS AND SECONDARY TEACHER/COACHES IN THE STATE OF WASHINGTON

Wu, Yao-tsung *see*
- ABIDING FAITH FOR A NATION IN CRISIS (CCC340)
- CHRISTIAN CHURCH IN CHINA (CCC334)
- CHRISTIANITY AND THE NEW CHINA (CCC333)
- THE JESUS I KNOW (CCC335)
- LIGHT AND DARKNESS (CCC336)
- NO MAN HATH SEEN GOD (CCC338)
- PROCEEDINGS (CCC337)
- THE SOCIAL GOSPEL (CCC341)
- TALKS ON CHRISTIAN FAITH (CCC339)

Wu, Yung-chuan *see* HSIU YANG WEI TI (CCC342)

Wuarin, Louis *see* L'AUTORITE DE JESUS:... SES DISCIPLES IMMEDIATS D'APRES LE TEMOIGNAGE... SYNOPTIQUES

WU-CH'UAN HSIEN-CHIH – 1825, 10. BCH-631 2 – 8 – ne IDC [950]

Wudtke, Alexander *see* EXPERIMENTELLE UNTERSUCHUNG DER ANTIBIOTIKAPRODUKTION SOWIE DES WACHSTUMS VON PILZEN BEI FERMENTATIONEN IM HUBSTRAHL-BIOREAKTOR

Wueest, Josef *see* ACHERLAND

Wuelfingen, Klaus Bock von *see* FRANZ KAFKA – DIE INSZENIERUNG UNMOEGLICHER UEBERSCHREITUNG IN "DER PROCESS" UND ANDEREN SCHRIFTEN

Wuelker, Richard Paul *see* FUENFZIG FELDPOSTBRIEFE EINES FRANKFURTERS

WUEMME-ZEITUNG – Bremen, Germany.12 Apr 1972- – 1 – gw Mikrofilm [072]

Wuensche, August *see*
- BIBLIOTHECA RABBINICA
- DIE FREUDE IN DEN SCHRIFTEN DES ALTEN BUNDES
- YISURE HA-MASHIAH, ODER, DIE LEIDEN DES MESSIAS

Wuensche, F O *see* FILICES SAXONICAE

Wuerfl, Christoph *see* EIN BEITRAG ZUR KENNTNIS DES SPRACHGEBRAUCHS KLOPSTOCKS

WUERRTEMBERGISCHE ARBEITERZEITUNG, SUEDDEUTSCHE ARBEITERZEITUNG – Zell, 1900-1917 – 3r – 1 – DM240.00 – gw Mikro Press [072]

Wuertele, Jonathan Saxton Campbell *see* DISCOURS PRONONCE LE 31 MAI 1880: DANS L'ASSEMBLEE LEGISLATIVE DE QUEBEC EN SECONDANT L'ADRESSE EN REPONSE AU DISCOURS DU TRONE

Wuerttemberg *see* JAHRBUECHER FUER STATISTIK UND LANDESKUNDE

Wuerttemberg. Landstande. Kammer der Abgeordneten *see*
- REGISTER
- VERHANDLUNGEN...PROTOKOLLE

Wuerttemberg. Landstande. Kammer des abgeordneten *see* VERHANDLUNGEN... BEILAGEN

Wuerttemberg. Landtag *see*
- VERHANDLUNGEN DER VERFASSUNGGEBENDEN LANDESVERSAMMLUNG...PROTOKOLLE
- VERHANDLUNGEN DER VERFASSUNGGEBENDEN LANDESVERSAMMLUNG...REGISTER

WUERTTEMBERG UND JANSSEN / Bossert, Gustav – Halle. Verein fuer Reformationsgeschichte, 1884. (Schriften des Vereins fuer Reformationsgeschichte; 5-6) – 1mf – 9 – us A.T.L.A. [240]

WUERTTEMBERGISCHE NACHRICHTEN *see* STUTTGARTER NACHRICHTEN

Wuerttembergische Nachrichten *see* STUTTGARTER NACHRICHTEN

WUERTTEMBERGISCHES SEEBLATT – (Title changes: Seeblatt fuer Stadt und Land, 1852; Seeblatt, 21 Dec 1864; Verbo Seeblatt, 1934; Donau-Bodensee-Zeitung, 1 Apr 1942; Seeblatt fuer Kreis und Stadt Friedrichshafen, 8 Sep 1945; Schwaebische Zeitung, 4 Dec 1945) – Friedrichshafen, Germany. 2 Jan 1975- – 1 – gw Mikrofilm [072]

WUERTTEMBERGISCHES WOCHENBLATT FUER LANDWIRTSCHAFT – Stuttgart. Germany. -w. 1 Jan 1949-16 Nov 1968. (47 reels) – 1 – uk British Libr Newspaper [072]

Wuerzburg, Konrad von *see* TROJANERKRIEG

WUERZBURGER ABENDBLATT – Wuerzburg, Germany. Febr. 1848-1849 – 1 – gw Mikrofilm [072]

WUERZBURGER JOURNAL – Wuerzburg, Germany. Jan-Nov 1849 – 1 – gw Mikrofilm [072]

WUERZBURGER STADT- UND LANDBOTE – Wuerzburg, Germany. 25 Sept 1848-49 – 1 – gw Mikrofilm [072]

DIE WUERZELN DER DEUTSCHEN VOLKSKRAFT / Blume, Wilhelm von – Tuebingen: Kloeres, 1917. 20p – 1 – us U.W. Library [943]

Wuest, Ernst *see* LEXICON ARISTOPHANEUM

Wuest, Paul *see* ENTSTEHUNG UND AUFBAU VON GOTTFRIED KELLERS SELDWYLER NOVELLE "KLEIDER MACHEN LEUTE"

Wuestenhoff, Conrad Kleefeld von *see* GRUENDUNG UND ENTWICKLUNG DER KREDITINSTITUTE IN MANNHEIM UND LUDWIGSHAFEN VON DER MITTE DES 19. JAHRHUNDERTS BIS 1911

Wuestling, Fritz *see* TIECKS WILLIAM LOVELL

WUHAN DAXUE XUEBAO – Zhexue Shehui Kexue Ban. Journal of Wuhan University, Philosophy & Social Science. In Chinese but Table of Contents in English in each issue. F p209 – 9 – $4.50f – cc Microforms [073]

WUHAN DAXUE XUEBAO – Ziran Kexue Ban. Wuhan University Journal, Natural Science. In Chinese but English abstracts to the main articles. F p176 – 9 – $3.50f – cc Microforms [073]

WUHAN JIAN CAI XUEYUAN XUEBAO – Journal of Wuhan Institute of Building Materials. In Chinese but English abstracts to the main articles. F p190 – 9 – $4.50f – cc Microforms [073]

WUHAN YIXUEYUAN XUEBAO – Acta Academiae Medicinae Wuhan. In Chinese but English abstracts to the main articles. F p145 – 9 – 4.00f – cc Microforms [073]

Wuhrmann, Willy *see* REGISTER; IM AUFTRAG DES ZWINGLI-VEREINS IN ZUERICH

Wukadinovic, Spiridion *see* GOETHE-PROBLEME

Wulf, Erich *see* AUGUST WILHELM SCHLEGEL ALS LYRIKER

Wulf, M de *see*
- HISTOIRE DE LA PHILOSOPHIE EN BELGIQUE
- HISTOIRE DE LA PHILOSOPHIE SCOLASTIQUE DANS LES PAYS-BAS ET LA PRINCIPAUTE DE LIEGE
- LES QUATRE PREMIERS QUODLIBETS DE GODEFROID DE FONTAINES
- LES QUODLIBET CINQ, SIX ET SEPT DE GODEFROID DE FONTAINES
- LE TRAITE "DE UNITATE FORMAE" DE GILLES DE LESSINES

Wulff Martin, Enrique *see* ASAMBLEA PLENARIA DEL CONSEJO ECONOMICO PROVINCIAL

WULI XUEBAO – Acta Physica Sinica. In Chinese but English abstracts to the main articles. F p 36 – 9 – $4.50f – cc Microforms [073]

Wulp, F. M. van der *see* CATALOGUE OF THE DESCRIBED DIPTERA FROM SOUTH ASIA

Wulsin, F R *see* THE PREHISTORIC ARCHAEOLOGY OF NORTH WEST AFRICA

WUNDER = THE MIRACLE / Bettex, Frederic – (In English) – Defiance [OH]: The Handbook Press, c1900 – 1mf – 9 – 0-8370-2317-3 – 1985-0317 – us A.T.L.A. [210]

DAS WUNDER IN DER WIES / Ziegler, Marianne von – Muenchen: P Hugendubel, 1934 – 1 – us U.W. Library [890]

DAS WUNDER UND DIE ERKENNBARKEIT GOTTES / Fluegel, Otto – (Includes bibliographical references) – Leipzig:Louis Pernitzsch, 1869 – 1mf – 9 – 0-8370-3158-3 – 1985-1158 – us A.T.L.A. [210]

Wunder, Uwe *see* ENTWICKLUNG EINES BIOSENSORS FUER GLUKARAT

DIE WUNDER VON LOURDES / Weninger, Alexander – Regensburg; New York: Friedrich Pustet, 1881 – 1mf – 9 – 0-8370-7113-5 – 1986-1113 – us A.T.L.A. [240]

DIE WUNDERBERICHTE UEBER ELIA UND ELISA IN DEN BUECHERN DER KOENIGE / Clemen, August – Grimma: C. Roessler, 1877. 1 fiche – 9 – us A.T.L.A. [220]

DIE WUNDERPFEIFE, ODER, DIE KINDER VON HAMELN : EIN GESCHICHTLICHES MAERCHEN / Nieritz, Gustav – Duesseldorf: F Bagel, [18–?] – 1r – 1 – us U.W. Library [390]

DIE WUNDERTHATEN DES HERRN: ZUM ERWEISE DES GLAUBENS / Steinmeyer, Franz Ludwig – Berlin: Wiegandt & Greiben, 1884. 1 fiche – 9 – us A.T.L.A. [240]

Wundt, Wilhelm Max *see*
- PHILOSOPHISCHEN MORALSYSTEME
- PRINCIPIEN DER SITTLICHKEIT
- TATSACHEN DES SITTLICHEN LEBENS

Wunsch, Hildrun *see* FEHLHALTUNG BEIM INSTRUMENTALSPIEL UND IHRE VERMEIDUNG

Wurmbrand, Irmgard *see* WETTERLEUCHTEN UM BARBARA

Wurster, Paul *see*
- DAS ENGLISCHE CHRISTENVOLK UND WIR
- DIE LEHRE VON DER INNEREN MISSION

Wurtz, Georges-Chr. *see* MOYENS DE RENDRE LA FRANCHE-MACONNERIE PLUS UTILE A L'HUMANITE...

Wurtz, Johann *see* DIE DINGELSTOCKS

Wurzbach, A von *see* ARNOLD HOUBRAKEN'S GROSSE SCHOUBURGH DER NIEDERLAENDISCHE MALER UND MALERINNEN

Wurzbach, C von *see* BIOGRAPHISCHES LEXIKON

WURZELUNTERSUCHUNGEN ZUM HEBRAEISCHEN UND ARAMAEISCHEN LEXIKON / Barth, Jakob – 1902. BNE-465 1 – 9 – ne IDC [470]

Wurzer, David J *see* THE EFFECTS OF GENDER ON ALT-PE MOTOR IN JUNIOR HIGH PHYSICAL EDUCATION

WU-SA T'UNG-SHIH – 1925 – 8 – BCH-852 2 – ne IDC [920]
WUSA YUNDONG SHILIAO, DIYI JUAN – Materials on the May 30th movement, v1. Comp. by the Institute of History, Shanghai Academy of Social Sciences. 1 reel.M-H138 – 5 – $23.00 – cc Microforms [950]
WUSI AIGUO YUNDONG DANGAN ZILIAO – Archival materials on the patriotic movement of 4 May 1919. Comp. by the Institute of Modern History, Chinese Academy of Social Sciences and the Second Chinese Archive of History. 1 reel. M-H119 – 5 – 35.00 – cc Microforms [950]
WUSI AIGUO YUNDONG, (SHANG-XIA CE). JINDAISHI ZILIAO LEIBIAN – Materials on modern history series: The Patriotic movement of 4 May, 1919. v1-2. Comp. by the Institute of Modern History, Chinese Academy of Social Sciences. 1 reel. M-H118 – 5 – $40.00 – cc Microforms [950]
WUSI SHIQI DE LISHI RENWU – Historical figures of the May 4th movement. Comp. by Hu Hua. 3 fiches. F-J27 – 9 – $13.50 – cc Microforms [920]
WUSI SHIQI QIKAN JIESHAO – An introduction to the periodicals of the May 4th movement of 1919. Comp. by Zhongyuang Bianyiju Yanjiushi. 2 reels. M-J14 – 5 – 70.00 – cc Microforms [073]
WUSI YUNDONG ZAI SHANDONG – The May 4th movement in Shandong. Comp. by the Shandong Institute of History and the History Department of Shandong University. 2 fiches. F-H123 – 9 – $9.00 – cc Microforms [950]
WUSI YUNDONG ZAI SHANDONG ZILIAO XUANJI – Selection of materials on the May 4th movement in Shandong. Comp. by Hu Wenben, Tian Kesheng. 7 fiches. F-H120 – 9 – $31.50 – cc Microforms [950]
WUSI YUNDONG ZAI SHANGHAI SHILIAO XUANJI – Selection of materials on the May 4th movement in Shanghai. Comp. by the Institute of History, Shanghai Academy of Social Sciences.1 reel. M-H122 – 5 – 35.00 – cc Microforms [950]
WUSI YUNDONG ZAI TIANJIN-LISHI ZILIAO XUANJI – The May 4th movement in Tianjin.Comp. by the History Department of Nankai University and the Tianjin Museum of History. 1 reel. M-H121 – 5 – $45.00 – cc Microforms [950]
WUSI YUNDONG ZAI WUHAN (SHILIAO XUANJI) – The May 4th movement in Wuhan. Comp. by Zhang Yinghui, Kong Xiangzheng. 4 fiches.F-H124 – 9 – $22.50 – cc Microforms [950]
Wustmann, Erich *see* GUNHILD DIE REITERIN
WUSUN JIANCE – Nondestructive Testing. 1985-86. F/P 286 – 9 – $4.50f – cc Microforms [073]
WUTAN YU HUATAN – Geophysical and geochemical exploration.1981-. F-P249 – 9 – $4.50f – cc Microforms [073]
Wuttke, Heinrich *see* ZUR VORGESCHICHTE DER BARTHOLOMAEUSNACHT
Wutz, F *see* ONOMASTICA SACRA
WUXU BIANFA DANGAN SHILIAO – Archival materials of the reform movement of 1898. Comp. by the First Chinese Archive of History. 7 fiches.F-H190 – 9 – 28.00 – cc Microforms [950]
WUXU DANGAN ZHONG DE TAIPING TIANGUO SHILIAO XUANJI – Selected historical materials of the Taiping Rebellion in the possession of Wu Xu. Comp. by Jing Wu, Zhong Ding. 2 fiches. F-H97 – 9 – $28.00 – cc Microforms [950]
WV SCHOOL JOURNAL : A PUBLICATION OF THE WEST VIRGINIA EDUCATION ASSOCIATION – (Cont: West Virginia Education Association. WVEA School Journal. Cont by: West Virginia School Journal) – Charleston. v109-118. jul 1980-jul 1990 1,9; v109 jul 1980-jun 1981. v110-118 jul 1981-jul 1990* 5 – 1,5,9 – D6948.02 – us UMI [370]
W.W. BUTCHER'S CANADIAN NEWSPAPER DIRECTORY / Butcher, W W – London, Ont.: "Speaker," 1886. 02005. (Pre-1900 Canadiana) – 9 – cn C.I.H.M. [072]
WWD – (Cont: Women's Wear Daily) – New York. feb 1976-1988*. v157-174 1989-97+ – 5,9 – D17278.02 – us UMI [640]
WYALONG ADVOCATE – Nov 7 1900-Dec 25 1915 – 9 – at Pascoe [072]
WYALONG STAR – Apr 1894-Dec 1895. Jan 1899- Dec 1907 – 9 – at Pascoe [072]
WYANDOT CHIEF – Upper Sandusky. 1885-1906 – 14r – 1 – $32.50r – us Archival [071]
Wyandot County. Ohio. Auditor *see*
– BLIND RELIEF DISBURSEMENTS
– SCHOOL FUND ACCOUNT RECORDS
– SCHOOL TREASURER'S REPORTS
Wyandot County. Ohio. Board of County Commissioners *see*
– COMMISSIONERS' JOURNALS
– INDEX TO JOURNALS
– SOLDIERS' BURIAL RECORDS
Wyandot County. Ohio. Board of Education *see* BOARD OF EXAMINERS' MINUTES
Wyandot County. Ohio. Board of Elections *see* POLL LISTS
Wyandot County. Ohio. Board of Railroad Appraisers *see* RAILROAD APPRAISEMENT RECORDS
Wyandot County. Ohio. Clerk of Courts *see*
– PARTNERSHIP AND TRADERS' RECORD
– POLL BOOKS AND TALLY SHEETS
– RECORD OF ESTRAYS
– RECORD OF FISHING LICENSES
– RECORD OF HUNTERS' LICENSES
– RECORD OF JUSTICE'S OATHS
Wyandot County. Ohio. Common Pleas. Civil Division *see*
– CHANCERY RECORDS
– COMPLETE RECORDS
– COMPLETE RECORDS, LAW RECORDS
– GENERAL INDEXES
– JUDGMENT INDEXES, DIRECT
– JUDGMENT INDEXES, REVERSE
– QUADRENNIAL ENUMERATIONS
Wyandot County. Ohio. County Home *see*
– DEATH RECORDS
– INVENTORY RECORD
– MINUTES
– PATIENTS' ACCOUNT RECORD
– RECEIPTS AND EXPENDITURES RECORD
– REGISTERS
Wyandot County. Ohio. District Court *see* COMPLETE RECORDS
Wyandot County. Ohio. Lovell. City Post Office *see* POSTMASTERS' ACCOUNT BOOK
Wyandot County. Ohio. Marseilles. City Post Office *see* REGISTER OF MONEY ORDERS
Wyandot County. Ohio. Probate Court *see*
– ADMINISTRATION DOCKETS
– CIVIL DOCKETS
– COMPLETE RECORDS
– JOURNALS
– MARRIAGE RECORDS
– REGISTER OF PATENTS
– STATEMENTS OF BIRTHS AND DEATHS
– WILL RECORDS
Wyandot County. Ohio. Recorder *see*
– DEED RECORDS
– GENERAL INDEX TO MORTGAGES
– MISCELLANEOUS RECORDS
– MORTGAGE RECORDS
– SOLDIERS' DISCHARGE RECORDS
– SOLDIERS' GRAVE RECORDS
Wyandot County. Ohio. Sheriff *see* JAIL REGISTER
Wyandot County. Ohio. Supreme Court *see*
– CHANCERY RECORDS
– COMPLETE RECORDS
– JOURNAL
Wyandot County, Ohio, Treasurer *see* JOURNAL OF WARRANTS REDEEMED
Wyandot County. Ohio. Upper Sandusky. City Council *see* MINUTES
Wyandot County. Ohio. Upper Sandusky. City Post Office *see* REGISTER OF MONEY ORDERS
WYANDOT COUNTY REPUBLICAN – Upper Sandusky Co. 1869-1903 – 13r – 1 – $32.50r – us Archival [071]
WYANDOT HERALD – Upper Sandusky, Co. 1853 – 1r – 1 – $32.50r – us Archival [071]
WYANDOT PIONEER – Upper Sandusky, Ohio. 1853-68 – 6r – 1 – $32.50r – us Archival [071]
WYANDOT TELEGRAPH – Upper Sandusky, Co. 1845 – 1r – 1 – $32.50r – us Archival [071]
WYANDOT TRIBUNE – Upper Sandusky, Co. 1848-50 – 1r – 1 – $32.50r – us Archival [071]
WYANDOT UNION – Upper Sandusky, Co. 1857-94 – 17r – 1 – $32.50r – us Archival [071]
WYANDOT UNION-REPUBLICAN – Upper Sandusky, Ohio. 1903-16 – 9r – 1 – $32.50r – us Archival [071]
Wyandott Indian Council *see* RECORDS
WYANDOTTE COUNTY AND KANSAS CITY, KANSAS – Chicago, 1890. Kansas Reel 13. (The Cox Library Collection) – 5 – us Americana [978]
Wyatt, T J *see* AN INVESTIGATION OF THE ORGANIZATIONAL STRUCTURE AND POTENTIAL FOR INTERGROUP CONFLICT BETWEEN PHYSICAL EDUCATION AND ATHLETIC DEPARTMENTS IN THREE SECONDARY SCHOOLS
Wycherley, R N *see* THE PAGEANTRY OF METHODIST UNION
Wychgram, J *see* FRAUENBILDUNG, 1. 1902-22. 1923 (HQ 23)
Wychgram, Jakob *see* SCHILLER DEM DEUTSCHEN VOLKE DARGESTELLT
WYCHODZCA – 1935-37 – 1r – 1 – inquire – us Ross [072]
WYCHODZTWO I OSADNICTWO POLSKIE PRZEDWOJNA SWIATOWA / Okolowicz, Jozef – Warszawa, 1920 – 1r – 1 – us I.H.R.C. [947]
"WYCHODZTWO POLSKIE" / Caro, Leopold – 1911 – 1r – 1 – us I.H.R.C. [947]
WYCHODZTWO POLSKIE W STANACH ZJEDNOCZONYCH AMERYKI / Szawleski, Mieczyslaw – Lwow, 1924 – 3r – 1 – us I.H.R.C. [947]
Wyckoff, DeWitt Campbell *see* BIBLIOGRAPHY IN CHRISTIAN EDUCATION FOR SEMINARY AND COLLEGE LIBRARIES
WYCLIFFE AND MOVEMENTS FOR REFORM / Poole, Reginald Lane – New York: A.D.F. Randolph, 1890 – 1mf – us A.T.L.A. [240]
WYCLIFFE AND THE HUGUENOTS / Hanna, William – 1860 – 9 – us A.T.L.A. [240]
Wycliffe, John *see*
– AN APOLOGY FOR LOLLARD DOCTRINES, ATTRIBUTED TO WYCLIFFE
– JOHANNIS DE WICLIF TRACTATUS DE OFFICIO PASTORALI E CODICE VINDOBONENSI
– TRACTS AND TREATISES OF JOHN DE WYCLIFFE
THE WYCLIFFE SEMI-MILLENNIAL BIBLE CELEBRATION / Convention of Bible Societies of New Jersey, 1880 – Newark, NJ: Amzi Pierson, [1880?] – 1mf – 9 – 0-8370-7288-3 – 1986-1288 – us A.T.L.A. [220]
Wydan, Mary E *see* AN ASSESSMENT OF THE POSSESSED QUALIFICATIONS AND IMPORTANT QUALIFICATIONS OF AQUATIC ADMINISTRATORS
Wydler, H *see* ESSAI MONOGRAPHIQUE SUR LES GENRES SCROPHULARIA
Wyeth, John *see* REPOSITORY OF SACRED MUSIC
Wyeth, Walter N *see* ISAAC MCCOY: EARLY INDIAN MISSIONS
WYKEHAM-MARTIN PAPERS / Kent County Archives. Maidstone – 1672-1820. BRRAM – 1 – uk Microform Academic [920]
Wykes, Boyd *see* RESOURCE PARTITIONING AND THE ROLE OF COMPETITION STRUCTURING IN LICHENOSTOMUS HONEYEATER AND BELL MINER COMMUNITIES IN SOUTHERN VICTORIA
Wyld, Henry Cecil Kennedy *see* A SHORT HISTORY OF ENGLISH. WITH A BIBLIOGRAPHY OF RECENT BOOKS ON THE SUBJECT, AND LISTS OF TEXTS AND EDITIONS
Wylie, David Gourley *see* THREE VIEWS OF THE PUBLIC SCHOOL QUESTION
Wylie, Ida Alena Ross *see* THE GERMANS
Wylie, Macleod (Mrs) *see* THE GOSPEL IN BURMAH
Wylie, Samuel S et al *see* HISTORY OF THE ROCKY SPRING CHURCH
Wylie, Theophilus A *see* INDIANA UNIVERSITY 1820-90
WYLLARD'S WEIRD / Braddon, Mary Elizabeth – British Fiction Archive: Unit 5 – 9 – uk Bell [830]
Wyman, Bruce *see*
– CASES ON RESTRAINT OF TRADE
– THE SPECIAL LAW GOVERNING PUBLIC SERVICE CORPORATIONS.
Wyman, J *see* FRESH-WATER SHELL MOUNDS OF THE ST JOHN'S RIVER, FLORIDA
WYMORE ARBOR STATE – Wymore, NE. -w. Jun 1895-Jul 1896, scattered issues missing; Sept 1896-Jan 1910; Jul 1911-Feb 1918; Jan-Sept 1919; Jan 1921 to date – 1 – us NE Hist [071]
WYNBERG TIMES – Cape Town, South Africa.6 Jan 1883-26 Dec 1908. 25 reels – 1, 16 diazo available at reduced price – sa SA Libr [072]
Wyndham, Edmund *see* ECOLOGY OF THE BUDGERYGAH
Wyneken, Gustav Adolf *see* AMOR DEI INTELLECTUALIS: EINE RELIGIONS-PHILOSOPHISCHE STUDIE
WYNKOOP GENEALOGY / Wynkoop, Richard – 1878 – 1 – $50.00 – us Presbyterian [920]
Wynkoop, Richard *see* WYNKOOP GENEALOGY
Wynn, R F *see* AN EXPLORATION OF THE LONG-TERM PROSPECTS FOR THE FURTHER DEVELOPMENT OF THE NILEWATERS IN THE SUDAN FOR IRRIGATION AND HYDROELECTRIC POWER
Wynne, F R et al *see* THE LITERATURE OF THE SECOND CENTURY
WYNOT TRIBUNE – Wynot, NE. -w. Jan 1918-Jan 1920; Jun 1926-Dec 1931 – 1 – us NE Hist [071]
WYOMING : SESSION LAWS OF AMERICAN STATES AND TERRITORIES – 1869-1995 – 9 – $509.00 set – us Hein [340]
WYOMING : STATUTES ANNOTATED – Charlottesville: Michie Co, 1957-Jan 1995 update – 9 – $1,581.00 set – us Hein [340]
Wyoming *see*
– REPORTS AND OPINIONS (A-G)
– REPORTS, POST-NRS
– REPORTS, PRE-NRS
WYOMING ATTORNEY GENERAL REPORTS AND OPINIONS – (6 1888-1970, 1976-1982 $140.00. 9 1977-1995 $103.00. 1971-1975 not available) – 1888-1995 – 6,9 – $243.00set – us Hein [340]
THE WYOMING DEMOCRAT – Tunkhannock, PA. -w 1890-1912; 1924-27. 9 rolls – 13 – $25.00r – us I.M.R. [071]
WYOMING FROM TERRITORIAL DAYS TO THE PRESENT / Beard, Frances B – Chicago: American Hist. Soc. Inc., 1933.v1-3. Wyoming reel 2.(Cox Library Collection) – 5 – us Americana [978]
WYOMING LAW JOURNAL *see* LAND AND WATER LAW REVIEW
WYOMING LAWYER – v1-18. 1976-95 – 9 – $152.00 set – us Hein [340]
WYOMING MAPS : CITIES AND TOWNS – 1883-1903. 191 maps. 17 towns. Sanborn Company Fire Insurance Maps – 1 – $40.00r – us Shkurkin [910]
Wyoming. State Bar Association *see* PROCEEDINGS
WYOMING STATE BAR ASSOCIATION PROCEEDINGS – 1915-37 (all publ) – 26mf – 9 – $39.00 – LLMC 84-692 – us L.L.M.C. [073]
WYOMING STATE BUSINESS DIRECTORY 1929 / The Gazetteer Publishing and Printing Co – (1930. Wyoming reel 3. 1937. Wyoming reel 3) – Wyoming reel 3. (Cox Library Collection) – 5 – us Americana [380]
Wyoming. Supreme Court *see* WYOMING SUPREME COURT REPORTS
WYOMING SUPREME COURT REPORTS / Wyoming. Supreme Court – (Pre-NRS: v1-2 1870-82 4mf $18.00. Updates planned) – v1-26. 1870-1920 – 38mf (1:42) 49mf (1:24) – 9 – $130.00 – LLMC 84-212 – us L.L.M.C. [340]
WYOMING TELESCOPE – Wyoming, NE. -w. Jun-Sept 1857, scattered issues missing; Mar-Sept 1859, scattered issues missing – 1 – us NE Hist [071]
WYONG ADVOCATE – Nov 21 1935-Dec 19 1935. Feb 18 1937-Feb 25 1937. Mar 3 1938. November 30 1939 – 9 – at Pascoe [072]
WYONG AND LAKES DISTRICT ADVOCATE – Jan 7 1932-Apr 3 1957 (impf) – 9 – at Pascoe [072]
WYONG MIRROR – Nov 4 1931. Jan 27 1932. Aug 26 1936. Feb 3 1937 – 9 – at Pascoe [072]
WYOTTENS EMBLEMATISCHER PARNASSUS / Woytt, L W M – O 806 1. 3 v. 1727-1730 – 9 – ne IDC [760]
Wyplel, Ludwig *see* ENGLANDS EINFLUSS AUF DIE LEHRDICHTUNG HALLERS
Wypyski, Eugene M *see* BANKRUPTCY REFORM ACT OF 1978
Wyss, Johann Rudolf *see* BLUMENLESE AUS DEN SAEMMTLICHEN WERKEN VON JOHANN RUDOLF WYSS DEM JUENGERN
Wytfliet, Cornelius *see* HISTOIRE UNIVERSELLE DES INDES ORIENTALES ET OCCIDENTALES
Wythe, Joseph Henry *see* THE AGREEMENT OF SCIENCE AND REVELATION
WYTHE'S CHANCERY REPORTS / Virginia. Supreme Court – (A Pre-NRS title) – 1v. 1788-1799 (all publ) – 6mf – 9 – $9.00 – LLMC 91-098 – us L.L.M.C. [340]
Wytsman, P A G *see*
– GENERA AVIUM
– GENERA INSECTORUM...

WZ/WESTDEUTSCHE ZEITUNG *see* GENERALANZEIGER DER STADT WUPPERTAL

X RAY *see* THE X-RAY

X3 (X3 INFORMATION PROCESSING SYSTEMS) – Printed index. Updated every 30 days – 9 – us Info Handling [000]

Xatard, Veronique *see* CATEGORIES GRAMMATICALES ET DISTRIBUTION

Xau, Fernand-Arthur-Pierre *see*
- CHEZ M. SULLY-PRUDHOMME
- EMILE ZOLA
- HISTOIRE BIOGRAPHIQUE ILLUSTREE DE NOS DEPUTES
- LA QUESTION DES HUISSIERS

Xavier, Humberto Flavio *see* PROBLEME DER UMSETZUNG DER RICHTLINIEN DER EUROPAEISCHEN GEMEINSCHAFT IN DAS NATIONALE RECHT PORTUGALS AM BEISPIEL DER WASSERRICHTLINIEN

Xavir, Manuel *see* PANEGYRICO FUNERAL PREDICADO EN LAS EXEQUIAS QUE LA CIUDAD DE PLASENCIA CELEBRO EN LA MEMORIA DEL SR. DON CARLOS 2

XAY DUNG – Saigon. South Vietnam. 1964-1966 – 1 – us UMI [072]

XENIA BERNARDINA – (Pars 1a, 1: Sermones de Tempore. 11mf; Pars 1a, 2:Sermones de Sanctis. 12mf; Pars 2a, 1: Handschriften-Verzeichnisse. 12mf; Pars 2a, 2: Handschriften-Verzeichnisse. 11mf; Pars 3a: Beitraege z. Geschichte der Cist. Stifte. 9mf; Pars 4a: Bibliographia Bernardina. 13mf) – Vindobonae. v1-5. 1891 – 8 – Dfl238.00 – ne Slangenburg [240]

Xenia, Ohio *see* MISCELLANEOUS EARLY NEWSPAPERS

XENIA ORCHIDACEA / Reichenbach, Heinrich G L – 3v. Leipzig. 1854-, 1858-1900. B-1261 2 – 8 – ne IDC [580]

Xenia. Presbytery (United Pres. Ch. of N.A.) *see* RECORDS, 1858-1911

XENOBIOTICA – The fate of foreign compounds in biological systems. v.1-5. 1971-75 – 9 – 2465.00; 2413.00v – uk Dawson [540]

XEUVERL : ROMAN / Pongratz, Alfons – Muenchen: Deutscher Volksverlag: 1941 – 1r – 1 – us U.W. Library [830]

Xi, Jianwei *see* PREDICTION OF ONE REPETITION MAXIMUM BENCH PRESS FROM PUSH-UPS IN ACTIVE YOUNG MALES

XIAMEN DAXUE XUEBAO – (1983 $3.50f; 1982, 1986- $4.50f) – Ziran Kexue Ban. Universitatis Amoiensis Acta Scientiarum Naturalium. In Chinese but English abstracts to the main articles. F p186 – 9 – cc Microforms [073]

XIAMEN DAXUE XUEBAO – (1984 $3.50f; 1978-83, 1986- $4.50f) – Zhexue Shehui Kexue Ban. Journal of Xiamen University, Philosophy & Social Science. In Chinese but Table of Contents in English in each issue. F p208 – 9 – cc Microforms [073]

XIAMEN RIBAO = XIAMEN DAILY – China. 1985-. M-D85 – 1 – $55.00r – cc Microforms [072]

XI'AN JIAOTONG DAXUE XUEBAO = JOURNAL OF XI'AN UNIVERSITY – 1981-. F-P226 – 9 – $4.50f – cc Microforms [073]

XIAN QU – 1922-Aug 1923. 2 ill. DL14f – 9 – 30.00 – cc Globe [073]

XIAN SHIBIAN ZILIAO DIYIJI (ZHONGGUO XIANDAI GEMING SHILIAO CONGKAN) – Series of materials on contemporary Chinese revolutionary history: materials on the Xi'an incident, Part 1. Comp. by the Institute of Contemporary History, Chinese Academy of Social Sciences. 3 fiches. F-H140 – 9 – $18.00 – cc Microforms [950]

XIAN WANBAO = EVENING POST – China. 1983- . M-D50 – 1 reel/y – 1 – $55.00r – cc Microforms [072]

XIANDAI HANYU CIDIAN – Contemporary Chinese dictionary.Comp. by the Institute of Linguistics, Chinese Academy of Social Sciences. 6 fiches.F-J32 – 9 – $4.00f – cc Microforms [480]

XIANG BAO – (Hunan Daily). China. Mar-Oct 1898. M B7 – 2r – 1 – $100.00 – cc Microforms [072]

XIANG DAO – China. A weekly newspaper published from 1922-27. 44 ill. DL48f – 210.00;+GM; 9 – cc Globe [072]

XIANG DAO = THE GUIDE WEEKLY – 13 Dec 1922-18 Jul 1927.2 reels. M-C67 – 1 – $160.00 – cc Microforms [073]

XIANQU – The Pioneer. 15 Jan 1922-15 Aug 1923. F C4. In Chinese – 9 – $9.00 – cc Microforms [073]

XIAO SHUO CIYU HUISHI – Explanations of words and phrases in Chinese novels and short stories. Comp. by Lu Danan. 1 reel. M-J35 – 5 – 35.00 – cc Microforms [480]

XIAORIBAO = THE TABLOID – Apr-May 1919. 2 fiches.F-C37 – 9 – $9.00 – cc Microforms [073]

XIAOSHUOJIA = NOVELIST – Oct-Dec 1936. 5 fiches.F-C57 – 9 – $22.50 – cc Microforms [830]

XIBEI DAXUE XUEBAO – (Zhexue Shehui Kexue Ban). (Journal of Northern China University, Philosophy & Social Science). In Chinese but Table of Contents in English in each issue. F p213 – 9 – $4.50f – cc Microforms [073]

XIBEI GONGYE DAXUE XUEBAO – Journal of Northwest Polytech University. In prep. F/P 305 – 9 – 4.00f – cc Microforms [073]

XIBEI SHI YUAN XUEBAO – (Zhexue Shehui Kexue Ban). Journal of Northwestern Teacher's College, Philosophy and Social Science. In Chinese but Table of Contents in English in each issue. F p224 – 9 – $3.50f – cc Microforms [073]

XIBEI WENHUA RIBAO – (Cultural Daily, Northwest China ed.). 1932-48. M B8 – 21r – 1 – $1,050.00 – cc Microforms [072]

XII Mezhdunarodnyi seminar po issledovaniiu semi *see* DINAMIKA IZMENENIIA POLOZHENIIA ZHENSHCHINY I SEMIA

XIJING RIBAO – Xijing Daily, Xian. China. 1934-46. M B11 – 27r – 1 – $1,350.00 – cc Microforms [072]

XILIANG YIGAO (ZOUGAO). (ZHONGGUO JINDAISHI ZILIAO CONGSHU) – Historical materials of modern China series: Posthumous manuscripts of Xiliang: Memorials to the emperor. Comp. by the Institute of History, Chinese Academy of Social Sciences. 1 reel. M-H186 – 5 – 20.00 – cc Microforms [950]

Ximenez, Francisco *see*
- HISTORIA DE LA PROVINCIA DE SAN VICENTE DE CHIAPA Y GUATEMALA, DE LA ORDEN DE PREDICACDORES. TOMO 1. GUATEMALA, 1929
- HISTORIA DE LA PROVINCIA DE SAN VICENTE DE CHIAPA Y GUATEMALA DE LA ORDEN DE PREDICADORES...TOMO 3

XIN CHAO – 5 issues from 1919. 12 ill. DL66f – 9 – 70.00 – cc Globe [073]

XIN HUA RI BAO – China. Published during the war with Japan and early Liberation War. The only public newspaper published during the period of Guo Ming Tang's Power.1938-Feb 1947.DL7 – 9 – 1220.00 – cc Globe [072]

XIN HUA SHE XIN WENG GAO – (Title change: Jin Ri Xin Wen. Sept 1957-Mar 1969. 2185.00; 9. Title change: Xin Hua She Xin Wen Gao. Apr 1969-1986. 6960 ill. 23,145.00; GM; 9) – Collection of news printed and broadcast daily in China and abroad. Includes articles in Chinese, English, French, Spanish, Russian and Arabic. 1948-57. Il1 – 9 – 1330.00 – cc Globe [950]

XIN JIAN SHE – A Political magazine published from 1949-1966. PW54 – 9 – 210.00 – cc Globe [073]

XIN JIANSHE = NEW CONSTRUCTION – 1949-66.F-P261 – 9 – $3.50f – cc Microforms [073]

XIN QIN NIAN – Five editions from Apr 1925-Jul 1926. 15 ill. DL45f – 9 – 75.00 – cc Globe [073]

XIN QIN NIAN – Monthly.Sept 1915-Jul 1922. 133 ill. DL43f – 9 – 620.00 – cc Globe [073]

XIN QIN NIAN – Quarterly. Four editions from Apr 1925-Jul 1926. 10 ill. DL44f – 9 – 50.00 – cc Globe [073]

XIN QINGNIAN = NEW YOUTH – No.1-4. -q. Jun 1923-Dec 1924.7 fiches. F-C77 – 9 – $38.50 – cc Microforms [073]

XIN QINGNIAN = NEW YOUTH – No.1-5. Apr 1925-Jul 1926. 11 fiches. F-C78 – 9 – $40.50 – cc Microforms [073]

XIN SHEHUI – The New Society. Nov 1919-May 1920. F C12. In Chinese – 9 – $13.50 – cc Microforms [073]

XIN SHI DAI – A monthly magazine published by Mao in Apr 1922.8 ill.DL69f – 9 – 35.00 – cc Globe [073]

XIN WEN JIAN BAO – China. Dec 1947-Feb 1948. 4 ill. DL27f – 9 – 30.00 – cc Globe [072]

XIN YULIN – New Literature Circles. Jul 1924-Oct 1934. 1 reel. M/C 81 – 1 – $55.00 – cc Microforms [480]

XIN ZHANG GUO – News Daily of the Central Committee of the Communist Party. February 1939 – May 1941. 18 ill. DL5f – $75.00 – cc Globe [950]

XIN ZHONG GUO – China. News daily of the Central Committee of the Communist Party. 1937-38. 10 ill. DL58f – 9 – 40.00 – cc Globe [072]

XIN ZHONG HUA BAO – China. News daily of the Central Committee of the Communist party. Feb 1939-May 1941.18 ill. DL5f – 9 – 75.00 – cc Globe [072]

XINAN JIAOTONG DAXUE XUEBAO – Journal of Southwest Jiaotong University. In prep. F/P 304 – 9 – 4.00f – cc Microforms [073]

XINCHAO – The Renaissance. Jan 1919-Mar 1922. M C2. In Chinese – 1 – $90.00 – cc Microforms [073]

XING HUA RI BAO – China. Sept-Dec 1948. 5 ill. DL11f – 9 – 30.00 – cc Globe [072]

XINGQI PINGLUN – Weekly Review. 1919. F C10. In Chinese – 9 – $30.00 – cc Microforms [073]

XINHAI GEMING KIANGSU DIQU SHILIAO – Historical materials on the Revolution of 1911 in Jiangsu. Comp. by the History Department of Yangzhou Normal College. 7 fiches. F-H108 – 9 – $31.50 – cc Microforms [950]

XINHAI GEMING QIANHOU-SHEN XUANHUAI DANGAN ZILIAO XUANJI ZHIYI – A selection of archival materials in the possession of Shen Xuan Huai, part 1: Before and after the Revolution of 1911. Comp. by Chen Xulu, etc. 5 fiches. F-H169 – 9 – 4.00f – cc Microforms [950]

XINHAI GEMING SHILIAO – Historical materials of the Revolution of 1911. Comp. by Zhang Guogan. 4 fiches. F-H102 – 9 – $18.00 – cc Microforms [950]

XINHAI GEMING WUCHANG SHOUYI SHILIAO JILU – Historical materials on the first uprising of the Revolution of 1911 at Wuchang. Comp. by the Hubei Library. 2 fiches. F-H105 – 9 – $9.00 – cc Microforms [950]

XINHAI GEMING ZAI GUANGXI (SHANG-XIA CE) – The Revolution of 1911 in Guangxi, v1-2.Comp. by the Guangxi Political Consultative sic Conference. 5 fiches. F-H110 – 9 – $22.50 – cc Microforms [950]

XINHAI GEMING ZAI HUBEI SHILIAO XUANJI – Selection of historical materials on the Revolution of 1911 in Hubei province. Comp. by Wuhan University. 8 fiches. F-H104 – 9 – $36.00 – cc Microforms [950]

XINHAI GEMING ZAI SHANGHAI SHILIAO XUANJI: XIUDING BEN – A selection of historical materials on the Revolution of 1911 in Shanghai. Rev. ed. comp. by the Institute of History, Shanghai Academy of Social Sciences. 1 reel. M-H107 – 5 – $34.00 – cc Microforms [950]

XINHAI GEMING ZHEJIANG SHILIAO XUANJI – A selection of historical materials on the Revolution of 1911 in Zhejiang. Comp. by the Society for the Study of the History of the Revolution of 1911, Zhejiang Provincial Library. 7 fiches. F-H109 – 9 – $31.50 – cc Microforms [950]

XINHAI GEMINGSHI ZHONGWEN SHUMU – A list of Chinese books on the 1911 Revolution. Comp. by the Library of the Institute of Modern History, Chinese Academy of Social Sciences. 1 fiche.F-J9 – 9 – $4.50f – cc Microforms [950]

XIN-HUA RIBAO – Xinhua Daily. China. In Chinese. Current subscription. Annual delivery. 1989- , 1 reel/y. M D19 – 1 – $55.00r – cc Microforms [072]

XINHUA RIBAO – (Huazhong Ban). (New China Daily, Central China ed.). Jan-Oct 1946, Jan 1948-Apr 1949. M B17 – 3r – 1 – $150.00 – cc Microforms [072]

XINHUA RIBAO – (Taihang Ban). (New China Daily, Taihang ed.). 1943-49. M B19 – 6r – 1 – $300.00 – cc Microforms [072]

XINHUA RIBAO – (Taiyue Ban). (New China Daily, Taiyue ed.). 1944-49. M B18 – 4r – 1 – $200.00 – cc Microforms [072]

XIN-HUA WENZHAI – New China's Digest. In Chinese. F p3 – 9 – $4.50f – cc Microforms [073]

XIN-HUA YUEBAO – New China Monthly. In Chinese. F p2 – 9 – $4.50f – cc Microforms [073]

XINJIANG JUNKEN BAO – China. Army reclamation of wasteland. 1984-. M-D69 – 1 reel/y – 1 – $34.00r – cc Microforms [073]

XINJIANG RIBAO – China. Xinjiang Daily. 1986-.M-D95 – 1 – $55.00r – cc Microforms [072]

XINLI XUEBAO – (Acta psychogica Sinica). In Chinese but English abstracts to the main articles. F p134 – 9 – 4.00f – cc Microforms [073]

XIN-MIN WANBAO – China. New People's Evening Post. 1983-. M-D38 – 2r/y – 1 – $55.00r – cc Microforms [072]

XINSHENG = NEW LIFE – Feb 1934-Jun 1935. -w. 2 reels. M-C47 – 1 – $68.00 – cc Microforms [073]

XINSHIDAI – New Era Monthly. Apr 1923-Jun 1923. F C7. In Chinese – 9 – $22.50 – cc Microforms [073]

XINWEN CHUBAN BAO = PRESS AND PUBLISHING JOURNAL – China. 1984-. -w. M-D59. As Zhongguo Baokan (The Chinese Press) until 1990 – 1 reel/y – 1 – $28.00r – cc Microforms [072]

XINWENXUE SHILIAO – (1981 $3.50f; 1982-$4.50f) – Historical Material of Modern Literature. In Chinese. F p27 – 9 – cc Microforms [480]

XINWENYI = LA NOUVELLE LITTERATURE – Sept 1929-Apr 1930. 2 reels. M-C42 – 1 – $68.00 – cc Microforms [480]

XITONG GONGCHENG LILUN YU SHIJIAN – Systems Engineering-Theory and Practice.1984. F/P 291 – 9 – $4.50f – cc Microforms [073]

XITONG KEXUE YU SHUXUE – Journal of Systems Science and Mathematical Sciences. In Chinese but English abstracts to the main articles. F p140 – 9 – $4.50f – cc Microforms [073]

XIWANG = HOPE – 1945-Aug 1946. 8 fiches. F-C65 – 9 – $36.00 – cc Microforms [073]

XIWANG = HOPE – Mar 1937. Semimonthly. 2 fiches. F-C58 – 9 – $9.00 – cc Microforms [073]

XIZANG RIBAO – Xizang Daily. 1986- . M/D 113 – 1 – $55.00r – cc Microforms [072]

XIZANG YANJIU – Tibetan Studies.1982-84. F/P 270 – 9 – $3.50f – cc Microforms [073]

XPERANXKI, I.A. MOT SO VAN DE VE HINH LUAT VIET NAM DAN CHU CONG HOA = CRIMINAL LAW ISSUES OF THE DEMOCRATIC REPUBLIC OF VIETNAM – Hanoi: The People's Supreme Court, 1964 – 2mf – 9 SEL-120/1 – ne IDC [340]

Xpycoctomika *see* STUDI E RICERCHE INTERNO A SAN GIOVANNI CRISOSTOMO

THE X-RAY – (Library has: v.4, no.43; v.5, no.20, 31, 34-37, 45; v.6, no.4, 8-12, 30, 33; v.7, no.33 (July 5, 1941-April 29, 1944)) – Muncie, Ind.: Court Asher, 1937 – 1 – CSUX89-S126 – us Hoover Inst Photo [073]

AN X-RAY ATLAS OF THE ROYAL MUMMIES / ed by Harris, James E & Wente, Edward F – (404p accompanying text) – Chicago, University of Chicago Press, 1980 – 5mf – 11 – $90.00f – 0-226-31745-5 – us Chicago [930]

X-RAY SPECTROMETRY – (1982-. 1,5,6,9) – v1-. 1972- – 1 – us UMI [073]

XUE DEN – 1922-27 – 9 – 350.00 – cc Globe [073]

XUESHU YUEKAN – Academic Monthly. In Chinese. F p13 – 9 – $4.50f – cc Microforms [073]

XUMO SHOUYI XUEBAO – Acta Veterinaria et Zootechnica Sinica. In Chinese but English abstracts to the main articles. F p58 – 9 – $4.50f – cc Microforms [073]

Xydias, N *see* VIENNE SUR LE RHONE

Y AHORA QUE? / Antonio, Jorge – [Buenos Aires]: Ediciones Verum et Militia, [1966] – 1 – CSUXADQ6610-B – us Hoover Inst Photo [972]

...Y AL OESTE PORTUGAL / Lorenzo, Pedro de – Madrid: Editora Nacional, 1946 – 1 – sp Bibl Santa Ana [946]

Y BRYTWN – Bala, Wales. -m. Feb 1837-July 1840. 28 ft – 1 – uk British Libr Newspaper [072]

Y CHWARELWR CYMREIG – Bangor, Wales. June 1893-March 1902 – 3r – 1 – uk British Libr Newspaper [072]

Y CLORIANYDD – Bangor, Wales. -w. Aug 1891-Dec 1898. 2 1 2 reels – 1 – uk British Libr Newspaper [072]

Y GROSSO : VEO EL CIELO ABIERTO... / Bayle, Constantino – Madrid: Razon y Fe, 1941 – sp Bibl Santa Ana [946]

Y PAPYR CYMRAEG NEWYDD – Caernarvon, Wales. 22 Sept 1836-8 Mar 1837 – 22ft – 1 – uk British Libr Newspaper [072]

Y PROTESTANT – Mold, Wales. -m. 24 May 1839-1 June 1848. 1 reel – 1 – uk British Libr Newspaper [072]

Y RHEDEGYDD – Blaenau Ffestiniog, Wales. -w. Sept 1885-Oct 1895. (1885 imperfect). 3 1 2 reels – 1 – uk British Libr Newspaper [072]

Y SEREN – Bala, Wales. -w. June 1889-Dec 1907. 7 1 2 reels – 1 – uk British Libr Newspaper [072]

YA – Madrid, Spain. -d. 19 Nov 1940-8 Nov 1945; 1 Jan-31 Dec 1947. Imperfect. 21 reels – 1 – uk British Libr Newspaper [072]

YA, CON EL PIE EN EL ESTRIBO / Sanchez-Arjona, Vicente – Sevilla: Imp. Alvarez, Tomo 1. 1959 – 1 – sp Bibl Santa Ana [810]

YA, CON EL PIE EN EL ESTRIBO / Sanchez-Arjona, Vicente – Sevilla: Imp. Alvarez, Tomo 2. 1959 – 1 – sp Bibl Santa Ana [810]

YA, CON EL PIE EN EL ESTRIBO / Sanchez-Arjona, Vicente – Sevilla: Imp. Alvarez, Tomo 3. 1959 – 1 – sp Bibl Santa Ana [810]

Yaari, A *see*
- MASSA MESHULLAM MI-VOLTERRA BE-EREZ-YISRA'EL BI-SHENAT 5241
- RA'ASH ZEFAT BI-SHENAT 5520
- SHELUHEI EREZ-YISRA'EL
- TE'UDOT LE-TOLEDOT HA-YISHUV BE-HEVRON

Yaari, M *see*
- ANALYSIS OF ZIONISM
- FROM VISION TO REALITY

YAB SRAS GSUNS 'BUM / ed by Zhol-pa-khan, Lhasa – Collected works of Tson-Kha-pa, Rgyal-tshab-rje and Mkhas-grub-rje. 1897 – 690mf – 9 – $300.00 – us I.A.S.W.R. [280]

Yablunosky, Matthew S *see* ANALYZING THE PRIVATE CONTRIBUTIONS AMONG COLLEGIATE LETTERWINNERS

A YACHT VOYAGE: LETTERS FROM HIGH LATITUDES, BEING SOME ACCOUNT OF A VOYAGE IN THE SCHOONER YACHT "FOAM", 85 O.M., TO ICELAND, JAN MAYEN, AND SPITZBERGEN, IN 1856 / Dufferin, Earl of & Dufferin, Ava, Hamilton-Temple-Blackwood, Frederick – Toronto; A yacht voyage of six thousand miles 02791 (Pre-1900 Canadiana) – 9 – cn C.I.H.M. [971]

YACHTING – (v. 125- 1969- 5,6. v. 127-1970- 9) – v. 1- 1907- – 1 – us UMI [790]

YACIMIENTOS PETROLIFEROS FISCALES / Argentina. Secretaria de Industria y Comercio – Buenos Aires, 1949 – 1 – CSUXADH3607-B – us Hoover Inst Photo [333]

YACKANDANDAH SHIRE MINUTES – 1865-19903 – 18r – 5,1 – at Corangamite [910]

YACKANDANDAH TIMES – 1890-1934. YT1-16 – 16 – 1 – at Corangamite [072]

YACKANDANDAH WATER BOARD MINUTES – 1987-1989. YWB2 – 1r – 5 – at Corangamite [910]

YAD AR EVANGELIUM? / Arbman, Per T – Upsala: Almquist & Wiksell, 1907. 1 fiche – 9 – us A.T.L.A. [240]

YAD VA SHEM... STUDIES IN JEWISH BIBLIOGRAPHY... IN MEMORY OF A.S. FREIDUS / Freidus, A S – New York, 1929 – 15mf – ne IDC [270]

YAD VASHEM: ARCHIVES OF THE DESTRUCTION – A photographic record of the Holocaust. 15,000 pictures on 245 fiches. Printed index – 9 – is I.T.T.I. [940]

YADKIN BAPTIST CHURCH. NORTH CAROLINA : CHURCH RECORDS – 1787-1946 – 1 – 21.76 – us Baptist [240]

YADKIN BAPTIST CHURCH. PATTERSON, NORTH CAROLINA : CHURCH RECORDS – 1787-1837; 1891-1946 – 1 – 24.48 – us Baptist [240]

Yague, Francisco *see* HISTORIA...DEL CASTANAR...BEJAR

YAH SRAS GSUNS 'BUM – 1897 – 690mf – $300.00 – us I.A.S.W.R. [280]

YAHVISM AND OTHER DISCOURSES / Moses, Adolph – Louisville: Coun. of Jewish Women, 1903.1 fiche – 9 – us A.T.L.A. [270]

YAHWEH : THE DIVINE NAME IN THE BIBLE / Parke-Taylor, G H – 1975 – $15.00 – 0-88920-045-9 – cn W.L.U. Press [220]

YAHWEH-ELOHIM: THE MEMORIAL NAME / Lasius, E J – Birmingham: Robert Roberts, 1883. 1 fiche – 9 – us A.T.L.A. [270]

YAKIMA FIRST SOUTHERN BAPTIST CHURCH (FORMERLY: BETHEL). YAKIMA, WASHINGTON : CHURCH RECORDS – 1932-49, 1955-72 – 1 – 21.87 – us Baptist [240]

YAKIMA RESERVATION NEWS – 1966-70. (American Indian Periodicals in the Princeton University Library). 5 fiches – 9 – $45.00 – us UPA [305]

Yale, Cyrus *see* THE GODLY PASTOR

YALE DIVINITY NEWS / Yale University.Divinity School – 1921-65 – 1 – us UMI [240]

YALE DIVINITY QUARTERLY – 1904-20 – 1 – us UMI [240]

YALE FRENCH STUDIES – v1- 1948- 1; v31-5,6; v53- 9 – us UMI [440]

YALE JOURNAL OF BIOLOGY AND MEDICINE – v. 16-21. 1943-1949 – 1,5,6 – us Princeton Micro [574]

YALE JOURNAL OF INTERNATIONAL LAW – (Title varies: v1-6 1974-1980 as Yale Studies in World Public Order. v7-9 1980-1983 as Yale Journal of World Public Order) – v1-20. 1974-95 – 9 – $291.00 set – us Hein [340]

YALE JOURNAL OF LAW AND LIBERATION – v1-3. 1989-92 – 9 – $40.00 set – us Hein [340]

YALE JOURNAL OF LAW AND THE HUMANITIES – v1-7. 1988-1995 – 9 – $100.00 set – us Hein [340]

YALE JOURNAL OF WORLD PUBLIC ORDER *see* YALE JOURNAL OF INTERNATIONAL LAW

YALE JOURNAL ON REGULATION – v1-12. 1983-95 – 9 – $209.00 set – us Hein [340]

YALE LAW AND POLICY REVIEW – v1-13. 1982-95 – 9 – $226.00 set – us Hein [340]

YALE LAW JOURNAL – (Add vols as copyright expires) – v1-29. 1891-1919/20 – 114mf – 9 – $294.00 – LLMC 84-693 – us L.L.M.C. [073]

YALE LAW JOURNAL – v1-106. 1891-1997 – 1,5,6,9 – $3,555.00 – us Hein [073]

THE YALE LAW LIBRARY BLACKSTONE COLLECTION : (BIOGRAPHY AND CRITICISM) – 44mf – 9 – LLMC 82-800 Titles 247-266 – us L.L.M.C. [340]

THE YALE LAW LIBRARY BLACKSTONE COLLECTION : (BLACKSTONE'S MISCELLANEOUS WORKS) – ca 35mf – 9 – LLMC 82-800 Titles 229-246 – us L.L.M.C. [340]

THE YALE LAW LIBRARY BLACKSTONE COLLECTION / Yale University. Law Library; ed by Cohen, Morris L – (Free descriptive catalog available on request. Full cataloguing as a major microform collectiion available from OCLC. Individual titles are not listed separately here but under broad block headings as guided by LLMC) – A full reprint of all the titles described in Eller's the William Blackstone Collection in the Yale Law Library: a bibliographic catalog. Over 264 separate titles – 2587mf – 9 – $3,750.00 – LLMC 82-800 – us L.L.M.C. [340]

THE YALE LAW LIBRARY BLACKSTONE COLLECTION *see*
- AN ANALYSIS OF THE LAWS OF ENGLAND
- BLACKSTONE'S COMMENTARIES ON THE LAWS OF ENGLAND
- THE COMIC BLACKSTONE
- COMMENTARIES ON THE LAWS OF ENGLAND
- REPORTS OF CASES DETERMINED IN THE SEVERAL COURTS OF WESTMINSTER-HALL, FROM 1746-1779

YALE LAW SCHOOL : STAGE 5 – 375mf – 9 – H-1781-1783/1 – ne IDC [340]

YALE REVIEW – Old Series, v. 1-19. 1892-1911. New Series, v. 1-34. 1911-1945 – 1 – us Princeton Micro [370]

YALE REVIEW – (v58- 1968- 5,6 v59- 1969-9) – v1- 1892- – 1 – us UMI [320]

YALE SCIENTIFIC MAGAZINE – v1- 1894- 1; v50- 5,6; v51- 9 – us UMI [500]

YALE STUDIES IN WORLD PUBLIC ORDER *see* YALE JOURNAL OF INTERNATIONAL LAW

YALE THEATER – (See also: Theater) – v1-8 1968-1977 1; v8 5,6,9 – us UMI [790]

YALE UNIVERSITY DIVINITY SCHOOL – 35mf – 9 – ne IDC [200]

Yale University Divinity School, New Haven, CT. *see* FINDING AIDS

Yale University. Law Library *see* THE YALE LAW LIBRARY BLACKSTONE COLLECTION

Yale University. Library *see* CATALOG OF THE YALE COLLECTION OF WESTERN AMERICANA

Yale University.Divinity School *see* YALE DIVINITY NEWS

YALKUT MAARABI – (New York). 1904 – 1 – us A.J.P.C. [073]

THE YALKUT ON ZECHARIAH / King, Edward George – (Includes bibliographical references) – Cambridge: Deighton, Bell, 1882 – 1mf – 9 – 0-8370-6070-2 – 1986-0070 – us A.T.L.A. [220]

YAMAGA YASUTARO PAPERS – Vancouver, BC: University of British Columbia Library, Facilities and Preservation Office, 1996 – 7r – 1 – Can$100.00 – cn U.B.C. Preserve [971]

Yamakami, Sogen *see* SYSTEMS OF BUDDHISTIC THOUGHT

Yamashita, Tomoyuki *see* BEFORE THE MILITARY COMMISSION CONVENED BY THE COMMANDING GENERAL, UNITED STATES ARMY FORCES, WESTERN PACIFIC. PROCEEDINGS

LE YAMASKA : WEEKLY BILINGUAL NEWSPAPER – Cowansville, Canada. 1 oct 1958-12 sep 1979 – 8r – 1 – Can$60.00r – cn Can Microfilming [072]

Yamaska Printing Co. *see* THE WEEKLY TIMES

YAMHILL COUNTY JOURNAL – Yamhill, OR. -w. 8 Nov 1929-11 Nov 1932. 1 roll – 1 – us U.O. Library [071]

YAMHILL COUNTY NEWS – Carlton, OR. -w. 7 Mar 1946-13 Nov 1947. 1 roll – 1 – us U.O. Library [071]

YAMHILL COUNTY REPORTER – McMinnville, OR. -w. 25 Apr 1879-11 Mar 1886; 5 Jan 1894-22 Jul 1904. 4 rolls – 1 – us U.O. Library [071]

YAMHILL RECORD – (Set incl. North Yamhill Record) – Yamhill, OR. -w. 5 Mar 1908-28 Feb 1929. – 6r – 1 – us U.O. Library [071]

YAMHILL REVIEW – Carlton, OR. -w. 25 Nov 1948-26 Dec 1974. – 10r – 1 – us U.O. Library [071]

Yamin, Muhammad *see*
- ATLAS SEDJARAH
- OPENING SPEECH OF THE STATE TEACHERS COLLEGE IN BANDUNG, INDONESIA, DELIVERED ON OCT. 20, 1954
- PERKEMBANGAN SEDJARAH NEGARA MADJAPAHIT (T.M. 1293-1525) DALAM EMPAT DEWASA MENURUT ADJARAN PROF. TOYNBEE
- SAPTA DHARMA
- SPEECH ON THE DRAFT FUNDAMENTAL LAW OF THE FIRST NATIONAL OVERALL DEVELOPMENT PLAN DELIVERED TO THE PRESIDENT OF INDONESIA ON 13 AUG. 1960

YAN' DARGENT, PEINTRE ET DESSINATEUR BRETON : SA VIE ET SES OEUVRES / Hanciau, G – Paris: Imp. reunies, 1889 – 1 – F50.00 – fr Armell [700]

Yan, Jin H *see* AGE-RELATED CHANGES IN THE RELEASE POINT, VELOCITY AND ACCELERATION IN GIRLS' OVERARM THROWING PERFORMANCE

YANAR DAG / Ortac, Yusuf Ziya – Istanbul: Marifet Matbaasi, 1928 – $20.00 – us MEDOC [470]

Yancey, Benjamin C *see* BENJAMIN C. YANCEY PAPERS

Yanez, Juan Vicente *see* COMPENDIO...NTRA. SRA. GUADALUPE

Yang, Chih-hsien *see* THE EFFECTS OF PERCEIVED DIRECTORS' LEADERSHIP BEHAVIORS AND SELECTED DEMOGRAPHIC VARIABLES ON PHYSICAL EDUCATION INSTRUCTORS' JOB SATISFACTION

Yang, Chou *see* CHINA'S NEW LITERATURE AND ART

Yang, Kuang *see* PELADJARAN BAHASA NIPPON CHUNGHUA INDONESIA. (OLEH) YANG KWONG

Yang, M-C *see* TRAVEL AND CULTURE SHOCK ADAPTATION AMONG CHINESE STUDENTS AT THE PENNSYLVANIA STATE UNIVERSITY

YANG TZU CHIANG SHUI TAO CHI K'AN / China – Nanking. 1931. BCH-1096 1 – 9 – ne IDC [324]

Yang, Tzu-hung *see* INTRODUCTORY CATECHISM, VOL 2 (CCC344)

Yang, W Y *see* METHODS OF FARM MANAGEMENT INVESTIGATIONS FOR IMPROVING FARM PRODUCTIVITY

YANGCHENG WANBAO = GANGAO HAIWAI BAN – China. Guangzhou Evening News, Supplement for Hong Kong, Macao and overseas. 1986-. M-D47A – 1 reel/y – 1 – $55.00r – cc Microforms [072]

YANGCHENG WANBAO = YANGCHENG EVENING POST – (1983-1987 (1 reel each year); 1988 (2r); 1989-1991 Consists of 1 reel for each year) – 1992- – $55.00r – cc Microforms [950]

YANGRU GENGXIN CUNGAO. JINDAISHI ZILIAO ZHUANKAN – Special series on modern history: Yang Rus collected documents, 1900-01. Comp. by the Institute of Modern History, Chinese Academy of Social Sciences. 4 fiches. F-H57 – 9 – $18.00 – cc Microforms [950]

YANJING XUEBAO – Yenching Journal of Chinese Studies. no.1-40. Jun 1927-Jun 1951. 5 reels.M-C76 – 5 – $200.00 – cc Microforms [073]

YANK – All editions – 1 – us NY Public [970]

YANK – All editions. 1942-45 – 40r – 1 – us Ross [072]

YANK LEGION NEWS – Portland OR. Mar 22-June 14 1945 – 1 – us U.O. Library [071]

YANK NEWS – Portland OR. Sep 13 1945-Dec 25 1947 – 1 – us U.O. Library [071]

YANKEE – Boston. Mass. 1812-1820 – 1,3 – us Readex [071]

YANKEE DOODLE – Batavia, OH, 18 Dec 1858 and 8 Jan 1859 – 1 reel – 1 – us Western Res [073]

YANKEE DOODLE WITH VARIATIONS / Hewitt, James – New York: J. Hewitt 181?. MUSIC 3082, Item 5 – 1 – us L of C Photodup [780]

YANKEE NOTIONS – New York. v10. 1861 – 1r – 1 – us Ross [073]

Yanshi County. China *see* HONGZHI YANSHI XIAN ZHI, 1504

YANSHI XUEBAO – Acta Petrologica Sinica. In prep – 9 – $4.00f – cc Microforms [660]

YANTAI RIBAO = YANTAI DAILY – China. 1984-. M-D65 – 1 reel/y – 1 – $55.00r – cc Microforms [072]

YANTU GONGCHENG XUEBAO – Chinese Journal of Geotechnical Engineering. In Chinese but English abstracts to the main articles. 105p – 9 – $4.00f – cc Microforms [629]

Yanuck, M *see* SOUTH ASIAN LIBRARY RESOURCES IN NORTH AMERICA

A YAO GRAMMAR / Sanderson, Meredith – London: Society for Promoting Christian Knowledge; New York: Macmillan, 1922 – us Res Libr [490]

YAO-CHOU CHIH – 1885, 11, 1. BCH-677 2 – 8 – ne IDC [950]

YAOWU FENXI ZAZHI – Chinese Journal of Pharmaceutical Analysis. In Chinese but English abstracts to the main articles. F p157 – 9 – 4.00f – cc Microforms [073]

YAOXUE XUEBAO – Acta Pharmaceutica Sinica. In Chinese but Table of Contents in English in each issue. F p51 – 9 – $4.50f – cc Microforms [073]

YAP DISTRICT CHARTER, 1978 : AS APPROVED BY THE SEVENTH CONGRESS OF MICRONESIA / Federated States of Micronesia – 2nd reg sess. Saipan: the Congress, 19 Feb 1978 – 2mf – 9 – $3.00 – LLMC 82-100H Title 4 – us L.L.M.C. [324]

YAP STATE CODE : 1988 EDITION / Federated States of Micronesia – (Only released in Jan 1988) – Yap: the Gov, 1987 – 8mf – 9 – $12.00 – LLMC 82-100H Title 13 – us L.L.M.C. [324]

Yap, Sylvia *see* SINGAPORE-MALAYSIA CONFERENCES ON HEALTH AND RELATED SCIENCES

YA-PI SHAN PAO – Jesselton. North Borneo. 1965-67 – 1 – us UMI [073]

YAPRAK – Ankara: Sahibi ve Yazi Isleri Mueduerue: Orhan Veli Kanik. Nos. 1-28 (1 Ocak 1949-15 Haziran 1950) – 2mf – 9 – $30.00 – us MEDOC [949]

YAQUINA BAY NEWS – Newport. Or. and News Recorder. 1901-44 – 1 – us UMI [071]

YAQUINA BAY NEWS – Newport, OR. And Yaquina Bay News-Reporter. -w. 1901-44 – 1 – 240.00 – us Oregon Hist [071]

YAQUINA BAY NEWS – (Set incl. Yaquina Bay News-Reporter (Newport)) – Newport, OR. -w. 29 Jun 1944-27 Nov 1947. – 2r – 1 – us U.O. Library [071]

YAQUINA BAY NEWS REPORTER – Newport OR. May 14 1908-Feb 2 1911, May 21 1908 – 1 – us U.O. Library [071]

YAQUINA MAIL – Newport OR. Nov 4 1884 – 1 – us U.O. Library [071]

YAQUINA POST – Toledo, OR. -w. 6 Aug 1898-19 Jul 1902. 1 roll – 1 – us U.O. Library [071]

YARA : PERIODICO HUMORISTICO, LITTERARIO, PHILOSOPHICO E NOTICIOSO – Manaos, Amazonas. 15 Out-30 Nov 1913 – 1,5,6 – bl Biblioteca [072]

YARIM TUERKLER / Guenduez, Aka – Istanbul: Kanaat Matbaasi, 1919 – $30.00 – us MEDOC [470]

YARIN – Sermuharriri: Arif Oruc, Mesul Mueduerue: Sueleyman Tevfik. Nos. 234-235, 239, 245-246, 253-257, 259-264 (12 Agustos-11 Eyluel 1930) – 9 – $70.00 – us MEDOC [956]

YARMOUK-JORDAN VALLEY PROJECT, THE HASHEMITE KINGDOM OF JORDAN MASTER PLAN / Michael Baker Jr., Inc – Report by Michael Baker Jr., Inc., Rochester Pa., and Harza Engineering Comapny, Chicago, Ill., consulting engineers. 8v (in 10). 1965. BNE-9753 1 – 9 – ne IDC [338]

YARMOUTH 1665-1890 – 50mf – 9 – us Holbrook [920]

YARMOUTH HERALD – Yarmouth, Canada. 1833-73 – 14r – 1 – $910.00 – cn Library Assoc [971]

YARMOUTH INDEPENDENT – Norfolk. 1861-1900 – 21r – 1 – uk Microform Academic [072]

YARMOUTH MERCURY – Norfolk. 1885-89, 1895-96, 1900-07, 1933-38 – 20r – 1 – uk Microform Academic [072]

YARMOUTH, NOVA SCOTIA: A SEQUEL TO CAMPBELL'S HISTORY / Brown, George Stayley – Boston: R. Avery, 1888. 00974. (Pre-1900 Canadiana) – 9 – cn C.I.H.M. [971]

YARMOUTH, NOVA SCOTIA: A SEQUEL TO CAMPBELL'S HISTORY / Brown, George Stayley – Boston: Rand Avery Co., Printers, 1888. Canada reel 6. (Cox Library Collection) – 5 – us Americana [971]

Yarrell, W *see* A HISTORY OF BRITISH FISHES

Yarrow, Henry Crecy *see* INTRODUCTION TO THE STUDY OF MORTUARY CUSTOMS AMONG NORTH AMERICAN INDIANS

YASS COURIER – Jan 3 1902-Mar 28 1929 – 9 – at Pascoe [072]

YATED NEEMAN – Israel, 1985- – 1 – $320.00y – us Ross [072]

Yates, W E *see* USE OF AIRCRAFT IN AGRICULTURE

YAVNEH / Klein, S & Assaf, S – Jerusalem. 1939, 1940. v. 1 dedicated to Samuel Klien, v. 2. dedicated to Simha Assaf. BJ-100-42 1 – 9 – ne IDC [920]

YAYASAN LEMBAGA BANTUAN HUKUM INDONESIA (YLBHI) = INDONESIAN LEGAL AID FOUNDATION – Jakarta. 1-45; 55-59 Doc. 1980-1990 – 25mf – 9 – ne IDC [340]

YAZAREYTU ITYOPYA – (Scattered issues lacking) – Addis Abada, Ethiopia. Jan 9 1952-Sept 10 1990 – 14r – 1 – us L of C Photodup [072]

YAZD, FACE A LA "MODERNISATION" (IRAN) / Kouban Hafezi, S – 9 – F100.00 – fr Ethnologie [360]

Yazdani, G *see*
– AMAL-I-SALIH
– BIDAR. ITS HISTORY AND MONUMENTS

Yazdi, Muhammad *see* NUR-I 'ILM

YAZOO BANNER – Benton. Miss. 1838-44 – 1 – us UMI [071]

Yazoo City, Mississippi *see* MISCELLANEOUS EARLY NEWSPAPERS

YCIIEXNOZNYECKNX HAYK – Years. 1954-1963 – 1 – us Princeton Micro [290]

YDELHEYD DES WERELDS VERCIERT MET ZINNEBEELDEN, RYM-DIGHTEN EN ZEDE-LEERINGEN / Poirters, Adrianus – Antwerpen, 1714 – 3mf – 9 – O-3157/1 – ne IDC [760]

YDELHEYT DES WERELTS / Poirters, Adrianus – 1st ed. Antwerpen, 1645 – 3mf – 9 – O-3156/1 – ne IDC [760]

DER YDISHER EKSPRES = JEWISH EXPRESS SUPPLEMENT – (In Yiddish) – Leeds, GB. v2 no110. 3 Sep 1899 – 1r – 1 – $25.00 – cn Can Microfilming [072]

YE HORNET – Vancouver: Hornet Print and Pub. Co, 1893- – 9 – cn C.I.H.M. [971]

YE LAST SWEET THING IN CORNERS: BEING YE FAITHFUL DRAMA OF YE ARTISTS' VENDETTA / Dixon, Frederick Augustus – Philadelphia: Duncan & Hall, 1880. 02724. (Pre-1900 Canadiana) – 9 – cn C.I.H.M. [820]

YE WU YUEH PAO / China. Ministry of Finance. Director of Salt Administration – Monthly Bulletin. 7 v. Nanking. 1942-48. Lacking: v. 1 (1-11) 1929; v. 2-4 (1-8) 1943-45; v. 7 (11-12) 1948. BCH-1099 1 – 9 – ne IDC [336]

Yeakel, Reuben *see*
– BISHOP JOSPH LONG
– JACOB ALBRIGHT AND HIS CO-LABORERS

YEAR BOOK OF LABOUR STATISTICS 1935-36 TO 1995 = ANUARIO DE ESTADISTICAS DEL TRABAJO / International Labour Organisation – (1935/36-64 Sfr65.00v. 1965-88 Sfr80.00v. 1989-91 Sfr120.00v. 1993-Sfr210.00v (sold together with Sources and Methods: Labour Statistics) – 54v – 9 – Sfr2800.00 – sz I.L.O. [331]

YEAR BOOK OF THE GENERAL CONFERENCE OF THE MENNONITE CHURCH OF N.A. – 1931-46 (complete) – 1r – 1 – ATLA 1993-S006 – us A.T.L.A. [240]

YEAR BOOKS OF THE REIGN OF KING EDWARD 1 (RS31A) / ed by Horwood, A J – (v1 1866 Dfl35.00. v2 1873 Dfl46.00. v3 1863 Dfl39.00. v4 1864 Dfl39.00. v5 1879 Dfl42.00) – ne Slangenburg [941]

YEAR BOOKS OF THE REIGN OF KING EDWARD 3 (RS31B) / ed by Horwood, A J & Pike, L O – (v1 1883 Dfl46.00. v2 1885 Dfl35.00. v3 1886 Dfl35.00. v4 1888 Dfl32.00. v5 1889 Dfl35.00. v6 1891 Dfl39.00. v7 1896 Dfl30.00. v8 1900 Dfl42.00. v9 1901 Dfl46.00. v10 1903 Dfl46.00. v11 1904 Dfl35.00. v12 1905 Dfl42.00. v13 1906 Dfl39.00. v14 1908 Dfl42.00. v15 1911 Dfl42.00) – ne Slangenburg [941]

A YEAR OF CHALLENGE / Sukarno, Pres. Indonesia – SE 10,337 1. Speech in commemoration of Independence Day, 17 Aug. 1958 – 9 – ne IDC [324]

THE YEAR OF GRACE : A HISTORY OF THE REVIVAL IN IRELAND, A.D. 1859 / Gibson, William – [American ed]. Boston: Gould & Lincoln, 1860 – 2mf – 9 – 0-8370-6257-8 – 1986-0257 – us A.T.L.A. [240]

THE YEAR OF GRACE : A HISTORY OF THE ULSTER REVIVAL OF 1859 / Gibson, William – Jubilee ed. Edinburgh: Oliphant, Anderson & Ferrier, [1908?] – 1mf – 9 – 0-8370-6258-6 – 1986-0258 – us A.T.L.A. [240]

A YEAR OF LIVING DANGEROUSLY / Sukarno, Pres. Indonesia – Provisional trans. SE 5755 1. Speech on 17 Aug. 1964 – 9 – ne IDC [324]

A YEAR OF SOUTH AMERICAN TRAVEL / Hazeltine, F A – Letters from the river Plate countries and Brazil. Philadelphia: J.B. Lippincott Co., 1891. 249p – 1 – us U.W. Library [972]

YEAR OF THE HARE / Paasilinna, Arto – 1994 – 136p – 9 – 92-3-103031-0 – Co-publ with Peter Owen/UNESCO Publishing – fr UNESCO [830]

YEARBOOK / American Council on Industrial Arts Teacher Education – (1976- . 5,6,9) – 1952- – 1 – us UMI [370]

YEARBOOK / Central Conference of American Rabbis – 1890-1959 – 1 – us A.J.P.C. [290]

YEARBOOK / Egypt. Federation Egyptienne de l'industrie – 20 v. 1949-76. (lacking 1958 59, 1971). BNE-4630 – 9 – ne IDC [330]

YEARBOOK / National Council for the Social Studies – 1931-1977 – 1 – us UMI [300]

YEARBOOK / National Council of Teachers of Mathematics – 1926- 1; 1977- 5,6,9 – us UMI [370]

YEARBOOK / National Council of Women of Canada – 1894-99 – 1 – $185.00 – cn McLaren [305]

YEARBOOK. COUNCIL ON TECHNOLOGY TEACHER EDUCATION *see* AMERICAN COUNCIL ON INDUSTRIAL ARTS TEACHER EDUCATION YEARBOOK

YEARBOOK OF AGRICULTURE / U.S. Department of Agriculture – 1894-1986. 753 fiches – 9 – 1000.00 – us Updata [630]

YEARBOOK OF CONSTRUCTION STATISTICS / United Nations – 1963-1985 – E/F.74 – 9 (ST/ESA/STAT/Ser.U/1-14) – us U.N. Pubs [690]

YEARBOOK OF CONSTRUCTION STATISTICS / United Nations – 59 fiches – 9 – 110.00; 1.90f – uk UNIMICRO [690]

YEARBOOK OF FISHERY STATISTICS – it F.A.O. [338]

YEARBOOK OF FOREST PRODUCTS STATISTICS – it F.A.O. [338]

YEARBOOK OF HUMAN RIGHTS / United Nations – (1946-1978. E.254 F.269; 1979-1981; 183-1985. E.33) – 9 – us U.N. Pubs [320]

YEARBOOK OF INDUSTRIAL STATISTICS / United Nations – 1950- . -ann. 366 fiches – 9 – 700.00; 1.90f – uk UNIMICRO [338]

YEARBOOK OF INDUSTRIAL STATISTICS / United Nations – 1974-1981 – E.208 – 9 (ST/STAT/Ser.P/12-20) – us U.N. Pubs [338]

YEARBOOK OF INTERNATIONAL AND ENVIRONMENTAL LAW – v1-5. 1990-94 – 9 – us Hein [340]

YEARBOOK OF INTERNATIONAL TRADE STATISTICS / United Nations – (1950-1974. ST/STAT/Ser.G/1-23. E.327; 1975-1977. ST/ESA/STAT/Ser.G/24-26. E.107; 1978-1987. ST/ESA/STAT/Ser.G/27-36. E/F.462) – 9 – us U.N. Pubs [380]

YEARBOOK OF INTERNATIONAL TRADE STATISTICS / United Nations – Published in 2v.277 fiches – 9 – 540.00; 1.90f – uk UNIMICRO [380]

YEARBOOK OF LABOUR STATISTICS / International Labour Organisation – v. 1-1935- – 9 – us UMI [331]

YEARBOOK OF NATIONAL ACCOUNTS STATISTICS / United Nations – (1957-1965. E/F.61; 1966-1970. E.101; 1971-1976. ST/STAT/Ser.O/1-6. E.215; 1977-1981. ST/ESA/STAT/Ser.O/7-11. E.215) – 9 – us U.N. Pubs [650]

YEARBOOK OF NATIONAL ACCOUNTS STATISTICS / United Nations – 601 fiches – 9 – 1180.00; 1.90f – uk UNIMICRO [310]

YEARBOOK OF SCHOOL LAW – (1971. 5,6,9) – 1967-71 – 1 – us UMI [340]

YEARBOOK OF THE INTERNATIONAL LAW COMMISSION / United Nations – 426mf – 9 – $820.00; $1.90f – uk UNIMICRO [340]

YEARBOOK OF THE INTERNATIONAL LAW COMMISSION / United Nations – (1949-1955. A/CN.4/Ser.A/1949-1955. E.69; 1956-1987. A/CN.4/Ser.A/1956-1987. E.399 F.414 S.415) – 9 – us U.N. Pubs [340]

YEARBOOK OF THE MINISTRY'S ACHIEVEMENTS, 1964 / Libya. Ministry of Agriculture and Livestock – BNE-1033 1 – 9 – ne IDC [338]

YEARBOOK OF THE UNITED NATIONS / United Nations – 631mf – 9 – $1200.00; $1.90f – uk UNIMICRO [327]

YEARBOOK OF THE UNITED NATIONS / United Nations – Vols 1-39. 1946-1985 – E.770 – 9 – us U.N. Pubs [320]

YEARBOOK OF WORLD AFFAIRS – 140mf – 9 – us UMI [327]

YEARBOOK OF WORLD ENERGY STATISTICS / United Nations – 1979-1981 – E/F.55 – 9 (ST/ESA/STAT/Ser.J/23-25) – us U.N. Pubs [333]

YEARBOOK ON HUMAN RIGHTS / United Nations – 254 fiches – 9 – 490.00; 1.90f – uk UNIMICRO [320]

YEARBOOKS / Baptist Woman's Missionary Union. Auxiliary to Southern Baptist Convention – 1912-80 – 1 – 254.87 – us Baptist [240]

YEARBOOKS / Charleston. South Carolina – 1880-1951. 66v.475 fiches – 9 – us South Carolina Historical [324]

YEARBOOKS / Great Britain – Maynard ed. 3 reels – 1 – $150.00 – us Trans-Media [340]

YEARBOOKS AND DIRECTORIES / Northern Baptist Convention/American Baptist Convention/American Baptist Churches in the U.S.A – 1907-80.Single reels available – 1 – $1090.80 – us A.B.H.S. [240]

YEARBOOKS-ANNUAL REPORTS / Association of the Bar of the City of New York – 1870-1977. After 1908 called: Yearbooks. Lacking: 1883, 1976 at this time. 84-408 – 9 – 256.00 – us L.L.M.C. [340]

YEARLY BULLETIN OF PRICE STATISTICS, 1964 / Libya. Ministry of Agriculture and Animal Wealth. Agricultural Planning and Economics Department. Statistics Division – Jul 1965. BNE-605 1 – 9 – ne IDC [630]

YEARLY SUMMARY OF FOREIGN TRADE / Kuwait. Central Statistical Office – Statistics. 3 v. in 1. 1965-67. BNE-9006 1 – 9 – ne IDC [310]

YEARS OF FREEDOM / India. National Congress – New Delhi. no. 1-10 1947 48-1956 57. Incomplete – 1 – us NY Public [950]

YEARS OF FREEDOM / Indian National Congress. All-India Congress Committee – v1-10. 1947-57 – 1r – 1 – us Ross [323]

YEARS ON THE AMAZON, 1891-1938 / Nelson, Erik – 660p – 1 – 23.10 – us Baptist [240]

YEAR'S WORK IN MODERN LANGUAGE STUDIES – (v. 1-16. $244.50v; v. 17-24. $2410.50v; v. 25-29. $2413.50v) – v. 1-29. 1929 30-1967. 1931-68. London – 9 – $24255.00 – uk Dawson [400]

Yeary, Mamie *see* REMIMISCENCES OF THE BOYS IN GRAY 1861-1865

YEAST – v1- 1985- – 1,5,6,9 – us UMI [660]

YEATES' REPORTS / Pennsylvania. Superior Court – (A Pre-NRS title) – v1-4. 1791-1808 (all publ) – 8mf – 9 – $36.00 – LLMC 84-193 – us L.L.M.C. [340]

Yeats, William Butler *see* JOHN SHERMAN, AND DHOYA. BY GANCONAGH [I.E. W.B. YEATS]

YEDA AM – Folklore. Tel Aviv. v. 1-17. 1948-74. BJ-91-83 1 – 9 – ne IDC [390]

YEDIAH MI-ZEFAT – (Ha-Levanon, 23rd Sivan 5629). 1869. BJ-27-223 1 – 9 – ne IDC [956]

YEDIES = BULLETIN (MINISTRY FOR JEWISH AFFAIRS) (HEBREW) – (In Hebrew) – Kaunas, LT. no1. Sep 1919 – 1r – 1 – $25.00 – cn Can Microfilming [072]

YEDIES = INFORMATION : FUN YIDISHN VISNSHAFTLEKHN INSTITUT / Jewish Scientific Institute (YIVO) – (In Yiddish) – Vilnius, LT. no28 24 Jan 1929-no83/84 Mar/Apr 1939 – 1r – 1 – $35.00 – cn Can Microfilming [072]

YEDIES FUN YIDISHN VISNSHAFTLEKHN INSTITUT – Vilne. n1-86. 1925-1939 – 12mf – 9 – ne IDC [947]

YEDIOT = NEWS – (In Hebrew) – Berlin, DE. no1. May 1923 – 1r – 1 – $25.00 – cn Can Microfilming [072]

YEDIOT AHARONOT – Tel Aviv. 1939-Available: 1960-76. BJ-91-84 3 – 1 – ne IDC [956]

YEDIOT CHADASHOT = THE LATEST NEWS – (In Hebrew – German) – Tel Aviv, IS. no3650. 16 May 1948 (Birth of Israel Issue) – 1r – 1 – $25.00 – cn Can Microfilming [072]

YEDIOT HACHARONOT – 1979- – 1 – $660.00y – us Ross [072]

YEDI'OT HA-HEVRAH LA-HAKIRAT EREZ YISRA'EL VE-ATTIKOTEHA – Jerusalem. 1933-67. BJ-91-85 1 – 9 – ne IDC [930]

YEDI-SEKIZ PASA – Istanbul: Seyhan Matbaasi, 1949. No. 1-4 (29 Nisan-20 Mayis 1949) – $20.00 – us MEDOC [073]

YEH CH'ENG TA KUAN. DJAKARTA DAHULU DAN SEKARANG / Wu, Shih-huang – SE 4659 1. 1951 – 9 – ne IDC [950]

YEH SU TI YEN CHIN (CCC258) / Pao, Kuang-lin – (In Chinese) – [s.l: s.n, 1928] – 1r – 1 – 1984-6597 – us A.T.L.A. [240]

Yeh, Tu *see* NOT "THEIR" JESUS (CCC345)

YEHUDEI EREZ-YISRA'EL BE-SOF HA-ME'AH HA-17 / Heyd, U – v. 4. Yerushalayim. 1953. BJ-27-68 1 – 9 – ne IDC [270]

YEHUDEI HA-MIZRAH BE-EREZ-YISRA'EL / Gaon, M D – Jersualem. pt 2. 1938 – 14mf – ne IDC [956]

YEHUDEI HA-MIZRAH BE-EREZ-YISRA'EL / Gaon, M D – pt. 2. Jerusalem. 1938. BJ-27-3 1 – 9 – ne IDC [270]

Yekta, Rauf *see* ESATIZ-I ELHAN

YELA UTRILLA, JUAN F. CATEDRATICO Y DOCTOR EN CIENCIAS HISTORICAS... / ed by Bayle, Constantino – Madrid: Razon y Fe, 1926 – 1 – sp Bibl Santa Ana [500]

Yellin, D *see*
– MINHAH LE-DAVID, SEFER HA-YOVEL LE DAVID YELLIN
– YERUSHALAYIM HA-YEHUDIT LIFENEI SHELOSH ME'OT SHANAH

YELLOW ADVERTISER (REDBRIDGE EDN) – (Also known as: Redbridge Yellow Advertiser; Ilford Yellow Advertiser) – Jan-Jun, Jul 10-Dec 18 1987; 1988-Jun, Jul 7-Dec 29 1995; 1996-Jun 1997 – 21r – 1 – uk British Libr Newspaper [072]

YELLOW ADVERTISER, WALTHAM FOREST ED – London, UK. 7 May 1982-1983. -w. 1 1/2 reels – 1 – uk British Libr Newspaper [072]

YELLOW CREEK BAPTIST CHURCH. SPRING CITY, TENNESSEE : CHURCH RECORDS – 1853-1961 – 1 – 38.25 – us Baptist [240]

THE YELLOW SHEET : 1911-1915 – 1995 – us NE Hist [370]

YELLOWKNIFER – Northwest Territories, CN. 1981-95 – 1 – cn Commonwealth Micro [072]

YELLOWSTONE LEADER – Big Timber. Mont. 1900-1905 – 1 – us UMI [071]

YELLOWSTONE NEWS – Billings. Mont – 1 – us UMI [071]

YELLOWSTONE VALLEY RECORDER – Billings. Mont. 1895-1896 – 1 – us UMI [071]

YELMO – v1- 1971- 1; v27- 5,6,9 – us UMI [370]

Yelvertone, E *see* THE MASS IN SWEDEN, ITS DEVELOPMENT FROM THE LATIN RITE, FROM 1531-1917

YELVINGTON BAPTIST CHURCH. OWENSBORO, KENTUCKY : CHURCH RECORDS – 1813-33, 1878-May 1883, 1909, 1917 – 1 – 19.17 – us Baptist [240]

YEMEN – (1299[1822], def' a 2. $190.00; 1305H/1303M[1887], def' a 4. $190.00) – 9 – us MEDOC [956]

Yemen *see*
- AL-JARIDAH AL-RASMIYAH
- OFFICIAL GAZETTE

Yemen. Central Bank of Yemen, Sana'a *see*
- ANNUAL REPORTS
- FOREIGN TRADE STATISTICS FOR THE YEMEN ARAB REPUBLIC FOR THE FISCAL YEAR
- REPUBLICAN DECREE CONCERNING LAW NO. 4 OF 1971, CONCERNING THE ESTABLISHMENT, FORMATION AND JURISDICTION OF THE CENTRAL BANK OF YEMEN

YEN CHUNG-P'ING – Chung-kuo mien-fang-chih shih kao, 1955 – 8 – BCH-850 2 – ne IDC [920]

Yen, J *see* THE ASSESSMENT OF DESTINATION AWARENESS OF INDIANA'S TOURISM POTENTIAL

YEN WU HUI K'AN / China. Ministry of Finance. Director of Salt Administration – Nanking. 1932-37. Lacking: (1-20) 1932-33; (41-60) 1934-35; (69-111) 1935-37. BCH-1098 1 – 9 – ne IDC [336]

YEN WU YUEH PAO / China. Ministry of Finance. Director of Salt Administration – Official gazette. Nanking. 1929-31. Lacking: (1-2) 1929; (17-33) 1930 31. BCH-1097 1 – 9 – ne IDC [336]

Yen, Y C James *see* FOUNDATION CHARACTERS, BK 1 (CCC128)

YENCHING JOURNAL OF SOCIAL STUDIES – Peking. v1-5. 1938-50 – 22mf – 9 – CH-1005/2 – ne IDC [300]

YENCHING JOURNAL OF SOCIAL STUDIES – Peking: Yenching University, 1938-50 – 1r – 1 – us Ross [300]

YENCHING NEWS – v11-29. 1932-50 (incomplete) – 1r – 1 – ATLA S0701E – us A.T.L.A. [073]

Yenching University. Library *see* YEN-CHING-TA-HSUEH T'U-SHU-KUAN PAO

YEN-CHING-TA-HSUEH T'U-SHU-KUAN PAO / Yenching University. Library – BULLETIN. 1-134. Peiping. 1931-39. Monthly. BCH-370 1 – 9 – ne IDC [020]

YENI ADANA – Adana, 1919-1928 – 9 – $10.00 – us MEDOC [956]

YENI ADIM – Iskece. Sermuharriri: Mehmed Hilmi; Mueduer-i Mes'ul: Sabri Ali, 1926-19? – 9 – $25.00 – us MEDOC [956]

YENI ADLI KANUNU / Tarik, Tevfik – Istanbul: Orhaniye Matbaasi, 1340M/1342H [1924] – 9 – $20.00 – us MEDOC [956]

YENI DUENYA – Istanbul. Nesriyat Mueduerue: Cami Baykurt. Nos. 1-3 (1-3 Aralik 1945) – 9 – $20.00 – us MEDOC [956]

YENI DUZEN – Nicosia, Cyprus. July 1991-Apr 1992; Oct 1992-Dec 1992 – 4r – 1 – us L of C Photodup [072]

YENI FELSEFE MECMUASI – Selanik: Rumeli Matbaasi. Mueessisleri: M. Zekeriya [Sertel], Nebizade Ahmed Hamdi; Mesul Mueduerue: Ahmed Hamdi, 1911. No. 7 (15 Tesrinisani 1911) – 9 – $25.00 – us MEDOC [956]

YENI FIKIR – (Mueessisleri: Edhem Nijad, A. Ferid. Nos. 1-6 (15 Kanunievvel 1327-15 Mayis 1328[1911-12]) – Manastir, Istanbul: Yeni Turan Matbaasi, Sems Matbaasi, 1911-? – 3mf – 9 – $50.00 – us MEDOC [949]

YENI FIKIR – Tiflis, Georgia: Zakafkasya Merkezi Icraiye Komitesi ve Halk Komiser Surasinin Nasir-i Efkaridir. Nos. 13, 94, 117, 120, 204 (22 Mart 1922-25 Sep 1923) – 9 – $20.00 – us MEDOC [956]

YENI GEVEZE – Istanbul: Bekir Efendi Matbaasi, Karabet Matbassi. Sahib-i Imtiyaz: Kirkor Faik, Mueduer-i Mes'ul: A. Sami, A. Rifki, 1910-1912. No. 2 (4 Mart 1326 [1910]) – 1mf – 9 – $10.00 – us MEDOC [949]

YENI GIRESUN – Giresun, 1921-19? – 9 – $10.00 – us MEDOC [956]

YENI HAYAT – Ankara, 1922 – 9 – $10.00 – us MEDOC [956]

YENI HAYAT – Izmir, 1913 – 9 – $10.00 – us MEDOC [956]

YENI KALEM – Nos. 1-25 (1927-1928) – 9mf – 9 – $52.50 – us MEDOC [949]

YENI MECMUA – (Includes supplement "Canakkale") – Istanbul: Hilal Matbaasi, 1917-1923 – 9 – $350.00 – us MEDOC [956]

YENI OSMANLI TARIH EDEBIYATI / Fuad, Koepruenluezade Mehmed & Sueleyman, Sihabeddin – Istanbul, Sirket-i Mertebiye Matbaasi, 1332 [1914] – $95.00 – us MEDOC [470]

YENI STRATEJI VE KALKINMA PLANI UCUNCU BES YIL 1973-1977 / Turkey. Devlet Planlama Teskilati – (New Strategy Development Plan, Third Five Year 1973-1977). Ankara. 1973. BD-1770 1 – 9 – ne IDC [338]

YENI ULKE – Istanbul, Turkey. Oct 20-27 1990-Dec 20-26 1992 – 1r – 1 – us L of C Photodup [072]

YENI YOL – Trabzon. Sahibi ve Basmuharriri: Bekir Suekuti. Nos. 140/240, 132/232, 151/251, 497/597, 756/856 (1 Haziran 1341 [1925]-24 Tesrinisani 1927) – 9 – $20.00 – us MEDOC [956]

YENICERI – (Sahib-i Imtiyaz ve Mueduer-i Mes'ul: Cemil H. No. 3 (5 Kanunievvel 1327[1911]) – Istanbul, 1911-1912 – 1mf – 9 – $12.00 – us MEDOC [949]

YEOPIN BAPTIST CHURCH. CHOWAN ASSOCIATION. NORTH CAROLINA : CHURCH RECORDS – 1791-1882 – 1 – 34.20 – us Baptist [240]

YEOPIN UNION BAPTIST CHURCH. CHOWAN ASSOCIATION. NORTH CAROLINA : CHURCH RECORDS – 1853-78 – 1 – 15.93 – us Baptist [240]

YERINGTON TIMES *see* THE BALLOT BOX

YERUSHALAYIM – Jerusalem. 1947-55. BJ-91-87 1 – 9 – ne IDC [956]

YERUSHALAYIM HA-YEHUDIT LIFENEI SHELOSH ME'OT SHANAH / Yellin, D – Ed. by le-Zekher A. M. Luncz, E. L. Sukenik and I. Peres. Yerushalayim. 1928. BJ-27-67 1 – 9 – ne IDC [025]

YERUSHALAYIM, LE-ZEKHER AVRAHAM MOSHEH LUNCZ / Luncz, A M – Jerusalem. 1928. BJ-100-72 1 – 9 – ne IDC [900]

YESHUOT VE-NEHAMOT – Amsterdam. 1649. BJ-43-1371 1 – 9 – ne IDC [956]

YESHUOT VE-NEHAMOT – Hanau. 1620. BJ-43-136 1 – 9 – ne IDC [956]

YESHURUN – Zeitschrift fuer die Wissenschaft des Juedenthums. Lemberg. Breslau, etc. 1856-78. Hebrew and German. BJ-100-117 1 – 9 – ne IDC [270]

YESIL GIRESUN – Giresun, 1924-19? – 9 – $10.00 – us MEDOC [956]

YETA 3 : PARAMOUNT CHIEF OF THE BAROTSE (NORTHERN RHODESIA) / MacKintosh, Catherine Winkworth – London: Pickering & Inglis, 1937 – us Res Libr [960]

YEVREISKAYA...EVREISKAIA LETOPIS – (Russian). Leningrad. v. 1-4. 1923-1926 – 1 – us NY Public [305]

YEVREYSKO-KHAZARSKAYA PEREPISKA V 10-OM VEKE / Kokovtsov, P K – L. 1932. BJ-421-27 1 – 9 – ne IDC [460]

Yewdall, Z *see* DIARIES, 1779-1781, 1784-1797, 1805-1809, 1817-1825

Yexley, Lionel *see* THE INNER LIFE OF THE NAVY...TOGETHER WITH A DETAILED ACCOUNT OF THE SYSTEMS OF VICTUALLING AND UNIFORM IN VOGUE DURING THE LATTER PART OF THE NINETEENTH AND OPENING YEARS OF THE TWENTIETH CENTURY

YEZIRAT ADAM – Lublin. 1624. BJ 43-138 1 – 9 – ne IDC [470]

YI ER JIU YUNDONG (ZHONGGUO XIANDAISHI ZILIAO CONGKAN) – Series of materials on contemporary Chinese history: The December Ninth Movement, 1935. Comp. by Renmin Chubanshe, 1954. 4 fiches. F/H128 – 9 – $14.00 – cc Microforms [950]

YI ZHONG DAO BAO – China. Oct 1946-Aug 1948. 54 ill. DL34f – 9 – 180.00 – cc Globe [072]

YICHUAN XUEBAO – (1977-84 $3.50f; 1986 $4.50f) – Acta Genetica Sinica. In Chinese but English abstracts to the main articles. F p101 – 9 – cc Microforms [073]

DER YID = THE JEW – (In Yiddish) – New York & Montreal. v1 no2 Mar 1918-v1 no5 20 Sep 1918 – 1r – 1 – $25.00 – cn Can Microfilming [071]

DER YID = THE JEW – Montreal, CN. v1 no 2. 1918 – 1r – 1 – Can$30.00 – cn Can Microfilming [072]

DER YID – New York. N.Y. 1959-67 – 1 – us A.J.P.C. [071]

DIE YIDDISCHE BIHNE – New York, NY. 1909-10. The Jewish Stage – 1 – us A.J.P.C. [430]

YIDDISCHE WELT = THE JEWISH WORLD – (In Yiddich) – Cincinnati, Cleveland, Columbus, OH. v2 n151. 1 Jul 1923-v17 n80. 4 Apr 1938 – 7r – 1 – $50.00r – cn Can Microfilming [071]

YIDDISH ARBEITER WELT – Jewish labor world. (Chicago). 1908-17 – 1 – us A.J.P.C. [331]

THE YIDDISH ART COMPANION – (Chicago). 1916 – 1 – us A.J.P.C. [700]

YIDDISH BOOKS FROM THE HARVARD COLLEGE LIBRARY – 1994/95 – ca 5,500mf (1:24) in 6 installments – 9 – diazo DM46,200.00 (silver DM62,100.00 ISBN: 3-598-33184-3) – 3-598-33176-2 – gw Saur [800]

YIDDISH CLASSICS ON MICROFICHE – (Indiv. titles: Isaac L. Peretz $375.00; Mendele Mocher Sforim $535.00; Sholem Aleichem $685.00) – Rare works in Yiddish and Hebrew. 152 titles. Includes printed guide – 444mf – 9 – $1,430.00 set – us UPA [430]

YIDDISH LITERATURE FROM THE YIVO INSTITUTE – Children's literature and Jewish folklore in Yiddish. 1023 titles. Includes printed guide – 1,373r – 9 – $5,445.00 – us UPA [800]

YIDDISH NEWS DIGEST – New York. N.Y. 1951; 1957-62; 1963 – 1 – us A.J.P.C. [071]

DIE YIDDISHE FOLKSSHTIME – Warsaw 1911? – 1 – us NY Public [943]

YIDDISHE NAYES = JEWISH NEWS – Toronto, CN. v1 no 1. 1956-1985 – 1r – 1 – Can$50.00 – cn Can Microfilming [072]

DIE YIDDISHE WOCHENSCHRIFT – New York. N.Y. 1912 – 1 – us A.J.P.C. [071]

DER YIDDISHER KAEMPFER – New York. v. 1 no. 1-v. 9 no. 25. Mar 30 1906-Aug 20 1920. Incomplete – 1 – us NY Public [305]

DER YIDDISHER KEMPFER = THE JEWISH FIGHTER – (In Yiddish. Weekly) – Paris, FR. v1 no18. Dec 1947 – 1r – 1 – $25.00 – cn Can Microfilming [072]

YIDDISHES TAGEBLATT – New York. N.Y. The Jewish daily news. 1888-1928 – 1 – us A.J.P.C. [071]

YIDISHE BURZHVAZIE UN YIDISHER PROLETARIAT IN ERSHTER HELFT FUN 19 YORHUNDERT / Yuditzki, A – Kiev. 1931. BJ-290-26 1 – 9 – ne IDC [940]

DOS YIDISHE FOLK = JEWISH PEOPLE – (In Yiddish) – New York City, NY. v27 no4 6 Mar 1942-v27 no10 Sep 1942 – 1r – 1 – $25.00 – cn Can Microfilming [071]

YIDISHE FOLKS SHTIME = JEWISH PEOPLES' VOICE – (In Jewish and English) – New York City, NY. v1 n1. Feb 1938-v1 n4. May 1938 – 1r – 1 – $25.00 – cn Can Microfilming [071]

YIDISHE ILLUSTRIERTE TSAYTUNG = JEWISH ILLUSTRATED JOURNAL – (Yiddish weekly) – Berlin, DE. no15. 29 Aug 1924 – 1r – 1 – $25.00 – cn Can Microfilming [072]

YIDISHE POST (JEWISH POST) *see* VOCHENZAITUNG (THE JEWISH WEEKLY)

YIDISHE PRESE = DE JOODSCHE PERS – (In Yiddish) – Antwerp, BE. v9 no3(418). 20 Jan 1933 – 1r – 1 – $25.00 – cn Can Microfilming [072]

DI YIDISHE PRESE IN DER GEVEZENER RUSLANDISHER IMPERIE / Kirzhnitz, A – Moscow, 1930 – 2mf – ne IDC [470]

DI YIDISHE PRESE IN RATNFARBAND / Kirzhnitz, A – Minsk. 1928. BJ-290-19 1 – 2mf – 9 – ne IDC [430]

YIDISHE SHRIFTN = JEWISH WRITINGS – (In Yiddish) – v3 no1-2 Jan/Feb 1948-no211 Dec 1964 – 1r – 1 – $50.00 – cn Can Microfilming [072]

YIDISHE SHTIME = JEWISH VOICE – (In Yiddish) – Munich, DE. v2 no5. 31 Oct 1947 – 1r – 1 – $25.00 – cn Can Microfilming [072]

YIDISHE TSAYTUNG = JEWISH NEWSPAPER – (In German) – Landsberg, DE. no159 9 Dec 1947-no184 9 Mar 1948 – 1r – 1 – $35.00 – cn Can Microfilming [072]

YIDISHE TSAYTUNG = JEWISH NEWSPAPER – (In Yiddish) – Landsberg, DE. no92(no160) 12 Dec 1947-no86(no250) 31 Dec 1948 – 1r – 1 – $35.00 – cn Can Microfilming [072]

YIDISHE TSAYTUNG – (Yiddish weekly) – Lwow, PL. v22 no14. 1 Aug 1884 – 1r – 1 – $25.00 – cn Can Microfilming [072]

DI YIDISHE VELT – Cleveland, Ohio: The Jewish world, 1913-52 – 1 – us A.J.P.C. [071]

YIDISHE VELT *see* DI YIDISHE VELT

YIDISHE VOKH = LA SEMAINE JUIVE – (In Yiddish. Weekly) – Paris, FR. no7 5 Dec 1948-no19 6 Mar 1949 – 1r – 1 – $30.00 – cn Can Microfilming [072]

YIDISHER AMERIKANER = THE JEWISH AMERICAN – New York, NY. 1906 – 1 – us A.J.P.C. [071]

YIDISHER INVALID = JEWISH INVALID – (In Yiddish) – Munich, DE. no1. 1948 – 1r – 1 – $25.00 – cn Can Microfilming [072]

YIDISHER KULTUR KONGRES = JEWISH CULTURAL CONGRESS – (In Yiddish) – Paris, FR. no2 May 1937-no5 Aug 1937 – 1r – 1 – $30.00 – cn Can Microfilming [072]

DER YIDISHER REKORDER – New York etc. v. 1-4 no. 100. Apr 3 1893-Mar 1 1895 – 1 – us NY Public [071]

YIDISHER REKORDER – New York. v1-4. 1893-95 – 1r – 1 – us Ross [071]

YIELD AND NUTRITIONAL VALUE OF THE COMMERCIALLY MORE IMPORTANT FISH SPECIES – 1989 – 192p – it F.A.O. [338]

YIELD RESPONSE TO WATER – 1981 – 201p – it F.A.O. [631]

YI-ER-JIU YUNDONG ZILIAO (DIYIJI) ZHONGGUO XIANDAI GEMING SHILIAO CONGKAN) – Series of materials on contemporary Chinese revolutionary history: Materials on the December Ninth Movement, part 1. Comp. by Renmin Chubanshe, 1981. 7 fiches. F/H139 – 9 – $31.50 – cc Microforms [950]

YI-ER-YI YUNDONG SHILIAO XUANBIAN (SHANG XIA) – Selection of materials on the December 1st student movement, v1-2. 7 fiches. F/H145 – 9 – $31.50 – cc Microforms [950]

YIHETUAN DANGAN SHILIAO, 1-2 – Archival materials on the Boxer Rebellion, v1-2. Compiled by the Imperial Palace archives. 1 reel. M-H88 – 5 – $40.00 – cc Microforms [950]

YIHETUAN YUNDONG SHILIAO CONGBIAN, 1-2 – Archival materials of the Boxer Rebellion series: v1-2. Compiled by the History Department of Beijing University. 7 fiches. F-H85 – 9 – $31.50 – cc Microforms [950]

YIHETUAN ZAI SHANXI DIQU SHILIAO – Archival materials on the Boxer Rebellion in the Shanxi region. Comp. by Qiao Zhiqiang. 2 fiches. F-H86 – 9 – $9.00 – cc Microforms [950]

YIK KHUAN POH – (In Chinese). Kuala Lumpur. Malaysia. -d. 24 Mar 1919-30 Nov 1934. (145 reels) – 1 – uk British Libr Newspaper [072]

YILDIZ – Izmir: Maarif Matbaasi, 1922 – 9 – $10.00 – us MEDOC [956]

YILIAO QIGIE – Medical Instruments. In Chinese but English abstracts to the main articles. F p160 – 9 – 4.00f – cc Microforms [616]

Yin, Tzu-heng *see*
- MY PHILOSOPHY OF RELIGION (CCC347)
- THE STORY OF MY BECOMING A CHRISTIAN (CCC346)

YIN WEN DIAN XUN GAO – Apr 1949-1982, 1986-87. H3 – 9 – 8835.00 – cc Globe [073]

Ying, Yuan-t'ao *see* CHRISTIANS AND WARTIME SERVICE (CCC311)

YING-TE HSIEN-CHIH – 1843, 16. BCH-604 2 – 8 – ne IDC [950]

YINGYANG XUEBAO – Acta Nutrimenta Sinica. 1983-84. F/P 294 – 9 – $4.50f – cc Microforms [073]

YINGYONG HUAXUE – Chinese Journal of Applied Chemistry. 1984, 1986. F- – 9 – 4.00f – cc Microforms [073]

YINGYONG KEXUE XUEBAO – (1983 $3.50f; 1984 $4.50f) – Journal of Applied Sciences. 1983, 1985. F/P 267 – 9 – cc Microforms [073]

YINGYONG SHENGXUE = APPLIED ACOUSTICS – 1982-. F-P256 – 9 – $4.50f – cc Microforms [073]

YINGYONG SHUXUE HE LIXUE – Applied Mathematics & Mechanics. In Chinese but English abstracts to the main articles. F p115 – 9 – 4.00f – cc Microforms [073]

YINGYONG SHUXUE XUEBAO = ACTA MATHEMATICAE APPLICATAE SINICA – (1981 $4.50f; 183 $3.50f) – 1981-. F-P252 – 9 – cc Microforms [073]

YIN-HANG CHOU-PAO – "Banker's Weekly". v. 1-33. Shanghai. 1917-49. Lacking: (1-26) 1917 24; v. 8 (33-47) 1924; v. 9 (5-50) 1925; v. 10 (1-14, 31) 1926; v. 12 (44-50) 1928; v. 15 (10-50) 1931; v. 16 (1, 23) 1932; v. 23 (1-50) 1939; v. 24 (41, 44, 47, 50) 1940; v. 25-29, 1942-45; v. 30 (1-38, 41, 44-50) 1946; v. 31 (1-36) 1947; v. 33 (17-50) 1949. BCH-373 1 9 ne IDC [073]

YIN-HANG TSA-CHIH – "The Banker's Semi-monthly". Hankow. 1923-27. Lacking: v. 1 (5-7, 18) 1923-24; v. 2 (14, 17) 1925; v. 3 (20-24) 1926-27. BCH-374 1 – 9 – ne IDC [073]

YIN-HANG YUEH-K'AN – "The Banker's Magazine". 8 v. Peking. 1921-28. Lacking: v. 1 (1) 1921; v. 7 (9) 1927. BCH-375 1 – 9 – ne IDC [073]

YIN-NI HUA CH'IAO HSUEEH SHENG LIEN HO TSUNG HUI, DJAKARTA – (Joint commemorative volume for the Conference of Overseas Chinese Students in Indonesia). SE 10,379 1. 1957 – 9 – ne IDC [370]

YIN-NI SHANG YEH NIEN CHIEN – Added title: Almanak Perdagangan Indonesia. The commercial year book of Indonesia. SE 2713 1 – 9 – ne IDC [380]

YIN-TU-NI-HSI-YA HUA CH'IAO MEI KUNG T'UAN TSO P'IN HSUAN CHI / ed by Lu, Shao-fei – A selection of the works of the Overseas Chinese in Indonesia. SE-3807 1. 1958 – 9 – ne IDC [480]

YIN-TU-NI-HSI-YA YUE YEN – (Indonesian tales). SE 5698 1. 1963 – 9 – ne IDC [390]

YIQI YIBIAO XUEBAO – (1980-1983, 1984- $4.50f; 1983 $3.50f) – Chinese Journal of Scientific Instrument. In Chinese but English abstracts to the main articles. F p109 – 9 – cc Microforms [073]

YISHUV EREZ HA-KODESH / Solomon, Y M – (Yehudah vi-Yerushalayim, Nr.2-3, 5-7, 14-16). BJ-27-231 1 – 9 – ne IDC [956]

YISRAEL SHELANU – Brooklyn, NY. 1979-84 – 1 – us A.J.P.C. [071]

YISURE HA-MASHIAH, ODER, DIE LEIDEN DES MESSIAS / Wuensche, August – Leipzig: Fues, 1870. 1 fiche – 9 – us A.T.L.A. [240]

YIUYUE YANJIU – Music Study. In Chinese but Table of Contents in English in each issue. F p29 – 9 – 4.00f – cc Microforms [073]

Yivo Institute *see* JEWISH DISPLACED PERSONS

YIWEN = TRANSLATED LITERATURE – Sept 1934-Sept 1935; Mar 1936-May 1937. 5 reels. M-C50 – 1 – $200.00 – cc Microforms [800]

YIWOBLETER, THE MONTHLY OF THE YIDDISH SCIENTIFIC INSTITUTE – Wilne. v1-14. 1931-1939 – 77mf – 9 – ne IDC [947]

YIZHOUJIAN = THE WEEKLY REVIEW – May-Jun 1934. 3 fiches.F-C48 – 9 – $13.50 – cc Microforms [073]

L'YMAGIER – I-II, no. 1-8. Paris. oct 1894-juil 1896 – 1 – fr A.C.R.P.P. [073]

YMCA : DOCUMENTS OF YMCA INTERNATIONAL COMMITTEE – 1903-1936 – 5r – 1 – us I.H.R.C. [060]

YMHA NEWS – Montreal, CN. v7 no 3, v12 no 7. 1943-1949 – 1r – 1 – cn Can Microfilming [072]

YO FUI TESTIGO ANTES, DURANTE Y DESPU ES DE LA SEGUNDA TIRANIA (MEMORIAS) / Garcia, Eduardo Augusto – Buenos Aires: Luis Lasserre, 2nd ed [1971] – 1 – CSUXADJ1259-B – us Hoover Inst Photo [920]

YO HE VISITADO FRAGOSA, EL GASCO Y MARTILANDRAN (HURDES) / Delgado Solis, Sebastian – Caceres: Tip. Vda. de Garcia Floriano, 1956 – 1 – sp Bibl Santa Ana [946]

YO MATE AL DIABLO / Perez Fernandez, Manuel – Badajoz: Tip. Vda. de A. Arqueros, s.a. – 1 – sp Bibl Santa Ana [240]

YO SOY... LENGUA ESPANOLA CURSO NO 6 / Garcia Carrasco, Francisco A et al – Madrid: Compania Bibliografica Espanola S.A., 1968 – 1 – sp Bibl Santa Ana [440]

YO TENGO UN ABRAZO PARA TI MIAJA / San Martin, Julio – Madrid, 193? Fiche W1155. (Blodgett Collection of Spanish Civil War Pamphlets) – 9 – us H.U. College Libr [946]

YO, Y MISAN ECDOTAS : RECUERDOS, CITAS RELATOS, EJEMPLOS, CONVERSACIONES / Camisado – Rosario, 1956 – 1 – CSUXAHZ5475-B – us Hoover Inst Photo [972]

YOGA JOURNAL – (1986-. 1,5,6) – 1982- – 9 – us UMI [790]

THE YOGACARA IDEALISM / Chatterjee, Ashok Kumar First ed. Varanasi: Banaras Hindu University, (1962). xii,309p – 1 – us U.W. Library [280]

THE YOGA-SYSTEM OF PATANJALI / Woods, James Haughton – or THE ANCIENT Hindu Doctrine of concentration of mind. Cambridge, Mass. 1914. BI-1070 1 – 9 – ne IDC [290]

YOKO UND DIE PHILOSOPHEN : NOVELLEN AUS JAPAN / Tjadens, Herbert – 4. Aufl. Leipzig: P Reclam, 1942 – 1r – 1 – us U.W. Library [830]

YOLANDE: THE STORY OF A DAUGHTER / Black, William – British Fiction Archive: Unit 4 – 9 – uk Bell [830]

YOLO COUNTY – 1992- – 3+ r – 1 – $150.00 – P00141 – us Library Micro [910]

YOLO COUNTY INCLUDING WOODLAND – Yolo Co, CA. 1870; 1878-1879; 1893-1894; 1904-1926; 1939; 1948-1949 – 12r – 1 – $600.00 – D107 – us Library Micro [978]

YOLO COUNTY RECORD – Woodland, CA. 1928-1930 – 1r – 1 – $50.00 – C03697 – us Library Micro [071]

YOLO INDEPENDENT – Broderick, CA. 1911-1922 – 6r – 1 – $300.00 – C03586 – us Library Micro [071]

YOM *see*
- HA-YOM

YOM HAD-DIN (THE DAY OF JUDGEMENT) – London, UK. 5 Sept 1930 – 1 – uk British Libr Newspaper [072]

YOM HAMEDINA = THE DAY OF THE STATE – (In Hebrew) – Tel Aviv, IS. 14 May 1948 (4 PM Edition – Birth of Israel Issue) – 1r – 1 – $25.00 – cn Can Microfilming [072]

YOM LE YOM – Israel, 1993- – 1 – $220.00y – us Ross [072]

YOMAN HA-PATENTIM / Israel. Ministry of Justice – 1953-76. (Appears together with Simmane ha-mishmar). Lacking: (1-6) 1952?-53. BJ-81-36 1 – 9 – ne IDC [340]

YOMIURI SHIMBUN : TOKYO EDITION – (1991- 36r per year Y309,000) – Nov 1874-Dec 1990 – 1291r – 1 – Y13,222,800 – ja Japan Micro [950]

YOMIURI SHIMBUN – (Yrly reel count varies) – Tokyo, 1874- – 1 – inquire – us Ross [072]

YONCALLA TIMES – Yoncalla, OR. -w. 1 Sept 1911-1 Nov 1912. 1 roll – 1 – us U.O. Library [071]

Yonekawa, Shin'ichi *see* GENERAL TRADING COMPANIES

Yonge, Charlotte Mary *see*
- CATHARINE OF ARAGON AND THE SOURCES OF THE ENGLISH REFORMATION
- MUSINGS OVER THE "CHRISTIAN YEAR" AND "LYRA INNOCENTIUM"

Yonge, J *see*
- CURRUS TRIUMPHALIS
- WOUNDS OF THE BRAIN PROVED CURABLE

Yong-Kil, Chung *see* DIE POLITISCHEN BEZIEHUNGEN NORDKOREAS ZUR VR CHINA UND ZUR SOWJETUNION IM HINBLICK AUF DIE WIEDERVEREINIGUNG KOREAS

YONGLE LEQING XIAN ZHI, APPROX. 1420 / Zhejiang Province. China – Records of Leqing County in the reign of Yongle. 8 vols. Comp. unknown. F A26. (Rare Local Records in Chinese...1420-1507) – 9 – $27.00 – cc Microforms [950]

YONGSHENG = ETERNAL LIFE – Mar-Jun 1936. -w. 5 fiches. F-C53 – 9 – $22.50 – cc Microforms [073]

Yonkers, New York *see* MISCELLANEOUS EARLY NEWSPAPERS

Yoo, Ho S *see* RELATIONSHIP BETWEEN PLAYING POSITION IN FOOTBALL AND SELECTED PSYCHOLOGICAL VARIABLES

Yoo, Seang L *see* A MODEL TO UNDERSTAND SPORT-CONFIDENCE AND SPORT COMPETITION ANXIETY OF COLLEGE VARSITY ATHLETES

YORBA LINDA STAR – Yorba Linda, CA. Jul 1920-Jun 1994 – 7r – 1 – $350.00 – HR03114 – us Library Micro [071]

YORCK : SCHAUSPIEL IN 5 AKTEN UND EINEM VORSPIEL / Lissauer, Ernst – Berlin: Oesterheld, 1921 – 1r – 1 – us U.W. Library [820]

YORICK OU LE VOYAGEUR BRETON DE 1788 / Bonnard du Hanlay, Sebastien-F – Landerneau [i.e. Nantes]: Cognard, [1804] – 1 – F95.83 – fr Armell [910]

YORK COUNTY FIRST BAPTIST CHURCH. YORK COUNTY. SOUTH CAROLINA : CHURCH RECORDS – 1866-1972 – 1 – 44.01 – us Baptist [240]

YORK COURANT – York, England. 1728-1805 – 18r – 1 – uk Microform Academic [072]

YORK DAILY – York, PA. -d 1871-1918 – 13 – $25.00r – us I.M.R. [071]

YORK DAILY NEWS-TIMES – York, NE. Jan 1911 to date – 1 – us NE Hist [071]

YORK DAILY RECORD – York, PA. -d 1971-1989 – 13 – $25.00r – us I.M.R. [071]

YORK DAILY TIMES – York, NE. Oct 1895-Feb 1896; Apr 1896-Aug 1898; Jan 1899-Sept 1902 – 1 – us NE Hist [071]

YORK DAILY VIDETTE – York, NE. Oct 1895-Feb 1896; May 1896 – 1 – us NE Hist [071]

YORK DEMOCRAT – York, NE. -w. Oct 1890; Dec 1892; Oct 1895-Nov 1898; Feb 1899-Jan 1907; Mar-Jul 1907; Oct 1907-Jul 1912; Sept 1912-Sept 1917, scattered issues missing; May 1919-Nov 1924 – 1 – us NE Hist [071]

YORK DEMOCRATIC PRESS – York, PA. -sw 1865-1901 – 13 – $25.00r – us I.M.R. [071]

York. England *see*
- CITY CHAMBERLAIN ACCOUNT BOOKS, 1446-1600
- CITY CHAMBERLAIN ROLLS, 1396-1600
- CORPORATION HOUSE BOOKS, 1490-1603

YORK EVENING PRESS – York, PA., 1900-1906 – 13 – $25.00r – us I.M.R. [071]

YORK GAZETTE – York, PA. (German Version) -w 1796-1900 – 13 – $25.00r – us I.M.R. [071]

YORK GAZETTE AND DAILY – York, PA. -d 1934-1935 – 13 – $25.00r – us I.M.R. [071]

YORK GAZETTEER, YORK JOURNAL AND THE PROTESTANT YORK COURANT – York. England. 1745-53 – 1 – uk Microform Academic [072]

YORK GOSPELS – (From a manuscript dated between 800 and 1100). Ms. Add 1. York Minster Library – 1 – uk Microform Academic [240]

YORK HERALD TIMES – Pennsylvania. -w 1907-1920; 1932-1939; 1941-1946 – 13 – $25.00r – us I.M.R. [071]

York. Holy Trinity *see* PARISH REGISTERS

York Minster *see* MUSIC MANUSCRIPTS

York Minster Library *see*
- MS 16. K16
- SHEFFIELD PLAYBILLS
- TORRE MANUSCRIPTS, 1690-94 FROM YORK MINSTER LIBRARY

YORK REPUBLICAN – York, NE. -w. Apr 1876-Jun 1955 – 1 – us NE Hist [071]

York, Sherril L *see* FITTING HUMAN PERFORMANCE DATA: A COMPARISON OF THREE METHODS OF DATA SMOOTHING WITH MLAB

York. St. Martin's-cum-Gregory *see* PARISH REGISTERS

YORK SUNDAY NEWS – Lancaster. Pa. 1960- – 1 – us UMI [071]

YORK TIMES – York, NE. -w. (-sw 1908-12). Apr-Jul 1886, scattered issues missing; Nov 1892; Dec 1895-May 1898; Feb 1899-Jul 1912 – 1 – us NE Hist [071]

YORK WEEKLY POST *see* UPPER CANADA GAZETTE OR AMERICAN ORACLE

Yorke, Peter C *see* THE YORKE-WENDTE CONTROVERSY

THE YORKE-WENDTE CONTROVERSY : LETTERS ON THE PAPAL PRIMACY AND THE RELATIONS OF CHURCH AND STATE / Wendte, CW & Yorke, Peter C – San Francisco: Monitor, 1896 – 1mf – us A.T.L.A. [240]

YORKSHIRE, 1822 : BRITISH ISLES CENSUS DIRECTORIES PROJECT, ENGLAND – (In prep) – at Vine [941]

YORKSHIRE, 1834 : BRITISH ISLES CENSUS DIRECTORIES PROJECT, ENGLAND – (In prep) – at Vine [941]

YORKSHIRE (ALL RIDINGS), 1841 : BRITISH ISLES CENSUS DIRECTORIES PROJECT, ENGLAND. VOL 232 – 3mf – 9 – A$21.00 – at Vine [941]

YORKSHIRE (ALL RIDINGS), 1854 : BRITISH ISLES CENSUS DIRECTORIES PROJECT, ENGLAND – at Vine [941]

YORKSHIRE (ALL RIDINGS), 1855 : BRITISH ISLES CENSUS DIRECTORIES PROJECT, ENGLAND – at Vine [941]

YORKSHIRE (BRADFORD, HALIFAX, HUDDERSFIELD, HULL, LEEDS, SHEFFIELD, WAKEFIELD AND YORK), 1805 : BRITISH ISLES CENSUS DIRECTORIES PROJECT, ENGLAND. VOL 167 – 1mf – 9 – A$9.00 – at Vine [941]

Yorkshire Dialect Society *see* TRANSACTIONS OF THE YORKSHIRE DIALECT SOCIETY

YORKSHIRE (EAST), 1867 : BRITISH ISLES CENSUS DIRECTORIES PROJECT, ENGLAND – at Vine [941]

YORKSHIRE (EAST AND NORTH), 1840 : BRITISH ISLES CENSUS DIRECTORIES PROJECT, ENGLAND – at Vine [941]

YORKSHIRE (EAST, EXC YORK), 1892 : BRITISH ISLES CENSUS DIRECTORIES PROJECT, ENGLAND. VOL 45 – 7mf – 9 – A$45.00 – at Vine [941]

YORKSHIRE (EAST RIDING), 1823 : BRITISH ISLES CENSUS DIRECTORIES PROJECT, ENGLAND – (In prep) – at Vine [941]

YORKSHIRE (EAST RIDING), 1846 : BRITISH ISLES CENSUS DIRECTORIES PROJECT, ENGLAND – at Vine [941]

YORKSHIRE EVENING POST – Leeds. 1958-to date – 1 – uk Microform Academic [072]

YORKSHIRE EVENING PRESS – Leeds. 1937-to date – 1 – uk Microform Academic [072]

YORKSHIRE FACTORY TIMES – Leeds. Jul 1889-Jun 1913 – 23r – 1 – uk Microform Academic [072]

YORKSHIRE FACTORY TIMES – (The Labour Pioneer). Huddersfield, Dewsbury and Heckmondwike. England. -w. Jul 1889-Apr 1926. (Wanting 1896, 1911). (28 reels) – 1 – uk British Libr Newspaper [331]

YORKSHIRE (FAR SOUTH WEST), 1832 : BRITISH ISLES CENSUS DIRECTORIES PROJECT, ENGLAND. VOL 194 – 1mf – 9 – A$9.00 – at Vine [941]

YORKSHIRE GAZETTE – England. 1819-26, 1889-91, 1899-1954 – 1819-26 6r; 1889-91, 1899-1954 71r – 1 – uk Microform Academic [072]

YORKSHIRE GAZETTE AND HERALD – England. 1954- – 1 – uk Microform Academic [072]

YORKSHIRE (HALIFAX, DEWSBURY AND HUDDERSFIELD), 1863 : BRITISH ISLES CENSUS DIRECTORIES PROJECT, ENGLAND. VOL 142 – 3mf – 9 – A$21.00 – at Vine [941]

YORKSHIRE HARLEQUIN – Yorkshire. 1896-98 – 1 – uk Microform Academic [072]

YORKSHIRE HERALD – England. 1891-Sep 1933 – 250r – 1 – uk Microform Academic [072]

YORKSHIRE (HUDDERSFIELD DISTRICT), 1879 : BRITISH ISLES CENSUS DIRECTORIES PROJECT, ENGLAND. VOL 141 – 3mf – 9 – A$21.00 – at Vine [941]

YORKSHIRE (HULL, LEEDS AND SHEFFIELD), 1837 : BRITISH ISLES CENSUS DIRECTORIES PROJECT, ENGLAND. VOL 191 – 1mf – 9 – A$9.00 – at Vine [941]

YORKSHIRE (LEEDS), 1798 : BRITISH ISLES CENSUS DIRECTORIES PROJECT, ENGLAND – at Vine [941]

YORKSHIRE (LEEDS), 1826 : BRITISH ISLES CENSUS DIRECTORIES PROJECT, ENGLAND. VOL 77 – 3mf – 9 – A$21.00 – at Vine [941]

YORKSHIRE (LEEDS AND SHEFFIELD), 1824 : BRITISH ISLES CENSUS DIRECTORIES PROJECT, ENGLAND – (In prep) – at Vine [941]

YORKSHIRE LEGENDS AND TRADITIONS AS TOLD BY HER ANCIENT CHRONICLERS, HER POETS, AND JOURNALISTS / Parkinson, Thomas – 2nd ser. London: E. Stock, 1889. x/246p – 1 – us U.W. Library [390]

YORKSHIRE (MIDDLESBOROUGH, YORK AND DISTRICT), 1916 : BRITISH ISLES CENSUS DIRECTORIES PROJECT, ENGLAND – (In prep) – at Vine [941]

THE YORKSHIRE MINERS, 1881-1926 : A STUDY IN LABOUR AND SOCIAL HISTORY / Neville, Robert G – 1974 – 11mf – 9 – $50.00 – us UMI [331]
YORKSHIRE NEWS – York, England. 1911, 1915 – 1 – us Res Libr [072]
YORKSHIRE (NORTH), 1890 : BRITISH ISLES CENSUS DIRECTORIES PROJECT, ENGLAND – at Vine [941]
YORKSHIRE (NORTH RIDING), 1823 : BRITISH ISLES CENSUS DIRECTORIES PROJECT, ENGLAND. VOL 154 – 2mf – 9 – A$15.00 – at Vine [941]
Yorkshire Parish Register Society *see* TRANSCRIPTS
YORKSHIRE (PART), 1816 : BRITISH ISLES CENSUS DIRECTORIES PROJECT, ENGLAND – (In prep) – at Vine [941]
THE YORKSHIRE POST – 1866- – 24r per y – 1 – $75.00r – us Ross [072]
YORKSHIRE POST – Leeds. 1866-to date – 1 – uk Microform Academic [072]
YORKSHIRE POST AND LEEDS INTELLIGENCER *see* LEEDS INTELLIGENCER
THE YORKSHIRE POST AND LEEDS MERCURY – Leeds, [England]: Yorkshire Conservative Newspaper Co Ltd, oct 1956-58 – us Res Libr [072]
YORKSHIRE (SEDBERGH, DENT AND GARSDALE), 1905 : BRITISH ISLES CENSUS DIRECTORIES PROJECT, ENGLAND. VOL 76 – 1mf – 9 – A$9.00 – at Vine [941]
YORKSHIRE (SHEFFIELD), 1787 : BRITISH ISLES CENSUS DIRECTORIES PROJECT, ENGLAND – at Vine [941]
YORKSHIRE (SHEFFIELD), 1857 : BRITISH ISLES CENSUS DIRECTORIES PROJECT, ENGLAND. VOL 86 – 2mf – 9 – A$15.00 – at Vine [941]
YORKSHIRE (SHEFFIELD AND ROTHERMAN), 1849 : BRITISH ISLES CENSUS DIRECTORIES PROJECT, ENGLAND – at Vine [941]
YORKSHIRE (SOUTH, INC SHEFFIELD), 1868 : BRITISH ISLES CENSUS DIRECTORIES PROJECT, ENGLAND. VOL 23 – 6mf – 9 – A$39.00 – at Vine [941]
YORKSHIRE (STH, INCLUDING SHEFFIELD) 1852 : BRITISH ISLES CENSUS DIRECTORIES PROJECT, ENGLAND. VOL 255 – 4mf – 9 – A$27.00 – at Vine [941]
YORKSHIRE TRIBUNE – England.1855-56. -w. 12 feet – 1 – uk British Libr Newspaper [072]
YORKSHIRE TRIBUNE – London. 1855-56 – 1 – uk Microform Academic [073]
YORKSHIRE (WEST INC LEEDS), 1853 : BRITISH ISLES CENSUS DIRECTORIES PROJECT, ENGLAND. VOL 11 – 5mf – 9 – A$33.00 – at Vine [941]
YORKSHIRE (WEST RIDING), 1822 : BRITISH ISLES CENSUS DIRECTORIES PROJECT, ENGLAND – at Vine [941]
YORKSHIRE (WEST RIDING), 1889 : BRITISH ISLES CENSUS DIRECTORIES PROJECT, ENGLAND – at Vine [941]
YORKSHIRE (WEST RIDING), 1900 : BRITISH ISLES CENSUS DIRECTORIES PROJECT, ENGLAND – at Vine [941]
YORKSHIRE (WEST RIDING), 1936 : BRITISH ISLES CENSUS DIRECTORIES PROJECT, ENGLAND – (In prep) – at Vine [941]
YORKSHIRE (WEST RIDING-PART 1), 1837 : BRITISH ISLES CENSUS DIRECTORIES PROJECT, ENGLAND. VOL 115 – 5mf – 9 – A$33.00 – at Vine [941]
YORKSHIRE (WEST RIDING-PART 2), 1838 : BRITISH ISLES CENSUS DIRECTORIES PROJECT, ENGLAND. VOL 116 – 5mf – 9 – A$33.00 – at Vine [941]
YORKVILLE ENQUIRER – Rock Hill. S.C. 1856-1928 – 1 – us UMI [071]
THE YORUBA COLLECTION OF WILLIAM AND BERTA BASCOM – New York: Norman Ross Pub, 1992 – 560mf – 9 – $3,000.00 – us Ross [060]
THE YORUBA COUNTRY, ITS PEOPLE, CUSTOMS, AND MISSIONS / Pinnock, Samuel G – n.d. 96p. (Nigerian Baptist Historical Materials) – 1 – us Baptist [960]
YORUBA HEATHENISM / Johnson, James – Exeter, [1899] – us Res Libr [290]
YO-SAN-FI-ROK, L'ART D'ELEVER LES VERS A SOIE AU JAPON / Ouekaki-Morikouni – Traduction du japonais. Paris: Vve Bouchard-Huzard. 1848 – 9 – $7.50 – fr Orientalistes [480]
Yoshioka, Carlton F *see* LEISURE SOCIALIZATION AND ADULT AND CHILD RELATED DECISION-MAKING INTERACTIONS IN FAMILY RECREATIONAL ACTIVITIES
YOSIFON – Zurich. 1546. BJ-43-139 1 – 9 – ne IDC [470]
YOST'S WEEKLY – Staunton. Va. 1892-1894 – 1 – us UMI [071]
YOU NAME IT – Madison, WI. 13 Oct 1943. Continued by: Hillelites – 1 – us A.J.P.C. [071]
Youatt, W *see* SHEEP, THEIR BREEDS, MANAGEMENT AND DISEASES
LA YOUGOSLAVIE – Belgrade, Yugoslavia. Nov 1929-Oct 1931; 16 Nov 1932 – 2r – 1 – us L of C Photodup [949]
LA YOUGOSLAVIE SOCIALISTE / Bobrowski, C – F50.00 – fr Ethnologie [335]
YOUJI HUAXUE – Organic Chemistry. In Chinese but English abstracts to the main articles. F p90 – 9 – $4.50f – cc Microforms [073]
Young, A *see* THE EXAMPLE OF FRANCE, A WARNING TO BRITAIN
YOUNG ADULT CATALOG OF THE BOSTON PUBLIC LIBRARY / Boston Public Library – (Available on microfilm by request) – 1972 – $200.00 export $240.00 – uk Hall [010]
YOUNG AFRICA – (Lacking: 1943. Cont: Young People's Inland Africa) – 1938-57 – 1r – 1 – ATLA S0710D – us A.T.L.A. [073]
YOUNG AFRICA *see* YOUNG PEOPLE'S INLAND AFRICA
Young, Alfred *see* CATHOLIC AND PROTESTANT COUNTRIES COMPARED
YOUNG ALLIES – Issue Nos. 1-5 Summer 1941-Fall 1942 – 5mf – 15 – $31,95 – us Comics [760]
YOUNG AMERICA – New York: National Reform Association, 1830-47 – 1r – 1 – us Ross [073]
YOUNG AMERICAN – Nevada City, CA. 1853-1854 – 1r – 1 – $50.00 – C03622 – us Library Micro [071]
YOUNG AMERICA'S COLLECTION OF INSTRUMENTAL MUSIC / Howe, Elias – consisting of the most popular polkas, schottisches, waltzes, redowas, marches, quicksteps, contra dances, hornpipes, songs, &c. Arranged in three parts: first, second, and bass. For wood, brass and stringed bands, amateur musical clubs, &c. Boston: Russell & Richardson, 1858. Includes: "Anvil Chorus" (from Il Trovatore), "Pop goes the weasel," "Wedding March" (from Lohengrin), and "Yankee Doodle." MUSIC 1989, Item 1 – 1 – us L of C Photodup [780]
Young, Andrew W *see*
- THE GOVERNMENT CLASS BOOK
- HISTORY OF CHAUTAUQUA COUNTY
- HISTORY OF WAYNE COUNTY

Young, Arthur *see* ARTHUR YOUNG'S TOUR IN IRELAND (1776-1779)
THE YOUNG AUSTRO AMERICAN *see* FORUM UND TRIBUNE
Young, Bennett H *see* A HISTORY OF JESSAMINE COUNTY
THE YOUNG BLUENOSE – Halifax, N.S.: G.E. Frye, v1 no 1(Mar 1878)- – 9 – cn C.I.H.M. [971]
YOUNG CANADA – Neil's Harbor, N.S.: W.S. McLean, v1 no 1(July 1887)- – 9 – cn C.I.H.M. [971]
YOUNG CANADA – Toronto: [s.n. 1860?-18–] – 9 – cn C.I.H.M. [971]
YOUNG CANADA'S REPLY TO ANNEXATION / Beers, William George – Montreal?, 1888?. 03546. (Pre-1900 Canadiana) – 9 – cn C.I.H.M. [971]
THE YOUNG CANADIAN – Montreal: Young Canadian Co, [1890?-1891] – 9 – cn C.I.H.M. [971]
Young, Charles Alexander *see* HISTORICAL DOCUMENTS ADVOCATING CHRISTIAN UNION
YOUNG CHILDREN – v1- 1945- 1; v29- 5,6,9 – us UMI [370]
YOUNG CHINA – San Francisco. Calif. 1955-59 – 1 – us UMI [071]
THE YOUNG CHINA DAILY – San Francisco, CA. Feb 1911-1959; Jun 1971-91 – 274r – 1 – $13,700.00 – C02868 – us Library Micro [071]
YOUNG CHRISTIAN WOMEN = NU CH'ING NIEN – (In Chinese) – v9 no 4-12-v12 no 14. 1930-35 (incomplete) – 2r – 1 – ATLA S0309 – us A.T.L.A. [073]
YOUNG CITIZEN – v.1-38. Sep 1941-Feb 1973. Continued by: yScholastic news citizen – 1 – us UMI [073]
THE YOUNG CITIZEN'S MANUAL; BEING A DIGEST OF THE LAWS OF THE STATE OF NEW YORK AND OF THE UNITED STATES, RELATING TO CRIMES AND THEIR PUNISHMENTS. / Conkling, Alfred – 2d ed. New York, Dean, 1839. 279 p. LL-1682 – 1 – us L of C Photodup [340]
Young Communist League *see*
- CHAMPION
- CLARITY
- YOUNG WORKER

YOUNG COMMUNIST REVIEW – New York. v. 1-8. no 27. Sept 1936-July 6 1943 – 1 – us NY Public [335]
Young County Federation of Women's Clubs. (Texas) *see* SCRAPBOOK OF YOUNG COUNTY
YOUNG CZECHOSLOVAKIA – London. (German ed.). (Einheit). -W. 15 May 1941-17 Nov 1945. (2 reels) – 1 – uk British Libr Newspaper [072]
YOUNG CZECHOSLOVAKIA – Sudeten German anti-fascist fortnightly.London. Title change 23 May 1942: Einheit.15 May 1941-17 Nov 1945 – 1 – gw Mikrofilm [072]
Young, D *see* THE ORIGIN AND HISTORY OF METHODISM IN WALES AND THE BORDERS
THE YOUNG DIANA / Corelli, Marie – British Fiction Archive: Unit 1 – 9 – uk Bell [830]
Young, E *see* THE FERNS OF WALES
Young, E J *see* MY SERVANTS THE PROPHETS
Young, E R *see* BY CANOE AND DOG-TRAIN AMONG THE CREE AND SALTEAUX INDIANS
Young, Edward *see* THE UNIVERSAL PASSION
Young, Elaine W *see* FACTORS WHICH INFLUENCE PATIENT SATISFACTION WITH SEXUALITY EDUCATION
YOUNG EMU AND ITS FAMILY LIFE IN CAPTIVITY / Curry, Peter – (MSc Thesis) – 1979 – microfiche – A$15.00 – at R.A.O.U. [590]
YOUNG ENGLAND – The social condition of the Empire. London. -w. 4 Jan-5 Apr 1845. (17 ft) – 1 – uk British Libr Newspaper [072]
YOUNG FABIAN PAMPHLETS / Fabian Society – Nos.1-50 – 24mf – 9 – uk Microform Academic [320]
THE YOUNG FRIEND'S MANUAL : CONTAINING A STATEMENT OF SOME OF DOCTRINES AND TESTIMONIES OF FRIENDS, AND OF THE PRINCIPLES OF TRUTH PROFESSED BY THAT SOCIETY / Hallowell, Benjamin – 3rd ed. Philadelphia: Friends' Book Association, 1884 – 1mf – 9 – 0-8370-8905-0 – 1986-2905 – us A.T.L.A. [240]
YOUNG FRIEND'S REVIEW – London [Ont: s.n. 1886-1899] – 9 – cn C.I.H.M. [971]
Young, George *see* THE POLITICAL AND OCCASIONAL POEMS OF WINTHROP MACKWORTH PRAED
Young, George Paxton *see* MISCELLANEOUS DISCOURSES AND EXPOSITIONS OF SCRIPTURE
YOUNG IRELAND – Dublin, Ireland.1917-23 – 1 – ie Microforms [072]
Young, John *see*
- THE CHRIST OF HISTORY
- THE PROVINCE OF REASON
- THE PROVINCE OF REASON: A CRITICISM OF...THE LIMITS OF RELIGIOUS THOUGHT

Young, Loyal *see* A COMMENTARY ON THE BOOK OF ECCLESIASTES
THE YOUNG MAN'S AFFAIRS / Brown, Charles Reynolds – New York: Thomas Y. Crowell, 1909. 160p. 1 fiche – 9 – us A.T.L.A. [240]
YOUNG MAN'S DIFFICULTIES WITH HIS BIBLE / Faunce, Daniel Webster – Philadelphia: American Baptist Publ., 1898. 1 fiche – 9 – us A.T.L.A. [240]
Young, Marnie J *see* FUNCTIONAL MOTOR SKILLS AND THE DEVELOPMENTALLY DISABLED
YOUNG MEN : FAULTS AND IDEALS: A FAMILIAR TALK WITH QUOTATIONS FROM LETTERS / Miller, James Russell – New York: Thomas Y Crowell, c1893 – 1mf – 9 – 0-8370-7249-2 – 1986-1249 – us A.T.L.A. [240]
THE YOUNG MEN AND THE CHURCHES : WHY SOME OF THEM ARE OUTSIDE, AND WHY THEY OUGHT TO COME IN / Gladden, Washington – Boston: Congregational Sunday-School and Pub. Society, 1885 – 1mf – us A.T.L.A. [240]
YOUNG MEN, HOBBIES, AVIATION, CAREERS *see* AMERICAN AIRCRAFT MODELER
THE YOUNG ORGANIST: A COMPLETE INSTRUCTOR / Getze, J – c.1859 – 1 – us Sibley [780]
YOUNG PEOPLE AND CULTURAL INSTITUTIONS : EIGHT YOUNG PEOPLE GIVE THEIR VIEWS ON THE CULTURAL INSTITUTIONS IN THEIR COUNTRIES. – 1980 – 9 – 92-3-101698-9 – fr UNESCO [305]
YOUNG PEOPLE'S BIBLE MEETING TOPICS – 1908 (complete) – 1r – 1 – ATLA 1994-S000 – us A.T.L.A. [220]
YOUNG PEOPLE'S ILLUSTRATED MONTHLY – London, UK. 1894. -m. 28 feet – 1 – uk British Libr Newspaper [072]
YOUNG PEOPLE'S INLAND AFRICA – (Cont by: Young Africa) – v5-16. 1926-37 (incomplete) – 1r – 1 – ATLA S0710C – us A.T.L.A. [073]
YOUNG PEOPLE'S INLAND AFRICA *see* YOUNG AFRICA
YOUNG PEOPLE'S LEADER – v. 1-3. 1894-96 – 1 – 38.50 – us Baptist [240]
YOUNG PEOPLE'S PAPER – (lacks: v8 no 1, 6) – v1-13. 1894-1906 – 2r – 1 – ATLA 1994-S014 – us A.T.L.A. [073]
Young People's Socialist League *see* CHALLENGE! YPSL
YOUNG POETS OF A NEW POLAND – 1993 – 254p – 9 – 92-3-102930-4 – Co-published with Forest Books – fr UNESCO [460]
YOUNG POETS OF GERMANY / ed by Gutzschhahn, Uwe-Michael – 1994 – 9 – 92-3-102952-5 – fr UNESCO [430]
Young, Robert *see*
- COMPLETE PARADIGMS OF THE SAMARITAN VERBS
- SAMARITAN WORD-BOOK
- SYRIAC ROOT-BOOK

THE YOUNG SOLDIER – [Toronto?: s.n. 1886?-189- or 19–] – 9 – cn C.I.H.M. [971]
YOUNG SPARTACUS / Communist League of America – 1-4 2+6 (all publ). 1931-1935 – 1 reel – 1 – $65.00 – us UPA [335]
YOUNG SUN – (In Chinese) – nos 198-267. 1959-61 (complete) – 1r – 1 – ATLA S0320 – us A.T.L.A. [073]
Young, T *see*
- AN INTRODUCTION TO MEDICAL LITERATURE INCLUDING A SYSTEM OF PRACTICAL NOSOLOGY
- AN INTRODUCTION TO MEDICAL LITERATURE, INCLUDING A SYSTEM OF PRACTICAL NOSOLOGY

Young, W *see* A COMMENTARY ON THE GREEK TEXT OF THE EPISTLE OF PAUL TO THE COLOSSIANS
Young, William *see*
- A COMMENTARY ON THE GREEK TEXT OF THE EPISTLES OF PAUL TO THE THESSALONIANS
- YOUNG'S HISTORY OF LAFAYETTE COUNTY

Young, William Henry *see* TACTOLOGY
YOUNG WORKER – New York: Young Workers' League of America. v1-14. 1922-36 – 2r – 1 – us Ross [331]
YOUNG WORKER / Young Communist League – 1-14 2+17 (all publ). 1922-1936 – 3r – 1 – $345.00 – us UPA [335]
Youngen, Lois J *see* MORAL JUDGMENT AND THE PERCEIVED LEGITIMACY OF INJURIOUS ACTS AMONG COLLEGIATE ATHLETES
YOUNGER'S CREEK BAPTIST CHURCH. ELIZABETHTOWN, KENTUCKY : CHURCH RECORDS – Dec 1876-Sept 1983 – 1 – 55.17 – us Baptist [240]
YOUNG'S HISTORY OF LAFAYETTE COUNTY / Young, William – Indianapolis: B.F. Bowen and Co., 1910. 2v. Missouri Reel 23. (The Cox Library Collection) – 5 – us Americana [978]
YOUNG'S VICE-ADMIRALTY DECISIONS / Nova Scotia. Canada; ed by Oxley – 1v. 1865-80 (all publ) – 4mf – 9 – $6.00 – LLMC 81-038 – us L.L.M.C. [340]
YOUNG'S VOCAL AND INSTRUMENTAL MUSICAL MISCELLANY; BEING A COLLECTION OF THE MOST APPROVED SONGS, DUETS, CATCHES AND GLEES; ADAPTED FOR THE VOICE, PIANO FORTE, VIOLIN AND GERMAN FLUTE – Philadelphia: For the Author 1793. MUSIC 1095 – 1 – us L of C Photodup [780]
Youngstedt, S D *see* DOES BODY TEMPERATURE MEDIATE ANXIOLYTIC EFFECTS AF ACUTE EXERCISE
YOUNGSTOWN, OHIO, TAXES, MS V.F.O. – (List of all property liable to appraisement for County taxes) – 1801-05 – 1r – 1 – us Western Res [978]
Younker, Bowman H *see* DIARY AND PERSONAL RECORDS

YOUR HEALTH AND SAFETY – 1984- – 1,5,6,9 – us UMI [615]

YOUR HONOR / Devitt, Edward J – Washington: FJC, 1986 – 1mf – 9 – $1.50 – LLMC 95-398 – us L.L.M.C. [340]

YOUR JEWISH CENTER NEWS – Los Angeles, CA.1944-45 – 1 – us A.J.P.C. [071]

YOUR PATIENT AND CANCER – v.1-. 1981- – 1,5,6,9 – us UMI [616]

YOUR RIGHTS / Bennett, John – 1986, Australian Civil Liberties Union, 4p – 9 – 1.00f – at Libertarian Micro [335]

YOUR TOWN – Salem, OR. -w. 6 Dec 1946-11 Jun 1948. 1 roll – 1 – us U.O. Library [071]

YOUSE JINSHU – Nonferrous Metals. In Chinese, with English abstracts to the main articles – 9 – $4.00f – cc Microforms [670]

THE YOUTH – (New York). 1910-21 – 1 – us A.J.P.C. [073]

YOUTH: A NARRATIVE : AND TWO OTHER STORIES / Conrad, Joseph – Edingburgh, London: William Blackwood, 1902 – 1 roll – 1 – 1-55879-911-7 – uk Libr Preservation [830]

YOUTH ALTERNATIVES – (v6- 1979- 5,6,9) – v1- 1974- – 1 – us UMI [305]

YOUTH AND VOCATION (CCC149) = CHING-KUO CH'ING-NIEN CHIH-YEH WEN-T'I / Ho, Ch'ing-ju – (In Chinese) – 1934 – 1r – 1 – 1984-B500 – us A.T.L.A. [240]

YOUTH IN THE 1980'S – 1981 – 320p – 9 – 92-3-101885-X – fr UNESCO [305]

YOUTH INSTITUTIONS AND SERVICES : PRESENT STATE AND DEVELOPMENT – 1977 – 51p – 9 – 92-3-101398-X – fr UNESCO [360]

YOUTH MOBILIZATION FOR DEVELOPMENT IN ASIAN SETTINGS – 1979 repr 1984 – 136p – 9 – 92-3-101686-5 – fr UNESCO [305]

THE YOUTH OF MADAME DE LONGUEVILLE, OR NEW REVELATIONS OF COURT AND CONVENT IN THE SEVENTEENTH CENTURY / Cousin, Victor – Trans. by F.W. Ricord. New York: D. Appleton & Co., 1854. 403p – 1 – us U.W. Library [944]

YOUTH SERVICE IN ENGLAND AND WALES: REPORT OF THE COMMITTEE APPOINTED BY THE MINISTER OF EDUCATION / Great Britain. Committee Appointed by the Minister of Education – Albemarle Report.1958 – 2mf – 9 – uk Microform Academic [324]

YOUTH, TRADITION AND DEVELOPMENT IN AFRICA – 1981 – 146p – 9 – 92-3-101918-X – fr UNESCO [305]

THE YOUTHS' BOOK-READING MOVEMENT (CCC199) = CH'ING NIEN TU SHU YUN TUNG / Hu, I-ku – (In Chinese) – [s.l: s.n, 1927] – 1r – 1 – 1984-B500 – us A.T.L.A. [240]

THE YOUTH'S COMPANION – Boston. Mass. 1879-1926 – 1 – us UMI [071]

THE YOUTH'S INSTRUCTOR – [Saint John, N.B.? : s.n. 1824] – 9 – cn C.I.H.M. [971]

THE YOUTH'S INSTRUCTOR IN THE ENGLISH TONGUE / Owen, John – 1732. 191p. (English Linguistics Series 1500-1800) – 9 – us UMI [420]

THE YOUTH'S LIBERAL GUIDE FOR THEIR MORAL CULTURE AND RELIGIOUS ENLIGHTENMENT / Kottinger, Hermann Marcus – Milwaukee: Trayser. 2v. 1877 – 2mf – 9 – 0-8370-8685-X – 1986-2685 – us A.T.L.A. [240]

YOUTH'S MONITOR – v1. 1883 (complete) – 1r – 1 – ATLA 1993-S018 – us A.T.L.A. [073]

YOUTH'S MONITOR AND MONTHLY MAGAZINE – [Toronto?: s.n. 1836?] – 9 – cn C.I.H.M. [305]

THE YOUTH'S PRECEPTOR – Halifax, N.S.: W Cunnabell, [1853?-18– or 19–] – 9 – cn C.I.H.M. [305]

YOZEREI HA-SIFRUT HA-IVRIT HA-HADASHAH / Zitron, S L – 1-2. Vilna. 2 pts. BJ-422-102 1 – 9 – ne IDC [470]

YOZEROT – Prague. 1605. BJ-43-141 1 – 9 – ne IDC [470]

O YPIRANGA – Sao Paulo, 1 Aug 1867-Dec 1868; Jan, Aug-12 Dec 1869 – 1,5,6 – bl Biblioteca [072]

O YPIRANGA – Sao Paulo, Brazil. Aug 1882-Oct 1883 – 1 – bl Biblioteca [072]

YPODIGMA NEUSTRIE (CHRONIA..7) / Thomas Walsingam – 1876 – Dfl46.00 – ne Slangenburg [240]

Y.P.S.L. CHALLENGE *see* CHALLENGE (YOUNG PEOPLE'S SOCIALIST LEAGUE OF AMERICA)

YR AMSERAU – Liverpool, England. -w. Aug 1843-Dec 1859 – 6r – 1 – uk British Libr Newspaper [072]

YR YSPIUR – Llangollen, Wales, UK. Feb-May 1845. 19 feet – 1 – uk British Libr Newspaper [072]

Yriarte, Charles *see* FLORENCE; ITS HISTORY, THE MEDICI, THE HUMANISTS, LETTERS, ARTS

Yriarte, Tomas de *see* FABLES LITTERAIRES...

YRIGOYEN Y PERON : ARQUETIPOS DE LA JUSTICIA SOCIAL; SU PARALELO HISTORICO Y SU ACCION PROSELITISTA EN EL MEDIO REVOLUCIONARIO – [Buenos Aires?, 1947?] – 1 – CSUXADL5931-B – us Hoover Inst Photo [320]

YSTADS ALLEHANDA – Ystad, Sweden. 1873- – 1 – sw Kungliga [072]

YTINERARIO DE NAVEGACION DE LOS MARES Y TIERRAS OCCIDENTALES... / Escalante de Mendoza, J – Sevilla, 1575; Madrid, 1583 – 12mf – 9 – sp Cultura [380]

Yu, Jeh-chang *see* INDIGENIZATION OF THE YMCA IN CHINA (CCC349)

Yu, Jin-Wen *see* THE ENERGY FLOW OF THE HUMAN BEING AND THE UNIVERSE

Yu, Mu-jen *see*
- CHRISTIAN WORK IN RURAL CHINA (CCC350)
- CHRISTIANITY AND THE RURAL RECONSTRUCTION MOVEMENT IN CHINA (CCC351)

Yu, mu-jen *see* A SHORT STUDY OF RELIGIONS (CCC183)

Yuan, Ting-an *see* PHILOSOPHY OF THEISM (CCC352)

YUANREN WENJI PIANMU FENLEI SUOYIN / Lu, Junling – Classified index of literary writings of the Yuan Dynasty. 6 fiches.F-J20 – 9 – $27.00 – cc Microforms [480]

YUANYI XUEBAO – Acta Horticulturae Sinica. In Chinese but English abstracts to the main articles. F p108 – 9 – 4.00f – cc Microforms [073]

YUANZIHE WULI – Chinese Journal of Nuclear Physics. In Chinese but English abstracts to the main articles. F p121 – 9 – $4.50f – cc Microforms [073]

YUBA CITY-HERALD – Yuba, CA. 1935-37; 1940-44 – 4r – 1 – $200.00 – B03125 – us Library Micro [071]

YUBA COLLEGE FORTY-NINER – Marysville, CA. 1929-61 – 1r – 1 – $50.00 – B02437 – us Library Micro [370]

YUBA COUNTY – Yuba Co, CA: Thompson & West, 1879 – 1r – 1 – $50.00 – B40287 – us Library Micro [978]

YUBA COUNTY INCLUDING MARYSVILLE – Yuba Co, CA. 1853-1861; 1870; 1878-1879; 1892-1904; 1925-1950 – 22r – 1 – $1,100.00 – D108 – us Library Micro [978]

YUBA/SUTTER COUNTIES – 1992- – 3+ r – 1 – $150.00 – P00142 – us Library Micro [910]

Yucatan. Mexico (State) *see*
- DIARIO OFICIAL
- DIARIO OFICIAL DEL GOBIERNO DEL ESTADO DE YUCATAN

YU-CHOU FENG – The Cosmic Winds. v. 1-152. Shanghai. 1935-47. semi-monthly. Lacking: v. 47-56, v. 58-60, v. 62-81, 1937-39; v. 118, v. 121-123, v. 126-131, 1941-43; v. 134-143, v. 147-148, v. 150, 1946-47. BCH-378 2 – 8 – ne IDC [073]

DER YUD – Krakau. v. 1-4. 1899-1902 – 1 – us NY Public [270]

YUDIN COLLECTION DRAWINGS OF CHINESE SUBJECTS / U.S. Library of Congress. Prints and Photographs Division – 333 drawings by unknown Russian artist working in Siberia and China circa 1860. 1 reel. P&P23 – 1 – 23.00r – us L of C Photodup [740]

YUDISCHE GAZETEN – New York. Aug 22 1890-Dec 30 1927. Not collated – 1 – us NY Public [071]

DI YUDISHE BIBIOTHEK – (Missing: 1891 v1(p73-104)) – Warzawa. 3v. 1891, 1892, 1895 – 12mf – ne IDC [470]

DOS YUDISHE FOLK = JEWISH PEOPLE – (In Yiddish) – Warsaw, PL. no199 12 Sep 1919; no205 19 Sep 1919 – 1r – 1 – $25.00 – cn Can Microfilming [072]

DI YUDISHE PRESE IN DER GEVEZENER RUSLANDISHER IMPERIE / Kirzhnitz, A – Moscow. 1930. BJ-290-18 1 – 9 – ne IDC [430]

DOS YUDISHE VOKHENBLAT = JEWISH WEEKLY – Bedzin, PL. v3 no32 1927-v5 no36 1929 – 1r – 1 – $25.00 – cn Can Microfilming [072]

YUDISHE VOKHENSHRIFT = JEWISH WEEKLY / ed by Peretz, I L – (In Yiddish) – Warsaw, PL. no1-no4. Jan-Mar 1909 – 1r – 1 – $25.00 – cn Can Microfilming [072]

YUDISHER POK – New York. v. 1-2. Nov 1894-June 1896 – 1 – us NY Public [071]

YUDISHER POK – New York. v1-2. 1894-96 – 2r – 1 – us Ross [270]

YUDISHER TELEGRAF = YIDDISH TELEGRAPH – (Yiddish daily) – Bucarest, RM. v2 no303. 22 May 1878 – 1r – 1 – $25.00 – cn Can Microfilming [072]

YUDISHER TERYAK – Hanau. 1615. BJ-43-142 1 – 9 – ne IDC [470]

YUDISHES FOLKSBLATT – Philadelphia. Pa. 1894 – 1 – us A.J.P.C. [071]

Yuditzki, A *see* YIDISHE BURZHVAZIE UN YIDISHER PROLETARIAT IN ERSHTER HELFT FUN 19 YORHUNDERT

Yue, Guang H *see* THE EFFECTS OF IMAGINARY MAXIMAL MUSCLE CONTRACTION TRAINING ON THE VOLUNTARY NEURAL DIRVE TO MUSCLE

YUEH HUA PAO – Saigon. South Vietnam. 1967 – 1 – us UMI [072]

YUEH-TUNG CH'ENG AN – (Includes index) – v1-38. 1832 – 8 – BCH-835 2 – ne IDC [920]

Yuen, Garry E *see* THE BACK HANDSPRING

YUGANTAR – Bombay, India. 1962-Jun 1964 – 1r – 1 – us L of C Photodup [072]

YUGANTHARA – Calcutta, India. 1981-1990 – 39r – 1 – us L of C Photodup [072]

YUGEND = YOUTH – (In German) – Apr 1918 – 1r – 1 – $25.00 – cn Can Microfilming [072]

YUGOSLAV LAW = DROIT YOUGOSLAVE – (v.4-. 1979- 5,6,9) – v.1-. 1975- – 1 – us UMI [073]

YUGOSLAV LIFE – Belgrade. 1966- – 1 – 23.00r – us L of C Photodup [949]

YUGOSLAV REVIEW – New York, v2, no 1, Oct. 1923 – 1r – 1 – us I.H.R.C. [978]

THE YUGOSLAV SOCIAL PLAN FOR 1964. THE LAW ON ECONOMIC PLANNING MEASURES IN 1964. THE LAW ON THE FEDERAL BUDGET FOR 1964. THE FEDERAL BUDGET FOR 1964 / Yugoslavia – 1964. BD-1787 1 – 9 – ne IDC [350]

THE YUGOSLAV SOCIAL PLAN FOR 1965. THE LAW ON ECONOMIC PLANNING MEASURES FOR 1965. THE LAW ON THE FEDERAL BUDGET FOR 1965. THE FEDERAL BUDGET FOR 1965 / Yugoslavia – 1965. BD-1788 1 – 9 – ne IDC [350]

YUGOSLAV STATISTICS, 1834-1919 / Palairet, M R – (With printed guide) – 86r – 13 – £5,460.00 – uk Chadwyck [949]

YUGOSLAVIA = ANNUAIRE STATISTIQUE 1929-1940 : STATISTICKI GODISNJAK 1929-1940 / Yugoslavia. Opsta Drzavna Statistika – (Coll title: European Official Statistical Serials, 1841-1984) – 58mf – 9 – £6.00f (set £1,100.00 174mf) – uk Chadwyck [949]

YUGOSLAVIA : STATISTICKI GODISNJAK 1954-1965 / Yugoslavia. Savezni Zavod zu Statistiku – (Coll title: European Official Statistical Serials, 1841-1984) – 116mf – 9 – £5.00f (set £1,100.00 174mf) – uk Chadwyck [949]

Yugoslavia *see*
- 1962 FEDERAL SOCIAL PLAN. THE 1962 FEDERAL BUDGET
- DRUSTVENI PLAN, 1964
- THE FIVE YEARS' DEVELOPMENT PLAN
- FIVE-YEAR PLAN OF ECONOMIC DEVELOPMENT OF YUGOSLAVIA, 1961-1965
- LAW ON THE FIVE YEAR PLAN FOR THE DEVELOPMENT OF THE NATIONAL ECONOMY OF THE FEDERATIVE PEOPLE'S REPUBLIC OF YUGOSLAVIA IN THE PERIOD FROM 1947 TO 1951
- PLAN SOCIAL DE DEVELOPPEMENT ECONOMIQUE DE LA YOUGOSLAVIE, 1961-1965
- SLUZBENE NOVINE
- SLUZBENI LIST SOCIJALISTICKE FEDERATIVNE REPUBLIKE JUGOSLAVIJE
- THE YUGOSLAV SOCIAL PLAN FOR 1964. THE LAW ON ECONOMIC PLANNING MEASURES IN 1964. THE LAW ON THE FEDERAL BUDGET FOR 1964. THE FEDERAL BUDGET FOR 1964
- THE YUGOSLAV SOCIAL PLAN FOR 1965. THE LAW ON ECONOMIC PLANNING MEASURES FOR 1965. THE LAW ON THE FEDERAL BUDGET FOR 1965. THE FEDERAL BUDGET FOR 1965

YUGOSLAVIA : PEOPLES, STATES AND SOCIETY – (With printed guide $125) – 109r – 1 – $9,990.00 coll $100.00r – us Ross [949]

YUGOSLAVIA EXPORT – Zagreb, Belgrade, Yugoslavia. International edition. -w. 10 Jan 1960-15 Sept 1964; March 1965-Dec 1970. 5 reels – 1 – uk British Libr Newspaper [949]

Yugoslavia. Laws, Statutes, etc *see* ZAKON O PROMETU ZEMLJISTA I ZGRADA

Yugoslavia. Ministarstvo prosvete *see* PROSVETNI GLASNIK

Yugoslavia. Opsta Drzavna Statistika *see* YUGOSLAVIA

Yugoslavia. Savezni Zavod zu Statistiku *see* YUGOSLAVIA

Yugoslavia. Treaties, etc *see* MEDUNARODNI UGOVORI I DRUGI SPORAZUMI

Yui, Tsunehiko *see* EIGYO HOKOKUSHO SHUSEI

YUIBUTSU RON KENKYU – GAKUGEI – Japan, 1932-38 – 8r – 1 – inquire – us Ross [072]

Yuji, Isobe *see* NJIOER MELAMBAI. (SEPATAH KATA PENJONGSONG, OLEH SOEKARNO)

YUKAN NIIGATA *see* NIIGATA NIPPO

YUKAN SHINSHU – Japan, 1946-49 – 7r – 1 – inquire – us Ross [072]

YUKAN SHINSHU – Jun 1946-Dec 1949 – 7r – 1 – Y49,000 – ja Japan Micro [950]

YUKON SUN AND KLONDIKE PIONEER – Dawson, Canada. 1899-1904 – 6r – 1 – $390.00 – cn Library Assoc [971]

YUKON WORLD – Dawson, Canada. 1904-09 – 8r – 1 – $520.00 – cn Library Assoc [971]

Yule, H *see*
- CATHAY AND THE WAY THITHER
- HOBSON-JOBSON
- HOBSON-JOBSON; A GLOSSARY OF COLLOQUIAL ANGLO-INDIAN WORDS AND PHRASES

Yun, Chi-Hong *see* PRE- AND POST-KNOWLEDGE OF RESULTS INTERVALS AND MOTOR PERFORMANCE OF MENTALLY RETARDED INDIVIDUALS

YUNG KUANG *see* THE LIGHT OF THE OCEAN

Yung, Tse *see* SERULING DEWATA DAN NAGA SAKTI (SIAN TIE SIN LIONG)

YUNG-CH'UN CHOU-CHIH – 1787, 16, 1. Lacking: pt. 8, ch. 12. BCH-580 2 – 8 – ne IDC [950]

YUNG-CH'UN HSIEN-CHIH – 1927; 1930, 28. BCH-581 2 – 8 – ne IDC [950]

DER YUNGER ARBETER = THE YOUNGER WORKER – Toronto, CN. v- no-. 1924 – 1r – 1 – Can$25.00 – cn Can Microfilming [072]

DER YUNGER DOR = THE YOUNG GENERATION – (In Yiddish. Bi-weekly) – London, GB. v1 no1 15 Sep 1922-no6 24 Nov 1922 – 1r – 1 – $25.00 – cn Can Microfilming [072]

YUNG-PEI FU-CHIH – 1765; 1766, Manuscript. 6-11. BCH-683 2 – 8 – ne IDC [950]

YUNGVALD = YOUNG FOREST – (In Yiddish) – Moscow, RU. v- no7(no30) Aug 1926-no32 Oct 1926 – 1r – 1 – $25.00 – cn Can Microfilming [072]

YUNG-YEN – Justice.Tientsin, 1912-14. 2v. BCH-376/1 – 9 – ne IDC [340]

DER YUNION ARBEITER / International Ladies Garment Workers' Union – New York. v. 1-2 no. 34. Dec 4 1925-Sept 26 1927 – 1 – us NY Public [331]

YUNION ARBEITER – New York: International Ladies' Garment Workers' Union. v1-2. 1925-27 – 1r – 1 – us Ross [331]

YUN-NAN HSIANG-SHIH LU – List of successful candidates in the imperial examination in Yunnan province: 1855, 1879, 1882, 1888, 1891, 1894, 1903. 1 reel – 1 – 14.00 – us Chinese Res [950]

YUN-NAN JIH-PAO – Kumming, Yunnan, China. Yunnan Daily. Jan, Jul 1951-1960; Mar 1961-May 1963; May, Jun, Sept 1964; Sept, Oct 1965. Loose issues. 23 reels – 1 – 590.00 – us Chinese Res [072]

Yunnan Mission (Pres. Ch. in the U.S.A.) *see* MINUTES, 1924-1934

YUNNAN RIBAO = YUNNAN DAILY – 1983- . M-D54 – 1 reel/y – 1 – $55.00r – cc Microforms [072]

YUN-NAN T'UNG-CHIH – 1736, 30, 1. BCH-660 2 – 8 – ne IDC [950]

YUNNAN XINHAI GEMING ZILIAO – Materials on the Revolution of 1911 in Yunnan. Comp. by Xie Benshu, Jin Dexin. 7 fiches. F-H111 – 9 – $31.50 – cc Microforms [950]

YUNNAN ZHIWU YANJIU – Acta Botanica Yunnanica. In Chinese but English abstracts to the main articles. F p84 – 9 – 4.00f – cc Microforms [073]

YUNOST – (Youth). Moscow. U.S.S.R. 1960- – 1 – us UMI [305]
YUTAN BREEZE – Yutan, NE. -w. Apr-Jun 1896; Sept 1896-Feb 1898; Apr 1898-Dec 1899, scattered issues missing; Dec 1901-May 1903 – 1 – us NE Hist [071]
YUYAN WENZI BAO = LINGUISTIC JOURNAL – China. As Hanyu Pinyin Bao (Journal of Chinese Phonetic Spelling) until 1992. -bim. 1985- . M-D92 – 1 reel/y – 1 – $28.00r – cc Microforms [480]
YU-YEN WEN-HSUEH CHUAN-K'AN – "Journal of Philology and Literature". v. 1 (1-2). Canton. 1936. Quarterly. BCH-379 1 – 9 – ne IDC [480]
Yvelin, Pierre *see*
- APOLOGIE POUR L'AUTHEUR DE L'EXAMEN DE LA POSSESSION DES RELIGIEUSES DE LOUVIERS
- EXAMEN DE LA POSSESSION DES RELIGIEUSES DE LOUVIERS

YWHA CLARION – Montreal, CN. v1 no 7, v7 no 3. 1928-1932; 1937 – 1r – 1 – cn Can Microfilming [072]
Y-Worth, William *see* CHYMICUS RATIONALIS: OR, THE FUNDAMENTAL GROUNDS OF THE CHYMICAL ART RATIONALLY STATED AND DEMONSTRATED
ZA ANTIFASHISTSKUI U DEMOKRATICHESKUI U GERMANII U = UM EIN ANTIFASCHISTISCH-DEMOKRATISCHES DEUTSCHLAND : SBORNIK DOKUMENTOV 1945-1949 GG / Ministerstvo inostrannykh del SSSRMinisterstvo inostrannykh del GDR – Moskva: Politizdat, 1969 – 1 – CSUX90-B5702 – us Hoover Inst Photo [320]
ZA CHETVERTVEKA. (1871-94). SBORNIK STATEI / Arsenev, K K – St. Petersburg. 1915. BR-10,546 1 – 9 – ne IDC [947]
ZA INDUSTRIALIZATIZIYU – Moscow. 1930-1936. Incomplete – 1 – us NY Public [330]
ZA INDUSTRIALIZATSII U SIBIRI – (Library has: Nov.-Dec. 1929; Jan.-May 1930) – Novosibirsk: Sibkra isovnarkhoz, 1929-1931. 3v – 1 – CSUX89-S826 – us Hoover Inst Photo [338]
ZA INDUSTRIALIZATSIIU – Moscow, 1930-36 – 1r – 1 – us Ross [072]
ZA KHLOPKOVUI U NEZAVISIMOST / Glavnogo khlopkovogo komiteta i Vsesoiuznogo tsentra khlopkovodchesko i kooperatsii – (Library has: Jan.-March, June-July, 1931) – Tashkent: Izdvo Vses. nauch.-issl. int po khlopkovodstvu i khlopkovo i promyshl., 1931- – 1 – CSUX89-S513 – us Hoover Inst Photo [320]
ZA KNIZHNOI – Obozrenie novyk knig i knizhnago dela. S. 1. 1906-07. BR-7634 2 – 8 – ne IDC [460]
ZA KOMMUNISTICHESKOE PROSVESHCHENIE – Moscow, USSR. 1934; June 22-Dec 1935 – 2r – 1 – us L of C Photodup [072]
ZA KOMMUNIZM / Furmanov, Dmitrii – Izd. 2-e. Moskva: Gos. izd-vo, 1928 – 1 – CSUX88-B7727 – us Hoover Inst Photo [320]
ZA KOOPERATIVNO ZEMEDELIE – Sofia, Bulgaria. May 1951-1958 – 8r – 1 – us L of C Photodup [949]
ZA OBORONU – (Library has: 1946; nos. 7/8-9, 13/14-23/24) – Moskva: Redizdat T SS Soiuza Osoaviakhim SSSR, 1939-1948. 10v – 1 – CSUX89-S951 – us Hoover Inst Photo [355]
ZA PROLETARSKUIU MUZYKU – Moscow, 1930-32 (bimonthly) – 25mf – 9 – us Ross [780]
ZA RUBEZHOM – Moscow. U.S.S.R. 1960- – 1 – us UMI [072]
ZA RUBEZHOM – Moscow, USSR. 1966-1992 – 28r – $1,400.00 – R63624 – us Library Micro [072]
ZA SMUTNYE GODY : PUBLITSISTICHESKIIA STATI I RIECHI A.A. BASHMAKOVA / Bashmakov, A A – S-Peterburg: Russko-Frant suzskai a tip., 1906 – 1 – CSUX88-B988 – us Hoover Inst Photo [947]
ZA SOTSYALISTICHKU JUGOSLAVYU – Moscow, U.S.S.R. -w. Jan 1953-Sept 1954. 1 reel – 1 – uk British Libr Newspaper [949]
ZA SVIATUIU RUS'. DUNY O RODNOI ZEMLE / Remizov, A – 1914. 59p. BR-856 2 – 8 – ne IDC [460]
ZA SVOBODU – Warsaw, Poland. Nov 1921-Jul 1922 – 1r – 1 – us L of C Photodup [943]
ZA UBEZHDENIE: IZ VOSPOMINANII SSYL'NAGO = FOR CONVICTION: FROM THE MEMOIRS OF AN EXILE / Timoshenko, Mikhail – Odessa: author, 1913. 140p – 1 – 5.60 – us Baptist [240]
ZA ULUCHSHENIE KOOPERATIVNYKH KADROV / Iakovlev, A I – M., 1929 – 1mf – 9 – COR-286/1 – ne IDC [334]
ZABAIKAL'SKII KHOZIAIN – (Missing: 1916 n20; 1916 n23-1917 n4) – Chita, 1912-17 n6 – 43mf – 9 – COR-591/1 – ne IDC [334]
ZABAIKAL'SKII KOOPERATOR – (Missing: 1924 n1-2) – Chita, 1924-25 n14 – 8mf – 9 – COR-592/1 – ne IDC [334]
Zabalza, A *see* THE DESTINATION AND EARLY CAREER PERFORMANCE OF SECONDARY SCHOOL GRADUATES IN COLOMBIA
ZABAN-I ZANAN – (Sal 23-25, shumarah 4 (1 Azar 1321-Tir 1324[Dec 1942-Jul 1945])) – Tehran: Sadiqah Dawlatabadi – 1 reel – 1 – $125.00 – us MEDOC [950]
Zabarella, Giacomo *see* DE REBVS NATVRALIBVS LIBRIS XXX: QVIBUS QVAESTIONES....
Zabelin, I *see* ISTORIIA GORODA MOSKVY
ZABER-NECKAR-POST – Heilbronn, Germany. 1960 – 1 – gw Mikrofilm [072]
Zabora, James R *see* JOURNAL OF PSYCHOSOCIAL ONCOLOGY
Zabriskie, Francis Nicoll *see* THE STORY OF A SOUL, OR, THOUGHTS ON THE PARABLE OF THE PRODIGAL SON
Zabriskie, James C *see* THE PUBLIC LAND LAWS OF THE UNITED STATES, 1796-1869.
Zacagnio, A *see* COLLECTANEA MONUMENTORUM VETERUM ECCLESIAE GRAECAE ET LATINAE
Zacatecas. Mexico (State) *see* PERIODICO OFICIAL
Zacconi, L *see*
- PRATTICA DI MUSICA UTILE ET NECESSARIA SI AL COMPOSITORE PER COMPORRE I CANTI SUOI REGOLATAMENTE
- PRATTICA DI MVSICA VTILE ET NECESSARIA SI ALCOMPOSITORE PER COMPORRE I CANTI SUO REGOLATAMENTE

Zacharia, Friedrich Wilhelm *see* DER RENOMIST
ZACHARIAH REGAN PAPERS *see* REGAN, ZACHARIAH, PAPERS, MS 4705
Zacharias, Alfred *see* DER BAUERNZORN
ZACHARIAS WERNERS DRAMEN : IHRE QUELLEN UND IHR VERHAELTNIS ZUR GESCHICHTE / Diekmann, Rudolf – (Includes bibliographical references) – Muenster: Der Westfale, 1913 – 1r – 1 – us U.W. Library [790]
ZACHARIAS WERNERS WEIHE DER KRAFT : EINE STUDIE ZUR TECHNIK DES DRAMAS / Fraenkel, Jonas – (Includes bibliographical references) – Hamburg: L Voss, 1904 – 1r – 1 – us U.W. Library [790]
ZACHARIE 9-14 / Lagrange, P – 1961 – 3mf – 8 – ne Slangenburg [220]
ZACHEM I KOMU NUZHNA POEZIIA / Aseev, N – M. 1961. BR-1975 2 – 8 – ne IDC [460]
Zachri, Rukiah *see* CRIME IN INDONESIA
Zachrisson, R E *see* THOMAS HARDY AS MAN, WRITER AND PHILOSOPHER
Zacot, F *see* ESPACES MELANESIENS
ZADACHI I OSNOVNYE PRINTSIPY ORGANIZATSII SOIUZOV KOOPERATIVOV (GLAVNYM OBRAZOM – POTREBITEL'NYKH) / Pekarskii, V F – Ed 2. Pg., 1915 – 1mf – 9 – COR-94/1 – ne IDC [334]
ZADACHI KOOPERATSII / Suponev, N A – L., 1924 – 1mf – 9 – COR-189/1 – ne IDC [334]
ZADACHI PROMYSHLENNOSTI V SVIAZI S VOINOI : DOKLAD KHARKOVSKOMU OTDI ELENII U IMPERATORSKAGO RUSSKAGO TEKHNICHESKAGO OBSHCHESTVA / Ditmar, Nikolai Fedorovich fon- – Kharkov: Tipo-lit. I U.M. Berkman, 1915 – 1 – CSUX88-B8165 – us Hoover Inst Photo [947]
ZADACHI RABOCHAGO KLASSA V RUSSKO I REVOLIUTSII : RI ECH, PROIZNESENNAI A 9 MAI A 1917 GODA NA NARODNOM SOBRANII V MOSKVIE / Goldman-Liber, M – Moskva: Izd. E.D. Trautsko i, 1917 – 1 – CSUX88-B1603 – us Hoover Inst Photo [320]
ZADACHI SEL'SKOKHOZIAISTVENNOI KREDITNOI KOOPERATSII V SSSR / Mesiatsev, P P – M., 1927 – 1mf – 9 – COR-393/1 – ne IDC [334]
ZADACHI SOVREMENNOI KOOPERATSII / Meshcheriakova, N L – M., 1922 – 1mf – 9 – COR-169/1 – ne IDC [334]
ZADACHI VNUTRENNEI TORGOVLI I KOOPERATSIIA / Kuibyshev, V V – Ed 2. M., 1924 – 1mf – 9 – COR-162/1 – ne IDC [334]
Zadah, Muhammad Sadiq Mufti *see* KURDISTAN
ZADE-I SA'IR / Celal, Mehmed – Istanbul, 1311 – 2mf – 9 – $12.00 – us MEDOC [949]
Zadelhoff, F van *see* DIEREN, SPANKEREN EN LAAG-SOEREN IN VROEGER TIJDEN
ZADRUGA – Belgrade, Yugoslavia. May 1946-1952; 1956-Jan 1960 (scattered issues) – 5r – 1 – us L of C Photodup [949]
ZADUSHEVNOE SLOVO – Chtenie dlia detei ot 5 do 8 let. n1-12. Spb. 1877 – 8 – BR-8193 2 – ne IDC [460]
ZADUSHEVNOE SLOVO – Chtenie dlia iunoshestva ot 12-16 let. (Pod red. V. Lapina). v12-16. Spb. 1877 – 8 – BR-8194 2 – ne IDC [460]
ZADUSHEVNOE SLOVO – Chtenie dlia mladshego vozrasta. (Pod red. S. Makarovoi). pt. 1 (1-12). M., Spb. 1879. BR-8195 2 – 8 – ne IDC [947]
ZADUSHEVNOE SLOVO – Chtenie dlia starshego vozrasta (Pod red. S.M. Makarovoi). v1-12. Spb. 1879 – 8 – BR-8196 2 – ne IDC [460]
ZADUSHEVNOE SLOVO – Semeinoe chtenie dlia vzroslykh. Romany, povesty, razskazy i puteshestviia luchshikh pisatelei. v. 1-12. M., Spb. 1877. BR-8197 2 – 8 – ne IDC [460]
Zaech, Alfred *see* GOTTFRIED KELLER IM SPIEGEL SEINER ZEIT
Zafara 72 *see* LA CASETA DE LA CORDIALIDAD. FERIA DE SAN MIGUEL, 1972. BAILES, ACTOS CULTURALES. CONCURSOS. CENA DE GALA
ZAFER – Trabzon, 1922-19? – 9 – $10.00 – us MEDOC [956]
Zafra. Ayuntamiento *see*
- 3 FERIA REGIONAL DEL CAMPO EXTREMENO
- 10TH FERIA REGIONAL DEL CAMPO EXTREMENO. OCTUBRE 1975
- REVISTA DE FERIA 1969
- ZAFRA Y SU FERIA 1945

Zafra, Manuel de *see* DIA FESTIVO...GUADALUPE...PROCESION
ZAFRA Y SU FERIA 1945 / Zafra. Ayuntamiento – Badajoz: Tipografia clasica, 1945 – sp Bibl Santa Ana [946]
Zafren, Daniel H *see*
- THE COMPACT OF FREE ASSOCIATION, FOREIGN POLITICAL PROVISIONS
- THE DRAFT GUAM COMMONWEALTH ACT

ZAGAR, INCORPORATED, RECORDS – (Corporate record books, including the articles of incorporation, shareholder meeting minutes, financial records, and annual reports of this drilling and tapping equipment manufacturer) – 1935-84 – 1r – 1 – us Western Res [622]
ZAGLEMBIER TSAYTUNG = ZAGLEM TIMES – (In Yiddish) – Bedzin, PL. v17 no41 1927; v17 no48 1927 – 1r – 1 – $25.00 – cn Can Microfilming [072]
Zagoskin, N F *see* STOLY RAZRIADNOGO PRIKAZA, PO KHRANIASCHIMSIA V MOSKOVSKOM ARKHIVE MINISTERSTVA IUSTITSII KNIGAM IKH
ZAGRANICHNYI VESTNIK – Ucheno-literaturnyi zhurnal. v. 1-6. Spb. 1881-83. B-1988 2 – 8 – ne IDC [073]
ZAGRANICHNYI VESTNIK – Zhurnal inostrannoi literatury, nauki i zhizni. v. 1-13. Spb. 1864-67. B-1987 2 – 8 – ne IDC [073]
ZAGREBER TAGBLATT – Zagreb, Yugoslavia. Oct 1925-May 1926 – 1r – 1 – us L of C Photodup [949]
ZAH VE-ADOM / Treves, R – Constantinople. 1740. BJ-27-30 1 – 9 – ne IDC [290]
Zahlan, Antwan *see* AL-ILM WA-AL-TIKNULUJIYA FI AL-SIRA AL-ARABI-AL-ISRAILI
Zahlbruckner, A *see*
- CATALOGUS LICHENUM UNIVERSALIS
- STUDIEN UEBER BRASILIANISCHE FLECHTEN

Zahm, John Augustine *see* BIBLE, SCIENCE, AND FAITH
Zahn, Adolph *see*
- DIE BEIDEN LETZTEN LEBENSJAHRE VON JOHANNES CALVIN
- ERNSTE BLICKE IN DEN WAHN DER MODERNEN KRITIK DES ALTEN TESTAMENTES: NEUE FOLGE
- ISRAELITISCHE UND JUEDISCHE GESCHICHTE
- DIE ZOEGLINGE CALVIN'S IN HALLE AN DER SAALE

Zahn, Ernst *see*
- ERNST ZAHNS GESAMMELTE WERKE
- GESAMMELTE WERKE
- LUKAS HOCHSTRASSERS HAUS
- MACHT DER HEIMAT
- DIE SAEGE VON MARIELS
- TITO
- DER WEG HINAUF

Zahn, Franz Ludwig *see* ZAHN'S BIBLISCHE HISTORIEN NACH DEM KIRCHENJAHRE GEORDNET
Zahn, Karl *see* UEBER 1,2-METHYL-PHENYLGLYCOLE
Zahn, Richard *see* LICHOEKOLOGISCHE UNTERSUCHUNGEN DER CHLOROPLASTENFARBSTOFFE PHOTOSTABILER UND PHOTOLABILER PFLANZEN (1952)
Zahn, Theodor *see*
- DIE BLEIBENDE BEDEUTUNG DES NEUTESTAMENTLICHEN KANONS FUER DIE KIRCHE
- EINIGE BEMERKUNGEN ZU ADOLF HARNACK'S PRUEFUNG DER GESCHICHTE DES NEUTESTAMENTLICHEN KANONS (ERSTER BAND. ERSTE HAELFTE)
- FORSCHUNGEN ZUR GESCHICHTE DES NEUTESTAMENTLICHEN KANONS UND DER ALTKIRCHLICHEN LITERATUR
- GRUNDRISS DER GESCHICHTE DES NEUTESTAMENTLICHEN KANONS
- DER HIRT DES HERMAS

Zahn, W *see* DIE ALTMARK IM DREISSIGJAEHRIGEN KRIEGE
ZAHNAERZTLICHE PRAXIS – Muenchen-Graefelfing. v1-25. 1952-74*. v26-31 1975-80. v32-45 1981-94*. v46-48 1995-97+ – 1 – D9845 – us UMI [617]
ZAHN'S BIBLISCHE HISTORIEN NACH DEM KIRCHENJAHRE GEORDNET / Zahn, Franz Ludwig – Philadelphia: Schaefer und Koradi, [18-?] – 1mf – 9 – 0-8370-9759-2 – 1986-3759 – us A.T.L.A. [220]
Zaidan, Jurji *see*
- A HISTORY OF EGYPT
- HISTORY OF EGYPT

Zain, Sutan M *see*
- ENGLISH DICTIONARY; ENGLISH-INDONESIAN
- KITAB SOERAT-MENJOERAT DALAM BAHASA INDONESIA

Zain-al-Din, Al-Ma'Bari *see* TOHFUT-UL-MUJAH IDEEN
ZAIRE COLONIAL DOCUMENTS : DE RYCK COLLECTION OF MATERIAL ON GENERAL ADMINISTRATION, EQUATEUR, KIVU, AND RUANDA-URUNDI. CA 1885-1954 – Chicago: Center for Research Libraries, [1982?] – us Res Libr [960]
ZAIRE (FORMERLY BELGIAN CONGO) : STATISTIQUES RELATIVES A L'ANNEE...1957 AND 1959 – (Coll title: African Official Statistical Serials, 1867-1982) – 3mf – 9 – £24.00 – uk Chadwyck [960]
ZAJEDNICAR – Allegheny, PA, Jan. 1907-Dec. 25, 1940 – 11r – 1 – us I.H.R.C. [975]
ZAJMY – Prague, Czechoslovakia. Aug 1934-May 1938 (incomplete) – 1r – 1 – us L of C Photodup [072]
Zak, L S *see*
- FORMY EKONOMICHESKOI SAMOPOMOSHCHI V OBLASTI REMESLENNOGO TRUDA
- OSNOVNYE NACHALA TEORII KREDITA I KREDITNOI KOOPERATSII

ZAKASPIISKII KRAI / Penkina, Z M – Sistematicheskii sbornik bibliograficheskikh ukazanii knig i statei o Zakaspiiskom krae i sopredel'nykh stranakh. Spb. 1888. BR-7207 2 – 8 – ne IDC [010]
ZAKELIJKE AANTEKENINGEN, DL.3, F. 1591-1911 JAVA EN MADURA, BUITENBEZITTINGEN, 1859-79 – Arch. Kol. BSD-108/1 mf. 18-28 – 9 – ne IDC [950]
ZAKELIJKE AANTEKENINGEN, DL.4,F – 1915-2099 Buitenbezittingen vervolg, 1859-79. Arch. Kol. BSD-108/1 mf. 29-34 – 9 – ne IDC [950]
ZAKELIJKE AANTEKENINGEN, SYSTEMATISCH INGEDEELDE OPGAVE VAN DE LITERATUR, DL.1 – Oost-Indie. c1820-59. Arch. Kol. BSD-108/1 mf.1-17 – 9 – ne IDC [950]
Zakhar'in, I N *see* ZHIZN, SLUZHBA I PRIKLIUCHENIIA MIROVOGO SUD'I
ZAKLINATEL'NITSA ZMEI / Sologub, F – Roman. Berlin. 1921. BR-885 2 – 8 – ne IDC [460]
ZAKON ARMIANSKOI SOVETSKOI SOTSIALISTICHESKOI RESPUBLIKI O ZDRAVOOKHRANENII / Armenian SSR – Erevan: Aiastan, 1971 – 1 – CSUX91-B2629 – us Hoover Inst Photo [947]

ZAKON AZERBA IDZHANSKO I SOVETSKO I SOTSIALISTICHESKO I RESPUBLIKI O SELSKOM, POSELKOVOM SOVETE DEPUTATOV TRUDI ASHCHIKHSI A AZERBA IDZHANSKO I SSR / Azerbaijan S.S.R. – Baku: Verkhovny i Sovet Azerba idzhansko i SSR, 1968 – 1 – CSUX91-B2118 – us Hoover Inst Photo [947]

ZAKON AZERBAIDZHANSKO I SOVETSKOI SOTSIALISTICHESKOI RESPUBLIKI O SELSKOM, POSELKOVOM SOVETE DEPUTATOV TRUDI ASHCHIKHSIA AZERBA IDZHANSKOI SSR : PRINIAT TRETEI SESSIE I VERKHOVNOGO SOVETA AZERBAIDZHANSKOI SSR SEDMOGO SOZYVA 21 MAI A 1968 G / Azerbaijan S.S.R. – Baku: Azerba idzhanskoe gos. izd-vo, 1972 – 1 – CSUX91-B2006 – us Hoover Inst Photo [947]

ZAKON I DIEISTVITELNOST V SOVIETSKOI ROSSII / Chubinskii, M P – Bielgrad: Izd. Vseslavi anskago knizhnago magazina M.I. Stefanovich, 1926, c1925 – 1 – CSUX89-B6660 – us Hoover Inst Photo [947]

ZAKON O GOSUDARSTVENNOM PLANE RAZVITII A NARODNOGO KHOZI A ISTVA SSSR *see* O GOSUDARSTVENNOM PLANE RAZVITII A NARODNOGO KHOZI A ISTVA SSSR

ZAKON O KOOPERATIVNYKH TOVARISHCHESTVAKH I IKH SOIUZAKH – M., 1917 – 1mf – 9 – COR-30/1 – ne IDC [334]

ZAKON O PIATILETNEM PLANE VOSSTANOVLENIA I RAZVITIIA NARODNOGO KHOZIAISTVA SSSR NA 1946-1950 GG / U.S.S.R. – M. 1946. BD-537 1 – 9 – ne IDC [947]

ZAKON O PROMETU ZEMLJISTA I ZGRADA / Yugoslavia. Laws, Statutes, etc – Zagreb, Narodni list, 1954. 14 p. LL-4051 – 1 – us L of C Photodup [340]

ZAKON O SUMAMA I ZAKON O LOVU / Croatia. (Federated Republic, 1945-) Laws, Statutes, etc – Zagreb, Sekija sumarstva i drvne industrije Drustva inzenjera i technicara, NR Hrvatske, 1949. 21 p. LL-4031 – 1 – us L of C Photodup [324]

ZAKON O ZHILISHCHNOI KOOPERATSII : POSTATEINYI KOMMENT / Berdichevskii, N G – M., 1925 – 1mf – 9 – COR-289/1 – ne IDC [334]

ZAKON OB USTROISTVE SEL'SKOGO KREDITA I ZEMSTVO / Kekuatov, K V – Pg., 1915 – 1mf – 9 – COR-45/1 – ne IDC [334]

ZAKON V SOVETSKOM GOSUDARSTVE / Arkhippov, K A – Moscow, 1926. 157p. BR-9376 1 – 9 – ne IDC [340]

ZAKONODATEL' STVO O VODOPOL'ZOVANII V SSSR; PROBLEMY SOVERSHENSTVOVANIIA SOVETSKOGO ZAKONODATEL' STVA OB ISPOL'ZOVANII VODNYKH RESURSOV / Kolbasov, Oleg Stepanovich – Moskva, IUrid. lit-ra, 1965. 166 p. LL-4206 – 1 – us L of C Photodup [340]

ZAKONODATEL'NYE AKTY VYZVANNYE VOINOI 1914-1917 GG; ZAKONY, MANIFESTY, RESKRIPTY... / ed by Averbakh, O I – Pg., Vilnius. 5v. 1915-1918 – 72mf – 9 – ne IDC [324]

ZAKONODATEL'NYE PAMIATNIKI 16 I 17 STOLETTII / Khitrovo, N P – Moscow, 1905. 448p. New ed. of Tatishchev-Mueller ed. of 1768 with some additional texts and history of legislation reproduced. BR-9723/1 or 2 – 8,9 – ne IDC [340]

ZAKONODATELSTVO O PECHATE (VELIKIIA REFORMY SHESTIDESIATYKH GODOV) / Arsenev, K K – St. Petersburg, 1903. 263p. BR-9788 2 – 8 – ne IDC [947]

ZAKONODATEL'STVO O PROMYSLOVOI KREDITNOI KOOPERATSII / Genkin, – M., 1928 – 2mf – 9 – COR-291/1 – ne IDC [334]

ZAKONODATEL'STVO O TRUDOVYKH ARTELIAKH / Provolovich, I A; ed by Danilova, E – M., 1926 – 1mf – 9 – COR-295/1 – ne IDC [334]

ZAKONY O CHAST NOI PROMYSHLENNOSTI : SBORNIK DEKRETOV, POSTANOVLENII, RAZ"IASNENII I INSTRUKTSII S KOMMENTARIEM / Vorms, A E & Mints, S V – M., 1924 – 2mf – 9 – COR-296/1 – ne IDC [334]

ZAKONY O FINANSAKH POTREBITEL'SKOI KOOPERATSII : PRAKT. UKAZANIIA / Lur'e, GI – M., 1925 – 1mf – 9 – COR-297/1 – ne IDC [334]

ZAKONY O KOOPERATSII : SISTEMATICHESKII SBORNIK DEKRETOV, POSTANOVLENII, INSTRUKTSII, PRIMERNYKH USTAVOV I PR. / Dolmatovskii, A M – M., 1924 – 5mf – 9 – COR-715/1 – ne IDC [334]

ZAKONY O PECHATI / Mseriants, Z M – Nastol'naia spravochnaia kniga dlia avtorov. Ed. 2. M. 1870. BR-10,072 1 – 9 – ne IDC [340]

ZAKONY O PECHATI / Mseriants, Z M – Nastol'naia spravochnaia kniga dlia avtorov. Ed. 3. M. 1873. BR-10,073 1 – 9 – ne IDC [340]

ZAKONY O PECHATI / Mseriants, Z M – Nastol'naia spravochnaia kniga dlia avtorov. Ed. 4. M. 1876. BR-10,074 1 – 9 – ne IDC [340]

ZAKONY O PECHATI / Mseriants, Z M – Nastol'naia spravochnaia kniga dlia avtorov. Ed. 5. M. 1888. BR-10,075 1 – 9 – ne IDC [340]

ZAKONY O PECHATI / Mseriants, Z M – Nastol'naia spravochnaia kniga dlia avtorov. Ed. 6. M. 1893. BR-10,076 1 – 9 – ne IDC [340]

ZAKONY O PECHATI / Mseriants, Z M – Nastol'naia spravochnaia kniga dlia avtorov. Ed. 7. M. 189? BR-10,077 1 – 9 – ne IDC [340]

ZAKONY O PECHATI / Mseriants, Z M – Nastol'naia spravochnaia kniga dlia avtorov. Ed. 8. M. 1899. BR-10,078 1 – 9 – ne IDC [340]

ZAKONY O PECHATI / Russia. Laws, statutes, etc – 8th ed. Moscow, 1899 – 1 – 35.00r – us Hoover Inst Photo [324]

ZAKONY O TRUDE V UCHREZHDENIIAKH SSSR ZA GRANITSEI / Kilinskii, A – Moscow, 1933. 80p. Applicable labor laws in Soviet institutions abroad. BR-9118/1 – 9 – ne IDC [340]

ZAKONY O TRUDEI SOTSIALNOM STRAKHOVANII NA STROITELNYKH RABOTAKH / Gringolts, A & Perlovagor, M – 3-e izd. ispr. i dop. Moskva: Sovetskoe zakonodatelstvo, 1931 – 1 – CSUX91-B581 – us Hoover Inst Photo [650]

Zakrevskh, I *see* O NASTOIASHCHEM I BUDUSHCHEM SUDA 21 PRISIAZHNYKH

ZALAI HIRLAP – Zalaegerszeg, Hungary. 1962-79 – 35r – 1 – us L of C Photodup [072]

ZALAMEA DE LA SERENA (BADAJOZ) JAMAS FUE "ILIPA" / Eguibar y Muniz, Juan Jose de – Badajoz: Dip. Provincial, 1969. Sep. REE – 1 – sp Bibl Santa Ana [946]

Zaleski, S S *see* POLAND. HER PEOPLE, HISTORY, INDUSTRIES, FINANCE, SCIENCE

Zaleski, S S J *see* JEZUICI W POLSCE

Zamacois, Eduardo *see* CRONICAS DE LA GUERRA

ZAMAN – Nalchik, USSR. Apr-Dec 1991; Feb-Nov 1992 – 2r – 1 – us L of C Photodup [072]

ZAMAN – Selanik. Sahib-i Imtiyaz: Abduelkerim; Mueduer-i Mes'ul: Ali Nihad; Umur-i Tahririyye: Yunus Nadi [Abalioglu], 1908-1910 – 9 – $25.00 – us MEDOC [956]

ZAMBESI MISSION RECORD : A MISSIONARY PUBLICATION FOR READERS AT HOME AND ABROAD – (Available: 1926, v8(111)-1934, v9(146)) – London – 21mf – 9 – A-715/2 – ne IDC [240]

ZAMBIA : STATISTICAL YEARBOOK 1967-1971 / Zambia. Central Statistical Office – (1967 not available. Coll title: African Official Statistical Serials, 1867-1982) – 12mf – 9 – £100.00 – uk Chadwyck [960]

Zambia *see* GOVERNMENT GAZETTE

Zambia. Adult Education Advisory Board *see* REPORT 1975-1976

Zambia. Central Planning Office *see* AN OUTLINE OF THE TRANSITIONAL DEVELOPMENT PLAN

Zambia. Central Statistical Office *see* ZAMBIA

Zambia. Commission of Inquiry University of Zambia *see* REPORT

Zambia. Department of Technical Education and Vocational Training *see* ANNUAL REPORT ... 1974-1976

Zambia. Educational and Occupational Assessment Service *see* ANNUAL REPORT 1967-1980

THE ZAMBIA JOURNAL *see* THE NORTHERN RHODESIAN JOURNAL

Zambia. Ministry of Development. Planning and National Guidance *see* SECOND NATIONAL DEVELOPMENT PLAN 1972-1976

Zambia. Ministry of Education *see*
- ANNUAL REPORT 1964-1971
- EDUCATION FOR DEVELOPMENT
- EDUCATIONAL DEVELOPMENT IN THE SECOND NATIONAL DEVELOPMENT PLAN 1972-1976
- EDUCATIONAL REFORM
- SUMMARY OF CONTRIBUTIONS TO THE NATIONAL DEBATE ON EDUCATION REFORM

Zambia. Ministry of Education and Culture *see* ANNUAL REPORT 1972-1981

Zambia. Ministry of Education and Culture. Development and Planning Unit *see* EDUCATIONAL STATISTICS 1972-1984

Zambia. Ministry of Education. Curriculum Development Centre *see* CURRICULUM DEVELOPMENT IN ZAMBIA, THE SEARCH FOR RELEVANCE 1964-1974

Zambia. Ministry of Education. Development and Planning Unit *see* STATISTICAL PROFILE OF ZAMBIAN EDUCATION 1976-1978

Zambia. Ministry of Education. Psychological Service *see* ANNUAL REPORT 1975-1977/78

ZAMBIA NEWS *see* SUNDAY TIMES OF ZAMBIA

Zambia. Office of National Development and Planning *see* FIRST NATIONAL DEVELOPMENT PLAN, 1966-1970

Zambia. University. Institute for African Studies. Manpower Research Unit *see* STRUCTURE AND SOCIAL CONTEXT OF NON-FORMAL TRAINING IN LUSAKA

ZAMBIAN HANDBOOK OF PASTURE AND FODDER CROPS – 1979 2nd print 1984 – 148p – it F.A.O. [631]

Zambornitskii, N M *see* NAPOLEONOVSKAIA EPOKHA

Zambrano, Juan *see* CONSULTA CANONICA, ECLESIASTICA, REGULAR Y CEREMONIAL POR LOS CONVENTOS...

Zambrano Villalobos, Sebastian *see* TERTIUS ARTICULUS QUE...

ZAMECHANIIA K PROEKTU OBSHCHEGO KOOPERATIVNOGO ZAKONA / Izgoev, A S – (Soveshchanie po razsmotreniiu kooperativnogo zakona. No. 1. 7p) – Pg., n.d. – 1mf – 9 – COR-33/1 – ne IDC [334]

ZAMECHATEL'NYE BOGATSTVA CHASTNYKH LITS V ROSSII / Karnovich, E P – (Ekonomichesko-istoricheskoe issledovanie). Ed. 2. Spb. 1885. BR-6051 2 – 8 – ne IDC [330]

ZAMETKI O RUSSKOI ADVOKATURE / Arsenev, K K – St. Petersburg, 1875. 2v. BR-9733 1 – 9 – ne IDC [947]

ZAMETKI O RUSSKOM FUTURIZME / Saianov, V – Ocherki po istorii russkoi poezii XX veka. Krasnaia gazeta. L. 1929. BR-3581 2 – 8 – ne IDC [460]

Zamora, Alonso de *see* HISTORIA DE LA PROVINCIA DE SAN ANTONIO DEL NUEVO REINO DE GRANADA. CARACAS, 1930

Zamora, Hermenegildo *see*
- LA BIBLIA DE GUADALUPE. UN INTERESANTE CODICE DESCONOCIDO (1)
- UN OPUSCULO BIBLICO DEL TOSTADO DESCONOCIDO

Zamosc, D *see* PILEGESH BE-GIVAH

Zampach, Della *see* MITTERNACHTSWALZER

Zamudio de Alfaro, A *see* ORDEN PARA LA CURA Y PRESERVACION DE LAS SECAS Y CARBUNCOS...

Zanardini, G A M *see*
- ICONOGRAPHIA PHYCOLOGICA ADRIATICA
- SYNOPSIS ALGARUM

ZANBUR – Baku, 1909-1910 (?) – 5mf – 9 – $125.00 – us MEDOC [949]

Zancudo y Barrado, Antonio *see* SATISFACION HISTORICO-JURIDICA...ORDEN DE ALCANTARA

Zanden, C M van der *see* ETUDE SUR LE PURGATOIRE DE SAINT PATRICE

Zander, Alfred *see* GERMANIEN, HEILIG HERZ EUROPAS

Zander, Maximilian *see* POLYCYCLIC AROMATIC COMPOUNDS

Zander, Walter *see* POUR SORTIR DU CHAOS MONETAIRE

Zandstra, Sidney *see* THE WITNESS OF THE VULGATE, PESHITTA AND SEPTUAGINT TO THE TEXT OF ZEPHANIAH

ZANESVILLE AND MUSKINGHAM COUNTY / Lewis, T W – Chicago: S. J. Clarke, 1927. Vols. 1-3. Ohio Reel 52. (The Cox Library Collection) – 5 – us Americana [978]

Zanesville. Presbytery (Pres. Ch. in the U.S.A.) *see* MINUTES, 1844-83

Zanetti, A M *see* DELLA PITTURA VENEZIANA E DELLE OPERE PUBBLICHE DE' VENEZIANI MAESTRI

Zanger, Johann *see* PRACTICAE MUSICAE PRAECEPTA

Zangwill, Israel *see*
- DREAMERS OF THE GHETTO
- GHETTO TRAGEDIES
- THE KING OF THE SCHNORRERS

ZAN-I RUZ – (Missing issues: shurmarah-i 960, 971-972, 980, 984-985, 987, 992-1068, 1070, 1081, 1091, 1166, 1181, 1184, 1193-96, 1298, 1390, 1409, 1416-1419, 1439, 1454) – Tehran. Shumarah-i 959-1255 (20 Isfand 1362-28 Bahman 1368 [10 Mar. 1984-17 Feb. 1990]); 1206-1307 (25 Farvardin 1369-25 Isfand 1369 [14 Apr 1990-16 Mar 1991]); 1308-1354 (31 Farvardin 1370-24 Isfand 1370 [20 Apr 1991-14 Mar 1992]); 1355-1402 (29 Farvardin 1371-25 Isfand 1371 [18 Apr 1992-16 Mar 1993]); 1403-1502 (21 Farvardin 1372-27 Isfand 1373 [9 April 1993-17 March 1995]); 1503-1550 (26 Farvardin 1374-26 Isfand 1374 [14 April 1995-15 March 1996]) – $750.00 – us MEDOC [470]

ZAN-I RUZ – (Shumarah-'i 959-1255 (20 Isfand 1362-28 Bahman 1368[10 Mar. 1984-17 Feb. 1990]); 1206-1307 (25 Farvardin 1369-25 Isfand 1369[14 Apr 1990-16 Mar 1991]); 1308-1354 (31 Farvardin 1370-24 Isfand 1370[20 Apr 1991-14 Mar 1992]); 1355-1402 (29 Farvardin 1371-25 Isfand 1371[18 Apr 1992-16 Mar 1993]); 1403-1502 (21 Farvardin 1372-27 Isfand 1373[9 April 1993-17 March 1995]). Missing issues: shumarah-'i 960, 971-972, 980, 984-985, 987, 992-1068, 1070, 1081, 1091, 1166, 1181, 1184, 1193-96, 1298, 1390, 1409, 1416-1419, 1439, 1454. Newly filmed material only: $300.00. 1403-1502 (21 Farvardin 1372-27 Isfand 1373[9 April 1993-17 March 1995]). Missing issues: 1409, 1416-1419, 1439, 1454) – Tehran – $600.00 – us MEDOC [956]

ZAN-I RUZ – (Some issues missing) – Tehran. Shumarah-'i 959-1255 (20 Isfand 1362-28 Bahman 1368 [10 Mar. 1984-17 Feb. 1990]); 1206-1307 (25 Farvardin 1369-25 Isfand 1369 [14 April 1990-16 March 1991]); 1308-1354 (31 Farvardin 1370-24 Isfand 1370 [20 April 1991-14 March 1992]); 1355-1402 (29 Farvardin 1371-25 Isfand 1371 [18 Apr 1992-16 Mar 1993]) – 9 – $300.00 – us MEDOC [956]

Zannius, F *see* ODE QVAM SVPER DIVINA AC FOELICISSIMA VICTORIA EX CELEBERRIMA PUGNA AD SCOPULOS ECHINEOS NONIS OCTOB. MDLXXI

ZANOZA – Zhurnal filosofskii, politicheskii, ekonomicheskii, sotsial'nyi, uchenyi i literaturnyi. Spb. 1863-65. Lacking: 1864, v. 33-37. BR-4179 2 – 8 – ne IDC [100]

Zanutto, A *see* MANOSCRITTI ETIOPICA

Zanutto, Silvio *see* BIBLIOGRAFIA ETIOPICA

Zanzibar *see*
- DEVELOPMENT PLAN, 1960-64
- GOVERNMENT PUBLICATIONS
- THE OFFICIAL GAZETTE

Zanzibar and East Africa *see* THE GAZETTE FOR ZANZIBAR AND EAST AFRICA

ZANZIBAR VOICE – Zanzibar, Tanzania. -w. Jan 1941-Nov 1951; Jan 1958-Dec 1962. 1941, 1942, 1947 very imperfect. 9 reels – 1 – uk British Libr Newspaper [072]

ZAOTH-REVUE – Rotterdam. v1-4. 1932-33 – 3mf – 9 – J-261-121/1 – ne IDC [073]

ZAPADNAIA MONGOLIIA I URIANKHANSKII KRAI / Grum-Grzhimailo, G E – v. 1-3. Spb., L. 1914-30. Lacking: v. 2. BU-725 2 – 8 – ne IDC [950]

ZAPADNOE SREDNEVEKOV'E V RUKOPISIAKH GOSUDARSTVENNOI BIBLIOTEKI SSSR IM. V.I. LENINA / Zhitomirskaia, S V – Srednie veka, v. 10, 1957. BR-11,006 1 – 9 – ne IDC [025]

ZAPADNOE VLIIANIE NA RUSSKII IAZYK V PETROVSKUIU EKOPHU / Smirnov, N A – 2v. Spb. 1910. B-785 2 – 8 – ne IDC [400]

ZAPADNOE VLIIANIE V NOVOI RUSSKOI LITERATURE / Veselovskii, A N – Ed. 5. M. 1916. BR-7949 2 – 8 – ne IDC [460]

ZAPADNOEVROPEISKIE RUKOPISI, KHRANIASHCHIESIA V SSSR / Liublinskaia, A D – BR-10,780/1 – 9 – ne IDC [025]

ZAPADNYI FRONT (19 FEVRALIA 1919 G.-8 APRELIA 1924 G.). KRATKII OBZOR FONDA NO. 104 / U.S.S.R. Army – Comp. by A. A. Ezhov. M. 1939. TsARKKA. BR-11,081 1 – 9 – ne IDC [355]

Zapadov, A V *see*
- MASTERSTVO DERZHAVINA
- RUSSKAIA PROZA 18 VEKA

ZAPASY ZERNOVYKH KHLEBOV I KORMOV V SAMARSKOI GUBERNII NA... / Samarskoe gubernskoe statisticheskoe biuro – (Includes c.1: 1919:Jan) – Samara: [Biuro], 191u – 1 – CSUXAKZ2008-S – us Hoover Inst Photo [640]

Zapata, D *see* VERDADERA APOLOGIA EN DEFENSA DE LA MEDICINA RACIONAL PHILOSOPHICA...

LA ZAPATERA PRODIGIOSA / Garcia Lorca, Federico – MS DE 1924-1926 – 2mf – 9 – sp Cultura [830]

Zapatilla, Lupianejo (pseud. de Adolfo de Castro) *see* CARTAS...BARTOLO GALLAR..

Zapf, J N *see* VARIATIONS, 7, SUR L'AIR BEGLUECKT DURCH DICH POUR LE PIANOFORTE

Zapirain, Luis *see* TERROR SOBRE ESPANA

ZAPISKI / Akademiia Nauk. URSR. Kiev. Istorichna Sektsiia – v1-38. 1908-30 – 3r – 1 – us Ross [947]

ZAPISKI / Akademiia Nauk. URSR. Kiev. Istorichno-Filologichnii Viddil – v1-26. 1919-31 – 4r – 1 – us Ross [460]

ZAPISKI / Daskova, E R – S prilozheniem 4-kh portretov, raznykh dokumentov, pisem i ukazatelia. Spb. 1907. BR-6013 2 – 8 – ne IDC [947]

ZAPISKI / Institut Lenina. Moscow – no1-3 1927-1928 – 1 – us NY Public [947]

ZAPISKI / Institut V I Lenina. Moscow – v1-3. 1927-28 – 1r – 1 – us Ross [335]

ZAPISKI – Kiev: Institut Narodn'oi Osviti. v1-4. 1926-30 – 1r – 1 – us Ross [460]

ZAPISKI / Nashchokin, V A – Spb, 1842 – 8 – BR-7722 2 – ne IDC [460]

ZAPISKI / Poroshin, S A – Spb, 1844 – 8 – BR-7784 2 – ne IDC [460]

ZAPISKI / Russkoe Arkheologicheskoe Obshchestvo. Leningrad. Klassicheskoe Otdelenie – v1-9 1904-1917 – 1 – us NY Public [930]

ZAPISKI / Russkoe Arkheologicheskoe Obshchestvo. Leningrad. Vostochnoe Otdelenie – v1-25 1886-1921 – 1 – us NY Public [930]

ZAPISKI CHERNIGOVSKOGO GUBERNSKOGO STATISTICHESKOGO KOMITETA – (Missing: 1972 v3) – Chernigov. v1-3. 1866-1872 – 11mf – 9 – RET-30/1 – ne IDC [947]

ZAPISKI CHUDAKA. 1-2 / Belyi, A – M., Berlin. 1922. BR-609 2 – 8 – ne IDC [460]

ZAPISKI EMIGRANTA / Gurovich, I – Petrograd: "Petrograd", 1923 – 1 – CSUX88-B4620 – us Hoover Inst Photo [920]

ZAPISKI GENERALA-EVREIA / Grulev, Mikhail Vladimirovich – Parizh: Impr. "Pascal", 1930 – 1 – CSUX89-B6749 – us Hoover Inst Photo [350]

ZAPISKI GLAVNOUGOVARIVAI USHCHEGO 293 PEKHOTNOGO IZHORSKOGO POLKA / Gippius Andrei – Moskva: Gos. izd-vo, 1930 – 1 – CSUX89-B1003 – us Hoover Inst Photo [460]

ZAPISKI I TRUDY OBSHCHESTVA ISTORII I DREVNOSTEI ROSSIISKIKH, UCHREZHDENNAGO PRI IMPERATORSKOM MOSKOVSKOM UNIVERSITETE / Moscow. University – v. 1-2. M. 1815-24. Trudy i zapiski. v. 3. M. 1826. Trudy i letopisi. v. 4-8. M. 1827-37. B-1990 2 – 8 – ne IDC [370]

ZAPISKI IMPERATORSKAGO KAZANSKAGO EKONOMICHESKAGO OBSHCHESTVA – Kazan'. 1854-61. Pages missing in the original: 1855, v. 1. BR-8198 2 – 8 – ne IDC [330]

ZAPISKI IMPERATORSKAGO KHAR'KOVSKOGO UNIVERSITETA / Khar'kov. University – Kahr'kov. 1896-1915. Lacking: 1914 (3); 1915 (1-2). B-1398 2 – 8 – ne IDC [073]

ZAPISKI IMPERATORSKAGO NOVOROSSIISKAGO UNIVERSITETA / Novorossiiskago. University – v. 1-113. Odessa. 1867-1914. B-1992 2 – 8 – ne IDC [947]

ZAPISKI IMPERATORSKAGO RUSSKAGO ARKHEOLOGICHESKAGO OBSHCHESTVA – Novaia seriia. v. 1-12. Spb. 1886-1902. B-1253 2 – 8 – ne IDC [930]

ZAPISKI IMPERATORSKAGO RUSSKAGO GEOGRAFICHESKAGO OBSHCHESTVA – Spb. 1861-64. B-1993 2 – 8 – ne IDC [910]

ZAPISKI IMPERATORSKAGO RUSSKAGO GEOGRAFICHESKAGO OBSHCHESTVA PO OTDELENIIU STATISTIKI – v. 1-14. Spb. 1867-1915. Lacking: 1900 (8: 3), 1900 (9). B-1996 2 – 8 – ne IDC [910]

ZAPISKI IMPERATORSKOGO RUSSKOGO GEOGRAFICHESKOGO OBSHCHESTVA PO OTDELENIIU ETNOGRAFII – (Missing: v37(2); v40(2)) – Spb. v1-43. 1867-1916, 1925 – 468mf – 9 – ne IDC [947]

ZAPISKI ISTORIKO-FILOLOGICHESKOGO FAKUL' TETA IMPERATORSKOGO S.-PETERBURGSKOGO UNIVERSITETA / St. Petersburg. University. Faculty of Historical Philology – v. 1-133. Spb. 1876-1916. Lacking: 1907 (84), 1914 (119). B-1999 – 8 – ne IDC [400]

ZAPISKI IUGO-ZAPADNOGO OTDELA IMPERATORSKOGO RUSSKOGO GEOGRAFICHESKOGO OBSHCHESTVA – v. 1-2. Kiev. 1874-75. B-2000 2 – 8 – ne IDC [910]

ZAPISKI KNIZHKA KOOPERATORA NA... – M., 1914-15 – 9mf – 9 – COR-593/1 – ne IDC [334]

ZAPISKI L'VA NIKOLAIEVICHA ENGEL'GARDTA – 1766-1836. Izd. Russkago Arkhiva. M. 1867. BR-10,536 2 – 8 – ne IDC [025]

ZAPISKI MECHTATELEI – v. 1-6. Spb. 1919-22. BR-1947 2 – 8 – ne IDC [073]

ZAPISKI MOSKOVSKAGO ARKHEOLOGICHESKAGO INSTITUTA / Moscow. Archaeological Institute – Cont. as: Zapiski Imperatorskago Moskovskago arkheologicheskago instituta imeni Imperatora Nikolaia II. v. 1-41. M., Sergiev Posad. 1909-17. Lacking: v. 4: 2, 1909; v. 35-36, 1914; v. 40, 1915; v. 41, 1917; v. 13, 16, 19, 21-22, 33-34 not published. B-2002 2 – 8 – ne IDC [930]

ZAPISKI NAPISANNYE V 1771 GODU / Danilov, M V – M. 1842. BR-6130 2 – 8 – ne IDC [920]

ZAPISKI NAUCHNOGO OBSHCHESTVA MARKSISTOV – (Library has: Jan.-June 1922, Jan.-Apr. 1923) – Peterburg: Gos. izdvo, 1922-1928. 7v – 1 – CSUX89-S810 – us Hoover Inst Photo [335]

ZAPISKI NEOFILOLOGICHESKOGO OBSHCHESTVA PRI S.-PETERBURGSKOM UNIVERSITETE – (Missing: 1892 v1-2(3-4); 1894 v3(3-4); 1913 v7) – Spb. v1-8. 1892-1915 – 28mf – 9 – 2003/2 – ne IDC [947]

ZAPISKI NEOFILOLOGICHESKOGO OBSHCHESTVA PRI S.-PETERSBURGSKOM UNIVERSITETE – (Missing: 1892 v1-2(3-4); 1894 v3(3-4); 1913 v7) – Spb. v1-8. 1892-1915 – 28mf – 9 – ne IDC [947]

ZAPISKI NOVOROSSIISKAGO UNIVERSITETA / Novorossiiskago. University. Faculty of Historical Philology – Istorikofilologicheskogo Fakul'teta. v. 1-13. Odessa. 1909-16. B-2004 2 – 8 – ne IDC [370]

ZAPISKI O ZHIZNI I SLUZHBE A.I. BIBIKOVA – 1817. BR-5990 2 – 8 – ne IDC [920]

ZAPISKI OBSHCHESTVA ISTORII FILOLOGII I PRAVA PRI VARSHAVSKOM UNIVERSITETE / Warsaw. University – v. 1-7. Warsaw. 1902-14. Lacking: v. 4, 6. B-1445 2 – 8 – ne IDC [400]

ZAPISKI OTDELA RUKOPISEI GOSUDARSTVENNOI BIBLIOTEKI SSSR IMENI V.I. LENINA / Lenin Library – v1-36. M. 1938-75. PKG-E-3 BR-10,287 1 – 9 – ne IDC [010]

ZAPISKI OTDELENIIA RUSSKOI I SLAVIANSKOI ARKHEOLOGII IMPERATORSKOGO RUSSKOGO ARKHEOLOGICHESKOGO OBSHCHESTVA – v. 1-11, 13. Spb. 1851-1916. B-2006 2 – 8 – ne IDC [930]

ZAPISKI PARTIZANA / Akovenko, Vasillii Grigorevich – Moskva: Gos. izdvo, 1925 – 1 – CSUX88-B5877 – us Hoover Inst Photo [320]

ZAPISKI PISATELIA / Lundberg, E – Izdatel'stvo pisatelei v Leningrade. v. 1-2. L. 1930. BR-1385 2 – 8 – ne IDC [460]

ZAPISKI PO GIDROGRAFII / Russia. (1923-U.S.S.R.). Gidrograficheskoe Upravlenie – 43v. 1887-1939 – 1 – $161.00 – us L of C Photodup [910]

ZAPISKI S 1682 PO 2 IIULIA 1709 / Zheliabuzhskii, I A – Spb. 1840. BR-7986 2 – 8 – ne IDC [947]

ZAPISKI SIBIRSKAGO OTDELA IMPERATORSKAGO RUSSKAGO GEOGRAFICHESKAGO OBSHCHESTVA – Irkutsk. 1856-86. Lacking: v. 8, v. 11. B-2009 2 – 8 – ne IDC [910]

ZAPISKI VILENSKOI ARKHEOGRAFICHESKOI KOMISSII – Vil'na. v1. 1856 – 2mf – 9 – ne IDC [930]

ZAPISKI VOSTCHNO-SIBIRSKAGO OTDELA IMP. RUSSKAGO GEOGRAFICHESKAGO OBSHCHESTVA – Po Otdeleniiu etnografii. v. 1 (1-3), v. 2 (1-2), v. 3 (1). Irkutsk. 1889-96. B-2011 2 – 8 – ne IDC [910]

ZAPISKI VOSTOCHNOGO OTDELENIIA IMPERATORSKOGO RUSSKOGO ARKHEOLOGICHESKOGO OBSHCHESTVA – v. 1-24. Spb. 1886-1917. B-1267 2 – 8 – ne IDC [930]

ZAPISKI ZAPADNO-SIBIRSKOGO OTDELA IMPERATORSKOGO RUSSKOGO GEOGRAFICHESKOGO OBSHCHESTVA – v 1-38. Omsk. 1879-1927. Lacking: 1892 (13(2-3), 14), 1893 (15(2), 16(2)), 1895-97 (18-24), 1912 (36 (2-3)). B-2012 2 – 289mf – 8 – ne IDC [910]

ZAPISNAIA KNIGA KREPOSTNYM AKTAM 15-16 VV., IAVLENNYM V NOVGORODE D'IAKU D. ALIABEVU / ed by Lappo-Danilevskii, A S – St. Petersburg, 1898. 215, 56p.BR-11,136/1 – 9 – ne IDC [947]

ZAPISNYE KNIGI I BUMAGI STARINNYKH DVORTSOVYKH PRIKAZOV. DOKUMENTY 18-19 VV. BYVSHEGO ARKHIVA ORUZHEINOI PALATY / Uspenskii, A I – Moscow, 1906. 247p. BR-10,715/1 – 9 – ne IDC [010]

ZAPISY O SCHUZICH / Czechoslovakia. Narodni shromazdeni Poslanecka snemova – Praha. 26 Apr 1920-16 Dec 1938.7 reels – 1 – 23.00r – us L of C Photodup [943]

Zapletal, Vincenz *see* DER BIBLISCHE SAMSON

Zappella, Jeannine *see* LA CONSTRUCTION DE L'OPINION PUBLIQUE DANS LE SONDAGE DE LA QUESTION AU DISCOURS DE REFORMULATION

ZAPYSKY / Kiev. Universytet – Kiev. v. 1-4. 1926-1930 – 1 – us NY Public [370]

ZAPYSKY / Naukove Tovaristvo Imeni Shevchenka – L'vov. v. 1-152, no. 3, v. 153, no. 1-4, v. 154-155, 157-165, 167. 1892-1958 – 1 – us NY Public [400]

ZAPYSKY FIZYCHNO-MATEMATYCHNOHO = BULLETIN DE LA CLASSE DES SCIENCES PHYSIQUES ET MATHEMATIQUES – 1-5, 1923-31. Kyiv. 5v in 3 – 1 – us U.W. Library [500]

ZAPYSKY ISTORYCHNO-FILOLOHICHNOHO VIDDILU UKRAJINS'KOI AKADEMIJI NAUK / Akademiia Nauk. Kiev – v. 1-25. Kiev. 1919-29. BR-3458 2 – 8 – ne IDC [400]

ZAR – Pardubice, Czechoslovakia. 1954-Mar 1960 – 2r – 1 – us L of C Photodup [072]

Zaragoza, Justo *see* LAS INSURRECCIONES EN CUBA

Zarandona, Aguilar et al *see* INDICE DEL ARCHIVO PARROQUIAL DE ZACUALPAN DE AMILPAS

Zaraza, Lorenzo A *see* FIGURONES Y ESTAMPAS. CARACAS, 1937

ZARIA – (Library has holdings (incomplete) from between Feb. 23, 1929 and Jan. 20, 1937) – Kharbin: "Zaria", 1920- – 1 – CSUX86-S487 – us Hoover Inst Photo [072]

ZARIA – Sofia, Bulgaria. Sept 1942-1944 (scattered issues) – 3r – 1 – us L of C Photodup [949]

ZARJA – Lubljana, Yugoslavia, 1912, 1914 – 5mf or 1 reel – 9,1 – us I.H.R.C. [947]

Zarka, Ch. *see* ASPECTS DE L'HABITAT DANS LES CENTRES MINIERS DE LA REGION DE GAFSA

Zarlino, G *see*
- DE TUTTE L'OPERE DEL R. M. GIOSEFFO ZARLINO DA CHIOGGIA
- DIMONSTRATIONI HARMONICHE
- DIMOSTRATIONI HARMONICHE..
- ISTITUTIONI HARMONICHE

Zarncke, Friedrich *see* LITERARISCHES ZENTRALBLATT FUER DEUTSCHLAND 1850-1945

ZARNITSY – Literaturno-politicheskii sbornik. v. 2. Spb. 1909. BR-3529 2 – 8 – ne IDC [320]

[Zarphanalian, G] *see* HAYKAKAN MATENAGITUT'IWN

ZARRAH-ZARRAH FISIKA MODERN.. / Johannes, H – 1952. Jajasan Fonds Universitit Gadjah Meda. Summary in English. 27p. SEM-3474/1 – 9 – ne IDC [999]

Zart, Gustav *see* DAS MENSCHLICH ANZIEHENDE IN DER ERSCHEINUNG JESU CHRISTI

ZARUMA – (Filmed with other Hausa newspapers) – Zaria, Nigeria: Gaskiya Corp, feb-mar 13, apr 24-may 22, jun 19-jul 2, jul 31-aug 14, spe 25-oct 9, nov 6-20, dec 4-31 1958; jan 11-mar 22 1959 – 1r – 1 – us Res Libr [072]

Zarusky, Juergen *see* WIDERSTAND ALS "HOCHVERRAT" 1933-1945

ZARYA – Stuttgart. no. 1-4. Apr 1901-Aug 1902 – 1 – us NY Public [073]

ZARYA BOSTOKA – Tblish (Georgia), USSR. 1962-1981 – 20r – $1,000.00 – B63596 – us Library Micro [072]

ZARYA VOSTOKA – (Tbilisi). Georgia. U.S.S.R. 1955- – 1 – us UMI [073]

Zarza de Alange *see*
- FERIA Y FIESTAS DE 1945
- FIESTAS DE SEPTIEMBRE DE 1970
- FIESTAS LOCALES Y FERIA DEGANADOS... LOS DIAS 1,2,3 Y 4 DE MAYO DE 1981

ZARZEWIE – Warsaw, Poland. -w. May 1957-Dec 1969. 15 reels – 1 – uk British Libr Newspaper [947]

ZASADY REWOLUCJI SOCJALISTYCZNEJ W ROSJI / Bukharin, Nikolai Ivanovich – Warszawa: Wydawn. Zarz adu g ownego Socjaldemokracji Krolestwa Polskiego i Litwy, 1918 – 1 – CSUX88-B2683 – us Hoover Inst Photo [320]

ZASEDANIIA SOVETA FEDERATSII – Moscow: Federal'noe sobranie Rossiiskoi Federatsii, 1994- – 50mf – 9 – $279.00y – us East View [320]

ZASEDANIIA VERKHOVNOGO SOVETA LITOVSKOI SSR 1940-1989 : CONV. 1-11 SESSION 12. STENOGRAFICHESKII OTCHET – (Missing: 1940-1946; Conv. 4 session 2, 4; Conv. 5 session 1) – Vilnius, 1941-1989 – 190mf – 9 – ne IDC [947]

ZASEDANIIA VERKHOVNOGO SOVETA SSSR 1938-1968 : CONV. 1-7 SESSION 4 – (Missing: Conv. 4 session 5) – Stenograficheskii Otchet. M., 1938-1968 – 224mf – 9 – R-18504/1 – ne IDC [947]

ZASELENIE NOVOROSSI / Kabuzan, V M – Moskva, 1976 – 4mf – 9 – ne IDC [947]

ZASHCHISHCHAITE SVOBODU ROSSII / Gurevich, Boris – Petrograd: K-vo M.A. I Asnago, 1917 – 1 – CSUX89-B6589 – us Hoover Inst Photo [947]

ZASTAW W PRAWIE LITEWSKIEM 15 I 16 WIEKU / Adamus, John – Lwow, 1925. 141 p. LL-4205 – 1 – us L of C Photodup [340]

ZASTROZZI : A ROMANCE / Shelley, Percy Bysshe – London: Printed for G. Wilkie and J. Robinson, 1810 – 1 roll – 1 – 1-55879-281-3 – uk Libr Preservation [830]

DER ZAUBERLEHRLING, ODER, DIE TEUFELSJAEGER / Ewers, Hanns Heinz – Muenchen: Mueller, 1923 – 1r – 1 – us U.W. Library [430]

ZAUBERSPRUECHE FUER MUTTER UND KIND / Erman, A – Berlin, 1901. (Koenigl. Preuss. Akademie Wissenschaften Berlin, Abhandlung) – 9 – ne IDC [390]

"ZAUMNYI IAZYK" I POEZIIA. SBORNIKI PO TEORII POETICHESKOGO IAZYKA / Shklovskii, V – I. Petrograd. 1916. BR-3585 2 – 8 – ne IDC [460]

Zaunert, Paul *see* BUERGERS VERSKUNST

Zaunslifer, P *see* TAFEREEL VAN OVERDEFTIGE ZINNEBEELDEN

Zausmer, Otto *see* GRILLPARZERS LYRIK ALS AUSDRUCK SEINES WESENS

Zavala, Silvio *see* SERVIDUMBRE NATURAL Y LIBERTAD CRISTIANA SEGUN LOS TRATADISTAS ESPANOLES DE LOS SIGLOS 16 Y 17. BUENOS AIRES, 1944

Zavala y Aunon, Miguel de *see* REPRESENTACION... FELIPE V...AUMENTO...ERARIO

ZAVETY – Literaturno-politicheskii zhurnal. Spb. 1912-14. B-2014 2 – 8 – ne IDC [320]

ZAVIETY – Leningrad. apr 1912-jul 1914 – 1 – D2669 – us UMI [073]

ZAVTRA / ed by Prokhanov, A – Moscow: Gazeta soiuza pisatelei, 1991- – 1mf – 9 – $89.95y – us East View [320]

ZAVVA'AT RABBI YEHUDAH – (Ha-Maggid, Lyck, 5619). 1859. BJ-27-218 1 – 9 – ne IDC [956]

ZAVVAOT R. ELIEZER HA-GADOL – Amsterdam. 1649. BJ-43-143 1 – 9 – ne IDC [470]

Zaydan, Jirji *see* PENGANTIN FERGANA

ZAZ-TRAZ! : JORNAL POLITICO-HUMORISTICO – Queluz de Minas, 14 Out 1917 – 1,5,6 – bl Biblioteca [073]

ZBIORY POLSKIE, ARCHIWA, BIBLIOTEKI, GABINETY, GALERJE, MUZEA I INNE ZBIORY PAMIATEK PRZESZLOSCI W OJCZYZNIE I NA OBCZYZNIE / Chwalewik, E – 2v Warszawa 1926-27 BR-9824 1 – 9 – ne IDC [010]

ZBIRNYK / Naukove Tovaristvo Imeni Shevchenka. Fil'ol'ogichna Sektsiia – L'vov. 1899-1929. v. 2-22 – 1 – us NY Public [400]

ZBIRNYK / Naukove Tovaristvo Imeni Shevchenka. Fil'ol'ogichna Sektsiia – Lvov. v2-22. 1899-1929 – 2r – 1 – us Ross [460]

ZBIRNYK (POLTAVS' KYI DERZHAVNY I MUZEI IM. V.G. KOROLENKA) – Poltava (Ukraine): The Museum, 1927-. Published out of order – 1 – us U.W. Library [060]

ZDA ABSTRACTS *see* ZINC ABSTRACTS

ZDRAVEN FRONT – Sofia, Bulgaria. Dec 1952-1969 – 5r – 1 – us L of C Photodup [949]

Zdravomyslov, K Ia. *see* ARKHIV I BIBLIOTEKA SV. SINODA I KONSISTORSKIE ARKHIVY

Zdziechowski, Marian *see* SPLYWY ROSYJSKIE NA DUSZE POLSKA

Zech, Paul *see*
- ROTES HERZ DER ERDE
- STEFAN ZWEIG

ZECHARIAH : HIS VISIONS AND WARNINGS / Alexander, William – London: James Nisbet, 1885 – 1mf – 9 – 0-8370-2069-7 – 1985-0069 – us A.T.L.A. [220]

THE ZECHARIAH CHAFEE, JR. PAPERS / Chafee, Zechariah Jr. – (Guide only $100.00) – $8,940.00 – 0-89093-817-2 – us UPA [340]

ZEDE- EN ZINNEBEELDEN OVER KONING DAVIDS HARPZANGEN, NEVENS DAAR OP TOEGEPASTE ZIEL-ZUCHTEN : DICHTKUNDIG ZAMENGESTELT DOOR KORNELIS ZWEERTS, MET HONDERT EN VYFTIG PRINTVERBEELDINGEN VERSIERT / Sweerts, C – Twede druk. Amsterdam, [c1765] – 4mf – 9 – O-3174/1 – ne IDC [760]

ZEDE-EN ZINNEBEELDEN OVER KONING DAVIDS HARPGEZANGEN / Sweerts, C – O 471. 1725 – 9 – ne IDC [780]

ZEDEKUNST, DAT IS WELLEVENSKUNSTE, UITG. B. BECKER / Coornhert, D V – Leiden, 1942 – 10mf – 8 – ne Slangenburg [100]

ZEDELYCK VERMAECK-VELDT OFT SESDE DEEL VAN HET SEDELYCK-VERMAECK-TONEEL VERTHOONENDE DEN LEERSAEMEN HANDEL VAN DE ONREDELYCKE DIEREN AEN DE VERKEERDE, EN BEESTAERDIGE WERELT VAN VERSCHEYDEN SOO GRIECKSE, ALS LATYNSCHE SCHRYVERS TEN THOON GESTELT,... / Moons, J – (Titlepage missing) – Antwerpen, 1701 – 4mf – 9 – O-3135/1 – ne IDC [760]

ZEDELYK VERMAEK TONNEEL VERTOONENDE DOOR ZINNE-BEELDEN DEN LEERZAEMEN HANDEL... / Moons, J – Den tweeden druk. Antwerpen, [c1764] – 5mf – 9 – O-3136/1 – ne IDC [760]

ZEDELYK VERMAEK-VELD VERTOONENDE DEN LEERSAMEN HANDEL VAN DE ONREDELIJKE DIEREN : AEN DE VERKEERDE, EN BEESTAERDIGE WERELD VAN VERSCHEYDEN SOO GRIEKSE, ALS LATYNSCHE SCHRYVERS TEN TOON GESTELT, VERDUYTST IN VERMAKELIJKE POESIE,... / Moons, J – Tweeden druk. Antwerpen, [c1764] – 4mf – 9 – O-3137/1 – ne IDC [760]

DE ZEDELYKE EN STICHTELYKE GEZANGEN / Luiken, J – O 351. 1709 – 9 – ne IDC [760]

ZEDELYKE LUST-WARANDE VERTOONENDE DOOR ZINNE-BEELDEN DEN LEERZAEMEN HANDEL... / Moons, J – Antwerpen, [c1764] – 6mf – 9 – O-3134/1 – ne IDC [760]

Zederbaum, A *see*
- KOHELET
- MELIZ EHAD MINNI ALEF

ZEDERRYKE ZINNEBEELDEN / Verryke, E – O 819. 1717 – 9 – ne IDC [740]

ZEDERYKE ZINNEBEELDEN / Verryke, E – O 793. 1713 – 9 – ne IDC [740]

ZEDERYKE ZINNEBEELDEN DER TONGE, DOOR MATTHEUS BROUERIUS VAN NIEDEK / Brouerius van Niedek, M – Amsterdam, 1764 – 5mf – 9 – ne IDC [700]

ZEDERYKE ZINNEBEELDEN DER TONGE, DOOR MATTHEUS BROUERIUS VAN NIEDEK / Brouerius van Niedek, M – Amsterdam, 1786 – 6mf – 9 – ne IDC [700]

ZEDERYKE ZINNEBEELDEN, VERTOONT IN KONSTPLATEN... / Verryke, E – 1st ed. Amsterdam, 1712 – 3mf – 9 – ne IDC [700]

Zedler, Johann Heinrich *see* GROSSES VOLLSTAENDIGES UNIVERSAL-LEXIKON ALLER WISSENSCHAFTEN UND KUENSTE (AEL, ABT 1;32)

Zedner, J *see* CATALOGUE OF THE HEBREW BOOKS IN THE LIBRARY OF THE BRITISH MUSEUM

Zedtwitz, Franz Xaver, Graf *see*
- FELDMUENSTER
- DER UNTERGANG DES SONNENREICHES

ZEE-ATLAS OFTE WATER WAERELD / Doncker, Hendrick – (With 14p bklet) – 1987 – 4 color mf – 15 – A$100.00 – 0-642-10421-2 – at Nat'l Libr [550]

ZEEDELYKE GESCHIEDENISSE OF AANGENAAM WINTER-GROEN / Abraham a Sancta Clara – Amsterdam, 1782 – 7mf – 9 – ne IDC [700]

ZEEMANSGIDS VOOR DE OOST-INDISCHE ARCHIPEL ED. BY MINISTERIE VAN MARINE, AFD. HYDROGRAFIE – Ed 8. 's-Gravenhage, 1947-1949. 2v – 19mf – 9 – SE-91/1 – ne IDC [950]

Zeeus, J *see*
- GEDICHTEN; MET VEELE KOPERE KUNSTPLATEN VERSIERT
- GEDICHTEN VAN JACOB ZEEUS, MET VEELE KOPERE KUNSTPLATEN VERSIERT

ZEEUSCHE NACHTEGAEL, ENDE DES SELFS DRIEDERLEY GHESANG : GEHEEL ANDERS IN DER WAERHEYDT VERTHOONT ALS DE SELVE VOOR DESEN BY SOMMIGE UYT ENCKEL MISVERSTANT VERKEERDIELIJCK GHEOORDEELT – Amsterdam, 1633 – 4mf – 9 – O-3026/1 – ne IDC [760]

ZEEUSCHE NACHTEGAEL, ENDE DES SELFS DRYDERLEY GESANG – Rotterdam, 1632 (1633) – 8mf – 9 – ne IDC [700]

Zeeuwsch Genootschap der Wetenschappen. Middelburg *see*
- NIEUWE VERHANDELINGEN
- NIEUWE WERKEN VAN HET ZEEUWSCH GENOOTSCHAP DER WETENSCHAPPEN

Zeeuwsch genootschap der wetenschappen, Middelburg *see* VERHANDELINGEN UITG. DOOR HET ZEEUWSCH GENOOTSCHAP DER WETENSCHAPPEN TE VLISSINGEN

ZEGEPRAAL DER GODDELYKE LIEFDE, VERTOONT IN ZEVEN EN VEERTIG ZIEL OPWEKKENDE ZINNEBEELDEN : IN ZANGMAAT VERVAT OP GELYK GETAL, VAN DE UITGELEZENSTE EN BEKWAAMSTE WYZEN, ENZ. DE TWEEDE DRUK, MERKELYK VERMEERDERD EN VERBETERD / Hoogstraten, J van – Amsterdam, 1728 – 3mf – 9 – O-3088/1 – ne IDC [760]

ZEHEN PREDIG VON DEN SECHS HAUPTSTUCKEN CHRISTLICHER LEHR... / Andreae d.A E, J – Tuebingen, 1561 – 2mf – 9 – ne IDC [240]

ZEHENERLEY KURTZE FORM ZU PREDIGEN / Huberinus, Caspar – [Nuernberg: Johann Daubmann, 1552]. [G.F.: 22.1] – 7mf – 9 – HUB-86/1 – ne IDC [240]

ZEHN ACTENSTUECKE UEBER DIE AMTSENTSETZUNG DES PROFESSORS HOFFMANN VON FALLERSLEBEN – Mannheim: F Bassermann, 1843 – 1r – 1 – us U.W. Library [920]

ZEHN FRAGEN UEBER DIE WAHRHEIT DES CHRISTLICHEN GLAUBENS / Bertling, O – Leipzig: J.C. Hinrichs, 1899. 1 fiche – 9 – us A.T.L.A. [240]

ZEHNTAUSEND MANN DIE ZOGEN INS MANOEVER : EIN ERLEBNISBERICHT / Teske, Hermann – Potsdam: L Voggenreiter, 1936 – 1r – 1 – us U.W. Library [890]

ZEICHEN DER ZEIT – (Chicago). 1869 – 1 – us A.J.P.C. [073]

DAS ZEICHEN DES MENSCHENSOHNES UND DER DOPPELSINN DES JONAZEICHENS / Runze, Georg – (Includes bibliographical references) – Berlin: R Gaertners, 1897 – 1mf – 9 – 0-8370-4999-7 – 1985-2999 – us A.T.L.A. [220]

ZEICHNUNGEN AUS DER SCHOENEN BAUKUNST ODER DARSTELLUNG IDEALISCHER UND AUSGEFUEHRTEN GEBAEUDE... / Stieglitz, C L – Leipzig, 1805 – 9 – ne IDC [720]

Zeidler, Paul Gerhard *see* FRANCESCO CRISPI, DER ADVOKAT ITALIENS

Zeidtler, C G *see* HISTORIA DAVIDIS GEORGI EJUSQUE ASSECLARUM

Zeiller, C R *see* DESCRIPTION DE LA FLORE FOSSILE

Zeiller, Jacques *see* LES ORIGINES CHRETIENNES DANS LA PROVINCE ROMAINE DE DALMATIE

Zeise, Heinrich *see* AUS MEINER LIEDERMAPPE

Zeiss, Karl *see* HEBBELS WERKE

Zeissberg, H von *see* QUELLEN ZUR GESCHICHTE DER DEUTSCHEN KAISERPOLITIK OESTERREICHS WAEHREND DER FRANZOESISCHEN REVOLUTIONSKRIEGE 1790-1801

DI ZEIT – New York. v. 1-2 no. 365, 487-599. Aug 29 1920-Aug 31 1921; Jan 4-Apr 26 1922 – 1 – us NY Public [071]

DI ZEIT – Wilna. v. 1 no. 1-64. Feb 14-May 7 1906 – 1 – us NY Public [072]

DIE ZEIT – (1923-1925 4r DM280.00) – Berlin, 1902-1903 – 1r – 1 – DM90.00 – gw Mikro Press [072]

DIE ZEIT – (1961-1992.-32r) – Toronto, 1993 – 1r – 1 – cn Preston [971]

DIE ZEIT – (1972-84 66r DM4,620.00. 1985-94 72r DM5,400.00. 1995 subsc mit magazin 7r DM420.00. Ohne magazin 4r DM240.00) – Hamburg, 1946-1971 – 1 – DM2,450.00 – gw Mikro Press [072]

DIE ZEIT – Berlin, apr-jun 1922, mar 1925 – 2r – 1 – Inquire at Mikrofilmarchiv for details – gw Misc Inst [072]

DIE ZEIT – Berlin. sep 20, 1896-sep 30, 1897 – 2r – 1 – gw Mikrofilm [072]

DIE ZEIT – (Die Zeit Magazin also available, 1995-) – Hamburg, 1946- – 4r per y – 1 – inquire – us Ross [072]

DIE ZEIT – Hamburg, DE. 1975-1984 – 20r – $1,000.00 – R63612 – us Library Micro [072]

DIE ZEIT – Hamburg, West Germany. Wochenzeitung f. Politik, Wirtschaft, Handel u. Kultur. Feb. 21, 1946- – 1 – gw Mikrofilm [072]

DIE ZEIT – Liberec, Czechoslovakia. Nov 1938-Feb 1945 (scattered issues) – 8r – 1 – us L of C Photodup [072]

DIE ZEIT – New York, NY. 1920-22. The Times – 1 – us A.J.P.C. [071]

DIE ZEIT – Prague, Czechoslovakia. 1 Oct 1935; Jul 1937-Sept 1938 – 6r – 1 – us L of C Photodup [072]

DIE ZEIT – Prague, Czechoslovakia. -d. 22 Dec 1935-14 Sept 1938. 12 reels – 1 – uk British Libr Newspaper [072]

DIE ZEIT – Vienna, Austria. -d. 1 July 1915-6 Aug 1919. Imperfect. 24 reels – 1 – uk British Libr Newspaper [072]

DIE ZEIT – Vilna, Russia. 1906 – 1r – 1 – us Ross [072]

DIE ZEIT : WOCHENZEITUNG FUER POLITIK, WIRTSCHAFT, HANDEL UND KULTUR – Hamburg. feb 21, 1946-65. apr 12-sep 27, 1968. 1975-dec 21, 1979. 1982 – 1 – gw Mikrofilm [072]

ZEIT : WIENER WOCHENSCHRIFT FUER POLITIK... – Wien. v2-38. 1895-1904 – 342mf – 9 – H-584/2 – ne IDC [073]

DIE ZEIT (1901) – Berlin, Germany.2 Oct 1902-24 Sept 1903 – 1 – gw Mikrofilm [072]

DIE ZEIT ALS EINBILDUNGSKRAFT DES DICHTERS : UNTERSUCHUNGEN ZU GEDICHTEN VON BRENTANO, GOETHE UND KELLER / Staiger, Emil – (Includes bibliographical references) – Zuerich: Atlantis Verlag, 1963, c1953 – 1 – us U.W. Library [430]

DIE ZEIT ALS EINBILDUNGSKRAFT DES DICHTERS : UNTERSUCHUNGEN ZU GEDICHTEN VON BRENTANO, GOETHE UND KELLER / Staiger, Emil – (Includes bibliographical references) – Zuerich: M. Niehan, c1939 – 1 – us U.W. Library [430]

DIE ZEIT CONSTANTIN'S DES GROSSEN / Burckhardt, Jakob – Leipzig: E.A. Seemann, 1880 – 2mf – us A.T.L.A. [940]

DIE ZEIT DES IGNATIUS UND DIE CHRONOLOGIE DER ANTIOCHENISCHEN BISCHOEFE BIS TYRANNUS : NACH JULIUS AFRICANUS UND DEN SPAETEREN HISTORIKERN / Harnack, Adolf von – Leipzig: J.C. Hinrichs [i.e. Hinrichs], 1878 – 1mf – us A.T.L.A. [240]

ZEIT (DIE) MIT MAGAZINE – 1946-1995 – 8 times per yr – 1 – DM400.00 – sz Infoprint [072]

ZEIT GEIST – New York. v1-3. sep 1905-jul 1908* – 1 – D6249 – us UMI [073]

ZEIT (HAMBURG) – 1946-1995 – 4 times per yr – 1 – DM220.00 – sz Infoprint [072]

ZEIT IM BILD – Berlin, jan-jun 1909, jul-dec 1914 – 1 – Inquire at Mikrofilmarchiv for details – gw Misc Inst [072]

ZEIT- UND HANDBUECHLEIN FUER FREUNDE DER THEOLOGISCHEN LEKTUERE – Bayreuth, 1775-85, 1792 – 1r – 1 – Dist. gw Mikrofilm – gw Misc Inst [240]

ZEITBILDER ODER ERINNERUNGEN AN MEINE VEREWIGTEN WOHLTHAETER / Konrad, Martin – Mainz, 1879. 192p – DM150.00 – 3-89349-234-8 – gw Hänsel [240]

ZEIT-ECHO – Crailsheim, Germany. Aug 1946-1948 – 1 – gw Mikrofilm [072]

DER ZEIT-GEIST – New York, NY. 1905-08. The Spirit of the Times – 1 – us A.J.P.C. [073]

DER ZEIT-GEIST – New York. v1-3. 1905-08 – 2r – 1 – us Ross [071]

DER ZEITGEIST – Milwaukee. 1880-82 – 1 – us A.J.P.C. [073]

DER ZEITGEIST – Stuttgart, Germany. May 1908-14 – 1 – gw Mikrofilm [072]

DER ZEITGEIST – Stuttgart, May 1908-14 – 2r – 1 – DM240.00 – gw Mikro Press [072]

ZEITGEIST – New York. v. 1-3. Sept 1 1905-July 3 1908 – 1 – us NY Public [071]

DER ZEITGEIST: MONATLICHES BILDUNGSORGAN DES DEUTSCHEN METALLARBEITER-VERBANDES – v1-7. 1908-14. Stuttgart: A. Schlicke. -m. illus. (Serial publications of German trade unions in the Memorial Library, University of Wisconsin-Madison.) – 1 – us U.W. Library [331]

ZEITGEIST UND BERNERGEIST / Gotthelf, Jeremias; ed by Bloesch, Hans – (Includes bibliographical references) – Erlenbach, Zuerich: E Rentsch, 1926 – 1 – us U.W. Library [890]

DER ZEITGEIST UND DAS CHRISTENTHUM / Schweitzer, Jean Baptist von – Leipzig: Otto Wigand, 1861. 1 fiche – 9 – us A.T.L.A. [240]

ZEITGENOSSEN, LEIPZIG UND ALTENBURG 1816-1841 : BIOGRAPHIEN UND CHARAKTERISTIKEN 1816-1828. EIN BIOGRAPHISCHES MAGAZIN FUER DIE GESCHICHTE UNSERER ZEIT 1829-1841. VERLAG: F.A.BROCKHAUS – 1994 – 157mf (1:24) – 9 – diazo DM3,200.00 (Silver DM3,900.00. ISBN: 3-598-32291-7) – 3-598-32290-9 – gw Saur [943]

ZEITGLOSSEN DES GESUNDEN MENSCHENVERSTANDES / Holtzendorff, Franz von – Muenchen: Ackermann, 1884 – 1r – 1 – us U.W. Library [840]

ZEITIGES AND STREITIGES / Ruettenauer, Benno – Heidelberg: G. Weiss, 1895 – 1 – us U.W. Library [430]

Zeitler, Adolf *see*
- BUSINESS AND FAMILY PAPERS RE ACTIVITIES IN THE NEW HEBRIDES
- CORRESPONDENCE AND OTHER PAPERS RE BUSINESS AND FAMILY ACTIVITIES IN THE NEW HEBRIDES

ZEITLICHE UND BEGRIFFLICHE ABGRENZUNG DER SPAETGOTIK INNERHALB DER ARCHITEKTUR VON DEUTSCHLAND, FRANKREICH, UND ENGLAND / Hoeltje, Georg – Halle, 1930 – 2mf – DM62.00 – 3-8267-3052-6 – gw Hänsel [720]

Zeitlin, W *see* BIBLIOTHEKA HEBRAICA PO MENDELSSOHNIANA, BIBLIOGRAPHISCHES HANDBUCH DER NEU HEBRAEISCHEN LITTERATUR... BIS ZUM JAHRE 1890

DIE ZEITLUPE – Leipzig, Jan-Sep 1931 – 1r – 1 – gw Mikrofilm [072]

ZEIT-MAGAZIN – Hamburg, West Germany. 1973$. Suppl. to yDie Zeit, Hamburg – 1 – gw Mikrofilm [072]

ZEITMORPHOLOGISCHE VERGLEICH VON HERMANN HESSES "DEMINAN," "SIDDHARTA," "NARZISS UND GOLDMUND" ZUR AUGWEISUNG TYPISCHER GESTALTZUEGE / Wagner, Marianne – Bonn 1952 – 1 – DM30.00 – gw Mikro Press [430]

ZEITSCHRIFT / Freiburger Geschichtsverein – Freiburg i. B. Bd. 1-15; 1867-99. Film Mas C 381 – 1 – us H.U. Library [073]

ZEITSCHRIFT / Gewerkschaft der Angestellten – v1-10. 1923-32. -m. (Serial publications of German trade unions in the Memorial Library, University of Wisconsin-Madison.) – 1 – us U.W. Library [330]

ZEITSCHRIFT / Harz-Verein fuer Geschichte und Altertumskunde – Wernigerode. Jahrg. 6-15; 1873-82. Film Mas C 364 – 1 – us H.U. Library [073]

ZEITSCHRIFT / Historische Gesellschaft fuer die Provenz Posen – Jahrg. 1-30; 1885-1918. Includes Namen- und Sachregister zu Jahrg. 1-10 (1885-95). Film Mas C 698 – 1 – us H.U. Library [073]

ZEITSCHRIFT / Historischer Verein. Niedersachsen, Hannover – Hannover. 1850-64, 1899-1923. Film Mas C 416 – 1 – us H.U. Library [073]

ZEITSCHRIFT / Prussia. Statistisches Landesamt – v. 1-72. 1860-1934. Erganzungsheft. v. 1-37. 1868-1919. 17 Scattered issues wanting – 1 – 589.00 – us L of C Photodup [943]

ZEITSCHRIFT / Verein Deutscher Ingenieure. Berlin – (Also known as V.D.I. Berichte). v1-85 1856-1941 – 1,5,6 – us Princeton Micro [620]

ZEITSCHRIFT / Verein fuer Thueringische Geschichte und Altertumskunde – Jena. Bd. 1-19; 1852-99. Film Mas C 421 – 1 – us H.U. Library [073]

ZEITSCHRIFT / Westpreussischer Geschichtsverein – Heft 1-47; 1880-1904. Film Mas C 386 – 1 – us H.U. Library [073]

ZEITSCHRIFT [ALLGEMEINE] FUER ENTOMOLOGIE *see* WOCHENSCHRIFT [ILLUSTRIERTE] FUER ENTOMOLOGIE

ZEITSCHRIFT DER DEUTSCHEN MORGENLAENDISCHE GESELLSCHAFT – 1(1847)-19(1865) – 254mf – 9 – Dfl889.00 – ne Slangenburg [073]

ZEITSCHRIFT DER DEUTSCHEN MORGENLAENDISCHEN GESELLSCHAFT... – Leipzig. v1-95. 1847-1941 – 1250mf – 9 – H-219c/2 – ne IDC [073]

ZEITSCHRIFT DER INTERNATIONALEN MUSIK-GESELLSCHAFT – Leipzig. 1899/1900-1913/14. v1-14. p-625/1 – 108mf – 9 – ne IDC [780]

ZEITSCHRIFT DER KOMMUNISTISCHEN INTERNATIONALE *see* KOMMUNISMUS

ZEITSCHRIFT DER SAVIGNY-STIFTUNG FUER RECHTSGESCHICHTE : GERMANISTISCHE ABTEILUNG – Weimar. v1-55. 1880-1935 – 710mf – 9 – H-585/2 – ne IDC [340]

ZEITSCHRIFT DER SAVIGNY-STIFTUNG FUER RECHTSGESCHICHTE : KANONISTISCHE ABTEILUNG – Weimar. v32-55. 1911-35 – 240mf – 9 – H-586/2 – ne IDC [340]

ZEITSCHRIFT DER SAVIGNY-STIFTUNG FUER RECHTSGESCHICHTE : ROMANISTISCHE ABTEILUNG – Weimar. v1-55. 1880-1935 – 419mf – 9 – H-587/2+1 – ne IDC [340]

ZEITSCHRIFT DES BERG-UND HUETTENMAENNISCHEN VEREINES FUER KAERNTEN – Klagenfurt, Austria. -f. 1870-76. 3 reels – 1 – uk British Libr Newspaper [073]

ZEITSCHRIFT DES DEUTSCHEN PALAESTINA-VEREINS – Leipzig, 1878-1920 – 264mf – 9 – H-588/2 – ne IDC [073]

ZEITSCHRIFT DES DEUTSCHEN PALAESTINA-VEREINS – v1-67. 1978-45 (complete) – Inquire – 1 – ATLA 1994-S504 – us A.T.L.A. [073]

ZEITSCHRIFT DES DEUTSCHEN PALESTINA-VEREINS – 1(1878)-42(1919) – 256mf – 9 – Dfl896.00 – ne Slangenburg [073]

ZEITSCHRIFT DES FERDINANDEUMS FUER TIROL UND VORARLBERG – Innsbruck. Folge 3, Bd. 1-60; 1853-1920. Film Mas C 706 – 1 – us H.U. Library [073]

ZEITSCHRIFT DES K. SAECHSISCHEN STATISTISCHEN LANDESAMTES – v. 1-86. 1855-1940 – 1 – 314.00 – us L of C Photodup [943]

ZEITSCHRIFT DES LANDWIRTSCHAFTLICHEN CENTRALVEREINS DER PROVINZ SACHSEN – (Cont as: Landwirtschaftliche Wochenschrift fuer die Provinz Sachsen 1899) – Halle S., 1852-55; 1857-58; 1864-1911; 1913-19 – 16r – 1 – DM1,600.00 – gw Mikro Press [072]

ZEITSCHRIFT DES LANDWIRTSCHAFTLICHEN CENTRALVERIENS DER PROVINZ SACHSEN – Halle, Saale, Germany. Title change (1899): Landwirtschaftliche Wochenschrift fuer die Provinz Sachsen. 1852-55; 1857-58; 1864-1911; 1913-19 – 1 – gw Mikrofilm [630]

ZEITSCHRIFT DES VEREINES FUER HESSISCHE GESCHICHTE UND LANDESKUNDE / Verein fuer Hessische Geschichte und Landeskunde – Kassel. 1-8, 11-63; 1837-1952. Vol. 11-20 are numbered N.F., 1-10, and v. 21-62 also numbered N.F., 11-52. Some vols also have special titles. Includes Index, v. 1-45; also Supplement, Bd. 1-10 and N.F., 1-15; 1840-1906. Incomplete: N.F. BD. 14 lacking. Film Mas C 688 – 1 – us H.U. Library [073]

ZEITSCHRIFT DES VEREINS FUER GESCHICHTE SCHLESIENS – v1-6, 8-10, 16-18, 20-23, 26-28, 31-35, 37-41, 46-51, 53-54, 60-62, 65-66; 1855-1932. Annual – 1 – us U.W. Library [943]

ZEITSCHRIFT DES VEREINS FUER THUERINGISCHE GESCHICHTE UND ALTERTUMSKUNDE – Band 9. NF Band 1(1879)-Band 16. NF Band 8(1893) Jena – 9 – Dfl266.00 – ne Slangenburg [073]

ZEITSCHRIFT (DES VEREINS) FUER VOLKSKUNDE – Berlin. v1-38. 1891-1928. N.S. v1-11. 1929-40 – 484mf – 9 – H-589/2 – ne IDC [073]

ZEITSCHRIFT DES VEREINS FUER VOLKSKUNDE – v1-38. 1891-1928 – 1 – us I.U. Libraries [390]

ZEITSCHRIFT FUEHRUNG UND ORGANISATION : ZFO – (Cont: Zeitschrift fuer Organisation) – Baden-Baden. v51-63 1982-94*. v64-66 1995-97+ – 1 – D5719.01 – us UMI [650]

ZEITSCHRIFT FUEHRUNG UND ORGANISATION – ZFO *see* ZEITSCHRIFT FUER ORGANISATION

ZEITSCHRIFT FUER AEGYPTISCHEN SPRACHE UND ALTERTUMSKUNDE – Leipzig. v1-62. 1863-1927 – 268mf – 9 – 348/2 – ne IDC [470]

ZEITSCHRIFT FUER ANALYTISCHE CHEMIE – (Cont by: Fresenius' Zeitschrift fuer analytische Chemie) – Muenchen. v1-127 1862-1944* – 1 – D13168 – us UMI [540]

ZEITSCHRIFT FUER ANGEWANDTE MATHEMATIK UND MECHANIK – v1-35. 1921-55 – 1 – us Princeton Micro [510]

ZEITSCHRIFT FUER ANGEWANDTE MATHEMATIK UND MECHANIK – (v24 n3-4 were not available for filming) – Berlin. v1-24. 1921-44 – 1 – D1144 – us UMI [620]

ZEITSCHRIFT FUER ANGEWANDTE MATHEMATIK UND PHYSIK = JOURNAL OF APPLIED MATHEMATICS AND PHYSICS – JOURNAL DE MATHEMATIQUES ET DE PHYSIQUE APPLIQUEES – Basel. v1-40 1950-89*. v41-48 1990-97+ – 1 – D13947 – us UMI [620]

ZEITSCHRIFT FUER ANORANISCHE UND ALLGEMEINE CHEMIE – (Cum index for v1-200 1892-1931 available) – Hamburg. v1-252. 1892-nov 1944 – 1 – D1145 – us UMI [540]

ZEITSCHRIFT FUER ANORGANISCHE UND ALLGEMEINE CHEMIE – v1-278. 1893-1955 – 1,5,6 – us Princeton Micro [540]

ZEITSCHRIFT FUER ARBEITERFRAGEN – Berlin, 1871-76 – 1 – Inquire at Mikrofilmarchiv for details – gw Misc Inst [331]

ZEITSCHRIFT FUER ARMENISCHE PHILOLOGIE – Marburg. 2v. 1903-05 – 8mf – 9 – AR-407/1 – ne IDC [460]

ZEITSCHRIFT FUER ASCESE UND MYSTIK – (20(1947)-: Geist und Leben) – 1(1925)-19(1944) – 120mf – 9 – Dfl420.00 – ne Slangenburg [073]

ZEITSCHRIFT FUER ASSYRIOLOGIE UND VERWANDTE GEBIETE – 1(1886)-43 NF: 9(1936) – 299mf – 9 – Dfl1,047.00 – ne Slangenburg [073]

ZEITSCHRIFT FUER ASSYRIOLOGIE UND VERWANDTE GEBIETE – Leipzig, Berlin. v1-46. 1886-1940. Ergaenzungshefte. Berlin, Weimar. v1-21. 1894-1900 – 375mv – 9 – H-592c/2 – ne IDC [073]

ZEITSCHRIFT FUER ASTRONOMIE AND VERWANDTE WISSENSCHAFTEN – Tubingen etc., 1816-18 – 3 – us Readex [520]

ZEITSCHRIFT FUER ASTROPHYSIK – Berlin. vol. 1-30. 1930-52 – 1 – 140.00 – us L of C Photodup [520]

ZEITSCHRIFT FUER ASTROPHYSIK – v.1-69, 1930-68 – 1,5,9 – us UMI [520]

ZEITSCHRIFT FUER ASZESE UND MYSTIK – Innsbrueck. v1-19. 1925-1944 – 120mf – 9 – ne IDC [210]

ZEITSCHRIFT FUER AUSLAENDISCHES OEFFENTLICHES RECHT UND VOELKERRECHT – Berlin, Leipzig. v1-12. 1929-44 – 137mf – 9 – IL-10/1 – ne IDC [340]

ZEITSCHRIFT FUER BAUWESEN – (1875: only atlas) – Berlin, 1875, 1876 – 1 – Inquire at Mikrofilmarchiv for details – gw Misc Inst [690]

ZEITSCHRIFT FUER BAUWESEN – Berlin. v1-81. 1851-1931. Atlases and year indexes – 794mf – 9 – OA-302/1 – ne IDC [073]

ZEITSCHRIFT FUER BELEUCHTUNGSWESEN – Berlin, DE. 1901-05 – 2r – 1 – uk British Libr Newspaper [073]

ZEITSCHRIFT FUER BILDENDE KUNST – (Indices. Beiblatt "Kunstchronik"; Beiblatt "Der Kunstmarkt". Leipzig. v1-12. 1904-1915) – Leipzig. v1-24. 1866-89; N.S. v1-33. 1890-1922 – 938mf – 9 – O-527/1 – ne IDC [700]

ZEITSCHRIFT FUER BIOLOGIE – v74-116.1921-71. Ceased publ. Jan 1971 – 1,5,6 – us Princeton Micro [574]

ZEITSCHRIFT FUER BUDDHISMUS – Trier, etc. 1913-28. Lacking: 1915-19, 1927. H-593/2 – 8 – ne IDC [280]

ZEITSCHRIFT FUER BUDDHISMUS UND VERWANDTE GEBIETE – 1(1913/14)-9(1931) – 61mf – 98 – Dfl214.00 – ne Slangenburg [073]

ZEITSCHRIFT FUER BUERSTEN – Leipzig, DE. Oct 1906-Sep 1912 – 5 1/2r – 1 – uk British Libr Newspaper [072]

ZEITSCHRIFT FUER CALCIUMCARBID-FABRIKATION UND ACETYLEN-BELEUCHTUNG – Berlin. Carbid und Acetylen. -m. April 1897-March 1923 – 8r – 1 – uk British Libr Newspaper [680]

ZEITSCHRIFT FUER CELTISCHE PHILOLOGIE – Halle. v1-17. 1897-1928 – 158mf – 9 – H-603/2 – ne IDC [490]

ZEITSCHRIFT FUER CHEMIE – Erlangen. 1858-71 – 3 – us Readex [073]

ZEITSCHRIFT FUER CHRISTLICHE KUNST – Duesseldorf. v1-34. 1888-1921 – 232mf – 9 – H-594/2 – ne IDC [700]

ZEITSCHRIFT FUER COMPRIMIRTE UND FLUESSIGE GASE – Weimar, Germany. -m. Apr 1897-Dec 1908 – 2r – 1 – uk British Libr Newspaper [660]

ZEITSCHRIFT FUER DAS GESAMMTE BRAUWESEN – Munich, DE. 1895-99 – 4r – 1 – uk British Libr Newspaper [660]

ZEITSCHRIFT FUER DAS GESAMTE HANDELSRECHT UND WIRTSCHAFTSRECHT – v1- 1858- 1; v137- 5,6; v139- 9 – us UMI [073]

ZEITSCHRIFT FUER DEMOGRAPHIE UND STATISTIK DER JUDEN – Berlin, 1905-16, 1919-20, 1923-27, 1930-31 – 2r – 1 – Inquire at Mikrofilmarchiv for details – gw Misc Inst [310]

ZEITSCHRIFT FUER DEMOGRAPHIE UND STATISTIK DER JUDEN – Berlin. v1-17, n.s.v1-6, 1905-16, 1919-23, 1924-31. Complete. B404 (Leo Baeck Institute. German-Jewish Periodicals, Pt 2) – 2r – 1 – $130.00 – us UPA [310]

ZEITSCHRIFT FUER DEMOGRAPHIE UND STATISTIK DER JUDEN – (Missing: 1914. Nos. 6, 9-12) – Berlin, 1905-14, 1919 – 116mf – 9 – H-595/2 – ne IDC [304]

ZEITSCHRIFT FUER DEUTSCHE FORSCHUNG – Hrsg. von der Freien Deutschen Hochschule in Paris. Paris. Jul 1938-Mar 1939 – 1 – gw Mikrofilm [073]

ZEITSCHRIFT FUER (DEUTSCHE) KULTURGESCHICHTE... – Nuernberg, etc. v1-4. 1856-59; S2: v1-4. 1872-75; S3: v1-3. 1891-93; S4: v1-9. 1894-1902 – 223mf – 9 – H-596/2 – ne IDC [943]

ZEITSCHRIFT FUER DEUTSCHE PHILOLOGIE – Stuttgart. v1-64. 1869-1939 – 602mf – 9 – H-400c/2 – ne IDC [430]

ZEITSCHRIFT FUER DEUTSCHE PHILOLOGIE – v. 1-61. 1869-1936 – 1 – us Princeton Micro [430]

ZEITSCHRIFT FUER DEUTSCHE SPRACHE – Hamburg, Paderborn. v1-10. 1887-1896/1897 – 93mf – 9 – H-597/2 – ne IDC [430]

ZEITSCHRIFT FUER DEUTSCHES ALTERTUM UND DEUTSCHE LITERATUR / ed by Haupt, Moritz et al – (Bis Bd. 18: Zeitschrift fuer deutsches Altertum. Verbunden mit: Anzeiger fuer dt. Altertum und dt. Literatur (Rezensionen)) – Leipzig und Berlin. v1-81. 1841-1944 – 700mf – 9 – subsc: DM3,800.00 diazo DM4,600.00 silver – gw Olms [430]

ZEITSCHRIFT FUER DEUTSCHES ALTERTUM UND DEUTSCHE LITERATUR / ed by Haupt, Moritz et al – Leipzig. v1-76. 1841-1939 – 889mf – 9 – H-404c/2 – ne IDC [430]

ZEITSCHRIFT FUER DEUTSCHES ALTERTUM UND DEUTSCHE LITERATUR – (Includes: Anzeiger fuer Deutsches Altertum) – Leipzig, Berlin, DE. 1841-1944; 1948-50 – 24r – 1 – DM2,400.00 – gw Mikro Press [430]

ZEITSCHRIFT FUER DEUTSCHES ALTERTUM UND DEUTSCHE LITERATUR – Leipzig Berlin, Germany. 1841-1950 – 1 – gw Mikrofilm [430]

ZEITSCHRIFT FUER DIE ALTTESTAMENTLICHE WISSENSCHAFT – 1(1881)-41(1923) – 245mf – 9 – Dfl858.00 – ne Slangenburg [073]

ZEITSCHRIFT FUER DIE ALTTESTAMENTLICHE WISSENSCHAFT / ed by Stade, B – Giessen. v1-52. 1881-1934. Index – 287mf – 9 – H-132/2 – ne IDC [220]

ZEITSCHRIFT FUER DIE ALTTESTAMENTLICHE WISSENSCHAFT *see* EIN APPARATUS CRITICUS ZUR PESITTO ZUM PROPHETEN JESAIA

ZEITSCHRIFT FUER DIE ENTOMOLOGIE / ed by Germar, E F – Leipzig. v1-5. 1839-44 – 41mf – 9 – Z-1015/2 – ne IDC [590]

ZEITSCHRIFT FUER DIE ENTOMOLOGIE – Leipzig, 1839-44. v.1-6 – 3 – us Readex [590]

ZEITSCHRIFT FUER DIE GESAMMTE LUTHERISCHE THEOLOGIE UND KIRCHE – 1(1840)-39(1878) – 539mf – 9 – Dfl1,887.00 – ne Slangenburg [073]

ZEITSCHRIFT FUER DIE GESAMMTE LUTHERISCHE THEOLOGIE UND KIRCHE – Leipzig. v1-39. 1840-1878 – 539mf – 9 – ne IDC [240]

ZEITSCHRIFT FUER DIE GESAMMTE ORNITHOLOGIE – Budapest. v1-4. 1884-88 – 33mf – 9 – Z-2045/1 – ne IDC [590]

ZEITSCHRIFT FUER DIE GESAMTE STAATSWISSENSCHAFT – Tuebingen. v1-102. 1844-1942 – 1361mf – 9 – H-423c/3 – ne IDC [073]

ZEITSCHRIFT FUER DIE GESCHICHTE DER JUDEN IN DEUTSCHLAND – Berlin, 1929-38 – 1r – 1 – Inquire at Mikrofilmarchiv for details – gw Misc Inst [943]

ZEITSCHRIFT FUER DIE GESCHICHTE DER JUDEN IN DEUTSCHLAND – Berlin. v1-8. 1929-38. Complete. B407 (Leo Baeck Institute. German-Jewish Periodicals, Pt 2) – 1r – 1 – $75.00 – us UPA [270]

ZEITSCHRIFT FUER DIE GESCHICHTE DER JUDEN IN DEUTSCHLAND / ed by Geiger, Ludwig – Braunschweig, 1886-91. Hildesheim, 1992 – 25mf – 9 – DM200.00 diazo DM250.00 silver – gw Olms [073]

ZEITSCHRIFT FUER DIE HISTORISCHE THEOLOGIE – 1(1832)-45(1875) – 517mf – 9 – Dfl1,810.00 – ne Slangenburg [073]

ZEITSCHRIFT FUER DIE HISTORISCHE THEOLOGIE – Leipzig. v1-45. 1832-1875 – 517mf – 9 – ne IDC [240]

ZEITSCHRIFT FUER DIE RELIGIOESEN INTERESSEN DES JUDENTHUMS / ed by Frankel, Zacharias – Berlin. 1844-46. v1-3. J-23-62/1 – 16mf – 9 – ne IDC [270]

ZEITSCHRIFT FUER DIE WISSENSCHAFT DER SPRACHE – Berlin, Greifswald. v1-4(1). 1846-53 – 30mf – 9 – H-599/2 – ne IDC [073]

ZEITSCHRIFT FUER ELECKTROTECHNIK – Vienna, Austria. -f. 1893-97. 4 reels – 1 – uk British Libr Newspaper [073]

ZEITSCHRIFT FUER ELEKTRISCHE INFORMATIONS- UND ENERGIETECHNIK – Leipzig. v1-13 1971-jun 1983* – 1 – D13019 – us UMI [073]

ZEITSCHRIFT FUER ENTOMOLOGIE – (N.S. v7 has not been published. Missing: 1928. v16/3-4)) – Breslau. v1-15. 1847-61; N.S. v1-32. 1870-1907. S3: v1-17. 1908-35. Yearbook – 137mf – 9 – Z-1014/2 – ne IDC [590]

ZEITSCHRIFT FUER ETHNOLOGIE UND IHRE HUELFSWISSENSCHAFTEN ALS LEHRE VOM MENSCHEN IN SEINEN BEZIEHUNGEN ZUR NATUR UND ZUR GESCHICHTE – (Missing: v67(p. 129-end); v68-69) – Berlin. v1-70. 1869-1938 – 1386mf – 9 – H-600c/2 – ne IDC [073]

ZEITSCHRIFT FUER EXACTE PHILOSOPHIE IM SINNE DES NEUERN PHILOSOPHISCHEN REALISMUS, 1. 1861 – 20. 1896 / ed by Allihn, F H Th & Ziller, T – Leipzig. 20 Bde. 1861-96 (mf ed 1997) – 60mf – 9 – DM1,260.00 – 3-89131-158-3 – gw Fischer [100]

ZEITSCHRIFT FUER FRANZOESISCHE SPRACHE UND LITERATUR – (v1-65. Dfl80.00v; Suppl. 1-15. Dfl30.00ea; Gen. Index 1-50. Dfl30.00) – Leipzig. v1-65 with suppl. 1-15 and Gen. Index 1-50. 1879-1944 – 5,9 – Dfl5,680.00 – ne Swets [440]

ZEITSCHRIFT FUER FRANZOESISCHE SPRACHE UND LITTERATUR *see* ZEITSCHRIFT FUER NEUFRANZOESISCHE SPRACHE UND LITERATUR...

ZEITSCHRIFT FUER GEBURTSHILFE UND PERINATOLOGIE – v1- 1877- 1; v179- 5,6,9 – us UMI [073]

ZEITSCHRIFT FUER GEOPHYSIK – (Publication suspended 1944-52. The micro-edition incl the suppl: Geographische Berichte. Cont by: Journal of Geophysics – Zeitschrift fuer Geophysik) – Heidelberg. v1-39. 1924-73* – 1 – D13187 – us UMI [550]

ZEITSCHRIFT FUER GESCHICHTSWISSENSCHAFT – 1977-1983 – 189mf – 1 – DM1,077.30 – gw Mikro Press [900]

ZEITSCHRIFT FUER GEWERBE – Beuthen, Germany. -m. 1870-79. 2 1 2 reels – 1 – uk British Libr Newspaper [073]

ZEITSCHRIFT FUER GEWERBE-HYGIENE UND UNFALL-VERHUTUNG – Wien. Jahrg. 4-40. 1897-33 – 1 – us NY Public [073]

ZEITSCHRIFT FUER HYGIENE – (Cont by: Zeitschrift fuer Hygiene und Infektionskrankheiten) – Heidelberg. v1-10. 1886-91* – 1 – D13123 – us UMI [613]

ZEITSCHRIFT FUER HYGIENE *see* ZEITSCHRIFT FUER HYGIENE UND INFEKTIONSKRANKHEITEN

ZEITSCHRIFT FUER HYGIENE UND INFEKTIONSKRANKHEITEN – (Cont: Zeitschrift fuer Hygiene. Cont by: Zeitschrift fuer Hygiene und Infektionskrankheiten, medizinische Mikrobiologie, Immunologie und Virologie) – Heidelberg. v11-147. 1892-1961* – 1 – D13123.01 – us UMI [613]

ZEITSCHRIFT FUER HYGIENE UND INFEKTIONSKRANKHEITEN *see*
- ZEITSCHRIFT FUER HYGIENE
- ZEITSCHRIFT FUER HYGIENE UND INFEKTIONSKRANKHEITEN, MEDIZINISCHE MIKROBIOLOGIE, IMMUNOLOGIE UND VIROLOGIE

ZEITSCHRIFT FUER HYGIENE UND INFEKTIONSKRANKHEITEN, MEDIZINISCHE MIKROBIOLOGIE, IMMUNOLOGIE UND VIROLOGIE – (Cont: Zeitschrift fuer Hygiene und Infektionskrankheiten. Cont by: Zeitschrift fuer medizinische Mikrobiologie und Immunologie) – Heidelberg. v148-151. oct 1961-dec 1965* – 1 – D13123.02 – us UMI [613]

ZEITSCHRIFT FUER HYGIENE UND INFEKTIONSKRANKHEITEN, MEDIZINISCHE MIKROBIOLOGIE, IMMUNOLOGIE UND VIROLOGIE *see*
- ZEITSCHRIFT FUER HYGIENE UND INFEKTIONSKRANKHEITEN
- ZEITSCHRIFT FUER MEDIZINISCHE MIKROBIOLOGIE UND IMMUNOLOGIE

ZEITSCHRIFT FUER IMMUNITAETS FORSCHUNG IMMUNOBIOLOGY – v1-118. 1909-59 – 1,5,6 – us Princeton Micro [073]

ZEITSCHRIFT FUER INDOLOGIE UND IRANISTIK / ed by Deutsche Morgenlaendische Gesellschaft – Leipzig. 1922-35/36. v1-10 H-601/2 – 60mf – 8 – ne IDC [073]

ZEITSCHRIFT FUER INDUKTIVE ABSTAMMUNGS- UND VERERBUNGSLEHRE – (Publication suspended 1944-47. Cont by: Zeitschrift fuer Vererbungslehre) – Heidelberg. v1-88. 1908-57* – 1 – D13207 – us UMI [572]

ZEITSCHRIFT FUER INDUKTIVE ABSTAMMUNGS- UND VERERBUNGSLEHRE *see* ZEITSCHRIFT FUER VERERBUNGSLEHRE

ZEITSCHRIFT FUER INSTRUMENTENBAU : CENTRALORGAN FUER DIE INTERESSEN DER FABRIKATION VON MUSIKINSTRUMENTEN UND DES HANDELS... / ed by Wit, P de – (Missing: 1915/1916, v36(32-33, p. 333-354); 1916/1917, v37(16, p. 161-176; 31, p. 317-332)) – Leipzig. v1-37. 1881-1916/1917 – 344mf – 9 – P-942/1 – ne IDC [690]

ZEITSCHRIFT FUER INTERNATIONALES PRIVAT- UND STRAFRECHT (T. NIEMEYER) / ed by Boehm, F – (Title varies. Widely known as Niemeyer's Zeitschrift) – Erlangen, Leipzig. v1-28. 1891-1920 – 200mf – 9 – H-1071/1 – ne IDC [340]

ZEITSCHRIFT FUER KATHOLISCHE THEOLOGIE – 1(1877)-68(1944) – 845mf – 9 – Dfl2,958.00 – ne Slangenburg [073]

ZEITSCHRIFT FUER KATHOLISCHE THEOLOGIE – Innsbrueck. v1-68. 1877-1944 – 845mf – 9 – ne IDC [240]

ZEITSCHRIFT FUER KEILSCHRIFTFORSCHUNG UND VERWANDTE GEBIETE – 1(1884)-2(1885) – 14mf – 9 – Dfl49.00 – ne Slangenburg [073]

ZEITSCHRIFT FUER KEILSCHRIFTFORSCHUNG UND VERWANDTE GEBIETE – Leipzig, 1884-85 – 15mf – 9 – H-602/2 – ne IDC [073]

ZEITSCHRIFT FUER KINDERHEILKUNDE – (Publication suspended sep 1944-jun 1947. Cont by: European Journal of Pediatrics) – Heidelberg. v1-120 1910-75* 1; v84-120 1960-75* 5; v65-120 1947-75 9 – 1,5,9 – D13113 – us UMI [618]

ZEITSCHRIFT FUER KIRCHENGESCHICHTE – 1(1877)-85(1974) – 844mf – 9 – Dfl2,954.00 – ne Slangenburg [073]

ZEITSCHRIFT FUER KIRCHENGESCHICHTE – Gotha, Tuebingen. v1-85. 1877-1974 – 844mf – 9 – ne IDC [240]

ZEITSCHRIFT FUER KIRCHLICHE WISSENSCHAFT UND KIRCHLICHES LEBEN – 1(1880)-10(1889) – 118mf – 9 – Dfl413.00 – ne Slangenburg [073]

ZEITSCHRIFT FUER KIRCHLICHE WISSENSCHAFT UND KIRCHLICHES LEBEN – Leipzig. Jahrg. 1-10; 1880-1889. No more published. Film Mas C 288 – 1 – us H.U. Library [073]

ZEITSCHRIFT FUER KOLONIALPOLITIK, KOLONIALRECHT UND KOLONIALWIRTSCHAFT – Berlin. Beitrage zur Kolonialpolitik und Kolonialwirtschaft. 1899-1911 (complete) – 1 – 35.00r – us Hoover Inst Photo [323]

ZEITSCHRIFT FUER KREBSFORSCHUNG – (Cont by: Zeitschrift fuer Krebsforschung und klinische Onkologie – Cancer Research and Clinical Oncology) – Heidelberg. v1-75. 1903-71* – 1 – D13119 – us UMI [616]

ZEITSCHRIFT FUER KREBSFORSCHUNG *see* ZEITSCHRIFT FUER KREBSFORSCHUNG UND KLINISCHE ONKOLOGIE

ZEITSCHRIFT FUER KREBSFORSCHUNG UND KLINISCHE ONKOLOGIE = CANCER RESEARCH AND CLINICAL ONCOLOGY – (Cont: Zeitschrift fuer Krebsforschung. Cont by: Journal of Cancer Research and Clinical Oncology) – Heidelberg. v76-92. 1971-78* – 1 – D13119.01 – us UMI [616]

ZEITSCHRIFT FUER KREBSFORSCHUNG UND KLINISCHE ONKOLOGIE – CANCER RESEARCH AND CLINICAL ONCOLOGY *see* ZEITSCHRIFT FUER KREBSFORSCHUNG

ZEITSCHRIFT FUER KRISTALLOGRAPHIE – Frankfurt. v56-61. jan 1921-jul 1925 – 1 – D1146 – us UMI [540]

ZEITSCHRIFT FUER KRISTALLOGRAPHIE, KRISTALLOGEOMETRIE, KRISTALLPHYSIK, KRISTALLCHEMIE – v. 1-102. 1877-1940 – 1,5,6 – us Princeton Micro [540]

ZEITSCHRIFT FUER LAERMBEKAEMPFUNG – v.8-28, 1961-81. ISSN:0022-8249 – 1,5,6,9,13 – 57.00v – us UMI [360]

ZEITSCHRIFT FUER LARYNGOLOGIE, RHINOLOGIE, OTOLOGIE UND IHRE GRENZGEBIETE – (Cont by: Laryngologie, Rhinologie, Otologie und ihre Grenzgebiete) – Stuttgart. 1948-73* – 1 – D10475 – us UMI [617]

ZEITSCHRIFT FUER LEBENSMITTELUNTERSUCHUNG UND -FORSCHUNG – v109-135 1962-1968 – 1,5,6 – us Princeton Micro [660]

ZEITSCHRIFT FUER LEBENSMITTELUNTERSUCHUNG UND -FROSCHUNG – v. 88-171. 1948-80 – 1,5,9 – 13,419.00 – us UMI [073]

ZEITSCHRIFT FUER MALAKOZOOLOGIE – Hannover. 10v. 1844-53 – 31mf – 9 – 2805/2 – ne IDC [590]

ZEITSCHRIFT FUER MATHEMATIK UND PHYSIK, 1. 1856 – 64. 1917 : MIT: LITERATURZEITUNG DER ZEITSCHRIFT FUER MATHEMATIK UND PHYSIK, 1. 1856 – 19. 1874; HISTORISCH-LITERARISCHE ABTEILUNG DER ZEITSCHRIFT FUER MATHEMATIK UND PHYSIK, 20. 1875 – 45. 1900; SUPPL / ed by Schloemilch, O et al – 1856-1917 (mf ed 1996) – 387mf – 9 – DM2,590.00 – 3-89131-229-6 – gw Fischer [510]

ZEITSCHRIFT FUER MATHEMATIK UND PHYSIK MIT LITERATURZEITUNG DER ZEITSCHRIFT FUER MATHEMATIK UND PHYSIK / ed by Schloemilch, Oskar & Witzschel, B – Leipzig. 64v. 1856-1917 – 469mf – 9 – subsc: DM2,600.00 diazo DM3,500.00 silver – gw Olms [073]

ZEITSCHRIFT FUER MEDIZINISCHE MIKROBIOLOGIE UND IMMUNOLOGIE – (Cont: Zeitschrift fuer Hygiene und Infektionskrankheiten, medizinische Mikrobiologie, Immunologie und Virologie. Cont by: Medical Microbiology and Immunology) – Heidelberg. v152-156. 1966-71* – 1 – D13123.03 – us UMI [613]

ZEITSCHRIFT FUER MEDIZINISCHE MIKROBIOLOGIE UND IMMUNOLOGIE *see* ZEITSCHRIFT FUER HYGIENE UND INFEKTIONSKRANKHEITEN, MEDIZINISCHE MIKROBIOLOGIE, IMMUNOLOGIE UND VIROLOGIE

ZEITSCHRIFT FUER MENSCHLICHE VEREBUNGS- UND KONSTITUTIONSLEHRE – v.29-37, 1949-64 – 1,5,9 – us UMI [573]

ZEITSCHRIFT FUER METALLKUNDE – (Publication suspended sep 1944-jun 1946. Former title: Internationale Zeitschrift fuer Metallographie 1911-18) – Leipzig. v1-39. 1911-48 – 1 – D293 – us UMI [660]

ZEITSCHRIFT FUER METALLKUNDE – v1-35. 1911-1943 – 1,5,6 – us Princeton Micro [660]

ZEITSCHRIFT FUER MISSIONSKUNDE UND RELIGIONSWISSENSCHAFT – v1-54. 1886-1939 (complete) – 7r – 1 – ATLA S0029 – us A.T.L.A. [073]

ZEITSCHRIFT FUER MISSIONSWISSENSCHAFT – 1(1911)-27(1937) – 170mf – 9 – Dfl595.00 – ne Slangenburg [073]

ZEITSCHRIFT FUER MISSIONSWISSENSCHAFT – Muenster. v1-27. 1911-1937 – 170mf – 9 – ne IDC [240]

ZEITSCHRIFT FUER MISSIONSWISSENSCHAFT – v1-17. 1911-27 (complete) – Inquire – 1 – ATLA 1993-S524 – us A.T.L.A. [073]

ZEITSCHRIFT FUER MISSIONSWISSENSCHAFT – v26-27. 1936-37 (complete) – Inquire – 1 – ATLA 1993-S526 – us A.T.L.A. [073]

ZEITSCHRIFT FUER MISSIONSWISSENSCHAFT UND RELIGIONSWISSENSCHAFT – v18-25. 1928-35 (complete) – Inquire – 1 – ATLA 1993-S525 – us A.T.L.A. [073]

ZEITSCHRIFT FUER MISSIONSWISSENSCHAFT UND RELIGIONSWISSENSCHAFT – v34-75. 1950-91 (complete) – Inquire – 1 – ATLA 1993-S528 – us A.T.L.A. [073]

ZEITSCHRIFT FUER MORPHOLOGIE DER TIERE – (Cont: Zeitschrift fuer Morphologie und Oekologie der Tiere. Cont by: Zoomorphologie) – Heidelberg. v61-81. nov 1967-nov 1975* – 1 – D13251.01 – us UMI [590]

ZEITSCHRIFT FUER MORPHOLOGIE DER TIERE *see*
- ZEITSCHRIFT FUER MORPHOLOGIE UND OEKOLOGIE DER TIERE
- ZOOMORPHOLOGIE

ZEITSCHRIFT FUER MORPHOLOGIE UND OEKOLOGIE DER TIERE – (Publication suspended aug 1944-may 1952. Cont by: Zeitschrift fuer Morphologie der Tiere) – Heidelberg. v1-60. apr 1924-sep 1967* – 1 – D13251 – us UMI [590]

ZEITSCHRIFT FUER MORPHOLOGIE UND OEKOLOGIE DER TIERE *see* ZEITSCHRIFT FUER MORPHOLOGIE DER TIERE

ZEITSCHRIFT FUER MUSIKWISSENSCHAFT / ed by Die Deutsche Musikgesellschaft – Leipzig. v1-15. 1918-33 – 254mf – 9 – H-605/1 – ne IDC [780]

ZEITSCHRIFT FUER MUSIKWISSENSCHAFT – Leipzig. 1918-35. Lacking: v.2, title pages; other – 1 – 113.00 – us L of C Photodup [780]

ZEITSCHRIFT FUER MUSIKWISSENSCHAFT – Leipzig: Deutsche Gesellschaft fuer Musikwissenschaft. v1-17. 1918-35 – 5r – 1 – us Ross [780]

ZEITSCHRIFT FUER MUSIKWISSENSCHAFT – Leipzig. v. 1-17. Oct 1918-1935 – 1 – us NY Public [780]

ZEITSCHRIFT FUER NATIONALOEKONOMIE – (Publication suspended 1945-apr 1948. Cont by: Journal of Economics) – Wien. v1-45. 1930-85* – 1 – D13285 – us UMI [330]

ZEITSCHRIFT FUER NATIONALOEKONOMIE/ JOURNAL OF ECONOMICS – v.12-41, 1948-81. ISSN:00044-3158 – 1,5,6,9,13 – 151.00v – us UMI [330]

ZEITSCHRIFT FUER NEUFRANZOESISCHE SPRACHE UND LITERATUR... – (Cont. as: Zeitschrift fuer franzoesische Sprache und Litteratur. Oppeln, Leipzig, 1889-1909. v11-35) – Oppeln, Leipzig. v1-10. 1879-88 – 390mf – 9 – H-606/2 – ne IDC [440]

ZEITSCHRIFT FUER NEUROLOGIE = JOURNAL OF NEUROLOGY – (Cont: Deutsche Zeitschrift fuer Nervenheilkunde. Cont by: Journal of Neurology) – Heidelberg. v198-206. 1970-74 – 9 – D13121.01 – us UMI [611]

ZEITSCHRIFT FUER NEUTESTAMENTLICHE WISSENSCHAFT – 1(1900)-41(1942) – 241mf – 9 – Dfl2,375.00 – ne Slangenburg [073]

ZEITSCHRIFT FUER NEUTESTAMENTLICHE WISSENSCHAFT UND DIE KUNDE DES URCHRISTENTUMS – Giessen. v1-24. 1900-25 – 147mf – 9 – H-232/2 – ne IDC [220]

ZEITSCHRIFT FUER NUMISMATIK – Berlin, 1874-1935 – 230mf – 9 – subsc: DM1,500.00 diazo DM1,800.00 silver – gw Olms [730]

ZEITSCHRIFT FUER NUMISMATIK – Berlin. v1-42. 1874-1932 – 333mf – 9 – H-607/2 – ne IDC [730]

ZEITSCHRIFT FUER OEFFENTLICHE WIRTSCHAFT – Berlin. v1-11 no 9-10 1934. Sep, Oct 1944 – 3r – 1 – DM300.00 – gw Mikro Press [073]

ZEITSCHRIFT FUER OEFFENTLICHE WIRTSCHAFT – (Suppl: 1936, 1937-44) – Berlin, DE. 1934-44 – 1 – gw Mikrofilm [073]

ZEITSCHRIFT FUER OEFFENTLICHE WIRTSCHAFT – (Suppl available: 1936 n4-12, 1937-44) – Berlin, 1934-44 – 1 – Inquire at Mikrofilmarchiv for details – gw Misc Inst [336]

ZEITSCHRIFT FUER OEFFENTLICHES RECHT – Wien. v5-23. 1926-42* – 1 – D13272 – us UMI [340]

ZEITSCHRIFT FUER ORGANISATION – (Cont by: Zeitschrift Fuehrung und Organisation – ZFO) – Berlin. v1-38 1951-69*. v39-50 1970-81 1; v41-42 1972-73. v43-46 1974-77*. v47-50 1978-81 5; v43-50 1974-81 9 – 1,5,9 – D5719 – us UMI [650]

ZEITSCHRIFT FUER ORGANISATION *see* ZEITSCHRIFT FUEHRUNG UND ORGANISATION

ZEITSCHRIFT FUER ORTHOPAEDIE – v1- 1891- 1; v111- 5,6; v113- 9 – us UMI [073]

ZEITSCHRIFT FUER ORTHOPAEDIE UND IHRE GRENZGEBIETE – Stuttgart. v1-129 1891-1991*. v130-135 1992-97+ – 1 – D10142 – us UMI [617]

ZEITSCHRIFT FUER OSTERREICHISCHE VOLKSKUNDE – v1-24. 1895-1918 – 1 – us I.U. Libraries [390]

ZEITSCHRIFT FUER OSTEUROPAEISCHE GESCHICHTE – Berlin. v1-5. 1911-31 – 59mf – 9 – R-5726/2 – ne IDC [947]

ZEITSCHRIFT FUER OSTEUROPAEISCHES RECHT *see* OSTRECHT

ZEITSCHRIFT FUER OSTRECHT *see* OSTRECHT

ZEITSCHRIFT FUER PARASITENKUNDE – Jena. 4v. 1869-75 – 17mf – 9 – 8592/1 – ne IDC [630]

ZEITSCHRIFT FUER PARASITENKUNDE – v. 14-63. 1949-80 – 1,5,9 – 6150.00 – us UMI [073]

ZEITSCHRIFT FUER PFLANZENERNAEHRUNG UND BODENKUNDE = JOURNAL OF PLANT NUTRITION AND SOIL SCIENCE – 1922-49, 1958-96 – 1,5,6,13 – us V.C.H. [580]

ZEITSCHRIFT FUER PFLANZENKRANKHEITEN – Stuttgart. v1-30. 1891-1920 – 356mf – 9 – 7370/2 – ne IDC [630]

ZEITSCHRIFT FUER PFLANZENZUECHTUNG – Berlin. v1-7. 1913-20 – 40mf – 9 – 7452/1 – ne IDC [631]

ZEITSCHRIFT FUER PHYSIK – (Publication suspended 1945-46. Split into: Zeitschrift fuer Physik. A, Atoms and Nuclei; Zeitschrift fuer Physik. B, Condensed Matter and Quanta; and: zeitschrift fuer Physik. C, Particles and Fields) – Heidelberg. v1-73 1920-31*. v74-116 1932-40. v117-271 1941-74* – 1 – D13246 – us UMI [530]

ZEITSCHRIFT FUER PHYSIK – v. 1-123. 1920-1944 – 1,5,6 – us Princeton Micro [530]

ZEITSCHRIFT FUER PHYSIK *see*
- ZEITSCHRIFT FUER PHYSIK. A
- ZEITSCHRIFT FUER PHYSIK. B
- ZEITSCHRIFT FUER PHYSIK. C

ZEITSCHRIFT FUER PHYSIK A – v. 1-298. 1920-80 – 1,5,9 – 29,502.00 – us UMI [073]

ZEITSCHRIFT FUER PHYSIK. A : ATOMIC NUCLEI – (Cont in part: Zeitschrift fuer Physik. A, Atoms and Nuclei. Cont by: Zeitschrift fuer Physik. A, Hadrons and Nuclei) – Berlin. v323-325 1986*. v326-331 1987-88. v332-334 1989*. v335-337 1990 1,9; v323-325 1986*. v326-328 1987. v329-337 1988-90* 5 – 1,5,9 – D17030 – us UMI [530]

ZEITSCHRIFT FUER PHYSIK. A : ATOMS AND NUCLEI – (With: Zeitschrift fuer Physik. B, Condensed Matter and Quanta; and: Zeitschrift fuer Physik. C, Particles and Fields; supersedes: Zeitschrift fuer Physik; and cont its numbering. Split into: Zeitschrift fuer Physik. A, Atomic Nuclei; and: Zeitschrift fuer Physik. D, Atoms, Molecules, and Clusters) – Berlin. v272-298. 1975-80* 1; v299-308 1981-nov 1982. v309-313 dec 1982-oct 1983*. v314-322 nov 1983-dec 1985 1,5,9 – 1,5,9 – D13246.01 – us UMI [530]

ZEITSCHRIFT FUER PHYSIK. A : HADRONS AND NUCLEI – (Cont: Zeitschrift fuer Physik. A, Atomic Nuclei) – Berlin. v338-349 1991-sep 1994*. v350-358 1995-97+ – 1,5,9 – D17030.01 – us UMI [530]

ZEITSCHRIFT FUER PHYSIK. A – ATOMIC NUCLEI *see* ZEITSCHRIFT FUER PHYSIK. A

ZEITSCHRIFT FUER PHYSIK. A -ATOMIC NUCLEI *see* ZEITSCHRIFT FUER PHYSIK. A

ZEITSCHRIFT FUER PHYSIK. A – ATOMS AND NUCLEI *see* ZEITSCHRIFT FUER PHYSIK. D

ZEITSCHRIFT FUER PHYSIK. A, ATOMS AND NUCLEI *see*
- ZEITSCHRIFT FUER PHYSIK
- ZEITSCHRIFT FUER PHYSIK. A

ZEITSCHRIFT FUER PHYSIK. A, HADRONS AND NUCLEI *see* ZEITSCHRIFT FUER PHYSIK. A

ZEITSCHRIFT FUER PHYSIK B – v. 1-39. 1962-80 – 1,5,9 – 3861.00 – us UMI [073]

ZEITSCHRIFT FUER PHYSIK. B : CONDENSED MATTER – (Cont: Zeitschrift fuer Physik. B, Condensed Matter and Quanta) – Heidelberg. v38-76 1980-sep 1989. v77-81 oct 1989-nov 1990*. v82-85 1991. v86-97 1992-94*. v98-109 1995-97+ 1,9; v38-76 1980-sep 1989. v77-97 1991-94*. v98-109 1995-97+ 5 – 1,5,9 – D13247.03 – us UMI [530]

ZEITSCHRIFT FUER PHYSIK. B : CONDENSED MATTER AND QUANTA – (Cont: Physics of Condensed Matter; while assuming the numbering and part of the content of: Zeitschrift fuer Physik. Cont by: Zeitschrift fuer Physik. B, Condensed Matter) – Heidelberg. v20-37. 1975-80* – 1 – D13247.02 – us UMI [530]

ZEITSCHRIFT FUER PHYSIK. B – CONDENSED MATTER *see* ZEITSCHRIFT FUER PHYSIK. B

ZEITSCHRIFT FUER PHYSIK. B – CONDENSED MATTER AND QUANTA *see*
- ZEITSCHRIFT FUER PHYSIK. A
- ZEITSCHRIFT FUER PHYSIK. B

ZEITSCHRIFT FUER PHYSIK. B, CONDENSED MATTER AND QUANTA *see* ZEITSCHRIFT FUER PHYSIK

ZEITSCHRIFT FUER PHYSIK. C : PARTICLES AND FIELDS – (Cont in pt: Zeitschrift fuer Physik) – Heidelberg. v1-6. 1979-80* 1; v7-40 dec 1980-sep 1988. v41-64 oct 1988-dec 1994*. v65-76 1995-97+ 1,5,9; v30-37. feb 1986-mar 1988* 5 – 1,5,9 – D13248 – us UMI [530]

ZEITSCHRIFT FUER PHYSIK. C – PARTICLES AND FIELDS *see* ZEITSCHRIFT FUER PHYSIK. A

ZEITSCHRIFT FUER PHYSIK. C, PARTICLES AND FIELDS *see* ZEITSCHRIFT FUER PHYSIK

ZEITSCHRIFT FUER PHYSIK. D : ATOMS, MOLECULES AND CLUSTERS – (Cont in pt: Zeitschrift fuer Physik. A, Atoms and Nuclei) – Berlin. v1-3 jan-oct 1986. v4-10 oct 1986-dec 1988*. v11-24 jan 1989-nov 1992. v29-45 1994-97+ 1,9; v1-17 1986-90*. v18-24 1991-nov 1992. v29-32 jan 1994-jan 1995*. v33-45 feb 1995-dec 1997+ 5 – 1,5,9 – D17031 – us UMI [530]

ZEITSCHRIFT FUER PHYSIK. D -ATOMS, MOLECULES, AND CLUSTERS *see* ZEITSCHRIFT FUER PHYSIK. A

ZEITSCHRIFT FUER PHYSIK UND MATHEMATIK – bd.1-bd.10. 1826-32 – 3 – us Readex [510]

ZEITSCHRIFT FUER PHYSIKALISCHE CHEMIE : ABT. A – Leipzig. v1-192 1887-1943 – 1 – D1148 – us UMI [540]

ZEITSCHRIFT FUER PHYSIKALISCHE CHEMIE : ABT. B – Leipzig, Berlin. v1-53. sep 1928-jul 1943 – 1 – D2732 – us UMI [540]

ZEITSCHRIFT FUER PHYSIKALISCHE CHEMIE – S.A. Leipzig. v147-186. 1930-40 – 358mf – 9 – 222c/2 – ne IDC [540]

ZEITSCHRIFT FUER PHYSIKALISCHE CHEMIE, ABTEILUNG A – v. 1-191. 1887-1942 – 1,5,6 – us Princeton Micro [540]

ZEITSCHRIFT FUER PHYSIKALISCHE CHEMIE, ABTEILUNG B – v. 1-53. 1928-1943 – 1,5,6 – us Princeton Micro [540]

ZEITSCHRIFT FUER PRAKTISCHE ANAESTHESIE UND WIEDERBELEBUNG *see* ZEITSCHRIFT FUER PRAKTISCHE ANAESTHESIE, WIEDERBELEBUNG UND INTENSIVTHERAPIE

ZEITSCHRIFT FUER PRAKTISCHE ANAESTHESIE, WIEDERBELEBUNG UND INTENSIVTHERAPIE – (Cont by: Praktische Anaesthesie, Wiederbelebung und Intensivtherapie. Former title: Zeitschrift fuer praktische Anaesthesie und Wiederbelebung 1966-71) – Stuttgart. v1-8 1966-73* – 1 – D10169 – us UMI [617]

ZEITSCHRIFT FUER PRAKTISCHE BAUKUNST – (Missing: Some plates of 1843, 1844, 1845, 1876) – Leipzig, Berlin. v1-41. 1841-81. Year Indexes – 239mf – 9 – OA-301/1 – ne IDC [720]

ZEITSCHRIFT FUER PRAKTISCHE GEOLOGIE MIT BESONDERER BERUECKSICHTIGUNG DER LAGERSTAETTENKUNDE – Berlin, Halle. v1-39. 1893-1931 – 591mf – 9 – 2519/2 – ne IDC [550]

ZEITSCHRIFT FUER PSYCHOANALYTISCHE PAEDAGOGIK – Herausgeber P. Federn, Anna Freud, H. Meng, E. Schneider, A.S. Storfer. 1926 27-1937 (t. I-XI) – 1 – fr A.C.R.P.P. [073]

ZEITSCHRIFT FUER RASSENKUNDE UND DIE GESAMTE FORSCHUNG AM MENSCHEN – Stuttgart, 1940-1941 – 1r – 1 – DM75.00 – gw Mikro Press [572]

ZEITSCHRIFT FUER RECHTSGESCHICHTE – Weimar. v1-13. 1861-78 – 118mf – 9 – H-608/2 – ne IDC [340]

ZEITSCHRIFT FUER RECHTSMEDIZIN = JOURNAL OF LEGAL MEDICINE – (Cont: Deutsche Zeitschrift fuer die gesamte gerichtliche Medizin. Cont by: International Journal of Legal Medicine) – Heidelberg. v67-103 1970-nov 1990* – 1 – D13249.01 – us UMI [614]

ZEITSCHRIFT FUER RECHTSMEDIZIN – v. 39-85. 1948-80 – 1,5,9 – 4688.00 – us UMI [073]

ZEITSCHRIFT FUER RELIGIONSPSYCHOLOGIE – v1-11. 1928-38 (complete) – Inquire – 1 – ATLA 1994-S507 – us A.T.L.A. [073]

ZEITSCHRIFT FUER ROMANISCHE PHILOLOGIE – 1905-. v28b never publ. Publ. suspended 1942-51 – 1 – us U.W. Library [440]

ZEITSCHRIFT FUER ROMANISCHE PHILOLOGIE – Tuebingen. v1-60. 1877-1940 – 778mf – 9 – 939c/2 – ne IDC [450]

ZEITSCHRIFT FUER SAEUGETIERKUNDE – Berlin. v7-8. 1932-33 – 19mf – 9 – 2396/2 – ne IDC [590]

ZEITSCHRIFT FUER SCHWEIZERISCHE KIRCHENGESCHICHTE – 58(1964) – 7mf – 9 – Dfl28.00 – ne Slangenburg [073]

ZEITSCHRIFT FUER SCHWEIZERISCHE KIRCHENGESCHICHTE – Stans. v1-36. 1907-42 – 219mf – 9 – H-402c/2 – ne IDC [240]

ZEITSCHRIFT FUER SEMITISTIK UND VERWANDTE GEBIETE / ed by Deutsche Morgenlaendische Gesellschaft – Leipzig. v1-10. 1922-35 – 58mf – 9 – H-609/2 – ne IDC [073]

ZEITSCHRIFT FUER SEMITISTIK UND VERWANDTE GEBIETE – v1-10. 1922-35 (complete) – Inquire – 1 – ATLA 1994-S502 – us A.T.L.A. [073]

ZEITSCHRIFT FUER SEXUALWISSENSCHAFT – Internationale Zentralblatt fuer die Biologie, Psychologie, Pathologie und Soziologie des Sexuallebens. Bonn. juil 1914-sept 931 (t. I-XVIII) – 1 – fr A.C.R.P.P. [073]

ZEITSCHRIFT FUER SEXUALWISSENSCHAFT, 1908 (HQ 27) / ed by Hirschfeld, Magnus – 1908 (mf ed 1997) – 9mf – 9 – DM150.00 – 3-89131-139-7 – gw Fischer [305]

ZEITSCHRIFT FUER SEXUALWISSENSCHAFT (HQ 8) / ed by Eulenberg, A & Bloch, I – Bonn, Berlin, Koeln. 1(1914)-18(1932) (mf ed 1992) – 96mf – 9 – DM780.00 – 3-89131-062-5 – gw Fischer [073]

ZEITSCHRIFT FUER SOZIALFORSCHUNG / ed by Institut fuer Sozialforschung – Leipzig, etc. v1-8(2). 1932-39 – 74mf – 9 – H-610/2 – ne IDC [073]

ZEITSCHRIFT FUER SOZIALFORSCHUNG – Paris, France. Title change 1939: Studies in Philosophy and Social Science. New York. Sept 1933-Mar 1941 – 1 – gw Mikrofilm [073]

ZEITSCHRIFT FUER SOZIALISMUS – Monatsschrift fuer die Probleme des Sozialismus.Karlsbad (Karlovy Vary), Czechoslovakia.Former title (Oct 1933-nr.1): Sozialistische Revolution. Oct 1933-Sept 1936 – 1 – gw Mikrofilm [073]

ZEITSCHRIFT FUER SOZIOLOGIE – (v. 4-1975- 5,6,9) – v. 1- 1972- – 1 – us UMI [073]

ZEITSCHRIFT FUER SPEKULATIVE PHYSIK – Jena and Leipzig. 1800-01 – 3 – us Readex [530]

ZEITSCHRIFT FUER SYSTEMATISCHE THEOLOGIE – v1-24. 1923-55 (complete) – Inquire – 1 – ATLA 1994-S509 – us A.T.L.A. [073]

ZEITSCHRIFT FUER TECHNISCHE PHYSIK – (Leipzig). (All published.) v. 1-24. 1920-1943 – 1,5,6 – us Princeton Micro [530]

ZEITSCHRIFT FUER THEOLOGIE UND KIRCHE – (1939-1949 nicht erschienen) – Alte Folge: 1(1891)-27(1917). Neue Folge: 1(1920)-19(1938) – 408mf – 9 – Dfl80.00 – ne Slangenburg [073]

ZEITSCHRIFT FUER THEOLOGIE UND KIRCHE – Tuebingen. v1-27. 1891-1917; S2 v1-19. 1920-1938 – 408mf – 9 – ne IDC [240]

ZEITSCHRIFT FUER TROPENMEDIZIN UND PARASITOLOGIE – (Cont by: Tropenmedizin und Parasitologie) – Stuttgart. v1-24 1949-73* – 1 – D10176 – us UMI [614]

ZEITSCHRIFT FUER VATERLAENDISCHE GESCHICHTE UND ALTERTUMSKUNDE – Muenster. Bd. 25-83; 1865-1925. Includes Historisch-geographisches Register, Bd. 1-50, 51-75. Film Mas C 409 – 1 – us H.U. Library [073]

ZEITSCHRIFT FUER VERBRAUCHERPOLITIK = JOURNAL OF CONSUMER POLICY – (Cont by: Journal of Consumer Policy) – Neuwied. v1-4 1977-81* – 1 – D14756 – us UMI [360]

ZEITSCHRIFT FUER VERERBUNGSLEHRE – (Cont: Zeitschrift fuer induktive Abstammungs- und Vererbungslehre. Cont by: Molecular and General Genetics) – Heidelberg. v89-98 1958-66* – 1 – D13207.01 – us UMI [575]

ZEITSCHRIFT FUER VERERBUNGS-LEHRE *see* ZEITSCHRIFT FUER INDUKTIVE ABSTAMMUNGS- UND VERERBUNGSLEHRE

ZEITSCHRIFT FUER VERGLEICHENDE ERDKUNDE – Magdeburg, 1842-50. v. 1-10 – 3 – us Readex [550]

ZEITSCHRIFT FUER VERGLEICHENDE LITTERATURGESCHICHTE UND RENAISSANCE LITTERATUR – Berlin. v1-18. 1887-1910 – 100mf – 9 – H-1401/1 – ne IDC [410]

ZEITSCHRIFT FUER VERGLEICHENDE PHYSIOLOGIE – (Suspended jun 1944-jul 1948. Cont by: Journal of Comparative Physiology) – Heidelberg. v1-76. 1924-72* 1; v20 1934. v21-25 1935-38*. v26-30 1938-44. v31-76 1948-72* 9 – 1,9 – D13120 – us UMI [570]

ZEITSCHRIFT FUER VERGLEICHENDE RECHTWISSENSCHAFT – (v. 75- 1975- 5,6,9) – v. 1- 1878- – 1 – us UMI [073]

ZEITSCHRIFT FUER VERGLEICHENDE SPRACHFORSCHUNG AUF DEM GEBIETE DER INDO-GERMANISCHEN SPRACHEN *see* ZEITSCHRIFT FUER VERGLEICHENDE SPRACHFORSCHUNG AUF DEM GEBIETE DES DEUTSCHEN, GRIECHISCHEN UND LATEINISCHEN

ZEITSCHRIFT FUER VERGLEICHENDE SPRACHFORSCHUNG AUF DEM GEBIETE DES DEUTSCHEN, GRIECHISCHEN UND LATEINISCHEN – (Cont. as: Zeitschrift fuer vergleichende Sprachforschung auf dem Gebiete der Indo-Germanischen Sprachen. 1877-1920. Berlin, etc., 1877-1920. v23-49) – Berlin, etc. v1-22. 1852-74 – 476mf – 9 – H-612/2 – ne IDC [410]

ZEITSCHRIFT FUER VERSICHERUNGSWESEN – Berlin, Germany. -w. 8 Nov 1916-18 Dec 1918. 1 reel – 1 – uk British Libr Newspaper [073]

ZEITSCHRIFT FUER VOELKERPSYCHOLOGIE UND SPRACHWISSENSCHAFT – Berlin etc. F. Duemmler. 1.-20. Bd.; 1860-90. Film Mas C 667 – 1 – us H.U. Library [150]

ZEITSCHRIFT FUER VOELKERRECHT UND BUNDESSTAATSRECHT / ed by Koehler, J – Breslau. v1-14. 1906-28 – 120mf – 9 – H-1077/1 – ne IDC [340]

ZEITSCHRIFT FUER VOLKSKUNDE – Hrsg. von Edmund Veckenstedt. Leipzig. Bd. 1-4; 1882-92. Film Mas 9356 – 1 – us H.U. Library [073]

ZEITSCHRIFT FUER VOLKSKUNDE – v39-48, 50-56. 1929-39, 1953-60 – 1 – us I.U. Libraries [390]

ZEITSCHRIFT FUER WAHRSCHEINLICHKEIT-STHEORIE UND VERWANDTE GEBIETE – (Cont by: Probability Theory and Related Fields) – Berlin. v1-70 apr 1962-oct 1985 1; v41-55 1977-apr 1981*. v56-61 apr 1981-dec 1982. v62-70 1983-85* 5; v26-33 1973-75. v41-61 1977-82. v62-64 jan-oct 1983*. v65-70 nov 1983-oct 1985 9 – 1,5,9 – D13250 – us UMI [510]

ZEITSCHRIFT FUER WISSENSCHAFTLICHE GEOGRAPHIE – Lahr etc. Bd. 1-8; 1880-91. Film Mas C 586 – 1 – us H.U. Library [910]

ZEITSCHRIFT FUER WISSENSCHAFTLICHE GEOGRAPHIE – Lahr, etc. v1-8. 1880-91 – 54mf – 9 – H-613/2 – ne IDC [900]

ZEITSCHRIFT FUER WISSENSCHAFTLICHE PHOTOGRAPHIE, PHOTOPHYSIK UND PHOTOCHEMIE – v. 12-38. 1913-1939 – 1,5,6 – us Princeton Micro [770]

ZEITSCHRIFT FUER WISSENSCHAFTLICHE THEOLOGIE – 1(1858)-55(1914) – 525mf – 9 – Dfl1,838.00 – ne Slangenburg [073]

ZEITSCHRIFT FUER WISSENSCHAFTLICHE THEOLOGIE / ed by Hilgenfeld, A – Jena. v1-55. 1858-1914 – 543mf – 9 – H-233/2 – ne IDC [240]

ZEITSCHRIFT FUER ZELLEN- UND GEWEBELEHRE – (Cont by: Zeitschrift fuer Zellforschung und mikroskopische Anatomie) – Heidelberg. v1. 1924* – 1 – D13110 – us UMI [574]

ZEITSCHRIFT FUER ZELLEN- UND GEWEBELEHRE *see* ZEITSCHRIFT FUER ZELLFORSCHUNG UND MIKROSKOPISCHE ANATOMIE

ZEITSCHRIFT FUER ZELLFORSCHUNG UND MIKROSKOPISCHE ANATOMIE : ABTEILUNG HISTOCHEMIE – (Cont by: Histochemie. Histochemistry. Histochimie) – Heidelberg. v1-3 mar 1958-mar 1964* – 1 – D13175 – us UMI [574]

ZEITSCHRIFT FUER ZELLFORSCHUNG UND MIKROSKOPISCHE ANATOMIE = CELL AND TISSUE RESEARCH – (Cont: Zeitschrift fuer Zellforschung und mikroskopische Anatomie. Cont by: Cell and Tissue Research) – Heidelberg. v125-147 1972-73* – 1 – D13110.02 – us UMI [574]

ZEITSCHRIFT FUER ZELLFORSCHUNG UND MIKROSKOPISCHE ANATOMIE – (Publication suspended apr 1945-dec 1947. Cont: Zeitschrift fuer Zellen- und Gewebelehre. Cont by: Zeitschrift fuer Zellforschung und mikroskopische Anatomie. Cell and tissue research) – Heidelberg. v2-124 1925-72* – 1 – D13110.01 – us UMI [574]

ZEITSCHRIFT FUER ZELLFORSCHUNG UND MIKROSKOPISCHE ANATOMIE *see*
- ZEITSCHRIFT FUER ZELLEN- UND GEWEBELEHRE
- ZEITSCHRIFT FUER ZELLFORSCHUNG UND MIKROSKOPISCHE ANATOMIE

ZEITSCHRIFT FUER ZELLFORSCHUNG UND MIKROSKOPISCHE ANATOMIE – CELL AND TISSUE RESEARCH *see* ZEITSCHRIFT FUER ZELLFORSCHUNG UND MIKROSKOPISCHE ANATOMIE

ZEITSCHRIFT ZUR RELIGIONSGESCHICHTE DES URCHRISTENTUMS – 1918-20 (complete) – 1r – 1 – ATLA 1994-S536 – us A.T.L.A. [073]

DER ZEITSCHRIFTEN VERLEGER – Berlin, 1933, jun 20 1934-38 – 1 – Inquire at Mikrofilmarchiv for details – gw Misc Inst [070]

ZEITSCHRIFTEN-DIENST – (Incl suppl 1940/41 and register 1939-41) – Berlin, 1939 (incomplete), oct 9 1942-mar 9 1945 – 1 – Inquire at Mikrofilmarchiv for details – gw Misc Inst [072]

ZEITSCHRIFTENINDEX (INDEX DEUTSCHSPRACHIGER ZEITSCHRIFTEN) : AUTOREN-, SCHLAGWORT-, UND REZENSIONENREGISTER ZU DEUTSCHSPRACHIGEN ZEITSCHRIFTEN 1750-1815 – (69 Seiten Beiheft in Archivmappe) – Hildesheim, 1989 – 28mf – 9 – DM980.00 – gw Olms [073]

ZEITTAFEL DES GELDES / Bayrische Vereinsbank – 1974. 4p – 9 – 1.00f – at Libertarian Micro [335]

ZEITTUNG (NEWE) WIE DIE STADT MUNSTER EINGENOMEN IST – BME-152 1 – 9 – ne IDC [240]

DIE ZEITUNG – London, 1941-1945 – 3r – 1 – DM225.00 – gw Mikro Press [072]

DIE ZEITUNG – London, England. Mar. 12, 1941-June 1, 1945 – 1 – gw Mikrofilm [072]

ZEITUNG AUS DEM FELDLAGER / ed by Welke, Martin – Bremen u.a., 1813-14. Hildesheim, 1979 – 1mf – 9 – DM20.00 – gw Olms [072]

ZEITUNG DER 10. ARMEE – Wilna (Vilnius, U.S.S.R.). 1917-18. Incompl – 1 – gw Mikrofilm [072]

ZEITUNG DES ARBEITER-VEREINS ZU KOELN – Koeln, Germany. 23 Apr-21 Sept 1848 – 1 – gw Mikrofilm [072]

ZEITUNG DES JUDENTUMS = JEWISH JOURNAL – (In German) – Berlin, DE. v74 no14 8 Apr-v74 no52 30 Dec 1910 – 1r – 1 – $35.00 – cn Can Microfilming [072]

ZEITUNG DES VEREINS DEUTSCHER EISENBAHN-VERWALTUNGEN – Berlin, Germany. -f. 1894-96; April 1918-June 1919. 4 reels – 1 – uk British Libr Newspaper [072]

ZEITUNG DES VEREINS DEUTSCHER EISENBAHN-VERWALTUNGEN – Leipzig, Berlin. 1874, 1878, 1880-82, 1884, 1886-87 – 8r – 1 – Inquire at Mikrofilmarchiv for details – gw Misc Inst [380]

ZEITUNG FUER DAS AMT RITZEBUETTEL – Ritzebuettel (Cuxhaven), Germany. 18 Oct 1843-14 Sept 1853 – 1 – gw Mikrofilm [072]

ZEITUNG FUER DAS DEUTSCHE VOLK *see*
- DEUTSCHE REICHS-ZEITUNG

ZEITUNG FUER DEN DEUTSCHEN ADEL – Leipzig, 1840 – 1r – 1 – gw Mikrofilm [943]

ZEITUNG FUER DIE ELEGANTE WELT – Leipzig, 1801, 1806-09, sep 1 1810-jun 30 1818, jan 17-dec 31 1825 (incomplete), oct 16-dec 29 1828, 1833-jul 31 1834 – 8r – 1 – gw Mikrofilm [390]

ZEITUNG FUER HINTERPOMMERN – Stolp, Germany. (Slupsk, Poland). 1895, nrn.78-105; 299-305 – 1 – gw Mikrofilm [072]

ZEITUNG FUER NORDDEUTSCHLAND – Hannover, 1848-53; 1854-64; 1865-69; 1870; 1871 – 27r – 1 – DM2,025.00 – gw Mikro Press [072]

ZEITUNG FUER NORDDEUTSCHLAND – (See also: Bremer Zeitung) – Hannover, Germany. Former title: Bremer Zeitung. 1848-Jun 1853; 1854-Jun 1864; 1865-69; May-Dec 1870; 27 Feb-Dec 1871 – 1 – gw Mikrofilm [072]

ZEITUNG FUER NORDDEUTSCHLAND *see*
- BREMER ZEITUNG

ZEITUNG FUER OSTPOMMERN – (With suppl: Ostpommersche Heimat) – Stolp, 1830 n5, 1931 n1-50, 1932 n 1-37, 1933 n1-40, 1934-39 n35, 1940 n1-2 – 2r – 1 – gw Mikrofilm [943]

ZEITUNG FUER STAEDTE, FLECKEN UND DOERFER – Braunschweig, Wolfenbuettel, Germany. 1848-49 – 1 – gw Mikrofilm [072]

ZEITUNG FUER STAEDTE, FLECKEN UND DOERFER – (Full title: Gnaedigst privilegirte Braunschweigische Zeitung fuer Staedte, Flecken und Doerfer besonders fuer den deutschen Landmann) – Braunschweig/ Wolfenbuettel, 1786-1809, 1811-21, 1823, 1825, 1828-47, 1848-49 – 27r – 1 – Inquire at Mikrofilmarchiv for details – gw Misc Inst [943]

ZEITUNG FUER STAEDTE, FLECKEN UND DOERFER, INSBESONDERHEIT FUER DIE LIEBEN LANDSLEUTE JUNG UND ALT : (AUCH GENANNT "ROTHE ZEITUNG") / ed by Braess, Dietrich (Herausgeber der Microfiche-Edition: Martin Welke) – Wolfenbuettel, 1786-1798. Hildesheim 1993 – 53mf – 9 – DM700.00 diazo DM800.00 silver – gw Olms [320]

DER ZEITUNGS-VERLAG – (Special issue "Die deutsche Zeitung": may 12 1928. Cont by: Deutsche Presse, apr 10 1943.) – Magdeburg, Berlin, Hannover, Liegnitz. oct 6 1900-sep 21 1905, 1906-44 – 1 – gw Mikrofilm [070]

DAS ZEITUNGSWESEN IN WESTFALEN VON DEN ERSTEN ANFAENGEN BIS ZUM JAHRE 1813 : IN SEINER GESCHICHTLICHEN ENTWICKLUNG UND KULTURELLEN BEDEUTUNG DARGESTELLT / D'Ester, Carl – Muenster, 1907 – xvi/222p – 9 – DM48.00 – 3-89349-068-X – gw Hänsel [072]

ZEITWENDE – (Former titles: Zeitwende jan 1925-jun 1953: Zeitwende – die neue Furche jul 1953-dec 1967) – Karlsruhe. v43-44 jan 1972-nov 1973. v47 jan-oct 1976. v50-51 jan 1979-oct 1980 1; v43 jan-nov 1972. v47 jan-oct 1976*. v50 jan-oct 1979*. v51 jan-oct 1980 5; v47 jan-oct 1976*. v50-51 jan 1979-oct 1980* 9 – 1,5,9 – D7165 – us UMI [073]

ZEITWENDE *see* ZEITWENDE

ZEITWENDE – DIE NEUE FURCHE *see* ZEITWENDE

ZEKA – Istanbul, 1 sene, 1-2 cilt, nu. 1-34 (5 Mart 1328-19 Haziram 1330 [1 Rebi' II 1330-? (20 Mar 1912-4 Jul. 1914)]) – 2mf – 9 – $75.00 – us MEDOC [949]

ZEKENIM IM NE'ARIM / Braudes, R A – Vienna. 1886. BJ-422-9 1 – 9 – ne IDC [470]

Zeki, Muvahhid *see* ARTVIN VILAYETI HAKKINDA MALUMAT-I UMUMIYE

Zeki [Pakalin], Mehmet *see* MAKTUL SEHZADELER

O ZELADOR : ORGAO DO PARTIDO NAMORISCO – Manaos, Amazonas. 31 Out 1909 – 1,5,6 – bl Biblioteca [072]

Zelak, Dominik *see* TIECK UND SHAKESPEARE

Zelaznik, Howard *see* DIFFERENCES IN MOVEMENT SPEED BETWEEN SIX YEAR OLD CHILDREN AND ADULTS ON THREE MOTOR TASKS

ZELENAIA ULITSA : STAT'I I ZAMETKI OB ISKUSSTVE / Shershenevich, V – 1915 – 8 – BR-1085 2 – ne IDC [700]

Zelenin, D K *see*
- BIBLIOGRAFICHESKII UKAZATEL' RUSSKOI ETNOGRAFICHESKOI LITERATURY O VNESHNEM BYTE NARODOV ROSSII. 1700-1910 GG
- OBZOR RUKOPISNYKH MATERIALOV UCHENOGO ARKHIVA VSESOIUZNOGO GEOGRAFICHESKOGO OBSHCHESTVA O NARODAKH PRIBALTIKI (LATYSHI, LITOVTSY, ESTY)
- OPISANIE RUKOPISEI UCHENOGO ARKHIVA IMPERATORSKOGO RUSSKOGO GEOGRAFICHESKOGO OBSHCHESTVA

Zelenin, DK *see* OBZOR RUKOPISNYKH MATERIALOV UCHENOGO ARKHIVA VSESOIUZNOGO GEOGRAFICHESKOGO OBSHCHESTVA O NARODAKH SSSR. I. BASHKIRY, BESERMIANE, BOLGARY, VENSY, EVREI, KALMYKI, KARELY, KOMI, KOMI-PERMIAKI

ZELENYI VERTOGRAD. SLOVA POTSELUINYIA. STIKHI / Bal'mont, K D – Spb. 1909. BR-550 2 – 8 – ne IDC [460]

ZELEZNICAR – Prague. Czechoslovakia. -w. 11 Apr 1967-21 Dec 1968. (1 reel) – 1 – uk British Libr Newspaper [072]

Zel'geim, V N *see* KREDIT I POTREBITEL'SKAIA KOOPERATSIIA

Zelicman, Cecilio *see* EL SEGUNDA PLAN QUINQUENAL EN LA ENSENANZA MEDIA

Zelinskii, K *see* NA RUBEZHE DVUKH EPOKH

Zeller, Alwin *see* DAS PFERD, DER ESEL UND DER HUND IN DER HEILIGEN SCHRIFT

Zeller, Bernhard *see* FESTGABE FUER EDUARD BEREND, ZUM 75. GEBURTSTAG, AM 5. DEZEMBER 1958

Zeller, Eduard *see*
- THE CONTENTS AND ORIGIN OF THE ACTS OF THE APOSTLES, CRITICALLY INVESTIGATED
- DREI ABHANDLUNGEN ZUR GESCHICHTE DER ALTEN PHILOSOPHIE UND IHRES VERHAELTNISSES ZUM CHRISTENTUM

Zeller, Gustav *see* DIE SYNTAX DES NOMENS BEI GEORG RUDOLF WECKHERLIN

Zeller, Hannah *see* FLEURS DE LA PALESTINE

Zeller, Paul *see* NEUESTE DOGMENGESCHICHTE

ZELLESCHER ANZEIGER – (Title change: Cellesche Zeitung und Anzeigen, 1 Feb 1869; Cellesche Zeitung, 1 Apr 1943) – Celle, Germany. Apr 1817-1968 – 220r – 1 – gw Mikrofilm [072]

ZELLESCHER ANZEIGER – (Title changes: 1869 Cellesche Zeitung und Anzeigen. 1943 Cellesche Zeitung) – Celle, DE. Apr 1817-1968 – 220r – 1 – gw Mikrofilm [072]

Zellinger, Johann B *see* DIE DAUER DER OEFFENTLICHEN WIRKSAMKEIT JESU

Zellner, J *see* TRIO '(IN CIS MOLL] FUER KLAVIER, VIOLINE UND VIOLA [ODER VIOLONCELL], OP. 46...

ZELLULAERE WIRKUNGEN VON ULTRASCHALLSTOSSWELLEN / Steinbach, Pia – 1994 – 2mf – DM80.00 – 3-89349-894-X – gw Hänsel [574]

Zelter, C *see* SAEMMTLICHE LIEDER, BALLADEN, UND ROMANZEN..

ZELUCO : VARIOUS VIEWS OF HUMAN NATURE, TAKEN FROM LIFE AND MANNERS, FOREIGN AND DOMESTIC / Moore, J – Chiswick, 1822. 2v – 6mf – 9 – ne IDC [100]

Zelzer, K *see* DIE ALTEN LATEINISCHEN THOMASAKTEN (T.U.U. 5-122)

ZEMEDELSKE NOVINY – Prague, Czechoslovakia. -d. Jan 1953-Dec 1955. Imperfect. 10 reels – 1 – uk British Libr Newspaper [072]

ZEMEDELSKO ZNAME – 1976- – 1r per y – 1 – us Ross [072]

ZEMEDELSKO ZNAME – Sofia, 1976-1991ff – 16r – 1 – DM1,200.00 – gw Mikro Press [949]

ZEMEDELSKO ZNAME – Sofia, Bulgaria. -d. Nov 1944-Oct 1945; Feb 1947-Jan 1948; June 1959-Dec 1970. 27 reels – 1 – uk British Libr Newspaper [949]

ZEMEDELSKO ZNAME – Sofia, Bulgaria. Sept 1944-1946 (scattered issues); 1947-76 – 39r – 1 – us L of C Photodup [949]

ZEMELNOE PRAVO V PERVYI GOD SOVETSKOI VLASTI (1917-18) / Abykeeva, A T – Voronezh, 1960. 46p. BR-8416 1 – 9 – ne IDC [947]

ZEMELNOE USTROISTVO TRUDI ASHCHIKHSI A EVREEV / Golde, I U – Moskva: T Sentr. Izd-vo narodov Soi uza S.S.R., 1925 – 1 – CSUX89-B5936 – us Hoover Inst Photo [947]

ZEMELNY I KODEKS ESTONSKO I SSR : OFITSIALNY I TEKST – Tallin: E esti raamat, 1970 – 1 – CSUX91-B2401 – us Hoover Inst Photo [340]

ZEMEL'NYI VOPOS V ROSSII I KOOPERATSIIA / Avaliani, S – Pg., 1917 – 1mf – 9 – COR-1/1 – ne IDC [334]

Zemenszky, Edith von *see* THE PAPERS OF GENERAL FRIEDRICH WILHELM VON STEUBEN, 1777-1794

ZEMER NA'EH LE-PURIM – Prague. c.1650? BJ-43-145 1 – 9 – ne IDC [270]

ZEMIROT VE-TUSHBAHOT – Basle. 1599. BJ-43-146 1 – 9 – ne IDC [470]

ZEMLIA I SVOBODA / Elpatevskii, Sergei I Akovlevich – Spb.: Izdatel P. Kulakov, 1906 (S.-Peterburg: Tip. t-vo "Obshchestvennai a polza") – 1 – CSUX88-B9831 – us Hoover Inst Photo [947]

ZEMLIA I VOLIA / Sotsialistov-Revoliutsionerov Partii. Petrogradskago oblastnago komiteta – Petrograd. Mar. 21-Aug. 31, 1917, nos. 1-69, 71-82, 85, 87-128, 130 – 1 – 35.00r – us Hoover Inst Photo [335]

ZEMLIA RODNAIA / Sologub, F – Vybrannye stikhi. M. n.d. BR-887 2 – 8 – ne IDC [460]

ZEMLIANKA / Kamenskii, V – Spb. 1911. BR-949 2 – 8 – ne IDC [460]

ZEMNOI PROSTOR / Pasternak, B – Stikhi. M. 1945. BR-1022 2 – 8 – ne IDC [460]

ZEMNYIA STUPENI. ELEGII, PESNI, POEMY / Baltrushaitis, Iu – M. 1911. BR-559 2 – 8 – ne IDC [460]

ZEMSKII LIBERALIZM / Iordanskh, N I – Ed. 2. 1906. BR-266 2 – 8 – ne IDC [320]

ZEMSKOE DVIZHENIE / Belokonskii, Ivan – 2e izd., ispr., znachitelno dop. i illi ustrirovannoe 260 portretami zemskikh i obshchestvennykh di ei atele i i gruppami. Moskva: Zadruga, 1914 – 1 – CSUX89-B425 – us Hoover Inst Photo [947]

ZEMSKOE DVIZHENIE / Belokonskii, Ivan – 2nd ed. M., 1914. 397p – 5mf – 9 – ne IDC [320]

ZEMSTVO – Ezhenedel'naia politicheskaia i obshchestvennaia gazeta. v. 1-57. M. 1881. BR-3530 2 – 8 – ne IDC [073]

ZEMSTVO I KONSTITUTSIIA : S RISUNKAMI, ISPOLNENNYMI INSTITUTOM BRUKMAN V MIUNKHENIE / Belokonskii, Ivan – Moskva: Izd. Moskovskago knigoizdatelskago t-va "Obrazovanie", 1910 – 1 – CSUX89-B1645 – us Hoover Inst Photo [947]

ZEMSTVO I KOOPERATSIIA / Blinovskii, Pl – Ekaterinburg, 1913 – 1mf – 9 – COR-8/1 – ne IDC [334]

ZEMSTVO I KOOPERATSIIA / Khizhniakov, V V – M., 1918 – 2mf – 9 – COR-137/1 – ne IDC [334]

ZEMSTVO I KOOPERATSIIA / Maslov, S L – M., 1916 – 1mf – 9 – COR-68/1 – ne IDC [334]

ZEMSTVO LIBRARY CARD CATALOGUE / The Saltykov-Shchedrin State Public Library, St. Petersburg. (Russian National Library) – (Includes printed guide and plastic binder) – 78mf – 9 – R-18497/1-R-18499/1 – ne IDC [020]

ZEMSTVO STATISTICS / ed by Pries, Anne – (Indiv. titles avail.) – 150 titles – 9 – ne IDC [304]

ZEN / Watts, Alan – Stanford, CA: J.L. Delkin, (c1948). 41p. illus. Title also in Chinese – 1 – us U.W. Library [280]

ZEN BOW – v. 1-11. 1967-79 – 1 – us UMI [180]

ZEN BOW NEWSLETTER – (See also: Zen Bow) – v1 1979- – 1,5,6,9 – us UMI [180]

Zen, S H, Chen *see* SYMPOSIUM ON CHINESE CULTURE

ZEN UND DER KRIMINALROMAN : EINE ZEN AESTHETIK DES ROMANS AM BEISPIEL DER KRIMINALROMANE JANWILLEM VAN DE WETERINGS / Patzer, Georg – 1992 – 9 – DM98.00 – 3-89349-500-2 – gw Hänsel [430]

ZENA V UMENI – no.1-12. 1907-1908 – 1 – us I.U. Libraries [073]

ZENAH U-RE'ENAH – Amsterdam. 1648. BJ-43-147 1 – 9 – ne IDC [470]

ZENAH U-RE'ENAH, HAMESH MEGILLOT VE-HAFTAROT – Hanau. 1922. BJ-43-148 1 – 9 – ne IDC [470]

THE ZEND-AVESTA : PART 1: THE VENDIDAD / ed by Mueller, Friedrich Max – (Translated by James Darmesteter) – 1880 – 6mf – 8 – ne Slangenburg [280]

THE ZEND-AVESTA : PART 2: THE SIROZAHS, YASTS, AND NYAYIS / ed by Mueller, Friedrich Max – (Translated by James Darmesteter) – 1883 – 7mf – 8 – ne Slangenburg [280]

THE ZEND-AVESTA : PART 3: THE YASNA, VISPARAD, AFRINAGAN, GAHS, AND MISCELLANEOUS FRAGMENTS / ed by Mueller, Friedrich Max – (Translated by L.H. Mills) – 1887 – 8mf – 8 – ne Slangenburg [280]

ZENGER'S – San Francisco, CA: SF State University, 1971-1980 – 3r – 1 – $150.00 – B03676 – us Library Micro [071]

ZENGERS *see* GOLDEN GATOR

Zenker, E V *see* ANARCHISM

Zenker, J C *see* PLANTAE INDICAE

Zenker, Wolfgang *see* ALLE WIPFEL RAUSCHEN HEIMAT

Zenkevich, M *see*
- DIKAIA PORFIRA
- SKVOZ' GROZY LET

ZENOBIA, QUEEN OF PALMYRA: A POEM / Dawson, Aeneas McDonell – s.l.: s.n., 1883 (Ottawa: C. Mitchell). 03978. (Pre-1900 Canadiana) – 9 – cn C.I.H.M. [810]

Zenos, Andrew Constantinides *see*
- THE ELEMENTS OF THE HIGHER CRITICISM
- THE TEACHING OF JESUS CONCERNING CHRISTIAN CONDUCT

ZENO-ZEITUNG *see*
- VOLKS-ZEITUNG FUER RHEINE UND UMGEBUNG

ZENSKA REVUE – v1-6, 9. 1906-1911, 1914 – 1 – us I.U. Libraries [073]

Zentner, Wilhelm *see* SCHEFFEL IN ITALIEN

Zentralarbeitsgemeinschaft der Industriellen und Gewerblichen Arbeitgeber und Arbeitnehmer Deutschlands. Zentralausschuss *see* NIEDERSCHRIFT DER KONSTITUIERENDEN SITZUNG...: ABGEHALTEN...12 DEC 1919..

ZENTRALBLATT DER CHRISTLICHEN GEWERKSCHAFTEN DEUTSCHLANDS – Krefeld, 1901-33 – 5r – 1 – DM650.00 – gw Mikro Press [072]

ZENTRALBLATT DER CHRISTLICHEN GEWERKSCHAFTEN DEUTSCHLANDS – Krefeld, Germany. 1901-1933 – 1 – gw Mikrofilm [072]

ZENTRALBLATT DER DEUTSCHEN DEMOKRATISCHEN REPUBLIK – Berlin, 1957-70 – 5r – 1 – us Ross [324]

ZENTRALBLATT FUER ARBEITSMEDIZIN, ARBEITSSCHUTZ UND PROPHYLAXE – Heidelberg. v27. 1977 – 1,5,9 – D7268.01 – us UMI [613]

ZENTRALBLATT FUER BAKTERIOLOGIE, PARASITENKUNDE, INFEKTIONSKRANKHEITEN UND HYGIENE – Originale. Reihe A. Medizinische Mikrobiologie und Parasitologie. v. 1-232. 1887-1973 – 1 – us UMI [610]

ZENTRALBLATT FUER BAKTERIOLOGIE, PARASITENKUNDE, INFEKTIONSKRANKHEITEN UND HYGIENE – Originale. Reihe B. Hygiene Praeventiv Medizin. v. 155-. 1971- – 1 – us UMI [616]
ZENTRALBLATT FUER BAKTERIOLOGIE, PARASITENKUNDE, INFEKTIONSKRANKHEITEN UND HYGIENE – Series 1, Referate. v. 31-144. 1902-1944 – 1,5,6 – us Princeton Micro [610]
ZENTRALBLATT FUER BAKTERIOLOGIE, PARASITENKUNDE, INFEKTIONSKRANKHEITEN UND HYGIENE – Series 2, v. 1-106. 1895-1945 – 1,5,6 – us Princeton Micro [576]
ZENTRALBLATT FUER BAKTERIOLOGIE, PARASITENKUNDE, INFEKTIONSKRANKHEITEN UND HYGIENE – v. 1-16. 1887-1894. Series 1, v. 17-30. 1895-1901. Series 1, Originale, v. 31-149. 1902-1943 – 1,5,6 – us Princeton Micro [610]
ZENTRALBLATT FUER BIBLIOTHEKSWESEN / ed by Vorstius, Joris – 1990 – 361mf (1:24) – 9 – diazo DM2,400.00 (silver DM3,200.00 ISBN 3-598-33001-4) – 3-598-33000-6 – gw Saur [020]
ZENTRALBLATT FUER CHIRURGIE – (Publication suspended nov 1944-47) – Leipzig. 1874-1988*. v114-115 1989-90. v116-119 1991-94*. v120-122 1995-97+ – 1 – D7403 – us UMI [617]
ZENTRALBLATT FUER DIE FILMINDUSTRIE – Magdeburg, aug 20-n4 1919 – 1 – gw Mikrofilm [790]
ZENTRALBLATT FUER DIE GESAMTE KINDERHEILKUNDE – v. 43-125. 1952-80 – 1,5,9 – 12,450.00 – us UMI [618]
ZENTRALBLATT FUER DIE GESAMTE NEUROLOGIE UND PSYCHIATRIE – v. 105-230. 1948-80 – 1,5,9 – 18,806.00 – us UMI [073]
ZENTRALBLATT FUER DIE GESAMTE OPHTHALMOLOGIE – v. 50-120. 1948-80 – 1,5,9 – 10,597.00 – us UMI [617]
ZENTRALBLATT FUER DIE GESAMTE RADIOLOGIE – v. 1-121. 1952-80 – 1,5,9 – 12,537.00 – us UMI [073]
ZENTRALBLATT FUER DIE GESAMTE RECHTSMEDIZIN – v. 1-20. 1970-80 – 1,5,9 – 2595.00 – us UMI [073]
ZENTRALBLATT FUER DIE GESAMTE UNTERRICHTSVERWALTUNG IN PREUSSEN – Berlin, 1933-44 – 1 – Inquire at Mikrofilmarchiv for details – gw Misc Inst [350]
ZENTRALBLATT FUER GYNAEKOLOGIE – (Publication suspended sep 1944-jan 1947) – Leipzig. v1-97 1877-1975*. v98-102 1976-80. v103-111 1981-89*. v112 1990. v113 1991*. v114-115 1992-93. v116 1994*. v117-119 1995-97+ – 1 – D7402 – us UMI [618]
ZENTRALBLATT FUER HALS-, NASEN- UND OHRENHEILKUNDE – v. 38-125. 1948-80 – 1,5,9 – 13,314.00 – us UMI [617]
ZENTRALBLATT FUER HAUT- UND GESCHLECHTSKRANKHEITEN – v. 72-144. 1948-80 – 1,5,9 – 10,841.00 – us UMI [073]
ZENTRALBLATT FUER INSTRUMENTALMUSIK, SOLO UND CHORGESANG – v. 1-16. 1885-1901 – 1 – 134.00 – us L of C Photodup [780]
ZENTRALBLATT FUER MATHEMATIK – v. 1-429. 1931-80 – 1,5,9 – 21,557.00 – us UMI [073]
ZENTRALBLATT FUER MATHEMATIK UND IHRE GRENZGEBIETE – (Duetschen Akademie der Wissenschaften Zu Berlin: Heildelberger Adademieder Wissenshaften.) v. 1-28. 1931-1944 – 1,5,6 – us Princeton Micro [370]
ZENTRALBLATT FUER MECHANIK – Goettingen etc. v. 1-10. Apr 1933-Aug 9 1941 – 1 – us NY Public [621]
ZENTRALBLATT FUER MECHANIK – v. 1-12. 1933-1944 – 1 – us Princeton Micro [621]
ZENTRALBLATT FUER PSYCHOANALYSE UND PSYCHOTHERAPIE – Medizinische Monatsschrift fuer Seelenkunde. Wiesbaden. 1910-13 (t. I-III) – 1 – fr A.C.R.P.P. [073]
ZENTRALBLATT GASTROENTEROLOGIE-STOFFWECHSEL - ENDOKRINOLOGIE – v. 319-325. 1973-76 – 1,5,9 – 677.00 – us UMI [073]
ZENTRALBLATT HAEMATOLOGIE-KLINISCHE ONKOLOGIE – v. 319-322. 1973-76 – 1,5,9 – 387.00 – us UMI [616]
ZENTRALBLATT IMMUNOLOGIE-TRANSPLANTATION – v. 319-323. 1973-76 – 1,5,9 – 484.00 – us UMI [616]
ZENTRALBLATT KARDIOLOGIE-NEPHROLOGIE – v. 319-325. 1973-76 – 1,5,9 – 677.00 – us UMI [616]
ZENTRALBLATT KINDERHEILKUNDE = PAEDIATRICS – Berlin. 1991-94*. 1995-97+ – 1,5,9 – D19696 – us UMI [618]
ZENTRALBLATT PNEUMONOLOGIE-TUBERKULOSE – v. 319-323. 1973-76 – 1,5,9 – 403.00 – us UMI [073]
ZENTRALBLATT PNEUMONOLOGIE UND TUBERKULOSE – v. 57-115. 1950-75 – 1,5,9 – 2124.00 – us UMI [073]
ZENTRALBLATT PRAKTISCHE INNERE MEDIZIN – v. 319-323. 1973-76 – 1,5,9 – 483.00 – us UMI [616]
DER ZENTRALE GEGENSTAND IM DRAMA LESSINGS, KLEISTS UND GRILLPARZERS : UNTERSUCHUNGEN ZUR DRAMATURGIE DES 18. UND 19. JAHRHUNDERTS / Wagner, Horst – Frankfurt a.M., 1967 – 3mf – 9 – DM76.00 – 3-89349-395-6 – gw Hänsel [430]
Zentralkomitees der Kommunistischen Partei Lettlands *see* DIE ROTE FAHNE
Zentralkommission der Maschinensetzer Deutschlands *see* BERICHT UND ABRECHNUNG
Zentralleitung der Arbeitslager in der Schweiz *see* UEBER DIE GRENZEN
ZENTRALORGAN FUER DIE GESAMTE CHIRURGIE – v. 111-217. 1948-76 – 1,5,9 – 3293.00 – us UMI [617]
Zentralverband aller in der Schmiederei beschaeftigten Personen *see* GESCHAEFTSBERICHT DES VORSTANDES
Zentralverband christlicher Lederarbeiter Deutschlands *see*
- BERICHT
- GESCHAEFTS- UND KASSENBERICHT

Zentralverband der Angestellten *see*
- GESCHAEFTSBERICHT
- PROTOKOLL

Zentralverband der Angestellten. Ortsgruppe Gross-Berlin *see* TATIGKEITSBERICHT
Zentralverband der Arbeitnehmer oeffentlicher Betriebe und Verwaltungen *see* GESCHAEFTSBERICHT
Zentralverband der Backer, Konditoren und verwandten Berufsgenossen Deutschlands *see* PROTOKOLL UEBER DIE VERHANDLUNGEN DES VERBANDSTAGES
Zentralverband der Fleischer und Berufsgenossen Deutschlands *see* PROTOKOLL DES VERBANDSTAGES
Zentralverband der Glasarbeiter und -Arbeiterinnen Deutschlands *see*
- JAHRES- UND RECHENSCHAFTSBERICHT
- PROTOKOLL DER ORDENTLICHEN GENERALVERSAMMLUNG

Zentralverband der Handels-, Transport-, und Verkehrsarbeiter und Arbeiterinnen Deutschlands *see* RECHENSCHAFTSBERICHT DES VORSTANDES
Zentralverband der Handlungsgehilfen *see* GESCHAEFTSBERICHT
Zentralverband der Hotel-, Restaurant-, und Cafeangestellten *see*
- BERICHT DER HAUPTVERWALTUNG
- PROTOKOLL

Zentralverband der Landarbeiter *see* VERHANDLUNGSBERICHT UEBER DEN VERBANDSTAG
Zentralverband der Lederarbeiter und Arbeiterinnen Deutschlands *see*
- GESCHAEFTSBERICHT
- JAHRESBERICHT
- PROTOKOLL

Zentralverband der Maurer Deutschlands *see*
- JAHRBUCH
- PROTOKOLL
- STATISTISCHE ERHEBUNGEN DES...FUER DIE ZEIT VOM 1. OKTOBER 1891 BIS 30 SEPTEMBER 1892

Zentralverband der Schiffszimmerer Deutschlands *see* PROTOKOLL DER GENERALVERSAMMLUNG
Zentralverband der Schuhmacher *see*
- JAHRBUCH
- PROTOKOLL UEBER DIE VERHANDLUNGEN DES ORDENTLICHEN VERBANDSTAGES

Zentralverband der Schuhmacher Deutschlands *see* GESCHAEFTSBERICHT DES ZENTRALVORSTANDES
Zentralverband der Schuhmacher Deutschlands. Betriebsrate-Kongress fuer die Schuhindustrie *see* PROTOKOLL DER VERHANDLUNGEN
Zentralverband der Schuhmacher Deutschlands. Bezirk 6 *see* BERICHT DER BEZIRKSVERWALTUNG FUER DAS JAHR.../BEZIRK 6, SITZ BERLIN
Zentralverband der Schuhmacher. Zahlstelle Berlin *see* JAHRESBERICHT DER ORTSVERWALTUNG FUER.../ ZENTRALVERBAND..
Zentralverband der Stukkateure Gipser, Pliesterer und Verwandten Berufsgenossen Deutschlands *see* PROTOKOLL DES VERBANDSTAGES
Zentralverband der Toepfer und Berufsgenossen Deutschlands *see* VERWALTUNGSBERICHT DES VORSTANDES
Zentralverband der Zimmerer und verwandten Berufsgenossen Deutschlands *see* PROTOKOLL
Zentralverband deutscher Konsumgenossenschaften *see* JAHRBUCH
Zentralverein Deutscher Staatsbuerger Juedischen Glaubens *see* ZENTRALVEREIN-ZEITUNG
Zentralverein fuer alle in der Hut- und Filzwareindustrie beschaeftigten Arbeiter und Arbeiterinnen *see* PROTOKOLL
ZENTRALVEREIN-ZEITUNG / Zentralverein Deutscher Staatsbuerger Juedischen Glaubens – Berlin. v1-17. 1922-38 – 7r – 1 – us Ross [072]
Zentralvorstandes der Liberal-Demokratischen Partei Deutschlands. Sekretariat *see* REFERATE UND DISKUSSIONSBEITRAEGE..
ZEOLITES – Woburn. v1-6 1981-86*. v7-17 1987-97+ 1,9; v1-9 1981-89*. v10 1990. v11-14 1991-94*. v15-17 1995-97+ 5 – 1,5,9 – D16651 – us UMI [073]
Zepeda y Vivero, Juan A *see* AGRICULTURA METODICA...NATURALEZA
UM ZEPTER UND KRONEN : ZEITROMAN / Samarow, Gregor – Stuttgart: Deutsche Verlags-Anstalt, 1904 – 1r – 1 – us U.W. Library [830]
ZERAMIM – Vilna. 1931-32. BJ-291-36 1 – 9 – ne IDC [470]
ZERAMIN – Vilna. 18 nos. 1931-1932 – 8mf – 9 – ne IDC [460]
DER ZERBROCHENE FRANZ : NEBST ANDEREN HUMORESKEN UND GESCHICHTEN / Hevesi, Lajos – Stuttgart: Adolf Bonz, 1900 – 1 – us U.W. Library [870]
DER ZERBROCHENE KRUG : NOVELLE / Zschokke, Heinrich; ed by Edward S Joynes – Boston: D C Heath, 1908 – 1r – 1 – us U.W. Library [830]
DER ZERBROCHNE KRUG / Kleist, Heinrich von – Berlin: A Hofmann, [1877] – 1r – 1 – us U.W. Library [820]
ZERI I POPULLIT – Tirane, 1976-79 – 2r – 1 – DM200.00 – gw Mikro Press [949]
ZERI I POPULLITT – Tirana, Albania. Nov 1948-Dec 1991 – 53r – 1 – us L of C Photodup [072]
ZERI I RINISE – Tirana, Albania. 1962-91 – 20r – 1 – us L of C Photodup [949]
ZERKALA / Gippius, Z N – Vtoraia kniga razskazov. Spb. 1898. BR-729 2 – 8 – ne IDC [460]
ZERKALO / Odoevsteva, I – Roman. Paris. 1939. BR-1227 2 – 8 – ne IDC [460]
Zerkaulen, Heinrich *see*
- BLAU IST DAS MEER
- DIE BRUECKEN
- HOERNERKLANG DER FRUEHE
- KOMM MIT NACH MADEIRA
- NARREN VON GESTERN – HELDEN VON HEUTE

Zerling, Jean Pierre *see* ASPECTS ARTICULATOIRES DE LA LABIALE VOCALIQUE EN FRANCAIS. CONTRIBUTION A LA MODELISATION A PARTIR DE LABIOPHOTOGRAPHIES
Zernial, U *see* PHILOTAS
Zernova, A S *see* NACHALO KNIGOPECHATANIIA V MOSKVE I NA UKRAINE
O ZERO – Muriae, Brazil. Sept-Oct 1922 – 1 – bl Biblioteca [072]
ZERT A PRAVDA – v22-25, 1898-1902 – 1 – us I.U. Libraries [073]
DIE ZERTANZTEN SCHUHE : FUER DIE MAERCHENSPIELE DER KUENSTLERISCHEN VOLKSBUEHNE SCHLICHT UND GETREU NACH DEM MAERCHEN DER GEBRUEDER GRIMM IN HANDLUNG UND REIM GEBRACHT: UNTER BENUTZUNG DER WEISE EINES ALTEN JOHANNISREIGENS VOM RHEIN UND EINER WEISE AUS DEN BERGKREYEN (1535) / Guembel-Seiling, Max – Leipzig: Breitkopf & Haertel, 1918 – 1r – 1 – us U.W. Library [820]
ZERUBABEL / Levinsohn, I B – Odessa. 1864. BJ-422-49 1 – 9 – ne IDC [290]
ZERUBABEL – (Yiddish monthly) – Lwow, PL. 1905 – 1r – 1 – $25.00 – cn Can Microfilming [072]
Zerwick, Chloe *see*
- A SHORT HISTORY OF GLASS

Zerzer, Julius *see* KRIEGSMESSE 1914
Zesen, Phillip von *see* MORALIA HORATIANA
ZESZYTY OSWIECIMSKIE – Oswiecim (Auschwitz), 1957-83 – 3r – 1 – inquire – us Ross [072]
ZETETIC – (Cont by: Skeptical Inquirer) – Buffalo. v1-2 fal 1976-fal 1977* – 1 – D18234 – us UMI [073]
ZETLAND TIMES – Lerwick, Scotland. Shetland Times. -w. 17 June 1872-Dec 1979. 88 1 2 reels – 1 – uk British Libr Newspaper [072]
Zetterberg, H L *see* SOCIOLOGY IN THE UNITED STATES OF AMERICA
Zetterstedt, J W *see* FAUNA INSECTORUM LAPPONICA
DIE ZEUGNISSE FUER DAS EVANGELIUM JOHANNIS / Riggenbach, Christoph Johannes – (Includes bibliographical references) – Basel: Bahnmaier, 1866 – 1mf – 9 – 0-8370-4906-7 – 1985-2906 – us A.T.L.A. [220]
DIE ZEUGNISSE VOM CHRISTENTUM IM SLAVISCHEN "DE BELLO JUDAICO" DES JOSEPHUS / Berendts, Alexander – Leipzig: J.C. Hinrichs, 1906. (Texte und Untersuchungen zur Geschichte der altchristlichen Literatur; der ganzen Reihe 29. Bd., 4. Heft: n.F., 14. Bd., 4. Heft) – 1mf – us A.T.L.A. [240]
DIE ZEUGNISSE VOM CHRISTENTUM IM SLAVISCHEN "DE BELLO JUDAICO" DES JOSEPHUS (T.U.U. 2-29/4) / Berendts, Alexander – Leipzig, 1905 – 2mf – 9 – ne Slangenburg [240]
Zeumer, K *see* MONUMENTA GERMANIAE HISTORICA (MGH)
ZEVAH TOV – Prague. 1628. BJ-43-150 1 – 9 – ne IDC [270]
Zevecotius, J *see* EMBLEMATA OFTE SINNE BEELDEN MET DICHTEN VERCIERT...
ZEVENER ZEITUNG – Zelinograd, U.S.S.R. 1981- – 1 – gw Mikrofilm [943]
ZEVENER ZEITUNG – Zeven, West Germany. 1981- – 1 – gw Mikrofilm [072]
ZEVENER ZEITUNG *see* BREMERVOERDER ZEITUNG
Zeydel, Edwin Hermann *see* LUDWIG TIECK AND ENGLAND
Zeyher, C LP *see* ENUMERATIO PLANTARUM AFRICAE AUSTRALIS
ZEYTTUNG (NEWE), WIE DIE STATT MUENSTER EROBERET VND GEWUNNEN WORDEN IST – BME-153 1 – 9 – ne IDC [240]
ZEYTUNG (NEWE) VON DEN WYDERTAUFFEREN ZU MUENSTER. AUFF DIE NEWE ZEYTUNG VON MUENSTER D. MART. LUTHER VORREDE. ETC – Nuernberg, Fr. Peypus. 1535. BME-154 1 – 9 – ne IDC [240]
Zezschwitz, Gerhard von *see*
- INNRE MISSION
- PROFANGRAECITAET UND BIBLISCHER SPRACHGEIST
- ZUR APOLOGIE DES CHRISTENTHUMS: NACH GESCHICHTE UND LEHRE

ZGA. VOLSHEBNYE RASSKAZY / Remizov, A – Prague. 1925. BR-857 2 – 8 – ne IDC [460]
ZGODA : MEN'S EDITION – Milwaukee, WI: aug 1910-mar 1911 – 1r – 1 – us Res Libr [071]
ZGODA – Milwaukee, WI: Polish National Alliance, [1887-90; 1892-94; 1896-99; jul 1900-06; 1908-10; 1912-82] – 30r – 1 – us Res Libr [071]
ZGODA : WOMEN'S EDITION – Milwaukee, WI: 1900-jun 1908; 1912-13 – 4r – 1 – us Res Libr [071]
Zhabin, A I *see* EKSPORT PROMYSLOVOI KOOPERATSII
ZHALO SMERTI / Sologub, F – Razskazy. M. 1904. BR-886 – 8 – ne IDC [460]
ZHANDI = BATTLEGROUND – Mar 1938. 3 fiches. F-C59 – 9 – $13.50 – cc Microforms [073]
Zhang, Jianhui *see* MODIFICATION AND REVISION OF THE LEADERSHIP SCALE FOR SPORT
Zhang, Q *see* GENDER DIFFERENCES IN PEAK BLOOD LACTATE CONCENTRATION AND BLOOD LACTATE REMOVAL FOLLOWING STRENUOUS EXERCISE
Zhang, Songning *see* SELECTED ASPECTS OF BIOMECHANICAL AND NEUROMUSCULAR RESPONSES TO LANDING PERFORMANCE
ZHANNA D'ARK / Merezhkovskii, Dimitrii – Berlin. 1938. BR-802 2 – 8 – ne IDC [460]

ZHAOHUA = MORNING FLOWER – No.1-20.Dec 1928-May 1929. -w. 2 fiches. F-C72 – 9 – $9.00 – cc Microforms [073]
ZHAOHUA XUNKAN = MORNING FLOWER – v1, no.1-12. Jun-Sept 1929. 3 issues per month. 5 fiches. F-C73 – 9 – $22.50 – cc Microforms [073]
ZHAR-PTITSA = THE FIRE-BIRD – Paris-Berlin: A Kogan's Russkoye Iskusstvo Publ, 1921-25 – 11mf – 9 – inquire – us Ross [700]
ZHAR-PTITSA. SVIREL' SLAVIANINA / Bal'mont, K D – M. 1907. BR-548 2 – 8 – ne IDC [460]
ZHAS ALASH – (250 issues per year) – 1921-1995 – 1 – sz Infoprint [947]
ZHATVA – Zhurnal literatury. M. 1911-16. B-2013 2 – 8 – ne IDC [073]
Zhdanov, A *see* DOKLAD O ZHURNALAKH "ZVEZDA" I "LENINGRAD"
Zhdanov, I *see* RUSSKII BYLEVOI EPOS
ZHEJIANG DAXUE XUEBAO – Journal of Zhijiang University. In Chinese but English abstracts to the main articles. F p175 – 9 – $4.50f – cc Microforms [073]
Zhejiang Province. China *see*
- JIAJING CHUN'AN XIAN ZHI, 1524
- JIAJING PUJIANG XIAN ZHI, 1556
- JIAJING TAIPING XIAN ZHI, 1540
- JIAJING WENZHOU FU ZHI, 1537
- JIAJING WUKANG XIAN ZHI, 1550
- JIAJING XINCHANG XIAN ZHI, 1579
- WANLI HUANGYAN XIAN ZHI, 1579
- YONGLE LEQING XIAN ZHI, APPROX. 1420

ZHEJIANG RIBAO – Zhejiang Daily. China. In Chinese. Current subscription. Annual delivery. 1980- , 1 reel/y. M D18 – 1 – $55.00r – cc Microforms [072]
ZHEJIANG ZHONGYI XUEYUAN XUEBAO – Journal of Zhejiang Traditional Chinese Medicine College. In Chinese but English abstracts to the main articles. F p169 – 9 – 4.00f – cc Microforms [616]
ZHELEZNODOROZHNIKI KAZAKHSTANA V PERVOI RUSSKOI REVOLIUTSII 1905-1907 GG / Asylbekov, M K – Alma-Ata, 1965 – 1 – 35.00r – us Hoover Inst Photo [947]
ZHELEZNODOROZHNOE POTREBITELSKOE DELO – Perm', 1912-13 n7 – 3mf – 9 – COR-587/1 – ne IDC [334]
ZHELEZNODOROZHNOE PRAVO PO ZAKONODATEL' STVU SSSR / Gusakov, A G – Moscow, 1929. 344p. An exhaustive treatise on Soviet railway legislation throughout the NEP period.BR-8460/1 – 9 – ne IDC [947]
ZHELEZNODOROZHNYI PROLETARIAT SIBIRI V REVOLIUTSII 1905-1907 GG / Belimov, I T – Novosibirsk, 1967 – 1 – 35.00r – us Hoover Inst Photo [335]
Zheleznova, N A *see* ISPOLZOVANIE IZBYTOCHNOSTI V INFORMATSIONNYKH SISTEMAKH
Zheliabuzhskii, I A *see* ZAPISKI S 1682 PO 2 IIULIA 1709
ZHEMCHUGA / Gumilev, Nikolai Sepanovich – Stikhi. M. 1910. BR-1158 2 – 8 – ne IDC [460]
ZHEN ZHI ZHOU KAN – Ed. by Mao Zedong. Dec 1928-Jun 1926 sic. 98 ill. DL50f – 9 – 30.00 – cc Globe [073]
ZHENGDE DAMING FU ZHI, APPROX. 1521 / Hebei Province. China – Records of Daming Prefecture during the reign of Zhengde. 10 vols. Comp. by Tang Jin. F A3. (Rare Local Records in Chinese...1420-1507) – 9 – $54.00 – cc Microforms [950]
ZHENGDE GUANGHUA XIAN ZHI, 1515 / Hubei Province. China – Records of Guanghua County in the reign of Zhengde. 6 vols. Comp. by Cao Lin. F A85. (Rare Local Records in Chinese...1420-1507) – 9 – $18.00 – cc Microforms [950]
ZHENGDE JIANCHANG FU ZHI, 1516 / Jiangxi Province. China – Records of Jianchang Prefecture in the reign of Zhengde. 19 vols. Comp. by Xia Liangsheng. F A45. (Rare Local Records in Chinese...1420-1507) – 9 – $54.00 – cc Microforms [950]
ZHENGDE KUIZHOU FU ZHI, 1513 / Sichuan Province. China – Records of Kuizhou Prefecture in the Reign of Zhengde. 12 vols. Compiled by Wu Xianzhi. F A98. (Rare Local Records in Chinese...1420-1507) – 9 – $31.50 – cc Microforms [950]
ZHENGDE NANKANG FU ZHI, 1515 / Jiangxi Province. China – Records of Nankang Prefecture in the reign of Zhengde. 10 vols. Comp. by Chen Lin. F A46. (Rare Local Records in Chinese...1420-1507) – 9 – $31.50 – cc Microforms [950]
ZHENGDE QIONGTAI ZHI, 1521 / Guangdong Province. China – Records of Qiongtai in the reign of Zhengde, 44 vols. Comp. by Tang Zhou. (Rare Local Records in Chinese...1420-1507). F A91 – 9 – $99.00 – cc Microforms [950]
ZHENGDE RUZHOU ZHI, 1506 / Henan Province. China – Records of Ruzhou in the reign of Zhengde. 8 vols. Comp. by Cheng Tiangui. F A65. (Rare Local Records in Chinese...1420-1507) – 9 – $22.50 – cc Microforms [950]
ZHENGDE XIN XIAN ZHI, 1515 / Shandong Province. China – Records of Xin Xian County in the reign of Zhengde. 10 vols. Comp. by Wu Zongqi. F A59. (Rare Local Records in Chinese...1420-1507) – 9 – $22.50 – cc Microforms [950]
ZHENGDE XINXIANG XIAN ZHI, 1506 / Henan Province. China – Records of Xinxiang County in the reign of Zhengde. 6 vols. Comp. by Li Jin. F A68. (Rare Local Records in Chinese...1420-1507) – 9 – $13.50 – cc Microforms [950]
ZHENGDE YINGZHOU ZHI, 1511 – Records of Yingzhou in the reign of Zhengde. 6 vols. Comp. by Liu Jie. F A32. (Rare Local Records in Chinese...1420-1507) – 9 – $13.50 – cc Microforms [950]
ZHENGDE YUANZHOU FU ZHI, 1514 / Jiangxi Province. China – Records of Yuanzhou Prefecture in the reign of Zhengde. 14 vols. Comp. by Yan Song. F A48. (Rare Local Records in Chinese...1420-1507) – 9 – $40.50 – cc Microforms [950]
ZHENGZHI SHENGHUO – The Political Life Weekly. 1924-26. 1 reel. M/C 86 – 1 – $55.00 – cc Microforms [073]
ZHENGZHI XIESHANG HUIYI ZILIAO – Materials on the Chinese people's political consultative conference. Comp. by Sichuan Renmin Chubanshe, 1981. 7 fiches. F-H143 – 9 – $31.50 – cc Microforms [950]
ZHENKONG KEXUE YU JISHU – (1983 $3.50f; 1984- $4.50f) – Vacuum Science and Technology. In Chinese but English abstracts to the main articles. F p146 – 9 – cc Microforms [073]
ZHENSHCHINA I VYBORY V UCHREDITELNOE SOBRANIE / Ancharova, Mariia – Moskva: Izd-vo "1917 god", [1917?] – 1 – CSUX89-B2282 – us Hoover Inst Photo [947]
ZHENSKAIA ZHIZN' – Moscow, 1914 n1-6; 1915 n1-24; 1916 n1-12 – 19mf – 9 – $120.00 – us Ross [640]
ZHENSKIE RABOTY – St Petersburg, 1872 n1-12; 1873 n1-24; 1874 n1-2 – 11mf – 9 – $90.00 – us Ross [640]
ZHENSKII VESTNIK – Ezhemesiachnyi obshchestvenno-nauchno-literaturnyi zhurnal, posviashchennyi zhenskomu voprosu. Spb. 1904-17. Lacking: 1904 (4-12), 1905 (4, 12), 1907 (7-8), 1913 (10), 1915 (2, 5-6, 11-12), 1916 (7-11), 1917 (3-12). B-2017 2 – 8 – ne IDC [073]
ZHENSKII VESTNIK – St Petersburg, 1866 n1-2; 1867 n3-9; 1868 n1 – 66mf – 9 – $460.00 – us Ross [640]
ZHENSKII ZHURNAL – Moscow, 1926-1930 – 48mf – 9 – $300.00 – us Ross [305]
ZHENSKOE OBRAZOVANIE – St Petersburg, 1876-1877; 1879-1891 – 255mf – 9 – $1,490.00 – us Ross [073]
ZHERNOVA – [Izd.] Komitet sotsial'noi zashchity. M., 1989-1990. Nos. 1-20 – 1mf – 9 – RI-2/1 – ne IDC [947]
ZHEXUE YANJIU – (1978-84 $3.50f; 1987- $4.50f) – Philosophical Research. In Chinese with Table of Contents in English in each issue. F p10 – 9 – cc Microforms [100]
ZHEZL PRAVLENIIA / Simeon Polotskii – 1753 – 8 – B-493 2 – ne IDC [947]
ZHI WAN ZHANZHENG – The wars between warlords of Hebei and Anhui. Comp. by the Second Chinese Archive of History. 4 fiches.F-H193 – 9 – $18.00 – cc Microforms [950]
ZHILENG XUEBAO – Journal of Chinese Association of Refrigeration.1979-. F-P253 – 9 – $4.50f – cc Microforms [073]
ZHILISHCHNAIA KOOPERATSIIA – (Missing: 1926 n14; 1930 n18; 1932 n4) – M., 1924-37 n6 – 236mf – 9 – COR-589/1 – ne IDC [334]
ZHILISHCHNAIA KOOPERATSIIA SSSR V 1924-25 GG. : STATISTIKO-EKONOMICHESKII OBZOR – M., 1926 – 3mf – 9 – COR-247/1 – ne IDC [334]
ZHILISHCHNOE DELO – L., 1924-30 – 55mf – 9 – COR-590/1 – ne IDC [334]
ZHILISHCHNYE ZAKONY / Alekseev, T D – Moscow, Leningrad, 1947. 240p. BR-8417 1 – 9 – ne IDC [947]
Zhirkevich, A V *see*
- SONNOE TSARSTVO VELIKIKH NACHINANII

Zhirmunskii, M M *see* SEL'SKOKHOZIAISTVENNAIA KOOPERATSIIA I GOSPROMYSHLENNOST'
Zhirmunskii, V M *see*
- GETE V RUSSKOI LITERATURE
- VALERII BRIUSOV I NASLEDIE PUSHKINA
- VOPROSY TEORII LITERATURY
- VVEDENIE V METRIKU: TEORIIA STIKHA

ZHITIE ALEKSANDRA NEVSKAGO / Mansikka, V – (Pamiatniki drevnei pis'mennosti i iskusstva, CLXXX). Spb. 1913. BR 4087 2 – 8 – ne IDC [920]
Zhitomirskaia, S V *see* ZAPADNOE SREDNEVEKOV'E V RUKOPISIAKH GOSUDARSTVENNOI BIBLIOTEKI SSSR IM V.I. LENINA
ZHITTIA I REVOLIUTSIIA – Kiev, 1929-34 – 1r – 1 – us Ross [335]
ZHIVAIA MYSL' – Ezhenedel'nyi khudozhestvenno-literaturnyi i nauchnyi zhurnal. v. 1-24. M. 1907. Lacking: v. 19-21, 24. B-2018 2 – 8 – ne IDC [073]
ZHIVAIA STARINA : PERIODICHESKOE IZDANIE OTDELENIIA ETNOGRAFII RUSSKOGO GEOGRAFICHESKOGO OBSHCHESTVA – Spb. v1-25. 1890-1916 – 289mf – 9 – ne IDC [947]
ZHIVOPISETS / Novikov, N I – 1772-73. (Ed. 7 by P. A. Efremova). Spb. 1864. BR-5783 2 – 8 – ne IDC [460]
ZHIVOPISNAIA ROSSIIA : ILLIUSTRIROVANNYI VESTNIK OTCHIZNOVEDENIIA, ISTORII, KUL'TURY, GOSUDARSTVENNOI, OBSHCHESTVENNOI I EKONOMICHESKOI ZHIZNI ROSSII – (Missing: 1905 v5) – Spb. v1-5. 1901-1905 – 162mf – 9 – 2021/2 – ne IDC [947]
ZHIVOPISNAIA ROSSIIA : OTECHESTVO NASHE V EGO ZEMEL'NOM, ISTORICHESKOM... ZNACHENII / ed by Semenov-Tianshanskii, P – St Petersburg: M Wolf Publ, 1881-1901 – 72mf – 9 – $490.00 – us Ross [947]
ZHIVOPISNAIA RUSSKAIA BIBLIOTEKA – v. 1-4. Spb. 1856-59. B-2022 2 – 8 – ne IDC [025]
ZHIVOPISNOE OBOZRENIE – Ezhenedel'nyi illiustrirovannyi zhurnal. Spb. 1872-1902, 1904-05. Available only from copy in Helsinki University Library. Lacking: 30& of the issues. B-2024 2 – 8 – ne IDC [073]
ZHIVOPISNOE OBOZRENIE – Ezhmesiachnyi literaturnyi i politicheskii zhurnal. Prilozhenie k ezhenedel'nomy zhurnalu "Zhivopisnoe obozrenie". Spb. 1882-1902. Lacking: 1882 (6), 1884 (2-3, 6-7, 10), 1886-97, 1900 (6-12), 1901 (1-12). B-2025 2 – 8 – ne IDC [320]
ZHIVOPISNOE OBOZRENIE – v. 1-9. M. 1836-44. Lacking: v. 9, 1843-44. B-2023 2 – 8 – ne IDC [460]
ZHIVOTNOVOD-KOOPERATOR – Iaroslavl', 1922 n1 – 1mf – 9 – COR-588/1 – ne IDC [334]
ZHIVYIA LITSA / Gippius, Z N – Blok Briusov Vyrubova Rozanov Sologub o mnogikh. 2 v. Prague. 1925. BR-1262 2 – 8 – ne IDC [460]
ZHIWU BAOHU – Plant Protection. 1982, 1984-85. F/P 279 – 9 – $4.50f – cc Microforms [073]
ZHIWU BINGLI XUEBAO – Acta Phytopathologica Sinica. In Chinese but English abstracts to the main articles. F p56 – 9 – 4.00f – cc Microforms [616]
ZHIWU FENLEI XUEBAO – Acta Phytotaxonomica Sinica. In Chinese but English abstracts to the main articles. F p44 – 9 – 4.00f – cc Microforms [073]
ZHIWU PAOHU XUEBAO – Acta Phytophylacica Sinica. In Chinese but English abstracts to the main articles. F p65 – 9 – $4.50f – cc Microforms [073]
ZHIWU SHENGLI XUEBAO – Acta Phytophysiologica Sinica. In Chinese but English abstracts to the main articles. F p71 – 9 – 4.00f – cc Microforms [073]
ZHIWU SHENGTAIXUE YU DI ZHIWUXUE CONGKAN – Acta Phytoecologica et Geobotanica Sinica. In Chinese but English abstracts to the main articles. F p85 – 9 – 4.00f – cc Microforms [073]
ZHIWU XUEBAO – Acta Botanica Sinica. In Chinese but English abstracts to the main articles. F p45 – 9 – $4.50f – cc Microforms [073]
ZHIWU YIANJU – Bulletin of Botanical Research. In Chinese but English abstracts to the main articles. F p83 – 9 – 4.00f – cc Microforms [073]
ZHIZN' – Literaturnyi, nauchnyi i politicheskii zhurnal. Spb. 1897-1901. Lacking: 1899 (3-4, 12), 1900 (1). B-1440 2 – 8 – ne IDC [320]
ZHIZN' – St. Petersburg. London. Geneva. Jan. 1897-Apr. 1901; Apr.-Sept. Dec. 1902 – 1 – 35.00r – us Hoover Inst Photo [073]
ZHIZN' (1764-1805) / Pishchevich, A S – v. 1-3. M. 1885. BR-7771 2 – 8 – ne IDC [947]
ZHIZN' BURYATII – Verkhneudinsk. v. 1, no. 4-6. v. 2, no. 1-8. Oct 1924-Aug 1925 – 1 – us NY Public [073]
ZHIZN' DLIA VSEKH – Literaturnyi, khudozhestvennyi, nauchno-populiarnyi i obshchestvennyi zhurnal. Spb. 1909-17. Lacking: 1914 (8-10), 1916 (3), 1917 (1-12). B-2028 2 – 8 – ne IDC [073]
ZHIZN' GENERAL-FEL'DMARSHALA GR / Chichagov, N – P. A. Rumiantsova Zadunaiskago. Spb. 1849. BR-6010 2 – 8 – ne IDC [947]
ZHIZN I RABOTA V.I. LENINA, 23 APRELI A 1870-21 I ANVARI A 1924 / Aroslavskii, Emelian – Moskva: Gos. izdvo, 3-e izd. [between 1924 and 1929?] – 1 – CSUX88-B7012 – us Hoover Inst Photo [335]
ZHIZN' I SMERT' / Otsup, N – Stikhi. 1-2. Paris. 1961. BR-1221 2 – 8 – ne IDC [460]
ZHIZN' I SOTSIALIZM – Literaturnyi, obshchestvennyi ekonomicheskii i politicheskii zhurnal. v. 1-5. Spb. 1906. B-2029 2 – 8 – ne IDC [330]
ZHIZN' MAIAKOVSKOGO / Koloskov, A – M. 1951. BR-1343 2 – 8 – ne IDC [460]
ZHIZN NATSIONALNOSTEI – Moscow. USSR. -w. 9 Nov 1918-26 Jan 1922. (1 reel) – 1 – uk British Libr Newspaper [947]
ZHIZN' NATSIONAL'NOSTEI – Moscow. Nov. 9, 1918-Sept. 11, 1922; Jan. 1923-Jan. 1924 – 1 – 35.00r – us Hoover Inst Photo [072]
ZHIZN' SIBIRI – (Library has: Jan.-Dec. 1930) – Novonikolaevsk [etc]: [s.n.], 1922-1931. 106v – 1 – CSUX89-S938 – us Hoover Inst Photo [072]
ZHIZN, SLUZHBA I PRIKLIUCHENIIA MIROVOGO SUD'I / Zakhar'in, I N – Spb, 1900 – 9 – BR-10 081 1 – ne IDC [947]
ZHIZN' ZAMECHATEL'NYKH LIUDEI / Vladislavlev, I V – (Chto Chitat', Vyp. 3). M. 1914. BR-5698 2 – 8 – ne IDC [947]
ZHIZNBORBA = DER WECKER : RAZSKAZ / Junger, Ewig – S.-Peterburg: bKn-vo "Novy i mir", 1906 – 1 – CSUX88-B824 – us Hoover Inst Photo [830]
O ZHIZNI EVREEV V ROSSII : ZAPISKA V GOSUDARSTVENNUIU DUMU / Gessen, I Ulii – S.-Peterburg: Tip. t-va "Obshchestvennai a polza", 1906 – 1 – CSUX89-B6095 – us Hoover Inst Photo [947]
ZHIZN'I LITERATURNAIA PEREPISKA PETRA IVANOVICHA RYCHKOVA / Perarskii, P P – Spb. 1867. BR-7752 2 – 8 – ne IDC [460]
ZHIZN'S MAIAKOVSKIM / Kamenskii, V – M. 1940. BR-950 2 – 8 – ne IDC [460]
Zhol-pa-khan, Lhasa *see* YAB SRAS GSUNS 'BUM
ZHONG GUO FU NU – 1981-82.24 ill. DT23f – 9 – 80.00 – cc Globe [073]
ZHONG GUO FU NU – Published by the Chinese Women's Association. Jul 1949-1966; 1978-80. 261 ill. PT23f – 9 – 875.00 – cc Globe [073]
ZHONG GUO JIAN SHE – English ed. 1952-81. 304 ill. DL7f – 9 – 1015.00 – cc Globe [073]
ZHONG GUO NONG MIN – Published as a guide for members of the farmers' movement. 1956-Jun 1957. 25 ill.DL51f – 9 – 120.00 – cc Globe [073]
ZHONG GUO QIN NIAN – The magazine of the Committee of China Youth during the first national war. Oct 1923-Oct 1927. 45 ill. DL46f – 9 – 240.00 – cc Globe [073]
ZHONG GUO WEN HUA – Academic magazine published in Yan An during the war with Japan.Feb 1940-Aug 1941.17 ill. DL57f – 9 – 70.00 – cc Globe [073]
ZHONG GUO XIN WEN – Transcripts of telexes sent to the foreign press, 1952-Sept 1981. G1 – 9 – 3300.00 – cc Globe [073]
ZHONG GUO YU WEN – An academic magazine published by the China Social and Science Academy, Jul 1952-1966.123 ill. SW6f – 9 – 415.00 – cc Globe [073]

ZHONG HUA YI XUE ZA ZHI – 1965-67; 1973-81. 105 ill. DL14f – 9 – 355.00 – cc Globe [073]

ZHONG SHAN RI BAO – China. 1928-30 – 9 – 900.00 – cc Globe [072]

ZHONG WAI RIBAO: UNIVERSAL GAZETTE – Shanghai, China. In Chinese. -d. Sept-Dec 1908. 2 reels – 1 – uk British Libr Newspaper [072]

ZHONGCAOYAO – Chinese Traditional and Herbal Drugs. 1986. F/P 273 – 9 – $4.50f – cc Microforms [073]

ZHONGGUO BAIKE NIANJIAN, 1980-81 – Yearbook of Chinese Encyclopedic Yearbook, 1980-81. Comp. by the Encyclopedic Publishing House.1 reel. M-J36 – 5 – $45.00 – cc Microforms [950]

ZHONGGUO BAOKAN *see* XINWEN CHUBAN BAO

ZHONGGUO CAIMO BAO *see* JINGTI RIBAO

ZHONGGUO CHUBAN NIANJIAN, 1980-81 – Yearbook of Chinese publications, 1980-81. Comp. by the Chinese Publishers Association. 1 reel. M-J37 – 5 – $23.00 – cc Microforms [070]

ZHONGGUO CONGSHU ZONGLU – Bibliography of Chinese serial works. Comp. by the Shanghai Library. 2 reels. M-J1 – 5 – 70.00 – cc Microforms [080]

ZHONGGUO DIANZI BAO = THE CHINESE ELECTRON JOURNAL – China. 1985-. -w. M-D73 – 1 reel/y – 1 – $28.00r – cc Microforms [072]

ZHONGGUO DIZHI BAO – China. Chinese Journal of Geology. -bim. 1986-. M-D100 – 1 – $28.00r – cc Microforms [073]

ZHONGGUO DIZHI SHILIAO – Materials for a geological history of China. Comp. by Wang Jiaying. 3 fiches. F-H156 – 9 – $13.50 – cc Microforms [950]

ZHONGGUO FANGZHI BAO – China. China Textiles. -w. 1986-. M-D99 – 1 – $28.00 – cc Microforms [072]

ZHONGGUO FAZHI BAO *see* FAZHI RIBAO

ZHONGGUO FUNU BAO = THE CHINESE WOMEN JOURNAL – China. 1985-. -w. M-D70 – 1 reel/y – 1 – $28.00r – cc Microforms [640]

ZHONGGUO GONGREN – Cina Laboristo. Yanan. Feb 1940-Mar 1941. 8 fiches. In Chinese. F/C18 – 9 – $36.00 – cc Microforms [073]

ZHONGGUO GONGREN – The Chinese Worker. Shanghai. Dec 1928-May 1929. 8 fiches. In Chinese. F/C17 – 9 – $36.00 – cc Microforms [073]

ZHONGGUO GONGREN – The Chinese Worker. Shanghai, Guangzhou. Oct 1924-Jul 1927. 4 fiches. F/C16. In Chinese – 9 – $18.00 – cc Microforms [073]

ZHONGGUO GONGSHANG BAO = CHINA INDUSTRIAL AND COMMERCIAL NEWS – China. 1985-. -w. M-D75 – 1 – $28.00r – cc Microforms [072]

ZHONGGUO GUDAI QINGTONGQI XIAO CICIAN – A concise dictionary of ancient Chinese bronze wares. Comp. by Du Naisong. 2 fiches. F-J30 – 9 – $9.00 – cc Microforms [930]

ZHONGGUO GUDIAN WENXUE PINLUN ZILIAO SUOYIN – Index to critical materials on classical Chinese literature. Comp. by the Chinese Department of Fujian Normal College. 2 fiches. F-J16 – 9 – $9.00 – cc Microforms [480]

ZHONGGUO HEYUN BAO = THE CHINESE RIVER TRANSPORT JOURNAL – China. 1985-. 2 issues per week. M-D78 – 1 – $34.00r – cc Microforms [072]

ZHONGGUO HEZUO JINGJI BAO – China. Chinese Cooperative Economics. -w. 1986-. M-D106 – 1 – $28.00r – cc Microforms [330]

ZHONGGUO HUANJING BAO = THE CHINESE ENVIRONMENTAL JOURNAL – China. 1984-. 2 issues a week. M-D60 – 1 reel/y – 1 – $28.00r – cc Microforms [580]

ZHONGGUO HUANJING KEXUE – Environmental Sciences in China.1984. F/P 280 – 9 – $4.50f – cc Microforms [073]

ZHONGGUO JIAOTONG BAO = THE CHINESE COMMUNICATION JOURNAL – China. 1985-. 2 issues per week. M-D72 – 1 reel/y – 1 – $28.00r – cc Microforms [072]

ZHONGGUO JIAOYU BAO = CHINESE JOURNAL OF EDUCATION – China. 1984-. 2 issues per week. M-D57 – 1 reel/y – 1 – $34.00r – cc Microforms [072]

ZHONGGUO JIDIAN BAO = CHINESE MACHINERY AND ELECTRONICS NEWS – China. 2 issues a week. 1984-. M-D58. As Zhongguo Jixie Bao (Chinese Journal of Machinery) until 1989 – 1 reel/y – 1 – $34.00r – cc Microforms [072]

ZHONGGUO JIGUANG – Chinese Journal of Lasers. 1979, 1986. F/P 112 – 9 – $4.50f – cc Microforms [073]

ZHONGGUO JIN BASHI NIAN MINGSHI LUNZHU MULU – A bibliography of writings on the history of the Ming Dynasty of the last 80 years.Comp. by the Institute of History, Chinese Academy of Social Sciences. 6 fiches. F-J8 – 9 – $22.50 – cc Microforms [950]

ZHONGGUO JINDAI DUIWAI MAOYISHI ZILIAO (ZHONGGUO JINDAI JINGJISHI CANKAO ZILIAO CONGKAN) – Series of reference materials on the economic history of modern China: Source materials for a history of modern China's foreign trade. Comp. by Yao Xian. 1 reel.M-H152 – 5 – $40.00 – cc Microforms [950]

ZHONGGUO JINDAI GONGYESHI ZILIAO, 1-2. (ZHONGGUO JINDAI JINGJISHI ZILIAO CANGKAN – Series of reference materials on the economic history of modern China: Source materials for an industrial history of modern China, v1-2. Comp. by Sun Yutang, Wang Jingyu. 2 reels. M-H149 – 5 – $80.00 – cc Microforms [950]

ZHONGGUO JINDAI HUOBISHI ZILIAO, (DIYIJI QING ZHENGFU TONGZHI SHIQI, 1840-1911) – Source materials for a monetary history of modern China, part 1: The Qing Dynasty, 1840-1911. Comp. by the Head Office of the People's Bank of China.1 reel. M-H153 – 5 – 35.00 – cc Microforms [950]

ZHONGGUO JINDAI JINGJISHI TONGJI ZILIAO XUANJI (ZHONGGUO JINDAI JINGJISHI CANKAO ZILIAO CONGKAN) – Series of reference materials on the economic history of modern China: A Collection of statistical materials on the economic history of modern China.Comp. by Yan Zhongping and others. 4 fiches. F-H147 – 9 – 4.00f – cc Microforms [950]

ZHONGGUO JINDAI NONGYESHI ZILIAO (ZHONGGUO JINDAI JINGJISHI CANKAO ZILIAO CONGKAN) – Series of reference materials on the economic history of modern China: Source materials for an agricultural history of modern China. Comp. by Li Wenzhi. 2 reels. M-H151 – 5 – 70.00 – cc Microforms [950]

ZHONGGUO JINDAI QIKAN PIANMU HUILU – Accumulative catalog of modern Chinese periodicals. Comp. by the Shanghai Library. 2 reels. M-J13 – 5 – $80.00r; $112.50f – cc Microforms [073]

ZHONGGUO JINDAI SHOUGONGYESHI ZILIAO, 1840-1949 (ZHONGGUO JINGJISHI ZILIAO CONGKAN) – Series of reference materials on the economic history of modern China: Source materials for a history of the handicraft industry in modern China, 1840-1949. Comp. by Peng Zeyi. 1 reel. M-H150 – 5 – $45.00 – cc Microforms [950]

ZHONGGUO JINDAI TIELUSHI ZILIAO.(ZHONGGUO JINDAI JINGJISHI CANKAO ZILIAO CONGKAN.) – Series of reference materials on the economic history of modern China: Source materials for a history of railroads in modern China. Comp. by Mi Rucheng. 1 reel. M-H154 – 5 – 35.00 – cc Microforms [950]

ZHONGGUO JINDAI XIANDAI CONGSHU MULU – A bibliography of modern and contemporary Chinese books in series. Comp. by Shanghai Library. 1 reel. M-J2 – 5 – 35.00 – cc Microforms [070]

ZHONGGUO JINDAISHI ZILIAO CONGKAN: DIERCI YAPIAN ZHANZHENG, 1-6 – Series on modern Chinese history: The Second opium war, v1-6. 2 reels.M-H73 – 5 – $80.00 – cc Microforms [950]

ZHONGGUO JINDAISHI ZILIAO CONGKAN: HUIMIN QIYI, 1-4 – Series on modern Chinese history: The Hui uprisings, v1-4. Comp. by the Chinese Historical Association. 1 reel. M-H67 – 5 – $40.00 – cc Microforms [950]

ZHONGGUO JINDAISHI ZILIAO CONGKAN: NIANJUN, 1-6 – Series on modern Chinese history: The Nian army, v1-6. Comp. by the Chinese Historical Association. 2 reels. M-H66 – 5 – $90.00 – cc Microforms [950]

ZHONGGUO JINDAISHI ZILIAO CONGKAN: TAIPING TIANGUO, 1-8 – Series on modern Chinese history: The Taiping Rebellion, v1-8. Comp. by the Chinese Historical Association.2 reels. M-H65 – 5 – $80.00 – cc Microforms [950]

ZHONGGUO JINDAISHI ZILIAO CONGKAN: WUXU BIANFA, 1-4 – Series on modern Chinese history: The Reform movement of 1898. Comp. by the Chinese Association of History. 1 reel. M-H71 – 5 – 35.00 – cc Microforms [950]

ZHONGGUO JINDAISHI ZILIAO CONGKAN: XINHAI GEMING, 1-8 – Series on modern Chinese history: The Revolution of 1911, v1-8. Comp. by the Chinese Historical Association.2 reels. M-H74 – 5 – $80.00 – cc Microforms [950]

ZHONGGUO JINDAISHI ZILIAO CONGKAN: YANGWU YUNDONG, 1-8 – Series on modern Chinese history: The Westernization movement, v1-8. Comp. by the Chinese Historical Association. 2 reels.M-H69 – 5 – 50.00 – cc Microforms [950]

ZHONGGUO JINDAISHI ZILIAO CONGKAN: YAPIAN ZHANZHENG, 1-6 – Series on modern Chinese history: The Opium war, v1-6. Comp. by the Chinese Historical Association. 2 reels. M-H64 – 5 – $80.00 – cc Microforms [950]

ZHONGGUO JINDAISHI ZILIAO CONGKAN: YIHETUAN, 1-4 – Series on modern Chinese history: The Boxer Rebellion, v1-4. Comp. by the Chinese Historical Association. 1 reel. M-H72 – 5 – 35.00 – cc Microforms [950]

ZHONGGUO JINDAISHI ZILIAO CONGKAN: ZHONGFA ZHANZHENG, 1-7 – Series on modern Chinese history: The Sino-French war, v1-7. Comp. by the Chinese Historical Association. 2 reels. M-H70 – 5 – 70.00 – cc Microforms [950]

ZHONGGUO JINDAISHI ZILIAO CONGKAN: ZHONGRI ZHANZHENG, 1-7 – Series on modern Chinese history: Sino-Japanese war, v1-7. Comp. by the Chinese Historical Association. 2 reels. M-H68 – 5 – 70.00 – cc Microforms [950]

ZHONGGUO JINGI WENTI – Chinese Economic Problems. In Chinese but Table of Contents in English in each issue. F p5 – 9 – 4.00f – cc Microforms [330]

ZHONGGUO JINGJISHI CHANGBIAN – Economic history of China, hand-written copy by Huang Xuwan. Original micropublication. 17 reels. M-H202 – 5 – 1020.00; 60.00r – cc Microforms [950]

ZHONGGUO JUNREN – The Chinese Armyman. Feb. 1925-Mar 1926. 6 fiches. F/C 24 – 9 – $27.00 – cc Microforms [072]

ZHONGGUO KEJI BAO – (1986 $40.00r; 1987-$55.00r) – China. China Science and Technology Gazette. Three issues per week. 1986-. M-D103 – 1 – cc Microforms [072]

ZHONGGUO KEXUE-JISHU DAXUE XUEBAO – Journal of China University of Science and Technology. In Chinese but English abstracts to the main articles. F p178 – 9 – 4.00f – cc Microforms [073]

ZHONGGUO LISHI RENWU SHENGZU NIANBIAO – Table of birth and death rates of Chinese historical figures. Comp. by Wu Hailin, Li Yanpei. 7 fiches. F-J23 – 9 – $52.50 – cc Microforms [310]

ZHONGGUO LISHIXUE NIANJIAN, 1980-81 = YEARBOOK OF CHINESE HISTORY, 1980-81 – (1979-80 $45.50; 1981 $24.50) – Comp. by editorial board of Yearbook of Chinese History.12 fiches. F-J38 – 9 – cc Microforms [950]

ZHONGGUO LUYOU BAO = CHINA TOURIST WEEKLY – China. 1983-. As Luyou Bao (Tourist Weekly) until 1985. M-D34 – 1 reel/y – 1 – $28.00r – cc Microforms [073]

ZHONGGUO MEISHUJIA RENMING CIDIAN – A dictionary of Chinese artists.Comp. by Yu Jianhua. 1 reel. M-J28 – 5 – 35.00 – cc Microforms [700]

ZHONGGUO MEITAN BAO – Journal of the Chinese Coal Industry. 2 issues per week. 1983- – 1 reel/y – 1 – $28.00r – cc Microforms [622]

ZHONGGUO MINGSHENG CIDIAN – A dictionary of scenic spots in China. Comp. by China National Bureau of Cultural Relics. 1 reel. M-J31 – 5 – 35.00 – cc Microforms [910]

ZHONGGUO MINGUO DANGAN ZILIAO HUIBIAN (DIYI JI) – (Zhonghua Minguo Dangan Shiliao Huibian (Er). v2. 6 fiches. F-H115. 12.00; MIM; 9) – Archival materials on the history of the Republic of China, v1. Comp. by the Second Chinese Archive of History. 3 fiches. F-H114 – 9 – $13.50 – cc Microforms [950]

ZHONGGUO NIANGZAO – China Brewing. 1983-85.F/P 282 – 9 – $4.50f – cc Microforms [073]

ZHONGGUO NONGYE HEZUOHUA YUNDONG SHILIAO – Materials on the history of the agricultural cooperative movement in China.Comp. by Shijingtang. 1 reel.M-H168 – 5 – $23.00 – cc Microforms [950]

ZHONGGUO NONGYE KEXUE – Chinese Agricultural Science. In Chinese but English abstracts to the main articles. F p40 – 9 – $4.50f – cc Microforms [630]

ZHONGGUO QICHE BAO = THE CHINESE AUTOMOBILE JOURNAL – China. -w 1985-. M-D76 – 1 – $28.00 – cc Microforms [072]

ZHONGGUO QINGGONGYE BAO – China. The Chinese light industry journal. -w.1985-. M-D71 – 1 – $28.00 – cc Microforms [072]

ZHONGGUO QINGNIAN = CHINESE YOUTH – Shanghai. Oct 1923-Oct 1927. 2 reels. M-C68 – 1 – $240.00 – cc Microforms [073]

ZHONGGUO QINGNIAN = CHINESE YOUTH – Yanan. Apr 1939-Mar 1941. 2 reels. M-C69 – 1 – $110.00 – cc Microforms [073]

ZHONGGUO QINGNIAN BAO – Chinese Youth Gazette. In Chinese. Current subscription. Annual delivery. Oct 1978-Dec 1979. 1 reel; 1980- . 1 reel per yr. M D4 – 1 – $55.00r – cc Microforms [072]

ZHONGGUO RENKOU BAO = CHINA DEMOGRAPHIC JOURNAL – China. As Jiankan Bao, Jihua Shengyu Bao until Jul 1987. As Zhongguo Jihua Shengyn Bao (Chinese Journal of Family Planning) until 1990. (Health Gazette, Birth Control Edition). -w. 1984-. 1 reel per yr. M-D6A – 1 – $40.00r – cc Microforms [072]

ZHONGGUO RENMIN GEMING ZHANZHENG DITUXUAN – A selection of maps of the Chinese people's revolutionary war. Comp. by the Military Museum of the Chinese People's Revolution. 1 fiche. F-J43 – 9 – $4.50f – cc Microforms [950]

ZHONGGUO SHANGYE BAO = THE CHINESE COMMERCE JOURNAL – China. 2 issues per week. 1985-. M-D74 – 1 – $34.00r – cc Microforms [072]

ZHONGGUO SHAONIAN BAO – Chinese Children's Journal. In Chinese. Current subscription. Annual delivery. Nov 1978-Dec 1979. 1 reel; 1980- . 1 reel per yr. M D5 – 1 – $28.00 – cc Microforms [073]

ZHONGGUO SHEDUI QIYE BAO *see* ZHONGGUO XIANGZHEN QIYE BAO

ZHONGGUO SHEHUI KEXUE – Social Sciences in China. In Chinese but Table of Contents in English in each issue. F p12 – 9 – $4.50f – cc Microforms [073]

ZHONGGUO SHENGWU YIXUE GONGCHENG XUEBAO – Chinese Journal of Biomedical Engineering. 1981, 1983-85. F/P 281 – 9 – $4.50f – cc Microforms [073]

ZHONGGUO SHI YANJIU – (1979, 1981-83 $3.50f; 1980, 1984- $4.50f) – Journal of Chinese Historical Studies. In Chinese but Table of Contents in English in each issue. F p15 – 9 – cc Microforms [073]

ZHONGGUO SHIPIN – China Food. 1980-84. F/P 266 – 9 – $4.00f – cc Microforms [640]

ZHONGGUO SHIPIN BAO = THE CHINESE FOOD JOURNAL – China. 1984-. M-D62 – 1 reel/y – 1 – $34.00r – cc Microforms [660]

ZHONGGUO SHIXUE LUNWEN SUOYIN – Index to Chinese papers on history. Comp. by the Institute of History, Chinese Academy of Science. 1 reel. M-J18 – 5 – $40.00 – cc Microforms [950]

ZHONGGUO TIYU BAO = CHINA SPORTS NEWS – (1977-79, 1981-89 $45.00r; 1990-91 $55.00r) – China. 4 issues per week. 1977-. Tiyu Bao (Sports News) until 1989. M-D30 – 1 – cc Microforms [072]

ZHONGGUO TUSHU YINSHUA KAPIAN LEIJI LIANHE MULU – A joint cumulative bibliography of Chinese books, 1974-78. Comp. by the Beijing Library. 1 reel. M-J45 – 5 – $35.00 – cc Microforms [020]

ZHONGGUO WENHUA BAO – Chinese Journal of Culture. 1987- . M/D 118 – 1 – $34.00r – cc Microforms [072]

ZHONGGUO XIANDAI WENXUE QIKAN MULU – Catalog of literary periodicals of contemporary China. Comp. by Xiandai Wenxu Qikan Lianhe Diaocha Xiaozu. 2 fiches. F-J15 – 9 – $4.00f – cc Microforms [480]

ZHONGGUO XIANDAISHI ZILIAO XUANBIAN 1-5 – Selection of historical materials on contemporary China, v1-5. Comp. by Wei Honggun. 2 reels. M-H125 – 5 – $80.00 – cc Microforms [950]

ZHONGGUO XIANGZHEN QIYE BAO = CHINA'S TOWNSHIP ENTERPRISES JOURNAL – (Continues Zhongguo Shedui Qiye Bao (China Commune Enterprises) after 1987) – China. 2 issues per week. 1982-. M-D31 – 1 – $34.00 – cc Microforms [072]

ZHONGGUO XIANGZHENQIYE BAO – Journal of Chinese Rural Enterprises. 1986- . M/D 115 – 1 – cc Microforms [630]

ZHONGGUO XIAOFEIZHE BAO – China. Consumer's Weekly. 1986-. M-D107 – 1 – $28.00r – cc Microforms [072]

ZHONGGUO XIQU QUYI CIDIAN – A dictionary of Chinese traditional operas and folk arts. Comp. by Shanghai Art Research Institute and Shanghai branch of Chinese Dramatists Association. 1 reel. M-J29 – 5 – $40.00 – cc Microforms [390]

ZHONGGUO XUESHENG ZHOUKAN – Chinese Student Weekly. Aug 1925-Mar 1927. 1 reel. M/C 85 – 1 – $55.00 – cc Microforms [073]

ZHONGGUO XUMUSHI ZILIAO – Materials on the history of animal husbandry in modern China. Comp. by Wang Yuhu. 5 fiches. F-H155 – 9 – $22.50 – cc Microforms [950]

ZHONGGUO YAOLI XUEBAO – Acta Pharmacologica Sinica. In Chinese but English abstracts to the main articles. F p156 – 9 – 4.00f – cc Microforms [073]

ZHONGGUO YIXUE KEXUEYUAN XUEBAO – Acta Academiae Medicinae Sinicae. In Chinese but English abstracts to the main articles. F p161 – 9 – 4.00f – cc Microforms [073]

ZHONGGUO YIXUE WENZHAI – Zhongyi. China Medical Abstracts, Traditional Chinese Medicine. In Chinese but Table of Contents in English in each issue. F p168 – 9 – 4.00f – cc Microforms [616]

ZHONGGUO YOUYI SHILIAO – Materials on the history of the Chinese courier system. Comp. by Lou Zuyi. 2 fiches. F-H157 – 9 – 4.00f – cc Microforms [950]

ZHONGGUO YUWEN – The Chinese Language. In Chinese but Table of Contents in English in each issue. F p22 – 9 – $4.50f – cc Microforms [480]

ZHONGGUO YUYIANXUE LUNWEN SUOYI – Index to Chinese papers on linguistics. Comp. by the Institute of Linguistics, Chinese Academy of Social Sciences. 2 fiches. F-J17 – 9 – $27.00 – cc Microforms [480]

ZHONGGUO ZAOZHI – China Pulp and Paper. 1982-84. F/P 262 – 9 – $4.50f – cc Microforms [073]

ZHONGGUO ZHENJIU – Chinese Acupuncture & Moxibustion. In Chinese but English abstracts to the main articles. F p159 – 9 – 4.00f – cc Microforms [616]

ZHONGGUO ZHEXUESHI YANJIU – (1982-84 $3.50f; 1981, 1987 $4.50f) – Studies on History of Chinese Philosophy. In Chinese with Table of Contents in English in each issue. F p11 – 9 – cc Microforms [180]

ZHONGGUO ZHIGONG YUNDONG KIANSHI (ZHONGGUO XIANDAISHI ZILIAO CONGKAN) – Series of materials on contemporary Chinese history: A Short history of the labour movement in China. Comp. by Deng Zhongxia.3 fiches. F-H132 – 9 – 4.00f – cc Microforms [950]

ZHONGHUA FANGSHE YIXUE YU FANGHU ZAZHI – Chinese Journal of Radiological Medicine and Protection. In Chinese but English abstracts to the main articles. F p155 – 9 – 4.00f – cc Microforms [616]

ZHONGHUA GUKE ZAZHI – Chinese Journal of Orthopedics. In Chinese but English abstracts to the main articles. F p152 – 9 – 4.00f – cc Microforms [616]

ZHONGHUA JIEHE HE HUXIXITONG JIBING ZAZHI – Chinese Journal of Tuberculosis and Respiratory Diseases. In Chinese but English abstracts to the main articles. F p154 – 9 – 4.00f. – cc Microforms [073]

ZHONGHUA MINGUO DANGAN ZILIAO HUIBIAN – (v2. (ER). 14 fiches. FH/115. $49.00; 9) – (Diyi Ji). Archival materials on the History of the Republic of China.Comp. by the Second Chinese Archive of History. v1. 3 fiches. FH/114 – 9 – $13.50 – cc Microforms [950]

ZHONGHUA NEIKE ZAZHI – Chinese Journal of Internal Medicine. In Chinese but English abstracts to the main articles. F p149 – 9 – $4.50f – cc Microforms [073]

ZHONGHUA PIFUKE ZAZHI – Chinese Journal of Dermatology. In Chinese but English abstracts to the main articles. F p148 – 9 – $4.50f – cc Microforms [073]

ZHONGHUA RENMIN GONGHEGUO GUOWUYUAN GONGBAO – Bulletins of the State Council of the People's Republic of China. 1980-86. F/P271 – 9 – $4.50f – cc Microforms [073]

ZHONGHUA WAIKE ZAZHI – Chinese Journal of Surgery. In Chinese but English abstracts to the main articles. F p153 – 9 – 4.00f – cc Microforms [616]

ZHONGHUA WEISHENGWUXUE HE MIANYIXUE ZAZHI – Chinese Journal of Microbiology and Immunology. In Chinese but English abstracts to the main articles. F p150 – 9 – 4.00f – cc Microforms [073]

ZHONGHUA XIN-XUEGUANBING ZAZHI – Chinese Journal of Cardiology. In Chinese but English abstracts to the main articles. F p147 – 9 – $3.50f – cc Microforms [073]

ZHONGHUA ZHONGLIU ZAZHI – Chinese Journal of Oncology. In Chinese but English abstracts to the main articles. F p151 – 9 – $4.50f – cc Microforms [073]

ZHONGLIU = MIDSTREAM – Sept 1936-Aug 1937. Semimonthly. 1 reel. M-C61 – 1 – $45.00 – cc Microforms [073]

ZHONG-NAN KUANG-YE XUEYUAN XUEBAO – Journal of Central-South Institute of Mining Metallurgy. In Chinese, with English abstracts to the main articles – 9 – $4.00f – cc Microforms [622]

ZHONGSHAN DAXUE XUEBAO – (1977-78, 1980-82 $4.50f; 1979, 1983-84 $3.50f) – Zhexue Shehui Kexue Ban. Journal of Zhongshan University, Philosophy and Social Science. In Chinese but Table of Contents in English in each issue. F p210 – 9 – cc Microforms [073]

ZHONGSHAN DAXUE XUEBAO – Ziran Kexue Ban. Acta Scientiarum Naturalium Universitatis Sunyatseni. In Chinese but English abstracts to the main articles. F p187 – 9 – $4.50f – cc Microforms [073]

ZHONGUO SHANGBAO = CHINA COMMERCIAL NEWS – 1992- – 1r per y – 1 – inquire – us Ross [072]

ZHONGWAI LISHI NIANBIAO – Chronological tables of Chinese and foreign histories. Comp. by Jian Bozan, Qi Sihe and others. 1 reel. M/J40 – 1 – 35.00 – cc Microforms [520]

ZHONGYI ZAZHI – (1979, 1984 $3.50f; 1980-83, 1986- $4.50f) – Journal of Traditional Chinese Medicine. In Chinese but Table of Contents in English in each issue. F p54 – 9 – cc Microforms [616]

ZHONGYUAN = THE CENTRAL PLAINS – Jun 1943-Oct 1945. -m. 7 fiches. F-C62 – 9 – $27.00 – cc Microforms [073]

ZHOUBAO = THE WEEKLY – Sept 1945-Aug 1946. 1 reel. M-C63 – 1 – $45.00 – cc Microforms [073]

ZHOUGGUO JUNREN – The Chinese Armyman. Feb 1925-Mar 1926. F C24. In Chinese – 9 – $27.00 – cc Microforms [073]

ZHUHAI TEQU BAO – China. Zhuhai Special Zone News. -w. 1985-. M-D98 – 1 – $28.00r – cc Microforms [072]

ZHUNGGUO JINDAI GONGYESHI ZILIAO, 1-4 – Source materials for a modern Chinese industrial history, v1-4. Comp. by Chen Zheng, etc. 2 reels. M-H146 – 5 – 70.00 – cc Microforms [950]

ZHURNAL / Moscow. Patriarchate – (Journal of Moscow Patriarchate). 1961- – 1 – us UMI [073]

ZHURNAL / Russia. Ministarstvo Narodnovo Prosveshcheniya – Ukazatel k Neoffotzial'noi chasti Povremenikh Izdanii Ministerstva Narodnago Prosveshcheniya zz 1803-1853 gody. Sanktpeterburg. 1856 – 1 – us NY Public [324]

ZHURNAL / Russia. Ministerstva Narodnago Prosveshcheniia – (Journal of the Ministry of Public Education). o.s. 326 v., 1834-1905; n.s. 72 v. 1906-17 – 3 – us Readex [324]

ZHURNAL DEPARTAMENTA NARODNOGO PROSVESHCHENNIA – Spb. 1821-24. B-2034 2 – 8 – ne IDC [380]

ZHURNAL DEZHURNYKH GENERAL A.D. IUDANTOV / ed by Evdokimov, L V – Tsarstvovanie Imperatritsy Elisavety Petrovny. Spb. 1897. BR-10,523 1 – 9 – ne IDC [947]

ZHURNAL DLIA KHOZIAEK – Moscow, 1913-18; 1922-26 – 102mf – 9 – $690.00 – us Ross [640]

ZHURNAL DLIA VSEKH – 1896-1906. Lacking: 1896-97 (1-12), 1898 (1, 3, 6-12), 1900 (7), 1901 (5, 8), 1906 (9-12). B-1405 2 – 8 – ne IDC [073]

ZHURNAL DLIA ZHENSHCHIN – Moscow, 1915 n3-4, 7-8; 1916 n6; 1917 n5-6; 1918 n10-12; 1922 n1-2, 5-7; 1923 n1-5; 1924 n1-12; 1925 n1-12; 1926 n1-6 – 37mf – 9 – $240.00 – us Ross [640]

ZHURNAL DREVNEI I NOVOI SLOVESNOSTI – Spb. 1818-19. B-2035 2 – 8 – ne IDC [073]

ZHURNAL EKSPERIMENTAL' NOI I TEORETICHESKOI FIZIKI – (Journal of experimental and theoretical physics). v. 1-45. 1931-1963 – 1,5,6 – us Princeton Micro [530]

ZHURNAL HEOLOHO-HEOHRAFICHNOHO TSYKLU = JOURNAL DU CYCLE DE GEOLOGIE ET DE GEOGRAPHIE – no.1-4 (8). 1932-34. Frequency varies.4v in 3. charts, maps, plates. Text in Ukrainian; English, French, or German summaries – 1 – us U.W. Library [550]

ZHURNAL IURIDICHESKAGO OBSHCHESTVA PRI IMP. S-PETERBURGSKOM UNIVERSITETE / St. Petersburg. University. Law Society – Spb. 1894-98. Journal of the Petersburg University Law Society; succeeded the vZhurnal vgrazhdanskogo vi vugolovnogo vprara (R-9568) and was in turn succeeded by vVestnik vprava (R-2386). BR-9569 1 – 9 – ne IDC [340]

ZHURNAL KIEVSKOGO GUBERNSKOGO EKONOMICHESKOGO SOVESHCHANIIA – (Includes c.1: no.2 1921:Oct) – Kiev: Gos. izdvo, 1921 – 1 – CSUXAKY5910-S – us Hoover Inst Photo [350]

ZHURNAL MINISTERSTVA NARODNAGO PROSVESHCHENIIA / Russia – St. Petersburg. o.s. 1834-1905. n.s. 1906-17 – 1 – us UMI [947]

ZHURNAL MINISTERSTVA NARODNOGO PROSVESHCHENIIA – 362 v. Spb. 1834-1905; 72 v. Spb. 1906-17. B-1203 2 – 8 – ne IDC [073]

ZHURNAL SOVESHCHANIIA TOVARISHCHEI MINISTROV VREMENNAGO PRAVITEL'STVA – Petrograd. June 14-Oct. 18, 1917, 1 volume, nos. 48, 77, 78, 101, 123, 124, 145, 254 – 1 – 35.00r – us Hoover Inst Photo [324]

ZHURNAL UGOLOVNAGO PRAVA I PROTESSA / International Association of Criminalists. Russian Group – 2v. Spb. 1912-13. Issued by the Russian Group of the International Association of Criminalists. Quarterly. (BEL 2887). BR-9341 1 – 9 – ne IDC [073]

ZHURNAL ZASEDANIIA VREMENNAGO PRAVITEL' STVA PO ZAKLIUCHENIIAM...SOVESHCHANIIA TOVARISHCHEI MINISTROV – Petrograd. Apr. 17-Oct. 1917, 2 volumes, nos. 1-252. Many issues missing – 1 – 35.00r – us Hoover Inst Photo [324]

ZHURNAL ZASEDANIIA VREMENNAGO PRAVITEL' STVA PROEKTY – Petrograd. Aug. 21-Oct. 2, 1917, 1 volume, nos. 158, 171, 172, 175-178, 180 – 1 – 35.00r – us Hoover Inst Photo [072]

ZHURNAL ZEMLEVLADEL'TSEV – Moscow. 1858-1859, nos. 1-22. Missing: nos. 23-24 – 1 – 35.00r – us Hoover Inst Photo [072]

ZHURNALIST = JOURNALIST : PUBLICATION OF THE PRINTERS UNION – Moscow, 1926-33 – 105mf – 9 – $600.00 – us Ross [070]

ZHURNALIST – Moscow. 1922, nos. 1-2; 1923, nos. 3-5; 1924, nos. 11-16; 1925, nos. 1-12; 1927, nos. 1-12 – 1 – 35.00r – us Hoover Inst Photo [380]

ZHURNALIST – Moscow. 1973-74 – 1 – D16263 – us UMI [070]

ZHURNAL'NAIA LETOPIS' – M. 1926-37. Cont. as: Letopis' zhurnal'nykh statei. M. 1938-72. Lacking: 1957 (36); 1965 (49); 1966 (index 40-52); 1971 (33). BR-10,419 1 – 9. 1973-74.; ; 9 – ne IDC [073]

ZHURNALY SEKRETNAGO I GLAVNAGO KOMITETOV PO KREST'IANSKOMU DELU / Russia. Gosudarstvennyi sovet. Arkhiv gosudarstvennago soveta – (Zhurnaly i Memorii Obshchego Sobraniia Soveta po Krest'ianskomu Delu) – Petrograd, 1915. 2 vols – 1 – 35.00r – us Hoover Inst Photo [324]

ZHURNALY ZASEDANII VREMENNAGO PRAVITEL' STVA – Petrograd. Mar. 4-Oct. 3?, 1917, nos. 1-181?. Index for April available. Missing: nos. 1, 2, 151, 171-180 – 1 – 35.00r – us Hoover Inst Photo [072]

ZHYTTA I REVOLUTZIYA – Kiev. 1920-1933. Incomplete – 1 – us NY Public [335]

ZHYTTIA I SLOVO = LIFE AND WORD – Toronto, 1965- – 1 – $130.00y – cn McLaren [072]

Ziaa Al-din Barni *see* TARIKH-I-FEROZ SHAHI

Zibrt, C *see*
– BIBLIOGRAFICHY PREHLED CESKYCH NARODNICH PISNI
– BIBLIOGRAFIE CESKE HISTORIE

ZICHRONOTH – Amsterdam. v1-4(5). 1933-1936 – 6mf – 9 – J-261-122/1 – ne IDC [073]

Zickel, S *see* DEUTSCH-AMERIKANISCHES HAND-LEXIKON DES ALLGEMEINEN WISSENS (AEL, ABT 1;12)

Zickendraht, Karl *see* DER STREIT ZWISCHEN ERASMUS UND LUTHER UEBER DIE WILLENSFREIHEIT

ZIDONGHUA XUEBAO – Acta Automatica Sinica. In Chinese but English abstracts to the main articles. F p68 – 9 – 4.00f – cc Microforms [073]

Zidouemba, Dominique *see* DIRECTORY OF DOCUMENTATION, LIBRARIES AND ARCHIVES SERVICES IN AFRICA

ZIDOVSKE SPRAY = JEWISH AFFAIRS – Prague, CS. v6 no21. 25 Apr 1923 – 1r – 1 – $25.00 – cn Can Microfilming [072]

Ziegelbauer, M *see* HISTORIA REI LITERARIAE O.S.B.

DER ZIEGELBRENNER – Munich. Sept. 1917-Apr. 1920, Vol. 1, no. 1-Vol. 4, nos. 26 34; Jan. 1930, no. 1. Missing: Vol. 3, no. 15, Feb. 1919 – 1 – 35.00r – us Hoover Inst Photo [073]

Ziegelmeier, Otto W *see* DER CHRISTLICHE FREIHEITSBEGRIFF

Ziegenfuss, T N *see* THE EFFECTS OF CONTINUOUS AND INTERMITTENT EXERCISE BOUTS OF EQUAL WORK OUTPUT ON POST-EXERCISE ENERGY EXPENDITURE

Ziegle, H *see* AFRIQUE EQUATORIALE FRANCAISE

Ziegler, F *see* A SCHOOL DICTIONARY

Ziegler, Friedrich *see* PRACTICAL KEY TO THE CANARESE LANGUAGE

Ziegler, Heinrich *see* DIE GEGENREFORMATION IN SCHLESIEN

Ziegler, I *see* DIE KOENIGSGLEICHNISSE DES MIDRASCH

Ziegler, Johannes Joachim *see* ZUR RELEVANZ KOMMUNIKATIVER FERTIGKEITEN IN DER AERZTLICHEN PRAXIS

Ziegler, Marianne von *see* DAS WUNDER IN DER WIES

Ziegler, Theobald *see* GOETHES WELT- UND LEBENSANSCHAUUNG

Ziehen, Eduard *see* DIE DEUTSCHE SCHWEIZERBEGEISTERUNG IN DEN JAHREN 1750-1815

Ziehnert, Widar *see* SACHSEN'S VOLKSSAGEN

Ziel, Rainer *see* UNTERSUCHUNGEN ZUR KENNTNIS VON ORDNUNGSVORGAENGEN IN FLUORIT-UEBERSTRUKTUR-PHASEN IM SYSTEM SrF_2-YbF_3

DIE ZIELE DER GEOGRAPHIE DES MENSCHEN / Schlueter, Otto – Muenchen: Oldenbourg, 1906. 63p – 1 – us U.W. Library [304]

ZIELE UND MITTEL DER VOLKSBILDUNG / Lippert, Julius – Prag: Verlag des deutschen Vereines zur Verbreitung gemeinnuetziger Vortraege, 1875 – 1r – 1 – us U.W. Library [370]

ZIELONY SZTANDAR – London, UK. 8 Nov 1942-24 Mar 1943 – 1 – uk British Libr Newspaper [072]

ZIELONY SZTANDAR – Warsaw, Poland. -sw. Aug 1951-Dec 1958. 8 reels – 1 – uk British Libr Newspaper [947]

ZIELSPRACHE DEUTSCH – v1- 1951- 1; 1976-5,6,9 – us UMI [430]

ZIELSPRACHE DEUTSCH – (Preceded by: Deutschunterricht fuer Auslaender) – Muenchen. v1-8. 1970-77. – 5,9 – Dfl240.00; Dfl30.00v – ne Swets [430]

ZIELSPRACHE ENGLISCH – 1972- 1; 1976-5,6,9 – us UMI [420]

ZIELSPRACHE FRANZOESISCH – Muenchen. 1978-79* – 1,5,9 – D11005 – us UMI [440]

ZIELSPRACHE SPANISCH – Muenchen. 1978 1; 1978* 5,9 – 1,5,9 – D11006 – us UMI [440]

ZIEMIA POMORSKA – Bydgoszcz, Poland. 1945; Oct 1948-1950 (scattered issues) – 4r – 1 – us L of C Photodup [943]

Zienkovskago, V V *see* DIETI EMIGRATSII

DIE ZIERDE DER GEISTLICHEN HOCHZEIT, UN DIE KLEINEREN SCHRIFTEN / Ruisbroeck, Jan van; ed by Huebner, Friedrich Markus – Leipzig, 1924 – 7mf – ne Slangenburg [290]

DIE ZIERDE DER GEISTLICHEN HOCHZEIT, UND DIE KLEINEREN SCHRIFTEN / Ruisbroeck, Jan van; ed by Huebner, Friedrich Markus – Leipzig, 1924 – 7mf – 8 – ne Slangenburg [290]

Zierer, Maria Steinmueller *see* BAUERNSCHRITT

Zierer, Otto *see* DER MANN OHNE HERZ

Ziesel, Kurt *see* VERWANDLUNG DER HERZEN

DER ZIGEUNER / Zillich, Heinrich – Muenchen: A Langen/G Mueller, 1933 – 1r – 1 – us U.W. Library [830]

ZIGEUNER CHRISTL : ROMAN / Wegrich, Arno – Nuernberg: Fanfaren Verlag, 1940 – 1r – 1 – us U.W. Library [830]

ZIG-ZAG – Bristol, England. 25 Aug 1881-25 May 1882. -w.1 reel – 1 – uk British Libr Newspaper [072]

ZIG-ZAG – Maceio, Alagoas. 14 Jan 1889 – 1,5,6 – bl Biblioteca [072]

ZIGZAG – Santiago, Chile.19 Feb 1905-18 Sept 1964 – 1 – us Res Libr [072]

ZIGZAG JOURNEYS IN ACADIA AND NEW FRANCE: A SUMMER'S JOURNEY OF THE ZIGZAG CLUB THROUGH THE HISTORIC FIELDS OF THE EARLY FRENCH SETTLEMENTS OF AMERICA / Butterworth, Hezekiah – Boston: Estes and Lauriat, 1884. 00372. (Pre-1900 Canadiana) – 9 – cn C.I.H.M. [910]

O ZIG-ZIG : PERIODICO ESQUIPATICO E FOLGAZAO – Perdoes, 15 Mar 1895 – 1,5,6 – bl Biblioteca [072]

ZIKHRON YA'AKOV / Lifshiz, Y – 3v. Kovna. 1924-30. BJ-290-16 1 – 9 – ne IDC [270]

ZIKHRONOT IR MOLADETI / Schulmann, E – St. Petersburg. 1895. BJ-422-75 1 – 9 – ne IDC [470]

ZIKHROYNES FUN A IDISHN SOTSIALIST / Michalevitch, B – 3v. Warsaw. 1921-23. BJ-290-28 1 – 9 – ne IDC [940]

ZIKKARON BE-SEFER / Letteris, M H – Vienna. 1869. Reminiscences of Jewish life. BJ-422-44 1 – 9 – ne IDC [270]

ZIKKARON LE-AVRAHAM ELIYYAHU FESTSCHRIFT. A. HARKAVY / Harkavy, A – St. Petersburg. 1908. BJ-100-41 1 – 9 – ne IDC [970]

Ziller, T *see* ZEITSCHRIFT FUER EXACTE PHILOSOPHIE IM SINNE DES NEUERN PHILOSOPHISCHEN REALISMUS, 1. 1861 – 20. 1896

Zillich, Heinrich *see*
- DER URLAUB
- WAELDER UND LATERNENSCHEIN
- DER WEIZENSTRAUSS
- DER ZIGEUNER
- ZWISCHEN GRENZEN UND ZEITEN

Zillier, Carl *see* HISTORY OF SHEYBOYGAN COUNTY

ZILLIONS – (Cont: Penny Power) – Mount Vernon. v1-8. aug 1990-jul 1998+ – 1,5,9 – D16119.01 – us UMI [073]

Zimansky, Paul E *see* OLD BABYLONIAN CONTRACTS FROM NIPPUR, VOL 1

Zimbabwe. Department of African Education *see* PEOPLE AND EDUCATION

ZIMBABWE (FORMERLY RHODESIA) : OFFICIAL YEARBOOK OF THE COLONY OF SOUTHERN RHODESIA CONTAINING GENERAL INFORMATION AND STATISTICS 1924-1952 / Zimbabwe (formerly Rhodesia). Department of Statistics – (Coll title: African Official Statistical Serials, 1867-1982) – 34mf – 9 – £7.00f (set £330.00 39mf) – uk Chadwyck [960]

Zimbabwe (formerly Rhodesia). Department of Statistics *see*
- ZIMBABWE (FORMERLY RHODESIA)
- ZIMBABWE. STATISTICAL YEARBOOK OF SOUTHERN RHODESIA

Zimbabwe. Ministry of Education *see* ANNUAL REPORT OF THE SECRETARY FOR EDUCATION 1978-1980

ZIMBABWE REVIEW : SUPPLEMENT – Cairo: Zimbabwe African People's Union. v1 n6 apr 20 1964; v1 n6 may 4 1964; special issue jul 14 1964; v2 n1-7/8 jan 12-jul/aug 1965 – 1r – 1 – us Res Libr [072]

ZIMBABWE. STATISTICAL YEARBOOK OF SOUTHERN RHODESIA : THE OFFICIAL ANNUAL OF THE SOCIAL AND ECONOMIC CONDITIONS OF THE COLONY 1938 AND 1947 / Zimbabwe (formerly Rhodesia). Department of Statistics – (Coll title: African Official Statistical Serials, 1867-1982) – 5mf – 9 – £7.00f (set £330.00 39mf) – uk Chadwyck [960]

Zimbe, Bartolomayo Musoke *see* BUGANDA AND KING

Zimmer, Friedrich *see*
- GALATERBRIEF UND APOSTELGESCHICHTE
- DAS GEBET: NACH DEN PAULINISCHEN SCHRIFTEN
- DER ROEMERBRIEF
- DER TEXT DER THESSALONICHERBRIEF

Zimmer, Fritz Alfred *see* JULIUS MOSEN

Zimmer, Hans *see* JUST FRIEDRICH WILHELM ZACHARIAE UND SEIN RENOMMIST

Zimmer, Heinrich *see* THE CELTIC CHURCH IN BRITAIN AND IRELAND

Zimmerman, Henry J *see* HISTORY OF THE MIT RADAR SCHOOL IN RELATION TO ARMY TRAINING FROM JUNE 23, 1941 TO JUNE 30, 1945

Zimmerman, M G *see*
- RUSSIAN-ENGLISH SCIENTIFIC AND TECHNICAL DICTIONARY OF USEFUL COMBINATIONS AND EXPRESSIONS

Zimmerman, Paul *see* PAPERS OF PAUL ZIMMERMAN

Zimmermann, Adolph *see* MIT DERNBURG NACH OSTAFRIKA

Zimmermann, B *see* ORDINAIRE DE L'ORDRE N.D. DU CARMEL PAR SIBERT DE BEKA (VERS 1312)

Zimmermann, Charlotte *see* DIE DEUTSCHE BEICHTE VOM 9. JAHRHUNDERT BIS ZU REFORMATION

Zimmermann, Curt *see* F.L.W. MEYER

Zimmermann, Felix *see*
- EFFET DE LA FIXATION D'EMETTEURS CHEZ LE POISSON
- NEUES LEBEN AUS KLOPSTOCK

Zimmermann, Heinrich *see* DIE PAEPSTLICHE LEGATION IN DER ERSTEN HAELFTE DES 13. JAHRHUNDERTS

Zimmermann, Hellmuth *see* ELOHIM: EINE STUDIE ZUR ISRAELITISCHEN RELIGIONS- UND LITTERATURGESCHICHTE

Zimmermann, Paul *see*
- FRIEDRICH WILHELM ZACHARIAE IN BRAUNSCHWEIG
- GOETHES BRIEFE AN E. TH. LANGER
- TROPFEN IN'S MEER

Zimmermann, Thomas *see* QUALITAETSMANAGEMENT IN DER UNTERNEHMUNGSBERATUNG

Zimmern, Heinrich *see*
- THE BABYLONIAN AND THE HEBREW GENESIS
- BABYLONISCHE BUSSPSALMEN
- BABYLONISCHE HYMNEN UND GEBETE
- BEITRAEGE ZUR KENNTNIS DER BABYLONISCHEN RELIGION
- BIBLISCHE UND BABYLONISCHE URGESCHICHTE
- ISTAR UND SALTU; EIN ALTAKKADISCHES LIED
- KOENIG LIPIT-ISTAR'S VERGOETTLICHUNG; EIN ALTSUMERISCHES LIED
- SUMERISCH-BABYLONISCHE TAMMUZLIEDER

Zimmert, J T *see* CATALOGUE OF THE EDWARD E. AYER ORNITHOLOGICAL LIBRARY

ZIMRAT HA-AREZ / Berab, J – Jerusalem. 1950. BJ-27-18 1 – 9 – ne IDC [956]

ZINC ABSTRACTS – (Cont by: Zincscan. Former title: ZDA Abstracts 1943-61) – London. v37-38. mar 1979-dec 1980 1,5,9; v37. 1979* 1 – 1,5,9 – D1430 – us UMI [670]

ZINC ABSTRACTS *see* ZINCSCAN

Zinc Development Association *see* ABSTRACTS

ZINCSCAN – (Cont: Zinc Abstracts) – London. v1-3 dec 1986-89* – 1 – D17374 – us UMI [670]

ZINCSCAN *see* ZINC ABSTRACTS

Zindler, Erwin *see* AUF BIEGEN UND BRECHEN

THE ZINGARI – Cape Town, South Africa. 4 Nov 1870-9 Jul 1875. 4 reels – 1, 16 diazo available at reduced price – sa SA Libr [072]

ZINGHA, REINE D'ANGOLA, HISTOIRE AFRICAINE / Castilhon, Jean-Louis – 1769. (Utopias in the Enlightenment Series). (African Library Series) – 9 – fr Hachette [920]

Zingler, Ute *see* STUDIEN ZUR ENTWICKLUNG DER ITALIENISCHEN VIOLONCELLSONATE VON DEN ANFAENGEN BIS ZUR MITTE DES 18. JAHRHUNDERTS

Zink, Georges... et al *see* HISTOIRE DE LA LITTERATURE ALLEMANDE

Zinker, B A *see* MILD IRON DEFICIENCY AND HORMONAL ALTERATIONS DURING REST AND EXHAUSTIVE EXERCISE

Zinkernagel, Franz *see* GOETHE UND HEBBEL

Zinn, J G *see*
- CATALOGUS PLANTARUM HORTI ACADEMICI ET AGRI GOTTINGENSIS
- OBSERVATIONES QUAEDAM BOTANICAE ET ANATOMICAE

ZINNEBEELDEN DER GODDELYKE LIEFDE / Veen, O van – O 449. 1703 – 9 – ne IDC [740]

ZINNE-BEELDEN DER LIEFDE / Elger, W den – 1703. O-598 1 – 9 – ne IDC [760]

ZINNE-BEELDEN DER LIEFDE / Elger, W den – 1725. O 243 – 9 – ne IDC [760]

ZINNE-BEELDEN DER LIEFDE / Elger, W den – 1732. O 599 – 9 – ne IDC [760]

ZINNE-BEELDEN, OFT ADAMS APPEL / Veen, J. van der – O 445. 1642 – 9 – ne IDC [760]

ZINNE-BEELDEN, OFT ADAMS APPEL : VERCIERT MET SEER AERDIGE KONST-PLATEN, MITSGADERS SIJNE OUDE EN NIEUWE ONGEMEENE BRUYLOFS ZEGEZANGEN, RAETSELEN, UYTGEBEELT MET ZIN-RIJCKE UYTLEGGINGEN; SIJN GULDEN EN YSEREN EEUW; ALS MEDE EEN NIKKERS-PRAETJE / Veen, J van der – Den tweeden druck. Amsterdam, 1660 – 7mf – 9 – O-3220/1 – ne IDC [760]

ZINNE-BEELDEN, OFT ADAMS APPEL : VERCIERT MET SEER AERDIGHE CONST-PLAETEN. MIDTSGADERS SIJNE OUDE ENDE NIEUWE ONGHEMEENE BRUYDT-LOFS ENDE ZEGHE-ZANGHEN / Veen, J van der – Amsterdam, 1646 – 5mf – 9 – O-3191/1 – ne IDC [760]

ZINNE-BEELDEN, OFT ADAMS APPEL, VERCIERT MET SEER AARDIGE KONST-PLATEN : MITSGADERS SYNE OUDE EN NIEUWE ONGEMEENE BRUYLOFS- EN ZEGEZAUGEN, RAATSELEN, UYTGEBEELDT MET ZIN-RYKE UYTLEGGINGEN;... / Veen, J van der – Amsterdam, 1703 – 8mf – 9 – O-3221/1 – ne IDC [760]

ZINNEBEELDEN. UIT HORATIUS FLACCUS / Veen, O van – O 446. 1683 – 9 – ne IDC [740]

ZINNE-EN MINNE-BEELDEN : SELFSTRYD: TOONEEL DER MANNELYKE AGTBAARHEIDT... / Cats, J – Amsterdam, 1717 – 8mf – 9 – ne IDC [700]

ZINNE-POPPEN : ALLE VERCIERT MET RIJMEN, EN SOMMIGHE MET PROZE: DOOR ZIJN DOCHTER ANNA ROEMERS / Visscher, R – Amsterdam, 1669 – 5mf – 9 – O-3222/1 – ne IDC [760]

DER ZINS UND DAS RECHT AUF DEN VOLLEN ARBEITSERTRAG / Beckerath, Ulrich von – 9 – 1.00f – at Libertarian Micro [335]

Zins, Wendy S *see* RELATIONSHIPS BETWEEN SOCIAL SUPPORT AND GENERAL WELL-BEING IN AN INTRODUCTORY HEALTH, FITNESS, AND RECREATION COURSE

Zinsser, Judith P *see* NEW PARTNERSHIP

ZINZENDORF UND SEIN CHRISTENTUM : IM VERHAELTNIS ZUM KIRCHLICHEN UND RELIGIOESEN LEBEN SEINER ZEIT / Becker, Bernhard – Leipzig: F. Jansa, 1900 – 2mf – us A.T.L.A. [240]

ZINZENDORFS FROEMMIGKEIT IM LICHT DER PSYCHOANALYSE : EINE KRITISCHE PRUEFUNG DES BUCHS VON DR. OSKAR PFISTER, "DIE FROEMMIGKEIT DES GRAFEN LUDWIG VON ZINZENDORF", UND EIN BEITRAG ZUM VERSTAENDNIS DER EXTRAVAGANTEN LEHRWEISE ZINZENDORFS / Reichel, Gerhard – Tuebingen: J.C.B. Mohr, 1911 – 1mf – us A.T.L.A. [240]

ZION : MONATSSCHRIFT FUER DIE NATIONALEN ITERESSEN DES JUEDISCHEN VOLKES. – v. 1-5. Berlin. 1895-98. BJ-23-64 1 – 24mf – 9 – ne IDC [270]

ZION BAPTIST CHURCH. SHELBY, NORTH CAROLINA : CHURCH RECORDS – 1817-1961 – 1 – 35.82 – us Baptist [240]

ZION EVANGELICAL LUTHERAN CHURCH RECORDS – (Membership lists, sacramental registers, attendence lists, minutes, bulletins, financial records, and publications of the Church, its Voters Assembly, and school, the first German Lutheran church in Cleveland) – Cleveland, Cuyahoga, OH. 1843-1994 – 24r – 1 – us Western Res [240]

ZION HILL BAPTIST CHURCH. BUFORD, GEORGIA : CHURCH RECORDS – Aug 1868 – Sept 1979. Incomplete – 1 – 64.44 – us Baptist [240]

ZION HILL BAPTIST CHURCH. SPARTANBURG, SOUTH CAROLINA : CHURCH RECORDS – (780p) – 1840-1864, 1868-1874, 1876-1946 – 1 reel – 1 – $35.10 – us Baptist [240]

Zion Lutheran Church (Waterville, Ohio) *see* RECORDS

ZIONISM – (Cont by: Studies in Zionism) – Tel Aviv. v1-2 1980-apr 1981* – 1 – D12231 – us UMI [270]

ZIONISM: A STATEMENT / Schechter, Solomon – New York. 1906. BJ-28-21 1 – 9 – ne IDC [956]

ZIONISM AND THE ARAB WORLD / Jewish Agency for Palestine. Jerusalem – Memorandum presented to the Anglo-American Committee of Inquiry on Palestine. Mar 1946. BJ-28-145 1 – 9 – ne IDC [956]

DER ZIONISMUS, SEIN WESEN UND SEINE ORGANISATION / Bernstein, Simon – Berlin, Judischer verlag, 1919 – 1 – us U.W. Library [270]

DER ZIONIST – New York, NY. 1897 – 1 – us A.J.P.C. [071]

ZIONIST BULLETIN – London, 1919-20 – 13mf – 9 – J-213-3/1 – ne IDC [270]

Zionist Congress. 1931 *see* THE ZIONIST MOVEMENT 1916-1931

Zionist Congress. (1907-1951) *see* REPORTS OF THE ZIONIST EXECUTIVE, ITS DEPARTMENTS AND AFFILIATED BODIES TO ZIONIST CONGRESSES

Zionist Congresses. 1897-1951 *see* PROTOKOLL DER VERHANDLUNGEN DES 1-23 ZIONISTEN CONGRESSES

THE ZIONIST MOVEMENT 1916-1931 / Zionist Congress. 1931 – A Statement of Policy, (by C. Weizmann). Submitted to the XVIIth Zionist Congress (1931). London. 1931. BJ-28-46 1 – 9 – ne IDC [956]

Zionist Organization. London *see*
- MANDATE FOR PALESTINE
- TRUTH ABOUT PALESTINE: A REPLY TO THE PALESTINE ARAB DELEGATION

Zionist Organization of America *see* REPORT OF THE PROCEEDINGS OF THE 24TH ANNUAL CONVENTION

THE ZIONIST REVIEW – (English monthly and weekly) – London, GB. v6 no2 Jun 1922-v7 no94 Feb 1942 – 1r – 1 – $25.00 – cn Can Microfilming [072]

ZIONISTISCHE NACHRICHTEN – Basel, 1947 n1-4, 1948 n1, 2, 8-11 – 1 – Dist. gw Mikrofilm – gw Misc Inst [956]

DE ZIONISTISCHE STEM – Amsterdam. Nos. 1-30. 1918-20 – 3mf – 9 – J-261-123/1 – ne IDC [270]

Zionistische Vereinigung fuer Deutschland *see* JUEDISCHE RUNDSCHAU

ZION'S FREUND – 1938-40 (complete) – 1r – 1 – ATLA S0664E – us A.T.L.A. [073]

ZION'S FRIEND – (Philadelphia). 1898-1905 – 1 – us A.J.P.C. [270]

ZION'S HARP – (Pages 1-14 lacking) – 1 – 13.09 – us Baptist [240]

ZION'S HERALD – Boston. v1-84. 1823-1906 – 1 – D4633 – us UMI [240]

ZION'S HERALD – v1-101. 1823-1923 (complete) – 59r – 1 – ATLA S0022 – us A.T.L.A. [073]

ZION'S TIDINGS – v1-33. 1921-53 (incomplete) – 3r – 1 – ATLA 1994-S033 – us A.T.L.A. [073]

DER ZIONSBOTE – 1866-68, 1870-78 – 1 – 43.26 – us Baptist [240]

ZIP – (Cont by: Zip Target Marketing) – Philadelphia. v1-2 1978-79*. v3-6 1980-mar 1983 1; v3 1980. v4-6 1981-mar 1983* 5; v3-6 1980-mar 1983 9 – 1,5,9 – D11927 – us UMI [073]

ZIP *see* ZIP TARGET MARKETING

ZIP TARGET MARKETING – (Cont: Zip. Cont by: Target Marketing) – Philadelphia. v6-9. apr 1983-jul 1986 1,9; v6 apr-dec 1983*. v7-9 jan 1984-jul 1986 5 – 1,5,9 – D11927.01 – us UMI [073]

ZIP TARGET MARKETING *see* ZIP

Zipper, Albert *see* THEODOR KOERNER

ZIRAN BIANZHENGFA TONGXUN – Dialectics of Nature Bulletin. In Chinese with English abstracts to the main articles. F p77 – 9 – $4.50f – cc Microforms [100]

ZIRAN KEXUE NIANJIAN, 1981 = YEARBOOK OF NATURAL SCIENCES, 1981 – Comp. by editorial dept. of Nature Magazine. 4 fiches. F-J39 – 9 – $24.50 – cc Microforms [580]
ZIRAN ZAZHI – Nature Journal. 1984-86. F/P 272 – 9 – $4.50f – cc Microforms [073]
ZIRAN ZIYUAN = NATURAL RESOURCES – 1982-. F-P254 – 9 – $4.50f – cc Microforms [580]
Zirbes, Peter *see* EIFELSAGEN, LIEDER UND GEDICHTE
Zirus, Werner *see*
– AHASVERUS
– AHASVERUS, DER EWIGE JUDE
Zisk, D M *see* THE PHYSIOLOGICAL COST OF PLYOMETRIC REBOUND JUMPING AT VARIED INTENSITIES
ZISKA / Corelli, Marie – British Fiction Archive: Unit 1 – 9 – uk Bell [830]
ZITHER UND HACKBRET : GEDICHTE IN OBERSTEIERISCHER MUNDART / Rosegger, Peter – 3. sehr verm. neub. Aufl; Graz: Verlag von "Leykam", 1884 – 1r – 1 – us U.W. Library [810]
ZITREK – Prague. Czechoslovakia. -w. 9 Oct 1968-26 Mar 1969. (1 reel) – 1 – uk British Libr Newspaper [072]
Zitron, S L *see* YOZEREI HA-SIFRUT HA-IVRIT HA-HADASHAH
Zittel, Emil *see*
– DIE ENTSTEHUNG DER BIBEL
– DIE REVISION DER LUTHERBIBEL
ZITU-GO KYAU. DO-ZI KYAU = L'ENSEIGNEMENT DE LA VERITE, ET L'ENSEIGNEMENT DE LA JEUNESSE / Kobaudaisi – Trans. from Japanese by Leon de Rosny. Paris: Imprimerie de la Revue Orientale et Americaine. 1876 – 9 – $7.50 – fr Orientalistes [180]
ZIVILE RECHTSHILFEERSUCHEN... / Daum, H – N.p., [1938] – 1mf – 1 – ILM-2229/1 – ne IDC [327]
ZIVOT CIRKEVNI V CECHACH / Winter, Zikmund – v. 1-2. Praha. 1895-96. BR-5091 2 – 8 – ne IDC [943]
ZIVOT STRANY – (Coll title: Czech/Slovakian Periodicals. Missing: 1954(5); 1956(15-24); 1957(19-21,23-24); 1958(3,16,20,23); 1959(4); 1963/18); 1986(17); 1987(8,11,19); 1989(22). In Czech) – 1954-1989 – 616mf – 9 – R-18221/1 – ne IDC [320]
ZIVYON / ed by Creizenach, M C & Jost, I M BJ-91-88 1 – 2v. Frankfurt a.Main. 1840-43. – 9 – ne IDC [270]
Ziya, Ahmet *see* MESRUTIYET UGRUNDA
ZIYA GOEKALP VE MEFKURE ARASINDAKI MUENASEBET VESILESIYLE BIR TETKIK TECRUEBESI / UErfi [Betin], Saffet – $55.00 – us MEDOC [470]
ZIYYON-ME'ASSEF – v. 1-6. Jerusalem. 1926-34. BJ-100-178 1 – 9 – ne IDC [270]
Zizek, Slavoj *see* BOLECINA RAZLIKE
ZIZKA : GESAENGE / Meissner, Alfred – Leipzig: F L Herbig, [185-?] – 1r – 1 – us U.W. Library [810]
ZIZN', LICHNOST' TVORCHESTVO / Esenin, Sergei – M. 1926. BR-2063 2 – 8 – ne IDC [460]
Z-J-FUNK – Bad Langensalza, 1925-26 – 1r – 1 – gw Mikrofilm [790]
Z.K. MATTHEWS (BOTSWANA) – 5r – 1 – sa Microfile [960]
ZLATOLIRA / Severianin, I – Poezy. Kn. III. ed. 4. M. 1915. BR-1042 2 – 8 – ne IDC [460]
ZLATOROG – v2, 4-24. 1921, 1923-1943 – 1 – us I.U. Libraries [073]
Zlobicka, Jadwiga *see* CZYTANIA DLA SZKOL POWSZECHNYCH
ZLYIA CHARY / Bal'mont, K D – M. 1906. BR-551 – 8 – ne IDC [460]
ZMEDELESKE NOVINY – (Cont as: Ceske a Moravskoslezske Zemedelske Noviny) – Prague, Czechoslovakia. Jun 1945-1980 – 76r – 1 – us L of C Photodup [072]
Zmeev, L F *see* RUSSKIE VRACHI PISATELI
ZMEINYE TSVETY. PUTEVYIA PIS'MA IZ MEKSIKI / Bal'mont, K D – Moscow, 1910. BR-552 2 – 8 – ne IDC [460]
ZNACHENIE SEL'SKOKHOZIAIST VENNYKH KOMMUN V SOVETSKOM STROITEL'STVE : TEORIIA I PRAKTIKA BOR'BY / Kalinin, M I – M., L., 1926 – 1mf – 9 – COR-153/1 – ne IDC [334]
ZNAK – v11-27, 35-36. 1959-75, 1983-84 – 1 – us I.U. Libraries [073]
ZNAME – Sofia, Bulgaria. Aug 1894-Apr 1898; Sept 1945-1946 (scattered issues) – 2r – 1 – us L of C Photodup [949]
Znamenskii, P *see* DUKHOVNYE SHKOLY V ROSSII DO REFORMY 1808 GODA
ZNAMJA TRUDA : ORGAN CENTRAL'NOGO KOMITETA PARTII LEVYCH SOCIALISTOV-REVOLJUCIONEROV – Paris, Petrograd, Berlin, 1907-14 – 1 – us Hoover Inst Photo [335]
ZNAMYA – (Banner). Moscow. U.S.S.R. 1961- – 1 – us UMI [073]
ZNAMYA YUNOSTI – Minsk (Belorussia), USSR. 1965-1981 – 17r – $850.00 – B63589 – us Library Micro [072]
ZNAMYA YUNOSTI – Minsk, U.S.S.R. -d. Jan 1960-March 1962. 2 reels – 1 – uk British Libr Newspaper [947]
ZNANIE – Ezhemesiachnyi nauchnyi i kritiko-bibliograficheskii zhurnal. Spb. 1870-77. Lacking: 1870 (1-9), 1875 (7-12), 1877 (5-12). B-2030 2 – 8 – ne IDC [073]
ZOA PUBLIC AFFAIRS MEMORANDUM – New York, NY. 1973-4 Dec 1980 – 1 – us A.J.P.C. [071]
ZOAR BAPTIST CHURCH. SHELBY, NORTH CAROLINA : CHURCH RECORDS – 1874-1963 – 1 – 5.00 – us Baptist [240]
ZOAR HUNT'S CORNERS UNITED CHURCH OF CHRIST – Huron County. Ohio. 1854-1981 – 1 reel – 1 – us Archival [240]
Zoar Hunt's Corners United Church of Christ (Huron County, Ohio) *see* RECORDS
Zobeltitz, Fedor Karl Maria Hermann August von *see* DIE JUNKER, ROMAN
Zobeltitz, Hanns von *see* DER BILDHAUER
Zobrist, George W *see* VLSI DESIGN
Zochowski, F *see* CZESCI MOWY ODMIENIAJACE SIE PRZEZ PRZYPADKI
Zoctizoum, Yarrise *see* TWO STUDIES ON UNEMPLOYMENT AMONG EDUCATED YOUNG PEOPLE
ZODIAC : A MONTHLY PERIODICAL, DEVOTED TO SCIENCE, LITERATURE AND THE ARTS – Albany. v1-2. jul 1835-jan 1837 – 1 – D4172 – us UMI [073]
ZODIACUS MEDICO-GALLICUS; SIVE, MISCELLANEORUM CURIOSORUM, MEDICO-PHYSICORUM SYLLOGE CONTINENS CELEBERRIMORUM VIRORUM TUM MEDICORUM & ALIORUM ERUDITORUM IN GALLIA – Geneva, 1680-85. v. 1-5 – 3 – us Readex [610]
THE ZODIAKE OF LIFE / Palingenius, Marcellus – 1576 – 9 – 20.00 – us Scholars' Facs [450]
ZOE – Athens. Greece. -w. 5 Mar 1935-29 Feb 1936, 12 Feb 1938-1 Apr 1941, 6 Feb 1946-29 Dec 1949. (3 reels) – 1 – uk British Libr Newspaper [949]
Zoeberlein, Hans *see* DER BEFEHL DES GEWISSENS
Zoeckler, Otto *see*
– THE BOOKS OF THE CHRONICLES
– DIE CHRISTLICHE APOLOGETIK IM NEUNZEHNTEN JAHRHUNDERT
– ECCLESIASTES, OR, KOHELETH
– PROPHET DANIEL
– THE PROVERBS OF SOLOMON
– THE SONG OF SOLOMON
– DIE SPRUECHE SALOMONIS
Zoega, G *see* CATALOGUS CODICUM COPTICORUM MANUSCRIPTORUM
DIE ZOEGLINGE CALVIN'S IN HALLE AN DER SAALE / Zahn, Adolph – Halle: R. Muhlmann, 1864 – 1mf – us A.T.L.A. [240]
Zoeller, Hugo *see* DIE DEUTSCHEN IM BRASILISCHEN URWALD
Zoete, Robert *see* DU RECRUTEMENT DES GENS DE MER; ETUDE HISTORIQUE ET CRITIQUE
Zoetmulder, Petrus Josephus *see* THE CULTURAL BACKGROUND OF INDONESIAN POLITICS
ZOHAR HA-TEVAH / Hanau, S Z – (Hebrew grammar). Ed. 1. Berlin. 1733. Ed. 7. Wilna. 1820. BJ-412-9 1 – 9 – ne IDC [470]
ZOIST : A JOURNAL OF CEREBRAL PHYSIOLOGY AND MESMERISM AND THEIR APPLICATIONS TO HUMAN WELFARE – London. v1-13 apr 1843-jan 1856 – 1 – D2845 – us UMI [130]
Zoller, Josepho *see* MIRA SATIS, AC SINE OMNI PECCATO MARIAE SANCTISSIMA CONCEPTIO
Zollinger, Friedrich *see* GOETHE IN ZUERICH
Zollinger, H *see* SYSTEMATISCHES VERZEICHNISS DER IM INDUSCHEN ARCHIPEL IN. 1842-1848 GESAMMELTEN SOWIE DER AUS JAPAN EMPFANGENEN PFLANZEN
Zollmann, Theodor *see* BIBEL UND NATUR IN DER HARMONIE IHRER OFFENBARUNGEN
ZOLNIERZ WOLNOSCI – (See: Polska Zbrojna) – Warsaw, Poland. Jul 1950-1986; 1988-92 – 85r – 1 – us L of C Photodup [943]
Zolotar, T P *see* SLAVIANSKIE KNIGI KIRILLOVSKOI PECHATI 15-18 VV
ZOLOTO V LAZURI / Belyi, A – M. 1904. BR-610 2 – 8 – ne IDC [460]
ZOLOTOE RUNO – Zhurnal. M. 1906-09. B-1526 2 – 8 – ne IDC [073]
ZOLOTOI SNOP BOLGARSKOI POEZII. NARODNYIA PESNI. / Bal'mont, K D – Sofia, 1930. BR-553 – 8 – ne IDC [460]
Zonarad, Ioannes *see* EPITOMAE HISTORIARUM LIBRI 18 (CSHB 50)
Zonarae, Joannis *see*
– ANNALES (CBH 22)
– ANNALES (CSHB 42, 43)
DIE ZONE – Der Querschnitt durch die deutsche Politik, Literatur, Kunst, Theater, Musik und Wissenschaft. Paris, France. 1933-Jul 1934 (Nrn.1-8) – 1 – gw Mikrofilm [073]
LA ZONE RURALE DE BROBO VUE A TRAVERS SON MARCHE HEBDOMADAIRE / Ancey, G – (Africa series). 1967 – 9 – fr Hachette [960]
ZONE RURALE DE SAN PEDRO. ENQUETES DEMOGRAPHIQUES / Trouchaud, J P – (Africa series). 1969 – 9 – fr Hachette [304]
LES ZONES D'ACTIONS PRIORITAIRES INTEGREES (ZAPIS) DE L'EST CAMEROUN / Lenglart, J – 9 – F120.00 – fr Ethnologie [960]
ZONES OF THE SOLAR SYSTEM – P/MS, University Park, PA. 1976 – 600p 24f – 9 – $0.50f – us Lawrence Pub [520]
LES ZONES RURALES ET LES CENTRES SECONDAIRES DE LA REGION DE BOUAKE / Chevassu, J & Michotte, J – Africa series. 1969 – 9 – fr Hachette [960]
ZONGULDAK – Zonguldak, 1923-1928 – 9 – $10.00 – us MEDOC [956]
ZONING COMMISSION MINUTES / Erie County, Ohio. Oxford Township. Board of Trustees – 1954-96 – 1r – 1 – $32.50r – us Archival [978]
ZONING DIGEST – (Cont by: Land Use Law & Zoning Digest) – Chicago. v1-25. 1949-73* – 1 – D10925 – us UMI [340]
ZONK – Johannesburg: African People's Pictorial, 1951-64 – 6r – 1 – us Ross [072]
ZOOLOGIA TYPICA, OR FIGURES OF NEW AND RARE MAMMALS AND BIRDS, IN THE ZOOLOGICAL SOCIETY OF LONDON / Fraser, L – 2044 2. 1849 – 8 – ne IDC [590]
ZOOLOGICA SCRIPTA – Stockholm. v11-26. 1982-97+ 1,5,9; v11-12. 1982-83* 9 – 1,5,9 – D49438 – us UMI [590]
ZOOLOGICAL JOURNAL – London; Edinburgh, 1824-34 – 3 – us Readex [073]
ZOOLOGICAL RECORD – (Former title: Record of Zoological Literature 1864-69) – London. v96-130. 1959-94 1; v96-98 1959-61*. v100 1963. v109-114 1972-77. v115-127 1978-91*. v128 1992. v129-130 1993-94* 5; v96 1959. v97 1960*. v98 1961. v111-130 1974-94 9 – 1,5,9 – D1286 – us UMI [590]
Zoological Society. London *see* THE ZOOLOGICAL WORKS OF SAMUEL RICHARD TICKELL
Zoological Society of London. Committee of Science and Correspondence *see* PROCEEDINGS
Zoological Society of London. Gardens *see* LIST OF THE VERTEBRATED ANIMALS EXHIBITED...1828-1927
THE ZOOLOGICAL WORKS OF SAMUEL RICHARD TICKELL / Zoological Society. London – 1987 – 52 colour mf – 15 – $1,980.00 – 0-907716-24-5 – uk Mindata [590]
ZOOLOGISCHE FORSCHUNGSREISEN IN AUSTRALIEN UND DEM MALAYISCHEN ARCHIPEL, 1891-1893 / ed by Semon, R – 2662 2. 3 v. 1893-1913 – 287mf – 8 – ne IDC [590]
ZOOLOGISCHER ANZEIGER – (v1-45. Dfl140.00v; v46-161. Dfl70.00v; v162-167. Dfl90.00v) – Leipzig. v1-167. 1878-1961 – 5,9 – Dfl14,960.00 – ne Swets [590]
ZOOLOGY – 211 serials – 9 – ne IDC [590]
ZOOLOGY AND BOTANY: PROGRESS REPORTS – 1841-42; 1845. Includes: I. Bonaparte, C. I. The State of Zoology in Europe as regards the Vertebrata. II. The Progress of Zoology in 1842. III. Link, H. F. The Progress of Physiological Botany in 1841 – 1,7 – uk Microform Academic [580]
ZOOLOGY OF NEW HOLLAND / Shaw, G – (Figures by James Sowerby). 2064 2. 1794 – 8 – ne IDC [590]
THE ZOOLOGY OF THE VOYAGE OF H.M.S. EREBUS AND TERROR, 1839-1843 / Richardson, J & Gray, J E – Z-189 2. 2 v. 1844-1875 – 8 – ne IDC [910]
THE ZOOLOGY OF THE VOYAGE OF H.M.S. SAMARANG DURING 1843-1846 / ed by Adams, Andrew Leith – (Contents: Crustacea, by A. Adams and A. White. 1848. Fishes, by J. Richardson. 1848. Mollusca, by A. Adams and L. Reeve. 1848. Vertebrata, by J.E. Gray. 1848) – Z 180/2. 1850 – 8 – ne IDC [590]
ZOOLOGY OF THE VOYAGE OF H.M.S. SULPHUR, 1836-1842 / Hinds, R B – 2v. 1844 – 8 – Z 181 2 – ne IDC [590]
ZOOLOGY-ENTOMOLOGY DEPARTMENT SERIES / Alabama. Agricultural Experiment Station – 1,5,6 – us Spaulding [630]
ZOOMORPHOLOGIE – (Cont: Zeitschrift fuer Morphologie der Tiere. Cont by: Zoomorphology) – Heidelberg. v82-95. 1975-80* – 1 – D13251.02 – us UMI [590]
ZOOMORPHOLOGIE *see*
– ZEITSCHRIFT FUER MORPHOLOGIE DER TIERE
– ZOOMORPHOLOGY
ZOOMORPHOLOGY – (Cont: Zoomorphologie) – Heidelberg. v96-108 1980-apr 1989*. v109-117 jun 1989-1997+ – 1 – D13251.03 – us UMI [590]
ZOOMORPHOLOGY *see* ZOOMORPHOLOGIE
ZOOPLANKTON FIXATION AND PRESERVATION / ed by Steedman, H F – 2nd impr 1985 – 350p – 9 – 92-3-101272-X – fr UNESCO [590]
ZOOPLANKTON SAMPLING – 3rd impr 1979 – 174p – 9 – 92-3-101194-4 – fr UNESCO [590]
Zopf, W *see*
– BEITRAEGE ZU EINER CHEMISCHEN MONOGRAPHIE DER CLADONIACEEN
– DIE FLECHTENSTOFFE IN CHEMISCHER BOTANISCHER, PHARMAKOLOGISCHER UND TECHNISCHER BEZIEHUNG
ZORA – Chicago, IL, 1901 – 2mf or 1 reel – 9,1 – us I.H.R.C. [975]
ZORA – Sofia, Bulgaria. Mar 1941-Sept 1944 (scattered issues) – 9r – 1 – us L of C Photodup [949]
ZORA SLOVANSKA *see* SLAVIANSKAIA ZARIA
ZORAM THUPUAN – (Assamese language) – Aijal (Assam), India. 1961-62 – 1r – 1 – us L of C Photodup [072]
Zoretti, Ludovic *see* L'EDUCATION NATIONALE ET LE MOUVEMENT OUVRIER EN FRANCE
ZORI NOI – Suceava, Romania. 1962-73; 1975-76; 1978-80; Mar-Dec 1981 – 27r – 1 – us L of C Photodup [949]
[ZORINSKI] A PIPER O'ER THE MEADOWS / Arnold, Samuel – London: Rt Birchall, 180- – 1 – us Sibley [780]
Zorita, Alonso de *see* HISTORIA DE LA NUEVA ESPANA
Zorita. Ayuntamiento *see*
– FERIAS Y FIESTAS DE LA VELADA, 1945
– FIESTAS DE LA VELA EN ZORITA...EN HONOR...LA VIRGEN DE FUENTE SANTA 1979
– LA VELADA. FIESTAS 1971 EN ZORITA
Zorn, Joseph *see* DIE MOTIVE DER STURM-UND DRANG-DRAMATIKER
ZORNITSA – Sofia, Bulgaria. 1929-Nov 1930 (scattered issues) – 1r – 1 – us L of C Photodup [949]
ZOROASTRE / Rameau, Jean-Philippe – Paris: La veuve Boivin; Leclair: Le Castagniere, [1749?] – 1 – us Sibley [780]
ZOROASTRIAN THEOLOGY: FROM THE EARLIEST TIMES TO THE PRESENT DAY / Dhalla, Maneckji Nusservanji – New York: s.l., 1914. xxxii,384p – 1 – us U.W. Library [290]
Zorraquin Becu, Horacio [et al] *see* CUATRO REVOLUCIONES ARGENTINAS
Zosimus *see* CORPUS SCRIPTORUM HISTORIAE BYZANTINAE (CSHB 30)
Zoterberg, H *see* CATALOGUES DES MANUSCRITS SYRIAQUES ET SABEENS (MANDAITES) DE LA BIBLIOTHEQUE NATIONALE
Zouch, Richard *see* THE DOVE; OR, PASSAGES OF COSMOGRAPHY; A POEM...REPRINTED FROM THE ORIGINAL ED. OF 1613.
ZOUTPANSBERG REVIEW – Smitsdorp, Pietersburg, South Africa. 1889-1962 – 1 – sa State Libr [072]
ZOVY DREVNOSTI.. / Bal'mont, K D – Berlin, 1923. BR-555 2 – 8 – ne IDC [460]
ZRITEL' – Ezhemesiachnoe izdanie. Spb, 1792 – 8 – B-2032 2 – ne IDC [790]

Zschaeck, F *see* LEVOLDI DE NORTHOF CHRONICA COMITUM DE MARKA (MGH 6: 6.BD)
Zscharnack, Leopold *see* DER DIENST DER FRAU IN DEN ERSTEN JAHRHUNDERTEN DER CHRISTLICHEN KIRCHE
Zschimmer, W *see* DR. E.L.TH. HENKE'S NACHGELASSENE VORLESUNGEN UEBER LITURGIK UND HOMILETIK
Zschokke, Emil *see*
- HEINRICH ZSCHOKKE
- POEMS

Zschokke, Heinrich *see*
- ADDRICH IM MOOS
- AUSGEWAEHLTE NOVELLEN
- GESAMMELTE SCHRIFTEN
- HEINRICH ZSCHOKKE'S NOVELLEN
- INCIDENTS OF SOCIAL LIFE AMID THE EUROPEAN ALPS
- SAEMMTLICHE NOVELLEN
- EINE SELBSTSCHAU
- TALES
- TALES FROM THE GERMAN OF HEINRICH ZSCHOKKE
- DER TOTE GAST
- DER ZERBROCHENE KRUG

Zschokke, Hermann *see*
- DIE BIBLISCHEN FRAUEN DES ALTEN TESTAMENTES
- DAS BUCH JOB

ZSHERMINAL (GERMINAL) – London, UK. 16 Mar 1900; Jan, Jun, Nov, Dec 1902; 1905-Sept 1908; Mar-May 1909 – 1 – uk British Libr Newspaper [072]
ZU DEN SCHRIFTEN DES MAKARIOS VON MAGNESIA / Schalkhausser, Georg – Leipzig: J.C. Hinrichs, 1907. (Texte und Untersuchungen zur Geschichte der altchristlichen Literatur; der ganzen Reihe 31. Bd., Heft 4: 3. Reihe, 1. Bd., Heft 4) – 1mf – us A.T.L.A. [240]
ZU DEN SCHRIFTEN DES MAKARIOS VON MAGNESIA (T.U.U. 3-31/4) / Schalkhausser, Georg – Leipzig, 1907 – 4mf – 9 – ne Slangenburg [240]
ZU GOETHE'S LEBEN UND WERKEN / Traumann, Ernst – Berlin: E Felber, 1909 – 1r – 1 – us U.W. Library [430]
ZU GOETHES WILHELM MEISTER : DIE HISTORISCHE STELLUNG BESONDERS DER WANDERJAHRE / Schoeps, Richard – (Includes bibliographical references) – Naumburg a.S.: H Sieling, 1906 – 1r – 1 – us U.W. Library [430]
ZU HEINRICH VON KLEIST'S WERKEN : DIE LESARTEN DER ORIGINALAUSGABEN UND DIE AENDERUNGEN LUDWIG TIECK'S UND JULIAN SCHMIDT'S / Koehler, Reinhold – Weimar: H Boehlau, 1862 – 1r – 1 – us U.W. Library [430]
ZU JESAJA 53: EIN ERKLAERUNGSVERSUCH / Bertholet, Alfred – Freiburg i.B.: J.C.B. Mohr, 1899. 1 fiche – 9 – us A.T.L.A. [240]
ZU LUDWIG UHLANDS GEDAECHTNIS : MITTHEILUNGEN AUS SEINER AKADEMISCHEN LEHRTHAETIGKEIT / Holland, Wilhelm Ludwig – Leipzig: S Hirzel, 1886 – 1 – 1 – us U.W. Library [430]
ZU SCHILLERS "DAS IDEAL UND DAS LEBEN" / Bartels, Rudolf – Halle: Verlag der Buchhandlung des Waisenhauses, 1907 – 1r – 1 – us U.W. Library [430]
Zuallart, H *see* IL DEVOTISSIMO VIAGGIO DIE GIERVSALEMME
Zubarovskii, N *see* SBORNIK ZAKONODATEL'NYKH MATERIALOV, INSTRUKTSII I RAZ"IASNENII PO KOOPERATSII INVALIDOV
ZUBATOVSHCHINA I GAPONOVSHCHINA / Ainzaft, Samuil Semenovich – Moskva: Izd. VT SSPS, 1922 – 1 – CSUX88-B744 – us Hoover Inst Photo [947]
Zube, David *see* THE NEED FOR AND FINANCING OF AN IDEAL MARKET FOR FREEDOM IDEAS AND FOR OTHER IDEALS AS WELL
Zube, John *see*
- 94 POINTS AGAINST COMPULSORY VOTING
- AN ABC AGAINST NUCLEAR WAR A HANDBOOK OF IDEAS ON THE PREVENTION OF NUCLEAR WAR MAINLY THROUGH THE EXTENSION OF RIGHTS AND LIBERTIES
- ANARCHISM AND CRIME
- DO ESP AND MICROGRAPHICS HAVE ANYTHING IN COMMON?
- INDUSTRIAL DEMOCRACY, WORKERS' PARTICIPATION, WORKERS' CONTROL, CO-OWNERSHIP, EXTENSIVE PROFIT-SHARING, COOPERATIVE PRODUCTION, VOLUNTARY SOCIALISM OR EXTENDED CAPITALISM
- LET FREEDOM PAY ITS WAY
- THE NEED FOR AND FINANCING OF AN IDEAL MARKET FOR FREEDOM IDEAS AND FOR OTHER IDEALS AS WELL
- NEUE BILDUNGSWEGE
- STOP THE 22 X00. MILLION LEGAL TENDER CRIME
- WAR OVER THE FALKLAND ISLANDS?
- WAS MUSS AN DEN STAATSVERFASSUNGEN GEAENDERT WERDEN DAMIT EIN ANDAUERNDER FRIEDE MOEGLICH WIRD, UND WIE KOENNEN DIESE REFORMEN DURCHGESETZT WERDEN?
- WHAT HAS TO BE CHANGED IN THE CONSTITUTIONS OF ALL STATES AND HOW CAN THESE REFORMS BE REALIZED?

Zube, John, et al *see* SLOGANS AND THOUGHTS FOR LIBERTY
Zubkova, N A *see* RUKOPISNYE FONDY PUBLICHNOI BIBLIOTEKI. PECHATNYE KATALOGI I OBZORY
Zuborg, Hermann *see* UEBER DEN ALTDEUTSCHEN MINNESANG
Zubov, Iu. S *see*
- SATIRA V.V. MAIAKOVSKOGO
- V.V. MAIAKOVSKII

Zuccarini, J G *see*
- FLORA JAPONICA
- PLANTARUM NOVARUM VEL MINUS COGNIATRUM IN HORTO BOTANICO HERBARIOQUE REGIO MONACENSI

Zuccaro, F *see* L'IDEA DE PITTORI, SCULTORI, ET ARCHITETTI
Zuchelli, A *see* MERCKWUERDIGE MISSIONS- UND REISE-BESCHREIBUNG NACH CONGO IN ETHIOPIEN
Zuchold, E A *see* ADDITAMENTA AD G. A. PRITZELII THESAURUM LITERATURAE BOTANICAE
Zuckermandel, M *see* GESAMMELTE AUFSAETZE
Zuckermann, Benedict *see* MATERIALIEN ZUR ENTWICKLUNG DER ALTJUEDISCHEN ZEITRECHNUNG IM TALMUD
Zuckmayer, Carl *see*
- BARBARA BLOMBERG
- DER FROEHLICHE WEINBERG
- KATHARINA KNIE
- SCHINDERHANNNES

Zueblin, Charles *see* THE RELIGION OF A DEMOCRAT
ZUEBUEK – Istanbul: Guenes Matbaacilik, 1962, Baslica yazari: Aziz Nesin; Sahibi: Meral Nesin. No. 1-43 (5 Subat-26 Kasim 1962) – $150.00 – us MEDOC [073]
ZUECHTER : GENETICS AND BREEDING RESEARCH – (The micro-edition incl: Zuechter, Sonderheft. Cont by: Theoretical and applied genetics) – Heidelberg. v1-37. 1929-67* – 1 – D13108 – us UMI [575]
ZUECHTER – SONDERHEFT *see* ZUECHTER
ZUEMRUED-I 'ANKA – Sene 1-2, nos. 1-224 (1339-1341) – 21mf – 9 – $225.00 – us MEDOC [949]
Zuendel, Friedrich *see* JESUS IN BILDERN AUS SEINEM LEBEN
Zuendt, Ernst Anton Joseph *see* EBBE UND FLUTH
ZUERICHER NOVELLEN / Keller, Gottfried – Stuttgart: Riederer, 1949 – 1 – us U.W. Library [830]
DIE ZUERICHER WIEDERTAEUFER ZUR REFORMATIONSZEIT : NACH DEN QUELLEN DES STAATSARCHIVS / Egli, Emil – Zuerich: Friedrich Schulthess, 1878 – 1mf – 9 – 0-8370-8895-X – 1986-2895 – us A.T.L.A. [240]
ZUFALLIGE GEDANCKEN UND NUSZLICHE BEDENCKEN UBER DEN STREIT / Stahl, Georg Ernst – Halle, 1747 – 1 – us U.W. Library [540]
DER ZUG DES HAUPTMANNS VON ERCKERT / Grimm, Hans – Feldpostausg. Muenchen: A Langen/G Mueller, 1943, c1936 – 1r – 1 – us U.W. Library [430]
ZUGAENGE / Penzoldt, Ernst – Berlin: Suhrkamp, 1947 – 1r – 1 – us U.W. Library [430]
Zugasti, Julian de *see*
- EL BANDOLERISMO
- EL BANDOLERISMO...TOMO 4. PARTE PRIMERA. ORIGENES DEL BANDOLERISMO

DER ZUGGEIST / Schmidt, Maximilian – Berlin: Hermann Hillger, [189-?] – 1r – 1 – us U.W. Library [830]
ZUHUR – Istanbul: 1890. Cikaran: OEmer Sevki. Nos. 1-129 (1 Mart-9 Temmuz 1306 [1890]) – $125.00 – us MEDOC [073]
ZUHURI – Cairo. Sahibi ve Mueduerue: Kemal Saadeddin. No. 1 (10 Mayis 1906) – 9 – $25.00 – us MEDOC [956]
DE ZUID AFRIKAAN *see* VOLKSVRIEND
DE ZUID-AFRIKAAN – (Title varies: De Zuid-Afrikaan vereenigd Met De Volksvriend 1871-94. De Zuid-Afrikaan Vereenigd met Ons Land 1894-1930. Suppressed: 1901-Jul 1902. Issued as Advertentieblad) – Cape Town, South Africa. 5 Jan 1860-8 Apr 1930 – 89r – 1 – sa SA Libr [072]
ZUID-AFRIKAANSCHE KRONIJK *see* SOUTH AFRICAN CHRONICLE
Zuidema, Floris C *see* IMPACT OF URBANIZATION AND INDUSTRIALIZATION ON WATER RESOURCES PLANNING AND MANAGEMENT
Zuidema, Floris C et al *see* MANUAL ON DRAINAGE IN URBANIZED AREAS
HET ZUID-WESTEN – Oudtshoorn, South Africa. 15 Oct 1900-24 Dec 1914 – 15r – 1, 16 diazo available at reduced price – sa SA Libr [072]
ZUKA : A JOURNAL OF EAST AFRICAN CREATIVE WRITING – Nairobi. n1-6. 1967-72 – 10mf – 9 – $5.00f – us Ross [073]
DIE ZUKUNFT – Berlin, 1877-78 – 1 – DM80.00 – gw Mikro Press [072]
DIE ZUKUNFT – Berlin, 1898 – 1 – Inquire at Mikrofilmarchiv for details – gw Misc Inst [072]
DIE ZUKUNFT – Berlin, Germany. Socialistische Revue. 1877-1878 – 1 – gw Mikrofilm [072]
DIE ZUKUNFT – Berlin. v. 1-118. 1892-1922 – 1 – 556.00 – us L of C Photodup [073]
DIE ZUKUNFT – New York. 1892-97 – 1 – us A.J.P.C. [073]
DIE ZUKUNFT – Paris, France. Ab 1939 Organ der Deutsch-Franzoesischen Union. 12 Oct 1938-10 May 1940 – 1 – gw Mikrofilm [073]
DIE ZUKUNFT : SOCIALISTISCHE REVUE – Berlin, 1877-78 – 1 – Inquire at Mikrofilmarchiv for details – gw Misc Inst [335]
DIE ZUKUNFT – Sozialistische Monatsschrift fuer Politik, Wissenschaft und Kultur. Wien, Austria – 1 – gw Mikrofilm [073]
DIE ZUKUNFT – Wien, 1949-51 – 1 – DM80.00 – gw Mikro Press [072]
ZUKUNFT – Prague, Czechoslovakia. Mar 1928-1932 – 1r – 1 – us L of C Photodup [072]
DIE ZUKUNFT DER NOTENDECKUNG DURCH HANDELSWECHSEL / Rittershausen, Heinrich – (Stirner, by H. Schultheiss, et al. 1922. 184p. Aufsatz und Literaturliste, by Mackay Gesellschaft. Literature List, by Liberty Classics) – 1945. 36p. 1 fiche (29x). Together with: – 9 – 1.00f – at Libertarian Micro [320]
DIE ZUKUNFT DIE KIRCHE : EINE WOCHENSCHRIFT – (Filmed with: Kirchenblatt fuer die Reformierte Schweiz) – 1845-54; 1938-70; 1972-86 (incomplete) – 11r – 1 – ATLA S0124A – us A.T.L.A. [073]
DIE ZUKUNFT DIE KIRCHE *see* KIRCHENBLATT FUER DIE REFORMIERTE SCHWEIZ
DAS ZUKUNFTSBILD DES JESAIA / Guthe, Hermann – Leipzig: Breitkopf & Haertel, 1885 – 9 – us A.T.L.A. [220]
DIE ZUKUNFTSERWARTUNG DES JESAIA / Hackmann, Heinrich Friedrich – (Includes bibliographical references) – Goettingen: Vandenhoeck und Ruprecht, 1893 – 1mf – 9 – 0-8370-3443-4 – 1985-1443 – us A.T.L.A. [220]
DIE ZUKUNFTSHOFFNUNGEN DES URCHRISTENTUMS / Knopf, Rudolf – Tuebingen: J.C.B. Mohr, 1907. (Religionsgeschichtliche Volksbuecher fuer die deutsche christliche Gegenwart; 1. Reihe, 13. Heft) – 1mf – us A.T.L.A. [240]
Zulaica Garate, Roman *see*
- LOS FRANCISCANOS Y LA IMPRENTA EN MEXICO
- LOS FRANCISCANOS Y LA IMPRENTA EN MEXICO EN EL SIGLO 16

DIE ZULASSIGKEIT NEUEN THATSACHLICHEN VORBRINGENS IN DEN HOHEREN INSTANZEN; EINE CIVILPROCESSUALISCHE ABHANDLUNG / Menger, Anton – Wien: Holder, 1873. 172p. LL-4078 – 1 – us L of C Photodup [340]
Zulia. Venezuela. (State) *see* GACETA OFICIAL DEL ESTADO ZULIA
ZULULAND AND THE ZULUS : THEIR HISTORY, BELIEFS, CUSTOMS, MILITARY SYSTEM, HOME LIFE, LEGENDS, ETC, AND MISSIONS TO THEM / Farrer, James Anson – 2nd ed. London: Kerby & Endean, 1879 – us Res Libr [305]
ZULULAND OBSERVER – South Africa. 14 Aug 1969- – 1 – sa State Libr [960]
ZULU-LAND, OR, LIFE AMONG THE ZULU-KAFIRS / Grout, Lewis – 1864 – 1 – $50.00 – us Presbyterian [305]
ZULULAND (SOUTH AFRICA) DIOCESAN RECORDS / United Society for the Propagation of the Gospel. Archives – 19th Century – 1 – uk Microform Academic [025]
ZULULAND TIMES – Eshowe, South Africa. 1907-1975 – 1 – sa State Libr [072]
ZUM BEGRIFF DER KAUSALITAET IN DER KRIEGSURSACHENFORSCHUNG : EINE ANALYSE AM BEISPIEL DES ZWEITEN GOLFKRIEGES / Hunger, Bertolt – 1993 – 1mf – 9 – DM75.00 – 3-89349-724-2 – gw Hänsel [320]
ZUM BEGRIFF DER REGEL IN DER PHILOSOPHIE DER UMGANGSSPRACHE UEBER WITTGENSTEIN, AUSTIN UND SEARLE / Wiggershaus, Rolf – Frankfurt a.M., 1974 – 2mf – 9 – DM62.00 – 3-89349-791-9 – gw Hänsel [190]
ZUM BERGARBEITERAUSSTAND IM RUHRREVIER / Hilbck, A – Koln, 1905 – 1 – DM30.00 – gw Mikro Press [331]
ZUM BEWEIS DES GLAUBENS / Peip, Albert – (Includes bibliographical references) – Guetersloh: C Bertelsmann, 1867 – 1mf – 9 – 0-8370-5208-4 – 1985-3208 – us A.T.L.A. [230]
ZUM EVANGELISCHEN LEBENSIDEAL IN SEINER LUTHERISCHEN UND REFORMIERTEN AUSPRAEGUNG *see* COLLECTED WORKS
ZUM EVANGELIUM DES PAULUS UND DES PETRUS : ALTES UND NEUES / Holsten, C – Rostock, 1868 – 8mf – 8 – ne Slangenburg [220]
ZUM EVANGELIUM DES PAULUS UND DES PETRUS; ALTES UND NEUES / Holsten, Earl J – 1868 – 9 – us A.T.L.A. [240]
ZUM GESETZ UND ZUM ZEUGNISS: EINE ABWEHR WIDER DIE NEU-KRITISCHE SCHRIFTFORSCHUNG / Boehl, Eduard – Wien: Wilhelm Braumueller, 1883.1 fiche – 9 – us A.T.L.A. [240]
ZUM GOETHE-PROBLEM : LITERARHISTORISCHE STUDIEN / Stockmann, Alois – Freiburg im Breisgau: Herder, 1920 – 1r – 1 – us U.W. Library [430]
ZUM IRDISCHEN AUSGANG VON GOETHES FAUSTDICHTUNG / Hohlfeld, A R – (Includes bibliographical references) – Weimar: Verlag der Goethe-Gesellschaft, 1936 – 1r – 1 – us U.W. Library [430]
ZUM KAMPF UM DAS APOSTOLIKUM : EINE STREITSCHRIFT WIDER D. HARNACK / Cremer, Hermann – Berlin: Wiegandt & Grieben, 1893 – 1mf – us A.T.L.A. [240]
ZUM STREIT UM DIE BUEHNE : EIN BERLINER TAGEBUCH / Mauthner, Fritz – Kiel: Lipsius und Tischer, 1893 – 1r – 1 – us U.W. Library [943]
ZUM VATER UNSER HEINRICHS VON KROLEWIZ / Thuemmler, Curt – Leipzig-Reudnitz, 1897 – 1mf – 9 – DM48.00 – 3-89349-351-4 – gw Hänsel [430]
ZUM VERHAELTNIS VON RELIGION UND MODERNER SCHULE : AKTUELLE DISKUSSIONEN IM SENEGAL UM DIE EINFUEHRUNG VON RELIGIONSUNTERRICHT IN DAS OEFFENTLICHE SCHULWESEN / Asdonk, Ben – 1995 – 2mf – 9 – DM80.00 – 3-8267-2172-1 – gw Hänsel [370]
ZUM VERSTAENDNIS VON BILDUNG UND AUSBILDUNG IN DER SOZIALLEHRE V. A. HUBERS (1800-1869) UNTER BESONDERER BERUECKSICHTIGUNG DER DIFFERENZ SEINER FRUEH UND SPAETSCHRIFTEN / Jansen, Brigitte E S – 1995 – 2mf – 9 – DM80.00 – 3-8267-2110-1 – gw Hänsel [370]
ZUM VICTORIA NYANZA; EINE ANTISKLAVEREI-EXPEDITION UND FORSCHUNGSREISE / Werther, C Waldemar – Berlin, 1894 – 1 – us Res Libr [960]
ZUM ZUSAMMENHANG VON IDENTIFIKATION MIT DEM GRUPPENREPRAESENTANTEN UND REGIONALER IDENTITAET : DER FALL MANFRED STOLPE UND DIE BRANDENBURGER / Bissels, Thomas & Keseberg, Kerstin – 1994 – 2mf – DM80.00 – 3-8267-2020-2 – gw Hänsel [150]

ZUM ZUSAMMENHANG VON SELBSTVERWIRKLICHUNG UND MORALITAET / Schmidt, Nicole D – 1993 – 2mf – 9 – DM80.00 – 3-89349-818-4 – gw Hänsel [170]

Zumbag de Koesfelt, C *see* INSTITUTIONES MUSICAE, OF KORTE ONDERWYZINGEN RAKENDE DE PRACTYK VAN DE MUZYK EN IN-ZONDERHEID VAN DEN GENERAALEN BAS OF BASSUS CONTINUUS, BENEVENS DE DAER UIT SPRUITENDE GRONDEN VAN DE COMPOSITIE, UITGEGEVEN DOOR EEN LIEFHEBBER VAN DEZE KUNST

Zumkeller, A *see* DAS MOENCHTUM DES HEILIGEN AUGUSTINUS

Zumpt, August Wilhelm *see* DAS GEBURTSJAHR CHRISTI

ZUMUTBARKEIT VON KERNENERGIERISIKEN : SOZIALWISSENSCHAFTLICHE ANALYSE DER KERNENERGIE-DEBATTE / Beker, Gabriele Heidelberg, 1978 – 6mf – 9 – DM118.00 – 3-89349-635-1 – gw Hänsel [320]

Zunft, Stefanie *see* ORGANISATIONSENTWICKLUNG UND BERATUNG IM NON-PROFIT-BEREICH

Zuni Day School *see* TOWN CRIER

LOS ZUNIGA, SENORES DE PLASENCIA / Paredes Guillen, Vicente – Caceres: Tip. Enc. y Lib. de Jimenez, 1909 – 1 – sp Bibl Santa Ana [946]

DIE ZUNKUNFT DER KIRCHE – EINE WOCHENSCHRIFT. 1845-46. Which is filmed with: Kirchenblatt fuer die reformierte Schweiz. v. 1-10. 1845-54 – 1 – us A.T.L.A. [073]

Zunz, L *see*
- GESAMMELTE SCHRIFTEN
- DIE JUEDISCHE DICHTER DER PROVENCE
- DIE RITUS DES SYNAGOGALEN GOTTESDIENSTES
- DIE SYNAGOGALE POESIE DES MITTELALTERS
- SYNAGOGAL-POESIEEN: HEBRAEISCHE TEXTE MIT DER DEUTSCHEN UEBERTRAGUNG... DES MITTELALTERS
- TIFERET SEIVAH, JUBELSCHRIFT. L. ZUNZ
- ZUR GESCHICHTE UND LITERATUR

ZUOJIA = THE WRITER – Apr-Nov 1936. 2 reels. M-C55 – 1 – $80.00 – cc Microforms [800]

ZUOWU XUEBAO – Acta Agronomica Sinica. In Chinese but English abstracts to the main articles. F p79 – 9 – 4.00f – cc Microforms [630]

ZUR ABERCIUS-INSCHRIFT (T.U.U. 1-12/4B) / Harnack, Adolf von – Leipzig, 1895 – 1mf – 9 – ne Slangenburg [240]

ZUR AELTESTEN GESCHICHTE DES PRIMATES IN DER KIRCHE / Friedrich, Johann – Bonn: P. Neusser, 1879 – 1mf – us A.T.L.A. [240]

ZUR ALTHEBRAEISCHEN STROPHIK / Perles, Felix – (Includes bibliographical references) – Wien: Alfred Hoelder, 1896 – 1mf – 9 – 0-8370-9261-2 – 1986-3261 – us A.T.L.A. [470]

ZUR ANALYSE VON FARBTRENDS : DARGESTELLT AM BEISPIEL VON TEPPICHBOEDEN / Spriwald, Dietmar – 1994 – 1mf – DM48.00 – 3-8267-2068-7 – gw Hänsel [650]

ZUR APOLOGIE DES CHRISTENTHUMS: NACH GESCHICHTE UND LEHRE / Zezschwitz, Gerhard von – Leipzig: J.C. Hinrichs, 1866. 1 fiche – 9 – us A.T.L.A. [240]

ZUR AUSLEGUNG DER STELLE PHILIPPER 2, 5-11...PAULINISCHEN CHRISTOLOGIE / Weiffenbach, Wilhelm – Karlsruhe: H. Reuther, 1884. 1 fiche. 8370-5740-X – 9 – us A.T.L.A. [240]

ZUR BARDESANISCHEN GNOSIS (T.U.U. 3-34/4) / Haase, Felix – Leipzig, 1910 – 2mf – 9 – ne Slangenburg [240]

ZUR BEDEUTUNG DER SOZIALPERSPEKTIVITAET IN DER MARKTPSYCHOLOGISCHEN IMAGEFORSCHUNG / Ebbecke, Dirk – 1995 – 2mf – 9 – DM80.00 – 3-8267-2201-9 – gw Hänsel [650]

ZUR BELEUCHTUNG DER SOCIALEN FRAGE / Rodbertus, Karl – I. Berlin, A. Schindler, 1875. 223 p. 1. Unveraenderter Abdruck meines sweiten und dritten socialen Briefes an Von Kirchmann. (No more published.) (Label pasted over imprint reads: Berlin, Puttkammer & Muehlbrecht.) Film Mas 8114 – 1 – us H.U. Library [300]

ZUR BEURTHEILUNG WIELANDS *see* FESTGABE ZUM NEUNZIGSTEN GEBURTSTAG LEOPOLDS VON RANKE

ZUR BIBLIOGRAPHIE DER GEDAECHTNIS- UND TRAUERVORTRAEGE IN DER HEBRAEISCHEN LITERATUR / Wachstein, B – Wien, 1922-1932 – 6mf – ne IDC [470]

ZUR BIOGRAPHIE FERDINAND RAIMUNDS / Frankl, Ludwig August – Wien: A Hartleben, 1884 – 1r – 1 – us U.W. Library [920]

ZUR BIOGRAPHIE FRANZ GRILLPARZER'S / Frankl, Ludwig August – 2., verm. Aufl. Wien: A Hartleben, 1884 – 1r – 1 – us U.W. Library [920]

ZUR BUEHNENTECHNIK ADOLPH MUELLNERS / Hugle, Richard Friedrich – (Includes bibliographical references (p.32)) – Leipzig: A Pries, 1922 – 1r – 1 – us U.W. Library [790]

ZUR CHARAKTERISTIK DES LUKAS : NACH SPRACHE UND STIL: EINE PHILOLOGISCHE LAIENSTUDIE / Vogel, Theodor – (Includes bibliographical references) – 2. voellig umgearb. Aufl Leipzig: Duerr, 1899 – 1mf – 9 – 0-8370-5651-9 – 1985-3651 – us A.T.L.A. [220]

ZUR CHRISTLICHEN ERKENNTNIS : VORTRAEGE UND AUFSAETZE FUER DENKENDE CHRISTEN / Mueller, Ernst Friedrich Karl – Leipzig: A Deichert (Georg Boehme), 1898 – 1mf – 9 – 0-8370-4533-9 – 1985-2533 – us A.T.L.A. [240]

ZUR CHRISTLICHEN KULTUS- UND KULTURGESCHICHTE : ABHANDLUNGEN UND VORTRAEGE / Kleinert, Paul – Berlin: H. Reuther, 1889 – 1mf – us A.T.L.A. [240]

ZUR CHRONOLOGIE DES LEBENS JESU / Mommert, Carl – Leipzig: E Haberland, 1909 – 1mf – 9 – 0-8370-4466-9 – 1985-2466 – us A.T.L.A. [240]

ZUR CHRONOLOGIE DES LEBENS JESU NACH DEN SYNOPTIKERN : EINE DISSERTATION / Sevin, Hermann – (Includes bibliographical references) – Heidelberg: A H Avenarius, 1870 – 1mf – 9 – 0-8370-5236-X – 1985-3236 – us A.T.L.A. [240]

ZUR CONCHYLIEN-FAUNA VON CHINA / Gredler, P V – Z-553 2. 1885 – 8 – ne IDC [590]

ZUR DEUTSCH-CHRISTLICHEN BILDUNG : POPULAR-THEOLOGISCHE VORTRAGE / Beyschlag, Willibald – (Ten of the 15 essays are new in this edition) – 2. Aufl. uberw. Halle a. S: Eugen Strien, [c1899] – 1mf – 9 – 0-8370-2330-0 – 1985-0330 – us A.T.L.A. [240]

ZUR DEUTSCHEN LITERATUR ALTLIVLANDS / Mackensen, Lutz – (Includes bibliographical references) – Wuerzburg: Holzner-Verlag, 1961 – 10r – 1 – us U.W. Library [430]

ZUR DEUTSCHEN SAGE UND DICHTUNG : GESAMMELTE AUFSAETZE / Golther, Wolfgang – (Includes bibliographical references) – Leipzig: Xenien-Verlag, 1911 – 1r – 1 – us U.W. Library [430]

ZUR DOGMATIK : SIEBEN ABHANDLUNGEN AUS DER "ZEITSCHRIFT FUER THEOLOGIE UND KIRCHE" / Kaftan, Julius – Tuebingen: J C B Mohr (Paul Siebeck), 1904 – 1mf – 9 – 0-8370-3830-8 – 1985-1830 – us A.T.L.A. [240]

ZUR EHRE GOTTES : EIN ZEITGEMAELDE / Sacher-Masoch, Leopold, Ritter von – Leipzig: E J Guenther, 1872 – 1 – us U.W. Library [830]

ZUR EINFUEHRUNG IN DAS AKADEMISCHE LEBEN UND STUDIUM DES THEOLOGEN / Luthardt, Christoph Ernst – 1892 – 1 – us A.T.L.A. [240]

ZUR EINLEITUNG IN DIE HALACHISCHEN MIDRASCHIM / Hoffmann, David – Berlin: M. Driesner, (1886). 1 fiche – 9 – us A.T.L.A. [270]

ZUR EMPFINDLICHKEIT DES TABAKKAEFERS LASIODERMA SERRICORNE (FABRICIUS) (COLEOPTERA: ANOBIIDAE) GEGENUEBER BEHANDLUNG MIT KOHLENSTOFFDIOXID UNTER HOCHDRUCK / Ulrichs, Christian – 1995 – 2mf – 9 – DM80.00 – 3-8267-2080-6 – gw Hänsel [590]

ZUR ENTSTEHUNGSGESCHICHTE DES CHRISTENTHUMS...SEPTUAGINTA ZUM EVANGELIUM / Friedlaender, Moriz – Wien: Alfred Hoelder, 1894. 1 fiche – 9 – us A.T.L.A. [240]

ZUR ENTSTEHUNGSGESCHICHTE DES KANONS IN DER ROEMISCHEN MESSE / Drews, Paul – Tuebingen: J.C.B. Mohr, 1902 – 1mf – us A.T.L.A. [240]

ZUR ENTSTEHUNGSGESCHICHTE VON GOETHE "TORQUATO TASSO" / Rueff, Hans – (Includes bibliographical references (3rd prelim. leaf) and index) – Marburg a.L.: N G Elwert, 1910 – 1r – 1 – us U.W. Library [430]

ZUR ENTSTEHUNGSGESCHICHTE VON GOETHES TORQUATO TASSO : WIDERLEGUNG DER HYPOTHESE KUNO FISCHERS / Beik, Kazimir – (Includes bibliographical references) – Leipzig: W Schunke, 1918 – 1r – 1 – us U.W. Library [430]

ZUR ENTWICKLUNG UND STRUKTUR EINIGER PTERIDOPHYTEN AUS JAVA / Westermaier, M – Freiburg, 1900 – 1mf – 9 – 7278/1 – ne IDC [950]

ZUR ENTWICKLUNGSGESCHICHTE DER FARRNKRAEUTER / Leszczyc-Suminski, J – Berlin. 1848. B-7212 1 – 9 – ne IDC [580]

ZUR ENTWICKLUNGSGESCHICHTE DER NOVELLENDICHTUNG LUDWIG TIECK'S / Garnier, T D – (Includes bibliographical references) – Giessen: E Roth, 1899 – 1r – 1 – us U.W. Library [430]

ZUR EPOCHENGESCHICHTE DES NATURKUNDLICHEN UNTERRICHTS IN HESSEN-DARMSTADT / Neusel, Manfred – Frankfurt a.M., 1977 – 4mf – 9 – DM90.00 – 3-89349-633-5 – gw Hänsel [370]

ZUR ERINNERUNG AN FUERST GEORG DEN GOTTSELIGEN ZU ANHALT : ZUM 400JAEHRIGEN GEBURTSTAGE AM 15. AUGUST 1907 / Westphal, F – Leipzig: Verein fuer Reformationsgeschichte, 1907. (Schriften des Vereins fuer Reformationsgeschichte; 25. Jahrg., Schrift 95) – 1mf – us A.T.L.A. [240]

ZUR ERINNERUNG AN GOTTHOLD EPHRAIM LESSING : BRIEFE UND AKTENSTUECKE AUS DEN PAPIEREN DER HERZOGLICHEN BIBLIOTHEK UND DEN AKTEN DES HERZOGLICHEN LANDESHAUPTARCHIVS ZU WOLFENBUETTEL / Lessing, Gotthold Ephraim; ed by Heinemann, O v. – Leipzig: S Hirzel, 1870 – 1r – 1 – us U.W. Library [920]

ZUR ERKLAERUNG DER PSALMEN SALOMOS / Perles, Felix – Berlin: Wolf Peiser, 1902. 1 fiche – 9 – us A.T.L.A. [240]

ZUR ERKLAERUNG DES POLYKARPMARTYRIUMS / Reuning, Wilhelm – 1917 – 1 – us A.T.L.A. [240]

ZUR ERKLAERUNG UND TEXTKRITIK DES 1. BUCHES TERTULLIANS, "ADVERSUS MARCIONEM" (T.U.U. 3-38/2) / Bill, A – Leipzig, 1911 – 2mf – 9 – ne Slangenburg [240]

ZUR ERZAEHLUNGSKUNST DER ANNETTE VON DROSTE-HUELSHOFF : DIE OBJEKTIVITAET IN DER "JUDENBUCHE" / Heitmann, Felix – 1995 – 1mf – 9 – DM48.00 – 3-8267-3117-4 – gw Hänsel [430]

ZUR FRAGE DER GOLDWAEHRUNG / Best, Dr – 9 – 1.00f – at Libertarian Micro [335]

ZUR FRAGE DES RENTIERNOMADISMUS / Flor, F – (Mitt. Anthropol. Gesellschaft in Wien, v. 55). 1930. BU-578 2 – 8 – ne IDC [306]

ZUR FRAGE NACH DEM URSPRUNG DES GNOSTIZISMUS (T.U.U. 1-15/4) / Anz, W – Leipzig, 1897 – 2mf – 9 – ne Slangenburg [240]

ZUR FRAGE NACH DER BEDEUTUNG DER HEILIGEN SCHRIFT : ZWEI VORLESUNGEN ZUM ZWECKE DER HABILITATION / Schulze, Martin – Halle (Saale): J Krause, 1894 – 1mf – 9 – 0-8370-6368-X – 1986-0368 – us A.T.L.A. [220]

ZUR FREIHEIT, ZUM FRIEDEN UND ZUR GERECHTIGKEIT AND JUSTICE = TOWARDS PEACE, FREEDOM AND JUSTICE / Beckerath, Ulrich von – Mostly in German, a collection of papers, notes and letters with contributions by several other writers on almost 5000 documents in 39 fiches. Still to be alphabetically indexed – 9 – 1.00f – at Libertarian Micro [335]

ZUR GEGENREFORMATION IN SCHLESIEN : TROPPAU, JAEGERNDORF, LEOBSCHUETZ : NEUE ARCHIVALISCHE AUFSCHLUESSE / Loesche, Georg – Leipzig: Verein fuer Reformationsgeschichte, 1915-1916. (Schriften des Vereins fuer Reformationsgeschichte; Jahrg. 32, 1.-3. Stueck, Nr. 117/8, 123) – 1mf – us A.T.L.A. [240]

ZUR GENETIK DER WAHRNEHMUNGS-GESCHWINDIGKEIT / Dittmar, Manuela – Frankfurt a.M., 1984 – 2mf – DM80.00 – 3-89349-914-8 – gw Hänsel [150]

ZUR GESCHICHTE DER ALTEVANGELISCHEN GEMEINDEN : VORTRAG / Keller, Ludwig – Berlin: E.S. Mittler, 1887 – 1mf – us A.T.L.A. [240]

ZUR GESCHICHTE DER DEUTSCHEN PROTESTANTEN, 1555-1559 / Wolf, Gustav – Nebst einem anhange von archivalischen beilagen. 1888 – 1 – us A.T.L.A. [240]

ZUR GESCHICHTE DER ERZAEHLENDEN SCHAEFERDICHTUNG IN DEUTSCHLAND / Schaumann, Ursula – Heidelberg, 1930 – 1mf – 9 – DM48.00 – 3-89349-799-4 – gw Hänsel [430]

ZUR GESCHICHTE DER JUEDISCHEN POESIE / Delitzsch, Franz – Leipzig. 1836. BJ-421-5 1 – 9 – ne IDC [470]

ZUR GESCHICHTE DER KIRCHLICHEN UNIONS- UND REFORMBESTREBUNGEN VON 1538 BIS 1542 / Cardauns, Ludwig – Rom: Loescher, 1910 – 1mf – us A.T.L.A. [240]

ZUR GESCHICHTE DER MAERCHENOPFER / Schmidt, Leopold – 1995 – 1mf – 9 – DM48.00 – 3-8267-3140-9 – gw Hänsel [780]

ZUR GESCHICHTE DER NEUESTEN THEOLOGIE / Schwarz, Carl – (Includes bibliographical references) – 4 enl rev ed. Leipzig: F A Brockhaus, 1869 – 2mf – 9 – 0-8370-8713-9 – 1986-2713 – us A.T.L.A. [240]

ZUR GESCHICHTE DER NEUTESTAMENTLICHEN SCHRIFT UND DES URCHRISTENTHUMS / Wieseler, Karl – Leipzig: J.C. Hinrichs, 1880. 1 fiche – 9 – us A.T.L.A. [240]

ZUR GESCHICHTE DER ORIENTALISCHEN FRAGE : BRIEFE AUS DEM NACHLASSE FRIEDRICHS VON GENTZ 1823-1829 / ed by Prokesch von Osten, A – Wien, 1877 – 3mf – 9 – ne IDC [943]

ZUR GESCHICHTE DER PALAESTINAENSISCHEN GEONIM / Poznanski, S A – (Zeitschrift deutschen morgenlaendischen Ges.). v. 68. 1914. BJ-32-39 1 – 9 – ne IDC [950]

ZUR GESCHICHTE DER SELGUQEN VON KERMAN / Houtsma, M Th. – 1885. BU-657 2 – 8 – ne IDC [950]

ZUR GESCHICHTE DER SONNTAGSSCHULEN UND KINDERGOTTESDIENSTE IN DEUTSCHLAND : FESTSCHRIFT ZU IHREM 25JAEHRIGEN JUBILAEUM IM AUFTRAG DES KOMITE FUER FOERDERUNG DER SONNTAGSSCHULSACHE IN DEUTSCHLAND / ed by Reinhard, Wilhelm – (Includes bibliographical references) – Berlin: Verlag der Buchh der Berliner Stadtmission, 1888 – 1mf – 9 – 0-8370-7577-7 – 1986-1577 – us A.T.L.A. [240]

ZUR GESCHICHTE DER SYRISCHEN PUNCTUATION / Nestle, Eberhard – (In German and Syriac. Includes bibliographical references) – [S.l.: s.n., 1876?] – 1mf – 9 – 0-8370-8601-9 – 1986-2601 – us A.T.L.A. [470]

ZUR GESCHICHTE DER WIEDERTAEUFER IN ROSTOCK / (Hofmeister, A) – Schwerin. 1885. BME-423 1 – 9 – ne IDC [240]

ZUR GESCHICHTE DES CHRISTENTUMS IN MITTEL-ASIEN BIS ZUR MONGOLISCHEN EROBERUNG / Barthold, W; ed by Stuebe, Rudolf – Tuebingen: J.C.B. Mohr, 1901 – 1mf – us A.T.L.A. [240]

ZUR GESCHICHTE DES CONCILS VON TRIENT (1559-63) : ACTENSTUECKE AUS OESTERREICHISCHEN ARCHIVEN / ed by Sickel, Th – (In Latin, Italian, and German) – Wien: Carl Gerold, 1872 – 2mf – 9 – 0-8370-8946-8 – 1986-2946 – us A.T.L.A. [240]

ZUR GESCHICHTE DES HUSITENTUMS : CULTURHISTORISCHE STUDIEN / Bezold, Friedrich von – Muenchen: T. Ackermann, 1874 – 1mf – us A.T.L.A. [900]

ZUR GESCHICHTE DES RASTADTER CONGRESSES / Vivenot, A von – Wien, 1871 – 6mf – 9 – ne IDC [943]

ZUR GESCHICHTE DES RELIGIOESEN ERKENNTNISPROBLEMS. ERSTER TEIL / Mayer, Gottlob – Leipzig: A. Deichert, 1897. 1 fiche – 9 – us A.T.L.A. [240]

ZUR GESCHICHTE SAULS UND DAWIDS / Steinthal, Heymann – (Includes bibliographical references & appendixes) – Berlin: Rosenthal, 1891 – 1mf – 9 – 0-8370-5395-1 – 1985-3395 – us A.T.L.A. [220]

ZUR GESCHICHTE UND GEOGRAPHIE OSTTURKESTANS / Lueders, H – Phil. Hist. Klasse. SPAW. 1922; SPAW. 1930. BU-620 2 – 8 – ne IDC [949]

ZUR GESCHICHTE UND KRITIK VON FRIEDRICH WILHELM GOTTER'S MEROPE / Schloesser, Rudolf – (Includes bibliographical references) – Leipzig: J B Hirschfeld, 1890 – 1r – 1 – us U.W. Library [430]

ZUR GESCHICHTE UND LITERATUR / Zunz, L – Berlin. 1845. BJ-32-45 1 – 9 – ne IDC [400]

ZUR GESELLSCHAFTLICHEN PRODUKTION VON ARMUT / Beger, Kai-Uwe – 1992 – 116p – 9 – DM98.00 – 3-89349-558-4 – gw Hänsel [360]

ZUR GRUND- UND BODENFRAGE / Liebknecht, Wilhelm – Leipzig, 1876 – 1 – DM60.00 – gw Mikro Press [943]

ZUR HANDSCHRIFTLICHEN UEBERLIEFERUNG DES CLEMENS ALEXANDRINUS (T.U.U. 2-20/4C) / Staehlin, Otto – Leipzig, 1901 – 1mf – 9 – ne Slangenburg [240]

ZUR HEIMATH – v1-7. 1885-81 (complete) – 1r – 1 – ATLA 1992-S000 – us A.T.L.A. [073]

ZUR IDENTIFIKATION KONTINUIERLICHER ZERKLEINERUNGSPROZESSE IM LABORBETRIEB / Bernhardt, Peter – 1993 – 2mf – 9 – DM80.00 – 3-89349-834-6 – gw Hänsel [620]

ZUR INFORMATION *see* INFORMATION

ZUR JOHANNEISCHEN FRAGE : BEITRAGE ZUR WURDIGUNG DES VIERTEN EVANGELIUMS GEGENUBER DEN ANGRIFFEN DER KRITISCHEN SCHULE / Beyschlag, Willibald – (Erweiterte Separatabdruck aus den "Theologischen Studien und Kritiken") – Gotha: Friedrich Andreas Perthes, 1876 – 1mf – 9 – 0-8370-2331-9 – 1985-0331 – us A.T.L.A. [220]

ZUR JUDENFRAGE IN DEUTSCHLAND / ed by Freund, W – Vom Standpunkte des Rechts und der Gewissenfreiheit. Berlin. 1843-44. BJ-23-38 1 – 9 – ne IDC [360]

ZUR KAISERWAHL 1619 / ed by Tadra, F – Wien, 1878 – 2mf – 9 – ne IDC [943]

ZUR KENNTNISS DER NEUHEBRAEISCHEN RELIGIOESEN POESIE / Dukes, L – Frankfurt am Main. 1842. BJ-421-6 1 – 9 – ne IDC [470]

ZUR KONSTRUKTION EINIGER SEMANTISCHER ANTINOMIEN / Pardey, Ulrich – Frankfurt a.M., 1975 – 1mf – 9 – DM48.00 – 3-89349-685-8 – gw Hänsel [410]

ZUR KONZEPTION EINER "SOCIALLY USEFUL ECONOMY" : DIE BRITISCHE DEBATTE IM KONTEXT DER STRUKTURPOLITIK DES GREATER LONDON COUNCIL 1981-1986 / Lorenz, Guenther – 1995 – 2v 8mf – 9 – DM136.00 – 3-8267-2202-7 – gw Hänsel [350]

ZUR KRIEGEZEIT DURCH CHINA, 1900-1901 / Wegener, Georg – 2nd ed. Berlin: Allgemeiner Verein fuer deutsche Litteratur, 1902. viii,405p. illus. map – 1 – us U.W. Library [950]

ZUR KRITIK UND GESCHICHTE DER UNTERSUCHUNGEN UEBER DAS ALGENGESCHLECHT / Pringsheim, N – Berlin. 1856. B-6396 1 – 9 – ne IDC [580]

ZUR LEHRE VON DER BEKEHRUNG UND VON DER PRAEDESTINATION : ZWEITE ENTGEGNUNG GEGEN MISSOURISCHE AUSFLUECHTE / Dieckhoff, A W – Rostock: G. Kahl, 1886 – 1mf – us A.T.L.A. [240]

ZUR LEHRE VON DER CHRISTLICHEN GEWISSHEIT: DREI ABHANDLUNGEN / Carlblom, August – Leipzig: E. Bidder, 1874. 1 fiche – 9 – us A.T.L.A. [240]

ZUR LEHRE VON DER GOTTHEIT JESU CHRISTI / Grass, Karl Konrad – (Includes bibliographical references) – Guetersloh: C Bertelsmann, 1900 – 1mf – 9 – 0-8370-4806-0 – 1985-2806 – us A.T.L.A. [240]

ZUR LOESUNG DER JUDENFRAGE DURCH DIE JUDEN: EIN JUEDISCHER OSTERABEND / Hezekia, Moses ben – Berlin: Wilhelm Jessleib, 1884 – 9 – us A.T.L.A. [270]

ZUR MORPHOLOGIE / Goethe, Johann Wolfgang von – Stuttgart u. Tuebingen, 1817, 1823. 2. v. in 1. Film Mas 8739 – 1 – us H.U. Library [590]

ZUR NATIONALFEIER : FESTREDE GEHALTEN AM 1. SEPTEMBER 1879 IM GROSSEN KATHHAUSSAALE ZU NUERNBERG / Kreppel, Friedrich – 2. Aufl. Nuernberg: J P Raw, 1879 – 1r – 1 – us U.W. Library [943]

ZUR NEUESTEN GESCHICHTE DES ONTOLOGISCHEN GOTTESBEWEISES / Bohatec, Josef – Leipzig: A. Deichert, 1906. 1 fiche – 9 – us A.T.L.A. [240]

ZUR ORNITHOLOGIE DER SUEDSEE-INSELN: I: DIE VOEGEL DER PALAU-GRUPPE / Finsch, F H O – Hamburg, 1875. 51p, 5pls. Z/1751/2 – 8 – ne IDC [590]

ZUR OSTDEUTSCHEN AGRARGESCHICHTE : EIN KOLLOQUIUM / Appelius, Erhard W et al – (Includes bibliographical references) – Wuerzburg: Holzner-Verlag, 1960 – 1 – us U.W. Library [943]

ZUR OST-EUROPAEISCHEN ARCHAEOLOGIE / Tallgren, A M – (FUF. v. 20). Helsinfors. 1929. BU-520 1 – 9 – ne IDC [930]

ZUR PHILOSOPHIE UND POESIE DES KAPITALISMUS / Mehring, Franz; ed by Raddatz, Fritz J – (Includes bibliographical references and index) – Darmstadt, Neuwied: Luchterhand, 1975 – 1r – 1 – us U.W. Library [330]

ZUR PROZESSKONZEPTION MUENDLICHEN DARSTELLENS IM AUSDRUCKSUNTERRICHT UNTER BESONDERER BERUECKSICHTIGUNG DER SUBJEKT-OBJEKT-DIALEKTIK / Polz, Marianne – 1992 – 9 – DM98.00 – 3-89349-474-X – gw Hänsel [400]

ZUR PSYCHOLOGIE DER VOREXILISCHEN PROPHETIE IN ISRAEL / Kurtz, Robert – Poessneck i.Th.: B. Feigenspan, 1904. 1 fiche – 9 – us A.T.L.A. [270]

ZUR QUELLENKRITIK DER GESCHICHTE DES GNOSTICISMUS / Harnack, Adolf von – Leipzig: E. Bidder, 1873-1874 – 1mf – us A.T.L.A. [240]

ZUR QUELLENKRITIK DES EPIPHANIOS / Lipsius, Richard Adelbert – Wien: W. Braumueller, 1865 – 3mf – us A.T.L.A. [240]

ZUR RECHTLICHEN NATUR DER VOELKERBUNDSMANDATE / Gsell-Truempi, F – Glarus, 1928 – 2mf – 1 – ILM-2143/1 – ne IDC [327]

ZUR RELEVANZ KOMMUNIKATIVER FERTIGKEITEN IN DER AERZTLICHEN PRAXIS / Ziegler, Johannes Joachim – 1994 – 2mf – DM80.00 – 3-89349-908-3 – gw Hänsel [610]

ZUR REVISION DER LUTHERBIBEL : OSTERPROGRAMM DER VEREINIGTEN FRIEDRICHS-UNIVERSITAET, HALLE-WITTENBERG / Riehm, Eduard – (Includes bibliographical references) – Halle (Saale): Buchdr des Waisenhauses, 1882 – 1mf – 9 – 0-8370-6348-5 – 1986-0348 – us A.T.L.A. [220]

ZUR ROLLE DER SORPTION BEIM VERHALTEN VON HERBIZIDEN IM BODEN / Heckrath, Goswin – 1994 – 1mf – DM60.00 – 3-8267-2016-4 – gw Hänsel [630]

ZUR SELIGSPRECHUNGS-FEIER DES SELIGEN PETER CANISIUS / Weninger, Francis Xavier – New York: Gebrueder Benziger, 1865 – 1mf – 9 – 0-8370-6875-4 – 1986-0875 – us A.T.L.A. [920]

ZUR SPRACHE DER EWE-NEGER : EIN BEITRAG ZUR SELLENKUNDE / Czermak, Wilhelm – (Filmed with: Bibliotheca Africana) – Innsbruck: F Rauch, [n.d.] – us Res Libr [470]

ZUR SPRACHE DES AEGIDIUS ALBERTINUS : BEITRAEGE ZUR GESCHICHTE DER MUENCHENER LITERATUR- UND DRUCKSPRACHE AM BEGINNE DES 17. JAHRHUNDERTS / Himmler, Gebhard – (Includes bibliographical references) – Passau: Druck von Ablassmayer & Penninger, 1903 – 1r – 1 – us U.W. Library [430]

ZUR SPRACHE DES AEGIDIUS ALBERTINUS : BEITRAEGE ZUR GESCHICHTE DER MUENCHENER LITERATUR- UND DRUCKSPRACHE AM BEGINNE DES 17. JAHRHUNDERTS / Himmler, Gebhard – Muenchen: Druck von H Kutzner, 1902 – 1r – 1 – us U.W. Library [430]

ZUR SPRACHE DES ALTEN GOETHE : EIN VERSUCH UEBER DIE SPRACHE DES EINZELNEN / Lewy, Ernst – (Includes bibliographical references) – 1r – 1 – us U.W. Library [430]

ZUR STELLUNG AVENCEBROLS IM ENTWICKLUNGSGANGE D. ARAB. PHILOSOPHIE : BGPHMA 6 / Wittmann, M – Muenster, 1905 – 2mf – 9 – ne Slangenburg [240]

ZUR SYMBOLFRAGE : ZWEI ABHANDLUNGEN / Achelis, Ernst Christian – Berlin: H. Reuther, 1892 – 1mf – us A.T.L.A. [240]

ZUR SYNTAX DER KASUS UND TEMPORA IN DEN TRAKTATEN DES HL. CYPRIAN : LAT. CHRIST. PRIMAEVA: 9 / Merkx, P A H J – 1939 – 4mf – 8 – ne Slangenburg [240]

ZUR SYNTAX DES KOREANISCHEN : TOPIK UND WORTSTELLUNG / Lim, Mija – 1995 – 3mf – 9 – DM98.00 – 3-8267-2148-9 – gw Hänsel [480]

ZUR TEXTGESCHICHTE DER CIVITAS DEI AUGUSTINS (T.U.U. 3-32/2A) / Dombart, B – Leipzig, 1908 – 1mf – 9 – ne Slangenburg [240]

ZUR TEXTGESCHICHTE UND ERKLAERUNG VON TERTULLIANS APOLOGETIKUM (T.U.U. 3-40/4) / Schroers, H – Leipzig, 1914 – 2mf – 9 – ne Slangenburg [240]

ZUR THEOLOGIE A. RITSCHL'S / Frank, H R – Erlangen: A. Deichert, 1891 – 1mf – us A.T.L.A. [240]

ZUR THEOLOGIE DER PSALMEN / Kurtz, Johann Heinrich – Dorpat: E.J. Karow, 1865. 1 fiche – 9 – us A.T.L.A. [220]

ZUR THEOLOGIE DES ALTEN TESTAMENTS / Kittel, Rudolf – Leipzig: J.C. Hinrichs, 1899. 1 fiche – 9 – us A.T.L.A. [240]

ZUR THEOLOGISCHEN ENCYKLOPAEDIE: KRITISCHE BETRACHTUNGEN / Raebiger, Julius Ferdinand – Wroclau: E. Morgenstern, 1882. 1 fiche – 9 – us A.T.L.A. [240]

ZUR THEORETISCHEN BESTIMMUNG UND PRAKTISCHEN NUTZUNG MUSIKERZIEHERISCHER POTENZEN DES MUSIKKRITISCHEN SCHRIFTTUMS / Koehler, Klaus – 1992 – 9 – DM98.00 – 3-89349-504-5 – gw Hänsel [780]

ZUR THEORIE DER BIBLISCHEN WEISSAGUNG UND ZUR CHARAKTERISTIK DES HEBRAEERBRIEFS : ZWEI VORTRAEGE / Klostermann, August – Noerdlingen: C H Beck, 1889 – 1mf – 9 – 0-8370-3934-7 – 1985-1934 – us A.T.L.A. [220]

ZUR THEORIEDISKUSSION IN DER WIRTSCHAFTSETHNOLOGIE / Riesebrodt, Martin – Heidelberg, 1973 – 2mf – 9 – DM62.00 – 3-89349-695-5 – gw Hänsel [170]

ZUR TYPOLOGIE DER GOETTIN ATHENA / Mathiopoulos, Elsie – Bonn 1968 – 1 – DM30.00 – gw Mikro Press [240]

ZUR UEBERLIEFERUNG DER MATTHAEUSERKLAERUNG DES ORIGENES (T.U.U. 4-47/2) / Klostermann, Erich & Benz, E – Leipzig, 1931 – 3mf – 9 – ne Slangenburg [240]

ZUR UEBERLIEFERUNG DES PHILOSTORGIOS (T.U.U. 2-17/3B2) / Jeep, I – Leipzig, 1899 – 1mf – 9 – ne Slangenburg [240]

ZUR UEBERLIEFERUNGSGESCHICHTE DER ALTCHRISTLICHEN LITTERATUR (T.U.U. 1-12/1B) / Harnack, Adolf von – Leipzig, 1894 – 1mf – 9 – ne Slangenburg [240]

ZUR UEBERWINDUNG DES ZWEIFELS / Jaeger, Paul – Tuebingen: J.C.B. Mohr, 1906. 1 fiche – 9 – us A.T.L.A. [240]

ZUR UEE-TSI-FRAGE / Haloun, G – In: ZDMG. v91. Leipzig. 1937 – 8 – BU-557 2 – ne IDC [999]

ZUR UNDOGMATISCHEN GLAUBENSLEHRE: VORTRAEGE UND ABHANDLUNGEN / Dreyer, Otto – Berlin: C.A. Schwetschke, 1901. 1 fiche – 9 – us A.T.L.A. [240]

ZUR VERSOEHNUNG DES BESITZES UND DER ARBEIT / Walcker, Karl & Schenckendorff, E von – Kiel: Lipsius und Tischer, 1891 – 1r – 1 – us U.W. Library [943]

ZUR VERSOEHNUNGSLEHRE : EINE DOGMATISCHE UNTERSUCHUNG / Haering, Theodor – Goettingen: Vandenhoeck & Ruprecht, 1893 – 1mf – 9 – 0-8370-5041-3 – 1985-3041 – us A.T.L.A. [240]

ZUR VERSTAENDIGUNG UEBER DEN CHRISTLICHEN VORSEHUNGSGLAUBEN / Beyschlag, Willibald – Halle a. S:Eugen Strien, 1888 – 1mf – 9 – 0-8370-2686-5 – 1985-0686 – us A.T.L.A. [210]

ZUR VERWENDBARKEIT VON STUTENMILCH, KUMYSS UND ESELMILCH ALS DIAETETIKA UND HEILMITTEL UNTER BESONDERER BERUECKSICHTIGUNG DER BEDUERFNISSE DES SAEUGLINGS UND DES FRUEHGEBORENEN / Buehlbaecker, Alexander – 1995 – 5mf – 9 – DM118.00 – 3-8267-2185-3 – gw Hänsel [618]

ZUR VORGESCHICHTE DER BARTHOLOMAEUSNACHT : HISTORISCH KRITISCHE STUDIE / Wuttke, Heinrich – Leipzig: T.O. Weigel, 1879 – 1mf – us A.T.L.A. [944]

ZUR WIRTSCHAFTSPOLITIK OBERSCHWAEBISCHER REICHSSTAEDTE IM AUSGEHENDEN MITTELALTER / Kleiber, Ludwig – Freiburg, 1921 – 1 – DM30.00 – gw Mikro Press [320]

ZUR WISSENSCHAFTSKRITIK BILDUNGSPOLITISCHER ANALYSEN – UNTER BESONDERER BERUECKSICHTIGUNG DES VERHAELTNISSES VON KRITISCH-FUNKTIONALISTISCHER UND HISTORISCH-MATERIALISTISCHER THEORIEBILDUNG / Baigger, Hans-Christoph – Frankfurt a.M., 1976 – 3mf – 9 – DM76.00 – 3-89349-713-7 – gw Hänsel [320]

ZUR WUERDIGUNG SCHILLER'S IN AMERIKA : ERINNERUNGSBLAETTER AN DIE HUNDERTSTE WIEDERKEHR VON SCHILLER'S TODESTAG / ed by Comite der Chicago Schiller Gedenkfeier, Mai 1905 – (Includes index) – Chicago: Koelling & Klappenbach, [1905] – 1 – us U.W. Library [430]

ZUR ZEIT JESU = IN THE TIME OF JESUS : HISTORICAL PICTURES / Seidel, Martin – (In English. Includes bibliographical references, appendixes and index) – New York: Anson D F Randolph, [1885?] – 1mf – 9 – 0-8370-5220-3 – 1985-3220 – us A.T.L.A. [220]

ZURBARAN / Gaya Nuno, Juan Antonio – Barcelona: Ediciones Aedos, 1948 – sp Bibl Santa Ana [946]

ZURBARAN EN SAN PABLO DE SEVILLA / Caturla, Maria Luisa – Badajoz: Imp. Diputacion Provincial, 1964 – sp Bibl Santa Ana [946]

Zurbitu, D *see*
- LA COLORINA. BADAJOZ, ARQUEROS, 1928
- UNA EXCURSION AL REAL MONASTERIO DE GUADALUPE. MADRID, 1927

Zurcher, George *see* THE APPLE OF DISCORD, OR TEMPORAL POWER IN THE CATHOLIC CHURCH

Zurhellen, Otto *see* DIE HEIMAT DES VIERTEN EVANGELIUMS

Zurhellen-Pfleiderer, Else *see* DIE RELIGION DER PATRIARCHENGESCHICHTEN

Zurich. (Canton). Laws, Statutes, etc. (Indexes) *see* GESAMMT-REGISTER ZU AMTSBLATT AND GESETZESSAMMLUNGEN DES KANTONS ZURICH

ZURICH CITIZEN NEWS – Ontario Prov., Canada. 1900-1981. Title varies – 1 – cn Commonwealth Micro [072]

Zurich. Kunsthaus *see* BILDER NACH SKULPTUREN UND GEMAELDEN DER SAMMLUNG

ZURUF AUS DER HEIMAT AN DIE DEUTSCH-LUTHERISCHE KIRCHE NORDAMERICAS / Loehe, Wilhelm – Stuttgart: S.G. Liesching, 1845 – 1mf – us A.T.L.A. [240]

ZUSAMMENHAENGE VON ALLGEMEINER WEHRPFLICHT UND VOLKSWIRTSCHAFT ALS GRUNDLAGE ZUR BEURTEILUNG DEUTSCHER WEHRPOLITIK : MIT EINEM ANHANG. DIE DEUTSCHEN RUESTUNGEN VON 1871-1914 / Wrede, Clemens, Freiherr von – 1995 – 1mf – 9 – DM48.00 – 3-8267-3170-0 – gw Hänsel [355]

ZUSAMMENHAENGE ZWISCHEN SOZIALSTUKTUR UND BELASTUNG BEI WEIBLICHEN HAUSMEERSCHWEINCHEN (CAVIA APEREA F. PORCELLUS) / Thyen, Yvonne – 1993 – 2mf – 9 – DM98.00 – 3-89349-716-1 – gw Hänsel [574]

ZUSAMMENHANG ZWISCHEN WISSENSCHAFT UND GLAUBEN / Mir, Miguel – Regensburg: Georg Joseph Manz, 1883. 1 fiche – 9 – us A.T.L.A. [240]

DER ZUSAMMENSCHLUSS : POLITISCHE MONATSSCHRIFT ZUR PFLEGE DER DEUTSCHEN EINTRACT – (Filmed in reverse sequence) – 1926-28 (complete) – 1r – 1 – ATLA S0048 – us A.T.L.A. [073]

DER ZUSAMMENSCHLUSS DES POLITISCHEN KATHOLIZISMUS IN DEUTSCHLAND IM JAHRE 1848 / Schnabel, Franz – Heidelberg, 1910 – xi/132p – 9 – DM48.00 – 3-89349-070-1 – gw Hänsel [320]

ZUSEHEN IST NICHT EXISTIEREN : ELEKTRONISCHE MEDIEN UND DIE NOTWENDIGKEIT SCHULISCHEN HANDELNS DARGESTELLT ANHAND DER PLANUNG, DURCHFUEHRUNG UND ANALYSE EINER UNTERRICHTSREIHE IM FACH SOZIALKUNDE FUER AUSZUBILDENDE... / Kolhoff, Ludger – 1993 – 1mf – 9 – DM60.00 – 3-89349-828-1 – gw Hänsel [370]

Zutphen *see* CONSUETUDINES SCI VICTORIS PARISIENSIS

ZUVERLAESSIGE NACHRICHTEN VON DEM GEGENWAERTIGEN ZUSTANDE, VERAENDERUNG UND WACHSTUM DER WISSENSCHAFTEN – Leipzig. bd 1-18. 1740-1757 (mf ed 1993) – 72mf – 9 – DM1,950.00 – 3-89131-096-X – gw Fischer [500]

ZVEN'IA. IZBRANNYE STIKHI. 1890-1912 / Bal'mont, K D – M. 1913. BR-556 2 – 8 – ne IDC [460]
ZVENIGOROD OKLIKANNYI. NIKOLINY PRITCHI / Remizov, A – Paris, 1924. 158, (3)p. BR-858 2 – 8 – ne IDC [460]
ZVENO – (Library has holdings (incomplete) from between Jan. 5, 1925 and June 1, 1928) – Paris: "Zveno", 1923-1928 – 1 – CSUX87-S257 – us Hoover Inst Photo [944]
Zverez, I D *see* TEACHING METHODS IN THE SOVIET SCHOOL
Zverintsev, L N *see* SISTEMATICHESKII BIBLIOGRAFICHESKII UKAZATEL' KNIG, BROSHIUR I ZHURNALOV PO VSEM OTRASLIAM TECHNIKI. VYSHEDSHIKH
ZVEZDA – Khudozhestvenno-literaturnyi zhurnal. Spb. 1886-1905. Available: 1886 (1-52), 1887 (1 33), 1889 (15-16). R-2041 2 – 8 – ne IDC [073]
ZVEZDA – Leningrad. 1961-74 – 1 – D16264 – us UMI [073]
ZVEZDA – (Star). Moscow. U.S.S.R. 1961- – 1 – us UMI [073]
ZVEZDA NEZVEZDNAIA / Remizov, A – Stella Maria Maris. Paris, 1928. 79p. BR-859 2 – 8 – ne IDC [460]
Zviagintsev *see* MOSKVA
ZVIAZDA – Minsk. U.S.S.R. 1961- – 1 – us UMI [072]
ZVIDOMLENNYA / Akademiia Nauk. URSR. Kiev. – 1921-1927 – 1 – us NY Public [073]
ZVIT I REZOLIUTSII Z' IZDU / Association of United Ukrainian Canadians – v1-16 1920-37 – 1 – $85.00 – cn McLaren [360]
Zwaardecroon, Hendrick *see* MEMOIR OF HENDRICK ZWAARDECROON, COMMANDEUR OF JAFFNAPATAM, 1697
DIE ZWANGSVOLLSTRECKUNG AUSLAENDISCHER URTEILE... / Diehl, H – Borna, Leipzig, 1911 – 1mf – 1 – ILM-2256/1 – ne IDC [327]
DIE ZWANGSVOLLSTRECKUNG AUSWAERTIGER RICHTERLICHER URTHEILE IN RUSSLAND / Engelmann, J – Leipzig, 1884 – 1mf – 1 – ILM-2270/1 – ne IDC [327]
ZWANGSVOLLSTRECKUNG WEGEN BAGATELLFORDERUNGEN / Schwab, Kai Michael – 1993 – 2mf – 9 – DM98.00 – 3-89349-694-7 – gw Hänsel [340]
ZWANZIG COMPONISTEN, EINE SKIZZE / Junker, C L – Bern. 1776. BP-336 1 – 9 – ne IDC [780]
ZWANZIG COMPONISTEN, EINE SKIZZE VON C. L. JUNKER / Junker, C L – 1776 – 9 – us Sibley [780]
ZWANZIG LIEDER VERMISCHTEN INHALTS / Flaschner, G B – Zittan & Leipzig: J D Schops, 1789 – 1 – us Sibley [780]
Zwarg, Leopold Fredrick *see* APPARATUS WORK FOR BOYS AND GIRLS; A COURSE OF GRADED INSTRUCTION...IN THE USE OF HORIZONTAL BARS, PARALLEL BARS, HORSES, RINGS, LADDERS..
Zwarts, J *see*
- DE JOODSCHE GEMEENTE VAN AMERSFOORT
- PORTUGEESCHE JODEN TE MAARSSEN EN MAARSSEVEEN IN DE 17DE EEUW
- DE SYNAGOGEN TE UTRECHT

DER ZWECK IM RECHT, VON RUDOLPH VON JHERING. / Jhering, Rudolf von – 4. aufl. 1. ausg. in volkstumlicher gestalt. Leipzig, Breitkopf und Hartel, 1904-05. 2 v. LL-4075 – 1 – us L of C Photodup [340]
"ZWECKMAESSIGKEIT" IN DER PATHOLOGIE / Ribbert, Hugo – Bonn: F Cohen, 1906 – us Res Libr [574]
HET ZWEEPJE – Amsterdam. Nos. 1-16. 1875-76 – 2mf – 9 – J-261-124/1 – ne IDC [949]
ZWEI AKADEMISCHE VORLESUNGEN UEBER GRUNDPROBLEME DER SYSTEMISCHEN THEOLOGIE / Wobbermin, Georg – Berlin: Alexander Duncker, 1899.1 fiche – 9 – us A.T.L.A. [240]
ZWEI APOSTOLISCHE ZEUGEN FUER DAS JOHANNES EVANGELIUM / Haussleiter, Johannes – Muenchen: C.H. Beck, 1904. 1 fiche – 9 – us A.T.L.A. [240]
ZWEI AUFSATZE ZUR RELIGIONSGESCHICHTE VORDERASIENS / Schneider, Hermann G – (Leipziger semitistische Studien. v. 5, pt. 1. Leipzig. 1914). Leipzig. 1909. BNE-20,116 1 – 9 – ne IDC [290]
ZWEI BISHER UNBEKANNTE ENTWUERFE DES WORMSER EDIKTES GEGEN LUTHER / Brieger, Theodor – Leipzig, 1910 – 1mf – 9 – DM38.00 – 3-89349-329-8 – gw Hänsel [240]
ZWEI BISHER UNVEROEFFENTLICHTE ZEITDOKUMENTE DES VERLAGS-ARCHIVES UEBER HEINES "REISEBILDER" UND "BUCH DER LIEDER" : AUS DEM VON ERNST ELSTER VORBEREITETEN "BRIEFWECHSEL ZWISCHEN HEINE UND CAMPE" / Campe, Julius – [Hamburg]: Hoffmann und Campe, 1925 – 1r – 1 – us U.W. Library [430]
ZWEI CALVIN-VORTRAEGE : RECHTFERTIGUNG UND HEILIGUNG NACH CALVIN, CALVIN UND DER MODERNE GEMEINDEGEDANKE / Lang, August – Guetersloh: C. Bertelsmann, 1911 – 1mf – us A.T.L.A. [240]
ZWEI FAMILIEN / Bauernfeld, Eduard von – Wien: A Mausberger; Leipzig: P Baumgaertner, 1840 – 1 – us U.W. Library [820]
ZWEI GOETHE-STUDIEN / Vincent, Ernst – Jena: W Biedermann, 1929 – 1r – 1 – us U.W. Library [430]
ZWEI GOETHEVORTRAEGE : DIE JUGENDSPRACHE GOETHES / Waetzoldt, Stephan – (Includes bibliographical references) – Berlin: R Wilhelmi, 1888 – 1r – 1 – us U.W. Library [430]
ZWEI GOETTINGER MACHZORHANDSCHRIFTEN / Techen, Ludwig – Goettingen: Dieterich, 1884 – 1mf – 9 – 0-8370-5580-6 – 1985-3580 – us A.T.L.A. [090]
ZWEI GRIECHISCHE APOLOGETEN / Geffcken, Johannes – Leipzig: B.G. Teubner, 1907 (Sammlung wissenschaftlicher Kommentare zu griechischen und roemischen Schriftstellern) – 1mf – us A.T.L.A. [240]
ZWEI ISLANDER-GESCHICHTEN – 1897 – 1 – us I.U. Libraries [390]
ZWEI JAHRE ARCHIVARBEIT IM REICHSKOMMISSARIAT OSTLAND / Dulfer, K – Mitteilungsblatt des (Preussischen Generaldirektors der Staatsarchive. 1943 (23 Dec). BR-9841 1 – 9 – ne IDC [943]
ZWEI SCHWAEBISCHE ERZAEHLER : MELCHIOR MEYR UND HERMANN KURZ / Golz, Bruno – Hamburg: Hanseatische Verlagsanstalt, [1925] – 1r – 1 – us U.W. Library [430]
ZWEI VORTRAEGE / Nitzsch, Carl Immanuel – Berlin: Wiegandt und Grieben, 1855 – 1mf – us A.T.L.A. [240]
ZWEIFEL? / Bettex, Frederic – 2. stark verm. Aufl. Stuttgart: J F Steinkopf, 1909 – 1mf – 9 – 0-8370-2321-1 – 1985-0321 – us A.T.L.A. [210]
Zweifel, J *see* EXPEDITION C. A. VERMINCK
Zweig, Arnold *see*
- EINSETZUNG EINES KOENIGS
- DIE NOVELLEN UM CLAUDIA
- SAEMTLICHE POETISCHE WERKE, NEBST EINER AUSWAHL SEINER BRIEFE
- DIE SENDUNG SEMAELS

Zweig, Stefan *see*
- AMOK
- DIE AUGEN DES EWIGEN BRUDERS
- BEGEGNUNGEN MIT MENSCHEN, BUECHERN, STAEDTEN
- BEN JONSONS VOLPONE
- ERSTES ERLEBNIS
- DIE FRUEHEN KRAENZE
- JEREMIAH
- JEREMIAS
- KLEINE CHRONIK
- SILBERNE SAITEN

DIE ZWEITE APOKALYPSE DES JACOBUS AUS NAG-MAMMADI-CODEX 5 (T.U.U. 5-119) / Funk, W-P – 1976 – 5mf – 9 – ne Slangenburg [220]
DER ZWEITE BRIEF AN DIE THESSALONICHER / Kloepper, Albert – Koenigsberg: Hartung, 1889. 1 fiche – 9 – us A.T.L.A. [240]
DER ZWEITE BRIEF DES PAULUS AN DIE KORINTHER / Bachmann, Philipp – 1909 – 1 – us A.T.L.A. [240]
DAS ZWEITE BUCH DER MEDIZINISCHEN BRIEFE DES ZUERICHER PHILOSOPHEN UND ARZTES KONRAD GESSNER / Tilemann, Hero – Duesseldorf, 1939 – 2mf – DM62.00 – 3-8267-3061-5 – gw Hänsel [610]
DIE ZWEITE GENERATION : ROMAN EINER KOLONIALEN JUGEND / Spiesser, Fritz – 3. Aufl. Muenchen: F Eher, 1942 – 1r – 1 – us U.W. Library [830]
DIE ZWEITE HELVETISCHE CONFESSION : EINE ANTRITTSREDE / Boehl, Eduard – (Includes bibliographical references) – Wien: Wilhelm Braumueller, 1864 – 1mf – 9 – 0-8370-8650-7 – 1986-2650 – us A.T.L.A. [240]
DER ZWEITE KORINTHERBRIEF DES APOSTELS PAULUS : GESCHICHTLICHE UND LITERARKRITISCHE UNTERSUCHUNGEN / Halmel, Anton – Halle: Max Niemeyer, 1904 – 1mf – 9 – 0-8370-3455-8 – 1985-1455 – us A.T.L.A. [220]
DIE ZWEITE ROEMISCHE GEFANGENSCHAFT DES APOSTELS PAULUS : EINE KIRCHENHISTORISCHE UND NEUTESTAMENTLICHE UNTERSUCHUNG / Steinmetz, Rudolf – (Includes bibliographical references) – Leipzig: A Deichert, 1897 – 1mf – 9 – 0-8370-9309-0 – 1986-3309 – us A.T.L.A. [220]
ZWEITER LANDRECHTSTEIL UND LEHNRECHT (MGH LEGES 3: 2.BD. 2.TEIL) – 1961 – Dfl30.00 – ne Slangenburg [240]
ZWEITSINN. VORSTUDIEN ZU EINER THEORIE DER SPRACHLICHEN / Kandler, Gunther – Andeutung. Bonn, 1950 – 1 – DM40.00 – gw Mikro Proc [400]
ZWELFF WICHTIGE VND STARCKE VRSACHEN HANSEN JEDELSHAUSERS VON VLM, WARUMB ER VON DEN WIDERTAUFFERN. SEY ABGETRETTEN / Erhard, Chr – Ingolstat, W. Eder. 1587. BME-140 1 – 9 – ne IDC [240]
Zwemer, Samuel Marinus *see*
- THE INFLUENCE OF ANIMISM ON ISLAM; AN ACCOUNT OF POPULAR SUPERSTITIONS
- ISLAM, A CHALLENGE TO FAITH
- THE MOSLEM DOCTRINE OF GOD
- THE UNOCCUPIED MISSION FIELDS OF AFRICA AND ASIA

Zwerenz, Carl *see* DER GEISTERBESCHWOERER
DIE ZWERGENSCHLACHT : EIN SOZIALER ROMAN / Ular, Alexander – Frankfurt a.M: Ruetten & Loening, 1910 – 1r – 1 – us U.W. Library [830]
DAS DIE ZWEY VND VIERZIG ANHALTISCHE ARGUMENT WIDER DER VBISQUISTEN TREWME NOCH FEST STEHEN... / Kirchner, T – Zerbst, 1584 – 6mf – ne IDC [240]
ZWEYTER VERSUCH IN FIGUTIRTEN CHORAELEN SOWOHL FUER DIE ORGEL, ALS FUER DAS CLAVICHORD / Marpurg, E W – Berlin, Amsterdam: J J Hummel, [179-?] – 1 – us Sibley [780]
ZWIASTUN – (Cont and filmed with: Straznica Ewangeliczna) – v16-43. 1961-88 (complete) – Inquire – 1 – ATLA S0382A – us A.T.L.A. [073]
ZWIASTUN *see* STRAZNICA EWANGELICZNA
ZWIAZKOWIEC – Warsaw, Poland. Jul 1949-1950 – 1r – 1 – us L of C Photodup [943]
ZWIAZKOWIEC – (Weekly, later semi-monthly Polish language fraternal newspaper) – Cleveland, OH. 4 Jan 1934-27 Dec 1990 – 17r – 1 – us Western Res [071]
DER ZWIEBELFISCH – Munich. 1909-1921, Jhrg. 1-12; 1946-1948, Jhg. 25, no. 1-9 – 1 – 35.00r – us Hoover Inst Photo [073]
ZWIEGESANG SELIGER GEISTER : ERZAEHLUNG / Peters, Friedrich Ernst – Goettingen: Deuerlich, 1944 – 1r – 1 – us U.W. Library [830]
ZWILAZKOWIEC = THE ALLIANCER – (In Polish. Some missing issues) – Canada, 1933-87 – 57r – 1 – cn Commonwealth Micro [072]
DER ZWINGER – Dresden, etc. Bd. 1-5; 1917-21. Film Mas C 289 – 1 – us H.U. Library [073]
Zwingli, H *see*
- IN CATABAPTISTARUM STROPHAS ELENCHUS
- VBER DOCTOR BALTHAZARS TOUFFBUECHLIN
- VOM DEM TOUFF. VOM WIDERTAUFF. VNND VOM KINDERTOUFF
- VON DEM PREDIG AMPT
- WELCHE VRSACH GEBIND ZE UFRUREN

Zwingli, Ulrich *see* SELECTED WORKS OF HULDREICH ZWINGLI, 1484-1531
ZWINGLI UND CALVIN / Lang, August – Bielefeld: Velhagen & Klasing, 1913 (Monographien zur Weltgeschichte; 31) – 1mf – us A.T.L.A. [940]
ZWINGLI UND ERASMUS : EINE REFORMATIONSGESCHICHTLICHE STUDIE / Usteri, Johann Martin – Zuerich: S Hoehr, 1885 – 1mf – us A.T.L.A. [940]
ZWINGLIS BEDEUTUNG NEBEN LUTHER : FESTREDE ZU ZWINGLIS 400JAEHRIGEM GEBURTSTAG, 1 JANUAR 1484 / Schweitzer, Alexander – Zuerich: F. Schulthess, 1884 – 1mf – us A.T.L.A. [240]
ZWINGLI'S STELLUNG ZUR SCHRIFT / Nagel, E – Freiburg I.B.: J.C.B. Mohr, 1896 – 1mf – us A.T.L.A. [240]
ZWISCHEN DEN ZEITEN – v1-11 n6. 1923-33 (complete) – 3r – 1 – ATLA S0011 – us A.T.L.A. [073]
ZWISCHEN FLUCHT UND MIGRATION : HINDUS AUS BANGLADESH IN EINEM WESTBENGALISCHEN DORF / Polzer, Claudia – 1992 – 125p – 9 – DM98.00 – 3-89349-622-X – gw Hänsel [304]
ZWISCHEN GESTERN UND MORGEN / Heuss, Theodor – Stuttgart: J Engelhorn, 1919 – 1r – 1 – us U.W. Library [840]
ZWISCHEN GRENZEN UND ZEITEN : ROMAN / Zillich, Heinrich – Muenchen: A Langen/G Mueller, 1943, c1939 – 1r – 1 – us U.W. Library [830]
ZWISCHEN HARZ UND WESER – Goettingen. feb 14, 1953-dec 28, 1961 – 1r – 1 – gw Mikrofilm [072]
ZWISCHEN HIMMEL UND ERDE : ERZAEHLUNG / Ludwig, Otto – Wiesbaden: Verlag des Volksbildungsvereins, 1910 – 1r – 1 – us U.W. Library [830]
ZWISCHEN POLEMIK UND KRITIK : DIE ZEITSCHRIFTEN DES AUGUST VON KOTZEBUE / Kotzebue, August von – 1786-1827 (mf ed 1997) – 235mf – 9 – DM4,550.00 – 3-89131-230-X – gw Fischer [430]
ZWISCHEN POLEMIK UND KRITIK: DIE ZEITSCHRIFTEN DES AUGUST VON KOETZEBUE *see* ERHEITERUNGEN, 1811-1827
ZWISCHEN POLEMIK UND KRITIK: DIE ZEITSCHRIFTEN DES AUGUST VON KOTZEBUE *see*
- DIE BIENE, 1808-1810
- DER FREIMUETHIGE, 1804-1811
- FUER GEIST UND HERZ, 1786
- DIE GRILLE, 1811-1812
- HEKATE, 1823
- LITERARISCHES WOCHENBLATT, 1818-1820
- POLITISCHE FLUGBLAETTER, 1814-1816

ZWISCHENSTAATLICHE STRAFRECHTSPOLITIK / Frank, H – N.p., 1935 – 1mf – 1 – ILM-2089/1 – ne IDC [327]
ZWITTAUER NACHRICHTEN – Zwittau, Czechoslovakia.1 Mai 1937-1938 – 1 – gw Mikrofilm [072]
ZWO PREDIGTEN VON ZWEIERLEY GERECHTIGKEIT, DES GESETZES UND DES EUANGELIJ... / Major, G – Wittemberg, 1550 – 1mf – ne IDC [240]
ZWOELF FREIHEITSLIEDER – Zuerich: Verlag des literarischen Comptoirs, 1843 – 1r – 1 – us U.W. Library [780]
DIE ZWOELF KLEINEN PROPHETEN / Hitzig, Ferdinand – 3. Aufl. Leipzig: S Hirzel, 1863 – 1mf – 9 – 0-8370-3599-6 – 1985-1599 – us A.T.L.A. [220]
ZWUESCHE TUER U ANGLE : E GESCHICHT US DER "GUETEN ALTEN ZYT" ZUM ENE DREIAKTIGE STUECK UMGMOEDELET / Balzli, Ernst – Aarau: A Breuninger Theaterverlag, [195-?] – 1 – us U.W. Library [830]
Zybura, John S *see* PRESENT-DAY THINKERS AND THE NEW SKOLASTICISM...
Zycha, H *see* MUCORINEAE
ZYCIE – London, UK. 18 May 1947-1959 – 1 – uk British Libr Newspaper [072]
ZYCIE BIALOSTOCKIE – Bialystok, Poland. Jul 1952-1959 – 15r – 1 – us L of C Photodup [943]
ZYCIE CZESTOCHOWY – Czestochowa, Poland. Aug 1951-1959 – 14r – 1 – us L of C Photodup [943]
ZYCIE LEBELSKIE – Lublin, Poland. Apr-May 1949; May 1952-Mar 1955 (incomplete) – 4r – 1 – us L of C Photodup [943]
ZYCIE LITERACKIE – (1980-1986 6r $85.00r) – 1954-71 – 18r – 1 – $85.00r – us Ross [072]
ZYCIE LITERACKIE – Cracow, Poland. -w. Sept 1951-Dec 1970. 19 reels – 1 – uk British Libr Newspaper [460]
ZYCIE OLSZTYNSKIE – (Some issues lacking) – Olsztyn, Poland. Oct 1949-1950; Jun-Dec 1951; Jul 1952-1959 – 18r – 1 – us L of C Photodup [943]
ZYCIE PARTII – Organ Komitetu Centralnego Polskiej Zjednoczonej Partii Robotniczej. Warszawa: Naktadem Robotniczoj Spotdzielni Wydawniczej Prasa. ill. Began in Mar 1949. Suspended 1952-Apr 1955 – 1 – us U.W. Library [073]
ZYCIE RADOMSKIE – Radom, Poland. 31 Oct 1949; Jul 1952-1959 – 14r – 1 – us L of C Photodup [943]
ZYCIE WARSZAWY – (Backfile through 1998 $85r) – 1999- – 12r per y – 1 – $960.00 – us Ross [306]

ZYCIE WARSZAWY – Warsaw, Poland. Feb 1945-1993 – 150r – 1 – us L of C Photodup [943]

ZYCIE WARSZAWY – (Backfile through 1998 $85r) – Poland, 1999- – 12r per y standing order – 1 – us Ross [072]

ZYCIE WARZAWY – 1993 – 1 – sz Infoprint [947]

ZYCIE WOLNE. WARSAW – v. 1-2. 1927-1928. Incomplete – 1 – us NY Public [943]

Zydowski Instytut Historyczny. Warsaw *see* BIULETYN

ZYDU BALSAS – (Missing: many numbers) – Kovno. v1-22. 1919-1940 – 38r – 1 – ne IDC [072]

Zyegler, C *see* VON DER WAREN NYESSUNG BEYD LEIBS UND BLUTS CHRISTI

ZYGON – Chicago. v1-30. 1966-97+ 1; v6-32. 1971-97+ 5; v13-32. 1978-97+ 9 – 1,5,9 – D2748 – us UMI [574]

ZYGOTE – Cambridge. v1-2 1993-94*. v3-5 1995-97+ – 1,5,9 – D21035 – us UMI [574]

Zyll de Jong, E van *see* THE NETHERLANDS EAST INDIES AND JAPAN

ZYMERGY LITERARY REVIEW – Montreal. v1-5. 1987-91 – 9 – Can$20.00y – cn Micromedia [420]

Zywicki, Scott S *see* THE ENERGY COST OF WOMEN WALKING WITH AND WITHOUT HAND WEIGHTS WHILE PERFORMING RHYTHMIC ARM MOVEMENTS